Car Section Contents

Unit Repair Contents

Car Models

CHILTON'S
1990
AUTOMOTIVE SERVICE MANUAL

Vice President & General Manager John P. Kushnerick
Editor-In-Chief Kerry A. Freeman, S.A.E.
Managing Editor Dean F. Morgantini, S.A.E. □ **Managing Editor** David H. Lee, A.S.E., S.A.E.
Senior Editor Richard J. Rivele, S.A.E. □ **Senior Editor** W. Calvin Settle, Jr., S.A.E.
Senior Editor Ron Webb
Project Manager Nick D'Andrea □ **Project Manager** Wayne A. Eiffes, A.S.E., S.A.E.
Service Editors Lawrence C. Braun, S.A.E., A.S.C., Dennis Carroll, Peter M. Conti, Jr.,
Thomas G. Gaeta, Ken Grabowski, A.S.E., Martin J. Gunther, Neil Leonard, A.S.E.,
Robert McAnally, Steven Morgan, Michael J. Randazzo, Richard T. Smith, Jim Steele,
Larry E. Stiles, Jim Taylor, Anthony Tortorici, A.S.E., S.A.E.
Editorial Consultants Edward K. Shea, S.A.E., Stan Stephenson

Manager of Production John J. Cantwell
Art & Production Coordinator Robin S. Miller
Supervisor Mechanical Paste-up Margaret A. Stoner
Mechanical Artist Cynthia Fiore
Special Projects Peter Kaprielyan

Sales Director Albert M. Kushnerick □ **Assistant** Jacquelyn T. Powers
Regional Sales Managers Joseph Andrews, David Flaherty

CHILTON BOOK COMPANY

*ONE OF THE **ABC PUBLISHING COMPANIES**,
A PART OF **CAPITAL CITIES/ABC, INC.***
Manufactured in USA ©1989 Chilton Book Company ● Chilton Way, Radnor, Pa. 19089
ISBN 0–8019–7955–2 Library of Congress Card Catalog Number 82–72944
1234567890 8765432109

Quick Locator Index

310-A

SAFETY NOTICE

Proper service and repair procedures are vital to the safe, reliable operation of all motor vehicles, as well as the personal safety of those performing repairs. This manual outlines procedures for servicing and repairing vehicles using safe, effective methods. The procedures contain many NOTES, CAUTIONS and WARNINGS which should be followed along with standard safety procedures to eliminate the possibilty of personal injury or improper service which could damage the vehicle or compromise its safety.

It is important to note that the repair procedures and techniques, tools and parts for servicng motor vehicles, as well as the skill and experience of the individual performing the work vary widely. It is not possible to anticipate all of the conceivable ways or conditions under which vehicles may be serviced, or to provide cautions as to all of the possible hazards that may result. Standard and accepted safety precautions and equipment should be used when handling toxic or flammable fluids, and safety goggles or other protection should be used during cutting, grinding, chiseling, prying, or any other process that can cause material removal or projectiles.

Some procedures require the use of tools specially designed for a specific purpose. Before substituting another tool or procedure, you must be completely satisfied that neither your personal safety, nor the performance of the vehicle will be endangered

PART NUMBERS

Part numbers listed in this reference are not recomendations by Chilton for any product by brand name. They are references that can be used with interchange manuals and aftermarket supplier catalogs to locate each brand supplier's discrete part number.

Although information in this manual is based on industry sources and is complete as possible at the time of publication, the possibilty exists that some car manufacturers made later changes which could not be included here. While striving for total accuracy, Chilton Book Company cannot assume responsibity for any errors, changes or omissions that may occur in the compilation of this data.

YEAR IDENTIFICATION

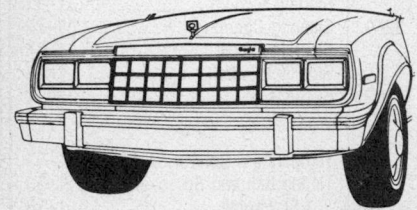

1986–87 Eagle

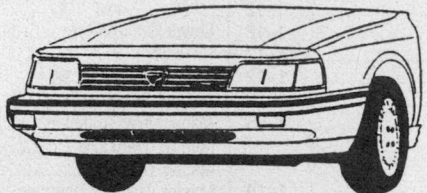

1988–90 Medallion

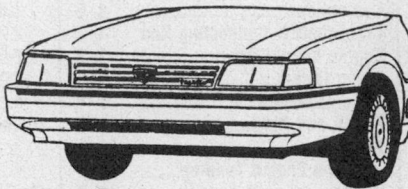

1988–90 Premier

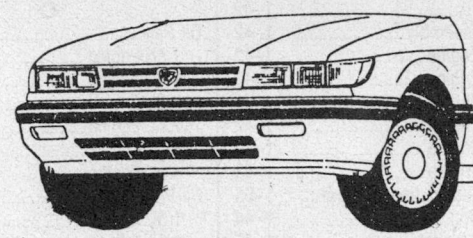

1989–90 Summit

VEHICLE IDENTIFICATION NUMBER (VIN)

It is important for servicing and ordering parts to be certain of the vehicle and engine identification. The VIN (vehicle identification number) is a 17 digit number visible through the windshield on the driver's side of the dash and contains the vehicle and engine identification codes. The tenth digit indicates model year and the fourth digit indicates engine code on all 1986–88 models. On 1989 and later models, the tenth digit indicates model year and the eighth digit indicates engine code. It can be interpreted as follows:

VEHICLE IDENTIFICATION CHART

It is important for servicing and ordering parts to be certain of the vehicle and engine identification. The VIN (vehicle identification number) is a 17 digit number visible through the windshield on the driver's side of the dash and contains the vehicle and engine identification codes. The tenth digit indicates model year and the fourth digit indicates engine code. It can be interpreted as follows:

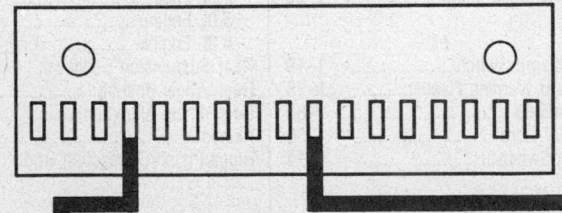

Engine Code						Model Year	
Code	Cu. In.	Liters	Cyl.	Fuel Sys.	Eng. Mfg.	Code	Year
C	258	4.2	6	2 bbl	AMC	G	1986
U	150	2.5	4	1 bbl	AMC	H	1987
Z	150	2.5	4	TBI	AMC	J	1988
F	132	2.2	4	MPI	Renault	K	1989
J	182	3.0	6	MPI	Renault		

VEHICLE IDENTIFICATION CHART

It is important for servicing and ordering parts to be certain of the vehicle and engine identification. The VIN (vehicle identification number) is a 17 digit number visible through the windshield on the driver's side of the dash and contains the vehicle and engine identification codes. The tenth digit indicates model year and the eighth digit indicates engine code. It can be interpreted as follows:

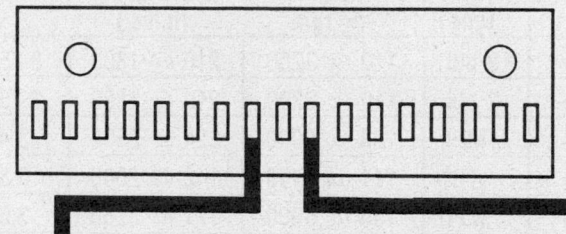

Engine Code

Code	Cu. In.	Liters	Cyl.	Fuel Sys.	Eng. Mfg.
X	96	1.5	4	MPI	Mitsubishi
Y	98	1.6	4	MPI	Mitsubishi
Z	98	1.6	4	MPI	Mitsubishi
F	132	2.2	4	MPI	Renault
H	150	2.5	4	TBI	AMC
U	182	3.0	6	MPI	Renault

Model Year

Code	Year
K	1989
L	1990

ENGINE IDENTIFICATION

Year	Model	Engine Displacement cu. in. (liter)	Engine Series Identification (VIN)	No. of Cylinders	Engine Type
1986	Eagle	6-258 (4.2)	C	6	OHV
1987	Eagle	6-258 (4.2)	C	6	OHV
1988	Eagle	6-258 (4.2)	C	6	OHV
	Medallion	4-132 (2.2)	F	4	SOHC
	Premier	4-150 (2.5)	Z	4	OHV
	Premier	6-182 (3.0)	J	6	DOHC
1989-90	Medallion	4-132 (2.2)	F	4	SOHC
	Premier	4-150 (2.5)	H	4	OHV
	Premier	6-182 (3.0)	U	6	DOHC
	Summit	4-96 (1.5)	X	4	SOHC
	Summit	4-98 (1.6)	Y	4	SOHC
	Summit	4-98 (1.6)	Z	4	DOHC

OHV Overhead Valve Engine
SOHC Single Overhead Cam Engine
DOHC Double Overhead Cam Engine

GENERAL ENGINE SPECIFICATIONS

Year	VIN	No. Cylinder Displacement cu. in. (liter)	Fuel System Type	Net Horsepower @ rpm	Net Torque @ rpm (ft.lbs.)	Bore × Stroke (in.)	Compression Ratio	Oil Pressure @ rpm
1986	C	6-258 (4.2)	2 bbl	110 @ 3200	210 @ 1800	3.75 × 3.900	9.2:1	46 @ 2000
1987	C	6-258 (4.2)	2 bbl	110 @ 3200	210 @ 1800	3.75 × 3.900	9.2:1	46 @ 2000
1988	F	4-132 (2.2)	MPI	103 @ 5000	124 @ 2500	3.46 × 3.50	9.2:1	44 @ 3000
	Z	4-150 (2.5)	TBI	111 @ 4750	142 @ 2500	3.87 × 3.18	9.2:1	55 @ 3500
	J	6-182 (3.0)	MPI	150 @ 5000	171 @ 3750	3.66 × 2.87	9.3:1	60 @ 4000
	C	6-258 (4.2)	2 bbl	110 @ 3200	210 @ 1800	3.75 × 3.900	9.2:1	46 @ 2000
1989-90	X	4-96 (1.5)	MPI	81 @ 65	91 @ 30	2.97 × 3.23	9.4:1	11.4 @ 750
	Y	4-98 (1.6)	MPI	113 @ 65	99 @ 50	3.24 × 2.95	9.2:1	11.4 @ 750
	Z	4-98 (1.6)	MPI	113 @ 65	99 @ 50	3.24 × 2.95	9.2:1	11.4 @ 750
	F	4-132 (2.2)	MPI	103 @ 5000	124 @ 2500	3.46 × 3.50	9.2:1	44 @ 3000
	H	6-150 (2.5)	TBI	111 @ 4750	142 @ 2500	3.88 × 3.19	9.2:1	13 @ 600
	U	6-182 (3.0)	MPI	150 @ 5000	171 @ 3750	3.66 × 2.87	9.3:1	60 @ 4000

MPI Multiport Injection
TBI Throttle Boby Injection

TUNE-UP SPECIFICATIONS
Refer to Section 34 for all spark plug recommendations

Year	VIN	No. Cylinder Displacement cu. in. (liter)	Spark Plugs Gap (in.)	Ignition Timing (deg.) MT	Ignition Timing (deg.) AT	Compression Pressure (psi)	Fuel Pump (psi)	Idle Speed (rpm) MT	Idle Speed (rpm) AT	Valve Clearance In.	Valve Clearance Ex.
1986	C	6-258 (4.2)	.035	9B①	9B①	120-150	5-6½	900	800	Hyd.	Hyd.
1987	C	6-258 (4.2)	.035	9B①	9B①	120-150	5-6½	900	800	Hyd.	Hyd.
1988	F	4-132 (2.2)	.035	③	③	②	34–36	800	700	.006	.008
	Z	4-150 (2.5)	.035	③	③	②	14–15	—	750	Hyd.	Hyd.
	J	6-182 (3.0)	.035	③	③	②	36–37	—	800	Hyd.	Hyd.
1989	X	4-96 (1.5)	.039–.043	⑦	⑦	137	47-50	650–850	650–850	.006	.010
	Y	4-98 (1.6)	.028–.031	⑧	⑧	171	47-50	650–850	650–850	Hyd.	Hyd.
	Z	4-98 (1.6)	.028–.031	⑧	⑧	149	47-50	650–850	650–850	Hyd.	Hyd.
	F	4-132 (2.2)	.035	⑥	⑥	⑤	34–36	800	700	.006	.008
	H	4-150 (2.5)	.035	⑥	⑥	⑤	14–15	⑥	⑥	Hyd.	Hyd.
	U	6-182 (3.0)	.035	⑥	⑥	⑤	28–30	⑥	⑥	Hyd.	Hyd.
1990					SEE UNDERHOOD SPECIFICATIONS STICKER						

① Eagle exc. Calif.—11B
② The lowest reading should be no less than 75% of the highest reading.
③ Refer to Underhood Sticker
⑤ The lowest reading should be no less than 75% of the highest reading,
⑥ Refer to Underhood Sticker
⑦ Base timing—5° BTDC
Actual timing—10° BTDC
⑧ Base timing—5° BTDC
Actual timing—8° BTDC

FIRING ORDERS

NOTE: To avoid confusion, always replace spark plug wires one at a time.

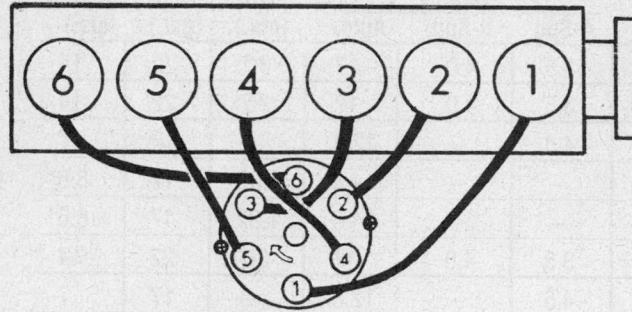

AMC 4.2L engine
Engine firig order: 1—5—3—6—2—4
Distributor rotation: clockwise

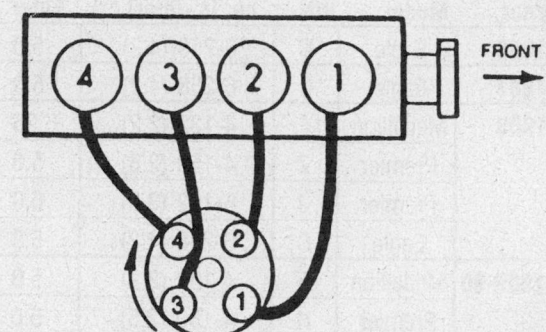

AMC 2.5L engine
Engine firing order: 1—3—4—2
Distributor rotation: clockwise

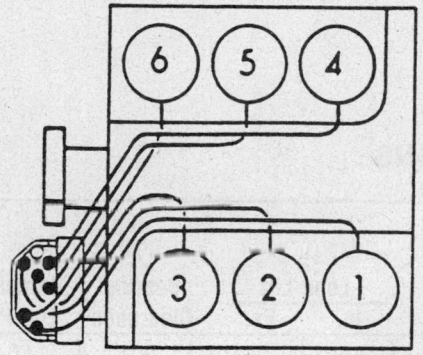

Renault 3.0L engine
Engine firing order: 1—6—3—5—2—4
Distributor rotation: counterclockwise

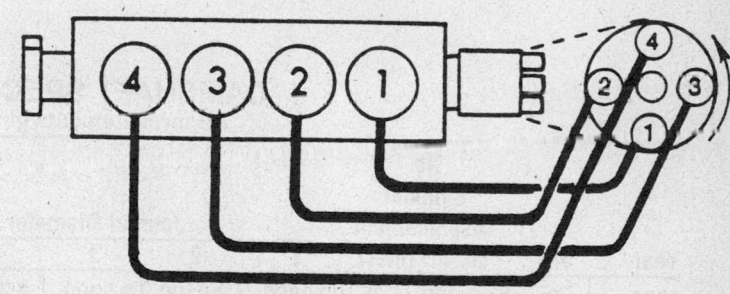

Renault 2.2L engine
Engine firing order: 1—3—4—2
Distributor rotation: counterclockwise

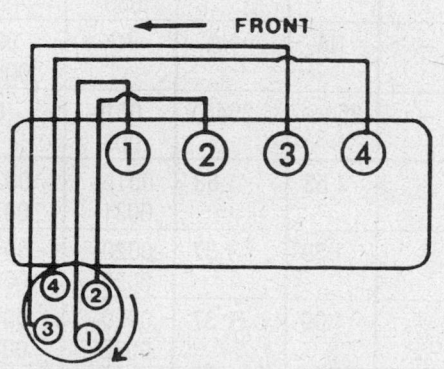

Mitsubishi 1.5L SOHC engine
Engine firing order: 1-3-4-2
Distributor rotation: clockwise

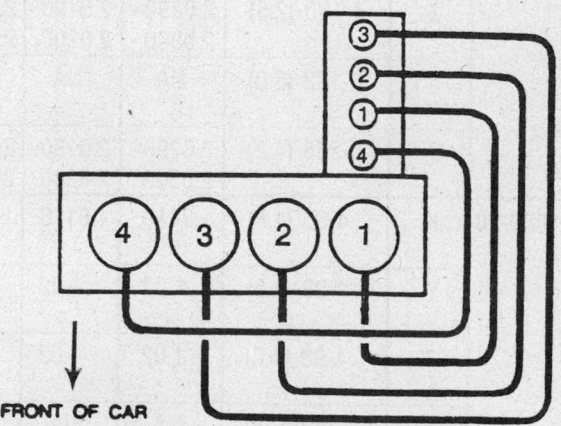

Mitsubishi 1.6L DOHC engine
Engine firing order: 1-3-4-2
Distributor rotation: clockwise

CAPACITIES

Year	Model	VIN	No. Cylinder Displacement cu. in. (liter)	Engine Crankcase with Filter	without Filter	Transmission (pts.) 4-Spd	5-Spd	Auto.	Drive Axle (pts.)	Fuel Tank (gal.)	Cooling System (qts.)
1986	Eagle	C	6-258 (4.2)	5.0	4.0	3.5	4.0	17	3②	22	14
1987	Eagle	C	6-258 (4.2)	5.0	4.0	3.5	4.0	17	3②	22	14
1988	Medallion	F	4-132 (2.2)	5.25	4.75	4.8	—	12.8	—	17	7
	Premier	Z	4-150 (2.5)	5.0	4.5	—	—	14.8	1.32	17	8.6
	Premier	J	6-182 (3.0)	6.0	5.5	—	—	14.8	1.32	17	8.6
	Eagle	C	6-258 (4.2)	5.0	4.0	3.5	4.0	17	3②	22	14
1989-90	Medallion	F	4-132 (2.2)	5.0	4.5	4.8	—	12.8	—	17	7
	Premier	H	4-150 (2.5)	5.0	4.5	—	—	14.8	1.32	17	8.6
	Premier	U	6-182 (3.0)	6.0	5.5	—	—	14.8	1.32	17	8.6
	Summit	X	4-96 (1.5)	4.0	3.5	3.6	①	13.0	—	13.2	5.3
	Summit	Y	4-98 (1.6)	5.0	4.5	3.6	①	13.0	—	13.2	5.3
	Summit	Z	4-98 (1.6)	5.0	4.5	3.6	①	13.0	—	13.2	5.3

① KM201—3.8 pt.   ② Front axle—2.5
   KM210—4.4 pt

CAMSHAFT SPECIFICATIONS
All measurements given in inches.

Year	VIN	No. Cylinder Displacement cu. in. (liter)	Journal Diameter 1	2	3	4	5	Lobe Lift In.	Ex.	Bearing Clearance	Camshaft End Play
1986	C	6-258 (4.2)	2.0290–2.0300	2.0190–2.0200	2.0090–2.0100	1.9990–2.0000	—	.254①	.254①	.001–.003	0
1987	C	6-258 (4.2)	2.0290–2.0300	2.0190–2.0200	2.0090–2.0100	1.9990–2.0000	—	.254①	.254①	.001–.003	0
1988	F	4-132 (2.2)	NA	NA	NA	NA	—	NA	NA	NA	.002–.005
	Z	4-150 (2.5)	2.0290–2.0300	2.0190–2.0200	2.0090–2.0100	1.9990–2.0000	—	.240	.250	.001–.003	0
	J	6-182 (3.0)	NA	NA	NA	NA	—	NA	NA	NA	.003–.0055
	C	6-258 (4.2)	2.0290–2.0300	2.0190–2.0200	2.0090–2.0100	1.9990–2.0000	—	.254①	.254①	.001–.003	0
1989-90	X	4-96 (1.5)	1.8110	1.8110	1.8110	1.8110	—	1.53	1.53	.0016–.0031	.0020–.0079
	Y	4-98 (1.6)	1.02	1.02	1.02	1.02	—	1.39	1.37	.0020–.0035	.0040–.0080
	Z	4-98 (1.6)	1.02	1.02	1.02	1.02	—	1.39	1.37	.0020–.0035	.0040–.0080
	F	4-132 (2.2)	NA	NA	NA	NA	—	NA	NA	NA	.002–.005
	H	4-150 (2.5)	2.0290–2.0300	2.0190–2.0200	2.0090–2.0100	1.9990–2.0000	—	.240	.250	.001–.003	0

CAMSHAFT SPECIFICATIONS
All measurements given in inches.

Year	VIN	No. Cylinder Displacement cu. in. (liter)	Journal Diameter 1	2	3	4	5	Lobe Lift In.	Ex.	Bearing Clearance	Camshaft End Play
1989-90	U	6-182 (3.0)	NA	NA	NA	NA	—	NA	NA	NA	.003–.0055

NA Not Available   ① 2 bbl carburetor — .248

CRANKSHAFT AND CONNECTING ROD SPECIFICATIONS
All measurements are given in inches.

Year	VIN	No. Cylinder Displacement cu. in. (liter)	Crankshaft Main Brg. Journal Dia.	Main Brg. Oil Clearance	Shaft End-play	Thrust on No.	Connecting Rod Journal Diameter	Oil Clearance	Side Clearance
1986	C	6-258 (4.2)	2.4996–2.5001	.0010–.0025	.0015–.0065	3	2.0934–2.0955	.0010–.0030	.005–.014
1987	C	6-258 (4.2)	2.4996–2.5001	.0010–.0025	.0015–.0065	3	2.0934–2.0955	.0010–.0030	.005–.014
1988	F	4-132 (2.2)	2.4660–2.4760	.0015–.0035	.002–.009	1	2.206–2.216	.0008–.0030	.012–.022
	Z	4-150 (2.5)	2.4996–2.5001	.0020	.0015–.0065	2	2.0934–2.0955	.0015–.0020	.010–.019
	J	6-182 (3.0)	2.7576–2.7583	.0015–.0035	.003–.010	1	2.3611–2.3618	.0008–.0030	.008–.015
	C	6-258 (4.2)	2.4996–2.5001	.0010–.0025	.0015–.0065	3	2.0934–2.0955	.0010–.0030	.005–.014
1989-90	X	4-96 (1.5)	1.8900	.0008–.0018	.0020–.0071	2	1.6500–	.0006–.0017	.0039–.0098
	Y	4-96 (1.6)	2.2400	.0008–.0020	.0020–.0071	2	1.7700–	.0008–.0020	.0039–.0098
	Z	4-96 (1.6)	2.2400	.0008–.0020	.0020–.0071	2	1.7700–	.0008–.0020	.0039–.0098
	F	4-132 (2.2)	2.4760	.0015–.0035	.005–.011	1	2.215	.0008–.0030	.012–.022
	H	4-150 (2.5)	2.4996–2.5001	.0020	.0015–.0065	2	2.0934–2.0955	.0015–.0020	.010–.019
	U	6-182 (3.0)	2.7576–2.7583	.0015–.0035	.0015–.0065	1	2.3611–2.3618	.0008–.0030	.008–.015

VALVE SPECIFICATIONS

Year	VIN	No. Cylinder Displacement cu. in. (liter)	Seat Angle (deg.)	Face Angle (deg.)	Spring Test Pressure (lbs.)	Spring Installed Height (in.)	Stem-to-Guide Clearance (in.) Intake	Exhaust	Stem Diameter (in.) Intake	Exhaust
1986	C	6-258 (4.2)	44.5	44	195 @ 1.411	$1^{13}/_{16}$	.0010–.0030	.0010–.0030	.3720	.3720
1987	C	6-258 (4.2)	44.5	44	195 @ 1.411	$1^{13}/_{16}$	.0010–.0030	.0010–.0030	.3720	.3720

AMC/JEEP-EAGLE
EAGLE • PREMIER • MEDALLION • SUMMIT

VALVE SPECIFICATIONS

Year	VIN	No. Cylinder Displacement cu. in. (liter)	Seat Angle (deg.)	Face Angle (deg.)	Spring Test Pressure (lbs.)	Spring Installed Height (in.)	Stem-to-Guide Clearance (in.) Intake	Stem-to-Guide Clearance (in.) Exhaust	Stem Diameter (in.) Intake	Stem Diameter (in.) Exhaust
1988	F	4-132 (2.2)	②	②	NA	NA	.0040	.0040	.3150	.3150
	Z	4-150 (2.5)	45	45	200 @ 1.216	$1\frac{11}{16}$	.001–.003	.001–.003	.312	.312
	J	6-182 (3.0)	45	45	155 @ 1.220	$1\frac{13}{16}$	NA	NA	.315	.315
	C	6-258 (4.2)	44.5	44	195 @ 1.411	$1\frac{13}{16}$	.0010–.0030	.0010–.0030	.3720	.3720
1989-90	X	4-96 (1.5)	44–44.5	45–45.5	NA	NA	.0008–.0020	.0020–.0035	.260	.260
	Y	4-98 (1.6)	44–44.5	45–45.5	NA	NA	.0008–.0019	.0020–.0033	.259	.257
	Z	4-98 (1.6)	44–44.5	45–45.5	NA	NA	.0008–.0019	.0020–.0033	.259	.257
	F	4-132 (2.2)	②	②	NA	NA	.0040	.0040	.3150	.3150
	H	4-150 (2.5)	①	45	200 @ 1.21	$1\frac{11}{16}$	.001–.003	.001–.003	.311–.312	.311–.312
	U	6-182 (3.0)	45	45	155 @ 1.220	$1\frac{13}{16}$	NA	NA	.315	.315

NA Not available

① Intake — 44½
   Exhaust — 40½

② Intake — 60
   Exhaust — 45

PISTON AND RING SPECIFICATIONS
All measurments are given in inches.

Year	VIN	No. Cylinder Displacement 00002n. (liter)	Piston Clearance	Ring Gap Top Compression	Ring Gap Bottom Compression	Ring Gap Oil Control	Ring Side Clearance Top Compression	Ring Side Clearance Bottom Compression	Ring Side Clearance Oil Control
1986	C	6-258 (4.2)	.0009–.0017	.010–.020	.010–.020	.010–.025	.0017–.0032	.0017–.0032	.0010–.0080
1987	C	6-258 (4.2)	.0009–.0017	.010–.020	.010–.020	.010–.025	.0017–.0032	.0017–.0032	.0010–.0080
1988	F	4-132 (2.2)	NA	①	①	①	NA	NA	NA
	Z	4-150 (2.5)	.0013–.0021	.010–.020	.010–.020	.015–.055	.0010–.0032	.0010–.0032	.0010–.0095
	J	6-182 (3.0)	NA	.016–.022	.016–.022	–	.0010–.0020	.0010–.0020	.0015–.0035
	C	6-258 (4.2)	.0009–.0017	.010–.020	.010–.020	.010–.025	.0017–.0032	.0017–.0032	.0010–.0080
1989-90	X	4-96 (1.5)	.0008–.0016	.0079–.0138	.0079–.0138	.0079–.0276	.0012–.0028	.0008–.0024	NA
	Y	4-98 (1.6)	.0008–.0016	.0098–.0157	.0138–.0197	.0079–.0276	.0012–.0028	.0012–.0028	NA
	Z	4-98 (1.6)	.0012–.0020	.0098–.0157	.0138–.0197	.0079–.0276	.0012–.0028	.0012–.0028	NA
	F	4-132 (2.2)	NA	①	①	①	NA	NA	NA
	H	4-150 (2.5)	.0013–.0021	.010–.020	.010–.020	.015–.055	.0010–.0032	.0010–.0032	.0010–.0085

PISTON AND RING SPECIFICATIONS
All measurments are given in inches.

Year	VIN	No. Cylinder Displacement cu. in. (liter)	Piston Clearance	Ring Gap			Ring Side Clearance		
				Top Compression	Bottom Compression	Oil Control	Top Compression	Bottom Compression	Oil Control
1989-90	U	6-182 (3.0)	.0013–0..21	.016–.022	.016–.022	NA	.0010–.0020	.0010–.0020	.0015–.0035

NA—Not Available

① The factory specifies only 1 type of ring for this engine. The ring gap is pre-adjusted.

TORQUE SPECIFICATIONS
All readings in ft. lbs.

Year	VIN	No. Cylinder Displacement cu. in. (liter)	Cylinder Head Bolts	Main Bearing Bolts	Rod Bearing Bolts	Crankshaft Pulley Bolts	Flywheel Bolts	Manifold		Spark Plugs
								Intake	Exhaust	
1986	C	6-258 (4.2)	80-90	75-85	30-35	70-90	95-115	18-28	18-28	7-15
1987	C	6-258 (4.2)	80-90	75-85	30-35	70-90	95-115	18-28	18-28	7-15
1988	F	4-132 (2.2)	①	69	46	96	44	11	13	11
	Z	4-150 (2.5)	100	80	33	80	48–54	23	23	28
	J	6-182 (3.0)	②	③	37	133	48–54	11	13	11
	C	6-258 (4.2)	80-90	75-85	30-35	70-90	95-115	18-28	18-28	7-15
1989-90	X	4-96 (1.5)	51-54	36-40	23-25	51 72	94-101	13-18	18-28	15-21
	Y	4-98 (1.6)	65-72	47-51	23-25	80-94	94-101	18-22	18-22	15-21
	Z	4-98 (1.6)	65-72	47-51	23-25	80-94	94-101	18-22	18-22	15-21
	F	4-132 (2.2)	①	69	46	96	44	11	13	11
	H	4-150 (2.5)	④	80	33	80	48–54	23	23	22
	U	6-182 (3.0)	52	80	35	125	48–54	11	13	11

① Torque in 3 steps, in sequence:
1st—37 ft. lbs.
2nd—59 ft. lbs.
3rd—69 ft. lbs.
Run engine for 15 minutes, shut off and allow to cool for 6 hours and re-check, should be 65–72 ft. lbs.

② Torque in 2 steps, in sequence:
1st—45 ft. lbs.
2nd—Angular tighten to 106 degrees
Run engine for 15 minutes, shut off and allow to cool for 6 hours. Angular tighten to 45 degrees.

③ Tighten in 2 steps, in sequence:
1st—20 ft. lbs.
2nd—Angular torque 75 degrees
④ No. 1-7 and No. 9-10—110 ft. lbs.
No. 8—100 ft. lbs.

WHEEL ALIGNMENT

Year	Model	Caster		Camber		Toe-in (in.)	Steering Axis Inclination (deg.)
		Range (deg.)	Preferred Setting (deg.)	Range (deg.)	Preferred Setting (deg.)		
1986	Eagle	2P–3P	2½P	⅛N–⅝P	¼P	¹⁄₁₆–³⁄₁₆③	11½
1987	Eagle	2P–3P	2½P	⅛N–⅝P	¼P	¹⁄₁₆–³⁄₁₆③	11½①
1988	Medallion	1½P–3½P	2½P	¹⁄₁₆P–¹³⁄₁₆P	⁷⁄₁₆P	⁵⁄₆₄③	12¾
	Premier	1⁵⁄₁₆P–2¹³⁄₁₆P	2⅛P	⁹⁄₁₆N–¹⁄₁₆N	⁵⁄₁₆N	⅛③	NA
	Eagle	2P–3P	2½P	⅛N–⅝P	¼P	¹⁄₁₆–³⁄₁₆③	11½①
1989-90	Medallion	1½P–3½P	2½P	¹⁄₁₆P–¹³⁄₁₆P	⁷⁄₁₆P	⁵⁄₆₄③	12¾
	Premier	1½P–3½P	2⅛P	⁹⁄₁₆N–¹⁄₁₆N	⁵⁄₁₆N	⅛③	NA
	Summit	1¹³⁄₁₆P–2¹³⁄₁₆P	2P	½N–½P	0	0	NA

P Positive ① Left—¾P-⅛P; Right—⅛P ② Left—¾P-⅛P; Right—½P-1P ③ Toe-out
N Negative

ELECTRICAL

NOTE: Disconnecting the negative battery cable on some vehicles may interfere with the functions of the on board computer systems and may require the computer to undergo a relearning process, once the negative battery cable is reconnected.

For testing and overhaul procedures on starters, alternators and voltage regulators, refer to the Unit Repair Section.

Charging System

ALTERNATOR

Removal and Installation

EAGLE

1. Disconnect the negative battery cable.
2. Disconnect the terminal wire connector and output wire from the rear of the alternator.
3. Loosen the alternator adjustment and mounting bolts. Remove the alternator belt.
4. Remove the mounting and adjustment bolts and remove the alternator.
5. Installation is the reverse of the removal procedure.
6. Adjust the belt tension to specification.

PREMIER

1. Disconnect battery negative cable.
2. On 2.5L engine, remove the power steering pump locking nut from mounting bracket.
    a. Loosen pivot bolt, adjusting bolt and 2 bolts located at rear of power steering pump.
    b. Remove alternator drive belt and disconnect electrical connectors from alternator.
    c. Remove pivot bolt, mounting bolts and alternator assembly.
3. On 3.0L engine, raise and support the vehicle safely. Remove the lower splash shield.
    a. Loosen alternator adjusting bolt to relieve the belt tension. Remove alternator drive belt, mounting bolt and pivot bolt.
    b. Disconnect electrical connectors from alternator and remove alternator assembly.
To install:
4. Position the alternator on engine and install pivot bolt and mounting bolts finger tight.
5. Reconnect electrical connectors and install the drive belt.
6. On 2.5L engine, install a belt tension gauge and tighten adjusting bolt to obtain the proper belt tension.
    a. Torque pivot bolt to 30 ft. lbs. (40 Nm).
    b. Torque the 2 rear power steering mounting bolts to 20 ft. lbs. (27 Nm).
    c. Torque the locking nut to 20 ft. lbs. (27 Nm).
7. On 3.0L engine, torque pivot bolt to 37 ft. lbs. (50 N.m).
    a. Tighten adjusting bolt to obtain the proper belt tension.
    b. Torque mounting bolt to 20 ft. lbs. (27 N.m).
    c. Install the lower splash shield and lower the vehicle.
8. Reconnect battery negative cable and check alternator operation.

MEDALLION

1. Disconnect the negative battery cable. Raise and support the vehicle safely.

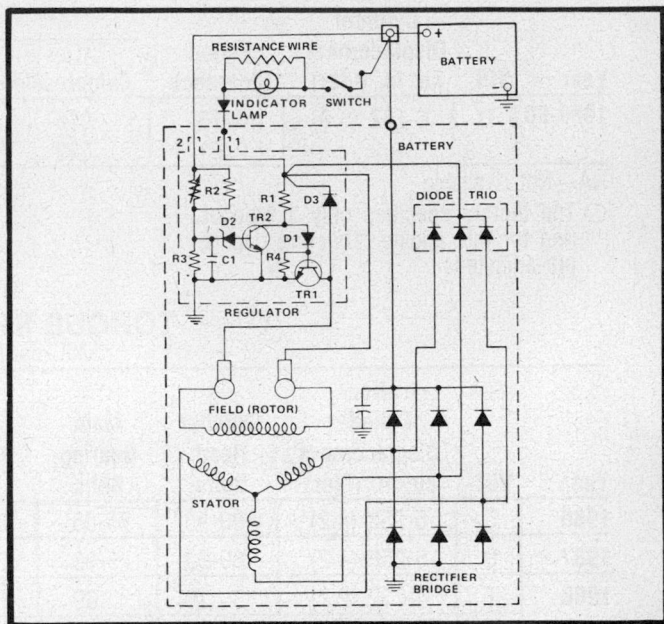

Delco S–10 charging system schematic

2. Remove the lower splash shield.
3. Loosen, but do not remove the locking bolt and adjusting nut from the drive belt tension adjuster.
4. Remove the lower alternator mounting nut. The nut is also used by the top tensioner mount.
5. Loosen the top alternator mounting bolt. Remove the tensioner from the alternator.

NOTE: Never use a sharp instrument to remove the drive belt from the pulley. The belt is made of synthetic material and may be damaged.

6. Remove the serpentine drive belt from the alternator pulley.
7. Disconnect and tag the alternator wiring. Remove the top alternator mounting bolt.
8. Remove the alternator from the engine.
To install:
9. Position alternator and install the top mounting bolt.
10. Install alternator lower mounting nut and tensioner. Tighten mounting nut finger tight.
11. Install electrical connectors. Install serpentine belt.
12. Tighten tensioner nut finger tight and tensioner adjuster nut to obtain proper belt tension.
13. Tighten all mounting bolts and nuts.
14. Install splash shield and lower vehicle.
15. Reconnect battery negative cable and check alternator operation.

SUMMIT

1. Disconnect negative battery cable.
2. Remove left hand under panel.
3. Remove the drive belts.
4. Remove water pump pulleys.
5. Remove alternator mounting bracket and pivot bolt.
6. On vehicle equipped with a 1.6L engine, remove the battery holder, battery, washer tank and battery tray. Remove the attaching bolts at top of radiator and move radiator to provide clearance. Do not remove the radiator hoses.

7. Disconnect alternator electrical connections and remove alternator.

8. Installation is the reverse of the removal procedure.

9. Adjust engine drive belts.

VOLTAGE REGULATOR

All models are equipped with an internal voltage regulator. Removal and installation requires alternator disassembly. Refer to the Unit Repair Section for the procedure.

BELT TENSION

Procedure

EAGLE

The serpentine drive belts are tensioned to a specific rating with the use of an appropriate belt tension gauge, placed on the belt midway between the pulleys. Install the gauge on the longest belt span possible. If the belt is notched on the inner surface, place the middle finger of the tensioner into 1 of the notches. Correct belt tension is 140–160 lbs.

PREMIER, MEDALLION AND SUMMIT

A single serpentine belt is used to drive all engine accessories. On Premier with 2.5L engine, the drive belt tension is adjusted with the power steering pump. On Premier with 3.0L engine, the drive belt tension is adjusted with the alternator. On Medallion and Summit, the drive belt tension is adjusted with the belt tension adjuster bolt, next to the alternator.

Place the tension gauge on the longest belt span between pulleys, when checking and adjusting belt tension.

Starting System

STARTER

Removal and Installation

EAGLE

1. Disconnect the negative battery cable.
2. Raise and support the vehicle safely.
3. Disconnect the starter motor wiring.
4. Remove the starter motor mounting bolts and remove the starter. Retain any shims which may have been used to align it with the ring gear.
5. Install the starter with any shims and tighten the mounting bolts to 18 ft. lbs.
6. Connect the starter motor wiring and lower the vehicle.
7. Connect the negative battery cable and check the starter motor operation.

PREMIER

1. Disconnect the negative battery cable. Raise and support the vehicle safely.
2. Disconnect and tag the starter motor wiring.
3. On 2.5L engine, remove the starter motor mounting bolts. Remove the starter motor from the engine and remove the bushing in the starter motor mounting plate.
4. On 3.0L engine, remove the starter motor mounting bolts. Remove the starter motor and mounting plate from the engine.
5. Installation is the reverse of the removal procedure. Check for proper operation.

MEDALLION

1. Disconnect the negative battery cable. Raise and support the vehicle safely.

DRIVE BELT ADJUSTMENT TENSIONS

	New Belt		Used Belt	
	Ft. Lbs.	Newtons	Ft. Lbs.	Newtons
Serpentine Drive Belt				
Four and Six Cylinder Engines	180-200	800-890	140-160	616-704
Alternator Drive Vee Belt				
Four and Six Cylinder Engines	125-155	556-689	90-115	400-512
Air Condition Compressor Vee Belt				
Four and Six Cylinder Engines	125-155	556-689	90-115	400-512
Air Pump Vee Belt				
Four Cylinder Engine	125-155	556-689	90-115	400-512
Six Cylinder Engine W/O P.S.	125-155	556-689	90-115	400-512
Six Cylinder Engine W/P.S.	65-75	289-334	60-70	267-311
Power Steering Vee Belt				
All Engines	125-155	556-689	90-115	400-512

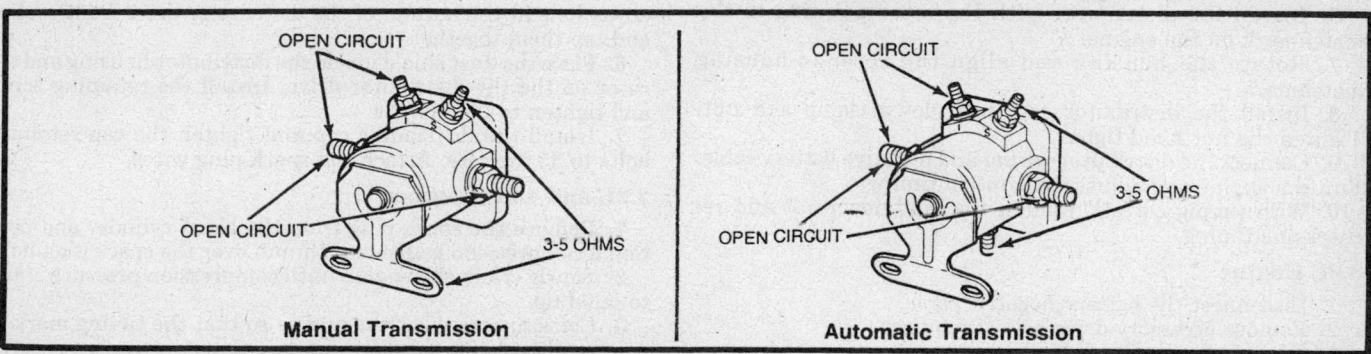

Starter solenoid ohmmeter check

2. Remove the 3 starter motor mounting bracket bolts and remove the bracket from the starter motor.

3. With the bracket removed, disconnect and tag the starter motor wiring.

4. Remove the rear starter motor mounting bolts.

5. Support the starter motor and remove the front mounting bolt.

6. Remove the starter motor and locating bushing from the engine.

7. Transfer the rear mount from the old starter motor to the new motor.

To install:

8. Place the bushing in the front starter motor mount on the engine.

9. Install the starter motor on the engine and tighten the mounting bolts.

10. Connect the starter motor wiring.

11. Install the starter motor mounting bracket and tighten the mounting bolts.

12. Lower the vehicle and connect the negative battery cable.

13. Check the starter motor operation when finished.

SUMMIT

1. Disconnect the negative battery cable.

2. Remove air cleaner assembly.

3. Remove heat shield from beneath intake manifold.

4. Disconnect and tag starter motor electrical connections.

5. Remove starter motor mounting bolts and remove starter.

To install:

6. Position starter motor and install mounting bolts.

7. Reconnect all electrical connections.

8. Install heat shield to intake manifold and install air cleaner assembly.

9. Reconnect battery negative cable and check starter motor operation.

Ignition System

DISTRIBUTOR

Removal and Installation

TIMING NOT DISTURBED

Except 3.0L Engine

1. Disconnect the negative battery cable. Remove the distributor cap with the wires attached.

2. Matchmark the position of the rotor tip to the distributor housing and engine.

3. Disconnect and tag the distributor wiring and vacuum hose(s).

4. Remove the distributor hold down bolt and pull the distributor up out of the engine. Note the position of the rotor in relation to the engine as the rotor stops rotating.

5. Do not rotate the engine with the distributor removed.

6. Install the distributor with the rotor pointing to the matchmark on the engine.

7. Rotate the housing and align the rotor-to-housing matchmark.

8. Install the distributor cap, hold down clamp and nut. Tighten the nut hand tight.

9. Connect the distributor wiring and negative battery cable. Run the engine and adjust the ignition timing.

10. With timing correct, tighten the hold down nut and recheck the timing.

3.0L Engine

1. Disconnect the battery negative cable.

2. Remove accessory drive belt, if required.

3. Remove the timing belt cover.

4. Remove the spark plug wires from the spark plugs.

5. Remove the screws retaining the distributor cap.

6. Remove the screw that attach the distributor drive to the rotor and remove the rotor. Remove the dust shield from inside the housing.

7. Separate the distributor drive front and rear sections. Remove the distributor housing attaching bolts and remove the housing and seal.

To install:

8. Lightly coat the seal lips with clean engine oil and install the seal and housing.

9. Install the distributor drive rear section through the back of the cover, past the seal and into the housing.

10. Line up the dowel in the top of the rear section with the dowel hole in the bottom of the distributor drive front section and tap them together.

11. Place the dust shield inside the distributor housing and the rotor on the the distributor drive. Install the retaining screw and tighten to 26 inch lbs.

12. Install the distributor cap and tighten the cap retaining bolts to 35 inch lbs. Attach the spark plug wires.

TIMING DISTURBED

1.5L and 1.6L Engines

1. Remove the spark plug from the No. 1 cylinder and position a compression gauge or a thumb over the spark plug hole.

2. Slowly crank the engine until compression pressure starts to build up.

3. Continue cranking the engine so that the timing mark or pointer aligns with the TDC mark.

4. Align the distributor housing mark with gear mating mark. The mating mark on the distributor is located at the lower edge of the distributor shaft housing.

5. Install the distributor while aligning the fine cut (groove or projection) on the distributor flange with the center of the distributor hold down stud.

6. Install distributor hold down nut, spark plug wires, electrical and vacuum connections. Recheck ignition timing.

NOTE: Some engines may be sensitive to the routing of the distributor sensor wires. If routed near the high-voltage coil wire or spark plug wires, the electromagnetic field surrounding the high-voltage wires could generate an occasional disruption of the ignition system operation.

3.0L ENGINE

1. Remove the spark plug from the No. 1 cylinder and position a compression gauge or a thumb over the spark plug hole.

2. Slowly crank the engine until compression pressure starts to build up.

3. Continue cranking the engine so that the timing mark or pointer aligns with the TDC mark.

4. Install the distributor drive rear section through the back of the cover, past the seal and into the housing.

5. Line up the dowel in the top of the rear section with the dowel hole in the bottom of the distributor drive front section and tap them together.

6. Place the dust shield inside the distributor housing and the rotor on the distributor drive. Install the retaining screw and tighten to 26 inch lbs.

7. Install the distributor cap and tighten the cap retaining bolts to 35 inch lbs. Attach the spark plug wires.

2.2L and 4.2L Engines

1. Remove the spark plug from the No. 1 cylinder and position a compression gauge or a thumb over the spark plug hole.

2. Slowly crank the engine until compression pressure starts to build up.

3. Continue cranking the engine so that the timing mark or pointer aligns with the TDC mark.

4. Install the distributor with its drive meshed, so that the ro-

tor points to the No. 1 terminal on the distributor cap with No. 1 cylinder piston at TDC.

5. Complete installation in the reverse order of removal and adjust the timing as required.

NOTE: Some engines may be sensitive to the routing of the distributor sensor wires. If routed near the high-voltage coil wire or spark plug wires, the electromagnetic field surrounding the high-voltage wires could generate an occasional disruption of the ignition system operation.

2.5L Engine

1. Rotate the engine until the No. 1 piston is at TDC compression.
2. Using an appropriate tool inserted in the distributor hole, rotate the oil pump gear so that the slot in the oil pump shaft is slightly past the 3 o'clock position, relative to the length of the engine block.
3. With the distributor cap removed, install the distributor

with the rotor at the 5 o'clock position, relative to the oil pump gear shaft slot. When the distributor is completely in place, the rotor should be at the 6 o'clock position. If not, remove the distributor and perform the entire procedure again.

4. Tighten the lockbolt.

IGNITION TIMING

Adjustment

1.5L AND 1.6L ENGINES

1. Run engine until normal operating temperature is reached.
2. Turn all accessories **OFF**. Place transaxle in **P** for automatic transaxles or **N** for manual transaxles.
3. Connect a timing light.
4. Insert a paper clip behind the tach terminal connector and connect a tachometer to the paper clip.

NOTE: Do not separate connector. The paper clip should be inserted along terminal surface.

5. Check and adjust curb idle speed.
6. Stop the engine and jumper ignition timing adjustment connector (located in engine compartment) to ground.
7. Start engine and run at curb idle. Check ignition timing.
8. On 1.5L engine, if ignition timing is not within specification, loosen the distributor hold down nut and adjust an necessary. Tighten hold down nut after adjustment. Stop the engine.
9. On 1.6L engine, if ignition timing is not within specification, loosen the crank angle sensor mounting nut and adjust by turning the crank angle sensor. Tighten the hold down nut after adjustment. Stop the engine.
10. Remove jumper wire from ignition timing adjustment connector. Start engine and recheck ignition timing. Adjust idle to specification.
11. Stop the engine. Remove tachometer and paper clip.

2.2L, 2.5L AND 3.0L ENGINES

Ignition timing on 2.2L and 3.0L engines is adjusted by the vehicle's Electronic Control Unit (ECU). The ECU uses input from sensors in the engine to determine various conditions during operation such as, manifold pressure, engine speed, manifold air temperature and coolant temperature. These inputs allow the ECU to adjust the timing under a variety of engine conditions. Therefore no timing adjustment is needed for normal vehicle service.

4.2L ENGINE

A scale located on the timing chain cover and a notch milled into the vibration damper are used as references to set ignition timing. Do not use the timing probe socket as a reference point to

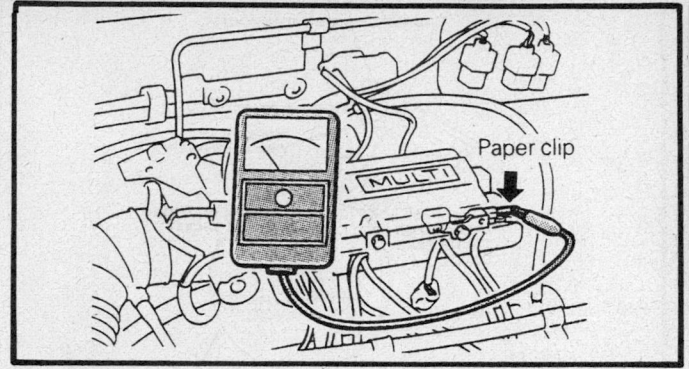

Tachometer connector typical (1.5L and 1.6L engines)

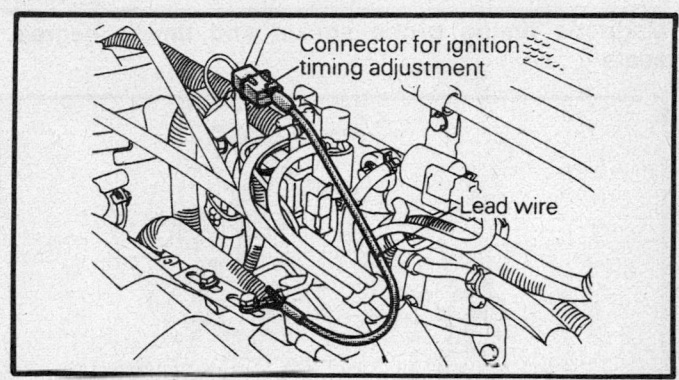

Ignition timing adjustment connector typical—(1.5L and 1.6L engines)

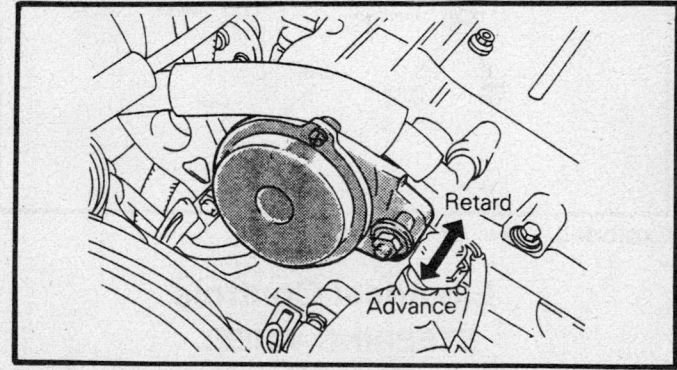

Crank angle sensor—1.6L engine

check the ignition timing when using a conventional timing light.

1. Have the engine at normal operating temperature.
2. Disconnect the 3 wire connector to the vacuum input switch.
3. Disconnect and plug the distributor vacuum advance hose.
4. Attach a timing light and a tachometer to the electrical system of the engine.
5. Start the engine and increase the speed to 1600 rpm while observing the initial timing with the timing light.
6. If necessary, adjust the ignition timing to specifications.

NOTE: If the specifications listed in the charts differ from the specifications on the emission control label, use the specifications as listed on the label.

7. Remove the timing light and the tachometer from the engine wiring.

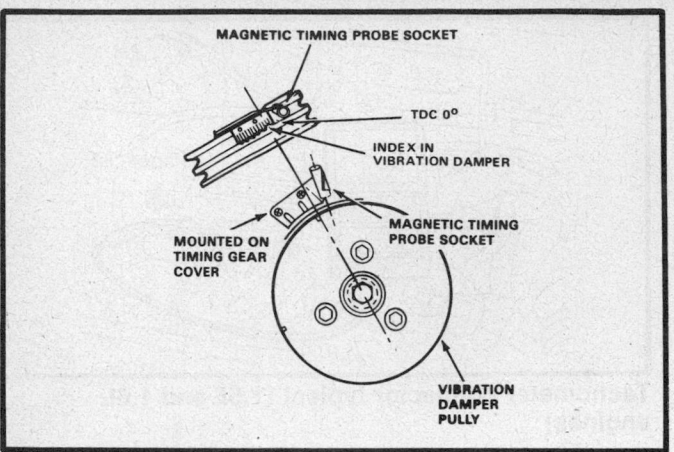

Magnetic timing probe socket and timing degree scale

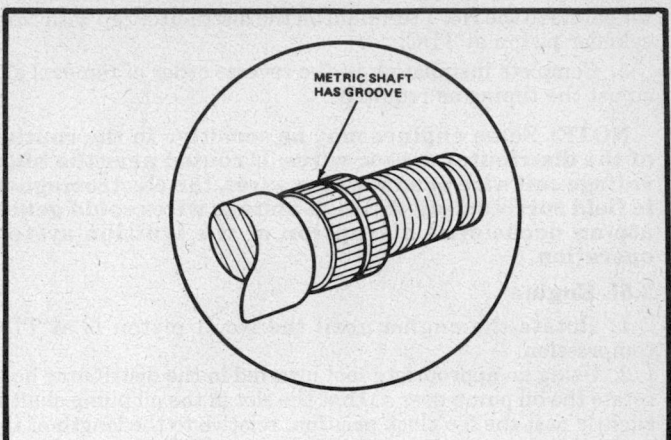

Identification of metric steering shaft

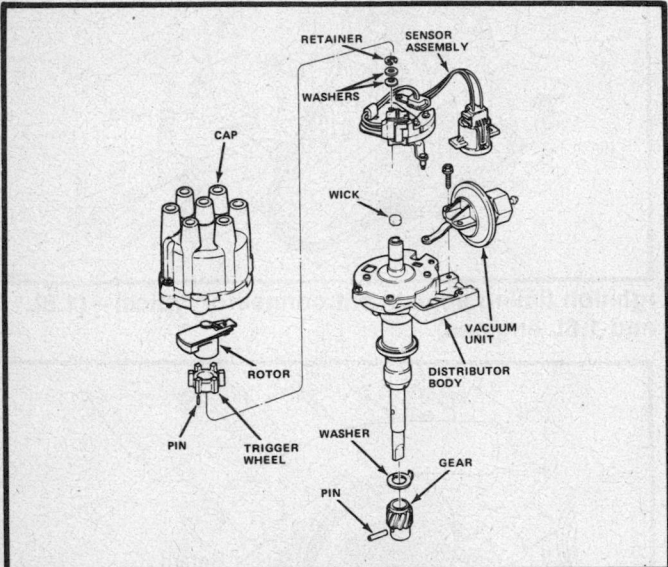

Exploded view of SSI distributor

Electrical Controls
STEERING WHEEL

Removal and Installation

EAGLE

1. Disconnect the negative battery cable.
2. Remove the horn button and disconnect the wires.
3. Remove the steering wheel center nut and washer. Before removing the wheel, note the position of the index marks on the wheel and the steering shaft. If none are present, paint an alignment mark on the shaft and wheel.
4. Remove the wheel with a puller.

NOTE: Do not hammer on the end of the steering shaft; the plastic retainers could shear, which maintain the rigidity of the energy-absorbing steering column.

5. Installation is the reverse of removal. Tighten the steering wheel nut to 20 ft. lbs.

NOTE: Some shafts have metric threads. These can be identified by a groove in the shaft splines. Metric nuts are coded blue.

PREMIER AND MEDALLION

1. Disconnect the negative battery cable.
2. Unsnap the horn button and disconnect the wires. Remove the horn button.
3. Note the position of the reference mark on the end of the steering shaft. Remove the nut and slide the wheel off the shaft. If required, use a suitable steering wheel puller.
4. Install the electrical connector. Align the pin on the turn signal cam with the pin bore in the steering wheel and slide the wheel into place.
5. Align the wheel with the reference mark on the steering shaft and install the nut. Tighten the nut to 52 ft. lbs.
6. Connect the negative battery cable.

SUMMIT

1. Disconnect battery negative cable.
2. Remove horn pad. Disconnect horn button connector.
3. Remove steering wheel attaching nut.
4. Make mating marks on the steering wheel and shaft for proper installation position.
5. Using a suitable puller, remove the steering wheel.

NOTE: Do not hammer on steering wheel to remove it. The collapsible column mechanism may be damaged.

To install:
6. Position the steering wheel on shaft with mating marks aligned.
7. Install the steering wheel attaching nut and torque to 33 ft. lbs. (45 Nm).
8. Reconnect the horn button and connector. Install the horn pad.
9. Reconnect battery negative cable.

HORN SWITCH

Removal and Installation

EAGLE

1. Disconnect the negative battery cable.
2. On steering wheels with center horn buttons, remove the button by first lifting it up and then pulling it out. On other types, remove the mounting screws at the back of the wheel and pull the horn wire plastic retainer out of the turn signal cancelling cam and remove the button.
3. Remove the steering wheel retaining nut.
3. Use a steering wheel puller to remove the steering wheel.
4. Remove the cancelling cam.

NOTE: Do not hammer on the end of shaft.

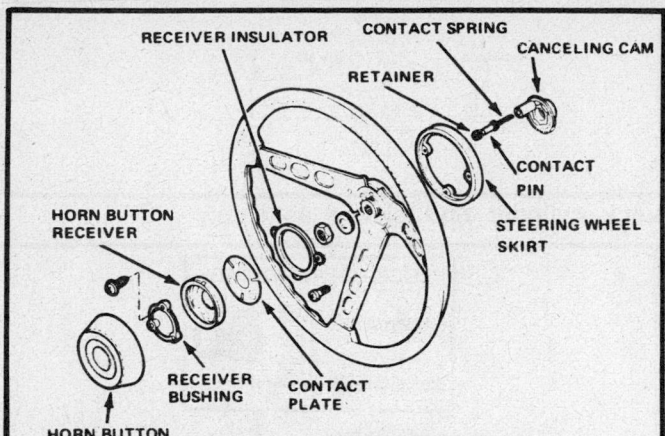

Sport steering wheel and horn switch components

5. Install in reverse order of the removal procedure.

PREMIER AND MEDALLION

1. Disconnect the negative battery cable.
2. Remove the horn pad from the center of the steering wheel and disconnect the electrical wires.
3. Connect the electrical leads and push the horn pad into place. Connect the negative battery cable.

SUMMIT

1. Disconnect battery negative cable.
2. Remove the horn pad.
3. Using a suitable puller, remove the steering wheel.

NOTE: Do not hammer on steering wheel to remove it. To do so may damage the collapsible mechanism.

4. Remove horn switch.
5. To install, reverse removal procedure.

IGNITION LOCK

Removal and Installation

EAGLE

1. Disconnect the negative battery cable. On vehicles equipped with tilt steering wheels, place the wheel in the straight ahead position. Remove the steering wheel.
2. Loosen the anti-theft cover attaching screws and remove the cover from the column.

NOTE: Do not hammer on the shaft. Do not move the screws from the cover; they are attached to it with plastic retainers.

3. To remove the lockplate, a special compressor is required. Depress the lockplate with the tool and pry the snapring from the groove in the steering shaft. Remove the tool, snapring, plate, turn signal cam, upper bearing preload spring and thrust washer from the shaft.
4. Place the turn signal lever in the right turn position and remove it.
5. Depress the hazard warning switch button and remove it by rotating it counterclockwise. Remove the package tray, (if equipped) and the lower trim panel.

NOTE: In the next steps, provision is made for pulling the direction signal switch wiring harness entirely out of the steering column to replace the lock cylinder. Many times, this is not necessary. Follow the first part of the procedure in Step 7, pulling the wiring upward using normal slack, in order to get the turn signal switch far enough away from the lock cylinder for clearance.

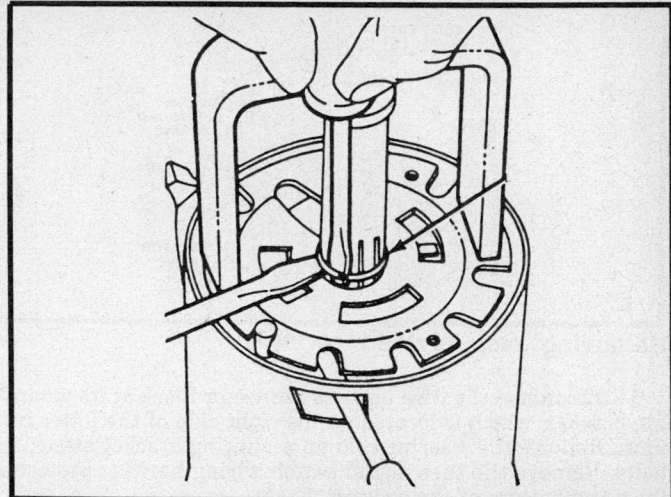

Removing lock plate retainer and snap ring

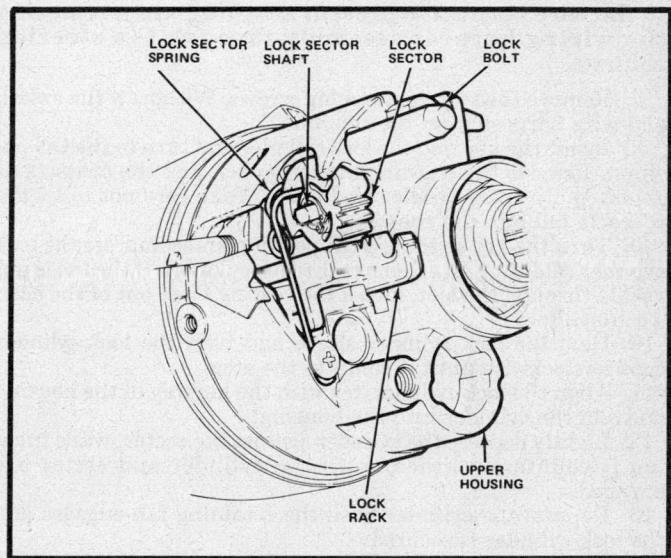

Position of lock sector tension spring

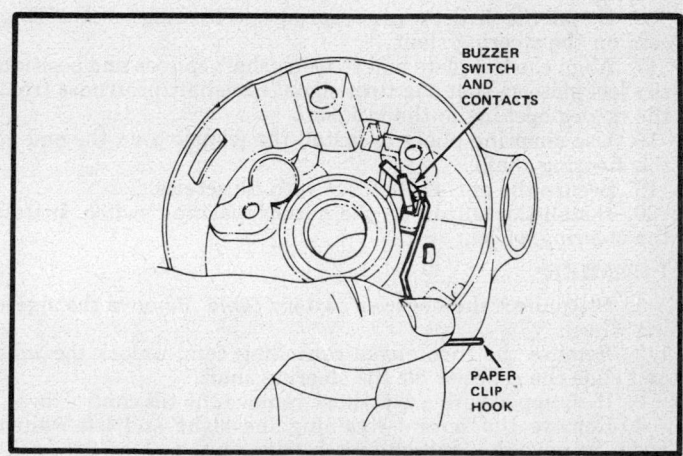

Removing buzzer switch and contacts

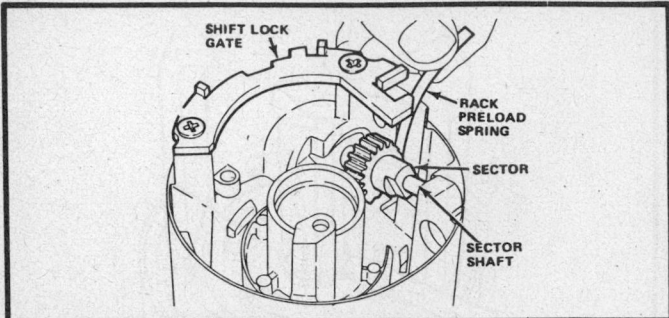

Removing rack preload spring

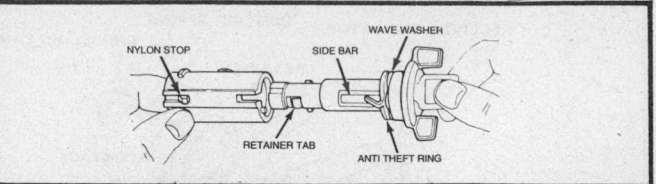

Lock cylinder and sleeve assembly

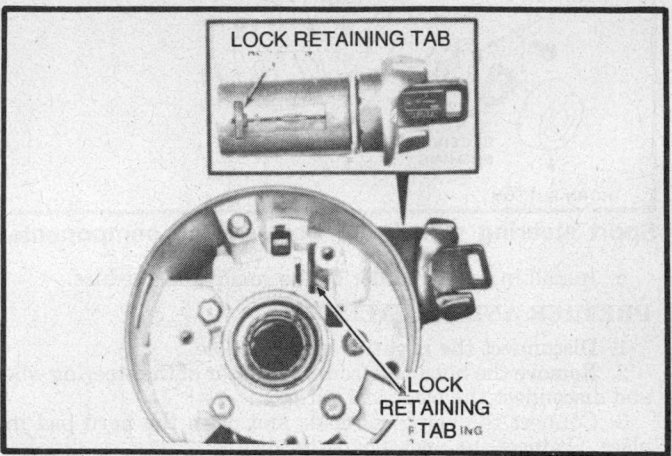

Ignition lock cylinder retaining tab. Insert small probe in access slot to release lock cylinder

6. Disconnect the wire harness connector block at its mounting bracket, which is located on the right side of the lower column. Remove the steering column mounting bracket attaching bolts. Remove the turn signal switch wiring harness protector from the bottom of the column.

NOTE: To aid in the removal and replacement of the directional switch harness, tape the harness connector to the wire harness to prevent snagging when removing the wiring harness assembly through the steering column.

7. Remove the switch attaching screws. Withdraw the switch and wire harness from the column.
8. Insert the key into the lock cylinder and turn to the **ON** position. Remove the warning buzzer switch and the contacts as an assembly using needlenosed pliers. Take care not to let the contacts fall into the column.
9. Turn the key to the **LOCK** position and compress the lock cylinder retaining tab. Remove the lock cylinder. If the tab is not visible through the slot, knock the casting flash out of the slot.
To install:
10. Hold the lock cylinder sleeve and turn the lock cylinder counterclockwise until it contacts the stop.
11. Align the lock cylinder key with the keyway in the housing and slip the cylinder into the housing.
12. Lightly depress the cylinder against the sector, while turning it counterclockwise, until the cylinder and sector are engaged.
13. Depress the cylinder until the retaining tab engages and the lock cylinder is secured.
14. Install the turn signal switch. Be sure that the actuating lever pivot is properly seated and aligned in the top of the housing boss, before installing it with its screws.
15. Install the turn signal lever and check the operation of the switch.
16. Install the thrust washer, spring and turn signal cancelling cam on the steering shaft.
17. Align the lockplate and steering shaft splines and position the lockplate so that the turn signal camshaft protrudes from the dogleg opening in the lockplate.
18. Use snapring pliers to install the snapring on the end of the steering shaft.
19. Secure the anti-theft cover with its screws.
20. Install the button on the hazard warning switch. Install the steering wheel.

PREMIER

1. Disconnect the negative battery cable. Remove the steering wheel.
2. Remove the turn signal cancelling cam, unlock the tabs and slide the canceler off the steering shaft.
3. If equipped with a tilt wheel, remove the tilt control lever.
4. Remove the screws retaining the right and left switch pods. Remove the ignition switch trim ring.
5. Remove the screws from the pod housing/column cover.

Remove the pod housing/column cover by pulling it up, guide the pods through the cover and remove the cover.
6. Insert the key into the ignition, lining up the key with groove in the lock cylinder housing. Push in the locking tab on the bottom of the housing, with a punch and remove the cylinder. Separate the switch from the wires by removing the screw retaining the connector.
To install:
7. Insert the key into the ignition lining up key with groove in lock cylinder housing.
8. Depress the tab, and install the lock cylinder.
9. Install the pod housing/column cover and install the pods. Install the ignition switch trim ring.

NOTE: The retaining clips on the left and right switch pods must be in place when the switches are installed.

10. Install the tilt lever, if equipped. Install the turn signal cam with pin bore in the steering wheel. Reconnect electrical connector.
11. Align the reference mark on the steering shaft and install the steering wheel. Reconnect the negative battery cable.

MEDALLION

1. Disconnect the negative battery cable.
2. Remove the screws from the lower steering column cover and remove the cover.
3. On vehicles equipped with cruise control, pull down on the piece of wire at the forward edge of the cover. This will pull the spring loaded cruise control commutator into its housing.
4. Remove the upper and lower steering column covers. Remove the screws retaining the lower instrument panel and remove the panel.
5. Remove the ignition switch cover. Remove the ignition switch mounting screw.
6. Insert the key into the ignition and turn it to the unmarked arrow on the switch. Push in the locking tabs on the side of the housing with a punch and remove the switch. Separate the switch from the wires by removing the screw retaining the connector.

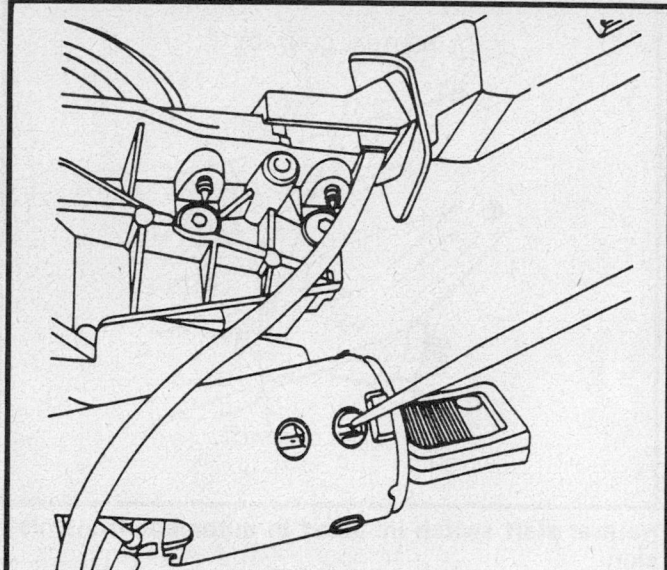

Removing lock cylinder—Medallion

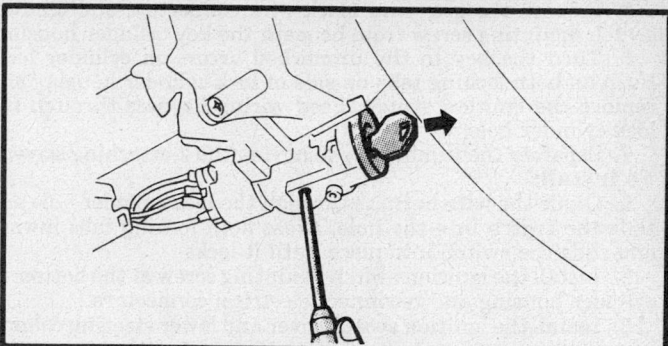

Removing lock cylinder—Summit

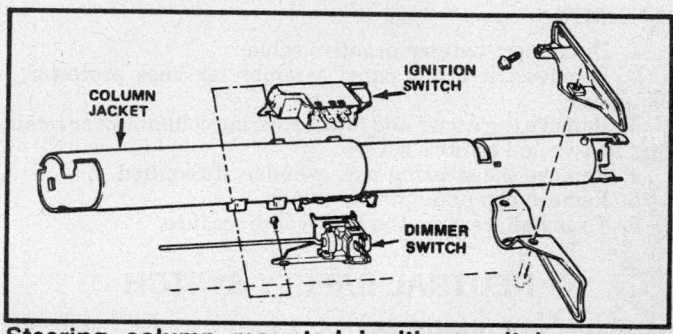

Steering column mounted ignition switch

7. Install the switch into the lock cylinder, push the wires through the cylinder hole. Push the locking tabs in and lock the switch in position.

8. Connect the electrical leads. Install the ignition switch cover. Install the trim covers.

9. Connect the negative battery cable.

SUMMIT

1. Disconnect battery negative cable.
2. Install the key into the ignition and turn to **ACC** position.
3. Using a cross-tip tool, push the lock pin on the lock cylinder inward and pull the lock cylinder from its housing.
4. Reverse removal procedure to install.

IGNITION SWITCH

Removal and Installation

EAGLE

The ignition switch is mounted on the lower steering column and is connected to the key lock by a remote lock rod.

1. Disconnect the negative battery cable.
2. With key in **OFF-LOCK** position, remove mounting screws, rod and wiring.
3. When installing, move slider to extreme left of switch pointing inward toward steering column. Put actuator rod in slider hole and install switch.
4. On tilt wheel columns, remove lash by pushing downward on switch before tightening mounting screws.

PREMIER

1. Disconnect battery negative cable.
2. Remove instrument panel lower cover attaching screws and remove cover.
3. Remove the horn pad. Disconnect the wires and remove the horn button.
4. Remove the steering wheel and the turn signal cancel cam.
5. If the vehicle is equipped with tilt wheel, remove the tilt lever.
6. Remove the screws retaining the right and left switch pods. Remove the ignition switch trim ring.
7. Remove the screws from the pod housing/column cover. Remove the pod housing/column cover by pulling it up, guide the pods through the cover and remove the cover.

8. Remove the lower column shroud attaching screws and remove lower shroud.
9. Remove the upper column shroud attaching screws and remove upper shroud.
10. Remove the ignition switch retaining screws and separate the switch from cylinder housing.
11. Cut the tie straps and remove the harness anchor.
12. Loosen the retaining nut in the center of the steering column connector and separate the switch pod connector by disengaging locking tabs.
13. Remove the electrical harness from the channels of steering column connector and remove the ignition switch assembly.
To install:
14. Slide the switch pod connectors into the ignition switch connector and install the nut.
15. Install the ignition switch and secure with retaining screws.
16. Route the wiring harness along the underside of steering column and secure with tie straps. Install the harness anchor and secure with retaining screw.
17. Follow the remaining removal procedure to complete installation.
18. When installing the steering wheel, align the pin on the turn signal cam with the pin bore on the steering wheel. Tighten the steering wheel nut to 52 ft. lbs. (70 Nm).
19. Reconnect battery negative cable.

MEDALLION

1. Disconnect battery negative cable.
2. Remove 4 screws from lower steering column cover.
3. On cruise control equipped vehicles, pull down on the wire at the forward edge of the lower cover. This allow the spring loaded commutator brush to be pull into its housing.

NOTE: If the lower steering cover is removed before the commutator brush is pulled into its housing, the brush will be broken off the cover.

4. Remove the upper steering column cover and ignition switch cover.

5. Remove the gray and black wire connectors and ignition switch mounting screw from beneath the key cylinder housing.

6. Turn the key to the unmarked arrow on cylinder lock. Push on both locking tabs on side of lock cylinder housing and remove the ignition switch. Feed wiring harness through the lock cylinder hole.

7. Separate the tumbler by removing the 2 attaching screws.

To install:

8. Guide the wire harness through the lock cylinder hole and slide the switch into the hole. Press both locking tabs inward and slide the switch into place until it locks.

9. Install the ignition switch mounting screw at the bottom of cylinder housing and reconnect electrical connectors.

10. Install the ignition switch cover and lower steering column cover.

11. Reconnect battery negative cable.

SUMMIT

1. Disconnect battery negative cable.

2. Remove the lower panel assembly or knee protector, if equipped.

3. Remove the upper and lower steering column cover retaining screws and remove covers.

4. Remove the steering lock cylinder, if required.

5. Remove clip and ignition switch.

6. To install, reverse the removal procedure.

NEUTRAL SAFETY SWITCH

Removal and Installation

EAGLE

1. Disconnect the negative battery cable.

2. Raise the vehicle and support safely.

3. Remove the 3 wire connector from the switch, located on the left side of the transmission.

4. Unscrew the switch from the case. Transmission fluid will drain from the case with the switch out.

5. Install the new switch and switch seal in the transmission case and torque to 24 ft. lbs.

6. Reconnect the 3 wire electrical connector.

7. Lower vehicle, test switch and correct the transmission fluid level.

PREMIER

1. Disconnect battery negative cable.

2. Disconnect the neutral switch harness connector located in the engine compartment.

3. Raise and support the vehicle safely. Remove the splash shield.

4. Remove the bolt attaching the switch bracket to transaxle case and remove switch from case.

To install:

5. Place a new O-ring on the switch and reverse removal procedure.

6. Lower the vehicle, reconnect switch harness connector and battery negative cable.

MEDALLION

A Multi-function switch located on the transaxle assembly allows the vehicle to start only in N and P positions.

1. Disconnect the negative battery cable.

2. Remove the electrical connection from switch.

3. Remove the switch mounting screws and remove the switch.

4. Installation is the reverse of the removal procedure.

SUMMIT

An Inhibitor switch located on the transaxle assembly allows the vehicle to start only in N and P positions.

1. Disconnect the negative battery cable.

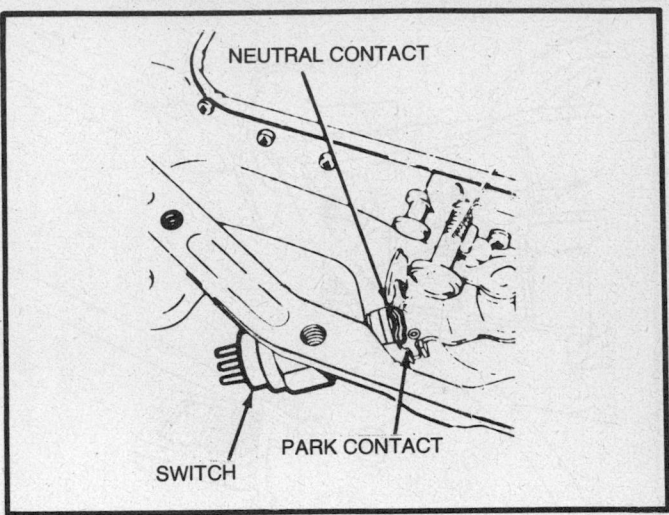

Neutral start switch installed in automatic transmission

2. Remove the electrical connection from switch.

3. Remove the switch mounting screws and remove the switch.

4. Installation is the reverse of the removal procedure.

Adjustment

SUMMIT

1. Place the selector lever in N position.

2. Loosen the control cable to manual control lever coupling adjusting nuts to set the cable and lever free.

3. Place the manual control lever in N position.

4. Turn inhibitor switch body until 0.47 in. wide end of manual control lever aligns with switch body flange 0.47 in. wide portion.

5. Tighten attaching bolts taking care not to allow the switch to change position.

STOPLIGHT SWITCH

Removal and Installation

EAGLE

1. Disconnect the negative battery cable.

2. Remove the package tray, if equipped.

3. Disconnect the electrical connector from the switch.

4. Remove the locknut from the switch assembly and remove the switch.

5. Install the new switch in the mounting bracket until it contacts the brake pedal stopper.

6. Depress the brake pedal several times to eliminate the vacuum in the power brake booster, then press the pedal down by hand and observe the amount of pedal free play. Free play should be ½ in.

7. After adjustment, secure the switch by tightening lock nut.

8. Connect the electrical wires to the switch. Connect the negative battery cable and check the operation of the brake lights.

PREMIER AND MEDALLION

1. Disconnect the negative battery cable.

2. Remove the bolt retaining the master cylinder pushrod to the brake pedal.

3. Disconnect the electrical wires from the stoplight switch and remove the switch.

4. Install the switch and the master cylinder pushrod to the brake pedal and install the retaining bolt.

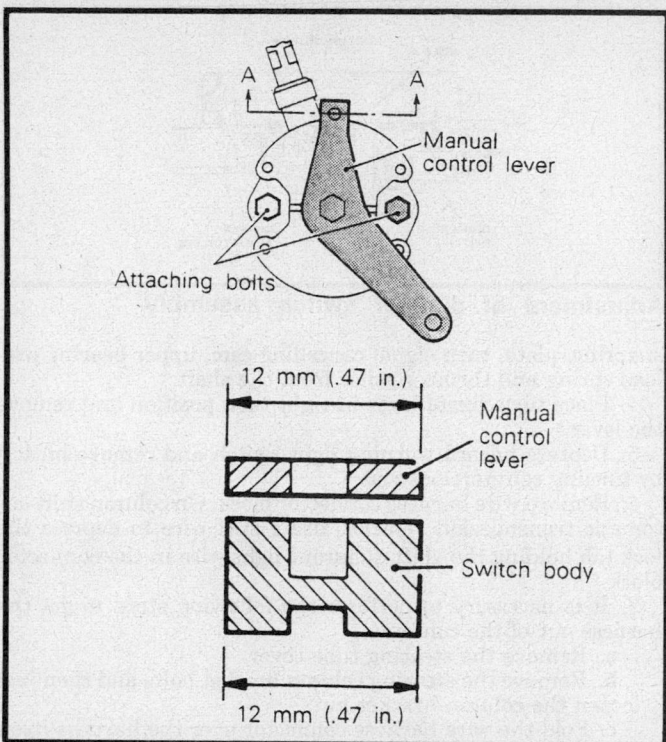

Inhibitor switch alignment—Summit

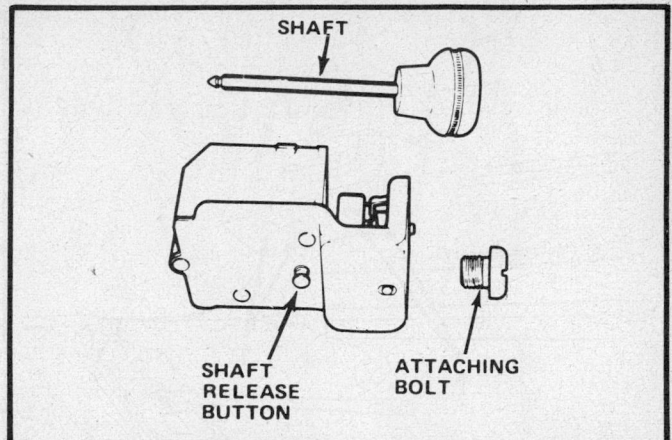

Light switch components—typical

5. Connect the electrical wires to the switch. Connect the negative battery cable and check the operation of the brake lights.

SUMMIT

1. Disconnect the negative battery cable.
2. Disconnect the stop light switch connector.
3. Loosen the switch locknut and remove switch.
4. Install the switch in until it contacts the brake pedal stopper.
5. Depress the brake pedal several times to eliminate the vacuum in the power brake booster, then press the pedal down by hand and observe the amount of pedal free play. Free play should be 0.1–0.3 in.
6. After adjustment, secure the switch by tightening lock nut.

HEADLIGHT SWITCH

Removal and Installation

EAGLE

1. Disconnect the negative battery cables.
2. Relocate anything preventing full access to switch such as instrument cluster bezel, package tray, speedometer cable or switch overlay assembly.
3. Remove screws and tilt cluster assembly away from instrument panel.
4. Place switch in full **ON** position. Pull on knob and press shaft release button to release shaft and knob assembly.
5. Remove mounting sleeve nut, wiring connector, ground wire and remove switch.
6. Installation is the reverse of the removal procedure.

SUMMIT

1. Disconnect battery negative cable.
2. Remove the sunglass pocket from side panel.
3. Remove the side panel or lower panel assembly, if necessary.

4. Remove knob and lock ring nut from switch. Remove switch.
5. To install, reverse removal procedure.

COMBINATION SWITCH

Removal and Installation

PREMIER

1. Disconnect the negative battery cable.
2. Remove instrument panel lower cover attaching screws and cover, if equipped.
3. Remove support bar attaching screws and remove support bar.
4. Move air duct aside and remove tie straps.
5. Loosen the retaining nut in center of steering column and separate column connector.
6. Separate the switch assembly connector from steering column connector by disengaging tab. Push on the wire side of left hand headlight switch pod connector and remove connector from channel.
7. Remove retaining screws from left hand switch pod and remove switch pod housing back cover. Pull the electrical harness through the housing and remove switch.
8. To install, reverse removal procedure.

MEDALLION

1. Disconnect the negative battery cable.
2. Remove the screws from the lower steering column cover and remove the cover.
3. On vehicles equipped with cruise control, pull down on the piece of wire at the forward edge of the cover. This will pull the spring loaded cruise control commutator into its housing.
4. Remove the upper and lower steering column covers.
5. Remove the 2 screws attaching the switch and remove the switch.
6. Disconnect the wire connectors.
7. Install the switch to the column and install the retaining screws. Install the steering column covers.
8. Install the lower steering column cover. Connect the negative battery cable.

SUMMIT

1. Disconnect battery negative cable.
2. Remove the lower panel assembly or knee protector, if equipped.
3. Remove the upper and lower steering column cover retaining screws and remove covers.
4. Remove the horn pad and steering wheel assembly.
5. Remove clip and switch assembly.
6. Installation is the reverse of the removal procedure.

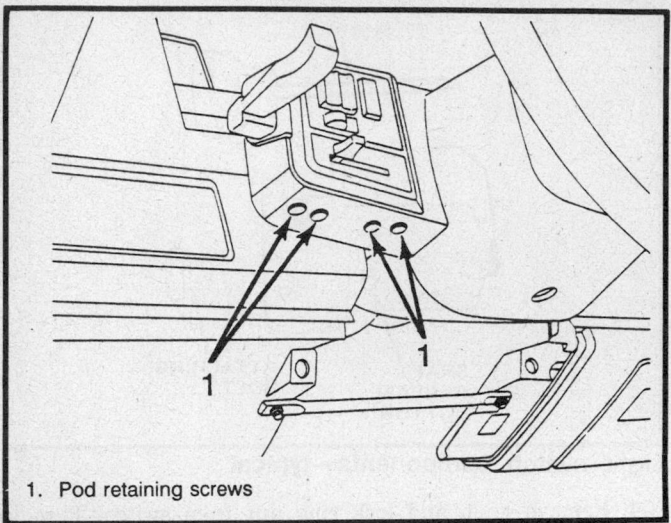

1. Pod retaining screws

Removing the pod assembly—Premier

DIMMER SWITCH

Removal and Installation

EAGLE

1. Disconnect the negative battery cable.
2. Remove the lower finish panel, tube cover and the package tray, if equipped.
3. Remove the wiring connector from the switch.
4. Tape the actuator rod to the column, remove the switch retaining screws and remove the switch by pulling it from the actuator rod.

To install:

5. Position the switch by pushing in onto the actuator rod and install the retaining screws.
6. Remove the tape holding the actuator rod to the column.
7. Adjust the switch by depressing it slightly and inserting a $\frac{3}{32}$ inch drill bit into the hole on the outer face of the switch. This prevents horizontal switch movement.
8. Move the switch towards the steering wheel to remove the lash from the actuator rod.
9. Tighten the switch retaining screws to 35 inch lbs. (4 Nm) torque.
10. Remove the drill bit and install the wiring connector.
11. Check the operation of the switch.
12. Install the finish panel, the tube cover and the package tray, if equipped.
13. Connect the negative battery cable.

TURN SIGNAL SWITCH

Removal and Installation

EAGLE

1. Disconnect the negative battery cable. On vehicles equipped with tilt steering wheels, place the wheel in the straight ahead position. Remove the steering wheel.
2. Loosen the anti-theft cover attaching screws and remove the cover from the column.

NOTE: Do not hammer on the shaft. Do not move the screws from the cover; they are attached to it with plastic retainers.

3. To remove the lockplate, a special compressor is required. Depress the lockplate with the tool and then pry the snapring from the groove in the steering shaft. Remove the tool,

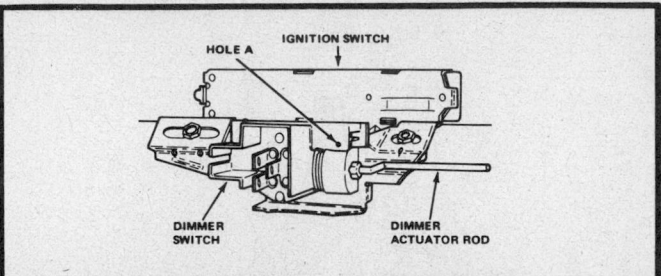

Adjustment of dimmer switch assembly

snapring, plate, turn signal cancelling cam, upper bearing pre-load spring and thrust washer from the shaft.

4. Place turn signal lever in right turn position and remove the lever.
5. Depress hazard warning light switch and remove button by turning counterclockwise.
6. Remove wire harness connector block. On column shift automatic transmission vehicles, use a stiff wire to depress the lock tab holding the shift quadrant light wire in the connector block.
7. It is necessary to perform the following steps to get the harness out of the column:
    a. Remove the steering tube cover.
    b. Remove the steering column bracket bolts and then just loosen the column bracket nuts.
    c. Fold the wire harness connector over the harness itself and then wrap it with tape to prevent snagging when it is removed.
8. Remove switch screws and pull the switch and wire harness out of the column. If necessary, lift the column when pulling the switch and harness out. If the vehicle has a tilt column, also remove the plastic harness protector when raising the column.
9. Install in reverse order. If the column nuts and bolts have been loosened, make sure to retorque the bolts to 15 ft. lbs. and the nuts to 10 ft. lbs.

WINDSHIELD WIPER SWITCH

Removal and Installation

EAGLE

1. Disconnect the negative battery cable.
2. Remove the control knob. A flat blade tool can be used to overcome the spring tension which holds the knob in place.
3. Separate switch from instrument panel and wiring. Remove the switch.
4. Install in reverse order.

WINDSHIELD WIPER MOTOR

Removal and Installation

EAGLE

1. Disconnect the negative battery cable.
2. Remove the wiper arms and blades.
3. Remove the attaching screws, the wiring connector and pull the motor and linkage out of the dash panel opening.
4. Raise up the lock tab of the drive link-to-crank stud retaining clip and slide the clip from the stud. Remove the wiper motor retaining bolts and remove the wiper motor assembly.
5. The installation is the reverse of the removal procedure. Check for positive retention of the retaining clip on the crank stud.

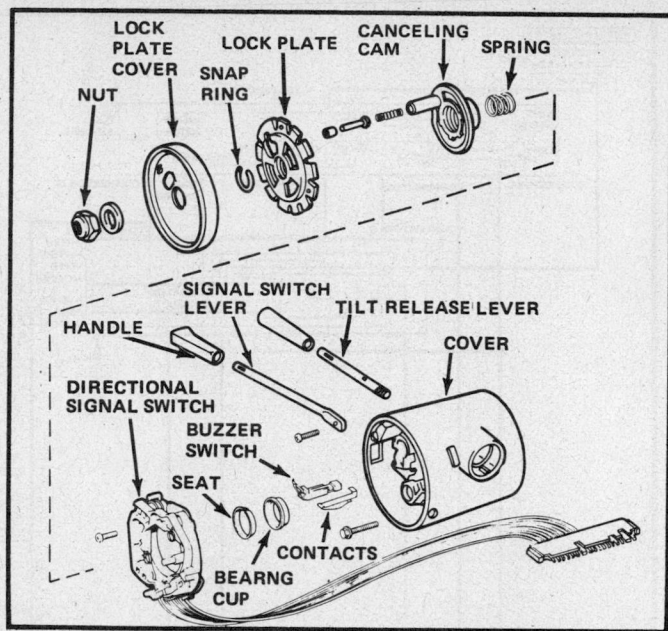

Turn signal switch and component parts

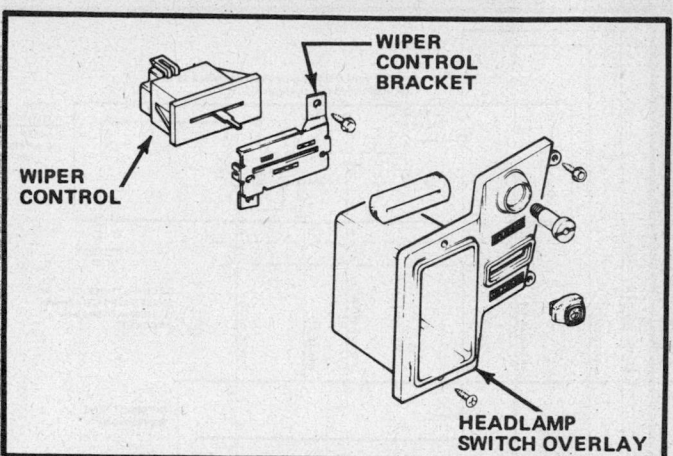

Wiper switch mounting components—typical

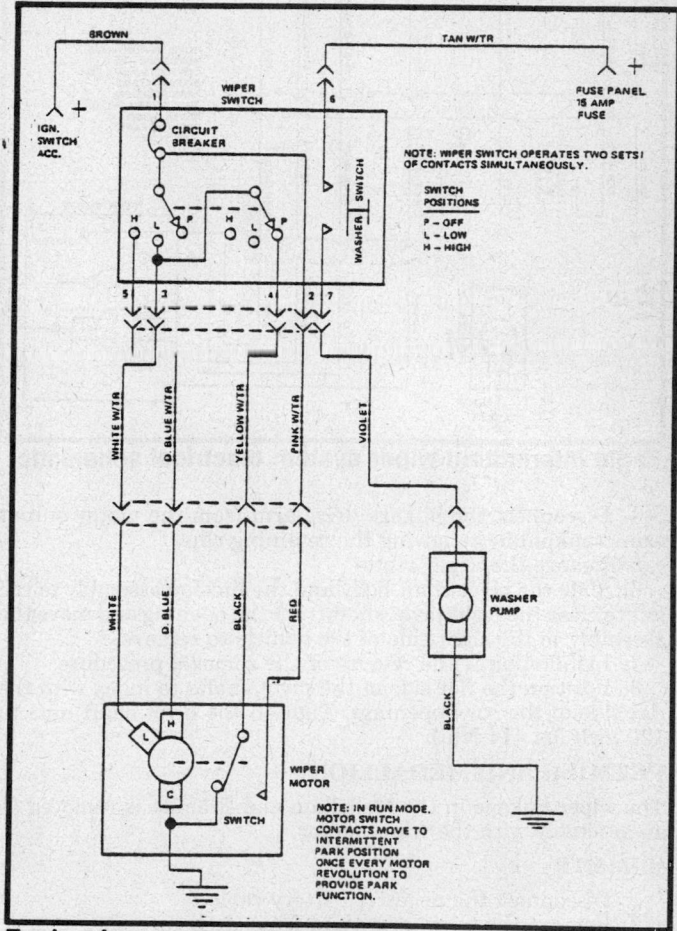

Eagle wiper system electrical schematic

6. Tighten the attaching screws to 25 inch lbs. (3 Nm).
7. After locating the park position of the motor, install the arms and blades.

PREMIER

1. Disconnect the negative battery cable.
2. Remove the wiper arms. Remove the screws retaining the left and right cowl screens and remove both screens.
3. Remove the motor and linkage mounting screws.
4. Disconnect the electrical connector and remove the motor and linkage as an assembly.
5. Install the motor/linkage assembly and connect the electrical leads.
6. Install the cowl screens and the wiper arms. Connect the negative battery cable.

MEDALLION

1. Disconnect the negative battery cable.
2. Remove the wiper arms. Remove the screws retaining the cowl in front of the windhield and remove the cowl.
3. Disconnect the electrical plug at the wiper motor. Remove the screws retaining the wiper motor and transmission and remove the assembly.
4. Install the wiper and transmission assembly. Connect the electrical plug to the wiper motor.
5. Install the cowl and the wiper arms.
6. Connect the negative battery cable.

SUMMIT

1. Disconnect the negative battery cable.
2. Remove the wiper arms and front deck garnish.
3. Remove windshield holder, clips, deck covers and air inlet garnish.
4. Disconnect the electrical connector.
5. Remove wiper motor mounting screws and remove motor assembly from linkage.
6. To install, reverse removal procedure.

DELAY WIPER CONTROLS

The delay wiper control provides a pause between wipe cycles for use during conditions of very slight precipitation.

WINDSHIELD WIPER LINKAGE

Removal and Installation

EAGLE

1. Disconnect the negative battery cable.
2. Remove the wiper arms and blades.
3. Remove the pivot shaft-to-cowl top attaching nuts and washers.

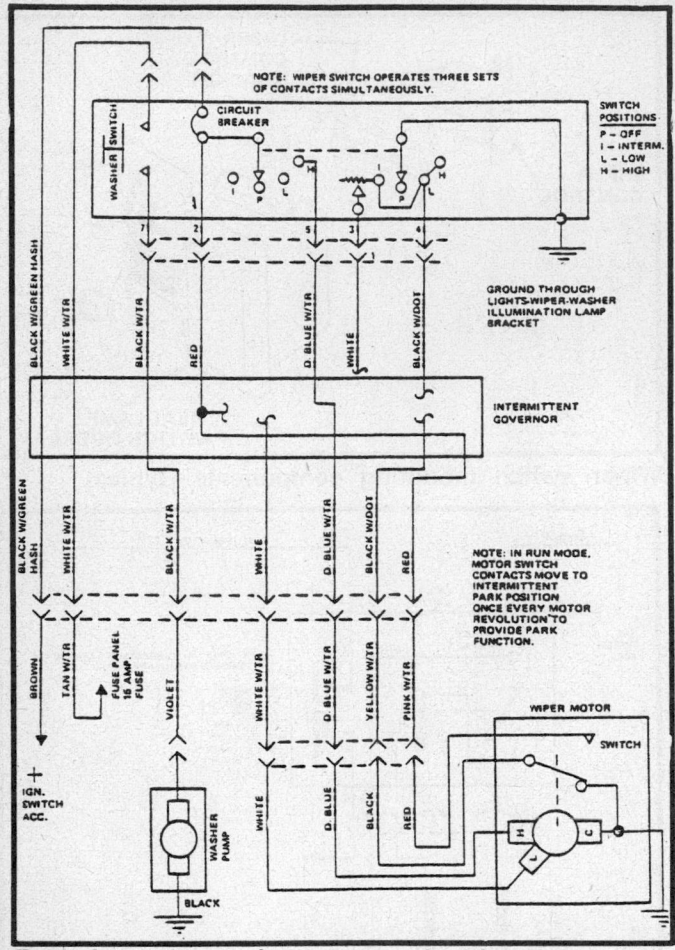

Eagle intermittent wiper system electrical schematic

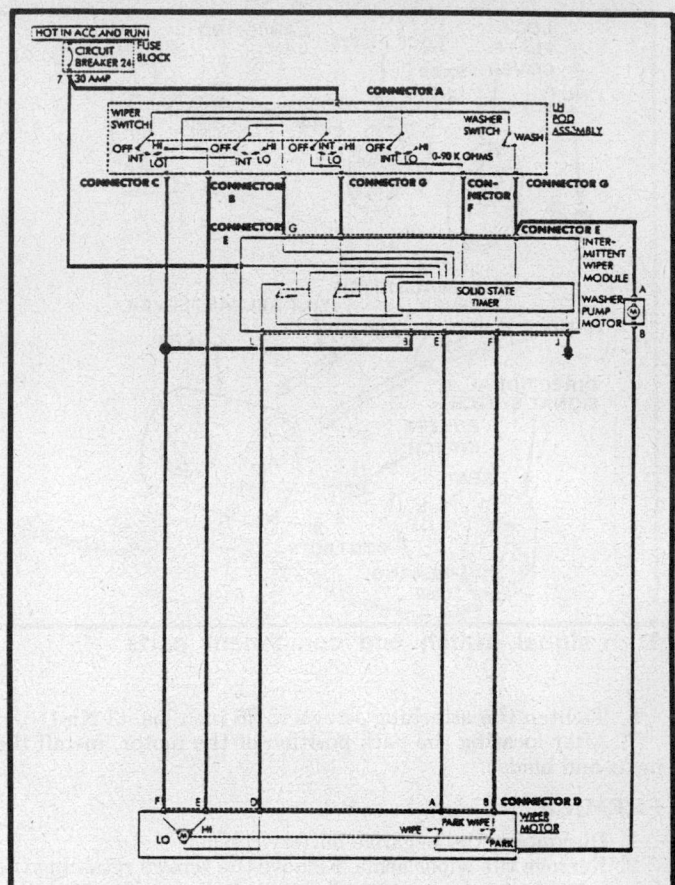

Premier intermittent wiper/washer electrical schematic

4. Disconnect the linkage drive arm from the motor output arm crankpin by removing the retaining clip.

5 Remove the wiper motor.

6. Slide the pivot shaft body and the linkage assembly to the left to clear the right pivot shaft from the opening and move the assembly to the right side of the vehicle to remove.

7. Installation is the reverse of the removal procedure.

8. Position the flat side of the pivot shafts to index with the flat side of the cowl openings. Tighten the pivot shaft nuts to 120 inch lbs. (14 Nm).

PREMIER AND MEDALLION

The wiper linkage in the Medallion and Premier is removed as an assembly with the wiper motor.

SUMMIT

1. Disconnect the negative battery cable.
2. Remove the wiper arms and front deck garnish.
3. Remove windshield holder, clips, deck cover and air inlet garnish.
4. Remove linkage to motor retaining screw and remove linkage.
5. Install is the reverse of the removal procedure.

Instrument Cluster

Removal and Installation

EAGLE

1. Disconnect the negative battery cable.

2. On certain vehicles, the lower steering column cover must be removed and the gear selector cable must be disconnected from the steering column shift shroud. Remove the package tray, if equipped.

3. Remove the bezel retaining screws across top, over radio and behind the glove box door. Disconnect wire to box light. Tip bezel outward at top and disengage bottom tabs.

4. Disconnect the speedometer cable and push down on the 3 illumination lamp housings above the bezel to clear the instrument panel.

5. Disconnect the headlamp switch, the wiper control connectors and the switch lamp. The headlamp switch is disconnected by lifting the 2 locking tabs to disconnect its electrical connector.

6. Remove the cluster illumination sockets and the instrument cluster wire connectors.

7. If equipped with clock or tachometer, remove their attaching screws. Disconnect the wiring harness from the printed circuit board.

8. Remove the cluster housing and circuit board to bezel attaching screws and remove the assembly from the bezel.

9. The installation is the reverse of the removal procedure. Make sure that the clock ground and feed wire terminals contact the foil beneath the circuit board mounting screws.

PREMIER

1. Disconnect the negative battery cable.
2. Remove the screws retaining the instrument cluster bezel and remove the bezel.
3. Remove the cluster retaining screws and tilt the cluster forward. Disconnect the electrical connectors.

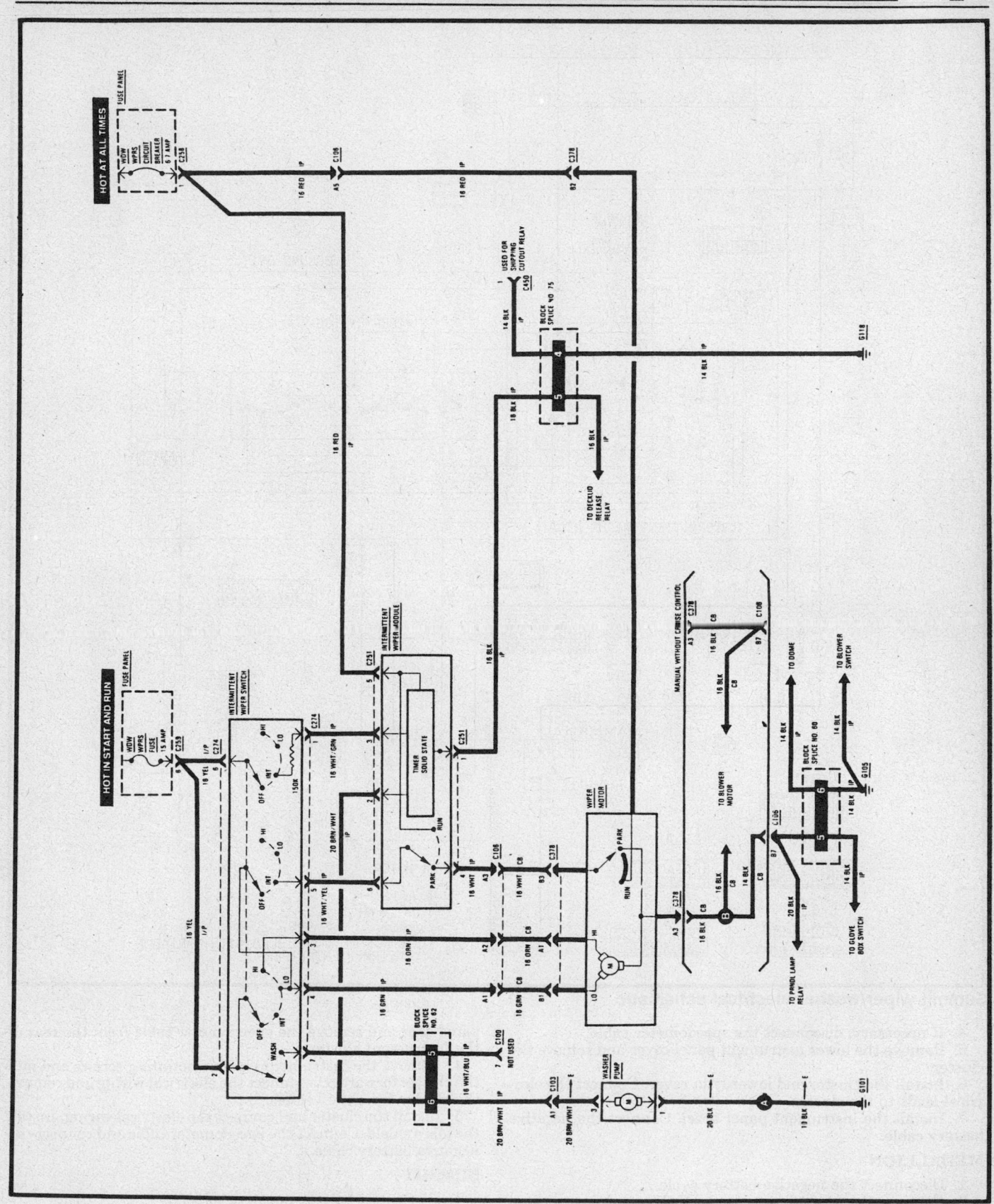

Medallion intermittent wiper system electrical schematic

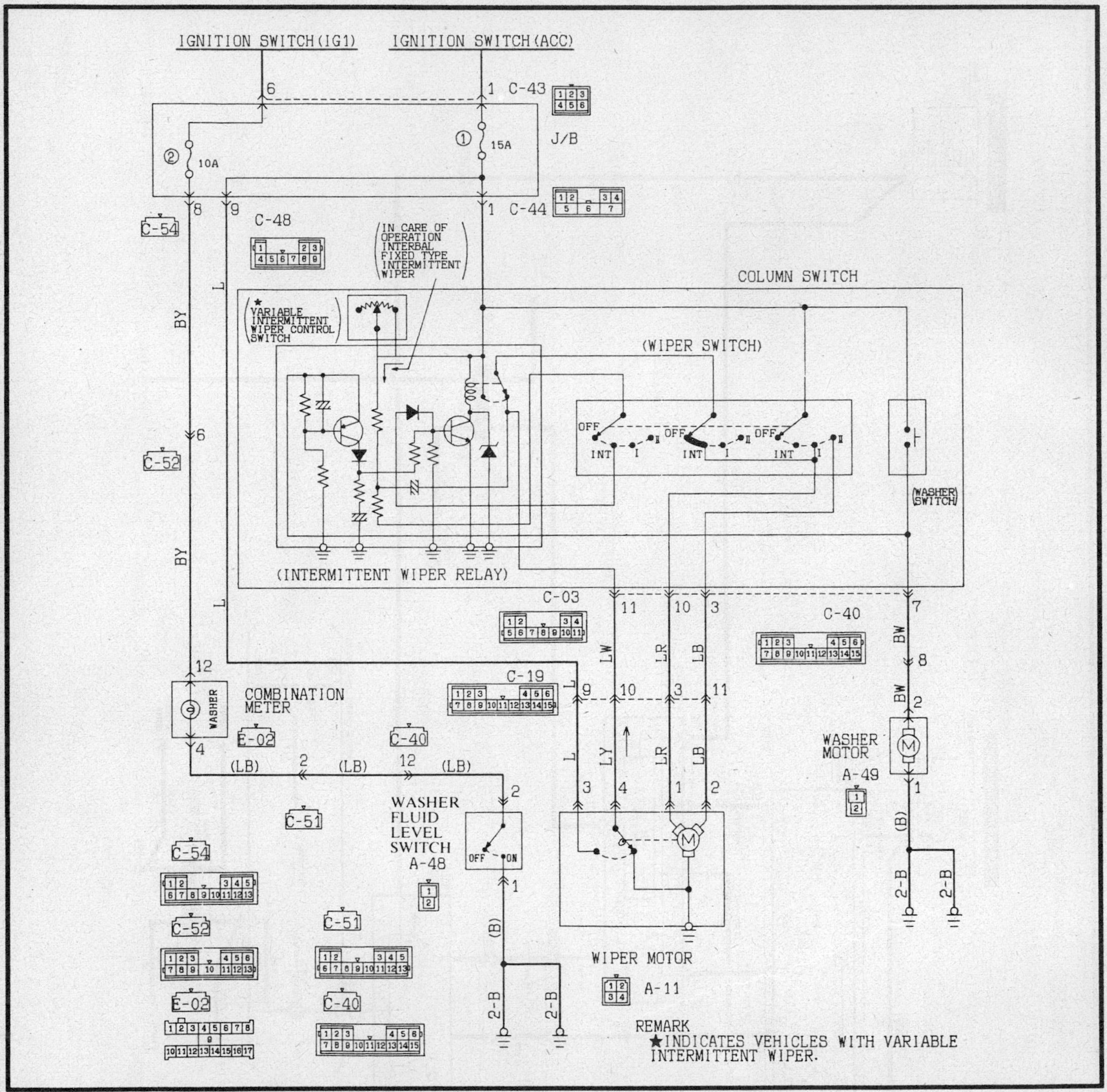

Summit wiper/washer electrical schematic

4. If necessary, disconnect the speedometer cable.

5. Remove the lower instrument panel cover and remove the cluster.

6. Install the cluster and lower trim cover. Connect the electrical leads to the cluster.

7. Install the instrument panel bezel. Connect the negative battery cable.

MEDALLION

1. Disconnect the negative battery cable.

2. Remove the instrument glare shield retaining screws. Press the holding tabs in and remove the glare shield.

3. Open the fuse panel access door, reach through the fuse

panel door and remove the speedometer cable from the rear of the instrument cluster.

4. Remove the instrument cluster mounting screws and pull the cluster forward. Disconnect the electrical wiring and remove the cluster from the vehicle.

5. Install the cluster and connect the electrical wiring. Install the glare shield. Connect the speedometer cable and connect the negative battery cable.

SUMMIT

1. Disconnect battery negative cable.

2. Remove the center panel.

3. Remove knee protector of lower panel assembly.

4. Remove the cluster bezel and cluster retaining screws.
5. Disconnect the speedometer cable at the transaxle.
6. Pull the cluster and speedometer cable slightly rearward and release the lock. Remove cluster assembly.
7. Installation is the reverse of the removal procedure.

SPEEDOMETER AND GAUGES

Removal and Installation

1. Disconnect the negative battery cable.
2. Remove the instrument cluster.
3. Remove the cluster housing and the printed circuit board, exposing the speedometer and the gauges, mounted to the cluster case.
4. Remove the speedometer and/or gauges as required.
5. Installation is the reverse of the removal procedure.

SPEEDOMETER CABLE

Removal and Installation
EAGLE, MEDALLION AND SUMMIT

1. The cable is attached to the rear of the speedometer with a threaded knurled nut or an adapter. Remove the instrument cluster screws and pull the instrument cluster forward.
2. Unscrew the speedometer cable from the speedometer. Push the cable through the firewall.
3. At the transmission or transaxle, unscrew the cable from the housing and remove the cable.
4. Installation is the reverse of the removal procedure.

PREMIER

The speedometer is operated by an electronic circuit. The Vehicle Speed Sensor (VSS) generates an AC signal which is proportional to the vehicle speed. This signal is sent to the speedometer circuit board. The solid state circuit drives the pointer of the speedometer.

Electrical Circuit Protectors

TURN SIGNAL FLASHER

The turn signal flasher in the Eagle, is located on the instrument panel behind the headlamp switch. The turn signal flasher in the Medallion, Premier and Summit is located behind the left side of the instrument panel.

HAZARD WARNING FLASHER

On the Eagle, the hazard warning flasher is plugged into the fuse panel. The hazard flasher in the Medallion, Premier and Summit is located behind the left side of the instrument panel.

FUSE PANEL

On the Eagle, the fuse panel is located on the left side of the passenger compartment, adjacent to the parking brake mechanism. The fuse panel in the Medallion, Premier and Summit is located above the parking brake release lever, under the instrument panel.

CIRCUIT BREAKERS

Circuit breakers are an integral part of the headlamp switch and the wiper switch, as well as the A/C circuit. They are used to protect each circuit from an overload.

FUSIBLE LINKS

Fusible links are used to prevent major wire harness damage in the event of a short circuit or an overload condition in the wiring circuits which are normally not fused, due to carrying high amperage loads or because of their locations within the wiring harness. Each fusible link is of a fixed value for a specific electrical load and should a link fail, the cause of the failure must be determined and repaired prior to installing a new fusible link of the same value.

NOTE: When replacing a protective electrical relay, be very sure to install the same type of relay. Verify that the schematic imprinted on the original and replacement relays are identical. Relay part numbers may change. Do not rely on them for identification. Instead, use the schematic imprinted on the relay for positive identification.

Speed Controls

Refer to "Chilton's Chassis Electronics Service Manual" for additional coverage.

CONTROL SWITCH

The cruise control switch assembly is integral with the turn signal switch and headlamp high/low beam switch lever. The switch is not repairable. The switch and harness assembly can be replaced only as a complete unit.

Removal and Installation
EAGLE

1. Disconnect the negative battery cable.
2. Remove the lower steering column cover.
3. Disconnect the 4-wire harness connector located under the instrument panel.
4. If equipped with a tilt steering column, remove the wires from the connector.
5. Fold back and tape 2 of the 4 wires to the wire harness.
6. Tie or tape string to the wire harness.
7. If equipped with a standard steering column, tie or tape string to the wire harness connector.
8. Remove the control switch assembly from the headlamp high/low beam (dimmer) switch by pulling straight out.
9. Carefully pull the wire harness up through and out of the steering column.
10. Remove the string from the wire harness.
11. Test the operation of the replacement cruise command control switch assembly by connecting it to the system before installing it in the steering column.
12. Remove the wires from the connector. Tape 2 of the 4 wires back along the wire harness (tilt column only) and tape or tie the harness to the string that was attached to the original wire harness before removal.
13. Pull the replacement harness down through the steering column. On tilt steering columns, the harness must pass through the hole on the left side of the steering shaft.
14. Install the control switch assembly.
15. Install the harness wires in the connector (tilt column only) and connect the connector to the system.
16. Install the lower steering column cover.
17. Test the Cruise Command operation.

PREMIER AND MEDALLION

The cruise control switch on the Medallion and Premier is located in the steering wheel cover.
1. Disconnect the negative battery cable.
2. Remove the steering wheel center pad. Disconnect the electrical leads.
3. Pry up on the switch panel and remove it.

Speed control continuity test—Eagle

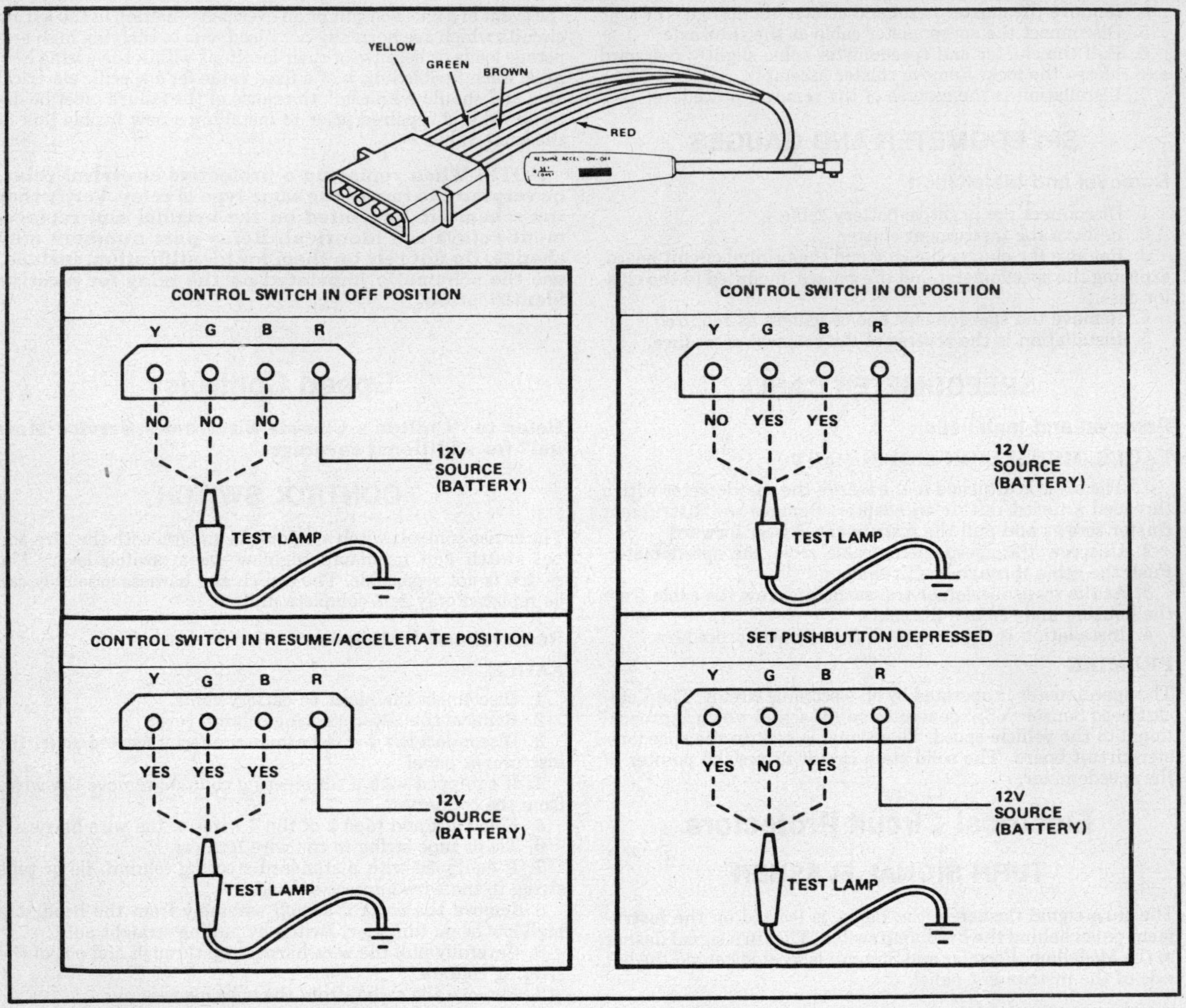

4. Install the switch panel to the steering wheel and connect the electrical leads.
5. Install the horn cover. Connect the negative battery cable.

SPEED SENSOR

Testing

1. Disconnect the speed sensor wire harness connector.
2. Connect a voltmeter set on the low AC scale to the speed sensor wire connector terminals.

3. Raise the vehicle and support it safely.
4. On the Eagle, be sure the vehicle is not in the 4WD mode.
5. Operate the engine (wheels spinning freely) at 30 mph and note the voltage. The voltage should be approximately 0.9 volt. Increases of 0.1 volt per each 10 mph increase in speed should also be indicated.
6. Turn **OFF** the engine and slowly stop the wheels.
7. Disconnect the voltmeter.
8. Replace the speed sensor, if defective.
9. Connect the speed sensor wire harness connector.
10. Remove the safety stands and lower the automobile.

COOLING AND HEATING SYSTEMS

Water Pump

Removal and Installation

1.5L AND 1.6L ENGINE

1. Disconnect the negative battery cable.
2. Drain the cooling system.
3. Remove the accessory drive belts.
4. Remove the water pump pulley and tension pulley bracket.
5. Remove the timing belt cover.
6. Remove the tensioner assembly, then remove the timing belt.
7. Remove the hoses from the pump, attaching bolts and remove the water pump.
8. Clean the gasket mating surfaces.
9. Install the pump to the engine block using a new gasket and O-ring. Tighten mounting bolts 9–11 ft. lbs (12–15 Nm). Complete installation by reversing removal procedure.
10. Fill the cooling system and connect the negative battery cable. Bleed the cooling system.

2.2L ENGINE

1. Disconnect the negative battery cable.
2. Drain the cooling system.
3. Remove the accessory drive belts.
4. Remove the timing belt cover.
5. Remove the water pump pulley bolt and remove the pulley.
6. Remove the timing belt and tensioner. Remove the hoses from the pump.
7. Remove the water pump attaching bolts and remove the water pump.
8. Clean the gasket mating surfaces.

To install:
9. Position the pump on the engine block using a new gasket. Tighten the bolts to 20 ft. lbs.
10. Install the timing belt and tensioner. Adjust the timing belt tension.
11. Install the timing belt cover. Install the water pump pulley and the accessory drive belts. Install the hoses.
12. Fill the cooling system and connect the negative battery cable. Bleed the cooling system.

2.5L ENGINE

1. Disconnect the negative battery cable.
2. Drain the cooling system. Remove the serpentine drive belt.
3. Disconnect the hoses from the engine. Remove the water pump pulley mounting bolts and remove the pulley.
4. Remove the water pump mounting bolts and remove the pump.
5. Clean the gasket mating surfaces. Install the water pump using a new gasket. Tighten the bolts to 13 ft. lbs.
6. Install the hoses and the water pump pulley. Tighten the pulley retaining bolts to 20 ft. lbs.
7. Install the accessory drive belt.

NOTE: It is important that the serpentine belt is installed correctly. If it is incorrectly routed, the water pump could be rotated in the wrong direction, causing the engine to overheat.

8. Fill the cooling system. Connect the negative battery cable. Start the engine and bleed the cooling system.

3.0L ENGINE

1. Disconnect the negative battery cable.
2. Drain the cooling system.
3. Remove the spark plug wire holder from the top of the thermostat housing. Remove the nuts holding the engine damper to the engine.
4. Remove the accessory drive belt. Remove the upper and lower radiator hoses from the radiator.
5. Disconnect the electrical lead to the coolant temperature sensor.
6. At the back of the water pump disconnect the hoses to the cylinder heads and the heater hoses.
7. Remove the water pump mounting bolts and remove the water pump.

To install:
8. Position the water pump to the block and tighten the mounting bolts to 13 ft. lbs.
9. Connect all of the hoses to the water pump, making sure that they are not kinked. Connect the electrical lead to the coolant temperature sensor.
10. Install the accessory drive belt and the engine damper. Adjust the drive belt tension.
11. Install the spark plug wire holder to the thermostat housing.
12. Fill the cooling system. Connect the negative battery cable. Start the engine and bleed the cooling system, check for leaks.

4.2L ENGINE

1. Disconnect the negative battery cable. Drain the cooling system.
2. Loosen the adjustment bolts from the alternator and the power steering pump, (if equipped). Remove the drive belts.
3. Unfasten the fan ring. Remove the fan and pump pulley assembly. Withdraw the fan ring (or shroud).
4. Remove the hoses at the pump.
5. Remove the water pump mounting bolts and withdraw the pump.

NOTE: Engines built for sale in California having a single, serpentine drive belt and viscous fan drive, have a reverse rotating pump and drive. These components are identified by the word REVERSE stamped on the drive cover and inner side of the fan and REV cast into the water pump body. Never interchange standard rotating parts with these.

6. Installation is in the reverse order of removal. Always use a new pump gasket.
7. Bleed the radiator by running the engine and opening the heater control valve. Run the engine long enough so that the thermostat opens. Check the coolant level.
8. The water pump securing bolts should be tightened to 13 ft. lbs. and the fan bolts to 18 ft. lbs. Adjust the belts.

Electric Cooling Fan

SYSTEM OPERATION

Premier, Medallion and Summit are equipped with electric cooling fan systems designed to operate automatically under different conditions. The system reacts with the changes in engine temperature. When the engine coolant temperature reaches 198°F (but below 212°F) the cooling fan switch low speed contacts close. This activates the cooling fan in low speed operation. When the coolant temperature exceeds 212°F the fan switch activates the fan in high speed operation. On vehicles equipped with A/C, the coolant fan switch automatically turns the cooling fan **ON** while the A/C is activated.

On Summit, if the engine coolant temperature rises to 185°F (85°C) or the refrigerant high pressure switch is **ON** due to high atmospheric temperature in the summer, the thermosensor contacts closes and current flow through the fan motor.

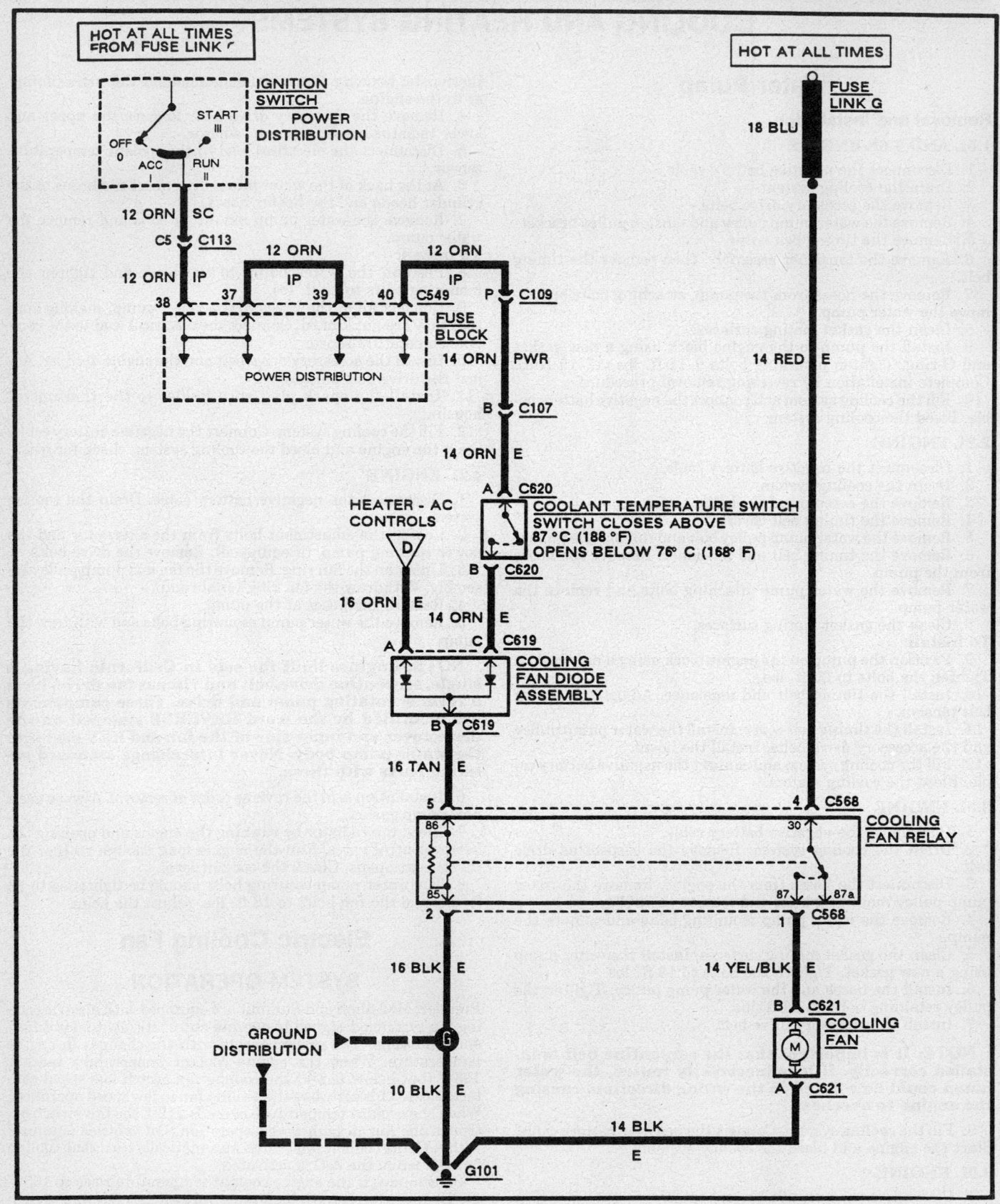

Cooling fan wiring schematic—Medallion and Premier

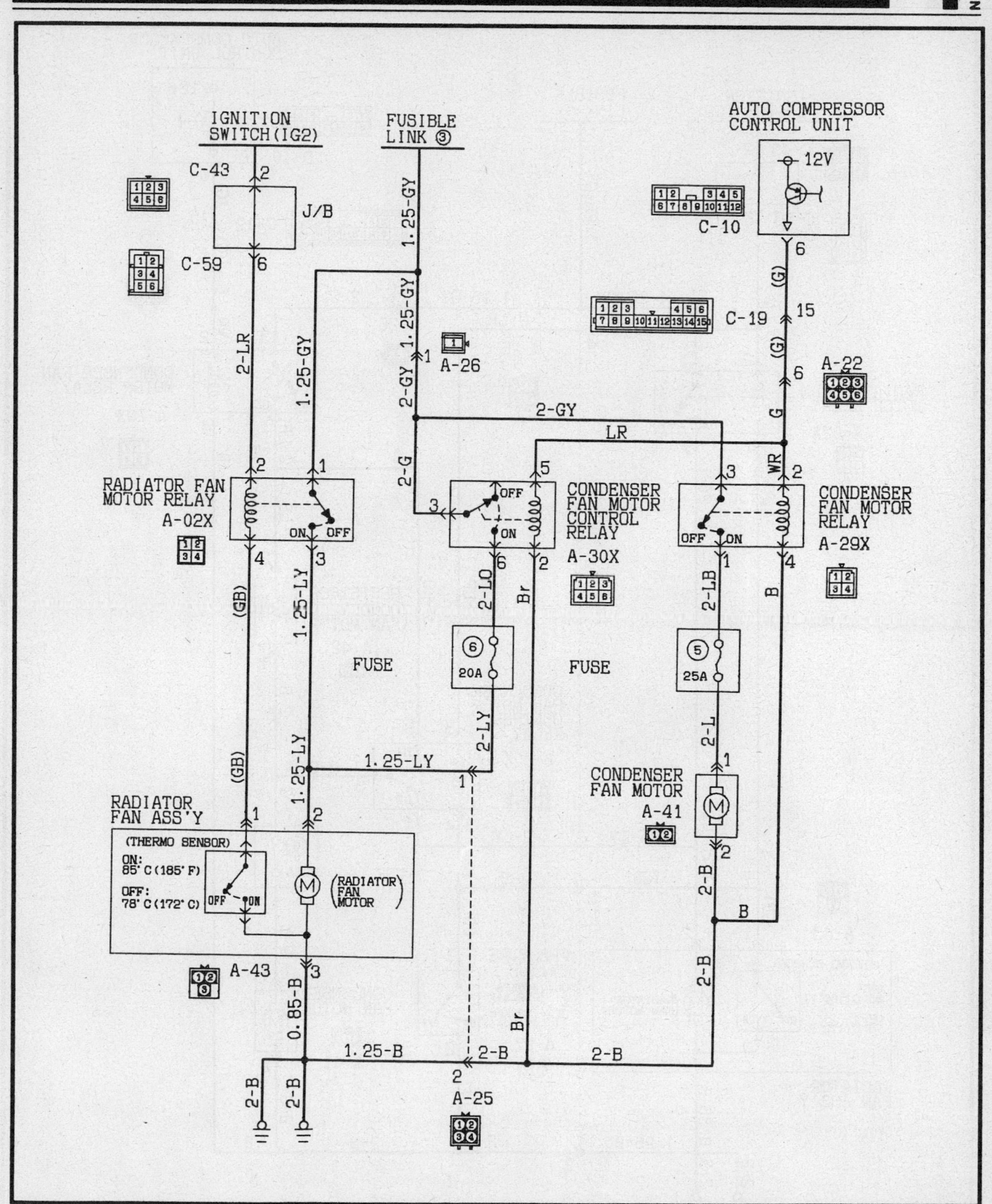

Cooling fan wiring schematic—Summit 1.5L engine

AUTO COMPRESSOR
CONTROL UNIT

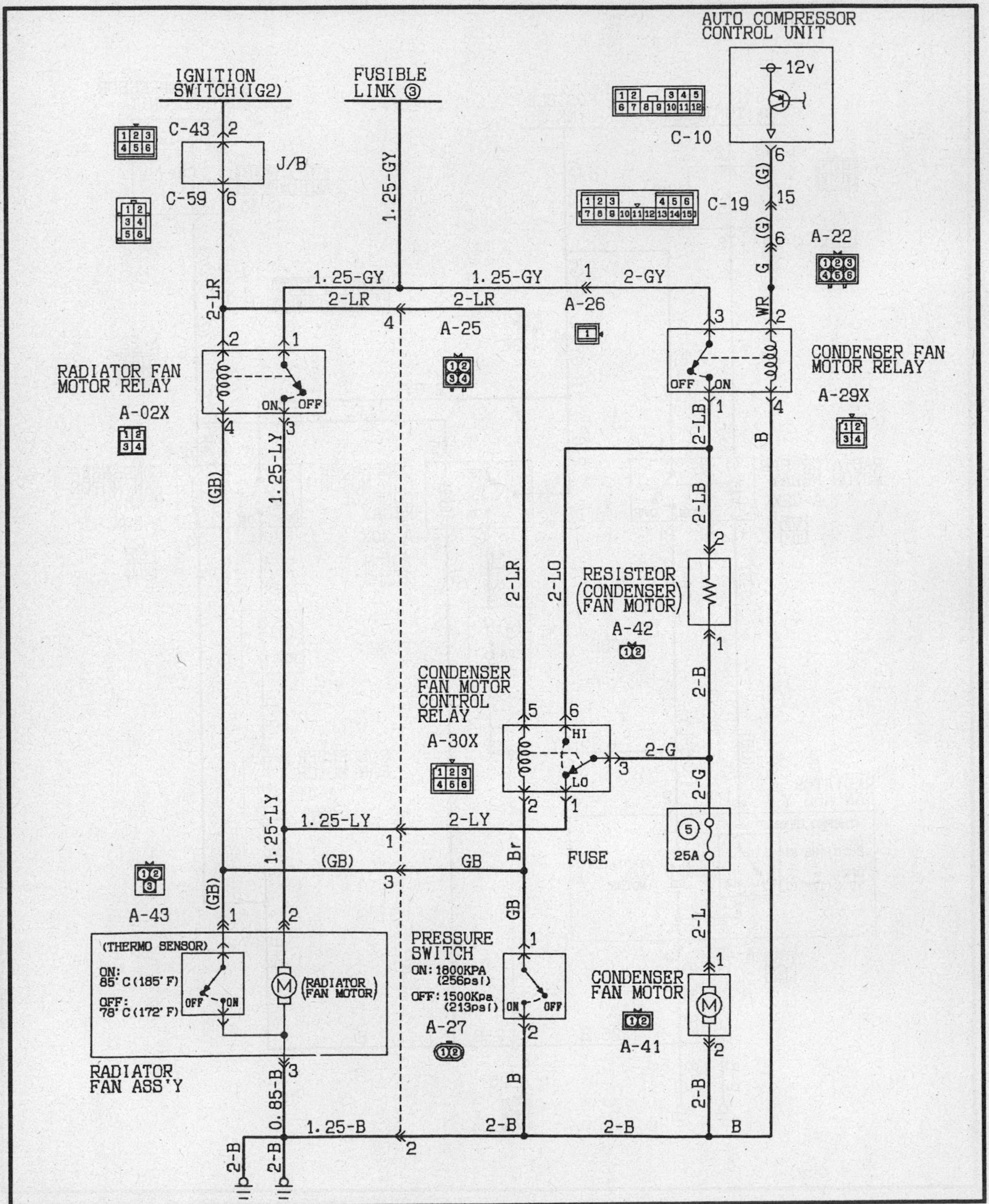

12v

C-10

IGNITION
SWITCH (IG2)

FUSIBLE
LINK ③

C-43   2

J/B

C-59   6

1.25-GY

C-19   15

A-22

1.25-GY   1.25-GY   1   2-GY

2-LR   2-LR   4   A-26

A-25

CONDENSER FAN
MOTOR RELAY

OFF ON

A-29X

RADIATOR FAN
MOTOR RELAY

A-02X

2   1

ON   OFF

4   3

RESISTEOR
(CONDENSER)
FAN MOTOR)

A-42

CONDENSER
FAN MOTOR
CONTROL
RELAY

A-30X

5   6   HI

LO   3   2-G

2   1

FUSE

25A

A-43

(THERMO SENSOR)
ON:
85°C (185°F)
OFF:
78°C (172°F)

OFF   ON

(M) (RADIATOR
FAN MOTOR)

RADIATOR
FAN ASS'Y

PRESSURE
SWITCH
ON: 1800KPA
(256psi)
OFF: 1500Kpa
(213psi)

A-27

1

ON   OFF

2

CONDENSER
FAN MOTOR

A-41

(M)

2

1.25-LY   1.25-LY   2-LY   1

(GB)   GB   Br

3

2-LR   2-LO

1.25-LY

(GB)

2-B 0.85-B   1.25-B   2-B   2-B   2-B   B

2   2

2-B   2-B

Cooling fan wiring schematic—Summit 1.6L engine

Removal and Installation

PREMIER AND MEDALLION

1. Disconnect the negative battery cable.
2. Remove the radiator support bracket screws. Remove the vibration cushion nuts.
3. Remove the upper radiator crossmember mounting screws and remove the crossmember.
4. Disconnect the electrical connectors from the fan. Remove the cooling fan and shroud mounting bolts and remove the fan by lifting upwards.
5. Install the fan into position and install the mounting bolts. Install the radiator crossmember and support bracket.
6. Connect the negative battery cable.

SUMMIT

1. Disconnect the battery cables. Remove the battery and battery holder.
2. Remove washer tank, shroud and bushings. On turbo-charge engines, remove the power steering oil cooler tube mounting bolt and hood latch assembly.
3. Disconnect fan electrical connector and resistor, if equipped. Remove fan mounting bolts and fan assembly.
To install:
4. Position the fan in vehicle and install the mounting bolts.
5. Reconnect fan electrical connection.
6. Install bushings, shroud and washer tank. On turbocharge engines, install the hood latch assembly and power steering oil cooler tube mounting bolt.
7. Install battery holder and reconnect negative battery cable. Check fan operation.

Blower Motor

Removal and Installation

EAGLE

1. Disconnect the negative battery cable.
2. Disconnect the wiring to the blower motor.
3. Remove the blower motor and fan assembly retaining bolts or nuts. Remove the blower motor and fan assembly from the housing.
4. To remove the blower fan from the motor shaft, squeeze and remove the blower retainer clip. Then, slide the blower hub off the motor shaft. This will give access to the nuts attaching the motor to the mounting plate. Remove them and remove them and then unbolt and remove the motor from the mounting plate.
5. Install the blower motor onto the mounting plate. Install the fan onto the motor shaft. Position the fan so that a 0.350 in. clearance exists between the mounting plate of the motor and the end of the blower fan.
6. Position the ears of the spring clip retainer over the flat surface of the motor shaft. The edge of the clip must be flush with the edge of the fan hub.
7. Install the blower motor into the housing and install the retaining bolts or nuts.
8. Connect the wiring to the motor and check operation of the motor and fan assembly.

PREMIER

1. Disconnect the negative battery cable.
2. Disconnect the electrical connector from the coolant reservoir.
3. Remove the coolant reservoir retaining strap and move the reservoir aside.
4. Remove the coolant reservoir mounting bracket. Disconnect the electrical wires from the blower motor.
5. Remove the blower motor mounting bolts and remove the blower motor.

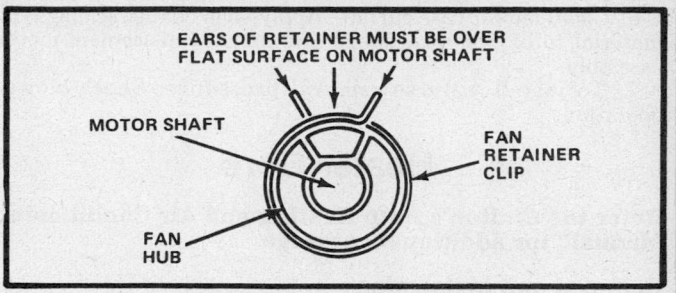

Blower fan retainer specification—Eagle

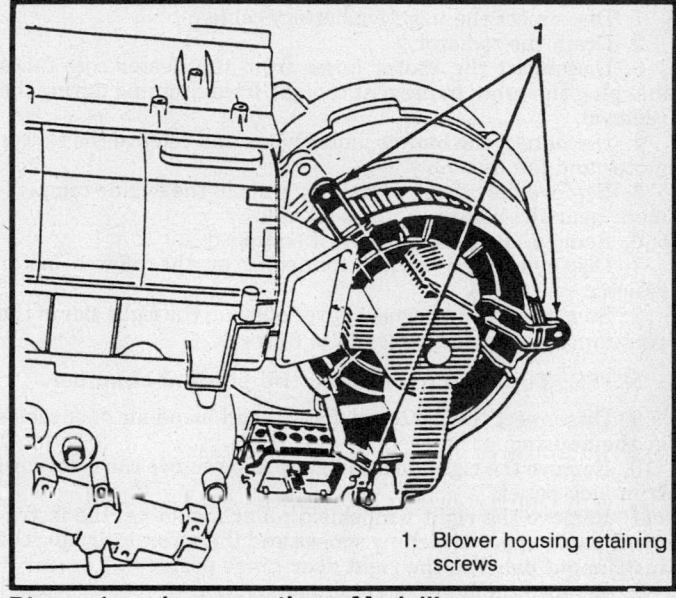

1. Blower housing retaining screws

Blower housing mounting—Medallion

6. Install the blower and mounting bolts. Connect the electrical leads and install the coolant reservoir.
7. Connect the negative battery cable.

MEDALLION

1. Disconnect the negative battery cable.
2. Remove the glove box door straps and remove the glove box door. Remove the inner glove box.
3. Unclip the ventilator outlet from the right side of the blower housing. Disconnect the electrical connector from the blower motor.
4. Remove the blower housing retaining screws and remove the housing.
5. Remove the fan assembly from the blower housing.
6. Install the fan assembly into the blower housing and install the retaining screws. Connect the electrical connector and the ventilator outlet.
7. Install the inner glove box and the glove box door.
8. Connect the negative battery cable.

SUMMIT

1. Disconnect the negative battery cable.
2. Remove the glove box and right hand speaker cover.
3. Remove the right hand cowl side trim, knee protector, and glove box frame.
4. Remove lap heater duct (vehicles without rear heater) or shower duct (vehicles with rear heater) and blower electrical connection.
5. Remove the MPI control unit, blower attaching screws and blower assembly.

6. Clean blower case surface. Apply strip chaulk sealing type material to blower case flange and install replacement motor assembly.

7. To install, reverse removal procedure. Check blower operation.

Heater Core

Refer to "Chilton's Auto Heating and Air Conditioning Manual" for additional coverage.

Removal and Installation

EAGLE WITHOUT AIR CONDITIONING

1. Disconnect the negative battery cable.
2. Drain the radiator.
3. Disconnect the heater hoses from the heater core tubes and plug the tubes to prevent coolant from draining during the removal.
4. Disconnect the blower motor wires and remove the blower motor and fan assembly.
5. Remove the housing retaining nuts in the engine compartment near the blower motor position.
6. Remove the package tray, if equipped.
7. Disconnect the wiring connector at the blower motor resistor.
8. Snap the wiring harness cover open on the right side of the plenum chamber and remove the harness.

NOTE: Tape the harness to the plenum chamber.

9. Disconnect the heater, defroster and blend-air door cables at the housing.
10. Remove the right door sill plate and remove the right cowl trim kick panel.
11. Remove the right windshield pillar moulding, the instrument panel upper attaching screws and the screw attaching the instrument panel to the right door hinge post.
12. Remove the housing retaining screws.
13. Pull the right side of the instrument panel slightly rearward and remove the housing.
14. Remove the cover and screws retaining the heater core to the housing and remove the heater core from the housing.
15. Installation is the reverse of the removal procedure.
16. Ensure the heater core seals are properly installed to prevent air leakage around the perimeter of the heater core.
17. Properly adjust the control cables during the installation.
18. Be sure air is expelled from the cooling system during the engine operation.

EAGLE WITH AIR CONDITIONING

1. Disconnect the negative battery cable and drain the cooling system.
2. Disconnect heater hoses and plug hoses, cover fittings.
3. Disconnect blower wires and remove motor and fan assembly.
4. Remove the housing attaching nut from the stud in the engine compartment.
5. Remove package shelf, if so equipped.
6. Disconnect wire at resistor, located below glove box.
7. Remove instrument panel center bezel, air outlet and duct, on A/C equipped models.
8. Disconnect air and defroster cables from damper levers.
9. Remove right-side windshield pillar molding, the instrument panel upper sheet metal screws and the capscrew at the right door post.
10. Remove the right cowl trim panel and door sill plate.
11. Remove right kick panel and heater housing attaching screws.
12. Pull right side of instrument panel outward slightly and remove housing.

13. Remove core, defroster and blower housing.
14. Remove core from housing.
15. Installation is in the reverse order of removal.

PREMIER AND MEDALLION

1. Disconnect the negative battery cable. Drain the cooling system.
2. Remove the lower instrument panel trim cover and support rod. Disconnect the shift cable from the column lever. Pull the plastic sleeve down on the lower steering column and expose the intermediate shaft joint. Matchmark the intermediate and steering shafts. Remove the bolt from the intermediate shaft.
3. Remove the bolts that hold the steering column to the instrument panel and lower the column. Disconnect the column electrical connector. Remove the column from the vehicle.
4. Remove the windshield defroster grill. Remove the parking brake assembly mounting screws and lower the assembly. Remove the ashtray and cigarette lighter.
5. Disconnect all of the electrical connectors behind the instrument panel. Remove the bolts that hold the instrument panel to the center floor bracket.
6. Lift up and rearward on the instrument panel and remove it from the vehicle.

NOTE: The A/C system must be discharged before disconnecting the refrigerant lines. The refrigerant will freeze anything it contacts including skin and eyes.

7. Disconnect the heater hoses, vacuum lines and electrical connectors.
8. Remove the nuts retaining the heater case to the firewall and remove the case from the vehicle.
9. Remove the plastic tabs retaining the heater core and remove the heater core from the case.

To install:

10. Install the heater core in the heater housing and secure with retaining tabs. Verify that the housing seals are in place and in good condition.
11. Position the heater housing to the dash panel being certain that the drain tube extends through its opening in the floor and all electrical wiring and vacuum lines extends through the dash panel.
12. Complete installation by reversing the removal procedure.
13. Connect the negative battery cable, refill the cooling system and recharge the A/C system.

SUMMIT

1. Disconnect the negative battery cable. Drain the cooling system and remove heater hoses.
2. Disconnect air selection control, temperature control, mode selection control connector and remove heater control assembly.
3. Disconnect electrical connector for ECI control relay. Remove instrument panel center stay assembly and rear heater duct.
4. Remove lap heater duct (vehicles without rear heater) or shower duct (vehicles with rear heater), foot duct, lap duct and center ventilation duct.
5. Remove the electronic level control unit, if equipped.
6. Remove heater assembly mounting nuts, evaporator mounting nuts and clips.
7. Remove the heater assembly.

NOTE: Be careful not to damage the liquid pipe and suction hose during removal of the heater unit.

8. Remove heater core plate and fastening clips. Remove heater core from heater unit.
9. Installation is the reverse of the removal procedure.
10. When installing the mode selection control wire, move the mode selection lever to **OUTWARD** position. With the lever in an outward direction, connect the inner cable of the mode selec-

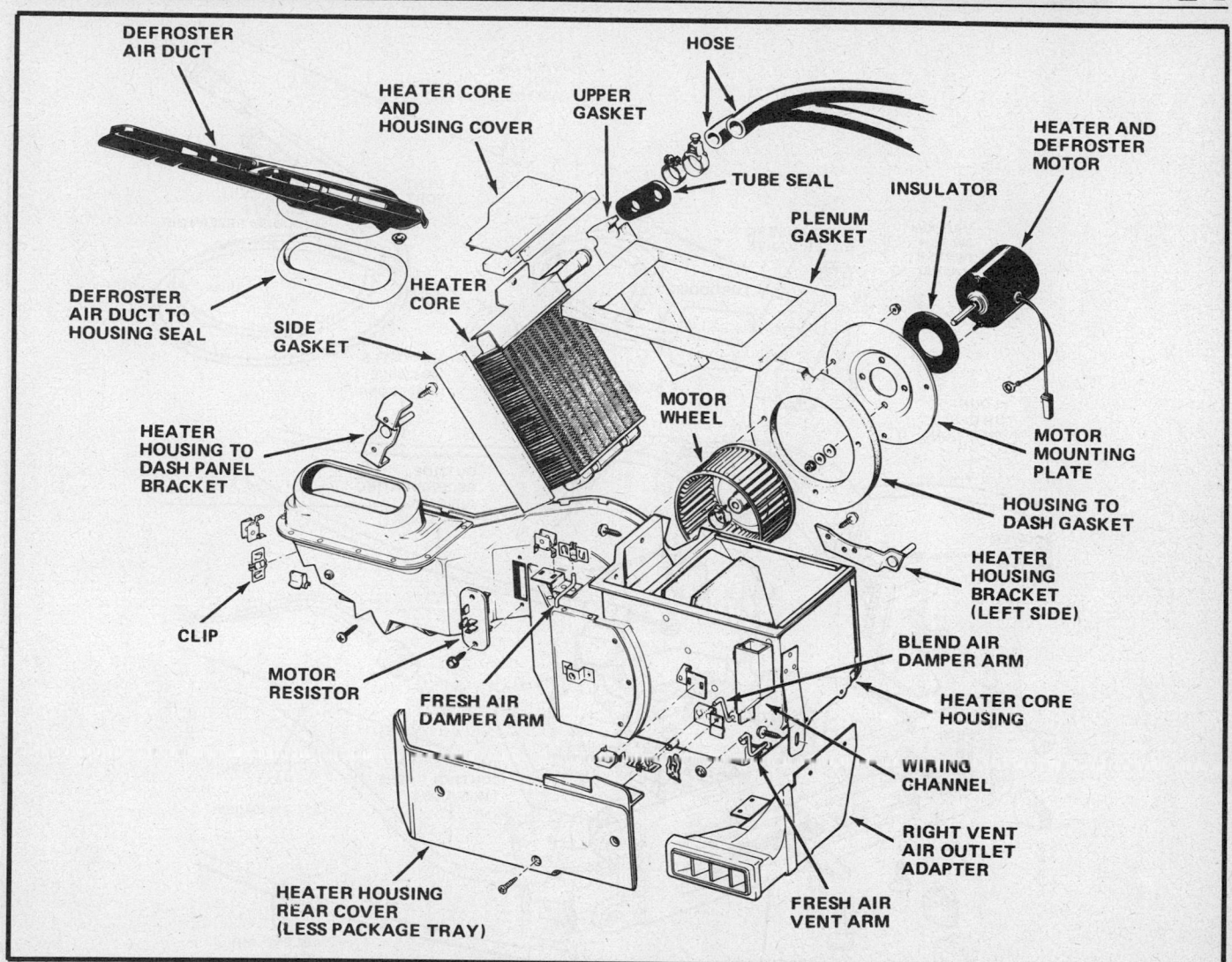

Exploded view of heater case assembly—Eagle

tion control wire to the end of the mode selection lever and secure with retaining clip.

11. When installing the temperature control wire, move the temperature control lever to the **COOL** position. With the blend air damper lever pressed completely downward, connect the inner cable of the temperature control wire to end of the blend air damper lever, and secure with retaining clip.

12. When installing the air selection control wire, move the air selection damper lever to the **INWARD** position. With the air selection damper lever pressed inward, connect the inner cable of the air selection control wire to the end of the air selection damper lever and secure with retaining clip.

13. Check for proper operation.

Temperature Control/Blower Switch

Removal and Installation

EAGLE

1. Disconnect the negative battery cable.
2. Remove the ash tray and retainer screws.
3. Remove the radio knobs and attaching nuts, if equipped.
4. Remove the instrument panel center housing and disconnect the electrical wiring and connections.

5. Remove the control panel attaching screws.
6. Remove the center upper discharge duct and remove the radio, if equipped.
7. Remove the attaching screws and lower control and disconnect the cables from control levers.
8. Disconnect the electrical connectors and vacuum hoses.
9. Remove the control panel.
10. The blower switch can be replaced with the control panel out of the dash assembly.

To install:

11. Position the control panel in place.
12. Install the electrical connectors and vacuum hoses.
13. Connect the cables to the control levers.

NOTE: The control cables must be installed with the colored tape in the center of the clips attached to the control panel.

14. Install the control panel retaining screws.
15. Complete installation by reversing the removal procedure.
16. Move the control levers to full travel in both directions to adjust the cables.
17. Connect the negative battery cable and check the system operation.

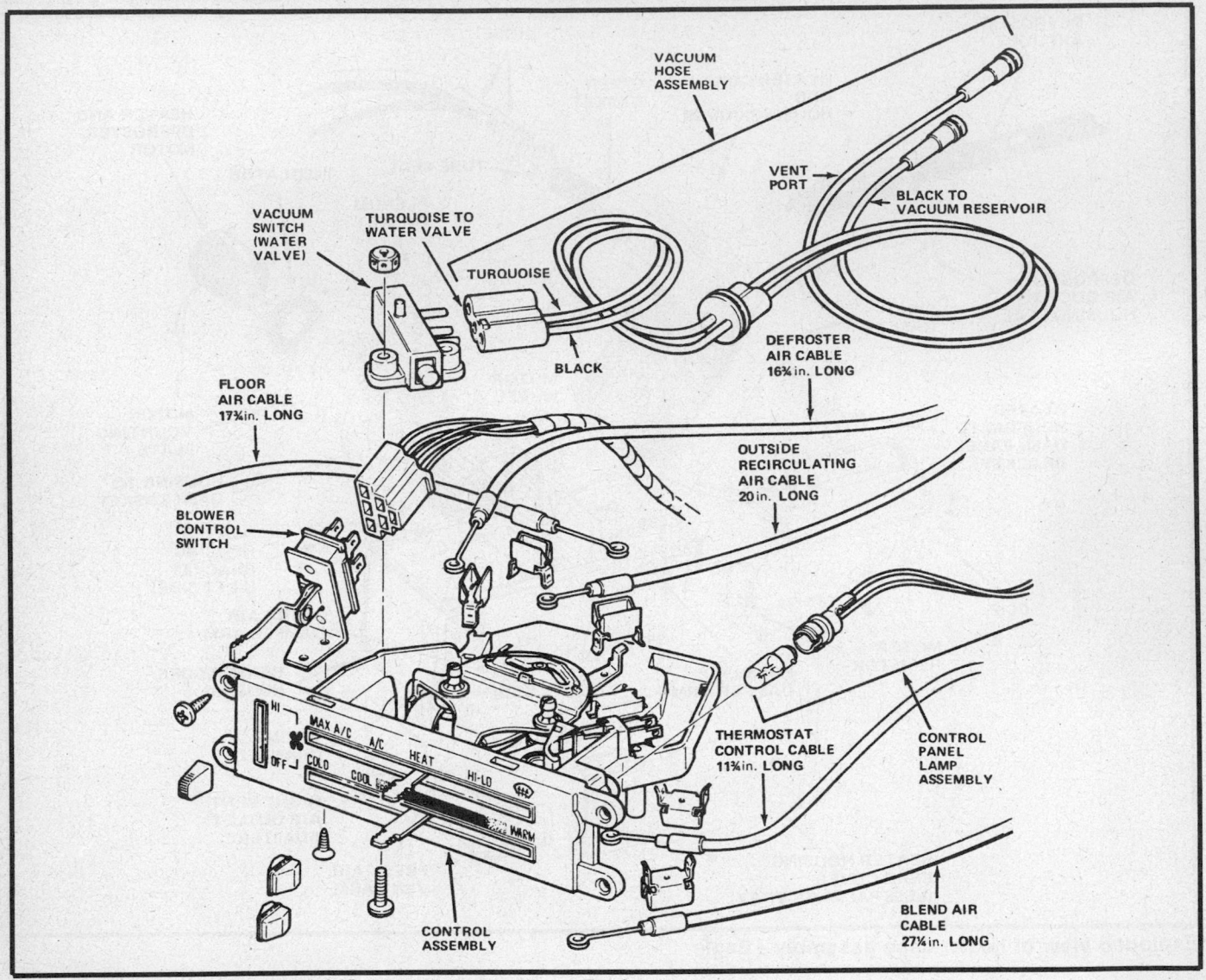

Exploded view of heater and A/C control assembly— Eagle

PREMIER

The temperature control switches are located in a pod on the right side of the steering column. The control assembly is removed with the pod assembly.

1. Disconnect the negative battery cable.
2. Remove the instrument panel lower cover. Remove the lower instrument panel support bar.
3. Pull the air duct out of the way. Separate the steering column electrical connector.
4. Remove the screws that retain the pod to the column and pull the pod part way out. Remove the 2 screws retaining the electrical connector to the pod casing.
5. Pull the harness out and through the pod.
6. Install the pod wiring connector and install the pod to the column. Connect the steering column connector and install the lower support. Connect the air duct.
7. Connect the negative battery cable.

MEDALLION

1. Disconnect the negative battery cable.
2. Remove the radio and the radio mounting bracket.
3. Remove the heater control knobs by pulling them off.

4. Remove the control panel retaining screw and lower the panel.
5. Disconnect the selector cables and remove all electrical connections.
6. Connect the selector cables and electrical connectors to the panel. Raise the panel into position and install the retaining screw.
7. Install the radio mounting bracket and the radio.
8. Connect the negative battery cable.

SUMMIT

1. Disconnect the negative battery cable.
2. Remove glove box and ashtray .
3. Remove heater control panel attaching screws and remove panel.
4. Remove radio.
5. Disconnect air selection control, temperature control and mode selection control connector.
6. Remove control assembly mounting screws and carefully pull rearward. Press out the upper and lower bracket from control assembly and remove control assembly.
7. Installation is the reverse of the removal procedure.

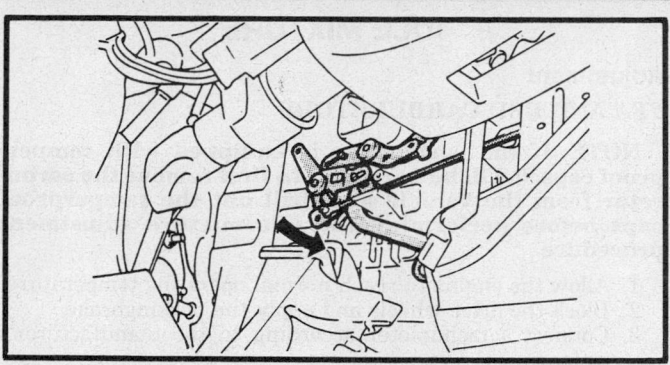

Mode selection control wire installation—Summit

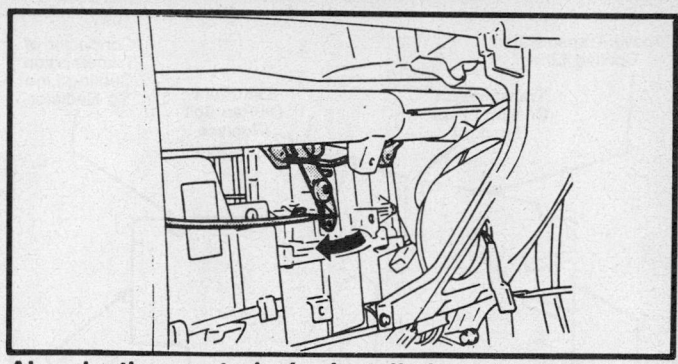

Air selection control wire installation—Summit

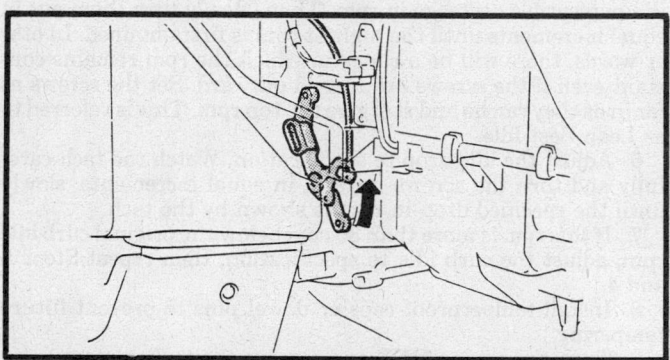

Temperature control wire installation—Summit

8. When installing the mode selection control wire, move the mode selection lever to **OUTWARD** position. With the lever in an outward direction, connect the inner cable of the mode selection control wire to the end of the mode selection lever and secure with retaining clip.

9. When installing the temperature control wire, move the temperature control lever to the **COOL** position. With the blend air damper lever pressed completely downward, connect the inner cable of the temperature control wire to end of the blend air damper lever, and secure with retaining clip.

10. When installing the air selection control wire, move the air selection damper lever to the **INWARD** position. With the air selection damper lever pressed inward, connect the inner cable of the air selection control wire to the end of the air selection damper lever and secure with retaining clip.

11. Check for proper operation.

CARBURETED FUEL SYSTEM

Fuel Pump

Removal and Installation

4.2L ENGINE

1. Disconnect the negative battery cable.
2. Disconnect the fuel lines from the fuel pump.
3. Remove the attaching bolts and the pump from the engine block.
4. Install the pump and the new gasket on the engine block. Retain with the 2 retaining bolts.

NOTE: Be sure the actuating arm of the pump is positioned on the top of the camshaft eccentric.

5. Install the fuel inlet and outlet lines to the fuel pump.
6. Install the negative battery cable.
7. Start the engine and check for leakage.

Carburetor

Removal and Installation

4.2L ENGINE

1. Allow the engine to cool. Disconnect the negative battery cable.
2. Remove the vacuum hoses, the air cleaner assembly and flange gasket. Mark the hoses to aid in assembly.
3. Disconnect the fuel line and vacuum hoses from the carburetor. Mark the hoses to aid in assembly.

4. Disconnect the throttle linkage and electrical wire connectors.
5. Remove the carburetor attaching bolts and nuts. Remove the carburetor from the intake manifold.
6. Clean the gasket surfaces on the carburetor base and the intake manifold.
7. The carburetor installation is the reverse of the removal procedure.

IDLE SPEED

Adjustment

YFA AND BBD CARBURETORS

1. Connect a tachometer to the engine and run the engine until normal operating temperature is reached. Block the drive wheels and apply the parking brake.
2. Position the transmission control lever according to the instruction on the underhood emission label.
3. Adjust the sol-vac vacuum actuator by removing the vacuum hose to the unit. Plug the hose.
4. Adjust the idle speed by using the vacuum actuator adjustment screw on the throttle lever. This adjustment is made with all accessories **OFF**.
5. Adjust the engine rpm to specification.
6. After the vacuum actuator adjustment is completed, leave the vacuum hose plugged and disconnected.
7. Adjust the curb idle using the ¼ in. hex-headed adjustment screw on the end of the sol-vac unit. Adjust to specifications.

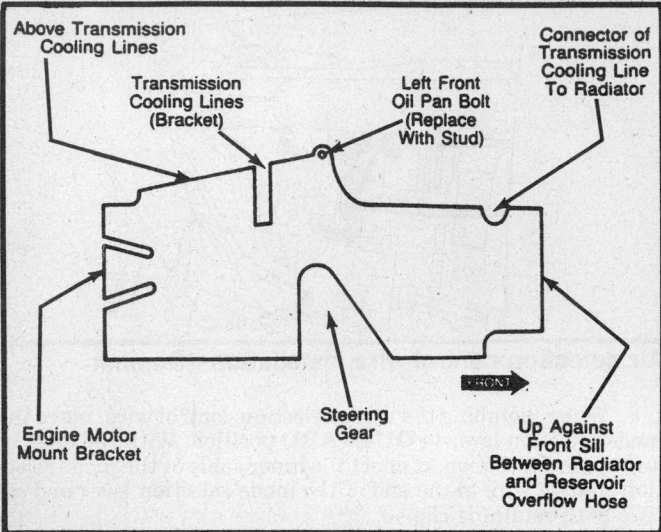

Labels on diagram:
Above Transmission Cooling Lines
Transmission Cooling Lines (Bracket)
Left Front Oil Pan Bolt (Replace With Stud)
Connector of Transmission Cooling Line To Radiator
Engine Motor Mount Bracket
Steering Gear
Up Against Front Sill Between Radiator and Reservoir Overflow Hose
FRONT

Install the splash shield (part No. 8983–100–047 or equivalent) fitting it into the engine compartment as shown on 4.2L engine

NOTE: The engine speed will vary 10–30 rpm during this mode due to being in the closed loop fuel control.

8. Turn the engine OFF and remove the tachometer.

IDLE MIXTURE

Adjustment

YFA AND BBD CARBURETORS

NOTE: If the carburetor is equipped with tamperproof caps, it will be necessary to first remove the carburetor from the vehicle and drill out the tamperproof caps before performing the idle mixture adjustment procedure.

1. Allow the engine to reach normal operating temperature.
2. Block the drive wheels and apply the parkingbrake.
3. Connect a tachometer according to the manufacturer's instructions.
4. Set the idle speed to specification.
5. Turn the mixture screws in in equal increments until there is a perceptible decrease in rpm. Then, slowly turn them out in equal increments until the highest rpm is first obtained. In other words, there will be a range in which the rpm remains constant even if the screws are turned outward. Set the screws as far in as they can be and still give the top rpm. This is referred to as Lean Best Idle.
6. Adjust the idle drop to specification. Watch the tach carefully and turn the screws inward, in equal increments, slowly until the specified drop in rpm is shown by the tach.
7. If this rpm is more than 30 rpm below the original curb idle rpm, adjust the curb idle to specification, then repeat Steps 3 and 4.
8. Install tamperproof caps or dowel pins to prevent future tampering.
9. Turn the engine OFF and remove the tachometer.

FUEL INJECTION SYSTEM

Refer to "Chilton's Electronic Engine Controls Manual" for addition coverage.

Description

There are 2 types of fuel injection systems used in Medallion, Premier and Summit vehicles. The 1.5L, 1.6L, 2.2L and 3.0L engines use a Multi-Point Injection system (MPI). The MPI system features 1 injector per cylinder injecting fuel directly above each intake valve port. The system uses a pressure-speed type injection system. The amount of fuel injected into the engine depends entirely on intake manifold pressure and engine speed. Other factors such as engine coolant temperature, manifold air temperature, throttle position, exhaust oxygen content and even battery voltage are monitored and used to calculate fuel injection. The systems Electronic Control Unit (ECU) controls ignition timing and operates the ignition power module.

The 2.5L engine uses a Throttle Body Injection system (TBI). The TBI system is a pulse time system that injects fuel through an electronically controlled fuel injector into the throttle body above the throttle plate. The ECU controls the duration of this injection and meters the fuel to the engine. The duration of the fuel pulse varies as engine operating conditions change, all monitored and controlled by the ECU.

IDLE SPEED

Adjustment

The idle speed on fuel injected vehicles is controlled by the ECU through the use of an Idle Speed Control motor (ISC) or an idle speed regulator. The ISC motor does not require periodic adjustment. If the ISC is removed or replaced, it must be adjusted to establish the initial position of the plunger. To adjust the ISC, use the following procedure:

1.5L AND 1.6L ENGINES

1. Start engine and run until normal operating temperature is reached.
2. Turn all lights, electric cooling fan and accessories OFF and place transaxle in N.
3. Connect a tachometer. Check ignition timing and adjust if necessary.
4. On 1.5L engine, connect the tachometer to the engine speed detection terminal.
   a. Run the engine for at least 5 seconds at 2000–3000 rpm.
   b. Return engine to idle and run for approximately 2 minutes.
   c. If the curb idle speed is not within specification, adjust the idle speed screw until the engine runs at the specified curb idle speed.
5. On 1.6L engine, disconnect the female connector from the connector for ignition timing adjustment and jumper to a known good ground.
   a. Connect terminal No. 10 of the self-diagnosis connector to a known good ground.
   b. Start the engine and let it run at idle.
   c. If the basic idle speed is not within specification, adjust the speed adjusting screw until the engine runs at the specified basic idle speed.
6. Stop the engine and turn ignition OFF.
7. On 1.5L engines, disconnect the tachometer from the engine speed detection terminal.

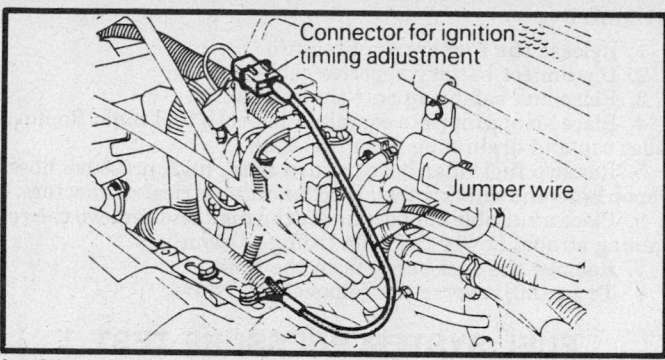

Ignition timing adjustment connector—1.6L engine

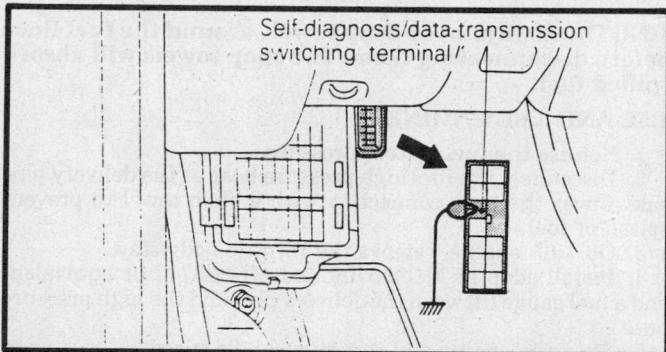

Self-diagnosis connector, terminal No. 10—1.6L engine

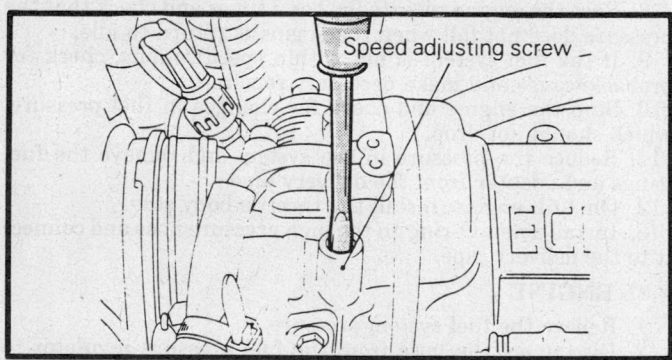

Speed adjusting screw—1.6L engine

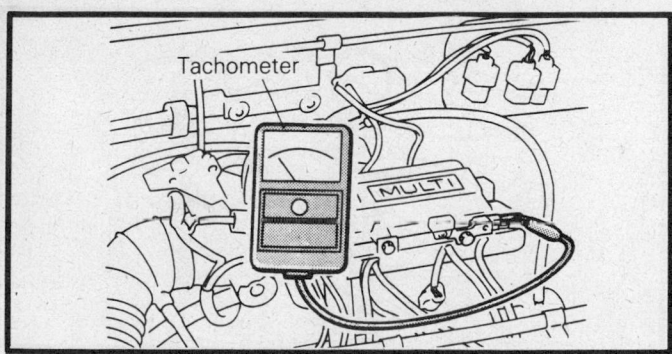

Engine speed detection terminal—1.5L engine

8. On 1.6L engines, disconnect grounding jumper wire from the diagnosis connector and ignition timing connector. Disconnect the tachometer.

2.2L AND 3.0L ENGINES

The idle speed on vehicles equipped with a 2.2L and 3.0L engines is controlled by an idle speed regulator. A permanent magnet motor inside the regulator regulates the valve between the fully open and fully closed positions. The ECU controls the idle speed regulator by alternately grounding its coils to adjust the air bypass flow rate to maintain proper idle speed.

The idle regulating valve cannot be adjusted. Idle mixture is adjusted at the factory and should not be attempted.

2.5L ENGINE

1. Start the engine and allow it to reach normal operating temperature.
2. Disconnect the ISC motor wire connector.
3. Locate the diagnostic terminals on the right side inner fender well. Connect a tachometer to terminals D1-1 and D1-3 of the diagnostic connector.
4. Modify the electrical connector of adapter harness tool Ele. AB.99, Ele. CT.02 or equivalent so it will connect to the ISC motor.
5. Using a sharp blade tool, cut a groove in terminal A, the same size and shape as the grooves in terminal D and B.
6. Attach adapter harness tool Ele. AB99 or equivalent to the ISC motor and fully extend the ISC motor plunger.
7. Adjust the plunger screw until the engine is running at 3500 rpm.
8. Remove adapter harness tool Ele. AB99, Ele. CT.02 or equivalent and reconnect the idle speed motor electrical connector. Idle speed should automatically return to normal.

FUEL SYSTEM PRESSURE RELIEF

Procedure

NOTE: Always wear eye protection when servicing the fuel system. Do not smoke or allow open flame near the fuel system or components during fuel system service.

Modern fuel injection systems operate under high pressure, this makes it necessary to first relieve the system of pressure before servicing. The pressurized fuel when released may ignite or cause personal injury. the following outlined steps may be used for most fuel systems:

1. Remove the fuel tank filler cap to relieve fuel tank pressure.
2. Disconnect fuel pump electrical harness connector at the fuel tank side.
3. Start engine and let it run until it stops. Turn ignition **OFF**.
4. Disconnect battery negative cable and reconnect fuel pump electrical harness.

NOTE: Always wrap shop towels around the fuel lines before disconnecting them. The shop towels will absorb spilled fuel.

Fuel Pump

The fuel pump used on both the TBI and MPI system is a positive displacement, single speed type pump. The pump (except models equipped with a 2.2L engine) is integral with the fuel sender unit and is suspended in the fuel tank.

Removal and Installation
PREMIER

1. Relieve the fuel system pressure.

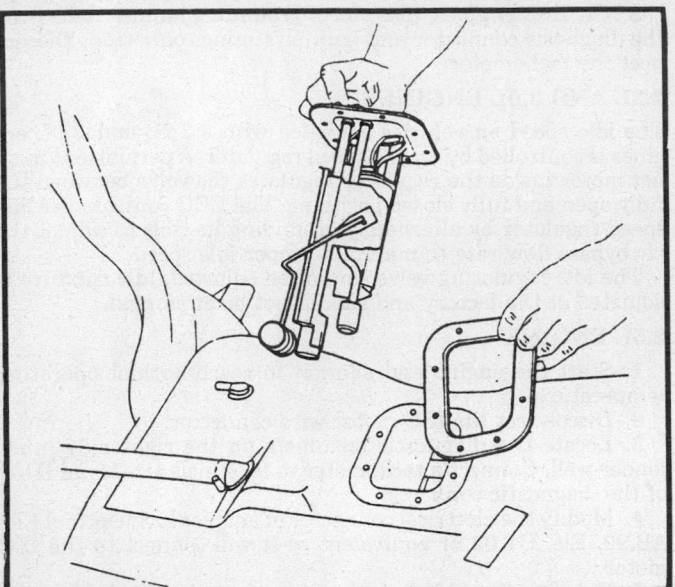

Removing in-tank fuel pump—typical

2. Disconnect the negative battery cable.

3. Drain the fuel from the fuel tank.

4. Raise and safely support the vehicle. Remove the right rear wheel and inner fender splash shield.

5. Disconnect the fuel lines at the fuel filter and the electrical connectors from the tank. Disconnect the fuel tank vent tube from the filler neck. Disconnect the ground wire from the body.

6. Place a suitable support under the tank and remove the retaining straps. Lower the tank from the vehicle.

7. Remove the bolts holding the tank sending unit to the tank. Pull the sending unit/pump from the tank, note the position of the gasket.

8. Disconnect electrical connectors from the terminals on fuel pump and remove the pump holding bracket.

9. Disconnect hose clamp at inlet port. Unscrew hose clamp and remove fuel pump.

NOTE: There is a tray in the bottom of the fuel tank that is contoured to hold the fuel filter. Be certain when installing the pump/sending unit that the filter correctly fits into the tray.

To install:

10. Position the gasket so that the holes in the gasket line up with bolts holes in the fuel tank.

11. Install the sending unit/pump into the fuel tank and install the retaining bolts.

12. To complete installation, follow the removal procedure.

MEDALLION
The fuel pump used on the 2.2L engine is mounted on a plate located under the vehicle if front of the rear axle assembly.

1. Release the fuel system pressure.

2. Disconnect battery negative cable.

3. Raise and support the vehicle safely.

4. Disconnect electrical connectors from pump.

5. Plug the pump inlet and outlet hoses to prevent fuel flow.

6. Disconnect fuel pump hoses. Wrap a shop towel around the hoses and remove hoses from fuel pump.

7. Remove the pump retaining strap and remove the fuel pump.

8. Installation is the reverse of the removal procedure.

NOTE: The pump terminals are different sizes to ensure the pump rotates in the correct direction.

SUMMIT
1. Release the fuel system pressure.

2. Disconnect battery negative cable.

3. Raise and safely support the vehicle.

4. Place an appropriate container beneath fuel tank. Remove filler cap and drain plug from fuel tank.

5. Remove fuel filler hose, return hose, high pressure hose, vapor hose and check valve. Disconnect electrical connectors.

6. Place a suitable support under the tank and remove the retaining straps. Lower the tank from the vehicle.

7. Remove the fuel pump from the tank.

8. To install, reverse the removal procedure.

FUEL SYSTEM PRESSURE TEST

The fuel pressure must be checked and, if necessary adjusted whenever the fuel pressure regulator has been replaced.

NOTE: Always wrap shop towels around the fuel lines before disconnecting them. The shop towels will absorb spilled fuel.

1.5L AND 1.6L ENGINE
1. Release the fuel system pressure.

2. Disconnect the fuel high pressure hose at the delivery pipe side. Cover the hose connection with a shop towel to prevent splash of fuel.

3. On 1.6L engine, remove the throttle body stay.

4. Install adapter MD998709 and MD998742 or equivalent and a fuel gauge between the delivery pipe and the high pressure hose.

5. Start the engine and run at curb idle speed.

6. Check the fuel system pressure. It should be approximately 36 psi.

7. Disconnect and plug the vacuum hose from the pressure regulator. The pressure should increase to 47–50 psi.

8. Race the engine repeatedly 2 or 3 times and check that the pressure does not fall when the engine is return to idle.

9. If the fuel system is not within specifications, check for probable cause and make necessary repairs.

10. Stop the engine and check for changes in fuel pressure, which should not drop.

11. Reduce the pressure in the system and remove the fuel gauge and adapter from the delivery pipe.

12. On 1.6L engine, install the throttle body stay.

13. Install a new O-ring on the high pressure hose and connect it to the delivery pipe.

2.2L ENGINE
1. Relieve the fuel system pressure.

2. Disconnect the hose from the fuel pressure regulator to fuel rail.

3. Disconnect the vacuum hose from the pressure regulator and connect it to a vacuum pump.

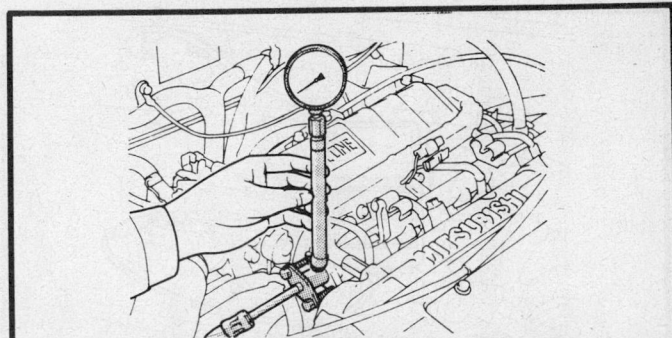

Checking fuel pressure—1.5L and 1.6L engines

4. Connect a fuel gauge to the fuel rail and start the engine.

5. Check the fuel pressure readings. It should be 36 ± 3 psi.

6. Apply 15 inches of vacuum to the pressure regulator. The pressure should drop to 29 ± 3 psi.

7. Turn the ignition **OFF**. Remove the fuel gauge from fuel rail.

8. Reconnect the vacuum hose to the pressure regulator and hose from the pressure regulator to the fuel rail.

2.5L ENGINE

NOTE: The throttle body has 2 port plugs on it. The test port is located on the side of the fuel pressure regulator next to the fuel return tube connection.

1. Allow the engine to cool down before removing the test port.

2. Relieve the fuel system pressure.

3. Placed a shop towel over test port to catch fuel and slowly remove the test port plug from the throttle body.

4. Install fuel pressure test adapter, tool 6173 or equivalent, along with a 0–30 psi (0–207 kpa) gauge into test port.

5. Start the engine and let it idle. Check the fuel pressure reading. The fuel pressure should be 14–15 psi (97–103 kpa). If the pressure is not within specifications adjust the fuel pressure regulator as followed:

    a. Locate the fuel pressure regulator adjusting screw behind the aluminum plug in th nose of the fuel pressure regulator casing.

    b. Lightly tap the plug with a small punch and hammer until it pops out.

    c. Run the engine at 750–800 rpm, then turn the adjustment screw until the fuel pressure is within specifications.

6. Turn the ignition switch **OFF**. Disconnect the fuel gauge and pressure test adapter tool 6173 or equivalent.

7. Install the plug in test port. Install the aluminum plug in front of the regulator adjusting screw.

8. Replace the fuel tank filler cap.

3.0L ENGINE

1. Relieve the fuel system pressure.

2. Remove the black fuel supply tube from the fuel rail using tool 6182 or equivalent. Slide the tool over the nipple and up into the connector until the handle fits the connector. Pull the fuel supply tube off the fuel rail.

3. Install fuel tube adapter 6175 or equivalent and a 0–60 psi gauge. Push the adapter female end with the quick connect fitting over the fuel rail. Push the male end with the nipple into the black fuel supply tube.

4. Start the engine and check the fuel pressure. It should be 28–30 psi (193–207 kpa).

NOTE: The fuel pressure regulator used on this system is non-adjustable.

5. If the fuel pressure is not within specifications. Check items such as a restricted fuel return hose, pressure regulator vacuum hose for leaks, faulty fuel pump or a faulty pressure regulator.

6. Remove the fuel tube adapter 6175 or equivalent.

7. Lightly lubricate the ends of the fuel supply tube with clean engine oil. Install the black fuel supply tube to fuel rail and grey fuel return tube to the pressure regulator.

FUEL INJECTOR

Removal and Installation

1.5L AND 1.6L ENGINES

1. Relieve the fuel system pressure.

2. Disconnect the negative battery cable.

3. Remove the high pressure fuel hose, fuel return hose and O-rings.

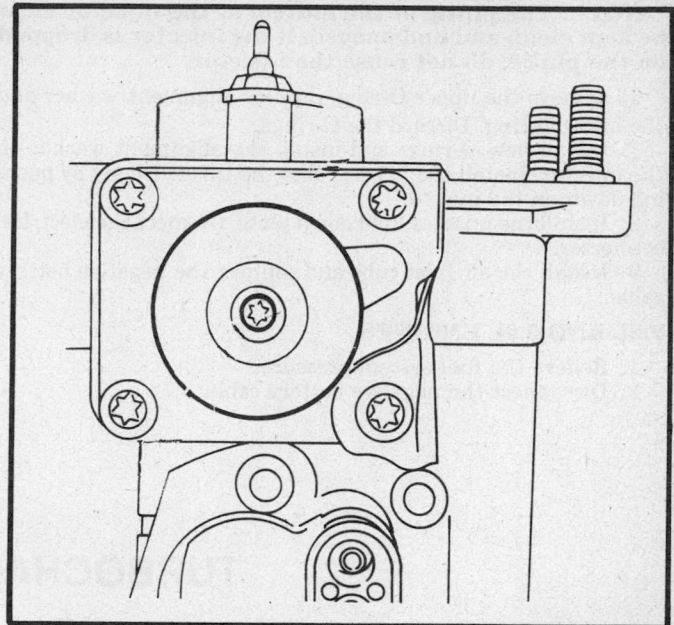

TBI fuel pressure adjustment screw

4. Disconnect vacuum hose connections.

5. Remove the pressure regulator attaching screws and remove pressure regulator and O-ring.

6. Disconnect and tag injector connectors.

7. Remove delivery pipe mounting bolts. Remove delivery pipe and insulators with injectors attached.

8. Remove injector, O-ring and grommet.

9. Installation is the reverse of the removal procedure.

10. When installing the fuel pressure regulator or high pressure fuel hose, apply petrol to the hose union and O-rings.

2.5L ENGINE

1. Relieve the fuel system pressure.

2. Disconnect the negative battery cable.

3. Remove the air inlet tube from the throttle body. Disconnect the electrical lead from the fuel injector.

4. Remove the screws attaching the injector hold down plate and remove the hold down plate.

5. Using an appropriate tool, grasp the top of the injector and pull the injector out of the throttle body.

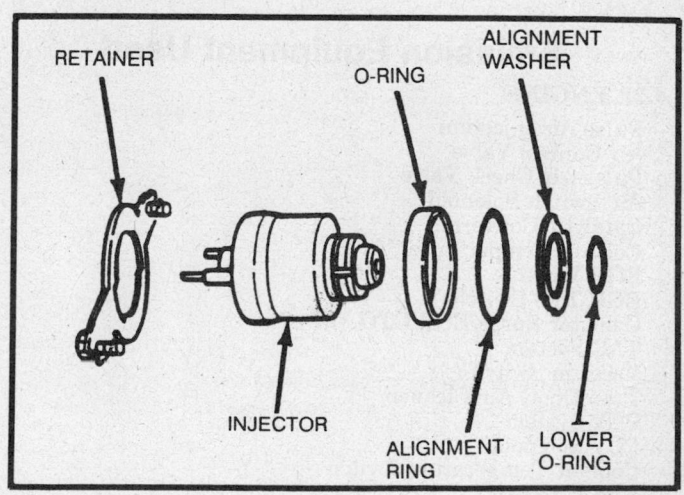

TBI fuel injector – 2.5L engine

NOTE: The pintle at the bottom of the injector must be kept clean and undamaged. If the injector is dropped on the pintle, do not reuse the injector.

6. Remove the upper O-ring, injector alignment washer and the lower O-ring. Discard the O-rings.

7. Install new O-rings and install the alignment washer on the injector. Install the injector into the throttle body by pushing down on the injector.

8. Install the injector hold down plate. Connect the electrical connector.

9. Install the air inlet tube and connect the negative battery cable.

2.2L AND 3.0L ENGINES

1. Relieve the fuel system pressure.
2. Disconnect the negative battery cable.

3. Disconnect the fuel lines from the fuel rail assembly.

4. Disconnect and tag the electrical leads from the fuel injectors and lay the harness aside.

5. Disconnect the accelerator cable from the the throttle body. On the 3.0L engine, remove the 4 screws attaching the engine cover and remove the cover.

6. Remove the fuel rail mounting bolts. Pull the fuel rail and injectors from the engine, using a back and forth twisting motion.

7. Install the fuel rail and injectors to the engine, be careful not to damage the O-rings on the injectors. Install the fuel rail hold down bolts and connect the fuel lines.

8. Connect the electrical leads to the injectors. Connect the throttle cable. On the 3.0L engine install the engine cover plate.

9. Connect the negative battery cable. Turn the ignition to the **ON** position to pressurize the fuel system and check for leaks.

TURBOCHARGER SYSTEM

Refer to "Chilton's Electronic Engine Controls Manual" for additional coverage.

TURBOCHARGER UNIT

Removal and Installation

1.6L ENGINE

1. Disconnect battery negative cable.
2. Drain the engine oil, cooling system and remove the radiator.
3. Disconnect the oxygen sensor electrical connector and remove the oxygen sensor.

4. Disconnect all vacuum and air hoses that interfere with the removal procedure.

5. Remove the heat shields from both the exhaust manifold and turbocharger.

6. Remove the engine hanger, eye bolt and gaskets.

7. Remove connection for water hose and water pipe.

8. Disconnect and separate the exhaust pipe from the turbocharger.

9. Remove the exhaust manifold and turbocharger assembly.

10. To install, reverse the removal procedure.

11. Fill the engine crankcase, cooling system and reconnect battery negative cable.

EMISSION CONTROL SYSTEM

Refer to "Chilton's Emission Diagnosis and Service Manual" for addition coverage.

Emission Equipment Used

4.2L ENGINE

Pulse Air Injection
Air Control Valve
Pulse Air Check Valve
Air Switch Solenoid
Catalytic Converter
Coolant Temperature Switch
EGR Valve
EGR TVS Switch
Canister Purge/EGR CTO Valve
TAC System
Vacuum Switch
Trap Door, Air Cleaner
PCV System
PCV Solenoid
Coolant Temperature Switch
Knock Sensor
Decel Valve (Calif. w/MT)

Oxygen Sensor
Microprocessor
Carburetor Vent to Canister
Electric Choke
Sol-Vac Idle Control Valve
Thermal Electric Switch
TAC Delay Valve and Check Valve
Ignition CTO Valve
Ignition Electronic Spark Retard

EXCEPT 4.2L ENGINE

Electronic Control Unit (ECU)
Fuel Injector
Manifold Absolute Pressure Sensor (MAP)
Manifold Air Temperature Sensor (MAT)
Coolant Temperature Sensor
Exhaust Gas Recirculation Valve (EGR)
Exhaust Gas Solenoid
Oxygen Sensor
Throttle Position Sensor (TPS)
Knock Sensor
Speed Sensor
Ignition Control Module (ICM)
Idle Speed Regulator

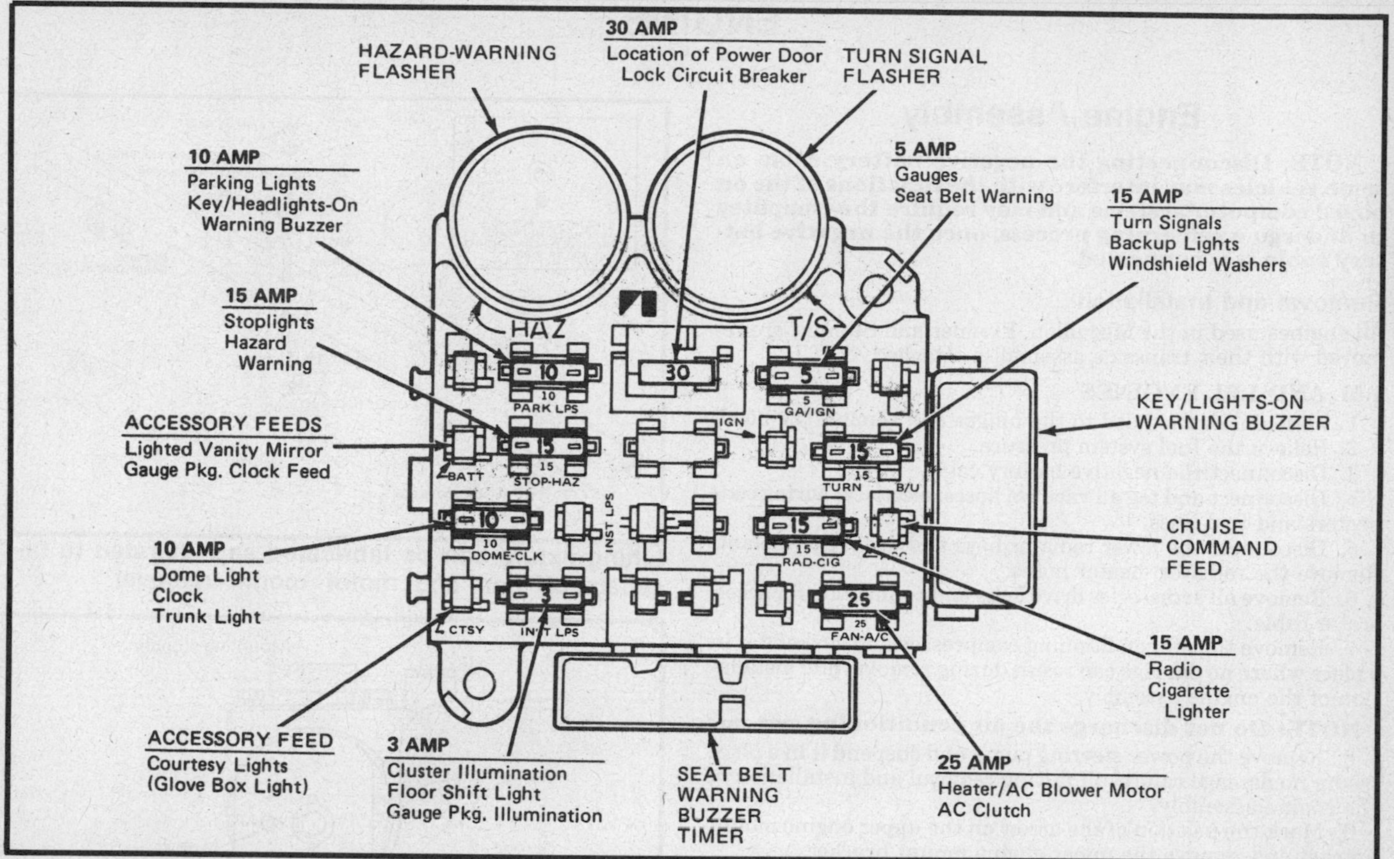

HAZARD-WARNING
FLASHER

30 AMP
Location of Power Door
Lock Circuit Breaker

TURN SIGNAL
FLASHER

10 AMP
Parking Lights
Key/Headlights-On
Warning Buzzer

5 AMP
Gauges
Seat Belt Warning

15 AMP
Turn Signals
Backup Lights
Windshield Washers

15 AMP
Stoplights
Hazard
Warning

KEY/LIGHTS-ON
WARNING BUZZER

ACCESSORY FEEDS
Lighted Vanity Mirror
Gauge Pkg. Clock Feed

CRUISE
COMMAND
FEED

10 AMP
Dome Light
Clock
Trunk Light

15 AMP
Radio
Cigarette
Lighter

ACCESSORY FEED
Courtesy Lights
(Glove Box Light)

3 AMP
Cluster Illumination
Floor Shift Light
Gauge Pkg. Illumination

SEAT BELT
WARNING
BUZZER
TIMER

25 AMP
Heater/AC Blower Motor
AC Clutch

HAZ   T/S

PARK LPS   IGN   GA/IGN
BATT   STOP-HAZ   TURN   B/U
DOME-CLK   INST LPS   RAD-CIG   A/C
CTSY   IN T LPS   FAN-A/C

Fuse panel and fuse locations — Eagle

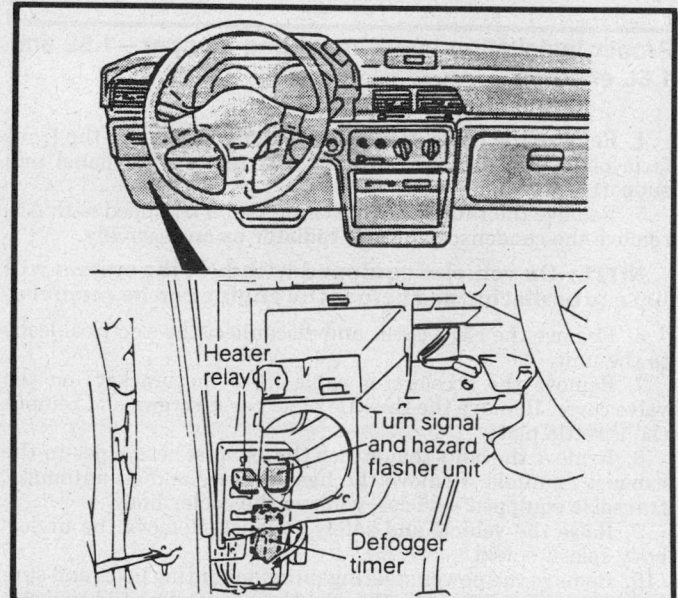

Heater
relay

Turn signal
and hazard
flasher unit

Defogger
timer

Turn signal and hazard flasher unit location — typical

Resetting Emission Warning Lamps

EAGLE

The 1000 hour emission maintenance E-Cell timer is located in
the passenger compartment within the wiring harness leading
to the microprocessor. It is a printed circuit board. The timer
must be replaced when the emission maintenance light illuminates, after service to the oxygen sensor has been completed.
Remove it from its enclosure and insert a replacment timer.

PREMIER

The Premier is equipped with an emission maintenance lamp
that is reset after 7500 miles. Push the **RESET** button on vehicle maintenance monitor.

SUMMIT

The Summit is equipped with a malfunction indicator light that
alerts the driver of any irregularity in the emission system. After the system has been service, turn the ignition switch **OFF**
and disconnect the negative battery cable for approximately 10
seconds. Then, reconnect the negative battery cable.

ENGINE

Engine Assembly

NOTE: **Disconnecting the negative battery cable on some vehicles may interfere with the functions of the on board computer systems and may require the computer to undergo a relearning process, once the negative battery cable is reconnected.**

Removal and Installation

All engines used in the Medallion, Premier and Summit are removed with their transaxle assemblies attached.

1.5L AND 1.6L ENGINES

1. Matchmark the hood to the hinges and remove the hood.
2. Relieve the fuel system pressure.
3. Disconnect the negative battery cable.
4. Disconnect and tag all vacuum hoses, electrical wiring connectors and fuel lines.
5. Disconnect the lower radiator hose and drain the coolant. Remove the radiator, heater hoses.
6. Remove all accessories drive belts and connection for accelerator cable.
7. Remove the air conditioning compressor and suspend it in a place where no damage can result during removal and installation of the engine assembly.

NOTE: **Do not discharge the air conditioning system.**

8. Remove the power steering pump and suspend it in a place where no damage can result during removal and installation of the engine assembly.
9. Mark the position of the arrow on the upper engine mount bracket and remove the upper engine mount bracket.
10. Install an engine support fixture.
11. Raise the vehicle and disconnect the exhust pipe at the exhaust manifold.
12. Remove the front and rear roll stopper bracket to engine connection bolt.
13. Mark the position of the arrow on the mounting stopper of the transaxle mounting and remove the transaxle mount bracket connection bolt.
14. Lower the vehicle and install an engine lift tool to the engine hooks.
15. Slowly raise the engine from the vehicle while checking to be sure all cables, hoses, harness connectors, etc. are disconnected from the engine assembly.
16. Installation is the reverse of the removal procedure.
17. When installing the transaxle mounting stopper on an automatic transaxle, be certain that the arrow is oriented with the mark made during removal.
18. When installing the engine front roll stopper bracket be certain the part where the round hole is made is facing the front of the vehicle.
19. On vehicles equipped with a manual transaxle, temporarily tighten the front roll stopper bracket bolt nut. Then, after the total weight of the engine has been placed on the vehicle body, finish tightening the nut with the distance between the lower edge of the bracket and the center hole of the insulator set to 2.5–2.6 in.
20. When installing the upper engine mounting stopper of an automatic transaxle vehicle, be certain that the arrow is in the direction with the mark made during removal.

2.2L, 2.5L AND 3.0L ENGINES

1. Matchmark the hood to the hinges and remove the hood.
2. Disconnect the negative battery cable, the coil wire, all vacuum and fuel lines.
3. Disconnect the lower radiator hose and drain the coolant. Remove the air cleaner.

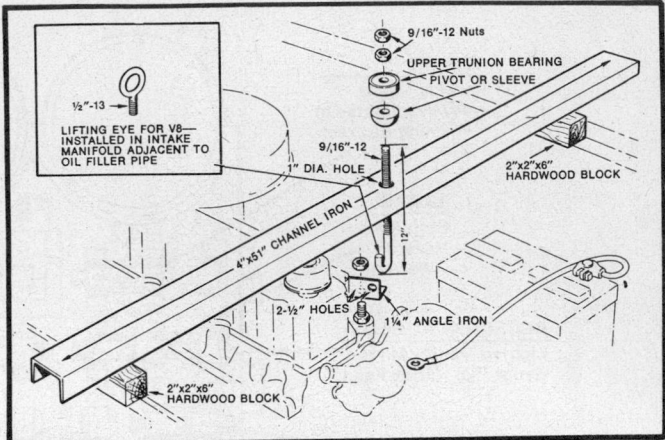

Lifting fixture can be fabricated as illustrated to facilitate oil pan and motor mount removal

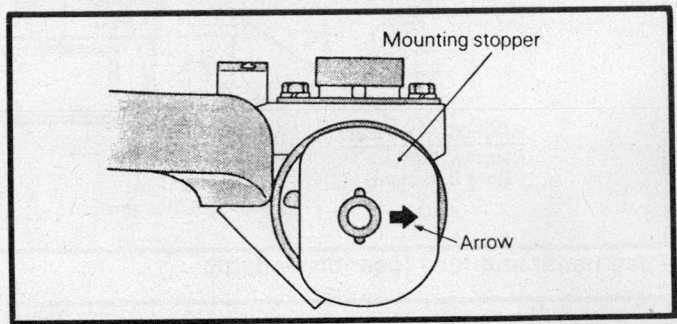

Proper installation upper mounting stopper—1.5L and 1.6L engines

4. Remove the grille. Remove the screws retaining the front facia panel and radiator support and remove the panel and support.
5. Remove the radiator and cooling fan, if equipped with A/C remove the condensor and the radiator as an assembly.

NOTE: **On vehicles equipped with A/C, the system will have to be discharged before the engine can be removed.**

6. Remove the ECU cover and disconnect the electrical leads to the unit.
7. Remove the accelerator cable from the brackets on the valve cover. Remove the throttle plate cover screws and remove the throttle plate.
8. Remove the bolts that attach the exhaust head pipes-to-the exhaust manifold. Remove the heater hoses and on automatic transaxle equipped vehicles, remove the cooler lines.
9. Raise the vehicle and safely support. Remove the underbody splash shield.
10. Remove the power steering pump mounting bolts and support the pump to the side. Remove the header pipe-to-converter bolts and remove the converter.
11. On vehicles equipped with automatic transaxle, disconnect the shifter linkages. On manual transaxle vehicles, disconnect the clutch cable at the transaxle.
12. Remove the wheel assemblies and remove the front stabilizer bar. Remove the brake calipers and support aside. Disconnect the ball joints from the steering knuckle. Remove the axle shaft retaining pin and remove the axle. Remove the strut-to-steering knuckle bolts.

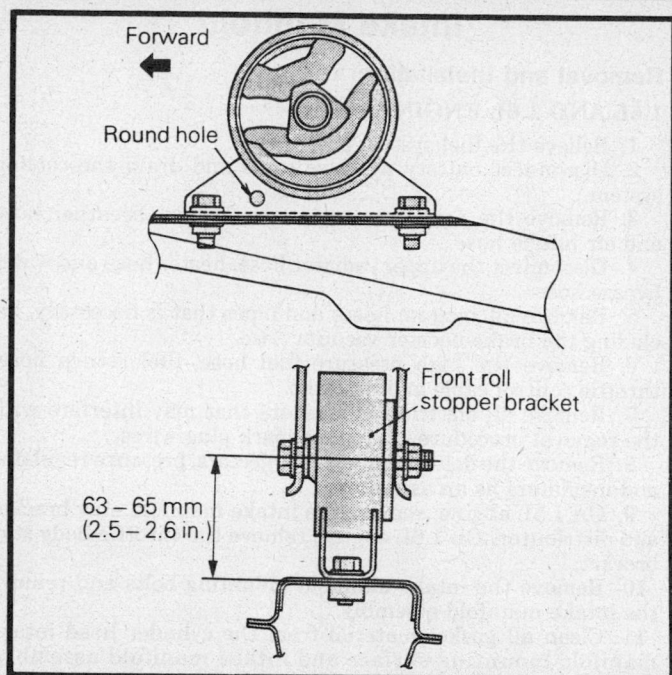

Proper installation front roll stopper bracket—1.5L and 1.6L engines

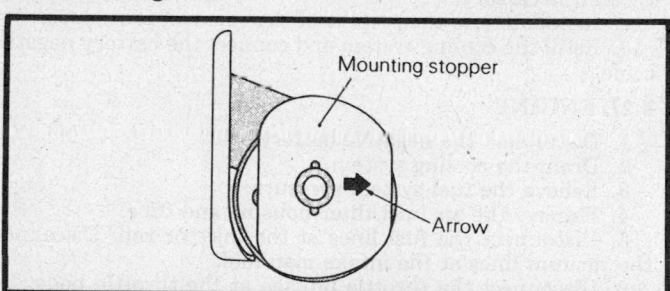

Proper installation automatic transaxles mounting stopper—1.5L and 1.6L engines

13. Loosen the upper strut mounting bolts and swing the axle/strut assembly aside, support the axles safely.

14. Disconnect the speedometer cable. Disconnect the vapor canister and remove it.

15. Loosen the bolts attaching the transmission support to the engine cradle. Remove the bolts attaching the left and right halves of the crossmember to the transaxle. Lower the vehicle.

16. Attach a suitable lifting device to the engine lifting eyes and lift the engine slightly, remove the engine support bolts and remove the engine/transaxle assembly. Lift the engine out at an angle, make sure the transaxle clears the engine compartment.

To Install:

17. Position the engine in vehicle and align the engine mounts with the engine cradle.

18. Install the engine mount bolts and remove the lifting device. Install the left and right sections of the crossmember.

19. Position and install the axle shafts to the transaxle, use new axle shaft retaining pins. Install the shock absorber-to-steering knuckle bolts and attach the tie rod ends. Attach the front stabilizer bar.

20. Install the brake calipers on the rotors and tighten the retaining bolts to 73 ft. lbs. Install the front wheels.

21. Install the converter to the header pipe. Install the power steering pump and adjust the belt tension. Connect the shift linkage and throttle cables.

22. Reconnect all electrical and vacuum leads. Install the can-ister and the air cleaner assemblies. Reconnect the fuel lines and coolant hoses.

23. Install the radiator and fan assemblies. Attach the front facia and support assembly. Install the grill.

24. Attach the negative battery cable and install the hood.

25. Check all fluid levels. Fill and bleed the cooling system.

4.2L ENGINE

NOTE: The engine is removed separately from the transmission.

1. Drain the coolant from the engine and radiator.

NOTE: Do not drain the cooling system until the coolant has cooled and the system pressure has been released.

2. Scribe the hood hinge locations and remove the hood.

3. Disconnect the battery cables and remove the battery.

4. Disconnect the wiring from the distributor, coil, distributor and the oil pressure sending switch.

5. Remove the vacuum switch assembly bracket from the cylinder head cover.

6. Disconnect the front fuel pipe from the fuel pump and insert a plug into the pipe.

7. Disconnect the right engine ground strap and remove the right front engine support cushion-to-bracket bolt.

8. If the vehicle is equipped with air conditioning, completely discharge the system and cap all openings. Disconnect the compressor clutch electrical connector.

9. Remove the electrical connectors from the starter motor.

10. Remove the air cleaner assembly. Tag hoses as necessary.

11. Disconnect the idle speed control solenoid wire connector, the fuel return hose from the fuel filter and the carburetor bowl vent hose from the canister.

12. Disconnect the throttle cable and remove from the bracket. Disconnect the throttle rod, if equipped. Disconnect the throttle rod at the bellcrank. Disconnect the stepper motor wire connector and oxygen sensor wire connector, if equipped.

13. If equipped, disconnect the heater control vacuum hose from the manifold and disconnect the temperature sending gauge wire connector.

14. Disconnect the upper and lower radiator hoses, the coolant hoses from the rear of the manifold and the thermostat housing.

15. Remove the fan shroud screws, disconnect the transmission oil cooler pipe fittings from the radiator, if equipped. Remove the radiator and the shroud.

16. Remove the fan assembly from the hub. Install a ⁵⁄₁₆ x ½ inch bolt through the fan pulley into the water pump flange to maintain alignment when the crankshaft is rotated.

17. Remove the power brake vacuum check valve, if equipped.

18. If the vehicle is equipped with power steering, disconnect the hoses from the steering gear fittings and drain the system.

19. Remove the transmission filler tube, if equipped.

20. Raise the vehicle and support safely. Remove the starter motor.

21. If equipped with automatic transmission, remove the converter access plate, matchmark the converter to the drive plate and remove the converter-to-drive plate bolts. Remove the exhaust pipe support brace from the converter housing.

NOTE: This brace also supports the inner end of the transmission linkage.

22. If equipped with manual transmission, remove the flywheel access cover and the clutch release bellcrank inner support screws. Disconnect the springs and remove the clutch release bellcrank. Remove the outer bellcrank-to-throw-out lever rod bracket retainer. Disconnect the back-up lamp switch wire harness under the hood at the firewall for access to the flywheel housing bolts.

23. Remove the engine mount cushion-to-bracket screws.

24. Disconnect both halfshafts and the front axle assembly.
25. Disconnect the exhaust pipe from the manifold, loosen the upper converter or flywheel housing-to-engine bolts and loosen the bottom bolts. Lower the vehicle.
26. Remove the A/C compressor idler pulley and the mounting bracket, if equipped.
27. Attach a lifting device to the engine and raise the engine off the front supports. Place a support stand under the converter or flywheel housing and remove the remaining bolts.
28. Remove the engine assembly from the engine compartment.
29. The installation of the engine assembly is the reverse of the removal procedure.
30. The following torques must be observed:
    a. Drive plate-to-converter bolts — 22 ft. lbs.
    b. Converter housing-to-engine bolts — 54 ft. lbs.
    c. Halfshafts-to-axle — 45 ft. lbs.

Engine Mounts

Removal and Installation

EAGLE

1. Disconnect the negative battery cable.
2. Remove the heated air tube and engine mount bracket-to-axle housing attaching bolts, if required.
3. Remove the engine mounts through bolts.
4. Raise the vehicle and support it safely.
5. Disconnect the axle tube at right side and axle at pinion support, if required.
6. Position a jack under the engine and carefully raise the engine.
7. Remove the engine mounts.
8. Install the replacement mounts and torque the attaching bolts to 33 ft. lbs. (45Nm).
9. Install the engine mount support bracket. Lower the engine and remove the jack.
10. If required, raise the axle into position and install the bolts at pinion and at axle tube.
11. Install the engine mounts through bolts and torque to 45 ft. lbs. (60Nm).
12. Lower the vehicle and reconnect the battery negative cable.

PREMIER AND MEDALLION

1. Disconnect the negative battery cable.
2. Remove the engine mount upper attaching bolt.
3. Remove the engine pitch restrictor (dog bone).
4. Raise the vehicle and support it safely.
5. Remove the engine mount bottom attaching bolt.
6. Carefully raise the engine and remove the engine mount.
7. Installation is the reverse of the removal procedure.

SUMMIT

1. Disconnect the negative battery cable.
2. Mark the position of the arrow on the engine mount mounting stopper. Remove the engine mount bracket and body connection bolt.
3. Remove the mounting stoppers bolt and stoppers.
4. Raise the vehicle and support it safely.
5. Place a wooden block between a jack and the oil pan.
6. Slightly raise the engine and remove the engine mount assembly.
7. Install the replacement mount assembly, lower the engine and remove the jack.
8. Install the engine mount bracket and body connection bolt and torque to 36–47 ft. lbs. (50–65Nm).
9. Install the mounting stoppers and attaching bolt and torque to 33–43 ft. lbs. (45–60Nm). Make certain the arrow is in the direction with the mark made during removal of the mounting stoppers.

Intake Manifold

Removal and Installation
1.5L AND 1.6L ENGINES

1. Relieve the fuel system pressure.
2. Disconnect battery negative cable and drain the cooling system.
3. Remove the accelerator cable connection, breather hose and air intake hose.
4. Disconnect the upper radiator hose, heater hose and water bypass hose.
5. Remove all vacuum hoses and pipes that is necessary, including the brake booster vacuum hose.
6. Remove the high pressure fuel hose, fuel return hose, throttle control cable and brackets.
7. Remove all electrical connectors that may interfere with the removal procedure, including spark plug wires.
8. Remove the delivery pipe, fuel injectors, pressure regulator and insulators as an assembly.
9. On 1.5L engine, remove the intake manifold stay bracket and distributor. On 1.6L engine, remove the throttle body stay bracket.
10. Remove the intake manifold mounting bolts and remove the intake manifold assembly.
11. Clean all gasket material from the cylinder head intake manifold mounting surface and intake manifold assembly. Check both surfaces for cracks and other damage. Check the intake manifold water passages and jet air passages for clogging. Clean if necessary.
12. Installation is the reverse of the removal procedure.
13. Refill the cooling system and connect the battery negative cable.

2.2L ENGINE

1. Disconnect the negative battery cable.
2. Drain the cooling system.
3. Relieve the fuel system pressure.
4. Remove the air inlet/filter housing and tube.
5. Disconnect the fuel lines at the injector rail. Disconnect the vacuum lines at the intake manifold.
6. Disconnect the throttle linkage at the throttle body. Remove the electrical connectors from the injectors.
7. Remove the intake manifold retaining bolts and remove the intake manifold.
8. Clean gasket mating surfaces.

To install:
9. Position the intake manifold on the head using a new gasket and insert the bolts. Torque the manifold bolts to 11 ft. lbs. in the proper sequence.
10. Connect the electrical leads to the injectors and the fuel lines to the fuel rail.
11. Connect the vacuum lines at the manifold and the throttle linkage at the throttle body.
12. Attach the air inlet to the throttle body. Fill the cooling system and connect the negative battery cable.
13. Run the engine, bleed the cooling system and check for leaks.

3.0L ENGINE

1. Relieve the fuel system pressure.
2. Disconnect the negative battery cable.
3. Remove the engine cover retaining bolts and remove the cover.
4. Remove the air inlet cover from the throttle body.
5. Disconnect the transmission kickdown cable, accelerator cable and cruise control cable from the throttle body. Remove the vacuum hoses from the intake manifold.
6. Remove the electrical connector from the throttle position sensor. Disconnect and tag the electrical connectors from the fuel injectors and lay the harness aside.

7. Remove the EGR tube. Remove the wire from the air temperature sensor.

8. Remove the fuel lines from the injector rails.

9. Remove the 4 bolts retaining the intake manifold and remove the manifold. Remove and discard the O-rings, from the cylinder heads.

NOTE: When the intake manifold has been removed the O-rings in the cylinder heads must be replaced.

10. Clean all gasket mating surfaces.

To install:

11. Use new O-rings and install the intake manifold. Torque the retaining bolts to 11 ft. lbs., tighten in an **X** pattern.

12. Install the fuel lines to the fuel rail assembly. Connect the electrical connectors to the fuel injectors. Connect all of the elctrical connectors and vacuum hoses removed.

13. Connect the EGR tube. Connect the transmission kickdown cable, accelerator and cruise control cables. Connect the negative battery cable.

14. Install the air inlet to the throttle body. Install the engine cover.

15. Run the engine and check for leaks.

Exhaust Manifold

Removal and Installation

1.5L ENGINE AND 1.6L ENGINE WITHOUT TURBOCHARGER

1. Disconnect battery negative cable.

2. Raise and support the vehicle safely.

3. Remove the exhaust pipe to exhaust manifold attaching nuts and separate exhaust pipe.

4. Lower vehicle.

5. On 1.6L engine, remove electric cooling fan assembly.

6. Remove outer exhaust manifold heat shield, engine hanger and disconnect oxygen sensor electrical connector and remove sensor.

7. Remove exhaust manifold mounting bolts, inner heat shield and remove exhaust manifold.

8. Clean all gasket material from mating surfaces.

9. When installing, use a new exhaust manifold and manifold to exhaust pipe gasket. Reverse the removal procedure to reinstall.

1.6L ENGINE WITH TURBOCHARGER

1. Disconnect battery negative cable. Drain the cooling system.

2. Raise and support the vehicle safely.

3. Remove the exhaust pipe to turbocharger attaching nuts and separate exhaust pipe.

4. Lower vehicle. Remove air intake and vacuum hose connections.

5. Remove upper exhaust manifold and turbocharger heat shields.

6. Remove engine hanger, eye bolt and gasket, water hose and water pipe.

7. Remove exhaust manifold mounting bolts. Remove exhaust manifold and gasket.

8. Clean all gasket material from mating surfaces.

9. When installing, use a new exhaust manifold and turbocharger to exhaust pipe gasket. Reverse the removal procedure to reinstall.

2.2L ENGINE

1. Disconnect the negative battery cable.

2. Remove the exhaust manifold heat shield and hot air tube.

3. Remove the EGR tube from the manifold.

4. Remove the bolts retaining the header pipe to the manifold.

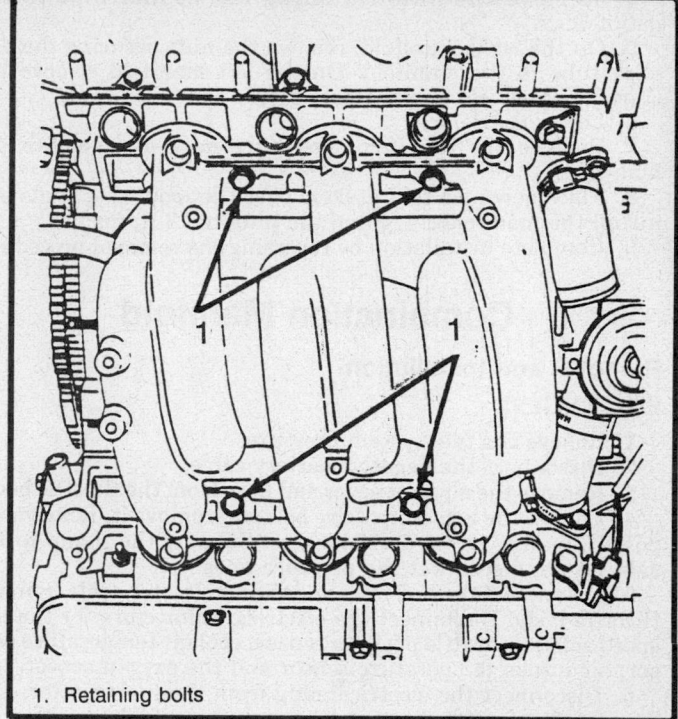

1. Retaining bolts

Install new O-rings before installing the manifold—3.0L engine

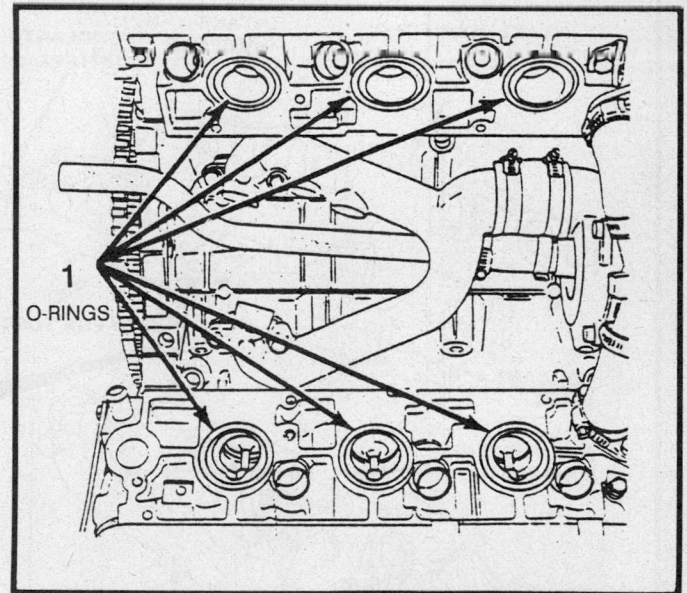

Install new O-rings before installing the manifold

5. Remove the manifold mounting nuts. Remove the manifold and gaskets.

6. To install, place the manifold gaskets and the manifold on the block and tighten the mounting nuts to 13 ft. lbs.

7. Install the heat shield and the EGR tube.

8. Connect the negative battery cable.

3.0L ENGINE

1. Disconnect the negative battery cable.

2. Disconnect the EGR tube from the right manifold.

3. Raise the vehicle and support it safely.

4. Remove the nuts retaining the header pipe to the manifolds.

5. On the right manifold, remove the nuts securing the dipstick tube to the manifold. On the left manifold remove the starter heat shield and the heat stove.

6. Lower the vehicle.

7. Remove the manifold mounting nuts and remove the manifolds.

8. Place new manifold gaskets over the mounting studs and install the manifolds. Tighten the nuts to 13 ft. lbs.

9. Complete installation by reversing the removal procedure.

Combination Manifold

Removal and Installation

2.5L ENGINE

1. Relieve the fuel system pressure.
2. Disconnect the negative battery cable.
3. Remove the air inlet cover and hose from the throttle body.
4. Loosen the accessory drive belt and remove it. Remove the power steering pump and brackets. Support the pump to the side, do not disconnect the pressure lines.
5. Disconnect the fuel lines and the accelerator cable from the throttle body. Disconnect the electrical connectors for the idle speed sensor, throttle position sensor, coolant temperature sensor, air intake temperature sensor and the oxygen sensor.
6. Disconnect the electrical plug from the fuel injector. Disconnect the vacuum lines at the intake manifold.

7. Remove the bolts supporting the EGR tube to the exhaust manifold. Remove the heater hoses from the intake manifold.

8. Remove the intake/exhaust manifold mounting bolts and remove the manifolds from the engine.

9. Clean all of the gasket mounting surfaces.

10. To install, position the new intake manifold gasket and the new exhaust manifold spacers over the locating dowels and install the manifold to the head. Tighten the bolts in sequence and to the specified torque.

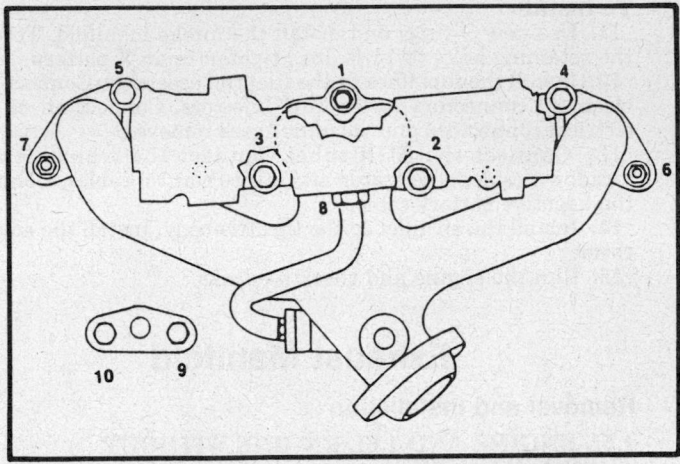

2.5L intake/exhaust manifold torque sequence

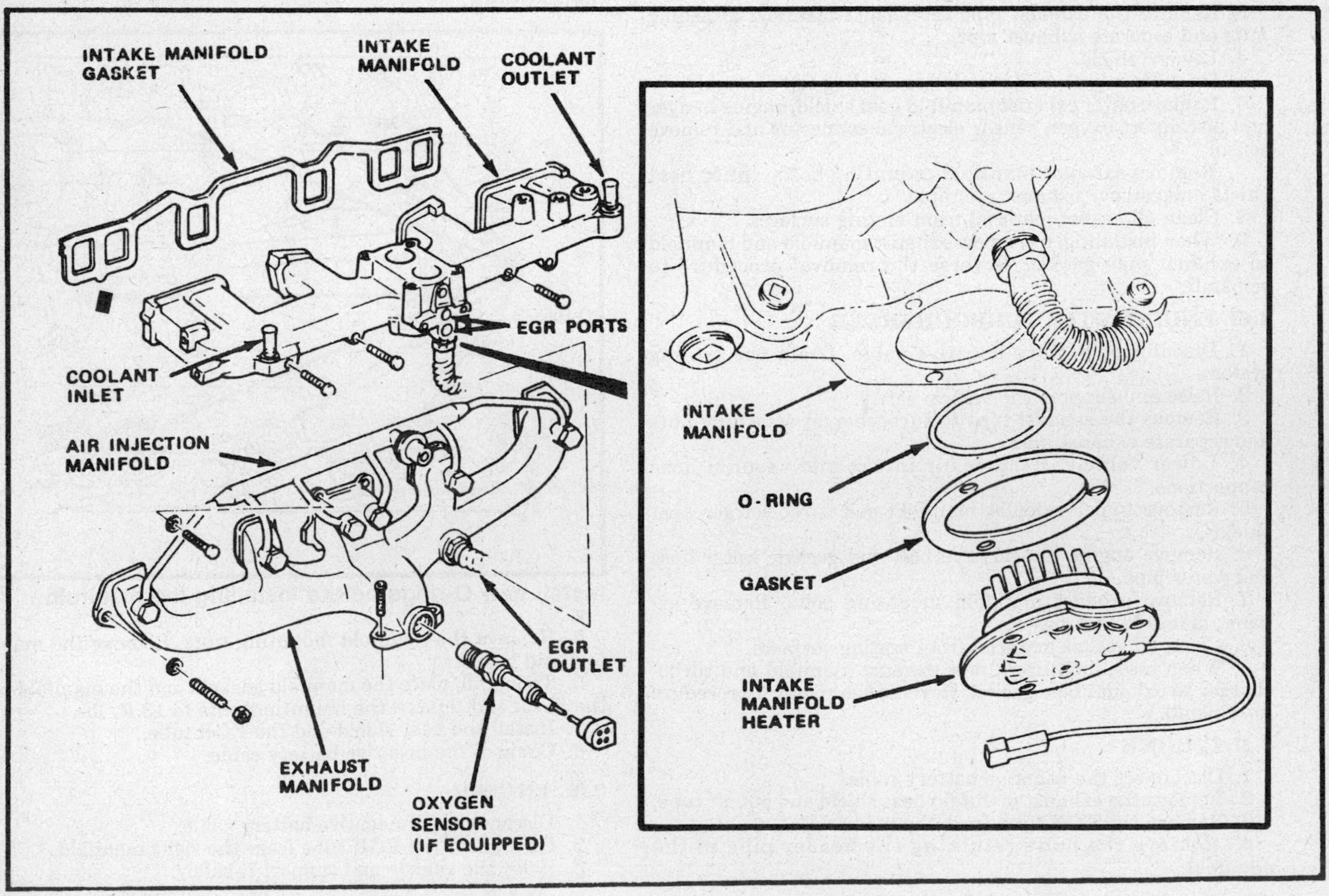

4.2L engine intake/exhaust manifold assembly

11. Install the EGR tube to the exhaust manifold. Connect the heater and vacuum hoses. Attach the fuel lines to the throttle body.

12. Reconnect all electrical connectors. Install the power steering pump and brackets.

13. Connect the accelerator cable. Install the accessory drive belt and adjust the tension. Install the air inlet tube and cover.

14. Connect the negative battery cable and fill the cooling system.

15. Run the engine and bleed the cooling system, check for leaks.

4.2L ENGINE

The intake manifold is mounted on the left-hand side of the engine and bolted to the cylinder head. A gasket is used between the intake manifold and the head; none is required for the exhaust manifold. Note that an improved clamp washer is supplied for this manifold. It is Part No. 8933 004 255 or equivalent and is used at bolt locations numbered 3 through 10. Do not use these washers at positions 1, 2, 11 and 12, where smaller, chamfered washers are used.

1. Disconnect the negative battery cable.

2. Remove the air cleaner. Disconnect the fuel line, vent hose and solenoid wire, if equipped.

3. Disconnect the accelerator cable from the accelerator bellcrank.

4. Disconnect the PCV vacuum hose from the intake manifold and the TCS solenoid and bracket, if so equipped.

5. Remove the spark CTO switch and EGR valve (or exhaust back-pressure sensor) vacuum lines from each of these components.

6. Disconnect the hoses from the air pump and the injection manifold check valve. Disconnect the vacuum line from the diverter valve and remove the diverter valve with hoses, if so equipped.

7. Remove the air pump and power steering bracket, if equipped and remove the air pump. Move the power steering pump aside, out of the way, without disconnecting the hoses.

8. Remove the air conditioning drive belt idler assembly from the cylinder head, if so equipped. On some vehicles it is necessary to remove the A/C compressor. Do not discharge the A/C system; just lay the compressor aside.

9. Disconnect the throttle valve linkage if equipped with automatic transmission.

10. Disconnect the exhaust pipe from the manifold.

11. On some vehicles, an oxygen sensor is screwed in the exhaust manifold just above the exhaust pipe connection. Disconnect the wire and remove the sensor, if so equipped.

12. Remove the manifold attaching bolts, nuts and clamps and remove the intake and exhaust manifold as an assembly. Discard the gasket. The 2 manifolds are separated at the heat riser.

13. To install the intake and exhaust manifolds:

    a. Clean all the mating surfaces on the cylinder head and the manifolds.

    b. Assemble the 2 manifolds together and tighten the heat riser retaining nuts to 5 ft. lbs.

    c. Position the manifold to the engine together with a new intake manifold gasket and tighten the manifold attaching bolts and nuts in the proper sequence to the specified torque.

    d. Install the remaining components in the reverse order of removal. Adjust the automatic transmission throttle linkage, if so equipped. Adjust the drive belt(s) tension.

Valve System

VALVE ADJUSTMENT

1.6L, 2.5L, 3.0L AND 4.2L ENGINES

Vehicles equipped with these engines uses hydraulic valve tappets, eliminating the need for valve lash adjustment. The tappet

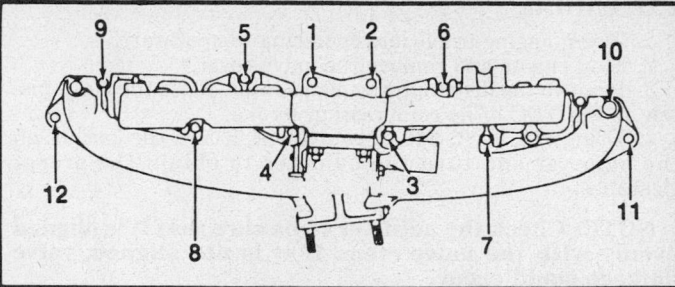

4.2L engine intake/exhaust manifold torque sequence

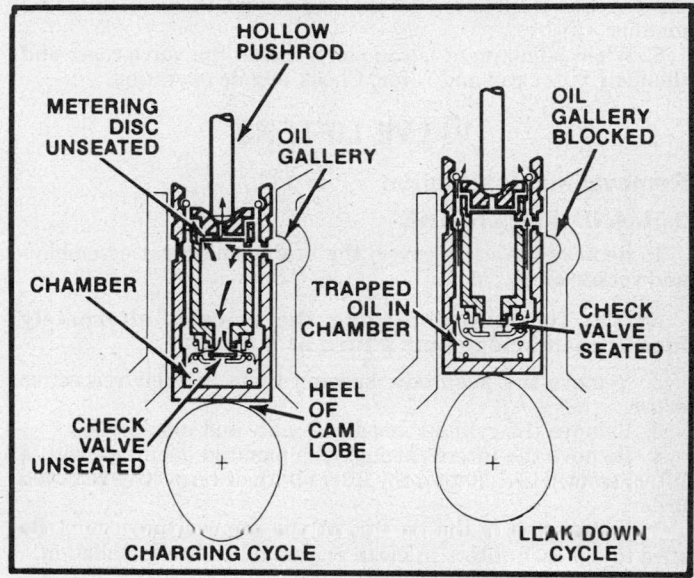

Hydraulic valve operation—typical

plunger is positioned to a pre-set dimension when the valve train is bolted into place, allowing for noiseless operation of the valve system.

1.5L ENGINE

1. Warm the engine to normal operating temperature.

2. Remove all spark plugs for easy operation.

3. Remove the rocker cover.

4. Rotate the crankshaft clockwise until the notch on the pulley is lined up with the **T** mark on the timing belt lower cover. This operation will bring No. 1 and No. 4 pistons at TDC.

5. Move the rocker arms by hand on either No. 1 or No. 4 cylinder to determine which cylinder is TDC on its compression stroke. If both the intake and exhaust rocker arms are movable, that cylinder is TDC on its compression stroke.

6. With No. 1 cylinder on TDC of its compression stroke, adjust No. 1 cylinder intake and exhaust, No. 2 intake and No. 3 exhaust valve clearance to specifications.

7. With No. 4 piston on TDC of its compression stroke, adjust No. 2 exhaust, No. 3 intake and No. 4 intake and exhaust valve clearance to specifications.

8. Perform adjustment as follows:

    a. Loosen the rocker arm locknut and adjust the clearance using a feeler gauge while turning the adjusting screw.

    b. After proper clearance is obtained, hold the adjusting screw to prevent it from turning and tighten the locknut.

    c. Turn the crankshaft through 360 degrees to line up the notch on the crankshaft pulley with the **T** mark on the timing belt lower cover.

    d. Repeat Steps a and b above.

9. Install the rocker cover, spark plugs and check engine operation.

2.2L ENGINE

1. Warm engine to normal operating temperature.
2. Stop engine and remove the valve cover.
3. Remove the distributor cap and rotor. Place the No. 1 piston on the TDC of its compression stroke.
4. Using tool MOT–647 or equivalent, loosen the locknut on the adjuster and turn the adjuster to obtain the proper clearance.

NOTE: Check the adjuster to be sure that it is aligned evenly with the valve stem. If it is not aligned, valve damage could occur.

5. Rotate the crankshaft to bring each set of valves to the TDC of its compression stroke and adjust them in the same manner.
6. When adjustment is complete, install the valve cover and the distributor cap and rotor. Check engine operation.

VALVE LIFTERS

Removal and Installation

2.5L AND 4.2L ENGINE

1. Remove the valve cover, the bridge and pivot assemblies and rocker arms.

NOTE: To avoid damaging the bridges, alternately loosen each bridge bolt a turn at a time.

2. Remove the pushrods, keeping them in their respective order.
3. Remove the cylinder head assembly and manifolds.
4. Remove the lifters through the pushrod openings, with a lifter removal tool. Retain the lifters in their respective removed order.
5. Installation is the reverse of the removal procedure. Be sure to dip each lifters in clean engine oil before installation.

NOTE: Install the used lifters into their original bores.

6. Install the cylinder head assembly onto the engine block using a new head gasket. Tighten in sequence to the proper torque specification. Install the manifolds, if removed separately.
7. Install the pushrods into their original positions and install the rocker arms and bridges and the pivot assemblies. Tighten the bridge bolts a turn at a time, alternately, to avoid damaging the bridges.
8. Pour the remaining oil supplement over the valve train.
9. Install the valve cover and complete the assembly as required.

3.0L ENGINE

1. Disconnect the negative battery cable.
2. Remove the rocker cover and the rocker shaft assembly.
3. On the rocker shaft, remove the retaining screw from the end of the shaft and carefully disassemble the rocker shaft components.
4. From the rocker arm, remove the lifter and the lifter thrust washer. Check the lifters for excess wear and check the rocker arm for blocked oil passages.
5. Lightly coat the lifter and thrust washer with clean engine oil. Install the lifter in the rocker arm.

NOTE: The lifter may tend to fall from the rocker arm. To prevent this use masking tape or wire to hold the tappet in place until the shaft assembly is installed.

6. Assemble the rocker shaft components in the order they were disassembled. Install the rocker shaft assembly on the cylinder head.
7. Install the rocker arm cover.

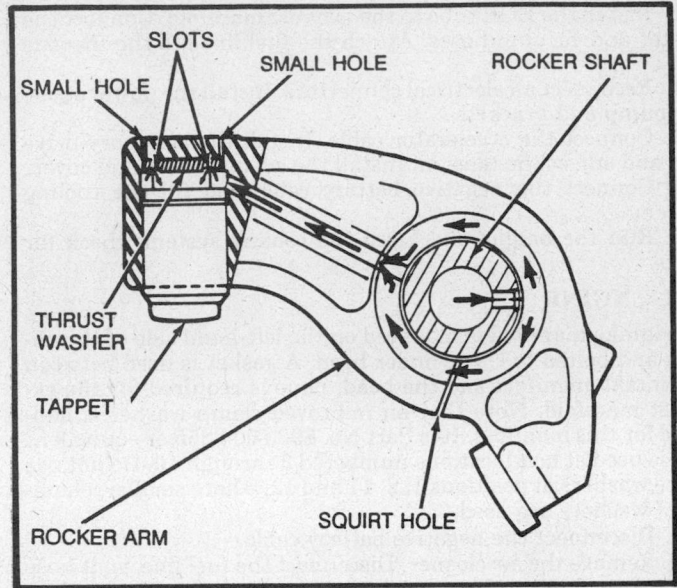

Hydraulic tappet and rocker arm—3.0L engine

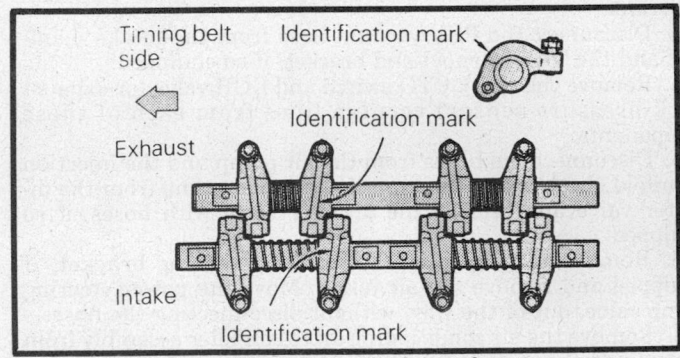

Rocker shaft identification—1.5L engine

VALVE ROCKER SHAFT/ARM ASSEMBLY

Removal and Installation

1.5L AND 1.6L ENGINE

1. Relieve the fuel system pressure.
2. Disconnect the negative battery cable.
3. Remove the accelerator cable, throttle cable, air intake hose, and air cleaner assembly.
4. Remove high pressure fuel hose and fuel return hose.
5. Remove and tag spark plug cables, vacuum hoses and electrical connections that is necessary.
6. Remove the rocker arm cover. On 1.6L engine, remove the semi-circular packing.
7. On 1.5L engine, remove the bolts retaining the rocker arm shafts to the cylinder head and remove intake/exhaust shafts. On 1.6L engine, remove each individual rocker arm.

NOTE: On 1.5L engine, the rocker arms for odd numbered cylinder are marked 1–3 and 2–4 for even number cylinders.

8. Clean all gasket material from rocker cover and cylinder head.
9. To install, position the rocker shafts assembly (1.5L engine) on cylinder head and tighten the rocker shaft retaining bolts to 14–20 ft. lbs. On 1.6L engine, install each individual rocker arm.
10. On 1.5L engine, use a new rocker cover gasket and install

the rocker cover. On 1.6L engine, when installing the rocker cover and semi-circular packing, apply a coating of sealant (Mopar part No. 4318034 or equivalent) to the semi-circular packing and the cylinder head top surfaces. Also, apply a coating of sealant to the rocker cover.

11. Complete installation by reversing the removal procedure.

2.2L ENGINE

1. Relieve the fuel system pressrue. Disconnect the negative battery cable.
2. Remove the rocker arm cover retaining bolts and remove the rocker cover.
3. Remove the bolts retaining the rocker arm shaft to the cylinder head.

To install:

4. Position the rocker shaft assembly on cylinder head and tighten the rocker shaft retaining bolts to obtain the following value.
   a. 2.2L engine—66 inch lbs.
   b. 3.0L engine—53 inch lbs.
5. Install the rocker cover using a new gasket.
6. Connect the negative battery cable and check engine operation.

3.0L ENGINE

1. Relieve the fuel system pressure. Disconnect the negative battery cable.
2. Remove the engine cover mounting bolts and remove the engine cover.
3. Disconnect vacuum hoses and electrical connectors, as required.

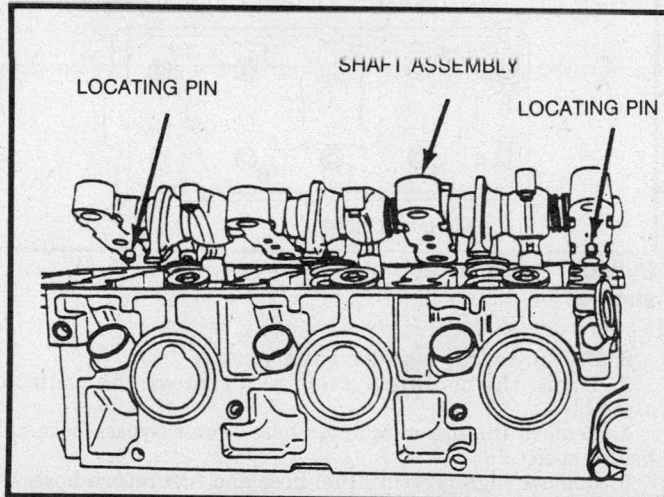

LOCATING PIN   SHAFT ASSEMBLY   LOCATING PIN

Rocker shaft assembly on the 2.5L and 3.0L engines

4. Remove the spark plug wire holder and loosen the accessory drive belt.
5. Remove the A/C compressor mounting bolts and position the compressor out of the way, if required.
6. Remove the power steering reservoir, idle speed regulator bracket, accelerator cable and bracket, if required. Lay to the side.
7. Remove the rocker arm cover attaching bolts and remove the rocker cover.
8. Remove the rocker arm shaft attaching bolts and remove the shaft assembly.

NOTE: Both left and right rocker shaft assemblies are identical and can be used on either cylinder head. Always install them on the same cylinder head that they were removed from.

To install:

9. Lightly coat the rocker shaft assembly with clean engine oil and position on the cylinder head. Tighten the attaching bolts to 53 inch lbs. (6 Nm).
10. Before installing the rocker cover, apply a light coating of sealer to the top of the timing case cover at cylinder head joints area. Complete installation by reversing the removal procedure.

2.5L AND 4.2L ENGINES

1. Disconnect the negative battery cable.
2. Disconnect and mark all vacuum hoses and electrical connections as required.
3. On 4.2L engine, disconnect the fuel pipe at the fuel pump. Remove the vacuum switch and bracket assembly. Remove the diverter valve and bracket assembly.
4. Remove the valve cover.
5. Remove the bolts at each bridge and pivot assembly. Alternately loosen each bolt a turn at a time to avoid damaging the bridges.
6. Remove the bridges, pivots and corresponding pairs of rocker arms and keep them in the order of removal.
7. Installation is the reverse of the removal procedure, with special emphasis on installing the components into their original positions.
8. At each bridge, tighten the bolts alternately a turn at a time, to avoid damage to the bridge. Tighten the bolts to 19 ft. lbs. with a re-torque of 16–26 ft. lbs.

Cylinder Head

Removal and Installation

1.5L ENGINE

1. Drain the cooling system and relieve the fuel system pressure.
2. Disconnect the negative battery cable. Remove the upper radiator hose and heater hose.
3. Remove the timing belt upper cover and rocker arm cover.

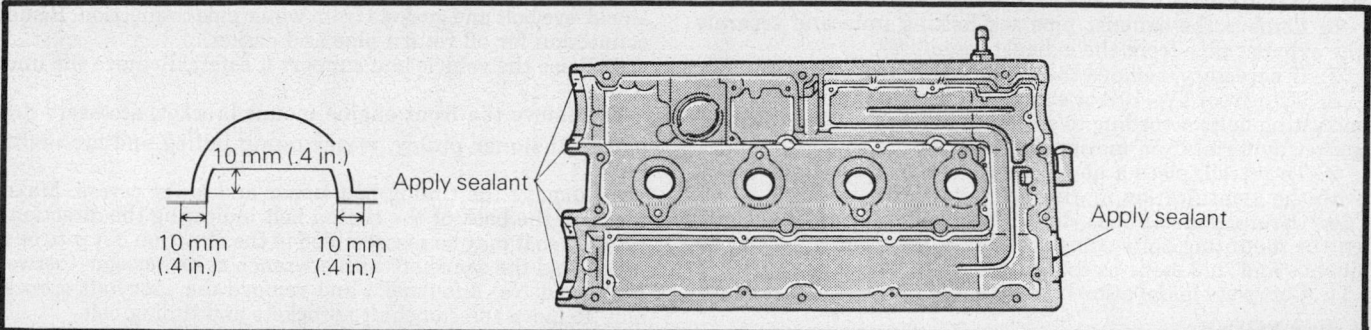

10 mm (.4 in.)

10 mm (.4 in.)   10 mm (.4 in.)

Apply sealant

Apply sealant

Applying sealant to rocker cover—1.6L engine

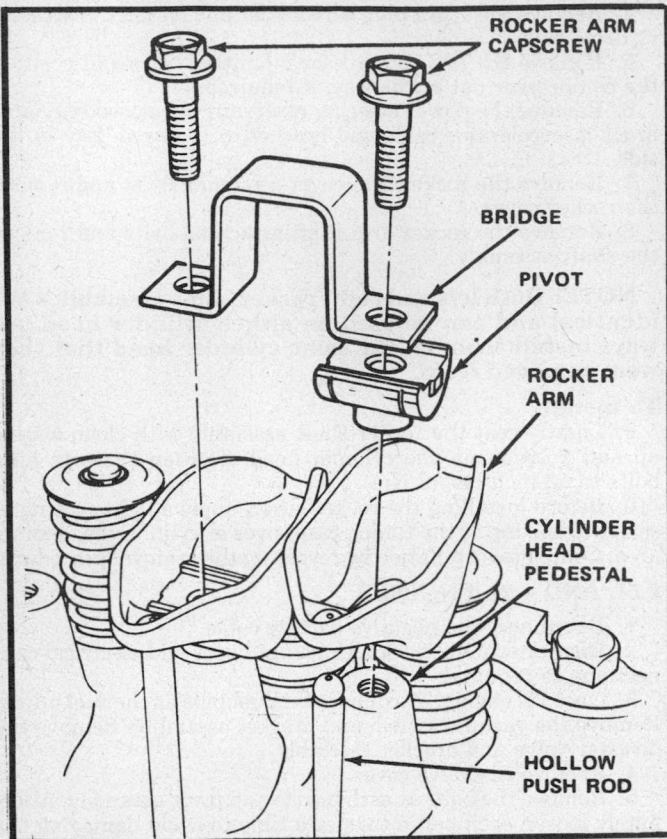

4.2L engine rocker and pivot assembly

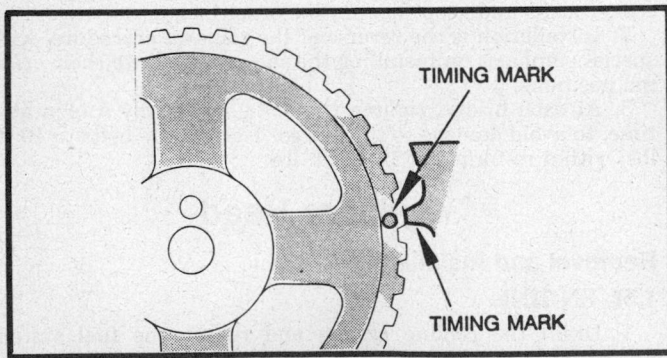

Camshaft sprocket timing mark—1.5L engine

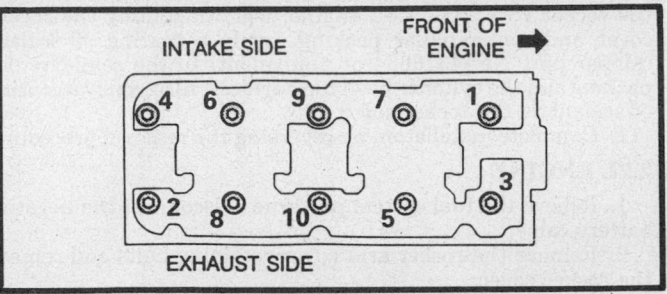

Cylinder head bolts removal sequence—1.5L engine

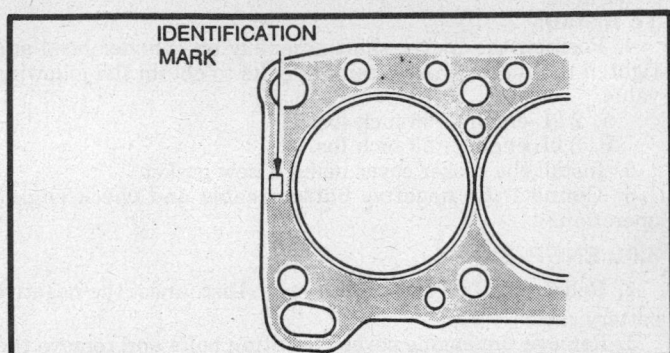

Cylinder head gasket identification mark—1.5L engine

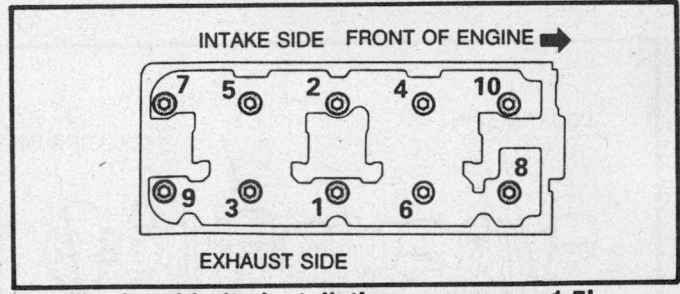

Cylinder head bolts installation sequence—1.5L engine

4. Rotate the crankshaft and align the timing marks.

5. Remove the camshaft sprocket together with the timing belt and support it with wire to prevent disturbing valve timing.

6. Remove the exhaust pipe self-locking nuts and separate the exhaust pipe from the exhaust manifold.

7. If necessary, remove the rocker shaft/arm assembly.

8. Using tool TW-10B or equivalent, loosen the cylinder head mounting bolts according to sequence in 2 or 3 cycles. Clean all gasket material from mating surfaces.

9. To install, place a new head gasket on the cylinder block with the identification marks facing upward.

10. Carefully install the cylinder head on cylinder block. Tighten the mounting bolts using tool TW-10B or equivalent in sequence and in 3 steps to specification.

11. Complete installation by reversing the removal procedure.

1.6L ENGINE

1. Relieve the fuel system pressure.

2. Disconnect the negative battery cable.

3. Drain the cooling system and remove the radiator assembly.

4. Remove the upper radiator hose, water bypass hose and heater hose.

5. Remove high pressure fuel hose and fuel return hose.

6. Remove the center cover, rocker cover, semi-circular packing and rubber plug.

7. On vehicles equipped with a turbocharger, remove the heat shield, eye bolt and gaskets from water pipe connection. Remove connection for oil return pipe and gasket.

8. Raise the vehicle and support it safely. Remove the under cover.

9. Remove the front engine mount bracket, accessory drive belts, tensioner pulley, water pump pulley and crankshaft pulley.

10. Remove the timing belt upper and lower covers. Make a mark on the back of the timing belt indicating the direction of rotation so it may be reassembled in the direction if it is to be reused. Hold the camshaft with a wrench at its hexagon (between No. 2 and No. 3 journals) and remove the camshaft sprocket bolt. Remove the camshaft sprockets and timing belt.

NOTE: Avoid contaminating the timing belt with en-

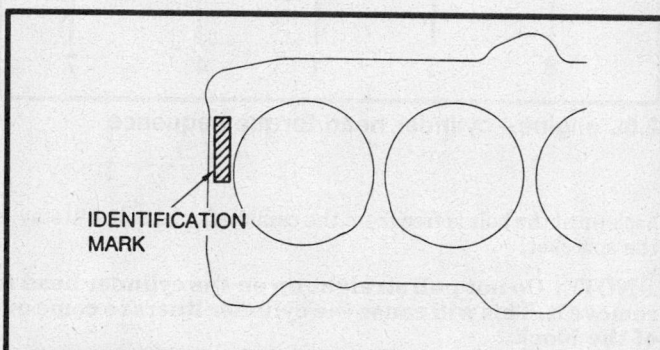

Cylinder head bolts removal sequence—1.6L engine

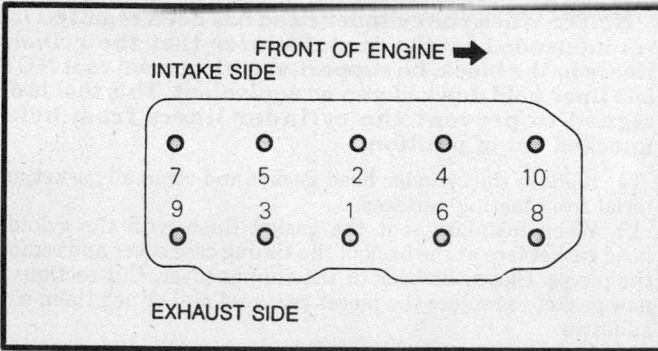

Cylinder head gasket identification mark—1.6L engine

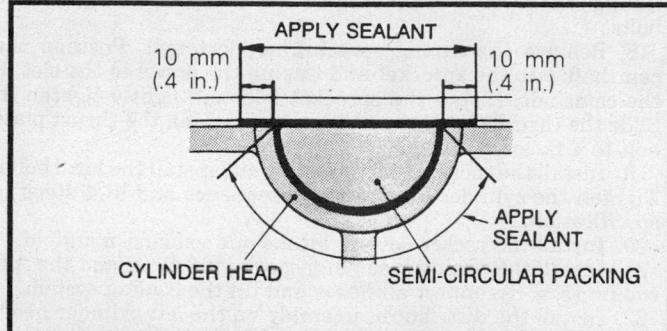

Cylinder head bolts installation sequence—1.6L engine

Applying sealant to semi-circular packing—1.6L engine

gine coolant or oil. These fluids drastically shorten the life of the timing belt.

11. Remove the self-locking nuts from exhaust pipe and separate the exhaust pipe from the exhaust manifold. On engine equipped with turbocharger, separate the exhaust pipe from turbocharger assembly.

12. Using tool MD998051 or equivalent, loosen and remove cylinder head mounting bolts and washers in the proper sequence and in 2 or 3 cycles. Remove the cylinder head assembly. Clean all gasket material from mating surfaces.

13. To install, position a new cylinder head gasket on the cylinder block with the identification mark at the front top. Install the cylinder head to the cylinder block and tighten all bolts with tool MD998051 or equivalent, to the specified torque in the proper sequence and in 2 or 3 cycles.

14. Install the camshaft sprockets, reset the engine valve timing, install and adjust the timing belt.

15. Complete installation by reversing the removal procedure.

2.2L ENGINE

1. Relieve the fuel system pressure.

2. Disconnect the negative battery cable and drain the cooling system. Remove the air inlet tube from the throttle body.

3. Remove the accessory drive belts. Remove the timing belt cover.

4. Loosen the bolts on the timing belt tensioner and remove the timing belt. Remove the spark plugs and wires.

5. Remove any hoses attached to the rocker cover and remove the rocker arm cover. Remove the distributor from the rear of the head.

6. Remove all of the cylinder head bolts except for the bolt at position No. 10 in the tightening sequence. Loosen the bolt at position No. 10 and pivot the cylinder head on that bolt. This can be done by tapping the opposite end of the head with an block of wood. This is necessary to free the cylinder head from the cylinder liners.

NOTE: When the cylinder head has been removed it is recommended by the manufacturer that the cylinder liners in the block, be supported with special tool MOT-588 liner hold down clamp or equivalent. This tool is designed to prevent the cylinder liners from being knocked out of position.

7. Once the head is free, remove the last bolt and remove the cylinder head. Clean all gasket material from mating surfaces.
To install:

8. Place the new cylinder head gasket on the block using the alignment dowel, on the block, to hold it in place.

9. Position the cylinder head on the block and insert the cylinder head bolts. Tighten the bolts in sequence and in 3 steps to specification.

10. Install the distributor to the head. Install the rocker arm cover, using a new gasket. Tighten the rocker cover bolts to 35 inch lbs.

11. Install the timing belt and adjust the belt tension. Install the timing belt cover. Install the spark plugs and wires.

12. Install the accessory drive belts and reconnect all hoses that were disconnected.

13. Install the air inlet tube. Fill the cooling system.

14. Reconnect the negative battery cable. Run the engine and bleed the cooling system. Check for leaks.

2.5L ENGINE

1. Relieve the fuel system pressure.

2. Disconnect the negative battery cable and drain the cooling system.

3. Loosen the accessory drive belt and remove it.

4. Remove the bolts attaching the A/C compressor and without disconnecting the pressure lines, move the compressor aside.

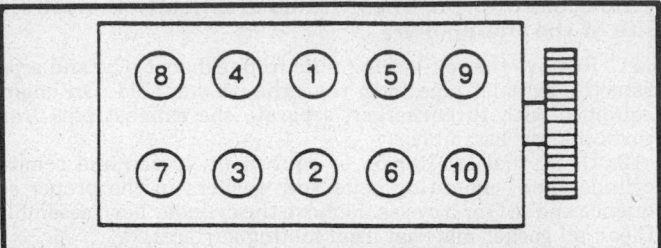

2.2L engine—cylinder head torque sequence

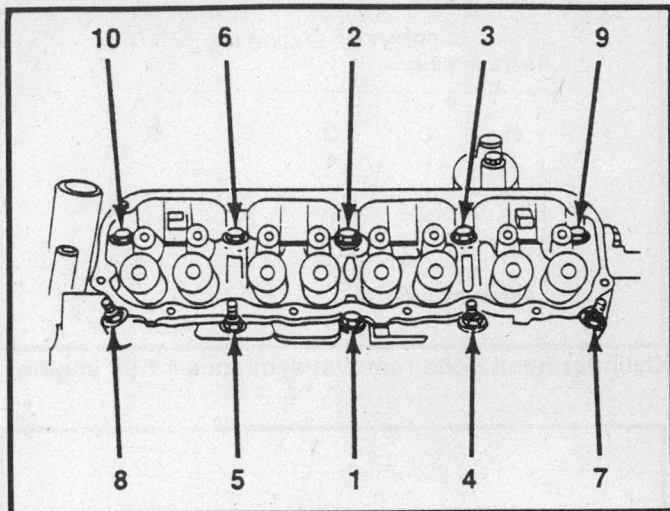

2.5L engine—cylinder head torque sequence

5. Disconnect the upper radiator hose and the heater hoses.

6. Remove the rocker arm cover. Remove the rocker arms and assemblies, keep all of the valve train components in their original order, for installation.

7. Remove the intake and exhaust manifolds.

8. Remove the cylinder head bolts and remove the cylinder head.

9. Clean all gasket material from mating surfaces.

To install:

10. To install, place the new cylinder had gasket on the block with the numbers facing **UP**.

NOTE: The cylinder head gasket used on this engine is a composite gasket and does not require the use of any sealing compound.

11. Place the cylinder head on the block and install the bolts. Tighten the bolts in 3 steps and in sequence to the correct torque.

12. Install the valve train components in their original sequence. Place a new gasket on the cylinder head and install the rocker cover.

13. Connect all of the hoses removed and install the A/C compressor, tighten the mounting bolts to 20 ft. lbs. Route the accessory drive belt and adjust the tension.

14. Connect the battery cable and fill the cooling system. Run the engine and bleed the cooling system, check for leaks.

3.0L ENGINE

1. Relieve the fuel system pressure.

2. Disconnect the negative battery cable and drain the cooling system.

3. Remove the accessory drive belt and remove the A/C compressor from the cylinder head cover.

4. Remove the intake and exhaust manifolds.

5. Remove the spark plug wires. Remove the rocker arm cover.

6. Remove the alternator mounting bracket and remove the top timing case bolts that thread into the cylinder head.

NOTE: The timing sprocket and chain must be supported in place and not allowed to drop into the timing case. If the chain and sprocket slip into the case the timing case will have to be removed.

7. Turn the engine over until the camshaft sprocket is straight up. Attach tool MOT–589 (timing chain support bracket) or equivalent, to the timing case cover. On the left cylinder head, remove the distributor assembly.

8. Remove the threaded plug on the front of the timing case cover to gain access to the camshaft sprocket bolt.

9. Remove the cylinder head bolts. Remove the rocker shaft assembly.

10. Remove the rear camshaft cover and gasket at the rear of the cylinder head.

11. Loosen the camshaft thrust plate screw (located behind the timing sprocket) and move the thrust plate up. This will allow the camshaft to move in the head.

12. Loosen the camshaft sprocket bolt and pull the camshaft

back until the bolt is free from the camshaft, the bolt will stay in the sprocket.

NOTE: Do not pull straight up on the cylinder head to remove it. This will cause the cylinder liners to come out of the block.

13. Position a block of wood on the intake manifold side of the head and strike it with a hammer, do the same on the exhaust manifold side of the head. Repeat this until the cylinder head is loose. Remove the cylinder head.

NOTE: When the cylinder head has been removed it is recommended by the manufacturer that the cylinder liners in the block, be supported with special tool MOT–588 liner hold down clamp or equivalent. This tool is designed to prevent the cylinder liners from being knocked out of position.

14. Remove the cylinder head gasket and clean all gasket material from mating surfaces.

15. When installing, cut the gasket flush with the cylinder head gasket face at the back of the timing case cover and remove the pieces. Clean the back of the timing cover. Cut sections of new gasket to replace the pieces removed and attach them with adhesive.

16. Install a new cylinder head gasket over the alignment dowels on the head. Place a small bead of RTV or equivalent at the point where the head gasket meets the timing case cover.

17. Place the cylinder head on the block and install the top timing case cover to cylinder head bolts, only finger tighten the bolts.

18. Remove the timing sprocket support tool. Position the camshaft into the sprocket and line up the dowel to the slot in the camshaft. Install the sprocket bolt and lightly tighten it. Slide the thrust plate into position and tighten the thrust plate bolt to 4 ft. lbs.

19. Install the rocker shaft assembly and install the head bolts. Tighten the cylinder head bolts in sequence and in 4 steps to specification.

20. Install the rocker covers, intake and exhaust manifold.

21. Install the timing case plug, spark plug wires and the A/C compressor. Reconnect all hoses and fill the cooling system.

22. Install the distributor assembly on the left cylinder head.

23. Install the accessory drive belt and adjust the tension. Connect the negative battery terminal. Start the engine and bleed the cooling system. Check for leaks.

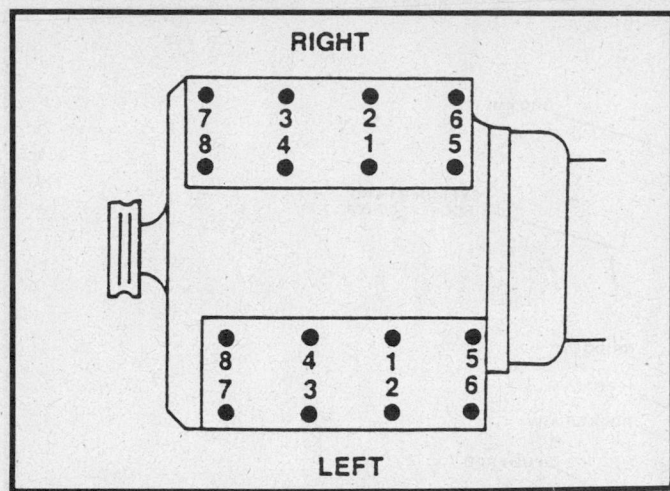

3.0L engine—cylinder head torque sequence

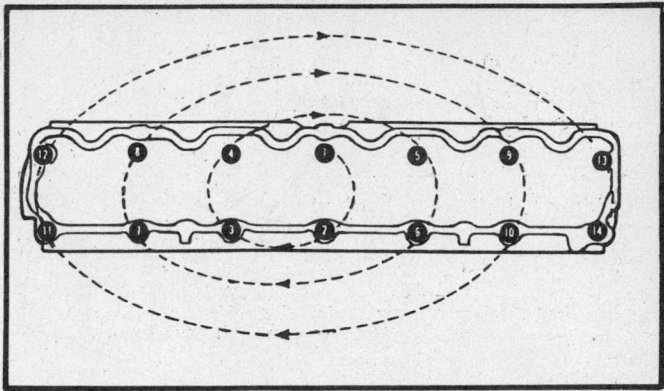

4.2L engine cylinder head bolt tightening sequence

4.2L ENGINE

1. Disconnect the negative battery cable.
2. After the cooling system has cooled, drain the engine block and the radiator. Disconnect the hoses at the thermostat housing.
3. Remove the air cleaner and its components.
4. Remove the air cleaner and the PCV valve moulded hose.
5. Disconnect the distributor vacuum advance hose from the CTO valve. Disconnect the fuel line at the fuel pump.
6. Disconnect the PCV valve from the cover rubber grommet and disconnect the PCV shutoff valve vacuum hose.
7. Remove the vacuum switch and bracket assembly, the diverter valve and bracket and the necessary vacuum hoses and electrical connections to provide clearance for cover removal.
8. Remove the cover retaining bolts and remove the valve cover.
9. Alternately loosen the bridge and rocker arm pivot bolts, 1 turn at a time, to prevent damage to the bridges. Remove the pushrods.

NOTE: Keep the pushrods, bridges, pivots and rocker arms in their order of removal for ease of installation.

10. Without disconnecting the hoses, disconnect the power steering pump bracket and set the assembly aside.
11. Remove the intake and exhaust manifolds from the cylinder head.
12. If equipped with air conditioning, complete the following:
   a. Remove the A/C compressor drive belt.
   b. Loosen the alternator belt and remove the A/C compressor/alternator bracket to head mounting bolt.
   c. Remove the bolts from the air compressor and set the compressor aside.

NOTE: The 4.2L engine serpentine drive belt tension is released by loosening the alternator.

13. Remove the spark plugs, disconnect the temperature sending wire connector and the negative battery cable. Remove the ignition coil and bracket.
14. Remove the cylinder head bolts and remove the cylinder head from the engine block.
15. After cleaning, inspection and overhaul, the cylinder head can be installed in the reverse order of its removal.
16. Apply an even coat of perfect seal sealing compound, or its equivalent, to both sides of the replacement head gasket. Position the gasket on the cylinder block with the word **TOP** facing upward.

NOTE: Do not apply sealing compound on the cylin-der head or engine block gasket surfaces. Do not allow sealer to enter the cylinder bores.

17. Tighten the cylinder head bolts in the proper sequence to 85 ft. lbs.

NOTE: The cylinder head gasket is made of an aluminum coated embossed steel and does not require retorquing of the cylinder head bolts.

18. During the completion of the cylinder head installation, torque the bridge bolts to 19 ft. lbs., turning each, alternately, 1 turn at a time until the specified torque has been reached. Install the cylinder head cover with a ⅛ inch bead of RTV sealer along the sealing surface of the head. Make sure not to delay more than 10 minutes in installing the cover onto the bead of sealer. Torque the cylinder head cover retaining bolts to 28 inch lbs.

Camshaft

Removal and Installation

1.5L ENGINE

1. Relieve the fuel system pressure.
2. Disconnect the battery negative cable.
3. Remove the distributor.
4. Remove the rocker cover, timing belt cover and timing belt.
5. Remove the camshaft sprocket and oil seal.
6. Loosen both rocker arms assembly uniformly and remove.
7. Remove the camshaft rear cover, rear cover gasket, thrust plate and camshaft thrust case. Remove the camshaft.
8. After the camshaft has been removed, check the following:
   a. Check the camshaft journals for wear or damage.
   b. Check the fuel pump drive eccentric cam and distributor drive gear tooth surfaces.
   c. Check the cam lobes for damage. Also, check the cylinder head oil holes for clogging.

To install:

9. Lubricate the camshaft with heavy engine oil and slide it into the head.
10. Insert the camshaft thrust case in cylinder head with the threaded hole facing upward and align the threaded hole with the bolt hole in the cylinder head. Install and firmly tighten the attaching bolt.
11. Check the camshaft endplay between the thrust case and camshaft. The camshaft endplay should be 0.0020–0.0080 inches (0.5–0.20mm). If the end play is not within specification, Replace the camshaft thrust case.
12. When installing the oil seal, coat the external surface with engine oil. Position the seal on the camshaft end and drive into place using tool MD998306 or equivalent.
13. Complete installation by reversing the removal procedure.

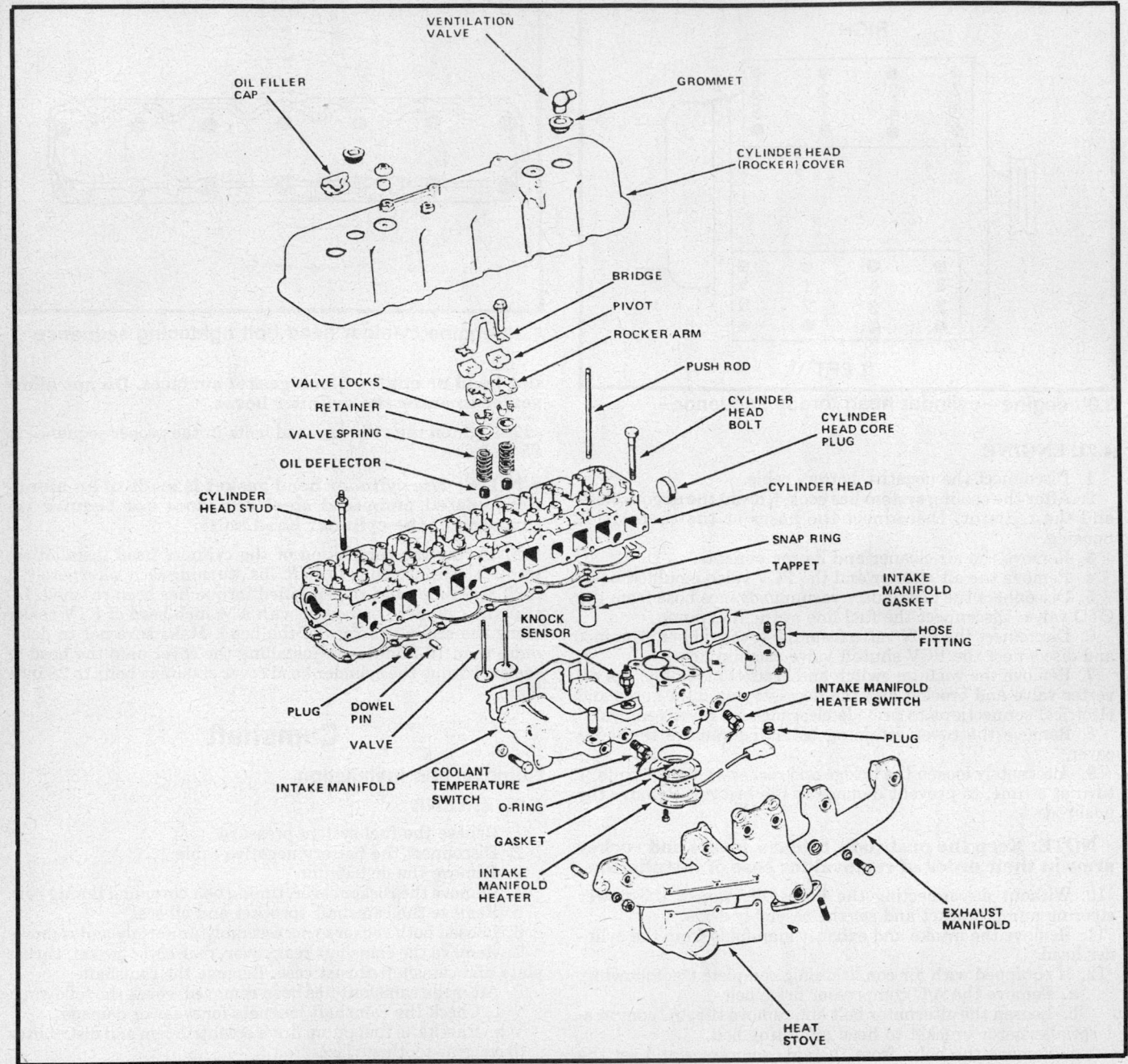

Exploded view of 4.2L engine cylinder head

1.6L ENGINE

1. Relieve the fuel system pressure.
2. Disconnect battery negative cable.
3. Remove the accelerator cable connection.
4. Remove the timing belt cover and timing belt.
5. Remove the center cover, breather and PCV hoses and spark plug cables.
6. Remove the rocker cover, semi-circular packing, throttle body stay, crankshaft angle sensor, both camshaft sprockets and oil seals.
7. Loosen the bearing cap bolts in 2 or 3 steps. Lable and re- move both camshaft bearing caps.

NOTE: If the bearing caps are difficult to remove, use a plastic hammer to gently tap the rear part of the camshaft.

8. Remove the intake and exhaust camshafts.
9. After the camshaft has been removed, check the following:
   a. Check the camshaft journals for wear or damage.
   b. Check the cam lobes for damage. Also, check the cylinder head oil holes for clogging.
10. To install, lubricate the camshafts with heavy engine oil and position the camshafts on the cylinder head.

NOTE: Do not confuse the intake camshaft with the exhaust camshaft. The intake camshaft has a split on its rear end for driving the crank angle sensor.

11. Make sure the dowel pin on both camshaft sprocket ends are located on the top.

12. Install the bearing caps. Tighten the caps in sequence and in 2 or 3 steps. No. 2 and 5 caps are of the same shape. Check the markings on the caps to identify the cap number and intake/exhaust symbol. Only **L** (intake) or **R** (exhaust) is stamped on No. 1 bearing cap. Also, make sure that the rocker arm is correctly mounted on the lash adjuster and the valve stem end.

13. Apply a coating of engine oil to the oil seal. Using tool MD998307 or equivalent, press-fit the seal into the cylinder head.

14. Align the punch mark on the crank angle sensor housing with the notch in the plate. With the dowel pin on the sprocket side of the intake camshaft at top, install the crank angle sensor on the cylinder head.

NOTE: The crank angle sensor can be installed with the punch mark positioned opposite the notch; however, that position will result in incorrect fuel injection and ignition timing.

15. Complete the installation by reversing the removal procedure.

2.2L ENGINE

1. Relieve the fuel system pressure.
2. Disconnect the negative battery cable. Drain the cooling system.
3. Remove the intake and exhaust manifolds.
4. Remove the rocker cover and remove the rocker shaft assembly.
5. Remove the accessory drive belt. Remove the timing belt cover.
6. Remove the timing belt. Remove the cylinder head retaining bolts and remove the cylinder head.
7. Remove the camshaft sprocket and the bolts retaining the camshaft thrust plate.
8. Pry the oil seal out from around the camshaft and slide the camshaft from the head. Use care not to damage the camshaft lobes or the bearings.

To install:

9. Lubricate the camshaft with heavy oil and slide it into the head.
10. Install the camshaft thrust plate. Install a new camshaft oil seal using tool MOT–791–10 or equivalent. Install the camshaft sprocket and tighten the retaining bolt to 37 ft. lbs.
11. Install the cylinder head using a new gasket, tighten all bolts in sequence, to the specified torque.
12. Install the timing belt and adjust the tension. Install the timing belt cover.
13. Install the rocker shaft assembly. Install the rocker cover, intake and exhaust manifolds.
14. Install the accessory drive belt and fill the cooling system. Connect the negative battery cable. Run the engine and bleed the cooling system.

2.5L ENGINE

1. Relieve the fuel system pressure.
2. Disconnect the negative battery cable. Drain the cooling system.
3. Remove the radiator.
4. Remove the fan and water pump pulley.
5. Remove the grille if necessary for clearance.
6. Remove the rocker cover, rocker arms and pushrods.
7. Remove the distributor, spark plugs and fuel pump.
8. Remove the lifters.
9. Remove the crankshaft hub and timing gear cover.
10. Remove the 2 camshaft thrust plate screws by working through the holes in the gear.
11. Remove the camshaft and gear assembly by pulling it through the front of the block. Be carefull not to damage the bearings.

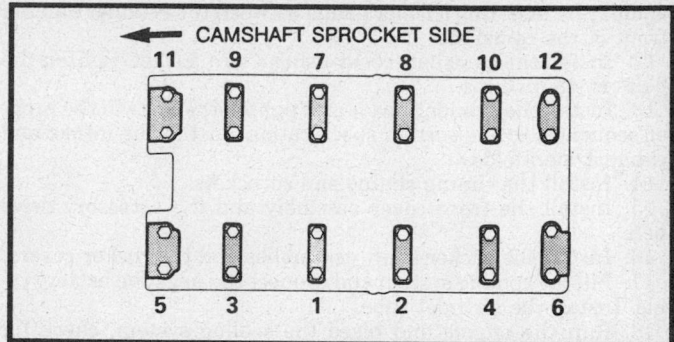
Camshaft bearing caps torque sequence—1.6L engine

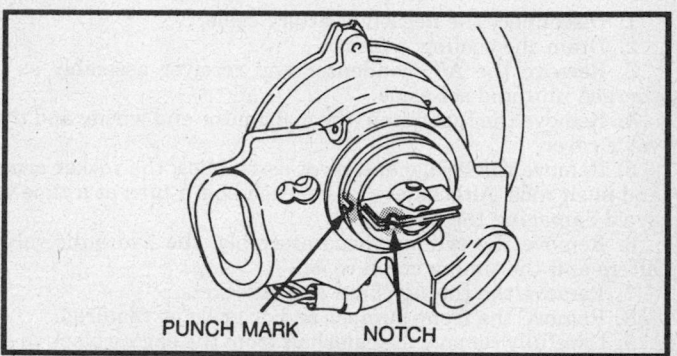
Proper cam angle sensor installation—1.6L engine

To install:

12. Lubricate the camshaft with heavy oil and install it into the block.
13. Install the timing chain and sprockets. Install the timing case cover.
14. Install the valve lifters and related components. Install the rocker cover.
15. Install the crankshaft hub and the water pump pulley. Install the accessory drive belts.
16. Position the distributor and tighten the hold down bolt, install the spark plugs.
17. Install the grille. Connect the negative battery cable.

3.0L ENGINE

The camshafts used in this engine are removed from the rear of the cylinder heads after the cylinder heads have been removed.

1. Relieve the fuel system pressure.
2. Disconnect the negative battery cable.
3. Drain the cooling system.
4. Remove the accessory drive belt. Remove the air inlet tube from the throttle body.
5. Remove the intake and exhaust manifolds.
6. Remove the front cover and remove the timing chains and sprockets.
7. Remove the rocker covers and the rocker shaft assemblies. Remove the cylinder head(s).
8. Remove the camshaft cover at the rear of the cylinder head. Loosen the camshaft retainer bolt and slide the retainer away from the camshaft.
9. Slide the camshaft out of the head, use care not to damage the camshaft lobes or bearings.

To install:

10. Coat the camshaft with heavy oil and slide it into the head. Position the retainer in the grove of the camshaft and tighten the mounting bolt to 9 ft. lbs.
11. Push the camshaft to the front and check the camshaft

endplay by inserting a feeler gauge between the retainer and the front of the camshaft.

12. Install the camshaft cover using a new gasket, tighten the bolts to 48 inch lbs.

13. Install the cylinder heads and tighten the bolts in the proper sequence, to the correct specification. Install the intake and exhaust manifolds.

14. Install the timing chains and sprockets.

15. Install the front cover assembly and the accessory drive belt.

16. Install the rocker shaft assemblies and the rocker covers.

17. Fill the cooling system and connect the negative battery cable. Install the air inlet tube.

18. Run the engine and bleed the cooling system, check for leaks.

4.2L ENGINE

1. Disconnect the negative battery cable.

2. Drain the cooling system.

3. Remove the A/C condenser and receiver assembly as a charged unit and set aside.

4. Remove the fuel pump, the distributor and wiring and the valve cover.

5. Remove the bridge and pivot assemblies, the rocker arms and push rods. Alternately loosen each bolt a turn at a time to avoid damaging the bridges.

6. Remove the cylinder head assembly, the hydraulic valve lifters and the timing chain cover.

7. Remove the timing chain and sprockets.

8. Remove the front bumper and/or grille as required.

9. Carefully remove the camshaft from the engine block so as not to damage the camshaft bearings.

To install:

10. Lubricate the camshaft with engine oil supplement, or its equivalent. Carefully install the camshaft into the engine to avoid damage to the camshaft bearings.

11. Install the timing chain and sprockets, with the timing marks aligned. Install the camshaft sprocket retaining bolt and torque to 50 ft. lbs.

12. Install the timing chain cover with the new seal and gasket. Install the vibration damper and pulley, the fan assembly and shroud and install the drive belts and tighten to specifications. Install the fuel pump.

13. Rotate the crankshaft a full revolution to place the No. 1 cylinder piston on its compression stroke. Install the distributor so that the rotor is aligned with the No. 1 spark plug terminal of the distributor cap.

NOTE: If the crankshaft/camshaft remains in position with the timing marks aligned, the No. 6 cylinder piston will be on its compression stroke.

14. Install the lifters, the cylinder head and gasket, the pushrods, the rocker arms, the bridges and pivots. Tighten each of the 2 bolts for each bridge alternately, a turn at a time, to avoid damage to the bridges.

NOTE: Lubricate the hydraulic valve train with engine oil supplement and allow it to remain with the engine oil for at least 1000 miles.

15. Install the valve cover, the A/C condenser and receiver assembly, the radiator and shroud and fill with coolant.

16. Install the front bumper/grille, as required.

17. Adjust the ignition timing and idle, as required.

Intermediate Shaft

Removal and Installation

2.2L ENGINE

1. Disconnect the negative battery cable.

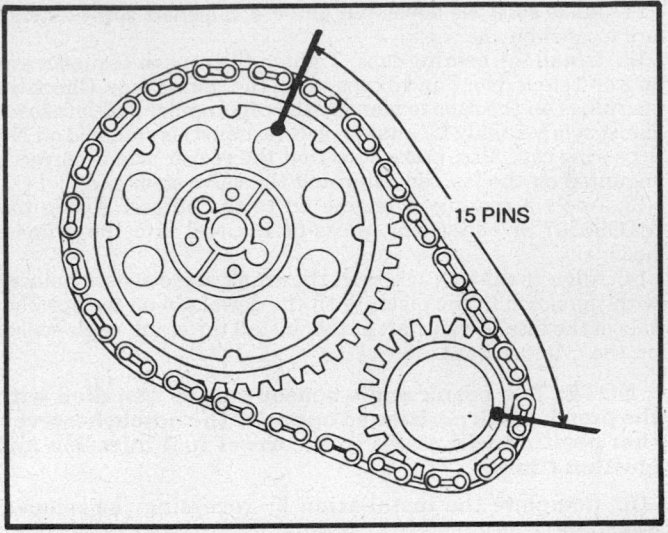

To verify correct installation, rotate crankshaft until camshaft sprocket timing mark is at about a one o'clock position. There must be 15 pins between the timing marks.

2. Remove the timing belt cover and the timing belt.

3. Remove the oil pump driveshaft cover (located on the side of the block).

4. Screw a piece of threaded rod into the top of oil pump driveshaft and remove it.

5. Remove the bolt retaining the intermediate shaft sprocket and remove the intermediate shaft sprocket.

6. Remove the bolts from the intermediate shaft cover. Remove the cover and gasket. Remove the bolt from the intermediate shaft retainer and pivot the retainer. Remove the intermediate shaft by pulling it from the block.

7. To Install, coat the shaft with heavy oil and slide it into the block. Pivot the retainer into position and tighten the bolt. Install the shaft cover and loosely install the retaining bolts.

8. Install the shaft oil seal and align the cover using tool MOT–790 or equivalent. Tighten the cover retaining bolts.

9. Install the sprocket and bolt, tighten the bolt to 37 ft. lbs.

10. Install the oil pump driveshaft and cover.

11. Install the timing belt and cover, check the belt tension.

12. Connect the negative battery cable.

Timing Case Cover/Oil Seal

Removal and Installation

1.5L AND 1.6L ENGINES

1. Disconnect the negative battery cable.

2. Raise the vehicle and support it safely. Remove the under panel.

3. Place a wooden block between a jack and the oil pan. Slightly raise the engine and remove the engine mount bracket.

4. Remove all accessory drive belts, tension pulley bracket, water pump pulley, crankshaft compressor pulley and crankshaft pulley.

5. Remove the upper and lower timing belt covers.

6. If removal of the front oil seal is necessary, pry the seal from the case cover.

7. On 1.5L engine, apply engine oil to the sufrace of seal installer tool MD998305 or equivalent and slide the new seal along the tool until it touches the front case. Tap the oil seal into place.

8. On 1.6L engine, install the crankshaft oil seal using tool MD998375 or equivalent.

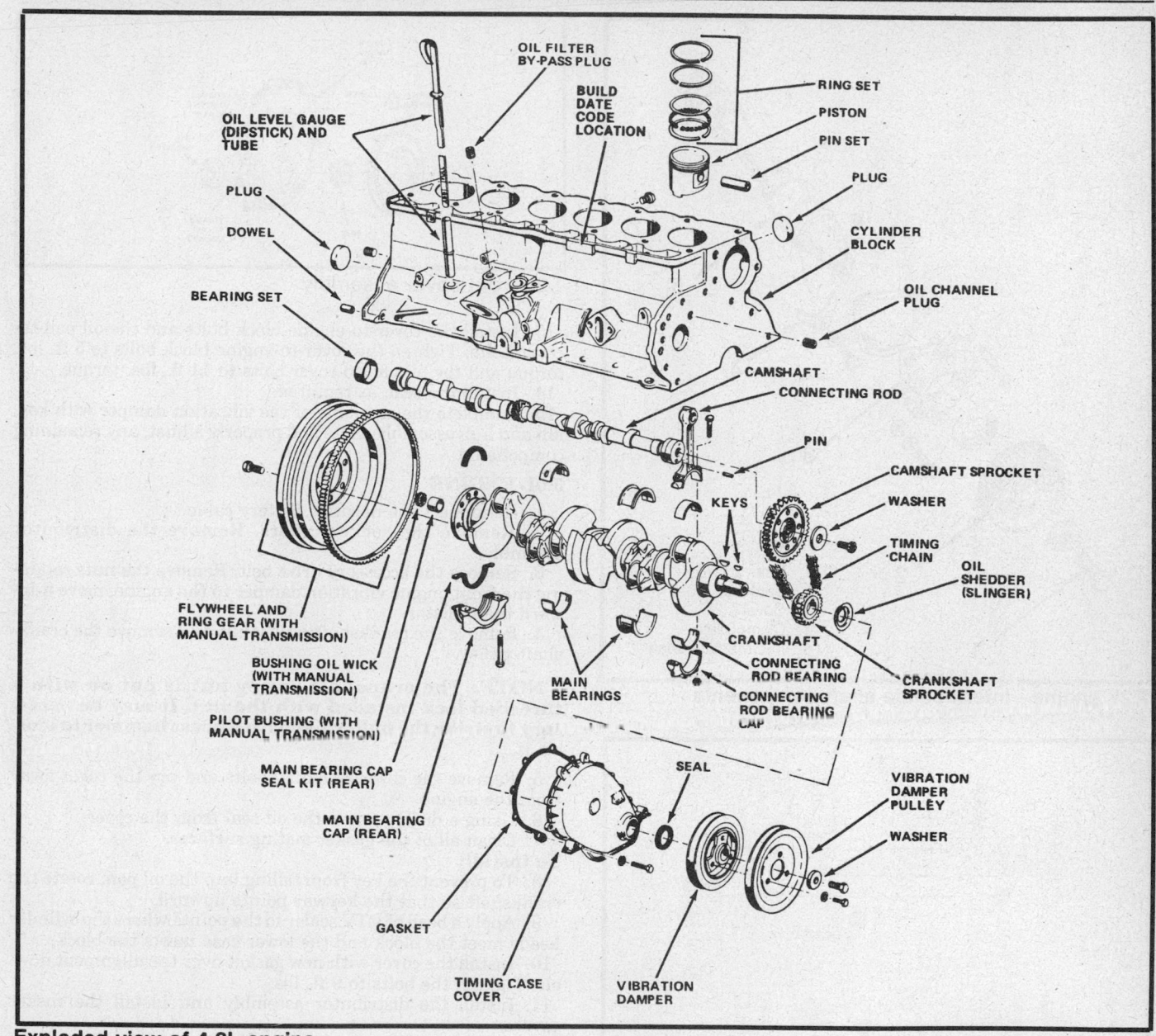

Exploded view of 4.2L engine

9. Complete installation by reversing the removal procedure. Adjust accessory drive belts tension.

2.2L, 2.5L AND 4.2L ENGINES

1. Disconnect the negative battery cable.
2. Remove the drive belts, engine fan and hub assembly, vibration damper, pulley and woodruff key.
3. Remove the A/C compressor and alternator bracket, if equipped.
4. Remove the oil pan to cover bolts and the cover to engine block bolts.
5. Remove the front cover assembly from the engine.
6. Cut off the oil pan side gasket end tabs flush with the front face of the cylinder block and remove the gasket tabs.
7. Remove the oil seal from the timing cover and clean all gasket material from the sealing surface.

To install:

8. Apply sealant to both sides of the gasket and install on the cover sealing surface.
9. Cut the end tabs from the replacement oil pan side gasket and cement the tabs on the oil pan.
10. Install new oil seal into the cover assembly.

NOTE: The oil seal can be installed after the cover has been installed on the engine block, depending upon the cover aligning tools available.

11. Coat the front cover seal end tab recesses with RTV sealant and position the seal on the cover bottom.
12. Position the cover on the engine block and position an alignment tool into the crankshaft opening.

NOTE: 2 different types of alignment tools are available, without seal in housing or with seal in housing.

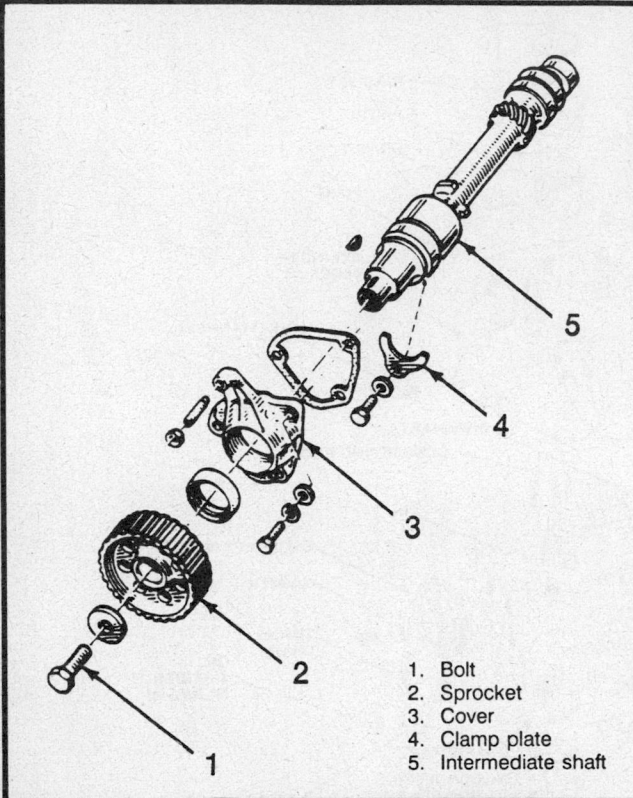

1. Bolt
2. Sprocket
3. Cover
4. Clamp plate
5. Intermediate shaft

2.2L engine—intermediate shaft components

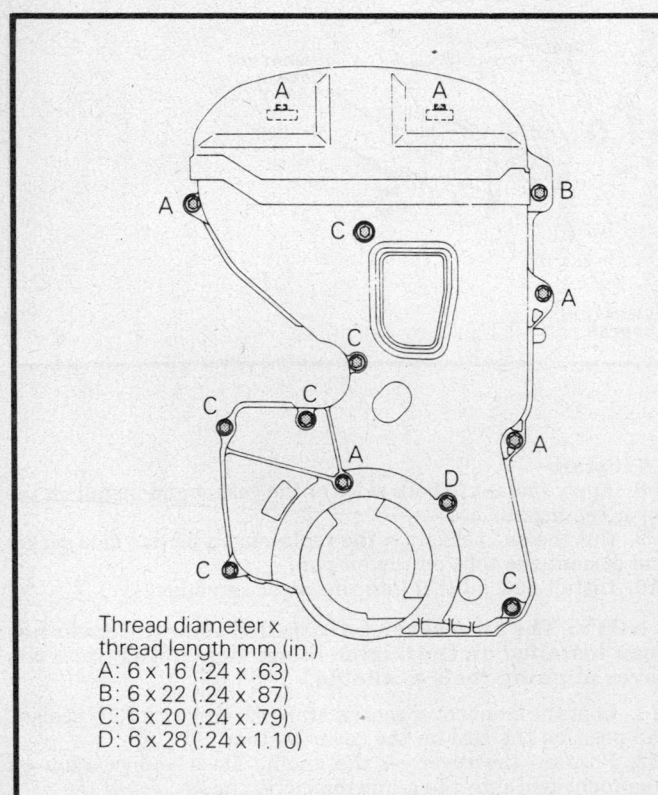

Thread diameter x
thread length mm (in.)
A: 6 x 16 (.24 x .63)
B: 6 x 22 (.24 x .87)
C: 6 x 20 (.24 x .79)
D: 6 x 28 (.24 x 1.10)

**Proper installation of timing belt upper/lower cover—
1.6L engine**

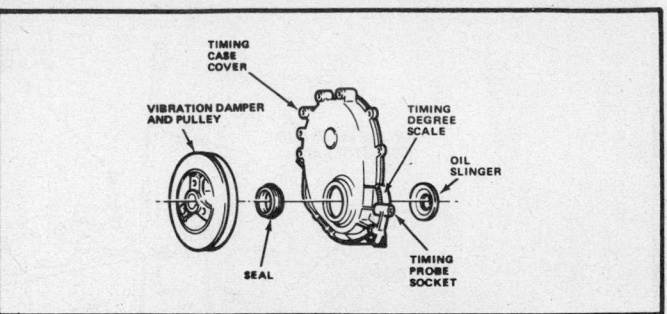

4.2L front cover assembly

13. Install the cover-to-engine block bolts and the oil pan-to-cover bolts. Tighten the cover-to-engine block bolts to 5 ft. lbs. torque and the oil pan-to-cover bolts to 11 ft. lbs. torque.

14. Install the seal, as required.

15. Complete the assembly of the vibration damper with key, fan and hub assembly, belts and properly adjust, any remaining components.

3.0L ENGINE

1. Disconnect the negative battery cable.

2. Remove the rocker covers. Remove the distributor assembly.

3. Remove the accessory drive belt. Remove the nuts retaining the front engine vibration damper to the engine, move it toward the radiator.

4. Remove the crankshaft pulley nut and remove the crankshaft pulley.

NOTE: The cranshaft pulley nut is put on with a threaded lock installed with the nut. It may be necessary to strike the pulley nut with a brass hammer to loosen it.

5. Remove the cover retaining bolts and pry the cover away from the engine.

6. Using a drift, remove the oil seal from the cover.

7. Clean all of the gasket mating surfaces.

To install:

8. To prevent the key from falling into the oil pan, rotate the crankshaft so that the keyway points upward.

9. Apply a bead of RTV sealer to the points where the cylinder heads meet the block and the lower case meets the block.

10. Install the cover with new gasket over the alignment dowels. Tighten the bolts to 9 ft. lbs.

11. Install the distributor assembly and install the rocker covers.

12. Install the crankshaft pulley, apply thread locking compound to the threads of the pulley nut and tighten to 133 ft. lbs.

13. Install the accessory drive belt and adjust the belt tension.

NOTE: It is very important the accessory drive belt is routed correctly. If it is incorrectly routed the water pump could be driven in the wrong direction, causing the engine to overheat.

14. Install the engine vibration damper. Connect the negative battery cable.

Timing Gears or Chain or Belts

Removal and Installation

1.5L ENGINE

1. Disconnect the negative battery cable.

2. Remove the front engine mount bracket and accessory drive belts.

3. Remove timing belt upper and lower covers.

4. Remove the tensioner spacer, tensioner spring and tensioner assembly.

5. Make a mark on the back of the timing belt indicating the direction of rotation so it may be reassembled in the same direction if it is to be reused. Remove the timing belt.

NOTE: If coolant or engine oil comes in contact with the timing belt, they will drastically shorten its life. Also, do not allow engine oil or coolant to contact the timing belt sprockets or tensioner assembly.

6. Inspect all parts for damage and wear. If any of the following is found, replacement is necessary:
   a. Timing belt—cracks on back surface, sides, bottom and separated canvas.
   b. Tensioner pulleys—turn the pulleys and check for binding, excessive play, unusual noise or if there is a grease leak.
7. To install, position the tensioner, tensioner spring and tensioner spacer on engine block. Install the mounting bolt and torque to 14–20 ft. lbs. (20–27 Nm).
8. Align the timing marks on the camshaft sprocket and crankshaft sprocket. This will position No. 1 piston on TDC on the compression stroke.
9. Position the timing belt on the crankshaft sprocket and keeping the tension side of the belt tight, set it on the camshaft sprocket.
10. Apply counterclockwise force to the camshaft sprocket to give tension to the belt and make sure all timing marks are lined up.
11. Perform the belt tension adjustment and complete installation by reversing the removal procedure.

1.6L ENGINE

1. Disconnect the negative battery cable.
2. Raise the vehicle and support it safely. Remove the under cover.
3. Remove the front engine mount bracket.
4. Loosen the water pump pulley and remove all accessory drive belts, tensioner pulley, water pump pulley and crankshaft pulley.
5. Remove the timing belt upper and lower covers.
6. Rotate the crankshaft clockwise and align the timing marks so No. 1 piston will be at TDC of the compression stroke. At this time the timing marks on the camshaft sprocket and the upper surface of the cylinder head should coincide, and the dowel pin of the camshaft sprocket should be at the upper side.

NOTE: Always rotate the crankshaft in a clockwise direction. Make a mark on the back of the timing belt indicating the direction of rotation so it may be reassembled in the same direction if it is to be reused.

7. Hold the camshaft with a wrench at its hexagon (between No. 2 and 3 journals) and remove the camshaft sprocket bolt. Remove the camshaft sprocket and timing belt.
8. Remove the timing belt tensioner pulley, tensioner arm, idler pulley, oil pump sprocket, special washer, flange and spacer.
9. Remove the timing belt rear right cover, upper rear left cover and lower rear left cover.
10. Inspect all parts for damage and wear. If any of the following is found, replacement is necessary:
   a. Timing belt—cracks on back surface, sides, bottom and separated canvas.
   b. Tensioner and idler pulleys—turn the pulleys and check for binding, excessive play, unusual noise or if there is a grease leak.
   c. Auto tensioner—measure the tensioner rod. If the rod protrude more than 0.47 of an inch, replace the auto tensioner. Clamp the auto tensioner in a vise in a level position. Do not allowed the plug at the bottom of the tensioner to come in direct contact with the vice. If the rod can be easily

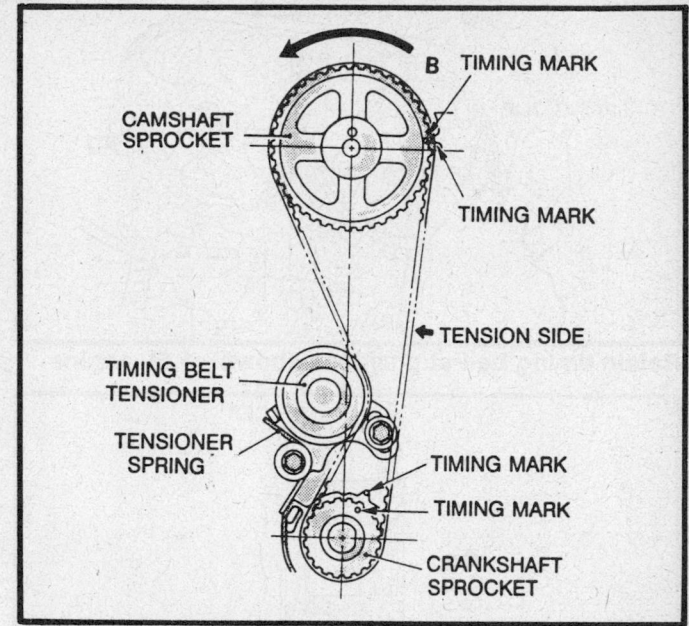

Timing marks alignment—1.5L engine

retracted, replace the auto tensioner. You should feel a fair amount of resistance when pushing the rod in. If the auto tensioner leaks, replace it.

11. During reassemble of the parts, the following should be observed:
   a. Pay special attention to the direction of the flange and crankshaft sprocket. If these parts are installed in the wrong direction, the timing bolt may be damaged.
   b. Carefully push the auto tensioner rod in until the set hole in the rod ligned up with the hole in the cylinder. Place a wire into the hole to retain the rod.
   c. Install the tensioner pulley onto the tensioner arm. Locate the pinhole in the tensioner pulley shaft to the left of the center bolt. Then, tighten the center bolt finger-tight.
12. When installing the timing belt, turn the 2 camshaft sprockets so their dowel pins are located on top. Align the timing marks facing each other with the top surface of the cylinder head. When you let go of the exhaust camshaft sprocket, it will rotate 1 tooth in the counter-clockwise direction. This should be taken into account when installing the timing belts on the sprocket.

NOTE: Both camshaft sprockets are used for the intake and exhaust camshafts and is provided with 2 timing marks. When the sprocket is mounted on the exhaust camshaft, use the timing mark on the right with the dowel pin hole on top. For the intake camshaft sprocket, use the one on the left with the dowel pin hole on top.

13. Align the crankshaft sprocket and oil pump sprocket timing marks. Install the timing belt as followed:
   a. Install the timing belt around the intake camshaft sprocket and retain it with a spring clip or binder clip.
   b. Install the timing belt around the exhaust sprocket, aligning the timing marks with the cylinder head top surface using 2 wrenches. Retain the belt wit a spring clip.
   c. Install the timing belt around the idler pulley, oil pump sprocket, crankshaft sprocket and the tensioner pulley. Remove the 2 spring clips.
   d. Lift upward on the tensioner pulley in a clockwise direction and tighten the center bolt. Make sure all timing marks are lined up.
   e. Rotate the crankshaft a ¼ turn counterclockwise. Then, turn in clockwise until the timing marks are lined up again.

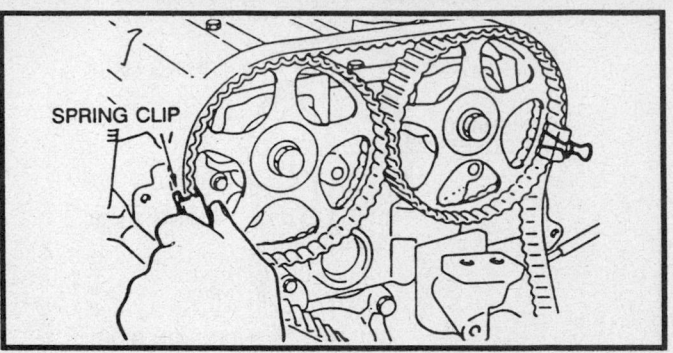

Retain timing belt at positions shown—1.6L engine

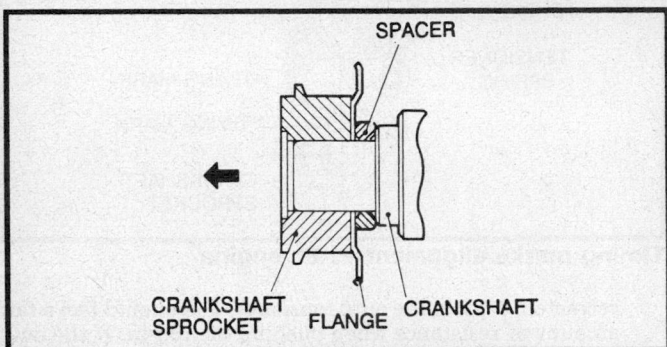

Proper installation of flange and crankshaft sprocket—1.6L engine

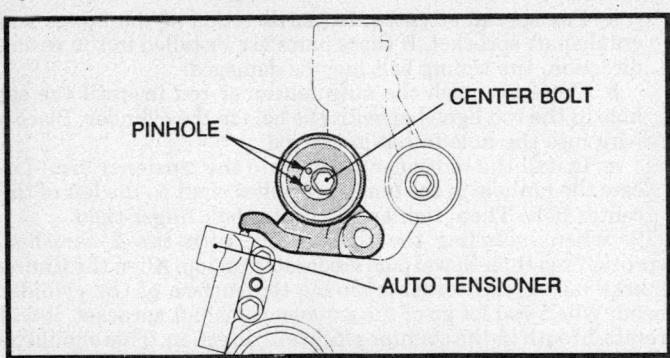

Proper installation of tensioner pulley—1.6L engine

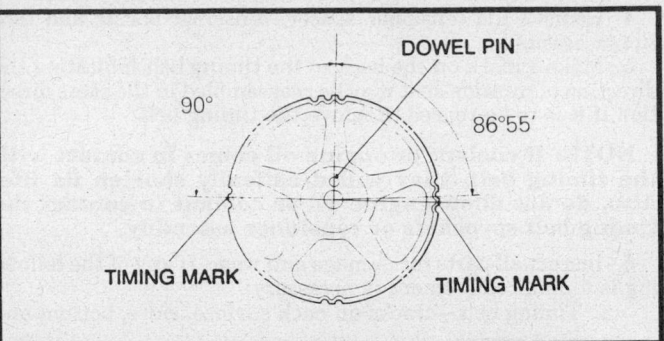

Crankshaft sprocket timing marks—1.6L engine

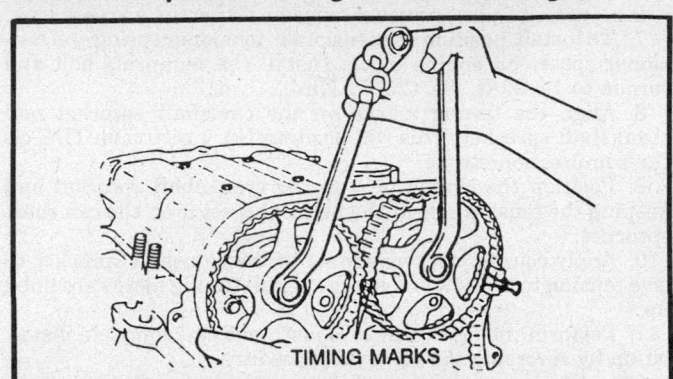

Aligning camshafts sprocket timing marks—1.6L engine

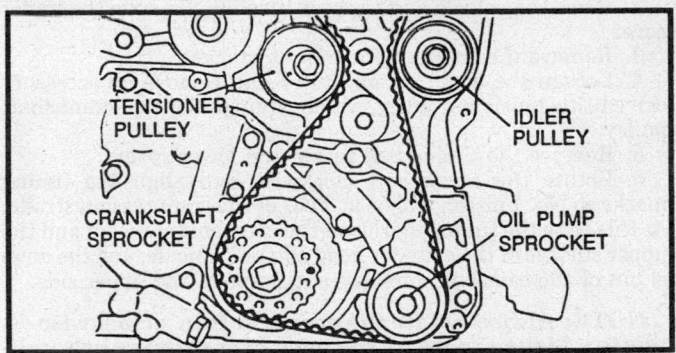

Proper timing marks alignment—1.6L engine

14. Perform the timing belt tension adjustment and remove the set wire attached to the auto tensioner.
15. Complete installation by reversing the removal procedure.

2.2L ENGINE

1. Disconnect the negative battery cable.
2. Remove the drive belts, vibration damper, pulley and woodruff key.
3. Remove the A/C compressor and alternator bracket, if equipped.
4. Remove the timing belt cover.
5. Make a mark on the back of the timing belt indicating the direction of rotation so it may be reassembled in the same direction if it is to be reused.
6. Loosen the timing belt tensioner pivot bolt and locking bolt.
7. Remove the timing belt.

NOTE: If coolant or engine oil comes in contact with the timing belt, they will drastically shorten its life. Also, do not allow engine oil or coolant to contact the timing belt sprockets or tensioner assembly.

8. Inspect all parts for damage and wear. If any of the following is found, replacement is necessary:
   a. Timing belt—cracks on back surface, sides, bottom and separated canvas.
   b. Tensioner pulleys—turn the pulleys and check for binding, excessive play, unusual noise or if there is a grease leak.
9. To install, position the camshaft sprocket timing index in line with the static timing mark.
10. Position the crankshaft so that No. 1 piston is at TDC on the compression stroke.
11. Remove the access hole plug in the cylinder block and insert tool Mot 861 (TDC rod) or equivalent into the TDC slot in the crankshaft counterweight.
12. Loosen the timing belt tensioner bolts. Push the tensioner pulley towards the water pump to compress the tensioner spring. Tighten the tensioner bolts. This allows for eaiser installation of the timing belt.
13. Install the timing belt on the sprockets. If the original timing belt is being reused, install the timing belt with the arrow previously made, pointing in the proper direction of rotation.

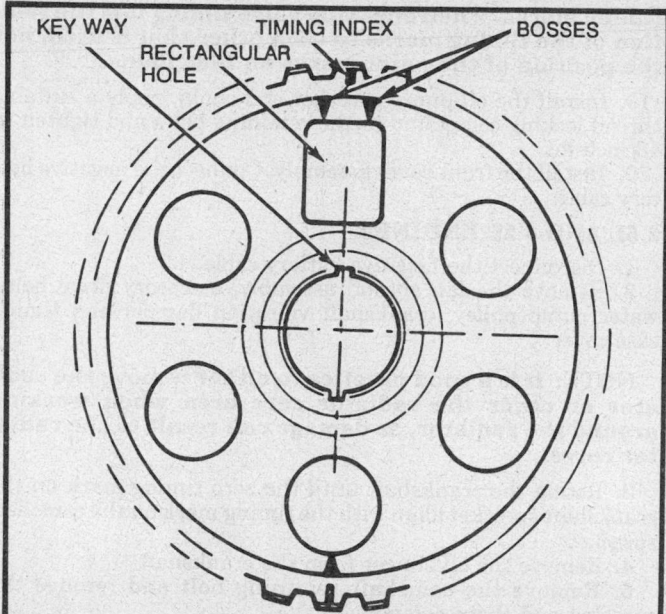

Camshaft sprocket timing marks alignment—2.2L engine

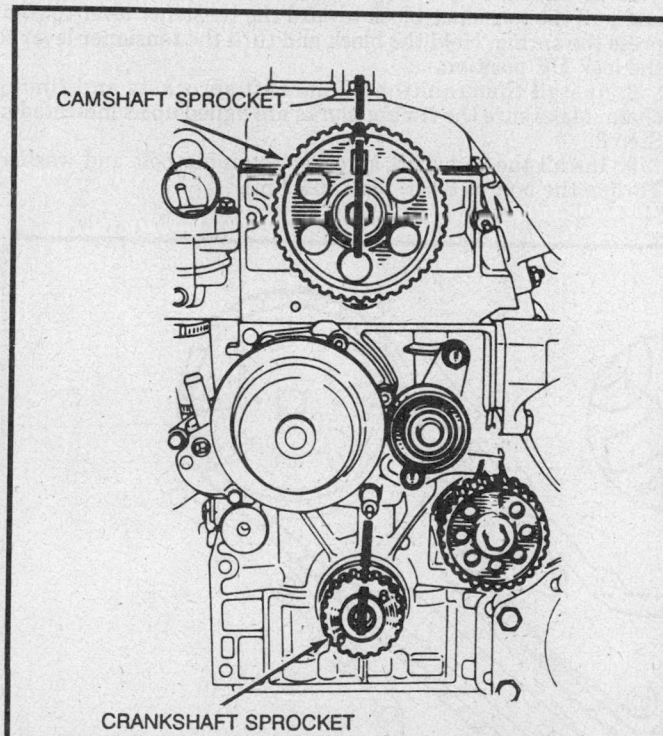

Timing index and timing marks alignment—2.2L engine

14. Loosen the tensioner bolts and allow the spring loaded tensioner to contact the belt. This will automatically tension the belt. Then, tighten the tensioner retaining bolts.

15. Position the timing belt cover over the sprockets and check the position of the camshaft sprocket timing mark with the index on the cover.

16. Remove tool Mot 861 or equivalent and install cylinder block plug, check the timing belt tension adjustment and complete installation by reversing the removal procedure.

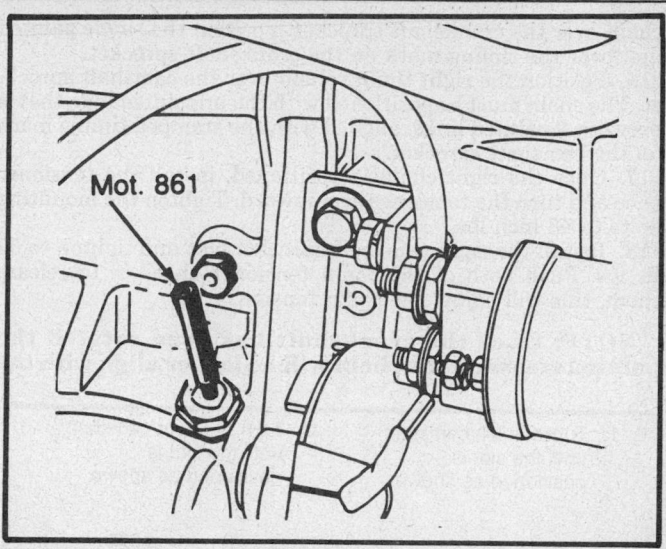

TDC access plug hole—2.2L engine

3.0L ENGINE

1. Disconnect the negative battery cable.
2. Remove the front cover assembly.
3. Remove the oil pump sprocket retaining bolts and remove the sprocket/chain assembly.
4. Remove the bolt attaching the right side camshaft sprocket to the camshaft. Remove the right side tensioner and let the tensioner shoe hang down.
5. Remove the right side timing chain and sprocket. Remove the right side chain guide and tensioner shoe.

NOTE: Keep all of the components from each side together. This will aid in installation.

6. Remove the bolt attaching the left side camshaft sprocket to the camshaft. Remove the left side tensioner and let the tensioner shoe hang down.
7. Remove the left side timing chain and sprocket. Remove the left side chain guide and tensioner shoe.
8. To install, place the left and right chain guides into position and tighten the bolts to 48 inch lbs. Install the tensioner shoes and tighten the mounting bolts to 9 ft. lbs.
9. Turn the left camshaft until the keyway slot is in the **11 o'CLOCK** position. Turn the right camshaft so that the keyway is in the **8 o'CLOCK** position.
10. Turn the crankshaft until the keyway is aligned with the centerline of the left cylinder head.

NOTE: The crankshaft has 3 sprockets on it. A sprocket each for the left and right timing chains and 1 for the oil pump drive. The timing mark is located on the center sprocket.

11. Install the left camshaft sprocket. Install the left timing chain on the crankshaft. Position the single painted link of the timing chain, on the tooth of the rear sprocket, that is directly behind the timing mark of the center sprocket.
12. Install the left timing chain over the camshaft sprocket. The chain must be positioned with the unpainted link, that is between 2 painted links, aligned with the stamped timing mark on the camshaft sprocket.
13. Once the left chain is positioned, install the tensioner shoe and turn the tensioner arm inward. Tighten the mounting bolts to 48 inch lbs.
14. Turn the crankshaft until the timing mark on the center sprocket is aligned with the lower oil pump mounting bolt.
15. Install the right camshaft sprocket. Install the right timing

chain over the crankshaft sprocket. Position the single painted link over the timing mark on the crankshaft sprocket.

16. Position the right timing chain over the camshaft sprocket. The chain must be positioned with the unpainted link, that is between 2 painted links, aligned with the stamped timing mark on the camshaft sprocket.

17. Once the right chain is positioned, install the tensioner shoe and turn the tensioner arm inward. Tighten the mounting bolts to 48 inch lbs.

18. Install the right camshaft sprocket bolt and tighten to 59 ft. lbs. Push both of the chain tensioner shoes in to release them, this will adjust the chain tension.

NOTE: Once the crankshaft has been rotated the painted marks on the chain will no longer align with the

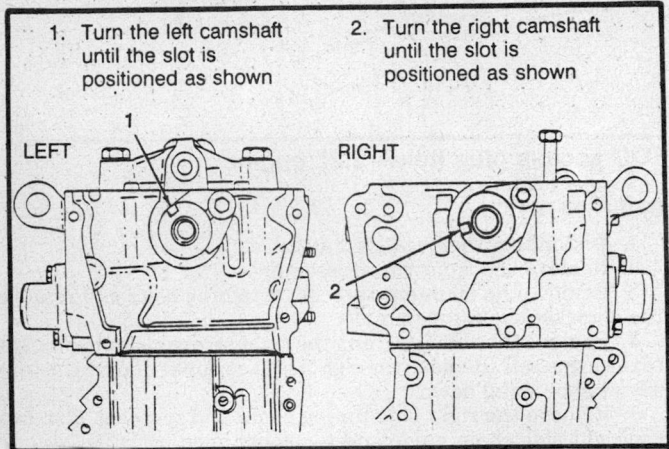

1. Turn the left camshaft until the slot is positioned as shown
2. Turn the right camshaft until the slot is positioned as shown

LEFT   RIGHT

3.0L engine—camshaft positioning for timing chain installation

timing marks. When checking valve timing it is the relation of the timing marks to each other that is used, not the position of the paint marks on the chains.

19. Install the oil pump sprocket and chain, apply a suitable thread locking compound to the retaining bolts and tighten to 48 inch lbs.

20. Install the front cover assembly. Connect the negative battery cable.

2.5L AND 4.2L ENGINES

1. Disconnect the negative battery cable.
2. Remove the fan shroud assembly, accessory drive belts, water pump pulley, crankshaft vibration damper and timing case cover.

NOTE: It is a good practice to either remove the radiator or cover the radiator core area when working around the radiator, as damage can result to the radiator cores.

3. Rotate the crankshaft until the zero timing mark on the crankshaft sprocket align with the timing mark on the camshaft sprocket.
4. Remove the oil slinger from the crankshaft.
5. Remove the camshaft retaining bolt and remove the sprocket and chain assembly.
6. On 2.5L engine, if the timing chain tensioner is to be replaced, the oil pan must also be remove.
7. To install, turn the tensioner lever to the unlock position and pull the tensioner block toward the tensioner lever to compress the spring. Hold the block and turn the tensioner lever to the lock **UP** position.
8. Install the crankshaft/camshaft sprockets and timing chain. Make sure the timing marks are ligned up as indicated in Step 3.
9. Install the camshaft sprocket retaining bolt and washer. Torque the bolt to 80 ft. lbs. (108 Nm).

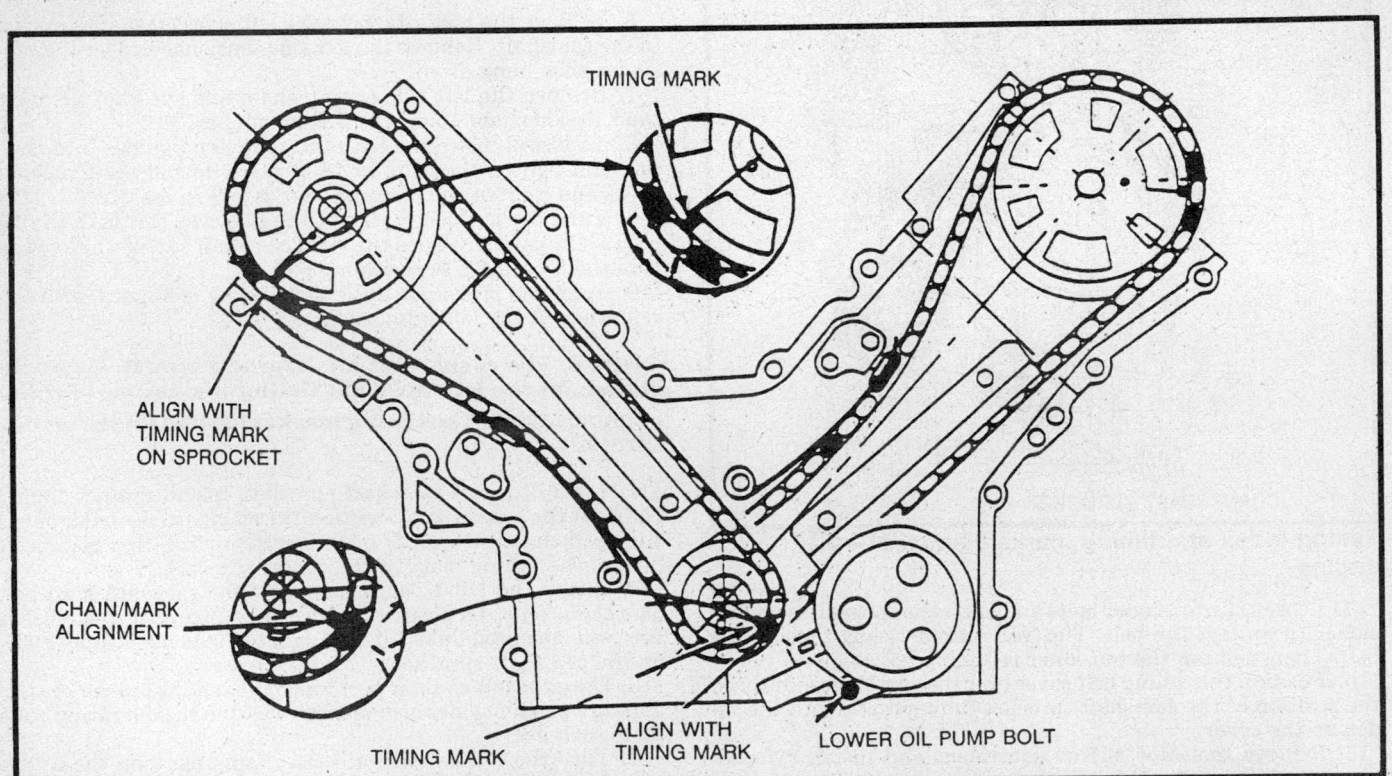

TIMING MARK

ALIGN WITH TIMING MARK ON SPROCKET

CHAIN/MARK ALIGNMENT

TIMING MARK   ALIGN WITH TIMING MARK   LOWER OIL PUMP BOLT

3.0L engine—timing chain and sprocket alignment

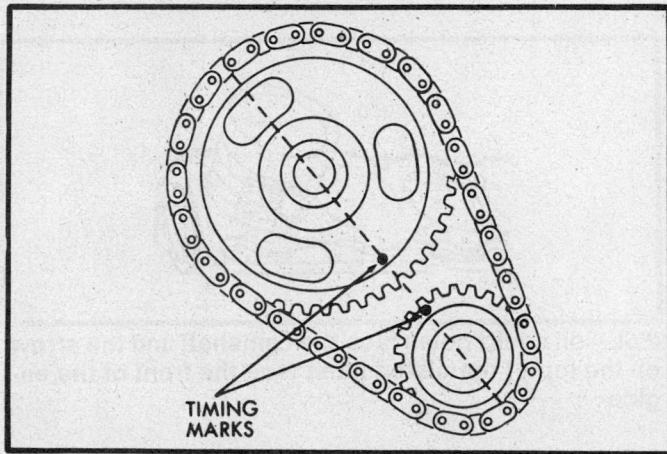

2.5L timing chain tensioner

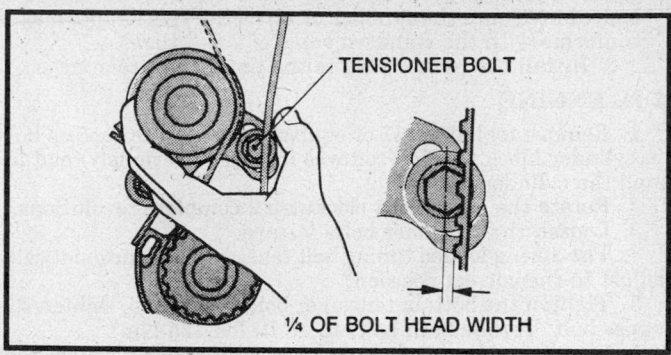

Checking belt tension—1.5L engine

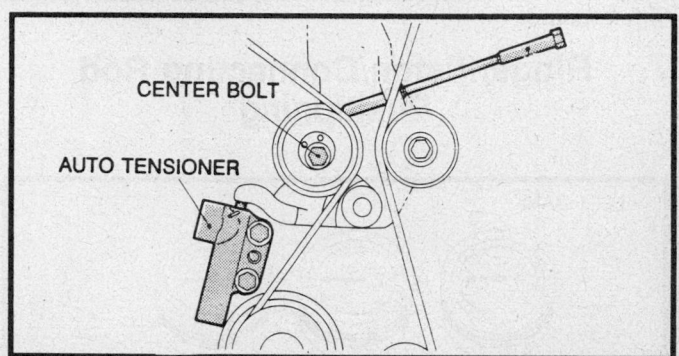

Tensioner pulley adjustment—1.6L engine

2.5L and 4.2L engines timing marks alignment

NOTE: To verify correct installation of the timing chain, rotate the crankshaft until the camshaft sprocket timing mark is approximately at the 1 o'clock position. There should be 20 pins between the marks.

10. Install the oil slinger and timing case cover using a new gasket.

11. Complete installation by reversing the removal procedure.

TIMING BELT TENSION

Adjustment

1.5L ENGINE

1. Loosen the pivot side tensioner bolt and then the slot side bolt.

2. Tighten the slot side tensioner bolt and then the pivot side bolt.

NOTE: If the pivot side bolt is tightened first, the tensioner could turn with bolt, causing overtension.

3. Turn the crankshaft clockwise. Loosen the pivot side tensioner bolt and then the slot side bolt. Tighten the slot bolt and then the pivot side bolt.

4. Check the belt tension by holding the tensioner and timing belt together by hand and give the belt a slight thumb pressure at a point level with tensioner center. Make sure the belt cog crest comes as deep as about ¼ of the width of the slot side tensioner bolt head.

1.6L ENGINE

1. After turning the crankshaft ¼ turn counterclockwise, turn it clockwise to move No. 1 cylinder to TDC.

2. Loosen the center bolt. Using tool MD998738 or equivalent, and a torque wrench, apply a torque of 1.88–2.03 ft. lbs. (2.6–2.8 Nm). Tighten the center bolt.

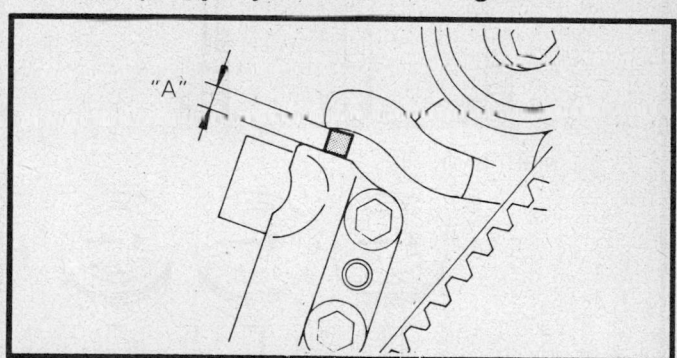

Point of measurement at tensioner arm and tensioner body—1.6L engine

3. Screw the special tool into the engine left support bracket until its end makes contact with the tensioner arm. At this point, screw the special tool in some more and remove the set wire attached to the auto tensioner, if wire was not previously removed. Then, remove the special tool.

4. Rotate the crankshaft 2 complete turns clockwise and let it sit for approximately 15 minutes. Then, measure the auto tensioner protrusion (the distance between the tensioner arm and auto tensioner body) to ensure that it is within 0.15–0.18 inches (3.8–4.5mm). If out of specification, repeat Step 1–4 until the specified value is obtained.

If the timing belt tension adjustment is being performed with the engine mounted in the vehicle, and clearance between the tensioner arm and the auto tensioner body cannot be measured, the following alternative method can be used:

a. Screw in special tool MD998738 or equivalent, until its end makes contact with the tensioner arm.

b. After the special tool makes contact with the arm, screw it in some more to retract the auto tensioner pushrod while counting the number of turns the tool makes until the tensioner arm is brought into contact with the auto tensioner body. Make sure the number of turns the special tool makes conforms with the standard value of 2.5–3 turns.

   c. Install the rubber plug to the timing belt rear cover.

2.2L ENGINE

1. Remove tool Mot 861 or equivalent from TDC access hole in cylinder block (if TDC rod was installed previously) and install the cylinder block plug.
2. Rotate the crankshaft clockwise 2 complete revolutions.
3. Loosen the tensioner bolts ¼ turn.
4. The spring loaded timing belt tensioner will automatically adjust to the correct position.
5. Tighten the bottom tensioner bolt first. Then, tighten the upper bolt. Torque both bolts to 18 ft. lbs. (25 Nm).
6. Check the timing belt tension with tension gauge tool Ele.346 or equivalent. The deflection should be 0.216–0.276 in. (5.5–7.0 mm).

Rings/Piston/Connecting Rod Positioning

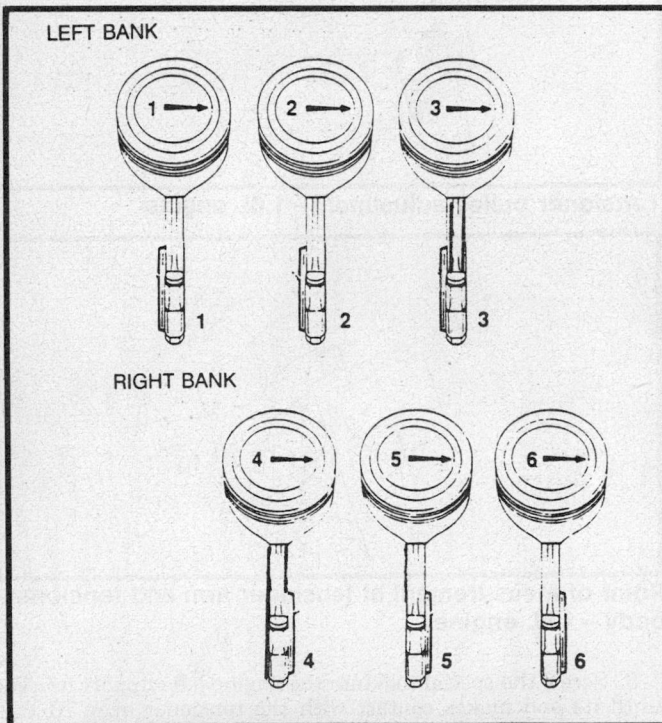

Piston positioning—3.0L engine

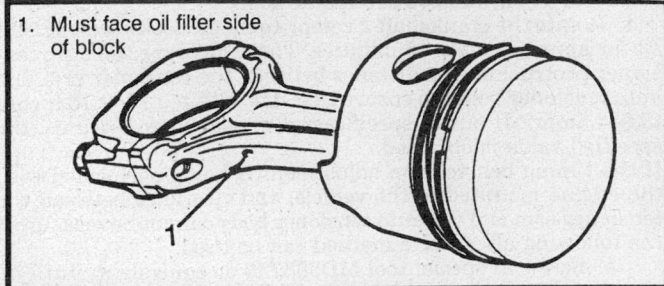

Piston positioning—2.2L engine

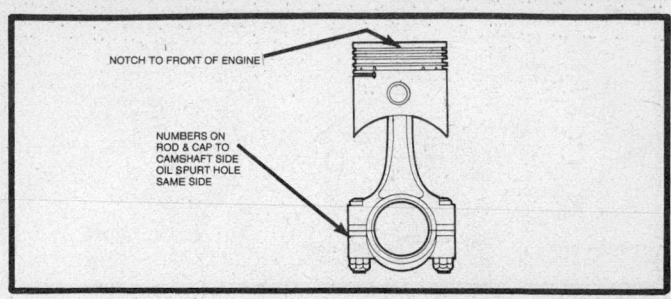

4.2L piston installation

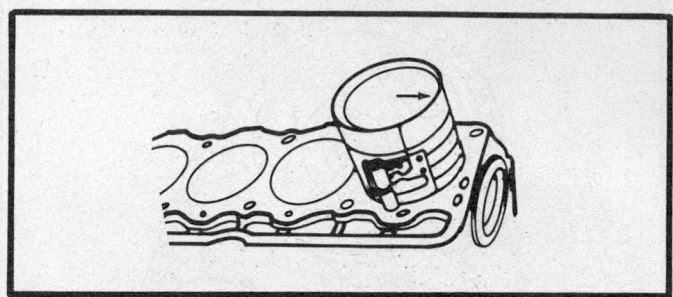

2.5L—oil squirt holes face the camshaft and the arrow on the top of the piston must face the front of the engine

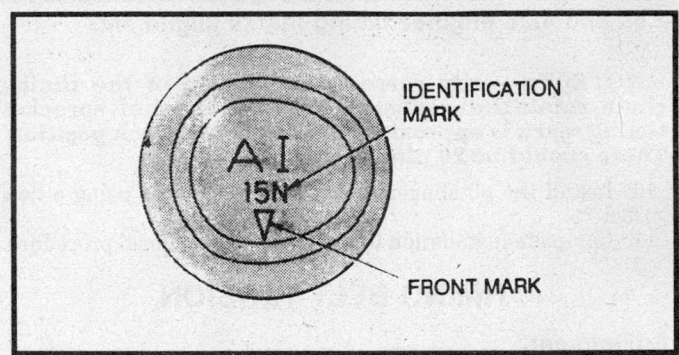

Piston identification marks face the front of engine—1.5L

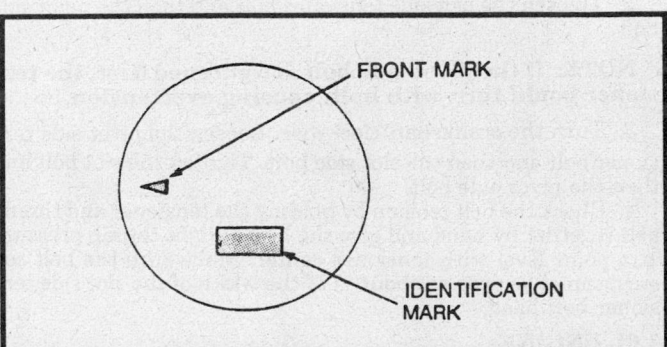

Piston identification marks face the front of engine—1.6L

ENGINE LUBRICATION SYSTEM

Oil Pan

Removal and Installation

1.5L AND 1.6L ENGINES

1. Disconnect the negative battery cable.
2. Raise the vehicle and support it safely.
3. Remove the oil pan drain plug and drain the engine oil. On 1.6L engine equipped with turbocharger, remove the oil return pipe and gasket.
4. Remove the oil pan mounting bolts, separate the engine oil pan and remove.
5. Clean all sealant from the oil pan and cylinder block.
6. To install, apply approximately 0.16 in. of sealant (MZ100168) or equivalent around the surface of the oil pan.
7. Assemble the oil pan to the cylinder block within 15 minutes after applying the sealant.
8. Install the oil pan mounting bolts and torque to 4–6 ft. lbs. (6–8 Nm). On 1.6L engine equipped with turbocharger, install the oil return pipe using a new gasket.
9. Install the oil pan drain plug.
10. Lower the vehicle and refill with engine oil.

2.2L ENGINE

1. Disconnect the negative battery cable.
2. Raise and safely support the vehicle.
3. Remove the underbody splash shield and drain the engine oil.
4. Remove the engine mount cushion nuts.
5. Lower the vehicle and position engine support tool MS–1900 or equivalent, on the inner fender flanges.
6. Tighten the support tool until the engine comes up enough to remove the oil pan.
7. Raise and safely support the vehicle. Remove the oil pan bolts and remove the oil pan.
8. Before installing, clean all the gasket mating surfaces with a suitable solvent and wipe dry.
9. Install the oil pan to the engine block using a new gasket. Do not use any sealer on the gasket, it must be installed dry.

NOTE: There are 3 sizes of bolts used to retain the oil pan on this engine. Note the location of each bolt when it is removed.

10. Tighten the oil pan bolts attaching the pan to the clutch/converter housing first, then tighten the remaining bolts. Tighten all of the bolts to 88 inch lbs.
11. Install the splash shield and lower the vehicle.
12. Remove the support tool and install the engine mount bolts.
13. Fill the engine with the required amount of oil.

2.5L AND 3.0L ENGINES

1. Disconnect the negative battery cable.
2. Raise and safely support the vehicle. Drain the oil.
3. Remove the front anti-sway bar retaining bolts and remove the sway bar.
4. Loosen the engine mount stud and nut assemblies. Remove the front tires.
5. Remove the lower ball joint retaining bolts and disengage the lower ball joints from the steering knuckles.
6. Remove the nuts at the center of the transaxle crossmember securing the rear of the transaxle to the crossmember.
7. Lower the vehicle and attach engine support tool MS–1900 to the engine.
8. With the vehicle down, loose the 4 sub-frame attaching nuts. Remove the front 2 first, allowing the sub-frame to pivot

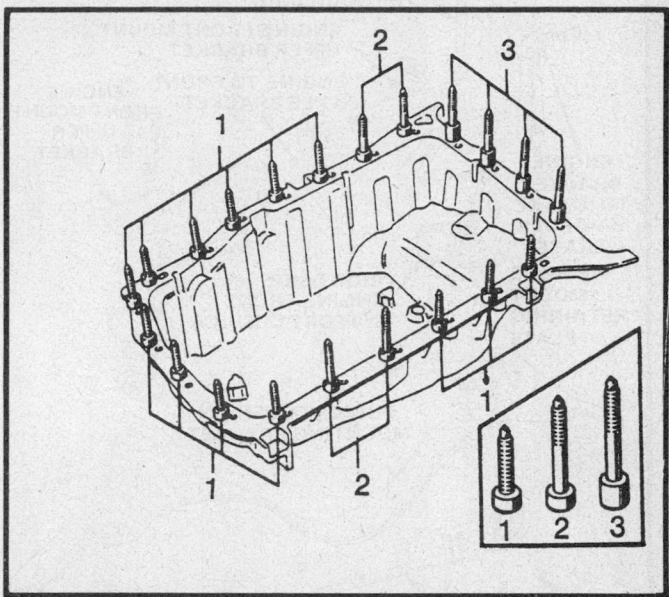

2.2L engine oil pan bolts — must be installed in correct position

to the ground. Support the rear of the sub-frame and remove the 2 rear nuts. Lower the sub-frame away from the vehicle.
9. Raise and support the vehicle. Remove the oil pan retaining bolts and remove the oil pan.
10. Before installing, clean all of the gasket mating surfaces. Install the oil pan using a new gasket. Do not use any sealer, the gasket must be installed dry.
11. Tighten all of the retaining bolts to 9 ft. lbs.
12. Install the sub-frame assembly and tighten the mounting nuts to 92 ft. lbs.
13. Connect the lower ball joints and tighten the attaching nut to 77 ft. lbs. Tighten the transaxle-to-crossmember bolts to 20 ft. lbs.
14. Remove the engine support tool. Attach the anti-sway bar and install the front wheels.
15. Lower the vehicle. Fill the crankcase with the appropriate quantity and grade of oil.

4.2L ENGINE

1. Disconnect the negative battery cable. Drain engine oil.
2. Lock steering wheel.
3. Remove air cleaner.
4. Support engine with holding fixture.
5. Raise the vehicle and support it safely.
6. Remove front axle universal joint clamp strap bolts.
7. Remove bolts at engine cushions.
8. Remove bolts from sill-to-crossmember brace bar at crossmember and rotate bar out of way.
9. Loosen pitman arm at gear.
10. Loosen idler arm at steering linkage.
11. Remove bolt from steering damper at crossmember.
12. Loosen sway bar bolts and lower sway bar.
13. Support axle and crossmember assembly.
14. Remove bolt from right bracket at axle tube bolt bars.
15. Remove bolts from left upper axle bracket at upper end.
16. Remove bolts from pinion end bracket at pinion.
17. Remove crossmember nuts and bolts.
18. Lower crossmember and axle assembly.
19. Remove starter motor.

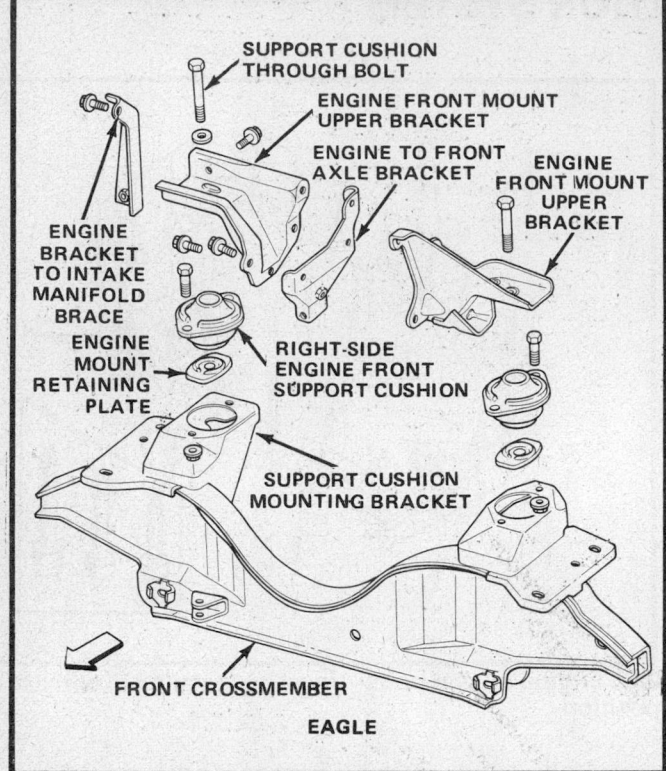

Eagle engine mounting brackets

20. Remove torque converter inspection shield.
21. Remove oil pan screws.
22. Remove oil pan by sliding it rearward.
23. Before installing, clean all gasket surfaces.
24. Install replacement oil pan front seal on timing case cover and apply sealant to tab ends.
25. Cement replacement oil pan side gaskets into position on engine block. Apply sealant to ends of gaskets.
26. Coat inside curved surface of replacement oil pan rear seal with soap. Apply sealant to gasket contacting surface of seal end tabs.
27. Install seal in recess of rear main bearing cap. Ensure it is fully seated.
28. Apply engine oil to oil pan contacting surface of front and rear oil pan seals.
29. Install oil pan and drain plug.
30. Install starter motor.
31. Install torque converter housing access cover.
32. Raise crossmember assembly.
33. Install crossmember nuts and bolts.
34. Install engine cushion bolts.
35. Install sill-to-crossmember brace bolts.
36. Install pitman arm (onto steering gear) and nut.
37. Install idler arm (onto steering linkage) and nut.
38. Tighten sway bar bolts with 25 ft. lbs. (34 Nm) torque.
39. Install steering damper on crossmember bolt. Tighten with 50 ft. lbs. (68 Nm) torque.
40. Raise and install front axle assembly. Connect at axle tube, upper left axle bracket and pinion bracket. Tighten all axle connections with 45 ft. lbs. (61 Nm) torque.
41. Install front universal clamp strap bolts. Tighten with 14 ft. lbs. (19 Nm) torque.
42. Connect both half shafts to front axle and tighten with 45 ft. lbs. (61 Nm) torque.
43. Remove engine holding fixture.
44. Install air cleaner.

45. Start engine and check for leaks.

Oil Pump

Removal and Installation

NOTE: Whenever the oil pump is disassembled or the cover removed, the gear cavity must be filled with petroleum jelly (vaseline) for priming purposes. Do not use grease.

1.5L AND 1.6L ENGINES

1. Disconnect the negative battery cable.
2. Remove the front engine mount bracket and accessory drive belts.
3. Remove timing belt upper and lower covers.
4. Remove the timing belt and crankshaft sprocket.
5. Remove the oil pan drain plug and drain the engine oil. On 1.6L engine equipped with turbocharger, remove the oil return pipe and gasket.
6. Remove the oil pan mounting bolts separate the engine oil pan and remove.
7. Remove the oil screen and gasket.
8. Remove and tag the front cover mounting bolts. All mounting bolts are of different length.
9. On 1.6L engine, remove the plug cap using tool MD998162 or equivalent and remove the oil pressure switch.
10. Remove the front case cover and oil pump assembly.

NOTE: On 1.5L engine, the outer gear do not have any marks indicating its installed direction. Make a mark on the reverse side of the outer gear so it can be reinstalled in its proper position.

11. Check the oil pump housing and gears for cracks, wear and other damage.
12. Remove the oil seal from the front cover.
13. Clean all gasket material from mounting surfaces.
14. To install, apply engine oil to the entire surface of the gears. On 1.5L engine, make sure the outer gear is installed in the same direction as before according to the mark made at the time of removal.
15. On 1.6L engine, install the drive/driven gears with the 2 timing marks aligned.
16. Assemble the front case cover and oil pump assembly to the engine block using a new gasket. On 1.6L engine, assemble the front case cover and oil pump assembly using tool MD998285 or equivalent on the front end of the crankshaft.
17. On 1.5L engine, apply engine oil to the surface of seal installer tool MD998305 or equivalent and slide the new seal along the tool until it touches the front case. Tap the oil seal into place.
18. On 1.6L engine, install the crankshaft oil seal using tool MD998375 or equivalent.
19. Complete installation by reversing the removal procedure.

2.2L ENGINE

1. Disconnect the negative battery cable.
2. Remove the oil pump drive cover plate bolts and remove the cover.
3. Using a threaded rod, thread it into the top of the pump driveshaft. Remove the pump driveshaft by pulling it out of the block.
4. Raise and safely support the vehicle. Drain the oil.
5. Remove the oil pan. Remove the oil pump mounting bolts and remove the pump.
6. Install the oil pump using a new gasket. Tighten the mounting bolts to 33 ft. lbs.
7. Install the oil pan. Fill the crankcase with the correct grade and quantity of oil.
8. Install the oil pump driveshaft and cover.

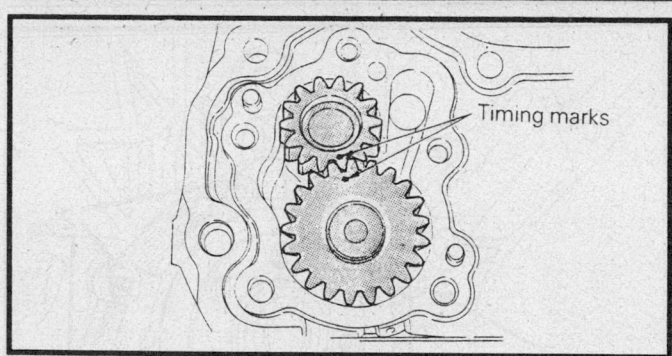

Oil pump gear timing marks alignment—1.6L engine

Timing marks

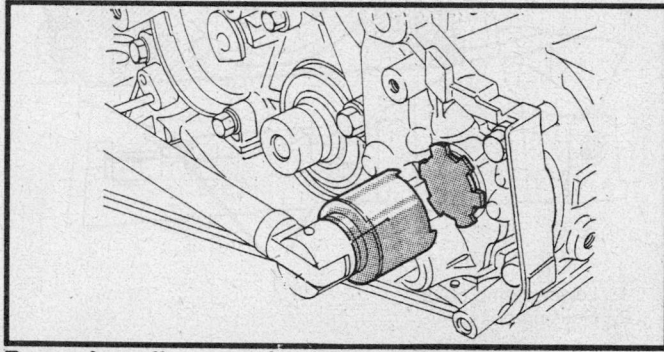

Removing oil pump plug cap—1.6L engine

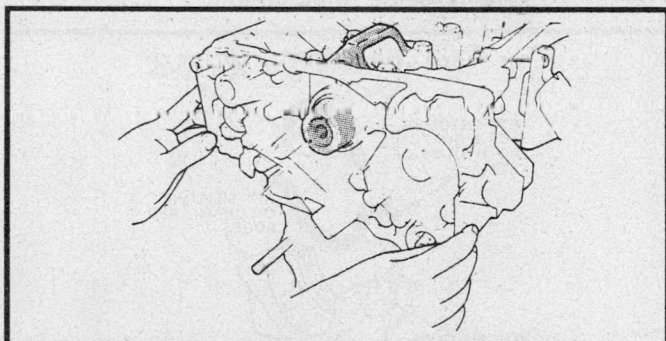

Installing front cover/oil pump assembly—1.6L engine

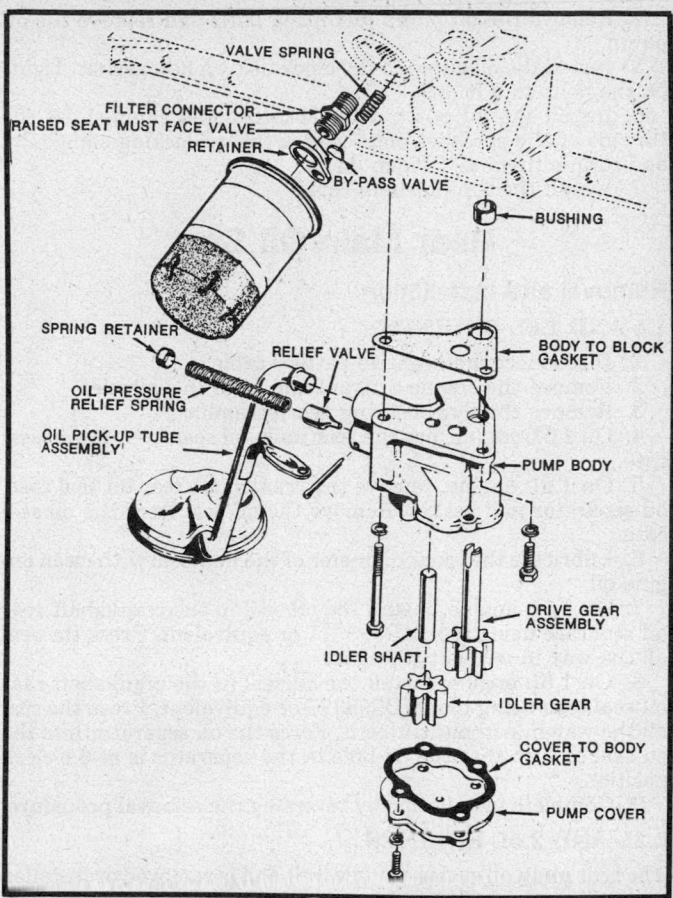

VALVE SPRING
FILTER CONNECTOR
RAISED SEAT MUST FACE VALVE
RETAINER
BY-PASS VALVE
BUSHING
SPRING RETAINER
RELIEF VALVE
BODY TO BLOCK GASKET
OIL PRESSURE RELIEF SPRING
OIL PICK-UP TUBE ASSEMBLY
PUMP BODY
DRIVE GEAR ASSEMBLY
IDLER SHAFT
IDLER GEAR
COVER TO BODY GASKET
PUMP COVER

Exploded view of the oil pump assembly—4.2L engine

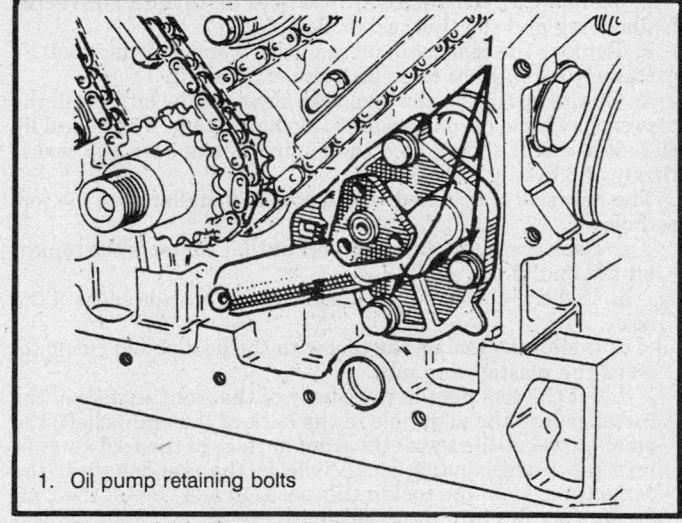

1. Oil pump retaining bolts

Oil pump mounting 3.0L engine

9. Start the vehicle and check for leaks.

2.5L AND 4.2L ENGINES

1. Disconnect the negative battery cable.
2. Raise the vehicle and support safely. Drain the engine oil and remove the oil pan.
3. Remove the oil pump retaining bolts, the oil pump and gasket.

NOTE: The oil pump removal and installation will not affect the distributor timing because the distributor drive gear remains meshed with the camshaft. Do not disturb the position of the oil inlet tube and strainer assembly in the pump body. If the tube is moved in the body, a replacement tube and strainer must be installed to assure an airtight seal.

4. To insure self priming, fill the gear cavity with petroleum jelly before installing the cover.
5. Install the pump with a new gasket. Tighten the short bolts to 10 ft. lbs. and the long bolts to 17 ft. lbs.

6. Install the oil pan using new gaskets and seals. Complete the assembly as required.

3.0L ENGINE

1. Disconnect the negative battery cable.
2. Remove the timing chain cover assembly.
3. Remove the bolts retaining the oil pump drive sprocket. Remove the sprocket and the oil pump drive chain.

4. Remove the oil pump mounting bolts and remove the oil pump.

5. Install the oil pump to the block using a new gasket. Tighten the bolts to 9 ft. lbs.

6. Install the oil pump drive sprocket and chain. Coat the threads of the sprocket bolts with a thread locking compound and torque them to 48 inch lbs.

7. Install the timing chain cover.

Rear Main Oil Seal

Removal and Installation

1.5 AND 1.6L ENGINES

1. Disconnect the negative battery cable.

2. Remove the engine or transaxle from the vehicle.

3. Remove the flywheel/ring gear assemble.

4. On 1.5L engine, pry the rear main oil seal from the oil seal case.

5. On 1.6L engine, remove the crankshaft rear oil seal case, oil separator and gasket. Remove the oil seal from the oil seal case.

6. Lubricate the inner diameter of the new seal with clean engine oil.

7. On 1.5L engine, install the oil seal in the crankshaft rear oil seal case using tool MD998011 or equivalent. Press the seal all the way in without tilting it.

8. On 1.6L engine, install the oil seal in the crankshaft rear oil seal case using tool MD998376 or equivalent. Press the seal all the way in without tilting it. Force the oil separator into the oil seal case so that the oil hole in the separator is at 6 o'clock position.

9. Complete installation by reversing the removal procedure.

2.2L AND 2.5L ENGINES

The rear main oil seal is a single unit and is removed or installed without removal of the oil pan or crankshaft.

1. Disconnect the negative battery cable.

2. Remove the transaxle, flywheel or torque converter bellhousing and the flywheel or flex plate.

3. Remove the rear main oil seal with a small prying tool. Be extremely careful not to scratch the crankshaft.

4. Oil the lips of the new seal with clean engine oil. Install the new seal by hand onto the rear crankshaft flange. The helical lip side of the seal should face the engine. Make sure the seal is firmly and evenly installed.

The new seal is installed with a special installer. Use the tool as follows:

   a. Back the plastic wing nut off until it contacts the capnut on the end of the shaft.

   b. Lightly lubricate both the inside and outside edges of the seal.

   c. Install the seal on the tool with the dust shield facing toward the plastic wing nut.

   d. Fit the tool pilot in the center of the front surface of the installer into the pilot hole in the back of the crankshaft; the small dowel at the top of the front surface of the tool must fit into the corresponding small hole in the crankshaft at the same time. Hold the tool in this position and thread the 2 attaching screws into the crankshaft.

   e. Turn the plastic wingnut in until it bottoms out to fully seat the seal. Unscrew the attaching nuts and remove the seal installer.

   f. Inspect the dust shield all around to make sure it is not curled under. If it is, gently to pull the lip out.

   g. Replace the flywheel or flexplate, bellhousing and transaxle.

3.0L ENGINE

1. Disconnect the negative battery cable.

2. Remove the transaxle assembly.

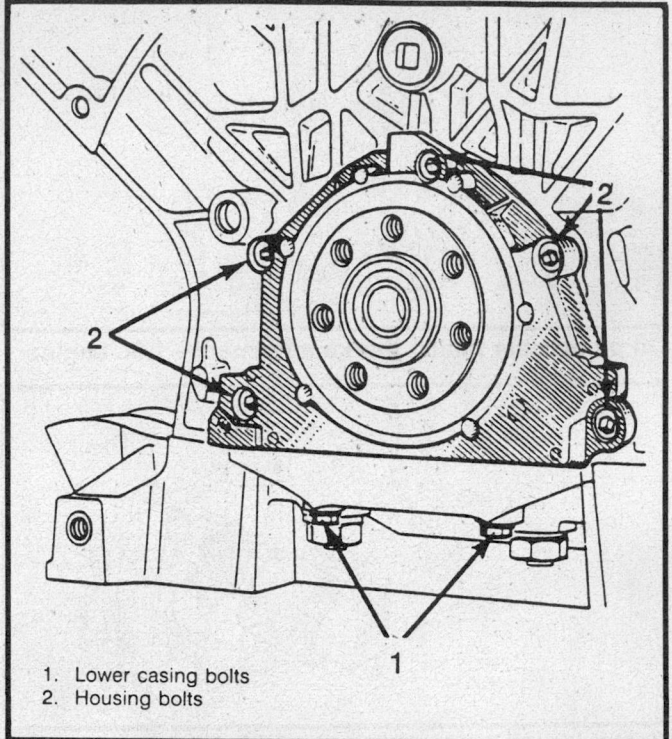

1. Lower casing bolts
2. Housing bolts

Rear main seal housing—3.0L engine

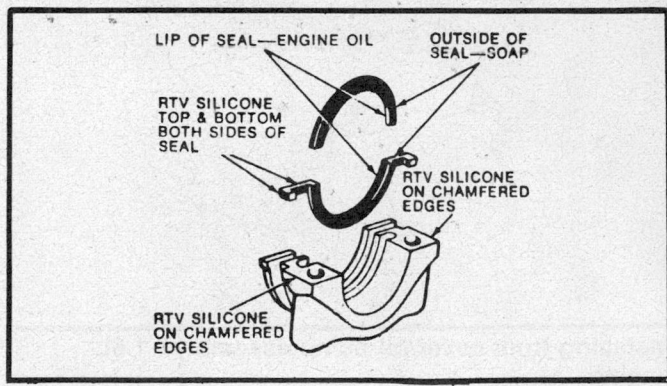

LIP OF SEAL—ENGINE OIL
OUTSIDE OF SEAL—SOAP
RTV SILICONE TOP & BOTTOM BOTH SIDES OF SEAL
RTV SILICONE ON CHAMFERED EDGES
RTV SILICONE ON CHAMFERED EDGES

Rear main bearing seal components—4.2L engine

3. Remove the bolts from the lower rear main seal housing.

4. Remove the rear main seal housing bolts and remove the housing.

5. Push the old rear main seal from the housing.

6. Clean the gasket mating surfaces.

7. Install the rear main seal housing on the block. Use a new housing gasket.

8. Tighten the seal housing-to-block bolts first, then tighten the lower bolts. Torque all bolts to 9 ft. lbs.

9. Install the new rear seal to tool MOT–259–01 or equivalent, lightly coat the inner edges of the seal with oil. Install the seal to the seal housing by lightly tapping on the installation tool.

10. Remove the installation tool. Install the transaxle assembly.

11. Connect the negative battery cable. Start the vehicle and check for leaks.

4.2L ENGINE

1. Disconnect the negative battery cable.

2. The crankshaft rear main bearing seal consists of 2 pieces, an upper and a lower seal, each with a single lip.

3. Raise the vehicle and support safely. Drain the engine oil and remove the oil pan.

4. Remove the lower rear main bearing cap and discard the oil seal.

5. Loosen all the main bearing caps. Tap the upper seal with a brass drift and hammer, or other suitable tool, until the seal protrudes enough to grasp it and pull it from the engine block.

6. To install the seal, coat the lip of the seal with engine oil and position the seal with the lip towards the front of the engine. Install the seal into the engine block.

7. Position the lower half of the seal into the rear main bearing cap, after coating both sides of the lower seal tabs with RTV sealant and the lip of the seal with engine oil. Coat the outer curved surface of the seal with soap. Seat the seal firmly into the rear main bearing cap.

8. Install the rear main bearing cap and torque the bolts to 80 ft. lbs.

9. Install the oil pan and its components. Complete the assembly in the reverse of the removal procedure.

Connecting Rod and Main Bearing

Replacement

Whenever a new or reconditioned crankshaft is installed, new connecting rod bearings and main bearings should be installed. To fit new bearings accurately:

1. Wipe the oil from the crankshaft journal and the outer and inner surfaces of the bearing shell. Place a piece of plastic gauging material in the center of the bearing. Use a floor jack or other means to hold the crankshaft against the upper bearing shell. This is necessary to obtain accurate clearance readings when using plastic gauging material.

2. Install the bearing cap and bearing. Place engine oil on the cap bolts and install. Torque the bolts to specification. Then, remove the bearing cap and determine the bearing clearance by comparing the width of the flattened plastic gauging material at its widest point with the graduations on the gauging material container. The number within the graduation on the envelope indicates the clearance in millimeters or thousandths of an inch. If the clearance is greater than allowed, replace both bearing shells as a set.

3. Recheck the clearance after replacing the shells. Main bearing clearances must be corrected by the use of selective upper and lower shells. Under no circumstances should the use of shims behind the shells to compensate for wear be attempted.

NOTE: In order to prevent the possibility of cylinder block and/or main bearing cap damage, the main bearing caps are to be tapped into their cylinder block cavity using a wood or rubber mallet before the bolts are installed. Do not use attaching bolts to pull the main bearing caps into their seats. Failure to observe this information may damage the cylinder block or a bearing cap.

4. When installing the thrust bearing cap, use a block of wood and bump the shaft in each direction to align the thrust flanges of the main bearing. After bumping the shaft in each direction, wedge the shaft to the front and hold it while torquing the thrust bearing cap bolts.

5. Check crankshaft endplay, using a flat feeler gauge.

FRONT SUSPENSION AND STEERING

For front suspension component removal and installation procedures, refer to the Unit Repair Section. For steering wheel removal and installation, refer to electrical control section.

Manual Steering Gear

Adjustment

WORM BEARING PRELOAD

1. Loosen the worm bearing adjuster locknut.

2. Carefully tighten the worm bearing adjuster until it bottoms, then back off adjuster ¼ turn.

3. Install a socket and torque wrench on the splined end of the wormshaft.

4. Rotate the wormshaft clockwise to its stop, noting the number of turns. Then, back off the shaft ½ the number of turns.

5. Tighten the worm bearing adjuster until the torque required to rotate the wormshaft is 5–8 inch lbs. (0.6–0.9Nm).

6. Tighten the worm bearing adjuster locknut and torque to 90 ft. lbs.

PITMAN SHAFT OVERCENTER DRAG TORQUE

1. Rotate the wormshaft from stop-to-stop and count the total number of turns.

2. Turn the wormshaft back ½ the total number of turns to place the ball nut and pitman shaft in centered position.

3. Install a socket and an torque wrench on the pitman shaft splines.

4. Tighten the pitman shaft adjuster screw while rotating the shaft back and forth overcenter until the torque required to rotate the shaft overcenter equals the worm bearing preload setting.

5. Rotate the shaft overcenter and continue tightening the adjuster screw until the drag torque is increased by an additional 4–10 inch lbs. (0.5–1 Nm), but do not exceed the total of 16 inch lbs. (2 Nm).

6. Hold the adjuster screw in position and tighten the adjuster screw locknut to 23 ft. lbs. (31 Nm). Do not allow the screw to turn while tightening the locknut.

Removal and Installation

EAGLE

1. Disconnect the negative battery cable.

2. Have the wheels in a straight-ahead position.

3. Remove the flexible coupling-to-intermediate shaft attaching nuts.

4. Raise and support the vehicle safely.

5. Remove the following:
   a. Skid plate, if equipped
   b. Left side crossmember-to-sill support brace
   c. Stabilizer bar brackets from the frame

6. Mark the pitman arm for alignment and remove using special puller.

7. Remove the steering gear mounting bolts and remove the steering gear assembly.

8. Installation is the reverse of the removal procedure. Check the steering gear worm bearing preload and pitman shaft overcenter drag torque adjustment.

NOTE: Always adjust the worm bearing preload first and the pitman shaft overcenter drag torque last.

Power Steering Gear

Adjustment
WORM BEARING PRELOAD

1. Seat the adjuster plug firmly in the housing using a spanner wrench. Approximately 20 ft. lbs. (27 Nm) is required to seat the housing.
2. Place an index mark on the gear housing opposite one of the holes in the adjuster plug.
3. Measure back counterclockwise $^3/_{16}$–$^1/_4$ in. (4.7–6.3 mm) from the index mark and remark the housing.
4. Turn the adjuster plug counterclockwise until the hole in the plug is aligned with the second mark on the housing.
5. Install the adjuster plug locknut and tighten it to 85 ft. lbs. (115 Nm). Be sure the adjuster plug does not turn when tightening the locknut.
6. Turn the stub shaft clockwise to stop, then turn the shaft back $^1/_4$ turn.
7. Using a torque wrench and a socket, measure the torque required to turn the stub shaft. Take the reading with the torque wrench at vertical position while turning the stub shaft at an ever rate. The torque required to turn the stub shaft should be 4–10 inch lbs. (0.45–1.13 Nm).

PITMAN SHAFT OVERCENTER DRAG TORQUE

1. Turn the pitman shaft adjuster screw counterclockwise until fully extended, then turn it back $^1/_2$ turn clockwise.
2. Rotate the stub shaft from stop-to-stop and count the total number of turns.
3. Turn the stub shaft back $^1/_2$ the total number of turns.

NOTE: When the gear is centered, the flat on the stub shaft should face upward and be parallel with the side cover and the master spline on the pitman shaft should be in line with the adjuster screw.

4. Using a torque wrench and a socket, measure the torque required to turn the stub shaft. Take the reading with the torque wrench at vertical position. Rotate the torque wrench 45 degrees each side of the center and record the highest drag torque measured on or near center.
5. Adjust the overcenter drag torque by turning the pitman shaft adjusting screw clockwise until the desired drag torque is obtained. Adjust the drag torque to the following limits:
   a. On new steering gears, add 4–8 inch lbs. (0.45–0.90 Nm) to previously measured worm bearing preload torque, but do not exceed a combined total of 18 inch lbs. (2 Nm) drag torque.
   b. On used steering gears, add 4–5 inch lbs. (0.5–0.6 Nm) to previously measured worm bearing preload torque, but do not exceed a combined total of 14 inch lbs. (2 Nm) drag torque.
6. Tighten the pitman shaft adjusting screw locknut to 35 ft. lbs. (47 Nm) after the adjusting overcenter drag torque.

Removal and Installation
EAGLE

1. Disconnect the negative battery cable.
2. Place wheels in straight-ahead position.
3. Position drain pan under steering gear.
4. Disconnect hoses at gear. Raise and secure hoses above pump fluid level to prevent excessive oil spillage and cap ends of hoses to keep out dirt.
5. Remove flexible coupling-to-intermediate shaft attaching nuts.
6. Raise the vehicle and support it safely. Remove the skid plate, if so equipped; the left side crossmember to still support brace; and the stabilizer bar brackets from the frame.
7. Paint alignment marks on pitman arm and pitman shaft for assembly reference.
8. Remove pitman arm using the proper tool.

9. Remove steering gear mounting bolts and remove steering gear.
10. Center steering gear. Turn stub shaft (using flexible coupling) from stop to stop and count total number of turns; then turn back from either stop $^1/_2$ total number of turns to center gear. At this point, flat on stub shaft should be facing upward.
11. Align flexible coupling and intermediate shaft flange.
12. Install gear mounting bolts in gear, install spacer on gear and mount gear on frame side-sill. Tighten gear mounting bolts to 65 ft. lbs. torque.
13. Install and tighten flexible coupling nuts and torque to 25 ft. lbs.
14. Install pitman arm. Index arm to the shaft using alignment marks made during removal.
15. Install pitman arm nut. Tighten nut to 115 ft. lbs. torque and stake the nut to the pitman shaft.

NOTE: The pitman arm nut must be staked to the shaft to retain it properly.

16. Install the stabilizer bar brackets, left side crossmember to sill support brace and skid plate, if so equipped. Lower the vehicle.
17. Align flexible coupling, if necessary.
18. Connect hoses to gear and tighten fittings to 25 ft. lbs. torque.
19. Fill pump reservoir with power steering fluid and bleed air from system.

Power Steering Rack and Pinion

Adjustment

1. Disconnect the negative battery cable.
2. Raise and support the vehicle safely.
3. Remove the steering rack assembly from the vehicle.
4. Secure the steering rack assembly in a vise. Do not clamp the vise jaws on the steering housing tubes. Clamp the vise jaws only on the housing cast metal.
5. Remove the steering gear housing endplug from the steering gear shaft bore using tool 6103 or equivalent.
6. Remove the preload adjustment cap locknut from the steering gear housing bore using tool 6097 or equivalent.
7. Loosen the preload adjustment cap. Retorque the preload adjustment cap to 45–50 inch lbs. (5–6Nm), then back off the plug by turning it 45–50 degrees counterclockwise.
8. Secure the preload adjustment cap with a new locknut using tool 6097 or equivalent. Do not allow the adjustment cap to rotate when tightening the locknut.
9. Install the endplug using tool 6103 or equivalent. Complete installation by reversing the removal procedure.

Removal and Installation
PREMIER AND MEDALLION

1. Disconnect the negative battery cable.
2. Unsnap the steering shaft boot flange from the dash panel opening and slide the boot upward.
3. Remove the intermediate steering shaft bolt. Reference mark the intermediate shaft and the steering gear shaft, separate the shafts.
4. Raise and support the vehicle safely.
5. In the engine compartment, remove the splash shield from the steering gear.
6. Fold back the lock tabs on the inner tie rod retaining bolts. Loosen the bolts that hold the steering gear to the body and remove the steering gear through the left fender well.
To install:
7. Position the steering gear and install the mounting nuts. Connect the tie rods to the steering knuckles turns. Disconnect the power steering lines and plug them.
8. Remove the steering gear mounting nut.

9. Raise and safely support the vehicle. Remove the left front wheel. Remove the nuts retaining the outer tie rods to the steering knuckle.

10. Tighten the bolts to 35 ft. lbs.

11. Connect the power steering lines. Tighten the bolts attaching the tie rods to the steering gear to 55 ft. lbs. and bend the lock tabs over the bolts.

12. Install the splash shield over the steering gear.

13. Inside the vehicle, align the intermediate shaft with the steering shaft and connect the shafts. Install the retaining bolt and tighten it to 25 ft. lbs.

14. Reposition the shaft boot. Connect the negative battery cable.

15. Fill and bleed the power steering system.

SUMMIT

1. Disconnect the negative battery cable.
2. Raise the vehicle and support it safely.
3. Drain the power steering fluid.
4. Remove the band from the steering joint cover.
5. Remove the joint assembly and gear box connecting bolt.
6. Remove the pressure and return hoses.
7. Separate the tie rod ends from the steering knuckles.
8. Remove the gear box mounting clamps and remove the gear box assembly.
9. To install, reverse the removal procedure.

Power Steering Pump

Removal and Installation

EAGLE

NOTE: The power steering pump on some 4.2L engine equipped vehicles sold in California, is driven by a single serpentine belt. Do not attempt to move the pump to adjust the belt. Use the adjusting hole in the alternator bracket and adjust the tension to 140 lbs. force.

1. Disconnect the negative battery cable. Remove the fan belt.

2. Place a container under the pump to catch fluid. Remove the fuel vapor storage canister and air cleaner, if necessary.

3. Disconnect the hoses and cap the outlets, so that the power steering unit does not lose fluid. Remove the air pump belt.

4. On vehicles equipped with air conditioning, loosen the idler pulley adjusting bolt and idler pulley, air pump adjusting strap mounting bolt and remove the compressor drive belt from the idler pulley. Loosen the 2 nuts that attach the upper leg of the aluminum idler pulley mounting bracket to the cylinder head and remove the bolt that attaches the lower leg of the mounting bracket to the engine front cover.

5. Remove the nut from the air pump mounting stud, remove the power steering pump-to-engine front cover front adapter plate (do not unbolt the adapter plate from the pump), remove the long adjusting bolt that passes through the adapter plate and remove the bolt hidden behind the flange in the rear adapter plate. Remove the pump, adapter plate and mounting bracket together.

6. After installation, fill the system with the approved power steering fluid. Bleed the system of air by raising the front of the car and turning the wheels from side to side without hitting the stops several times. Check the level frequently.

PREMIER, MEDALLION AND SUMMIT

1. Disconnect the negative battery cable.
2. Raise and safely support the vehicle.
3. Remove the underbody splash shield. Loosen the accessory drive belt.
4. Disconnect and plug the power steering fluid lines.
5. Remove the pump mounting bolts and remove the pump.

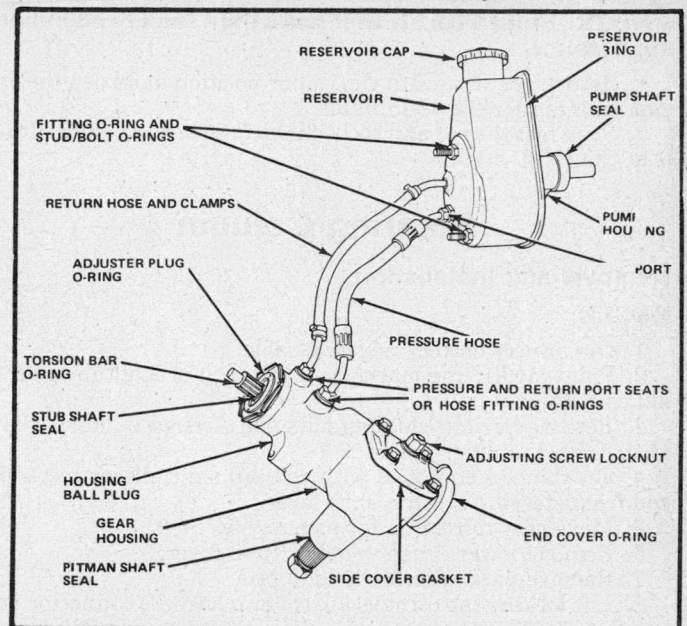

Power Steering system—typical

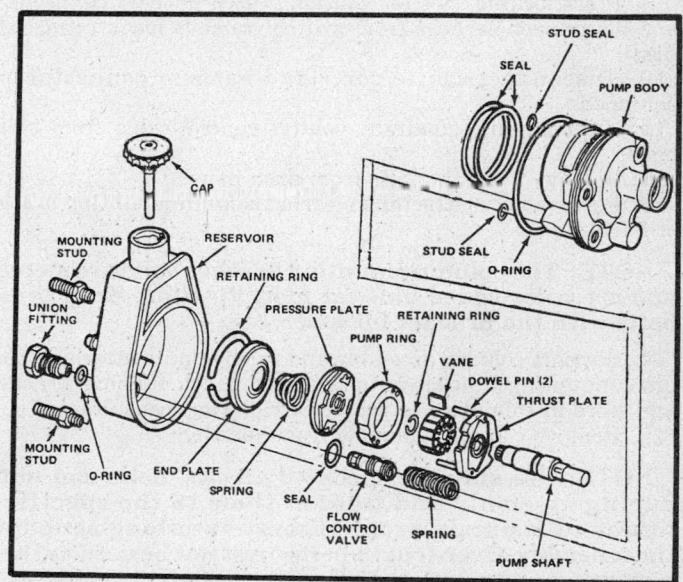

Exploded view of power steering pump—typical

On the 1.5 and 3.0L engine, remove the pump with the mounting brackets attached.

6. On 1.6L engine, remove the heat protector.

7. On 1.5 and 1.6L engines, remove the oil reservoir and bracket.

8. Install the pump to the engine and connect the pressure lines. Install the accessory drive belt and adjust the tension.

9. Lower the vehicle. Fill and bleed the system.

Bleeding System

1. With the wheels turned all the way to the left, add power steering fluid to the **COLD** mark on the fluid level indicator.

2. Start the engine and run at fast idle momentarily, shut engine **OFF** and recheck fluid level. If necessary add fluid to to bring level to the **COLD** mark.

3. Start the engine and bleed the system by turning the wheels from side to side without hitting the stops.

NOTE: Fluid with air in it has a light tan or red bubbly appearance.

4. Return the wheels to the center position and keep the engine running for 2 or 3 minutes.

5. Road test the car and recheck the fluid level making sure it is at the **HOT** mark.

Steering Column

Removal and Installation

EAGLE

1. Disconnect battery negative cable.

2. Paint identifying marks on intermediate shaft and gear to aid assembly.

3. Remove flexible coupling nuts and disengage intermediate shaft from coupling.

4. On vehicles equipped with column shift, disconnect shift rod from steering column shift lever.

5. Move seat to rear as far as possible.

6. Remove lower finish panel or tube cover.

7. Remove package tray, if equipped.

8. Lift locking tab on steering column harness connector and separate column harness from instrument panel harness connector.

9. Press locking tabs on ignition switch harness connectors and disconnect harness from switch (remove black connector first).

10. Disconnect cruise command harness connector, if equipped.

11. Unhook shift quadrant pointer control cable from shift bowl.

12. Remove toe plate bolts from dash panel.

13. Remove bolts attaching steering column mounting bracket-to-column.

NOTE: The column mounting bracket bolts are metric and are color-coded blue for identification. Keep these bolts with the bracket for assembly.

14. Support column assembly and remove nuts attaching column mounting bracket-to-instrument panel. Remove bracket and store in safe place to protect break-away capsules.

15. Remove column assembly from vehicle.

NOTE: Use only the specified screws, bolts and nuts during assembly and tighten them to the specified torque to maintain proper energy-absorbing action of the assembly. Over-length bolts must not be used as they may prevent a portion of the assembly from compressing under impact. The bolts or nuts attaching the column mounting bracket to the instrument panel must be tightened to the specified torque so the column mounting bracket will break away under impact.

16. Remove column holding fixture and install mounting bracket on column. Tighten bracket attaching bolts to 20 ft. lbs. torque.

17. If intermediate steering shaft was removed, install shaft on column using alignment marks made during removal.

18. Install column in vehicle.

19. Engage intermediate shaft flange with steering gear flexible coupling and loosely install 2 column mounting bracket-to-instrument panel attaching nuts. Finger-tighten nuts only.

20. Install toe plate gasket, toe plate and toe plate attaching bolts. Finger-tighten bolts only.

21. Install flexible coupling nuts and tighten to 30 ft. lbs. torque.

22. Install remaining column mounting bracket-to-instrument panel attaching nuts. Finger-tighten nuts only.

23. Position column so flexible coupling is flat and not distorted and tighten column mounting bracket-to-instrument panel attaching nuts to 10 ft. lbs. torque.

24. Align toe plate, clamp and tighten attaching bolts to 10 ft. lbs. torque.

25. Connect shift linkage and check operation. Adjust if necessary.

26. Connect quadrant cable-to-shift-bowl, if equipped.

27. Connect ignition switch harness, steering column harness and cruise command connector, if equipped.

28. Install lower finish panel, tube cover, or package tray, if equipped.

29. Remove protective covering from column painted areas.

30. Connect battery negative cable.

PREMIER AND MEDALLION

1. Disconnect the negative battery cable.

2. Remove the lower instrument panel trim covers and support rod.

3. Disconnect the steering column electrical connector.

4. Disconnect the shift cable from the shift lever. Unsnap the steering column boot and slide it up the shaft to gain access to the intermediate shaft bolt.

5. Matchmark the steering column shaft and the intermediate shaft. Remove the bolt from the intermediate shaft.

6. Remove the steering column-to-instrument panel bolts. Lower the column assembly to the floor, separate the column from the intermediate shaft and remove it from the vehicle.

7. To install, align the intermediate shaft and the steering shaft, using the matchmarks made earlier and loosely install the retaining bolt.

8. Lift the column into position and install the column-to-instrument panel bolts and tighten to 35 ft. lbs.

9. Tighten the intermediate shaft retaining bolt. Attach the shift cable to the shift lever.

10. Attach the electrical connectors and install the instrument panel support rod. Install the trim covers.

11. Slide the steering shaft boot into position. Connect the negative battery cable.

SUMMIT

1. Disconnect the negative battery cable.

2. Remove the instrument under cover.

3. Remove the trim clip, foot shower duct and lap shower duct.

4. Remove the horn pad, steering wheel and column upper and lower cover.

5. Remove the band from the steering joint cover and remove the joint assembly and gear box connecting bolt.

6. Remove the lower and upper column mounting brackets.

7. Remove the steering column assembly.

8. Installation is the reverse of the removal procedure.

Front Wheel Bearings

FRONT WHEEL DRIVE

Removal and Installation

PREMIER AND MEDALLION

1. Raise and safely support the vehicle.

2. Remove the wheel.

3. Remove the brake caliper and support it to the side. Do not disconnect the brake lines or support the caliper by the brake line.

4. Push the axleshaft out of the hub. If it does not push out easily use tool TAV–1050 or equivalent, on the hub.

5. Remove the brake rotor. Working through the access hole in the hub, remove the bolts that retain the bearing assembly. Remove the hub and wheel bearing as an assembly using tool TAV–1050 or equivalent, to pull the hub off the knuckle.

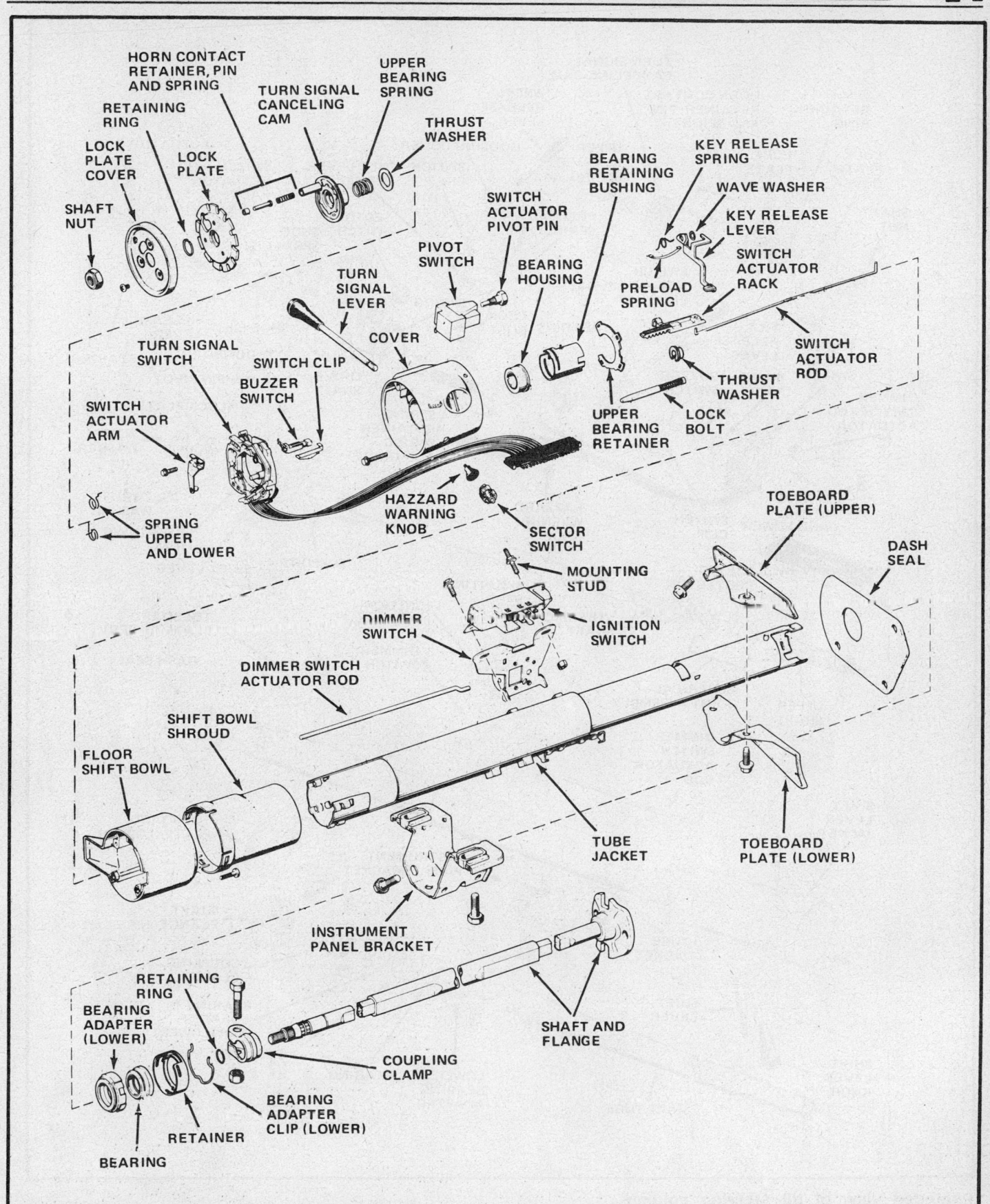

Exploded view of standard type column

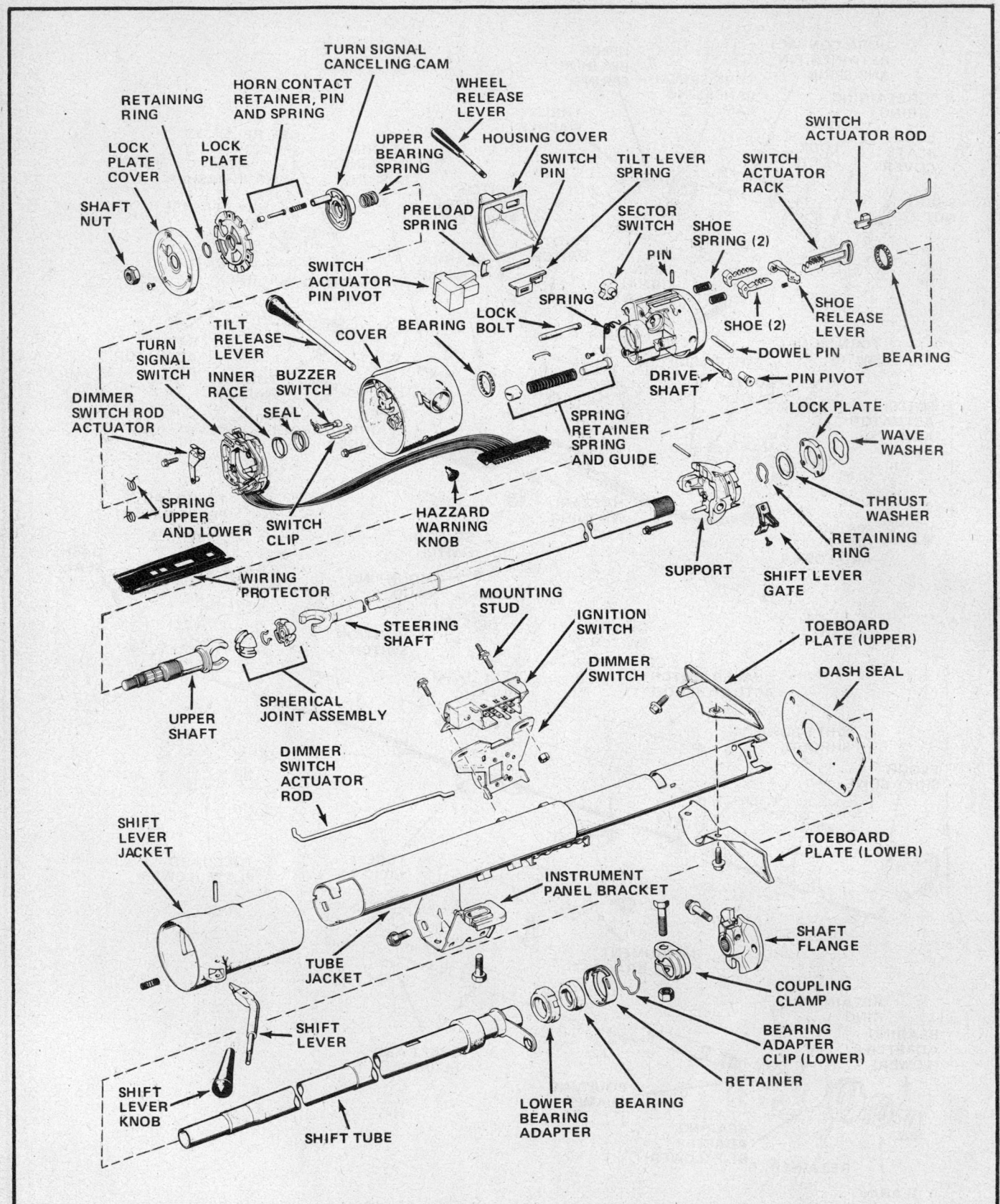

TURN SIGNAL
CANCELING CAM

HORN CONTACT
RETAINER, PIN
AND SPRING

WHEEL
RELEASE
LEVER

SWITCH
ACTUATOR ROD

RETAINING
RING

UPPER
BEARING
SPRING

HOUSING COVER

SWITCH
PIN

TILT LEVER
SPRING

SWITCH
ACTUATOR
RACK

LOCK
PLATE
COVER

LOCK
PLATE

PRELOAD
SPRING

SECTOR
SWITCH

SHOE
SPRING (2)

SHAFT
NUT

SWITCH
ACTUATOR
PIN PIVOT

PIN

SHOE (2)

SHOE
RELEASE
LEVER

BEARING

TILT
RELEASE
LEVER

COVER

BEARING

LOCK
BOLT

SPRING

DOWEL PIN

BEARING

TURN
SIGNAL
SWITCH

INNER
RACE

BUZZER
SWITCH

DRIVE
SHAFT

PIN PIVOT

DIMMER
SWITCH ROD
ACTUATOR

SEAL

SPRING
RETAINER
SPRING
AND GUIDE

LOCK PLATE

WAVE
WASHER

SPRING
UPPER
AND LOWER

SWITCH
CLIP

HAZZARD
WARNING
KNOB

THRUST
WASHER

RETAINING
RING

WIRING
PROTECTOR

SUPPORT

SHIFT LEVER
GATE

MOUNTING
STUD

IGNITION
SWITCH

TOEBOARD
PLATE (UPPER)

STEERING
SHAFT

DIMMER
SWITCH

DASH SEAL

UPPER
SHAFT

SPHERICAL
JOINT ASSEMBLY

DIMMER
SWITCH
ACTUATOR
ROD

TOEBOARD
PLATE (LOWER)

SHIFT
LEVER
JACKET

INSTRUMENT
PANEL BRACKET

SHAFT
FLANGE

TUBE
JACKET

COUPLING
CLAMP

SHIFT
LEVER

BEARING
ADAPTER
CLIP (LOWER)

SHIFT
LEVER
KNOB

RETAINER

SHIFT TUBE

LOWER
BEARING
ADAPTER

BEARING

Exploded view of tilt steering column

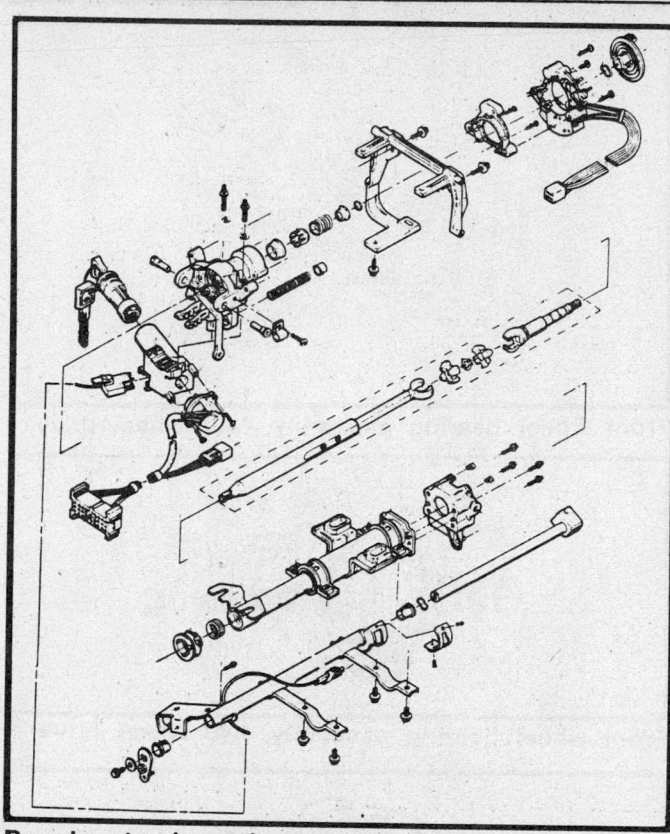

Premier steering column assembly

6. If the wheel bearing is being replaced, remove it from from the hub by pulling on it. Discard the bearing race.

7. Remove the ball joint key bolt and disconnect the ball joint from the knuckle. Remove the 2 bolts that attach the strut to the steering knuckle.

8. Remove the steering knuckle.

To install:

9. Insert the ball joint into the steering knuckle and install the ball joint key bolt, tightening to 77 ft. lbs. Position the steering knuckle to the strut and install the retaining bolts, tightening to 123 ft. lbs.

10. Install the wheel bearing over the rear of the hub and install the hub/bearing assembly over the axleshaft.

11. Working through the access hole in the hub, install the bearing retaining bolts, tightening to 11 ft. lbs.

12. Install the axle retaining nut and tighten it to 181 ft. lbs.

NOTE: It is essential that the axle retaining nut be tightened to the specified torque. The nut sets the wheel bearing preload besides retaining the axle.

13. Install the brake rotor and the caliper.

14. Install the wheel and lower the vehicle.

SUMMIT

1. Raise the vehicle and support it safely.

2. Remove both front wheels from the vehicle.

3. Remove the cotter pin, driveshaft retaining nut and washer.

4. Remove the caliper assembly and support it out of the way.

5. Remove the self-locking nut and separate the lower arm ball joint connection.

6. Remove the tie rod from the steering knuckle.

7. Mark the position of the hub and knuckle in relationship to the strut assembly connection. Remove the driveshaft and strut assembly connection.

8. Remove the hub and knuckle.

9. Mount the hub and knuckle assembly in a vise.

10. Separate the hub and brake disc using tools MB991056 and MB990998 or their equivalent.

11. Remove the outer bearing inner race, hub oil seal, outer bearing inner race, driveshaft oil seal, inner bearing outer race and dust cover from the steering knuckle.

To install:

12. Apply Mopar lubricant (Part No. 2525035) or equivalent to the outside surface of the bearing outer races. Drive the bearing outer races into the knuckle using tools C–3893 and MB990776–A or their equivalent.

13. Apply Mopar lubricant (Part No. 2525035) or equivalent to the bearings and inside surface of the hub. Place the outside bearing inner race into the knuckle. Apply lubricant to the lip of the oil seal and to the surfaces of the oil seal which contact the hub. Drive the oil seal into the knuckle using tools C–4171 and MB991015 or their equivalent.

14. Install the hub into the knuckle using tool MB990998 or equivalent. After the hub has been completely inserted, tighten the nut on the tool to 144–188 ft. lbs. (200–260 Nm). Rotate the front hub to seat the bearings.

15. Measure the wheel bearing starting torque using an inch pound torque wrench and tool MB990998 or equivalent. The starting torque must be 11 inch lbs. or less, and must not feel rough when rotated.

16. Check and make sure the hub endplay is .008 inch or less.

17. Apply Mopar lubricant (Part No. 2525035) or equivalent to the inner bearing, inside of the knuckle and the lip of oil seal. Drive the driveshaft side oil seal into the knuckle until it contacts the inner bearing outer race using tools C–4171 and MB991015 or their equivalent.

18. Assembly the hub and knuckle to the strut assembly and complete installation by reversing the removal procedure.

Adjustment

The wheel bearing adjustment on Premier, Medallion and Summit vehicles are pre-set to specification by design and therefore cannot be adjusted.

REAR WHEEL DRIVE

Removal and Installation

EAGLE

1. Raise and support the vehicle safely.

2. Remove wheel, caliper and rotor.

3. Remove bolts attaching axle shaft flange-to-halfshaft.

4. Remove cotter pin, nut lock and axle hub nut.

5. Remove halfshaft.

6. Remove steering arm from steering knuckle.

7. Remove caliper anchor plate from steering knuckle.

8. Remove 3 Torx® head bolts retaining hub assembly using tool set J–25359 or equivalent.

9. Remove hub assembly from steering knuckle.

10. Clean grease from steering knuckle cavity.

To install:

11. Partially fill hub cavity of steering knuckle with chassis lubricant and install hub assembly.

12. Tighten hub Torx® head bolts to 75 ft. lbs. (102 Nm) torque.

13. Install caliper anchor plate and plate retaining bolts.

14. Tighten caliper anchor plate retaining bolts to 100 ft. lbs. (136 Nm) torque.

15. Install halfshaft. Install axle flange-to-shaft bolts and install hub nut.

16. Tighten halfshaft-to-flange bolts to 45 ft. lbs. (61 Nm) torque.

17. Tighten hub nut to 175 ft. lbs. (237 Nm) torque.

18. Install nut lock and cotter pin.

19. Install rotor, caliper and wheel.

Adjustment

TWO WHEEL DRIVE

1. Raise and support the vehicle safely.
2. Remove the hub cap, grease cap and O-ring, cotter pin and nutlock.
3. On vehicle with styled wheels, remove the wheel and hub cap and reinstall the wheel.
4. Tighten the spindle nut to 25 ft. lbs. (34 Nm) while rotating the wheel to seat the bearings.
5. Loosen the spindle nut $1/3$ of a turn and while rotating the wheel, tighten the spindle nut to 6 inch lbs. (0.7 Nm).
6. Install the nutlock on the spindle nut so cotter pin hole in nutlock and spindle are aligned.
7. Install a new cotter pin, grease cap and O-ring and hub cap.
8. On vehicles with styled wheels, remove the wheel and install the hub cap and wheel.
9. Lower the vehicle.

FOUR WHEEL DRIVE

4WD vehicles have a unique front axle hub and bearing assembly. The assembly is sealed and does not require lubrication, periodic maintenance, or adjustment. The hub has ball bearings which seat in races machined directly into the hub. There are darkened areas surrounding the bearing race areas of the hub. These darkened areas are from a heat treatment process, are normal and should not be mistaken for a problem condition.

FOUR WHEEL DRIVE

SELECT DRIVE

EAGLE

The select drive gives the operator the option of driving in the 2WD or 4WD modes, merely by changing a switch, located on the dash. The model 30 front axle is used with the select drive system, having the 2WD disconnect mechanism located on the right hand axle tube.

A second disconnect mechanism is located on the transfer case. Both the axle and transfer case disconnect mechanisms are operated by vacuum controlled servo type motors. The vacuum shift motors are not interchangeable. The axle shift motor is vented to prevent lubrication from being drawn out of the axle by vacuum, should the shift motor seals become worn or damaged. The transfer case shift motor is not vented.

During the changes in the drive mode, the axle and the transfer case are shifted into the selected mode in sequence, not simultaneously. When the 4WD mode is selected, the axle is shifted first. When the 2WD mode is selected, the transfer case is shifted first.

OPERATION

NOTE: It may be necessary to move the vehicle forward or backward slightly, to fully engage or disengage the axle and transfer case.

When shifted to the 4WD mode, the axle shift motor is operated first. As complete axle engagement occurs, vacuum is directed from the axle shift motor to the transfer case motor, activating the motor and cause the transfer case to shift into the 4WD mode.

When shifted into the 2WD mode, vacuum is routed to the transfer case shift motor, opposite of the apply, which is vented and the transfer case is disengaged. As the transfer case shift motor disengages the transfer case, a vacuum port is opened to the axle shift motor, causing it also to disengage in the same manner as the shift motor of the transfer case. Each shift motor

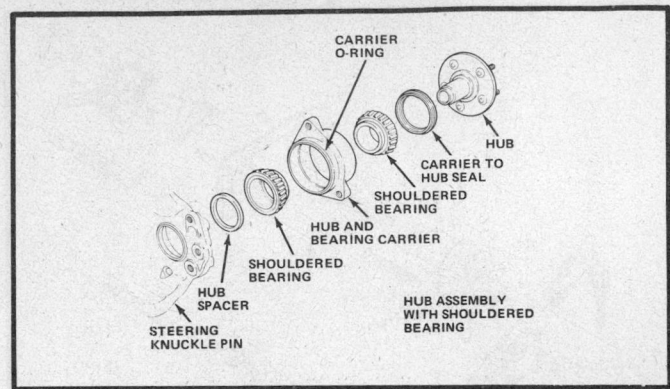

Front wheel bearing assembly, four wheel drive

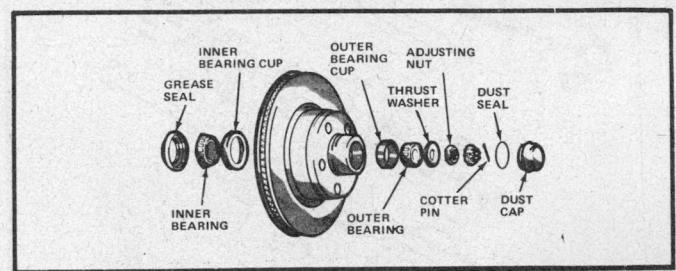

Front wheel bearing assembly, two wheel drive

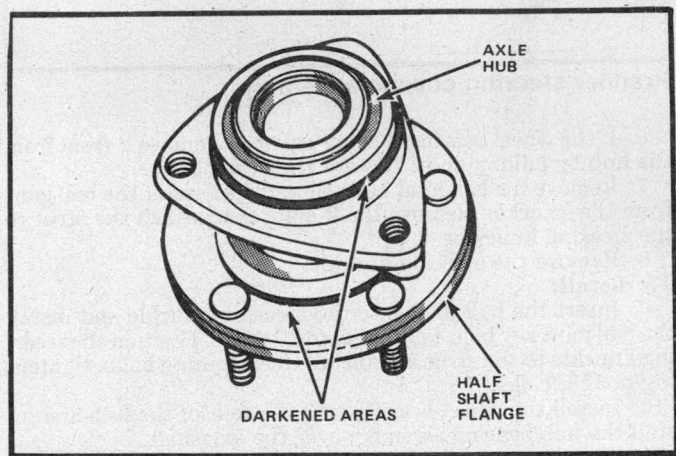

Darkened area locations on four wheel drive front wheel bearing

is dependent upon the other to engage or disengage, depending upon the drive mode selected by the operator. One-way check valves incorporated in the system ensure that the axle and transfer case shift in the correct sequence and are vented properly. The check valves are located in the vacuum lines.

NOTE: The vehicle must be at a complete stop when changing driving modes and may require a backward or forward motion of the vehicle to engage the axle and/or transfer case.

Trouble Diagnosis

TRANSFER CASE SHIFT MOTOR

1. Disconnect the vacuum harness from the transfer case shift motor. Connect a controlled vacuum source to the shift motor from port.
2. Apply 15 inch Hg. of vacuum to the shift motor while rotat-

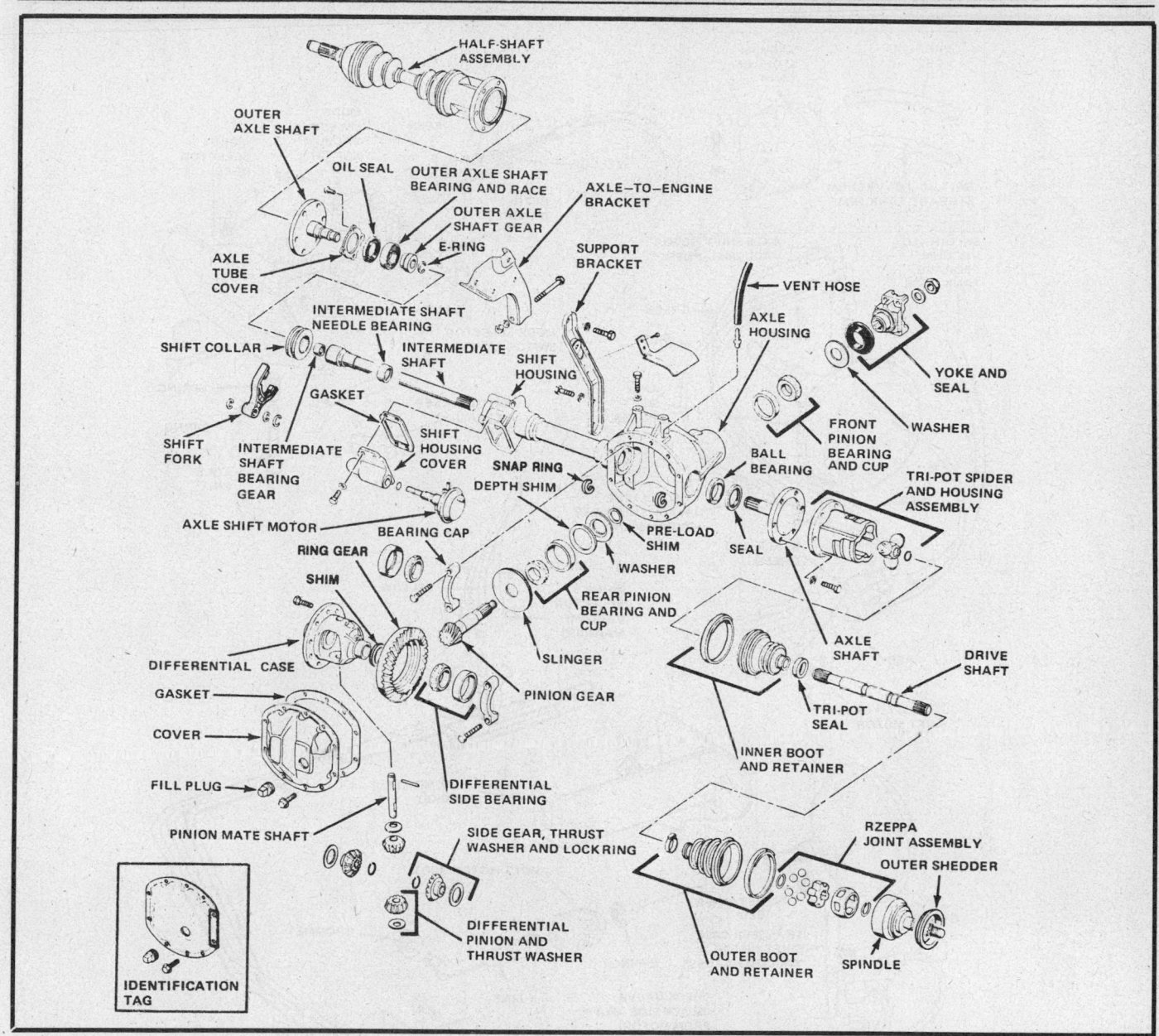

Exploded view of front axle assembly—Select Drive System

ing the rear propeller shaft to fully engage the transfer case in the 4WD mode.

3. The shift motor should maintain the applied vacuum for a minimum of 30 seconds. If the vacuum is not held, replace the motor.

4. If the motor holds the vacuum, connect the controlled vacuum source to the rear port of the shift motor and plug the front axle connecting port. Apply 15 inch Hg to the rear port.

5. If vehicle is equipped with automatic transmission, shift into the **P** position. If equipped with manual transmission, shift into first gear. The shift motor should maintain vacuum applied for a minimum of 30 seconds. If vacuum is not held, replace the motor.

6. If the motor holds the vacuum, remove the cap from the shift motor axle connecting port and check for vacuum at the port. If there is no vacuum at the port, rotate the rear propeller shaft as necessary, to ensure complete transfer case engagement.

NOTE: The transfer case must be completely engaged before the shift motor stem will extend fully and open the axle interconnecting port.

7. If vacuum is present at the shift motor axle connecting port after fully engaging the transfer case, the unit is operating properly.

8. If vacuum is still not present at the shift motor axle connecting port, slide the boot away from the shift motor stem and measure the distance the stem has extended. The stem should be extended a distance of $5/8$ inch from the edge of the shift motor housing to the E-ring on the stem.

9. If the stem has not extended to its specification, check the mode selector switch and vacuum harness. If the shift motor stem has extended to specifications, but vacuum is still not present at the axle connecting port, replace the shifting motor.

AXLE SHIFT MOTOR

1. Disconnect the vacuum harness from the axle shift motor.

VACUUM HOSE

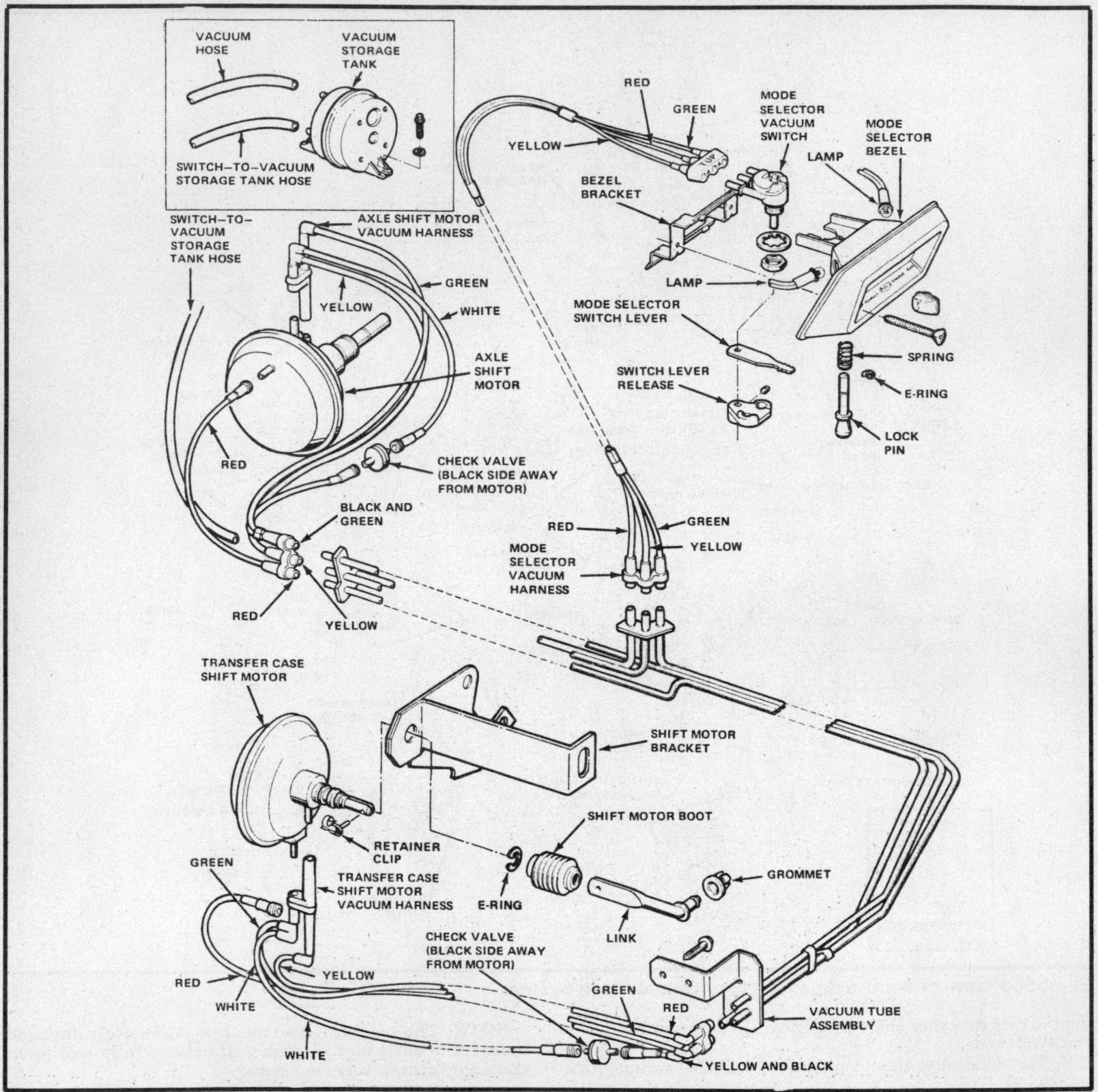

VACUUM STORAGE TANK

SWITCH—TO—VACUUM STORAGE TANK HOSE

SWITCH—TO—VACUUM STORAGE TANK HOSE

AXLE SHIFT MOTOR VACUUM HARNESS

GREEN

YELLOW

WHITE

AXLE SHIFT MOTOR

RED

CHECK VALVE (BLACK SIDE AWAY FROM MOTOR)

BLACK AND GREEN

RED

YELLOW

TRANSFER CASE SHIFT MOTOR

RED

GREEN

YELLOW

MODE SELECTOR VACUUM HARNESS

BEZEL BRACKET

MODE SELECTOR VACUUM SWITCH

MODE SELECTOR BEZEL

LAMP

LAMP

MODE SELECTOR SWITCH LEVER

SWITCH LEVER RELEASE

SPRING

E-RING

LOCK PIN

RETAINER CLIP

TRANSFER CASE SHIFT MOTOR VACUUM HARNESS

E-RING

SHIFT MOTOR BRACKET

SHIFT MOTOR BOOT

GROMMET

LINK

GREEN

RED

WHITE

YELLOW

WHITE

CHECK VALVE (BLACK SIDE AWAY FROM MOTOR)

GREEN

RED

VACUUM TUBE ASSEMBLY

YELLOW AND BLACK

Vacuum control components—Select Drive System

Connect a controlled vacuum source to the shift motor front port.

2. Apply 15 inch Hg to the shift motor and rotate the right front wheel to fully disengage the axle.

3. The shift motor should retain the applied vacuum for a minimum of 30 seconds. If the vacuum is not held, replace the motor.

4. If the shift motor holds the vacuum properly, disconnect the vacuum source from the front port on the shift motor. Connect the vacuum source to the shift motor rear port and cap the transfer case connecting port and apply 15 inch Hg to the shift motor.

5. The shift motor should maintain the applied vacuum to the rear port for a minimum of 30 seconds. If the shift motor does not hold the vacuum, replace the motor.

6. If the motor retains the vacuum, remove the cap from the shift motor transfer case connecting port and check for vacuum at this port. If vacuum is present, shift motor is operating properly.

7. If vacuum is not present, rotate the right front wheel as necessary, to be sure the axle has shifted completely. The axle must shift completely in order for the connecting port to open completely.

8. If vacuum is still not present at the shift motor transfer

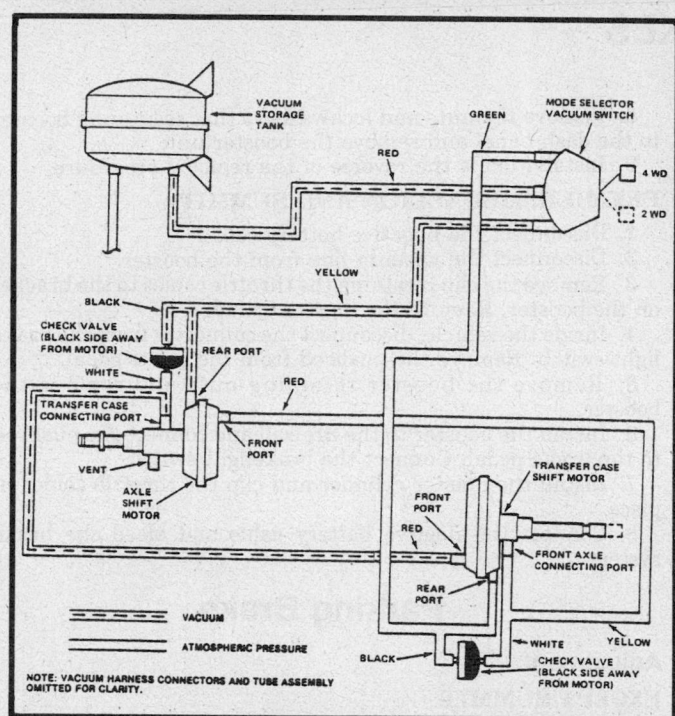

Vacuum schematic with Select Drive System in the four wheel drive mode

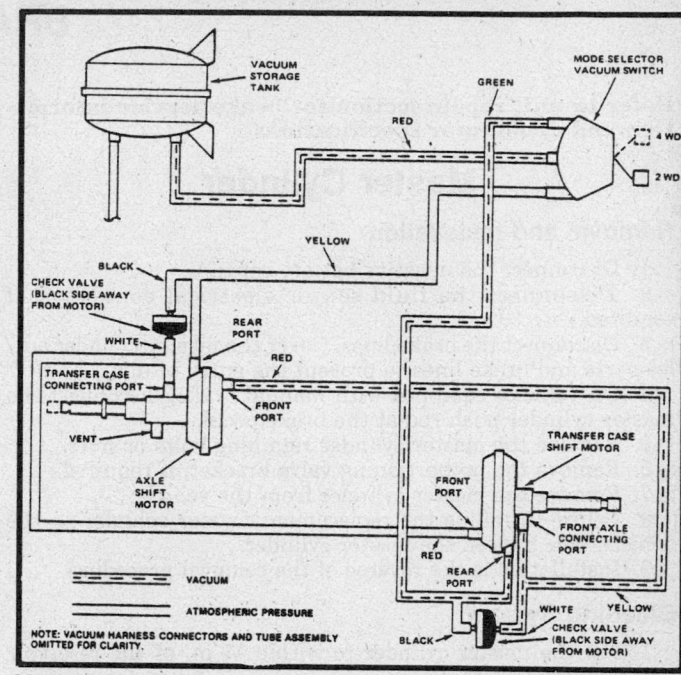

Vacuum schematic with Select Drive System in the two wheel drive mode

case connecting port, replace the motor. If vacuum is present, the unit is operating properly.

Alignment

Procedures

NOTE: The front suspension assembly must be free of worn, loose or damaged parts prior to measurement of front wheel alignment.

CASTER AND CAMBER

Eagle

Adjust the camber by turning the lower control arm inner eccentric pivot bolt. Tighten the pivot bolt locknuts to 110 ft. lbs. (149 Nm) after completing the camber adjustment.

Adjust the caster by loosening the strut rod jamnut and turning the rod adjusting nuts in or out to move the lower control arm forward or rearward to obtain the desired caster angle. After completing the caster adjustment tighten the adjusting nut to 65 ft. lbs. (88 Nm) and the jamnut to 75 ft. lbs. (102 Nm).

PREMIER, MEDALLION AND SUMMIT

The camber and caster are pre-set at the factory an cannot be adjusted. If the camber and caster are not within the standard value, replace the bend or damaged parts.

TOE-IN

Eagle

1. Place the front wheels in straight ahead position and center the steering wheel and gear.
2. Turn the tie rod adjusting tubes equally in opposite directions to obtain the desired toe-in setting.
3. If the steering wheel spoke position was disturbed during the toe-in adjustment, correct spoke position by turning the tie rod tubes equally in the same direction until the desired position is obtained.

Premier, Medallion and Summit

1. Remove the clamp from the steering gear box bellows.
2. Loosen the tie rod end locking nuts.
3. Turn the left and right tie rods the same amount in either direction. The toe will move out as the left tie rod is turned in the forward direction and the right tie rod is turned in the reverse direction. The toe can aslo be changed approximately 0.48 in. (12mm) by turning both tie rods half a turn each.
4. After adjustment, tighten the tie rod end locking nuts and reinstall the clamp on the steering gear box bellows.

BRAKES

Refer to unit repair section for brake service information and drum/rotor specifications.

Master Cylinder

Removal and Installation

1. Disconnect the negative battery cable.
2. Disconnect the fluid sensor electrical connector, if required.
3. Disconnect the brake lines. Cover the master cylinder outlet ports and brake lines to prevent the entry of dirt.
4. On vehicles equipped with manual brake, disconnect the master cylinder push rod at the brake pedal.
5. Remove the master cylinder retaining bolts or nuts.
6. Remove the proportioning valve bracket, if required.
7. Remove the master cylinder from the vehicle.
8. Before installing the replacement master cylinder on the vehicle, bench bleed the master cylinder.
9. Installation is the reverse of the removal procedure.

Bleeding System

1. Fill the master cylinder to within ¼ in. of the reservoir rim.
2. Raise and support the vehicle safely.

NOTE: The rear wheels on Premier, Medallion and Summit vehicles must be at normal ride height for satisfactory bleeding. Do not allow the rear wheels to hang free.

3. Bleed the system in the following sequence:—right rear, left rear, right front and left front.
4. Bleed 1 wheel at a time.
5. Install a rubber hose on the bleeder screw of the caliper or wheel cylinder to be bled and place the opposite end of the hose in a container partially fill with brake fluid.
6. Open the bleeder screw ¾ turn. Have a helper press the brake pedal to the floor, then tighten the bleeder screw. Have the helper slowly release the brake pedal.
7. Repeat the bleeding operation until clear brake fluid flows without air bubbles.

NOTE: Check the master cylinder fluid level frequently during the bleeding procedure and refill if necessary.

8. After bleeding operation is completed, discard the fluid in the container. Fill the master cylinder to ¼ in. from the reservoir rim and check the brake operation.

Power Brake System

BRAKE BOOSTER

Removal and Installation

EAGLE

1. Disconnect the negative battery cable.
2. Disconnect the booster unit push rod and brakelamp switch at the brake pedal.
3. Remove the vacuum hose from the booster check valve.
4. Remove the master cylinder attaching nuts and lockwashers. Seperate the master cylinder from the booster. Do not disconnect the brake lines.

5. Remove the nuts and lockwashers that secure the booster to the dash panel and remove the booster unit.
6. Installation is the reverse of the removal procedure.

PREMIER, MEDALLION AND SUMMIT

1. Disconnect the negative battery cable.
2. Disconnect the vacuum line from the booster.
3. Remove the clip retaining the throttle cables to the bracket on the booster. Remove the master cylinder.
4. Inside the vehicle, disconnect the connector from the brake light switch. Remove the pushrod from the brake pedal.
5. Remove the booster retaining nuts and remove the booster.
6. Install the booster to the firewall and connect the pushrod to the brake pedal. Connect the brakelight switch.
7. Install the master cylinder and clip the throttle cables in place.
8. Connect the negtive battery cable and bleed the brake system.

Parking Brake

Adjustment

EXCEPT SUMMIT

1. Check the rear brake shoe to drum clearance, adjust if necessary.
2. On Eagle vehicle, apply the brakes several times while backing up to adjust the drum brakes. Make 1 forward application for each reverse application to equalize the adjustment.
3. Fully apply and release the parking brake about 10 times. Set the pedal on the first notch from the released position.
4. Raise and support the vehicle safely.
5. Tighten the cable at the equalizer so that the wheels can just barely be turned forward. Be sure to hold the end of the cable screw to prevent the cable from turning.
6. Release the parking brake and check for rear brake drag. The wheels should rotate freely with the parking brake **OFF**.

SUMMIT

1. Pull the parking brake lever with a force of approximately 45 lbs. and count the number of notches. If the lever extend beyound 5–7 notches, adjustment is necessary.
2. Remove the console box, hold the adjusting nut in position with a spanner, and loosen the locknut.
3. Loosen the adjusting nut to the end of the cable and free the parking brake cable.
4. On vehicles equipped with rear drum brake, pull the parking brake lever back with a force of approximately 44 lbs. until the lever stroke ceases to change. If the lever stroke does not change, the automatic adjustment mechanism is functioning normally, and the shoe to drum clearance is correct.
5. On vehicles equipped with rear disc brake, start the engine and forcefully depress the brake pedal several times and confirm that the pedal stroke stops changing. If the pedal stroke stops changing, it indicates that the automatic adjusting mechanism is functioning normally, and the shoe to drum clearance is correct. Check to be the clearance between the stopper and the parking brake lever at the caliper side is 0.078 in. (2mm) or less.
6. Rotate the adjusting nut to obtain the standard value of 5–7 notches.
7. After completing adjustment, jack up the rear of the vehicle. With the parking brake lever in the release position, rotate the rear wheels to confirm that the rear brakes are not dragging.

CLUTCH AND TRANSMISSION/TRANSAXLE

Refer to "Chilton's Transmission Service Manual" for additional coverage.

Clutch Linkage

Adjustment

EAGLE AND PREMIER

All Eagle and Summit models have hydraulically actuated clutch systems with no provision for adjustment.

MEDALLION

All Medallion uses a cable operated, self adjusting clutch mechanism. The adjustment is automatically set during operation by a quadrant mechanism on the clutch pedal assembly.

SUMMIT

1. Measure the clutch pedal height from the face of the pedal pad to the firewall. If the pedal height is not within 6.70–6.89 inches (170–175mm), adjustment is necessary.
2. Measure the clutch pedal clevis pin play at the face of the pedal pad. If the clutch pedal clevis pin play are not within 0.04–0.12 inches (1–3mm), adjustment is necessary.
3. If the clutch pedal height or clevis pin play are not within the standard value, adjust as follows:
   a. For vehicles without cruise control, turn and adjust the bolt so that the pedal height is the standard value, and then secure by tightening the locknut.
   b. Vehicles with auto-cruise control system, disconnect the clutch switch connector and turn the switch to obtain the standard clutch pedal height. Then, lock with the locknut.
   c. Turn the pushrod to adjust the clutch pedal clevis pin play to agree with the standard value and then secure the pushrod with the locknut.

NOTE: When adjusting the clutch pedal height or th clutch pedal clevis pin play, be careful not to push the pushrod toward the master cylinder.

   d. Check that when the clutch pedal is depressed all the way 5.9 in. (149mm), the interlock switch switches over from **ON** to **OFF**.

HYDRAULIC CLUTCH

System Bleeding

1. Fill the reservoir with brake fluid.
2. Loosen the bleed screw, have the clutch pedal pressed to the floor.
3. Tighten the bleed screw and release the clutch pedal.
4. Repeat the bleeding operation until the fluid is free of air bubbles.

NOTE: It is suggested to attach a hose to the bleeder and place the other end into a container at least one-half full of brake fluid during the bleeding operation. Do not allow the reservoir to run out of fluid during the bleeding operation.

Clutch Plate/Pressure Plate

Removal and Installation

NOTE: The flywheel bolts must not be reused.

EAGLE

1. Disconnect the negative battery cable.

2. Remove the transmission, starter motor and throwout bearing.
3. Disconnect the clutch linkage at the housing and remove the housing.
4. Mark the clutch cover and flywheel for reassembly.
5. Remove the clutch cover and the driven plate by loosening the bolts alternately and in several stages.
6. Remove the pilot bushing lubricating wick and soak the wick in engine oil.
7. Inspect the parts for signs of overheating (blue color), distortion, scoring, or wear. Overheated or deeply scored or worn parts should be replaced. Light wear may be cleaned up by sanding or refacing.
8. Installation is the reverse of removal. Use an alignment tool to position the driven plate on the flywheel. Tighten the cover bolts alternately and in several stages.

MEDALLION AND SUMMIT

1. Disconnect the negative battery cable.
2. Remove the transaxle assembly from the vehicle.
3. Remove the pressure plate attaching bolts.
4. Remove the pressure plate release bearing assembly and the clutch disc.
5. Inspect the condition of the clutch components and replace any worn parts.

NOTE: The release bearing and pressure plate are not serviced separately. The bearing is permanently attached to the pressure plate diaphragm fingers. The pressure plate and bearing must be serviced as an assembly.

6. Inspect the flywheel for heat damage or cracks. Replace it if necessary.
7. Install the clutch disc to the flywheel. Install alignment tool EMB–786–01 or equivalent. Install the pressure plate assembly and tighten the pressure plate bolts evenly to 18 ft. lbs. Remove the alignment tool.
8. Install the transaxle assembly and check the clutch operation.

Manual Transmission

Removal and Installation

EAGLE

1. Disconnect the negative battery cable.
2. Shift transmission into **N**.
3. Remove screws attaching gearshift lever bezel and boot-to-floorpan.
4. Slide bezel and boot upward on gearshift lever to provide access to lever attaching bolts.
5. Remove bolts attaching gearshift lever-to-lever mounting cover on transmission adapter housing and remove gearshift lever.
6. Remove bolts attaching gearshift lever mounting cover-to-transmission adapter and remove mounting cover to provide access to transfer case upper mounting stud nut in transmission adapter housing.
7. Remove nut from transfer case upper mounting stud located inside transmission adapter housing.
8. Raise the vehicle.
9. Remove the skid plate.
10. Remove speedometer adapter retainer bolt and remove retainer, adapter and cable. Discard adapter O-ring and plug adapter opening in transfer case to prevent excessive oil spillage.

NOTE: Matchmark the position of the speedometer adapter for assembly alignment, before removing it.

11. Matchmark the driveshafts and axle yokes for assembly alignment and disconnect propeller shafts at transfer case.

12. Disconnect backup lamp switch wire.

13. Place support stand under the engine.

14. Support transmission and transfer case using suitable transmission jack.

15. Remove rear crossmember.

16. Remove catalytic converter bracket from transfer case and brace rod from racket.

17. Remove bolts attaching transmission-to-clutch housing.

18. Remove transmission and transfer case as an assembly.

19. Remove nuts from transfer case mounting studs and remove transmission from transfer case.

To install:

20. Position the transmission on transfer case. Install and tighten all transfer case mounting stud nuts to 26 ft. lbs. torque.

21. Support transmission-transfer case assembly on suitable transmission jack.

22. Align transmission clutch shaft with throwout bearing and clutch disc splines and seat transmission against clutch housing.

23. Install and tighten transmission-to-clutch housing attaching bolts to 55 ft. lbs. torque.

24. Connect propeller shafts-to-transfer case yokes. Tighten clamp strap bolts to 15 ft. lbs. torque.

25. Install brace rod and rear crossmember. Tighten attaching bolts to 30 ft. lbs. torque.

26. Connect backup lamp switch wire.

27. Install replacement O-ring on speedometer adapter and install adapter and cable and retainer. Tighten retainer bolt to 100 inch lbs.

NOTE: Do not attempt to reuse the original adapter O-ring. The ring is designed to swell in service to improve its sealing qualities and could be cut or torn during installation if reuse is attempted.

28. Attach catalytic converter bracket-to-transfer case. Tighten skid plate attaching bolts to 30 ft. lbs. torque. Check and correct lubricant levels in transmission and transfer case, if necessary.

29. Install skid plate. Tighten skid plate attaching bolts to 30 ft. lbs. torque.

30. Remove stand used to support engine and remove transmission jack, if not removed previously.

31. Lower the vehicle.

32. Clean mating surfaces of gearshift lever mounting cover and of transmission adapter housing.

33. Apply RTV-type sealant to gearshift lever mounting cover, install cover bolts and torque to 13 ft. lbs. torque.

34. Install gearshift lever on mounting cover. Before tightening lever attaching bolts make certain lever is engaged with shift rail. Tighten lever attaching bolts to 18 ft. lbs. torque.

35. Position gearshift lever boot and bezel in floorpan and install bezel attaching screws.

Manual Transaxle

Removal and Installation

MEDALLION

1. Disconnect the negative battery cable.

2. Disconnect and remove the flexible heat tube from the engine.

3. Remove the TDC sensor retaining bolt and remove the sensor.

4. Remove the bolts retaining the steering bracket and remove the bracket.

5. Remove the bolts attaching the crossmember to the side sill and body.

6. Raise and safely support the vehicle.

7. Remove the front wheels. Disconnect and remove the passenger side tie rod.

8. Loosen the bolt retaining the coolant expansion tank and move the tank aside.

9. Attach engine support tool MS-1900 or equivalent, to the engine and tighten the adjuster nut until there is no slack in the chain.

10. Remove the bolts attaching the exhaust head pipe to the manifold. Remove the bolts attaching the exhaust head pipe to the converter and remove the head pipe.

11. Remove the crossmember by turning it and taking out through the passenger side wheel well.

12. Disengage the clutch cable. Remove the upper steering knuckle mounting bolt and loosen the lower bolt.

13. Remove the driveshaft retaining pin. Swing each rotor and steering knucle outward and slide the driveshafts from the transaxle.

14. Disconnect the reverse lockout cable and disconnect the shift rod from the lever. Disconnect the speedometer cable. Disconnect the ground strap at the transaxle.

15. Support the transaxle. Remove the transaxle support cushion nuts. Remove the bolts that attach the 2 transaxle mounting brackets to the transaxle.

16. Disconnect the wiring harness connector and remove the starter. Remove the bolts attaching the clutch housing to the engine.

17. Pull the transaxle straight back until the clutch shaft is clear of the engine and lower the transaxle.

To install:

18. Raise and position the transaxle into the vehicle. Align the release bearing and the release fork.

19. Install the transaxle-to-engine mounting bolts. Tighten to 37 ft. lbs.

20. Install the starter and connect the electrical connectors. Slightly raise the transaxle and install the mounting brackets. Align the transaxle support cushion bolts and install the retaining nuts.

21. Connect the speedometer cable and the shift rods. Connect the clutch cable.

22. Install the axleshafts by tilting the steering knuckle in, install the upper bolt and tighten both bolts to 148 ft. lbs.

23. Install the axle retaining pins. Connect the ground strap to the case.

24. Install the crossmember through the wheel well opening and position it on the side sills. Install and tighten the bolts.

25. Connect the tie rods to the steering bracket and tighten the mounting bolts to 25 ft. lbs. Connect the steering gear bracket to the steering rack and tighten the bolts to 30 ft. lbs.

26. Install the front wheels. Install the TDC sensor and the heat tube. Connect the exhaust header pipe to the converter and manifold.

27. Check and fill the transaxle fluid. Remove the engine support tool and connect the battery.

28. Check the operation of the shift mechanism.

SUMMIT

1. Disconnect the negative battery cable.

2. Remove the battery and battery tray.

3. Remove the air pipe and air hose.

4. Raise the vehicle and support it safely.

5. Drain the transaxle oil.

6. Remove the tension rod on vehicle equipped with dual overhead cam (DOHC) engine.

7. Remove the control cable connection (cable control type).

8. Remove the clutch release cylinder connection (hydraulic control type).

9. Remove the backup lamp switch connector, speedometer cable connection and starter motor.

10. Remove the transaxle mounting bolts and bracket. Remove the transaxle assembly.

11. To install, reverse the removal procedure.

Automatic Transmission

Removal and Installation

EAGLE

1. Disconnect the negative battery cable.
2. Open the engine hood and disconnect the fan shroud. Remove the fill tube attaching bolt.
3. Raise the vehicle and support safely.
4. Remove the skid plate.
5. Matchmark and remove the driveshaft(s).
6. Remove or loosen necessary exhaust system components and bracing brackets.
7. Remove the starter assembly. Remove stiffening braces.
8. Matchmark and remove speedometer adapter and cable assembly.
9. Disconnect the shift and throttle linkage. On column shift vehicles, remove the bellcrank bracket bolt at the converter housing.
10. Disconnect the neutral start and back-up light switch connector. Remove the TCS switch oil line, if equipped.
11. Remove cover in front of the converter, if equipped and matchmark converter to the converter drive plate.
12. Remove the converter-to-drive plate bolts.
13. Support the transmission assembly with a lifting and lowering device. Safety chain the transmission assembly to the device. The transfer case will be removed with the transmission.
14. Remove bolt(s) at the rear support cushion.
15. Remove the rear crossmember and groundstrap, if equipped with strap.
16. Move the transmission as necessary and remove the oil cooler lines.
17. Place a support stand under the engine as required.
18. Remove transmission fill tube, as required.

NOTE: **Transmission fluid will drain out. Plug fill tube hole.**

Remove bolts attaching transmission to the engine.

19. Move the transmission assembly rearward and while holding the converter in position, lower the assembly from under the vehicle.

To install:

20. Reverse of the removal procedure. However, varied steps must be accomplished or checked before and during the installation of the unit.

   a. If the torque converter was removed or inadvertently separated from the transmission, a new pump seal should be installed and the pump rotor drive lugs re-aligned with an aligning tool, before the converter is re-installed.

   b. With a lifting device, raise the transmission assembly and align the converter housing with the engine attaching flange dowel pins. Match the marks between the converter and the drive plate. Install the attaching bolts, seat the converter housing flush with the engine flange before tightening the bolts.

NOTE: **Drive plate bolts must not be reused.**

   c. Install the oil cooler lines, the rear engine crossmember and the mount bolt(s).

   d. Complete the assembly and check the fluid level of the transfer case lubricant.

   e. Lower the vehicle and complete the assembly topside.

   f. Fill the transmission with fluid and correct the level as necessary.

   g. Road test the vehicle and check the transmission operation.

Automatic Transaxle

Removal and Installation

PREMIER

1. Disconnect the negative battery cable.
2. Loosen the throttle valve cable adjusting nut and remove the cable from the engine bracket.
3. Disengage the shift cable and support it to the side. Remove the upper steering knuckle mounting bolt and loosen the lower bolt.
4. Remove the driveshaft retaining pin. Swing each rotor and steering knuckle outward and slide the driveshafts from the transaxle.
5. Remove the underbody splash shield.
6. Remove the converter housing covers. Remove the converter-to-driveplate bolts. Support the transaxle.
7. Remove the nuts attaching the crossmember to the side sills. Remove the large bolt and nut that attach the rear cushion to the support bracket.
8. Remove the support bracket and rear cushion.
9. Disconnect the header pipes from the exhaust manifold and the catalytic converter.
10. Loosen the engine cradle bolts. Remove the starter, plate and dowel. Disconnect the shift cable from the transmission lever. Remove the cable bracket bolts and separate the bracket from the case.
11. Disconnect and remove the TDC sensor, disconnect the speedometer sensor. Disconnect the transaxle cooling lines.
12. Remove the transaxle-to-engine bolts, pull the transaxle back and away from the engine.

To install:

13. Position the transaxle to the engine. Install the transaxle-to-engine bolts and tighten to 31 ft. lbs.
14. Connect all electrical leads, install the TDC sensor. Connect the speedometer. Install the transaxle cooler lines.
15. Attach the shift bracket to the case and tighten the bolts to 125 inch lbs. Install the shift cable into the bracket.
16. Install the starter. Connect the exhaust head pipes to the manifolds and he converter.
17. Install the rear support and cushion, install the mounting bolts and tighten to 49 ft. lbs.
18. Tighten the engine cradle bolts to 92 ft. lbs. Connect the driveshafts.
19. Install the converter-to-driveplate bolts and tighten to 24 ft. lbs. Install the converter housing covers.
20. Tilt the steering knuckles in and install the top bolts, tighten all to 148 ft. lbs.
21. Install the front wheels. Install the under body splash shield. Attach the throttle valve cable.
22. Connect the negative battery cable. Check the fluid level.

MEDALLION

1. Disconnect the negative battery cable.
2. Disconnect and remove the flexible heat tube from the engine.
3. Remove the TDC sensor retaining bolt and remove the sensor.
4. Remove the bolts retaining the steering bracket and remove the bracket.
5. Remove the bolts attaching the crossmember to the side sill and body.
6. Raise and safely support the vehicle.
7. Remove the front wheels. Disconnect and remove the passenger side tie rod.
8. Loosen the bolt retaining the coolant expansion tank and move the tank aside.
9. Attach engine support tool MS-1900 or equivalent, to the engine and tighten the adjuster nut until there is no slack in the chain.

10. Remove the bolts attaching the exhaust head pipe to the manifold. Remove the bolts attaching the exhaust head pipe to the converter and remove the head pipe. Disconnect the coolant lines to the heat exchanger.

11. Remove the crossmember by turning it and taking out through the passenger side wheel well.

12. Disengage the shift cable and support it to the side. Remove the upper steering knuckle mounting bolt and loosen the lower bolt.

13. Remove the driveshaft retaining pin. Swing each rotor and steering knuckle outward and slide the driveshafts from the transaxle.

14. Disconnect the speedometer cable. Disconnect the ground strap at the transaxle. Disconnect the BVA module harness.

15. Support the transaxle. Remove the transaxle support cushion nuts. Remove the bolts that attach the 2 transaxle mounting brackets to the transaxle.

16. Disconnect the wiring harness connector and remove the starter. Remove the converter-to-flywheel bolts. Remove the transaxle-to-engine bolts.

17. Pull the transaxle straight back until the converter is clear of the engine and lower the transaxle. Install converter retainer BVI–465 or equivalent, to keep the converter from falling out.

To install:

18. Raise and position the transaxle into the vehicle. Apply a small amount of grease to the torque converter pilot. Align the painted marks on the converter with the painted marks on the flywheel. Install the converter to flywheel bolts, tighten to 34 ft. lbs.

19. Install the transaxle-to-engine mounting bolts. Tighten to 37 ft. lbs.

20. Install the starter and connect the electrical connectors. Slightly raise the transaxle and install the mounting brackets. Align the transaxle support cushion bolts and install the retaining nuts.

21. Connect the speedometer cable and the shift cable.

22. Install the axleshafts by tilting the steering knuckle in, install the upper bolt and tighten both bolts to 148 ft. lbs.

23. Install the axle retaining pins. Connect the ground strap to the case.

24. Install the crossmember through the wheel well opening and position it on the side sills. Install and tighten the bolts.

25. Connect the tie rods to the steering bracket and tighten the mounting bolts to 25 ft. lbs. Connect the steering gear bracket to the steering rack and tighten the bolts to 30 ft. lbs. Connect the cooling lines.

26. Install the front wheels. Install the TDC sensor and the heat tube. Connect the exhaust header pipe to the converter and manifold. Connect the BVA wiring.

27. Check and fill the transaxle fluid. Remove the engine support tool and connect the battery.

SUMMIT

1. Disconnect the negative battery cable.

2. Remove the battery and battery tray.

3. Remove the air pipe and air hose.

4. Raise the vehicle and support it safely.

5. Drain the transaxle oil.

6. Remove the tension rod on vehicle equipped with dual overhead cam (DOHC) engine.

7. Remove the control cable connection and cooler lines connections.

8. Remove the throttle control cable connection (3–Speed transaxle).

9. Remove the shift control solenoid valve connector connection (4–Speed transaxle).

10. Remove the inhibitor switch connector and kickdown servo switch connector (4–Speed transaxle).

11. Remove the pulse generator connector and oil temperature sensor connector (4–Speed transaxle).

12. Remove the speedometer cable connection and starter.

13. Remove the transaxle mounting bolts and bracket. Remove the transaxle assembly and properly support it.

14. To install, reverse the removal procedure.

Transfer Case

EAGLE

Torque Bias Test

This test may be performed to determine the condition of the viscous coupling, which is the "heart" of the AMC transfer case. Note that if a malfunction in the coupling is observed, the coupling cannot be repaired in any way, but must be replaced. The following procedure is an in-vehicle test. If the transfer case is to be disassembled, test the coupling as outlined within the overhaul procedure (bench test) in the Unit Repair section.

1. Drive the vehicle onto a level surface, turn the engine **OFF** and place the transmission shift lever in **N**. Place the Select Drive lever in the 4WD position.

2. Raise 1 of the front wheels off of the floor, then remove the wheel cover from the raised wheel.

3. Attach a socket (of the same size as the lug nuts) to a torque wrench. Install the socket and torque wrench to any 1 of the lug nuts of the raised wheel.

4. Rotate the wheel with the torque wrench and note the amount of torque required to turn the wheel.

5. A reading of 45 ft. lbs. minimum should be obtained. If a reading of less than 45 ft. lbs. was obtained, the transfer case must be disassembled and the bench test of the coupling should be performed. If the reading was 45 ft. lbs. or more, the coupling is operating properly.

6. Remove the torque wrench and socket, install the wheel cover and lower the vehicle.

Removal and Installation

MANUAL TRANSMISSION

1. Disconnect the negative battery cable.

2. Raise the vehicle and support safely.

3. Remove the skid plate and rear brace rod at the transfer case. Support engine/transmission assembly.

4. Remove the speedometer adapter and cable, after match marking the adapter to the housing.

5. Matchmark the driveshafts and remove from the transfer case yokes.

6. Remove the vacuum shift motor harness.

7. Support the transfer case and remove the retaining nuts from the studs and remove the transfer case.

8. The installation of the transfer case assembly is the reverse of the removal procedure.

9. Make all connections and check the fluid level in the transfer case.

AUTOMATIC TRANSMISSION

1. Disconnect the negative battery cable.

2. Raise the vehicle and support safely.

3. Support the engine/transmission assembly.

4. Disconnect catalytic converter support bracket at the adapter housing, if equipped.

5. Remove the skid plate and rear brace rod at the transfer case.

6. Matchmark the speedometer adapter and remove it and the speedometer cable.

7. Matchmark the driveshafts and disconnect from the transfer case yokes.

8. Disconnect the gearshift and throttle linkage at the transmission. Support the transfer case.

9. Lower the rear crossmember.

10. Remove the retaining case-to-adapter housing stud nuts and remove the transfer case.

11. The installation is the reverse of the removal procedure.
12. Install new speedometer adapter O-ring and correct the fluid levels of the transmission and transfer case.

NOTE: If the transfer case has been disassembled and repaired, fill the transfer case to the bottom edge of the filler hole with appropriate lubricant and install the plug. Drive the vehicle approximately 8–10 miles and recheck the lubricant level. Refill as necessary. This method results in a more accurate lubricant fill.

DRIVEAXLE AND HALFSHAFTS

Driveshaft (RWD)

Removal and Installation

EAGLE

1. Disconnect the negative battery cable.
2. Place the transmission in **N**.
3. Raise the vehicle and support safely.
4. Mark the axle and driveshaft yokes for assembly reference.
5. Disconnect the driveshaft at the axle yoke and from the transfer case.

NOTE: The axle yoke is attached to the drive pinion nut. Do not loosen this nut.

6. Remove the driveshaft.
7. Installation is the reverse of the removal procedure. Tighten the clamp strap bolts to 17 ft. lbs. (23 Nm).

Front Drive Axle (FWD)

Refer to the unit repair section for overhaul procedures.

Removal and Installation

PREMIER

1. Raise the vehicle and support it safely.
2. Remove the wheels.
3. Remove the brake caliper. Do not disconnect the brake hose from the caliper.
4. Remove the driveshaft hub nut.
5. Using a drift type tool, remove the driveshaft to transaxle roll pin.

NOTE: Before proceeding to the next step, be certain the front suspension is hanging free. The strut body to suspension knuckle bolts are splined. Remove the bolts only as instructed in the following steps.

6. Remove the 2 splined bolts that attach the strut body to the suspension knuckle. Loosen and turn the nuts until they are almost at the end of the bolt threads. Tap the nuts with a brass hammer to loosen the bolts and disengage the splines. Remove the nuts and slide the bolts out of the strut body and suspension knuckle.
7. Place a drain pan under the transaxle end of the driveshaft.

8. Wrap a shop towel around the driveshaft outer rubber boot to prevent damaging the boot.
9. Tilt the suspension knuckle out and away from the strut body and remove the driveshaft.
10. During installation, mate the driveshaft with the transaxle shaft and align the roll pin holes in each shaft.

NOTE: One side of the roll pin hole in the transaxle shaft is beveled. Align the beveled side of that hole with the side of the hole in the CV joint housing that is located in the housing "valley."

11. Insert the driveshaft to transaxle shaft roll pin and seat it with a hammer and a drift type tool.
12. Complete installation by reversing the removal procedure.

MEDALLION

1. Disconnect the negative battery cable.
2. Raise the vehicle and support it safely.
3. Remove the front wheels.
4. Remove the driveshaft nut.
5. Remove the double roll pins that attach the driveshaft to the side gear shaft with tool B.Vi. 31.01 or equivalent.
6. Remove the tie rod end.
7. Remove the upper bolt that attaches the knuckle to the strut. Then, loosen but do not remove the lower bolt.

NOTE: The driveshaft splines are secured to the hub splines with Loctite. Use tool T.Av. 1050 or equivalent to break the shaft loose from the hub. Do not attempt to loosen the shaft with a hammer.

8. Tilt the rotor/knuckle outward and remove the driveshaft.
9. To install, reverse the removal procedure.

SUMMIT

1. Disconnect the negative battery cable.
2. Raise the vehicle and support it safely.
3. Remove the front wheels.
4. Remove the cotter pin, driveshaft nut and washer.
5. Remove the self-locking nut and separate the lower arm ball joint.
6. Remove the tie rod end.
7. Using tool CT–1003 or equivalent, remove the driveshaft from the front hub.
8. Tap the tripod joint case of the driveshaft and inner shaft lightly with a plastic hammer and remove the driveshaft and inner shaft from the transaxle.
9. To install, reverse the removal procedure.

REAR AXLE AND REAR SUSPENSION

Refer to the unit repair section for axle overhaul procedures and rear suspension service.

Rear Axle Assembly

Removal and Installation

EAGLE

1. Apply the parking brake to lock the rear wheels. Remove the axle shaft nuts.

2. Raise the vehicle and support safely. Remove the rear wheels.

NOTE: The brake drums and axle shafts can be removed at this time, or can be removed after the axle assembly has been removed from the vehicle.

3. Disconnect the flexible brake line at the body floorpan bracket. Release and disconnect the parking brake cables at the equalizer.

4. Mark the driveshaft and yokes for assembly reference.

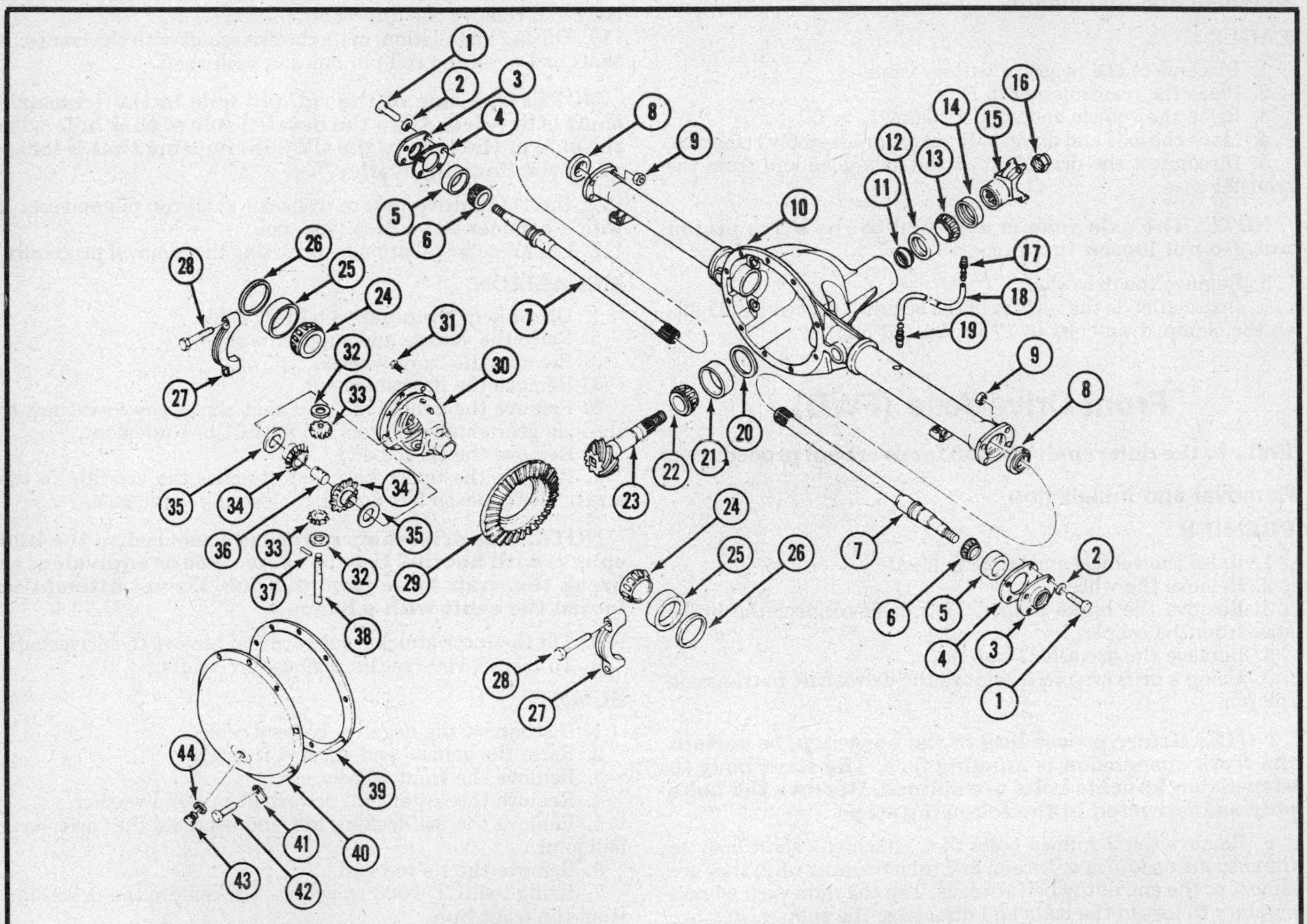

1. BOLT	16. PINION NUT	30. DIFFERENTIAL CASE
2. WASHER	17. BREATHER	31. RING GEAR BOLT
3. AXLE SHAFT OIL SEAL AND RETAINER ASSEMBLY	18. BREATHER HOSE	32. DIFFERENTIAL PINION WASHER
4. AXLE SHAFT BEARING SHIM	19. BREATHER	33. DIFFERENTIAL PINION
5. AXLE SHAFT BEARING CUP	20. PINION DEPTH ADJUSTING SHIM	34. DIFFERENTIAL SIDE GEAR
6. AXLE SHAFT BEARING	21. PINION REAR BEARING CUP	35. DIFFERENTIAL SIDE GEAR THRUST WASHER
7. AXLE SHAFT	22. PINION BEARING-REAR	36. DIFFERENTIAL PINION SHAFT THRUST BLOCK
8. AXLE SHAFT INNER OIL SEAL	23. PINION GEAR	37. DIFFERENTIAL PINION SHAFT PIN
9. NUT	24. DIFFERENTIAL BEARING	38. DIFFERENTIAL PINION SHAFT
10. AXLE HOUSING	25. DIFFERENTIAL BEARING CUP	39. AXLE HOUSING COVER GASKET
11. COLLAPSIBLE SPACER	26. DIFFERENTIAL BEARING SHIM	40. AXLE HOUSING COVER
12. PINION BEARING CUP-FRONT	27. DIFFERENTIAL BEARING CAP	41. AXLE IDENTIFICATION TAG
13. PINION BEARING-FRONT	28. DIFFERENTIAL BEARING CAP BOLT	42. BOLT
14. PINION OIL SEAL	29. RING GEAR	43. AXLE HOUSING COVER FILL PLUG
15. UNIVERSAL JOINT YOKE		44. WASHER

Rear axle with standard differential — 7⁹⁄₁₆ axle

5. Remove the stabilizer bar, if equipped.

6. Disconnect the axle vent hose and support the rear axle with a lifting device.

7. Disconnect the shock absorbers at the spring tie plates.

8. Remove the spring U-bolts, spring plates and spring clip plate if equipped with the stabilizer bar.

9. Lower the axle assembly and remove from under the vehicle.

10. The installation of the rear axle is in the reverse of the removal procedure.

11. Tighten the U-bolt nuts to 55 ft. lbs. torque.

NOTE: The driveshaft is a balanced unit; care must be used in handling. Do not bend or distort the tube or yokes, or vibration will result.

PREMIER AND MEDALLION

1. Raise and safely support the vehicle.

2. Remove the rear wheels.

3. Remove the parking brake cables from the body support.

4. Disconnect and plug the brake hoses at the axle. Remove the shock absorbers.

5. Support the axle assembly and remove the support bracket bolts. Lower the axle assembly and remove.

6. Position the axle under the vehicle and raise it into place. Install and tighten the support bracket bolts, tighten to 68 ft. lbs.

7. Connect the brake hoses at the axle. Connect the parking brake cables. Install the shock absorbers, tighten the upper shock bolt to 60 ft. lbs. and the lower bolt to 85 ft. lbs.

8. Install the rear wheels, bleed the brake system and adjust the parking brake cable.

SUMMIT WITH REAR DRUM BRAKES

1. Remove the trunk side trim on vehicle equipped with hatchback.

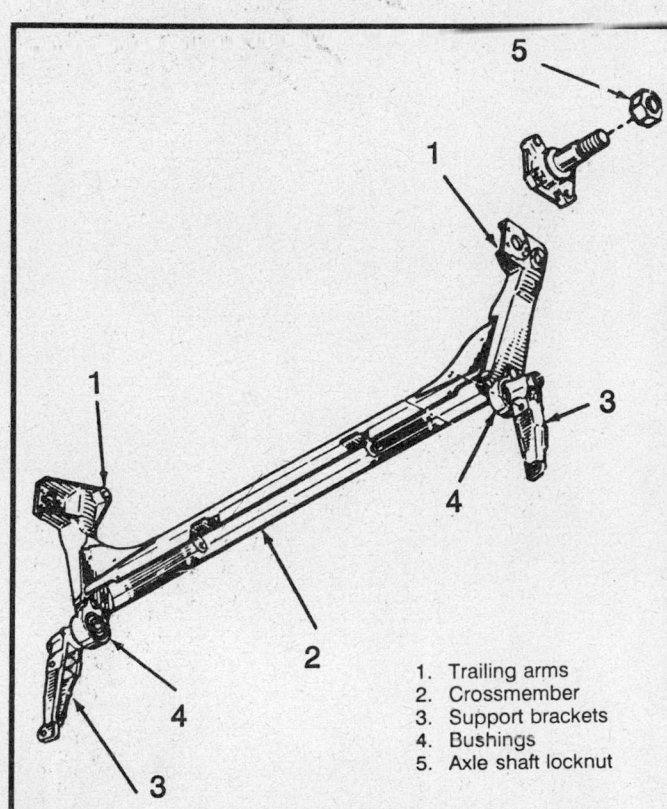

1. Trailing arms
2. Crossmember
3. Support brackets
4. Bushings
5. Axle shaft locknut

Rear axle assembly (FWD)—typical

2. Raise the vehicle and support it safely.

3. Remove the rear wheels.

4. Remove the hub cap, wheel bearing nut and outer wheel bearing inner race.

5. Remove the rear brake drum, parking brake cable, brake hose and tube bracket.

6. Remove the lateral rod mounting bolt and nut and secure the lateral rod to the axle beam with a piece of wire.

7. Place a wooden block on a jack and slightly raise the torsion axle and arm assembly. Remove the cap and upper mounting nuts from the shock absorber.

8. Remove the trailing arm bolts and remove the rear suspension assembly.

9. To install, reverse the removal procedure. Adjust the parking brake.

SUMMIT WITH REAR DISC BRAKES

1. Remove the trunk side trim on vehicle equipped with hatchback.

2. Raise the vehicle and support it safely.

3. Remove the parking brake cable, brake hose and tube bracket.

4. Remove the rear disc brake, hub cap and wheel bearing nut.

5. Remove the outer wheel bearing inner race, rear hub assembly, dust shield and brake adapter.

6. Remove the lateral rod mounting bolt and nut and secure the lateral rod to the axle beam with a piece of wire.

7. Place a wooden block on a jack and slightly raise the torsion axle and arm assembly. Remove the cap and upper mounting nuts from the shock absorber.

8. Remove the trailing arm bolts and remove the rear suspension assembly.

9. To install, reverse the removal procedure. Adjust the parking brake.

Rear Axle Shaft, Bearing and Seal

Removal and Installation

EAGLE

1. The hub and drum are separate units and are removed after the wheel is removed. The hub and axle shaft are serrated together on the taper. An axle shaft key assures proper alignment during assembly.

2. With the wheel on the ground and the parking brake applied, remove and discard the axle shaft nut cotter pin and remove the nut. Raise the vehicle and remove the wheel. Release the parking brakes and remove the drum.

3. Attach a puller to the rear hub and remove the hub. The use of a knock-out puller should be discouraged, since it may result in damage to the axle shaft, wheel bearings or differential thrust block.

4. Disconnect the parking brake cable at the equalizer.

5. Disconnect the brake tube at the wheel cylinder and remove the brake support plate assembly, oil seal and axle shims. Note that the axle shims are located on the left side only.

6. Using a screw type puller, remove the axle shaft and bearings from the axle housing.

NOTE: On twin-grip axles, rotating the differential with a shaft removed will misalign the side gear splines, preventing installation of the replacement shaft.

7. Remove the axle shaft inner oil seal and install new seals at assembly.

8. The bearing is a press fit and should be removed with an arbor press.

9. The axle shaft bearings have no provision for lubrication after assembly. Before installing the bearings, they should be packed with a good quality wheel bearing lubricant.

10. Press the axle shaft bearings onto the axle shaft with the small diameter of the cone toward the outer (tapered) end of the shaft.

11. Soak the inner axle shaft seal in light lubricating oil. Coat the outer surface of the seal retainer with sealant.

12. Install the inner oil seal.

13. Install the axle shafts, indexing the splined end with the differential side gears.

14. Install the outer bearing cup.

15. Install the brake support plate. Sealant should be applied to the axle housing flange and brake support mounting plate.

16. Install the original shims, oil seal and brake support plate. Torque the nuts to 30–35 ft. lbs.

NOTE: The oil seal and retainer go between the axle housing flange and the brake support plate.

17. To adjust the axle shaft endplay, strike the axle shafts with a lead mallet to seat the bearings. Install a dial indicator on the brake support plate and check the play while pushing and pulling the axle shaft. Endplay should be 0.004–0.008 in. Add shims to the left side only to decrease the play and remove shims to increase the play.

18. Slide the hub onto the axle shafts aligning the serrations and the keyway on the hub with the axle shaft key.

19. Replace the hub and drum, install the wheel, lower the car onto the floor and tighten the axle shaft nut to 250 ft. lbs. If the cotter pin hole is not aligned with a castellation on the nut, tighten the nut to the next castellation.

NOTE: A new hub must be installed whenever a new axle shaft is installed. Install 2 thrust washers on the shaft. Tighten the new hub onto the shaft until the hub is 1 3/16 inch (30.14mm) from the end of the shaft. Remove the nut; remove 1 thrust washer. Install the nut and torque to 250 ft. lbs. New hubs do not have serrations on the axle shaft mating surface. The serrations are cut when the hub is installed to the axle shaft.

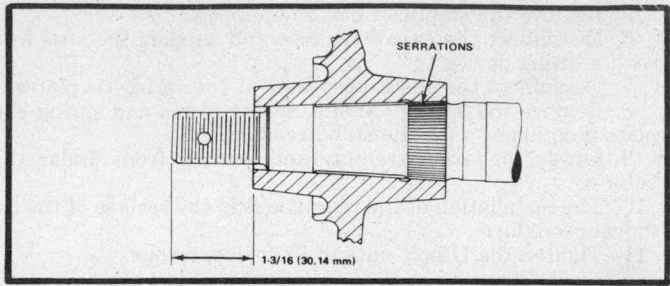

Measurement for replacement hub installation onto axle shaft

20. Connect the parking brake cable at the equalizer.

21. Connect the brake tube at the wheel cylinder and bleed the brakes.

PREMIER, MEDALLION AND SUMMIT

The rear wheel bearings and hubs are replaced as assemblies only. They are non-adjustable. The maximum allowable bearing endplay is 0.001 in. If the end play exceeds this the bearing/hub assembly must be replaced.

1. Raise and safely support the rear of the vehicle. Remove the wheel.

2. Remove the brake drum from the axle shaft hub.

3. Remove the axle shaft hub nut and remove the hub/bearing assembly.

4. Lightly oil the axle shaft before installing the hub/bearing assembly. Install the hub to the axle shaft using a NEW nut. Tighten the nut to 123 ft. lbs.

5. Install the brake drum. Install the wheel and lower the vehicle.

YEAR IDENTIFICATION

1986–90 Omni

1986 Omni GLH

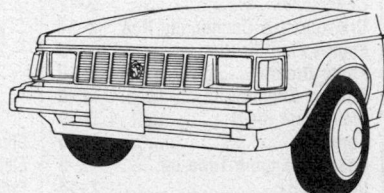

1986–90 Horizon

1986–87 Turismo

1986 Turismo Duster

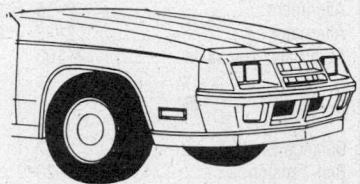

1986–87 Charger

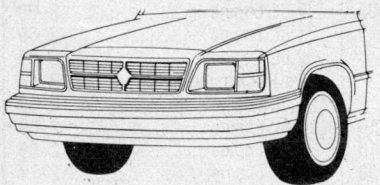

1986–90 Aries

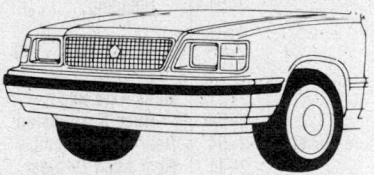

1986–90 Reliant

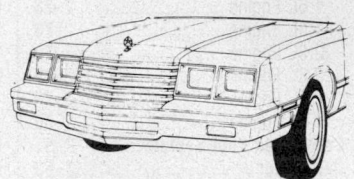

1986 Dodge 400, 600

1987-88 Dodge 600

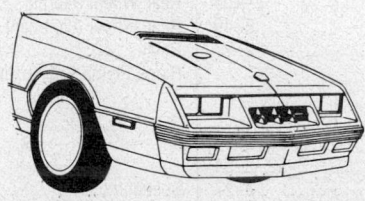

1986 Daytona Turbo

1986 Daytona

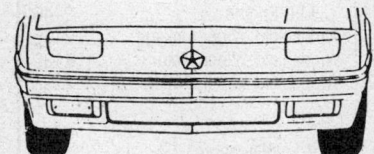

1987-88 Daytona

1989–90 Daytona

1986 Shelby Charger

YEAR IDENTIFICATION

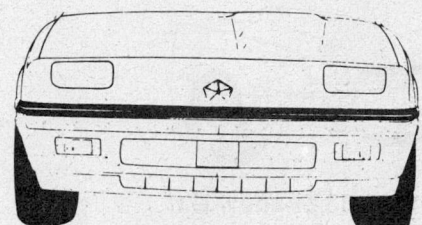

1987-88 Shelby Z

1986 Laser

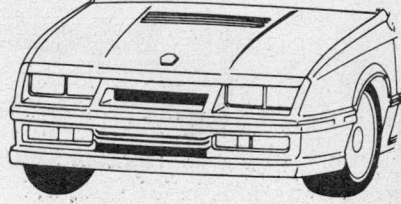

1986 Laser XE

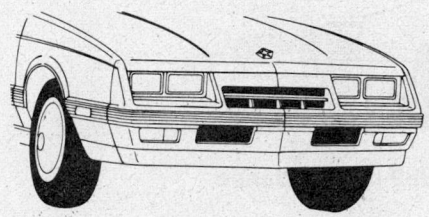

1986–88 Lancer

1989–90 Dodge Lancer

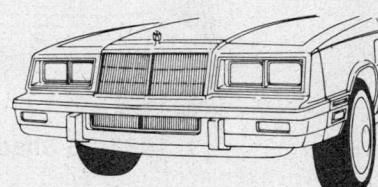

1986 New Yorker

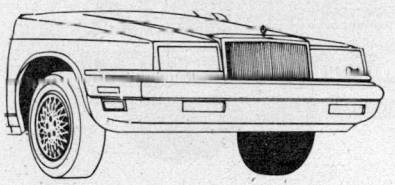

1989–90 New Yorker/Landau

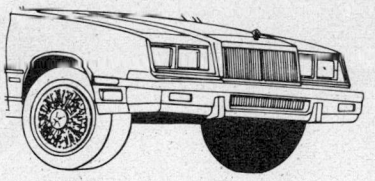

1988 New Yorker Turbo

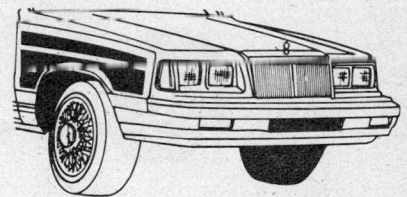

1988 Town & Country

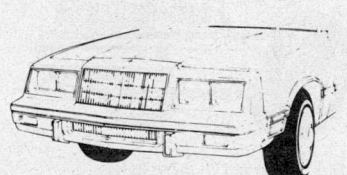

1986 LeBaron, E-Class

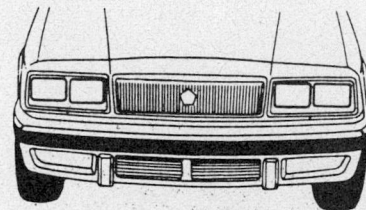

1986–88 LeBaron GTS

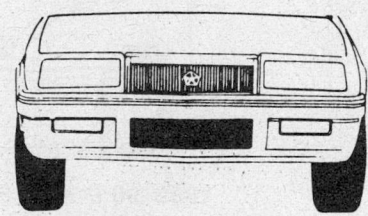

1986–90 LeBaron Coupe, GTC

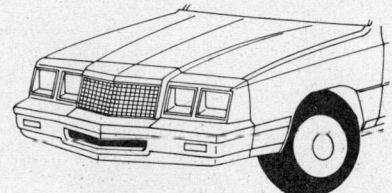

1986 Caravelle

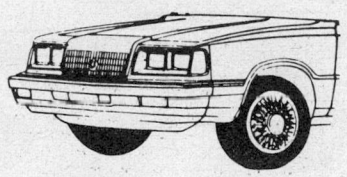

1987-88 Caravelle SE

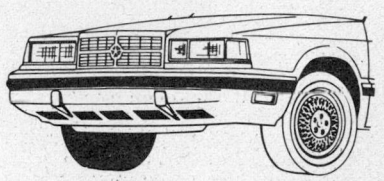

1988–90 Dynasty

YEAR IDENTIFICATION

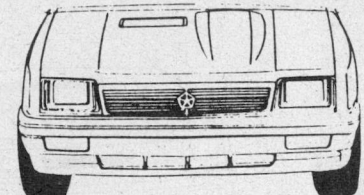

1987-88 Shadow

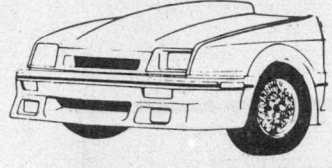

1987-88 Shadow D.C.

1989–90 Shadow ES

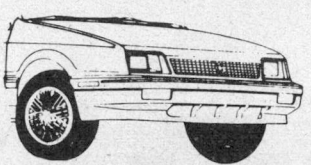

1989–90 Sundance

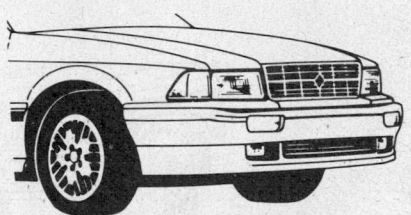

1989–90 Dodge Spirit

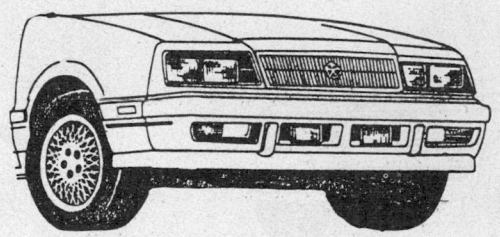

1989–90 LeBaron GTS

1989–90 Dodge Shelby

1989–90 Plymouth Acclaim

1989–90 Laser

VEHICLE IDENTIFICATION CHART

It is important for servicing and ordering parts to be certain of the vehicle and engine identification. The VIN (vehicle identification number) is a 17 digit number visible through the windshield on the driver's side of the dash and contains the vehicle and engine identification codes. The tenth digit indicates model year and the eigth digit indicates engine code. It can be interpreted as follows:

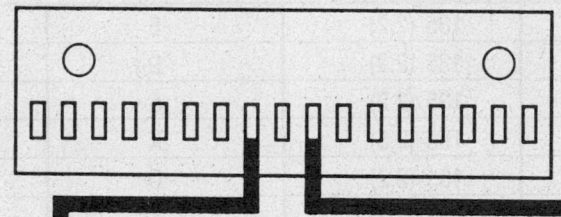

\ Engine Code						\ Model Year	
Code	**Cu. In.**	**Liters**	**Cyl.**	**Fuel Sys.**	**Eng. Mfg.**	**Code**	**Year**
A ('86)	98	1.6	4	Carb.	Peugeot	G	1986
T ('89–'90)	107	1.8	4	MPI	Mitsubishi	H	1987
R ('89–'90)	122	2.0	4	MPI	Mitsubishi	J	1988
U ('89–'90)	122	2.0	4	MPI-Turbo	Mitsubishi	K	1989
A ('89–'90)	135	2.2	4	Turbo II	Chrysler	L	1990
C ('86–'87)	135	2.2	4	Carb.	Chrysler		
C ('88–'90)	135	2.2	4	EFI	Chrysler		
D ('86–'89)	135	2.2	4	EFI	Chrysler		
E ('86–'89)	135	2.2	4	Turbo	Chrysler		
J ('89–'90)	153	2.5	4	Turbo I	Chrysler		
K ('86–'90)	153	2.5	4	EFI	Chrysler		
3 ('88–'90)	181	3.0	6	EFI	Mitsubishi		

ENGINE IDENTIFICATION

Year	Model	Engine Displacement cu. in. (liter)	Engine Series Identification (VIN)	No. of Cylinders	Engine Type
1986	LeBaron	135 (2.2)	D	4	OHC
	LeBaron	135 (2.2)	E	4	OHC
	LeBaron	153 (2.5)	K	4	OHC
	Town & Country	135 (2.2)	D	4	OHC
	Town & Country	135 (2.2)	E	4	OHC
	Town & Country	153 (2.5)	K	4	OHC
	Laser	135 (2.2)	D	4	OHC
	Laser	135 (2.2)	E	4	OHC
	Laser	153 (2.5)	K	4	OHC
	New Yorker	135 (2.2)	E	4	OHC
	New Yorker	153 (2.5)	K	4	OHC
	Omni	98 (1.6)	A	4	OHC
	Omni	135 (2.2)	C	4	OHC
	Omni	135 (2.2)	E	4	OHC
	Charger	98 (1.6)	A	4	OHC
	Charger	135 (2.2)	C	4	OHC

ENGINE IDENTIFICATION

Year	Model	Engine Displacement cu. in. (liter)	Engine Series Identification (VIN)	No. of Cylinders	Engine Type
1986	Charger	135 (2.2)	E	4	OHC
	600	135 (2.2)	D	4	OHC
	600	135 (2.2)	E	4	OHC
	600	153 (2.5)	K	4	OHC
	Aries	135 (2.2)	D	4	OHC
	Aries	153 (2.2)	K	4	OHC
	Lancer	135 (2.2)	D	4	OHC
	Lancer	135 (2.2)	E	4	OHC
	Lancer	153 (2.5)	K	4	OHC
	Daytona	135 (2.2)	D	4	OHC
	Daytona	135 (2.2)	E	4	OHC
	Daytona	153 (2.5)	K	4	OHC
	Horizon	98 (1.6)	A	4	OHC
	Horizon	135 (2.2)	C	4	OHC
	Turismo	98 (1.6)	A	4	OHC
	Turismo	135 (2.2)	C	4	OHC
	Caravelle	135 (2.2)	D	4	OHC
	Caravelle	135 (2.2)	E	4	OHC
	Caravelle	153 (2.5)	K	4	OHC
	Reliant	135 (2.2)	D	4	OHC
	Reliant	153 (2.5)	K	4	OHC
1987	LeBaron	135 (2.2)	D	4	OHC
	LeBaron	135 (2.2)	E	4	OHC
	LeBaron	135 (2.2)	C	4	OHC
	LeBaron	153 (2.5)	K	4	OHC
	Town & Country	135 (2.2)	E	4	OHC
	Town & Country	153 (2.5)	K	4	OHC
	New Yorker	135 (2.2)	E	4	OHC
	New Yorker	153 (2.5)	K	4	OHC
	Omni	135 (2.2)	C	4	OHC
	Omni	135 (2.2)	E	4	OHC
	Charger	135 (2.2)	C	4	OHC
	Charger	135 (2.2)	E	4	OHC
	600	135 (2.2)	D	4	OHC
	600	135 (2.2)	E	4	OHC
	600	153 (2.5)	K	4	OHC
	Aries	135 (2.2)	D	4	OHC
	Aries	153 (2.5)	K	4	OHC
	Lancer	135 (2.2)	D	4	OHC
	Lancer	135 (2.2)	E	4	OHC
	Lancer	153 (2.5)	K	4	OHC

ENGINE IDENTIFICATION

Year	Model	Engine Displacement cu. in. (liter)	Engine Series Identification (VIN)	No. of Cylinders	Engine Type
1987	Daytona	135 (2.2)	E	4	OHC
	Daytona	153 (2.5)	K	4	OHC
	Shadow	135 (2.2)	D	4	OHC
	Shadow	135 (2.2)	E	4	OHC
	Horizon	135 (2.2)	C	4	OHC
	Turismo	135 (2.2)	C	4	OHC
	Sundance	135 (2.2)	D	4	OHC
	Sundance	135 (2.2)	E	4	OHC
	Caravelle	135 (2.2)	D	4	OHC
	Caravelle	135 (2.2)	E	4	OHC
	Caravelle	153 (2.5)	K	4	OHC
	Reliant	135 (2.2)	D	4	OHC
	Reliant	153 (2.5)	K	4	OHC
1988	LeBaron	135 (2.2)	C	4	SOHC
	LeBaron	135 (2.2)	D	4	SOHC
	LeBaron	135 (2.2)	E	4	SOHC
	New Yorker	135 (2.2)	E	4	SOHC
	New Yorker	181 (3.0)	3	6	SOHC
	New Yorker Landau	181 (3.0)	3	6	SOHC
	Omni	135 (2.2)	C	4	SOHC
	600	135 (2.2)	C	4	SOHC
	600	135 (2.2)	D	4	SOHC
	600	153 (2.5)	K	4	SOHC
	Aries	135 (2.2)	C	4	SOHC
	Aries	135 (2.2)	D	4	SOHC
	Lancer	135 (2.2)	A	4	SOHC
	Lancer	135 (2.2)	C	4	SOHC
	Lancer	135 (2.2)	E	4	SOHC
	Lancer	153 (2.5)	K	4	SOHC
	Daytona	135 (2.2)	C	4	SOHC
	Daytona	135 (2.2)	E	4	SOHC
	Daytona	153 (2.5)	K	4	SOHC
	Shadow	135 (2.2)	A	4	SOHC
	Shadow	135 (2.2)	C	4	SOHC
	Shadow	153 (2.5)	K	4	SOHC
	Horizon	135 (2.2)	D	4	SOHC
	Sundance	135 (2.2)	A	4	SOHC
	Sundance	135 (2.2)	C	4	SOHC
	Sundance	153 (2.5)	K	4	SOHC
	Caravelle	135 (2.2)	D	4	SOHC
	Caravelle	135 (2.2)	E	4	SOHC

ENGINE IDENTIFICATION

Year	Model	Engine Displacement cu. in. (liter)	Engine Series Identification (VIN)	No. of Cylinders	Engine Type
1988	Caravelle	153 (2.5)	K	4	SOHC
	Reliant	135 (2.2)	D	4	SOHC
	Reliant	153 (2.5)	K	4	SOHC
1989-90	LeBaron	135 (2.2)	A	4	SOHC
	LeBaron	135 (2.2)	D	4	SOHC
	LeBaron	153 (2.5)	J	4	SOHC
	LeBaron	153 (2.5)	K	4	SOHC
	New Yorker	181 (3.0)	3	6	SOHC
	New Yorker Landau	181 (3.0)	3	6	SOHC
	Omni	135 (2.2)	D	4	SOHC
	Aries	135 (2.2)	D	4	SOHC
	Aries	153 (2.5)	K	4	SOHC
	Spirit	153 (2.5)	J	4	SOHC
	Spirit	153 (2.5)	K	4	SOHC
	Spirit	181 (3.0)	3	6	SOHC
	Lancer	135 (2.2)	A	4	SOHC
	Lancer	135 (2.2)	D	4	SOHC
	Lancer	153 (2.5)	J	4	SOHC
	Lancer	153 (2.5)	K	4	SOHC
	Daytona	135 (2.2)	A	4	SOHC
	Daytona	153 (2.5)	J	4	SOHC
	Daytona	153 (2.5)	K	4	SOHC
	Shadow	135 (2.2)	D	4	SOHC
	Shadow	153 (2.5)	K	4	SOHC
	Shadow	153 (2.5)	J	4	SOHC
	Dynasty	153 (2.5)	K	4	SOHC
	Dynasty	181 (3.0)	3	6	SOHC
	Horizon	135 (2.2)	D	4	SOHC
	Sundance	135 (2.2)	D	4	SOHC
	Sundance	153 (2.5)	J	4	SOHC
	Sundance	153 (2.5)	K	4	SOHC
	Acclaim	153 (2.5)	K	4	SOHC
	Acclaim	153 (2.5)	J	4	SOHC
	Acclaim	181 (3.0)	3	6	SOHC
	Reliant	135 (2.2)	D	4	SOHC
	Reliant	153 (2.5)	K	4	SOHC
	Laser	107 (1.8)	T	4	SOHC
	Laser	122 (2.0)	R	4	DOHC
	Laser	122 (2.0)	U	4	DOHC

OHC Over Head Cam
SOHC Single Over Head Cam
DOHC Double Over Head Cam

GENERAL ENGINE SPECIFICATIONS

Year	VIN	No. Cylinder Displacement cu. in. (liter)	Fuel System Type	Net Horsepower @ rpm	Net Torque @ rpm (ft.lbs.)	Bore × Stroke (in.)	Compression Ratio	Oil Pressure @ rpm
1986	A	4-98 (1.6)	2 bbl	64 @ 4800	87 @ 2800	3.17 × 3.07	8.8:1	65 @ 3000
	C	4-135 (2.2)	2 bbl	96 @ 5200	119 @ 3200	3.44 × 3.62	9.5:1	50 @ 2000
	D	4-135 (2.2)	EFI	99 @ 5600	121 @ 3200	3.44 × 3.62	9.5:1①	50 @ 2000
	E	4-135 (2.2)	Turbo	146 @ 5200	168 @ 3600	3.44 × 3.62	8.5:1	50 @ 2000
	K	4-153 (2.5)	EFI	100 @ 4800	133 @ 2800	3.44 × 4.09	9.0:1	80 @ 3000
1987	C	4-135 (2.2)	2 bbl	96 @ 5200	119 @ 3200	3.44 × 3.62	9.5:1	50 @ 2000
	D	4-135 (2.2)	EFI	99 @ 5600	121 @ 3200	3.44 × 3.62	9.5:1①	50 @ 2000
	E	4-135 (2.2)	Turbo	146 @ 5200	170 @ 3600	3.44 × 3.62	8.0:1	50 @ 2000
	K	4-153 (2.5)	EFI	100 @ 4800	133 @ 2800	3.44 × 4.09	9.0:1	80 @ 3000
1988	C	4-135 (2.2)	EFI	99 @ 5600	121 @ 3200	3.44 × 3.62	9.5:1	80 @ 3000
	D	4-135 (2.2)	EFI	99 @ 5600	121 @ 3200	3.44 × 3.62	9.5:1	80 @ 3000
	E	4-135 (2.2)	Turbo	146 @ 5200	170 @ 3600	3.44 × 3.62	8.0:1	80 @ 3000
	K	4-153 (2.5)	EFI	100 @ 4800	133 @ 2800	3.44 × 4.09	9.0:1	80 @ 3000
	3	6-181 (3.0)	EFI	136 @ 4800	168 @ 2800	3.59 × 2.99	8.85:1	80 @ 3000
1989-90	T	4-107 (1.8)	MPI	92 @ 5000	105 @ 3500	3.17 × 3.39	9.0:1	12 @ idle
	R	4-122 (2.0)	MPI	135 @ 6000	125 @ 5000	3.35 × 3.46	9.0:1	12 @ idle
	U	4-122 (2.0)	Turbo	190 @ 6000	203 @ 3000	3.35 × 3.46	7.8:1	12 @ idle
	A	4-135 (2.2)	Turbo	146 @ 5200	170 @ 3600	3.44 × 3.62	8.1:1	80 @ 3000
	C	4-135 (2.2)	EFI	99 @ 5600	121 @ 3200	3.44 × 3.62	9.5:1	80 @ 3000
	D	4-135 (2.2)	EFI	99 @ 5600	121 @ 3200	3.44 × 3.62	9.5:1	80 @ 3000
	E	4-135 (2.2)	Turbo	146 @ 5200	170 @ 3600	3.44 × 3.62	8.1:1	80 @ 3000
	K	4-153 (2.5)	EFI	100 @ 4800	135 @ 2800	3.44 × 4.09	8.9:1	80 @ 3000
	J	6-153 (2.5)	Turbo	150 @ 4800	180 @ 2000	3.44 × 4.09	7.8:1	80 @ 3000
	3	6-181 (3.0)	EFI	141 @ 5000	171 @ 2000	3.59 × 2.99	8.85:1	80 @ 3000

① 10:1 — Shelby and Hi-Performance

ENGINE TUNE-UP SPECIFICATIONS
Refer to Section 34 for all spark plug recommendations

Year	VIN	No. Cylinder Displacement cu. in. (liter)	Spark Plugs Gap (in.)	Ignition Timing (deg.) MT	Ignition Timing (deg.) AT	Compression Pressure (psi)	Fuel Pump (psi)	Idle Speed (rpm) MT	Idle Speed (rpm) AT	Valve Clearance In.	Valve Clearance Ex.
1986	A	4-98 (1.6)	0.035	①	①	100③	4.5–6.0	850	850	.012C	.014C
	C	4-135 (2.2)	0.035	①	①	100③	4.5–6.0	800④	900	Hyd.	Hyd.
	D	4-135 (2.2)	0.035	①	①	100③	15	900	800	Hyd.	Hyd.
	E	4-135 (2.2)	0.035	①	①	100③	55	900	800	Hyd.	Hyd.
	K	4-153 (2.5)	0.035	①	①	100③	15	800	700	Hyd.	Hyd.

2–9

ENGINE TUNE-UP SPECIFICATIONS
Refer to Section 34 for all spark plug recommendations

Year	VIN	No. Cylinder Displacement cu. in. (liter)	Spark Plugs Gap (in.)	Ignition Timing (deg.) MT	AT	Compression Pressure (psi)	Fuel Pump (psi)	Idle Speed (rpm) MT	AT	Valve Clearance In.	Ex.
1987	C	4-135 (2.2)	0.035	12B	12B	100③	4.5–6.0	800④	900	Hyd.	Hyd.
	D	4-135 (2.2)	0.035	12B	12B	100③	15	900	700	Hyd.	Hyd.
	E	4-135 (2.2)	0.035	12B	12B	100③	55	900	800	Hyd.	Hyd.
	K	4-153 (2.5)	0.035	12B	12B	100③	15	900	900	Hyd.	Hyd.
1988	C	4-135 (2.2)	0.035	12B	12B	100③	15	800④	900	Hyd.	Hyd.
	D	4-135 (2.2)	0.035	12B	12B	100③	15	900	700	Hyd.	Hyd.
	E	4-135 (2.2)	0.035	12B	12B	100③	55	900	800	Hyd.	Hyd.
	K	4-153 (2.5)	0.035	12B	12B	100③	15	900	900	Hyd.	Hyd.
	3	6-181 (3.0)	0.040	—	12B	178②	48	—	700	Hyd.	Hyd.
1989	T	4-107 (1.8)	0.040	10B	10B	131	47.6	850	650	Hyd.	Hyd.
	R	4-122 (2.0)	0.030	8B	8B	137	47.6	850	650	Hyd.	Hyd.
	U	4-122 (2.0)	0.030	8B	8B	114	36.3	850	650	Hyd.	Hyd.
	A	4-135 (2.2)	0.035	12B	12B	100③	55	900	900	Hyd.	Hyd.
	C	4-135 (2.2)	0.035	12B	12B	100③	15	850	850	Hyd.	Hyd.
	D	4-135 (2.2)	0.035	12B	12B	100③	15	850	850	Hyd.	Hyd.
	E	4-135 (2.2)	0.035	12B	12B	100③	55	900	900	Hyd.	Hyd.
	J	4-153 (2.5)	0.035	12B	12B	100③	55	900	725	Hyd.	Hyd.
	K	4-153 (2.5)	0.035	12B	12B	100③	15	850	850	Hyd.	Hyd.
	3	6-181 (3.0)	0.040	—	12B	178②	48	—	700	Hyd.	Hyd.
1990			SEE UNDERHOOD SPECIFICATIONS STICKER								

NOTE: The underhood specifications sticker often reflects tune-up specification changes made in production. Sticker figures must be used if they disagree with those in this chart. Part numbers in this chart are not recommendations by Chilton for any product by brand name

Hyd. Hydraulic

C Cold

① Refer to emission control label on vehicle

② @ 250 rpm
③ Minimum
④ Canada—900 rpm

FIRING ORDERS

NOTE: To avoid confusion, always replace spark plug wires one at a time.

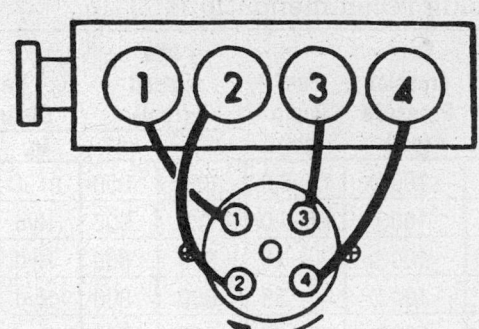

Chrysler (2.2L/2.5L) Firing order: 1-3-4-2
Distributor rotation: clockwise

FIRING ORDERS

NOTE: To avoid confusion, always replace spark plug wires one at a time.

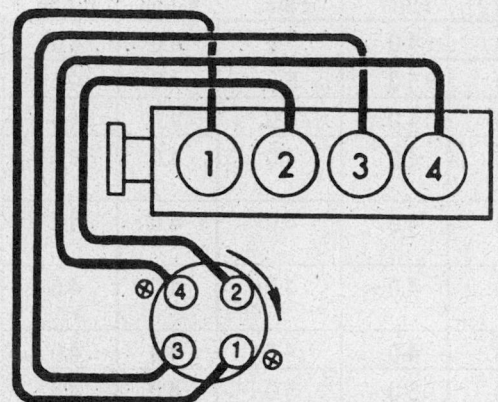

Chrysler 4 cyl (Mitsubishi 2.6L)
Firing order: 1-3-4-2
Distributor rotation clockwise

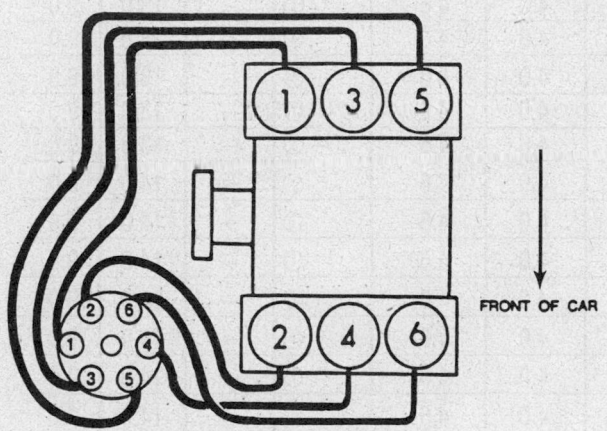

Chrysler Corp. 3.0L Engine
Firing Order: 1-2-3-4-5-6
Distributor rotation: Counterclockwise

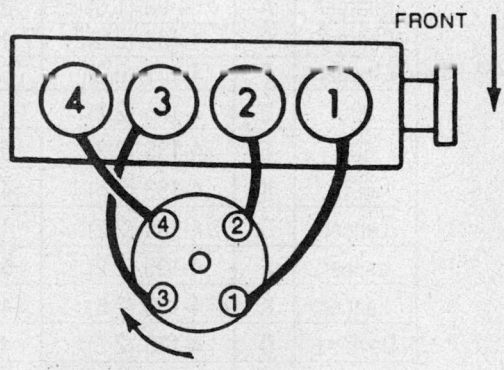

Chrysler: 1.6L
Firing order: 1-3-4-2
Distributor rotation: clockwise

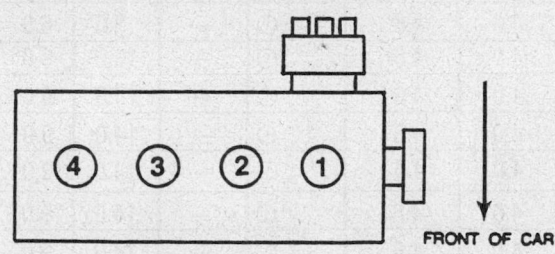

Chrysler Corp. 1.8L Engine
Firing Order: 1-3-4-2

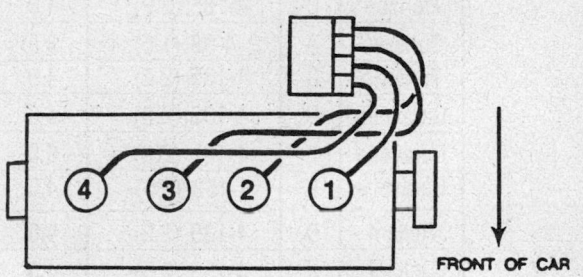

Chrysler Corp. 2.0L Engine
Firing Order: 1-3-4-2

CAPACITIES

Year	Model	VIN	No. Cylinder Displacement cu. in. (liter)	Engine Crankcase with Filter	without Filter	Transmission (pts.) 4-Spd	5-Spd	Auto.	Drive Axle (pts.)	Fuel Tank (gal.)	Cooling System (qts.)
1986	LeBaron	D	4-135 (2.2)	4.0	4.0	4.0	4.6	①	—	14.0	9.0
	LeBaron	E	4-135 (2.2)	5.0	5.0	4.0	4.6	①	—	14.0	9.0
	LeBaron	K	4-153 (2.5)	4.0	4.0	4.0	4.6	①	—	14.0	9.0
	Town & Country	D	4-135 (2.2)	4.0	4.0	4.0	4.6	①	—	14.0	9.0
	Town & Country	E	4-135 (2.2)	4.0	4.0	4.0	4.6	①	—	14.0	9.0
	Town & Country	K	4-153 (2.5)	4.0	4.0	4.0	4.6	①	—	14.0	9.0
	Laser	D	4-135 (2.2)	4.0	4.0	4.0	4.6	①	—	14.0	9.0
	Laser	E	4-135 (2.2)	5.0	5.0	4.0	4.6	①	—	14.0	9.0
	Laser	K	4-153 (2.5)	4.0	4.0	4.0	4.6	①	—	14.0	9.0
	New Yorker	E	4-135 (2.2)	5.0	5.0	4.0	4.6	①	—	14.0	9.0
	New Yorker	K	4-153 (2.5)	4.0	4.0	4.0	4.6	①	—	14.0	9.0
	Omni	A	4-98 (1.6)	3.5	3.0	4.0	4.6	①	—	13.0	6.8
	Omni	C	4-135 (2.2)	4.0	4.0	4.0	4.6	①	—	13.0	9.0
	Omni	E	4-135 (2.2)	5.0	5.0	4.0	4.6	①	—	13.0	9.0
	Charger	A	4-98 (1.6)	3.5	3.0	4.0	4.6	①	—	13.0	6.8
	Charger	C	4-135 (2.2)	4.0	4.0	4.0	4.6	①	—	13.0	9.0
	Charger	E	4-135 (2.2)	5.0	5.0	4.0	4.6	①	—	13.0	9.0
	600	D	4-135 (2.2)	4.0	4.0	4.0	4.6	①	—	14.0	9.0
	600	E	4-135 (2.2)	5.0	5.0	4.0	4.6	①	—	14.0	9.0
	600	K	4-153 (2.5)	4.0	4.0	4.0	4.6	①	—	14.0	9.0
	Lancer	D	4-135 (2.2)	4.0	4.0	4.0	4.6	①	—	14.0	9.0
	Lancer	E	4-135 (2.2)	5.0	5.0	4.0	4.6	①	—	14.0	9.0
	Lancer	K	4-153 (2.5)	4.0	4.0	4.0	4.6	①	—	14.0	9.0
	Daytona	D	4-135 (2.2)	4.0	4.0	4.0	4.6	①	—	14.0	9.0
	Daytona	E	4-135 (2.2)	5.0	5.0	4.0	4.6	①	—	14.0	9.0
	Daytona	K	4-153 (2.5)	4.0	4.0	4.0	4.6	①	—	14.0	9.0
	Aries	D	4-135 (2.2)	4.0	4.0	4.0	4.6	①	—	14.0	9.0
	Aries	K	4-153 (2.5)	4.0	4.0	4.0	4.6	①	—	14.0	9.0
	Horizon	A	4-98 (1.6)	3.5	3.0	4.0	4.6	①	—	13.0	6.8
	Horizon	C	4-135 (2.2)	4.0	4.0	4.0	4.6	①	—	13.0	9.0
	Turismo	A	4-98 (1.6)	3.5	3.0	4.0	4.6	①	—	13.0	6.8
	Turismo	C	4-135 (2.2)	4.0	4.0	4.0	4.6	①	—	13.0	9.0
	Caravelle	D	4-135 (2.2)	4.0	4.0	4.0	4.6	①	—	14.0	9.0
	Caravelle	E	4-135 (2.2)	5.0	5.0	4.0	4.6	①	—	14.0	9.0
	Caravelle	K	4-153 (2.5)	4.0	4.0	4.0	4.6	①	—	14.0	9.0
	Reliant	D	4-135 (2.2)	4.0	4.0	4.0	4.6	①	—	14.0	9.0
	Reliant	K	4-153 (2.5)	4.0	4.0	4.0	4.6	①	—	14.0	9.0

CAPACITIES

Year	Model	VIN	No. Cylinder Displacement cu. in. (liter)	Engine Crankcase with Filter	Engine Crankcase without Filter	Transmission (pts.) 4-Spd	Transmission (pts.) 5-Spd	Transmission (pts.) Auto.	Drive Axle (pts.)	Fuel Tank (gal.)	Cooling System (qts.)
1987	LeBaron	C	4-135 (2.2)	4.0	4.0	—	4.6	①	—	14.0	9.0
	LeBaron	D	4-135 (2.2)	5.0	5.0	—	4.6	①	—	14.0	9.0
	LeBaron	E	4-135 (2.2)	5.0	5.0	—	4.6	①	—	14.0	9.0
	LeBaron	K	4-153 (2.5)	4.0	4.0	—	4.6	①	—	14.0	9.0
	Town & Country	E	4-135 (2.2)	5.0	5.0	—	4.6	①	—	14.0	9.0
	Town & Country	K	4-153 (2.5)	4.0	4.0	—	4.6	①	—	14.0	9.0
	New Yorker	E	4-135 (2.2)	5.0	5.0	—	4.6	①	—	14.0	9.0
	New Yorker	K	4-153 (2.5)	4.0	4.0	—	4.6	①	—	14.0	9.0
	Omni	C	4-135 (2.2)	4.0	4.0	—	4.6	①	—	13.0	9.0
	Omni	E	4-135 (2.2)	5.0	5.0	—	4.6	①	—	14.0	9.0
	Charger	C	4-135 (2.2)	4.0	4.0	—	4.6	①	—	13.0	9.0
	Charger	E	4-135 (2.2)	5.0	5.0	—	4.6	①	—	13.0	9.0
	600	D	4-135 (2.2)	4.0	4.0	—	4.6	①	—	14.0	9.0
	600	E	4-135 (2.2)	5.0	5.0	—	4.6	①	—	14.0	9.0
	600	K	4-153 (2.5)	4.0	4.0	—	4.6	①	—	14.0	9.0
	Lancer	D	4-135 (2.2)	4.0	4.0	—	4.6	①	—	14.0	9.0
	Lancer	E	4-135 (2.2)	5.0	5.0	—	4.6	①	—	14.0	9.0
	Lancer	K	4-153 (2.5)	4.0	4.0	—	4.6	①	—	14.0	9.0
	Daytona	E	4-135 (2.2)	5.0	5.0	—	4.6	①	—	14.0	9.0
	Daytona	K	4-153 (2.5)	4.0	4.0	—	4.6	①	—	14.0	9.0
	Shadow	E	4-135 (2.2)	5.0	5.0	—	4.6	①	—	14.0	9.0
	Shadow	D	4-135 (2.2)	4.0	4.0	—	4.6	①	—	14.0	9.0
	Aries	D	4-135 (2.2)	4.0	4.0	—	4.6	①	—	14.0	9.0
	Aries	K	4-153 (2.6)	4.0	4.0	—	4.6	①	—	14.0	9.0
	Horizon	C	4-135 (2.2)	4.0	4.0	—	4.6	①	—	13.0	9.0
	Turismo	C	4-135 (2.2)	4.0	4.0	—	4.6	①	—	13.0	9.0
	Sundance	D	4-135 (2.2)	4.0	4.0	—	4.6	①	—	14.0	9.0
	Sundance	E	4-135 (2.2)	5.0	5.0	—	4.6	①	—	14.0	9.0
	Caravelle	D	4-135 (2.2)	4.0	4.0	—	4.6	①	—	14.0	9.0
	Caravelle	E	4-135 (2.2)	5.0	5.0	—	4.6	①	—	14.0	9.0
	Caravelle	K	4-153 (2.5)	4.0	4.0	—	4.6	①	—	14.0	9.0
	Reliant	D	4-135 (2.2)	4.0	4.0	—	4.6	①	—	14.0	9.0
	Reliant	K	4-153 (2.5)	4.0	4.0	—	4.6	①	—	14.0	9.0
1988	LeBaron	C	4-135 (2.2)	4.0	4.0	—	4.6	①	—	14.0	9.0
	LeBaron	D	4-135 (2.2)	4.0	4.0	—	4.6	①	—	14.0	9.0
	LeBaron	E	4-135 (2.2)	5.0	5.0	—	4.6	①	—	14.0	9.0
	New Yorker	E	4-135 (2.2)	5.0	5.0	—	4.6	①	—	16.0	9.0
	New Yorker	3	4-181 (3.0)	4.0	4.0	—	—	①	—	16.0	9.5
	New Yorker Landau	3	4-181 (3.0)	4.0	4.0	—	—	①	—	16.0	9.5

CAPACITIES

Year	Model	VIN	No. Cylinder Displacement cu. in. (liter)	Engine Crankcase with Filter	Engine Crankcase without Filter	Transmission (pts.) 4-Spd	Transmission (pts.) 5-Spd	Transmission (pts.) Auto.	Drive Axle (pts.)	Fuel Tank (gal.)	Cooling System (qts.)
1988	Omni	C	4-135 (2.2)	4.0	4.0	—	4.6	①	—	13.0	9.0
	Aries	C	4-135 (2.2)	4.0	4.0	—	4.6	①	—	14.0	9.0
	Aries	D	4-135 (2.2)	4.0	4.0	—	4.6	①	—	14.0	9.0
	600	C	4-135 (2.2)	4.0	4.0	—	4.6	①	—	14.0	9.0
	600	D	4-135 (2.2)	4.0	4.0	—	4.6	①	—	14.0	9.0
	600	K	4-153 (2.5)	4.0	4.0	—	4.6	①	—	14.0	9.0
	Lancer	A	4-135 (2.2)	4.0	4.0	—	4.6	①	—	14.0	9.0
	Lancer	C	4-135 (2.2)	4.0	4.0	—	4.6	①	—	14.0	9.0
	Lancer	E	4-135 (2.2)	5.0	5.0	—	4.6	①	—	14.0	9.0
	Lancer	K	4-153 (2.5)	4.0	4.0	—	4.6	①	—	14.0	9.0
	Daytona	C	4-135 (2.2)	4.0	4.0	—	4.6	①	—	14.0	9.0
	Daytona	E	4-135 (2.2)	5.0	5.0	—	4.6	①	—	14.0	9.0
	Daytona	K	4-153 (2.5)	4.0	4.0	—	4.6	①	—	14.0	9.0
	Shadow	A	4-135 (2.2)	4.0	4.0	—	4.6	①	—	14.0	9.0
	Shadow	C	4-135 (2.2)	4.0	4.0	—	4.6	①	—	14.0	9.0
	Shadow	K	4-153 (2.5)	4.0	4.0	—	4.6	①	—	14.0	9.0
	Dynasty	3	4-181 (3.0)	4.0	4.0	—	—	①	—	16.0	9.5
	Horizon	D	4-135 (2.2)	4.0	4.0	—	4.6	①	—	13.0	9.0
	Sundance	A	4-135 (2.2)	4.0	4.0	—	4.6	①	—	14.0	9.0
	Sundance	C	4-135 (2.2)	4.0	4.0	—	4.6	①	—	14.0	9.0
	Sundance	K	4-153 (2.5)	4.0	4.0	—	4.6	①	—	14.0	9.0
	Reliant	D	4-135 (2.2)	4.0	4.0	—	4.6	①	—	14.0	9.0
	Reliant	K	4-153 (2.5)	4.0	4.0	—	4.6	①	—	14.0	9.0
	Caravelle	D	4-135 (2.2)	4.0	4.0	—	4.6	①	—	14.0	9.0
	Caravelle	E	4-135 (2.2)	5.0	5.0	—	4.6	①	—	14.0	9.0
	Caravelle	K	4-153 (2.5)	4.0	4.0	—	4.6	①	—	14.0	9.0
1989-90	LeBaron	A	4-135 (2.2)	4.0	4.0	—	4.6	②	—	14.0	9.0
	LeBaron	D	4-135 (2.2)	4.0	4.0	—	4.6	②	—	14.0	9.0
	LeBaron	J	4-153 (2.5)	4.0	4.0	—	4.6	②	—	14.0	9.0
	LeBaron	K	4-153 (2.5)	4.0	4.0	—	4.6	②	—	14.0	9.0
	Aries	D	4-135 (2.2)	4.0	4.0	—	4.6	②	—	14.0	9.0
	Aries	K	4-153 (2.5)	4.0	4.0	—	4.6	②	—	14.0	9.0
	New Yorker	3	4-181 (3.0)	4.0	4.0	—	—	②	—	16.0	9.5
	New Yorker Landau	3	4-181 (3.0)	4.0	4.0	—	—	②	—	16.0	9.5
	Omni	D	4-135 (2.2)	4.0	4.0	—	4.6	②	—	13.0	9.0
	Spirit	J	4-153 (2.5)	4.0	4.0	—	4.6	②	—	14.0	9.0
	Spirit	K	4-153 (2.5)	4.0	4.0	—	4.6	②	—	14.0	9.0
	Spirit	3	4-181 (3.0)	4.0	4.0	—	—	②	—	14.0	9.0
	Lancer	A	4-135 (2.2)	4.0	4.0	—	4.6	②	—	14.0	9.0
	Lancer	D	4-135 (2.2)	4.0	4.0	—	4.6	②	—	14.0	9.0

CAPACITIES

Year	Model	VIN	No. Cylinder Displacement cu. in. (liter)	Engine Crankcase with Filter	Engine Crankcase without Filter	Transmission (pts.) 4-Spd	Transmission (pts.) 5-Spd	Transmission (pts.) Auto.	Drive Axle (pts.)	Fuel Tank (gal.)	Cooling System (qts.)
1989-90	Lancer	J	4-153 (2.2)	4.0	4.0	—	4.6	②	—	14.0	9.0
	Lancer	K	4-153 (2.5)	4.0	4.0	—	4.6	②	—	14.0	9.0
	Daytona	A	4-135 (2.2)	4.0	4.0	—	4.6	②	—	14.0	9.0
	Daytona	J	4-153 (2.5)	4.0	4.0	—	4.6	②	—	14.0	9.0
	Daytona	K	4-153 (2.5)	4.0	4.0	—	4.6	②	—	14.0	9.0
	Shadow	D	4-135 (2.2)	4.0	4.0	—	4.6	②	—	14.0	9.0
	Shadow	K	4-153 (2.5)	4.0	4.0	—	4.6	②	—	14.0	9.0
	Shadow	J	4-153 (2.5)	4.0	4.0	—	4.6	②	—	14.0	9.0
	Dynasty	3	4-181 (3.0)	4.0	4.0	—	—	②	—	16.0	9.5
	Dynasty	K	4-153 (2.5)	4.0	4.0	—	4.6	②	—	16.0	9.0
	Horizon	D	4-135 (2.2)	4.0	4.0	—	4.6	②	—	13.0	9.0
	Sundance	D	4-135 (2.2)	4.0	4.0	—	4.6	②	—	14.0	9.0
	Sundance	K	4-153 (2.5)	4.0	4.0	—	4.6	②	—	14.0	9.0
	Sundance	J	4-153 (2.5)	4.0	4.0	—	4.6	②	—	14.0	9.0
	Reliant	D	4-135 (2.2)	4.0	4.0	—	4.6	②	—	14.0	9.0
	Reliant	K	4-153 (2.5)	4.0	4.0	—	4.6	②	—	14.0	9.0
	Acclaim	J	4-153 (2.5)	4.0	4.0	—	4.6	②	—	14.0	9.0
	Acclaim	K	4-153 (2.5)	4.0	4.0	—	4.6	②	—	14.0	9.0
	Acclaim	3	4-181 (3.0)	4.0	4.0	—	—	①	—	14.0	9.5
	Laser	T	4-107 (1.8)	4.1	3.6	—	3.8	12.9	—	15.9	6.6
	Laser	R	4-122 (2.0)	4.6	4.1	—	3.8	12.9	—	15.9	7.6
	Laser	U	4-122 (2.0)	4.6	4.1	—	4.6	—	—	15.9	7.6

① A413, A415L, A470 except fleet—17.8 pts.
  A413, A555 fleet—18.4 pts.
② A413 except fleet—17.8 pts.
  A413 fleet—18.4 pts.
  A413 lockup—17.0 pts.
  A604 electronic—18.2 pts.

CAMSHAFT SPECIFICATIONS
All measurements given in inches.

Year	VIN	No. Cylinder Displacement cu. in. (liter)	Journal Diameter 1	2	3	4	5	Lobe Lift In.	Lobe Lift Ex.	Bearing Clearance	Camshaft End Play
1986	C	4-135 (2.2)	1.375–1.376	1.375–1.376	1.375–1.376	1.375–1.376	1.375–1.376	0.430	0.430	0.010 Max	0.006
	D	4-135 (2.2)	1.375–1.376	1.375–1.376	1.375–1.376	1.375–1.376	1.375–1.376	0.430	0.430	0.010 Max	0.006
	E	4-135 (2.2)	1.375–1.376	1.375–1.376	1.375–1.376	1.375–1.376	1.375–1.376	0.430	0.430	0.010 Max	0.006

CAMSHAFT SPECIFICATIONS
All measurements given in inches.

Year	VIN	No. Cylinder Displacement cu. in. (liter)	Journal Diameter 1	2	3	4	5	Lobe Lift In.	Ex.	Bearing Clearance	Camshaft End Play
1986	K	4-153 (2.5)	1.375–1.376	1.375–1.376	1.375–1.376	1.375–1.376	1.375–1.376	0.430	0.430	0.010 Max	0.006
1987	C	4-135 (2.2)	1.375–1.376	1.375–1.376	1.375–1.376	1.375–1.376	1.375–1.376	0.430	0.430	0.010 Max	0.006
	D	4-135 (2.2)	1.375–1.376	1.375–1.376	1.375–1.376	1.375–1.376	1.375–1.376	0.430	0.430	0.010 Max	0.006
	E	4-135 (2.2)	1.375–1.376	1.375–1.376	1.375–1.376	1.375–1.376	1.375–1.376	0.430	0.430	0.010 Max	0.006
	K	4-153 (2.5)	1.375–1.376	1.375–1.376	1.375–1.376	1.375–1.376	1.375–1.376	0.430	0.430	0.010 Max	0.006
1988	C	4-135 (2.2)	1.375–1.376	1.375–1.376	1.375–1.376	1.375–1.376	1.375–1.376	0.430	0.430	0.010 Max	0.006
	D	4-135 (2.2)	1.375–1.376	1.375–1.376	1.375–1.376	1.375–1.376	1.375–1.376	0.430	0.430	0.010 Max	0.006
	E	4-135 (2.2)	1.375–1.376	1.375–1.376	1.375–1.376	1.375–1.376	1.375–1.376	0.430	0.430	0.010 Max	0.006
	K	4-153 (2.5)	1.375–1.376	1.375–1.376	1.375–1.376	1.375–1.376	1.375–1.376	0.430	0.430	0.010 Max	0.006
1989-90	T	4-107 (1.8)	1.336–1.337	1.336–1.337	1.336–1.337	1.336–1.337	1.336–1.337	NA	NA	0.002–0.004	0.004–0.008
	R	4-122 (2.0)	1.022–1.023	1.022–1.023	1.022–1.023	1.022–1.023	1.022–1.023	NA	NA	0.002–0.004	0.004–0.008
	U	4-122 (2.0)	1.022–1.023	1.022–1.023	1.022–1.023	1.022–1.023	1.022–1.023	NA	NA	0.002–0.004	0.004–0.008
	A	4-135 (2.2)	1.375–1.376	1.375–1.376	1.375–1.376	1.375–1.376	1.375–1.376	0.430	0.430	0.010 Max	0.005–0.013
	C	4-135 (2.2)	1.375–1.376	1.375–1.376	1.375–1.376	1.375–1.376	1.375–1.376	0.430	0.430	0.010 Max	0.005–0.013
	D	4-135 (2.2)	1.375–1.376	1.375–1.376	1.375–1.376	1.375–1.376	1.375–1.376	0.430	0.430	0.010 Max	0.006
	E	4-135 (2.2)	1.375–1.376	1.375–1.376	1.375–1.376	1.375–1.376	1.375–1.376	0.430	0.430	0.010 Max	0.005–0.013
	J	4-153 (2.5)	1.375–1.376	1.375–1.376	1.375–1.376	1.375–1.376	1.375–1.376	0.430	0.430	0.010 Max	0.005–0.013
	K	4-153 (2.5)	1.375–1.376	1.375–1.376	1.375–1.376	1.375–1.376	1.375–1.376	0.430	0.430	0.010 Max	0.005–0.013

CRANKSHAFT AND CONNECTING ROD SPECIFICATIONS
All measurements are given in inches.

Year	VIN	No. Cylinder Displacement cu. in. (liter)	Crankshaft				Connecting Rod		
			Main Brg. Journal Dia.	Main Brg. Oil Clearance	Shaft End-play	Thrust on No.	Journal Diameter	Oil Clearance	Side Clearance
1986	A	4-98 (1.6)	2.046	0.0009–0.0031	0.004–0.011	3	1.612	0.0010–0.0025	0.006–0.009
	C	4-135 (2.2)	2.362–2.363	0.0003–0.0031	0.002–0.007	3	1.968–1.969	0.0008–0.0031	0.005–0.013
	D	4-135 (2.2)	2.362–2.363	0.0003–0.0031	0.002–0.007	3	1.968–1.969	0.0008–0.0034	0.005–0.013
	E	4-135 (2.2)	2.362–2.363	0.0004–0.0023	0.002–0.007	3	1.968–1.969	0.0008–0.0031	0.005–0.013
	K	4-153 (2.5)	2.362–2.363	0.0003–0.0031	0.002–0.007	3	1.968–1.969	0.0008–0.0034	0.005–0.013
1987	C	4-135 (2.2)	2.362–2.363	0.0003–0.0031	0.002–0.007	3	1.968–1.969	0.0008–0.0031	0.005–0.013
	D	4-135 (2.2)	2.362–2.363	0.0003–0.0031	0.002–0.007	3	1.968–1.969	0.0008–0.0034	0.005–0.013
	E	4-135 (2.2)	2.362–2.363	0.0004–0.0023	0.002–0.007	3	1.968–1.969	0.0008–0.0031	0.005–0.013
	K	4-153 (2.5)	2.362–2.363	0.0003–0.0031	0.002–0.007	3	1.968–1.969	0.0008–0.0034	0.005–0.013
1988	C	4-135 (2.2)	2.362–2.363	0.0003–0.0031	0.002–0.007	3	1.968–1.069	0.0008–0.0031	0.005–0.013
	D	4-135 (2.2)	2.362–2.363	0.0003–0.0031	0.002–0.007	3	1.968–1.969	0.0008–0.0034	0.005–0.013
	E	4-135 (2.2)	2.362–2.363	0.0004–0.0023	0.002–0.007	3	1.968–1.969	0.0008–0.0031	0.005–0.013
	K	4-153 (2.5)	2.362–2.363	0.0003–0.0031	0.002–0.007	3	1.968–1.969	0.0008–0.0034	0.005–0.013
	3	6-181 (3.0)	2.361–2.363	0.0006–0.0020	0.002–0.010	3	1.968–1.969	0.0008–0.0028	0.004–0.010
1989-90	T	4-107 (1.8)	2.240	0.0008–0.0020	0.002–0.007	3	1.770	0.0008–0.0020	0.004–0.001
	R	4-122 (2.0)	2.2434–2.244	0.0008–0.0020	0.002–0.007	3	1.771–1.772	0.0008–0.0020	0.004–0.0098
	U	4-122 (2.0)	2.243–2.244	0.0008–0.0020	0.002–0.007	3	1.771–1.772	0.0008–0.0020	0.004–0.001
	A	4-135 (2.2)	2.362–2.363	0.0004–0.0023	0.002–0.010	3	1.968–1.969	0.0008–0.0031	0.005–0.013
	C	4-135 (2.2)	2.362–2.363	0.0003–0.0031	0.002–0.010	3	1.968–1.969	0.0008–0.0031	0.005–0.013
	D	4-135 (2.2)	2.362–2.363	0.0003–0.0031	0.002–0.010	3	1.968–1.969	0.0008–0.0034	0.005–0.013
	E	4-135 (2.2)	2.362–2.363	0.0004–0.0023	0.002–0.010	3	1.968–1.969	0.0008–0.0031	0.005–0.013

CRANKSHAFT AND CONNECTING ROD SPECIFICATIONS
All measurements are given in inches.

Year	VIN	No. Cylinder Displacement cu. in. (liter)	Crankshaft Main Brg. Journal Dia.	Main Brg. Oil Clearance	Shaft End-play	Thrust on No.	Connecting Rod Journal Diameter	Oil Clearance	Side Clearance
1989-90	J	4-153 (2.5)	2.362–2.363	0.0004–0.0023	0.002–0.010	3	1.968–1.969	0.0008–0.0034	0.005–0.013
	K	4-153 (2.5)	2.362–2.363	0.0003–0.0031	0.002–0.010	3	1.968–1.969	0.0008–0.0034	0.005–0.013
	3	6-181 (3.0)	2.361–2.363	0.0006–0.0020	0.002–0.010	3	1.968–1.969	0.0008–0.0028	0.004–0.010

VALVE SPECIFICATIONS

Year	VIN	No. Cylinder Displacement cu. in. (liter)	Seat Angle (deg.)	Face Angle (deg.)	Spring Test Pressure (lbs.)	Spring Installed Height (in.)	Stem-to-Guide Clearance Intake	Exhaust	Stem Diameter Intake	Exhaust
1986	A	4-98 (1.6)	45	45	–	1.65	0.0005–0.0018	0.0013–0.0026	0.3140–0.3146	0.3132–0.3138
	C	4-135 (2.2)	45	45	150 @ 1.22	1.65	0.0009–0.0026	0.0030–0.0047	0.3124	0.3103
	D	4-135 (2.2)	45	45	150 @ 1.22	1.65	0.0009–0.0026	0.0030–0.0047	0.3124	0.3103
	E	4-135 (2.2)	45	45	175 @ 1.22	1.65	0.0009–0.0026	0.0030–0.0047	0.3124	0.3103
	K	4-153 (2.5)	45	45	150 @ 1.22	1.65	0.0009–0.0026	0.0030–0.0047	0.3124	0.3103
1987	C	4-135 (2.2)	45	45	150 @ 1.22	1.65	0.0009–0.0026	0.0030–0.0047	0.3124	0.3103
	D	4-135 (2.2)	45	45	150 @ 1.22	1.65	0.0009–0.0026	0.0030–0.0047	0.3124	0.3103
	E	4-135 (2.2)	45	45	175 @ 1.22	1.65	0.0009–0.0026	0.0030–0.0047	0.3124	0.3103
	K	4-153 (2.5)	45	45	150 @ 1.22	1.65	0.0009–0.0026	0.0030–0.0047	0.3124	0.3103
1988	C	4-135 (2.2)	45	45	150 @ 1.22	1.65	0.0009–0.0026	0.0030–0.0047	0.3124	0.3103
	D	4-135 (2.2)	45	45	150 @ 1.22	1.65	0.0009–0.0026	0.0030–0.0047	0.3124	0.3103
	E	4-135 (2.2)	45	45	175 @ 1.22	1.65	0.0009–0.0026	0.0030–0.0047	0.3124	0.3103
	K	4-153 (2.5)	45	45	150 @ 1.22	1.65	0.0009–0.0026	0.0030–0.0047	0.3124	0.3103
	3	6-181 (3.0)	44–44.3	45–45.5	73 @ 1.59	1.99	0.0010–0.0020	0.0019–0.0030	0.3140	0.3125
1989-90	T	4-107 (1.8)	44–44.5	45–45.5	62 @ 1.47	1.469	0.0012–0.0024	0.0020–0.0035	0.3100	0.3100

VALVE SPECIFICATIONS

Year	VIN	No. Cylinder Displacement cu. in. (liter)	Seat Angle (deg.)	Face Angle (deg.)	Spring Test Pressure (lbs.)	Spring Installed Height (in.)	Stem-to-Guide Clearance (in.)		Stem Diameter (in.)	
							Intake	Exhaust	Intake	Exhaust
1989-90	R	4-122 (2.0)	44–44.5	45–45.5	53 @ 1.40	NA	0.0008–0.0019	0.0020–0.0038	0.2585–0.2591	0.2571–0.2579
	U	4-122 (2.0)	44–44.5	45–45.5	53 @ 1.40	NA	0.0008–0.0019	0.0020–0.0038	0.2585–0.2591	0.2571–0.2579
	A	4-135 (2.2)	45	45	108 @ 1.65	1.65	0.0009–0.0026	0.0030–0.0047	0.3124	0.3103
	C	4-135 (2.2)	45	45	100 @ 1.65	1.65	0.0009–0.0026	0.0030–0.0047	0.3124	0.3103
	D	4-135 (2.2)	45	45	100 @ 1.65	1.65	0.0009–0.0026	0.0030–0.0047	0.3124	0.3103
	E	4-135 (2.2)	45	45	108 @ 1.65	1.65	0.0009–0.0026	0.0030–0.0047	0.3124	0.3103
	J	4-153 (2.5)	45	45	100 @ 1.65	1.65	0.0009–0.0026	0.0030–0.0047	0.3124	0.3103
	K	4-153 (2.5)	45	45	100 @ 1.65	1.65	0.0009–0.0026	0.0030–0.0047	0.3124	0.3103
	3	6-181 (3.0)	44.3	45.5	73 @ 1.59	1.99	0.0010–0.0020	0.0019–0.0030	0.3140	0.3125

PISTON AND RING SPECIFICATIONS
All measurments are given in inches.

Year	VIN	No. Cylinder Displacement cu. in. (liter)	Piston Clearance	Ring Gap			Ring Side Clearance		
				Top Compression	Bottom Compression	Oil Control	Top Compression	Bottom Compression	Oil Control
1986	A	4-98 (1.6)	0.0016–0.0020	0.012–0.018	0.012–0.018	0.010–0.016	0.0018–0.0028	0.0018–0.0020	0.008 Max.
	C	4-135 (2.2)	0.0005–0.0015	0.011–0.021	0.011–0.021	0.015–0.055	0.0015–0.0031	0.0015–0.0037	0.008 Max.
	D	4-135 (2.2)	0.0005–0.0015	0.011–0.021	0.011–0.021	0.015–0.055	0.0015–0.0031	0.0015–0.0037	0.008 Max.
	E	4-135 (2.2)	0.0015–0.0025	0.010–0.020	0.009–0.018	0.015–0.055	0.0015–0.0031	0.0015–0.0037	0.008 Max.
	K	4-153 (2.5)	0.0005–0.0015	0.011–0.021	0.011–0.021	0.015–0.055	0.0015–0.0031	0.0015–0.0037	0.008 Max.
1987	C	4-135 (2.2)	0.0005–0.0015	0.011–0.021	0.011–0.021	0.015–0.055	0.0015–0.0031	0.0015–0.0037	0.008 Max.
	D	4-135 (2.2)	0.0005–0.0015	0.011–0.021	0.011–0.021	0.015–0.055	0.0015–0.0031	0.0015–0.0037	0.008 Max.
	E	4-135 (2.2)	0.0015–0.0025	0.010–0.020	0.009–0.018	0.015–0.055	0.0015–0.0031	0.0015–0.0037	0.008 Max.
	K	4-153 (2.5)	0.0005–0.0015	0.011–0.021	0.011–0.021	0.015–0.055	0.0015–0.0031	0.0015–0.0037	0.008 Max.

PISTON AND RING SPECIFICATIONS
All measurments are given in inches.

Year	VIN	No. Cylinder Displacement cu. in. (liter)	Piston Clearance	Ring Gap			Ring Side Clearance		
				Top Compression	Bottom Compression	Oil Control	Top Compression	Bottom Compression	Oil Control
1988	C	4-135 (2.2)	0.0005–0.0015	0.011–0.021	0.011–0.021	0.015–0.055	0.0015–0.0031	0.0015–0.0037	0.008 Max.
	D	4-135 (2.2)	0.0005–0.0015	0.011–0.021	0.011–0.021	0.015–0.055	0.0015–0.0031	0.0015–0.0037	0.008 Max.
	E	4-135 (2.2)	0.0015–0.0025	0.010–0.020	0.009–0.018	0.015–0.055	0.0015–0.0031	0.0015–0.0037	0.008 Max.
	K	4-153 (2.5)	0.0005–0.0015	0.011–0.021	0.011–0.021	0.015–0.055	0.0015–0.0031	0.0015–0.0037	0.008 Max.
	3	6-181 (3.0)	0.0008–0.0015	0.012–0.018	0.010–0.016	0.012–0.035	0.0020–0.0035	0.0008–0.0020	—
1989-90	T	4-107 (1.8)	0.0004–0.0012	0.012–0.018	0.008–0.138	NA	0.0018–0.0033	0.0008–0.0024	NA
	R	4-122 (2.0)	0.0008–0.0016	0.010–0.018	0.014–0.020	NA	0.0012–0.0028	0.0012–0.0028	NA
	U	4-122 (2.0)	0.0012–0.0020	0.010–0.018	0.014–0.020	NA	0.0012–0.0028	0.0012–0.0028	NA
	A	4-135 (2.0)	0.0005–0.0015	0.010–0.020	0.009–0.019	0.015–0.055	0.0016–0.0030	0.0016–0.0035	0.008
	C	4-135 (2.2)	0.0005–0.0015	0.010–0.021	0.011–0.020	0.015–0.055	0.0015–0.0031	0.0015–0.0031	0.008 Max.
	D	4-135 (2.2)	0.0005–0.0015	0.011–0.021	0.011–0.021	0.015–0.055	0.0015–0.0031	0.0015–0.0031	0.008 Max.
	E	4-135 (2.2)	0.0015–0.0025	0.010–0.020	0.009–0.018	0.015–0.055	0.0015–0.0031	0.0015–0.0037	0.008 Max.
	K	4-153 (2.5)	0.0005–0.0015	0.011–0.021	0.011–0.021	0.015–0.055	0.0015–0.0031	0.0015–0.0031	0.008 Max.
	J	4-153 (2.5)	0.0006–0.0018	0.010–0.020	0.008–0.019	0.015–0.055	0.0016–0.0030	0.0016–0.0030	0.008 Max.
	3	6-181 (30.0)	0.0008–0.0015	0.012–0.018	0.010–0.016	0.012–0.035	0.0020–0.0035	0.0008–0.0020	—

NA Not available

TORQUE SPECIFICATIONS
All readings in ft. lbs.

Year	VIN	No. Cylinder Displacement cu. in. (liter)	Cylinder Head Bolts	Main Bearing Bolts	Rod Bearing Bolts	Crankshaft Pulley Bolts	Flywheel Bolts	Manifold		Spark Plugs
								Intake	Exhaust	
1986	A	4-98 (1.6)	52	48	28	110	70	11	15	22
	C	4-135 (2.2)	②	30①	40①	50	70	17	17	26
	D	4-135 (2.2)	②	30①	40①	50	70	17	17	26
	E	4-135 (2.2)	②	30①	40①	50	70	17	17	26
	K	4-153 (2.5)	②	30①	40①	50	70	17	17	26

TORQUE SPECIFICATIONS
All readings in ft. lbs.

Year	VIN	No. Cylinder Displacement cu. in. (liter)	Cylinder Head Bolts	Main Bearing Bolts	Rod Bearing Bolts	Crankshaft Pulley Bolts	Flywheel Bolts	Manifold Intake	Manifold Exhaust	Spark Plugs
1987	C	4-135 (2.2)	②	30①	40①	50	70	17	17	26
	D	4-135 (2.2)	②	30①	40①	50	70	17	17	26
	E	4-135 (2.2)	②	30①	40①	50	70	17	17	26
	K	4-153 (2.5)	②	30①	40①	50	70	17	17	26
1988	C	4-135 (2.2)	②	30①	40①	50	70	17	17	26
	D	4-135 (2.2)	②	30①	40①	50	70	17	17	26
	E	4-135 (2.2)	②	30①	40①	50	70	17	17	26
	K	4-153 (2.5)	②	30①	40①	50	70	17	17	26
	3	6-181 (3.0)	70	60	38	110	70	17	17	20
1989-90	T	4-107 (1.8)	52	38	25	12	98	12	12	18
	R	4-122 (2.0)	68	50	35	18	98	12	20	18
	U	4-122 (2.0)	68	50	35	18	98	12	20	18
	A	4-135 (2.2)	②	30①	40①	50	70	17	17	26
	C	4-135 (2.2)	②	30①	40①	50	70	17	17	26
	D	4-135 (2.2)	②	30①	40①	50	70	17	17	26
	E	4-135 (2.2)	②	30①	40①	50	70	17	17	26
	J	4-153 (2.5)	②	30①	40①	50	70	17	17	26
	K	4-153 (2.5)	②	30①	40①	50	70	17	17	26
	3	6-181 (3.0)	70	60	38	110	70	17	17	20

① Plus ¼ turn more
② 4 step torque sequence—45, 65, 65 plus ¼ turn more

WHEEL ALIGNMENT

Year	Model		Caster Range (deg.)	Caster Preferred Setting (deg.)	Camber Range (deg.)	Camber Preferred Setting (deg.)	Toe-in (in.)	Steering Axis Inclination (deg.)
1986	Omni, Horizon	Front	—	1⅞P	¼N–¾P	⁵⁄₁₆P	¹⁄₁₆①	13⅜
	Turismo, Charger	Rear	—	—	1¼N–¼N	¾N	³⁄₃₂	—
	Aries, Reliant	Front	—	1³⁄₁₆P	¼N–¾P	⁵⁄₁₆P	¹⁄₁₆①	13⁵⁄₁₆P
	400, 600, E-Class, New Yorker, LeBaron, Daytona, Laser, LeBaron GTS, Lancer	Rear	—	—	1¼N–¼N	½N	0	—
1987	Omni, Horizon	Front	—	1⅔P	¼N–¾P	⁵⁄₁₆P	¹⁄₁₆	—
	Turismo, Charger	Rear	—	—	1¼N–¼N	¾N	³⁄₃₂	—

WHEEL ALIGNMENT

Year	Model		Caster Range (deg.)	Caster Preferred Setting (deg.)	Camber Range (deg.)	Camber Preferred Setting (deg.)	Toe-in (in.)	Steering Axis Inclination (deg.)
1987	Aries, Reliant 400, 600, E-Class, New Yorker, LeBaron, Daytona, Laser, LeBaron GTS, Lancer, Shadow, Sundance	Front	—	1⅔P	¼N–¾P	5/16P	1/16	—
		Rear	—	—	1¼N–¼P	½N	0	—
1988	Omni, Horizon	Front	—	1⅔P	¼N–¾P	5/16P	1/16	—
		Rear	—	—	1¼N–¼N	¾N	3/32	—
	Reliant, 600, Caravelle, Sundance, Lancer, Shadow, LeBaron, New Yorker, Daytona, Dynasty	Front	—	1⅓P	¼N–¾P	5/16P	1/16	—
		Rear	—	—	1¼N–¼P	½N	0	—
1989-90	Omni, Horizon	Front	—	1⅔P	¼N–¾P	5/16P	1/16	—
		Rear	—	—	1¼N–¼N	¾N	3/32	—
	New Yorker, LeBaron, Aries, Shadow, Dynasty, Reliant, Daytona, Sundance, Spirit, Acclaim	Front	—	1⅔P	¼N–¾P	5/16P	1/16	—
		Rear	—	—	1¼N–¼P	½N	0	—
	Lancer	1.8L	1 5/6P–2 5/6P	2⅓P	4/15N–11/15P	7/30P	0	—
		2.0L	1 7/10P–9/10P	⅖P	5/6N–1 1/6	1/12N	0	—

① Toe-out

ELECTRICAL

NOTE: Disconnecting the negative battery cable on some vehicles may interfere with the functions of the on board computer systems and may require the computer to undergo a relearning process, once the negative battery cable is reconnected.

For testing and overhaul procedures on starters, alternators and voltage regulators, refer to the Unit Repair Section.

Charging System

ALTERNATOR

Removal and Installation

NOTE: To perform the alternator adjustment on some models, it may be necessary to raise the vehicle and remove the splash shield.

1. Disconnect the negative battery cable.
2. Disconnect and label the wires from the alternator.
3. On the 3.0L engine, insert a ½ in. breaker bar into the tensioner, rotate it counterclockwise (to release belt tension) and remove the drive belt from the alternator pulley.
4. On all other engines, loosen the belt tension adjusting bolt, disconnect the drive belt(s) and remove the supporting nuts and bolts. Remove the alternator from the engine.
To Install:
5. Check the clearance between the alternator housing and the mount. If more than 0.008 in. clearance exists, install shims.
6. On all other engines, adjust the belt tension to ¼–⅜ in. deflection between the longest span between 2 pulleys, using moderate thumb pressure.
7. On the 3.0L engine, insert a ½ in. breaker bar into the tensioner, rotate it counterclockwise, install the drive belt and remove the breaker bar; the tensioner is designed to maintain proper tension on the belt at all times.

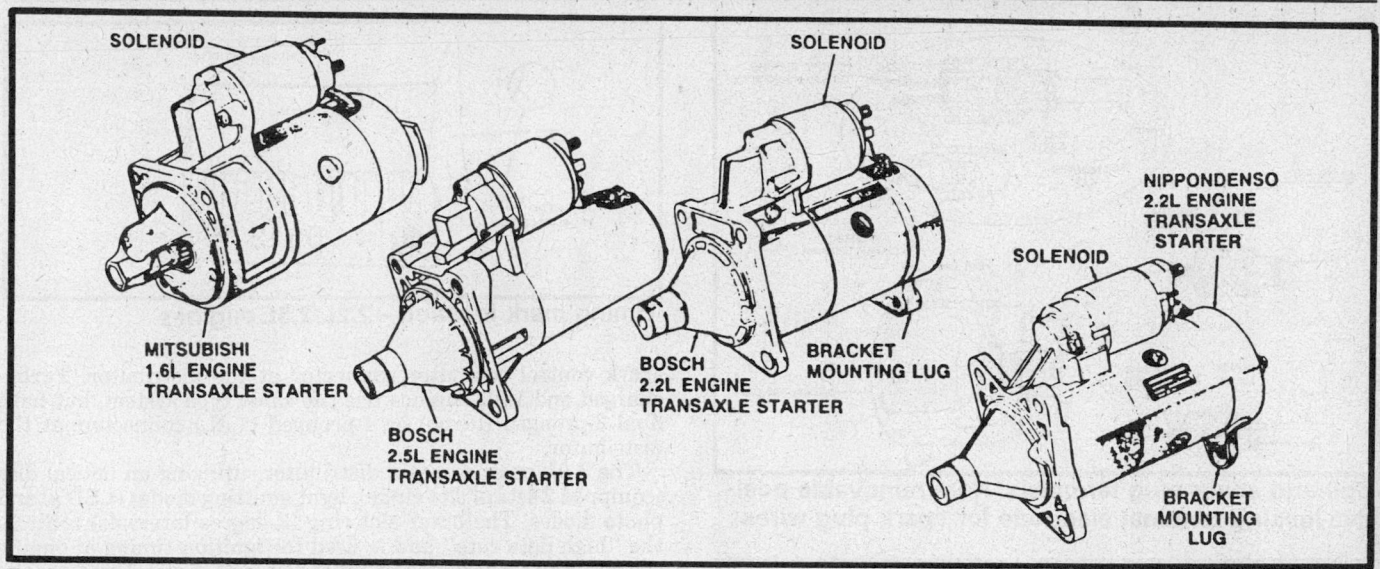

MITSUBISHI 1.6L ENGINE TRANSAXLE STARTER

SOLENOID

BOSCH 2.5L ENGINE TRANSAXLE STARTER

SOLENOID

BOSCH 2.2L ENGINE TRANSAXLE STARTER

BRACKET MOUNTING LUG

SOLENOID

NIPPONDENSO 2.2L ENGINE TRANSAXLE STARTER

BRACKET MOUNTING LUG

Typical starters used with varied engine applications

VOLTAGE REGULATOR

Removal and Installation

EXTERNAL TYPE

1. Disconnect the negative battery cable.
2. Disconnect the connector from the regulator.
3. Remove the sheet metal screws and the regulator.
4. To install, reverse the removal procedures. Make sure regulator has a clean mounting contact.

IN-CIRCUIT TYPE

The in-circuit type can only be serviced by replacing the power/logic module.

INTERNAL TYPE
Bosch

1. Disconnect the negative battery cable.
2. At the rear of the alternator, remove the regulator mounting screws.
3. Remove the regulator/brush holding assembly from the alternator.
4. To install, reverse the removal procedures.

Mitsubishi

To remove the regulator, the alternator must be removed from the vehicle and disassembled.

BELT TENSION

DRIVEBELTS

On the 3.0L engine, the drive belt is equipped with an automatic tensioner and is self-adjustable. The following procedure is for 4 cylinder vehicles only.

Satisfactory performance of the belt driven accessories depends upon proper drive belt tension. Three tensioning methods are given in order of preference:
1. Belt tension gauge method
2. Torque equivalent method
3. Belt deflection method
Due to space limitations in the engine compartment, the belt tension gauge method is usually restricted to use after the vehicle has been raised and the splash shield has been removed.

GAUGE METHOD EXCEPT 2.2L ENGINE AIR PUMP
1. For conventional belts, affix the tension gauge to the belt.

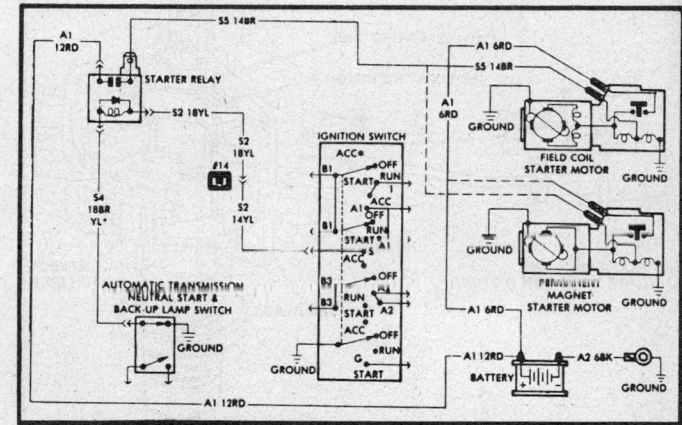

Typical starting system circuit

2. For V-belts (1.6L engine, alternator/water pump belt when equipped with Bosch alternator) use a Poly-V Burroughs gauge.

TORQUE METHOD

Each adjustable accessory bracket is provided with a ½ in. square hole for torque wrench use. Equivalent torque values for adjusting each accessory drive belt are specified.

BELT DEFLECTION METHOD

Place a straight edge across 2 adjacent pulleys and adjust belt tension with a force (push-pull) of 10 lbs., applied at the mid point, to produce a belt deflection. A small spring scale can be used to establish the 10 lbs. reading.

Starting System

STARTER

Removal and Installation

1. Disconnect the negative battery cable. Raise and safely support the vehicle, if necessary.
2. Remove the starter motor heat shield, if equipped.
3. With the 2.2L or 2.5L engine, loosen the air pump tube at the exhaust manifold and swivel the tube bracket away from the starter.

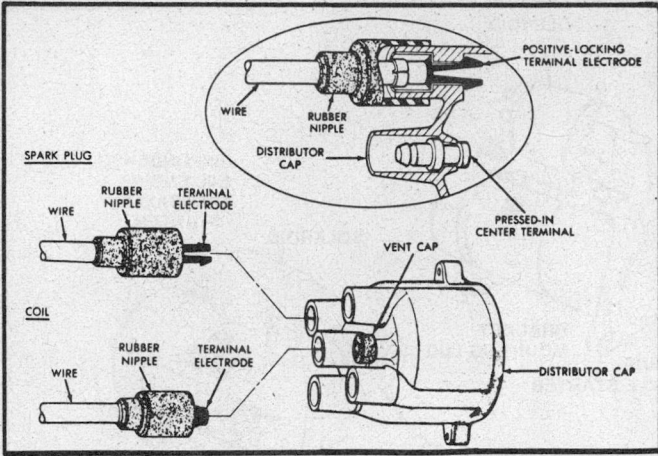

Coil and spark plug terminals. Note removable positive locking terminal electrode for spark plug wires

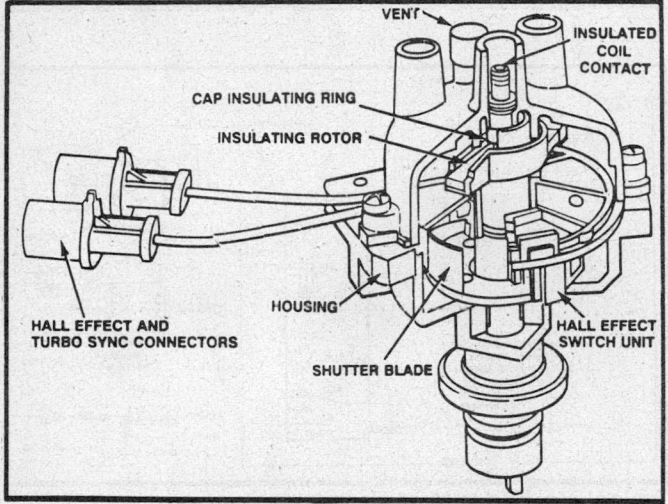

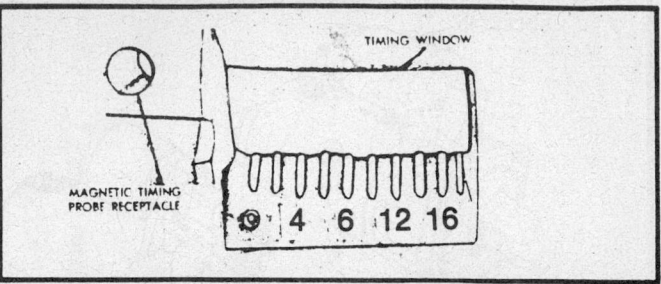

Timing mark location – 2.2L/2.5L engines

spark control computer connector at the distributor. Turbocharged and 1.8L engines use the same type system, but have dual 3-pronged (turbo) or 4-pronged (1.8L) connectors at the distributor.

The 3.0L engine uses a distributor, utilizing an optical disc (equipped 2 sets of slot rings), light emitting diodes (LED's) and photo diodes. The outer slot ring (2 degree intervals) controls the "high data rate" and is used for ignition timing at engine speeds up to 1200 rpm. The inner slot ring (6 slots) controls the "low data rate", each slot indicates the TDC of each piston and is used for ignition timing at engine speeds above 1200 rpm. As the distributor rotates, the **ON** and **OFF** light pulses are converted into electrical pulses and sent to the Single Board Engine Controller (SBEC). The SBEC controls the firing of the ignition coil and the distributor the high voltage to the desired spark plug.

The 2.0L engine uses a coil pack, a transistor, a crank angle sensor and an engine control unit to produce ignition voltage to the spark plugs.

To remove the spark plug cables from the distributor cap (except 1.8L), remove the distributor cap and squeeze the inside retaining prongs together to remove the cables.

Removal and Installation
TIMING NOT DISTURBED

1.8L Engine

1. Disconnect the negative battery cable and the distributor pickup lead wire at the harness connector. Remove the spark plug cables from the distributor cap.
2. Remove the vacuum hose from the the vacuum control unit.
3. Remove the hold-down nut and the distributor assembly.
To Install:
4. Install the distributor by performing the following procedures:
   a. Align the mating mark (line) with the mating punch mark on the distributor gear.
   b. Install the distributor to the cylinder head. Align the distributor flange mating mark with the center of the distributor hold-down stud.
5. To complete the installation, reverse the removal procedures. Start the engine. Check and adjust the timing, if necessary.

Except 1.8L Engine

1. Disconnect the negative battery cable.
2. Disconnect the distributor pickup lead wire at the harness connector. If equipped, remove the the splash shield.
3. Remove the retaining screws and the distributor cap.
4. Rotate the engine crankshaft (in the direction of normal rotation) until No. 1 cylinder is at TDC on the compression stroke. Make a mark on the block and the distributor housing where the rotor points for installation reference.
5. Remove the hold-down bolt and clamp.

4. On the 1.8L and 2.0L, remove the battery, battery tray and the intake manifold stay.
5. Disconnect and label the starter motor wiring.
6. Support the starter and remove the mounting bolts. Remove the starter from the flywheel housing and transaxle support bracket.
7. To install, reverse the removal procedures.

Ignition System

Refer to the underhod Vehicle Emission Information Label for the latest service procedures or specification change information.

Vehicles with 1.6L, 2.2L, 2.5L and 3.0L engines, are equipped with a Lean Burn/Electronic Spark Control system. This system consists of a spark control computer, various engine sensors and a specially calibrated carburetor or fuel injection system. The function of the system is to help the engine burn an unusually lean fuel/air mixture.

DISTRIBUTOR

All engines, except the 2.0L and 3.0L, are equipped with a computer controlled Hall Effect ignition system and use a 3-pronged

Timing mark location—1.6L engine

6. Carefully lift the distributor from the engine. The shaft on some engines may rotate slightly as the distributor is removed.

To Install:

7. Lower the distributor into the engine, engaging the gears and making sure that the O-ring is properly seated in the block. The rotor should align with the marks made before removal.

8. Tighten the hold-down bolt and connect the wires (make sure they snap into place).

9. To complete the installation, reverse the removal procedures. Start the engine. Check and adjust the ignition timing, if necessary.

TIMING DISTURBED

1. If the engine has been rotated while the distributor was removed, rotate the crankshaft until the No. 1 cylinder is at TDC on the compression stroke. This will be align the **0** mark on the flywheel or crankshaft pulley, with the pointer on the clutch housing, or engine front cover.

2. Position the rotor just ahead of the No. 1 terminal of the cap and lower the distributor into the engine. With the distributor fully seated, the rotor should be directly under the No. 1 terminal.

3. Tighten the hold-down screw, only enough so the distributor can be rotated to adjust the timing and connect the wiring.

4. Run the engine adjust the ignition timing.

5. Tighten the hold-down screw and recheck the timing.

NOTE: 1.6L, 2.2L, 2.5L and 3.0L engines use a distributor cap with positive locking secondary wires. These wire locks must be released from inside the distributor cap if the wires need to be replaced.

IGNITION TIMING

Adjustment

On all engines, except the 1.6L and 3.0L, the ignition is timed using the No. 1 cylinder at the left side of the engine, facing the vehicle. The 1.6L engine, the No. 1 cylinder is on the right (flywheel) side. The 3.0L engine has the No. 1 cylinder at the left rear, when facing the vehicle.

NOTE: 1986–87 vehicles equipped with 2.2L (EFI) and automatic transaxle, may exhibit erratic idle when the air conditioning compressor is engaged. If equipped with one of the logic module part numbers listed below, it will be necessary to retard the ignition timing 4 degrees; from 12 degrees BTDC to 8 degrees BTDC.

1986 FEDERAL—5227505, 5227505, 5227893
1986 CALIFORNIA—5227508, 5227510
1987 FEDERAL—5227579, 5227880
1987 CALIFORNIA—5227581, 5227882

Procedure

EXCEPT 1.8L AND 2.0L ENGINES

1. Connect a timing light according to the manufacturer's in-

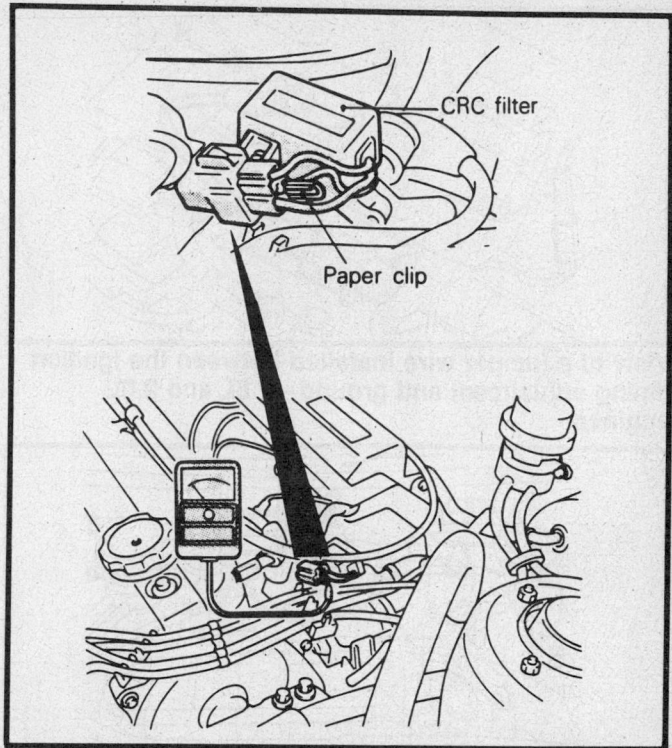

View of a paper clip and a tachometer installed to the CRC filter connector—1.8L engine

structions. Connect the red lead of a tachometer to the negative coil terminal and the black lead to ground. Place the cylinder selector switch in the appropriate position for the engine tested.

2. Start and run the engine until it reaches normal operating temperature.

3. Momentarily open the throttle and release it. Make sure there is no binding of the throttle linkage and the idle speed screw (on carburetor models) is against the stop.

NOTE: On EFI models, disconnect and reconnect the coolant temperature sensor connector on the thermostat housing. The loss of power lamp on the instrument panel and the radiator fan should turn ON and stay ON.

4. On carburetor models (equipped with a carburetor switch), connect a jumper wire between the carburetor switch and ground. At the Spark Control Computer (SCC), disconnect and plug the vacuum line.

5. Using the 1000 rpm scale, read the curb idle speed. If the rpm is not within specifications, adjust the idle speed screw on top of the solenoid (carburetor) or perform the On-Board Diagnostics for the throttle body minimum air flow check procedure (1988 and later EFI systems).

6. Loosen the distributor hold-down bolt so the distributor can be rotated.

7. Aim the timing light or read the magnetic timing unit. Carefully rotate the distributor until the timing marks are aligned.

NOTE: For the 2.2L and 2.5L engines, remove the timing hole access cover on the bell housing or read the magnetic timing unit. The timing marks, for the 1.6L and 3.0L engines, are on the crankshaft pulley and front cover.

8. Tighten the distributor hold-down bolt and recheck the timing. Check and adjust the idle speed, if necessary.

9. For carburetor models, unplug and reconnect the vacuum

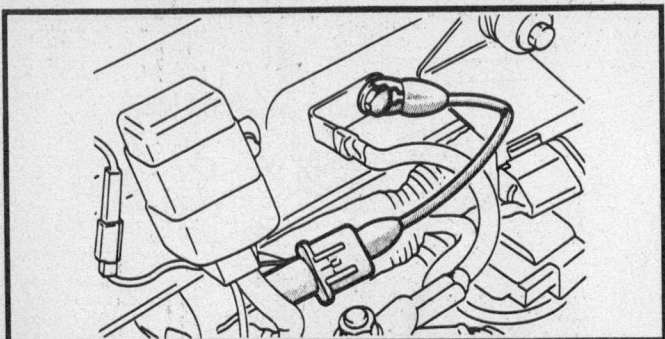

View of a jumper wire installed between the ignition timing adjustment and ground—1.8L and 2.0L engines

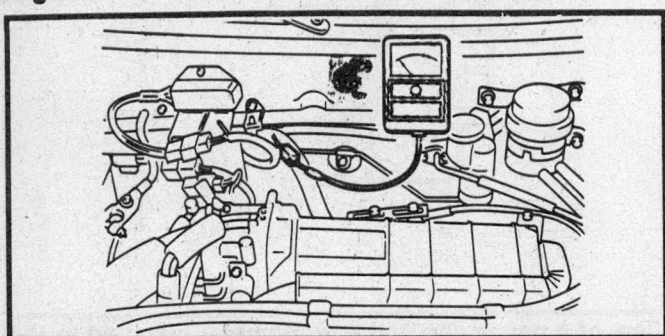

View of a paper clip and a tachometer installed in the engine revolution speed detection terminal—2.0L engine

hose to the Spark Control Computer. For EFI models, reconnect the coolant temperature sensor connector and erase the fault codes using the erase code mode on the Diagnostic Readout Box II (DRBII).

1.8L AND 2.0L ENGINES

1. Operate the engine until normal operating temperatures are reached. Turn **OFF** all accessories, lights and cooling fan. Place the steering wheel in the **N** and the transaxle in the **N** or **P** positions.
2. Connect a timing light to the engine.
3. Using a paper clip, insert it in the CRC filter connector (1.8L) or engine revolution speed detection terminal (2.0L) and connect a tachometer lead to it. Check the curb idle speed; it should be 600–800 rpm (1.8L) or 650–850 rpm (2.0L).
4. Stop the engine. Using a jumper wire, connect it between the ignition adjustment terminal and ground.
5. Start the engine and operate it at curb idle speed. Aim the timing light at the timing plate at the front of the engine and check the basic ignition timing; it should be 5 degrees BTDC, adjust it (if necessary).
6. If the timing is not 5 degrees BTDC, loosen the distributor (1.8L) or crank angle sensor (2.0L) mounting nut, turn the distributor/sensor to adjust the timing, tighten the nut and recheck the setting.

NOTE: **When tightening the nut, be sure the distributor or sensor does not move.**

7. Stop the engine and disconnect the jumper wire.
8. Start the engine, run it at curb idle speed and check the ignition timing; the timing should be 10 degrees BTDC (1.8L) or 8 degrees BTDC (2.0L).

NOTE: **Actual ignition timing may vary, depending upon the control mode of the engine control unit; should**

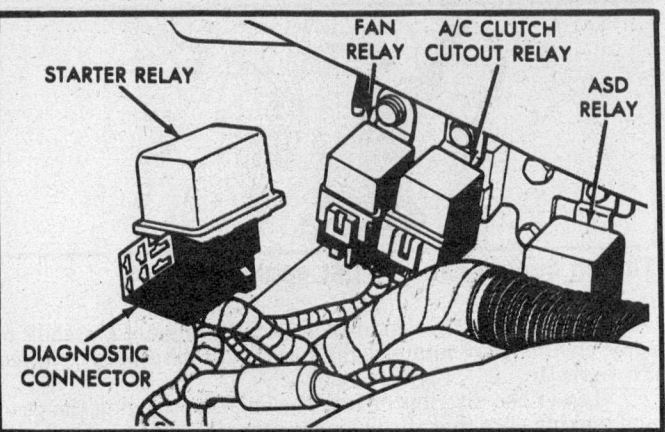

Location of the Diagnostic Readout Box II (DRBII)— EFI engines

the timing vary, recheck the basic ignition timing. At altitudes of more than 2300 ft., the actual ignition timing is further advanced to ensure good combustion.

THROTTLE BODY MINIMUM AIR FLOW CHECK

This procedure is used with 1988 and later EFI systems.
1. Using a Diagnostic Readout Box II (DRBII), connect it to the diagnostic connector located in the engine compartment near the starter relay.
2. Remove the air cleaner assembly and plug the heated air door vacuum hose.
3. Place the transaxle in **P** or **N**, operate the engine until normal operating temperatures are reached and the cooling fan has cycled **ON** and **OFF** at least once.
4. Connect a power timing light or magnetic timing probe and a tachometer to the engine.
5. Disconnect the coolant temperature sensor connector at the thermostat housing and set the basic timing to 10–14 degrees BTDC.
6. Turn the engine **OFF** and reconnect the coolant temperature sensor connector.
7. At the intake manifold, disconnect the PCV valve hose from the nipple and attach the special tool C-5004 or equivalent, to the nipple; a 0.125 in. orifice should be inside the attached hose.
8. Start the engine and allow it idle for at least 1 minute.
9. Using the DRBII, access the minimum airflow idle speed; the following should occur:
   a. The AIS motor will fully close.
   b. The idle spark advance will become fixed.
   c. The idle fuel will become enriched—single point fuel injection only.
   d. The engine idle rpm will be displayed on the DRBII.
10. Using the tachometer, check the idle rpm. If the odometer reading is under 1000 miles, the idle speed should be 700–1300 rpm (2.2L), 650–1250 rpm (2.5L) or 600–900 rpm (3.0L); if the odometer reading is over 1000 miles, the idle speed should be 1100–1300 rpm (2.2L), 1050–1250 rpm (2.5L) or 650–900 rpm (3.0L). If the idle speed is not within specifications, replace the throttle body.
11. Turn the engine **OFF** and disconnect the test equipment. Reinstall the air cleaner and connect the heated air door vacuum hose.

Electrical Controls
STEERING WHEEL

Removal and Installation

1. Disconnect the negative battery cable and the wiring con-

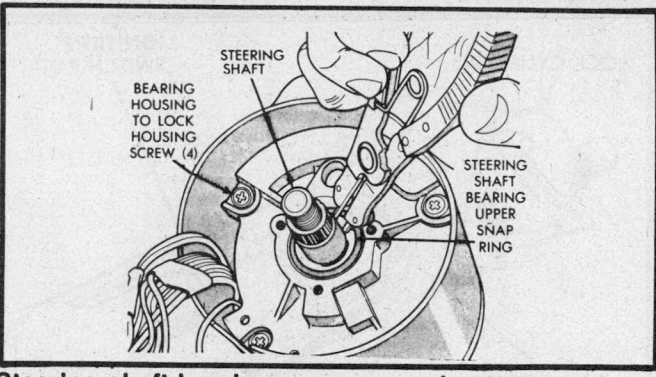

Steering shaft bearing upper snap ring removal

nector at the steering column, if necessary.

2. Remove the horn button or the pad and the horn switch.

NOTE: On the Laser, the horn pad is held in place with a screw, located under the steering wheel.

3. Remove the steering wheel nut and washer.
4. Using a steering wheel puller, remove the steering wheel.

To Install:

5. Align the master serration in the wheel hub with the missing tooth on the shaft. Torque the shaft nut to 45 ft. lbs. (all except Laser) or 25–33 ft. lbs. (Laser).

NOTE: To avoid possible damage, do not tighten the nut against the steering column lock.

6. Replace the horn switch and button.

HORN SWITCH

Removal and Installation

1. Disconnect the negative battery cable and the turn signal switch electrical connector.
2. Remove the horn button by lifting it out.

NOTE: On the Laser, the horn pad is held in place with a screw, located under the steering wheel.

3. Remove the steering wheel nut and the horn switch.

NOTE: On 4 spoke steering wheels, remove the screws from the rear of the steering wheel in order to remove the horn pad.

4. Installation is the reverse of the removal procedure.

IGNITION LOCK

Removal and Installation

OMNI, HORIZON, TURISMO AND CHARGER

1. Disconnect the negative battery cable.
2. Place the cylinder in the **LOCK** position and remove the key.
3. Remove the steering wheel, the column cover screws, the covers, the sound deadener panel and the turn signal switch.
4. Using a hacksaw blade, cut the upper ¼ in. from the key cylinder retainer pin boss.
5. Using a drift punch, drive the roll pin from the housing and remove the key cylinder.
6. To install, insert the cylinder into the housing, make sure it engages the lug on the ignition switch driver, install the roll pin and reverse the removal procedures. Check the cylinder for free operation.

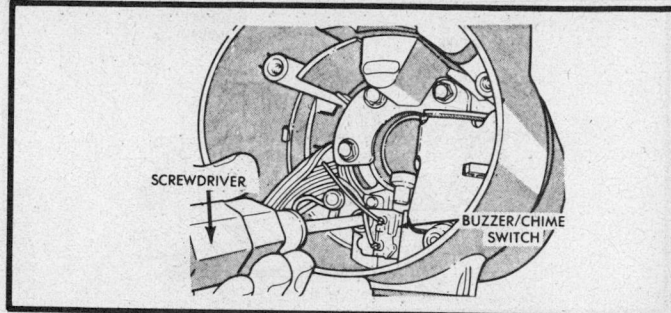

Removing ignition key buzzer/chime switch

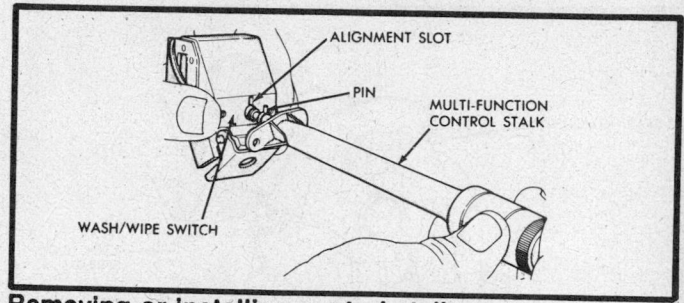

Removing or installing control stalk

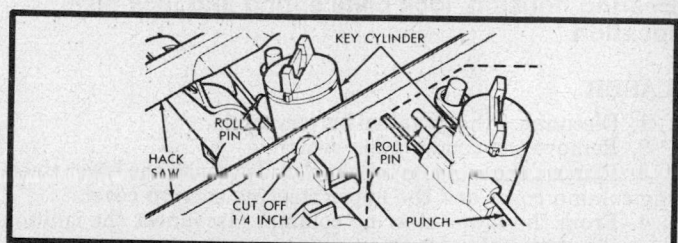

Cutting retainer pin boss to remove key cylinder

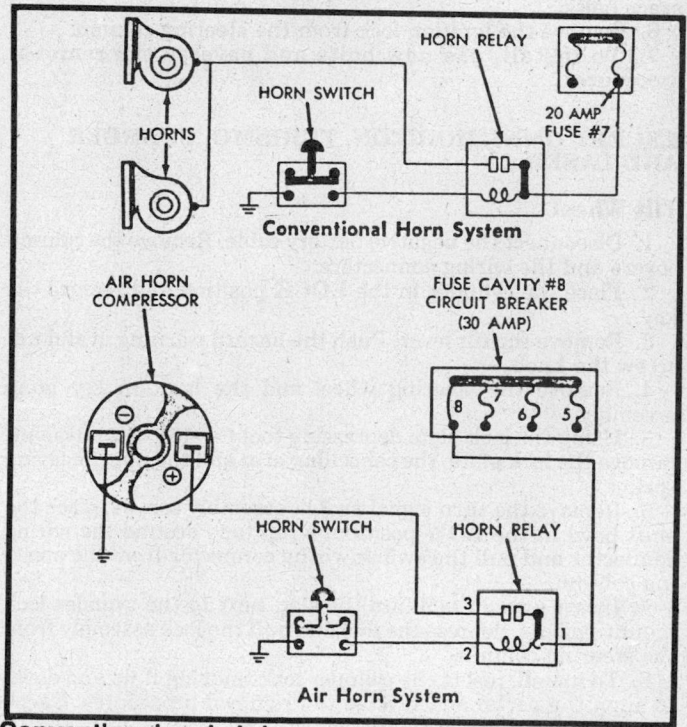

Conventional and air horn system electrical schematic

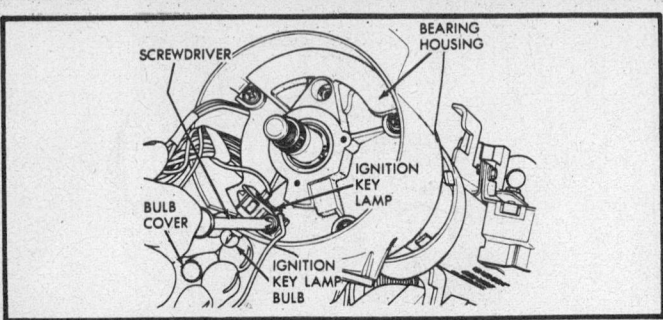

Ignition key lamp removal

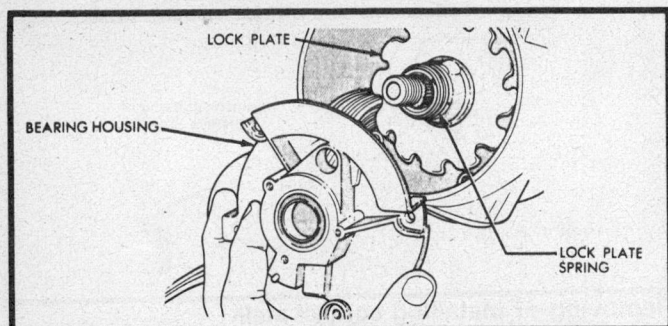

Bearing housing, lock plate spring and lock plate location

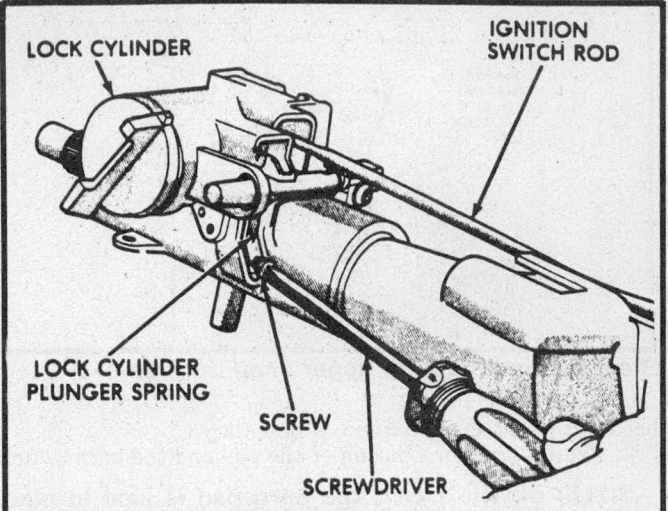

Removing lock cylinder plunger spring

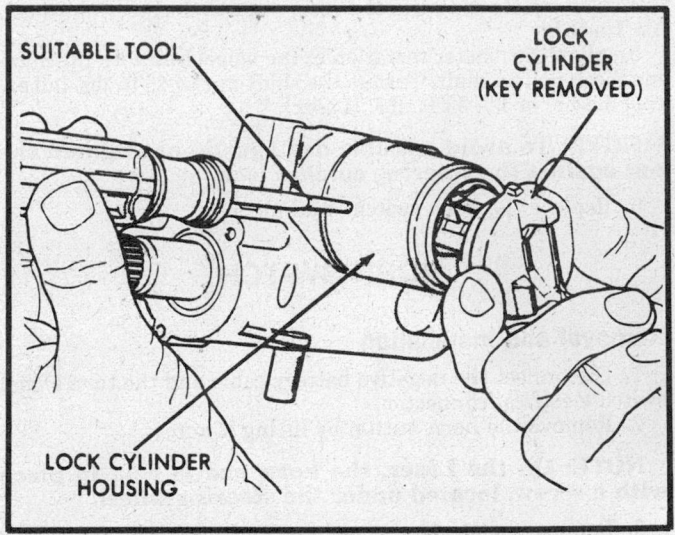

Depressing retainer to allow lock cylinder removal

LASER

1. Disconnect the negative battery cable.
2. Remove the combination switch.
3. Remove the instrument panel under cover, the lower steering column cover and the upper steering column cover.
4. From the lower steering column, disconnect the ignition switch's electrical connector.
5. Using a hacksaw, cut the ignition lock-to-steering lock brace bolts.
6. Remove the ignition lock from the steering column.
7. To install, use new bolts and reverse the removal procedures.

EXCEPT OMNI, HORIZON, TURISMO, CHARGER AND LASER

Tilt Wheel

1. Disconnect the negative battery cable. Remove the column covers and the wiring connectors.
2. Place the cylinder in the **LOCK** position and remove the key.
3. Remove the tilt lever. Push the hazard warning in and unscrew the knob.
4. Remove the steering wheel and the ignition key lamp assembly.
5. Using the lock plate depressing tool C–4156 or equivalent, remove the lock plate, the cancelling arm and the upper bearing spring.
6. Remove the turn signal switch assembly screws, place the shift bowl in the **LOW** position, wrap tape around the wiring connector and pull the switch/wiring connector from the steering column.
7. Insert a small tool into the slot, next to the cylinder lock mounting boss, depress the tool and pull the lock assembly from the steering column.
8. To install, insert the cylinder lock (moving it up and down to align the parts) and reverse the removal procedures. Check the operation of the cylinder lock.

Except Tilt Wheel

1. Disconnect the negative battery cable and remove the column covers.
2. Place the cylinder in the **LOCK** position and remove the key.
3. Remove the steering wheel, the combination switch assembly, the upper bearing retaining plate, the lock plate spring and the lock plate from the steering column.
4. Remove the buzzer/chime switch screw and the switch.
5. Remove the ignition switch-to-column screws and the switch, slide off the actuating rod.
6. Remove the dimmer switch screws and disengage from the actuating rod.
7. Remove the bellcrank screws and slide it up into the lock housing to disengage it from the ignition actuator rod.
8. Insert a small diameter tool into both cylinder lock release holes, push in on the tools and pull the lock cylinder out of the housing.
9. To install, reverse the removal procedures. Check the operation of the cylinder lock.

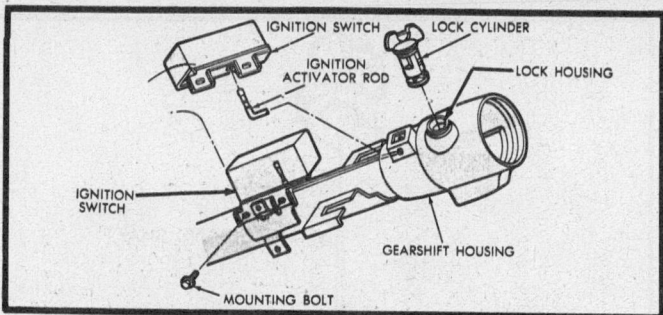

Ignition switch location, typical of all models

Floor Shift Column

1. Disconnect the negative battery cable.
2. Remove the upper and lower steering column covers.
3. From underneath the lock cylinder, remove the lock cylinder plunger spring and screw.
4. Using a small rod, depress the release plunger through the small access hole in the top of the lock cylinder housing.
5. With the release plunger depressed, pull the lock cylinder (without key) from the lock cylinder housing.

To Install:

6. Insert the assembly into the housing until the plunger engages the lock cylinder and retains it in the lock cylinder bore.
7. To complete the installation, reverse the removal procedures.

IGNITION SWITCH

Removal and Installation

OMNI, HORIZON, TURISMO AND CHARGER

1. Disconnect the negative battery cable.
2. Remove the connector from the switch.
3. Place the key in the **LOCK** position.
4. Remove the key.
5. Remove the switch screws and allow the switch (with pushrod) to drop below the jacket.
6. Rotate the switch 90 degrees to permit removal of the switch from the pushrod.

To Install:

7. Position the switch in **LOCK** (2nd detent from the top).
8. Place the switch at right angles to the column and insert the pushrod.
9. Align the switch on the bracket and install the screws.
10. With a light rearward load on the switch, tighten the screws. Check for proper operation.

EXCEPT OMNI, HORIZON, TURISMO AND CHARGER

1. Disconnect the negative battery cable.
2. Remove steering column cover.
3. Remove under panel sound deadener.
4. Loosen the ignition switch mounting plate screws to adjust switch by pushing up gently on the switch to take up rod system slack.
5. Remove speed control switch and/or wires, as required.
6. Lower and support the steering column, if necessary for switch replacement.
7. Remove the switch-to-column screws.
8. Rotate switch to 90 degrees and pull up to disengage from ignition switch rod.

To Install:

9. Rotate switch to 90 degrees and push up to engage to ignition switch rod.
10. Install the ignition switch mounting plate screws, but do not tighten.
11. Adjust the switch by pushing up gently on the switch to

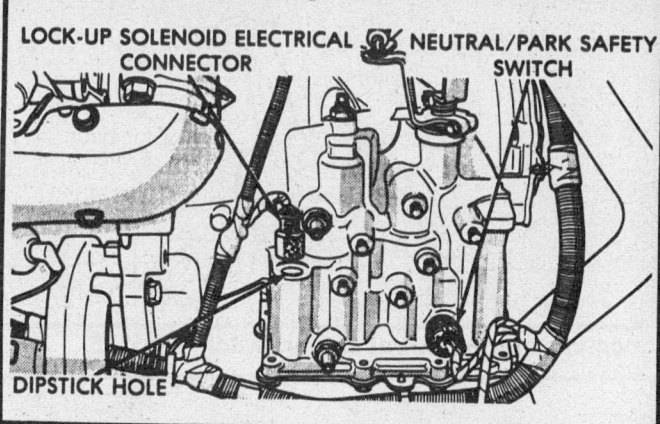

Location of the neutral safety switch—all transxles except A-604 and KM175

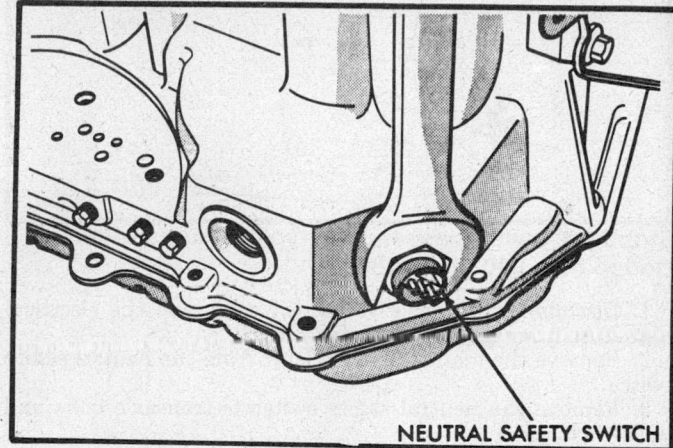

Location of the neutral safety switch—A-604

take up rod system slack. Tighten the switch-to-column screws.
12. Install the steering column to dash, if removed.
13. Install the speed control switch and/or wires.
14. Install the steering column cover.
15. Install the under panel sound deadener.

NEUTRAL SAFETY SWITCH

Removal and Installation

EXCEPT KM175 TRANSAXLE

The neutral safety switch is located on the left rear side of the transaxle.

1. Disconnect the negative battery cable and the electrical connector from the neutral safety switch.
2. To test for continuity, connect an ohmmeter between the center pin and the case; continuity should only exist when the transaxle is in **P** or **N**.
3. Using a wrench, remove the switch from the transaxle and allow the fluid to drain from the case.
4. Move the selector to **P** and to **N** positions and make sure the switch operating levers are centered in the switch hole.
5. To install, use a new seal, torque the switch to 24 ft. lbs. (33 Nm). Add fluid to the transaxle.

KM175 TRANSAXLE

The neutral safety (inhibitor) switch is located on the upper right side of the transaxle.

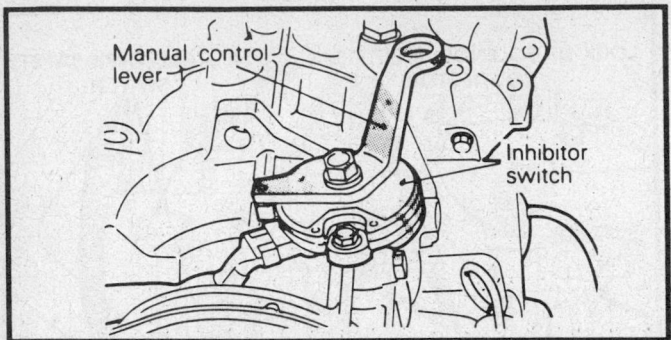

Location of the neutral safety switch—KM175

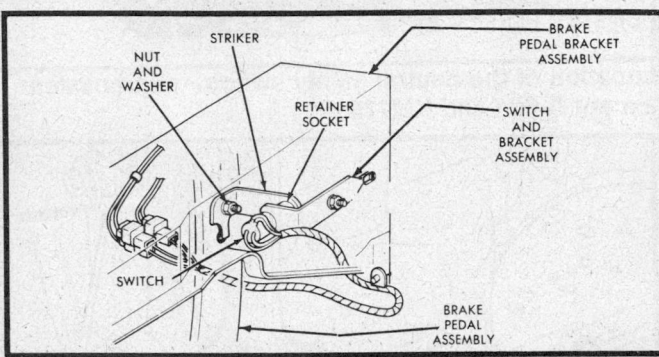

Stoplight switch assembly, typical Aries, Reliant, Dodge 400, 600 and LeBaron

1. Disconnect the negative battery cable and the electrical connector from the neutral safety switch.
2. Remove the manual control lever from the neutral safety switch.
3. Remove the neutral safety switch-to-transaxle bolts and the switch.

To Install:

4. Place the shift selector and the manual control lever into the **N** positions.
5. Mount the neutral safety switch to the transaxle but do not torque the bolts.
6. Turn the neutral safety switch to align the 0.47 in. (12mm) hole with the manual control lever 0.47 in. (12mm) hole. Once aligned, torque the switch-to-transaxle bolts to 7–9 ft. lbs. (10–12 Nm).

STOPLIGHT SWITCH

Adjustment

OMNI, HORIZON, TURISMO AND CHARGER

1. Loosen the switch-to-pedal bracket attaching screw and slide the assembly away from the pedal blade.
2. Push the brake pedal down and allow to return on it's own. Do not pull the pedal back.
3. Place a 0.130 in. spacer gauge on the pedal blade and slide the switch toward the pedal blade until the switch plunger is fully depressed against the spacer gauge.
4. Torque the switch bracket screw to 75 inch lbs. torque and remove the spacer.
5. Operate the brake pedal and be sure the brake light switch does not prevent full pedal return.

EXCEPT OMNI, HORIZON, TURISMO AND CHARGER

The stoplight switch is self-adjusting during the installation.

1. Install the switch in the retaining bracket and push the switch forward as far as it will go.
2. The brake pedal will move forward slightly. Pull the pedal

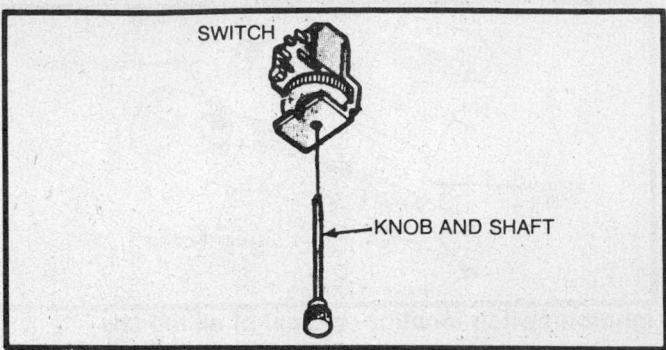

Typical headlamp switch with shaft and knob

back, bringing the striker back towards the switch until the pedal will go no further.
3. This movement of the pedal will cause the switch to ratchet backwards to the correct position. Very little movement is required and no further adjustment is necessary.

Removal and Installation

1. Disconnect the negative battery cable and lower the steering column.
2. Remove the nut located on the inboard side of the brake support bracket which fastens the switch to the bracket.
3. Remove the wiring from the dash and disconnect the wiring connector.
4. Remove the switch.
5. To install, reverse removal procedures and adjust the switch.

HEADLAMP SWITCH

Removal and Installation

OMNI, HORIZON, TURISMO AND CHARGER

1. Disconnect the negative battery cable.
2. Pull the headlight knob from the switch.
3. Unscrew the collar from the instrument panel side of the switch.
4. Push the switch through the panel and let it drop; disconnect the wires.
5. Installation is the reverse of removal.

EXCEPT OMNI, HORIZON, TURISMO AND CHARGER

1. Disconnect the negative battery cable.
2. Snap out headlight switch bezel out of instrument panel.
3. Remove the screws securing the headlight switch mounting plate to the base panel.
4. Push the switch and plate rearward and disconnect the wiring connector.
5. Depress the button on the switch and remove the knob and stem.
6. Snap out the mounting plate cover, then remove the nut that attaches the switch to the mounting plate.
7. Installation is the reverse of removal.

CONCEALED HEADLAMPS

Manual Operation

DAYTONA

1. Disconnect the negative battery cable.
2. Lift hood and look through the access hole in the sight shield (located behind the bumper facia).

NOTE: The vehicle is equipped with 2 headlamp motors; 1 on each side of the vehicle.

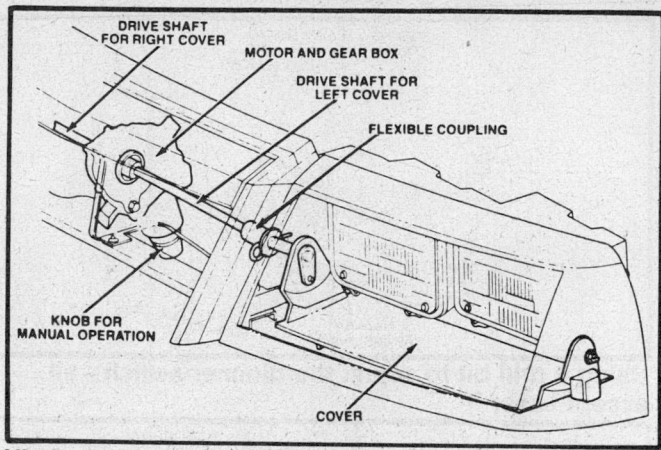

View of the concealed headlight motor assembly— LeBaron, New Yorker, New Yorker Landau and Dynasty

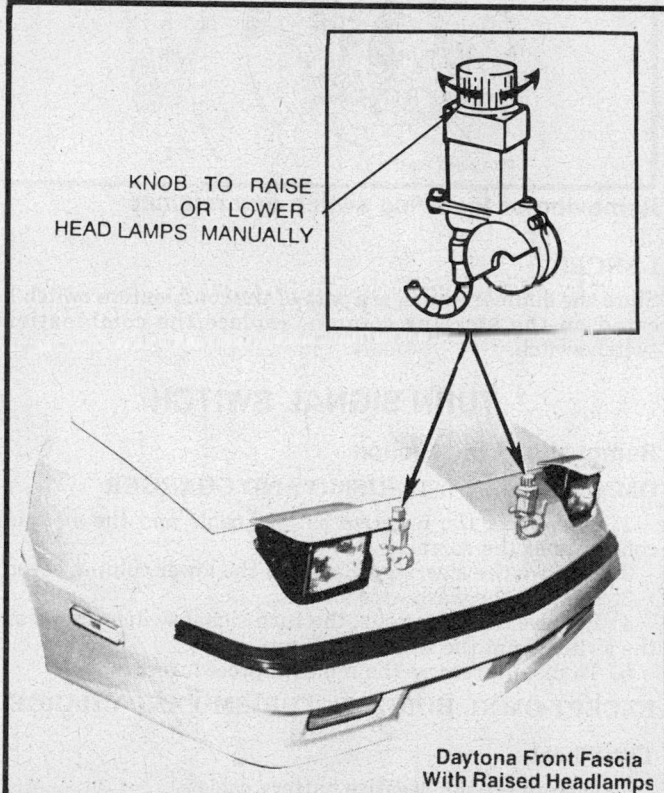

Daytona Front Fascia With Raised Headlamps

View of the concealed headlight motor assemblies— Daytona

3. Remove the hand wheel cover boot.
4. Turn the manual override hand wheel to raise the headlamps.

LEBARON, NEW YORKER LANDAU AND DYNASTY

1. Disconnect the negative battery cable.
2. Look under the center of the front bumper.
3. Remove the hand wheel cover boot.
4. Turn the manual override hand wheel to raise the headlamps.

LANCER

1. Disconnect the negative battery cable.

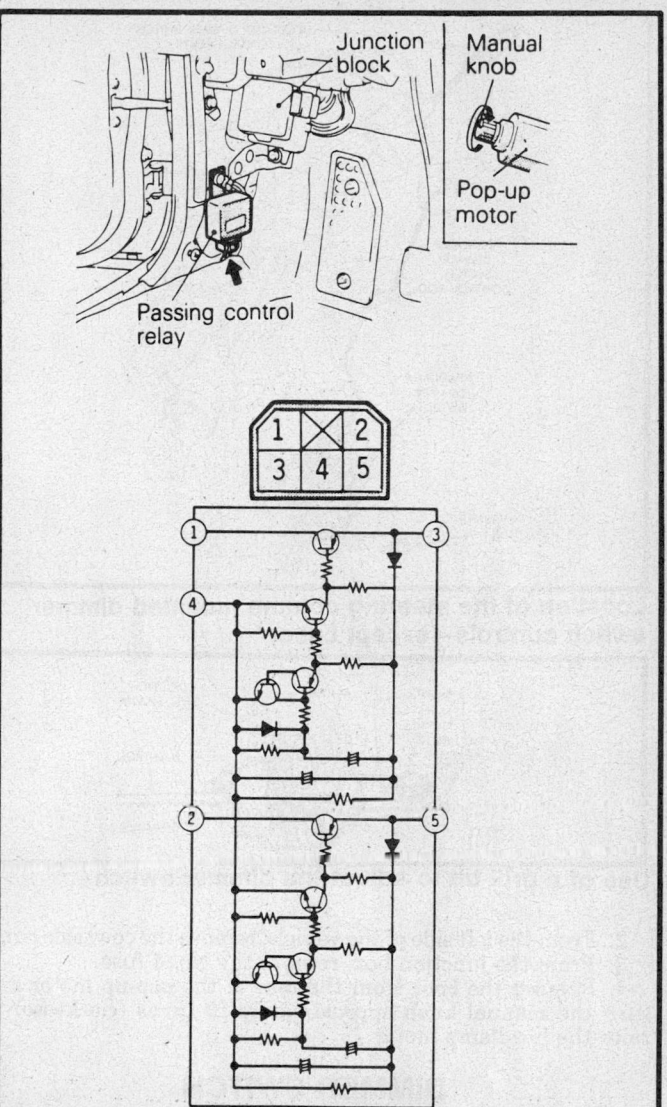

View of the headlight pop-up motor knob and electrical circuit—Laser

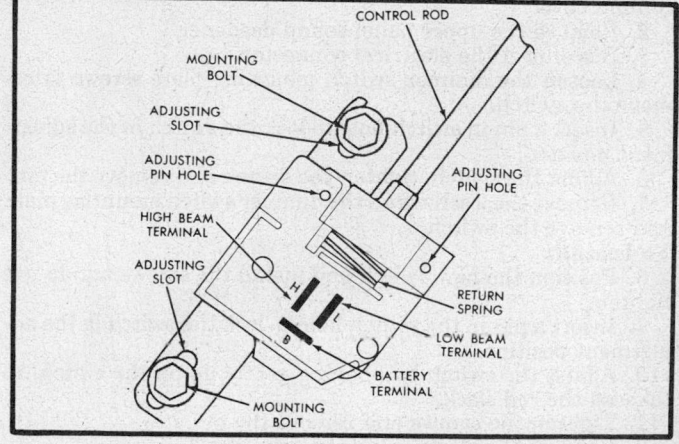

View of the steering column mounted headlight dimmer switch—except Laser

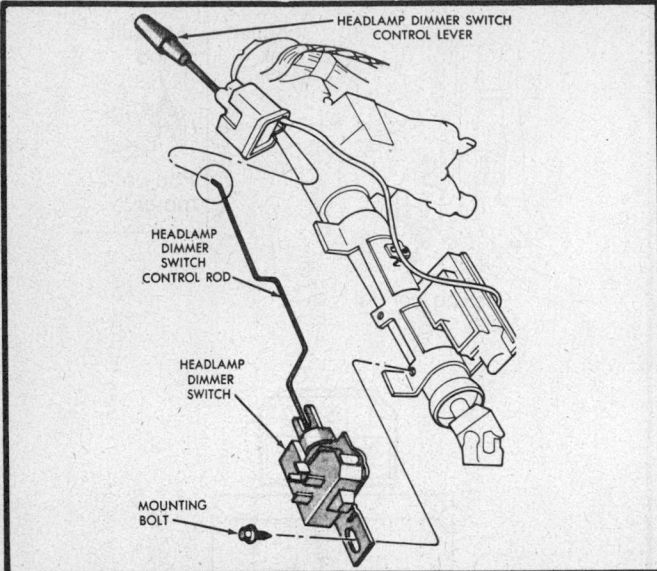

Location of the steering column mounted dimmer switch controls — except Laser

Use of a drill bit to adjust the dimmer switch

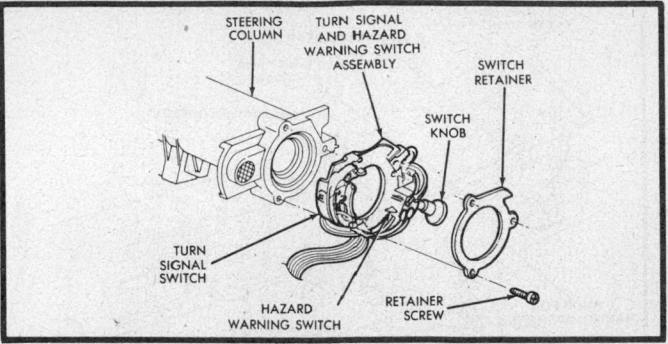

Using a drill bit to adjust the dimmer switch — all except Laser

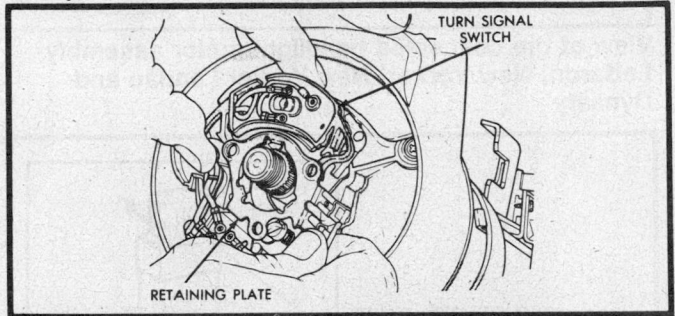

Removing or installing switch and retainer

2. From the left side of the vehicle, remove the cowl side trim.
3. From the junction box, remove the No. 4 fuse.
4. Remove the boot from the rear of the pop-up motor and turn the manual knob approximately 10 turns (clockwise) to raise the headlamp motor.

DIMMER SWITCH

Removal and Installation
EXCEPT LANCER

1. Disconnect the negative battery cable. Remove steering column cover.
2. Remove the upper panel sound deadener.
3. Disconnect the electrical connector.
4. Loosen the dimmer switch mounting plate screws to remove the switch.
5. Insert a pin in switch hole to lock the switch in the adjustment position.
6. Adjust the switch, tighten the screws and remove the pin.
7. Remove the 2 screws on the dimmer switch mounting plate and remove the switch.

To Install:
8. Position the new switch and install the screws but do not tighten.
9. Insert a pin in the switch hole to lock the switch in the adjustment position.
10. Adjust the switch by pushing gently up on the switch, to take up the rod slack.
11. Tighten the screws and remove the pin.
12. Connect the electrical connector.
13. Install the upper panel sound deadener.
14. Install the steering column cover.

LANCER

Since the dimmer switch is a part of the combination switch located on the steering column, replace the combinations switch.switch.

TURN SIGNAL SWITCH

Removal and Installation
OMNI, HORIZON, TURISMO AND CHARGER

1. Disconnect the negative battery cable and the electrical connector at the column.
2. Remove the steering wheel and the lower column cover.
3. Remove the wash/wipe switch.
4. Remove the wiring clip, the turn signal switch screws and the switch from the steering column.
5. To install, reverse the removal procedures.

EXCEPT OMNI, HORIZON, TURISMO AND CHARGER

Tilt Wheel

1. Disconnect the negative battery cable.
2. Remove the steering wheel, the column under cover and the lower instrument panel bezel.
3. Pry out the wiring trough plastic retainers and lift out the trough.
4. Position the gearshift lever to the full clockwise position.
5. Disconnect the turn signal wiring connectors at the steering column.
6. If equipped, remove the plastic cover from the lock plate. Using tool C-4156 or equivalent, depress the lock plate and pry out the retaining ring.
7. Remove the lock plate, the cancelling cam and the upper bearing spring.
8. Place the turn signal switch in the right turn position and remove the turn signal-to-wash/wiper switch pivot screw.
9. Remove the hazard warning switch knob screw and the turn signal switch-to-steering column screws.

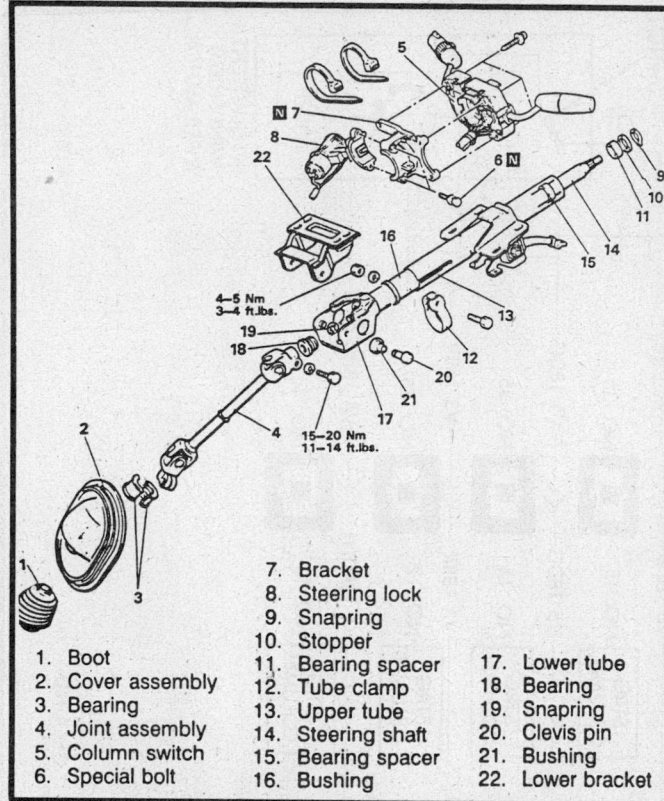

1. Boot	7. Bracket	11. Bearing spacer	17. Lower tube
2. Cover assembly	8. Steering lock	12. Tube clamp	18. Bearing
3. Bearing	9. Snapring	13. Upper tube	19. Snapring
4. Joint assembly	10. Stopper	14. Steering shaft	20. Clevis pin
5. Column switch		15. Bearing spacer	21. Bushing
6. Special bolt		16. Bushing	22. Lower bracket

Exploded view of the steering column–Laser

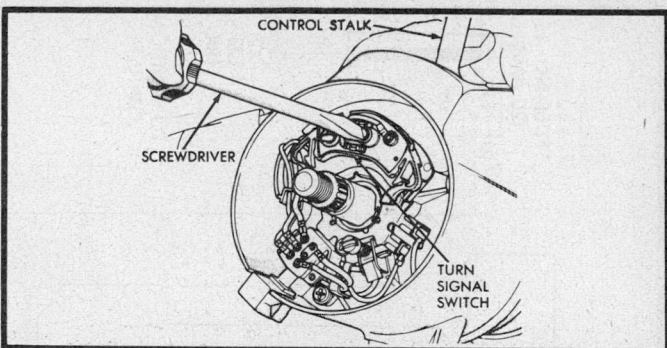

Wash/wipe switch removal and installation, all models except Omni and Horizon

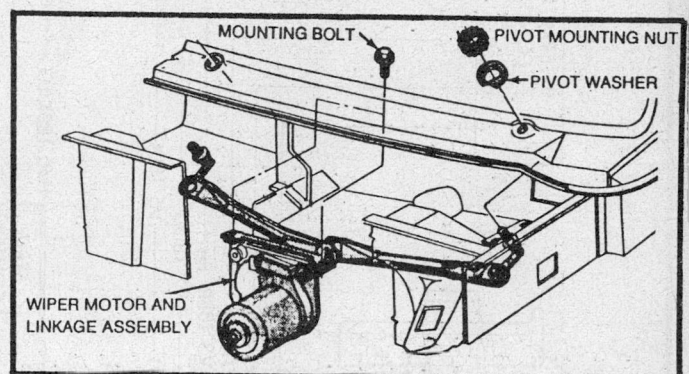

Wiper motor and linkage—typical

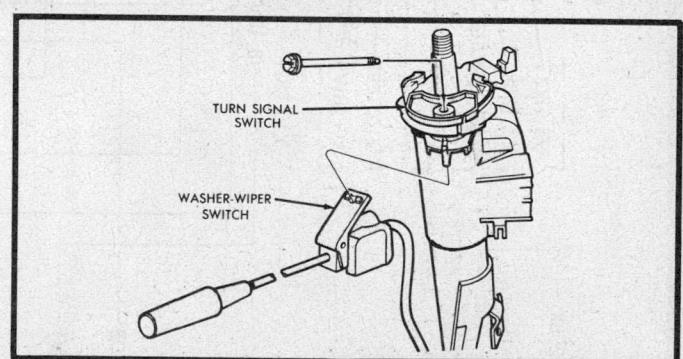

Steering column windshield wiper switch, typical

10. Remove the turn signal/hazard warning switch assembly by pulling the switch up the column, while straightening and guiding the wires up through the column opening.

11. To install, reverse the removal procedures. Lubricate the switch pivot with light grease. Place the switch in the right turn position, when installing. Use tool C–4156 or equivalent, to install the upper bearing spring, the cancelling cam and the lock plate.

Except Tilt Wheel

1. Disconnect the negative battery cable.
2. Remove the steering wheel, the column under cover and the lower instrument panel bezel.
3. Pry out the wiring trough plastic retainers and lift out the trough.
4. Position the gearshift lever to the full clockwise position.
5. Disconnect the turn signal wiring connectors at the steering column.
6. Remove the wash/wipe switch-to-turn signal switch pivot screw.

NOTE: Leave the turn signal lever in the installed position.

7. Remove the turn signal switch-to-upper bearing housing screws.
8. Remove the turn signal/hazard warning switch assembly by pulling the switch up the column, while straightening and guiding the wires up through the column opening.
9. To install, reverse the removal procedures. Lubricate the switch pivot with light grease.

COMBINATION SWITCH

Removal and Installation

LASER

1. Disconnect the negative battery cable and remove the steering wheel.
2. From the lower steering column, disconnect the electrical connector.

NOTE: To disconnect the electrical connector, it may be necessary to remove some of the steering column cover panels.

3. Remove the combination switch-to-steering column screws and the switch.
4. To install, reverse the removal procedures and check the switch operation.

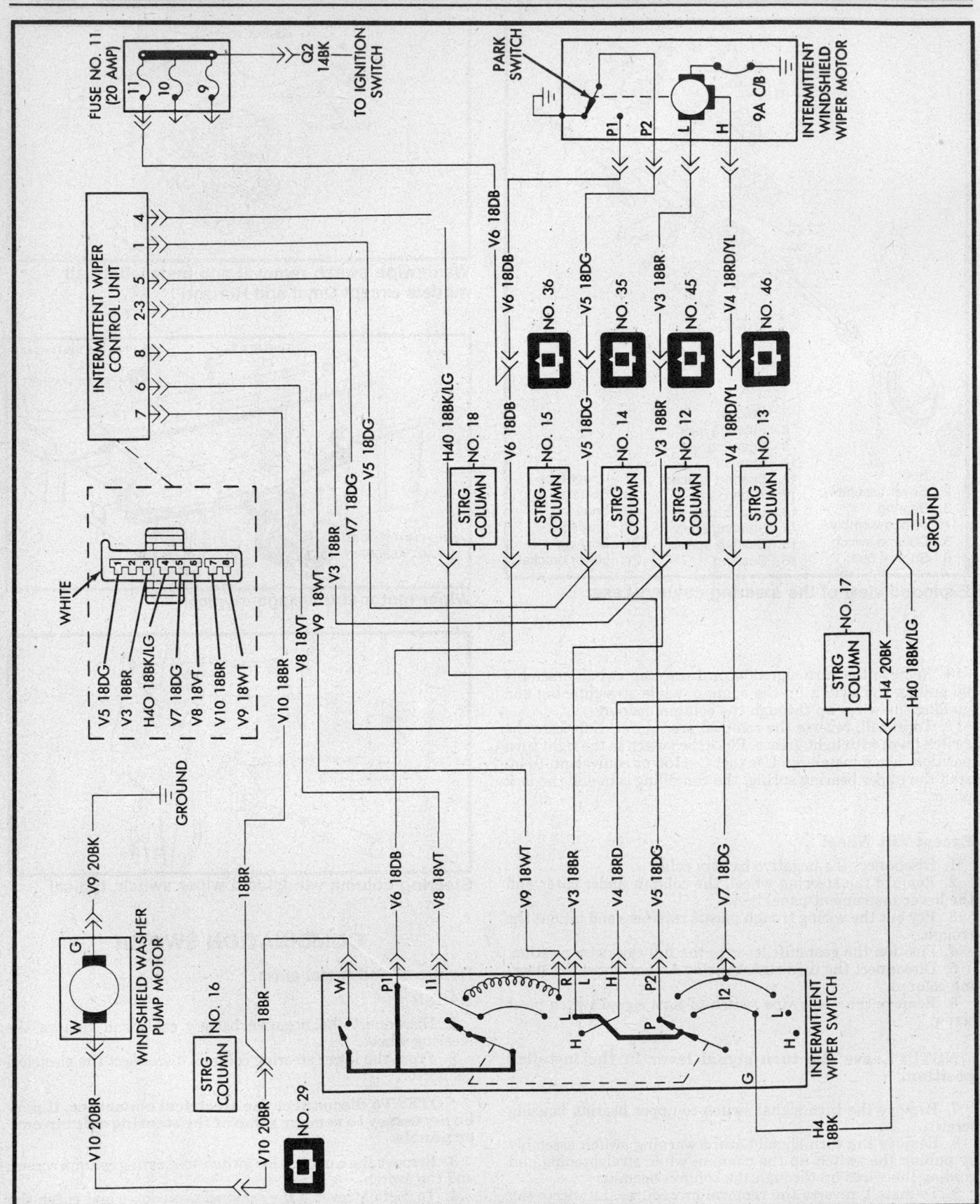

Typical schematic of the windshield wiper system except Laser

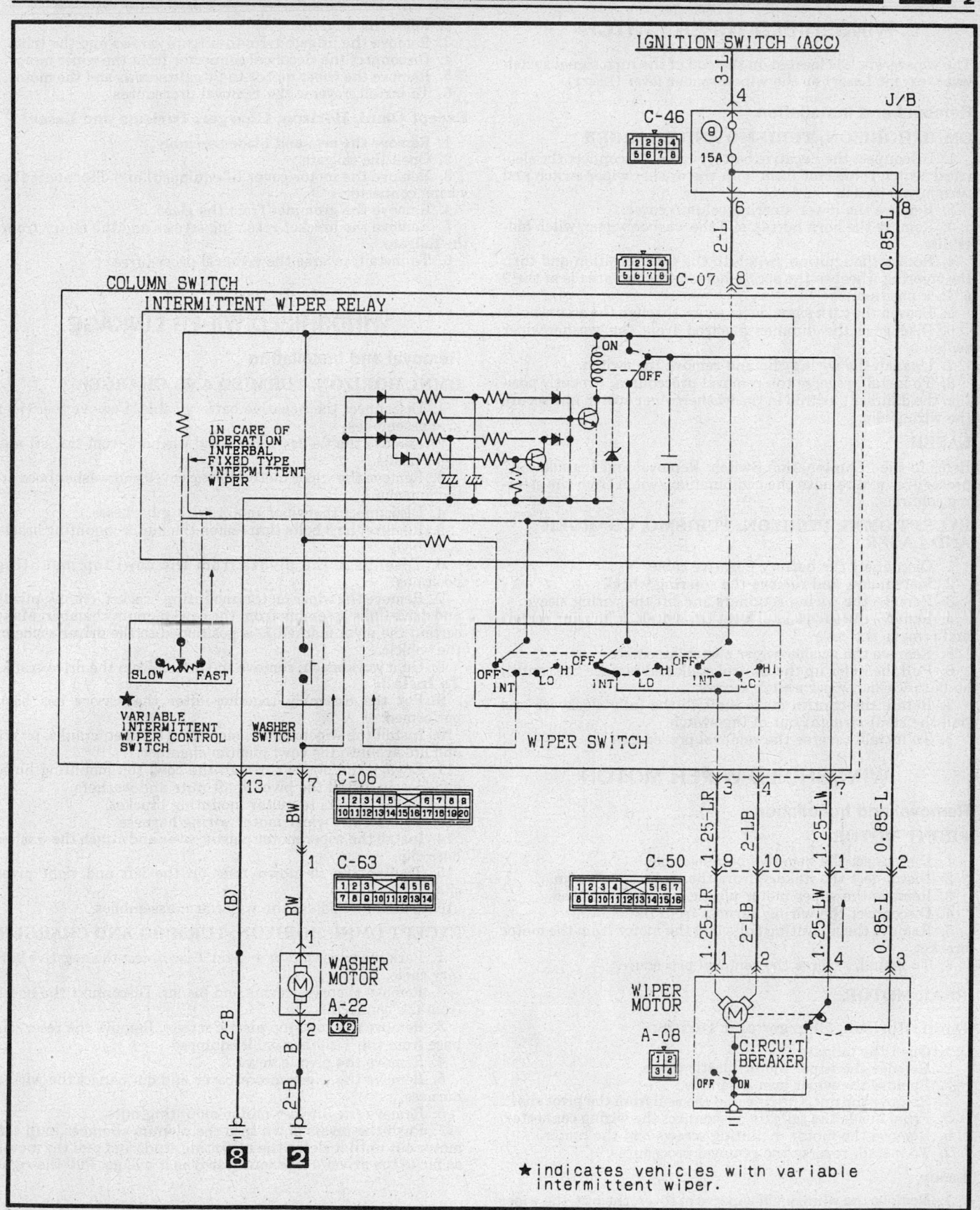

Schematic of the windshield wiper system—Laser

WINDSHIELD WIPER SWITCH

The wiper switch is located on the end of the turn signal switch lever (except Laser) or the wiper/washer lever (Laser).

Removal and Installation

OMNI, HORIZON, TURISMO AND CHARGER

1. Disconnect the negative battery cable. Disconnect the electrical switch connector from both the washer/wiper switch and turn signal switch.
2. Remove the lower steering column cover.
3. Remove the horn button and the washer/wiper switch hider disc.
4. Rotate the ignition switch to the **OFF** position and turn the steering wheel so the access hole in the hub area is at the 9 o'clock position.
5. Loosen the turn signal lever screw through the access hole.
6. Disengage the dimmer pushrod from the washer/wiper switch.
7. Unsnap the wiring clip and remove the switch.
8. To install, reverse the removal procedures. Properly position the dimmer pushrod in the washer/wiper switch and secure the wiring clip.

LASER

Refer to the "Combination Switch, Removal and Installation" procedures and remove the combination switch from the steering column.

EXCEPT OMNI, HORIZON, TURISMO, CHARGER AND LASER

1. Disconnect the battery negative cable.
2. Matchmark and remove the steering wheel.
3. Remove the wiring retainers and lift the wiring sleeve.
4. Remove the turn signal lever cover-to-lock housing screws and remove the cover.
5. Remove the washer/wiper switch assembly.
6. Pull the hider up the control stalk and remove the control stalk-to-washer/wiper switch screws.
7. Rotate the control stalk shaft to the fully clockwise and pull the shaft straight out of the switch.
8. To install, reverse the removal procedures.

WINDSHIELD WIPER MOTOR

Removal and Installation

FRONT MOTOR

1. Disconnect the negative battery cable.
2. Disconnect the linkage from the motor crank arm.
3. Remove the wiper motor plastic cover, if equipped.
4. Disconnect the wiring harness from the motor.
5. Remove the mounting bolts and the motor from the motor bracket.
6. To install, reverse the removal procedures.

REAR MOTOR

Omni, Horizon, Charger and Turismo

1. Open the tailgate.
2. Remove the wiper motor plastic cover.
3. Remove the wiper arm assembly.
4. Remove the nut, the ring and the seal from the pivot shaft.
5. From inside the tailgate, disconnect the wiring connector.
6. Remove the motor mounting screws and the motor.
7. To install, reverse the removal procedures.

Laser

1. Remove the windshield wiper arm cover, the nut, the wiper arm and the grommet.

2. Raise the liftgate.
3. Remove the liftgate trim-to-liftgate screws and the trim.
4. Disconnect the electrical connector from the wiper motor.
5. Remove the wiper motor-to-liftgate screws and the motor.
6. To install, reverse the removal procedures.

Except Omni, Horizon, Charger, Turismo and Laser

1. Remove the arm and blade assembly.
2. Open the tailgate.
3. Remove the motor cover (if equipped) and disconnect the wiring connector.
4. Remove the grommet from the glass.
5. Remove the bracket retaining screws and the motor from the tailgate.
6. To install, reverse the removal procedures.

WINDSHIELD WIPER LINKAGE

Removal and Installation

OMNI, HORIZON, TURMISO AND CHARGER

1. Disconnect the negative battery cable. Remove the wiper arm assemblies.
2. Remove the tie down nuts and washers from the left and right pivots.
3. Remove the wiper motor plastic cover and washer hose attaching clip.
4. Disconnect the wiper motor wiring harness.
5. Remove the 3 bolts that fasten the motor mounting bracket to body.
6. Disengage the pivots from the cowl top mounting positions.
7. Remove the wiper motor, mounting bracket, cranks, pivots and drive links assembly from the cowl plenum chamber. Make certain the pivot marked **L** is positioned to the driver's side of the vehicle.
8. On a workbench, remove the motor from the drive crank.
To Install:
9. Put the assembly together after the service has been performed.
10. Install the wiper motor, mounting bracket, cranks, pivots and linkage into the cowl plenum chamber.
11. Engage the pivots through the cowl top mounting holes and loosely install the pivot shaft nuts and washers.
12. Install 3 bolts to motor mounting bracket.
13. Connect the wiper motor wiring harness.
14. Install the wiper motor plastic cover and attach the washer hose clip.
15. Tighten the tie down nuts on the left and right pivot shafts.
16. Install and adjust the wiper arm assemblies.

EXCEPT OMNI, HORIZON, TURMISO AND CHARGER

1. Park the wiper motor system. Disconnect the negative battery cable.
2. Remove the wiper arms and blades. Disconnect the hoses from the connector.
3. Remove the cowl top plastic screen. Remove the reservoir hose from the T-connector, if equipped.
4. Remove the pivot screws.
5. Remove the wiper motor cover and disconnect the wiring harness.
6. Remove the 3 wiper motor mounting nuts.
7. Push the pivots down into the plenum chamber, pull the motor out until it clears the mounting studs and pull the motor as far to the driver's side (outboard) as it will go. Pull the right

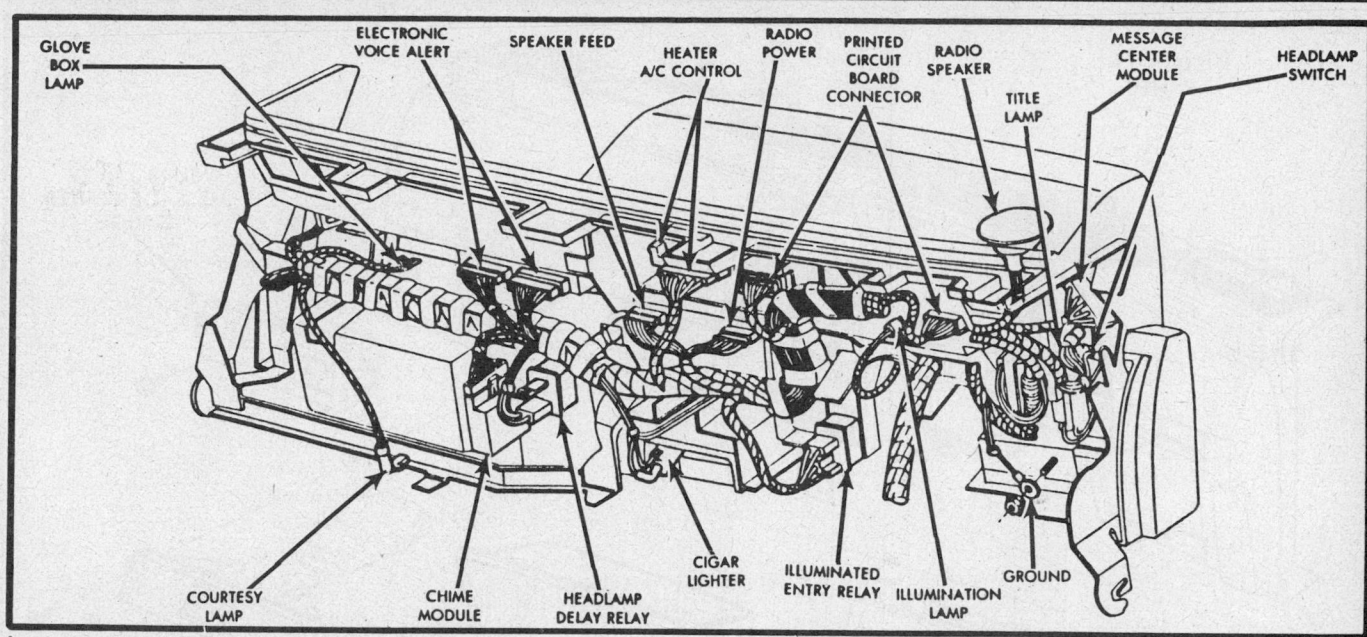

Instrument panel component location, Lancer and LeBaron

pivot and link out through the opening and shift the motor to opposite side (inboard) of the opening to remove the motor, left link and pivot.

8. Clamp the motor crank in a vise and remove the nut from the end of the motor shaft. Do not rotate the motor output shaft from the park position.

To Install:

9. Assemble the linkage to the motor. Make sure the crank fits over the D slot on the motor shaft. Tighten the mounting nut 95 inch lbs. Be sure the motor is still in the park position before assembling to linkage. If not, temporarily connect the motor to wiring and operate the switch to position the motor into park before assembling linkage.

10. Place the left pivot and link into the plenum chamber and slide it all the way to the left (outboard) until the motor clears the studs and crank is behind the sheetmetal. Push the right pivot and link through the opening. Move the assembly right and position the motor on the studs.

11. Install 3 motor mounting nuts and tighten to 55 inch lbs.

12. Connect the wiring to the motor.

13. Install the motor cover and tighten the screws to 35 inch lbs.

14. Attach the reservoir hose to the T-connector (if equipped), through the hole provided in the cowl screen.

15. Use plastic fasteners to install the cowl screen (if equipped).

16. Install the arm and blade assemblies. Connect the arm washer hoses to the T-connector.

17. Connect the negative battery cable and check the starter motor operation.

Instrument Cluster

Refer to "Chilton's Electronic Instrumentation Service Manual" for additional coverage.

Removal and Installation

NOTE: On certain models, after the bezel and mask-lens assemblies have been removed, the gauges are accessible for replacement as required. Extreme care must be exercised to avoid damage to the instrument panel components.

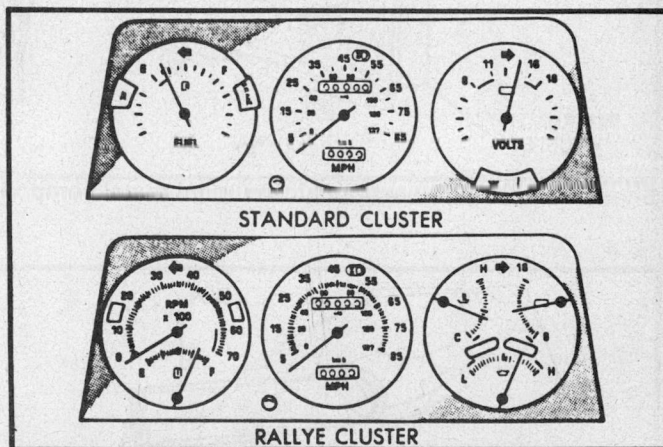

Two types of instrument panel clusters for Omni, Horizon, Turismo, Charger, TC3 and 024 models

OMNI, HORIZON, TURISMO AND CHARGER

1. Disconnect the negative battery cable.

2. Remove the cluster bezel. Remove the masks/lens lower screws, allow the mask/lens to drop slightly and remove, as required.

3. If the cluster is being removed, the mask/lens would be removed with the cluster.

4. Remove the cluster-to-instrument panel screws.

5. Pull the cluster away from the panel, disconnect the speedometer and the wiring connector.

6. Remove the cluster assembly from the instrument panel.

7. To install, reverse the removal procedures.

ARIES, RELIANT, DODGE 400 AND LEBARON

1. Remove the negative battery cable.

2. Place the shift lever in the **1ST** detent position.

3. Remove the upper left and lower cluster bezel screws.

4. Remove the instrument cluster bezel by snapping the bezel off the retaining clips.

5. Remove the instrument panel cluster mask by snapping the mask off the retaining clips.

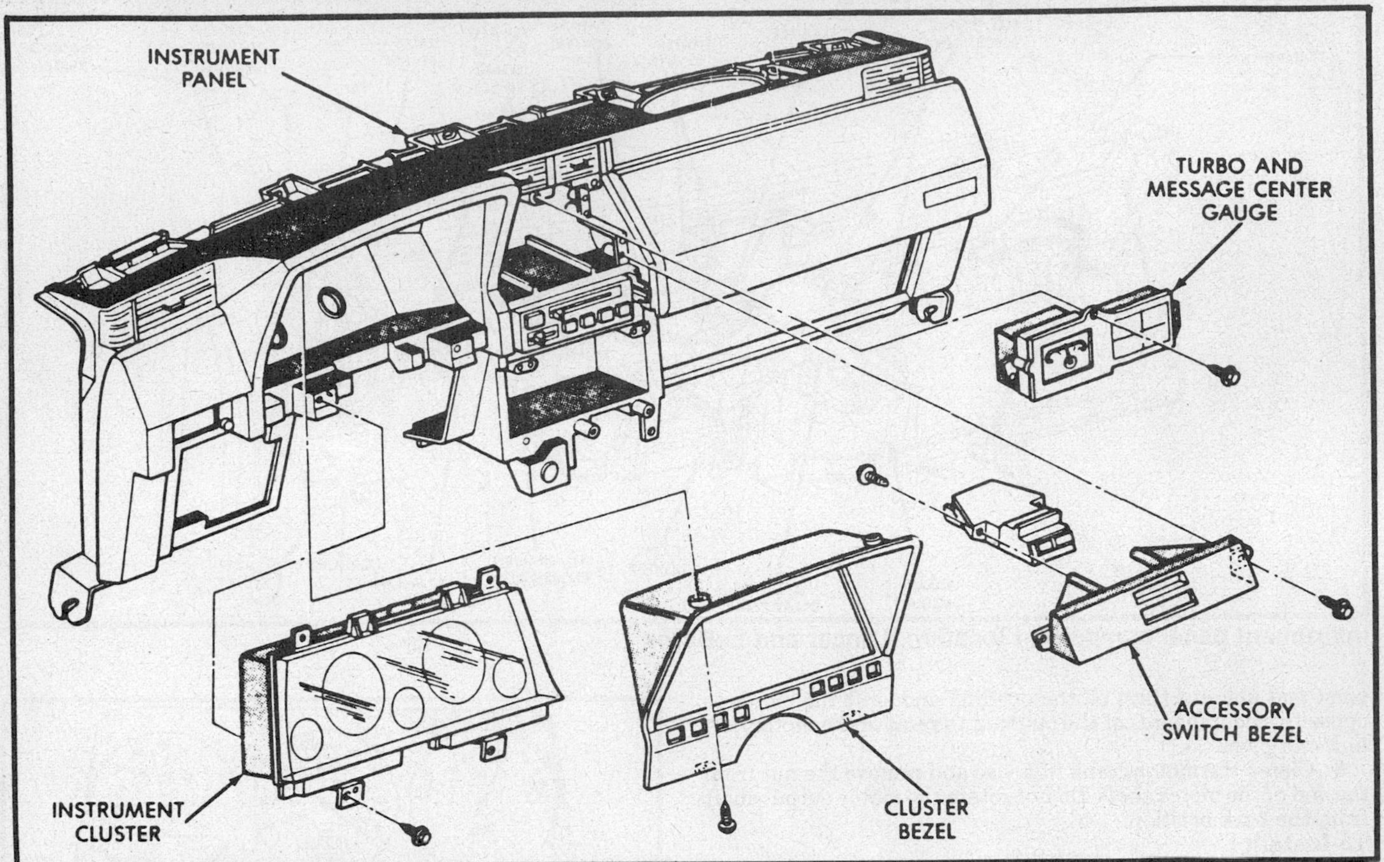

INSTRUMENT PANEL

TURBO AND MESSAGE CENTER GAUGE

ACCESSORY SWITCH BEZEL

INSTRUMENT CLUSTER

CLUSTER BEZEL

Shadow and Sundance upper instrument panel components

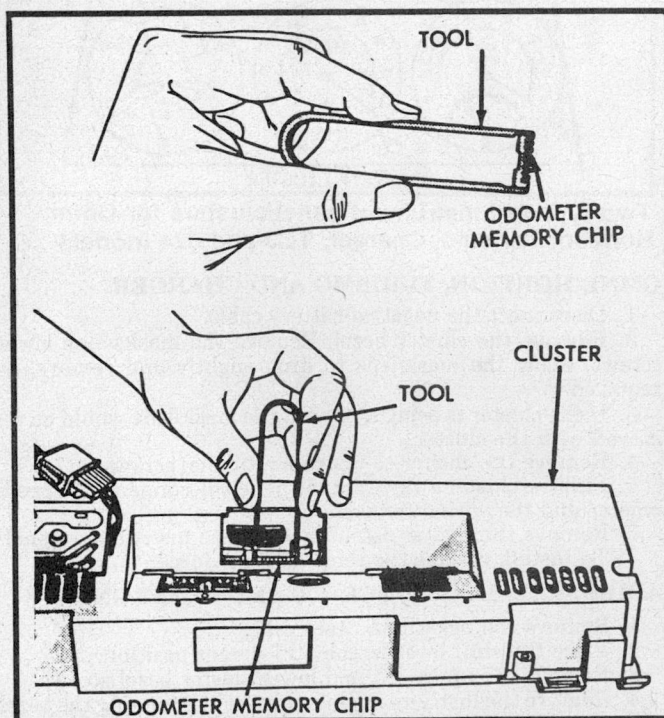

TOOL

ODOMETER MEMORY CHIP

CLUSTER

TOOL

ODOMETER MEMORY CHIP

Removal or installation of odometer memory chip in the electronic cluster assembly

6. Remove the instrument panel top cover mounting screws and lift the edge of the top panel to remove the screws attaching the cluster housing to the base panel.

7. Lift the rearward edge of the top panel and slide the cluster housing rearward.

NOTE: Rearward direction is toward the rear of the vehicle.

8. Reach behind the cluster assembly and disconnect the right and left printed circuit board connector.

9. Disconnect the speedometer cable and remove the cluster assembly.

10. To install, reverse the removal procedures.

CARAVELLE, LANCER, LEBARON GTS, LEBARON, DYNASTY, 600, E-CLASS AND NEW YORKER

NOTE: The electronic cluster is serviced as an assembly. The individual gauges cannot be serviced separately.

1. Disconnect the negative battery cable.

2. Place the shift lever in 1 detent position.

3. Remove the radio knobs and the cluster bezel screws.

4. Remove the bezel by snapping the bezel off of the retaining clips.

5. Remove the cluster mask by snapping the mask off the retaining clips.

NOTE: The electronic cluster is removed and installed in the same manner as the conventional cluster, except for the speedometer cable. When replacing the electronic cluster, the odometer memory chip must be installed into another electronic cluster.

CAVITY	FUSE/COLOR	ITEMS FUSED
1	4 AMP PK	CLUSTER ILLUMINATION, A/C & HEATER, RADIO, EBL SWITCH, TURBO GAUGE, CIGAR LIGHTER, ASH RECEIVER & CONSOLE GEAR SELECTOR
2	20 AMP YL	FUEL PUMP
3		OPEN
4	5 AMP TN	BRAKE WARNING, POWER LOSS, OIL, SEAT BELT & ECONO SHIFT LAMPS; FUEL, TEMPERATURE & VOLTAGE GAUGES; SEAT BELT BUZZER, HEATER, TACHOMETER & SPEED CONTROL
5	20 AMP YL	HAZARD FLASHER
6	10 AMP RD	BACK-UP LAMPS, RADIATOR FAN & EBL RELAYS
7	30 AMP LGN 20 AMP YL	A/C BLOWER MOTOR HEATER BLOWER MOTOR
8	30 AMP C/BRKR	POWER WINDOWS
9	20 AMP YL	GLOVE BOX LAMP, HORN, HORN RELAY, CHIMES, RADIO (MEMORY) & CIGAR LIGHTER
10	20 AMP YL	LICENSE, SIDE MARKER, PARK & TAIL LAMPS, RADIO DISPLAY INTENSITY
11	30 AMP C/BRKR	POWER DOOR LOCKS
12	20 AMP YL	CHMSL, STOP, KEY-IN, DOME, MAP & CARGO LAMPS; TIME DELAY RELAY & POWER MIRRORS
13		OPEN

CAVITY	FUSE/COLOR	ITEMS FUSED
14	20 AMP YL	WINDSHIELD WIPER & WASHER MOTOR
15	10 AMP RD	TURN SIGNALS
16	10 AMP RD	RADIO

AMPS	FUSE	COLOR CODE
3	VT	VIOLET
4	PK	PINK
5	TN	TAN
10	RD	RED
20	YL	YELLOW
25	NAT	NATURAL
30	LG	LIGHT GREEN

Fuse panel and corresponding circuit coverage for Shadow and Sundance

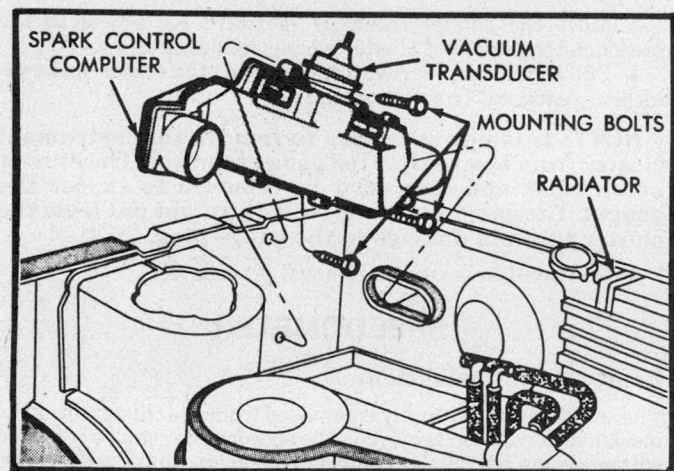

Spark Control Computer (SCC)—typical

6. Remove the rearward screw from the instrument panel upper pad assembly.

7. Lift the rearward edge of the instrument panel upper pad and remove the screws from the top of the cluster.

8. Remove the screws from the bottom of the cluster and lift the rearward edge of the upper pad and pull the cluster outwards.

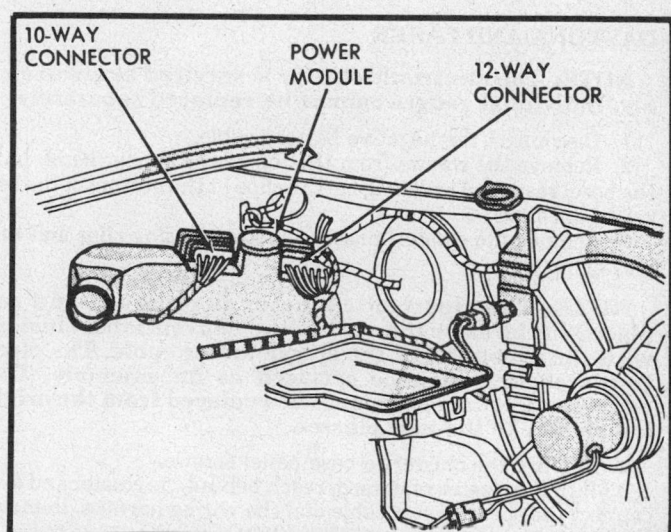

Power module location—EFI models

9. Disconnect the wiring and the speedometer cable from the cluster. Remove the cluster assembly.

10. To install, reverse the removal procedures.

CAVITY	FUSE/COLOR	ITEMS FUSED
1	20 AMP YL	HAZARD FLASHER
2	20 AMP YL	BACK-UP LAMPS, TRIP NAVIGATOR, ELAPSED TIMER FAN RELAY COIL ELECTRONIC VOICE ALERT (11 FUNCTION) TRANSMISSION PRESSURE SWITCH (24 FUNCTION)
3	30 AMP C/BRKR SILVER CAN	POWER WINDOW MOTORS
4	30 AMP LG	A/C, ATC OR HEATER BLOWER MOTOR
5	20 AMP YL	CAVITY 12 (CLUSTER), PARK, TAIL, SIDE MARKER & LICENSE LAMPS; ELECTRONIC DISPLAY INTENSITY & TAIL LAMP OUTAGE
6	20 AMP YL	STOP, DOME, MAP AND CARGO LAMPS; TIME DELAY RELAY, ATC MEMORY ELECTRONIC MONITOR (C-P-24) ELECTRONIC VOICE ALERT (24 FUNCTION), STOP LAMP OUTAGE TOROIDS, BRAKE SENSE, POWER MIRROR MOTORS AND ILLUMINATED ENTRY COIL AND LAMP AND TBI OR TURBO LOGIC MODULE
7	20 AMP YL	GLOVE BOX LAMP; CIGAR LIGHTER, MEMORY FOR RADIO AND ELAPSED TIMER-TRIP NAVIGATOR, ELECTRONIC VOICE ALERT (11 OR 24 FUNCTION), CHIMES, ELECTRONIC CLUSTER, HORN AND RELAY
8	30 AMP C/BRKR SILVER CAN	AIR HORNS & RELAY, POWER SEAT MOTOR & POWER DOOR LOCKS
9	10 AMP TN	RADIO
10	20 AMP YL	TURN SLIGNAL LAMPS; HEATED REAR WINDOW REALY ATC CONTROL AND IN CAR SENSOR
11	20 AMP YL	FRONT WINDSHIELD WIPER AND WASHER AND INTERMITTENT WIPE MODULE

CAVITY	FUSE/COLOR	ITEMS FUSED
12	5 AMP TN	CLUSTER ILLUMINATION LAMPS MECHANICAL OR ELECTRONIC CLUSTER HEATED REAR WINDOW, REAR WASH AND WIPE, A/C AND HEATER CONTROL, RADIO, ASH RECEIVER, CIGAR LIGHTER, ELAPSED TIMER, NAVIGATOR, MESSAGE CENTER, CONSOLE GEAR SELECTOR AND ELECTRONIC DIMMING
13	5 AMP TN	CLUSTER PRINTED CIRCUIT BOARD GAUGES AND WARNING LAMPS, CHIMES, SPEED CONTROL SERVO, INCANDESCENT MESSAGE CENTER, ELECTRONIC VOICE ALERT (11 OR 24 FUNCTION) ELECTRONIC MONITOR ILLUMINATED ENTRY SEAT BELT LAMP ELECTRONIC CLUSTER
14	6 AMP C/BRKR GOLD CAN	REAR WASH WIPE & LIFTGATE RELEASE SOLENOID
15		
16		

AMPS	FUSE	COLOR CODE
3	VT	VILOET
4	PK	PINK
5	TN	TAN
10	RD	RED
20	YL	YELLOW
25	NAT	NATURAL
30	LG	LIGHT GREEN

Fuse panel and corresponding circuit coverage for Daytona and Laser

DAYTONA AND LASER

NOTE: The electronic cluster is serviced as an assembly. Individual gauges cannot be replaced separately.

1. Disconnect the negative battery cable.
2. Remove the screws from the top of the cluster bezel, pull the bezel rearward to disengage the clips at the bottom of the bezel and remove.
3. Remove the cluster mast-to-cluster housing clips and the cluster mask.

NOTE: The electronic cluster is removed and replaced in the same manner as the conventional cluster, with the exception of the speedometer cable. The electronic cluster must be serviced as an assembly. The odometer memory chip must be replaced from the original cluster to the new cluster.

4. Remove the cluster-to-base panel screws.
5. Pull the cluster rearward, reach behind the cluster and disconnect the speedometer cable and the wiring harness. Remove the cluster assembly.
6. To install, reverse the removal procedures.

SHADOW AND SUNDANCE

1. Disconnect the negative battery cable. Remove the instrument cluster bezel.
2. Remove the instrument cluster retaining screw.

3. Move the cluster assembly rearward for access to the speedometer cable and cluster wiring connectors.
4. Pull the cluster rearward and towards the center of the vehicle to remove it from the dash.

NOTE: It is not necessary to remove the instrument cluster from the vehicle for gauge removal. The cluster bezel, mask and lens must be removed to expose the gauges. The gauges must be pulled straight put from the cluster to avoid damage to the gauge pins.

5. To install, reverse the removal procedures.

SPEEDOMETER

Removal and Installation

The speedometer assembly is removed from the cluster after the mask/lens have been removed. The speedometer can be removed without complete cluster removal on certain models. However, because of working clearance, it is suggested to remove the complete cluster assembly and disassemble it on a clean work bench to avoid loss of parts or dropped components.

MEMORY CHIP REPLACEMENT

The odometer memory chip is located on the back of the electronic cluster.

The odometer memory chip must be removed from the electronic cluster assembly and installed into a new cluster, retain-

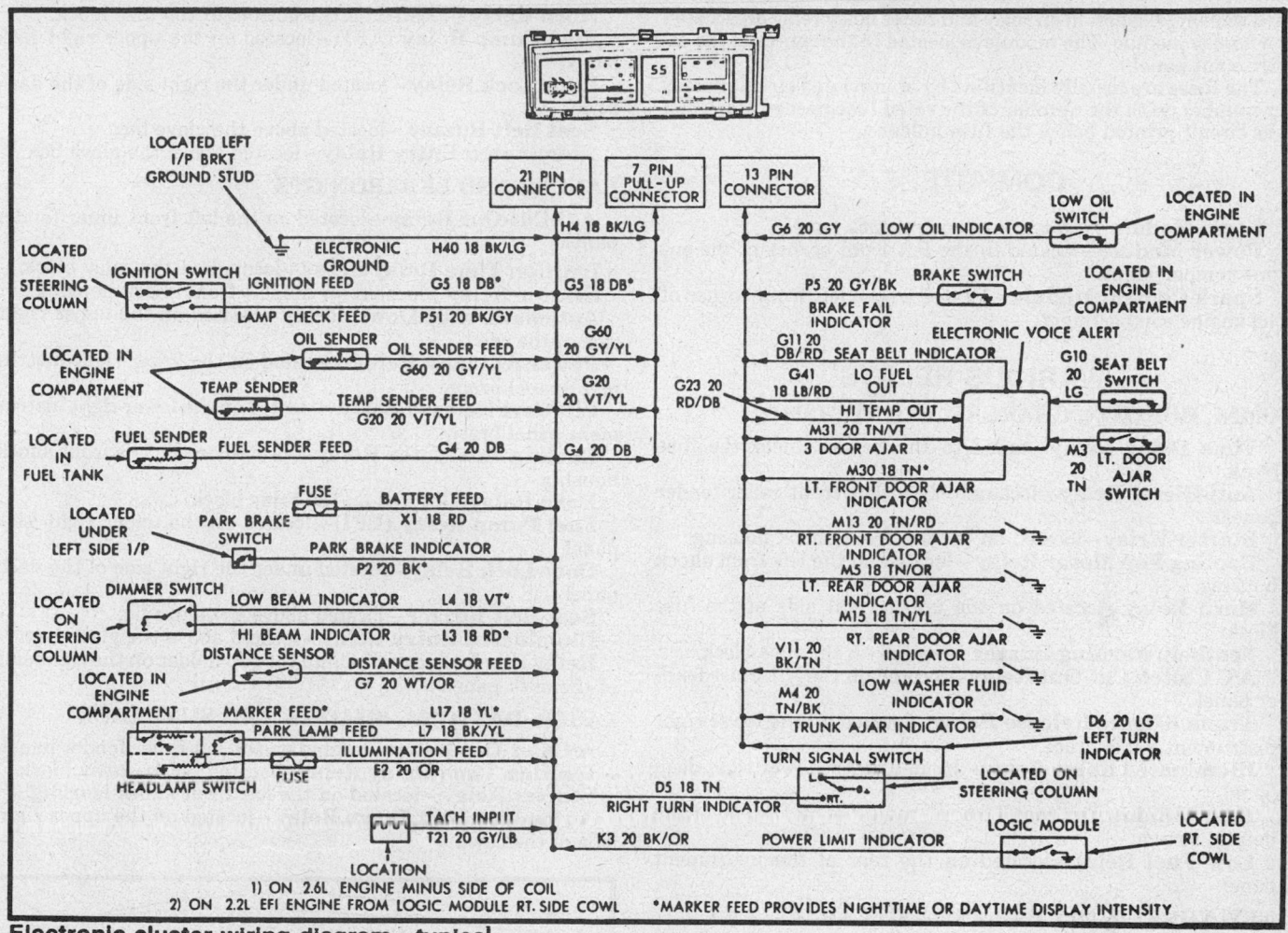

Electronic cluster wiring diagram—typical

ing the vehicle's accumulated mileage. A special tweezer type tool must be used for the removal and installation of the memory chip and its installed position must be noted for proper installation.

ELECTRONIC SPEED SENSOR

The distance sensor is located on the transaxle end of the speedometer. The speed sensor is located on the left inner fender panel.

SPEEDOMETER CABLE

Removal and Installation

The Omni, Turismo, Charger and Horizon use a plastic ferrule which is attached to the panel and is held in place by a metal spring clip. The remaining models use a ferrule on the speedometer cable end which must be released before the cable can be removed.

The speedometer assembly must be removed before servicing of the core or replacement of the housing assembly can be accomplished.

Electrical Circuit Protectors

FUSIBLE LINKS

Fusible links are used to prevent major wire harness damage in

the event of a short circuit or an overload condition in the wiring circuits which are normally not fused, due to carrying high amperage loads or because of their locations within the wiring harness. Each fusible link is of a fixed value for a specific electrical load and should a link fail, the cause of the failure must be determined and repaired prior to installing a new fusible link of the same value. The fusible links are located in the left front fender, below the starter relay.

CIRCUIT BREAKERS

Circuit breakers are used along with the fusible links to protect the various components of the electrical system, such as the headlight, the windshield wipers, electric windows, tailgate front switch and tailgate rear switch. The circuit breakers are located either in the switch or mounted on or near the lower lip of the instrument panel, to the right or left of the steering column.

FUSE PANELS

The fuse panel is used to house the fuses that protect the individual or combined electrical circuits within the vehicle. On most models, the turn signal flasher, the hazard warning flasher and the seat belt warning buzzer/timer are located on the fuse panel for quick identification and replacement. On Sundance, Shadow, LeBaron GTS and Lancer, the turn signal flasher, hazard warning flasher, horn relay and timer delay relay are located on a relay module. The module is located in the center of the instrument panel.

The fuses are usually identified by abbreviated circuit names or number, with the number of the rated fuse needed to protect the circuit printed below the fuse holder.

COMPUTERS

Logic Module—located in the right kick panel.
Power Module—located in the left front corner of the engine compartment.
Spark Control Module—located in the left front corner of the engine compartment.

VARIOUS RELAYS

OMNI, HORIZON, CHARGER AND TURISMO

Time Delay Relay—taped to the harness near the fuse block.
Anti-Diesel Relay—located on the left front inner fender panel.
Starter Relay—located on the left front shock housing.
Cooling Fan Motor Relay—located on the left front shock housing.
Horn Relay—located on the upper right side of the fuse block.
Seatbelt Warning Buzzer—located on the fuse block.
A/C Clutch Cut-Out Relay—located on the left inner fender panel.
Trunk/liftgate Release Relay—located on the lower right instrument panel brace.
Illuminated Entry Relay—located on the lower right dash panel.
Rear Window Defrost Timer—mounted on the end of the defrost switch.
Low Fuel Relay—located on the rear of the instrument panel

NEW YORKER, 600, E CLASS AND CARAVELLE

A/C Cut-Out Relay—located on the left front inner fender panel.
Ignition Time Delay Relay—located on the bottom of the fuse block.
Starter Relay—located on the left front shock housing.
Automatic Shut Down Relay—located on the upper right side of the cowl.
Power antenna Relay—located on the lower right instrument panel brace.
Lift Gate Release Relay—located on the lower right instrument panel brace.
Cooling Fan Motor Relay—located on the left front shock housing.
Horn Relay—located on the bottom of the fuse block.
Fuel Pump Relay (EFI)—located on the upper right kick panel.

ARIES, LEBARON AND RELIANT

A/C Cut-Out Relay—located on the left front inner fender panel.
Ignition Time Delay Relay—located above the fuse block.
Starter Relay—located on the left front shock housing.
Automatic Shut Down Relay—located on the upper right side of the cowl.
Power Antenna Relay—located on the lower right instrument panel brace.
Lift Gate Release Relay—located on the lower right instrument panel brace.
Cooling Fan Motor Relay—located on the left front shock housing.

Horn Relay—located on the bottom of the fuse block.
Fuel Pump Relay (EFI)—located on the upper right kick panel.
Door Lock Relay—located under the right side of the dash panel.
Seat Belt Buzzer—located above the glove box.
Illuminated Entry Relay—located above the glove box.

LANCER AND LEBARON GTS

A/C Cut-Out Relay—located on the left front inner fender panel.
Ignition Time Delay Relay—located on the relay block.
Starter Relay—located on the left front shock housing.
Automatic shut Down Relay—located on the upper right side of the cowl.
Power Antenna Relay—located on the lower right instrument panel brace.
Lift Gate Release Relay—located on the lower right instrument panel brace
Cooling Fan Motor Relay—located on the left front shock housing.
Horn Relay—located on the relay block.
Fuel Pump Relay (EFI)—located on the upper right kick panel.
Door Lock Relay—located under the right side of the dash panel.
Seat Belt Buzzer—located above the glove box.
Illuminated Entry Relay—located above the glove box.
Relay Block—located behind the cup holder on the right side of the dash panel.

LASER, DAYTONA, SHADOW AND SUNDANCE

A/C Cut-Out Relay—located on the left inner fender panel.
Ignition Time Delay Relay—located on the relay block.
Starter Relay—located on the left front shock housing.
Automatic Shut Down Relay—located on the upper right side of the cowl.

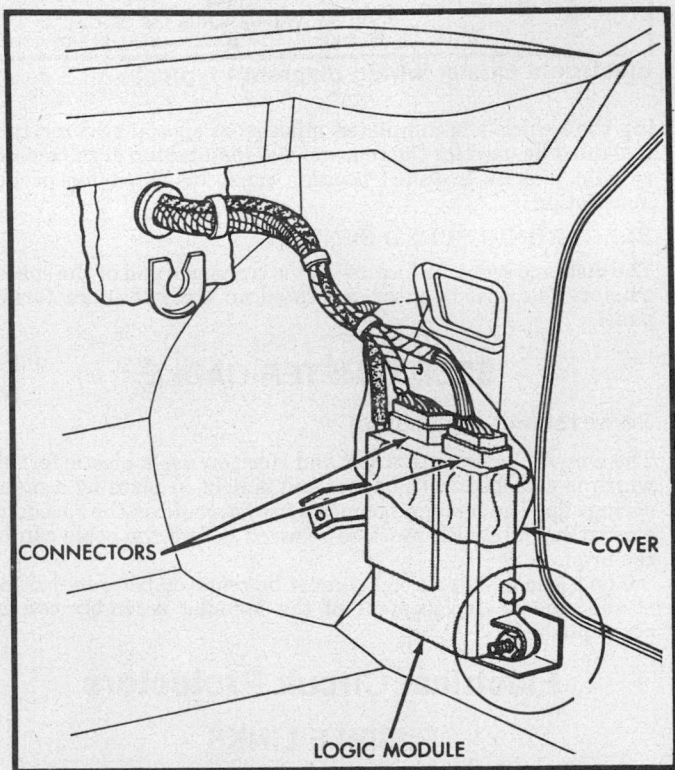

CONNECTORS   COVER

LOGIC MODULE

Logic module location—typical

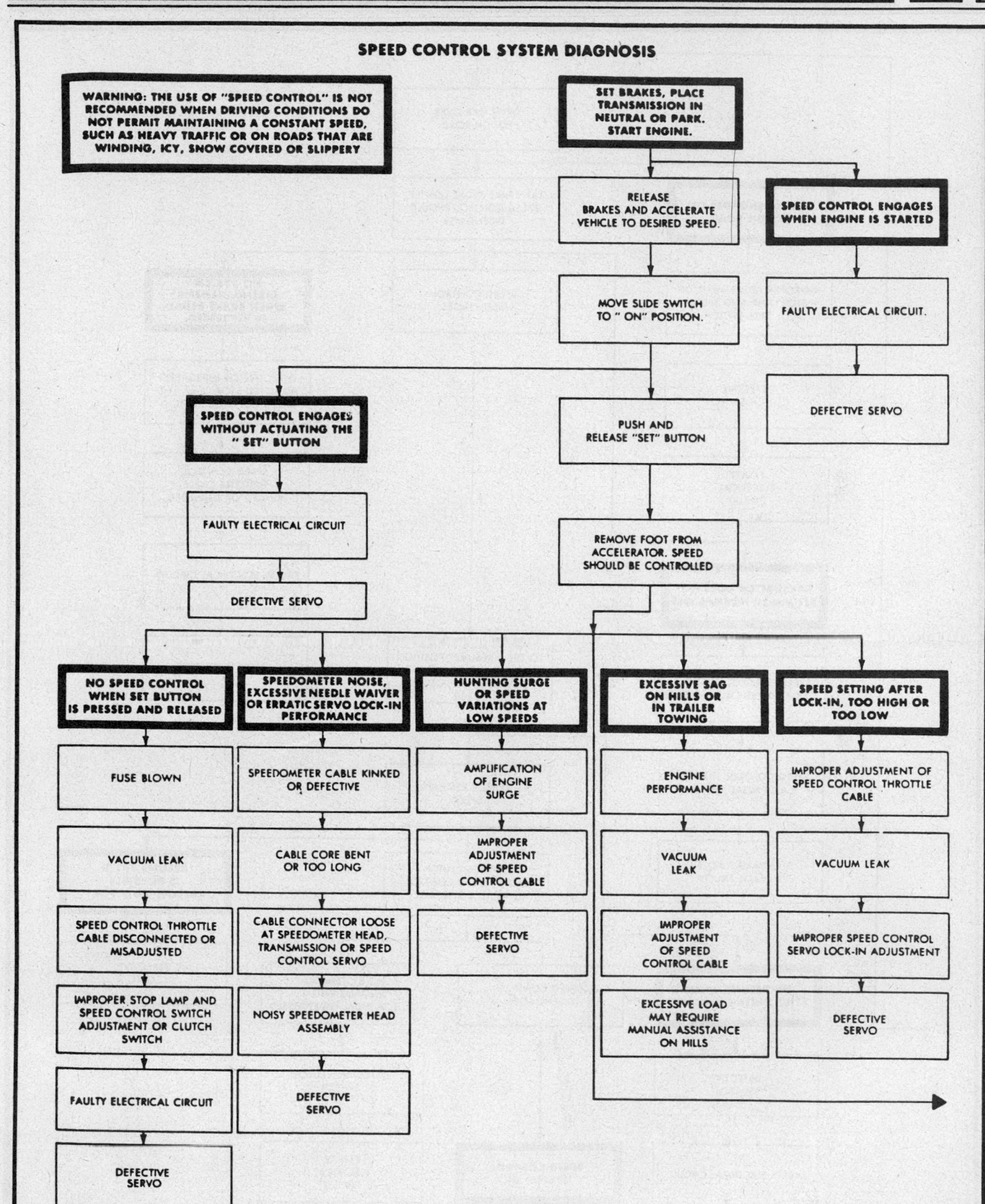

Speed control troubleshooting chart

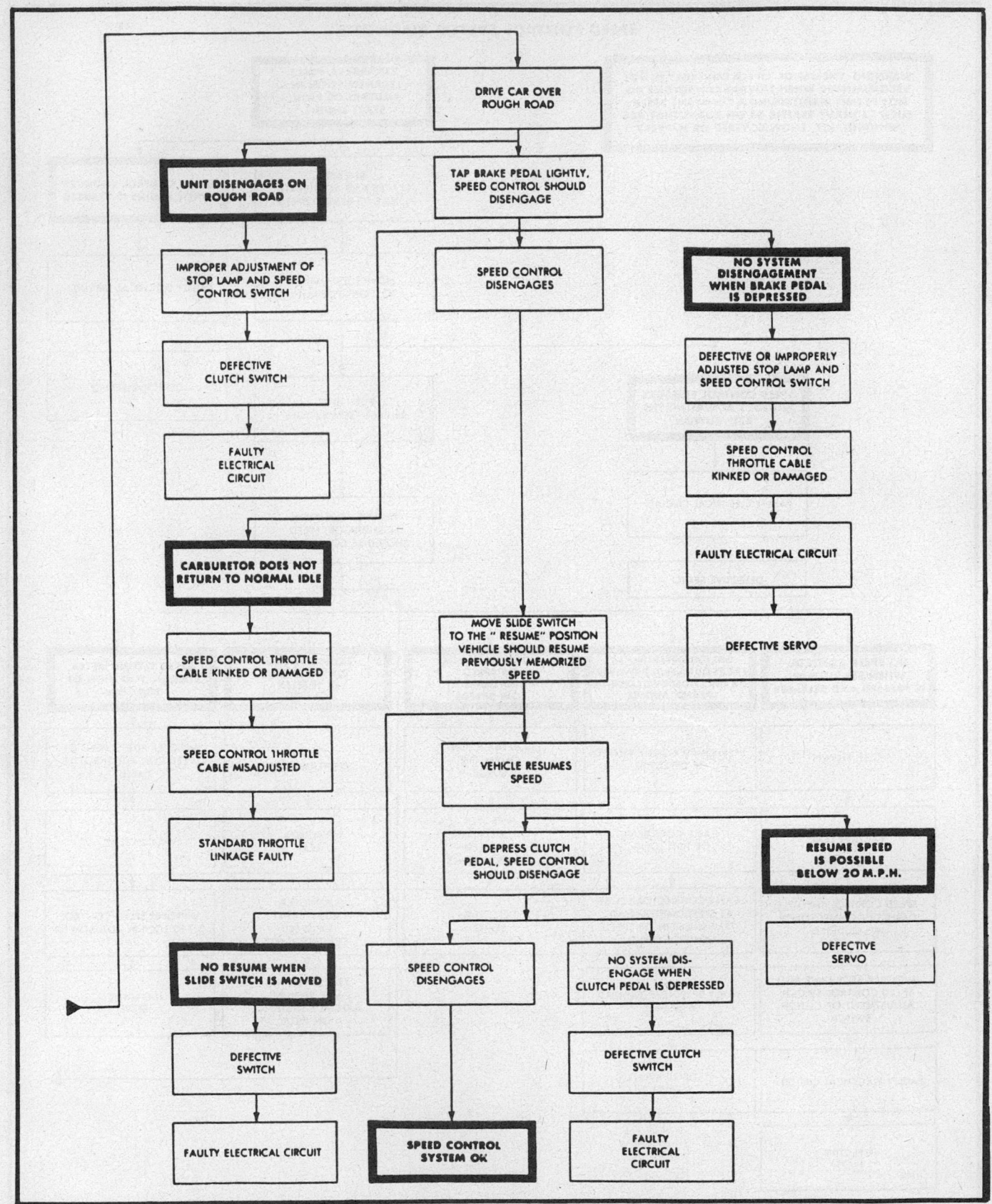

Speed control troubleshooting chart, continued

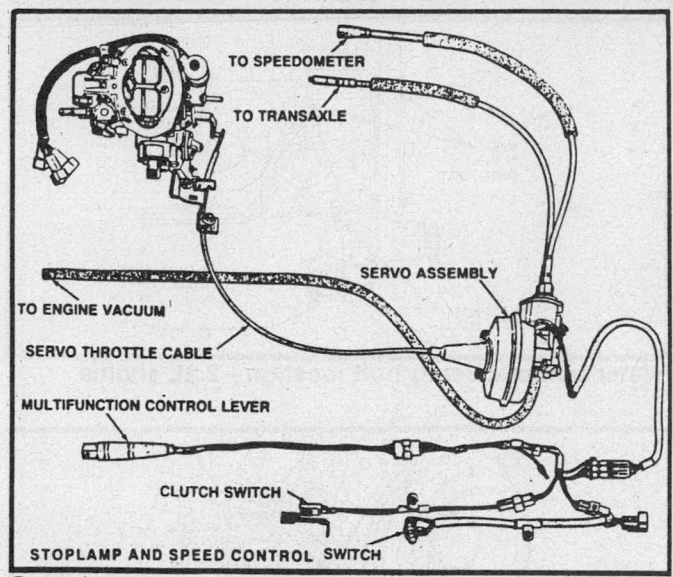

TO SPEEDOMETER

TO TRANSAXLE

SERVO ASSEMBLY

TO ENGINE VACUUM

SERVO THROTTLE CABLE

MULTIFUNCTION CONTROL LEVER

CLUTCH SWITCH

STOPLAMP AND SPEED CONTROL SWITCH

Speed control components—typical

Power Antenna Relay—located on the lower right instrument panel brace.

Lift Gate Release Relay—located on the lower right instrument panel brace.

Cooling Fan Motor Relay—located on the left front shock housing.

Horn Relay—located on the relay block.

Fuel Pump Relay (EFI)—located on the upper right kick panel.

Door Lock Relay—located under the right side of the dash panel.

Seat Belt Buzzer—located above the glove box.

Illuminated Entry Relay—located above the glove box.

Relay Block—located above the glove box.

Relay Block—located behind the cup holder on the right side of the dash panel.

TURN SIGNAL FLASHER

On the Omni, Horizon, Charger and Turismo, the turn signal flasher is located on the upper right side of the fuse block.

On the Aries, LeBaron, Reliant, New Yorker, Dynasty, 600, E-Class and Caravelle, the turn signal flasher is located on the bottom of the fuse block.

On the Lancer, LeBaron GTS, Laser, Daytona, Shadow and Sundance, the turn signal flasher is located on the relay block.

HAZARD WARNING FLASHER

On the Omni, Horizon, Charger and Turismo, the hazard flasher is located on the upper right side of the fuse block.

On the Aries, LeBaron, Reliant, New Yorker, 600, E-Class and Caravelle, the hazard flasher is located on the bottom of the fuse block.

On the Lancer, LeBaron GTS, Laser, Daytona, Shadow and Sundance, the hazard flasher is located on the relay block.

Speed Controls

Refer to "Chilton's Chassis Electronics Service Manual" for additional coverage.

COMPONENTS

Cable Adjustment

1. Start and run the engine until it reaches normal operating temperature.
2. Remove the snapring from the cable clevis to throttle lever stud.
3. The clearance between the throttle lever stud and the cable clevis should be $\frac{1}{16}$ in. (1.66mm).
4. To adjust, loosen the cable retaining clamp nut, located approximately 7 in. from the throttle lever stud.
5. Pull all slack out of the cable, using the head of the throttle stud as a gauge.

NOTE: Do not pull the cable so tight that it moves the throttle away from the curb idle position.

6. Torque the retaining clamp nut to 45 ft. lbs. and move the cable clevis back on the round portion of the throttle lever stud.
7. Install the snapring.

Servo Lock-In Screw Adjustment

NOTE: This screw should not be adjusted to compensate for abnormal conditions, such as poor engine performance, power to weight ratio (trailering) or improper slack in throttle control cable.

1. If the speed drops more than 2–3 mph when the speed control is activated, turn the lock-in screw, located on the servo, counterclockwise approximately ¼ turn per 1 mph correction required.
2. If the speed increases 2–3 mph when the speed control is activated, the lock-in screw should be turned clockwise approximately ¼ turn per 1 mph correction required.

NOTE: This adjustment must not exceed 2 turns in either direction or damage to the unit may occur.

COOLING AND HEATING SYSTEMS

Water Pump

Removal and Installation

1.6L ENGINE

1. Disconnect the negative battery cable.
2. Remove the radiator cap and drain the cooling system through the water pump drain plug.
3. Disconnect the coolant hose at the pump.
4. Loosen the water pump drive belt. Remove the retaining screws and remove the water pump pulley.
5. Remove the pump-to-engine extension screws and remove the water pump assembly.

To Install:

6. Using a new gasket, reverse the removal procedures. Torque the pump extension bolts to 9 ft. lbs. and the pump drain plug to 13 ft. lbs.
7. Adjust the belt tension, so it can be depressed ¼ in., under light thumb pressure, on the longest span between the 2 pulleys.

1.8L ENGINE

The water pump is located on the right side of the engine under the timing cover.

1. Disconnect the negative battery cable.
2. Remove the crankshaft sprocket.

Exploded view of the water pump—1.8L engine

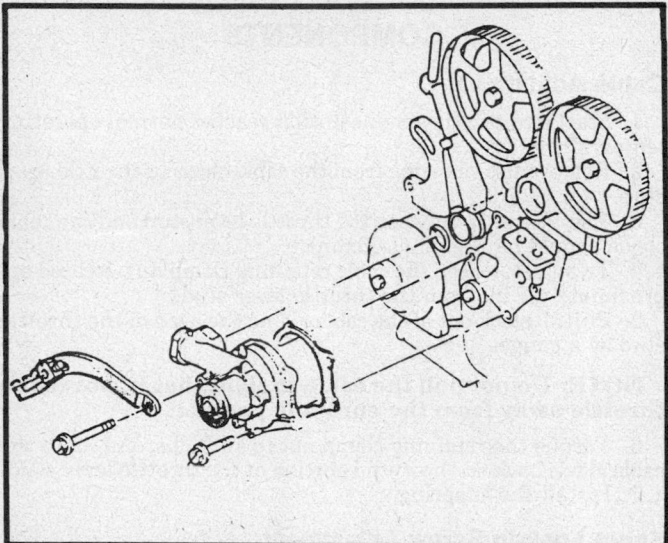

Exploded view of the water pump—2.0L engine

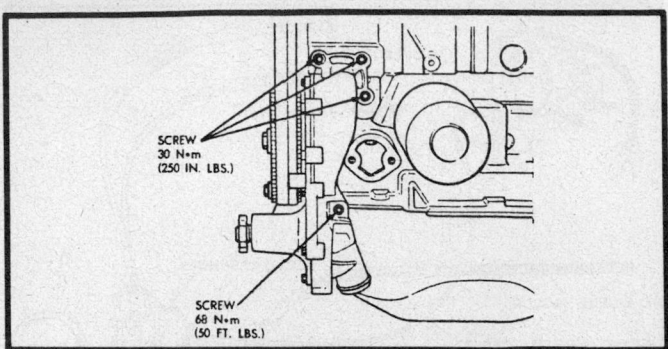

SCREW
30 N•m
(250 IN. LBS.)

SCREW
68 N•m
(50 FT. LBS.)

Water pump/housing bolt location—2.2L engine

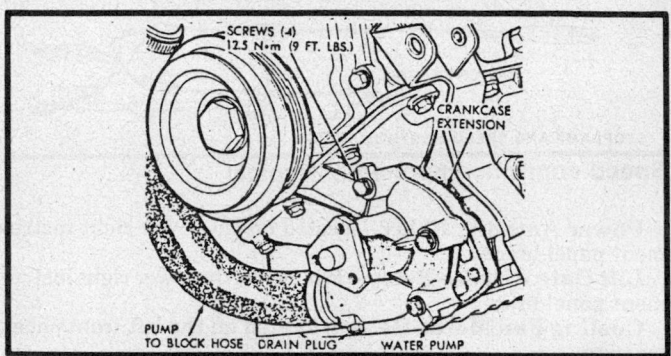

SCREWS (4)
12.5 N•m (9 FT. LBS.)

CRANKCASE
EXTENSION

PUMP
TO BLOCK HOSE   DRAIN PLUG   WATER PUMP

Water pump location—1.6L engine

3. Drain the cooling system. Remove the inner (small) timing belt and tensioner.

4. Remove the radiator hose from the water pump.

5. Remove the water pump-to-engine bolts, the pump from the engine and the O-ring from the water pipe.

6. Clean the gasket mounting surfaces. Inspect the water pump for cracks, wear and/or damage; replace the pump, if necessary.

To Install:

7. Using a new gasket and an new O-ring (coat it with water), reverse the removal procedures. Torque the water pump-to-engine bolts to 9–10 ft. lbs. (12–15 Nm) and the alternator brace/water pump-to-engine bolt to 15–19 ft. lbs. (20–27 Nm).

8. Refill the cooling system. Start the engine, allow it to reach normal operating temperatures and check for leaks.

2.0L ENGINE

The water pump is located on the right side of the engine under the timing cover.

1. Disconnect the negative battery cable.

2. Remove the crankshaft sprocket.

3. Drain the cooling system. Remove the inner (small) timing belt and tensioner.

4. Remove the radiator hose from the water pump.

5. Remove the alternator brace, the water pump-to-engine bolts and the pump from the engine.

6. Clean the gasket mounting surfaces. Inspect the water pump for cracks, wear and/or damage; replace the pump, if necessary.

To Install:

7. Using a new gasket, reverse the removal procedures. Torque the:

Water pump-to-engine bolts to 9–10 ft. lbs. (12–15 Nm).

Alternator brace/water pump-to-engine bolt to 15–19 ft. lbs. (20–27 Nm).

8. Refill the cooling system. Start the engine, allow it to reach normal operating temperatures and check for leaks.

2.2L AND 2.5L ENGINES

1. Disconnect the negative battery cable and drain the cooling system.

2. Remove the upper radiator hose.

3. Without discharging the air conditioning system, remove the compressor from the engine brackets and support it out of the way.

4. Remove the alternator from the engine and support it aside.

5. Disconnect the lower radiator and bypass hoses. Remove the water pump mounting bolts and the water pump.

To Install:

6. Reverse the removal procedures. Torque the top retaining screws to 20 ft. lbs. and the lower screw to 50 ft. lbs.

7. Adjust the belt tension, so the belt can be depressed ¼ in., under light thumb pressure, on the longest span between the 2 pulleys.

3.0L ENGINE

The water pump is driven by the timing belt on this engine. To service the water pump the timing cover and the timing belt must first be removed.

1. Disconnect the negative battery cable. Remove the timing belt from the water pump pulley.

2. Drain the cooling system.

3. Remove the water pump mounting bolts, separate the pump from the water inlet pipe and remove the pump from the engine.

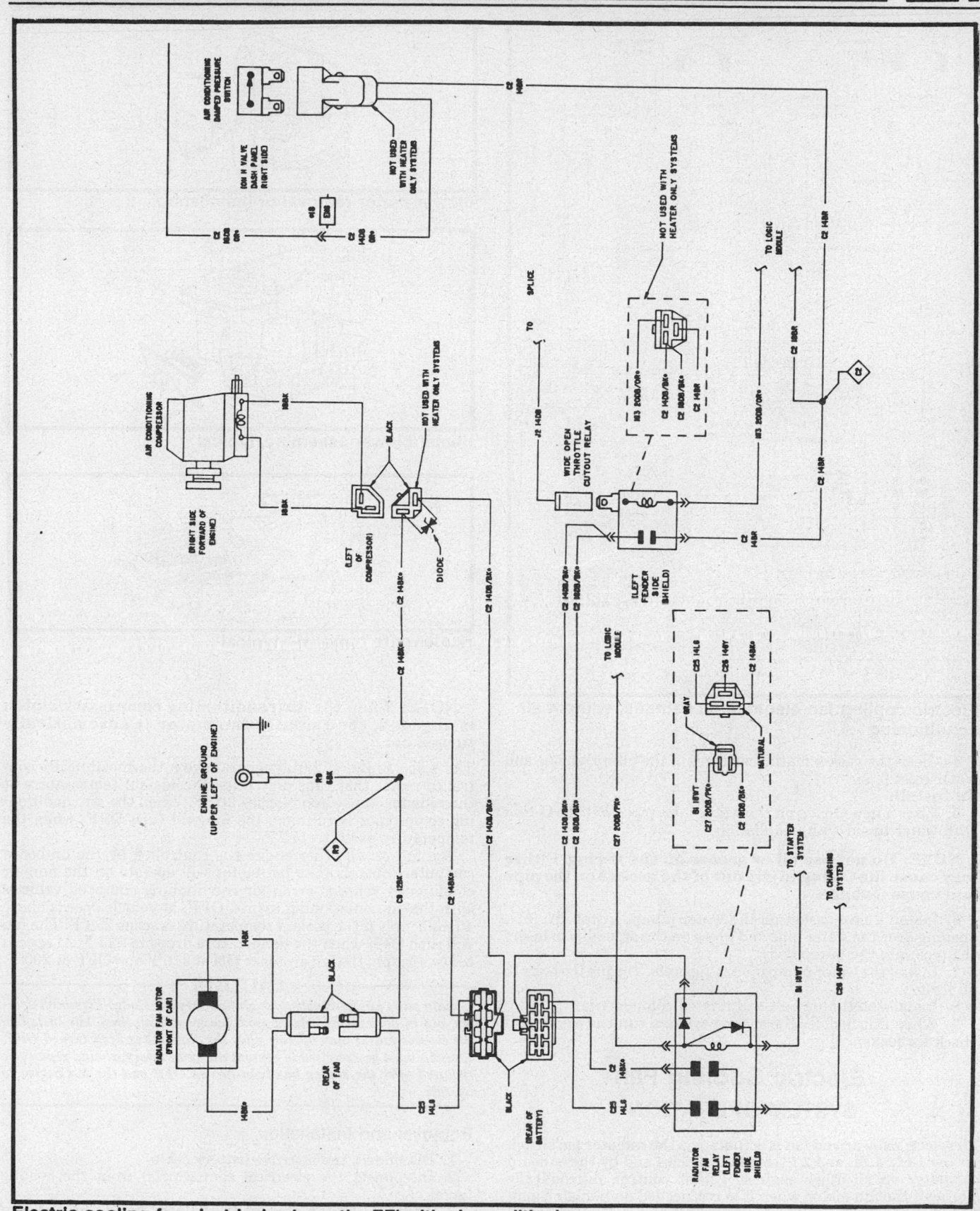

Electric cooling fan electrical schematic, EFI with air conditioning

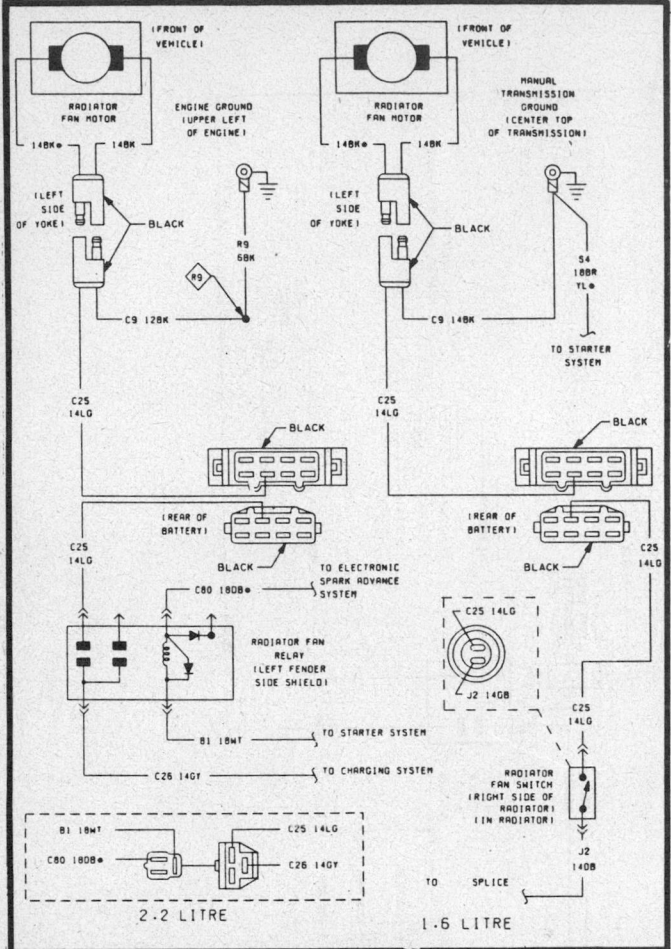

Electric cooling fan electrical schematic, without air conditioning

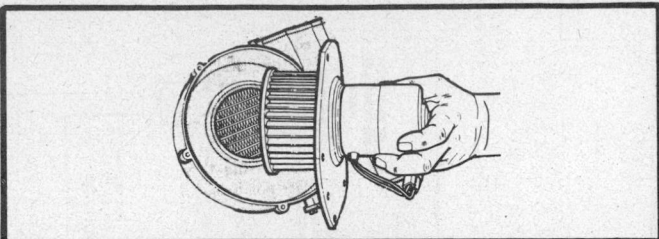

Blower motor removal or installation

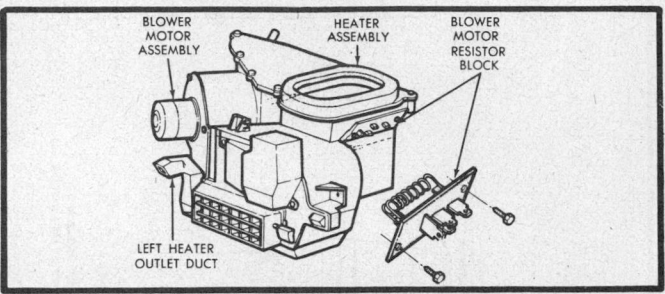

Heater/blower assembly, typical

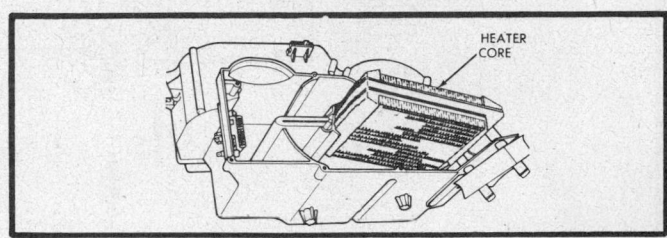

Heater core removal—typical

4. Clean the gasket mating surfaces of the pump, engine and water inlet pipe.

To Install:

5. Place a new O-ring on the water inlet pipe. Wet the O-ring with water to aid with installation.

NOTE: Do not use oil or grease on the O-ring. Either may cause the O-ring to slip out of the groove on the pipe and cause leakage.

6. Install a new gasket on the water pump. Install the inlet opening over the water pipe and press on the assembly to insert the pipe into the pump body.

7. Install the water pump mounting bolts. Torque the bolts to 20 ft. lbs.

8. Install the timing belt and related components.

9. When finished, fill the cooling system, run the engine and check for leaks.

Electric Cooling Fan
SYSTEM OPERATION

The electrically driven fan is actuated by the radiator fan switch on the 1.6L, 1.8L and 2.0L engine vehicles and by the onboard computer on all other engines. Either control automatically shuts off the fan motor when it is not needed on non-air conditioned vehicles, or air conditioned vehicles when the air condition is turned **OFF**.

NOTE: When the air conditioning compressor clutch is engaged, the radiator fan motor is automatically turned on.

The 1.6L, 1.8L and 2.0L engines have a thermostatically controlled motor that runs only when the coolant temperature at the radiator fan switch reaches 207°F. When the air conditioning compressor is running, the fan will turn **OFF**, when the temperature drops to 175°F.

The fan on all other engines is controlled by the on-board computer controls. The fan motor will operate on the non-air conditioned vehicles or on air conditioning equipped vehicles with the air conditioning turned **OFF**, at vehicle speeds above 40 mph, only if the coolant temperature reaches 230°F. The fan will turn **OFF** when the temperature drops to 220°F. At speeds below 40 mph, the fan switches **ON** at 210°F and **OFF** at 200°F.

─────────────── **CAUTION** ───────────────

Certain parts kits available through the Chrysler/Dodge/Plymouth dealers, aid in driveability related modifications. With these kits installed, the electric fan(s) may operate after the engine has been turned OFF. Caution must be exercised to prevent personal injury, should repairs be required after the engine has been turned OFF and the fan begins to operate.

Removal and Installation

1. Disconnect the negative battery cable.
2. Disconnect the electrical connector(s) from the cooling fan(s).
3. Remove the fan/shroud-to-radiator bolts and the fan/shroud assembly.

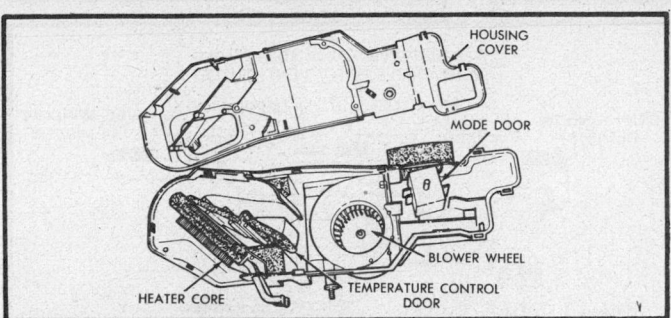

HOUSING COVER

MODE DOOR

BLOWER WHEEL

HEATER CORE

TEMPERATURE CONTROL DOOR

Heater core location—typical

4. If necessary, remove the cooling fan(s) from the shroud.
5. To install, reverse the removal procedures.

Testing

1. Disconnect the negative battery cable and the fan motor connector.
2. Connect jumper wires to 12V battery source observing polarities.
3. If the fan runs, the motor is functioning properly. If fan does not run, replace the motor.

RADIATOR FAN SWITCH

1.6L, 1.8L and 2.0L Engines

The radiator fan switch is located in the left hand radiator tank and is internally isolated from the radiator. The switch is normally open and contains a bi-metal contact arm to close the switch when the coolant temperature reaches a temperature of approximately 200°F.

NOTE: If the fan motor turns OFF and ON, the fan switch does not have to be tested.

To check the fan motor switch, use the following procedure:
1. Disconnect the negative battery cable. and the wiring connector to the fan switch and install a jumper wire in the female connector. This will simulate a closed fan switch at any temperature.
2. If the fan does not operate with the ignition switch **ON**, the problem is elsewhere.

Switch Calibration

1. Disconnect the negative battery cable.
2. Remove the switch from the radiator and immerse the conduction portion of the switch (not the electrical terminals) into a circulation oil bath, heater to 212°F.
3. Use a continuity light to determine if the switch is closed.
4. Using a continuity light, lower the temperature to at least 170°F, to assure that the switch opens.

2.2L AND 2.5L ENGINES

1986–89 2.2L engines no longer use a temperature sensing switch in the radiator. For both the 2.2L and 2.5L engines, the fan is controlled by the on-board computer, as the coolant temperature is sensed by the computer's temperature sensor. This sensor is the same for turbocharged and TBI, but with carbureted engines, 2 thermistor sensors are used, 1 of which is for the cooling system fan.

Switching through the on-board computer provides fan control for the following conditions:
1. The fan will not operate during cranking until the engine starts, no matter what the coolant temperature is.
2. The fan will always run when the air conditioning clutch is engaged as on the previous models.
3. On non-air conditioned vehicles or with air conditioning **OFF**, the fan will run at vehicle speeds above approximately 40

mph, only if the coolant temperature reaches 230°F and will turn **OFF** when the temperature drops to approximately 220°F.
4. Models with turbochargers or TBI engines also include a method to help prevent steaming (water evaporated by hot water circulating through the radiator, evaporating moisture on the outside of the radiator and when there is no ram air to blow it under the vehicle) the fan will operate only between 100–195°F coolant temperature and only at idle, below 60°F ambient temperature and at 0 vehicle speed for only 3 minutes.
5. On turbocharged or TBI engines equipped with on-board diagnostic indicators, the circuitry and temperature sensors are diagnosed by the diagnostic indicator.

Removal and Installation

1. Disconnect the negative battery cable.
2. Remove the switch connector.
3. Remove fan switch.
4. Reverse procedure for installation.

ELECTRIC FAN RELAY

Testing

1.6L, 1.8L AND 2.0L ENGINES

The relay is mounted on the left shock housing. If the fan is not operating and the relay is suspected, replace it with a good relay. Remove the connector from the radiator fan switch and insert jumper wires into both connector terminals. This operation eliminates the need to raise the coolant temperature to 193–207°F., in order to close the radiator fan switch. Turn the ignition key to the **ACC** position. If the fan operates correctly, the replaced relay is at fault. It must be understood that the fan also operates whenever the air conditioning compressor operates, regardless of the engine coolant temperature.

2.2, 2.5L AND 3.0L ENGINES

The relay is mounted on the left shock housing. If the fan is not operating and the relay is suspected, replace it with a good relay. Turn the ignition switch and air conditioner **ON**. If the fan operates correctly, the replaced relay is at fault.

Blower Motor

NOTE: If equipped with air conditioning, the blower motor is located inside the heater/evaporator unit. The unit must be removed from the vehicle and disassembled to remove the blower motor.

Removal and Installation

1. Disconnect the negative battery cable.
2. Remove the blower motor feed and ground wires. The ground wire is attached to the A/C unit support brace screw.
3. Remove the wires from the retaining clip on the recirculating housing.
4. Remove the blower motor vent tube from the air conditioning unit, if equipped. The vent tube will remain attached to the blower motor.
5. Remove the blower motor mounting nuts and remove the motor assembly from the recirculating housing unit.
6. Remove the spring tension clip from the blower motor shaft and lift off the fan cage.
To Install:
7. Install the fan cage and retaining clip on the new motor. Make sure the motor rotates freely and the clip is on tight.
8. Installation is the reverse of the removal procedure.

Heater Core

Refer to "Chilton's Auto Heating and Air Conditioning Manual" for additional coverage.

Removal and Installation

WITH AIR CONDITIONING

Omni, Horizon, Turismo and Charger

1. Discharge the air conditioning refrigerant system.
2. Drain the cooling system.
3. Disconnect the negative battery cable.
4. Disconnect the temperature door cable from evaporator heater assembly.
5. Remove the glove box and door.
6. Disconnect the blower motor feed wire and anti-diesel relay wires.
7. Remove the central air duct cover from the central air distributor duct.
8. Remove the screws securing the central air conditioning air distributor duct. Remove the duct from under the dash panel.
9. Remove the defroster duct adaptor.
10. Disconnect the heater hoses. Remove the condenser drain tube from unit.
11. Disconnect the vacuum lines at the engine intake manifold and water valve.
12. Remove the unit to dash retaining nuts.
13. Remove the panel support bracket.
14. Remove the right side cowl lower panel. Remove the top cover of the instrument panel. Remove all but the left panel-to-fenceline screws.
15. Remove the instrument panel pivot bracket screw from the right side.
16. Remove the screws securing the lower instrument panel and steering column, if required.
17. Pull the carpet rearward as far as possible.
18. Remove the nut from the air conditioning-to-plenum mounting brace and blower motor ground cable.
19. Support the unit and remove the brace from its stud.
20. Lift the unit and pull it rearward as far as possible to clear the dash panel and liner. Pull rearward on the lower instrument panel to gain enough clearance to remove the unit.

NOTE: This operation may require assistance.

21. Slowly lower the unit to floor and slide it rearward, out from the under dash panel.
22. Remove the unit from the vehicle.
23. With the unit on a workbench, remove the nut from the mode door actuator arm, on the top cover. Remove the retaining clips from the front edge of the cover.
24. Remove the mode door actuator-to-cover screws and the actuator.
25. Remove the cover-to-heater evaporator assembly screws and the cover.
26. Lift the mode door out of the unit.
27. Remove the heater core tube retaining bracket and screw. Lift the heater core out of the unit.
28. To install, reverse the removal procedures. Refill the cooling system, run the engine, check for leaks and check the heater operation when finished.

Except Omni, Horizon, Turismo and Charger

1. Disconnect the negative battery cable. Discharge the air conditioning system and drain the cooling system.
2. Disconnect the heater hoses at the heater core. Plug the core tube and hose openings.
3. Disconnect the vacuum lines at the intake manifold and water valve.
4. Remove the right side scuff plate and cowl side trim panel.
5. Remove the glove box assembly, air conditioning controls, console and the forward console mounting bracket, if equipped.
6. Remove the center distribution tube and pull the defroster adapter from under the panel.

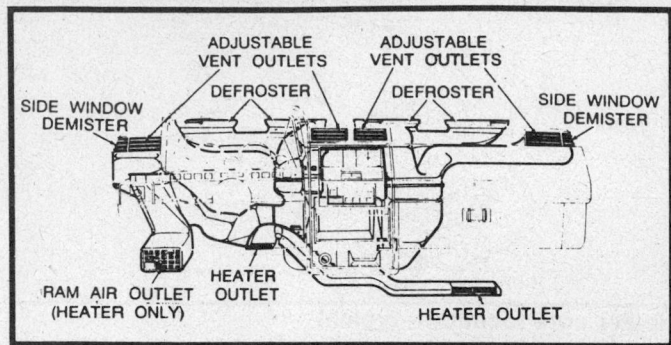

Heating and ventilating system—Sundance and Shadow

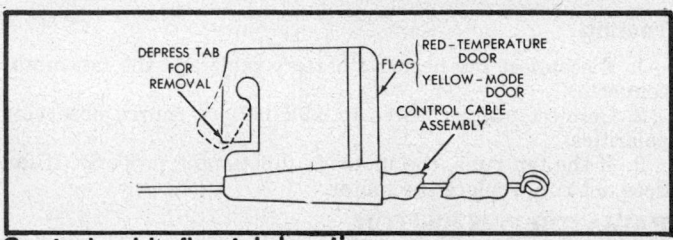

Control cable flag tab location

7. Remove the Corbin clamp (spring clamp) and condensation drain tube.
8. Disconnect the unit from the wiring harness.
9. Remove and label the control cables by depressing the tab on the flag and pulling the flag out of the receiver on the evaporator/heater assembly.
10. Remove the right side cowl to plenum brace.
11. Pull the carpet back from the underside of the unit.
12. Remove the hanger strap-to-unit screw and the unit-to-firewall nuts from the engine side.
13. Pull the unit rearward until the studs clear the dash liner. Allow the unit to drop vertically, until it comes in contact with the converter tunnel.
14. Rotate the unit around the instrument panel lower reinforcement, making sure not to allow the unit to slide in either direction.
15. Remove the mode door actuator arm nut from the top cover and the retaining clips from the front edge of the cover.
16. Remove the cover-to-assembly screws, the cover and the mode door.
17. Remove the heater core tube retaining bracket screw and lift the core from the housing.
18. The assembly of the unit is the reverse of the removal procedure.

NOTE: During assembly, be careful of the vacuum lines to prevent their hanging up on the accelerator or becoming trapped between the assembly and the dash.

19. To complete the installation, reverse the removal procedures.

WITHOUT AIR CONDITIONING

Omni, Horizon, Turismo and Charger

1. Disconnect the negative battery cable.
2. Drain the cooling system.
3. Remove the ash tray.
4. Depress the tab on the temperature control cable flag and pull the cable out of the receiver on the heater assembly.
5. Disconnect the blower motor wiring connector.
6. Disconnect the heater hoses at the core connections. Plug the core holes.

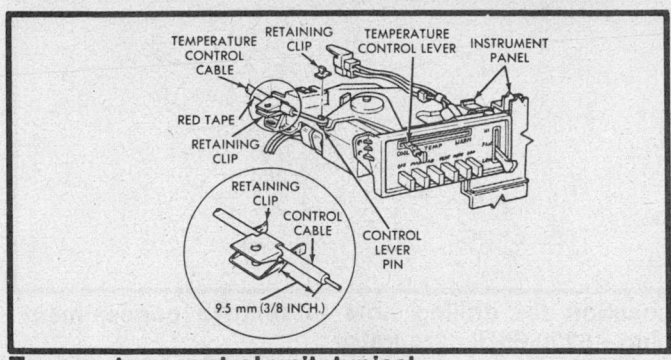

Temperature control unit, typical

7. Remove the unit-to-dash nuts.
8. Remove the glove box and glove box door.
9. Remove the heater brace bracket-to-instrument panel screw.
10. Remove the unit support strap nut and the strap from the plenum stud. Lower the heater unit from under the dash panel.
11. Disconnect the mode control cable and remove the unit from the vehicle.
12. Remove the heater core cover and the core.
13. To install, reverse the removal procedures. Refill the cooling system, run the engine, check for leaks and check the heater operation, when finished.

Except Omni, Horizon, Turismo and Charger

NOTE: Due to various models differences, minor sequence differences may be encountered during removal procedure of the heater core.

1. Disconnect the negative battery cable. Drain the cooling system.
2. Disconnect and label the blower motor electrical wiring.
3. From under the heater assembly, depress the tab on the mode door and temperature control cables. Pull the flags from the receivers and remove the self-adjusting clip from the crank arm.
4. Remove the glove box assembly.
5. Remove the heater hoses at the unit on the engine side. Plug the hoses and core outlets.
6. Remove the screw attaching the hanger strap to the heater assembly through the glove box opening. Remove hanger strap.

7. Remove the demister adapter from the top of the heater assembly, if equipped.
8. On the engine side of the firewall, remove the retaining nuts for the heater assembly to dash panel.
9. Slide the heater assembly from under the instrument panel. It may be necessary to loosen the bottom of the instrument panel for room.
10. To install, reverse the removal procedures.

TEMPERATURE CONTROL/BLOWER SWITCH

Removal and Installation

OMNI, HORIZON, TURISMO AND CHARGER

1. Disconnect the negative battery cable.
2. Remove the light switch and left switch bezel.
3. Remove the control mounting screws and pull the control outward.
4. Disconnect and label the electrical leads, vacuum lines and control cable.
5. Remove the controls from the vehicle.
6. To install, reverse the removal procedures.

EXCEPT OMNI, HORIZON, TURISMO AND CHARGER

Left Side of Instrument Panel

1. Disconnect the negative battery cable.
2. Remove the headlight switch knob.
3. Remove the bezel screw, roll the bezel out and lift up to free the bezel locking lugs.
4. Remove the control mounting screws and remove the control from the dash.
5. Disconnect the cables, vacuum hoses and electrical wiring.
6. To install, reverse the removal procedures.

Center of Instrument Panel

1. Disconnect the negative battery cable.
2. Remove the bezel attaching screws.
3. Remove the bezel by rolling out and lifting up to free bezel locking feet.
4. Remove the control retaining screws and slide the control outward.
5. Disconnect and label the cables, vacuum hose and wiring.
6. To install, reverse the removal procedures.

CARBURETED FUEL SYSTEM

Fuel Pump

NOTE: The mechanical fuel pump is located on the left side of the engine near distributor.

FUEL SYSTEM SERVICE PRECAUTION

When working with the fuel system certain precautions should be taken;
1. Always work in a well ventilated area
2. Keep a dry chemical (Class B) fire extinguisher near the work area
3. Always disconnect the negative battery cable
4. Do not make any repairs to the fuel system until all the necessary steps for repair have been reviewed

FUEL SYSTEM PRESSURE RELIEF

Procedure

1. Remove the fuel tank cap.
2. Place a shop towel around the fuel line to catch the excess fuel.
3. Disconnect the fuel line.
4. To install, reverse the removal procedures.

Pressure Testing

1. Insert a T fitting in fuel line at carburetor.
2. Connect a 6 in. piece of hose between T fitting and gauge.
3. Vent the pump for a few seconds to relieve air trapped in fuel chamber. If this is not done, the pump will not operate at

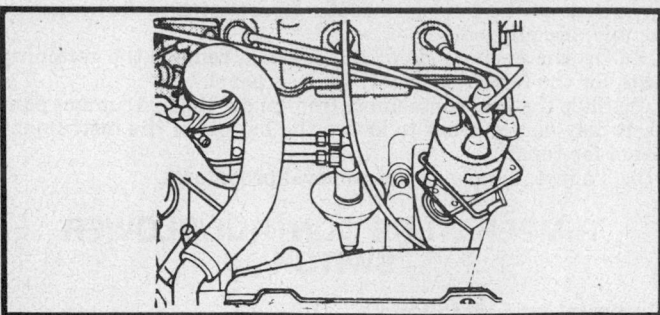

Mechanical fuel pump location — typical

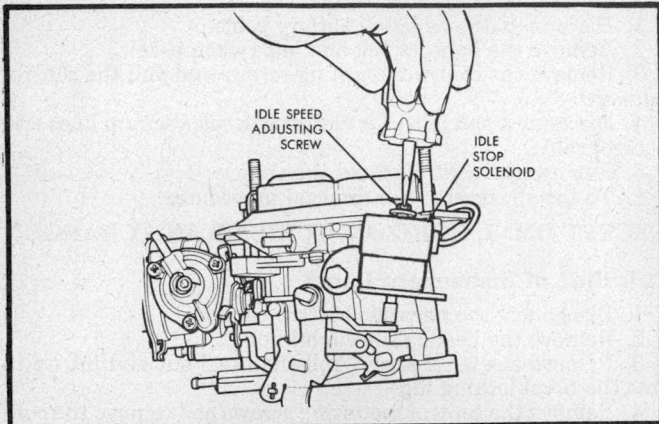

IDLE SPEED ADJUSTING SCREW

IDLE STOP SOLENOID

Idle RPM adjustment — 5220/6520 carburetor

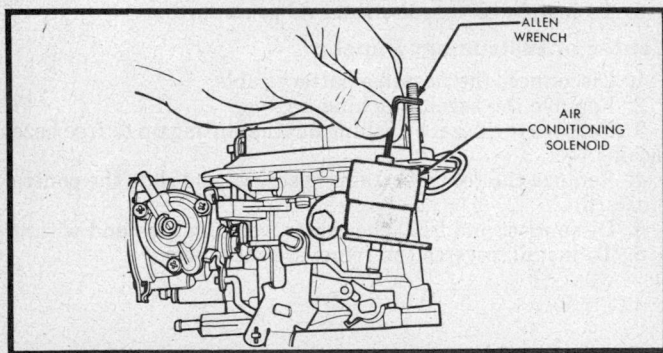

ALLEN WRENCH

AIR CONDITIONING SOLENOID

Air conditioning idle speed adjustment — 5220/6520 carburetor

full capacity and a low pressure reading will result.

4. Connect a tachometer, start engine and run at idle. The reading should be as shown in specifications (depending on pump) and remain constant.

NOTE: The mechanical fuel pump is not adjustable. If found to be defective, it must be replaced. A return to 0 indicates a leaky outlet valve. If pressure is too low, a weak diaphragm main spring, or improper assembly of diaphragm may be the cause. If pressure is to high, the main spring is too strong or the air vent is plugged.

Removal and Installation

---------------- CAUTION ----------------

Keep all possible heat and ignition sources away from fuel drainage and spills. Wipe up spilled fuel promptly and dispose of any fuel soaked rags in a suitable container.

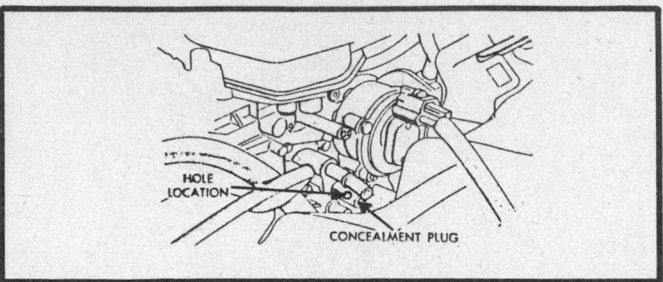

HOLE LOCATION

CONCEALMENT PLUG

Location for drilling hole to remove concealment plug — 5220/6520 carburetor

1. Disconnect the negative battery cable.
2. Disconnect the fuel and vapor lines at the pump.
3. Remove the fuel pump to engine mounting bolts and remove the pump.
4. Clean the gasket mating surfaces of the engine and pump.
To Install:
5. Using a new gasket and install the pump on the engine.
6. Tighten the mounting bolts, connect the fuel lines, run the engine and check for leaks.

Carburetor
Removal and Installation

---------------- CAUTION ----------------

Do not attempt to remove the carburetor from the engine of a vehicle that has just been road tested. Allow the engine to cool sufficiently, to prevent accidental fuel ignition and/or personal injury.

1.6L AND 2.2L ENGINES

1. Disconnect the negative battery cable.
2. Remove the air cleaner assembly.
3. Remove the fuel tank filler cap. The fuel tank could be under a small amount of pressure.
4. Place a container under fuel inlet fitting to catch any fuel that may be trapped in fuel line.
5. Disconnect the fuel inlet line. Disconnect and label all wiring.
6. Disconnect the throttle linkage. Disconnect and label all hoses.
7. Remove the carburetor-to-manifold nuts and the carburetor from the engine.
8. Clean the mating surfaces of the isolator and carburetor.
9. To install, use a new gasket and reverse the removal procedures. Torque the mounting nuts to 200 inch lbs.

IDLE SPEED

Adjustment
HOLLEY 5220/6520 CARBURETORS EXCEPT 2.2L ENGINE
Without Air Conditioning

NOTE: Before checking or adjusting any idle speed, check ignition timing and adjust, if necessary.

1. Disconnect and plug vacuum connector at the Coolant Vacuum Switch Cold Closed (CVSCC).
2. Unplug connector at radiator fan and install jumper wire so fan will run continuously.
3. Remove PCV valve and allow valve to draw underhood air.
4. Connect tachometer to engine.
5. Ground carburetor switch with jumper wire.
6. Disconnect oxygen system test connector located on left fender shield on 6520 equipped vehicles.

7. Start and run engine until normal operating temperature is reached.

8. If tachometer indicates rpm is not to specifications, turn idle speed screw until correct idle speed is obtained.

9. Reconnect PCV valve, oxygen connector and vacuum connector.

10. Remove jumper wire and reconnect radiator fan.

NOTE: After Steps 9 and 10 are completed, the idle speed may change slightly. This is normal and engine speed should not be readjusted.

HOLLEY 5220/6520 CARBURETORS—2.2L ENGINE

With Air Conditioning

These vehicles are equipped with either a vacuum kicker or a solenoid kicker. It is not necessary to set the air conditioning idle speed, but the kicker operation should be checked.

1. Start and run engine until normal operating temperature is reached.

2. Set temperature control lever to **MAX COLD** position and turn **ON** air conditioning.

3. As the air conditioning compressor clutch cycles **OFF** and **ON**, the kicker plunger should move in and out. If so, proceed to Step 5. If not, proceed to Step 4. The air cleaner may be removed to allow the kicker to be more visible.

4. Check the kicker system for vacuum leaks in the hoses. Check the operation of the vacuum solenoid. If no problems are found replace the kicker and repeat Steps 1–3.

5. Turn off the air conditioning.

6. Turn off the engine and install air cleaner, if removed.

ANTI-DIESELING CONTROL

Adjustment

HOLLEY 5220/6520 CARBURETORS

NOTE: Anti-dieseling, on some models, is controlled by either an idle stop solenoid or solenoid kicker, while anti-dieseling is controlled on the remaining models by the high run ignition timing.

1. With the engine fully warmed, place the transaxle in **N** and set parking brake. Turn the headlights off.

2. Ground the idle stop carburetor switch with a jumper wire.

3. Remove the red wire terminal from the 6-way connector on the carburetor side of connector.

4. Adjust the throttle stop screw to 700 rpm.

5. Reconnect the wire at connector and remove the jumper wire from the idle stop carburetor switch.

CONCEALMENT PLUGS

Removal

HOLLEY 5220/6520 CARBURETORS

1. Disconnect the negative battery cable. Remove the air cleaner crossover assembly.

2. Remove the canister purge and diverter valve vacuum hoses.

3. Make a center punch at a point ¼ in. from the end of the mixture screw housing.

4. Drill through the outer housing with a ³⁄₁₆ in. drill bit.

5. Pry out the concealment plug. Save the plug for reinstallation.

IDLE MIXTURE

Propane Adjustment

HOLLEY 5220/6520 CARBURETORS

NOTE: Tampering with the carburetor is a violation of Federal law. Adjustment of the carburetor idle air/fuel mixture can only be done under certain circumstances and should only be used if an idle defect still exists after normal diagnosis has revealed no other faulty condition, such as incorrect idle speed, incorrect basic timing, faulty hose or wire connections, etc. It is also important to make sure the combustion computer systems are operating properly. Adjustment of the air/fuel mixture should also be performed after a major carburetor overhaul.

1. Set the parking brake and place transaxle in **N**. Turn off all lights and accessories. Connect a tachometer to the engine. Start the engine and allow it to warm up on the 2nd highest step on the fast idle cam until normal operating temperature is reached. Return the engine to curb idle.

2. Disconnect and plug the vacuum hose at the EGR valve. Disconnect and plug the vacuum connection at the CCEGR/CVSCC. Disconnect the vacuum hose to the heated air door sensor at the 3-way connector. In it's place, install the supply hose from the propane bottle. Make sure both valves are fully closed and that the bottle is upright and in a safe location.

3. Unplug the connector at the radiator fan and install a jumper wire so the fan will run continuously. Remove the PCV valve from the molded rubber connector and allow the valve to draw under hood air. Disconnect and plug the ³⁄₁₆ in. diameter control hose at the canister. Connect a jumper wire between the carburetor switch and to ground. On Holley 6520 models, disconnect the oxygen test connector located on the left fender shield.

4. Open the propane main valve. With the air cleaner in place, slowly open the propane metering valve until maximum engine rpm is reached. When too much propane is added, engine speed will decrease. Fine tune the metering valve for the highest engine rpm.

5. With the propane still flowing, adjust the idle speed screw on top of the solenoid to get the specified propane rpm. Fine tune the propane metering valve to get the highest engine rpm. If there has been a change in the maximum rpm, readjust the idle speed screw to the specified propane rpm.

6. Turn off the propane main valve and allow the engine speed to stabilize. With air cleaner in place, slowly adjust the mixture screw to obtain the specified idle set rpm. Pause between adjustment to allow the engine speed to stabilize.

NOTE: An Allen wrench should be used to turn the idle mixture screw.

7. Turn on the propane main valve. Fine tune the metering valve to get the highest engine rpm. If the maximum engine speed is more than 25 rpm different than the specified propane rpm, repeat Steps 4–7.

8. Turn off both valve on the propane bottle. Remove the propane supply hose and reinstall the vacuum hose. Connect the radiator fan wiring.

9. If not equipped with air conditioning, perform the fast idle speed adjustment and reinstall the concealment plug. The plug can be installed with the carburetor on the engine.

10. If equipped with air conditioning, perform the air conditioning idle speed, idle set rpm and fast idle speed adjustments. Replace the concealment plug. The plug can be installed with the carburetor on the engine.

FUEL INJECTION SYSTEM

Refer to "Chilton's Electronic Engine Controls Manual" for additional coverage.

Description

SINGLE POINT FUEL INJECTION

The Electronic Fuel Injection (SPFI) System is a computer regulated single point fuel injection system that provides precise air/fuel ratio for all driving conditions. At the center of this system is a digital pre-programmed computer known as a Logic Module that regulates ignition timing, air-fuel ratio, emission control devices and idle speed. This component has the ability to update and revise its programming to meet changing operating conditions.

Various sensors provide the input necessary for the logic module to correctly regulate the fuel flow at the fuel injector. These include the Manifold Absolute Pressure (MAP), Throttle Position Sensor (TPS), Oxygen Feedback, Coolant Temperature Sensor (CTS) and Vehicle Speed Sensor (VSS). In addition to the sensors, various switches also provide important information. These include the neutral-safety, heated backlite, air conditioning, air conditioning clutch switches and an electronic idle switch.

All inputs to the logic module are converted into signals sent to the power module. These signals cause the power module to change either the fuel flow at the injector or ignition timing or both.

The logic module test many of its own input and output circuits. If a fault is found in a major system, this information is stored in the logic module. Information on this fault can be displayed to a technician by means of the instrument panel power loss lamp or by connecting a diagnostic read out and reading a numbered display code which directly relates to a general fault.

MULTI POINT FUEL INJECTION (TURBO)

The turbocharged multi point Electronic Fuel Injection (MPFI) system combines an electronic fuel and spark advance control system with a turbocharged intake system.

At the center of this system is a digital pre-programmed computer known as a logic module that regulates ignition timing, air-fuel ratio, emission control devices and idle speed. This component has the ability to update and revise its programming to meet changing operating conditions.

Various sensors provide the input necessary for the logic module to correctly regulate fuel flow at the fuel injectors. These include the Manifold Absolute Pressure (MAP), Throttle Position (TPS), Oxygen Feedback, Coolant Temperature (CTS), Charge Temperature and Vehicle Speed Sensors (VSS). In addition to the sensor, various switches also provide important information. These include the transaxle neutral-safety, heated backlite, air conditioning and the air conditioning clutch switches.

Inputs to the logic module are converted into signals sent to the power module. These signals cause the power module to change either the fuel flow at the injector or ignition timing or both.

The logic module tests many of its own input and output circuits. If a fault is found in a major circuit, this information is stored in the logic module. Information on this fault can be displayed to a technician by means of the instrument panel power loss lamp or by connecting a diagnostic readout and observing a numbered display code which directly relates to a general fault.

IDLE SPEED

Adjustment

The idle speed is controlled by the automatic idle speed motor (AIS) which is controlled by the logic module. The logic module gathers data from various sensors and switches in the system and adjusts the engine idle to a predetermined speed. Idle speed specifications can be found on the vehicle emission control information (VECI) label located in the engine compartment.

IDLE MIXTURE

Adjustment

Idle mixture is adjusted at the factory and should not be attempted.

FUEL SYSTEM PRESSURE RELIEF

Procedure

NOTE: Whenever working on or around any part of the fuel system, take precautions to avoid the risk of fire. The fuel system is under constant pressure which must be relieved before attempting any service procedures.

EXCEPT LASER

1. To release the pressure, remove the fuel tank cap and the wiring connector from the fuel injector (SFI) or any fuel injector (MFI).
2. Connect a jumper wire from a fuel injector (No. 1) terminal-to-ground and a 2nd jumper wire from the other injector terminal-to-positive battery terminal for 10 seconds (1986–88) or 5 seconds (1989–90); the injector will open, allowing the fuel pressure to be relieved.
3. With the fuel pressure reduced, remove the jumper wires and continue with the fuel system service.

LASER

1. From the rear of the fuel tank, disconnect the fuel pump's electrical harness connector.
2. Start the engine and operate it until it stops; turn the ignition switch OFF.
3. Disconnect the negative battery cable.
4. Reconnect the fuel pump electrical harness connector.

Fuel Pump

PRESSURE TESTING

EXCEPT LASER

1. Relieve the fuel system pressure. Disconnect the negative battery cable.
2. If equipped with SPI and MPI, disconnect $5/16$ in. fuel supply line from throttle body. If equipped with a Turbo, remove protective cover from service valve on the fuel rail.
3. Connect pressure tester C–3292 and C–4749 or equivalent, between the fuel supply hose and throttle body (SPI) or to the fuel rail service valve (MPI).
4. Using ATM tester C–4805 or equivalent, with the ignition in run position, depress the ATM button. This will activate the fuel pump and pressurize the system. Reading should be 14.5 psi (100 Kpa) on SPI and 55 psi (380 kpa) on MPI and Turbo.

LASER

1. Relieve the fuel pressure. Disconnect the negative battery cable.
2. If equipped with a 2.0L engine, remove the throttle body stay.
3. Disconnect the high pressure fuel line from the delivery pipe; be sure to use a shop towel to collect the residual fuel.

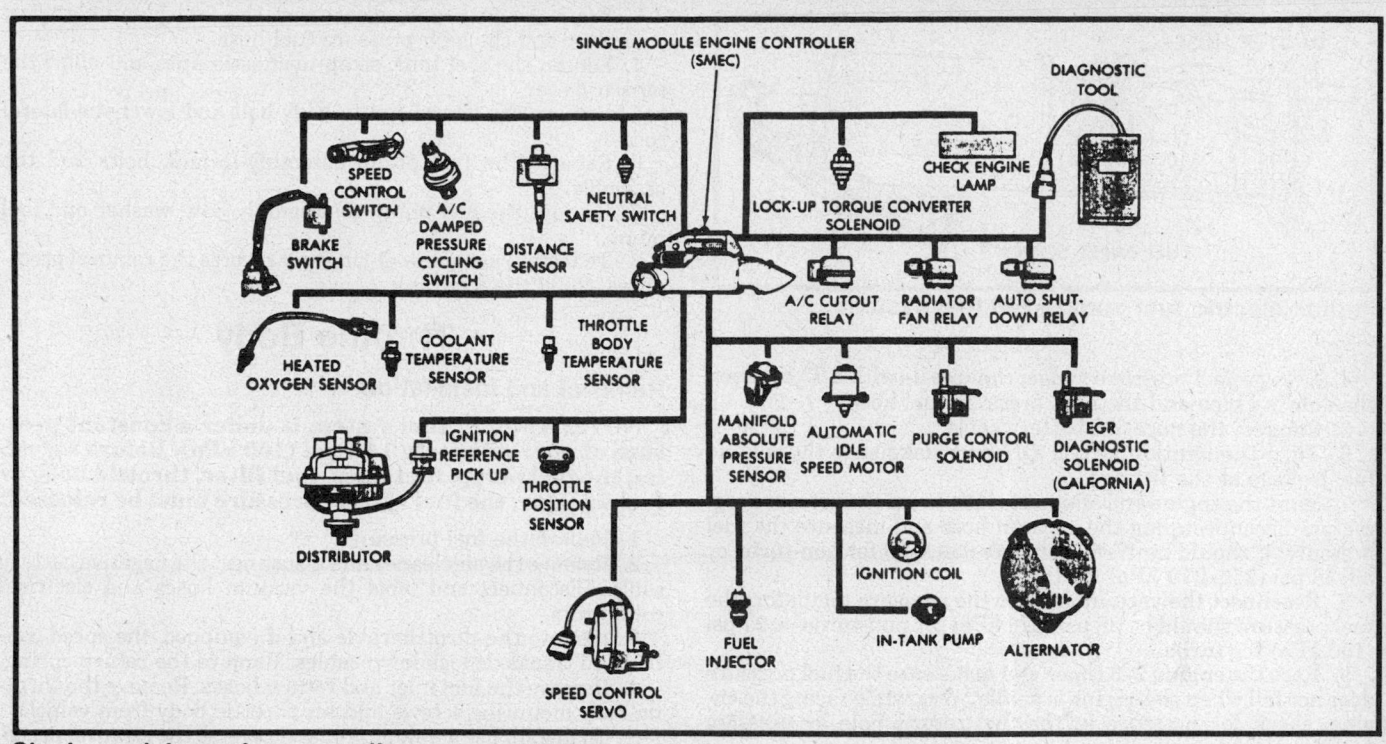

Single module engine controller components

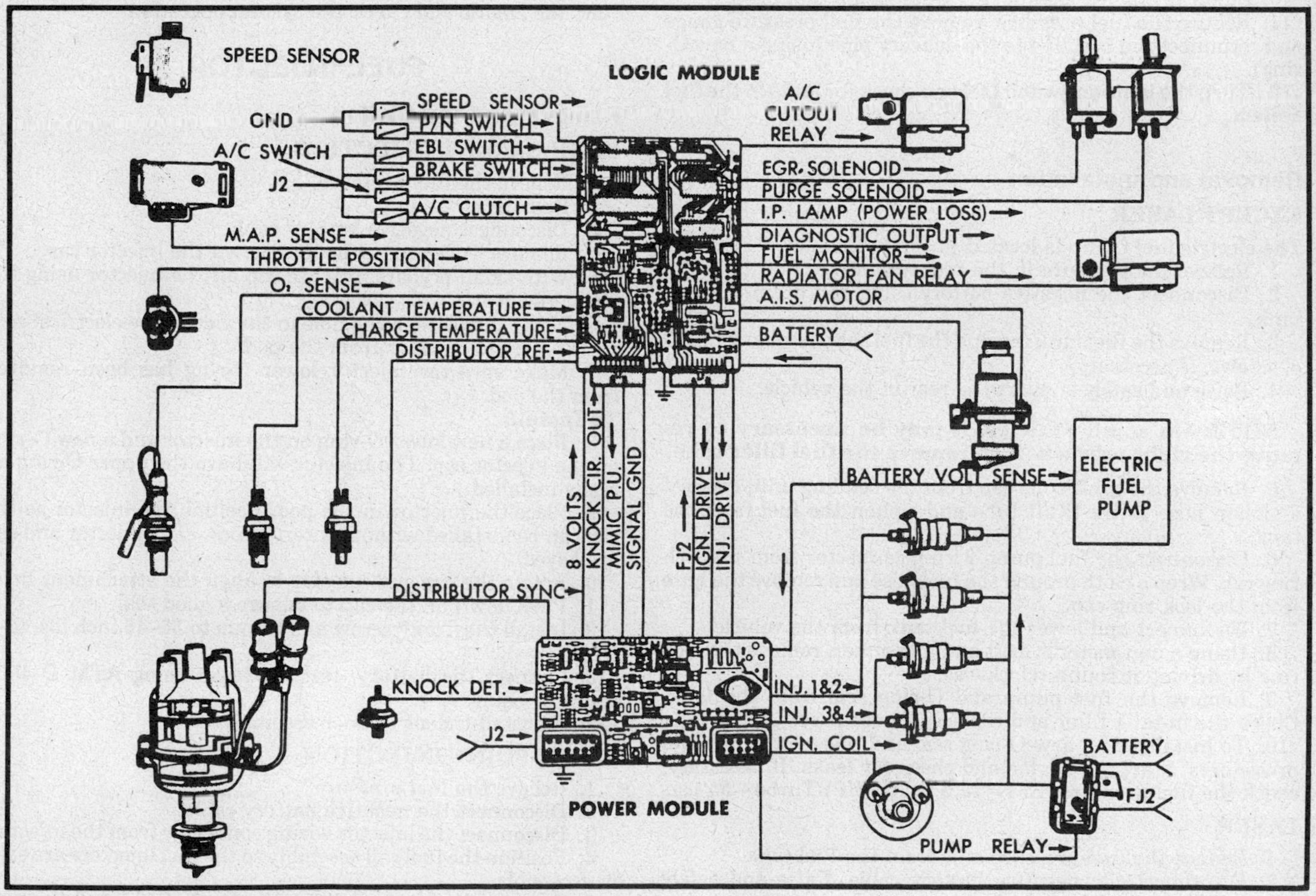

Multi-point EFI fuel system (turbo) components

In-tank electric fuel pump—EFI fuel system

4. Using a fuel pressure gauge, connect it (with a **T**) between the delivery pipe and the high pressure fuel hose.

5. Connect the negative battery cable.

6. Turn the ignition switch **ON** and make sure there is no fuel leakage at the fittings.

7. Start the engine and allow it to idle. From the pressure regulator, disconnect/plug the vacuum hose and measure the fuel pressure; it should be 47–50 psi (330–350 kPa) for non-turbo or 36–38 psi (250–270 kPa) for turbo.

8. Reconnect the vacuum hose to the pressure regulator; the fuel pressure should be 38 psi (270 kPa) for non-turbo or 27 psi (190 kPa) for turbo.

9. Race the engine 2–3 times and make sure the fuel pressure does not fall when the engine is at idle. Also, while racing the engine, check for pressure in the fuel return hole by pressing (gently) on the return hose.

10. Stop the engine, the fuel pressure should not drop.

11. Reduce the fuel pressure, remove the fuel pressure gauge and reconnect the fuel line to the delivery pipe (using a new O-ring).

12. Turn the ignition switch **ON** and check for leaks in the fuel system.

Removal and Installation
EXCEPT LASER

The electric fuel pump is located in the fuel tank.

1. Relieve the pressure in the fuel system.

2. Disconnect the negative battery cable and drain the fuel tank.

3. Remove the fuel tank cap and the fuel tube-to-quarter panel screws, if necessary.

4. Raise and safely support the rear of the vehicle.

NOTE: On some vehicles, it may be necessary to remove the right rear wheel to remove the fuel filler tube.

5. Remove the draft tube cap from the sending unit, connect a siphon hose to the draft tube and siphon the fuel from the tank.

6. Disconnect the fuel pump wiring connector from the lock ring cap. Wrap a cloth around the fuel hose and remove the hose from the lock ring cap.

7. Disconnect and lower the fuel tank from the vehicle.

8. Using a non-metallic drift and a hammer, remove the lock ring by driving it counterclockwise.

9. Remove the fuel pump and O-ring seal from the tank. Check the in-tank filter and replace, if necessary.

10. To install, use a new O-ring seal and reverse the removal procedures. Start the engine and check for leaks. If necessary, check the fuel pressure: EFI—14.5 psi or MPI/Turbo—55 psi.

LASER

1. Reduce the fuel pressure and drain the fuel tank.

2. Disconnect the negative battery cable. Raise and safely support the rear of the vehicle.

3. From the fuel tank, disconnect the fuel pump electrical connector and the high pressure fuel hose.

4. Loosen the fuel tank strap-to-chassis nuts and allow the tank to lower.

5. Remove the lateral rod-to-body bolt and lower the lateral rod.

6. Remove the fuel pump assembly-to-tank bolts and the assembly.

7. Remove the fuel pump-to-assembly bolt, washer and fuel pump.

8. To install, use a new O-ring and reverse the removal procedures. Refill the fuel tank.

Throttle Body

Removal and Installation

NOTE: The EFI fuel system is under a constant pressure of approximately 14.5 psi (100 kPa). Before servicing the fuel pump, fuel lines, fuel filter, throttle body or fuel injector, the fuel system pressure must be released.

1. Relieve the fuel pressure.

2. Remove the air cleaner and disconnect the negative battery cable. Disconnect and label the vacuum hoses and electrical connectors.

3. Remove the throttle cable and if equipped, the speed control and transaxle kickdown cables. Remove the return spring.

4. Remove the fuel inlet and return hoses. Remove the throttle body mounting screws and lift throttle body from vehicle.

5. To install, use a new gasket and reverse the removal procedures. Torque the mounting screws to 200 inch lbs. (23 Nm). Start the engine and check the system operation.

FUEL INJECTOR

Removal and Installation
SINGLE POINT INJECTION

1. Relieve the fuel pressure.

2. Remove air cleaner.

3. Disconnect negative battery cable.

4. Remove Torx® screw holding down the injector cap.

5. With small prybars, pry the cap off the injector using the slots provided.

6. Using the place in the hole in the side of the electrical connector, pry the injector from the pod.

7. Make sure the injector lower O-ring has been removed from the pod.

To Install:

8. Place a new lower O-ring on the injector and a new O-ring on the injector cap. The injector will have the upper O-ring already installed.

9. Place the injector in the pod. Position the injector so the cap can be installed without interference. (The injector and cap are keyed).

10. Rotate the cap and injector to align the attachment hold.

11. Push down on the cap to ensure a good seal.

12. Install the Torx® screw and torque to 35–45 inch lbs. (4–5 Nm).

13. Connect the battery, test for leaks using ATM C-4805 testor or equivalent.

14. Reinstall the air cleaner assembly.

MULTI-POINT INJECTION

1. Relieve the fuel pressure.

2. Disconnect the negative battery cable.

3. Disconnect the injector wiring connector from the injector.

4. Position the fuel rail assembly so the fuel injectors are easily accessible.

5. Remove the injector clip from the fuel rail and injector.

Pull the injector straight out of the fuel rail receiver cup.

6. Check the injector O-ring for damage. If the O-ring is damaged, replace it. If the injector is being reused, install a protective cap on the injector tip to prevent damage.

7. Repeat the procedure for the remaining injectors.

To Install:

8. Before installing an injector the rubber O-ring must be lubricated with a drop of clean engine oil to aid in installation.

9. Install injector top end into fuel rail receiver cup.

NOTE: Be careful not to damage O-ring during installation.

10. Install injector clip by sliding open end into top slot of the injector and onto the receiver cup ridge into the side slots of clip.

11. Repeat the Steps for the remaining injectors.

TURBOCHARGER SYSTEM

Refer to "Chilton's Electronic Engine Control Manual" for additional coverage.

Description

The turbocharger is basically an air compressor or air pump. It consists of a turbine or hot wheel, a shaft, a compressor or cold wheel, a turbine housing, a compressor housing and a center housing which contains bearings, a turbine seal assembly and a compressor seal assembly.

Turbochargers are installed on an engine to put more and denser air into the engine combustion chambers. Because of the increased volume and weight of compressed air more fuel can be scheduled to produce more horsepower from a given size engine. The turbocharged version of an engine will also maintain a higher level of power output than the non-turbocharged version when operated at altitudes above sea level.

TURBOCHARGER UNIT

Removal and Installation

NOTE: The turbo boost pressure is 9 psi for manual transaxle vehicles and 10 psi for automatic transaxle vehicles.

2.0L ENGINE (1989–90)

1. Drain the cooling system and the crankcase. Disconnect the negative battery cable.

2. If equipped with air conditioning, remove the condenser fan motor.

3. Remove both exhaust manifold covers. Disconnect the electrical connector from the oxygen sensor.

4. Remove the dipstick, the dipstick tube and the O-ring. Disconnect the air intake hose, the vacuum hoses and the A air hose.

5. Loosen the power steering pump and remove the drive belt, the power steering pump and the bracket.

6. From the rear of the engine, remove the turbocharger's oil tube-to-engine bolt and gaskets. Disconnect the water hose and pipe from the turbocharger.

7. Remove the turbocharger-to-exhaust pipe nuts and separate the exhaust pipe from the turbocharger. Remove the turbocharger from the exhaust manifold.

8. Clean the gasket mounting surfaces. Inspect the for cracks, flatness and/or damage.

NOTE: Before installing the turbocharger assembly, be sure it is first charged with oil. Failure to do this may cause damage to the assembly.

9. To install, use new gaskets and reverse the removal procedures. Torque the turbocharger-to-exhaust manifold nuts/bolt to 40–47 ft. lbs. and the turbocharger-to-exhaust pipe nuts to

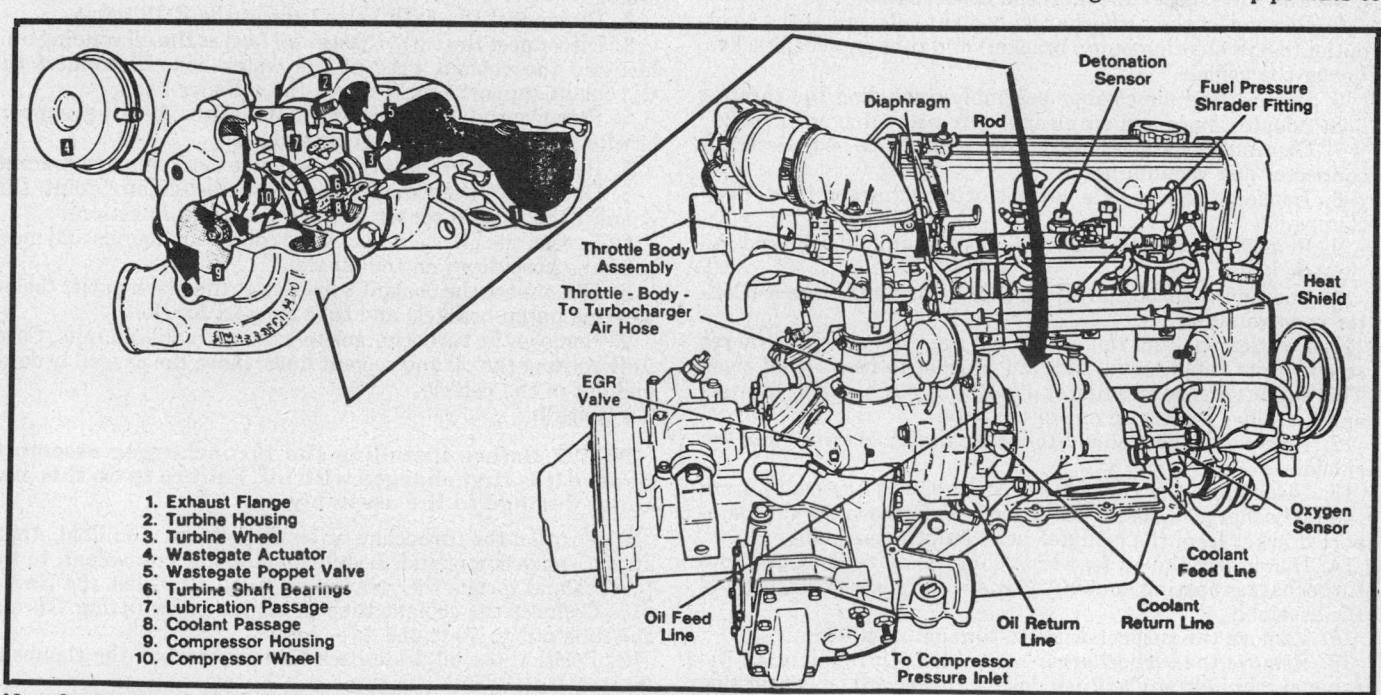

1. Exhaust Flange
2. Turbine Housing
3. Turbine Wheel
4. Wastegate Actuator
5. Wastegate Poppet Valve
6. Turbine Shaft Bearings
7. Lubrication Passage
8. Coolant Passage
9. Compressor Housing
10. Compressor Wheel

Key features of 2.2L turbo engine

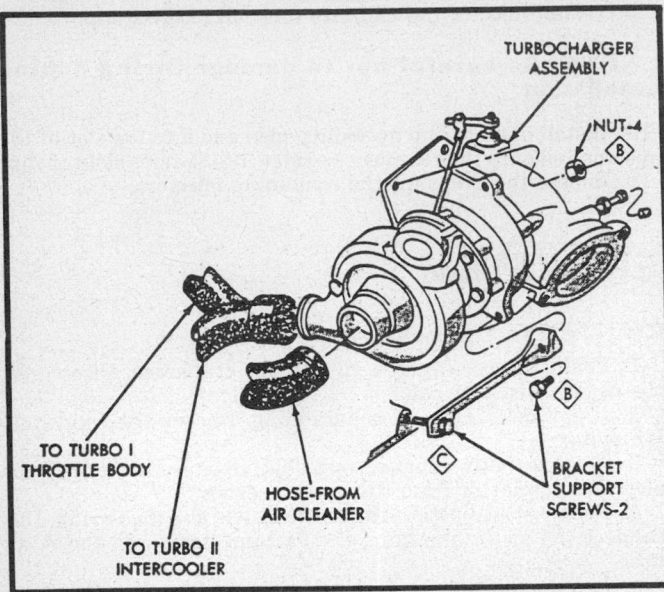

TURBOCHARGER ASSEMBLY

NUT-4 B

TO TURBO I THROTTLE BODY

TO TURBO II INTERCOOLER

HOSE-FROM AIR CLEANER

C

BRACKET SUPPORT SCREWS-2 B

View of the turbocharger (I and II)—2.2L and 2.5L engines

29–43 ft. lbs. Refill the cooling system and the crankcase. Start the engine, allow it to reach normal operating temperatures and check it for leaks and engine performance.

2.2L ENGINE (1986–87)

1. Disconnect the negative battery cable. Drain the cooling system. Raise and safely support the vehicle.
2. Disconnect the exhaust pipe at the articulated joint. Disconnect the oxygen sensor at the electrical connector.
3. Remove the turbocharger housing to engine block support bracket.
4. Loosen the oil drain back tube connector hose clamps and move the tube (hose) down on the block nipple.
5. Disconnect the turbocharger coolant tube nut at the block outlet (below steering pump bracket) and tube support bracket. Lower the vehicle.
6. Remove the air cleaner assembly, including the throttle body adaptor, hose and air cleaner box with support bracket.
7. Disconnect the accelerator linkage, throttle body electrical connector and vacuum hoses.
8. Loosen the throttle body-to-turbocharger inlet hose clamps.
9. Remove the throttle body-to-intake manifold bolts and the throttle body.
10. Loosen the turbocharger discharge hose end clamps. (Center band retains).
11. Position the fuel rail out of the way. Remove the bracket screws from intake manifold and bracket-to-heat shield clips. This will lift and secure fuel rail (with injectors, wiring harness and fuel lines intact) up out of the way.
12. Remove the heat shield-to-intake manifold screws and the shield.
13. Disconnect the coolant return tube/hose assembly from the turbocharger housing to water box. Remove the tube support bracket from the cylinder head and the assembly.
14. Disconnect the oil feed line from the oil sending unit and turbocharger bearing housing. Remove the support bracket and the assembly.
15. Remove the turbocharger-to-exhaust manifold nuts.
16. Remove the turbocharger assembly by lifting it off of the exhaust manifold studs. Push downward toward passenger side (of unit) up and out of engine compartment.

NOTE: Before installing the turbocharger assembly, be sure it is first charged with oil. Failure to do this may cause damage to the assembly.

To Install:

17. Position the turbocharger assembly on the exhaust manifold studs. Make sure the turbocharger discharge tube is in position between the intake manifold and turbocharger.
18. Apply anti-seize compound to threads and torque the nuts to 30 ft. lbs. (41 Nm).
19. Torque the oil feed line tube nuts (to sending unit hex tee and turbocharger center housing) to 125 inch lbs. (14 Nm). Install and tighten the support bracket screw.
20. Torque the:
   Heat shield-to-intake manifold screws to 105 inch lbs. (12 Nm).
   Coolant tube nuts to 30 ft. lbs. (41 Nm).
   Fuel rail bracket-to-intake manifold screws to 250 inch lbs. (28 Nm).
   Discharge tube (hose) clamp to 35 inch lbs. (4.1 Nm).
   Throttle body-to-intake manifold screws to 250 inch lbs. (28 Nm).
   Throttle body hose clamps to 35 inch lbs. (4.1 Nm).
21. Reconnect the accelerator linkage, electrical connector and vacuum hoses.
22. Torque the:
   Hose adaptor-to-throttle body screws to 55 inch lbs. (6 Nm).
   Air cleaner box support bracket screw to 40 ft. lbs. (54 Nm).
   Coolant tube nut to block connector to 30 ft. lbs. (41 Nm).
   Oil drain back hose clamps to 30 inch lbs. (3 Nm).
   Turbocharger-to-block support bracket screw to 40 ft. lbs. (54 Nm).
   Turbocharger housing screw to 20 ft. lbs. (27 Nm).
   Articulated joint shoulder bolts to 250 inch lbs. (28 Nm).
23. Refill the cooling system and reconnect the battery.

2.2L ENGINE (1988–90) AND 2.5L (1989–90) ENGINE

The turbochargers are removed from under the vehicle.

1. Disconnect the negative battery cable. Drain the cooling system.
2. Disconnect the EGR valve tube at the EGR valve.
3. Disconnect the turbocharger oil feed at the oil sending unit hex and the coolant tube at the water box. Disconnect the oil/coolant support bracket from the cylinder head.
4. Remove the right intermediate shaft, bearing support bracket and outer driveshaft assemblies.
5. Remove the turbocharger-to-engine block support bracket.
6. Disconnect the exhaust pipe at the articulated joint. Disconnect the oxygen sensor at the electrical connection.
7. Loosen the oil drain-back tube connector clamps and move the tube hose down on the nipple.
8. Disconnect the coolant tube nut at the block outlet (below steering pump bracket) and tube support bracket.
9. Remove the turbocharger-to-exhaust manifold nuts. Carefully routing the oil and coolant lines, move the assembly down and out of the vehicle.

To Install:

NOTE: Before installing the turbocharger assembly, be sure it is first charged with oil. Failure to do this may cause damage to the assembly.

10. Position the turbocharger on the exhaust manifold. Apply an anti-seize compound, Loctite® 771–64 or equivalent, to the threads and torque the retaining nuts to 40 ft. lbs. (54 Nm).
11. Connect the coolant tube to engine block fitting. Torque the tube nut to 30 ft. lbs. (41 Nm).
12. Position the oil drain-back hose and torque the clamps to 30 inch lbs. (3 Nm).
13. Install and torque the:

Turbocharger-to-engine support bracket block screw to 40 ft. lbs. (54Nm).

Turbocharger housing screw to 20 ft. lbs. (27 Nm).

Articulated joint shoulder bolts to 250 inch lbs. (28 Nm).

14. Install the right driveshaft assemblies, the starter and the oil feed line at the sending unit hex. Torque the oil feed tube nut to 125 inch lbs. (14 Nm) and the EGR tube-to-EGR valve nut to 60 ft. lbs. (81 Nm).

15. Refill the cooling system and reconnect battery.

TURBOCHARGER WASTEGATE UNIT

Removal and Installation

1. Disconnect the negative battery cable.
2. Remove the vacuum hose from the wastegate.
3. Remove the control linkage from the turbocharger assembly.
4. Remove the wastegate.
5. To install, reverse the removal procedures.

EMISSION CONTROL SYSTEMS

Refer to "Chilton's Emission Diagnosis and Service Manual" for additional coverage.

List of Equipment Used

Heated Inlet Air
Positive Crankcase Ventilation System
Carburetor Calibration
Distributor Calibration
Initial Timing
Air Pump
Exhaust Gas Recirculation System
Electric Choke
Evaporation Control System with canister
Catalytic Converter, Mini and Regular
Electronic Feedback Carburetor
Jet Air Control Valve
Pulse Air Feeder System
Aspirator Air System

Resetting Emission Warning Lamps

Vehicles equipped with the Spark Control Computer (SCC) have the capability of on board diagnostics. If a problem occurs in the system it will be indicated by the power loss lamp.

Procedures
1986–87 VEHICLES

1. To retrieve the fault codes, turn the ignition switch **ON/OFF/ON/OFF** within 5 seconds.
2. The power loss lamp will turn **ON** for 2 seconds as a lamp check and turns **OFF**.
3. Immediately following the lamp check will be a display of flashing code number(s); flash-flash-flash-flash-pause-flash = Code 41.
4. If other codes exist, they will follow in numerical order.

NOTE: The logic module is programmed to erase the fault code memory automatically after 20–40 start ups.

5. To immediately erase the fault codes, disconnect the negative battery cable, reconnect it and start the engine.

1988–90 VEHICLES

1. To retrieve the fault codes, turn the ignition switch to the **RUN** position (without starting the engine) and count the possible flashes of the Check Engine lamp (in the instrument cluster); flash-pause-flash-flash = Code 12.
2. If other codes exist, they will follow in numerical order.
3. To erase the fault codes, turn the ignition switch **ON/OFF** between 50–100 times.

ENGINE

NOTE: Disconnecting the negative battery cable on some vehicles may interfere with the functions of the on board computer systems and may require the computer to undergo a relearning process, once the negative battery cable is reconnected.

Engine Assembly

Removal and Installation

1.8L AND 2.0L ENGINES

1. Release the fuel pressure. Remove the battery cables (negative first) and the battery. Mark the hood hinge outline on the hood and remove the hood. Remove the air cleaner duct from the throttle body or turbocharger (2.0L).
2. Move the temperature control to the **HOT** position. Remove the radiator cap, loosen the drain plug and drain the cooling system.
3. If equipped with an automatic transaxle, disconnect and plug the oil cooler lines from the radiator.

4. Remove the radiator-to-engine hoses, the fan/shroud assembly and the radiator from the vehicle.
5. Disconnect and plug the fuel line(s) from the engine. Label and disconnect the vacuum hoses and electrical connectors from the engine. If equipped with cruise control, disconnect the actuator and bracket; move it aside.
6. Disconnect the electrical connectors from the starter and remove the starter from the transaxle.
7. Raise and safely support the vehicle under the frame. Remove the front wheel/tire assemblies. Remove the undercover from the vehicle. Drain the fluid from the transaxle and the engine. Disconnect the speedometer cable from the transaxle.
8. Disconnect the exhaust pipe from the exhaust manifold.
9. Disconnect and remove the shift lever cables from the transaxle. Disconnect any electrical connectors from the transaxle. If equipped with a manual transaxle, remove the clutch slave cylinder and move it aside; do not disconnect the hydraulic line.
10. If equipped with an automatic transaxle, remove the bell housing cover, matchmark the torque converter to the flexplate, remove the torque converter-to-flexplate bolts and push the converter into the transaxle.

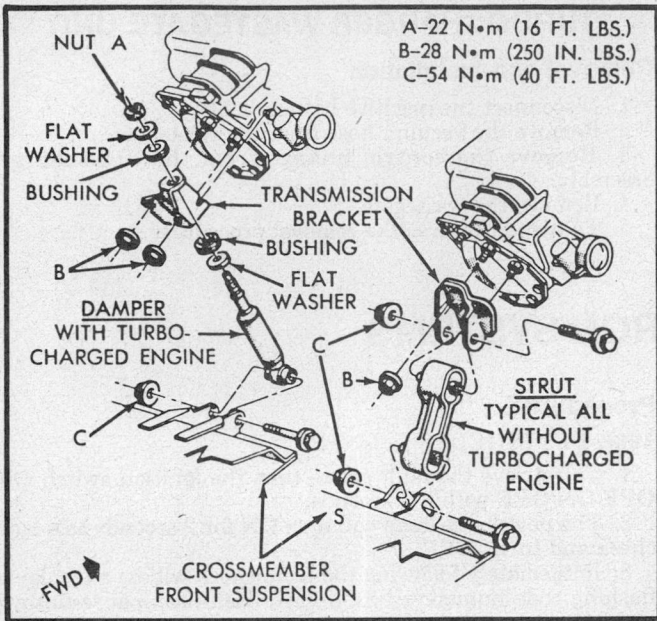

Engine anti-roll strut/damper components

A—22 N•m (16 FT. LBS.)
B—28 N•m (250 IN. LBS.)
C—54 N•m (40 FT. LBS.)

NOTE: When removing the torque converter bolts, rotate the crankshaft (using a wrench on the crankshaft pulley bolt) to expose the bolts.

11. To remove the transaxle, perform the following procedures:

   a. Remove the cotter pin and nut from the tie rod end-to-steering knuckle and the lower ball joint-to-steering knuckle connections. Using a steering linkage puller tool or equivalent, separate the tie rod end and lower ball joint from the steering knuckle.

   b. Using a small pry bar, insert it between the halfshaft and transaxle, gently pry the halfshaft to disengage it from the transaxle by pulling the steering knuckle outward. Using a piece of wire, support the halfshaft.

NOTE: Do not pull on the halfshaft, for the inboard joint may become damaged. Be careful not to damage the oil seal.

   c. Using a transmission jack, secure it to the transaxle. Remove the transaxle-to-engine bolts, move the transaxle from the engine and lower it from the vehicle.

12. Remove the power steering pump (with the hose attached) and support it aside.

13. If equipped with air conditioning, remove the compressor from the bracket and secure it with a wire (with the hoses attached).

14. Using an engine lifting device, secure it to the engine and take the weight off the mounts. Remove the upper engine mount-to-chassis bracket and the lower engine bracket-to-chassis bolts.

15. Carefully, lift the engine from the vehicle; be sure all hoses, electrical connectors and cables are free of the engine.

To Install:

16. Reverse the removal procedures. Torque the:
   Lower engine bracket-to-chassis bolts to 36–47 ft. lbs.
   Upper engine bracket-to-chassis bolt to 22–29 ft. lbs.
   Exhaust pipe-to-manifold nuts to 22–29 ft. lbs.

Transaxle-to-engine bolts to 32–39 ft. lbs. (manual) or 22–25 ft. lbs. (automatic).
   Torque converter-to-flexplate bolts to 33–38 ft. lbs.
   Tie rod end-to-steering knuckle nut to 17–25 ft. lbs.
   Lower ball joint-to-steering knuckle nut to 43–52 ft. lbs.
   Starter-to-transaxle bolts to 20–25 ft. lbs.

17. Reconnect the hoses, electrical connectors and cables to the engine/transaxle assembly. Adjust the drive belt tensions. Refill the cooling system, the engine and transaxle. Start the engine, check it's operation and leaks.

1.6L, 2.2L AND 2.5L ENGINES

1. Disconnect the negative battery cable and all engine ground straps.

2. Mark the hood hinge outline on the hood and remove the hood.

3. Drain the cooling system. Remove the radiator hoses, fan assembly, radiator shroud and radiator.

4. Remove the air cleaner, duct hoses and oil filter.

5. If equipped, remove the air conditioning compressor and move it aside.

6. If equipped, remove the power steering pump mounting bolts and set the pump aside, without disconnecting any fluid lines.

7. Disconnect and label the electrical connectors from the engine, alternator and carburetor or fuel injection system.

NOTE: If equipped with a fuel injection system, it will be necessary to relieve the pressure in the fuel system before disconnecting the fuel lines.

8. Disconnect the fuel line, heater hoses and accelerator linkage.

9. If equipped, disconnect the air pump lines and remove the pump.

10. Remove the alternator from the engine.

11. Disconnect the shift linkage(s), clutch linkage (as required) and speedometer cables.

12. Raise and safely support the front of the vehicle.

13. If equipped with a manual transaxle, perform the following procedures:

   a. Disconnect the clutch cable.

   b. Remove the lower cover from the transaxle case.

   c. Remove the exhaust pipe-to-exhaust manifold bolts. Separate the pipe from the manifold.

   d. Remove the starter and support it out of the way.

   e. Using a transmission holding tool, secure it to the transaxle.

   f. If equipped, remove the anti-roll strut or damper (turbocharged) from the transaxle.

14. If equipped with an automatic transaxle, perform the following procedures:

   a. Remove the lower cover from the transaxle case.

   b. Remove the exhaust pipe-to-exhaust manifold bolts. Separate the pipe from the manifold.

   c. Remove the starter and set it aside.

   d. Mark the flex plate to the torque converter, for installation purposes.

   e. Remove the torque converter-to-flex plate bolts. Separate the converter from the flex plate.

   f. Using a C-clamp, secure the bottom of the torque converter to the transaxle so it will not fall out.

   g. Using a transmission holding tool, secure it to the transaxle.

15. If may be necessary to remove the right inner splash shield. Attach an engine lifting fixture and vertical lift to the engine.

16. To lower the engine, separate the right side engine bracket from the yoke bracket. To raise the engine, remove the yoke/insulator long bolt.

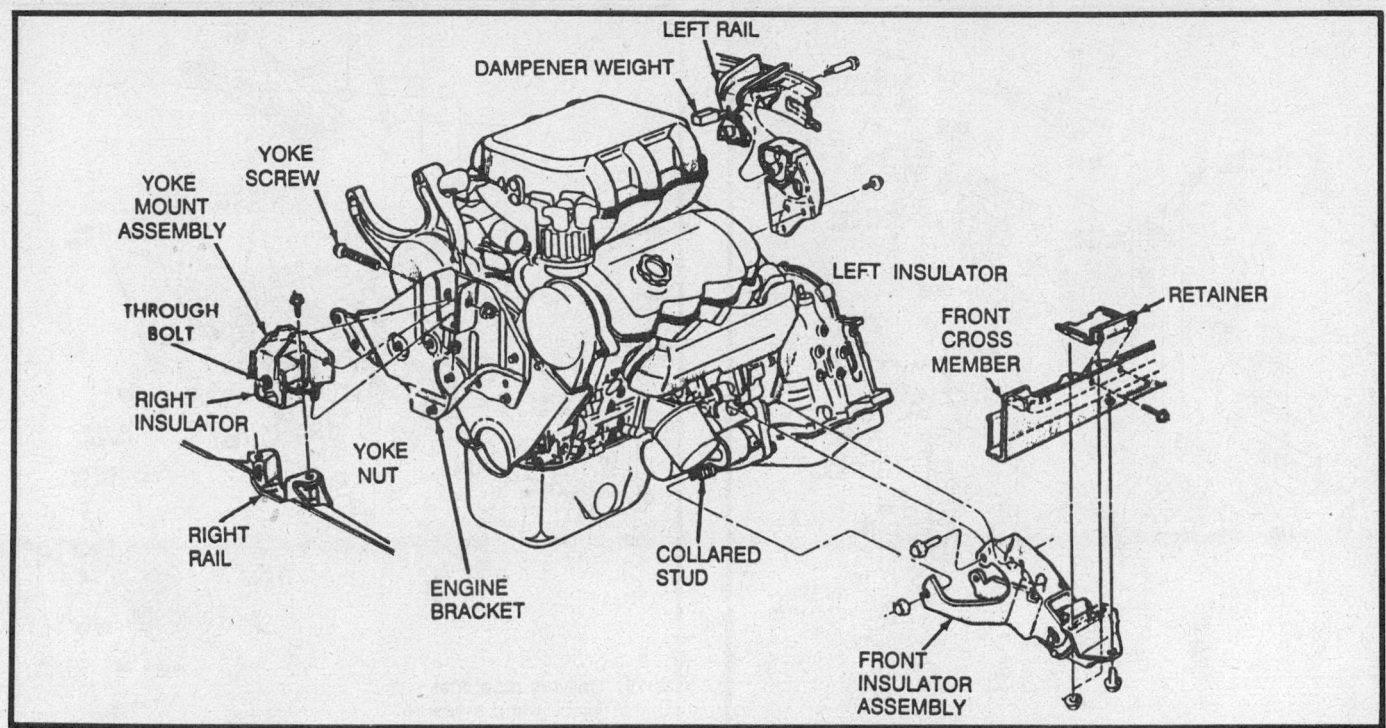

3.0L engine mounting

NOTE: If removing the insulator-to-rail screws, first mark the position of the insulator on the side rail to insure proper alignment during reinstallation.

17. Remove the transaxle-to-engine bolts, front engine mount nut/bolt and the left insulator through bolt (from inside the wheelhouse) or the insulator bracket-to-transaxle bolts.
18. Lift the engine from the vehicle.

To Install:

19. Reverse the removal procedures. Loosely install all of the mounting bolts. With all bolts installed, torque the:
   Engine-to-mount bolts to 40 ft. lbs.
   Engine-to-transaxle bolts to 70 ft. lbs.
   Torque converter-to-flex plate bolts to 40 ft. lbs.
20. Refill the cooling system. Start the engine, allow it to reach normal operating temperature. Check for leaks. Check the ignition timing and adjust if necessary. Adjust the idle speed/mixture (if possible) and the transaxle linkage.

3.0L ENGINE

1. Disconnect the negative battery cable.
2. Matchmark the hinge-to-hood position and remove the hood.
3. Drain the cooling system. Disconnect and label all engine electrical connections.
4. Remove the coolant hoses from the radiator and engine. Remove the radiator and cooling fan assembly.
5. Relieve the fuel pressure and disconnect the fuel lines from the engine. Disconnect the accelerator cable from the engine. Remove the air cleaner assembly.
6. Raise and safely support the vehicle. Drain the engine oil.
7. Remove the air conditioning compressor mounting bolts, the drive belt and support the compressor aside. Disconnect the exhaust pipe from the exhaust manifold.
8. Remove the transaxle inspection cover, matchmark the converter to the flexplate and remove the converter bolts. Attach a C-clamp on the bottom of the converter to prevent the converter from falling out.
9. Remove the power steering pump mounting bolts and set the pump aside, upright, with the fluid lines attached.
10. Remove the lower transaxle-to-engine bolts. Disconnect and label the starter motor wiring and remove the starter motor from the engine.
11. Lower the vehicle. Disconnect and label the vacuum hoses and engine ground straps.
12. Install a transmission holding fixture to the transaxle. Attach an engine lifting fixture to the engine and support the engine.
13. Remove the upper transaxle-to-engine bolts.
14. To separate the engine mounts from the insulators, perform the following procedures:
   a. Mark the right insulator-to-right frame support and remove the mounting bolts.
   b. Remove the front engine mount through bolt.
   c. Remove the left insulator through bolt, from inside the wheel housing.
   d. Remove the insulator bracket-to-transaxle bolts.
15. Lift and remove the engine from the vehicle.

To Install:

16. Lower the engine into the engine compartment. Align the engine mounts and install the bolts; do not tighten the bolts until all bolts have been installed. Torque the through bolts to 75 ft. lbs.
17. Install the upper transaxle-to-engine mounting bolts and torque to 75 ft. lbs. Remove the engine lifting fixture from the engine.
18. Raise and safely support the vehicle. Remove the C-clamp from the converter housing.
19. Align the converter marks, install the flex plate-to-converter bolts and torque to 55 ft. lbs. Install the transaxle inspection cover.
20. Connect the exhaust pipe to the exhaust manifold. Install the starter motor and connect the wiring.
21. Install the power steering pump and air conditioning compressor, adjust the drive belt tension.
22. Lower the vehicle. Reconnect all vacuum hoses and electrical connections to the engine.

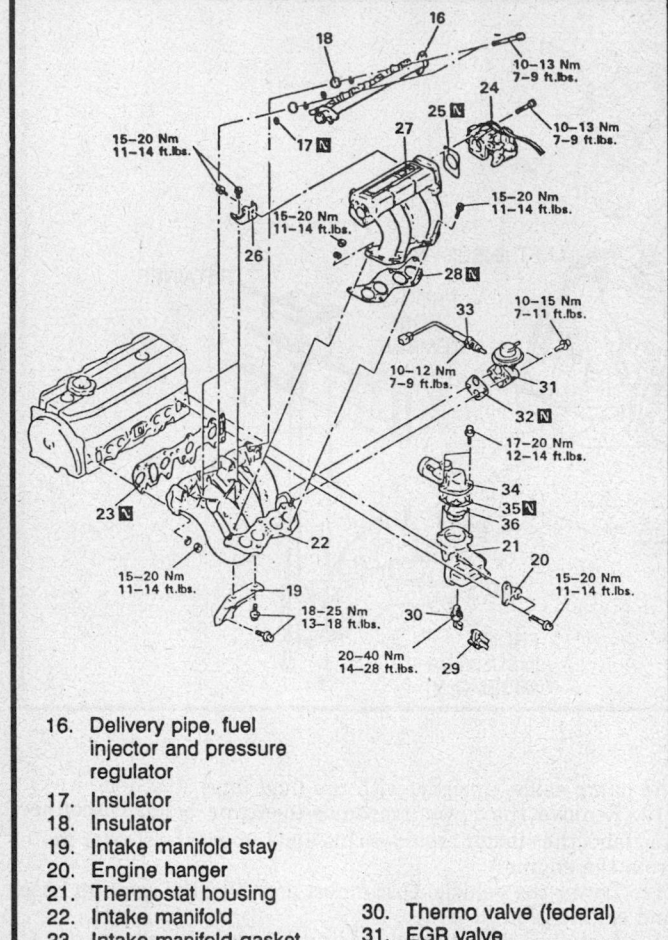

16. Delivery pipe, fuel injector and pressure regulator
17. Insulator
18. Insulator
19. Intake manifold stay
20. Engine hanger
21. Thermostat housing
22. Intake manifold
23. Intake manifold gasket
24. Throttle body assembly
25. Gasket
26. Air intake plenum stay
27. Air intake plenum
28. Air intake plenum gasket
29. Vacuum hose (federal)
30. Thermo valve (federal)
31. EGR valve
32. EGR gasket
33. EGR temperature sensor (calif.)
34. Water outlet fitting
35. Gasket
36. Thermostat

Exploded view of the intake manifold assembly—1.8L engine

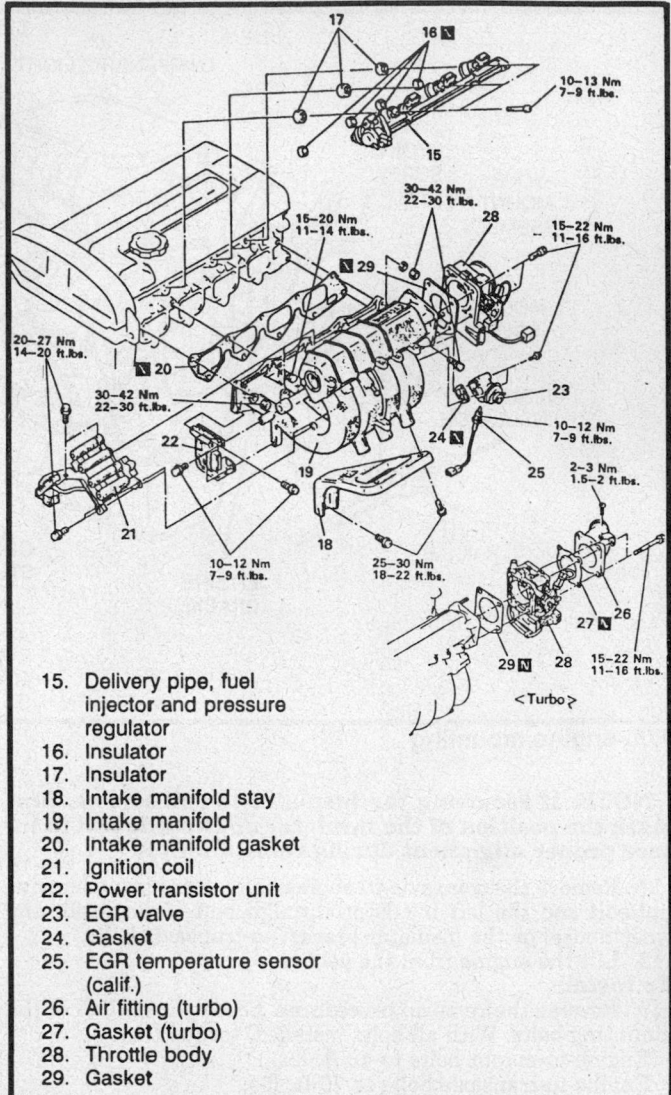

<Turbo>

15. Delivery pipe, fuel injector and pressure regulator
16. Insulator
17. Insulator
18. Intake manifold stay
19. Intake manifold
20. Intake manifold gasket
21. Ignition coil
22. Power transistor unit
23. EGR valve
24. Gasket
25. EGR temperature sensor (calif.)
26. Air fitting (turbo)
27. Gasket (turbo)
28. Throttle body
29. Gasket

Exploded view of the intake manifold assembly—2.0L engine

23. Connect the fuel lines and accelerator cable.
24. Install the radiator and fan assembly. Connect the fan motor wiring. Connect the radiator hoses and refill the cooling system.
25. Refill the engine with the proper oil to the correct level.
26. Connect the engine ground straps. Install the hood and align the matchmarks. Connect the battery.
27. Start and run the engine until it reaches normal operating temperatures and check for leaks. Adjust the transaxle linkage, if necessary.

Engine Mounts

Removal and Installation

The engine mounts can be removed and installed by first supporting the engine/transaxle assembly from below.

Insulator location on frame rail (right side) and transaxle bracket (left side) are adjustable to allow right/left drive train adjustment, in relation to driveshaft assembly length.

Check and reposition the right engine mount insulator. The left engine mount insulator centers itself with engine weight removed. Adjust the drive train position if required, for the following conditions:

   a. Driveshaft distress
   b. Any front end structural damage (after repair)
   c. Insulator replacement

Adjustment

1. Remove the engine weight from the engine mounts by carefully supporting the engine and transaxle assembly, from below.
2. Loosen the right engine mount insulator vertical fasteners and the front engine mount bracket to front crossmember fasteners.

NOTE: The left engine mount insulator is sleeved over the shaft. The long support bolt provides lateral movement adjustment with the engine weight removed from the mount.

3. Using a pry bar, pry the engine right and left, as required to achieve the proper driveshaft assembly length.
4. Torque the right side engine mount insulator vertical bolts

to 250 inch lbs. (28 Nm). Torque the front engine mount fasteners to 40 ft. lbs. (54 Nm) and center the left engine mount insulator.

5. Recheck the driveshaft length.

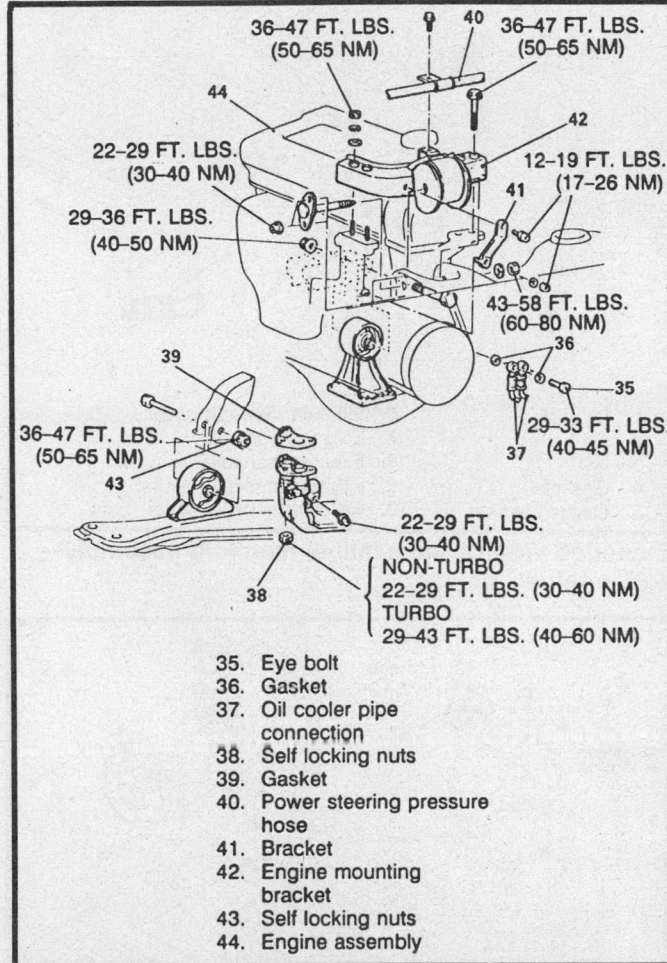

36–47 FT. LBS. (50–65 NM)
40
36–47 FT. LBS. (50–65 NM)
44
22–29 FT. LBS. (30–40 NM)
42
12–19 FT. LBS. (17–26 NM)
41
29–36 FT. LBS. (40–50 NM)
43–58 FT. LBS. (60–80 NM)
39
36
35
29–33 FT. LBS. (40–45 NM)
37
36–47 FT. LBS. (50–65 NM)
43
22–29 FT. LBS. (30–40 NM)
NON-TURBO
22–29 FT. LBS. (30–40 NM)
TURBO
29–43 FT. LBS. (40–60 NM)
38

35. Eye bolt
36. Gasket
37. Oil cooler pipe connection
38. Self locking nuts
39. Gasket
40. Power steering pressure hose
41. Bracket
42. Engine mounting bracket
43. Self locking nuts
44. Engine assembly

Exploded view of the engine mounts and related components—1.8L and 2.0L engines

Intake Manifold

Removal and Installation

1.6L ENGINE

1. Disconnect the negative battery cable. Relieve the fuel pressure.
2. Remove the air cleaner. Disconnect and label all vacuum lines, electrical wiring and fuel lines from carburetor.
3. Drain the cooling system. Disconnect inlet hose.
4. Disconnect the EGR tube at the manifold.
5. Remove the intake manifold-to-engine nuts and washers and the manifold.
6. Remove carburetor from intake manifold.
7. Clean the gasket mounting surfaces.

To Install:

8. Using new gaskets, reverse the removal procedures. Torque the carburetor-to-intake manifold nuts to 133 inch lbs. (15 Nm).
9. Refill the cooling system, run the engine and check for leaks.

1.8L ENGINE

1. Disconnect the negative battery cable. Relieve the fuel pressure. Drain the cooling system to a level below the intake manifold.
2. Remove the air intake duct and disconnect the accelerator cable. Disconnect the upper radiator hose, the overflow tube, the water bypass hose, the water hose and the heater hose.
3. Label and disconnect the brake booster hose, other vacuum hoses, the vacuum pipe and the PCV hose.
4. Disconnect the fuel high pressure hose (remove the O-ring), the fuel return hose, the delivery pipe, the fuel injector and the pressure regulator.
5. Disconnect the engine wiring harness electrical connector.
6. Remove the intake manifold stay, the engine hanger and the thermostat housing. Remove air intake plenum stay, the plenum and gasket.
7. Remove the intake manifold-to-engine nuts/bolts, the manifold and the gasket.
8. Clean the gasket mounting surfaces. Inspect the manifold and plenum for cracks, flatness and/or damage; replace them, if necessary.

To Install:

9. Using new gaskets, reverse the removal procedures. Torque the:
Intake manifold-to-engine nuts/bolts to 11–14 ft. lbs.
Plenum-to-intake manifold nuts/bolts to 11–14 ft. lbs.
10. Using a new O-ring, connect the fuel high pressure connector. Refill the cooling system. Start the engine, allow it to reach normal operating temperatures and check for leaks and engine performance.

2.0L ENGINE

1. Disconnect the negative battery cable. Relieve the fuel pressure. Drain the cooling system to a level below the intake manifold.
2. Remove the air intake duct (non-turbo) or the air hose (turbo). Disconnect the accelerator cable and the wiring harness connector(s). Remove the throttle body stay. Disconnect the water bypass hose and the water hose.
3. Label and disconnect the brake booster hose, other vacuum hoses and the PCV hose.
4. Disconnect the fuel high pressure hose (remove the O-ring), the fuel return hose, the delivery pipe, the fuel injector and the pressure regulator.
5. Disconnect the spark plug cables.
6. Remove the intake manifold stay, the intake manifold-to-engine nuts/bolts, the manifold and the gasket.
7. Clean the gasket mounting surfaces. Inspect the manifold for cracks, flatness and/or damage; replace it, if necessary.
8. To install, use new gaskets and reverse the removal procedures. Torque the intake manifold-to-engine nuts/bolts to 11–14 ft. lbs. (inner) or to 22–30 ft. lbs. (outer). Using a new O-ring, connect the fuel high pressure connector. Refill the cooling system. Start the engine, allow it to reach normal operating temperatures and check for leaks and engine performance.

3.0L ENGINE

1. Disconnect the negative battery cable. Relieve the fuel system pressure.
2. Drain the cooling system.
3. Remove the throttle body-to-air cleaner hose.
4. Remove the throttle body and transaxle kickdown linkage.
5. Remove the automatic idle speed (AIS) motor and throttle position sensor (TPS) wiring connectors from the throttle body.
6. Remove and label the vacuum hose harness from the throttle body.
7. From the air intake plenum, remove the PCV and brake booster hoses and the EGR tube flange.

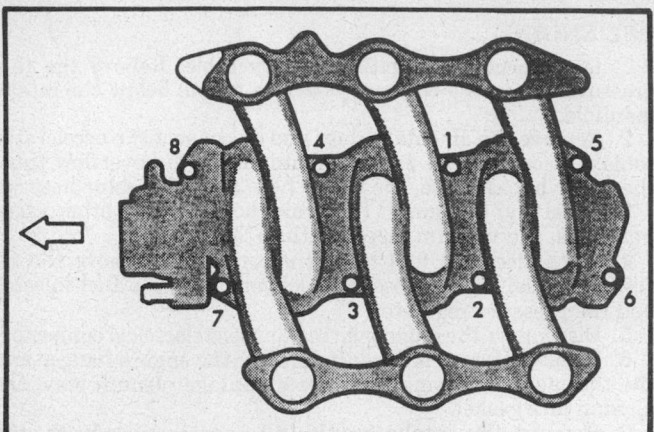

3.0L intake manifold tightening sequence

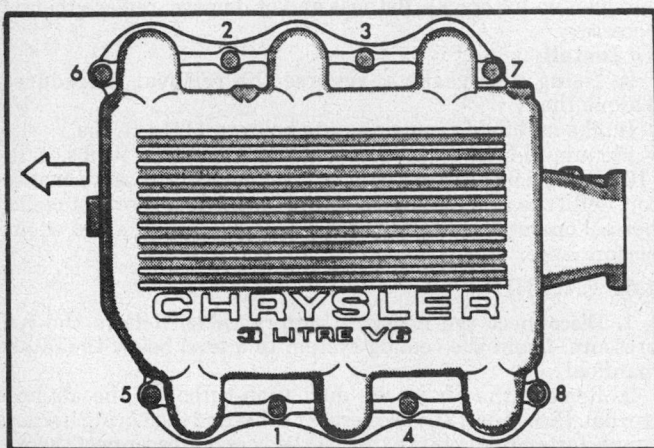

3.0L intake plenum tightening sequence

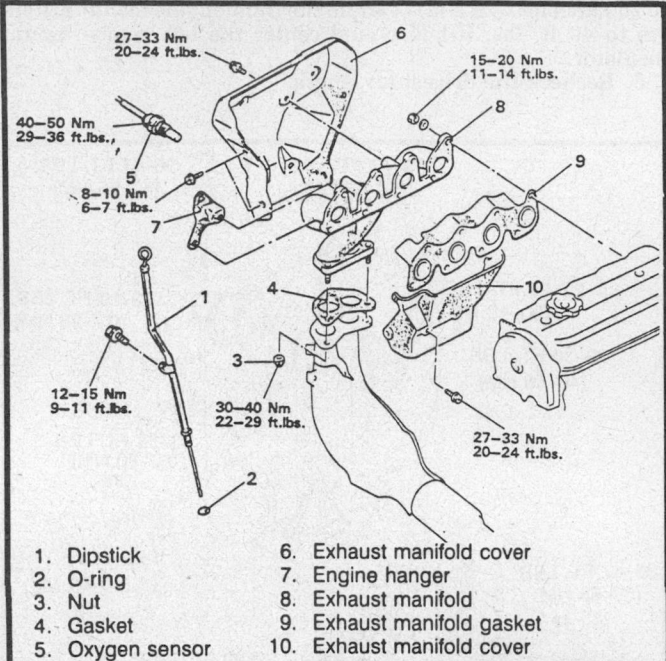

1. Dipstick
2. O-ring
3. Nut
4. Gasket
5. Oxygen sensor
6. Exhaust manifold cover
7. Engine hanger
8. Exhaust manifold
9. Exhaust manifold gasket
10. Exhaust manifold cover

Exploded view of the exhaust manifold assembly— 1.8L engine

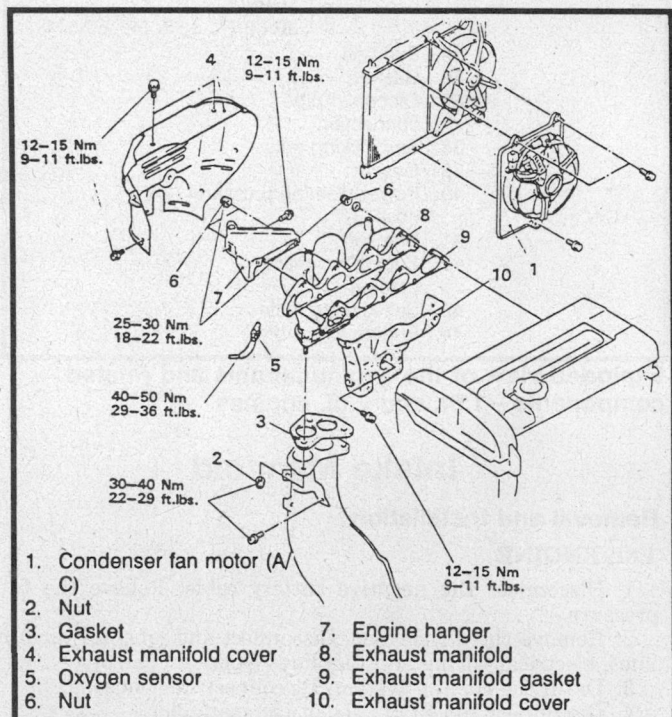

1. Condenser fan motor (A/C)
2. Nut
3. Gasket
4. Exhaust manifold cover
5. Oxygen sensor
6. Nut
7. Engine hanger
8. Exhaust manifold
9. Exhaust manifold gasket
10. Exhaust manifold cover

Exploded view of the exhaust manifold assembly— 2.0L engine

8. Disconnect and label the charge and temperature sensor wiring at the intake manifold.

9. Remove the vacuum connections from the air intake plenum vacuum connector.

10. Remove the fuel hoses from the fuel rail.

11. Remove the air intake-to-plenum mounting bolts and the plenum.

NOTE: When servicing the engine with the air intake plenum removed, cover the intake manifold holes with a clean cloth when servicing.

12. Remove the vacuum hoses from the fuel rail and pressure regulator.

13. Disconnect the fuel injector wiring harness from the engine wiring harness.

14. Remove the fuel pressure regulator mounting bolts and remove the regulator from the fuel rail.

15. Remove the fuel rail mounting bolts and remove the fuel rail from the intake manifold.

16. Separate the radiator hose from the thermostat housing and heater hoses from the heater pipe.

17. Remove the intake manifold mounting bolts and the manifold from the engine.

18. Clean the gasket mounting surfaces on the engine and intake manifold.

To Install:

19. Using new gaskets, position the intake manifold on the engine and install the mounting nuts and washers.

20. Torque the nuts (in sequence) to 174 inch lbs. (20 Nm).

21. Make sure the injector holes are clean. Lubricate the injector O-rings with a drop of clean engine oil and install the injector assembly onto the engine.

22. Install and torque the fuel rail mounting bolts to 115 inch lbs.

23. Install the fuel pressure regulator onto the fuel rail. Torque the mounting bolts to 95 inch lbs.

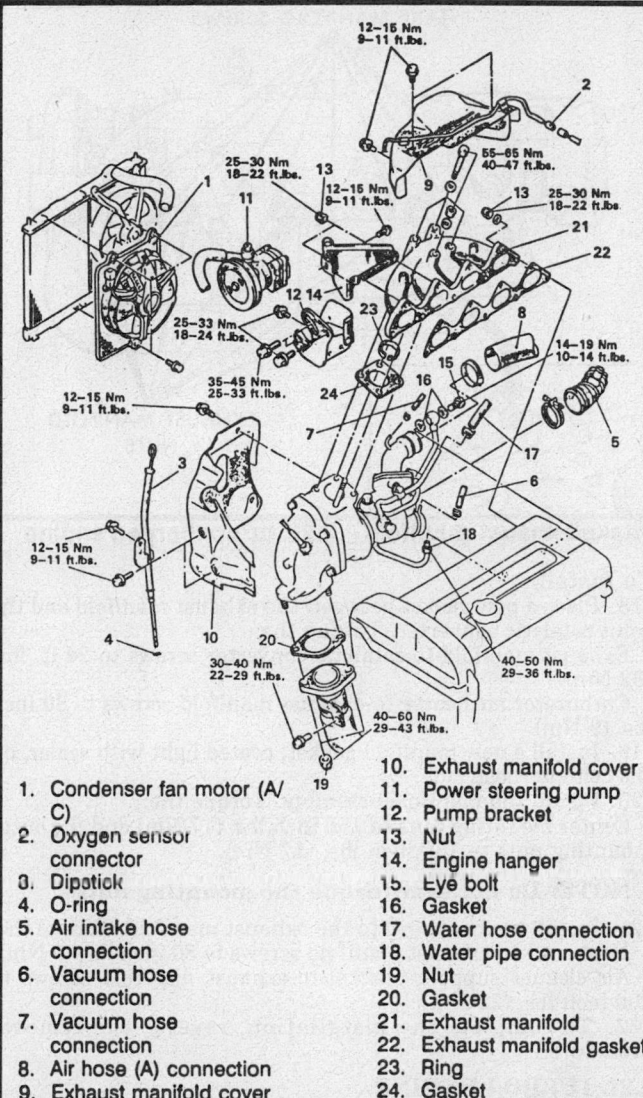

1. Condenser fan motor (A/C)	10. Exhaust manifold cover
2. Oxygen sensor connector	11. Power steering pump
3. Dipstick	12. Pump bracket
4. O-ring	13. Nut
5. Air intake hose connection	14. Engine hanger
6. Vacuum hose connection	15. Eye bolt
7. Vacuum hose connection	16. Gasket
8. Air hose (A) connection	17. Water hose connection
9. Exhaust manifold cover	18. Water pipe connection
	19. Nut
	20. Gasket
	21. Exhaust manifold
	22. Exhaust manifold gasket
	23. Ring
	24. Gasket

Exploded view of the exhaust manifold assembly— 2.0L turbo engine

24. Install the fuel supply and return tube and the vacuum crossover hold-down bolt. Torque the bolt to 95 inch lbs.

25. Connect the fuel injection wiring harness to the engine wiring harness.

26. Connect the vacuum harness to the fuel pressure regulator and fuel rail assembly.

27. Remove the cover from the lower intake manifold and clean the mating surface.

28. Place the intake manifold gasket with the beaded sealant side **UP**, on the intake manifold. Install the air intake plenum and torque the mounting bolts to 115 inch lbs.

29. To complete the installation, reverse the removal procedures. Refill the cooling system. Start the engine, allow it to reach normal operating temperatures and check for leaks.

Exhaust Manifold

Removal and Installation

1.6L ENGINE

1. Disconnect the negative battery cable.

2. Separate the carburetor air heater tube from the exhaust manifold heat stove.

3. Remove the oxygen sensor from the exhaust manifold. If equipped with an AIR system, disconnect the AIR pipe from the exhaust manifold.

4. Separate the EGR assembly from the exhaust manifold.

5. Raise and safely support the vehicle. Remove the exhaust pipe-to-exhaust manifold nuts and separate the pipe from the manifold.

6. Remove the exhaust manifold mounting nuts and the exhaust manifold. Remove the carburetor air heater from the exhaust manifold, if necessary.

7. Clean the gasket mating surfaces.

8. To install, use new gaskets and reverse the removal procedures. Torque the exhaust manifold mounting bolts to 15 ft. lbs.

NOTE: When tightening the manifold bolts, start with the center bolt and work outwards.

1.8L ENGINE

1. Disconnect the negative battery cable.

2. Remove the dipstick, the dipstick tube and the O-ring.

3. Remove the exhaust manifold cover, the engine hanger and the exhaust manifold-to-exhaust pipe nuts.

4. Disconnect the electrical connector from the oxygen sensor.

5. Remove the exhaust manifold-to-cylinder head nuts, the manifold and the gasket.

6. Clean the gasket mounting surfaces. Inspect the manifold for cracks or damage; replace it, if necessary.

7. To install, use new gaskets and reverse the removal procedures. Torque the exhaust manifold-to-cylinder head nuts to 11–14 ft. lbs.

2.0L ENGINE

Except Turbocharger

1. Disconnect the negative battery cable.

2. If equipped with air conditioning, remove the condenser fan motor.

3. Remove the exhaust manifold cover and the exhaust manifold-to-exhaust pipe nuts.

4. Disconnect the electrical connector from the oxygen sensor.

5. Remove the engine hanger, the exhaust manifold-to-engine nuts, the manifold and gasket.

6. Clean the gasket mounting surfaces. Inspect the manifold for cracks or damage; replace it, if necessary.

To Install:

7. Using new gaskets, reverse the removal procedures. Torque the:

Exhaust manifold-to-engine nuts to 18–22 ft. lbs.

Exhaust manifold-to-exhaust pipe nuts to 22–29 ft. lbs.

Turbocharger

1. Disconnect the negative battery cable.

2. Drain the cooling system and the crankcase. If equipped with air conditioning, remove the condenser fan motor.

3. Remove both exhaust manifold covers. Disconnect the electrical connector from the oxygen sensor.

4. Remove the dipstick, the dipstick tube and the O-ring. Disconnect the air intake hose, the vacuum hoses and the **A** air hose.

5. Loosen the power steering pump and remove the drive belt, the power steering pump and the bracket.

6. Remove the engine hanger. From the rear of the engine, remove the turbocharger's oil tube-to-engine bolt and gaskets. Disconnect the water hose and pipe from the turbocharger.

7. Remove the turbocharger-to-exhaust pipe nuts and separate the exhaust pipe from the turbocharger. Remove the turbocharger from the exhaust manifold.

8. Remove the exhaust manifold-to-engine nuts, the manifold and gasket.

9. Clean the gasket mounting surfaces. Inspect the manifold for cracks, flatness and/or damage.

To Install:

10. Using new gaskets, reverse the removal procedures. Torque the:

Exhaust manifold-to-engine nuts to 18–22 ft. lbs.
Turbocharger-to-exhaust manifold nuts/bolt to 40–47 ft. lbs.
Turbocharger-to-exhaust pipe nuts to 29–43 ft. lbs.

11. Refill the cooling system and the crankcase. Start the engine, allow it to reach normal operating temperatures and check it for leaks and engine performance.

3.0L ENGINE

1. Disconnect the negative battery cable. Raise and safely support the vehicle.

2. Disconnect the exhaust pipe from the rear exhaust manifold, at the articulated joint.

3. Disconnect the EGR tube from the rear manifold and the oxygen sensor wire.

4. Remove the cross-over pipe-to-manifold bolts.

5. Remove the rear manifold-to-cylinder head nuts and the manifold.

6. Lower the vehicle and remove the heat shield from the manifold.

7. Remove the front manifold-to-cylinder head nuts and the manifold.

8. Clean the gasket mounting surfaces. Inspect the manifolds for cracks, flatness and/or damage; replace them, if necessary.

To Install:

9. Using new gaskets, reverse the removal procedures. Torque the:

Manifold-to-cylinder head nuts to 175 inch lbs.

NOTE: When installing, the numbers 1–3–5 on the gaskets are used with the rear cylinders and 2–4–6 are on the gasket for the front cylinders.

Cross-over pipe-to-manifold nuts to 51 ft. lbs.
Exhaust manifold-to-exhaust pipe nuts to 250 inch lbs.

10. Start the engine and check for exhaust leaks.

Combination Manifold

Removal and Installation

2.2L AND 2.5L ENGINES EXCEPT TURBOCHARGED

1. Disconnect the negative battery cable.

2. Drain the cooling system.

3. Remove the air cleaner and disconnect all vacuum lines, electrical wiring and fuel lines from the carburetor.

4. Disconnect the throttle linkage.

5. Loosen the power steering pump and remove the drive belt.

6. Remove the power brake vacuum hose from the intake manifold.

7. On Canadian models, remove the coupling hose from the diverter valve to the exhaust manifold air injection tube assembly. Remove the water hoses from the water crossover.

8. Remove the water hoses from the water crossover.

9. Raise and safely support the vehicle. Disconnect the exhaust pipe from the exhaust manifold.

10. Remove the power steering pump and set it aside.

11. Remove the intake manifold support bracket.

12. Remove the EGR tube.

13. On Canadian models, remove the air injection tube bolts and the air injection tube assembly.

14. Remove the intake manifold bolts.

15. Lower the vehicle and remove the intake manifold.

16. Remove the exhaust manifold nuts.

17. Remove the exhaust manifold.

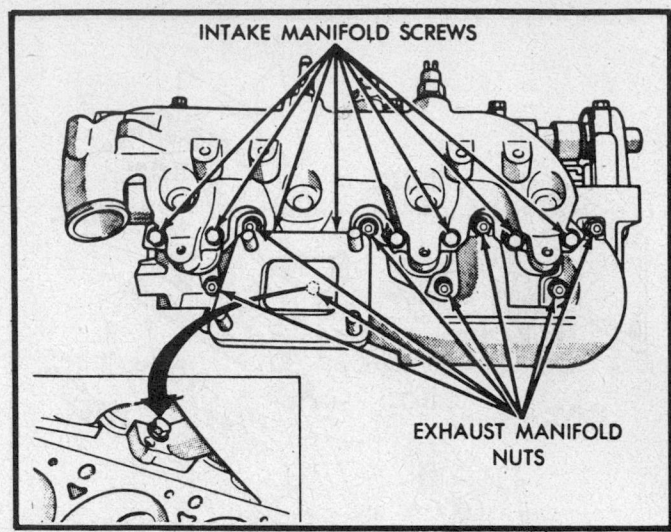

Intake/exhaust manifold—2.2L turbocharged engine

To Install:

18. Place a new gasket between the exhaust manifold and the front catalytic converter. Torque the:

Exhaust manifold-to-catalytic converter screws to 24 ft. lbs. (32 Nm).
Carburetor air heater-to-exhaust manifold screws to 80 inch lbs. (9 Nm).

19. Install a new manifold gasket, coated light with sealer, on the cylinder head side.

20. Install the manifold assembly. Torque the:

Center mounting nuts to 150 inch lbs. (17 Nm) and the outer mounting nuts to 150 inch lbs. (17 Nm).

NOTE: Do not over-torque the mounting nuts.

21. Install the heat cowl to the exhaust manifold. Torque the:

Heat cowl-to-exhaust manifold screws to 80 inch lbs. (9 Nm).
Air cleaner support bracket-to-exhaust manifold screws to 200 inch lbs. (23 Nm).

22. To complete the installation, reverse the removal procedures.

2.2L TURBO I ENGINE

1. Disconnect the negative battery cable. Drain the cooling system. Raise and safely support the vehicle.

2. Disconnect the exhaust pipe at the articulated joint. Disconnect the oxygen sensor at the electrical connection.

3. Remove the turbocharger-to-engine support bracket.

4. Loosen the oil drain back tube connector hose clamps. Move the tube down on the engine block fitting.

5. Disconnect the turbocharger coolant inlet tube from the engine block and disconnect the tube support bracket.

6. Remove the air cleaner assembly, including the throttle body adaptor, hose and air cleaner box with support bracket.

7. Disconnect the accelerator linkage, throttle body electrical connector and vacuum hoses.

8. Relocate the fuel rail assembly. Remove the bracket-to-intake manifold screws and the bracket-to-heat shield clips. Lift and secure the fuel rail (with injectors, wiring harness and fuel lines intact) up and out of the way.

9. Disconnect the turbocharger oil feed line at the oil sending unit Tee fitting.

10. Disconnect the upper radiator hose from the thermostat housing.

11. Remove the cylinder head, manifolds and turbocharger as an assembly.

12. With the assembly on a workbench, loosen the upper turbocharger discharge hose end clamp.

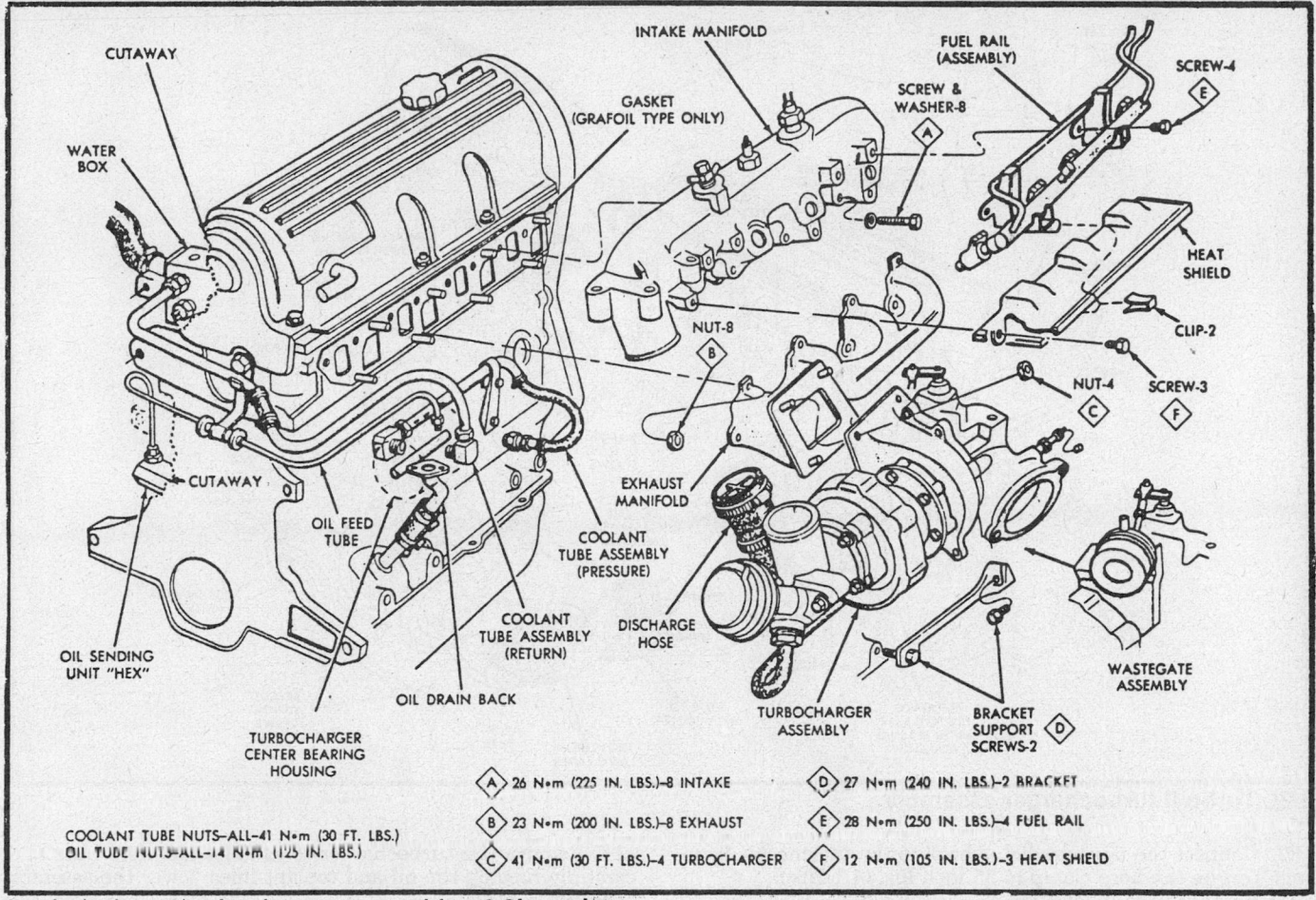

Intake/exhaust/turbocharger assembly—2.2L engine

NOTE: Do not disturb the center deswirler retaining clamp.

13. Remove the throttle body-to-intake manifold screws and throttle body assembly. Disconnect the turbocharger coolant return tube from the water box. Disconnect the retaining bracket on the cylinder head.

14. Remove the heat shield-to-intake manifold screws and the heat shield.

15. Remove the turbocharger-to-exhaust manifold nuts and the turbocharger assembly.

16. Remove the intake manifold bolts and the intake manifold.

17. Remove the exhaust manifold nuts and the exhaust manifold.

To Install:

18. Place a new two-side Grafoil or equivalent, intake/exhaust manifold gasket; do not use sealant.

19. Position the exhaust manifold on the cylinder head. Apply anti-seize compound to threads, install and torque the retaining nuts, starting at center and progressing outward in both directions, to 200 inch lbs. (23 Nm). Repeat this procedure until all nuts are at 200 inch lbs. (23 Nm).

20. Position the intake manifold on the cylinder head. Install and torque the retaining screws, starting at center and progressing outward in both directions, to 225 inch lbs. (26 Nm). Repeat this procedure until all screws are at 225 inch lbs. (26 Nm).

21. Connect the turbocharger outlet to the intake manifold inlet tube. Position the turbocharger on the exhaust manifold. Apply anti-seize compound to threads and torque the nuts to 30 ft. lbs. (41 Nm). Torque the connector tube clamps to 30 inch lbs. (41 Nm).

22. Install the tube support bracket to the cylinder head.

23. Install the heat shield on the intake manifold. Torque the screws to 105 inch lbs. (12 Nm).

24. Install the throttle body air horn into the turbocharger inlet tube. Install and torque the throttle body-to-intake manifold screws to 250 inch lbs. (28 Nm). Torque the tube clamp to 30 inch lbs. (3 Nm).

25. Install the cylinder head/manifolds/turbocharger assembly on the engine.

26. Reconnect the turbocharger oil feed line to the oil sending unit Tee fitting and bearing housing, if disconnected. Torque the tube nuts to 125 inch lbs. (14 Nm).

27. Install the air cleaner assembly. Connect the vacuum lines and accelerator cables.

28. Reposition the fuel rail. Install and torque the bracket screws to 250 inch lbs. (28 Nm). Install the air shield-to-bracket clips.

29. Connect the turbocharger inlet coolant tube to the engine block. Torque the tube nut to 30 ft. lbs. (41 Nm). Install the tube support bracket.

30. Install the turbocharger housing-to-engine block support bracket and the screws hand tight. Torque the block screw 1st to 40 ft. lbs. (54 Nm). Torque the screw to the turbocharger housing to 20 ft. lbs. (27 Nm).

31. Reposition the drain back hose connector and tighten the hose clamps. Reconnect the exhaust pipe.

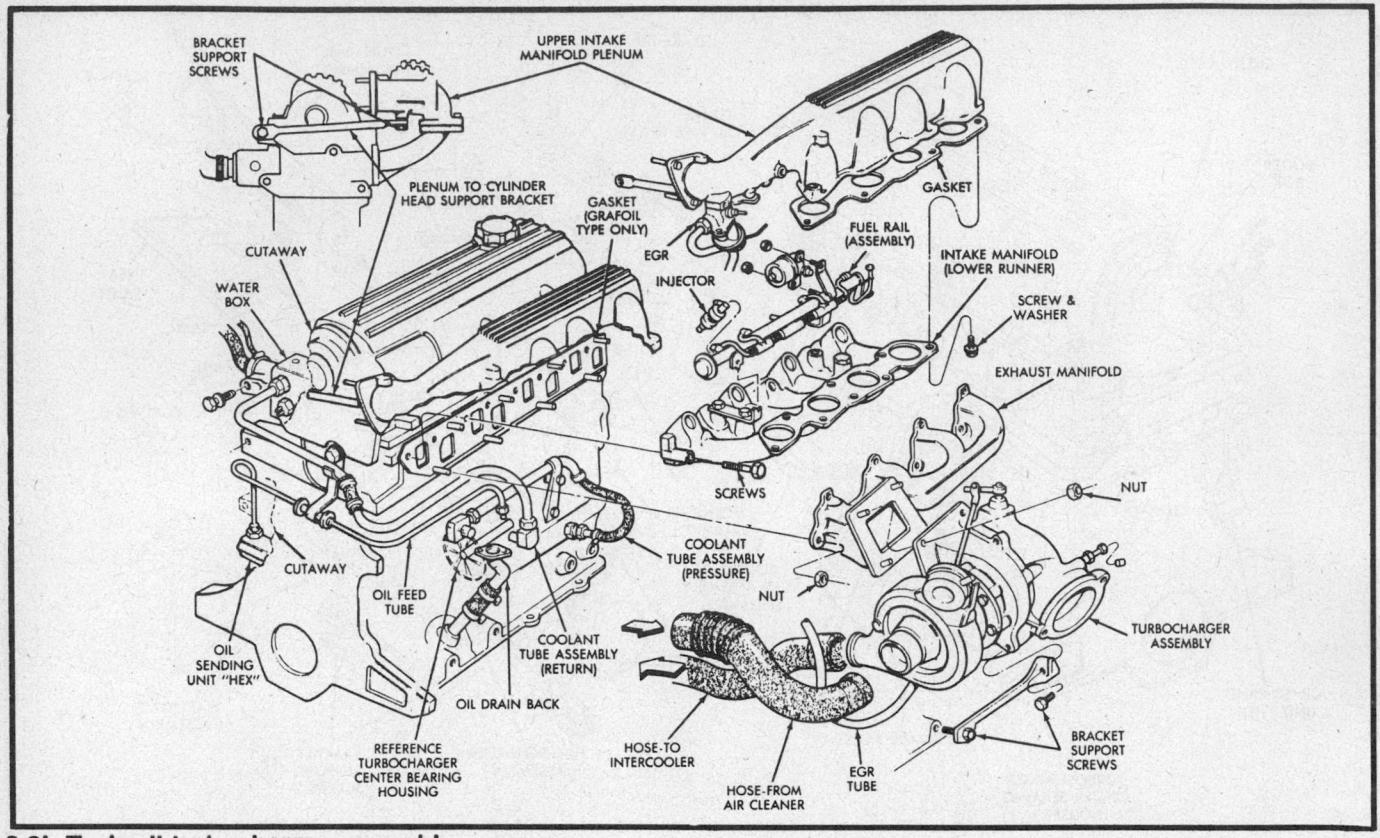

2.2L Turbo II turbocharger assembly

32. Connect the upper radiator hose to the thermostat housing. Torque the hose clamp to 35 inch lbs. (4.1 Nm).

33. Refill the cooling system.

2.2L AND 2.5L TURBO II ENGINE

1. Disconnect the negative battery cable. Drain the cooling system.

2. Remove the air cleaner assembly. Remove the intake manifold upper plenum-to-cylinder head support bracket.

3. Separate the throttle body assembly from the intake manifold. Disconnect the EGR vacuum line from the valve, PCV, MAP and brake booster vacuum supply hoses. Disconnect the charge temperature sensor electrical connector.

4. Disconnect the starter wiring and remove the starter.

5. Remove the screw to separate the upper intake manifold plenum from the lower intake runner.

6. Remove the upper plenum and the plenum-to-runner gasket.

NOTE: Do not allow any debris to enter runner.

7. Remove the cowl mounted heat shield and the fuel rail.

8. Disconnect the turbocharger oil feed at the oil sending unit. Disconnect the coolant tube at the water box and the oil/coolant support bracket from the cylinder head.

9. Raise and safely support the vehicle. Remove the right side intermediate shaft, bearing support bracket and outer driveshaft assembly.

10. Remove the turbocharger-to-engine block support bracket.

11. Disconnect the exhaust pipe at the articulated joint and the oxygen sensor at the electrical connection.

12. Loosen the oil drain-back tube connector clamps and move the tube hose down on the nipple.

13. Disconnect the coolant tube nut at the block outlet, below the steering pump bracket and tube support bracket.

14. Remove the turbocharger-to-exhaust manifold nuts and, carefully routing the oil and coolant lines, lower the assembly from the vehicle.

15. Remove the intake manifold screws and washer assemblies. Remove the lower runner.

16. Remove the exhaust manifold nuts and the exhaust manifold.

To Install:

17. Install a new Grafoil or equivalent, intake/exhaust manifold gasket; do not use sealant.

18. Position the intake manifold runner, install and torque retaining screws, starting at the center and progressing outward in both directions, to 200 inch lbs. (23 Nm).

19. Repeat this procedure until all screws are at 200 inch lbs. (23 Nm).

20. Set the exhaust manifold in place. Install and torque the retaining nuts, starting at center and progressing outward in both directions, to 200 inch lbs. (23 Nm).

21. Repeat this procedure until all nuts are at 200 inch lbs. (23 Nm).

22. Install the fuel rail.

23. Install the cowl mounted heat shield.

24. Install a new gasket on the lower intake manifold runner. Install the upper intake manifold plenum. Install and torque the 7 screws to 200 inch lbs. (54 Nm).

25. Install the upper plenum-to-cylinder head support bracket and torque the screws to 40 ft. lbs. (54 Nm).

26. Position the turbocharger on the exhaust manifold, apply an anti-seize compound (Loctite® 771–64 or equivalent) to threads. Torque the nuts to 40 ft. lbs. (54 Nm).

27. Connect the coolant tube to the engine block fitting. Torque the tube nut to 30 ft. lbs. (41 Nm).

28. Position the oil drain-back hose and torque the clamps to 30 inch lbs. (3 Nm).

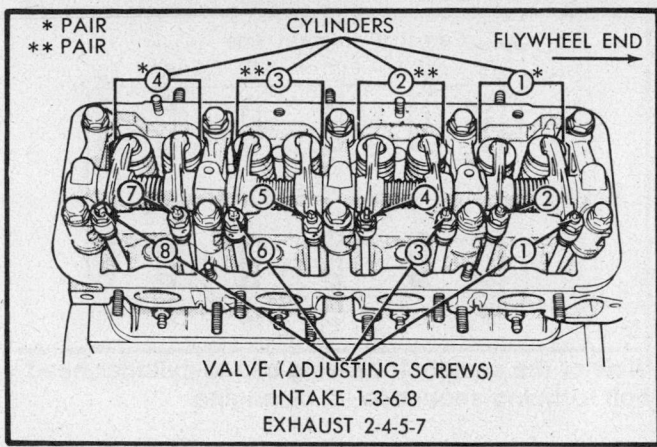

Adjusting valve clearance—1.6L engine

Valves 'Rocking' on Cylinder Number	Adjust Valves on Cylinder Number
4	1
2	3
1	4
3	2

29. Install and tighten the turbocharger-to-engine block support bracket and install screws hand tight. Torque the block screw 1st to 40 ft. lbs. (54 Nm) and the screw to the turbocharger housing to 20 ft. lbs. (27 Nm).

30. Connect the exhaust pipe. Torque the articulated joint shoulder bolt to 250 inch lbs. (28 Nm).

31. Install the right side driveshaft assembly.

16. Install the starter and connect the wiring.

32. Install the oil feed line at the sending unit. Torque the tube nut to 125 inch lbs. (14 Nm).

33. Connect the EGR tube at the EGR valve. Torque the tube nut to 60 ft. lbs. (81 Nm).

34. Connect the PCV, MAP, brake booster vacuum supply hoses and the charge temperature sensor electrical connection.

35. Refill the cooling system and reconnect battery.

Valve System

VALVE ADJUSTMENT

Procedure

1.6L ENGINE

NOTE: Valve clearance must be set with the engine cold and the piston at TDC on the compression stroke.

1. Disconnect the negative battery cable.

2. Remove the valve cover. Rotate the crankshaft and watch movement of exhaust valves. When 1 is closing, (moving upward) continue rotating the crankshaft slowly, until the inlet valve on the same cylinder just starts to open. This is the "valve rocking" position. The piston in the opposite cylinder is now at TDC of it's compression stroke and the valve lash can be checked and adjusted.

3. Example: To check valve clearances on No. 1 cylinder, position the valves on the companion cylinder No. 4, in the "rocking" position as follows:

   a. Observe rockers on companion cylinder No. 4. Turn crankshaft until exhaust valve rocker is moving upward

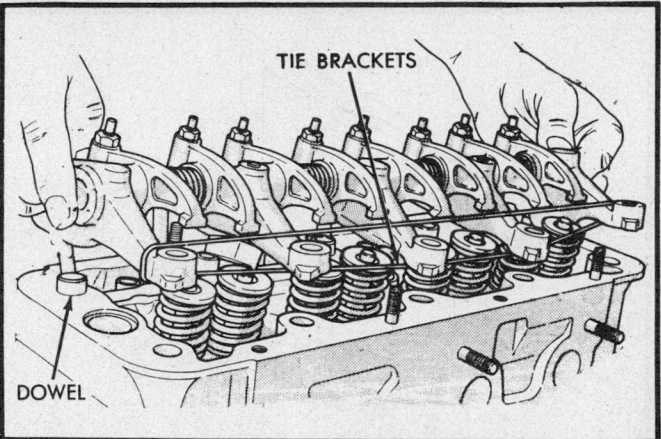

Removing rocker arm assembly—1.6L engine

(valve closing)—keep turning slowly until intake valve rocker just starts to move down (valve opening)—stop.

   b. Check both valve clearances on No. 1 cylinder.

4. After checking both valve clearances, rotate the crankshaft ½ turn, the next cylinder in the firing order should have its valves "rocking" and the companion cylinder can be adjusted.

5. Adjust the valves to obtain the following specifications: Intake 0.010 in. and Exhaust 0.012 in.

1.8L, 2.0L, 2.2L, 2.5L AND 3.0L ENGINES

These engines use hydraulic lash adjusters. No periodic adjustment or checking is necessary.

VALVE ROCKER SHAFT/ARM ASSEMBLY

Removal and Installation

1.6L ENGINE

1. Disconnect the negative battery cable. Relieve the fuel pressure.

2. Remove the valve cover.

3. Remove the rocker arm assembly.

4. With the rocker arm assemblies removed from the engine, slide the end brackets, rocker arms and springs from the rocker arm shafts.

NOTE: Store all parts in the order of removal. The rocker arms are assembled in pairs.

5. Inspect all items for wear and/or distortion. Make sure the oil holes are clear.

6. To install, use new gaskets, lubricate the parts and reverse the removal procedures.

1.8L ENGINE

1. Relieve the fuel pressure. Disconnect the negative battery cable.

2. Disconnect the breather hose, the PVC hose and the brake booster vacuum hose.

3. Disconnect the spark plug cables. Remove the upper engine mounting bracket.

4. Remove the rocker arm cover, the gasket and the upper front timing belt cover.

5. If necessary, use a wrench on the crankshaft pulley bolt, rotate the crankshaft (clockwise) to align the camshaft timing mark with the timing notch in the rear upper timing belt cover.

6. Remove the rear timing belt cover-to-rocker arm/shaft assembly bolts.

7. Using the lash adjuster retaining clip tools MD998443 or equivalent, place them on the rocker arms to keep the lash adjusters from falling out.

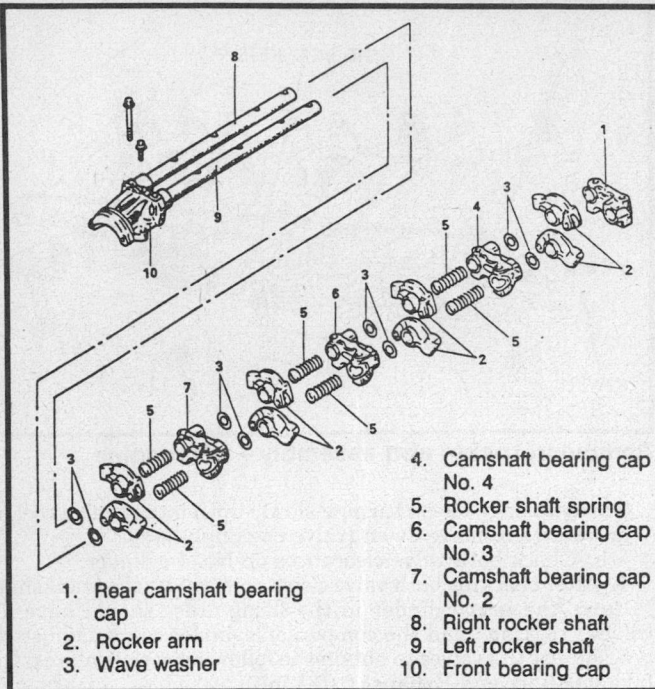

4. Camshaft bearing cap No. 4
5. Rocker shaft spring
6. Camshaft bearing cap No. 3
7. Camshaft bearing cap No. 2
8. Right rocker shaft
9. Left rocker shaft
10. Front bearing cap

1. Rear camshaft bearing cap
2. Rocker arm
3. Wave washer

Exploded view of the rocker arm/shaft assembly— 1.8L engine

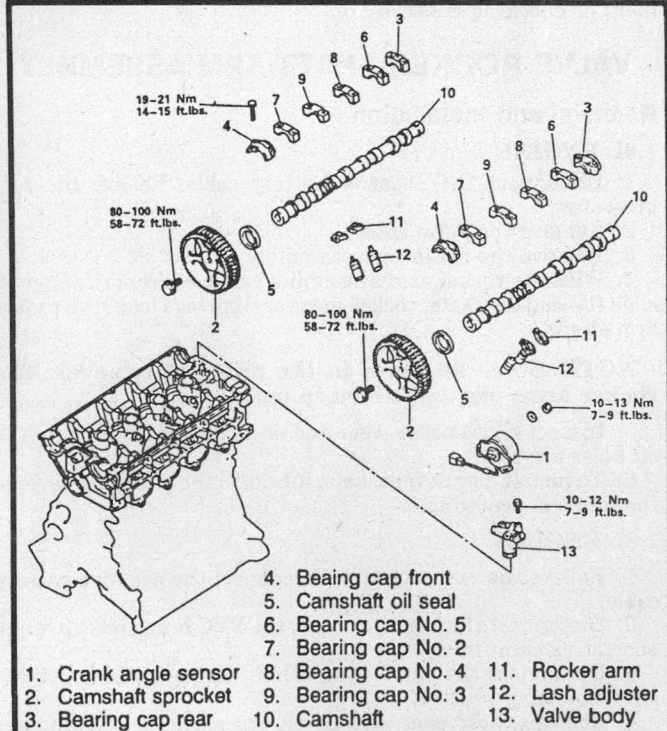

4. Beaing cap front
5. Camshaft oil seal
6. Bearing cap No. 5
7. Bearing cap No. 2
8. Bearing cap No. 4
9. Bearing cap No. 3
10. Camshaft
11. Rocker arm
12. Lash adjuster
13. Valve body

1. Crank angle sensor
2. Camshaft sprocket
3. Bearing cap rear

Exploded view of the rocker arm/shaft assembly— 2.0L engine

8. Remove the rocker arm/shaft assembly-to-cylinder head bolts and lift the assembly from the cylinder head.

9. To disassemble the rocker arm/shaft assembly, remove the mounting bolts and slide the rocker arms, the wave washers and springs from the rocker arm shafts; be sure to keep the parts in order for reinstallation purposes.

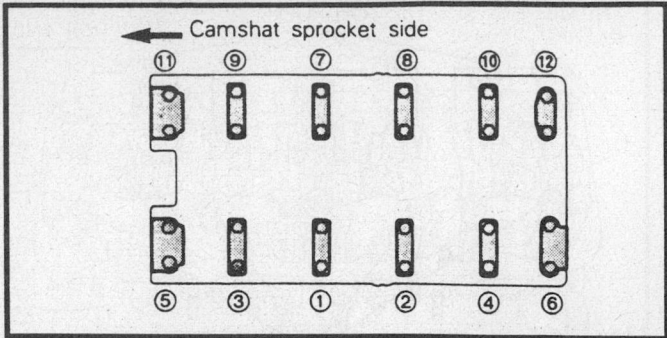

View of the camshaft bearing cap-to-cylinder head bolt torquing sequence—2.0L engine

10. Clean the gasket mounting surfaces. Check the parts for damage and/or wear and the rocker for smooth operation; replace the parts, if necessary.

To Install:

11. Using a new semi-circular packing, lubricate it with sealant and install it into the rear of the cylinder head.

12. Align the camshaft sprocket and the sprocket's timing mark with the timing mark on the rear timing belt cover.

13. To assemble the rocker arm/shaft assembly, install the wave washers, the rocker arms, the springs, the bearing caps and the mounting bolts.

14. Torque the rocker arm/shaft assembly-to-cylinder head bolts to 14–20 ft. lbs. (long) or 14–15 ft. lbs. (short).

15. To complete the installation, use a new gasket and reverse the removal procedures. Start the engine, allow it to reach normal operating temperatures and check the engine operation.

2.0L ENGINE

1. Relieve the fuel system pressure. Disconnect the negative battery cable.

2. Disconnect the high pressure fuel hose, the O-ring and the fuel return hose.

3. Disconnect the vacuum hoses, the PVC hose and the brake booster vacuum hose.

4. Disconnect the spark plug cables and the electrical connectors from the fuel injector (turbo) and the crankshaft angle sensor.

5. Disconnect the vacuum hoses (turbo). Disconnect the engine ground cable and the control wiring harness. Remove the power steering pressure hose-to-engine clamp and the upper engine mounting bracket. Using a floor jack, place a block of wood between the oil pan and the jack, raise the engine slightly; be careful not to place excessive loads on various parts.

6. To remove the timing belt, perform the following procedures:

a. Remove the rocker arm cover and gasket.

b. Remove the drive belt from the alternator, power steering air conditioner compressor. Remove the tensioner pulley bracket, the water pump pulley and the crankshaft pulley.

c. Remove the upper/lower front timing belt cover and the center cover.

d. Using a wrench on the crankshaft pulley bolt, rotate the crankshaft (clockwise) to position the No. 1 piston at the TDC of it's compression stroke; the camshaft timing marks should be facing each other and aligned with the upper surface of the cyinder head. The crankshaft and oil pump sprockets timing notches should be aligned with their timing pointer.

e. Mark the timing belt with an arrow to determine the direction of rotation; this is so the belt can be installed in the same direction.

f. Remove the auto tensioner and the timing belt.

7. From the rear of the engine, remove the crank angle sensor.

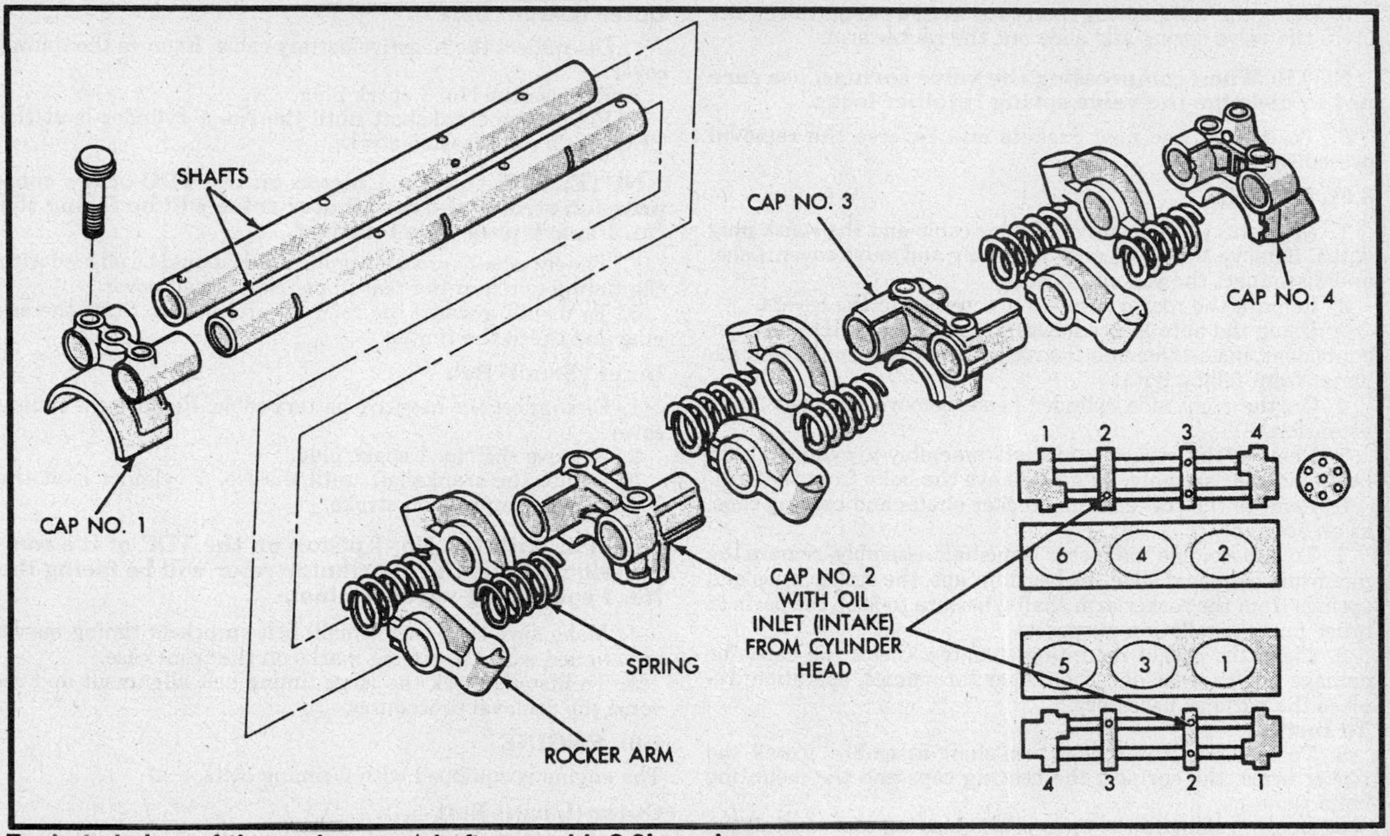

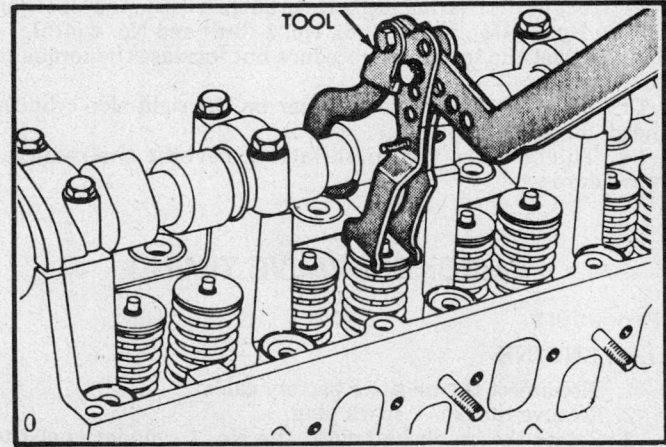

Exploded view of the rocker arm/shaft assembly 3.0L engine

8. Remove the camshaft bearing caps-to-cylinder head bolts, the bearing caps the camshafts and the rocker arms.

9. Clean the parts and the gasket mounting surfaces; be sure to keep the coolant and oil passages clean. Inspect the parts for damage and/or wear; replace the parts, if necessary.

To Install:

10. Install the rocker arms, the camshafts, the bearing caps and the bearing caps-to-cylinder head bolts; torque the bearing caps-to-cylinder head bolts (in sequence) to 14–15 ft. lbs.

11. Using a new semi-circular packing, lubricate it with sealant and install it into the rear of the cylinder head.

12. Install a new O-ring to the high pressure fuel hose delivery pipe, lubricate it with gasoline and install it onto the delivery pipe.

13. Align the camshaft sprocket timing marks with each other and the upper edge of the cylinder head. Install the timing belt and the automatic tensioner.

14. To adjust the timing belt tension, perform the following procedures:

    a. Rotate the crankshaft ¼ turn counterclockwise and clockwise to move the No. 1 piston to the TDC position.

    b. Loosen the tensioner pulley center bolt. Using the tool MD998752 or equivalent, and a 0–2.2 inch lbs. torque wrench, apply 1.88–2.03 ft. lbs. pressure to the tensioner pulley.

    c. While holding pressure on the pulley, tighten the center bolt.

    d. Using the tool MD998738 or equivalent, screw it into the left engine support bracket until it makes contact with the tensioner arm. Turn the screw inward and remove the set wire from the auto tensioner.

    e. Remove the screw tool.

    f. Rotate the crankshaft 2 complete revolutions (clockwise), allow it to stand for 15 minutes and measure the distance between the tensioner arm and the tensioner body; it

Valve spring removal—2.2L/2.5L engines

should be 0.15–0.18 in. If it is not within specifications, repeat the adjustment procedures.

15. To complete the installation, use new gaskets and reverse the removal procedures. Start the engine, allow it to reach normal operating temperatures and check the engine operation.

2.2L AND 2.5L ENGINES

1. Relieve the fuel system pressure. Disconnect the negative battery cable.

2. Remove the PCV module from the rocker cover by turning it counterclockwise.

3. Remove the rocker arm cover bolts and the cover.

4. Rotate the crankshaft until the base circle of the camshaft journal is in contact with the rocker arm.

5. Using the valve spring compression tool or equivalent, depress the valve spring and slide out the rocker arm.

NOTE: When compressing the valve springs, use care not to dislodge the valve spring retainer locks.

6. To install, use new gaskets and reverse the removal procedures.

3.0L ENGINE

1. Disconnect the negative battery cable and the spark plug wires. Remove the air cleaner assembly and valve cover. Label and disconnect the vacuum hoses.

2. Remove the rocker arm cover screws and the covers.

3. Using the auto lash adjuster retainer tools MD998443 or equivalent, install them on the rocker arms to keep the lash adjuster from falling out.

4. On the right side cylinder head, remove the distributor extension.

5. Remove the rocker arm/shaft assembly-to-cylinder head bolts and the assembly; do not remove the bolts from the caps.

6. Remove the rocker arms, rocker shafts and bearing caps, as an assembly.

7. To disassemble the rocker arm/shaft assembly, remove the mounting bolts and slide the bearing caps, the rocker arms and springs from the rocker arm shafts; be sure to keep the parts in order for reinstallation purposes.

8. Clean the gasket mounting surfaces. Check the parts for damage and/or wear and the rocker for smooth operation; replace the parts, if necessary.

To Install:

9. To assemble the rocker arm/shaft assembly, install the rocker arms, the springs, the bearing caps and the mounting bolts.

10. Apply sealant to the ends of the bearing caps. Install the rocker arm/shaft assembly, make sure the arrow mark on the cap and the arrow mark on the cylinder head are aligned.

11. Torque the bearing cap bolts to 85 inch lbs. in the following order: No. 3 (1st), No. 2 (2nd), No. 1 (3rd) and No. 4 (4th).

12. Repeat the torquing procedure but increase the torque to 180 inch lbs.

13. Install the distributor adapter on the right side cylinder head, if removed.

14. To complete the installation, reverse the removal procedures.

CHECKING VALVE TIMING

Procedure

1.6L ENGINE

1. Disconnect the negative battery cable.

2. Remove the No. 1 spark plug.

3. Rotate the crankshaft until the No. 1 cylinder is at the TDC of it's compression stroke.

NOTE: With the No. 1 piston on the TDC of it's compression stroke, the distributor rotor will be facing the No. 1 spark plug wire terminal.

4. Remove the timing chain cover.

5. Make sure the timing marks on the camshaft and crankshaft sprockets are facing each other; if they are not, the timing chain may need to be replaced.

6. Check and/or adjust the valve clearances; they should be 0.010 in. (intake) and 0.012 in. (exhaust).

7. After checking, reverse the removal procedures. Start the engine and check the operation.

1.8L ENGINE

The engine is equipped with 2 timing belts.

Outer (Large) Belt

1. Disconnect the negative battery cable. Remove the timing cover.

2. Remove the No. 1 spark plug.

3. Rotate the crankshaft until the No. 1 cylinder is at the TDC of it's compression stroke.

NOTE: With the No. 1 piston on the TDC of it's compression stroke, the distributor rotor will be facing the No. 1 spark plug wire terminal.

4. The camshaft sprocket timing mark should be aligned with the timing notch in the rear upper timing belt cover.

5. To install, reverse the removal procedures. Start the engine and check the timing.

Inner (Small) Belt

1. Disconnect the negative battery cable. Remove the timing cover.

2. Remove the No. 1 spark plug.

3. Rotate the crankshaft until the No. 1 cylinder is at the TDC of it's compression stroke.

NOTE: With the No. 1 piston on the TDC of it's compression stroke, the distributor rotor will be facing the No. 1 spark plug wire terminal.

4. Make sure the inner (small) belt sprockets timing marks are aligned with the timing marks on the front case.

5. To install, check the large timing belt alignment and reverse the removal procedures.

2.0L ENGINE

The engine is equipped with 2 timing belts.

Outer (Large) Belt

1. Disconnect the negative battery cable. Remove the timing cover.

2. Remove the No. 1 spark plug.

3. Rotate the crankshaft until the No. 1 cylinder is at the TDC of it's compression stroke.

NOTE: With the No. 1 piston on the TDC of it's compression stroke, the distributor rotor will be facing the No. 1 spark plug wire terminal. The camshaft sprockets timing marks should be facing each other and aligned with the top of the cylinder head; the timing marks on the crankshaft and oil pump sprockets should be aligned with the timing indicators on the engine.

4. To install, reverse the removal procedures. Start the engine and check the engine timing.

Inner (Small) Belt

1. Disconnect the negative battery cable. Remove the timing cover.

2. Remove the No. 1 spark plug.

3. Rotate the crankshaft until the No. 1 cylinder is at the TDC of it's compression stroke.

NOTE: With the No. 1 piston on the TDC of it's compression stroke, the distributor rotor will be facing the No. 1 spark plug wire terminal.

4. Make sure the inner (small) belt sprockets timing marks are aligned with the timing marks on the front case.

5. To install, check the large timing belt alignment and reverse the removal procedures.

2.2L AND 2.5L ENGINES

1. Disconnect the negative battery cable. Remove the timing covers.

2. Remove the No. 1 spark plug.

3. Rotate the crankshaft until the No. 1 cylinder is at the TDC of it's compression stroke.

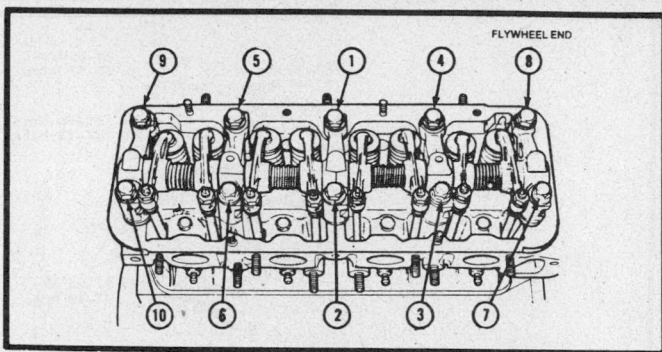

Head bolt tightening sequence—1.6L engine

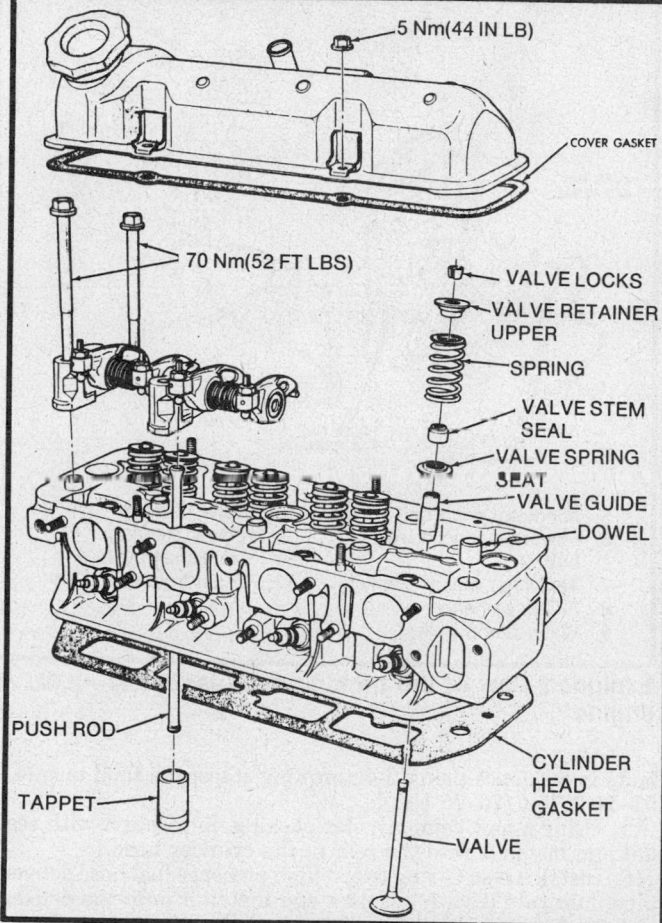

Exploded view of cylinder head assemby –1.6L engine

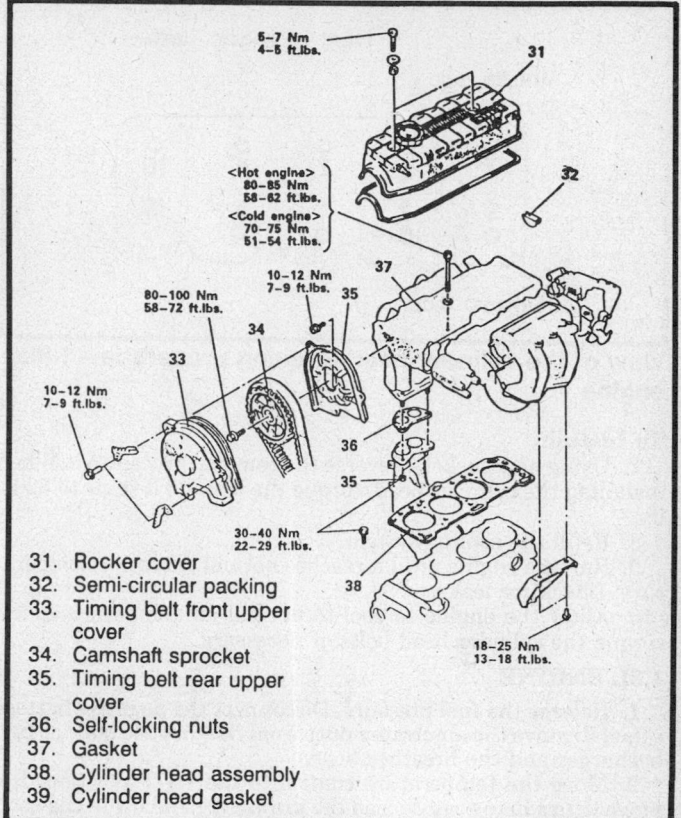

31. Rocker cover
32. Semi-circular packing
33. Timing belt front upper cover
34. Camshaft sprocket
35. Timing belt rear upper cover
36. Self-locking nuts
37. Gasket
38. Cylinder head assembly
39. Cylinder head gasket

Exploded view of the cylinder head—1.8L engine

2. Remove the No. 1 spark plug.

3. Rotate the crankshaft until the No. 1 cylinder is at the TDC of it's compression stroke.

NOTE:With the No. 1 cylinder at the TDC of it's compression stroke, the sprockets timing marks should be aligned with the engine's timing mark indicators.

4. To install, reverse the removal procedures. Start the engine and check the engine timing.

Cylinder Head

Removal and Installation

1.6L ENGINE

NOTE: The engine must be cold before cylinder head removal, to avoid distortion.

1. Disconnect the negative battery cable. Remove the valve cover. Drain the cooling system. Relieve the fuel pressure.

2. Remove the cylinder head bolts evenly, starting at the ends and working toward the center. The brackets supporting the rocker assembly are located on dowels and are retained by the cylinder head bolts. Only brackets No. 2 and 4 are pinned to the rocker arm shafts.

3. Move and support the end brackets and remove the rocker assembly.

4. Remove the pushrods, noting their position so they can be installed in the same position.

5. Remove the cylinder head from the engine.

6. Clean the cylinder head and engine block gasket surfaces.

NOTE: When installing the head gasket, the word DESSUS or TOP must be facing upward.

NOTE: At this point the valves for the No. 1 cylinder will be closed and the timing mark will be aligned with the pointer on the flywheel housing. Make sure the arrows on the camshaft sprocket are aligned with the camshaft cap/cylinder head line.

4. Verify that the dot mark on the crankshaft pulley aligns with the line mark on the intermediate shaft.

5. To install, reverse the removal procedures. Start the engine and check the ignition timing.

3.0L ENGINE

1. Disconnect the negative battery cable. Remove the timing covers from the engine.

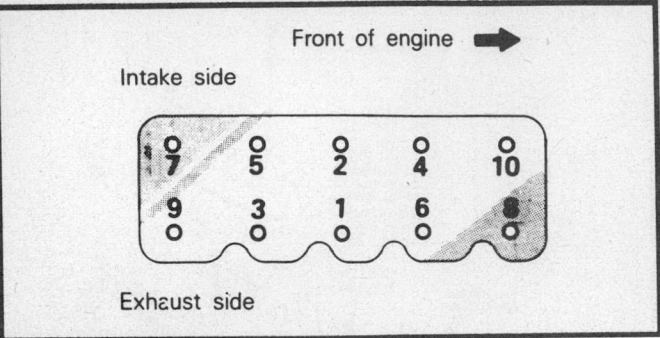

View of the cylinder head torquing procedure—1.8L engine

To Install:

7. Using new gaskets, reverse the removal procedures. When installing the cylinder head, torque the bolts in 3 steps to 52 ft. lbs.

8. Refill the cooling system.

9. Run the engine until it reaches normal operating temperature. Check for leaks.

10. Allow the engine to cool to normal air temperature. Retorque the cylinder head bolts, if necessary.

1.8L ENGINE

1. Release the fuel pressure. Disconnect the negative battery cable. Remove the air cleaner duct from the throttle body or turbocharger and the breather hose.

2. Move the temperature control to the **HOT** position. Remove the radiator cap, loosen the drain plug and drain the cooling system.

3. Disconnect the accelerator cable and the cruise control cable, if equipped. Disconnect the high pressure fuel hose, the O-ring and the fuel return hose.

4. Disconnect the upper radiator hose, the water breather hose, the water bypass hose and the heater hose. Disconnect the vacuum hose, the PVC hose and the brake booster vacuum hose.

5. Disconnect the spark plug cables. Disconnect the electrical connectors from the oxygen sensor, the temperature gauge unit, the water temperature sensor, the ISC, the TPS, the distributor, the MPS, the fuel injector, the EGR temperature sensor (Calif.), the power transistor and the condenser.

6. Disconnect the engine ground cable and the control wiring harness. Remove the power steering pressure hose-to-engine clamp and the upper engine mounting bracket. Using a floor jack, place a block of wood between the oil pan and the jack, raise the engine slightly; be careful not to place excessive loads on various parts.

7. Remove the rocker arm cover, the gasket and the upper front timing belt cover.

8. Using a wrench on the crankshaft pulley bolt, rotate the crankshaft (clockwise) to align the camshaft timin mark with the timing notch in the rear upper timing belt cover.

9. Remove the camshaft sprocket bolt, the sprocket with the timing belt and position the belt on the lower timing belt cover.

10. Remove the intake manifold-to-support bracket bolts and the exhaust pipe-to-manifold nuts.

11. Using a cylinder head bolt wrench tool MD998360 or equivalent, remove the cylinder head bolts by reversing the torquing sequence. Remove the cylinder head and the gasket.

12. Clean the gasket mounting surfaces; be sure to keep the coolant and oil passages clean.

To Install:

13. Install a new cylinder head gasket on the engine with it's identification mark at the front and facing upwards.

14. Install the cylinder head. Using the cylinder head bolt torquing tool TW-10B or equivalent, torque the cylinder head

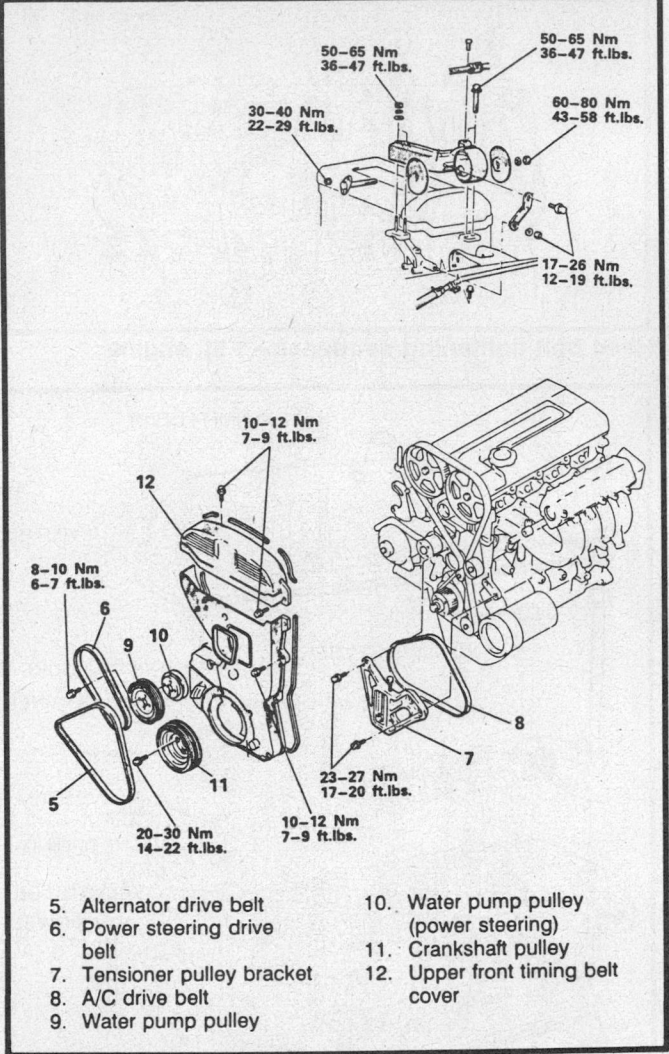

5. Alternator drive belt
6. Power steering drive belt
7. Tensioner pulley bracket
8. A/C drive belt
9. Water pump pulley
10. Water pump pulley (power steering)
11. Crankshaft pulley
12. Upper front timing belt cover

Exploded view of the timing cover assembly—2.0L engine

bolts in sequence using 2–3 torquing steps; the final torque is 51–54 ft. lbs. (70–75 Nm).

15. Using a new semi-circular packing, lubricate it with sealant and install it into the rear of the cylinder head.

16. Install a new O-ring to the high pressure fuel hose delivery pipe, lubricate it with gasoline and install it onto the delivery pipe.

17. Align the camshaft sprocket with the timing belt and the sprocket's timing mark with the timing mark on the rear timing belt cover. Install the camshaft sprocket bolt and torque to 58–72 ft. lbs.

18. To complete the installation, use new gaskets and reverse the removal procedures. Refill the cooling system, start the engine, allow it to reach normal operating temperatures and check for leaks and engine operation.

2.0L ENGINE

1. Release the fuel pressure. Disconnect the negative battery cable. Remove the air cleaner duct from the throttle body or turbocharger and the breather hose.

2. Move the temperature control to the **HOT** position. Remove the radiator cap, loosen the drain plug and drain the cooling system.

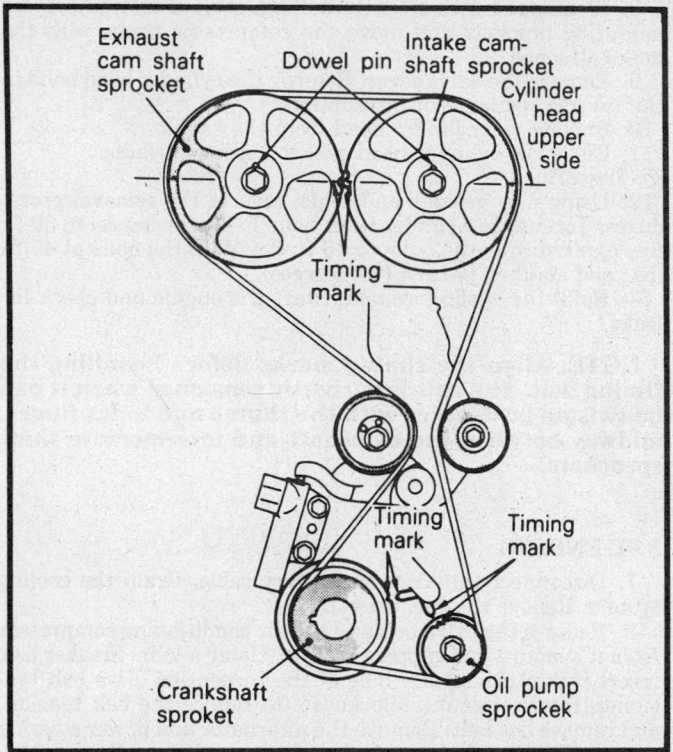

View of the engine timing and sprocket locations— 2.0L engine

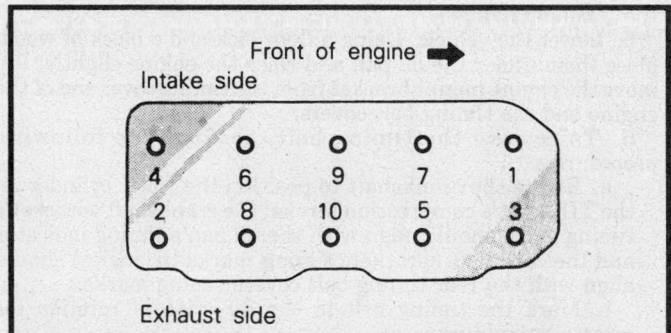

View of the cylinder head torque sequence—2.0L engine

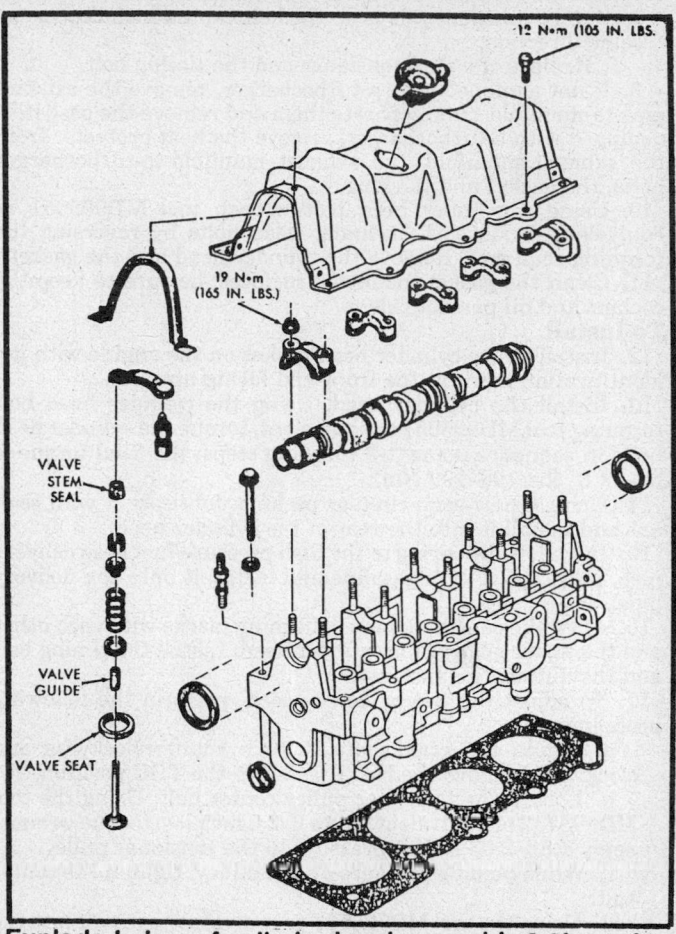

Exploded view of cylinder head assembly 2.2L engine

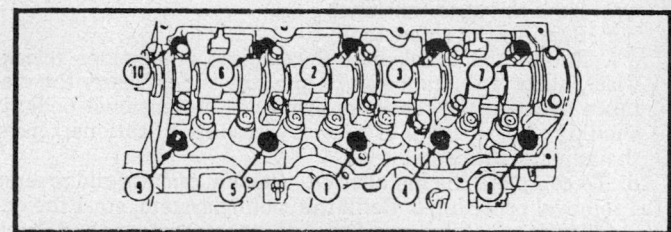

Head bolt tightening sequence—2.2L/2.5L engine

3. Disconnect the accelerator cable and the cruise control cable, if equipped. Disconnect the high pressure fuel hose, the O-ring and the fuel return hose.

4. Disconnect the upper radiator hose, the overflow hose, the water bypass hose, the heater hose and the water hose (turbo). Disconnect the vacuum hoses, the PVC hose and the brake booster vacuum hose.

5. Disconnect the spark plug cables. Disconnect the electrical connectors from the oxygen sensor, the temperature gauge unit, the water temperature sensor, the ISC, the TPS, the engine coolant temperature switch (air conditioning), the fuel injector, the ignition coil, the power transistor, the EGR temperature sensor (Calif.), the knock sensor (turbo), the noise filter and the crankshaft angle sensor.

6. Disconnect the air intake hose (turbo), the breather hose, the air intake hose, the vacuum hoses (turbo). If equipped with a turbocharger, remove the oil feed line eye bolt, gasket and move the line aside.

7. Disconnect the engine ground cable and the control wiring

harness. Remove the power steering pressure hose-to-engine clamp and the upper engine mounting bracket. Using a floor jack, place a block of wood between the oil pan and the jack, raise the engine slightly; be careful not to place excessive loads on various parts.

8. To remove the timing belt, perform the following procedures:

a. Remove the rocker arm cover and gasket.

b. Remove the drive belt from the alternator, power steering air conditioner comperssor. Remove the tensioner pulley bracket, the water pump pulley and the crankshaft pulley.

c. Remove the upper and lower front timing belt covers.

d. Using a wrench on the crankshaft pulley bolt, rotate the crankshaft (clockwise) to position the No. 1 piston at the TDC of it's compression stroke; the camshaft timing marks should be facing each other and aligned with the upper surface of the cyinder head. The crankshaft and oil pump sprockets timing notches should be aligned with their timing pointer.

e. Mark the timing belt with an arrow to determine the di-

rection of rotation; this is so the belt can be installed in the same direction.

    f. Remove the auto tensioner and the timing belt.

    9. If not equipped with a turbocharger, remove the exhaust pipe-to-manifold nuts, separate them and remove the gasket. If equipped with a turbocharger, remove the heat protector from the exhaust manifold, the exhaust manifold-to-turbocharger bolts, the gasket and the ring.

    10. Using a cylinder head bolt wrench tool MD998051 or equivalent, remove the cylinder head bolts by reversing the torquing sequence. Remove the cylinder head and the gasket.

    11. Clean the gasket mounting surfaces; be sure to keep the coolant and oil passages clean.

To Install:

    12. Install a new cylinder head gasket on the engine with it's identification mark at the front and facing upwards.

    13. Install the cylinder head. Using the cylinder head bolt torquing tool MD998051 or equivalent, torque the cylinder head bolts in sequence using 2–3 torquing steps; the final torque is 62–72 ft. lbs. (90–100 Nm).

    14. Using a new semi-circular packing, lubricate it with sealant and install it into the rear of the cylinder head.

    15. Install a new O-ring to the high pressure fuel hose delivery pipe, lubricate it with gasoline and install it onto the delivery pipe.

    16. Align the camshaft sprocket timing marks with each other and the upper edge of the cylinder head. Install the timing belt and the automatic tensioner.

    17. To adjust the timing belt tension, perform the following procedures:

        a. Rotate the crankshaft ¼ turn counterclockwise and clockwise to move the No. 1 piston to the TDC position.

        b. Loosen the tensioner pulley center bolt. Using the tool MD998752 or equivalent, and a 0–2.2 inch lbs. torque wrench, apply 1.88–2.03 ft. lbs. pressure to the tensioner pulley.

        c. While holding pressure on the pulley, tighten the center bolt.

        d. Using the tool MD998738 or equivalent, screw it into the left engine support bracket until it makes contact with the tensioner arm. Turn the screw inward and remove the set wire from the auto tensioner.

        e. Remove the screw tool.

        f. Rotate the crankshaft 2 complete revolutions (clockwise), allow it to stand for 15 minutes and measure the distance between the tensioner arm and the tensioner body; it should be 0.15–0.18 in. If it is not within specifications, repeat the adjustment procedures.

    18. To complete the installation, use new gaskets and reverse the removal procedures. Refill the cooling system, start the engine, allow it to reach normal operating temperatures and check for leaks and engine operation.

2.2L AND 2.5L ENGINES

NOTE: The engine must be cold before cylinder head removal, to prevent warping the cylinder head.

    1. Disconnect the negative battery cable. Drain the cooling system.

    2. Remove the air cleaner assembly. Disconnect and label all coolant hoses.

    3. Disconnect and label the vacuum lines, hoses and wiring connectors from the manifold(s), carburetor or throttle body and from the cylinder head.

    4. Disconnect the accelerator linkage, the converter and the exhaust pipe. Remove the intake and exhaust manifolds with the carburetor or throttle body.

    5. Remove the upper part of the front timing case cover.

    6. Rotate the engine by hand, until the timing marks align (No. 1 piston at TDC).

    7. With the timing marks aligned, loosen the timing belt tensioner and remove the belt from the camshaft sprocket.

    8. If equipped with air conditioning, remove the compressor mounting brackets and move the compressor aside, with the hoses attached.

    9. Remove the valve cover. Remove the cylinder head bolts in the reverse sequence of installation.

    10. Remove the cylinder head from the engine.

    11. Clean the cylinder head gasket mating surfaces.

To Install:

    12. Using new gaskets and seals, reverse the removal procedures. Torque the cylinder head bolts in the sequence, to 30 ft. lbs. Again torque the bolts to 45 ft. lbs. With the bolts at 45 ft. lbs., add another ¼ turn (90 degrees).

    13. Refill the cooling system. Start the engine and check for leaks.

NOTE: Align the timing marks before installing the timing belt. The belt is correctly tensioned when it can be twisted 90 degrees with the thumb and index finger, midway between the camshaft and intermediate shaft sprockets.

3.0L ENGINE

    1. Disconnect the negative battery cable. Drain the cooling system. Relieve the fuel pressure.

    2. Remove the drive belt and the air conditioning compressor from it's mount and support it aside. Using a ½ in. breaker bar, insert it into the square hole of the serpentine drive belt tensioner, rotate it counterclockwise (to reduce the belt tension) and remove the belt. Remove the alternator and power steering pump (if equipped) from the bracket(s) and move them aside.

    3. Raise and safely support the front of the vehicle. Remove the right front wheel assembly and the right inner splash shield.

    4. Lower the vehicle and remove the crankshaft pulleys and the torsional damper.

    5. Lower the vehicle. Using a floor jack and a block of wood, place them under the oil pan and raise the engine slightly. Remove the engine mount bracket from the timing cover end of the engine and the timing belt covers.

    6. To remove the timing belt, perform the following procedures:

        a. Rotate the crankshaft to position the No. 1 cylinder on the TDC of it's compression stroke; the crankshaft sprocket's timing mark should align with the oil pan's timing indicator and the camshaft sprockets timing marks (triangles) should align with the rear timing belt covers timing marks.

        b. Mark the timing belt in the direction of rotation for reinstallation purposes.

        c. Loosen the timing belt tensioner and remove the timing belt.

NOTE: When removing the timing belt from the a camshaft sprocket, make sure the belt does not slip off of the other camshaft sprocket. Support the belt so it can not slip off of the crankshaft sprocket and opposite side camshaft sprocket.

    7. Remove the air cleaner assembly. Label and disconnect the spark plug wires and the vacuum hoses.

    8. Remove the rocker arm covers.

    9. Install auto lash adjuster retainers tool MD998443 or equivalent, on the rocker arms.

    10. From the right cylinder head, mark the rotor-to-distributor housing and the housing-to-distributor extension locations. Remove the distributor and the distributor extension.

    11. Remove the camshaft bearing assembly-to-cylinder head bolts (do not remove the bolts from the assemby); the rocker arms, rocker shafts and bearing caps are an assembly. Remove the camshafts from the cylinder head and inspect them for damage.

    12. To remove the intake manifold assembly, perform the fol-

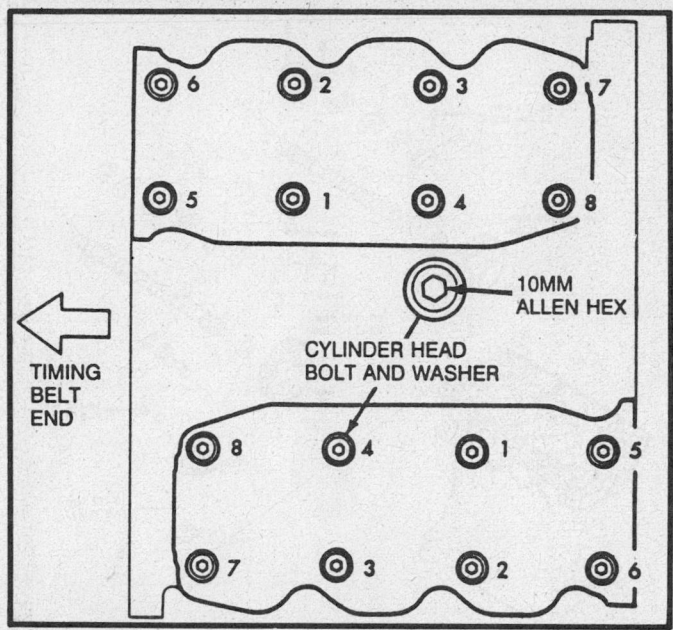

3.0L cylinder head torque sequence

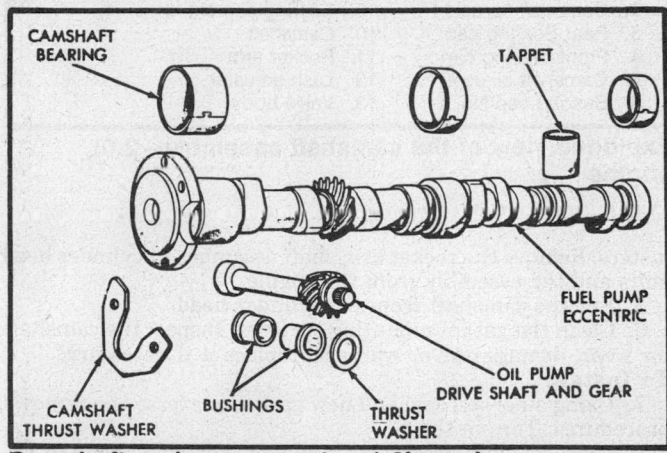

Camshaft and components—1.6L engine

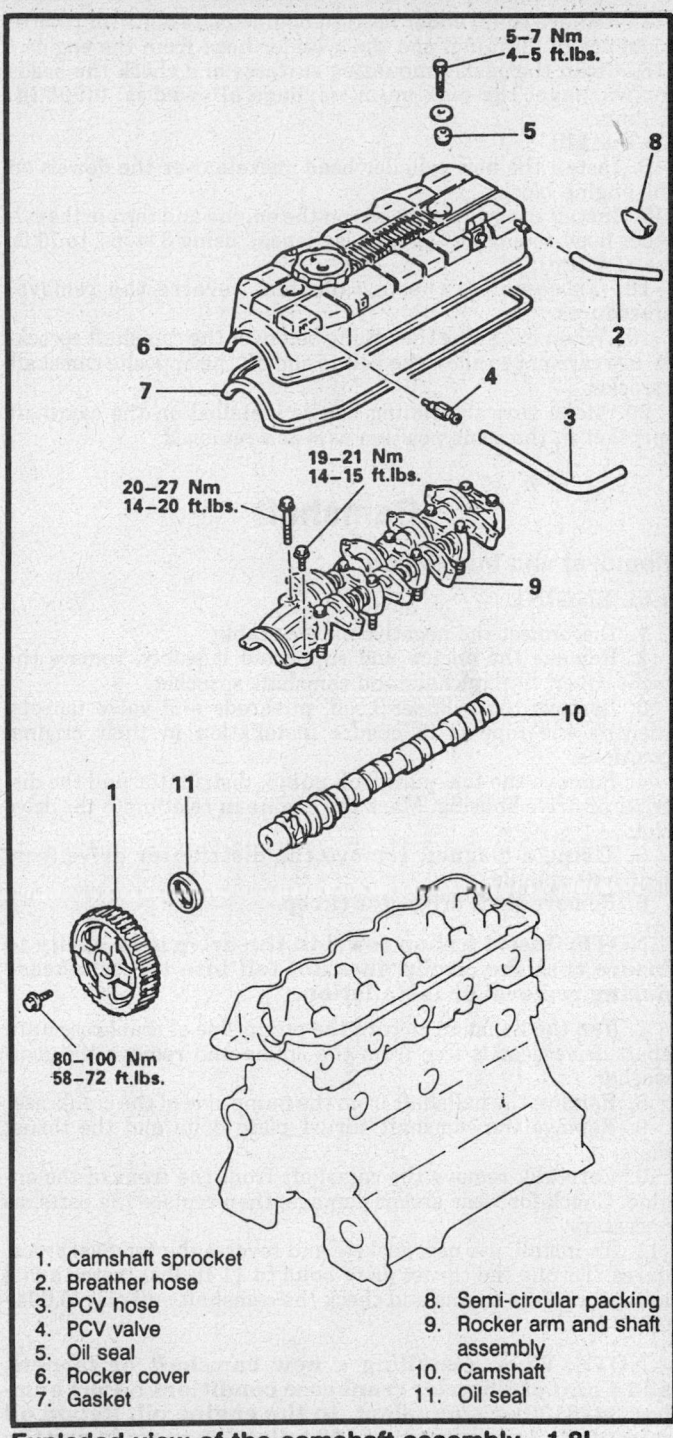

1. Camshaft sprocket
2. Breather hose
3. PCV hose
4. PCV valve
5. Oil seal
6. Rocker cover
7. Gasket
8. Semi-circular packing
9. Rocker arm and shaft assembly
10. Camshaft
11. Oil seal

Exploded view of the camshaft assembly—1.8L engine

lowing procedures:

   a. Remove the throttle cable and the transaxle kickdown linkage.

   b. Remove the electrical connectors from the automatic idle speed (AIS) motor, the throttle position sensor (TPS) from the throttle body, the charge temperature sensor and the coolant temperature sensor.

   c. Remove the EGR tube flange from the intake plenum.

   d. Remove the air intake plenum-to-intake manifold bolts, the plenum and gaskets.

   f. Disconnect the vacuum hoses from the fuel rail and the fuel pressure regulator. Disconnect the fuel injector wiring harness connector.

   g. Remove the fuel pressure regulator bolts and the regulator; be careful not to damage the O-ring.

   h. Remove the fuel rail-to-intake manifold bolts and the fuel rail.

   i. Remove the intake manifold-to-engine bolts and the manifold/gaskets.

13. To remove the exhaust manifolds, perform the following procedures:

   a. Raise and safely support the vehicle. From the cowl side, disconnect the exhaust pipe-to-exhaust manifold bolts.

   b. Disconnect the EGR tube and the oxygen sensor wire from the rear manifold.

   c. Remove the cross-over pipe from both exhaust manifolds and the pipe.

   d. Remove the rear manifold-to-cylinder head nuts and the manifold.

   e. Lower the vehicle. Remove heat shield from the front manifold.

   d. Remove the front mainfold-to-cylinder nuts and the manifold.

14. Remove the cylinder head-to-engine bolts bolts (in reverse sequence of torquing) and the cylinder head from the engine.

15. Clean the gasket mounting surfaces and check the heads for warpage; the maximum warpage allowed is: 0.008 in. (0.2mm).

To install:

16. Install the new cylinder head gaskets over the dowels on the engine block.

17. Install the cylinder heads on the engine and torque the cylinder head-to-engine bolts (in sequence), using 3 steps, to 70 ft. lbs. (95 Nm).

18. To complete the installation, reverse the removal procedures.

19. When installing the timing belt over the camshaft sprocket, use care not to allow the belt to slip off the opposite camshaft sprocket.

20. Make sure the timing belt is installed on the camshaft sprocket in the same position as when removed.

Camshaft

Removal and Installation

1.6L ENGINE

1. Disconnect the negative battery cable.

2. Remove the engine and supported it safely, remove the front cover, timing chain and camshaft sprocket.

3. Remove the cylinder head, pushrods and valve tappets. Identify the tappets to ensure installation in their original positions.

4. Remove the fuel pump, oil pump, distributor and the distributor drive housing. Mark the engine in relation to the drive slot.

5. Using a magnet, remove the distributor drive from halfshaft spindle.

6. Remove shaft drive gear circlip.

NOTE: Insert a shop towel in the drive gear cavity to insure that the circlip does not fall into the crankcase during removal or installation.

7. Tap the halfshaft toward the pump side of crankcase until shaft drive gear is free from the spline and remove the gear/washer.

8. Remove the halfshaft from the pump side of the crankcase.

9. Remove the camshaft thrust plate bolts and the thrust plate.

10. Carefully remove the camshaft from the front of the engine. Check for wear and/or damage, then replace the parts, as necessary.

11. To install, use new gaskets and reverse the removal procedures. Torque the thrust plate bolts to 11 ft. lbs. Install a dial indicator to the engine and check the camshaft end play (0.004–0.008 in.).

NOTE: When installing a new camshaft or tappets, add 1 pint of Chrysler crankcase conditioner, Part number 3419130 or equivalent, to the engine oil. Retain oil mixture for a minimum of 500 miles. When replacing the camshaft, use a straight edge to check all tappet faces for wear. Replace tappets with negative crown or dishing.

1.8L ENGINE

1. Disconnect the negative battery cable. Relieve the fuel pressure.

2. Remove the timing belt (with camshaft sprocket) and the rocker arm cover from the cylinder head.

3. Remove the distributor from the cylinder head.

4. Using the lash adjuster retainer tools MD998443 or equivalent, install them on the rocker arms to support the lash ad-

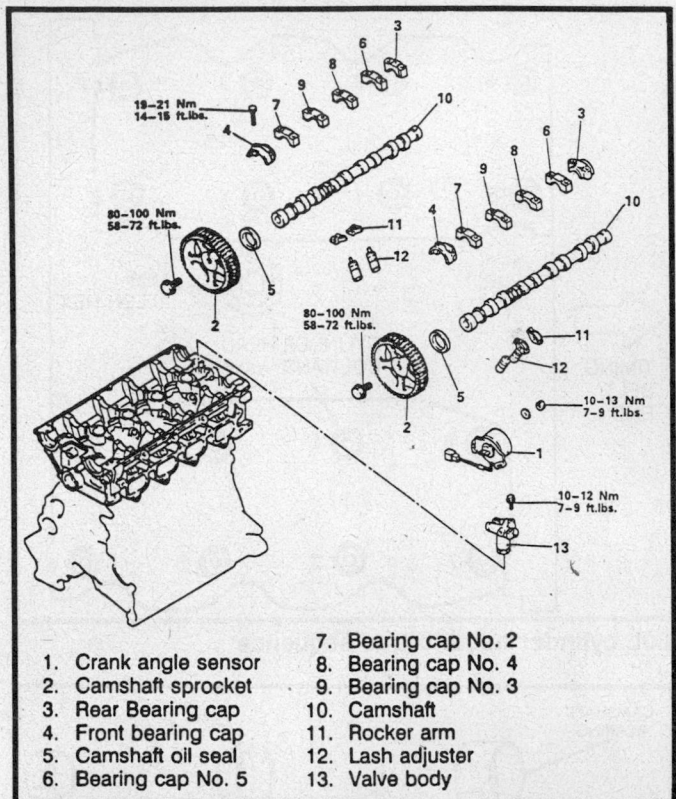

1. Crank angle sensor	7. Bearing cap No. 2
2. Camshaft sprocket	8. Bearing cap No. 4
3. Rear Bearing cap	9. Bearing cap No. 3
4. Front bearing cap	10. Camshaft
5. Camshaft oil seal	11. Rocker arm
6. Bearing cap No. 5	12. Lash adjuster
	13. Valve body

Exploded view of the camshaft assembly—2.0L engine

justers. Remove the rocker arm/shaft assembly-to-cylinder head bolts and the assembly from the engine.

5. Lift the camshaft from the cylinder head.

6. Clean the gasket mounting surfaces. Inspect the camshaft for wear, damage and/or warpage; replace it if necessary.

To Install:

7. Using a new oil seal and new gaskets, reverse the removal procedures. Torque the:

Rocker arm/shaft assembly-to-cylinder head long bolts to 14–20 ft. lbs. (20–27 Nm) and the short bolts to 14–15 ft. lbs. (19–21 Nm).

Camshaft sprocket-to-camshaft bolt to 58–72 ft. lbs. (80–100 Nm).

8. Start the engine and check the engine timing and operation.

2.0L ENGINE

1. Disconnect the negative battery cable. Relieve the fuel pressure.

2. Remove the camshafts from the cylinder head.

3. From each camshaft, remove the sprocket-to-camshaft bolt and the sprocket.

4. Clean the gasket mounting surfaces. Inspect the camshafts for wear, damage and/or warpage; replace it if necessary.

To Install:

5. Using a new oil seal and new gaskets, reverse the removal procedures. Torque the:

Camshaft bearing caps-to-cylinder head bolts to 14–15 ft. lbs. (19–21 Nm).

Camshaft sprocket-to-camshaft bolts to 58–72 ft. lbs. (80–100 Nm).

6. Start the engine and check the engine timing and operation.

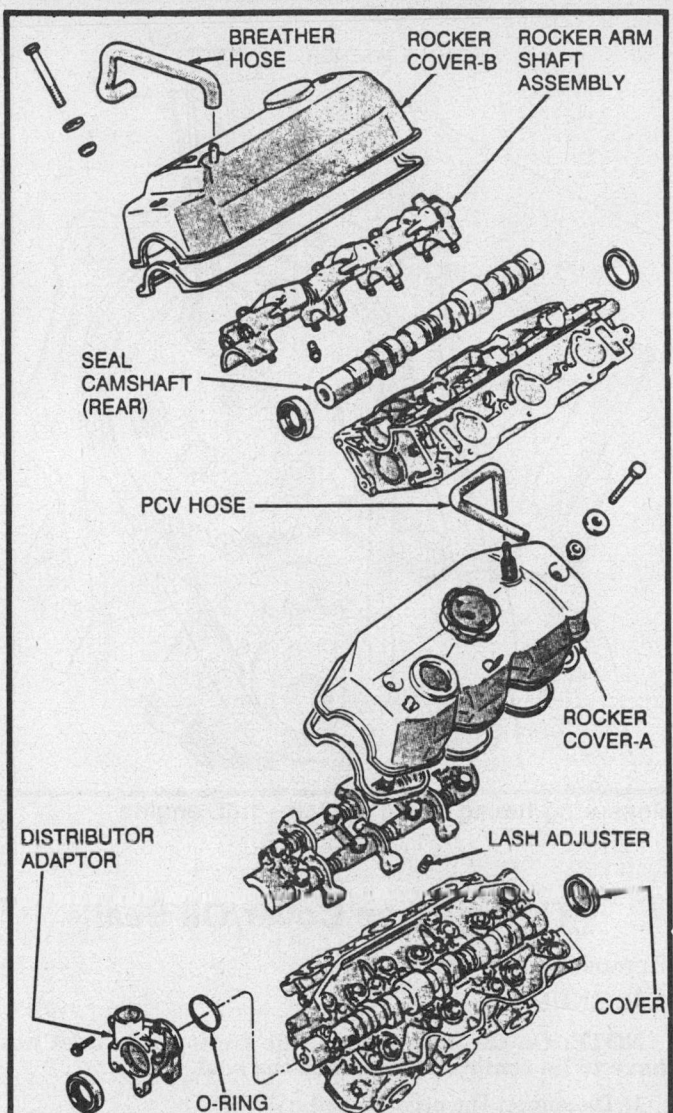

3.0L cylinder head and valve train assemblies

2.2L AND 2.5L ENGINES

1. Disconnect the negative battery cable. Relieve the fuel pressure.

2. Remove the timing case covers and turn the crankshaft so the No. 1 piston is at the TDC of the compression stroke.

3. Remove the timing belt, the camshaft sprocket bolt and the sprocket.

4. Remove the PCV module (by turning it counterclockwise) from the cylinder head cover. Remove the cylinder head cover screws and the cover.

5. Mark the rocker arms for installation identification and loosen the camshaft bearing bolts, several turns each.

6. Using a soft mallet, rap the rear of the camshaft, a few times, to break the bearing caps loose.

7. Remove the bolts and bearing caps, be careful that the camshaft does not cock. Cocking the camshaft could cause damage to the bearings.

8. Check the oil holes for blockages and the parts for wear and/or damage, replace the parts, if necessary. Clean the gasket mounting surfaces.

To Install:

9. Lubricate the camshaft, place the bearing caps with No. 1

at the timing belt end and No. 5 at the transaxle end. The camshaft bearing caps are numbered and have arrows facing forward. Torque the camshaft bearing bolts to 18 ft. lbs.

NOTE: Apply RTV silicone gasket material to the No. 1 and 5 bearing caps. Install the bearing caps before the seals are installed.

10. Mount a dial indicator to the front of the engine and check the camshaft endplay. Play should not exceed 0.006 in.

11. To complete the installation, use new gaskets/seals and reverse the removal procedures. Check the ignition timing.

3.0L ENGINE

1. Disconnect the negative battery cable. Remove the air cleaner assembly and valve covers.

2. Install auto lash adjuster retainers MD998443 or equivalent on the rocker arms.

3. From the right side cylinder head, remove the distributor extension.

4. Remove the camshaft bearing caps but do not remove the bolts from the caps.

5. Remove the rocker arms, rocker shafts and bearing caps, as an assembly.

6. Remove the camshaft from the cylinder head.

7. Inspect the bearing journals on the camshaft, cylinder head and bearing caps.

To Install:

8. Lubricate the camshaft journals and camshaft with clean engine oil and install the camshaft in the cylinder head.

9. Align the camshaft bearing caps with the arrow mark (depending on cylinder numbers) and in numerical order.

10. Apply sealer at the ends of the bearing caps and install the assembly.

11. Torque the bearing cap bolts, in the following sequence: No. 3, No. 2, No. 1 and No. 4 to 85 inch lbs.

12. Repeat torquing steps and increase the torque to 180 inch lbs.

13. Install the distributor drive assembly, if removed.

14. To complete the installation, reverse the removal procedures.

Timing Cover

1.8L ENGINE

1. Disconnect the negative battery cable.

2. Remove the power steering pressure hose-to-engine clamp and the upper engine mounting bracket. Using a floor jack, place a block of wood between the oil pan and the jack, raise the engine slightly; be careful not to place excessive loads on various parts.

3. Remove the drive belts from the alternator, the power steering pump and the air compressor, if equipped. Remove the alternator, the power steering pump and the air compressor, if equipped.

4. Remove the upper front timing belt cover.

5. Using a wrench on the crankshaft pulley bolt, rotate crankshaft (clockwise) to align the camshaft timing mark with the timing notch in the rear upper timing belt cover.

6. Remove the crankshaft pulley bolt and the pulley.

7. Remove the lower timing belt cover-to-engine screws and the cover.

8. To install, reverse the removal procedures. Torque the crankshaft pulley-to-crankshaft bolts to 11–13 ft. lbs. Adjust the drive belt tensions.

2.0L ENGINE

1. Disconnect the negative battery cable. Disconnect the spark plug cables.

2. Remove the power steering pressure hose-to-engine clamp and the upper engine mounting bracket. Using a floor jack,

place a block of wood between the oil pan and the jack, raise the engine slightly; be careful not to place excessive loads on various parts.

3. Remove the drive belts from the alternator, the power steering pump and the air compressor, if equipped. Remove the alternator, the power steering pump and the air compressor, if equipped.

4. Remove the upper front timing belt cover.

5. Using a wrench on the crankshaft pulley, rotate the crankshaft (clockwise) to position the No. 1 piston at the TDC of it's compression stroke; the camshaft timing marks should be facing each other and aligned with the upper surface of the cylinder head. The crankshaft and oil pump sprockets timing notches should be aligned with their timing pointer.

6. Remove the water pump pulley, the crankshaft pulley bolts and the pulley.

7. Remove the lower timing belt cover-to-engine screws and the cover.

8. To install, reverse the removal procedures. Torque the crankshaft pulley-to-crankshaft bolts to 14–22 ft. lbs. and the water pump pulley bolt to 7–9 ft. lbs. Adjust the drive belt tensions.

2.2L AND 2.5L ENGINES

1. Disconnect the negative battery cable.

2. If equipped with air conditioning, remove the mounting bracket bolts and move the compressor aside. Remove the water pump and power steering pump drive belts.

3. Remove the crankshaft pulley bolt and remove the pulley.

4. Remove the upper and lower timing belt covers.

5. To install, reverse the removal procedures. Torque the front cover-to-engine bolts to 40 inch lbs. and the crankshaft pulley bolt to 21 ft. lbs.

3.0L ENGINE

1. Disconnect the negative battery cable.

2. If equipped with air conditioning, loosen the adjustment pulley locknut, turn the jack screw counterclockwise (to reduce the drive belt tension) and remove the belt.

3. To remove the serpentine drive belt, insert a ½ in. breaker bar in to the square hole of the tensioner pulley, rotate it counterclockwise (to reduce the drive belt tension) and remove the belt.

4. Remove the air conditioning compressor and the air compressor bracket (if equipped), power steering pump and alternator from the mounts; support them aside. Remove power steering pump/alternator automatic belt tensioner bolt and the tensioner.

5. Raise and safely support the vehicle. Remove the right inner fender splash shield.

6. Using a wrench on the crankshaft pulley, rotate the crankshaft to position the No. 1 cylinder of the TDC of it's compression stroke. Remove the crankshaft pulley bolt and the pulley/damper assembly from the crankshaft.

7. Lower the vehicle and place a floor jack under the engine to support it.

8. Separate the front engine mount insulator from the bracket. Raise the engine slightly and remove the mount bracket.

9. Remove the timing belt cover bolts and upper/lower covers from the engine.

10. To install, reverse the removal procedures. Torque the:
Timing belt covers-to-engine bolts to 115 inch lbs.
Engine mount-to-engine bolts to 35 ft. lbs.
Insulator-to-frame bolts to 250 inch lbs. (1988) or 50 ft. lbs. (1989–90).
Engine mount through bolt to 75 ft. lbs. (1988) or 100 ft. lbs. (1989–90).

NOTE: The engine mount through bolt must be torqued with the engine support removed and the engine's weight on the mount.

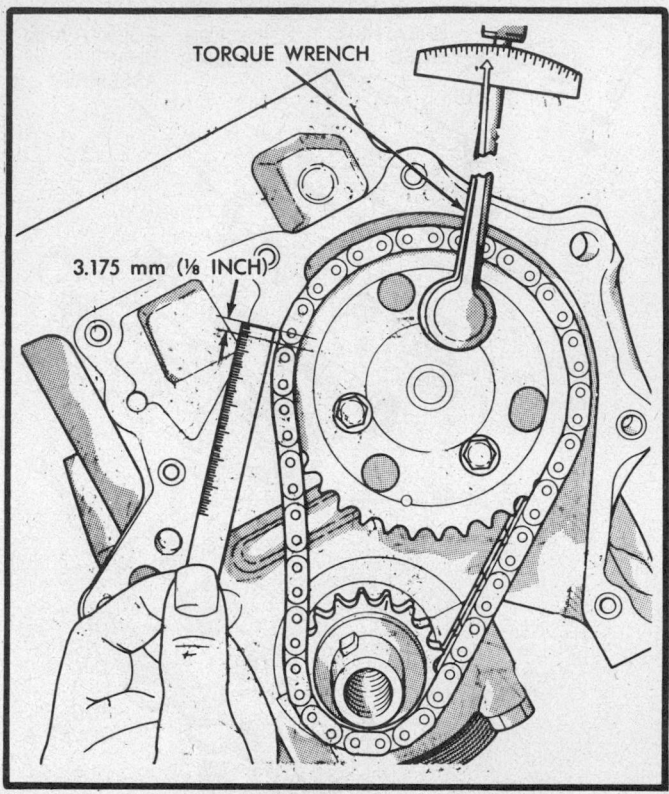

Measuring timing chain stretch—1.6L engine

Timing Case Cover/Oil Seal

Removal and Installation

1.6L ENGINE

NOTE: On the 1.6L engine, the front cover does not have to be removed to replace the seal.

1. Disconnect the negative battery cable.

2. Remove the air pump and alternator drive belts. Remove the air pump mounting bracket.

3. Raise and safely support the vehicle. Remove the right inner splash shield.

4. Remove the crankshaft pulley bolt and washer. Remove the pulley.

5. Install the seal remover tool C–748 or equivalent, over the crankshaft nose and turn, tightly into the seal.

6. Tighten the thrust screw to remove the seal.

NOTE: If the front cover is removed from the engine, tap the side of the thrust screw to remove the seal.

To Install:

7. Using the oil seal installation tool C–4761 or equivalent, drive the new seal into the front cover.

8. To complete the installation, reverse the removal procedures. Torque the crankshaft pulley bolt to 110 ft. lbs.

Timing Gears and Chain

Removal and Installation

1.6L ENGINE

1. Disconnect the negative battery cable.

2. Remove the air pump and alternator belts.

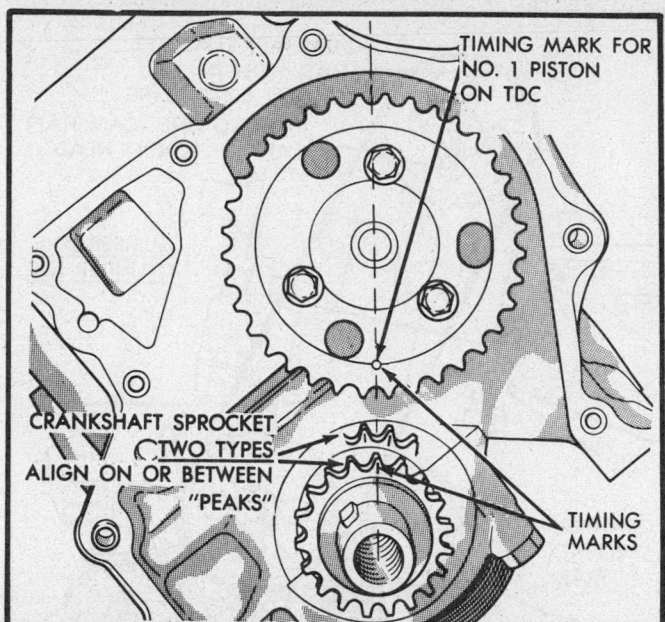

Timing mark alignment, 1.6L engine. Note two different types of sprockets used and their markings

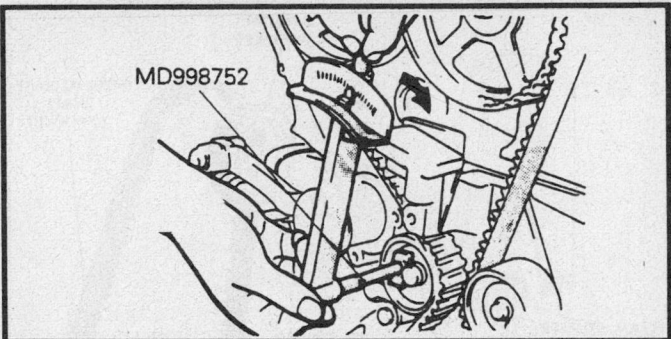

Applying torque to the tensioner pulley—2.0L engine

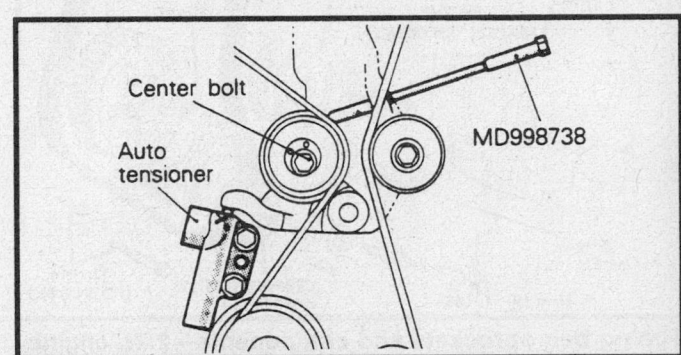

Applying pressure to the tensioner arm—2.0L engine

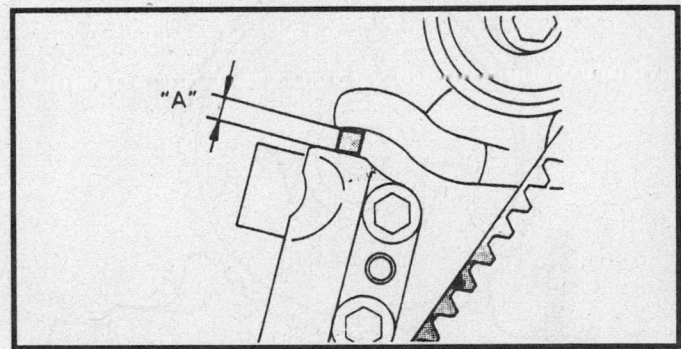

Measuring the distance between the tensioner arm and the tensioner body—2.0L engine

3. Raise and safely support the vehicle. Remove right inner splash shield.

4. Remove crankshaft pulley bolt, washer and pulley.

5. Drain the cooling system through water pump drain plug. Remove water pump to timing cover hose.

6. Raise slightly and carefully support engine (timing cover end).

7. Remove the engine mount bracket-to-timing cover/block bolts.

8. Remove crankcase extension-to-cover and cover-to-block screws. Two cover block screws pass through tubular locating dowels; make sure dowels do not fall into crankcase extension during cover removal. Remove timing cover.

9. Rotate camshaft sprocket so 1 (of 3) bolt head is located at the top of a centerline drawn through the camshaft and crankshaft sprockets.

10. With torque wrench and socket installed on the top bolt head, apply torque in the direction of crankshaft rotation to take up slack; 30 ft. lbs. cylinder head installed or 15 ft. lbs. cylinder head removed. Do not allow crankshaft to rotate during this procedure.

11. Holding a ruler even with the idle of a chain link, apply the same torque, described above, in the reverse direction and note amount of chain movement. If chain movement exceeds ⅛ in., install a new chain.

12. Remove the timing gear bolts, timing gear and chain.

13. Installation is the reverse of removal. Align the timing marks. Torque the camshaft bolt to 113 inch lbs.

Timing Belt And Tensioner

Adjustment

1.8L ENGINE

Inner (Small) Belt

1. Disconnect the negative battery cable. Remove the timing cover.

2. Loosen the tensioner pulley bolt.

3. On the longest span between 2 pulleys, depress the timing belt to make sure the deflection is 0.20–0.28 in. (5–7mm); if the

deflection is not correct, adjust the tensioner pulley and tighten the pulley bolt.

4. After adjustment, inspect and/or adjust the outer (large) timing belt.

5. To install, reverse the removal procedures.

Outer (Large) Belt

1. Disconnect the negative battery cable. Remove the timing cover.

2. Loosen the tensioner mounting nut; the spring will move the tensioner and apply tension on the belt.

3. Check each sprocket's mark to make sure the timing is correct.

4. Move the crankshaft (clockwise) by 2 teeth on the camshaft sprocket.

NOTE: This procedure will apply the proper tension of the timing belt; be sure to not to rotate the crankshaft counterclockwise or apply pressure on the belt to check the amount of tension.

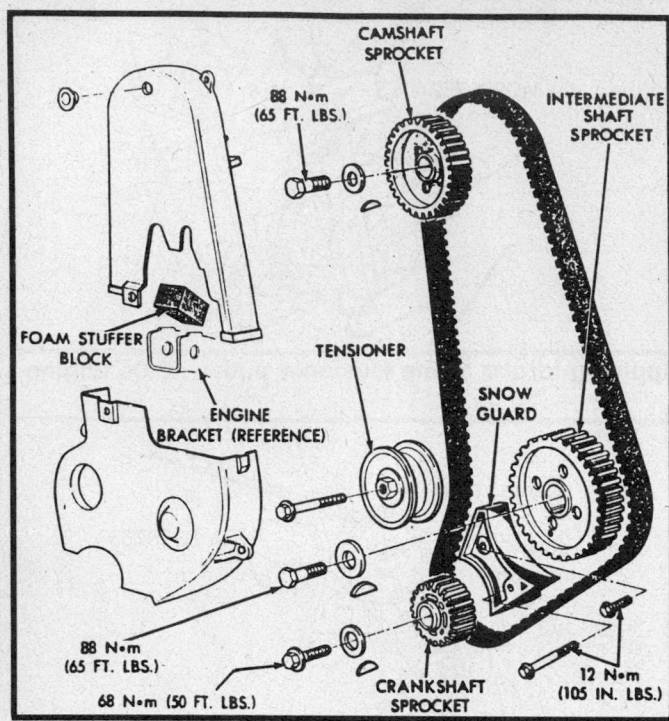

Timing belt sprockets and components—2.2L engine

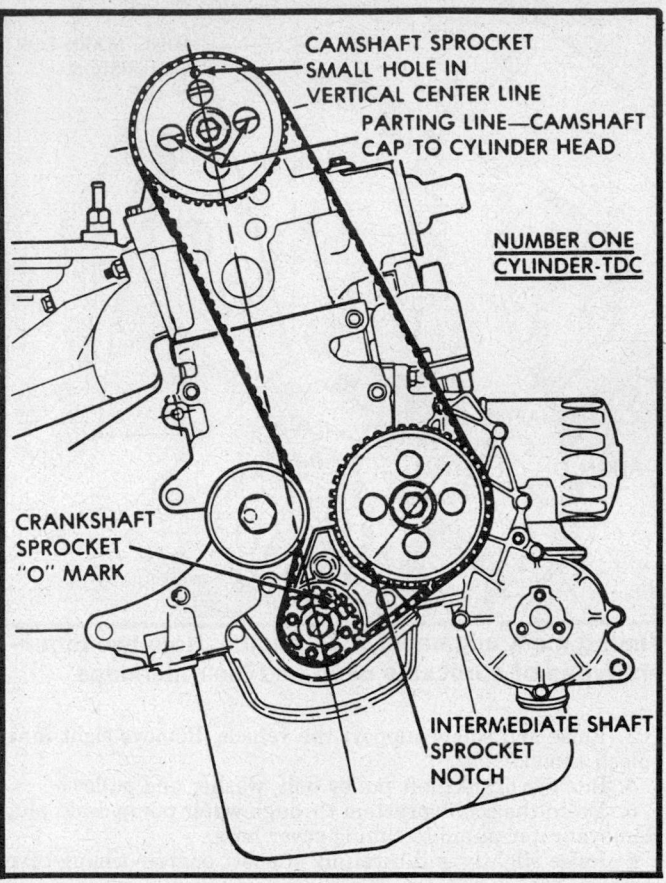

Engine valve timing and sprocket alignment—2.2L/2.5L

Arrows on cam sprocket hub must be in line with No.1 camshaft cap to cylinder head line, with small hole in sprocket, at the top and in the top to bottom engine vertical line—2.2L engine

5. Apply pressure on the tensioner toward the turning direction so no portion of the belt raises off the camshaft sprocket; make sure the belt sprocket teeth are fully engaged with the camshaft sprocket.

6. Tighten the tensioner installation bolt and the tensioner spacer, in that order.

NOTE: If the tensioner spacer is tightened first, the tensioner will rotate with it and the belt tension will be thrown out of adjustment.

7. Move the center part of the belt, on the longest span between pulleys, to make sure the clearance between the belt and the cover is within 0.40 in. (12mm).

8. To install, reverse the removal procedures.

2.0L ENGINE

Inner (Small) Belt

1. Disconnect the negative battery cable. Remove the timing cover.

2. Loosen the tensioner pulley bolt.

3. On the longest span between 2 pulleys, depress the timing belt to make sure the deflection is 0.20–0.28 in. (5–7mm); if the deflection is not correct, adjust the tensioner pulley and tighten the pulley bolt.

4. After adjustment, inspect and/or adjust the outer (large) timing belt.

5. To install, reverse the removal procedures.

Outer (Large) Belt

1. Disconnect the negative battery cable. Remove the timing cover.

2. Rotate the crankshaft ¼ turn counterclockwise and clockwise to move the No. 1 cylinder to the TDC of it's compression stroke.

3. Loosen the tensioner pulley center bolt. Using the tool MD998752 or equivalent, and a torque wrench, apply 1.88–2.03 ft. lbs. (2.6–2.8 Nm) and tighten the center bolt.

NOTE: If the body interferes with the torque wrench and tool, raise the engine slightly.

4. Using the tool MD998738 or equivalent, screw it into the left engine support bracket until it makes contact with the tensioner arm and screw the tool in some more.

5. Remove the set wire and the tool.

6. Rotate the crankshaft 2 complete clockwise revolutions and allow it to stand for 15 minutes. After 15 minutes, measure the auto tensioner protrusion **A** (distance between the tensioner arm and the auto tensioner body); it must be within 0.15–0.18 in. (3.8–4.5mm) or repeat the adjustment steps.

7. If the clearance between the tensioner are and the auto tensioner body is difficult to measure, perform the following procedures:

    a. Using the tool MD998738 or equivalent, screw it into the left engine support bracket until it contacts the tensioner arm.

    b. Screw it in further until the auto tensioner body pushrod moves backward and the tensioner arm contacts the auto tensioner body; make sure the number of turns is equal to 2.5–3 turns.

    c. Install the rubber plug into the timing belt rear cover.

    d. To complete the installation, reverse the removal procedures.

2.2L AND 2.5L ENGINES

1. Disconnect the negative battery cable. Remove the timing covers.

2. While holding the large hex wrench on the tension pulley, loosen the pulley nut.

3. Adjust the tensioner by turning the large tensioner hex to the right.

NOTE: The tension is correct when the belt can be twisted 90 degrees with the thumb and finger midway between the camshaft and the intermediate pulleys.

4. Torque the tensioner locknut to 32 ft. lbs.

5. To complete the installation, reverse the removal procedures. Torque the timing cover bolts to 40 inch lbs. and the crankshaft pulley bolt to 21 ft. lbs.

3.0L ENGINE

NOTE: The 3.0L engine is equipped with a spring-loaded timing belt tensioner. The tensioner will compensate in either direction as necessary. No adjustments are possible. If the timing belt is loose and the tensioner is out of it's travel range, check the condition of the belt, tensioner and/or tensioner spring.

Removal and Installation

1.8L ENGINE

The engine is equipped with 2 timing belts.

Outer (Large) Belt

1. Disconnect the negative battery cable. Remove the timing cover.

2. Using a wrench on the crankshaft pulley bolt, rotate the crankshaft (clockwise) to align the camshaft timing mark with the timing notch in the rear upper timing belt cover.

3. Place an arrow on the timing belt indicating the direction of rotation.

4. Loosen the timing belt tensioner-to-engine nut and bolt. Move the tensioner toward the water pump side and lightly secure the bolt.

5. Remove the large (outer) timing belt.

6. To install, adjust the outer (large) timing belt tension and reverse the removal procedures. Start the engine and check the engine timing.

Inner (Small) Belt

1. Disconnect the negative battery cable. Remove the timing cover.

2. Remove the outer (large) belt.

3. Make sure the inner (small) belt sprockets timing marks are aligned with the timing marks on the front case.

4. Place an arrow on the timing belt indicating the direction of rotation.

5. Loosen and remove the tensioner pulley bolt. Remove the inner (small) timing belt.

6. To install, adjust the inner (small) timing belt tension and reverse the removal procedures.

2.0L ENGINE

The engine is equipped with 2 timing belts.

Outer (Large) Belt

1. Disconnect the negative battery cable. Remove the timing cover.

2. Using a wrench on the crankshaft pulley bolt, rotate the crankshaft (clockwise) to align the camshaft timing marks (facing each other and aligned with the top of the cylinder head; the timing marks on the crankshaft and oil pump sprockets should be aligned with the timing indicators on the engine.

3. Place an arrow on the timing belt indicating the direction of rotation.

4. Remove the auto tensioner-to-engine bolts and the tensioner.

5. Remove the large (outer) timing belt.

6. To install, adjust the outer (large) timing belt tension and reverse the removal procedures. Start the engine and check the engine timing.

Inner (Small) Belt

1. Disconnect the negative battery cable. Remove the timing cover.

2. Remove the outer (large) belt.

3. Make sure the inner (small) belt sprockets timing marks are aligned with the timing marks on the front case.

4. Place an arrow on the timing belt indicating the direction of rotation.

5. Loosen and remove the tensioner pulley bolt. Remove the inner (small) timing belt.

6. To install, adjust the inner (small) timing belt tension and reverse the removal procedures.

2.2L AND 2.5L ENGINES

1. Disconnect the negative battery cable. Remove the timing covers.

2. While holding the large hex wrench on the tension pulley, loosen the pulley nut.

3. Remove the timing belt from the tensioner.

4. Slide the belt off the 3 toothed sprockets.

5. Using the larger bolt on the crankshaft pulley, turn the engine until the No. 1 cylinder is at TDC of the compression stroke. At this point the valves for the No. 1 cylinder will be closed and the timing mark will be aligned with the pointer on the flywheel housing. Make sure the arrows on the camshaft sprocket are aligned with the camshaft cap/cylinder head line.

6. Verify that the dot mark on the crankshaft pulley aligns with the line mark on the intermediate shaft.

7. Install the timing belt on the toothed sprockets.

8. Adjust the timing belt tension.

9. To complete the installation, reverse the removal procedures. Torque the tensioner locknut to 32 ft. lbs., the timing cover-to-engine bolts to 40 inch lbs. and the crankshaft pulley bolt to 21 ft. lbs. Check the ignition timing.

3.0L ENGINE

1. Disconnect the negative battery cable. Remove the timing covers from the engine.

2. If the same timing belt will be reused, mark the direction of the timing belt's rotation, for installation in the same direction.

3. Make sure the engine is positioned so the No. 1 cylinder is

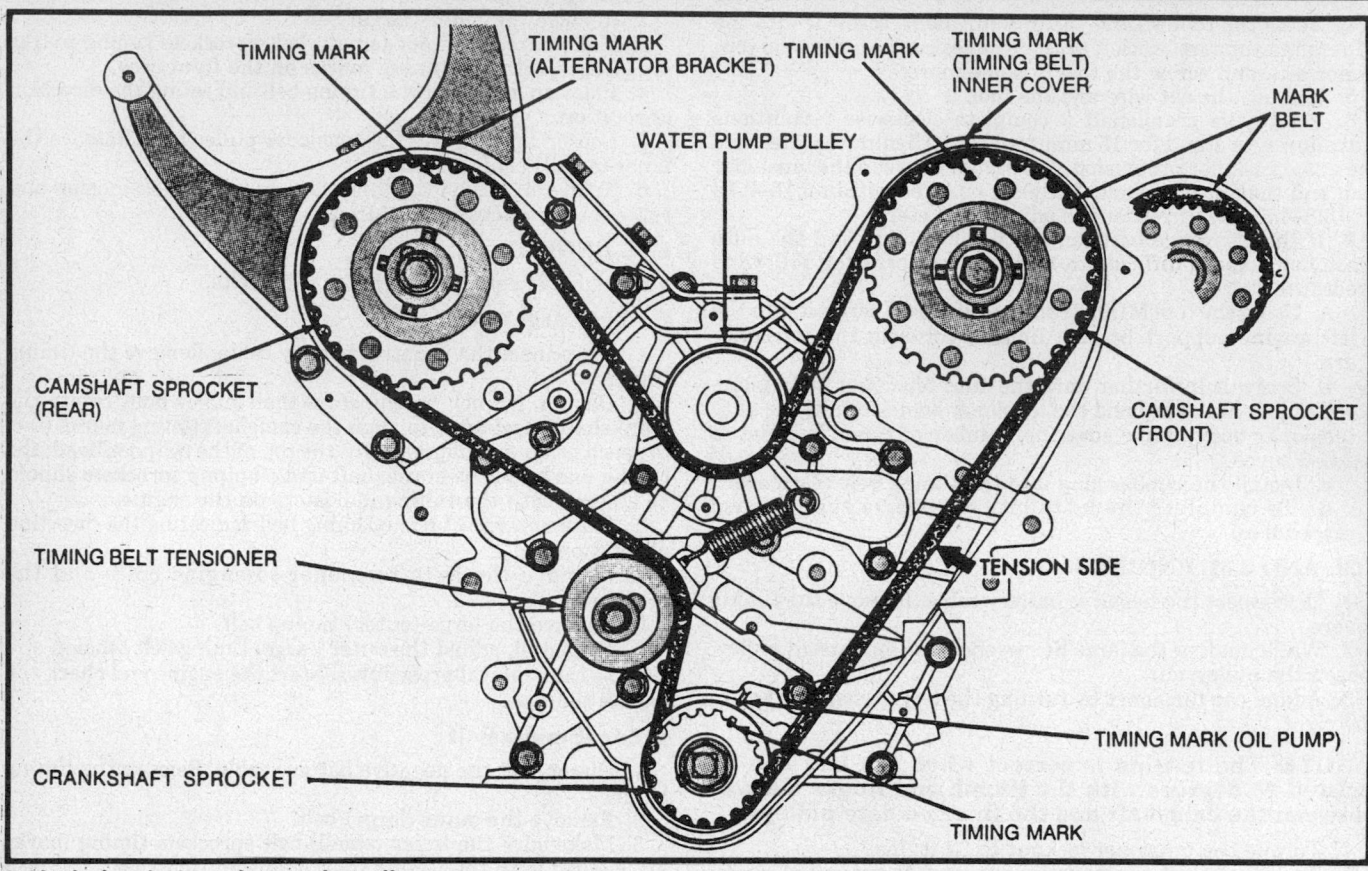

TIMING MARK TIMING MARK (ALTERNATOR BRACKET) TIMING MARK TIMING MARK (TIMING BELT) INNER COVER

MARK BELT

WATER PUMP PULLEY

CAMSHAFT SPROCKET (REAR)

CAMSHAFT SPROCKET (FRONT)

TIMING BELT TENSIONER

TENSION SIDE

TIMING MARK (OIL PUMP)

CRANKSHAFT SPROCKET

TIMING MARK

3.0L timing belt and sprocket alignment

at the TDC of it's compression stroke and the sprockets timing marks are aligned with the engine's timing mark indicators.

4. Install the timing belt. Rotate the tensioner counterclockwise and tighten the bolt.

5. Rotate the engine by hand, 2 revolutions and check the timing marks are still aligned.

6. Loosen the tensioner to place tension on the belt. Torque the tensioner lock bolt to 23 ft. lbs.

7. To complete the installation, reverse the removal procedures. Start the engine and inspect the engine timing and operation.

Timing Sprockets

Removal and Installation

1.8L ENGINE

1. Disconnect the negative battery cable. Remove both timing belts.

2. Remove the outer crankshaft sprocket bolt, washer, outer sprocket, flange and inner sprocket from the crankshaft.

3. Remove the camshaft sprocket bolt, washer and sprocket.

4. To remove the oil pump sprocket, perform the following procedures:

    a. On the left side of the engine, remove the plug.

    b. Using a 0.31 in. (8mm) rod, insert it into the through the block hole and into the left silent shaft hole (to lock the shaft).

    c. Remove the oil pump sprocket nut and the sprocket.

5. To remove the right silent shaft sprocket, secure the sprocket, remove the sprocket-to-shaft bolt, washer and the sprocket.

To Install:

6. Reverse the removal procedures. Torque the:

Right side silent shaft sprocket bolt to 26–29 ft. lbs. (34–40 Nm).

Oil pump sprocket bolt to 26–29 ft. lbs. (34–40 Nm).

Camshaft sprocket bolt to 58–72 ft. lbs. (80–100 Nm).

Crankshaft sprocket bolt to 80–94 ft. lbs. (110–130 Nm).

7. Align the sprockets timing marks. Install and adjust the timing belt.

8. To complete the installation, use new gaskets and reverse the removal procedures. Start the engine and check the engine's timing and operation.

2.0L ENGINE

1. Disconnect the negative battery cable. Remove both timing belt.

2. Remove the rocker arm cover.

3. Using a wrench, position it on each camshaft's hexagon surface (between the No. 2 and No. 3 journals) to hold the camshaft. Remove the camshaft sprocket bolt and the sprocket.

4. Remove the outer crankshaft sprocket bolt, washer, outer sprocket, flange and inner sprocket from the crankshaft.

5. To remove the oil pump sprocket, perform the following procedures:

    a. On the left side of the engine, remove the plug.

    b. Using a 0.31 in. (8mm) rod, insert it into the through the block hole and into the left silent shaft hole (to lock the shaft).

    c. Remove the oil pump sprocket nut and the sprocket.

6. To remove the right silent shaft sprocket, secure the sprocket, remove the sprocket-to-shaft bolt, washer and the sprocket.

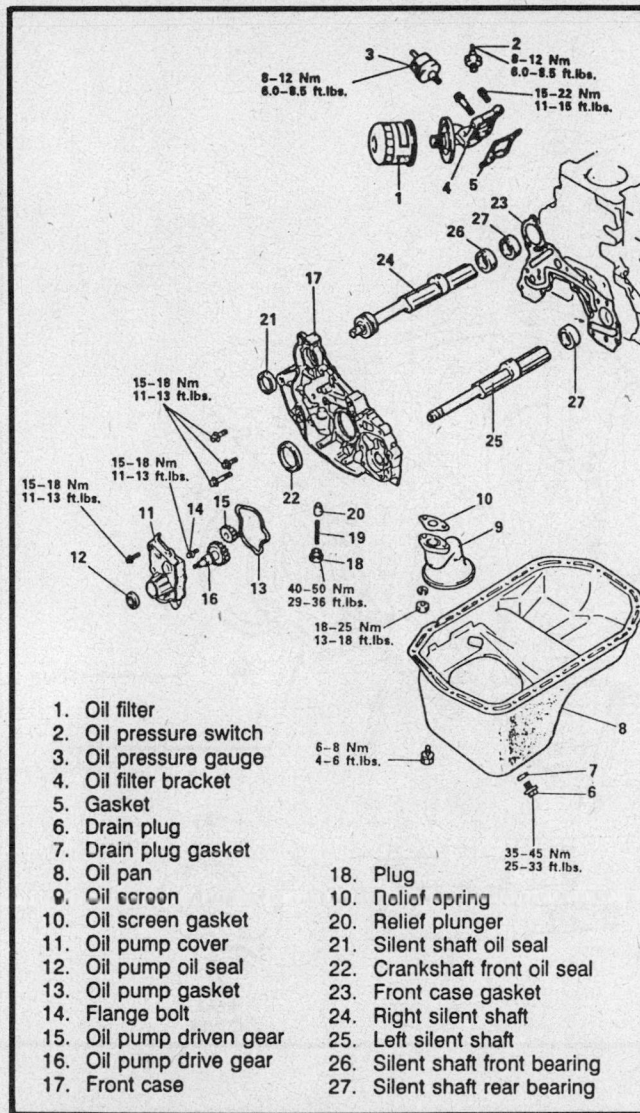

1. Oil filter
2. Oil pressure switch
3. Oil pressure gauge
4. Oil filter bracket
5. Gasket
6. Drain plug
7. Drain plug gasket
8. Oil pan
9. Oil screen
10. Oil screen gasket
11. Oil pump cover
12. Oil pump oil seal
13. Oil pump gasket
14. Flange bolt
15. Oil pump driven gear
16. Oil pump drive gear
17. Front case
18. Plug
19. Relief spring
20. Relief plunger
21. Silent shaft oil seal
22. Crankshaft front oil seal
23. Front case gasket
24. Right silent shaft
25. Left silent shaft
26. Silent shaft front bearing
27. Silent shaft rear bearing

Exploded view of the balance (silent) shaft assemblies—1.8L engine

To Install:

7. Reverse the removal procedures. Torque the:
   Right side silent shaft sprocket bolt to 25–29 ft. lbs. (34–40 Nm).
   Oil pump sprocket bolt to 36–43 ft. lbs. (50–60 Nm).
   Camshaft sprocket bolts to 58–72 ft. lbs. (80–100 Nm).
   Crankshaft sprocket bolt to 80–94 ft. lbs. (110–130 Nm).
8. Align the sprockets timing marks. Install and adjust the timing belt.
9. To complete the installation, use new gaskets and reverse the removal procedures. Start the engine and check the engine's timing and operation.

2.2L AND 2.5L ENGINES

1. Disconnect the negative battery cable. Remove the timing belt.
2. Remove the crankshaft sprocket bolt. Using the puller tool C–4685 or equivalent and the button from tool L–4524 or equivalent, remove the crankshaft sprocket.
3. Using the tool C–4687 or equivalent, hold the camshaft and/or intermediate sprocket, remove the center bolt(s) and the sprocket(s).

4. To install, use new gaskets and reverse the removal procedures. Torque the camshaft and intermediate sprocket bolts to 65 ft. lbs. and the crankshaft sprocket bolt to 50 ft. lbs. Adjust the timing belt tension.

3.0L ENGINE

1. Disconnect the negative battery cable. Remove the timing belt from the engine.
2. Remove the crankshaft sprocket, the shield and the sprocket.
3. To remove the camshaft sprocket(s), use camshaft holding tool MB990775 or equivalent, and remove the camshaft sprocket bolt(s) and sprocket(s).

To Install:

4. Install the camshaft sprocket, hold the camshaft with tool MB990775 or equivalent, and torque the bolt to 70 ft. lbs. (95 Nm).
5. Install the crankshaft sprocket, the shield and the bolt onto the crankshaft. Torque the crankshaft sprocket bolt to 110 ft. lbs. (150 Nm).
6. To complete the installation, reverse the removal procedures. Start the engine and check the engine timing and opertation.

Oil Seal

Removal and Installation

1.8L AND 2.0L ENGINES

Several oil seals are located at the front of the engine: crankshaft seal, the camshaft seal(s), the balance (silent) shaft seal and the oil pump seal. The seals can be replaced when the front case is removed or by performing the following procedures.

1. Disconnect the negative battery cable. Remove both timing belts.
2. Remove the sprockets from the crankshaft, the camshaft(s), the balance (silent) shaft and the oil pump.
3. Using a small prybar, pry the oil seal(s) from the engine, front case or oil pump (oil pump seal); be careful not to damage the seal(s) mounting surface(s).

To Install:

4. Using an oil seal installation tool or equivalent, lubricate the new seal with engine oil and drive the seal into the block, front case or oil pump until it seats.
5. To complete the installation, reverse the removal procedures. Start the engine and check for leaks. Check and/or adjust the ignition timing.

2.2L AND 2.5L ENGINES

1. Disconnect the negative battery cable. Remove the timing sprockets.
2. Using the tool C–4679 or equivalent, remove the crankshaft, the camshaft and/or intermediate seal(s).

To Install:

3. Before installing the oil seals, polish the shafts with 400 grit emery paper, use the oil seal installation tool C–4680 or equivalent and drive the seal into it's seat.

NOTE: If the seal has a steel case, lightly coat the seal with Loctite Stud N' Bearing Mount® or equivalent. If the seal case is rubber coated, apply soap and water to facilitate the installation.

4. To complete the installation, use new gaskets and reverse the removal procedures. Torque the camshaft and intermediate sprocket bolts to 65 ft. lbs. and the crankshaft sprocket bolt to 50 ft. lbs. Adjust the timing belt tension.

3.0L ENGINE

1. Disconnect the negative battery cable. Remove the timing sprockets.

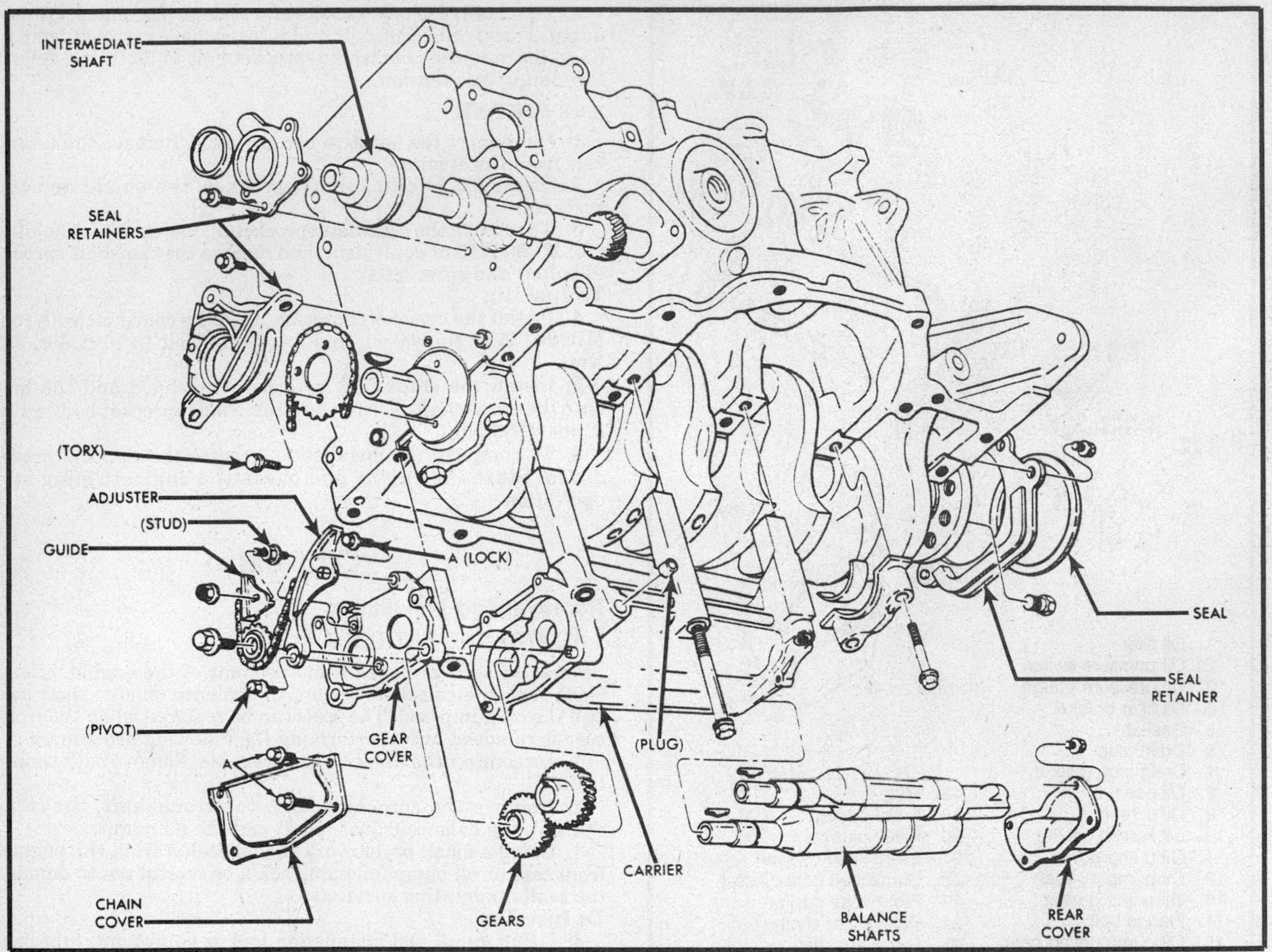

INTERMEDIATE SHAFT

SEAL RETAINERS

(TORX)

ADJUSTER

(STUD)

GUIDE

A (LOCK)

(PIVOT)

GEAR COVER

(PLUG)

CHAIN COVER

GEARS

CARRIER

BALANCE SHAFTS

REAR COVER

SEAL

SEAL RETAINER

Balance shafts and intermediate shaft locations—2.5L engine

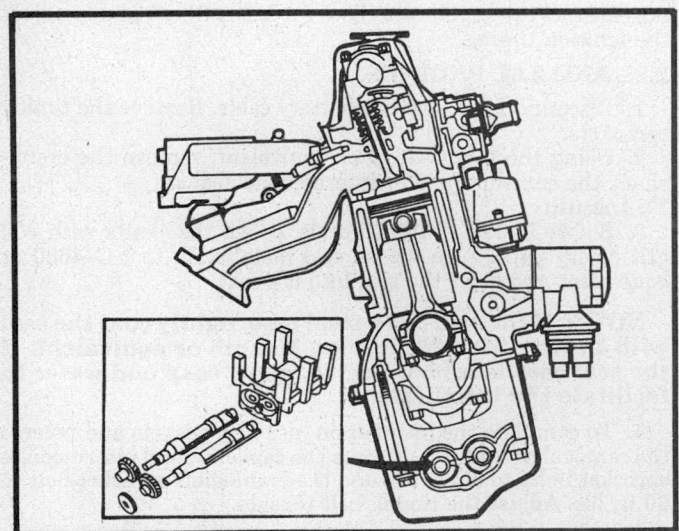

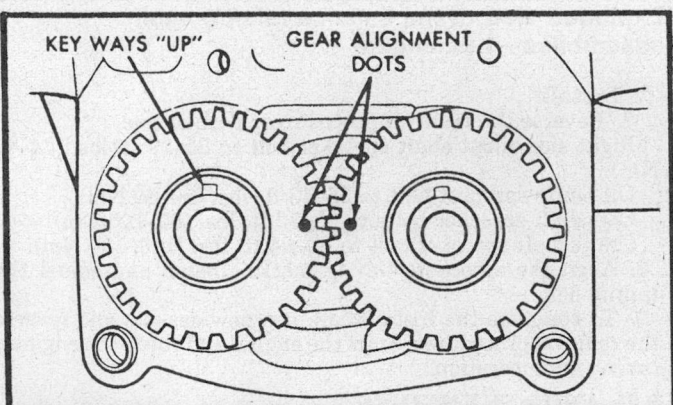

KEY WAYS "UP"

GEAR ALIGNMENT DOTS

Alignment of balance shaft gear sprockets—2.5L engine

2. Remove the oil pump assembly from the front of the engine and pry the oil seal from the oil pump housing.

3. Using a small prybar, pry the oil seals from the camshafts.

To Install:

4. Lubricate the new seals with engine oil. Using the oil seal

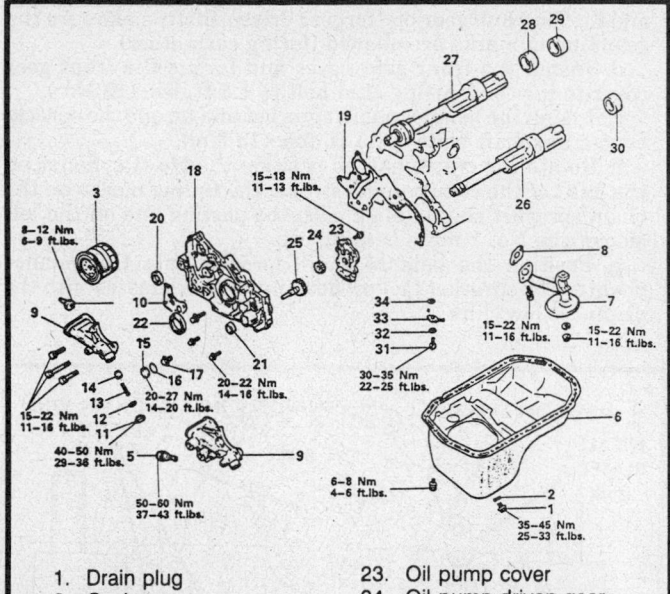

1. Drain plug
2. Gasket
3. Oil filter
4. Oil pressure switch
5. Oil cooler bypass valve (turbo)
6. Oil pan
7. Oil screen
8. Gasket
9. Oil filter bracket
10. Gasket
11. Relief plug
12. Gasket
13. Relief spring
14. Relief plunger
15. Plug cap
16. O-ring
17. Driven gear bolt
18. Front case
19. Gasket
20. Oil seal
21. Silent shaft oil seal
22. Crankshaft front oil seal
23. Oil pump cover
24. Oil pump driven gear
25. Oil pump drive gear
26. Left silent shaft
27. Right silent shaft
28. Silent shaft front bearing
29. Right silent shaft rear bearing
30. Left silent shaft rear bearing
31. Check valve (turbo)
32. Gasket (turbo)
33. Oil jet (turbo)
34. Gasket (turbo)

Exploded view of the balance (silent) shaft assemblies—2.0L engine

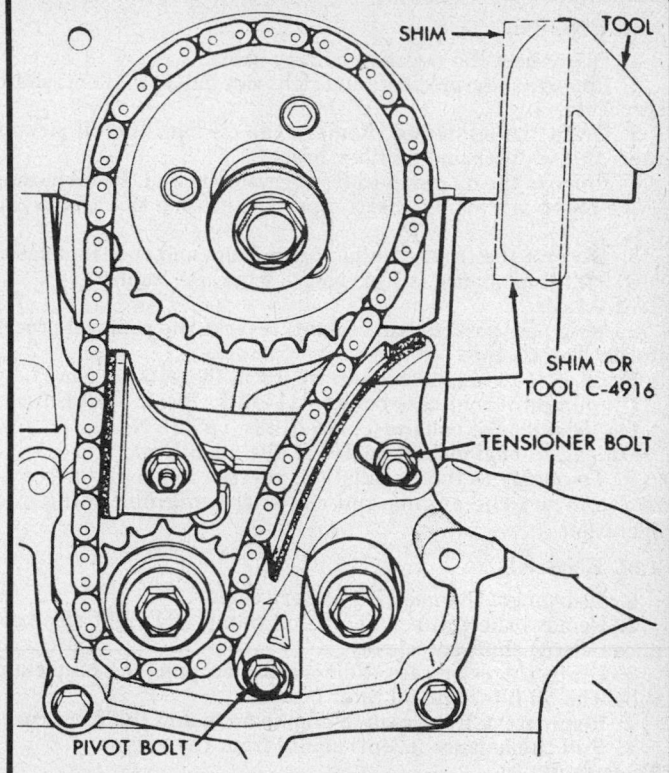

Adjustment of chain tensioner—2.5L engine

installer tool MD998713 or equivalent, drive the new camshaft seals into the cylinder head until they seat.

5. Using the oil seal installer tool MB998306 or equivalent, lubricate the new seal with engine oil and drive it into the oil pump housing until it seats.

6. Using a new gasket, install the oil pump housing to the engine and torque the bolts to 120 inch lbs. (13 Nm).

7. To complete the installation, reverse the removal procedures. Start the engine and check the engine timing and operation.

Balance Shafts

The 1.8L and 2.0L engines are equipped with 2 "Balance (Silent) Shafts" which cancel the vertical vibrating force of the engine and the secondary vibrating forces, which include the sideways rocking of the engine due to the turning direction of the crankshaft and other rolling parts. The balance (silent) shafts are operated indirectly by 2 separate timing belts. The left shaft is operated (through gears) connected to the oil pump.

The 2.5L engine is equipped with a pair of dual counter-rotating balance shafts, below and on both sides of the crankshaft, at almost a center position. The 2 counter-rotating eccentric balance shafts, interconnected by gears, are driven by a short chain from the crankshaft. They turn at twice the engine speed to offset the reciprocating mass of the pistons and connecting rods. This achieves the desired balancing effect. The balance shafts are enclosed in an aluminum housing, mounted beneath the crankshaft. The housing is bolted to the bottom of the main bearing webs of the engine block and rests in the oil supply of an enlarged oil pan. When the engine is running, the balance shafts pump oil out of the housing to minimize the drag which would occur if the shafts spun in the oil.

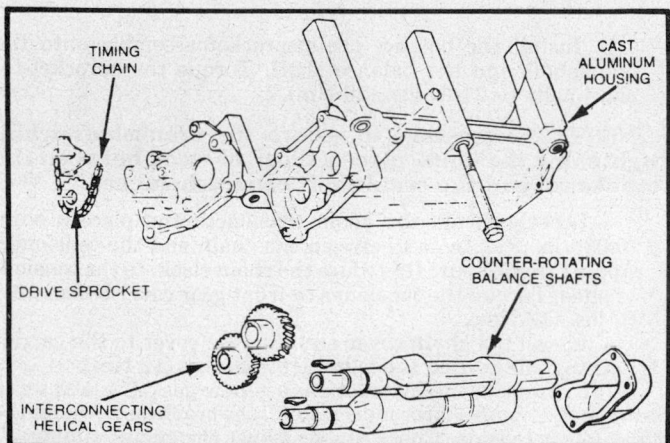

Balance shafts and housings—2.5L engine

Removal and Installation

1.8L ENGINE

1. Disconnect the negative battery cable.
2. Remove the crankshaft and right side balance (silent) shaft sprockets.
3. Drain the crankcase. Remove the oil pan, the oil pickup tube, the oil filter and oil filter bracket.
4. Remove the oil pump-to-front case bolts and the oil pump; if the pump is sticking, insert a prybar into the slot and pry it free.
5. Remove the front case-to-engine bolts and the front case.
6. Pull the balance (silent) shafts from the engine.

To Install:

7. Using new gaskets and sealant, reverse the removal procedures. Torque the:
   Front case-to-engine bolts to 11–13 ft. lbs. (15–18 Nm).
   Oil pump-to-front case bolts to 11–13 ft. lbs. (15–18 Nm).
   Oil pickup tube bolts to 11–16 ft. lbs. (15–22 Nm).
   Oil pan-to-engine bolts to 4–6 ft. lbs. (6–8 Nm).
8. To complete the installation, reverse the removal procedures. Start the engine and check the engine timing and operation.

2.0L ENGINE

1. Disconnect the negative battery cable.
2. Remove the crankshaft, the oil pump and right side balance (silent) shaft sprockets.
3. Drain the crankcase. Remove the oil pan, the oil pickup tube, the oil filter and oil filter bracket.
4. Remove the front case-to-engine bolts and the front case.
5. Pull the balance (silent) shafts from the engine.

To Install:

6. Using new gaskets and sealant, reverse the removal procedures. Torque the:
   Front case-to-engine bolts to 11–13 ft. lbs. (15–18 Nm).
   Oil pickup tube bolts to 11–16 ft. lbs. (15–22 Nm).
   Oil pan-to-engine bolts to 4–6 ft. lbs. (6–8 Nm).
7. To complete the installation, reverse the removal procedures. Start the engine and check the engine timing and operation.

2.5L ENGINE

The balance shaft chain assembly is installed in a carrier attached to the lower crankcase. The balance shaft chain assembly is located behind the timing belt assembly. The timing belt must be removed before removing the balance chain assembly.

1. Disconnect the negative battery cable. Remove the timing belt.
2. Raise and safely support the vehicle. Remove the oil pan, the oil pickup, the crankshaft belt sprocket and the front crankshaft oil seal retainer.
3. Remove the balance shaft chain cover, the guide and the tensioner.
4. Remove the balance shaft sprocket-to-shaft bolt, the gear cover-to-balance shaft bolt and the crankshaft sprocket-to-crankshaft bolts, then the sprockets with the balance chain.
5. Remove the front gear cover-to-carrier housing stud, the gear cover and the balance shaft drive gears.
6. Remove the rear gear cover-to-carrier housing bolts, the rear cover and the balance from the rear of the carrier.
7. If necessary, remove the carrier housing-to-crankcase bolts and the housing.

To Install:

8. Install the balance shaft/carrier assembly by performing the following procedures:
   a. If the carrier housing is being installed, torque the carrier housing-to-crankcase bolts to 40 ft. lbs. (54 Nm).
   b. Rotate the balance shafts until the keyways are facing upward (parallel to the vertical centerline of the engine).

c. Install the short hub gear on the sprocket driven shaft and the long hub gear on the gear driven shaft; make sure the gear timing marks are aligned (facing each other).
   d. Install the front gear cover and torque the front gear cover-to-carrier housing stud bolt to 8.5 ft. lbs. (12 Nm).
   e. Install the balance chain sprocket and torque the sprocket-to-crankshaft bolts to 11 ft. lbs. (13 Nm).
   f. Rotate the crankshaft to position the No. 1 cylinder on the TDC of the compression stroke; the timing marks on the chain sprocket should align with the parting line on the left side of the No. 1 main bearing cap.
   g. Position the balance shaft sprocket into the balance chain so the sprocket (yellow dot) timing mark mates with the chain (yellow) link.

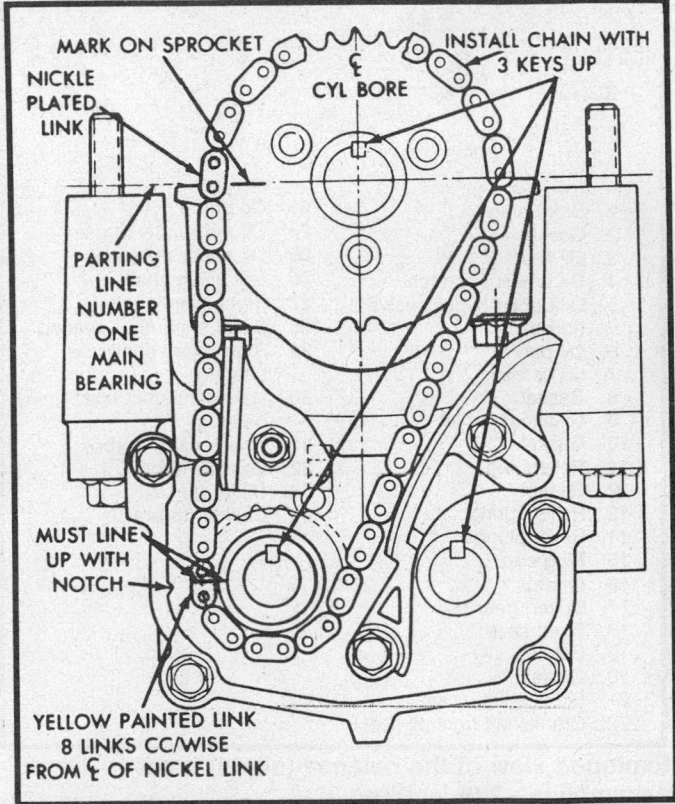

Balance shaft sprocket timing to crankshaft sprocket—2.5L engine

h. Install the balance chain/sprocket assembly onto the crankshaft and the balance shaft. Torque the sprocket-to-shaft bolts to 21 ft. lbs. (28 Nm).

NOTE: If necessary to secure the crankshaft while tightening the bolts, place a block of wood between the crankcase and the crankshaft counterbalance.

i. Loosely install the chain tensioners and place a shim (0.039 in. × 2.75 in.) between the chain and the tensioner. Apply firm pressure (to reduce the chain slack) to the tensioner shoe. Torque the tensioner-to-front gear cover bolts to 8.5 ft. lbs. (12 Nm).
   j. Install the chain cover and the rear cover to the carrier housing and torque the bolts to 8.5 ft. lbs. (12 Nm).
9. To complete the installation, use new gasket, sealant and reverse the removal procedures. Refill the crankcase. Adjust the timing belt tension. Check and/or adjust the engine timing.

Pistons/Rings/Connecting Rod Positioning

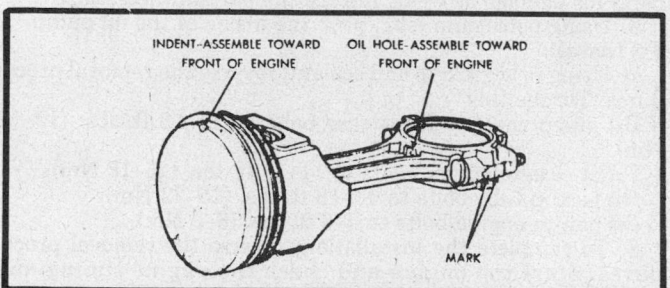

Piston and connecting rod positioning—2.2L engine

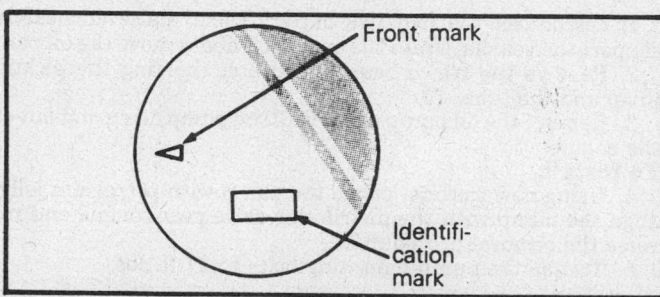

View of the piston head identification and alignment marks—1.8L and 2.0L engines

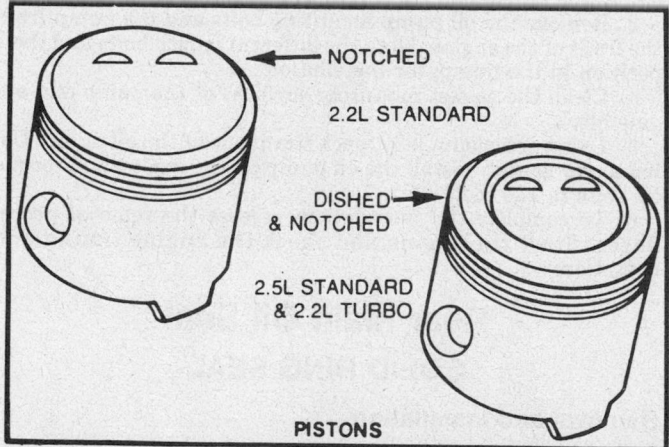

2.2L and 2.5L engine piston differences

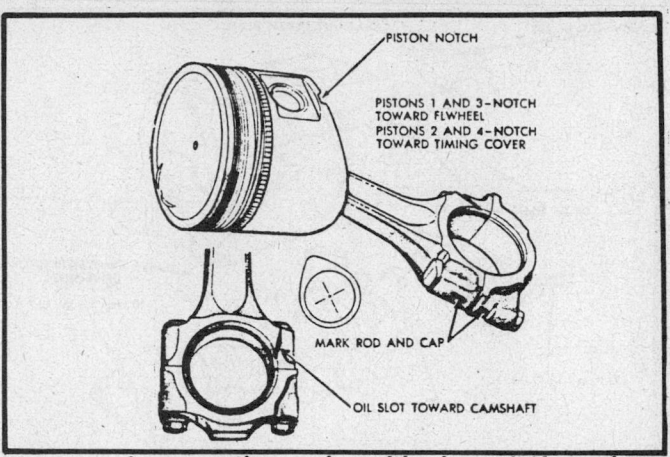

Piston and connecting rod positioning—1.6L engine

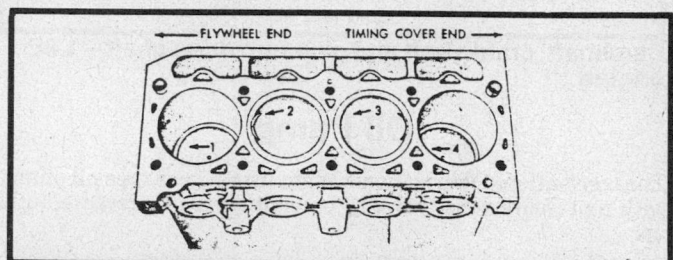

Cylinder and piston identification—1.6L engine

The piston crown is marked with an arrow which must point toward the timing belt or chain end of the engine when installed. On 2.2L and 2.5L engines, the connecting rod and cap are marked with rectangular forge marks which must be mated when assembled and be on the intermediate shaft side of the engine when installed.

In the 1.6L engine, the No. 1 and No. 3 pistons are installed with the piston skirt notch facing the flywheel, while No. 2 and No. 4 piston skirt notches are toward the timing cover.

Engines equipped with light connecting rods will have the letter **LW** ink-stamped on the engine block core plug, nearest the distributor. Lightweight rods will have the letters **LW** cast in the rod shank.

On the 3.0L engine, the pistons are marked with an **R** for cylinder Nos. 1, 3 and 5 and with an **L** for cylinder Nos. 2, 4 and 6. The connecting rod must be numbered when removed. Mark both halves of the cap for proper installation.

NOTE: Lightweight connecting rods cannot be mixed with the heavyweight rods, as engine vibrations will result. The connecting rods must be used in sets only, either all lightweights or all heavyweights.

ENGINE LUBRICATION SYSTEM

Oil Pan

Removal and Installation

1. Disconnect the negative battery cable.
2. Raise and safely support the vehicle. Drain the engine oil.
3. Support the oil pan and remove the mounting bolts.
4. Remove the oil pan and discard the gaskets.
5. Clean the oil pan and gasket mounting surfaces.

To Install:

6. Using a new gasket and sealant (1.8L and 2.0L engines), reverse the removal procedures. Torque the oil pan bolts to:
7 ft. lbs.—1.6L.
4–6 ft. lbs.—1.8L and 2.0L.
17 ft. lbs.—2.2L and 2.5L.
51 inch lbs.—3.0L.
7. Refill the engine oil, run the engine and check for leaks.

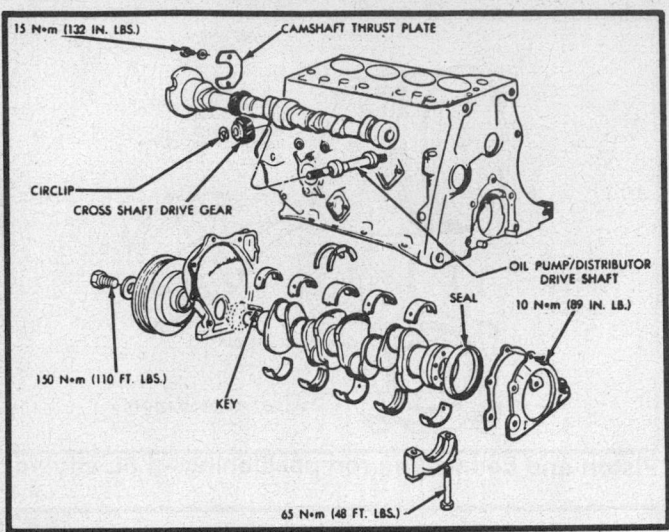

15 N•m (132 IN. LBS.)   CAMSHAFT THRUST PLATE

CIRCLIP

CROSS SHAFT DRIVE GEAR

OIL PUMP/DISTRIBUTOR DRIVE SHAFT

SEAL

10 N•m (89 IN. LB.)

150 N•m (110 FT. LBS.)   KEY

65 N•m (48 FT. LBS.)

Camshaft, crankshaft and oil pump drive shaft – 1.6L engine

Oil Pump

The conventional lubrication system uses a gear type oil pump, with a pressure relief valve to prevent extreme pressure build up.

Removal and Installation

1.6L ENGINE

The oil pump is located on the right side of the engine block.
1. Disconnect the negative battery cable. Remove the oil filter.
2. Holding the oil pump cover and housing together, remove the bolts and pull the assembly away from the engine.
3. Remove the gaskets. Clean the gasket mating surfaces.
To Install:
4. Prime the pump body with petroleum jelly. Use new gaskets and place sealer on the mounting bolt threads.
5. Insert the bolts to align the pump body with the housing. Align the pump with the engine. Engage the driving shaft gear tongue with the slot in the halfshaft and torque the mounting bolts to 9 ft. lbs.
6. Run the engine and check for leaks.

1.8L ENGINE

1. Disconnect the negative battery cable. Remove the timing belts.
2. Remove the oil pump shaft sprocket.
3. Remove the oil pump-to-front case bolts and the oil pump; if the pump is sticking, insert a prybar into the slot and pry it free.
4. Using petroleum jelly, pack the inside of the oil pump.
To Install:
5. Using new gaskets and sealant, reverse the removal procedures. Torque the oil pump-to-front case bolts to 11–13 ft. lbs. (15–18 Nm).
6. To complete the installation, reverse the removal procedures. Start the engine and check the engine timing and operation.

2.0L ENGINE

1. Disconnect the negative battery cable. Remove the crankshaft, the oil pump and the right side balance (silent) shaft sprockets.
2. Drain the crankcase. Remove the oil pan, the oil pickup tube, the oil filter and oil filter bracket.

3. Remove the front case-to-engine bolts and the front case.
4. From the rear of the front case, remove the oil pump cover-to-front case bolts, the cover, the drive gear and the driven gear.
5. Clean the gasket mounting surfaces. Inspect the oil pump parts for damage or wear; replace the parts, if necessary.
6. Using petroleum jelly, pack the inside of the oil pump.
To Install:
7. Using new gaskets and sealant, reverse the removal procedures. Torque the:
Oil pump cover-to-front case bolts to 11–13 ft. lbs. (15–18 Nm).
Front case-to-engine bolts to 11–13 ft. lbs. (15–18 Nm).
Oil pickup tube bolts to 11–16 ft. lbs. (15–22 Nm).
Oil pan-to-engine bolts to 4–6 ft. lbs. (6–8 Nm).
8. To complete the installation, reverse the removal procedures. Start the engine and check the engine timing and operation.

2.2L AND 2.5L ENGINES

1. Disconnect the negative battery cable. Raise and safely support the vehicle. Drain the engine oil and remove the oil pan.
2. Remove the No. 3 bearing cap bolt (holding the pickup tube) and the tube.
3. Remove the oil pump bolts. Pull the pump down and out of the engine.
To Install:
4. Using new gaskets, prime the pump with petroleum jelly, align the pump with the distributor drive gear tongue and reverse the removal procedures.
5. Torque the pump mounting bolts to 17 ft. lbs.

3.0L ENGINE

1. Disconnect the negative battery cable. Remove the timing belt from the engine.
2. Remove the balancer and crankshaft sprocket from the end of the crankshaft.
3. Remove the oil pump mounting bolts and the pump from the front of the engine. Note the different length bolts and their position in the pump, for installation.
4. Clean the gasket mounting surfaces of the pump and engine block.
5. Using petroleum jelly, pack the inside of the oil pump. Using a new gasket, install the oil pump on the engine and torque all bolts to 130 inch lbs.
6. To complete the installation, reverse the removal procedures. Start the engine and check the engine timing and operation.

Rear Main Oil Seal
SOLID RING SEAL

Removal and Installation

1.6L ENGINE

NOTE: In order to replace the rear main bearing oil seal, the engine assembly must be removed from the vehicle.

1. Remove the engine and position it in a holding fixture. Remove the flywheel or drive plate from the crankshaft.
2. Remove the rear oil seal housing mounting bolts and the housing.
3. Place the housing inner surface on blocks of wood, allowing clearance for the seal removal.
4. Using the seal removal/installation tool or equivalent, drive the seal from the housing.
To Install:
5. Invert the seal housing and place it on a smooth surface. Using the seal removal/installation tool or equivalent, drive the new seal into the housing until it seats.

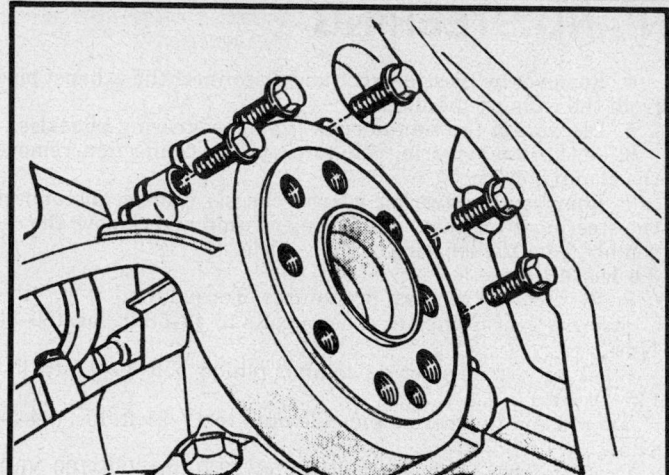

3.0L rear main seal assembly

6. To complete the installation, use a new gasket, lubricate the seal lips and reverse the removal procedures. Torque the seal housing mounting bolts to 9 ft. lbs.

1.8 AND 3.0L ENGINE

1. Disconnect the negative battery cable. Remove the transaxle from the vehicle.
2. If equipped with a manual transaxle, remove the flywheel from the crankshaft. If equipped an automatic transaxle, remove the adapter plate, the drive plate and the adapter plate from the crankshaft.
3. Remove the rear oil seal retainer from the rear of the engine.
4. Using a seal driver, place the retainer on 2 blocks of wood and drive the seal from the retainer.
5. Clean and inspect the retainer for damage. Clean the gasket mating surfaces.

To Install:
6. Using seal driver tool MB998718 or equivalent, drive the new seal into the retainer, with the lip facing inward, until it bottoms out.
7. Apply RTV sealer to the retainer mating surface and lightly coat the seal lip with clean engine oil.
8. Install the seal retainer on the engine. Torque the mounting bolts to 7–9 ft. lbs. (1.8L) or 104 inch lbs. (3.0L)
9. Install the transaxle in the vehicle.
10. When finished, run the engine and check for leaks.

2.0L ENGINE

The rear main bearing oil seal is located in a housing on the rear of the block. To replace the seal, remove the transaxle and work from underneath the vehicle. The engine can also be removed from the vehicle.

1. Disconnect the negative battery cable.
2. If equipped with a manual transaxle, remove the flywheel from the crankshaft. If equipped an automatic transaxle, remove the adapter plate, the drive plate and the adapter plate from the crankshaft.
3. Remove the oil seal housing-to-engine mounting bolts. Remove the housing from the engine.
4. Remove the separator from the oil seal housing.
5. Using a small pry bar, pry the old seal from the housing.
6. Clean the gasket mating surfaces.

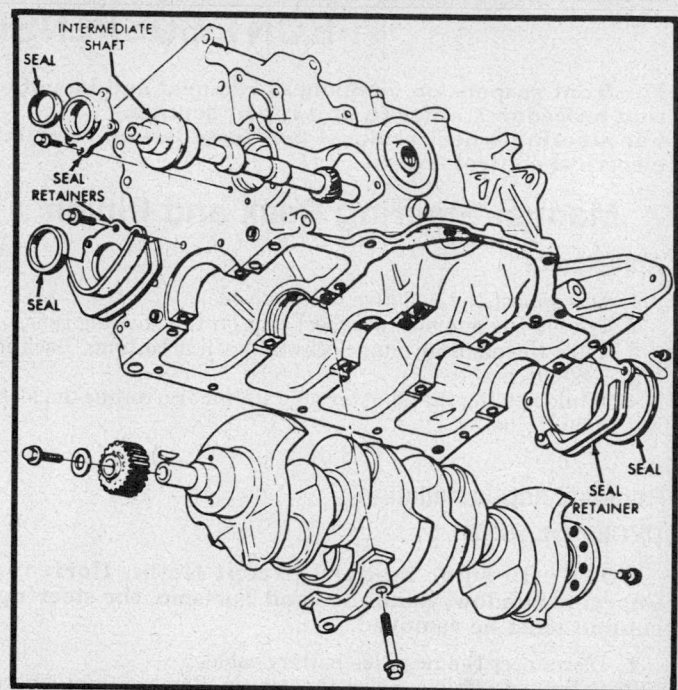

Crankshaft and intermediate shaft seals—2.2L engine

To Install:
7. Using new gaskets/seals, lubricate the new oil seal and seat it in the housing. Install the separator with the oil hole facing down.
8. To complete the installation, reverse the removal procedures.

2.2L AND 2.5L ENGINES

The rear main seal is located in a housing on the rear of the block. To replace the seal the engine must be removed.
1. Remove the engine and position it in a holding fixture. Remove the flywheel or the drive plate from the crankshaft.

NOTE: Before removing the transaxle, align the dimple on the flywheel with the pointer on the flywheel housing. The transaxle will not mate with the engine during installation, unless this alignment is observed.

2. Using a small pry bar, carefully pry the old seal from the oil seal housing.
3. Coat the new seal with Loctite® Stud N' Bearing Mount (4057987) or equivalent and drive it into place, using the installation tool or equivalent. Take care not to scratch the seal or the crankshaft.
4. To install, reverse the removal procedures.

Connecting Rod and Main Bearings

Replacement

Engine bearings are of the precision insert type, they are available for in standard and undersizes. Upper and lower bearing inserts may be different. Be careful to align holes. Do not obstruct any oil passages. Bearing inserts must not be shimmed. Do not touch the bearing surface of the insert with bare fingers. Skin oil and acids will etch the bearing surface.

FRONT SUSPENSION AND STEERING

For front suspension component removal and installation procedures, refer to unit repair section.
For steering wheel removal and installation, refer to electrical control section.

Manual Steering Rack and Pinion

Adjustment

1. Disconnect the negative battery cable.
2. Loosen the adjuster plug lock nut on the steering gear.
3. Turn the adjuster plug clockwise until it bottoms. Back it off 40–60 degrees.
4. While holding the adjuster plug stationary, torque the lock nut to 50 ft. lbs.

Removal and Installation
EXCEPT LASER

NOTE: On some models, except Omni, Horizon, Charger, Shadow, Sundance and Turismo, the steering column must be removed.

1. Disconnect the negative battery cable.
2. Raise and safely support the vehicle. Remove front wheel assemblies.
3. Remove the cotter pins, castle nuts and tie rod ends (using a ball joint puller) from the steering knuckles.
4. Except for the Omni, Horizon, Charger, Shadow, Sundance and Turismo, remove the steering column-to-steering gear coupling pin; follow the procedures in Step 6, this will expose the coupling pin so it can be driven out. If equipped, remove the anti-rotational link from the crossmember and the air diverter valve bracket, from the left side of the crossmember.

NOTE: The lower universal joint is removed with the steering gear.

5. On the Omni, Horizon, Charger, Shadow, Sundance and Turismo, drive out the lower roll pin attaching the pinion shaft to the lower universal joint. Use a back-up, to protect the universal joint, while driving the roll pin.
6. On the Omni, Horizon, Charger, Shadow, Sundance and Turismo, support the front suspension crossmember with a hydraulic jack. Remove the rear nuts attaching the crossmember to the frame. Loosen the front bolts attaching the crossmember to the frame and lower the crossmember slightly for access to the boot seal shields.
7. Except for the Omni, Horizon, Charger, Shadow, Sundance and Turismo, remove the front suspension crossmember attaching bolts and the lower front suspension crossmember, using a transaxle jack, so the steering gear can be removed from the crossmember.
8. Remove the splash and the boot seal shields.
9. Remove the steering gear bolts from the front suspension crossmember.
10. Remove the steering gear from the left side of the vehicle.
To Install:
11. Reverse the removal procedures. The right rear crossmember bolt is a pilot bolt that correctly locates the crossmember, tighten it first. Torque the crossmember bolts to 90 ft. lbs. and the steering gear attaching bolts to 21 ft. lbs.

LASER

1. Disconnect the negative battery cable.
2. Position the wheels in the straight ahead position.
3. Raise and safely support the front of the vehicle. Remove the front wheels.

4. Remove the crossmember and disconnect the exhaust pipe from the exhaust manifold.
5. Disconnect the tie rod ends from the steering knuckles.
6. At the lower steering column-to-pinion connection, remove the clamp bolt.
7. Remove the steering gear-to-chassis clamps, disconnect the steering gear from the steering column and remove the assembly from the left side of the vehicle.
To Install:
8. Reverse the removal procedures. Torque the:
Steering gear clamps-to-chassis bolts to 43–58 ft. lbs. (60–80 Nm).
Steering gear-to-steering column pinion bolt 11–14 ft. lbs. (15–20 Nm).
Tie rod end-to-steering knuckle nuts to 17–25 ft. lbs. (24–34 Nm).
Crossmember-to-chassis bolts to 58–72 ft. lbs. (80–100 Nm).
Front roll stopper bolt to 36–47 ft. lbs. (50–65 Nm).
Exhaust pipe-to-exhaust manifold nuts to 22–29 ft. lbs. (30–40 Nm).
9. Check and/or adjust the front wheel alignment.

POWER RACK AND PINION

Adjustment

1. Disconnect the negative battery cable.
2. Loosen the adjuster plug lock nut on the steering gear.
3. Turn the adjuster plug clockwise until it bottoms. Back it off 40–60 degrees.
4. While holding the adjuster plug stationary, torque the lock nut to 50 ft. lbs.

Removal and Installation
EXCEPT LASER

NOTE: On some models, except Omni, Horizon, Charger, Shadow, Sundance and Turismo, the steering column must be removed.

1. Disconnect the negative battery cable.
2. Raise and safely support the vehicle. Remove front wheel assemblies.
3. Remove the cotter pins, castle nuts and tie-rod ends (using a ball joint puller) from the steering knuckles.
4. Except for the Omni, Horizon, Charger, Shadow, Sundance and Turismo, remove the steering column-to-steering gear coupling pin; follow the procedures in Step 6, this will expose the coupling pin so it can be driven out. If equipped, remove the anti-rotational link from the crossmember and the air diverter valve bracket, from the left side of the crossmember.

NOTE: The lower universal joint is removed with the steering gear.

5. Disconnect and plug the oil pressure lines from the power steering pump.
6. On the Omni, Horizon, Charger, Shadow, Sundance and Turismo, drive out the lower roll pin attaching the pinion shaft to the lower universal joint. Use a back-up, to protect the universal joint, while driving the roll pin.
7. On the Omni, Horizon, Charger, Shadow, Sundance and Turismo, support the front suspension crossmember with a hydraulic jack. Remove the rear nuts attaching the crossmember to the frame. Loosen the front bolts attaching the crossmember to the frame and lower the crossmember slightly for access to the boot seal shields.
8. Except for the Omni, Horizon, Charger, Shadow, Sundance and Turismo, remove the front suspension cross-

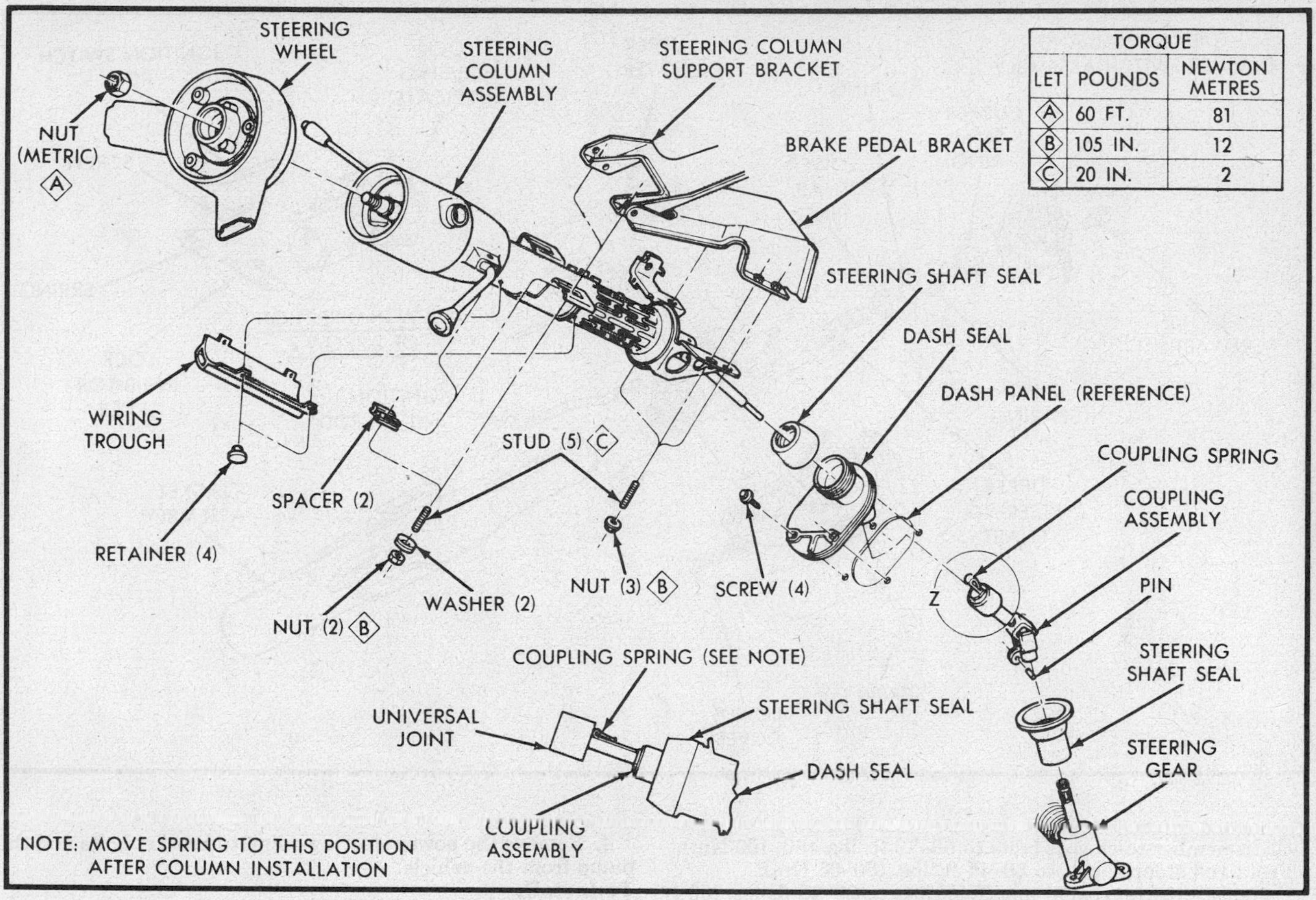

STEERING WHEEL

STEERING COLUMN ASSEMBLY

STEERING COLUMN SUPPORT BRACKET

TORQUE		
LET	POUNDS	NEWTON METRES
A	60 FT.	81
B	105 IN.	12
C	20 IN.	2

NUT (METRIC) A

BRAKE PEDAL BRACKET

STEERING SHAFT SEAL

DASH SEAL

DASH PANEL (REFERENCE)

COUPLING SPRING

COUPLING ASSEMBLY

WIRING TROUGH

STUD (5) C

SPACER (2)

PIN

STEERING SHAFT SEAL

RETAINER (4)

NUT (3) B

SCREW (4)

Z

STEERING GEAR

WASHER (2)

NUT (2) B

COUPLING SPRING (SEE NOTE)

UNIVERSAL JOINT

STEERING SHAFT SEAL

DASH SEAL

COUPLING ASSEMBLY

NOTE: MOVE SPRING TO THIS POSITION AFTER COLUMN INSTALLATION

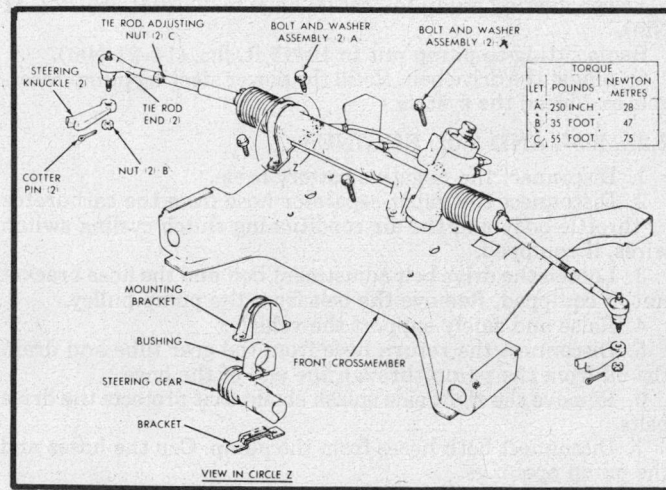

TIE ROD ADJUSTING NUT (2) C

BOLT AND WASHER ASSEMBLY (2) A

BOLT AND WASHER ASSEMBLY (2) A

STEERING KNUCKLE (2)

TIE ROD END (2)

	TORQUE	
LET	POUNDS	NEWTON METRES
A	250 INCH	28
B	35 FOOT	47
C	55 FOOT	75

COTTER PIN (2)

NUT (2) B

Z

MOUNTING BRACKET

BUSHING

FRONT CROSSMEMBER

STEERING GEAR

BRACKET

VIEW IN CIRCLE Z

Steering gear mounting, typical of all models.

member attaching bolts and the lower front suspension crossmember, using a transaxle jack, so the steering gear can be removed from the crossmember.

9. Remove the splash and the boot seal shields.
10. Remove the steering gear bolts from the front suspension crossmember.

11. Remove the steering gear from the left side of the vehicle.
12. To install, reverse the removal procedures. The right rear crossmember bolt is a pilot bolt that correctly locates the crossmember, tighten it first. Torque the crossmember bolts to 90 ft. lbs. and the steering gear attaching bolts to 21 ft. lbs. Refill the power steering pump. Bleed the power steering system.

LASER
1. Disconnect the negative battery cable.
2. Position the wheels in the straight ahead position.
3. Raise and safely support the front of the vehicle. Remove the front wheels.
4. Disconnect the power steering lines from the power steering gear and drain the fluid.
5. Remove the crossmember and disconnect the exhaust pipe from the exhaust manifold.
6. Disconnect the tie rod ends from the steering knuckles.
7. At the lower steering column-to-pinion connection, remove the clamp bolt.
8. Remove the steering gear-to-chassis clamps, disconnect the steering gear from the steering column and remove the assembly from the left side of the vehicle.
To Install:
9. Reverse the removal procedures. Torque the:
Steering gear clamps-to-chassis bolts to 43–58 ft. lbs. (60–80 Nm).
Steering gear-to-steering column pinion bolt 11–14 ft. lbs. (15–20 Nm).
Tie rod end-to-steering knuckle nuts to 17–25 ft. lbs. (24–34 Nm).

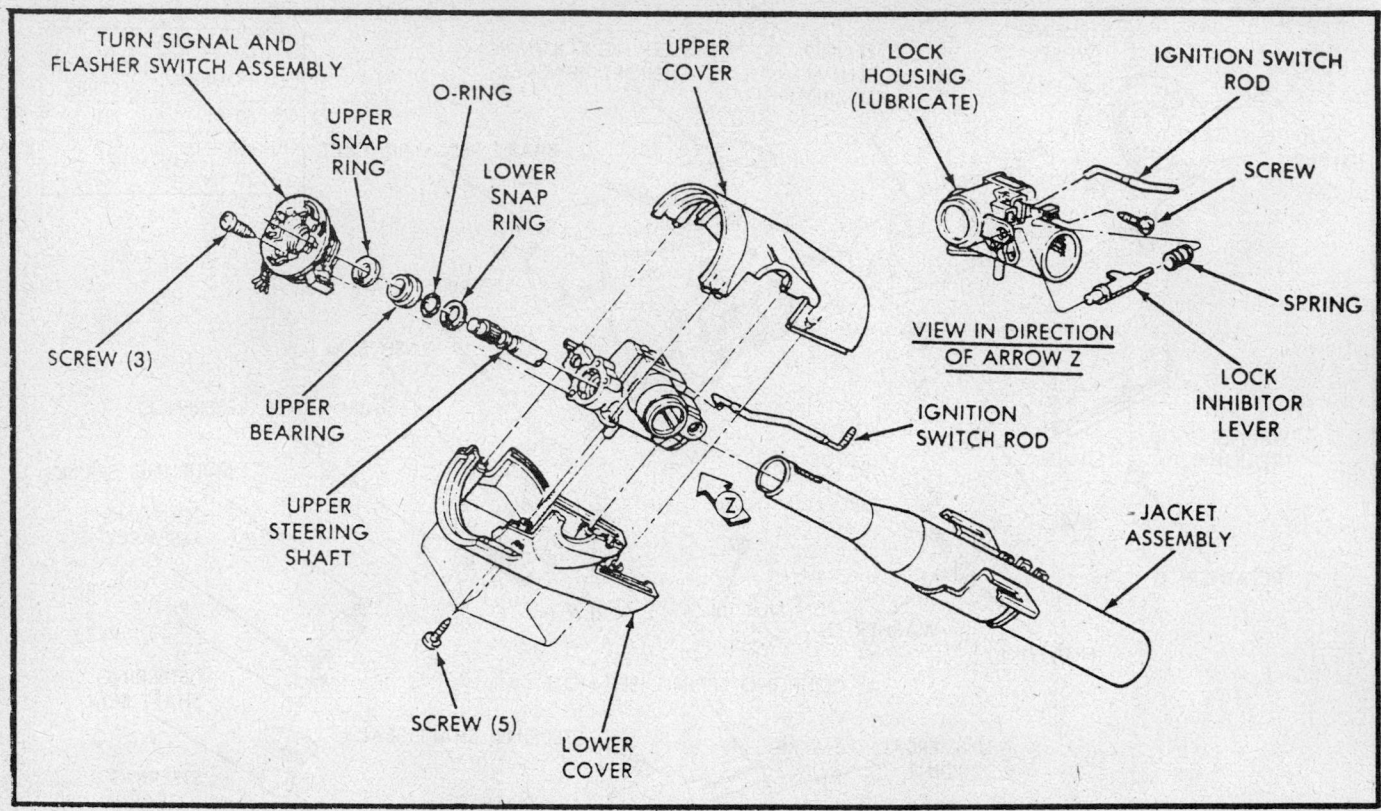

Crossmember-to-chassis bolts to 58–72 ft. lbs. (80–100 Nm).
Front roll stopper bolt to 36–47 ft. lbs. (50–65 Nm).
Exhaust pipe-to-exhaust manifold nuts to 22–29 ft. lbs. (30–40 Nm).

10. Refill the power steering reservoir and bleed the power steering system. Check and/or adjust the front wheel alignment.

Power Steering Pump

Removal and Installation

1.6L ENGINE

1. Disconnect the negative battery cable.
2. Loosen, but do not remove, the power steering pump pressure hose.
3. Remove the belt adjustment nut and loosen the locking nuts from the rear pump studs.
4. Place a container on the radiator yoke to catch the power steering fluid.
5. Remove the drive belt and locking nuts. Lift the pump, bracket and rubber isolator (as an assembly) from the engine.
6. Remove the pump reservoir cap and pour the fluid into the container.
7. Remove and plug the hoses and pump openings.
8. To install, reverse the removal procedures. Adjust the drive belt tension, refill the reservoir with power steering fluid and torque the locking nuts to 21 ft. lbs. Bleed the power steering system.

1.8L AND 2.0L ENGINES

1. Disconnect the negative battery cable.
2. Remove the pressure hoses from the power steering pump and drain the system.
3. Loosen the power steering pump and remove the drive belt.

4. Remove the power steering pump-to-bracket bolts and the pump from the vehicle.

To Install:

5. Using new pressure tube washers, reverse the removal procedures. Torque the:
Power steering pump-to-bracket bolts to 20–30 ft. lbs. (27–41 Nm).
Banjo fitting-to-pump nut to 10–15 ft. lbs. (14–21 Nm).
6. Adjust the drive belt. Refill the power steering pump reservoir and bleed the system.

2.2L, 2.5L AND 3.0L ENGINES

1. Disconnect the negative battery cable.
2. Disconnect the vapor separator hose from the carburetor or throttle body and the air conditioning clutch cycling switch wires, if equipped.
3. Loosen the drive belt adjustment bolt and the hose bracket nut, if equipped. Remove the belt from the pump pulley.
4. Raise and safely support the vehicle.
5. Disconnect the return hose from the gear tube and drain the oil from the pump through the end of the hose.
6. Remove the right side splash shield that protects the drive belts.
7. Disconnect both hoses from the pump. Cap the hoses and the pump openings.
8. Remove the lower stud nut and the pivot bolt from the pump.
9. Lower the vehicle and remove the drive belt from the pulley.
10. Move the pump rearward, to clear the mounting bracket and remove the adjusting bracket.
11. Rotate the pump clockwise, so the pump pulley faces the rear of the vehicle and pull upwards to remove the pump from the vehicle.
12. To install, use new O-rings on the pressure hose and re-

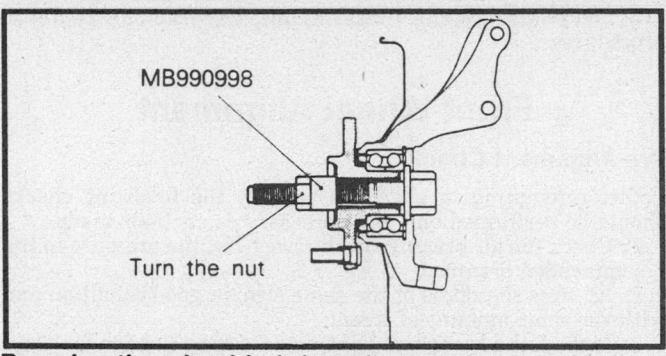

Pressing the wheel hub into the steering knuckle—Laser

MB990998

Turn the nut

verse the removal procedures. Adjust the belt to the correct tension and refill the pump reservoir to the proper level with power steering fluid. Torque the adjustment bolt to 30 ft. lbs., the lower stud nut and the pivot bolt to 40 ft. lbs. Bleed the power steering system.

Belt Adjustment
EXCEPT LASER

1. Disconnect the negative battery cable.
2. Working on top of the vehicle, loosen the top power steering pump-to-bracket bolt. Working under the vehicle, loosen the bottom power steering pump-to-bracket bolt.
3. Using a ½ in. breaker bar, place it into the square hole on the adjusting bracket and turn the adjusting bracket to apply pressure to the belt.
4. Using a straight edge and thumb pressure, at the center of the belt, establish a belt deflection of ¼ in. (new) or $\frac{7}{16}$ in. (used).
5. When the correct deflection is established, torque the top (1st) and the bottom (2nd) power steering pump-to-bracket bolt to 40 ft. lbs.

LASER

1. Disconnect the negative battery cable.
2. Loosen the power steering pump-to-bracket bolts.
3. While applying pressure on the power steering pump check the belt deflection; it should be 0.24–0.35 in. (6–9mm) under 22 lbs. of pressure.
4. When the correct deflection is established, torque the power steering pump-to-bracket bolts to 25–33 ft. lbs. (35–45 Nm).

Bleeding System

1. Check and/or refill the power steering pump reservoir.
2. Raise and safely support the vehicle.
3. Start the engine and turn the steering wheel from side-to-side (lock-to-lock) several times, to bleed the air from the system.
4. Check and/or refill the power steering pump reservoir.

NOTE: If air bubbles are still present in the oil, repeat the bleeding procedure until the system is free of air bubbles.

Steering Column

Removal and Installation
OMNI, TURISMO, CHARGER AND HORIZON

1. Disconnect the negative battery cable and all column wiring connectors.
2. Remove the lower roll pin from the upper universal joint.

3. Remove the column-to-instrument panel screws.
4. Remove the steering column from vehicle.
5. To install the steering column, reverse the removal procedure.

EXCEPT OMNI, TURISMO, CHARGER AND HORIZON

1. Disconnect the negative battery cable.
2. If equipped with a column shift, disconnect the cable rod, remove the cable clip and the cable from the lower bracket.
3. Disconnect all the wiring connectors at the steering column.
4. Remove the steering wheel and components.
5. Remove the instrument panel steering column cover and lower dash reinforcement. Disconnect the bezel, exposing the steering column brackets.
6. Remove the indicator set screw and the shaft indicator pointer from the shaft housing, if equipped.
7. Remove the steering column bracket-to-instrument panel support nuts and lower the bracket support.

NOTE: Do not remove the roll pin to remove the steering column assembly.

8. Firmly pull the steering column rearward, disconnecting the lower stub shaft from the steering gear coupling. If equipped with speed control and manual transaxle, do not damage the clutch pedal speed control switch.
9. Reinstall the anti-rattle coupling spring back into the lower coupling tube. Be sure the anti-rattling spring snaps into the slot in the coupling.
10. Remove the column assembly out through the passenger compartment.
To Install:
11. Install a new grommet from the rod side of the shift lever whenever the rod is disconnected from the lever.
12. To install the steering column, reverse the removal procedure.

Front Wheel Bearings

Removal and Installation
EXCEPT 1989–90 LASER

1. Raise and safely support the vehicle. Remove the halfshaft from the steering knuckle assembly.
2. Attach the hub removal tool C–4811 or equivalent, and the triangular adapter, to the 3 rear threaded holes of the steering knuckle housing with the thrust button inside the hub bore.
3. Tighten the bolt in the center of the tool, to press the hub from the steering knuckle. Remove the removal tools.
4. Remove the bolts and bearing retainer from the outside of the steering knuckle.
5. Carefully pry the bearing seal from the machined recess of the steering knuckle and clean the recess.
6. Insert the tool C–4811 or equivalent, through the hub bearing and install bearing removal adapter to the outside of the steering knuckle. Tighten the tool to press the hub bearing from the steering knuckle. Discard the bearing and the seal.
To Install:
7. Use tool C–4811 or equivalent, and the bearing installation adapter to press in the hub bearing into the steering knuckle.
8. Install a new seal, the bearing retainer and the bolts to the steering knuckle. Torque the bearing retainer bolts to 20 ft. lbs.
9. Use the tool C–4811 or equivalent, and the hub installation adapter, to press the hub into the hub bearing.
10. Using the bearing installation tool C–4698 or equivalent, drive the new dust seal into the rear of the steering knuckle.
11. To complete the installation, reverse the removal procedures. Torque the tie rod-to-steering knuckle nut to 35 ft. lbs., the control arm-to-steering knuckle bolt to 70 ft. lbs., the hub nut bolt to 180 ft. lbs. and the brake caliper-to-steering knuckle bolts to 160 ft. lbs.

SECTION 2
CHRYSLER/DODGE/PLYMOUTH
FRONT WHEEL DRIVE—ALL MODELS

1989–90 LASER

1. Raise and safely support the vehicle. Remove the steering knuckle assembly and secure it in a vise.
2. Using a wheel hub pressing tool or equivalent, press the wheel hub front the steering knuckle; do not use a hammer, for the wheel bearings may become damaged.
3. Using a small prybar, pry the oil seal from the inner side of the steering knuckle assembly.
4. At the wheel hub, crush the oil seal in 2 places so a wheel puller tool can catch the wheel bearing inner race. Using a wheel puller tool, press the inner race from the wheel hub.
5. From the steering knuckle, remove the internal snapring and press the wheel bearing from knuckle.

To Install:

6. Using multi-mileage grease, pack the wheel bearing and lubricate the bearing surface of the steering knuckle.
7. Using the wheel bearing installation tool MB990085 or equivalent, and a shop press, press the wheel bearing into the steering knuckle until it seats. Install the internal snapring.
8. Using an oil seal installation tool, drive the new oil seal into the hub side of the steering knuckle until it is flush with the surface. Using multi-mileage grease, lubricate the seal lip and the seal surface which contacts the front hub.
9. Using the hub installation tool MB990998 or equivalent, press the hub into the steering knuckle; torque the tool to 144–188 ft. lbs. (200–260 Nm) and rotate the hub in order to seat the bearing.
10. Using an inch lb. torque wrench, check the turning torque of the hub/steering knuckle assembly; it should be 16 inch lbs. (1.8 Nm) or less.
11. Using a dial indicator, position it to the front of the hub, check the hub endplay; it should be less than 0.008 in. (0.2mm).
12. Using an oil seal installation tool or equivalent, drive a new oil seal into the inner side of the steering knuckle and lubricate the lip with multi-mileage grease.
13. To complete the installation, reverse the removal procedures.

Front Wheel Alignment

Pre-Alignment Check

Before attempting to align the vehicle, the following checks should be performed and any necessary corrections made.

1. Check the air pressure in the tires. Set the pressure to the recommended pressure.
2. All tires should be of the same size, in good condition and with the same amount of tread.
3. Inspect the lower ball joint and steering linkage for play.
4. Check for broken or sagging, front and rear springs.

Adjustment

CAMBER

Camber is adjusted by loosening the cam and knuckle bolts and rotating the cam bolt until the proper specification is obtained.

CASTER

Caster is not adjustable. If the caster is out of specifications, check for worn, loose or broken suspension and/or steering components.

TOE

Toe is adjusted by changing the tie rod length. Loosen the right and left tie rod end lock nuts first and then turn left and right tie rods by the same amount to align toe to specification.

NOTE: Before turning the tie rods, apply grease between tie rods and rack boots so the boots won't be twisted. After adjustment, tighten lock nuts to specified torque and make sure the rack boots are not twisted.

BRAKES

Refer to unit repair section for brake service information and drum/rotor specifications.

Master Cylinder

Removal and Installation
POWER BRAKES

Except Laser

1. Disconnect the negative battery cable.
2. Disconnect the primary and secondary brake tubes from the master cylinder. Plug the tubes and the cylinder openings.
3. Remove the master cylinder-to-power brake booster nuts.
4. Slide the master cylinder straight out, away from the booster.
5. To install, reverse the removal procedures. Align the pushrod with the master cylinder piston and torque the nuts to 16 ft. lbs. Connect the brake tubes and bleed the brakes.

Laser

1. Disconnect the negative battery cable.
2. Remove the reservoir tubes from the master cylinder and drain the reservoir.
3. Disconnect the primary and secondary brake tubes from the master cylinder. Plug the tubes and the cylinder openings.
4. Remove the master cylinder-to-power brake booster nuts.
5. Slide the master cylinder straight out, away from the booster.
6. To install, reverse the removal procedures. Align the pushrod with the master cylinder piston and torque the nuts to 6–9 ft. lbs. (8–12 Nm). Connect the brake tubes and bleed the brakes.

EXCEPT POWER BRAKES

1. Disconnect the negative battery cable.
2. Disconnect the primary and secondary brake lines and install plugs in the master cylinder openings.
3. Disconnect the stoplight switch mounting bracket from under the instrument panel.
4. Pull the brake pedal backward to disengage the pushrod from the master cylinder piston.

NOTE: This will destroy the grommet.

5. Remove the master cylinder-to-firewall nuts.
6. Slide the master cylinder out and away from the firewall. Be sure to remove all pieces of the broken grommet.

To Install:

7. Install the boot on the pushrod.
8. Install a new grommet on the pushrod.
9. Apply a soap and water solution to the grommet and slide it firmly into position in the primary piston socket. Move the pushrod from side-to-side to make sure it's seated.
10. From the engine side, press the pushrod through the master cylinder mounting plate and align the mounting studs with the holes in the cylinder.
11. Install the nuts and torque them to 16 ft. lbs.
12. From under the instrument panel, place the pushrod on the pin on the pedal and install a new retaining clip.

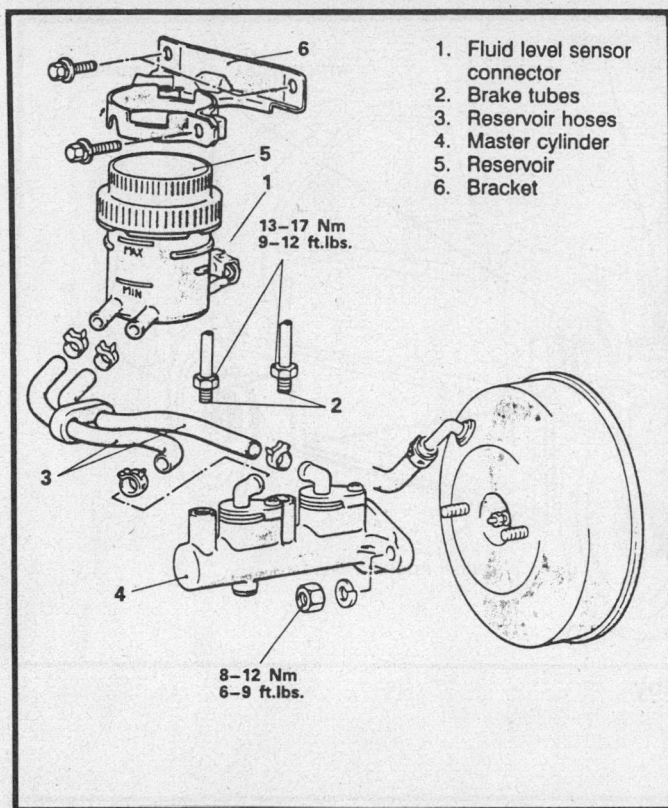

1. Fluid level sensor connector
2. Brake tubes
3. Reservoir hoses
4. Master cylinder
5. Reservoir
6. Bracket

13–17 Nm
9–12 ft.lbs.

8–12 Nm
6–9 ft.lbs.

Exploded view of the master cylinder and reservoir— Laser

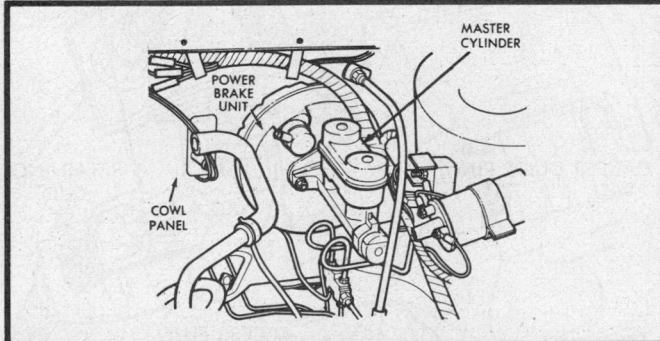

Master cylinder and power brake unit location

NOTE: Be sure to lubricate the pin.

13. Install the brake lines on the master cylinder.
14. Bleed the brake system.

Bleeding System

1. Carefully clean all dirt from around the master cylinder filler cap.
2. If a bleeder tank is used, follow the manufacturer's instructions.
3. Remove the filler cap and refill the master cylinder to the lower edge of the filler neck.
4. Clean off the bleeder connections at all of the wheel cylinders or disc brake calipers. Attach the bleeder hose and fixture to the right rear wheel cylinder bleeder screw and place the end of the tube in a glass jar, submerged in brake fluid.
5. Open the bleeder valve ½–¾ turn. Have an assistant de-

press the brake pedal and allow it to return slowly. Continue this pumping action to force any air out of the system.
6. When bubbles cease to appear at the end of the bleeder hose, close the bleeder valve and remove the hose. Check the level of the brake fluid in the master cylinder and add fluid, if necessary.
7. After the bleeding operation at each caliper or wheel cylinder has been completed, refill the master cylinder reservoir and replace the filler plug.

NOTE: Never reuse brake fluid which has been removed from the lines through the bleeding process because it contains air bubbles and dirt.

Power Brake Booster

Removal and Installation

1. Disconnect the negative battery cable.
2. Remove the master cylinder, it can be pulled aside, far enough, to allow booster removal without disconnecting the brake lines.
3. Disconnect the vacuum hose from the booster.
4. Under the instrument panel, pry the retaining clip center tang over the end of the brake pedal pin and pull the retainer clip from the pin. Discard the clip.
5. Remove the booster-to-cowl nuts and the booster from the vehicle.

To Install:

6. Position the booster on the firewall and torque the nuts to 20 ft. lbs.
7. Carefully position the master cylinder on the booster, install the nuts and torque them to 18 ft. lbs.
8. Connect the vacuum hose to the booster.
9. Lubricate the bearing surface of the pedal pin with chassis lube. Connect the pushrod to the pedal pin and install a new clip.
10. Check the stoplight operation. With vacuum applied to the power brake unit and pressure applied to the pedal, the master cylinder should vent (force a jet of fluid through the front chamber vent port).

NOTE: Do not attempt to disassemble the power brake unit. The booster is serviced as a complete assembly only.

Bleeding System

BOOSTER BLEEDING

Booster bleeding must be performed whenever the pressure hose, the return hose or the pump/motor is replaced or when the reservoir is emptied or removed.

1. Depressurize the hydraulic accumulator by performing the following procedures:
   a. Turn the ignition switch **OFF**, disconnect the electrical connector from the sensor block on the hydraulic assembly, pump the brake pedal at least 25 times (using at least 50 lbs. force); a noticable change in the brake pedal will occur when the accumulator is discharged.
   b. If a definite increase in pedal pressure is felt, stroke the pedal a few more times; this should remove all the pressure from the system.

—————————— CAUTION ——————————

Failure to depressurize the hydraulic accumulator, prior to performing this operation, may result in personal injury and/or damage to the painted surface.

——————————————————————————————

2. Make sure the pump/motor and hydraulic electrical connections are connected; the brake lines and hose connections must be tight.

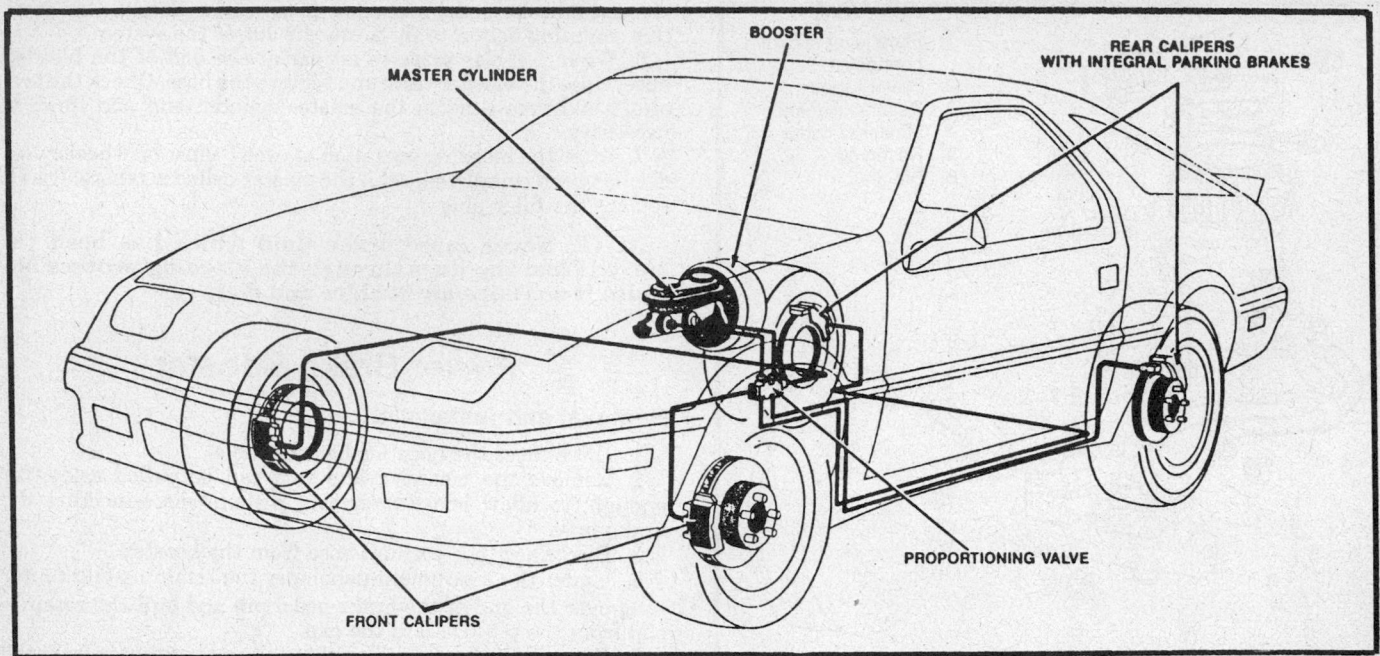

Four-wheel disc brake system of Dodge Daytona Shelby

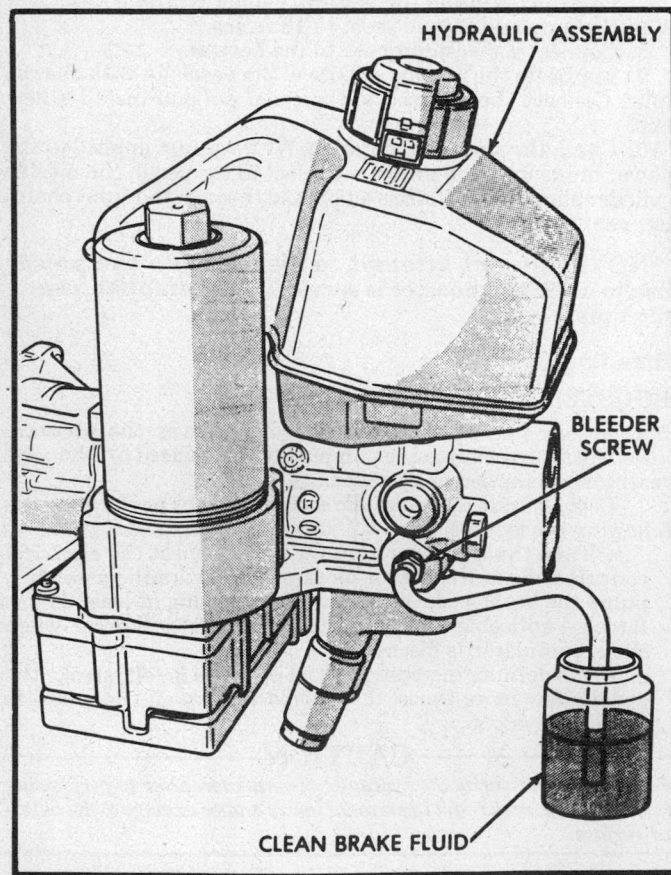

Bleeding the hydraulic accumulator—anti-lock brake control system

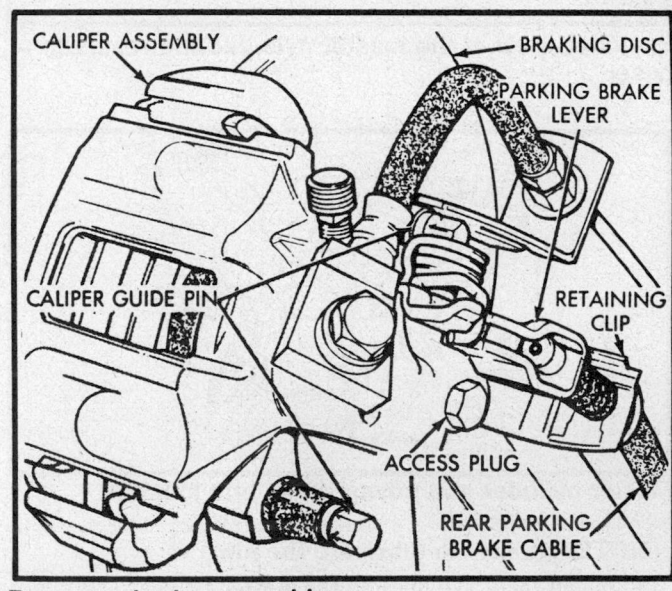

Rear disc brake assembly

3. Fill the reservoir to the full level.

4. Connect a transparent hose to the bleeder screw on the right side of the hydraulic assembly and place the other end in a clear container to receive the brake fluid.

5. Open the bleeder screw ½–¾ turn.

6. Turn the ignition switch **ON** (the pump/motor should run) and discharge the fluid into the container; bleed it until the fluid is bubble free.

7. Turn the ignition switch **OFF**, tighten the bleeder screw to 7.5 ft. lbs. (10 Nm) and remove the hose.

8. Refill the reservoir to the **FULL** mark.

9. Turn the ignition switch **ON** and allow the pump to charge the accumulator; it should take approximately 30 seconds.

MANUAL BLEEDING

This procedure is performed when the brake lines or hoses are disconnected from the system.

1. Depressurize the hydraulic accumulator by performing the following procedures:

a. Turn the ignition switch **OFF**, disconnect the electrical connector from the sensor block on the hydraulic assembly, pump the brake pedal at least 25 times (using at least 50 lbs. force); a noticeable change in the brake pedal will occur when the accumulator is discharged.

b. If a definite increase in pedal pressure is felt, stroke the pedal a few more times; this should remove all the pressure from the system.

——————— CAUTION ———————

Failure to depressurize the hydraulic accumulator, prior to performing this operation, may result in personal injury and/or damage to the painted surface.

2. Connect a transparent hose to the caliper bleeder screw and place the other end into a clear container of brake fluid.

3. Slowly, pump the brake pedal several times (using full strokes) and allow 5 seconds between pedal strokes. After 2–3 strokes, continue to hold pressure on the pedal (at the bottom of it's travel).

4. With pressure on the pedal, have an assistant open the bleeder screw ½–¾ turn; allow the screw to be open until fluid no longer runs it. Tighten the screw and allow the pedal to return.

5. Repeat this procedures 3–4 times, until the fluid is clear (no bubbles).

6. Repeat the above procedure, in sequence, on each of the following calipers: left rear, right rear, left front and right front.

Parking Brake

Adjustment

NOTE: The service brakes must be properly adjusted before adjusting the parking brakes.

1. Raise and safely support the vehicle. Fully release the parking brake.

2. Clean the threads of the adjusting nut with a wire brush and lubricate with grease.

3. Loosen the adjusting nut until there is slack in the cable.

4. Check service brakes for proper adjustment. Adjust if necessary.

5. Tighten the adjusting nut until a slight drag in the brakes are felt while rotating the wheels.

6. Loosen the cable adjusting nut until both rear wheels turn freely. Back-off the nut 2 full turns.

7. Apply and release the parking brake several times to make sure the wheels rotate freely.

CLUTCH AND TRANSAXLE

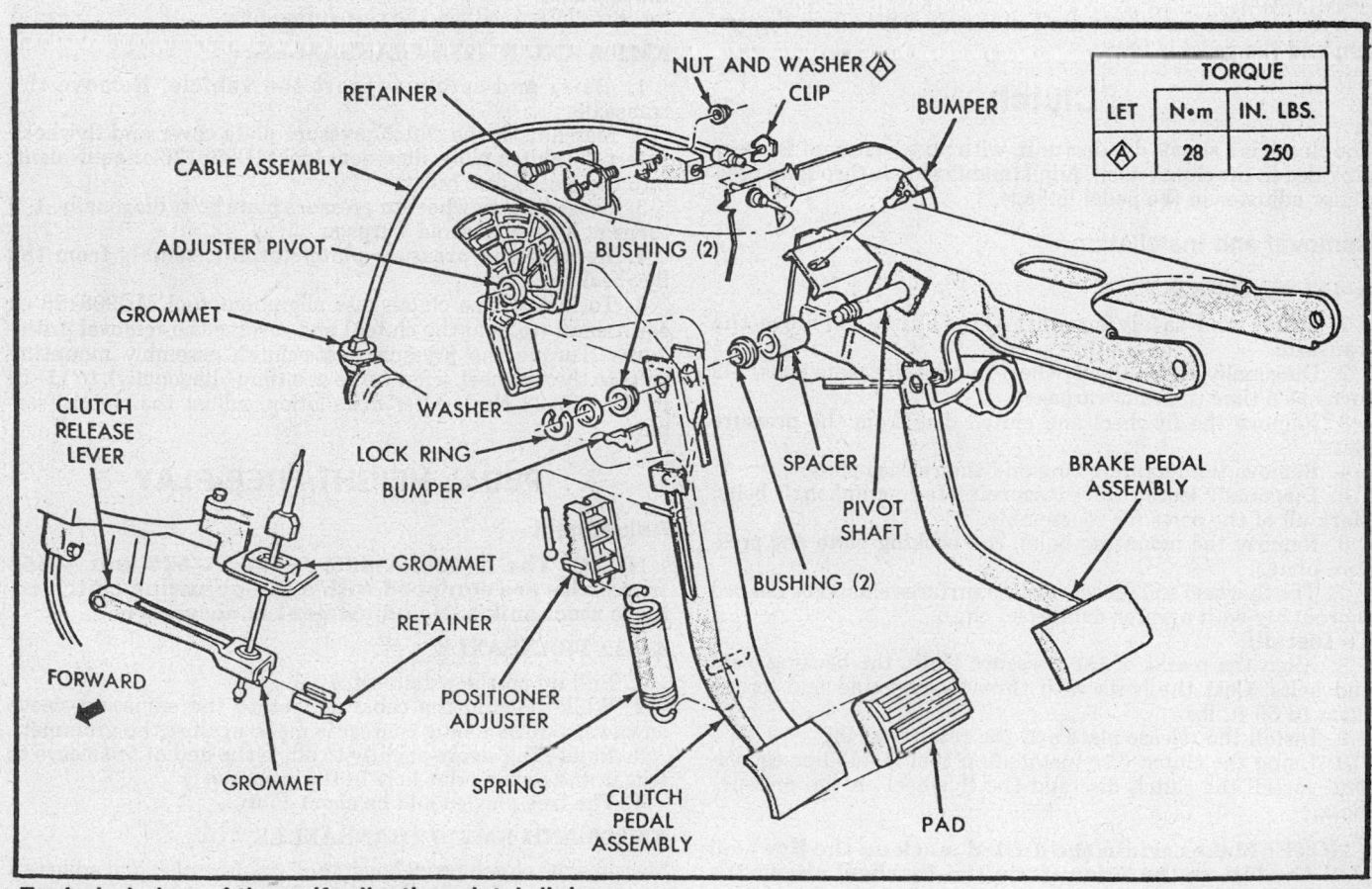

TORQUE		
LET	N•m	IN. LBS.
◇	28	250

Exploded view of the self adjusting clutch linkage

Refer to "Chilton's Transmission Service Manual" for additional coverage.

Clutch Linkage
CABLE

Adjustment

1. Remove clip from shock tower mount and remove cable from bracket.
2. Remove retainer from clutch release lever at transaxle.
3. Pry out ball end of cable from positioner adjuster and remove cable.
4. Reverse the above procedure for installation.
5. After installation, push the clutch pedal 2–3 times to adjust the cable.

HYDRAULIC

Bleeding

1. Check and/or add hydraulic fluid to the master cylinder reservoir.

NOTE: An assistant is needed to perform the following procedure.

2. At the slave cylinder, loosen the bleeder screw, slowly depress the clutch pedal (until it bottoms), tighten the bleeder screw and release the clutch pedal. Be sure to check and/or add more fluid to the master cylinder reservoir.
3. Loosen the bleeder screw, slowly depress the clutch pedal (until it bottoms), tighten the bleeder screw and release the clutch pedal.
4. Repeat this procedure until all the air is bled from the system and the pedal is firm.

Clutch

The clutch is a simple dry disc unit, with no adjustment for wear provided in the clutch itself. Adjustment is made through a positioner adjuster in the pedal linkage.

Removal and Installation

A–412 TRANSAXLE

1. Raise and safely support the vehicle. Remove the transaxle.
2. Diagonally loosen the flywheel-to-pressure plate bolts, 1–2 turns at a time to avoid warpage.
3. Remove the flywheel and clutch disc from the pressure plate.
4. Remove the retaining ring and the release plate.
5. Diagonally loosen the pressure plate-to-crankshaft bolts. Mark all of the parts for reassembly.
6. Remove the mounting bolts, the backing plate and pressure plate.
7. The flywheel and pressure plate surfaces should be cleaned thoroughly with a water dampened cloth.
To Install:
8. Align the marks of the pressure plate, the backing plate and bolts. Coat the bolts with thread compound and torque them to 55 ft. lbs.
9. Install the release plate and the retaining ring.
10. Using the clutch disc installation tool L–4533 or equivalent, install the clutch disc and the flywheel on the pressure plate.

NOTE: Make certain the drilled mark on the flywheel is at the top, so the 2 dowels on the flywheel align with the proper holes of the pressure plate.

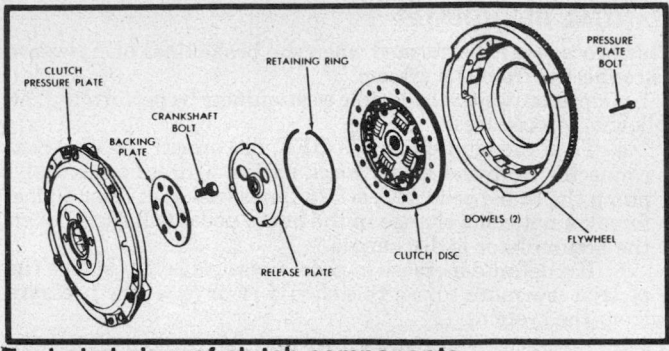

Exploded view of clutch components

11. To complete the installation, torque the flywheel bolts to 15 ft. lbs. and reverse the removal procedures.

A–460, A–465, A–520, A–525 AND A–555 TRANSAXLES

1. Raise and safely support the vehicle. Remove the transaxle.
2. Match mark the clutch/pressure plate cover and flywheel. Insert the clutch plate alignment tool C–4676 or equivalent, into the clutch disc hub.
3. Loosen the flywheel-to-pressure plate bolts diagonally, 1–2 turns at a time to avoid warpage.
4. Remove the pressure plate/clutch assembly from the flywheel.
5. To install, use clutch disc alignment tool C–4676 or equivalent, (to hold the clutch) and reverse the removal procedures. Torque the pressure plate/clutch assembly mounting bolts to the flywheel, a few turns at a time (diagonally), to 21 ft. lbs. After installation, adjust the clutch free-play.

KM206 AND KM215 TRANSAXLES

1. Raise and safely support the vehicle. Remove the transaxle.
2. Matchmark the clutch/pressure plate cover and flywheel. Insert the clutch plate alignment tool MD998126 or equivalent, into the clutch disc hub.
3. Loosen the flywheel-to-pressure plate bolts diagonally, 1–2 turns at a time to avoid warpage.
4. Remove the pressure plate/clutch assembly from the flywheel.
5. To install, use clutch disc alignment tool MD998126 or equivalent, (to hold the clutch) and reverse the removal procedures. Torque the pressure plate/clutch assembly mounting bolts to the flywheel, a few turns at a time (diagonally), to 11–16 ft. lbs. (15–22 Nm). After installation, adjust the clutch free-play.

PEDAL HEIGHT/FREE-PLAY

Adjustment

NOTE: The A–460, A–465, A–520, A–525 and A–555 transaxles are equipped with a self-adjusting clutch release mechanism. No adjustment is necessary.

A–412 TRANSAXLE

1. Pull up on the clutch cable.
2. While holding the cable up, rotate the adjusting sleeve downward until a snug contact is made against the grommet.
3. Rotate the sleeve slightly to allow the end of the sleeve to seat in the rectangular hole in the grommet.
4. The free-play should be about ¼ in.

KM206 AND KM215 TRANSAXLES

Measure the clutch pedal height and the free-play and adjust (if necessary); the height should be 6.93–7.13 in. (176–181mm)

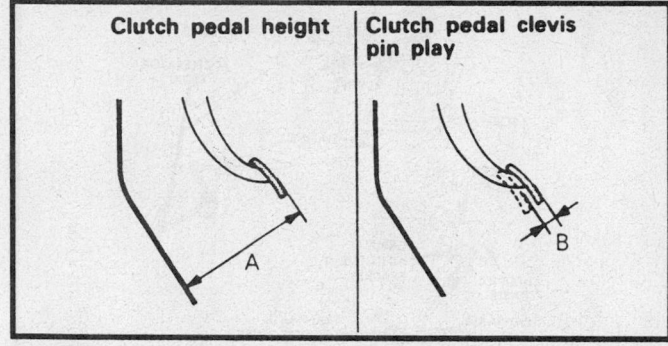

Clutch pedal height	Clutch pedal clevis pin play

View of the clutch pedal free-play and pedal height — Laser

and the free-play should be 0.04–0.12 in. (1–3mm).

1. If not equipped with cruise control, loosen the locknut and adjust the bolt (top of the clutch pedal) to the desired pedal height and tighten the locknut.

2. If equipped with cruise control, disconnect the clutch switch connector, loosen the locknut, adjust the switch to the desired pedal height, tighten the locknut and reconnect the electrical connector.

3. To adjust the free-play, loosen the pushrod's locknut, adjust the pushrod to the desired free-play and tighten the locknut.

NOTE: When performing these adjustments, be careful not to move the pushrod toward the master cylinder.

4. Depress the clutch pedal and measure it's full stroke; if not 6 in. (151mm), loosen the locknut and readjust.

5. Depress the clutch pedal and measure the distance from the firewall to the center of the pedal; if not at least 2.2 in. (55mm), check for air in the hydraulic system or a defective master cylinder or clutch.

Manual Transaxle

Removal and Installation

NOTE: Whenever the differential cover is removed, a new gasket should be formed using RTV sealant.

A–412 TRANSAXLE

1. Disconnect the negative battery cable. Disconnect and label the starter wires and backup light switch wire.

2. Remove the starter mounting bolts and remove the starter.

3. Disconnect the shift linkage rods and clutch cable.

4. Remove the speedometer cable retaining bolt and remove the cable from the transaxle.

5. Using a vertical hoist or fabricated support fixture, support the engine from above. Loosen the left wheel hub nut. Raise and safely support the vehicle.

6. Disconnect the right halfshaft and support it. Remove the left halfshaft and support it.

7. Remove the left splash shield. Remove the large and small dust cover bolts at the bell housing.

8. Drain the transaxle. Place a transmission jack under the transaxle and chain the transaxle in place.

9. Unbolt the left engine mount and remove the transaxle-to-engine bolts.

10. Slide the transaxle to the left until the mainshaft clears and lower it from the vehicle.

11. To install, reverse the removal procedures. Adjust the clutch cable and the shift linkage with the transaxle installed. Refill the transaxle and road test.

A–460, A–465, A–520, A–525 AND A–555 TRANSAXLES

1. Disconnect the negative battery cable.

2. Install an engine lifting eye fixture on the No. 4 cylinder exhaust manifold bolt and support the engine.

3. Disconnect the shift and the throttle linkages.

4. Remove the hub castle locknut and cotter pin from both front wheels. Raise and safely support the vehicle. Remove both front wheels.

5. Remove the left front splash shield and left engine/transaxle mount.

6. Remove the upper bell housing bolts.

7. Remove the speedometer cable bolt and disconnect the cable from the transaxle.

8. Disconnect the sway bar. Remove the right and left lower ball joint bolts. Using a pry bar, separate the lower ball joints from the steering knuckles.

9. Disconnect the halfshafts from both hubs. Remove the halfshafts from the vehicle.

10. At the right splash shield, remove the access plug, so a wrench can be placed on the crankshaft bolt to rotate the engine.

11. Remove the engine mount bracket from the front crossmember and the front engine mount insulator through bolt.

12. Place a transmission jack under the transaxle and secure it with a chain.

13. Remove the starter and lower bell housing bolts.

14. Lower the transaxle and separate it from the engine.

15. To install, reverse the removal procedures. Refill the transaxle with SAE 5W–30 engine oil. Adjust the shift and throttle linkages.

KM206 AND KM215 TRANSAXLES

1. Disconnect the negative battery cable.

2. Disconnect the electrical connectors from the starter and remove the starter from the transaxle.

3. Raise and safely support the vehicle under the frame. Remove the front wheel and tire assemblies. Remove the undercover from the vehicle. Drain the fluid from the transaxle. Disconnect the speedometer cable from the transaxle.

4. Disconnect the exhaust pipe from the exhaust manifold.

5. Disconnect and remove the shift lever cables from the transaxle. Disconnect any electrical connectors from the transaxle. Remove the clutch slave cylinder and move it aside; do not disconnect the hydraulic line.

6. Remove the cotter pin and nut from the tie rod end-to-steering knuckle and the lower ball joint-to-steering knuckle connections. Using a steering linkage puller tool or equivalent, separate the tie rod end and lower ball joint from the steering knuckle.

7. Using a small pry bar, insert it between the halfshaft and transaxle, gently pry the halfshaft to disengage it from the transaxle by pulling the steering knuckle outward. Using a piece of wire, support the halfshaft.

NOTE: Do not pull on the halfshaft, for the inboard joint may become damaged. Be careful not to damage the oil seal.

8. Using a transmission jack, secure it to the transaxle. Remove the transaxle-to-engine bolts, move the transaxle from the engine and lower it from the vehicle.

To Install:

9. Reverse the removal procedures. Torque the:
Exhaust pipe-to-manifold nuts to 22–29 ft. lbs.
Transaxle-to-engine bolts to 32–39 ft. lbs.
Tie rod end-to-steering knuckle nut to 17–25 ft. lbs.
Lower ball joint-to-steering knuckle nut to 43–52 ft. lbs.
Starter-to-transaxle bolts to 20–25 ft. lbs.

10. Check and/or adjust the shift cables.

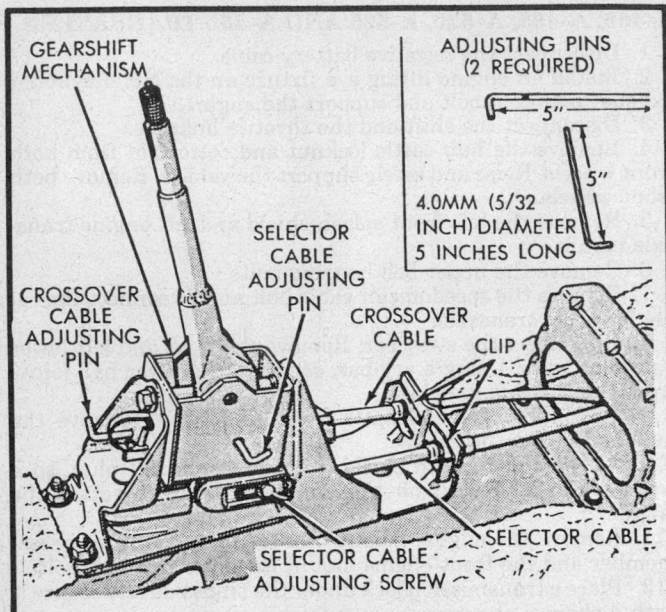

Fabricating transmission cable adjusting pins and adjusting the selector cable on console shifter

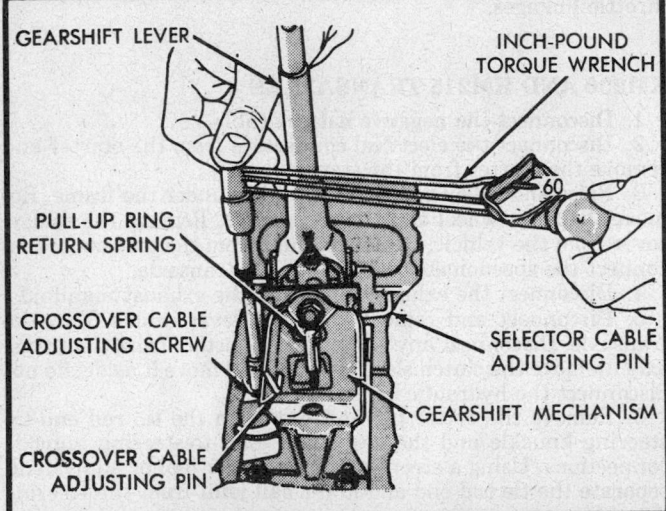

Console shifter crossover cable adjustment

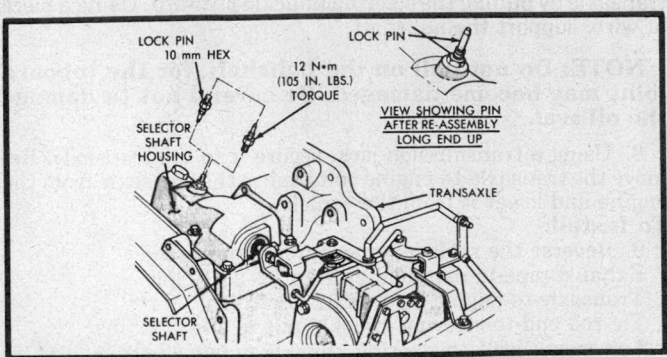

Adjustment of gearshift linkage on the A—460 manual transaxle

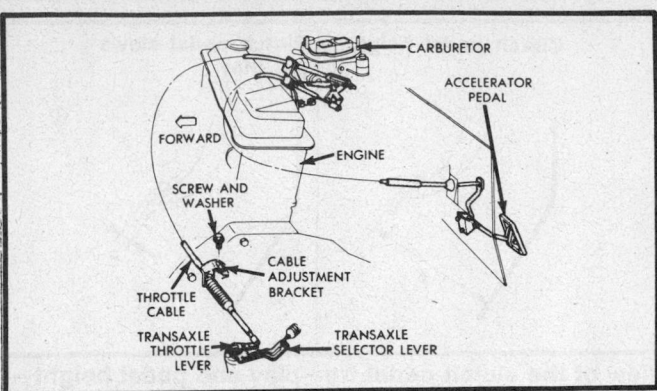

Throttle control cable components

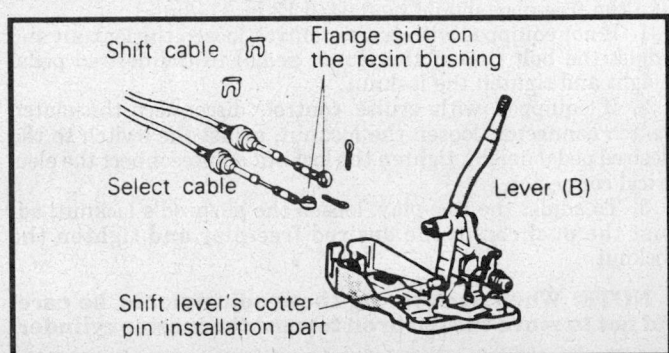

Exploded view of the shift selector and shift cables— Laser

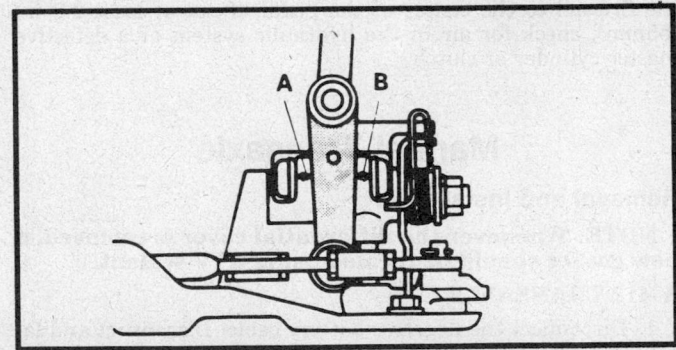

Adjusting the shift cable to make shift selector's dimension A and B equal—Laser

Adjustment

A-412 TRANSAXLE

1. Place the transaxle in **N** at the 3–4 position.
2. Loosen the shift tube clamp.
3. Place a ¾ in. spacer between the shift tube flange and the yoke at the shift base.
4. Tighten the shift tube clamp and remove the spacer.

NOTE: While tightening the shift tube clamp nut, no force should be exerted upward. No adjustments are possible on other transaxles.

A-460, A-465, A-520, A-525 AND A-555 TRANSAXLES

Rod Operated Type

1. Working over the left front fender, remove the lock pin from the transaxle selector shaft housing.
2. Reverse the lock pin (long end down) and insert the lock

pin into same threaded hole while pushing the selector shaft into the selector housing.

3. A hole in the selector shaft will align with the lock pin, allowing the lock pin to be screwed into the housing. This operation locks the selector shaft in the 1–2 and NEUTRAL position.

4. Raise and safely support the vehicle.

5. Loosen the clamp bolt that secures the gearshift tube to the gearshift connector.

6. Check that the gearshift connector slides and turns freely in the gearshift tube.

7. Position the shifter mechanism connector assembly so the isolator is contacting the upstanding flange and that the rib on the isolater is aligned in both directions with the hole in the blockout bracket. Hold the connector isolator in this position while torquing the clamp bolt on the gearshift tube to 170 inch lbs. (19 Nm). No significant force should be exerted on the linkage during this operation.

8. Lower the vehicle.

9. Remove the lock pin from the selector shaft housing and reinstall the lock pin (long end up) in the selector shaft housing. Torque the lock pin to 105 inch lbs. (12 Nm).

10. Check the 1st/reverse shifting and the blockout into **R**.

Cable Operated Type

1. Working over the left front fender, remove the lock pin from the transaxle selector shaft housing.

2. Reverse the lock pin (long end down) and insert lock pin into same threaded hole while pushing the selector shaft into the selector housing. A hole in the selector shaft will align with the lock pin, allowing the lock pin to be screwed into the housing. This operation locks the selector shaft in the 1–2 and NEUTRAL position.

3. Remove the gearshift knob, the retaining nut and the pull–up ring from the gearshift lever.

4. If necessary, remove the shift lever boot and console to expose the gearshift linkage.

5. Fabricate 2 cable adjusting pins: 3/16 in. dia. × 5 in. long with a 1/2 in. 90 degrees bend at one end.

6. Place a pin in the hole provided at the right side and the other in the hole provided at the rear side of the shifting mechanism (make sure the alignment holes match). Torque the selector (right side) and the crossover (left side) adjusting bolts, to 4–5 ft. lbs.

7. Remove the lock pin from the selector shaft housing and reinstall the lock pin (with the long end up) in the selector shaft housing. Torque the lock pin to 105 inch lbs. (12 Nm).

8. Check the first/reverse shifting and blockout into **R**.

9. Reinstall the console, boot, pull–up ring, retaining nut and knob.

KM206 AND KM215 TRANSAXLES

1. Remove the console assembly from the vehicle.

2. At the shift selector assembly, remove the shift cable-to-shift selector cotter pins and disconnect the shift cables from the shift selector assembly.

3. Move the transaxle shift selector and shift selector into the **N** positions.

4. If necessary, turn the shift cable adjuster to adjust the cable(s) length to align with lever **B** in the **N** position. Connect the shift cable (flange side of the resin bushing should face cotter pin side of the shift lever) with lever **B** and install a new cotter pin.

5. At the shift selector, make sure dimensions **A** and **B** are equal; if they are not, turn the cable adjuster to make the necessary adjustment.

6. Adjust the other cable in the same fashion.

7. Move the shift selector into each position to make sure it is shifting smoothly.

Automatic Transaxle

The automatic transaxle combines a torque converter, fully automatic transaxle, final drive gearing and differential, into a compact front wheel drive system. Officially, the various transaxles are designated as the Torqueflite Automatic Transaxles.

In 1989, an A–604, 4 speed, electronic transaxle was introduced; it is the first to use fully adaptive controls. The controls perform their functions based on real time feedback sensor information, similar to the system used by the antilock brake system. Although, the transaxle is conventional in design, it's functions are controlled by the ECM.

Since the A–604 is equipped with a learning function, each time the battery cable is disconnected, the ECM memory is lost. In operation, the transaxle must be shifted many times for the learned memory to be reinstalled in the ECM; during this period, the vehicle will experience rough operation.

Removal and Installation

The transaxle can be removed with the engine installed in the vehicle but, the transaxle and torque converter must be removed as an assembly. Otherwise the drive plate, pump bushing or oil seal could be damaged. The drive plate will not support a load. No weight should be allowed on the drive plate.

A–404, A–413, A–415L, A–470 AND A–604 TRANSAXLES

1. Disconnect the negative battery cable. If equipped, disconnect the electrical connectors from the transaxle.

2. Install an engine lifting eye fixture on the No. 4 cylinder exhaust manifold bolt and support the engine.

3. Disconnect the shift and the throttle linkages.

4. Remove the hub castle locknut and the cotter pin from both front wheels. Raise and safely support the vehicle. Remove both front wheels.

5. Remove the left front splash shield and the left engine/transaxle mount.

6. Remove the upper transaxle-to-engine bolts.

7. Remove the speedometer cable bolt and disconnect the cable from the transaxle.

8. Disconnect the sway bar. Remove the lower ball joint-to-steering knuckle bolts from both sides. Using a pry bar, separate the lower ball joints from the steering knuckles.

9. Disconnect the halfshafts from both hubs and remove them from the vehicle.

10. Matchmark the torque converter to the drive plate. Remove the torque converter mounting bolts.

11. Remove the oil cooler tubes and neutral safety switch wire.

12. At the right splash shield, remove the access plug, so a wrench can be placed on the crankshaft bolt to rotate the engine.

13. Remove the engine mount bracket from the front crossmember and the front engine mount insulator through bolt.

14. Place a transmission jack under the transaxle and secure it with a chain.

15. Remove the starter and the lower bell housing bolts.

16. Lower the transaxle and separate it from the engine.

17. To install, reverse the removal procedures. Refill the transaxle with Dexron® II automatic transmission fluid. Adjust the shift and throttle linkages, if necessary.

KM175 AND KM177 TRANSAXLES

1. Disconnect the negative battery cable and the electrical connectors from the starter. Remove the starter from the transaxle.

2. Raise and safely support the vehicle under the frame. Remove the front wheel/tire assemblies. Remove the undercover from the vehicle. Drain the fluid from the transaxle. Disconnect the speedometer cable from the transaxle.

3. Disconnect the exhaust pipe from the exhaust manifold.

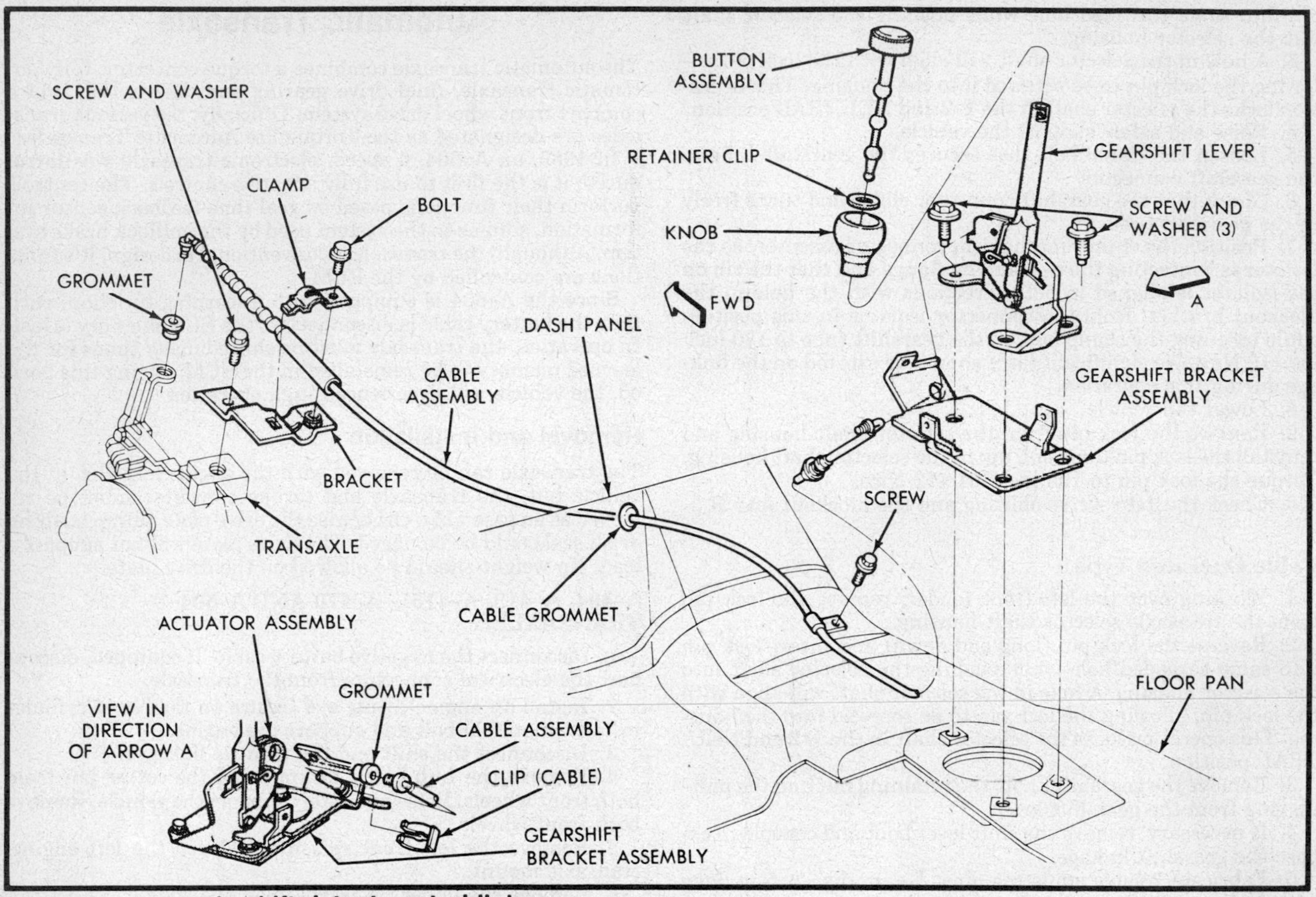

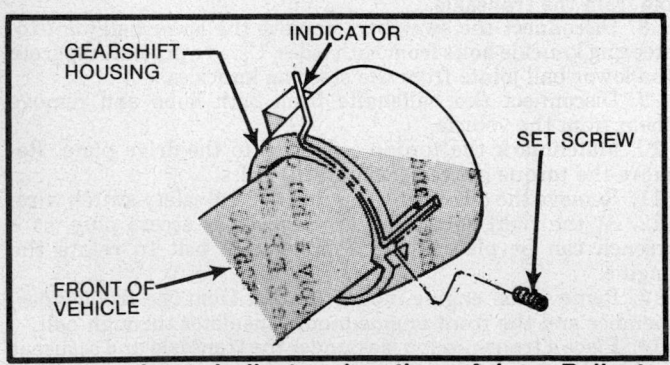

Automatic transaxle shift detent control linkage

Shift quadrant indicator location—Aries, Reliant, LeBaron, 400, 600 and E Class

4. Disconnect and remove the shift lever cables from the transaxle. Disconnect any electrical connectors from the transaxle.

5. Remove the bell housing cover, matchmark the torque converter to the flexplate, remove the torque converter-to-flexplate bolts and push the converter into the transaxle.

NOTE: When removing the torque converter bolts, rotate the crankshaft (using a wrench on the crankshaft pulley bolt) to expose the bolts.

6. Remove the cotter pin and nut from the tie rod end-to-steering knuckle and the lower ball joint-to-steering knuckle

connections. Using a steering linkage puller tool or equivalent, separate the tie rod end and lower ball joint from the steering knuckle.

7. Using a small pry bar, insert it between the halfshaft and transaxle, gently pry the halfshaft to disengage it from the transaxle by pulling the steering knuckle outward. Using a piece of wire, support the halfshaft.

NOTE: Do not pull on the halfshaft, for the inboard joint may become damaged. Be careful not to damage the oil seal.

8. Using a transmission jack, secure it to the transaxle. Remove the transaxle-to-engine bolts, move the transaxle from the engine and lower it from the vehicle.

To Install:

9. Reverse the removal procedures. Torque the:
Exhaust pipe-to-manifold nuts to 22–29 ft. lbs.
Transaxle-to-engine bolts to 22–25 ft. lbs.
Torque converter-to-flexplate bolts to 33–38 ft. lbs.
Tie rod end-to-steering knuckle nut to 17–25 ft. lbs.
Lower ball joint-to-steering knuckle nut to 43–52 ft. lbs.
Starter-to-transaxle bolts to 20–25 ft. lbs.

10. Refill the transaxle.

Adjustment

THROTTLE CABLE

1. Perform transaxle kickdown cable adjustment while engine is at normal operating temperature or make sure the carburetor is not on fast idle cam by disconnecting choke.

2. Loosen adjustment bracket lock screw. Bracket must slide freely in it's slot. The bracket should be positioned with both bracket alignment tabs touching the transaxle cast surface.

3. Slide bracket to the left (toward engine) to the limit of it's travel.

4. Release the bracket and move throttle lever full right to it's internal stop; this will pull the bracket back to it's correct position. Torque adjustment screw to 105 inch lbs. (12 Nm).

5. On carbureted models, when correctly adjusted, the transaxle throttle lever will move with the slightest carburetor throttle opening and will come to within 0.080 in. (2mm) of full travel at wide open throttle.

SHIFT LINKAGE

NOTE: When it is necessary to disconnect the linkage cable from the lever, which uses plastic grommets as retainers, the grommets should be replaced.

1. Set the parking brake.
2. Move the shift lever into **P**.
3. Loosen the clamp bolt on the gearshift cable bracket.
4. On the column shift models, make sure the preload adjustment spring engages the fork on the transaxle bracket.
5. Pull the shift lever all the way to the front detent position **P** and torque the lock screw to 100 inch lbs. (11 Nm).
6. Check the following conditions:
   a. The detent positions for **N** and **D** should be within limits of hand lever gate stops.
   b. Key start must occur ONLY when the shift lever is in **P** or **N** positions.

HALFSHAFTS

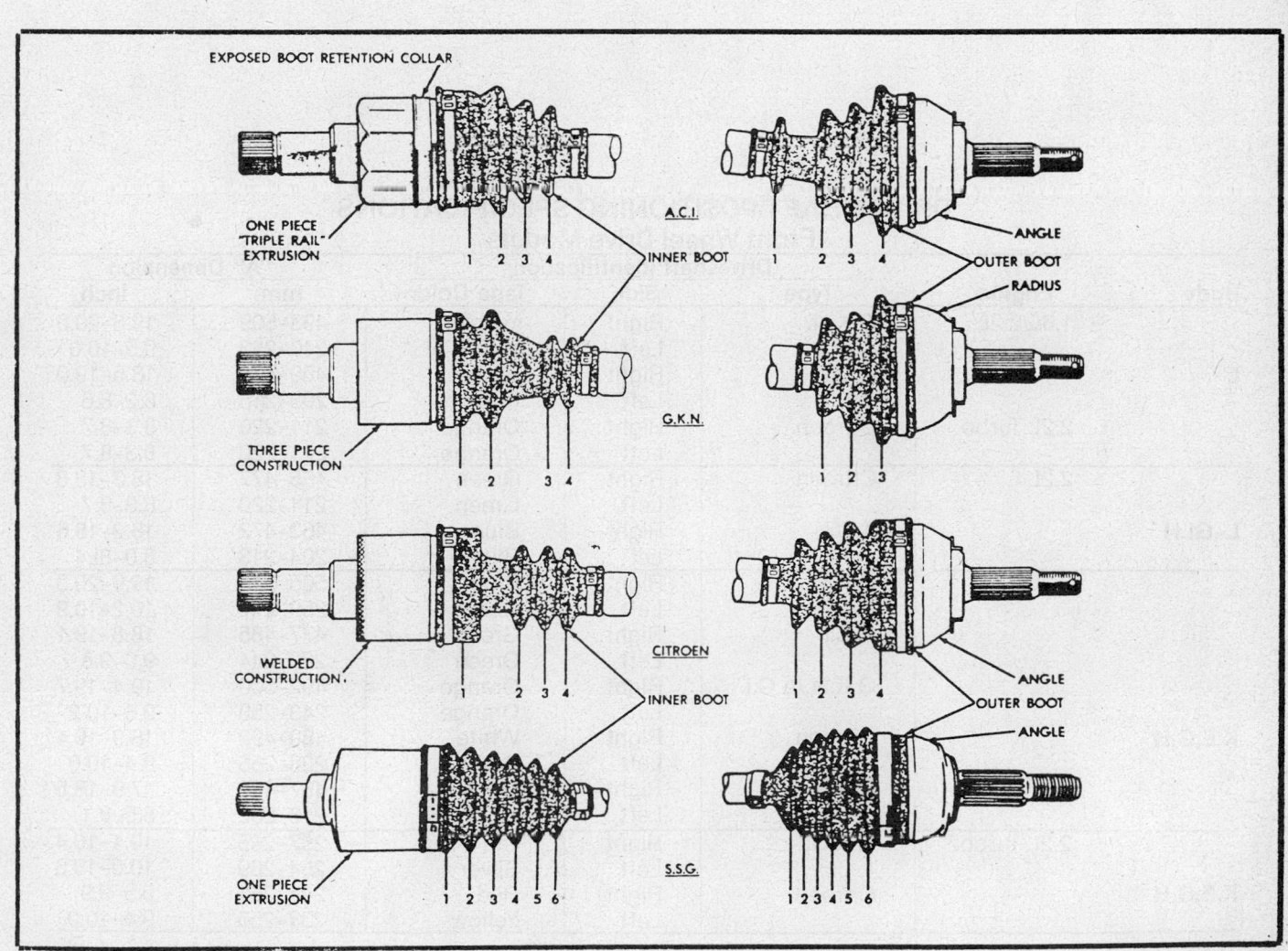

Halfshaft Identification

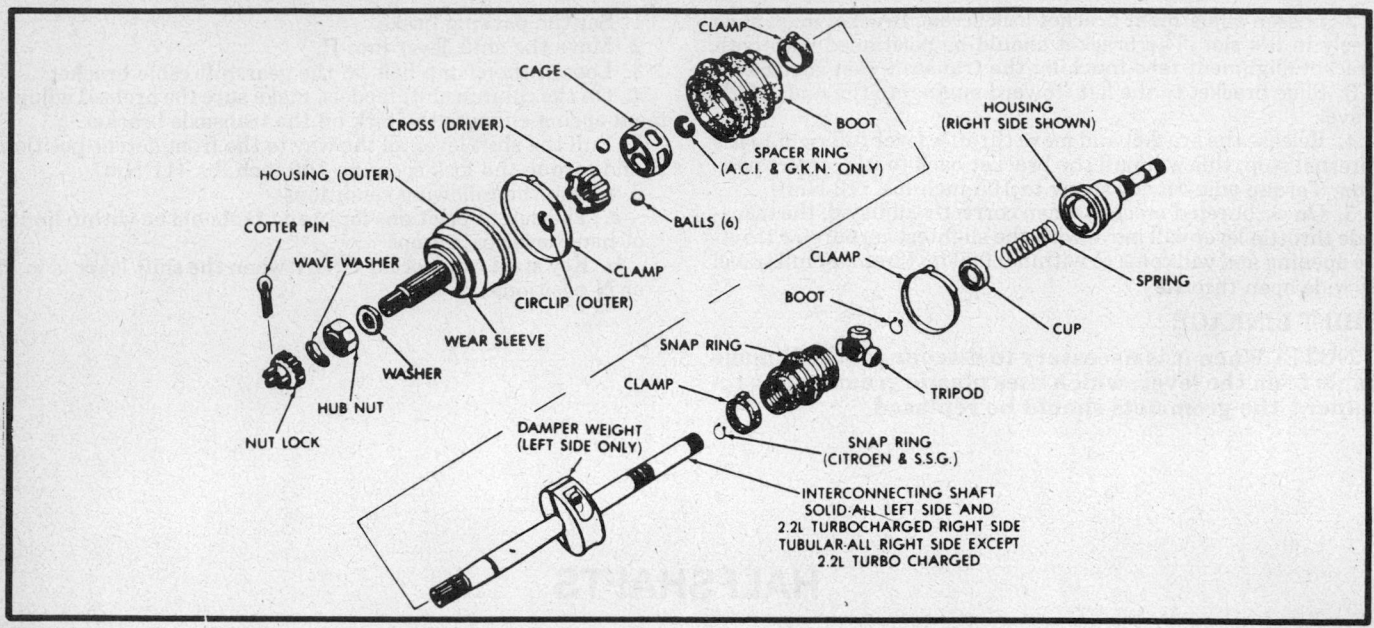

Exploded view of halfshaft components—typical

DRIVE SHAFT POSITIONING SPECIFICATIONS
Front Wheel Drive Models

| Body | Engine | Driveshaft Identification | | | "A" Dimension | |
		Type	Side	Tape Color	mm	Inch
L	1.6L/2.2L	G.K.N.	Right	Yellow	498–509	19.6–20.0
			Left	Yellow	240–253	9.5–10.0
		A.C.I.	Right	Red	469–478	18.5–19.0
			Left	Red	208–218	8.2–8.6
	2.2L Turbo	Citroen	Right	Orange	211–220	8.3–8.7
			Left	Orange	211–220	8.3–8.7
L-GLH	2.2L	Citroen	Right	Green	465–477	18.3–18.8
			Left	Green	211–220	8.3–8.7
		A.C.I.	Right	Blue	463–472	18.2–18.6
			Left	Blue	204–213	8.0–8I.4
K,E,G,H	2.2L/2.5L	G.K.N.	Right	Blue	505–515	19.9–20.3
			Left	Blue	259–277	10.2–10.9
		A.C.I.	Right	Green	477–485	18.8–19.1
			Left	Green	229–244	9.0–9.6
		G.K.N./A.C.I.	Right	Orange	492–500	19.4–19.7
			Left	Orange	243–258	9.6–10.2
		Citroen	Right	White	480–492	18.9–19.4
			Left	White	238–255	9.4–10.0
		S.S.G.	Right	Gold	457–469	17.9–18.5
			Left	Gold	216–232	8.5–9.1
K,E,G,H	2.2L Turbo	G.K.N.	Right	Tan	257–265	10.1–10.4
			Left	Silver	254–269	10.0–10.6
		Citroen	Right	Red	241–251	9.5–9.9
			Left	Yellow	238–255	9.4–10.0

DRIVE SHAFT POSITIONING SPECIFICATIONS
Front Wheel Drive Models

Body	Engine	Driveshaft Identification			"A" Dimension	
		Type	Side	Tape Color	mm	Inch
P	2.2L	G.K.N.	Right	Blue	505–515	19.9–20.3
			Left	Blue	259–277	10.2–10.9
		A.C.I.	Right	Green	477–485	18.8–19.1
			Left	Green	229–244	9.0–9.6
		G.K.N./A.C.I.	Right	Orange	492–500	19.4–19.7
			Left	Orange	243–258	9.6–10.2
		Citroen	Right	White	480–492	18.9–19.4
			Left	White	238–255	9.4–10.0
		S.S.G.	Right	Gold	457–469	17.9–18.5
			Left	Gold	216–232	8.5–9.1
P	2.2L Turbo	G.K.N.	Right	Tan	257–265	10.1–10.4
			Left	Silver	254–269	10.1–10.6
		Citroen	Right	Red	241–251	9.5–9.9
			Left	Yellow	238–255	9.4–10.0
		S.S.G.	Right	Turquoise	219–228	8.6–9.0
			Left	Gold	216–232	8.5–9.1

Body Identification
L—Horizon, Turismo, Omni, Charger, Shelby Charger
G—Daytona, (and Turbo), Laser
H—Lancer, LeBaron GTS
K—Aries, Reliant, Caravelle (Canada), 600 LeBaron, Executive Sedan
E—Caravelle (U.S.), 600, New Yorker
P—Shadow, Sundance

Front Drive Axle

DRIVESHAFT IDENTIFICATION

Driveshafts are identified as "ACI", "GKN", "SSG" or "CITROEN" assemblies. Vehicles can be equipped with any of these 4 assemblies. However, the assemblies should not be interchanged.

Removal and Installation

EXCEPT LASER

NOTE: Drain some of the fluid from the transaxle to prevent oil spillage when the halfshafts are removed from the transaxle.

1. With the vehicle on the ground, remove the cotter pin, castle hub nut lock, spring washer, hub nut and washer.
2. Raise and safely support the vehicle.
3. Before removing the right side halfshaft, disconnect the speedometer cable and remove the cable assembly from the transaxle.
4. Remove the ball joint stud-to-steering knuckle clamp bolt.
5. Using a pry bar, separate the ball joint stud from the steering knuckle, by prying against the knuckle leg and control arm.
6. Separate the outer CV-joint splined shaft from the hub by holding the CV housing and moving the hub away. Do not pry on the slinger or the outer CV-joint.
7. When removing the halfshaft from the transaxle, support the shaft at the CV-joints and pull on the inner shaft. Do not pull on the halfshaft. If equipped with the flange type halfshaft, remove the Allen head screws from the transaxle drive flange and separate the halfshaft from the transaxle.

To Install:
8. Reverse the removal procedures. Torque the:
Halfshaft flange bolts to 37 ft. lbs. (50 Nm).
Steering knuckle/ball joint bolt to 70 ft. lbs. (95 Nm).
Hub nut to 180 ft. lbs. (245 Nm).

NOTE: When torquing the hub nut, have an assistant apply the foot brake for added holding power.

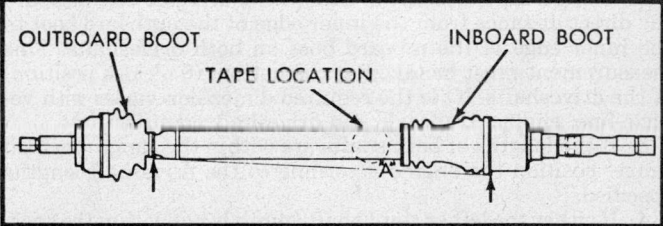

Halfshaft positioning measurement location

LASER

1. From both front wheels, remove the grease cup, the cotter pin, the hub nut and the washer.
2. Raise and safely support the vehicle under the frame. Remove the front wheel and tire assemblies. Remove the undercover from the vehicle.
3. Remove the cotter pin and nut from the tie rod end-to-steering knuckle and the lower ball joint-to-steering knuckle connections. Using a steering linkage puller tool or equivalent, separate the tie rod end and lower ball joint from the steering knuckle.
4. Using a pressing tool, attach it to the wheel hub and press the halfshaft from the hub; be sure to support the halfshaft after removal.
5. Using a small pry bar, insert it between the halfshaft and transaxle, gently pry the halfshaft to disengage it from the transaxle by pulling the steering knuckle outward.

NOTE: Do not pull on the halfshaft, for the inboard joint may become damaged. Be careful not to damage the oil seal.

To Install:
6. To install the halfshaft, insert it into the transaxle and push it inward until the snapring secures it.
7. To complete the installation, reverse the removal procedures. Torque the:
Tie rod end-to-steering knuckle nut to 17–25 ft. lbs. (24–34 Nm).

Lower ball joint-to-steering knuckle nut to 43–52 ft. lbs. (62–72 Nm).

8. Lower the vehicle to the ground, the weight of the vehicle must be resting on the wheels, torque the hub nut to 144–188 ft. lbs. (200–260 Nm) and install a new cotter pin.

NOTE: When torquing the hub nut, have an assistant apply the foot brake for added holding power.

HALFSHAFT

Positioning Specifications

Front wheel drive vehicles have the engine mounted with slotted holes allowing for side-to-side positioning of the engine. If the vertical bolts on the right or left upper engine mount have been loosened (e.g. engine removal and installation) for any reason or if the vehicle has experienced front structural damage, driveshaft lengths must be checked and corrected (if necessary). A shorter than required driveshaft length can result in objectionable noise. A longer than required driveshaft length may result in potential damage.

Use of the following procedure will insure satisfactory driveshaft engagement under all normal vehicle operating conditions.

1. The vehicle must be completely assembled. Front wheels must be properly aligned and in the straight ahead position. The vehicle must be in a position so the full weight of the body is distributed on the tires; a platform hoist, or front end alignment rack, is recommended.

2. Using a tape measure or other measuring device, measure the direct distance from the inner edge of the outboard boot to the inner edge of the inboard boot on both driveshafts. This measurement must be taken at the bottom (6 o'clock position) of the driveshafts. Note the required dimension varies with vehicle-line, engine, transaxle and driveshaft manufacturer.

3. If the lengths of both shafts are within the range specified range, position the engine according to the driveshaft lengths specified.

4. If either the left or right shaft length is not within the specified range, position the engine according to the driveshaft lengths specified.

5. If proper driveshaft lengths cannot be achieved within the travel limits available in the slotted engine mounts, check for any condition that could effect the side-to-side position of the measurement locations (e.g. engine support brackets, siderail alignments, etc).

6. After insuring proper driveshaft lengths, the transmission shift linkage must be readjusted to insure proper operation.

Boot

Handling and Cleaning

It is vitally important during any service procedures requiring boot handling that care be taken not to puncture or tear by overtightening clamps or misuse of tool(s) or pinching the boot. Pinching can occur by rotating the CV-joints (especially the tripod) beyond normal working angles.

The rubber material in driveshaft boots is not compatible with oil, gasoline or cleaning solvents; care must be taken that boots never come in contact with any of these.

NOTE: The only acceptable cleaning agent for driveshaft boots is soap and water. After washing, the boot must be thoroughly rinsed and dried before reusing.

Inspection

Noticeable amounts of grease on areas adjacent and on the exterior of the CV-joint boot is the first indication that a boot is punctured, torn or that a clamp has loosened. When a CV-joint is removed for service, the boot should be properly cleaned and inspected for cracks, tears and scuffed areas on interior surfaces. If any of these conditions exist, boot replacement is recommended.

Installation

Different boot clamping methods are used on the various driveshaft assemblies. ACI and GKN units generally use metal "ladder" type clamps. A small rubber clamp may also be used. Citroen units use a 2 piece clamp consisting of a strap and buckle. This clamp is used at all boot attachment points and can also be used for ACI and AKN applications.

SSG CV-joints use 2 types of boots, 1 made of plastic and the other of rubber. The plastic boot requires a heavy duty clamp and installer tool C-4975 or equivalent. The soft boot requires a clamp with a rounded edge to prevent the clamp from cutting the boot.

ACI and GKN boot installations require the use of a clamp installer tool C-4124 or equivalent, to compress the clamp bridge. Proceed with boot installation as follows:

1. If equipped, slide small rubber clamp onto the shaft.
2. Slide the small end of the boot over the shaft, position as follows:
   a. Right inner CV-joint—align the small end of the boot lip face with the mark on the shaft.
   b. Left inner and outer CV-Joint Boots—position the small end of the boot in the groove provided.
3. Fasten the small boot end by placing the rubber clamp over the boot groove or fit the metal clamp in the boot groove. Make sure the boot is properly located on the shaft. Locate the clamp tangs in the slots making the clamp as tight as possible by hand.
4. Clamp bridge with tool C-4124 or equivalent, and squeeze to complete tightening.

NOTE: During this procedure, care must be taken not to cut through the clamp bridge or damage the boot.

5. After attaching the boot to the shaft, install the inner or outer CV-joint.
6. Locate the large end of the boot in the housing groove and over the retaining shoulder, making sure the boot is not twisted. Install the metal spring clamp or fit the metal ladder clamp in the boot groove and locate the clamp tangs in the slots. Make the ladder clamp as tight as possible by hand.
7. Clamp bridge with tool C-4124 or equivalent, and squeeze to complete tightening.

NOTE: During this procedure, care must be taken not to cut through clamp bridge or damage boot. Seal/Wear Sleeve Lubrication—During any service procedures where knuckle and driveshaft are separated, clean seal and wear sleeve and relubricate both components prior to reinstalling driveshaft. Lubricate wear sleeve and seal with MOPAR multi-purpose lubricant part 2932524 or equivalent.

8. Apply on the full circumference of the wear sleeve, a bead of lubricant that is ¼ in. (6mm) wide, to seal contact area. Fill lip to housing cavity on seal, complete circumference and lubricate the seal lip.

CITROEN BOOT

Citroen boot installation requires use of clamp installer tool C-4653 or equivalent, to tighten and cut the strap type clamp. Proceed with boot installation as follows:

1. Slide the small end of the boot over the shaft. If installing an outer CV-joint boot, position the vent sleeve under the boot clamp groove. Position as follows:
   a. Right inner CV-Joint boot—align the boot lip face with the inboard edge of the part number label. If the label is no longer attached, align the edge of the boot lip with the mark

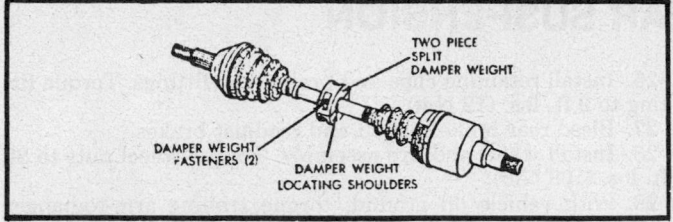

Installation of damper weight

remaining on the shaft where the previous boot was attached.

b. Left inner and outer CV-joint boots—position the boot between the locating shoulders and align the edge of the boot lip with the mark remaining on the shaft where the previous boot was attached.

NOTE: Boot clamping procedures are the same for attachment to the shafts or CV-joints.

2. Wrap a binding strap around boot twice, plus 2½ in. (63mm).

3. Pass the strap through the buckle and fold it back about 1⅛ in. (29mm) on the inside of the buckle.

4. Put the strip around the boot with the eye of the buckle toward the front. Wrap the strip around the boot once and pass it through the buckle. Wrap it around a 2nd time, also passing it through the buckle.

5. Fold the strip back slightly to prevent it from slipping backwards.

6. Open the tool all the way and place strip in narrow slot approximately ½ in. (13mm) from buckle.

7. Hold the binding strip with the left hand, push the tool forward, slightly upward and fit the hook of the tool into the eye of the buckle.

8. Tighten the strip by closing the tool handles. Rotate the tool handles downward while slowly releasing the pressure on the tool handles. Allow the tool handles to open progressively. Open the tool entirely and remove the sideways.

9. If the strap is not tight enough, re-engage the tool a 2nd or 3rd time, always about ½ in. (13mm) from the buckle. When tightening always make sure the strap slides in a straight line and without resistance in the buckle; without making a fold. An effective grip will be obtained only by following the above instructions.

10. If the strip is tight enough, remove the tool sideways and cut off the strap ⅛ in. (3mm), so it does not overlap the edge of the buckle. Complete job by folding the strip back neatly.

NOTE: During any service procedures where knuckle and driveshaft are separated, thoroughly clean the seal and wear sleeve with solvent and relubricate both components at reassembly; do not allow solvent to contact boot.

11. Lubricate wear sleeve and seal with MOPAR multi-purpose lubricant or equivalent, as follows:

a. Wear sleeve—apply a full circumference ¼ in. (6mm) bead of lubricant to seal contact area.

b. Seal—fill lip to housing cavity (full circumference) and lubricate the seal lip with oil.

12. Complete installation of inner or outer CV-joint and remaining end of boot by following installation procedures for clamping.

TYPE SSG WITH PLASTIC BOOT
(LEFT INNER, LEFT AND RIGHT OUTER CV-JOINT)

1. With the axle assembly removed from the vehicle and disassembled, remove the plastic and rubber boots from the shaft assembly. Prepare the assembly before installing the boot.

To Install:

2. To install the plastic boot, slide the small clamp onto the shaft.

3. Position the small end of the boot over the shaft with the lip of the boot in the 3rd groove, towards the center of the shaft.

4. Position the clamp evenly over the boot, place the clamp installer tool C–4975 or equivalent, over the bridge of the clamp and tighten the nut until the jaws of the tool are completely closed, face-to-face.

5. After attaching the boot to the shaft, assemble and install the CV-joint.

6. Position the large end of the boot on the housing and install the clamp. Crimp the bridge of the clamp with the tool.

NOTE: Use only the clamps provided in the boot package for this application, otherwise damage to the boot or CV-joint may occur.

TYPE SSG WITH RUBBER BOOT
(RIGHT INNER CV-JOINT)

1. With the axle assembly removed from the vehicle and disassembled, remove the rubber boot. Prepare the assembly before installing the boot.

2. Slide the small clamp onto the shaft assembly.

3. Install the boot onto the shaft and position the flat between the locating shoulders.

4. Position the clamp on the boot and crimp the bridge of the clamp with tool C–3250 or equivalent.

5. Install the CV-joint assembly. Position the large end of the boot on the housing, install the clamp and crimp the bridge of the clamp with the tool.

NOTE: During any service procedures where the knuckle and the driveshaft are separated, thoroughly clean the seal and wear sleeve with solvent. Relubricate both components at time of reassembly.

6. Apply a full circumference bead (¼ in.) of lubricant to the seal contact area of the wear sleeve.

7. Fill the seal lip to housing cavity and lubricate the seal lip with lubricant.

DAMPER WEIGHTS

Damper weights are used on the left driveshaft assemblies of all front wheel drive vehicles. These weights are attached to the interconnecting shaft and are not available as a separate service part. However, they can be removed from the driveshaft assembly during driveshaft positioning specifications procedures. When the weights are reattached between the locating shoulders, torque the fasteners to the following specifications:

ACI—8 ft. lbs. (11Nm)
CITROEN and S.S.G.—21 ft. lbs. (28 Nm)
GKN—23 ft. lbs. (30 Nm)

CV-Joints

Refer to Unit Repair Section for CV-joint overhaul.

REAR AXLE AND REAR SUSPENSION

Refer to the Unit Repair Section for axle overhaul procedures and rear suspension services.

Rear Axle Assembly

Description

OMNI, HORIZON, TURISMO AND CHARGER

A trailing, independent arm assembly, with integral sway bar is used. The wheel spindles are attached to 2 trailing arms which extend rearward from mounting points on the body where they are attached with shock absorbing, oval bushing. A crossmember is welded to the trailing arms, just to the rear of the bushing. A coil spring over shock absorber strut assembly, similar to the front suspension, is used.

EXCEPT OMNI, HORIZON, TURISMO AND CHARGER

These models use a flexible beam axle with trailing links and coil springs. One shock absorber on each side is mounted outside the coil spring and attached to the body and the beam axle. Wheel spindles are bolted to the outer ends of the axle.

Removal and Installation

OMNI, HORIZON, TURISMO AND CHARGER

1. Raise and safely support the vehicle. Remove the wheel assembies.
2. Remove brake fittings and retaining clips holding flexible brake line.
3. Remove parking brake cable adjusting connection nut.
4. Release both parking brake cables from brackets by slipping ball-end of cables through brake connectors. Pull parking brake cable through bracket.
5. Pry off grease cap.
6. Remove cotter pin and castle lock.
7. Remove adjusting nut and brake drum.
8. Remove brake assembly and spindle bolts.
9. Set spindle aside and using a piece of wire, hang brake assembly aside.
10. Place supports under rear crossmember to support the rear suspension.
11. Remove shock absorber brackets.
12. Remove trailing arm-to-hanger bracket bolts.
13. Lower jack and remove axle assembly.
To Install:
14. Using jacks, position the rear axle assembly under vehicle.
15. Install trailing arm-to-hanger mounting bracket, finger tighten bolts only.
16. Install shock absorber bolts loosely.
17. Place spindle and brake assembly in position; install bolts finger-tight.
18. Torque the bolts to 45 ft. lbs. (60 Nm).
19. Install brake drum.
20. Install washer and nut. Torque adjusting nut to 20–25 ft. lbs. (27–34 Nm) while rotating wheel. Back off adjusting nut to completely release bearing pre-load. Finger-tighten adjusting nut.
21. Position nut lock with a pair of slots aligned with cotter pin hole. Install cotter pin. The endplay should be 0.001–0.003 in. (0.025–0.076mm). Clean and install the grease cap.
22. Put parking brake cable through the bracket.
23. Slip ball-end of parking brake cables through brake connectors on parking brake bracket.
24. Install both retaining clips.
25. Install parking brake cable adjusting connection nut. Tighten until all slack is removed from cables.
26. Install retaining clips and brake tube fittings. Torque fitting to 9 ft. lbs. (12 Nm).
27. Bleed rear brake system and readjust brakes.
28. Install wheel and tire assembly. Torque wheel nuts to 80 ft. lbs. (108 Nm).
29. With vehicle on ground, torque trailing arm-to-hanger bracket mounting bolts to 40 ft. lbs. (55 Nm).
30. Torque shock absorber mounting bolts to 40 ft. lbs. (55 Nm) torque.

EXCEPT OMNI, HORIZON, TURISMO AND CHARGER

1. Raise and safely support the vehicle. Remove the wheel assemblies.
2. Separate the parking brake cable at the connector and cable housing at the floor pan bracket.
3. Separate the brake tube assembly from the brake hose at the training arm bracket and remove the lock.
4. Remove the lower shock absorber through bolts and the track bar-to-axle through bolts. Support the track bar end with wire to keep it aside.
5. Lower the axle until the spring and isolator assemblies can be removed.
6. Support the pivot bushing end of the trailing arms and remove the pivot bushing hanger bracket-to-frame screws. Carefully lower the axle assembly and remove it from the vehicle.
To Install:
7. Raise and safely support the axle assembly.
8. Attach the pivot bushing hanger brackets-to-frame rail bolts and tighten.
9. Install the springs and isolators and carefully raise the axle assembly.
10. Install the shock absorber and track bar through bolts; do not tighten.
11. Position the spindle and brake support to the axle while routing the parking brake cable through the trailing arm opening and the brake tube over the trailing arm. Torque to 45 ft. lbs. (60 Nm).
12. Install the hub and drum, if removed.
13. Route the parking brake cable through the fingers in the bracket and lock housing end into the floor pan bracket. Install the cable end into the intermediate connector.
14. Install the brake hose end fitting into the bracket and install the lock. Tighten.
15. Install wheel assemblies and lower vehicle to floor. Torque the lower shock absorber bolts to 40 ft. lbs. (55 Nm) and the track bar bolt to 80 ft. lbs. (108 Nm).
16. Bleed the brake system.

Rear Wheel Bearings

Removal and Installation

REAR DRUM BRAKES

1. Raise and safely support the vehicle.
2. Remove the grease cap, cotter pin, locknut, hub nut, washer and outer wheel bearing.
3. Pull the brake drum and wheel assembly from the axle spindle.
4. From inside the brake drum, remove the dust seal and inner wheel bearing.
5. If necessary, remove the wheel bearing races, by using a brass drift and a hammer to drive the races from the opposite side of the drum.
6. Clean and inspect the bearings and races for damage; replace it, if necessary.
7. Repack the bearings with clean wheel bearing grease. Drive the races into the hub until seated, coat the inside of the

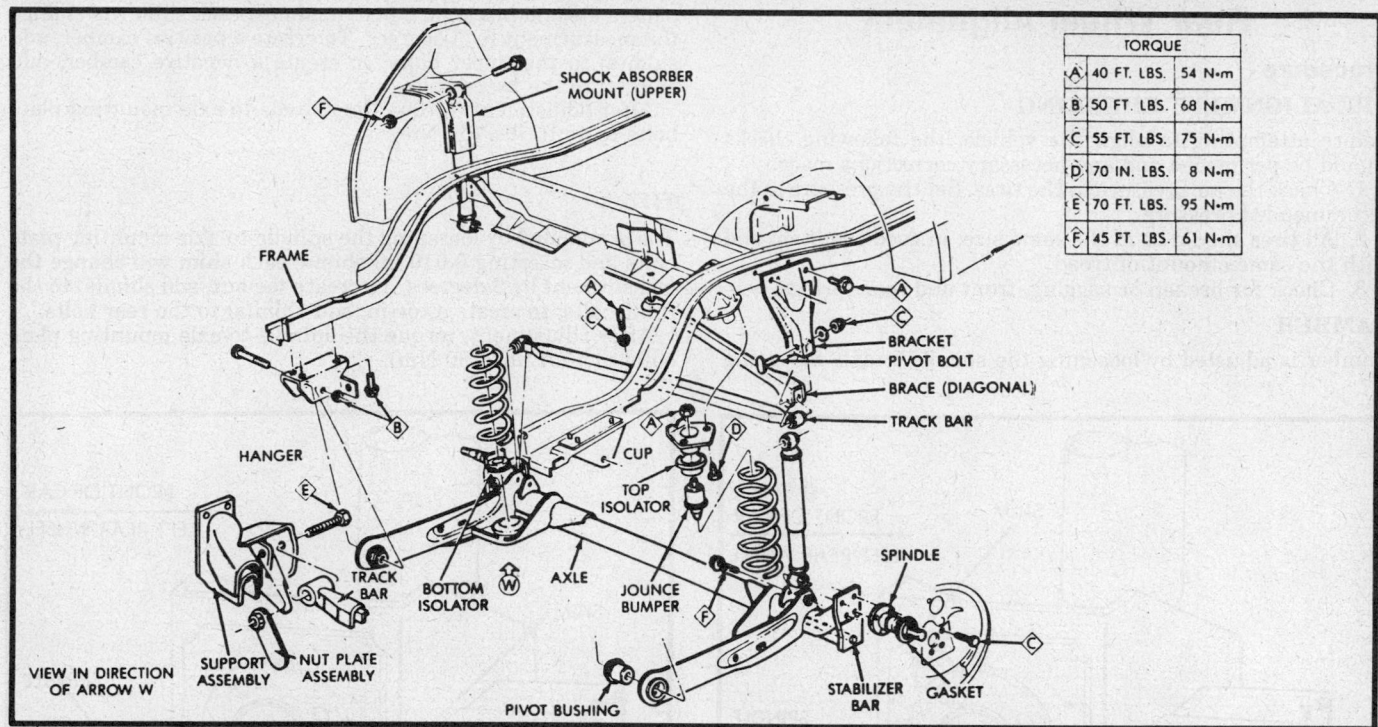

TORQUE		
Ⓐ	40 FT. LBS.	54 N•m
Ⓑ	50 FT. LBS.	68 N•m
Ⓒ	55 FT. LBS.	75 N•m
Ⓓ	70 IN. LBS.	8 N•m
Ⓔ	70 FT. LBS.	95 N•m
Ⓕ	45 FT. LBS.	61 N•m

Trailing Arm Rear Suspension

drum with grease, install the inner bearing and a new dust seal (flush with the drum).

8. To install, reverse the removal procedures. Adjust the wheel bearings.

REAR DISC BRAKES

Except Laser

1. Raise and safely support the vehicle. Remove the brake caliper from the mount and remove the brake rotor.
2. Remove the grease cap, cotter pin, locknut, hub nut, washer and outer wheel bearing.
3. Pull the hub assembly off of the spindle.
4. From inside the hub assembly, remove the dust seal and inner wheel bearing.
5. If necessary, remove the wheel bearing races, by using a brass drift and a hammer to drive the races from the opposite side of the hub.
6. Clean and inspect the bearings and races for damage. Replace, if necessary.
7. Repack the bearings with clean wheel bearing grease. Drive the races into the hub until seated, coat the inside of the hub with grease, install the inner bearing and a new dust seal (flush with the hub).
8. To install, reverse the removal procedures.
9. Adjust the wheel bearings when finshed.

Laser

1. Remove the grease cap, the hub nut and the thrust washer.
2. Raise and safely support the rear of the vehicle. Remove the wheel assembly.
3. Remove the brake caliper-to-knuckle bolts and support the caliper with a wire; do not disconnect the brake hose.
4. Remove the brake disc and the wheel bearing/hub unit.

To Install:

5. Reverse the removal procedures. To tighten the wheel bearing hub nut, lower the vehicle to the ground and torque the hub nut to 144–188 ft. lbs. (200–260 Nm).

6. Raise and safely support the rear of the vehicle. Make sure the wheel turns freely.

7. After adjustment crimp the hub nut into the spindle's indentation. Install the grease cap and lower the vehicle.

Adjustment

NOTE: Wheel bearings should be properly packed with approved wheel bearing grease before adjustments are made.

WITH DRUM BRAKES

1. Raise and safely support the vehicle.
2. Remove the grease cap, cotter pin and locknut.
3. Tighten the hub nut until it is snug and it back off slightly.
4. Install locknut and a new cotter pin.
5. Rotate the wheel assembly to make sure it rotates freely.

WITH DISC BRAKES

Except Laser

1. Raise and safely support the vehicle.
2. Remove the grease cap, cotter pin and locknut.
3. Tighten the hub nut until it is snug and it back off slightly.
4. Install locknut and a new cotter pin.
5. Rotate the wheel assembly to make sure it rotates freely.

Laser

1. Remove the grease cap and back off the hub nut.
2. Retorque the hub nut to 144–188 ft. lbs. (200–260 Nm).
3. Raise and safely support the rear of the vehicle. Make sure the wheel turns freely.
4. After adjustment crimp the hub nut into the spindle's indentation. Install the grease cap and lower the vehicle.

Rear Wheel Alignment

Procedure

PRE-ALIGNMENT CHECKING

Before attempting to align the vehicle, the following checks should be performed and any necessary corrections made.

1. Check the air pressure in the tires. Set the pressure to the recommended pressure.

2. All tires should be of the same size, in good condition and with the same amount of tread.

3. Check for broken or sagging, front and rear springs.

CAMBER

Camber is adjusted by loosening the spindle-to-axle mounting plate bolts and inserting 0.010 in. shims; each shim will change the measurment by 3 degrees. To create a positive camber, add shim(s) to the upper bolts; to create a negative camber, add shim(s) to the lower bolts.

After adjustment, torque the spindle-to-axle mounting plate bolts to 45 ft. lbs. (60 Nm).

TOE

Toe is adjusted by loosening the spindle-to-axle mounting plate bolts and inserting 0.010 in. shims; each shim will change the measurment by 3 degrees. To create toe-out, add shim(s) to the front bolts; to create a toe-in, add shim(s) to the rear bolts.

After adjustment, torque the spindle-to-axle mounting plate bolts to 45 ft. lbs. (60 Nm).

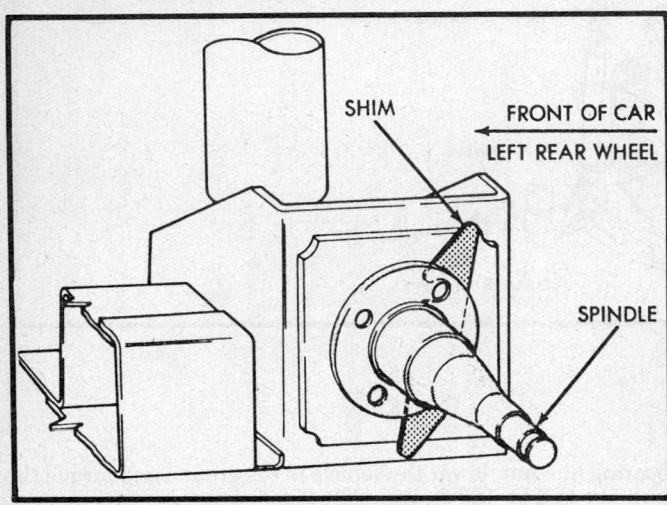

Shim installation for toe-in adjustment

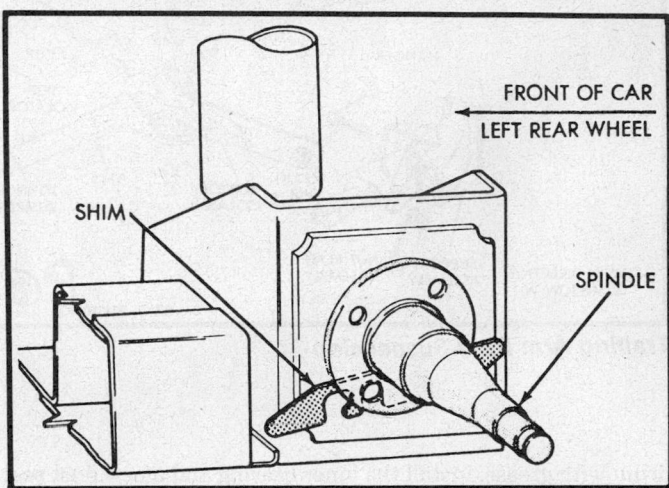

Shim installation for negative camber adjustment

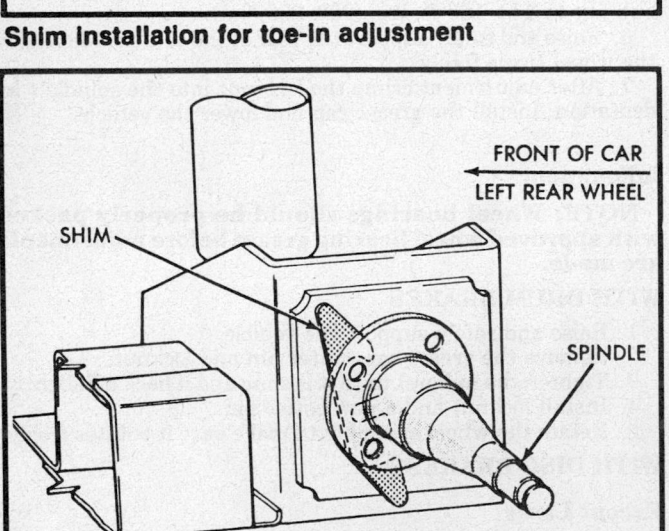

Shim installation for toe-out adjustment

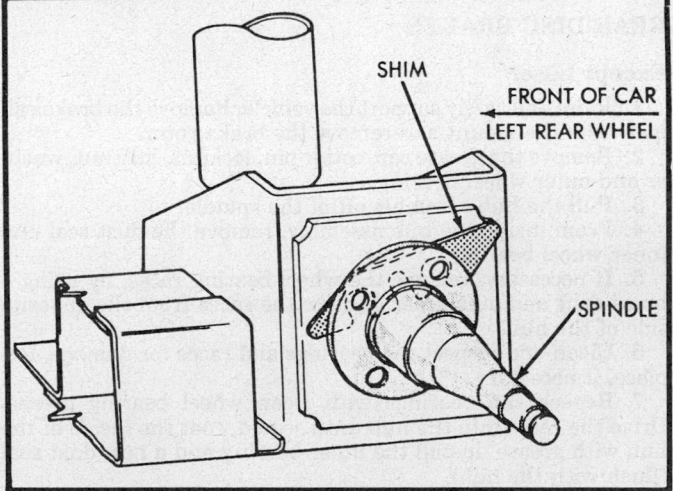

Shim installation for positive camber adjustment

3 Chrysler/Dodge/Plymouth 3

FIFTH AVENUE • NEWPORT • DIPLOMAT • GRAN FURY • CARAVELLE (RWD)

YEAR IDENTIFICATION

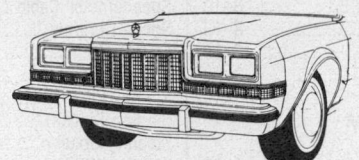

1986–89 Gran Fury

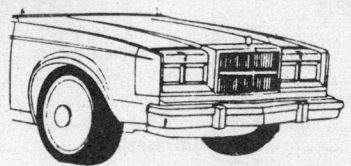

1986–89 Diplomat

1986–89 Fifth Avenue

VEHICLE IDENTIFICATION

It is important for servicing and ordering parts to be certain of the vehicle and engine identification. The VIN (vehicle identification number) is a 17 digit number visible through the windshield on the driver's side of the dash and contains the vehicle and engine identification codes. The tenth digit indicates model year, and the eighth digit indicates engine code. It can be interpreted as follows:

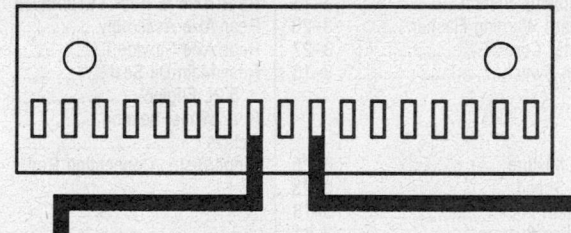

Engine Code						Model Year	
Code	Cu. In.	Liters	Cyl.	Fuel Sys.	Eng. Mfg.	Code	Year
P	318	5.2	8	2 bbl	Chrysler	G	1986
R	318	5.2	8	4 bbl	Chrysler	H	1987
S	318 HD	5.2	8	4 bbl	Chrysler	J	1988
4	318	5.2	8	4 bbl	Chrysler	K	1989

HD Heavy Duty

ENGINE IDENTIFICATION

Year	Model	Engine Displacement cu. in. (liter)	Engine Series Identification (VIN)	No. of Cylinders	Engine Type
1986	Diplomat	318 (5.2)	P	8	OHV
	Gran Fury/Caravelle①	318 (5.2)	P	8	OHV
	Gran Fury/Caravelle①	318 (5.2)	R	8	OHV
	Gran Fury/Caravelle①	318 (5.2)	S	8	OHV

ENGINE IDENTIFICATION

Year	Model	Engine Displacement cu. in. (liter)	Engine Series Identification (VIN)	No. of Cylinders	Engine Type
1986	Fifth Avenue/Newport	318 (5.2)	P	8	OHV
	Fifth Avenue/Newport	318 (5.2)	R	8	OHV
	Fifth Avenue/Newport	318 (5.2)	S	8	OHV
1987	Diplomat	318 (5.2)	P	8	OHV
	Gran Fury/Caravelle ①	318 (5.2)	P	8	OHV
	Gran Fury/Caravelle ①	318 (5.2)	R	8	OHV
	Gran Fury/Caravelle ①	318 (5.2)	S	8	OHV
	Fifth Avenue/Newport	318 (5.2)	P	8	OHV
	Fifth Avenue/Newport	318 (5.2)	R	8	OHV
	Fifth Avenue/Newport	318 (5.2)	S	8	OHV
1988	Diplomat	318 (5.2)	P	8	OHV
	Gran Fury/Caravelle ①	318 (5.2)	P	8	OHV
	Gran Fury/Caravelle ①	318 (5.2)	4	8	OHV
	Gran Fury/Caravelle ①	318 (5.2)	S	8	OHV
	Fifth Avenue/Newport	318 (5.2)	P	8	OHV
	Fifth Avenue/Newport	318 (5.2)	4	8	OHV
	Fifth Avenue/Newport	318 (5.2)	S	8	OHV
1989	Diplomat	318 (5.2)	P	8	OHV
	Gran Fury/Caravelle ①	318 (5.2)	P	8	OHV
	Gran Fury/Caravelle ①	318 (5.2)	4	8	OHV
	Gran Fury/Caravelle ①	318 (5.2)	S	8	OHV
	Fifth Avenue/Newport	318 (5.2)	P	8	OHV
	Fifth Avenue/Newport	318 (5.2)	4	8	OHV
	Fifth Avenue/Newport	318 (5.2)	S	8	OHV

① Caravelle – Canada only

GENERAL ENGINE SPECIFICATIONS

Year	VIN	No. Cylinder Displacement cu. in. (liter)	Fuel System Type	Net Horsepower @ rpm	Net Torque @ rpm (ft.lbs.)	Bore × Stroke (in.)	Compression Ratio	Oil Pressure @ rpm
1986	P	8-318 (5.2)	2 bbl	140 @ 3600	265 @ 1600	3.910 × 3.310	9.0:1	80 @ 3000
	R	8-318 (5.2)	4 bbl	165 @ 4000	240 @ 2000	3.910 × 3.310	8.6:1	80 @ 3000
	S	8-318 (5.2)HD	4 bbl	175 @ 4000	250 @ 3200	3.910 × 3.310	8.0:1	80 @ 3000
1987	P	8-318 (5.2)	2 bbl	140 @ 3600	265 @ 1600	3.910 × 3.310	9.0:1	80 @ 3000
	R	8-318 (5.2)	4 bbl	165 @ 4000	240 @ 2000	3.910 × 3.310	8.6:1	80 @ 3000
	S	8-318 (5.2)HD	4 bbl	175 @ 4000	250 @ 3200	3.910 × 3.310	8.0:1	80 @ 3000
1988	P	8-318 (5.2)	2 bbl	140 @ 3600	265 @ 1600	3.910 × 3.310	9.0:1	80 @ 3000
	4	8-318 (5.2)	4 bbl	165 @ 4000	240 @ 2000	3.910 × 3.310	8.6:1	80 @ 3000
	S	8-318 (5.2)HD	4 bbl	175 @ 4000	250 @ 3200	3.910 × 3.310	8.0:1	80 @ 3000

GENERAL ENGINE SPECIFICATIONS

Year	VIN	No. Cylinder Displacement cu. in. (liter)	Fuel System Type	Net Horsepower @ rpm	Net Torque @ rpm (ft.lbs.)	Bore × Stroke (in.)	Compression Ratio	Oil Pressure @ rpm
1989	P	8-318 (5.2)	2 bbl	140 @ 3600	265 @ 1600	3.910 × 3.310	9.0:1	80 @ 3000
	4	8-318 (5.2)	4 bbl	140 @ 3600	265 @ 2000	3.910 × 3.310	9.0:1	80 @ 3000
	S	8-318 (5.2)HD	4 bbl	175 @ 4000	250 @ 3200	3.910 × 3.310	8.0:1	80 @ 3000

HD Heavy Duty

GASOLINE ENGINE TUNE-UP SPECIFICATIONS
Refer to Section 34 for all spark plug recommendations

Year	VIN	No. Cylinder Displacement cu. in. (liter)	Spark Plugs Gap (in.)	Ignition Timing (deg.) MT	Ignition Timing (deg.) AT	Compression Pressure (psi)	Fuel Pump (psi)	Idle Speed (rpm) MT	Idle Speed (rpm) AT	Valve Clearance In.	Valve Clearance Ex.
1986	P	8-318 (5.2)	.035	—	7B	100	5.75-7.25	—	680	Hyd.	Hyd.
	R	8-318 (5.2)	.035	—	16B	100	5.75-7.25	—	750	Hyd.	Hyd.
	S	8-318 (5.2)	.035	—	16B	100	5.75-7.25	—	750	Hyd.	Hyd.
1987	P	8-318 (5.2)	.035	—	7B	100	5.75-7.25	—	680	Hyd.	Hyd.
	R	8-318 (5.2)	.035	—	16B	100	5.75-7.25	—	750	Hyd.	Hyd.
	S	8-318 (5.2)	.035	—	16B	100	5.75-7.25	—	750	Hyd.	Hyd.
1988	P	8-318 (5.2)	.035	—	7B	100	5.75-7.25	—	680	Hyd.	Hyd.
	4	8-318 (5.2)	.035	—	16B	100	5.75-7.25	—	750	Hyd.	Hyd.
	S	8-318 (5.2)	.035	—	16B	100	5.75-7.25	—	750	Hyd.	Hyd.
1989	P	8-318 (5.2)	.035	—	7B	100	5.75-7.25	—	680	Hyd.	Hyd.
	4	8-318 (5.2)	.035	—	16B	100	5.75-7.25	—	750	Hyd.	Hyd.
	S	8-318 (5.2)	.035	—	16B	100	5.75-7.25	—	750	Hyd.	Hyd.

NOTE: The underhood specifications sticker often reflects tune-up specification changes made in production. Sticker figures must be used if they disagree with those in this chart.

FIRING ORDERS

NOTE: To avoid confusion, always replace spark plug wires one at a time.

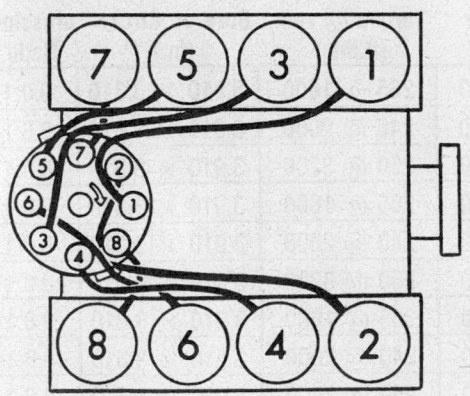

Chrysler Corp. 318, V8
Engine firing order: 1–8–4–3–6–5–7–2
Distributor rotation: clockwise

CAPACITIES

Year	Model	VIN	No. Cylinder Displacement cu. in. (liter)	Engine Crankcase with Filter	Engine Crankcase without Filter	Transmission (pts.) 4-Spd	Transmission (pts.) 5-Spd	Transmission (pts.) Auto.	Drive Axle (pts.)	Fuel Tank (gal.)	Cooling System (qts.)
1986	Diplomat	P	8-318 (5.2)	5	4	—	—	16.4	②	18	15.5③
	Gran Fury/Caravelle①	P	8-318 (5.2)	5	4	—	—	16.4	②	18	15.5③
	Gran Fury/Caravelle①	R	8-318 (5.2)	5	4	—	—	16.4	②	18	15.5③
	Gran Fury/Caravelle①	S	8-318 (5.2)	5	4	—	—	16.4	②	18	15.5③
	Fifth Avenue/Newport	P	8-318 (5.2)	5	4	—	—	16.4	②	18	15.5③
	Fifth Avenue/Newport	R	8-318 (5.2)	5	4	—	—	16.4	②	18	15.5③
	Fifth Avenue/Newport	S	8-318 (5.2)	5	4	—	—	16.4	②	18	15.5③
1987	Diplomat	P	8-318 (5.2)	5	4	—	—	16.4	②	18	15.5③
	Gran Fury/Caravelle①	P	8-318 (5.2)	5	4	—	—	16.4	②	18	15.5③
	Gran Fury/Caravelle①	R	8-318 (5.2)	5	4	—	—	16.4	②	18	15.5③
	Gran Fury/Caravelle①	S	8-318 (5.2)	5	4	—	—	16.4	②	18	15.5③
	Fifth Avenue/Newport	P	8-318 (5.2)	5	4	—	—	16.4	②	18	15.5③
	Fifth Avenue/Newport	R	8-318 (5.2)	5	4	—	—	16.4	②	18	15.5③
	Fifth Avenue/Newport	S	8-318 (5.2)	5	4	—	—	16.4	②	18	15.5③
1988	Diplomat	P	8-318 (5.2)	5	4	—	—	16.4	②	18	15.5③
	Diplomat	4	8-318 (5.2)	5	4	—	—	16.3	16.4	18	15.5③
	Diplomat	S	8-318 (5.2)	5	4	—	—	16.3	16.4	18	15.5③
	Gran Fury/Caravelle①	P	8-318 (5.2)	5	4	—	—	16.4	②	18	15.5③
	Gran Fury/Caravelle①	4	8-318 (5.2)	5	4	—	—	16.3	16.4	18	15.5③
	Gran Fury/Caravelle①	S	8-318 (5.2)	5	4	—	—	16.3	16.4	18	15.5③
	Fifth Avenue/Newport	P	8-318 (5.2)	5	4	—	—	16.4	②	18	15.5③
	Fifth Avenue/Newport	4	8-318 (5.2)	5	4	—	—	16.3	16.4	18	15.5③
	Fifth Avenue/Newport	S	8-318 (5.2)	5	4	—	—	16.3	16.4	18	15.5③
1989	Diplomat	P	8-318 (5.2)	5	4	—	—	16.4	②	18	15.5③
	Diplomat	4	8-318 (5.2)	5	4	—	—	16.3	16.4	18	15.5③
	Diplomat	S	8-318 (5.2)	5	4	—	—	16.3	16.4	18	15.5③
	Gran Fury/Caravelle①	P	8-318 (5.2)	5	4	—	—	16.4	②	18	15.5③

CAPACITIES

Year	Model	VIN	No. Cylinder Displacement cu. in. (liter)	Engine Crankcase with Filter	Engine Crankcase without Filter	Transmission (pts.) 4-Spd	Transmission (pts.) 5-Spd	Transmission (pts.) Auto.	Drive Axle (pts.)	Fuel Tank (gal.)	Cooling System (qts.)
1989	Gran Fury/Caravelle①	4	8-318 (5.2)	5	4	—	—	16.3	16.4	18	15.5③
	Gran Fury/Caravelle①	S	8-318 (5.2)	5	4	—	—	16.3	16.4	18	15.5③
	Fifth Avenue/Newport	P	8-318 (5.2)	5	4	—	—	16.4	②	18	15.5③
	Fifth Avenue/Newport	4	8-318 (5.2)	5	4	—	—	16.3	16.4	18	15.5③
	Fifth Avenue/Newport	S	8-318 (5.2)	5	4	—	—	16.3	16.4	18	15.5③

① Caravelle-Canada only
② 7¼ in. axle—2.5 pts.
　8¼ in. axle—4.4 pts.
　9¼ in axle—4.5 pts.
③ Add 1 qt. for models with air conditioning

CAMSHAFT SPECIFICATIONS
All measurements given in inches.

Year	VIN	No. Cylinder Displacement cu. in. (liter)	Journal Diameter 1	Journal Diameter 2	Journal Diameter 3	Journal Diameter 4	Journal Diameter 5	Lobe Lift In.	Lobe Lift Ex.	Bearing Clearance	Camshaft End Play
1986	P	8–318 (5.2)	1.998–1.999	1.982–1.983	1.967–1.968	1.951–1.952	1.5605–1.5615	0.373	0.400	0.001–0.003	0.002–0.010
	R	8–318 (5.2)	1.998–1.999	1.982–1.983	1.967–1.968	1.951–1.952	1.5605–1.5615	0.373	0.400	0.001–0.003	0.002–0.010
	S	8–318 (5.2)	1.998–1.999	1.982–1.983	1.967–1.968	1.951–1.952	1.5605–1.5615	0.373	0.400	0.001–0.003	0.002–0.010
1987	P	8–318 (5.2)	1.998–1.999	1.982–1.983	1.967–1.968	1.951–1.952	1.5605–1.5615	0.373	0.400	0.001–0.003	0.002–0.010
	R	8–318 (5.2)	1.998–1.999	1.982–1.983	1.967–1.968	1.951–1.952	1.5605–1.5615	0.373	0.400	0.001–0.003	0.002–0.010
	S	8–318 (5.2)	1.998–1.999	1.982–1.983	1.967–1.968	1.951–1.952	1.5605–1.5615	0.373	0.400	0.001–0.003	0.002–0.010
1988	P	8–318 (5.2)	1.998–1.999	1.982–1.983	1.967–1.968	1.951–1.952	1.5605–1.5615	0.373	0.400	0.001–0.003	0.002–0.010
	4	8–318 (5.2)	1.998–1.999	1.982–1.983	1.967–1.968	1.951–1.952	1.5605–1.5615	0.373	0.400	0.001–0.003	0.002–0.010
	S	8–318 (5.2)	1.998–1.999	1.982–1.983	1.967–1.968	1.951–1.952	1.5605–1.5615	0.373	0.400	0.001–0.003	0.002–0.010
1989	P	8–318 (5.2)	1.998–1.999	1.982–1.983	1.967–1.968	1.951–1.952	1.5605–1.5615	0.373	0.400	0.001–0.003	0.002–0.010
	4	8–318 (5.2)	1.998–1.999	1.982–1.983	1.967–1.968	1.951–1.952	1.5605–1.5615	0.373	0.400	0.001–0.003	0.002–0.010
	S	8–318 (5.2)	1.998–1.999	1.982–1.983	1.967–1.968	1.951–1.952	1.5605–1.5615	0.373	0.400	0.001–0.003	0.002–0.010

CRANKSHAFT AND CONNECTING ROD SPECIFICATIONS
All measurements are given in inches.

Year	VIN	No. Cylinder Displacement cu. in. (liter)	Crankshaft				Connecting Rod		
			Main Brg. Journal Dia.	Main Brg. Oil Clearance	Shaft End-play	Thrust on No.	Journal Diameter	Oil Clearance	Side Clearance
1986	P	8–318 (5.2)	2.4995–2.5005	①	.002–.010	3	2.1240–2.1250	.0005–.0022	.006–.014
	R	8–318 (5.2)	2.4995–2.5005	①	.002–.010	3	2.1240–2.1250	.0005–.0022	.006–.014
	S	8–318 (5.2)	2.4995–2.5005	①	.002–.010	3	2.1240–2.1250	.0005–.0022	.006–.014
1987	P	8–318 (5.2)	2.4995–2.5005	①	.002–.010	3	2.1240–2.1250	.0005–.0022	.006–.014
	R	8–318 (5.2)	2.4995–2.5005	①	.002–.010	3	2.1240–2.1250	.0005–.0022	.006–.014
	S	8–318 (5.2)	2.4995–2.5005	①	.002–.010	3	2.1240–2.1250	.0005–.0022	.006–.014
1988	P	8–318 (5.2)	2.4995–2.5005	①	.002–.010	3	2.1240–2.1250	.0005–.0022	.006–.014
	4	8–318 (5.2)	2.4995–2.5005	①	.002–.010	3	2.1240–2.1250	.0005–.0022	.006–.014
	S	8–318 (5.2)	2.4995–2.5005	①	.002–.010	3	2.1240–2.1250	.0005–.0022	.006–.014
1980	P	8–318 (5.2)	2.4995–2.5005	①	.002–.010	3	2.1240–2.1250	.0005–.0022	.006–.014
	4	8–318 (5.2)	2.4995–2.5005	①	.002–.010	3	2.1240–2.1250	.0005–.0022	.006–.014
	S	8–318 (5.2)	2.4995–2.5005	①	.002–.010	3	2.1240–2.1250	.0005–.0022	.006–.014

① No. 1 – .0005–.0015;
No. 2–5 – .0005–.0020

VALVE SPECIFICATIONS

Year	VIN	No. Cylinder Displacement cu. in. (liter)	Seat Angle (deg.)	Face Angle (deg.)	Spring Test Pressure (lbs. @ inch)	Spring Installed Height (in.)	Stem-to-Guide Clearance (in.)		Stem Diameter (in.)	
							Intake	Exhaust	Intake	Exhaust
1986	P	8–318 (5.2)	45	45	177 @ 1.31	$1\frac{21}{32}$	.0010–.0030	.0020–.0040	.3725	.3715
	R	8–318 (5.2)	45	45	177 @ 1.31	$1\frac{21}{32}$	.0010–.0030	.0020–.0040	.3725	.3715
	S	8–318 (5.2)	45	45	193 @ 1.25	$1\frac{21}{32}$	.0015–.0035	.0025–.0045	.3720	.3710
1987	P	8–318 (5.2)	45	45	177 @ 1.31	$1\frac{21}{32}$	.0010–.0030	.0020–.0040	.3725	.3715
	R	8–318 (5.2)	45	45	177 @ 1.31	$1\frac{21}{32}$	.0010–.0030	.0020–.0040	.3725	.3715

VALVE SPECIFICATIONS

Year	VIN	No. Cylinder Displacement cu. in. (liter)	Seat Angle (deg.)	Face Angle (deg.)	Spring Test Pressure (lbs. @ inch)	Spring Installed Height (in.)	Stem-to-Guide Clearance (in.)		Stem Diameter (in.)	
							Intake	Exhaust	Intake	Exhaust
1987	S	8–318 (5.2)	45	45	193 @ 1.25	$1^{21}/_{32}$	.0015–.0035	.0025–.0045	.3720	.3710
1988	P	8–318 (5.2)	45	45	177 @ 1.31	$1^{21}/_{32}$	.0010–.0030	.0020–.0040	.3725	.3715
	4	8–318 (5.2)	45	45	177 @ 1.31	$1^{21}/_{32}$	.0010–.0030	.0020–.0040	.3725	.3715
	S	8–318 (5.2)	45	45	193 @ 1.25	$1^{21}/_{32}$	.0015–.0035	.0025–.0045	.3720	.3710
1989	P	8–318 (5.2)	45	45	177 @ 1.31	$1^{21}/_{32}$	.0010–.0030	.0020–.0040	.3725	.3715
	4	8–318 (5.2)	45	45	177 @ 1.31	$1^{21}/_{32}$	.0010–.0030	.0020–.0040	.3725	.3715
	S	8–318 (5.2)	45	45	193 @ 1.25	$1^{21}/_{32}$	.0015–.0035	.0025–.0045	.3720	.3710

PISTON AND RING SPECIFICATIONS
All measurments are given in inches.

Year	VIN	No. Cylinder Displacement cu. in. (liter)	Piston Clearance	Ring Gap			Ring Side Clearance		
				Top Compression	Bottom Compression	Oil Control	Top Compression	Bottom Compression	Oil Control
1986	P	8–318 (5.2)	.0005–.0015 ①	.010–.020	.010–.020	.015–.055	.0015–.0030	.0015–.0030	.0002–.0050
	R	8–318 (5.2)	.0005–.0015 ①	.010–.020	.010–.020	.015–.055	.0015–.0030	.0015–.0030	.0002–.0050
	S	8–318 (5.2)	.0005–.0015 ①	.010–.020	.010–.020	.015–.055	.0015–.0030	.0015–.0030	.0002–.0050
1987	P	8–318 (5.2)	.0005–.0015 ①	.010–.020	.010–.020	.015–.055	.0015–.0030	.0015–.0030	.0002–.0050
	R	8–318 (5.2)	.0005–.0015 ①	.010–.020	.010–.020	.015–.055	.0015–.0030	.0015–.0030	.0002–.0050
	S	8–318 (5.2)	.0005–.0015 ①	.010–.020	.010–.020	.015–.055	.0015–.0030	.0015–.0030	.0002–.0050
1988	P	8–318 (5.2)	.0005–.0015 ①	.010–.020	.010–.020	.015–.055	.0015–.0030	.0015–.0030	.0002–.0050

PISTON AND RING SPECIFICATIONS
All measurments are given in inches.

Year	VIN	No. Cylinder Displacement cu. in. (liter)	Piston Clearance	Ring Gap			Ring Side Clearance		
				Top Compression	Bottom Compression	Oil Control	Top Compression	Bottom Compression	Oil Control
1988	4	8–318 (5.2)	.0005–.0015 ①	.010–.020	.010–.020	.015–.055	.0015–.0030	.0015–.0030	.0002–.0050
	S	8–318 (5.2)	.0005–.0015 ①	.010–.020	.010–.020	.015–.055	.0015–.0030	.0015–.0030	.0002–.0050
1989	P	8–318 (5.2)	.0005–.0015 ①	.010–.020	.010–.020	.015–.055	.0015–.0030	.0015–.0030	.0002–.0050
	4	8–318 (5.2)	.0005–.0015 ①	.010–.020	.010–.020	.015–.055	.0015–.0030	.0015–.0030	.0002–.0050
	S	8–318 (5.2)	.0005–.0015 ①	.010–.020	.010–.020	.015–.055	.0015–.0030	.0015–.0030	.0002–.0050

① High Performance engines — .001–.002

TORQUE SPECIFICATIONS
All readings in ft. lbs.

Year	VIN	No. Cylinder Displacement cu. in. (liter)	Cylinder Head Bolts	Main Bearing Bolts	Rod Bearing Bolts	Crankshaft Pulley Bolts	Flywheel Bolts	Manifold		Spark Plugs
								Intake	Exhaust	
1986	P	8-318 (5.2)	105	85	45	100	55	45	②	30
	R	8-318 (5.2)	105	85	45	100	55	45	②	30
	S	8-318 (5.2)	105	85	45	100	55	45	②	30
1987	P	8-318 (5.2)	105	85	45	100	55	45	②	30
	R	8-318 (5.2)	105	85	45	100	55	45	②	30
	S	8-318 (5.2)	105	85	45	100	55	45	②	30
1988	P	8-318 (5.2)	105	85	45	100	55	45	②	30
	4	8-318 (5.2)	105	85	45	100	55	45	②	30
	S	8-318 (5.2)	105	85	45	100	55	45	②	30
1989	P	8-318 (5.2)	105	85	45	100	55	45	②	30
	4	8-318 (5.2)	105	85	45	100	55	45	②	30
	S	8-318 (5.2)	105	85	45	100	55	45	②	30

② Nuts — 15 ft. lbs., bolts — 20 ft.lb

WHEEL ALIGNMENT

Year	Model	Caster Range (deg.)	Caster Preferred Setting (deg.)	Camber Range (deg.)	Camber Preferred Setting (deg.)	Toe-in (in.)	Steering Axis Inclination (deg.)
1986	Fifth Avenue/Newport, Gran Fury/Caravelle①, Diplomat	1¼P-3¾P	2½P	¼N-1¼P	½P	⅛	8
1987	Fifth Avenue/Newport, Gran Fury/Caravelle①, Diplomat	1¼P-3¾P	2½P	¼N-1¼P	½P	⅛	8
1988	Fifth Avenue/Newport, Gran Fury/Caravelle, Diplomat	1¼P-3¾P	2½P	¼N-1¼P	½P	⅛	8
1989-90	Fifth Avenue/Newport, Gran Fury/Caravelle①, Diplomat	1¼P-3¾P	2½P	¼N-1¼P	½P	⅛	8

① Caravelle—Canada only

ELECTRICAL

NOTE: Disconnecting the negative battery cable on some vehicles may interfere with the functions of the on board computer systems and may require the computer to undergo a relearning process, once the negative battery cable is reconnected.

For testing and overhaul procedures on starters, alternators and voltage regulators, refer to the Unit Repair section.

Charging System

ALTERNATOR

Removal and Installation

1. Disconnect the negative battery terminal.

2. Loosen the alternator mounting nut and bolt, the belt tensioner bracket bolt and remove the drive belt.

3. Remove the alternator mounting nut and bolt, the belt tensioner bracket bolt and spacer.

4. Disconnect the battery, field and ground leads from the alternator.

5. Disconnect the harness from the alternator and remove the alternator from the vehicle.

6. Position the harness to the alternator and reconnect the battery, field and ground leads to the alternator.

7. Position the alternator spacer between the end shields and install the mounting nut.

8. Install the adjustment bracket bolt and drive belt.

9. Adjust the drive belt tension.

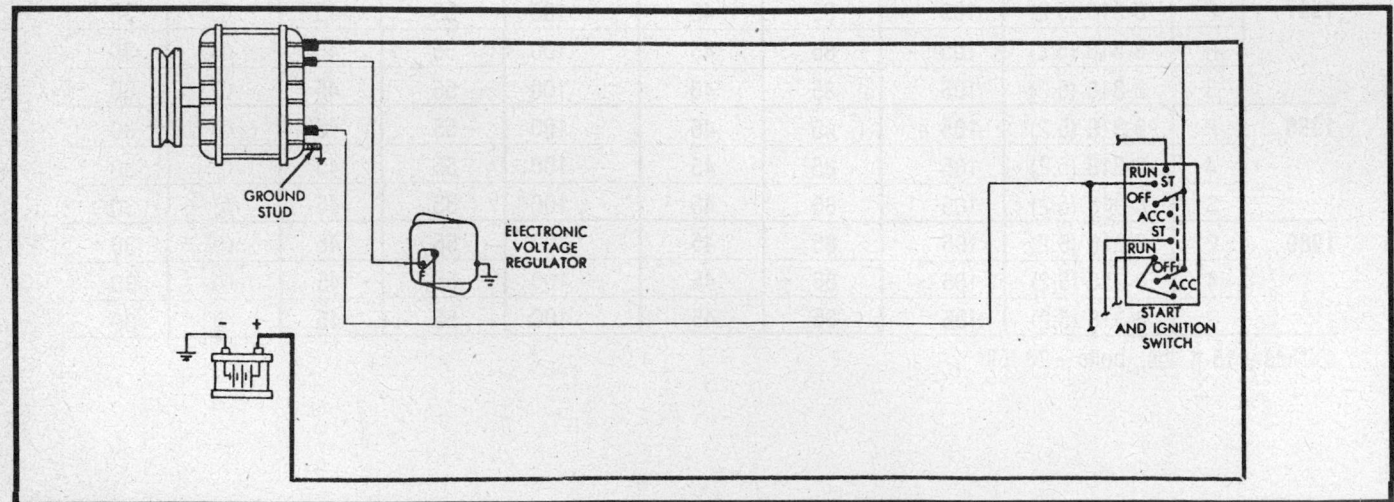

Schematic of typical charging circuit

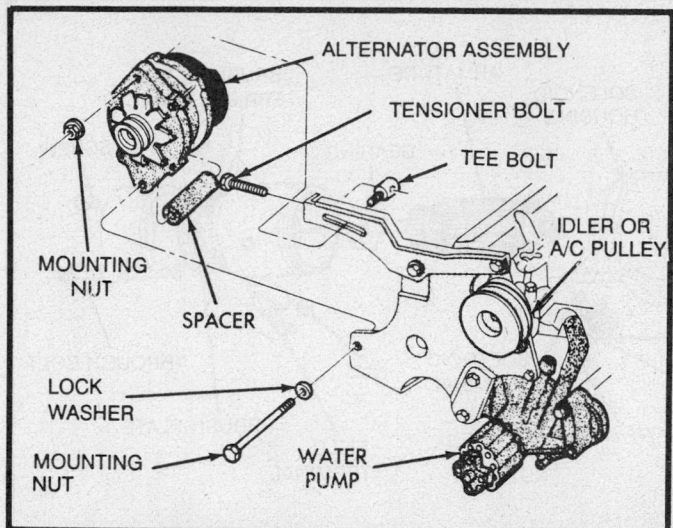

Alternator mounting

VOLTAGE REGULATOR

Removal and Installation

1. Disconnect the negative battery cable. Disconnect the wiring harness plug from the voltage regulator.
2. Remove the mounting screws from the voltage regular base and remove the regulator.
3. Prior to installing the voltage regulator, clean the mounting surface of any dirt or corrosion build-up. (The regulator must have a good ground contact).
4. Position the voltage regulator to the mounting surface and install the mounting screws.
5. Connect the wiring harness plug to the voltage regulator. Test the system for proper operation.

BELT TENSION SPECIFICATIONS
Torque Method
All measurements in ft. lbs.

	New Belt	Used Belt
Alternator		
With A/C	75 (101 Nm)	50 (68 Nm)
Without A/C	75 (101 Nm)	40 (54 Nm)
Power Steering		
With A/C ①	120 (163 Nm)	60 (81 Nm)
Without A/C	50 (68 Nm)	40 (54 Nm)

① Initial orientation of torque wrench is approximately horizontal

BELT TENSION

Satisfactory performance of the belt driven accessories depends on proper belt tension. The 2 tensioning methods are given in order of preference:
1. Belt tension gauge method
2. Torque equivalent method

Belt Tension Gauge Method

For this method, the belt is adjusted by measuring the tension of the belts with a belt tension gauge. Check belt tension in the middle of the span, between the 2 pulleys.

Torque Equivalent Method

Each adjustable accessory bracket is provided with a ½ in. (13mm) square hole for torque wrench use. Equivalent torque values for adjusting each accessory drive belt are specified.

Starting System
STARTER

Removal and Installation

1. Disconnect the negative battery cable. Raise and support the vehicle safely.
2. Remove the cable from the starter and heat shield.
3. Disconnect the solenoid leads at the solenoid terminals.
4. Remove the starter securing bolts and remove the starter from the engine flywheel housing.
5. On vehicles with automatic transmissions, the fluid cooler tube bracket may interfere with starter removal. In this case, remove the starter securing bolts, slide the cooler tube bracket off the stud and remove the starter.
6. Installation is the reverse order of the removal procedure. Be sure the starter and flywheel housing mating surfaces are free of dirt and oil.
7. When tightening the bolt and nut, hold the starter away from the engine to ensure proper alignment during its seating as the bolt is tightened. Do not damage the flywheel housing seal, if so equipped.

Ignition System
DISTRIBUTOR

Removal and Installation
TIMING NOT DISTURBED

1. Disconnect the negative battery cable.
2. Remove the cap and wire assembly.
3. Disconnect the vacuum line at the distributor governor-vaccum unit (if equipped).
4. Disconnect the lead wire at the harness connector.
5. Mark the relative positions of the distributor and rotor on the engine block or distributor housing edge.
6. Loosen the distributor mounting and lift out the distributor. Should the distributor shaft rotate slightly during the removal, make a second matchmark to indicated rotor positioning for installation.

NOTE: To simplify reinstallation, do not disturb the engine while the distributor is out.

7. Re-install by reversing the above procedure, aligning the distributor rotor and the mark on the block when installing the distributor.
8. Start the engine and check the ignition timing. Refer to the underhood Vehicle Emission Information Label for correct timing specifications.

TIMING DISTURBED

1. Rotate the crankshaft until No. 1 cylinder is at TDC.
2. The pointer on the timing chain case cover should be over the 0 mark on the crankshaft pulley.
3. The slot in the intermediate shaft which carries the gear that drives the oil pump and the distributor should be parallel (or nearly so) to the crankshaft.
4. Hold the distributor over the mounting pad on the cylinder block so the distributor body flange coincides with the mounting

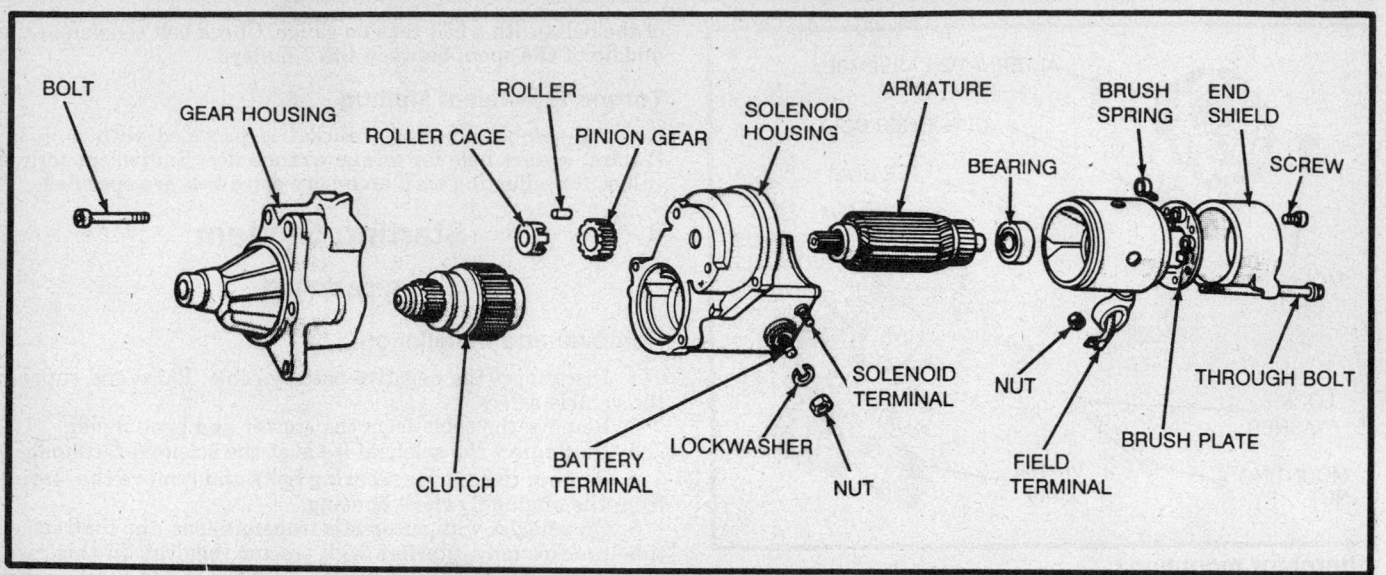

Exploded view of starter

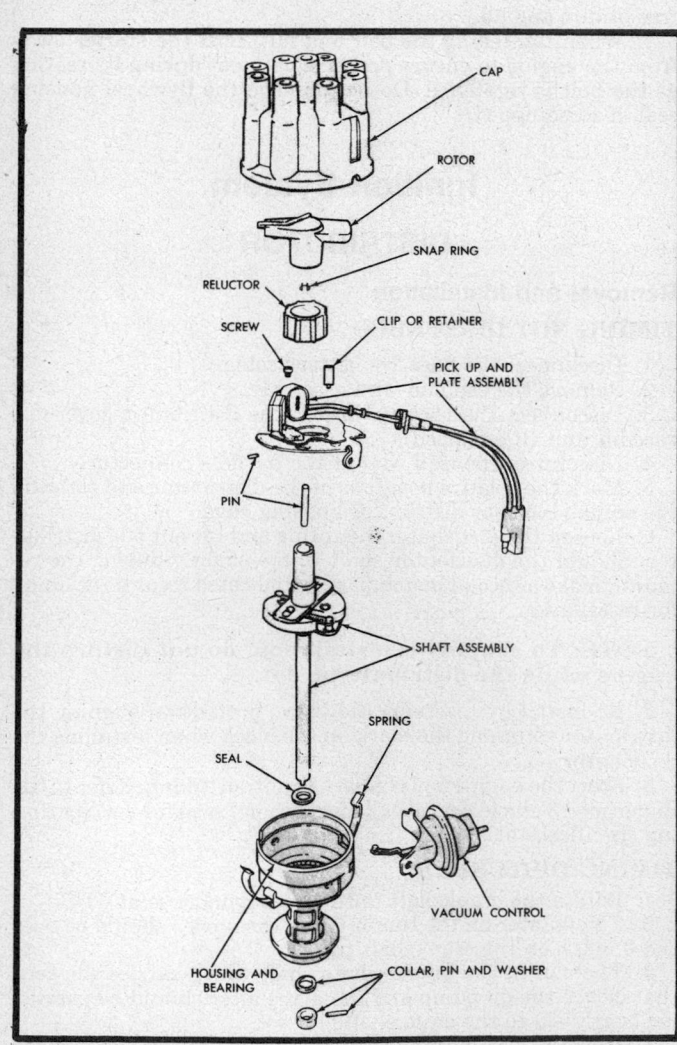

Exploded view of single pick-up distributor, typical

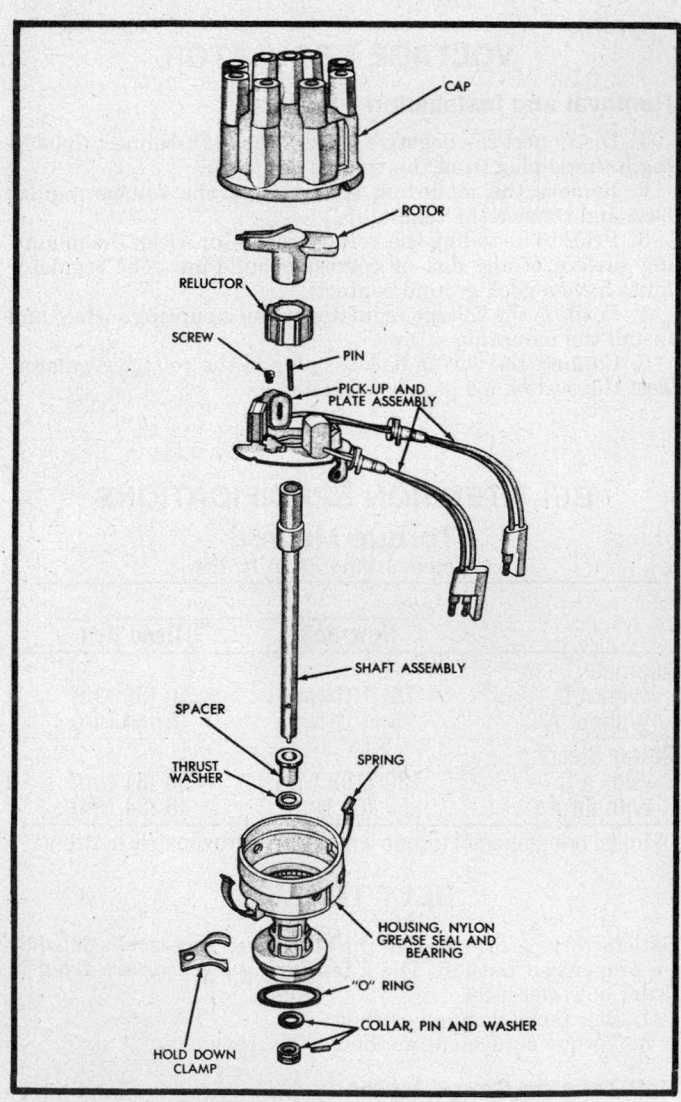

Exploded view of ESA dual pick-up distributor

pad and the rotor points to the No. 1 cylinder firing position.

5. Install the distributor while holding the rotor in position, allowing it to move only enough to engage the slot in the drive gear.

6. Install the cap, snug down the retaining bolt and check the ignition timing. Refer to the underhood Vehicle Emission Information Label for correct timing specifications.

IGNITION TIMING

Adjustment

The ignition timing test indicates correct timing of the engine only at idle and with the engine hot. Check timing as follows:

1. Connect tachometer and timing light. A magnetic timing probe receptacle is mounted to timing indicator and may be advisable to use.

2. Set parking brake and place transmission in **P** or **N** position. Start the engine and run until normal operating temperature is reached.

3. If equipped with carburetor ground switch, connect jumper wire between switch and ground. If the engine is not equipped with a spark control computer, disconnect and plug the vacuum line at the distributor.

4. Adjust engine idle if necessary. Check ignition timing.

5. If timing is out of allowed specifications, loosen and rotate distributor housing.

6. Turn the distributor housing in the direction of rotor-rotation to retard the timing. Rotate the distributor housing against rotor rotation to advance the timing.

7. Tighten distributor locking bolt securely.

8. Recheck engine idle and remove test equipment.

Electrical Controls

STEERING WHEEL

Removal and Installation

——————— CAUTION ———————

A driver air bag restraint system is available on late model 1988–89 vehicles. Improper maintenance, including incorrect removal and installation of related components, can lead to personal injury caused by unintentional activation of the airbag. Disconnect the negative battery cable and isolate whenever the airbag system is being serviced in any way.

NOTE: All vehicles are equipped with collapsible steering columns. A sharp blow or excessive pressure on the column will cause it to collapse. Do not hammer on the steering wheel.

1. Disconnect the negative battery cable.

2. Remove the padded center assembly. This center assembly is often held on only by spring clips. There are usually holes in the back of the wheel so the pad can be pushed off. However, on some deluxe steering wheel pads, it is held on by screws behind the arms of the wheel. Remove the horn wire, if necessary.

3. On the tilt and telescoping steering column, remove the locking lever knob by releasing the clip on its underside. Remove the locking lever screws and the lever.

4. Remove the large center nut. Mark the steering wheel and steering shaft so the wheel may be replaced in its original position. In most cases, the wheel can only go on one way.

5. Using a puller, pull the steering wheel from the steering shaft.

6. Reverse the procedure to install the wheel. When placing the wheel on the shaft, make sure the front tires are in the straight ahead position and the steering wheel and shaft are properly aligned. Tighten the retaining nut to 45 ft. lbs.

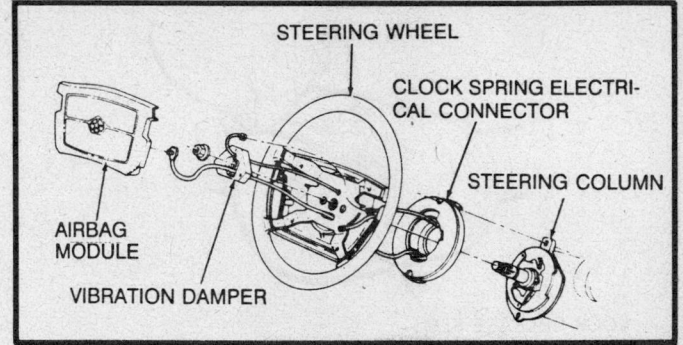

Exploded view of steering column—air bag system

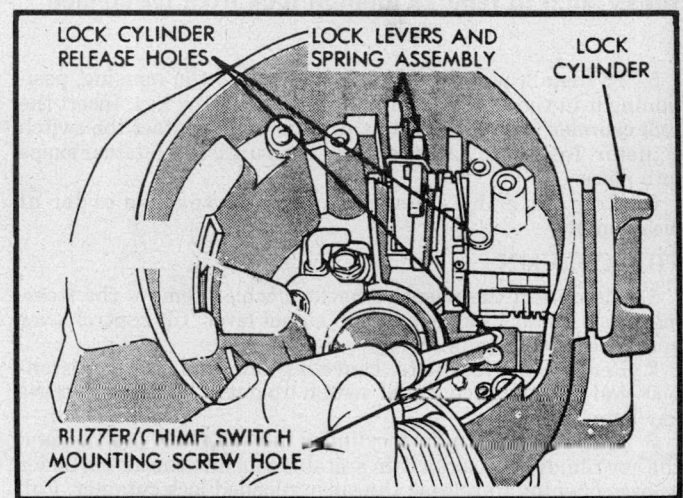

Releasing the ignition lock—standard column

HORN SWITCH

Removal and Installation

1. Disconnect the negative battery cable.

2. Remove the horn pad by prying from the bottom, being carefull not to mar the steering wheel surface.

3. Remove the electrical lead from the horn ring terminal.

4. Remove the screws retaining each horn switch to the steering wheel.

5. Carefully lift the both horn switches from steering wheel.

6. Installation is the reverse order of the removal procedure.

IGNITION LOCK

Removal and Installation

STANDARD COLUMN

1. Disconnect the negative battery cable. Remove the steering wheel and turn signal lever. Pull the turn signal switch up out of the way.

2. Remove the retaining snapring and pry the upper bearing housing off the steering shaft.

3. Press out the pin attaching the lockplate to the steering shaft and remove the lockplate. Remove the lock lever guide plate. Remove the buzz/chime switch.

4. With the ignition lock cylinder in the **LOCK** position and the ignition key removed, insert 2 small diameter tools into the lock cylinder release openings to release the spring-loaded lock retainer. Pull the lock cylinder out of its housing.

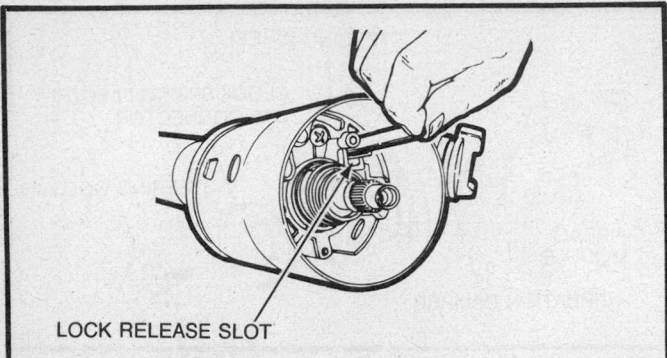

Slide a thin probe into the lock release and depress latch to remove ignition lock from tilt column

5. To install, place the lock cylinder into the housing, positioning it in the **LOCK** position and remove the key. Insert the lock cylinder far enough into the housing to contact the switch actuator. Insert the key, press and turn until the retainer snaps into place.

6. Complete the reassembly in the reverse order of disassembly.

TILT COLUMN

1. Disconnect the negative battery cable. Remove the steering wheel, shaft lock cover, turn signal lever, tilt control lever and hazard warning knob.

2. Remove the lockplate, canceling cam and spring, disconnect and pull the turn signal switch up out of the way. Remove key lamp.

3. With the ignition lock cylinder in the **LOCK** position and the key removed, insert a thin suitable tool into the lock cylinder release opening to release the spring-loaded lock retainer. Pull the lock cylinder out of its housing.

4. To install, place the lock cylinder in its housing, positioning it in the **LOCK** position and remove the key. Insert the cylinder into the housing until it contacts the switch actuator. Move the switch actuator rod up and down to align the parts. When aligned, move the lock cylinder inward and snap into place.

5. Complete the reassembly in the reverse order of disassembly.

IGNITION SWITCH

Removal and Installation

1. Disconnect the negative battery cable.
2. Remove the instrument panel steering column bracket cover and lower reinforcement.
3. Remove the connector from the switch.
4. Place the key in the **LOCK** position.
5. Remove the key.
6. Remove the mounting screws from the switch and allow the switch and pushrod to drop below the jacket.
7. Rotate the switch 90 degrees to permit removal of the switch from the pushrod.
8. Install the switch by positioning it in the **LOCK** position (2nd detent from the top).
9. Place the switch at right angles to the column and insert the pushrod.
10. Rotate the switch 90 degrees to lock the actuator rod, align the switch on the bracket and install the screws.
11. With a light rearward load on the switch, tighten the screws. Check for proper operation.

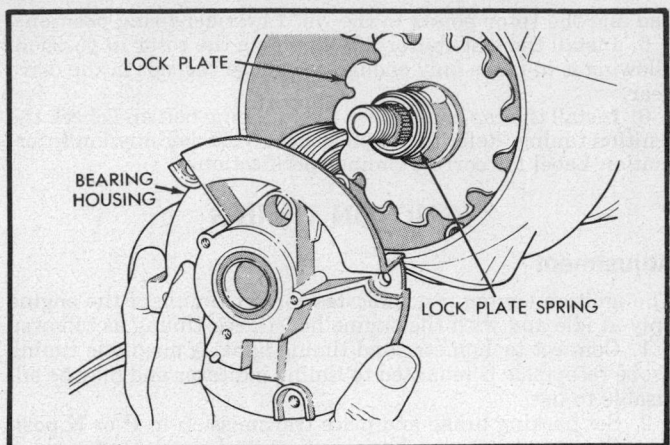

Removal of bearing housing, lock plate spring and lock plate

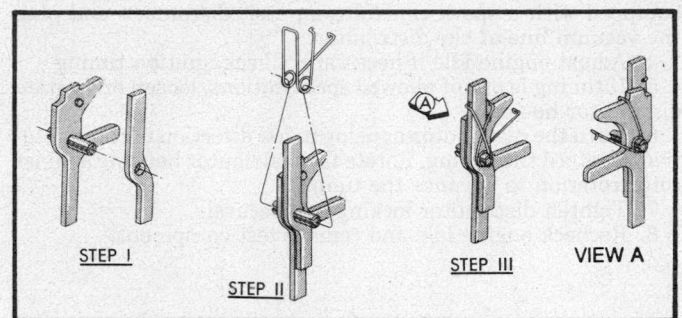

Assembling lock levers and spring

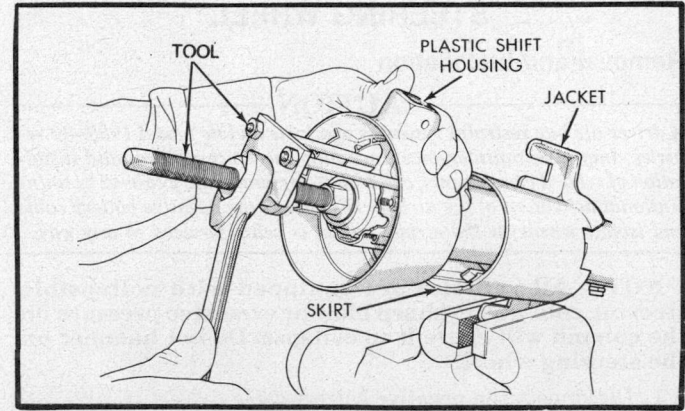

Removal of plastic shift housing

NEUTRAL SAFETY SWITCH

Removal and Installation

1. Disconnect the negative battery terminal.
2. Raise the vehicle and support it safely.
3. The neutral safety switch is located on the left side of the automatic transmission case. Fluid will drain from the transmission when the switch is unscrewed and removed.
4. Clean any dirt or grease from around the area of the switch.

NOTE: Care must be taken as not to allow dirt to enter the transmission.

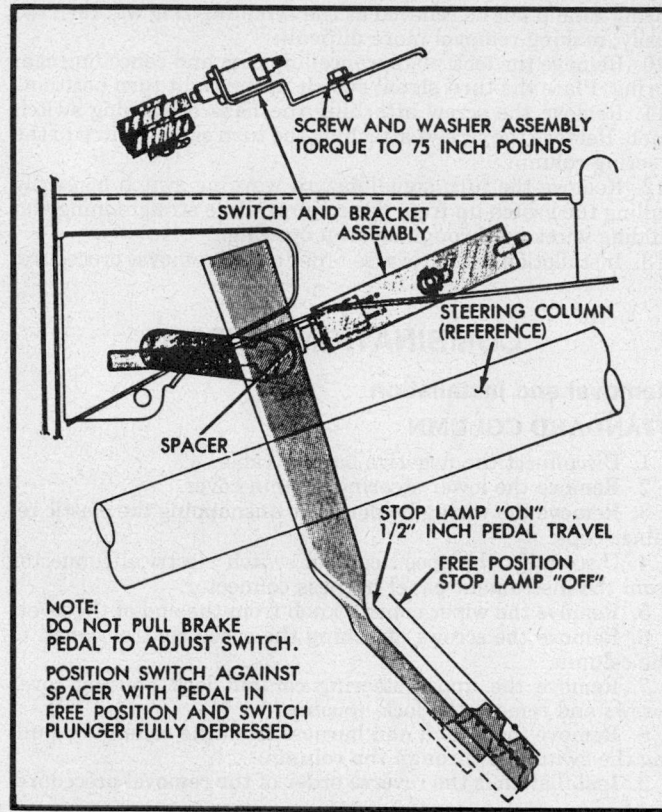

SCREW AND WASHER ASSEMBLY
TORQUE TO 75 INCH POUNDS

SWITCH AND BRACKET
ASSEMBLY

STEERING COLUMN
(REFERENCE)

SPACER

STOP LAMP "ON"
1/2" INCH PEDAL TRAVEL

FREE POSITION
STOP LAMP "OFF"

NOTE:
DO NOT PULL BRAKE
PEDAL TO ADJUST SWITCH.

POSITION SWITCH AGAINST
SPACER WITH PEDAL IN
FREE POSITION AND SWITCH
PLUNGER FULLY DEPRESSED

Stoplight switch adjustment—typical

5. Place a drain pan under the transmission, unscrew the neutral safety switch and allow the fluid drain out.

6. When installing the neutral safety switch, install a new seal and screw the neutral safety switch into the transmission. Torque the neutral safety switch to 25 ft. lbs. and replenish lost fluid.

STOPLIGHT SWITCH

The stoplight switch or stop light/speed control switch and mounting bracket, are attached to the brake pedal bracket. (Vehicles equipped with speed control, the stop light switch is a combined unit).

Adjustment

1. Loosen the switch assembly pedal-to-bracket screw and slide the assembly away from the pedal blade or striker plate.

2. Depress the brake pedal and allow it to return to free position, do not pull the brake pedal back at any time.

3. Position a spacer gauge on the pedal striker plate. A clearance of 0.130–0.150 in. (3.302–3.810mm) is required for vehicles without speed control and 0.060–0.080 (1.542–2.032mm) is required for vehicles equipped with cruise control.

4. Slide the switch assembly toward the pedal striker until the switch plunger is fully depressed against the spacer gauge (on heavy duty or stop light/speed control switches, depress the plunger until the switch body contacts the feeler gauge).

5. Tighten the switch bracket screw to 75 inch lbs. (8 Nm).

6. Remove the spacer gauge and check operation. Be sure the stop light switch does not prevent full pedal return.

Removal and Installation

1. Disconnect the negative battery cable.

2. Remove the switch assembly pedal-to-bracket attaching screw and remove the switch and bracket as an assembly.

3. Remove the switch-to-bracket retaining nut and disassemble the switch from the bracket.

4. Installation is the reverse order of the removal procedure. Adjust the switch.

HEADLAMP SWITCH

Removal and Installation

1. Disconnect negative battery cable.
2. Remove the instrument cluster bezel.
3. Remove the mounting screws from switch module and pull assembly away from panel.
4. To remove the knob and stem assembly, depress the headlight switch stem release button and pull assembly from switch.
5. Disconnect electrical wiring.
6. Remove the switch from the vehicle.
7. Installation is the reverse order of the removal procedure.

DIMMER SWITCH

Removal and Installation

1. Disconnect the negative battery cable.
2. Remove the steering column lower cover.
3. Disconnect the electrical connector from the switch.
4. Remove the dimmer switch retaining nuts. Disengage the switch from the actuating rod. Remove the switch from the vehicle.
5. Install the switch to its proper mounting. Insert two $3/32$ in. drill shanks through the alignment holes.
6. Install the actuator rod into the washer/wiper switch pocket. Once the switch is installed, remove the drill shanks.

TURN SIGNAL SWITCH

Removal and Installation

STANDARD COLUMN

1. Disconnect the negative battery cable. Remove the steering wheel and the steering column cover.

2. Remove sound deadening insulation panel and lower instrument panel bezel.

3. Loosen the Allen screw on the gearshift housing and remove the gearshift indicator.

4. Place the gearshift lever in full clockwise position.

5. Pry out the plastic buttons retaining wiring the harness holder to the column. Remove the harness holder.

6. Disconnect wiring connector from switch. Wrap the connector with tape to prevent snagging when removing the switch.

7. Remove the screw holding the turn signal lever assembly to the turn signal switch pivot. Leave the assembly in its installed location.

8. Remove the screws and bearing retainer fastening the turn signal switch to the upper bearing housing.

9. Remove the turn signal/hazard warning switch by gently pulling the switch up from the column while straightening and guiding wires up through column opening.

10. Installation is the reverse order of the removal procedure.

TILT COLUMN

1. Disconnect the negative battery cable. Remove the steering wheel and the steering column cover.

2. Remove the sound deadening insulation panel and lower instrument panel bezel.

3. Loosen the Allen screw on the gearshift housing and remove the gearshift indicator.

4. Place the gearshift lever in full clockwise position and tilt position at mid-point.

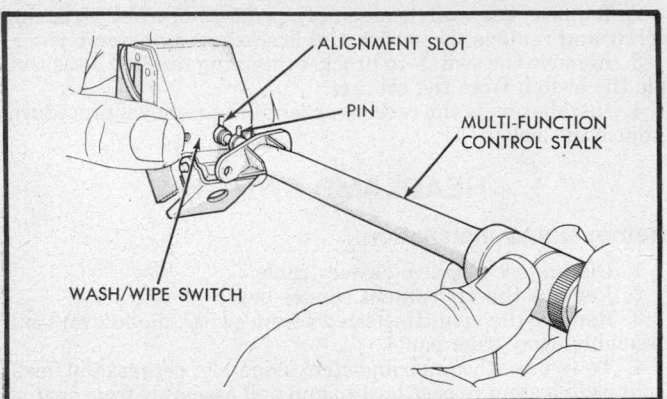

Multi-function control stalk removal or installation

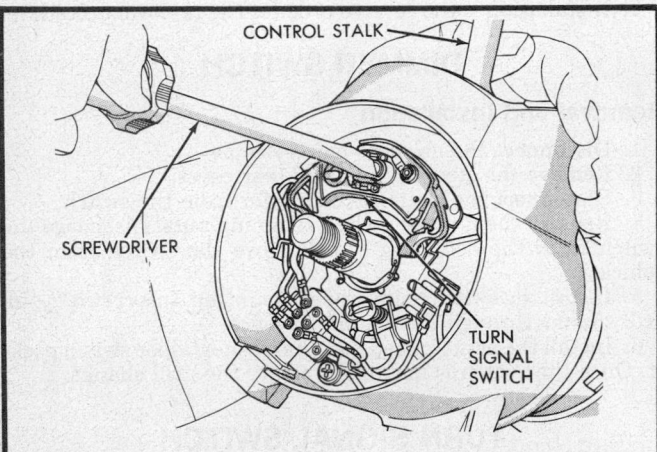

Turn signal switch removal or installation

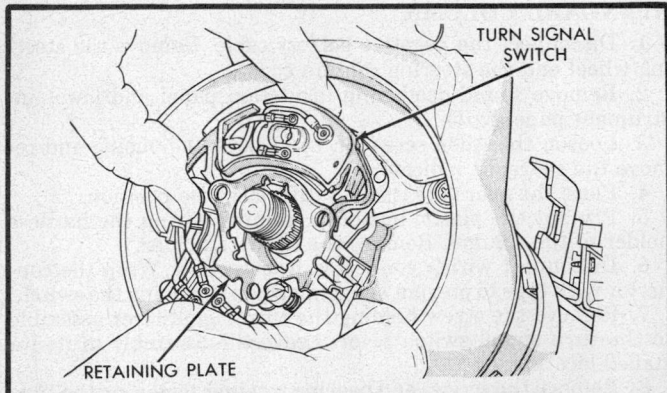

Removal or installation of retainer and turn signal switch

5. Remove the nuts retaining the column to the lower panel reinforcement.

6. Remove the steering column mounting bracket retaining bolts and remove the bracket from the column.

7. Pry out plastic buttons retaining wiring holder to the column and remove the holder.

8. Disconnect wiring connector from switch. Wrap the connector with tape to prevent snagging when removing the switch.

9. Remove the plastic cover from the lock plate. Depress the lock plate using a lock plate depressing tool and pry the retaining ring out of the groove. The full load of the upper bearing

spring should not be relieved as the retaining ring will turn too easily, making removal more difficult.

10. Remove the lock plate, cancelling cam and cancelling cam spring. Place the turn signal switch in the right turn position.

11. Remove the screw attaching the hazard warning switch knob. Remove the screws attaching the turn signal switch to the steering column.

12. Remove the turn signal/hazard warning switch by gently pulling the switch up from the column while straightening and guiding wires up through column opening.

13. Installation is the reverse order of the removal procedure.

COMBINATION SWITCH

Removal and Installation
STANDARD COLUMN

1. Disconnect the negative battery cable.

2. Remove the lower steering column cover.

3. Remove the wiring holder after unsnapping the plastic retainer clips.

4. Disconnect the speed control switch electrical connector from the instrument panel harness connector.

5. Remove the wiper control knob from the end of the lever.

6. Remove the screws attaching the speed control switch to the column.

7. Remove the upper steering column lock housing cover screws and remove the lock housing.

8. Remove the switch and harness from the column by pulling the switch up through the column.

9. Installation is the reverse order of the removal procedure.

TILT COLUMN

1. Disconnect the negative battery cable.

2. Remove the lower steering column cover.

3. Remove the steering column mounting nuts and lower the column down from the instrument panel taking care not to damage the gear indicator wire.

4. Remove the plastic screws attaching the support bracket to the column jacket.

5. Unsnap the plastic retainer clips and remove the wiring harness holder.

6. Disconnect the speed control switch electrical connector from the instrument panel harness connector.

7. Remove the wiper control knob from the end of the lever.

6. Remove the screws attaching the speed control switch to the column.

8. Remove the steering wheel and attach a flexible guide wire to the lower end of the speed control switch harness.

9. Pull the switch wires up through the lock housing between the lock plate and side of the housing.

10. Disconnect the guide wire from the harness and remove the switch.

11. Installation is the reverse order of the removal procedure.

WINDSHIELD WIPER SWITCH

Removal and Installation

1. Disconnect the negative battery cable.

2. Remove the steering wheel.

3. With tilt wheel only, remove the lock plate cover and the lock plate.

4. Remove the lower instrument panel bezel.

5. With tilt wheel only:
   a. Remove the gear shift indicator.
   b. Remove the nuts retaining the column to the lower panel reinforcement.
   c. Remove the mounting bracket from the steering column after removing the retaining bolts.

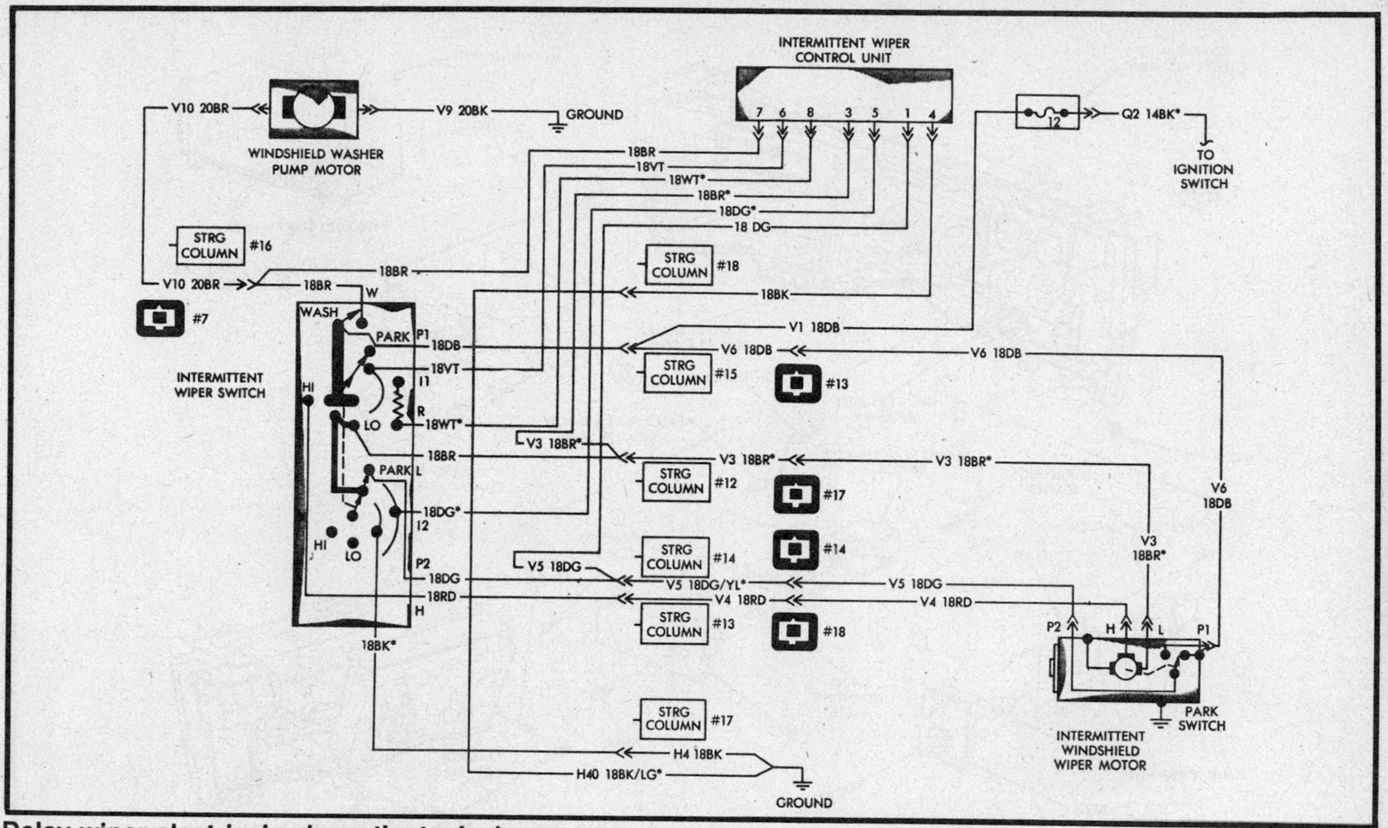

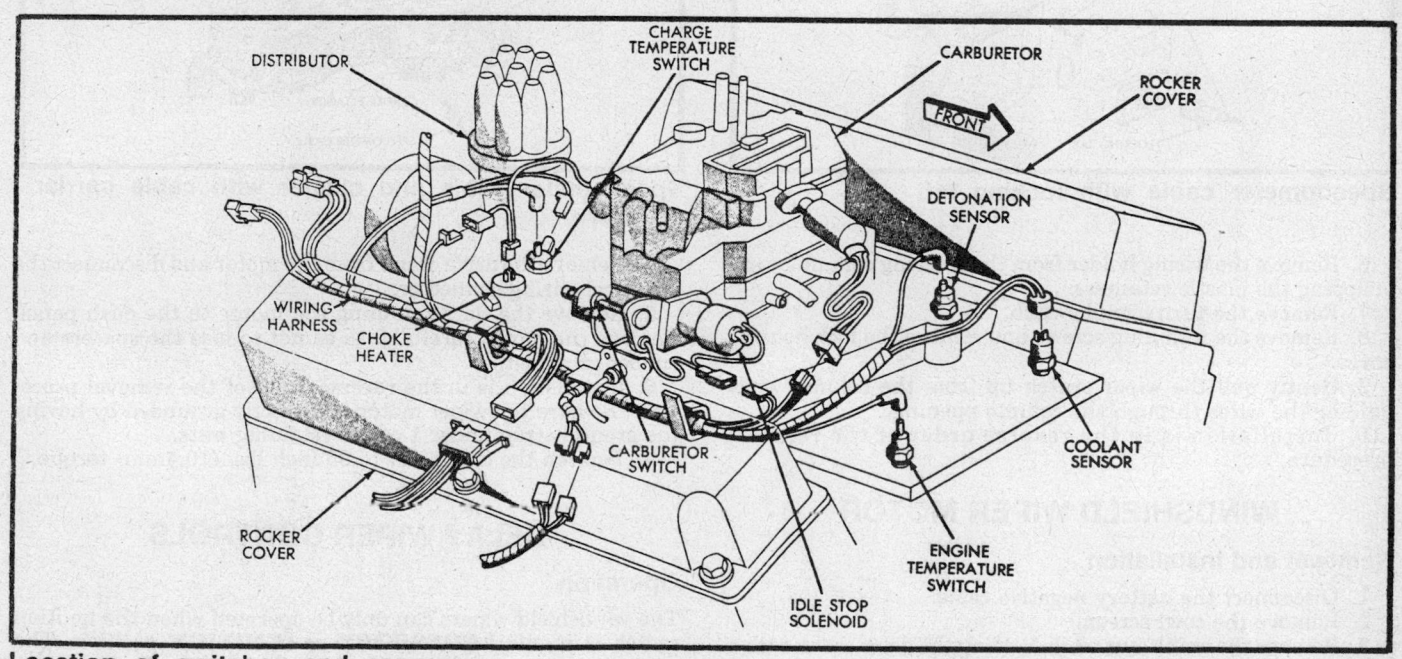

Delay wiper electrical schematic, typical

Location of switches and sensors

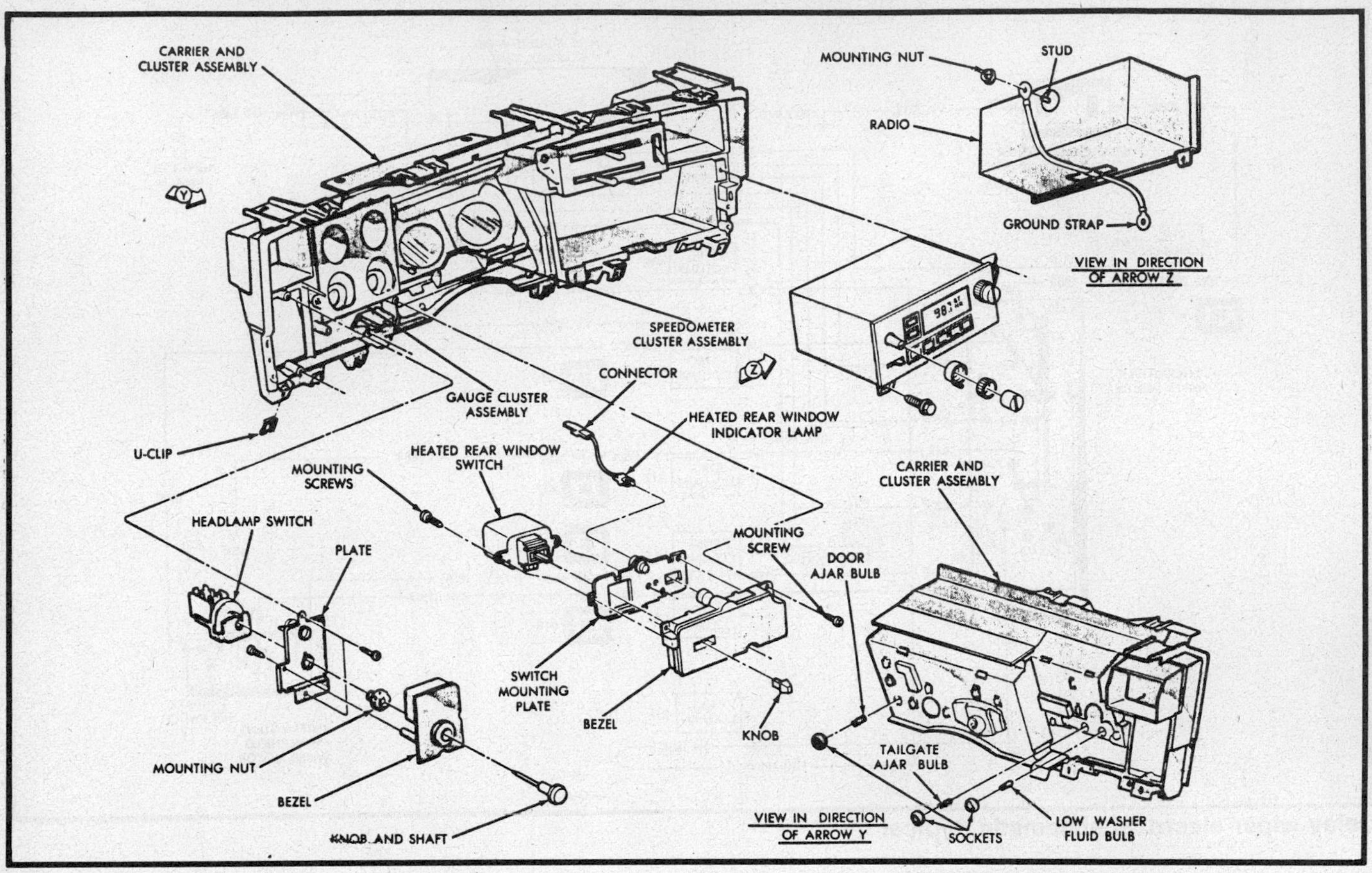

Instrument panel, typical

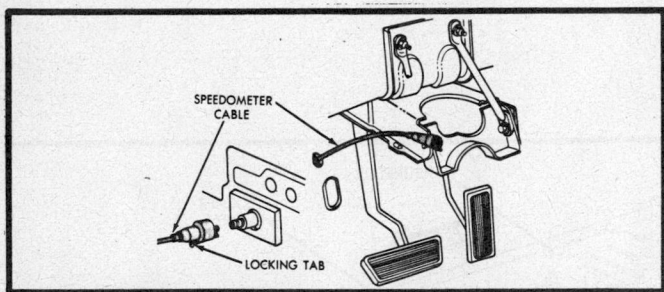

Speedometer cable with locking tab

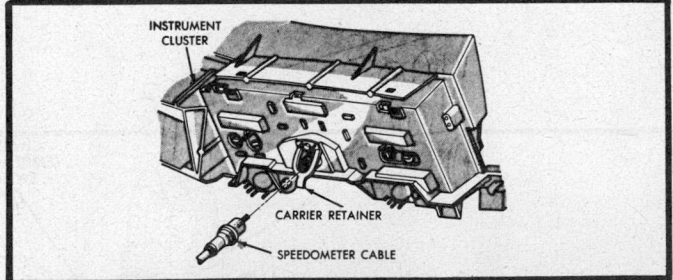

Speedometer cable and cluster with cable carrier retainer

6. Remove the wiring holder from the steering column by unsnapping the plastic retainers.

7. Remove the turn signal switch.

8. Remove the retaining screws and remove the lock housing cover.

9. Gently pull the wiper switch up from the column while guiding the wires through the column opening.

10. Installation is in the reverse order of the removal procedure.

WINDSHIELD WIPER MOTOR

Removal and Installation

1. Disconnect the battery negative cable.

2. Remove the cowl screen.

3. Remove the crank-nut while holding the drive crank with a wrench to prevent overloading the gears.

4. Remove the drive crank from the motor and disconnect the electrical wiring connector.

5. Remove the nuts retaining the motor to the dash panel. Remove the motor carefully, so as not to lose the spacers and rubber grommet.

6. Installation is in the reverse order of the removal procedure. Be sure the wiper motor is correctly grounded by having the ground strap under 1 of the retaining nuts.

7. Tighten the crank nut to 95 inch lbs. (10.4mm) torque.

DELAY WIPER CONTROLS

Operation

The windshield wipers can only be operated when the ignition switch is in the **ACCESSORY** or **IGNITION** position. The wiper motor incorporates permanent magnet fields. The wiper

CAVITY	FUSE/COLOR	ITEMS FUSED
1	20 AMP YL	HAZARD FLASHERS
2	5 AMP TN / 20 AMP YL	HEATED REAR WINDOW & SPEED CONTROL ELECTRIC DECKLID RELEASE
3	30 AMP C/BRKR SILVER CAN	POWER WINDOWS & ILLUMINATED ENTRY RELAY
4	30 AMP LG	A/C & HEATER WITH HI-LO (B) BLOWER MOTOR
5	20 AMP YL	CAV 13, PARK SIDE MARKER, OPERA, TAIL & LICENSE LAMPS, ELECTRONIC SEARCH TUNE, DISPLAY INTENSITY
6	20 AMP YL	STOP, DOME, DOOR & UNDERPANEL COURTESY, MAP, VANITY MIRROR, TRUNK, CARGO & DOOR KEY CYLINDER LAMPS IGNITION TIME DELAY RELAY, KEY-IN BUZZER & ELECTRONIC CHIMES, ILLUMINATED ENTRY
7	20 AMP YL	GLOVE BOX LAMP HORNS, HORN RELAY, CIGAR LIGHTER, AUTOMATIC POWER ANTENNA CONTROLLER, CLOCK & SEARCH TUNE RADIO MEMORY
8	30 AMP C/BRKR SILVER CAN	POWER DOOR LOCKS & SEATS
9	20 AMP YL	RIGHT SPOT LIGHT
10	20 AMP YL	LEFT SPOT LIGHT
11	5 AMP TN	BRAKE WARNING, LOW OIL PRESSURE, SEAT BELT DOOR AJAR & LIFTGATE AJAR LAMPS FUEL & TEMPERATURE GAUGE, VOLTAGE LIMITER & SEAT BELT BUZZER
12	20 AMP YL	WINDSHIELD WIPER
13	3 AMP VT	CLUSTER, HEADLAMP SWITCH, A/C & HEATER CONTROL, HEATED REAR WINDOW, ASH RECEIVER, RADIO LAMPS, CLOCK, SEARCH TUNE RADIO DISPLAY DIMMING

CAVITY	FUSE/COLOR	ITEMS FUSED
14	6 AMP C/BRKR GOLD CAN / 20 AMP YL	POLICE RELAY PACKAGE / ELECTRIC DECK LID RELEASE
15	5 AMP TN	RADIO, CLOCK DISPLAY & POWER ANTENNA CONTROLLER SENSE
16	20 AMP YL	BACK-UP & TURN SIGNAL LAMPS A/C CLUTCH & SOLENOID IDLE STOP

AMPS	FUSE	COLOR CODE
3	VT	VIOLET
4	PK	PINK
5	TN	TAN
10	RD	RED
20	YL	YELLOW
25	NAT	NATURAL
30	LG	LIGHT GREEN

FUSE BLOCK AND RELAY BANK
HAZARD FLASHER
TIME DELAY RELAY
30 AMP CIRCUIT BREAKERS
TURN SIGNAL FLASHER
6 AMP CIRCUIT BREAKER
HORN RELAY

Fuse block and relay module, typical

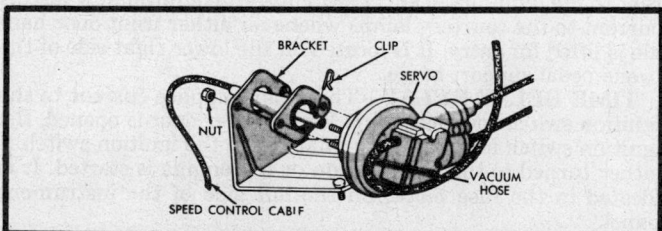

Removal of throttle cable cover

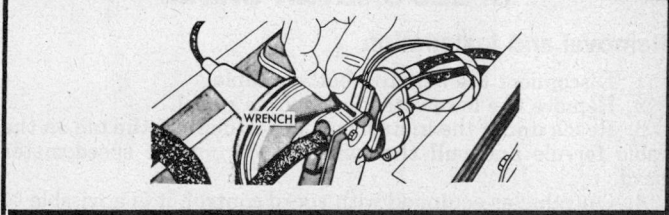

Adjusting lock-in screw

Inspecting for engine vacuum

motor speeds are determined by current flow to the appropriate set of brushes.

The intermittent wipe system in addition to the low and high speed, has a delay mode. The delay mode has a range of 2–15 seconds. This is accomplished by a variable resister in the wiper switch and is controlled electrically by a relay.

The intermittent wiper module is located on the lower reinforcement, directly below the instrument cluster. To test the intermittent wiper switch, first disconnect the switch wires from the body wiring at the connector. Using a continuity tester or an ohmmeter, test for continuity between the terminals.

WINDSHIELD WIPER LINKAGE

Removal and Installation

1. Remove the drive crank from the wiper motor and the drive link.
2. Remove the pivot assembly mounts and remove the linkage assembly.
3. Installation is the reverse order of the removal procedure.

Instrument Cluster

Refer to "Chilton's Electronic Instrumentation Service Manual" for additional coverage.

Removal and Installation

1. Disconnect the negative battery cable.
2. Remove the instrument cluster bezel.

3. Loosen the shift pointer set screw and remove the pointer.
4. From under the dash, disconnect the speedometer cable.

NOTE: The speedometer cables are attached to the speedometer by a snap-on plastic ferrule, which attaches directly to the speedometer head and must be disconnected before the speedometer or cluster can be removed.

5. Remove the cluster retaining screws and pull the cluster away from the carrier. Disconnect the electrical wiring.
6. Remove the cluster assembly from the dash.
7. Installation is the reverse order of the removal procedure.

SPEEDOMETER

Removal and Installation

NOTE: The disassembly of the cluster and speedometer will vary to a small degree from each car line to another. It is most important to mask surfaces which may become scratched or damaged during the disassembly or assembly procedures. Extreme care should be exercised when handling the internal components of the speedometer/cluster assembly. The electronic units cannot be repaired, but must be replaced.

1. Disconnect the negative battery cable. Remove the instrument cluster.
2. Remove the cluster and the printed circuit board assembly from the carrier.
3. Remove the trip odometer knob from the shaft.
4. Remove the plastic pins and pull the lens and mask assembly away from the cluster housing.
5. Remove the screws retaining the speedometer to the cluster housing and the remove speedometer.
6. Disconnect the connector-to-odometer switch, if equipped.
7. Installation is the reverse order of the removal procedure.

SPEEDOMETER CABLE

Removal and Installation

1. Disconnect the negative battery cable.
2. Remove the lower steering column panel.
3. Reach under the instrument panel, depress the tab on the cable ferrule and pull the cable away from the speedometer head.
4. On vehicles equipped with speed control, it is advisable to first disconnect the cable from the speed control in order to provide additional working cable length at the speedometer head.
5. Installation is the reverse order of the removal procedure.

Electrical Circuit Protectors

FUSIBLE LINKS

The fusible links are used to prevent major damage to wire harnesses in the event of a short circuit or an overload condition in the wiring circuits which normally are not fused, due to carrying high amperage loads or because of their locations within the wiring harness. Each fusible link is of a fixed value for a specific electrical load and should the link fail, the cause of the failure must be determined and repaired prior to installing a new fusible link of the same value.

When replacing fusible links connected to the battery terminal or starter relay, they should be serviced with the same type of prefabricated fusible link. All other fusible links can be replaced with fusible link wire cut from bulk rolls.

NOTE: When replacing fusible links, use only rosin core solder. Do not use acid core solder.

CIRCUIT BREAKERS

Circuit breakers are used in varied circuits to control amperage surges and if the circuit is opened, to re-set themselves as the heat from the current flow load has diminished. Should a continual interruption of power be experienced when operation of a controlled electrical component is attempted, repairs to the circuits/components or replacement of the component must be accomplished. Circuit breakers are located in the fuse panel and, if necessary, can be changed quickly by pulling the assembly from the fuse panel and inserting a new one in its place.

FUSE PANEL

The relays and circuit breakers are located on the fuse panel. The fuse panel is located on the left side of the passenger compartment, either mounted to the underside of the dash panel or to the inner side of the firewall panel.

COMPUTER

The computer is located on the carburetor air cleaner. Should it become necessary to replace the computer, remove the mounting screws from inside the air cleaner. Do not take the computer apart for any reason. It is not serviceable and must be replaced as an assembly.

VARIOUS RELAYS

ACCESSORY POWER RELAY—This relay supplies current to the dash bulk head and related accessories. It is located on the left side of the brake pedal support bracket.

STARTER RELAY—This relay supplies current directly from the battery to the starter solenoid. It is located in the upper left side of the firewall.

ILLUMINATED ENTRY RELAY—This relay supplies current to the illuminated entry switches, which ultimately directs current to the courtesy lamps whenever either front door handle is lifted for entry. It is located on the lower right side of the brake pedal support brace.

TIME DELAY RELAY—This relay supplies current to the ignition switch courtesy lamp. When either door is opened, the ignition switch lamp will illuminate until the ignition switch is either turned to the **ON** position or the engine is started. It is located in the fuse block, on the left side of the instrument panel.

HORN RELAY—This relay supplies current to the horn switch. The horn relay is located in the fuse block on the left side of the instrument panel.

TURN SIGNAL FLASHER/HAZARD WARNING FLASHER—Both the turn signal and hazard warning system flashers are mounted to the fuse panel. Both can be removed and replaced by simply pulling the flasher from the fuse panel and installing a new one in its place.

SPEED CONTROLS

Refer to "Chilton's Chassis Electronics Service Manual" for additional coverage.

Adjustment
SPEED CONTROL CABLE

1. Have the engine at normal operating temperature with the choke off and the engine speed at curb idle.
2. Remove the spring clip from the lost motion link stud. The clearance between the stud and the cable clevis should be $1/16$ in.
3. Insert a gauge pin ($1/16$ in.) between the cable clevis and the stud. Loosen the clip at the cable support bracket.

4. Pull all the slack from the cable, but do not pull the throttle away from the curb idle position.

5. Tighten the clip at the cable support bracket to 45 inch lbs. torque.

6. Remove the gauge pin and install the spring clip on the stud of the lost motion link.

SERVO LOCK-IN SCREW

1. If the set speed drops more than 2–3 mph, or speed increase of more than 2–3 mph when the speed control is activated, the lock-in adjusting screw can be adjusted.

2. It must be remembered that lock-in accuracy will be affected by poor engine performance, power to weight ratio (loaded or empty vehicle), or improper slack in the throttle control cable.

3. Adjust the lock-in screw counterclockwise for an increase in speed correction of approximately 1 mph per ¼ turn of the lock-in screw.

4. Adjust the lock-in screw clockwise for a decrease in speed correction of approximately 1 mph per ¼ turn of the lock-in screw.

NOTE: This adjustment must not exceed 2 turns in either direction, or damage to the servo unit may occur.

Troubleshooting

ROAD TEST

A road test should be made to determine what malfunctions are occurring to the speed control system. Particular attention should be directed to the speedometer operation, which should be smooth and without flutter at all speeds. Speedometer problems must be corrected before other repairs to the system are made.

ELECTRICAL TEST

The electrical input should be checked at the servo with the use of a test lamp tool. Typical electrical schematics are included to aid in the electrical diagnosis.

VACUUM TEST

With the engine operating and a vacuum gauge attached to the servo vacuum feed hose, a minimum of 10 in. Hg. must be present.

COOLING AND HEATING SYSTEM

Water Pump

Removal and Installation

1. Disconnect the negative battery cable. Drain the cooling system.

2. Remove the fan shroud screws and move the shroud out of the way.

3. It may be necessary to remove the radiator on some vehicles to obtain the working clearance necessary to remove the water pump.

4. Loosen the alternator mounting bolts. Loosen the mounting bolts for the power steering pump, idler pulley, air conditioning compressor and air pump, if equipped. Remove all the accessory belts.

5. Remove the fan, spacer or fluid drive and the pulley.

NOTE: For fluid-coupled fan drives, do not set the drive unit down with its shaft pointing downward. Keep the unit in a vertical position as installed on the engine. This will prevent the silicone fluid from leaking out.

6. On some vehicles, it may be necessary to remove the alternator or compressor mounting bracket bolts from the water pump to swing the alternator or compressor out of the way. Keep the compressor in an upright position.

7. On some vehicles, it may be necessary to unbolt the power steering pump and set it aside, leaving the hoses connected. Also remove the air pump and brackets, if so equipped.

8. Detach the hoses from the water pump. Remove the bolts which secure the water pump body to its engine block housing. Remove the water pump and discard the gasket.

9. Install the bypass hose to the pump with the second clamp temporarily in the center of the hose. Install the water pump with a new gasket, using sealer. Torque the bolts to 30 ft. lbs. (40.7 Nm).

10. Rotate the pump shaft by hand to be sure it rotates freely. Install the alternator or compressor mounting bracket to the pump if either was removed. Install the pulley, spacer or fluid drive and the fan. Torque the nuts to 15 ft. lbs. (20.3 Nm).

11. Reinstall all accessory drive belts. Adjust them to get about ½ in. of play under moderate thumb pressure on the longest run of belt between pulleys.

12. Install the radiator if previously removed.

13. Install the fan shroud. Fill the cooling system to 1¼ in. below the filler neck with correct water and antifreeze mixture, without a coolant reserve tank. With a reserve tank, fill the radiator and fill the tank to the indicated level. Warm up the engine with the heater on and inspect the water pump for any leaks. Check the coolant level and add as required.

Blower Motor

NOTE: Blower motor service is accomplished from inside the vehicle, under the right side of the instrument panel.

Removal and Installation

FIFTH AVENUE, DIPLOMAT AND GRAN FURY EXCEPT NEWPORT

1. Disconnect the battery ground cable.

2. Remove the blower motor feed and ground wires at the connector.

3. Remove the blower motor mounting nuts from the bottom of the recirculation housing or separate lower blower housing from upper housing.

4. Lower the blower motor assembly downward from under the instrument panel.

5. Remove the blower motor mounting plate screws.

6. Separate the blower motor housing from the blower motor and fan assembly housing.

7. When installing, set the blower motor and fan assembly into the blower motor housing and install the housing to mounting plate screws.

8. Position the blower assembly up into the recirculation housing and install the retaining nuts.

9. Install the blower motor feed and ground wire connector.

10. Install the battery ground cable.

11. Test the blower motor operation on all fan speeds.

NEWPORT

1. Disconnect the negative battery cable.

2. Remove the glove box assembly.

3. Disconnect the blower motor feed and ground wires at the resistor block.

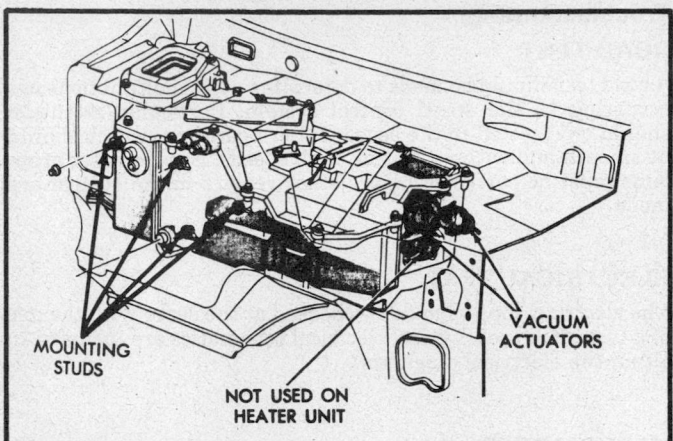

Front view of the heater and A/C system—Fury/Diplomat

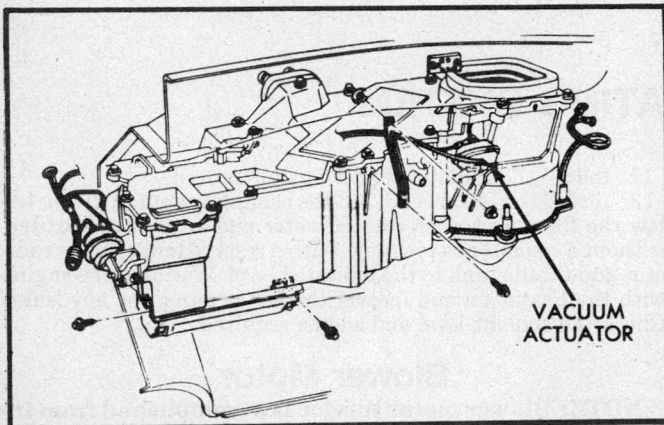

Rear view of the heater and A/C system—Fury/Diplomat

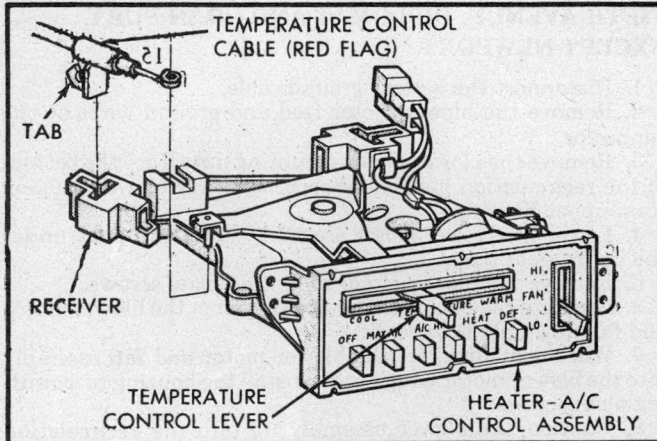

Temperature control, pushbutton type

4. Remove the heater assembly to plenum mounting brace.
5. Remove the screws fastening the blower motor assembly to the heater housing.
6. Remove the blower motor assembly.
7. When installing the blower motor, position and fasten the blower motor assembly to the heater housing.
8. Install the brace from the heater assembly to plenum.

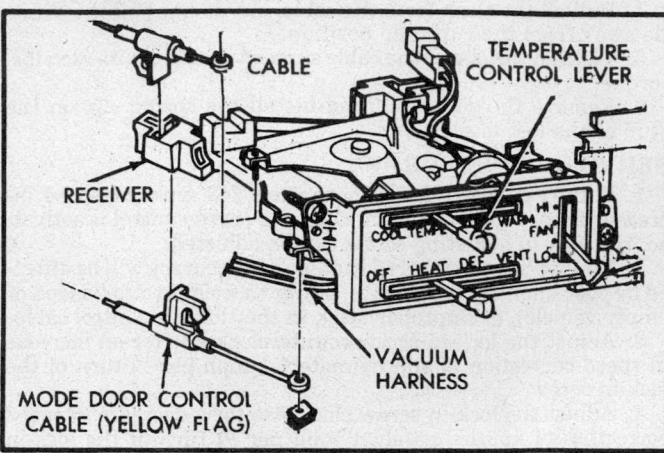

Temperature control, lever type

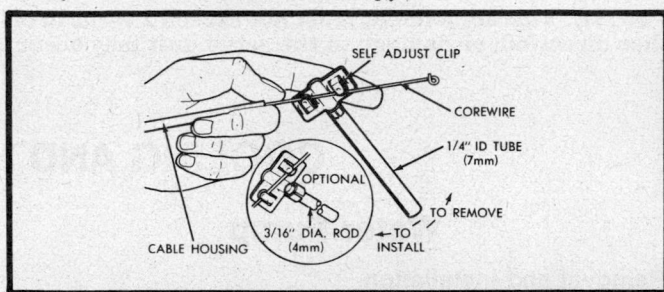

Removing or installing self-adjusting clip using an assist rod

9. Install the blower motor feed and ground wires on the resistor block.
10. Install the glove box assembly.
11. Install the negative battery cable and check the operation of the blower motor.

Heater Core

Refer to "Chilton's Auto Heating and Air Conditioning Manual" for additional coverage.

Removal and Installation

1. Disconnect the negative battery cable.
2. Discharge the air condition system.
3. Drain the radiator coolant.
4. Remove the air cleaner and disconnect the heater hoses. Plug the core tubes to prevent spillage.
5. Remove the H-type expansion valve.
6. Slide the front seat all the way back.
7. Remove the instrument cluster bezel assembly.
8. Remove the instrument panel upper cover by removing the mounting screws at the top inner surface of the glove box, above the instrument cluster, at the left end cap mounting, at the right side of the pad brow and in the defroster outlets.
9. Remove the steering column cover (the instrument panel piece under the column).
10. Remove the right intermediate side cowl trim panel. Remove the lower instrument panel (the part with the glove box). Remove the instrument panel center to lower reinforcement.
11. Remove the floor console, if so equipped.
12. Remove the right center air distribution duct. Detach the locking tab on the defroster duct.
13. Disconnect the temperature control cable from the housing. Disconnect the blower motor resistor block wiring.
14. Detach the vacuum lines from the water valve and tee in

the engine compartment. Detach the wiring from the evaporator housing. Remove the vacuum lines from the inlet air housing and disconnect the vacuum harness coupling.

15. Remove the drain tube in the engine compartment. Remove the mounting nuts from the firewall.

16. Remove the hanger strap from the rear of the evaporator and plenum stud.

17. Roll the heater/air condition unit back so the pipes clear and remove it.

18. Remove the blend air door lever from the shaft. Remove the screws and lift off the top cover. Lift the heater core out.

19. When installing the heater core, place the evaporator housing on the front floor under the instrument panel.

20. Tip the evaporator housing up under instrument panel and press mounting studs through the dash panel, making sure the defroster duct and air condition distribution duct is properly seated on unit and gasket is installed properly. Connect the locking tab on the defroster duct.

21. While holding the housing in position, place the mounting bracket in position to the plenum stud and install the nut.

22. In engine compartment, install retaining nuts and tighten securely. Install condensate drain tube.

23. Connect electrical connectors to the resistor block and connect the control cable.

24. Connect vacuum lines in engine compartment, making sure the grommet is seated. Connect vacuum lines to inlet air housing and vacuum harness coupling.

25. Install right center air distribution duct.

26. Install instrument panel center to lower reinforcement.

27. Install lower instrument panel.

28. Install right intermediate side cowl trim panel.

29. Install steering column cover.

30. Install instrument panel upper cover.

31. Install cluster bezel assembly.

32. From engine compartment, remove plugs from core tubes and connect hoses to heater. Install condensate tube and Corbin clamp.

33. Install H-valve and install refrigerant lines to valve. Replace gaskets.

34. Fill cooling system and inspect for leaks.

35. Install air cleaner and connect battery negative cable.

After the evaporator heater housing assembly is installed in the vehicle, it will be necessary to evacuate and recharge the system with the proper amount of refrigerant. It is recommended, operation of all controls be tested and an overall performance test be made after the repair or replacement of the evaporator assembly.

TEMPERATURE CONTROL BLOWER SWITCH

Removal and Installation

1. Disconnect the negative battery cable.

2. Remove the necessary cluster bezels, radio, if necessary, accessory switch bezel, lower, right or left trim panels and necessary air ducts to expose the heater/air conditioning control unit.

3. Remove the retaining screws and separate the control linkage, vacuum and electrical leads from the control unit. Remove the unit from the dash.

4. To install the control unit, install the control linkage, vacuum and electrical leads to the control unit, install it on the dash and complete the installation in the reverse of the removal order.

CARBURETED FUEL SYSTEM

Fuel Pump

Removal and Installation

1. Disconnect the negative battery cable.

2. Remove the fuel lines from the fuel pump. It may be necessary to plug the line from the tank to prevent fuel from leaking out.

3. Remove the pump-to-block mounting bolts.

4. Remove the pump.

5. Remove the old gasket from the pump and replace with a new gasket during reinstallation.

6. Installation is the reverse order of removal procedure.

FUEL SYSTEM PRESSURE RELIEF

Procedure

1. Place a container under the fuel inlet fitting to catch any fuel that may be trapped in the fuel line.

2. Relieve the fuel pressure by slowly loosening the fuel inlet line, using 2 wrenches to avoid twisting the line.

3. Fuel will spray slightly from the line into the container. Wrap a shop towel around the connection to avoid the spray of fuel.

4. When repairs have been completed, tighten the fuel lines and inspect for fuel leaks.

FUEL FILTER

Removal and Installation

Locate the filter in the fuel line between the fuel pump and the carburetor. Using hose-clamp pliers, remove the attaching clamps and pull the filter off. Reverse this procedure for installation. Be sure the arrow on the filter is pointing toward the carburetor (direction of fuel flow).

NOTE: Some filters have a third line, the purpose of which is to prevent vapor lock by allowing fuel vapors to return to the tank.

Carburetor

Removal and Installation

1. Be sure that the engine is cold before removing the carburetor from the engine. Disconnect the negative battery cable.

2. Remove the air cleaner.

3. Remove the fuel tank pressure vacuum filler cap.

4. Place a container under the fuel inlet fitting to catch any be remaining in the fuel line.

5. Disconnect fuel inlet line using a line wrench and a open end wrench to avoid twisting the line.

6. Disconnect the throttle linkage, choke linkage and all vacuum hoses.

7. Remove the carburetor mounting bolts or nuts and carefully remove the carburetor from the engine compartment. Hold the carburetor level to avoid spilling fuel from fuel bowl.

IDLE SPEED

Adjustment

NOTE: Before checking or adjusting any idle speed, check ignition timing and adjust if necessary.

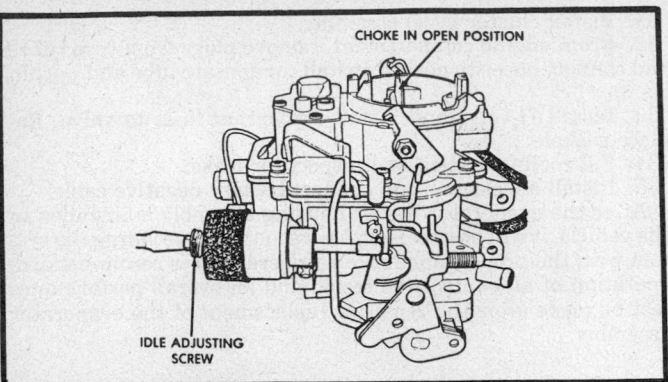

Idle adjustment, Holley 2280/6280

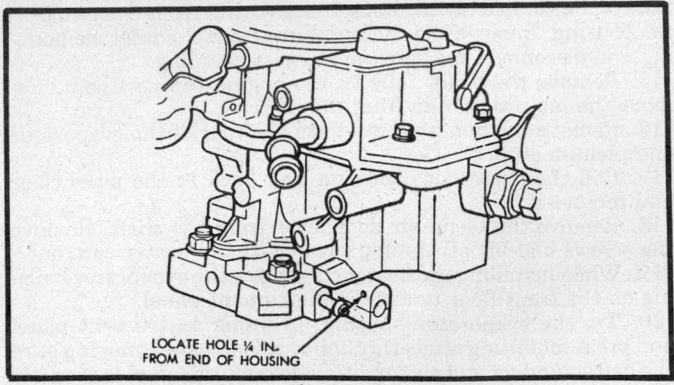

Concealment plug removal, Holley 2280/6280

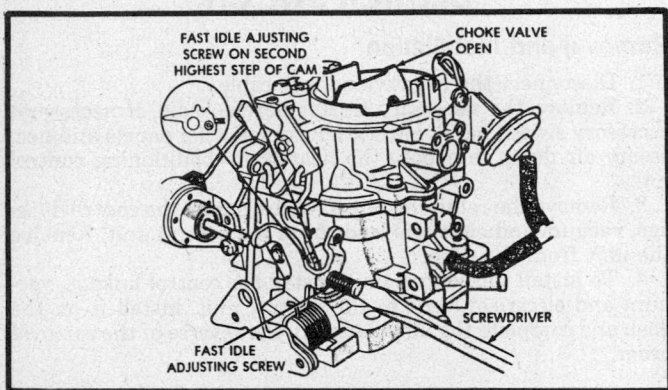

Fast idle adjustment, Holley 2280/6280

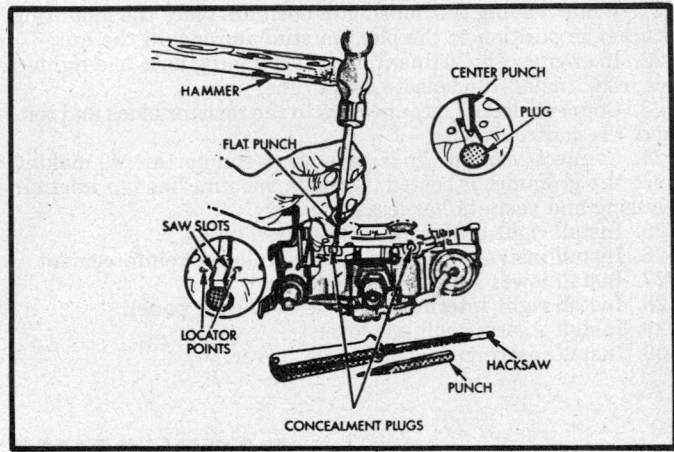

Concealment plug removal, Rochester Quadrajet

HOLLEY 6280 ELECTRONIC FEEDBACK CABURETOR

NOTE: Before checking or adjusting any idle speed, check ignition timing and adjust if necessary.

1. Disconnect and plug the vacuum hose at the EGR valve. Disconnect and plug the hose from the carburetor at the heated air temperature sensor. Remove air cleaner and disconnect and plug the canister purge hose at the canister and plug the vacuum hose at the ESA unit. Remove the PCV valve from the valve cover and allow the valve to draw underhood air. Install tachometer, start and run engine until normal operating temperature is reached. Turn off engine. Disconnect, then reconnect, fusible link at battery.

2. Ground the carburetor switch. Disconnect the engine harness lead from the oxygen sensor and ground the engine harness lead.

NOTE: Care should be exercised so that no pulling force is put on the wire attached to the O₂ sensor. The bullet connector to be disconnected is approximately 4 in. from the sensor. Use care in working around the sensor as the exhaust manifold is extremely hot.

3. Start the engine and allow it to run to fully warm up.
4. Connect a jumper wire between the positive battery terminal and the solenoid idle stop lead wire. Be sure to attach the wire to the right solenoid or damage to the wiring harness will occur.
5. Open throttle slightly to allow solenoid plunger to extend. Remove solenoid outer screw and spring. Insert a ⅛ in. Allen wrench into solenoid and adjust solenoid idle speed.
6. Install the screw and spring. Turn the screw in until it lightly bottoms out. Remove jumper wire. Set the idle speed by turning out solenoid screw.

7. The solenoid rpm is 900 and the idle rpm is 680.
8. Remove the tachometer. Unplug and reconnect all hoses. Reinstall the PCV valve and the air cleaner.

ROCHESTER QUADRAJET ELECTRONIC FEEDBACK CARBURETOR

NOTE: Before checking or adjusting any idle speed, check ignition timing and adjust if necessary.

1. Disconnect and plug the vacuum hose at the EGR valve.
2. Disconnect and plug the hose from the carburetor at the heated air temperature sensor.
3. Remove air cleaner and disconnect and plug the canister purge hose at the canister.
4. Remove the PCV valve from the valve cover and allow the valve to draw underhood air.
5. Install tachometer and start and run engine until normal operating temperature is reached.
6. Disconnect carburetor electrical connector. Attach a jumper wire between the ground switch terminal of the wiring harness connector (violet wire) and a good ground.
7. Attach a jumper wire between solenoid coil terminal of the carburetor connector (red wire) and battery positive post. Open throttle slightly to allow solenoid plunger to extend.
8. Remove outer screw and spring from solenoid. Insert a ⅛ in. Allen wrench into solenoid and adjust solenoid idle speed.
9. The solenoid rpm specification is 800. The idle rpm specification is 750.
10. Install screw and spring and turn in the outer screw until it lightly bottoms out. Remove jumper wire from carburetor connector and battery. Turn the outer solenoid screw until correct idle rpm is obtained.

11. Remove remaining jumper wire and reconnect carburetor connector. Remove tachometer, unplug and reconnect all hoses, reinstall the PCV valve and air cleaner.

IDLE MIXTURE

Adjustment

Tampering with the carburetor is a violation of Federal law. Adjustment of the carburetor idle air/fuel mixture can only be done under certain circumstances, as explained below. Upon completion of the carburetor adjustment, it is important to restore plugs and/or roll pins removed during the servicing of the carburetor.

This procedure should only be used if an idle defect still exists after normal diagnosis has revealed no other faulty condition, such as incorrect basic timing, incorrect idle speed, faulty wire or hose connections, etc. It is also important to make sure the combustion computer system is operating properly. Adjustment of the carburetor air/fuel mixture should be performed, if necessary, after a major carburetor overhaul.

Make all adjustments with engine fully warmed up, transmission in neutral, headlights off, air conditioning compressor not operating, idle stop carburetor switch (if so equipped) grounded with a jumper wire and the vacuum hose at EGR valve (if so equipped) and distributor or spark control unit disconnect and plugged. On ESC equipped vehicles, wait 1 minute after returning to idle before checking timing.

NOTE: Refer to the underhood Emission Control Specification label for any further requirements or late changes in specifications before making carburetor or engine adjustments.

HOLLEY 6280 ELECTRONIC FEEDBACK CARBURETOR

1. Disconnect the negative battery cable.
2. Remove the concealment plug as follows:
   a. Remove air cleaner.
   b. Disconnect all hoses from front of carburetor base.
   c. Remove the carburetor from the engine.
   d. Center punch at a point ¼ in. from end of mixture screw housing.
   e. Drill through outer housing at punch mark with a $^3/_{16}$ in. drill bit.
   f. Pry out and save concealment plug for reinstallation.
   g. Repeat operation on opposite side.
   h. Install the carburetor on the engine.
   i. Install all hoses to the carburetor and proceed to the idle mixture adjustment.
3. Set the parking brake and place the transmission in neutral. Reconnect the negative battery cable. Turn all lights and accessories off. Connect a tachometer to the engine.
4. Start the engine and allow it to warm up on the 2nd highest Step of the fast idle cam until normal operating temperature is reached. Return the engine to idle and turn off engine.
5. Disconnect and plug the vacuum hoses at the EGR valve and ESA computer. No vacuum is to be applied to the computer. Disconnect and plug canister purge hose at canister.
6. Ground carburetor switch. Disconnect, then reconnect, battery fusible link.
7. Disconnect engine harness lead from sensor and ground engine harness lead.

NOTE: Care should be used so that no pulling force is put on the wire attached to the sensor. The bullet connector to be disconnect is approximately 4 in. from the sensor. Use care in working around the sensor, as the exhaust manifold is extremely hot.

8. Start and run engine for at least 4 minutes.
9. Disconnect the vacuum supply hose from the choke dia-

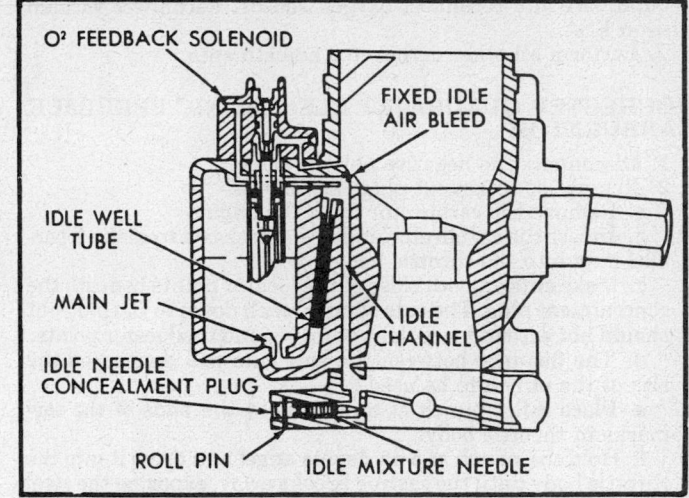

Idle system

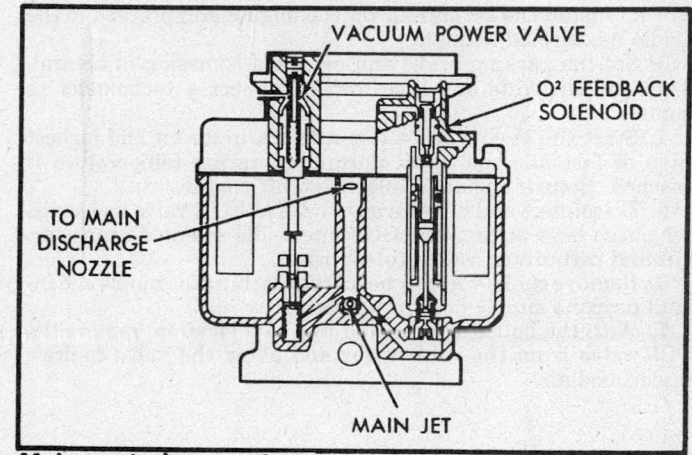

Main metering system

phragm at the carburetor and install the propane supply hose in its place. Other connections at the tee must remain in place.

10. With the propane bottle upright and in a safe location, remove the PCV valve from the valve cover and allow the valve to draw underhood air.

11. Open the propane main valve. Slowly open the propane metering valve until the maximum engine rpm is reached. When too much propane is added, engine rpm will decrease. Fine tune the metering valve to obtain the highest engine rpm.

12. With the propane still flowing, adjust the idle speed screw on the solenoid to obtain the correct propane rpm. Again, Fine tune the metering valve to obtain the highest engine rpm. If there has been a change in the maximum rpm, readjust the idle speed screw to the specified propane rpm.

13. Turn off the propane main valve and allow the engine speed to stabilize. Slowly adjust the mixture screws by equal amounts, pausing between adjustments to allow engine speed to stabilize, to obtain the smoothest idle at the correct idle rpm.

14. The idle rpm specification is 680. The propane rpm is 740.

15. Turn on the propane main valve and Fine tune the metering valve to obtain the highest engine rpm. If the maximum engine speed is more than 25 rpm different than the specified propane rpm, repeat Steps 8–12.

16. Turn off propane main and metering valves. Remove the propane supply hose and reinstall the heated air sensor hose. Reinstall new concealment plugs. If installed, remove sensor

ground wire and reconnect oxygen sensor. Reconnect vacuum line on ESA.

17. Perform all other carburetor adjustments.

ROCHESTER QUADRAJET ELECTRONIC FEEDBACK CARBURETOR

1. Disconnect the negative battery cable.
2. Remove concealment plugs as follows:
    a. Remove the carburetor from the engine.
    b. Invert the carburetor and use a hacksaw to make 2 parallel cuts into the throttle body.
    c. Make cuts on both sides of the locator points beneath the concealment plug. The cuts should reach down to the plug but should not extend more than ⅛ in. beyond the locater points.
    d. The distance between the saw cuts will depend on the size of the punch to be used.
    e. Place a flat punch at a point near the ends of the saw marks in throttle body.
    f. Hold the punch at a 45 degree angel and drive it into the throttle body until the casting breaks away, exposing the steel plug.
    g. Repeat the procedure for the other concealment plug.
    h. Install the carburetor on the engine and proceed to the idle mixture adjustment.
3. Set the parking brake and place transmission in neutral. Turn off all lights and accessories, connect a tachometer to engine.
4. Start the engine and allow it to warm up on 2nd highest Step of fast idle cam until normal operating temperature is reached. Return engine to idle. Turn off engine.
5. Disconnect and plug vacuum hose at EGR valve and canister purge hose at canister. Disconnect idle solenoid connector. Ground carburetor switch (black wire).
6. Remove choke vacuum hose from carburetor nipple and install propane supply hose in its place.
7. With the bottle upright and in a safe location, remove the PCV valve from the valve cover and allow the valve to draw underhood air.

8. Disconnect the engine harness lead from the oxygen sensor and ground the engine harness lead.

NOTE: Care should be used so that no pulling force is put on the wire attached to the oxygen sensor. The bullet connector to be disconnected is approximately 4 in. from the sensor. Use care in working around the sensor, as the exhaust manifold is extremely hot.

9. Reconnect the negative battery cable. Start and run engine for at least 2 minutes to allow effect of disconnecting the sensor to take place. Open propane main valve.
10. Slowly open propane metering valve until maximum engine rpm is reached. When too much propane is added, engine rpm will decrease. Fine tune the metering valve to obtain the highest rpm.
11. With propane still flowing, adjust the idle speed screw on the solenoid to achieve the specified propane rpm. Again, fine tune the metering valve to obtain the highest engine rpm. If there has been a change in the maximum rpm, readjust the idle speed screw on the solenoid to the specified propane rpm.
12. The rpm specification for propane is 800. The rpm specification for idle is 750.
13. Turn off propane main valve and allow engine speed to stabilize. Slowly adjust the idle mixture screws by equal amounts, pausing between adjustments to allow engine speed to stabilize, to achieve the smoothest idle at the specified rpm.
14. Turn on propane main valve. Fine tune the metering valve to obtain the highest engine rpm. If the maximum speed is more than 25 rpm different than the specified rpm, repeat Steps 7–9.
15. Turn off propane main and metering valves. Remove the propane supply hose. Install the PCV valve. Unplug and reconnect all hoses. Remove the jumper wire and reconnect the oxygen sensor.
16. After adjustments are complete, seal the mixture screws in the throttle body using silicone sealant. The sealer is required to discourage unnecessary adjustments of the setting and to prevent fuel vapor loss in that area.
17. Perform all other carburetor adjustments.

EMISSION CONTROL SYSTEMS

Refer to "Chilton's Emission Diagnosis and Service Manual" for additional coverage.

EQUIPMENT USED
Closed crankcase ventilation valve
Heated inlet air system
Evaporation control system with canister storage
Exhaust gas recirculation system
Emission calibrated carburetor

Emission calibrated distributor
Catalytic converter
Fuel tank rollover valve
Electric choke
Orifice spark advance system
Air injection system
Air aspirator system
Pressure-vacuum filler cap
Trap door air cleaner (California)

ENGINE

NOTE: Disconnecting the negative battery cable on some vehicles may interfere with the functions of the on board computer systems and may require the computer to undergo a relearning process, once the negative battery cable is reconnected.

Engine Assembly

Removal and Installation
1. Scribe hood hinge positions and remove the hood.

2. Drain cooling system, remove the battery and carburetor air cleaner.
3. Remove the radiator/heater hoses and remove radiator. Set the fan shroud aside.
4. Remove the air conditioning compressor and set aside without removing lines.
5. Remove vacuum lines, distributor cap and wiring.
6. Remove the carburetor linkage, starter wires and oil pressure wire.
7. Remove the power steering hoses, if so equipped.

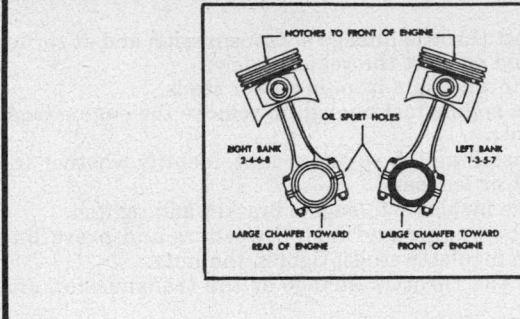

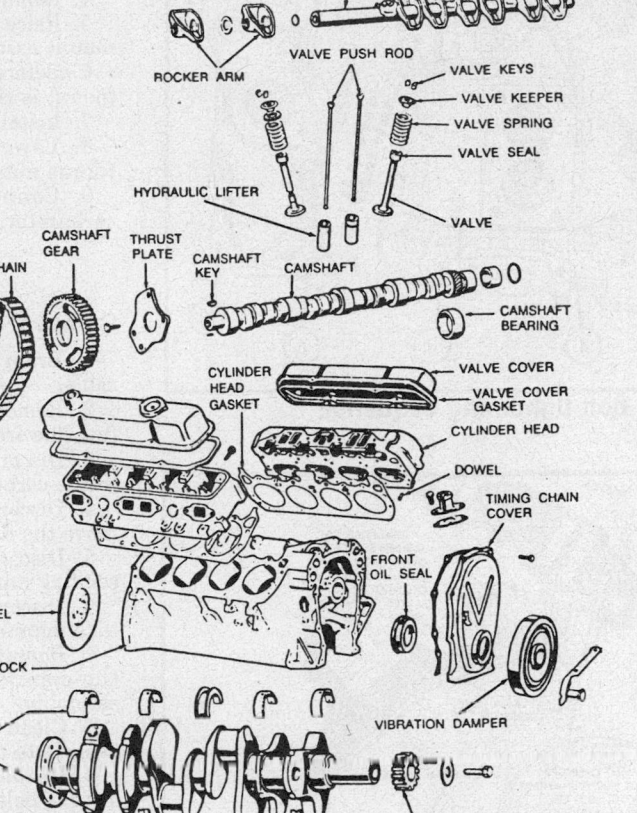

Chrysler V8 engine—exploded view

8. Remove the starter motor, alternator, charcoal canister and horns.

9. Raise and support the vehicle safely.

10. Remove the exhaust pipe at the manifold.

11. Remove the bell housing bolts and inspection plate.

12. Remove the torque converter drive plate bolts from torque converter drive plate. Mark the converter and drive plate to aid in re-assembly.

13. Support the transmission with a transmission stand tool. Attach a C-clamp on front bottom of transmission torque converter housing. This will assure that the torque converter will be retained in proper position in the transmission housing.

14. Disconnect the engine from the torque converter drive plate.

15. Install engine lifting fixture. Attach a chain hoist to fixture eyebolt.

16. Remove engine front mount bolts.

17. Remove engine from engine compartment and support it safely on a engine repair stand.

18. After all repairs have been made, remove engine from repair stand and install in engine compartment.

19. Install bell housing bolts and inspection plate. Remove stand from transmission.

20. Install torque converter drive plate bolts and front end mounts. Remove C-clamp. Install inspection plate.

21. Remove engine lifting fixture and install carburetor and lines.

22. Install starter motor, alternator, charcoal canister and lines.

23. Install vacuum lines, distributor cap and wiring.

24. Install exhaust pipe. Torque to 24 ft. lbs. (33 Nm). Tighten nuts alternately so space between manifold flange and exhaust pipe flange is approximately equal.

25. Connect carburetor linkage and wiring to engine.

26. Install radiator, radiator hoses and heater hoses.

27. Install fan shroud. Fill cooling system.

28. Fill the engine crankcase with approved SAE rated oil.

29. Install the battery and carburetor air cleaner. Connect vacuum hose and power steering hoses, if so equipped.

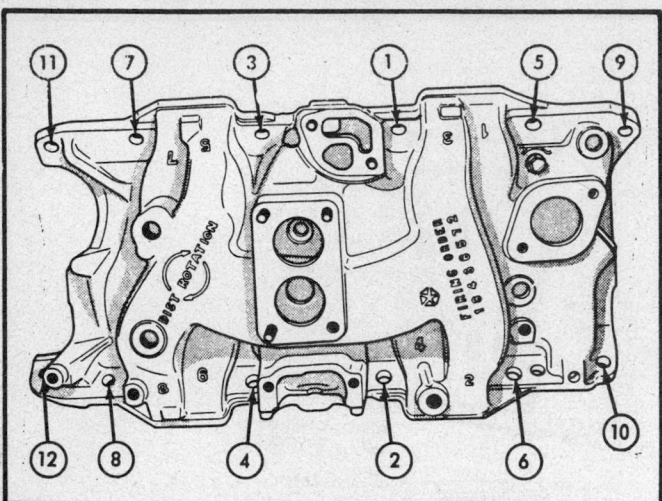

Intake manifold bolt tightening sequence

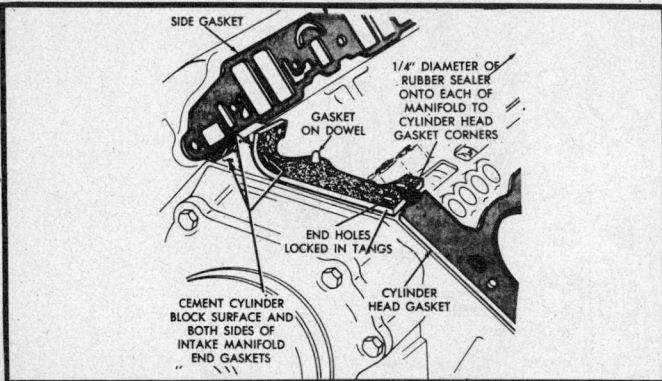

Sealing intake manifold at gasket ends

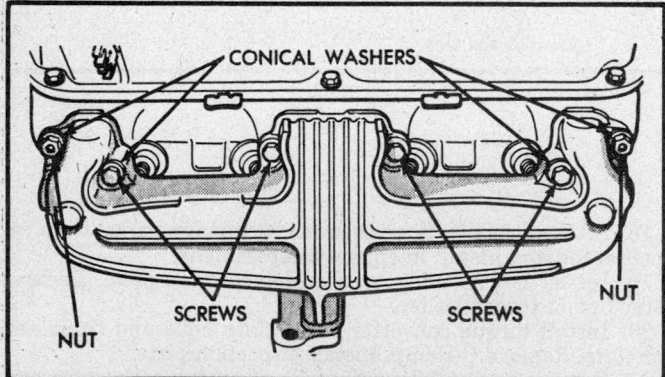

Exhaust manifold fastener locations

30. Install air conditioning equipment, if so equipped.
31. Run engine until full operating temperature is reached and adjust carburetor as necessary.
32. Install hood.
33. Road test vehicle.

Engine Mounts

Removal and Installation

1. Disconnect the negative battery cable.

2. Position the fan to clear the radiator hose and radiator top tank.
3. Disconnect throttle linkage at transmission and at carburetor. Raise and support the vehicle safely.
4. Remove torque nuts from insulator studs.
5. Raise the engine just enough to remove the engine front mount assembly.
6. Before installing the engine mount, identify whether the mount is right or left hand.
7. Install the insulator to engine bracket and tighten.
8. Lower the engine and install washers and prevailing torque nuts to insulator studs; tighten the nuts.
9. Connect the throttle linkage at the transmission and carburetor.

Intake Manifold

Removal and Installation

1. Drain the cooling system. Disconnect the negative battery cable.
2. Remove the alternator, the air cleaner and disconnect the fuel line from the carburetor.
3. Disconnect all vacuum lines and throttle linkage attached to the carburetor and intake manifold.
4. Disconnect the spark plug wires from the plugs and remove the distributor cap and wires as an assembly.
5. Disconnect the wires from the coil and the temperature sending unit.
6. Disconnect the heater hose and by pass hose from the intake manifold.
7. Remove the intake manifold attaching bolts and remove the manifold, carburetor, and coil from the engine as an assembly.
8. Clean all gasket mounting surfaces and firmly cement new gaskets to the engine.
9. Installation is the reverse order of the removal procedure. Torque bolts to 45 ft. lbs. (61 Nm) in 3 passes, in the sequence.

Exhaust Manifold

Removal and Installation

1. Disconnect the negative battery cable.
2. Raise and support the vehicle safely.
3. Disconnect the exhaust manifold at the pipe flange. Access to these bolts is from underneath the vehicle.
4. If so equipped, disconnect the air injection nozzles and carburetor heated air stove.
5. Disconnect any components of the EGR system which are in the way. Remove the exhaust manifold by removing the securing bolts and washers.
6. When the exhaust manifold is removed, sometimes the securing studs will come out with the nuts. If this occurs, studs must be replaced with the aid of sealing compound on the coarse thread ends. If this is not done, water leaks may develop at the studs.
7. Installation is the reverse order of the removal procedure. Torque the bolts to 20 ft. lbs. (27 Nm) and the nuts to 15 ft. lbs. (20 NM).

NOTE: On the center branch of the manifold, no conical washers are used.

Valve System

VALVE ADJUSTMENT

All engines use hydraulic lifters and non-adjustable rocker arms. The lifters take up lash automatically and no adjustment is possible. After engine re-assembly, these lifters adjust themselves shortly after oil pressure builds up.

VALVE LIFTERS

Removal and Installation

EXCEPT ROLLER LIFTERS

1. Disconnect the negative battery cable.
2. Remove valve cover, rocker assembly and pushrods and identify pushrods to insure installation in original location.
3. Slide a lifter extractor tool through the opening in the cylinder head and seat the tool firmly in the head of lifter.

NOTE: Although it is possible to remove the valve lifters without removing the intake manifold, it is recommended the manifold be removed.

4. Pull the lifter out of the bore with a twisting motion. If all lifters are to be removed, identify lifters to insure installation in original locations.

NOTE: The plunger and lifter bodies are not interchangeable. The plunger and valve must always be installed to the original body. It is advisable to work on 1 lifter at a time to avoid mixing of parts. Mixed parts are not compatible. Do not disassemble a lifter on a dirty work bench.

5. To install the lifters, lubricate lifters completely with engine oil.
6. Install lifters and pushrods in their original positions.
7. Install the rocker arm and shaft assembly.
9. Install the valve cover.
9. Start and operate engine. Warm up to normal operating temperature.

NOTE: To prevent damage to valve mechanism, engine must not be run above fast idle until all hydraulic lifters have filled with oil and have become quiet.

ROLLER LIFTERS

1. Disconnect the negative battery cable.
2. Remove the valve cover. Remove the rocker assembly and pushrods. Identify the pushrods to insure proper installation.
3. Remove the intake manifold. Remove the valve lifter yoke retainer and aligning yokes.
4. Remove the valve lifters using a valve lifter removal tool. Identify the lifters to insure proper installation.
5. Repair or replace the valve lifters as required.
6. Installation is the reverse order of the removal procedure.
7. When installing the aligning yokes, make sure the arrow points toward the camshaft. Torque the retaining bolt to 200 inch lbs. (23 Nm).

NOTE: Some vehicles built prior to 10/29/87, may exhibit lifter related noise. This condition can be identified as a single or multiple ticking noise in 1 or both cylinder banks. Remove the head covers on the noisy bank(s) 1 at a time. Check the rocker shaft fastener torques. If loose, retorque and re-check the engine noise. If noise is still present, replace lifters, pushrods and gaskets.

ROCKER ARMS AND SHAFT ASSEMBLY

Removal and Installation

1. Disconnect the negative battery cable.
2. Disconnect the spark plug wires by pulling on the boot straight out in line with the plug.
3. Disconnect closed crankcase ventilation system and evaporation control system from valve cover.

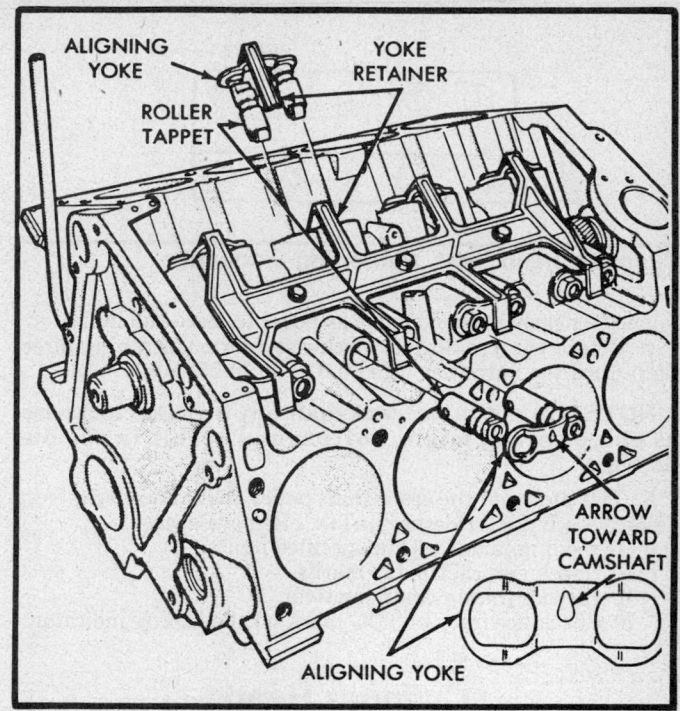

Valve lifter installation

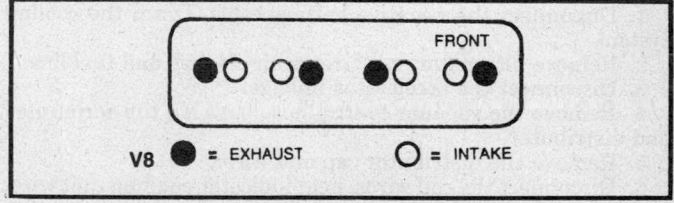

Valve arrangement

4. Remove the valve cover and gasket.
5. Remove rocker shaft bolts and retainers.
6. Remove rocker arms and shaft assembly.
7. Before installing the rocker arm assemblies, check the oil drain holes for blockage.
8. Install the rocker arm and shaft assemblies with the notch of rocker shaft pointing to centerline of engine and toward front of engine on the left bank and to the rear on right bank, making sure to install the long stamped steel retainers in the No. 2 and NO. 4 positions. Tighten bolts to 200 inch lbs. (23 Nm).
9. Clean the valve cover gasket surface. Inspect cover for distortion and flatten if necessary.
10. Clean the head rail if necessary. Install the valve cover and tighten bolts to 80 inch lbs. (9 Nm).
11. Install closed crankcase ventilation system and evaporation control system.

VALVE TIMING

Procedure

1. Remove the valve cover.
1. Turn crankshaft until the No. 6 exhaust valve is closing and No. 6 intake valve is opening.
2. Insert a ¼ in. (6.35mm) spacer between rocker arm pad and stem tip of No. 1 intake valve. Allow spring load to bleed lifter down, giving in effect a solid lifter.
3. Install a dial indicator so plunger contacts valve spring re-

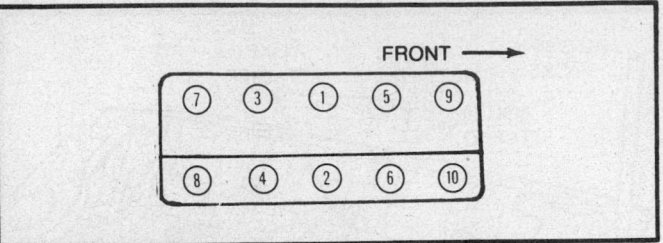

Cylinder head bolt tightening sequence

tainer as nearly perpendicular as possible. Zero the indicator.

4. Rotate the crankshaft clockwise (normal running direction) until the valve has lifted 0.010 in. (0.254mm).

NOTE: Do not turn crankshaft any further clockwise, as valve spring might bottom and result in serious damage.

5. The timing of the crankshaft pulley should now read from 10 degrees BTDC–2 degrees ATDC. Remove spacer.

6. If reading is not within specified limits:
   a. Check sprocket index marks.
   b. Inspect timing chain for wear.
   c. Check accuracy of TDC mark on the timing indicator.

Cylinder Head

Removal and Installation

1. Disconnect the negative battery cable. Drain the cooling system.

2. Remove alternator, carburetor air cleaner and fuel line.

3. Disconnect the accelerator linkage.

4. Remove the vacuum control hose between the carburetor and distributor.

5. Remove the distributor cap and wires.

6. Disconnect the coil wires, heat indicator sending unit wire, heater hoses and by-pass hose.

7. Remove the closed ventilation system, evaporation control system and valve covers.

8. Remove the intake manifold, ignition coil and carburetor as an assembly.

9. Remove the exhaust manifolds.

10. Remove the rocker arm and shaft assemblies. Remove the pushrods and identify to insure installation in original location.

11. Remove the head bolts from each cylinder head and remove the cylinder heads.

12. Prior to installing the cylinder heads, clean all gasket surfaces of cylinder block and cylinder heads.

13. Inspect all surfaces with a straightedge if there is any reason to suspect leakage. If out of flatness exceeds 0.004 in., either machine or replace the head.

14. Remove cylinder heads from holding fixtures, install gaskets and place heads on engine.

15. Clean pipe sealant from bolt threads and bolt holes. Apply Mopar Lock N' Seal® or equivalent to bolt threads. Install cylinder head bolts. Starting at top center, tighten all cylinder head bolts to 50 ft. lb. (68 Nm) in sequence. Repeat procedure, re-tighten all cylinder head bolts to specified torque.

16. Inspect pushrods and replace worn or bent rods.

17. Install the pushrods, rocker arm and shaft assemblies with the notch on the end of rockershaft pointing to centerline of engine and toward front of engine on the left bank and to the rear on right bank, making sure to install the long stamped steel retainers in the No. 2 and NO. 4 positions, tighten to 200 inch lbs. (23 Nm).

18. Do not use any sealer on side composition gaskets.

19. Install side gaskets to cylinder head.

20. Clean the cylinder block front and rear gasket surfaces using an approved solvent.

21. Apply a thin, uniform coating of a quick dry cement to the intake manifold front and rear gaskets and cylinder block gasket surface. Allow to dry 4–5 minutes or until tack free.

NOTE: When installing gaskets, the center hole in the gasket must engage the dowels in block. End holes in seals must be locked into tangs of head gasket.

22. Carefully install the front and rear intake manifold gaskets.

23. Place a drop (approximately ¼ in. diameter) of rubber sealer onto each of the 4 manifold to cylinder head gasket corners.

24. Carefully lower intake manifold into position on the cylinder block and cylinder heads. After the intake manifold is in place, inspect to make sure end seals are in place.

25. Install the finger tight. Tighten the intake manifold bolts in 3 stages in sequence. The 1st stage to 25 ft. lbs. (34 Nm), the 2nd stage to 40 ft. lbs. (54 Nm) and 3rd stage to 45 ft. lbs. (61 Nm).

26. Install exhaust manifolds and tighten screws to 20 ft. lbs. (27 Nm) and nuts to 15 ft. lbs. (20 Nm).

27. Adjust spark plug gap and install the plugs, tightening to 30 ft. lbs. (41 Nm).

28. Install the ignition wires, heat indicator sending unit wire, heater hoses and by-pass hose.

29. Install the vacuum control hoses between carburetor and distributor.

30. Install the throttle linkage and adjust as necessary.

31. Install the distributor cap and wires.

32. Install the fuel line, alternator and drive belt. Tighten the alternator mounting bolt to 30 ft. lbs. (41 Nm) and adjusting strap bolt to 200 inch lbs. (23 Nm).

33. Be certain the valve covers are not distorted at screw holes—flatten if necessary.

34. Place the new valve cover gaskets in position and install valve covers. Tighten to 80 inch lbs. (9 Nm) using load spreader fasteners.

35. Install the closed crankcase ventilation system and evaporation control system.

36. Fill the cooling system and install battery ground cable.

Camshaft

Removal and Installation

1. Disconnect the negative battery cable. Drain the cooling system. Position the engine at TDC on the compression stroke.

2. Remove the air cleaner assembly. Remove the valve covers. Remove the rocker arm and shaft assemblies. Remove the distributor.

3. Remove the intake manifold assembly. Remove the pushrods and lifters. Be sure to identify the components, so that each part will be replaced in its original location.

4. Remove the radiator assembly. Remove the front cover assembly. Remove the camshaft gear and timing chain.

5. As required, remove the air conditioning condenser. Before removing this component, properly discharge the system.

NOTE: On some vehicles it may be necessary to remove the grille assembly to allow enough room to remove the camshaft.

6. Install a long bolt into front of camshaft to facilitate removal of the camshaft. Remove the camshaft, being careful not to damage cam bearings with the cam lobes.

NOTE: To reduce internal leakage and help maintain higher oil pressure at idle, cup plugs have been pressed into the oil galleries behind the camshaft thrust plate.

7. Prior to installing the camshaft, lubricate the camshaft

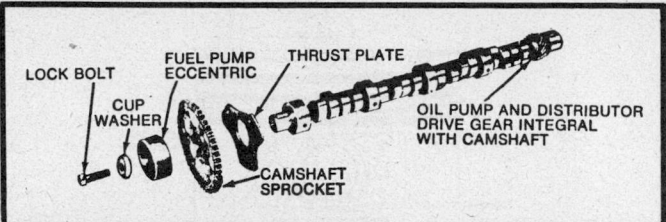

Camshaft and sprocket assembly

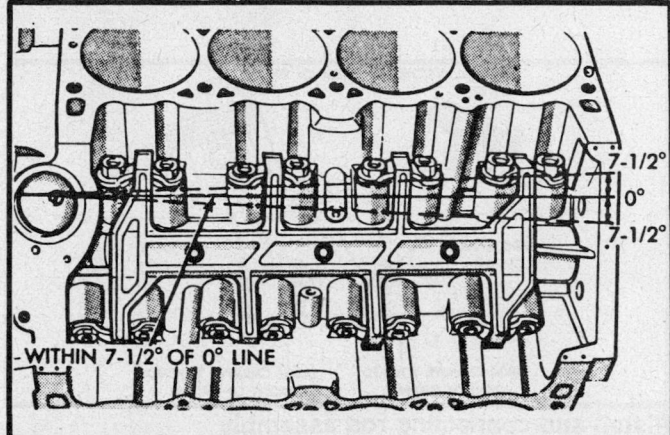

Drive gear installation

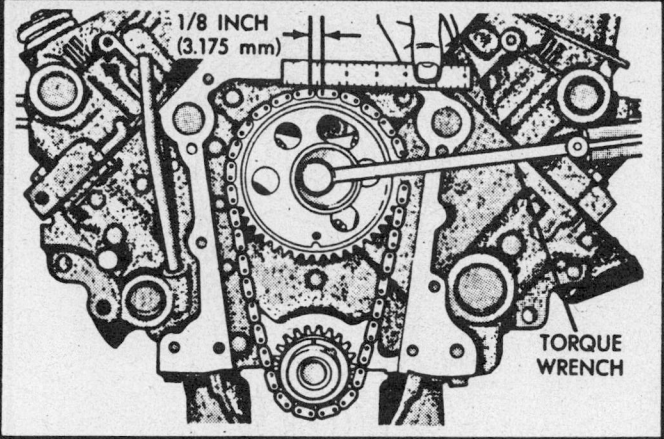

Measuring timing chain wear and stretch

lobes and camshaft bearing journals and insert the camshaft to within 2 in. (50.8mm) of its final position in cylinder block.8. When installing the camshaft thrust plate and chain oil tab. Make sure the tang enters the lower right hole in the thrust plate. Tighten to 210 inch lbs. (24 Nm). The top edge of the tab should be flat against the thrust plate in order to catch oil for chain lubrication.

9.Check the camshaft for 0.002–0.006 in. endplay with a new thrust plate and up to 0.010 in. endplay with a used thrust plate. If not within limits install a new thrust plate.

10. The installation is the reverse of the removal procedure. Be sure to torque the intake manifold bolts to specification and in the proper sequence.

11. Be sure to use new gaskets or RTV sealant, as required.

Timing Case Cover/Oil Seal

COVER

Removal and Installation

1. Disconnect the negative battery cable.
2. Drain the cooling system.
3. Remove the water pump.
4. Remove the power steering pump.
5. Remove the pulley from the vibration damper and bolt and washer securing the vibration damper on the crankshaft.
6. Using a vibration damper pulling tool, remove the vibration damper from end of crankshaft.
7. Remove the fuel lines and fuel pump.
8. Loosen the oil pan bolts and remove the front bolt at each side.
9. Remove the chain case cover and gasket using extreme caution to avoid damaging the oil pan gasket.
10. Prior to installing the timing cover, be sure mating surfaces of chain case cover and cylinder block are clean and free from burrs.
11. Using a new cover gasket, carefully install the chain case

cover to avoid damaging oil pan gasket. A ⅛ in. diameter bead of sealer is recommended on the oil pan gasket. Do not tighten the chain case cover bolts at this time.

12. Lubricate the seal lip with lubriplate, position vibration damper hub slot on crankshaft. Damper will act as a pilot for the crankshaft seal.

13. Press the vibration damper on the crankshaft.

14. Tighten the chain case cover screws to 30 ft. lbs. (41 Nm) first, tighten the oil pan screws to 200 inch lbs. (23 Nm).

15. Install the vibration damper bolt with the washer and tighten to 135 ft. lbs. (183 Nm).

16. Position the pulley on the vibration damper and attach with bolts and lockwashers. Tighten to 200 inch lbs. (23 Nm).

17. Install the fuel pump and fuel lines.

18. Install the water pump and housing assembly, using new gaskets. Tighten bolts to 30 ft. lbs. (41 Nm).

19. Install the power steering pump.

20. Install the fan/belt assembly, hoses and close drains.

21. Fill the cooling system.

OIL SEAL

Removal and Installation

1. Disconnect the negative battery cable.
2. Loosen and remove the belts from the crankshaft pulley.
3. Remove the radiator shroud screws and set the shroud back over the engine.
4. Remove the fan and shroud from the engine.
5. Remove the crankshaft pulley and vibration damper bolt and washer from the end of the crankshaft.
6. Pull the vibration damper from the end of crankshaft.
7. Using a seal removing tool behind the lips of the oil seal, pry outward, being careful not to damage the crankshaft seal surface of cover.
8. Install the new seal by installing the threaded shaft part of the installing tool into the threads of the crankshaft.
9. Place the seal into the opening, with the seal spring toward the inside of the engine.
10. Place the installing tool with the thrust bearing and nut on the shaft. Tighten nut until tool is flush with the timing chain cover.
11. Lubricate the damper hub and install the vibration damper.
12. Install the vibration damper bolt and washer and torque to 135 ft. lbs. (183 Nm).
13. Install the pulley on the vibration damper and torque to 200 inch lbs. (23 Nm).
14. Set the radiator shroud back over engine and install the fan and belts.

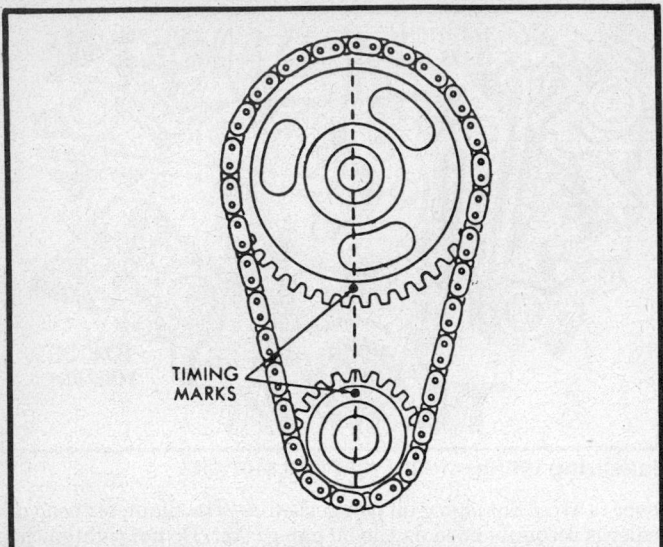

Timing mark alignment

15. Install the radiator shroud to the radiator.
16. Connect the negative battery cable.

TIMING CHAIN

Removal and Installation

1. Position the engine at TDC on the compression stroke.
2. Disconnect the negative battery cable.
3. Remove the front timing cover.
4. Remove the camshaft sprocket attaching cup washer, fuel pump eccentric and remove timing chain with crankshaft and camshaft sprockets.
5. Place both camshaft sprocket and crankshaft sprocket on the bench with timing marks on exact imaginary center line through both camshaft and crankshaft bores.
6. Place the timing chain around both sprockets.
7. Turn the crankshaft and camshaft to line up with keyway location in crankshaft sprocket and in camshaft sprocket.
8. Lift the sprockets and chain, keep the sprockets tight against the chain in position as described.
9. Slide both sprockets evenly over their respective shafts and use a straight edge to check alignment of the timing marks.
10. Install the fuel pump eccentric, cup washer and camshaft bolt. Tighten bolt to 35 ft. lbs. (47 Nm).
11. Check the camshaft for 0.002–0.006 in. (0.051–0.0152mm) endplay with a new thrust plate and up to 0.010 in. (0.254mm) endplay with a used thrust plate. If not within these limits, install a new thrust plate.
12. Continue the installation in the reverse order of the removal procedure.

Chain Slack Measurement

TIMING COVER REMOVED

1. Place a scale next to the timing chain so taht any movement of the chain can be measured.
2. Position a torque wrench and socket over the camshaft

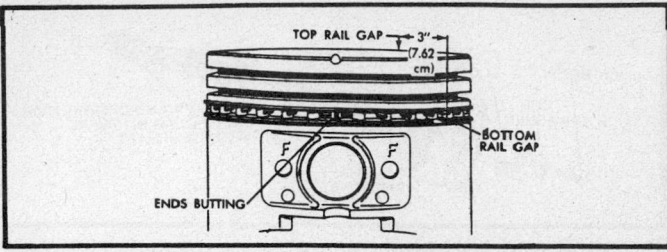

Oil ring position

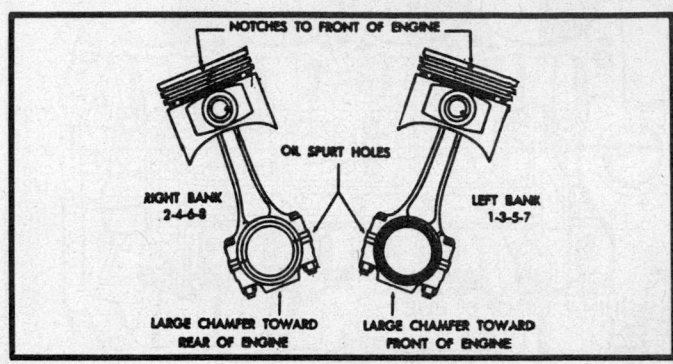

Piston and connecting rod assembly

sprocket lock bolt, and apply torque in the direction of crankshaft rotation to take up the chain slack.
3. Specification should be 30 ft. lbs., with the cylinder head installed and 15 ft. lbs. with the cylinder head removed from the engine.

NOTE: When torque is applied to the camshaft sprocket bolt the crankshaft should not be permitted to move.

4. Holding the scale with dimensional reading even with the edge of the chain link, apply torque in the reverse direction and note the amount of chain movement.
5. Specification should be 30 ft. lbs., with the cylinder head installed and 15 ft. lbs. with the cylinder head removed from the engine.
6. If the timing chain movement is more than $1/8$ in., replace the chain.

Rings/Piston/Connecting Rod Positioning

1. When installing the piston assemblies, stagger the compression ring gaps, so that they do not line up with the oil ring gaps.
2. Make sure the oil ring expander ends are butted and the rail gap ends are located as shown in the illustration.
3. A V groove is cut into the parting bearing face. When installing, make sure that the groove in the rod aligns with the groove in the cap (the groove provides for lubrication of the cylinder wall in the opposite bank).

LUBRICATION

Oil Pan

Removal and Installation

1. Disconnect the negative battery cable and remove dipstick.
2. Raise the vehicle, support it safely and drain the oil from the pan.
3. Remove the exhaust crossover pipe. Disconnect and lower center steering link.
4. Remove the starter nut and bolt and remove the starter.
5. Remove the torque converter inspection plate.
6. Remove the engine oil pan retaining bolts and remove the oil pan.
7. Inspect alignment of the oil strainer. The bottom of the strainer must be parallel with the machined surface of the cylinder block. The bottom of the strainer must touch the bottom of oil pan with $\frac{1}{16}$–$\frac{1}{8}$ in. (1.587–3.175mm) interference desirable.
8. Using a new pan gasket, add a drop of sealer at corners of rubber and cork.
9. Install the oil pan and torque the screws to 200 inch lbs. (23 Nm).
10. Install the torque converter inspection plate.
11. Install the starter and starter mounting nut and bolt.
12. Install the crossover pipe. Torque to 24 ft. lbs. (33 Nm).
13. Connect the center steering link.
14. Lower the vehicle, install dipstick and fill the engine with motor oil.
15. Connect the negative battery cable, start engine and check for leaks.

Oil Pump

Removal and Installation

1. Disconnect the negative battery cable.
2. Raise the vehicle and support it safely.
3. Remove the oil pan.
4. Remove the oil pump from the rear main bearing cap.
5. Prime the oil pump before installation by filling the rotor cavity with engine oil and rotating the shaft.
6. Install the oil pump on the rear main bearing cap and tighten the retaining bolts to 30 ft. lbs. (41 Nm).

Rear Main Oil Seal

SPLIT RUBBER TYPE

Removal and Installation

1. Disconnect the negative battery cable.
2. Raise the vehicle and support it safely.
3. Remove the oil pan.
4. Remove the rear main bearing cap.
5. Remove lower oil seal by pushing the end with a small punch tool.
6. Remove upper oil seal by pressing with a small punch tool on the end of the seal, being careful not to damage the crankshaft.

NOTE: Always wipe crankshaft surface clean and oil lightly before installing a new seal.

6. Insert cap seals into slots in bearing cap.
7. If this is not done, oil leakage will occur. Install seal edge toward inside of shoulder.
8. Lightly oil the lips of the crankshaft seals.
9. Rotate the half seal into the cylinder block with paint

Oil pan gasket

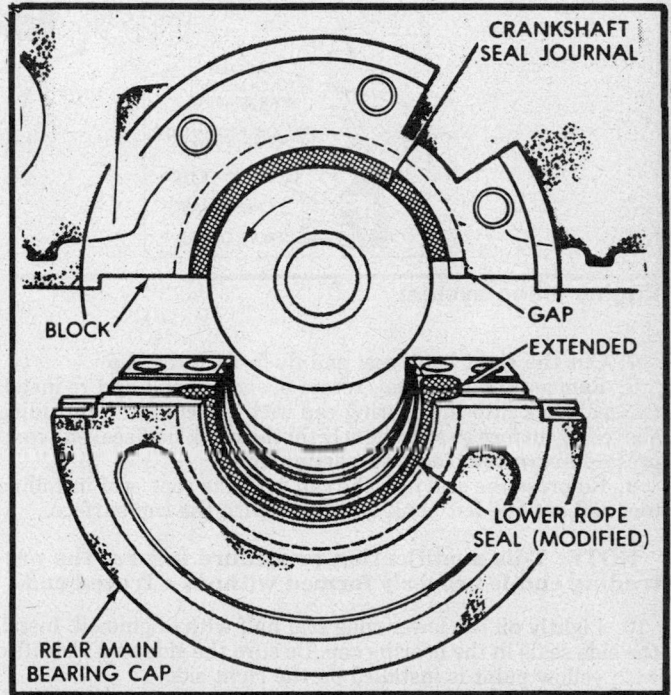
Modifying lower rear main bearing cap rope seal

stripe toward rear. Be careful not to shave or cut the outer surface of the seal.
10. Place the other half seal in bearing cap with paint stripe toward rear.
11. Assemble the bearing cap to cylinder block. Install cleaned and oiled cap bolts and torque to 85 ft. lbs. (115 Nm).
12.
Continue the installation in the reverse order of the removal procedure.

ROPE TYPE

Removal and Installation

1. Disconnect the negative battery cable.
2. Raise the vehicle and support it safely.
3. Remove the oil pan.
4. Remove the rear main bearing cap.
5. Remove the lower rope oil seal by prying from the side of the bearing cap with a small pry tool.
6. Install a new lower seal half in the cap. Tap the seal down into position with a rope seal installing tool.

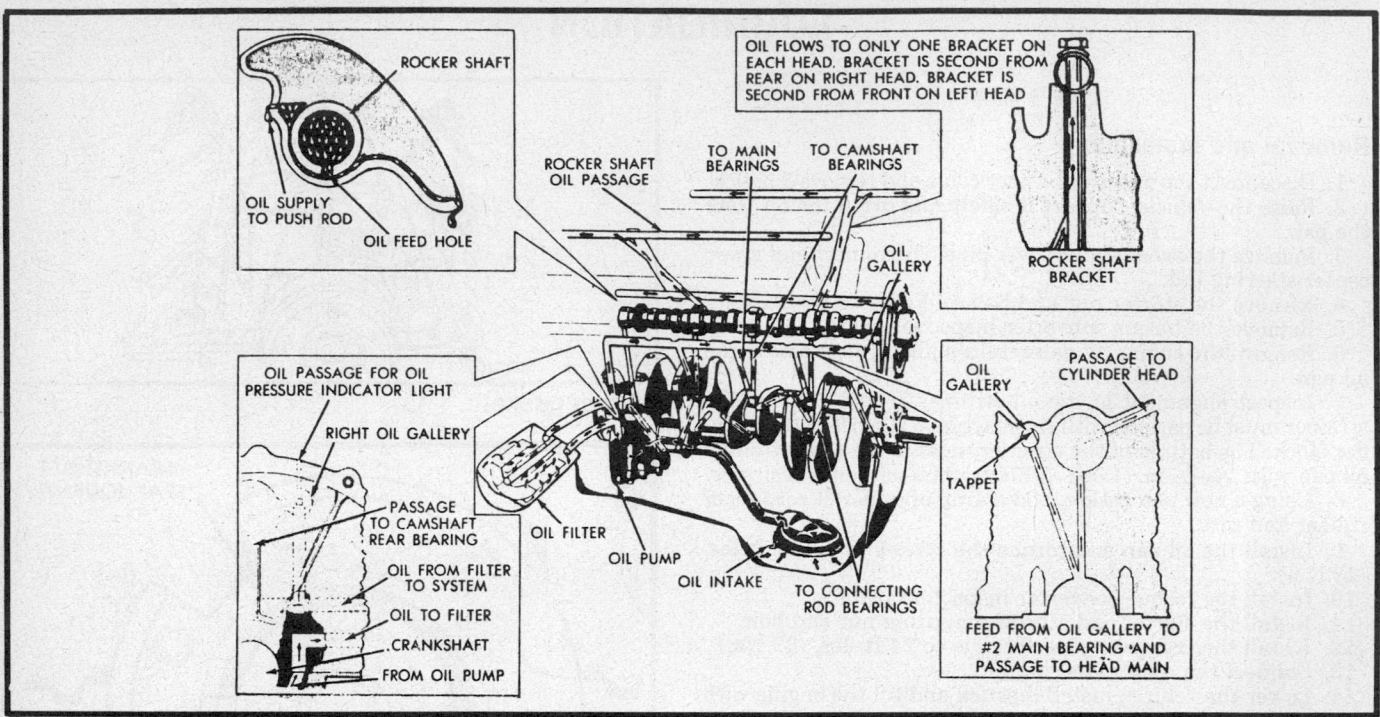

Engine oiling system

7. Cut the right bank seal end flush with the cap.

8. Remove the rope seal, rotate it end for end and re-install the seal back into the bearing cap with the cut end protruding above the surface so as to tightly fill the block half seal end compressed above the block/cap parting line.

9. Re-press the seal into the cap with the rope seal installing tool and cut the left bank side flush with the cap surface.

NOTE: This modification procedure insures the protruding end is properly formed without a frayed end.

10. Lightly oil the lower rope seal half with engine oil. Install the side seals in the bearing cap. Be sure the side seal identified with yellow paint is installed on the right side.

11. Remove the upper seal half with a rope seal remover tool.

12. Screw the tool into the seal, being careful not to damage the crankshaft. Pull the seal out with the tool while rotating the crankshaft.

13. Lightly lubricate the new seal before installing it.

14. Install the upper rope seal using a rope seal installer tool. Carefully trim the upper seal after installation.

15. Install the rear main bearing cap, being careful not to crimp the extended side of the oil seal between the cap and the block.

16. Install the main bearing bolts and torque to 85 ft. lbs. (115 Nm).

17. Complete the assembly of the oil pump and oil pan assembly. Add sealer at the bearing cap to block joint to provide oil pan end sealing.

Connecting Rod and Main Bearing

Bearing caps are not interchangeable and should be marked at removal to insure correct assembly. Upper and lower bearing halves are not interchangeable. The upper and lower number 3 bearing halves are flanged to carry the crankshaft thrust loads. All bearing cap bolts removed during service procedures are to be cleaned and oiled before reinstallation. Bearing shells are available in standard and the following undersizes: 0.001 in. (0.25mm), 0.002 in. (0.051mm), 0.003 in. (0.076), 0.010 in. (0.254mm) and 0.012 in. (0.305mm).

NOTE: Never install an undersize bearing shell that will reduce clearance below specifications.

FRONT SUSPENSION AND STEERING

For front suspension component removal and installation procedures, refer to unit repair section.
For steering wheel removal and installation, refer to electrical control section.

Steering Gear

Adjustment

1. Disconnect the center link from the steering gear arm.
2. Start the engine and run at idle speed.

3. Turn the steering wheel gently from 1 stop to stop counting the number of turns. Then turn the wheel back exactly half way, to center position.

4. Loosen the sector shaft adjusting screw until backlash is evident in steering gear arm. Feel backlash by holding the end of the steering gear arm between thumb and forefinger with a light grip. Tighten the adjusting screw until backlash just disappears.

5. Continue to tighten to ⅜–½ turn from this position and tighten locknut to 28 ft. lbs. (38 Nm) to maintain this setting.

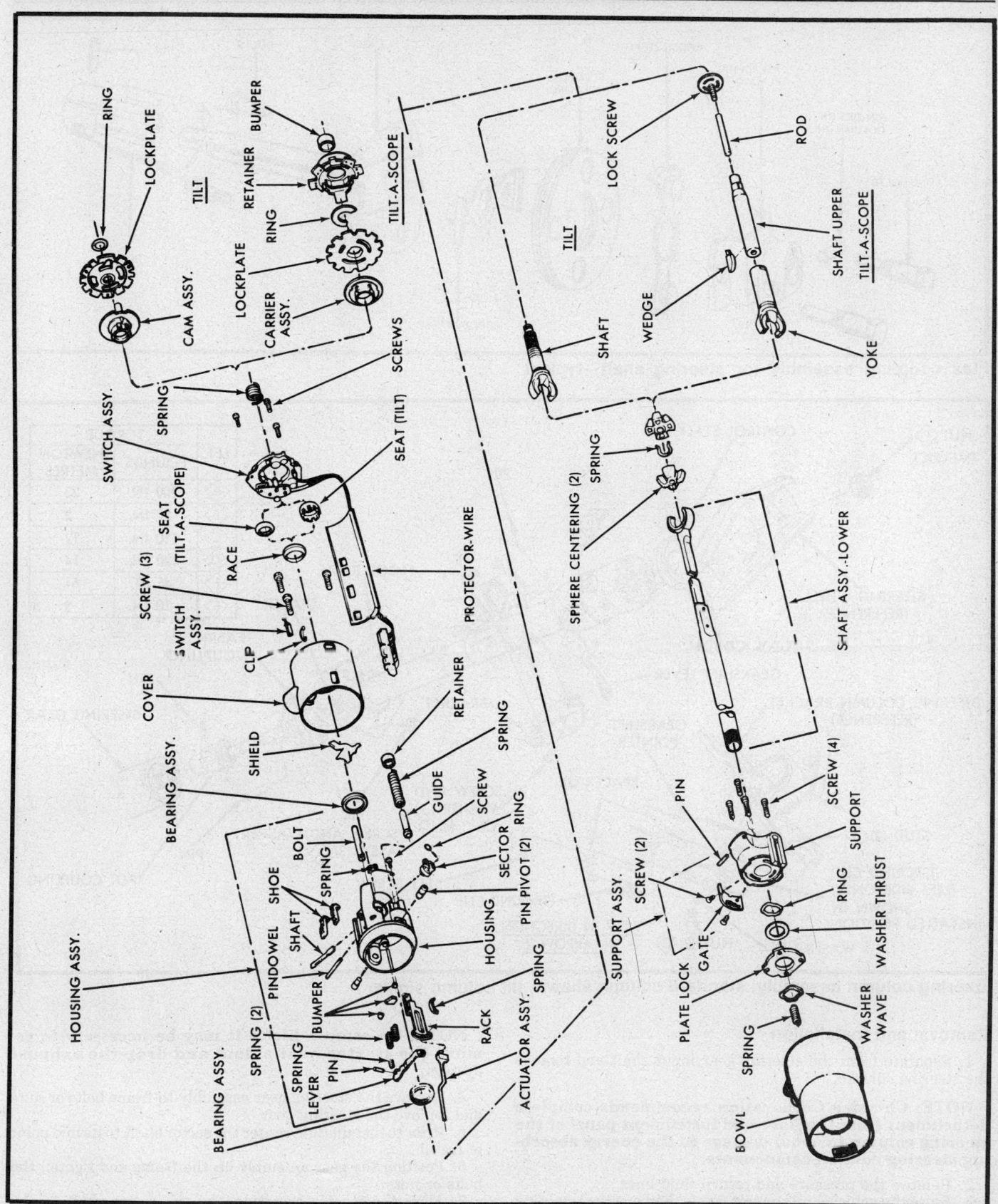

Exploded view of tilt steering column—typical

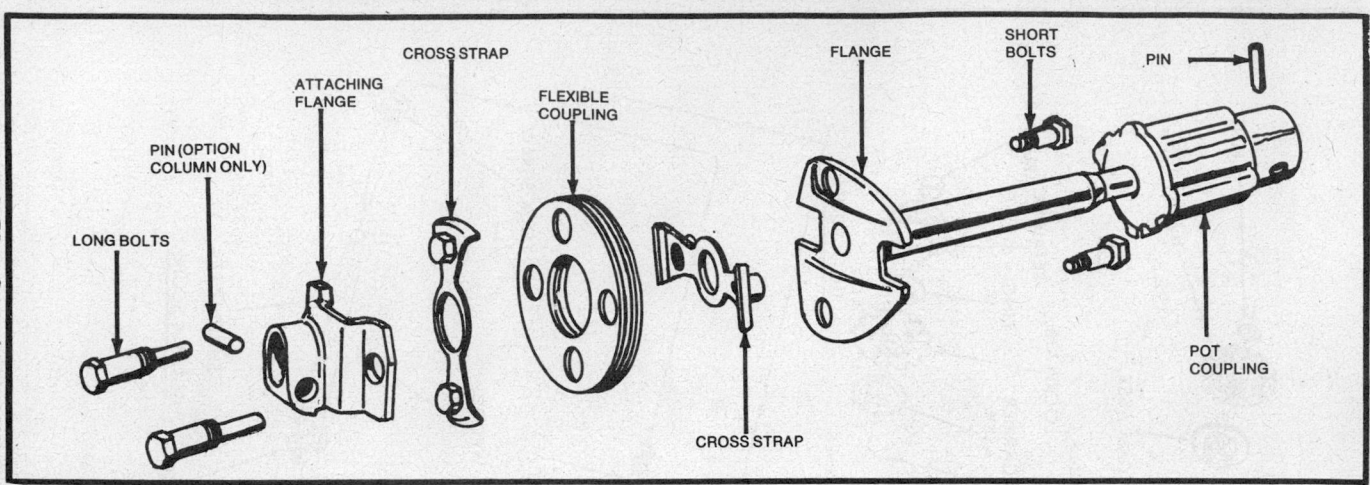

Flex coupling assembly for steering shaft—typical

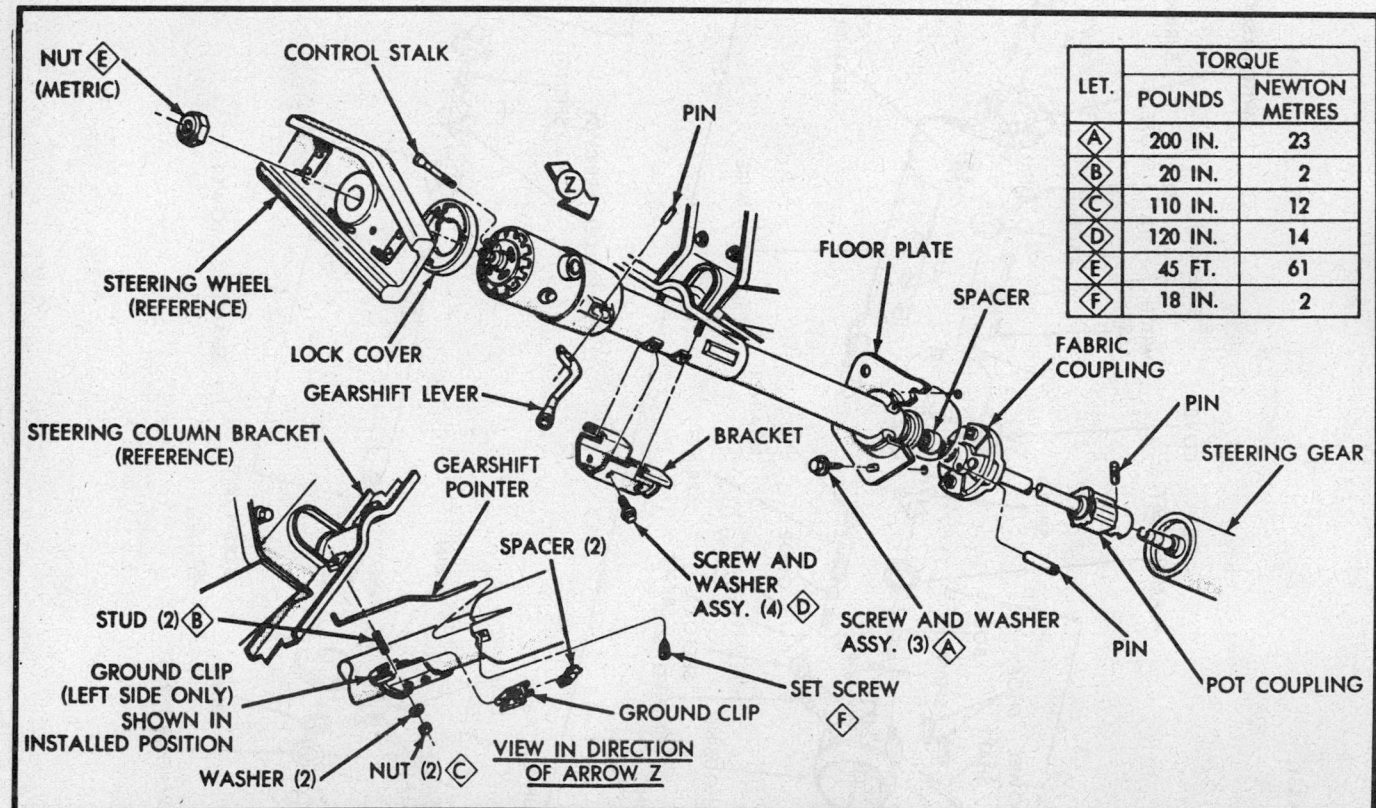

LET.	TORQUE	
	POUNDS	NEWTON METRES
A	200 IN.	23
B	20 IN.	2
C	110 IN.	12
D	120 IN.	14
E	45 FT.	61
F	18 IN.	2

Steering column assembly, standard column shown, tilt column similar

Removal and Installation

1. Separate from the steering gear input shaft and remove the steering column.

NOTE: Chrysler Corporation recommends complete detachment from the floor and instrument panel of the steering column to avoid damage to the energy absorbing steering column components.

2. Remove the pressure and return fluid lines.
3. Raise the vehicle and support safely. Remove the retaining nut and washer from the steering gear arm sector shaft. With a puller tool, remove the steering gear arm.

NOTE: On some vehicles it may be necessary to remove the starter heat shield and drop the exhaust system.

4. Remove the steering gear assembly-to-frame bolts or nuts and remove the steering gear.
5. Prior to installation, center the sector shaft to its mid point of travel.
6. Position the gear assembly on the frame and tighten the bolts or nuts.
7. Align the master serrations on the sector shaft to the splines in the steering arm, install and tighten the nut and washer.

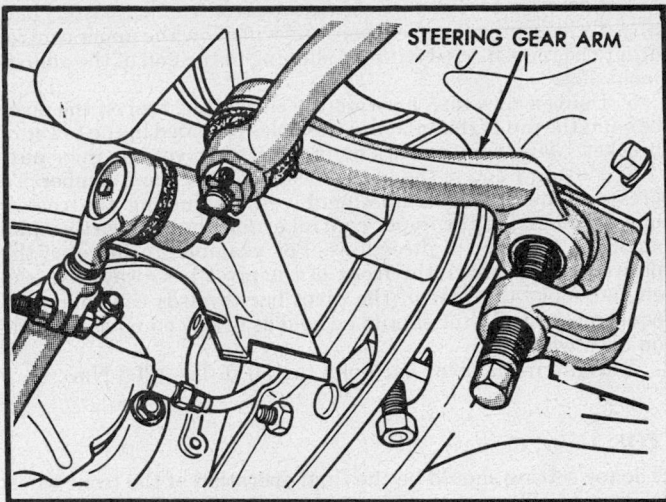

STEERING GEAR ARM

Removing the steering gear arm

8. Lower the vehicle and install the pressure and return fluid lines.

9. Install the steering column, fill the reservoir with fluid, start the engine and turn the steering wheel several times from stop to stop to bleed the system of air.

Power Steering Pump

Removal and Installation

1. Back off the pump mounting and locking bolts. Remove the pump drive belt.

2. Disconnect all hoses at the pump.

3. Remove the pump bolts and pump with the bracket.

4. To install the pump, place the pump in position and install the mounting bolts.

5. Install the pump drive belt and adjust. There should be no more than ½ in. of play, under moderate thumb pressure, on the longest run of belt. Some pump brackets have a ½ in. square hole for use in tensioning the belt. Torque the mounting bolts to 30 ft. lbs.

6. Connect the pressure and return hoses. Replace the pressure hose O-ring, if so equipped.

7. Fill the pump with power steering fluid.

NOTE: Do not use transmission fluid, use only recommended power steering fluid.

8. Start the engine and rotate the steering wheel from stop to stop several times. This will bleed the system. Check the pump fluid level and fill as required.

9. Be certain the hoses are away from the exhaust manifolds and are not kinked or twisted.

Bleeding System

Whenever the power steering system has been serviced, it is necessary to bleed the system. Start the engine and rotate the steering wheel from stop to stop several times. This will bleed the system. A noticeable winding noise is heard when air is in the system or fluid level is low. The system is free from air when the winding noise has dissipated and fluid is free of bubbles and foam.

NOTE: Do not hold the steering to either extreme for more than 5 seconds at a time. This can damage the pump and the gear seals by overheating the fluid.

Steering Column
Removal and Installation

CAUTION

A driver air bag restraint system will be available on late model 1988–89 vehicles. Improper maintenance, including incorrect removal and installation of related components, can lead to personal injury caused by unintentional activation of the Airbag. Disconnect the negative battery cable and isolate whenever the airbag system is being serviced in any way. Always point airbag module away from the body to minimize injury in the event of accidental deployment.

NOTE: Due to variations from vehicle to vehicle, this removal and installation procedure is to be used as a guide. Certain procedures may be accomplished in another sequence than listed.

1. Disconnect the negative battery cable.

2. On vehicles equipped with column shift, disconnect the link by prying the shift rod out of the grommet in the shift lever.

3. Remove the steering shaft lower coupling to worm shaft roll pin.

4. Disconnect the wiring connectors at the steering column jacket.

5. Remove the steering wheel center pad assembly and disconnect the horn switch, if applicable.

6. Remove the steering wheel retaining nut and remove the steering wheel from the steering shaft.

NOTE: Do not bump or hammer on the steering shaft to remove the steering wheel.

7. Remove the floor plate to floor pan attaching screws.

8. To expose the steering column bracket retaining screws, remove instrument panel steering column cover and lower reinforcements.

9. Remove the nuts holding the steering column bracket to the instrument panel supports.

10. Carefully remove the lower coupler from the steering gear wormshaft, then remove the column assembly out through the passenger compartment.

NOTE: Do not damage the paint or trim during the removal procedure.

11. Should a new grommet be needed in the shift rod, install from the rod side of the lever.

12. The installation of the steering column is the reverse procedure of the removal.

Front Wheel Bearings

Adjustment

1. Raise the vehicle and support it safely.

2. Remove the grease cup, cotter pin and locknut.

3. Back off on the adjusting nut.

4. Check for free wheel rotation.

5. While rotating the wheel, tighten the wheel bearing adjustment nut to 240–300 inch lbs.

6. Loosen the nut ¼ turn (90 degrees). Retighten the nut so that it is finger tight.

7. Position the nut lock so 1 pair of the slots is in line with the cotter pin hole and install the cotter pin. This adjustment should give 0.001–0.003 in. endplay.

8. Install the rest of the components removed.

Removal and Installation

1. Raise the vehicle and support it safely.

2. Remove the tire and wheel assembly.

3. Remove the brake caliper assembly (do not disconnect the brake line) and move to the side.

NOTE: Avoid strain on the flexible brake hose.

4. Remove the grease cup, cotter pin and locknut.
5. Remove the adjusting nut and washer.
6. Remove the outer bearing and remove brake disc from spindle.
7. Remove the inner bearing by removing the bearing seal with a seal remover tool.
8. Installation is the reverse order of the removal procedure.
9. Adjust the wheel bearing and use a new cotter pin.

Alignment

Refer to the wheel alignment specifications at the front of this section.

Procedures
CAMBER

1. Prepare the vehicle for measuring the wheel alignment.
2. Determine the initial camber/caster readings to confirm the variance to specifications before loosening the pivot bar bolts.
3. Remove any foreign material from the exposed threads of the pivot bar bolts.
4. Loosen nuts slightly holding the pivot (camber/caster) bar. Slightly loosening the pivot bar nuts will allow the upper control arm to be repositioned without slipping to the end of the adjustment slots.
5. Using a claw tool, position the claw of the tool on the pivot bar and the pin of the tool into the holes provided in the tower of bracket. Make adjustments by moving the pivot bar in or out.
6. Move both ends of the upper control arm in or out equal amounts until desired adjustment specification is achieved.
7. If caster readings are within specifications at this time, tighten the pivot bar bolts to 150 ft. lbs. (203 Nm).

CASTER

1. Prepare the vehicle for measuring the wheel alignment.
2. Determine the initial caster readings to confirm the variance to specifications before loosening the pivot bar bolts.
3. Remove any foreign material from the exposed threads of the pivot bar bolts.

4. Loosen nuts slightly holding the pivot (camber/caster) bar. Slightly loosening the pivot bar nuts will allow the upper control arm to be repositioned without slipping to the end of the adjustment slots.
5. Using a claw tool, position the claw of the tool on the pivot bar and the pin of the tool into the holes provided in the tower of bracket. Make adjustments by moving the pivot bar in or out.
6. Moving 1 end of the bar will change caster and camber. To preserve the camber adjustment while adjusting the caster, move each end of the upper control arm pivot bar exactly equal amounts in opposite directions. For example, to increase the positive caster, move the front of the pivot bar away from the engine, move the rear of the pivot bar towards the engine an equal amount. Caster should be held as nearly equal as possible on both wheels.
7. Tighten the pivot bar bolts to 150 ft. lbs. (203 Nm).

TOE

The toe setting should be the final operation of the front wheel alignment adjustments.
1. Secure the steering wheel in the straight ahead position. On vehicles equipped with power steering, start the engine before centering the steering wheel.

NOTE: The Manufacturer recommends that the engine be kept running while adjusting toe. Care should be exercised as damage to both the technician and the vehicle may occur.

2. Loosen the tie rod clamp bolts.
3. Adjust the toe by turning the tie rod sleeves.

NOTE: To avoid a binding condition in either tie rod assembly, rotate both tie rod ends in the direction of sleeve travel during the adjustment. This will ensure both ends will be in the center of their travel when tightening the sleeve clamps. Shut the engine down, as required.

4. Position the sleeve clamps so the ends do not locate in the sleeve slot, tighten the clamp bolts. Be sure the clamp bolts are indexed at or near the bottom to avoid possible interference with the torsion bars when the vehicle is in full jounce.

BRAKES

Refer to unit repair section for brake service information and drum/rotor specifications.

Master Cylinder

Removal and Installation

1. Disconnect the negative battery cable.
2. Disconnect the brake lines from the master cylinder. Plug the brake line outlets to prevent fluid loss.
3. Remove the master cylinder-brake-booster nuts.
4. Slide the master cylinder straight out and off the brake booster.
5. Installation is the reverse order of the removal procedure.

Bleeding System

Complete bleeding will require a residual valve on outlet of each bleeder tube. Obtain an bleeder tool equipped with at least 1 residual valve on primary outlet tube. To modify secondary outlet tube use a flaring tool to flare the tube outlet and install residual the valve.
1. Clamp master cylinder in a vise and attach bleeding tubes.
2. Fill both reservoirs with approved brake fluid.

3. Using a brass rod or wood dowel depress pushrod slowly and allow the pistons to return under pressure of springs. Do this several times until all air bubbles are expelled.
4. Remove bleeding tubes from cylinder, plug outlets to prevent spillage and install caps.
5. Remove from vise and install master cylinder on vehicle.

Power Brake Booster

Removal and Installation

1. Disconnect the negative battery cable.
2. Remove the master-cylinder-brake booster nuts and position the master cylinder out of the way without disconnecting the lines. Use care not to kink the brake lines.
3. Disconnect the vacuum hose from the brake booster.
4. Working under the dash, remove the nut and bolt or retainer clip attaching the brake booster pushrod to the brake pedal.
5. Remove the brake booster attaching nuts and washers.
6. Remove booster assembly from the vehicle.
7. Installation is the reverse order of the removal. Torque mounting nuts to 200–250 inch lbs. (22–28 Nm) and pushrod nut/bolt to 30 ft. lbs. (41 Nm).

Parking Brake

Adjustment

1. Raise the vehicle and support it safely.
2. Insert an adjusting tool through the rear brake adjusting hole and rotate the star wheel until a slight drag is felt while rotating the wheels. Back off the star wheel until no drag is felt with the aid of a welding rod type probe, to move the adjusting lever out of engagement with the star wheel.
3. Tighten the cable adjusting nut until a slight drag is felt in the rear wheels when the rear wheels are rotated. Loosen the cable adjusting nut until the rear wheels can be rotated freely. Back off the cable adjusting nut 2 additional turns.
4. Apply and release the parking brake several times and check to verify the rear wheels rotate freely, without any brake drag.

TRANSMISSION

Refer to "Chilton's Transmission Service Manual" for additional coverage.

Automatic Transmission

Removal and Installation

1. The transmission and torque converter must be removed as an assembly; otherwise, the converter drive plate, pump bushing, or oil seal may be damaged. The drive plate will not support a load; therefore, none of the weight of the transmission should be allowed to rest on the plate during removal.
2. Disconnect negative battery cable. Raise the vehicle and support it safely.
3. Some vehicles require the exhaust system be dropped for clearance.
4. Remove engine to transmission braces, if so equipped.
5. Remove cooler lines at transmission.
6. Remove starter motor and cooler line bracket.
7. Remove torque converter access cover.
8. Loosen oil pan bolts and tap the pan to break it loose, allowing fluid to drain.
9. Re-install the pan.
10. Mark torque converter and drive plate to aid in re-assembly. The crankshaft flange bolt circle, inner and outer circle of holes in the drive plate and the 4 tapped holes in front face of the torque converter all have 1 hole offset so these parts will be installed in the original position. This maintains balance of the engine and torque converter.
11. Rotate engine to position the bolts attaching torque converter to drive plate and remove bolts.
12. Mark parts for re-assembly, then disconnect propeller shaft at rear universal joint. Carefully pull shaft assembly out of the extension housing.
13. Disconnect wire connector from the back-up lamp and neutral safety switch.
14. Disconnect gearshift rod and torque shaft assembly from transmission.

NOTE: When it is necessary to disassemble linkage rods from levers using plastic grommets as retainers, the grommets should be replaced with new grommets. Use a prying tool to force rod from grommet in lever, then remove the old grommet. Use pliers to snap new grommet into lever and rod into grommet.

15. Disconnect throttle rod from lever at the left side of transmission. Remove linkage bellcrank from transmission, if so equipped.
16. Remove oil filler tube and speedometer cable.
17. Install engine support fixture with frame hooks or a suitable substitute, that will support rear of the engine.
18. Raise the transmission slightly with service jack to relieve load on the supports.
19. Remove bolts securing transmission mount to crossmember and crossmember to frame, remove the crossmember.
20. Remove all bell housing bolts.
21. Carefully work the transmission and torque converter as-

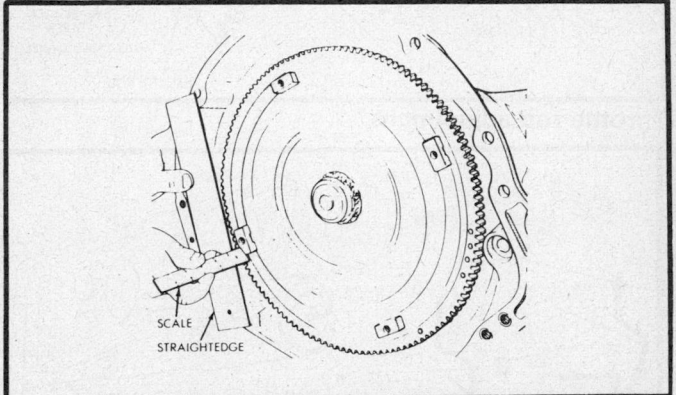

Measuring converter face for full engagement in front pump gears

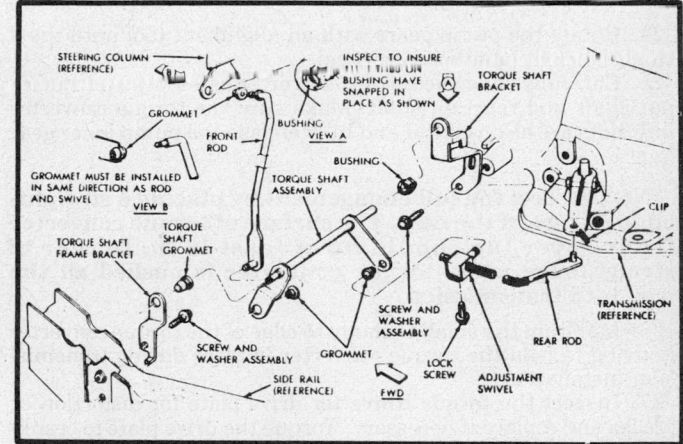

Column gearshift linkage

sembly rearward off engine block dowels and disengage converter hub from the end of the crankshaft. Attach a small C-clamp to the edge of the bell housing to hold the torque converter in place during transmission removal.
22. Lower the transmission and remove the assembly from under the vehicle.
23. To remove the torque converter assembly, remove the C-clamp from the edge of the bell housing, carefully slide the assembly out of the transmission.

NOTE: The transmission and torque converter must be installed as an assembly; otherwise, the torque converter drive plate, pump bushing and oil seal will be damaged. The drive plate will not support a load; therefore, none of the weight of transmission should be allowed to rest on the plate during installation.

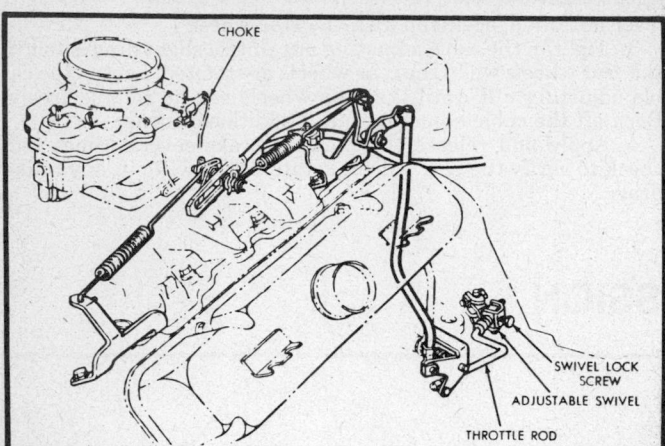

Throttle rod adjustment

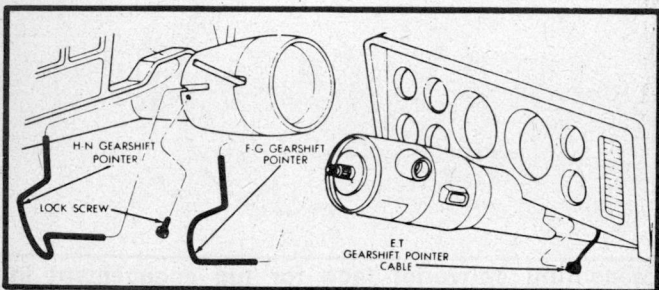

Gearshift pointer wire

24. Rotate the pump gears with an alignment tool until the 2 small holes in handle are vertical.

25. Carefully slide the torque converter assembly over the input shaft and reaction shaft. Make sure the torque converter hub slots are also vertical and fully engage the pump inner gear lugs.

NOTE: Test for full engagement by placing a straightedge on face of the case. The surface of torque converter front cover lug should be at least ½ in. to rear of straightedge when torque converter is pushed all the way into transmission.

26. Maintain the small C-clamp to edge of the torque converter housing to hold the torque converter in place during transmission installation.

27. Inspect the torque converter drive plate for distortion or cracks and replace if necessary. Torque the drive plate to crankshaft bolts to 55 ft. lbs. (75 Nm). When the drive plate replacement has been necessary, make sure both transmission dowel pins are in the engine block and they are protruding far enough to hold the transmission in alignment.

28. Coat the converter hub hole in the crankshaft with multipurpose grease. Place transmission and torque converter assembly on a service jack and position assembly under vehicle for installation. Raise or tilt as necessary until the transmission is aligned with the engine.

29. Rotate the torque converter so the mark on the torque converter (made during removal) will align with the mark on the drive plate. The offset holes in plate are located next to ⅛ in. hole in the inner circle of plate. Carefully work the transmission assembly forward over the engine block dowels with the torque converter hub entering the crankshaft opening.

30. After the transmission is in position, install the converter housing bolts and tighten to 30 ft. lbs (41 Nm). If so equipped, re-install vibration damper weight on rear of the extension housing.

31. Install the crossmember to frame and lower transmission to install mount on extension to the crossmember. Tighten bolts.

32. The engine support fixture may now be removed.

33. Install the oil filler tube and speedometer cable.

34. Connect the throttle rod to the transmission lever.

35. Connect the gearshift rod and torque shaft assembly to the transmission lever and frame.

36. Place the wire connector on the combination back-up lamp and neutral/park starter switch.

37. Carefully guide the sliding yoke into the extension housing and on the output shaft splines. Align marks made at removal. Connect the propeller shaft to the rear axle pinion shaft yoke.

38. Rotate the crankshaft clockwise with socket wrench on the vibration dampener bolt, as needed to install the torque converter to drive plate bolts, matching marks made at removal. Tighten to 270 inch lbs. (31 Nm).

39. Install the torque converter access cover.

40. Install the starter motor and cooler line bracket.

41. Tighten the cooler lines to the transmission fittings.

42. Install the engine-to-transmission struts, if so equipped. Tighten the bolts holding strut to transmission before the strut to engine bolts.

43. Replace the exhaust system, if it was disturbed and adjust for clearance.

44. Adjust the shift and throttle linkage.

45. Refill the transmission with Dexron®II type automatic transmission fluid.

CONTROL LINKAGE

Adjustment

NOTE: Chrysler Corporation recommends, when it is necessary to disassemble linkage rods from their levers which use plastic grommets for retainers, the grommets should be replaced with new ones.

COLUMN SHIFT

1. Make sure all linkage is free, especially the adjustable slide on the shift rod, so the pre-load spring action is not reduced by friction. Disassemble, clean and lube if necessary.

2. Put the shift lever in the **P** position.

3. With the adjustable swivel loose, move the shift lever all the way to the rear-most detent position, which is **P**.

4. Tighten swivel lock bolts to 90 inch lbs. (10 Nm).

5. Verify the vehicle will only start in **P** or **N**.

CONSOLE SHIFT

1. Adjustment is similar to above, but no pre-load spring is used. Make sure that with the shift handle in **P**, the transmission lever is in the rear-most detent position, which is **P**.

2. Tighten swivel lock bolt with no load applied in either direction on the linkage to 90 inch lbs. (10 Nm).

3. Verify the vehicle will only start in **P** or **N**.

THROTTLE LINKAGE

Adjustment

1. Perform transmission throttle rod adjustment while engine is at normal operating temperature. Otherwise, make sure carburetor is not on fast idle cam.

2. Raise the vehicle and support it safely.

3. Loosen adjustment swivel lock screw.

4. To insure proper adjustment, the swivel must be free to slide along the flat end of the throttle rod, this will insure the preload spring action is not restricted. Disassemble and clean or repair parts to assure free action, if necessary.

5. Hold transmission lever firmly forward against its internal stop and tighten swivel lock screw to 100 inch lbs. (11 Nm).

6. The adjustment is finished and linkage backlash was automatically removed by the preload spring.

7. Lower the vehicle, reconnect the choke if disconnected and test the linkage freedom of operation by moving the throttle rod rearward, slowly releasing it to confirm it will return fully forward.

SHIFT QUADRANT POINTER

Adjustment

WIRE TYPE

NOTE: **Always check for proper automatic transmission linkage adjustment before changing the adjustment of the shift quadrant indicator.**

1. Remove the instrument panel steering column cover. Set the shift lever in **P** position.

2. Loosen the set screw holding the indicator wire and adjust the wire to align with **P**.

3. Re-tighten the set screw and install the steering column cover.

4. Check for indicator alignment from **L** position through **P** and readjust if necessary.

CABLE TYPE

1. Set the shift lever in **P** position.

2. Adjust the clip on the steering column to insure the indicator is centered on the **P**.

3. Check the alignment of the indicator in all position.

DRIVESHAFT AND U-JOINTS

The driveshaft is a one-piece tubular shaft with 2 universal joints, one at each end. The front joint yoke serves as a slip yoke on the transmission output shaft. The rear universal joint is the type that must be disassembled to be removed.

Driveshaft

Removal and Installation

1. Raise and support the vehicle safely.

2. Matchmark the driveshaft, U-joint and pinion flange before disassembly. These marks must be realigned during reassembly to maintain the balance of the driveline. Failure to align them may result in excessive vibration.

3. Remove both of the clamps from the differential pinion yoke and slide the driveshaft forward slightly to disengage the U-joint from the pinion yoke. Tape the 2 loose U-joint bearings together to prevent them from falling off.

NOTE: **Do not disturb the bearing assembly retaining strap. Never allow the driveshaft to hang from either of the U-joints. Always support the unattached end of the shaft to prevent damage to the joints.**

4. Lower the rear end of the driveshaft and gently slide the front yoke/driveshaft assembly rearward disengaging the assembly from the transmission output shaft. Be careful not to damage the splines or the surface with the output shaft seal rides on.

5. Check the transmission output shaft seal for sign of leakage.

6. Installation is the reverse order of the removal procedure. Be sure to align the matchmarks. The torque for the clamp bolts is 14 ft. lbs. (19 Nm).

Universal Joints

Refer to the unit repair section for overhaul procedures.

REAR AXLE AND SUSPENSION

Refer to the unit repair section for axle overhaul procedures and rear suspension services.

Rear Axle Assembly

Removal and Installation

1. Raise the vehicle and support it safely. Install suitable stands at the front of the rear springs.

2. Block the brake pedal in the up position, using a wooden block or equivalent.

3. Drain the lubricant from differential housing.

4. Loosen and remove rear wheels. Do not removed drum retaining spring clips or brake drums.

5. Disconnect hydraulic brake lines at wheel cylinders and cap fittings to prevent loss of brake fluid.

6. Disconnect the parking brake cables.

7. Disconnect the driveshaft at differential pinion flange and secure in a near horizontal position to prevent damage to front universal joint.

8. Remove the shock absorbers from the spring plate studs and loosen rear spring U-bolt nuts and remove U-bolts.

9. Remove the axle assembly from vehicle.

10. Installation is the reverse order of the removal procedure.

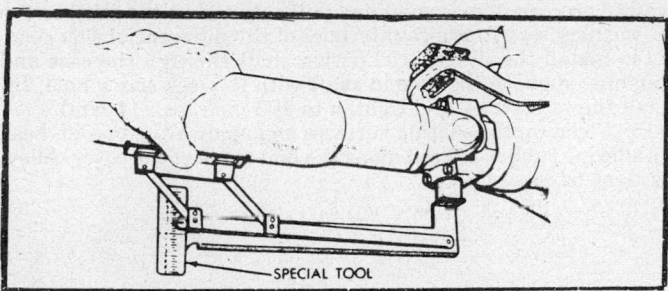

Measuring rear joint angle

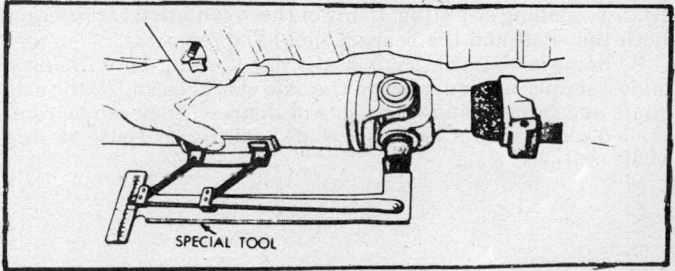

Measuring front joint axle

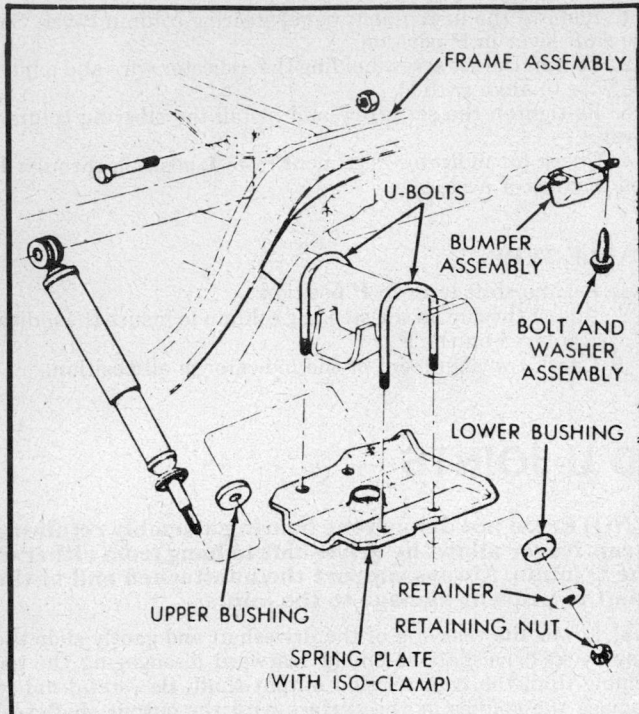

Rear shock absorber mounting

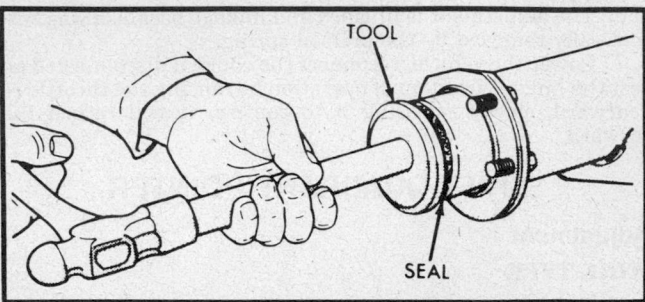

Installing axle shaft oil seal

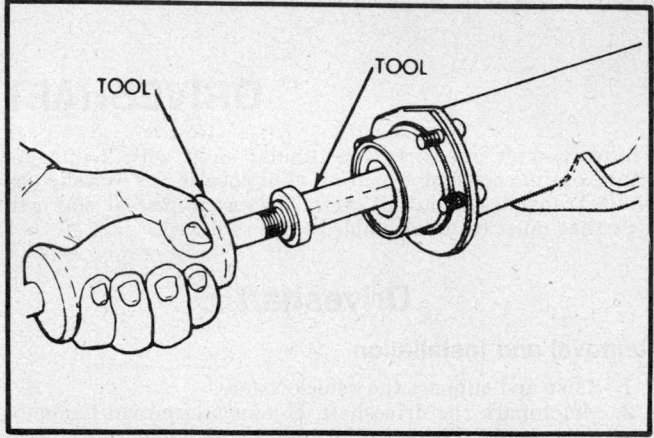

Removing axle shaft bearing

Axle Shaft, Bearing or Oil Seal

Removal and Installation

NOTE: Under no circumstances should rear axle bearing cones, cups, bores or journals be subjected to heating with a torch, hitting with a hammer or any other abnormal abuse, permanent damage may result.

1. Raise the vehicle and support it safely.
2. Remove the wheel cover and wheel and tire assembly. Remove the brake drum.
3. Loosen the housing cover and drain the lubricant from the rear axle. Remove the cover.
4. Turn the differential case to make the differential pinion shaft lock screw is accessible and remove the lock screw and pinion shaft.
5. Push the axle shafts toward the center of vehicle and remove the C-washers from the recessed groove of the axle shaft.
6. Remove the axle shaft from housing being careful not to damage the straight roller-type axle shaft bearing which will remain in the rear axle housing.
7. Inspect the axle shaft bearing surfaces for signs of imperfection, spalling or pitting. If any of these conditions are present both the shaft and the bearing should be replaced.
8. Remove the axle shaft seal from housing bore. Using a slide hammer motion, remove the axle shaft bearing. If the axle shaft and bearing show no signs of distress, they can be reinstalled along with a new axle shaft seal. Never reuse an axle shaft seal.

NOTE: Inspect housing bearing shoulder for burrs and remove any if present.

9. Wipe the axle shaft bearing cavity of axle housing clean. The axle shaft oil seal bores at both ends of the housing should be smooth and free of rust and corrosion. This also applies to the brake support plate and housing flange face surface.
10. Insert the axle shaft bearing into cavity making sure it bottoms against the shoulder and it is not cocked in bore.

NOTE: Under no circumstances should the seal be used to position or bottom the bearing in its bore as this would damage the seal.

11. Install the axle shaft bearing seal using bearing installer tool, until the outer flange of tool bottoms against housing flange face. This positions the seal to the proper depth beyond the end of the flange face.
12. Lubricate the bearing and seal area of the axle shaft, slide the axle shaft into place being careful the splines of the shaft do not damage the oil seal and properly engage with the splines of differential side gears.
13. With the axle shaft in place, install the C-washers in recessed grooves of axle shaft and pull outward on the shaft so the C-washers seat in the counterbore of the differential side gear.
14. Install the differential pinion shaft through the case and pinions, aligning the hole in shaft with the lock screw hole. Install the lock screw and tighten to 100 inch lbs. (11 Nm).
15. Clean up the mating surfaces and apply a $1/16$-$3/32$ in. bead of silicone rubber sealant along the bolt circle of the cover. Allow sealant to cure.

YEAR IDENTIFICATION

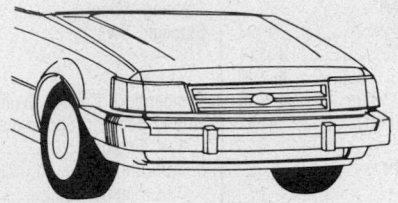

1986-87 Escort

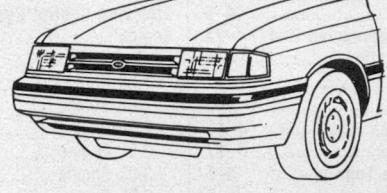

1988–90 Escort

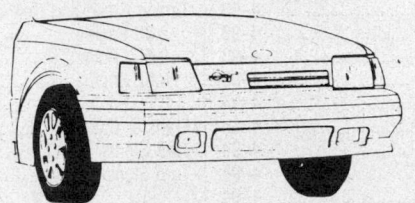

1989–90 Escort GT

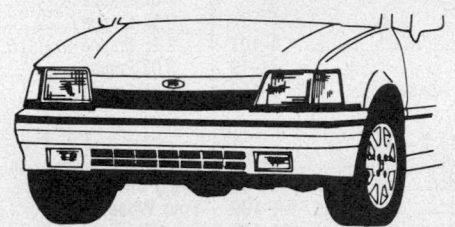

1989 Escort GT

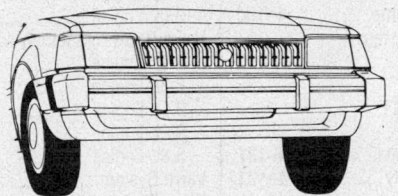

1986–88 Lynx

1986-88 Lynx XR3

1986-87 Topaz

1988–90 Topaz

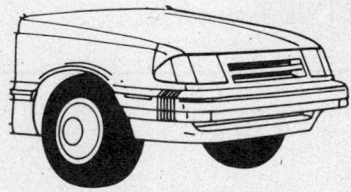

1986-88 Tempo

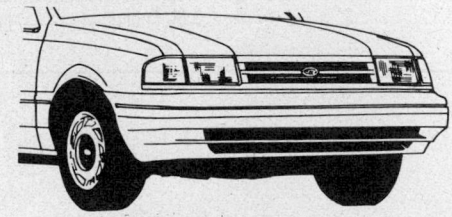

1989–90 Tempo

1987–90 Taurus

YEAR IDENTIFICATION

1987–90 Sable

1988–90 Lincoln Continental

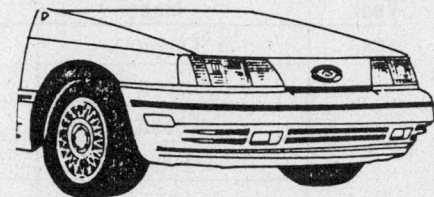

1990 Taurus SHO

VEHICLE IDENTIFICATION

It is important for servicing and ordering parts to be certain of the vehicle and engine identification. The VIN (vehicle identification number) is a 17 digit number visible through the windshield on the driver's side of the dash and contains the vehicle and engine identification codes. The tenth digit indicates model year, and the eighth digit indicates engine code. It can be interpreted as follows:

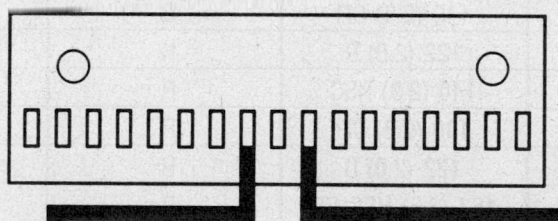

			Engine Code				Model Year	
Code	Cu. In.	Liters	Cyl.	Fuel Sys.	Eng. Mfg.		Code	Year
9	116	1.9	4	2 bbl	Ford		G	1986
9	116	1.9	4	CFI	Ford		H	1987
J	116	1.9 HO	4	EFI	Ford		J	1988
H	122	2.0	4	Diesel	Toyo Kogyo		K	1989
R	140	2.3 HSC	4	EFI	Ford		L	1990
X	140	2.3 HSC	4	CFI/EFI	Ford			
S	140	2.3 HSO	4	CFI	Ford			
D	154	2.5	4	CFI	Ford			
U	182	3.0	6	EFI	Ford			
Y	182	3.0 SHO	6	SEFI	Yamaha			
4	232	3.8	6	EFI	Ford			

HO High Output
HSO High Specific Output
HSC High Swirl Combustion
MHO Methanol High Output
EFI Electronic Fuel Injection
CFI Central Fuel Injection

ENGINE IDENTIFICATION

Year	Model	Engine Displacement cu. in. (liter)	Engine Series Identification (VIN)	No. of Cylinders	Engine Type
1986	Escort	116 (1.9)	9	4	OHC
	Escort	116 (1.9) EFI	J	4	OHC
	Escort	122 (2.0) D	H	4	OHC
	Lynx	116 (1.9)	9	4	OHC
	Lynx	116 (1.9) EFI	J	4	OHC
	Lynx	122 (2.0) D	H	4	OHC
	Tempo	140 (2.3) HSC	R	4	OHC
	Tempo	140 (2.3) HSC-CF	X	4	OHC
	Tempo	122 (2.0) D	H	4	OHC
	Topaz	140 (2.3) HSC	R	4	OHC
	Topaz	140 (2.3) HSC-CF	X	4	OHC
	Topaz	122 (2.0) D	H	4	OHC
1987	Escort	116 (1.9) CFI	9	4	OHC
	Escort	116 (1.9) EFI	J	4	OHC
	Escort	122 (2.0) D	H	4	OHC
	Lynx	116 (1.9) CFI	9	4	OHC
	Lynx	116 (1.9) EFI	J	4	OHC
	Lynx	122 (2.0) D	H	4	OHC
	Tempo	140 (2.3) HSC	R	4	OHC
	Tempo	140 (2.3) CFI	R	4	OHC
	Tempo	122 (2.0) D	H	4	OHC
	Topaz	140 (2.3) HSC	R	4	OHC
	Topaz	140 (2.3) CFI	R	4	OHC
	Topaz	122 (2.0) D	H	4	OHC
	Taurus	153 (2.5) HSG-CFI	D	4	OHV
	Taurus	182 (3.0) EFI	U	6	OHV
	Sable	153 (2.5) HSG-CFI	D	4	OHV
	Sable	182 (3.0) EFI	U	6	OHV
1988	Escort	116 (1.9) CFI	9	4	OHC
	Escort	116 (1.9) EFI	J	4	OHC
	Tempo	140 (2.3) HSO-EFI	S	4	OHC
	Tempo	140 (2.3) EFI	X	4	OHC
	Topaz	140 (2.3) HSO-EFI	S	4	OHC
	Topaz	140 (2.3) EFI	X	4	OHC
	Taurus	153 (2.5) HSG-CFI	D	4	OHV
	Taurus	182 (3.0) EFI	U	6	OHV
	Taurus	232 (3.8) EFI	4	6	OHV
	Sable	153 (2.5) HSG-CFI	D	4	OHV
	Sable	182 (3.0) EFI	U	6	OHV
	Sable	232 (3.8) EFI	4	6	OHV
	Continental	232 (3.8) EFI	4	6	OHV

ENGINE IDENTIFICATION

Year	Model	Engine Displacement cu. in. (liter)	Engine Series Identification (VIN)	No. of Cylinders	Engine Type
1989-90	Escort	116 (1.9) CFI	9	4	OHC
	Escort	116 (1.9) EFI	J	4	OHC
	Tempo	140 (2.3) HSO-EFI	S	4	OHC
	Tempo	140 (2.3) CFI	X	4	OHC
	Topaz	140 (2.3) HSO-EFI	S	4	OHC
	Topaz	140 (2.3) CFI	X	4	OHC
	Taurus	153 (2.5) HSG-CFI	D	4	OHV
	Taurus	182 (3.0) EFI	U	6	OHV
	Taurus SHO	182 (3.0) EFI	U	6	DOHC
	Taurus	232 (3.8) EFI	4	6	OHV
	Sable	153 (2.5) HSG-CFI	D	4	OHV
	Sable	182 (3.0) EFI	U	6	OHV
	Sable	232 (3.8) EFI	4	6	OHV
	Continental	232 (3.8) EFI	4	6	OHV

HO High Output
HSC High Swirl Combustion
M-HO Methanol High Output
D Diesel
CFI Central Fuel Injection
EFI Electronic Fuel Injection
OHC Overhead Cam

GENERAL ENGINE SPECIFICATIONS

Year	VIN	No. Cylinder Displacement cu. in. (liter)	Fuel System Type	Net Horsepower @ rpm	Net Torque @ rpm (ft.lbs.)	Bore × Stroke (in.)	Compression Ratio	Oil Pressure @ rpm
1986	9	4-116 (1.9)	2 bbl	86 @ 4800	100 @ 3000	3.23 × 3.46	9.0:1	35-65 @ 2000
	J	4-116 (1.9)	EFI	108 @ 5200	114 @ 4000	3.23 × 3.46	9.0:1	35-65 @ 2000
	H	4-122 (2.0)	Diesel	52 @ 4000	82 @ 2400	3.39 × 3.39	22.7:1	55-60 @ 2000
	R	4-140 (2.3)	1 bbl	84 @ 4600	118 @ 2600	3.70 × 3.30	9.0:1	35-65 @ 2000
	X	4-140 (2.3)	CFI	100 @ 4600	125 @ 3200	3.70 × 3.30	9.0:1	55-10 @ 2000
	D	4-154 (2.5)	CFI	88 @ 4600	130 @ 2800	3.68 × 3.62	9.7:1	40-60 @ 2000
	U	6-182 (3.0)	EFI	140 @ 4800	160 @ 3000	3.50 × 3.15	9.3:1	55-70 @ 2000
1987	9	4-116 (1.9)	CFI	86 @ 4800	100 @ 3000	3.23 × 3.46	9.0:1	35-65 @ 2000
	J	4-116 (1.9)	EFI	108 @ 5200	114 @ 4000	3.23 × 3.46	9.0:1	35-65 @ 2000
	H	4-122 (2.0)	Diesel	52 @ 4000	82 @ 2400	3.39 × 3.39	22.7:1	55-60 @ 2000
	R	4-140 (2.3)	1 bbl	84 @ 4600	118 @ 2600	3.70 × 3.30	9.0:1	35-65 @ 2000
	X	4-140 (2.3)	CFI	100 @ 4600	125 @ 3200	3.70 × 3.30	9.0:1	55-70 @ 2000
	D	4-154 (2.5)	CFI	88 @ 4600	130 @ 2800	3.68 × 3.62	9.7:1	55-70 @ 2000
	U	6-182 (3.0)	EFI	140 @ 4800	160 @ 3000	3.50 × 3.15	9.3:1	40-60 @ 2000

GENERAL ENGINE SPECIFICATIONS

Year	VIN	No. Cylinder Displacement cu. in. (liter)	Fuel System Type	Net Horsepower @ rpm	Net Torque @ rpm (ft.lbs.)	Bore × Stroke (in.)	Compression Ratio	Oil Pressure @ rpm
1988	9	4-116 (1.9)	CFI	90 @ 4600	106 @ 3400	3.23 × 3.46	9.0:1	35-65 @ 2000
	J	4-116 (1.9)	EFI	110 @ 5400	115 @ 4200	3.23 × 3.46	9.0:1	35-65 @ 2000
	X	4-140 (2.3)	EFI	98 @ 4400	124 @ 2200	3.70 × 3.30	9.0:1	35-65 @ 2000
	S	4-140 (2.3)	EFI	100 @ 4400	130 @ 2600	3.70 × 3.30	9.0:1	55-70 @ 2000
	D	4-153 (2.5)	CFI	90 @ 4400	130 @ 2600	3.68 × 3.30	9.0:1	55-70 @ 2000
	U	6-182 (3.0)	EFI	140 @ 4800	160 @ 3000	3.50 × 3.10	9.0:1	40-60 @ 2000
	4	6-232 (3.8)	EFI	140 @ 3800	215 @ 2200	3.81 × 3.39	9.0:1	40-60 @ 2000
1989-90	9	4-116 (1.9)	CFI	90 @ 4600	106 @ 3400	3.23 × 3.46	9.0:1	35-65 @ 2000
	J	4-116 (1.9)	EFI	110 @ 5400	115 @ 4200	3.23 × 3.46	9.0:1	35-65 @ 2000
	X	4-140 (2.3)	EFI	98 @ 4400	124 @ 2200	3.70 × 3.30	9.0:1	35-65 @ 2000
	S	4-140 (2.3)	EFI	100 @ 4400	130 @ 2600	3.70 × 3.30	9.0:1	55-70 @ 2000
	D	4-153 (2.5)	CFI	90 @ 4400	130 @ 2600	3.68 × 3.30	9.0:1	55-70 @ 2000
	U	6-182 (3.0)	EFI	140 @ 4800	160 @ 3000	3.50 × 3.10	9.0:1	40-60 @ 2000
	Y	6-182 (3.0)	SEFI	NA	NA	3.50 × 3.15	NA	12.8 @ 800
	4	6-232 (3.8)	EFI	140 @ 3800	215 @ 2200	3.81 × 3.39	9.0:1	40-60 @ 2000

EFI Electronic Fuel Injection
CFI Central Fuel Injection
SEFI Sequential Fuel Injection
NA Not available

GASOLINE ENGINE TUNE-UP SPECIFICATIONS
Refer to Section 34 for all spark plug recommendations

Year	VIN	No. Cylinder Displacement cu. in. (liter)	Spark Plugs Gap (in.)	Ignition Timing (deg.) MT	Ignition Timing (deg.) AT	Compression Pressure (psi)	Fuel Pump (psi)	Idle Speed (rpm) MT	Idle Speed (rpm) AT	Valve Clearance In.	Valve Clearance Ex.
1986	9	4-116 (1.9)	0.044	10B	10B	—	4-6	750	750	Hyd.	Hyd.
	J	4-116 (1.9)	0.044	10B	10B	—	35-45	900	800	Hyd.	Hyd.
	R	4-140 (2.3)	0.044	10B	10B	—	4-6	800	750	Hyd.	Hyd.
	X	4-140 (2.3)	0.044	10B	10B	—	35-46	750	650	Hyd.	Hyd.
	D	4-154 (2.5)	0.044	10B	10B	—	35-45	725	650	Hyd.	Hyd.
	U	6-182 (3.0)	0.044	—	10B	—	35-45	—	625	Hyd.	Hyd.
1987	9	4-116 (1.9)	0.044	10B	10B	—	4-6	750	750	Hyd.	Hyd.
	J	4-116 (1.9)	0.044	10B	10B	—	35-45	800	750	Hyd.	Hyd.
	R	4-140 (2.3)	0.044	10B	10B	—	4-6	800	750	Hyd.	Hyd.
	X	4-140 (2.3)	0.044	10B	10B	—	35-45	750	650	Hyd.	Hyd.
	D	4-154 (2.5)	0.044	10B	10B	—	35-45	725	650	Hyd.	Hyd.
	U	6-182 (3.0)	0.044	—	10B	—	35-45	—	625	Hyd.	Hyd.
1988	9	4-116 (1.9)	0.044	①	①	—	30-45	950	950	Hyd.	Hyd.
	J	4-116 (1.9)	0.044	①	①	—	13-17	950	950	Hyd.	Hyd.
	X	4-140 (2.3)	0.044	①	①	—	45-60	②	③	Hyd.	Hyd.

GASOLINE ENGINE TUNE-UP SPECIFICATIONS
Refer to Section 34 for all spark plug recommendations

Year	VIN	No. Cylinder Displacement cu. in. (liter)	Spark Plugs Gap (in.)	Ignition Timing (deg.) MT	Ignition Timing (deg.) AT	Compression Pressure (psi)	Fuel Pump (psi)	Idle Speed (rpm) MT	Idle Speed (rpm) AT	Valve Clearance In.	Valve Clearance Ex.
1988	S	4-140 (2.3)	0.044	①	①	—	45-60	②	③	Hyd.	Hyd.
	D	4-153 (2.5)	0.044	—	①	—	13-17	—	650	Hyd.	Hyd.
	U	6-182 (3.0)	0.044	①	—	—	30-45	750	—	Hyd.	Hyd.
	4	6-232 (3.8)	0.052	—	①	—	30-45	①	—	Hyd.	Hyd.
1989	9	4-116 (1.9)	0.044	①	①	—	30-45	950	950	Hyd.	Hyd.
	J	4-116 (1.9)	0.044	①	①	—	13-17	950	950	Hyd.	Hyd.
	X	4-140 (2.3)	0.044	①	①	—	45-60	②	③	Hyd.	Hyd.
	S	4-140 (2.3)	0.044	①	①	—	45-60	②	③	Hyd.	Hyd.
	D	4-153 (2.5)	0.044	—	①	—	13-17	—	650	Hyd.	Hyd.
	U	6-182 (3.0)	0.044	①	—	—	30-45	750	—	Hyd.	Hyd.
	Y	6-182 (3.0)	0.044	10B	—	NA	36-39	800	—	④	④
	4	6-232 (3.8)	0.054	—	①	—	30-45	①	—	Hyd.	Hyd.
1990					SEE UNDERHOOD SPECIFICATIONS STICKER						

B Before Top Dead Center
① Refer to Vehicle Emission Control Information Decal for specification
② Manual transaxle—1500-1600
③ Automatic transaxle—975-1075
④ Shim set bucket type valve lifter is used

FIRING ORDERS

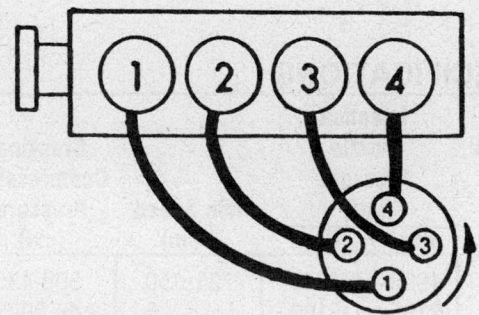

Ford 1.9L 4 cyl engine
Firing order 1-3-4-2
Distributor rotation: counterclockwise

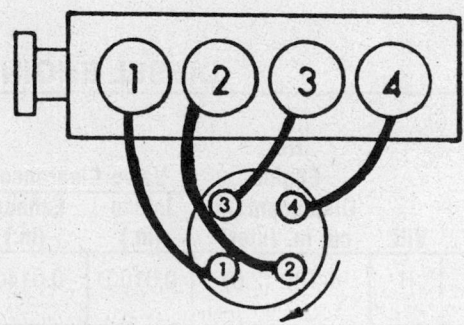

Ford 2.3L 4 cyl engine
Firing order 1-3-4-2
Distributor rotation: clockwise

FIRING ORDERS

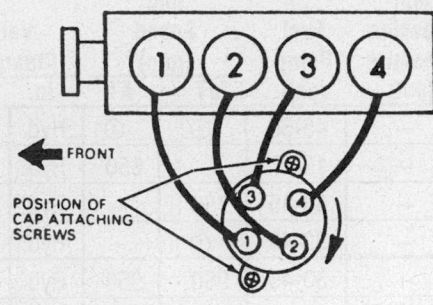

Ford 2.5L 4 cyl engine
Firing order 1–3–4–2
Distributor rotation: clockwise

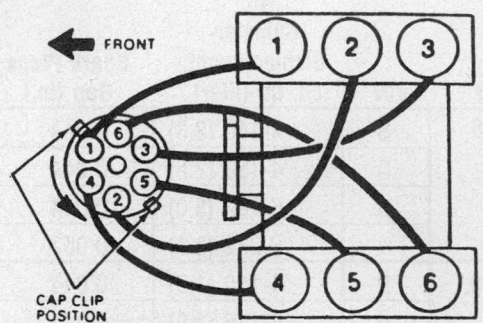

Ford 3.0L 6 cyl engine
Firing order 1–4–2–5–3–6
Distributor rotation: counterclockwise

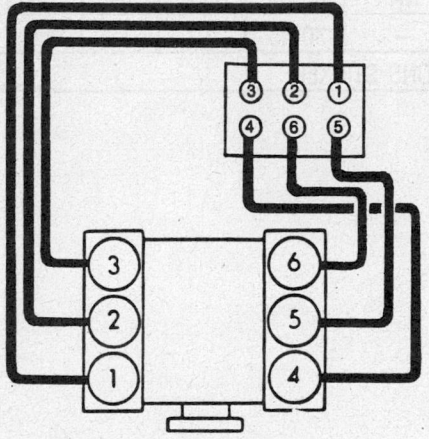

Ford 3.0L V6 SHO engine
Firing order 1–4–2–5–3–6
Distributorless ignition system

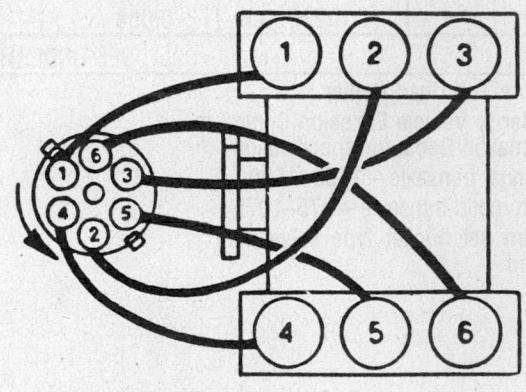

Ford 3.8L V6 engine
Firing order 1–4–2–5–3–6
Distributor rotation: counterclockwise

DIESEL ENGINE TUNE-UP SPECIFICATIONS

Year	VIN	No. Engine Displacement cu. in. (liter)	Valve Clearance Intake (in.)	Exhaust (in.)	Intake Valve Opens (deg.)	Injection Pump Setting (deg.)	Injection Nozzle Pressure (psi) New	Used	Idle Speed (rpm)	Cranking Compression Pressure (psi)
1986	H	4-122 (2.0)	0.010①	0.014①	13	TDC Hot	1990–2105	1849–2105	725 ± 50	390-435 @ 2000
1987	H	4-122 (2.0)	0.010①	0.014①	13	TDC Hot	1990–2105	1849–2105	725 ± 50	390-435 @ 2000

① The valve clearance specifications are set cold
TDC Top Dead Center

CAPACITIES

Year	Model	VIN	No. Cylinder Displacement cu. in. (liter)	Engine Crankcase with Filter	Engine Crankcase without Filter	Transmission (pts.) 4-Spd	Transmission (pts.) 5-Spd	Transmission (pts.) Auto.	Drive Axle (pts.)	Fuel Tank (gal.)	Cooling System (qts.)
1986	Escort	9	4-116 (1.9)	4.0	3.5	5	6.2	16.6	②	③	④
	Escort	J	4-116 (1.9)	4.0	3.5	5	6.2	16.6	②	③	④
	Escort	H	4-122 (2.0)	7.2	7.0	5	6.2	16.6	②	③	④
	Lynx	9	4-116 (1.9)	4.0	3.5	5	6.2	16.6	②	③	④
	Lynx	J	4-116 (1.9)	4.0	3.5	5	6.2	16.6	②	③	④
	Lynx	H	4-122 (2.0)	7.2	7.0	5	6.2	16.6	②	③	④
	Tempo	R	4-140 (2.3)	5.0	4.0	5.0	6.2	⑤	②	15.4⑥	⑦
	Tempo	X	4-140 (2.3)	5.0	4.0	5.0	6.2	⑤	②	15.4⑥	⑦
	Tempo	H	4-122 (2.0)	7.2	7.0	5.0	6.2	⑤	②	15.4⑥	⑦
	Topaz	R	4-140 (2.3)	5.0	4.0	5.0	6.2	⑤	②	15.4⑥	⑦
	Topaz	X	4-140 (2.3)	5.0	4.0	5.0	6.2	⑤	②	15.4⑥	⑦
	Topaz	H	4-122 (2.0)	7.2	7.0	5.0	6.2	⑤	②	15.4⑥	⑦
	Taurus	D	4-153 (2.5)	5.0	4.5	—	6.2	16.6	②	⑧	8.3
	Taurus	U	6-182 (3.0)	4.5	4.0	—	6.2	21.8	②	⑧	⑨
	Sable	D	4-153 (2.5)	5.0	4.5	—	6.2	16.6	②	⑧	8.3
	Sable	U	6-182 (3.0)	4.5	4.0	—	6.2	21.8	②	⑧	⑨
1987	Escort	9	4-116 (1.9)	4.0	3.5	5	6.2	16.6	②	13	⑨
	Escort	J	4-116 (1.9)	4.0	3.5	5	6.2	16.6	②	13	⑨
	Escort	H	4-122 (2.0)	7.2	7.0	5	6.2	16.6	②	③	④
	Lynx	9	4-116 (1.9)	4.0	3.5	5	6.2	16.6	①	13	⑨
	Lynx	J	4-116 (1.9)	4.0	3.5	5	6.2	16.6	②	13	⑨
	Lynx	H	4-122 (2.0)	7.2	7.0	5	6.2	16.6	②	③	④
	Tempo	R	4-140 (2.3)	5.0	4.0	—	6.2	⑤	⑩	⑪	⑦
	Tempo	X	4-140 (2.3)	5.0	4.0	—	6.2	⑤	⑩	⑪	⑦
	Tempo	H	4-12 (2.0)	7.2	7.0	—	6.2	⑤	②	15.4	⑦
	Topaz	R	4-140 (2.3)	5.0	4.0	—	6.2	⑤	⑩	⑪	⑦
	Topaz	X	4-140 (2.3)	5.0	4.0	—	6.2	⑤	⑩	⑪	⑦
	Topaz	H	4-122 (2.0)	7.2	7.0	—	6.2	⑤	②	15.4	⑦
	Taurus	D	4-153 (2.5)	5.0	4.5	—	6.2	16.6	②	⑧	8.3
	Taurus	U	6-182 (3.0)	4.5	4.0	—	6.2	21.8	②	⑧	⑨
	Sable	D	4-153 (2.5)	5.0	4.5	—	6.2	16.6	②	⑧	8.3
	Sable	U	6-182 (3.0)	4.5	4.0	—	6.2	21.8	②	⑧	⑨
1988	Escort	9	4-116 (1.9)	4.0	3.5	6.2	6.2	16.6	②	13	⑫
	Escort	J	4-116 (1.9)	4.0	3.5	6.2	6.2	16.6	②	13	⑫
	Tempo	S	4-140 (2.3)	5.0	4.0	—	6.2	⑤	⑩	⑪	⑬
	Tempo	X	4-140 (2.3)	5.0	4.0	—	6.2	⑤	⑩	⑪	⑬
	Topaz	S	4-140 (2.3)	5.0	4.0	—	6.2	⑤	⑩	⑪	⑬
	Topaz	X	4-140 (2.3)	5.0	4.0	—	6.2	⑤	⑩	⑪	⑫
	Taurus	D	4-153 (2.5)	5.0	4.5	—	6.2	16.6	②	⑧	8.3
	Taurus	U	6-182 (3.0)	4.5	4.0	—	6.2	21.8	②	⑧	11
	Taurus	4	6-232 (3.8)	5.0	4.5	—	—	26.2	②	⑧	12.1
	Sable	D	4-153 (2.5)	5.0	4.5	—	6.2	16.6	②	⑧	8.3
	Sable	U	6-182 (3.0)	4.5	4.0	—	6.2	21.8	②	⑧	8.3

CAPACITIES

Year	Model	VIN	No. Cylinder Displacement cu. in. (liter)	Engine Crankcase with Filter	Engine Crankcase without Filter	Transmission (pts.) 4-Spd	Transmission (pts.) 5-Spd	Transmission (pts.) Auto.	Drive Axle (pts.)	Fuel Tank (gal.)	Cooling System (qts.)
1988	Sable	4	6-232 (3.8)	5.0	4.5	—	—	26.2	②	⑧	12.1
	Continental	4	6-232 (3.8)	4.5	—	—	26.2		②	18.6	12.1	—
1989-90	Escort	9	4-116 (1.9)	4.0	3.5	6.2	6.2	16.6	②	⑭	⑫
	Escort	J	4-116 (1.9)	4.0	3.5	6.2	6.2	16.6	②	⑭	⑫
	Tempo	S	4-140 (2.3)	5.0	4.0	—	6.2	⑤	⑩	⑪	⑬
	Tempo	X	4-140 (2.3)	5.0	4.0	—	6.2	⑤	⑩	⑪	⑬
	Topaz	S	4-140 (2.3)	5.0	4.0	—	6.2	⑤	⑩	⑪	⑬
	Topaz	X	4-140 (2.3)	5.0	4.0	—	6.2	⑤	⑩	⑪	⑬
	Taurus	D	4-153 (2.5)	5.0	4.5	—	6.2	16.6	②	⑧	8.3
	Taurus	U	6-182 (3.0)	4.5	4.0	—	6.2	25.6	②	⑧	11
	Taurus	4	6-232 (3.8)	5.0	4.5	—	—	25.6	②	⑧	12.1
	Sable	D	4-153 (2.5)	5.0	4.5	—	6.2	16.6	②	⑧	8.3
	Sable	U	6-182 (3.0)	4.5	4.0	—	6.2	21.8	②	⑧	③
	Sable	4	6-232 (3.8)	5.0	4.5	—	—	26.2	②	⑧	12.1
	Continental	4	6-232 (3.8)	4.5	—	—	25.6		②	18.6	12.1	—

① 122 (2.0) Diesel
② Included in transaxle capacity
③ Standard tank—13 gals.
  Fuel economy leader—10 gals.
④ Standard models without air conditioning—7.9 qts.
  Manual transaxle with air conditioning—6.8 qts.
  Automatic transaxle with air conditioning—7.3 qts.
⑤ All models except the all wheel drive—16.6 pts.
⑥ All wheel drive models—20 pts.
⑦ All models without air conditioning—8.3 qts.
  Manual tranaxle with air conditioning—7.3 qts.
  Automatic transaxle with air conditioning—7.8 qts.
⑧ Standard—16 gal.
  Optional extended range—18.6
⑨ All models except station wagon with air conditioning—11 qts.
  Station wagon with air conditiong—11.8 qts.

⑩ Included in transaxle capacity. The all wheel drive model rear axle capacity is 13pts.
⑪ All models except the all wheel drive—15.4 gal.
  All wheel drive model—14.2 gal.
⑫ All models without air conditioning—8.3 qts.
  Manual transaxle with air conditioning—6.8 qts.
  Automatic transaxle with air conditioning—7.3 qts.
⑬ Manual transaxle—7.3 qts.
  Automatic transaxle—7.8 qts.
⑭ Standard—13 gal.
  All other models—11.5 gal.

CAMSHAFT SPECIFICATIONS
All measurements given in inches.

Year	VIN	No. Cylinder Displacement cu. in. (liter)	Journal Diameter 1	2	3	4	5	Lobe Lift	Bearing Clearance	Camshaft End Play
1986	9	4-116 (1.9)	1.8017–1.8007	1.8017–1.8007	1.8017–1.8007	1.8017–1.8007	1.8017–1.8007	0.240	0.0013–0.0033	0.0018–0.0060
	J	4-116 (1.9)	1.8017–1.8007	1.8017–1.8007	1.8017–1.8007	1.8017–1.8007	1.8017–1.8007	0.240	0.0013–0.0033	0.0018–0.0060
	H	4-122 (2.0)	1.2582–1.2589	1.2852–1.2589	1.2582–1.2589	1.2582–1.2589	1.2582–1.2589	—	0.0001–0.0026	0.0008–0.0059
	R	4-140 (2.3)	2.0060–2.0080	2.0060–2.0080	2.0060–2.0080	2.0060–2.0080	2.0060–2.0080	①	0.0010–0.0030	0.0090
	X	4-140 (2.3)	2.0060–2.0080	2.0060–2.0080	2.0060–2.0080	2.0060–2.0080	2.0060–2.0080	①②	0.0010–0.0030	0.0090
	D	4-154 (2.5)	2.0060–2.0080	2.0060–2.0080	2.0060–2.0080	2.0060–2.0080	2.0060–2.0080	①	0.0010–0.0030	0.0090–
	U	6-182 (3.0)	2.0074–2.0084	2.0074–2.0084	2.0074–2.0084	2.0074–2.0084	2.0074–2.0084	0.260	0.0010–0.0030	①
1987	9	4-116 (1.9)	1.8017–1.8007	1.8017–1.8007	1.8017–1.8007	1.8017–1.8007	1.8017–1.8007	0.240	0.0013–0.0033	0.0018–0.0060
	J	4-116 (1.9)	1.8017–1.8007	1.8017–1.8007	1.8017–1.8007	1.8017–1.8007	1.8017–1.8007	0.240	0.0013–0.0033	0.0018–0.0060
	H	4-122 (2.0)	1.2582–1.2589	1.2582–1.2589	1.2582–1.2589	1.2582–1.2589	1.2582–1.2589	—	0.0001–0.0026	0.0008–0.0059
	R	4-140 (2.3)	2.0060–2.0080	2.0060–2.0080	2.0060–2.0080	2.0060–2.0080	2.0060–2.0080	①	0.0010–0.0030	0.0090
	X	4-140 (2.3)	2.0060–2.0080	2.0060–2.0080	2.0060–2.0080	2.0060–2.0080	2.0060–2.0080	①②	0.0010–0.0030	0.0090
	D	4-154 (2.5)	2.2030–2.2040	2.1860–2.1870	2.1860–2.1870	2.2030–2.2040	2.0060–2.0080	③	0.0010–0.0030	0.0090
	U	6-182 (3.0)	2.0074–2.0084	2.0074–2.0084	2.0074–2.0084	2.0074–2.0084	2.0074–2.0084	0.260	0.0010–0.003	0.005
1988	9	4-116 (1.9)	1.8017–1.8007	1.8017–1.8007	1.8017–1.8007	1.8017–1.8007	1.8017–1.8007	0.240	0.0013–0.0033	0.0006–0.0018
	J	4-116 (1.9)	1.8166–1.8156	1.8166–1.8156	1.8166–1.8156	1.8166–1.8156	1.8166–1.8156	0.240	0.0013–0.0033	0.0006–0.0018
	X	4-140 (2.3)	2.0100–2.0090	2.0100–2.0190	2.0100–2.0190	2.0100–2.0190	2.0100–2.0190	①	0.0010–0.0030	0.0090
	S	4-140 (2.3)	2.0100–2.0190	2.0100–2.0190	2.0100–2.0190	2.0100–2.0190	2.0100–2.0190	②	0.0010–0.0030	0.0090
	D	4-154 (2.5)	2.2030–2.2040	2.1860–2.1870	2.1860–2.1870	2.2030–2.2040	—	①	0.0010–0.0030	0.0090
	U	6-182 (3.0)	2.0074–2.0084	2.0074–2.0084	2.0074–2.0084	2.0074–2.0084	—	0.260	0.0010–0.0030	0.0050
	4	6-232 (3.8)	2.0505–2.0515	2.0505–2.0515	2.0505–2.0515	2.0505–2.0515	—	④	0.0010–0.0030	—

CAMSHAFT SPECIFICATIONS
All measurements given in inches.

Year	VIN	No. Cylinder Displacement cu. in. (liter)	Journal Diameter 1	2	3	4	5	Lobe Lift	Bearing Clearance	Camshaft End Play
1989-90	9	4-116 (1.9)	1.8017–1.8007	1.8017–1.8007	1.8017–1.8007	1.8017–1.8007	1.8017–1.8007	0.240	0.0013–0.0033	0.0006–0.0018
	J	4-116 (1.9)	1.8166–1.8156	1.8166–1.8156	1.8166–1.8156	1.8166–1.8156	1.8166–1.8156	0.240	0.0013–0.0033	0.0006–0.0018
	X	4-140 (2.3)	2.0100–2.0090	2.0100–2.0190	2.0100–2.0190	2.0100–2.0190	2.0100–2.0190	①	0.0010–0.0030	0.0090
	S	4-140 (2.3)	2.0100–2.0190	2.0100–2.0190	2.0100–2.0190	2.0100–2.0190	2.0100–2.0190	②	0.0010–0.0030	0.0090
	D	4-154 (2.5)	2.2030–2.2040	2.1860–2.1870	2.1860–2.1870	2.2030–2.2040	—	①	0.0010–0.0030	0.0090
	U	6-182 (3.0)	2.0074–2.0084	2.0074–2.0084	2.0074–2.0084	2.0074–2.0084	—	0.260	0.0010–0.0030	0.0050
	Y	6-182 (3.0)	1.2189–1.2195	1.2189–1.2195	1.2189–1.2195	1.2189–1.2195	1.2189–1.2195	⑤	0.0010–0.0026	0.0120
	4	6-232 (3.8)	2.0505–2.0515	2.0505–2.0515	2.0505–2.0515	2.0505–2.0515	—	④	0.0010–0.0030	—

① Intake — 0.249 in.
Exhaust — 0.239 in.
② 2.3L HO engine — 0.2625 in.
③ Intake — 0.392
Exhaust — 0.377

④ Intake — 0.240
Exhaust — 0.241
⑤ Intake 0.335
Exhaust 0.315

CRANKSHAFT AND CONNECTING ROD SPECIFICATIONS
All measurements are given in inches.

Year	VIN	No. Cylinder Displacement cu. in. (liter)	Crankshaft Main Brg. Journal Dia.	Main Brg. Oil Clearance	Shaft End-play	Thrust on No.	Connecting Rod Journal Diameter	Oil Clearance	Side Clearance
1986	9	4-116 (1.9)	2.2827–2.2835	0.0008–0.0015	0.004–0.008	3	1.8854–1.8862	0.0008–0.0015	0.004–0.011
	J	4-116 (1.9)	2.2827–2.2835	0.0008–0.0015	0.004–0.008	3	1.8854–1.8862	0.0008–0.0015	0.004–0.011
	H	4-122 (2.0)	2.3598–2.3605	0.0012–0.0020	0.002–0.0011	3	2.0055–2.0061	0.0010–0.0020	0.004–0.010
	R	4-140 (2.3)	2.2489–2.2490	0.0008–0.0015	0.004–0.008	3	2.1232–2.1240	0.0008–0.0015	0.004–0.011
	X	4-140 (2.3)	2.2489–2.2490	0.0008–0.0015	0.004–0.008	3	2.1232–2.1240	0.0008–0.0015	0.004–0.011
	D	4-154 (2.5)	2.2489–2.2490	0.0008–0.0015	0.004–0.008	3	2.1232–2.1240	0.0008–0.0015	0.004–0.011
	U	6-182 (3.0)	2.5190–2.5198	0.0010–0.0014	0.004–0.008	3	2.1253–2.1261	0.0010–0.0014	0.006–0.014

CRANKSHAFT AND CONNECTING ROD SPECIFICATIONS
All measurements are given in inches.

Year	VIN	No. Cylinder Displacement cu. in. (liter)	Crankshaft				Connecting Rod		
			Main Brg. Journal Dia.	Main Brg. Oil Clearance	Shaft End-play	Thrust on No.	Journal Diameter	Oil Clearance	Side Clearance
1987	9	4-116 (1.9)	2.2821–2.2835	0.0008–0.0015	0.004–0.008	3	1.8854–1.8862	0.0008–0.0015	0.004–0.011
	J	4-116 (1.9)	2.2827–2.2835	0.0008–0.0015	0.004–0.008	3	1.8854–1.8862	0.0008–0.0015	0.004–0.011
	H	4-122 (2.0)	2.3598–2.3605	0.0012–0.0020	0.002–0.001	3	2.0055–2.0061	0.0010–0.0020	0.004–0.010
	R	4-140 (2.3)	2.2489–2.2490	0.0008–0.0015	0.004–0.008	3	2.1232–2.1240	0.0008–0.0015	0.004–0.011
	X	4-140 (2.3)	2.2489–2.2490	0.0008–0.0015	0.004–0.008	3	2.1232–2.1240	0.0008–0.0015	0.004–0.011
	D	4-154 (2.5)	2.2489–2.2490	0.0008–0.0015	0.004–0.008	3	2.1232–2.1240	0.0008–0.0015	0.004–0.011
	U	6-182 (3.0)	2.5190–2.5198	0.0010–0.0014	0.004–0.008	3	2.1253–2.1261	0.0010–0.0014	0.006–0.014
1988	9	4-116 (1.9)	2.2827–2.2835	0.0008–0.0015	0.004–0.008	3	1.7287–1.7279	0.0008–0.0015	0.004–0.011
	J	4-116 (1.9)	2.2827–2.2835	0.0008–0.0015	0.004–0.008	3	1.7287–1.7279	0.0008–0.0015	0.004–0.011
	X	4-140 (2.3)	2.2489–2.2490	0.0008–0.0015	0.004–0.008	3	2.1232–2.1240	0.0008–0.0015	0.004–0.011
	S	4-140 (2.3)	2.2489–2.2490	0.0008–0.0015	0.004–0.008	3	2.1232–2.1240	0.0008–0.0015	0.004–0.011
	D	4-154 (2.5)	2.2489–2.2490	0.0008–0.0015	0.004–0.008	3	2.1232–2.1240	0.0008–0.0015	0.004–0.011
	U	4-182 (3.0)	2.5190–2.5198	0.0010–0.0014	0.004–0.008	3	2.1253–2.1261	0.0010–0.0014	0.006–0.014
	4	6-232 (3.8)	2.5190–2.5198	0.0010–0.0014	0.004–0.008	3	2.3103–2.3111	0.0010–0.0014	0.005–0.011
1989-90	9	4-116 (1.9)	2.2827–2.2835	0.0008–0.0015	0.004–0.008	3	1.7287–1.7279	0.0008–0.0015	0.004–0.011
	J	4-116 (1.9)	2.2827–2.2835	0.0008–0.0015	0.004–0.008	3	1.7287–1.7279	0.0008–0.0015	0.004–0.011
	X	4-140 (2.3)	2.2489–2.2490	0.0008–0.0015	0.004–0.008	3	2.1232–2.1240	0.0008–0.0015	0.004–0.011
	S	4-140 (2.3)	2.2489–2.2490	0.0008–0.0015	0.004–0.008	3	2.1232–2.1240	0.0008–0.0015	0.004–0.011
	D	4-154 (2.5)	2.2489–2.2490	0.0008–0.0015	0.004–0.008	3	2.1232–2.1240	0.0008–0.0015	0.004–0.011
	U	4-182 (3.0)	2.5190–2.5198	0.0010–0.0014	0.004–0.008	3	2.1253–2.1261	0.0010–0.0014	0.006–0.014
	Y	6-182 (3.0)	2.5187–2.5197	0.0011–0.0022	0.0008–0.0087	3	2.0463–2.0472	0.0009–0.0022	0.006–0.012
	4	6-232 (3.8)	2.5190–2.5198	0.0010–0.0014	0.004–0.008	3	2.3103–2.3111	0.0010–0.0014	0.005–0.011

VALVE SPECIFICATIONS

Year	VIN	No. Cylinder Displacement cu. in. (liter)	Seat Angle (deg.)	Face Angle (deg.)	Spring Test Pressure (lbs. @ in.)	Spring Installed Height (in.)	Stem-to-Guide Clearance (in.) Intake	Stem-to-Guide Clearance (in.) Exhaust	Stem Diameter (in.) Intake	Stem Diameter (in.) Exhaust
1986	9	4-116 (1.9)	45	45	200 @ 1.09	1.44–1.48	0.0008–0.0027	0.0018–0.0037	0.3160	0.3150
	J	4-116 (1.9)	45	45	216 @ 1.02	1.44–1.48	0.0008–0.0027	0.0018–0.0037	0.3160	0.3150
	H	4-122 (2.0)	45	45	—	1.78	0.0016–0.0029	0.0018–0.0031	0.3138	0.3138
	R	4-140 (2.3)	45	45.5	182 @ 1.10	1.40	0.0018	0.0023	0.3160	0.3150
	X	4-140 (2.3)	45	45.5	182 @ 1.10	1.40	0.0018	0.0023	0.3160	0.3150
	D	4-154 (2.5)	45	45	182 @ 1.03	1.49	0.0018	0.0023	0.3415–0.3422	0.3411–0.3418
	U	6-182 (3.0)	45	44	185 @ 1.11	1.58	0.0010–0.0028	0.0015–0.0033	0.3126–0.3134	0.3121–0.3129
1987	9	4-116 (1.9)	45	45	200 @ 1.09	1.48–1.44	0.0008–0.0027	0.0018–0.0037	0.3160	0.3150
	J	4-116 (1.9)	45	45	216 @ 1.02	1.48–1.44	0.0008–0.0027	0.0018–0.0037	0.3160	0.3150
	H	4-122 (2.0)	45	45	—	1.78	0.0016–	0.0018–	0.3138	0.3138
	R	4-140 (2.3)	45	45.5	182 @ 1.10	1.49	0.0018	0.0023	0.3160	0.3150
	X	4-140 (2.3)	45	45.5	182 @ 1.10	1.49	0.0018	0.0023	0.3160	0.3150
	D	4-154 (2.5)	45	45	182 @ 1.03	1.49	0.0018	0.0023	0.3415–0.3422	0.3411–0.3418
	U	6-182 (3.0)	45	44	185 @ 1.11	1.58	0.0010–0.0028	0.0015–0.0033	0.3126–0.3134	0.3121–0.3129
1988	9	4-116 (1.9)	45	46	200 @ 1.09	1.44–1.486	0.0008–0.0027	0.0018–0.0037	0.3170	0.3150
	J	4-116 (1.9)	45	45	216 @ 1.02	1.44–1.48	0.0008–0.0027	0.0018–0.0037	0.3170	0.3150
	X	4-140 (2.3)	44.5	44.5	181 @ 1.07	1.49	0.0018–	0.0023–	0.3415–0.3422	0.3411–0.3418
	S	4-140 (2.3)	44.5	44.5	181 @ 1.07	1.49	0.0018	0.0023	0.3415–0.3422	0.3411–0.3418
	D	4-154 (2.5)	45	45	182 @ 1.13	1.49	0.0018	0.0023	0.3415–0.3422	0.3411–0.3418
	U	4-182 (3.0)	45	45	185 @ 1.11	1.85	0.0010–0.0028	0.0015–0.0033	0.3126–0.3134	0.3121–0.3219
	4	6-232 (3.8)	46	46	190 @ 1.28	2.02	0.0010–0.0028	0.0015–0.0033	0.3423–0.3415	0.3418–0.3410

VALVE SPECIFICATIONS

Year	VIN	No. Cylinder Displacement cu. in. (liter)	Seat Angle (deg.)	Face Angle (deg.)	Spring Test Pressure (lbs. @ in.)	Spring Installed Height (in.)	Stem-to-Guide Clearance (in.) Intake	Stem-to-Guide Clearance (in.) Exhaust	Stem Diameter (in.) Intake	Stem Diameter (in.) Exhaust
1989-90	9	4-116 (1.9)	45	46	200 @ 1.09	1.44–1.49	0.0008–0.0027	0.0018–0.0037	0.3170	0.3150
	J	4-116 (1.9)	45	45	216 @ 1.02	1.44–1.48	0.0008–0.0027	0.0018–0.0037	0.3170	0.3150
	X	4-140 (2.3)	44.5	44.5	181 @ 1.07	1.49	0.0018–	0.0023–	0.3415–0.3422	0.3411–0.3418
	S	4-140 (2.3)	44.5	44.5	181 @ 1.07	1.49	0.0018	0.0023	0.3415–0.3422	0.3411–0.3418
	D	4-154 (2.5)	45	45	182 @ 1.13	1.49	0.0018	0.0023	0.3415–0.3422	0.3411–0.3418
	U	4-182 (3.0)	45	45	185 @ 1.11	1.85	0.0010–0.0028	0.0015–0.0033	0.3126–0.3134	0.3121–0.3219
	Y	6-182 (3.0)	45	45.5	121 @ 1.19	1.76	0.0010–0.0023	0.0012–0.0025	0.2346–0.2356	0.23444–0.2350
	4	6-232 (3.8)	46	46	190 @ 1.28	2.02	0.0010–0.0028	0.0015–0.0033	0.3423–0.3415	0.3418–0.3410

PISTON AND RING SPECIFICATIONS
All measurments are given in inches.

Year	VIN	No. Cylinder Displacement cu. in. (liter)	Piston Clearance	Ring Gap Top Compression	Ring Gap Bottom Compression	Ring Gap Oil Control	Ring Side Clearance Top Compression	Ring Side Clearance Bottom Compression	Ring Side Clearance Oil Control
1986	9	4-116 (1.9)	0.0016–0.0024	0.010–0.020	0.010–0.020	0.016–0.055	0.002–0.003	0.002–0.004	Snug
	J	4-116 (1.9)	0.0016–0.0024	0.010–0.020	0.010–0.020	0.016–0.055	0.002–0.003	0.002–0.004	Snug
	H	4-122 (2.0)	0.0012–0.0020	0.008–0.016	0.008–0.016	0.008–0.016	0.002–0.004	0.002–0.003	Snug
	R	4-140 (2.3)	0.0013–0.0021	0.008–0.016	0.008–0.016	0.0015–0.055	0.002–0.004	0.002–0.004	Snug
	X	4-140 (2.3)	0.0013–0.0021	0.008–0.016	0.008–0.016	0.015–0.055	0.002–0.004	0.002–0.004	Snug
	D	4-154 (2.5)	0.0012–0.0022	0.008–0.016	0.008–0.016	0.015–0.055	0.002–0.004	0.002–0.004	Snug
	U	6-182 (3.0)	0.0014–0.0022	0.010–0.020	0.010–0.020	0.010–0.049	0.001–0.003	0.001–0.003	Snug

PISTON AND RING SPECIFICATIONS
All measurments are given in inches.

Year	VIN	No. Cylinder Displacement cu. in. (liter)	Piston Clearance	Ring Gap			Ring Side Clearance		
				Top Compression	Bottom Compression	Oil Control	Top Compression	Bottom Compression	Oil Control
1987	9	4-116 (1.9)	0.0016–.0024	0.010–0.020	0.010–0.020	0.016–0.055	0.002–0.003	0.002–0.004	Snug
	J	4-116 (1.9)	0.0016–0.0024	0.010–0.020	0.010–0.020	0.016–0.055	0.002–0.003	0.002–0.004	Snug
	H	4-122 (2.0)	0.0013–0.0020	0.008–0.016	0.008–0.016	0.008–0.016	0.002–0.0034	0.002–0.003	Snug
	R	4-140 (2.3)	0.0013–0.0021	0.008–0.016	0.008–0.016	0.015–0.055	0.002–0.004	0.002–0.004	Snug
	X	4-140 (2.3)	0.0013–0.0021	0.008–0.016	0.008–0.016	0.015–0.055	0.002–0.004	0.002–0.004	Snug
	D	4-154 (2.5)	0.0012–0.0022	0.008–0.016	0.008–0.016	0.015–0.055	0.002–0.004	0.002–0.004	Snug
	U	6-182 (3.0)	0.0014–0.0022	0.010–0.020	0.010–0.020	0.010–0.049	0.001–0.003	0.001–0.003	Snug
1988	9	4-116 (1.9)	0.0016–0.0024	0.010–0.020	0.010–0.020	0.016–0.055	0.002–0.003	0.002–0.004	Snug
	J	4-116 (1.9)	0.0016–0.0024	0.010–0.020	0.010–0.020	0.016–0.055	0.002–0.003	0.002–0.004	Snug
	X	4-140 (2.3)	0.0012–0.0022	0.008–0.016	0.008–0.016	0.015–0.055	0.002–0.004	0.002–0.004	Snug
	S	4-140 (2.3)	0.0012–0.0022	0.008–0.016	0.008–0.016	0.015–0.055	0.002–0.004	0.002–0.004	Snug
	D	4-154 (2.5)	0.0012–0.0022	0.008–0.016	0.008–0.016	0.015–0.055	0.002–0.004	0.002–0.004	Snug
	U	6-182 (3.0)	0.0014–0.0022	0.010–0.020	0.010–0.020	0.010–0.049	0.001–0.003	0.001–0.003	Snug
	4	6-232 (3.8)	0.0014–0.0032	0.010–0.020	0.010–0.020	0.015–0.058	0.002–0.004	0.002–0.004	—
1989-90	9	4-116 (1.9)	0.0016–0.0024	0.010–0.020	0.010–0.020	0.016–0.055	0.002–0.003	0.002–0.003	Snug
	J	4-116 (1.9)	0.0016–0.0024	0.010–0.020	0.010–0.020	0.016–0.055	0.002–0.003	0.002–0.004	Snug
	X	4-140 (2.3)	0.0012–0.0022	0.008–0.016	0.008–0.016	0.015–0.055	0.002–0.004	0.002–0.004	Snug
	S	4-140 (2.3)	0.0012–0.0022	0.008–0.016	0.008–0.016	0.015–0.055	0.002–0.004	0.002–0.004	Snug
	D	4-154 (2.5)	0.0012–0.0022	0.008–0.016	0.008–0.016	0.015–0.055	0.002–0.004	0.002–0.004	Snug
	U	6-182 (3.0)	0.0014–0.0022	0.010–0.020	0.010–0.020	0.010–0.049	0.001–0.003	0.001–0.003	Snug
	Y	6-182 (3.0)	0.0012–0.0020	0.012–0.018	0.012–0.018	0.008–0.020	0.001–0.002	0.001–0.002	0.0024–0.0059
	4	6-232 (3.8)	0.0014–0.0032	0.010–0.020	0.010–0.020	0.015–0.0583	0.002–0.004	0.002–0.004	—

TORQUE SPECIFICATIONS
All readings in ft. lbs.

Year	VIN	No. Cylinder Displacement cu. in. (liter)	Cylinder Head Bolts	Main Bearing Bolts	Rod Bearing Bolts	Crankshaft Pulley Bolts	Flywheel Bolts	Manifold Intake	Manifold Exhaust	Spark Plugs
1986	9	4-116 (1.9)	①	67-80	19-25	74-90	59-69	12-15②	15-20	8-15
	J	4-116 (1.9)	①	67-80	19-25	74-90	59-69	12-15②	15-20	8-15
	H	4-122 (2.0)	⑧	61-65	51-54	115-123	130-137	12-16	16-19	—
	R	4-140 (2.3)	④	51-56	21-26	140-170	54-64	15-23	③	5-10
	X	4-140 (2.3)	④	51-66	21-26	140-170	54-64	15-23	③	5-10
	D	4-154 (2.5)	70-76	51-66	21-26	140-170	54-64	15-23	20-30	5-10
	U	6-182 (3.0)	63-80	65-81	⑤	141-169	54-64	⑥	20-30	5-10
1987	9	4-116 (1.9)	①	67-80	19-25	74-90	59-69	12-15	15-20	8-15
	J	4-116 (1.9)	①	67-80	19-25	74-90	59-69	12-15	15-20	8-15
	H	4-122 (2.0)	⑧	61-65	51-54	115-123	130-137	12-16	16-19	—
	R	4-140 (2.3)	④	51-66	21-26	140-170	54-64	15-23	③	5-10
	X	4-140 (2.3)	④	51-66	21-26	140-170	54-64	15-23	③	5-10
	D	4-154 (2.5)	70-76	51-66	21-26	140-170	54-64	15-23	20-30	5-10
	U	6-182 (3.0)	63-80	65-81	⑤	141-169	54-64	⑥	20-30	5-10
1988	9	4-116 (1.9)	①	67-80	19-25	74-90	54-64	12-15	15-20	8-15
	J	4-116 (1.9)	①	67-80	19-25	74-90	54-64	12-15	15-20	8-15
	X	4-140 (2.3)	④	51-66	21-26	140-170	54-64	15-23	③	5-10
	S	4-140 (2.3)	④	51-66	21-26	140-170	54-64	15-23	⑦	6-10
	D	4-154 (2.5)	70-76	51-66	21-26	140-170	54-64	15-23	③	5-10
	U	6-182 (3.0)	63-80	65-81	⑤	141-169	54-64	⑥	20-30	5-10
	4	6-232 (3.8)	⑦	65-81	31-36	93-121	54-64	⑨	16-24	5-11
1989-90	9	4-116 (1.9)	①	67-80	26-30	74-90	54-64	12-15	15-20	8-15
	J	4-116 (1.9)	①	67-80	19-25	26-30	54-64	12-15	15-20	8-15
	X	4-140 (2.3)	④	51-66	21-26	140-170	54-64	15-23	③	5-10
	S	4-140 (2.3)	④	51-66	21-26	140-170	54-64	15-23	③	5-10
	D	4-154 (2.5)	70-76	51-66	21-26	140-170	54-64	15-23	③	5-10
	U	6-182 (3.0)	63-80	65-81	⑤	141-169	54-64	⑥	20-30	5-10
	Y	6-182 (3.0)	61-69	58-65	33-36	112-127	51-58	12-17	26-38	16-20
	4	6-232 (3.8)	⑦	65-81	31-36	93-121	54-64	⑨	16-24	5-11

① Tighten bolts to 44 ft. lbs., then loosen 2 turns. Tighten bolts again to 44 ft. lbs., then turn all bolts another ¼ turn. Turn all bolts again a final ¼ turn
② Manifold stud nuts—12-13 ft. lbs.
③ Tighten in 2 stages—5–7 ft. lbs.; 20–30 ft. lbs.
④ Tighten in 2 steps—52-59 ft. lbs. and then the final torque of 70-76 ft. lbs.
⑤ Step 1—Torque to 20-28 ft. lbs.
   Step 2—Back off at least 2 full turns
   Step 3—Torque to 20-26 ft. lbs.
⑥ Step 1—11 ft. lbs.
   Step 2—18 ft. lbs.
   Step 3—24 ft. lbs.
⑦ Tighten in 4 steps:
   Step 1—37 ft. lbs.
   Step 2—45 ft. lbs.

TORQUE SPECIFICATIONS
All readings in ft. lbs.

Year	VIN	No. Cylinder Displacement cu. in. (liter)	Cylinder Head Bolts	Main Bearing Bolts	Rod Bearing Bolts	Crankshaft Pulley Bolts	Flywheel Bolts	Manifold Intake	Manifold Exhaust	Spark Plugs

Step 3—52 ft. lbs.
Step 4—59 ft. lbs.

⑧ Tighten bolts to 22 ft. lbs., then using painted reference marks, tighten each bolt another 90–105 degrees; then another 90–105 degrees following sequence each time

⑨ Tighten in 3 steps:
Step 1—7 ft. lbs.
Step 2—15 ft. lbs.
Step 3—24 ft. lbs.

WHEEL ALIGNMENT

Year	Model	Caster Range (deg.)	Caster Preferred Setting (deg.)	Camber Range (deg.)	Camber Preferred Setting (deg.)	Toe-in (in.)	Steering Axis Inclination (deg.)
1986	Escort, Lynx	$1\frac{11}{16}P$-$3\frac{3}{16}P$	$2\frac{7}{16}P$	①	③	$\frac{7}{32}N$-$\frac{1}{64}P$	⑤
	Tempo, Topaz	$1\frac{11}{16}P$-$3\frac{3}{16}P$	$2\frac{7}{16}P$	⑥⑩	⑦⑪	⑧	⑨
	Taurus, Sable	3P-6P	4P	⑬	$\frac{1}{2}N$	$\frac{7}{32}N$-$\frac{1}{64}P$	$15\frac{3}{8}$
1987	Escort, Lynx	$1\frac{5}{8}P$-$3\frac{1}{8}P$	$2\frac{3}{8}P$	②	④	$\frac{1}{4}N$-0	⑤
	Tempo, Topaz	$1\frac{11}{16}P$-$3\frac{3}{16}P$	$2\frac{7}{16}P$	⑫	⑬⑭	0	⑯
	Taurus, Sable	3P-6P	4P	⑰㉑	㉒	㉓	$15\frac{3}{8}$
1988	Escort	$1\frac{5}{8}P$-$3\frac{1}{8}P$	$2\frac{3}{8}P$	②	④	$\frac{1}{4}N$-0	⑤
	Tempo, Topaz	$1\frac{11}{16}P$-$3\frac{3}{16}P$	$2\frac{7}{16}P$	⑫	⑬⑭	⑮	⑯
	Taurus, Sable	3P-6P	4P	⑰㉑	㉒	㉓	$15\frac{3}{8}$
	Continental	4P-$5\frac{5}{8}P$	$4\frac{13}{16}$	㉙	㉚	㉛	$15\frac{1}{2}$
1989-90	Escort	$1\frac{5}{8}P$-$3\frac{1}{8}P$	$2\frac{3}{8}P$	②	④	$\frac{1}{4}N$-0	⑤
	Tempo, Topaz	$1\frac{11}{16}P$-$3\frac{3}{16}P$	$2\frac{7}{16}P$	⑫	⑬⑭	⑮	⑯
	Taurus, Sable	㉔	㉕	㉖	㉗	㉘	$15\frac{1}{2}$
	Continental	$3\frac{5}{8}P$-$5\frac{1}{8}$	$4\frac{3}{8}P$	㉜	㉝	㉞	$15\frac{1}{2}$

N Negative
P Positive

① Left—$\frac{5}{8}P$-$2\frac{1}{8}P$
   Right—$\frac{3}{16}P$-$1\frac{11}{16}P$

② Left—$\frac{3}{8}P$-$1\frac{7}{8}P$
   Right—0-$1\frac{1}{8}P$

③ Left—$2\frac{3}{8}P$
   Right—$\frac{15}{16}P$

④ Left—$1\frac{1}{8}P$
   Right—$\frac{3}{4}P$

⑤ Left—$14\frac{21}{32}$
   Right—$15\frac{3}{32}$

⑥ Front left—$\frac{13}{32}P$-$1\frac{29}{32}P$
   Right—$\frac{1}{32}P$-$1\frac{15}{32}P$

⑦ Front left—$1\frac{5}{32}P$
   Right—$\frac{23}{32}P$

⑧ Front—$\frac{7}{32}N$-$\frac{1}{64}P$
   Rear—$\frac{3}{16}N$-$\frac{3}{16}P$

⑨ Left—$14\frac{21}{32}$
   Right—$15\frac{3}{32}$

⑩ Rear—$1\frac{1}{32}P$-$\frac{15}{32}$

⑪ Rear—$\frac{9}{32}P$

⑫ Front left—$\frac{21}{32}P$-$2\frac{5}{32}P$
   Right—$\frac{7}{32}P$-$1\frac{23}{32}P$

⑬ Front—$1\frac{13}{32}P$
   Right—$\frac{31}{32}P$

⑭ Rear (FWD)—$\frac{5}{32}N$
   Rear (AWD)—$1\frac{7}{32}N$

⑮ Front—$\frac{1}{4}P$-0
   Rear—$\frac{3}{16}N$-$\frac{3}{16}P$

⑯ Left—$14\frac{21}{32}$
   Right—$15\frac{3}{32}$

⑰ Front—$1\frac{3}{32}N$-$\frac{3}{32}P$

⑱ Not used

⑲ Not used

⑳ Not used

㉑ Rear sedan—$1\frac{5}{8}$-$\frac{1}{4}N$
   Rear wagon—$1\frac{5}{16}N$-$\frac{1}{16}N$

㉒ Front—$\frac{1}{2}N$
   Rear sedan—$\frac{15}{16}N$
   Rear wagon—$\frac{5}{8}N$

㉓ Front—$\frac{7}{16}N$-$\frac{1}{32}N$
   Rear—$\frac{1}{8}N$-$\frac{3}{8}P$

㉔ Sedan-$2\frac{13}{16}P$-$5\frac{13}{16}P$
   Wagon—$2\frac{11}{16}P$-$5\frac{11}{16}P$⑯

㉕ Sedan—$3\frac{13}{16}P$
   Wagon—$3\frac{11}{16}$

㉖ Front sedan—$1\frac{1}{8}N$-$\frac{1}{8}P$
   Front wagon—$1\frac{7}{8}N$-$\frac{1}{8}P$
   Rear—$1\frac{5}{8}N$-$\frac{7}{32}N$

㉗ Front sedan—$\frac{1}{2}N$
   Front wagon—$\frac{7}{8}N$
   Rear—$\frac{15}{16}N$

㉘ Front—$\frac{7}{32}N$-$\frac{1}{32}P$
   Rear—$\frac{1}{16}N$-$\frac{3}{16}P$

㉙ Front—$1\frac{1}{2}N$-$\frac{5}{16}P$
   Rear—$2N$-$\frac{5}{8}N$

㉚ Front—$\frac{7}{8}N$
   Rear—$1\frac{5}{16}$

㉛ Front—$\frac{21}{64}N$-$\frac{1}{32}P$
   Rear—$\frac{1}{32}N$-$\frac{7}{32}P$

㉜ Front—$1\frac{11}{16}N$-$\frac{1}{2}N$
   Rear—$2N$-$\frac{5}{8}N$

㉝ Front—$1\frac{1}{8}N$ •
   Rear—$1\frac{5}{16}N$

㉞ Front—$\frac{7}{32}N$-$\frac{1}{32}P$
   Rear—$\frac{1}{32}N$-$\frac{7}{32}P$

ELECTRICAL

For alternator, starter and regulator testing and overhaul procedures, refer to the Unit Repair section.

Charging System

ALTERNATOR

Removal and Installation

1. Disconnect the negative battery cable and remove the pulley cover shield, if equipped.
2. Loosen the alternator pivot bolt and remove the adjustment bracket-to-alternator bolt. Slide the alternator downward and remove the drive belt.
3. Identify, tag and disconnect the alternator wiring.

NOTE: Some vehicles use a push-on wiring connector on the field and stator connections. Pull or push straight when removing or installing the connector. Be careful not to damage the connector.

4. Remove the pivot bolt and the alternator.
5. On installation, position the alternator assembly on the engine and install the pivot bolt, but do not tighten until the belt is tensioned.
6. Install the drive belt over the alternator pulley.
7. Adjust the belt tension and tighten the adjuster and pivot bolts.
8. Connect the wiring to the alternator.
9. Install the pulley cover shield, if equipped. Connect the negative battery cable.

VOLTAGE REGULATOR

Removal and Installation

EXTERNAL TYPE

NOTE: There are three different types of regulators being used, depending on the vehicle, engine, alternator output and type of dash mounted charging indicator used (light or ammeter). The regulators are 100% solid state and are calibrated and preset by the manufacturer. No adjustments are required or possible on these regulators.

1. Disconnect the negative battery cable.
2. Disconnect the electrical connectors from the wiring harness.
3. Remove the regulator mounting screws and remove the regulator.
4. Installation is the reverse of the removal procedure.
5. Test the system for proper voltage regulation.

INTERNAL TYPE

Some vehicles are equipped with an integral type regulator. It is component of the alternator. To repair or replace the integral type regulator, the alternator must be removed and disassembled.

BELT TENSION

Adjustment

CONVENTIONAL AND COGGED BELTS
Except 2.3L HSC Engine

1. Disconnect the negative battery cable.
2. Loosen the alternator adjustment and pivot bolts.
3. Apply pressure on the alternator, using the belt adjusting

hole in the alternator bracket and use care not to damage the alternator housing.
4. Properly tighten the adjustment bolts. Release the pressure and tighten the pivot bolt to specifications.
5. Check the belt tension and readjust if necessary.

2.3L HSC Engine

1. Disconnect the negative battery cable.
2. Loosen the alternator adjustment and pivot bolts.
3. Using adjustable pliers or equivalent, apply tension to the belt. Position the bottom jaw of the pliers under the alternator adjustment boss and the top jaw in the notch at the top of the alternator adjustment bracket.
4. Squeeze the pliers together and using a belt tension gauge, set the belt to the proper tension. Tension should be 160 lbs. for a new belt and 140 lbs. for a used belt.
5. Maintaining proper belt tension, tighten the alternator adjustment bolt to 26 ft. lbs.

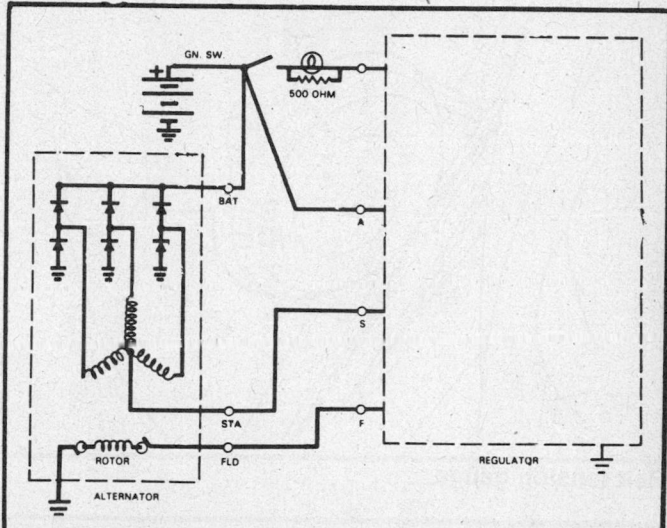

Charging system schematic with electronic regulator and indicator lamp

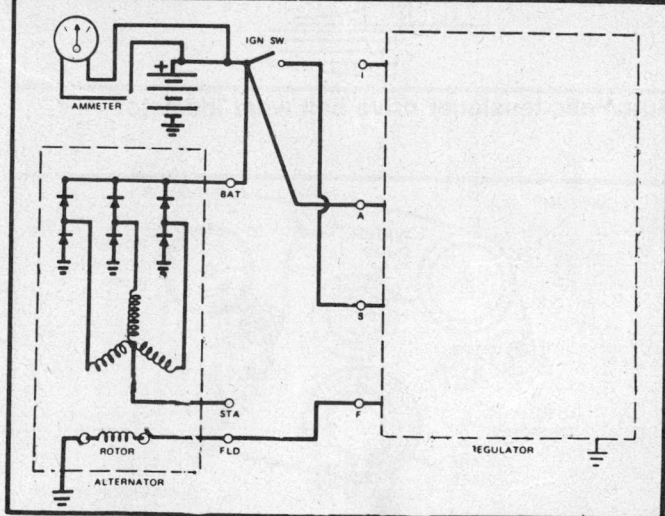

Charging system schematic with electronic regulator and ammeter

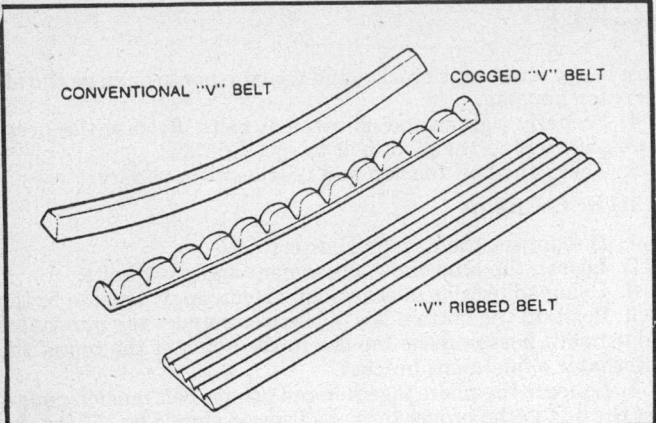

Types of drive belts

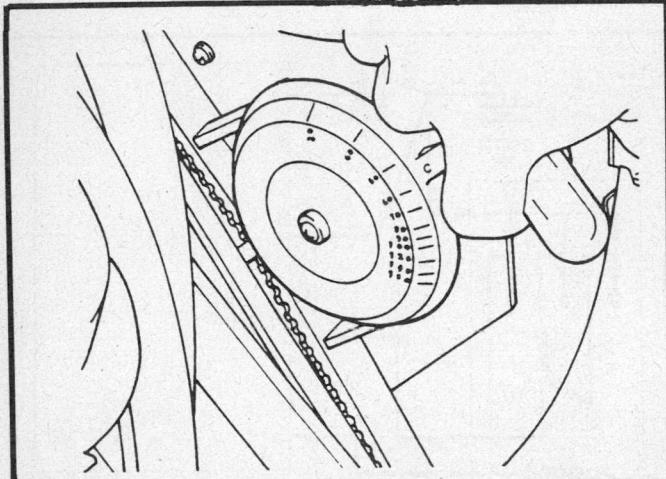

Belt tension gauge

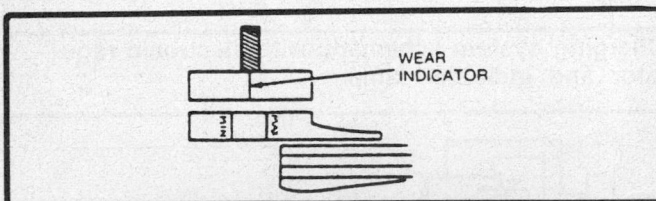

Automatic tensioner drive belt wear Indicator

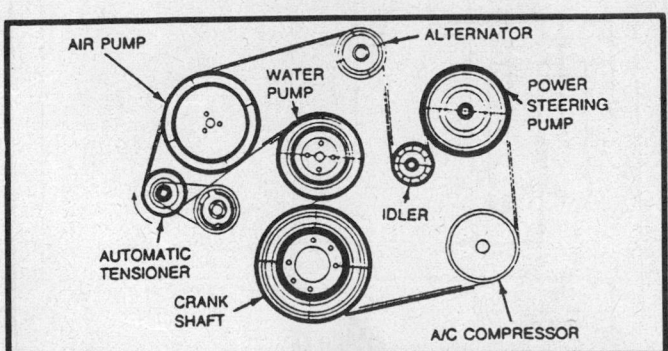

Alternator and accessory drive belt arrangement— 3.8L engine

6. Remove the belt tension gauge and idle the engine for 5 minutes.

7. With the engine **OFF**, tension gauge in place and tension being applied to the adjustable pliers so that the existing tension is not lost, loosen the alternator adjustment bolt to allow the belt tension to increase to 160 lbs. for a new belt and 140 lbs. for a used belt.

8. Then tighten the adjustment bolt to 26 ft. lbs. Tighten the alternator pivot bolt to 52 ft. lbs.

RIBBED BELTS

The V-ribbed belts used on some engines utilize an automatic belt tensioner whose function is to maintain the proper belt tension for the life of the belt. The automatic belt tensioners used on the 2.5L and 3.8L engines incorporate wear indicator **MINIMUM** and **MAXIMUM** marks.

1. Inspect the wear indicator marks with the engine off (not running).

2. If the indicator mark is not within the 2 marks, the belt is worn or an improper belt is installed.

3. A loose or improper belt will result in slippage which will in turn cause a noise complaint or improper accessory operation.

4. Automatic tensioners do not require removal when making a drive belt replacement.

5. When removing a drive belt, rotate the tensioner away from the belt.

1.9L ENGINE

1. Disconnect the negative battery cable.

2. Loosen the alternator adjustment and pivot bolts.

3. Install a ½ in. breaker bar or equivalent to the support bracket that is located behind the alternator.

4. Apply tension to the belt using the breaker bar. Using a belt tension gauge, set the belt to the proper tension. The tension should be 160 lbs. for a new belt and 130 lbs. for a used belt.

5. While maintaining proper belt tension, tighten the alternator adjustment bolt to 30 ft. lbs.

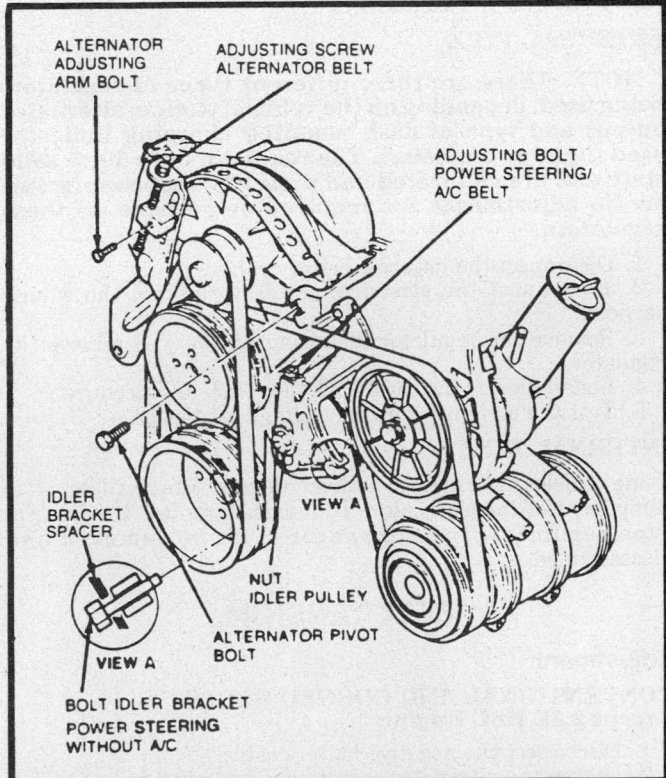

Belt tension adjustment 3.0L engine

6. Remove the belt tension gauge and breaker bar and idle the engine for 5 minutes.

7. With the engine **OFF**, check the belt tension. If the tension is below 120 lbs., retension the belt.

8. Tighten the adjustment bolt to 30 ft. lbs. Tighten the pivot bolt to 50 ft. lbs. and the support bracket bolt to 35 ft. lbs.

3.0L ENGINE

1. Disconnect the negative battery cable.
2. Loosen the alternator adjustment and pivot bolts.
3. Apply tension to the belt using the adjusting screw.
4. Using a belt tension gauge, set the belt to the proper tension. The tension should be 150 lbs. for a new belt and 120 lbs. for a used belt.
5. When the belt is properly tensioned, tighten the alternator adjustment bolt to 27 ft. lbs. (37 Nm).
6. Remove the tension gauge and run the engine for 5 minutes.
7. With the engine **OFF** and the belt tension gauge in place, check that the adjusting screw is in contact with the bracket before loosening the alternator adjustment bolt. Rotate the adjustment screw until the belt is tensioned to 120 lbs.
8. Tighten the alternator adjustment bolt to 27 ft. lbs. (37 Nm) and the pivot bolt to 51 ft. lbs. (69 Nm).

3.0L SHO ENGINE

1. Disconnect the negative battery cable.
2. Loosen the idler pulley bracket bolts.
3. Turn the adjusting bolt until the belt is adjusted properly.

NOTE: Turning the wrench to the right tightens the belt adjustment and turning the wrench to the left loosens the belt tension.

4. Tighten the idler pulley bracket bolts and check the belt tension.

5. Recheck the belt tension and adjust if necessary.

Starting System

STARTER

Removal and Installation

ESCORT, LYNX, TEMPO AND TOPAZ EXCEPT DIESEL ENGINE

1. Disconnect the negative battery cable.
2. Raise the vehicle and support safely.
3. Disconnect the starter cable at the starter terminal.
4. Remove the 2 bolts attaching the starter rear support bracket, remove the starter.
5. On vehicles equipped with roll restricter brace-to-starter studs on the transaxle housing, remove the nuts and remove the brace.
6. On Tempo and Topaz, remove the cable support.
7. For installation, reverse the removal procedure. Tighten the attaching studs or bolts to 30–40 ft. lbs. (41–54 Nm).

ESCORT, LYNX, TEMPO AND TOPAZ WITH DIESEL ENGINE

1. Remove the battery cover and disconnect the negative battery cable.
2. Disconnect the starter cable assembly from the starter relay and starter solenoid, located on the fender apron.
3. Remove the upper starter mounting stud bolt. Raise and support the vehicle safely.
4. Disconnect the vacuum hose from the vacuum pump.
5. Remove the 3 starter support bracket screws and bracket. Remove the power steering hose bracket.

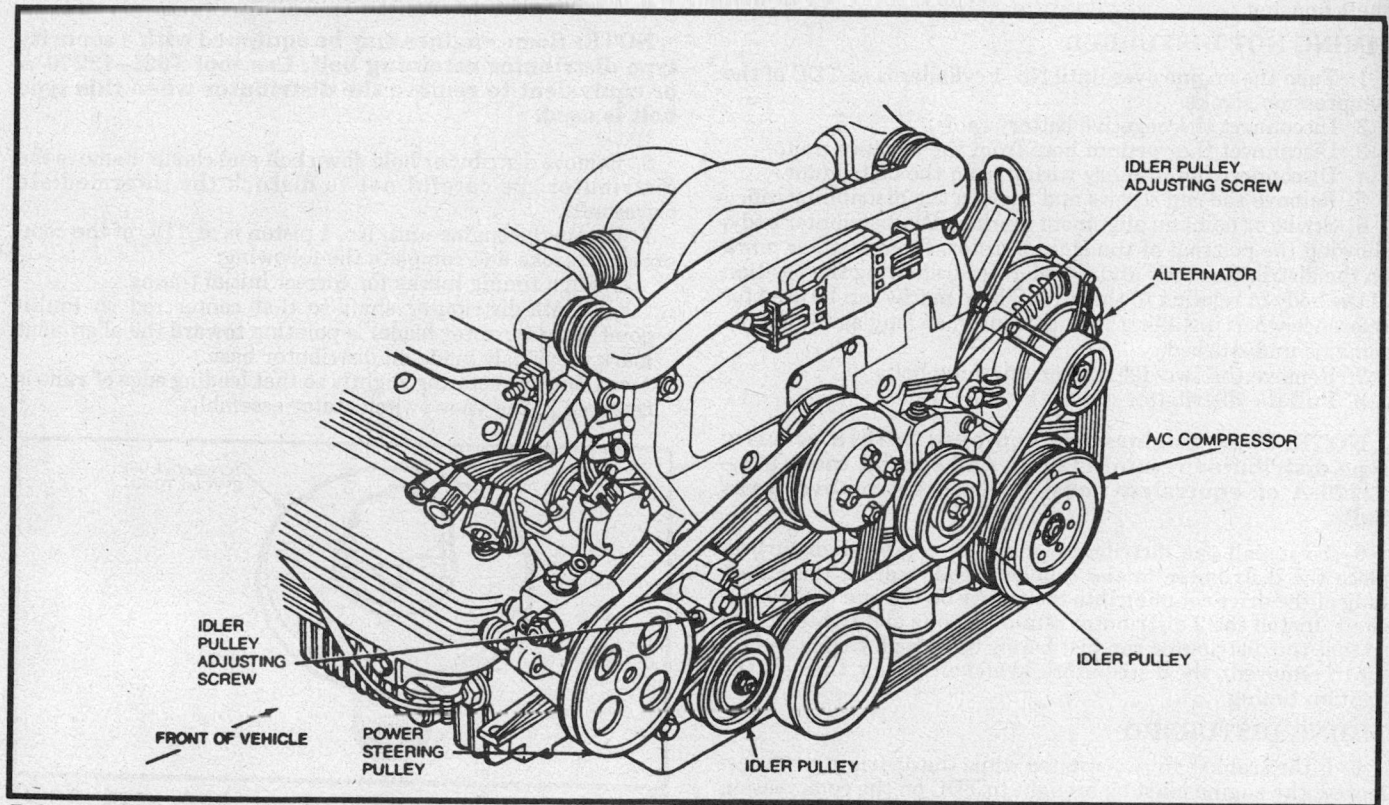

Drive belt arrangement 3.0L SHO engine

6. Remove the ground wire assembly and cable support on the starter bolt studs.

7. Remove the 2 starter mounting studs and position the them out of the way of the starter.

8. Remove the vacuum pump bracket. Remove the starter from the vehicle.

9. Installation is the reverse order of the removal procedure.

TAURUS, SABLE AND CONTINENTAL

1. Disconnect the negative battery cable and the cable connection at the starter.

2. Raise and support the vehicle safely.

3. Remove the cable support and ground cable connection from the upper starter stud bolt.

4. Remove the starter brace from the cylinder block and the starter.

5. On the 2.5L and 3.8L engines, remove 3 starter-to-bell housing bolts.

6. On the 3.0L engine, remove the 2 starter-to-bell housing bolts.

7. Remove the starter between the sub-frame and radiator on the automatic transaxle vehicles. Remove the starter between the sub-frame and the engine on the manual transaxle vehicles.

8. For installation, reverse the removal procedure. Torque the starter mounting bolts to 30–40 ft. lbs.

Ignition System

DISTRIBUTOR

Removal and Installation

1.9L ENGINE

The camshaft-driven distributor is located at the rear of the cylinder head. It is retained by 2 bolts at the base of the distributor shaft housing.

TIMING NOT DISTURBED

1. Turn the engine over until No. 1 cylinder is at TDC of the compression stroke.

2. Disconnect the negative battery cable.

3. Disconnect the vacuum hose from the advance unit.

4. Disconnect the primary wiring from the distributor.

5. Remove the cap screws and remove the distributor cap.

6. Scribe or paint an alignment mark on the distributor body, showing the position of the ignition rotor. Place another mark on the distributor body and cylinder head, showing the position of the body in relation to the head. These marks can be used for reference when installing the distributor, as long as the engine remains undisturbed.

7. Remove the two distributor retaining bolts.

8. Pull the distributor out of the head.

NOTE: Some engines are equipped with a security type distributor retaining bolts and special tool T82L–12270–A or equivalent must be used to remove these bolts.

9. To install the distributor with the engine undisturbed, place the distributor in the cylinder head, seating the off-set tang of the drive coupling into the groove on the end of the camshaft. Install the 2 distributor retaining bolts and tighten them so that the distributor can just barely be moved. Install the rotor (if removed), the distributor cap and all wiring, then set the ignition timing.

TIMING DISTURBED

1. If the crankshaft was rotated while the distributor was removed, the engine must be brought to TDC on the compression stroke of the No. 1 cylinder.

2. Remove the No. 1 spark plug. Place finger over the hole

and rotate the crankshaft slowly (use a wrench on the crankshaft pulley bolt) in the direction of normal engine rotation, until engine compression is felt.

NOTE: Turn the engine only in the direction of normal rotation. Backward rotation will cause the cam belt to slip or lose teeth, altering engine timing.

3. When engine compression is felt at the spark plug hole, indication that the piston is approaching TDC, continue to turn the crankshaft until the timing mark on the pulley is aligned with the **0** mark (timing mark) on the engine front cover.

4. Turn the distributor shaft until the ignition rotor is at the No.1 firing position.

5. Install the distributor into the cylinder head.

EXCEPT 1.9L AND 3.0L SHO ENGINES

The distributor used with these engines is a new universal design which is gear driven and has a die cast base that incorporates in integrally mounted TFI-IV (Thick Film Ignition) ignition module, a Hall Effect vane switch stator assembly and provision for fixed octane adjustment. The new design deletes the conventional centrifugal and vacuum advance mechanisms.

NOTE: No distributor calibration is required. Initial timing is a normal adjustment.

1. Disconnect the negative battery cable.

2. Disconnect the primary wiring connector from distributor.

NOTE: Before removing the distributor cap, mark the position of the No. 1 wire tower on the distributor base for assembly reference.

3. Remove distributor cap and position it and the attached wires aside as not to interfere with removing distributor.

4. Remove the rotor.

5. Remove TFI-IV harness connector.

NOTE: Some engines may be equipped with a security type distributor retaining bolt. Use tool T82L–12270–A or equivalent to remove the distributor when this type bolt is used.

6. Remove distributor hold down bolt and clamp. Remove the distributor. Be careful not to disturb the intermediate driveshaft.

7. Rotate the engine until No. 1 piston is at TDC of the compression stroke and complete the following:

   a. Align timing marks for correct initial timing.

   b. Rotate distributor shaft so that center rod on multipoint rotor (or rotor blade) is pointing toward the alignment mark previously made on distributor base.

   c. Continue rotating slightly so that leading edge of vane is centered in the vane switch stator assembly.

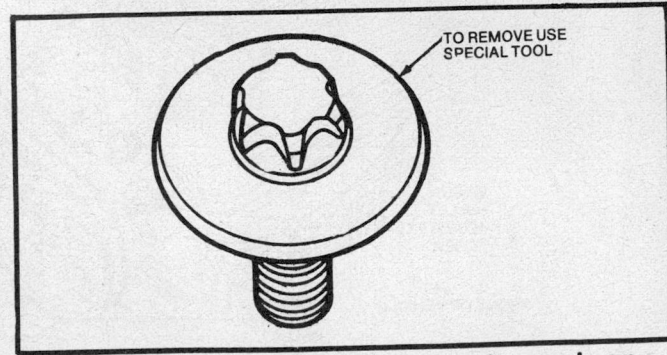

Security distributor hold down bolt used on some Tempo/Topaz models

d. Rotate distributor in block to align leading edge and the vane switch stator assembly and verify that the rotor is pointing at No. 1 cap terminal.

e. Install distributor retaining bolt and clamp. Do not tighten at this time.

8. If the vane and vane switch stator cannot be aligned by rotating the distributor in the block, pull distributor out of block enough to disengage distributor gear and rotate distributor shaft to engage a different distributor gear tooth. Repeat Step 1 as necessary.

9. Connect distributor to wiring harness.

10. Install distributor cap, rotor and ignition wires. Check that ignition wires are securely connected to the distributor cap and spark plugs. Tighten distributor cap screws to 18–35 inch lbs.

11. Set initial timing with a suitable timing light.

12. Tighten distributor retaining bolt to 17–25 ft. lbs. on all engines except the 3.8L engine.

13. On 3.8L engine, torque the retaining bolt to 40 ft. lbs.

14. Recheck initial timing. Adjust if necessary.

3.0L SHO ENGINE

This engine is equipped with a distributorless ignition system (DIS) which consists of the following components:

Crankshaft timing sensor
Camshaft sensor
DIS ignition module
Ignition coil pack
The spark angle portion of the EEC IV module

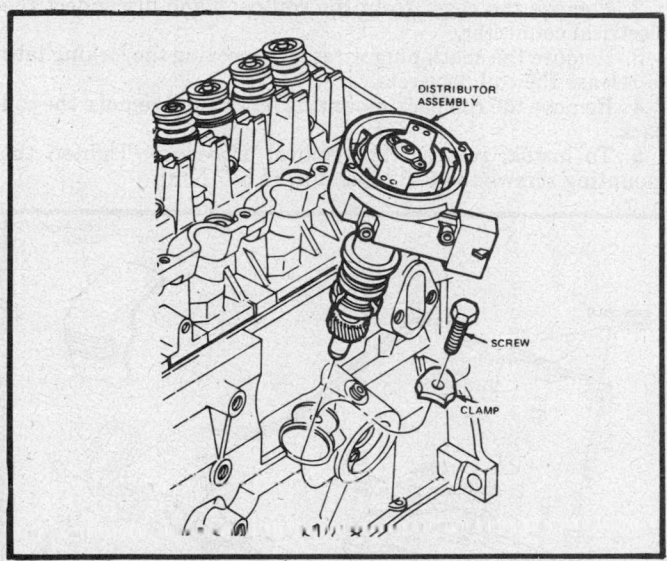

Tempo/Topaz distributor mounting

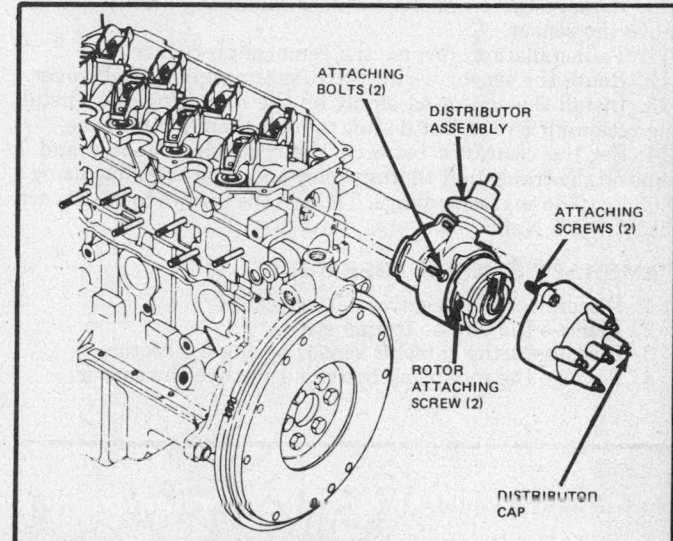

Distributor location Escort and Lynx

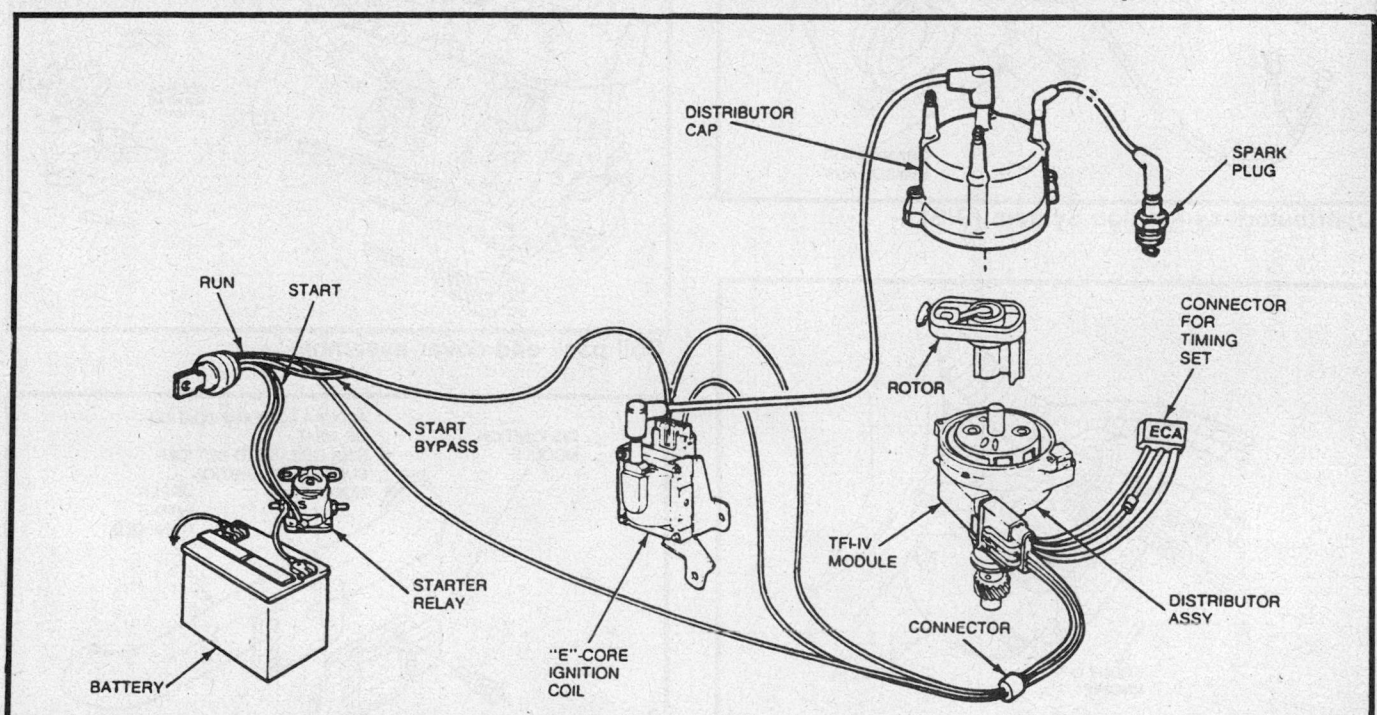

Ignition system all except the 3.0L SHO engine

Removal and Installation

CRANKSHAFT TIMING SENSOR

1. Disconnect the negative battery cable.
2. Loosen the tensioner pulleys for the A/C compressor and the power steering pump belts.
3. Remove the belts from the crankshaft pulley.
4. Remove the upper timing belt cover.
5. Disconnect the sensor wiring harness at the connector and route the wiring harness through the belt cover.
6. Raise the vehicle and support it safely.
7. Remove the RH front wheel and tire assembly.
8. Remove the crankshaft pulley using universal puller T67L–3600–A or equivalent.
9. Remove the lower timing belt cover.
10. Remove the crankshaft sensor mounting screws and remove the sensor.
11. To installation, reverse the removal procedure.
12. Route the sensor wiring harness through the belt cover.
13. Install the sensor assembly on the mounting pad. Install the retaining screws but do not tighten them at this time.
14. Set the clearance between the crankshaft sensor and 1 vane on the crankshaft timing pulley and vane assembly using a 0.03 in. (0.8mm) feeler gauge. Tighten the screws to 22–31 inch lbs. (2.5–3.5 Nm).

CAMSHAFT SENSOR ASSEMBLY

1. Disconnect the negative battery cable.
2. Remove the engine torque strut.
3. Disconnect the camshft sensor wiring connector.
4. Remove the mounting bolts and remove the sensor.

5. To install, reverse the removal procedure. Tighten the mounting bolts to 22–31 inch lbs. (2.5–3.5 Nm).

DIS IGNITION MODULE

1. Disconnect the negative battery cable.
2. Disconnect the wiring connectors at the module.
3. Remove the module mounting bolts and remove the module.
4. To install, reverse the removal procedure. Apply a uniform coating of Heat Sink grease to the mounting surface of the DIS module before installing it. Tighten the mounting bolts to 22–31 inch lbs. (2.5–3.5 Nm).

IGNITION COIL PACK

1. Disconnect the negative battery cable.
2. Remove the cover from the coil pack and disconnect the electrical connector.
3. Remove the spark plug wires by squeezing the locking tabs to release the coil boot retainers.
4. Remove the coil pack mounting screws and remove the coil pack.
5. To install, reverse the removal procedure. Tighten the mounting screws to 40–62 inch lbs. (4.5–7 Nm).

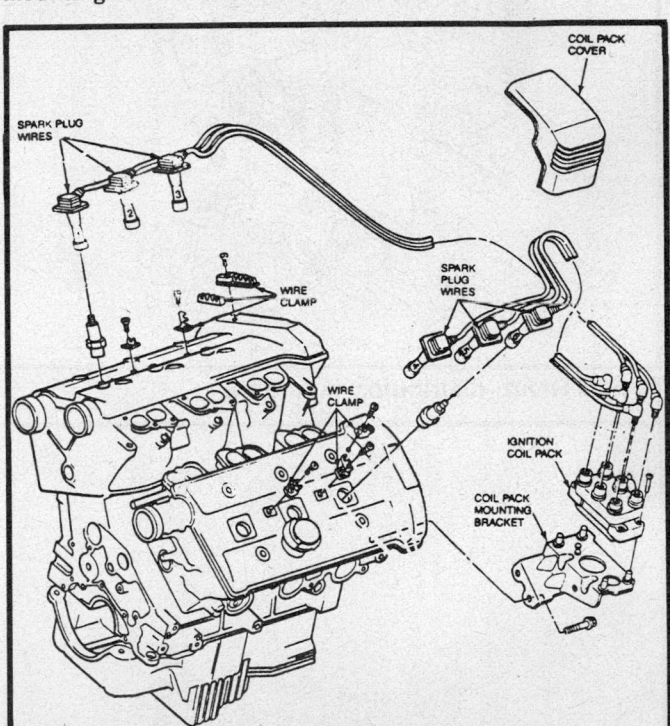

Coil pack and cover assembly

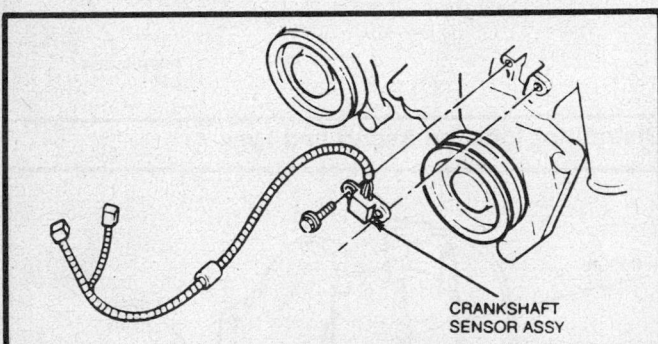

Distributorless Ignition System (DIS)

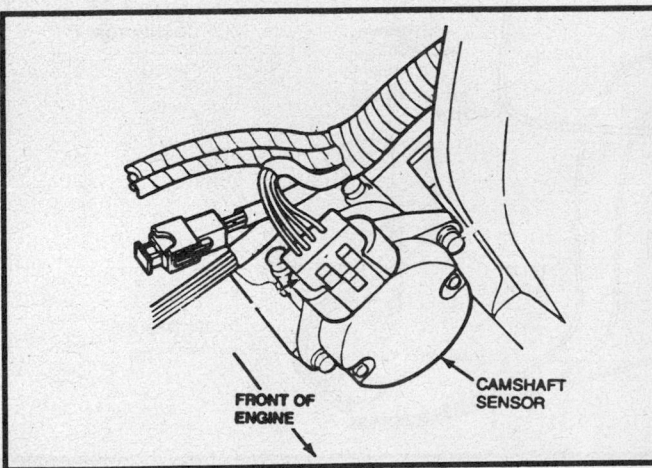

DIS camshaft sensor

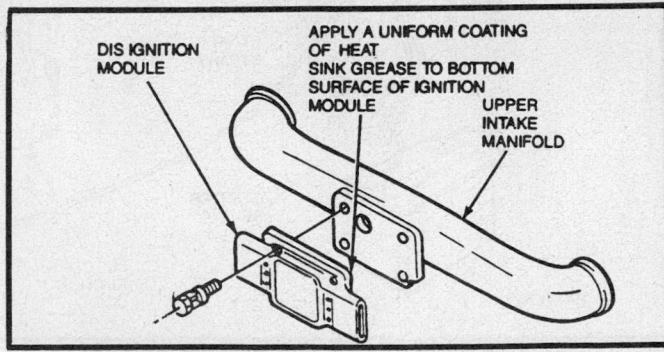

DIS Ignition module

Diesel Glow Plugs

Removal and Installation

1. Disconnect the negative battery cable, located in the luggage compartment.
2. Disconnect the glow plug harness from the glow plugs.
3. Using a 12mm deepwell socket, remove the glow plugs.
4. Install the glow plugs, using a 12mm deepwell socket. Tighten the glow plugs to 11–15 ft. lbs.
5. Connect the glow plug harness to the glow plugs. Tighten the nuts to 5–7 ft. lbs.
6. Connect the battery ground cable to the battery.
7. Check the glow plug system operation.

IGNITION TIMING

Adjustment

1.9L ENGINE

1. Ignition timing marks consist of a notch on the crankshaft pulley and a graduated scale molded into the camshaft belt cover. The number of degrees before or after TDC represented by each mark in the scale can be interpreted according to the decal affixed to the top of the belt cover.
2. With white paint or chalk, mark the notch in the crankshaft pulley and the appropriate mark in the degree scale. See the underhood emission control decal for timing specifications.
3. Warm the engine until it reaches normal operating temperature.
4. Shut off the engine. Disconnect and plug the vacuum hose from the distributor advance diaphragm. Make sure the transaxle is in **P** or **N**, apply the parking brake and block the wheels. Place the air conditioning/heater control switch in the **OFF** position.
5. Connect a suitable timing light to the engine. Connect a suitable tachometer to the engine.
6. If the vehicle is equipped with a barometric pressure switch, disconnect it from the ignition module and place a jumper wire across the pins at the ignition module connector yellow and black wire.
7. Start the engine and allow to reach normal operating temperature. Aim the light at the marks. If they are not aligned, loosen the distributor clamp bolts slightly and rotate the distributor body until the marks are aligned under timing light illumination.
8. Tighten the distributor clamp bolts and recheck the ignition timing. Connect the single wire connector and check the timing advance, to verify the distributor is advancing beyond the initial setting. Readjust idle speed.
9. Shut off the engine and connect the vacuum hoses. Remove the jumper from the ignition connector and connect if applicable. Remove all test equipment.

EXCEPT 1.9L ENGINE

On engines equipped with a manual transaxle, the timing marks are located on the flywheel and visible through an access hole in the transaxle case. The timing cover plate must be removed in order to view the timing marks and adjust the timing.

On engines equipped with an automatic transaxle, the timing marks are visible through an access hole in the transaxle case. There is no cover plate. To adjust the timing, align the pointer in the transaxle case with the mark on the flywheel. The 3.0L and 3.8L engine employ timing degree numbers on the crankshaft pulley and a timing pointer near the pulley.

NOTE: Some distributor retaining bolts have a security type head and can not be loosened to adjust timing, unless special tool T82L-12270-A or equivalent is available.

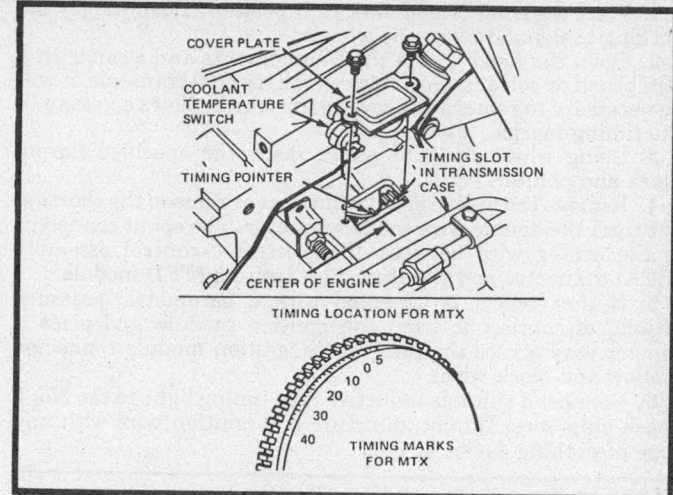
Tempo/Topaz manual transaxle timing marks

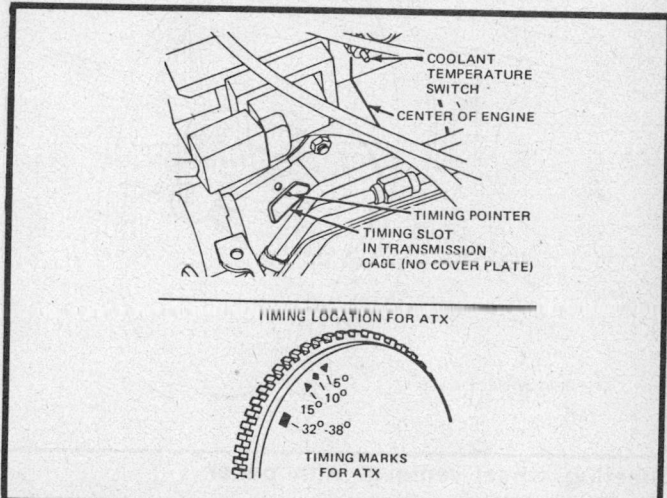
Tempo/Topaz automatic transaxle timing marks

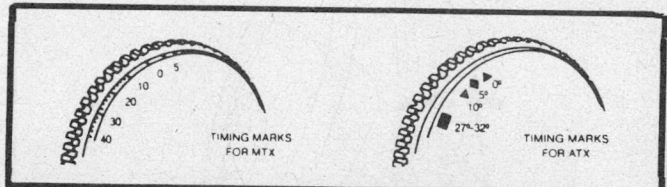
Timing mark locations for the 3.0L engine

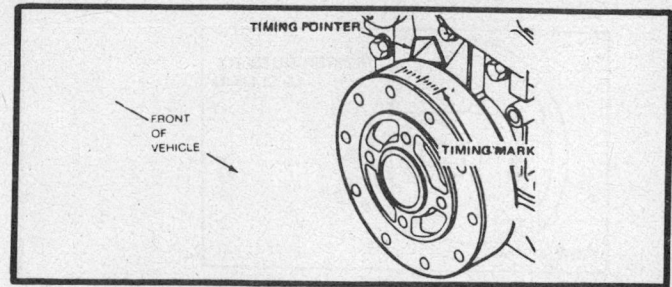
Timing mark locations for the 2.5L engine

1. Place the transaxle in the **P** or **N** position. Firmly apply the parking brake and block the wheels.

2. Open the hood, locate the timing marks and clean with a stiff brush or solvent. On vehicles with manual transaxle, it will be necessary to remove the cover plate which allows access to to the timing marks.

3. Using white chalk or paint, mark the specified timing mark and pointer.

4. Remove the in-line spout connector or remove the shorting bar from the double wire spout connector. The spout connector is the center wire between the electronic control assembly (ECA) connector and the thick film ignition (TFI) module.

5. If the vehicle is equipped with a barometric pressure switch, disconnect it from the ignition module and place a jumper wire across the pins at the ignition module connector (yellow and black wire).

6. Connect a suitable inductive type timing light to the No. 1 spark plug wire. Do not, puncture and ignition wire with any type of probing device.

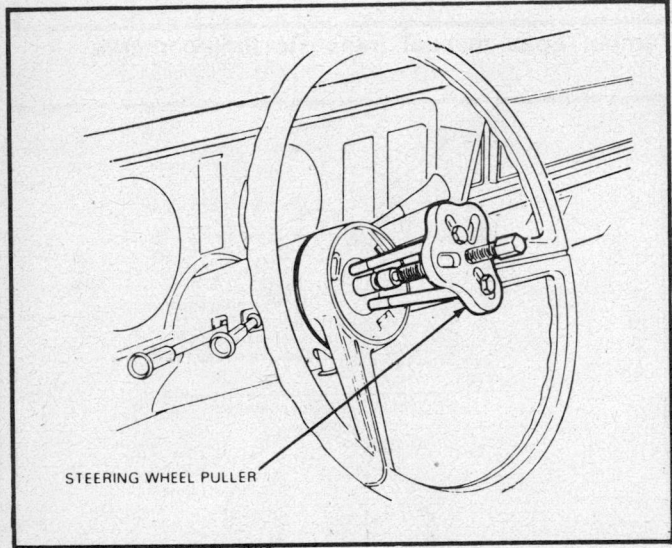

Steering wheel removal with puller

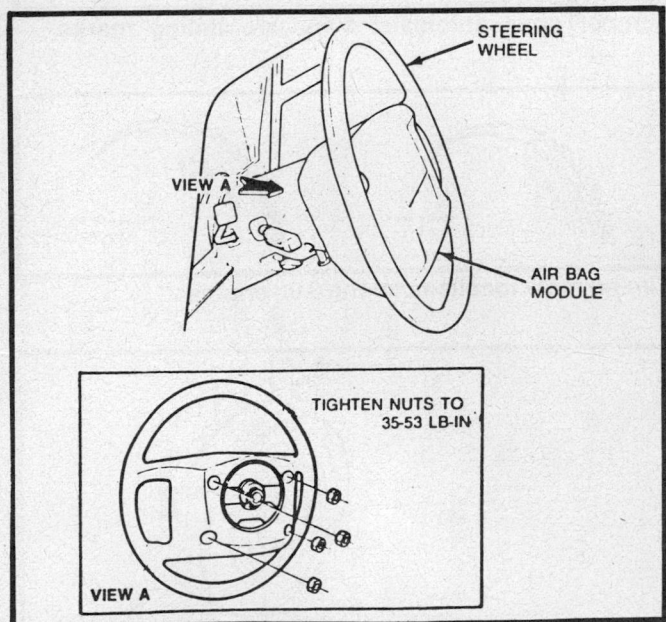

Typical air bag module on new models

NOTE: The high ignition coil charging currents generated in the EEC IV ignition system may falsely trigger timing lights with capacitive or direct connect pick-ups. It is necessary that an inductive type timing light be used in this procedure.

7. Connect a suitable tachometer to the engine. The ignition coil connector allows a test lead with an alligator clip to be connected to the Distributor Electronic Control (DEC) terminal without removing the connector.

8. Start the engine and let it run until it reaches normal operating temperature.

9. Check the engine idle rpm if it is not within specifications, adjust as necessary. After the rpm has been adjusted or checked, aim the timing light at the timing marks. If they are not aligned, loosen the distributor clamp bolts slightly and rotate the distributor body until the marks are aligned under timing light illumination.

10. Tighten the distributor clamp bolts and recheck the ignition timing. Readjust the idle speed. Shut the engine off, remove all test equipment, reconnect the in-line spout connector to the distributor and reinstall the cover plate on the manual transaxle vehicles.

Electrical Controls

STEERING WHEEL

Removal and Installation

1. Disconnect the negative battery cable. Remove the steering wheel center horn pad cover by removing the retaining screws from the steering wheel assembly.

NOTE: The emblem assembly is removed after the horn pad cover is removed, by pushing it out from the backside of the emblem.

2. Remove the energy absorbing foam from the wheel assembly, if equipped. Remember the energy absorbing foam must be installed when the steering wheel is assembled. Disconnect the horn pad wiring connector.

3. On vehicles equipped with air bag restraint System, remove the 4 nuts holding the air bag module to the steering wheel (the nuts are located on the back of the steering wheel).

4. Lift the air bag module from the wheel and disconnect the air bag module to slip-ring clock spring connector.

5. On all vehicles, loosen and remove the center mounting nut and on the vehicles equipped with speed control system, remove the electrical connectors. Discard the center nut and replace with new.

6. Remove the steering wheel with a suitable puller. Do not use a knock-off type puller, because it will cause damage to the collapsible steering column. On the Taurus, Sable and Continental vehicles, the use of a steering wheel puller is not required. Grasp the rim of the steering wheel and pull the steering wheel from the upper shaft.

NOTE: The multi-switch lever switch must be in the NEUTRAL position before installing the steering wheel or damage to the switch cam may result.

7. Position the steering wheel on the end of the steering wheel shaft. Align the mark on the steering wheel with the mark on the shaft to assure the straight-ahead steering wheel position corresponds to the straight-ahead position of the front wheels.

8. Install a new service wheel locknut or bolt. Torque the nut to 50–60 ft. lbs. and the bolt to 23–33 ft. lbs. Connect all the electrical connectors on the vehicles equipped with speed control.

9. On vehicles equipped with air bags, connect the air bag module wire to slip ring connector and place the module on the steering wheel with the 4 attaching nuts, torque the nuts to 35–33 inch lbs.

10. On the other vehicles install the steering wheel hub cover and torque the nuts to 13–20 inch lbs.

11. Reconnect the negative battery cable and check the steering wheel for proper operation.

HORN SWITCH

Removal and Installation

NOTE: If the horn switch is installed in the multifunction switch, refer to "Combination Switch, Removal and Installation" procedure.

1. Disconnect the negative battery cable.

2. Remove the screws from the back of the steering wheel and lift off the horn cover pad.

3. Remove the foam pad, if equipped. Remove the wire connectors from the steering wheel terminals and remove the horn switch.

4. Complete the installation of the horn switch by reversing the removal procedure.

IGNITION LOCK CYLINDER

Removal and Installation

1. Disconnect the negative battery cable from the battery.

2. On vehicles equipped with a tilt steering column, remove the upper extension shroud by unsnapping the shroud from the retaining clip at the 9 o'clock position.

3. Remove the steering column lower shroud on Escort and Lynx. On Tempo and Topaz, remove the trim halves. On vehicles equipped with tilt steering wheel, remove the upper extension shroud by unsnapping from a retaining clip that is located at the 9 o'clock position.

4. Disconnect the warning buzzer electrical connector. With the lock cylinder key, rotate the cylinder to the **RUN** position.

5. Take a ⅛ in. diameter pin or small wire punch and push on the cylinder retaining pin. The pin is visible through a hole in the mounting surrounding the key cylinder. Push on the pin and withdraw the lock cylinder from the housing.

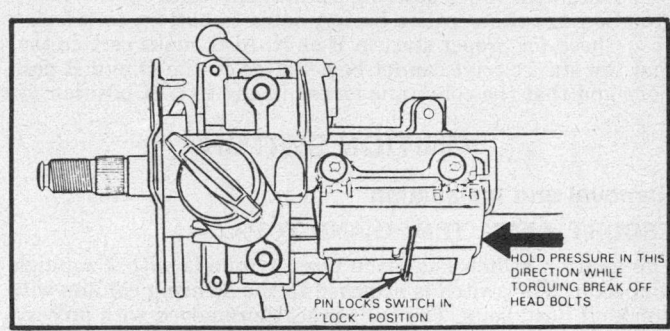

Ignition switch installation

Removing casting from steering shaft

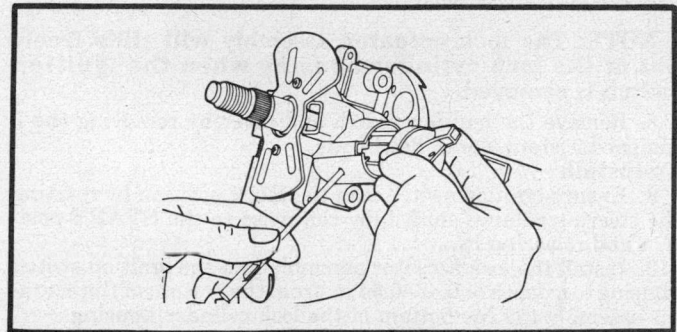

Removing lock cylinder

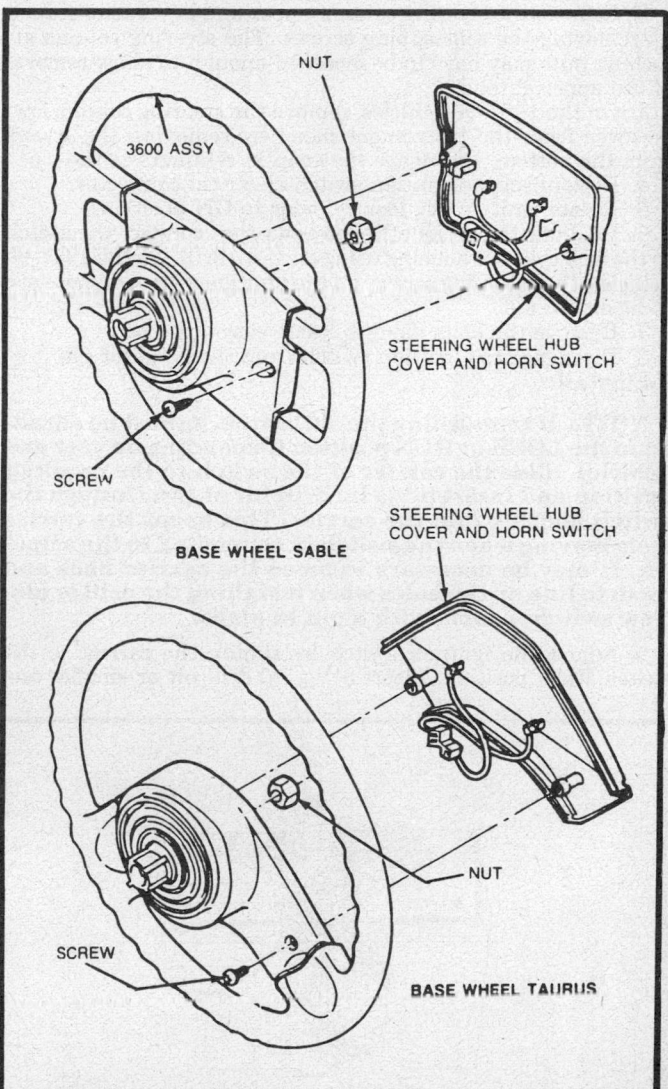

Horn switch removal and installation—Taurus/Sable

6. Install the lock cylinder by turning it to the **RUN** position and depressing the retaining pin. Be sure the lock cylinder is fully seated and aligned in the interlocking washer before turning the key to the **OFF** position. This action will permit the cylinder retaining pin to extend into the cylinder housing hole.

7. Rotate the lock cylinder, using the lock cylinder key, to ensure correct mechanical operation in all positions.

8. Install the electrical connector for the key warning buzzer.

9. Install the lower steering column shroud.

10. Connect the negative battery cable to battery terminal.

11. Check for proper start in **P** or **N**. Also, make certain that that the start circuit cannot be actuated in the **D** and **R** positions and that the column is locked in the **LOCK** position.

IGNITION SWITCH

Removal and Installation
ESCORT, LYNX, TEMPO AND TOPAZ

The ignition switch has blade type terminals with 1 multiple connector. The switch is attached to the steering column with break-off head bolts. The bolts must be removed with an easy-out tool or other means.

1. Disconnect the negative battery cable.

2. Remove the steering column upper and lower trim shroud by removing the self-tapping screws. The steering column attaching nuts may have to be loosened enough to allow removal of the upper shroud.

3. On the 1987–90 vehicles, remove the steering column lower cover from the instrument panel by removing the screws from the bottom. Disengage the snap-in retainers at the top.

4. Disconnect the ignition switch electrical connector.

5. Rotate ignition key lock cylinder to **ON** position.

6. Drill out the break-off head bolts that connect the switch to the lock cylinder housing using an ⅛ in. drill. On the 1987–90 vehicles, the retaining screws on the ignition switch do not have to be drilled out.

7. Remove the bolts using suitable easy-out tool.

8. Disengage the ignition switch from the actuator pin.

To install:

NOTE: If reinstalling the old switch, it must be adjusted to the LOCK or RUN position (depending on year and vehicle). Slide the carrier of the switch to the required position and insert a ¹/₁₆ in. drill bit or pin through the switch housing into the carrier. This keeps the carrier from moving when the switch in connected to the actuator. It may be necessary to move the carrier back and forth to line up the holes when installing the drill or pin. New switches come with a pin in place.

9. Adjust the ignition switch by sliding the carrier to the switch **RUN** position. Insert a ¹/₁₆ in. drill bit or smaller tool

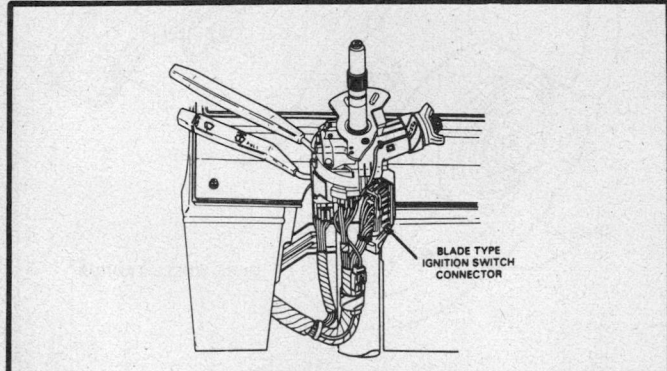

Blade type ignition switch connector

through the switch housing and into the carrier to prevent movement of the carrier with respect to the switch housing. It may be necessary to move the carrier slightly back and forth to align the carrier and housing adjustment holes.

NOTE: A new replacement switch assembly will be pre-set in the RUN position.

10. Make certain that the ignition key lock cylinder is in approximately the **RUN** position. The **RUN** position is achieved by rotating the key lock cylinder approximately 90 degrees from the **LOCK** position.

11. Install the ignition switch onto the actuator pin. It may be necessary to move the switch slightly back and fourth to align the switch mounting holes with the column lock housing threaded holes.

12. Install the new break-off head bolts (or attaching bolts) and hand tighten.

13. Move the ignition switch up the steering column until all the travel in the screw slots in used. Hold the switch in this position and tighten the break-off head bolts until the heads break off.

14. Remove the adjustment drill bit or pin, if used.

15. Connect the electrical connector to the ignition switch. Connect the negative battery cable and check the ignition switch for proper function including **START** and **ACC** positions. Also make certain that the steering column is in the **LOCK** position.

16. Align the steering column mounting holes with the support bracket and install the bolts and nuts. Install the steering column trim shrouds.

17. Install the steering column lower cover on the instrument panel, if equipped.

18. Check the ignition switch for proper starting in **P** or **N**. Also make certain that the start circuit can not be actuated in the **D** or **R** position and that the column is locked in the **LOCK** position.

TAURUS, SABLE AND CONTINENTAL

1. Disconnect the negative battery cable.

2. Rotate the ignition lock cylinder to the **RUN** position and depress the lock cylinder retaining pin through the access hole in the shroud with a ⅛ in. drift punch or wire pin. Push on the pin and pull out on the lock cylinder.

3. On vehicles equipped with tilt streering columns, remove the tilt release lever by removing the Allen head cap screw that holds the tilt lever to the steering column.

4. On all vehicles, remove the lower steering column/instrument panel cover by removing the 4 Torx® head sheet metal screws.

5. Remove the steering column shroud.

6. Remove the bolts and nuts that attach the steering column to support bracket and lower column. Disconnect the ignition switch electrical connector.

7. Remove the lock actuator cover plate by removing the tamper resistant Torx® head bolt.

NOTE: The lock actuator assembly will slide freely out of the lock cylinder housing when the ignition switch is removed.

8. Remove the ignition switch and cover by removing the 2 tamper-resistant Torx® head bolts.

To install:

9. Ensure ignition switch is in the **RUN** position by rotating the steering column shaft fully clockwise to the **START** position and releasing it.

10. Install the lock actuator assembly into the ignition switch housing to a depth of 0.46–0.54 in. from the bottom of the actuator assembly top the bottom of the lock cylinder housing.

11. While holding the actuator assembly at the proper depth, install the ignition switch.

12. Install the ignition switch and cover. Torque the cover retaining screws to 30–48 inch lbs.

13. Install the lock cylinder. Rotate the ignition switch to the **LOCK** position and measure the depth of the actuator assembly. The actuator must be 0.92–1.00 in. inside the lock cylinder housing. If the actuator depth does not meet specifications, it must be removed and reinstalled.

14. Install the lock actuator cover plate with the Torx® head screw and torque the screw to 30–48 inch lbs. Install the ignition switch electrical connector.

15. Connect the negative (ground) battery cable to the battery terminal. Check the ignition switch for proper starting in all positions including **START** and **ACC**.

16. Check the column function as follows:

a. With the column shift lever in the **P** position or with the

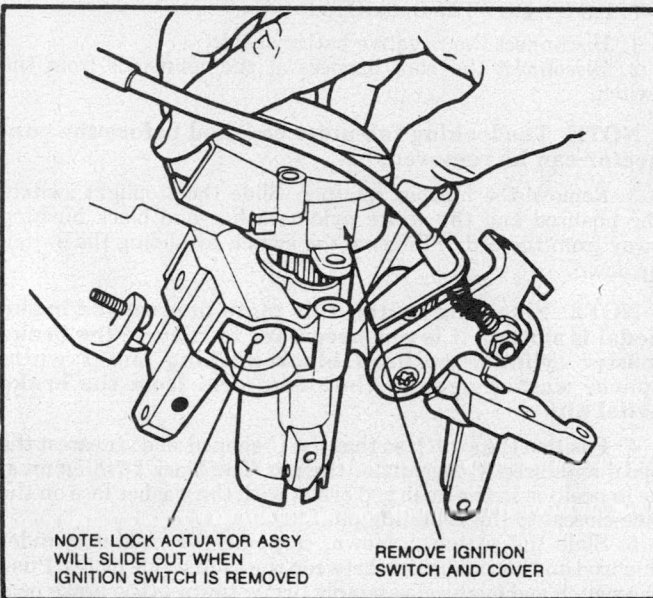

NOTE: LOCK ACTUATOR ASSY WILL SLIDE OUT WHEN IGNITION SWITCH IS REMOVED

REMOVE IGNITION SWITCH AND COVER

Removing the ignition switch and cover—Taurus/Sable and Continental

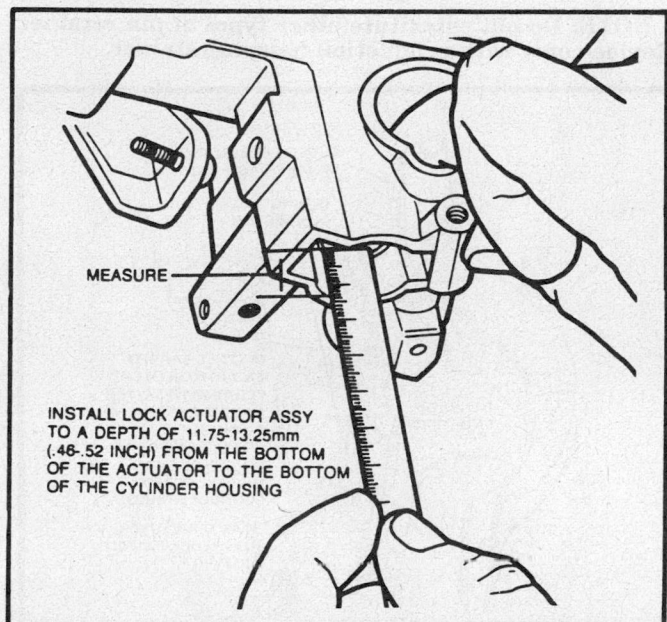

MEASURE

INSTALL LOCK ACTUATOR ASSY TO A DEPTH OF 11.75-13.25mm (.46-.52 INCH) FROM THE BOTTOM OF THE ACTUATOR TO THE BOTTOM OF THE CYLINDER HOUSING

Measuring cylinder lock depth—Taurus/Sable and Continental

floor shift key release button depressed and with the ignition lock cylinder in the **LOCK** position, make certain that the steering column locks.

b. Position the column shift lever in the **D** position or the floor shift key release button fully extended and rotate the cylinder lock to the **RUN** position. Continue to rotate the cylinder toward the **LOCK** position until it stops. In this position make certain that engine electrical off has been acheived and that the steering shaft does not lock.

c. Turn the radio power button on. Rotate the cylinder counterclockwise to the **ACC** position to verify that the radio is energized.

d. Place the shift lever in **P** and rotate the cylinder clockwise to the **START** position to verify that the starter energizes.

17. Align the steering column mounting holes with the support bracket and center the column in the instrument panel opening. Install and tighten the 4 retaining nuts to 15–25 ft. lbs.

18. Install the 3 self-tapping screws and install the column trim shrouds. Install the instrument panel lower cover with 4 Torx® head sheet metal screws.

19. On vehicles equipped with tilt steering columns, install the tilt release lever and socket head screw. Install the lock cylinder.

21. On vehicles equipped with tilt steering columns, check column travel through the entire range to ensure that there is no interference between the column and the instrument panel.

NEUTRAL SAFETY SWITCH

Removal and Installation

AUTOMATIC TRANSAXLE

1. Disconnect the battery negative cable.
2. Remove the 2 valve supply rear hoses and all the vacuum hoses from the managed air valve, if necessary.
3. Remove the managed air valve supply hose band to intermediate shift control bracket attaching screw, if necessary.
4. Remove the air cleaner assembly.
5. Disconnect the wire connector from the neutral safety switch.
6. Remove the retaining screws from the neutral start switch and remove the switch.
7. To install the switch, place the switch on the manual shift shaft and loosely install the retaining bolts. Place the transaxle in **N**.

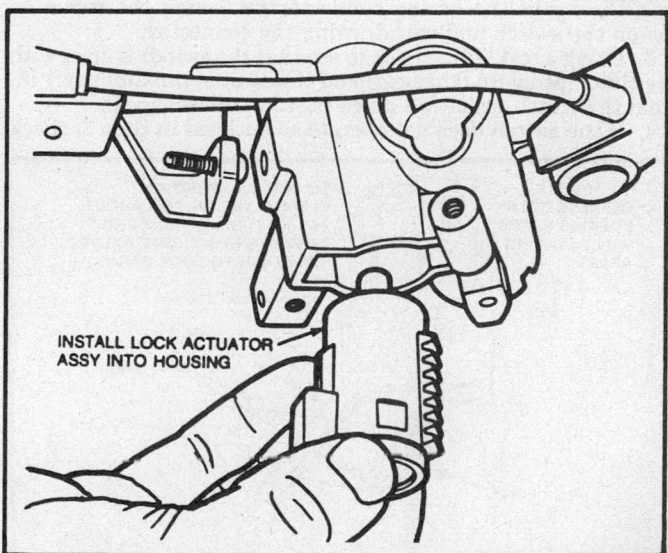

INSTALL LOCK ACTUATOR ASSY INTO HOUSING

Installing the lock cylinder—Taurus/Sable

8. Use a No. 43 drill (0.089 in.) and insert it into the switch to set the contacts.

9. Tighten the retaining screws of the switch, remove the drill and complete the assembly by reversing the removal procedure.

10. Check the ignition switch for proper starting in **P** or **N**. Also make certain that the start circuit can not be actuated in the **D** or **R** position and that the column is locked in the **LOCK** position.

STARTER/CLUTCH INTERLOCK SWITCH

Removal and Installation

MANUAL TRANSAXLE

1. Disconnect the negative battery cable.
2. Remove panel above clutch pedal, if equipped.
3. Disconnect the switch wiring connector.
4. Remove lower speed switch attachment to bracket, if equipped.
5. Remove clutch interlock attaching screw (and hairpin clip, if equipped) and allow switch to rotate down.
6. Depress barb at end of rod and withdraw rod from clutch pedal.

NOTE: Always install the switch with the self-adjusting clip about 1 in. from the end of the rod. The clutch pedal must be fully up (clutch engaged). Otherwise, the switch may be misadjusted.

7. Insert barbed end of rod into bushing on clutch pedal (or insert the eyelet end of the rod over the clutch pedal pin and secure with the hairpin clip, if equipped).
8. Swing switch around to line up hole in mounting boss with corresponding hole in bracket. Attach with screw.
9. Install speed control/EFI/diesel switch, if equipped and adjust.
10. Reset clutch interlock switch by pressing clutch pedal to floor.
11. Connect wiring connector.
12. Install the panel above the clutch, if equipped.

Adjustment

1. Remove panel above clutch pedal on the Tempo, Topaz, Taurus and Sable vehicles.
2. Disengage the wiring connector by flexing the retaining tab on the switch and withdrawing the connector.
3. Using a test light, check to see that the switch is open with the clutch pedal up (engaged) and closed at approximately 1 in. from the clutch pedal full down position (disengaged).
4. If the switch does not operate as outlined in Step 3, check

to see if the self-adjusting clip is out of position on the rod. It should be near the end of the rod.

5. If the self-adjusting clip is out of position, remove and reposition the clip approximately 1 in. from the end of the rod.

6. Reset the switch by pressing the clutch pedal to the floor. Repeat Step 3. If the switch is damaged or the clips do not remain in place replace the switch.

STOPLIGHT SWITCH

The mechanical stoplight switch assembly is installed on the pin of the brake pedal arm, so that it straddles the master cylinder pushrod.

Removal and Installation

WITHOUT POWER BRAKES

1. Disconnect the negative battery cable.
2. Disconnect the wire harness at the connector from the switch.

NOTE: The locking tab must be lifted before the connector can be removed.

3. Remove the hairpin retainer. Slide the stoplight switch, the pushrod and the white nylon washer and black bushing away from the pedal. Remove the switch by sliding the switch up/down.

NOTE: Since the switch side plate nearest the brake pedal is slotted, it is not necessary to remove the brake master cylinder pushrod black bushing and 1 white spacer washer nearest the pedal arm from the brake pedal pin.

4. Position the switch so that the U-shaped side is nearest the pedal and directly over/under the pin. The black bushing must be in position in the push rod eyelet with the washer face on the side closest to the retaining pin.
5. Slide the switch up/down, trapping the master cylinder pushrod and black bushing between the switch side plates. Push the switch and pushrod assembly firmly towards the brake pedal arm. Assemble the outside white plastic washer to pin and install the hairpin retainer to trap the whole assembly.

NOTE: Do not substitute other types of pin retainer. Replace only with production hairpin retainer.

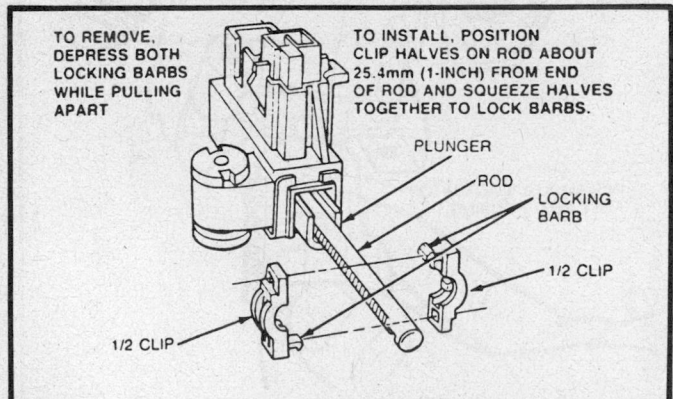

TO REMOVE, DEPRESS BOTH LOCKING BARBS WHILE PULLING APART

TO INSTALL, POSITION CLIP HALVES ON ROD ABOUT 25.4mm (1-INCH) FROM END OF ROD AND SQUEEZE HALVES TOGETHER TO LOCK BARBS.

PLUNGER
ROD
LOCKING BARB
1/2 CLIP
1/2 CLIP

Adjusting the starter/clutch interlock switch

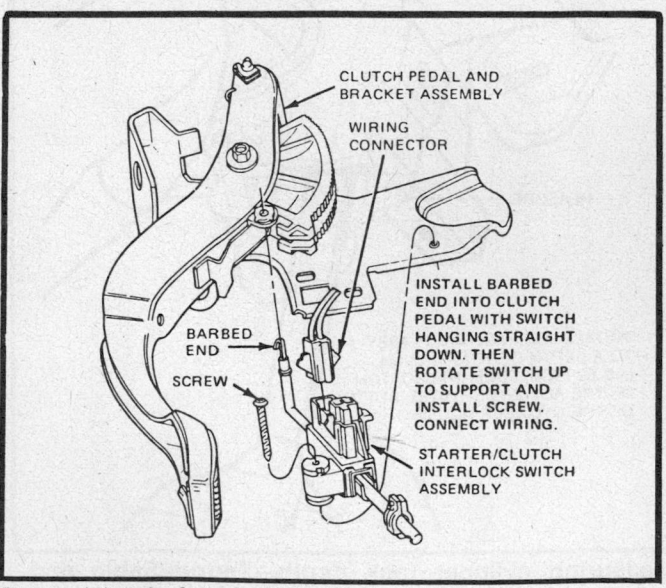

CLUTCH PEDAL AND BRACKET ASSEMBLY
WIRING CONNECTOR
BARBED END
SCREW
INSTALL BARBED END INTO CLUTCH PEDAL WITH SWITCH HANGING STRAIGHT DOWN. THEN ROTATE SWITCH UP TO SUPPORT AND INSTALL SCREW. CONNECT WIRING.
STARTER/CLUTCH INTERLOCK SWITCH ASSEMBLY

Starter/clutch interlock switch installation

6. Connect the wire harness connector to the switch.

7. Check the stoplight switch for proper operation. stoplights should illuminate with less than 6 lbs. applied to the brake pedal at the pad.

NOTE: The stoplight switch wire harness must have sufficient length to travel with the switch during full stroke at the pedal.

WITH POWER BRAKES

1. Disconnect the negative battery cable.

2. Disconnect the stoplight switch wire connector from the switch.

3. Remove the hairpin retainer and outer white nylon washer from the pedal pin. Slide the stoplight switch off the brake pedal pin just far enough for the outer side plate of the switch to clear the pin. Remove the switch and replace with new.

4. Position the new stoplight switch so that it straddles the pushrod, with the slot on the pedal pin and the switch outer frame hole just clearing the pin. Slide the switch downward onto the pin and pushrod. Slide the assembly inboard toward the brake pedal arm.

5. Install the outer white nylon washer and the hairpin retainer.

6. Connect the stoplight switch wire connector to the switch. Connect the negative battery cable.

7. Check the stoplights for proper operation with the engine running. Stoplights should illuminate with less than 6 pounds applied to the brake pedal at the pad.

HEADLAMP SWITCH

Removal and Installation

ESCORT, LYNX, TEMPO AND TOPAZ

1. Disconnect the negative battery cable.

2. On vehicles without A/C, remove the left hand side air vent control cable retaining screws and lower the cable to the floor.

3. Remove the fuse panel bracket retaining screws. Move the fuse panel assembly aside to gain access to the headlamp switch.

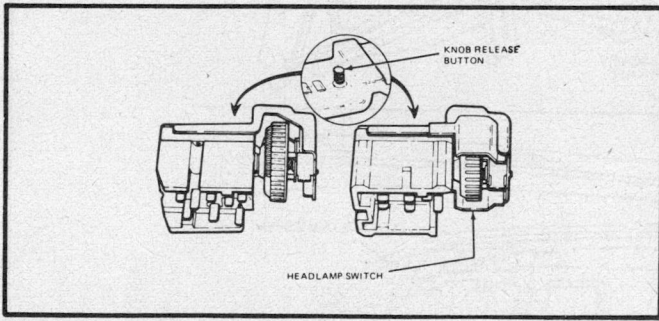

Headlamp switch knob release button Escort and Lynx

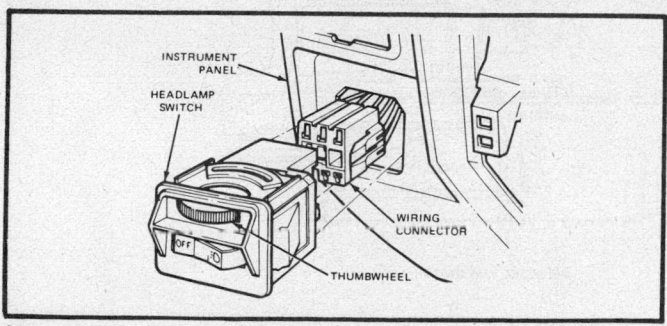

Headlamp switch mounting on Tempo/Topaz

4. Pull the headlamp knob out to the **ON** position. Depress the headlamp knob and shaft retainer button, which is located on the bottom of the headlight switch. Remove the knob and the shaft assembly from the switch.

5. Remove the headlamp switch retaining bezel. Disconnect the multiple connector plug and remove the switch from the instrument panel.

6. Install the headlamp switch into the instrument panel. Connect the multiple connector and install the headlamp switch retaining bezel.

7. Install the knob and shaft assembly by inserting the shaft into the headlamp switch gently pushing until the shaft is in the lock position.

8. Move the fuse panel back into position and install the fuse panel bracket with the two retaining screws.

9. On vehicles without A/C, install the left hand side air vent control cable and bracket. Install the negative battery cable and check the headlamp switch for the proper operation.

TAURUS, SABLE AND CONTINENTAL

1. Disconnect the negative battery cable. On the Taurus and Continental, remove the headlamp switch knob.

2. On the Taurus, remove the bezel retaining nut and remove the bezel. On the Sable and Continental, remove the lower left finish panel from the instrument panel On the Continental, remove the moulding above the finish panel.

3. On the Taurus, remove the instrument cluster finish panel and remove the 2 screws retaining the headlamp switch to the instrument panel. Pull the switch out of the instrument panel and disconnect the electrical connector. Remove the switch from the vehicle.

4. On the Sable and Continental, remove the 2 screws retaining the headlamp switch to the finish panel, disconnect the electrical connector and remove the switch from the vehicle.

5. Complete the installation of the headlamp switch by reversing the removal procedure.

COMBINATION SWITCH

Removal and Installation

ESCORT, LYNX, TEMPO AND TOPAZ

1. Disconnect the negative battery cable.

2. Remove the lower shroud.

3. Loosen the steering column attaching nuts enough to allow the removal of the upper trim shroud.

4. Remove the upper shroud.

5. Remove the turn signal switch lever by pulling the lever straight out from the switch. To make removal easier, work the outer end of the lever around with a slight rotary movement before pulling it out.

6. Peel back the foam sight shield from the turn signal switch.

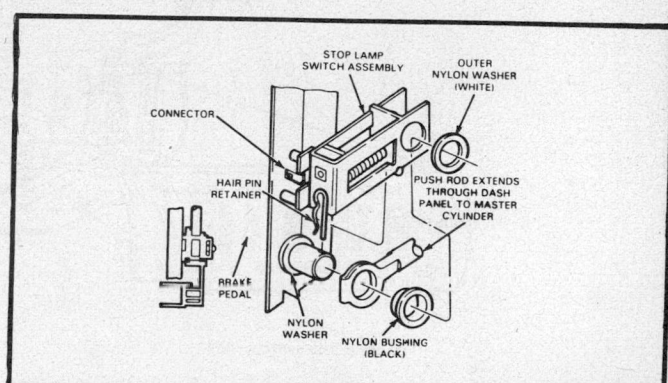

Stoplamp switch components

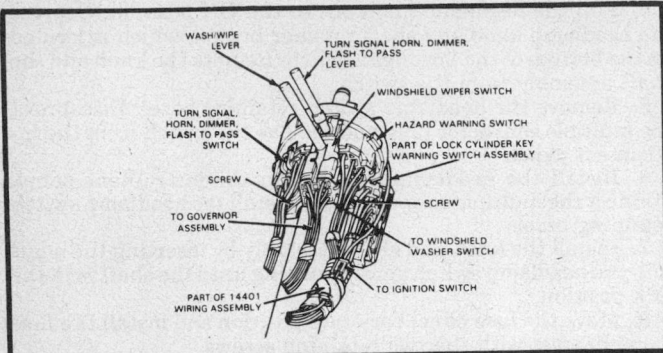

Stalk mounted switch levers and wiring harnesses Escort, Lynx, Tempo and Topaz

7. Disconnect the turn signal switch electrical connectors.

8. Remove the self-tapping screws that attach the turn signal switch to the lock cylinder housing and disengage the switch from the housing.

9. Transfer the ground brush located in the turn signal switch canceling cam to the new switch assembly on vehicles equipped with speed control.

To install:

10. Align the turn signal switch mounting holes with the corresponding holes in the lock cylinder housing and install 2 self-tapping screws until tight.

11. Apply the foam sight shield to the turn signal switch.

12. Install the turn signal switch lever into the switch by aligning the key on the lever with the keyway in the switch and pushing the lever toward the switch to full engagement.

13. Install turn signal switch electrical connectors to full engagement.

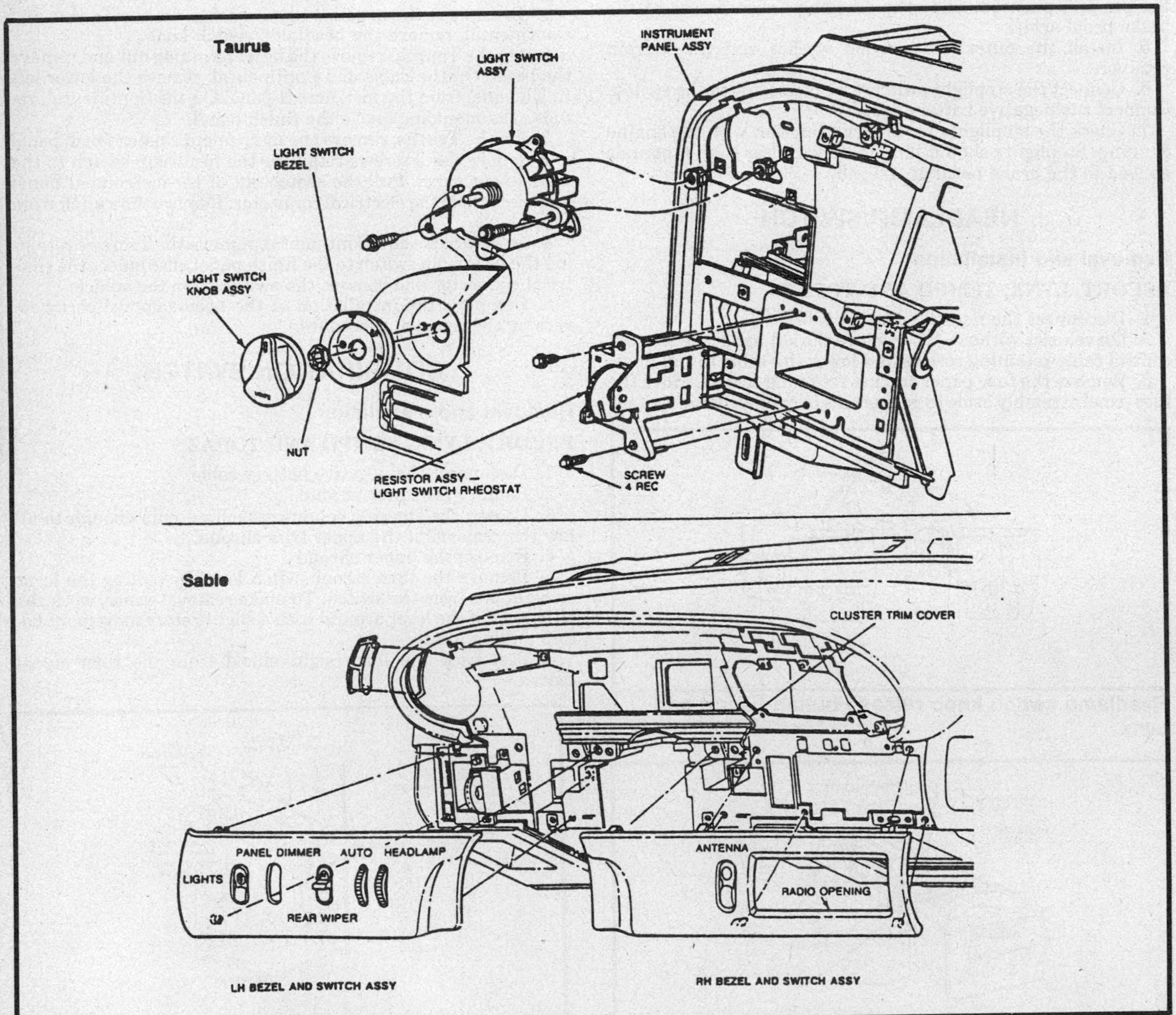

Headlight switch removal and installation—Taurus/Sable

14. Install the steering column trim shrouds.
15. Torque the steering column attaching nuts to 17–25 ft. lbs.
16. Connect the negative battery cable.
17. Check the steering column for proper operation.

TAURUS, SABLE AND CONTINENTAL

1. Disconnect the negative battery cable. If equipped with a tilt steering column, set the tilt column to its lowest position and remove the tilt lever by removing the Allen head retaining screw.

2. Remove the ignition lock cylinder. Remove the steering column shroud screws and remove the upper and lower shrouds.

3. Remove the wiring harness retainer and disconnect the 3 electrical connectors.

4. Remove the self tapping screws attaching the switch to the steering column and disengage the switch from the steering column casting.

5. Align the turn signal switch mounting holes with the corresponding holes in the steering column and install self-tapping screws. Torque the screws to 18–27 inch lbs.

6. Install the electrical connectors and install the wiring harness retainer.

7. Install the upper and lower steering column shroud and shroud retaining screws, torque the screws to 6–10 inch lbs.

8. Install the ignition lock cylinder. Attach the tilt lever, if removed and torque the tilt lever Allen head retaining screw to 6–9 inch lbs.

9. Connect the negative battery cable. Check the switch and the steering column for proper operation.

WINDSHIELD WIPER SWITCH

The standard and interval front wiper and washer systems on 1988–90 Tempo and Topaz vehicles feature an instrument panel-mounted rotary switch for wiper and washer control, whereas the switch on earlier vehicles was integral with the column mounted switch handle. On the Escort vehicles with non-tilt steering columns, the switch handle is an integral part of the switch and can not be removed separately. On the Taurus, Sable and Continental vehicles, the wiper switch is incorporated in the multi-function switch on the steering column. If there is any need for repairs to the wiper switch, the multi-function switch must be replaced as an assembly.

Removal and Installation
ESCORT AND LYNX
Except Tilt Steering Wheel

1. Disconnect the negative battery cable.
2. Loosen the steering column attaching nuts enough to remove the upper trim shroud.
3. Remove the trim shrouds.
4. Disconnect the quick connect electrical connector.
5. Peel back the foam sight shield. Remove the hex-head screws holding the switch and remove the wash/wipe switch.
6. Position the switch on the column and install the hex-head screws. Replace the foam sight shield over the switch.
7. Connect the quick connect electrical connector.
8. Install the upper and lower trim shrouds.
9. Tighten the steering column attaching nuts to 17–25 ft. lbs.
10. Connect the negative battery cable.
11. Check the steering column and wiper switch for proper operation.

Tilt Steering Wheel

1. Disconnect the negative battery cable.
2. Remove the steering column shroud.
3. Peel back the side shield and disconnect the switch wiring connector.

4. Remove the screw attaching the wiring retainer to the steering column.

5. Grasp the switch handle and pull straight out to disengage the wiper switch from the turn signal switch.

6. Complete the installation of the switch by reversing the removal procedure.

TEMPO AND TOPAZ
Column Mounted

1. Disconnect the negative battery cable.

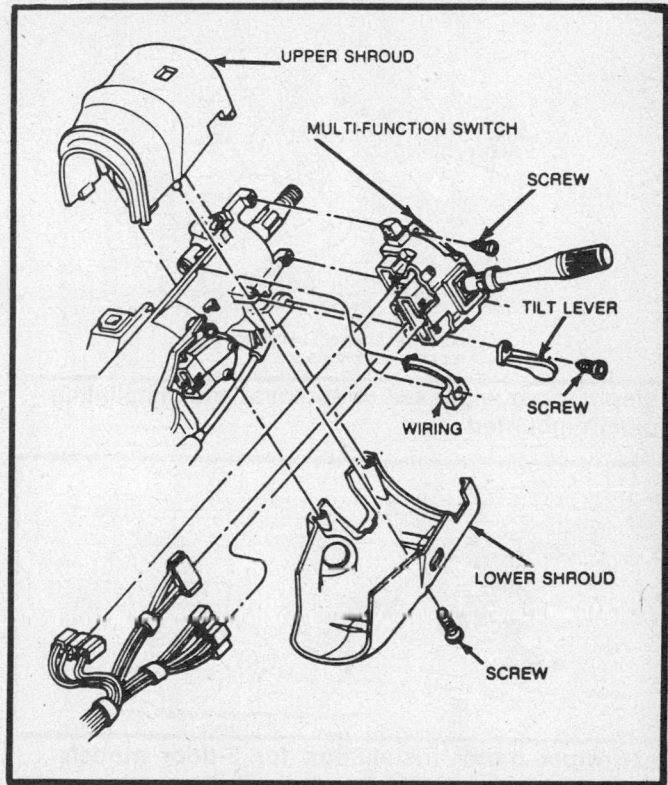

Multi-function switch removal and installation—Taurus/Sable

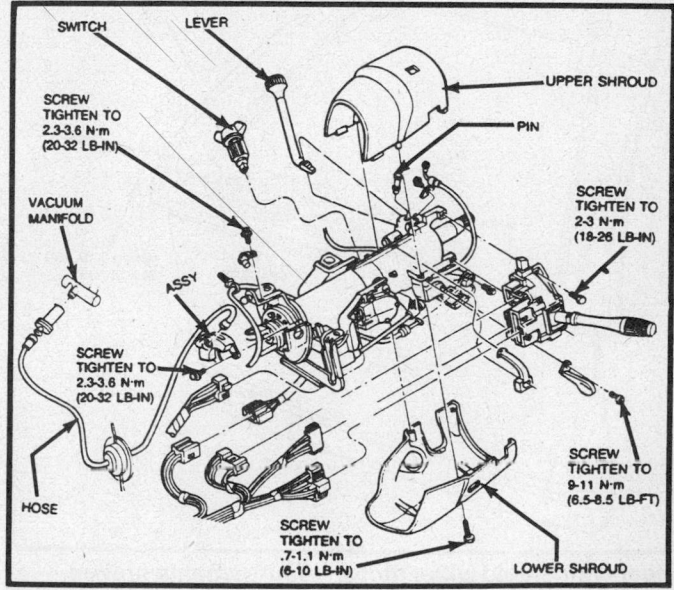

Multi-function switch assembly—Continental

2. Remove the instrument panel finish panel.
3. Remove the wiper switch housing retaining screws and remove the switch housing from the instrument panel.
4. Remove the wiper switch knob. Disconnect the electrical connectors from the switch assembly.
5. Remove the screws holding the wiper switch in the switch housing plate and remove the switch.
6. Complete the installation of the switch by reversing the removal procedure.

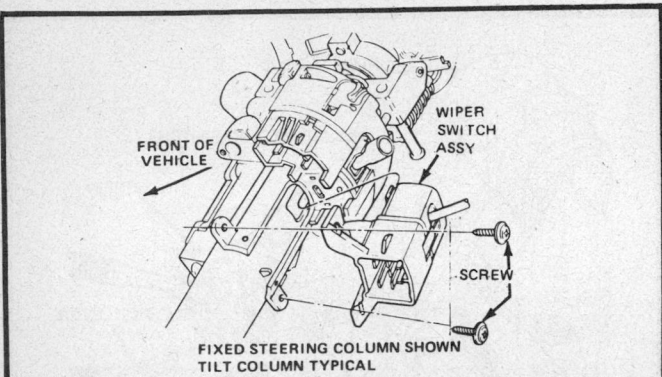

Tempo/Topaz wiper switch removal and installation— column mounted

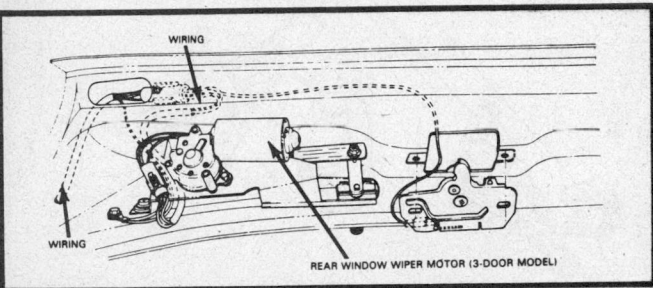

Rear wiper motor installation for 3-door models

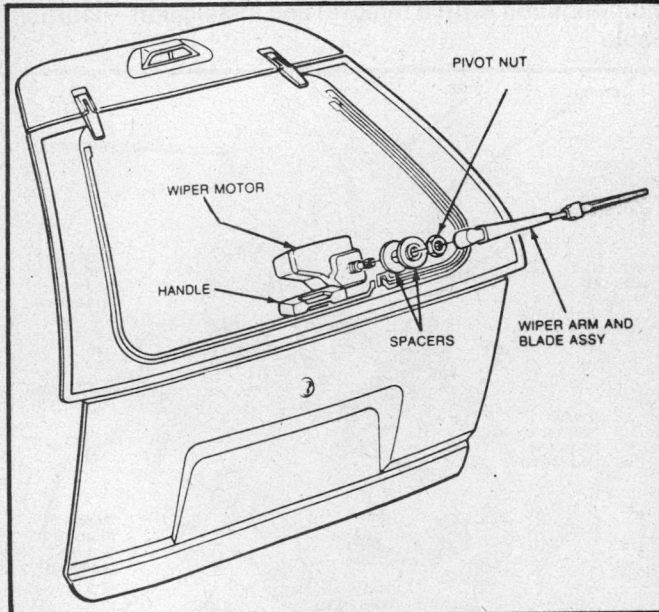

Rear windshield wiper motor—Taurus/Sable station wagon

Except Column Mounted

1. Disconnect the negative battery cable.
2. Insert a suitable prying tool into the small slot on top of the switch bezel.
3. Push down on the tool to work the top of the switch away from the instrument panel.
4. Work the bottom portion of the switch from the panel and completely remove the switch from the panel opening. Hold the switch and pull the wiring at the rear of the switch until the switch connector can be easily disconnected. Disconnect the connector and allow the wiring to hang from the switch mounting opening.
5. Connect the wiring connector to the new switch and route the wiring back into the mounting opening. Insert the switch into the opening so that the graphics are properly aligned.
6. Push on the switch until the bezel seats against the instrument panel and the clips lock the switch into place.

TAURUS, SABLE AND CONTINENTAL

The standard and interval wiper systems used on these vehicles feature a rotary actuated switch which is part of the turn signal lever of the multi-function switch. To replace the wiper switch, refer to "Combination Switch, Removal and Installation".

WINDSHIELD WIPER MOTOR

Removal and Installation

1. Disconnect the negative battery cable.
2. Lift the water shield cover from the cowl on the passenger side.
3. Disconnect the power lead from the motor.
4. Remove the linkage retaining clip from the operating arm on the motor.
5. Remove the attaching screws from the motor and bracket assembly and remove.
6. Remove the operating arm from the motor. Unscrew the 3 bolts and separate the motor from the mounting bracket.
7. Complete the installation of the wiper motor by reversing the removal procedures.

WIPER LINKAGE

Removal and Installation

The wiper linkage is mounted below the cowl top panel and can be reached by raising the hood.

1. Remove the wiper arm and blade assembly from the pivot shaft. Pry the latch (on the arm) away from the shaft to unlock the arm from the pivot shaft.
2. Raise the hood and disconnect the negative battery cable. Remove the right and left leaf screens if so equipped.
3. Remove the clip and disconnect the linkage drive arm from the motor crank pin.
4. On Tempo and Topaz, remove the cowl top grille.
5. On Tempo and Topaz, remove the screws retaining the pivot assemblies to the cow.
6. On Escort and Lynx, remove the large pivot retainer nuts from each pivot shaft.
7. On the Taurus, Sable and Continental, remove the screws attaching the pivot assemblies to the cowl panel.
8. Remove the linkage and pivot assembly from the cowl chamber.
9. Complete the installation of the linkage assembly by reversing the removal procedure.

Instrument Cluster

Refer to "Chilton's Electronic Instrumentation Service Manual" for additional coverage.

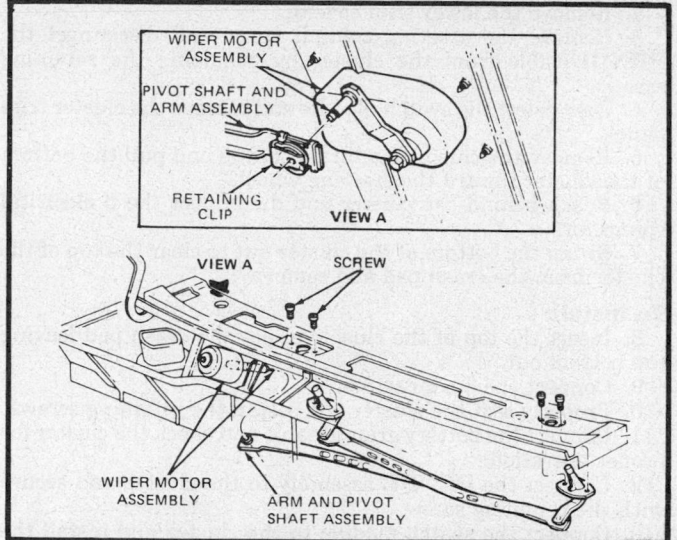

Tempo/Topaz wiper pivot shaft and linkage

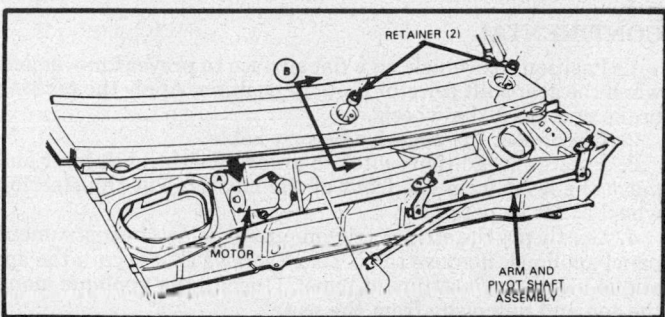

Wiper motor linkage removal and installation Escort and Lynx

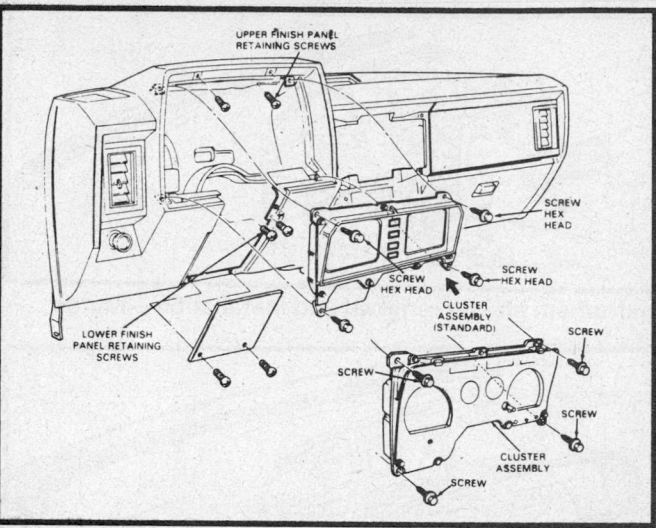

Instrument cluster assembly Escort and Lynx

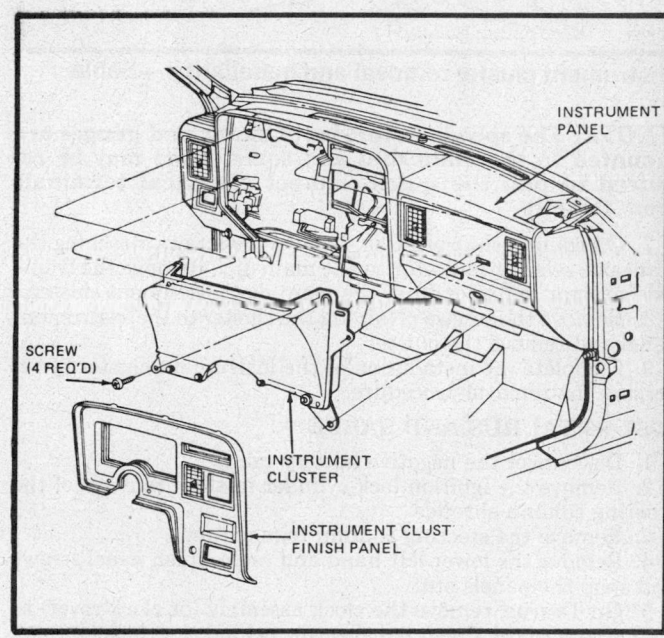

Tempo/Topaz instrument cluster removal and installation

CONVENTIONAL

Removal and Installation

EXCEPT TAURUS AND SABLE

1. Disconnect the negative battery cable.
2. Remove the 2 retaining screws at the bottom of the steering column and snap the steering column cover out.
3. On 1988–90 Tempo and Topaz, remove the steering column trim shroud and the snap-in lower cluster finish panels.
4. On the Tempo and Topaz, remove the instrument panel finish screws, radio knobs and remove the finish panel. On the 1988–90 Tempo and Topaz, remove the cluster opening finish panel retaining screws and pull the panel rearward. Also, disconnect the speedometer cable from the transaxle at this time.
5. On the Escort and Lynx, remove the cluster opening finish panel retainer screws and remove the finish panel.
6. Remove the upper and lower screws and retaining cluster to remove the instrument panel. On the 1988–90 Tempo and Topaz, carefully pull the instrument panel rearward enough to disengage the speedometer cable.
7. From under the instrument panel, disconnect the speedometer cable by pressing the flat surface of the plastic quick connector, as required.
8. Pull the cluster away from the instrument panel and disconnect the electrical feed plug to the cluster from its receptacle in the printed circuit.
9. Complete the installation of the instrument cluster by reversing the removal procedure.

1986 TAURUS AND SABLE

1. Disconnect the negative battery cable.
2. Disconnect the speedometer cable by dropping the fuse panel on its hinge to allow access to the speedometer cable latch attachment. Press the cable latch to disengage the cable from the speedometer head, while pulling the cable away from the speedometer.
3. Remove the instrument cluster finish panel retaining screws and remove the finish panel.
4. Remove the steering column shroud. On Sable vehicles with a tachometer cluster, remove the lower trim panel attaching screws and remove the trim panel.
5. Remove the mask and lens mounting screws and remove the mask and lens. On Sable vehicles equipped with a tachometer cluster, remove the lower floodlamp bulb and socket assemblies.
6. Lift the main dial assembly from the backplate.

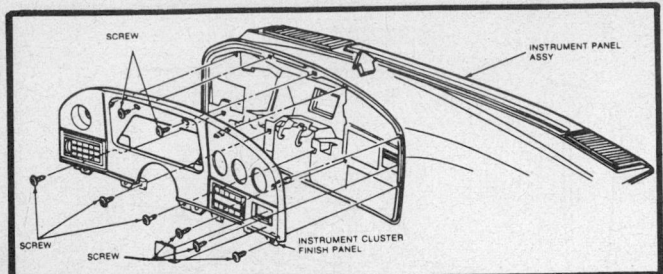

Instrument cluster removal and installation—Taurus

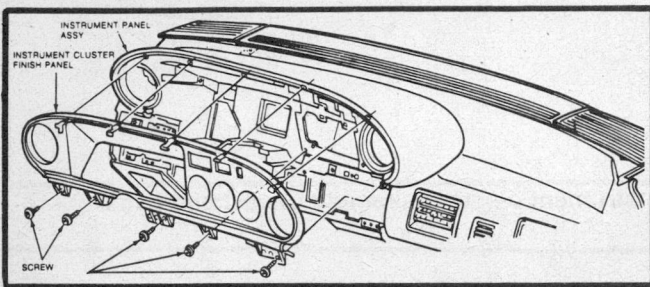

Instrument cluster removal and installation—Sable

NOTE: The speedometer, tachometer and gauges are mounted to the main dial and some effort may be required to pull the quick-connect electrical terminals from the clip.

7. On column shift vehicles, remove the screws attaching the transaxle selector indicator to the main dial. Remove the transaxle selector indicator from the main dial/instrument cluster.

8. Remove the screws retaining the cluster to the instrument panel and remove the cluster.

9. Complete the installation of the instrument cluster by reversing the removal procedure.

1987–90 TAURUS AND SABLE

1. Disconnect the negative battery cable.
2. Remove the ignition lock cylinder to allow removal of the steering column shrouds.
3. Remove the steering column trim shrouds.
4. Remove the lower left hand and radio finish panel screws and snap the panels out.
5. On Taurus, remove the clock assembly (or clock cover) to gain access to the finish panel screw behind the clock.
6. Remove the cluster opening finish panel retaining screws and jam nut behind the headlamp switch. Remove the finish panel by rocking the edge upward and outward.
7. On column shift vehicles, disconnect the transaxle selector indicator from the column by removing the retaining screw.
8. Disconnect the speedometer cable at the transaxle.
9. Remove the 4 cluster-to-instrument panel retaining screws and pull the cluster assembly forward.
10. Disconnect the cluster electrical connector and speedometer cable. Press the cable latch to disengage the cable from the speedometer head while pulling the cable away from the cluster. Remove the cluster.
11. Complete the installation of the instrument panel by reversing the removal procedure.

ELECTRONIC

Removal and Installation

TAURUS AND SABLE

1. Disconnect the negative battery cable.

2. Remove the lower trim covers.
3. Remove the steering column cover and disconnect the **PRNDL** cable from the cluster by removing the retaining screws.
4. Disconnect the switch module and remove the cluster trim panel.
5. Remove the cluster mounting screws and pull the bottom of the cluster toward the steering wheel.
6. Reach behind the cluster and disconnect the 3 electrical connectors.
7. Swing the bottom of the cluster out to clear the top of the cluster from the crash pad and remove.

To install:

8. Insert the top of the cluster under the crash pad leaving the bottom out.
9. Connect the 3 connectors.
10. Properly seat the cluster and install the retaining screws.
11. Connect the battery ground cable and check the cluster for proper operation.
12. Connect the **PRNDL** assembly to the cluster and secure with the retaining screw.
13. Connect the switch module to the cluster and install the cluster trim panel.
14. Install the lower trim covers.

CONTINENTAL

1. Position the vehicle on a flat surface to prevent movement when the gear shift selector is out of position. Apply the parking brake and block the wheels.
2. Disconnect the negative battery cable.
3. Rotate the ignition switch to unlock the the shift lever and move the lever from the front of the cluster. Tilt the steering wheel as far as possible.
4. Gently pry the strip of trim mounted below the instrument panel applique. Remove the 5 Torx® screws that secure the applique below the instrument panel. Unsnap the applique along the top and pull away from the panel.
5. Disconnect the switch assembly connector from the instrument cluster. Disconnect the warning lamp and clock connector. Set the applique aside.
6. Remove the 2 Torx® screws (below the instrument cluster) that secure the reinforcement strip (metal support) to the substructure. Set the metal support aside.
7. Remove the screws from the bottom of the steering column shroud. Remove the tilt lever.
8. Raise the top section of the shroud to release a clip located on the left hand side of the steering wheel. Separate the upper section of the shroud from the side section near the ignition switch. Remove the upper section from the shift lever.
9. Gently pull the gap cover from below the instrument cluster.
10. Remove the 4 Torx® screws attaching the instrument cluster to the substructure.
11. Tilt the bottom of the instrument cluster slightly toward the rear of the vehicle. Disconnect the **PRNDL** assembly from the cluster by undoing the 2 snaps located beneath the cluster. Pull the **PRNDL** assembly down and to the right and position off to the side.
12. Place a clean, soft cloth on the steering column to prevent scratching the surface of the steering column as the instrument cluster is removed.
13. Push the bottom of the instrument cluster into the instrument panel cavity. Tilt the top of the instrument cluster toward the rear of the vehicle. Push the cluster up and out of the cavity.
14. Reach around the back of the instrument cluster to disconnect the 4 connectors (1 on the right side, 2 in the middle and 1 on the left). The connectors have locking tabs that must be pressed in to release.
15. Complete the installation of the instrument cluster by reversing the removal procedure.

SPEEDOMETER

Removal and Installation
ESCORT, LYNX, TEMPO AND TOPAZ

1. Disconnect the negative battery cable.
2. Reach under the instrument panel and disconnect the speedometer cable by pressing on the flat surface of the plastic connector.
3. Remove screws that retain the lens and mask to the backplate.
4. Remove the nuts retaining the fuel gauge assembly to the back plate. Remove the fuel gauge assembly and then remove the speedometer assembly.
5. Prior to installing the speedometer, apply a $^3/_{16}$ in. bead of silicone damping grease part number D7AZ–19A331–A or equivalent in the drive hole of the speedometer head. Install speedometer head assembly into cluster.

NOTE: The speedometer is calibrated at the time of manufacture. Excessive rough handling of the speedometer may disturb the calibration.

6. Install retaining screws to retain the lens and mask to the backplate.
7. Install instrument cluster.
8. Connect battery ground and check operation of speedometer.

TAURUS AND SABLE

1. Disconnect the negative battery cable.
2. Remove the instrument cluster finish panel retaining screws and remove the finish panel.
3. Remove the mask-and-lens mounting screws and remove the mask and lens. On Sable, remove the lower floodlamp bulb and socket assemblies.
4. Remove the entire dial assembly from the instrument cluster by carefully pulling it away from the cluster backplate.

NOTE: The speedometer, tachometer and gauges are mounted to the main dial and some effort may be required to pull the quick-connect electrical terminals from the clip.

5. On column shift vehicles, remove the screws attaching the transaxle selector indicator to the main dial. Remove the transaxle selector indicator from the main dial/instrument cluster. On Sable, remove the odometer drive jack shaft and remove the attachment clip at the odometer, slip the jack shaft out of the odometer bracket and speedometer bridge.
6. Pull the reset knob from the trip odometer, if equipped. To remove the speedometer from the main dial, manually rotate the speedometer pointer to align it with the slot in the dial. Remove the mounting screws and carefully pull the speedometer away from the dial, making sure to guide the pointer through the slot.
7. Complete the installation of the speedometer by reversing the removal procedure.

CONTINENTAL

The display of speedometer/odometer and fuel/multigauge information is accomplished by a remote Cluster Control Assembly (CCA) module that is integral with the electronic instrument cluster assembly.

1. Disconnect the negative battery cable.
2. Remove the electronic instrument cluster.
3. Locate and undo the Message Center Control Assembly (MCCA) module retaining snap and lift the module enough to clear the snap. Undo the bottom snap and remove the module.
4. Remove the Cluster Control Assembly (CCA) button assembly connector from the mask.
5. Undo the Cluster Control Assembly (CCA) housing snap on the left hand side of the module. Lift the end a small amount to clear the snap.
6. Remove the remaining snap and remove the module from the cluster assembly.
7. Complete the installation of the new Cluster Control Assembly (CCA) module with the cluster assembly by reversing the removal procedure.

SPEEDOMETER CABLE

Removal and Installation

1. Disconnect the negative battery cable.

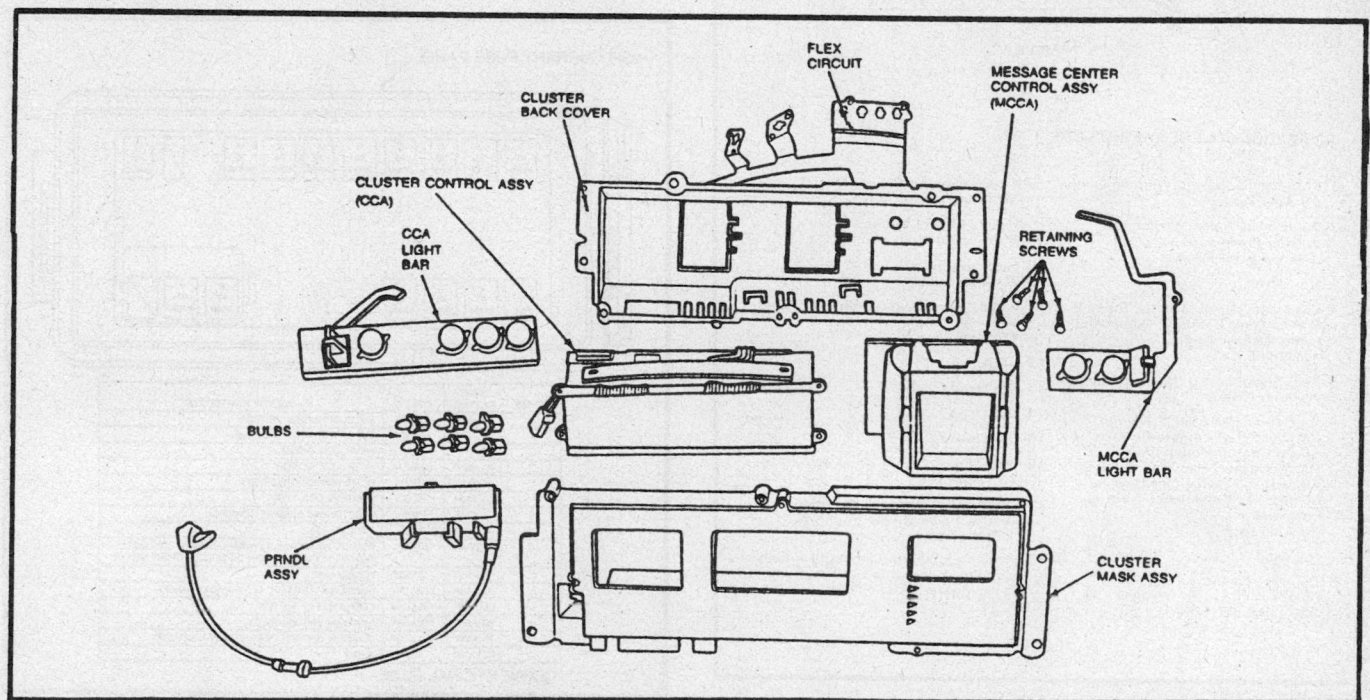

Electronic Instrument Cluster (EIC) assembly—Continental

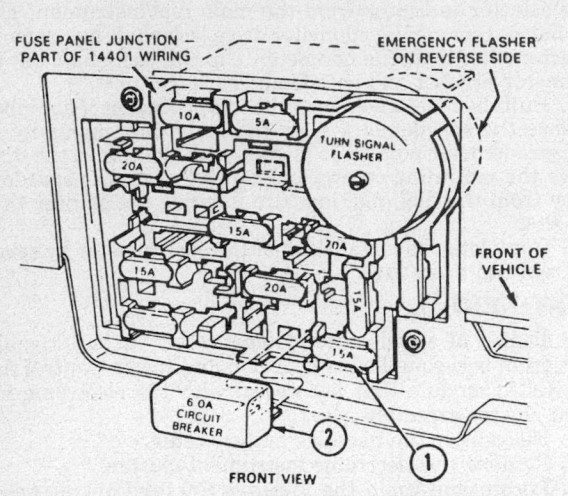

FRONT VIEW

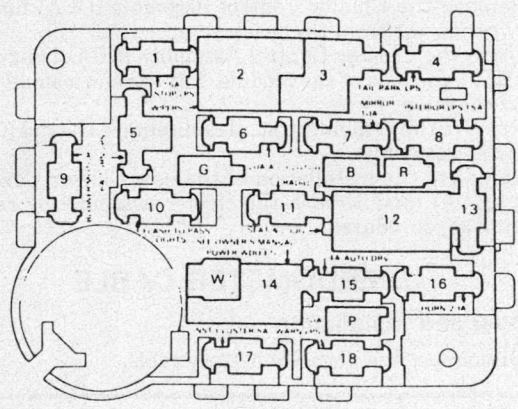

REAR VIEW

FUSE/CIRCUIT BREAKER USAGE

1. Stop Lamps, Hazard Warning Lamps
   15 Amp Fuse

2. Windshield Wiper, Windshield
   Washer Pump, Interval Wiper
   6 Amp Circuit Breaker

3. Not Used

4. Taillamps, Parking Lamps, Side
   Marker Lamps, Cluster Illumination
   Lamp, License Lamp.
   15 Amp Fuse

5. Turn Signal Lamps, Back up Lamps
   15 Amp Fuse

6. Air Conditioner Clutch, Heated
   Backlite Relay, Liftgate Release,
   Speed Control Module, Rear
   Wiper/Washer, Electronic Digital
   Clock Display, Graphics Display
   Module, Air Conditioner Throttle
   Positioner.
   20 Amp Fuse

7. Not used

8. Courtesy Lamps, Key Warning
   Buzzer
   15 Amp Fuse

9. Air Conditioner Blower Motor
   30 Amp Fuse

   Heater Blower Motor
   15 Amp Fuse

10. Flash to pass
    20 Amp Fuse

11. Radio, Tape Player, Premium Sound
    with one Amplifier.
    15 Amp Fuse

12. Not Used

13. Not Used

14. Not Used

15. Not Used

16. Horn, Front Cigar Lighter
    20 Amp Fuse

17. Instrument Cluster Illumination
    Lamps, Radio, Climate Control
    5 Amp Fuse

18. Warning Indicator Lamps, Low Fuel
    Module, Auto Lamp System, Dual
    Timer Buzzer, Tachometer.

Fuse and circuit breaker locations, typical

2. Reach under the instrument panel and disconnect the speedometer cable housing by pressing on the flat surface of the plastic connector.

3. Pull speedometer cable out of the upper end of the casing.

4. If cable is broken, raise the vehicle and support it safely. Remove cable from transaxle or speed control speed sensor if equipped.

5. Remove the lower part of the broken cable from low end of the casing.

6. Determine the exact length of the old core and cut the new core following the instructions included in the core kit.

7. Install the new cable into casing, inserting it from the speedometer end.

8. Connect the speedometer casing to the transaxle and speedometer.

Electrical Circuit Protectors

FUSIBLE LINKS

Fusible links are used to prevent major wire harness damage in the event of a short circuit or an overload condition in the wiring circuits that are normally not fused, due to carrying high amperage loads or because of their locations within the wiring harness. Each fusible link is of a fixed value for a specific electrical load and should a fusible link fail, the cause of the failure must be determine and repaired prior to installing a new fusible link of the same value. Please be advised that the color coding of replacement fusible links may vary from the production color coding that is outlined in the text that follows.

ESCORT, LYNX, TEMPO AND TOPAZ

Green 14 Gauge Wire—On Escort and Lynx equipped with diesel engine, there are 2 links (1 for Tempo and Topaz) located in the glow plug wiring to protect the glow plug control.

Black 16 Gauge Wire—On Escort and Lynx, there is 1 link located in the wiring for the rear window defogger. On Tempo and Topaz, there is 1 link located in the wiring for the anti-theft system.

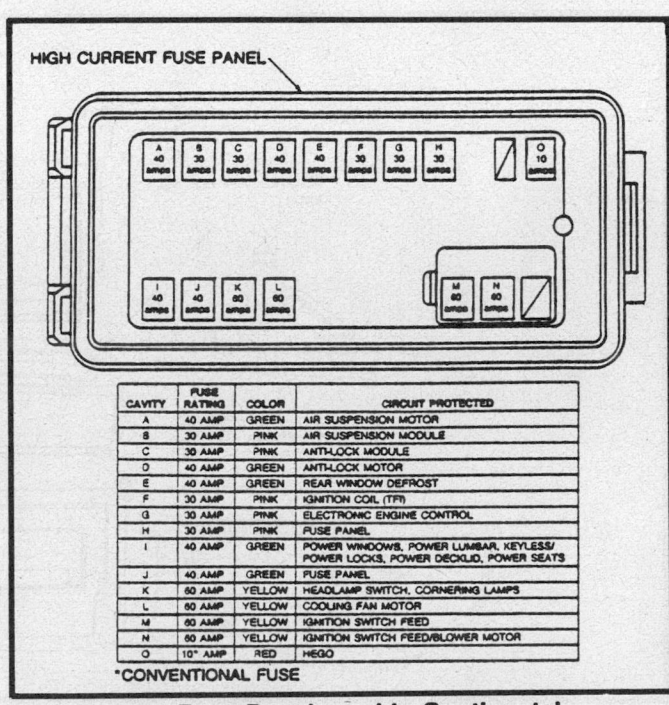

CAVITY	FUSE RATING	COLOR	CIRCUIT PROTECTED
A	40 AMP	GREEN	AIR SUSPENSION MOTOR
B	30 AMP	PINK	AIR SUSPENSION MODULE
C	30 AMP	PINK	ANTI-LOCK MODULE
D	40 AMP	GREEN	ANTI-LOCK MOTOR
E	40 AMP	GREEN	REAR WINDOW DEFROST
F	30 AMP	PINK	IGNITION COIL (TFI)
G	30 AMP	PINK	ELECTRONIC ENGINE CONTROL
H	30 AMP	PINK	FUSE PANEL
I	40 AMP	GREEN	POWER WINDOWS, POWER LUMBAR, KEYLESS/POWER LOCKS, POWER DECKLID, POWER SEATS
J	40 AMP	GREEN	FUSE PANEL
K	60 AMP	YELLOW	HEADLAMP SWITCH, CORNERING LAMPS
L	60 AMP	YELLOW	COOLING FAN MOTOR
M	60 AMP	YELLOW	IGNITION SWITCH FEED
N	60 AMP	YELLOW	IGNITION SWITCH FEED/BLOWER MOTOR
O	10* AMP	RED	HEGO

*CONVENTIONAL FUSE

High-Current Fuse Panel used in Continental

Red 18 Gauge Wire—On Tempo and Topaz equipped with gasoline engines, there is 1 link used to protect the carburetor circuits. On the Escort and Lynx equipped with diesel engines, there is 1 link located in the heater fan wiring to protect the heater fan motor circuit.

Brown 18 Gauge Wire—On Tempo and Topaz, there is 1 link used to protect the rear window defogger and the fuel door release. On the Escort and Lynx, there is 1 link used to protect the heater fan motor circuit. There is 1 link used to protect the EEC module on Tempo, Topaz, Escort and Lynx with the 2.3L engine.

Blue 20 Gauge Wire—On Escort and Lynx with gasoline engines, there are 2 links in the wire between the starter relay and the EFE heater. On Tempo and Topaz there is link located in the wire between the ignition switch and the A/C-heater cooling fan. On Tempo and Topaz, there is 1 link located in the wire between the battery and the engine compartment light. On 1988–90 Escort, Tempo and Topaz, a fusible link is installed in the engine compartment near the starter relay and protects the passive restraint module circuit. On Escort, Lynx, Tempo and Topaz equipped with diesel engine, there is 1 link used to protect the vacuum pump circuit. On the Tempo and Topaz, there is 1 link used to protect the heater fan motor circuit.

TAURUS AND SABLE

Green 14 Gauge Wire—This fusible link is located in the wiring going to the starter relay and it protects the starter circuit.

Black 16 Gauge Wire—This fusible link is located in the wiring going to the starter relay and it protects the rear window defrost circuit.

Black 16 Gauge Wire—This fusible link is located on the left front inner fender panel, near the voltage regulator and is used to protect the voltage regulator and alternator circuit.

Black 16 Gauge Wire—This fusible link is located in the wiring going to the starter relay and it protects the starter and alternator circuit. On the 1988–90 vehicles this fusible link is located in the vicinity of the left hand shock tower and protects the battery feed to headlamp switch and fuse panel circuits.

Orange 16 Gauge Wire—This fusible link used on the 1988–90 vehicles is located in the vicinity of the left hand shock tower and functions to protect the battery feed to ignition switch and fuse panel circuits.

Blue 20 Gauge Wire—This fusible link is located on the starter relay and protects the electrical system in general. On the 1988–90 vehicles this fusible link is located on the left hand shock tower and protects the ignition coil, ignition module and cooling fan controller.

CONTINENTAL

The Continental does not use fusible links. The fusible links have been replaced by a high current fuse panel. The high current fuse panel is located in the engine compartment on the left hand fender apron.

NOTE: Always disconnect the negative battery cable before servicing the high current fuses or serious personal injury may result.

CIRCUIT BREAKERS

Circuit breakers are used to protect the various components of the electrical system, such as headlights and windshield wipers. The circuit breakers are located either in the control switch or mounted on or near the fuse panel.

TEMPO AND TOPAZ

Headlights and Highbeam Indicator—One 18 amp circuit breaker (22 amp in the 86–87 vehicles) incorporated in the lighting switch.

Front and Rear Marker, Side Parking, Rear and License Lamps—One 15 amp circuit breaker incorporated in the lighting switch.

Windshield Wiper and Rear Window Circuit—One 4.5 amp circuit breaker located in the windshield wiper switch.

Power Windows—There are two 20 amp circuit breakers located in the starter relay and the fuse block.

Power Seats and Power Door Locks—One 20 amp circuit breaker located in the fuse block.

Station Wagon Power Back Window (Tail light switch)—One 20 amp circuit breaker located in the fuse block.

Intermittent 2-Speed Windshield Wiper—One 8.25 amp circuit breaker located in the fuse block.

Door Cigar Lighter—One 20 or 30 amp circuit breaker located in the fuse block.

Liftgate Wiper—One 4.5 amp circuit breaker located in the instrument panel.

ESCORT, LYNX, TAURUS AND SABLE

Headlights and High Beam Indicator—One 22 amp circuit breaker incorporated in the lighting switch.

Liftgate Wiper—One 4.5 amp circuit breaker located in the instrument panel to the left of the radio.

Windshield Wiper and Wiper Pump Circuit—One 6 amp circuit breaker (8.25 amp on the Escort and Lynx) located in the in the fuse block.

The Taurus and Sable have 3 circuit breakers all located in the fuse block. The 6 amp circuit breaker is used for the windshield wiper circuit and one 20 amp circuit breaker is used for the instrument illumination. There is also an in-line 30 amp circuit breaker for the power windows.

CONTINENTAL

Windshield Wiper Circuit—One 6 amp circuit breaker is located in the fuse panel and protects the windshield wiper governor, switch, motor, washer motor and fluid level switch.

VARIOUS RELAYS

ESCORT AND LYNX

Air Conditioning Fan Controller—is located on the right side of the dash, behind the glove box.

Cold Start Module (Carbureted with automatic transaxle)—is located at the left rear corner of the engine compartment.

Cooling Fan Relay—is located on the left hand side of the instrument panel.

Electronic Control Assembly (ECA)—is located at the front of the console.

Electronic Engine Control (EEC) Power Relay—is located at the left hand side of the instrument panel.

EFE Heater Relay—is mounted on the left hand side fender apron.

Fuel Pump Relay—is located at the left hand side of the instrument panel.

Horn Relay—is located behind the instrument panel on the left side of the radio.

RPM Module—is located behind the glove box.

Starter Relay—located on the left hand side of the fender apron in front of the shock tower.

TEMPO AND TOPAZ

Cooling Fan Controller—is located behind the left side of the instrument panel.

Cooling Fan Controller Module—is located behind the right side of the instrument panel.

Cooling Fan Relay—is located in the air conditioning cooling fan control module.

Electronic Control Assembly—is located under the left side of the instrument panel.

Electronic Engine Control Power Relay—is located behind the glove box on the right side of the instrument panel.

Fuel Pump Relay—is located behind the glove box.

Horn Relay—is located in the fuse block.

Speed Sensor—is located at the left rear side of the transaxle.

Speed Control Servo—is located on the left front shock tower.

Speed Control Amplifier—is located under the left side of the instrument panel.

Starter Relay—is located on the left front fender apron in front of the shock tower.

TAURUS, SABLE AND CONTINENTAL

Alternator Output Control Relay (3.0L and 3.8L engines with heated windshield)—is located between the right front inner fender panel and splash shield.

Alternator Output Control Relay—is located between the right front inner fender and the fender splash shield.

ATC Blower Motor Speed Controller—is located in the evaporator case, upstream of the evaporator core.

ATC High Blower Relay—is located on the upper half of the evaporator case.

Electronic Control Assembly—is located under the right side of the instrument panel.

Electronic Automatic Temperature Control Unit—is located behind the instrument panel.

Horn Relay—is located under the left side of the instrument panel.

Idle Speed Controller (3.0L engine)—is located on the left hand side of the engine.

Self-Test Connector—is located in the wiring harness behind the alternator.

Speed Control Servo—is attached to the electronic control assembly.

Speed Control Switch—is located in the steering wheel.

Starter Relay—is located on the left front fender apron in front of the shock tower.

Upshift Relay (Manual transaxle)—is located on the support brace under the instrument panel.

Vehicle Speed Sensor—is located near the electronic control assembly.

Heated Rear Window Defroster System Relay—is mounted to the instrument panel.

Speed Control Switch—is located in the steering wheel.

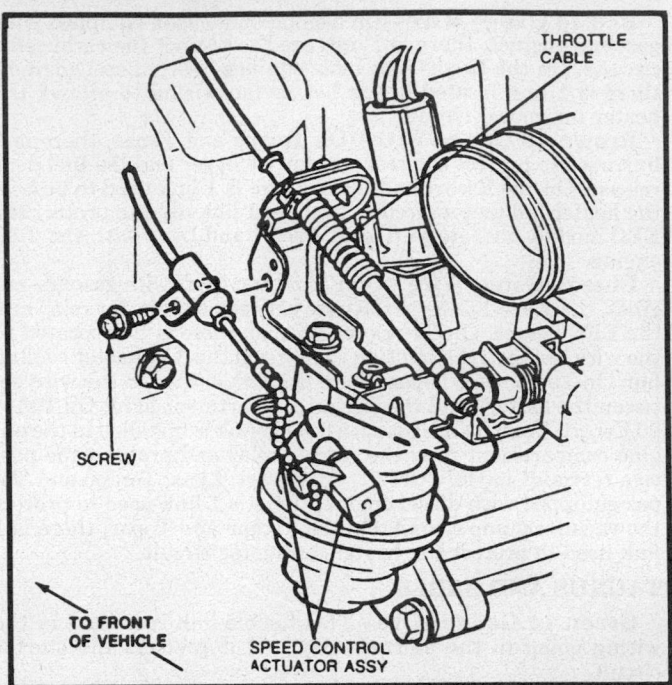

Speed control actuator cable assembly—Taurus/Sable with 2.5L engine

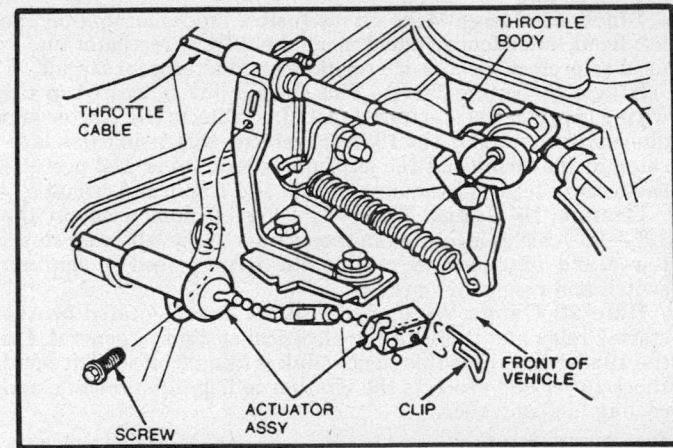

Speed control actuator cable assembly—Escort with CFI manual transaxle

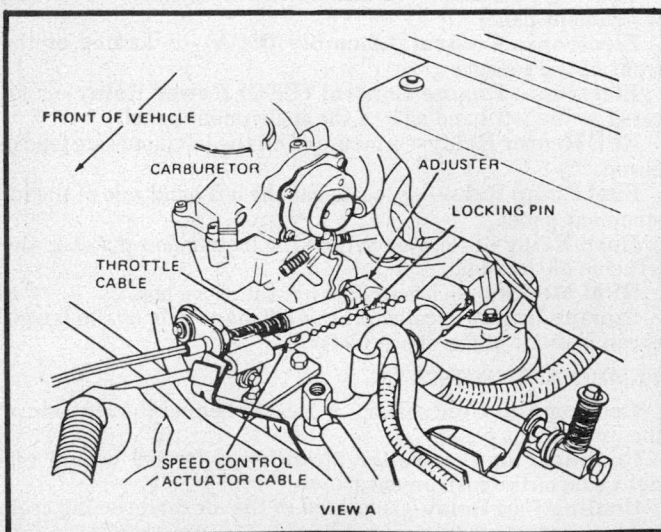

Speed control actuator cable assembly—Tempo and Topaz

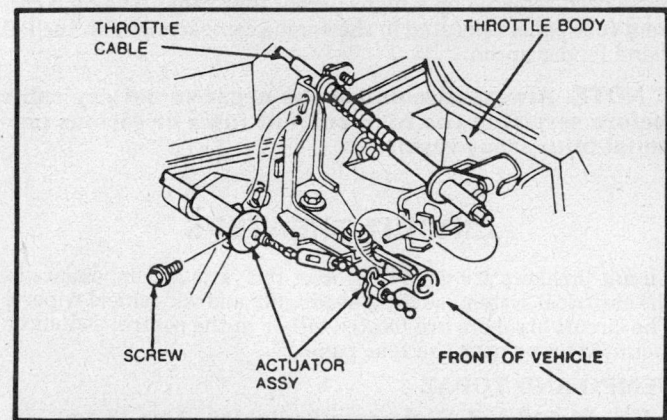

Speed control actuator cable assembly—Escort with CFI automatic transaxle

TURN SIGNAL/HAZARD WARNING FLASHERS

EXCEPT CONTINENTAL

The turn signal flasher is located on the front side of the fuse panel. The hazard flasher is located on the rear of the fuse panel behind the turn signal flasher.

CONTINENTAL

An electronic combination turn signal and emergency warning flasher is attached by a bracket to the lower left hand instrument panel reinforcement above the fuse panel.

Speed Controls

Refer to "Chilton's Chassis Electronics Service Manual" for additional coverage.

ACTUATOR CABLE

Adjustment

TEMPO AND TOPAZ
TAURUS AND SABLE WITH 2.5L ENGINE

1. With engine off, set carburetor so that throttle plate is closed and choke linkage is de-cammed.
2. Remove locking pin.
3. Pull bead chain through adjuster.
4. Insert locking pin in best hole of adjuster for tight bead chain without opening throttle plate.

ESCORT, LYNX AND CONTINENTAL
TAURUS AND SABLE WITH 3.0L ENGINE

1. Remove cable retaining clip.
2. Disengage throttle positioner (Escort and Lynx).
3. Set carburetor at hot idle (Escort and Lynx).
4. Pull or push on actuator cable end tube to take up any slack. Maintain a light tension on cable.
5. While holding cable, insert cable retaining clip and snap securely.

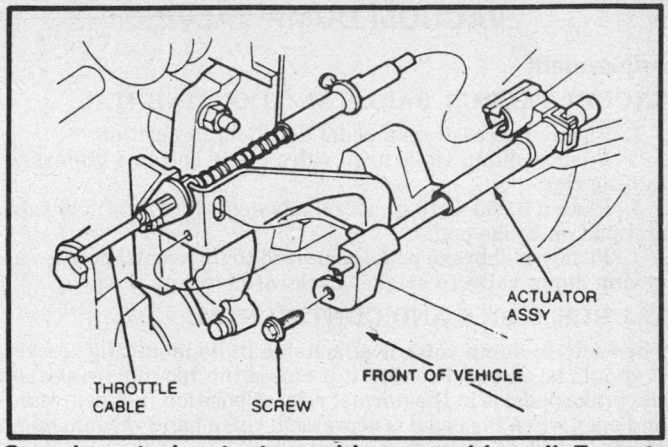

Speed control actuator cable assembly—all Escort with EFI

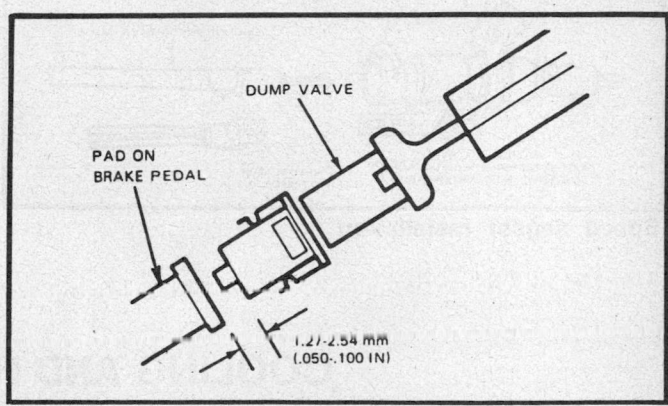

Dump valve—correctly adjusted

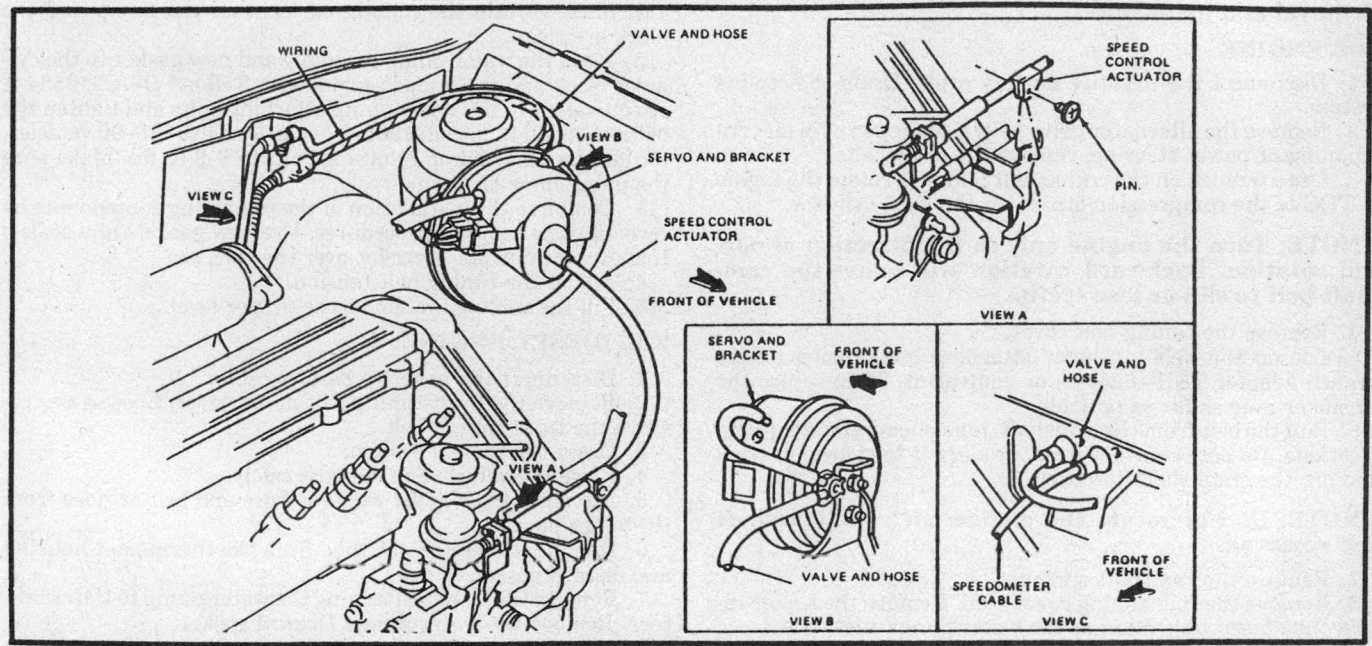

Speed control 2.0L diesel engine

VACUUM DUMP VALVE

Adjustment

EXCEPT TAURUS, SABLE AND CONTINENTAL

1. Firmly depress brake pedal and hold in position.
2. Push in dump valve until valve collar bottoms against retaining clip.
3. Place a 0.050–0.10 in. shim between white button of valve and pad on brake pedal.
4. Firmly pull brake pedal rearward to its normal position allowing dump valve to ratchet backwards in retaining clip.

TAURUS, SABLE AND CONTINENTAL

The vacuum dump valve is adjustable in its mounting bracket. It should be adjusted so that it is closed (no vacuum leak) when the brake pedal is in the normal release position (not depressed) and open when the pedal is depressed. Use a hand vacuum pump or equivalent to make this adjustment.

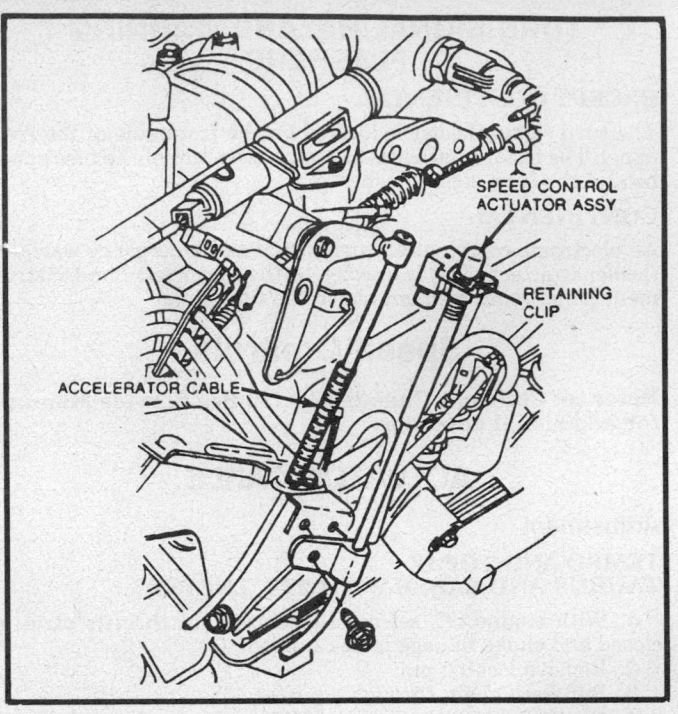

Speed control actuator cable assembly – Taurus/sable with 3.0L engine

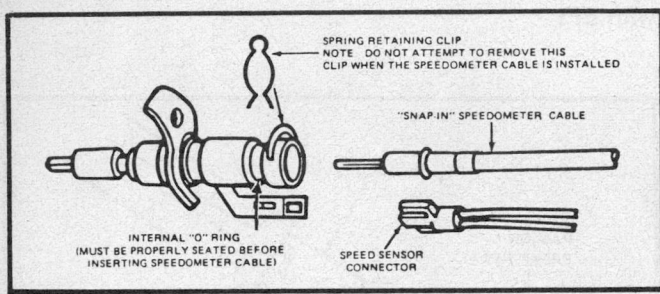

Speed sensor installation

COOLING AND HEATING SYSTEMS

Water Pump

Removal and Installation

1.9L ENGINE

1. Disconnect the negative battery cable. Drain the cooling system.
2. Remove the alternator drive belt. If equipped with air conditioning or power steering, remove the drive belts.
3. Use a wrench on the crankshaft pulley to rotate the engine to TDC of the compression stroke on the No.1 cylinder.

NOTE: Turn the engine only in the direction of normal rotation. Backward rotation will cause the camshaft belt to slip or lose teeth.

4. Remove the timing belt cover.
5. Loosen the belt tensioner attaching bolts, using torque wrench adapter T81P-6254-A or equivalent. Then secure the tensioner over as far as possible.
6. Pull the belt from the camshaft, tensioner and water pump sprockets. Do not remove it from, or allow it to change its position on, the crankshaft sprocket.

NOTE: Do not rotate the engine with the camshaft belt removed.

7. Remove the camshaft sprocket.
8. Remove the rear timing cover stud. Remove the heater return tube hose connection at the water pump inlet tube.
9. Remove the water pump inlet tube fasteners and the inlet tube and gasket.

10. Remove the water pump to cylinder block bolts and remove the water pump and its gasket.
11. Make certain the mating surfaces on the pump and the block are clean.
12. Place the water pump assembly and new gasket to the cylinder block and apply pipe sealant with Teflon® D8AZ-19554-A or equivalent to the water pump attaching bolts and tighten the bolts to 30–40 ft. lbs. on 1986–87 vehicles. On 1988–90 vehicles, torque the water pump retaining bolts to 6–9 ft. lbs. Make sure the pump impeller turns freely.
13. Complete the installation of the remaining components by reversing the removal procedures. Use new gaskets and sealer. Install the camshaft sprocket over the cam key.
14. Adjust the timing belt tension.
15. Fill the cooling system to the proper level.

2.0L DIESEL ENGINE

1. Disconnect the negative battery cable.
2. Remove the front timing belt upper cover. Loosen and remove the front timing belt.
3. Drain the cooling system.
4. Raise the vehicle and support safely.
5. Disconnect the lower radiator hose and heater hose from the water pump.
6. Disconnect the coolant tube from the thermostat housing and discard gasket.
7. Remove the 3 bolts attaching the water pump to the crankcase. Remove the water pump. Discard gasket.
8. Clean the water pump and crankshaft gasket mating surfaces.

9. Install the water pump, using a new gasket. Tighten bolts to 23–34 ft. lbs.

10. Connect the coolant tube from the thermostat housing on the water pump using a new gasket. Tighten bolts to 5–7 ft. lbs.

11. Connect the heater hose and lower radiator hose to the water pump.

12. Lower vehicle.

13. Fill and bleed the cooling system.

14. Install and adjust the front timing belt.

15. Run the engine and check for coolant leaks.

16. Install the front timing belt upper cover.

2.3L ENGINE

1. Drain the cooling system.

2. Disconnect the negative battery cable.

3. Loosen thermactor pump adjusting bolt and remove belt.

4. Remove thermactor pump hose clamp located below the thermactor pump.

5. Remove the thermactor pump bracket bolts.

6. Remove thermactor pump and bracket as an assembly.

7. Loosen water pump idler pulley and remove the belt from the water pump pulley.

8. Disconnect the heater hose at the water pump.

9. Remove the water pump retaining bolts. Remove the water pump from its mounting.

To install:

10. Thoroughly clean both gasket mating surfaces on the water pump and cylinder block.

11. Coat the new gasket on both sides with a water resistant sealer and position on the cylinder block.

12. Install the water pump retaining bolts. Tighten to 15–22 ft. lbs.

13. Connect the heater hose on the water pump.

14. Install water pump belt on the pulley and adjust the tension. Install thermactor pump and bracket.

15. Install thermactor pump hose located on the bottom of the pump.

16. Install thermactor pump belt to the pulley and adjust the belt tension.

17. Connect the negative ground cable.

18. Replace engine coolant. Operate the engine until normal operating temperature is reached. Check for leaks and recheck the coolant level.

2.5L ENGINE

1. Disconnect the negative battery cable.

2. Remove the radiator cap and position a drain pan under the bottom radiator hose.

3. Raise and support the vehicle safely. Remove the lower radiator hose from the radiator and drain the coolant into the drain pan.

4. Remove the water pump inlet tube. Loosen the belt tensioner by inserting a ½ inch flex handle in the square hole of the tensioner and rotate the tensioner counterclockwise and remove the the belt from the pulleys.

5. Disconnect the heater hose from the water pump. Remove the water pump retaining bolts and remove the pump from the engine.

6. Complete the installation of the water pump by reversing the removal procedure. Torque the water pump-to-engine block retaining bolts to 15–22 ft. lbs.

7. Refill the cooling system to the proper level. Start the engine and allow to reach normal operating temperature and check for leaks.

3.0L ENGINE EXCEPT SHO AND 3.8L ENGINE EXCEPT CONTINENTAL

NOTE: These engines use aluminum components that require a special rust inhibitor coolant formulation to avoid radiator damage. The cooling system should be filled with a 50/50 mix of water and antifreeze, with the addition of 2 cooling system protector pellets D9AZ–19558–A or equivalent.

1. Disconnect the negative battery cable and place a suitable drain pan under the radiator drain cock.

NOTE: Drain the system with the engine cool and the heater temperature control set at the maximum heat position. Attach a ⅜ in. hose to the drain cock so as to direct the coolant into the drain pan.

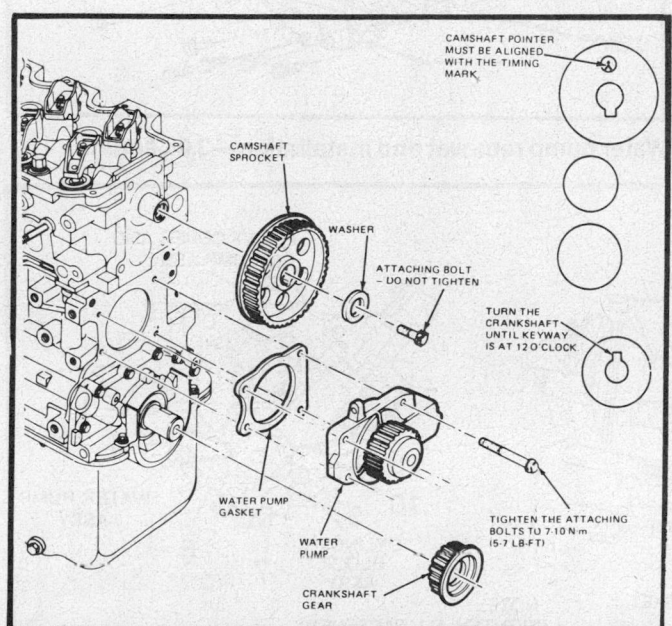

Water pump location and timing gear alignment for timing belt installation Escort and Lynx

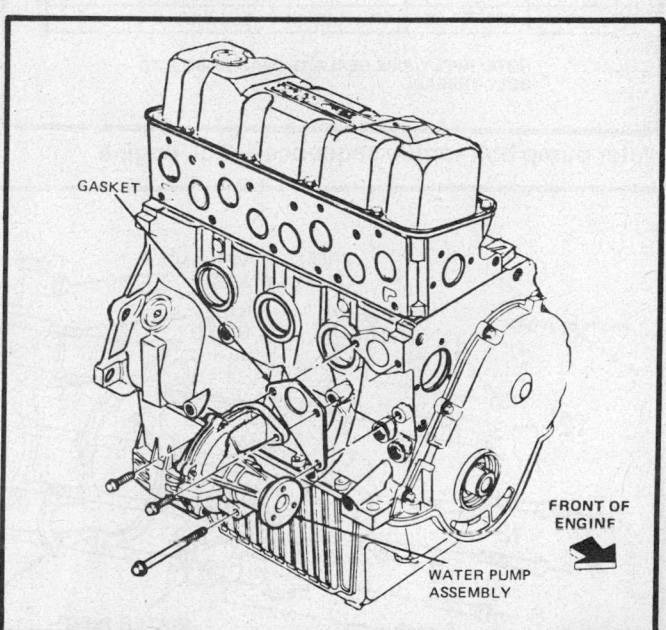

2.3L HSC engine, water pump removal and installation

2. Remove the radiator cap, open the drain cock on the radiator and drain the cooling system.

3. Loosen the accessory drive belt idler pulley and remove the drive belts.

4. Disconnect the idler pulley bracket from the engine. Disconnect the heater hose from the water pump.

5. Remove the 4 pulley-to-pump hub bolts. The pulley will remain loose on the hub due to the insufficient clearance between the inner fender and the water pump.

6. Remove the water pump to engine block attaching bolts and lift the water pump and pulley out of the vehicle.

7. Complete the installation of the water pump by reversing the removal procedure. Torque the water pump-to-engine block bolts as follows: there are 2 size bolts the metric class M8 bolt which is torqued to 15–22 ft. lbs. the other bolt is metric class M6 which is torqued to 6–8 ft. lbs. Be sure to apply a suitable thread sealer to the bolts prior to installation.

3.8L ENGINE CONTINENTAL

NOTE: This engine uses an aluminum cylinder head and requires special corrosion inhibiting coolant to avoid radiator damage.

1. Disconnect the negative battery cable. Drain the cooling system.

2. Remove the lower nut on both right hand engine mounts. Raise and safely support the engine.

3. Loosen the accessory drive belt idler. Remove the drive belt and water pump pulley.

4. Remove the air suspension pump.

5. Remove the power steering pump mounting bracket attaching bolts. Leaving hoses connected, place pump/bracket assembly aside in a position to prevent fluid from leaking out.

6. If equipped with air conditioning, remove the compressor front support bracket.

7. Leave the compressor in place, if removed.

8. Disconnect coolant bypass and heater hoses at the water pump.

9. Remove the water pump-to-engine block attaching bolts and remove the pump from the vehicle. Discard the gasket and replace with new.

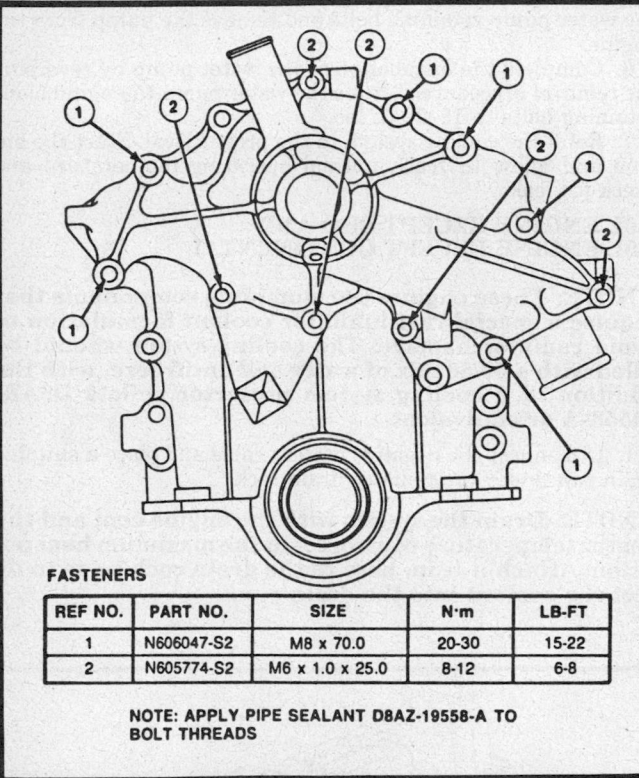

FASTENERS

REF NO.	PART NO.	SIZE	N·m	LB-FT
1	N606047-S2	M8 x 70.0	20-30	15-22
2	N605774-S2	M6 x 1.0 x 25.0	8-12	6-8

NOTE: APPLY PIPE SEALANT D8AZ-19558-A TO BOLT THREADS

Water pump bolt torque sequence—3.0L engine

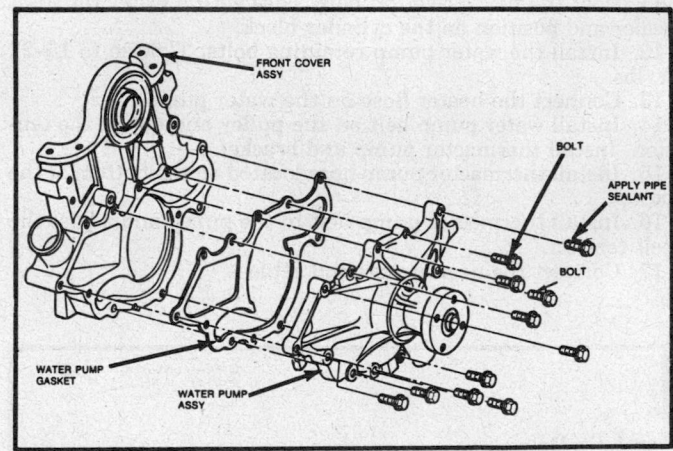

Water pump removal and installation—3.0L engine

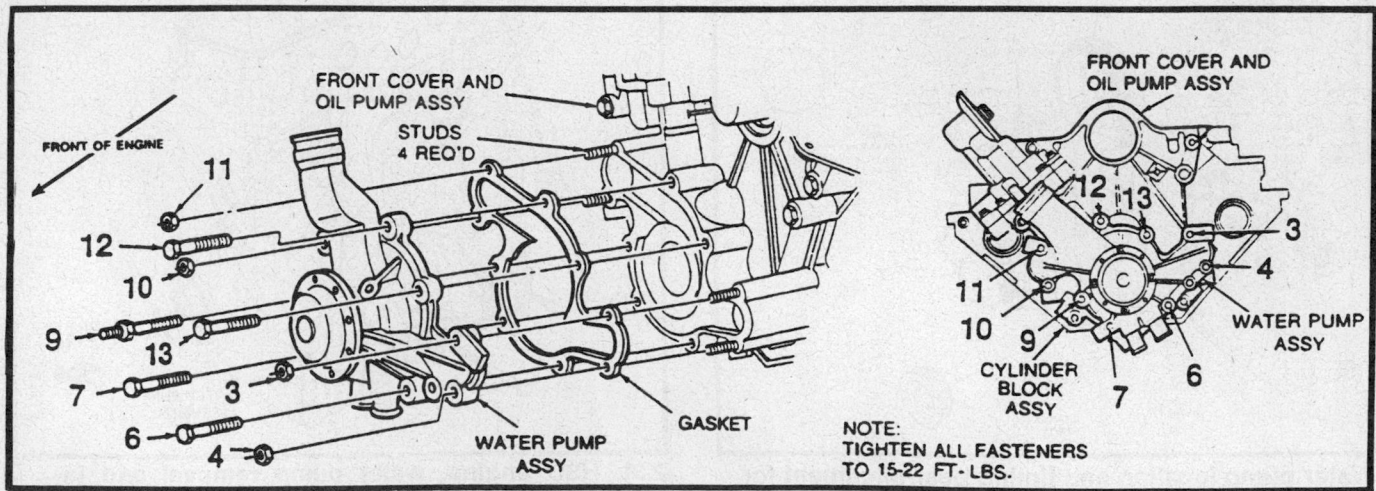

Water pump bolt torque sequence—3.8L engine

To install:

10. Lightly oil all bolt and stud threads before installation except those that require sealant. Thoroughly clean the water pump and front cover gasket contact surfaces.

11. Apply a coating of contact adhesive to both surfaces of the new gasket. Position a new gasket on water pump sealing surface.

12. Position water pump on the front cover and install attaching bolts.

13. Tighten the attaching bolts to 15–22 ft. lbs.

14. Connect the cooling bypass hose, heater hose and radiator lower hose to water pump and tighten the clamps.

15. If equipped with air conditioning, install compressor front support bracket.

16. Install the air suspension pump.

17. Position the accessory drive belt over the pulleys.

18. Install the water pump pulley, fan/clutch assembly and fan shroud. Cross-tighten fan/clutch assembly attaching bolts to 12-18 ft. lbs.

19. Position accessory drive belt over pump pulley and adjust drive belt tension.

20. Lower the engine.

21. Install and tighten the lower right hand engine mount nuts.

22. Fill cooling system to the proper level.

23. Start engine and check for coolant leaks.

3.0L SHO ENGINE

1. Disconnect the battery cables.
2. Remove the battery and the battery tray.
3. Drain the cooling system.
4. Remove the accessory drive belts.
5. Remove the bolts retaining the A/C and alternator idler pulley and bracket assembly.

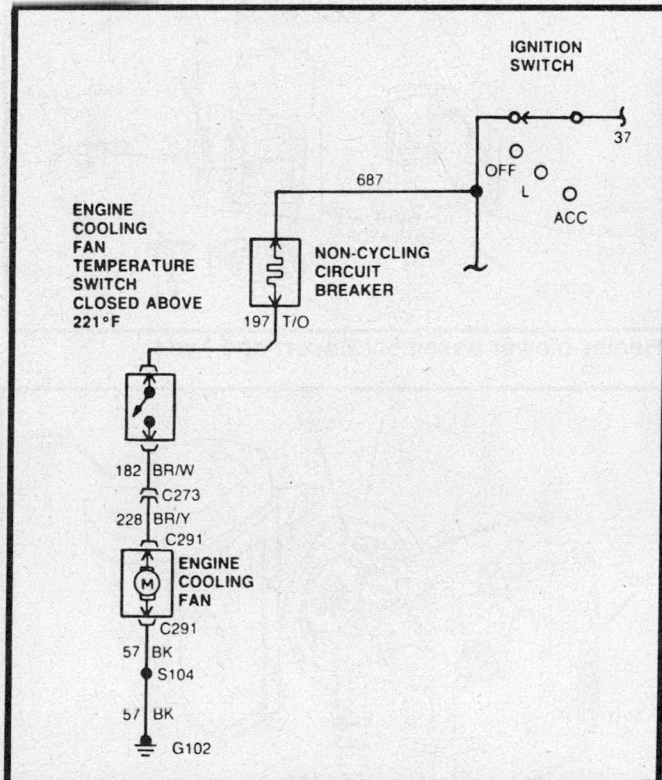

Electric cooling fan wiring schematic Escort and Lynx

6. Disconnect the electrical connector from the ignition module and ground strap.

7. Loosen the clamps on the upper intake connector tube and remove the retaining bolts.

8. Remove the upper intake connector tube.

9. Remove the right hand wheel and tire assembly.

10. Remove the splash shield.

11. Remove the upper timing belt cover.

12. Remove the crankshaft pulley.

13. Remove the lower timing belt cover.

14. Remove the bolts from the center timing belt cover and position it out of the way.

15. Remove the water pump attaching bolts and remove the water pump.

16. To install, reverse the removal procedure. Tighten the water pump bolts to 12–16 ft. lbs. (15–23 Nm). Tighten the crankshaft pulley bolt to 113–126 ft. lbs. (152–172 Nm).

Electric Cooling Fan

SYSTEM OPERATION

ESCORT, LYNX, TEMPO AND TOPAZ

The cooling fan system uses a coolant temperature switch mounted in the thermostat housing. On the Escort and Lynx, the cooling fan will operate only when the temperature switch is closed. On Tempo and Topaz, the cooling fan operates only when the ignition switch is in the **RUN** position. Vehicles equipped with air conditioning feature a cooling fan controller and a cooling fan relay. Vehicles using the standard heater power the cooling fan through the cooling fan relay. The cooling fan operates when the engine coolant temperature exceeds 210°F (84.7°C) or when the air conditioning system is energized.

TAURUS, SABLE AND CONTINENTAL

The low and high speed electro-drive cooling fan is wired to operate only when the ignition switch in the **RUN** position thus preventing cycling of the fan, after the engine is shut off. The cooling fan low speed is controlled during vehicle operation by the integrated relay control assembly and the EEC-IV module which will energize the cooling fan if the following conditions are met: engine temperature exceeds 215°F (102°C), air conditioner is in use and the vehicle speed does not provide sufficient airflow (will energize the fan at approximately 43 mph). An engine temperature above 230°F (110°C) will cause the fan to operate in the high speed mode.

Removal and Installation

1. Disconnect negative battery cable.

2. Disconnect the wiring connector from the fan motor. Disconnect the wire loom from the clip on the shroud. (Push down on the lock fingers, pull the connector from the motor end). On the Taurus, Sable and Continental vehicles, remove the integrated relay control assembly from the radiator support.

3. Remove the nuts retaining the fan motor and shroud assembly and remove the component. On the Taurus, Sable and Continental, rotate the fan and shroud assembly and remove upwards past the radiator.

4. Remove the retaining clip from the motor shaft and remove the fan.

NOTE: A metal burr may be present on the motor shaft after the retaining clip has been removed. If necessary, remove burr to facilitate fan removal.

5. Unbolt and withdraw the fan motor from the shroud.

To install:

6. Install the fan motor in position in the fan shroud. Install the retaining nuts and washers and tighten to 44–66 inch lbs.

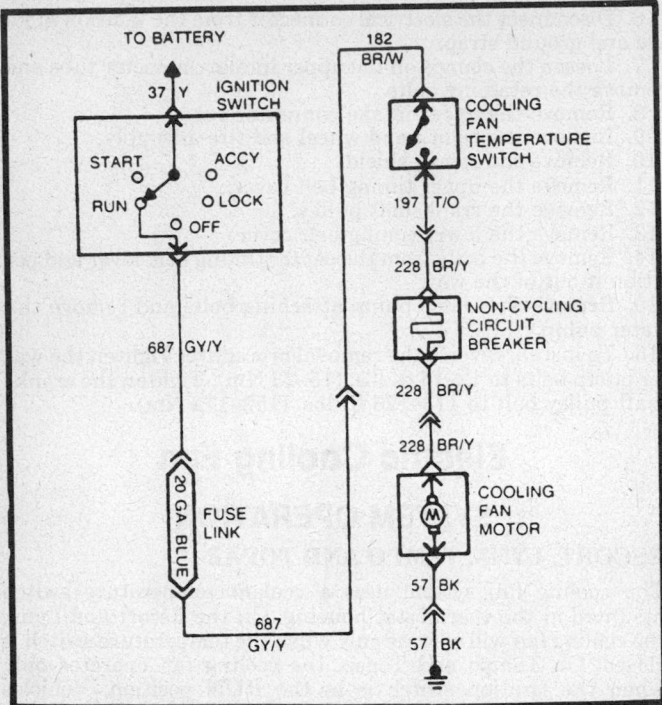

Electric cooling fan wiring schematic—Tempo/Topaz without A/C

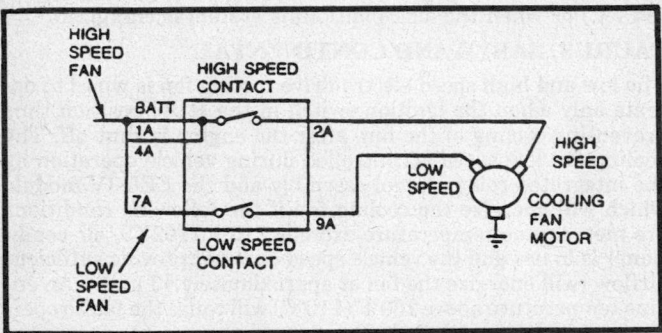

Partial wiring schematic of the integrated relay control circuit—Taurus/Sable and Continental

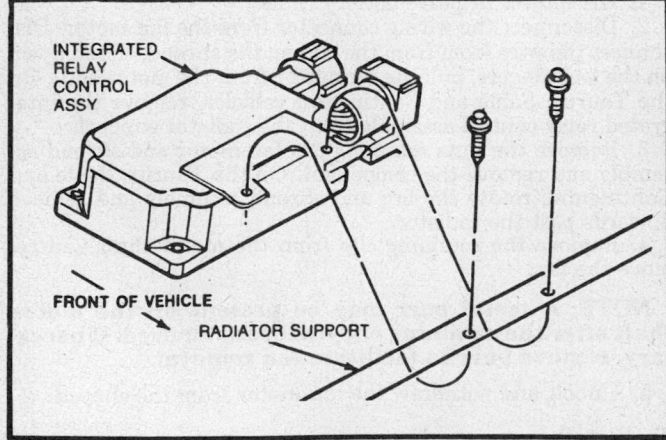

Exploded view of the integrated relay control assembly—Taurus/Sable

7. Position the fan assembly on the motor shaft and install the retaining clip.

8. Position the fan, motor and shroud as an assembly in the vehicle. Install the retaining nuts and tighten to 35–45 inch lbs. on Escort and Lynx and 23–33 inch lbs. on Tempo, Topaz, Taurus, Sable and Continental.

9. Install the fan motor wire loom in the clip provided on the fan shroud. Connect the wiring connector to the fan motor. (Be sure the lock fingers on the connector snap firmly into place.) On the Taurus, Sable and Contenental, install the integrated relay control assembly located on the radiator support.

10. Reconnect battery cable.

11. Check the fan for proper operation.

Blower Motor

Removal and Installation

WITHOUT AIR CONDITIONING
ESCORT, LYNX, TEMPO AND TOPAZ

1. Disconnect the negative battery cable.

2. On Escort and Lynx, remove the air inlet duct assembly. On Tempo and Topaz, remove the right ventilator assembly.

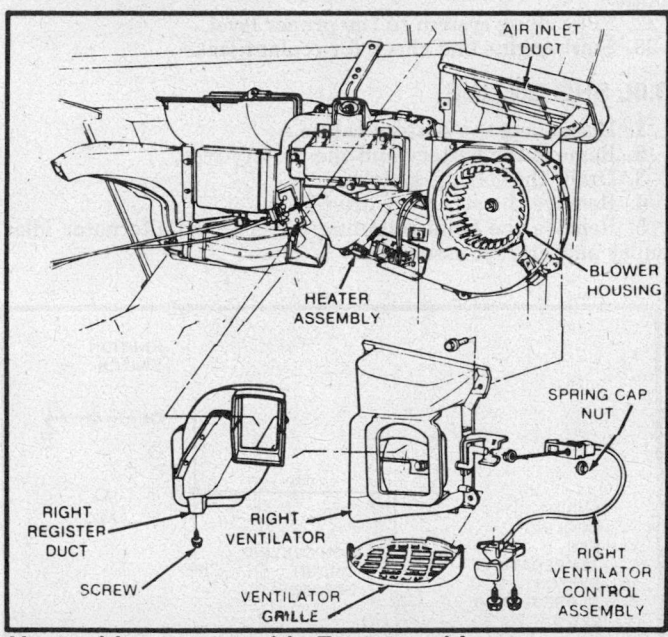

Heater blower assembly Escort and Lynx

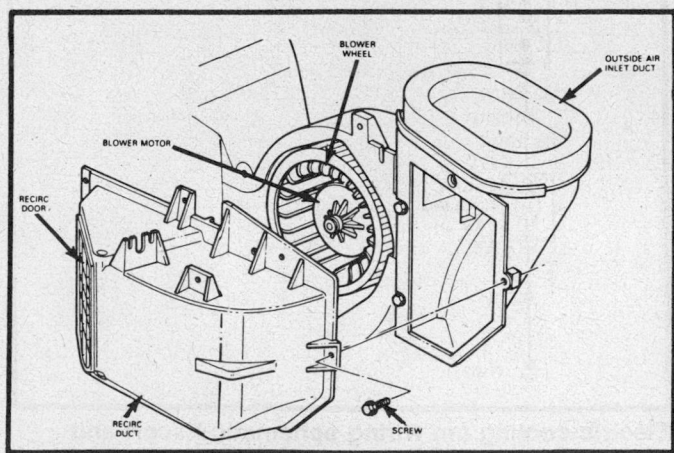

Taurus/Sable and Continental

3. Remove the hub clamp spring from the blower wheel hub. Pull the blower wheel from the blower motor shaft.

4. Remove the blower motor flange attaching screws located inside the blower housing.

5. Pull the blower motor out from the blower housing (heater case) and disconnect the blower motor wires from the motor.

6. Connect the wires to the blower motor and position the motor in the blower housing.

7. Install the blower motor attaching screws.

8. Position the blower wheel on the motor shaft and install the hub clamp spring.

9. Install the air inlet duct assembly and the right ventilator assembly.

10. Check the system for proper operation.

WITH AIR CONDITIONING
ESCORT, LYNX, TEMPO AND TOPAZ

1. Disconnect the negative battery cable.

2. Remove the glove compartment door and glove compartment.

3. Disconnect the blower motor wires from the blower motor resistor.

4. Loosen the instrument panel at the lower right hand side prior to removing the motor through the glove compartment opening.

5. Remove the blower motor and mounting plate from the evaporator case.

6. Rotate the motor until the mounting plate flat clears the edge of the glove compartment opening and remove the motor.

7. Remove the hub clamp spring from the blower wheel hub. Then, remove the blower wheel from the motor shaft.

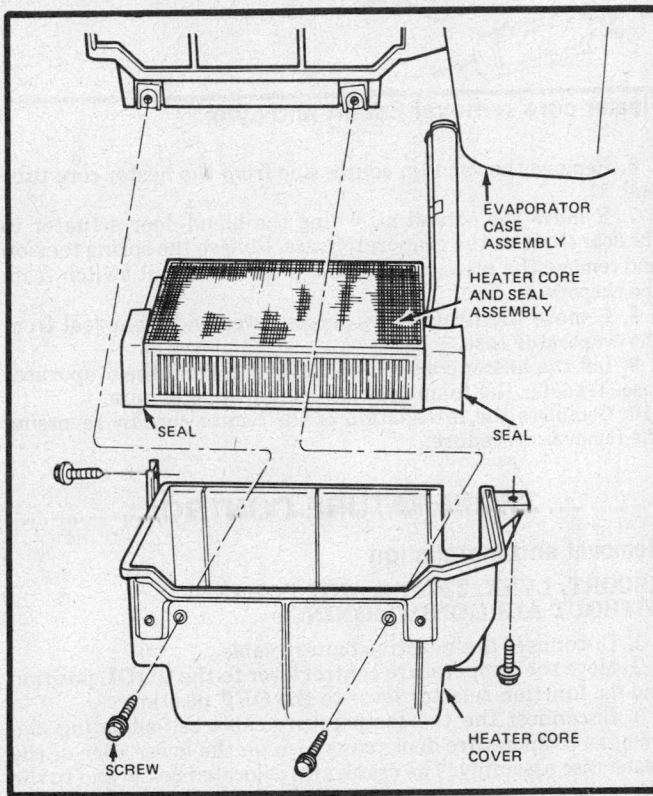

Tempo/Topaz heater core removal

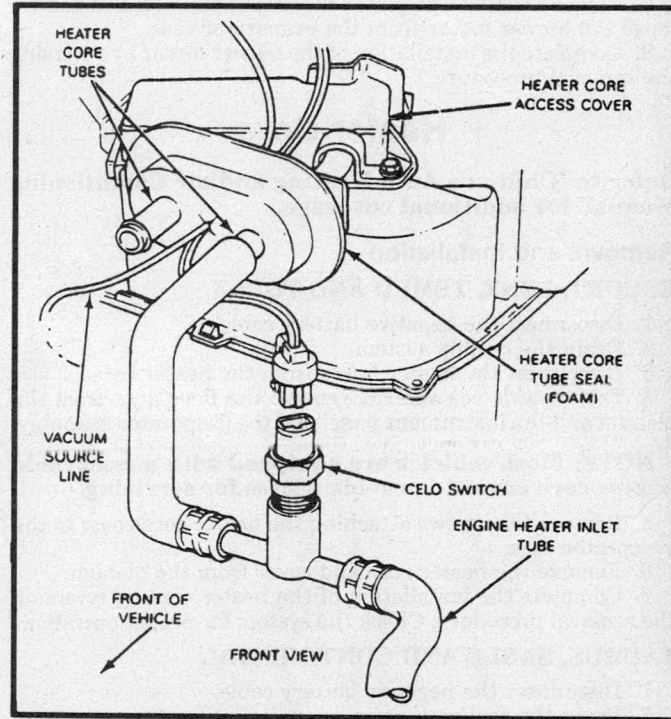

Heater core assembly with cold engine lock out switch—Continental

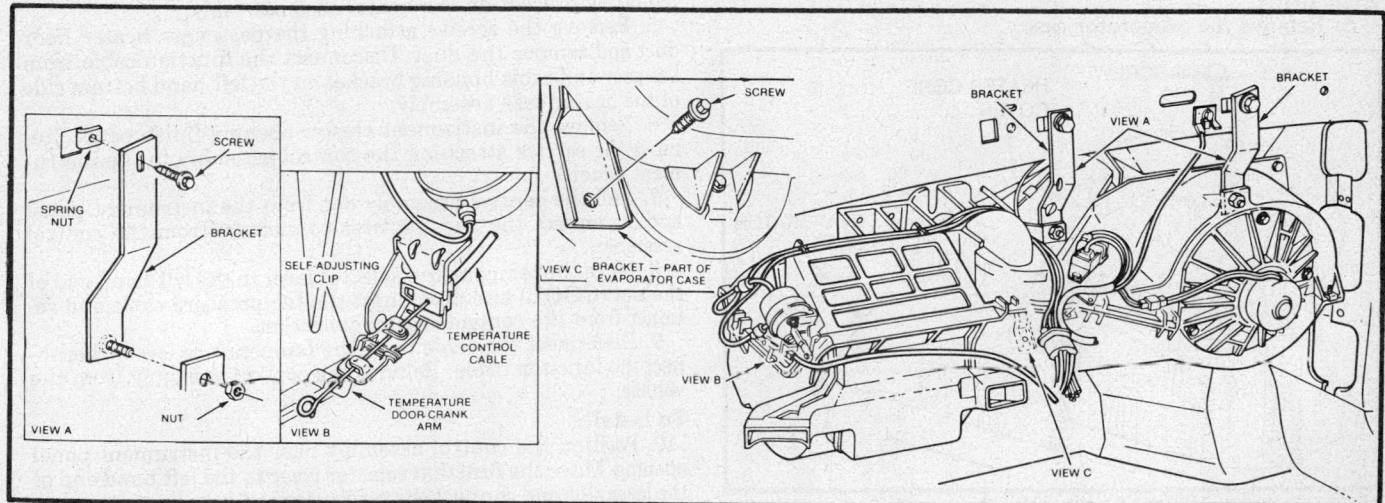

Heater and A/C case Escort and Lynx

8. Complete the installation of the blower motor by reversing the removal procedure.

TAURUS, SABLE AND CONTINENTAL

1. Disconnect the negative battery cable.
2. Open the glove compartment door, release the door retainers and lower the door.
3. Remove the screw attaching the recirculation duct support bracket to the instrument panel cowl.
4. Remove the vacuum connection to the recirculation door vacuum motor. Remove the screws attaching the recirculation duct to the heater assembly.
5. Remove the recirculation duct from the heater assembly, lowering the duct from between the instrument panel and the heater case.
6. Disconnect the blower motor electrical lead. Remove the blower motor wheel clip and remove the blower motor wheel.
7. Remove the blower motor mounting plate screws and remove the blower motor from the evaporator case.
8. Complete the installation of the blower motor by reversing the removal procedure.

Heater Core

Refer to "Chilton's Auto Heating and air Conditioning Manual" for additional coverage.

Removal and Installation
ESCORT, LYNX, TEMPO AND TOPAZ

1. Disconnect the negative battery cable.
2. Drain the cooling system.
3. Disconnect the heater hoses from the heater core.
4. From inside the vehicle, remove the floor duct from the plenum and the instrument panel and the evaporator assembly.

NOTE: Most vehicles are equipped with a removable heater core cover to provide access for servicing.

5. Remove the screws attaching the heater core cover to the evaporator case.
6. Remove the heater core and cover from the plenum.
7. Complete the installation of the heater core by reversing the removal procedure. Check the system for proper operation.

TAURUS, SABLE AND CONTINENTAL

1. Disconnect the negative battery cable.
2. Drain the cooling system.
3. Disconnect the heater hoses from the heater core.
4. Remove the instrument panel assembly and lay it on the front seat.
5. Remove the evaporator case.

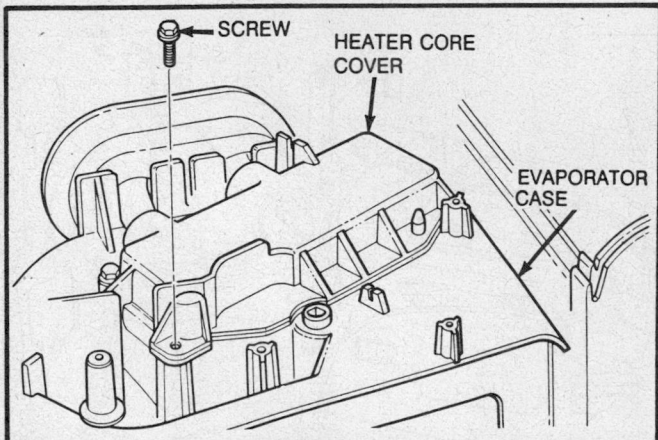

SCREW — HEATER CORE COVER

EVAPORATOR CASE

Heater core access cover on the Taurus/Sable

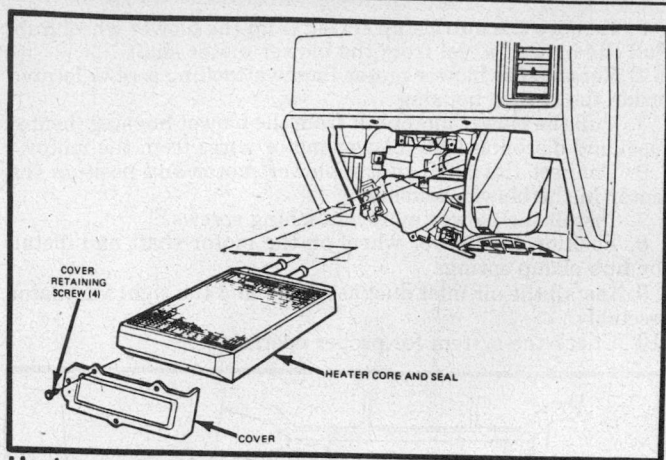

COVER RETAINING SCREW (4)

HEATER CORE AND SEAL

COVER

Heater core removal Escort and Lynx

6. Remove the vacuum source line from the heater core tube seal.
7. Remove the screws attaching the blend door actuator to the door shaft on the evaporator case. Relieve the spring tension and remove the actuator and cold engine lock out switch from the evaporator case.
8. Remove the heater core access cover and foam seal from the evaporator case.
9. Lift the heater core with 3 foam seals from the evaporator case. Transfer the foam seals to the new heater core.
10. Complete the installation of the heater core by reversing the removal procedure.

TEMPERATURE CONTROL

Removal and Installation
ESCORT, LYNX, TEMPO AND TOPAZ
WITHOUT AIR CONDITIONING

1. Disconnect the negative battery cable.
2. Move the temperature control lever to the **COOL** position and the function selector lever to the **OFF** position.
3. Disconnect the the temperature cable self-adjusting clip from the temperature door crank arm on the lower edge of the heater case assembly. The crank arm is located below and to the left of the heater core compartment cover.
4. Disconnect the temperature cable housing from the mounting bracket on the heater case assembly.
5. Remove the screws attaching the passenger heater floor duct and remove the duct. Disconnect the function cable from the gear and cable housing bracket on the left hand bottom side of the heater case assembly.
6. Remove the instrument cluster opening finish panel. Remove the screws attaching the control assembly to the instrument panel.
7. Pull the control assembly out from the instrument panel and disconnect the wire harness connectors from the control assembly.
8. Move the temperature selector lever to the left hand end of the slot (**COOL**) and disconnect the temperature cable end retainer from the control assembly bracket.
9. Disconnect the cable from the temperature lever. Disconnect the function cable. Remove the control assembly from the vehicle.

To install:
10. Position the control assembly near the instrument panel opening. Move the function selector lever to the left hand end of the lever slot and connect the cable wire and housing to the control assembly.

11. Install the passenger heater floor duct. Connect the temperature cable to the control assembly.

12. Connect the wire harness connectors to the control assembly. Position the control assembly to the instrument panel and secure with attaching screws.

13. Move the temperature control lever and function lever to the left hand side. Position the self-adjusting clip on the control cable. Connect the control cable housing to the mounting bracket on the heater case assembly and adjust the cable.

14. Connect the function cable to the gear and cable housing bracket. Check the airflow for proper operation.

15. Reinstall the instrument finish panel.

ESCORT, LYNX, TEMPO AND TOPAZ WITH AIR CONDITIONING

1. Disconnect the negative battery cable.

2. Move the A/C Norm selector lever to the **MAX A/C** position and disconnect the air inlet cable housing end retainer from the A/C case bracket. Disconnect the cable from the inlet door cam.

3. Move the temperature control lever to the **COOL** position and disconnect the temperature control cable housing retainer from the A/C case bracket.

4. Move the function selector lever to the panel position and disconnect the function selector cable housing end retainer from the A/C case bracket. Disconnect the cable self-adjust clip from the cam pin.

5. Remove the instrument panel center finish panel. Remove the screws attaching the control assembly to the instrument panel.

6. Pull the control assembly out of the instrument panel. Move the temperature control and the outside recirculation control levers to **COOL** and **RECIRC** positions respectively.

7. Disconnect the temperature cable housing from the control mounting bracket. Disconnect the temperature cable wire from the control lever.

8. Disconnect the cables from the control. Disconnect the electrical connectors from the control assembly and remove the assembly.

To install:

9. Position the control assembly near the instrument panel opening. Connect the electrical connectors to the control assembly.

10. Move the control levers to **COOL** and **RECIRC** positions, respectively.

11. Connect the function cable wire and then the cable housing to the control assembly.

12. Connect the cables to the control assembly. Position the control assembly to the instrument panel and secure with attaching screws. Install the instrument panel finish center.

13. Move the **MAX/A/C/NORM** door lever to the **MAX/A/C** position. Place the cable end loop over the pin on the air door cam and position the wire under the tab of the cam. Slide the cable housing end retainer into the plenum cable bracket to secure the cable housing to the evaporator.

14. Move the temperature control lever to the **COOL** position. Connect the self-adjusting clip of the temperature control cable to the temperature door crank arm. Slide the cable housing end retainer into the evaporator case bracket and engage the tabs of the cable and retainer with the bracket.

15. Move the temperature control lever to the Warm position to adjust the cable assembly. Move the function selector lever to the Panel position. Connect the self-adjusting clip of the function cable to the cam pin on the side of the plenum.

16. Slide the cable housing end and retainer into the plenum cable bracket and push to engage the tabs of the cable end retainer with the bracket.

17. Move the function selector lever to the **DEFROST** (full right) position to adjust the cable assembly. Check for the proper operation of all control assembly levers.

TAURUS AND SABLE WITHOUT ELECTRONIC AUTOMATIC TEMPERATURE CONTROL

1. Disconnect the negative battery cable.

2. Remove the retaining screws attaching the control assembly to the instrument panel.

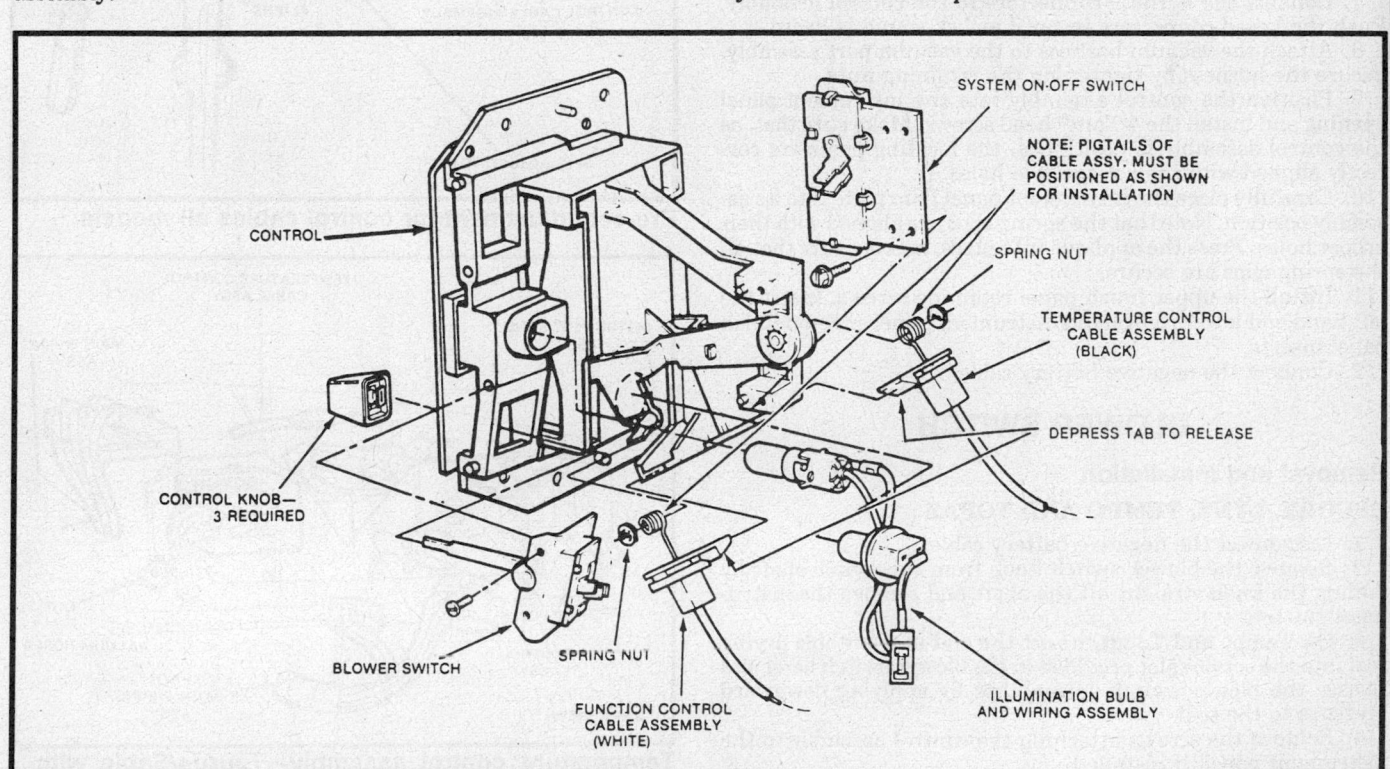

Heater core assembly Escort, Lynx, Tempo and Topaz

3. Pull the control assembly from the instrument panel. Disconnect the wire connectors from the rear of the control assembly.

4. Disconnect the temperature control cable and vacuum lines from the control assembly.

5. Discard the push nuts retaining the vacuum harness and replace with new. Remove the temperature control assembly.

6. Complete the installation of the temperature control assembly by reversing the removal procedure.

NOTE: When installing the new vacuum harness retaining nuts, do not try to screw them onto the posts as they must be pushed in.

TAURUS, SABLE AND CONTINENTAL WITH ELECTRONIC AUTOMATIC TEMPERATURE CONTROL

NOTE: On Continental, Ectronic Automatic Temperature Control (ETAC) is standard equipment.

1. Disconnect the negative battery cable.

2. Pull out the lower left hand and lower right hand instrument panel snap-on finish panel inserts. Remove the eight screws retaining the upper finish panel.

3. Pull the lower edge of the upper finish panel away from the instrument panel. It is best to grasp the finish panel from the lower left hand corner and pull the panel away by walking hands around the panel in a clockwise direction.

4. Remove the 4 Torx® head screws retaining the control assembly. Pull the control assembly away from the instrument panel into a position which provides access to the rear connections.

5. Disconnect the 2 harness connectors from the control assembly by depressing the latches at the top of the connectors and pulling.

6. Remove the vacuum harness retaining nuts. Pull the control assembly away from the instrument panel.

To install:

7. Connect the harness connectors to the control assembly. Push the keyed connectors in until a click sound is heard.

8. Attach the vacuum harness to the vacuum port assembly. Secure the harness by tightening the retaining nuts.

9. Position the control assembly into the instrument panel opening and install the 4 Torx® head screws. Make sure that, as the control assembly is positioned, the locating posts are correctly aligned with their respective holes.

10. Carefully place the instrument panel trim plate into its assembly position. Note that the spring clips are aligned with their proper holes. Press the applique into place, making sure that all the spring clips are secure.

11. Install the upper finish panel retaining screws. Insert the left hand and lower right hand instrument panel snap-on finish panel inserts.

12. Connect the negative battery cable.

BLOWER SWITCH

Removal and Installation

ESCORT, LYNX, TEMPO AND TOPAZ

1. Disconnect the negative battery cable.

2. Remove the blower switch knob from the switch shaft by pulling the knob straight off the shaft and remove the instrument cluster.

3. On Tempo and Topaz, insert the end of a suitable prying tool into the service slot provided in the blower switch bezel and release the blower switch spring clips by applying downward pressure to the tool.

4. Remove the screws attaching the control assembly to the instrument panel, if installed.

5. Pull the control assembly out from the instrument panel and disconnect the harness connectors from the blower switch and the A/C push button switch.

6. Remove the blower switch and A/C button switch attaching screw and remove the blower switch assembly.

7. Complete the installation of the blower and A/C push button switch by reversing the removal procedure.

TAURUS AND SABLE

1. Disconnect the negative battery cable.

2. Remove the control assembly from the instrument panel.

3. Remove the blower switch knob.

4. Remove the screws attaching the control assembly to the instrument panel.

5. Remove the retaining screw from the back side of the control assembly which attaches the blower switch to the control assembly.

6. Disconnect the wire connector from the switch and remove the switch.

7. Complete the installation of the switch by reversing the removal procedure.

NOTE: On Taurus and Sable equipped with electronic automatic temperature control, there is a blower motor controller installed behind the glove box and mounted to the evaporator case. This controller can be removed by dropping the glove box door and working through the glove box opening.

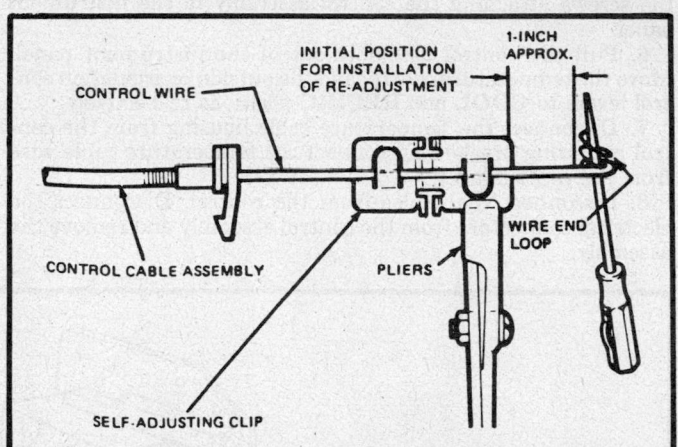

Pre-set adjustment for control cables all models

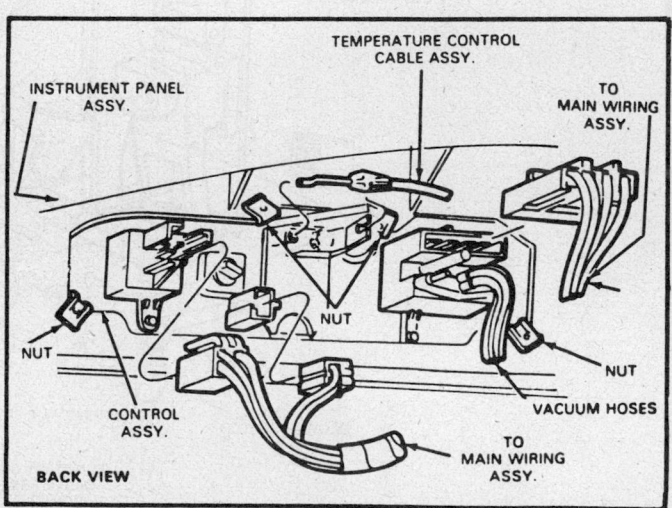

Temperature control assembly—Taurus/Sable without ETAC

CARBURETED FUEL SYSTEM

FUEL SYSTEM SERVICE PRECAUTION

When working with the fuel system certain precautions should be taken:

Always work in a well ventilated area

Keep a fire extinguisher near the work area

Always disconnect the negative battery cable

Do not make any repairs to the fuel system until all necessary steps for repair have been reviewed

Fuel Pump

Removal and Installation

1.9L AND 2.3L ENGINES

1. Disconnect the negative battery cable.
2. Loosen the threaded fuel line connection(s) a small amount. Do not remove lines at this time.
3. Loosen mounting bolts approximately 2 turns. Apply force with hand to loosen fuel pump if gasket is stuck. Rotate the engine until the fuel pump cam lobe is near its low position. The tension on the fuel pump will be greatly reduced at the low cam position.
4. Disconnect the fuel pump inlet and outlet lines.
5. Remove the fuel pump attaching bolts and remove the pump and gasket. Discard the old gasket and replace with new.
6. Measure the fuel pump pushrod length. It should be 3.88 in. minimum on the 1.9L engine. On 2.3L engine, it should be 2.34 in. minimum. Replace if worn or out of specification.
7. To install, remove all fuel pump gasket material from the engine and the fuel pump if installing the original pump.
8. Install the attaching bolts into the fuel pump and install a new gasket. Position the fuel pump to the mounting pad. Tighten the attaching bolts alternately and evenly and tighten to 11–19 ft.lb.
9. Install fuel lines to fuel pump. Start the threaded fitting by hand to avoid cross threading. Tighten outlet nut to 15–18 ft. lb.
10. Start engine and observe for fuel leaks.
11. Stop engine and check all fuel pump fuel line connections for fuel leaks by running a finger under the connections. Check for oil leaks at the fuel pump mounting gasket.

Idle Speed and Mixture

CURB IDLE RPM

Adjustment

1.9L ENGINE WITH 740–2V WITHOUT IDLE SPEED CONTROL

1. Place the transaxle in **N** or **P**.
2. Bring engine to normal operating temperature.
3. Disconnect and plug vacuum hose at thermactor air control valve bypass section.
4. Place the fast idle adjustment screw on the second step of the fast idle cam. Run engine until cooling fan comes on.
5. Slightly depress throttle to allow fast idle cam to rotate. Adjust the curb idle rpm.

NOTE: Engine cooling fan must be running when checking curb idle rpm.

6. Increase the engine rpm momentarily. Check the idle speed and readjust if required.
7. If vehicle is equipped with a dashpot, check/adjust clearance to specification shown on the calibration sticker located under the hood.

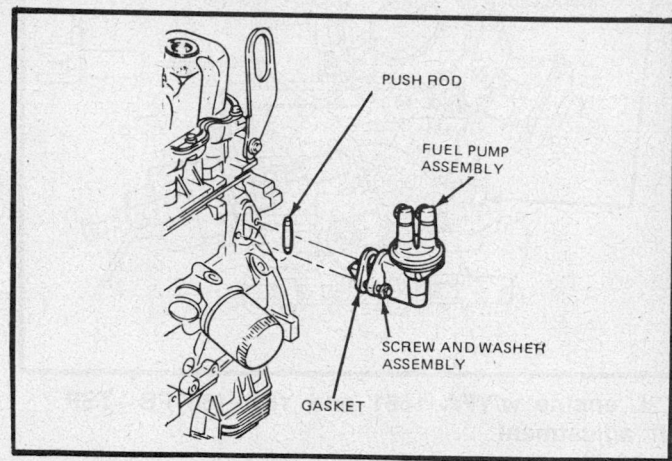

2.3L HSC engine, fuel pump removal and installation

8. Remove plug from hose at thermactor air control valve bypass section and reconnect.

1.9L ENGINE WITH 740–2V AND 5740–2V MECHANICAL VACUUM IDLE SPEED CONTROL (ISC)

1. Place the transaxle in **N** or **P**.
2. Bring engine to normal operating temperature.
3. Disconnect and plug vacuum hose at thermactor air control valve by pass section.
4. Place the fast idle adjustment screw on the second step of the fast idle cam. Run engine until cooling fan comes on.
5. Slightly depress throttle to allow fast idle cam to rotate. Check curb idle speed making certain that the cooling fan is running. If adjustment is required, proceed with the following:

    a. Place transaxle in **P**, deactivate the ISC by removing the vacuum hose at the ISC and plugging the hose.

    b. Connect a vacuum pump the ISC and supply sufficient vacuum to retract ISC plunger clear of the ISC adjustment screw.

    c. Check the curb idle speed. If rpm is not at 720 rpm (fan on), adjust rpm by turning the throttle stop adjusting screw.

    d. Remove vacuum pump from ISC, remove plug from ISC vacuum line and reconnect to ISC.

    e. Recheck the curb idle speed. If rpm is not at 750 rpm (fan on), adjust by turning the ISC adjustment screw.

6. Increase engine speed momentarily and recheck curb idle rpm. Readjust the curb idle speed, if required.
7. Remove plug from thermactor air control valve bypass section hose and reconnect.

2.3L ENGINE WITH YFA-IV AND YFA-IV FB

NOTE: A/C-ON RPM is non-adjustable and TSP-OFF RPM is not required.

1. Place the transaxle in **N** or **P**.
2. Bring engine to normal operating temperature.
3. Place A/C selector in the **OFF** position.
4. Check/adjust curb idle rpm. If adjustment is required, turn the hex head adjustment at the rear of the TSP or VOTM/TSP housing.
5. Increase the engine rpm momentarily. Check the curb idle speed and readjust if required.
6. Stop the engine.
7. Check/adjust the bowl vent setting as follows:

    a. Turn ignition key to the **ON** position to activate the TSP

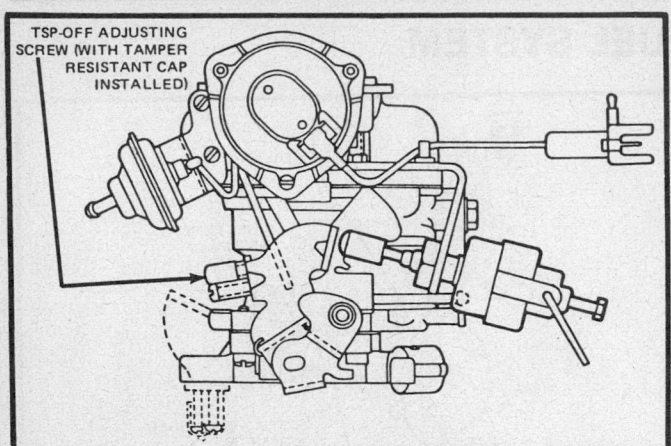

2.3L engine w/YFA–1661 and YFA–1661FB—TSP off adjustment

(engine not running). Open throttle so that the TSP plunger extends.

b. Secure the choke plate in the wide open position.

c. Open throttle so that the throttle vent lever does not touch the bowl vent rod. Close the throttle to the idle set position and measure the travel of the fuel bowl vent rod from the open throttle position.

d. Travel of the bowl vent rod should be within 0.100–0.150 in.

e. If out of specification, bend the throttle vent lever at notch, to obtain required travel.

8. Install air cleaner assembly.

2.3L ENGINE WITH 1949 OR 6149 FB CARBURETOR

NOTE: A/C-ON RPM is non-adjustable and TSP-OFF RPM adjustment is not required. Verify that TSP plunger extends with ignition key ON.

1. Place the transaxle in **N** or **P** and remove the air cleaner assembly.

2. Disconnect the throttle kicker vacuum line and plug.

3. Bring the engine to normal operating temperature. (Cooling fan should cycle).

4. Place the A/C selector in the **OFF** position.

5. Activate the cooling fan by grounding the control wire with a jumper wire.

6. Check/adjust curb idle rpm. If adjustment is required, turn curb idle adjusting screw.

7. Increase the engine speed momentarily. Check the curb idle rpm and readjust if required.

8. Reconnect the cooling fan wiring.

9. Turn the ignition key to the **OFF** position.

10. Reconnect the vacuum line to the throttle kicker.

11. Install the air cleaner assembly.

2.3L HSC ENGINE WITH 1949 CARBURETOR

NOTE: Verify that the TSP plunger extends with the ignition key in the ON position. The idle specifications can be found on the calibration sticker located under the hood.

1. Place the transaxle in **N** or **P**. Remove the air cleaner assembly, disconnect and plug the throttle kicker vacuum line.

2. Start the engine and let it run until it reaches normal operating temperature, then turn the engine off. Connect a suitable tachometer.

3. Place the A/C selector in the **OFF** position and activate the cooling fan by grounding the control wire with a jumper wire.

4. Check and adjust the curb idle rpm. If adjustment is re-

quired, turn the curb idle adjusting screw. Increase engine speed for 1 minute and recheck the curb idle rpm. Readjust the curb idle if necessary.

5. Reconnect the cooling fan wiring. Stop the engine and turn the ignition key to the **OFF** position. Reconnect the vacuum line to the throttle kicker and remove all test equipment.

1.9L ENGINE WITH 740–2V VACUUM OPERATED THROTTLE MODULATOR (VOTM)

1. Place the transaxle in **N** or **P**.

2. Bring engine to normal operating temperature.

3. Place A/C heat selector in **HEAT** position and the blower switch on **HIGH**.

4. Disconnect vacuum hose from VOTM and plug, install slave vacuum hose from intake manifold vacuum to VOTM.

5. Disconnect and plug vacuum hose at thermactor air control valve-bypass section.

6. Run engine until cooling fan comes on.

7. Check/adjust VOTM rpm to specification shown on the calibration sticker located under the hood.

NOTE: Engine cooling fan must be running when checking VOTM rpm. Adjust rpm by turning screw on VOTM.

8. Remove slave vacuum hose. Remove plug from VOTM vacuum hose and reconnect hose to VOTM.

9. Return intake manifold supply source to original location.

10. Remove plug from vacuum hose at thermactor air control valve by pass section and reconnect.

FAST IDLE RPM

Adjustment

1.9L ENGINE WITH 740–2V

1. Place the transaxle in **N** or **P**.

2. Bring engine to normal operating temperature.

3. Disconnect the vacuum hose at the EGR and plug.

4. Place the fast idle adjustment screw on the second step of the fast idle cam. Run engine until cooling fan comes on.

5. Check/adjust fast idle rpm to specification shown on the calibration sticker located under the hood. If adjustment is required, loosen locknut, adjust and retighten.

NOTE: Engine cooling fan must be running when checking fast idle rpm.

6. Remove plug from EGR hose and reconnect.

2.3L ENGINE WITH YFA-IV AND YFA/IV FB

1. Place transaxle in **N** or **P**.

2. Bring engine to normal operating temperature.

3. Turn the ignition key to the **OFF** position.

4. Put A/C selector in the **OFF** position.

5. Disconnect vacuum hose at the EGR valve and plug.

6. If equipped, disconnect wire to electric PVS.

7. Place the fast idle adjusting screw on the specified step of the fast idle cam.

8. Start engine without touching the accelerator pedal. Check/adjust fast idle rpm to specifiction shown on the calibration sticker located under the hood.

9. Increase the engine speed momentarily, allowing engine to return to idle and turn ignition key to **OFF** position.

10. Remove plug from the EGR vacuum hose and reconnect.

11. If equipped, reconnect wire to electric PVS.

2.3L ENGINE WITH 1949 OR 6149 FB CARBURETOR

1. Place the transaxle in **N** or **P**.

2. Bring the engine to normal operating temperature with the carburetor set on second step of fast idle cam.

3. Return the throttle to normal idle position.

4. Place the A/C selector in the **OFF** position.

5. Disconnect the vacuum hose at the EGR valve and plug.

6. Place the fast idle adjusting screw on the specified step of the fast idle cam.

7. Check/adjust the fast idle rpm to specification.

8. Increase the engine speed momentarily, allowing engine to return to idle. Stop the engine and turn ignition key to the **OFF** position.

9. Remove the plug from the EGR vacuum hose and reconnect.

Removal and Installation
MOTORCRAFT MODEL 740

1. Disconnect the negative battery cable. Remove the air cleaner assembly.

2. Disconnect the throttle cable and speed control cable, if equipped.

3. Identify, tag and disconnect the bowl vent tube, altitude compensator tubes (idle, primary and secondary, if equipped), air conditioning and/or power steering vacuum kicker (if equipped).

4. Identify, tag and disconnect the EGR vacuum tube, venturi vacuum tube, distributor vacuum tube, ISC vacuum tube (if equipped), choke pulldown motor vacuum tube and fuel inlet line at filter.

5. Disconnect the idle solenoid wire an choke cap terminal connectors.

6. Remove the automatic transaxle throttle valve (TV) linkage, if equipped.

7. Remove the carburetor flange nuts. If equipped, remove WOT A/C cut out switch.

8. Remove the carburetor from the manifold.

To install:

9. Clean all gasket surfaces. Replace any gasket(s) as necessary.

10. Position the carburetor on the spacer and install the WOT A/C cut out switch, if equipped. Install and tighten the attaching nuts.

11. Install the automatic transaxle throttle valve (TV) linkage, if equipped.

12. Connect the choke cap and the idle solenoid terminal connectors.

13. Connect the fuel inlet line at the filter and tighten to 22 ft. lbs.

14. Connect the distributor vacuum line, venturi vacuum line, EGR vacuum line, choke pulldown motor line and ISC vacuum line, if equipped.

15. Connect the air conditioning and /or power steering kicker vacuum line (if equipped).

16. Connect the altitude compensator vacuum lines: idle, primary and secondary, if so equipped.

17. Connect the bowl vent line.

18. Connect the throttle cable. Connect the speed control cable.

19. Start the engine and check for leaks.

20. Install the air cleaner assembly.

21. Check and/or adjust the curb idle and fast idle speed as necessary.

MOTORCRAFT MODEL 1949 NON-FEEDBACK AND 6149 FEEDBACK

1. Disconnect the negative battery cable. Remove the air cleaner assembly.

2. Disconnect the throttle cable from the throttle lever.

3. Disconnect the automatic transaxle TV rod from the throttle lever, if equipped.

4. Disconnect the distributor vacuum line (if equipped), EGR vacuum line (if equipped), venturi vacuum line (if equipped),

purge vacuum lines, PCV vacuum line, solenoid kicker vacuum line and fuel line. Use a back-up wrench on the fuel inlet fitting when removing the fuel line to avoid changing the float level.

NOTE: Identify all vacuum lines before removing to aid in installation.

5. Disconnect the TSP electrical connection at the connector. Disconnect the electric choke wire at the connector.

6. Disconnect the canister vent hose at the bowl vent tube.

7. Disconnect the throttle position sensor electrical lead at the connector (Model 6949 carburetor).

8. Disconnect the WOT A/C cut-off switch electrical lead at the connector (Model 1949, if equipped).

9. Remove EGR sensor wire from clip on pulldown diaphragm assembly mounting screw, (Model 6149).

10. Remove the carburetor attaching nuts and remove the carburetor from the intake manifold. Remove carburetor mounting gasket.

To install:

11. Clean the gasket mounting surfaces of the intake manifold and the carburetor. Place a new gasket on the intake manifold. Position the carburetor on the gasket and install the attaching nuts. To prevent leakage, distortion, or damage to the carburetor body flange, snug the nuts and then tighten each nut to 20 ft. lbs.

12. Install EGO sensor wire into clip on pulldown diaphragm assembly mounting screw (Model 6149).

13. Connect WOT A/C cut-off switch electrical lead at the connector (Model 6149).

14. Connect the canister vent hose at the bowl vent tube.

15. Connect the TSP electrical connection and the electric choke wire at the connector.

16. Connect the distributor vacuum line (if equipped), EGR vacuum line (if equipped), venturi vacuum line (if equipped), purge vacuum line, solenoid kicker vacuum line and fuel line. Use a back-up wrench on the fuel inlet fitting when installing the fuel line to avoid changing the float level.

17. Connect the automatic transaxle TV rod to the throttle lever.

18. Connect the throttle cable to the throttle lever.

19. Install the air cleaner assembly.

20. Check and adjust if necessary the curb idle speed, idle fuel mixture and fast idle speed.

MOTORCRAFT 5740

1. Disconnect the negative battery cable and remove the air cleaner assembly.

2. Disconnect the throttle cable and speed control cable, if equipped.

3. Identify, tag and disconnect the bowl vent tube and altitude compensator tubes (idle, primary and secondary if equipped).

4. Identify, tag and disconnect the EGR vacuum line, distributor vacuum line, ISC vacuum line, choke pulldown motor vacuum line and fuel inlet line at the filter.

5. Disconnect the idle solenoid wire and choke cap terminal connectors. Remove the automatic transaxle throttle valve linkage, if equipped.

6. Remove the carburetor flange nuts using carburetor wrench T74P-9510-A or equivalent. Remove the wide open throttle A/C cutout switch bracket, if equipped.

7. Remove the carburetor from the intake manifold. Clean all gasket surfaces. Replace any gaskets as necessary.

To install:

8. Position the carburetor on the spacer and install the wide open throttle A/C cutout switch bracket, if equipped. Install and tighten the attaching nuts.

NOTE: To prevent leakage, distortion or damage to the carburetor body flange, alternately tighten each nut to 14 ft. lbs.

9. Install the automatic transaxle throttle valve linkage (if equipped). Connect the choke cap and idle solenoid terminal connectors. Connect the fuel inlet line at the filter and torque it to 22 ft. lbs.

10. Connect all the vacuum lines, the throttle cable, speed control cable and reconnect the negative battery cable. Start the engine and check for fuel leaks.

11. Install the air cleaner assembly.

12. Check and adjust if necessary the curb idle speed, idle fuel mixture and fast idle speed.

FUEL INJECTION SYSTEM

Refer to "Chilton's Professional Electronic Engine Control Manual" for additional coverage.

Description

ELECTRONIC FUEL INJECTION (EFI)

The Electronic Fuel Injection system (EFI) is classified as a multi-point, pulse time, mass air flow fuel injection system. Fuel is metered into the intake air stream in accordance with engine demand through four injectors mounted on a tuned intake manifold.

An on board vehicle Electronic Engine control (EEC) computer accepts input from various engine sensors to compute the required fuel flow rate necessary to maintain a prescribed air/fuel ratio throughout the entire engine operational range. The computer then outputs a command to the fuel injectors to meter the approximate quantity of fuel.

SEQUENTIAL ELECTRONIC FUEL INJECTION (SEFI)

The Sequential Electronic Fuel Injection (SEFI) system is a multi-point, pulse time, speed density control, fuel injection system. Fuel is metered into each intake port in sequence in accordance with engine demand through 6 injectors mounted on a tuned intake manifold.

An on board vehicle Electronic Engine control (EEC) computer accepts input from various engine sensors to compute the required fuel flow rate necessary to maintain a prescribed air/fuel ratio throughout the entire engine operational range. The computer then outputs a command to the fuel injectors to meter the approximate quantity of fuel.

CENTRAL FUEL INJECTION (CFI)

The Ford Central Fuel Injection (CFI) System is a single point, pulse time modulated injection system. Fuel is metered into the air intake stream according to engine demands by solenoid injection valves mounted in a throttle body on the intake manifold. Fuel is supplied from the fuel tank by a high pressure, electric fuel pump alone or in conjunction with a low-pressure pump. The fuel is filtered and sent to the air throttle body where a regulator keeps the fuel delivery pressure at a constant 39 psi. Either one or two injector nozzles are mounted vertically above the throttle plates and connected in parallel (or in series if one injector nozzle is used) with the fuel pressure regulator. Excess fuel supplied by the pump but not needed by the engine, is returned to the fuel tank by a steel fuel return line.

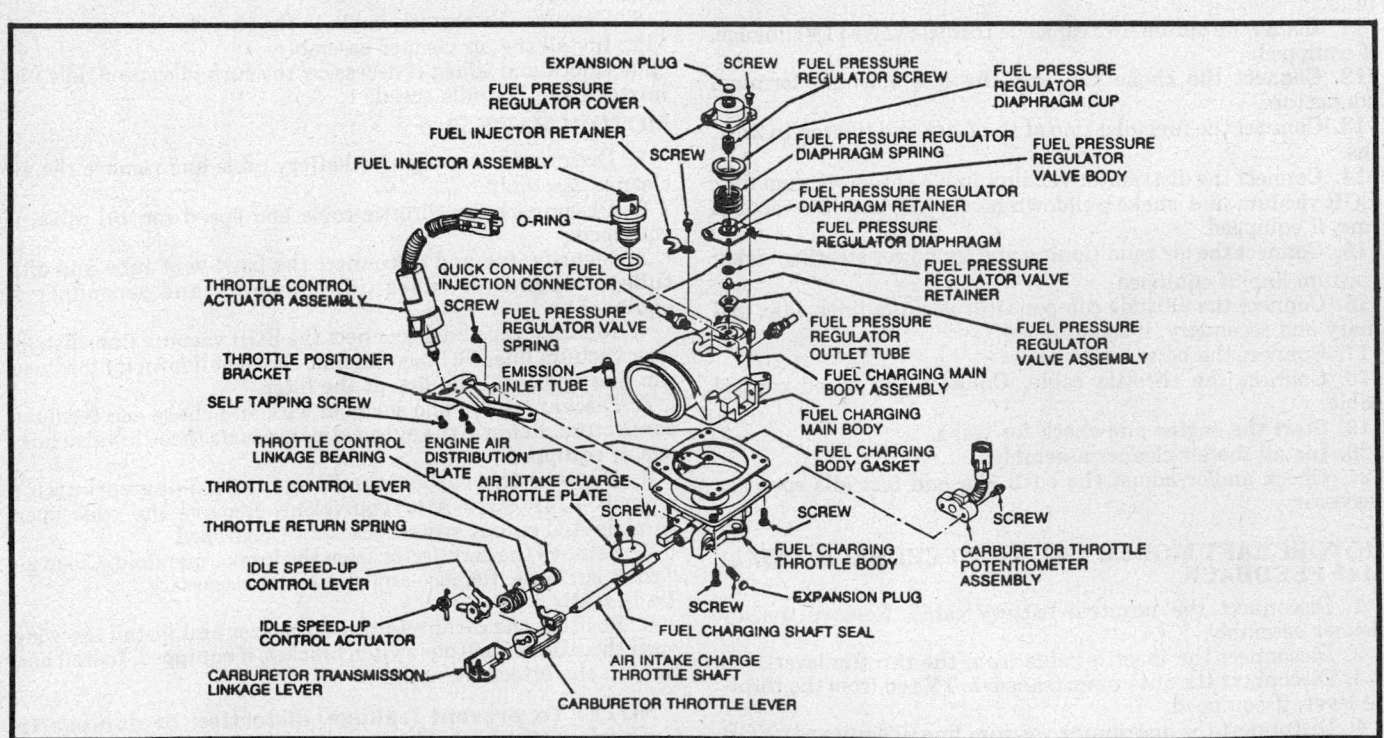

Exploded view of the central fuel injection

IDLE SPEED

Adjustment

1.9L ENGINE WITH EFI

The purpose of this procedure is to provide a means by verifying the initial engine rpm setting with the ISC disconnected.

NOTE: Curb idle rpm is controlled by the EEC IV processor and the Idle Speed Control (ISC) device as part of the fuel charging assembly.

1. Place the transaxle in **N** or **P**. Apply the parking brake and block the wheels.
2. Bring the engine to normal operating temperature and shut off.
3. Disconnect vacuum connector at EGR solenoid and plug both lines.
4. Disconnect idle speed control (ISC) power lead.
5. Electric cooling fan must be on during idle speed set procedure.
6. Start engine and operate at 2000 rpm for 60 seconds.
7. Set hand brake and place transaxle in **N** or **D**, check/adjust initial engine rpm within a period of 2 minutes by adjusting throttle plate screw.
8. If idle adjustment is not completed within the 2 minute time limit, stop engine, restart and repeat Steps 6–7.
9. Stop the engine and remove plugs from EGR vacuum lines at EGR solenoid and reconnect.
10. Reconnect idle speed control (ISC) power lead.

2.3L ENGINES WITH EFI

1. Apply the parking brake, block the drive wheels and place the vehicle in **D** or **N**.
2. Start the engine and let it run until it reaches normal operating temperature, then turn the engine off. Connect a suitable tachometer.
3. Disconnect the idle speed control air bypass valve power lead. Start the engine and run the engine at 2000 rpm for 120 seconds.

NOTE: If the electric cooling fan comes on during the idle speed adjusting procedures, wait for the fan to turn off before proceeding.

4. Allow the engine to idle and check the base idle, it should be at 750±50 rpm . If it is not, adjust as necessary.
5. Adjust the engine rpm to 750±50 rpm by adjusting the throttle stop screw.
6. Shut the engine off and reconnect the power lead to the idle speed control air bypass valve. Disconnect all test equipment.

1.9L, 2.3L AND 2.5L HSC ENGINES WITH CFI

NOTE: If for any reason the battery is disconnected or the vehicle has to be jump started, it may be necessary to perform this following procedure.

1. Apply the parking brake, block the drive wheels and place the vehicle in **P** or **N**.
2. Start the engine and let it run until it reaches normal operating temperature, then turn the engine off. Connect a suitable tachometer.
3. Start the engine and place the transaxle in **D** or **N**, let the engine run at idle for 120 seconds. The idle rpm should now return to the specified idle speed (The idle specifications can be found on the calibration sticker located under the hood).
4. Place the transaxle in **N** or **P** and the engine rpm should increase by approximately 100 rpm. Now lightly step on and off the accelerator. The engine rpm should return to the specified idle speed. If the rpm remains high, repeat the sequence. Remember it may take the the system approximately 2 minutes to

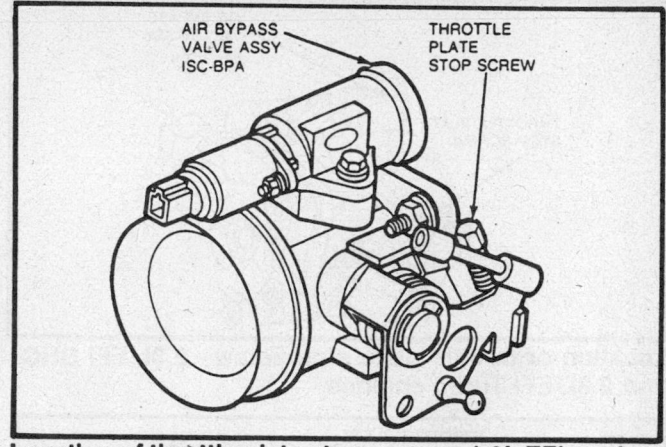
Location of throttle plate stop screw – 1.9L EFI engine

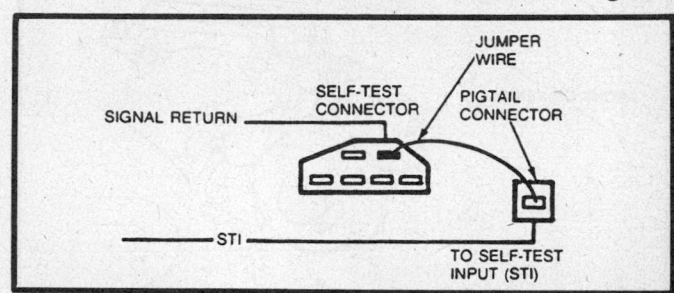
Jumper wire terminal connection points – 1.9L CFI and 2.5L CFI HSC engines

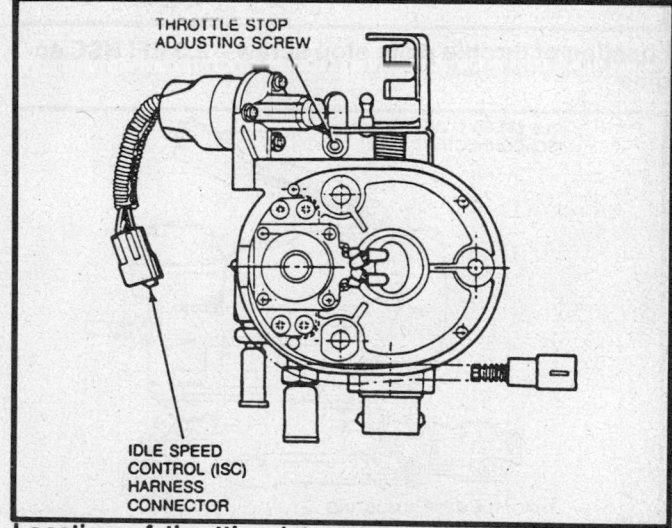
Location of throttle plate stop screw – 1.9L CFI engines

adjust. If the vehicle does not respond as previously described, perform the following adjustment. On the 1.9L CFI engine, removal of the CFI assembly is not required to adjust the idle speed at this point in the procedure. On these engines proceed directly to Step 5.

  a. Shut the engine off and remove the air cleaner. Locate the self-test connector and self-test input connector in the engine compartment.
  b. Connect a jumper wire between the self-test input connector and the signal return pin (is the top right terminal) on the self-test connector.
  c. Place the ignition key in the **RUN** position and be careful

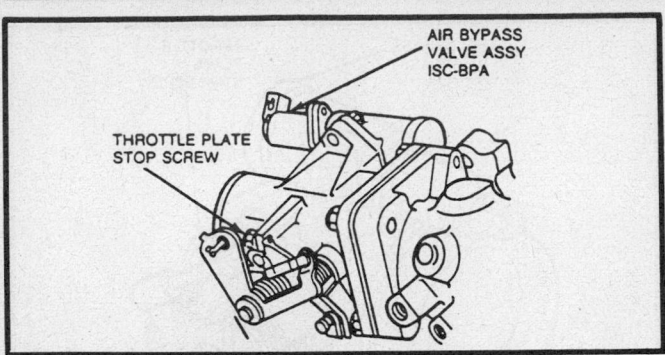

Location of throttle plate stop screw—2.3L EFI OHC and 2.3L EFI Turbo engines

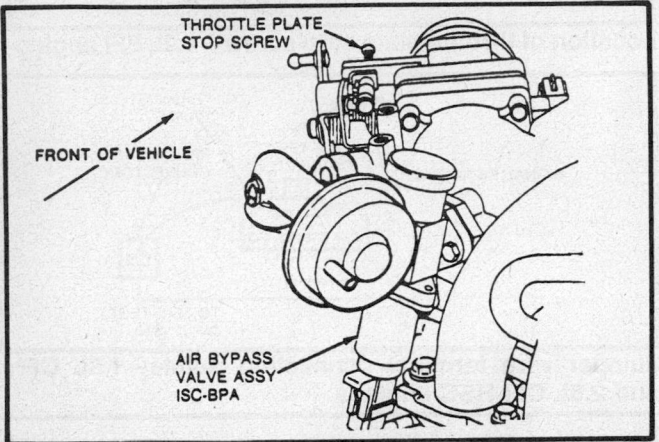

Location of throttle plate stop screw—2.3 EFI HSC engine

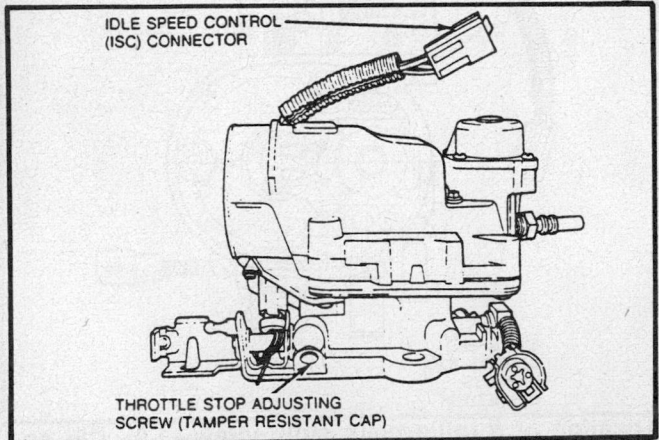

Location of throttle plate stop screw—2.5L CFI HSC engines

not to start the engine. The ISC plunger will retract, so wait approximately 10–15 seconds until the ISC plunger is fully retracted. Turn the ignition key to the off position and wait 10–15 seconds.

d. Remove the jumper wire and unplug the ISC motor from the wire harness. Now perform the throttle stop adjustment as follows:

e. Remove the CFI assembly from the vehicle.

f. Use a small punch or equivalent to punch through and remove the aluminum plug which covers the throttle stop adjusting screw.

g. Remove and replace the throttle stop screw. Reinstall the CFI assembly onto the vehicle.

5. Start the engine and allow to the idle to stabilize. Set the idle rpm to the specifications (listed on the calibration decal located under the hood) on the throttle stop adjusting screw.

6. Shut off the engine. Reconnect the ISC motor wire harness, remove all test equipment and reinstall the air cleaner assembly.

3.0L ENGINE

NOTE: The curb idle speed rpm is controlled by the EEC IV computer (ECM) and the idle speed control (ISC) air bypass valve assembly. The throttle stop screw is factory set and does not directly control the idle speed. Adjustment to this setting should be performed only as part of a full EEC IV diagnosis of irregular idle conditions or idle speeds. Failure to accurately set the throttle plate stop position as described in the following procedure could result in false idle speed control.

1. Apply the parking brake, turn the A/C control selector **OFF** and block the wheels.

2. Connect a tachometer and an inductive timing light to the engine. Start the engine and allow it to reach normal operating temperatures.

3. Unplug the spout line (at the distributor), the check and/or adjust the ignition timing to 8–12 degrees BTDC.

4. On the 3.0L EFI engine, remove the PCV entry line from the PCV valve. Using the orifice (0.200 in. dia.) tool No. T86P-9600-A or equivalent, install it in the PCV entry line.

5. On the 3.0L SEFI engine, remove the PCV hose from the throttle body and plug it. Remove the CANP hose from the throttle body and connect it to the PCV connector of the throttle body.

6. Stop the engine and disconnect the electrical connector from the air bypass valve assembly.

7. Start the engine. Place the transaxle in **D** or **N**. Disconnect the electrical connector from the electric cooling fan.

8. Check and/or adjust (if necessary) the idle speed to 740–780 rpm on the 3.0L EFI engine and 770–830 rpm on the 3.0L SEFI engine by turning the throttle plate stop screw.

9. After adjusting the idle speed, stop the engine and disconnect the battery for 3 minutes minimum.

10. Reconnect all hoses and electrical connections with the engine **OFF**.

11. Make sure that the throttle plate is not stuck in the bore and that the throttle plate stop screw is setting on the rest pad with the throttle closed. Correct any condition that will not allow the throttle to close to the stop set position.

12. Start the engine and confirm that the idle speed is now adjusted to specifications, if not, readjust as necessary.

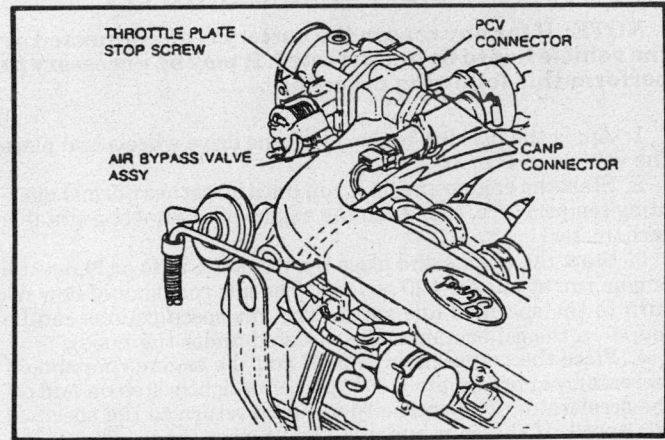

3.0L SEFI engine

Location of throttle plate stop screw—3.8L engine

3.8L ENGINE WITH EFI

1. Apply the parking brake, block the drive wheels and place the vehicle in **D** or **N**.

2. Start the engine and let it run until it reaches normal operating temperature, then turn the engine off. Connect a suitable tachometer.

3. Start the engine and run the engine at 2500 rpm for 30 seconds.

4. Allow the engine idle to stabilize.

5. Adjust the engine idle rpm to the specification shown on the vehicle emission control label by adjusting the throttle stop screw.

6. After the idle speed is within specification, repeat Steps 3–5 to ensure that the adjustment is correct.

7. Stop the engine and reconnect the power lead to the idle speed control air bypass valve. Disconnect all test equipment.

FUEL SYSTEM PRESSURE RELIEF

Procedure

1. The pressure in the fuel system must be released before attempting to remove the fuel pump.

2. A special valve is incorporated in the fuel rail assembly for the purpose of relieving the pressure in the fuel system.

3. Remove the air cleaner.

4. Attach pressure gauge tool No. T80L–9974–A or equivalent to the fuel pressure valve on the fuel rail assembly and release the pressure from the system.

Fuel Pump

Removal and Installation

1986 ESCORT AND LYNX

1. Disconnect the negative battery cable. Depressurize the fuel system and raise and support the vehicle safely.

2. Locate the fuel pump at the right rear, near the fuel tank and remove the assembly from the vehicle by loosening the mounting bolt until the assembly can slide off of the mounting bracket.

3. Remove the parking brake cable from the clip on the pump and disconnect the electrical connector and fuel pump outlet fitting.

4. Disconnect the fuel pump inlet line and remove the pump from under the vehicle. Be sure to either drain the fuel tank or raise the end of the fuel pump inlet line above the level in the tank to prevent siphon action.

5. Complete the installation of the fuel pump by reversing the removal procedure, also observe the following procedures:

   a. After installation is complete, install the fuel pressure gauge tool T80L9974–A or equivalent on the fuel rail pressure fitting.

b. Turn the ignition switch **ON** and **OFF** for 2 second intervals until the pressure gauge reads 35 psi.

c. Remove the pressure gauge tool, start the engine and check for fuel leaks.

EXCEPT 1986 ESCORT AND LYNX

— CAUTION —

Extreme caution should be taken when removing the fuel tank from the vehicle. Ensure that all removal procedures are conducted in a well ventilated area. Have a sufficient amount of absorbent material in the vicinity of the work area to quickly contain fuel spillages should they occur. Never store waste fuel in an open container as it may present a serious fire hazard.

1. Depressurize the fuel system as follows:

   a. Disconnect the electrical connector at the inertia switch.

   b. Crank the engine for a minimum of 15 seconds to reduce the fuel pressure pressure in the lines.

   c. Remove the air cleaner and attach pressure gauge tool T80L–9974–A or equivalent to the fuel pressure valve on the fuel rail assembly and release the pressure from the system.

2. Disconnect the negative battery cable and remove the fuel from the fuel tank by pumping it out through the filler neck. Use care to prevent combustion from any fuel spillage.

3. Raise and support the vehicle safely and remove the fuel filler tube (neck). On all wheel drive vehicles, remove the exhaust system and rear axle assembly.

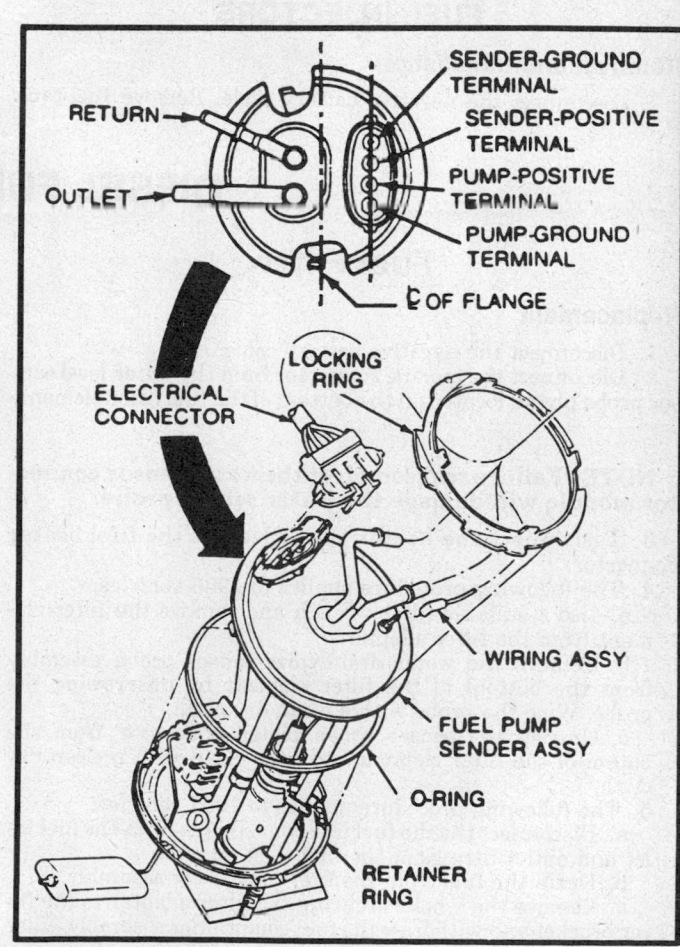

Electric fuel pump assembly with terminal connection points Escort (1987–90), Tempo, Topaz and Continental

4. Support the fuel tank and remove the fuel tank straps, lower the fuel tank enough to be able to remove the fuel lines, electrical connectors and vent lines from the tank.

5. Remove the fuel tank from under the vehicle and place it on a suitable work bench. Remove any dirt around the fuel pump attaching flange.

6. Turn the fuel pump locking ring counterclockwise and remove the lock ring.

7. Remove the fuel pump from the fuel tank and discard the flange gasket.

8. On all wheel drive vehicles, partially raise the sender unit and disconnect the jet pump line and resistor electrical connector. Remove the fuel pump and bracket assembly with seal gasket. Remove the seal gasket and replace with new. Remove the jet pump assembly.

9. Complete the installation of the fuel pump (and jet pump) by reversing the removal procedure, also observe the following procedures:

    a. Lightly coat the new seal ring gasket with a suitable lubricant compound part number C1AZ–19590–B or equivalent to hold the gasket in place during installation.

    b. Install the fuel pressure gauge and turn the ignition to the **ON** and **OFF** positions for 3 second intervals, (5 to 10 times) until the pressure gauge reads 13 psi on the CFI vehicles and 35 psi on the EFI vehicles.

    c. Remove the pressure gauge, start the engine and check for fuel leaks. Correct all fuel leaks immediately.

FUEL INJECTORS

Removal and Installation

1. Disconnect the negative battery cable. Remove fuel tank cap and release pressure from the fuel system at the fuel pressure relief valve. On 3.8L engine, remove the upper intake mainfold.

2. Disconnect fuel supply and return lines.

3. Remove vacuum line from fuel pressure regulator.

4. Disconnect the fuel injector wiring harness.

5. Remove fuel injector supply manifold assembly.

6. Carefully remove connectors from individual injectors(s) as required.

7. Grasping the injector's body, pull up while gently rocking the injector from side-to-side.

8. Inspect the injector O-rings (2 per injector) for signs of deterioration. Replace as required.

9. Inspect the injector "plastic hat" (covering the injector pintle) and washer for signs of deterioration. Replace as required. If hat is missing, look for it in intake manifold.

To install:

10. Lubricate new O-rings and install two on each injector (use a light grade oil).

11. Install the injector(s). Use a light, twisting, pushing motion to install the injector(s).

12. Carefully seat the fuel injector manifold assembly on the injectors and secure the manifold with the attaching bolts. Tighten to 15–22 ft. lbs. On the 3.8L engines, torque the retaining bolts to 5–8 ft. lbs.

13. Connect the vacuum line to the fuel pressure regulator.

14. Connect fuel injector wiring harness. On the 3.8L engines, install the upper intake manifold.

15. Connect fuel supply and fuel return lines. Tighten fuel return line to 15–18 ft. lbs.

16. Check entire assembly for proper alignment and seating.

DIESEL FUEL SYSTEM

Fuel Filter

Replacement

1. Disconnect the negative battery cable.

2. Disconnect the module connector from the water level sensor probe pigtail located on the bottom of the fuel filter element.

NOTE: Failure to disconnect the water sensor connector/module will damage the water sensor probe.

3. Disconnect the heater power lead at the fuel heater connector.

4. The following procedure applies to 1986 vehicles:

    a. Use a suitable filter wrench and remove the filter element from the filter adapter.

    b. Remove the water drain/valve sensor probe assembly from the bottom of the filter element by unscrewing the probe. Wipe the probe with a clean dry cloth.

    c. Unsnap the sensor probe pigtail connector from the botom of the filter element and wipe clean with a clean dry cloth.

5. The following procedure applies to 1987 vehicles:

    a. Disconnect the the fuel line connections from the fuel inlet and outlet fittings of the fuel filler adapter.

    b. Drain the fuel from the fuel condtioner assembly.

    c. Remove the 2 bolts securing the filter adapter to the filter bracket and withdraw the fuel conditioner assembly (filler adapter and filter element).

    d. Secure the filter adapter into a suitable vise. Using a suitable filter wrench, remove the filter element from the filter adapter.

NOTE: Position the filter adapter in the vise to prevent rotation during element disassembly. Do not position the filter adapter in such a manner as to cause stress to the fuel filter fittings or filter adapter flange, as damage to the filter adapter casting mat occur.

    e. Remove the water drain/valve sensor probe assembly from the bottom of the filter element by unscrewing the probe. Wipe the probe with a clean dry cloth.

    f. Unsnap the sensor probe pigtail connector from the botom of the filter element and wipe clean with a clean dry cloth.

6. Installation is the reverse order of the removal procedure. On 1987 vehicles, torque the 2 filter adapter to filter bracket bolts to 13–16 ft. lbs.

7. Clean the filter mounting surfaces. Coat the gasket of the new filter with clean diesel fuel.

8. Tighten the filter until the gasket touches the filter header, then tighten an additional ½ turn.

9. Air-Bleed the fuel system using the following procedure:

    a. Open the water drain valve on the bottom of the fuel filter conditioner (2–3 turns).

    b. Press in the fuel bypass button and hold it down tightly. Pump the priming pump on the top of the filter adapter. Continue pumping until clear fuel, free from air bubbles, flows from the water drain valve.

    c. Depress the priming pump and hold down while closing the water drain valve.

10. Start the engine and check for fuel leaks.

NOTE: To avoid fuel contamination do not add fuel directly to the new filter.

Draining Water From The System

NOTE: The fuel filter/conditioner must be serviced (water purged) at each engine oil change interval (7500 miles) as follows.

1. Make sure that the engine and the ignition switch are in the **OFF** position.
2. Place a suitable container under the fuel filter/conditioner water drain tube under the vehicle.
3. Open the water drain valve on the bottom of the filter.
4. Press in the bypass button and hold it tightly seated, while pumping the priming pump on the top of the filter.
5. Continue to pump until the water is purged from the filter and clear diesel fuel is visible.
6. Close the water vent valve.

Fuel Injection Pump

Removal and Installation

1. Disconnect battery ground cable from the battery, located in the luggage compartment.
2. Properly relieve the fuel system pressure.
3. Disconnect the air inlet duct from the air cleaner and intake manifold. Install protective cap in intake manifold.
4. Remove rear timing belt cover and flywheel timing mark cover. Remove rear timing belt as follows:
   a. Remove rear timing belt cover.
   b. Remove flywheel timing mark cover from clutch housing.
   c. Rotate crankshaft until the flywheel timing mark is at TDC on No. 1 cylinder.
   d. Check that the injection pump and camshaft sprocket timing marks are aligned.
   e. Loosen tensioner locknut. With a prybar, or equivalent tool, inserted in the slot provided, rotate the tensioner clockwise to relieve belt tension. Tighten locknut snug.
   f. Remove timing belt.
5. Disconnect throttle cable and speed cable, if so equipped.
6. Disconnect vacuum hoses at the altitude compensator and cold start diaphragm.
7. Disconnect fuel cut-off solenoid connector.
8. Disconnect fuel supply and fuel return hoses at injection pump.
9. Remove injection lines at the injection pump and nozzles. Cap all lines and fittings.
10. Rotate injection pump sprocket until timing marks are aligned. Install 2 bolts in the holes to hold the injection pump sprocket. Remove sprocket retaining nut.
11. Remove injection pump sprocket using a suitable gear puller with 2 bolts installed in the threaded holes in the sprocket.
12. Remove bolt attaching the injection pump to the pump front bracket.
13. Remove the 2 bolts attaching the injection pump to the pump rear bracket and remove the pump.
14. Install injection pump in position on the pump brackets.
15. Install 2 nuts attaching the pump to the rear bracket and tighten to 23–34 ft. lbs.
16. Install bolt attaching the pump to the front bracket and tighten to 12–16 ft. lbs.
17. Install injection pump sprocket. Hold the sprocket in place using the procedure described in Step 10. Install the sprocket retaining nut and tighten to 51–58 ft. lbs.
18. Remove protective caps and install the fuel lines at the injection pump and nozzles. Tighten the fuel line capnuts to 18–22 ft. lbs.
19. Connect fuel supply and fuel return hoses at the injection pump.
20. Connect fuel cut-off solenoid connector.
21. Connect vacuum lines to the cold start diaphragm and altitude compensator.
22. Connect throttle cable and speed control cable, if so equipped.
23. Install the rear timing belt. Loosen tensioner locknut and adjust timing belt. Install rear timing belt cover and tighten bolts to 5–7 ft. lbs.
24. Remove protective cap and install the air inlet duct to the intake manifold and air cleaner.
25. Connect battery ground cable to battery.
26. Air bleed fuel system.
27. Check and adjust the injection pump timing.
28. Run engine and check for fuel leaks.
29. Check and adjust engine idle.

Injection Timing

Adjustment

NOTE: Engine coolant temperature must be above 176°F (80°C) before the injection timing can be checked and/or adjusted.

1. Disconnect the battery ground cable from the battery located in luggage compartment.
2. Remove the injection pump distributor head plug bolt and sealing washer.

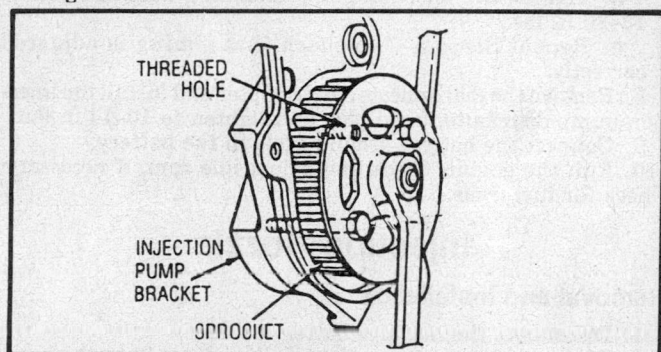

Injection pump sprocket removal and installation 2.0L diesel engine

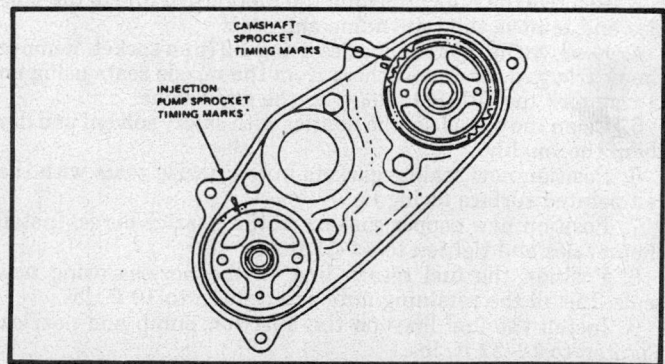

Camshaft and injector pump timing marks 2.0L diesel engine

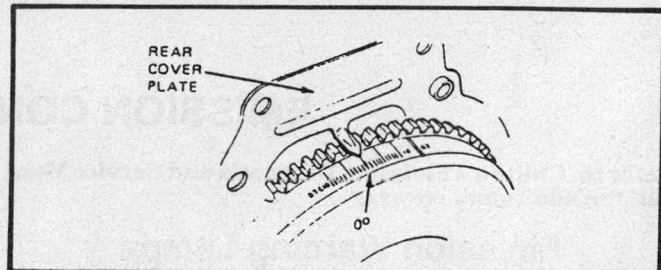

Flywheel timing mark 2.0L diesel engine

4-59

3. Install static timing gauge adapter, Rotunda tool 14-0303 or equivalent with a metric dial indicator gauge tool, so that indicator pointer is in contact with injection pump plunger.

4. Remove timing mark cover from transaxle housing. Align timing mark (TDC) with pointer on the rear engine cover plate.

5. Rotate the crankshaft pulley slowly, counterclockwise until the dial indicator pointer stops moving (approximately 30–50 degrees BTDC).

6. Adjust dial indicator to zero.

NOTE: Confirm that dial indicator pointer does not move from zero by slightly rotating crankshaft left and right.

7. Turn crankshaft clockwise until crankshaft timing mark aligns with indicator pin. Dial indicator should read 1 ± 0.02mm (0.04 ± 0.0008 in.). If reading is not within specification, adjust as follows:

   a. Loosen injection pump attaching bolt and nuts.

   b. Rotate the injection pump toward the engine to advance timing and away from the engine to retard timing.

   c. Rotate the injection pump until the dial indicataor reads 0.04 ± 0.0008 in. (1 ± 0.02mm).

   d. Tighten the injection pump attaching nuts and bolt to 13–20 ft. lbs.

   e. Repeat Steps 5–7 to check that timing is adjusted correctly.

8. Remove the dial indicator and adapter and install the injection pump distributor head plug and tighten to 10–14 ft. lbs.

9. Connect the battery ground cable to the battery.

10. Run the engine, check and adjust idle rpm, if necessary. Check for fuel leaks.

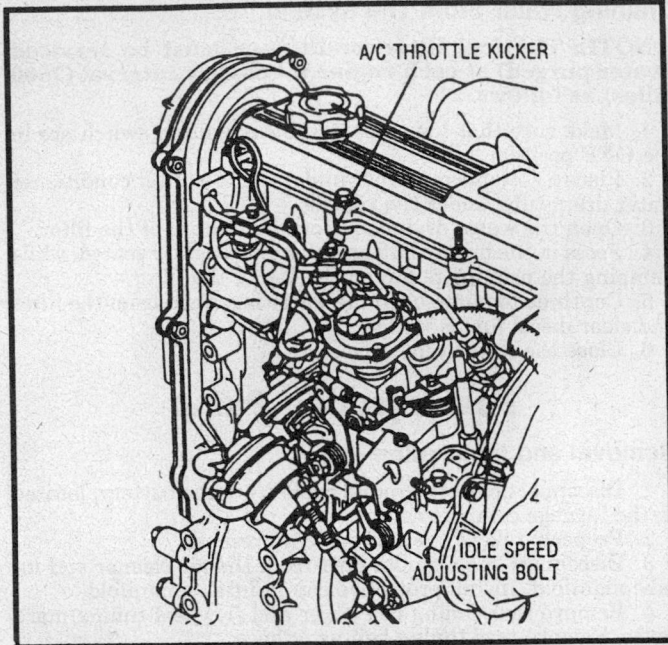

Adjusting the idle speed 2.0L diesel engine

Injection Nozzle

Removal and Installation

1. Disconnect the negative battery cable.

2. Disconnect and remove the injection lines from the injection pump and nozzles. Cap all lines and fitting to prevent dirt contamination.

3. Remove the nuts attaching the fuel return line to the nozzles and remove the return line and seals.

4. Remove the injector nozzles using a 27mm socket. Remove the nozzle gaskets and washers from the nozzle seats using an O-ring pick tool T71P-19703-C or the equivalent.

5. Clean the outside of the nozzles with safety solvent and dry them thoroughly.

6. Position new sealing gaskets in the nozzle seats with the red painted surface facing up.

7. Position new copper gaskets in the nozzles bores. Install the nozzles and tighten to 44–51 ft. lbs.

8. Position the fuel return line on the nozzles using new seals. Install the retaining nuts and tighten to 10 ft. lbs.

9. Install the fuel lines on the injection pump and nozzles. Tignten to 18–22 ft. lbs.

10. Air bleed the fuel system. Run the engine and check for fuel leaks.

Idle Speed

Adjustment

1. Place the transaxle in the **N** detent.

2. Bring the engine up to normal operating temperature. Stop engine.

3. Remove the timing hole cover. Clean the flywheel surface and install reflective tape.

4. Idle speed is measured with manual transaxle in the **N** detent.

5. Check curb idle speed, using Rotunda hand-held tachometer No. 99–0001 or equivalent. Curb idle speed is specified on the vehicle emissions control information decal. Adjust to specification by loosening the locknut on the idle speed adjusting bolt. Turn the idle speed adjusting bolt clockwise to increase, or counterclockwise to decrease engine idle speed. Tighten the locknut.

6. Place transaxle in **N**. Increase the engine speed momentarily and recheck the curb idle rpm. Readjust if necessary.

7. Turn air conditioner **ON**. Check the idle speed. Adjust to specification by loosening nut on the air conditioner throttle kicker and rotating screw.

EMISSION CONTROL SYSTEMS

Refer to "Chilton's Emission Diagnosis and Service Manual" for additional coverage.

Emission Warning Lamps

These vehicles have a "Check Engine" lamp that will light when there is a fault in the engine control system. This light can not be reset without diagnosing the fault in the system. When the system has been diagnosed and the problem corrected, the light will go out.

ENGINE

NOTE: Disconnecting the negative battery cable on some vehicles may interfere with the functions of the on board computer systems and may require the computer to undergo a relearning process, once the negative battery cable is reconnected.

Engine Assembly

Removal and Installation

1.9L ENGINE

1. Mark position of hood hinges and remove hood.
2. Relieve the fuel system pressure. Remove air cleaner, air intake duct and heat tube.
3. Disconnect negative battery cable.
4. Drain the cooling system. Remove the secondary wire from the ignition coil.
5. Remove the alternator drive belt. Remove alternator mounting bolts and lay alternator aside.
6. Disconnect and remove thermactor air pump, if equipped.
7. Disconnect radiator hoses and oil cooler lines if equipped with automatic transaxle.
8. Remove radiator cooling fan and shroud as an assembly.
9. Remove the transaxle cooler line routing clip located at the radiator, if equipped with automatic transaxle. Remove the radiator and disconnect the heater at the metal tube.
10. Indentify, tag and disconnect heater hoses, electrical connections and vacuum hoses as necessary. Disconnect the fuel pump supply and return lines. If equipped with power assist brakes, disconnect the power boost vacuum hose at the engine.
11. Disconnect kickdown rod at carburetor or fuel charging assembly, if equipped with automatic transaxle.
12. Disconnect accelerator cable at the fuel charging assembly and remove the cable routing bracket attaching screws. Disconnect the vapor hose at the carbon canister tube.
13. Raise the vehicle and support safely.
14. Remove the clamp frm the heater supply and return hose. Remove knee brace at front of starter motor and remove battery cable from starter.
15. Disconnect exhaust inlet pipe at manifold.
16. Remove support bracket in front of converter cover if equipped with automatic transaxle (inspection cover for manual transaxle) and remove cover.
17. Remove cranskshaft pulley and damper.
18. Remove torque converter to flywheel nuts, if equipped with automatic transaxle.
19. Remove timing belt cover lower attaching bolts, if equipped with manual transaxle.
20. Remove converter housing, if equipped with automatic transaxle or flywheel housing, if equipped with manual transaxle.
21. Remove 2 oil pan-to-transaxle attaching bolts. Disconnect coolant bypass hose from intake manifold. If equipped, remove the bolt attaching the battery negative cable to the cylinder block.
22. Remove nut and bolt attaching insulator bracket to the engine bracket at front of engine.
23. Lower vehicle.
24. Install suitable lifting brackets on engine.

NOTE: The top rear bolt attaching the thermactor pump bracket to the engine can be removed and used as a lifting bracket attaching point.

25. Use a suitable lifting device connected to the engine lifting brackets and raise engine just enough to remove the through bolt from the front engine insulator and remove insulator.
26. Remove the remaining timing belt cover bolts and remove the cover, if eqipped with manual transaxle.
27. Remove insulator attaching bracket from engine.

28. Position a jack under the transaxle. Raise jack just enough to support the weight of the transaxle.
29. Remove the converter housing, flywheel housing upper attaching bolts.
30. Remove engine assembly from vehicle.
31. Complete the installation of the engine by reversing the removal procedure.

2.0L DIESEL ENGINE

NOTE: Be sure to use the proper equipment when removing the engine and transaxle assembly, as the assembly is removed from underneath the vehicle.

1. Mark the position of the hood hinges and remove the hood.
2. Remove the negative ground cable from battery that is located in luggage compartment.
3. Properly relieve the fuel system pressure. Remove the air cleaner assembly.
4. Position a drain pan under the lower radiator hose. Remove the hose and drain the engine coolant.
5. Remove the upper radiator hose from the engine.
6. Disconnect the cooling fan at the electrical connector.
7. Remove the radiator shroud and cooling fan as an assembly. Remove the radiator.
8. Remove the starter cable from the starter.
9. Discharge air conditioning system, if equipped. Remove the pressure and suction lines from the air conditioning compressor. Cover or plug the line openings to prevent the entry of moisture and dirt.
10. Identify and disconnect all vacuum lines as necessary.
11. Disconnect the engine harness connectors (2) at the dash panel. Disconnect the glow plug relay connectors at the dash panel.

NOTE: Connectors are located under the plastic shield on the dash panel. Remove and save plastic retainer pins. Disconnect the alternator wiring connector on right hand fender apron.

12. Disconnect the clutch cable from the shift lever on transaxle.
13. Disconnect the injection pump throttle linkage.
14. Disconnect the fuel supply and return hoses on the engine.
15. Disconnect the power steering pressure and return lines at the power steering pump, if equipped. Remove the power steering lines bracket at the cylinder head.
16. Install engine support tool D79P-8000-A or equivalent to existing engine lifting eye.
17. Raise the vehicle and support it safely.
18. Remove the bolt attaching the exhaust pipe bracket to the oil pan.
19. Remove the 2 exhaust pipes to exhaust manifold attaching nuts.
20. Pull the exhaust system out of rubber insulating grommets and set aside.
21. Remove the speedometer cable from the transaxle.
22. Position a drain pan under the heater hoses. Remove 1 heater hose from the water pump inlet tube. Remove the other heater hose from the oil cooler.
23. Remove the bolts attaching the control arms to the body. Remove the stabilizer bar bracket retaining bolts and remove the brackets.
24. Halfshaft assemblies must be removed from the transaxle at this time.
25. On manual transaxle equipped vehicles, remove the shift stabilizer bar-to-transaxle attaching bolts. Remove the shift mechanism to shift shaft attaching nut and bolt at the transaxle.
26. Remove the left rear insulator mount bracket from body bracket by removing the 2 nuts.
27. Remove the left front insulator to transaxle mounting bolts.

28. Lower the vehicle. Install lifting equipment to the 2 existing lifting eyes on engine.

NOTE: Do not allow front wheels to touch floor.

29. Remove engine support tool D79L-8000-A or equivalent.
30. Remove right insulator intermediate bracket to engine bracket bolts, intermediate bracket to insulator attaching nuts and the nut on the bottom of the double ended stud attaching the intermediate bracket to engine bracket. Remove the bracket.
31. Carefully lower the engine and transaxle assembly to the floor.

To install:

32. Raise the vehicle support safely.
33. Position the engine and transaxle assembly directly below the engine compartment.
34. Slowly lower the vehicle over the engine and transaxle assembly.

NOTE: Do not allow the front wheels to touch floor.

35. Install the lifting equipment to both existing engine lifting eyes on engine.
36. Raise the engine and transaxle assembly up through engine compartment and position accordingly.
37. Install right insulator intermediate attaching nuts and intermediate bracket to engine bracket bolts. Install nut on bottom of double ended stud attaching intermediate bracket to engine bracket. Tighten to 75–100 ft. lbs.
38. Install engine support tool D79L-8000-A or equivalent to the engine lifting eye.
39. Remove the lifting equipment.
40. Raise the vehicle.
41. Position a suitable floor or transaxle jack under engine. Raise the engine and transaxle assembly into mounted position.
42. Install insulator to bracket nut and tighten to 75–100 lbs.
43. Tighten the left rear insulator bracket to body bracket nuts to 75–100 ft. lbs.
44. Install the lower radiator hose and install retaining bracket and bolt.
45. Install the shift stabilizer bar to transaxle attaching bolt. Tighten to 23–35 ft. lbs.
46. Install the shift mechanism to input shift shaft (on transaxle) bolt and nut. Tighten to 7–10 ft. lbs.
47. Install the lower radiator hose to the radiator.
48. Install the speedometer cable to the transaxle.
49. Connect the heater hoses to the water pump and oil cooler.
50. Position the exhaust system up and into insulating rubber grommets located at the rear of the vehicle.
51. Install the exhaust pipe to exhaust manifold bolts.
52. Install the exhaust pipe bracket to the oil pan bolt.
53. Place the stabilizer bar and control arm assembly into position. Install control arm to body attaching bolts. Install the stabilizer bar brackets and tighten all fasteners.
54. Halfshaft assemblies must be installed at this time.
55. Lower the vehicle.
56. Remove the engine support tool D79L-6000-A or equivalent.
57. Connect the alternator wiring at the right fender apron.
58. Connect the engine harness to main harness and glow plug relays at dash panel. Reinstall the plastic shield.
59. Connect the vacuum lines.
60. Install the air conditioning discharge and suction lines to air conditioning compressor, if so equipped. Do not charge system at this time.
61. Connect the fuel supply and return lines to the injection pump.
62. Connect the injection pump throttle cable.
63. Install the power steering pressure and return lines. Install bracket.

64. Connect the clutch cable to shift lever on transaxle.
65. Connect the battery cable to starter.
66. Install the radiator shroud and coolant fan assembly. Tighten attaching bolts.
67. Connect the coolant fan electrical connector.
68. Install the upper radiator hose to engine.
69. Fill and bleed the cooling system.
70. Install the negative ground battery cable to battery.
71. Install the air cleaner assembly.
72. Install the hood.
73. Charge air conditioning system, if so equipped.
74. Check and refill all fluid levels, (power steering, engine and transaxle).
75. Start the vehicle. Check for leaks.

2.3L ENGINE

NOTE: This procedure describes the removal and installation of the engine and transaxle as an assembly.

1. Mark position of hood hinges and remove hood.
2. Remove negative ground cable from battery.
3. Relieve the fuel system pressure. Remove air cleaner.
4. Remove lower radiator hose to drain engine coolant.
5. Remove upper radiator hose and disconnect transaxle cooler lines at rubber hoses below radiator, if equipped with automatic transaxle.
6. Remove coil and disconnect coolant fan at electrical connection.
7. Remove radiator shroud and cooling fan as an assembly. Remove radiator.
8. Discharge air conditioning system, if equipped and remove pressure and suction lines from compressor.

NOTE: Use extreme care when discharging air conditioning system, as the refrigerant is under high pressure.

9. Identify, tag and disconnect all electrical and vacuum lines as necessary.
10. Disconnect T.V. linkage or clutch cable at transaxle.
11. Disconnect accelerator linkage and fuel lines.
12. Disconnect thermactor pump discharge hose at pump.
13. Disconnect power steering lines at pump, if equipped.
14. Install engine support tool to existing engine lifting eye.
15. Raise vehicle and support safely.
16. Remove battery cable from starter and remove hose from catalytic converter.
17. Remove bolt attaching exhaust pipe bracket to oil pan an exhaust pipe to manifold attaching nuts.
18. Pull exhaust system out of rubber insulating grommets and set aside.
19. Remove speedometer cable from transaxle.
20. Remove on heater hose from water pump inlet tube and the other from the steel tube on intake manifold.
21. Remove water pump inlet tube clamp bolt at engine block and clamp bolts at underside of oil pan. Remove inlet tube.
22. Remove bolts attaching control arms to body. Remove stabilizer bar brackets retaining bolts and remove brackets.
23. Halfshaft assemblies must be removed from transaxle at this time.
24. On manual transaxle equipped vehicles, remove roll restrictor nuts from transaxle. Pull roll restrictor from mounting bracket.
25. On manual transaxle equipped vehicles, remove shift stabilizer bar to transaxle attaching bolts. Remove shift mechanism to shift shaft attaching nut an bolt at transaxle.
26. On automatic transaxle equipped, disconnect manual shift cable clip from lever on transaxle. Remove manual shift linkage bracket bolts from transaxle and remove bracket.
27. Remove the left rear insulator mount bracket from body bracket.

28. Remove the left front insulator to transaxle mounting bolts.

29. Lower the vehicle. Install lifting equipment to the two existing lifting eyes on engine.

NOTE: Do not allow front wheels to touch floor.

30. Remove engine support tool.

31. Remove right No. 3A insulator intermediate bracket to engine bracket bolts, intermediate bracket to insulator attaching nuts and the nut on the bottom of the double ended stud which attaches the intermediate bracket to engine bracket. Remove bracket.

32. Carefully lower engine and transaxle assembly to the floor.

33. Complete the installation of the engine/transaxle assembly by reversing the removal procedure.

2.5L ENGINE

1. Relieve the fuel system pressure. First disconnect the electrical connector at the inertia switch and crank the engine for 15 seconds.

2. On vehicles equipped with automatic transaxle, remove the transaxle timing window cover and rotate the engine until the flywheeel timing marker is aligned with the timing pointer.

3. Place a reference mark on the crankshaft pulley at the 12 o'clock position (TDC) then rotate the crankshaft pulley mark to the 6 o'clock postion (BTDC).

4. Disconnect the negative battery cable and mark the position of the hood.

5. Remove the air cleaner assembly and drain the cooling system.

6. Disconnect the upper radiator hose at the engine.

7. Identify, tag and disconnect all electrical wiring and vacuum hoses as required.

8. Disconnect the crankcase ventilation hose at the valve cover and intake manifold.

9. Disconnect the fuel lines and heater hoses at the throttle body.

10. Disconnect the engine ground wire.

11. Disconnect the accelerator and throttle valve control cables at the throttle body.

12. Evacuate the air conditioning system and remove the suction and discharge lines from the compressor, if equipped.

13. On manual transaxle equipped vehicles, remove the engine damper brace.

14. Remove the driver belt and water pump pulley.

15. Remove the air cleaner-to-canister hose.

16. Raise the vehicle and support safely.

17. Drain the engine oil and remove the oil filter.

18. Disconnct the starter cable and remove the starter motor.

19. On automatic transaxle equipped vehicles, remove the converter nuts and align the previously made reference mark as close to the 6 o'clock (BTDC) position as possible with the converter stud visible.

NOTE: The flywheel timing marker must be in the 6 o'clock (BDC) position for proper engine removal and installation.

20. Remove the engine insulator nuts.

21. Disconnect the exhaust pipe from the manifold.

22. Disconnect the canister and halfshaft brackets from the engine.

23. Remove the lower engine-to-transaxle retaining bolts.

24. Disconnect the lower radiator hose.

25. Lower the vehicle and position a suitable floor jack under the transaxle.

26. Disconnect the power steering lines from the pump.

27. Install engine lifting eyes tool D81L–6001–D or equivalent and engine support tool No. T79P–6000–A or equivalent.

28. Connect suitable lifting equipment to support the engine and remove the upper engine-to-transaxle retaining bolts.

29. Remove the engine from the vehicle and support on a suitable holding fixture.

30. Complete the installation of the engine assembly by reversing the removal procedure.

3.0L ENGINE

1. Disconnect the battery cables and drain the cooling system. Remove the engine hood.

2. Evacuate the A/C system safely and properly. Relieve the fuel system pressure. Remove the air cleaner assembly. Remove the battery and the battery tray.

3. Remove the integrated relay controller, cooling fan and radiator with fan shroud. Remove the engine bounce damper bracket on the shock tower.

4. Remove the evaporative emission line, upper radiator hose, starter brace and lower radiator hose.

5. Remove the exhaust pipes from both exhaust manifolds. Remove and plug the power steering pump lines.

6. Remove the fuel lines and remove and tag all necessary vacuum lines.

7. Disconnect the ground strap, heater lines, accelerator cable linkage, throttle valve linkage and speed control cable.

8. Disconnect and label the following wiring connectors; alternator, A/C clutch, oxygen sensor, ignition coil, radio frequency supressor, cooling fan voltage resistor, engine coolant temperature sensor, Thick film ignition module, injector wiring harness, ISC motor wire, throttle position sensor, oil pressure sending switch, ground wire, block heater (if equipped), knock sensor, EGR sensor and oil level sensor.

9. Raise the vehicle and support it safely. Remove the engine mount bolts and engine mounts. Remove the transaxle to engine mounting bolts and transaxle brace assembly.

10. Lower the vehicle. Install a suitable engine lifting plate onto the engine and use a suitable engine hoist to remove the engine from the vehicle. Remove the main wire harness from the engine.

11. Installation is the reverse order of the removal procedure. Torque the transaxle brace assembly bolts to 40–55 ft. lbs. Torque the engine mount nuts to 55–75 ft. lbs. and torque the engine mount bolts to 40–55 ft. lbs.

12. Torque the engine mount nuts and engine mount bolts to 70–96 ft. lbs.

3.8L ENGINE

1. Drain the cooling system and disconnect the battery ground cable. Properly relieve the fuel system pressure.

2. Disconnect the underhood lamp wiring connector. Mark position of hood hinges and remove hood.

3. Remove the oil level indicator tube.

4. Disconnect alternator to voltage regulator wiring assembly.

5. Remove the radiator upper sight shield. Remove the engine cooling fan motor relay retaining bolts and position cooling fan motor relay out of the way.

6. Remove the air cleaner assembly. Identify, tag and disconnect all vacuum lines as necessary.

7. Disconnect the radiator electric fan and motor assembly. Remove fan shroud.

8. Remove upper radiator hose.

9. Disconnect the transaxle oil cooler inlet and outlet tubes and cover the openings to prevent the entry of dirt and grease. Disconnect the heater hoses.

10. Disconnect the power steering pressure hose assembly.

11. Disconnect the air conditioner compressor clutch wire assembly. Discharge the air conditioning system and disconnect the compressor-to-condenser line.

12. Remove the radiator coolant recovery reservoir assembly. Remove the wiring shield.

13. Remove accelerator cable mounting bracket.

14. Disconnect fuel inlet and return hoses.

15. Disconnect power steering pump pressure and return tube brackets.

16. Disconnect the engine control sensor wiring assembly.

17. Identify, tag and disconnect all necessary vacuum hoses.

18. Disconnect the ground wire assembly. Remove the duct assembly.

19. Disconnect one end of the throttle control valve cable. Disconnect the bulkhead electrical connector and transaxle pressure switches.

20. Remove transaxle support assembly retaining bolts and remove transaxle and support assembly from vehicle.

21. Loosen the front wheel lug nuts. Raise the vehicle and support safely. Drain the engine oil and remove the filter.

22. Disconnect the heated exhaust gas oxygen sensor assembly.

23. Loosen and remove drive belt assembly. Remove the crankshaft pulley and drive belt tensioner assemblies.

24. Remove the starter motor assembly. Remove the converter housing assembly and remove the inlet pipe converter assembly.

25. Remove the engine left and right front support insulator retaining nuts.

26. Remove the converter-to-flywheel nuts.

27. Disconnect the oil level indicator sensor. Remove crankshaft pulley assembly.

28. Disconnect the lower radiator hose.

29. Remove the engine-to-transaxle bolts and partially lower engine. Remove the wheel assemblies.

30. Remove the water pump pulley retaining bolts and remove water pump from the vehicle.

31. Remove the distributor cap and position out of the way. Remove distributor rotor.

32. Remove the exhaust manifold bolt lock retaining bolts. Remove the thermactor air pump retaining bolts and remove the thermactor air pump.

33. Disconnect the oil pressure engine unit gauge assembly.

34. Install engine lifting eyes and connect suitable lifting equipment to the lifting eyes.

35. Position a suitable jack under the transaxle and raise the transaxle a small amount.

36. Remove the engine from the vehicle and position in a suitable holding fixture.

37. Complete the installation of the engine assembly by reversing the removal procedure.

Engine Mounts

Removal and Installation

1.9L, 2.0L AND 2.3L ENGINES
Right Engine Insulator (No. 3A)

1. Disconnect the negative battery cable. Place a floor jack and a block of wood under the engine oil pan. Raise the engine approximately ½ in. or enough to take the load off of the insulator.

2. Remove the lower support casting attaching nut (bottom of the double ended stud) and bolt. Remove the insulator to support casting attaching nuts. Do not remove the nut on top of the double ended stud.

3. Remove the insulator support casting from the vehicle. Remove the insulator attaching nuts through the right hand front wheel opening.

4. Remove the insulator attaching bolts through the engine compartment. Work the insulator out of the body and remove it from the vehicle.

5. Complete the installation of the insulator by reversing the removal procedure. Torque the insulator attaching nuts 75–100 ft. lbs. and torque the bolts to 37–55 ft. lbs. Torque the insulator support casting to insulator attaching nuts to 55–75 ft. lbs. and torque the lower support bracket nut to 60–90 ft. lbs.

Left Rear Engine Insulator (No. 4)

1. Disconnect the negative battery cable. Raise the vehicle and support safely. Place a transaxle jack and a block of wood under the transaxle.

2. Raise the transaxle approximately ½ in. or enough to take the load off of the insulator.

3. Remove the insulator attaching nuts from the support bracket. Remove the 2 through bolts and remove the insulator from the transaxle.

4. Complete the installation of the insulator by reversing the removal procedure. Torque the insulator through bolts to 30–45 ft. lbs. Torque the insulator-to-support bracket attaching nuts to 80–100 ft. lbs.

NOTE: To remove the left rear support bracket, remove the left rear engine insulator No. 4. Then remove the support bracket attaching bolts. When installing the support bracket, torque the attaching bolts to 45–65 ft. lbs.

Left Front Engine Insulator (No. 1)

1. Disconnect the negative battery cable. Raise and the vehicle and support safely. Place a transaxle jack and a block of wood under the transaxle. Raise the transaxle approximately ½ in. or enough to take the load off of the insulator.

2. Remove the insulator-to-support bracket attaching nut. Remove the insulators and transaxle attaching bolts and remove the insulator from the vehicle.

3. Complete the installation of the insulator by reversing the removal procedure. Torque the insulator to transaxle attaching bolts to 25–37 ft. lbs. Torque the insulator to support bracket nut to 45–65 ft. lbs. (80–100 ft. lbs. on the 2.3L engine).

2.5L AND 3.0L ENGINES
Right Rear Engine Insulator (No. 3)

1. Disconnect the negative battery cable. Remove the lower damper nut from the right side of the engine on manual transaxle equipped vehicles. Raise and support the vehicle safely.

2. Place a suitable jack and a block of wood the engine block.

3. Remove the nut attaching the right hand front and rear insulators to the frame.

4. Raise the engine with the jack until enough of a load is taken off of the insulator.

5. Remove the insulator retaining bolts and remove the insulator from the engine support bracket.

6. Complete the installation of the insulator by reversing the removal procedure. Torque the insulator to engine support bracket to 40–55 ft. lbs. Torque the nut attaching the right, front and rear insulators to frame to 55–75 ft. lbs.

Left Engine Insulator and
Support Assembly Automatic Transaxle

1. Disconnect the negative battery cable. Raise and support the vehicle safely. Remove the wheel assemblies.

2. Place a suitable jack and a block of wood under the tranmission and support the transaxle.

3. Remove the nuts attaching the insulator to the support assembly. Remove the through bolts attaching the insulator to the frame.

4. Raise the transaxle with the jack enough to relieve the weight on the insulator.

5. Remove the bolts attaching the support assembly to the transaxle. Remove the insulator and/or transaxle support assembly.

6. Complete the installation of the insulator by reversing the removal procedure. Torque the support assembly retaining bolts to 40–55 ft. lbs. Torque the insulator-to-frame nuts and bolts to 70–96 ft. lbs.

Left Engine Insulator and Support Assembly Manual Transaxle

1. Disconnect the negative battery cable. Raise and support the vehicle safely. Remove the wheel assemblies.
2. Place a suitable jack and a block of wood under the tranmission and support the transaxle.
3. Remove the bolts attaching the insulator to the frame.
4. Raise the transaxle with the jack enough to relieve the weight on the insulator.
5. Remove the bolts attaching the insulator to the transaxle. Remove the insulator and or transaxle support assembly.
6. Complete the installation of the insulator by reversing the removal procedure. Torque the support assembly retaining bolts to 70–96 ft. lbs. Torque the insulator-to-frame nuts and bolts to 70–96 ft. lbs.

Right Front Engine Insulator (No. 2)

1. Disconnect the negative battery cable. Remove the lower damper nut from the right side of the engine on vehicles equipped with manual transaxle. Raise and support the vehicle safely.
2. Place a suitable jack and a block of wood the engine block.
3. Remove the nut attaching the right hand front and rear insulators to the frame.
4. Raise the engine with the jack until enough of a load is taken off of the insulator.
5. Remove the bolts and remove the insulator from the engine A/C bracket.
6. Complete the installation of the insulator by reversing the removal procedure. Torque the insulator-to- engine A/C bracket to 40–55 ft. lbs. Torque the nut attaching the right hand front and right hand rear insulators to frame to 55–75 ft. lbs.

3.8L ENGINE
Right Front Engine Insulator

1. Disconnect the negative battery cable. Remove the compressor-to-engine mounting bracket mounting bolts and position the compressor to the side. Do not discharge the air conditioning system.
2. Raise the vehicle and support safely.
3. Remove nut attaching engine mount to air conditioning compressor bracket.
4. Temporarily attach the air conditioning compressor to the mounting bracket with the 2 lower bolts.
5. Position a jack and wood block in a convenient location under the engine block.
6. Remove the upper and lower nuts attaching the right front and left rear insulators to the frame.
7. Raise the engine with the jack enough to relieve the load on the insulator.
8. Remove insulator assembly. Remove heat shield from insulator.
9. Complete the installation of the insulator assembly by reversing the removal procedure. Torque the upper insulator stud retaining nut to 40–55 ft. lbs. and the lower retaining nut to 55–75 ft. lbs.

Right Rear Engine Insulator (No. 3)

1. Disconnect the negative battery cable. Raise the vehicle and support safely.
2. Loosen retaining nuts on the No. 2 right front and No. 3 left rear insulators.
3. Remove the front and back exhaust retaining bolts at manifold and at flexible coupling. Remove the catalytic converter.
4. Lower the vehicle and use engine support bar No. D87L-6000-A or equivalent to support engine. Install a J-hook on alternator bracket. Raise the engine approximately 1 in.
5. Loosen the retaining nut on No. 3 insulator (LH rear) and heat shield assembly.
6. Raise the vehicle and support safely.

7. Loosen the sub-frame retaining bolts (4).
8. Remove No. 3 insulator retaining nut. Remove No. 3 insulator and heat shield assembly.
9. Install the insulator and position the No. 3 mount and heat shield assembly upper stud and anti-rotation pin to the transaxle support bracket. Complete the remainder of the insulator installation by reversing the removal procedure. Torque the sub-frame retaining bolts to 50–70 ft. lbs. Torque the RH front and LH rear insulator retaining nuts to 70–96 ft. lbs.
10. Check the front end alignment and adjust if necessary.

Left Engine Insulator and Support Assembly

1. Disconnect the negative battery cable. Remove the air cleaner tray from fender apron on Continental.
2. Remove nut and bolt which retain the upper transaxle support bracket to transaxle on Continental.
3. Remove the bolts which retain the upper transaxle support bracket to lower support bracket.
4. Raise the vehicle and support safely.
5. Remove the wheel assembly.
6. Position a jack and wood block in a convenient location under the transaxle and support.
7. Remove the nut retaining the insulator to the support assembly.
8. Remove the through bolts retaining insulator to frame.
9. Raise the transaxle enough to relieve the load from the insulator.
10. Remove the bolts retaining the support assembly to the transaxle.
11. Remove insulator and/or transaxle support assembly.
12. Complete the installation of the support assembly by reversing the removal procedure. Torque the transaxle support retaining nut to 20–25 ft. lbs. Torque the transaxle support retaining bolts to 34–44 ft. lbs.

Intake Manifold

Removal and Installation

1.9L ENGINE

1. Raise and secure the hood in the open position.
2. Install protective fender covers.
3. Properly relieve the fuel system pressure. Disconnect the negative battery cable.

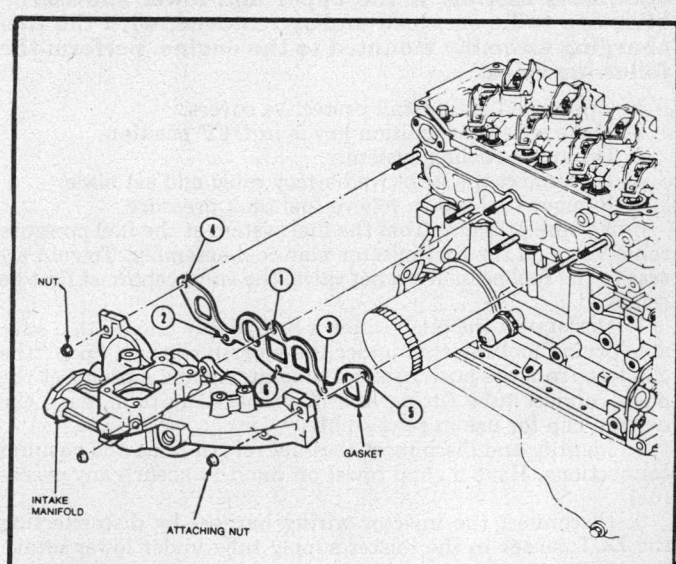

Intake manifold assembly 1.9L EFI engine

4. Partially drain the cooling system and disconnect the heater hose at the fitting located under the intake manifold.

5. Remove air cleaner assembly.

6. Identify, tag and disconnect the vacuum hoses.

7. Identify, tag and disconnect wiring connectors at the following points:
   a. Choke cap wire
   b. Bowl vent
   c. Idle fuel solenoid
   d. Coolant temperature sensor
   e. Air charge temperature sensor

8. Remove EGR supply tube.

9. Raise the vehicle and support safely.

10. Remove the PVS hose connectors. Label the connectors and set aside.

11. Remove 4 of the 7 lower intake manifold retaining nuts.

12. Lower the vehicle.

13. Disconnect fuel lines at the fuel filter (and or the throttle body) and the return line at the carburetor.

14. Disconnect accelerator and, if equipped, the speed control cable.

15. Disconnect the throttle valve linkage at the carburetor and remove the cable bracket attaching bolts on vehicles equipped with automatic transaxle.

16. If equipped with power steering, remove the thermactor pump drive belt, the pump, the pump mounting bracket and the thermactor bypass hose.

17. Remove the fuel pump.

18. Remove the remaining 3 intake manifold attaching nuts, intake manifold and gasket.

NOTE: Do not lay the intake manifold flat as the gasket surfaces may be damaged.

19. Make sure the mating surfaces on the intake manifold and the cylinder head are clean and free of gasket material.

20. Install a new intake manifold gasket.

21. Position the intake manifold on the engine and install the attaching nuts. Tighten the nuts to 12–13 ft. lbs.

22. Complete the installation of the remaining intake manifold components by reversing the removal procedure.

1.9L HO ENGINE

NOTE: The air intake manifold used on these engine is a 2 piece (upper intake and lower intake manifold) aluminum casting. If the upper and lower sub-assemblies are to be serviced and/or removed, with the fuel charging assembly mounted to the engine, perform the following steps.

1. Open hood and install protective covers.

2. Make sure that ignition key is in **OFF** position.

3. Drain the cooling system.

4. Disconnect the negative battery cable and set aisde.

5. Remove fuel cap to relieve fuel tank pressure.

6. Release pressure from the fuel system at the fuel pressure relief valve on the fuel injector manifold assembly. To gain access to the fuel pressure relief valve, the valve cap must first be removed.

7. Disconnect the push connect fuel supply line. With a suitable prying tool inserted under the hairpin clip tab, "pop" the clip free from the push connect tube fitting and disconnect the push connect tube fitting and disconnect the tube. Save the hairpin clip for use in reassembly.

8. Identify and disconnect the fuel return lines and vacuum connections. Have a shop towel on hand to absorb any excess fuel.

9. Disconnect the injector wiring harness by disconnecting the ECT sensor in the heater supply tube under lower intake manifold and the electronic engine control harness.

10. Disconnect air bypass connector from EEC harness.

NOTE: Not all assemblies may be serviceable while on the engine. In some cases, removal of the fuel charging assembly may facilitate service of the various sub-assemblies. Remove the fuel charging assembly as required and proceed with the following steps:

11. Disconnect the engine air cleaner outlet tube from the air intake throttle body.

12. Unplug the throttle position sensor from the wiring harness.

13. Unplug the air bypass valve connector.

14. Remove the upper manifold retaining bolts.

15. Remove upper manifold assembly and set it aside.

16. Remove and discard the gasket from the lower manifold assembly.

NOTE: If scraping is necessary, be careful not to damage the gasket surfaces of the upper and lower manifold assemblies, or allow material to drop into lower manifold.

17. Ensure that the gasket surfaces of the upper and lower intake manifolds are clean.

18. Place a new service gasket on the lower manifold assembly and mount the upper intake manifold to the lower, securing it with the retaining bolts. Torque the bolts to 15–22 ft. lbs.

19. Ensure the wiring harness in properly installed.

20. Connect electrical connectors to air bypass valve and throttle position sensor and the vacuum hose to the fuel pressure regulator.

21. Connect the engine air cleaner outlet tube to the throttle body intake securing it with a hose clamp tighten to 15–25 inch lbs.

2.0L DIESEL ENGINE

1. Disconnect the negative battery cable. Disconnect the air inlet duct from the intake manifold and install a protective cap in the intake manifold.

2. Disconnect the glow plug resistor electrical connector.

3. Disconnect the breather hose.

4. Drain the cooling system.

5. Disconnect the upper radiator hose at the thermostat housing.

6. Disconnect the two-coolant hoses at the thermostat housing.

7. Disconnect the connectors to the temperature sensors in the thermostat housing.

8. Remove the bolts attaching the intake manifold to the cylinder head and remove the intake manifold.

9. Clean the intake manifold and cylinder head gasket mating surfaces.

10. Install the intake manifold, using a new gasket, and tighten the bolts to 12–16 ft. lbs.

11. Connect the temperature sensor connectors.

12. Connect the lower coolant hose to the thermostat housing and tighten the hose clamp.

13. Connect the upper coolant tube, using a new gasket and tighten bolts to 5–7 ft. lbs.

14. Connect the upper radiator hose to the thermostat housing.

15. Connect the breather hose.

16. Connect the glow plug resistor electrical connector.

17. Remove the protective cap and install the air inlet duct.

18. Fill and bleed the cooling system.

19. Run the engine and check for intake air leaks and coolant leaks.

2.3L AND 2.5L ENGINES

1. Open and secure the hood.

2. Disconnect the negative battery cable. Properly relieve the fuel system pressure.

3. Drain the cooling system.

4. Remove accelerator cable.

5. Remove air cleaner assembly and heat stove tube at heat shield.

6. Remove required vacuum lines.

7. Remove thermactor belt from pulley. Remove hose below thermactor pump. Remove thermactor pump.

8. Disconnect the exhaust pipe to exhaust manifold retaining nuts.

9. Remove exhaust manifold heat shield. Disconnect the oxygen sensor wire at the connector.

10. Disconnect EGR sensor wire at connector.

11. Disconnect thermactor check valve hose at tube assembly. Remove bracket-to-EGR valve attaching nuts.

12. Disconnect the water inlet tube at the intake manifold.

13. Disconnect EGR tube at EGR valve.

14. Remove the intake manifold retaining bolts. Remove the intake manifold. Remove the gasket and clean the gasket contact surfaces.

To install:

15. Install intake manifold with gasket and retaining bolts. Torque the retaining bolts to 15–22 ft. lbs.

16. Connect water inlet tube at intake manifold.

17. Connect thermactor check valve hose at tube assembly. Install bracket to EGR valve attaching nuts.

18. Connect EGR sensor wire and the oxygen sensor wire at their proper connector.

19. Connect EGR tube to EGR valve.

20. Install exhaust manifold studs.

21. Connect exhaust pipe to exhaust manifold.

22. Install thermactor pump hose to pump. Install thermactor pump and thermactor pump drive belt.

23. Install vacuum lines.

24. Install air cleaner assembly and heat stove tube.

25. Install accelerator cable.

26. Connect negative ground cable and fill the cooling system.

27. Start engine and check for leaks.

3.0L EXCEPT SHO ENGINE

1. Disconnect the negative battery cable and drain the engine cooling system.

2. Loosen the hose clamp attaching the flex hose to the throttle body. Remove the air cleaner flex hose. Remove the air intake throttle body assembly with gasket. Discard the gasket and replace with new.

3. Identify, tag and disconnect and all vacuum connections to the throttle body.

4. Disconnect the EGR valve assembly. Disconnect the throttle linkage, throttle position sensor, air charge temperature sensor and idle speed control.

5. Disconnect the PCV hose and disconnect the alternator support brace.

6. Remove the throttle body attaching bolts and remove the throttle body.

7. Disconnect the fuel lines. Remove the fuel injection wiring harness from the engine. Disconnect and tag the spark plug wires and remove the rocker arm covers (It will be necessary to remove the heater hoses in order to remove the right hand side rocker cover).

8. Disconnect the upper radiator hose, the water outlet heater hose and the thermostat housing. Mark and remove the distributor assembly.

9. Remove the intake manifold attaching bolts and studs. Remove the manifold assembly with the fuel rails and injectors in place. Remove the manifold side gaskets and end seals. Discard the gaskets and seals and replace with new.

To install:

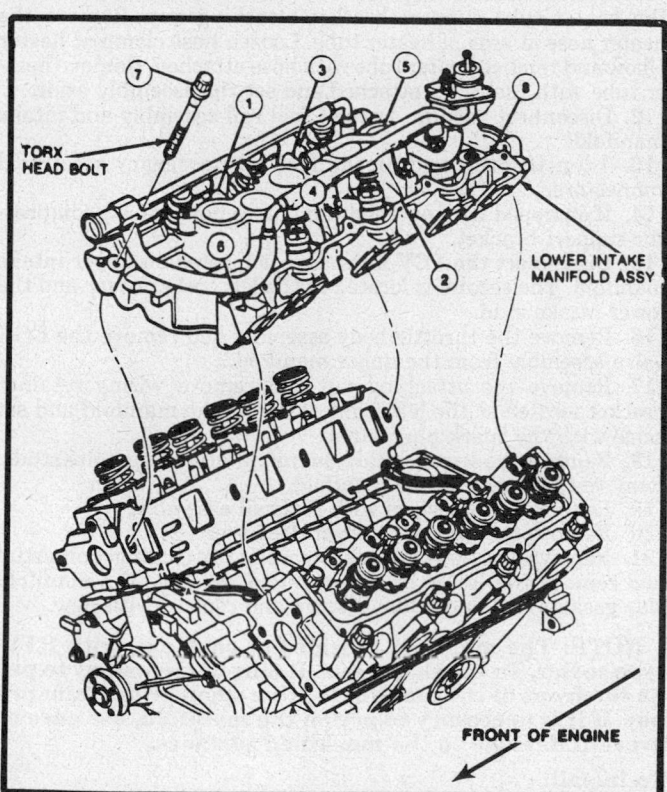

Intake manifold removal and installation—3.0L engine

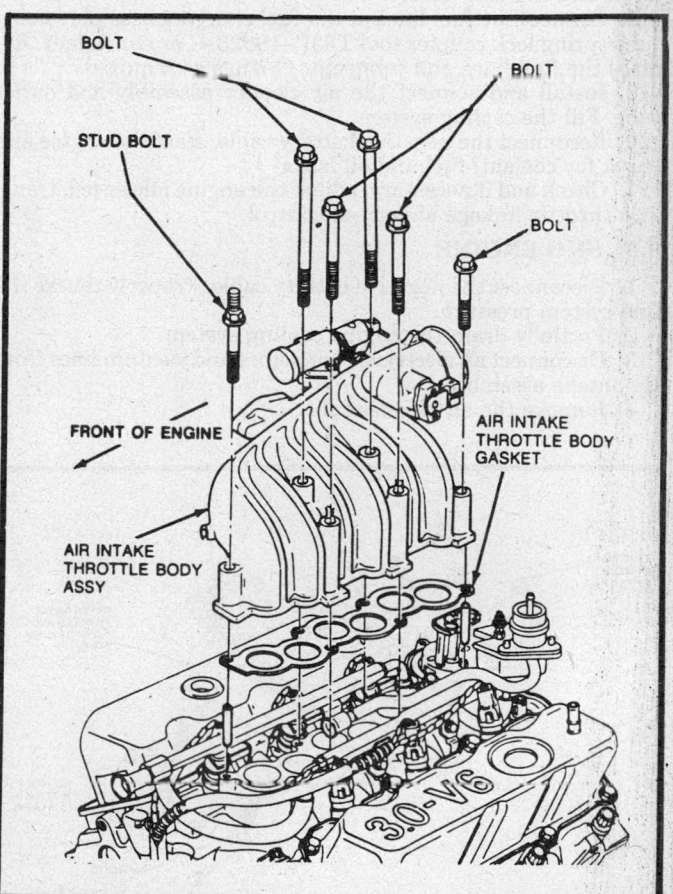

Air intake throttle assembly manifold removal and installation—3.0L engine

NOTE: Lightly oil all the attaching bolts and stud threads before installation. When using a silcone rubber sealer, assembly must occur within 15 minutes after the sealer has been applied. After this time, the sealer may start to set-up and its sealing quality may be reduced. In high temperature/humidty conditions, the sealant will start to set up in approxitmately 5 minutes.

10. The intake manifold, cylinder head and cylinder block mating surfaces should be clean and free of old silicone rubber sealer. Use a suitable solvent to clean these surfaces.

11. Apply a suitable silicone rubber sealer to the intersection of the cylinder block assembly and head assembly on the each corner of the 2 manifold end seals.

12. Install the front intake manifold gaskets in place and insert the locking tabs over the tabs on the cylinder head gaskets. Apply a suitable silicone sealer over gasket in the same places as before on the manifold end seals.

13. Carefully lower the intake manifold into position on the cylinder block and cylinder heads to prevent smearing the silicone sealer and causing gasket voids.

14. Install the retaining bolts and torque the bolts to 11 ft. lbs. then retorque to 18 ft. lbs.

15. Install the thermostat housing with a new thermostat and gasket, torque the attaching bolts to 6 to 8 ft. lbs.

16. Connect the PCV line at the PCV valve and exhaust manifold. Connect all necessary electrical connections. Connect the EGR valve assembly and all necessary vacuum lines. Apply a suitable silicone sealer to split between the head and the intake manifold (4 places).

17. Install the rocker arm covers (with new gaskets), heater hoses and radiator hose.

18. Connect the fuel lines at the fuel charging assembly using tube spring lock coupler tool T83P–19623–C or equivalent. Replace the fuel lines and connector O-rings as required.

19. Install and connect the air cleaner assembly and outlet tube. Fill the cooling system.

20. Reconnect the negative battery cable, start the engine and check for coolant, fuel and oil leaks.

21. Check and if necessary, adjust the engine idle speed, transaxle throttle linkage and speed control.

3.0L SHO ENGINE

1. Disconnect the negative battery cable. Properly relieve the fuel system pressure.

2. Partially drain the engine cooling system.

3. Disconnect all electrical connectors and vacuum lines from the intake assembly.

4. Remove the air cleaner tube.

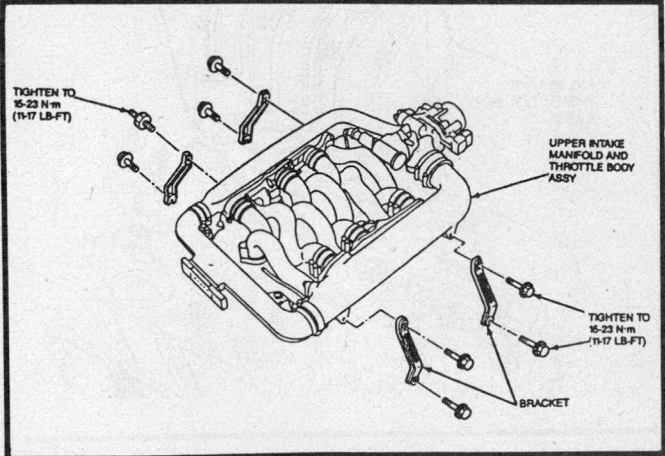

TIGHTEN TO
15-23 N·m
(11-17 LB-FT)

UPPER INTAKE
MANIFOLD AND
THROTTLE BODY
ASSY

TIGHTEN TO
15-23 N·m
(11-17 LB-FT)

BRACKET

Intake manifold 3.0L SHO engine

5. Disconnect the coolant lines and cables from the throttle body.

6. Remove the bolts retaining the upper intake brackets.

7. Loosen the lower bolts and remove the brackets.

8. Remove the bolts retaining the intake to the cylinder heads.

9. Remove the intake assembly and the gaskets.

10. Installation is the reverse of the removal procedure.

11. Lightly oil the attaching bolts and stud threads before installation.

NOTE: The intake gasket is reuseable.

12. Install the retaining bolts and tighten to 11–17 ft. lbs. (15–23 Nm).

3.8L ENGINE

1. Disconnect the negative battery cable. Drain the cooling system.

2. Properly relieve the fuel system pressure. Remove the air cleaner assembly including air intake duct and heat tube.

3. Disconnect the accelerator cable at throttle body assembly. Disconnect speed control cable, if equipped.

4. Disconnect the transaxle linkage at the upper intake manifold.

5. Remove the attaching bolts from accelerator cable mounting bracket and position cables aside.

6. Disconnect the thermactor air supply hose at the check valve.

7. Disconnect the flexible fuel lines from steel lines over rocker arm cover.

8. Disconnect the fuel lines at injector fuel rail assembly.

9. Disconnect the radiator hose at thermostat housing connection.

10. Disconnect the coolant bypass hose at manifold connection.

11. Disconnect the heater tube at the intake manifold. Remove the heater tube support bracket attaching nut. Remove the heater hose at rear of heater tube. Loosen hose clamp at heater elbow and remove heater tube with hose attached. Remove heater tube with fuel lines attached and set the assembly aside.

12. Disconnect vacuum lines at fuel rail assembly and intake manifold.

13. Identify, tag and disconnect all necessary electrical connectors.

14. If equipped with air conditioning, remove the air compressor support bracket.

15. Disconnect the PCV lines. One is located on upper intake manifold. The second is located at the left rocker cover and the lower intake stud.

16. Remove the throttle body assembly and remove the EGR valve assembly from the upper manifold.

17. Remove the attaching nut and remove wiring retainer bracket located at the left front of the intake manifold and set aside with the spark plug wires.

18. Remove the upper intake manifold attaching bolts/studs. Remove the upper intake manifold.

19. Remove the injectors with fuel rail assembly.

20. Remove the heater water outlet hose.

21. Remove the lower intake manifold attaching bolts/stud and remove the lower intake manifold. Remove the manifold side gaskets and end seals. Discard and replace with new.

NOTE: The manifold is sealed at each end with RTV-type sealer. To break the seal, it may be necessary to pry on the front of the manifold with a small or medium pry bar. If it is necessary to pry on the manifold, use care to prevent damage to the machined surfaces.

To install:

22. Lightly oil all attaching bolt and stud threads before installation.

NOTE: When using silicone rubber sealer, assembly must occur within 15 minutes after sealer application. After this time, the sealer may start to set-up and its sealing effectiveness may be reduced. The lower intake manifold, cylinder head and cylinder block mating surfaces should be clean and free of oil gasketing material. Use a suitable solvent to clean these surfaces.

23. Apply a bead of contact adhesive part number D7AZ-19B508-A or equivalent to each cylinder head mating surface. Press the new intake manifold gaskets into place, using locating pins as necessary to aid in assembly alignment.

24. Apply a ⅛ inch bead of silicone sealer part number D6AZ-19562-B or equivalent at each corner where the cylinder head joins the cylinder block.

25. Install the front and rear intake manifold end seals.

26. Carefully lower the intake manifold into position on cylinder block and cylinder heads. Use locating pins as necessary to guide the manifold.

27. Install the retaining bolts and stud bolts in their original locations. Torque the retaining bolts in numerical sequence to the following specifications in 3 steps.
   a. Step 1 — 8 ft. lbs.
   b. Step 2 — 15 ft. lbs.
   c. Step 3 — 24 ft. lbs.

28. Connect the rear PCV line to upper intake tube and install the front PCV tube so the mounting bracket sits over the lower intake stud.

29. Install the injectors and fuel rail assembly.

30. Position the upper intake gasket and manifold on top of the lower intake. Use locating pins to secure position of gasket between manifolds.

31. Install bolts and studs in their original locations. Tighten the 4 center bolts, then tighten the end bolts. Repeat Step 27.

32. Install the EGR valve assembly on the manifold. Tighten the attaching bolt to 15-22 ft. lbs.

33. Install the throttle body. Cross-tighten the retaining nuts to 15-22 ft. lbs.

34. Connect the rear PCV line at PCV valve and upper intake manifold connections. If equipped with air conditioning, install the compressor support bracket. Tighten attaching fasteners to 15-22 ft. lbs.

35. Connect all electrical connectors and vacuum hoses.

36. Connect the heater tube hose to the heater elbow. Position the heater tube support bracket and tighten attaching nut to 15-22 ft. lbs. Connect the heater hose to the rear of the heater tube and tighten hose clamp.

37. Connect coolant bypass and upper radiator hoses and secure with hose clamps.

38. Connect the fuel line(s) at injector fuel rail assembly and connect the flexible fuel lines to steel lines.

39. Position the accelerator cable mounting bracket and install and tighten attaching bolts to 15-22 ft. lbs.

40. Connect the speed control cable, if equipped. Connect the transaxle linkage at upper intake manifold.

41. Fill the cooling system to the proper level.

42. Start the engine and check for coolant or fuel leaks.

43. Check and, if necessary, adjust engine idle speed, transaxle throttle linkage and speed control.

44. Install the air cleaner assembly and air intake duct.

Exhaust Manifold

Removal and Installation

1.9L ENGINE

1. Disconnect the negative battery cable.
2. Remove the air cleaner tray.
3. Disconnect the electric fan wire.
4. Remove the radiator shroud bolts and radiator shroud.
5. Disconnect the EGR tube at the exhaust manifold.

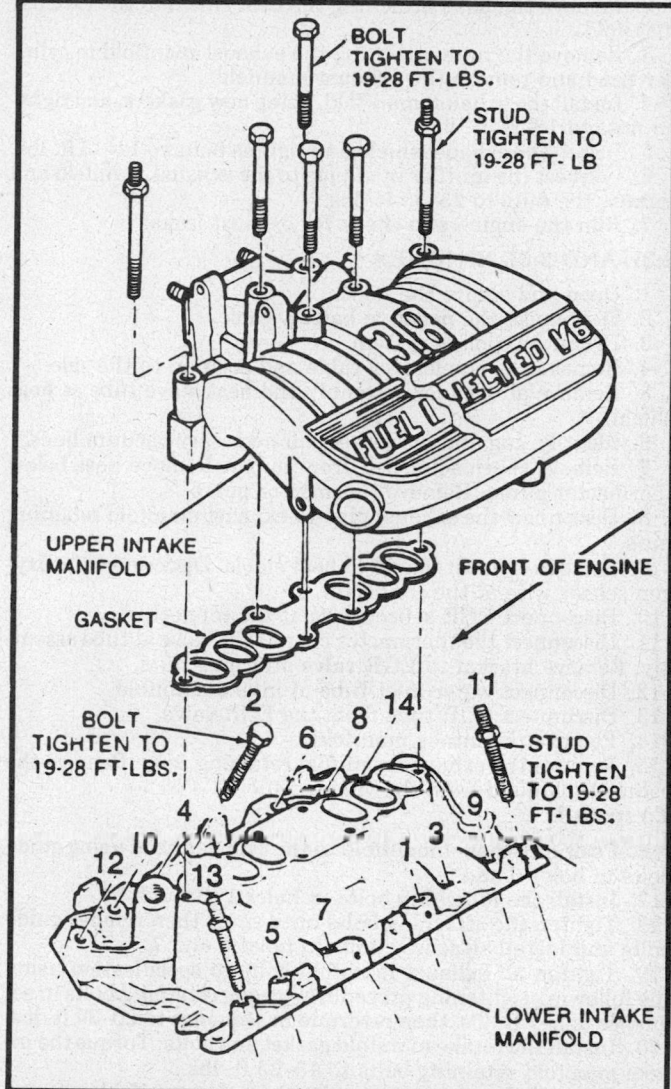

Upper and lower intake manifold assembly used on 3.8L engines. Torque lower intake manifold in sequence as shown

6. Disconnect thermactor tube at the exhaust manifold. Remove the air conditioning hose bracket.

7. Remove exhaust manifold heat stove. Remove the oxygen sensor from the exhaust manifold.

8. Remove exhaust manifold retaining nuts.

9. Raise vehicle and support safely.

10. Remove the anti-roll brace.

11. Disconnect the water tube brackets.

12. Disconnect the exhaust pipe at the catalytic converter.

13. Remove the exhaust manifold and gasket. Discard the gasket and replace with new.

14. Clean the exhaust manifold gasket contact areas.

15. Position the gasket and exhaust manifold.

16. Complete the installation of the exhaust manifold by reversing the removal procedure. Be sure to torque the retaining bolts to specification and in the proper sequence.

2.0L DIESEL ENGINE

1. Disconnect the negative battery cable. Remove the nuts attaching the muffler inlet pipe to the exhaust manifold.

2. Remove the bolts attaching the heat shield to the exhaust manifold.

3. Remove the nuts attaching the exhaust manifold to cylinder head and remove the exhaust manifold.

4. Install the exhaust manifold, using new gaskets, and tighten nuts to 16–20 ft. lbs.

5. Install the exhaust shield and tighten bolts to 12–16 ft. lbs.

6. Connect the muffler inlet pipe to the exhaust manifold and tighten the nuts to 25–35 ft. lbs.

7. Run the engine and check for exhaust leaks.

2.3L AND 2.5L ENGINES

1. Open and secure the hood.
2. Disconnect the negative battery cable.
3. Drain the cooling system.
4. Remove the accelerator cable and position to the side.
5. Remove air cleaner assembly and heat stove tube at heat shield.
6. Identify, tag and disconnect all necessary vacuum lines.
7. Remove thermactor belt from pulley. Remove hose below thermactor pump. Remove thermactor pump.
8. Disconnect the exhaust pipe-to-exhaust manifold retaining nuts.
9. Remove exhaust manifold heat shield. Disconnect the oxygen sensor wire at the connector.
10. Disconnect EGR sensor wire at the connector.
11. Disconnect the thermactor check valve hose at tube assembly. Remove bracket-to-EGR valve attaching nuts.
12. Disconnect water inlet tube at intake manifold.
13. Disconnect EGR tube from the EGR valve.
14. Remove the intake manifold.
15. Remove the exhaust manifold retaining nuts. Remove the exhaust manifold from the vehicle.

To install:

16. Position exhaust manifold to the cylinder head using guide bolts in holes 6 and 7.
17. Install the attaching bolts in holes 1 through 5.
18. Tighten the attaching bolts until snug, then remove guide bolts and install attaching bolts in holes 6 and 7.
19. Tighten all exhaust manifold bolts to specification using the following tightening procedure: torque retaining bolts in sequence to 5–7 ft. lbs. then retorque in sequence to 20–30 ft. lbs.
20. Install the intake manifold gasket and bolts. Torque the intake manifold retaining bolts to 15–23 ft. lbs.
21. Connect the water inlet tube at intake manifold.
22. Connect thermactor check valve hose at tube assembly. Install bracket to EGR valve attaching nuts.
23. Connect the EGR sensor wire and the oxygen sensor wire at their proper connector.
24. Connect the EGR tube to EGR valve.
25. Install exhaust manifold studs.
26. Connect exhaust pipe to exhaust manifold.

27. Install thermactor pump hose to pump. Install thermactor pump and thermactor pump drive belt.
28. Install vacuum lines.
29. Install air cleaner assembly and heat stove tube.
30. Install accelerator cable.
31. Connect the negative battery cable.
32. Fill the cooling system.
33. Start engine and check for leaks.

3.0L ENGINE
Left Side

1. Disconnect the negative battery cable. Remove the oil level indicator support bracket.
2. Remove the power steering pump pressure and return hoses. Remove the manifold exhaust pipe attaching nuts and remove the exhaust pipe from the exhaust manifold.
3. Raise the vehicle and support it safely. Remove the exhaust manifold attaching bolts and remove the manifold from the vehicle.
4. Clean all mating surfaces and lightly oil all bolt and stud threads prior to installation. Complete the installation of the left hand exhaust manifold by reversing the removal procedure. Torque the exhaust manifold retaining bolts to 15–22 ft. lbs. and torque the exhaust pipe attaching nuts to 16–24 ft. lbs.

Right Side

1. Disconnect the negative battery cable. Remove the heater hose support bracket.
2. Disconnect and plug the heater hoses. Remove the EGR tube from the exhaust manifold. Use a back-up wrench on the lower adapter.
3. Raise the vehicle and support it safely. Remove the manifold-to-exhaust pipe attaching nuts and remove the pipe from the manifold.
4. Remove the exhaust manifold attaching bolts and remove the exhaust manifold from the vehicle.
5. Clean all mating surfaces and lightly oil all bolt and stud threads prior to installation. Complete the installation of the right hand exhaust manifold by reversing the removal procedure. Torque the exhaust manifold retaining bolts to 15–22 ft. lbs. and torque the exhaust pipe attaching nuts to 16–24 ft. lbs. Torque the EGR tube to the exhaust manifold to 25–36 ft. lbs.

3.8L ENGINE
Left Side

1. Disconnect the negative battery cable. Remove the oil level dipstick tube support bracket.
2. Tag and disconnect the spark plug wires.
3. Raise the vehicle and support safely.
4. Remove the manifold-to-exhaust pipe attaching nuts.
5. Lower the vehicle.
6. Remove the exhaust manifold retaining bolts and remove the manifold from vehicle. Discard the gasket and replace with new.
7. Lightly oil all bolt and stud threads before installation. Clean the mating surfaces on the exhaust manifold, cylinder head and exhaust pipe so that they are free of the old gasket material.
8. Position the gasket and exhaust manifold on the cylinder head. Install pilot bolt (lower front bolt hole on No. 5 cylinder).
9. Install the remaining manifold retaining bolts. Torque the bolts 15–22 ft. lbs.

NOTE: A slight warpage in the exhaust manifold may cause a misalignment between the bolt holes in the head and the manifold. Elongate the holes in the exhaust manifold as necessary to correct the misalignment, if apparent. Do not elongate the pilot hole (lower front bolt on No. 5 cylinder).

10. Raise the vehicle and support safely.

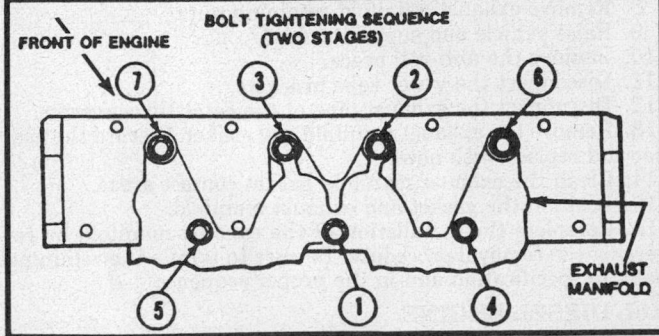

Exhaust manifold bolt torque sequence—2.3 and 2.5L engines

11. Connect the exhaust pipe to the manifold. Torque the attaching nuts to 16–24 ft. lbs.

12. Lower the vehicle.

13. Connect the spark plug wires. Install dipstick tube support bracket attaching nut. Tighten to 15-22 ft. lbs.

14. Start the engine and check for exhaust leaks.

Right Side

1. Disconnect the negative battery cable. Remove the air cleaner outlet tube assembly. On Taurus and Sable, disconnect the thermactor hose from the downstream air tube check valve.

2. Tag and disconnect the coil secondary wire from coil and the wires from spark plugs.

3. Disconnect the EGR tube.

4. Raise the vehicle and support safely.

5. Remove the transaxle dipstick tube. On the Taurus and Sable, remove the thermactor air tube by cutting the tube clamp at the underbody catalyst fitting with a suitable cutting tool.

6. Remove the manifold-to-exhaust pipe attaching nuts.

7. Lower the vehicle.

8. Remove the exhaust manifold retaining bolts. Remove the manifold and heat shroud on Taurus and Sable. Discard the gasket and replace with new.

9. Lightly oil all bolt and stud threads before installation. Clean the mating surfaces on exhaust manifold cylinder head and exhaust pipe so that they are free of the old gasket material.

10. Position the gasket, inner half of the heat shroud (if equipped) and exhaust manifold on cylinder head. Start 2 attaching bolts to align the manifold with the cylinder head. Install the remaining retaining bolts and torque to 15–22 ft. lbs.

11. Raise the vehicle and support safely.

12. Connect the exhaust pipe to manifold. Torque the attaching nuts to 16-24 ft. lbs. On the Taurus and Sable, position the thermactor hose to the downstream air tube and clamp tube to the underbody catalyst fitting.

13. Install the transaxle dipstick tube and lower vehicle.

14. Connect wires to their respective spark plugs and connect coil secondary wire to coil.

15. Connect the EGR tube. On the Taurus and Sable, connect the thermactor hose to the downstream air tube and secure with clamp. Install the air cleaner outlet tube assembly.

16. Start the engine and check for exhaust leaks.

Valve System

The intake and exhaust valves are driven by the camshaft, working through hydraulic valve lifters and rocker arms (1.9L engine), hydraulic lifters, pushrods and rocker arms (2.3L, 2.5L, 3.0L and 3.8L engines) or through hydraulic valve lifters only (3.0L SHO engine). The hydraulic lifters eliminate the need for periodic valve lash adjustments. Hydraulic valve components can be best maintained through regular and scheduled oil and filter changes.

Cam lobe-to-hydraulic lifter or valve stem-to-rocker arm clearance should be within specification with the hydraulic valve lifter completely collapsed. To determine the rocker arm to valve lifter clearance, make the following checks.

COLLAPSED LIFTER CLEARANCE CHECK

Procedure

1.9L Engine

To determine the rocker arm-to-tappet clearance, make the following check:

1. Connect an auxiliary starter switch in the starting circuit. Crank the engine with the ignition switch **OFF** until the No. 1 piston is on TDC after the compression stroke.

2. With the crankshaft in position, place the hydraulic lifter compressor tool on the rocker arm. Slowly apply pressure to bleed down the lifter until it completely bottoms. Hold the lifter in this position and check the available clearance between the rocker arm and the valve stem tip with a feeler gauge. The feeler gauge width must not exceed ⅜ in., in order to fit between the rails on the rocker arm. If the clearance is less than specifications, check the following for wear:

The fulcrum
The valve lifter
The camshaft lobe
The valve tip

3. With the No. 1 piston on TDC at the end of the compression stroke (Position No. 1), check the following valves:
   a. No. 1 Intake, No. 1 Exhaust
   b. No. 2 Intake

4. Rotate the crankshaft to Position No. 2 and check the following valves: No. 3 Intake, No. 3 Exhaust.

5. Rotate the crankshaft another 180 degrees from position No. 2 back to TDC and check the following valves:
   a. No. 4 Intake, No. 4 Exhaust.
   b. No. 2 Exhaust

6. The collapsed lifter clearance should be 0.059–0.194 in. On the 1987–90 1.9L CFI engine, the collapsed lifter clearance should be 0.047–0.138. On the 1987–90 1.9L EFI engine, the collapsed lifter clearance should be 0.059–0.150 in.

2.3L AND 2.5L ENGINES

1. Set the No. 1 piston on TDC on the compression stroke. The timing marks on the camshaft and crankshaft gears will be together. Check the clearance in No. 1 intake, No. 1 exhaust, No. 2 intake and No. 3 exhaust valves.

2. Rotate the crankshaft 1 complete turn (180 degrees for the camshaft gear). Check the clearance in No. 2 exhaust, No. 3 intake, No. 4 intake and No. 4 exhaust.

3. The clearance between the rocker arm and the valve stem tip should be 0.072–0.174 in. (1.80–4.34mm) with the lifter on the base circle of the cam.

3.0L EXCEPT SHO ENGINE
3.8L ENGINE

1. Rotate the engine until the number one cylinder is at TDC of its compression stroke and check that the following valves are in the open (down) position.

Checking the collapsed lifters clearance on the 1.9L engine

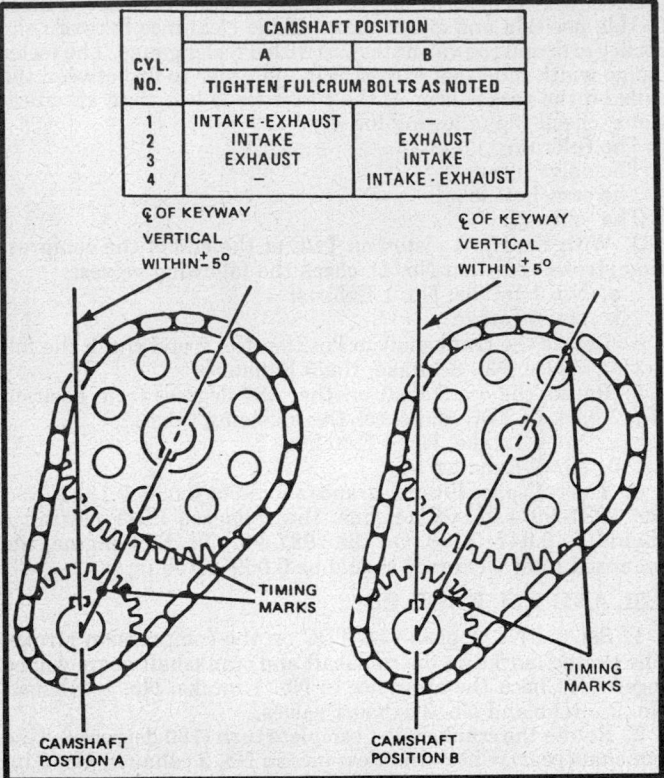

CYL. NO.	CAMSHAFT POSITION	
	A	B
	TIGHTEN FULCRUM BOLTS AS NOTED	
1	INTAKE-EXHAUST	—
2	INTAKE	EXHAUST
3	EXHAUST	INTAKE
4	—	INTAKE-EXHAUST

Collapsed tappet clearance 2.3L engine

   a. No.1 intake and No.1 exhaust
   b. No.3 intake and No.2 exhaust
   c. No.6 intake and No.4 exhaust
   2. Rotate the crankshaft 360 degrees and check to see that the following valves are in the open (down) position.
   a. No.2 intake and No.3 exhaust
   b. No.4 intake and No.5 exhaust
   c. No.5 intake and No.6 exhaust

3.0L SHO ENGINE

   1. Remove the valve cover.

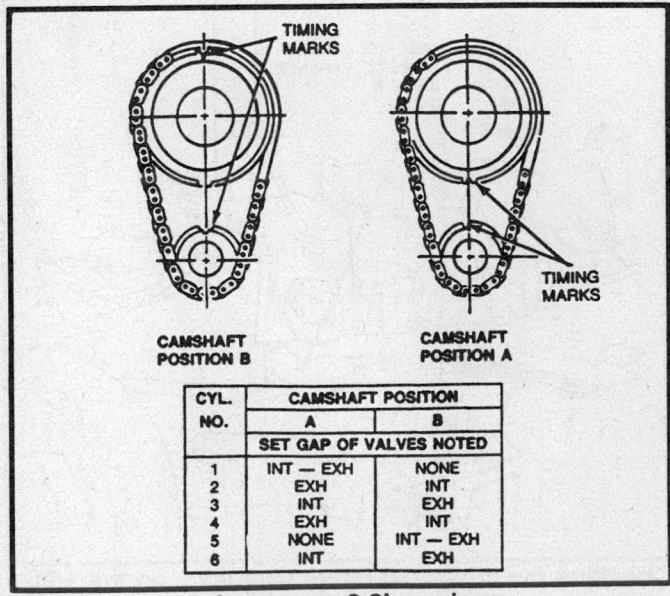

CYL. NO.	CAMSHAFT POSITION	
	A	B
	SET GAP OF VALVES NOTED	
1	INT — EXH	NONE
2	EXH	INT
3	INT	EXH
4	EXH	INT
5	NONE	INT — EXH
6	INT	EXH

Checking valve clearance—3.8L engines

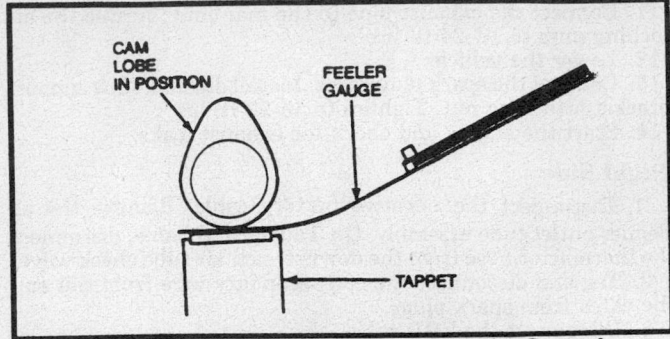

Checking valve clearance on the 3.0L SHO engine

   2. Remove the intake manifold assembly.
   3. Insert a feeler gauge under the cam lobe at a 90 degree angle to the camshaft. Clearance for the intake valves should be 0.006–0.010 in. (0.15–0.25mm). Clearance for the exhaust valves should be 0.010–0.014 in. (0.25–0.35mm).

NOTE: **The cam lobes must be directed 90 degrees or more away from the valve lifters.**

VALVE ADJUSTMENT

2.0L DIESEL ENGINE

   1. Warm up the engine and allow to reach normal operating temperature.
   2. Remove the valve cover.
   3. Set No. 1 cylinder to TDC on the compression stroke and check the valve clearance of No. 1 and No. 2 intake and No. 1 and No. 3 exhaust valves.
   4. Clearance for intake valves should be 0.008–0.011 in.. Exhaust valve clearance should be 0.011–0.015 in..
   5. Rotate the crankshaft 360 degrees and check the clearance of the No. 3 and No. 4 intake and No. 2 and No. 4 exhaust valves.
   6. If adjustment is necessary, rotate the crankshaft until the cam lobe of the valve requiring adjustment is down against the cam follower.
   7. Position the special cam follower retainer tool T84P-6513-B or equivalent under the cam between the lobes so that the edge contacts the cam follower needing adjustment.
   8. Rotate the camshaft until the cam lobe (of valve needing adjustment) is on its base circle (lobe pointing straight up).
   9. Pry the adjusting shim out of the cam follower and replace with a new shim.

NOTE: **Valve shims are available in thicknesses ranging from 3.40mm–4.60mm. If the valve was too tight or loose, install a shim of the appropriate size. Shim thickness is stamped on the valve shim. Install the shim with the numbers down to avoid wearing the numbers off.**

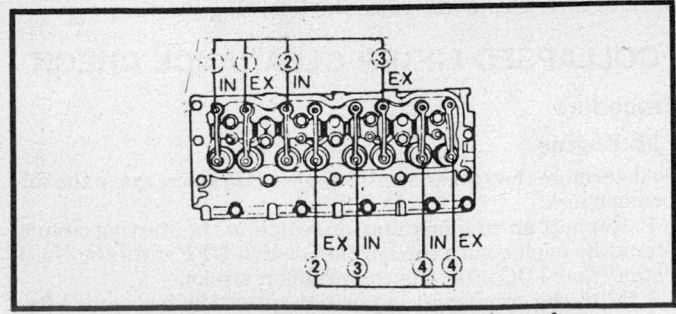

Valve adjustment sequence 2.0L diesel engine

Valve lifter compressor tool

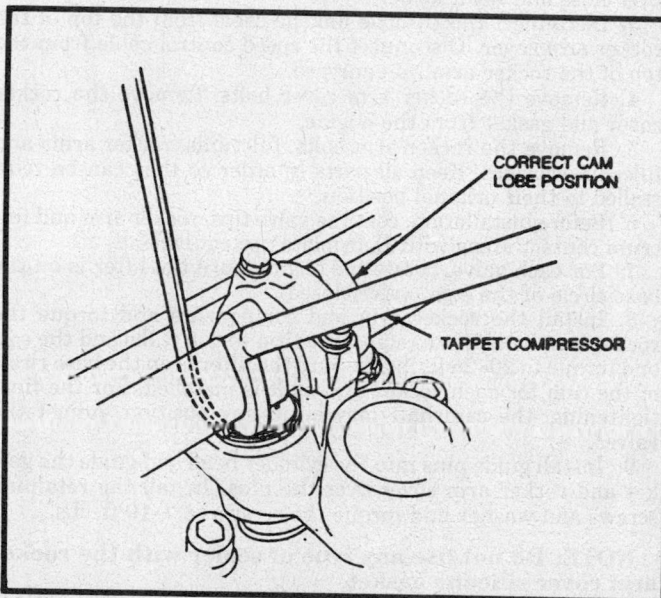

Valve lifter holding tool

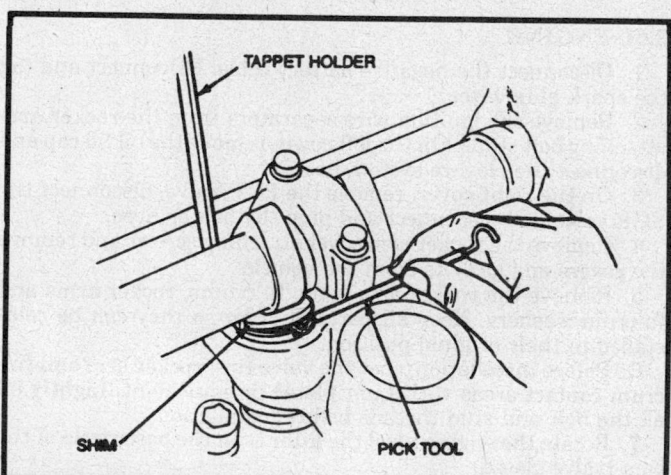

Removing the shim from the valve lifter

10. Rotate the camshaft until the lobe is down and remove the retainer tool.

11. Recheck the valve clearance by repeating the previous steps.

12. Install the valve cover using a new gasket. Tighten the retaining bolts to 5–7 ft. lbs.

3.0L SHO ENGINE

1. Disconnect the negative battery cable.
2. Remove the valve cover.
3. Remove the intake manifold assembly.
4. Install lifter compressor tool T89P–6500–A or equivalent, under the camshaft next to the lobe and rotate it downward to depress the valve lifter.
5. Install valve lifter holding tool T89P–6500–B or equivalent, and remove the compressor tool.
6. Using pick tool T71P–19703–C or equivalent, lift the adjusting shim and remove the shim with a magnet.
7. Determine the size of the shim by the numbers on the bottom face of the shim or by measuring with a micrometer.
8. Install the replacement shim with the numbers down. Make sure the shim is properly seated.
9. Release the lifter holder tool by installing the compressor tool.
10. Repeat the procedure for each valve by rotating the crankshaft as necessary.

VALVE LIFTERS

Removal and Installation

2.0L, 2.3L, 2.5L AND 3.0L ENGINES

1. Disconnect the negative battery cable. Remove the cylinder head and related parts.
2. Using a magnet, remove the lifters. Identify, tag and place the tappets in a rack so they can be installed in the original positions.
3. If the lifters are stuck in their bores by excessive varnish or gum, it may be necessary to use a hydraulic lifter puller tool to remove the lifters. Rotate the lifters back and forth to loosen any gum and varnish which may have formed. Keep the assemblies intact until the are to be cleaned.
4. Install new (or cleaned) hydraulic lifters through the pushrod openings with a magnet.
5. Install the cylinder head and related parts.

3.8L ENGINE

1. Disconnect the negative battery cable. Disconnect the secondary ignition wires at the spark plugs.
2. Remove the plug wire routing clips from mounting studs on the rocker arm cover attaching bolts. Lay plug wires with routing clips toward the front of engine.
3. Remove the upper intake manifold, rocker arm covers and lower intake manifold.
4. Sufficiently loosen each rocker arm fulcrum attaching bolt to allow the rocker arm to be lifted off the pushrod and rotated to one side.
5. Remove the pushrods. The location of each pushrod should be identified and labeled. When engine is assembled, each rod should be installed in its original position.
6. Remove the lifters using a magnet. The location of each lifters should be identified and labeled. When engine is assembled, each lifter should be installed in its original position.

NOTE: If lifters are stuck in bores due to excessive varnish or gum deposits, it may be necessary to use a hydraulic lifter puller tool to aid removal. When using a remover tool, rotate lifter back and forth to loosen it from gum or varnish that may have formed on the tappet.

7. Lightly oil all bolt and stud threads before installation. Using solvent, clean the cylinder head and valve rocker arm cover sealing surfaces.
8. Lubricate each lifter and bore with oil conditioner or heavy engine oil.

9. Install each lifter in bore from which it was removed. If a new tappet(s) is being installed, check new lifter for a free fit in bore.

10. Dip each pushrod end in oil conditioner or heavy engine oil. Install pushrods in their orignial positions.

11. For each valve, rotate crankshaft until lifter rests onto heel (base circle) of camshaft lobe. Position rocker arms over pushrods and install the fulcrums. Initially torque the fulcrum attaching bolts to 44 inch lbs. maximum.

12. Lubricate all rocker arm assemblies a suitable heavy engine oil.

13. Finally torque the fulcrum bolts to 19–25 ft. lbs. For the final tightening, the camshaft may be in any position.

NOTE: Fulcrums must be fully seated in the cylinder head and pushrods must be seated in rocker arm sockets prior to the final tightening.

14. Complete the installation of the lower intake manifold, valve rocker arm covers and the upper intake manifold by reversing the removal procedure.

15. Install the plug wire routing clips and connect wires to the spark plugs.

16. Start the engine and check for oil or coolant leaks.

Valve Rocker Assembly

Removal and Installation

1.9L ENGINE

1. Disconnect the negative battery cable and remove the air cleaner assembly.

2. Remove and tag all necessary vacuum hoses from the rocker cover. Remove the rocker cover from the cylinder head.

3. Remove the rocker cover and gasket from the engine.

4. Remove the rocker arm nuts, fulcrums, rocker arms and fulcrum washers. Keep all parts in order so they can be reinstalled to their original position.

5. Before installation, coat the valve tips, rocker arm and fulcrum contact areas with Lubriplate® or equivalent.

6. Rotate the engine until the lifter is on the base circle of the cam (valve closed).

NOTE: Be sure to turn the engine only in the normal rotation. Backward rotation will cause the camshaft belt to slip or lose teeth, altering the valve timing and causing serious engine damage.

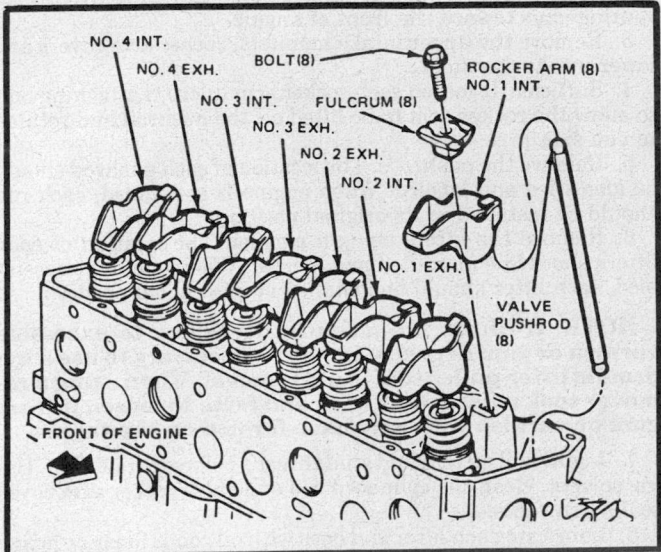

Rocker arm, fulcrum and pushrod removal

7. Install the rocker arm and components and torque the rocker arm nuts to 15–19 ft. lbs. Be sure the lifter is on the base circle of the cam for each rocker arm as it is installed. Adjust the valves.

8. Install guide pins into the cylinder head and guide the gasket and rocker arm cover over the pins. Install the retaining screws and washer and torque the screws to 6–8 ft. lbs.

NOTE: Do not use any type of sealer with the rocker arm cover silicone gasket.

2.3L, 2.5L AND 3.8L ENGINES

1. Disconnect the negative battery cable and remove the air cleaner assembly.

2. Remove and tag all necessary vacuum hoses from the rocker cover. Remove the oil fill cap and set it aside. Disconnect the PCV hose and set it aside.

3. Disconnect the throttle linkage cable from the top of the rocker arm cover. Disconnect the speed control cable from the top of the rocker arm , if equipped.

4. Remove the rocker arm cover bolts. Remove the rocker cover and gasket from the engine.

5. Remove the rocker arm bolts, fulcrums, rocker arms and fulcrum washers. Keep all parts in order so they can be reinstalled to their original position.

6. Before installation, coat the valve tips, rocker arm and fulcrum contact areas with Lubriplate® or equivalent.

7. For each valve, rotate the engine until the lifter is on the base circle of the cam (valve closed).

8. Install the rocker arm and components and torque the rocker arm bolts in two steps, the first to 6–8 ft.lbs and the second torque to 20–26 ft. lbs. Be sure the lifter is on the base circle of the cam for each rocker arm as it is installed. For the final tightening, the camshaft may be in any position. Adjust the valves.

9. Install guide pins into the cylinder head and guide the gasket and rocker arm cover over the pins. Install the retaining screws and washer and torque the screws to 7–10 ft. lbs.

NOTE: Do not use any type of sealer with the rocker arm cover silicone gasket.

3.0L ENGINE

1. Disconnect the negative battery cable. Disconnect and tag the spark plug wires.

2. Remove the ignition wire separators from the rocker arm attaching bolt studs. On the left cover, remove the oil fill cap and disconnect the closure system hose.

3. On the right cover, remove the PCV Valve, disconnect the EGR valve and disconnect and plug the heater hose.

4. Remove the rocker arm cover attaching screws and remove the covers and gaskets from the vehicle.

5. Remove the rocker arm bolts, fulcrums, rocker arms and fulcrum washers. Keep all parts in order so they can be reinstalled to their original position.

6. Before installation, coat the valve tips, rocker arm and fulcrum contact areas with Lubriplate® or equivalent. Lightly oil all the bolt and stud threads before installation.

7. Rotate the engine until the lifter is on the base circle of the cam (valve closed).

8. Install the rocker arm and components and torque the rocker arm fulcrum bolts to 19–29 ft. lbs. Be sure the lifter is on the base circle of the cam for each rocker arm as it is installed. Adjust the valves.

9. Install guide pins into the cylinder head and guide the gaskets and rocker arm covers over the pins. Install the attaching screws and washer and torque the screws to 7–10 ft. lbs. Torque the EGR tube to 25–36 ft. lbs.

NOTE: Apply a bead of RTV silicone sealer or equivalent at the cylinder head to intake manifold rail step (two places per rail) before installing the gasket. Do not use any type of sealer with the silicone (rubber) gasket.

Cylinder Head

Removal and Installation

1.9L ENGINE

NOTE: The engine must be cold before removing the cylinder head, to reduce the possibility of warpage or distortion.

1. Disconnect the negative battery cable. Properly relieve the fuel system pressure.
2. Drain the cooling system and disconnect the heater hose at the fitting located under the intake manifold.
3. Disconnect the radiator upper hose at the cylinder head.
4. Disconnect the wiring terminal from the cooling fan switch.
5. Remove the air cleaner assembly.
6. Remove the PVC hose.
7. Identify, tag and disconnect the required vacuum hoses.
8. Remove the rocker arm cover.
9. Disconnect all accessory drive belts.
10. Remove the crankshaft pulley using the proper puller tool.
11. Remove the timing belt cover.
12. Set the engine No. 1 cylinder to TDC prior to removing the timing belt.
13. Remove the distributor cap and spark plug wires as an assembly.
14. Loosen both belt tensioner attaching bolts using torque wrench adapter T81P-6254-A or equivalent.
15. Secure the belt tensioner as far left as possible.
16. Remove the timing belt.
17. Disconnect the EGR tube at the EGR valve.
18. Disconnect the PVS hose connectors, using Tool T81P-8564-A or equivalent. Label the connectors and set aside.
19. Disconnect the choke cap wire.
20. Disconnect the fuel supply and return lines at the metal connectors, located on the right side of the engine, set rubber lines aside.
21. Disconnect the accelerator cable and if equipped, the speed control cable.
22. Disconnect the altitude compensator, if equipped from the dash panel and place on the heater/AC air intake.

NOTE: Caution should be taken not to damage the altitude compensator.

23. Disconnect the alternator air intake tube and the alternator wiring harness.
24. Remove the alternator and its mounting bracket.
25. If equipped with power steering, remove the thermactor pump drive belt, the pump and the pump mounting bracket.
26. Raise the vehicle and support safely.
27. Disconnect the exhaust system at the exhaust pipe.
28. Lower the vehicle.
29. Remove the cylinder head bolts and washers. Discard the bolts. They cannot be reused.

NOTE: Do not reuse the cylinder head retaining bolts. Use new bolts when installing head.

30. Remove the cylinder head with the exhaust and intake manifolds attached. Discard the cylinder head gasket.

NOTE: Do not lay the cylinder head flat. Damage to the spark plug or gasket contact surfaces may result.

To install:
31. Clean all gasket material from the mating surfaces on the cylinder head and block.

NOTE: Rotate the camshaft until the camshaft gear pointer is aligned with the timing mark on the cylinder head and the camshaft keyway is at the 6 o'clock position. Position the No. 1 piston 90 degrees BTDC (pulley keyway at 9 o'clock position), during the cylinder head installation. After the cylinder head has been installed, rotate the crankshaft to bring No. 1 piston to TDC on its compression stroke. The crankshaft keyway should then be at the 12 o'clock position. With the distributor cap removed, the rotor should be pointing toward the No.1 spark plug tower in the cap. Install the timing belt and proceed with the cylinder head installation.

32. Position the cylinder head gasket on the cylinder block.
33. Install the cylinder head and install new bolts and washers in the following order:
   a. Apply a light coat of engine oil to the threads of the new cylinder head bolts and install the new bolts into the head.
   b. Torque the cylinder head bolts in sequence to 44 ft. lbs.
   c. Loosen the cylinder head bolts approximately 2 turns and then torque then again to 44 ft. lbs. using the same torque sequence.
   d. After setting the torque again, turn the head bolts 90 degrees in sequence and to complete the head bolt installation, turn the head bolts an additional 90 degrees in the same torque sequence.

NOTE: The cylinder head attaching bolts cannot be tightened to the specified torque more than once and must therefore be replaced when installing a cylinder head.

34. Raise the vehicle and support safely.
35. Connect the exhaust system at the exhaust pipe.
36. Lower the vehicle.
37. Install the thermactor pump mounting bracket, pump and drive belt, if removed.

NOTE: Apply Loctite® (or equivalent) to the attaching bolts.

38. Install the alternator mounting bracket and the alternator. Connect the alternator wiring harness and alternator air intake tube.
39. Connect the altitude compensator, if equipped.
40. Connect the accelerator cable and, if equipped, the speed control cable.
41. Connect the fuel supply and return lines at the metal connector, located on the right side of the engine.
42. Connect the choke cap wire. Connect the EGR tube to the EGR valve.
43. Install the timing belt, the timing belt cover and the crankshaft pulley.
44. Install the distributor cap and spark plug wires.
45. Apply a $^{3}/_{16}$ in. bead of sealer to the valve cover flange.
46. Tighten the attaching bolts to 6–8 ft. lbs.
47. Connect the required vacuum hoses.
48. Connect the wiring terminal to the cooling fan switch.
49. Connect the radiator upper hose at the cylinder head.
50. Connect the heater hose to the fitting located below the intake manifold.
51. Fill the cooling system to the proper level and connnect the negative battery cable.
52. Start the engine and check for leaks.
53. After engine has reached operating temperature, check and, if necessary, add coolant.
54. Adjust the ignition timing and connect the distributor vacuum line.

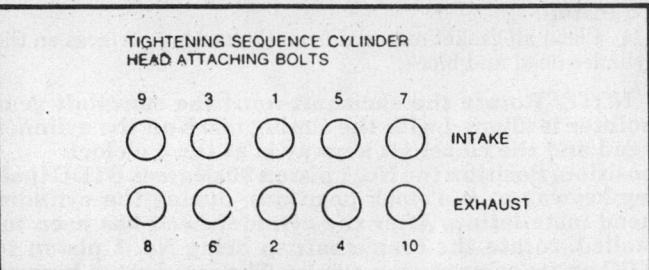

Cylinder head bolt torque sequence 1.9L engine

55. Install the PVS hose.
56. Install the air cleaner assembly.

2.0L DIESEL ENGINE

1. Disconnect the battery ground cable from the battery, which is located in the luggage compartment.
2. Properly relieve the fuel system pressure. Drain the cooling system.
3. Remove the camshaft cover, front and rear timing belt covers, and front and rear timing belts.
4. Raise the vehicle and safely support.
5. Disconnect the muffler inlet pipe at the exhaust manifold. Lower the vehicle.
6. Disconnect the air inlet duct at the air cleaner and intake manifold. Install a protective cover.
7. Disconnect the electrical connectors and vacuum hoses to the temperature sensors located in the thermostat housing.
8. Disconnect the upper and lower coolant hoses, and the upper radiator hose at the thermostat housing.
9. Disconnect and remove the injection lines at the injection pump and nozzles. Cap all lines and fittings.
10. Disconnect the glow plug harness from the main engine harness.
11. Remove the cylinder head bolts in the proper sequence. Remove the cylinder head.
12. Remove the glow plugs. Then remove pre-chamber cups from the cylinder head using a brass drift.
13. Clean the pre-chamber cups, pre-chambers in the cylinder heads and all gasket mounting surfaces on the cylinder head and engine block.
14. Install the pre-chambers in the cylinder heads making sure the locating pins are aligned with the slots provided.
15. Install the glow plugs and tighten to 11–15 ft. lbs. Connect glow plug harness to the glow plugs. Tighten the nuts to 5–7 ft. lbs.

NOTE: Carefully blow out the head bolt threads in the crankcase with compressed air. Failure to thoroughly clean the thread bores can result in incorrect cylinder head torque or possible cracking of the crankcase.

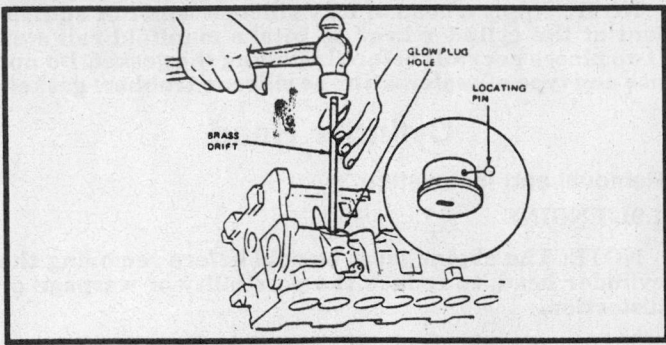

Pre-chamber removal 2.0L diesel engine

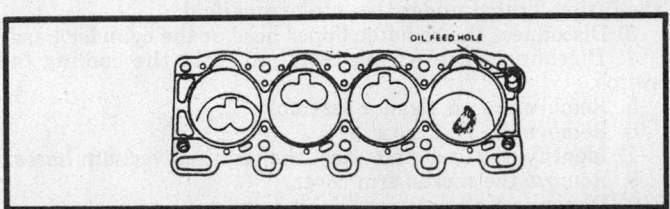

Cylinder head gasket identification 2.0L diesel engine

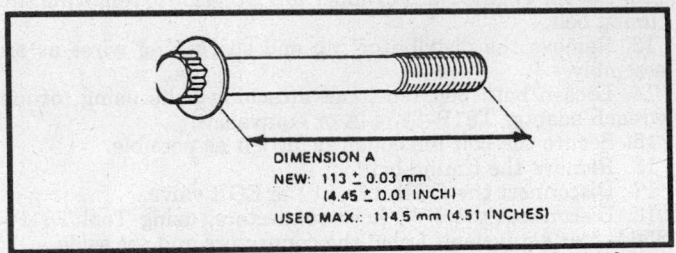

DIMENSION A
NEW: 113 ± 0.03 mm
(4.45 ± 0.01 INCH)
USED MAX.: 114.5 mm (4.51 INCHES)

Cylinder head bolt measurement 2.0L diesel engine

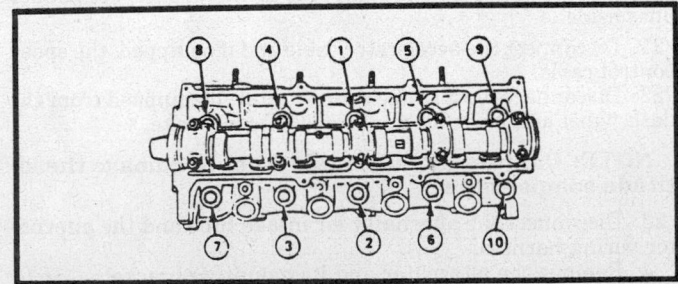

Cylinder head bolt tightening sequence 2.0L diesel engine

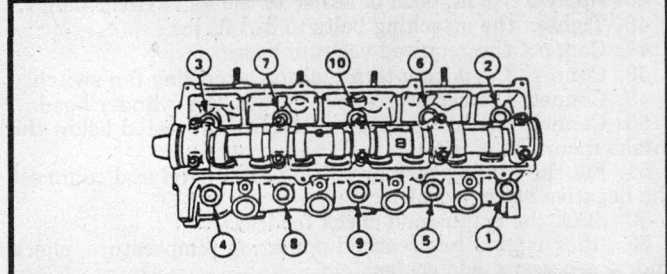

Cylinder head bolt removal 2.0L diesel engine

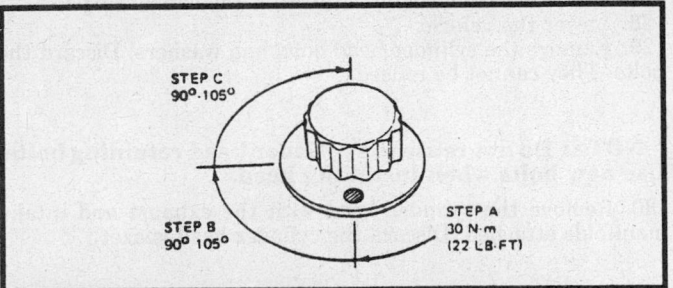

STEP C
90°-105°

STEP B
90° 105°

STEP A
30 N·m
(22 LB·FT)

Cylinder head bolt tightening steps 2.0L diesel engine

16. Position a new cylinder head gasket on the crankcase making sure the cylinder head oil feed hole is not blocked.

17. Measure each cylinder head bolt dimension A. If the measurement is more than 114.5mm (4.51 in.), replace the head bolt. Rotate the camshaft in the cylinder head until the cam lobes for No. 1 cylinder are at the base circle (both valves closed). Then, rotate the crankshaft clockwise until No. 1 piston is halfway up in the cylinder bore toward TDC. This is to prevent contact between the pistons and valves.

18. Install the cylinder head.

NOTE: Before installing the cylinder head bolts, paint a white reference dot on each one, and apply a light coat of engine oil on the bolt threads.

19. Tighten cylinder head bolts as follows:
   a. Tighten bolts in sequence to 22 ft. lbs.
   b. Using the painted reference marks, tighten each bolt in sequence another 90 degrees to 105 degrees.
   c. Repeat Step b by turning the bolts another 90–105 degrees.
20. Connect the glow plug harness to main engine harness.
21. Remove the protective caps and install injection lines to the injection pump and nozzles. Tighten capnuts to 18–20 ft. lbs.
22. Air bleed the system.
23. Connect the upper and lower coolant hoses, and the upper radiator hose to the thermostat housing. Tighten upper coolant hose bolts to 5–7 ft. lbs.
24. Connect the electrical connectors and the vacuum hoses to the temperature sensors in the thermostat housing.
25. Remove the protective cover and install the air inlet duct to the intake manifold and air cleaner.
26. Raise the vehicle and support it safely. Connect the muffler inlet pipe to the exhaust manifold. Tighten nuts to 25–35 ft. lbs.
27. Lower the vehicle.
28. Install and adjust the front timing belt.
29. Install and adjust the rear timing belt.
30. Install the front upper timing belt cover and rear timing belt cover. Tighten the bolts to 5–7 ft. lbs.
31. Check and adjust the valves. Install the valve cover and tighten the bolts to 5–7 ft. lbs.
32. Fill and bleed the cooling system.
33. Check and adjust the injection pump timing.
34. Connect battery ground cable to battery. Run engine and check for oil, fuel and coolant leaks.

2.3L AND 2.5L ENGINES

1. Disconnect the negative battery cable. Drain the cooling system.
2. Remove the air cleaner assembly. Properly relieve the fuel system pressure.
3. Disconnect the heater hose at the fitting located under the intake manifold. Disconnect the upper radiator hose at the cylinder head.
4. Disconnect distributor cap and spark plug wire and remove as an assembly.
5. Remove spark plugs, if necessary.
6. Disconnect and tag required vacuum hoses.
7. Remove dipstick. Disconnect the choke cap wire.
8. Remove rocker cover retaining bolts and remove cover. Disconnect the EGR tube at the EGR valve.
9. Disconnect the fuel supply and return lines at the rubber connections. Disconnect the accelerator cable and speed control cable, if equipped.
10. Loosen the thermactor pump belt pulley. Raise and support the vehicle safely.
11. Disconnect the exhaust system at the exhaust pipe, hose and tube. Lower the vehicle.
12. Remove the cylinder head bolts. Remove the cylinder head and gasket with thermactor pump, exhaust manifold and intake

manifold. On the 2.3L, engine the thermactor pump can be removed before removing the cylinder head.

To install:
13. Clean all gasket material from the mating surface of the cylinder head and block. Position the cylinder head gasket on the cylinder block, using a suitable sealer to retain the gasket.
14. Before installing the cylinder head, thread 2 cylinder head alignment studs, using exhaust manifold alignment studs T84P-6065-A or equivalent through the head bolt holes in the gasket and into the block at opposite corners of the block.
15. Install the cylinder head and cylinder head bolts. Run down several head bolts and remove the 2 guide bolts. Replace them with the remaining head bolts. Torque the cylinder head bolts to 52–59 ft. lbs. and retorque the bolts to 70–76 ft. lbs.

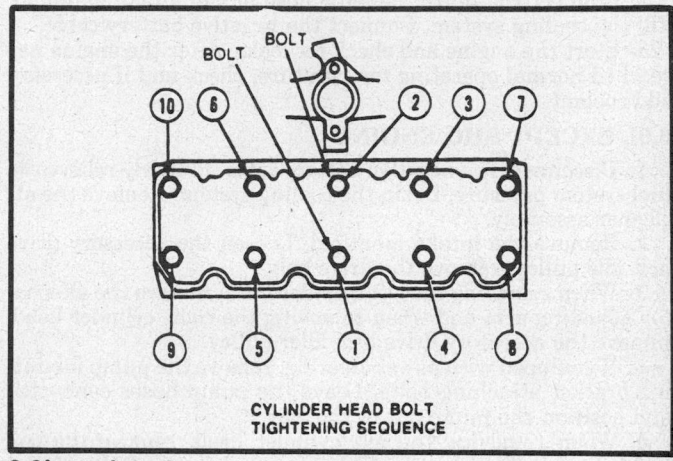

CYLINDER HEAD BOLT
TIGHTENING SEQUENCE

2.3L and 2.5L engine cylinder head bolt torque sequence

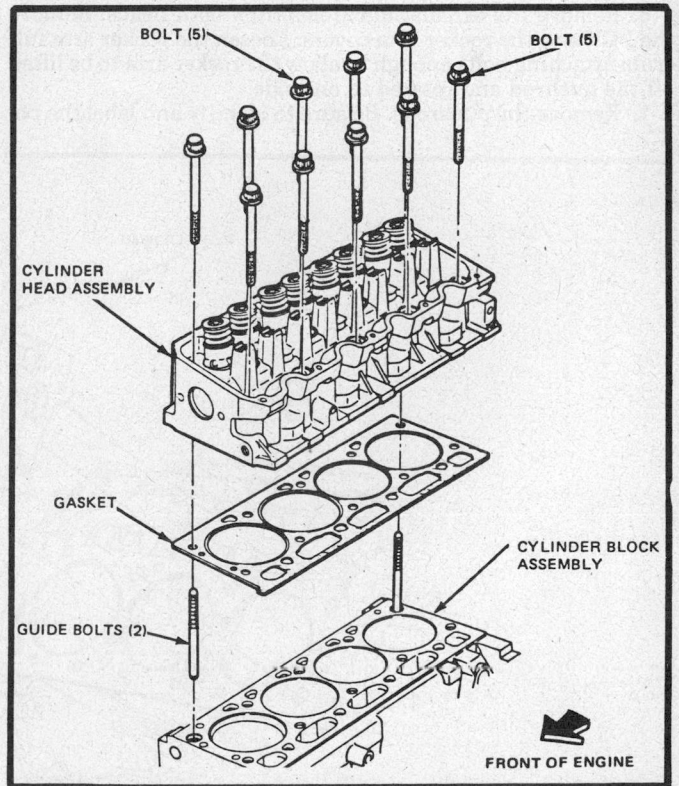

Cylinder head installation 2.3L engine

16. Raise and support the vehicle safely. Connect the exhaust system at the exhaust pipe and hose to metal tube.

17. Lower the vehicle and install the thermactor pump drive belt. Connect the accelerator cable and speed control cable, if equipped.

18. Connect the fuel supply and return lines. Connect the choke cap wire.

19. Connect the EGR tube at the EGR valve. Install the distributor cap and spark plug wires as an assembly . Install the spark plugs, if removed.

20. Connect all accessory drive belts. Install the rocker arm cover.

21. Connect the required vacuum hoses. Install the air cleaner assembly. Connect the electric cooling fan switch at the connector.

22. Connect the upper radiator hose at the intake manifold. Fill the cooling system. Connect the negative battery cable.

23. Start the engine and check for leaks. After the engine has reached normal operating temperature, check and if necessary add coolant.

3.0L EXCEPT SHO ENGINE

1. Disconnect the negative battery cable. Properly relieve the fuel system pressure. Drain the cooling system. Remove the air cleaner assembly.

2. Remove the intake manifold. Loosen the accessory drive belt idle pulley, remove the drive belt.

3. When removing the left cylinder head, remove the alternator adjusting arm and when removing the right cylinder head, remove the accessory drive belt idler pulley.

4. If equipped with power steering, remove the pump mounting bracket attaching bolts. Leave the pump hoses connected and position the pump out of the way.

5. When removing the left cylinder head, remove the coil bracket and dipstick tube. When removing the RH cylinder head, remove the grounding strap throttle cable support bracket.

6. Remove the exhaust manifolds from both heads. Remove the PCV and the rocker arm covers. Loosen the rocker arm fulcrum attaching bolts enough to allow the rocker arm to be lifted off the pushrod and rotated to one side.

7. Remove the pushrods. Be sure to identify and label the position of each pushrod. The rods should be installed in their original position during reassembly.

8. Remove the cylinder head attaching bolts and remove the cylinder heads from the engine. Remove and discard the old cylinder head gaskets.

To install:

9. Lightly oil all bolt and stud bolt threads before installation. Clean the cylinder head, intake manifold, rocker arm cover and cylinder head gasket contact surfaces. If the cylinder head was removed for a cylinder head gasket replacement, check that the flatness of the cylinder head and block gasket surfacers.

NOTE: If the flat surface of the cylinder head is warped, do not plane or grind off more than 0.010 in. If the head is machined past its resurface limit, the head will have to be replaced with a new one.

10. Position new head gaskets on the cylinder block using the dowels in the engine block for alignment. If the dowels are damaged, they must be replaced.

11. Position the cylinder head on the cylinder block. Tighten the cylinder head attaching bolts in 2 steps following the proper torque sequence. The first step is 48–54 ft. lbs. and the second step is 63–80 ft. lbs.

NOTE: When cylinder head attaching bolts have been tightened using the above procedure, it is not necessary to retighten the bolts after extended engine operation. The bolts can be rechecked for tightness if so desired.

12. Dip each pushrod end in oil conditioner or heavy engine oil. Install the pushrods in their original position.

13. Before installation, coat the valve tips, rocker arm and fulcrum contact areas with Lubriplate® or equivalent. Lightly oil all the bolt and stud threads before installation.

14. Rotate the engine until the lifter is on the base circle of the cam (valve closed).

15. Install the rocker arm and components and torque the rocker arm fulcrum bolts to 19–29 ft. lbs. Be sure the lifter is on the base circle of the cam for each rocker arm as it is installed. Adjust the valves.

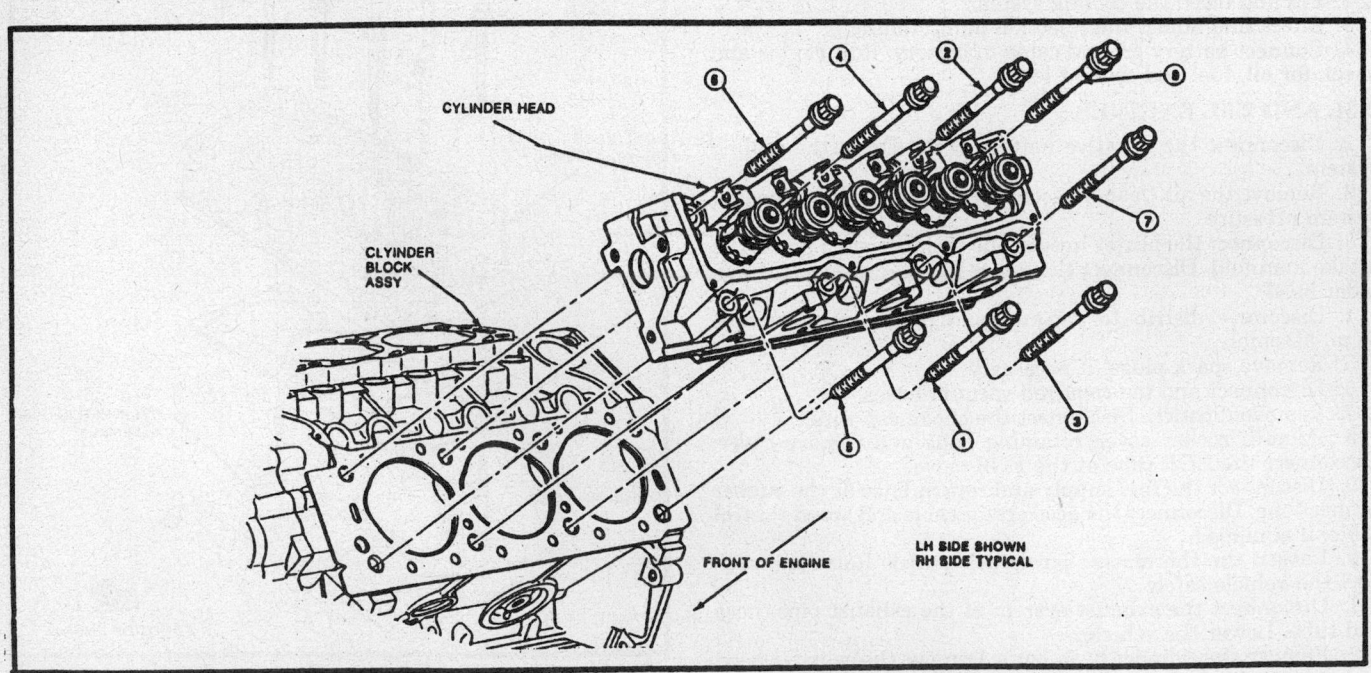

Cylinder head removal and installation—3.0L engine

NOTE: The fulcrums must be fully seated in the cylinder head and the pushrods must be seated in the rocker arm sockets prior to the final tightening.

16. Install the exhaust manifolds, the oil dipstick tube. Install the intake manifold. Complete the installation of the remaining components by reversing the removal procedure.

17. Start the engine and check for leaks.

18. Check and if necessary, adjust the transaxle throttle linkage and speed control. Install the air cleaner outlet tube duct.

3.0L SHO ENGINE

1. Disconnect the negative battery cable.

2. Drain the cooling system. Properly relieve the fuel system pressure.

3. Remove the air cleaner outlet tube.

4. Remove the intake manifold.

5. Loosen the accessory drive belt idlers and remove the drive belts.

6. Remove the upper timing belt cover.

7. Remove the left idler pulley and bracket assembly.

8. Raise the vehicle and support it safely.

9. Remove the right wheel and inner fender splash shield.

10. Remove the crankshaft damper pulley.

11. Remove the lower timing belt cover.

12. Align both camshaft pulley timing marks with the index marks on the upper steel belt cover.

13. Release the tension on the belt by loosening the tensioner nut and rotating the tensioner with a hex head wrench. When tension is released, tighten the nut.

14. Disconnect the crankshaft sensor wiring assembly.

15. Remove the center cover assembly.

16. Remove the timing belt noting the location of the letters **KOA** on the belt. The belt must be installed in the same direction.

17. Remove the valve rocker arm covers.

18. Remove the camshaft timing pulleys.

19. Remove the upper rear and the center rear timing belt covers.

20. If the left cylinder head is being removed, remove the DIS coil bracket and the oil dipstick tube. If the right cylinder head is being removed, remove the coolant outlet hose.

21. Remove the exhaust manifold on the left cylinder head. On the right cylinder head the exhaust manifold must be removed with the head.

22. Remove the cylinder head to block retaining bolts.

23. Remove the cylinder head.

24. Install in the reverse order of removal.

25. Lightly oil all bolt and stud bolt threads before installation.

26. When installing the cylinder head bolts, tighten in 2 steps following the sequence to 37–50 ft. lbs. (49–69 Nm) and then to 62–68 ft. lbs. (83–93 Nm).

3.8L ENGINE

1. Drain the cooling system and disconnect the negative battery cable.

2. Properly relieve the fuel system pressure. Remove the air cleaner assembly including air intake duct and heat tube.

3. Loosen the accessory drive belt idler and remove the drive belt.

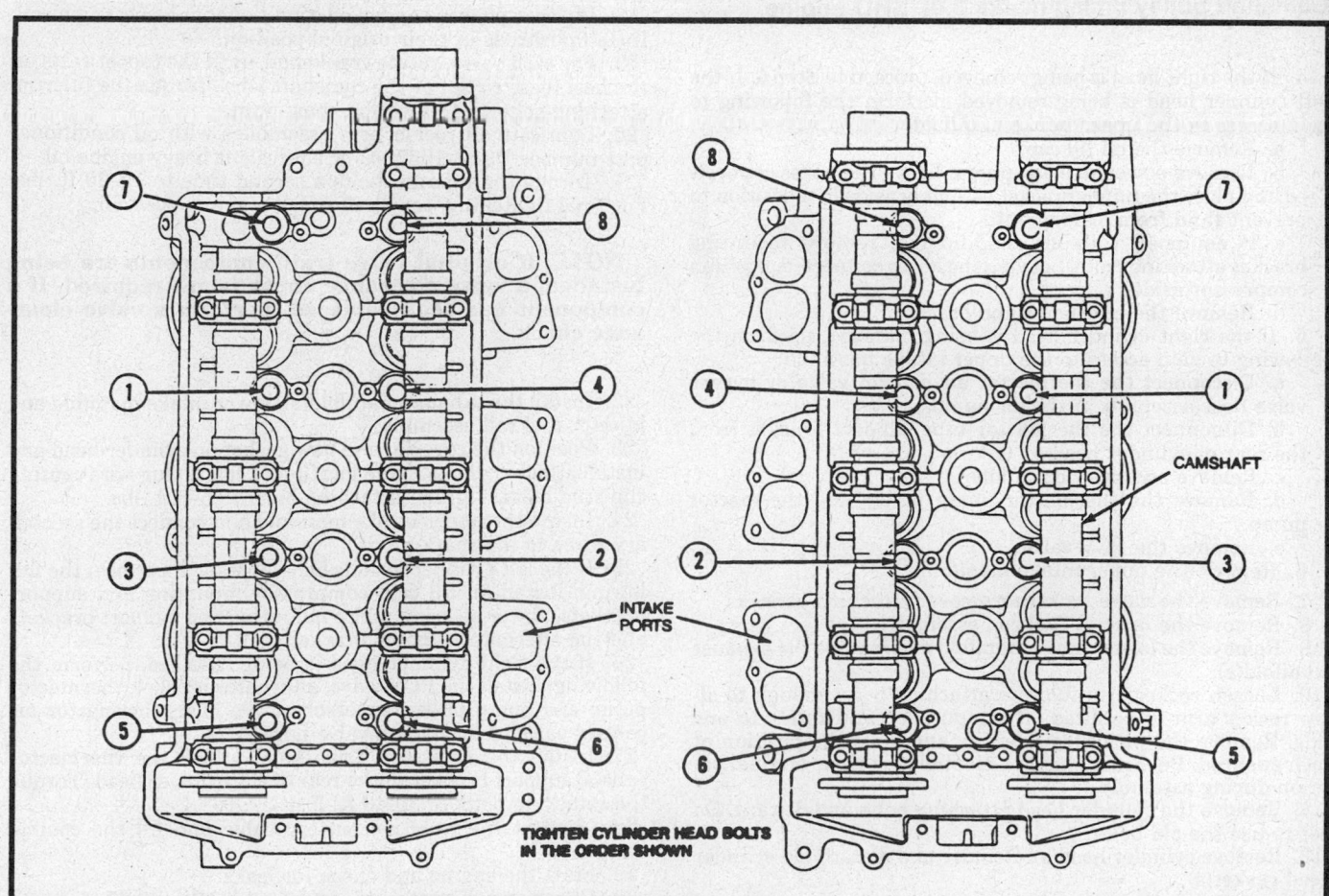

INTAKE PORTS

CAMSHAFT

TIGHTEN CYLINDER HEAD BOLTS IN THE ORDER SHOWN

Cylinder head bolt tightening sequence 3.0L SHO engine

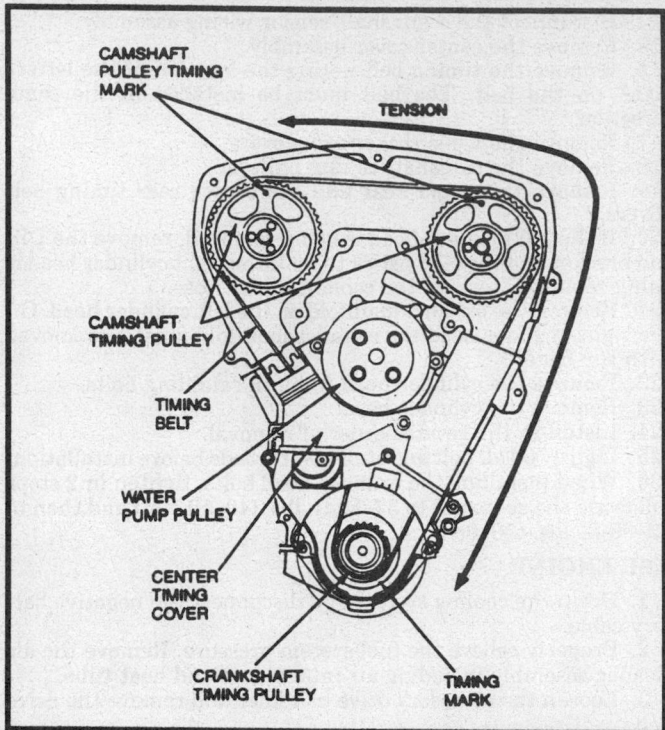

Camshaft pulley timing marks 3.0L SHO engine

4. If the right head is being removed, proceed to Step 5. If the left cylinder head is being removed, perform the following to gain access to the upper intake manifold:

    a. Remove the oil fill cap.

    b. Remove power steering pump. Leave the hoses connected and place the pump/bracket assembly aside in a position to prevent fluid from leaking out.

    c. If equipped with air conditioning, remove mounting bracket attaching bolts. Leaving the hoses connected, position compressor aside.

    d. Remove the alternator and bracket.

5. If the right cylinder head is being removed, perform the following to gain access to the upper intake manifold:

    a. Disconnect the thermactor air control valve or bypass valve hose assembly at the air pump.

    b. Disconnect the thermactor tube support bracket from the rear of cylinder head.

    c. Remove accessory drive idler.

    d. Remove the thermactor pump pulley and thermactor pump.

    e. Remove the PCV valve.

6. Remove the upper intake manifold.

7. Remove the valve rocker arm cover attaching screws.

8. Remove the injector fuel rail assembly.

9. Remove the lower intake manifold and remove the exhaust manifold(s).

10. Loosen rocker arm fulcrum attaching bolts enough to allow rocker arm to be lifted off the pushrod and rotate to one side. Remove the pushrods. Identify and label the position of each pushrod. Pushrods should be installed in their original position during assembly.

11. Remove the cylinder head attaching bolts and discard. Do not re-use the old bolts.

12. Remove cylinder head(s). Remove and discard old cylinder head gasket(s).

To install:

13. Lightly oil all bolt threads before installation.

14. Clean cylinder head, intake manifold, valve rocker arm cover and cylinder head gasket contact surfaces. If cylinder head was removed for a cylinder head gasket replacement, check flatness of cylinder head and block gasket surfaces.

15. Position the new head gasket(s) onto cylinder block using dowels for alignment. Position cylinder head(s) onto block.

16. Apply a thin coating of pipe sealant with Teflon® to threads of short cylinder head bolts (nearest to the exhaust manifold). Do not apply sealant to the long bolts. Install cylinder head bolts (8 each side).

NOTE: Always use new cylinder head bolts to ensure a leak-tight assembly. Torque retention with used bolts can vary, which may result in coolant or compression leakage at the cylinder head mating surface area.

17. Tighten cylinder head attaching bolts the following sequence:

    Step 1—37 ft. lbs.

    Step 2—45 ft. lbs.

    Step 3—52 ft. lbs.

    Step 4—59 ft. lbs.

    Step 5—Back-off each attaching bolt 2 to 3 turns

    Step 6—Repeat Steps 1–4

NOTE: When cylinder head attaching bolts have been tightened using the above procedure, it is not necessary to retighten bolts after extended engine operation. However, bolts can be checked for tightness if desired.

18. Dip each pushrod end in oil conditioner or heavy engine oil. Install pushrods in their original position.

19. For each valve, rotate crankshaft until the tappet rests on the heel (base circle) of the camshaft lobe. Torque the fulcrum attaching bolts to 43 inch lbs. maximum.

20. Lubricate all rocker arm assemblies with oil conditioner part number D9AZ-19579-C or equivalent heavy engine oil.

21. Torque the fulcrum bolts a second time to 19–25 ft. lbs. For final tightening, camshaft may be in any position.

NOTE: If original valve train components are being installed, a valve clearance check is not required. If a component has been replaced, perform a valve clearance check.

22. Install the exhaust manifold(s), lower intake manifold and injector fuel rail assembly.

23. Position the cover(s) and new gasket on cylinder head and install attaching bolts. Note location of spark plug wire routing clip stud bolts. Tighten attaching bolts to 6–8 ft. lbs.

24. Install the upper intake manifold and connect the secondary wires to the spark plugs.

25. If the left cylinder head is being installed, perform the following: install oil fill cap, compressor mounting and support brackets, power steering pump mounting and support brackets and the alternator/support bracket.

26. If the right cylinder head is being installed, perform the following: install the PCV valve, alternator bracket, thermactor pump and pump pulley, accessory drive idler, thermactor air control valve or air bypass valve hose.

27. Install the accessory drive belt. Attach the thermactor tube(s) support bracket to the rear of the cylinder head. Torque the attaching bolts to 30-40 ft. lbs.

28. Connect the negative battery cable and fill the cooling system.

29. Start the engine and check for leaks.

30. Check and, if necessary, adjust curb idle speed.

31. Install the air cleaner assembly including air intake duct and heat tube.

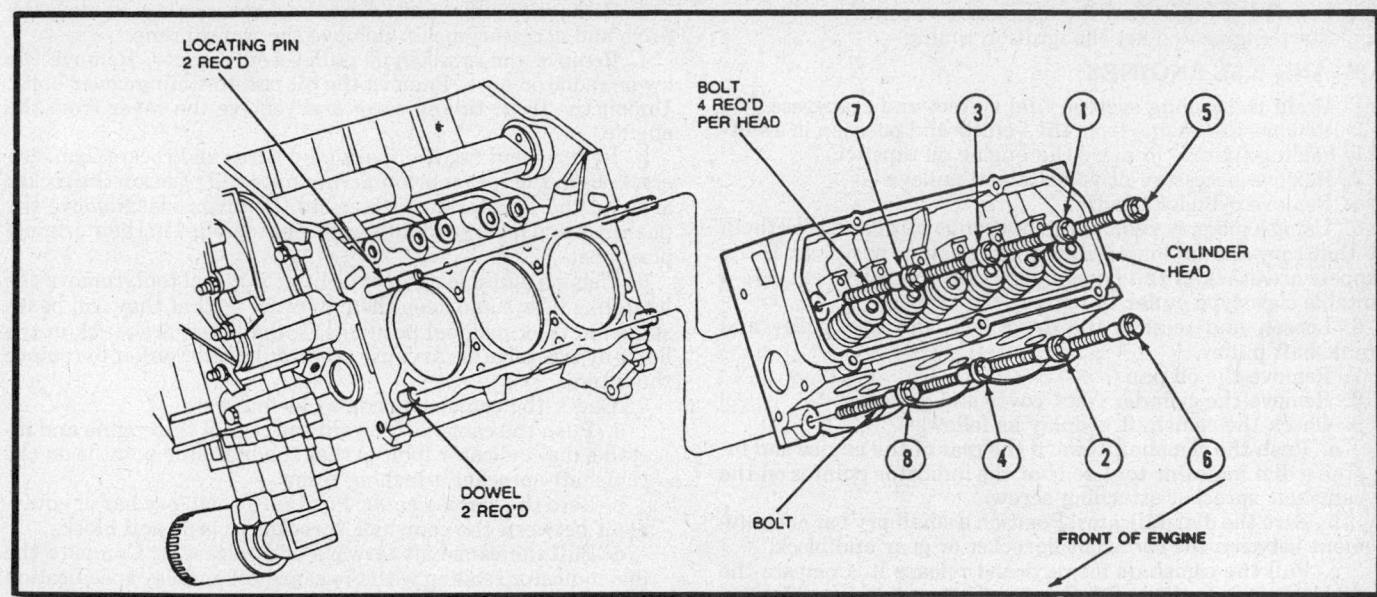

Cylinder head assembly with bolt torque sequence—3.8L engines

Camshaft

Removal and Installation

1.9L ENGINE

1. Disconnect the negative battery cable.
2. Properly relieve the fuel system pressure. Remove the air cleaner and PCV hose.
3. Remove the accessory drive belts and crankshaft pulley.
4. Remove the timing belt cover and valve cover.
5. Set the engine No. 1 cylinder at TDC prior to removing timing belt.

NOTE: Make sure the crankshaft is positioned at TDC and do not turn the crankshaft until the timing belt is installed.

6. Remove rocker arms and lifters as follows:
   a. Remove hex flange nuts.
   b. Remove fulcurms.
   c. Remove rocker arms.
   d. Remove fulcrum washer.
   e. Remove lifters.
7. Remove the distributor assembly.
8. Loosen both timing belt tensioner attaching bolts using torque wrench adapter or equivalent.
9. Remove timing belt.
10. Remove the camshaft sprocket, key and thrust plate.
11. Remove the fuel pump.
12. Remove the ignition coil and coil bracket.
13. Remove the camshaft through the back of the head toward the transaxle.
14. Inspect camshaft seal. Replace the seal if it shows any signs of wear or damage.

To install:

15. Thoroughly coat the camshaft bearing journals, cam lobe surfaces and thrust plate groove with a suitable lubricant compound.
16. Install camshaft through the rear of the cylinder head. Rotate camshaft during installation.
17. Install the camshaft thrust plate. Tighten attaching bolts to 7–11 ft. lbs.
18. Align and install the cam sprocket over the cam key. Install

attaching washer and bolt. While holding camshaft stationary, tighten the bolt to 37–46 ft. lbs.
19. Install the timing belt.
20. Install the timing belt cover.
21. Install the fuel pump.
22. Install the rocker arm assembly as follows:

NOTE: Replace used hex flange nuts with new ones. Lubricate all the parts with a heavy engine oil before installation.

   a. Install the lifters.
   b. Install the fulcrum washers.
   c. Install the rocker arms.
   d. Install the fulcrums.
   e. Install new rocker arm stud hex flange nuts. Tighten to 15–19 ft. lbs.
23. Install the distributor assembly.
24. Apply a $3/16$ in. bead of sealer to the valve cover flange.

NOTE: Make sure the surfaces on the cylinder head and valve cover are clean and free of sealant material.

25. Install the rocker arm cover attaching bolts and studs. Tighten bolts and studs to 6–8 ft. lbs.

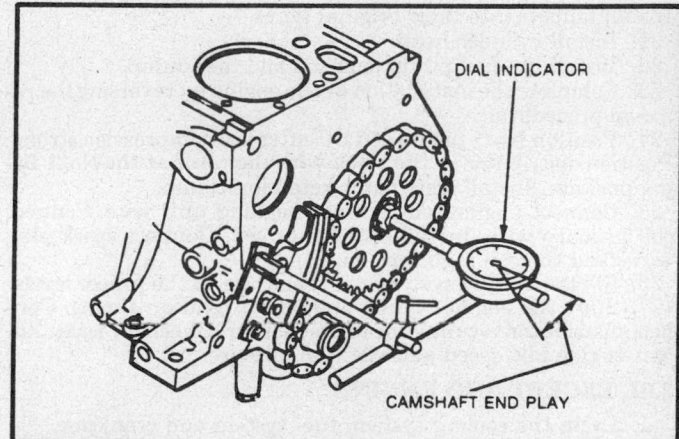

Checking the camshaft end-play

26. Install PCV hose and the air cleaner assembly.

27. Start engine and set the ignition timing.

2.3L AND 2.5L ENGINES

1. Drain the cooling system, fuel system and crankcase.

2. Remove the engine from the vehicle and position in a suitable holding fixture. Remove the engine oil dipstick.

3. Remove necessary drive belts and pulleys.

4. Remove cylinder head.

5. Using a magnet, remove the hydraulic lifter and label them so that they can be installed in their original positions. If the tappets are stuck in the bores by excessive varnish, etc., use a suitable claw-type puller to remove the tappets.

6. Loosen and remove the drive belt, fan and pulley and crankshaft pulley.

7. Remove the oil pan.

8. Remove the cylinder front cover and gasket.

9. Check the camshaft endplay as follows:

   a. Push the camshaft toward the rear of the engine and install a dial indicator tool, so that the indicator point is on the camshaft sprocket attaching screw.

   b. Zero the dial indicator. Position a small pry bar or equivalent between the camshaft sprocket or gear and block.

   c. Pull the camshaft forward and release it. Compare the dial indicator reading with the camshaft endplay specification of 0.009 in.

   d. If the camshaft endplay is over the amount specified, replace the thrust plate.

10. Remove the fuel pump, gasket and fuel pump pushrod.

11. Remove the timing chain, sprockets and timing chain tensioner.

12. Remove camshaft thrust plate. Carefully remove the camshaft by pulling it toward the front of the engine. Use caution to avoid damaging bearings, journals and lobes.

To install:

13. Clean and inspect all parts before installation.

14. Lubricate camshaft lobes and journals with heavy engine oil. Carefully slide the camshaft through the bearings in the cylinder block.

15. Install the thrust plate. Tighten attaching bolts to 6–9 ft. lbs.

16. Install the timing chain, sprockets and timing chain tensioner.

17. Install the cylinder front cover and crankshaft pulley.

18. Clean the oil pump inlet tube screen, oil pan and cylinder block gasket surfaces. Prime oil pump by filling the inlet opening with oil and rotate the pump shaft until oil emerges from the outlet tube. Install oil pump, oil pump inlet tube screen and oil pan.

19. Install the accessory drive belts and pulleys.

20. Lubricate the lifters and lifter bores with heavy engine oil. Install tappets into their original bores.

21. Install cylinder head.

22. Install the fuel pump pushrod and fuel pump.

23. Complete the installation of the engine by reversing the removal procedure.

24. Position No. 1 piston at TDC after the compression stroke. Position distributor in the block with the rotor at the No. 1 firing position. Install distributor retaining clamp.

25. Connect engine temperature sending unit wire. Connect coil primary wire. Install distributor cap. Connect spark plug wires and the coil high tension lead.

26. Fill the cooling system and crankcase to the proper levels.

27. Start the engine. Check and adjust ignition timing. Connect distributor vacuum line to distributor. Check for leaks. Adjust engine idle speed and idle fuel mixture.

3.0L EXCEPT SHO ENGINE

1. Drain the cooling system, fuel system and crankcase.

2. Remove the engine from the vehicle and position in a suitable holding fixture.

3. Remove the idler pulley and bracket assembly. Remove the drive and accessory belts. Remove the water pump.

4. Remove the crankshaft pulley and damper. Remove the lower radiator hose. Remove the oil pan to timing cover bolts. Unbolt the front timing cover and remove the cover from the engine.

5. Remove and tag the spark plug wires and rocker arm covers. Loosen the rocker arm fulcrum nuts and position the rocker arms to the side for easy access to the pushrods. Remove the pushrods and label so that they may be installed in their original positions.

6. Using a suitable magnet or lifter removal tool, remove the hydraulic lifters and keep them in order so that they can be installed in their original positions. If the lifters are stuck in the bores by excessive varnish use a hydraulic lifter puller to remove the lifters.

7. Check the camshaft endplay as follows:

   a. Push the camshaft toward the rear of the engine and install a dial indicator tool, so that the indicator point is on the camshaft sprocket attaching screw.

   b. Zero the dial indicator. Position a small pry bar or equivalent between the camshaft sprocket or gear and block.

   c. Pull the camshaft forward and release it. Compare the dial indicator reading with the camshaft endplay specification of 0.009 in.

   d. If the camshaft endplay is over the amount specified, replace the thrust plate.

8. Remove the timing chain and sprockets.

9. Remove the camshaft thrust plate. Carefully remove the camshaft by pulling it toward the front of the engine. Remove it slowly to avoid damaging the bearings, journals and lobes.

To install:

10. Clean and inspect all parts before installation.

11. Lubricate camshaft lobes and journals with heavy engine oil. Carefully insert the camshaft through the bearings in the cylinder block.

12. Install the thrust plate.

13. Install the timing chain and sprockets. Check the camshaft sprocket bolt for blockage of drilled oil passages prior to installation.

14. Install the front timing cover and crankshaft damper and pulley. Install the water pump as previously outlined.

15. Lubricate the lifters and lifter bores with a heavy engine oil. Install the lifters into their original bores. Install the cylinder head throttle body, intake manifold, valve rocker arm, pushrods and rocker arm covers.

16. Install the accessory drive belts and pulleys. Complete the installation of the engine by reversing the removal procedure.

17. Install the spark plug wires. Fill and the cooling system and crankcase to the proper level.

18. Start the engine. Check and adjust the ignition timing and engine idle speed as necessary. Check for leaks of any kind.

3.0L SHO ENGINE

1. Disconnect the negative battery cable. Properly relieve the fuel system pressure.

2. Set the engine on TDC on No. 1 cylinder.

3. Remove the intake manifold assembly.

4. Remove the timing cover and belt.

5. Remove the valve rocker arm covers.

6. Remove the camshaft pulleys, noting the location of the dowel pins.

7. Remove the upper rear timing belt cover.

8. Uniformly loosen the camshaft bearing caps.

NOTE: If the camshaft bearing caps are not uniformly loosened, camshaft damage may result.

9. Remove the bearing caps.

10. Remove the camshaft chain tensioner mounting bolts.

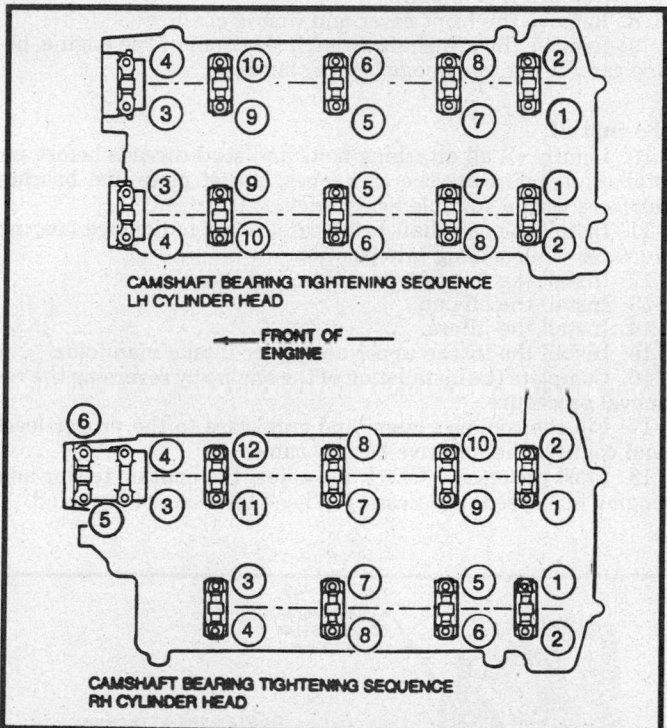

Aligning the chain with the timing marks 3.0L SHO engine

Camshaft bearing tightening sequence 3.0L SHO engine

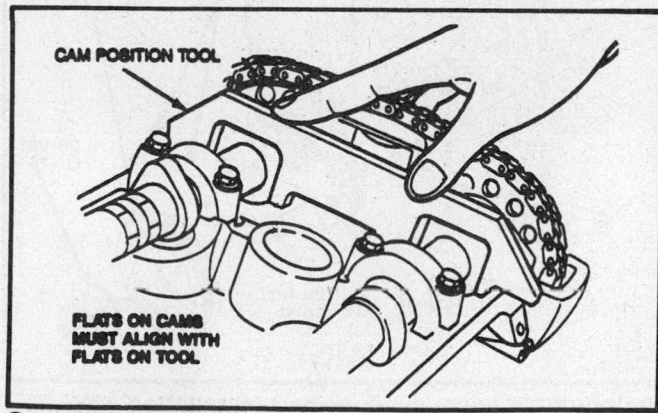

Camshaft positioning tool

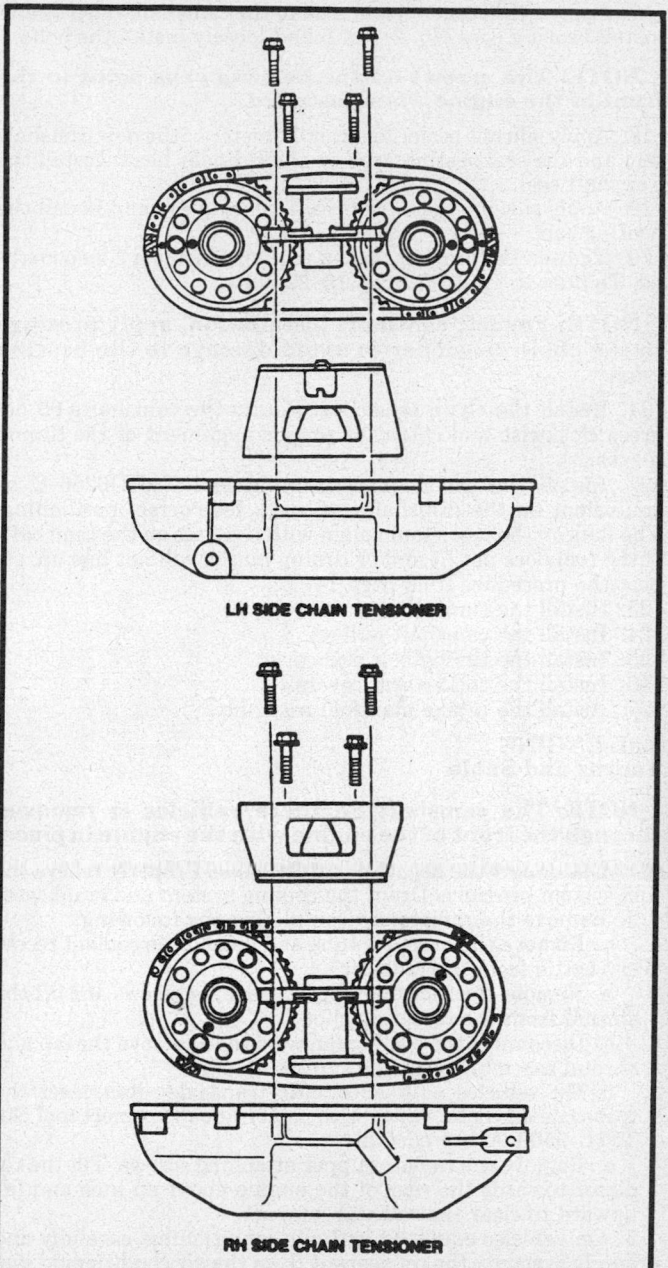

Installing the chain tensioners 3.0L SHO engine

11. Remove the camshafts together with the chain and tensioner.

12. Remove and discard the camshaft oil seal.

13. Remove the chain sprocket from the camshaft.

14. When installing the camshafts, align the timing marks on the chain sprockets with the camshaft and install the sprockets. Tighten the bolts to 10–13 ft. lbs. (14–18 Nm).

15. Install the chain over the camshaft sprockets. Align the white painted link with the timing mark on the sprocket.

16. Rotate the camshafts 60 degrees counterclockwise. Set the chain tensioner between the sprockets and install the camshafts on the cylinder head.

NOTE: The left and right chain tensioners are not interchangeable.

17. Apply a thin coat of engine oil to the camshaft journals and install bearing caps No. 2–No. 5 and loosely install the bolts.

NOTE: The arrows on the bearing caps point to the front of the engine when installed.

18. Apply silicone sealer to outer diameter of the new camshaft seal and the seal seating area on the cylinder head. Install the camshaft seal.

19. Apply silicone sealer the No. 1 bearing cap and install the bearing cap.

20. Tighten the bearing caps in sequence using a 2 step method. Tighten to 12–16 ft. lbs. (16–22 Nm).

NOTE: For left camshaft installation, apply pressure to the chain tensioner to avoid damage to the bearing caps.

21. Install the chain tensioner. Rotate the camshafts 60 degrees clockwise and check for proper alignment of the timing marks.

22. Install the camshaft positioning tool T89P–6256–C or equivalent on the camshafts to check for correct positioning. The flats on the tool should align with the flats on the camshaft. If the tool does not fit and/or timing marks will not line up, repeat the procedure from Step 14.

23. Install the timing belt rear cover.
24. Install the camshaft pulleys.
25. Install the timing belt and cover.
26. Install the rocker arm covers.
27. Install the intake manifold assembly.

3.8L ENGINE
Taurus and Sable

NOTE: The camshaft on these vehicles is removed through the front of the engine with the engine in place.

1. Disconnect the negative battery cable. Properly relieve the fuel system pressure. Drain the cooling system and crankcase.

2. Remove the radiator by completing the following:

   a. Remove the overflow tube and detach the coolant recovery bottle from the radiator.

   b. Remove the 2 shroud upper attaching screws and lift the shroud from the retaining clips.

   c. Disconnect the cooling fan wires and remove the fan and shroud assembly from the vehicle.

   d. On vehicles with automatic transaxle, disconnect the transaxle oil cooling lines with cooler line disconnect tool No. T82L–9500–AH or equivalent.

   e. Remove the radiator upper attaching screws. Tilt the radiator towards the rear of the engine about an inch and lift upward to clear the radiator support.

3. On vehicles equipped with air conditioning, carefully and properly evacuate the refrigerant from the air conditioning system. Disconnect the refrgerant lines from the right side of the radiator by undoing the spring lock couplings. Unbolt and remove the condenser from the radiator support.

4. Remove the grille.
5. Remove the intake manifold.
6. Remove the valve covers, rocker arms, pushrods and lifters.
7. Remove the front timing cover and timing chain.
8. Withdraw the camshaft through the front of the engine being careful not to damage the the bearing surfaces.

To install:
9. Lubricate the cam lobes, thrust plate and bearing surfaces with a suitable heavy engine oil prior to installation.
10. Insert the camshaft into the front of the engine in the manner as it was removed being careful not to damage the bearing surfaces.
11. Install the front cover and timing chain.
12. Install the oil pan.
13. Install the lifters.

14. Install the intake manifolds.
15. Install the grille.
16. Complete the installlation of the condenser and radiator by reversing the removal procedure.
17. Fill the cooling system and crankcase to the proper level and connect the negative battery cable.
18. Start the engine. Check and adjust the ignition timing and engine idle speed as necessary. Check for leaks of any kind.

Continental

1. Disconnect the negative battery cable.
2. Properly relieve the fuel system pressure.
3. Drain the cooling system and crankcase.
4. Remove the engine from the vehicle and position in a suitable holding fixture.
5. Remove the intake manifold.
6. Remove the valve covers, rocker arms, pushrods and lifters.
7. Remove the oil pan.
8. Remove the front cover and timing chain.
9. Remove the camshaft through the front of the engine, being careful not to damage bearing surfaces.

To install:
10. Lightly oil all attaching bolts and stud threads before installation. Lubricate the cam lobes, thrust plate and bearing surfaces with a suitable heavy engine oil.
11. Install the camshaft being careful not to damage bearing surfaces while sliding into position.
12. Install the front cover and timing chain.
13. Install the oil pan.
14. Install the lifters.
15. Install the intake upper and lower intake manifolds.
16. Complete the installation of the engine by reversing the removal procedure.
17. Fill the cooling system and crankcase to the proper level and connect the negative battery cable.
18. Start the engine. Check and adjust the ignition timing and engine idle speed as necessary. Check for leaks of any kind.

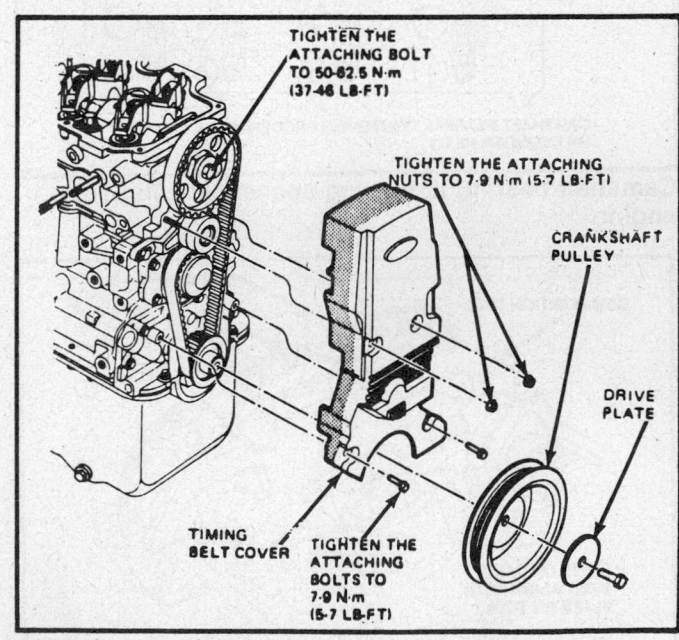

Timing chain cover removal and installation 1.9L engine

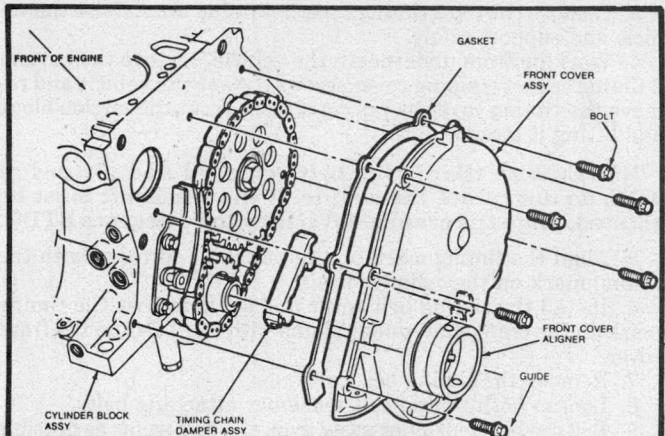

Front cover removal and installation—2.3L and 2.5L engines

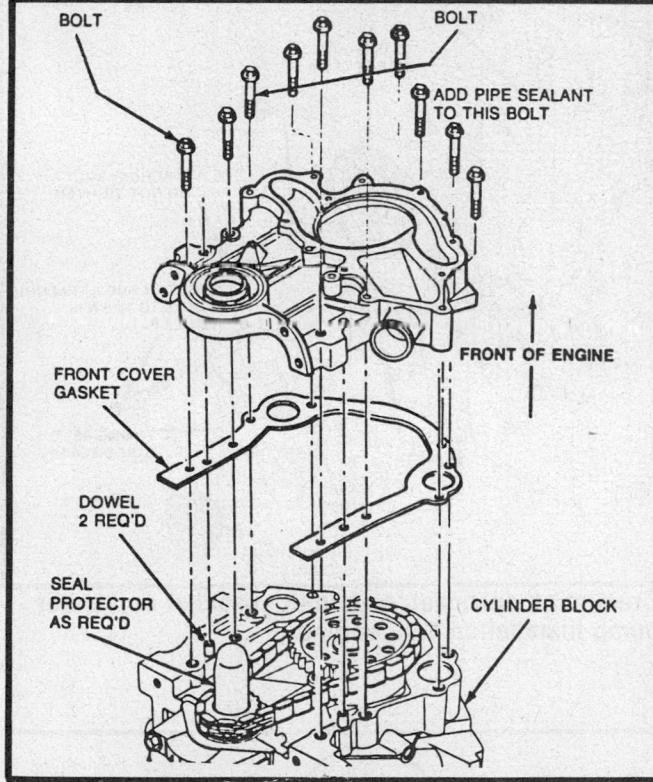

Front cover removal and installation—3.0L engine

Timing Case Cover/Oil Seal

Removal and Installation

1.9L ENGINE

1. Disconnect the negative battery cable.
2. Remove the accessory drive belts.
3. Remove the timing belt cover.
4. Remove the crankshaft front seal. Coat the new seal with clean engine oil.
5. Install the crankshaft front seal using a suitable seal installer tool.
6. Adjust the drive belt tension and connect the negative battery cable.

2.3L AND 2.5L ENGINES

NOTE: **The removal and installation of the front cover oil seal on these engines can only be accomplished with the engine removed from the vehicle.**

1. Remove the engine from the vehicle and position in a suitable holding fixture.
2. Remove bolt and washer at crankshaft pulley.
3. Remove the crankshaft pulley.
4. Remove the front cover oil seal.
5. Coat a new seal with grease. Install and drive the seal until it is fully seated. Check the seal after installation to be sure the spring is properly positioned in the seal.
6. Install crankshaft pulley, attaching bolt and washer. Torque the crankshaft pulley bolt to 140–170 ft. lbs.

3.0L EXCEPT SHO ENGINE

1. Disconnect the negative battery cable and loosen the accessory drive belts.
2. Raise and the front of the vehicle and support safely and remove the right front wheel.
3. Remove the pulley-to-damper attaching bolts. Disengage the accessory drive belts and remove the crankshaft pulley.
4. Remove the damper from the crankshaft using a damper removal tool.
5. Pry the seal from the timing cover with a suitable tool and be careful not to damage the front cover and crankshaft.

NOTE: **Before installation, inspect the front cover and shaft seal surface of the crankshaft damper for damage, nicks, burrs or other roughness which may cause the new seal to fail. Service or replace components as necessary.**

6. Lubricate the seal lip with clean engine oil and install the seal using a seal installer tool.
7. Coat the crankshaft damper sealing surface with clean engine oil. Apply RTV to the keyway of the damper prior to installation. Install the damper using a damper seal installer tool.
8. Position the crankshaft pulley and install the attaching bolts. Torque the attaching bolts to 19–28 ft. lbs.
9. Position the drive belt over the crankshaft pulley. Check the drive belt for proper routing and engagement in the pulleys.
10. Reconnect the negative battery cable and start the engine and check for oil leaks.

3.0L SHO ENGINE

NOTE: **The front cover on the 3.0L SHO engine is made up of 3 sections.**

1. Disconnect the negative battery cable.
2. Remove the left idler pulley and bracket assembly.
3. Remove the drive and accessory belts.
4. Remove the right front wheel and the inner fender panel splash panel.
5. Disconnect the electrical connector from the ignition module.
6. Loosen the hose clamps and remove the bolts from the intake connector tube and remove the tube.
7. Remove the upper timing belt cover.
8. Remove the crankshaft damper using the proper puller tool.
9. Remove the lower timing belt cover.
10. Disconnect the crankshaft sensor wire assembly and position it out of the way.
11. Remove the center timing belt cover.
12. Install in the reverse order of removal.

3.8L ENGINE

1. Disconnect the negative battery cable.
2. On Taurus and Sable, remove the fan shroud attaching screws and position the shroud back over the fan.

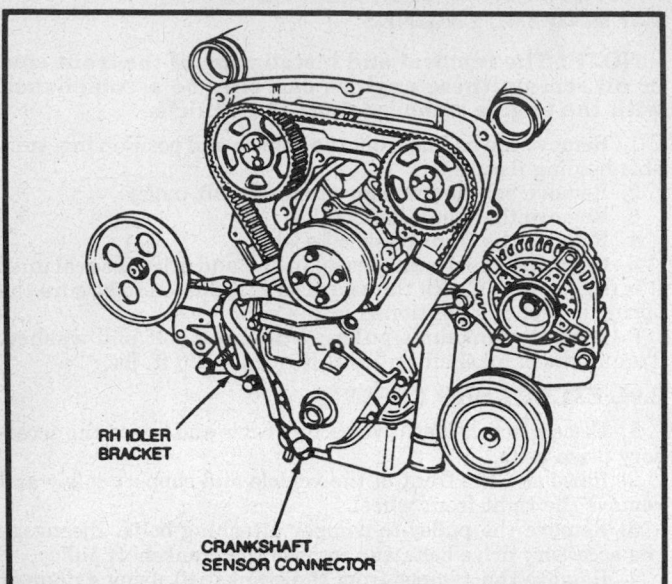

Center and lower timing covers 3.0L SHO engine

3. On Tarus and Sable, unbolt the fan clutch assembly and remove.

4. Loosen the accessory drive belt idler.

5. Raise the vehicle and support safely.

6. Disengage the accessory drive belt and remove crankshaft pulley.

7. Remove the crankshaft damper.

8. Remove the seal from the front cover with a suitable prying tool. Use care to prevent damage to front cover and crankshaft.

To install:

NOTE: Inspect the front cover and crankshaft damper for damage, nicks, burrs or other roughness which may cause the seal to fail. Service or replace components as necessary.

9. Lubricate the seal lip with clean engine oil and install the seal using suitable seal installer.

10. Lubricate the seal surface on the damper with clean engine oil. Install damper and pulley assembly. Install the damper attaching bolt and torque to 103–132 ft. lbs.

11. Position accessory drive belt over crankshaft pulley.

12. Lower the vehicle.

13. Check accessory drive belt for proper routing and engagement in the pulleys. Adjust the drive belt tension.

14. On Taurus and Sable, install the fan/clutch assembly and reposition the fan shroud with the attaching screws.

15. Connect the negative battery cable. Start the engine and check for leaks.

Timing Gears or Chain or Belt

TIMING BELT

Removal and Installation

1.9L ENGINE

1. Disconnect the negative battery cable. Remove all the drive belts.

2. Remove the alternator, if necessary to allow enough room to reach the top cover retaining bolts. Position the A/C compressor out of the way, if equipped to allow enough room to reach the bottom cover retainer bolts.

3. Remove the top 2 timing cover retaining nuts. Raise the vehicle and support safely.

4. Working from underneath the vehicle, remove the bottom 2 timing cover retaining cover screws. Lower the vehicle and remove the timing cover by prying it loose from the engine block and lifting it straight out.

NOTE: With the timing belt removed and pistons at TDC, do not rotate the engine. If the camshaft must be rotated, align the crankshaft pulley to 90 degrees BTDC.

5. Align the timing mark on the camshaft sprocket with the timing mark on the cylinder head.

6. Install the timing belt cover and confirm that the timing mark on the crankshaft pulley aligns with the **TDC** on the front cover.

7. Remove the timing belt cover.

8. Loosen both timing belt tensioner attaching bolts.

9. Pry the belt tensioner away from the belt as far as possible and tighten 1 of the tensioner attaching bolts.

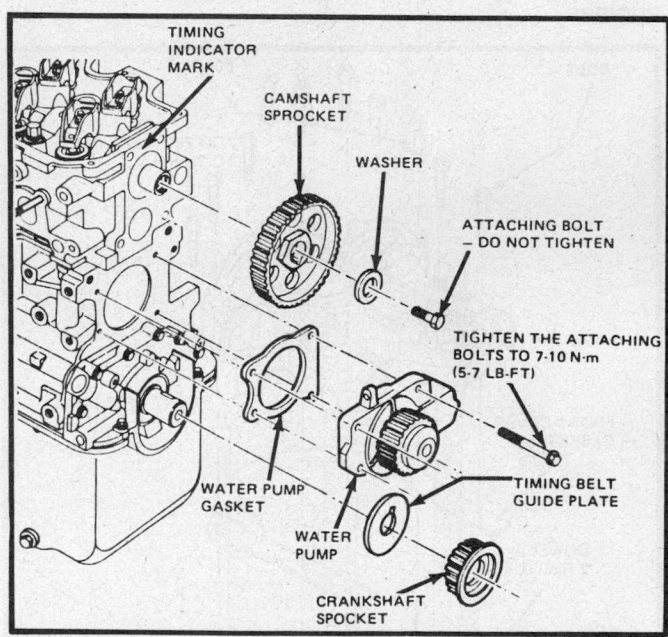

Crankshaft sprocket, camshaft sprocket and water pump installation 1.9L engine

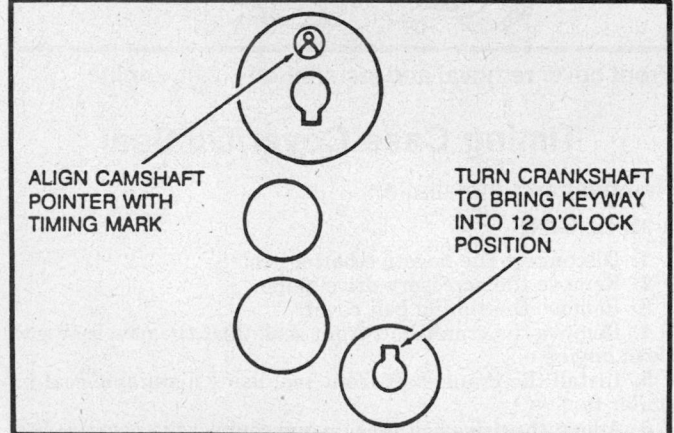

Installing the timing belt on the 1.9L engine

10. Remove crankshaft pulley (damper) and remove the timing belt.

To install:

NOTE: **Prior to installing the timing belt, make certain that the timing pointers on the spockets are aligned with the timing marks on the cylinder head and oil pump.**

11. After the timing sprockets are properly aligned, install the timing belt over the sprockets in a counterclockwise direction starting at the crankshaft. Keep the belt span from the crankshaft to the camshaft tight as the belt is installed over the remaining sprocket.

12. Loosen belt tensioner attaching bolts and allow the tensioner to snap against the belt.

13. Tighten 1 of the tensioner attaching bolts.

14. Install the crankshaft pulley, drive plate and pulley attaching bolt. Hold the crankshaft pulley stationary and tighten the pulley attaching bolt to 74–90 ft. lbs.

15. To seat the belt on the sprocket teeth, complete the following:

   a. Connect cable to the battery negative terminal.

   b. Crank engine for 30 seconds.

   c. Disconnect cable from the battery negative terminal.

   d. Turn camshaft, as necessary, to align the timing pointer on the cam sprocket with the timing mark on the cylinder head.

   e. Position the timing belt cover on the engine and check to see that the timing mark on the crankshaft aligns with the TDC pointer on the cover. If the timing marks do not align, remove the belt, align the timing marks and return to Step 11.

16. Loosen the belt tensioner attaching bolt tightened in Step 13.

17. Hold the crankshaft stationary and position a suitable torque wrench onto the camshaft sprocket bolt.

18. Turn the camshaft sprocket counterclockwise. Tighten the belt tensioner attaching bolt when the torque wrench reads as follows:

   a. New belt—27–32 ft. lbs.

   b. Used belt (30 days or more in service)—10 ft. lbs.

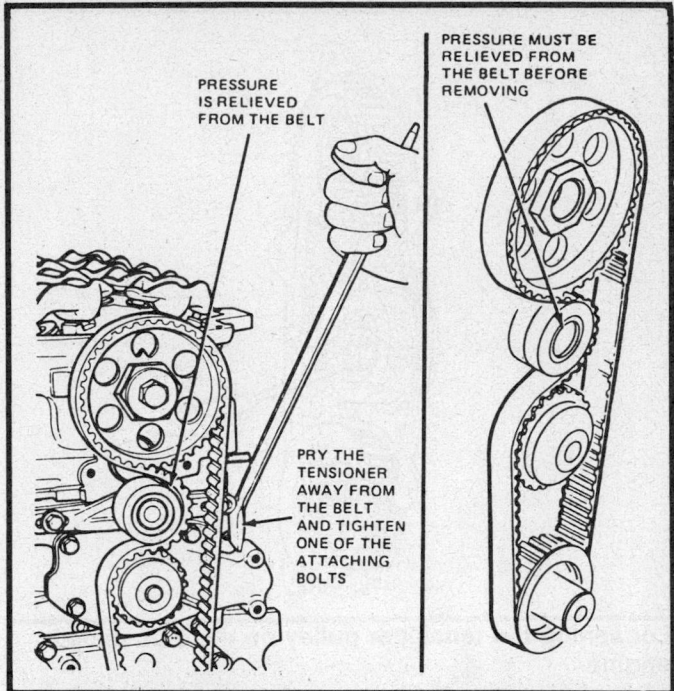

Timing belt tension adjustment 1.9L engine

NOTE: **The engine must be at room temperature when the torque is applied to the cam sprocket. Do not set torque on a hot engine.**

19. Install timing belt cover.

20. Install accessory drive belts and adjust the belt tension.

21. Connect negative battery cable.

2.0L DIESEL ENGINE
Rear Belt

1. Remove the rear timing belt cover.

2. Remove the flywheel timing mark cover from clutch housing.

3. Rotate the crankshaft until the flywheel timing mark is at TDC on No. 1 cylinder.

4. Check that the injection pump and camshaft sprocket timing marks are aligned.

5. Loosen the tensioner locknut. With a suitable tool inserted in the slot provided, rotate the tensioner clockwise to relieve belt tension. Tighten locknut snug.

6. Remove the timing belt.

7. Install the belt.

8. Loosen the tensioner locknut and adjust timing belt.

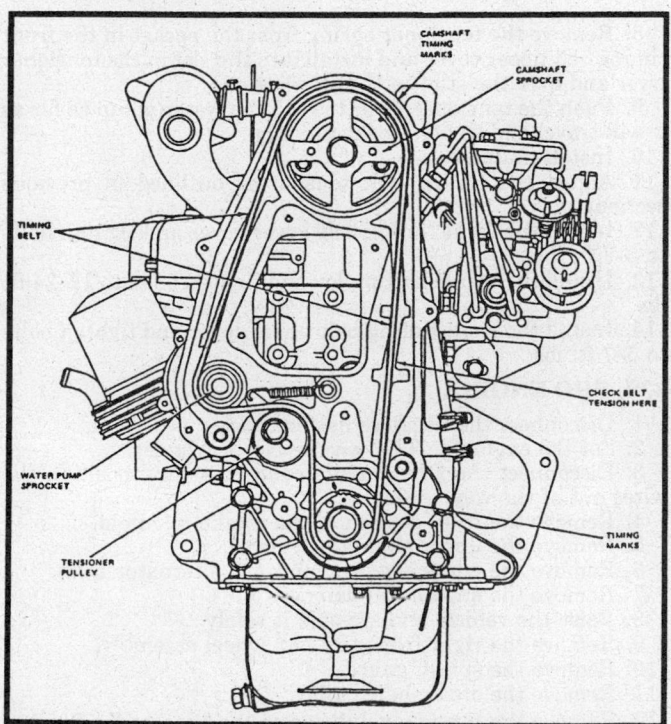

Timing belt installation 2.0L diesel engine

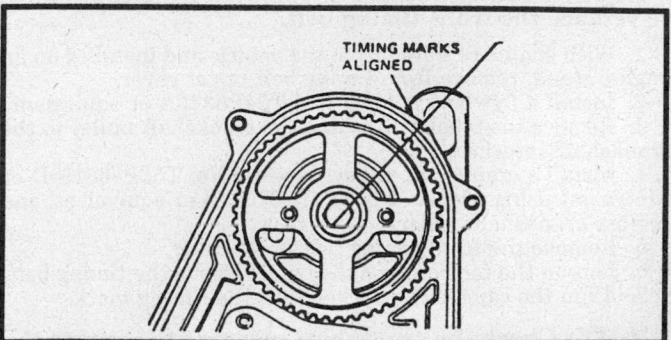

Camshaft timing mark 2.0L diesel engine

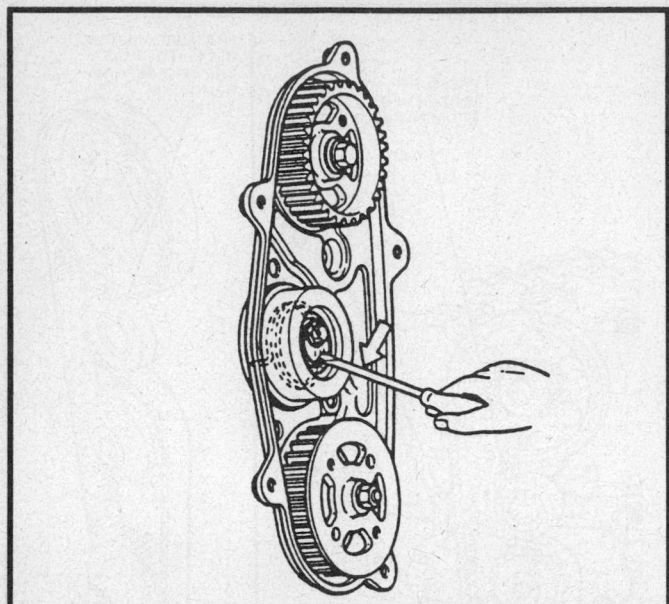

Loosening the tensioner pulley on the 2.0L diesel engine

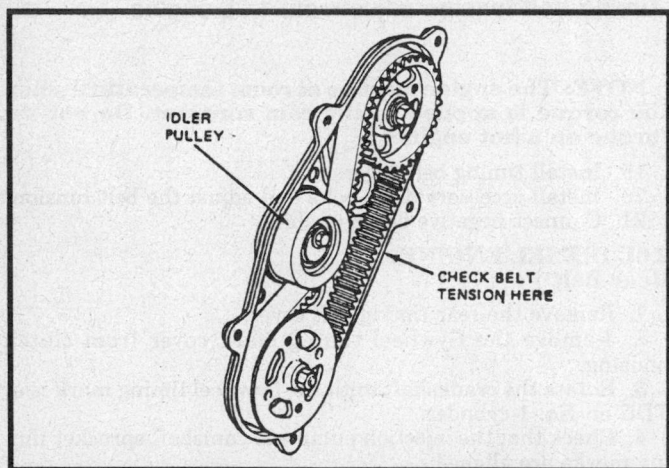

Timing belt tensioner rear belt 2.0L diesel engine

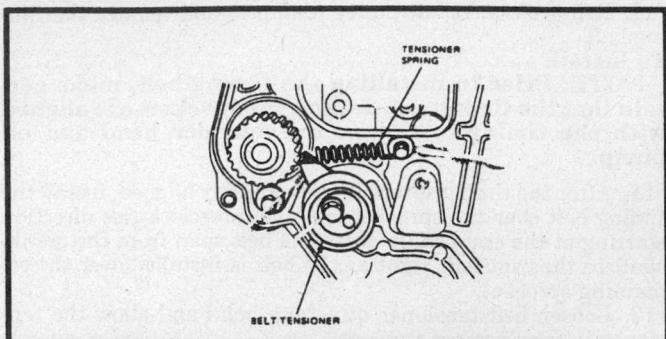

Front timing belt tensioner spring installation 2.0L diesel engine

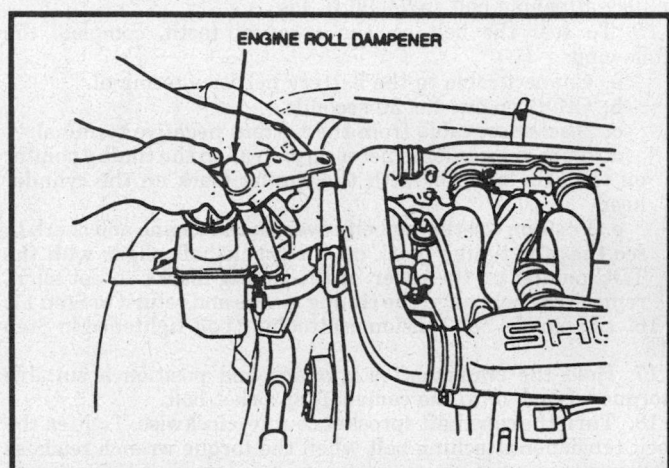

Removing the timing belt 3.0L SHO engine

9. Install rear timing belt cover and tighten bolts to 5–7 ft. lbs.

Front Belt

NOTE: The engine must be removed from the vehicle to replace the front timing belt.

1. With engine removed from the vehicle and installed on an engine stand, remove from timing belt upper cover.
2. Install a flywheel holding tool T84P6375A or equivalent.
3. Remove the 6 bolts attaching the crankshaft pulley to the crankshaft sprocket.
4. Install a crankshaft pulley remover No. T58P-6316-D or equivalent using adapter No. T74P-6700-B or equivalent, and remove crankshaft pulley.
5. Remove the front timing belt lower cover.
6. Loosen the tensioning pulley and remove the timing belt.
7. Align the camshaft sprocket with the timing mark.

NOTE: Check the crankshaft sprocket to see that the timing marks are aligned.

8. Remove the tensioner spring from the pocket in the front timing belt upper cover and install it in the slot in the tensioner lever and over the stud in the crankcase.
9. Push the tensioner lever toward the water pump as far as it will travel and tighten lockbolt snug.
10. Install timing belt.
11. Adjust the timing belt tension as outlined in previous section.
12. Install the front timing belt lower cover and tighten bolts to 5–7 ft. lbs.
13. Install the crankshaft pulley and tighten bolts to 17–24 ft. lbs.
14. Install the front timing belt upper cover and tighten bolts to 5–7 ft. lbs.

3.0L SHO ENGINE

1. Disconnect the negative battery cable.
2. Set the engine on TDC on the No. 1 cylinder.
3. Disconnect the DIS module connectors and position the wires out of the way.
4. Remove the front section of the intake manifold.
5. Remove the upper timing belt cover.
6. Remove the power steering and A/C alternator belts.
7. Remove the engine roll damper.
8. Raise the vehicle and support it safely.
9. Remove the right front tire and wheel assembly.
10. Remove the splash guard.
11. Remove the crankshaft pulley.
12. Remove the tensioner pulley and the bracket for the A/C alternator belt.

13. Remove the center timing belt cover.

14. Remove the lower timing belt cover.

15. Release tension at the automatic tensioner pulley and remove the timing belt.

16. Install in the reverse order of removal.

17. With the engine at TDC on the No. 1 cylinder, check that the camshaft pulley marks line up with the index marks on the upper steel belt cover.

18. Install the timing belt on the crankshaft pulley and then route it to the camshaft pulleys. The lettering on the belt **KOA** should be readable from the rear of the engine.

19. Tighten the crankshaft pulley bolt to 71–85 ft. lbs. (97–116 Nm).

TIMING CHAIN

Removal and Installation

2.3L AND 2.5L ENGINES

1. Remove the engine and transaxle from the vehicle as an assembly and position in a suitable holding fixture. Remove the dipstick.

2. Remove accessory drive pulley, if equipped, Remove the crankshaft pulley attaching bolt and washer and remove pulley.

3. Remove front cover attaching bolts from front cover. Pry the top of the front cover away from the block.

4. Clean any gasket material from the surfaces.

5. Check timing chain and sprockets for excessive wear. If the timing chain and sprockets are worn, replace with new.

6. Check timing chain tensioner blade for wear depth. If the wear depth exceeds specification, replace tensioner.

7. Turn engine over until the timing marks are aligned. Remove camshaft sprocket attaching bolt and washer. Slide both sprockets and timing chain forward and remove as an assembly.

8. Check timing chain vibration damper for excessive wear. Replace if necessary (the damper is located inside the front cover).

9. Remove the oil pan.

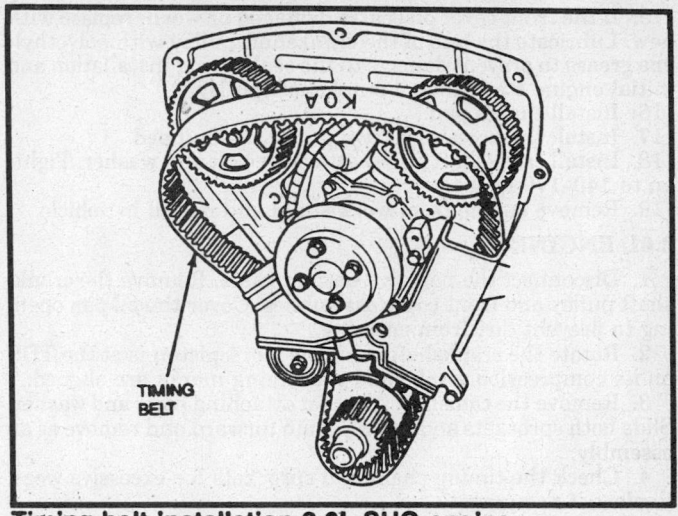

Timing belt Installation 3.0L SHO engine

To install:

10. Clean and inspect all parts before installation. Clean the oil pan, cylinder block and front cover of gasket material and dirt.

11. Slide both sprockets and timing chain onto the camshaft and crankshaft with timing marks aligned. Install camshaft bolt and washer and tighten 41–56 ft. lbs. Oil timing chain, sprockets and tensioner after installation with clean engine oil.

12. Apply oil resistant sealer to a new front cover gasket and position gasket into front cover.

13. Remove the front cover oil seal and position the front cover on the engine.

14. Position front cover alignment tool T84P-6019-C or equivalent onto the end of the crankshaft, ensuring the crank key is aligned with the keyway in the tool. Bolt the front cover to the engine and torque bolts to 6–8 ft. lbs. Remove the front cover alignment tool.

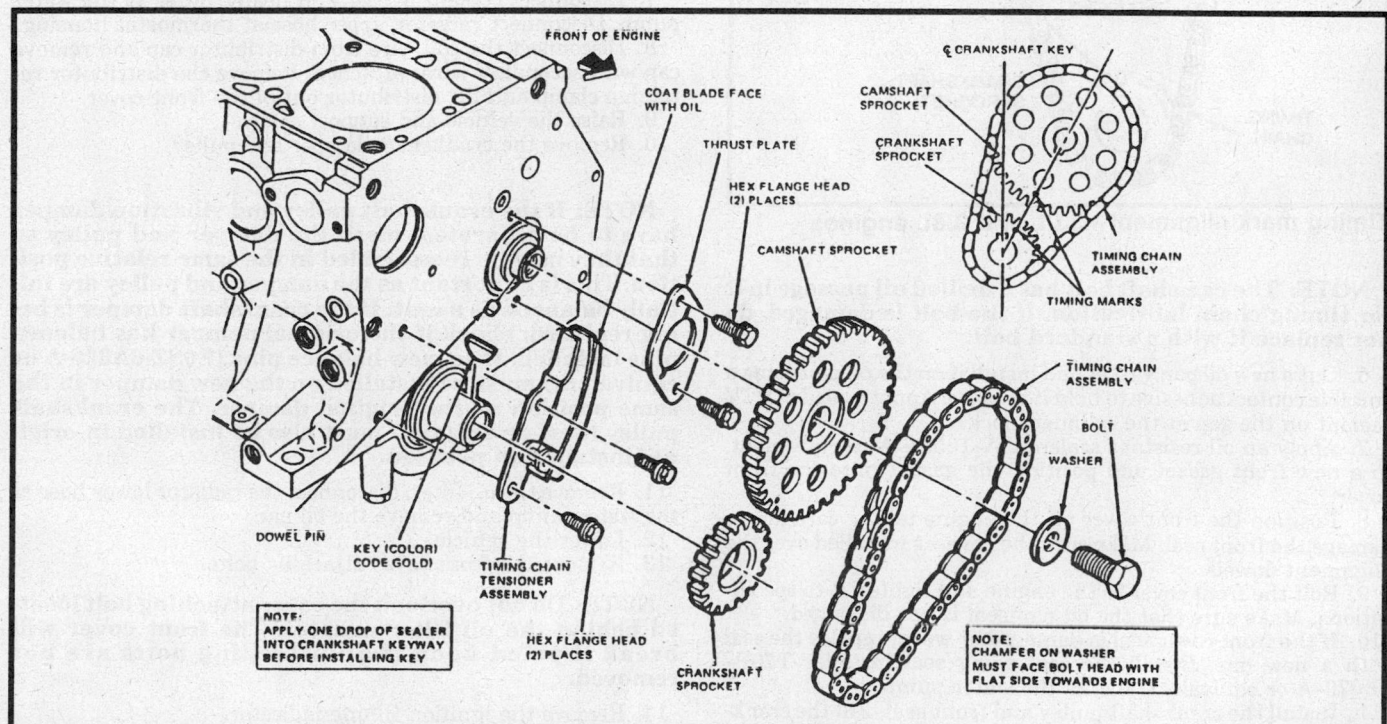

Timing chain tensioner, sprockets and timing chain installation 2.3L engine

15. If the front cover oil seal is damaged or worn, replace with new. Lubricate the hub of the crankshaft pulley with polyethylene grease to prevent damage to the seal during installation and initial engine start. Install crankshaft pulley.

16. Install the oil pan.

17. Install the accessory drive pulley, if equipped.

18. Install crankshaft pulley attaching bolt and washer. Tighten to 140–170 ft. lbs.

19. Remove engine from work stand and install in vehicle.

3.0L ENGINE

1. Disconnect the negative battery cable. Remove the crankshaft pulley and front cover assemblies. Cover the oil pan opening to prevent dirt from entering.

2. Rotate the crankshaft until the No. 1 piston is at the TDC on its compression stroke and the timing marks are aligned.

3. Remove the camshaft sprocket attaching bolts and washer. Slide both sprockets and timing chain forward and remove as an assembly.

4. Check the timing chain and sprockets for excessive wear. Replace if necessary.

NOTE: Before installation, clean and inspect all parts. Clean the gasket material and dirt from the oil pan, cylinder block and front cover.

5. Slide both sprockets and timing chain onto the camshaft and crankshaft with the timing marks aligned. Install the camshaft bolt and washer and torque to 40–51 ft. lbs. Apply clean engine oil to the timing chain and sprockets after installation.

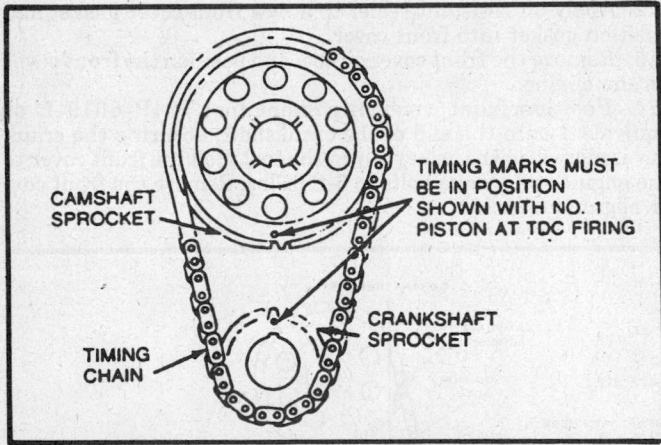

Timing mark alignment—3.0L and 3.8L engines

NOTE: The camshaft bolt has a drilled oil passage in it for timing chain lubrication. If the bolt is damaged, do not replace it with a standard bolt.

6. Cut a new oil pan gasket and install it on the oil pan using a suitable contact adhesive to hold it in place. Apply a bead of RTV sealant on the gap at the cylinder block.

7. Apply an oil resistant sealer B5A–19554–A or equivalent, to a new front gasket and position the gasket onto the front cover.

8. Position the front cover on the engine taking care not to damage the front seal. Make sure the cover is installed over the alignment dowels.

9. Bolt the front cover to the engine and tighten it to specifications. Make sure that the oil pan seal is not dislodged.

10. If the front cover seal is damaged or worn, replace the seal with a new one. Install the seal using seal installer T70P–6B070–A or equivalent. Install the water pump.

11. Install the crankshaft pulley and front seal. Fill the crankcase with the correct viscosity and amount of engine oil. Fill and bleed the cooling system.

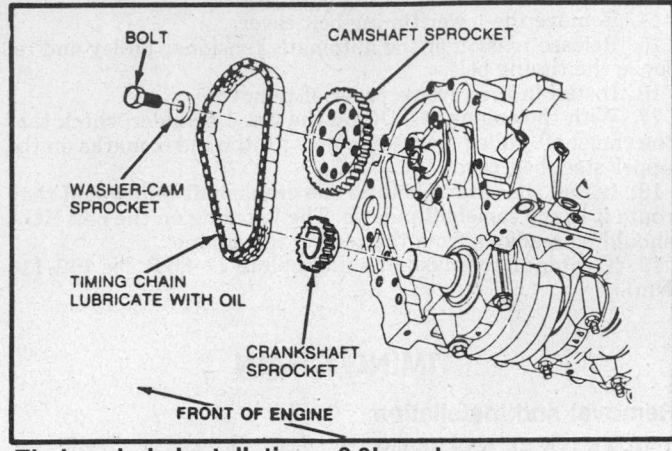

Timing chain installation—3.0L engine

12. Start the engine and check for oil and coolant leaks.

3.8L ENGINE

1. Disconnect the negative battery cable. Drain the cooling system and crankcase.

2. Remove the air cleaner assembly and air intake duct.

3. Remove the fan shroud attaching screws and unbolt the fan/clutch assembly. On Taurus and Sable, remove the fan/clutch assembly from the vehicle.

4. Loosen the accessory drive belt idler. Remove the drive belt and water pump pulley.

5. Remove the power steering pump mounting bracket attaching bolts. Leaving the hoses connected, place the pump/bracket assembly in a position that will prevent the loss of power steering fluid.

6. If equipped with air conditioning, remove the compressor front support bracket. Leave the compressor in place.

7. Disconnect coolant bypass and heater hoses at the water pump. Disconnect radiator upper hose at thermostat housing.

8. Disconnect the coil wire from distributor cap and remove cap with secondary wires attached. Remove the distributor retaining clamp and lift distributor out of the front cover.

9. Raise the vehicle and support safely.

10. Remove the crankshaft damper and pulley.

NOTE: If the crankshaft pulley and vibration damper have to be separated, mark the damper and pulley so that they may be reassembled in the same relative position. This is important as the damper and pulley are initially balanced as a unit. If the crankshaft damper is being replaced, check if the original damper has balance pins installed. If so, new balance pins (E0SZ–6A328–A or equivalent) must be installed on the new damper in the same position as the original damper. The crankshaft pulley (new or orignial) must also be installed in original installation position.

11. Remove the oil filter, disconnect the radiator lower hose at the water pump and remove the oil pan.

12. Lower the vehicle.

13. Remove the front cover attaching bolts.

NOTE: Do not overlook the cover attaching bolt located behind the oil filter adapter. The front cover will break if pried upon if all attaching bolts are not removed.

14. Remove the ignition timing indicator.

15. Remove the front cover and water pump as an assembly. Remove the cover gasket and discard.

16. Remove the camshaft bolt and washer from end of the camshaft. Remove the distributor drive gear.
17. Remove the camshaft sprocket, crankshaft sprocket and timing chain.

NOTE: The front cover houses the oil pump. If a new front cover is to be installed, remove the water pump and oil pump from the old front cover.

To install:
18. Lightly oil all bolt and stud threads before installation. Clean all gasket surfaces on the front cover, cylinder block and fuel pump. If reusing the front cover, replace crankshaft front oil seal.
19. If a new front cover is to be installed, complete the following:
    a. Install the oil pump gears.
    b. Clean the water pump gasket surface. Position a new water pump gasket on the front cover and install water pump. Install the pump attaching bolts and torque 15-22 ft. lbs.
20. Rotate the crankshaft as necessary to position piston No. 1 at TDC.
21. Lubricate timing chain with clean engine oil. Install the camshaft sprocket, crankshaft sprocket and timing chain. Make certain the timing marks are positioned across from each other.
22. Install the distributor drive gear.
23. Install the washer and bolt at end of camshaft and torque to 54–67 ft. lbs.
24. Lubricate the crankshaft front oil seal with clean engine oil.
25. Position a new cover gasket on the cylinder block and install the front cover/water pump assembly using dowels for proper alignment. A suitable contact adhesive (No. D7AZ-19B508-A or equivalent) is recommended to hold the gasket in position while the front cover is installed.
26. Position the ignition timing indicator.
27. Install the front cover attaching bolts. Apply Loctite® or equivalent to the threads of the bolt installed below the oil filter housing prior to installation. This bolt is to be installed and tightened last. Tighten all bolts to 15–22 ft. lbs.
28. Raise the vehicle and support safely.
29. Install the oil pan. Connect the radiator lower hose. Install a new oil filter.
30. Coat the crankshaft damper sealing surface with clean engine oil.
31. Position the crankshaft pulley key in the crankshaft keyway.
32. Install the damper with damper washer and attaching bolt. Torque bolt to 104–132 ft. lbs.
33. Install the crankshaft pulley and torque the attaching bolts 19-28 ft. lbs.
34. Lower the vehicle.
35. Connect the coolant bypass hose.
36. Install the distributor with rotor pointing at No. 1 distributor cap tower. Install the distributor cap and coil wire.
37. Connect the radiator upper hose at thermostat housing.
38. Connect the heater hose.
39. If equipped with air conditioning, install compressor and mounting brackets.
40. Install the power steering pump and mounting brackets.
41. Position the accessory drive belt over the pulleys. On the Taurus and Sable, install the fan/clutch assembly and fan shroud. Cross tighten the attaching bolts to 12–18 ft. lbs.
42. Install the water pump pulley. Position the accessory drive belt over water pump pulley and tighten the belt.
43. Connect battery ground cable. Fill the crankcase and cooling system to the proper level.
44. Start the engine and check for leaks.
45. Check the ignition timing and curb idle speed, adjust as required.
46. Install the air cleaner assembly and air intake duct.

Crankshaft pulley timing marks 2.0L diesel engine

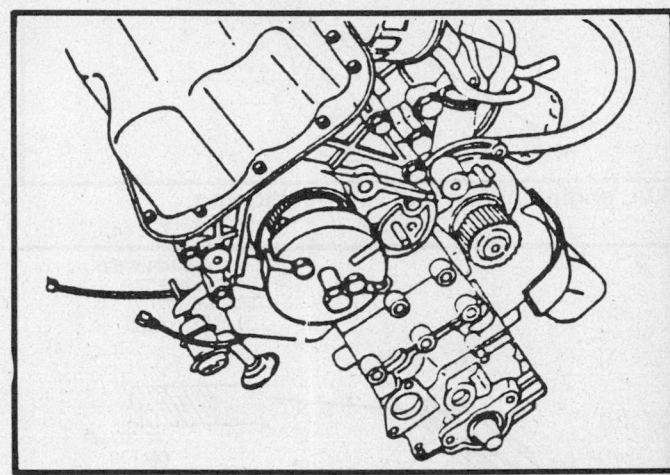

Crankshaft sprocket removal 2.0L diesel engine

Pistons and Rod Positioning

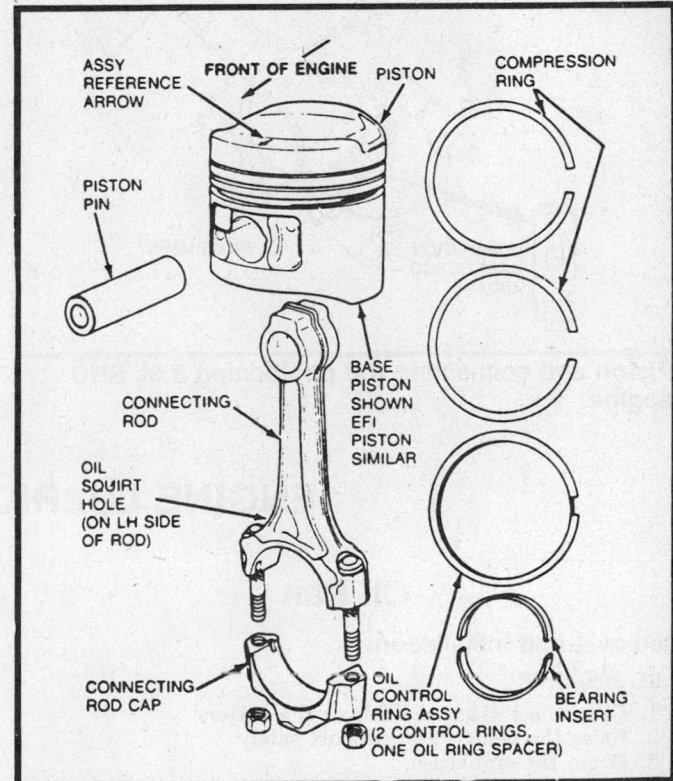

1.9L piston and rod assembly

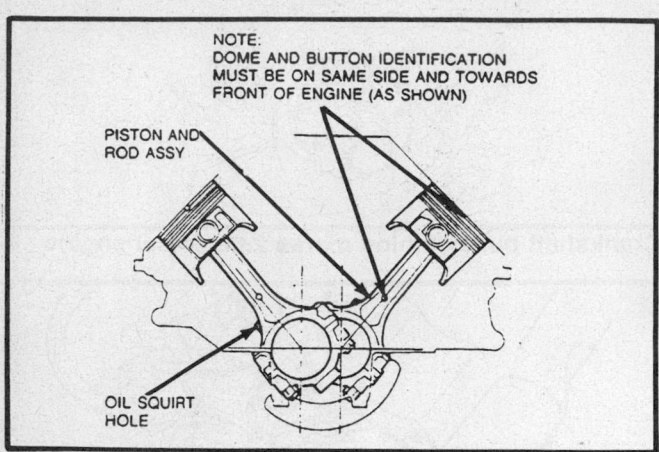

3.8L engine piston and rod positioning

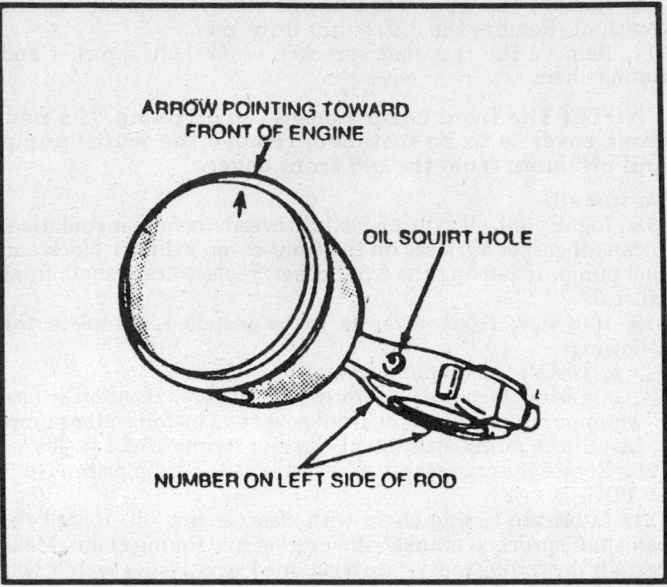

Piston and rod 2.3L engine

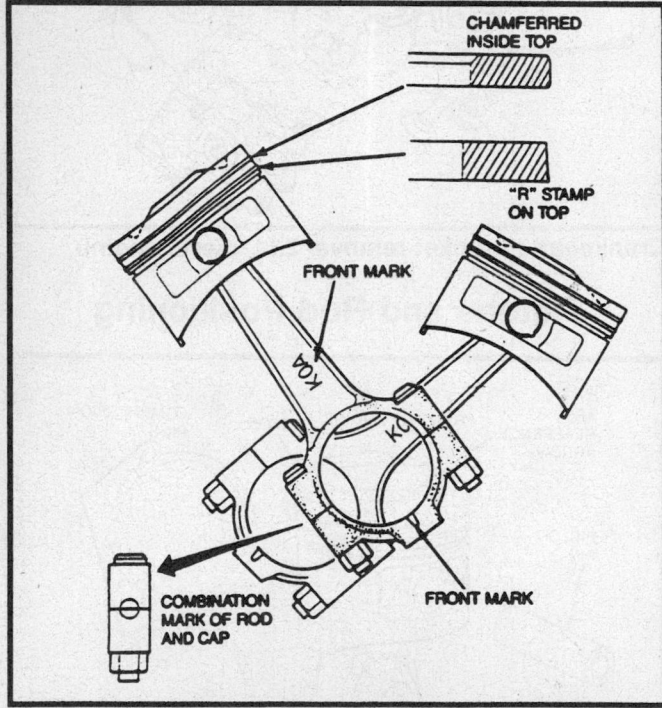

Piston and connecting rod positioning 3.0L SHO engine

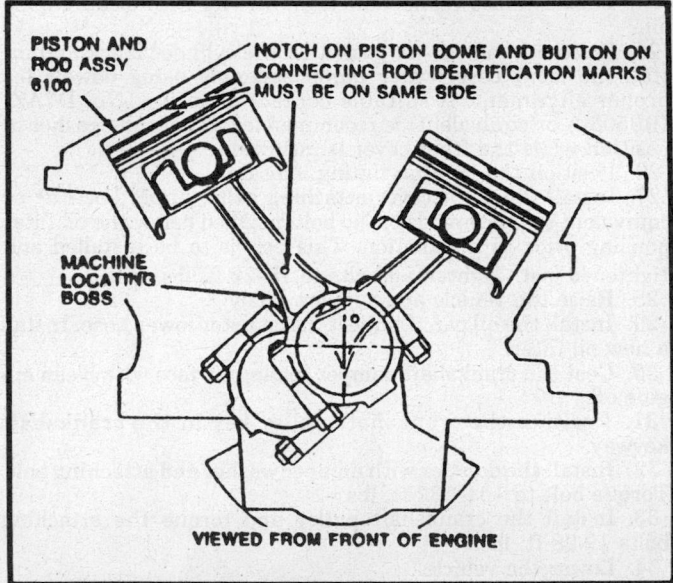

3.0L piston and rod assembly

ENGINE LUBRICATION SYSTEM

Oil Pan

Removal and Installation

1.9L ENGINE

1. Disconnect negative cable at the battery.
2. Raise the vehicle and support safely.
3. Drain the crankcase.
4. Disconnect cable at the starter.
5. Remove knee-brace located at the front of the starter.
6. Remove starter attaching bolts and starter.
7. Remove knee-braces at the transaxle.
8. Disconnect the exhaust inlet pipe at the manifold and converter. Remove pipe.
9. Remove oil pan retaining bolts and oil pan.
10. Remove oil pan front seal, rear seal and both oil pan side gaskets. 1987–90 vehicles use a 1 piece gasket with press fit tabs. Discard the gasket(s) and replace with new.

To install:
11. Clean the oil pan gasket surface and the mating surface on

the cylinder block. Wipe the oil pan rail with a solvent-soaked cloth to remove oil traces.

12. Remove the clean the oil pump pick up tube and screen assembly. Install tube and screen assembly.

13. Apply a bead of suitable silicone rubber sealer at the corner of the oil pan front and rear seals and at the seating point of the oil pump to the block retainer joint.

14. Install the front oil pan seal by pressing firmly into the oil pump slot cut into the bottom of the oil pump. Install the oil pan rear seal by pressing firmly into the slot cut into the rear retainer assembly. On the 1987–90 vehicles, make certain that the press fit tabs are fully engaged in the oil pan gasket channel.

15. Apply adhesive evenly to the oil pan flange and to the pan side of the gaskets. Allow the adhesive to dry past the "wet" stage and then install the gaskets on the oil pan. Sealant application is not required if a 1 piece gasket is installed.

16. Install and bolt the oil pan on the cylinder block. Torque the oil pan attaching bolts in sequence to 6–8 ft lbs. On 1987–90 vehicles, torque the 2 M-10 oil pan-to-transaxle bolts to 30–40 ft. lbs. then back off ½ turn, torque the M-8 oil pan-to-cylinder block bolts in sequence to 15–22 ft. lbs. and retorque the "M-10" bolts to 30–40 ft. lbs.

17. Install the starter, knee brace at the starter and connect the starter cable.

18. Install the exhaust inlet pipe. Lower the vehicle and fill the crankcase.

19. Connect negative battery cable.

20. Start the engine and check for oil leaks.

2.0L DIESEL ENGINE

1. Disconnect the negative battery cable.
2. Raise the vehicle and support it safely.
3. Drain the engine oil.
4. Remove the bolts attaching the pan to the crankcase and remove the pan.
5. Clean the oil pan and crankcase gasket mating surfaces.

To install:

6. Apply silicone sealer on the oil pan–to–crankcase mating surface.
7. Install the oil pan and tighten the bolts to 5–7 ft. lbs. (7–10 Nm).
8. Lower the vehicle and fill the crankcase with the specified quantity of engine oil.
9. Run the engine and check for oil leaks.

2.3L AND 2.5L ENGINES

1. Disconnect the negative battery cable. Raise the vehicle and support safely.
2. Drain the crankcase and drain the cooling system by removing the lower radiator hose.
3. Remove the roll restrictor on manual transaxle equipped vehicles.
4. Raise the vehicle and support it safely. Disconnect the starter cable.
5. Remove the starter.
6. Disconnect the exhaust pipe from oil pan.
7. Remove the engine coolant tube located from the lower radiator hose, water pump and at the tabs on the oil pan. Position air conditioner line off to the side. Remove the retaining bolts and remove the oil pan.

To install:

8. Clean both mating surfaces of oil pan and cylinder block making certain that all traces of RTV sealant are removed. On the 2.3L engine, ensure that the block rails, front cover and rear cover retainer are also clean.
9. Remove and clean oil pump pick-up tube and screen assembly. After cleaning, install tube and screen assembly.
10. Insert the oil pan gasket into the groove in the pan. On the 2.5L engine, coat the cylinder block surface with clean engine oil and bolt the pan to the block. On the 2.3L engine, place a bead of

sealant onto the rear joint cylinder block, rear oil seal retainer assembly/front joint cylinder block and front cover assembly. Once the sealant is applied, immediately raise the pan to the block and install the attaching bolts finger tight until the 2 pan-to-transaxle bolts can be installed.

11. Torque the pan-to-transaxle bolts to 30–39 ft. lbs. to align the pan with the transaxle then back off ½ turn.

12. Torque all pan flange bolts on 2.3L engine to 15–22 ft. lbs. Torque the pan flange bolts on 2.5L engine to 6–8 ft. lbs.

13. Complete the installation of the remaining components by reversing the removal procedure.

14. Fill the crankcase and cooling system to the proper level.

15. Start the engine and inspect for leaks.

3.0L EXCEPT SHO ENGINE

1. Disconnect the negative battery cable and remove the oil level dipstick.
2. Raise the vehicle and support safely. If equipped with a low level sensor, remove the retainer clip at the sensor. Remove the electrical connector from the sensor.
3. Drain the crankcase. Remove the starter motor and disconnect the electrical connector from the oxygen sensor.
4. Remove the catalyst and pipe assembly. Remove the lower engine/flywheel dust cover from the torque converter housing.
5. Remove the oil pan attaching bolts and slowly remove the oil pan from the engine block. Remove the oil pan gasket.

To install:

6. Clean the gasket surfaces on the cylinder block and oil pan. Apply a ⅕ in. bead of silicone sealer to the junction of the rear main bearing cap and cylinder block junction of the front cover assembly and cylinder block.

NOTE: When using a silicone sealer, the assembly process should occur within 15 minutes after the sealer has been applied. After this time, the sealer may start to set-up and its sealing effectiveness may be affected.

7. Position the oil pan gasket over the oil pan and secure the gasket with a suitable sealer contact adhesive.
8. Position the oil pan on the engine block and install the oil pan attaching bolts. Torque the bolts to 71 to 106 inch lbs.
9. Install the lower engine/flywheel dust cover to the torque converter housing. Install the catalyst and pipe assembly. Connect the oxygen sensor connector.
10. Install the starter motor. Install the low oil level sensor connector to the sensor and install the retainer clip. Lower the vehicle and replace the oil level dipstick.
11. Connect the negative battery cable. Fill the crankcase. Start the engine and check for oil and exhaust leaks.

3.0L SHO ENGINE

1. Disconnect the negative battery cable.
2. Remove the oil level dipstick.
3. Remove the accessory drive belts.
4. Remove the timing belt.
5. Raise the vehicle and support it safely.
6. If equipped with a low oil level sensor, remove the retainer clip and the electrical connector from the sensor.
7. Drain the engine oil.
8. Remove the starter motor.
9. Disconnect the HEGO sensors.
10. Remove the catalyst and pipe assembly.
11. Remove the lower flywheel dust cover from the converter housing.
12. Remove the oil pan attaching bolts and the pan.
13. To install, reverse the removal procedure. Tighten the pan attaching bolts to 11–17 ft. lbs. (15–23 Nm).

3.8L ENGINE

1. Disconnect the negative battery cable.
2. Raise the vehicle and support safely.
3. Drain the crankcase and remove the oil filter element.

4. Remove the converter assembly, starter motor and converter housing cover.

5. Remove the retaining bolts and remove the oil pan.

6. Clean the gasket surfaces on cylinder block, oil pan and oil pickup tube.

7. Trial fit oil pan to cylinder block. Ensure enough clearance has been provided to allow oil pan to be installed without sealant being scraped off when pan is positioned under engine.

8. Apply a bead of silicone rubber sealer part number D6AZ–19562–A or equivalent to the oil pan flange. Also apply a bead of sealer to the front cover/cylinder block joint and fill the grooves on both sides of the rear main seal cap.

NOTE: When using silicone rubber sealer, assembly must occur within 15 minutes after sealer application. After this time, the sealer may start to harden and its sealing effectiveness may be reduced.

9. Install the oil pan and secure to the block with the attaching screws. Torque the screws to 7–9 ft. lbs.

10. Install a new oil filter element. Install the converter housing cover and starter motor.

11. Install the converter assembly and lower the vehicle.

12. Fill the crankcase and connect the negative battery cable.

13. Start the engine and check for leaks.

Oil Pump

Removal and Installation

1.9L ENGINE

1. Disconnect the negative cable at the battery.

2. Loosen the alternator bolt on the alternator adjusting arm.

3. Lower the alternator to remove the accessory drivebelt from the crankshaft pulley.

4. Remove the timing belt cover.

5. Loosen both belt tensioner attaching bolts. Using a pry bar of other suitable tool, pry the tensioner away from the belt. While holding the tensioner away from the belt, tighten one of the tensioner attaching bolts.

NOTE: Set No. 1 cylinder at TDC prior to timing belt removal.

6. Disengage timing belt from camshaft sprocket, water pump sprocket and crankshaft sprocket.

7. Raise the vehicle and support safely.

8. Drain the crankcase.

9. Using a crankshaft pulley wrench, remove the crankshaft pulley attaching bolt.

10. Remove the timing belt.

11. Remove the crankshaft drive plate assembly.

12. Remove the crankshaft pulley.

13. Remove the crankshaft sprocket.

14. Disconnect the starter cable at the starter.

15. Remove the knee-brace from the engine.

16. Remove the starter.

17. Remove rear section of the knee-brace and inspection plate at the transaxle.

18. Remove oil pan retaining bolts and oil pan.

19. Remove front and rear oil pan seals. On 1987–90 vehicles, a 1 piece gasket is used.

20. Remove oil pan side gaskets.

21. Remove oil pump attaching bolts, oil pump and gasket.

22. Remove oil pump seal.

To install:

23. Make sure the mating surfaces on the cylinder block and the oil pump are clean and free of gasket material.

24. Remove the oil pick-up tube and screen assembly from the pump for cleaning.

25. Lubricate the outside diameter of the oil pump seal with clean engine oil.

26. Install the oil pump seal using a suitable seal installer tool.

27. Install pick-up tube and screen assembly on the oil pump. Tighten attaching bolts to 6–9 ft. lbs.

28. Lubricate the oil pump seal lip with light engine oil.

29. Position the oil pump gasket over the locating dowels.

30. Position the oil pump. Install attaching bolts and tighten to 5–7 ft. lbs.

31. Apply a bead of sealer approximately ⅛ in. wide at the corner of the front and ear oil pan seals and at the seating point of the oil pump to the block retainer joint.

32. Install front oil pan by pressing firmly into the slot cut into the bottom of the pump.

33. Install the rear oil seal by pressing firmly into the slot cut into rear retainer assembly.

NOTE: Install the seal before the sealer has cured.

34. Apply adhesive evenly to oil pan flange and to the oil pan side of the gaskets. Allow the adhesive to dry past the "wet" stage and then install the gaskets on the oil pan.

35. Position the oil pan on the cylinder block. Install oil pan attaching bolts and tighten bolts in the proper sequence to 6–8 ft. lbs. On 1987–90 vehicles, torque the 2 M–10 oil pan-to-transaxle bolts to 30–40 ft. lbs. then back off ½ turn, torque the M–8 oil pan-to-cylinder block bolts in sequence to 15–22 ft. lbs. and retorque the M–10 bolts to 30–40 ft. lbs.

36. Position the transaxle inspection plate and the rear section of the knee-brace on the transaxle. Install the 2 attaching bolts and tighten to specification.

37. Install starter, knee-brace and connect the starter cable.

38. Install crankshaft gear and crankshaft pulley. Install the crankshaft drive plate assembly.

39. Install timing belt over the crankshaft pulley.

40. Using the crankshaft pulley wrench, install the crankshaft pulley attaching bolt.

41. Lower the vehicle and install the engine front timing cover.

42. Position the accessory drive belts over the alternator and crankshaft pulleys and tighten.

43. Connect the negative battery cable and fill the crankcase.

44. Start the engine and check for oil leaks.

2.0L DIESEL ENGINE

1. Disconnect the negative battery cable.

2. Raise the vehicle and support it safely.

3. Drain the engine oil and remove the oil pan.

4. Remove the front timing belt.

5. Remove the bolts attaching the oil pump to the crankcase and remove the pump.

6. Remove the crankshaft front oil seal.

7. Clean the oil pump and crankcase gasket mating surfaces.

To install:

8. Apply a bead of silicone sealer on the oil pump-to-crankcase mating surface.

9. Install a new O-ring.

10. Install the oil pump, ensuring that the oil pump inner gear engages with the splines on the crankshaft. Tighten the 10mm bolts to 23–34 ft. lbs. (32–47 Nm) and the 8mm bolts to 12–16 ft. lbs. (16–23 Nm).

11. Install a new crankshaft oil seal.

12. Apply a bead of silicone sealer to the oil pan-to-crankcase mating surface. Install the oil pan and tighten the bolts to 5–7 ft. lbs. (7–10 Nm).

13. Install the front timing belt and tensioner.

14. Fill the crankcase with the specified quantity of engine oil.

15. Run the engine and check for leaks.

2.3L AND 2.5L ENGINES

1. Remove oil pan as outlined.

2. Remove oil pump attaching bolts and remove oil pump and intermediate driveshaft.

3. Prime oil pump by filling inlet port with engine oil. Rotate pump shaft until oil flows from outlet port.

4. If screen and cover assembly have been removed, replace gasket. Clean screen and reinstall screen and cover assembly and tighten attaching bolts and nut.

5. Position intermediate driveshaft into distributor socket.

6. Insert intermediate driveshaft into oil pump. Install pump and shaft as an assembly.

CAUTION

Do not attempt to force the pump into position if it will not seat. The shaft hex may be mis-aligned with the distributor shaft. To align, remove the oil pump and rotate the intermediate driveshaft into a new position.

7. Tighten the oil pump attaching bolts to 15–22 ft. lbs.

8. Complete the installation of the oil pan by reversing the removal procedure.

9. Fill the crankcase. Start engine and check for leaks.

3.0L EXCEPT SHO ENGINE

1. Remove the oil pan.

2. Remove the oil pump attaching bolts. Lift the oil pump off the engine and withdraw the oil pump driveshaft.

3. Prime the oil pump by filling either the inlet or the outlet port with engine oil. Rotate the pump shaft to distribute the oil within the oil pump body cavity.

4. Insert the oil pump driveshaft into the block with the pointed end facing inward. The pointed end is the closest to the pressed on flange. On 1987–89 vehicles, insert the oil pump intermediate shaft assembly into the hex drive hole in the oil pump assembly until the retainer "clicks" into place. Place the oil pump in the proper position with a new gasket and install the attaching bolts.

5. Torque the oil pump attaching bolts to 30–37 ft. lbs. Clean and install the oil pump inlet tube and screen assembly with a new gasket. Torque the oil pump inlet tube to pump bolts to 6–10 ft. lbs. and torque the oil inlet tube support to main bearing cap (nut) to 12–15 ft. lbs.

6. Install the oil pan with new gasket.

7. Fill the crankcase. Start engine and check for leaks.

3.0L SHO ENGINE

1. Disconnect the negative battery cable.

2. Remove the oil level dipstick.

3. Remove the accessory drive belts.

4. Remove the timing belt.

5. Raise the vehicle and support it safely.

6. If equipped with a low oil level sensor, remove the retainer clip and the electrical connector from the sensor.

7. Drain the engine oil.

8. Remove the starter motor.

9. Disconnect the HEGO sensors.

10. Remove the catalyst and pipe assembly.

11. Remove the lower flywheel dust cover from the converter housing.

12. Remove the oil pan attaching bolts and the pan.

13. Remove the pan gasket.

14. Remove the crankshaft timing belt pulley.

15. Remove the sump to oil pump bolts.

16. Remove the oil pump to block bolts and remove the pump.

17. To install, reverse the removal procedure. Tighten the oil pump bolts to 11–17 ft. lbs. (15–23 Nm). Tighten the sump to pump bolts to 6–8 ft. lbs. (7–11 Nm). Tighten the pan attaching bolts to 11–17 ft. lbs. (15–23 Nm).

3.8L ENGINE

NOTE: The oil pump, oil pressure relief valve and drive intermediate shaft are contained in the front cover assembly.

1. Disconnect the negative battery cable. Drain the cooling system and crankcase.

2. Remove the air cleaner assembly and air intake duct.

3. Remove the fan shroud attaching screws and unbolt the fan/clutch assembly. Remove the fan/clutch assembly from the vehicle (Taurus and Sable).

4. Loosen the accessory drive belt idler. Remove the belt and water pump pulley (Taurus and Sable).

5. Remove the power steering pump mounting bracket attaching bolts. Leaving the hoses connected, place the pump/bracket assembly in a position that will prevent the loss of power steering fluid.

6. If equipped with air conditioning, remove the compressor front support bracket. Leave the compressor in place.

7. Disconnect coolant bypass and heater hoses at the water pump. Disconnect radiator upper hose at thermostat housing.

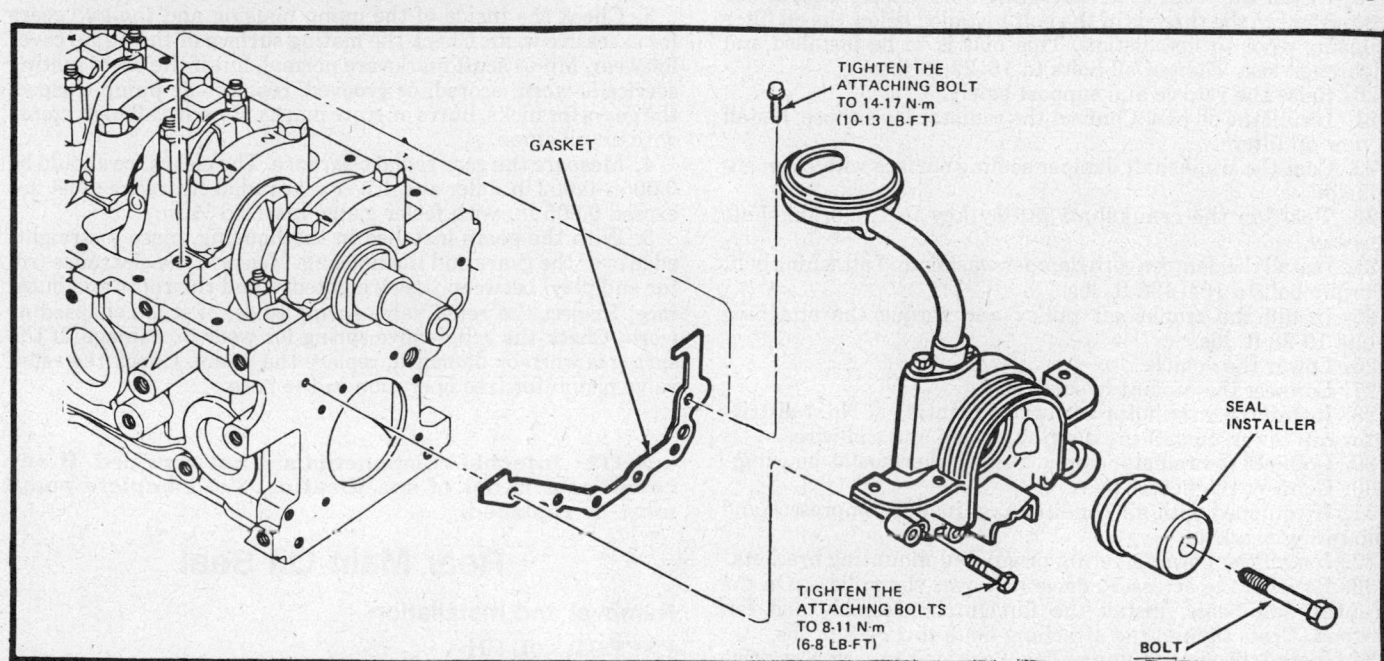

GASKET

TIGHTEN THE ATTACHING BOLT TO 14-17 N·m (10-13 LB-FT)

SEAL INSTALLER

TIGHTEN THE ATTACHING BOLTS TO 8-11 N·m (6-8 LB-FT)

BOLT

Oil pump assembly 1.9L engine

8. Disconnect the coil wire from distributor cap and remove cap with secondary wires attached. Remove the distributor hold-down clamp and lift distributor out of the front cover.

9. Raise the vehicle and support safely.

10. Remove the crankshaft damper and pulley.

NOTE: If the crankshaft pulley and vibration damper have to be separated, mark the damper and pulley so that they may be reassembled in the same relative position. This is important as the damper and pulley are initially balanced as a unit. If the crankshaft damper is being replaced, check if the original damper has balance pins installed. If so, new balance pins (E0SZ-6A328-A or equivalent) must be installed on the new damper in the same position as the original damper. The crankshaft pulley (new or orignial) must also be installed in original installation position.

11. Remove the oil filter, disconnect the radiator lower hose at the water pump and remove the oil pan.

12. Lower the vehicle.

13. Remove the front cover.

NOTE: Do not overlook the cover attaching bolt located behind the oil filter adapter. The front cover will break if pried upon if all attaching bolts are not removed.

14. Remove the oil pump cover attaching bolts and remove the cover. Lift the pump gears off the front cover pocket. Remove the cover gasket and replace with new.

To install:

15. Clean the front cover gasket contact surface. Place a straight edge across the front cover mounting surface and check for wear or warpage using a feeler gauge. If the surface is out of flat by more than 0.0016 in., replace the cover.

16. Lightly pack the gear pocket with petroleum jelly or coat all pump gear surfaces with oil conditioner D9AZ–19579–C or equivalent.

17. Install the gears in the pocket. Make certain that the petroleum jelly fills the gap between the gears and the pocket.

18. Position the cover gasket and install the front cover. Torque the cover retaining bolts to 18–22 ft. lbs.

19. Install the front cover attaching bolts. Apply Loctite® or equivalent to the threads of the bolt installed below the oil filter housing prior to installation. This bolt is to be installed and tightened last. Tighten all bolts to 15–22 ft. lbs.

20. Raise the vehicle and support safely.

21. Install the oil pan. Connect the radiator lower hose. Install a new oil filter.

22. Coat the crankshaft damper sealing surface with clean engine oil.

23. Position the crankshaft pulley key in the crankshaft keyway.

24. Install the damper with damper washer and attaching bolt. Torque bolt to 104–132 ft. lbs.

25. Install the crankshaft pulley and torque the attaching bolts 19-28 ft. lbs.

26. Lower the vehicle.

27. Connect the coolant bypass hose.

28. Install the distributor with rotor pointing at No. 1 distributor cap tower. Install the distributor cap and coil wire.

29. Connect the radiator upper hose at thermostat housing.

30. Connect the heater hose.

31. If equipped with air conditioning, install compressor and mounting brackets.

32. Install the power steering pump and mounting brackets.

33. Position the accessory drive belt over the pulleys. On the Taurus and Sable, install the fan/clutch assembly and fan shroud. Cross tighten the attaching bolts to 12–18 ft. lbs.

34. Install the water pump pulley. Position the accessory drive belt over water pump pulley and tighten the belt.

35. Connect battery ground cable. Fill the crankcase and cooling system to the proper level.

36. Start the engine and check for leaks.

37. Check the ignition timing and curb idle speed, adjust as required.

38. Install the air cleaner assembly and air intake duct.

Inspection
EXCEPT 3.8L ENGINE

NOTE: Oil pump internal components are not servicable, except for 3.0L engine. If any component is out of specification, the pump must be replaced.

1. Remove the oil pump from the vehicle.

2. Inspect the inside of the pump housing for damage or excessive wear.

3. Check the mating surface for wear. Minor scuff marks are normal, but if the cover, gears or housing are excessively worn, scored or grooved, replace the pump.

4. Inspect the rotor for nicks, burrs, or score marks. Remove minor imperfections with an oil stone.

5. Measure the inner-to-outer rotor tip clearance. On 1.9L and 2.0L engines, the clearance should be 0.002–0.007 in. On 2.3L, 2.5L and 3.0L engines the clearance must not exceed 0.010 in. with a feeler gauge inserted ½ in. minimum with the rotors removed from the pump housing.

6. With the rotor assembly installed in the housing, place a straight edge across the rotor assembly and housing. Measure the clearance (rotor endplay) between the the inner and outer rotors. On 1.9L engine, this clearance should be 0.0005–0.0035 in. On the 2.0L engine, the maximum clearance is 0.006 in. On 2.3L, 2.5L and 3.0L engines, the clearance is 0.04 in. maximum.

7. Check the relief valve spring tension. If the spring is worn or damaged, replace the pump. Check the relief valve piston for freedom of movement in the bore.

3.8L ENGINE

1. Remove the oil pump from the vehicle.

2. Wash all parts in a solvent and dry them thoroughly with compressed air. Use a brush to clean the inside of the pump housing and the pressure relief valve chamber. Ensure all dirt and metal particles are removed.

3. Check the inside of the pump housing and the two gears for excessive wear. Check the mating surface of the pump cover for wear. Minor scuff marks are normal, but if the cover mating service is worn, scored, or grooved, replace the pump. Inspect the gears for nicks, burrs or score marks. Remove all high points with an oil stone.

4. Measure the gear radial clearance. The clearance should be 0.0055–0.002 in. Idler and driver gear radial clearance must not exceed 0.005 in. with feeler gauge inserted ½ in.

5. With the gears installed in the housing, place a straightedge over the gears and the housing. Measure the clearance (rotor end play) between the straightedge and the rotor and outer race. Inspect the relief valve spring to see if it is collapsed or worn. Check the relief valve spring for wear or damage. If the spring is worn or damaged, replace the pump. Check the relief valve piston for free operation in the bore.

NOTE: Internal components are not serviced. If any component is out of specification, the complete pump must be replaced.

Rear Main Oil Seal

Removal and Installation
EXCEPT 3.0L SHO

1. Disconnect the negative battery cable.

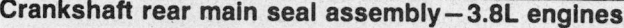

Crankshaft rear main seal assembly—3.8L engines

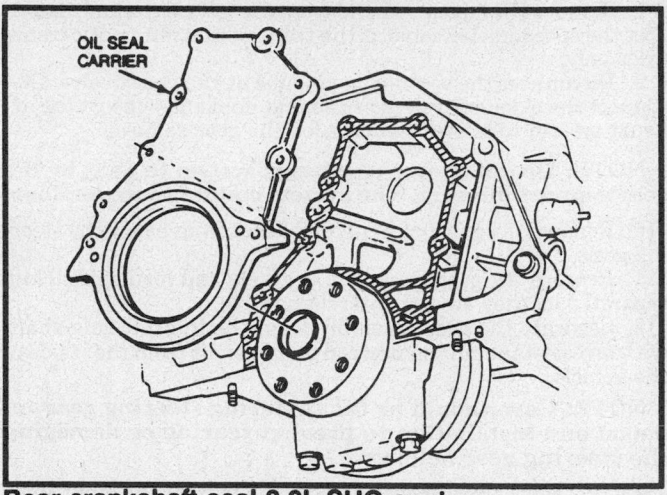

Rear crankshaft seal 3.0L SHO engine

2. Raise the vehicle and support it safely. Remove the transaxle.
3. Remove flywheel.
4. With a suitable tool, remove the oil seal.

NOTE: Use caution to avoid damaging the oil seal surface.

5. Inspect the crankshaft seal area for any damage which may cause the seal to leak. If damage is evident, service or replace the crankshaft as necessary.
6. Coat the crankshaft seal area and the seal lip with engine oil.
7. Using a seal installer tool, install the seal. Tighten the 2 bolts of the seal installer tool evenly so that the seal is straight and seats without mis-alignment.
8. Install the flywheel. Tighten attaching bolts to 54–64 ft. lbs.
9. Install rear cover plate.
10. Complete the installation of the transaxle by reversing the removal procedure.

3.0L SHO ENGINE

1. Disconnect the negative battery cable.
2. Raise the vehicle and support it safely.
3. Remove the sub-frame.
4. Remove the transaxle.
5. Remove the clutch cover, disc and flywheel.
6. Remove the oil pan.

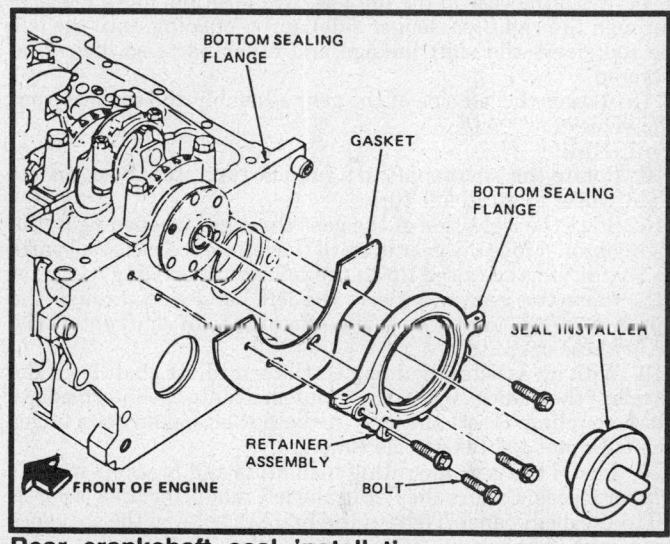

Rear crankshaft seal installation

7. Remove the oil baffle plate and the oil pickup tube.
8. Remove the oil seal carrier.
9. Remove the rear crankshaft oil seal using tool T87P–3504–N or equivalent.
10. Install a new rear crankshaft seal in the carrier and reverse the removal procedure for installation.

FRONT SUSPENSION AND STEERING

For front suspension component removal and installation procedures, refer to the Unit Repair section. For steering wheel removal and installation, refer the electrical control section.

Steering Gear
MANUAL RACK AND PINION

Removal and Installation
ESCORT, LYNX, TEMPO AND TOPAZ

1. Disconnect the negative battery cable.

2. Turn the ignition key to the **RUN** position.
3. Remove the access trim panel from below the steering column.
4. Remove the intermediate shaft bolts at the rack and pinion input shaft and the steering column shaft.
5. Spread the slots enough to loosen the intermediate shaft at both ends. They cannot be separated at this time.
6. Raise the vehicle and support it safely. Separate the tie rod ends from the steering knuckles, using tool 3290-C or equivalent. Turn the steering wheel a full left turn so that the tie rod will clear the shift linkage for removal.
7. Separate the tie rod ends from the steering knuckles. Turn the right wheel to the full left turn position.

8. Remove the left tie rod end from the left tie rod and disconnect the speedometer cable at the transaxle on automatic transaxles only.

9. Disconnect the secondary air tube at the check valve. Disconnect the exhaust system at the manifold and support the exhaust system to allow clearance for the gear removal.

NOTE: Do not allow the exhaust system to hang by the rear support hangers. The system could fall to the floor.

10. Remove the exhaust hanger bracket from below the steering gear.

11. Remove the gear mounting brackets and insulators. Keep separated as they are not interchangeable.

12. Separate the gear assembly from the intermediate shaft, with an assistant pulling upward on the shaft from the inside of the vehicle.

NOTE: Care should be taken during steering gear removal and installation to prevent tearing or damaging the steering gear bellows.

13. Rotate the gear forward and down to clear the input shaft through the dash panel opening.

14. With the gear in the full left turn position, move the gear through the right (passenger side) apron opening until the left tie rod clears the shift linkage and other parts so it may be lowered.

15. Lower the left side of the gear assembly and remove from the vehicle.

To install:

16. Rotate the input shaft to a full left turn stop. Position the right wheel to a full left turn.

17. Start the right side of the gear through the opening in the right apron. Move the gear in until the left tie rod clears all parts so that it may be raised up to the left apron opening.

18. Raise the gear and insert the left hand side through the apron opening. Rotate the gear so that the joint shaft enters the dash panel opening.

19. With an assistant guiding the intermediate shaft from the inside of the vehicle, insert the input shaft into the intermediate shaft coupling. Insert the intermediate shaft clamp bolts finger tight. Do not tighten at this time.

20. Install the gear mounting insulators and brackets in their proper places. Ensure the flat in the left mounting area is parallel to the dash panel. Tighten the bracket bolts in the sequence as described below:

a. Tighten the left (driver's side) upper bolt halfway.

b. Tighten the left hand lower bolt.

c. Tighten the left hand upper bolt.

d. Tighten the right hand bolts.

e. Do not forget that the right hand and left hand insulators and brackets are not interchangeable side to side.

21. Attach the tie rod ends to the steering knuckles. Tighten the castellated nuts to minimum specifications, then tighten the nuts until the slot aligns with the cotter pin hole. Insert a new cotter pin.

22. Install the exhaust system. Install the speedometer cable, if removed.

23. Tighten the gear input shaft to intermediate shaft coupling clamp bolt first. Then, tighten the upper intermediate shaft clamp bolt.

24. Install the access panel below the steering column. Turn the ignition key to the **OFF** position.

25. Check and adjust the toe. Tighten the tie rod end jam nuts, check for twisted bellows.

POWER RACK AND PINION

Removal and Installation

ESCORT, LYNX, TEMPO AND TOPAZ

1. Disconnect the negative battery cable.

2. Turn the ignition key to the **RUN** position.

3. Remove access panel from dash below the steering column.

4. Remove screws from steering column boot at the dash panel and slide boot up intermediate shaft.

5. Remove intermediate shaft bolt at gear input shaft and loosen the bolt at the steering column shaft joint.

6. With a suitable tool, spread the slots enough to loosen intermediates shaft at both ends. The intermediate shaft and gear input shaft cannot be separated at this time.

7. Remove the air cleaner.

8. On Escort and Lynx with A/C, wire the air conditioner liquid line above the dash panel opening. Doing so provides clearance for gear input shaft removal and installation.

9. Separate pressure and return lines at intermediate connections and drain fluid.

10. On Tempo and Topaz without diesel engine, remove the pressure switch.

11. Disconnect the exhaust secondary air tube at check valve. Raise the vehicle and support it safely. Disconnect exhaust system at exhaust manifold and remove exhaust system.

12. Separate tie rod ends from steering knuckles.

13. Remove left tie rod end from tie rod on manual transaxle vehicles. This will allow tie rod to clear the shift linkage.

NOTE: Mark location of rod end prior to removal.

14. Disconnect speedometer cable at transaxle on vehicles equipped with automatic transaxle. Remove the vehicle speed sensor.

15. Remove transaxle shift cable assembly at transaxle on vehicles equipped with automatic transaxle.

16. Turn steering wheel to full left turn stop for easier gear removal.

17. On Escort and Lynx, remove screws holding the heater water tube to shake brace below the oil pan.

18. On Escort and Lynx, remove nut from the lower of 2 bolts holding engine mount support bracket to transaxle housing. Tap bolt out as far as it will go.

19. Remove the gear mounting brackets and insulators.

20. Drape cloth towel over both apron opening edges to protect bellows during gear removal.

21. Separate gear from intermediate shaft by either pushing up on shaft with a bar from underneath the vehicle while pulling the gear down, or with an assistant removing the shaft from inside the vehicle.

22. Rotate gear forward and down to clear the input shaft through the dash panel opening.

23. Make sure input shaft is in full left turn position. Move gear through the right (passenger) side apron opening until left tie rod clears left apron opening and other parts so it may be lowered. Guide the power steering hoses around the nearby components as the gear is being removed.

24. Lower the left hand side of the gear and remove the gear out of the vehicle. Use care not to tear the bellows.

To install:

25. Rotate the input shaft to a full left turn stop. Position the right road wheel to a full left turn.

26. Start the right side of the gear through the opening in the right apron. Move the gear in until the left tie rod clears all parts so that it may be raised up to the left apron opening.

27. Raise the gear and insert the left hand side through the apron opening. Move the power steering hoses into their proper position at the same time. Rotate the gear so that the joint shaft enters the dash panel opening.

28. With an assistant guiding the intermediate shaft from the inside of the vehicle, insert the input shaft into the intermediate shaft coupling. Insert the intermediate shaft clamp bolts finger tight. Do not tighten at this time.

29. Install the gear mounting insulators and brackets in their proper places. Ensure the flat in the left mounting area is paral-

lel to the dash panel. Tighten the bracket bolts in the sequence as described below:

   a. Tighten the left (driver's side) upper bolt halfway.
   b. Tighten the left hand lower bolts.
   c. Tighten the left hand upper bolts.
   d. Tighten the right hand bolts.
   e. Do not forget that the right hand and left hand insulators and brackets are not interchangeable side to side.

30. Attach the tie rod ends to the steering knuckles. Tighten the castellated nuts to minimum specification, then tighten the nuts until the slot aligns with the cotter pin hole. Insert a new cotter pin.

31. On the Escort and Lynx, install the engine mount nut.

32. On the Escort and Lynx, install the heater water tube to the shake brace.

33. Install the exhaust system. Install the speedometer cable, if removed. Install the vehicle speed sensor and the transaxle shift cable.

34. Connect the secondary air tube at the check valve. Connect the pressure and return lines at the steering gear. Install the pressure switch , if removed.

35. Tighten the gear input shaft to intermediate shaft coupling clamp bolt first. Then, tighten the upper intermediate shaft clamp bolt.

36. Install the access panel below the steering column. Turn the ignition key to the **OFF** position.

37. Fill the system. Check and adjust the toe. Tighten the tie rod end jam nuts, check for twisted bellows.

TAURUS AND SABLE

1. Disconnect the negative battery cable. Working from inside the vehicle, remove the nuts retaining the steering shaft weather boot to the dash panel.

2. Remove the bolts retaining the intermediate shaft to the steering column shaft. Set the weather boot aside.

3. Remove the pinch bolt at the steering gear input shaft and remove the intermediate shaft. Raise the vehicle and support safely.

4. Remove the left hand side front wheel assembly. Remove the heat shield. Cut the bundling strap retaining the lines to the gear.

5. Remove the tie rod ends from the spindles. Place a drain pan under the vehicle and remove the hydraulic pressure and return lines from the steering gear.

NOTE: The pressure and return lines are on the front of the housing. Do not confuse them with the transfer lines on the side of the valve.

6. Remove the nut from the gear mounting bolts. The bolts are pressed into the gear housing and should not be removed during gear removal.

7. Push the weather boot end into the vehicle and lift the gear out of the mounting holes. Rotate the gear so the input shaft will pass between the brake booster and the floor pan. Carefully start working the steering gear out through the LH fender apron opening.

8. Rotate the input shaft so that it clears the left fender apron opening and complete the removal of the steering gear. If the steering gear seems to be stuck, check the right tie rod to ensure the stud is not caught on anything.

To install:

9. Install new plastic seals on the hydraulic line fittings.

10. Insert the steering gear through the left fender apron. Rotate the input shaft forward to completely clear the fender apron opening.

11. To allow the gear to pass between the brake booster and the floorpan, rotate the input shaft rearward. Align the steering gear bolts to the bolt holes. Install the mounting nuts and torque them to 85–100 ft. lbs. Lower the vehicle.

12. From inside the engine compartment, install the hydraulic

Power steering rack and pinion assembly

pressure and return lines. Tighten the pressure line to 20–25 ft. lbs. and the return line to 15–20 ft. lbs. Swivel movement of the lines is normal when the fittings are properly tightened.

13. Raise the vehicle and support safely. Secure the pressure and return lines to the transfer tube with the bundle strap. Install the heat shield.

14. Install the tie rod ends to spindles. Torque the castle nuts to 35 ft. lbs. and if necessary, torque the nuts a little bit more to align the slot in the nut for the cotter pin. Install the cotter pin.

15. Install the left front wheel assembly and lower the vehicle. Working from inside the vehicle, pull the weather boot end out of the vehicle and install it over the valve housing. Install the intermediate shaft to the steering gear input shaft. Install the the inner weather boot to the floor pan.

16. Install the intermediate shaft to the steering column shaft. Fill the power steering system.

17. Check the system for leaks and proper operation. Adjust the toe setting as necessary.

CONTINENTAL

The Variable Assist Power Steering System (VAPS) used on the Continental consists of a micro-procesor based module, a power rack and pinion steering gear, an actuator valve assembly, hose assemblies and a high efficiency power steering pump.

1. Disconnect the negative battery cable. Remove the primary steering column attachments.

2. Remove the intermediate shaft retaining bolts and remove the intermediate shaft.

3. From inside the passenger compartment, remove the secondary steering column boot.

4. Raise the vehicle and support safely. Remove the front wheels. Support the vehicle under the rear edge of the subframe.

5. Remove the tie rod cotter pins and nuts. Remove the tie rod ends from the spindle.

6. Remove the tie rod ends from the shaft. Mark the position of the jam nut to maintain the alignment.

7. Remove the nuts from the gear-to-sub-frame attaching bolts.

8. Remove both height sensor attachments.

9. Remove the rear sub-frame-to-attaching bolts.

10. Remove the exhaust pipe-to-catalytic converter attachment.

11. Lower the vehicle approximately 4 inches or until the subframe separates from the body.

12. Remove the heat shield band and fold the shield down.

13. Disconnect the VAPS electrical connector from the actuator assembly.

14. Rotate the gear to clear the bolts from the sub-frame and pull to the left to facilitate line fitting removal.

15. Position a drain pan under the vehicle and remove the line fittings. Remove the o-rings from the fiting connections and replace with new.

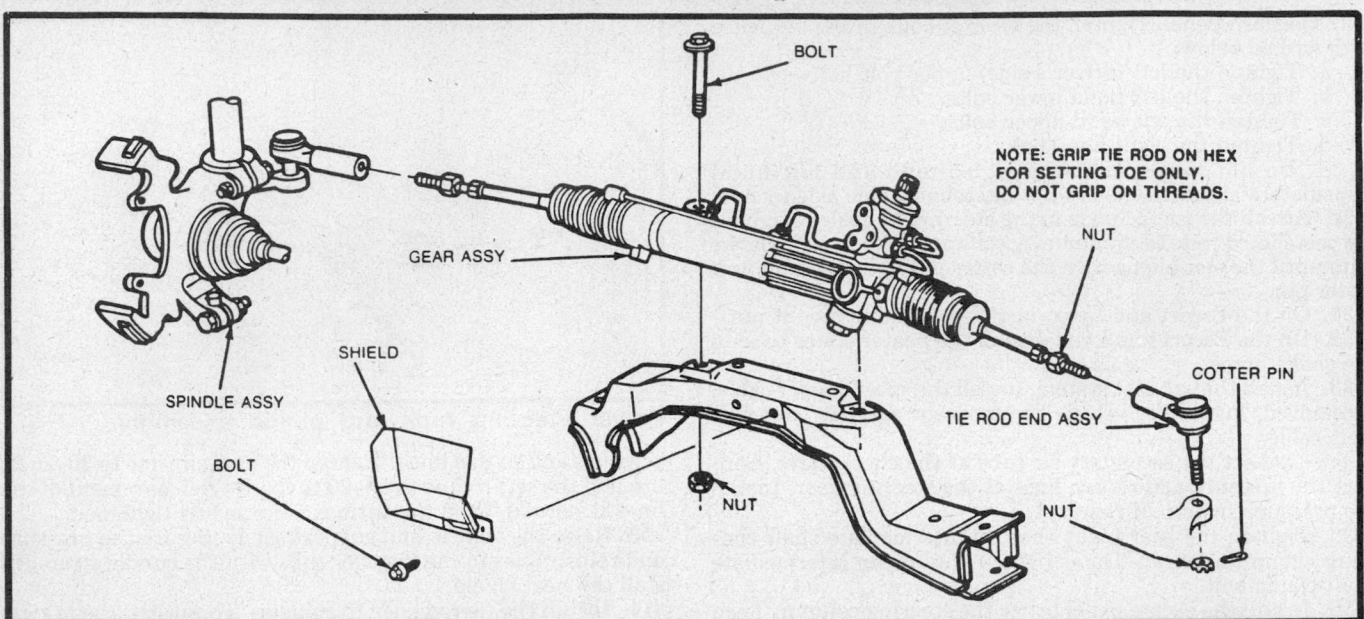

Power rack and pinion steering gear—Taurus/Sable

16. Remove the left sway bar.

17. Remove the steering gear assembly through the LH wheel well.

To install:

18. Install new o-rings into the line fittings.

19. Place the gear attachment bolts in the gear housing.

20. Install the steering gear assembly through the LH wheel well.

21. Connect and tighten the line fittings to the steering gear assembly.

22. Connect the VAPS electrical connector.

23. Position the steering gear into the sub-frame.

24. Install the tie rod ends onto the shaft.

25. Install the heat shield band.

26. Attach the tie rod ends onto the spindle. Install the nuts and secure with new cotter pins.

27. Attach the sway bar links.

28. Raise the vehicle until the sub-frame contacts the body. Install the sub-frame attaching bolts.

29. Install the gear-to-sub-frame nuts and torque to 85–100 ft. lbs.

30. Attach the exhaust pipe to the catalytic converter.

31. Attach the height sensors, install the wheels and lower the vehicle.

32. Fill the power steering system.

33. Install the secondary steering column boot and attach the intermediate shaft to the steering column.

34. Bleed the system and align the front end.

Power Steering Pump

Removal and Installation
ESCORT AND LYNX

1. Disconnect the negative battery cable. Remove the air cleaner, thermactor air pump and belt. Remove the reservoir filler extension and cover the hole to prevent dirt from entering.

2. On vehicles equipped with EFI and remote reservoir, remove the reservoir supply hose at the pump, drain the fluid and plug or cap the opening at the pump to prevent entry of contaminants during removal.

3. From under the vehicle, loosen 1 pump adjusting bolt. Remove 1 pump to bracket mounting bolt and disconnect the fluid return line.

4. From above the vehicle, loosen 1 adjusting bolt and the pivot bolt. Remove the drive belt and the 2 remaining pump to bracket mounting bolts.

5. Remove the pump by passing the pulley through the adjusting bracket opening. Remove the pressure hose from the pump assembly.

6. Complete the installation of the pump assembly by reversing the removal procedure. Fill the pump with fluid and check the system for proper operation.

TEMPO AND TOPAZ

1. Disconnect the negative battery cable. Loosen the alternator and remove the drive belt. Pivot the alternator to it most upright position.

2. Remove the radiator overflow bottle. Loosen and remove the power steering pump drive belt. Mark the pulley and pump drive hub with paint or grease pencil for location reference.

3. Remove the pulleys from the pump shaft.

4. Remove the return line from the pump. Be prepared to catch any spilled fluid in a suitable container.

5. Back off the pressure line attaching nut completely. The line will separate from the pump connection when the pump is removed.

6. Remove the pump mounting bolts and remove the pump.

7. Complete the installation of the pump by reversing the removal procedure. Fill the pump with fluid and check the system for proper opreation.

TAURUS, SABLE WITH 2.5L AND 3.8L ENGINES AND CONTINENTAL

1. Disconnect the negative battery cable. Loosen the tensioner pulley attaching bolts and using the ½ inch drive hole provided in the tensioner pulley, rotate the tensioner pulley clockwise and remove the belt from the alternator and power steering pulley.

2. Position a drain pan under the power steering pump from underneath the vehicle. Disconnect the hydraulic pressure and return lines.

3. Remove the pulley from the pump shaft using hub puller

T69L–10300–B or equivalent. Remove the bolts retaining pump to bracket and remove the power steering pump.

4. Complete the installation of the pump assembly by reversing the removal procedure. Fill the pump with fluid and check the system for proper operation.

NOTE: To install the power steering pump pulley, use steering pump pulley replacer T65P–3A733–C or equivalent. When using this tool, the small diameter threads must be fully engaged in the pump shaft before pressing on the pulley. Hold the head screw and turn the nut to install the pulley. Install the pulley face flush with the pump shaft within ± 0.100 in.

TAURUS AND SABLE WITH 3.0L ENGINES

1. Disconnect the negative battery cable. Loosen the idler pulley and remove the power steering belt.
2. Remove the radiator overflow bottle in order to gain access to the 3 screws attaching the pulleys to the pulley hub.
3. Matchmark both pulley to hub positions.
4. Remove the pulleys from the pulley hub.
5. Remove the return line from the pump. Be prepared to catch any spilled fluid in a suitable container.
6. Back off the pressure line attaching nut completely. The line will separate from the pump connection when the pump is removed.
7. Remove the pump mounting bolts and remove the pump.
8. Complete the installation of the pump assembly by reversing the removal procedure. Fill the pump with fluid and check for proper operation.

Bleeding System

If air bubbles are present in the power steering fluid, bleed the system by performing the following:

1. Fill the reservoir to the proper level.
2. Operate the engine until the fluid reaches normal operating temperature (165–175°F).
3. Turn the steering wheel all the way to the left then all the way to the right several times. Do not hold the steering wheel in the far left or far right position stops.
4. Check the fluid level and recheck the fluid for the presence of trapped air. If apparent that air is still in the system, fabricate or obtain a vacuum tester and purge the system as follows:
   a. Remove the pump dipstick cap assembly.
   b. Check and fill the pump reservoir with fluid to the **COLD FULL** mark on the dipstick.
   c. Disconnect the ignition wire and raise the front of the vehicle and support safely.
   d. Crank the engine with the starter and check the fluid level. Do not turn the steering wheel at this time.
   e. Fill the pump reservoir to the **COLD FULL** mark on the dipstick. Crank the engine with the starter while cycling the steering wheel lock-to-lock. Check the fluid level.
   f. Tightly insert a suitable size rubber stopper and air evacuator pump into the reservoir fill neck. Connect the ignition coil wire.
   g. With the engine idling, apply a 15 in. Hg vacuum to the reservoir for 3 minutes. As air is purged from the system, the vacuum will drop off. Maintain the vacuum on the system as required throughout the 3 minutes.
   h. Remove the vacuum source. Fill the reservoir to the **COLD FULL** mark on the dipstick.
   i. With the engine idling, re-apply 15 in. Hg vacuum source to the resrevoir. Slowly cycle the steering wheel to lock-to-lock stops for approximately 5 minutes. Do not hold the steering wheel on the stops during cycling. Maintain the vacuum as required.
   j. Release the vacuum and disconnect the vacuum source. Add fluid as required.
   k. Start the engine and cycle the wheel slowly and check for leaks at all connections.

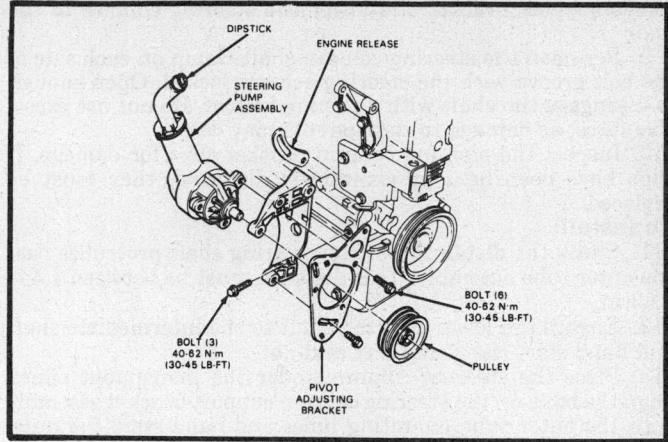

Power steering pump components

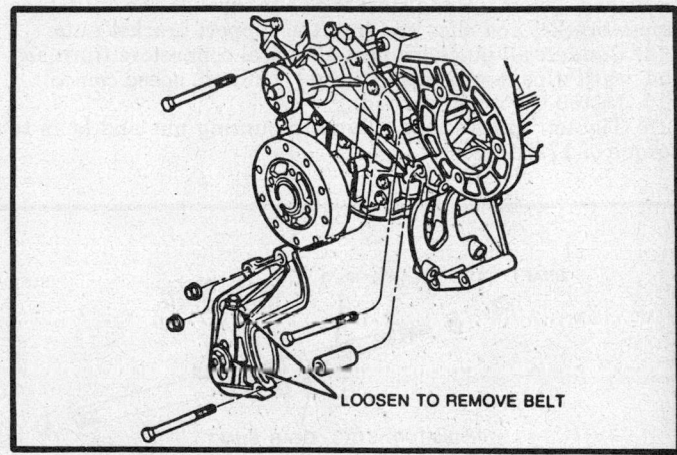

Power steering pump and bracket removal and installation—3.0L engine

l. Lower the front wheels.
5. In cases of severe aeration, repeat the procedure.

Steering Column

NOTE: All steering column components are assembled with fasteners that are designed with a thread locking system to prevent loosening due to vibrations associated with normal vehicle operation.

Removal and Installation

ESCORT, LYNX, TEMPO, AND TOPAZ

1. Disconnect the negative battery cable.
2. Remove the steering column cover on the lower portion of the instrument panel to expose the instrument panel reinforcement section.
3. Remove the instrument panel reinforcement section. Remove the speed control module, if equipped.
4. Remove the lower steering column shroud.
5. Loosen, but do not remove, the nuts and bolts retaining the steering column to the support bracket. Remove upper shroud.
6. Disconnect and label all steering column electrical connections (ignition, wash/wipe, turn signal, key warning buzzer and speed control).
7. Loosen the steering column to intermediate shaft clamp connection and remove the bolt or nut.
8. Remove the nuts and bolts retaining the steering column

to the support bracket and lower the steering column to the floor.

9. Pry open the steering column shaft clamp on each side of the bolt groove with the steering column locked. Open enough to disengage the shaft with a minimal effort. Do not use excessive force, as damage to components may result.

10. Inspect the steering column bracket clips for damage. If clips have been bent or excessively distorted, they must be replaced.

To install:

11. Check the distance that the steering shaft protrudes past the outer tube assembly. This distance must be between 1.44–1.63 in.

12. Engage the lower steering shaft to the intermediate shaft and hand start the clamp bolt and nut.

13. Place the steering column under the instrument panel, align the bolts on the steering column support bracket assembly with the outer tube mounting holes and hand start the nuts. Check for the presence of the clips on the outer bracket. The clips must be present to insure adequate performance of vital parts and systems. Hand start the bolts through the outer tube upper bracket and clips and into the support bracket nuts.

14. Connect all quick connect electrical connectors (turn signal, wash/wipe, key warning buzzer, ignition, speed control).

15. Install the upper shroud.

16. Tighten the steering column mounting nut and bolts to torque of 17–25 ft. lbs.

17. Cycle the steering column one turn left and one turn right to align the intermediate shaft into the column shaft. (vehicles with power steering must have the engine running). Torque the steering shaft clamp nut to 20–30 ft. lbs.

TAURUS, SABLE AND CONTINENTAL

1. Disconnect the negative battery cable.

2. Remove the steering column cover from lower portion of instrument panel by removing self-tapping screws.

3. On vehicles equipped with tilt steering columns, remove the tilt release lever by removing the Allen head cap screw that holds the tilt lever to the steering column.

4. Rotate the ignition lock cylinder to the **RUN** position and depress the lock cylinder retaining pin through the access hole in the shroud with a ⅛ in. punch. Push on the pin pull out on the lock cylinder.

5. Remove horn pad and steering wheel assembly. On vehicles equipped with column shift perform the following steps:

   a. Disconnect the **PRNDL** cable from the lock cylinder housing by removing the retaining screw. Disconnect the **PRNDL** cable from the shift socket. Remove the hood release cable from the handle.

   b. Remove the **PRNDL** cable from the retaining hook on the bottom of the lock cylinder housing.

6. Disconnect the speed control/horn brush wiring connector from the main wiring harness.

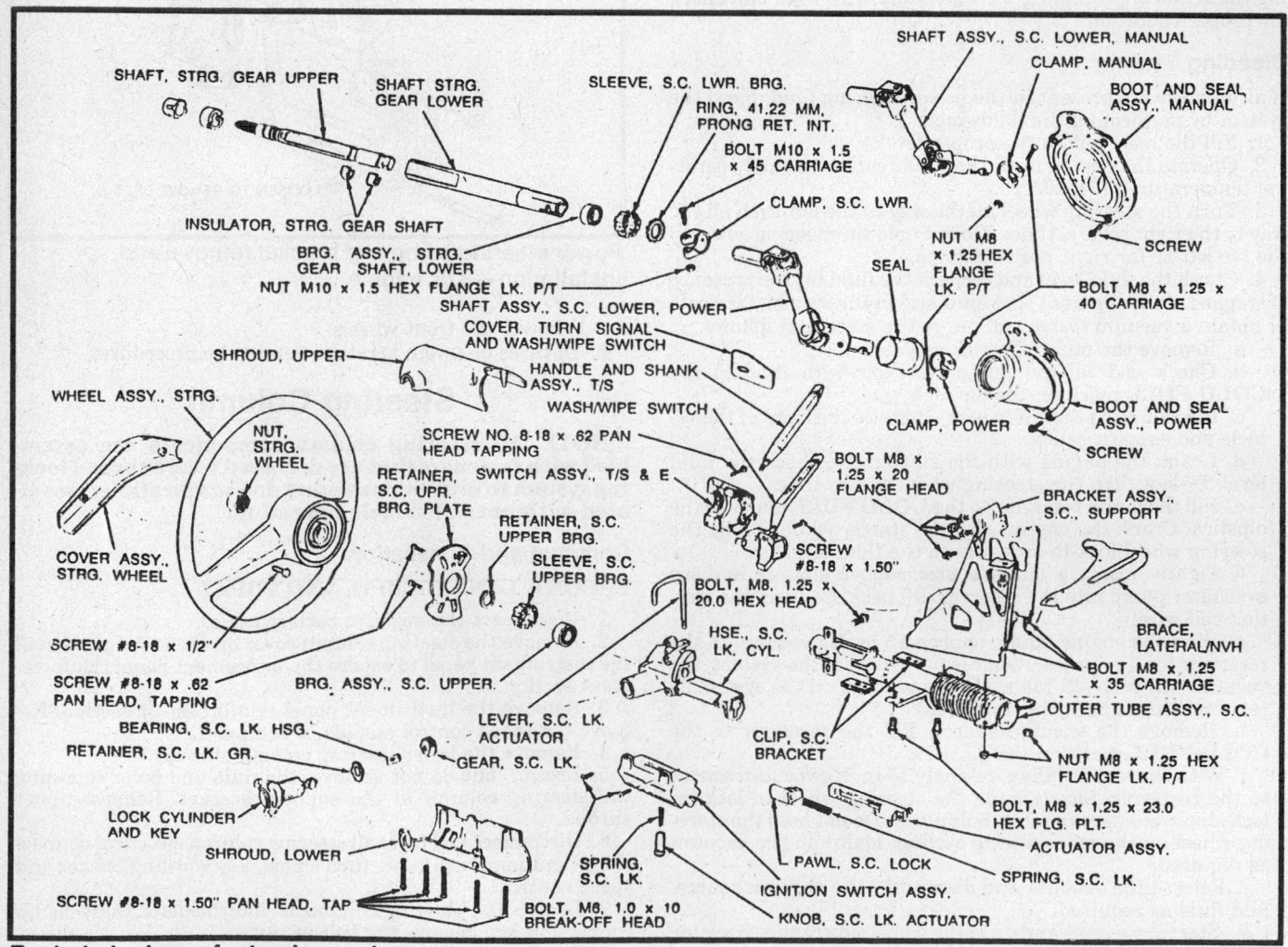

Exploded view of steering column assembly

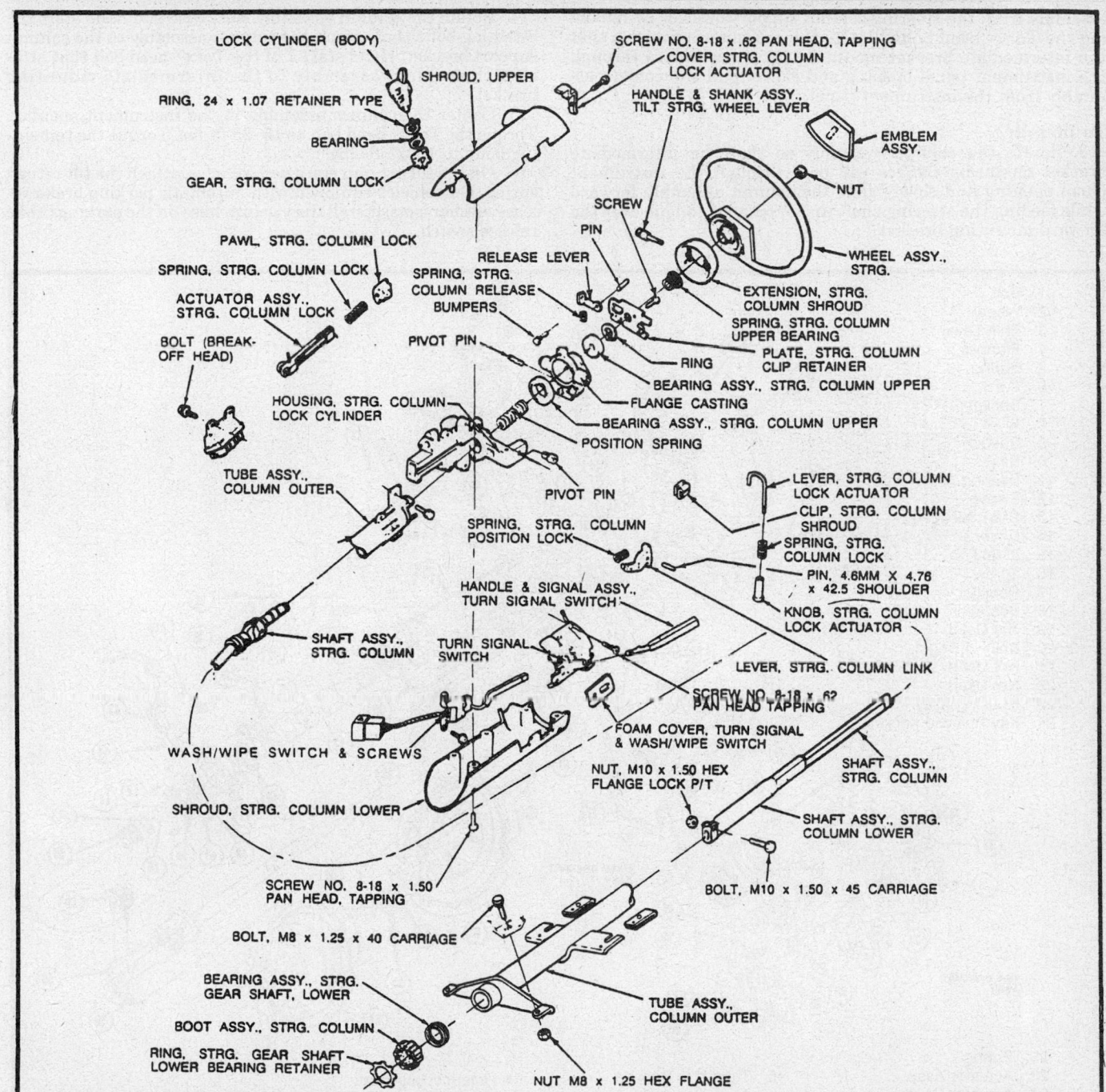

Tilt steering column—exploded view

7. Remove the multi-function switch wiring harness retainer from the lock cylinder housing by squeezing the end of the retainer and pushing out. Disconnect the multi-function switch connector from the switch and remove the multi-function switch from the lock cylinder housing by removing the self-tapping screws.

8. Disconnect the key warning buzzer switch wiring connector from the main wiring harness. Disconnect the wiring connector from the ignition switch.

9. Disconnect the steering shaft from the intermediate shaft by removing the 2 nuts and 1 U-clamp. On vehicles equipped with column shift, perform the following steps:

  a. Remove the shift cable plastic terminal from the column

selector lever pilot ball using a suitable tool to pry between the plastic terminal and the selector lever. Make certain not to damage the cable during or after assembly.

  b. Remove the shift cable (with the shift cable still attached) from the lock cylinder housing by removing the retaining screws.

10. On vehicles equipped with an automatic parking brake release mechanism, remove the vacuum hose from the parking brake release switch. On vehicles equipped with tilt columns, remove the tilt return spring.

11. Unbolt the column assembly from the mounting bracket by removing the Torx® head retaining bolt.

12. While supporting the column assembly, unbolt the column

assembly from the steering column support bracket by removing the Torx® head bolts. Rotate the column assembly so that the intermediate bracket mounting flanges will pass through the instrument panel opening and slowly pull the column assembly from the instrument panel.

To install:

13. Rotate the column assembly so that the intermediate bracket mounting flanges will pass through the instrument panel opening and slowly slide the column assembly forward while feeding the steering shaft universal joint tongue over the forward mounting bracket.

14. Rotate the column assembly clockwise and hand start the retaining bolts that attach the column assembly to the column support bracket. Hand start 1 of the Torx® head bolt that attaches the column assembly to the intermediate mounting bracket.

15. Center the column assembly in the instrument opening. Torque the Torx® head bolt to 15–25 ft. lbs. Torque the remaining bolts to 15–25 ft. lbs.

16. On the tilt column equipped vehicles, attach the tilt return spring. On vehicles equipped with automatic parking brake release mechanisms, install the vacuum hose on the parking brake release switch.

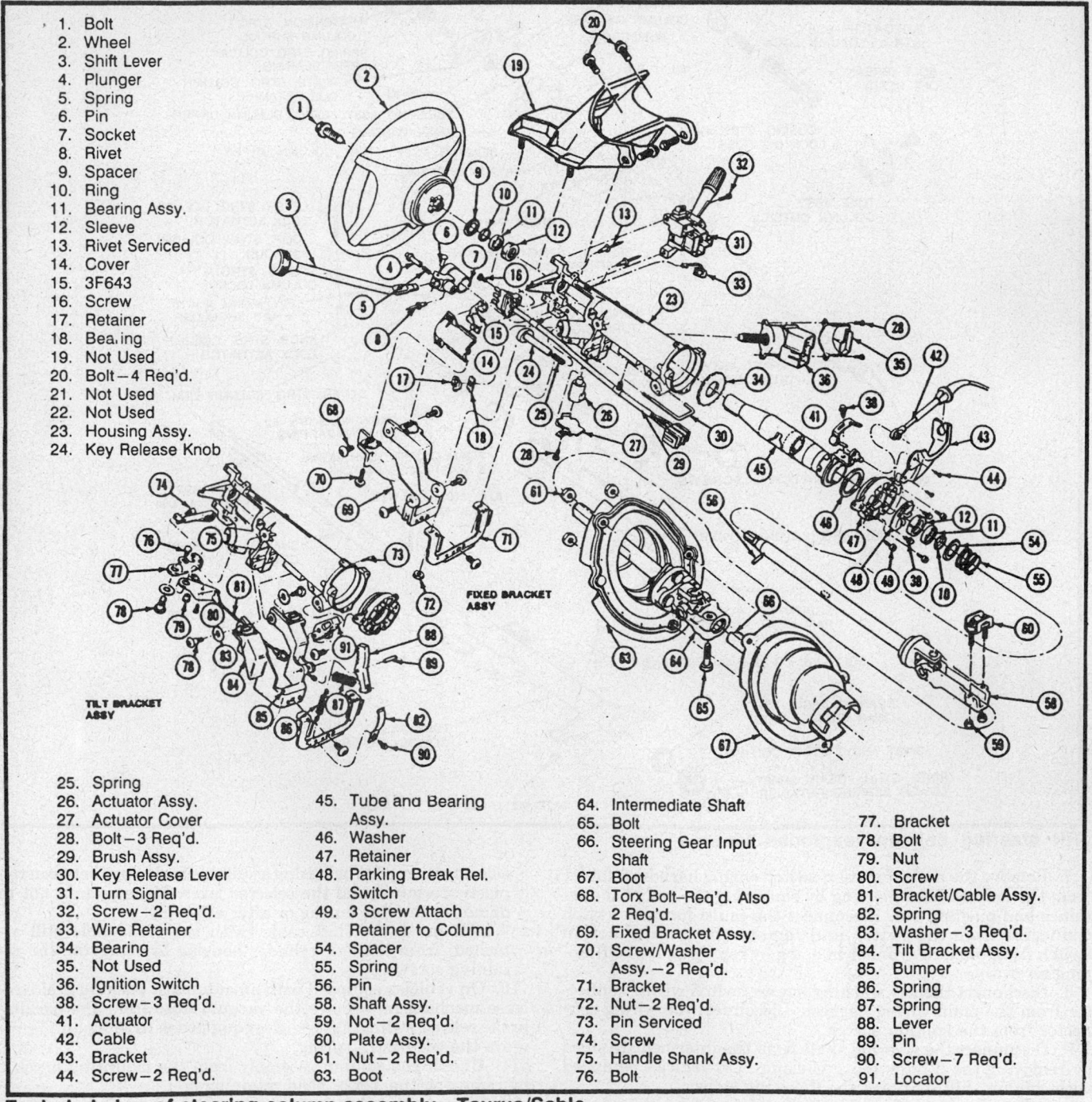

1. Bolt
2. Wheel
3. Shift Lever
4. Plunger
5. Spring
6. Pin
7. Socket
8. Rivet
9. Spacer
10. Ring
11. Bearing Assy.
12. Sleeve
13. Rivet Serviced
14. Cover
15. 3F643
16. Screw
17. Retainer
18. Bearing
19. Not Used
20. Bolt—4 Req'd.
21. Not Used
22. Not Used
23. Housing Assy.
24. Key Release Knob

25. Spring
26. Actuator Assy.
27. Actuator Cover
28. Bolt—3 Req'd.
29. Brush Assy.
30. Key Release Lever
31. Turn Signal
32. Screw—2 Req'd.
33. Wire Retainer
34. Bearing
35. Not Used
36. Ignition Switch
38. Screw—3 Req'd.
41. Actuator
42. Cable
43. Bracket
44. Screw—2 Req'd.

45. Tube and Bearing Assy.
46. Washer
47. Retainer
48. Parking Break Rel. Switch
49. 3 Screw Attach Retainer to Column
54. Spacer
55. Spring
56. Pin
58. Shaft Assy.
59. Not—2 Req'd.
60. Plate Assy.
61. Nut—2 Req'd.
63. Boot

64. Intermediate Shaft
65. Bolt
66. Steering Gear Input Shaft
67. Boot
68. Torx Bolt—Req'd. Also 2 Req'd.
69. Fixed Bracket Assy.
70. Screw/Washer Assy.—2 Req'd.
71. Bracket
72. Nut—2 Req'd.
73. Pin Serviced
74. Screw
75. Handle Shank Assy.
76. Bolt

77. Bracket
78. Bolt
79. Nut
80. Screw
81. Bracket/Cable Assy.
82. Spring
83. Washer—3 Req'd.
84. Tilt Bracket Assy.
85. Bumper
86. Spring
87. Spring
88. Lever
89. Pin
90. Screw—7 Req'd.
91. Locator

Exploded view of steering column assembly—Taurus/Sable

17. On vehicles equipped with column shift, perform the following steps.

a. Attach the shift cable bracket (with the shift cable attached) to the lock cylinder housing with the retaining screws. Torque the screws to 30–60 inch lbs.

b. Snap the transaxle shift cable terminal to the selector lever pivot ball on the steering column.

18. Connect the steering shaft to the intermediate shaft with the U-clamp and hex nuts. Torque them to 15–25 ft. lbs. On the tilt column equipped vehicles, the column must be in the middle tilt position before the nuts are tightened.

19. Install the main harness wiring connector to the ignition switch. Install the key warning buzzer switch wiring connector to the main wiring harness.

20. Install the multi-function switch to the lock cylinder housing with the self-tapping screws. Torque the screws to 18–26 inch lbs. Install the multi-function switch wiring harness retainer over the shroud mounting boss and snap it into the slot in the lock cylinder housing.

21. Connect the speed control/horn brush wiring connector to the main harness. On shift column equipped vehicles, perform the following steps:

a. Install the **PRNDL** cable into the retaining hook on the cylinder housing. Connect the **PRNDL** cable to the shift socket.

b. Loosely install the **PRNDL** cable onto the lock cylinder housing with one retaining screw. Adjust the **PRNDL** cable as follows: Place the shift lever in the **D** position with the regular transaxles and **OD** position with overdrive transaxles. Adjust the cable until the **PRNDL** pointer is centered on the **D** position or the **OD** position depending on the type of transaxle. Tighten the hex head screw to 18–30 inch lbs.

22. Install the steering wheel and horn pad. Install the steering column shrouds with retaining screws. On tilt column equipped vehicles, install the tilt release lever with one socket head capscrew.

23. Install the ignition lock cylinder. Install the steering column cover from the lower portion of the instrument panel with self-tapping screws.

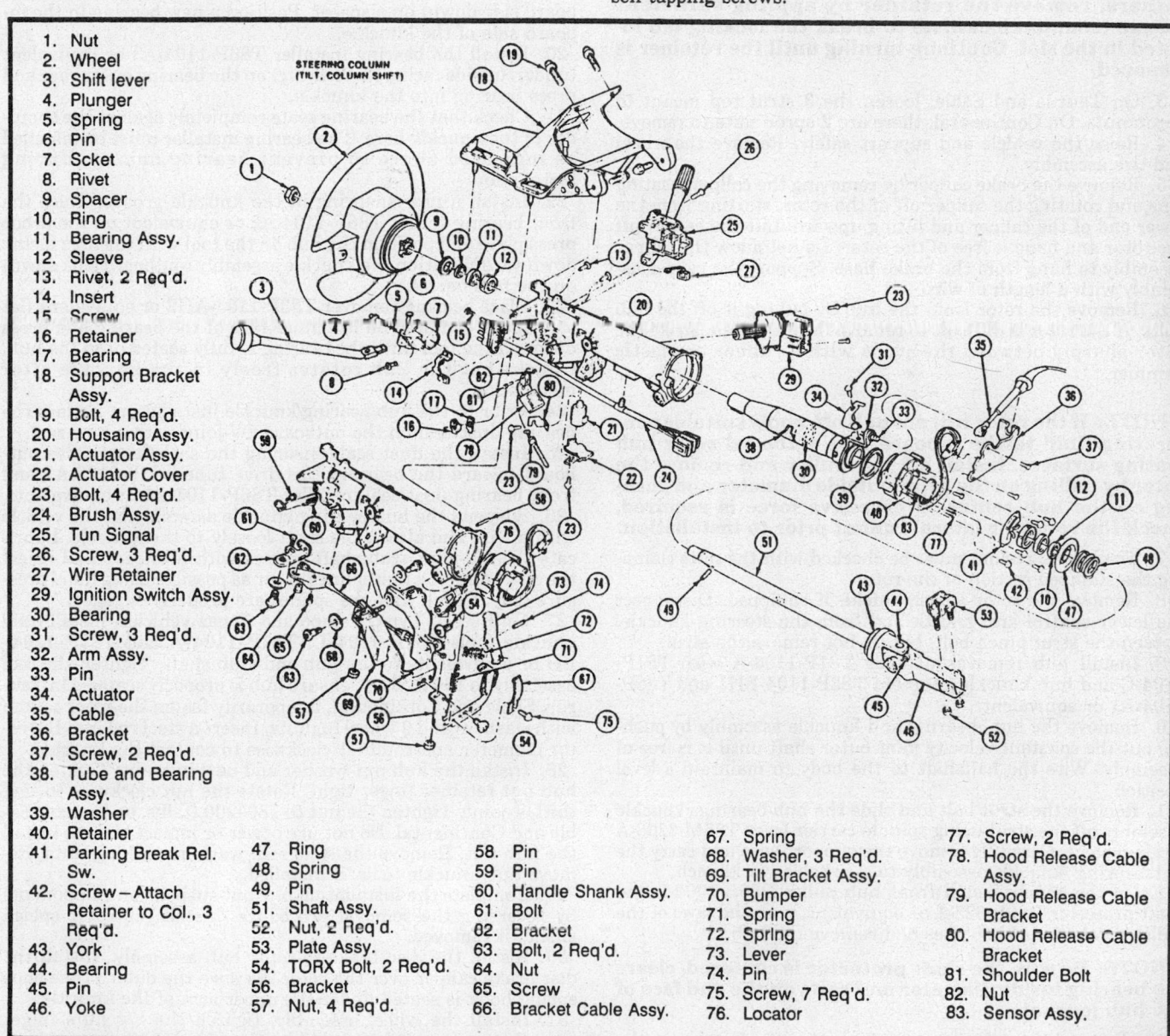

1. Nut
2. Wheel
3. Shift lever
4. Plunger
5. Spring
6. Pin
7. Scket
8. Rivet
9. Spacer
10. Ring
11. Bearing Assy.
12. Sleeve
13. Rivet, 2 Req'd.
14. Insert
15. Screw
16. Retainer
17. Bearing
18. Support Bracket Assy.
19. Bolt, 4 Req'd.
20. Housaing Assy.
21. Actuator Assy.
22. Actuator Cover
23. Bolt, 4 Req'd.
24. Brush Assy.
25. Tun Signal
26. Screw, 3 Req'd.
27. Wire Retainer
29. Ignition Switch Assy.
30. Bearing
31. Screw, 3 Req'd.
32. Arm Assy.
33. Pin
34. Actuator
35. Cable
36. Bracket
37. Screw, 2 Req'd.
38. Tube and Bearing Assy.
39. Washer
40. Retainer
41. Parking Break Rel. Sw.
42. Screw—Attach Retainer to Col., 3 Req'd.
43. York
44. Bearing
45. Pin
46. Yoke

47. Ring
48. Spring
49. Pin
51. Shaft Assy.
52. Nut, 2 Req'd.
53. Plate Assy.
54. TORX Bolt, 2 Req'd.
56. Bracket
57. Nut, 4 Req'd.

58. Pin
59. Pin
60. Handle Shank Assy.
61. Bolt
62. Bracket
63. Bolt, 2 Req'd.
64. Nut
65. Screw
66. Bracket Cable Assy.

67. Spring
68. Washer, 3 Req'd.
69. Tilt Bracket Assy.
70. Bumper
71. Spring
72. Spring
73. Lever
74. Pin
75. Screw, 7 Req'd.
76. Locator

77. Screw, 2 Req'd.
78. Hood Release Cable Assy.
79. Hood Release Cable Bracket
80. Hood Release Cable Bracket
81. Shoulder Bolt
82. Nut
83. Sensor Assy.

Exploded view of steering column assembly—Continental

24. Reconnect the negative battery cable and check the steering column and its components for proper operation.

Front Wheel Bearings

The front wheel bearings are located in the front knuckle and have a set-right design that requires no scheduled maintenance or adjustment. If the bearings are disassembled for any reason, they must be replaced as a unit.

Removal and Installation

1. Loosen the lug nuts.
2. Remove the hub retaining nut and washer by applying sufficient torque to the nut to overcome the prevailing torque feature of the crimp in the nut collar. Do not use an impact type tool to remove the hub nut. The hub nut must be discarded after removal.

NOTE: On vehicles equipped with locking tab type retainers, remove the retainer by appling sufficient torque (counterclockwise) to break the locking tab located in the slot. Continue turning until the retainer is removed.

3. On Taurus and Sable, loosen the 3 strut top mount to apron nuts. On Continental, there are 2 apron nuts to remove.
4. Raise the vehicle and support safely. Remove the wheel and tire assembly.
5. Remove the brake caliper by removing the caliper locating pins and rotating the caliper off of the rotor, starting from the lower end of the caliper and lifting upward. Lift the caliper off the rotor and hang it free of the rotor. Do not allow the caliper assembly to hang from the brake hose. Support the caliper assembly with a length of wire.
6. Remove the rotor from the hub by pulling it off the hub bolts. If the rotor is difficult to remove from the hub, strike the rotor sharply between the studs with a rubber or plastic hammer.

NOTE: If the rotor will not pull off, apply suitable penetrating fluid to the inboard and outboard rotor hub mating surfaces. Install a 3 jaw puller and remove the rotor by pulling on the rotor outside diameter and pushing on the hub center. If excessive force is required, check the rotor for lateral runout prior to installation.

7. The lateral runout must be checked with the nuts clamping the stamped section of the rotor.
8. Remove the rotor splash shield, if equipped. Disconnect the lower control arm and tie rod from the steering knuckle. Loosen the strut pinch bolt, but do not remove the strut.
9. Install hub remover/installer T81P-1104-A with T81P-1104-C and hub knuckle adapters T83P-1104-BH1 and T86P-1104-A1 or equivalent.
10. Remove the hub, bearing and knuckle assembly by pushing out the constant velocity joint outer shaft until it is free of assembly. Wire the halfshaft to the body to maintain a level position.
11. Remove the strut bolt and slide the hub/bearings/knuckle assembly off the strut using spindle carrier lever T85M-3206-A or equivalent. Carefully remove the support wire and carry the hub/bearing/knuckle assembly to a suitable workbench.
12. On the bench, install front hub puller D80L-1002-L and shaft protector D80L-625-1 or equivalent, with the jaws of the puller on the knuckle bosses and remove the hub.

NOTE: Be sure the shaft protector is centered, clears the bearing inside diameter and rests on the end face of the hub journal.

13. Remove the snapring, which retains the bearing in the knuckle assembly, with the snapring pliers and discard.

14. Using a suitable hydraulic press, place the front bearing spacer T86P-1104-A2 or equivalent step side up on the press plate and position the knuckle (outboard side up) on the spacer.
15. Install bearing remover T83P-1104-AH2 or equivalent centered on the bearing inner race and press the bearing out of the knuckle. Discard the old bearing.
16. Remove the halfshaft and place it in a suitable vise.
17. Remove the bearing dust seal by equally tapping on the outer edge with a light duty hammer and a suitable tool. Discard the dust seal.

To install:
18. Thoroughly clean the knuckle bearing bore and hub bearing journal to ensure the correct seating of a new bearing.

NOTE: If the hub bearing journal is scored or damaged, replace the hub. Do not attempt to service a bad hub.

19. Place the front bearing spacer T86P-1104-A or equivalent step side down on a press plate and position the knuckle (outboard side down) on a spacer. Position a new bearing in the inboard side of the knuckle.
20. Install the bearing installer T86P-1104-A3 or equivalent (undercut side facing the bearing) on the bearing outer race and press bearing into the knuckle.
21. Check that the bearing seats completely against the shoulder of the knuckle bore. The bearing installer must be installed as indicated above to prevent bearing damage during installation.
22. Install a new snapring in the knuckle groove. Place the front bearing spacer T86P-1104-A2 or equivalent on the arbor press plate and position the hub on the tool with the lugs facing downward. Position the knuckle assembly (outboard side down) on the hub barrel.
23. Place bearing remover T83P-1104-AH2 or equivalent flat side down, centered on the inner race of the bearing and press down on the tool until the bearing is fully seated onto the hub. Check that the hub rotates freely in the knuckle after installation.
24. Prior to the hub/bearing/knuckle installation, replace the bearing dust seal on the outboard CV-joint with a new seal.
25. Install the dust seal, ensuring the seal flange faces outboard toward the bearing. Use drive tube T83P-3132-A1 and front bearing dust seal installer T86P-1104-A4 or equivalent.
26. Suspend the hub/bearing/knuckle assembly on the vehicle with a wire and attach the strut loosely to the knuckle. Lubricate the CV-joint stub shaft splines with lubricant and insert the shaft onto the hub splines as far as possible using hand pressure only. Check that the splines are properly engaged.
27. On Escort, Lynx, Tempo and Topaz vehicles, install hub/knuckle tools T81P-1104-C, T81P-1104-A and T83P-1104-BH or equivalents to the hub and stub shaft. Tighten the tool assembly to 120 ft. lbs to ensure hub is properly seated. On Taurus, Sable and Continental, temporarily fasten the rotor to hub with washers and 2 wheel lugnuts. Insert a steel rod into the rotor diameter and rotate it clockwise to contact the knuckle.
28. Install the hub nut washer and new hub nut. Tighten the hub nut retainer finger tight. Rotate the nut clockwise to seat the CV-joint. Tighten the nut to 180–200 ft. lbs. on Taurus, Sable and Continental. Do not use power or impact tools to install the hub nut. Remove the steel rod, washers and lug nuts. Remove the hub/knuckle tools, if installed.
29. Complete the installation of front suspension components by reversing the removal procedure. Install the rotor splash shield, if removed.
30. Install the disc brake-to-rotor hub assembly. Install the disc brake caliper over the rotor. Be sure the outer brake shoe spring hook is seated under the upper arm of the knuckle.
31. Install the wheel assembly, tighten the lug nuts finger tight. Lower the vehicle and block the wheels to prevent the vehicle from moving. Tighten the lug nuts to 80–105 ft. lbs.

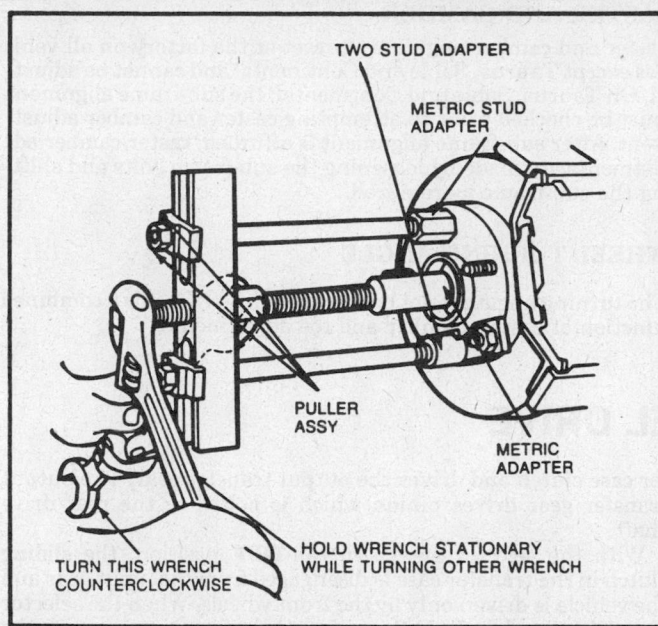

Removing the hub

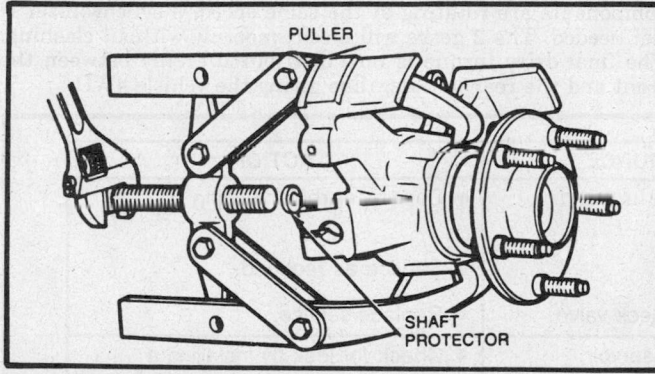

Typical front hub puller

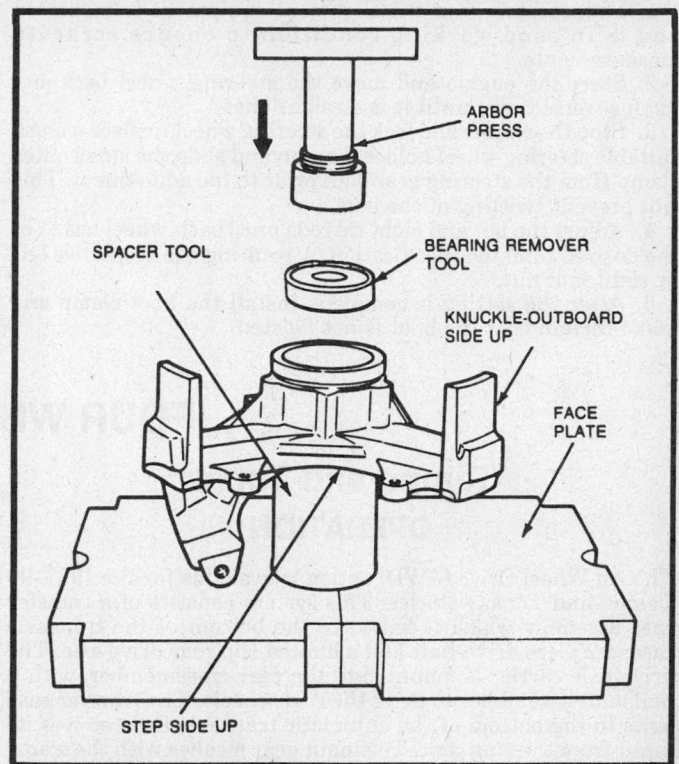

Pressing out the old bearing

NOTE: Replacement lug nuts or studs must be of the same type and size as those being replaced.

32. On Escort, Lynx, Tempo and Topaz, manually thread the hub retainer assembly onto the CV output shaft as far as possible. Torque the retainer nut assembly to 180–200 ft. lbs. Never use power tool to tighten the hub nut and do not move the vehicle before the retainer is tightened. During the tightening, an audible click should will indicate a proper ratchet of the retainer. As the retainer tightens, be sure that one of the 3 locking tabs is in the slot of the CV joint shaft. If the hub retainer assembly is damaged or more than 1 locking tab is broken, replace the retainer.

NOTE: On Escort, Lynx, Tempo and Topaz, when installing the retainer, if a locking tab does not engage in a shaft slot, or a tab breaks during installation, service the retainer as follows: Using a suitable pair of needle nose pliers, place the plier tips between the ratchet tabs and rotate in a counterclockwise direction until the next locking tab falls into slot. If 2 or more locking tabs are broken during installation, replace the retainer.

33. Install the wheel cover or hub cover. Lower the vehicle completely to the ground and remove wheel blocks. Road test the vehicle and check to see if the vehicle is operating properly.

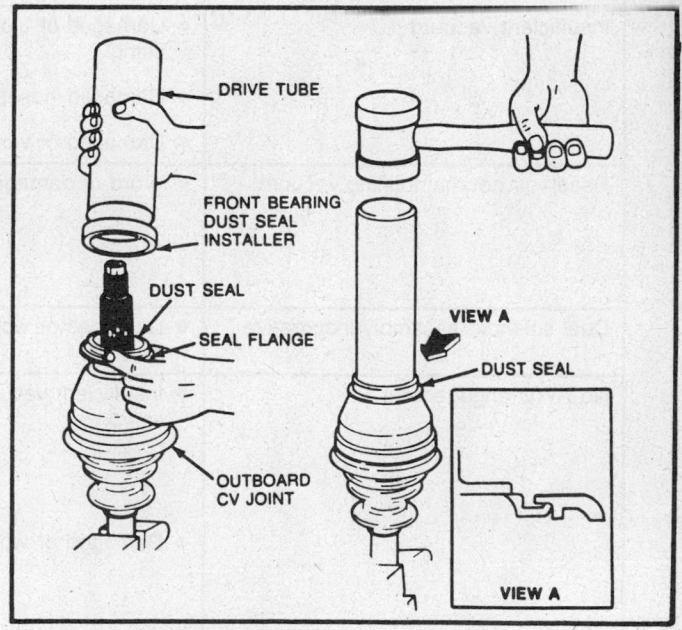

Installing the dust seal

Alignment

Procedure

TOE

NOTE: The toe adjustment may be performed at normal ride height.

1. Make certain that the alignment equipment is calibrated and is in good working condition to ensure accurate measurements.

2. Start the engine and move the steering wheel back and forth several times until it is straight ahead.

3. Stop the engine and lock the steering wheel in place using a suitable steering wheel holder. Loosen and slide the small outer clamp from the steering gear boot prior to toe adjustment. This will prevent twisting of the boot.

4. Adjust the left and right tie rods until each wheel has ½ of the desired total toe specification by rotating the respective left or right jam nut.

5. After the setting is complete, install the boot clamp and make certain that the boot is not twisted.

CASTER AND CAMBER

Caster and camber angles are preset at the factory on all vehicles except Taurus, Sable and Continental and cannot be adjusted. On Taurus, Sable and Continental, the sub-frame alignment must be checked prior to attempting caster and camber adjustment. After sub-frame alignment is affirmed, caster/camber adjustments are made by loosening the sub-frame bolts and shifting the sub-frame as required.

WHEEL TURNING ANGLE

The turning angle cannot be adjusted directly as it is a combined function of caster, camber and toe adjustments.

FOUR WHEEL DRIVE

Tempo and Topaz
OPERATION

The All Wheel Drive (AWD) option is available for the 1987–90 Tempo and Topaz vehicles. This system consists of a transfer case assembly which is bolted to the bottom of the transaxle case, a 2 piece driveshaft and a limited slip rear drive axle. The drive axle carrier is mounted to the rear crossmember, with 2 halfshaft assemblies to drive the rear wheels. The transfer case bolts to the bottom of the automatic transaxle and receives its input from the ring gear. The input gear meshes with the transfer case clutch and drives the output transfer gear. The output transfer gear drives pinion which is bolted to the rear drive shaft.

With the selector switch in the OFF position, the sliding clutch in the transfer case is disengaged from the input gear and the vehicle is driven only by the front wheels. When the selector switch is moved to the ON position, the vacuum servo moves the sliding clutch sleeve to engage the input gear. Because both components are rotating at the same speed, a synchronizer is not needed. The 2 gears will mesh smoothly without clashing. The final drive torque is now distributed evenly between the front and the rear wheels, thus giving the vehicle 4WD.

CONDITION	POSSIBLE SOURCE	ACTION
Insufficient vacuum	• Damaged or clogged manifold fitting.	• Service or replace fitting.
	• Damaged hoses.	• Service as required.
	• Damaged or worn check valve.	• Replace/service.
Reservoir not maintaining vacuum	• Worn or damaged reservoir.	• Check for leak by installing a vacuum gauge at rubber tee (input to dual solenoids). Gauge should rear 54-67 kPa (16-20 inches) vacuum.
Dual solenoid assembly inoperative	• Damaged or worn solenoid assembly.	• Check for vacuum at solenoids as outlined.
No AWD engagement	• Insufficient vacuum at vacuum servo.	• Disconnect vacuum harness at single to double connector and install a vacuum gauge. With engine running and AWD switch in proper position, check for vacuum.
	• Damaged or worn vacuum servo.	• Place transaxle in NEUTRAL. Raise vehicle on a hoist and disconnect vacuum harness at single to double connector. Install a hand vacuum pump onto red tube connector and block off black connector. Apply 54-67 kPa (16-20 inches) vacuum at servo end of harness. While rotating front wheels, note that rear wheels also rotate. If rear wheels do not rotate, replace vacuum servo.

All Wheel Drive vacuum diagnosis chart

BRAKES

NOTE: Refer to the unit repair section for brake service information and drum/rotor specifications.

Master Cylinder

Removal and Installation

EXCEPT POWER BRAKES

1. Disconnect the negative battery cable.
2. Working under the instrument panel, disconnect the master cylinder pushrod from the brake pedal.
3. Disconnect the stoplight switch and remove it.
4. Inside the engine compartment, disconnect the brake lines from the master cylinder.
5. Unbolt the master cylinder from the firewall and remove it. Be careful not to damage the firewall grommet.
6. Complete the installation of the master cylinder by reversing the removal procedure. Leave the brake tubes slightly loose at the master cylinder fittings.
7. Fill the master cylinder with fresh brake fluid. Use the foot pedal to bleed the master cylinder. Tighten the brake line fittings. Bleed the system.

POWER BRAKES

1. Disconnect the negative battery cable.
2. Disconnect the brake lines from the primary and secondary outlet ports of the master cylinder and the pressure control valve.
3. Remove the nuts attaching the master cylinder to the brake booster assembly. Disconnect the brake warning lamp wire.
4. Slide the master cylinder forward and upward from the vehicle.
5. To install, mount the master cylinder on the booster. Attach the brake fluid lines to the master cylinder, but leave the fittings slightly loose.
6. Install the brake warning lamp wire.
7. Fill the reservoirs with fresh brake fluid. Use the foot pedal to bleed the master cylinder. Tighten the brake line fittings. Bleed the system.

ANTI-LOCK BRAKE SYSTEM (ABS)

The Continental is equipped with a 4 wheel Anti-lock Brake System (ABS). The ABS consists of the following major components: hydraulic actuation unit, electric pump assembly, solenoid valve block assembly, electric controller, brake control valve and pressure switch, proportioning valve and brake fluid reservoir/level indicator assembly. The hydraulic actuation unit contains the master cylinder and brake booster sections arranged in fore and aft sequence.

NOTE: Before the actuation assembly is removed, the hydraulic pressure must be discharged from the system. To discharge the hydraulic pressure from the system, turn the ignition switch to the OFF position and pump the brake pedal a minimum of 20 times until an increase in pedal pressure is felt.

Removal and Installation

1. Disconnect the negative battery cable.
2. Remove the air cleaner housing and duct assembly.
3. Disconnect and label the following component electrical connectors: fluid level indicator, main valve, solenoid valve block, pressure waring switch, hydraulic pump motor and ground connector from the master cylinder portion of the actuation assembly.

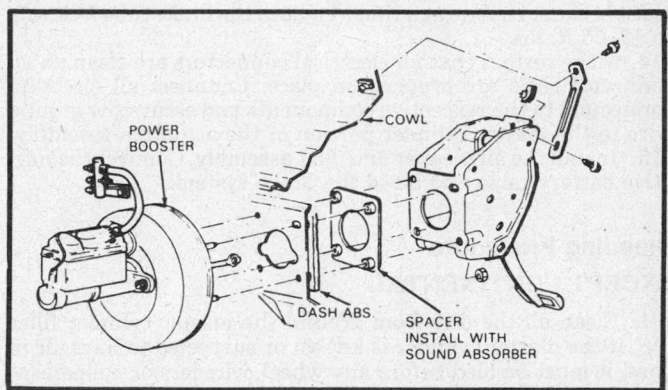

Power brake booster and master cylinder installation

4. Disconnect the 3 brake tube fittings from the solenoid block valve connections. Cover or plug the openings immediately to prevent the loss of fluid and contamination.

NOTE: Do not allow brake fluid to come in contact with any of the electrical connectors.

5. Remove the trim panel under the steering column.
6. Disconnect the actuation rod from the brake pedal by removing the hairpin connector adjacent to the stoplight switch. Slide the switch, pushrod and plastic bushings off the pedal pin.
7. Remove the retaining nuts that fasten the actuation assembly to the brake pedal support bracket. Remove the actuation assembly from the vehicle.

To install:

8. Inspect the foam gasket and rubber boot for damage and replace with new as required.
9. Position the actuation assembly with foam gasket and rubber boot onto the engine side of the dash panel by aligning the mounting studs and pushrod with the proper dash panel holes.
10. From inside the passenger compartment, attach the actuation assembly to the pedal support bracket with the retaining nuts and make finger tight.
11. Connect the pushrod, flanged plastic bushing and washer to the brake pedal pin. Position the stoplight switch so that the slot on the switch bracket straddles the brake pedal pin (with the hole on the opposite leg of the switch bracket just clearing the pin). Slide the switch until it bottoms on the pin then install the outer nylon bushing. Secure the assembly with the hairpin retainer.

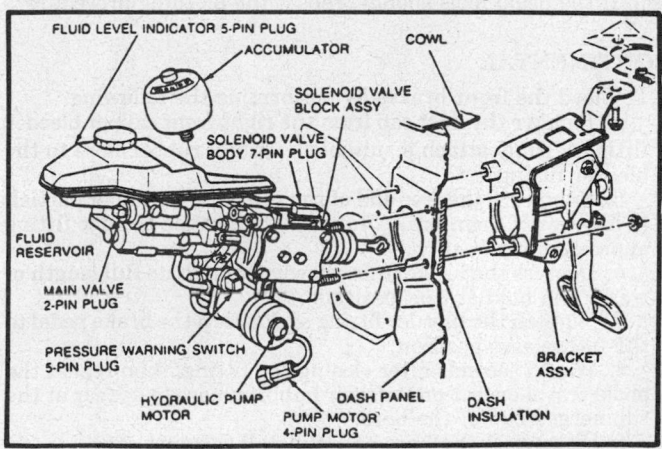

Hydraulic actuation unit assembly—Continental

12. Tighten the actuating/support bracket retaining nuts to 13–25 ft. lbs.

13. From inside the engine compartment, connect the solenoid block brake tubes one at a time. Tighten the brake tube locknuts to 13–25 ft. lbs.

14. Make certain that all electrical connectors are clean an all connector seals are properly in place. Connnect all electrical connectors to the respective components and secure the ground wire to the master cylinder portion of the actuation assembly.

15. Install the air cleaner and duct assembly. Connect the negative battery cable and bleed the brake system.

Bleeding Procedure

EXCEPT CONTINENTAL

1. Clean all the dirt from around the master cylinder filler cap. If the master cylinder is known or suspected to have air in bore, it must be bled before any wheel cylinders or calipers.

2. To bleed the master cylinder, loosen the upper secondary left front outlet fitting aproximately ¾ turn. Have an assistant push the brake pedal down slowly through full travel. Close the outlet fitting, then return the pedal slowly to the full released position. Wait 5 seconds, then repeat the operation until the air bubbles cease to appear.

3. Loosen the upper primary right front outlet fitting approximately ¾ turn. and repeat Step 2.

4. To continue to bleed the system, remove the rubber cap dust cap from the wheel cylinder bleeder fitting or caliper fitting. Check to make sure the bleeder fitting is positioned at the upper half on the front of the caliper, if not the caliper is located on the wrong side.

5. Attach a suitable length of rubber hose to the fitting. Submerge the free end of the hose in a container partially filled with clean brake fluid and loosen the bleeder fitting approximately ¾ of a turn.

6. Have the assistant push brake pedal down slowly through full travel. Close the bleeder fitting, then return the pedal to the full release position. Wait 5 seconds, then repeat this operation until the air bubbles cease to appear at the submerged end of the bleeder hose.

7. When the fluid is completely free of air bubbles, properly tighten the bleeder fitting and reinstall the rubber dust cap. Repeat this process on the opposite diagonal system. Refill the master cylinder reservoir after each wheel cylinder or caliper is bled and reinstall the master cylinder cap.

8. When the bleeding operation is completed, the fluid level should be filled to the maximum fill level indicated on the reservoir. Always ensure the disc brake pistons are returned to their normal positions by depressing the brake pedal several times until the normal pedal travel is established. Check the pedal feel. If the pedal feels spongy, repeat the bleeding procedure.

CONTINENTAL

1. Bleed the front brakes by performing the following:
   a. Remove the dust cap from the right front caliper bleeder fitting. Firmly attach a suitable length of rubber hose to the bleeder fitting.
   b. Submerge the free end of the tube in a container partially filled with clean brake fluid and loosen the bleeder fitting approximately ¾ turn.
   c. Depress the brake pedal slowly through its full length of travel and hold at that position.
   d. Tighten the bleeder fitting and return the brake pedal to the full release position.
   e. Wait 5 seconds after closing the fitting, then repeat the pedal travel operation until air bubbles cease to appear at the submerged end of the hose.
   f. Disconnect the hose and reinstall the dust cap.
   g. Repeat the bleeding procedure for the left front caliper.

2. Bleed the rear brakes by performing the following:
   a. Remove the dust cap from the right rear caliper bleeder fitting. Firmly attach a suitable length of rubber hose to the bleeder fiting. Place the free end of the hose in an empty container.
   b. Turn the ignition switch to the **RUN** position. This will energize the electric pump that will in turn fully charge the accumulator.
   c. Hold the brake pedal in the applied position and loosen the right caliper bleeder fitting for 10 seconds at a time until an air-free stream of brake fluid is observed.

NOTE: Care must be exercised when opening the bleeder fitting due the high pressure generated by a fully charged accumulator.

   d. Repeat the bleeding procedure for the left rear caliper.

NOTE: If the pump motor is allowed to run continuously for approximately 20 minutes, a thermal safety switch inside the motor will shut the motor off to prevent overheating. If that happens, a 2–10 minute cool down period is required until normal pump operation can resume.

Power Brake Booster

Removal and Installation

EXCEPT CONTINENTAL

1. Disconnect the battery ground cable and remove the brake lines from the master cylinder.

2. Remove the retaining nuts and remove the master cylinder.

3. From under the instrument panel, remove the stoplight switch wiring connector from the switch. Remove the pushrod retainer and outer nylon washer from the brake pin, slide the stoplight switch along the brake pedal pin, far enough for the outer hole to clear the pin.

4. Remove the switch by sliding it upward. Remove the booster to dash panel retaining nuts. Slide the booster pushrod and pushrod bushing off the brake pedal pin.

5. On Taurus and Sable, remove the screws and position the vacuum tee out of the way. Position the wire harness out of the way. Remove the transaxle shift cable and bracket.

6. Disconnect the manifold vacuum hose from the booster check valve and move the booster forward until the booster studs clear the dash panel and remove the booster.

7. Complete the installation of the power booster assembly by reversing the removal procedure. Bleed the brake system.

NOTE: On vehicles equipped with speed control, the vacuum dump valve must be adjusted if the brake booster has been removed.

8. To adjust the vacuum dump valve, complete the following:
   a. Firmly depress and hold the brake pedal.
   b. Push in the dump valve until the valve collar bottoms against the retaining clip.
   c. Place a 0.050–0.10 in. shim between the white button of the valve and the pad on the brake pedal.
   d. Firmly pull the brake pedal rearward to its normal position, allowing the dump valve to ratchet backward in the retaining clip.

CONTINENTAL

The power booster and the master cylinder are contained in the hydraulic actuation unit. To remove the power booster/master cylinder assembly, refer to Anti-Lock Brake System information.

Parking Brake

Adjustment
ESCORT, LYNX, TEMPO AND TOPAZ

1. Apply the service brake approximately 3 times (with the engine running, on vehicles equipped with power brakes) before adjusting the parking brake.

2. Place the parking brake control assembly in the 12th notch position (2 notches from full application). Tighten the adjusting nut until the rear wheel brakes drag slightly when the control assembly is fully released. Repeat as necessary.

3. Reposition the control assembly in the 12th notch. Loosen the adjusting nut just enough to eliminate rear brake drag when the control assembly is fully released.

TAURUS, SABLE AND CONTINENTAL

1. Make sure the parking brake is fully released. Place the transaxle in the **N** position.

2. Raise the vehicle and support safely. Tighten the adjusting nut against the cable equalizer or cable adjuster bracket (Continental). Then loosen the adjusting nut until the rear brakes are fully released. There should be no brake drag.

3. If the brake cables were replaced , stroke the parking brake several times, then release control and repeat Step 2.

4. Check for operation of the parking brake with the vehicle supported and the parking brake fully released. If there is any slack in the cables or if the rear brakes drag when the wheels are turned, adjust as required.

5. Lower the vehicle.

CLUTCH AND TRANSAXLE

Refer to "Chilton's Transmission Service Manual" for additional coverage.

Clutch Linkage

Adjustment

The free play in the clutch is adjusted by a built in mechanism that allows the clutch controls to be self-adjusted during normal operation. The self-adjusting feature should be checked every 5000 miles. This is accomplished by insuring that the clutch

pedal travels to the top of its upward position. Grasp the clutch pedal with hand or put foot under the clutch pedal, pull up on the pedal until it stops. Very little effort is required (about 10 lbs.). During the application of upward pressure, a click may be heard which means an adjustment was necessary and has been accomplished.

Clutch

Removal and Installation

1. Disconnect the negative battery cable. Raise the vehicle and support it safely. Remove the transaxle.

2. Mark the pressure plate assembly and the flywheel so that they can be assembled in the same position.

3. Loosen the attaching bolts 1 turn at a time, in sequence, until spring tension is relieved to prevent pressure plate cover distortion.

4. Support the pressure plate and remove the bolts. Remove the pressure plate and clutch disc from the flywheel.

5. Inspect the flywheel, clutch disc, pressure plate, throwout bearing and the clutch fork for wear. Replace parts as required. If the flywheel shows any signs of overheating (blue discoloration) or if it is badly grooved or scored, it should be refaced or replaced.

6. Clean the pressure plate and flywheel surfaces thoroughly. Position the clutch disc and pressure plate into the installed position, aligning the marks made previously. Support them with a suitable dummy shaft or clutch aligning tool.

7. Install the pressure plate-to-flywheel bolts. Tighten them gradually in a cross pattern to 20–24 ft. lbs. Remove the alignment tool.

8. Lubricate the release bearing and install it in the fork.

9. Complete the installation of the transaxle by reversing the removal procedure.

Manual Transaxle

Removal and Installation

1. Disconnect the negative battery cable. Wedge a wood block approximately 7 in. long under the clutch pedal to hold the pedal up slightly beyond its normal position. Grasp the clutch cable and pull forward, disconnecting it from the clutch release shaft assembly. Remove the clutch casing from the rib on the top surface of the transaxle case.

2. Remove the 2 top transaxle-to-engine mounting bolts. Remove the air cleaner. On the Escort and Lynx, remove the top bolt that secures the air management valve bracket to the transaxle.

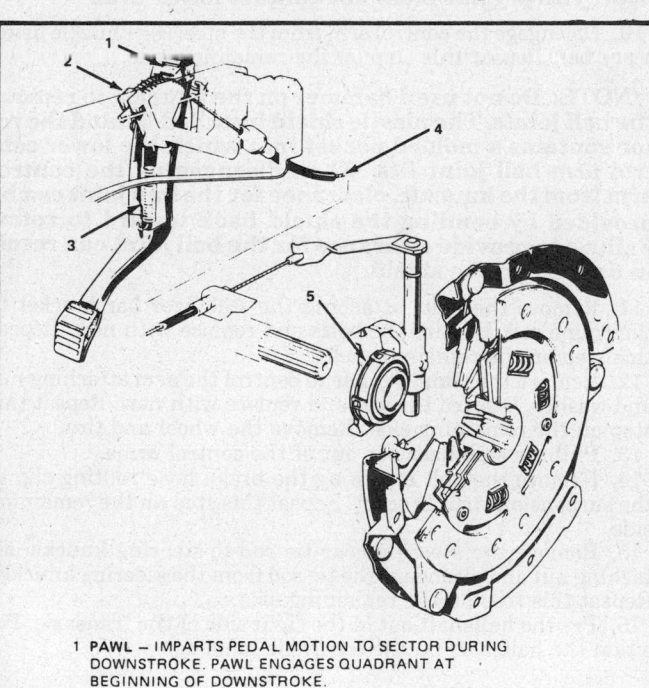

1 **PAWL** — IMPARTS PEDAL MOTION TO SECTOR DURING DOWNSTROKE. PAWL ENGAGES QUADRANT AT BEGINNING OF DOWNSTROKE.

2 **QUADRANT**—ACTUATES CABLE DURING PEDAL DOWN-STROKE FOLLOWING CABLE CORE AS CORE IS MOVED DURING DISC FACING WEAR.

3 **ADJUSTER SPRING** – KEEPS SECTOR IN FIRM CONTACT WITH CABLE. KEEPS RELEASE BEARING IN CONTACT WITH CLUTCH RELEASE FINGERS THROUGH CABLE LINKAGE WITH PEDAL IN UP POSITION.

4 **CABLE**

5 **RELEASE BEARING**

Self-adjusting clutch components

3. Raise the vehicle and support safely. Remove the front stabilizer bar-to-control arm attaching nut and washer (drivers side). Discard the attaching nut. Remove the front stabilizer bar mounting brackets. Discard the bolts.

4. Remove the nut and bolt that secures the lower control arm ball joint to the steering knuckle assembly. Discard the nut and bolt. Repeat this procedure on the opposite side.

5. Using a large pry bar, pry the lower control arm away from the knuckle.

NOTE: Exercise care not to damage or cut the ball joint boot. Pry bar must not contract the lower arm.

6. Using a large pry bar, pry the left inboard CV-joint assembly from the transaxle.

NOTE: Plug the seal opening to prevent lubricant leakage.

7. Remove the inboard CV-joint from the transaxle by grasping the left-hand steering knuckle and swinging the knuckle and halfshaft outward from the transaxle. If the CV-joint assembly cannot be pried from the transaxle, insert differential rotator tool T81P–4026–A or equivalent, through the left side and tap the joint out. Tool can be used from either side of transaxle.

8. Wire the halfshaft assembly in a near level position to prevent damage to the assembly during the remaining operations. Repeat this procedure on the opposite side.

9. Disengage the locking tabs and remove the backup lamp switch connector from the transaxle backup lamp switch.

10. Remove the nuts from the starter mounting studs which hold the engine roll restrictor bracket. Remove the engine roll restrictor.

11. Remove the starter stud bolts.

12. Remove the shift mechanism to shift shaft attaching nut and bolt and control selector indicator switch arm. Remove the shift shaft.

13. Remove the shift mechanism stabilizer bar-to-transaxle attaching bolt. Remove the $^7/_{32}$ in. sheet metal screw and the control selector indicator switch and bracket assembly.

14. Remove the speedometer cable from the transaxle.

15. Remove the stiffener brace attaching bolts from the oil pan to clutch housing.

16. Position a suitable jack under the transaxle. Remove the 2 nuts that secure the left hand rear No. 4 insulator to the body bracket.

17. Remove the bolts that secure the left hand front No.1 insulator to the body bracket. Lower the transaxle jack until the transaxle clears the rear insulator. Support the engine with the proper equipment.

18. Remove the remaining engine-to-transaxle attaching bolts. One of these bolts attaches the ground strap and wiring loom stand off bracket.

19. Remove the transaxle from the rear face of the engine and lower transaxle from the vehicle.

20. Complete the installation of the transaxle by reversing the removal procedure. Fill the transaxle.

NOTE: Prior to starting the engine after transaxle removal and installation, set the hand brake and pump the clutch pedal several times to ensure proper clutch adjustment.

Automatic Transaxle

Removal and Installation

EXCEPT TEMPO, TOPAZ, TAURUS AND SABLE WITH 2.3L HSC ENGINE AND CONTINENTAL

1. Disconnect the negative battery cable.

NOTE: Due to automatic transaxle case configuration, the right halfshaft assembly must be removed first.

The differential service tool T81P–4026–A or equivalent is then inserted into the transaxle to drive the lefthand inboard CV-joint assembly from the transaxle.

2. Remove the bolts attaching the managed air valve to the automatic transaxle valve body cover. Remove the air cleaner assembly, as required.

3. Disconnect the wiring harness connector from the neutral safety switch.

4. Disconnect the throttle valve linkage and the manual lever cable at their respective levers.

NOTE: Failure to disconnect the linkage during transaxle removal and allowing the transaxle to hang will fracture the throttle valve cam shaft joint (which is located under the transaxle cover).

5. Cover up the timing window in the converter housing to prevent contamination. Remove the bolts retaining the thermactor hoses, if equipped.

6. Remove the ground strap located above the upper engine mount, if equipped. Remove the coil and bracket assembly, if equipped.

7. Remove the transaxle-to-upper engine attaching bolts. The bolts are located below and on either side of the distributor. Raise the vehicle and support safely. Remove the front wheels.

8. Remove the nut from the control arm to steering knuckle attaching bolt (at the ball joint).

9. Drive the bolt out of the knuckle using a punch and hammer. Repeat this step on the remaining side. The nut and bolt must be discarded and replaced with new.

NOTE: Exercise care not to damage or cut ball joint boot. The pry bar must not contact lower arm.

10. Disengage the control arm from the steering knuckle using a pry bar. Repeat this step on the remaining side.

NOTE: Do not use a hammer on the knuckle to remove the ball joints. The plastic shield installed behind the rotor contains a molded pocket into which the lower control arm ball joint fits. When disengaging the control arm from the knuckle, clearance for the ball joint can be provided by bending the shield back toward to rotor. Failure to provide clearance for the ball joint can result in damage to the shield.

11. Remove the bolts attaching the stabilizer bar bracket to the frame rail. Discard the bolts and replace with new. Repeat this step on the remaining side.

12. Remove the stabilizer bar to control the arm attaching nut and washer. Discard the nut and replace with new. Repeat this step on the remaining side. Remove the wheel and tire.

13. Pull the stabilizer bar out of the control arms.

14. Remove the bolt attaching the brake hose routing clip to the suspension strut bracket. Repeat this step on the remaining side.

15. Remove the steering gear tie rod-to-steering knuckle attaching nut and disengage the tie rod from the steering knuckle. Repeat this step on the remaining side.

16. Pry the halfshaft out of the right side of the transaxle. Position the halfshaft on the transaxle housing.

NOTE: It is normal for some fluid to leak from the transaxle when the halfshaft is removed.

17. Disengage the left halfshaft from the differential side gear using driver T81P–4026–A or equivalent.

18. Pull the halfshaft out of the transaxle. Support the end of the shaft by suspending if from a convenient underbody component with a length of wire.

NOTE: Do not allow the shaft to hang unsupported, as damage to the outboard CV-joint may result.

19. Install seal plugs into the differential seals.

20. Remove the starter support bracket and disconnect the starter cable.

21. Remove the starter attaching bolts and the starter. On throttle body equipped vehicles, remove the 2 hose and bracket bolts on the starter and 1 bolt attached to the converter and disconnect the hoses.

22. Remove the transaxle support bracket.

23. Remove the dust cover from the torque converter housing.

24. Remove the torque converter to flywheel attaching nuts. Turn the crankshaft pulley bolt to bring the attaching nuts into an accessible position.

25. Remove the nuts attaching the left front insulator to the body bracket.

26. Remove the bracket to body attaching bolts and remove the bracket.

27. Remove the left rear insulator bracket attaching nut.

28. Disconnect the transaxle cooler lines.

29. Remove the bolts attaching the manual lever bracket to the transaxle case.

30. Position a transaxle jack under the transaxle and remove the 4 remaining transaxle to engine attaching bolts.

31. Before the transaxle can be lowered out of the vehicle, the torque converter studs must be clear of the flywheel.

32. Insert a suitable tool between the flywheel and the converter and carefully move the transaxle and converter away from the engine. When the converter studs are clear of the flywheel, lower the transaxle about 2–3 in.

33. Disconnect the speedometer cable and finish lowering the transaxle.

NOTE: When moving the transaxle away from the engine, watch the No. 1 insulator. If it contacts the body before the converter studs clear the flywheel, remove the insulator.

34. Complete the installation of the automatic transaxle by reversing the removal procedure. During installation ensure to observe the following:

　a. Prior to installaing the halfshaft in the transaxle, replace the circlip on the CV-joint stub.

　b. To install the halfshaft in the transaxle, carefully align the splines of the CV-joint with the splines in the differential. During installation, push the CV-joint into the differential until the circlip is felt to seat in the differential side gear. Use care to prevent damage to the differential oil seal.

　c. Attach the lower ball joint to the steering knuckle, taking care not to damage or cut the ball joint boot. Insert a new service pinch and attach new nut. While holding the bolt with a second wrench, tighten the nut to 37–44 ft. lbs. torque. Tightening of the bolt is not required.

TEMPO AND TOPAZ WITH 2.3L HSC ENGINE

The automatic transaxle and the 2.3L HSC engine on Tempo and Topaz must be removed and installed as an assembly. If any attempt is made to remove either component separately, it will cause damage to the transaxle or the lower engine compartment metal structure.

TAURUS, SABLE AND CONTINENTAL WITH AXOD

1. Disconnect the negative battery cable. Raise and support the vehicle safely. Remove the air cleaner assembly.

2. Remove the bolt retaining the shift cable and bracket assembly to the transaxle.

NOTE: Hold the bracket with a pry bar in the slot to prevent the bracket from moving.

3. Remove the shift cable bracket bolts and bracket from the transaxle. Disconnect the electrical connector from the neutral safety switch.

4. Disconnect the electrical bulkhead connector from the rear

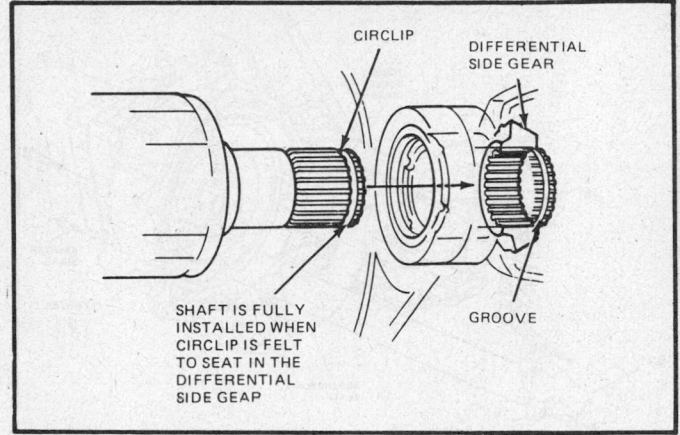

Halfshaft installation into differential side gears

of the transaxle. Unsnap the throttle valve cable from the throttle body lever. Remove the throttle valve cable from the transaxle case.

5. Carefully pull up on the throttle valve cable and disconnect the throttle valve cable from the T.V. link.

NOTE: Pulling to hard on the throttle valve may bend the internal T.V. bracket.

6. Remove the bolt and nut from the LH engine support strut. Remove the converter housing bolts from the top of the transaxle.

7. Position a suitable engine hoist over the engine and attach the hooks of the hoist to the engine lift points. Lift the engine slightly.

8. Remove both front wheels. Remove each tie rod end from its spindle.

9. Remove the lower ball joint attaching nuts and bolts. Remove the lower ball joints and remove the lower control arms from each spindle. Remove stabilizer bar nuts.

10. Remove the rack and pinion from the sub frame. Support the steering gear with a piece of wire from the tie rod end to the coil spring. Secure the housing of the gear to a suitable support to hold it in position.

11. Remove the nuts from the engine mounts. Disconnect the oxygen sensor electrical connection. Remove the exhaust Y-pipe from the engine and rear portion of the exhaust system.

12. Remove the sub frame by performing the following:

　a. Disconnect the exhaust system at the flex coupling and drop it down. Disconnect the lower control arm at the pinch bolts to the ball joints. Remove the two nuts that attach the steering gear to the number two crossmember.

　b. Remove the attaching nuts from the right front engine mount and right rear engine mount to subframe. Remove the stabilizer bar link attachment to the stabilizer bar.

　c. Remove the left engine mount insulator at the through bolts to subframe. Support the subframe with adjustable suitable jack stands at the subframe body mount location points. Remove the 4 body mount attaching bolts.

　d. With an assistant, lower the adjustable jacks and allow the subframe to lower. Rotate the front of the subframe down and pick up the rear of the subframe off the exhaust pipe. Work the subframe rearward until it can be lowered down past the exhaust pipe.

13. Remove the bolts from the sub-frame ataching points. Remove the bolts from the left engine support mount and lower the sub-frame.

14. Position a suitable transaxle jack under the oil pan of the transaxle. Remove the vehicle speed sensor from the transaxle.

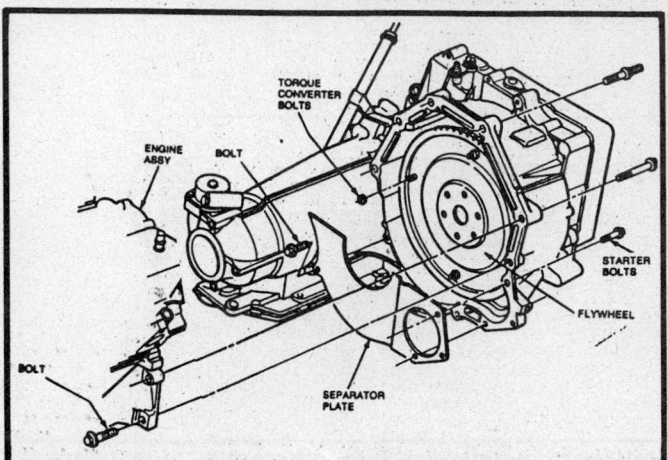

AXOD automatic transaxle – Taurus/Sable and Continental

NOTE: Vehicles equipped with electronic instrument clusters do not use a speedometer cable.

15. Remove the bolts from the transaxle mount. Remove the left engine support. Unbolt the separator plate.
16. Remove the starter ataching bolts and position the starter out of the way. Remove the separator plate.
17. Rotate the crankshaft pulley bolt to align the torque converter bolts with the starter drive hole. Then remove the torque converter-to-flywheel attaching nuts.
18. Disconnect the transaxle cooler lines. Remove the halfshafts.
19. Remove the remaining torque converter housing bolts. Separate the transaxle from the engine and carefully lower the transaxle out of the vehicle.
20. Complete the installation of the transaxle by reversing the removal procedure.

TAURUS AND SABLE WITH ATX

1. Disconnect the negative battery cable and remove the air cleaner assembly.
2. Position the engine control wiring harness away from the transaxle converter housing.
3. Disconnect the T.V. linkage and manual lever cable at the respective levers. Failure to disconnect the linkage during transaxle removal and allowing the transaxle to hang will fracture the throttle valve cam shaft joint (which is located under the transaxle cover).
4. Remove the power steering hose brackets.
5. Remove the upper transaxle-to-engine attaching bolts.
6. Install suitable engine lifting brackets to the right and left areas of the cylinder head and attach with bolts. Install 2 suitable engine support bars.

NOTE: An engine support bar may be fabricated from a length of 4×4 wood cut to 57 in.

7. Place 1 of the engine support bars across the vehicle in front of each engine shock tower. Place another support bar across the vehicle approximately between the alternator and valve cover. Attach chains to the lifting brackets. Raise the vehicle and support safely. Remove the wheel and tire assemblies.
8. Remove the catalytic converter inlet pipe and disconnect the exhaust air hose assembly.
9. Separate the lower ball joints from the struts and remove the lower control arm from each spindle.
10. Disconnect the stabilizer bar by removing the retaining nuts.
11. Disconnect and remove the rack and pinion and auxiliary cooler from the sub-frame. Position the rack and pinion away from the sub-frame and secure with wire.
12. Remove the right front bearing support assembly retaining bolts.
13. Remove the halfshaft and link shaft assembly out of the right side of the transaxle.
14. Disengage the left halfshaft from the differential side gear. Pull the halfshaft from the transaxle.

NOTE: Support and secure the halfshaft from an underbody component with a length of wire. Do not allow the halfshafts to hang unsupported.

15. Plug the seal holes.
16. Remove the front support insulator and position the left front spalsh shield aside.
17. Properly support the sub-frame and lower the vehicle onto the sub-frame support. Remove the sub-frame and disconnect the neutral start switch wire assembly.
18. Raise the vehicle after the sub-frame is removed. Disconnect the speedometer cable.
19. Disconnect and remove the shift cable from the transaxle.
20. Disconnect the oil cooler lines and remove the starter.
21. Remove the dust cover from the torque converter housing and remove the torque converter-to-flywheel housing nuts.
22. Position a suitable transaxle jack under the transaxle.
23. Remove the remaining transaxle-to-engine attaching bolts.

NOTE: Before the transaxle can be lowered from the vehicle, the torque converter studs must be clear of the flywheel. Insert a suitable tool between the flywheel and converter and carefully guide the transaxle and converter away from the engine.

24. Lower the transaxle from the engine.
25. Complete the installation of the transaxle by reversing the removal procedure. During installation ensure to observe the follwing:
   a. Clean the transaxle oil cooler lines.
   b. Install new circlips on the CV-joint seals.
   c. Carefully install the halfshafts in the transaxle by aligning the splines of the CV joint with the splines of the differential.
   d. Attach the lower ball joint to the steering knuckle with a new nut and bolt. Torque the nut to 37–44 ft. lbs. Torquing of the bolt is not required.
   e. When installing the transaxle to the engine, verify that the converter-to-transaxle engagement is maintained. Prevent the converter from moving forward and disengaging during installation.
   f. Adjust the T.V. and manual linkages. Check the transaxle fluid level.
   g. Tighten the following bolts to the torque specifications listed:
Transaxle-to-engine bolts, 25–33 ft. lbs. (34–45 Nm)
Control arm-to-knuckle bolts, 36–44 ft. lbs. (50–60 Nm)
Stabilizer U-clamp-to-bracekt bolts, 60–70 ft. lbs. (81–95 Nm)
Tie rod-to-knuckle nut, 23–35 ft. lbs. (31–47 Nm)
Starter-to-transaxle bolts, 30–40 ft. lbs. (41–54 Nm)
Converter-to-flywheel bolts, 23–39 ft. lbs. (31–53 Nm)
Insulator-to-bracket bolts, 55–70 ft. lbs. (75–90 Nm)

Transfer Case

Removal and Installation
TEMPO AND TOPAZ

1. Disconnect the negative battery cable.
2. Raise the vehicle and support it safely.
3. Drain the oil by removing the drive housing lower left hand retaining bolt.

4. Remove the vacuum line retaining bracket bolt.

5. Remove the driveshaft front retaining bolts and caps. Disengage the front driveshaft from the drive yoke.

6. If the transfer case is to be disassembled, check the backlash through the cup plug opening before removal in order to reset to existing backlash at installation. The backlash should be 0.012–0.024 in. on a 3 in. radius.

7. Remove the bolts retaining the vacuum motor shield and remove the shield.

8. Remove the vacuum lines from the vacuum servo.

9. Remove the bolts retaining the transfer case to the transaxle. Note and record the length and locations of the bolts.

10. Remove the the transfer case from the vehicle.

To install:

11. Position the transfer case to the transaxle.

12. Install the transfer case bolts in the proper positions. Torque the bolts in sequence to 23–38 ft. lbs. On 1988–90 vehicles, torque the bolts to 15–19 ft. lbs.

13. Install the vacuum motor supply hose connector. Position the vacuum motor shield and install the three retaining bolts. Torque the bolts to 7–12 ft. lbs.

14. Position the driveshaft to the drive yoke. Install the retaining bolts and torque the bolts to 15–17 ft. lbs. Install the vacuum line retaining bracket and bolt and torque it to 7–12 ft. lbs.

15. Fill the transaxle and lower the vehicle. Road test the vehicle and check the performance of the transfer case.

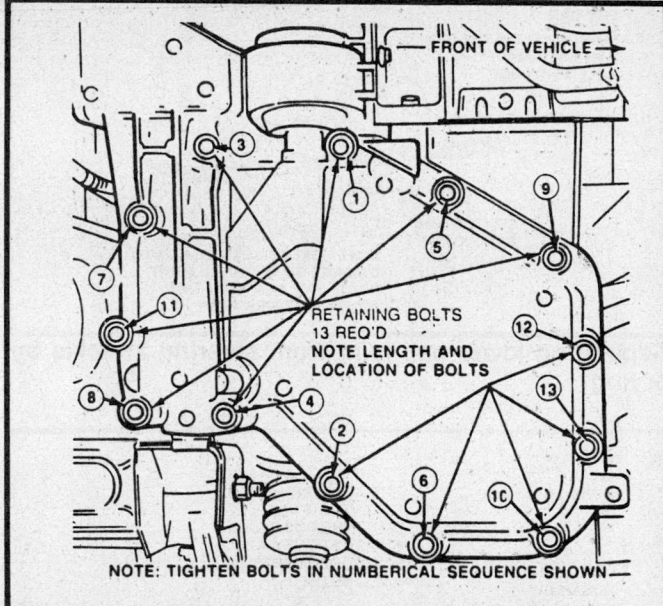

Transfer case retaining bolt torque sequence

DRIVESHAFTS/HALFSHAFTS

Front Drive Axle

When removing both the left and right halfshafts, install suitable shipping plugs to prevent dislocation of the differential side gears. Should the gears become misaligned, the differential will have to be removed from the transaxle to re-align the side gears.

NOTE: Due to the automatic transaxle case configuration, the right halfshaft assembly must be removed first. Differential Rotator T81P–4026–A or equivalent is then inserted into the transaxle to drive the left inboard CV-joint assembly from the transaxle. If only the left halfshaft assembly is to be removed for service, remove only the right halfshaft assembly from the transaxle. After removal, support it with a length of wire. Then drive the left halfshaft assembly from the transaxle.

Removal and Installation

ESCORT, LYNX AND TEMPO, TOPAZ WITH 2WD

1. Remove the cap from the hub and loosen the hub nut. Set the parking brake to prevent the vehicle from rolling while the nut is loosened. The nut must be loosened without unstaking. The use of a chisel or similar tool may damage the spindle thread.

2. Raise the vehicle and support it safely. Remove the wheel and tire assembly. Remove the hub nut and washer. Discard the nut, as it must not be reused.

3. Remove the bolt attaching the brake hose routing clip to the suspension strut.

4. Remove the nut from the ball joint to steering knuckle attaching bolt. Drive the bolt out of the steering knuckle using a punch and hammer. Discard the bolt and nut. They are of a torque prevailing design and cannot be reused.

5. Separate the ball joint from the steering knuckle using a pry bar. Position the end of the pry bar outside of the bushing pocket to avoid damage to the bushing. Use care to prevent damage to the ball joint boot.

NOTE: The lower control arm ball joint fits into a pocket formed in the plastic disc brake rotor shield. This shield must be bent back away from the ball joint while prying the ball joint out of the steering knuckle.

6. Remove the halfshaft from the differential housing using a pry bar. Position the pry bar between the case and the shaft, but be careful not to damage the dust deflector location between the shaft and the case.

NOTE: If extreme resistance is encountered when using a pry bar to remove the halfshafts from the differential, then do not use the pry bar to remove them. Avoid damage to the transaxle case and oil pan. Remove the oil pan and use a large pry bar to dislodge the circlip from between the pinion shaft and the inboard CV-joint. This will free the haftshaft from the differential.

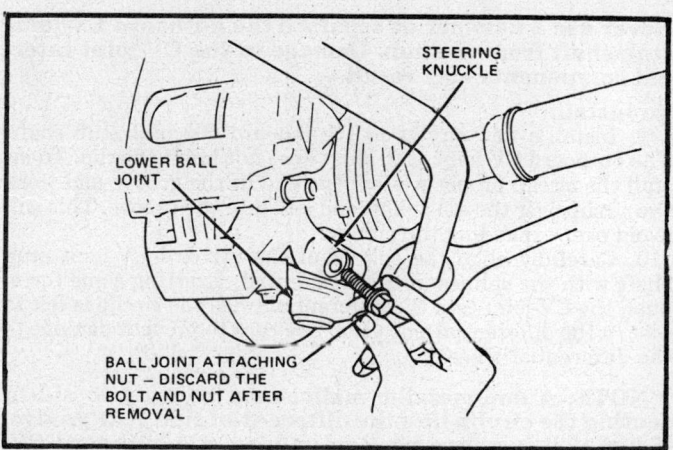

Removing lower ball joint pinch bolt

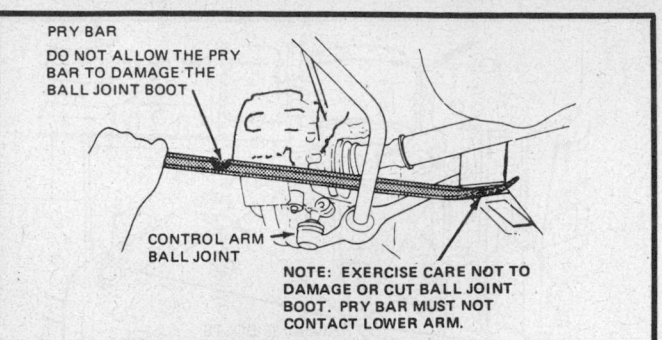

Separating lower ball joint from steering knuckle by prying

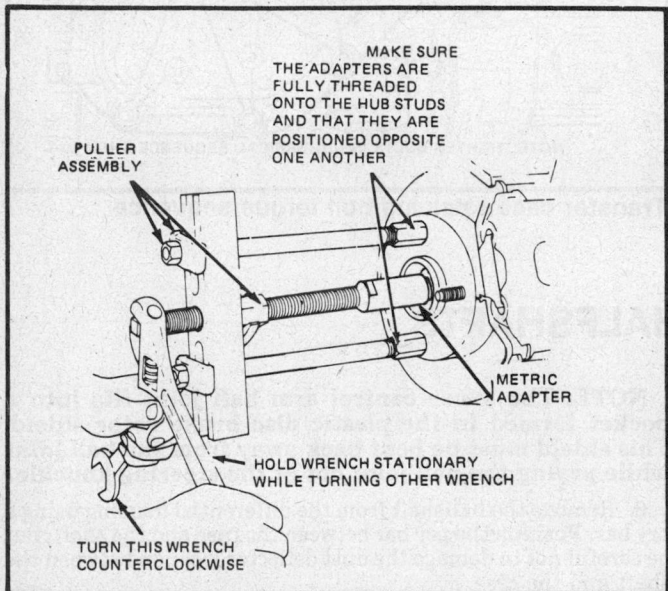

Removing hub from shaft assembly

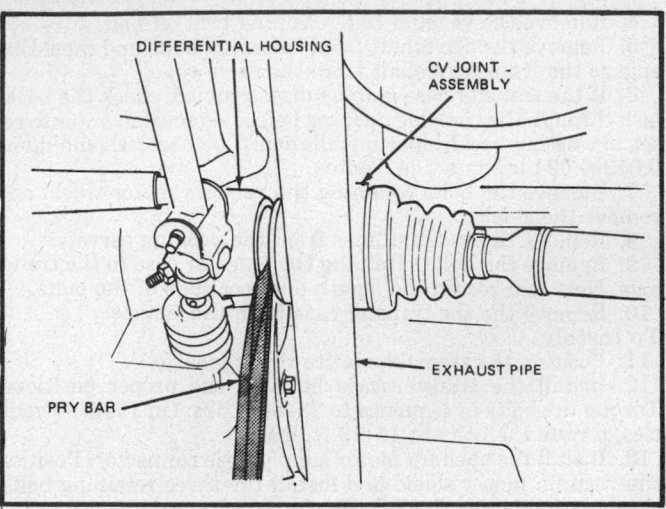

Removing halfshaft from transaxle assembly

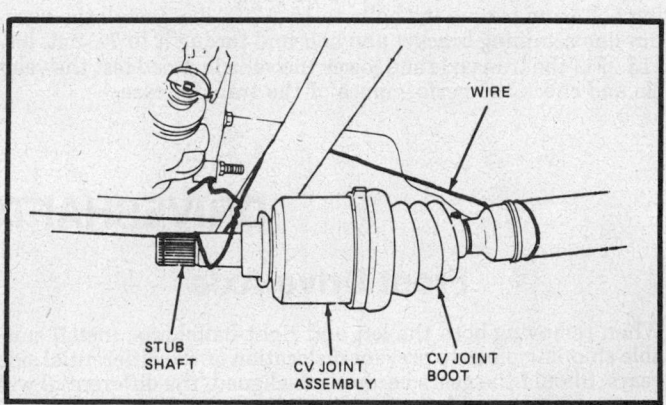

Support halfshaft by wiring to body

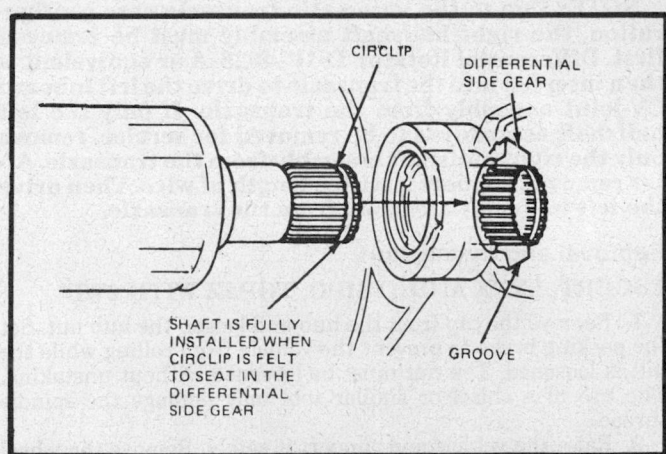

Seating circlip in transaxle differential side gear

7. Support the end of the shaft by suspending it from a convenient underbody component with a length of wire.

NOTE: Do not allow the shaft to hang unsupported, as damage to the outboard CV-joint may result.

8. Separate the outboard CV-joint from the hub.

Never use a hammer or separate the outboard CV-joint stub shaft from the hub. Damage to the CV-joint internal components may result.

To install:

9. Install a new circlip on the inboard CV-joint stub shaft. The outboard CV-joint stub shaft does not have a circlip. To install the circlip properly, start one end in the groove and work the circlip over the stub shaft end and into the groove. This will avoid over expanding the circlip.

10. Carefully align the splines of the inboard CV-joint stub shaft with the splines in the differential. Exerting some force, push the CV-joint into the differential until the circlip is felt to seat in the differential side gear. Use care to prevent damage to the differential oil seal.

NOTE: A non-metallic mallet may be used to aid in seating the circlip into the differential side gear groove. if a mallet is necessary, tap only on the outboard CV-joint stub shaft.

11. Carefully align the splines of the outboard CV-joint stub shaft with the splines in the hub and push the shaft into the hub as far as possible.

12. Connect the control arm to the steering knuckle and install a new nut and bolt.

13. Position the brake hose routing clip on the suspension strut and install the attaching bolts.

14. Install the hub nut washer and a new hub nut.

15. Install the wheel and tire assembly and lower the vehicle.

16. Tighten the wheel nuts to specifications.

TAURUS, SABLE AND CONTINENTAL

1. Remove the wheel cover/hub cover from the wheel and tire assembly and loosen the wheel nuts. Remove the hub retainer and washer. The nut must be discarded after removal.

2. Raise the vehicle and support safely. Remove the wheel assembly, remove the hub nut and washer. Discard the old hub nut. Remove the nut from the ball joint to steering knuckle attaching bolts.

3. Drive the bolt out of the steering knuckle using a suitable punch and hammer. Discard this bolt and nut after removal. Separate the ball joint from the steering knuckle using a suitable pry bar. On Continental, remove the anti-lock brake sensor from the steering knuckle and remove the height sensor link at the lower arm ball stud attachment.

4. Position the end of the pry bar outside of the bushing pocket to avoid damage to the bushing. Use care to prevent damage to the ball joint boot. Remove the stabilizer bar link at the stabilizer bar.

5. The following removal procedure applies to the right side halfshaft/link shaft for the automatic transaxle and the manual transaxle on the Taurus and Sable. For the Continental, proceed to Step 6:

    a. Remove the bolts attaching the bearing support to the bracket. Slide the link shaft out of the transaxle. Support the end of the shaft by suspending it from a convenient underbody component with a piece of wire. Do not allow the shaft to hang unsupported, damage to the outboard CV-joint may occur.

    b. Separate the outboard CV-joint from the hub.

NOTE: Never use a hammer to separate the outboard CV-joint stub shaft from the hub. Damage to the CV-joint threads and internal components may result. The right side link shaft and halfshaft assembly is removed as a complete unit.

6. The following removal procedure applies to the right and left side halfshafts for the automatic overdrive transaxle (Taurus, Sable and Continental) and the left side halfshaft on the manual transaxle (Taurus and Sable):

    a. Install the CV-joint puller tool T86P-3514-A1 or equivalent between CV-joint and transaxle case. Turn the steering hub and or wire strut assembly out of the way.

    b. Screw extension tool T86P-3514-A2 or equivalent, into the CV-Joint puller and hand tighten. Screw an impact slide hammer onto the extension and remove the CV-joint.

    c. Support the end of the shaft by suspending it from a convenient underbody component with a piece of wire. Do not allow the shaft to hang un-supported, damage to the outboard CV joint may occur.

    d. Separate the outboard CV joint from the hub using front hub remover tool T81P-1104-C or equivalent and metric

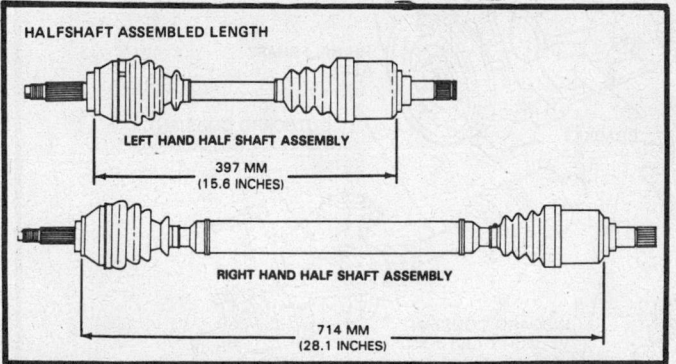

Dimensions for left and right halfshaft assembled lengths

HALFSHAFT ASSEMBLED LENGTH

LEFT HAND HALF SHAFT ASSEMBLY
397 MM
(15.6 INCHES)

RIGHT HAND HALF SHAFT ASSEMBLY
714 MM
(28.1 INCHES)

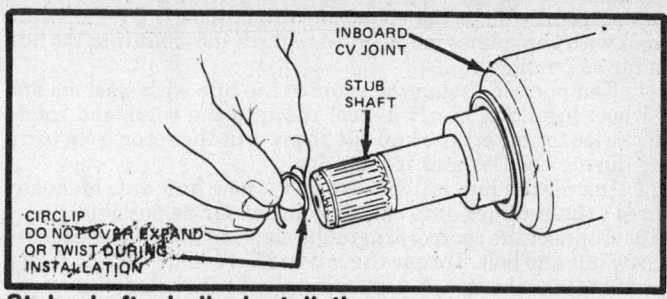

Stub shaft circlip installation

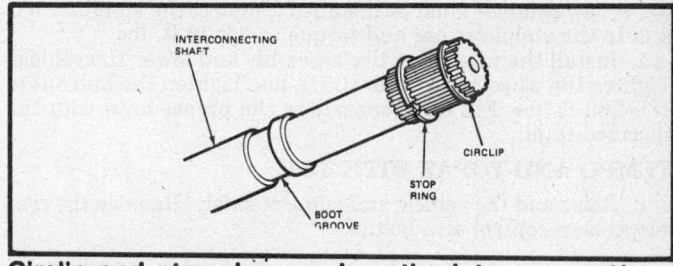

Circlip and stop ring used on the inter connecting shafts

adapter tools T83-P-1104-BH, T86P-1104-Al and T81P-1104-A or equivalent.

    e. Remove the halfshaft assembly from the vehicle.

7. The following removal procedure applies to the left side halfshaft for the automatic transaxle:

NOTE: Due to the automatic transaxle case configuration, the right halfshaft assembly must be removed first. Differential rotator tool T81P-4026-A or equivalent is then inserted into the transaxle to drive the left inboard CV-joint assembly from the transaxle. If only the left halfshaft assembly is to be removed for service, remove only the right halfshaft assembly from the transaxle. After removal, support it with a length of wire. Then drive the left halfshaft assembly from the transaxle.

    a. Support the end of the shaft by suspending it from a convenient underbody component with a piece of wire. Do not allow the shaft to hang unsupported as damage to the outboard CV-joint may occur.

    b. Separate the outboard CV-joint from the hub.

    c. Remove the halfshaft assembly from the vehicle.

To install:

8. Install a new circlip on the inboard CV-joint stub shaft and or link shaft. The outboard CV-joint does not have a circlip. When installing the circlip, start one end in the groove and work the circlip over the stub shaft end into the groove. This will avoid over expanding the circlip.

NOTE: The circlip must not be re-used. A new circlip must be installed each time the inboard CV-joint is installed into the transaxle differential.

9. Carefully align the splines of the inboard CV-joint stub shaft with the splines in the differential. Exerting some force, push the CV-joint into the differential until the circlip is felt to seat in the differential side gear. Use care to prevent damage to the differential oil seal. Torque the link shaft bearing to 16-23 ft. lbs.

NOTE: A non-metallic mallet may be used to aid in seating the circlip into the differential side gear groove. If a mallet is necessary, tap only on the outboard CV-joint stub shaft.

10. Carefully align the splines of the outboard CV-joint stub shaft with the splines in the hub and push the shaft into the hub as far as possible.

11. Temporarily fasten the rotor to the hub with washers and 2 wheel lug nuts. Insert a steel rod into the rotor and rotate clockwise to contact the knuckle to prevent the rotor from turning during the CV-joint installation.

12. Install the hub nut washer and a new hub nut. Manually thread the retainer onto the CV-joint as far as possible.

13. Connect the control arm to the steering knuckle and install a new nut and bolt. Torque the nut to 37–44 ft. lbs.(40–55 ft. lbs. on 1988–90 vehicles). A new bolt must be installed also.

14. Install the hub retainer washer and a new hub retainer. Manually thread the retainer onto the CV-joint as far as possible. A new retainer must be installed. Connect the stabilizer bar link to the stabilizer bar and torque to 35–38 ft. lbs.

15. Install the wheel and tire assembly and lower the vehicle. Tighten the wheel nuts to 80–105 ft. lbs. Tighten the hub nut to 180–200 ft. lbs. Fill the transaxle to the proper level with the specified fluid.

TEMPO AND TOPAZ WITH 4WD

1. Raise and the vehicle and support safely. Remove the rear suspension control arm bolt.

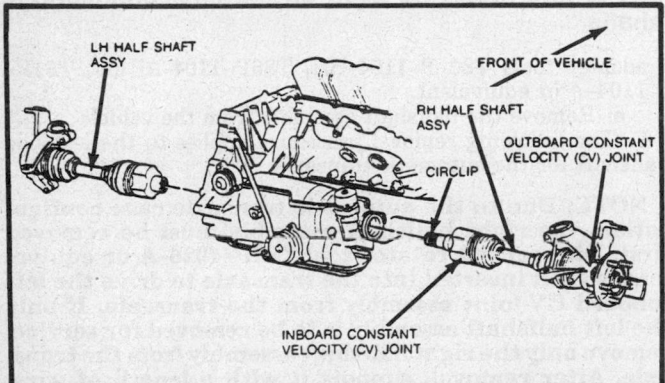

Assembly view of AXOD LH and RH halfshafts—Continental

2. Remove the outboard U-joint retaining bolts and straps. Remove the inboard U-joint retaining bolts and straps.

3. Slide the shaft together. Do not allow the splined shafts to contact with excessive force. Remove the halfshafts. Do not drop the halfshafts as the impact may cause damage to the U-joint bearing cups.

4. Retain the bearing cups. Inspect the U-joint assemblies for wear or damage, replace the U-joint if necessary.

5. Install the halfshaft at the inboard U-joint. The inboard shaft has a larger diameter than the outboard shaft. Install the U-joint retaining caps and bolts and torque them to 15–17 ft. lbs.

6. Install the halfshaft at the outboard U-joint. Install the U-joint retaining caps and bolts and torque them to 15–17 ft. lbs.

7. Install the rear suspension control arm bolt and torque it to 60–86 ft. lbs.

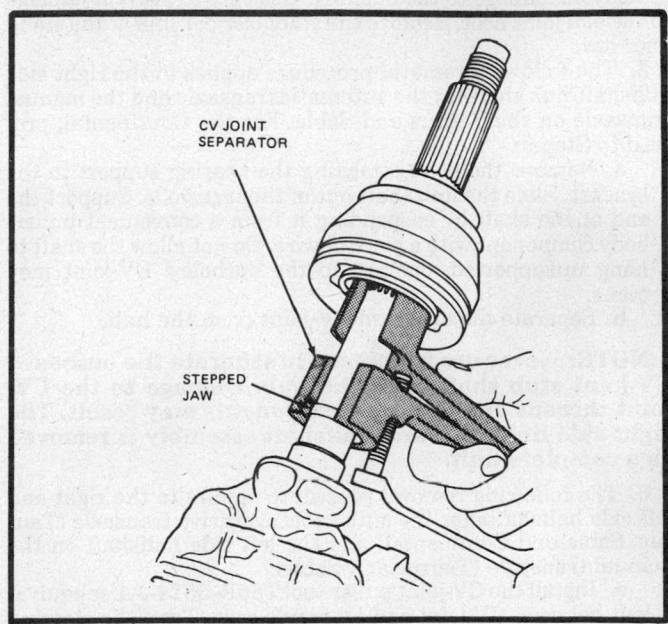

Separating CV-joint with special tool

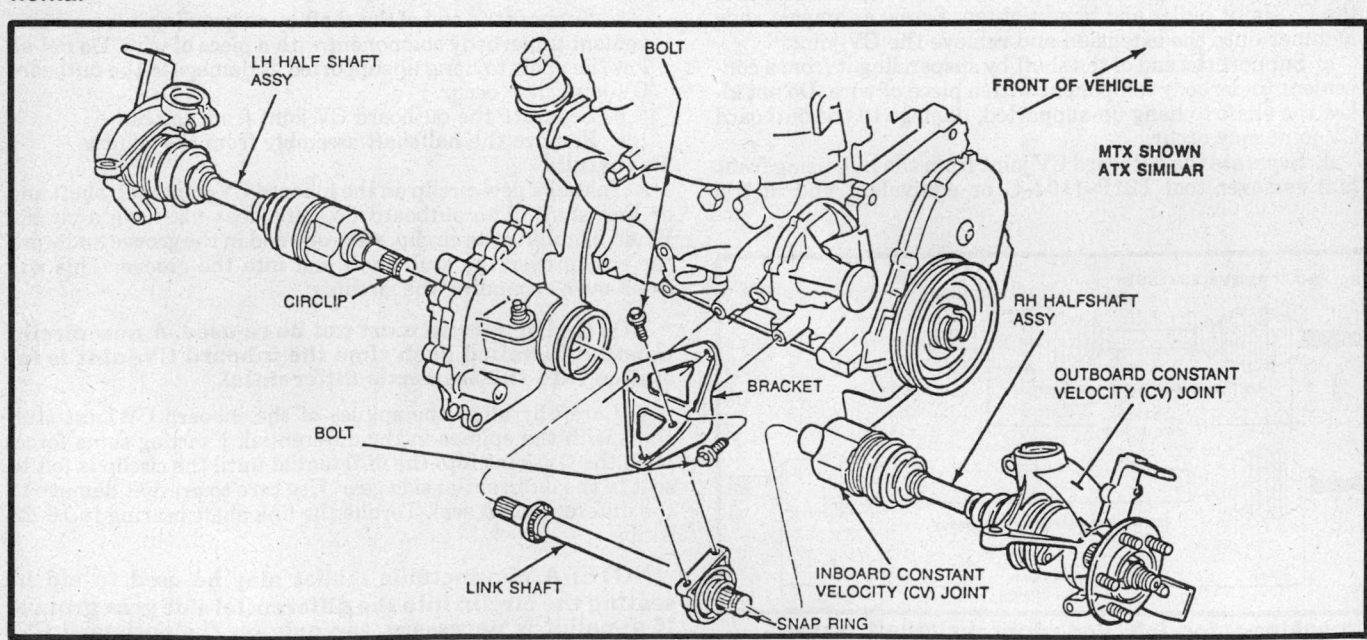

LH and RH halfshaft assembly removal and installation—Taurus/Sable

Driveshaft

Removal and Installation

TEMPO AND TOPAZ WITH 4WD

1. Raise the vehicle and support safely. Be sure to support the driveshaft using a suitable jack or hoist under the center bearing during removal and installation.

2. To maintain the driveshaft balance, mark the U-joints so they may be installed in their original position.

3. Remove the U-joint retaining bolts and straps. Slide the driveshaft toward the rear of the vehicle to disengage it.

4. Remove the rear U-joint bolts and retaining the driveshaft, from the torque tube yoke flange.

5. Slide the driveshaft toward the front of the vehicle to disengage. Do not allow the splined shafts to contact with excessive force.

6. Remove the center bearing retaining bolts. Remove the driveshaft and retain the bearing cups with tape, if necessary.

7. Inspect the U-joint assemblies for wear and or damage, replace the U-joint if necessary.

To install:

8. Install the driveshaft at the rear torque yoke flange. Ensure that the U-joint is in its original position.

9. Install the U-joint retaining bolts and caps. Torque them to 15–17 ft. lbs. Position the front U-joint. Install the U-joint retaining caps and bolts. Torque them to 15–17 ft. lbs.

10. Install the center bearing and retaining bolts. Torque to

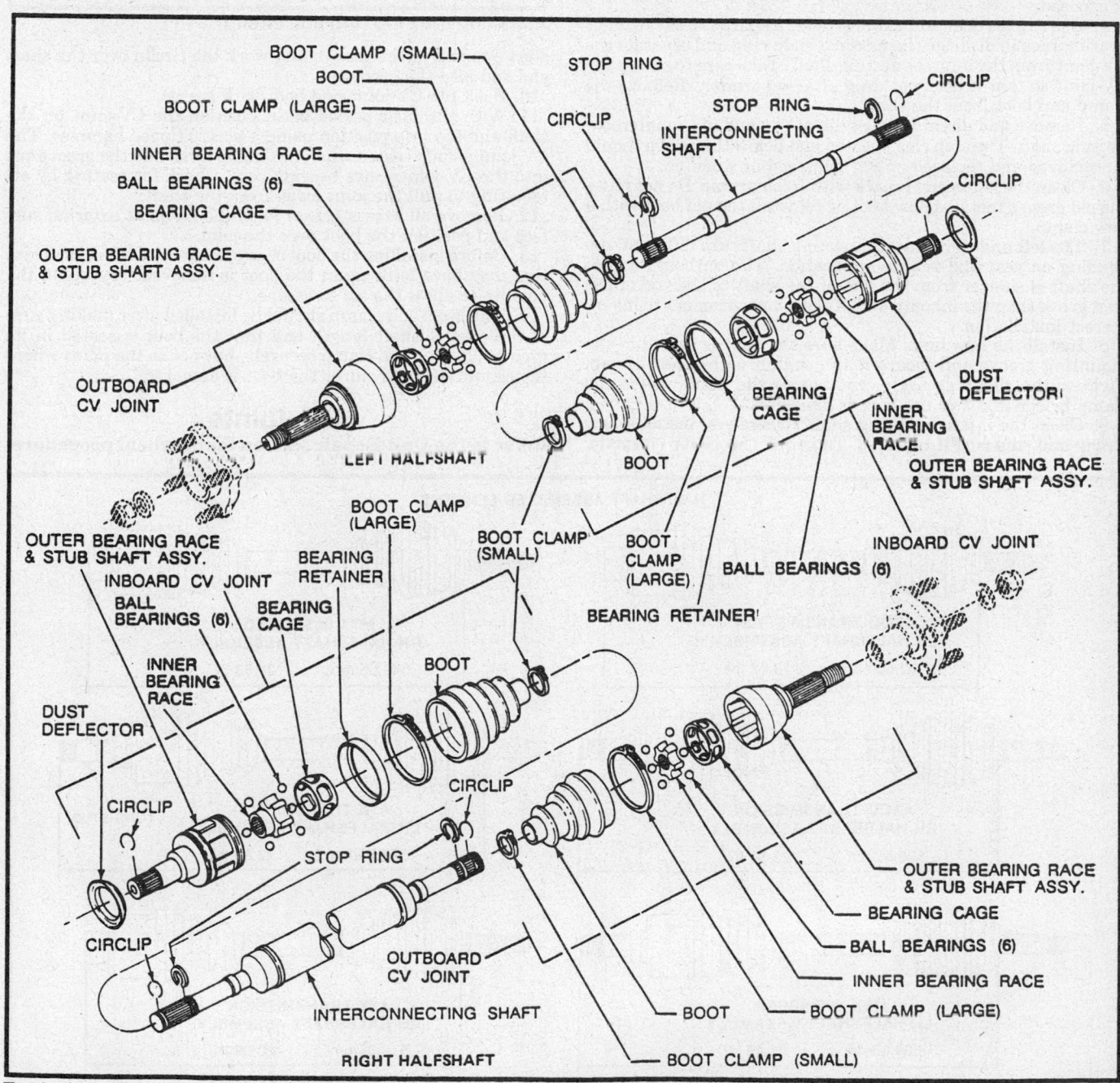

Exploded view of the left and right halfshafts and CV–joints

23–30 ft. lbs. Do not drop the assemble driveshafts as the impact may cause damage to the U-joint bearing cups.

Boot

Removal and Installation

1. Clamp the halfshaft in a vise that is equipped with soft jaw covers. Do not allow the vise jaws to contact the boot or boot clamp.

2. Cut the large boot clamp with a pair of side cutters and peel the clamp away from the boot. Roll the boot back over the shaft after the clamp has been removed.

3. Clamp the interconnecting shaft in a soft jawed vise with the CV-joint pointing downward so that the inner bearing race is exposed.

4. Use a brass drift and hammer, give a sharp tap to the inner bearing race to dislodge the internal snap ring and separate the CV-joint from the interconnecting shaft. Take care to secure the CV-joint so that it does not drop after separation. Remove the clamp and boot from the shaft.

5. Remove and discard the circlip at the end of the interconnecting shaft. The stop ring, located just below the circlip should be removed and replaced only if damaged or worn.

6. Clean the joints and repack with fresh grease. Do not reuse the old grease Install a new boot or reinstall the old boot with a new clamp.

7. The left and right interconnecting shafts are different, depending on year and vehicle application. The outboard end of the shaft is shorter from the end of the shaft to the end of the boot grove than the inboard end. Take a measurement to insure correct installation.

8. Install the new boot. Make sure the boot is seated in the mounting groove and secure it in position with a new clamp. Tighten the clamp securely, but not to the point where the clamp bridge is cut or the boot is damaged.

9. Clean the interconnecting shaft splines and install a new circlip and stop ring if removed. To install the circlip correctly,

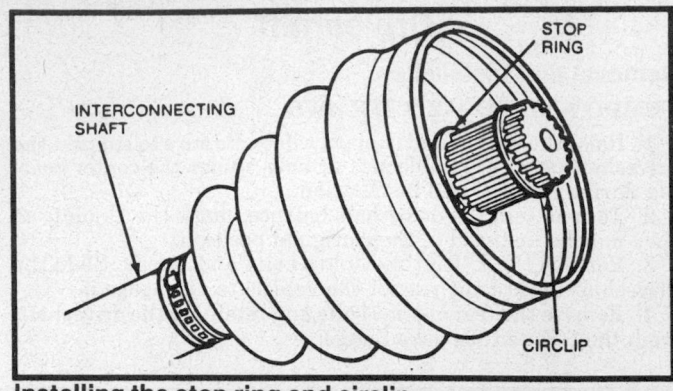

Installing the stop ring and circlip

start one end in the groove and work the circlip over the shaft end and into the groove.

10. Pack the CV joint and boot with grease.

11. With the boot peeled back, position the CV-joint on the shaft and tap into position using a plastic tipped hammer. The CV-joint is fully seated when the circlip locks into the groove cut into the CV-joint inner bearing race. Check for seating by attempting to pull the joint away from the shaft.

12. Remove all excess grease form the CV-joint external surface and position the boot over the joint.

13. Before installing the boot clamp, make sure all air pressure that may have built up in the boot is removed. Pry up on the boot lip to allow the air to escape.

14. The large end clamp should be installed after making sure of the correct shaft length and that the boot is seated in its groove. Tighten the clamp securely, but not to the point where the clamp bridge is cut or the boot is damaged.

CV-Joints
Refer to the Unit Repair section for overhaul procedure.

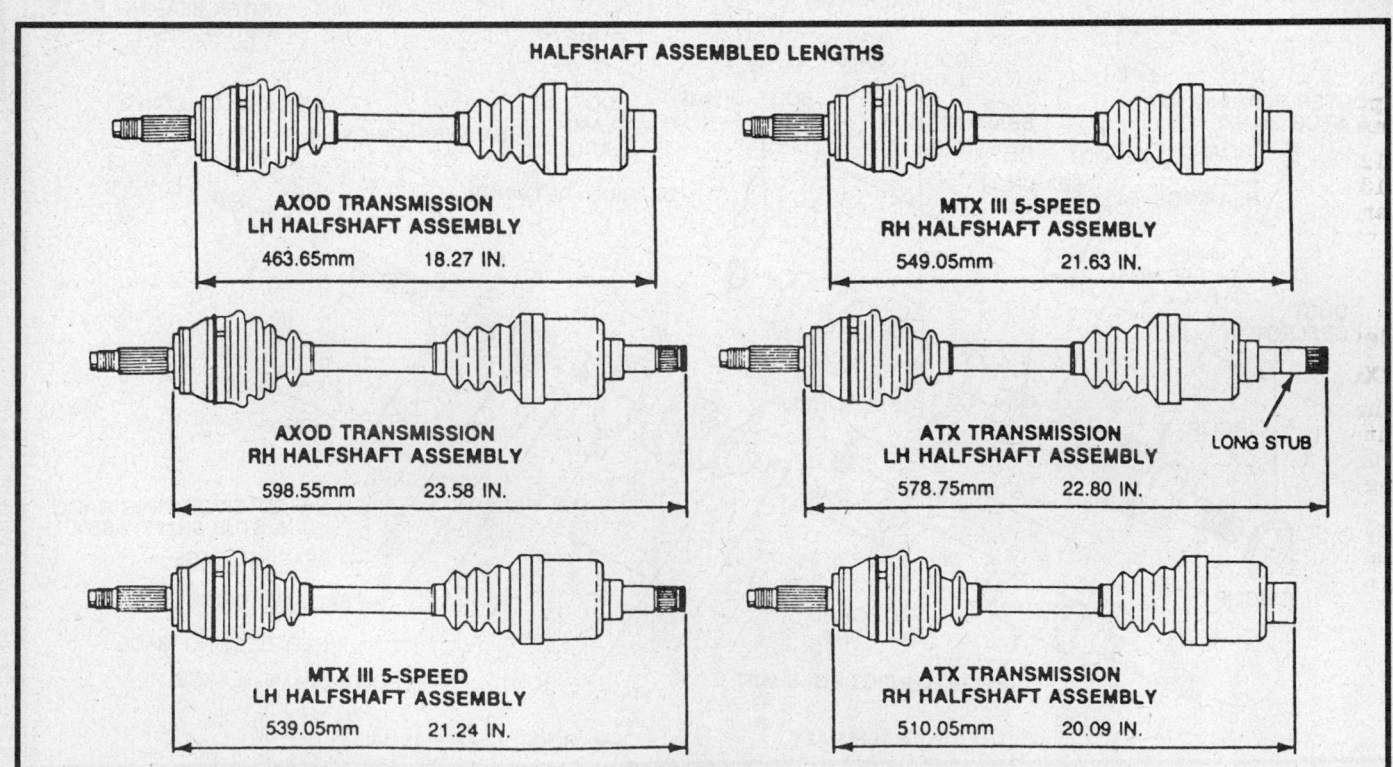

HALFSHAFT ASSEMBLED LENGTHS

AXOD TRANSMISSION
LH HALFSHAFT ASSEMBLY
463.65mm   18.27 IN.

MTX III 5-SPEED
RH HALFSHAFT ASSEMBLY
549.05mm   21.63 IN.

AXOD TRANSMISSION
RH HALFSHAFT ASSEMBLY
598.55mm   23.58 IN.

ATX TRANSMISSION
LH HALFSHAFT ASSEMBLY
578.75mm   22.80 IN.   LONG STUB

MTX III 5-SPEED
LH HALFSHAFT ASSEMBLY
539.05mm   21.24 IN.

ATX TRANSMISSION
RH HALFSHAFT ASSEMBLY
510.05mm   20.09 IN.

Halfshaft assembly lengths—Taurus/Sable and Continental

REAR AXLE AND REAR SUSPENSION

Refer to the Unit Repair Section for axle overhaul procedures and rear suspension services.

Rear Axle Assembly

Removal and Installation

TEMPO AND TOPAZ WITH 4WD

1. Raise the vehicle and support safely. Position a hoist or a suitable transaxle jack under the rear axle housing.
2. Remove the exhaust system.
3. Remove the rear U-joint bolts and straps retaining the driveshaft, from the torque tube yoke flange. Lower and support the driveshaft.
4. Remove the retaining bolts from the torque tube support bracket. Remove the axle retaining bolt from the left hand differential support bracket.
5. Remove the axle retaining bolt from the center differential support bracket.
6. Lower the axle assembly and remove the inboard U-joint retaining bolts and straps from each of the halfshaft. Remove and wire the halfshaft assemblies out of the way.
7. Lower the jack and remove the rear axle from the vehicle.
8. Position the rear axle assembly under the vehicle. Raise the rear axle far enough for the U-joint and halfshaft assemblies to be installed.
9. Position each inboard U-joint to the rear axle. Install the U-joint straps and retaining bolts. Using a T-30 Torx® bit, torque the bolts to 15–17 ft. lbs. to each halfshaft.
10. Raise the rear axle into position and install the bolts attaching the differential housing to the left hand center differential support bracket. Torque to 70–80 ft. lbs.
11. Position the torque tube and mounting bracket to the crossmember. Install the attaching bolts and torque to 28–35 ft lbs. Install the driveshaft and retaining bolts to the torque tube yoke flange. Using a T-30 Torx® bit, torque the bolts to 15–17 ft. lbs.

NOTE: Whenever a U-joint retaining bolt is removed, apply Loctite® or equivalent to the bolt threads prior to installation.

12. Install the exhaust system.
13. Check the lubricant level in the rear axle and add if necessary. Lower the vehicle and road test to check the rear axle for proper operation.

Rear Wheel Bearing

Removal and Installation

EXCEPT TEMPO AND TOPAZ WITH 4WD

The rear wheel bearings are located in the brake drum hub. The inner wheel bearing is protected by a grease seal. A washer and spindle nut retain the hub/drum assembly and control the bearing endplay.

1. Raise the vehicle and support safely. Remove wheel, dust cover, cotter pin nut retainer, adjusting nut and keyed flat washer from the spindle except Continenetal. On Continental, remove the brake caliper by removing the bolts that attach the caliper support to the cast iron brake adapter. Lift the caliper from the rotor and support with a piece of wire. Do not allow the caliper to hang by the brake hose.
2. Pull the hub and drum assembly off the spindle being careful not to drop the outer bearing assembly. On the Continental, remove the rotor from the hub by pulling it off the hub bolts and remove the grease cap, cotter pin, nut retainer, adjusting nut and keyed flatwasher from the spindle. Discard the cotter pin and replace with new.

3. Remove the outer bearing assembly. Using seal remover tool 1175-AC or equivalent, remove the grease seal. Remove the inner bearing assembly from the hub.
4. Wipe all lubricant from the spindle and the inside of the hub.
5. Clean both bearing assemblies and cups using a suitable solvent. Inspect the bearing assemblies and cups for excessive wear, scratches, pits or other damage. Replace all worn and damaged parts as necessary. Thoroughly clean all spindle and bearing surfaces.

NOTE: Be sure to allow the solvent to dry before repacking the bearings. Do not spin dry the bearings with air pressure.

6. If the cups are to be replaced, remove them with a slide hammer and bearing cup puller.
7. Pack the bearings with a multi-purpose grease.
8. Coat the cups with a thin film of grease. Install the inner bearings and a new grease seal. Ensure the retainer flange is seated all around.
9. Coat the bearing surfaces of the spindle with a thin film of grease. Slowly and carefully slide the drum and hub over the spindle and brake shoes. Keep the hub centered on the spindle to prevent damage to the grease seal and spindle threads. Install the outer bearing over the spindle and into the hub and install the keyed flat washer and adjusting nut on the spindle.
10. Adjust the bearing(s) and install a new cotter pin. On Continental, install the disc brake rotor to the hub assembly and install the disc brake caliper over the rotor.
11. Install the wheel assembly. Lower the car and tighten the wheel lugs to 80–105 ft. lbs.

TEMPO AND TOPAZ WITH 4WD

1. Raise and support the vehicle safely. Remove the tire and wheel assembly.
2. Remove the brake drum. Remove the parking brake cable from the brake backing plate.
3. Remove the brake line from the wheel cylinder. Remove the outboard U-joint retaining bolts. Remove the outboard end of the halfshaft from the wheel stub shaft yoke and wire it to the control arm.
4. Remove and discard the control arm to spindle bolt, washer and nut. Remove the tie rod nut, bushing and washer and discard the nut.
5. Remove and discard the 2 bolts retaining the spindle to the strut. Remove the spindle from the vehicle. Mount the spindle and backing plate assembly in a suitable vise.
6. Remove the cotter pin and nut attaching the stub shaft yoke to the stub shaft. Discard the cotter pin.
7. Remove the spindle and backing plate assembly from the vise. Remove the stub shaft yoke using a 2 jaw puller and shaft protector.
8. Position the spindle and backing plate assembly into a vise and remove the wheel stub shaft.
9. Remove the snapring retaining the bearing. Remove the bolts retaining the spindle to the backing plate and remove the backing plate.
10. Remove the spindle from the vise and mount it into a suitable press. With the spindle side facing upward, carefully press out the bearing from the spindle, using a driver handle and bearing cup driver. Discard the bearing after removal.

To install:

11. Mount the spindle in a press, spindle side facing down. Position a new bearing in the outboard side of the spindle and carefully press in the new bearing using a driver handle and bearing installer.
12. Remove the spindle from the press and mount it in a vise.

Install the snapring retaining the bearing. Position the backing plate to the spindle and install the retaining bolts.

13. Install the wheel stub shaft. Install the stub shaft yoke and attaching nut. Torque the nut to 120–150 ft. lbs. install a new cotter pin.

14. Remove the spindle and backing plate assembly from the vise. Position the spindle onto the tie rod and then into the strut lower bracket. Insert 2 new strut-to-spindle bolts, but do not tighten at this time.

15. Install the tie rod bushing washer and new nut. Install the new control arm to spindle bolt, washers and nut. Do not tighten them at this time.

16. Install a jack stand to support the suspension at the normal curb height before tightening the fasteners.

17. Torque the spindle to strut bolts to 70–96 ft. lbs. Torque the tie rod nut to 52–74 ft. lbs. Torque the control arm to spindle nut to 60–86 ft. lbs.

18. Position the outboard end of the halfshaft to the wheel stub shaft yoke. Install the retaining caps and bolts and torque them to 15–17 ft. lbs.

19. Install the brake line to wheel cylinder. Install the parking brake cable and brake drum. Install the wheel assembly, torque the lugs nuts to 80–105 ft. lbs.

20. Lower the vehicle and bleed the brake system. Check and adjust the toe, if necessary.

Adjustment

NOTE: Bearings on 4WD vehicles are not adjustable.

1. Raise the vehicle and support it safely.
2. Remove the wheel covers. Remove the grease cap from the hub being careful not to damage the cap.

NOTE: Styled steel wheels and aluminum wheels require removal of the wheel assembly to remove the dust cover.

3. Remove the cotter pin and nut retainer. Discard the cotter pin and replace with new.
4. Back-off the adjusting nut a full turn making certain that the nut rotates freely on the spindle thread. Correct any binding condition that may exist.

5. Tighten the adjusting nut to 17–25 ft. lbs. while rotating the hub and drum assembly to seat the bearings. Back-off the adjusting nut ½ turn (¼ turn on Continental). Then retighten it to between 10–15 inch lbs. (24–28 inch lbs. on Continental).

6. Position the nut retainer on the nut and install the cotter pin so tha the slots in the ntu retainer flange are aligned with the cotter pin hole in the spindle.

7. Spread the ends of the cotter pin and bend then around the nut retainer.

8. Check the hub rotation. If the hub rotates freely, install the grease cap. If binding occurs, check the bearing for damage and replace as necessary.

9. Install the wheels and lower the vehicle.

Rear Wheel Alignment

Procedure

REAR TOE
Escort and Lynx

1. Raise the vehicle and support it safely.
2. Loosen the tie rod nut (that faces the front of the vehicle) and slide the tie rod toward the rear of the vehicle to increase the amount of toe-out.
3. Loosen the tie rod nut (that faces the rear of the vehicle) and slide the tie rod toward the front of the vehicle to increase the amount of toe-in.
4. After adjusting the toe to specifications, hold the tie rod flat with a wrench and tighten the tie rod nut (that faces the rear of the vehicle) to 6–12 ft. lbs. and torque the tie rod nut (that faces the front of the vehicle) to 52–74 ft. lbs.

Tempo, Topaz, Taurus, Sable and Coantinental

1. Raise the vehicle and support it safely.
2. On Tempo and Topaz, loosen the bolt attaching the rear control arm to the body and rotate the alignment cam until the required alignment setting is obtained. Torque the control arm attaching bolts to 40–55 ft. lbs.
3. On Taurus, Sable and Continental, loosen the nut and bolt attaching the spindle to the lower suspension arm. Turn the adjusting cam to obtain the alignment setting. While holding the adjusting cam in position, torque the attaching nut to 60–86 ft. lbs.

YEAR IDENTIFICATION

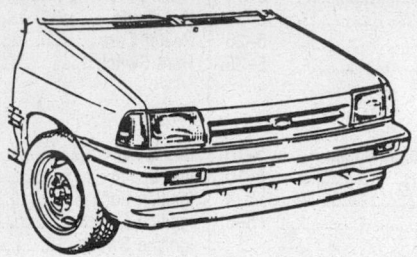

1988–90 Festiva

VEHICLE IDENTIFICATION

It is important for servicing and ordering parts to be certain of the vehicle and engine identification. The VIN (vehicle identification number) is a 20 digit number visible through the windshield on the driver's side of the dash and contains the vehicle and engine identification codes. The tenth digit indicates model year and the eighth digit indicates engine code. It can be interpreted as follows:

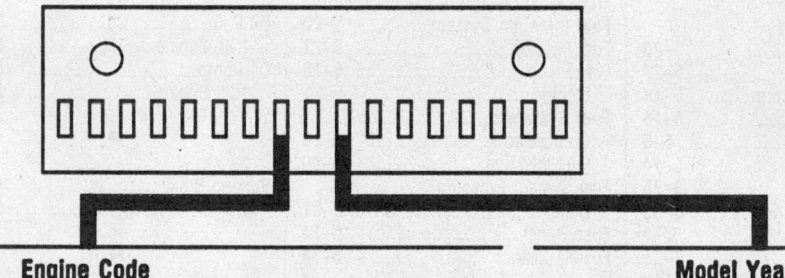

		Engine Code					Model Year	
Code	Cu. In.	Liters	Cyl.	Fuel Sys.	Eng. Mfg.		Code	Year
K	81	1.3	4	2 bbl	Kia Motors		J	1988
H	81	1.3	4	EFI	Kia Motors		K	1989
							L	1990

ENGINE IDENTIFICATION

Year	Model	Engine Displacement cu. in. (liter)	Engine Series Identification (VIN)	No. of Cylinders	Engine Type
1988	Festiva	81 (1.3)	K	4	OHC
1989	Festiva	81 (1.3)	K	4	OHC
	Festiva	81 (1.3)	H	4	OHC
1990	Festiva	81 (1.3)	K	4	OHC
	Festiva	81 (1.3)	H	4	OHC

GENERAL ENGINE SPECIFICATIONS

Year	VIN	Displacement cu. in. (liter)	Fuel System Type	Net Horsepower @ rpm	Net Torque @ rpm (ft.lbs.)	Bore × Stroke (in.)	Compression Ratio	Oil Pressure @ rpm
1988	K	81 (1.3)	2 bbl	58 @ 5000	73 @ 3500	2.78 × 3.29	9.7:1	50–64 @ 3000
1989-90	K	81 (1.3)	2 bbl	58 @ 5000	73 @ 3500	2.78 × 3.29	9.7:1	50–64 @ 3000
	H	81 (1.3)	EFI	58 @ 5000	73 @ 3500	2.78 × 3.29	9.7:1	50–64 @ 3000

GASOLINE ENGINE TUNE-UP SPECIFICATIONS
Refer to Section 34 for all spark plug recommendations

Year	VIN	Displacement cu. in. (liter)	Spark Plugs Gap (in.)	Ignition Timing (deg.) MT	Ignition Timing (deg.) AT	Compression Pressure (psi)	Fuel Pump (psi)	Idle Speed (rpm) MT	Idle Speed (rpm) AT	Valve Clearance In.	Valve Clearance Ex.
1988	K	81 (1.3)	.040	TDC	—	①	3–6	700–750	—	.012	.012
1989	K	81 (1.3)	.040	TDC②	TDC②	①	3–6	700–750	700–750	.012	.012
	H	81 (1.3)	.040	2BTDC	2BTDC②	①	NA	800–900	800–900	Hyd.	Hyd.
1990				SEE UNDERHOOD SPECIFICATIONS							

① The lowest cylinder pressure should be within 75% of the highest cylinder pressure reading. For example, if the highest cylinder is 134 psi, the lowest cylinder should be 101 psi. Engine should be at normal operating temperature with throttle body valve in the wide open position

② ± 1 degree

FIRING ORDERS

NOTE: To avoid confusion, always replace spark plug wires one at a time.

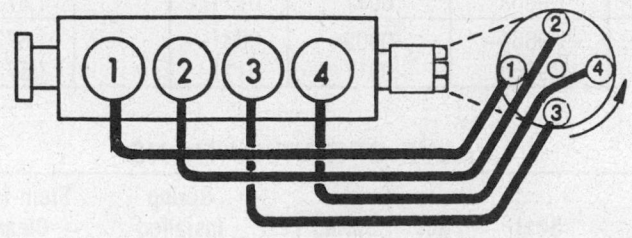

Ford Festiva 1.3L, 4 cylinder engine
Firing order 1–3–4–2
Distributor rotation: counterclockwise

CAPACITIES

Year	Model	Displacement cu. in. (liter)	Engine Crankcase with Filter	Engine Crankcase without Filter	Transmission (pts.) 4-Spd	Transmission (pts.) 5-Spd	Transmission (pts.) Auto.	Drive Axle (pts.)	Fuel Tank (gal.)	Cooling System (qts.)
1988	Festiva	81 (1.3)	3.9	3.6	5.2	5.2	—	—	10	5.3
1989-90	Festiva	81 (1.3)	3.9	3.6	5.2	5.2	11.0	—	10	5.3
	Festiva	81 (1.3)	3.9	3.6	5.2	5.2	11.0	—	10	5.3

CAMSHAFT SPECIFICATIONS
All measurements given in inches.

Year	VIN	Displacement cu. in. (liter)	Journal Diameter 1	2	3	4	5	Lobe Lift In.	Ex.	Bearing Clearance	Camshaft End Play
1988	K	81 (1.3)	1.7103–1.7112	1.7091–1.7100	1.7103–1.7112	—	—	1.4188–1.4224	1.4185–1.4224	.0026–.0045 ①	.002–.007 ②
1989-90	K	81 (1.3)	1.7103–1.7112	1.7091–1.7100	1.7103–1.7112	—	—	1.4188–1.4224	1.4185–1.4224	.0026–.0045 ①	.002–.007 ②
	H	81 (1.3)	1.7103–1.7112	1.7091–1.7100	1.7103–1.7112	—	—	1.4188–1.4224	1.4331–1.4371	.0026–.0045 ①	.002–.007 ②

① Center bearing oil clearance shown. Front and rear bearing oil clearance—.0014–.0033
② In service limit—.008

CRANKSHAFT AND CONNECTING ROD SPECIFICATIONS
All measurements are given in inches.

Year	VIN	Displacement cu. in. (liter)	Main Brg. Journal Dia.	Main Brg. Oil Clearance	Shaft Endplay	Thrust on No.	Journal Diameter	Oil Clearance	Side Clearance
1988	K	81 (1.3)	1.9661–1.9668	0009–.0017	.0031–.0111	—	1.5724–1.5731	.0009–.0017	.012
1989-90	K	81 (1.3)	1.9661–1.9668	0009–.0017	.0031–.0111	—	1.5724–1.5731	.0009–.0017	.012
	H	81 (1.3)	1.9661–1.9668	0009–.0017	.0031–.0111	—	1.5724–1.5731	.0009–.0017	.012

VALVE SPECIFICATIONS

Year	VIN	Displacement cu. in. (liter)	Seat Angle (deg.)	Face Angle (deg.)	Spring Test Pressure (lbs.)	Spring Installed Height (in.)	Stem-to-Guide Clearance Intake	Exhaust	Stem Diameter Intake	Exhaust
1988	K	81 (1.3)	45	45	—	1.717	.008	.008	.2744–.2750	.2742–.2748

VALVE SPECIFICATIONS

Year	VIN	Displacement cu. in. (liter)	Seat Angle (deg.)	Face Angle (deg.)	Spring Test Pressure (lbs.)	Spring Installed Height (in.)	Stem-to-Guide Clearance (in.)		Stem Diameter (in.)	
							Intake	Exhaust	Intake	Exhaust
1989-90	K	81 (1.3)	45	45	–	1.717	.008	.008	.2744–.2750	.2742–.2748
	H	81 (1.3)	45	45	–	1.717	.008	.008	.2744–.2750	.2742–.2748

PISTON AND RING SPECIFICATIONS
All measurments are given in inches.

Year	VIN	Displacement cu. in. (liter)	Piston Clearance	Ring Gap			Ring Side Clearance		
				Top Compression	Bottom Compression	Oil Control	Top Compression	Bottom Compression	Oil Control
1988	K	81 (1.3)	.006	.006–.012	.006–.012	.008–.028	.0602–.0608	.0598–.0604	.1583–.1591
1989-90	K	81 (1.3)	.006	.006–.012	.006–.012	.008–.028	.0602–.0608	.0598–.0604	.1583–.1591
	H	81 (1.3)	.006	.006–.012	.006–.012	.008–.028	.0602–.0608	.0598–.0604	.1583–.1591

TORQUE SPECIFICATIONS
All readings in ft. lbs.

Year	VIN	Displacement cu. in. (liter)	Cylinder Head Bolts	Main Bearing Bolts	Rod Bearing Bolts	Crankshaft Pulley Bolts	Flywheel Bolts	Manifold		Spark Plugs
								Intake	Exhaust	
1988	K	81 (1.3)	①	②	③	11–15	71–76	14–19	12–17	11–17
1989-90	K	81 (1.3)	①	②	③	11–15	71–76	14–19	12–17	11–17
	H	81 (1.3)	①	②	③	11–15	71–76	14–19	12–17	11–17

① Torque cylinder head bolts in sequence as follows:
Step 1: 35–40 ft. lbs.
Step 2: 56–60 ft. lbs.

② Torque main bearing cup bolts in sequence as follows:
Step 1: 22–27 ft. lbs.
Step 2: 40–43 ft. lbs.

③ Torque rod bearing nuts in sequence as follows:
Step 1: 11–13 ft. lbs.
Step 2: 22–25 ft. lbs.

WHEEL ALIGNMENT

Year	Model	Caster		Camber		Toe-in (in.)	Steering Axis Inclination (deg.)
		Range (deg.)	Preferred Setting (deg.)	Range (deg.)	Preferred Setting (deg.)		
1988	Festiva	1⁵⁄₁₆P–1¹¹⁄₁₆P	1⁹⁄₁₆	¼N–1⁹⁄₁₆P	¹¹⁄₁₆P	¹⁄₃₂–½①	14³⁄₁₆P
1989-90	Festiva	1⁵⁄₁₆P–1¹¹⁄₁₆P	1⁹⁄₁₆	¼N–1⁹⁄₁₆P	¹¹⁄₁₆P	¹⁄₃₂–½①	14³⁄₁₆P

P Positive
N Negative
① Prefered setting – ⁵⁄₁₆

ELECTRICAL

NOTE: Disconnecting the negative battery cable on some vehicles may interfere with the functions of the on board computer systems and may require the computer to undergo a relearning process, once the negative battery cable is reconnected.

For testing and overhaul procedures pertaining to starters and alternators, refer to the Unit Repair section.

Charging System

ALTERNATOR

Removal and Installation

1. Disconnect the negative battery cable.
2. Pull the rubber boot away from the **B** terminal to expose the terminal nut. Remove the nut and electrical lead from the terminal post.
3. Remove the alternator adjusting bracket bolt.
4. Disconnect the electrical connectors from the rear of the alternator housing.
5. Loosen the alternator pivot bolt enough to allow for alternator movement. It may be necessary to raise the vehicle in order to gain access to the retaining bolts.
6. Move the alternator toward the engine enough to raise the drive belt from the alternator pulley. Allow the drive belt to remain suspended from the water pump and crankshaft pulleys.
7. Support the alternator by hand and remove the pivot bolt. Remove the alternator from the engine.
8. Installation is the reverse of the removal procedure. Torque the pivot bolt to 27–30 ft. lbs. Torque the adjusting bolt to 35–45 ft. lbs.

BELT TENSION

Adjustment

1. Inspect the condition of the drive belt prior to adjustment. If the inspection reveals a severely glazed, frayed, oil contaminated or cracked belt, the belt must be replaced.
2. Raise the vehicle and support it safely.
3. Loosen the alternator mounting bolt and pivot bolt enough to allow for alternator movement.
4. Lower the vehicle.
5. Position a suitable pry bar between the alternator and an area in the vicinity of the through bolt, and apply moderate pressure to the bar. Do not pry against the stator frame.

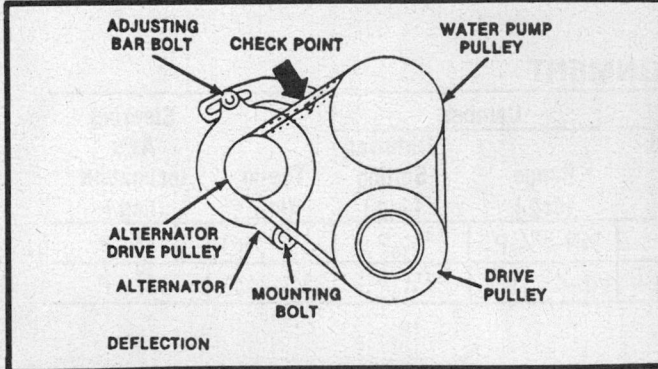

Alternator drive belt adjustment point

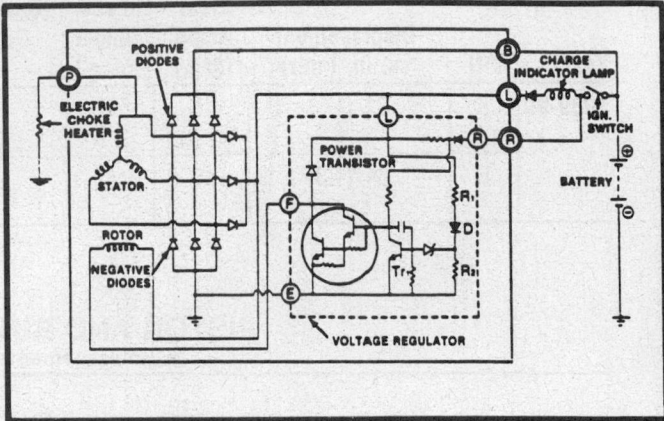

Charging system wiring schematic

6. Position a ruler perpendicular to center of the belt span between the alternator pulley and water pulley. The belt deflection may be determined through visual approximation by depressing the center of the belt with the thumb and observing the amount of deflection on the ruler.
7. For a used belt, belt deflection should be adjusted to 0.35–0.39 in. and re-checked after the engine has been run for approximately 10 minutes. New belts require no engine run time and belt deflection should be within 0.31–0.35 in.
8. When the correct belt deflection is obtained, torque the adjusting bolt to 14–19 ft. lbs. and the pivot bolt to 27–46 ft. lbs.

Starting System

STARTER

Removal and Installation

1. Disconnect the negative battery cable. Raise and support the vehicle safely.
2. Disconnect the wires from the starter **B** and **S** terminals and position the wires off to the side.
3. Unbolt the starter motor bracket from the transaxle.
4. Support the starter by hand and remove the bolts attaching the starter motor to the transaxle clutch housing.
5. Remove the starter with support bracket from the engine.
6. Position the starter against the transaxle housing and install the mounting bolts. Torque the mounting bolts to 23–34 ft. lbs.
7. Align the support bracket and transaxle mounting holes and install the attaching bolts. Torque the attaching bolts to 23–34 ft. lbs.
8. Reconnect the wires to their respective terminal posts.
9. Reconnect the negative battery cable.

Ignition System

DISTRIBUTOR

Removal and Installation

TIMING NOT DISTURBED

NOTE: If the distributor cap is being replaced, identify the spark plug wires and the cap towers with their respective cylinder numbers to ensure that the correct firing order will be retained when the new cap is installed.

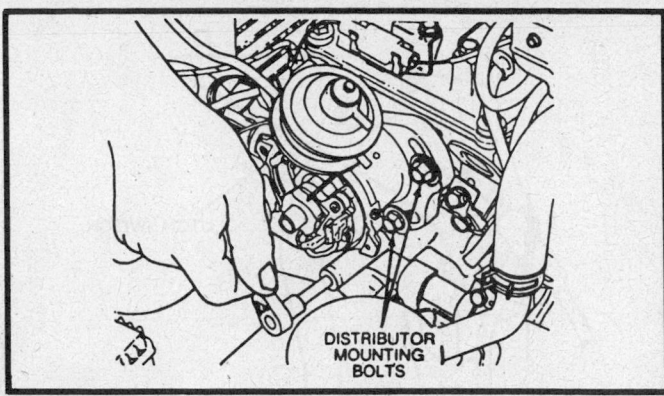
Distributor mounting bolt location

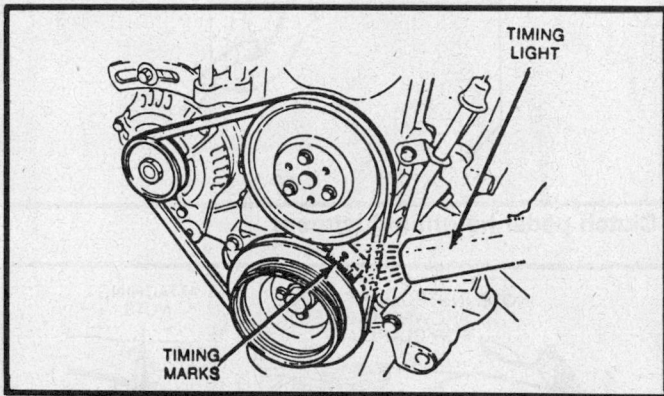
Ignition timing mark location

1. Disconnect the negative battery cable.
2. Disconnect the spark plug wires from the distributor cap by gently twisting and pulling on the rubber boots.
3. Remove the cap to housing attaching screws and remove the cap.
4. Disconnect the vacuum hose connecting from the carburetor spark port to the lower chamber nipple on the vacuum advance and the hose from the intake manifold to the upper chamber nipple.
5. Disconnect the ECM connector from the distributer wiring harness.
6. Remove the coil positive terminal nut and disconnect the distributor harness connector and supression capacitor wire. Pull the distributor connector off the coil ground terminal post. Separate the harness routing clip tabs and free the coil primary wiring harness.
7. Scribe a timing reference mark across the distributor mounting flange and cylinder head surface to ensure that the distributor will be installed without altering the timing.
8. Loosen the base flange mounting bolts and remove the distributor assembly from its mounting bore.
9. Remove the flange base O-ring and inspect for damage. Replace the O-ring as required. Coat the O-ring with clean engine oil and install into the flange base.
To install:
10. Insert the distributor assembly into the cylinder head mounting bore. Rotate the distributor until the offset drive tang aligns and engages with the camshaft slot.
11. After the distributor is engaged with the camshaft, align the timing reference marks scribed across the flange base and cylinder head. When the timing marks are aligned, install and tighten the mounting bolts.
12. Position the distributor-to-coil primary harness and the supression capacitor lead in the harness routing clip and close

the clip. Connect the harness to the coil primary terminals. Connect the supression capacitor and battery leads to the positive terminal. Connect the ECM connector to the distributor wiring harness.
13. Install the distributor cap, spark plug wires and reconnect the vacuum hoses to the vacuum advance unit.
14. Connect the negative battery cable.

TIMING DISTURBED

1. If the engine has been rotated while the distributor was removed, rotate the crankshaft until the No. 1 cylinder is at TDC, on the compression stroke.
2. The engine will be at TDC, when the **TC** mark on the belt cover is in alignment with the notch on the crankshaft pulley.
3. Insert the distributor assembly into the cylinder head mounting bore. Rotate the distributor until the offset drive tang aligns and engages with the camshaft slot.
4. Continue the installation in the reverse order of the removal procedure.

IGNITION TIMING

ADJUSTMENT

1. Start the engine and allow to reach normal operating temperature.
2. Stop the engine and connect a tachometer. Start the engine and check the idle speed. Adjust the idle speed, if necessary.
3. Disconnect the vacuum hoses from the vacuum advance unit and plug the hose openings. As required, disconnect the white altitude connector at the distributor.
4. Turn off all electrical accessories. As required, disconnect the barometric pressure switch (mounted high on the firewall on the right side of the engine).
5. Connect the timing light to the engine. Start the engine.
6. With the timing light, observe the timing marks on the crankshaft pulley and timing case.
7. If the timing is not as specified, loosen the distributor mounting bolts and rotate the distributor clockwise to advance the timing and counterclockwise to retard the timing.
8. When the timing is adjusted to specification, tighten the distributor mounting bolts.
9. Stop the engine. Remove the timing light. Unplug the vacuum hoses and connect them to the vacuum advance unit. Connect the barometric pressure switch, if removed.
10. Start the engine and check the idle speed. Adjust the idle speed as required.

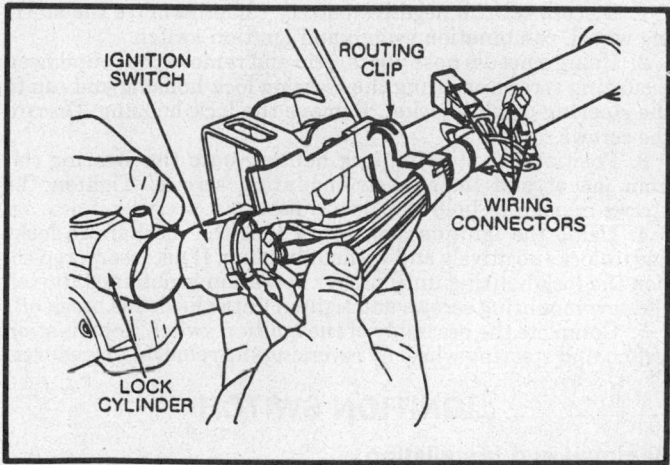
Ignition switch with wiring harness connections

Electrical Controls

STEERING WHEEL

Removal and Installation

1. Disconnect the negative battery cable. With the proper tool, pry the trim insert in the center of the steering wheel cover. Take care not to damage the cover.
2. Remove the steering wheel nut.
3. Remove the screws from the back of the steering wheel spokes. This will free the steering wheel cover assembly, cover bracket and horn buttons. Disconnect the horn wire from the horn button leads and remove the cover assembly.
4. Matchmark the steering wheel and steering column shaft for assembly reference. Using a steering wheel puller tool, remove the steering wheel.
5. Installation is the reverse of the removal procedure. Position the steering wheel onto the steering column shaft and align the matchmarks.

NOTE: When installing the steering wheel, make certain that the cutouts in the rear cover engage the turn signal cancelling cam. If necessary, use the steering wheel nut to seat the steering wheel onto the cancelling cam cutouts, then remove the nut.

HORN SWITCH

Removal and Installation

1. Disconnect the negative battery cable. Remove the steering wheel cover attaching screws located under the steering wheel spokes.
2. Pull the cover away from the steering wheel and disconnect the horn switch wire.
3. Remove the horn contacts, contact insulator, horn button and return spring.
4. Install the return spring, horn button, horn contacts and contact insulator.
5. Install the horn switch wire and the contact set attaching screws.
6. Connect the horn switch wire and position the cover on the steering wheel.
7. Install the steering wheel cover attaching screws.
8. Inspect the horn for proper operation.

IGNITION LOCK

Removal and Installation

1. Disconnect the negative battery cable. Remove the steering wheel, combination switch and ignition switch.
2. Using a needle nose pliers, grip and remove the round head mounting screws securing the steering lock housing and cap to the steering column jacket. Remove the lock housing. Discard the screws.
3. Position the steering lock housing onto the steering column jacket and install new mounting screws. Tighten the screws enough to hold the lock in postion.
4. Using the ignition key, verify that the mechanism locks and unlocks positively and without binding. If necessary, reposition the lock housing until proper operation is obtained. Install the new mounting screws and tighten until the heads break off.
5. Complete the assembly of the ignition switch, combination switch and steering wheel by reversing the removal procedures.

IGNITION SWITCH

Removal and Installation

1. Disconnect the battery negative cable.

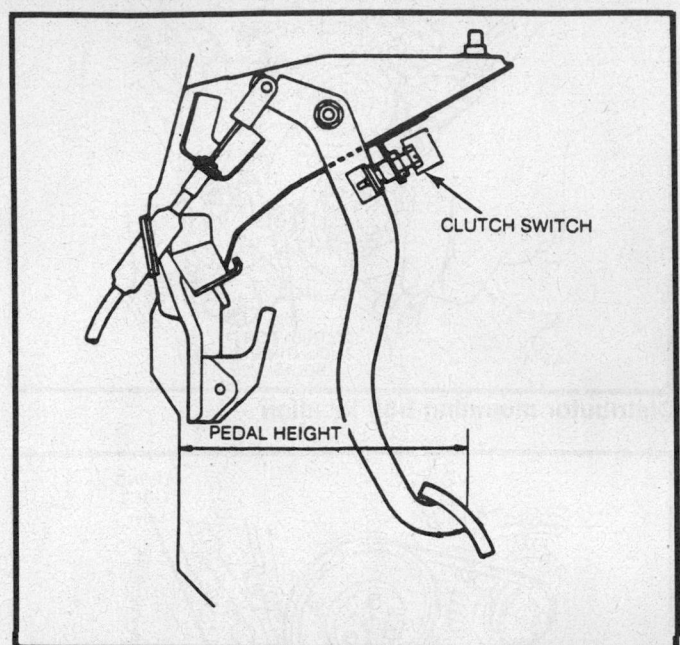

Clutch pedal height adjustment

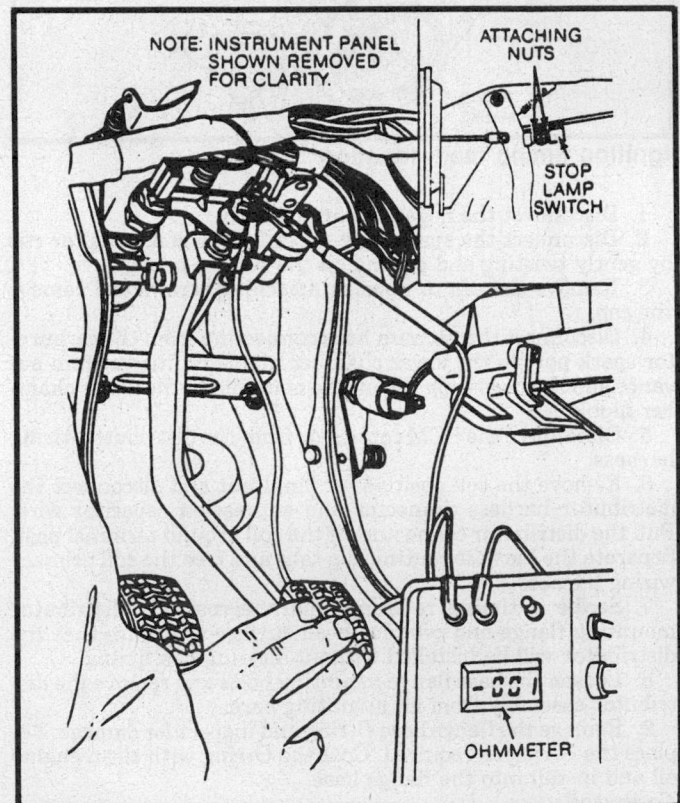

Adjusting the stoplamp switch

2. Remove the upper and lower steering column covers by removing the attaching screws from the lower cover.
3. Remove the instrument panel spacer brace.
4. Remove the air discharge duct located below the steering column.
5. Remove the steering column attaching nuts and lower the

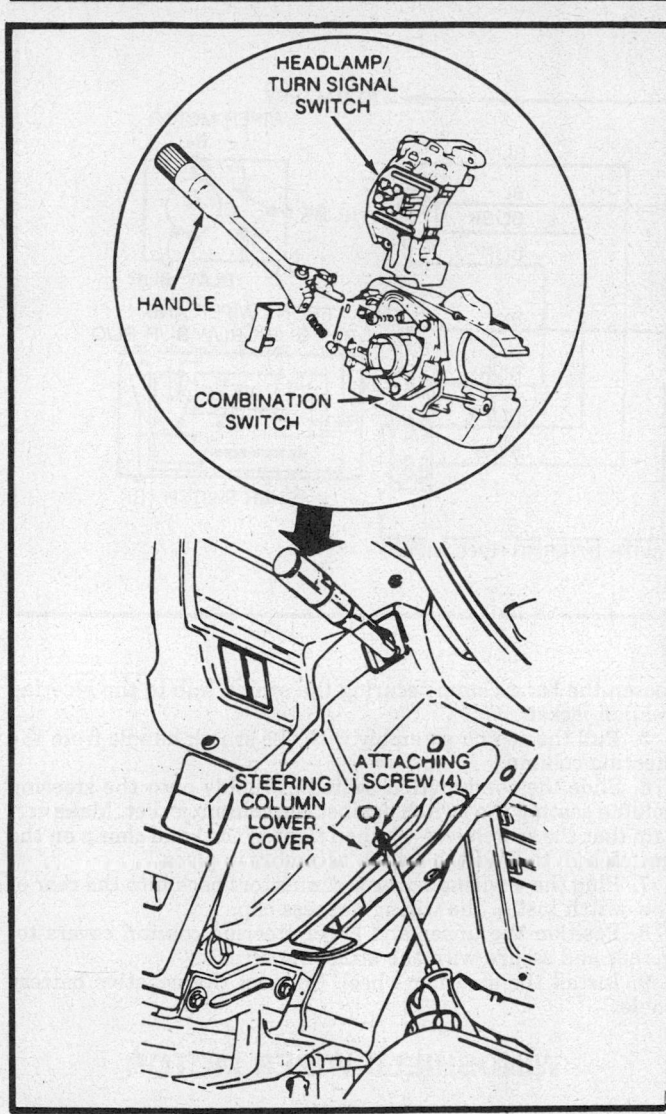

Combination switch assembly

steering column from its normal operating position.

6. Remove the tie strap securing the key warning buzzer switch wires to lock the cylinder housing. Discard the tie strap.

7. Remove the ignition switch retaining screw to release the switch from the steering column lock housing.

8. Remove the switch harness from the routing clip.

9. Separate the ignition switch wiring connectors and remove the ignition switch from the cylinder lock housing.

10. Installation is the reverse of the removal procedure.

NEUTRAL SAFETY SWITCH

Removal and Installation

1. Disconnect the negative battery cable. Raise and support the vehicle safely.

2. Disconnect the neutral safety switch electrical wires.

3. Place a drain pan under the transaxle, to catch any excess transaxle fluid.

4. Remove the neutral safety switch from its mounting.

5. Installation is the reverse of the removal procedure. Be sure to replace any lost fluid.

CLUTCH START SWITCH

Adjustment

1. To eliminate the possibility that the clutch cable is affecting the pedal height, loosen the cable adjusting nut and disengage the cable pin from the transaxle release lever.

2. Move the floor carpet and insulation out of the way of the dash panel to gain sufficient room for an accurate measurement.

3. With a machinist's ruler, measure the distance from the upper center of the pedal to the dash panel. The pedal height should be 8.209–8.304 in.

4. If the pedal height is within this range, no adjustment is necessary. If the pedal height is not within specification, it must be adjusted.

5. Remove the instrument panel bracket and air duct from under the instrument panel.

6. Locate the clutch switch and loosen the attaching nuts. Thread the switch in or out until the pedal height is within specification. Tighten the attaching nuts.

7. Connect the clutch cable to the transaxle release lever and adjust the pedal free play.

8. Measure the clutch pedal height. If the pedal height has changed after connecting the clutch cable, check for binding along the cable route.

9. Install the air inlet duct and instrument panel bracket. Place the insulation and floor carpet in their original positions.

Removal and Installation

1. Disconnect the negative battery cable. Move the floor carpet out of the way.

2. Remove the instrument panel bracket located under the steering column and remove the air duct.

3. Disconnect the clutch switch wiring connector.

4. Loosen the switch upper attaching nut and lower the switch from the mounting bracket. Remove the lower attaching nut from the switch and transfer to the new switch.

5. Position the switch into the mounting bracket and install the upper attaching nut.

STOPLIGHT SWITCH

Adjustment

1. Disconnect the negative battery cable. Disconnect the switch wiring connector.

2. Loosen the upper and lower attaching nuts enough to allow for rotation of the switch.

3. Connect an ohmmeter across the switch terminals.

4. Rotate the switch until the ohmmeter indicates continuity.

5. Slowly rotate the switch toward the brake pedal until the ohmmeter indicates that the switch is open (infinite resistance).

6. Rotate the switch toward the brake pedal ½ additional turn and tighten the attaching nuts to retain the adjustment.

7. Connect the switch wiring connector and check the switch for proper operation.

Removal and Installation

1. Disconnect the negative battery cable. Disconnect the stop lamp switch wiring connector.

2. Remove the upper attaching nut and lower the switch from the bracket.

3. Remove the lower attaching nut from the switch. Replace the switch as required.

4. Transfer the lower attaching nut onto the new switch and install the switch into the mounting bracket. Install the upper attaching nut. Do not tighten the nuts or reconnect the wiring connector at this time.

5. Adjust the switch.

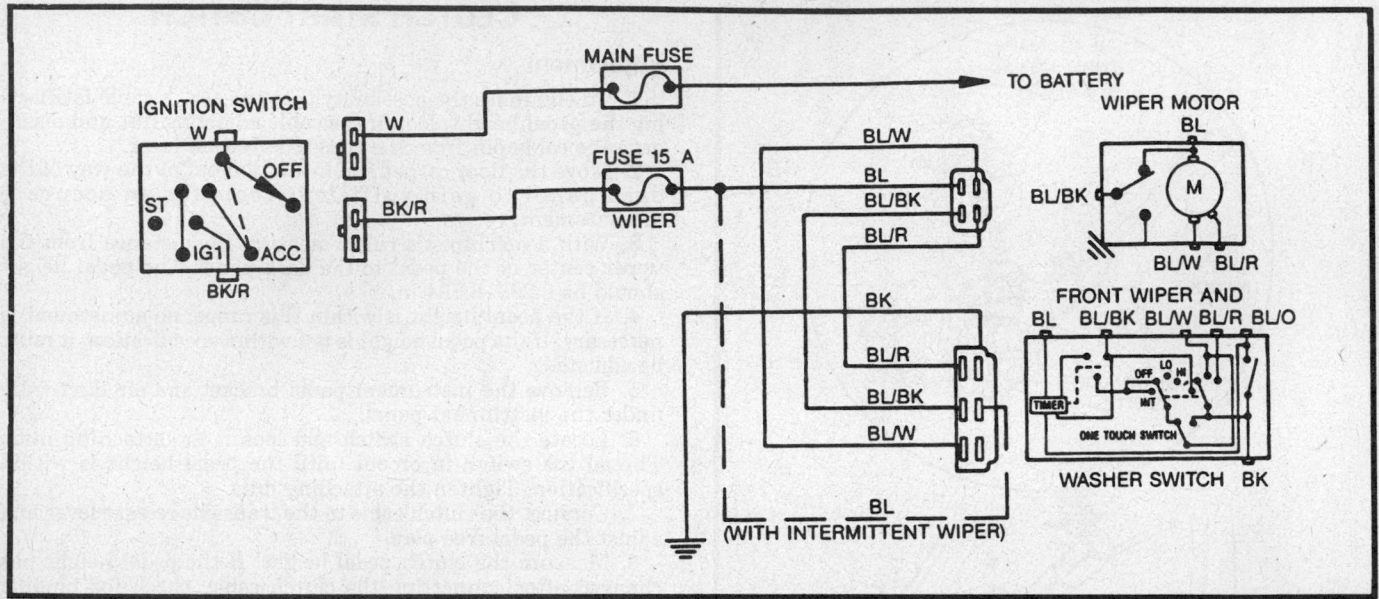

Windshield wiper electrical schematic

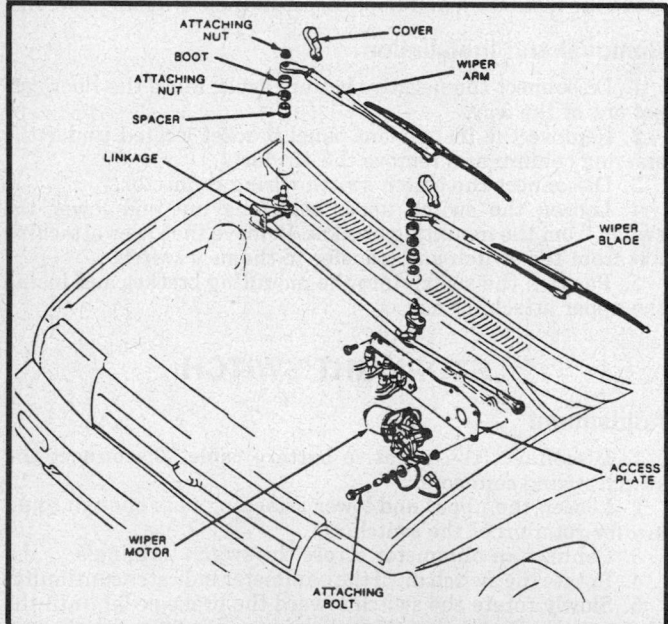

Wiper motor, wiper arm and linkage assembly

6. Connect the switch wiring connector.
7. Check the switch for proper operation.

COMBINATION SWITCH

Removal and Installation

1. Disconnect the negative battery cable.
2. Remove the steering wheel.
3. Remove the steering column lower cover attaching screws. Separate and remove the upper and lower steering column covers.
4. Compress the locking tabs and release the wiring harness clip. Unplug the 4 wiring harness connectors from the rear of the combination switch. From underneath the steering column,

loosen the band clamp securing the switch hub to the steering column jacket.
5. Pull the switch assembly with the switch handle from the steering column.
6. Slide the combination switch assembly onto the steering column seating the switch against the column jacket. Make certain that the switch is level, then tighten the band clamp on the switch hub to hold the switch assembly in place.
7. Plug the 4 wiring harness connectors back into the rear of the switch install the wiring harness clip.
8. Position the upper and lower steering column covers together and secure with the attaching screws.
9. Install the steering wheel. Connect the negative battery cable.

WINDSHIELD WIPER MOTOR

Removal and Installation

1. Disconnect the negative battery cable. Disconnect the wiring at the wiper motor.
2. Remove the wiper motor attaching bolts. Remove the wiper motor ground wire attaching bolt and remove the wire from the bolt.
3. Remove the mounting plate attaching screws and pull the plate away from the dash panel.
4. With the proper tool, disengage the linkage pivot from the output arm. Remove the wiper motor from the vehicle.
5. Position the motor on the mounting plate and connect the output arm to the linkage pivot.
6. Position the mounting plate and install the attaching screws.
7. Install the wiper motor attaching bolts. Connect the ground wire to the top right attaching bolt and install.
8. Connect the wiper motor wiring connector. Check the wiper motor for proper operation and linkage movement.

DELAY WIPER CONTROLS

Operation

The delay wiper switch has 3 detented positions for the interval delay wipe, slow wipe and fast wipe. The switch assembly is part of the combination switch. The switch also features a spring

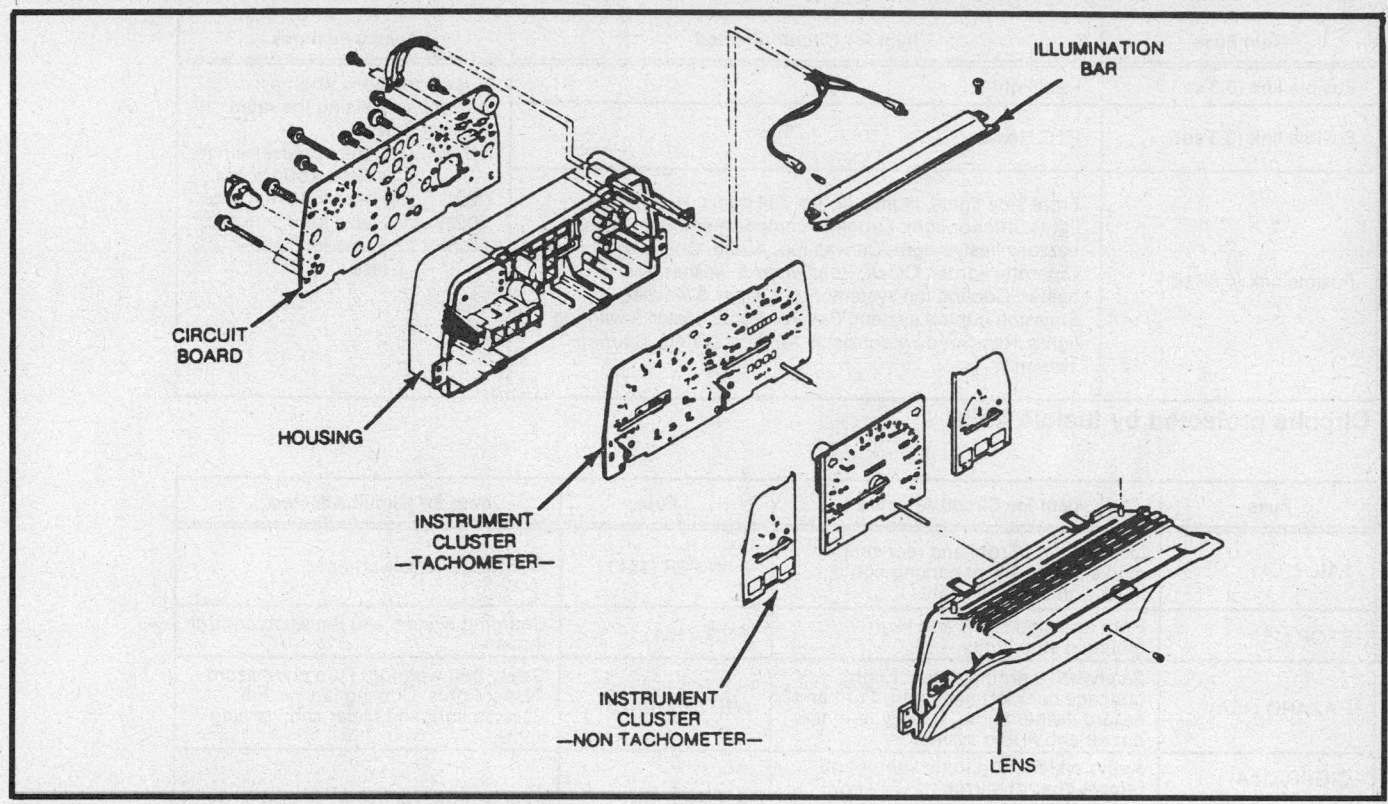

Exploded view of the instrument panel cluster

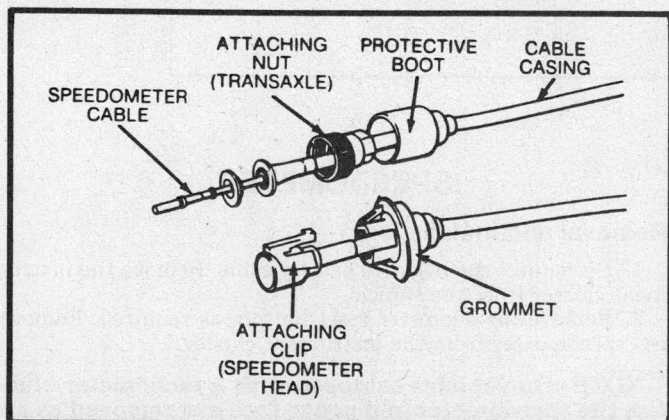

Speedometer cable showing instrument cluster and transaxle attachment points

loaded position. When the handle is pushed toward the instrument panel, the wiper will cycle until the handle is released at which time the spring will return the handle to the **OFF** position.

WINDSHIELD WIPER LINKAGE

Removal and Installation

1. Disconnect the negative battery cable. Remove the wiper motor.
2. Remove the attaching nut cover and remove the wiper arm attaching nut. Remove the wiper arm from the pivot by carefully prying on the arm to disengage it from the shaft. Repeat the procedure for the remaining wiper arm.

3. Remove the wiper linkage pivot assembly boots, attaching nuts and spacers.
4. Remove the wiper linkage assembly through the access opening in the dash panel.
5. Install the wiper linkage assembly through the access opening.
6. Install the pivot assembly spacers and attaching nuts. During installation of the spacers and attaching nuts, reach through the access opening and hold the linkage stationary.
7. Install the pivot assembly boots.
8. Install the wiper arms.

NOTE: Prior to installing the wiper arms, turn the ignition switch to the ON postion. Turn the wiper motor on and allow it to cycle several times and then turn the system off. This cycling should locate the linkage pivot shaft in the wiper park position and allow for proper wiper positioning.

9. Complete the assembly of the wiper motor by reversing the removal procedure.

Instrument Cluster

Removal and Installation

1. Disconnect the battery negative cable.
2. If equipped with tilt wheel, release the tilt lock and lower the steering column. If not equipped with tilt wheel, remove the steering column upper and lower covers.
3. Remove the screws securing the instrument cluster bezel to the instrument cluster.
4. Pull the instrument cluster bezel away from the instrument cluster.
5. If equipped with rear window defogger, disconnect the wiring from the switch.

Main Fuse	Item for Circuit Affected	Fusing Features
Fusible link (0.3 sq.)	Headlight	Fuse conditions when a current surpassing the rated current flows.
Fusible link (0.3 sq)	PTC Heater	100% . . . . Does not fuse within a period of 4 hours.
Fusible link (0.85 sq.)	Front side lights, Illume. lights, Tail lights, Horn & stop lights, Interior light, Luggage compartment light, Turn & hazzard flasher light, Canvas top, Audio, Charging system, Cigarette lighter, Clock, Rear wiper & washer, Air con & heater, Cooling fan system, Front wiper & washer, Emission control system, Reverse lights, Meter & warning lights, Rear window defroster, Ignition system, Starting system	200% . . . . Fuses for 5-100 sec. 300% . . . . Fuses for 0.5-15 sec. 500% . . . . Fuses for 1 sec. or less

Circuits protected by fusible links

Fuse	Item for Circuit Affected	Fuse	Item for Circuit Affected
TAIL (15A)	License light, Front and rear side marker lights, Front parking lights, Illum. lights and tail light	F. WIPER (15A)	Front wiper and washer
STOP (15A)	Horn and stop lights and High mounted stop lights	ENG. (10A)	Charging system and Emission control system
HAZARD (15A)	Safety belt warning, Interior light, Luggage compartment light, Turn and hazzard flasher lights, 1G Bey reminder buzzer and Audio system	METER (10A)	Safety belt warning, Turn and hazard flasher lights, Cooling fan system, Reverse light and Meter and warning lights
CIGAR (15A)	Audio system, Cigarette lighter and remote control mirror	R. DEF. (15A)	Rear window defroster
R. WIPER (15A)	Rear wiper and washer		
HEATER (15A)	Heater and Air conditioner		
FAN (15A)	Heater and air conditioner and Cooling fan system		

Circuits protected by fuses

6. If equipped with rear window wiper, disconnect the wiring from the switch.

7. Remove the screws securing the instrument cluster in the instrument panel.

8. Pull the cluster away from the instrument panel.

9. Reach behind the cluster, lift the lock tab and disconnect the speedometer cable.

10. Lift the lock tab and disconnect the electrical connectors from the back of the instrument cluster.

11. Remove the instrument cluster from the vehicle.

To install:

12. Position the instrument cluster in the instrument panel opening.

13. Connect the electrical connectors to the back of the instrument cluster.

14. Slide the instrument cluster into the instrument panel.

15. Connect the speedometer cable.

16. Install and tighten the instrument cluster attaching screws.

17. Position the instrument cluster bezel on the instrument cluster. If necessary, connect the rear defogger and rear wiper switch wiring.

18. Install and tighten the instrument cluster bezel attaching screws.

19. If equipped with tilt wheel, raise the steering column and lock in desired position.

20. Connect the battery negative cable.

21. Check the operation of all instruments, gauges, and indicator lights.

SPEEDOMETER

Removal and Installation

1. Disconnect the negative battery cable. Remove the instrument cluster from the vehicle.

2. Remove the odometer reset button, as required. Remove the speedometer from the instrument cluster.

NOTE: On vehicles equipped with a tachometer cluster, the speedometer and gauge face are removed as an assembly. If the speedometer is being replaced on these type clusters, transfer the tachometer and gauges to the new gauge face. On vehicles without a tachometer, the speedometer cluster is a separate module that can be removed and installed without removing the gauges.

3. Installation is the reverse of the removal procedure. Check the speedometer for proper operation.

SPEEDOMETER CABLE

Removal and Installation

1. Disconnect the negative battery cable. Remove the instrument cluster. Disconnect the speedometer cable casing from the rear of the instrument cluster by pressing the locking tab and releasing the instrument panel cluster.

2. At the transaxle end, disengage the speedometer protective boot from the sleeve and slide up the cable casing.

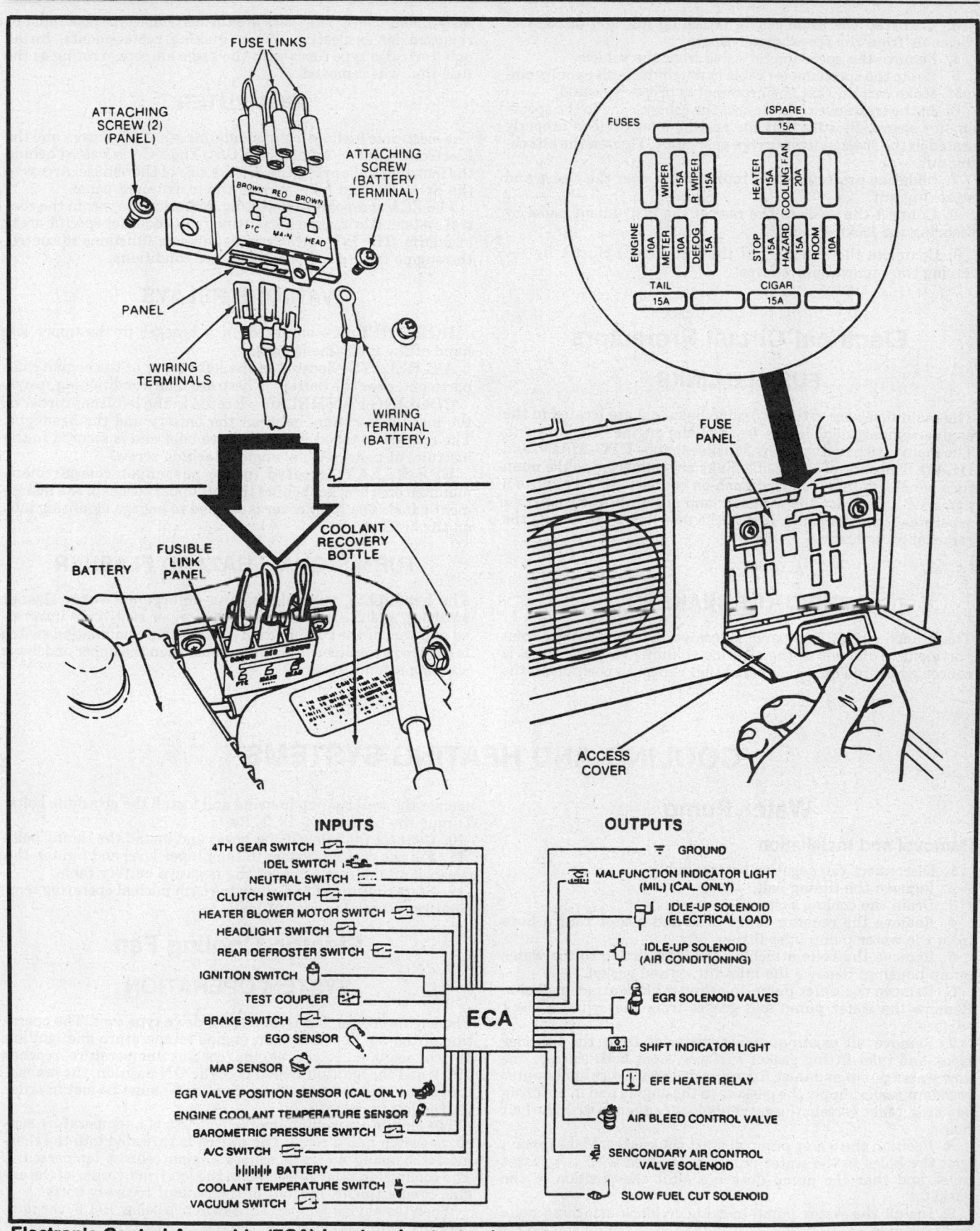

Electronic Control Assembly (ECA) input and output schematic

3. Unthread the cable casing attaching nut and disconnect the cable from the speedometer sleeve.

4. Remove the speedometer cable from the vehicle.

5. Route the speedometer cable through the dash panel grommet. Make certain that the grommet is properly seated.

6. At the transaxle end, connect the cable casing to the speedometer sleeve. Be sure that the speedometer cable is properly seated in the speedometer driven gear shaft. Tighten the attaching nut.

7. Slide the protective boot into position over the sleeve and attaching nut.

8. Connect the cable to the rear of the instrument panel by securing the locking tab.

9. Complete the assembly of the instrument cluster by reversing the removal procedures.

Electrical Circuit Protectors

FUSIBLE LINKS

The main fuses are actually fusible links and are located in the engine compartment in the front of the engine compartment. The main fuse panel contains 3 fusible links—**PTC**, **MAIN**, and **HEAD**. The ends of the fusible links are connected to the main fuse panel through standard push-on connectors. To remove a damaged link, grasp the insulator and pull until the connector separates from the panel. Install the new link by reversing the removal procedure.

CIRCUIT BREAKERS

The branch circuit fuse panel is located in the passenger compartment to the left of the steering column. The fuse panel is concealed behind an access panel that clips into position on the instrument panel. The fuses are the cartridge type that must be removed for inspection. When making replacements, install only cartridge type fuses with the same amperage rating as the fuse that was removed.

COMPUTER

The electronic fuel control system consists of 10 sensors and the Electronic Control Assembly (ECA). The ECA is located behind the instrument panel on the drivers side of the vehicle. Access to the ECA is gained by removing the instrument panel.

The ECA is capable of detecting malfunctions within the control system, storing and outputting fault codes for specific areas of failure. The ECA incorporates fail-safe functions to control the engine during component failure conditions.

VARIOUS RELAYS

HORN RELAY—mounted on a bracket in the upper left hand of the instrument panel.

A/C RELAYS—located in the left corner of the engine compartment, near the battery. There are 3 air conditioning relays.

COOLING FAN RELAY—located in the left front corner of the instrument panel between the battery and the headlight. The relay is installed in a protective boot and is secured to the instrument panel with a single attaching screw.

EFE RELAY—located in the passenger compartment mounted on a bracket behind the left upper corner of the instrument panel. The relay cover is formed to engage mounting tabs on the bracket.

TURN SIGNAL/ HAZARD FLASHER

The headlights, turn signal and emergency 4-way flasher switches, and the windshield washer wiper switch are integrated and part of the combination switch. The combination switch is located in the steering column in between the upper and lower steering column covers.

COOLING AND HEATING SYSTEMS

Water Pump

Removal and Installation

1. Disconnect the negative battery cable.
2. Remove the timing belt.
3. Drain the cooling system.
4. Remove the radiator lower hose and heater return hose from the water pump inlet fitting.
5. Remove the bolts attaching the inlet fitting to the water pump housing. Remove the inlet fitting and gasket.
6. Remove the water pump-to-cylinder block attaching bolts. Remove the water pump and gasket from the cylinder block surface.
7. Remove all existing gasket material from the cylinder block and inlet fitting gasket surfaces. Coat both sides of the new water pump and inlet fitting gaskets with a suitable water resistant sealer. Apply the gaskets to the engine and inlet fitting surfaces. Make certain the gasket holes are aligned with the bolt holes.
8. Position the water pump against the gasket. Make certain that the holes in the water pump are aligned with the gasket holes and that the pump does not shift the position of the gasket.
9. Install the water pump-to-cylinder block attaching bolts and torque to 14–19 ft. lbs. Position the inlet fitting and gasket against the water pump housing and install the attaching bolts. Torque the bolts to 14–19 ft. lbs.
10. Connect the inlet fitting hoses and install the timing belt.
11. Fill the cooling system to the proper level and tighten the expansion tank cap. Connect the negative battery cable.
12. Start the engine and allow to reach normal operating temperature. Check for coolant leaks.

Electric Cooling Fan

SYSTEM OPERATION

The engine cooling fan is an electro-drive type unit. The operation of the fan depends upon engine temperature and ignition switch position. If the engine coolant temperature reaches 207°F and the ignition switch is in the **ON** position, the fan motor circuit is completed. These conditions must be met in order for the fan to operate.

The circuit controlling the fan consists of a temperature sensitive switch and a relay. The switch is threaded into the thermostat housing where it senses engine coolant temperature. The cooling fan relay is located in the left front corner of the engine compartment, in front of the coolant recovery bottle.

When the engine temperature switch is below 194°F, the temperature switch is closed and the relay contacts are held open by

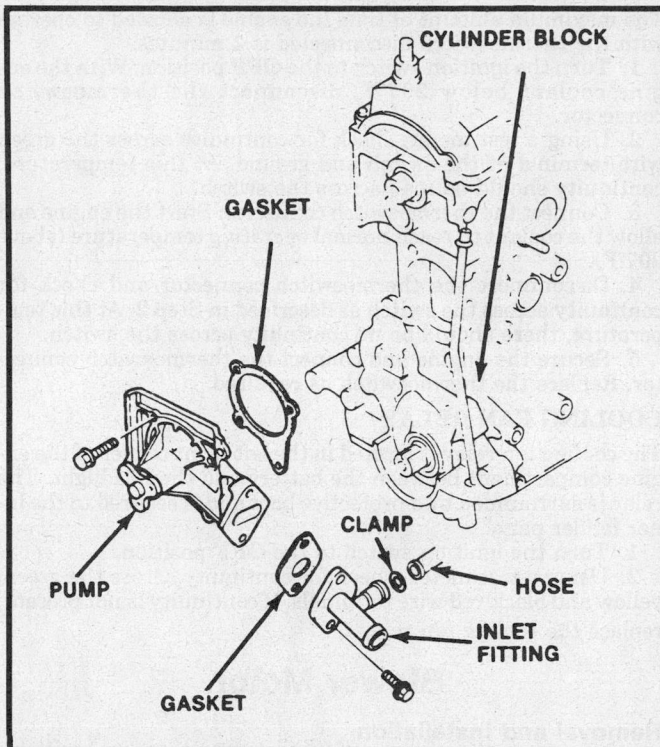

Water pump assembly

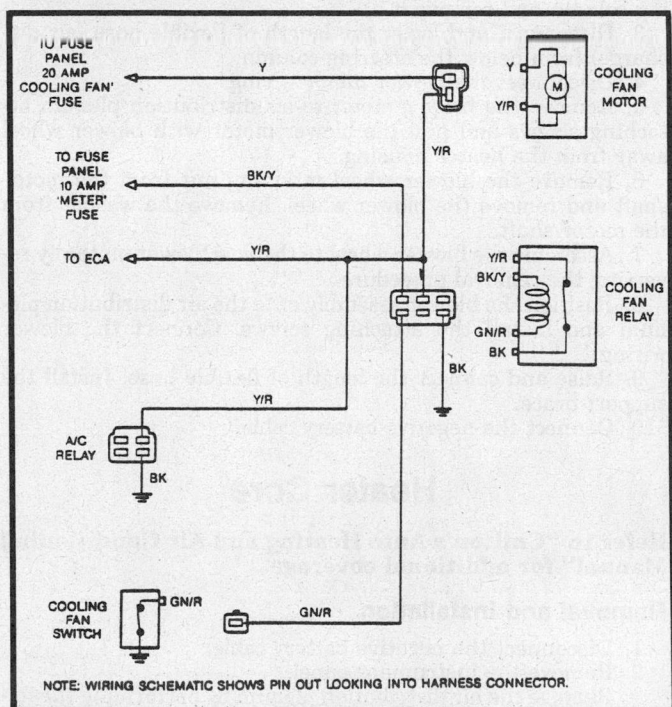

Electric cooling fan schematic

NOTE: WIRING SCHEMATIC SHOWS PIN OUT LOOKING INTO HARNESS CONNECTOR.

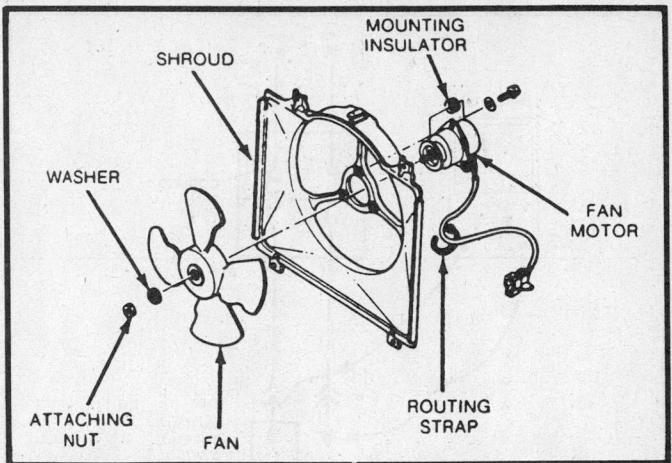

Cooling fan assembly

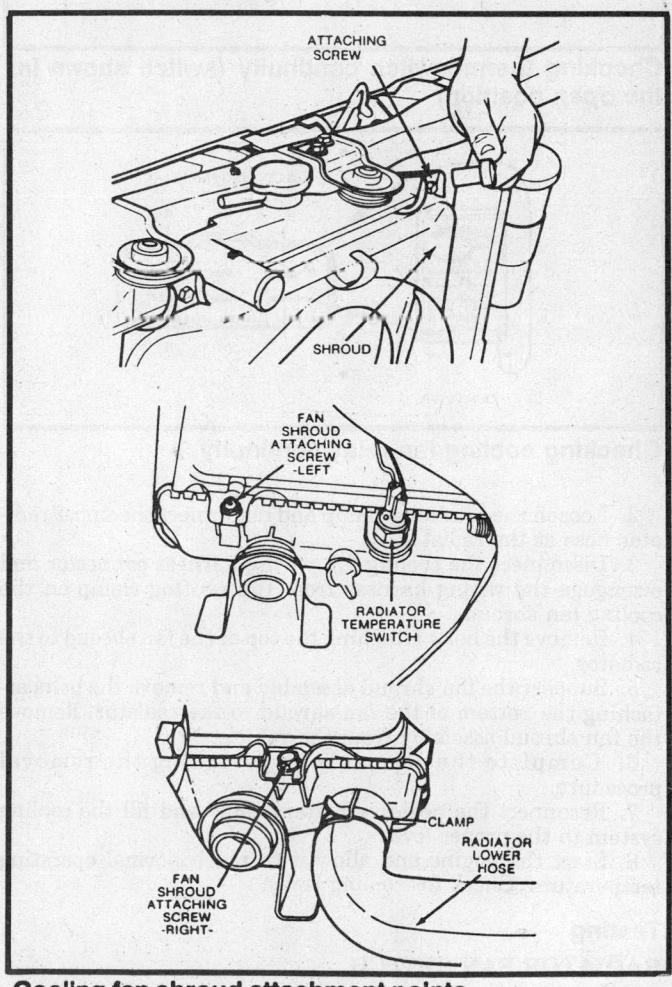

Cooling fan shroud attachment points (upper and lower)

the magnetism produced in the relay coil. When the switch is opened by increased engine temperatures, the coil circuit opens allowing spring pressure to close the relay contacts.

If the vehicle is equipped with air conditioning, an additional relay is installed in the cooling fan circuit. The air conditioning relay bypasses the engine temperature portion of the circuit.

The bypass allows the fan to operate whenever the air conditioning switch is engaged.

Removal and Installation
1. Disconnect the negative battery cable.

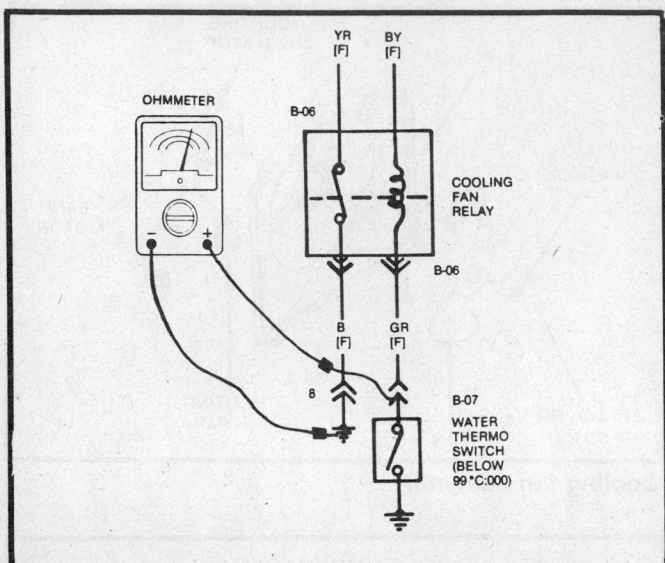

Checking thermoswitch continuity (switch shown in the open position)

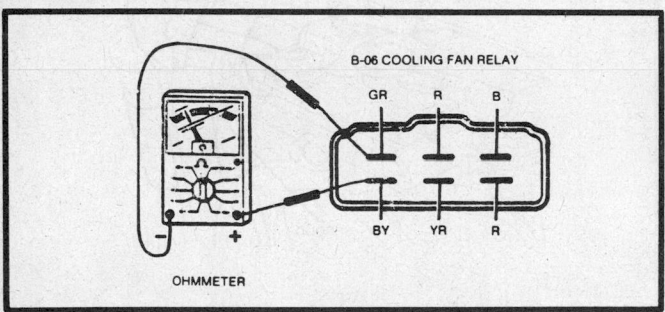

Checking cooling fan relay continuity

2. Loosen the retaining clamp and disconnect the upper radiator hose at the radiator.

3. Disconnect the cooling fan wiring harness connector and disengage the wiring harness from the routing clamp on the cooling fan shroud.

4. Remove the bolts attaching the top of the fan shroud to the radiator.

5. Support the fan shroud assembly and remove the bolts attaching the bottom of the fan shroud to the radiator. Remove the fan shroud assembly from the vehicle.

6. Complete the assembly by reversing the removal procedure.

7. Reconnect the negative battery cable and fill the cooling system to the proper level.

8. Start the engine and allow it to reach normal operating temperature. Check for cooling leaks.

Testing

RADIATOR FAN SWITCH

The cooling fan temperature switch is threaded into the front side of the thermostat housing. The themoswitch continuity test should be conducted when the coolant temperature is above and below the normal cut-in point of the switch (207°F).

To avoid the possibly of personal injury or damage to the vehicle, make certain that the ignition switch is in the **OFF** position before disconnecting the wire from the cooling fan temperature switch. If the wire is disconnected from the switch with the ignition switch in the **ON** position, the cooling fan may come on.

The maximum amount of time the engine is allowed to operate with the thermoswitch disconnected is 2 minutes.

1. Turn the ignition switch to the **OFF** position. With the engine coolant below 207°F, disconnect the thermoswitch connector.

2. Using a test meter, check for continuity across the green wire terminal of the switch and ground. At this temperature, continuity should be read across the switch.

3. Connect the thermoswitch connector. Start the engine and allow the coolant to reach normal operating temperature (above 207°F).

4. Disconnnect the thermoswitch connector and check for continuity across the switch as described in Step 2. At this temperature, there should be no continuity across the switch.

5. Secure the engine and connect the thermoswitch connector. Replace the thermoswitch as required.

COOLING FAN RELAY

The cooling fan relay is located in the left front corner of the engine compartment between the battery and the headlight. The relay is surrounded by a protective boot and is secured to the inner fender panel.

1. Turn the ignition switch to the **OFF** position.

2. Using a test meter, check for continuity across the green/yellow and black/red wire terminals. If continuity is not present, replace the cooling fan relay.

Blower Motor

Removal and Installation

1. Disconnect the negative battery cable.

2. Locate the instrument panel spacer brace below the steering column and remove it.

3. Disconnect and lower the length of flexible hose (air discharge) from below the steering column.

4. Disconnect the blower motor wiring.

5. Remove the blower motor-to-air distribution plenum attaching screws and pull the blower motor with blower wheel away from the heater housing.

6. Remove the blower wheel retaining nut from the motor shaft and remove the blower wheel. Remove the washer from the motor shaft.

7. Assemble the blower wheel to the new blower motor by reversing the removal procedure.

8. Position the blower assembly onto the air distribution plenum and install the attaching screws. Connect the blower wiring.

9. Raise and connect the length of flexible hose. Install the support brace.

10. Connect the negative battery cable.

Heater Core

Refer to "Chilton's Auto Heating and Air Conditioning Manual" for additional coverage.

Removal and Installation

1. Disconnect the negative battery cable.

2. Remove the instrument panel.

3. Remove the air distribution plenum by performing the following steps:

   a. Disconnect the heater hoses from inside the engine compartment.

   b. Disconnect the blower motor and blower resistor wiring.

   c. Disengage the wiring harness and antenna lead from the routing bracket on the front of the air distribution housing.

   d. Loosen the clamp screw securing the connector duct to the air inlet housing.

   e. Remove the upper and lower plenum attaching nuts.

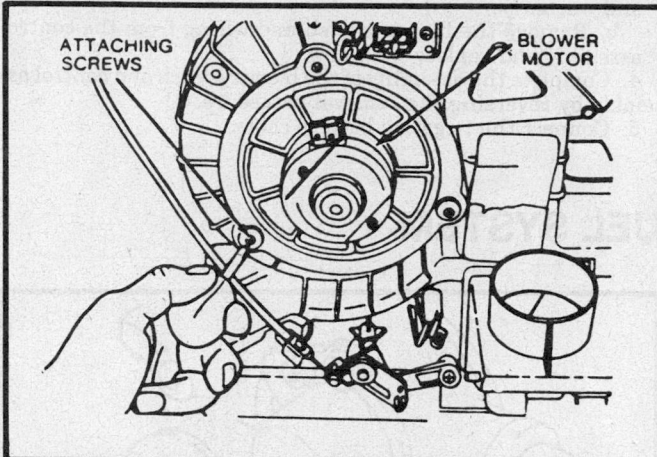

Blower motor mounting to air distribution plenum

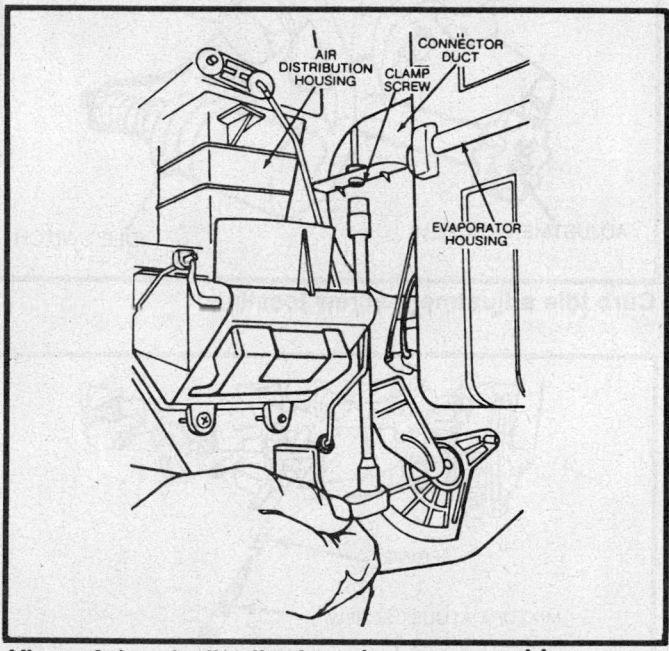

View of the air distribution plenum assembly

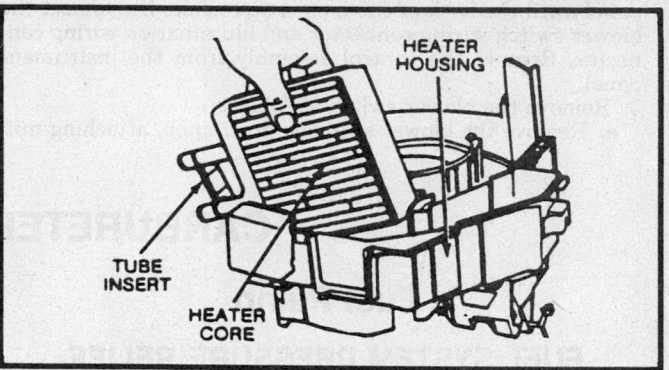

Positioning heater core in plenum half

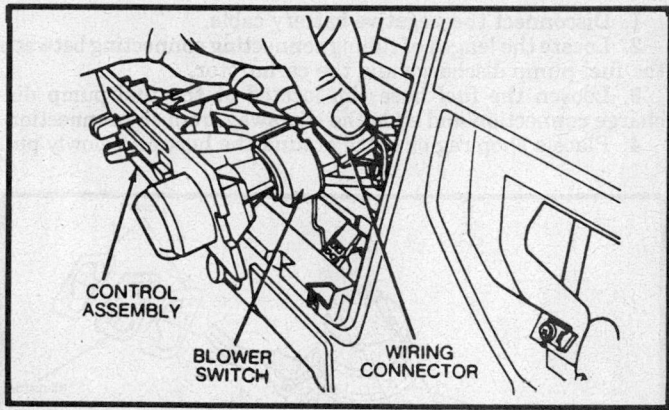

Removing blower switch/control assembly from instrument panel

Disengage the plenum from the defroster ducts and remove from the vehicle.

4. Disconnect the link from the 2 defroster doors.

5. Locate and remove the screws just above and to the right of the blower resistor. Turn the plenum around and remove the screw located to the left of the blower motor opening.

6. Remove the retaining clips that secure the the plenum halves. Separate the plenum halves.

7. Remove the heater core and tube insert/stiffener. Remove the tube insert/stiffener from the heater core and transfer to the new unit. Install the new heater core.

8. Complete the assembly and installation of the heater core and distribution plenum by reversing the disassembly and removal procedures.

9. Install the instrument panel.

10. Connect the negative battery cable.

TEMPERATURE CONTROL/ BLOWER SWITCH

Removal and Installation

1. Disconnect the negative battery cable.

2. Remove the control assembly by performing the following steps:

   a. Remove the screws attaching the accessory bezel (that surrounds the radio and temperature control assembly) to the instrument panel. Remove the accessory bezel from the instrument panel.

   b. Remove the radio attaching screws and pull the radio from the instrument panel until the back of the unit is accessible. Disconnect the antenna lead. Identify, tag and disconnect the 4 radio wiring connectors. Remove the rubber insulator from the radio ground stud. Remove the ground stud nut and pull the wire from the terminal post.

   c. Remove the screws attaching the control assembly to the instrument panel. Lower the glove box and remove the attaching screws. Remove the glove box.

   d. Through the glove box opening, locate the outside/recirculation air door cable. Remove the cable retaining clip and disconnect the cable from the operating lever.

   e. Locate the function control lever on the left side of the air distribution panel near the blower motor. Disconnect the cable from the operating lever.

   f. Pull the control assembly away from the instrument

panel until the back of the unit is accessible. Disconnect the blower switch wiring connector and illumination wiring connector. Remove the control assembly from the instrument panel.

3. Remove the blower switch as follows:
    a. Remove the blower switch control knob, attaching nut,

and washers.
    b. Remove the blower switch and wiring from the control assembly and replace with new.

4. Complete the assembly of the blower switch and control assembly by reversing the removal procedure.
5. Connect the negative battery cable.

CARBURETED FUEL SYSTEM

Fuel Pump

FUEL SYSTEM PRESSURE RELIEF

Procedure

1. Disconnect the negative battery cable.
2. Locate the length of tubing connecting connecting between the fuel pump discharge and the carburetor.
3. Loosen the fuel hose clip located at the fuel pump discharge connection and slide the clip away from the connection.
4. Place a shop rag or towel around the hose and slowly pull

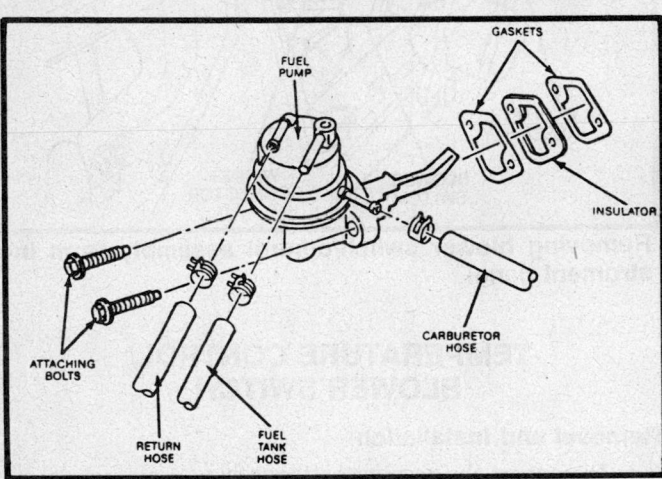

Fuel pump assembly

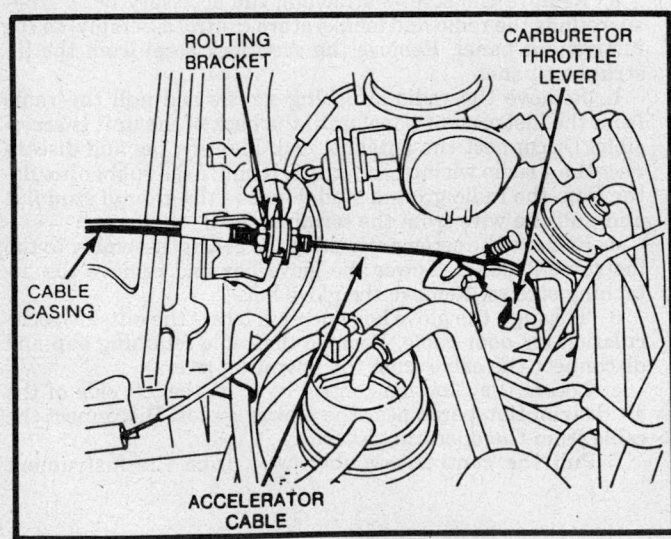

Accelerator cable-to-carburetor linkage

Curb idle adjustment screw location

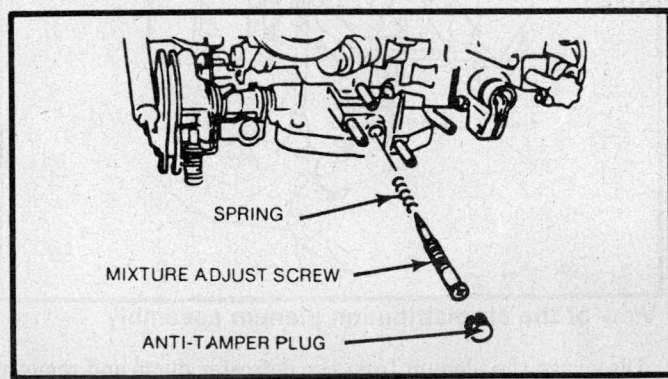

Idle mixture adjustment screw location

the hose away from the connection allowing the residual fuel pressure to be relieved. Allow the rag or towel to remain in place until all the excess fuel is absorbed.

Removal and Installation

1. Disconnect the negative battery cable. Remove the air cleaner assembly. Identify and tag all vacuum hoses as required.
2. Relieve the fuel system pressure.
3. Tag and disconnect the fuel pump inlet, outlet and return hoses.
4. Loosen the fuel pump retaining bolts to allow for movement of the pump on the cylinder head mounting. Place the fuel pump arm on the low side of the cam circle.
5. Loosen the pump retaining bolts.
6. Remove the pump from the mounting pad with insulator and gaskets. Replace the gaskets as required.

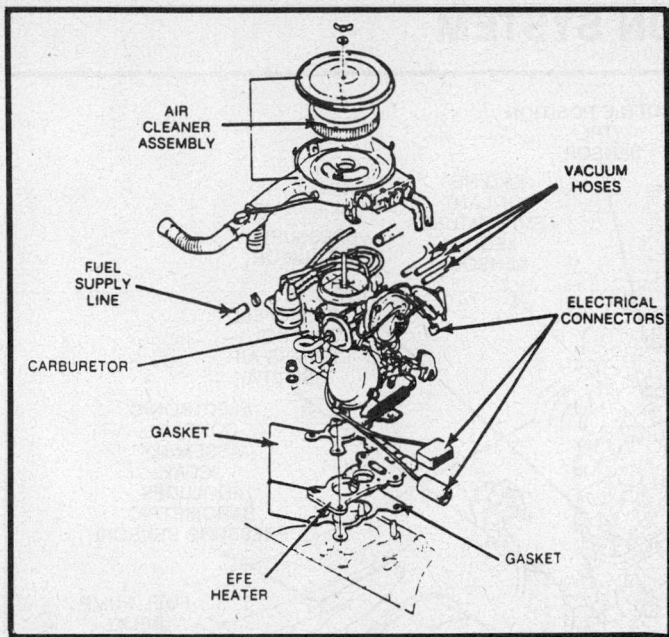

Carburetor with air cleaner assembly, electrical and vacuum connections

7. Clean the cylinder head and insulator gasket contact surfaces.

8. Install the pump, insulator and gaskets. Install the retaining bolts and torque to 17–22 ft. lbs.

9. Connect and secure the inlet, outlet and fuel return hoses to the fuel pump.

10. Complete the assembly of the air cleaner by reversing the removal procedure.

11. Start the engine and inspect for fuel leaks. Correct all fuel leaks immediately.

Carburetor

IDLE SPEED

Adjustment

1. Disconnect the cooling fan electrical connector. Check the ignition timing and adjust if necessary. Adjust the idle mixture, as required.

2. Place the transmission selector lever in **N** and firmly apply the parking brake. Make certain the air conditioning system is **OFF**. Be sure that all electrical accessories are **OFF**.

3. Connect a tachometer to the engine.

4. Start the engine and allow to reach normal operating temperature. Make certain that the choke is fully open.

5. Allow the engine to remain at idle and observe the idle speed reading. The idle speed should be 700–750 rpm.

6. If the idle speed is not within specifications, rotate the idle speed adjusting screw located on the right side of the carburetor as required until the correct idle speed is obtained.

IDLE MIXTURE

Adjustment

Adjustment of the idle mixture screw is normally unnecessary due to the fact that the adjustment has been made at the fac-

tory. The mixture adjust screw is sealed with an anti-tamper plug and roll pin to discourage adjustment. If the adjustment is required, proceed as follows with the use of an exhaust gas analyzer.

1. Disconnect the negative battery cable.

2. Remove the carburetor from the engine and position in a suitable holding fixture.

3. Remove the anti-tamper plug from the mixture adjust screw bore and discard the plug. Gently tap the roll pin from the mixture adjusting screw bore.

4. Install the carburetor and connect the negative battery cable. Leave the secondary injection hose disconnected at this time.

5. Insert the sensing probe of an exhaust gas analyzer in the secondary injection hose elbow opening. Plug the hose around the area of the probe lead to prevent the leakage of exhaust gas past the probe.

6. Start the engine and allow to reach normal operating temperature.

7. Observe the exhaust gas analyzer indicator reading. Rotate the mixture adjust screw until the analyzer registers a carbon monoxide concentration of 1.5–2.5%.

8. Check the idle speed and adjust if necessary.

9. Install a new anti-tamper plug over the mixture adjust screw and tap into position.

10. Remove the analyzer sensing probe and connect the secondary injection hose.

Removal and Installation

1. Disconnect the negative battery cable. Relieve the fuel system pressure.

2. Remove the air cleaner assembly.

3. Remove the retaining clip and disconnect the fuel supply line. Plug the hose opening to prevent contamination and the entry of foreign matter.

4. Disconnect the vacuum hoses from the carburetor. Identify each hose with its respective opening to ensure proper installation.

5. Disconnect the carburetor wiring connectors.

6. Disconnect the choke heater wire at the choke cap.

7. Move the throttle to the wide open position and disengage the throttle cable from the throttle lever.

8. Remove the carburetor retaining nuts and washers. Lift the carburetor upward from the intake manifold studs. Disconnect the idle up diaphragm link from the carburetor linkage. If the EFE heater sticks to the carburetor base, gently remove it. Discard the carburetor flange gaskets and replace with new.

9. Thoroughly clean the carburetor, EFE heater and intake manifold gasket contact surfaces and install new gaskets.

10. Position the carburetor over the intake manifold mounting studs and support by hand. While supporting the carburetor, connect the idle up diaphragm link to the carburetor linkage. Install and tighten the mounting nuts and washers.

11. Move the throttle to the wide open position and connect the throttle cable to the throttle lever.

12. Connect the choke heater wire.

13. Connect the carburetor wires to their respective connectors.

14. Connect the vacuum hoses to their original openings.

15. Connect the the fuel supply line and install the retaining clip.

16. Install the air cleaner assembly and connect the negative battery cable.

17. Start the engine and adjust the idle speed, if necessary.

FUEL INJECTION SYSTEM

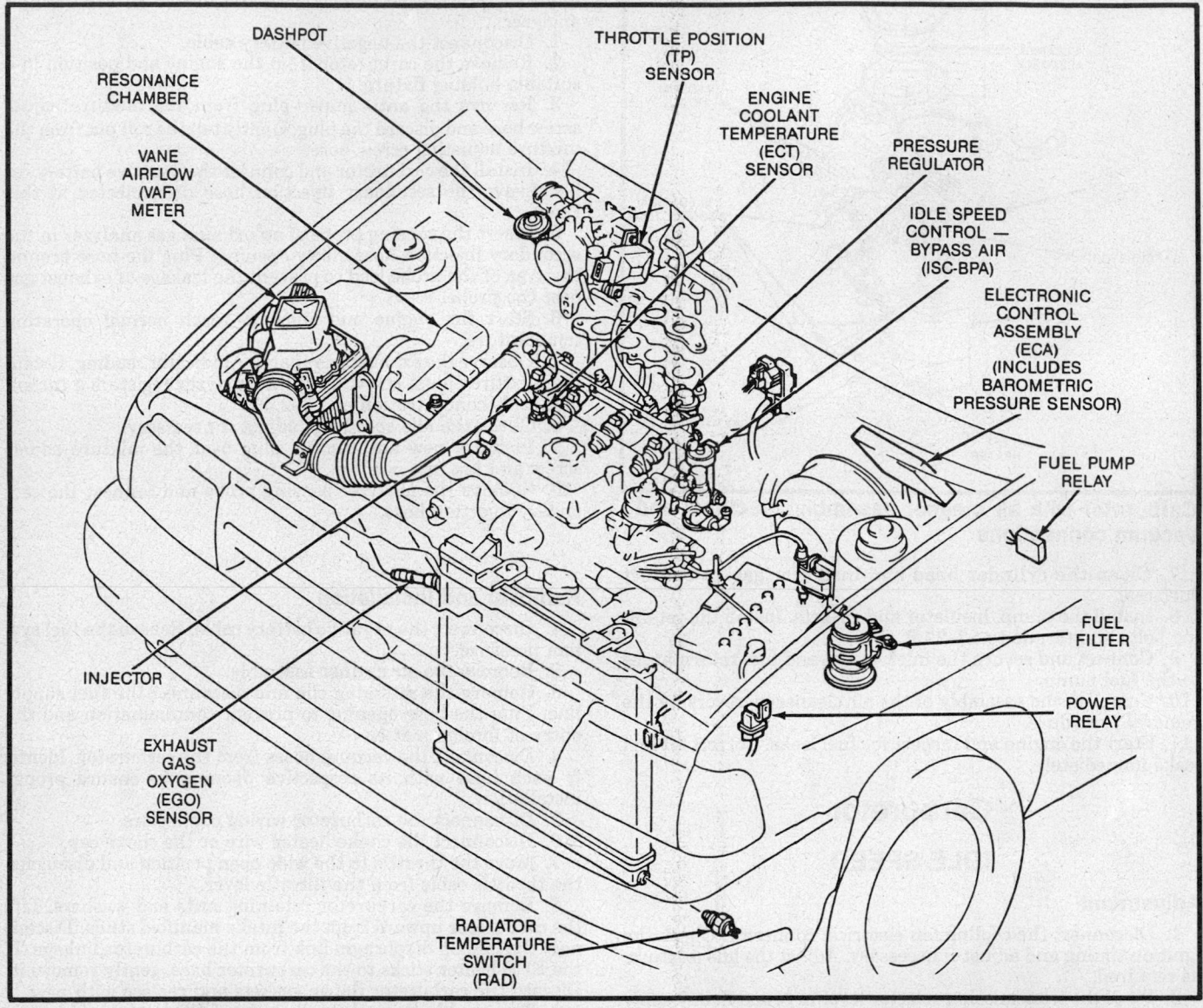

Fuel injection system component location

Refer to "Chilton's Electronic Engine Controls Manual" for additional coverage.

Description

The electronic fuel injection system meters fuel into the intake air system through 4 injectors, which are mounted on a tuned intake manifold. This system is classified as a multi point pulse injection system.

The components that make up this system are a fuel rail, a fuel pressure regulator, 4 fuel injectors, a vane air flow meter, a pressure regulator control solenoid, a power relay, a fuel filter, a fuel pump relay, a fuel pump and the fuel tank.

IDLE SPEED

Adjustment

1. Disconnect the cooling fan electrical connector. Check the ignition timing and adjust if necessary. Adjust the idle mixture, as required.

2. Apply the parking brake. Make certain the air conditioning system is **OFF**. Be sure that all electrical accessories are **OFF**.

3. Connect a tachometer to the test connector (clear pin No. 1). Check the idle speed.

4. If adjustment is required, connect a jumper wire between the test connector (black pin No. 1) and ground and turn the air adjustment screw to obtain the correct specification. Specification should be 800–900 rpm.

5. After adjustment is made, remove the jumper wire.

IDLE MIXTURE

Adjustment

Adjustment of the idle mixture screw is normally unnecessary due to the fact that the adjustment has been made at the factory. The idle mixture can not be adjusted.

FUEL SHUT OFF SWITCH

A fuel pump shut off switch is connected in series with the fuel pump switch circuit. In the event of an accident the switch will trigger and cut off the fuel supply. The reset button must be pushed after the switch has been triggered. The reset button is located on the left rear panel assembly and is accessible from inside of the vehicle.

This reset switch button should be checked in the event that the vehicle is unable to be started.

FUEL SYSTEM PRESSURE RELIEF

Procedure

1. Remove the rear seat cushion.
2. Run the engine while disconnecting the fuel pump electrical connector.
3. Allow the engine to stall.

Fuel Pump

Removal and Installation

1. Relieve the fuel system pressure. Disconnect the negative battery cable.
2. Remove the rear seat. Remove the rear carpet holddown pins.

3. Remove the fuel tank sending unit access cover.
4. Lift the plate and disconnect the sending unit electrical wiring.
5. Disconnect and plug the fuel line from the sending unit.
6. Remove the sending unit retaining screws. Remove the sending unit. Discard the gasket.
7. Remove the fuel filter from the pump. Remove the fuel pump wires from the sending unit.
8. Remove the retaining clamp screw. Remove the pump outlet hose clamp.
9. Remove the fuel pump from the sending unit.
10. Installation is the reverse of the removal procedure.

FUEL INJECTORS

1. Relieve the fuel system pressure. Disconnect the negative battery cable.
2. Remove the intake plenum. Remove the fuel inlet line from the fuel rail.
3. Disconnect the fuel return line from the fuel rail. Disconnect the electrical connections at the injectors.
4. Remove the pressure regulator. Remove the fuel rail retaining bolts. Remove the fuel rail.
5. Remove the fuel injectors. Discard the O-rings.
6. Installation is the reverse of the removal procedure. Be sure to lubricate the new O-rings with clean gasoline.

EMISSION CONTROL SYSTEMS

Refer to "Chilton's Emission Diagnosis and Service Manual" for additional coverage.

The emission system can be essentially divided into 2 groups: the Electronic Control Assembly controlled system (ECA) and the non-ECA controlled system. The components of the ECA control system are primarily tied in with the electronic control of the air/fuel ratio in the feedback carburetor.

Air bleed control valve
Air filter
Air inlet valve vacuum motor
Altitude compensator
Barometric sensor switch
Bowl vent solenoid valve
Carbon canister
Catalytic converter
Choke pull-off
Clutch and switches
Coolant temperature valve
Deceleration fuel shut-off valve
Electronic control assembly (ECA)
Electronic fuel evaporator (EFE) heater
Engine coolant temperature sensor and sensor switch
Exhaust gas oxygen (EGO) sensor
Exhaust gas recirculation (EGR) valve
Exhaust gas recirculation (EGR) valve position sensor
Exhaust gas recirculation (EGR) vacuum valve
Exhaust gas recirculation (EGR) modulator valve
Fast idle cam breaker
Fuel filter
Fuel pump
Fuel vapor separator

Heated air inlet system
Idle compensator
Idle switch
Idle up vacuum diaphragm
Inlet air temperature sensor
Inlet air valve vacuum check valve
Malfunction indicator lamp (MIL): California vehicles only
Manifold absolute pressure sensor
No. 1 purge control valve
No. 2 purge control valve
PCV valve
Reed valves
Roll over check valve
Secondary air control diaphragm
Three-way solenoid valve
Vacuum switch
Vacuum switch valve
Venturi vacuum amplifier

Emission Control Malfunction Indicator Lamp

The malfunction indicator lamp (MIL) is a dual function lamp that informs the driver of possible engine malfunctions and emission system failure. The MIL is controlled by the ECA. The ECA functions to monitor engine, ignition, and emission related components and signals the driver when the engine is running improperly or emmissions are unsatisfactory. If the MIL illuminates during vehicle operation, the cause of the fault or malfunction must be determined and corrected.

ENGINE

Engine Assembly

NOTE: Disconnecting the negative battery cable on some vehicles may interfere with the functions of the on board computer systems and may require the computer to undergo a relearning process, once the negative battery cable is reconnected.

Removal and Installation

NOTE: The engine and transaxle are removed as an assembly.

1. Disconnect the battery cables. Remove the battery and battery tray.
2. Mark the hinge location and remove the hood.
3. Drain the radiator coolant.
4. Drain the engine oil. drain the transaxle fluid. If equipped with automatic transaxle, disconnect and plug the fluid cooler lines.
5. Remove the air cleaner assembly and oil level dipstick. Remove the cooling fan and radiator as an assembly. Disconnect the accelerator cable at the carburetor and routing bracket, if equipped.
6. Disconnect the speedometer cable. Disconnect and remove all fuel hoses. Plug or cover the hose openings to prevent contamination from entering the system.
7. On fuel injected engines disconnect the transaxle vacuum hoes. On automatic transaxles, remove the nut that connects the shift lever to the manual shaft assembly. Remove the shift cable from the transaxle.
8. Disconnect the heater hoses, brake booster vacuum hose, carburetor to chassis or body hoses and canister hoses.
9. Remove the engine harness connectors coil, distributor, fan temperature switch, temperature sending unit, starter, backup lamp, neutral start, alternator, carburetor, EGO sensor and EGR position sensor. Identify and tag all electrical wiring connectors to ensure proper installation.
10. Disconnect and remove the engine ground. Disconnect the upper and lower radiator hoses.
11. Raise the vehicle and support safely.
12. Remove the catalytic converter.
13. If equipped, loosen the air conditioning compressor from its mounting and position to the side. Do not disconnect refrigeration hoses.
14. Disconnect lower control arms from the steering knuckles. Separate the transaxle halfshafts and install the differential side gear holding tools.
15. Remove the clutch control cable and shift control cable rod.
16. Remove the stabilizer bar from the transaxle, as necessary.
17. Properly support the engine.
18. Remove the rear crossmember mount bolts at the chassis.
19. Remove the front engine mount nut through hole in the crossmember. Remove the rear engine mount nuts at the crossmember. Remove the crossmember.
20. Lower the vehicle and attach engine lifter hooks. Remove right engine mount bolt.
21. Carefully remove the engine and transaxle as an assembly through the bottom of the vehicle.

To install:

22. Attach a lifting sling to the engine and transaxle assembly. Connect the sling to a suitable chain hoist.
23. Raise the engine assembly into place in the vehicle engine compartment and install the engine mount bolts through the mounts.
24. Support the engine in the chassis. Raise and support the vehicle safely.
25. Install the front engine mount nut and torque to 27–46 ft. lbs.
26. Position the crossmember onto the mounts and chassis. Attach the rear nut and torque 27–46 ft. lbs. Install the mount to crossmember nuts and torque to 27–46 ft. lbs.
27. Remove the differential side gear holding tools and install the halfshafts into the transaxle.
28. Connect the lower control arms to the steering knuckles. Attach the shift control rod and stabilizer bar to the transaxle. Attach the clutch cable, if equipped.
29. Attach the the air conditioning compressor to its mounting, if removed.
30. Connect the catalytic converter.
31. Lower the vehicle.
32. Install the radiator upper and lower hoses. Attach the engine ground wire.
33. Connect the engine electrical harness connectors coil, distributor, fan, temperature switch, starter, back-up light, neutral start switch, alternator, carburetor, EGO sensor, EGR position sensor, and the carburetor heater.
34. Connect the carbon canister hoses, carburetor hoses, brake booster vacuum hose, heater hoses and fuel hoses.
35. Attach the speedometer cable. Connect the accelerator cable brackets at the carburetor, as required. If equipped with automatic transaxle, install the shift cable.
36. Install the cooling fan and radiator assembly. If equipped with automatic transaxle, install the fluid cooler lines. Install the air cleaner assembly.
37. Install the battery and tray.
38. Fill the engine with the proper weight and grade of engine oil to the proper level.
39. Fill the transaxle with the proper grade of fluid to the specified level.
40. Fill the cooling system with the proper coolant mixture to the correct level.
41. Install the hood. Connect the battery cable. Start the engine, check for leaks and proper fluid levels.

Engine Mounts

Removal and Installation
FRONT MOUNT

1. Disconnect the negative battery cable. Remove the front mount through bolt attaching nut.
2. Properly support the engine.
3. Raise and support the vehicle safely.
4. Remove the front mount to crossmember attaching nuts.
5. Raise the vehicle as required to gain sufficient clearance to remove the front mount. Remove the front mount from the crossmember. Note and record the position of the mount to ensure proper installation.
6. Install the engine mount onto the crossmember in the original installation position.
7. Secure the mount to the crossmember with the attaching nuts. Torque the attaching nuts to 27–46 ft. lbs.
8. Lower the vehicle.
9. Move the engine as necessary until the holes in the mount align with the holes in the engine bracket. Install the through bolt and attaching nut. Torque the nut to 27–46 ft. lbs.
10. Remove the engine support.

REAR MOUNT

1. Disconnect the negative battery cable. Raise the vehicle and support safely.
2. Properly support the engine.
3. Remove the mount to crossmember attaching nut.
4. Remove the mount to engine attaching bolts.

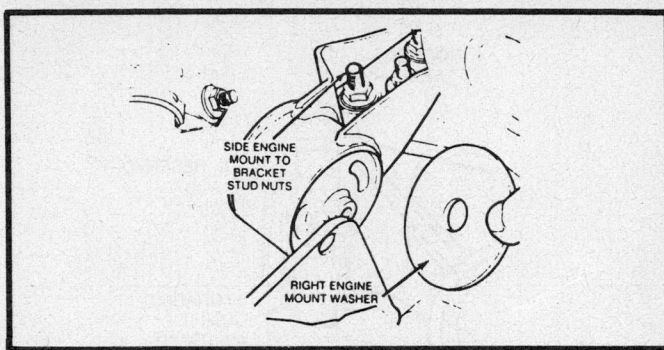

Side engine mount positioning

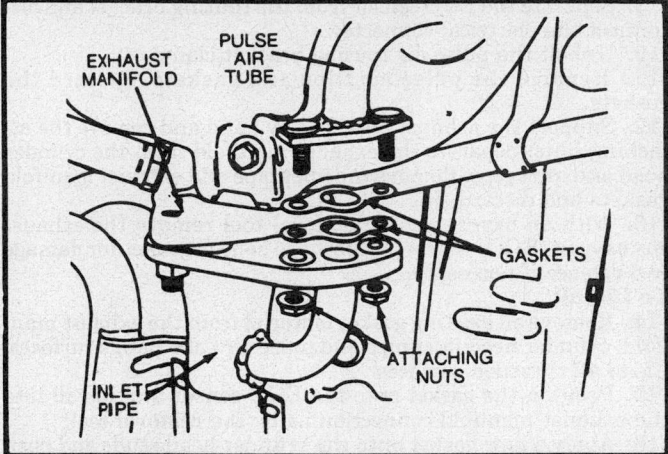

Exhaust manifold with pulse air tube and catalytic converter inlet pipe connections

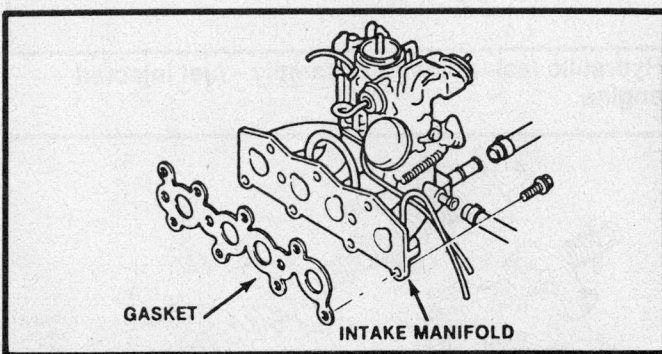

Exploded view of the Intake manifold assembly

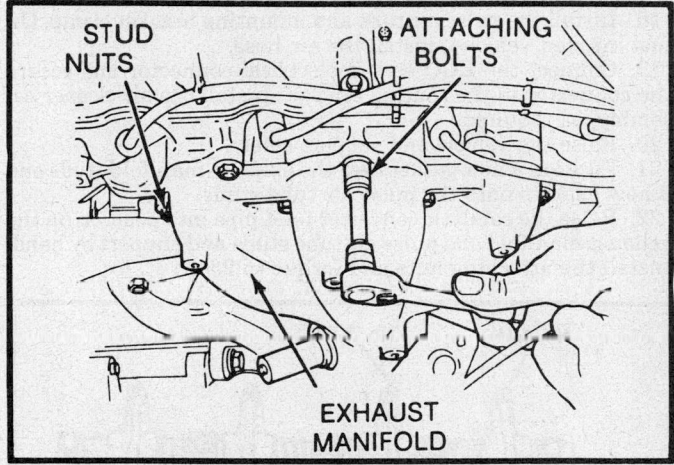

Exhaust manifold-to-cylinder head mounting

5. If necessary, raise the engine to gain access to the rear mount. Remove the mount from the crossmember.
6. Position the mount onto the rear engine bracket.
7. Install the mount to engine bracket bolts. Torque the bolts to 27–46 ft. lbs.
8. Lower the engine and mount onto the crossmember.
9. Install the attaching nut and torque to 27–46 ft. lbs.
10. Remove the engine support.

SIDE MOUNT

1. Disconnect the negative battery cable. Properly support the engine.
2. Remove the through bolt, nut and washer.
3. Remove the bracket to engine attaching nuts.
4. Remove the side mount and bracket as an assembly.
5. Position the engine mount and bracket onto the engine.
6. Install the engine to bracket attaching nuts. Torque the nuts to 27–46 ft. lbs.
7. Position the washer against the mount. Install the through bolt and nut. Torque the nut and bolt to 27–46 ft. lbs.
8. Remove the engine support.

Intake Manifold

Removal and Installation

1. Disconnect the negative battery cable. Drain the cooling system.
2. Remove the air cleaner assembly, on vehicles equipped with a carburetor. On vehicles equipped with fuel injection, remove the intake manifold bracket.
3. Disconnect the accelerator cable.
4. Identify, tag and disconnect all vacuum hoses and electrical wiring required to provide sufficient clearance to remove the intake manifold.
5. Support the intake manifold by hand and remove the retaining bolts. Remove the intake manifold from the cylinder head.

6. Remove the old gasket material and thoroughly clean the intake manifold and cylinder head surfaces. Apply a new gasket to the cylinder head surface and hold in place.
7. Position the intake manifold onto the new gasket and install the retaining bolts. Make the bolts hand tight. Torque the retaining bolts to specification.
8. Connect the vacuum hoses and electrical wiring to their respective connections. Install the accelerator cable.
9. Install the air cleaner assembly, as required. Install the intake manifold bracket, as required.
10. Refill the cooling system to the proper level. Install the radiator cap. Connect the negative battery cable.

Exhaust Manifold

Removal and Installation

1. Disconnect the negative battery cable.
2. Raise and safely support the vehicle.
3. Disconnect the catalytic converter inlet pipe from the exhaust manifold by removing the 3 attaching nuts.
4. Disconnect the pulse air tube from the air inlet pipe flange by removing the attaching nuts.
5. Unbolt the catalytic converter support bracket.
6. Lower the vehicle.
7. Remove the air cleaner assembly, as required. On fuel injected vehicles remove the air hose.
8. Remove the exhaust manifold heat shroud.

9. Separate the EGO sensor from the routing bracket and disconnect the electrical connector.

10. Unbolt the pulse air routing bracket clamp.

11. Remove the pulse air tube and gaskets. Discard the gaskets.

12. Support the exhaust manifold by hand and remove the attaching nuts. Separate the exhaust manifold from the cylinder head and inlet pipe. Remove the inlet pipe and exhaust manifold gaskets and discard.

13. With an oxygen sensor removal tool remove the exhaust gas oxygen (EGO) sensor. Inspect the sensor gasket for damage and replace if necessary.

To install:

14. Remove all existing gasket material from the exhaust manifold, cylinder head inlet pipe and pulse air tube flange surfaces. Clean all threaded surfaces.

15. Position the gasket onto the EGO sensor and install into the exhaust manifold connection using the removal tool.

16. Apply a new gasket onto the cylinder head studs and position the exhaust manifold onto the gasket. Install the attaching nuts and torque to 12-17 ft. lbs.

17. Install the heat shroud.

18. Install the pulse air tube and mounting bracket clamp. On fuel injected vehicles, install the air hose.

19. Connect the EGO sensor electrical connector and secure the connector in the routing bracket. Install the air cleaner assembly, as required.

20. Raise the vehicle and support safely.

21. Position a new gasket over the exhaust manifold studs and 2 new gaskets onto the pulse air tube studs.

22. Raise the catalytic converter inlet pipe into position on the exhaust manifold and pulse air tube studs and support by hand. Install the attaching nuts and torque to 23-34 ft. lbs.

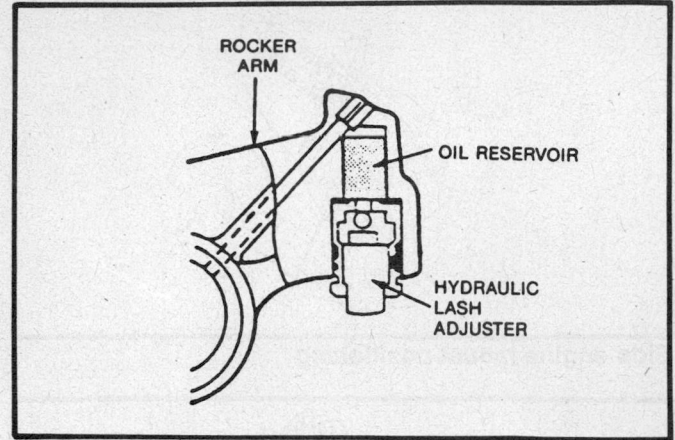

Hydraulic lash adjuster assembly—fuel injected engine

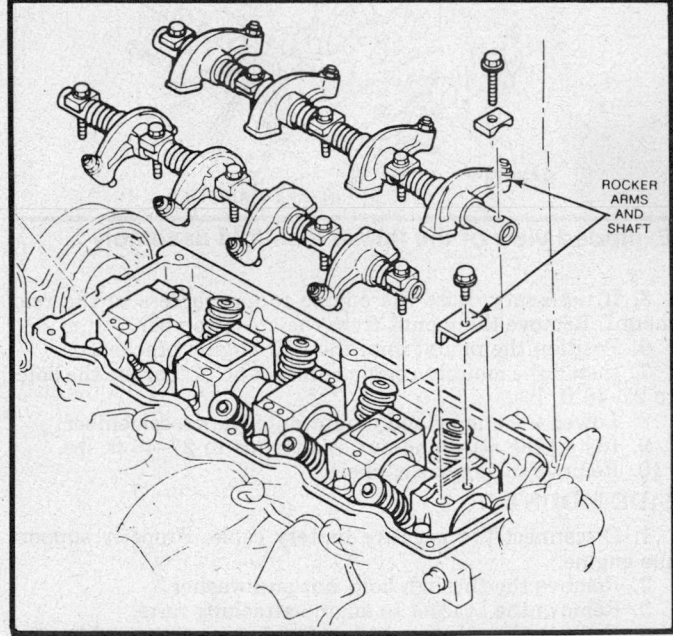

Rocker arm/shaft assembly

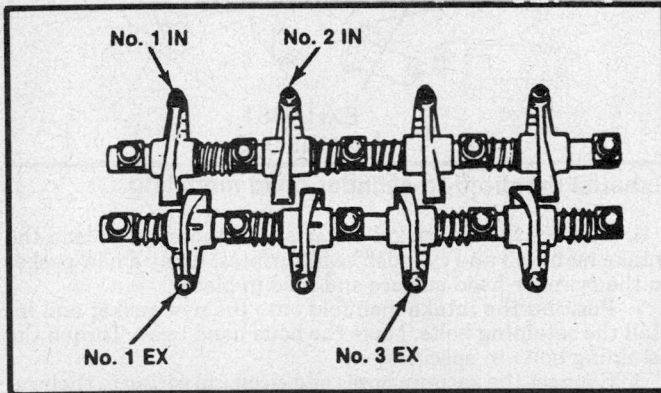

Intake and exhaust valve arrangement

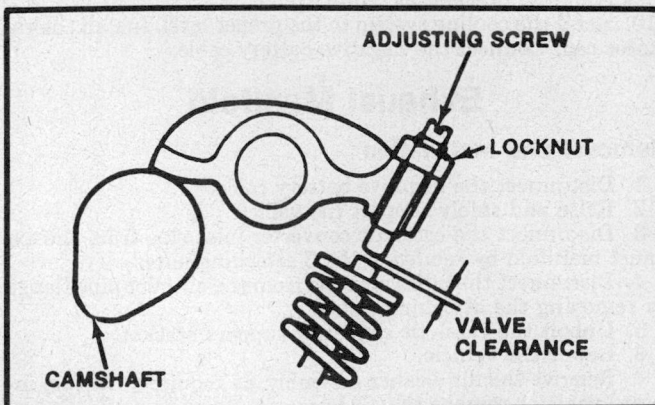

Valve clearance adjustment

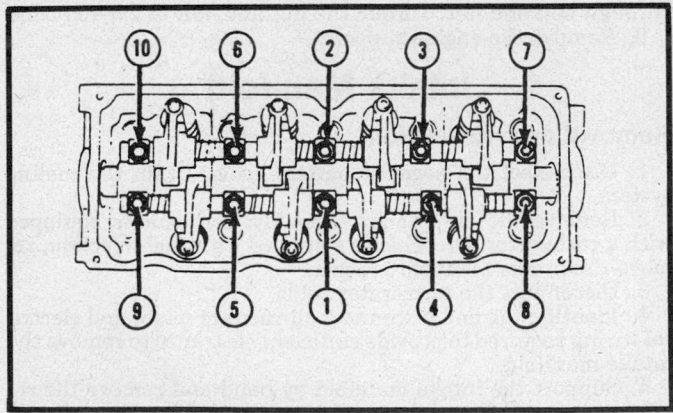

Rocker arm/shaft bolt torque sequence

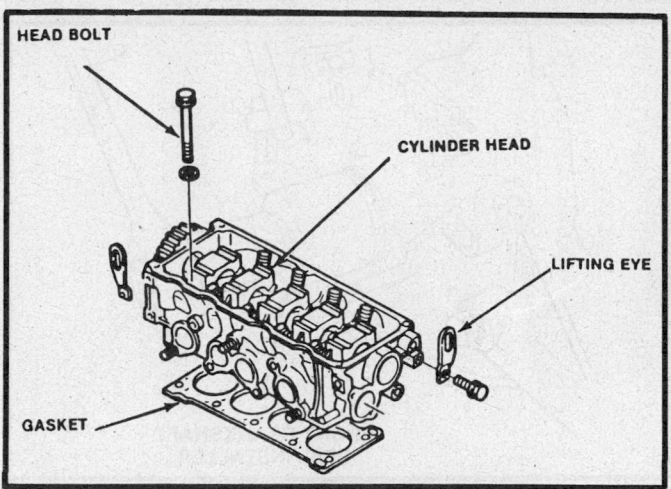
Exploded view of the cylinder head assembly

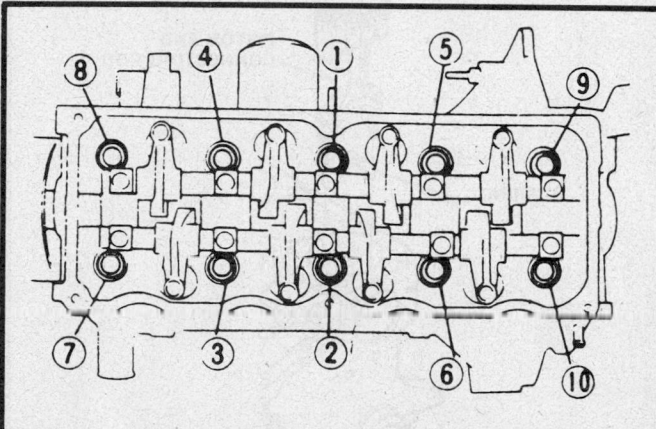
Cylinder head bolt torque sequence

23. Install the catalytic converter inlet pipe support bracket.
24. Lower the vehicle and connect the negative battery cable.
25. Start the engine and inspect for exhaust gas leaks.

Valve System

VALVE ADJUSTMENT

CARBURETED ENGINE

1. Start the engine and allow to reach normal operating temperature.
2. Set the No.1 piston to **TDC** by rotating the crankshaft until the **TC** mark on the belt cover aligns with the notch on the crankshaft pulley.
3. Remove the valve cover.
4. Adjust the No. 1 and No. 2 intake valves to specification. Adjust the No. 1 and No. 3 exhaust valves to specification.
5. Rotate the crankshaft 360 degrees so that the No. 4 piston is at TDC of the compression stroke. Adjust the remaining valves to specification.
6. Install the valve cover. Be sure to use a new gasket or RTV sealant, as required.

FUEL INJECTED ENGINE

1. Disconnect the negative battery cable. Remove the valve cover.
2. Inspect the lash adjuster operation by pushing down on

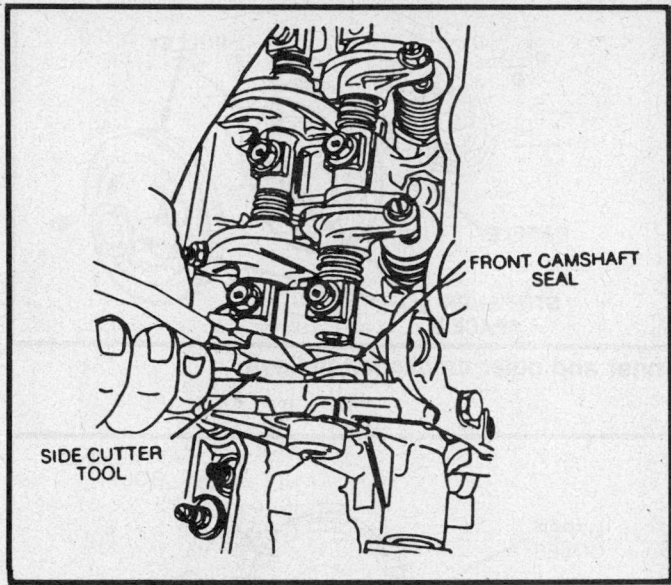
Removing the camshaft sprocket oil seal

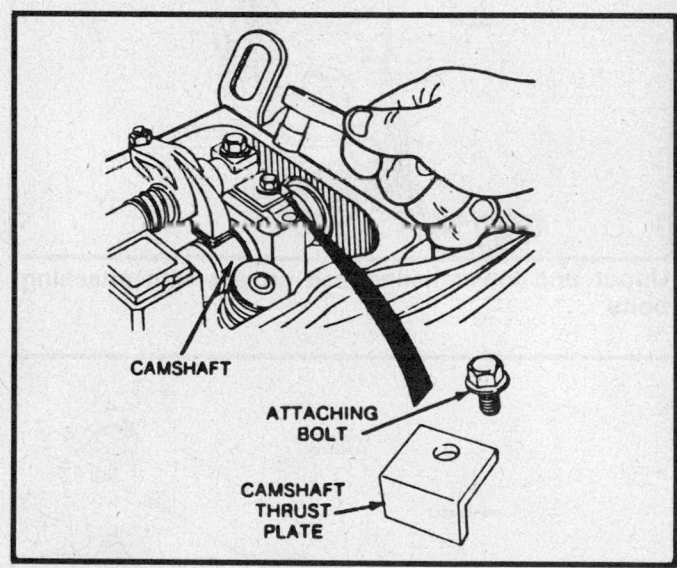
Camshaft with thrust plate

each rocker arm. If the rocker arm moves down, replace the lash adjuster.
3. Remove the rocker arm shaft assemblies.
4. Remove the hydraulic lash adjuster from the rocker arm.
5. Installation is the reverse of the removal procedure.
6. Be sure to coat the new lash adjuster with clean engine oil. Fill the oil reservoir in the rocker arm with clean engine oil.
7. Be careful not to damage the O-ring when installing the lash adjuster.
8. When installing the valve cover be sure to use new gaskets or RTV sealant, as required.

VALVE ROCKER SHAFT/ARM ASSEMBLY

Removal and Installation

1. Disconnect the negative battery cable.
2. Remove the air cleaner assembly, as required. On engines

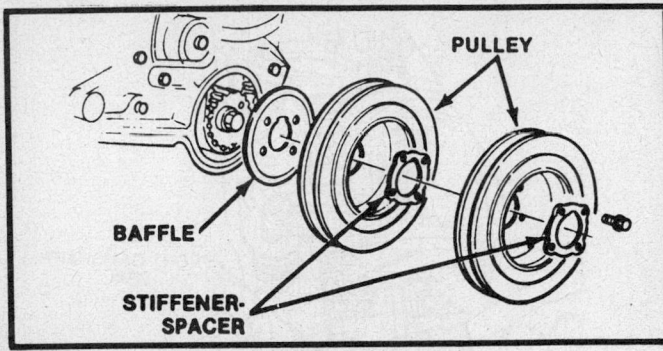

Inner and outer crankshaft pulleys

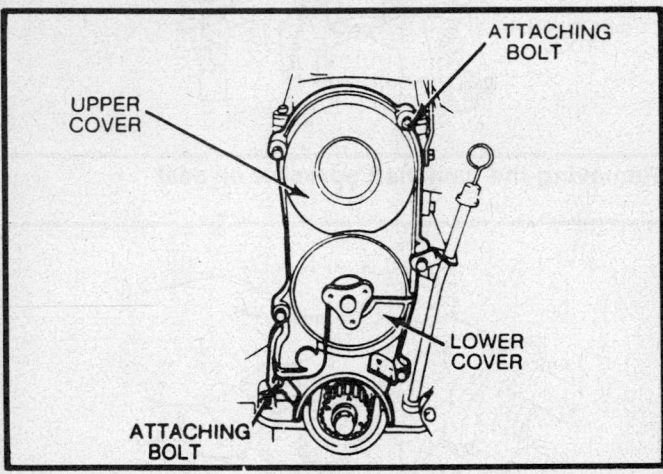

Upper and lower timing belt covers with attaching bolts

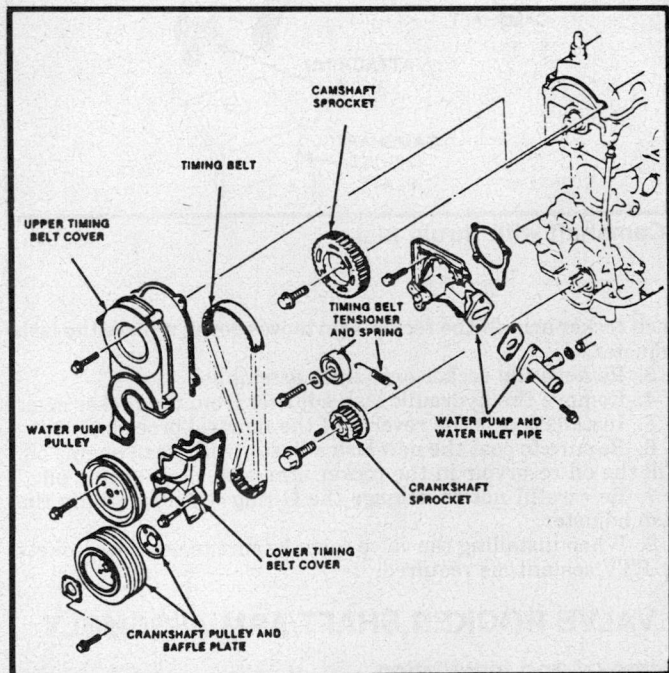

Exploded view of the camshaft and crankshaft sprockets with related components.

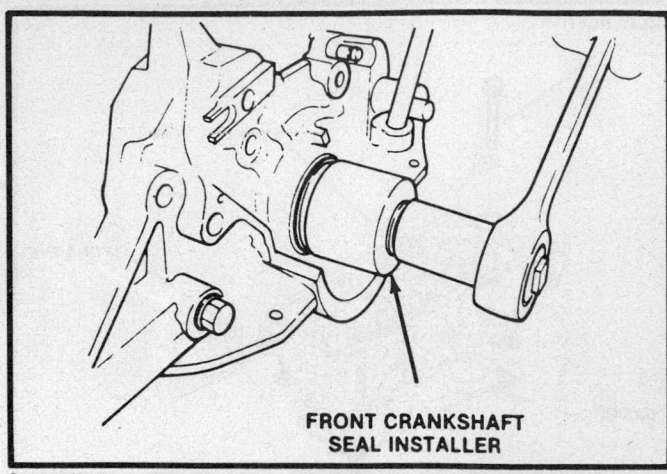

Install the oil pump/front crankshaft seal as illustrated

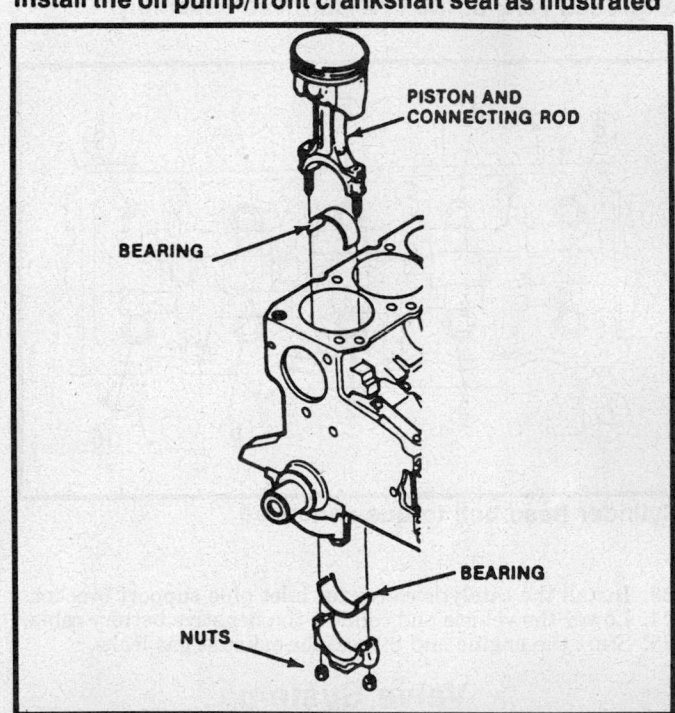

Piston and connecting rod assembly

equipped with fuel injection, remove the air hose and the resonance chamber.

3. Disconnect the accelerator cable from the throttle lever bracket. Remove the PCV valve.

4. Remove the spark plug wires from the routing clips. Remove the upper timing belt cover.

5. Remove the valve cover retaining bolts. Remove the valve cover. Discard the gasket.

6. Remove the rocker arm assembly retaining bolts. Remove the rocker arm assemblies from the engine.

7. Installation is the reverse of the removal procedure. Be sure to use new gaskets or RTV sealant, as required. Torque the rocker arm bolts in sequence to 16–21 ft. lbs.

Cylinder Head

Removal and Installation

1. Disconnect the negative battery cable. Drain the cooling system.

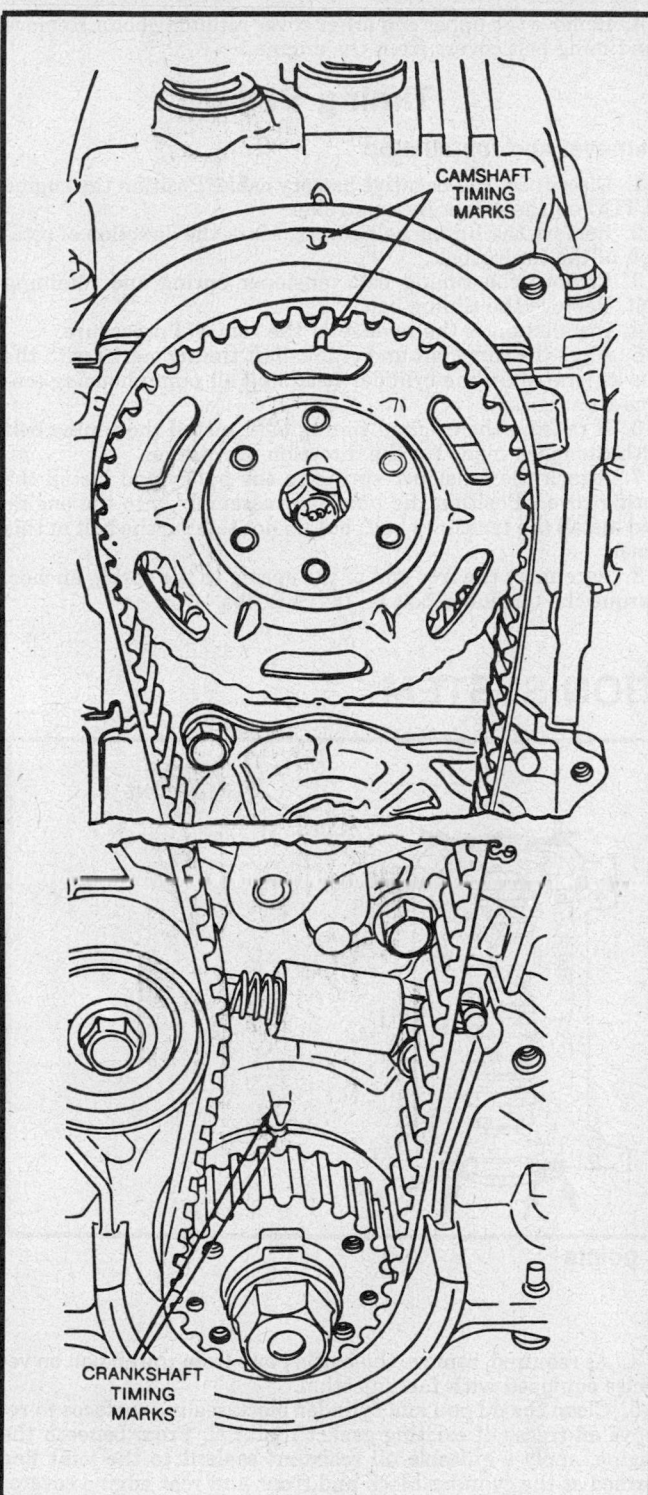

Camshaft and crankshaft timing mark alignment

2. Position the engine at TDC on the compression stroke.
3. Remove the valve cover. Remove the timing belt cover.
4. Remove the exhaust manifold. Remove the intake manifold.
5. Remove the spark plug wires and spark plugs. Remove the distributor.

6. Remove the front and rear engine lift hangers. Remove the engine ground wire.
7. Remove the wiring harness connector. Remove the upper radiator hose. Remove the bypass hose and bracket.
8. Remove the cylinder head retaining bolts. Remove the cylinder head from the engine. Discard the gasket.
9. Installation is the reverse of the removal procedure. Be sure to use new gaskets or RTV sealant, as required.
10. Be sure to torque the cylinder head to specification and in the proper sequence.

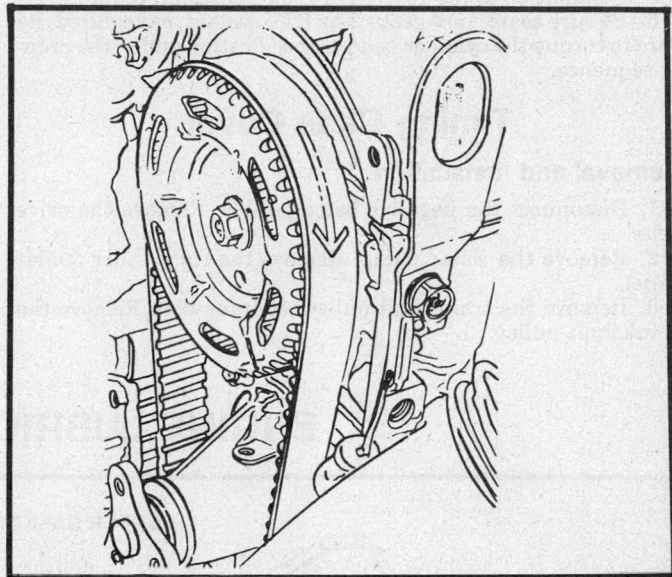

Timing belt rotation arrow. Normal direction of rotation is clockwise

Pistons, Rings and Rod Positioning

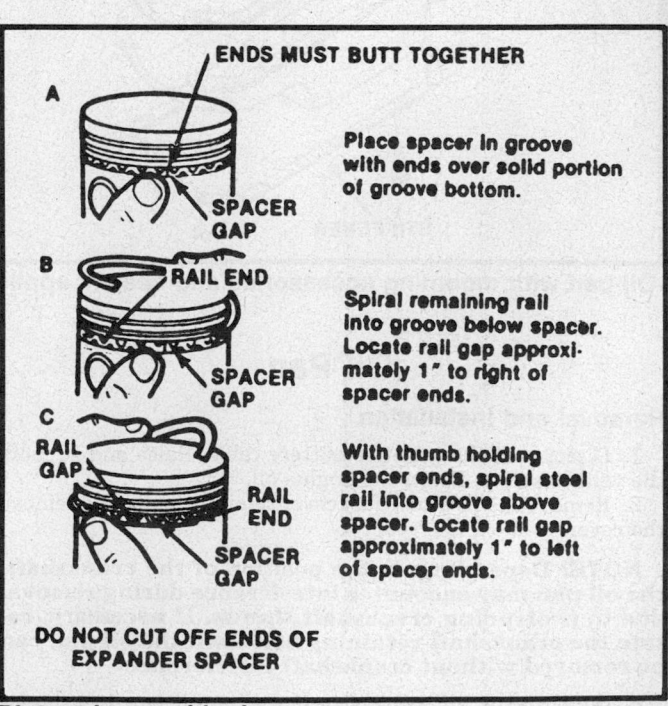

ENDS MUST BUTT TOGETHER

A — SPACER GAP

Place spacer in groove with ends over solid portion of groove bottom.

B — RAIL END — SPACER GAP

Spiral remaining rail into groove below spacer. Locate rail gap approximately 1" to right of spacer ends.

C — RAIL GAP — RAIL END — SPACER GAP

With thumb holding spacer ends, spiral steel rail into groove above spacer. Locate rail gap approximately 1" to left of spacer ends.

DO NOT CUT OFF ENDS OF EXPANDER SPACER

Piston ring positioning

Camshaft

Removal and Installation

1. Disconnect the negative battery cable. Drain the cooling system.
2. Remove the cylinder head from the engine.
3. Position the cylinder head in a suitable holding fixture. Remove the camshaft gear.
4. Remove the camshaft from the cylinder head.
5. Installation is the reverse of the removal procedure.
6. Be sure to use new gaskets or RTV sealant, as required. Be sure to torque the cylinder head to specification and in the proper sequence.

Timing Case Cover

Removal and Installation

1. Disconnect the negative battery cable. Remove the drive belts.
2. Remove the water pump. Remove the right inner fender panel.
3. Remove the crankshaft pulley retaining bolt. Remove the crankshaft pulley.

4. Remove the upper and lower cover retaining bolts. Remove the timing belt covers from the engine.

Timing Belt

Removal and Installation

1. Disconnect the negative battery cable. Position the engine at TDC on the compression stroke.
2. Remove the timing belt covers. Mark the direction of rotation of the timing belt.
3. Remove the timing belt tensioner spring and retaining bolt. Remove the timing belt.
4. Installation is the reverse of the removal procedure.
5. Align the camshaft and crankshaft timing marks with the marks located on the cylinder head and oil pump housing (engine front cover).
6. If reusing the original timing belt, install the timing belt with the mark made for the direction of rotation.
7. Attach the tensioner spring to the pulley and install the spring cover. Position the tensioner assembly onto the engine and install the tensioner bolt, but do not tighten the bolt at this time.
8. Reconnect the free end of the spring to the spring anchor. Torque the tensioner bolt to 14–19 ft. lbs.

ENGINE LUBRICATION SYSTEM

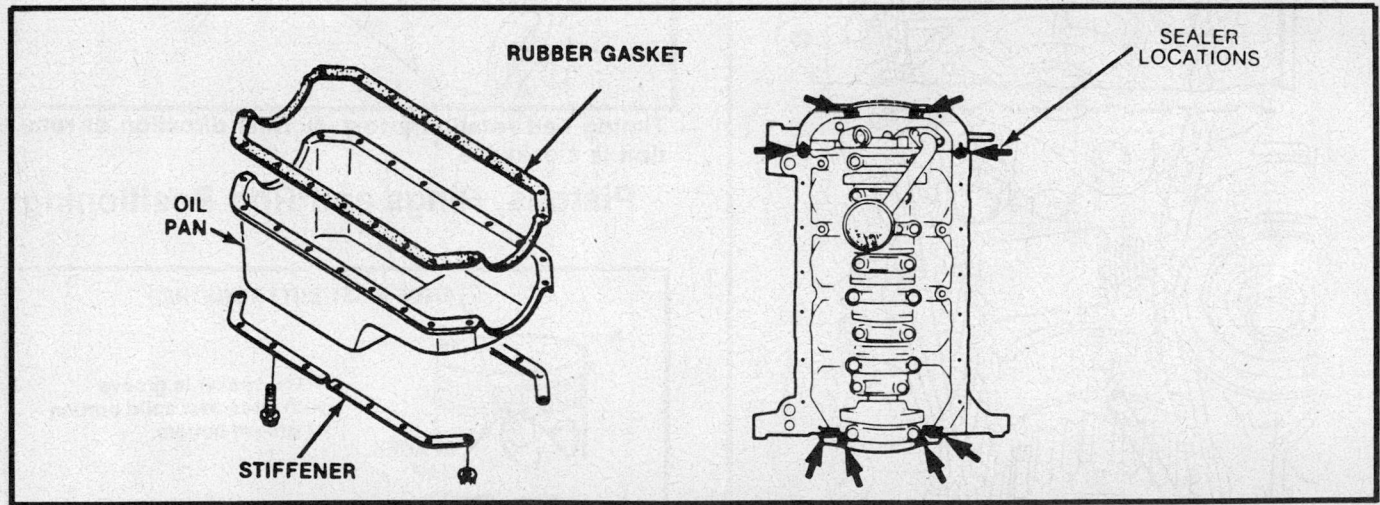

RUBBER GASKET

SEALER LOCATIONS

OIL PAN

STIFFENER

Oil pan with mounting accessories and sealant application points

Oil Pan

Removal and Installation

1. Disconnect the negative battery cable. Raise and support the vehicle safely. Drain the engine oil.
2. Remove the flywheel dust cover retaining bolts and remove the cover.

NOTE: Depending on the position of the crankshaft, the oil pan may encounter interference during removal due to protruding crankshaft throws. If necessary, rotate the crankshaft retaining bolt until the oil pan can be removed without crankshaft interference.

3. Support the oil pan and remove the oil pan to cylinder block bolts, nuts and stiffeners. Lower the oil pan. Discard the oil pan gasket.

4. As required, remove the baffle plate from the oil pan on vehicles equipped with fuel injection.
5. Clean the oil pan and cylinder block sealing surfaces to remove all traces of existing gasket material. From beneath the engine, apply a suitable oil resistant sealant to the joint line formed at the cylinder block and front and rear engine covers.
6. Apply the new rubber gasket to the oil pan.
7. Raise the oil pan and gasket against the cylinder block. Install the stiffeners, bolts and nuts. Torque the oil pan bolts in an alternate pattern to 5–7 ft. lbs.
8. Install the flywheel dust cover and attaching bolts. Torque the bolts to 13–20 ft. lbs.
9. Install the oil pan drain plug and fill the crankcase to the proper level. Connect the negative battery cable.
10. Start the engine and allow the oil to reach normal operating temperature. Check for oil leaks and correct as required.

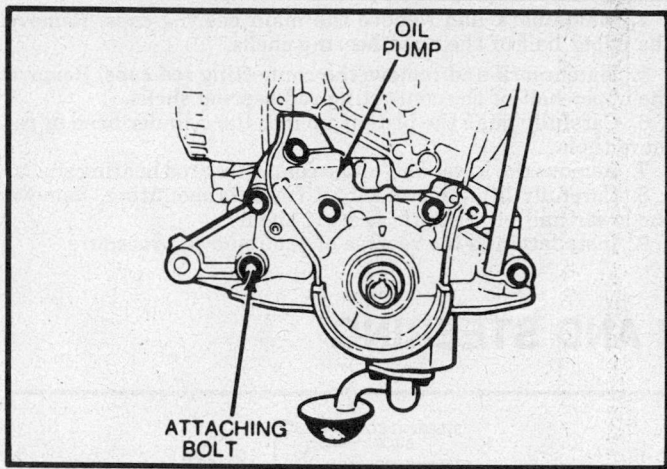
Oil pump assembly

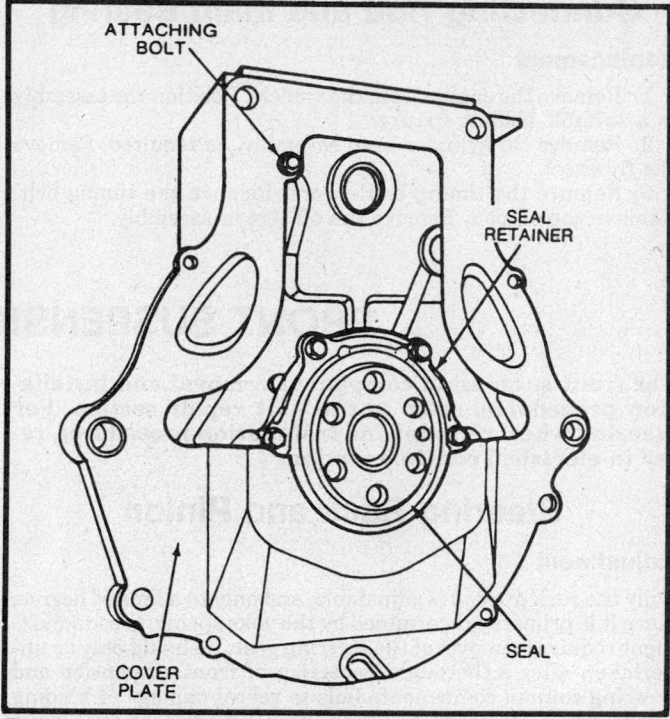
Rear crankshaft oil seal

Oil Pump

Removal and Installation

1. Disconnect the negative battery cable. Raise and support the vehicle safely. Remove the crankshaft sprocket.
2. Drain the engine oil. Remove the oil pan.
3. Remove the oil pump assembly retaining bolts. Remove the oil pump assembly and gasket from the engine. Discard the gasket.
4. As required, remove the pickup tube and screen.
5. Remove the screws from the oil pump cover. Remove the cover. Remove the oil pump gears.
6. Remove the front seal from the pump assembly. Remove the cotter pin, spring and relief valve from the oil pump body.
7. Installation is the reverse of the removal procedure.
8. Clean the oil pump and cylinder block contact surfaces to remove the old gasket material and sealent. Thoroughly coat both sides of the new oil pump gasket with a suitable sealant compound. Apply the gasket to the oil pump and remove any excess sealant. Pack the pump cavity with petroleum jelly.

NOTE: Do not allow the sealant compound to enter the oil pump discharge opening once the gasket is in place. This opening must be free and clear before the oil pump is installed onto the cylinder block.

9. Position the oil pump against the cylinder block surface and install the retaining bolts. Torque the bolts to 14–19 ft. lbs.
10. Install a new gasket onto the oil pump inlet and bolt the pickup tube to the oil pump. Torque the bolts to 6–8 ft. lbs.
11. Complete the assembly of the remaining components by reversing the removal procedure. Fill the crankcase to the proper level with engine oil. Connect the negative battery cable.
12. Start the engine and allow the oil to reach normal operating temperature. Check for leaks and correct as required.

Inspection

1. Remove the oil pump assembly from the vehicle.
2. Measure the inner gear tip to outer gear clearance at the minimum clearance point. The clearance should be 0.0078 in. maximum.
3. Inspect the oil pump body for scoring in the outer gear bore. A slight amount of scoring is acceptable.
4. Measure the housing-to-outer gear clearance with a feeler gauge. The clearance should be no more than 0.0087 in.
5. Measure the gear end play. Gear end play should not exceed 0.0055 in. If the pump clearances are not within specification, replace the gears or the body. Clean the relief valve

internals and inspect for nicks, burrs or binding operation. Clean the pickup tube and screen.
6. Assemble the oil pump relief valve into the bore. Install the spring, retainer and cotter pin.
7. Press or drive a new oil seal into the oil pump body bore.
8. Coat the cover attaching screws with a suitable thread locking compound and install the cover.
9. Install the oil pump assembly in the vehicle.

Rear Main Oil Seal

ONE PIECE SEAL

Removal and Installation

1. Disconnect the negative battery cable.
2. Remove the transaxle from the vehicle.
3. Remove the flywheel. If necessary, remove the cover plate.
4. Remove the seal retainer. Remove the crankshaft seal.
To install:
5. Using tool T87C-6701-A or equivalent, drive the seal into the retainer with the hollow portion of the seal facing the engine.
6. Install the gasket onto the retainer and position the retainer against the engine surface. Install the attaching bolts and torque to 6–8 ft. lbs. Trim the excess gasket material (if any) from the edge of the retainer after it has been fastened to the engine.
7. With a wire brush, remove all the old sealer from the flywheel bolts. Coat the threads of the bolts with stud and bearing mounting sealer, part number E0AZ–19954–B or equivalent.
8. Position the flywheel against the crankshaft and support by hand. Install the flywheel-to-crankshaft retaining bolts and tighten so that the flywheel no longer requires support. Install the flywheel locking tool to prevent the flywheel from turning.
9. Torque the flywheel retaining bolts in an alternate pattern to 71–76 ft. lbs.
10. Continue the installation in the reverse order of the removal procedure.

Connecting Rod and Main Bearing

Replacement

1. Remove the engine from the vehicle. Position the assembly in a suitable holding fixture.
2. Remove the cylinder head assembly, as required. Remove the flywheel.
3. Remove the timing belt covers. Remove the timing belt. Remove the oil pan. Remove the oil screen assembly.
4. Matchmark and remove the main bearing caps. Remove the upper half of the main bearing shells.
5. Matchmark and remove the connecting rod caps. Remove the upper half of the connecting rod bearing shells.
6. Carefully push the pistons up into the cylinder head or remove them.
7. Remove the lower half of the connecting rod bearing shells.
8. Carefully lift the crankshaft from its mounting. Remove the lower half of the main bearing shells.
9. Installation is the reverse of the removal procedure.

FRONT SUSPENSION AND STEERING

For front suspension component removal and installation procedures, refer to the unit repair section. For steering wheel removal and installation procedures, refer to electrical controls section.

Steering Rack and Pinion

Adjustment

Only the rack preload is adjustable, and only to a limited degree, since it is primarily determined by the yoke spring. Since adjustment requires removal of the steering gear, it should only be undertaken after a thorough inspection of front suspension and steering column components fails to reveal damage or binding elsewhere. If necessary, adjust the rack yoke preload as follows:

1. Remove the steering rack from the vehicle.
2. Center the steering rack in a protected jaw vise (equal left and right tie rod extension).
3. Measure the pinion operating torque with an inch lb. torque wrench and pinion torque adapter tool T87C–3504–C, or equivalent. Within 90 degrees of the centered rack position, pinion torque should be 8–11 inch lbs. Beyond 90 degrees, left or right, pinion torque should not exceed 13.3 inch lbs.
4. If the pinion torque is not within the specified limits, tighten or loosen the rack adjusting screw to increase or decrease rack preload.

NOTE: Do not loosen the adjusting screw so that it no longer makes contact with the yoke spacer. Any clearance at this point will allow the rack to deflect under load, resulting in reduced tooth engagement with the pinion.

5. When the pinion operating torque is within specification, tighten the jam nut on the adjusting screw. With a suitable adapter, torque the jam nut to 7–11 ft. lbs. to retain the adjustment.
6. Complete the assembly of the steering gear by reversing the removal procedure.

Removal and Installation

1. Disconnect the negative and positive battery cables and remove the battery from the vehicle.
2. Matchmark the steering column lower universal joint and steering rack pinion for assembly reference. Remove the steering column and intermediate shaft assembly from the vehicle.
3. Cut the plastic tie wrap securing the steering column boot to the steering rack.
4. Raise the vehicle and support safely. Remove the front tire and wheel assemblies.
5. Using the proper tool, separate both tie rod ends from the steering knuckles.
6. Remove the catalytic converter.
7. Cut and remove the plastic tie rod splash shield from the right inner fender.
8. Remove the steering rack mounting bolts and lower the

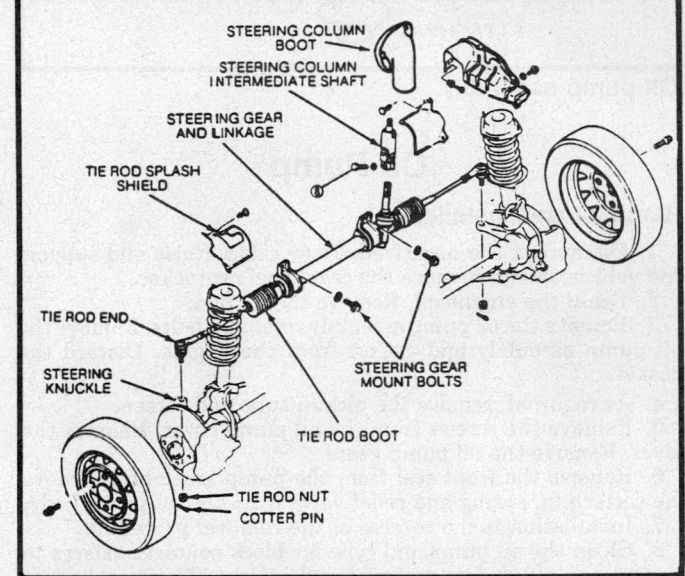

Rack and pinion steering assembly

steering rack until it is free of the steering column boot. Slide the rack to the right, through the inner fender tie rod opening, until the left tie rod is clear of the left inner fender, then lower the left end until the steering rack assembly can be withdrawn from the left side of the vehicle.

NOTE: While maneuvering the tie rod boots in and out of the inner fender openings, guide the steering rack assembly carefully to avoid cutting or nicking the boots.

9. From under the vehicle, insert the right side tie rod through the right inner tie rod opening, far enough to allow raising the left end of the assembly to enter the left fender opening. Shift the assembly to the left taking care not to catch the boots.
10. Align the steering rack pinion shaft housing with the steering column boot. Raise the steering rack into the boot.
11. Install the steering rack mounting bolts from left to right. Torque the bolts to 23–34 ft. lbs.
12. Connect the tie rod ends to the steering knuckles. If the tie rod ends are not properly aligned with the knuckle ends during installation, release the small end boot clips before rotating the tie rods. This is done to avoid twisting the boots.
13. Attach the right side tie rod splash shield on the right inner fender panel.
14. Install the catalytic converter.
15. Install the tire and wheel assemblies and lower the vehicle.
16. Secure the steering column boot to the steering rack housing with a new tie wrap.
17. Align the matchmarks made on the steering column lower

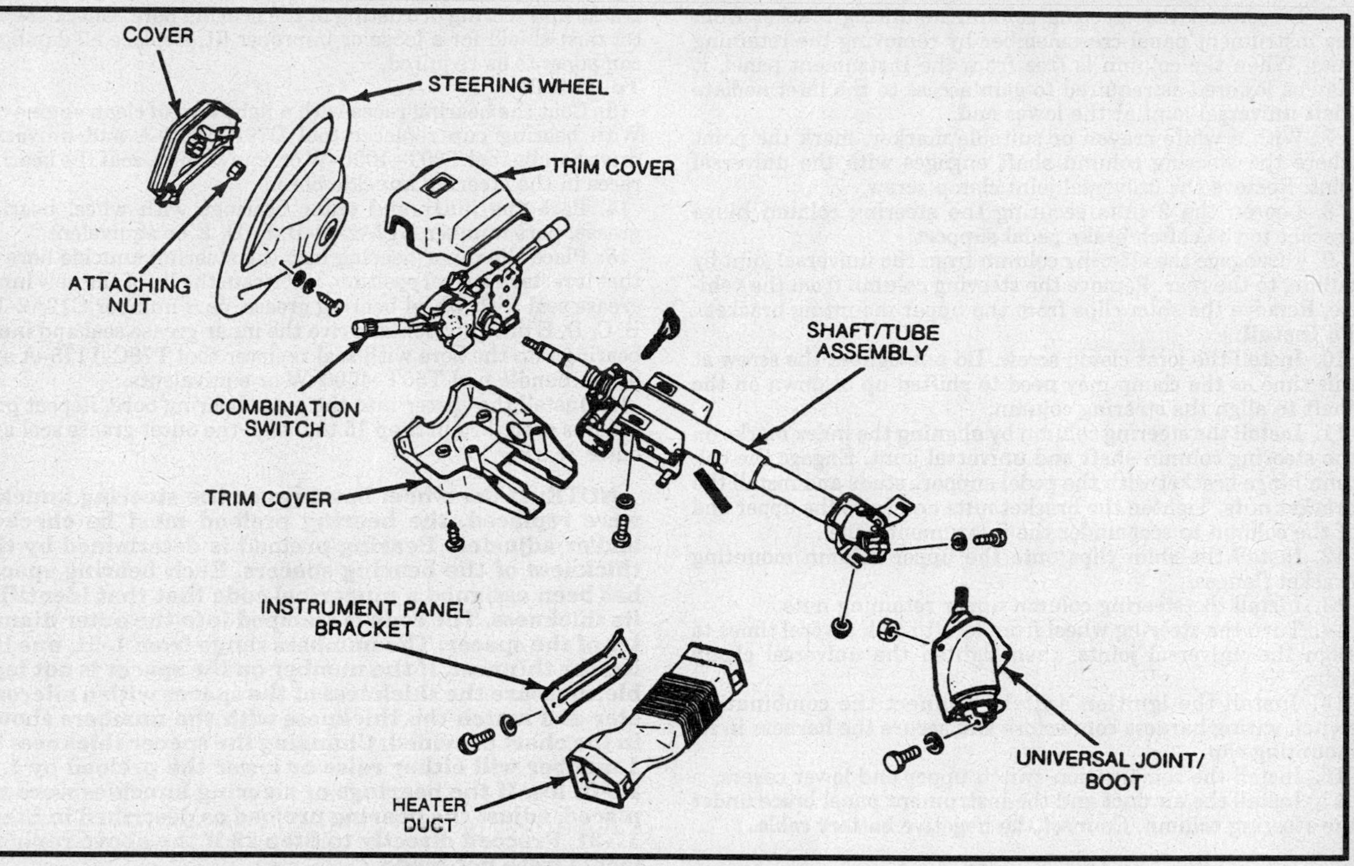

Exploded view of the steering wheel and steering column assembly

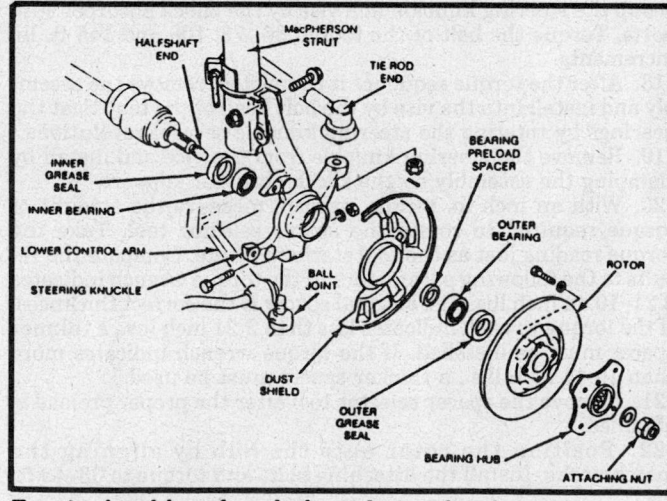

Front wheel bearing, hub and steering knuckle assembly

Stamped Mark	Thickness in. (mm)
1	0.2474 (6.285)
2	0.2490 (6.325)
3	0.2506 (6.365)
4	0.2522 (6.405)
5	0.2538 (6.445)
6	0.2554 (6.485)
7	0.2570 (6.525)
8	0.2586 (6.565)
9	0.2602 (6.605)
10	0.2618 (6.645)
11	0.2634 (6.685)
12	0.2650 (6.725)
13	0.2666 (6.765)
14	0.2682 (6.805)
15	0.2698 (6.845)
16	0.2714 (6.885)
17	0.2730 (6.925)
18	0.2746 (6.965)
19	0.2762 (7.005)
20	0.2778 (7.045)
21	0.2794 (7.085)

universal joint and the steering rack pinion shaft. Install the steering column when the proper alignment is acheived.

18. Install the battery.

Steering Column

Removal and Installation

1. Disconnect the negative battery cable.
2. Remove the instrument panel brace below the steering column and remove the air duct.

3. Remove the combination switch upper and lower covers by removing the lower cover attaching screws.
4. Release the combination switch wiring harness clip and unplug the 4 connectors from the rear of the switch.
5. Remove the ignition switch.

6. Disconnect the steering column mounting bracket from the instrument panel crossmember by removing the retaining nuts. When the column is free from the instrument panel, it may be lowered as required to gain access to the intermediate shaft universal joint at the lower end.

7. With a white crayon or suitable marker, mark the point where the steering column shaft engages with the universal joint. Remove the universal joint clamp screw.

8. Loosen the 2 nuts securing the steering column hinge bracket to the clutch/brake pedal support.

9. Disengage the steering column from the universal joint by pulling to the rear. Remove the steering column from the vehicle. Remove the shim clips from the upper mounting bracket.

To install:

10. Install the joint clamp screw. Do not tighten the screw at this time as the clamp may need to shifted up or down on the shaft to align the steering column.

11. Install the steering column by aligning the index marks on the steering column shaft and universal joint. Engage the column hinge bracket with the pedal support studs and install the bracket nuts. Tighten the bracket nuts and raise the upper end of the column to seat under the instrument panel.

12. Install the shim clips onto the upper column mounting bracket flanges.

13. Install the steering column upper retaining nuts.

14. Turn the steering wheel from lock to lock several times to align the universal joints, then tighten the universal clamp bolts.

15. Install the ignition switch. Connect the combination switch wiring harness connectors and secure the harness in its mounting clip.

16. Install the combination switch upper and lower covers.

17. Install the air duct and the instrument panel brace under the steering column. Connect the negative battery cable.

Front Wheel Bearings

Removal and Installation

1. Disconnect the negative battery cable.
2. Raise the vehicle and support it safely.
3. Remove the steering knuckle/rotor hub assembly from the vehicle.
4. With knuckle puller T87C–1104–A or equivalent, remove the wheel hub/rotor assembly from the steering knuckle.

NOTE: The dust shield is press fitted onto the steering knuckle and is not normally removed as part of the front wheel bearing replacement procedure. Do not attempt to remove the dust shield from the steering knuckle.

5. Remove the outer bearing preload spacer from the hub and set the spacer aside.
6. Position the rotor/hub assembly in a vise with protective jaws.
7. Scribe or paint alignment marks on the hub and rotor for assembly reference.
8. Remove the attaching bolts and separate the rotor from the hub.
9. Press the outer and inner bearings from the hub using bearing splitter tool D84L–1123–A, shaft protector D80L–625–2 or equivalents.
10. Remove the outer grease seal from the hub. With a suitable prying tool, pry the inner grease seal from the steering knuckle bore. Discard the seals regardless of condition.
11. With bearing puller tool T77F–1102–A and slide hammer T–50T–100 or equivalents, remove the bearing races from the steering knuckle.
12. Inspect the inner and outer bearings for abnormal wear patterns. Inspect the rotor hub for cracks, damage to the casting, abnormal wear at the oil seal contact surface, and scoring or rusting of the bearing bore. Inspect the steering knuckle for

cracks and scoring or rusting of the bearing bore. Check the rotor dust shield for a loose or improper fit. Replace all damaged components as required.

To install:

13. Coat the bearing races with a light film of clean engine oil. With bearing cup replacer tool D79P–1202–A and universal drive handle tool T80T–4000–W or equivalents, seat the bearing races in the steering knuckle bore.

14. Pack the inner and outer bearings with wheel bearing grease, part number C12A2–D–B, C, D, E or equivalent.

15. Place the inner bearing into the steering knuckle bore so that it rests in a level position. Lubricate the lip of the new inner grease seal with wheel bearing grease, part number C12A2–D–B, C, D, E or equivalents. Drive the inner grease seal and inner bearing into the bore with seal replacer tool T78C–1175–A and driver handle tool T80T–4000–W or equivalents.

16. Install the spacer into the outer bearing bore. Repeat procedures described in Step 15 to install the outer grease seal and outer bearing.

NOTE: If the wheel bearings or the steering knuckle were replaced, the bearing preload must be checked and/or adjusted. Bearing preload is determined by the thickness of the bearing spacers. Each bearing spacer has been assigned a numerical code that that identifies its thickness. The code is stamped into the outer diameter of the spacer. The numbers range from 1–21, one being the thinnest. If the number on the spacer is not legible, measure the thickness of the spacer with a micrometer and match the thickness with the numbers shown in the chart provided. Changing the spacer thickness by 1 number will either raise or lower the preload by 1.7–3.5 ft. lbs. If the bearings or steering knuckles were replaced, adjust the bearing preload as described in Steps 17–21. Proceed directly to Step 22 if the above replacements were not made.

17. Install spacer selection tool T87C–1104B or equivalent and clamp the steering knuckle in a vise by the shock absorber supports. Torque the bolt of the tool in 36, 72, 108 and 145 ft. lb. increments.

18. After the torque sequence is completed, remove the assembly and install into the vise by the bolt head of the tool. Seat the bearings by rotating the steering knuckle several revolutions.

19. Remove the steering knuckle from the vice and install by clamping the assembly by the shock absorber support.

20. With an inch lb. torque wrench, measure the amount of torque required to rotate the spacer selector tool. Take the torque reading just as the tool starts to rotate. Compare the results to the following parameters: If the torque wrench indicates 2.21–10.44 inch lbs., the original spacer is the correct thickness. If the torque wrench indicates less than 2.21 inch lbs., a thinner spacer must be installed. If the torque wrench indicates more than 10.44 inch lbs., a thicker spacer must be used.

21. Remove the spacer selector tool after the proper preload is obtained.

22. Position the rotor onto the hub by aligning the matchmarks. Install the attaching bolts and torque to 33–40 ft. lbs.

23. Position the rotor/hub assembly into the steering knuckle bore and place the assembly onto a suitable press. Press the steering knuckle into the hub/rotor assembly using a suitable adapter.

24. Complete the assembly of the steering knuckle by reversing the removal procedure.

25. Connnect the negative battery cable.

Alignment

Refer to the wheel alignment specifications at the front of this section.

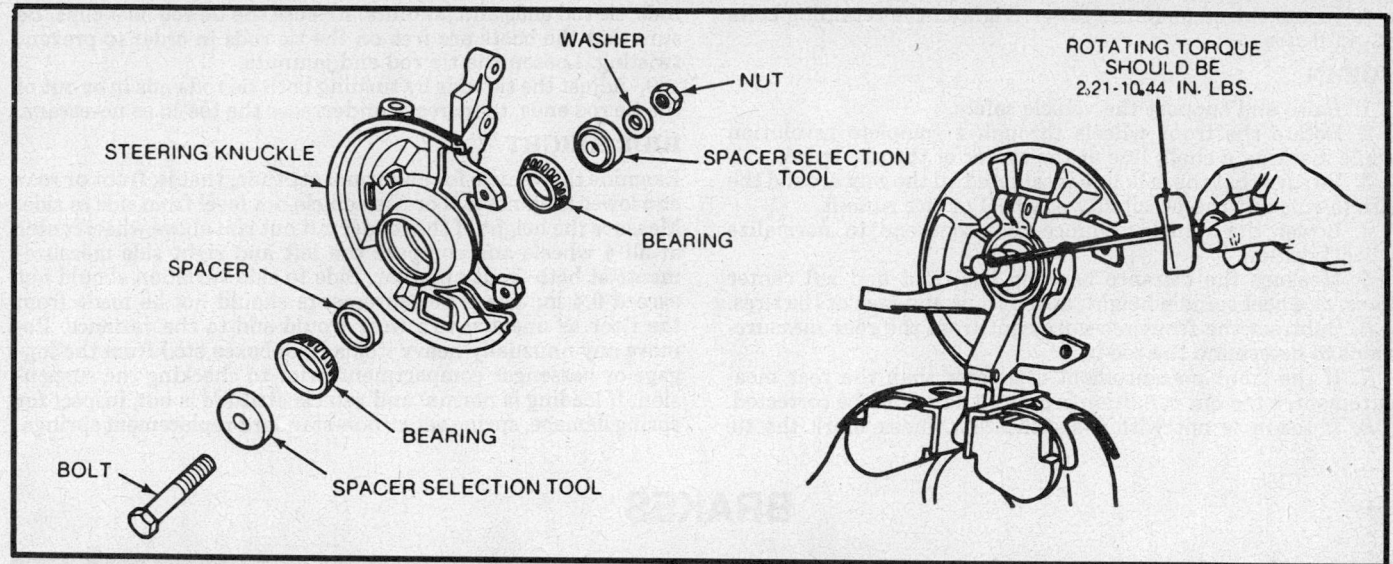

View of the spacer selection tool. Set bearing preload by rotating torque

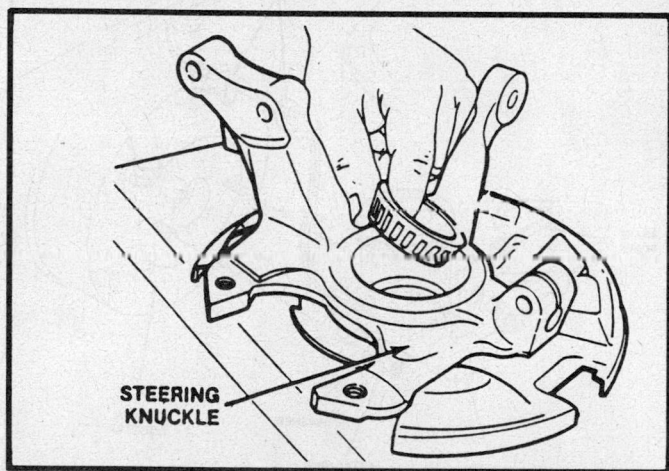

Positioning bearing in steering knuckle bore (typical)

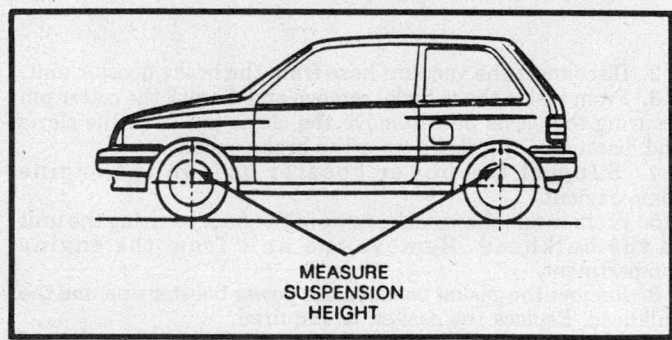

Suspension height inspection points

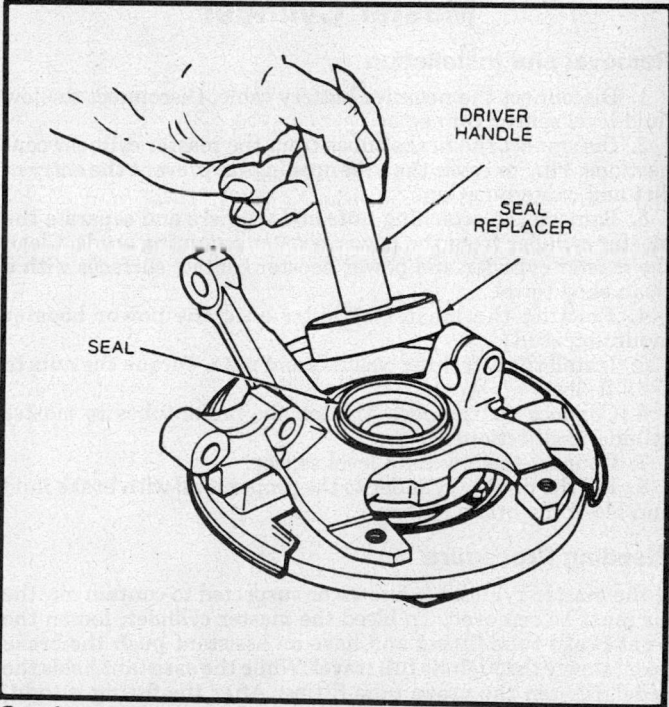

Seating grease seal and bearing

Procedure

CASTER

Caster is controlled by fixed vehicle demensions and is not adjustable. However the caster should be checked as a possible cause of a variety of suspension system problems.

CAMBER

The front suspension struts can be mounted in the strut towers 2 ways, which will result in a camber difference of about ½ degree. White alignment marks on the strut upper mounting blocks indicate which setting is in effect. From the factory the marks should be set on the outboard side of the struts.

To change the setting proceed as follows:

1. Remove the strut mounting nuts at the top of the strut tower.

2. Raise and support the vehicle safely. Remove the tire and wheel assembly.

3. Lower the strut to clear the mounting studs. Rotate the mounting block 180 degrees.

4. Install the strut in the tower. Tighten the retaining bolts 32–45 ft. lbs.

TOE-IN

1. Raise and support the vehicle safely.
2. Rotate the front wheels through a complete revolution while marking a chalk line at the center of the tire tread.
3. Be sure that the calk line is centered all the way around the tire to rule out the possibility of wheel or tire runout.
4. Lower the vehicle. Bounce the front end to normalize wheel position.
5. Measure the distance between the right and left center lines, at wheel spindle height, at the front and rear of the tires.
6. Subtract the front measurement from the rear measurement to determine the toe-in.
7. If the front measurement is greater than the rear measurement, a toe-out condition is present and must be corrected.
8. If toe-in is not within specification, index mark the tie rods, tie rod ends and jamnuts. Release the tie rod boot clips. Be sure that the boots are free on the tie rods in order to prevent twisting. Loosen the tie rod end jamnuts.
9. Adjust the tie rods by turning both tie rod ends in or out of the tie rod ends, to increase or decrease the toe-in as necessary.

RIDE HEIGHT

Examine the vehicle for abnormal attitude, that is, front or rear end lower than normal or the vehicle not level from side to side. Measure the height of the fender cut out rim above wheel center at all 4 wheels and compare the left and right side measurements at both front and rear. Side to side variation should not exceed 0.4 in. These measurements should not be made from the floor as unequal tire wear would add to the variance. Remove any unusually heavy items (tool boxes etc.) from the luggage or passenger compartment prior to checking the suspension. If loading is normal and vehicle attitude is not, inspect for spring damage, spring set or non-standard replacement springs.

BRAKES

Refer to the unit repair section for brake service information and drum/rotor specifications.

Master Cylinder

Removal and Installation

1. Disconnect the negative battery cable. Disconnect the low fluid level sensor connector.
2. Disconnect the brake tubes from the master cylinder connections. Plug or cover the tube openings to prevent the entry of dirt and contamination.
3. Remove the attaching nuts and washers and separate the master cylinder from the power booster mounting studs. Clean the master cylinder and power booster contact surfaces with a clean shop towel.
4. Position the master cylinder onto the power booster mounting studs.
5. Install the attaching washers and nuts. Torque the nuts to 7–12 ft. lbs.
6. Connect and properly tighten the brake tubes to master cylinder connections.
7. Connect the low fluid level sensor.
8. Fill the master cylinder to the proper level with brake fluid and bleed the brake system.

Bleeding Procedure

If the master cylinder is known or suspected to contain air, the air must be removed. To bleed the master cylinder, loosen the front brake tube fitting and have an assistant push the brake pedal slowly through its full travel. While the assistant holds the pedal, tighten the brake tube fitting. After the fitting is tight, the assistant may release the brake pedal. Repeat the procedure for the rear brake tube. Repeat the entire process several times to ensure all air is removed from the master cylinder. Add brake fluid as required. Do not allow the brake fluid to spill on the vehicle painted surface, or damage to the paint will occur.

Power Brake Booster

Removal and Installation

1. Disconnect the negative battery cable. Remove the master cylinder.

NOTE: It may be necessary to remove the master cylinder from the booster assembly without disconnecting the brake lines from the cylinder. If possible, position the master cylinder to the side.

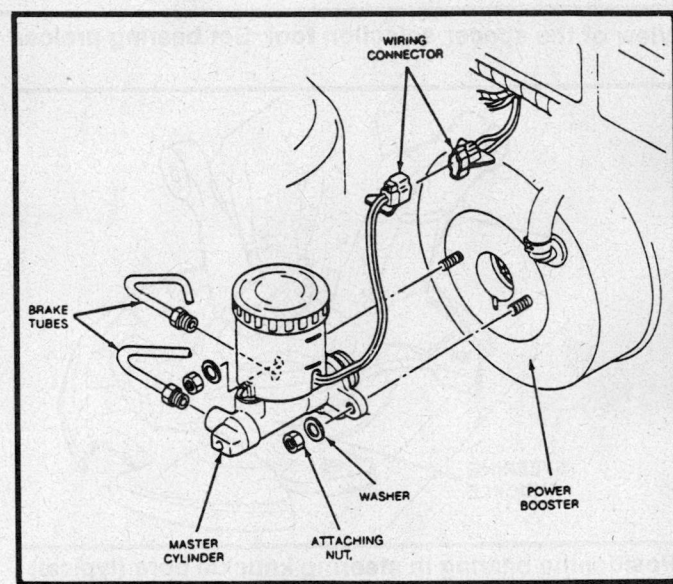

Master cylinder assembly

2. Disconnect the vacuum hose from the brake booster unit.
3. From inside the vehicle, remove and discard the cotter pin securing the clevis pin. Remove the clevis pin from the clevis and disconnect the clevis from the brake pedal.
4. Support the power booster unit in the engine compartment.
5. From inside the vehicle, remove the nuts securing the unit to the bulkhead. Remove the unit from the engine compartment.
6. Remove the gasket between the power booster unit and the bulkhead. Replace the gasket, as required.
7. Position the gasket onto the power brake booster studs and have a second technician position the unit against the bulkhead.
8. From inside the vehicle, secure the power booster to the bulkhead with the 4 retaing nuts. Torque the retaining nuts to 12–17 ft. lbs.
9. Lubricate the clevis with a coating of white lithium grease or equivalent. From inside the vehicle, attach the clevis to the brake pedal with the clevis pin. Secure the clevis pin with a new cotter pin.
10. Connect the vacuum to the power brake booster.

11. Complete the assembly of the master cylinder by reversing the removal procedure.

12. Bleed the brake system.

Bleeding Procedure

The brake hydraulic circuits form a split diagonal hydraulic system. The left front and right rear form 1 circuit while the right front and left rear form the other circuit. When bleeding 1 of these circuits, bleed the rear wheel first then bleed the front wheel at the opposite corner. Use heavy duty brake fluid when filling the master cylinder.

1. Clean all dirt and grease from the master cylinder filler cap. Remove the filler cap.

2. Fill the master cylinder to the proper level with the specified brake fluid. The master cylinder must not be allowed to run dry during the bleeding procedure.

3. Bleed the master cylinder.

4. Remove the bleeder cap from the appropriate rear wheel cylinder.

5. Attach a length of rubber hose to the bleeder fitting. Make certain that the hose fits snugly onto the fitting.

6. Submerge the free end of the hose into a container partially filled with clean brake fluid.

7. Loosen the bleeder fitting approximately ¾ turn.

8. Push the brake pedal through its full travel and hold it in that position.

9. Close the bleeder fitting and have the assistant release the brake pedal.

10. Repeat Steps 6–8 until air bubbles cease to appear from the submerged end of the hose.

11. When the fluid entering the container is free of bubbles, tighten the bleeder screw and remove the length of rubber hose.

12. Repeat Steps 3–10 for the appropriate diagonal front brake caliper.

13. Check the master cylinder fluid level. If necessary, refill the master cylinder to the proper level with the specified brake fluid.

Parking Brake

Adjustment

1. Make certain that the parking brake is fully released.

2. Remove the parking brake console insert.

3. Remove the locking clip from the cable adjuster nut located at the base of the parking brake handle.

4. Raise and support the vehicle safely.

5. Tighten the cable adjuster nut until there is a slight brake drag when the rear wheels are rotated.

6. Back off on the adjuster nut until the brake drag disappears.

7. Check the operation of the parking brake. The rear brakes should be fully applied when the brake lever is pulled upward 11–16 notches.

CLUTCH AND TRANSAXLE

Refer to "Chilton's Transmission Service Manual" for additional coverage.

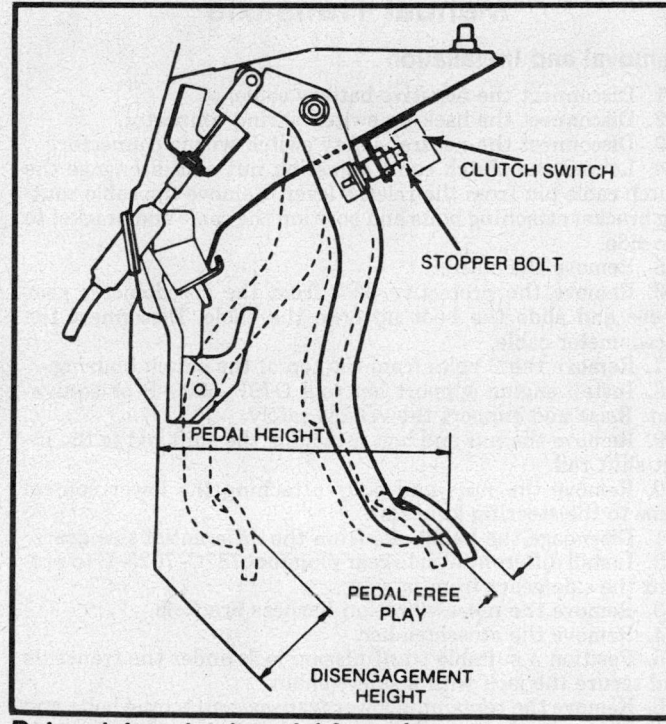

Determining clutch pedal free-play

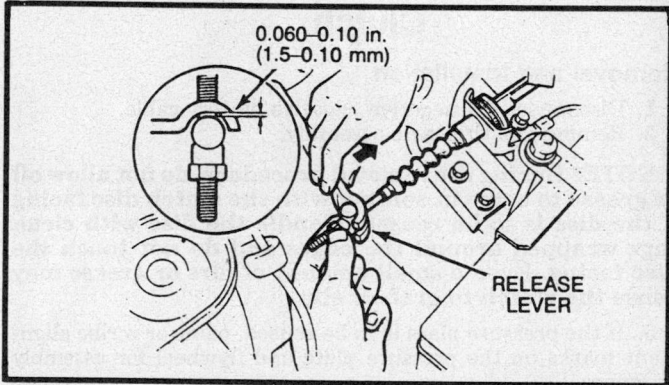

Measuring clearance between release lever and cable pin

Clutch Linkage

CABLE

Adjustment

1. Carefully move the clutch pedal back and forth and measure the amount of travel by visual approximation. If the clutch pedal free play is from 0.160–0.280 in., no adjustment is necessary.

2. If the free play is not within specification, proceed as follows. Pull back the transaxle release lever and measure the clearance between the lever and the cable pin. The clearance should be from 0.060–0.100 in. Loosen and rotate the cable ad-

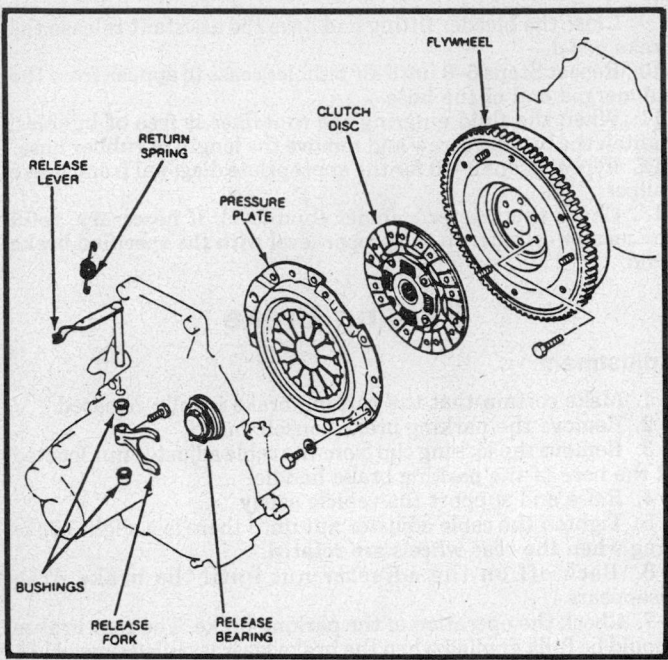

Exploded view of the clutch assembly

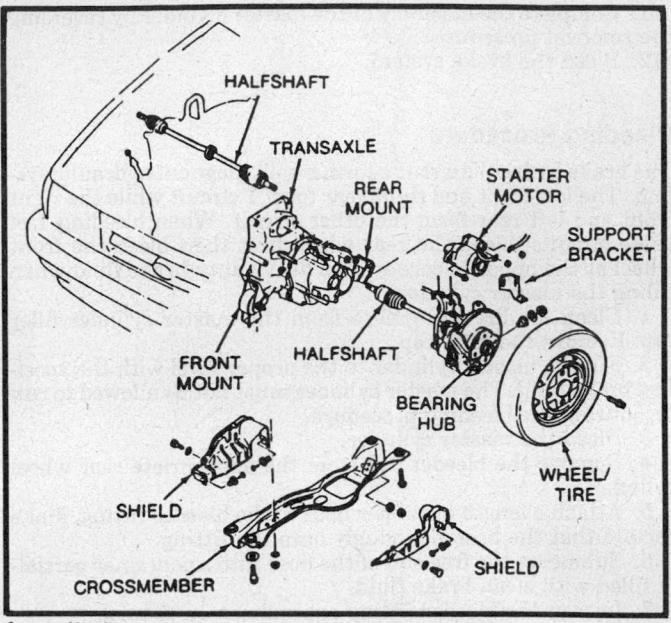

Installation view of the manual transaxle

juster nut until the clearance between the pin and the lever is within specification.

3. When the proper clearance is obtained, tighten the adjuster nut.

4. Repeat the procedure described in Step 1 to ensure that the free play travel is correct.

Clutch

Removal and Installation

1. Disconnect the negative negative battery cable.
2. Remove the transaxle assembly.

NOTE: During the removal procedure, do not allow oil or grease to come in contact with the clutch disc facing if the disc is to be reused. Handle the disc with clean rags wrapped around the edges and do not touch the disc facing. Even a small amount of dirt or grease may cause the clutch to grab or slip.

3. If the pressure plate is to be reused, paint or scribe alignment marks on the pressure plate and flywheel for assembly reference.

4. Install a locking tool to prevent the flywheel from turning.

5. Loosen the pressure plate attaching bolts in an alternate pattern 1 turn at a time. This will relieve the pressure plate spring tension evenly and prevent distortion of the pressure plate. Remove the pressure plate and clutch disc after the bolts are removed. Replace all clutch components as required.

6. Position the clutch disc on the flywheel and install a clutch alignment tool to hold the disc in place.

NOTE: When installing the clutch disc, make certain that the disc dampener springs are facing away from the flywheel. A new disc will be stamped FLYWHEEL to indicate the correct installation postion.

7. Align the reference marks, if present, and position the pressure plate on the flywheel and install the attaching bolts. Torque the bolts evenly in an alternate pattern to 13–20 ft. lbs. The bolts must be tightened in this manner to prevent distortion of the pressure plate.

8. Remove the clutch alignment tool.

9. Clean the clutch disc splines on the input shaft with a dry rag and coat the spline surfaces with clutch grease, part number C1AZ–19590–B or equivalent.

10. Complete the assembly of the transaxle by reversing the removal procedure.

11. Connect the negative battery cable.

12. Adjust the clutch pedal free play.

Manual Transaxle

Removal and Installation

1. Disconnect the negative battery cable.
2. Disconnect the back-up switch wiring connector.
3. Disconnect the neutral safety switch wiring connector.
4. Loosen the clutch cable adjusting nut and disengage the clutch cable pin from the release lever. Remove the cable routing bracket attaching bolts and position the cable and bracket to the side.
5. Remove the starter.
6. Remove the protective boot from the speedometer gear sleeve and slide the boot up onto the cable. Disconnect the speedometer cable.
7. Remove the 2 bolts from the top of the clutch housing.
8. Install engine support bar tool D79P–6000–B or equivalent. Raise and support the vehicle safely.
9. Remove the nut and bolt attaching the shift rod to the input shift rail.
10. Remove the nuts and bolts attaching the lower control arms to the steering knuckles.
11. Disengage the halfshafts from the differential side gears.
12. Install differential side gear plug tool 787C–7025–C to prevent the side gears from moving.
13. Remove the noise vibration harness brackets.
14. Remove the crossmember.
15. Position a suitable transmission jack under the transaxle and secure the jack with a safety chain.
16. Remove the remaining lower transaxle attaching bolts and pull the transaxle away from the engine. Lower the transaxle

from the vehicle and position the assembly in a suitable mounting fixture.

17. Clean the transaxle housing and rear engine contact surfaces. Apply a $\frac{1}{16}$ in. bead of gasket eliminator sealing compound to the transaxle housing. To ensure proper sealing, make certain the sealant encircles the bolt holes during application.

To install:

18. Raise the transaxle into position and seat against the rear of the engine.

19. Install the lower transaxle attaching bolts. Torque the bolts to 47–66 ft. lbs.

20. Install the noise vibration harness brackets and remove the transmission jack.

21. Install the crossmember and remove the differential plugs. Torque the crossmember to chassis and engine mount nuts to 27–46 ft. lbs.

22. Remove and discard the old halfshaft circlips. Replace the circlips with new ones. Engage the halfshafts with the differential side gears.

23. Connect the lower control arms to the steering knuckles. Install the lower control arm attaching clamp bolts and nuts. Hold the clamp bolt stationary and torque the nut to 32–40 ft. lbs.

24. Position the shift rod on the input shift rail and install the attaching bolt and nut.

25. Lower the vehicle and remove the engine support bar.

26. Install the 2 bolts at the top of the clutch housing. Torque the bolts 47–66 ft. lbs.

27. Install the starter.

28. Install the clutch cable bracket and engage the clutch cable with the release lever. Connect the neutral and back-up switch wiring connectors.

29. Remove the speedometer driven gear from the transaxle case bore. With a clean rag, wipe the driven gear and reinsert into the transaxle case. Visually inspect the the oil level on the driven gear. The oil level should be between the **F** and **L** marks on the gear sleeve. If the level is not within the normal operating range, add oil through the speedometer bore as required. Ensure that the oil meets Ford specification ESW-M2C–33F (ATF) or ESR-M2C–163A (ATF) Dexron®II.

30. Install the speedometer gear and connect the speedometer cable. Replace the rubber boot.

31. Connect the negative battery cable.

32. Adjust the clutch pedal free play.

Automatic Transaxle

Removal and Installation

1. Disconnect the negative battery cable. Loosen the front wheel lug nuts.

2. Drain the transaxle fluid. Disconnect the speedometer cable from the transaxle.

3. Disconnect the transaxle electrical connectors, which are located next to the governor.

4. Disconnect the transaxle ground wire. Disconnect the transaxle vacuum hose.

5. Remove the nut which connects the shift lever to the manual shaft assembly.

6. Remove the shift cable from the transaxle. Support the engine using tool D87L6000A or equivalent.

7. Raise and support the vehicle safely. Remove the tire and wheel assemblies.

8. Remove the left splash shield. Remove the stabilizer mounting nuts and brackets. Remove the left stabilizer body bracket.

9. Remove the lower arm clamp bolts and nuts. Pull the lower arms downward, separating the lower arms from the knuckles.

10. Remove the cotter pin and nut. Disconnect the tie rod end from the knuckle.

11. Remove the halfshafts. Install differential plugs tool T87C7025C or equivalent between the differential side gears.

12. Disconnect and plug the oil cooler lines. Remove the crossmember. Remove the gusset plate to transaxle bolts.

13. Remove the flywheel cover. Remove the torque converter retaining bolts. Remove the starter.

14. Properly support the transaxle assembly with the proper equipment.

15. Remove the engine to transaxle retaining bolts. Carefully remove the transaxle from the vehicle.

16. Installation is the reverse of the removal procedure. Be sure to fill the transaxle to specification with the proper fluid.

HALFSHAFTS

Front Drive Axle

HALFSHAFT

Removal and Installation

1. Disconnect the negative battery cable.

2. Raise the vehicle and support it safely.

3. Drain the transaxle fluid.

4. Remove the front tire and wheel assemblies. Remove the splash shields.

5. Bend back the lockwasher tab on the halfshaft locknut slot. Lock the brakes and loosen, but do not remove, the halfshaft locknut.

6. Remove the stabilizer bar control link from the lower suspension control arm.

7. Remove the clamp bolt and nut from the lower suspension control arm. With a suitable pry bar, pry the lower suspension control arm downward to disconnect the ball joint. Be careful not to tear or puncture the dust boot when disconnecting the ball joint.

8. With the proper tool, separate the halfshaft from the transaxle.

NOTE: The halfshaft must be separated from the transaxle gradually. If the halfshaft is pulled or jerked suddenly, the differential and wheel hub oil seals may be damaged. If necessary, use a suitable puller to push the drive shaft from the wheel hub.

9. Remove and discard the halfshaft locking nut and lockwasher.

10. Withdraw the halfshaft from the wheel hub and the transaxle. Wrap tape around the inboard and outboard splines to prevent damage.

11. Install differential plug tool T87C–7025–C or equivalent to prevent the side gear from moving.

To install:

12. Inspect the differential and wheel hub oil seals for damage and replace the seals as required.

13. Remove the protective tape. Remove the circlips from the inboard halfshaft spline gear ends and replace with new. Coat the inboard and outboard halfshaft spline ends with grease.

14. Remove the differential gear holding plugs.

NOTE: If the right halfshaft is being installed at this point in the procedure, the position of the dynamic damper assembly must be checked. Push the outboard

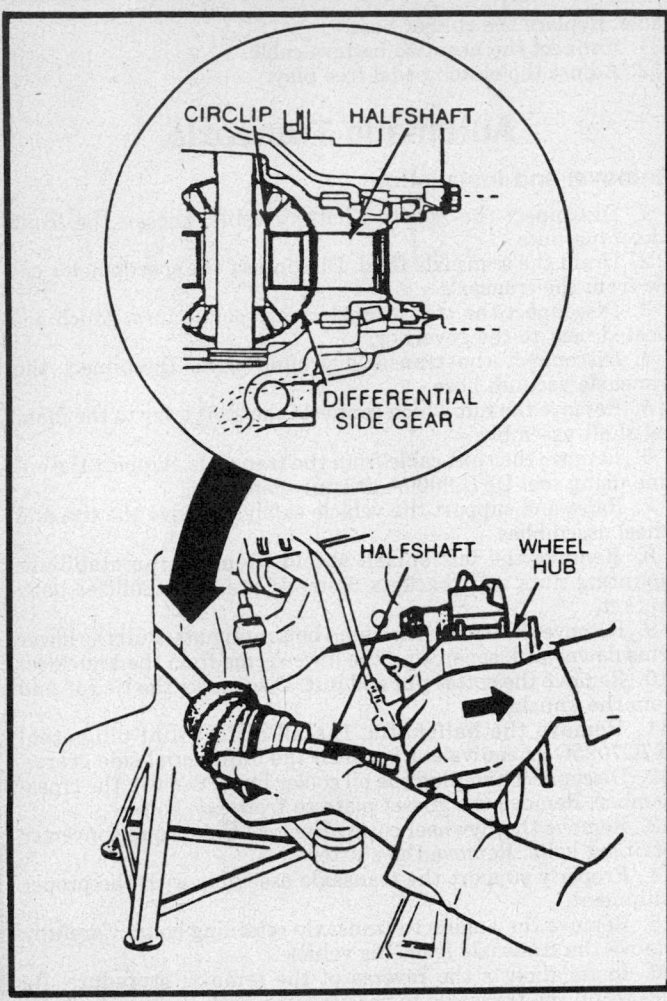

Disengaging outboard halfshaft section from wheel hub

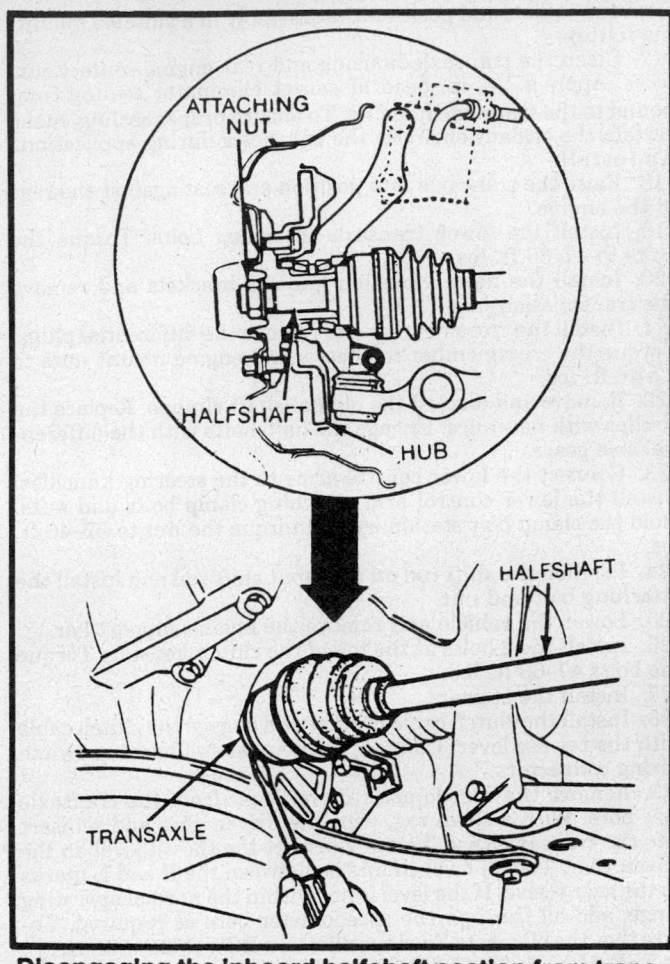

Disengaging the inboard halfshaft section from trans-axle

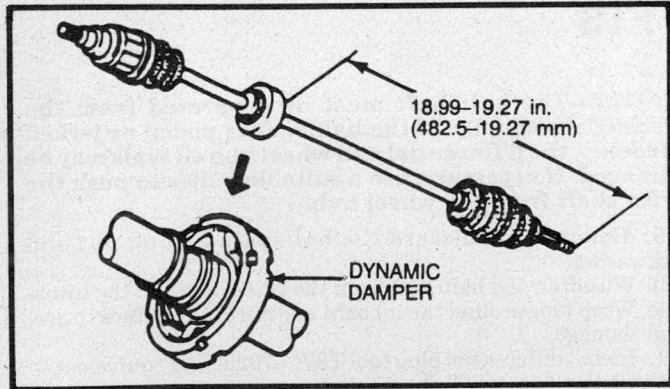

Positioning the dynamic damper—right halfshaft only

end of the halfshaft fully into the outboard CV joint and measure the distance from the end of the shaft to the edge of the damper. The correct distance is 19.27–19.99 in. Adjust the position of the damper on the shaft as required to obtain the proper orientation. The left halfshaft does not incorporate a dynamic damper.

15. Position and install the inboard end of the halfshaft into the differential side gear. Take care not to damage the differential oil seal.

16. Position and install the outboard end of the halfshaft into the wheel hub. Take care not to damage the wheel hub oil seal.

17. Install the halfshaft lockwasher and locknut onto the halfshaft and tighten by hand.

18. Raise the lower suspension control arm and connect the arm to the ball joint. Take care not to damage the ball joint dust boot.

19. Install the lower suspension arm clamp nut and bolt. Hold the bolt stationary and torque the nut to 33–40 ft. lbs.

20. Make certain the brakes are still locked and torque the outboard halfshaft locknut to 116–174 ft. lbs. Bend a tab of the the lockwasher into a slot in the locknut with the proper tool.

NOTE: Do not stake the locking tab with a pointed tool. Make certain that the locking tab is depressed at least 0.16 in. into the locknut slot to ensure proper locking capabilty. After the lockwasher is locked into place, grasp the wheel hub and pull to ensure that the halfshaft is installed properly. Rotate the wheel hub by hand to ensure that the wheel hub turns smoothly.

21. Install the splash shields. Install the tire and wheel assemblies. Install and tighten the transaxle drain plug.

22. Fill the transaxle with the proper grade and type fluid to specification. Lower the vehicle.

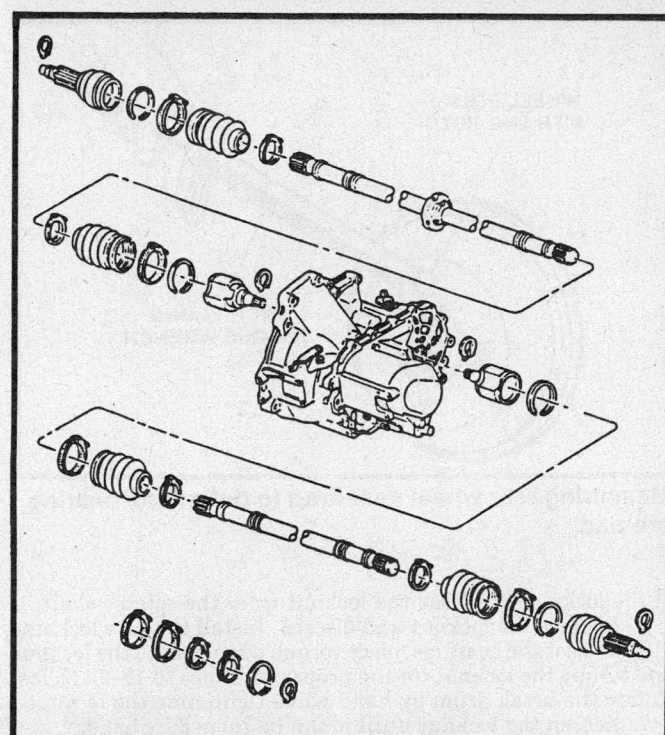

Assembly view of the front wheel driveshaft and CV-joint asemblies

Boot

RZEPPA JOINT

Removal and Installation

INBOARD AND OUTBOARD

1. Disconnect the negative battery cable. Raise and support the vehicle safely.
2. Remove the halfshaft from the vehicle. Support the assembly in a vise with protective jaws.

NOTE: During disassembly and assembly, do not allow dust or similar foreign matter to enter the halfshaft joints.

3. Using the the proper tool, pry the locking clip of the boot bands upward. Grasp the end of the bands with pliers and remove. Discard the bands and remove the boot from the joint.
4. Matchmark the outer ring with the shaft for assembly reference. Do not use a punch to make the alignment marks.

NOTE: The ball joint is located to the joint outer ring with an expandable circlip. Removal of this circlip is not required to release the joint from the halfshaft. Remove the circlip only if damage is evident and replace with new.

5. Withdraw the ball joint from the outer ring. Matchmark the halfshaft and ball joint inner ring for proper alignment at reassembly. Do not use a punch to make the alignment marks.
6. Remove the snapring securing the halfshaft in the ball joint inner ring. Remove the ball joint assembly from the halfshaft.
7. Matchmark the inner ring and cage for reassembly reference. Do not use a punch to make the alignment marks.
8. Insert a flat bladed tool between the ball cage and the inner ring to remove the balls. Be careful not to loose the balls.
9. Turn the cage about 30° to separate it from the inner ring. Remove the Rzeppa CV joint end boot. On the right halfshaft remove the dynamic damper.
10. Remove the Birfield CV joint end boot. Do not remove the Birfield joint, it is not repairable and the complete joint must be replaced should a problem arise.
11. Installation is the reverse of the removal procedure.

TRIPOT JOINT

Removal and Installation

INBOARD AND OUTBOARD

1. Disconnect the negative battery cable. Raise and support the vehicle safely.
2. Remove the halfshaft from the vehicle. Support the assembly in a vise with protective jaws.

NOTE: During disassembly and assembly, do not allow dust or similar foreign matter to enter the halfshaft joints.

3. Remove the large boot clamp. Roll the boot back over the shaft. Remove the wire ring bearing retainer. Remove the outer race.

NOTE: Before removing the outer race, matchmark the outer race and tripot bearing for reassembly.

4. Matchmark the tripot bearing and the shaft. Remove the tripot bearing snapring.
5. As required, remove the small clamp and the CV joint boot from the halfshaft.
6. Installation is the reverse of the removal procedure.

Universal Joints

Refer to the unit repair section for overhaul procedures.

REAR SUSPENSION

Refer to the unit repair section for axle overhaul procedures and rear suspension services.

Rear Wheel Bearing

Removal and Installation

1. Disconnect the negative battery cable.
2. Raise the vehicle and support it safely. Make certain that the parking brake is fully released.

3. Remove the wheel and tire assembly.
4. Remove the grease/dust cap.
5. With a small chisel, carefully raise the staked portion of the locknut to release the locknut from the spindle shaft.

NOTE: The drum/hub locknuts are threaded left and right. The left hand threaded locknut is located on the right hand side of the vehicle. Turn this locknut clockwise to loosen. The right hand threaded locknut is turned counterclockwise to loosen.

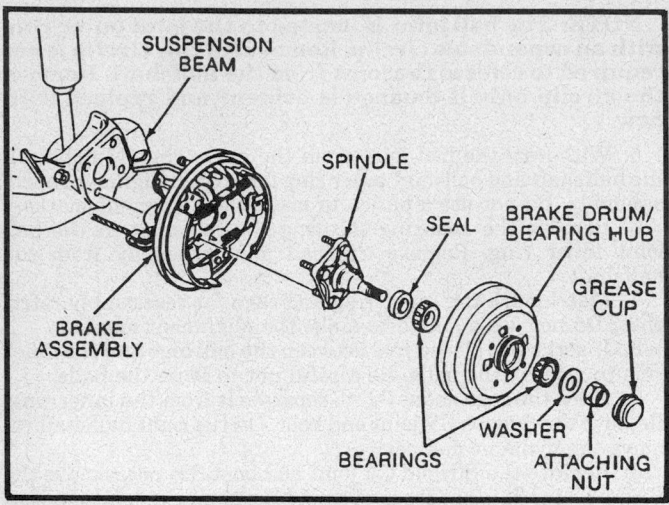

Rear wheel hub and bearing assembly

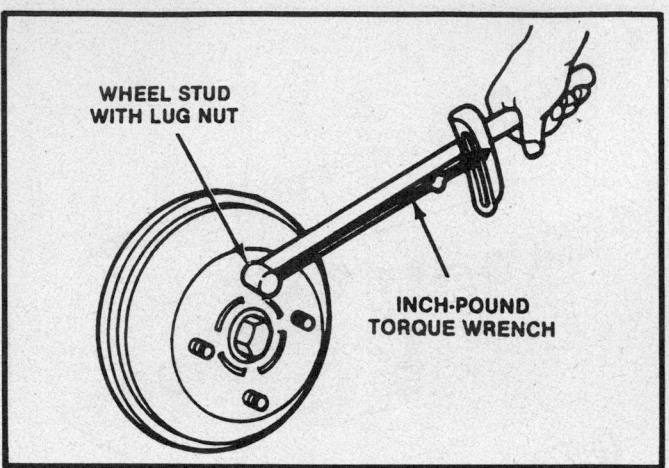

Measuring rear wheel seal drag to determine bearing preload.

6. Remove the locknut and washer. Discard the locknut.

7. Pull the brake drum bearings and hub assembly away from the spindle shaft. Take care not to damage the spindle shaft threads.

8. With a small roll head pry bar or equivalent, remove the bearing grease seal from the bearing hub. Discard the seal regardless of condition.

9. Remove the inner and outer bearings from the bearing hub. If the bearings are to be reused, identify and tag each bearing for installation reference. Replace worn or damaged bearings as required. Wipe all bearing hub surfaces with a clean shop towel.

10. Pack the bearings with an ample amount of wheel bearing grease.

To install:

11. Position the inner bearing in the hub. Install and seat a new grease seal with a suitable driving tool.

12. Position the brake drum and hub assembly on the spindle. Keep the hub centered during positioning to prevent damage to the new grease seal and spindle threads.

13. Install the outer bearing, lockwasher and new locknut.

14. Adjust the bearing preload.

15. Install the grease cap and wheel and tire assembly.

16. Lower the vehicle and connect the negative battery cable.

Adjustment

A staked attaching nut and a flat washer are used to hold the bearings and hub in position on the spindle shaft. The attaching nuts are left and right hand thread. The right hand threaded nut (located on the left side of the vehicle) must be turned clockwise to tighten and the left hand threaded nut must be turned counterclockwise to tighten.

1. Make certain that the parking brake is fully released.

2. Raise the vehicle and support it safely. Remove the wheel and tire assembly.

3. Remove the grease cap. Rotate the brake drum to ensure freedom of rotation.

4. With a small cape chisel, carefully raise the staked portion

of the locknut to release the locknut from the spindle shaft.

5. Remove the locknut and discard. Install the new locknut.

6. To seat the bearings, place torque wrench onto the locknut and torque the locknut (in the proper rotation) to 18–22 ft. lbs. Rotate the break drum by hand while tightening the locknut.

7. Loosen the locknut until it can be turned by hand.

8. Before the bearing preload can be set, the amount of seal drag must be measured and added to the the required preload. To measure the seal drag proceed as follows:

   a. Install the proper size nut onto a wheel stud and rotate the brake drum untilt the stud is in the 12 o'clock position.

   b. Place an inch lb. torque wrench onto the nut to measure the amount of force required to rotate the break drum.

   c. Pull the torque wrench and note and record the torque reading at which rotation begins. This value will be used to calculate the bearing preload range.

9. The required preload range, without seal drag, is 1.3–4.3 inch lbs. (1.3, minimum; 4.3, maximum). To calculate the preload, add the seal drag value obtained in Step 8.c to the minimum and maximum preload specifications. For example, if the seal drag was 2.2 inch lbs, then the minimum preload specification would be 1.3 inch lbs. + 2.2 inch lbs. = 3.5 inch lbs and the maximum preload specification would be 4.3 inch lbs. + 2.2 inch lbs. = 6.5 inch lbs. Therefore, for a seal drag of 2.2 inch lbs. the bearing preload should be within the range of 3.5–6.5 inch lbs.

10. After the preload range is determined, tighten the locknut a slight amount.

11. Rotate the brake drum until the nut and wheel are returned to the twelve o'clock position. Position the inch lb. torque wrench onto the nut and measure the amount of pull required to rotate the brake drum. Tighten the locknut until the torque shown on the torque wrench is within the range that was calculated in Step 9.

12. With the proper tool, stake the locknut in place. Take care not to damage the nut during staking.

13. Install the grease cap.

14. Install the wheel and tire assembly. Connect the negative battery cable.

YEAR IDENTIFICATION

1987–90 Mercury Tracer

VEHICLE IDENTIFICATION

It is important for servicing and ordering parts to be certain of the vehicle and engine identification. The VIN (vehicle identification number) is a 17 digit number visible through the windshield on the driver's side of the dash and contains the vehicle and engine identification codes. The tenth digit indicates model year and the eighth digit indicates engine code. It can be interpreted as follows:

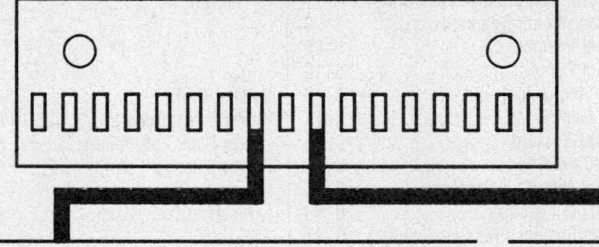

	Engine Code						Model Year	
Code	Cu. In.	Liters	Cyl.	Fuel Sys.	Eng. Mfg.		Code	Year
7	98	1.6	4	2 bbl	Ford①		H	1987
5	98	1.6	4	EFI	Ford①		J	1988
① Mexico							K	1989
							L	1990

ENGINE IDENTIFICATION

Year	Model	Engine Displacement cu. in. (liter)	Engine Series Identification (VIN)	No. of Cylinders	Engine Type
1987	Tracer	98 (1.6)	7	4	OHC
	Tracer	98 (1.6)	5	4	OHC
1988	Tracer	98 (1.6)	7	4	OHC
	Tracer	98 (1.6)	5	4	OHC
1989-90	Tracer	98 (1.6)	7	4	OHC
	Tracer	98 (1.6)	5	4	OHC

GENERAL ENGINE SPECIFICATIONS

Year	VIN	No. Cylinder Displacement cu. in. (liter)	Fuel System Type	Net Horsepower @ rpm	Net Torque @ rpm (ft.lbs.)	Bore × Stroke (in.)	Compression Ratio	Oil Pressure @ rpm
1987	5	4-98 (1.6)	EFI	61 @ 5000	125 @ 2500	3.07 × 3.29	9.3:1	50–64①
	7	4-98 (1.6)	2 bbl	NA	NA	3.07 × 3.29	9.3:1	50–64①
1988	5	4-98 (1.6)	EFI	61 @ 5000	125 @ 2500	3.07 × 3.29	9.3:1	50–64①
	7	4-98 (1.6)	2 bbl	NA	NA	3.07 × 3.29	9.3:1	50–64①
1989-90	5	4-98 (1.6)	EFI	61 @ 5000	125 @ 2500	3.07 × 3.29	9.3:1	50–64①
	7	4-98 (1.6)	2 bbl	NA	NA	3.07 × 3.29	9.3:1	50–64①

NA Not available

① 3000 rpm — hot

FIRING ORDER

NOTE: To avoid confusion, replace the spark plugs and wires one at a time.

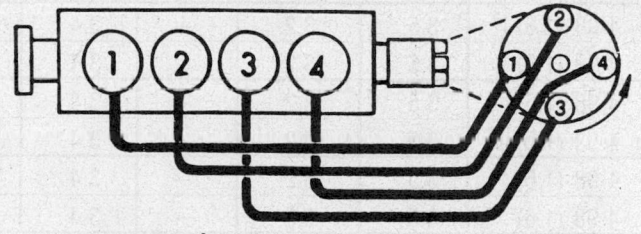

Ford 98 cu. in. (1.6L)
Firing order: 1–3–4–2
Distributor rotation: Counterclockwise

GASOLINE ENGINE TUNE-UP SPECIFICATIONS
Refer to Section 34 for all spark plug recommendations

Year	VIN	No. Cylinder Displacement cu. in. (liter)	Spark Plugs Gap (in.)	Ignition Timing (deg.) MT	Ignition Timing (deg.) AT	Compression Pressure (psi)	Fuel Pump (psi)	Idle Speed (rpm) MT	Idle Speed (rpm) AT	Valve Clearance In.	Valve Clearance Ex.
1987	5	4-98 (1.6)	0.044	7B③	7B③	134–250⑤	64–85	800–900①	950–1050②	.012H	.012H
	7	4-98 (1.6)	0.044	1–3B④	1–3B④	134–250⑤	4–5	800–900	950–1050	.012H	.012H
1988	5	4-98 (1.6)	0.044	7B③	7B③	134–250⑤	64–85	800–900	800–900	.012H	.012H
	7	4-98 (1.6)	0.044	1–3B④	1–3B④	134–250⑤	4–5	800–900	950–1050	.012H	.012H

GASOLINE ENGINE TUNE-UP SPECIFICATIONS
Refer to Section 34 for all spark plug recommendations

Year	VIN	No. Cylinder Displacement cu. in. (liter)	Spark Plugs Gap (in.)	Ignition Timing (deg.) MT	AT	Compression Pressure (psi)	Fuel Pump (psi)	Idle Speed (rpm) MT	AT	Valve Clearance In.	Ex.
1989	5	4-98 (1.6)	0.044	7B③	7B③	134–250⑤	64–85	800–900	800–900	.012H	.012H
	7	4-98 (1.6)	0.044	1–3B④	1–3B④	134–250⑤	4–5	800–900	950–1050	.012H	.012H
1990		SEE UNDERHOOD SPECIFICATIONS STICKER									

H Hot
① Idle-up; Pre Nov. '87
   Air conditioning—1250–1350 rpm
   Power steering—1000–1100 rpm
   Electrical load—900–950

② Idle-up; Pre Nov. '87
   Air conditioning—1250–1550 rpm
   Power steering—1150–1250 rpm
   Electrical load—1050–1100

③ Vacuum hose connected
④ Vacuum hose disconnected
⑤ All cylinders must be within 75% of each other

CAPACITIES

Year	Model	VIN	No. Cylinder Displacement cu. in. (liter)	Engine Crankcase with Filter	without Filter	Transmission (pts.) 4-Spd	5-Spd	Auto.	Drive Axle (pts.)	Fuel Tank (gal.)	Cooling System (qts.)
1987	Tracer	5	4-98 (1.6)	3.5	3.2	—	3.4	6.0	NA	11.9	①
	Tracer	7	4-98 (1.6)	3.5	3.2	—	3.4	6.0	NA	11.9	①
1988	Tracer	5	4-98 (1.6)	3.5	3.2	—	3.4	6.0	NA	11.9	①
	Tracer	7	4-98 (1.6)	3.5	3.2	—	3.4	6.0	NA	11.9	①
1989-90	Tracer	5	4-98 (1.6)	3.5	3.2	—	3.4	6.0	NA	11.9	①
	Tracer	7	4-98 (1.6)	3.5	3.2	—	3.4	6.0	NA	11.9	①

① Manual transaxle—5.3 qts.
   Automatic transaxle—6.3 qts.

CAMSHAFT SPECIFICATIONS
All measurements given in inches.

Year	VIN	No. Cylinder Displacement cu. in. (liter)	Journal Diameter 1	2	3	4	5	Lobe Lift In.	Ex.	Bearing Clearance	Camshaft End Play
1987	5	4-98 (1.6)	1.7103–1.7112	1.6870–1.7091	1.7103–1.7112	—	—	NA	NA	0.006	0.002–0.007
	7	4-98 (1.6)	1.7103–1.7112	1.6870–1.7091	1.7103–1.7112	—	—	NA	NA	0.006	0.002–0.007
1988	5	4-98 (1.6)	1.7103–1.7112	1.6870–1.7091	1.7103–1.7112	—	—	NA	NA	0.006	0.002–0.007
	7	4-98 (1.6)	1.7103–1.7112	1.6870–1.7091	1.7103–1.7112	—	—	NA	NA	0.006	0.002–0.007
1989-90	5	4-98 (1.6)	1.7103–1.7112	1.6870–1.7091	1.7103–1.7112	—	—	NA	NA	0.006	0.002–0.007
	7	4-98 (1.6)	1.7103–1.7112	1.6870–1.7091	1.7103–1.7112	—	—	NA	NA	0.006	0.002–0.007

NA Not available

CRANKSHAFT AND CONNECTING ROD SPECIFICATIONS

All measurements are given in inches.

Year	VIN	No. Cylinder Displacement cu. in. (liter)	Crankshaft				Connecting Rod		
			Main Brg. Journal Dia.	Main Brg. Oil Clearance	Shaft End-play	Thrust on No.	Journal Diameter	Oil Clearance	Side Clearance
1987	5	4-98 (1.6)	1.9661–1.9668	0.0011–0.0027	0.0031–0.0111	4	1.7693–1.7699	0.0009–0.0017	0.012
	7	4-98 (1.6)	1.9661–1.9668	0.0011–0.0027	0.0031–0.0111	4	1.7693–1.7699	0.0009–0.0017	0.012
1988	5	4-98 (1.6)	1.9661–1.9668	0.0011–0.0027	0.0031–0.0111	4	1.7693–1.7699	0.0009–0.0017	0.012
	7	4-98 (1.6)	1.9661–1.9668	0.0011–0.0027	0.0031–0.0111	4	1.7693–1.7699	0.0009–0.0017	0.012
1989-90	5	4-98 (1.6)	1.9661–1.9668	0.0011–0.0027	0.0031–0.0111	4	1.7693–1.7699	0.0009–0.0017	0.012
	7	4-98 (1.6)	1.9661–1.9668	0.0011–0.0027	0.0031–0.0111	4	1.7693–1.7699	0.0009–0.0017	0.012

VALVE SPECIFICATIONS

Year	VIN	No. Cylinder Displacement cu. in. (liter)	Seat Angle (deg.)	Face Angle (deg.)	Spring Test Pressure (lbs.)	Spring Installed Height (in.)	Stem-to-Guide Clearance (in.)		Stem Diameter (in.)	
							Intake	Exhaust	Intake	Exhaust
1987	5	4-98 (1.6)	45	45	NA	NA	0.008	0.008	0.2744–0.2750	0.2742–0.2748
	7	4-98 (1.6)	45	45	NA	NA	0.008	0.008	0.2744–0.2750	0.2742–0.2748
1988	5	4-98 (1.6)	45	45	NA	NA	0.008	0.008	0.2744–0.2750	0.2742–0.2748
	7	4-98 (1.6)	45	45	NA	NA	0.008	0.008	0.2744–0.2750	0.2742–0.2748
1989-90	5	4-98 (1.6)	45	45	NA	NA	0.008	0.008	0.2744–0.2750	0.2742–0.2748
	7	4-98 (1.6)	45	45	NA	NA	0.008	0.008	0.2744–0.2750	0.2742–0.2748

NA Not available

PISTON AND RING SPECIFICATIONS

All measurments are given in inches.

Year	VIN	No. Cylinder Displacement cu. in. (liter)	Piston Clearance	Ring Gap			Ring Side Clearance		
				Top Compression	Bottom Compression	Oil Control	Top Compression	Bottom Compression	Oil Control
1987	5	4-98 (1.6)	0.006	0.006–0.012	0.006–0.012	0.008–0.028	0.001–0.003	0.001–0.003	Snug
	7	4-98 (1.6)	0.006	0.006–0.012	0.006–0.012	0.008–0.028	0.001–0.003	0.001–0.003	Snug

PISTON AND RING SPECIFICATIONS
All measurments are given in inches.

Year	VIN	No. Cylinder Displacement cu. in. (liter)	Piston Clearance	Ring Gap			Ring Side Clearance		
				Top Compression	Bottom Compression	Oil Control	Top Compression	Bottom Compression	Oil Control
1988	5	4-98 (1.6)	0.006	0.006–0.012	0.006–0.012	0.008–0.028	0.001–0.003	0.001–0.003	Snug
	7	4-98 (1.6)	0.006	0.006–0.012	0.006–0.012	0.008–0.028	0.001–0.003	0.001–0.003	Snug
1989-90	5	4-98 (1.6)	0.006	0.006–0.012	0.006–0.012	0.008–0.028	0.001–0.003	0.001–0.003	Snug
	7	4-98 (1.6)	0.006	0.006–0.012	0.006–0.012	0.008–0.028	0.001–0.003	0.001–0.003	Snug

TORQUE SPECIFICATIONS
All readings in ft. lbs.

Year	VIN	No. Cylinder Displacement cu. in. (liter)	Cylinder Head Bolts①	Main Bearing Bolts①	Rod Bearing Nuts	Crankshaft Pulley Bolts	Flywheel Bolts	Manifold		Spark Plugs
								Intake	Exhaust	
1987	5	4-98 (1.6)	56–60	40–43	37–41	71–76	71–76	14–19	12–20	11–17
	7	4-98 (1.6)	56–60	40–43	37–41	71–76	71–76	14–19	12–20	11–17
1988	5	4-98 (1.6)	56–60	40–43	37–41	71–76	71–76	14–19	12–20	11–17
	7	4-98 (1.6)	56–60	40–43	37–41	71–76	71–76	14–19	12–20	11–17
1989-90	5	4-98 (1.6)	56–60	40–43	37–41	71–76	71–76	14–19	12–20	11–17
	7	4-98 (1.6)	56–60	40–43	37–41	71–76	71–76	14–19	12–20	11–17

① Using 2 steps

WHEEL ALIGNMENT

Year	Model		Caster		Camber		Toe-in (in.)	Steering Axis Inclination (deg.)
			Range (deg.)	Preferred Setting (deg.)	Range (deg.)	Preferred Setting (deg.)		
1987	Tracer	Front	$5/6$P–$2^2/3$P	$1^7/12$P	$1/20$P–$1^{11}/20$P	$12/15$P	0.04N–0.20P	—
		Rear	—	—	$3/4$N–$3/4$P①	0	0–0.16	—
1988	Tracer	Front	$5/6$P–$2^2/3$P	$1^7/12$P	$1/20$P–$1^{11}/20$P	$12/15$P	0.04N–0.20P	—
		Rear	—	—	$3/4$N–$3/4$P①	0	0–0.16	—
1989-90	Tracer	Front	$5/6$P–$2^2/3$P	$1^7/12$P	$1/20$P–$1^{11}/20$P	$12/15$P	0.04N–0.20P	—
		Rear	—	—	$3/4$N–$3/4$P①	0	0–0.16	—

① Not adjustable

ELECTRICAL

NOTE: Disconnecting the negative battery cable on some vehicles may interfere with the functions of the on board computer systems and may require the computer to undergo a relearning process, once the negative battery cable is reconnected.

For testing and overhaul procedures on starters, alternators and voltage regulators, refer to Unit Repair Section.

Charging System

ALTERNATOR

Removal and Installation
1. Disconnect the negative battery cable.
2. Label and disconnect each alternator wiring connector.
3. Remove the alternator-to-adjusting bracket bolt. Loosen the alternator through bolt and allow it to pivot. Shift the alternator toward the block and remove the drive belt.
4. Remove the through bolt and the alternator.
5. To install, reverse the removal procedures. Torque the alternator through bolt to 27–38 ft. lbs. and the adjusting bracket bolt to 35–45 ft. lbs. Start the engine and check the operation.

VOLTAGE REGULATOR

The voltage regulator is a component of the alternator and cannot be adjusted. If the voltage regulator becomes faulty, it must be replaced.

Removal and Installation
1. Disconnect the negative battery cable.
2. Remove the alternator.
3. Remove the nut and terminal insulator.
4. Remove the nuts and the end cover.
5. Remove the screws, brush holder and IC regulator.
6. Using a soldering iron, separate the stator leads from the brush holder/regulator assembly.
7. To install, solder the leads onto the brush holder/regulator assembly and reverse the removal procedures.

BELT TENSION

Deflection Method
The belt tension adjusted by moving the alternator within the range of the slotted bracket. Check the belt tension every 12 months or 10,000 miles. Push in on the drive belt about midway between the water pump and alternator pulleys. Belt deflection should be 0.31–0.35 in. (new) or 0.35–0.39 in. (used).
1. Loosen the adjustment nut and bolt in the slotted bracket. Slightly loosen the pivot bolt.
2. Pull (don't pry) the component outward to increase tension. Push inward to reduce tension. Tighten the adjusting nut/bolt and the pivot bolt.
3. Recheck the drive belt tension and readjust (if necessary). Torque the alternator mounting bolt to 27–38 ft. lbs. and the alternator pivot bolt to 14–19 ft. lbs.

Starting System

STARTER

Removal and Installation
1. Disconnect the negative battery cable.

2. Disconnect the electrical connectors from the starter terminals.
3. Remove the starter-to-bracket bolts, the support bracket bolts and the brackets.
4. Remove the starter-to-transaxle bolts and the starter from the vehicle.
5. To install, reverse the removal procedures. Torque the starter-to-engine bolts to 23–30 ft. lbs. and the support bracket through bolt to 54–71 inch lbs.

Ignition System

DISTRIBUTOR

Removal and Installation
TIMING NOT DISTURBED
1. Disconnect the negative battery cable.
2. Remove the distributor cap-to-distributor screws and move the cap (wires attached) aside. Remove the gasket.
3. Disconnect the vacuum hose (carbureted) or hoses (EFI) from the distributor vacuum advance.

NOTE: On the EFI, label the hoses for reinstallation purposes.

4. Disconnect the electrical connector(s) from the distributor; note the wire locations for reinstallation purposes.
5. Mark the relationship of the distributor-to-engine and the rotor-to-distributor housing for reinstallation purposes.
6. Remove the distributor-to-engine hold-down bolts and the distributor from the engine. Remove and discard the O-ring from the distributor.
7. To install, use a new O-ring (lubricate with clean engine oil), align the matchmarks and reverse the removal procedures; be sure to align the distributor with the camshaft dog. Check and/or adjust the engine timing.

TIMING DISTURBED
1. Remove the No. 1 spark plug.
2. Rotate the crankshaft to position the No. 1 piston on the TDC of its compression stroke.

NOTE: To locate the TDC of the compression stroke of the No. 1 piston, hold a finger over the spark plug hole. Rotate the crankshaft until compression is noticed and adjust the crankshaft pulley notch to align the with the 1–3 degree mark on the timing plate.

3. Rotate the rotor to position it with the No. 1 spark plug wire on the distributor cap and reinstall the distributor; be sure to align the distributor with the camshaft dog.
4. To complete the installation, reverse the removal procedures. Check and/or adjust the timing.

IGNITION TIMING

Adjustment
1. Operate the engine until normal operating temperature is reached.
2. Check and/or adjust the idle speed.
3. Turn OFF all of the accessories.
4. Disconnect and plug the vacuum line (carbureted) or lines (EFI) from the distributor vacuum advance.

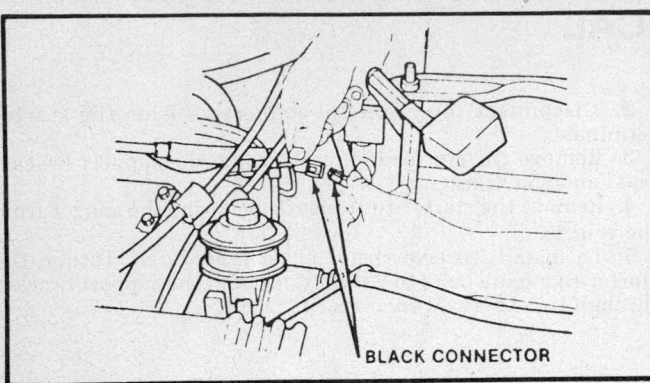

Disconnect the black electrical connector near the distributor when adjusting basic timing—EFI models

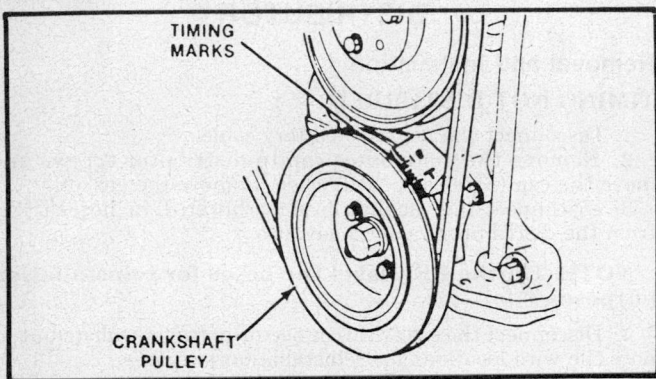

View of the ignition timing marks

NOTE: If using 2 vacuum lines, be sure to mark them for installation purposes.

5. If equipped with EFI, disconnect the black electrical connector at the distributor.

6. Using a timing light, connect it to the engine.

7. Aim the timing light at the crankshaft pulley/timing plate location; the crankshaft pulley notch should align with the 1–3 degree BTDC mark on the timing plate.

8. If necessary to adjust the ignition timing, perform the following procedures:

    a. Loosen the distributor hold-down bolts, just enough so the distributor can be turned.

    b. Rotate the distributor clockwise (to advance) or counterclockwise (to retard) the timing.

    c. With the timing corrected, tighten the distributor hold-down bolts.

    d. Recheck the timing.

9. To complete the operation, reverse the removal procedures. Check and/or adjust the idle speed.

Electrical Controls

STEERING WHEEL

Removal and Installation

1. Disconnect the negative battery cable.

2. From the rear of the steering wheel, remove the cover pad-to-steering wheel screws and the pad.

3. Remove the steering wheel-to-steering column nut.

4. Remove the steering wheel cover pad bracket-to-steering wheel screws and the bracket.

5. Using white paint, matchmark the steering wheel-to-steering column position.

6. Using a steering wheel puller tool, press the steering wheel from the steering column.

7. To install, align the matchmarks and reverse the removal procedures.

HORN SWITCH

Removal and Installation

1. Disconnect the negative battery cable.

2. From the rear of the horn pad, remove the retaining screws.

3. Rotate the pad upward and remove it.

4. Remove the horn switch bracket-to-steering wheel pad screws and the rear horn switch/ground wire-to-steering wheel pad screws.

5. Remove the center horn switch/button-to-steering pad screw, the switch, the button and the springs; be careful not to lose the springs.

6. To install, reverse the removal procedures. Check the operation of the horn.

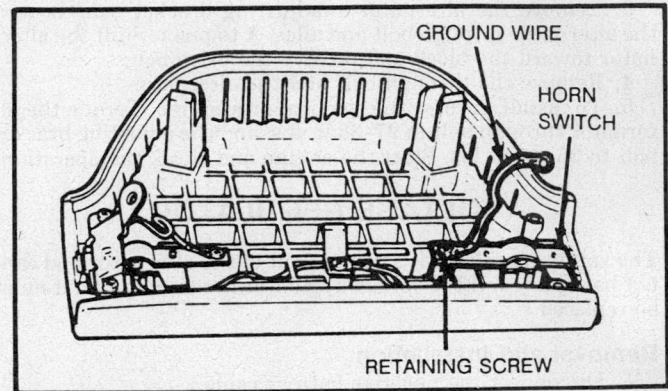

View of the horn switch/pad assembly

IGNITION SWITCH

Removal and Installation

1. Disconnect the negative battery cable.

2. Grasp the black trim ring around the ignition lock switch and pull it straight out.

3. From the driver's side, remove the sound deadening panel and the lap duct cover.

4. If equipped with air conditioning, remove the air conditioning duct assembly-to-access panel support bracket center screw, the access panel support bracket screws and the bracket.

5. From under the steering column, grasp the side window defogger duct ends, pull it outward, while twisting it slightly. From the ignition switch, located under the steering column, disengage the plastic strap connector locking tang and remove the plastic strap.

6. Remove the steering column-to-instrument panel bolts and lower the column.

7. Lift the upper steering column shroud and remove it from the steering column.

8. Remove the ignition switch-to-ignition switch housing screw, grasp the ignition switch body and pull it straight outward.

9. To disengage the electrical connectors from the ignition switch, perform the following procedures:

    a. Disengage the electrical connector locking tang.

    b. Grasp an electrical connector in each hand and pull them straight apart.

NOTE: **Be aware of the electrical connector cavity position for reassembly purposes.**

10. Using a straightened paper clip, disengage the 2 in-key buzzer wires from the 4-terminal connector; the wire colors are red and red wire/orange tracer.

11. To install, wires and connector, perform the following procedures:

　　a. Align the wire end flat sides with the grooved portion of the connector and push the wire inward until the locking tang engages wire end.

　　b. Push the 4-terminal connector into the housing connector until the locking tangs are in place.

　　c. Using electrical tape, wrap it around the ignition switch wires.

12. Install the ignition switch-to-ignition switch housing screw and the plastic snap connector around the ignition switch wiring. Attach the connector peg to the steering column mounting bracket.

13. Using electrical tape, wrap it around the ignition switch wiring and steering column.

14. To complete the installation, reverse the removal procedures. Check the ignition switch operation.

NEUTRAL SAFETY SWITCH

The neutral safety switch is mounted on the top right side of the automatic transaxle. No adjustment is possible on the neutral safety switch. If the engine will not start while the selector lever is in the **P** or **N** positions and the back-up lamps do not operate, check the shift control cable for proper adjustment. If shift cable adjustment is correct, the switch is defective and must be replaced.

Removal and Installation

1. Disconnect the negative battery cable.
2. Raise and support the vehicle safely.
3. Disconnect the electrical connector from the neutral safety switch.
4. Using a wrench, remove the switch from the transaxle.
5. To install, apply sealant to the switch threads and reverse the removal procedures. Torque the neutral safety switch-to-transaxle to 14–19 ft. lbs.

STOPLIGHT SWITCH

The stoplight switch is attached to the top of the brake pedal and controls the brake pedal height.

Removal and Installation

1. Disconnect the negative battery cable.
2. Disconnect the electrical connector from the stoplight switch.
3. Remove the stoplight switch-to-bracket nut and unscrew the switch from the bracket.
4. To install, screw the stoplight into the bracket until the brake pedal height is 8.62–8.82 in.

NOTE: **Brake pedal height is the distance from the cowl to the front center of the brake pedal.**

5. Tighten the switch locknut and install the electrical connector. Test the switch operation.

HEADLAMP SWITCH

The headlight/dimmer switch is a part of the combination switch which is attached to the steering column.

Removal and Installation

1. Disconnect the negative battery cable.

2. Remove the combination switch from the steering column and place it on a work table.

3. Remove the turn signal/headlight switch lever-to-combination switch screws and carefully lift the lever from the combination switch.

4. To install, reverse the removal procedures. Inspect the headlight operation.

COMBINATION SWITCH

The combination switch consists of the turn signal, hazard flasher, wiper/washer and headlight switches and is mounted on the steering column.

Removal and Installation

1. Disconnect the negative battery cable and remove the steering wheel.
2. Remove the steering column covers-to-steering column screws and the covers.
3. Depress the small tang on the electrical harness clip and disconnect the clip; move the electrical harness aside.
4. Loosen the combination switch-to-steering column clamp, slide the switch slightly forward and disconnect the electrical connector from the rear of the combination switch.
5. Remove the combination switch from the steering column.
6. To install, reverse the removal procedures. Check the switch operations.

WINDSHIELD WIPER SWITCH

Removal and Installation

FRONT

The windshield wiper switch is a part of the combination switch.

1. Disconnect the negative battery cable. Remove the combination switch from the steering column and place it on a work table.
2. Remove the turn signal/headlight switch lever-to-combination switch screws and carefully lift the lever from the combina-

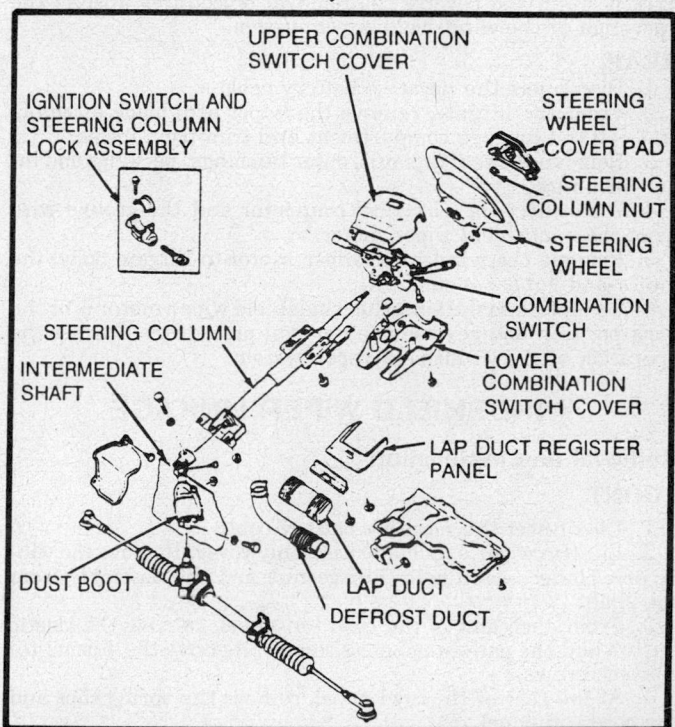

Exploded view of the steering column assembly

tion switch; be careful not to loose the detent balls and springs.

3. Remove the turn signal/headlight switch from the combination switch.

4. Remove the windshield wiper switch-to-combination switch screws and the wiper switch.

NOTE: If removing the windshield wiper switch lever from the combination switch, be careful not to loose the retaining pin, the O-ring, the detent plunger and the spring.

5. To install, reverse the removal procedures. Inspect the operation of the wiper system.

REAR

The rear windshield wiper switch is located on the left side of the instrument panel.

1. Disconnect the negative battery cable.

2. Using a small pry bar, gently pry the switch from the instrument panel and pull it outward.

3. Disconnect the electrical harness connector(s) from the rear of the switch.

4. To install, reverse the removal procedures. Inspect the operation of the rear wiper system.

WINDSHIELD WIPER MOTOR

Removal and Installation

FRONT

1. Disconnect the negative battery cable.

2. From the top left side of the cowl, remove the windshield wiper motor shield-to-chassis plastic retainers and the shield.

3. From the windshield wiper motor shaft, remove the drive link nut and split washer.

4. Disconnect the electrical connector from the windshield wiper motor.

5. Remove the windshield wiper motor-to-cowl bolts, the motor and rubber insulators.

6. To install, make sure the windshield wiper motor is in the park position and reverse the removal procedures. Inspect the operation of the windshield wiper system.

REAR

1. Disconnect the negative battery cable.

2. From the liftgate, remove the wiper arm/blade assembly and pull the luggage compartment end trim from inside.

3. Remove the seal cap, nut, outer bushings, packings and inner bushings.

4. Disconnect the electrical connector and the ground wire from the windshield wiper motor.

5. Remove the windshield wiper motor-to-liftgate bolts, the motor and rubber insulators.

6. To install, make sure the windshield wiper motor is in the park position and reverse the removal procedures. Inspect the operation of the windshield wiper system.

WINDSHIELD WIPER LINKAGE

Removal and Installation

FRONT

1. Disconnect the negative battery cable.

2. Lift the wiper arm/blade assembly cover. Remove the wiper arm/blade assembly-to-linkage nut and the assembly from the shaft.

3. From each end of the cowl top panel, remove the plastic button and the panel-to-chassis screws. Remove the 4 panel-to-chassis screws.

4. At the rear of the cowl panel, remove the spring clips and the cowl top panel.

5. From the washer jets, disconnect the hoses.

6. Remove the transmission link-to-motor nut/washer and disconnect the link.

7. Remove the 4 linkage pivot shaft-to-chassis bolts and the linkage from the vehicle.

8. To install, reverse the removal procedures. Check the operation the wiper assembly.

REAR

1. Using a piece of chalk, mark the position of the wiper blade/arm assembly-to-liftgate position.

2. From the liftgate, remove the seal cap, nut and the wiper arm/blade assembly.

3. To install, align the wiper blade/arm assembly and reverse the removal procedures. Inspect the operation of the windshield wiper system.

Instrument Cluster

Removal and Installation

1. Disconnect the negative battery cable.

2. Remove the steering wheel.

3. Remove the instrument cluster bezel-to-instrument panel screws and bezel.

4. Remove the instrument cluster-to-instrument panel screws.

5. From under the dash, depress the speedometer lock tab and pull the speedometer cable from the instrument cluster.

6. Pull the instrument cluster outward, depress the lock tab (located in the center of the connector) of the 3 electrical harness connectors and pull the connectors from the cluster.

7. To install, reverse the removal procedures. Inspect the operation of the instruments.

SPEEDOMETER

Removal and Installation

1. Disconnect the negative battery cable.

2. Remove the instrument cluster.

3. Remove the lens from the instrument cluster.

4. Remove the indicator lamp overlay from the instrument cluster.

5. Remove the speedometer-to-instrument cluster screws and the speedometer.

6. To install, reverse the removal procedures. Check the operation of the speedometer.

SPEEDOMETER CABLE

The speedometer cable consists of 2 pieces which are joined under the hood.

Removal and Installation

1. Disconnect the negative battery cable.

2. If necessary, remove both sound deadening panels and lap duct panels from under the dash.

3. From behind the instrument panel, depress the speedometer cable-to-speedometer lock tab and pull the cable from the speedometer.

4. Raise the hood and locate the speedometer cable connector. Slide the rubber grommet from the connector. Unscrew the connector and separate the cables from each other.

5. To remove the lower speedometer cable, unscrew it from the transaxle's driven gear and remove it from the vehicle.

6. To remove the upper speedometer cable, slide the grommet from the cable and pull the cable toward the inside of the vehicle.

7. To install, reverse the removal procedures and secure the locking tab onto the speedometer. Check the operation of the speedometer.

Electrical Circuit Protectors

CIRCUIT BREAKERS

A circuit breaker is mounted on the interior fuse panel which is located above the left side kick panel. This breaker controls vehicle electrical system components.

FUSE PANELS

The main fuse panel is located on the right side of the engine compartment.

An electrical equipment panel is located on under the left side of the instrument panel; it is part of the fuse panel and incorporates plug-in relays, a flasher, a buzzer and a circuit breaker.

RPM CONTROL MODULE

The rpm control module is located on the cowl behind the radio.

VARIOUS RELAYS

The door buzzer, entry timer, stoplamp checker and buzzer relays are mounted on the main fuse panel, located on the main fuse panel at the right side of the engine compartment.

TURN SIGNAL/HAZARD FLASHER—The turn signal/hazard flasher is installed on the main fuse panel which located on the right side of the engine compartment.

HORN RELAY—The horn relay is located in the engine compartment on the left inner fender.

A/C CUT-OUT RELAY—Located in the front of the left front shock tower in the engine compartment.

A/C RELAY NO. 1—Located on the left front shock tower in the engine compartment.

A/C RELAY NO. 2—Located on the left front shock tower in the engine compartment.

A/C RELAY NO. 3—Located on the left front shock tower in the engine compartment.

COOLING FAN RELAY—Located in the left front side of the engine compartment, next to the coolant recovery bottle.

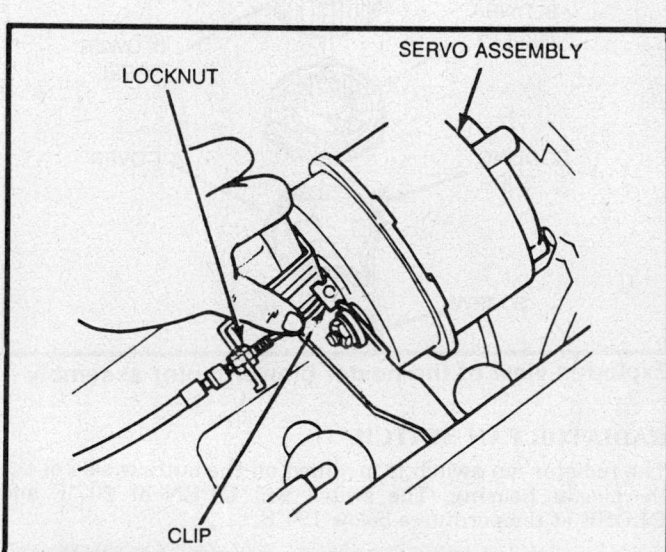
Speed control actuator inner cable adjustment

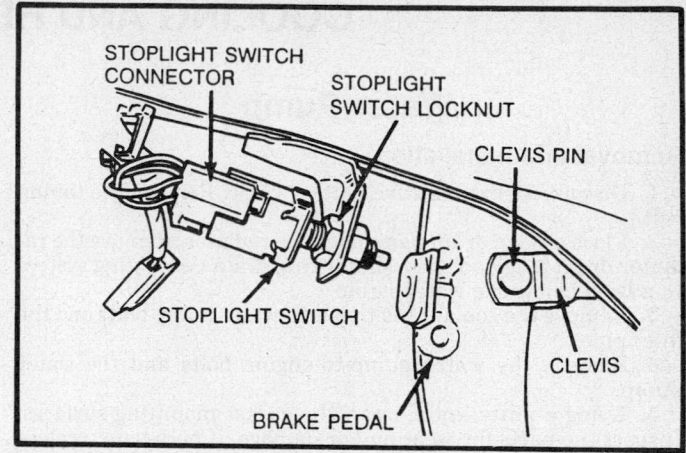
Stoplight switch adjustment for pedal height

DOOR BUZZER RELAY—Located in the electrical equipment panel, above the fuse block.

FUEL PUMP RELAY—Mounted under the center of the instrument panel.

PTC HEATER RELAY—Located in the engine compartment on the inner fender apron, next to the coolant recovery reservoir.

SPEED CONTROLS

Refer to "Chilton's Chassis Electronics Service Manual" for additional coverage.

Adjustment
ACTUATOR INNER CABLE FREE-PLAY

1. With the engine off, remove the clip from the actuator cable and adjust the locknut while pressing down on the cable until free-play is 0.04–0.12 in. (1–3mm).

CLUTCH PEDAL HEIGHT
Pedal height is the distance from the cowl to the center of the clutch pedal pad.

1. Remove the necessary instrument panel components which block access to the clutch pedal.
2. Loosen the clutch pedal locknut.
3. Turn the stop bolt to obtain the correct pedal height of 8.4–8.6 in. Tighten the locknut.
4. If components from the instrument panel were removed, reinstall them.

BRAKE PEDAL HEIGHT

Measure the distance from the center of the brake pedal to lower dash panel. Pedal height must be 8.62–8.82 in. (214.5–219.5mm). If the brake pedal height is not within these specifications, adjustment is necessary.

1. Disconnect the negative battery cable.
2. Adjust the pedal height by adjusting the stop light switch.
3. Disconnect the connector on the stop light switch.
4. Loosen the stop light switch locknut and rotate the switch until the pedal height is 8.62–8.82 in. (214.5–219.5mm).
5. Tighten the switch locknut.
6. Connect the stop light switch connector.
7. Connect the negative battery cable and check stop light operation.

COOLING AND HEATING SYSTEMS

Water Pump

Removal and Installation

1. Disconnect the negative battery cable. Remove the timing belt.
2. Place a clean drain pan under the radiator. Remove the radiator drain plug and the radiator cap; drain the cooling system to a level below the water pump.
3. Remove the coolant inlet pipe-to-water pump bolts and the inlet pipe.
4. Remove the water pump-to-engine bolts and the water pump.
5. Using a putty knife, clean the gasket mounting surfaces. Inspect the parts for wear and/or damage, if necessary, replace the parts.
6. To install, use new gaskets, sealant and reverse the removal procedures. Torque the water pump-to-engine bolts to 14–19 ft. lbs., the water inlet pipe-to-water pump bolts to 14–19 ft. lbs. and the water pump pulley-to-water pump bolts to 11–13 ft. lbs. Refill the cooling system. Start the engine, allow it to reach normal operating temperature and check for leaks.

Electric Cooling Fan

SYSTEM OPERATION

Removal and Installation

1. Disconnect the negative battery cable.
2. Disconnect the fan electrical wiring harnesses from the clamps.
3. Disconnect the electrical connector from the cooling fan.
4. Remove the fan shroud-to-radiator screws and the shroud/fan assembly from the vehicle.
5. Remove the fan from the shroud.
6. To install, reverse the removal procedures. Start the engine, allow it to reach normal operating temperature and the system operation.

Testing

1. Disconnect the negative battery cable. Disconnect the fan electrical connector.
2. Using a 12V DC power supply, connect it to the electrical connector (fan side); the fan should operate.
3. If the fan does not operate, inspect the temperature coolant switch and/or the fan relay.

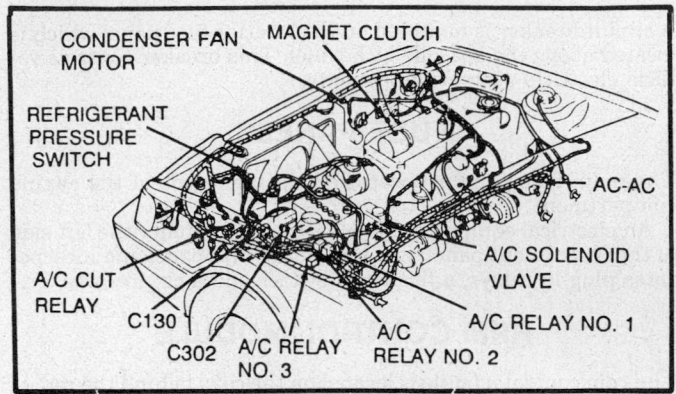

Location of the radiator fan and auxiliary fan components

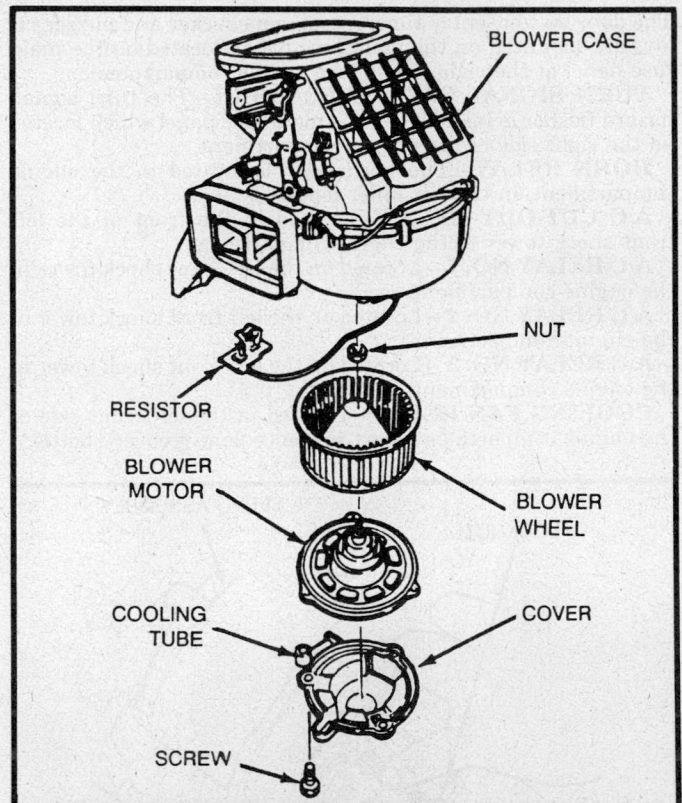

Exploded view of the heater blower motor assembly

RADIATOR FAN SWITCH

The radiator fan switch is mounted on the outflow side of the thermostat housing. The switch will **OPEN** at 207°F and **CLOSE** at temperatures below 194°F.

   NOTE: **The cooling fan will turn ON if a wire is disconnected from the coolant temperature switch when the ignition switch is in the ON position.**

ELECTRIC FAN RELAY

The electric fan relay is located on the front corner of the left fender between the coolant recovery bottle and the horn relay.

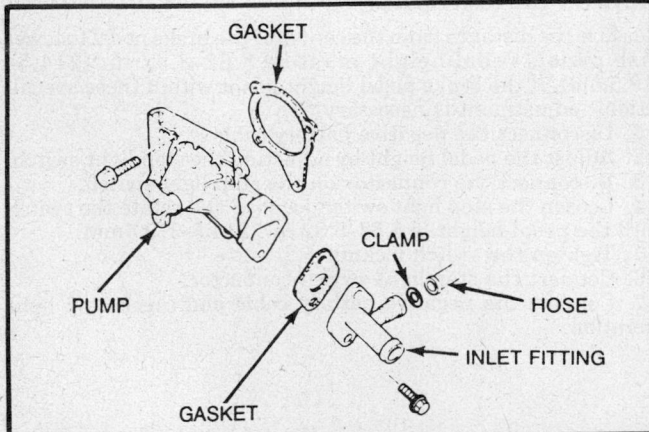

Exploded view of the water pump

Auxiliary Electric Cooling Fan

If equipped with air conditioning, an auxiliary electric cooling fan is located in front of the condenser. When the air conditioning system is turned **ON** and the compressor magnetic clutch is engaged, both fans operate simultaneously.

Testing

Visually check the condenser fan motor integrity (opens, shorts, bad fuses, bad connections). Repair as required. Start the engine, allow it to reach normal operating temperature and inspect the system operation.

Removal and Installation

1. Disconnect the negative battery cable.
2. Remove the front grille.
3. Disconnect the electrical connector from the auxiliary cooling fan.
4. Remove the auxiliary cooling fan mounting bolts and the fan.
5. To install, reverse the removal procedures. Start the engine, turn the air conditioning system **ON** and inspect the fan operation.

Blower Motor

Removal and Installation

1. Disconnect the negative battery cable.
2. From the passenger's side, remove the sound deadening panel.
3. Disconnect the electrical connector from the blower motor assembly.
4. Remove the blower motor-to-blower case screws, the cover, the cooling tube and the motor.
5. Remove the blower wheel-to-motor nut and pull the wheel straight off the motor. Remove the gasket from the motor.
6. To install, reverse the removal procedures. Check the blower motor operation.

Heater Core

Refer to "Chilton's Auto Heating and Air Conditioning Manual" for additional coverage.

Removal and Installation

The heater core is mounted in the heater case inside the vehicle behind the instrument panel.

1. Disconnect the negative battery cable.
2. From under the instrument panel, remove both sound deadening panels and the lap duct register panel.
3. From the blower motor case and heater case, disconnect the 3 air door control cables.
4. From behind the instrument cluster, depress the speedometer lock tab and pull the speedometer cable from the cluster.
5. From behind the instrument cluster, depress the lock tab (located in the center of the connector) of the 3 electrical harness connectors and pull the connectors from the cluster.
6. From under the steering column, remove the lap duct brace-to-instrument panel screws, the brace, the lap duct and the driver's deminster tube.
7. Remove the lower cover-to-steering column screws and the lower cover.

8. Remove the steering column-to-instrument panel bolts and lower the steering column.
9. Remove the glove box-to-instrument panel screws and the glove box.
10. Remove the hood release-to-instrument panel nut and move the release cable aside.
11. Remove the center floor console-to-chassis screws and the cover.
12. From below the radio, remove the lower trim panel-to-instrument panel screws and the lower panel.
13. Using a small pry bar, pry the instrument panel-to-chassis bolt covers from the perimeter of the instrument panel. Remove the instrument panel-to-chassis nuts/bolts. Lift and pull the panel out slightly.
14. Disconnect the electrical connector from the blower motor assembly.
15. From the rear of the radio, disconnect the antenna cable.
16. From the left corner of the instrument panel, disconnect the 3 instrument panel harness connectors and remove the instrument panel.
17. Using a clean drain pan, place it under the radiator, open the radiator drain cock, remove the radiator cap and drain the cooling system to a level below the heater case.
18. Disconnect and plug the heater hoses from the heater case.
19. Remove the defroster tubes-to-heater case push pins and the defroster tubes from the heater case. Remove the main air duct-to-heater case push pins and the main air duct.
20. From under the heater case, remove the lower carpet panel push pins, screw and the panel.
21. From the heater case, disconnect the electrical harness braces and remove the lower brace screws and brace.
22. Remove the heater case-to-chassis nut and bolts. Remove the lower duct-to-heater case push pins and lower duct. Remove the heater case by pulling it straight out; be careful not to damage the extension tubes.
23. Remove the heater core cover-to-heater case screws and the cover. Remove the tube braces and pull the heater core straight out.
24. Remove the outlet extension tube clip and tube. Loosen the inlet extension tube clamp and the extension tube.
25. To install, use a new O-ring (outlet extension tube) and reverse the removal procedures. Refill the cooling system. Start the engine, allow it to reach normal operating temperature and turn the heater control to **FULL HEAT**. Inspect the system for leakage and operations.

TEMPERATURE CONTROL PANEL

Removal and Installation

1. Disconnect the negative battery cable.
2. Remove the ash tray.
3. Remove the facia panel-to-dash screws, pull the facia outward and move it aside.
4. Pull the blower switch knob straight outward.
5. Remove the blower switch-to-control panel screws.
6. Remove both sound deadening panels.
7. From the air control doors, remove the 3 heater control cables.

NOTE: When removing the control panel, be sure to note the routing of the control cables.

8. Remove the heater control panel-to-dash screws and pull the panel outward.
9. To install, reverse the removal procedures. Adjust the heater control cables. Inspect the operation of the heater control assembly.

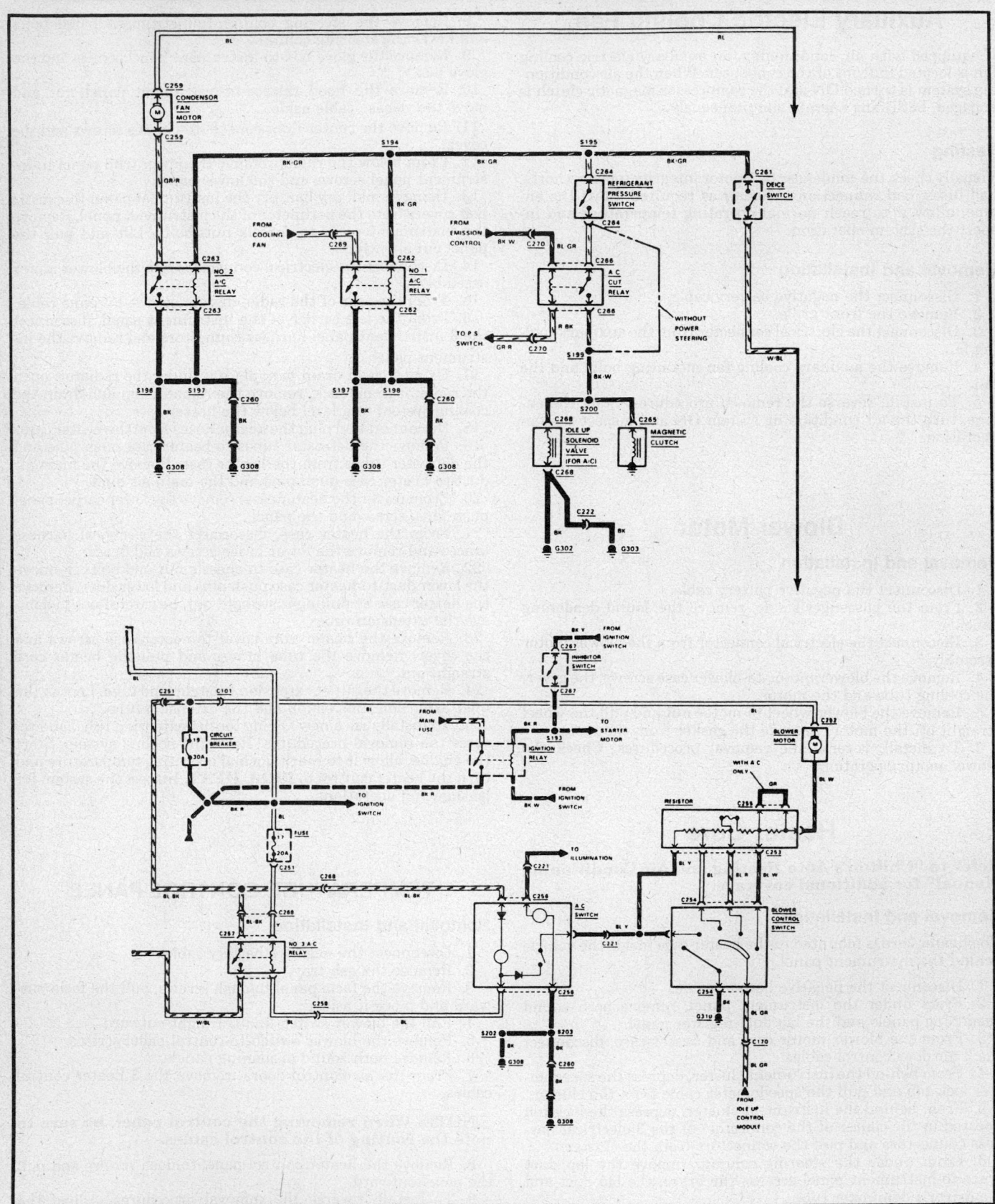

Schematic of the radiator fan and auxiliary fan

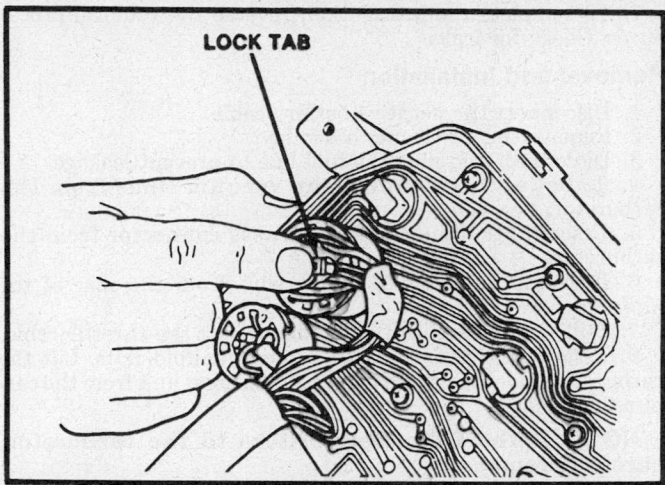

Depressing the electrical connector lock tab located at the rear of the Instrument cluster

BLOWER SWITCH

Removal and Installation

1. Disconnect the negative battery cable.
2. Remove the ash tray.
3. Remove the facia panel-to-dash screws, pull the appearance cover outward and move it aside.
4. Pull the blower switch knob straight outward.
5. Remove the blower switch-to-control panel screws.
6. Remove the blower switch-to-dash screws.
7. Remove the glove box-to-dash screws and the glove box.
8. Remove the glove box upper panel/latch assembly-to-dash screws and the upper panel/latch assembly.
9. Reaching behind the dash, through the glove box opening, remove the blower switch electrical harness-to-dash brace.
10. Pull the blower switch outward and disconnect the electrical connector.
11. To install, reverse the installation procedures. Check the switch operation.

CARBURETED FUEL SYSTEM

CAUTION

Do not carry an open flame or smoke during fuel pump removal and installation. Have a good supply of rags on hand to clean up any gasoline spillage and dispose of all used rags properly. Remember, gasoline is extremely flammable and can cause serious injury.

Carburetor

IDLE SPEED

Adjustment

NOTE: The idle mixture and timing must be adjusted before the idle speed is adjusted; adjustment must be done with cooling fan inoperative.

1. Place the transaxle in **N** or **P**.
2. Start the engine and allow it to reach normal operating temperature.
3. Turn **OFF** all light and accessories.
4. Using a tachometer, install it to the engine.
5. Check the idle speed; if necessary, to adjust the idle speed, turn the idle speed screw at the base of the carburetor.
6. If equipped with a manual transaxle, adjust the dashpot.

DASHPOT

Removal and Installation

1. Operate the engine until normal operating temperature is reached.
2. Using a tachometer, install it to the engine.
3. Loosen the dashpot jam nut.
4. Increase the engine speed to 3000 rpm and slowly reduce the engine speed to 2400–2600 rpm.
5. Screw in the dashpot until contact is made with the carburetor linkage and tighten the jam nut.

IDLE MIXTURE

The carburetor is equipped with a non-tamperable feature: A roll pin blocks the entry to the idle mixture screw and cannot be driven downward.

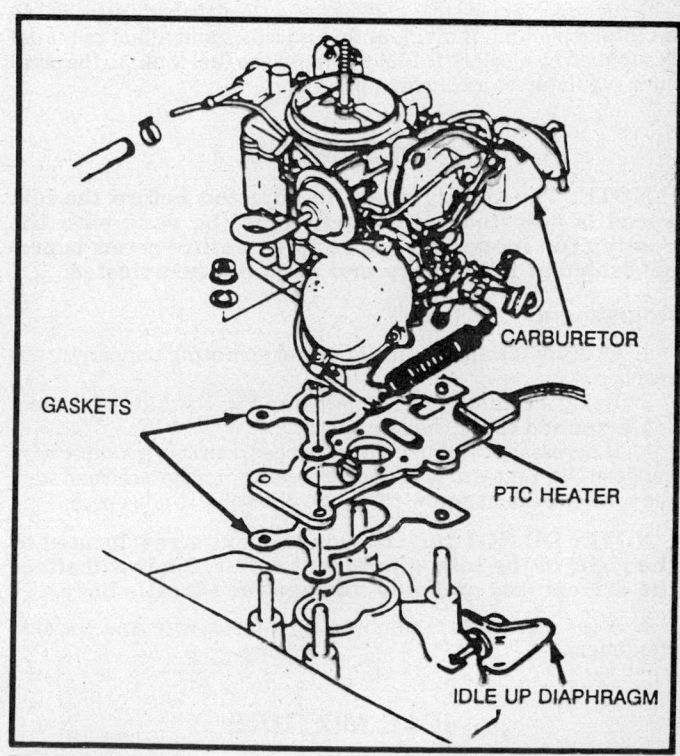

Exploded view of the carburetor and base components

Adjustment

1. To remove the roll pin from the carburetor's idle mixture screw, perform the following procedures.
   a. Remove the carburetor.
   b. Invert the carburetor.
   c. Using a pin punch and a hammer, drive the roll pin toward the top of the carburetor.
   d. Using new gaskets, reinstall the carburetor and the air filter (secure the wing nut).
2. At the air filter housing, disconnect air injection hoses; plug the front air injection hose. Using an Exhaust Gas Analyzer tool, install and seal the probe into the rear air injection hose to prevent leakage.
3. Start the engine and allow it to reach normal operating temperature.
4. Turn the idle mixture screw to obtain a carbon monoxide (CO) reading of 1.5–2.5%.
5. Adjust the idle speed.
6. When the idle speed and idle mixture are balanced, perform the following procedures:
   a. Remove the air cleaner housing.
   b. Using a hammer and a punch, install the roll pin to block the idle mixture screw.

7. To complete the installation, reverse the removal procedures. Check for leaks.

Removal and Installation

1. Disconnect the negative battery cable.
2. Remove the air cleaner assembly.
3. Disconnect and plug the fuel line to prevent leakage.
4. Label and disconnect the vacuum lines from the carburetor.
5. Disconnect the electrical harness connector from the carburetor.
6. Disconnect the choke heater wire from the rear of the alternator.
7. Fully open the throttle and disconnect the throttle cable.
8. Remove the carburetor-to-intake manifold nuts. Lift the carburetor and remove the idle-up diaphragm link from the carburetor linkage.

NOTE: If the PTC heater sticks to the carburetor, carefully remove it.

9. Clean the gasket mounting surfaces.
10. To install, use new gaskets and reverse the removal procedures. Start the engine. Check and/or adjust the idle mixture and idle speed. Check the fuel float level.

FUEL INJECTION SYSTEM

Refer to "Chilton's Electronic Engine Controls Manual" for additional coverage.

Description

The fuel injection system consists of a throttle body attached to an intake plenum, individual fuel injectors and a fuel rail. Fuel is supplied by an electric fuel pump (in the fuel tank) to the pressure regulator at a constant pressure.

IDLE SPEED

NOTE: The timing must be adjusted before the idle speed is adjusted; adjustment must be done with the cooling fan inoperative. The idle mixture screw is preset/sealed at the factory and must not be adjusted.

Adjustment

1. Operate the engine until normal operating temperature is reached.
2. Using a tachometer, connect it to Pin 1 (white) of the test connector and check the idle speed.
3. If necessary to adjust the idle speed, connect a jumper wire between Pin 1 (green) of the test connector and ground and turn the air adjustment screw to obtain the correct idle speed.

NOTE: DO NOT turn the adjustment screw located to the right of the idle adjustment screw, for it will affect the driveability and may damage the throttle body.

4. After adjustment, remove the jumper wire and the test equipment.

IDLE MIXTURE

NOTE: Idle mixture is adjusted at the factory and should not be attempted.

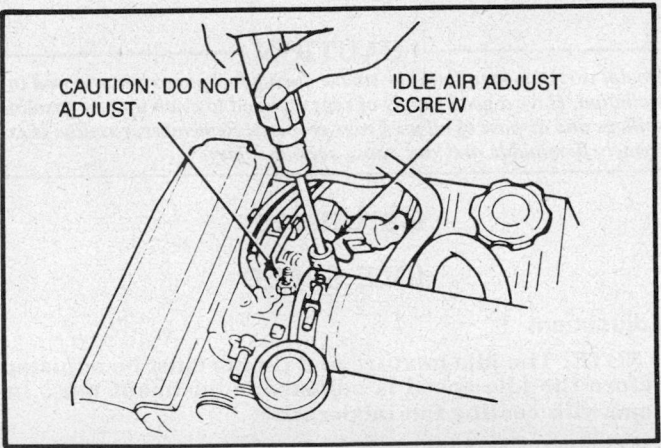

Adjusting the idle speed by turning the idle air adjusting screw—EFI engines

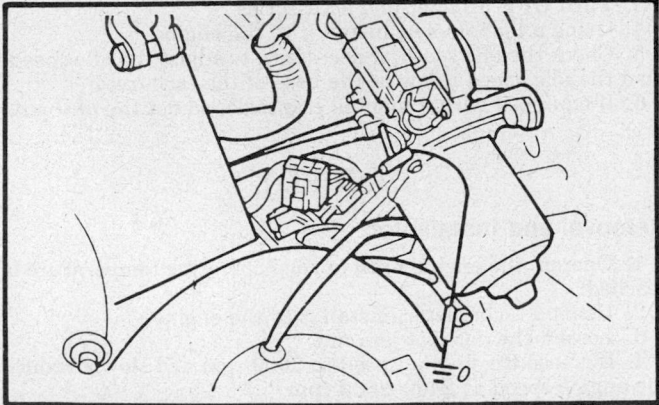

View of the jumper wire connected to the test connector—EFI engines

FUEL SYSTEM PRESSURE RELIEF

Procedure

The fuel system remains under high pressure, even when the engine is not in operation.

VANE FLOW AIR METER METHOD

1. Start the engine and disconnect the vane air flow meter.
2. When the engine stalls, turn the ignition switch **OFF**.
3. Reconnect the vane air flow meter.

FUEL PUMP CONNECTOR METHOD

1. Remove the back seat cushion.
2. Operate the engine.
3. Disconnect the fuel pump electrical connector.
4. Allow the engine to stall.
5. Turn the ignition switch **OFF** and reconnect the electrical connector.

Fuel Pump

The electric fuel pump is located in the fuel tank.

A fuel pump shut-off switch (inertia switch) is connected in series with the fuel pump switch circuit; the inertia switch will open and the fuel pump will cease operation in the event of the roll-over or a major collision. The switch must be pushed to activate the fuel pump.

On the 3 or 5 door vehicles, the inertia switch is located on the left side of the spare tire well. On the station wagon, the inertia switch is located inside the axle jack storage compartment at the right rear side.

Removal and Installation

1. Relieve the fuel pressure. Disconnect the negative battery cable.
2. Disconnect the fuel lines from the fuel sending unit at the fuel tank.
3. Remove the fuel sending unit-to-fuel tank bolts and the sending unit.
4. Remove the fuel filter from the fuel pump.
5. Disconnect the electrical connectors from the fuel pump.
6. Remove the retaining clamp screw, the outlet hose clamp and the fuel pump.
7. To install, use a new sending unit-to-fuel tank gasket and reverse the removal procedures.

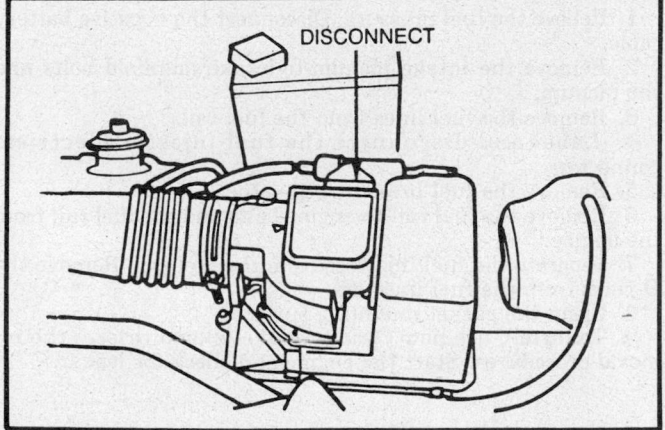

View of the vane air flow meter with electrical connector—EFI system

TIMING SENSORS

AIR CHARGE TEMPERATURE SENSOR (ACT)—Located inside the vane air flow meter.

COOLANT TEMPERATURE SENSOR (ECT)—Mounted into the intake manifold coolant passage.

EXHAUST GAS OXYGEN SENSOR (EGO)—Mounted into the exhaust manifold.

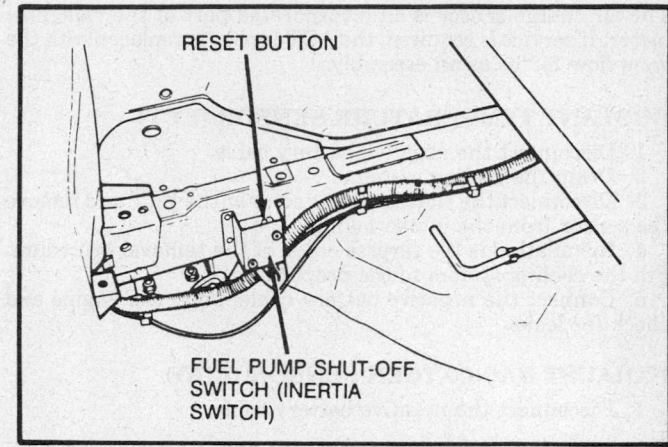

View of the fuel pump inertia switch—EFI equipped 3 and 5 door models

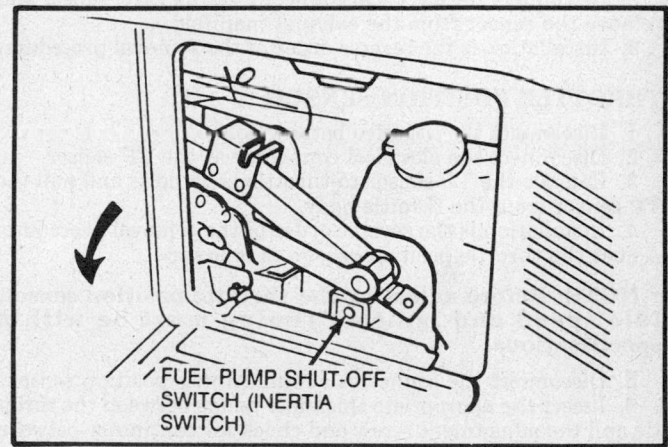

View of the fuel pump inertia switch—EFI equipped station wagon models

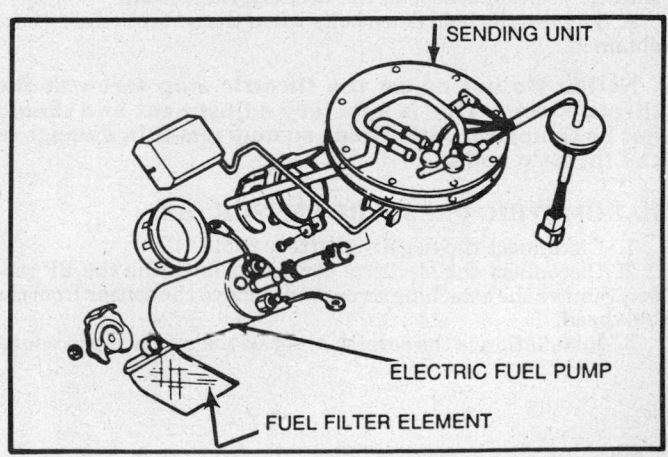

Exploded view of the electric fuel pump—EFI models

THROTTLE POSITION SENSOR (TP)—Located on the side of the throttle body.

BAROMETRIC PRESSURE SENSOR (BP)—Located on the bulkhead at the right rear portion of the engine compartment.

Removal and Installation

AIR CHARGE TEMPERATURE SENSOR (ACT)

The air charge sensor is an incorporated part of the vane flow meter. If service is required, the ACT sensor is replaced with the vane flow meter as an assembly.

COOLANT TEMPERATURE SENSOR (ECT)

1. Disconnect the negative battery cable.
2. Drain the cooling system.
3. Disconnect the electrical connector at the ECT and remove the sensor from the intake manifold.
4. Installation is the reverse order of the removal procedure. Fill the cooling system to the proper level.
5. Connect the negative battery cable, start the engine and check for leaks.

EXHAUST GAS OXYGEN SENSOR (EGO)

1. Disconnect the negative battery cable.

NOTE: Allow the engine to cool sufficiently before attempting to remove the oxygen sensor.

2. Disconnect the electrical connector at the EGO sensor and remove the sensor from the exhaust manifold.
3. Installation is the reverse order of the removal procedure.

THROTTLE POSITION SENSOR

1. Disconnect the negative battery cable.
2. Disconnect the electrical connector at the TP sensor.
3. Remove the TP sensor-to-throttle body bolts and pull the TP sensor from the throttle body.
4. Installation is the reverse order of the removal procedure. Adjust the throttle position sensor as follows:

NOTE: Before adjusting the throttle position sensor, idle speed and ignition timing must be within specifications.

5. Disconnect the connector at the throttle position sensor.
6. Insert the appropriate thickness gauge between the throttle and the adjustment screw and check for continuity between the terminals.
7. Loossen the the TP sensor hold down bolts and rotate the throttle position sensor in the necessary direction.
8. Tighten the hold down bolts when the correct readings are obtained.

NOTE: Do not adjust the throttle stop screw at the throttle lever. This is a factory adjustment and should not be tampered with. Doing so may result in damage to the throttle body.

BAROMETRIC PRESSURE SENSOR (BP)

1. Disconnect the negative battery cable.
2. Disconnect the electrical connector from the the BP sensor, remove the attaching screw and remove the sensor from the bulkhead.
3. Installation is the reverse order of the removal procedure.

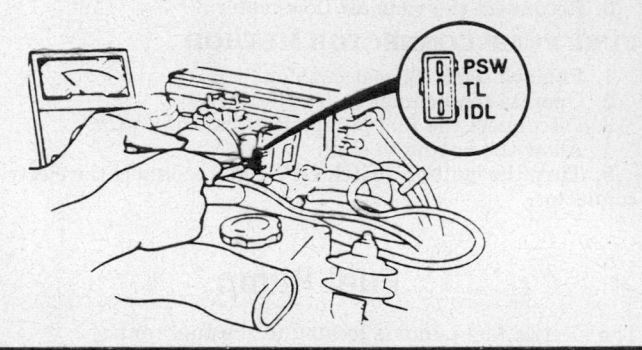

Insert thickness gauge between the throttle adjust screw and stop lever.	Continuity between terminals	
	IDL – TL	PSW – TL
0.02 in (0.5 mm)	Yes	No
0.027 in (0.7 mm)	No	No
Fully open throttle lever	No	Yes

Adjusting the throttle position sensor

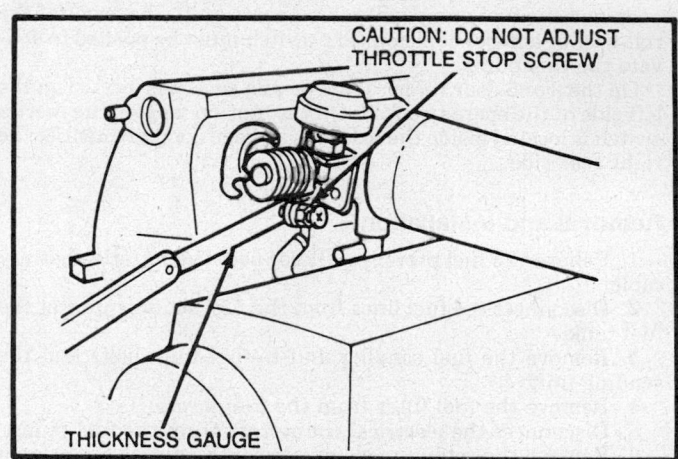

CAUTION: DO NOT ADJUST THROTTLE STOP SCREW

THICKNESS GAUGE

Factory adjustment throttle stop screw

FUEL INJECTOR

Removal and Installation

1. Relieve the fuel pressure. Disconnect the negative battery cable.
2. Remove the intake plenum-to-intake manifold bolts and the plenum.
3. Remove the fuel lines from the fuel rail.
4. Label and disconnect the fuel injector electrical connectors.
5. Remove the fuel pressure regulator.
6. Remove the fuel rail-to-engine bolts and the fuel rail from the engine.
7. Separate the fuel injectors from the fuel rail. Remove the O-rings from the fuel injectors.
8. Clean the gasket mounting surfaces.
9. To install, use new O-rings, gasket(s) and reverse the removal procedures. Start the engine and check for leaks.

EMISSION CONTROL SYSTEMS

Refer to "Chilton's Emission Diagnosis and Service Manual" for additional coverage.

CARBURETED ENGINE

The air injection hoses are connected to the air filter housing and consist of a pair of reed valves which control air flow to the exhaust manifold and the cataylic converter.

Positive Crankcase Ventilation
Evaporative Emission Control
Carbon Canister
Catalytic Converter
Exhaust Gas Recirculation
RPM Control Module
Deceleration Control System
Air Injection System
Temperature Activated Vacuum Valve
Cooling Fan Relay
Inlet Air Temperature Sensor
Rollover/Vent Valve
Anti-Afterburn Valve
Carbon Canister
Barometric Pressure Sensor
Dashpot
Oxygen Sensor
Clutch Switch

Idle Switch
RPM Control Module
Secondary Injection Pipes
Vacuum Delay Valve
Vacuum Switch Valve
Dashpot—Manual Transaxle

FUEL INJECTION

Positive Crankcase Ventilation
Evaporative Emission Control
Catalytic Converter
Exhaust Gas Recirculation
Electronic Control Assembly
Deceleration Control System
Secondary Air Injection System
Temperature Activated Vacuum Valve
Clutch Switch
Fuel Injectors
Cooling Fan Relay
Vacuum Delay Valve
Engine Coolant Temperature Sensor
Oxygen Sensor
Rollover/Vent Valve
Mass Air Flow System

ENGINE

Engine Assembly

NOTE: Disconnecting the negative battery cable on some vehicles may interfere with the functions of the on board computer systems and may require the computer to undergo a relearning process, once the negative battery cable is reconnected.

Removal and Installation

1. Using a scratch awl, matchmark the hood hinges to the hood. Remove the hood-to-hinge bolts and the hood.
2. If equipped with EFI, relieve the fuel pressure by performing the following procedures:
   a. Remove the back seat cushion.
   b. While the engine is operating, disconnect the electrical harness connector from the fuel pump.
   c. When the engine stalls, the fuel pressure will be relieved.
3. Disconnect the cables from the battery; negative cable first. Remove the battery-to-vehicle bolts and the tray.
4. Using a clean drain pan, place it under the radiator. Remove the cooling system expansion tank cap, open the drain cock and drain the cooling system.
5. Drain the engine crankcase and the transaxle; discard the fluids.
6. Remove the air cleaner assembly and the dipstick.
7. Disconnect the electrical connector from the fan. Remove the fan shroud-to-radiator bolts, the fan and the shroud.
8. Disconnect the accelerator cable, the speedometer cable and the speed control cable, if equipped.
9. If equipped with a mechanical fuel pump, place a shop rag under fuel pump to catch the excess fuel. Disconnect and plug the fuel lines.
10. Disconnect the heater hoses and the radiator hoses from the engine.

11. From the power brake booster, disconnect the vacuum hose.
12. Disconnect the idle-up solenoid hoses and the carbon canister hoses.
13. Disconnect the engine ground wire and the electrical harness connectors which will interfere with the engine removal.
14. If equipped with a carburetor, remove the secondary air pipe.
15. Remove the exhaust pipe-to-exhaust manifold bolts and separate the pipe from the manifold.
16. If equipped with air conditioning, remove the compressor from the engine bracket and move it aside.
17. If equipped with power steering, remove the pump from the engine bracket and move it aside; do not disconnect pressure hoses.
18. If equipped with a manual transaxle, disconnect the clutch control cable. Disconnect the shift control cable (automatic) or rod (manual).
19. Raise and support the vehicle safely.
20. Remove the engine splash shield-to-vehicle bolts and the shield. Remove the inner fender panel.
21. To remove the halfshafts from the transaxle, perform the following procedures:
   a. Remove the lower ball joint-to-steering knuckle assembly nut and bolt. Using a medium pry bar, pry the lower ball joint (downward) to separate it from the steering knuckle assembly.
   b. Turn the steering knuckle assembly and pull the halfshaft from the transaxle. If necessary, separate the tie rod end from the steering knuckle.

NOTE: If difficulty is experienced, place a pry bar between the halfshaft/transaxle assembly and pry the halfshaft from the transaxle.

c. With the halfshaft separated, support it on a wire.

22. Using a vertical lifting device, attach it to the engine and support its weight.

23. Remove the engine mount bolts and lift the engine/transaxle assembly from the vehicle. After removal, separate the engine from the transaxle.

24. To install, reverse the removal procedures. Refill the cooling system, the crankcase and the transaxle. Start the engine, allow it to reach normal operating temperature and check for leaks.

Engine Mounts

Removal and Installation

1. Disconnect the negative battery cable.

2. Raise and support the vehicle safely. Drain the cooling system.

3. Disconnect the upper and lower radiator hoses.

4. Position and jack with and block of wood, under the engine.

5. Remove the engine-to-mount bolts and the mount-to-frame bolts.

6. Relieve the pressure from the mount by jacking the engine until the mount can be removed. Remove the mount.

7. Installation is the reverse order of the removal procedure.

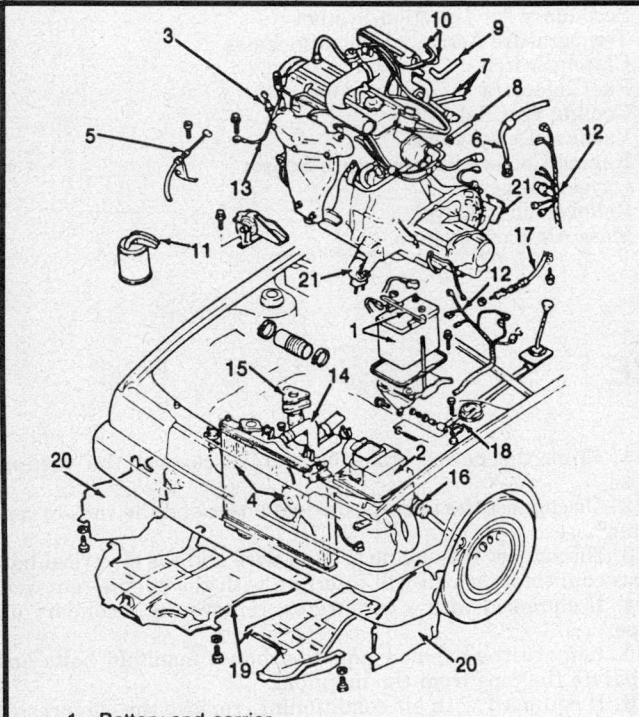

1. Battery and carrier
2. Air cleaner assembly
3. Dipstick
4. Cooling fan and radiator cowling
5. Accelerator cable and cruise control cable (if equipped)
6. Speedometer cable
7. Fuel hoses
8. Heater hoses
9. Brake vacuum hose
10. Idle-up solenoid valve hoses
11. Canister hoses
12. Engine harness connectors
13. Engine ground
14. Upper and lower radiator hose
15. Exhaust pipe
16. Halfshafts
17. Clutch control cable (manual transaxle)
18. Shift control rod
19. Engine splash shield
20. Inner fender panel
21. Engine mounts

Exploded view of the engine/transaxle assembly removal and installation—EFI

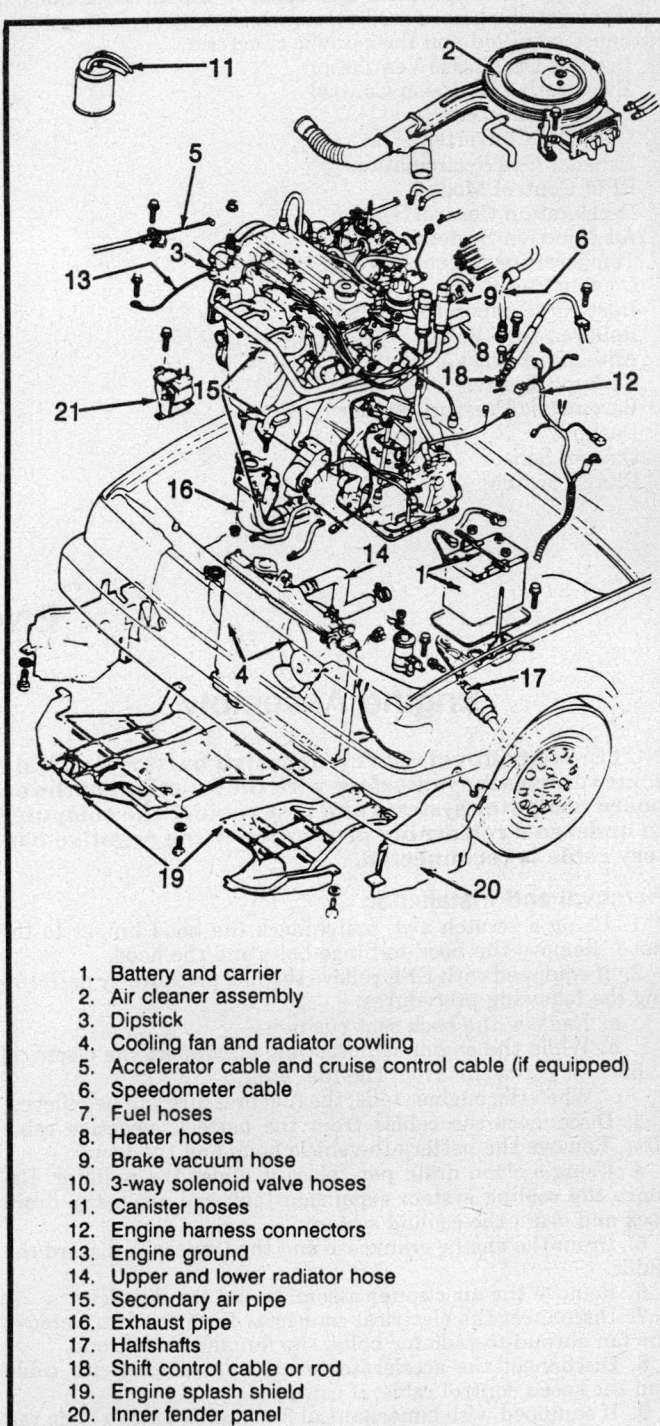

1. Battery and carrier
2. Air cleaner assembly
3. Dipstick
4. Cooling fan and radiator cowling
5. Accelerator cable and cruise control cable (if equipped)
6. Speedometer cable
7. Fuel hoses
8. Heater hoses
9. Brake vacuum hose
10. 3-way solenoid valve hoses
11. Canister hoses
12. Engine harness connectors
13. Engine ground
14. Upper and lower radiator hose
15. Secondary air pipe
16. Exhaust pipe
17. Halfshafts
18. Shift control cable or rod
19. Engine splash shield
20. Inner fender panel
21. Engine mounts

Exploded view of the engine/transaxle assembly removal and installation—carbureted

8. Fill the cooling system to correct level. Connect the negative battery cable.

9. Road test the vehicle and check mounts for looseness.

Intake Manifold

Removal and Installation

1. Disconnect the negative battery cable.

2. Using a clean drain pan, place it under the radiator. Remove the cooling system expansion tank cap, open the drain cock and drain the cooling system.

3. Disconnect the accelerator cable.

4. Label and disconnect all of the necessary wiring and hoses which may interfere with the intake manifold removal.

5. Remove the carburetor if equipped. Remove the throttle body and the intake plenum if equipped.

6. Remove the intake manifold-to-cylinder head bolts, the intake manifold and the gasket.

7. Clean the gasket mounting surfaces. Clean and inspect the parts for damage and/or wear; replace the parts, if necessary.

8. To install, use new gaskets and reverse the removal procedures. Torque the intake manifold-to-cylinder head bolts to 14–19 ft. lbs. Refill the cooling system. Start the engine, allow it to reach normal operating temperature and check for leaks.

Exhaust Manifold

Removal and Installation

1. Disconnect the negative battery cable.

2. If equipped with a carburetor, remove air cleaner and the air injection pipes from the exhaust manifold.

3. If equipped with EFI, disconnect the electrical connector from the oxygen sensor.

4. Remove the exhaust insulators-to-exhaust manifold bolts and the insulators.

5. Remove the exhaust pipe-to-exhaust manifold nuts and separate the exhaust pipe from the manifold.

6. Remove the exhaust manifold-to-cylinder head bolts, the manifold and the gasket.

7. Clean the gasket mounting surfaces. Inspect the parts for damage and replace them if necessary.

8. To install, use new gaskets and reverse the removal procedures. Torque the exhaust manifold-to-cylinder head bolts to 23–34 ft. lbs. and the air injection pipes-to-exhaust manifold bolts to 12–20 ft. lbs. Start the engine and check for exhaust leaks.

Valve System

VALVE ADJUSTMENT

The engine uses hydraulic lifters which operates with zero clearance in the valve train. The rocker arms are non-adjustable. The lifter will compensate for slack in the system but if there is excessive play, the entire system should be checked.

If the valve guides are found to be worn past allowable limits, new ones can be installed.

VALVE ARRANGEMENT

Right Side—I–I–I–I (front-to-rear)

Left Side—E–E–E–E (front-to-rear)

VALVE ROCKER/SHAFT ASSEMBLY

Removal and Installation

1. Disconnect the negative battery cable. Remove the upper front cover.

2. Remove the air cleaner (carbureted) or air duct (EFI).

3. Remove the accelerator and cruise control cables, if equipped from the rocker arm cover.

4. Disconnect the vent hose from the rocker arm cover and the spark plug wires from their clips.

5. Remove the rocker arm cover-to-cylinder head bolts, the cover and the gasket.

6. Remove the rocker arm shaft(s)-to-cylinder head bolts and the rocker arm shaft assemblies.

7. If necessary to separate the rocker arms from the rocker arm shafts, perform the following procedures:

   a. Remove the bolts from the rocker arm(s).

   b. Slide the rocker arm and springs from the shafts.

View of the intake manifold—carbureted engines

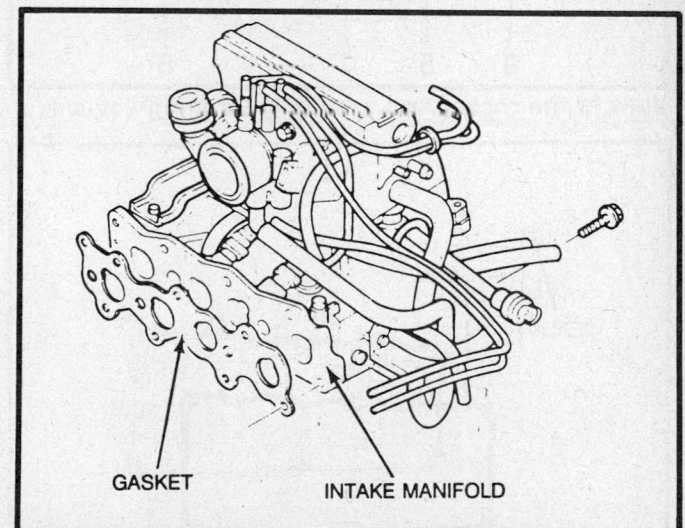

View of the intake manifold—EFI engines

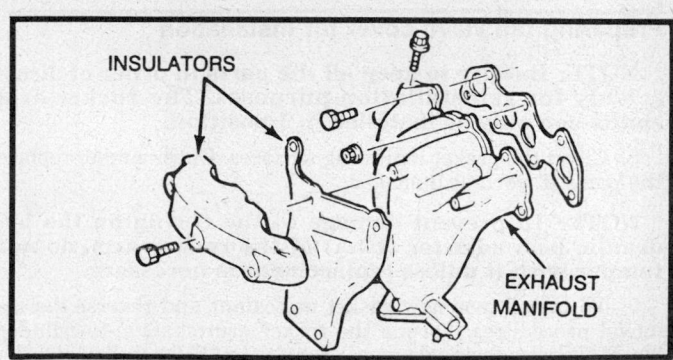

Exploded view of the exhaust manifold

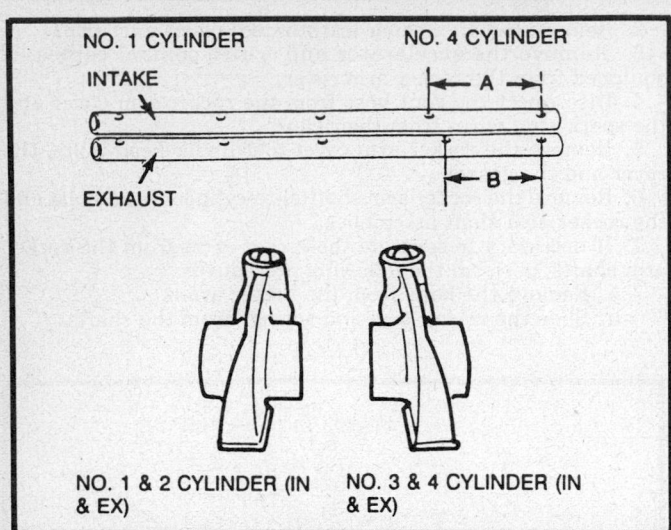

View of the rocker arm shafts and rocker arms

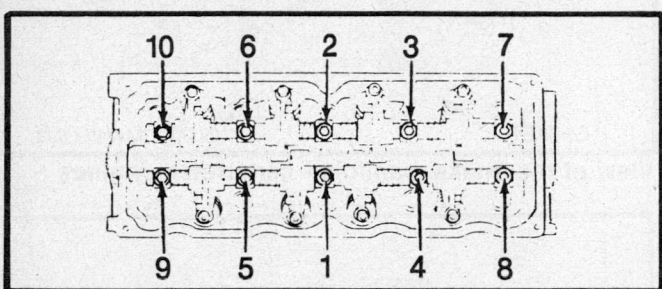

View of the rocker arm assembly torquing sequence

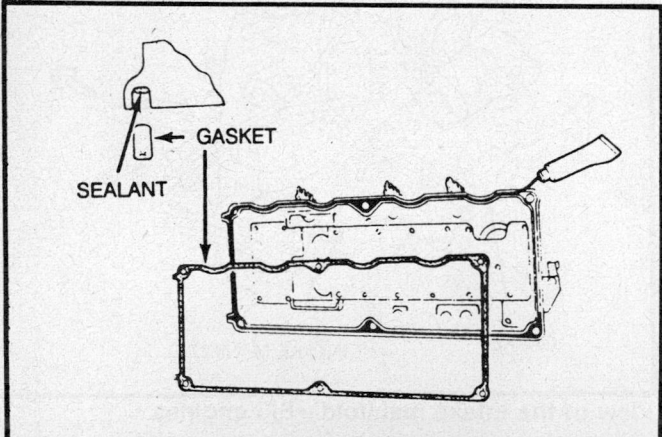

Preparing the valve cover for installation

NOTE: Be sure to keep all the parts in order of disassembly for reinstallation purposes. The rocker arm shafts can only be installed in 1 position.

8. Clean the gasket mounting surfaces. Check and/or replace the parts if worn or damaged.

NOTE: To prevent damage to the O-ring on the hydraulic lash adjuster (HLA) of the rocker arm, do not tamper with it unless replacement is necessary.

9. To install, use new gasket or sealant and reverse the removal procedures. Torque the rocker arm shaft(s)-to-cylinder head (oil holes facing downward) bolts to 16–21 ft. lbs. and the rocker arm cover-to-cylinder head bolts to 44–79 inch lbs.

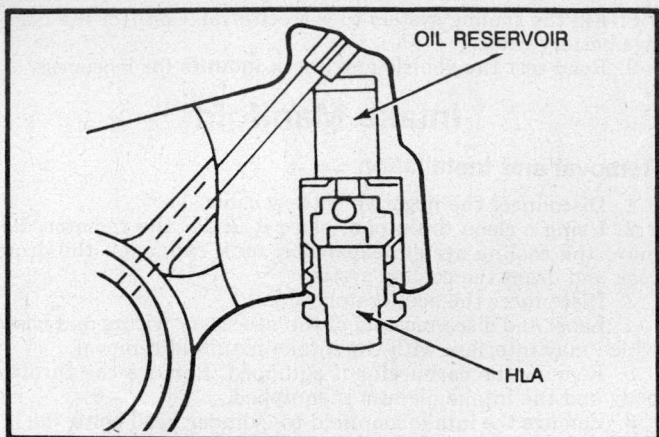

Cross-sectional view of the rocker arm, showing the Hydraulic Lash Adjuster (HLA)

NOTE: When torquing the rocker arm shaft(s)-to-cylinder head bolts, start in the center and move outwards in both directions.

10. To complete the installation, reverse the removal procedures. Start the engine and check for leaks.

Cylinder Head

Removal and Installation

1. Disconnect the negative battery cable.
2. Remove the timing belt and rocker arm assembly.
3. Remove the exhaust manifold.
4. Using a clean drain pan, place it under the radator. Open the drain cock and drain the cooling system.
5. Remove the spark plug wires and the spark plugs.
6. Remove the distributor-to-cylinder head bolts and the distributor from the engine.
7. From the front/rear of the engine, remove the engine lifting eyes. Disconnect the ground wire from the engine.
8. Disconnect the electrical harness connectors which may interfere with the cylinder head removal.
9. Remove the upper radiator hose, the water bypass hose and bracket.
10. Remove the cylinder head-to-engine bolts and the cylinder head.
11. Clean the gasket mounting surfaces. Check and/or replace the damaged or worn parts.
12. Prior to installation, clean the mating surfaces of the cylinder head and cylinder block throughly of any gasket material.
13. Position the cylinder head gasket on the engine block and install the cylinder head.
14. Coat the cylinder head bolts with oil and install them into the head. Tighten the cylinder head bolts in sequence to 50–60 ft. lbs. (75–81 Nm) in 2 steps.
15. Install the water bypass hose and bracket and upper radiator hose.
16. Reconnect the wire harness connectors.
17. Install the front and rear engine lifting eyes to the cylinder head and the engine ground wire.
18. Install the distributor, spark plugs and spark plug wires.
19. Install the intake and exhaust manifolds. Torque the intake manifold-to-cylinder head bolts to 14–19 ft. lbs. and the exhaust manifold-to-cylinder head bolts to 23–34 ft. lbs.
20. Install the rocker arm cover, timing belt and timing belt cover.
21. Install the water pump pulley and drive belts.
22. Fill the cooling system to the correct level.

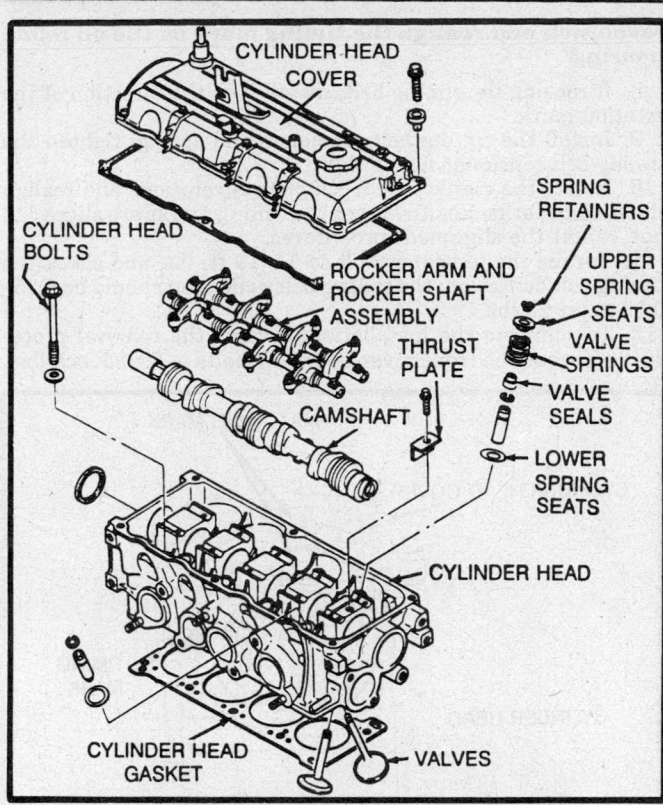

Exploded view of the cylinder head assembly

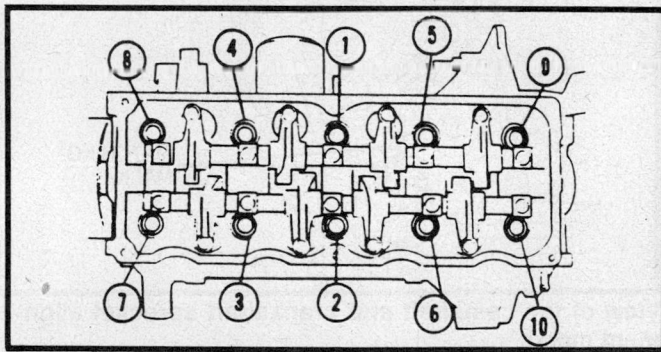

View of the cylinder head torque sequence

23. The remainder of the installation is the reverse order of the removal procedure.
24. Torque the air injection pipes-to-exhaust manifold bolts to 12–20 ft. lbs.
25. Connect the negative battery cable.
26. Start the engine, allow it to reach normal operating temperature and check for leaks.

Camshaft

Removal and Installation

1. Disconnect the negative battery cable.
2. Remove the timing belt and rocker arm assembly.
3. Matchmark the distributor housing-to-cylinder head and rotor-to-distributor housing. Remove the distributor hold-down bolts and the distributor from the rear end of the camshaft.
4. Using a medium pry bar (to prevent the camshaft from turning), remove the camshaft sprocket-to-camshaft bolt and the sprocket.

5. Using a small pry bar, pry the camshaft oil seal from the cylinder.
6. From the rear camshaft bearing journal, remove the thrust plate-to-cylinder head bolt and the thrust plate.
7. Slide the camshaft forward and from the cylinder head; be careful not to damage the journals and/or the lobes.
8. Clean the gasket mounting surfaces. Clean and inspect the parts for damage and/or wear; replace the parts, if necessary.
9. To install, lubricate the parts with clean engine oil, use new gaskets or sealant and reverse the removal procedures. Torque the camshaft thrust plate bolt to 6–9 ft. lbs., the camshaft sprocket-to-camshaft bolt to 36–45 ft. lbs., the distributor hold-down bolt to 14–22 ft. lbs.
10. To complete the installation, reverse the removal procedures. Refill the cooling system. Check the ignition timing. Start the engine, allow it to reach normal operating temperature and check for leaks.

Timing Cover

Removal and Installation
UPPER COVER

1. Disconnect the negative battery cable.
2. Remove the drive belt(s) from the front of the engine.
3. Remove the water pump pulley-to-water pump bolts and the pulley.
4. Remove the upper front cover-to-engine bolts and the cover.
5. Clean the gasket mounting surfaces.
6. To install, use a new gasket and reverse the removal procedures. Torque the front cover-to-engine bolts to 69–95 inch lbs.

LOWER COVER

1. Disconnect the negative battery cable.
2. Remove the drive belt(s) from the front of the engine.
3. Remove the water pump pulley-to-water pump bolts and the pulley.
4. To remove the crankshaft pulley, perform the following procedures:
   a. Remove the right inner fender panel.
   b. Remove the crankshaft pulley-to-crankshaft bolts, outer spacer, outer pulley, inner spacer, inner pulley and baffle.
5. Remove the upper/lower front cover-to-engine bolts and the covers.
6. Clean the gasket mounting surfaces.
7. To install, use a new gasket and reverse the removal procedures. Torque the front cover-to-engine bolts to 69–95 inch lbs., the crankshaft pulley-to-crankshaft bolts to 36–45 ft. lbs. and the water pump pulley-to-water pump bolts to 36–45 ft. lbs.

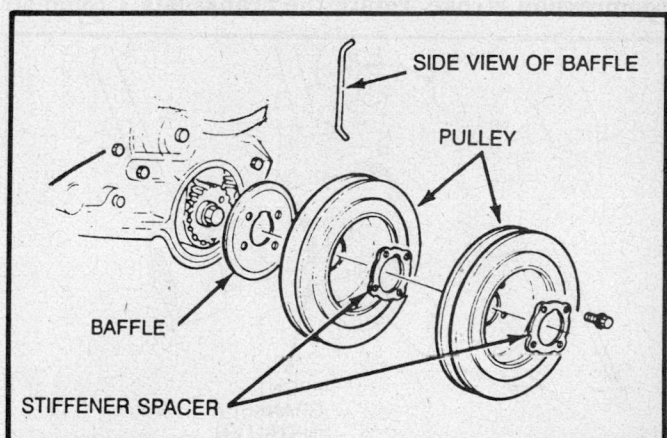

Exploded view of the crankshaft pulley assembly

Front Cover Oil Seal

The front oil seal is actually the front seal of the oil pump.

Removal and Installation

OIL PUMP INSTALLED

1. Disconnect the negative battery cable. Remove the timing belt.
2. Remove the crankshaft sprocket-to-crankshaft bolt, the sprocket and Woodruff key.
3. Using a small pry bar, pry the oil seal from the oil pump housing.
4. Using a clean shop cloth, clean the oil seal bore.
5. Lubricate the new oil seal with clean engine oil.
6. Using a front crankshaft seal installer tool, press the oil seal into the oil pump bore.
7. To complete the installation, check and/or adjust the engine timing and reverse the removal procedures. Start the engine and check for oil seal leaks.

OIL PUMP REMOVED

1. With the oil pump removed.
2. Using a small pry bar, pry the oil seal from the oil pump.
3. Using a clean shop cloth, clean the oil seal bore.
4. Lubricate the new oil seal with clean engine oil.
5. Using a oil seal driver tool, drive the new oil seal into the oil pump bore.
6. To complete the installation, pack the oil pump with petroleum jelly, check and/or adjust the engine timing and reverse the removal procedures. Start the engine and check for oil seal leaks.

Timing Belt

Removal and Installation

1. Disconnect the negative battery cable. Remove the front covers.
2. Remove the No. 1 spark plug. Rotate the crankshaft to position the No. 1 cylinder on the TDC of its compression stroke.
3. Using a piece of chalk, mark the rotation direction on the timing belt.
4. Remove the timing belt tensioner spring, mounting bolt and tensioner.
5. Remove the timing belt.
6. Inspect the timing belt tensioner and sprockets for signs wear or oil contamination, clean or replace the parts.
7. Check and/or align the camshaft and crankshaft sprockets with the cylinder head and oil pump alignment marks.

NOTE: If the No. 1 cylinder is not on the TDC of its compression stroke, rotate the crankshaft 1 complete

revolution and realign the timing mark on the oil pump housing.

8. If reusing the timing belt, install it in the direction of the rotation mark.
9. Install the timing belt tensioner and spring; tighten the timing belt tensioner finger tight.
10. Rotate the crankshaft 2 complete revolutions and realign the timing marks. Reaffirm that the timing marks are aligned, if not, repeat the alignment procedures.
11. Torque the tensioner bolt to 14–19 ft. lbs. and check the timing belt deflection; the timing belt deflection should be 0.35–0.39 in. at 22 lbs.
12. To complete the installation, reverse the removal procedures. Torque the front cover-to-engine bolts to 69–95 inch lbs.,

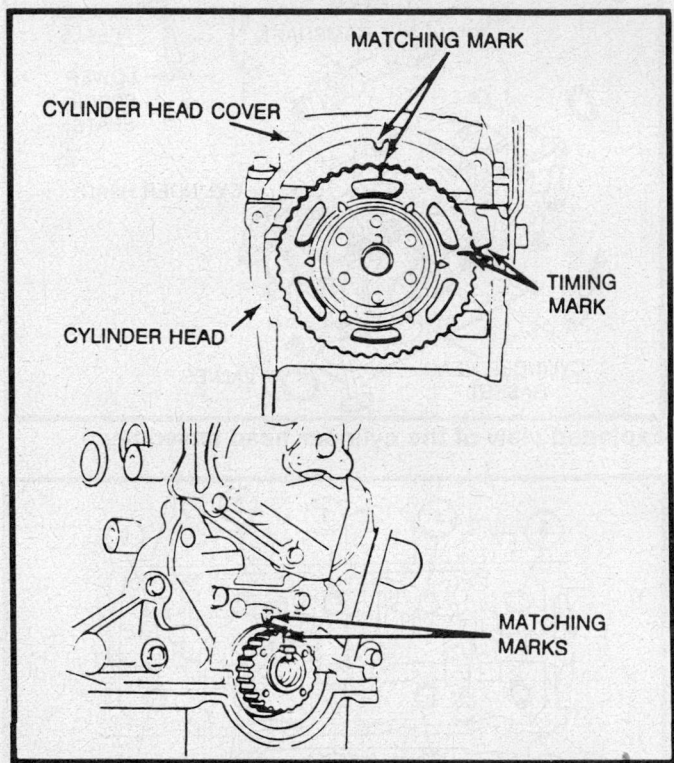

View of the camshaft and crankshaft sprocket alignment marks

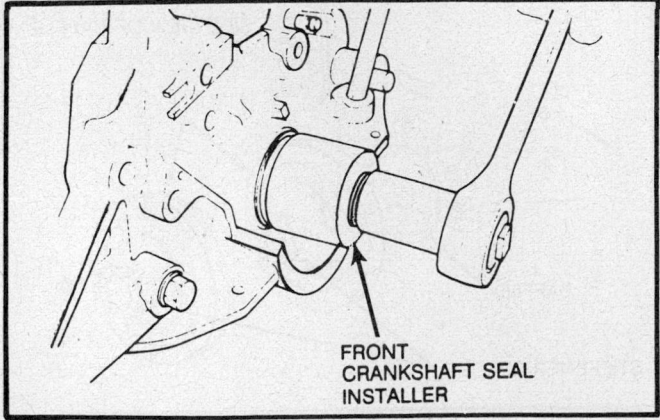

Pressing the new front oil seal into the oil pump

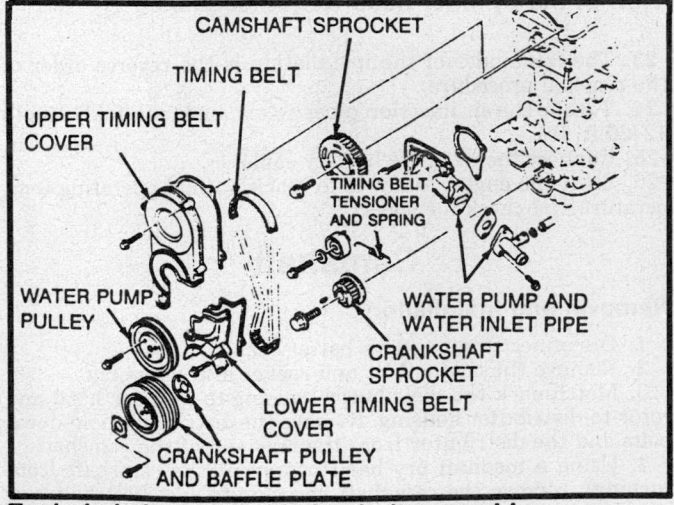

Exploded view of the timing belt assembly

the crankshaft pulley-to-crankshaft bolts to 36–45 ft. lbs. and the water pump pulley-to-water pump bolts to 36–45 ft. lbs. Start the engine and allow it to reach normal operating temperature. Check and/or adjust the ignition timing.

Pistons, Rings and Rod Positioning

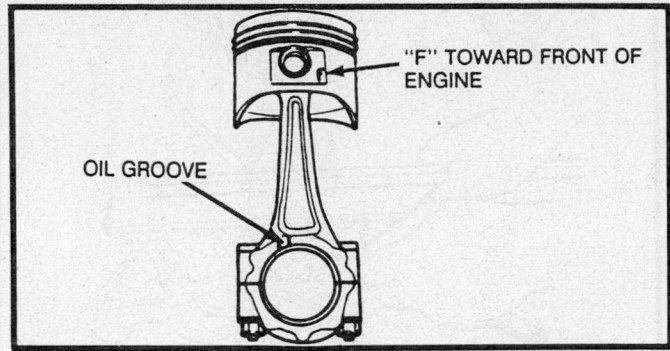

View of the piston and connecting rod positioning

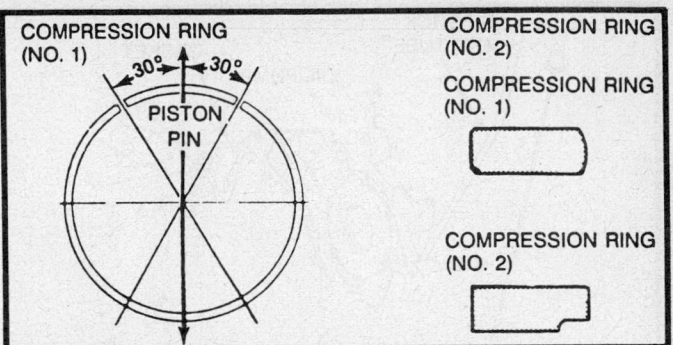

Positioning the compression rings

ENGINE LUBRICATION SYSTEM

Oil Pan

Removal and Installation

1. Disconnect the negative battery cable.
2. Raise and support the vehicle safely.
3. Remove the under engine splash shields and the right front inner fender panel.
4. Using a drain pan, place it under the engine, remove the oil pan plug and drain the crankcase.
5. Remove the flywheel-to-engine support housing bracket and the dust cover from the flywheel housing.
6. Remove the oil pan-to-engine nuts, bolts and stiffeners.

NOTE: If might be necessary to rotate the crankshaft to clear the oil pan.

7. Clean the gasket mounting surfaces. Clean and inspect the parts for damage; replace the parts, it necessary.
8. To install, use new gaskets, sealant (at the mating surfaces) and reverse the removal procedures. Torque the oil pan-to-engine nuts/bolts to 69–79 inch lbs., the flywheel housing dust cover bolts to 13–20 ft. lbs. and the flywheel housing support bracket bolts to 69–86 ft. lbs. Refill the crankcase with clean engine oil. Start the engine and check for leaks.

Oil Pump

The oil pump is located at the front of the engine behind the crankshaft pulley.

Removal and Installation

1. Disconnect the negative battery cable.
2. Remove the timing belt and the oil pan.
3. Remove the crankshaft sprocket-to-crankshaft bolt and the sprocket.
4. Remove the oil pickup tube-to-oil pump bolts and the tube. Remove the dipstick and the dipstick tube.
5. Remove the oil pump-to-engine bolts and the oil pump.
6. Clean the gasket mounting surfaces. Clean and inspect the parts for wear and/or damage, replace the parts (if necessary).

NOTE: When the oil pump is removed, it is recommended to replace the oil seal.

7. Using petroleum jelly, pack the pump cavity.
8. To install, use new gaskets, sealant and reverse the removal procedures. Torque the oil pump-to-engine bolts to 14–19 ft. lbs. Refill the crankcase with clean engine oil. Start the engine and check for leaks.

Inspection

1. With the oil pump disassembled, inspect the body for scoring damage and/or wear; if necessary, discard the worn parts.
2. Using a feeler gauge, inspect the pump body-to-outer gear clearance; it should not be greater than 0.0087 in.
3. Using a feeler gauge, inspect the inner gear tip-to-outer gear clearance; the maximum clearance should be 0.0078 in.
4. Using a feeler gauge, inspect the gears-to-pump housing endplay; the clearance should be no greater than 0.0055 in.

Apply sealant to oil pan-to-engine mating surfaces

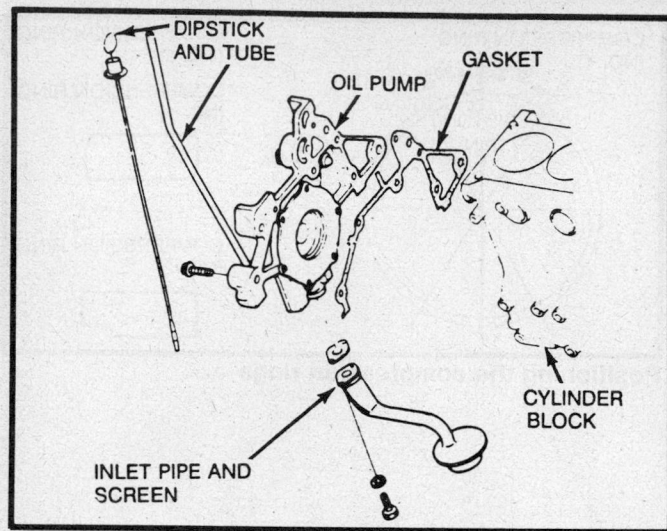

Exploded view of the oil pump assembly

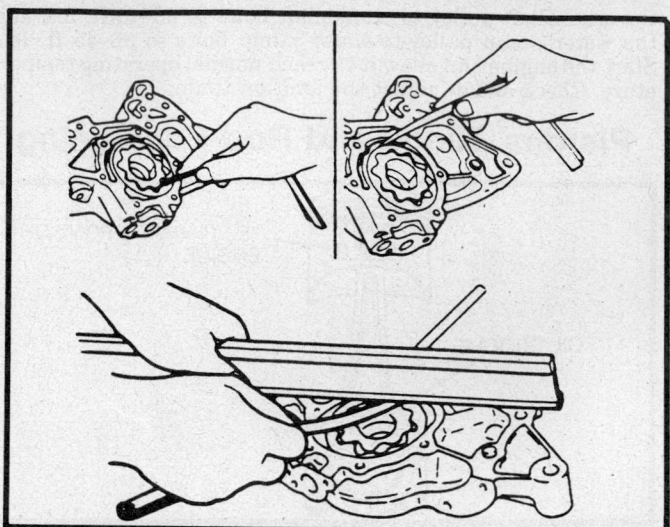

Using feeler gauges to inspect the oil pump components

NOTE: If the above measurements are not within limits, replace the necessary parts.

5. Be sure to clean the relief valve, the screen and the pick-up tube.

Rear Main Oil Seal

Removal and Installation

RETAINER REMOVED

1. Disconnect the negative battery cable. Raise and support the vehicle safely. Remove the transaxle.
2. If equipped with a manual transaxle, perform the following procedures:
   a. Matchmark the clutch assembly-to-flywheel.
   b. Remove the pressure plate-to-flywheel bolts (evenly) a little at a time and the clutch assembly.
3. Remove the flywheel-to-crankshaft bolts, the flywheel and the spacer plates (automatic transaxle).
4. If necessary, remove the rear engine plate-to-engine bolts and the plate.
5. Remove the rear oil seal retainer-to-engine bolts, the oil pan-to-rear oil seal retainer bolts and the retainer.
6. Using a pry bar, press the oil seal from the rear oil seal retainer.
7. Clean the gasket mounting surfaces. Using a clean shop cloth, clean the oil seal bore.
8. Using a new oil seal, lubricate it with clean engine oil and press it into the retainer until seats.
9. To install, use new gaskets, sealant and reverse the remove procedures. Torque the flywheel-to-crankshaft bolts to 71–76 ft. lbs. and the transaxle-to-engine bolts to 16–40 ft. lbs. (manual) or 47–66 ft. lbs.

RETAINER INSTALLED

1. Disconnect the negative battery cable. Raise and support the vehicle safely. Remove the transaxle.
2. If equipped with a manual transaxle, perform the following procedures:
   a. Matchmark the clutch assembly-to-flywheel.
   b. Remove the pressure plate-to-flywheel bolts (evenly) a little at a time and the clutch assembly.
3. Remove the flywheel-to-crankshaft bolts, the flywheel and the spacer plates (automatic transaxle).
4. If necessary, remove the rear engine plate-to-engine bolts and the plate.

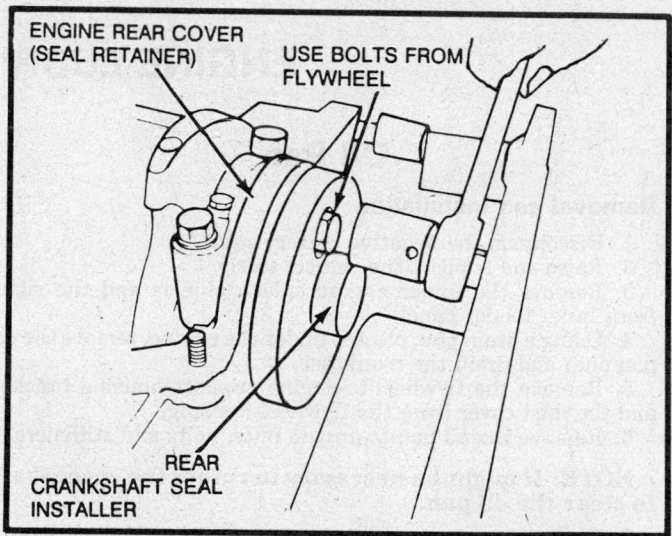

Using the oil seal installation tool to install the rear main oil seal.

5. Using a pry bar, pry the oil seal from the rear oil seal retainer.
6. Using a clean shop cloth, clean the oil seal bore.
7. Lubricate the new seal with clean engine.
8. Using a rear main seal installer tool, press the new oil seal into the retainer until it seats.
9. To complete the installation, reverse the removal procedures. Torque the flywheel-to-crankshaft bolts to 71–76 ft. lbs. and the transaxle-to-engine bolts to 16–40 ft. lbs. (manual) or 47–66 ft. lbs. (automatic).

Connecting Rod and Main Bearing

Replacement

Note the locations of main bearings. The bearing shells are grooved for distribution of oil to the connecting rods. Thrust is taken by half moon washer shaped bearings located on the upper side of the No. 4 bearing; they are designed to ride in recesses in the block.

The original fillet radius (point where the journal meets the crankshaft cheek) must be maintained; otherwise, crankshaft breakage may occur. The fillet radius should be 0.12 in.

Engine bearings are of the precision insert type. They are available for service in standard and various undersizes. Upper and lower bearing inserts may be different. Be careful to align the oil holes; do not obstruct any oil passages. Bearing inserts must not be shimmed. Do not touch the bearing surface of the insert with bare fingers. Skin oil and acids will etch the bearing surface.

NOTE: Bearing failure, other than normal wear, must be investigated carefully. Inspect the crankshaft, connecting rods and the bearing bores. Avoid damage to the crankshaft journals during removal and installation.

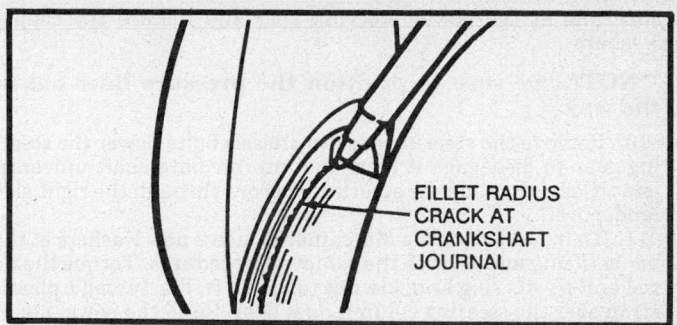

FILLET RADIUS
CRACK AT
CRANKSHAFT
JOURNAL

View of breakage occuring at the crankshaft fillet radius

FRONT SUSPENSION AND STEERING

For front suspension component removal and installation procedures, refer to unit repair section. For steering wheel removal and installation, refer to electrical control section.

Manual Steering Gear

Adjustment

1. Remove the steering gear from the vehicle and place it in a vise.
2. Using an inch lb. Torque wrench and a pinion torque adapter tool place the assembly on the pinion and measure the pinion turning torque; the torque should be 8–11 inch lbs.
3. To adjust the pinion torque, perform the following procedures:
   a. Loosen the adjusting bolt locknut.
   b. Make sure the rack is centered in the housing.
   c. Move the adjusting bolt slightly and recheck the pinion torque.
   d. When the pinion torque of 8–11 inch lbs. is reached, retorque the adjusting bolt locknut to 7–11 ft. lbs.
4. To install the steering gear, reverse the removal procedures. Check the steering operation.

Removal and Installation

1. Disconnect the terminals from the battery (negative cable first) and remove the battery from the vehicle.
2. Raise and support the vehicle safely. Remove the front wheel assemblies.
3. Remove the tie rod end-to-steering knuckle cotter pins and nuts. Using a tie rod separator tool, separate the tie rod end from the steering knuckle.
4. From the right side lower inner fender, remove the plastic dust shield.
5. Using a pair of diagonal cutters, cut the steering column dust boot-to-steering gear plastic wire tie clamp. Pull the dust boot back. Have an assistant turn the steering wheel until the steering column shaft bolt is accessible and lock the steering column.
6. Using white paint, matchmark the steering gear pinion shaft-to-intermediate lower shaft universal joint.
7. Remove the steering gear pinion shaft-to-intermediate lower shaft universal joint clamp bolt.
8. Remove the steering gear-to-chassis bolts, lower the steering gear to disengage it from the intermediate shaft universal joint. Carefully slide the steering gear out through the right side fender well.

9. To install, align the matchmarks and reverse the removal procedures. Torque the tie rod end-to-steering knuckle nut to 25–30 ft. lbs. Install a plastic strap over the steering column dust boot. Inspect the steering operation.

Power Steering Gear

Adjustment

1. Remove the power steering gear from the vehicle and place it in a vise.
2. Using an inch lb. torque wrench and a pinion torque adapter tool, place the assembly on the pinion and measure the pinion turning torque, the torque should be 0.52–1.3 inch lbs.
3. To adjust the pinion torque, perform the following procedures:
   a. Loosen the adjusting bolt locknut.
   b. Make sure the rack is centered in the housing.
   c. Move the adjusting bolt slightly and recheck the pinion torque.
   d. When the pinion torque of 0.52–1.3 inch lbs. is reached, retorque the adjusting bolt locknut to 29–36 ft. lbs.
4. To install the steering gear, reverse the removal procedures. Check the steering operation.

Removal and Installation

1. Disconnect the terminals from the battery (negative cable first) and remove the battery from the vehicle.
2. Raise and support the vehicle safely. Remove the front wheel assemblies.
3. Remove the tie rod end-to-steering knuckle cotter pins and nuts. Using a tie rod separator tool, separate the tie rod end from the steering knuckle.
4. From the right side lower inner fender, remove the plastic dust shield.
5. Using a pair of diagonal cutters, cut the steering column dust boot-to-steering gear plastic wire tie clamp. Pull the dust boot back. Have an assistant turn the steering wheel until the steering column shaft bolt is accessible and lock the steering column.
6. Using white paint, matchmark the steering gear pinion shaft-to-intermediate lower shaft universal joint.
7. Remove the steering gear pinion shaft-to-intermediate lower shaft universal joint clamp bolt.
8. Using a 17mm crowfoot tubing wrench, disconnect and plug the fluid return line from the power steering gear.
9. Using a 14mm socket, remove the banjo bolt from the pres-

sure line at the power steering gear and discard the copper washers.

NOTE: Be sure to position the pressure lines out of the way.

10. Remove the steering gear-to-chassis bolts, lower the steering gear to disengage it from the intermediate shaft universal joint. Carefully slide the steering gear out through the right side fender well.

11. To install, align the matchmarks, use 2 new washers at the banjo fitting and reverse the removal procedures. Torque the tie rod end-to-steering knuckle nut to 22–33 ft. lbs. Install a plastic strap over the steering column dust boot. Refill the power steering reservoir. Bleed the power steering system. Inspect the steering operation.

Power Steering Pump

Removal and Installation

1. Disconnect the negative battery cable.
2. At the power steering pump, loosen the locknut and adjuster bolt. Move the pump toward the engine and remove the drive belt.
3. From the engine lifting eye, remove the ground wire.
4. Disconnect and plug the hoses from the power steering pump. Disconnect the electrical connector from the pump's pressure switch.
5. Remove the adjusting screw, nut, block, pivot bolt and pump; if necessary, remove the pump pulley.
6. To install, reverse the removal procedures. Adjust the drive belt tension. Using Dexron II automatic transmission fluid, fill the power steering pump reservoir. Bleed the power steering system.

Belt Adjustment

1. Inspect the condition of the drive belt; replace it, if necessary.
2. At the power steering pump, loosen the locknut and adjuster bolt.
3. Using a drive belt tension gauge tool, position it between the power steering pump pulley and the crankshaft pulley. The drive belt deflection should be 0.31–0.35 in. (new belt) or 0.35–0.39 in. (used belt) at 22 lbs. pressure.

NOTE: A used belt is one that has at least 10 minutes run time.

4. If the power steering pump locknut was loosened, torque it to 32–45 ft. lbs.

Bleeding System

1. Raise and support the vehicle safely.
2. Using Dexron II automatic transmission fluid, fill the power steering reservoir to the **L** mark on the dipstick.
3. Start the engine and allow it to reach normal operating temperature.
4. Slowly turn the steering wheel (back and forth) lock-to-lock about 10 times, until all of the air is bled from the system and the reservoir is maintaining a full level.

NOTE: When bleeding the system, be sure to refill the reservoir several times.

5. Position the wheels in the straight ahead position and turn the engine **OFF**.
6. Refill the power steering reservoir until the fluid level is between the **L** and the **H** marks on the dipstick.
7. Lower the vehicle, start the engine, check for leaks and road test the vehicle.

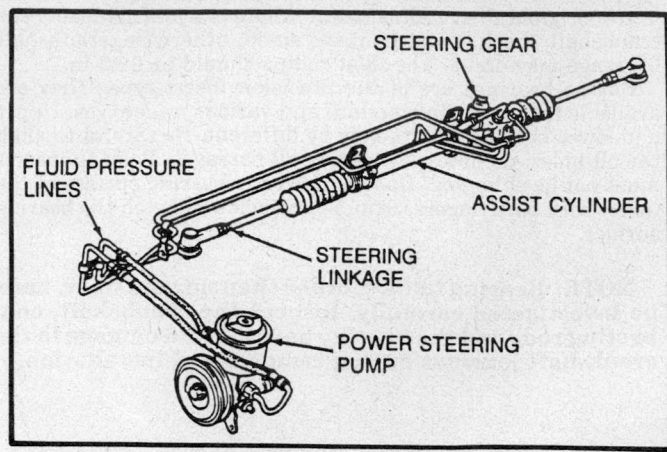

View of the power steering system

Steering Column

Removal and Installation

1. Disconnect the negative battery cable.
2. Remove the lap duct register panel screws, the lap duct brace screws, the brace and the lap duct.
3. Remove the combination switch lower cover screws and the cover.
4. Using paint, matchmark the lower universal joint-to-intermediate shaft.
5. Remove the lower steering column nuts, the lower steering column universal joint bolt and the upper steering column bolts.
6. Lower the steering column and disconnect the electrical harness connectors from the lower steering column.
7. Remove the steering column from the vehicle.
8. To install, align the universal joint-to-intermediate shaft and reverse the removal procedures. Inspect the operation of the steering column.

Front Wheel Bearings

The front wheel hub, steering knuckle and wheel bearings are all integral of each other and must be removed as an assembly.

Removal and Installation

1. Disconnect the negative battery cable. Raise and support the vehicle safely. Remove the halfshaft.
2. Disconnect the U-shaped clip from the center section of the caliper hose; do not disconnect the hose from the caliper. Remove the brake caliper-to-steering knuckle bolts and support the caliper on a length of wire; do not allow the caliper to hang by the brake hose.
3. Remove the tie rod-to-steering knuckle ball joint cotter pin and nut. Using a hammer and a tie rod separator tool, separate the tie rod end from the steering knuckle.
4. Using a scratch awl, mark the camber alignment cam bolt for reassembly. Remove the cam bolt and the upper attaching bolt from the strut and spindle.
5. Pull the steering knuckle assembly from the strut bracket.
6. To remove the rotor or the wheel bearings the steering knuckle assembly must be disassembled.
7. Using a hub removal tool, separate the steering knuckle from the hub assembly.
8. From the rear of the hub assembly, remove the bearing preload spacer.

NOTE: The bearing spacer, located between the bearings, determines the bearing preload; do not discard it.

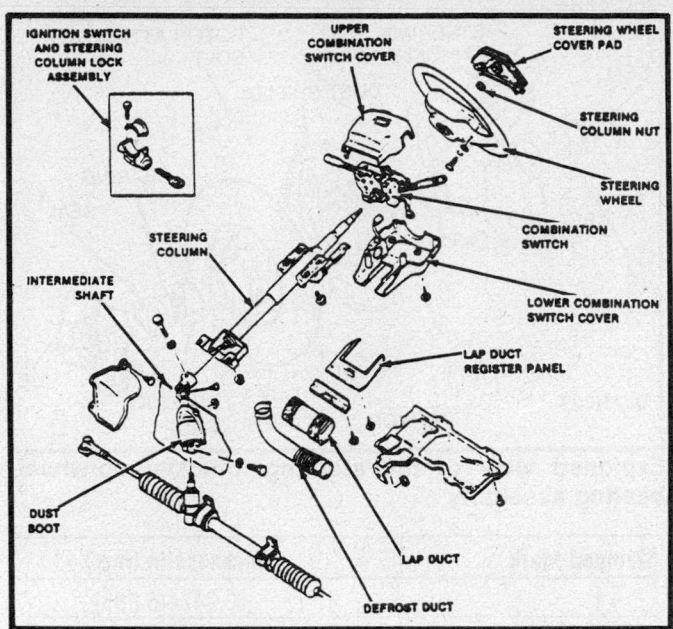

Exploded view of the steering column

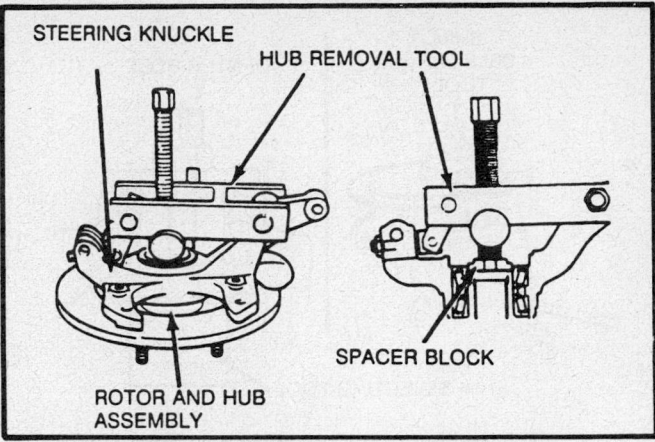

Separating the hub from the steering knuckle

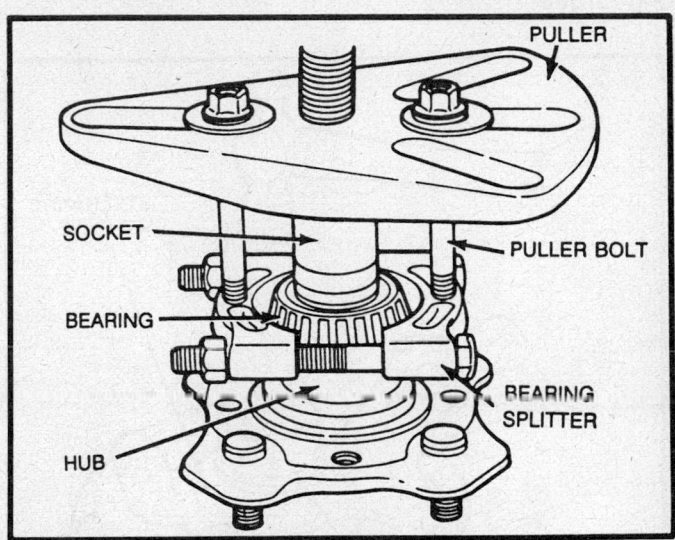

Pressing the wheel bearing from the hub

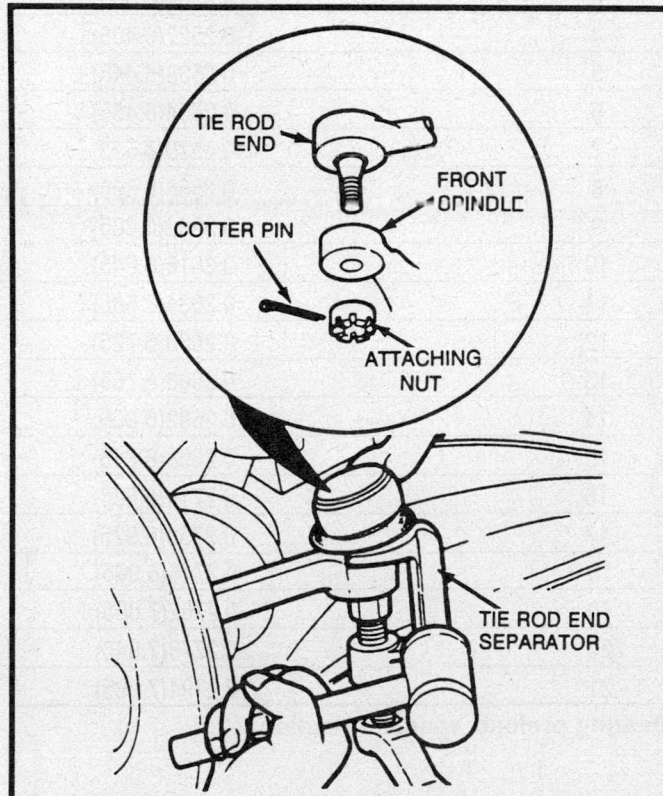

Separating the tie rod end from the steering knuckle

hub. A socket may have to be used to complete the bearing removal. Remove the outer grease seal from the hub and discard it.

Using a small pry bar at the inner side of the steering knuckle, pry the grease seal from the knuckle and discard it. Lift the inner wheel bearing from the steering knuckle.

13. If necessary to replace the bearing races in the steering knuckle, perform the following procedures:

    a. Using a brass drift and a hammer, drive the bearing races from the steering knuckle.

    b. Clean and inspect the steering knuckle for wear and/or damage, replace the steering knuckle, if necessary.

    c. To install, new or used bearing races, lubricate them with wheel bearing grease. Assemble the parts into the steering knuckle.

    d. Using a bearing race driver tool and a spacer selector tool, install the tools onto the steering knuckle assembly and the assembly onto a vise. Tighten the tool's center bolt (in increments) to 36, 72, 108 and 145 ft. lbs. After the final torque is reached, rotate the steering knuckle to seat the bearings. Retorque the center bolt to 145 ft. lbs.

    f. Remove the assembly from the vise and reinstall the steering knuckle into the vise; mount it by means of the shock absorber mount.

    g. Using a socket and an inch lb. torque wrench, position it

9. Using paint or chalk, matchmark the rotor-to-hub alignment for reassembly purposes.

10. Unless the brake disc is damaged, it should remain attached to the hub. Remove the rotor-to-hub bolts and the rotor.

11. Using the Bearing Puller Attachment tool No. D–1123–A or equivalent and the Puller tool No. D80L–927–A or equivalent, or a Bearing Splitter tool, press the wheel bearing from the

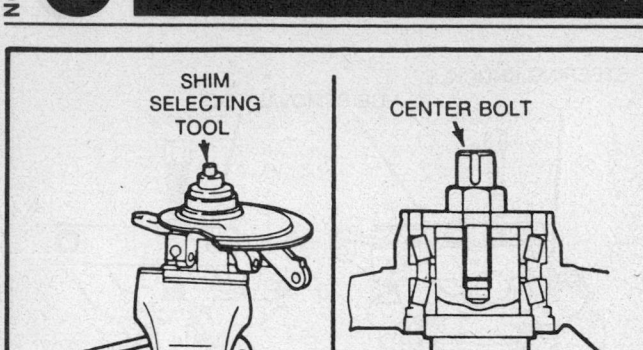

Installing wheel bearing races and adjusting the rotating torque

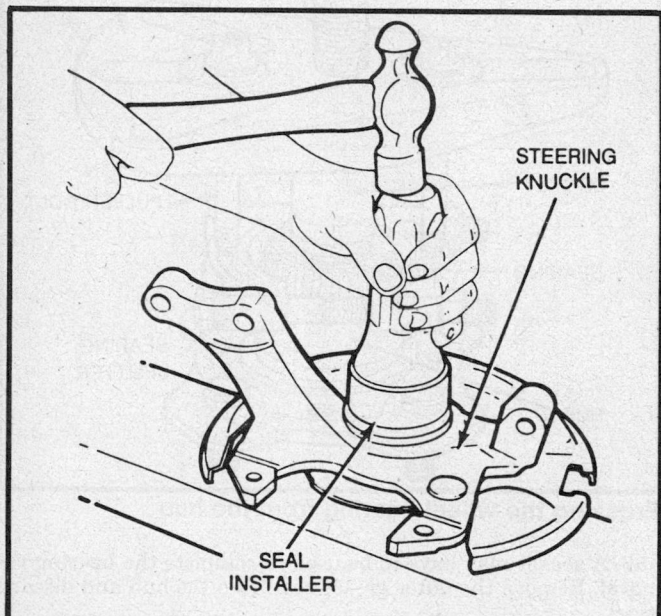

Driving the new grease seal into the steering knuckle

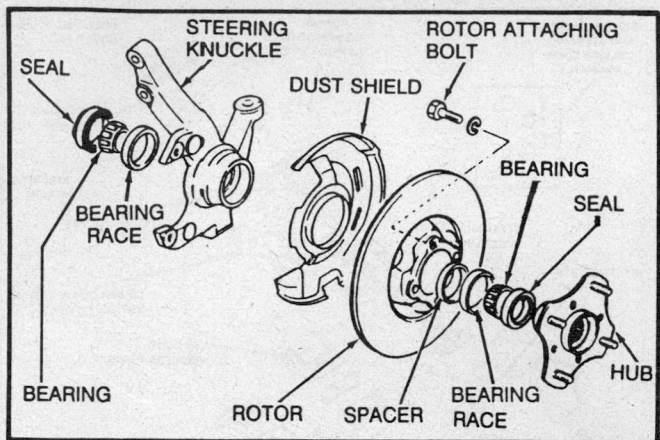

Exploded view of the steering knuckle/hub/wheel bearing assembly

Stamped Mark	Thickness in.(mm)
1	0.2474(6.285)
2	0.2490(6.325)
3	0.2506(6.365)
4	0.2522(6.405)
5	0.2538(6.445)
6	0.2554(6.485)
7	0.2570(6.525)
8	0.2586(6.565)
9	0.2602(6.605)
10	0.2618(6.645)
11	0.2634(6.685)
12	0.2650(6.725)
13	0.2666(6.765)
14	0.2682(6.805)
15	0.2698(6.845)
16	0.2714(6.885)
17	0.2730(6.925)
18	0.2746(6.965)
19	0.2762(7.005)
20	0.2778(7.045)
21	0.2794(7.085)

Bearing preload spacer selection

on the space selector tool. Measure the torque required to just move the assembly. The torque should be 2.21–10.44 inch lbs. If the torque is less than 2.21 inch lbs., a thinner spacer should be used; if the torque is more than 10.44 inch lbs., a thicker spacer should be used.

14. Clean and inspect all of the parts for wear and/or damage; replace the parts, if necessary. Using new wheel bearing grease, pack the inside of the steering knuckle.

15. Install a greased inner bearing into the steering knuckle. Using a new inner grease seal, lubricate with wheel bearing grease and drive it into the steering knuckle using a seal installer tool.

16. Lubricate and position the bearing preload spacer and the outer wheel bearing in the steering knuckle.

17. If the rotor was removed from the hub, align the matchmarks and install the hub-to-rotor bolts. Torque the hub-to-rotor bolts to 33–40 ft. lbs.

18. Position the hub/rotor assembly onto the steering knuckle. Using a hydraulic press, press the assembly together until the parts seat.

20. To install the hub/rotor assembly, use a new cotter pin (tie rod end) and reverse the removal procedures. Torque the steering knuckle-to-strut bolts to 69–86 ft. lbs., the lower control arm-to-steering knuckle clamp bolt to 32–40 ft. lbs., the tie rod-to-steering knuckle nut to 22–33 ft. lbs. and the caliper-to-steering knuckle bolts to 29–36 ft. lbs.

21. Lower the vehicle to the ground and torque the hub nut to 116–174 ft. lbs.(157–235 Nm); stake the hub nut. Check and/or adjust the front wheel alignment.

BRAKES

Refer to unit repair section for brake service information and drum/rotor specifications

Master Cylinder

Removal and Installation

1. Disconnect the negative battery cable. Disconnect the low fluid level sensor wiring connector.
2. Disconnect and plug the brake tubes from the master cylinder. Cap the master cylinder tube openings.
3. Remove the master cylinder-to-cowl (manual brakes) or master cylinder-to-power booster (power brakes) nuts and the master cylinder from the vehicle.
4. To install, reverse the removal procedures. Torque the master cylinder mounting nuts to 15–25 ft. lbs. Using DOT 3 brake fluid, fill the master cylinder reservoir. Bleed the brake system.

Bleeding System

1. Using DOT 3 brake fluid, check and/or refill the master cylinder reservoir until it is at least ½ full.
2. If the master cylinder has air trapped in the bore, perform the following procedures:
   a. Disconnect the front brake tube from the master cylinder and allow the fluid to flow from the master cylinder port.
   b. Reconnect and tighten the tube-to-master cylinder.
   c. Have an assistant depress the brake pedal (slowly) and hold it. Loosen the front tube-to-master cylinder, allow the air to purge, retighten the connection and release the pedal (slowly).
   d. After the air has been purged from the front tube, bleed the rear tube in the same manner.
3. To bleed the wheel cylinders or calipers, perform the following procedures:
   a. Connect a clear tube to the bleeder screw of the wheel cylinder or caliper.
   b. Have an assistant pump the brake pedal repeatedly and hold it. Loosen the bleeder screw, allow the air/fluid mixture to escape, retighten the screw and release the brake pedal (slowly). Perform this Step repeatedly until all air is removed from the fluid.
   c. Bleed all of the wheel cylinders or calipers using the following sequence: right rear, left front, left rear and right front.
4. After bleeding, check the pedal for sponginess. Check and/or refill the master cylinder reservoir.

Power Brake Booster

Removal and Installation

1. Remove the cables from the battery (negative cable first) and the battery from the vehicle.

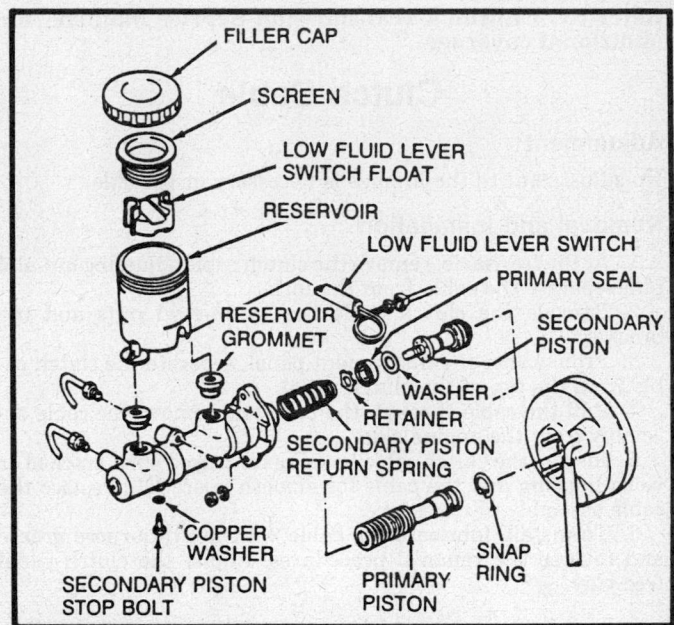

Exploded view of the master cylinder

2. Remove the master cylinder and move it aside; if possible, do not disconnect the brake tubes from the master cylinder.
3. Remove the vacuum hose from the brake booster.
4. From under the instrument panel, remove the spring clip and the clevis pin from the brake pedal.
5. Remove the brake booster-to-cowl nuts and the brake booster.
6. To install, reverse the removal procedures. If necessary, adjust the master cylinder pushrod. Check the brake operation. If the brake tubes were disconnected from the master cylinder, bleed the brake system.

Parking Brake

Adjustment

The parking brake lever adjusting nut is located on the left side of the hand brake lever under the console.
1. Remove the center console-to-chassis screws and the console.
2. Tighten the adjusting nut until the hand brake lever can only be actuated 10 clicks to lock the parking brakes.
3. With the vehicle on a flat surface, make sure it rolls with little effort and the brakes are not dragging.
4. Reinstall the center console.

CLUTCH AND TRANSAXLE

Refer to "Chilton's Transmission Service Manual" for additional coverage.

Clutch Cable

Adjustment

No adjustment to the linkage is necessary or possible.

Removal and Installation

1. At the transaxle, remove the clutch cable adjusting nut and pin; separate the cable from the fork.
2. Remove the clutch cable bracket-to-cowl nuts and the bracket.
3. From under the instrument panel, separate the clutch cable from the top of the clutch pedal.
4. Pull the cable through the cowl and remove the cable assembly from the engine side.
5. Inspect the clutch cable housing for frayed wire, cracked or worn housing and the cable for smooth operation; replace the cable assembly, if necessary.
6. To install, lubricate the cable with multi-purpose grease and reverse the removal procedures. Adjust the clutch pedal free-play.

Clutch

Removal and Installation

1. Disconnect the negative battery cable. Raise and support the vehicle safely. Remove the transaxle.
2. Using a flywheel locking tool, install it onto the engine, engage the flywheel ring gear tooth (to secure the flywheel). Using a clutch aligning tool, install it into the clutch disc and pilot shaft; this will support the clutch assembly.
3. Matchmark the pressure plate-to-flywheel for reinstallation purposes.
4. Remove the pressure plate-to-flywheel bolts, evenly, a little at a time.
5. Remove the pressure plate and clutch disc.
6. Inspect the pilot bearing, the flywheel, the pressure plate and clutch disc for wear and/or damage; replace the parts, if necessary.
7. To install, reverse the removal procedures. Torque the flywheel-to-crankshaft bolts to 71–75 ft. lbs., the pressure plate-to-flywheel bolts to 13–20 ft. lbs. Adjust the clutch pedal free-play.

Pedal Height/Free-Play Adjustment

PEDAL HEIGHT

Pedal height is the distance from the cowl to the center of the clutch pedal pad.

1. Remove the necessary instrument panel components which block access to the clutch pedal.
2. Loosen the clutch pedal locknut.
3. Turn the stop bolt to obtain the correct pedal height of 8.4–8.6 in. and tighten the locknut.
4. If components from the instrument panel were removed, reinstall them.

FREE-PLAY

Free-play is the distance the clutch pedal moves without engaging it.

1. Depress the clutch pedal and pull the pin away from the clutch lever (at the transaxle).
2. Turn the cable locknut to adjust the clutch pedal free-play of 0.35–0.59 inch.
3. Depress the pedal and check the disengagement height of

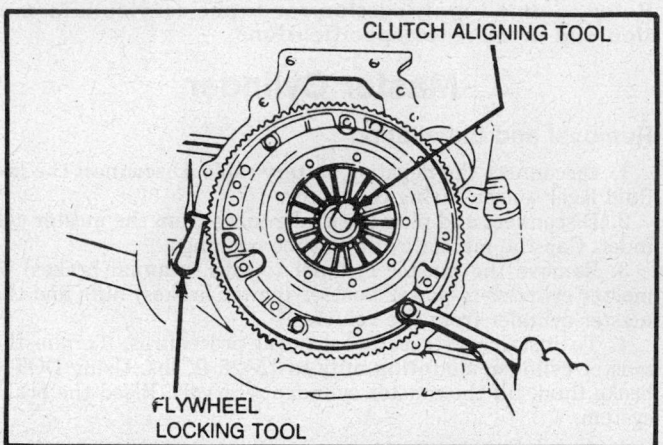

Using tools to replace the clutch assembly

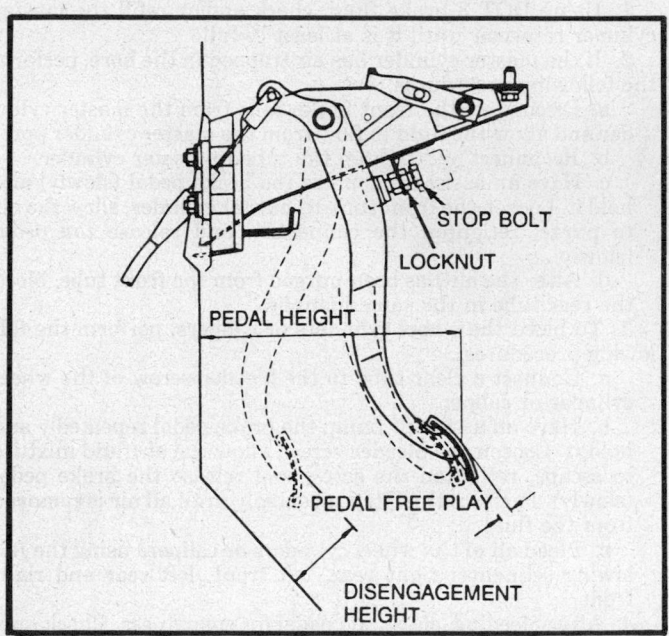

Adjusting the clutch pedal height and free-play

3.3 or more inches; the distance from the floor and the center of the clutch pedal pad.

Manual Transaxle

Removal and Installation

1. Disconnect the negative battery cable.
2. Remove the air cleaner. Loosen the front wheel lug nuts.
3. From the transaxle, disconnect the speedometer cable.
4. From the clutch release lever, remove the adjusting nut, pin and the clutch cable. Remove the clutch cable bracket-to-transaxle bolts and the bracket. Remove the ground wire bolt and ground wire.
5. Remove the coolant pipe bracket bolt and the bracket.
6. Remove the secondary air pipe, the EGR pipe bracket and the electrical harness clip.
7. Disconnect the neutral switch/back-up light switch coupler and the body ground connector.

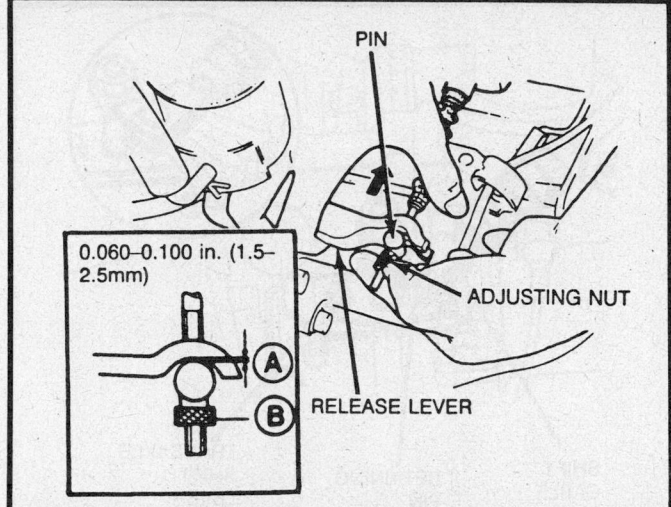

Adjusting the clutch pedal free-play

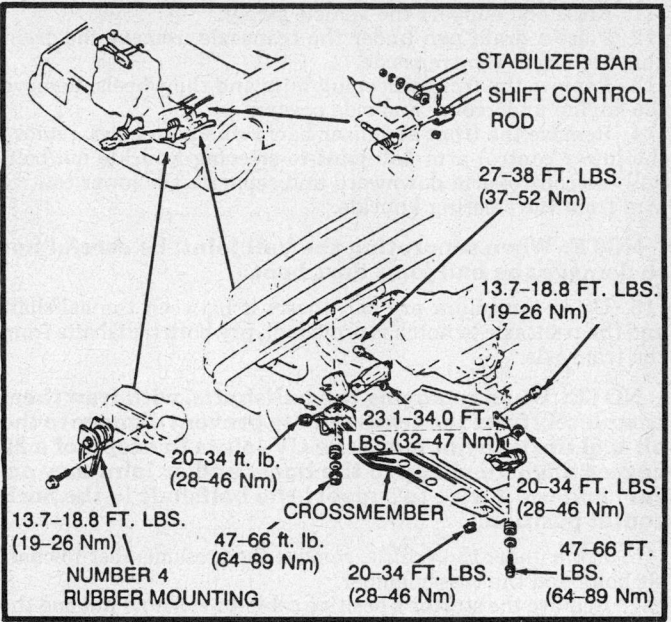

Exploded view of the crossmember and bracket assemblies

8. Remove the upper 2 transaxle-to-engine bolts.
9. Using a engine support bar tool, attach it to the rear engine lifting hook and support the engine's weight.
10. Raise and support the vehicle safely.
11. Place a drain pan under the transaxle, remove the drain plug and drain the transaxle.
12. Remove the front wheel lug nuts and the wheels. Remove the engine undercover and side covers.
13. Remove the front stabilizer bar. From both sides, remove the lower control arm ball joint-to-steering knuckle nut/bolt, pull the control arm downward and separate the lower control arm from the steering knuckle.

NOTE: When separating the ball joint, be careful not to damage the ball joint dust boot.

14. Using both hands, grasp the steering knuckle/hub assembly, apply even pressure (gradually increasing), pull both halfshafts from the transaxle.

NOTE: When removing the halfshafts, withdraw them completely from the transaxle (to prevent damage to the oil seal lips), do not move the CV-joints in excess of a 20 degree angle (damage to the boots and/or joint may occur) and use a wire to support the halfshaft in the horizontal position.

15. From under the vehicle, remove the crossmember-to-chassis bolts and the crossmember.
16. Remove the shift control rod-to-transaxle nut/bolt and slide the control rod aside. Remove the shift extension bar-to-bracket bolt and slide the extension bar off the bracket.
17. Remove the starter's positive cable-to-solenoid nut and the solenoid wire by pulling the wire from the connector.
18. Remove the starter-to-engine bolts and the starter. Remove the dust cover-to-clutch housing bolts and the cover.
19. Loosen the bracket bar on the engine support tool to lower the transaxle. Using a floor jack, support the transaxle.
20. Remove the No. 2 engine mount-to-transaxle nut/bolt, the transaxle-to-engine bolts and lower the transaxle from the vehicle.
21. To install the transaxle, perform the following procedures:
  a. Apply a small amount of clutch grease to the input shaft spline and reverse the removal procedures.
  b. Torque the transaxle-to-engine bolts to 47–66 ft. lbs., the No. 2 engine mount-to-transaxle nut/bolt to 27–38 ft. lbs., the starter to engine bolts to 23–34 ft. lbs., the extension bar-

to-transaxle bracket bolt to 23–34 ft. lbs., the control rod-to-transaxle nut/bolt to 12–17 ft. lbs., the crossmember-to-chassis bolts to 47–66 ft. lbs., the rear engine mount-to-crossmember nut to 20–34 ft. lbs.
  c. Refill the transaxle with Dexron®II or equivalent.
22. To install the halfshaft into the transaxle, perform the following procedures:
  a. Install a new locking clip on the halfshaft spline; be sure the gap in the clip is at the top of the clip groove.
  b. Slide the halfshafts into the transaxle bore; be careful not to damage the oil seal lip.
  c. Push firmly on the hub assembly, making sure the circlip snaps into place.
  d. After installation, pull the front hub outward to confirm that the circlips are engaged.
23. To complete the installation, reverse the removal procedures. Torque the lower control arm ball joint-to-steering knuckle nut/bolt to 32–40 ft. lbs., the stabilizer bar-to-chassis nuts/bolts to 23–33 ft. lbs., stabilizer bar-to-lower control arm nuts to 9–13 ft. lbs. Adjust the clutch pedal free-play. Test the vehicle performance.

Automatic Transaxle

Removal and Installation

1. Disconnect the negative battery cable.
2. Remove the air cleaner. Loosen the front wheel lug nuts.
3. From the transaxle, disconnect the speedometer cable.
4. Disconnect the shift control cable-to-transaxle clip and 2 bracket bolts. Remove the ground wire from the cylinder head.
5. Remove the water pipe bracket bolt and the bracket.
6. Remove the secondary air pipe, the EGR pipe bracket and the electrical harness clip.
7. Disconnect the electrical connectors from the inhibitor switch, the neutral switch and the kickdown solenoid. Disconnect the body ground connector.
8. Remove the upper 2 transaxle-to-engine bolts.
9. Remove the vacuum hose from the vacuum diaphragm line. Disconnect and plug the oil cooler line at the transaxle.
10. Using a engine support bar tool, attach it to the rear engine lifting hook and support the engine's weight.

11. Raise and support the vehicle safely.

12. Place a drain pan under the transaxle, remove the drain plug and drain the transaxle.

13. Remove the front wheel lug nuts and the wheels. Remove the engine undercover and side covers.

14. Remove the front stabilizer bar. From both sides, remove the lower control arm ball joint-to-steering knuckle nut/bolt, pull the control arm downward and separate the lower control arm from the steering knuckle.

NOTE: When separating the ball joint, be careful not to damage the ball joint dust boot.

15. Using a medium pry bar, insert it between the halfshaft and the transaxle (a notch is provided), pry both halfshafts from the transaxle.

NOTE: When removing the halfshafts, withdraw them completely from the transaxle (to prevent damage to the oil seal lips), do not move the CV-joints in excess of a 20 degree angle (damage to the boots and/or joint may occur) and use a wire to support the halfshaft in the horizontal position.

16. From under the vehicle, remove the crossmember-to-chassis bolts and the crossmember.

17. Remove the starter's positive cable-to-solenoid nut and the solenoid wire by pulling the wire from the connector.

18. Remove the starter-to-engine bolts and the starter. Remove the dust cover-to-clutch housing bolts and the cover.

19. Matchmark the torque converter-to-flexplate location. Remove the torque converter-to-flexplate bolts and slide the torque converter back into the transaxle.

20. Loosen the bracket bar on the engine support tool to lower the transaxle. Using a floor jack, support the transaxle.

21. Remove the No. 2 engine mount-to-transaxle nut/bolt, the transaxle-to-engine bolts and lower the transaxle from the vehicle.

22. To install the transaxle, reverse the removal procedures. Torque the transaxle-to-engine bolts to 47–66 ft. lbs., the No. 2 engine mount-to-transaxle nut/bolt to 27–38 ft. lbs., the starter to engine bolts to 23–34 ft. lbs., the crossmember-to-chassis bolts to 47–66 ft. lbs., the rear engine mount-to-crossmember nut to 20–34 ft. lbs. Refill the transaxle with Dexron®II or equivalent.

23. To install the halfshaft into the transaxle, perform the following procedures:

   a. Install a new locking clip on the halfshaft spline; be sure the gap in the clip is at the top of the clip groove.

   b. Slide the halfshafts into the transaxle bore; be careful not to damage the oil seal lip.

   c. Push firmly on the hub assembly, making sure the circlip snaps into place.

   d. After installation, pull the front hub outward to confirm that the circlips are engaged.

24. To complete the installation, reverse the removal procedures. Torque the lower control arm ball joint-to-steering knuckle nut/bolt to 32–40 ft. lbs., the stabilizer bar-to-chassis nuts/bolts to 23–33 ft. lbs., stabilizer bar-to-lower control arm nuts to 9–13 ft. lbs. Test the vehicle performance.

Adjustment

MANUAL SHIFT LINKAGE

1. Place the gear selector lever in the **N** position.

2. At the transaxle, remove the shift cable trunnion-to-transaxle shift lever spring clip and pin.

3. Rotate the transaxle shift lever fully counterclockwise to place it in the **P** position.

4. Move the transaxle shift lever clockwise 2 detents to place it in the **N** position.

NOTE: When moving the transaxle shift lever, be sure

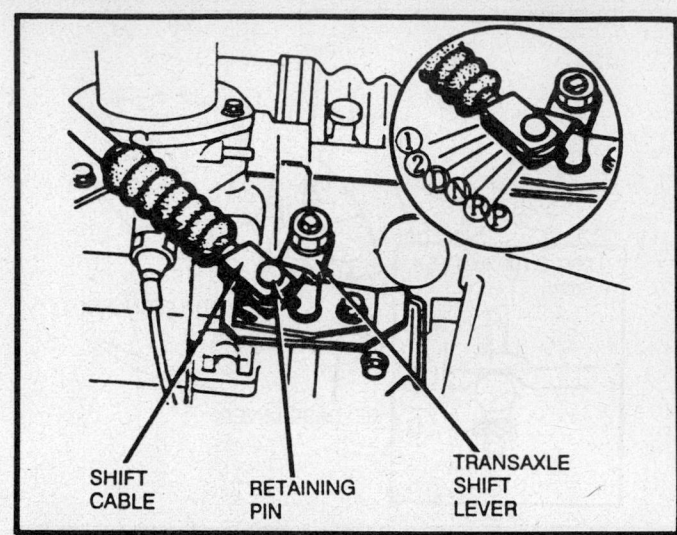

View of the shift cable trunnion/transaxle shift lever assembly

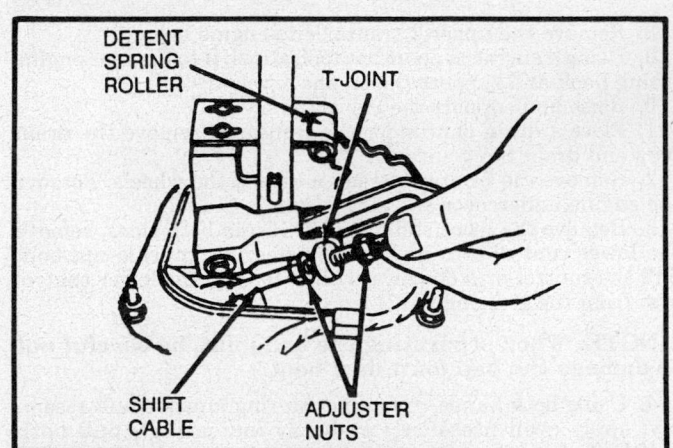

Adjusting the shift cable adjuster nuts

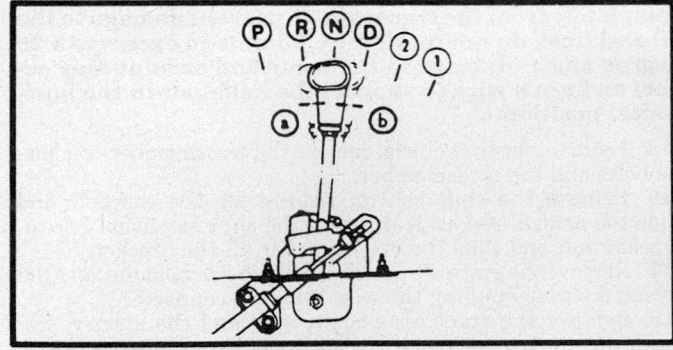

Checking the shift selector lever movement

to position it between the ends of the shift cable trunnion.

5. If the trunnion holes align with the shift lever hole, the cable is adjusted, replace the pin and spring clip. If the holes are not aligned, proceed with the remaining adjustment procedures.

6. From inside the vehicle, remove the shift quadrant bezel-to-console screws. Lift the front of the bezel to disengage it from the console and rotate it to provide access to the cable adjusting nuts.

7. At the shift cable, loosen the adjusting nuts.

8. Position the gear selector lever in the **P** position and inspect the detent spring roller. If the spring is not centered, perform the following procedures:

    a. Loosen the detent spring roller screws and move the spring to center it in the **P** position.

    b. Position the shift quadrant in the **P** position and reinstall the screws.

9. Move the shift selector lever to the **N** position.

10. Move the shift cable adjuster nuts until the holes in the cable trunnion and transaxle shift lever are aligned. Torque the shift cable adjuster nuts to 69–95 inch lbs.

11. Recheck the cable trunnion and transaxle shift lever holes for alignment. If aligned, install the pin and spring clip.

12. Using an assistant to watch the transaxle shift lever movement, start with the gear selector lever in the **N** position, push the shift interlock button and carefully move the shift lever rearward until the transaxle shift lever begins to move; note the amount of shift selector movement.

13. If the shift selector lever forward movement **a** does not equal the rearward movement **b**, turn the adjuster nuts until the movement is equal.

14. To complete the installation, reverse the removal procedures.

HALFSHAFTS

Front Drive Axle

HALFSHAFT

Removal and Installation

1. Raise and support the vehicle safely.

2. Remove the necessary splash covers from under the vehicle.

3. Remove the stabilizer bar-to-lower control arm nuts, bolt, washers and bushing.

4. Remove the wheel/tire assembly and the hub grease cap.

5. Using a stake chisel and a hammer, raise the staked portion of the hub nut.

6. Using an assistant to apply the brakes, loosen the hub nut.

7. Remove the lower control arm ball joint-to-steering knuckle clamp bolt, pull the lower control arm downward to separate the ball joint from the steering knuckle.

NOTE: When separating the ball joint, be careful not to damage the ball joint dust boot.

8. If equipped with a manual transaxle, use both hands, grasp the steering knuckle/hub assembly, apply even pressure (gradually increasing), pull both halfshafts from the transaxle. If equipped with an automatic transaxle, insert a medium pry bar between the halfshaft and the transaxle (a notch is provided), pry both halfshafts from the transaxle.

NOTE: When removing the halfshafts, withdraw them completely from the transaxle (to prevent damage to the oil seal lips), do not move the CV-joints in excess of a 20 degree angle (damage to the boots and/or joint may occur) and use a wire to support the halfshaft in the horizontal position.

9. Remove the hub nut (discard it) and washer. Pull the halfshaft from the steering knuckle assembly.

NOTE: If the wheel hub binds on the halfshaft splines, use a puller tool, to press the halfshaft from the wheel hub. Never use a hammer to separate the halfshaft from the wheel hub, for damage to the CV joint may occur.

10. Using differential plug tool(s), plug the transaxle bore(s) to prevent oil leakage.

11. Check the halfshaft for damage, wear and/or good working order; replace the halfshaft, if necessary.

12. To install the halfshaft into the transaxle, perform the following procedures:

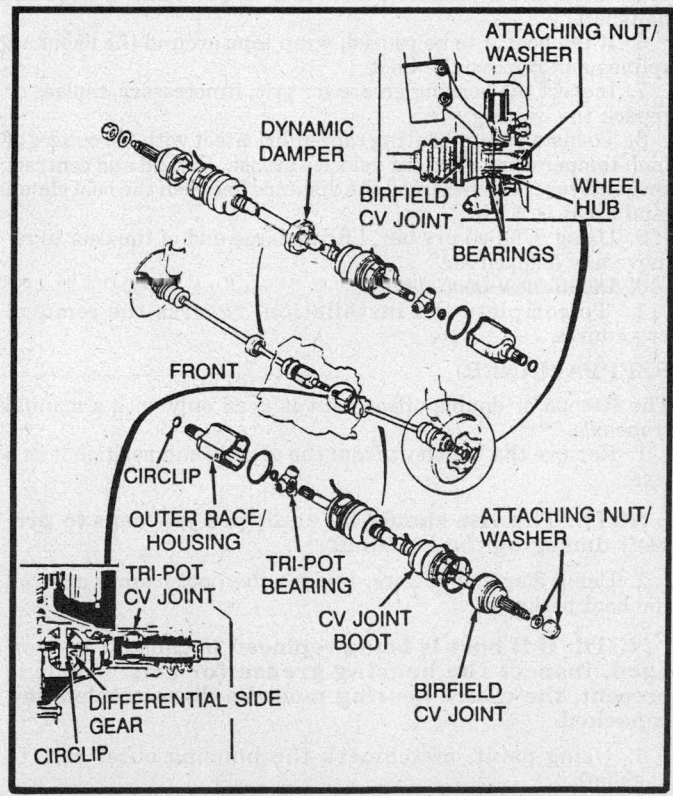

Exploded view of the halfshaft assemblies

    a. Install a new locking clip on the halfshaft spline; be sure the gap in the clip is at the top of the clip groove.

    b. Slide the halfshafts into the transaxle bore; be careful not to damage the oil seal lip.

    c. Push firmly on the hub assembly, making sure the circlip snaps into place.

    d. After installation, pull the front hub outward to confirm that the circlips are engaged.

13. Using multi-purpose grease, lubricate the halfshaft splines, lightly.

14. To complete the installation, reverse the removal procedures. Torque the lower control arm ball joint-to-steering

knuckle bolt to 32–40 ft. lbs. and a new halfshaft nut to 157–235 ft. lbs. Using a cold chisel (with the cutting edge rounded), stake the hub nut.

Boots

Removal and Installation

TRI-POT (INNER)

The Tri-pot joints are used only with an automatic transaxle.

1. Remove the halfshaft from the vehicle and position it in a vise.

NOTE: The vise should be equipped with jaw caps to prevent damaging the halfshaft.

2. Using diagonal cutters, remove the boot clamps and roll the boot backward.
3. Using paint, matchmark the bearing outer race, the tri-pot bearing and the halfshaft.
4. Using a pair of needle-nose pliers, remove the wire ring bearing retainer from the bearing outer race. Remove the outer race.
5. Remove the tri-pot bearing-to-halfshaft snapring. Using a brass drift and a hammer, drive the tri-pot bearing from the halfshaft.
6. If the boot is to be reused, wrap tape around the halfshaft splines and remove the boot.
7. Inspect the bearing grease for grit; if necessary, replace or repack the bearing.
8. To install outer bearing race, lubricate it with 3.5 ounces of high temperature constant velocity grease. Extend and contract the joint several times until the distance between the boot clamp land areas is 3.5 in.
9. Using a dulled pry bar, lift the large end of the boot to remove any trapped air.
10. Install new boot clamps.
11. To complete the installation, reverse the removal procedures.

RZEPPA (INNER)

The Rzeppa or double-offset joint is used only with a manual transaxle.

1. Remove the halfshaft from the vehicle and position it in a vise.

NOTE: The vise should be equipped jaw caps to prevent damaging the halfshaft.

2. Using diagonal cutters, remove the boot clamps and roll the boot backward.

NOTE: If it boot is being replaced because it is damaged, inspect the bearing grease for grit. If grit is present, the entire bearing must be disassembled and repacked.

3. Using paint, matchmark the housing outer race to halfshaft.
4. Using a small pry bar, remove the wire ring bearing retainer from the housing outer race. Remove the outer race.
5. Using paint, matchmark the inner bearing race-to-halfshaft.
6. Remove the inner bearing race-to-halfshaft snapring. Remove the inner bearing race, the cage and the ball bearings as an assembly.
7. If separating the inner bearing race assembly, perform the following procedures:
    a. Carefully pry ball bearings from the cage with a blunt pry bar.

NOTE: Be careful not to damage the ball bearings.

    b. Matchmark the inner race-to-cage.

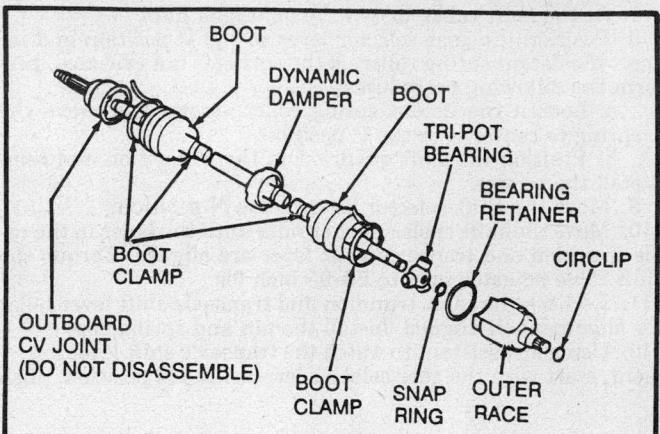

Exploded view of the Tri-Pot CV joint

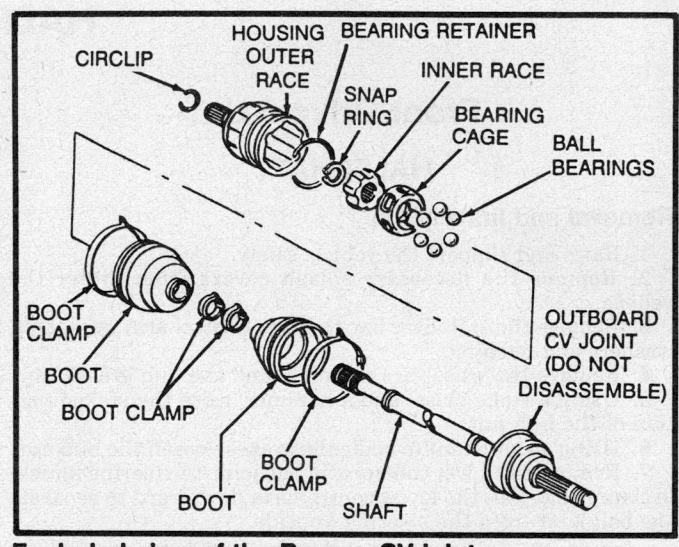

Exploded view of the Rzeppa CV joint

    c. Rotate the inner race to align the bearing lands with the cage windows and separate them.
8. Inspect the bearing grease for grit; if necessary, replace or repack the bearing.
9. If the boot is to be reused, wrap tape around the halfshaft splines and remove the boot.
10. To assemble bearing inner race assembly, perform the following procedures:
    a. Lubricate the parts with high temperature constant velocity grease.
    b. Align and install the inner race into the cage.

NOTE: Make sure inner race the chamfered splines are facing the large end of the cage.

    c. Using the heel portion of hand, press the ball bearings into the cage windows.
11. Install the boot onto the halfshaft.
12. Align the matchmarks and install the inner race assembly onto the halfshaft, secure it with the snapring.
13. To install housing outer race, lubricate it with 1.4–2.1 oz. of high temperature constant velocity grease and install it.
14. Lubricate the housing outer race with another 0.7–1.0 oz. of high temperature constant velocity grease and install the wire ring bearing retainer.
15. Slide the boot over the housing outer race.
16. Extend and contract the joint several times until the distance between the boot clamp land areas is 3.5 in.

17. Using a dulled pry bar, lift the large end of the boot to remove any trapped air.

18. Install new boot clamps.

19. To complete the installation, reverse the removal procedures.

BIRFIELD (OUTER)

The Birfield joint is outer joint used with either automatic or manual transaxles. The joint is not to be disassembled.

1. Remove the halfshaft from the vehicle and position it in a vise.

NOTE: The vise should be equipped with jaw caps to prevent damaging the halfshaft.

2. Using diagonal cutters, remove the boot clamps.

3. Remove the inner joint assembly from the halfshaft.

4. Slide the outer boot from the inboard side of the halfshaft.

5. To install, reverse the removal procedures.

Universal Joints

Refer to Unit Repair Section for overhaul procedures.

REAR AXLE AND REAR SUSPENSION

Refer to the unit repair section for axle overhaul procedures and rear suspension services.

Rear Axle Spindle

Removal and Installation

1. Raise and support the vehicle safely. Remove the wheel assembly and the brake drum/backing plate or the rotor assembly.

2. Remove the spindle-to-strut nut/bolt and the outer rear control arm common nut/bolt.

3. Remove the spindle from the strut.

4. Inspect the spindle for wear and/or damage; replace the spindle if necessary.

5. To install, reverse the removal procedures. Torque the spindle-to-strut nut/bolt to 69–86 ft. lbs. and the outer rear control arm common nut/bolt to 69–86 ft. lbs.

Rear Wheel Bearings

Removal and Installation

1. Raise and support the rear of the vehicle safely.

2. Remove the wheel and tire assembly.

3. Remove the grease cup from the rear wheel hub.

4. Using a small cape chisel and a hammer, carefully raise the staked portion of locknut; remove the discard the locknut.

NOTE: The locknuts are threaded for left and right hand applications; be sure to acquire the right one.

5. Remove the outer wheel bearing from the hub and the brake drum/bearing hub assembly.

6. Using a small pry bar, pry the grease seal from the rear of the drum. Remove the inner wheel bearing from the hub.

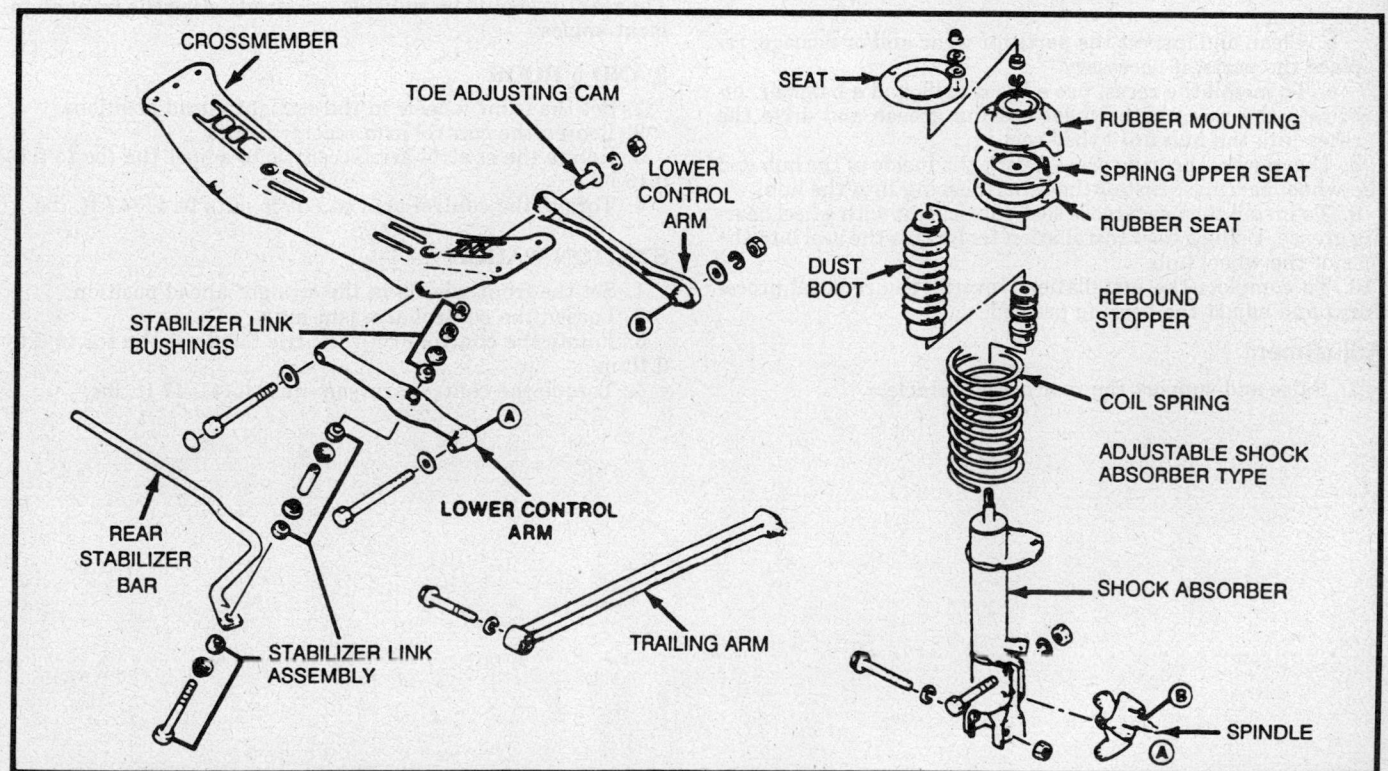

Exploded view of the rear suspension system—3 and 5 door models

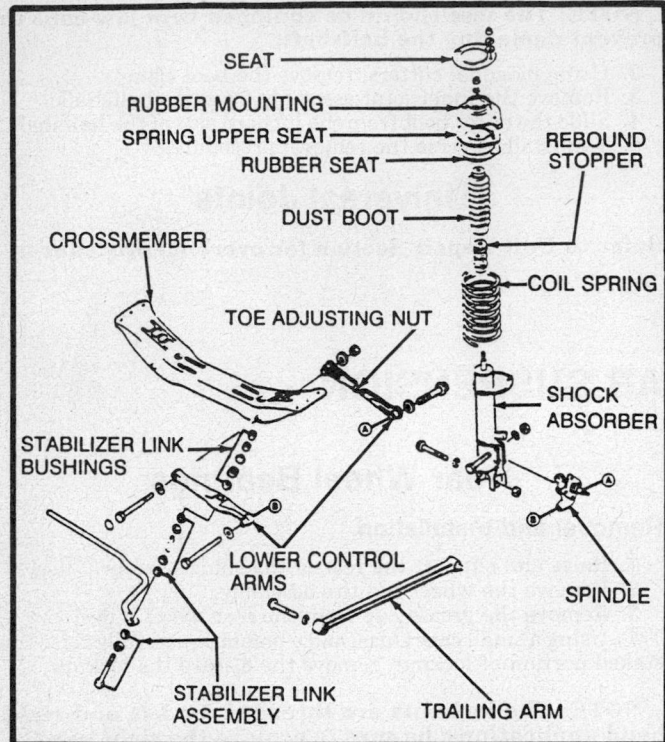

Exploded view of the rear suspension system—station wagon models

SEAT

RUBBER MOUNTING

SPRING UPPER SEAT

RUBBER SEAT

REBOUND STOPPER

DUST BOOT

CROSSMEMBER

COIL SPRING

TOE ADJUSTING NUT

SHOCK ABSORBER

STABILIZER LINK BUSHINGS

LOWER CONTROL ARMS

SPINDLE

STABILIZER LINK ASSEMBLY

TRAILING ARM

7. To replace the bearing races, perform the following procedures:

    a. Using a brass drift and a hammer, drive the races from the drum.

    b. Clean and inspect the parts for wear and/or damage; replace the parts, if necessary.

    c. To install the races, use a brass drift and a hammer, lubricate the races with wheel bearing grease and drive the races into the hub until they seat.

8. Using wheel bearing grease, pack the inside of the hub and the wheel bearings. Install the inner bearing into the hub.

9. To install the new grease seal, lubricate it with wheel bearing grease. Using a Seal Installation tool, drive the seal into the rear of the wheel hub.

10. To complete the installation, reverse the removal procedures and adjust the bearing preload.

Adjustment

1. Raise and support the rear of the vehicle.

2. Remove the wheel and tire assembly.

3. Remove the grease cup from the rear wheel hub.

4. Rotate the brake drum to make sure there is no brake drag; if there is drag, adjust the brake shoes.

5. Using a small cape chisel and a hammer, carefully raise the staked portion of locknut; remove the discard the locknut.

NOTE: The locknuts are threaded for left and right hand applications; be sure to acquire the right one.

6. Install the new locknut, rotate the drum and torque it to 18–21 ft. lbs.; loosen the locknut (slightly) until it can be turned by hand.

NOTE: Before the bearing preload can be set, the amount of seal drag must be measured and added to the preload torque.

7. Using an inch lb. torque wrench, position it (12 o'clock position) on 1 of the lug nuts and measure the torque necessary to start the wheel hub to turn.

8. To calculate the new torque, perform the following procedures:

    a. The required preload torque is 1.3–4.3 inch lbs.

    b. If the measure (seal drag) turning torque is 2.2 inch lbs., add it to the lowest and highest preload torque.

    c. The newly calculated preload torque is 3.5–6.5 inch lbs.

9. Torque the wheel bearing locknut slightly and recheck the wheel hub turning torque. When the wheel bearing torque falls within the newly calculated torque range, the torquing sequence is complete. Using a rounded cold chisel, stake the wheel locknut and reverse the removal procedures.

Rear Wheel Alignment

Toe Adjustment

The rear toe should be adjusted before adjusting the front alignment angles.

3 AND 5 DOOR

1. Set the front wheels in the straight ahead positioin.

2. Loosen the control arm eccentric nuts.

3. Rotate the control arm eccentric to adjust the toe to 0.0–0.16 in.

4. Torque the control arm eccentric nuts to 41–47 ft. lbs.

STATION WAGON

1. Set the front wheels in the straight ahead position.

2. Loosen the control arm jam nuts.

3. Rotate the control arm eccentric to adjust the toe to 0.0–0.16 in.

4. Torque the control arm jam nuts to 41–47 ft. lbs.

YEAR IDENTIFICATION

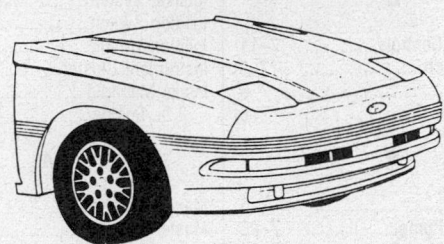

1989–90 Probe

VEHICLE IDENTIFICATION

It is important for servicing and ordering parts to be certain of the vehicle and engine identification. The VIN (vehicle identification number) is a 17 digit number visible through the windshield on the driver's side of the dash and contains the vehicle and engine identification codes. The tenth digit indicates model year and the eighth digit indicates engine code. It can be interpreted as follows:

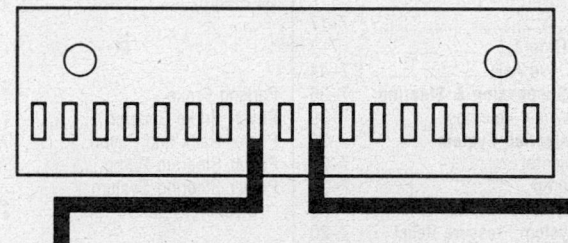

Engine Code						Model Year	
Code	Cu. In.	Liters	Cyl.	Fuel Sys.	Eng. Mfg.	Code	Year
C	133	2.2	4	MPFI	Mazda	K	1989
L	133	2.2	4	MPFI①	Mazda	L	1990

MPFI Multiport Fuel Injection
① Turbocharged engine

ENGINE IDENTIFICATION

Year	Model	Engine Displacement cu. in. (liter)	Engine Series Identification (VIN)	No. of Cylinders	Engine Type
1989–90	Probe GL	133 (2.2)	C	4	OHC
	Probe LX	133 (2.2)	C	4	OHC
	Probe GT	133 (2.2)	L①	4	OHC

OHC Overhead Cam
① Turbocharged engine

GENERAL ENGINE SPECIFICATIONS

Year	VIN	No. Cylinder Displacement cu. in. (liter)	Fuel System Type	Net Horsepower @ rpm	Net Torque @ rpm (ft.lbs.)	Bore × Stroke (in.)	Compression Ratio	Oil Pressure @ rpm
1989-90	C	4-133 (2.2)	MPFI	110 @ 4700	130 @ 3000	3.39 × 3.75	8.6:1	57 @ 3000
	L	4-133 (2.2)	MPFI	145 @ 4300	190 @ 3500	3.39 × 3.75	7.8:1	57 @ 3000

MPFI Multiport Fuel Injection

GASOLINE ENGINE TUNE-UP SPECIFICATIONS
Refer to Section 34 for all spark plug recommendations

Year	VIN	No. Cylinder Displacement cu. in. (liter)	Spark Plugs Gap (in.)	Ignition Timing (deg.) MT	AT	Compression Pressure (psi)	Fuel Pump (psi)	Idle Speed (rpm) MT	AT	Valve Clearance In.	Ex.
1989-90	C	4-133 (2.2)	0.040	5–7①	5–7①③	—	36	725–775	③④	Hyd.	Hyd.
	L	4-133 (2.2)	0.040	8–10②	—	—	36	725–775	—	Hyd.	Hyd.

① Distributor vacuum hoses disconnected and plugged
② Test connector grounded
③ Transaxle in Park
④ 725–775 rpm

FIRING ORDERS

NOTE: To avoid confusion, always replace spark plugs and wires one at a time.

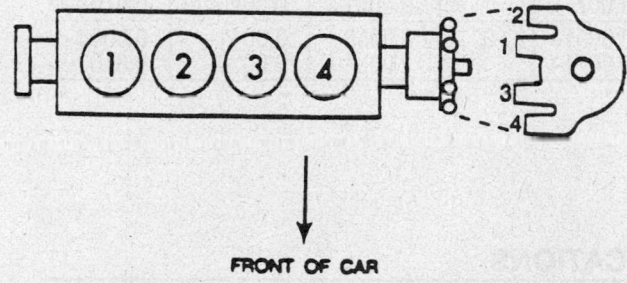

FRONT OF CAR

Ford Motor Co. (Mazda) 2.2L OHC engine
Firing order: 1-3-4-2
Non-turbocharged engine

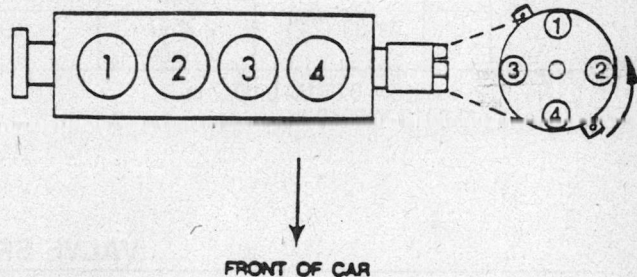

FRONT OF CAR

Ford Motor Co. (Mazda) 2.2L OHC engine
Firing order: 1-3-4-2
Turbocharged engine

CAPACITIES

Year	Model	VIN	No. Cylinder Displacement cu. in. (liter)	Engine Crankcase with Filter	without Filter	Transmission (pts.) 4-Spd	5-Spd	Auto.	Drive Axle (pts.)	Fuel Tank (gal.)	Cooling System (qts.)
1989-90	Probe	C	4-133 (2.2)	5.4	4.9	—	7.1	14.4	—	15.1	7.9
	Probe	L	4-133 (2.2)	5.4	4.9	—	7.7	—	—	15.1	7.9

CAMSHAFT SPECIFICATIONS
All measurements given in inches.

Year	VIN	No. Cylinder Displacement cu. in. (liter)	Journal Diameter 1	2	3	4	5	Lobe Lift In.	Ex.	Bearing Clearance	Camshaft End Play
1989–90	C	4-133 (2.2)	1.2575–1.2585	1.2563–1.2573	1.2563–1.2573	1.2563–1.2573	1.2575–1.2585	—	—	①	0.003–0.006
	L	4-133 (2.2)	1.2575–1.2585	1.2563–1.2573	1.2563–1.2573	1.2563–1.2573	1.2575–1.2585	—	—	①	0.003–0.006

① Front and rear—0.0014–0.0030 in.
Center journals—0.0026–0.0045 in.

CRANKSHAFT AND CONNECTING ROD SPECIFICATIONS
All measurements are given in inches.

Year	VIN	No. Cylinder Displacement cu. in. (liter)	Crankshaft Main Brg. Journal Dia.	Main Brg. Oil Clearance	Shaft End-play	Thrust on No.	Connecting Rod Journal Diameter	Oil Clearance	Side Clearance
1989–90	C	4-133 (2.2)	2.3597–2.3604–	①	0.0031–0.0071–	3	2.0055–2.0061–	0.0011–0.0026	0.0004–0.0103–
	L	4-133 (2.2)	2.3597–2.3604–	①	0.0031–0.0071–	3	2.0055–2.0061–	0.0011–0.0026	0.0004–0.0103–

① No. 1, 2, 4 and 5—0.0010–0.0017 in.
No. 3—0.0012–0.0019 in.

VALVE SPECIFICATIONS

Year	VIN	No. Cylinder Displacement cu. in. (liter)	Seat Angle (deg.)	Face Angle (deg.)	Spring Test Pressure (lbs.)	Spring Installed Height (in.)	Stem-to-Guide Clearance (in.) Intake	Exhaust	Stem Diameter (in.) Intake	Exhaust
1989-90	C	4-133 (2.2)	45	45	—	—	0.008	0.008	0.2744–0.2750	0.2742–0.2748
	L	4-133 (2.2)	45	45	—	—	0.008	0.008	0.2744–0.2750	0.2742–0.2748

PISTON AND RING SPECIFICATIONS
All measurments are given in inches.

Year	VIN	No. Cylinder Displacement cu. in. (liter)	Piston Clearance	Ring Gap Top Compression	Bottom Compression	Oil Control	Ring Side Clearance Top Compression	Bottom Compression	Oil Control
1989-90	C	4-133 (2.2)	0.0014–0.0030	0.008–0.014	0.006–0.012	0.012–0.035	0.001–0.003	0.001–0.003	—
	L	4-133 (2.2)	0.0014–0.0030	0.008–0.014	0.006–0.012	0.006–0.014	0.001–0.003	0.001–0.003	—

TORQUE SPECIFICATIONS
All readings in ft. lbs.

Year	VIN	No. Cylinder Displacement cu. in. (liter)	Cylinder Head Bolts	Main Bearing Bolts	Rod Bearing Bolts	Crankshaft Sprocket Bolts	Flywheel Bolts	Manifold Intake	Manifold Exhaust	Spark Plugs
1989-90	C	4-133 (2.2)	59–64	61–65	48–51	108–116	71–76	14–22	16–21	11–17
	L	4-133 (2.2)	59–64	61–65	48–51	108–116	71–76	14–22	16–21	11–17

WHEEL ALIGNMENT

Year	Model		Caster Range (deg.)	Caster Preferred Setting (deg.)	Camber Range (deg.)	Camber Preferred Setting (deg.)	Toe-in (in.)	Steering Axis Inclination (deg.)
1989-90	Probe GL	Front	0.47P–1.97P	1.22P	0.47N–1.03P	0.28P	0–0.24	12.78
		Rear	—	—	0.25N–1.25P	0.50P	0.12N–0.12P	—
	Probe LX	Front	0.47P–1.97P	1.22P	0.47N–1.03P	0.28P	0–0.24	12.78
		Rear	—	—	0.25N–1.25P	0.50P	0.12N–0.12P	—
	Probe GT	Front	0.47P–1.97P	1.22P	0.47N–1.03P	0.28P	0–0.24	12.78
		Rear	—	—	0.25N–1.25P	0.50P	0.12N–0.12P	—

N Negative
P Positive

ELECTRICAL

NOTE: Disconnecting the negative battery cable on some vehicles may interfere with the functions of the on board computer systems and may require the computer to undergo a relearning process, once the negative battery cable is reconnected.

For testing and overhaul procedures on starters, alternators and voltage regulators, refer to Unit Repair Section.

Charging System

ALTERNATOR

Removal and Installation

1. Disconnect the negative battery cable. Raise and safely support the front of the vehicle.
2. Remove the catalytic converter by performing the following procedures:
   a. From both ends of the converter, remove the flange nuts and washers.
   b. Remove the resonator pipe-to-body insulators.
   c. Push the rear exhaust assembly rearward and remove the converter with the gaskets.
3. From the rear of the alternator, depress the lock tab(s) and disconnect the electrical connectors.
4. Loosen the alternator's adjusting and through bolts, tilt it and remove the drive belt.
5. Remove the alternator's adjusting bracket lock bolt and through bolt.
6. While supporting the alternator, slide (lower) it between the steering gear and the right halfshaft.

To Install:

7. Reposition the alternator and install the mounting bolts (finger tight).
8. Install the drive belt, turn the alternator bracket's jack screw to adjust the drive belt tension; the belt deflection should be 0.24–0.31 in. (6–8mm).
9. After adjustment, torque the:
   Through bolt to 27–38 ft. lbs. (37–52 Nm)
   Lock bolt to 13–18 ft. lbs. (18–25 Nm)
10. To complete the installation, reverse the removal procedures. Start the engine and check the alternator's operation.

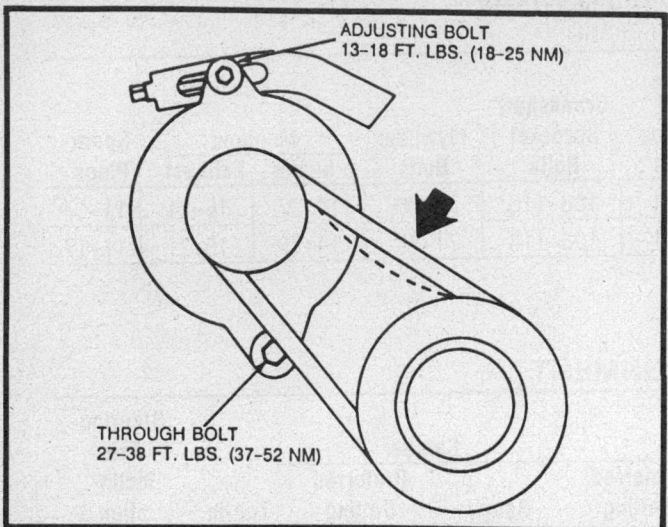

ADJUSTING BOLT
13–18 FT. LBS. (18–25 NM)

THROUGH BOLT
27–38 FT. LBS. (37–52 NM)

Adjusting the alternator's drive belt tension

VOLTAGE REGULATOR

The voltage regulator is an internal electronic type and can only be replaced when the alternator is disassembled.

BELT TENSION

Deflection Method
1. Disconnect the negative battery cable.
2. Loosen the alternator's lock bolt and through bolt.
3. Rotate the alternator bracket's jack screw to adjust the drive belt tension; the belt deflection should be 0.24–0.31 in. (6–8mm).
4. After adjustment, torque the:
Through bolt to 27–38 ft. lbs. (37–52 Nm)
Lock bolt to 13–18 ft. lbs. (18–25 Nm)

Starting System

STARTER

Removal and Installation
1. Disconnect the negative battery cable. Raise and safely support the front of the vehicle.
2. If equipped with a manual transaxle, remove the exhaust pipe bracket.
3. Remove the transaxle-to-engine bracket and intake manifold-to-engine bracket.
4. Disconnect the electrical connectors from the starter.
5. Remove the starter-to-engine bolts and the starter.
To Install:
6. Install the starter and torque the bolts to 23–34 ft. lbs. (31–46 Nm).
7. Connect the electrical connectors to the starter and torque the battery cable-to-starter nut to 90–110 inch lbs. (10–12 Nm).
8. Install the intake manifold-to-engine bracket bolts to 14–22 ft. lbs. (19–30 Nm).
9. If equipped with an automatic transaxle, torque the:
Transaxle-to-engine bracket bellhousing bolt to 66–86 ft. lbs. (89–117 Nm)
All other bolts to 27–38 ft. lbs. (37–52 Nm)
10. If equipped with a manual transaxle, torque the:
Transaxle-to-engine bracket bolts to 32–45 ft. lbs. (43–61 Nm)
Transaxle-to-exhaust pipe bracket bolts to 32–45 ft. lbs. (43–61 Nm)

11. To complete the installation, reverse the removal procedures. Check the starter operation.

Ignition System

DISTRIBUTOR

Removal and Installation
TIMING NOT DISTURBED
1. Disconnect the negative battery cable.
2. Remove the distributor cap screws, the cap and move it aside.
3. If not equipped with a turbocharger, perform the following procedures:
   a. Disconnect and label the vacuum lines from the distributor vacuum diaphragm.
   b. Disconnect the distributor electrical connectors from the ignition coil.
4. If equipped with a turbocharger, disconnect the distributor wiring harness connector (located near the upper side of the distributor.
5. Using a wrench on the crankshaft pulley, rotate the crankshaft to position the No. 1 piston on the TDC of it's compression stroke; the crankshaft pulley notch should align with the timing plate indicator.
6. Using chalk or paint, mark the relationship of the distributor housing-to-cylinder head and the rotor-to-distributor housing; this will assist in installation.
7. Remove the distributor hold-down bolts and the distributor.
8. Inspect the O-ring and replace it (if necessary).
To Install:
9. Using engine oil, lubricate the O-ring.
10. Align the rotor-to-distributor housing and the distributor housing-to-cylinder head.
11. Install the distributor and make sure to engage the drive dog with the camshaft slot. Tighten the distributor hold-down bolts finger tight.
12. Start the engine and check or adjust the ignition base timing.

TIMING DISTURBED
1. Disconnect the negative battery cable.
2. Remove the ditributor cap screws, the cap and move it aside.
3. If not equipped with a turbocharger, perform the following procedures:
   a. Disconnect and label the vacuum lines from the distributor vacuum diaphragm.
   b. Disconnect the distributor electrical connectors from the ignition coil.
4. If equipped with a turbocharger, disconnect the distributor wiring harness connector (located near the upper side of the distributor.
5. Remove the distributor hold-down bolts and the distributor.
6. Inspect the O-ring and replace it (if necessary).
To Install:
7. Using engine oil, lubricate the O-ring.
8. Remove the spark plug from the No. 1 cylinder and press your thumb over the opening.
9. Using a wrench on the crankshaft pulley, rotate the crankshaft to position the No. 1 piston on the TDC of it's compression stroke; pressure will be felt at the spark plug hole and the crankshaft pulley notch should align with the timing plate indicator.
10. Align the rotor to the No. 1 spark plug wire terminal of the distributor cap.

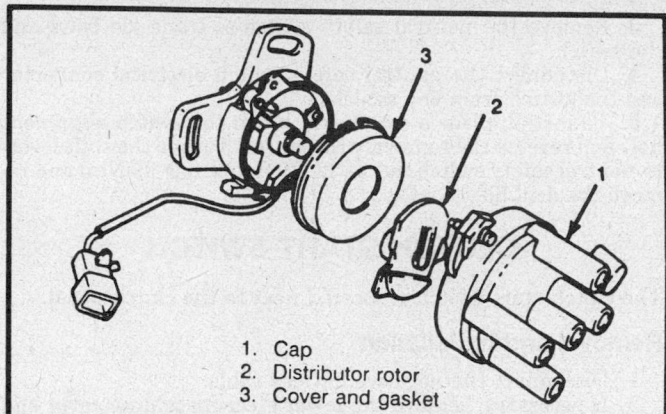

1. Cap
2. Distributor rotor
3. Cover and gasket

Exploded view of the distributor assembly—turbocharged

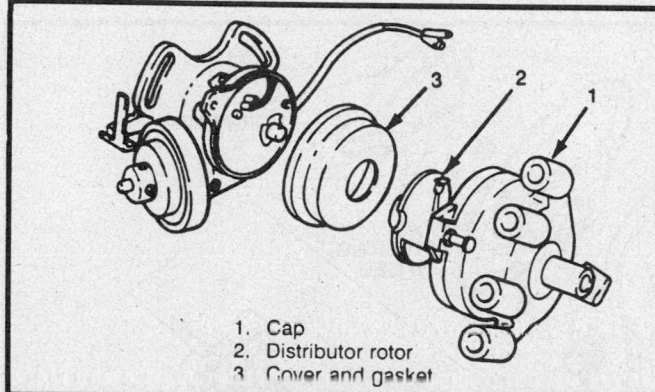

1. Cap
2. Distributor rotor
3. Cover and gasket

Exploded view of the distributor assembly—non-turbocharged

11. Install the distributor and make sure to engage the drive dog with the camshaft slot. Tighten the distributor hold-down bolts finger tight.

12. Start the engine and check or adjust the ignition base timing.

IGNITION TIMING

Adjustment

NOTE: Before performing this procedure, be sure the idle speed is set correctly.

1. Turn OFF all of the accessories.
2. Firmly set the parking brake and position the gear shift selector in P (automatic) or N (manual).
3. Start and operate the engine until normal operating temperatures are reached.
4. If not equipped with a turbocharger, disconnect and plug both vacuum hoses from the distributor vacuum diaphragm. If equipped with a turbocharger, connect a jumper wire between the test connector pin No. 1 and ground.
5. Using a timing light, point it at the timing plate (crankshaft pulley area), connect it to the engine and check the ignition timing; the timing should be 5–7 degrees BTDC (non-turbo) or 8–10 degrees BTDC (turbo).
6. If the ignition timing is not within specifications, loosen the distributor hold-down bolts, rotate the distributor to align the timing marks and tighten the hold-down bolts.

Grounding the test connector to check the ignition timing—turbocharged

Electrical Controls

STEERING WHEEL

Removal and Installation

1. Position the wheels in the straight ahead position. Disconnect the negative battery cable.
2. From the rear of the steering wheel, remove the horn pad-to-steering wheel screws, the horn pad and disconnect the horn electrical connector.
3. Remove the steering wheel-to-cloumn nut. Using paint or chalk, match-mark the steering wheel to the steering column.
4. Using a steering wheel puller, press the steering wheel from the steering shaft.
5. To install, align the match-mark and reverse the removal procedures. Torque the steering wheel-to-shaft nut to 29–36 ft. lbs. (39–49 Nm).

HORN SWITCH

A horn switch is mounted at 2 points on each rear side of the horn pad.

Removal and Installation

1. Disconnect the negative battery cable.
2. From the rear of the steering wheel, remove the horn pad-to-steering wheel screws, the horn pad and disconnect the horn electrical connector.
3. Remove the horn switch(s) from the horn pad.
4. To install, reverse the removal procedures. Check the horn operation.

IGNITION LOCK/SWITCH

Removal and Installation

1. Disconnect the negative battery cable. Remove the steering wheel.
2. Remove the steering column cover-to-instrument cover screws and the cover.
3. Remove the instrument cover-to-instrument cluster cover screws, pull the cover forward, disconnect the electrical connectors (from the rear) and remove the cover.
4. Remove the instrument cluster cover-to-dash screws and the cover.
5. Remove the lower panel, the lap duct and the defrost duct.
6. Remove the lower hinge bracket support nuts.
7. Remove the upper steering column-to-support bracket nuts/bolts and lower the steering column (allow it hang).
8. Remove the ignition switch-to-ignition switch housing screw.
9. At the left side of the steering column, disconnect the ignition switch snap connectors and the protective looming from the ignition switch wires.

10. Note the position of each wire in the 4-wire terminal connector. From the 4-wire connector, disconnect the key-in warning buzzer wires: green wire and the red wire/orange tracer.

NOTE: Use a paper clip or equivalent, to disengage the wire tangs from the 4-wire connector.

11. To install, reverse the removal procedures. Check the ignition switch's operation.

NEUTRAL SAFETY SWITCH

The neutral safety switch is located on top left side of the transaxle.

Removal and Installation

1. Disconnect the negative battery cable.
2. Remove the shift lever-to-neutral safety switch nut and lever.

3. Remove the neutral safety switch-to-transaxle bolts and the switch.
4. Disconnect the neutral safety switch electrical connector and the switch from the vehicle.
5. To install, place a small drill bit in the switch alignment hole and reverse the removal procedures. Torque the shift lever-to-neutral safety switch nut to 22–29 ft. lbs. (29–39 Nm) and remove the drill bit.

CLUTCH START SWITCH

The clutch start switch is located next to the clutch pedal.

Removal and Installation

1. Disconnect the negative battery cable.
2. If necessary, remove the lower steering column cover and ducts.
3. Using an ohmmeter, inspect the switch operation. When the switch rod is pushed in, the ohmmeter should show continu-

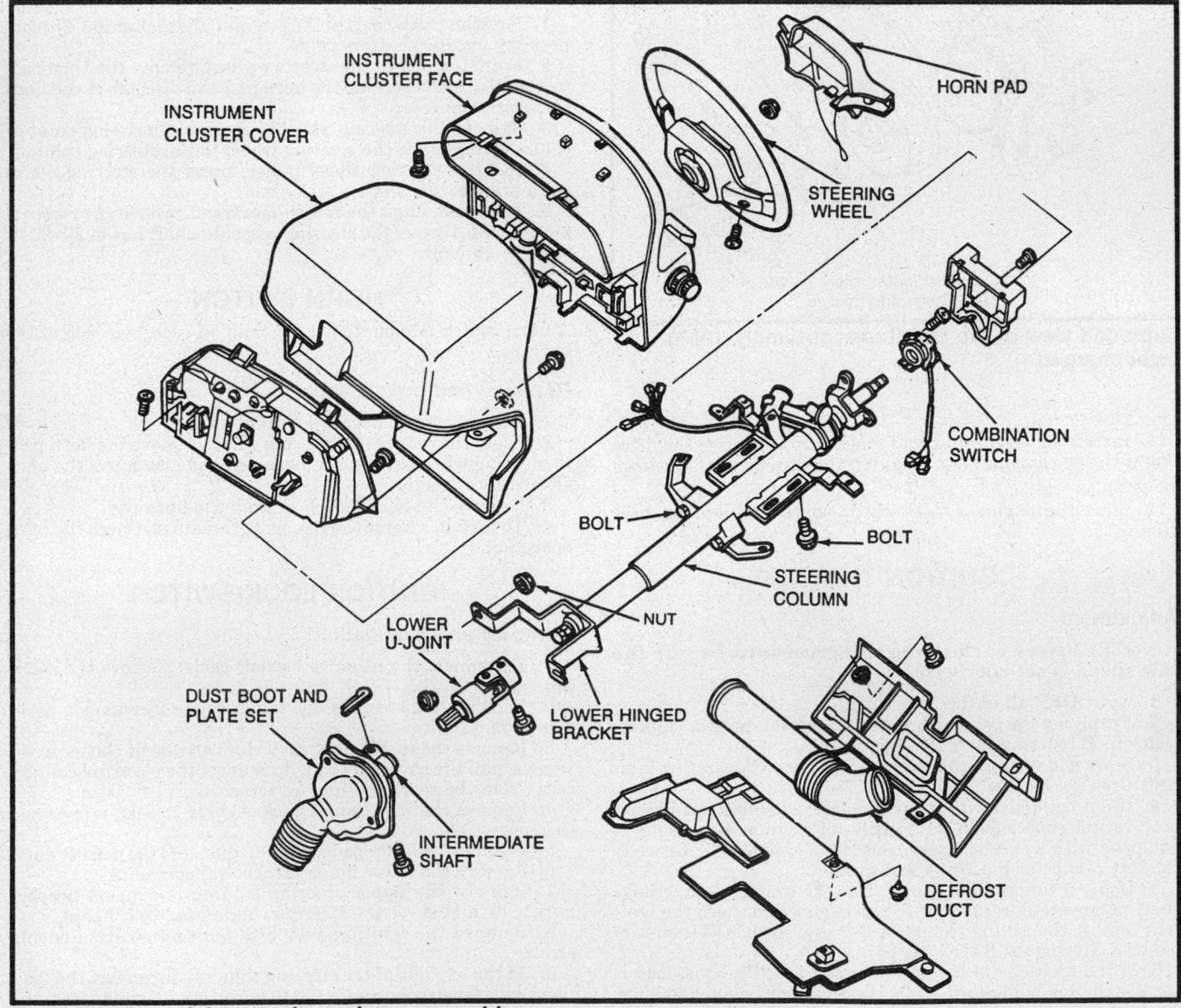

Exploded view of the steering column assembly

ity; when the switch rod is released, the ohmmeter should show no continuity.

4. If necessary, replace the switch.
5. To install, reverse the removal procedures.

STOPLIGHT SWITCH

The stoplight switch is located at the top of the brake pedal and is used to adjust the brake pedal height.

Adjustment

1. If necessary, remove the lower steering column cover and ducts.
2. Disconnect the electrical connector from the stoplight switch.
3. Loosen the stoplight switch locknut.
4. Turn the stoplight switch until the brake pedal height 8.54–8.74 in. (217–222mm) from the center of the pedal pad to the firewall.
5. Tighten the stoplight switch locknut, reconnect the electrical connector and check the stoplight operation.

Removal and Installation

1. If necessary, remove the lower steering column cover and ducts.
2. Disconnect the electrical connector from the stoplight switch.
3. Remove the stoplight switch locknut and the switch.
4. To install, turn the stoplight switch until the brake pedal height 8.54–8.74 in. (217–222mm) from the center of the pedal pad to the firewall.
5. Tighten the stoplight switch locknut, reconnect the electrical connector and check the stoplight operation.

HEADLAMP SWITCH

The headlamp switch is located on the left side of the instrument panel. When the headlamp switch is rotated to the **2ND** position, all of the accessory lights are activated. When the switch is rotated to the **3RD** position, the headlamp retractors will raise the headlamps and the headlamps are turned **ON**. When the switch is rotated to the **4TH** position, the headlamp retractors will remain in the raised position and the headlamps will turn **OFF**; this position is used for servicing.

The high beam dimmer switch is located on the turn signal switch lever located on the instrument cluster module cover.

Removal and Installation

1. Disconnect the negative battery cable. Remove the turn signal switch.
2. Gently, pull the rotary knob from the headlamp switch.
3. From the rear of the instrument cluster module cover, remove the rotary switch housing screws and the switch.
4. To install, reverse the removal procedures. Check the headlamp switch operation.

CONCEALED HEADLAMPS

Manual Operation

A manual control knob is located under each headlamp retractor motor and is accessible from under the front fasica. The retractor motor is mounted on a bracket which is attached to the radiator support.

To raise the headlamp(s), remove the retractor motor control knob's rubber boot, rotate the knob to lift the headlamp.

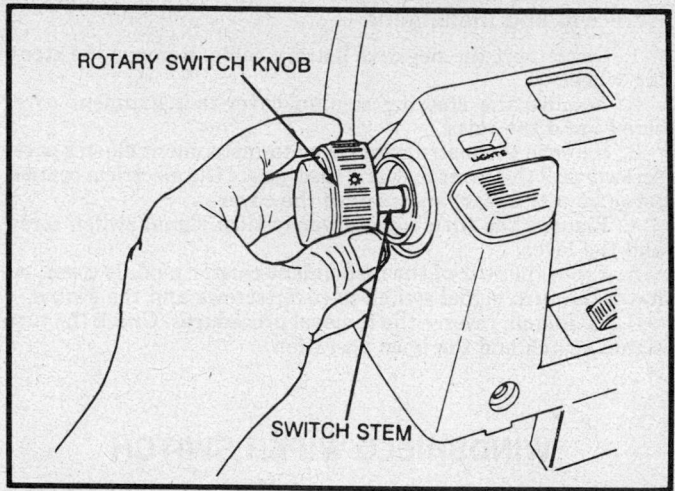

Removing the headlight switch from the instrument cluster module cover

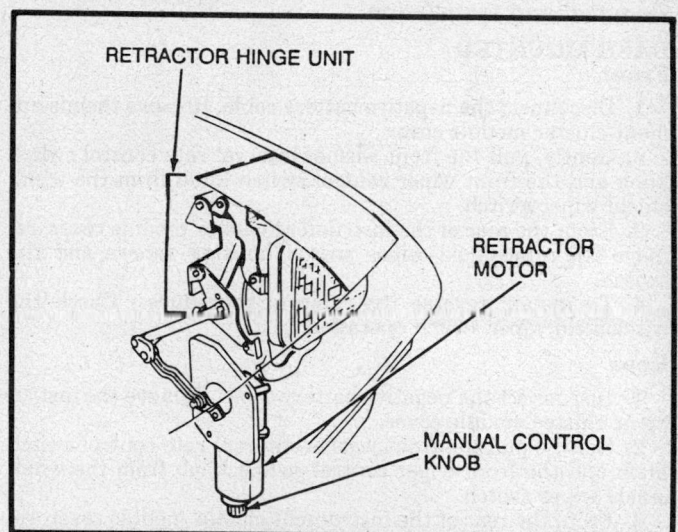

View of the headlight retractor motor assembly

DIMMER SWITCH

The high beam dimmer switch is located on the turn signal switch lever located on the instrument cluster module cover.

Removal and Installation

1. Disconnect the negative battery cable. Remove the steering wheel.
2. Remove the steering column cover-to-instrument cover screws and the cover.
3. Remove the instrument cover-to-instrument cluster cover screws, pull the cover forward, disconnect the electrical connectors (from the rear) and remove the cover.
4. Remove the turn signal lever-to-turn signal switch screw and the lever.
5. From the rear of the instrument cluster module cover, remove the turn signal switch-to-cover screws and the switch.
6. To install, reverse the removal procedures. Check the turn signal switch and the horn operation.

TURN SIGNAL SWITCH

The turn signal switch is located on the left side of the instrument cluster module cover.

Removal and Installation

1. Disconnect the negative battery cable. Remove the steering wheel.
2. Remove the steering column cover-to-instrument cover screws and the cover.
3. Remove the instrument cover-to-instrument cluster cover screws, pull the cover forward, disconnect the electrical connectors (from the rear) and remove the cover.
4. Remove the turn signal lever-to-turn signal switch screw and the lever.
5. From the rear of the instrument cluster module cover, remove the turn signal switch-to-cover screws and the switch.
6. To install, reverse the removal procedures. Check the turn signal switch and the horn operation.

WINDSHIELD WIPER SWITCH

The windshield wiper switches are mounted on the right side of the instrument cluster module cover.

Removal and Installation

DASH MOUNTED
Front

1. Disconnect the negative battery cable. Remove the instrument cluster module cover.
2. Gently, pull the front washer/interval rate control switch knob and the front wiper control switch knob from the windshield wiper switch.
3. From the rear of the instrument cluster module cover, remove the windshield wiper switch housing screws and the switch.
4. To install, reverse the removal procedures. Check the windshield wiper switch operation.

Rear

1. Disconnect the negative battery cable. Remove the instrument cluster module cover.
2. Gently, pull the front washer/interval rate control switch knob and the front wiper control switch knob from the windshield wiper switch.
3. From the rear of the instrument cluster module cover, remove the windshield wiper switch housing screws and the switch.
4. Remove the rear wiper/washer switch-to-instrument cluster module cover screws.
5. While depressing the control button switch tangs (at the rear), remove the switch cover from the front of the instrument cover. Remove the rear wiper/washer switch from the rear of the instrument cover.
6. To install, reverse the removal procedures. Check the windshield wiper/washer switch and the rear wiper/washer switch operation.

WINDSHIELD WIPER MOTOR

Removal and Installation

FRONT

1. Disconnect the negative battery cable.
2. Unscrew the retaining cap and remove the wiper blade/arm assemblies.
3. Disconnect the hose from the washer jets.
4. Remove the lower moulding and wiper linkage cover.
5. Pull the wiper linkage off the wiper motor output arm.
6. Disconnect the electrical connectors from the wiper motor.

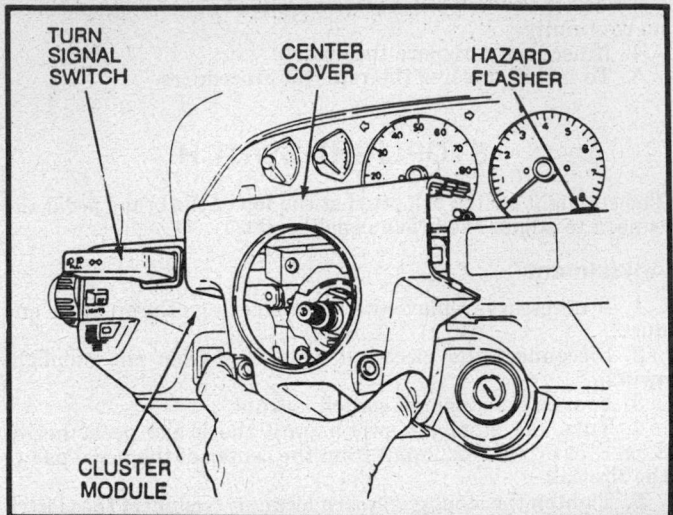

View of the turn signal switch location

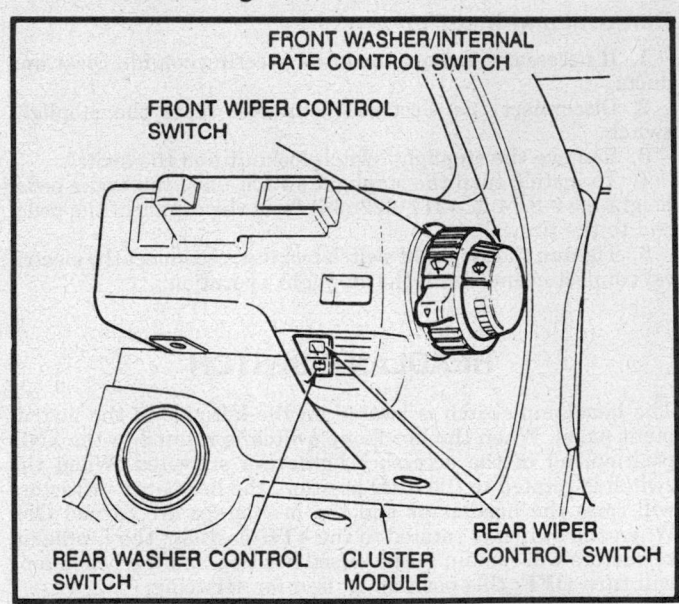

View of the windshield and rear window wiper/washer switch locations

7. Remove the wiper motor-to-chassis bolts and the motor from the vehicle.
8. To install, reverse the removal procedures. Check the wiper motor operation.

REAR

1. Disconnect the negative battery cable.
2. Lift the cover and remove the wiper blade/arm assembly-to-pivot arm nut and the assembly.
3. From the pivot arm, remove the boot, the retaining nut and the mount.
4. From the inner side of the tailgate, pry off the trim panel.
5. Disconnect the electrical connector from the wiper motor.
6. Remove the wiper motor-to-chassis bolts and the motor from the vehicle.
7. To install, reverse the removal procedures. Check the wiper motor operation.

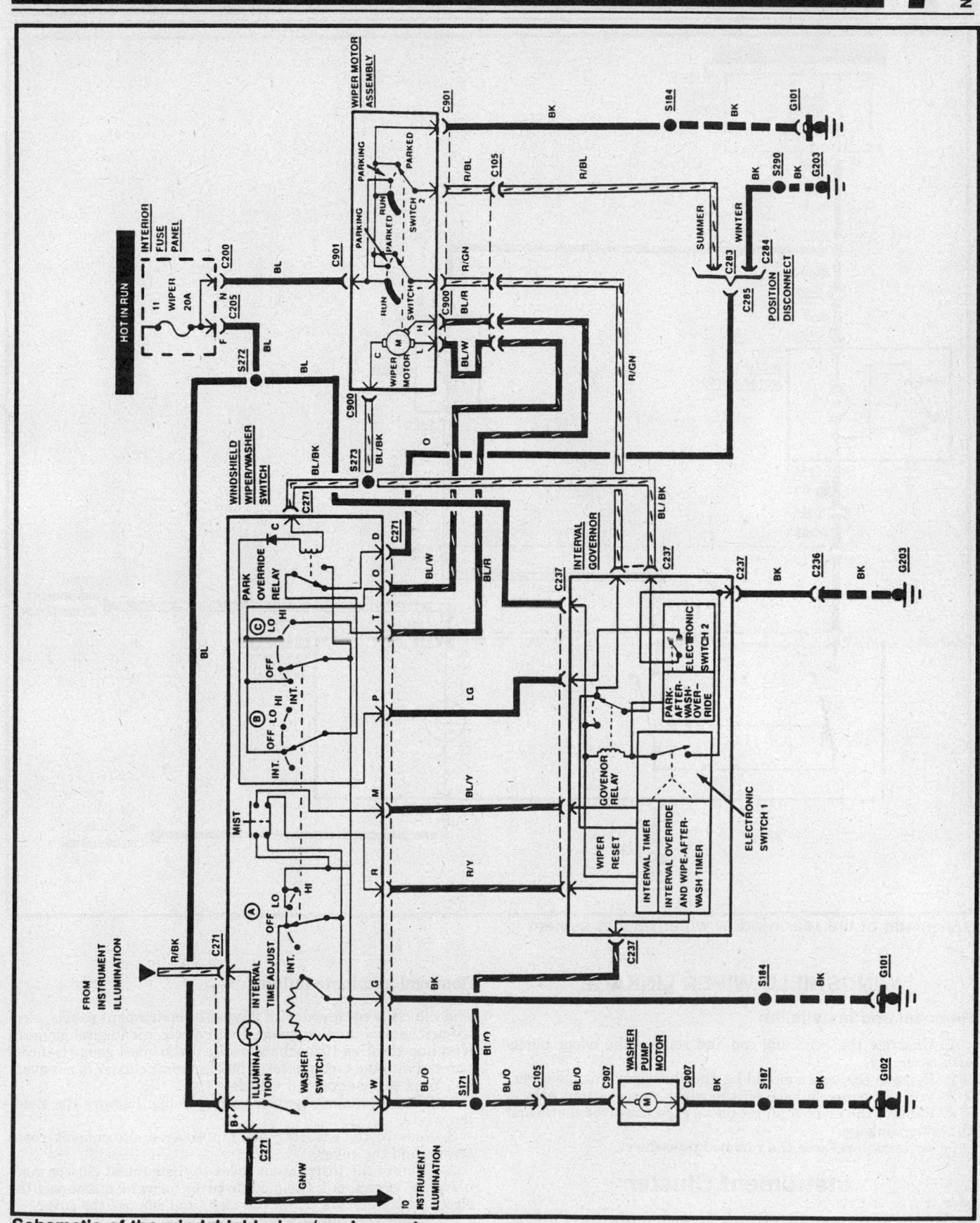

Schematic of the windshield wiper/washer system

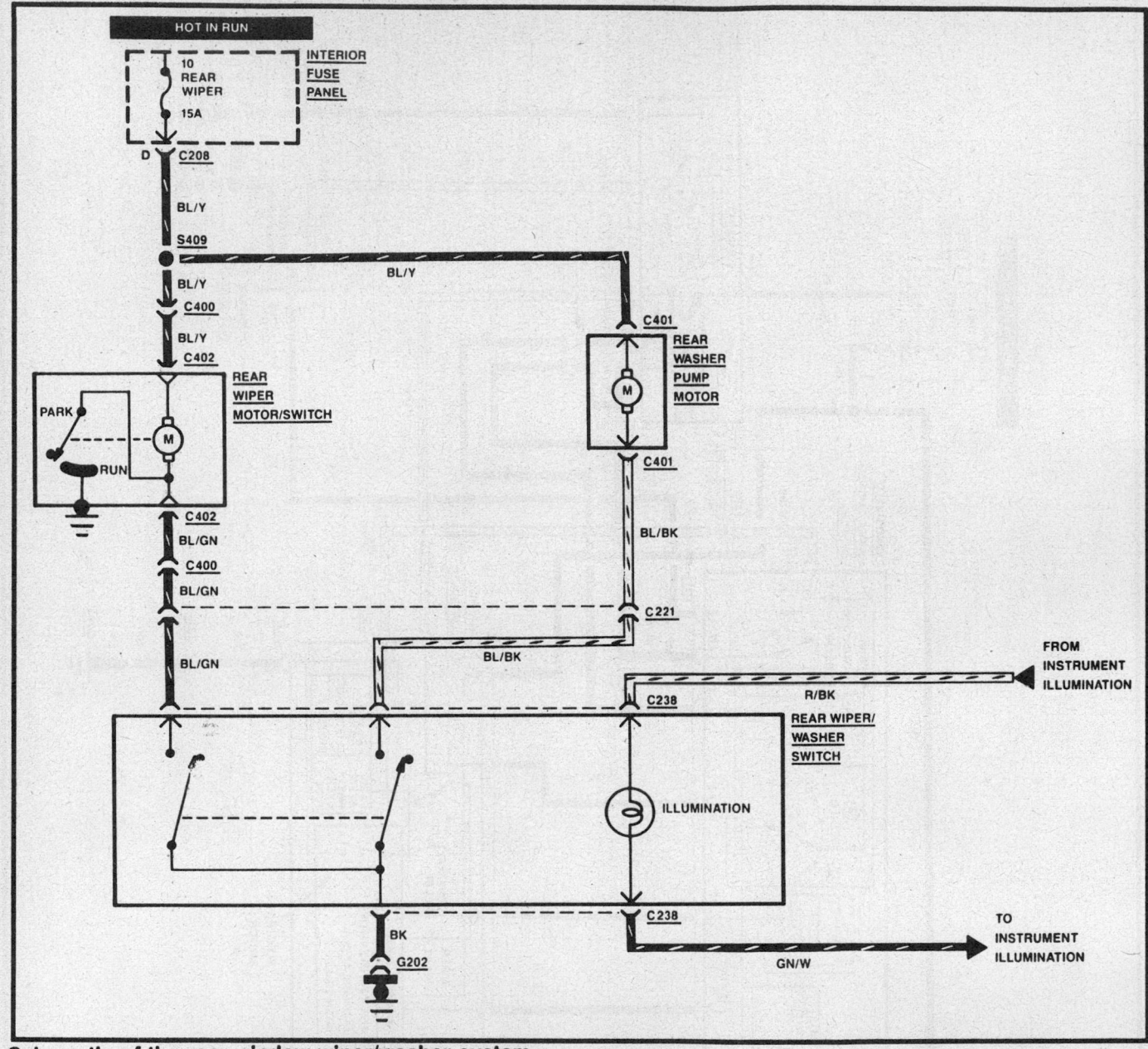

Schematic of the rear window wiper/washer system

WINDSHIELD WIPER LINKAGE

Removal and Installation

1. Unscrew the retaining cap and remove the wiper blade/arm assembly.
2. Remove the lower moulding and the wiper linkage cover.
3. Pull the wiper linkage off the wiper motor output arm.
4. Remove the pivot shaft retaining caps, the pivot shafts and the wiper linkage.
5. To install, reverse the removal procedures.

Instrument Cluster

Refer to "Chilton's Electronic Instrumentation Service Manual" for additional coverage.

Removal and Installation

The vehicle is equipped with 2 types of instrument panels: electro-mechanical (analog gauges) and electronic (digital gauges). If equipped with a turbocharger, the turbo boost gauge is incorporated into the tachometer. The electronic cluster is not available on a turbo equipped vehicle.

1. Disconnect the negative battery cable. Remove the steering wheel.
2. Remove the steering column cover-to-instrument cover screws and the cover.
3. Remove the instrument cover-to-instrument cluster module cover screws, pull the module cover forward, disconnect the electrical connectors (from the rear) and remove the cover.
4. Remove the instrument cluster cover-to-dash screws and the cover.

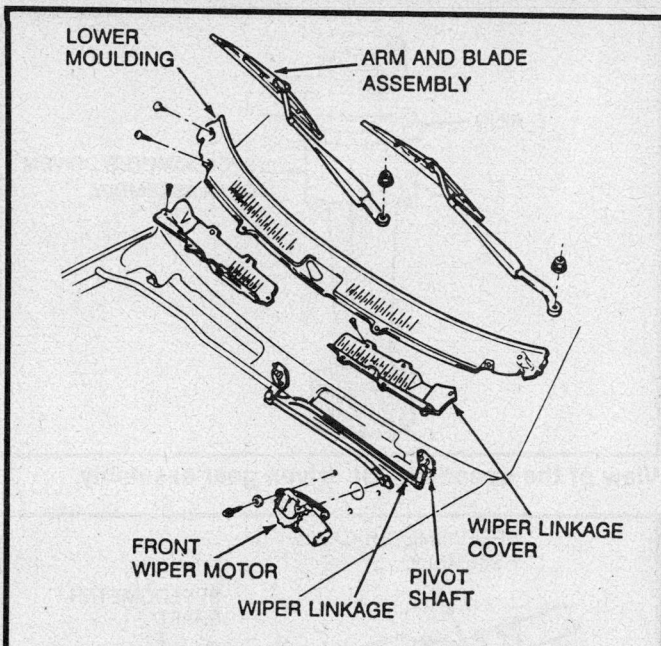

Exploded view of the windshield wiper assembly

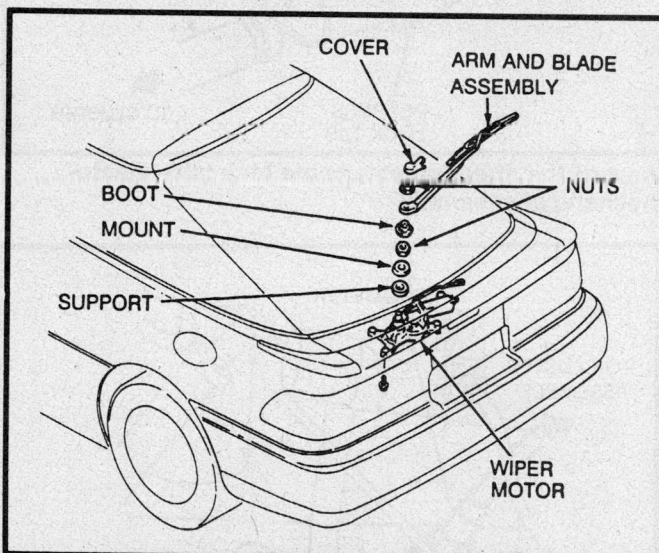

Exploded view of the rear window wiper assembly

5. Remove the lower cluster panel screws and the panel.

6. Remove the instrument cluster-to-dash screws, pull the cluster forward, disconnect the electrical connectors from the rear of the cluster and remove the cluster.

NOTE: If equipped with an electro-mechanical cluster, disconnect the speedometer cable from the rear of the cluster.

7. To install, reverse the removal procedures. Check all gauges, speedometer and tachometer for proper operation.

SPEEDOMETER

Removal and Installation

ELECTRONIC

The electronic speedometer is not servicable. If a problem is de-

tected within the speedometer circuitry or supporting logic circuitry, replace the electronic instrument cluster.

ELECTRO-MECHANICAL

The electro-mechanical speedometer subassembly is not servicable. If a problem is detected within the speedometer or supporting logic circuitry, replace the subassembly.

A speed sensor, used by the anti-lock brake system 4EAT (automatic transaxle), the speed sensing electronically controlled power steering and the programmed ride control system is located in the speedometer subassembly.

1. Disconnect the negative battery cable. Remove the instrument cluster.

2. Remove the lens assembly from the instrument cluster.

3. Remove the speedometer subassembly-to-instrument cluster screws and the subassembly from the cluster.

4. To install, reverse the removal procedures.

ELECTRONIC SPEED SENSOR

The electronic speed sensor is mounted on the transaxle and is used with the electronic instrument cluster.

1. Disconnect the negative battery cable and the electrical connector from the speed sensor.

2. Remove the sensor-to-transaxle bolt and pull the sensor straight out of the transxle.

3. To install the sensor, push it in until it seats and reverse the removal procedures. Check the speedometer operation.

SPEEDOMETER DRIVEN GEAR

The speedometer driven gear is mounted on the transaxle and is used with the electro-mechanical speedometer.

1. Disconnect the negative battery cable.

2. Pull the dust boot away from the speedometer cable connector.

3. Disconnect the cable from the speedometer driven gear.

4. Remove the speedometer drive gear-to-transaxle bolt, the driven gear and the O-ring.

NOTE: If may be necessary to gently, pry the driven gear away from the transaxle housing.

5. To install, use a new O-ring and reverse the removal procedures. Check the speedometer operation.

SPEEDOMETER CABLE

A 2 piece speedometer cable is used with the electro-mechanical speedometer.

Removal and Installation

UPPER CABLE

1. Disconnect the negative battery cable. Remove the upper and lower cluster cover panels from the cluster assembly.

2. Reach behind the instrument panel, depress the lock tab and pull the speedometer cable from the instrument cluster.

3. In the engine compartment, locate the upper/lower speedometer connector and unscrew it.

4. At the bulkhead, pry out the rubber grommet and slide it down the cable.

5. Gently, pry the retaining ring from the bulkhead and pull the speedometer cable through the bulkhead into the engine compartment.

6. To install, reverse the removal procedures. Check the speedometer operation.

LOWER CABLE

1. Disconnect the negative battery cable.

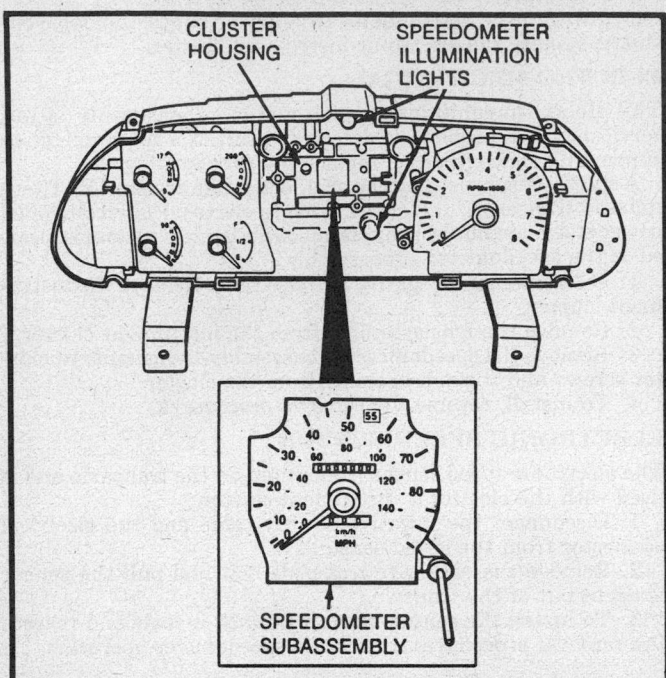

View of the electro-mechanical speedometer sub-assembly

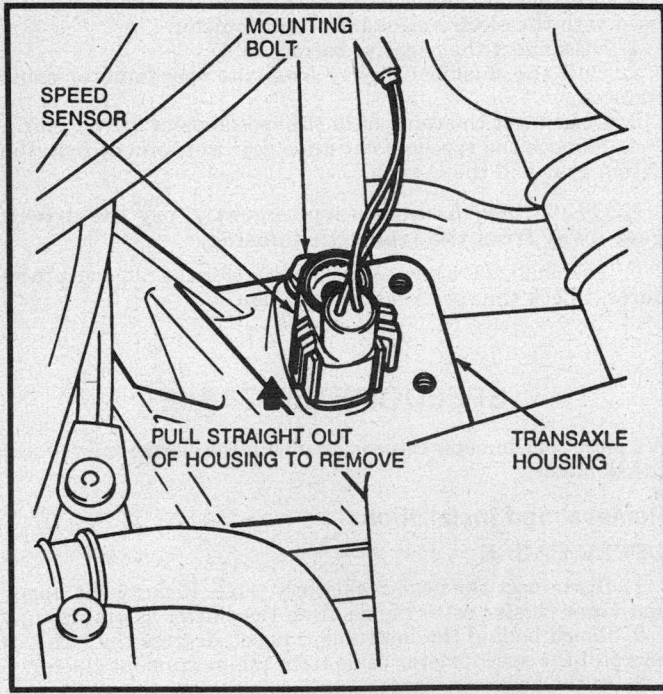

View of the electronic speed sensor

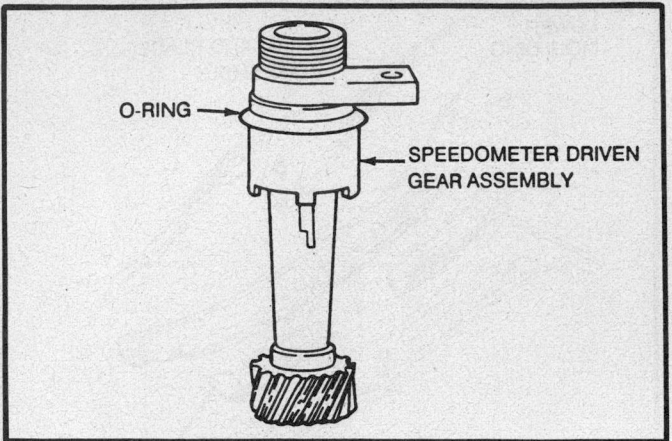

View of the speedometer driven gear assembly

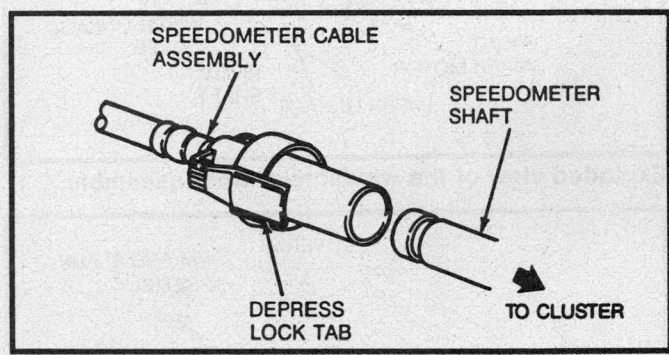

View of the speedometer cable lock tab—electo-mechanical assembly

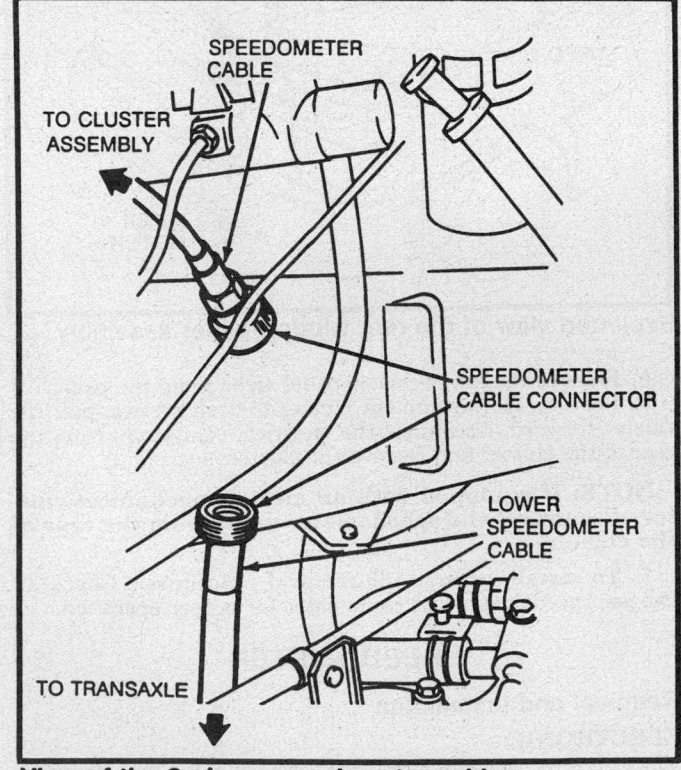

View of the 2 piece speedometer cables

2. In the engine compartment, locate the upper/lower speedometer connector and unscrew it.

3. Pull the dust boot away from the speedometer cable connector.

4. Disconnect the lower cable from the speedometer driven gear and remove the lower cable.

5. To install, reverse the removal procedures. Check the speedometer operation.

Electrical Circuit Protectors

CIRCUIT BREAKER

The vehicle is equipped with a rear window defroster circuit breaker which is mounted near the interior fuse block and central processing unit (CPU).

FUSE PANELS

MAIN FUSE BLOCK

The main fuse block is located in the left side of the engine compartment near the battery.

INTERIOR FUSE BLOCK

The interior fuse block is located above the left side kick panel. The fuses are a plug in type and are color-coded by amp rating.

COMPUTER

The central processing unit (CPU) is located above the left side kick panel.

RELAY BOXES

MAIN RELAY BOX

The main relay box is located on the upper left side of the bulkhead. It contains 2—EFI main relays, a horn relay and 2—cooling fan relays.

NOTE: **The cooling fan relay No. 1 is used only on vehicles equipped an electronically controlled automatic transaxle (4EAT).**

RELAY BOX

The relay box is mounted inside the vehicle, under the left side of the instrument panel on the bulkhead. It contains the turn signal/hazard flasher, fuel pump relay, the rear window defroster relay, the intermittent wiper relay, the stoplight/tail-light checker relay and the foglight relay.

VARIOUS RELAYS

EFI Main Relays (2)—located on the main relay box
Horn Relay—located on the main relay box
Cooling Fan Relay No. 1—located on the main relay box

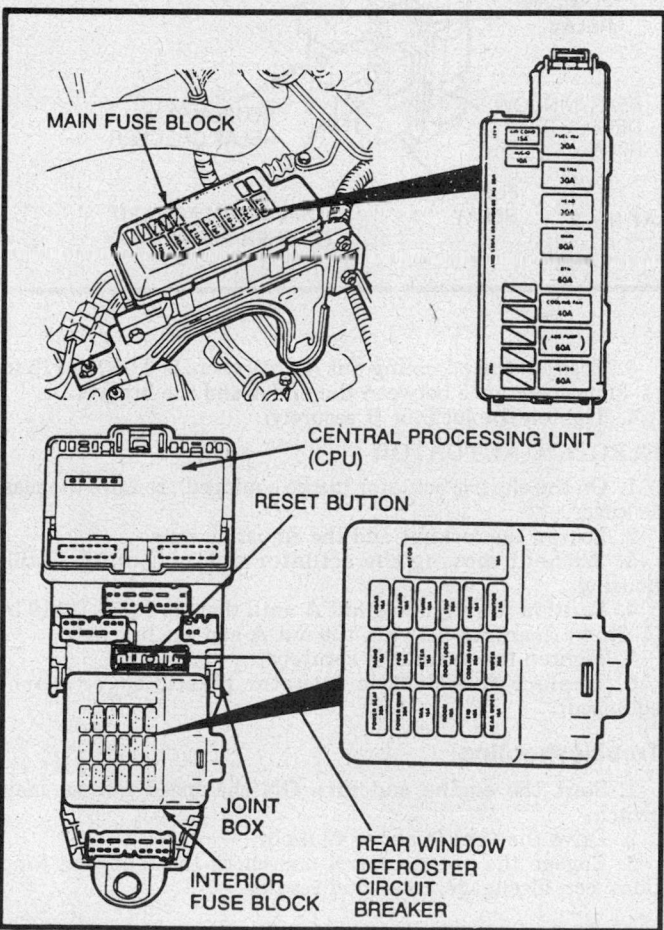

View of the central processing unit (CPU), the interior fuse block, the rear window defroster circuit breaker and the main fuse panel

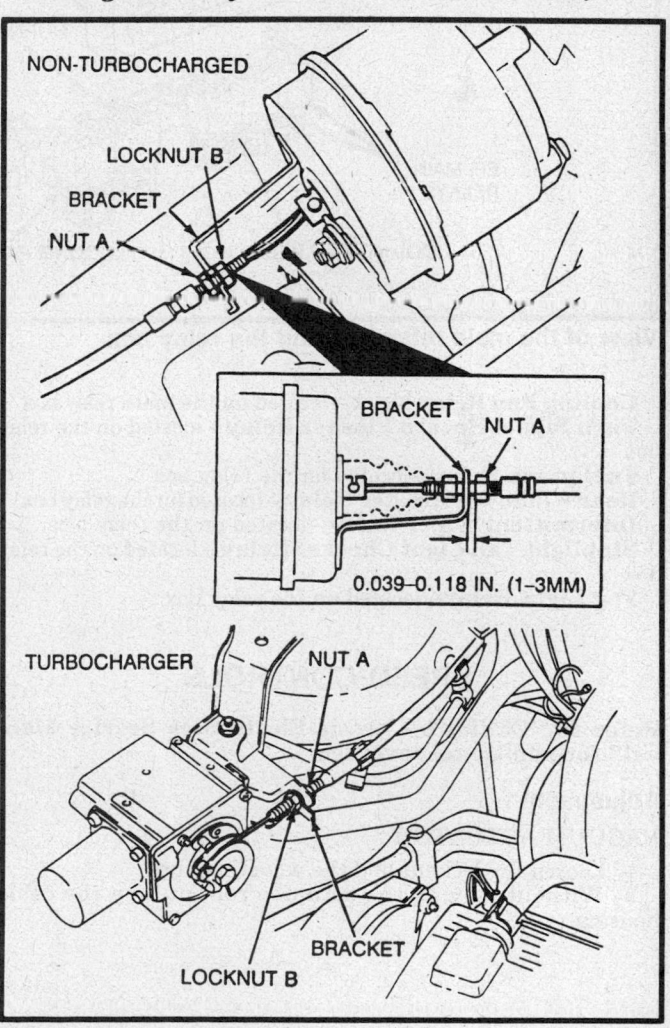

Adjusting the speed control actuators

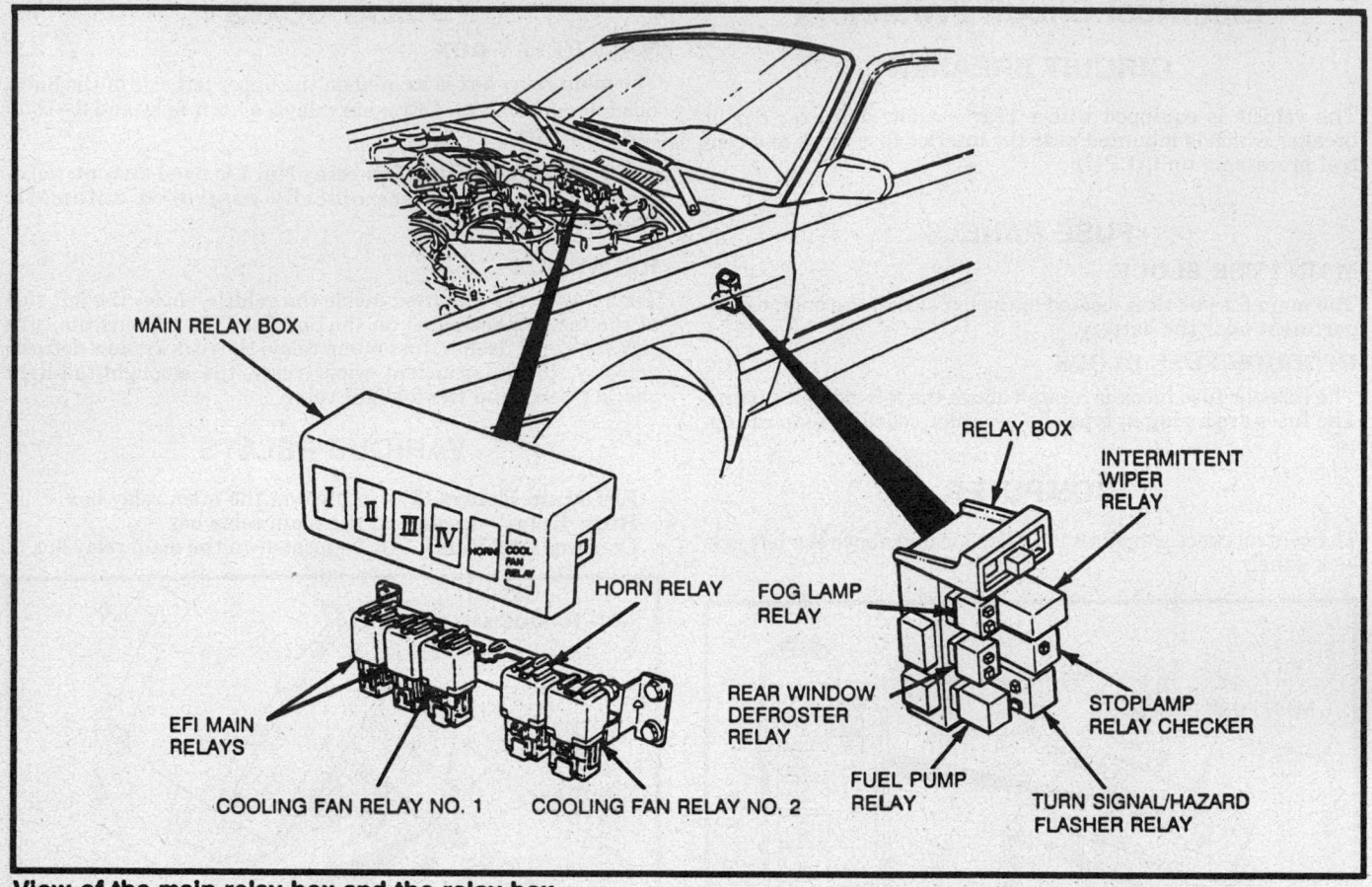

View of the main relay box and the relay box

Cooling Fan Relay No. 2—located on the main relay box
Turn Signal/Hazard Flasher Relay—located on the relay box
Fuel pump Relay—located on the relay box
Rear Window Defroster Relay—located on the relay box
Intermittent Wiper Relay—located on the relay box
Stoplight/Tail Light Checker Relay—located on the relay box
Fog Light Relay—located on the relay box

SPEED CONTROLS

Refer to "Chilton's Chassis Electronics Service Manual" for additional coverage.

Adjustment
VACUUM ACTUATOR

1. Loosen the locknut and the adjusting nuts.
2. Without moving the actuator rod, pull on the cable housing.

3. Position the adjusting nut **A** until there is 0.039–0.118 in. (1–3mm) clearance between the nut **A** and the bracket.
4. Tighten the locknut **B** securely.

ELECTRIC ACTUATOR

1. On the electric actuator (turbo equipped), remove the plastic cover.
2. Loosen the locknut and the adjusting nuts.
3. Without moving the actuator rod, pull on the cable housing.
4. Position the adjusting nut **A** until there is 0.039–0.118 in. (1–3mm) clearance between the nut **A** and the bracket.
5. Tighten the locknut **B** securely.
6. Replace the electric actuator plastic cover (turbo equipped).

Troubleshooting

1. Start the engine and turn **ON** the speed control main switch.
2. Drive the vehicle above 40 mph.
3. Engage the speed control and check the following functions: set, disengage, coast and resume.

COOLING AND HEATING SYSTEMS

Water Pump

The water pump is located at the front of the engine, behind the timing belt cover.

Removal and Installation

1. Disconnect the negative battery cable. Remove the timing belt.
2. Remove the timing belt tensioner pulley spring and the tensioner pulley.
3. Drain the cooling system to a level below the water pump.
4. Remove the water pump-to-engine bolts, the water pump and the O-ring (discard it).
5. Clean the gasket mounting surfaces.

To Install:

6. Using a new water pump O-ring, install it onto the water pump.
7. Install the water pump and torque the bolts 14–19 ft. lbs. (19–25 Nm).
8. To complete the installation, reverse the removal procedures. Refill the cooling system. Start the engine, allow it to reach normal operating temperatures and check for leaks. Check the timing.

Electric Cooling Fan

SYSTEM OPERATION

Removal and Installation

1. Disconnect the negative battery cable.
2. Disconnect the cooling fan electrical connectors.
3. Remove the fan shroud-to-radiator screws and the fan/shroud assembly.
4. If removing the fan motor from the shroud, perform the following procedurs:
   a. Remove the fan blade-to-motor nut and washer.
   b. Remove the fan motor-to-shroud bolts and the motor.
5. To install, reverse the removal procedures. Torque the:
   Fan motor-to-shroud bolts to 23–46 inch lbs. (2.6–5.2 Nm)
   Fan blade-to-motor nut to 69–95 inch lbs. (8–11 Nm)
   Fan/shroud assembly-to-radiator bolts to 61–87 inch lbs. (7–10 Nm)

Component Location

RADIATOR FAN SWITCH

The radiator fan switch is located in the thermostat housing.

ELECTRIC FAN RELAY

A cooling fan relay No. 2 is located in the main relay box in the engine compartment attached to the left side of the bulkhead. If equipped with an automatic transaxle, another cooling fan relay No. 1 is used with the cooling fan relay No. 2 and is positioned along side the cooling fan relay No. 2.

Blower Motor

Removal and Installation

1. Disconnect the negative battery cable.
2. Remove the sound deadening panel from the passenger side.
3. Remove the glove box assembly and the brace.
4. Remove the cooling hose from the blower motor assembly.
5. Disconnect the electrical connector from the blower motor.

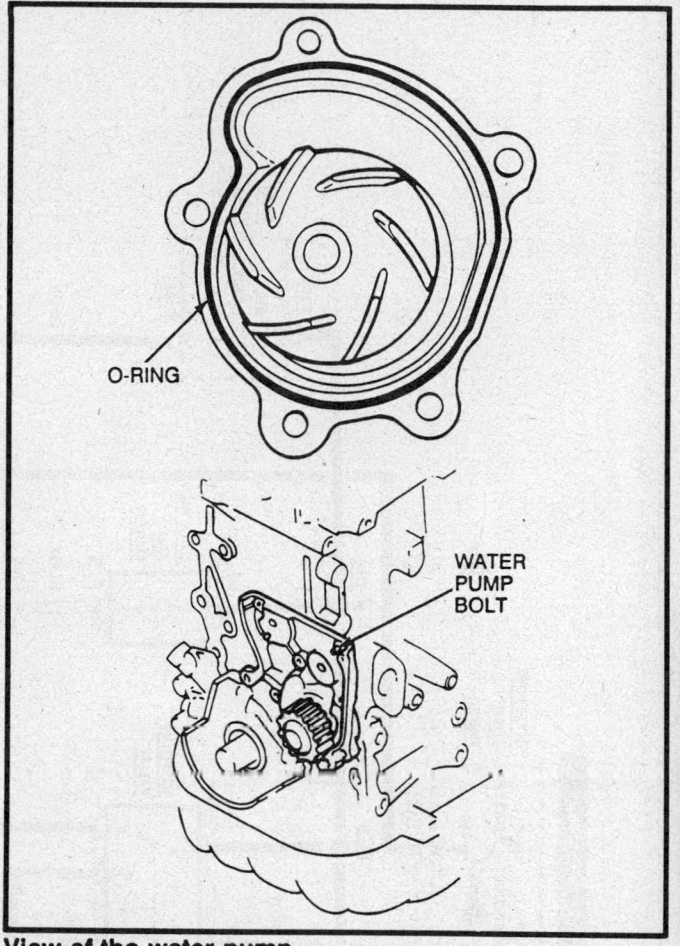

View of the water pump

6. Remove the blower motor-to-blower motor housing screws and blower motor.
7. If necessary, remove the blower wheel-to-blower motor clip and the wheel.
8. To install, reverse the removal procedures and check the blower motor operation.

Heater Core

Refer to "Chilton's Auto Heating and Air Conditioning Manual" for additional coverage.

Removal and Installation

WITH AIR CONDITIONING

1. Disconnect the negative battery cable. Remove the instrument panel.
2. Drain the cooling system to a level below the heater core.
3. Discharge the air conditioning system. Disconnect and plug the refrigerant lines from the evaporator case.
4. Disconnect the electrical connectors from the air conditioning relays at the top of the evaporator case.
5. Remove the charcoal canister from the vehicle.
6. From both ends of the evaporator case, remove the air duct bands. Remove the drain hose from the evaporator case.
7. Remove the evaporator case-to-chassis nuts and the case from the vehicle.

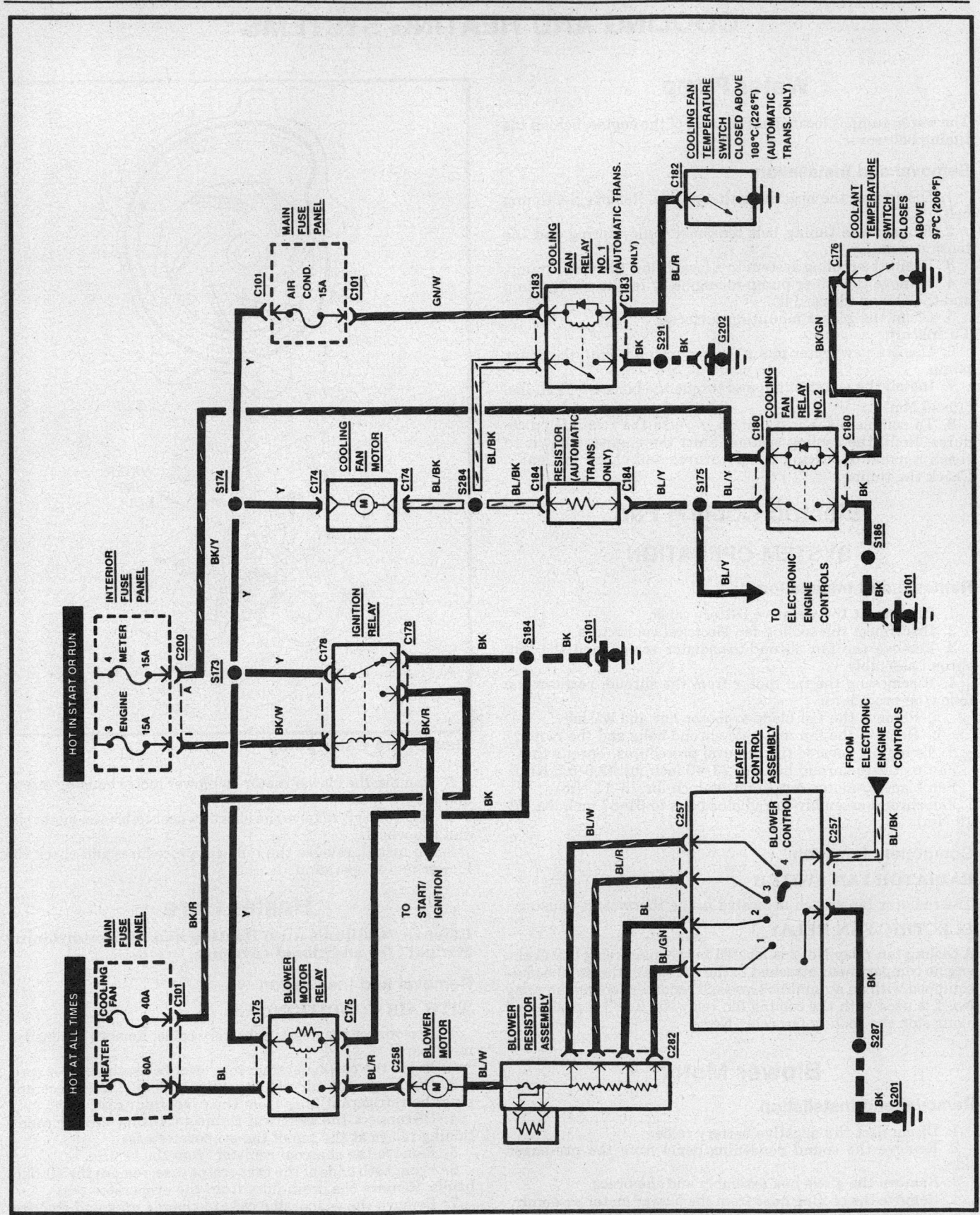

Schematic of the cooling system

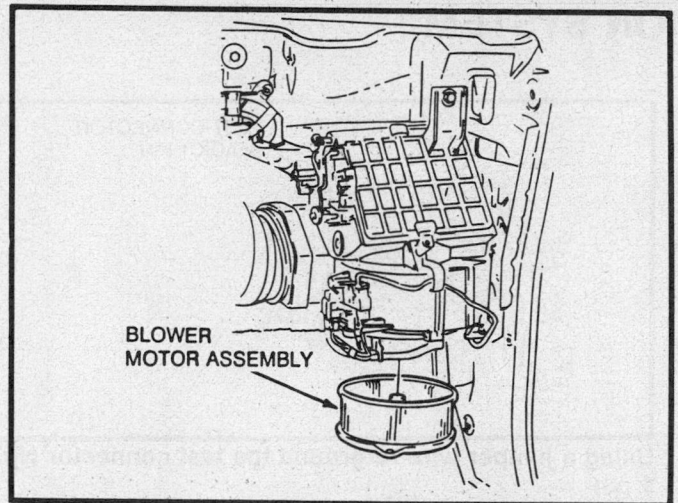

Exploded view of the blower motor assembly

8. Disconnect and plug the hoses from the heater core.

9. Remove the heater case-to-chassis bolts and pull the heater case straight; be careful not to damage the heater core extension tubes.

10. Remove the heater core tube braces-to-heater case screws and the tube braces.

11. Lift the heater core straight up and out of the heater case.

12. To install, reverse the removal procedures. Refill the cooling system and charge the air conditioning system.

13. Start the engine, allow it to reach normal operating temperatures and check the heater/air conditioning system operation and leaks.

WITHOUT AIR CONDITIONING

1. Disconnect the negative battery cable. Remove the instrument panel.

2. Drain the cooling system to a level below the heater core.

3. Disconnect and plug the hoses from the heater core.

4. Remove the main air duct from the heater case.

5. Remove the heater case-to-chassis screws and pull the heater case straight; be careful not to damage the heater core extension tubes.

6. Remove the heater core tube braces-to-heater case screws and the tube braces.

7. Lift the heater core straight up and out of the heater case.

8. To install, reverse the removal procedures. Refill the cooling system. Start the engine, allow it to reach normal operating temperatures and check the heater operation and leaks.

TEMPERATURE CONTROL/BLOWER SWITCH

The temperature control/blower switch assembly is located in the center of the instrument panel.

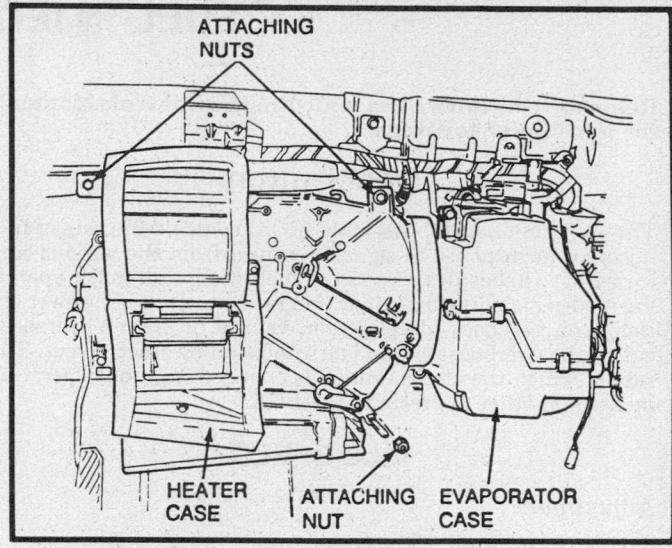

View of the heater case assembly—with air conditioning

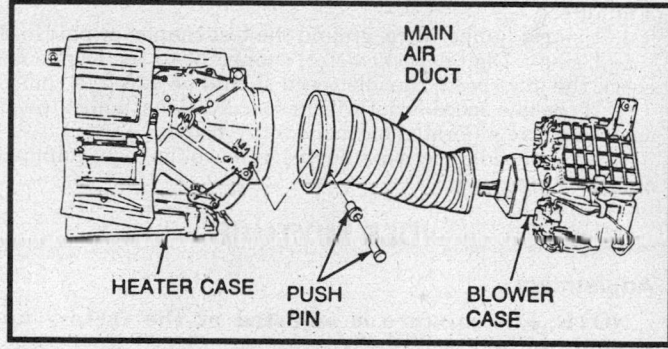

Exploded view of the main air duct and heater case assembly—without air conditioning

Removal and Installation

1. Disconnect the negative battery cable.

2. Remove the bezel cover from the control assembly face.

3. Remove the control assembly-to-instrument panel screws and pull the assembly forward. Disconnect the electrical connectors and control cables from the assembly.

4. Remove the control assembly from the vehicle.

5. If necessary to remove the blower switch from the control assembly, perform the following procedures:

   a. Pull the blower switch knob straight off the shaft.

   b. Remove the blower switch-to-control assembly nut and the switch from the control housing.

6. To install, reverse the removal procedures. Check the operation of the control housing.

FUEL INJECTION SYSTEM

Refer to "Chilton's Electronic Engine Controls Manual" for additional coverage.

Description

The electronic control assembly (ECA) controls the rate of fuel injection in response to signals received from the various sensors and switches. It corrects the fuel rate for all major operating modes including basic injection rate, acceleration, power enrichment, feedback, deceleration, vehicle or engine overspeed cut, turbo overboost cut and air conditioning start-up cut. The rate at which the air/fuel ration is changed from one operating mode to another is preset in the ECA.

IDLE SPEED

Adjustment

1. Turn **OFF** all of the accessories.
2. Firmly set the parking brake and position the gear shift selector in **P** (automatic) or **N** (manual).
3. Start and operate the engine at 2500–3000 rpm for at least 3 minutes.
4. Using a jumper wire, ground the test connector pin No. 1.
5. Using a Digital Tachometer, connect it to the engine and check the idle speed; the idle speed should be 725–775 rpm.
6. If the idle speed is not within specifications, adjust the air adjusting screw (located on the throttle body).
7. After the idle speed is adjusted, remove the test equipment and the jumper wire.

IDLE MIXTURE

Adjustment

NOTE: Idle mixture is adjusted at the factory and should not be attempted.

SYSTEM PRESSURE RELIEF

——————— CAUTION ———————
Keep all possible heat and ignition sources away from fuel drainage and spills. Wipe up spilled fuel promptly and dispose of any fuel soaked rags in a suitable container.
————————————————————

Procedure

1. Start the engine.
2. From under the instrument panel, disconnect the fuel pump relay from the junction block.
3. After the engine stalls, turn the ignition swtich **OFF** and reconnect the fuel pump relay to the junction block.

Fuel Pump

The fuel pump is attached to the fuel pump sending unit and is located in the fuel tank.

Removal and Installation

1. Release the fuel pressure and disconnect the negative battery cable.
2. Remove the rear seat and disconnect the electrical connector from the fuel tank sending unit.
3. Remove the sending unit cover-to-chassis screws and the cover.
4. Disconnect and plug the fuel hoses from the sending unit.

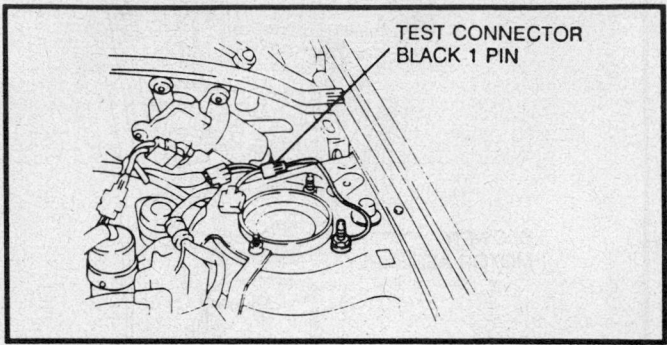

Using a jumper wire to ground the test connector No. 1 pin

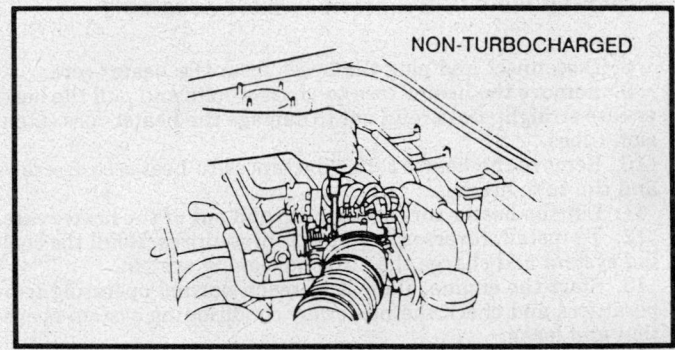

Turning the air adjusting screw to adjust the engine idle speed

5. Remove the sending unit-to-fuel tank screws and the sending unit from the fuel tank.
6. To install, reverse the removal procedures. Start the engine and check the engine operation.

TIMING SENSORS

Testing
CRANKSHAFT POSITION SENSOR (CPS)—TURBO

The crankshaft position sensor (CPS) is located withing the distributor. For each 2 crankshaft rotations, 24 pulses are created by the crankshaft sensor coil; the pulses are used by the ECA to determine engine speed and to set the ignition and fuel injection timing.

CYLINDER IDENTIFICATION SENSOR (CID)—TURBO

Two cylinder identification sensors (CID) are located within the distributor; the cylinder identification sensor **B** signal detects the No. 1 cylinder's TDC (compression) and the cylinder identification sensor **A** signal detects the No. 4 cylinder's TDC (compression). The signals, created by the distributor coils are sent to the ECA, which uses the signals to control the electronic spark advance (ESA) control system and the electronic fuel injection (EFI) system.

If a signal fails, the ECA uses the other signal to control the engine systems, with no change to the engine performance or operation.

KNOCK SENSOR—TURBO

The knock sensor is mounted on the engine block near the left side of the oil filter. It detects engine knocking and sends a signal to the knock control unit which in turn sends a signal to the ECA.

EXHAUST GAS RECIRCULATION (EGR) SENSOR TURBO AND NON-TURBO (CALIF.)

The exhaust gas recirculation (EGR) sensor consists of a variable resistor and is located on the EGR valve near the right side of the intake plenum. It detects the EGR control valve position and provides this information to the ECA.

EXHAUST GAS OXYGEN SENSOR (EGO)

The exhaust gas oxygen sensor (EGO) is mounted in the exhaust manifold and detects the amount of oxygen in the exhaust gas. It sends information to the ECA for used in determining fuel injection amounts.

BAROMETRIC PRESSURE SENSOR (BP)

The barometric pressure sensor (BP) is mounted at the right rear of the engine compartment on the bulkhead. It senses atmospheric pressure and sends the information to the ECA.

VANE AIR TEMPERATURE SENSOR (AT)

The vane air temperature sensor (AT) is a thermistor which is mounted inside the vane airflow meter and senses the intake air temperature. The information is sent to the ECA for calculating the fuel injection amount.

ENGINE COOLANT TEMPERATURE SENSOR (ECT)

The engine coolant temperature sensor (ECT) is mounted on the cylinder head (non-turbo) or intake manifold (turbo); it is used to detect the coolant temperature and sends information to the ECA to determine the fuel injection amount.

THROTTLE POSITION SENSOR (TPS)

The throttle position sensor (TPS) is a variable resistor type sensor; it is mounted on the left side of the throttle body and consists of a lever fitted coaxially of the throttle valve and a variable resistor. It detects the throttle valve position and sends signals to the ECA.

VEHICLE SPEED SENSOR—NON-TURBO

The vehicle speed sensor (VSS) is mounted within the instrument panel cluster. It sends information to the ECA, the 4EAT and the programmed ride control system to determine vehicle speed and fuel cut-off operation.

SWITCHES/RELAYS

Various other switches/relays are used by the ECA to determine the fuel injection amounts and fuel cut-off operations, are:

Brake On-Off Switch—located near top of brake pedal
Electrical Load (E/L) Control Unit—located under the center console in front of the ECA unit
Power Steering Pressure Switch—located on the right side of te power steering rack
Air Conditioning Cut-Off Relay—located on top of the evaporator case (non-turbo) or near the front of the battery on the left side of the radiator (turbo)
Ignition Switch (Start Position)—located on the steering column
Neutral Safety Switch (ATX)—located on top of the transaxle assembly (non-turbo)
Neutral Gear Switch (MTX)—located on the transaxle
Clutch Engage Switch (MTX)—located above the clutch pedal
Engine Coolant Temperature Switch—located on the radiator
Idle Switch—located on the right side of the throttle body
Vane Air Flow Meter (VAF)—located on the air intake system
Fifth Gear Switch (MTX)—located on the manual transaxle housing (non-turbo)

Removal and Installation
THROTTLE POSITION SENSOR (TPS)

1. Disconnect the negative battery cable.
2. Remove the air duct from the throttle body.
3. Disconnect the electrical connector from the TPS.
4. Carefully, bend back the TPS wire retaining brackets and the wire.
5. Remove the TPS-to-throttle body screws and pull the TPS from the throttle body.

To Install:

6. Position the TPS into the throttle body and tighten the screws finger tight.
7. To adjust the TPS, perform the following procedures:

   a. Using an unshielded male side TPS connector, attach it to the female connector.

   b. Turn the ignition switch to the **ON** position.

   c. Using a voltmeter, connect it to the BLACK and RED leads and record the reading; the reading should be between 4.5–5.5V.

   d. Move the voltmeter lead from the RED lead to the WHITE lead.

   e. Loosen the TPS mounting screws and adjust the TPS until the reading in the relationship chart is compared to the RED lead. Tighten the mounting screws and recheck the reading.

RED wire voltage (V)	WHITE wire voltage (V)	RED wire voltage (V)	WHITE wire voltage (V)
4.50–4.59	0.37–0.54	5.10–5.19	0.42–0.61
4.60–4.69	0.38–0.55	5.20–5.29	0.43–0.62
4.70–4.79	0.39–0.56	5.30–5.39	0.44–0.63
4.80–4.89	0.40–0.57	5.40–5.49	0.44–0.64
4.90–4.99	0.40–0.58	5.50	0.44–0.66
5.00–5.09	0.41–0.60		

TPS voltage relationship between the red and white wires—throttle valve fully closed

RED wire voltage (V)	WHITE wire voltage (V)	RED wire voltage (V)	WHITE wire voltage (V)
4.50–4.59	3.58–4.23	5.10–5.19	4.05–4.79
4.60–4.69	3.66–4.32	5.20–5.29	4.13–4.88
4.70–4.79	3.74–4.41	5.30–5.39	4.21–4.98
4.80–4.89	3.82–4.51	5.40–5.49	4.29–5.07
4.90–4.99	3.90–4.60	5.50	4.29–5.17
5.00–5.09	3.97–4.70		

TPS voltage relationship between the red and white wires—throttle valve fully open

NOTE: If the WHITE wire voltage cannot be adjusted to the relationship, replace the TPS and repeat the procedure.

   f. Hold the throttle valve **FULLY OPEN** and measure the voltage of the RED wire. With the throttle valve **FULLY OPEN**, measure the WHITE wire voltage; it should be within specifications provided in the relationship chart in comparison to the RED wire.

NOTE: If the WHITE wire voltage cannot be adjusted to the relationship, replace the TPS and repeat the procedure.

   g. Turn the ignition switch **OFF** and remove the test connector.
8. To complete the installation, reverse the removal procedures.

ELECTRICAL LOAD (EL) UNIT

The electrical load (EL) unit is located under the center console in front of the ECA unit.
1. Disconnect the negative battery cable.
2. Disengage the push pin retainers from both sides of the inner kick panels and remove the panels.
3. Remove the ECA unit-to-floorpan bracket bolts and the ECA unit.
4. Move the ECA toward the driver's side, disconnect the electrical connectors and remove the unit from the vehicle.
5. Remove the EL unit-to-floorpan bracket bolts and the EL unit.
6. To install, reverse the removal procedures.

VANE AIR FLOW METER

1. Disconnect the negative battery cable and the electrical connector from the vane airflow meter.
2. Remove the air duct from the air filter cover.
3. Remove the air cleaner cover bolts and the air cleaner.
4. From inside the air cleaner cover, remove the vane air flow meter nuts and the meter.
5. To install, reverse the removal procedures.

EXHAUST GAS OXYGEN SENSOR (EGO)

1. Disconnect the negative battery cable.
2. Disconnect the electrical connector from the sensor.
3. Using an EGO sensor wrench No. T79P-9472-A or equivalent, remove the EGO sensor from the exhaust manifold.
4. To install, reverse the removal procedures.

BAROMETRIC PRESSURE SENSOR

1. Disconnect the negative battery cable.
2. Disconnect the electrical connector from the sensor.
3. Remove the mounting nut and the sensor.
4. To install, reverse the removal procedures.

FUEL INJECTOR

Removal and Installation

1. Relieve the fuel pressure and disconnect the negative battery cable.
2. Drain the cooling system.
3. Disconnect the accelerator cables from the throttle body.
4. Remove the air duct from the throttle body.
5. Label and disconnect the vacuum lines and coolant hoses from the throttle body.
6. Disconnect the electrical connectors from the TPS, the idle switch and the bypass air control valve.
7. Remove the engine lifting bracket mounting bolts from the throttle body and the engine block.
8. Disconnect the coolant line/EGR hose bracket from the throttle body and the throttle cable brackets from the intake plenum.
9. Remove the wire loom bracket and the EGR back-pressure transducer bracket from the right side of the plenum.
10. Remove the PCV hose and the vacuum line assembly bracket from the intake plenum.
11. Label and disconnect the vacuum lines from the intake plenum.
12. Remove the plenum-to-intake manifold nuts/bolts, the plenum and the gasket.

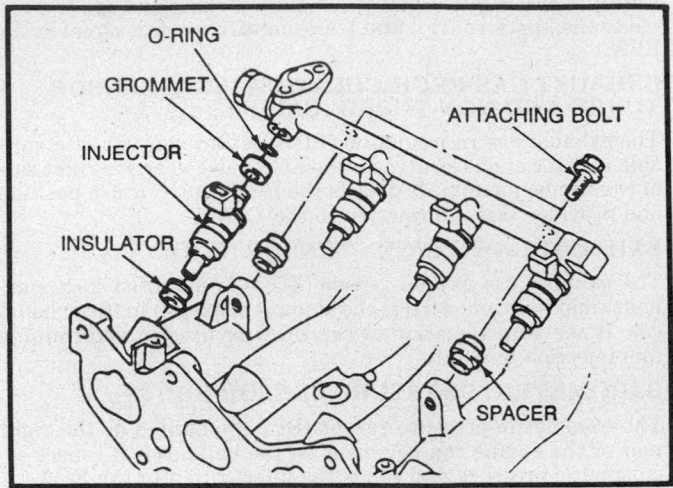

Exploded view of the fuel rail and fuel injectors

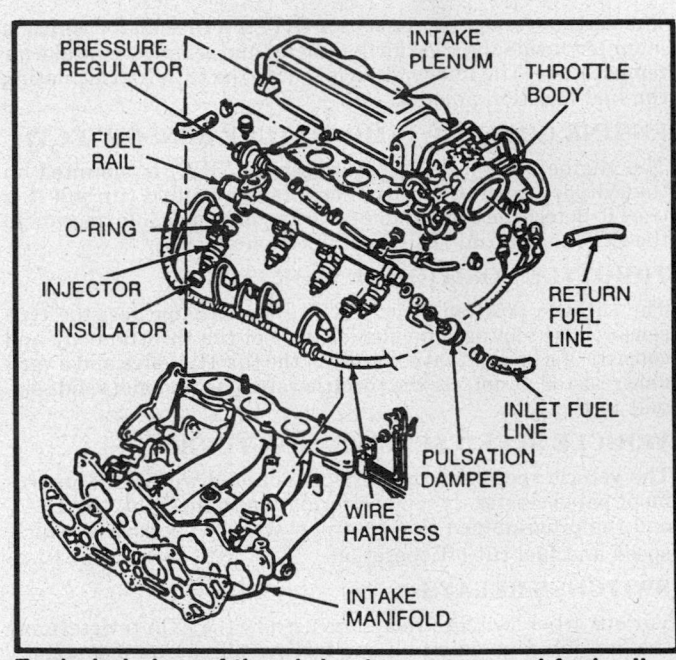

Exploded view of the air intake system and fuel rail assembly

13. Disconnect the electrical connectors from the fuel injectors.
14. Carefully, bend the wire harness retainer brackets away from the wire harness and move the harness assembly away from the intake manifold.
15. Remove the fuel supply tube from the pulsation damper.
16. Remove the fuel return line bracket from the intake manifold, the clamp and the fuel return line from the bracket.
17. Remove the fuel rail-to-intake manifold bolts and the fuel rail (with pressure regulator and pulsation damper attached).
18. Remove the fuel injectors, the grommet and the O-rings from the fuel rail. Remove the O-rings from the fuel injectors and discard it.

To Install:
19. Using new O-rings, lubricate them with engine oil and install the fuel injectors into the fuel rail.
20. Install the fuel injector/rail assembly into the intake manifold and torque the bolts to 14–19 ft. lbs. (19–25 Nm). Connect the electrical connectors to the fuel injectors.

21. Install the fuel return line bracket onto the intake manifold and the return line at the bracket (secure with a clamp).

22. Install the fuel supply line onto the pulsation damper and secure with a clamp.

23. Using a new gasket, install the intake plenum onto the intake manifold and torque the nuts/bolts to 14–19 ft. lbs. (19–25 Nm).

24. Install with the wiring harness onto the retainer brackets and carefully bend the brackets toward the wire harness.

25. To complete the installation, reverse the removal procedures. Refill the cooling system. Start the engine, allow it to reach normal operating temperatures and check for leaks and engine operation.

TURBOCHARGER SYSTEM

Refer to "Chilton's Electronic Engine Controls Manual" for additional coverage.

Description

The turbocharger is attached to the exhaust manifold and uses the exhaust gases to turn a small high speed turbine/air compressor assembly. The compressor receives air from the air cleaner and pumps it through an intercooler to the intake plenum. A compressor bypass valve responds to high vacuum during deceleration and opens to relieve excessive high pressure air and noise. Under heavy load or acceleration, the boost pressure is controlled by an exhaust bypass device or wastegate. A solenoid valve, governed by the ECA, controls the turbocharger boost pressure applied to the wastegate actuator. If a fault develops in the wastegate actuator (solenoid valve) resulting in excessive boost pressures, an overboost warning chime will sound; the chime is activated by the vane air flow meter through the ECA. The knock sensor and knock control unit combine to retard the engine spark advance when engine knocking occurs due to overboost by the turbocharger system.

TURBOCHARGER UNIT

Removal and Installation

1. Disconnect the negative battery cable.
2. Drain the cooling system to a level below the turbocharger.
3. Remove the air inlet and outlet hoses from the turbocharger's compressor.
4. Remove the heat shields from the exhaust manifold and turbocharger.
5. From above the distributor, disconnect the exhaust gas oxygen sensor (EGO) electrical connector and place the wire over the front of the vehicle (away from the heat shield).
6. From the top of the turbocharger, remove the oil feed line. From the lower portion of the turbocharger, remove oil return line and gasket.
7. Label and disconnect the coolant inlet and outlet hoses from the turbocharger.
8. From the exhaust manifold, remove the EGR tube. From the air bypass valve joint pipe area, disconnect the turbo boost control solenoid valve electrical connector.
9. From the turbo boost control solenoid valve at the turbocharger outlet air hose, remove the air tube.
10. From under the turbocharger, remove the retaining bracket-to-turbocharger bolt.
11. Discharge the air conditioning system and remove the refrigerant line from the head of the compressor.
12. Remove the exhaust gas oxygen sensor (EGO) from the exhaust manifold.
13. Disconnect the exhaust pipe from the turbocharger. Remove the exhaust manifold-to-cylinder head bolts, the exhaust manifold/turbocharger assembly and the gasket from the vehicle.

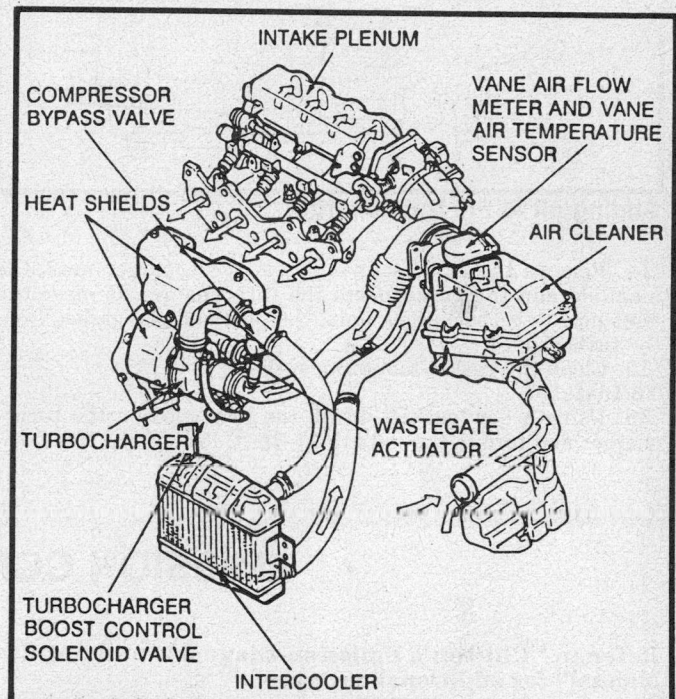

View of the turbocharger system

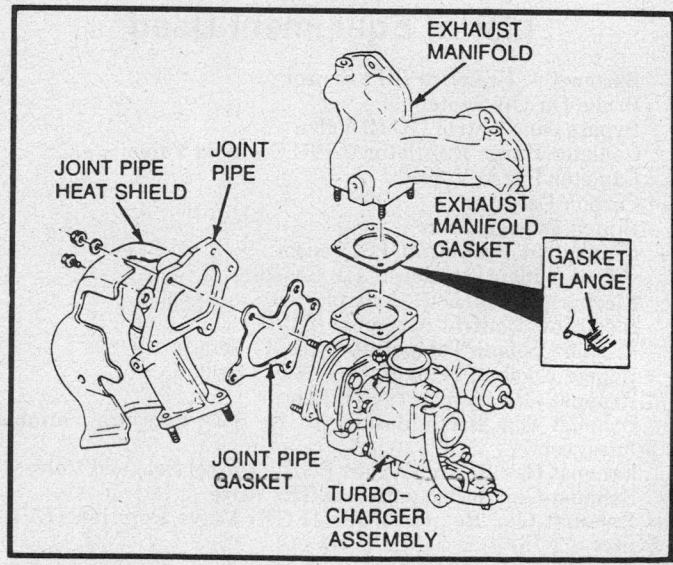

Exploded view of the turbocharger/exhaust manifold assembly

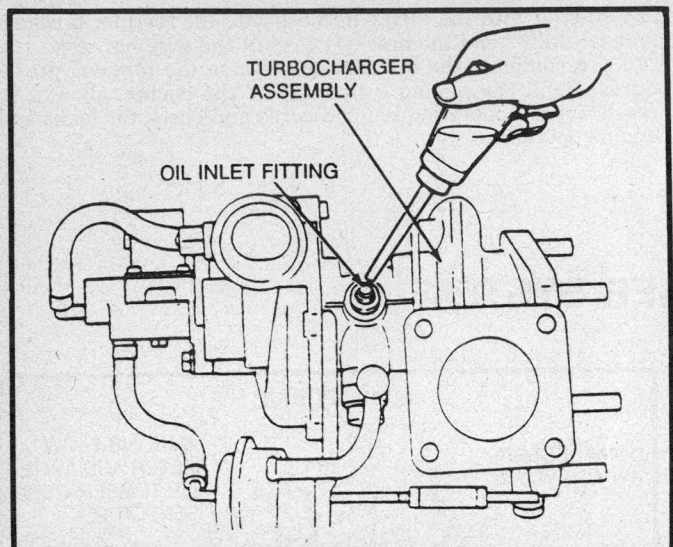

Adding oil to the turbocharger

14. Remove the exhaust manifold-to-turbocharger nuts, the manifold and the gasket from the turbocharger. Remove the joint pipe-to-turbocharger nuts, the pipe and the gasket from the turbocharger.

15. Clean the gasket mounting surfaces.

To Install:

16. Using a new gasket, install the joint pipe on the turbocharger and torque the nuts to 27–46 ft. lbs. (37–63 Nm).

17. Using a new gasket, install exhaust manifold on the turbocharger and torque the nuts to 20–29 ft. lbs. (27–39 Nm).

18. Using a new gasket, position the exhaust manifold/turbocharger assembly onto the cylinder head and torque the nuts to 16–21 ft. lbs. (22–28 Nm).

19. Using a new gasket, install the exhaust pipe to the turbocharger and torque the nuts to 23–34 ft. lbs. (31–46 Nm).

20. Install the coolant lines and oil return line to the turbocharger. Using 0.85 oz. (25 ml) of engine oil, insert it through the turbocharger oil feed passage.

21. To complete the installation, reverse the removal procedures. Refill the cooling system. Recharge the air conditioning system.

22. After replacing the turbocharger, perform the following procedures:

    a. Disconnect the electrical connector from the ignition coil.

    b. Crank the engine for approximately 20 seconds.

    c. Reconnect the electrical connector to the ignition coil.

    d. Start the engine and operate it at idle for approximately 30 seconds.

    e. Stop the engine, disconnect the negative battery cable and depress the brake pedal for at least 5 seconds to cancel the malfunction code.

    f. Reconnect the negative battery cable.

23. Start the engine, allow it to reach normal operating temperatures and check for leaks and engine operation.

TURBOCHARGER WASTEGATE UNIT

The wastegate unit is not servicable, if replacement of the wastegate unit is necessary, replace the turbocharger assembly as a unit.

EMISSION CONTROL SYSTEMS

Refer to "Chilton's Emission Diagnosis and Service Manual" for additional coverage.

List of Equipment Used

Barometric Pressure (BP) Sensor
Brake On-Off Switch
Bypass Air Control (BAC) Valve
Canister Purge Regulator (CPR) Solenoid Valve
Canister Purge Valve
Carbon Canister
Clutch Engage Switch
Crankshaft Position (CPS) Sensor
Cylinder Identification (CID) Sensors
Electrical Load (E/L) Control Unit
Electronic Control Assembly (ECA)
Engine Coolant Temperature (ECT) Sensor
Engine Coolant Temperature (ECT) Switch
Exhaust Gas Oxygen (EGO) Sensor
Exhaust Gas Recirculation (EGR) Back-Pressure Variable Transducer
Exhaust Gas Recirculation (EGR) Control Solenoid Valve
Exhaust Gas Recirculation (EGR) Valve
Exhaust Gas Recirculation (EGR) Valve Position (EVP) Sensor
Fuel Pressure Regulator
Idle Switch
Neutral Safety Switch

Knock Control Unit
Knock Sensor
Malfunction Indication Light (MIL)
Neutral Gear Switch
Positive Crankcase Ventilation (PCV) Valve
Power Relays
Power Steering (P/S) Pressure Switch
Pressure Regulator Control (PRC) Solenoid Valve
Rollover/Vent Valve
Self-Test Output/Self-Test Input Connectors
Three-Way Check Valve
Throttle Position Sensor
Turbo Boost Control Solenoid Valve
Vacuum Control Valve
Vacuum Delay Valve
Vacuum Reservoir
Vane Air Flow Meter
Vane Air Temperature (VAT) Sensor
Vapor Separator

Resetting Emission Warning Lamp

A malfunction indicator light (MIL) is located on the lower right side of the instrument cluster; it turns **ON** to signal the driver that the ECA system is malfunctioning.

When the self-test input (STI), located in the engine compartment near the driver's strut tower, connector is grounded, the

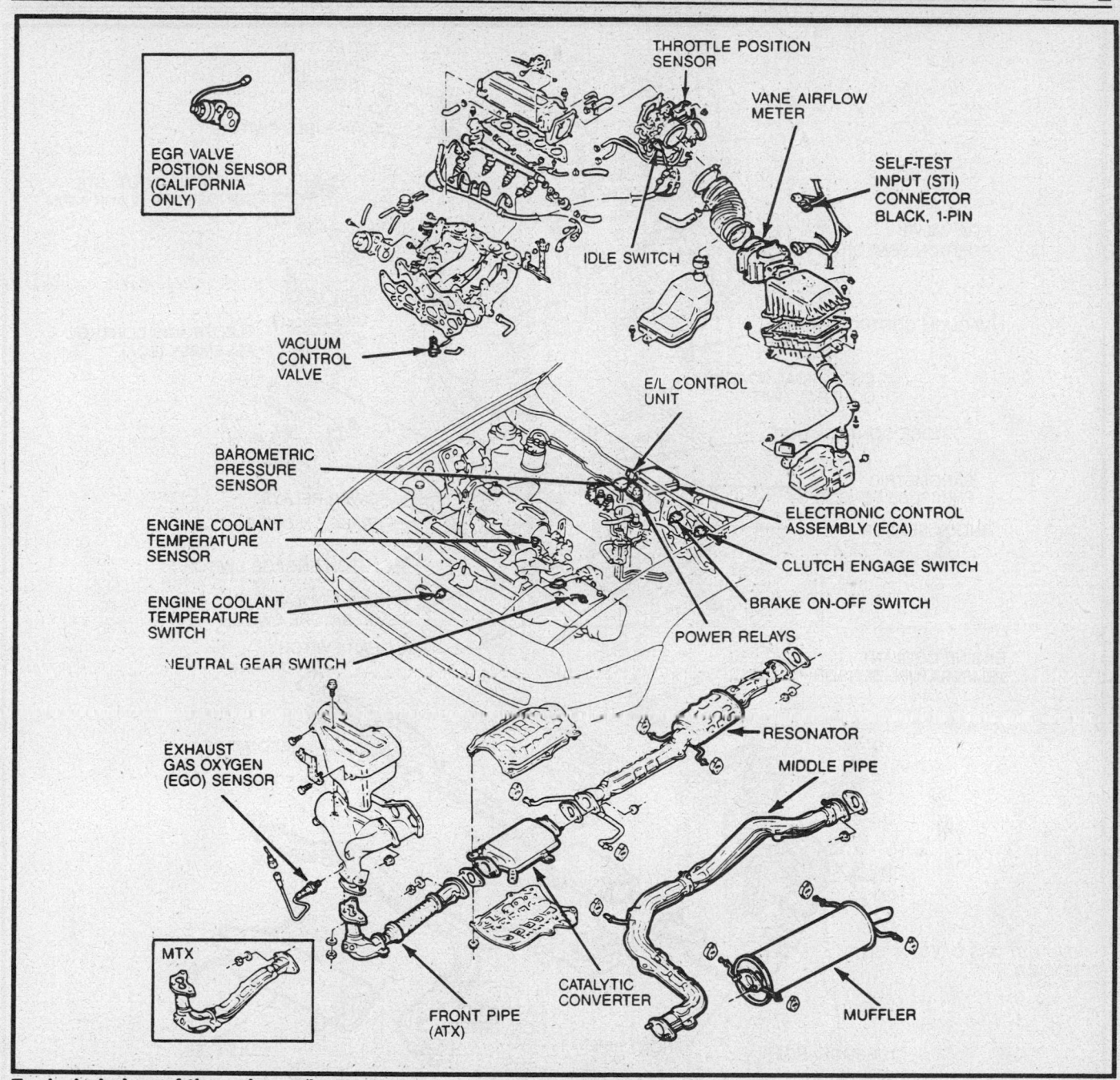

EGR VALVE POSTION SENSOR (CALIFORNIA ONLY)

THROTTLE POSITION SENSOR

VANE AIRFLOW METER

SELF-TEST INPUT (STI) CONNECTOR BLACK, 1-PIN

IDLE SWITCH

VACUUM CONTROL VALVE

E/L CONTROL UNIT

BAROMETRIC PRESSURE SENSOR

ENGINE COOLANT TEMPERATURE SENSOR

ENGINE COOLANT TEMPERATURE SWITCH

NEUTRAL GEAR SWITCH

ELECTRONIC CONTROL ASSEMBLY (ECA)

CLUTCH ENGAGE SWITCH

BRAKE ON-OFF SWITCH

POWER RELAYS

RESONATOR

MIDDLE PIPE

EXHAUST GAS OXYGEN (EGO) SENSOR

MTX

CATALYTIC CONVERTER

FRONT PIPE (ATX)

MUFFLER

Exploded view of the exhaust/input devices—non-turbocharged

light provides a flashing signal indicating the test mode condition.

The self-test output (STO), 6-pin connector, is used to retrieve service codes which where stored while the vehicle was in normal operation.

Procedure

To eliminate the codes from the memory, disconnect the negative battery cable, depress the brake pedal for 5–10 seconds, reconnect the negative battery cable and recheck to make sure the codes have been eliminated.

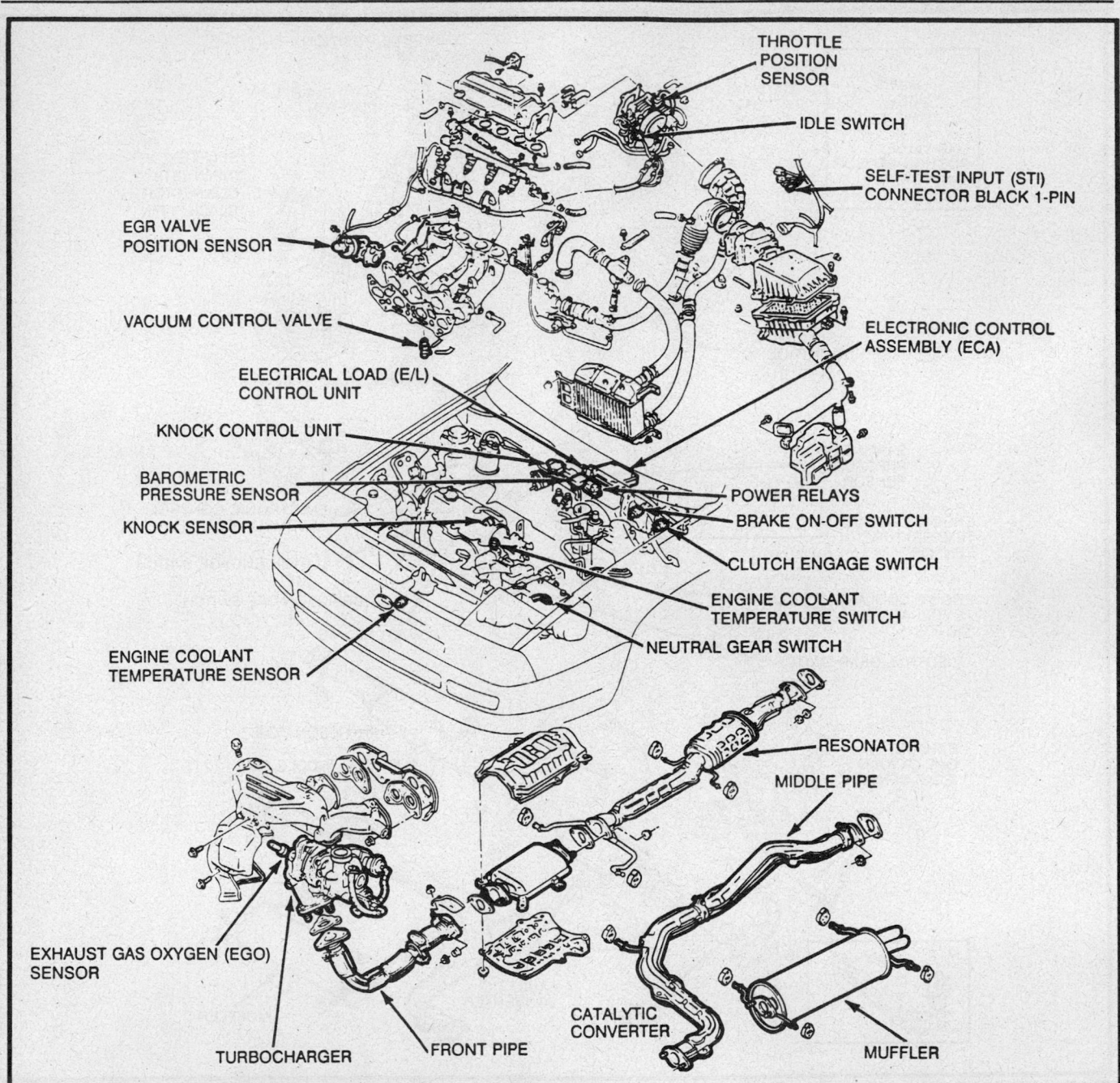

THROTTLE
POSITION
SENSOR

IDLE SWITCH

SELF-TEST INPUT (STI)
CONNECTOR BLACK 1-PIN

EGR VALVE
POSITION SENSOR

ELECTRONIC CONTROL
ASSEMBLY (ECA)

VACUUM CONTROL VALVE

ELECTRICAL LOAD (E/L)
CONTROL UNIT

KNOCK CONTROL UNIT

BAROMETRIC
PRESSURE SENSOR

POWER RELAYS

KNOCK SENSOR

BRAKE ON-OFF SWITCH

CLUTCH ENGAGE SWITCH

ENGINE COOLANT
TEMPERATURE SWITCH

NEUTRAL GEAR SWITCH

ENGINE COOLANT
TEMPERATURE SENSOR

RESONATOR

MIDDLE PIPE

EXHAUST GAS OXYGEN (EGO)
SENSOR

TURBOCHARGER

FRONT PIPE

CATALYTIC
CONVERTER

MUFFLER

Exploded view of the exhaust/input devices— turbocharged

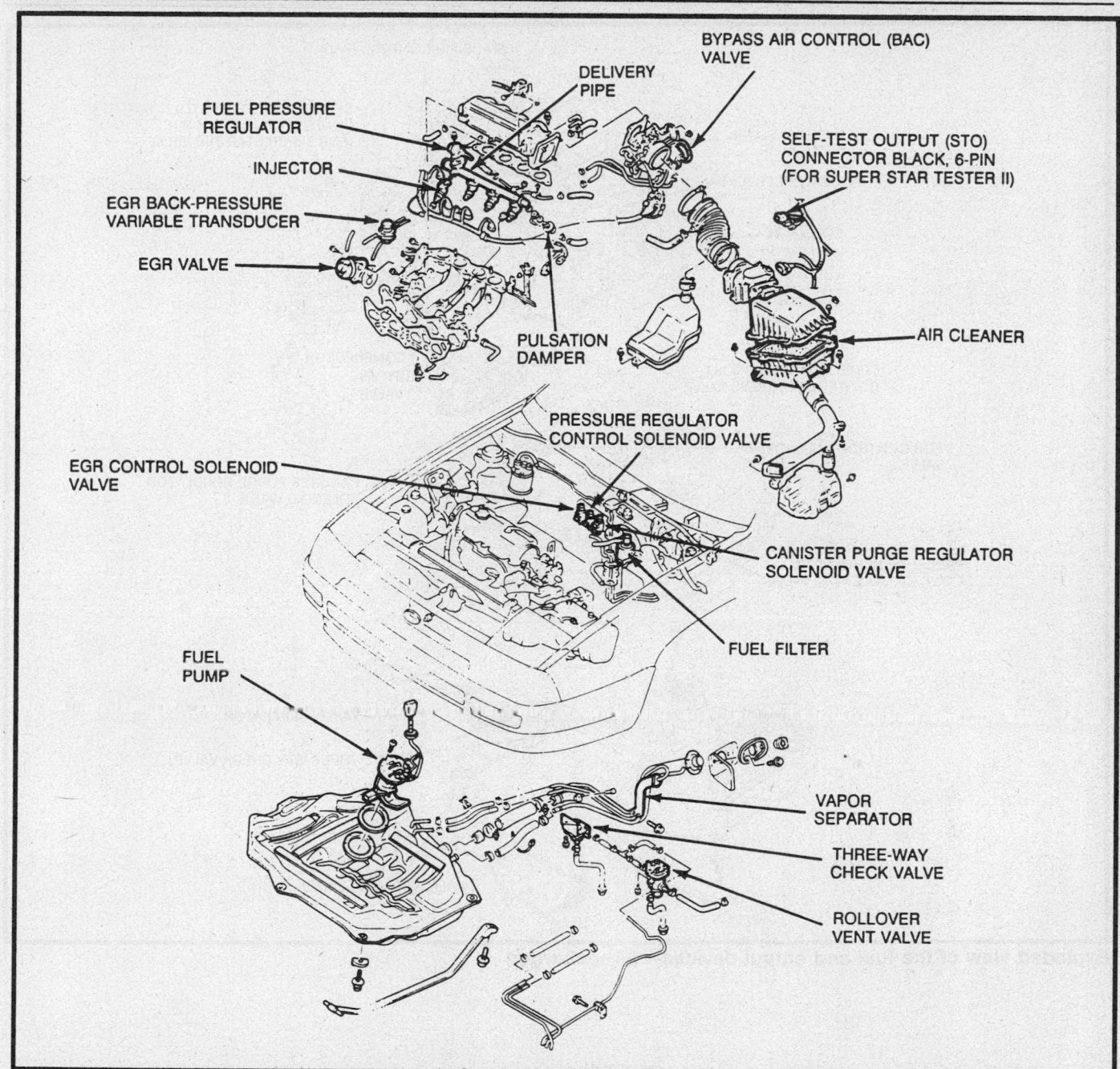

FUEL PRESSURE REGULATOR

INJECTOR

EGR BACK-PRESSURE VARIABLE TRANSDUCER

EGR VALVE

DELIVERY PIPE

BYPASS AIR CONTROL (BAC) VALVE

SELF-TEST OUTPUT (STO) CONNECTOR BLACK, 6-PIN (FOR SUPER STAR TESTER II)

PULSATION DAMPER

AIR CLEANER

EGR CONTROL SOLENOID VALVE

PRESSURE REGULATOR CONTROL SOLENOID VALVE

CANISTER PURGE REGULATOR SOLENOID VALVE

FUEL FILTER

FUEL PUMP

VAPOR SEPARATOR

THREE-WAY CHECK VALVE

ROLLOVER VENT VALVE

Exploded view of the fuel and output devices—non-turbocharged

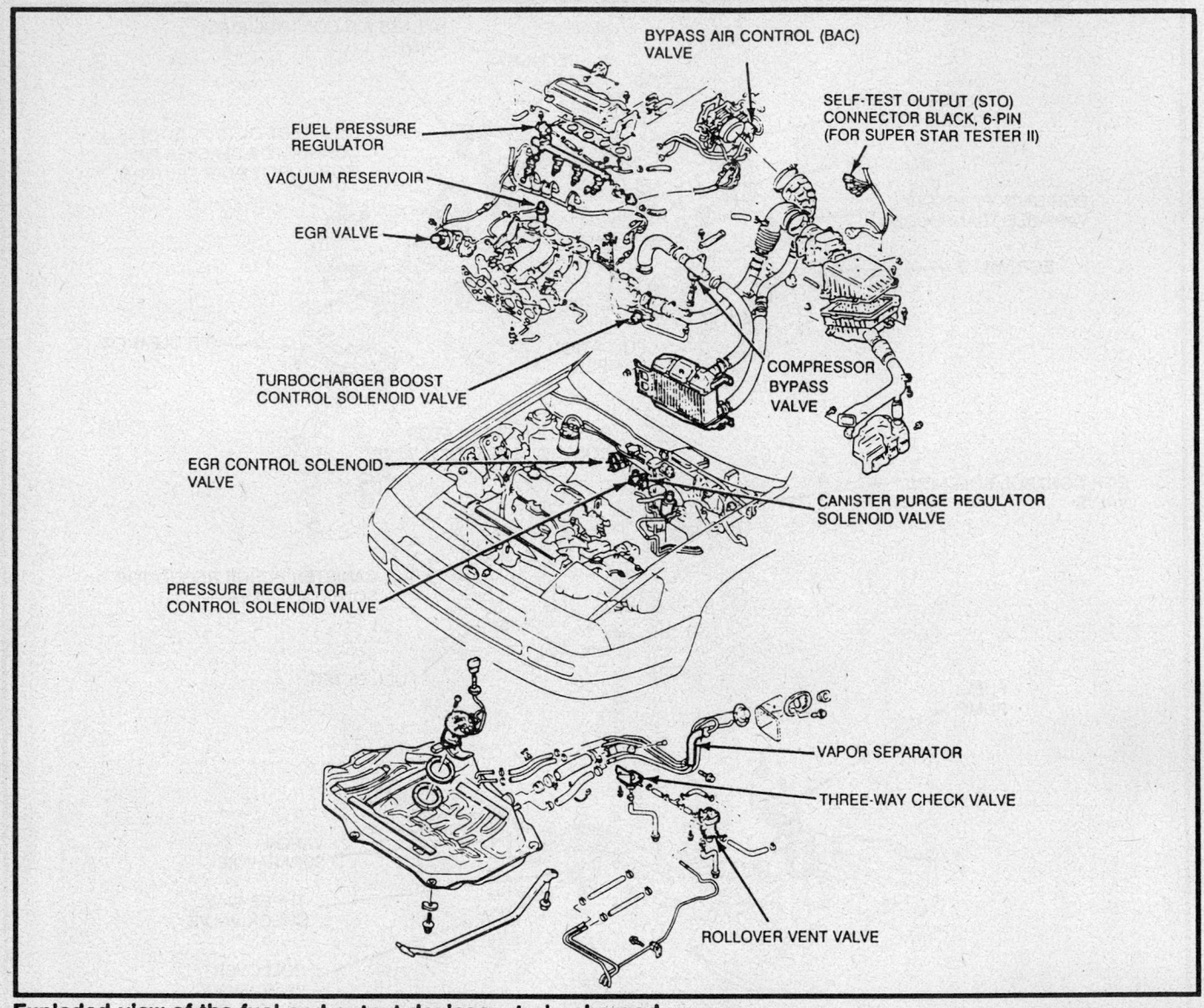

Exploded view of the fuel and output devices — turbocharged

ENGINE MECHANICAL

NOTE: Disconnecting the negative battery cable on some vehicles may interfere with the functions of the on board computer systems and may require the computer to undergo a relearning process, once the negative battery cable is reconnected.

Engine Assembly

Removal and Installation

1. Release the fuel pressure and disconnect the negative battery cable. Raise and safely support front of the vehicle.

2. Mark the hood hinge-to-hood location and remove the hood.

3. Drain the cooling system, the engine oil and the transaxle fluid (ATX).

4. Remove the battery, the battery carrier and the fuse holder.

5. Remove the air filter assembly and ducts. Disconnect the accelerator cable and the cruise control cable (if equipped).

6. Label and disconnect the electrical connectors from the electronic fuel injection system, the ignition coil, the thermostat

housing sensors, the O_2 sensor, the radiator sensors and the cooling fan assembly.

7. If equipped with an automatic transaxle, disconnect and plug the cooler lines from the radiator. Remove the radiator cooling fan assembly and the radiator.

8. If equipped with a manual transaxle, remove the clutch release cylinder and move it aside.

9. Remove the front exhaust pipe-to-exhaust manifold nuts, the exhaust pipe-to-catalytic converter nuts and the front exhaust pipe.

10. Discharge the air conditioning system and remove the air conditioning lines from the compressor. Disconnect the electrical connector from the compressor clutch.

11. Disconnect and plug the power steering lines from the power steering pump.

12. Disconnect the ground strap from the engine.

13. Disconnect and plug the heater hoses and the fuel lines.

14. Label and disconnect the vacuum lines from the brake booster chamber, the carbon canister, the bulkhead mounted solenoids and the distributor.

15. If equipped with an automatic transaxle, label and disconnect the electrical connectors from the transaxle.

16. Disconnect the speedometer cable from the transaxle.

17. If equipped with a turbocharger, disconnect the hoses/pipes and cover it with a clean rag.

18. To separate the halfshafts from the transaxle, perform the following procedures:

   a. Remove both front wheels and both inner fender splash guards.

   b. Disconnect the stabilizer bar from the lower control arms.

   c. Separate the lower ball joints and the tie rod ends from the steering knuckles.

   d. Positioning a pry bar between the transaxle and halfshaft, pry each halfshaft from the transaxle and suspend them on a wire.

19. Depending on which transaxle is used, disconnect the shift control cable or rod from the transaxle.

20. Using an engine lifting device, attach it to the engine and support it's weight.

21. Disconnect the engine mount bolts and remove the engine/transaxle assembly from the vehicle.

22. If necessary, remove the transaxle-to-engine bolts and support the engine on an engine stand.

To Install:

23. If the transaxle was removed from the engine, install it and torque the bolts to 66–86 ft. lbs. (89–117 Nm).

24. Lower the engine/transaxle assembly into the vehicle and secure the engine mount bolts.

25. To install the halfshafts, perform the following procedures:

   a. Install the halfshafts into the transaxle until the retaining ring snaps into place.

   b. Install the tie rod ends and the lower ball joints onto the steering knuckles.

   c. Install the stabilizer bar onto the lower control arms.

   d. Install the wheels.

26. Depending on which transaxle the vehicle is equipped with, connect the shift cable control or rod. If equipped with a manual transaxle, install the clutch release cylinder. If equipped with an automatic transaxle, connect the electrical connectors to the transaxle.

27. Connect the speedometer cable to the transaxle and the power steering lines to the power steering pump.

28. If equipped with air conditioning, use new O-rings and connect the high pressure and suction lines to the compressor. Reconnect the electrical connector to the compressor clutch.

29. Connect the engine ground strap. On a non-turbocharged vehicle, install the front exhaust pipe. If equipped with a turbocharger, connect the oil pipe and hoses to the turbocharger.

30. Install the radiator and the cooling fan assembly and reconnect the electrical connectors. If equipped with an automatic transaxle, reconnect the oil cooler lines to the radiator.

31. Connect the vacuum lines to the carbon canister, the bulkhead mounted solenoids, distributor and the brake booster.

32. Connect the heater hoses to the engine and the fuel lines to the fuel system. Connect the electrical connectors to the thermostat housing sensors, the coil and the electronic fuel injection assembly.

33. Install the accelerator cable and the cruise control cable (if equipped). Install the air filter and ducts.

34. Refill the cooling system, the crankcase and the transaxle (ATX). Charge the air conditioning system. Refill the power steering reservoir and bleed the system.

35. Start the engine, allow it to reach normal operating temperatures and check for leaks.

Engine Mounts

Removal and Installation

1. Disconnect the negative battery cable.

2. If necessary, raise and safely support the front of the vehicle.

3. Using an engine lifting device, attach it to the engine and support it's weight.

4. Remove the engine mount(s)-to-engine bolts, the engine mount(s)-to-chassis bolts and the mounts.

5. To install, reverse the removal procedures. Remove the engine lift.

Intake Manifold

Removal and Installation

1. Relieve the fuel pressure and disconnect the negative battery cable.

2. Drain the cooling system.

3. From the bottom of the intake manifold, remove the water hose.

4. Disconnect the accelerator cables from the throttle body.

5. Remove the air duct from the throttle body.

6. Label and disconnect the vacuum lines and coolant hoses from the throttle body.

7. Disconnect the electrical connectors from the TPS, the idle switch and the bypass air control valve.

8. Remove the engine lifting bracket mounting bolts from the throttle body and the engine block.

9. Disconnect the coolant line/EGR hose bracket from the throttle body and the throttle cable brackets from the intake plenum.

10. Remove the wire loom bracket and the EGR back-pressure transducer bracket from the right side of the plenum.

11. Remove the PCV hose and the vacuum line assembly bracket from the intake plenum.

12. Label and disconnect the vacuum lines from the intake plenum.

13. Remove the plenum-to-intake manifold nuts/bolts, the plenum and the gasket.

14. Disconnect the electrical connectors from the fuel injectors.

15. Carefully, bend the wire harness retainer brackets away from the wire harness and move the harness assembly away from the intake manifold.

16. Remove the fuel supply tube from the pulsation damper.

17. Remove the fuel return line bracket from the intake manifold, the clamp and the fuel return line from the bracket.

18. Remove the fuel rail-to-intake manifold bolts and the fuel rail (with pressure regulator and pulsation damper attached).

19. Remove the fuel injectors, the grommet and the O-rings

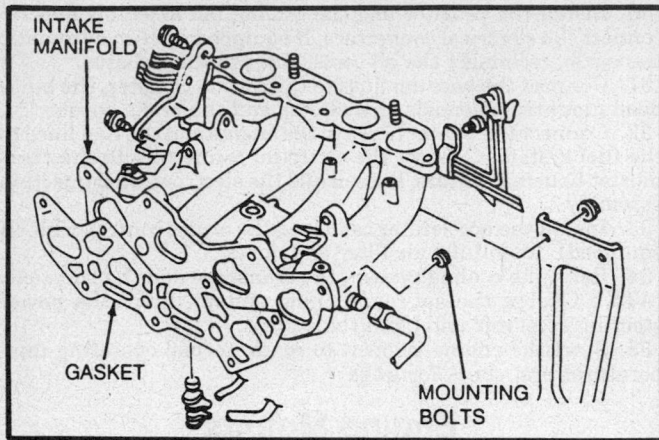

INTAKE
MANIFOLD

GASKET

MOUNTING
BOLTS

Exploded view of the intake manifold

from the fuel rail. Remove the O-rings from the fuel injectors and discard it.

20. Disconnect the EGR pipe from the intake manifold. Label and disconnect any electrical connectors and hoses from the intake manifold.

21. Remove the intake manifold bracket-to-manifold nuts and the bracket. Remove the intake manifold-to-cylinder head nuts/bolts, the manifold and gasket.

22. Clean the gasket mounting surfaces.

To Install:

23. Using a new gasket, position the intake manifold on the cylinder head studs and torque the nuts/bolts to 14–22 ft. lbs. (19–30 Nm).

24. Install the intake manifold bracket-to-manifold nuts to 14–22 ft. lbs. (19–30 Nm).

25. Using new O-rings, lubricate them with engine oil and install the fuel injectors into the fuel rail.

26. Install the fuel injector/rail assembly into the intake manifold and torque the bolts to 14–19 ft. lbs. (19–25 Nm). Connect the electrical connectors to the fuel injectors.

27. Install the fuel return line bracket onto the intake manifold and the return line at the bracket (secure with a clamp).

28. Install the fuel supply line onto the pulsation damper and secure with a clamp.

29. Using a new gasket, install the intake plenum onto the intake manifold and torque the nuts/bolts to 14–19 ft. lbs. (19–25 Nm).

30. Install with the wiring harness onto the retainer brackets and carefully bend the brackets toward the wire harness.

31. To complete the installation, reverse the removal procedures. Refill the cooling system . Start the engine, allow it to reach normal operating temperatures and check for leaks and engine operation.

Exhaust Manifold

Removal and Installation

WITHOUT TURBOCHARGER

1. Disconnect the negative battery cable.

2. Disconnect the electrical connector from the exhaust gas oxygen sensor and remove the sensor from the exhaust manifold.

3. Remove the exhaust pipe-to-exhaust manifold nuts, the exhaust pipe-to-catalytic converter nuts and the pipe from the vehicle.

4. Remove the outer heat shield.

5. Remove the exhaust manifold-to-cylinder head nuts, the manifold and the gasket.

To Install:

6. Clean the gasket mounting surfaces.

7. Using new gaskets, the raised gasket ridge must face the exhaust manifold, reverse the removal procedures. Torque the exhaust manifold-to-cylinder head nuts to 16–21 ft. lbs. (22–28 Nm).

8. Install the outer heat shield-to-exhaust manifold bolts to 14–22 ft. lbs. (19–30 Nm). Install the oxygen sensor and connect the electrical connector.

9. Connect the exhaust pipe-to-exhaust manifold and torque the nuts to 23–34 ft. lbs. (31–46 Nm). Start the engine and check for leaks.

10. To complete the installation, reverse the removal procedures.

WITH TURBOCHARGER

1. Disconnect the negative battery cable. Remove the turbocharger.

2. Remove the exhaust manifold-to-cylinder head nuts, the manifold and the gaskets.

3. Clean the gasket mounting surfaces.

4. Using new gaskets, the raised gasket ridge must face the exhaust manifold, install the exhaust manifold and torque the manifold-to-cylinder head nuts to 16–21 ft. lbs. (22–28 Nm).

5. To complete the installation, reverse the removal procedures. Start the engine and check for leaks.

Valve System

The rocker arms ride directly on the camshaft and are equipped with hydraulic lash adjusters; no valve adjustment is necessary or possible.

VALVE ROCKER SHAFT/ARM ASSEMBLY

Removal and Installation

1. Disconnect the negative battery cable. Remove the vent hose and the PCV valve from the rocker arm cover.

2. Remove the spark plug wire clips and move the wires aside.

3. Remove the rocker arm cover-to-cylinder head bolts, the rocker arm cover and the gasket.

4. Remove the rocker arm shaft assemblies-to-cylinder head bolts and the assemblies from the cylinder head.

5. If necessary, separate the rocker arms and springs from the shafts; be sure to keep the parts in order for reinstallation purposes.

6. Clean the gasket mounting surfaces. Inspect the parts for wear and/or damage; replace the parts (if necessary).

To Install:

7. Assemble the rocker arms and springs onto the shafts in the reverse order of removal.

NOTE: When installing the rocker arm shafts onto the cylinder head, pay attention to the notches at the ends of the shafts, they are different and cannot be interchanged.

8. Install the rocker arm/shaft assemblies onto the cylinder head and torque the rocker arm shaft-to-cylinder head bolts to 13–20 ft. lbs. (18–26 Nm), using 2 steps.

9. Using a new gasket, position it onto the cylinder head, apply silicone sealant to the shaded areas at both ends of the cylinder head and install the rocker arm cover. Torque the rocker arm cover-to-cylinder head bolts to 52–69 inch lbs. (6–8 Nm).

10. To complete the installation, reverse the removal procedures. Start the engine and check for leaks.

Cylinder Head

Removal and Installation

1. Disconnect the negative battery cable. Remove the timing belt and the intake manifold.

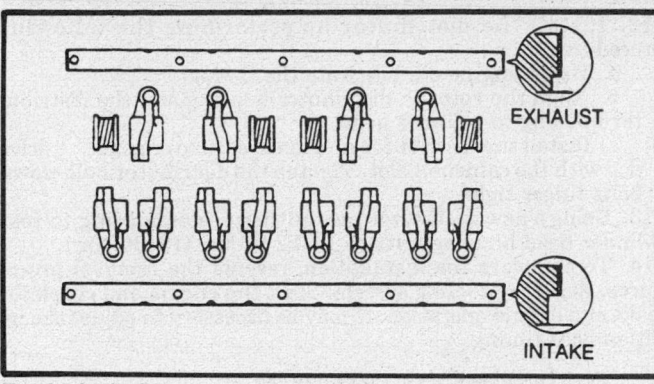

Exploded view of the rocker arm/shaft assemblies

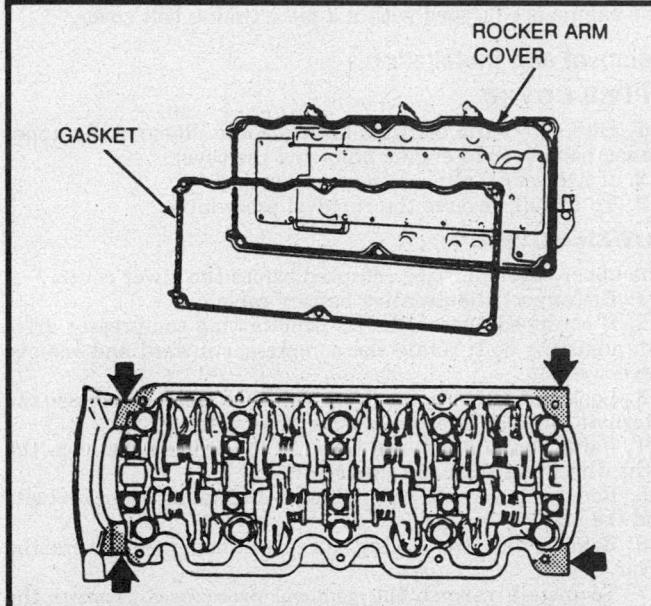

Exploded view of the rocker arm cover assembly

2. Remove the exhaust manifold and the distributor.

3. Remove rocker arm/shaft assemblies by performing the following procedures:

   a. Remove the vent hose and the PCV valve from the rocker arm cover.

   b. Remove the spark plug wire clips, the spark plugs and move the wires aside.

   c. Remove the rocker arm cover-to-cylinder head bolts, the rocker arm cover and the gasket.

   d. Remove the rocker arm shaft assemblies-to-cylinder head bolts and the assemblies from the cylinder head.

4. Remove the camshaft sprocket by performing the following procedures:

   a. Using a small pry bar, insert it through a hole in the camshaft sprocket (to lock it).

   b. Remove the camshaft sprocket-to-camshaft bolt and the sprocket.

5. Remove the rear timing belt cover-to-cylinder head nut/bolt and the cover.

6. Disconnect the electrical connectors from the thermostat housing sensors. Remove the upper radiator hose and the water bypass hose.

7. Remove the rear housing-to-cylinder head nut/bolts, the housing and gasket.

8. Remove the cylinder head bolts, a little at a time, in the re-verse order of installation. Remove the cylinder head and the gasket (discard it).

9. Clean the gasket mounting surfaces. Check the cylinder head for warpage, cracks and/or damage; replace it, if necessary.

To Install:

10. Using a new cylinder head gasket, position it on the engine block, install the cylinder head and torque the bolts to 59–64 ft. lbs. (80–86 Nm), using 2 steps, in sequence.

11. Using new gaskets, install and torque the:

   Rear timing belt cover-to-cylinder head nut/bolt to 14–19 ft. lbs. (19–25 Nm)

   Rear housing-to-cylinder head nut/bolts to 14–19 ft. lbs. (19–25 Nm)

12. Install the distributor by performing the following procedures:

   a. Using engine oil, lubricate the O-ring.

   b. Align the rotor-to-distributor housing and the distributor housing-to-cylinder head.

   c. Install the distributor and make sure to engage the drive dog with the camshaft slot. Tighten the distributor hold-down bolts finger tight.

13. Using a new gasket, torque the thermostat housing-to-rear cylinder head housing nuts to 14–22 ft. lbs. (19–30 Nm).

14. Install the exhaust manifold by performing the following procedures:

   a. Using new gaskets, the raised gasket ridge must face the exhaust manifold, reverse the removal procedures. Torque the exhaust manifold-to-cylinder head nuts to 16–21 ft. lbs. (22–28 Nm).

   b. If equipped with a turbocharger, install the turbocharger assembly.

   c. Install the outer heat shield-to-exhaust manifold bolts to

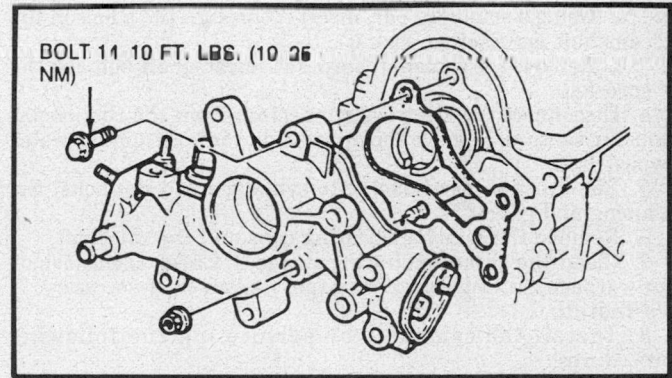

Exploded view of the rear cylinder head housing

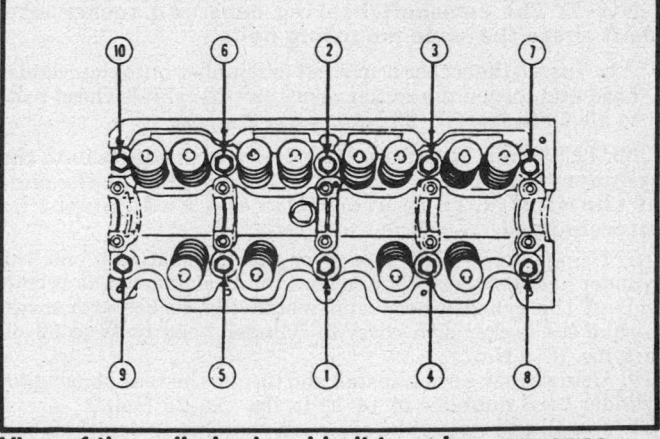

View of the cylinder head bolt torquing sequence

14–22 ft. lbs. (19–30 Nm). Install the oxygen sensor and connect the electrical connector.

d. If not equipped with a turbocharger, connect the exhaust pipe-to-exhaust manifold and torque the nuts to 23–34 ft. lbs. (31–46 Nm).

15. Install the rocker arm/shaft assemblies by performing the following procedures:

a. Install the rocker arm/shaft assemblies onto the cylinder head and torque the rocker arm shaft-to-cylinder head bolts to 13–20 ft. lbs. (18–26 Nm), using 2 steps.

NOTE: When installing the rocker arm shafts onto the cylinder head, pay attention to the notches at the ends of the shafts, they are different and cannot be interchanged.

b. Using a new gasket, position it onto the cylinder head, apply silicone sealant to the shaded areas at both ends of the cylinder head and install the rocker arm cover. Torque the rocker arm cover-to-cylinder head bolts to 52–69 inch lbs. (6–8 Nm).

16. To complete the installation, reverse the removal procedures. Refill the cooling system. Start the engine and check for leaks and engine operation. If may be necessary to adjust the ignition base timing.

Camshaft

Removal and Installation

1. Disconnect the negative battery cable. Remove the timing belt.
2. Remove rocker arm/shaft assemblies and the distributor.
3. Remove the camshaft sprocket by performing the following procedures:

a. Using a small pry bar, insert it through the a hole in the camshaft sprocket (to lock it).

b. Remove the camshaft sprocket-to-camshaft bolt and the sprocket.

4. Disconnect the electrical connectors from the thermostat housing sensors. Remove the upper radiator hose and the water bypass hose.
5. Remove the rear housing-to-cylinder head nut/bolts, the housing and gasket.
6. Remove the camshaft bearing caps and the camshaft.
7. Clean the gasket mounting surfaces. Check the camshaft for warpage, scoring and/or damage; replace it, if necessary.

To Install:

8. Install the camshaft by performing the following procedures:

a. Using new camshaft oil seals, install the camshaft and the bearing caps.

NOTE: The camshaft bearing caps and rocker arm/shaft share the same mounting bolts.

b. Install the rocker arm/shaft assemblies onto the cylinder head and torque the rocker arm shaft-to-cylinder head bolts to 13–20 ft. lbs. (18–26 Nm), using 2 steps.

NOTE: When installing the rocker arm shafts onto the cylinder head, pay attention to the notches at the ends of the shafts, they are different and cannot be interchanged.

9. Using a new rocker arm cover gasket, position it onto the cylinder head, apply silicone sealant to the shaded areas at both ends of the cylinder head and install the rocker arm cover. Torque the rocker arm cover-to-cylinder head bolts to 52–69 inch lbs. (6–8 Nm).
10. Using a new gasket, install and torque the rear housing-to-cylinder head nut/bolts to 14–19 ft. lbs. (19–25 Nm).
11. Install and torque the camshaft sprocket-to-camshaft bolt to 35–48 ft. lbs. (47–65 Nm).

12. Install the distributor by performing the following procedures:

a. Using engine oil, lubricate the O-ring.

b. Align the rotor-to-distributor housing and the distributor housing-to-cylinder head.

c. Install the distributor and make sure to engage the drive dog with the camshaft slot. Tighten the distributor hold-down bolts finger tight.

13. Using a new gasket, torque the thermostat housing-to-rear cylinder head housing nuts to 14–22 ft. lbs. (19–30 Nm).
14. To complete the installation, reverse the removal procedures. Refill the cooling system. Start the engine and check for leaks and engine operation. If may be necessary to adjust the ignition base timing.

Timing Belt Cover

The engine is equipped with a 2 piece timing belt cover.

Removal and Installation

UPPER COVER

1. Disconnect the negative battery cable. Remove the upper timing belt cover-to-engine bolts and the cover.
2. If necessary, remove the cover gasket.
3. To install, reverse the removal procedures.

LOWER COVER

The upper cover must be removed before the lower cover.

1. Disconnect the negative battery cable.
2. If equipped, loosen the air conditioning compressor drive belt adjusting bolt, rotate the compressor inward and remove the drive belt.
3. Loosen the alternator drive belt adjusting bolt, rotate the alternator inward and remove the drive belt.
4. Raise and support the front of the vehicle. Remove the right wheel and the right inner panel.
5. Remove the crankshaft pulley-to-crankshaft sprocket bolts and the pulley.
6. Remove the lower timing belt cover-to-engine bolts and the cover.
7. To install, reverse the removal procedures. Torque the crankshaft pulley-to-crankshaft sprocket bolts to 109–152 inch lbs. (12–7 Nm). Adjust the drive belt tensions.

Timing Belt

Removal and Installation

1. Disconnect the negative battery cable. Remove the timing belt covers.
2. Rotate the crankshaft to align the notch on the crankshaft pulley with the TDC mark on the timing cover. Make sure the No. 1 arrow mark, on the camshaft sprocket, is aligned with the pointer at the top of the rear timing belt cover; if not aligned, rotate the crankshaft 180 degrees.

NOTE: With the timing marks aligned, the No. 1 cylinder will be on the TDC of it's compression stroke.

3. Remove the timing belt tensioner spring, the tensioner pulley bolt and the pulley.
4. On the timing belt, mark an arrow to indicate the direction of rotation. Remove the timing belt.

To Install:

5. With the timing marks aligned, install the timing belt onto the sprockets.
6. Install the tensioner pulley and torque the bolt to 27–38 ft. lbs. (37–52 Nm); attach the spring. Make sure the timing belt is not loose at the water pump and idler pulley side.
7. Rotate the crankshaft 2 revolutions and realign the timing marks; if not aligned, reperform the installation procedures.

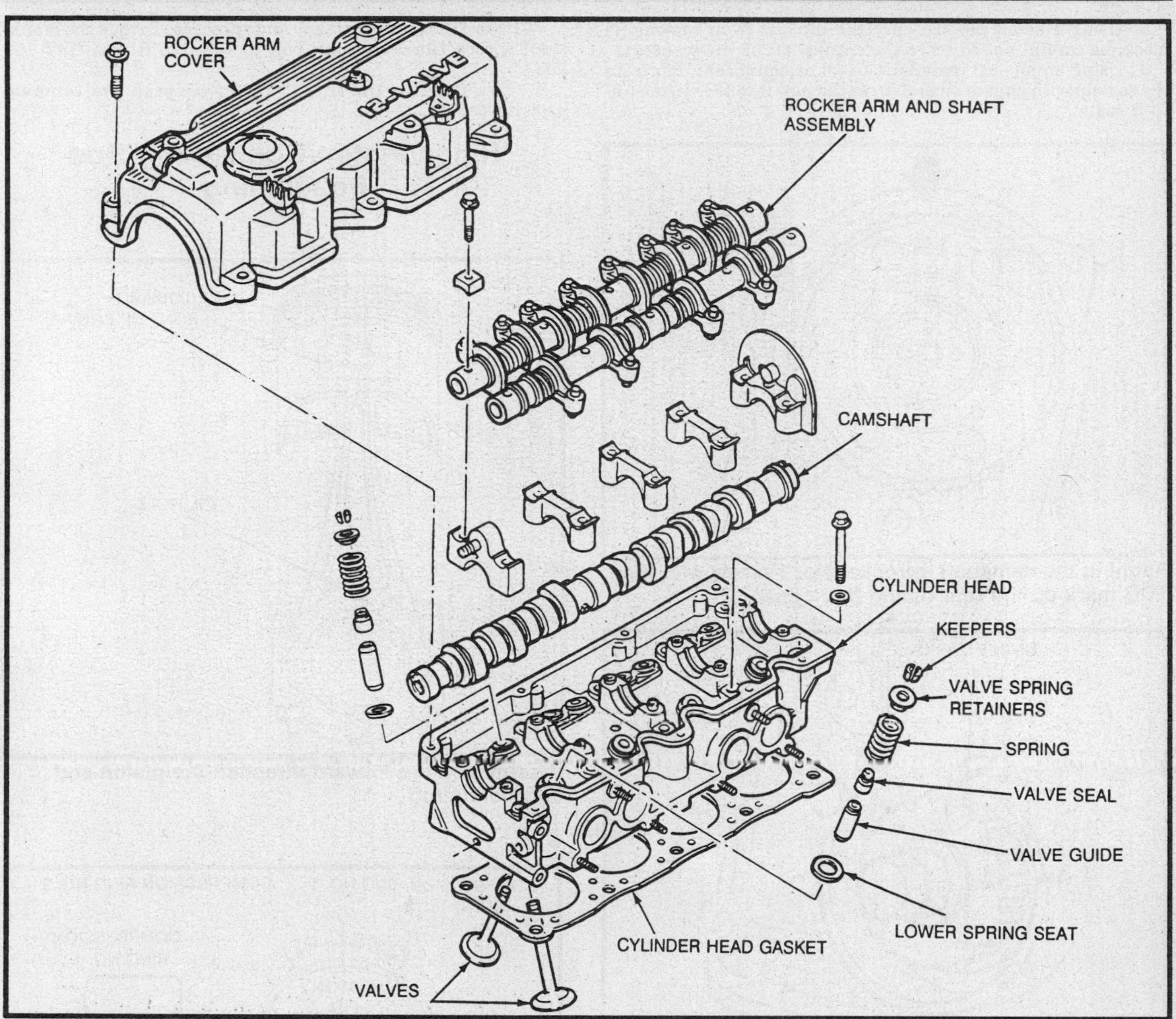

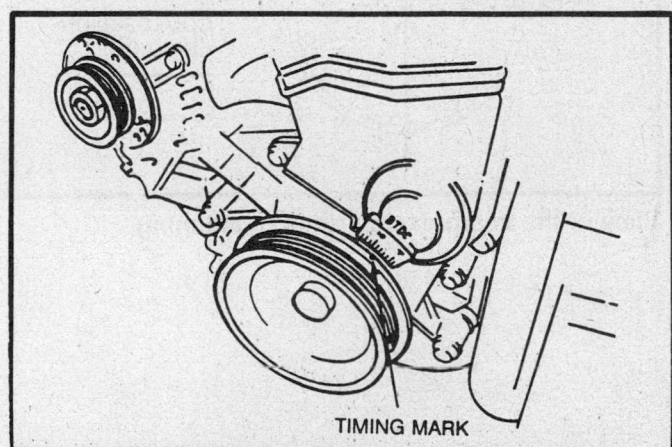

Exploded view of the cylinder head assembly

ROCKER ARM COVER

ROCKER ARM AND SHAFT ASSEMBLY

CAMSHAFT

CYLINDER HEAD

KEEPERS

VALVE SPRING RETAINERS

SPRING

VALVE SEAL

VALVE GUIDE

LOWER SPRING SEAT

CYLINDER HEAD GASKET

VALVES

Aligning the crankshaft pully notch with the TDC mark on the timing cover

TIMING MARK

8. Measure the timing belt deflection between the camshaft and crankshaft sprockets; if it is not 0.30–0.33 in. (7.5–8.5mm) at 22 lbs. (98 N), loosen the tensioner pulley bolt and repeat the adjustment or replace the tensioner.

9. To complete the installation, reverse the removal procedures. Adjust the drive belt tension(s). Start the engine and check and/or adjust the engine timing.

Timing Belt Oil Seal

Removal and Installation

1. Disconnect the negative battery cable. Remove the timing belt.

2. If equipped with a manual transaxle, place the shift lever in the 4TH gear and firmly apply the parking brake.

3. If equipped with an automatic transaxle, remove the lower flywheel cover and install the flywheel locking tool, onto the flywheel ring.

4. Remove the crankshaft sprocket-to-crankshaft bolt, the sprocket and the key.

5. Using a small pry bar, pry the oil seal from the engine block; be careful not to score the crankshaft or the seal seat.

6. Using an oil seal installation tool or equivalent, lubricate the seal lip with engine oil and drive the new into the engine until it seats.

7. Install the crankshaft key and sprocket. Torque the crankshaft sprocket-to-crankshaft bolt to 108–116 ft. lbs. (147–157 Nm).

8. To complete the installation, reverse the removal procedures.

Rings/Piston/Connecting Rod Positioning

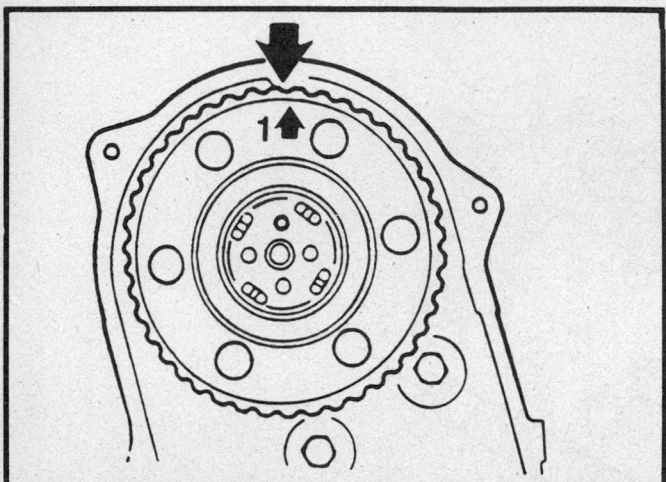

Aligning the camshaft sprocket No. 1 arrow with the TDC mark on the rear timing belt cover

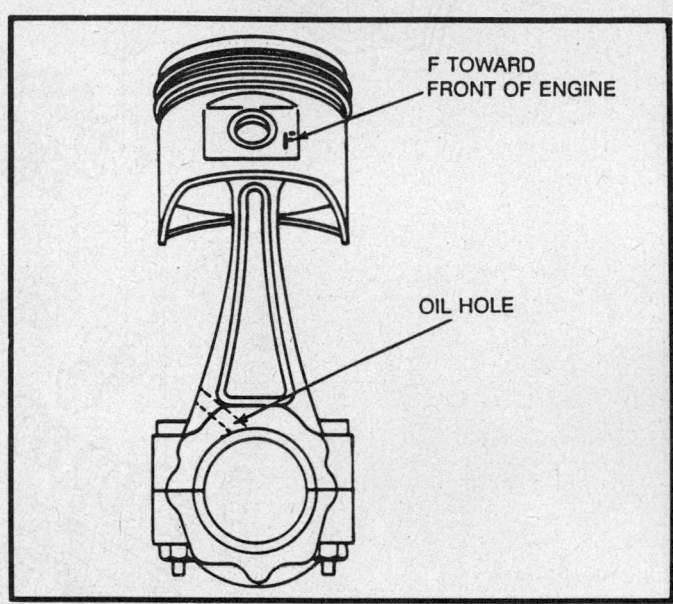

Determining the forward direction the piston and connecting rod

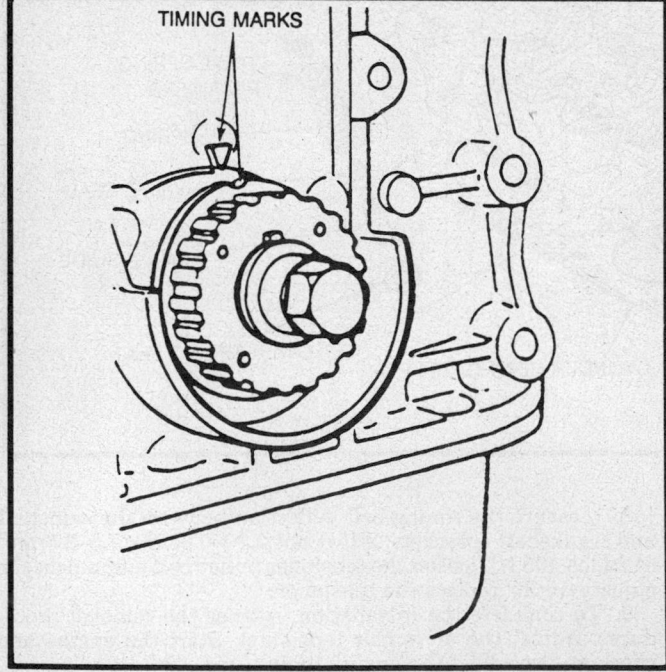

Aligning the crankshaft sprocket notch with the case timing mark

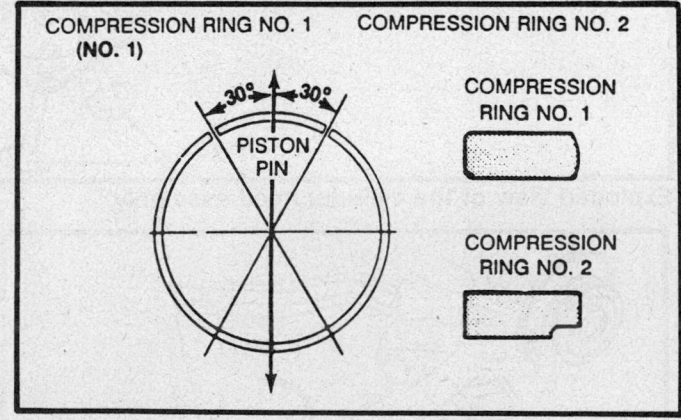

View of the compression rings positioning

ENGINE LUBRICATION

Oil Pan

Removal and Installation

1. Disconnect the negative battery cable.
2. Raise and support the front of the vehicle.
3. Remove the right wheel and the right inner splash shield.
4. Drain the crankcase.
5. Remove the engine-to-flywheel housing support bracket, the flywheel housing dust cover bolts and cover.
6. Remove the front exhaust pipe and the exhaust pipe support bracket.
7. Remove the oil pan-to-engine bolts, the oil pan, the oil pickup tube and the stiffener.
8. Clean the gasket mounting surfaces.

To Install:

9. Using silicone sealant, apply a continuous bead on both sides of the stiffener, along the inside of the bolt holes.
10. To install, reverse the removal procedures. Torque the:
Oil pan-to-engine bolts to 69–104 inch lbs. (8–12 Nm)
Flywheel housing dust cover bolts to 49–95 inch lbs. (8–11 Nm)
Flywheel housing support bracket-to-flywheel housing bolts to 27–38 ft. lbs. (37–52 Nm)
Flywheel housing support bracket-to-engine bolts to 27–38 ft. lbs. (37–52 Nm)
11. Refill the crankcase. Start the engine and check for leaks.

Oil Pump

The oil pump is located at the front of the engine and houses the front oil seal.

Removal and Installation

1. Disconnect the negative battery cable. Raise and safely support the vehicle.
2. Remove the crankshaft sprocket and the oil pan.
3. Remove the oil pump pickup tube-to-oil pump bolts, the tube and gasket.
4. Remove the oil pump-to-cylinder block bolts, the pump and gasket.
5. Using a small pry bar, pry the oil seal from the pump and clean the seal bore.
6. Clean the gasket mounting surfaces. Inspect the pump and gears for wear; if necessary, replace the parts.

To Install:

7. Using a new oil seal, press it into the oil pump until it seats and lubricate the seal lip with engine oil. Install a new O-ring into the oil pump.
8. Using petroleum jelly, pack the oil pump cavity. Using RTV sealant, apply a continuous bead to the oil pump gasket surface.

NOTE: When using sealant, do not allow the sealant to squeeze into the pump's outlet hole in the pump or cylinder block.

9. Install the oil pump to the cylinder block; be careful not to cut the oil seal lip. Torque the:
Upper oil pump-to-cylinder block bolts to 14–19 ft. lbs. (19–25 Nm)
Lower oil pump-to-cylinder block bolts to 27–38 ft. lbs. (37–52 Nm)
10. Using silicone sealant, apply a continuous bead on both sides of the stiffener, along the inside of the bolt holes.
11. To complete the installation, reverse the removal procedures. Torque the:

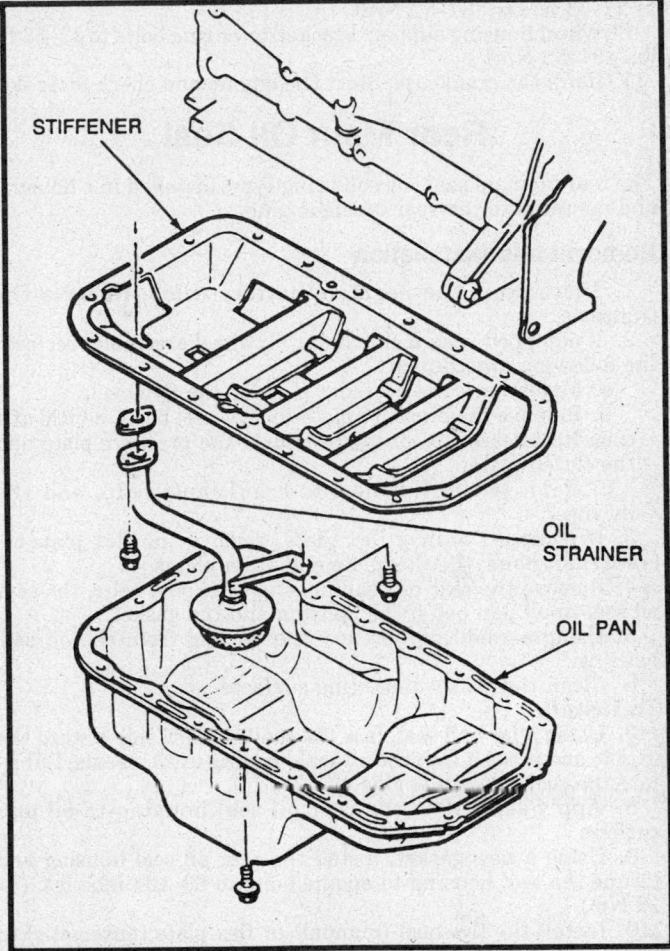

Exploded view of the oil pan, pickup tube and stiffener

STIFFENER

OIL STRAINER

OIL PAN

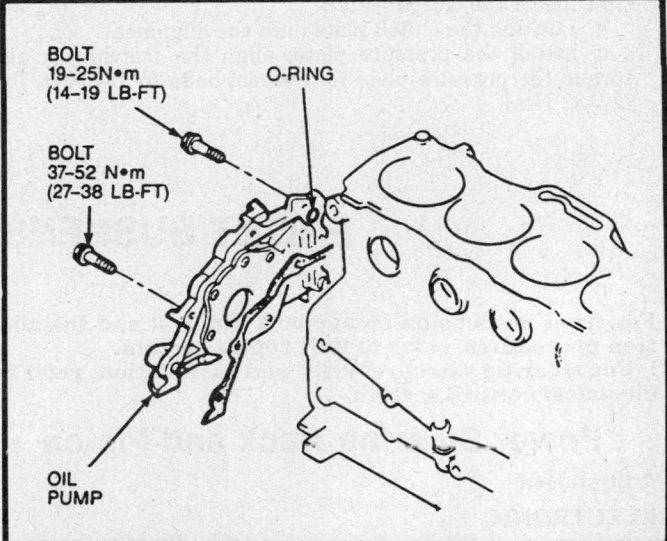

BOLT
19–25 N•m
(14–19 LB-FT)

O-RING

BOLT
37–52 N•m
(27–38 LB-FT)

OIL PUMP

Exploded view of the oil pump assembly

Oil pan-to-engine bolts to 69–104 inch lbs. (8–12 Nm)
Flywheel housing dust cover bolts to 49–95 inch lbs. (8–11 Nm)
Flywheel housing support bracket-to-flywheel housing bolts to 27–38 ft. lbs. (37–52 Nm)
Flywheel housing support bracket-to-engine bolts to 27–38 ft. lbs. (37–52 Nm)

11. Refill the crankcase. Start the engine and check for leaks.

Rear Main Oil Seal

The rear main oil seal is a solid ring type, installed in a housing and mounted to the rear of the engine.

Removal and Installation

1. Disconnect the negative battery cable. Remove the transaxle.
2. If equipped with a clutch and flywheel assembly, perform the following procedures:
   a. Matchmark the pressure plate to the flywheel.
   b. Remove the pressure plate-to-flywheel bolts, a little at a time (to release the spring pressure) the pressure plate and the clutch plate.
   c. Remove the flywheel-to-crankshaft bolts and the flywheel.
3. If equipped with a flex plate, remove the flex plate-to-crankshaft bolts, the flex plate and shim plates.
4. Remove the rear oil seal housing-to-engine bolts, the rear oil seal-to-oil pan bolts, the housing and the gasket.
5. Using a small prybar, pry the oil seal from the oil seal housing.
6. Clean the gasket mounting surfaces.
To Install:
7. Using a new oil seal, face the seal's hollow side toward the engine and press it into the oil seal housing until it seats. Lubricate the seal lip with engine oil.
8. Apply sealant to the rear oil seal housing-to-oil pan surface.
9. Using a new gasket, install the rear oil seal housing and torque the seal housing-to-engine bolts to 69–104 inch lbs. (8–12 Nm).
10. Install the flywheel (manual) or flex plate (automatic) to crankshaft bolts to 71–76 ft. lbs. (96–103 Nm).
11. If equipped with a clutch plate, perform the following procedures:
   a. Insert a clutch plate alignment tool into the pilot bearing (to support the clutch plate).
   b. Position the clutch plate onto the alignment tool.
   c. Install the pressure plate, align the matchmark and torque the pressure plate-to-flywheel bolts to 16–24 ft. lbs. (22–32 Nm).

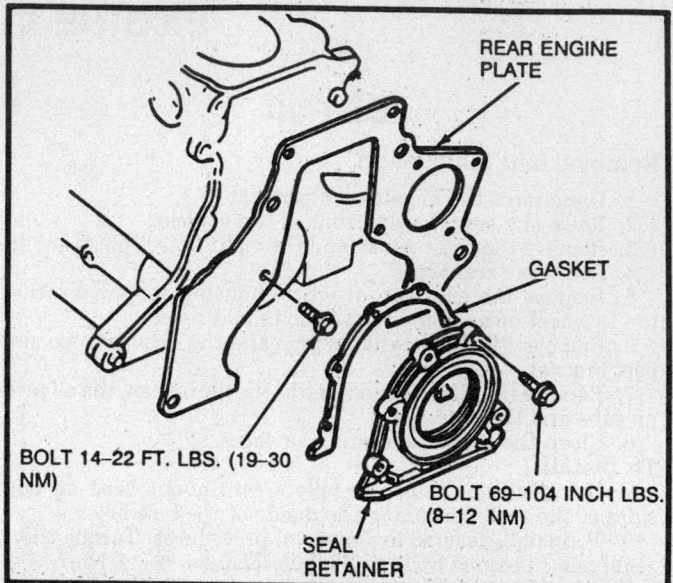

REAR ENGINE PLATE

GASKET

BOLT 14–22 FT. LBS. (19–30 NM)

BOLT 69–104 INCH LBS. (8–12 NM)

SEAL RETAINER

Exploded view of the rear oil seal assembly

12. To complete the installation, reverse the removal procedures.

Connecting Rod and Main Bearing

Replacement

Note the locations of the main bearings. The upper bearings are grooved for distribution of the oil to the connecting rods, while the lower mains are plain. Thrust is taken by the thrust bearing located at the center (No. 3) bearing cap.

Engine bearings are of the precision insert type. They are available for service in standard and various undersizes. Upper and lower bearing inserts may be different. Be careful to align the oil holes; do not obstruct any oil passages. Bearing inserts must not be shimmed. Do not touch the bearing surface of the insert with bare fingers. Skin oil and acids will etch the bearing surface.

NOTE: Bearing failure, other than normal wear, must be investigated carefully. Inspect the crankshaft, connecting rods and the bearing bores. Avoid damage to the crankshaft journals during removal and installation.

FRONT SUSPENSION AND STEERING

For front suspension component removal and installation procedures, refer to unit repair section.
For steering wheel removal and installation, refer to electrical control section.

Power Steering Rack and Pinion

Adjustment
ELECTRONIC
1. Disconnect the negative battery cable. Remove the steering assembly from the vehicle and place it in a holding fixture.

2. Using a pinion torque adapter tool and an inch lb. torque wrench, check the pinion turning torque; it should be 89–124 inch lbs. (10–14 Nm).
3. If the torque is not to specifications, loosen the locknut.
4. Using a yoke torque gauge tool, torque the adjusting cover to 39–48 inch lbs. (4.5–5.5 Nm) and loosen the cover 35 degrees.
5. Using a yoke locknut wrench tool, torque the locknut to 29–36 ft. lbs. (40–50 Nm).
6. Install the steering assembly. Refill the power steering reservoir. Start the engine and bleed the system. Test drive and check the steering operation.

STANDARD

1. Disconnect the negative battery cable. Remove the steering assembly from the vehicle and place it in a holding fixture.
2. Using a pinion torque adapter tool and an inch lb. torque wrench, check the pinion turning torque; it should be 89–124 inch lbs. (10–14 Nm).
3. If the torque is not to specifications, loosen the locknut.
4. Using a yoke torque gauge tool, torque the adjusting cover to 7.2 ft. lbs. (9.8 Nm), loosen the cover, retorque to 3.6 ft. lbs. (4.9 Nm) and loosen the cover 45 degrees.
5. Using a yoke locknut wrench tool, torque the locknut to 36–43 ft. lbs. (49–59 Nm).
6. Install the steering assembly. Refill the power steering reservoir. Start the engine and bleed the system. Test drive and check the steering operation.

Removal and Installation

ELECTRONIC

The variable assist power steering (VAPS) system automatically adjusts the power steering pressure. It provides light steering effort during low speed and parking maneuvers and higher steering effort at higher speeds for improved road feel.

The completely automatic system (no driver controls) consists of: a VAPS control unit, a steering angle sensor, a vehicle speed sensor, a solenoid valve, a test connector and inter-connecting wiring.

1. Disconnect the negative battery cable.
2. Raise and safely support the vehicle. Remove the front wheel and tire assemblies.
3. Disconnect the tie rod ends from the steering knuckles.
4. From both sides of the vehicle, remove the lower inner fender plastic dust shield.
5. At the steering assembly, pull back the steering column dust boot, turn the steering shaft until the clamp bolt is accessible and lock the steering column. Using paint, matchmark the steering column pinion shaft-to-intermediate shaft lower universal joint location.
6. Remove the clamp bolt from the intermediate shaft lower universal joint.
7. Disconnect the electrical connector from the solenoid valve and the power steering pressure switch.
8. Disconnect and plug the 3 hydraulic lines from the steering assembly; discard both copper washers from each fitting and move the lines aside.
9. Remove the steering assembly-to-chassis bolts. Lower the steering assembly (until it clears the bulkhead), slide it toward the right side (until the left tie rod clears the lower left control arm), move it toward the left side and from the vehicle.

To Install:

10. Move the steering assembly into position, so the pinion shaft is just below the intermediate shaft universal joint.
11. Raise the steering assembly into position, align the pinion shaft-to-intermediate universal joint matchmark and install the steering assembly-to-chassis bolts. Torque the steering assembly-to-chassis bolts to 27–40 ft. lbs. (36–54 Nm).
12. Install the pinion shaft-to-intermediate universal joint clamp bolt and torque to 13–20 ft. lbs. (18–26 Nm).
13. Using new copper washers, connect the hydraulic lines to the steering assembly.
14. Connect the tie rod ends to the steering knuckles.
15. To complete the installation, reverse the removal procedures. Lower the vehicle. Refill the power steering reservoir. Start the engine, bleed the power steering system and check for leaks.

STANDARD

1. Disconnect the negative battery cable.
2. Raise and safely support the vehicle. Remove the front wheel and tire assemblies.

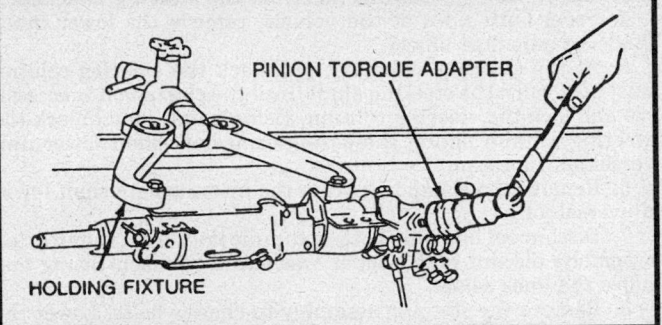

Checking the pinion turning torque of the power steering assembly

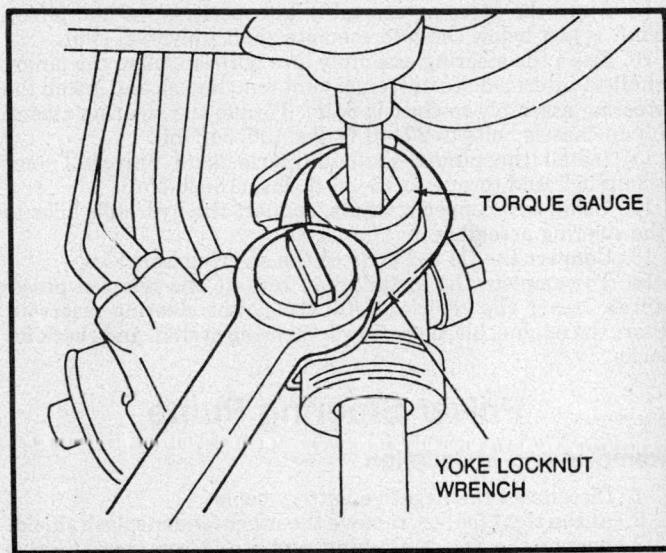

Torquing the locknut of the power steering assembly

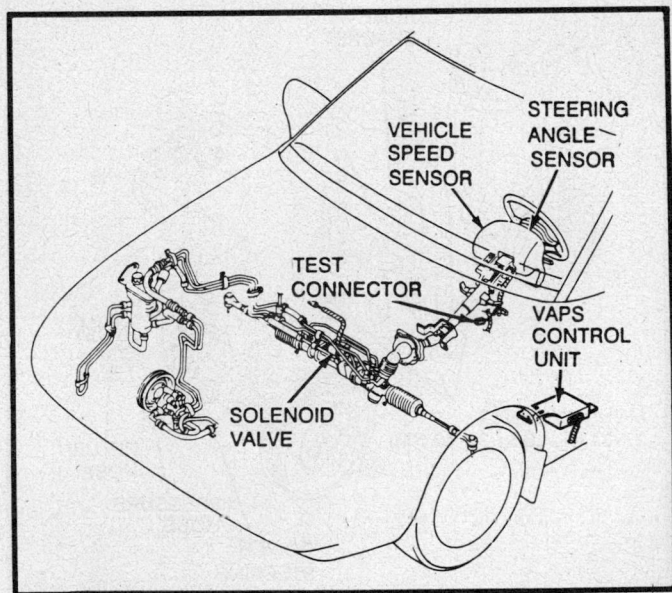

View of the variable assist power steering (VAPS) system

3. Disconnect the tie rod ends from the steering knuckles.

4. From both sides of the vehicle, remove the lower inner fender plastic dust shield.

5. At the steering assembly, pull back the steering column dust boot, turn the steering shaft until the clamp bolt is accessible and lock the steering column. Using paint, matchmark the steering column pinion shaft-to-intermediate shaft lower universal joint location.

6. Remove the clamp bolt from the intermediate shaft lower universal joint.

7. Disconnect and plug both hydraulic lines from the steering assembly; discard both copper washers from each fitting and move the lines aside.

8. Remove the steering assembly-to-chassis bolts. Lower the steering assembly (until it clears the bulkhead), slide it toward the right side (until the left tie rod clears the lower left control arm), move it toward the left side and from the vehicle.

To Install:

9. Move the steering assembly into position, so the pinion shaft is just below the intermediate shaft universal joint.

10. Raise the steering assembly into position, align the pinion shaft-to-intermediate universal joint matchmark and install the steering assembly-to-chassis bolts. Torque the steering assembly-to-chassis bolts to 27–40 ft. lbs. (36–54 Nm).

11. Install the pinion shaft-to-intermediate universal joint clamp bolt and torque to 13–20 ft. lbs. (18–26 Nm).

12. Using new copper washers, connect the hydraulic lines to the steering assembly.

13. Connect the tie rod ends to the steering knuckles.

14. To complete the installation, reverse the removal procedures. Lower the vehicle. Refill the power steering reservoir. Start the engine, bleed the power steering system and check for leaks.

Power Steering Pump

Removal and Installation

1. Disconnect the negative battery cable.
2. At the right fender, remove the inner fender splash shield.
3. Loosen the power steering pump and remove the drive belt.

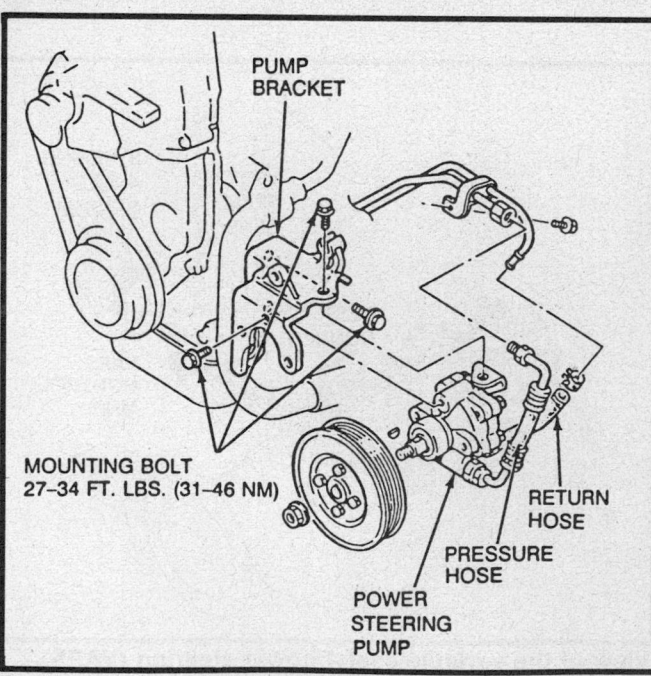

Exploded view of the power steering pump

PUMP BRACKET

MOUNTING BOLT 27–34 FT. LBS. (31–46 NM)

RETURN HOSE

PRESSURE HOSE

POWER STEERING PUMP

4. Disconnect and plug the pressure and return hoses from the pump.

5. Remove the pump-to-bracket bolts and the pump; if necessary, remove the drive pulley from the pump.

To Install:

6. Position the pump on the bracket and torque the bolts to 27–34 ft. lbs. (31–46 Nm).

7. Connect the pressure and return hoses to the pump.

8. Install the drive belt. Refill the power steering reservoir. Start the engine and bleed the system.

Bleeding System

1. Raise and safely support the front of the vehicle.
2. Disconnect the coil wire. Refill the power steering pump reservoir to the specified level.
3. Crank the engine. Check and refill the reservoir.
4. Crank the engine and rotate the steering wheel from lock-to-lock. Check and refill the power steering pump reservoir.
5. Connect the coil wire, start the engine and allow it to run for several minutes.
6. Rotate the steering wheel from lock-to-lock several times, until the air bubbles are eliminated from the fluid.
7. Turn the engine **OFF**. Check and/or refill the reservoir.
8. Disconnect the negative battery cable, depress the brake pedal for at least 5 seconds and reconnect the negative battery cable.

Steering Column

Removal and Installation

1. Disconnect the negative battery cable.
2. Remove the steering wheel.
3. Remove the column cover screws and the cover.
4. Remove the instrument cover-to-instrument cluster cover screws. Carefully, pull the cover outward and disconnect the electrical connectors from the cover. Remove the ignition illumination bulb and the instrument cover.
5. Loosen the instrument cluster cover-to-hinge screws, remove the instrument cluster-to-dash screws and the instrument cluster cover.
6. Remove the lower panel, the lap duct and the defrost duct.
7. Disconnect the electrical connectors from the turn signal switch assembly.
8. Remove the U-joint cinch bolt from the lower end of the steering shaft.
9. Remove the mounting nuts and the hinge bracket.
10. Remove the cluster support nuts and the upper steering column brackets nuts/bolts and the steering shaft assembly.
11. At the steering rack, lift the boot from the intermediate shaft U-joint and remove the U-joint cinch bolt.
12. Remove the intermediate shaft dust cover assembly nut, the intermediate shaft, the dust cover assembly and the steering column.

To Install:

13. Using an assistant to support the intermediate shaft and dust cover assembly, guide the lower U-joint onto the steering rack pinion.

14. Install the lower intermediate shaft U-joint cinch bolt and torque it to 13–20 ft. lbs. (18–26 Nm). Install the dust cover nut.

15. Using an assistant to support the steering column, guide the column into the upper intermediate U-joint; do not install the cinch bolt.

16. Install the hinge bracket nuts; do not tighten the nuts. Install the upper column bracket bolts. Torque the:

Hinge bracket nuts to 12–17 ft. lbs. (16–23 Nm)
Upper bracket bolts to 12–17 ft. lbs. (16–23 Nm)
Cluster support nuts to 6.5–10 ft. lbs. (8.8 Nm)

17. Connect the electrical connectors at the ignition switch. Install the instrument cluster cover.

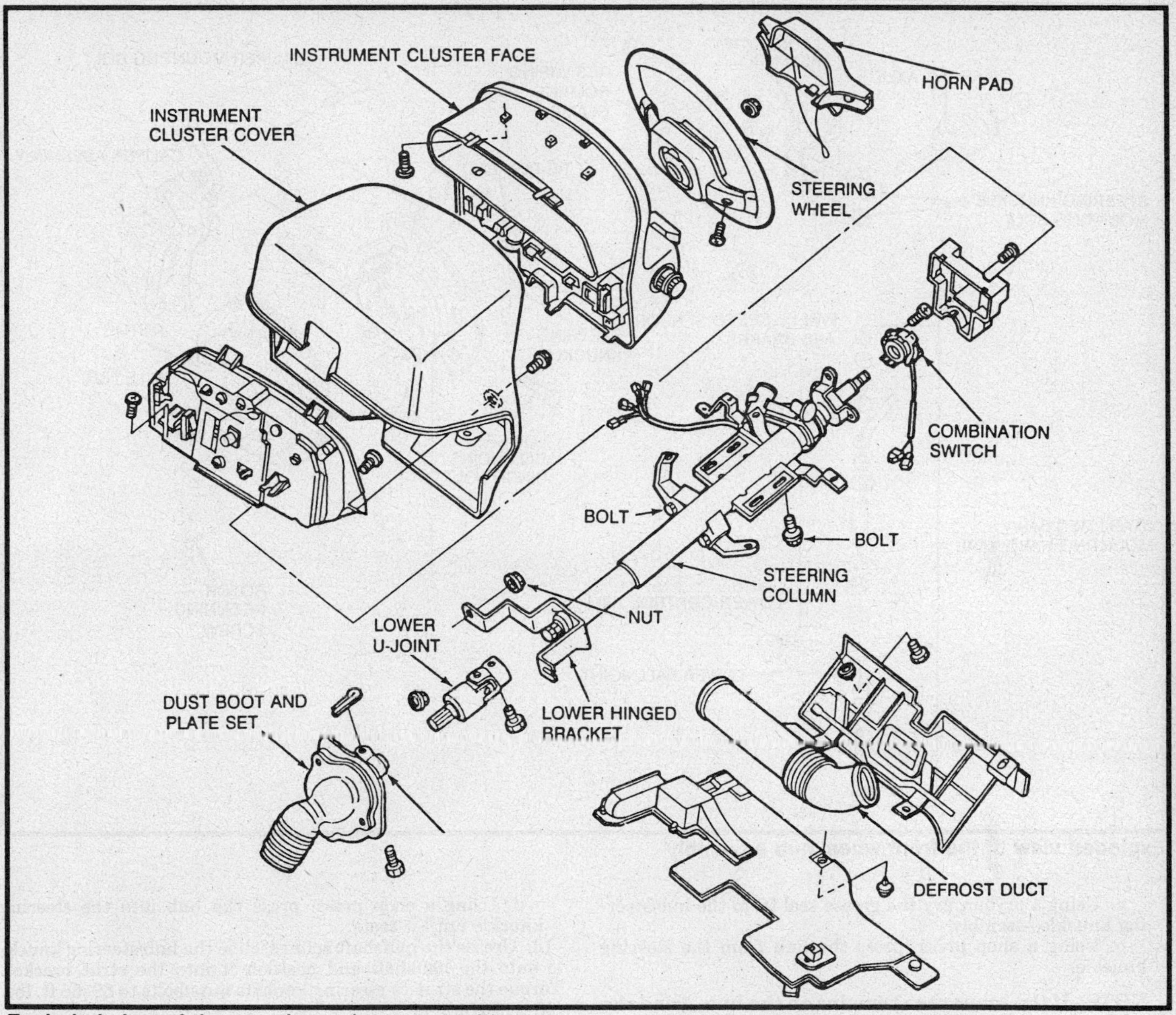

INSTRUMENT CLUSTER FACE

INSTRUMENT CLUSTER COVER

HORN PAD

STEERING WHEEL

COMBINATION SWITCH

BOLT

BOLT

STEERING COLUMN

NUT

LOWER U-JOINT

LOWER HINGED BRACKET

DUST BOOT AND PLATE SET

DEFROST DUCT

Exploded view of the steering column assembly

18. Connect the electrical connectors to the instrument cover and install the cover.

19. To install the steering wheel, align the match-mark and reverse the removal procedures. Torque the steering wheel-to-shaft nut to 29–36 ft. lbs. (39–49 Nm). Reconnect the negative battery cable.

Front Wheel Bearings

Removal and Installation

1. Raise and safely support the vehicle. Remove the front wheel and tire assembly and the grease cap.

2. Using a small cape chisel and a hammer, raise the staked portion of the hub nut.

3. Have an assistant apply the brakes and remove the hub nut (discard it).

4. Remove the stabilizer bar-to-control arm, bolt, nut, washers and bushings.

5. At the tie rod end, remove the cotter pin and nut. Using a

tie rod end separator tool or equivalent, separate the tie rod end from the steering knuckle.

6. Remove the caliper support-to-steering knuckle bolts and support the caliper assembly on a wire.

7. Remove the rotor-to-hub screws and the rotor.

8. Remove the lower control arm ball joint clamp nut/bolt. Using a prybar, pry the lower control arm downward and separate the ball joint from the steering knuckle.

9. Remove the steering knuckle-to-strut nuts/bolts and slide the steering knuckle assembly from the strut bracket.

10. Slide the steering knuckle assembly from the halfshaft and support the halfshaft on a wire; be careful not to damage the seals. Should the wheel hub bind on the halfshaft, use a plastic hammer to jar it free.

NOTE: If the halfshaft splines bind in the hub, it may be necessary to use a 2-jawed wheel puller to separate them.

11. Remove the wheel bearing by performing the following procedures:

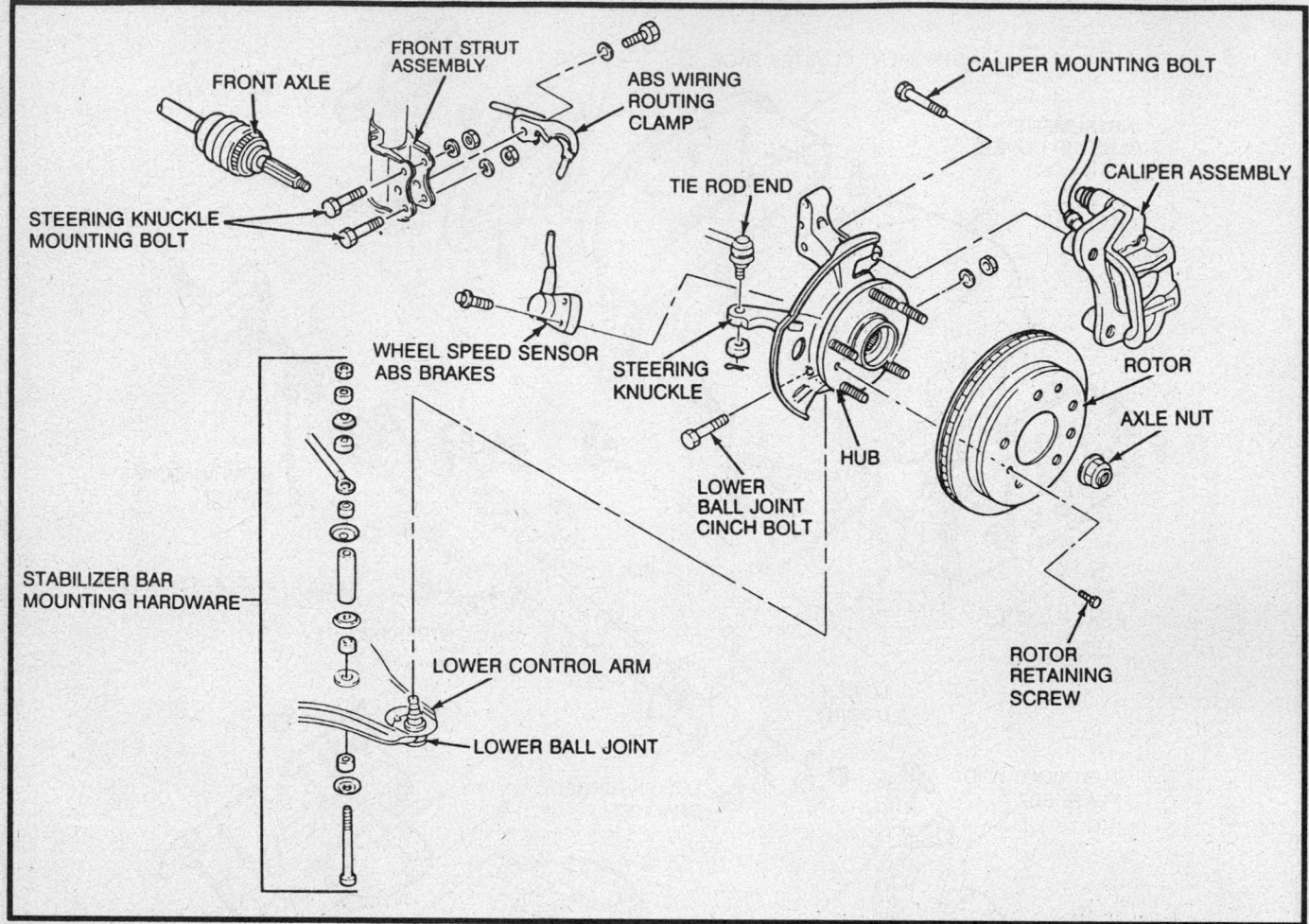

Exploded view of the front wheel hub assembly

a. Using a prybar, pry the grease seal from the hub/steering knuckle assembly.

b. Using a shop press, press the hub from the steering knuckle.

NOTE: If the inner race remains on the hub, grind the inner race to approximately 0.020 in. (0.5mm) and use a chisel to remove it.

c. Remove the snapring from the steering knuckle.

d. Using a shop press, press the wheel bearing from the steering knuckle.

NOTE: Unless the disc brake dust shield is damaged, it should be left on the steering knuckle; it is pressed on and is hard to get off without damaging.

To Install:

12. Install the wheel bearing by performing the following procedures:

a. Using a shop press, press the wheel bearing into the steering knuckle.

b. Install the snapring to secure the wheel bearing.

c. Using a new grease seal, lubricate the lip with grease. Using a seal installer tool or equivalent, drive the new seal into the steering knuckle until it seats.

d. Using a shop press, press the hub into the steering knuckle until it seats.

13. Grease the halfshaft splines, slide the hub/steering knuckle onto the halfshaft and position it into the strut bracket. Torque the strut-to-steering knuckle nuts/bolts to 69–86 ft. lbs. (93–117 Nm).

14. Push the lower control arm ball joint into the steering knuckle and torque the clamp bolt to 32–40 ft. lbs. (43–54 Nm).

15. Install the brake rotor and secure with the retaining screw.

16. Install the caliper anchor bracket-to-steering knuckle bolts and torque to 58–72 ft. lbs. (78–98 Nm).

17. Using a new hub nut, have an assistant apply the brakes and torque the nut to 116–174 ft. lbs. (157–235 Nm). Using a rounded edge cold chisel, stake the hub nut.

18. Connect the tie rod end to the steering knuckle, torque the nut to 22–33 ft. lbs. (29–44 Nm) and install a new cotter pin.

NOTE: Should the slots of the nut not align with the cotter pin hole, tighten the nut; never loosen it.

19. Connect the stabilizer bar to the lower control arm and tighten the nut until 0.79 in. (20mm) of the bolt threads are exposed beyond the nut.

20. Install the wheel and torque the lug nuts to 65–87 ft. lbs. (88–118 Nm).

BRAKES

Refer to unit repair section for brake service information and drum/rotor specifications.

Master Cylinder

Removal and Installation

1. Disconnect the negative battery cable and low fluid level sensor connector from the master cylinder.
2. Disconnect and plug the fluid lines from the master cylinder.
3. Remove the master cylinder-to-power booster nuts and the cylinder.
4. To install, reverse the removal procedures. Refill the master cylinder reservoir. Bleed the brake system.

Bleeding

This procedure is used to bench bleed the master cylinder.
1. Refill the master cylinder reservoir.
2. Push the plunger several times to force fluid into the piston.
3. Continue pumping the plunger until the fluid is free of the air bubbles.

Power Brake Booster

Removal and Installation

1. Disconnect the negative battery cable.
2. Remove the master cylinder and move it aside; it may not be necessary to disconnect the brake tubes from the master cylinder.
3. Disconnect the intake manifold-to-power brake booster rubber hose.
4. From under the instrument panel, remove the spring clip from the brake pedal clevis pin and the clevis pin.
5. Remove the power brake booster-to-firewall nuts and the booster.
6. To install, reverse the removal procedures. If the brake tubes were disconnected from the master cylinder, bleed the brake system.

Bleeding System

The vehicle uses a diagonally split system. The left front and the right rear are on 1 circuit; the right front and the left rear are on the other circuit.
1. Clean the dirt from the master cylinder filler cap.
2. Using a rubber hose, connect it to the rear wheel bleeder screw and submerge the other end in a partially filled container of brake fluid.
3. If equipped with power brakes or an anti-lock brake system, set the parking brake, position the shift selector in **P** (automatic) or **N** (manual) and start the engine.
4. Have an assistant pump the brake pedal 5–10 times and maintain pressure on the pedal after the last stroke.
5. Loosen the bleeder screw ¾ turn, allow the pedal to drop to the floor and close the bleeder screw.

NOTE: **Make sure the assistant maintains constant pressure on the pedal until the bleeder screw is closed or air may be drawn into the system. Be sure to check and refill the master cylinder reservoir occasionally.**

6. Repeat the procedure until all of the air bubbles are removed from the system.
7. Move the front (opposite) side of the vehicle and repeat the bleeding procedure; this procedure will bleed 1 circuit.
8. The other circuit can be bleed by starting at the other rear wheel cylinder and finishing at the other front wheel.

Parking Brake

The parking brake adjustment is performed at the parking brake lever.

Adjustment

1. Remove the center console-to-chassis screws and the console.
2. Adjust the parking brake lever nut so the brakes are fully applied when the parking brake lever can be lifted to 7–10 notches.
3. Reinstall the center console.

CLUTCH AND TRANSAXLE

Refer to "Chilton's Transmission Service Manual" for additional coverage.

Clutch Pedal

Adjustment

1. Remove the lower dash panel and air ducts.
2. Loosen the pushrod locknut and turn the stopper bolt until the clutch pedal height (distance from the firewall to the center of the clutch pedal is 8.524–8.720 in. (216.5–221.5mm).
3. Tighten the locknut. Reinstall the air ducts and the lower dash panel.

Clutch Pedal Free-Play

Adjustment

1. Remove the lower dash panel and air ducts.
2. Loosen the pushrod locknut and turn the pushrod until the clutch pedal free-play is 0.20–0.51 in. (5–13mm).
3. Tighten the locknut. Reinstall the air ducts and the lower dash panel.

Clutch Return Spring

The clutch return spring is located at the top of the clutch pedal.

Adjustment

1. Remove the lower dash panel and air ducts.
2. Turn the adjusting nut until the spring length is 1.52–1.56 in. (38.6–39.6mm) for non-turbo or 1.46–1.50 in. (37.1–38.1mm) for turbo.
3. Reinstall the air ducts and the lower dash panel.

HYDRAULIC

Adjustment/Bleeding

1. Disconnect the negative battery cable.
2. Check and/or refill the clutch master cylinder reservoir.
3. At the slave cylinder, remove the bleeder screw cap. Using a vinyl hose, connect it to the bleeder screw and submerge the other end in a container of brake fluid.
4. Have an assistant slowly pump the clutch pedal several times and maintain pressure.
5. With the clutch pedal depressed, open the bleeder screw. After the pedal has dropped, close the screw and release the pedal; repeat the procedure until the fluid is free of air bubbles.

Clutch

Removal and Installation

1. Disconnect the negative battery cable and remove the transaxle.
2. Using a clutch alignment tool or equivalent, position it through the pressure plate, clutch plate and into the pilot bushing; this will keep the assembly from dropping.
3. Using paint or chalk, matchmark the pressure plate-to-flywheel position.
4. Remove the pressure plate-to-flywheel bolts, a little at a time, evenly, to relieve the spring pressure.
5. Remove the pressure plate, clutch disc and alignment tool from the engine.
6. Inspect the parts for wear, damage and/or cracks; replace the parts, if necessary.

To Install:

7. Using clutch grease, apply a small amount to the clutch disc and input shaft splines.
8. Install the clutch plate and alignment tool.
9. Align the pressure plate to the flywheel matchmark. Install the pressure plate-to-flywheel bolts and torque, evenly, a little at a time, to 13–20 ft. lbs. (18–26 Nm).
10. To complete the installation, reverse the removal procedures.

Manual Transaxle

Removal and Installation

1. Disconnect the battery cables (negative cable first). Remove the battery and the battery tray.
2. Disconnect the main fuel block and coil wire from the distributor.
3. Disconnect the electrical connector from the air flow meter and remove the air cleaner assembly.
4. On non-turbo vehicles, remove the resonance chamber and bracket. On turbo vehicles, remove the throttle body-to-intercooler air hose and the air cleaner-to-turbocharger air hose.
5. Disconnect the speedometer cable (analog) or harness (digital).
6. Disconnect both ground wires from the transaxle. Raise and safely support the vehicle.
7. Remove the front wheels and the splash shields. Drain the transaxle.
8. Remove the slave cylinder and move it aside.
9. Remove the tie rod ends-to-steering knuckle cotter pins and nuts. Disconnect the tie rod ends from the steering knuckle.
10. Remove the stabilizer link assemblies from the lower control arm.
11. Remove the lower control ball joint-to-steering knuckle nut/bolt. Using a prybar, pry the lower control arm downward to separate the ball joint from the steering knuckle.
12. At the right halfshaft, remove the halfshaft-to-engine bracket.

13. Position a prybar between the halfshaft and transaxle case; pry the halfshaft(s) from the transaxle and suspend them on a wire.
14. Using transaxle plugs or equivalent, install them into the halfshaft openings of the transaxle case; this will keep the differential side gears from becoming mispositioned.
15. Remove the gusset plate-to-transaxle bolts. Disconnect the extension bar and shift control rod.
16. Remove the flywheel-to-transaxle inspection plate, the starter and the access brackets.
17. Using an engine support bar or equivalent, attach to the engine and support it's weight.
18. Remove the center transaxle mount/bracket, the left transaxle mount and the right transaxle mount-to-frame nut/bolt.
19. Remove the crossmember and the left lower arm as an assembly.
20. Using a transmission jack or equivalent, attach it to the transaxle.
21. Remove the transaxle-to-engine bolts, lower the transaxle and remove it from the vehicle.

To Install:

22. Using clutch grease, apply a small amount to the input shaft splines.
23. Raise and position the transaxle. Install the transaxle-to-engine bolts and torque to 66–86 ft. lbs. (89–117 Nm).
24. Install the center transaxle mount/bracket and torque the bolts to 27–40 ft. lbs. (36–54 Nm) and the nuts to 47–66 ft. lbs. (64–89 Nm); do not install the throttle air hose bracket nut.
25. Install the torque the:

Left transaxle-to-mount bolts—non-turbo to 27–38 ft. lbs. (37–52 Nm)

Left transaxle-to-mount bolts—turbo to 49–69 ft. lbs. (67–93 Nm)

Mount-to-bracket nut and bolt to 49–69 ft. lbs. (67–93 Nm)

Crossmember and left lower arm bolts to 27–40 ft. lbs. (36–54 Nm)

Crossmember and left lower arm nuts to 55–69 ft. lbs. (75–93 Nm)

Right transaxle mount nut and bolt to 63–86 ft. lbs. (85–117 Nm)

Flywheel inspection cover bolts to 69–95 inch lbs. (8–11 Nm)
Slave cylinder bolts to 14–19 ft. lbs. (19–26 Nm)
Gusset plate-to-transaxle bolts to 27–38 ft. lbs. (37–52 Nm)

26. On the end of each halfshaft, install a new retaining clip.
27. Remove the transaxle plugs and install the halfshaft until the retaining clips snap into place.
28. Install and torque the:

Tie rod end-to-steering knuckle nut to 22–33 ft. lbs. (29–44 Nm)

Lower control arm ball joint-to-steering knuckle nut and bolt to 32–40 ft. lbs. (43–54 Nm)

29. Install the stabilizer link assembly-to-lower control arm. Turn the upper nuts (on each assembly) until 1.0 inch (25.4mm) of the bolt can be measured above the nuts. When the length is reached, secure the upper nut and torque the lower nut to 12–17 ft. lbs. (16–23 Nm).
30. Install the splash shields and the front wheels; torque the lug nuts to 65–87 ft. lbs. (88–118 Nm).
31. On non-turbo vehicles, install the resonance chamber and bracket; torque to 69–95 inch lbs. (8–11 Nm). On turbo vehicles, install the throttle body-to-intercooler air hose and torque the bracket-to-mount bolt to 47–66 ft. lbs. (64–89 Nm).
32. To complete the installation, reverse the removal procedures. Refill the transaxle. Start the engine and check for leaks.

Automatic Transaxle

Removal and Installation

1. Disconnect the battery cables (negative cable first). Remove the battery and the battery tray.

2. Disconnect the main fuel block and coil wire from the distributor.

3. Disconnect the electrical connector from the air flow meter and remove the air cleaner assembly.

4. Remove the resonance chamber and bracket.

5. Disconnect the speedometer cable (analog) or harness (digital).

6. Disconnect the 5 transaxle electrical connectors and separate the harness from the transaxle clips.

7. Disconnect both ground wires, the range selector cable and the kickdown cable from the transaxle. Raise and safely support the vehicle.

8. Remove the front wheels and the splash shields. Drain the transaxle.

9. Disconnect and plug the oil cooler hoses from the transaxle.

10. Remove the tie rod ends-to-steering knuckle cotter pins and nuts. Disconnect the tie rod ends from the steering knuckle.

11. Remove the stabilizer link assemblies from the lower control arm.

12. Remove the lower control ball joint-to-steering knuckle nut/bolt. Using a prybar, pry the lower control arm downward to separate the ball joint from the steering knuckle.

13. At the right halfshaft, remove the halfshaft-to-engine bracket.

14. Position a prybar between the halfshaft and transaxle case; pry the halfshaft(s) from the transaxle and suspend them on a wire.

15. Using transaxle plugs or equivalent, install them into the halfshaft openings of the transaxle case; this will keep the differential side gears from becoming mispositioned.

16. Remove the gusset plate-to-transaxle bolts.

17. Remove the torque converter-to-transaxle cover, the starter and the access brackets.

18. Using paint or chalk, matchmark the torque converter-to-flexplate position.

19. Using an engine support bar or equivalent, attach to the engine and support it's weight.

20. Remove the center transaxle mount/bracket, the left transaxle mount and the right transaxle mount-to-frame nut/bolt.

21. Remove the crossmember and the left lower arm as an assembly.

22. Using a transmission jack or equivalent, attach it to the transaxle.

23. Using a prybar, position it between the torque converter and flexplate; pry the torque converter off the studs an move it into the transaxle.

24. Remove the transaxle-to-engine bolts, lower the transaxle and remove it from the vehicle.

To Install:

25. Raise and position the transaxle, align the torque converter-to-flexplate matchmark and studs. Install the transaxle-to-engine bolts and torque to 66–86 ft. lbs. (89–117 Nm).

26. Install the center transaxle mount/bracket and torque the bolts to 27–40 ft. lbs. (36–54 Nm) and the nuts to 47–66 ft. lbs. (64–89 Nm); do not install the throttle air hose bracket nut.

27. Install and torque the:
Left transaxle-to-mount nut to 63–86 ft. lbs. (85–117 Nm)
Mount-to-bracket nut and bolt to 49–69 ft. lbs. (67–93 Nm)
Crossmember and left lower arm bolts to 27–40 ft. lbs. (36–54 Nm)
Crossmember and left lower arm nuts to 55–69 ft. lbs. (75–93 Nm)
Right transaxle mount nut and bolt to 63–86 ft. lbs. (85–117 Nm)
Torque converter-to-flexplate nuts to 32–45 ft. lbs. (43–61 Nm)
Torque converter cover bolts to 69–95 inch lbs. (8–11 Nm)
Gusset plate-to-transaxle bolts to 27–38 ft. lbs. (37–52 Nm)

28. On the end of each halfshaft, install a new retaining clip.

29. Remove the transaxle plugs and install the halfshaft until the retaining clips snap into place.

30. Install and torque the:
Tie rod end-to-steering knuckle nut to 22–33 ft. lbs. (29–44 Nm)
Lower control arm ball joint-to-steering knuckle nut and bolt to 32–40 ft. lbs. (43–54 Nm)

31. Install the stabilizer link assembly-to-lower control arm. Turn the upper nuts (on each assembly) until 1.0 inch (25.4mm) of the bolt can be measured above the nuts. When the length is reached, secure the upper nut and torque the lower nut to 12–17 ft. lbs. (16–23 Nm).

32. Install the oil cooler hoses to the transaxle.

33. Install the splash shields and the front wheels; torque the lug nuts to 65–87 ft. lbs. (88–118 Nm).

34. Connect and adjust the kickdown cable. Connect the range selector cable and torque the bolt to 22–29 ft. lbs. (29–39 Nm).

35. Install the resonance chamber and bracket; torque to 69–95 inch lbs. (8–11 Nm).

36. To complete the installation, reverse the removal procedures. Refill the transaxle. Start the engine and check for leaks.

Adjustment

KICKDOWN CABLE

1. From the left front wheel well, remove the splash shield.

2. At the transaxle, remove the square head plug, marked **L**, and install an adapter and a pressure gauge in the hole.

3. Rotate the kickdown cable locknuts to the furthest point from the throttle cam to loosen the cable all the way.

4. Place the transaxle into the **P** position and warm the engine; the idle speed should be 700–800 rpm.

5. Rotate the locknuts toward the throttle cam until the line pressure exceeds 63–66 psi, rotate the locknuts away from the throttle cam until the line pressure is 63–66 ft. lbs. and tighten the locknuts.

6. Turn the engine **OFF**, install the square head plug and torque to 43–87 inch lbs. (5–10 Nm).

NOTE: If installing a new kickdown cable, fully open the throttle valve, crimp the pin with the protector installed and remove the protector.

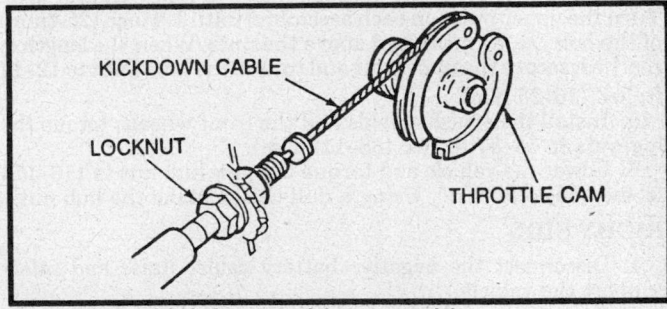

View of the kickdown cable assembly

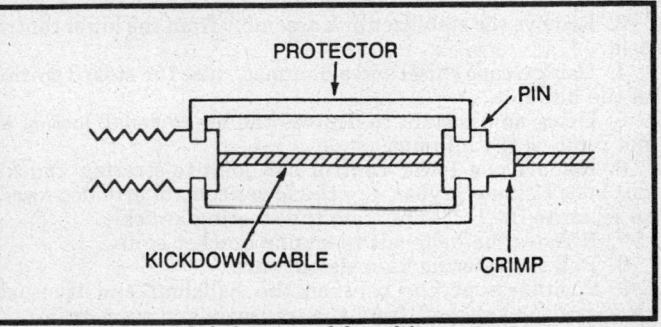

View of a new kickdown cable with protector

HALFSHAFTS

Front Drive Axle

Removal and Installation

LEFT SIDE

1. Disconnect the negative battery cable. Raise and safely support the vehicle.
2. Remove the left front wheel, the hub grease cup and the left splash shield.
3. Remove the stabilizer link assembly from the lower control arm.
4. Using a cape chisel and a hammer, raise the staked portion of the hub nut.
5. Using an assistant to depress the brake pedal, loosen, do not remove, the hub nut.
6. Remove the lower control ball joint-to-steering knuckle nut/bolt. Using a prybar, pry the lower control arm downward to separate the ball joint from the steering knuckle.
7. Pull the steering knuckle outward.
8. Position a prybar between the halfshaft and transaxle case; pry the halfshaft from the transaxle and support it.
9. Remove the hub nut (discard it) and slide the halfshaft from the steering knuckle.

NOTE: If the halfshaft binds in the hub splines, use a plastic hammer to bump it out or a wheel puller to press it out.

10. Using transaxle plugs or equivalent, install them into the halfshaft openings of the transaxle case; this will keep the differential side gears from becoming mispositioned.

To Install:
11. On the end of each halfshaft, install a new retaining clip.
12. Slide the halfshaft into the steering knuckle assembly.
13. Remove the transaxle plugs and install the halfshaft into the transaxle until the retaining clips snap into place.
14. Install and torque the lower control arm ball joint-to-steering knuckle nut and bolt to 32–40 ft. lbs. (43–54 Nm).
15. Install the stabilizer link assembly-to-lower control arm. Turn the upper nuts (on each assembly) until 1.0 inch (25.4mm) of the bolt can be measured above the nuts. When the length is reached, secure the upper nut and torque the lower nut to 12–17 ft. lbs. (16–23 Nm).
16. Install the splash shields and the front wheels; torque the lug nuts to 65–87 ft. lbs. (88–118 Nm).
17. Lower the vehicle and torque the new hub nut to 116–174 ft. lbs. (157–235 Nm). Using a dull chisel, stake the hub nut.

RIGHT SIDE

1. Disconnect the negative battery cable. Raise and safely support the vehicle.
2. Remove the right front wheel, the hub grease cup and the right splash shield.
3. Remove the stabilizer link assembly from the lower control arm.
4. Using a cape chisel and a hammer, raise the staked portion of the hub nut.
5. Using an assistant to depress the brake pedal, loosen, do not remove, the hub nut.
6. Remove the lower control ball joint-to-steering knuckle nut/bolt. Using a prybar, pry the lower control arm downward to separate the ball joint from the steering knuckle.
7. Remove the halfshaft-to-engine bracket bolts.
8. Pull the steering knuckle outward.
9. Position a prybar between the halfshaft and transaxle case; pry the halfshaft from the transaxle and support it.
10. Slide the halfshaft from the steering knuckle.

NOTE: If the halfshaft binds in the hub splines, use a plastic hammer to bump it out or a wheel puller to press it out.

11. Using transaxle plugs or equivalent, install them into the halfshaft openings of the transaxle case; this will keep the differential side gears from becoming mispositioned.

To Install:
12. On the end of each halfshaft, install a new retaining clip.
13. Slide the halfshaft into the steering knuckle assembly.
14. Remove the transaxle plugs and install the halfshaft into the transaxle until the retaining clips snap into place.
15. Torque the halfshaft-to-engine bracket bolts to 31–46 ft. lbs.
16. Install and torque the lower control arm ball joint-to-steering knuckle nut and bolt to 32–40 ft. lbs. (43–54 Nm).
17. Install the stabilizer link assembly-to-lower control arm. Turn the upper nuts (on each assembly) until 1.0 inch (25.4mm) of the bolt can be measured above the nuts. When the length is reached, secure the upper nut and torque the lower nut to 12–17 ft. lbs. (16–23 Nm).
18. Install the splash shields and the front wheels; torque the lug nuts to 65–87 ft. lbs. (88–118 Nm).
19. Lower the vehicle and torque the hub nut to 116–174 ft. lbs. (157–235 Nm).

Boot

Removal and Installation

INNER
Rzeppa

1. Remove the halfshaft from the vehicle and position it in a soft jawed vise, do not allow the vise to contact the boot.
2. Using a pair of side cutters, cut inner joint the boot clamps and move the boot rearward.
3. Using paint or chalk, matchmark the outer race to the halfshaft.
4. Using a small pry bar, pry the wire ring bearing retainer from the joint and remove the outer race.
5. Using paint or chalk, matchmark the bearing assembly to the halfshaft. Using a pair of snapring pliers, remove the outer snapring. Remove the inner race, cage and the ball bearings as an assembly.
6. Remove the boot.
7. Check the grease for grit; if necessary, clean the parts and regrease the assembly.

To Install:
8. Install the new boot on the shaft; be careful not to cut the boot on the shaft splines.
9. Align the matchmarks and install the inner race, cage and ball bearings as an assembly. Install the snapring.
10. Align the matchmarks and install the outer race and the large wire snapring.
11. Position the boot over the outer race so it is extended to 3.5 in. (90mm) between the clamps. Using a dull blade prybar, lift the boot end to expell the trapped air.
12. Using new boot clamps, wrap them around the boots in a clockwise direction, pull them tight (with pliers) and bend the locking tabs to secure them in place.
13. Work the CV-joint through it's full range of travel at various angles; it should flex, extend and compress smoothly.
14. Install the halfshaft into the vehicle.

Tripot

1. Remove the halfshaft from the vehicle and position it in a soft jawed vise, do not allow the vise to contact the boot.

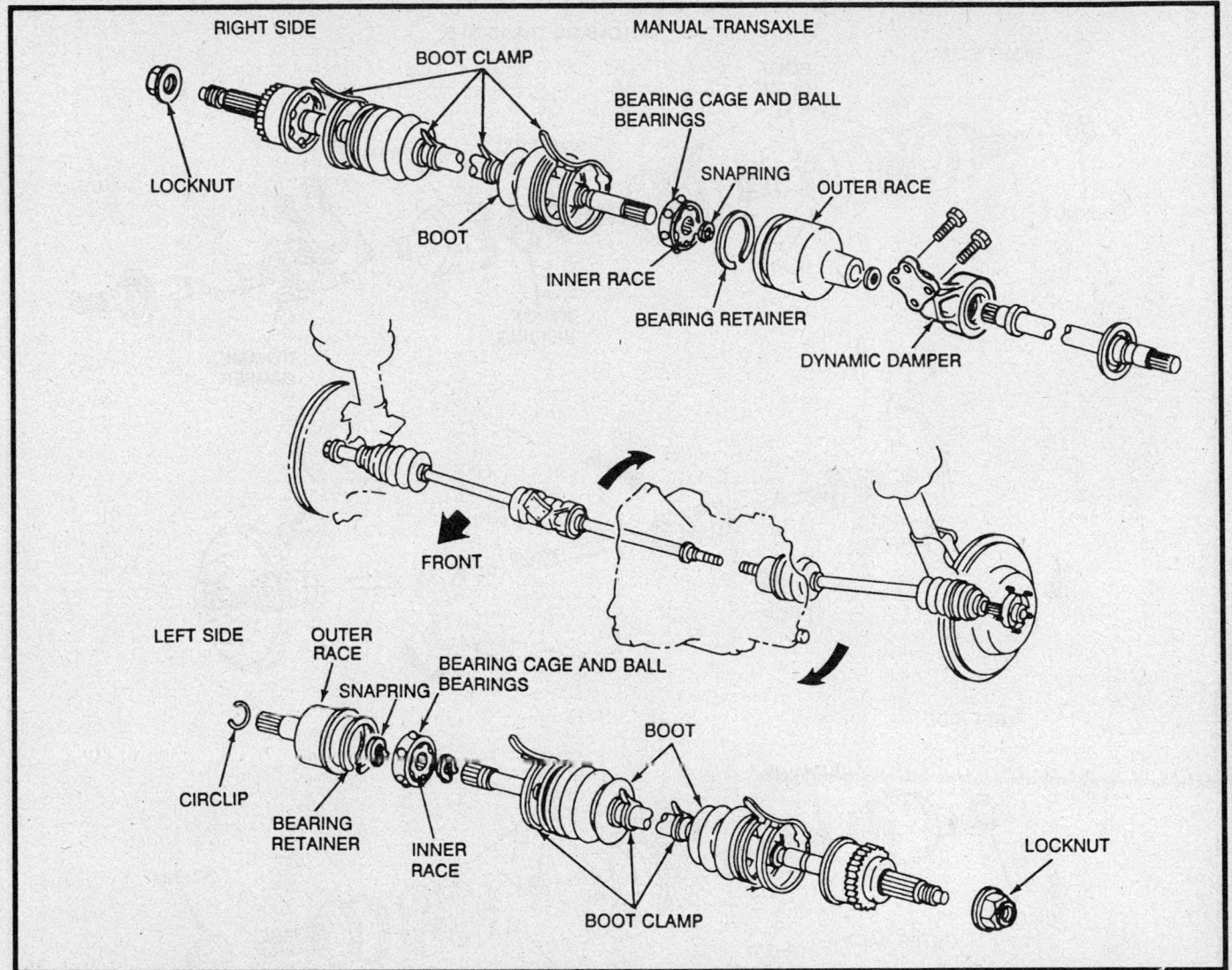

Exploded view of the halfshafts—manual transaxles

2. Using a pair of side cutters, cut inner joint the boot clamps and move the boot rearward.

3. Using paint or chalk, matchmark the outer race to the halfshaft.

4. Using a small pry bar, pry the wire ring bearing retainer from the joint and remove the outer race.

5. Using paint or chalk, matchmark the tripot bearing to the halfshaft. Using a pair of snapring pliers, remove the outer snapring.

6. Using a brass drift and a hammer, drive the tripot bearing assembly from the halfshaft.

7. Wrap tape around the shaft splines and remove the boot.

8. Check the grease for grit; if necessary, clean the parts and regrease the assembly.

To Install:

9. Install the new boot on the shaft; be careful not to cut the boot on the shaft splines.

10. Align the tripot bearing-to-halfshaft matchmarks. Using a brass drift and a hammer, drive the bearing assembly onto the halfshaft. Install the snapring.

11. Fill the CV-joint outer race with 3.5 oz. of grease.

12. Align the matchmarks and install the outer race and the large wire snapring.

13. Position the boot over the outer race so it is extended to 3.5 in. (90mm) between the clamps. Using a dull blade prybar, lift the boot end to expell the trapped air.

14. Using new boot clamps, wrap them around the boots in a clockwise direction, pull them tight (with pliers) and bend the locking tabs to secure them in place.

15. Work the CV-joint through it's full range of travel at various angles; it should flex, extend and compress smoothly.

16. Install the halfshaft into the vehicle.

OUTER

The outer joint are not servicable and must be replaced with the shaft as an assembly.

1. Remove the inner joint and boot assembly from the halfshaft.

2. Using a pair of side cutters, cut outer joint the boot clamps and remove the boot from the halfshaft.

3. Position the outer boot over the outer race so it is extended

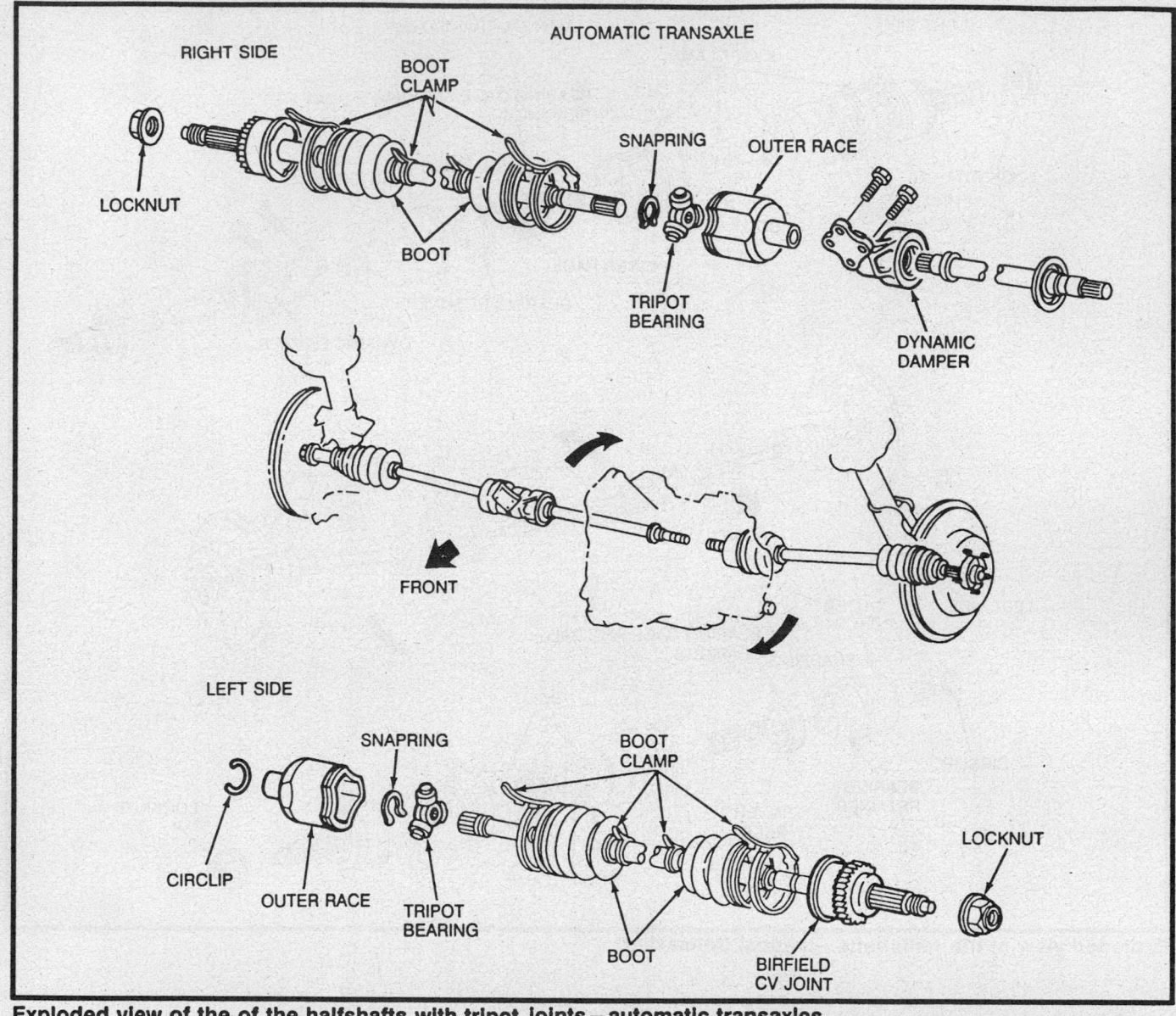

Exploded view of the of the halfshafts with tripot joints—automatic transaxles

to 3.5 in. (90mm) between the clamps. Using a dull blade prybar, lift the boot end to expell the trapped air.

4. Using new boot clamps, wrap them around the boots in a clockwise direction, pull them tight (with pliers) and bend the locking tabs to secure them in place.

5. To complete the installation, reverse the removal procedures. Install the halfshaft into the vehicle.

Universal Joints

Refer to unit repair section for overhaul procedures.

REAR AXLE AND REAR SUSPENSION

Refer to the unit repair section for axle overhaul procedures and rear suspension services.

Rear Axle Assembly

Removal and Installation

1. Raise and safely support the rear of the vehicle.

2. Remove the rear wheels.

3. Remove the upper trunk side garnish and lower trunk side trim to gain access to the strut assembly.

4. If equipped with a programmed ride control module, disconnect the electrical connector and remove the module from the upper strut.

5. If equipped, remove the ABS harness and bracket.

6. Disconnect and plug the brake lines from the wheel cylinders or calipers.

7. Remove the brake line U-clip from the strut housing.

8. Remove the trailing arm-to-spindle bolts.

9. Using a floor jack, position it under the rear axle assembly and support it's weight.

10. Remove the strut-to-chassis nuts and lower the rear axle assembly from the vehicle.

To Install:

11. Position and raise the rear axle assembly into position.

12. Install the strut-to-chassis nuts and torque the nuts to 34–46 ft. lbs. (48–63 Nm).

13. If equipped with a programmed ride control module, install it and reconnect the electrical connector.

14. If equipped with ABS, install the brake harness and bracket.

15. Install and torque the trailing arm-to-spindle bolts to 64–86 ft. lbs. (86–117 Nm).

16. Install the wheels and torque the lug nuts to 65–87 ft. lbs. (88–118 Nm).

17. Check and/or adjust the rear toe.

Rear Wheel Bearing

Removal and Installation

1. Raise and safely support the rear of the vehicle.
2. Remove the wheel and the grease cup.
3. Using a cape chisel and a hammer, raise the staked portion of the hub nut.
4. Remove and discard the hub nut.
5. Pull the brake drum assembly from the spindle.
6. Using a small prybar, pry the grease seal from the brake drum and discard it.
7. Remove the snapring. Using a chop press, press the wheel bearing from the brake drum.

To Install:

8. Using a shop press, press the new wheel bearing into the brake drum until it seats and install the snapring.
9. Using a grease seal installation tool or equivalent, lubricate the seal lip with grease and drive it into the brake drum until it seats.
10. Position the brake drum assembly onto the wheel spindle.
11. Using a new locknut, torque it to 73–101 ft. lbs. (98–117 Nm).
12. Check the wheel bearing freeplay.
13. Using a dull cold chisel, stake the locknut.
14. To complete the installation, reverse the removal procedures.

Adjustment

1. Raise and safely support the rear of the vehicle.
2. Remove the wheel and the grease cup.
3. Using a cape chisel and a hammer, raise the staked portion of the hub nut.
4. Remove and discard the hub nut.

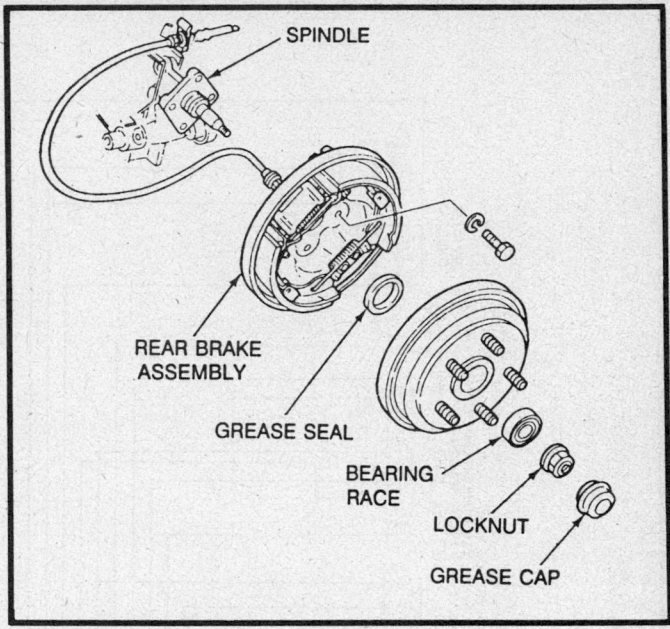

Exploded view of the rear wheel assembly

To Install:

5. Using a new locknut, torque it to 73–101 ft. lbs. (98–117 Nm).
6. Check the wheel bearing freeplay.
7. Using a dull cold chisel, stake the locknut.
8. To complete the installation, reverse the removal procedures.

Rear Wheel Alignment

CAMBER

Rear wheel camber is 0.25N–1.25P degrees but it is not adjustable.

TOE

1. Raise and safely support the rear of the vehicle.
2. Loosen the jam nuts clockwise (right control arm) or counterclockwise (left control arm).
3. To increase the toe-in, turn the right control arm rod counterclockwise and the left control arm rod clockwise.
4. To decrease the toe-in, turn the right control arm clockwise and the left control arm counterclockwise.

NOTE: When adjusting the control arm rods, turn each an equal amount of turns.

5. After adjustment, torque the control arm jam nuts 41–59 ft. lbs. (55–80 Nm).

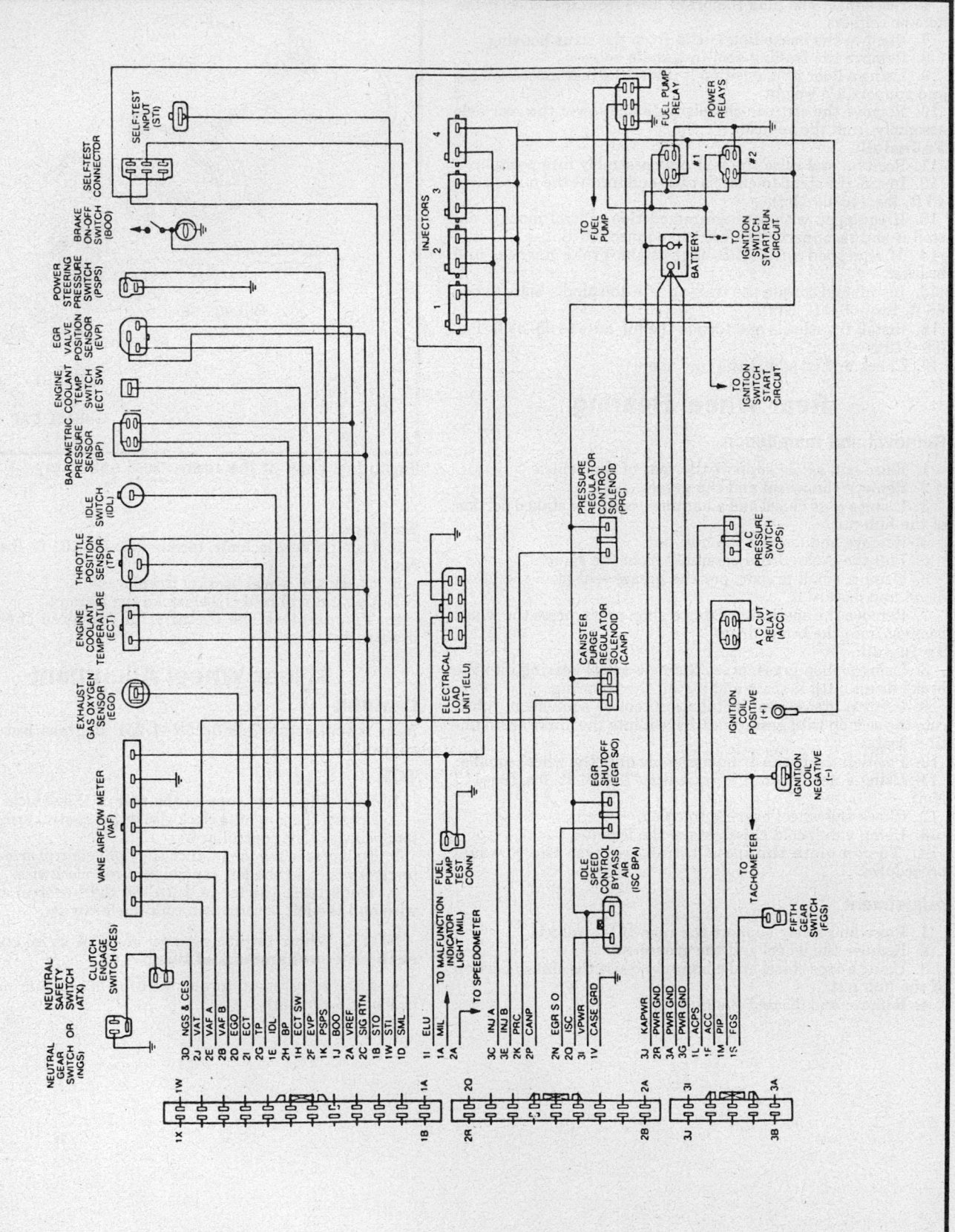

Underhood electrical schematic

YEAR IDENTIFICATION

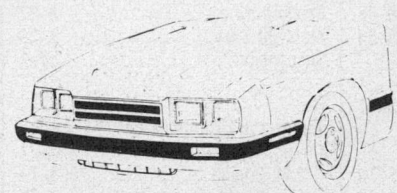

1986 Capri

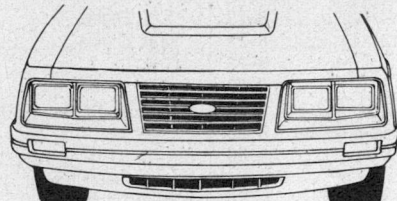

1986 Mustang

1987–90 Mustang

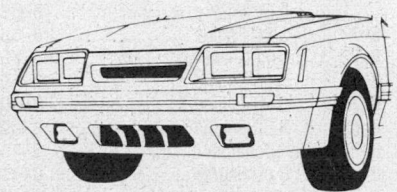

1986 Mustang GT

1987–90 Mustang GT

1986 Mustang SVO

1986 Thunderbird

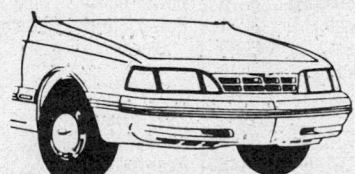

1987-88 Thunderbird

1989–90 Thunderbird

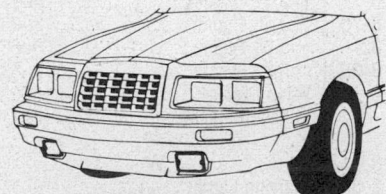

1986 Thunderbird Turbo

1987-88 Thunderbird Turbo

1989–90 Thunderbird Super Coupe

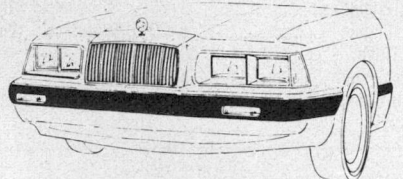

1986 Cougar

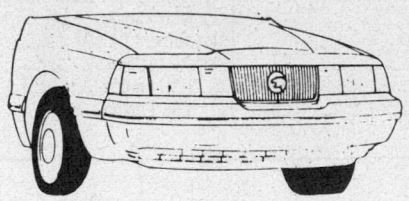

1987-88 Cougar

YEAR IDENTIFICATION

1989–90 Cougar

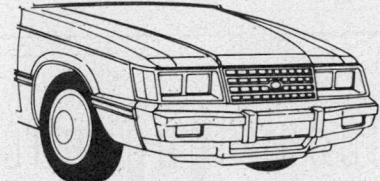

1986 LTD

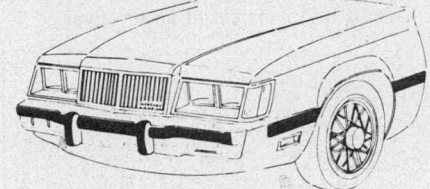

1986 Marquis

1986–90 Grand Marquis and Colony Park

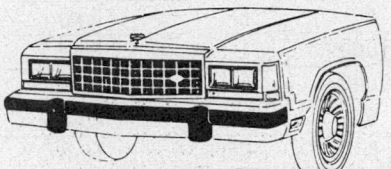

1986 Crown Victoria

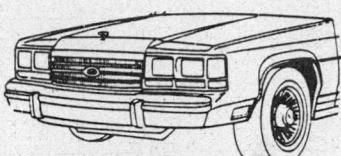

1987–90 Crown Victoria and Country Squire

1986–90 Lincoln Town Car

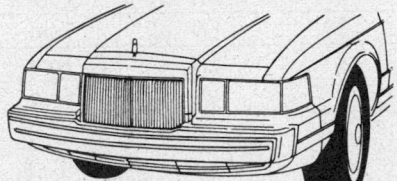

1986 Mark VII

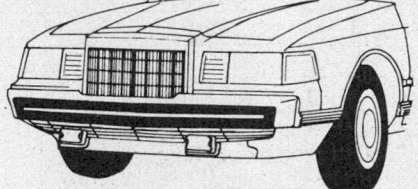

1986 Mark VII LSC

1987–90 Mark VII LSC

1989–90 Cougar XR7

VEHICLE IDENTIFICATION

It is important for servicing and ordering parts to be certain of the vehicle and engine identification. The VIN (vehicle identification number) is a 17 digit number visible through the windshield on the driver's side of the dash and contains the vehicle and engine identification codes. The tenth digit indicates model year and the eighth digit indicates engine code. It can be interpreted as follows:

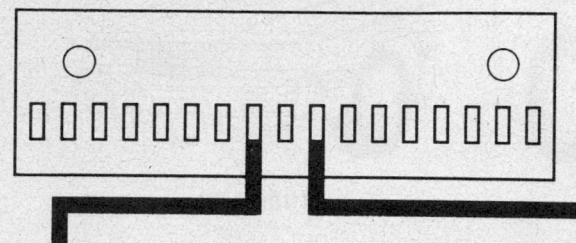

Engine Code

Code	Cu. In.	Liters	Cyl.	Fuel Sys.	Eng. Mfg.
A	140	2.3	4	1 bbl	Ford
A	140	2.3	4	EFI	Ford
T	140	2.3	4 (Turbo)	EFI	Ford
W	140	2.3	4 (Turbo)	EFI	Ford
C	232	3.8	6	2 bbl	Ford
3	232	3.8	6	CFI	Ford
3	232	3.8	6	EFI	Ford
R	232 (SC)	3.8	6	EFI	Ford
C	232 (SC)	3.8	6	EFI	Ford
F	302	5.0	8	VV	Ford
F	302	5.0	8	CFI	Ford
F	302	5.0	8	EFI	Ford
M	302 (HO)	5.0	8	CFI	Ford
M	302 (HO)	5.0	8	EFI	Ford
E	302 (HO)	5.0	8	EFI	Ford
G	351 (HO)	5.8	8	VV	Ford

Model Year

Code	Year
G	1986
H	1987
J	1988
K	1989
L	1990

EFI Electronic Fuel Injection
CFI Central Fuel Injection
HO High Output
SC Supercharged
VV Variable Venturi

ENGINE IDENTIFICATION

Year	Model	Engine Displacement cu. in. (liter)	Engine Series Identification (VIN)	No. of Cylinders	Engine Type
1986	Mustang	140 (2.3)	A	4	OHC
	Mustang	140 (2.3)	W	4	OHC-Turbo
	Mustang	232 (3.8)	3	6	OHV
	Mustang	302 (5.0)	F	8	OHV
	Mustang	302 (5.0) HO	M	8	OHV
	Capri	140 (2.3)	A	4	OHC
	Capri	140 (2.3)	W	4	OHC-Turbo
	Capri	232 (3.8)	3	6	OHV
	Capri	302 (5.0)	F	8	OHV
	Capri	302 (5.0) HO	M	8	OHV

ENGINE IDENTIFICATION

Year	Model	Engine Displacement cu. in. (liter)	Engine Series Identification (VIN)	No. of Cylinders	Engine Type
1986	LTD	140 (2.3)	A	4	OHC
	LTD	232 (3.8)	3	6	OHV
	Marquis	140 (2.3)	A	4	OHC
	Marquis	232 (3.8)	3	6	OHV
	Thunderbird	140 (2.3)	W	4	OHC-Turbo
	Thunderbird	232 (3.8)	3	6	OHV
	Thunderbird	302 (5.0)	F	8	OHV
	Cougar	140 (2.3)	W	4	OHC-Turbo
	Cougar	232 (3.8)	3	6	OHV
	Cougar	302 (5.0)	F	8	OHV
	Crown Victoria	302 (5.0)	F	8	OHV
	Crown Victoria	351 (5.8)	G	8	OHV
	Grand Marquis	302 (5.0)	F	8	OHV
	Grand Marquis	351 (5.8)	G	8	OHV
	Continental	302 (5.0)	F	8	OHV
	Continental	302 (5.0) HO	M	8	OHV
	Mark VII	302 (5.0)	F	8	OHV
	Mark VII	302 (5.0) HO	M	8	OHV
	Town Car	302 (5.0)	F	8	OHV
1987	Mustang	140 (2.3)	A	4	OHC
	Mustang	302 (5.0) HO	M	8	OHV
	Thunderbird	140 (2.3)	W	4	OHC-Turbo
	Thunderbird	232 (3.8)	3	6	OHV
	Thunderbird	302 (5.0)	F	8	OHV
	Cougar	232 (3.8)	3	6	OHV
	Cougar	302 (5.0)	F	8	OHV
	Crown Victoria	302 (5.0)	F	8	OHV
	Crown Victoria	351 (5.8)	G	8	OHV
	Grand Marquis	302 (5.0)	F	8	OHV
	Grand Marquis	351 (5.8)	G	8	OHV
	Continental	302 (5.0)	F	8	OHV
	Continental	302 (5.0) HO	M	8	OHV
	Mark VII	302 (5.0)	F	8	OHV
	Mark VII	302 (5.0) HO	M	8	OHV
	Town Car	302 (5.0)	F	8	OHV
1988	Mustang	140 (2.3)	A	4	OHC
	Mustang	302 (5.0)	F	8	OHV
	Mustang	302 (5.0) HO	M	8	OHV
	Thunderbird	140 (2.3)	W	4	OHC-Turbo
	Thunderbird	232 (3.8)	3	6	OHV
	Thunderbird	302 (5.0)	F	8	OHV

ENGINE IDENTIFICATION

Year	Model	Engine Displacement cu. in. (liter)	Engine Series Identification (VIN)	No. of Cylinders	Engine Type
1988	Cougar	232 (3.8)	3	6	OHV
	Cougar	302 (5.0)	F	8	OHV
	Crown Victoria	302 (5.0)	F	8	OHV
	Crown Victoria	351 (5.8)	G	8	OHV
	Grand Marquis	302 (5.0)	F	8	OHV
	Grand Marquis	351 (5.8)	G	8	OHV
	Continental	302 (5.0)	F	8	OHV
	Continental	302 (5.0) HO	M	8	OHV
	Mark VII	302 (5.0)	F	8	OHV
	Mark VII	302 (5.0) HO	M	8	OHV
	Town Car	302 (5.0)	F	8	OHV
1989-90	Mustang	140 (2.3)	A	4	OHC
	Mustang	302 (5.0) HO	M	8	OHV
	Thunderbird	232 (3.8)	3	6	OHV
	Thunderbird	232 (3.8) SC	R	6	OHV
	Cougar	232 (3.8)	3	6	OHV
	Cougar	232 (3.8) SC	R	6	OHV
	Crown Victoria	302 (5.0)	F	8	OHV
	Crown Victoria	351 (5.8)	G	8	OHV
	Grand Marquis	302 (5.0)	F	8	OHV
	Grand Marquis	351 (5.8)	G	8	OHV
	Mark VII	302 (5.0) HO	M	8	OHV
	Town Car	302 (5.0)	F	8	OHV

OHC Overhead Camshaft
OHV Overhead Valve
HO High Output
SC Supercharged

GENERAL ENGINE SPECIFICATIONS

Year	VIN	No. Cylinder Displacement cu. in. (liter)	Fuel System Type	Net Horsepower @ rpm	Net Torque @ rpm (ft.lbs.)	Bore × Stroke (in.)	Compression Ratio	Oil Pressure @ 2000 rpm
1986	A	4-140 (2.3)	2 bbl	88 @ 4200	122 @ 2600	3.781 × 3.126	9.0:1	40-60
	T	4-140 (2.3)T③	EFI	145 @ 4400	180 @ 3000	3.781 × 3.126	8.0:1	40-60
	W	4-140 (2.3)T	EFI	155 @ 4600	190 @ 2800	3.781 × 3.126	8.0:1	40-60
	3	6-232 (3.8)	CFI①	120 @ 3600	205 @ 1600	3.810 × 3.390	8.7:1	40-60
	F	8-302 (5.0)	EFI	150 @ 3200	270 @ 2000	4.000 × 3.000	8.9:1	40-60
	M	8-302 (5.0)HO	4 bbl	210 @ 4400	265 @ 3200	4.000 × 3.000	8.3:1	40-60
	G	8-351 (5.8)	VV	180 @ 3600	285 @ 2400	4.000 × 3.500	8.3:1	40-60
1987	A	4-140 (2.3)OHC	EFI	88 @ 4200	122 @ 2600	3.781 × 3.126	9.0:1	40-60
	W	4-140 (2.3)T	EFI	155 @ 4600	190 @ 2800	3.781 × 3.126	8.0:1	40-60

GENERAL ENGINE SPECIFICATIONS

Year	VIN	No. Cylinder Displacement cu. in. (liter)	Fuel System Type	Net Horsepower @ rpm	Net Torque @ rpm (ft.lbs.)	Bore × Stroke (in.)	Compression Ratio	Oil Pressure @ 2000 rpm
1987	3	6-232 (3.8)	EFI	120 @ 3600	205 @ 1600	3.810 × 3.390	8.7:1	40-60
	E	8-302 (5.0)	EFI	150 @ 3200	270 @ 2000	4.000 × 3.000	8.9:1	40-60
	F	8-302 (5.0)	EFI	150 @ 3200	270 @ 2000	4.000 × 3.000	8.9:1	40-60
	M	8-302 (5.0)HO	EFI	210 @ 4400	265 @ 3200	4.000 × 3.000	8.3:1	40-60
	G	8-351 (5.8)HO④	VV	180 @ 3600	285 @ 2400	4.000 × 3.500	8.3:1	40-60
1988	A	4-140 (2.3)	EFI	88 @ 4200	122 @ 2600	3.780 × 3.126	9.0:1	40-60
	T	4-140 (2.3)T	EFI	155 @ 4600	190 @ 2800	3.780 × 3.126	8.0:1	40-60
	4	6-232 (3.8)	EFI	120 @ 3600	205 @ 1600	3.810 × 3.390	8.7:1	40-60
	F	8-302 (5.0)	EFI	150 @ 3200	270 @ 2000	4.000 × 3.000	8.9:1	40-60
	E	8-302 (5.0)HO	EFI	220 @ 4400	265 @ 3200	4.000 × 3.000	8.3:1	40-60
	G	8-351 (5.8)HO	VV	180 @ 3600	285 @ 2400	4.000 × 3.500	8.3:1	40-60
1989-90	A	4-140 (2.3)	EFI	88 @ 4200	122 @ 2600	3.780 × 3.126	9.0:1	40-60
	T	4-140 (2.3)T	EFI	155 @ 4600	190 @ 2800	3.780 × 3.126	8.0:1	40-60
	4	6-232 (3.8)	EFI	120 @ 3600	205 @ 1600	3.810 × 3.390	8.7:1	40-60
	R	6-232 (3.8)SC	EFI	210 @ 2000	315 @ 2600	3.810 × 3.390	8.2:1	40-60
	C	6-232 (3.8)SC	EFI	210 @ 2000	315 @ 2600	3.810 × 3.390	8.2:1	40-60
	F	8-302 (5.0)	EFI	150 @ 3200	270 @ 2000	4.000 × 3.000	8.9:1	40-60
	E	8-302 (5.0)HO	EFI	220 @ 4400	265 @ 3200	4.000 × 3.000	8.3:1	40-60
	G	8 351 (5.8)HO	VV	100 @ 3000	285 @ 2400	4.000 × 3.500	8.3:1	40-60

■ Horsepower and torque are SAE net figures. They are measured at the rear of the transmission with all accessories installed and operating. Since the figures vary when a given engine is installed in different models, some are representative rather than exact.

T Turbocharger
EFI Electronic Fuel Injection
HO High Output
HSC High Swirl Combustion
CFI Central Fuel Injection
VV Variable Venturi carburetor
SC Supercharged

① Canadian models are equipped with a 2 bbl carburetor
③ SVO
④ Canada and police only

GASOLINE ENGINE TUNE-UP SPECIFICATIONS
Refer to Section 34 for all spark plug recommendations

Year	VIN	No. Cylinder Displacement cu. in. (liter)	Spark Plugs Gap (in.)	Ignition Timing (deg.) MT	Ignition Timing (deg.) AT	Compression Pressure (psi)	Fuel Pump (psi)	Idle Speed (rpm) MT	Idle Speed (rpm) AT	Valve Clearance In.	Valve Clearance Ex.
1986	A	4-140 (2.3)	.044	①	①	NA	6-8	750	750	Hyd.	Hyd.
	T	4-140 (2.3)T	.034	①	①	NA	39	825–975	825	Hyd.	Hyd.
	W	4-140 (2.3)T	.034	①	①	NA	39	825–975	825	Hyd.	Hyd.
	3	6-232 (3.8)	.044	①	①	NA	39	—	550	Hyd.	Hyd.
	F	8-302 (5.0)	.044	①	①	NA	39	①	①	Hyd.	Hyd.
	M	8-302 (5.0)HO	.044	①	①	NA	6-8	700	700	Hyd.	Hyd.
	G	8-351 (5.8)	.044	①	①	NA	6-8	650	650	Hyd.	Hyd.

GASOLINE ENGINE TUNE-UP SPECIFICATIONS
Refer to Section 34 for all spark plug recommendations

Year	VIN	No. Cylinder Displacement cu. in. (liter)	Spark Plugs Gap (in.)	Ignition Timing (deg.) MT	Ignition Timing (deg.) AT	Com-pression Pressure (psi)	Fuel Pump (psi)	Idle Speed (rpm) MT	Idle Speed (rpm) AT	Valve Clearance In.	Valve Clearance Ex.
1987	A	4-140 (2.3)	.044	①	①	NA	35	750	750	Hyd.	Hyd.
	W	4-140 (2.3)T	.034	①	①	NA	35	825–975	825–975	Hyd.	Hyd.
	3	6-232 (3.8)	.044	①	①	NA	35	—	550	Hyd.	Hyd.
	E	8-302 (5.0)	.044	①	①	NA	39	①④	①	Hyd.	Hyd.
	F	8-302 (5.0)	.044	①	①	NA	35	①	①	Hyd.	Hyd.
	M	8-302 (5.0)HO	.044	①	①	NA	35	700	700	Hyd.	Hyd.
	G	8-351 (5.8)	.044	①	①	NA	6-8	650	650	Hyd.	Hyd.
1988	A	4-140 (2.3)	.044	①	①	NA	35	750	750	Hyd.	Hyd.
	T	4-140 (2.3)	.034	①	①	NA	35	825–975	825–975	Hyd.	Hyd.
	4	6-232 (3.8)	.044	①	①	NA	39	—	550	Hyd.	Hyd.
	F	8-302 (5.0)	.044	①	①	NA	39	①	①	Hyd.	Hyd.
	E	8-302 (5.0)HO	.044	①	①	NA	39	700	700	Hyd.	Hyd.
	G	8-351 (5.8)	.044	①	①	NA	6-8	650	650	Hyd.	Hyd.
1989	A	4-140 (2.3)	.044	①	①	NA	35	750	750	Hyd.	Hyd.
	T	4-140 (2.3)	.034	①	①	NA	35	825–975	825–975	Hyd.	Hyd.
	4	6-232 (3.8)	.044	①	①	NA	39	—	550	Hyd.	Hyd.
	R	6-232 (3.8)SC	.044	①	①	NA	39	650	550	Hyd.	Hyd.
	C	6-232 (3.8)SC	.044	①	①	NA	39	650	550	Hyd.	Hyd.
	F	8-302 (5.0)	.044	①	①	NA	39	①	①	Hyd.	Hyd.
	E	8-302 (5.0)HO	.044	①	①	NA	39	700	700	Hyd.	Hyd.
	G	8-351 (5.8)	.044	①	①	NA	6-8	650	650	Hyd.	Hyd.
1990		SEE UNDERHOOD SPECIFICATIONS STICKER									

NOTE: The underhood specifications sticker often reflects tune-up specifications changes made in production. Sticker figures must be used if they disagree with those in this chart.

T Turbocharger
B Before top dead center
HO High Output
— Not applicable
HSC High Swirl Combustion

① Calibrations vary depending upon the model; refer to the underhood sticker

④ Electronic engine control models. The ignition timing, idle speed and idle mixture are not adjustable

FIRING ORDERS

NOTE: To avoid confusion, always replace spark plug wires one at a time.

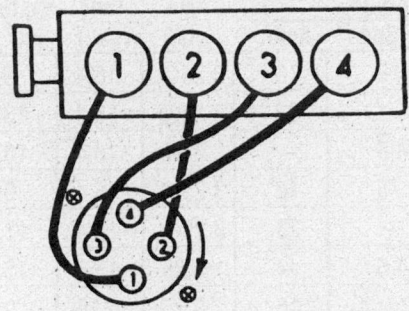

FORD MOTOR CO. 2300 cc 4-cyl.
Engine firing order: 1–3–4–2
Distributor rotation: clockwise

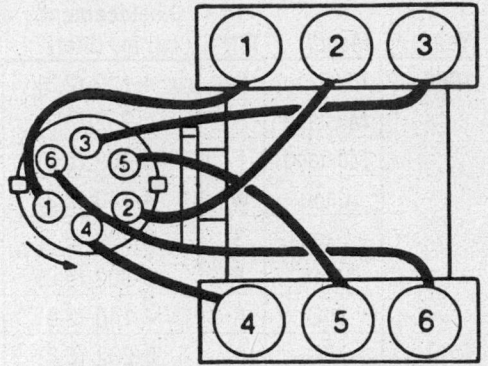

FORD MOTOR CO. 232 V6
Engine firing order 1–4–2–5–3–6
Distributor rotation: counterclockwise

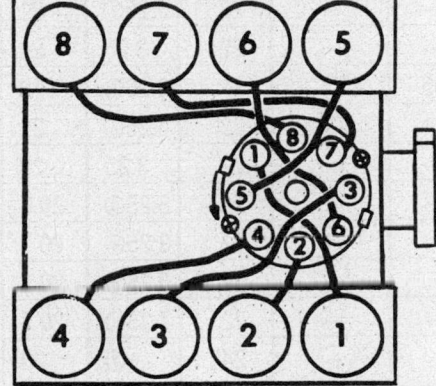

FORD MOTOR CO. 255, 302 (exc. HO) 460
V8 Engine firing order: 1–5–4–2–6–3–7–8
Distributor rotation: counterclockwise

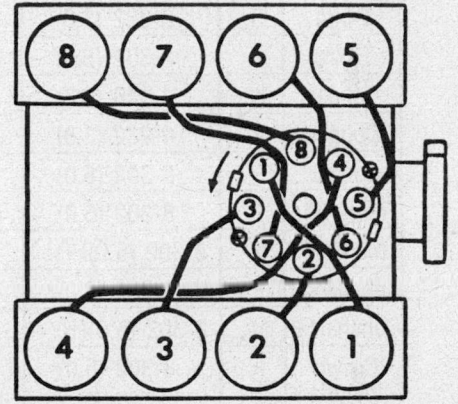

FORD MOTOR CO. 302HO, 351,400 V8
Engine firing order: 1–3–7–2–6–5–4–8
Distributor rotation: counterclockwise

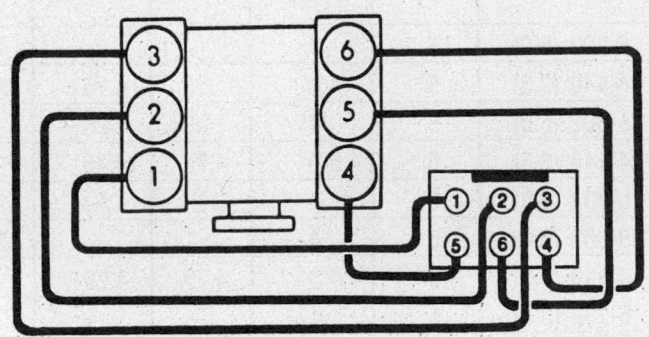

Ford Motor Co. 3.8L V6
Engine Firing Order: 1–4–2–5–3–6
Distributorless Ignition System

CAPACITIES

Year	Model	VIN	No. Cylinder Displacement cu. in. (liter)	Engine Crankcase with Filter	without Filter	Transmission (pts.) 4-Spd	5-Spd	Auto.	Drive Axle (pts.)	Fuel Tank (gal.)	Cooling System (qts.)
1986	Mustang	W	4-140 (2.3)	5	4②	2.8	4.75	16	3.25⑥	15.4	9.4
	Mustang	3	6-232 (3.8)	5	4	–	–	22	3.25⑥	15.4	13.4
	Mustang	F	8-302 (5.0)	5	4	4.5	4.5	–	3.25	15.4	13.4
	Capri	W	4-140 (2.3)	5	4②	2.8	4.75	16	3.25⑥	15.4	9.4
	Capri	3	6-232 (3.8)	5	4	–	–	22	3.25⑥	15.4	13.4
	Capri	F	8-302 (5.0)	5	4	4.5	4.5	–	3.25	15.4	13.4
	LTD	A	4-140 (2.3)	5	4	2.8	–	16	3.25	16	9.4
	LTD	3	6-232 (3.8)	5	4	–	–	22	3.25⑥	16	10.8
	Marquis	A	4-140 (2.3)	5	4	2.8	–	16	3.25	16	9.4
	Marquis	3	6-232 (3.8)	5	4	–	–	22	3.25⑥	16	10.8
	T-bird	W	4-140 (2.3)	5	4.5⑦	4.75	4.75	–	3.25⑥	18	8.7
	T-bird	3	6-232 (3.8)	5	4	–	–	22	3.25⑥	21	10.7
	T-bird	F	8-302 (5.0)	5	4	–	–	22	3.25	20	13.4
	Cougar	W	4-140 (2.3)	5	4.5⑦	4.75	4.75	–	3.25⑥	18	8.7
	Cougar	3	6-232 (3.8)	5	4	–	–	22	3.25⑥	21	10.7
	Cougar	F	8-302 (5.0)	5	4	–	–	22	3.25	20	13.4
	Mark VII	F	8-302 (5.0)	5	4	–	–	22	3.25⑥	20.7	13.4
	Mark VII	M	8-302 (5.0)HO	5	4	–	–	22	3.25⑥	20.7	13.4
	Continental	F	8-302 (5.0)	5	4	–	–	22	3.25⑥	20.7	13.4
	Continental	M	8-302 (5.0)HO	5	4	–	–	22	3.25⑥	20.7	13.4
	Crown Victoria	F	8-302 (5.0)	5	4	–	–	24	②	20	15
	Crown Victoria	G	8-351 (5.8)	5	4	–	–	24	②	20	16
	Grand Marquis	F	8-302 (5.0)	5	4	–	–	24	②	20	15
	Grand Marquis	G	8-351 (5.8)	5	4	–	–	24	②	20	16
	Town Car	F	8-302 (5.0)	5	4	–	–	24	②	20	10
1987	Mustang	A	4-140 (2.3)	5	4②	2.8	4.75	16	3.25⑥	15.4	9.4
	Mustang	M	8-302 (5.0)	5	4	4.5	4.5	–	3.25	15.4	13.4
	T-bird	W	4-140 (2.3)	5	4.5⑦	4.75	4.75	–	3.25⑥	18	8.7
	T-bird	3	6-232 (3.8)	5	4	–	–	22	3.25⑥	21	10.7
	T-bird	F	8-302 (5.0)	5	4	–	–	22	3.25	20	13.4
	Cougar	W	4-140 (2.3)	5	4.5⑦	4.75	4.75	–	3.25⑥	18	8.7
	Cougar	3	6-232 (3.8)	5	4	–	–	22	3.25⑥	21	10.7
	Cougar	F	8-302 (5.0)	5	4	–	–	22	3.25	20	13.4
	Mark VII	E	8-302 (5.0)	5	4	–	–	22	3.25⑥	20.7	13.4
	Mark VII	M	8-302 (5.0)HO	5	4	–	–	22	3.25⑥	20.7	13.4
	Continental	E	8-302 (5.0)	5	4	–	–	22	3.25⑥	20.7	13.4
	Continental	M	8-302 (5.0)HO	5	4	–	–	22	3.25⑥	20.7	13.4

CAPACITIES

Year	Model	VIN	No. Cylinder Displacement cu. in. (liter)	Engine Crankcase with Filter	Engine Crankcase without Filter	Transmission (pts.) 4-Spd	Transmission (pts.) 5-Spd	Transmission (pts.) Auto.	Drive Axle (pts.)	Fuel Tank (gal.)	Cooling System (qts.)
1987	Crown Victoria	F	8-302 (5.0)	5	4	—	—	24	②	20	15
	Crown Victoria	G	8-351 (5.8)	5	4	—	—	24	②	20	16
	Grand Marquis	F	8-302 (5.0)	5	4	—	—	24	②	20	15
	Grand Marquis	G	8-351 (5.8)	5	4	—	—	24	②	20	16
	Town Car	E	8-302 (5.0)	5	4	—	—	24	②	20	10
1988	Mustang	A	4-140 (2.3)	5	4	3.7	3.7	22	4.5	15.4	10
	Mustang	M	8-302 (5.0)	5	4	3.7	3.7	22	3.25	15.4	14.1
	T-bird	T	4-140 (2.3)	5	4.5⑦	4.75	4.75	16	3.25⑥	18	10
	T-bird	4	6-232 (3.8)	5	4	—	—	22	3.25⑥	21	11.8
	T-bird	F	8-302 (5.0)	5	4	—	—	22	3.25⑥	20.7	14.1
	Cougar	T	4-140 (2.3)	5	4.5⑦	4.75	4.75	16	3.25⑥	18	10
	Cougar	4	6-232 (3.8)	5	4	—	—	22	3.25⑥	21	11.8
	Cougar	F	8-302 (5.0)	5	4	—	—	22	3.25⑥	20.7	14.1
	Mark VII	E	8-302 (5.0)	5	4	—	—	22	3.25	20.7	14.1
	Crown Victoria	F	8-302 (5.0)	5	4	—	—	24	②	20	15
	Crown Victoria	G	0-351 (5.8)	5	4	—	—	24	②	20	16
	Grand Marquis	F	8-302 (5.0)	5	4	—	—	24	②	20	15
	Grand Marquis	G	8-351 (5.8)	5	4	—	—	24	②	20	16
	Town Car	F	8-302 (5.0)	5	4	—	—	24	②	20	16
1989-90	Mustang	A	4-140 (2.3)	5	4	3.7	3.7	22	4.5	15.4	10
	Mustang	E	8-302 (5.0)	5	4	3.7	3.7	22	3.25	15.4	14.1
	T-bird	4	6-232 (3.8)	5	4	—	—	22	3.25⑥	21	11.8
	T-bird	R	8-232 (3.8)SC	5	4	—	6.3	24	3.25⑥	18.8	11.8
	T-bird	C	8-232 (3.8)SC	5	4	—	6.3	24	3.25⑥	18.8	11.8
	Cougar	4	6-232 (3.8)	5	4	—	—	22	3.25⑥	21	11.8
	Cougar	R	8-232 (3.8)SC	5	4	—	6.3	24	3.25⑥	18.8	11.8
	Mark VII	E	8-302 (5.0)	5	4	—	—	22	3.25	20.7	14.1
	Crown Victoria	F	8-302 (5.0)	5	4	—	—	24	②	20	15
	Crown Victoria	G	8-351 (5.8)	5	4	—	—	24	②	20	16
	Grand Marquis	F	8-302 (5.0)	5	4	—	—	24	②	20	15

CAPACITIES

Year	Model	VIN	No. Cylinder Displacement cu. in. (liter)	Engine Crankcase with Filter	Engine Crankcase without Filter	Transmission (pts.) 4-Spd	Transmission (pts.) 5-Spd	Transmission (pts.) Auto.	Drive Axle (pts.)	Fuel Tank (gal.)	Cooling System (qts.)
	Grand Marquis	G	8-351 (5.8)	5	4	—	—	24	②	20	16
	Town Car	F	8-302 (5.0)	5	4	—	—	24	②	20	16

② 6.75 in. axle—2.5 pts.
7.5 in. axle—3.5 pts.
8.5 in axle—4.0 pts.

⑥ Traction-lok—3.55 pts.

⑦ Turbo 4.5—add .5 with filter

CAMSHAFT SPECIFICATIONS
All measurements given in inches.

Year	VIN	No. Cylinder Displacement cu. in. (liter)	Journal Diameter 1	Journal Diameter 2	Journal Diameter 3	Journal Diameter 4	Journal Diameter 5	Lobe Lift In.	Lobe Lift Ex.	Bearing Clearance	Camshaft End Play
1986	A	4-140 (2.3)	1.7713–1.7720	1.7713–1.7720	1.7713–1.7720	1.7713–1.7720	—	.400	.400	.001–.003	.001–.007
	T	4-140 (2.3)	1.7713–1.7720	1.7713–1.7720	1.7713–1.7720	1.7713–1.7720	—	.400	.400	.001–.003	.001–.007
	W	4-140 (2.3)	1.7713–1.7720	1.7713–1.7720	1.7713–1.7720	1.7713–1.7720	—	.400	.400	.001–.003	.001–.007
	3	6-232 (3.8)	2.0515–2.0505	2.0515–2.0505	2.0515–2.0505	2.0515–2.0505	—	.240	.241	.001–.003	①
	F	8-302 (5.0)	2.0805–2.0815	2.0655–2.0665	2.0505–2.0515	2.0355–2.0365	2.0205–2.0515	.2375 ②	.2474 ②	.001–.003	.001–.007
	M	8-302 (5.0)	2.0805–2.0815	2.0655–2.0665	2.0505–2.0515	2.0355–2.0365	2.0205–2.0515	.2375 ②	.2474 ②	.001–.003	.001–.007
	G	8-351 (5.8)	2.0805–2.0815	2.0655–2.0665	2.0505–2.0515	2.0355–2.0365	2.0505–2.0515	.2780	.2830	.001–.003	.001–.007
1987	A	4-140 (2.3)	1.7713–1.7720	1.7713–1.7720	1.7713–1.7720	1.7713–1.7720	—	.400	.400	.001–.003	.001–.007
	W	4-140 (2.3)	1.7713–1.7720	1.7713–1.7720	1.7713–1.7720	1.7713–1.7720	—	.400	.400	.001–.003	.001–.007
	3	6-232 (3.8)	2.0515–2.0505	2.0515–2.0505	2.0515–2.0505	2.0515–2.0505	—	.240	.241	.001–.003	①
	E	8-302 (5.0)	2.0805–2.0815	2.0655–2.0665	2.0505–2.0515	2.0355–2.0365	2.0205–2.0215	.2375 ②	.2474 ②	.001–.003	.001–.007
	F	8-302 (5.0)	2.0805–2.0815	2.0655–2.0665	2.0505–2.0515	2.0355–2.0365	2.0205–2.0215	.2375 ②	.2474 ②	.001–.003	.001–.007
	M	8-302 (5.0)	2.0805–2.0815	2.0655–2.0665	2.0505–2.0515	2.0355–2.0365	2.0205–2.0215	.2375 ②	.2474 ②	.001–.003	.001–.007

CAMSHAFT SPECIFICATIONS
All measurements given in inches.

Year	VIN	No. Cylinder Displacement cu. in. (liter)	Journal Diameter					Lobe Lift		Bearing Clearance	Camshaft End Play
			1	2	3	4	5	In.	Ex.		
1987	G	8-351 (5.8)	2.0805–2.0815	2.0655–2.0665	2.0505–2.0515	2.0355–2.0365	2.0205–2.0215	.2780	.2830	.001–.003	.001–.007
1988	A	4-140 (2.3)	1.7713–1.7720	1.7713–1.7720	1.7713–1.7720	1.7713–1.7720	–	.400	.400	.001–.003	.001–.007
	T	4-140 (2.3)	1.7713–1.7720	1.7713–1.7720	1.7713–1.7720	1.7713–1.7720	–	.400	.400	.001–.003	.001–.007
	4	6-232 (3.8)	2.0515–2.0505	2.0515–2.0505	2.0515–2.0505	2.0515–2.0505	–	.240	.241	.001–.003	①
	F	8-302 (5.0)	2.0805–2.0815	2.0655–2.0665	2.0505–2.0515	2.0355–2.0365	2.0205–2.0215	.2375 ②	.2474 ②	.001–.003	.001–.007
	E	8-302 (5.0)	2.0805–2.0815	2.0655–2.0665	2.0505–2.0515	2.0355–2.0365	2.0205–2.0215	.2375 ②	.2474 ②	.001–.003	.001–.007
	G	8-351 (5.8)	2.0805–2.0815	2.0655–2.0665	2.0505–2.0515	2.0355–2.0365	2.0205–2.0215	.2375 ②	.2474 ②	.001–.003	.001–.007
1989-90	A	4-140 (2.3)	1.7713–1.7720	1.7713–1.7720	1.7713–1.7720	1.7713–1.7720	–	.400	.400	.001–.003	.001–.007
	T	4-140 (2.3)	1.7713–1.7720	1.7713–1.7720	1.7713–1.7720	1.7713–1.7720	–	.400	.400	.001–.003	.001–.007
	4	6-232 (3.8)	2.0515–2.0505	2.0515–2.0505	2.0515–2.0505	2.0515–2.0505	–	.240	.241	.001–.003	①
	R	6-232 (3.8)SC	2.0515–2.0505	2.0515–2.0505	2.0515–2.0505	2.0515–2.0505	–	.245	.259	.001–.003	①
	C	6-232 (3.8)SC	2.0515–2.0505	2.0515–2.0505	2.0515–2.0505	2.0515–2.0505	–	.245	.259	.001–.003	①
	F	8-302 (5.0)	2.0805–2.0815	2.0655–2.0665	2.0505–2.0515	2.0355–2.0365	2.0205–2.0215	.2375 ②	.2474 ②	.001–.003	.001–.007
	E	8-302 (5.0)	2.0805–2.0815	2.0655–2.0665	2.0505–2.0515	2.0355–2.0365	2.0205–2.0215	.2375 ②	.2474 ②	.001–.003	.001–.007
	G	8-351 (5.8)	2.0805–2.0815	2.0655–2.0665	2.0505–2.0515	2.0355–2.0365	2.0205–2.0215	.2375 ②	.2474 ②	.001–.003	.001–.007

① The endplay is controlled by the button and spring on the camshaft end

② On the 1986–89 H.O. engine, intake lobe lift is .2780, exhaust is .2780

CRANKSHAFT AND CONNECTING ROD SPECIFICATIONS
All measurements are given in inches.

Year	VIN	No. Cylinder Displacement cu. in. (liter)	Crankshaft Main Brg. Journal Dia.	Crankshaft Main Brg. Oil Clearance	Crankshaft Shaft End-play	Crankshaft Thrust on No.	Connecting Rod Journal Diameter	Connecting Rod Oil Clearance	Connecting Rod Side Clearance
1986	A	4-140 (2.3)	2.3990–2.3982	0.0008–0.0015	0.004–0.008	3	2.0464–2.0472	0.0008–0.0015	0.0035–0.0105
	T	4-140 (2.3)	2.3990–2.3982	0.0008–0.0015	0.004–0.008	3	2.0464–2.0472	0.0008–0.0015	0.0035–0.0105
	W	4-140 (2.3)	2.3990–2.3982	0.0008–0.0015	0.004–0.008	3	2.0464–2.0472	0.0008–0.0015	0.0035–0.0105
	3	6-232 (3.8)	2.5190	0.0001–0.0010	0.004–0.008	3	2.3103–2.3111	0.0008–0.0026	0.0047–0.0114
	F	8-302 (5.0)	2.2482–2.2490	0.0004–0.0015	0.004–0.008	3	2.1228–2.1236	0.0008–0.0015	0.010–0.020
	M	8-302 (5.0)	2.2482–2.2490	0.0004–0.0015	0.004–0.008	3	2.1228–2.1236	0.0008–0.0015	0.010–0.020
	G	8-351 (5.8)	2.2994–3.0002	0.0008–0.0015 ③	0.004–0.008	3	2.3103–2.3111	0.0008–0.0015	0.010–0.020
1987	A	4-140 (2.3)	2.3990–2.3982	0.0008–0.0015	0.004–0.008	3	2.0464–2.0472	0.0008–0.0015	0.0035–0.0105
	W	4-140 (2.3)	2.3990–2.3982	0.0008–0.0015	0.004–0.008	3	2.0464–2.0472	0.0008–0.0015	0.0035–0.0105
	3	6-232 (3.8)	2.5190	0.0001–0.0010	0.004–0.008	3	2.3103–2.3111	0.0008–0.0026	0.0047–0.0114
	F	8-302 (5.0)	2.2482–2.2490	0.0004–0.0015	0.004–0.008	3	2.1228–2.1236	0.0008–0.0015	0.010–0.020
	M	8-302 (5.0)	2.2482–2.2490	0.0004–0.0015	0.004–0.008	3	2.1228–2.1236	0.0008–0.0015	0.010–0.020
	E	8-302 (5.0)	2.2482–2.2490	0.0004–0.0015	0.004–0.008	3	2.1228–2.1236	0.0008–0.0015	0.010–0.020
	G	8-351 (5.8)	2.2994–3.0002	0.0008–0.0015 ③	0.004–0.008	3	2.3103–2.3111	0.0008–0.0015	0.010–0.020
1988	A	4-140 (2.3)	2.3990–2.3982	0.0008–0.0015	0.004–0.008	3	2.0464–2.0472	0.0008–0.0015	0.0035–0.0105
	T	4-140 (2.3)	2.3990–2.3982	0.0008–0.0015	0.004–0.008	3	2.0464–2.0472	0.0008–0.0015	0.0035–0.0105
	4	6-232 (3.8)	2.5190	0.0001–0.0010	0.004–0.008	3	2.3103–2.3111	0.0008–0.0026	0.0047–0.0114
	F	8-302 (5.0)	2.2482–2.2490	0.0004–0.0015	0.004–0.008	3	2.1228–2.1236	0.0008–0.0015	0.010–0.020
	E	8-302 (5.0)HO	2.2482–2.2490	0.0004–0.0015	0.004–0.008	3	2.1228–2.1236	0.0008–0.0015	0.010–0.020
	G	8-351 (5.8)	2.2994–3.0002	0.0008–0.0015	0.004–0.008	3	2.3103–2.3111	0.0008–0.0015	0.010–0.020

CRANKSHAFT AND CONNECTING ROD SPECIFICATIONS
All measurements are given in inches.

Year	VIN	No. Cylinder Displacement cu. in. (liter)	Crankshaft Main Brg. Journal Dia.	Main Brg. Oil Clearance	Shaft End-play	Thrust on No.	Connecting Rod Journal Diameter	Oil Clearance	Side Clearance
1989-90	A	4-140 (2.3)	2.3990–2.3982	0.0008–0.0015	0.004–0.008	3	2.0464–2.0472	0.0008–0.0015	0.0035–0.0105
	T	4-140 (2.3)	2.3990–2.3982	0.0008–0.0015	0.004–0.008	3	2.0464–2.0472	0.0008–0.0015	0.0035–0.0105
	4	6-232 (3.8)	2.5190	0.0001–0.0010	0.004–0.008	3	2.3103–2.3111	0.0008–0.0026	0.0047–0.0114
	R	6-232 (3.8)SC	2.5194–2.5186	0.0009–0.0026	0.004–0.008	3	2.4226–2.4274	0.0008–0.0026	0.0047–0.0114
	C	6-232 (3.8)SC	2.5194–2.5186	0.0009–0.0026	0.004–0.008	3	2.4226–2.4274	0.0008–0.0026	0.0047–0.0114
	F	8-302 (5.0)	2.2482–2.2490	0.0004–0.0015	0.004–0.008	3	2.1228–2.1236	0.0008–0.0015	0.010–0.020
	E	8-302 (5.0)HO	2.2482–2.2490	0.0004–0.0015	0.004–0.008	3	2.1228–2.1236	0.0008–0.0015	0.010–0.020
	G	8-351 (5.8)	2.2994–3.0002	0.0008–0.0015	0.004–0.008	3	2.3103–2.3111	0.0008–0.0015	0.010–0.020

NA Not available
③ No. 1 — 0.0001–0.0005

VALVE SPECIFICATIONS

Year	VIN	No. Cylinder Displacement cu. in. (liter)	Seat Angle (deg.)	Face Angle (deg.)	Spring Test Pressure (lbs. @ in.)	Spring Installed Height (in.)	Stem-to-Guide Clearance (in.) Intake	Exhaust	Stem Diameter (in.) Intake	Exhaust
1986	A	4-140 (2.3)	45	44	154 @ 1.12	1 9/16	0.0010–0.0027	0.0015–0.0032	0.3420	0.3415
	T	4-140 (2.3)	45	44	154 @ 1.12	1 9/16	0.0010–0.0027	0.0015–0.0032	0.3420	0.3415
	W	4-140 (2.3)	45	44	154 @ 1.12	1 9/16	0.0010–0.0027	0.0015–0.0032	0.3420	0.3415
	3	6-232 (3.8)	44.5	45.8	215 @ 1.79	1 3/4	0.0010–0.0027	0.0015–0.0032	0.3420	0.3415
	F	8-302 (5.0)	45	45	205 @ 1.36	1 3/4	0.0010–0.0027	0.0015–0.0032	0.3420	0.3420
	M	8-302 (5.0)	45	45	205 @ 1.36	1 3/4	0.0010–0.0027	0.0015–0.0032	0.3420	0.3420
	G	8-351 (5.8)	45	45	204 @ 1.33	1 49/64 ③	0.0010–0.0027	0.0015–0.0027	0.3416–0.3423	0.3411–0.3418
1987	A	4-140 (2.3)	45	44	154 @ 1.12	1 9/16	0.0010–0.0027	0.0015–0.0032	0.3420	0.3415

VALVE SPECIFICATIONS

Year	VIN	No. Cylinder Displacement cu. in. (liter)	Seat Angle (deg.)	Face Angle (deg.)	Spring Test Pressure (lbs. @ in.)	Spring Installed Height (in.)	Stem-to-Guide Clearance (in.)		Stem Diameter (in.)	
							Intake	Exhaust	Intake	Exhaust
1987	T	4-140 (2.3)	45	44	154 @ 1.12	$1\frac{9}{16}$	0.0010–0.0027	0.0015–0.0032	0.3420	0.3415
	3	6-232 (3.8)	44.5	45.8	215 @ 1.79	$1\frac{3}{4}$	0.0010–0.0027	0.0015–0.0032	0.3420	0.3415
	E	8-302 (5.0)	45	45	205 @ 1.36	$1\frac{3}{4}$	0.0010–0.0027	0.0015–0.0032	0.3420	0.3420
	F	8-302 (5.0)	45	45	205 @ 1.36	$1\frac{3}{4}$	0.0010–0.0027	0.0015–0.0032	0.3420	0.3420
	M	8-302 (5.0)	45	45	205 @ 1.36	$1\frac{3}{4}$	0.0010–0.0027	0.0015–0.0032	0.3420	0.3420
	G	8-351 (5.8)	45	45	204 @ 1.33	$1\frac{49}{64}$③	0.0010–0.0027	0.0015–0.0027	0.3416–0.3423	0.3411–0.3418
1988	A	4-140 (2.3)	45	44	154 @ 1.12	$1\frac{9}{16}$	0.0010–0.0027	0.0015–0.0032	0.3420	0.3415
	T	4-140 (2.3)	45	44	154 @ 1.12	$1\frac{9}{16}$	0.0010–0.0027	0.0015–0.0032	0.3420	0.3415
	4	6-232 (3.8)	44.5	45.8	215 @ 1.79	$1\frac{3}{4}$	0.0010–0.0027	0.0015–0.0032	0.3420	0.3415
	F	8-302 (5.0)	45	45	205 @ 1.36	$1\frac{3}{4}$	0.0010–0.0027	0.0015–0.0032	0.3420	0.3420
	E	8-302 (5.0)HO	45	45	205 @ 1.36	$1\frac{3}{4}$	0.0010–0.0027	0.0015–0.0032	0.3420	0.3420
	G	8-351 (5.8)	45	45	204 @ 1.33	$1\frac{49}{64}$③	0.0010–0.0027	0.0015–0.0027	0.3416–0.3423	0.3411–0.3418
1989-90	A	4-140 (2.3)	45	44	154 @ 1.12	$1\frac{9}{16}$	0.0010–0.0027	0.0015–0.0032	0.3420	0.3415
	T	4-140 (2.3)	45	44	154 @ 1.12	$1\frac{9}{16}$	0.0010–0.0027	0.0015–0.0032	0.3420	0.3415
	4	6-232 (3.8)	44.5	45.8	215 @ 1.79	$1\frac{3}{4}$	0.0010–0.0027	0.0015–0.0032	0.3420	0.3415
	R	6-232 (3.8)SC	45.8	45.8	220 @ 1.18	$1\frac{3}{4}$	0.0010–0.0028	0.0015–0.0033	0.3423	0.3418–0.3418
	C	6-232 (3.8)SC	45.8	45.8	220 @ 1.18	$1\frac{3}{4}$	0.0010–0.0028	0.0015–0.0033	0.3423	0.3418–0.3418
	F	8-302 (5.0)	45	45	205 @ 1.36	$1\frac{3}{4}$	0.0010–0.0027	0.0015–0.0032	0.3420	0.3420
	E	8-302 (5.0)HO	45	45	205 @ 1.36	$1\frac{3}{4}$	0.0010–0.0027	0.0015–0.0032	0.3420	0.3420
	G	8-351 (5.8)	45	45	204 @ 1.33	$1\frac{49}{64}$③	0.0010–0.0027	0.0015–0.0027	0.3416–0.3423	0.3411–0.3418

③ Exhaust – $1\frac{37}{64}$

PISTON AND RING SPECIFICATIONS
All measurments are given in inches.

Year	VIN	No. Cylinder Displacement cu. in. (liter)	Piston Clearance	Ring Gap Top Compression	Ring Gap Bottom Compression	Ring Gap Oil Control	Ring Side Clearance Top Compression	Ring Side Clearance Bottom Compression	Ring Side Clearance Oil Control
1986	A	4-140 (2.3)	0.0030–0.0038	0.010–0.020	0.010–0.020	0.015–0.055	0.002–0.004	0.002–0.004	Snug
	T	4-140 (2.3)	0.0030–0.0038	0.010–0.020	0.010–0.020	0.015–0.055	0.002–0.004	0.002–0.004	Snug
	W	4-140 (2.3)	0.0030–0.0038	0.010–0.020	0.010–0.020	0.015–0.055	0.002–0.004	0.002–0.004	Snug
	3	6-232 (3.8)	0.0014–0.0032	0.010–0.022	0.010–0.022	0.015–0.055	0.002–0.004	0.002–0.004	Snug
	F	8-302 (5.0)	0.0018–0.0026	0.020	0.020	0.055	0.004	0.004	Snug
	M	8-302 (5.0)	0.0018–0.0026	0.020	0.020	0.055	0.004	0.004	Snug
	G	8-351 (5.8)	0.0022–0.0030	0.020	0.020	0.055	0.004	0.004	Snug
1987	A	4-140 (2.3)	0.0030–0.0038	0.010–0.020	0.010–0.020	0.015–0.055	0.002–0.004	0.002–0.004	Snug
	W	4-140 (2.3)	0.0030–0.0038	0.010–0.020	0.010–0.020	0.015–0.055	0.002–0.004	0.002–0.004	Snug
	3	6-232 (3.8)	0.0014–0.0032	0.010–0.022	0.010–0.022	0.015–0.055	0.002–0.004	0.002–0.004	Snug
	F	8-302 (5.0)	0.0018–0.0026	0.020	0.020	0.055	0.004	0.004	Snug
	E	8-302 (5.0)	0.0018–0.0026	0.020	0.020	0.055	0.004	0.004	Snug
	M	8-302 (5.0)	0.0018–0.0026	0.020	0.020	0.055	0.004	0.004	Snug
	G	8-351 (5.8)	0.0022–0.0030	0.020	0.020	0.055	0.004	0.004	Snug
1988	A	4-140 (2.3)	0.0030–0.0038	0.010–0.020	0.010–0.020	0.015–0.055	0.002–0.004	0.002–0.004	Snug
	T	4-140 (2.3)	0.0030–0.0038	0.010–0.020	0.010–0.020	0.015–0.055	0.002–0.004	0.002–0.004	Snug
	4	6-232 (3.8)	0.0014–0.0032	0.010–0.022	0.010–0.022	0.015–0.055	0.002–0.004	0.002–0.004	Snug
	F	8-302 (5.0)	0.0018–0.0026	0.020	0.020	0.055	0.004	0.004	Snug
	E	8-302 (5.0)HO	0.0018–0.0026	0.020	0.020	0.055	0.004	0.004	Snug
	G	8-351 (5.8)	0.0022–0.0030	0.020	0.020	0.055	0.004	0.004	Snug
1989-90	A	4-140 (2.3)	0.0030–0.0038	0.010–0.020	0.010–0.020	0.015–0.055	0.002–0.004	0.002–0.004	Snug
	T	4-140 (2.3)	0.0030–0.0038	0.010–0.020	0.010–0.020	0.015–0.055	0.002–0.004	0.002–0.004	Snug

PISTON AND RING SPECIFICATIONS
All measurments are given in inches.

| Year | VIN | No. Cylinder Displacement cu. in. (liter) | Piston Clearance | Ring Gap | | | Ring Side Clearance | | |
				Top Compression	Bottom Compression	Oil Control	Top Compression	Bottom Compression	Oil Control
1989-90	4	6-232 (3.8)	0.0014–0.0032	0.010–0.022	0.010–0.022	0.015–0.055	0.002–0.004	0.002–0.004	Snug
	R	6-232 (3.8)SC	0.0047–0.0014	0.0610–0.0602	0.0610–0.0602	0.1587–0.0602	0.0016–0.0034	0.0016–0.0034	Snug
	C	6-232 (3.8)SC	0.0047–0.0014	0.0610–0.0602	0.0610–0.0602	0.1587–0.0602	0.0016–0.0034	0.0016–0.0034	Snug
	F	8-302 (5.0)	0.0018–0.0026	0.020	0.020	0.055	0.004	0.004	Snug
	E	8-302 (5.0)HO	0.0018–0.0026	0.020	0.020	0.055	0.004	0.004	Snug
	G	8-351 (5.8)	0.0022–0.0030	0.020	0.020	0.055	0.004	0.004	Snug

TORQUE SPECIFICATIONS
All readings in ft. lbs.

| Year | VIN | No. Cylinder Displacement cu. in. (liter) | Cylinder Head Bolts | Main Bearing Bolts | Rod Bearing Bolts | Crankshaft Pulley Bolts | Flywheel Bolts | Manifold | | Spark Plugs |
								Intake	Exhaust	
1986	A	4-140 (2.3)	④	⑧	⑨	100–120	54–64	14–21③	16–23	5–10
	T	4-140 (2.3)	④	⑧	⑨	100–120	54–64	14–21	16–23	5–10
	3	6-232 (3.8)	②	65–81	31–36	85–100	75–85	⑤	15–22	5–11
	F	8-302 (5.0)	65–72	60–70	19–24	70–90	75–85	23–25①	18–24	10–15
	G	8-351 (5.8)	105–112	95–105	40–45	70–90	75–85	23–25①	18–24	10–15
1987	A	4-140 (2.3)	④	⑧	⑨	103–133	54–64	14–21③	20–30	5–10
	3	6-232 (3.8)	②	65–81	31–36	20–28	54–64	⑤	15–22	5–11
	E	8-302 (5.0)	65–72	60–70	19–24	70–90	75–85	23–25①	18–24	10–15
	F	8-302 (5.0)	65–72	60–70	19–24	70–90	75–85	23–25①	18–24	10–15
	G	8-351 (5.8)	105–112	95–105	40–45	70–90	75–85	23–25①	18–24	10–15
1988	A	4-140 (2.3)	④	⑧	⑨	103–133	54–64	14–21③	20–30	5–10
	T	4-140 (2.3)	④	⑧	⑨	103–133	54–64	13–18	20–30	5–10
	4	6-232 (3.8)	②	65–81	31–36	20–28	54–64	⑤	15–22	5–11
	R	6-232 (3.8)	⑩	65–81	31–36	20–28	54–64	⑪	15–22	5–11
	C	6-232 (3.8)	⑩	65–81	31–36	20–28	54–64	⑪	15–22	5–11
	F	8-302 (5.0)	65–72	60–70	19–24	70–90	75–85	23–25①	18–24	10–15
	E	8-302 (5.0)HO	65–72	60–70	19–24	70–90	75–85	23–25①	18–24	10–15
	G	8-351 (5.8)	105–112	95–105	40–45	70–90	75–85	23–25①	18–24	10–15

TORQUE SPECIFICATIONS
All readings in ft. lbs.

Year	VIN	No. Cylinder Displacement cu. in. (liter)	Cylinder Head Bolts	Main Bearing Bolts	Rod Bearing Bolts	Crankshaft Pulley Bolts	Flywheel Bolts	Manifold Intake	Manifold Exhaust	Spark Plugs
1989-90	A	4-140 (2.3)	④	⑧	⑨	103–133	54–64	14–21③	20-30	5-10
	T	4-140 (2.3)	④	⑧	⑨	103–133	54–64	13–18	20-30	5-10
	4	6-232 (3.8)	②	65–81	31–36	20–28	54–64	⑤	15–22	5–11
	F	8-302 (5.0)	65–72	60–70	19–24	70–90	75–85	23–25①	18–24	10–15
	E	8-302 (5.0)HO	65–72	60–70	19–24	70–90	75–85	23–25①	18–24	10–15
	G	8-351 (5.8)	105–112	95–105	40–45	70–90	75–85	23–25①	18–24	10–15

① Retorque with engine hot
② a. Tighten in 4 steps:
  37 ft. lbs. (50 Nm)
  45 ft. lbs. (60 Nm)
  52 ft. lbs. (70 Nm)
  59 ft. lbs. (80 Nm)
  b. Back-off all bolts 2–3 revolutions
  c. Repeat Step a (above)
③ Turbo: 5–7 ft. lbs., then 13–18 ft. lbs.
④ Tighten in 2 steps: 50–60 ft. lbs. and then 80–90 ft. lbs.
⑤ Tighten in 3 steps:
  7 ft. lbs. (10 Nm)
  15 ft. lbs. (20 Nm)
  24 ft. lbs. (32 Nm)
⑧ Tighten in 2 steps: 50–60 ft. lbs. and then 75–85 ft. lbs.
⑨ Tighten in 2 steps: 25–30 ft. lbs. and then 30–36 ft. lbs.
⑩ a. Tighten in 4 steps:
  32 ft. lbs. (50 Nm)
  45 ft. lbs. (60 Nm)
  52 ft. lbs. (70 Nm)
  59 ft. lbs. (80 Nm)
  b. Back off all bolts 2–3 revolutions
  c. Repeat Step a (above) to 52 ft. lbs.
  d. In sequential order, rotate bolts an additional 90 degrees
⑪ Tighten in 2 steps:
  7.5 ft. lbs. and then
  11 ft. lbs.

WHEEL ALIGNMENT

Year	Model	Caster Range (deg.)	Caster Preferred Setting (deg.)	Camber Range (deg.)	Camber Preferred Setting (deg.)	Toe-in (in.)	Steering Axis Inclination (deg.)
1986	Mustang/Capri	½P–2P	1¼P	¾N–¾P	0	1/16–5/16	—
	Thunderbird Mark VII	½P–2	1¼P	½N–1P	¼P	1/16–5/16	—
	LTD/Marquis (Sedan)	1⅛P–2⅛P	1⅝P	5/16N–1 3/16	7/16P	1/16–5/16	—
	(Wagon)	⅛N–1⅞P	⅞P	¼N–1¼P	½P	1/16–5/16	—
	Crown Victoria Grand Marquis	2¼P–3¾P	3P	¼N–1¼P	½P	1/16–3/16	10 31/32
	Town Car	2¼P–4P	3P	¼N–1¼P	½P	1/16–3/16	11
	Continental Mark VII	⅝P–2¾P	1½P	¾N–¾P	0	0–¼	11
1987	Mustang	½P–2P	1¼P	¾N–¾P	0	1/16–5/16	—
	Thunderbird Cougar	½P–2	1¼P	½N–1P	¼P	1/16–5/16	—
	Crown Victoria Grand Marquis	2¼P–3¾P	3P	¼N–1¼P	½P	1/16–3/16	10 31/32
	Town Car	2¼P–4P	3P	¼N–1¼P	½P	1/16–3/16	11

WHEEL ALIGNMENT

Year	Model	Caster Range (deg.)	Caster Preferred Setting (deg.)	Camber Range (deg.)	Camber Preferred Setting (deg.)	Toe-in (in.)	Steering Axis Inclination (deg.)
1987	Continental Mark VII	$5/8$P–$2\frac{3}{4}$P	$1\frac{1}{2}$P	$3/4$N–$3/4$P	0	0–$1/4$	11
	Thunderbird Turbo	$\frac{13}{32}$P–$1\frac{29}{32}$P	$1\frac{5}{32}$P	$\frac{9}{16}$N–$\frac{31}{32}$P	$1\frac{5}{32}$P	$\frac{3}{16}$	—
1988	Mustang	$1/2$P–2P	$1\frac{1}{4}$P	$3/4$N–$3/4$P	0	$\frac{1}{16}$–$\frac{5}{16}$	—
	Thunderbird Cougar	$1/2$P–2	$1\frac{1}{4}$P	$1/2$N–1P	$1/4$P	$\frac{1}{16}$–$\frac{5}{16}$	—
	Crown Victoria Grand Marquis	$2\frac{1}{4}$P–$3\frac{3}{4}$P	3P	$1/4$N–$1\frac{1}{4}$P	$1/2$P	$\frac{1}{16}$–$\frac{3}{16}$	$10\frac{31}{32}$
	Town Car	$2\frac{1}{4}$P–4P	3P	$1/4$N–$1\frac{1}{4}$P	$1/2$P	$\frac{1}{16}$–$\frac{3}{16}$	11
	Mark VII	$5/8$P–$2\frac{3}{4}$P	$1\frac{1}{2}$P	$3/4$N–$3/4$P	0	0–$1/4$	11
	Thunderbird Turbo	$\frac{13}{32}$P–$1\frac{29}{32}$P	$1\frac{5}{32}$P	$\frac{9}{16}$N–$\frac{31}{32}$P	$1\frac{5}{32}$P	$\frac{3}{16}$	—
1989-90	Mustang	$1/2$P–2P	$1\frac{1}{4}$P	$3/4$N–$3/4$P	0	$\frac{1}{16}$–$\frac{5}{16}$	—
	Thunderbird Cougar	$1/8$P–$1/4$P	$1/8$P	$3/4$N–$3/4$P	0	$1/8$–$1/4$	—
	Thunderbird Turbo	$\frac{13}{32}$P–$1\frac{29}{32}$P	$1\frac{5}{32}$P	$\frac{9}{16}$N–$\frac{31}{32}$P	$1\frac{5}{32}$P	$\frac{3}{16}$	—
	Crown Victoria Grand Marquis	$2\frac{1}{4}$P–$3\frac{3}{4}$P	3P	$1/4$N–$1\frac{1}{4}$P	$1/2$P	$\frac{1}{16}$–$\frac{3}{16}$	$10\frac{31}{32}$
	Town Car	$2\frac{1}{4}$P–4P	3P	$1/4$N–$1\frac{1}{4}$P	$1/2$P	$\frac{1}{16}$–$\frac{3}{16}$	11
	Mark VII	$5/8$P–$2\frac{3}{4}$P	$1\frac{1}{2}$P	$3/4$N–$3/4$P	0	0–$1/4$	11

P Positive
N Negative

ELECTRICAL

NOTE: Disconnecting the negative battery cable on some vehicles may interfere with the functions of the on board computer systems and may require the computer to undergo a relearning process, once the negative battery cable is reconnected.

For testing and overhaul procedures on starters, alternators and voltage regulators, refer to the unit repair section.

Charging System

ALTERNATOR

Removal and Installation

1. Disconnect the negative battery cable.
2. Loosen the alternator pivot bolt and remove the adjustment arm to alternator bolt. On vehicles with sepentine drive belts and on supercharged vehicles, release the belt tension at the automatic tensioner and remove the belt from the pulley.

3. Disengage the alternator drive belt from the drive pulley.
4. Disconnect the wiring terminals from the back of the alter-

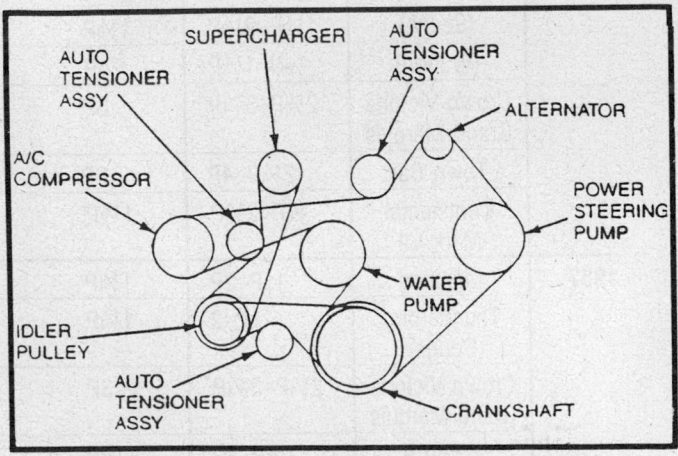

Serpentine belt arrangement—3.8L SC engine

nator. The stator and field wiring terminals are the push-on type. The push-on type terminal should be pulled straight off the terminal to prevent damage.

5. Remove the alternator pivot bolt.
6. Remove the alternator.
7. Installation is the reverse order of the removal procedure.

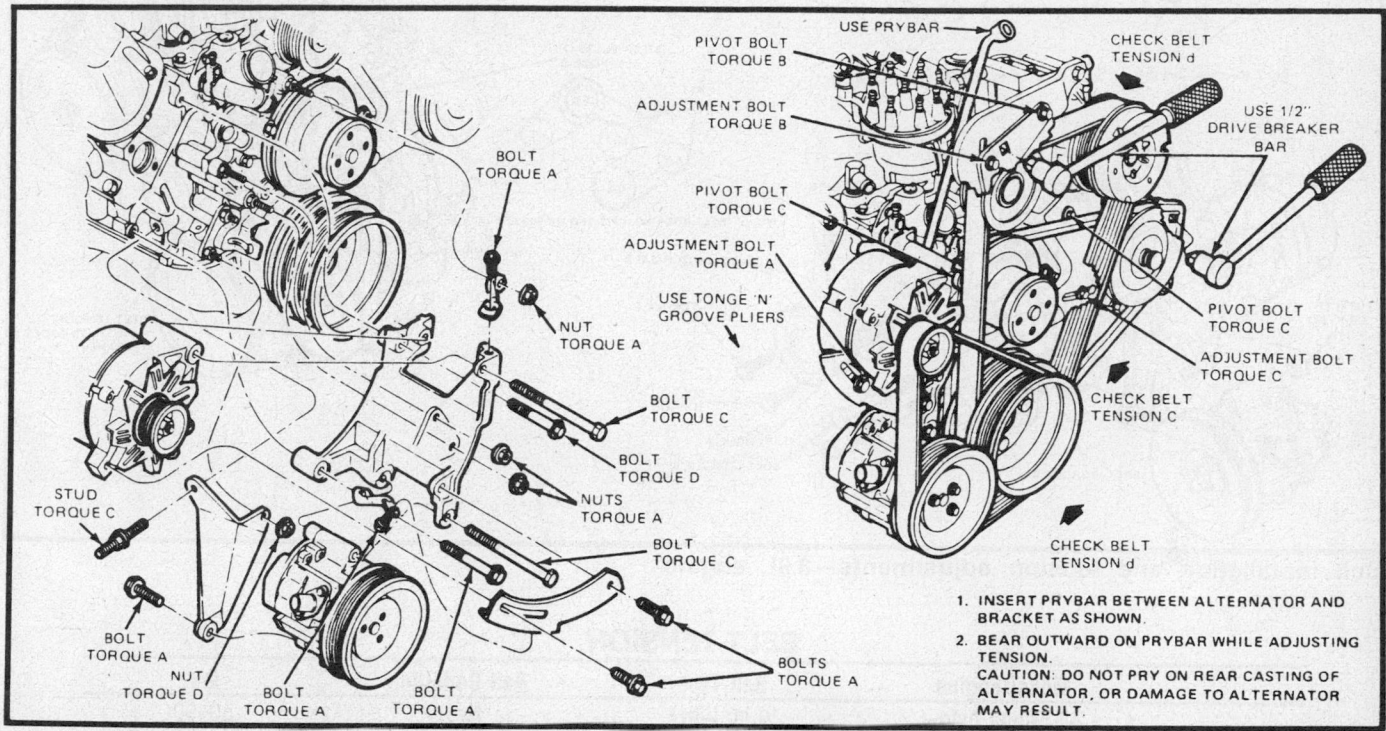

1. INSERT PRYBAR BETWEEN ALTERNATOR AND BRACKET AS SHOWN.
2. BEAR OUTWARD ON PRYBAR WHILE ADJUSTING TENSION.
CAUTION: DO NOT PRY ON REAR CASTING OF ALTERNATOR, OR DAMAGE TO ALTERNATOR MAY RESULT.

Belt installation and tension adjustments—Mark VII/Continental, Thunderbird/Cougar, 5.0L engine

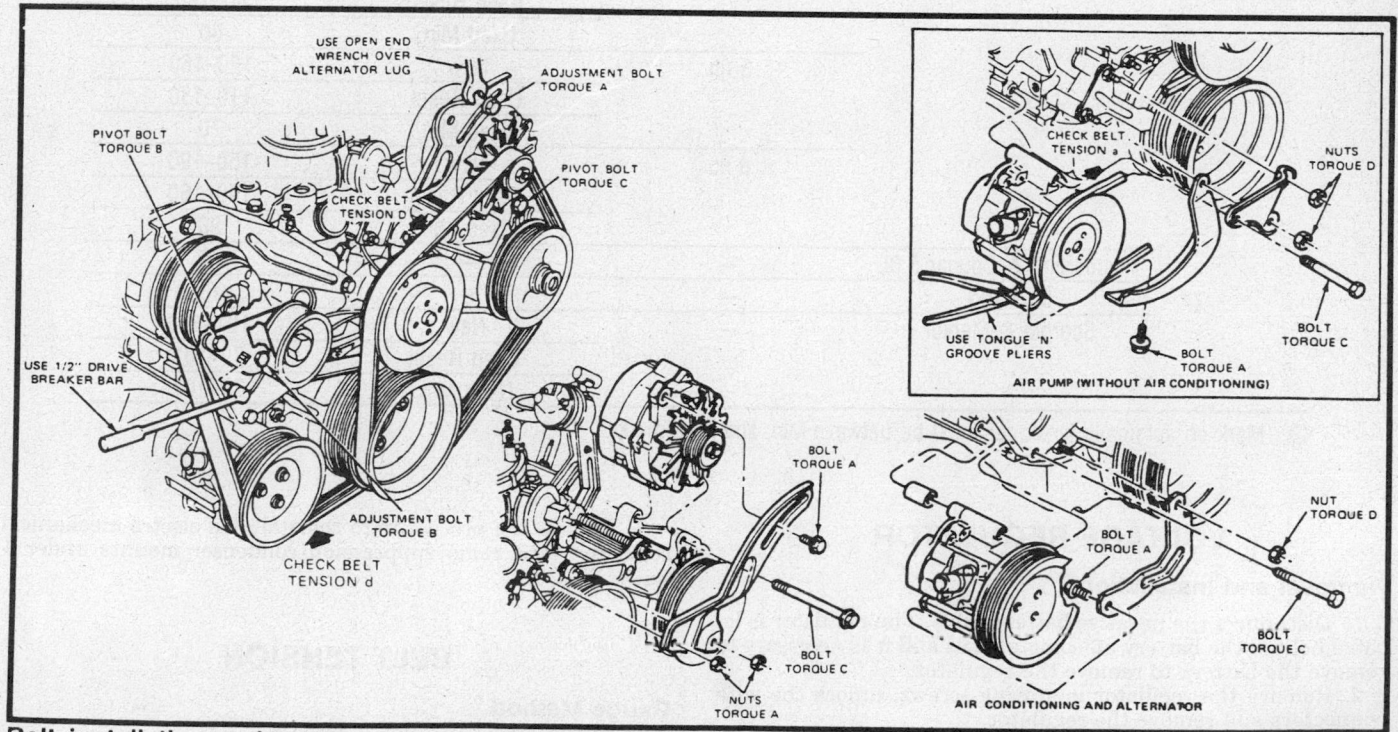

Belt installation and tension adjustment—Lincoln Town Car, Ford Crown Victoria/Mercury Grand Marquis, 5.0L and 5.8L engines

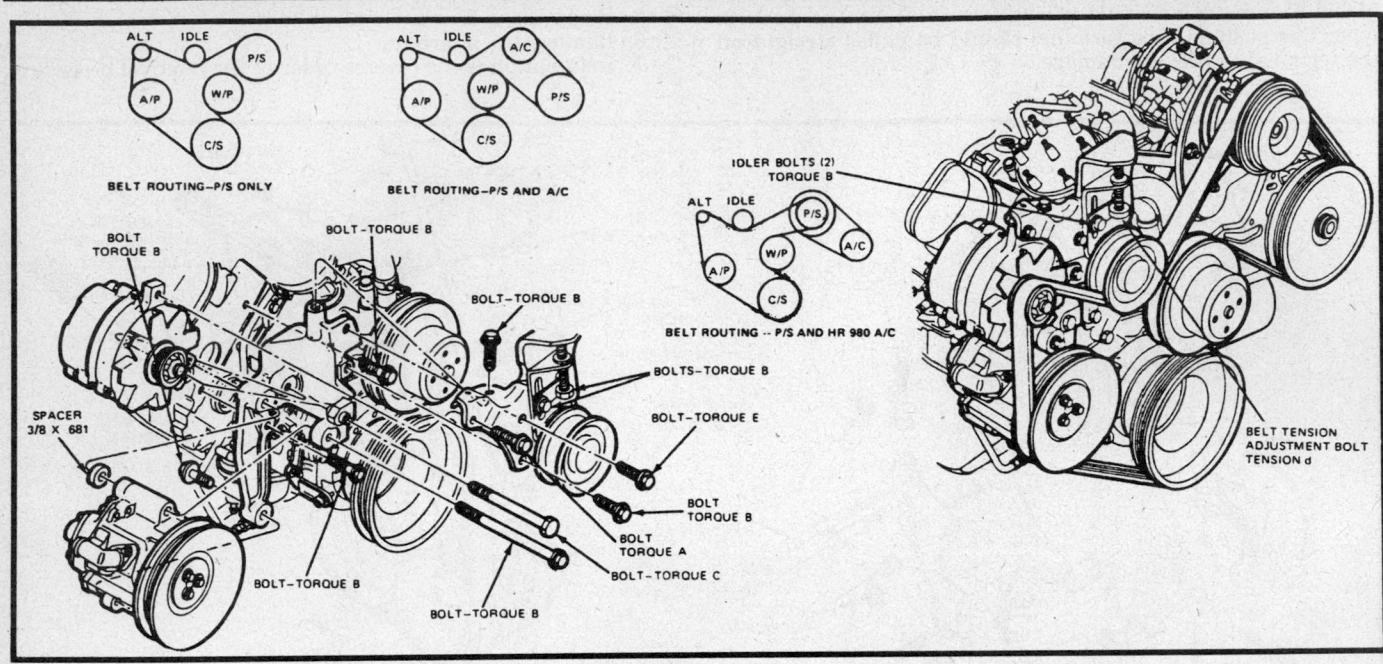

Belt installation and tension adjustments—3.8L engine

BELT TENSION

Model/Engine	Belt Type	Belt Condition	lbs.
All except below	¼ in. V-belt	New	50–90
		Used Reset	40–60
		Used Min.	40
	⅜ in. V-belt or 4000	New	90–130
		Used Reset	80–100
		Used Min.	60
	5 rib	New	120–160
		Used Reset	110–130
		Used Min.	70
	6 rib	New	150–190
		Used Reset	140–160
		Used Min.	90
Thunderbird & Cougar 5.0L	—	—	①
Mustang	—	—	①
Scorpio & Merkur	—	New	101–123
		Used Reset	79–101
		Used Min.	79–101

① Mark on automatic tensioner must be between Min. and Max. marks

VOLTAGE REGULATOR

Removal and Installation

1. Disconnect the negative battery cable. The regulator is located behind the battery on some models and it is necessary to remove the battery to remove the regulator.

2. Remove the regulator mounting screws, unlock the wire connectors and remove the regulator.

NOTE: Always disconnect the connector plug from the regulator before removing the mounting screws.

3. Reverse the procedure to reinstall. On electro-mechanical regulators, the radio suppression condenser mounts under 1 screw.

BELT TENSION

Gauge Method
EXCEPT SERPENTINE BELT

Using belt tension gauge Tool T631–8620–A or equivalent, ad-

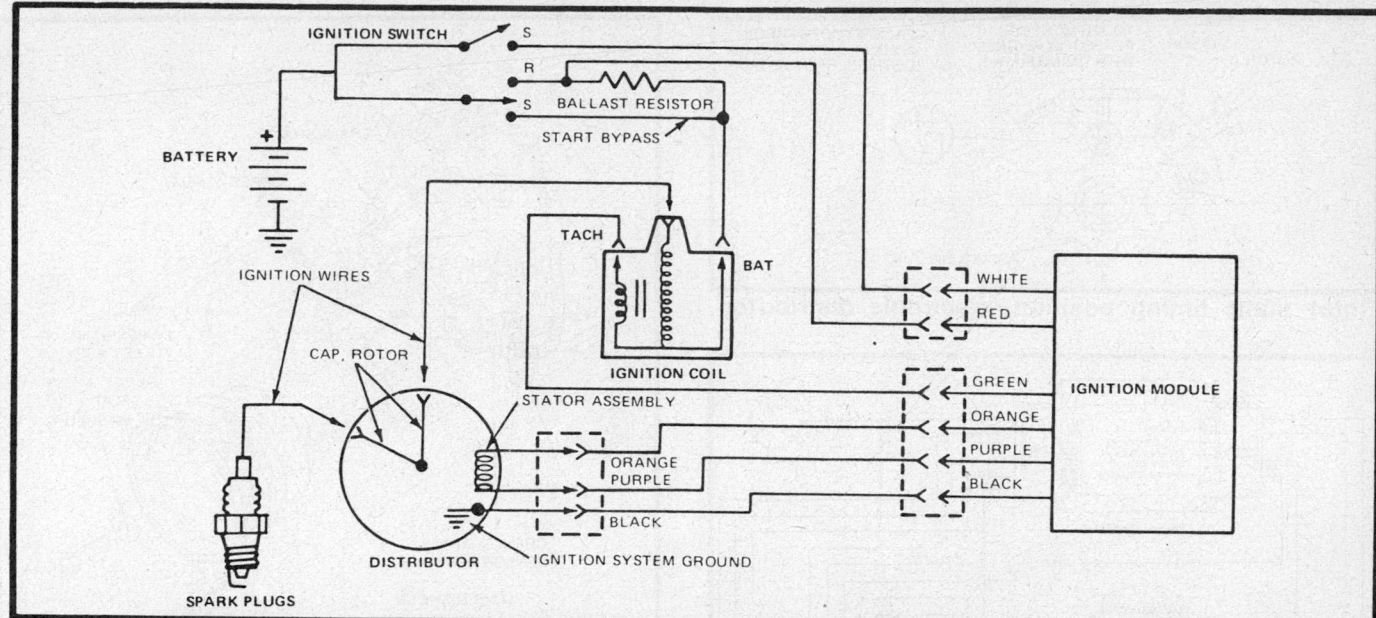

Typical schematic of the ignition system

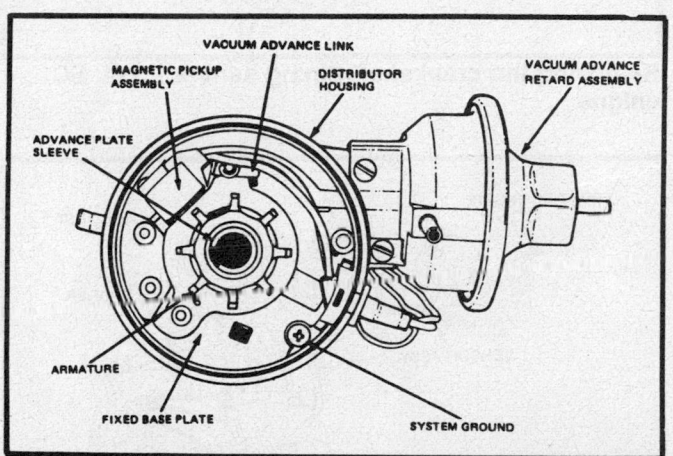

Breakerless ignition distributor used with the eight cylinder engines

just the alternator belt if the tension is below 300N, as indicated on the gauge. If the belt is used, the correct belt tension is 350N, as indicated on the gauge. If the belt is new, the correct tension is 575N, as indicated on the gauge.

SERPENTINE BELT

The correct belt tension is indicated on the indicator mark of the belt tensioner. If the indicator mark is not within specification, replace the belt or the tensioner.

Starting System

STARTER

Removal and Installation

1. Disconnect the negative battery cable.
2. Raise the vehicle and support it safely.
3. Disconnect the starter cable from the starter.
4. On some vehicles equipped with the 5.0L engine it may be necessary to remove the right engine mount and raise the engine. On some vehicles with the 3.8L engine, it may be necessary

to remove the wish-bone brace. On Mustang, remove the cross-member from under the bell housing and remove the steering gear assembly from the side rail. On Thunderbird, Cougar, LTD, Marquis and Continental models, remove the cross brace.

5. Disconnect and tag the electrical wiring. Remove the starter housing bolts and crossmember from under the engine. Remove the heat shield, if equipped.
6. Manipulate the starter so that it can be lowered through the steering linkage. On some engine/chassis combinations, this can be accomplished by turning the front wheels either right or left, or by removing the idler arm bracket attaching bolts and lowering the steering linkage away from the engine.
7. Install the starter by sliding it into position. On 4 and 6 cylinder in-line engines, removal of a thermactor (air) pump mounting bolt and drive belt will allow the pump to be moved to the side and permit access to the distributor. If necessary, disconnect the thermactor air filter and lines as well.
8. On the block, tighten the mounting bolts to 15–20 ft. lbs. Reconnect the electrical leads.

Ignition System

DISTRIBUTOR

Removal and Installation

EXCEPT VEHICLES WITH DISTRIBUTORLESS IGNITION

Timing Not Disturbed

1. Disconnect the negative battery cable. Remove the air cleaner on V6 and V8 engines.
2. Remove the distributor cap and position the cap and ignition wires to the side.
3. Disconnect the wiring harness plug from the distributor connector. Disconnect and plug the vacuum hoses from the vacuum diaphragm assembly, if equipped.
4. Rotate the engine (in normal direction of rotation) until No. 1 piston is on Top Dead Center (TDC) of the compression stroke. The TDC mark on the crankshaft pulley and the pointer should align. Rotor tip pointing at the No. 1 spark plug wire position on the distributor cap.

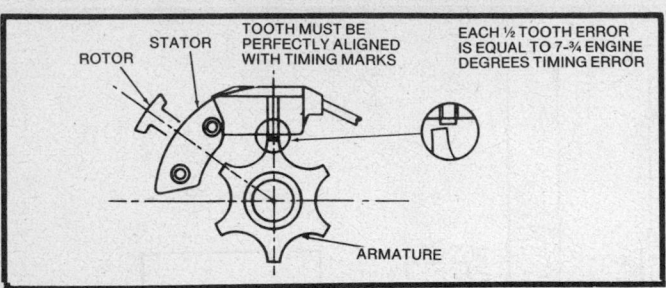

Rotor static timing position, electronic distributor

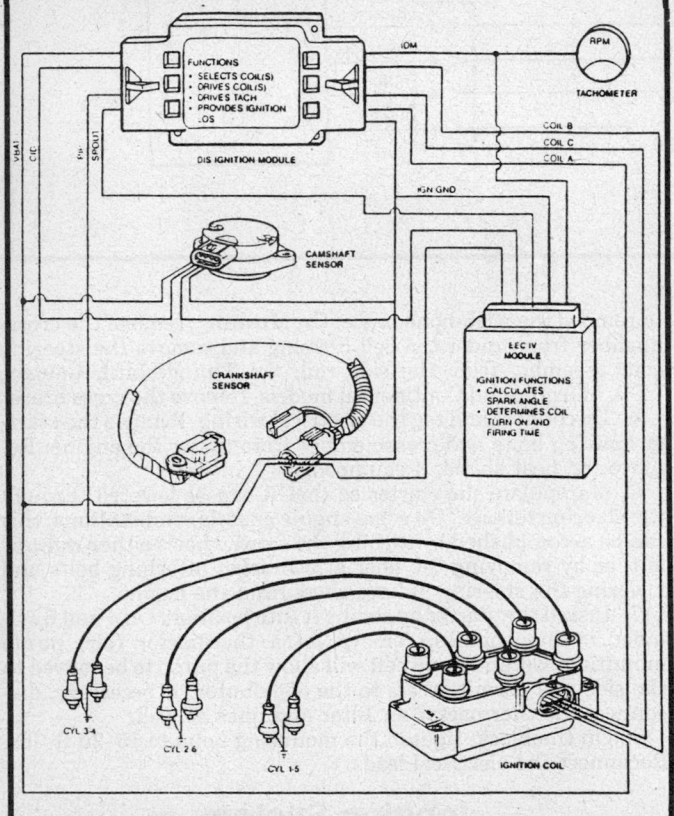

Distributorless ignition system (DIS) components

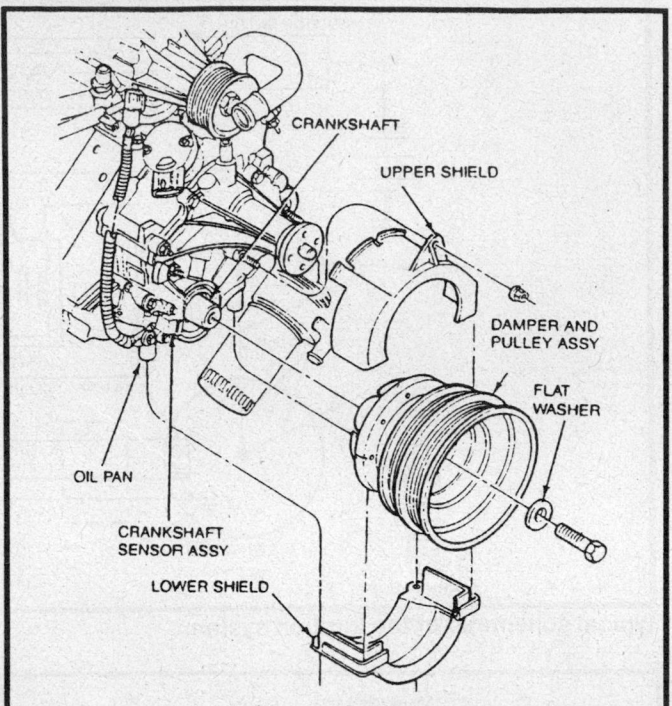

Removing the crankshaft timing sensor — 3.8L SC enigne

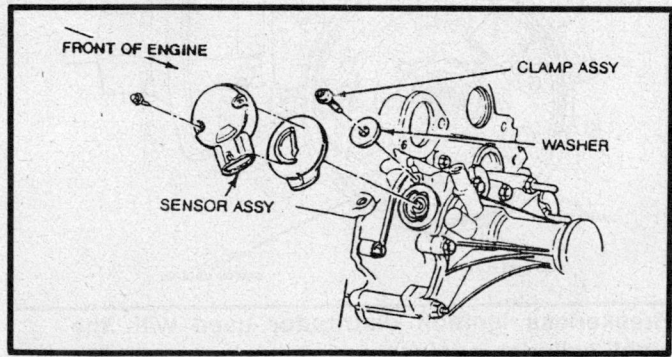

Removing the camshaft sensor assembly — 3.8L SC engine

5. On Dura Spark I or II equipped engines, turn the engine slightly past the No. 1 spark plug position to align the stator (pick-up coil) assembly pole with an armature pole (the closest one). On Dura Spark III, the distributor sleeve groove (when looking down from the top) and the cap adaptor alignment slot should align. On vehicles equipped with EEC IV, remove the rotor (2 screws) and note the position of the "polarizing square" and shaft plate for reinstallation reference.

6. Scribe a mark on the distributor body and the engine block to indicate the position of the rotor tip and the position of the distributor in the engine. Dura Spark III and some EEC IV system distributors are equipped with a notched base and will only locate at 1 position on the engine.

7. Remove the holddown bolt and clamp located at the base of the distributor. Some Dura Spark III and EEC IV system distributors are equipped with a special holddown bolt that requires a Torx head wrench for removal. Remove the distributor from the engine. Pay attention to the direction the rotor tip points if it moves from the No. 1 position when the drive gear disengages. For reinstallation purposes, the rotor should be at this point to insure proper gear mesh and timing.

8. Avoid turning the engine, if possible, while the distributor is removed. If the engine is turned from TDC position, TDC timing marks will have to be reset before the distributor is installed.

To install:

9. Position the distributor in the engine with the rotor aligned to the marks made on the distributor, or at the position the rotor pointed when the distributor was removed. The stator and armature or "polarizing square" and shaft plate should also be aligned. Engage the oil pump intermediate shaft and insert the distributor until fully seated on the engine, if the distributor does not fully seat, turn the engine slightly to fully engage the intermediate shaft.

10. On engines equipped with an indexed distributor base, make sure when positioning the distributor that the slot in the distributor base will engage the block tab and the sleeve/adaptor slots are aligned.

11. After the distributor has been fully seated into the block, recheck the timing mark and rotor alignment. Install the holddown bracket and bolt. On models equipped with an indexed base, tighten the mounting bolt. On other engines, snug the mounting bolt so the distributor can be turned for ignition timing purposes.

12. On 4 cylinder engines, reinstall the thermactor pump belt and adjust the tension. On V6 and V8 engines, install the air cleaner assembly. Connect all electrical and vacuum leads. Check and reset the ignition timing.

NOTE: A silicone compound is used on rotor tips, distributor cap contacts and on the inside of the connectors on the spark plugs cable and module couplers. Always apply Silicone Dielectric Compound after servicing any component of the ignition system.

Timing Disturbed

If the engine was cranked with the distributor removed, it will have to be put into its compression stroke with the No. 1 cylinder at TDC. The following procedure will enable the proper setting of the timing.

1. Remove the No. 1 spark plug.
2. Place a finger over the spark plug hole and crank the engine slowly until compression is felt.
3. Align the timing mark on the crankshaft pulley with the **0** degree mark on the timing scale. This places the No. 1 cylinder at the TDC of its compression stroke.
4. Turn the distributor shaft until the rotor points to the No. 1 spark plug tower on the cap.
5. Install the distributor into the engine, aligning the marks made on the block and the distributor housing.
6. Tighten the distributor hold down bolt and connect all electrical wires and vacuum lines. Check and adjust the timing.

DISTRIBUTORLESS IGNITION SYSTEM (DIS)

The 3.8L supercharged engine used in 1989-90 Thunderbird SC and Cougar XR7, uses an distributorless ignition system.

The DIS system uses various electronic sensors in place of the distributor and uses an coil that fires 2 cylinders at the same time. The various components in the system are as follows:

Crankshaft Timing Sensor—the crankshaft timing sensor is a single Hall effect magnetic switch. It is activated by 3 vanes on the crankshaft damper and pulley assembly. The signal provided by this sensor feeds base timing and rpm information to the DIS module and EEC-IV module. Base timing is set at 10 degrees BTDC and is not adjustable.

Camshaft Sensor—This sensor is driven by the camshaft and provides cylinder position information for the ignition coil and fuel system

DIS Ignition Module—This module receives the signal from the crankshaft sensor, the camshaft sensor and spark signal from the EEC-IV module. The main purpose of this module is to take the information supplied to it and control the ignition coils so that they fire at the correct sequence. The DIS module also controls the engine dwell.

Ignition Coil Pack—The ignition coil pack contains 3 separate ignition coils which are controlled by the DIS module, through 3 coil leads. Each ignition coils fires 2 spark plugs at the same time, 1 on the compression stroke and 1 on the exhaust stroke.

Removal and Installation

CRANKSHAFT TIMING SENSOR

1. Disconnect the negative battery cable.
2. Loosen the accessory drive belt tensioners for both the air conditioning compressor and the supercharger. Remove the belts from the crankshaft pulley.

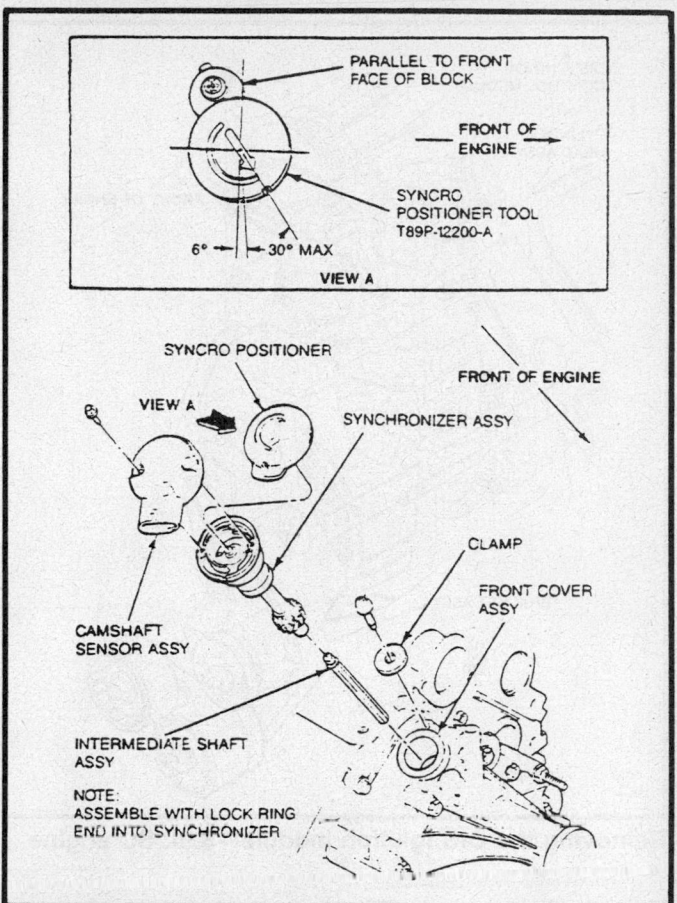

Installing the synchronizer assembly—3.8L SC engine

3. Disconnect the electrical connector from the sensor wiring.
4. Raise and safely support the front of the vehicle. Remove the upper and lower crankshaft damper covers.
5. Remove the crankshaft pulley and damper using a suitable puller.
6. Remove the 2 sensors mounting bolts and remove the sensor.
7. To install the sensor, position it on its mount and install the retaining bolts. Torque the retaining bolts to 31 inch lbs.
8. Install the crankshaft damper and pulley, tightening the pulley bolt to 103-132 ft. lbs.
9. Install the upper and lower damper covers and lower the vehicle.
10. Reconnect the sensor wiring and install the accessory drive belts.

CAMSHAFT SENSOR

1. Disconnect the negative battery cable.
2. Disconnect the electrical leads from the camshaft sensor.
3. Remove the sensor mounting screws and remove the sensor.
4. Install the sensor in position and install the mounting screws, tightening to 31 inch. lbs.
5. Reconnect the electrical leads and connect the negative battery cable.

SYNCHRONIZER ASSEMBLY

NOTE: Before starting this procedure, set the No. 1 cylinder to 26 degrees after TDC of the compression stroke. Then note the position of the camshaft sensor

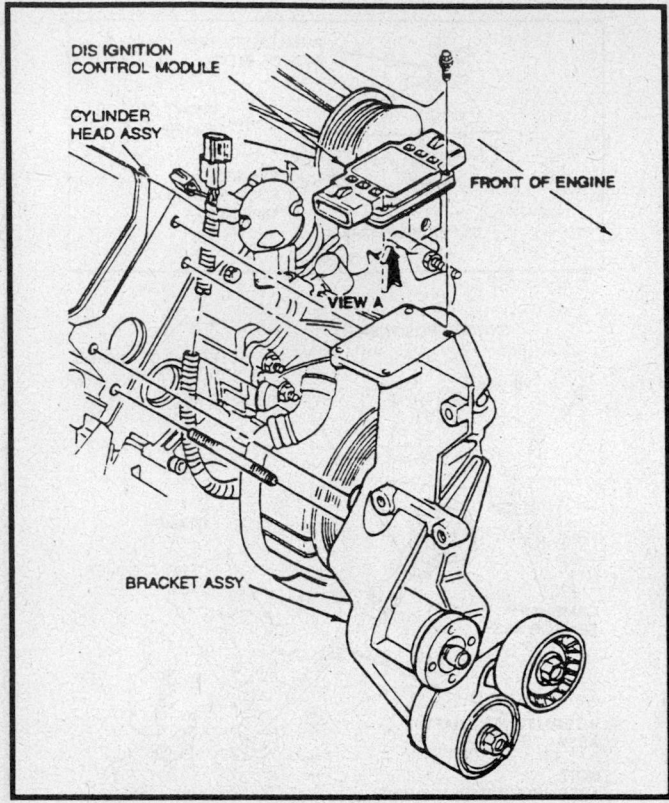

DIS IGNITION CONTROL MODULE

CYLINDER HEAD ASSY

FRONT OF ENGINE

VIEW A

BRACKET ASSY

Removing the DIS ignition module—3.8L SC engine

electrical connector. The installation procedure requires that the connector be located in the same position.

1. Disconnect the negative battery cable.
2. Remove the camshaft sensor assembly.
3. Remove the synchronizer clamp, bolt and washer.
4. Remove the synchronizer from the front engine cover, by pulling it out. The oil pump intermediate shaft will come out with the assembly.

NOTE: If the replacement synchronizer does not contain a plastic locator cover tool, a special service tool such as the synchro positioner T89P-12200-A or equivalent, must be used to install the synchronizer. Failure to use this special tool will cause the synchronizer timing to be out of adjustment, this could lead to engine damage.

5. To install the synchronizer, position the synchronizer so that gear engagement occurs when the arrow on the locator tool is pointed 30 degrees counterclockwise from the front face of the engine block. This will locate the camshaft sensor electrical connector to the position it was in before removal.
6. Install the synchronizer base clamp and tighten the mounting bolt to 15–22 ft. lbs.
7. Remove the positioner tool and install the camshaft sensor. Connect the sensor electrical lead and connect the negative battery cable.

IGNITION MODULE

1. Disconnect the negative battery cable.
2. Disconnect both electrical connectors from the module.
3. Remove the module retaining bolts and remove the module.
4. To install the module, apply a uniform coating of heatsink

grease or equivalent to the mounting surface of the module.
5. Install the module and tighten the mounting bolts to 22–31 inch lbs.
6. Reconnect the electrical connectors and connect the negative battery cable.

IGNITION COIL PACK

1. Disconnect the negative battery cable.
2. Disconnect the electrical connector from the coil.
3. Remove the spark plug wires from the coil by squeezing the lock tabs to release the boot.
4. Remove the coil mounting screws and remove the coil.
5. To install the coil, position it and install the mounting screws. Tighten the mounting screws to 40–62 inch lbs.
6. Reconnect the electrical lead and connect the spark plug wires.

IGNITION TIMING

Adjustment

EXCEPT WITH DISTRIBUTORLESS IGNITION

The engines are timed by the monolithic timing method during assembly. The monolithic system uses a timing receptacle on the front of the engine which can be connected to digital readout equipment, which electronically determines timing. Timing can also be adjusted in the conventional way.

NOTE: Requirements vary from vehicle to vehicle. Always refer to the Emissions Specifications Sticker for exact timing procedures.

1. Locate the timing marks and pointer on the lower engine pulley and engine's front cover.
2. Clean the marks and apply chalk or bright-colored paint to the pointer.
3. If the ignition module has (–12A244–) as a basic part number, disconnect the 2 wire connector (yellow and black wires). On engines equipped with the EEC IV system, disconnect the single white (black on some vehicles) wire connector near the distributor.
4. Attach a timing light and tachometer according to manufacturer's specifications.
5. Disconnect and plug all vacuum lines leading to the distributor.
6. Start the engine, allow it to warm to normal operating temperature, then set the idle to the specifications given on the underhood sticker (for timing).
7. On vehicles equipped with the ignition module, place a jumper wire between the pins (for the yellow and black wires) in the module connector. If the vehicle is equipped with a barometric pressure switch, disconnect it from the ignition module and place a jumper wire across the pins at the ignition module connector (yellow and black wire.)
8. Aim the timing light at the timing mark and pointer on the front of the engine. If the marks align when the timing light flashes, remove the timing light, set the idle to its proper specification and connect the vacuum lines at the distributor. If the marks do not align when the light flashes, turn the engine off and loosen the distributor holddown clamp slightly.
9. Start the engine again and observe the alignment of the timing marks. To advance the timing, turn the distributor clockwise, for the 3.8L and all V8 engines. When the timing marks are aligned, turn the engine off and tighten the distributor holddown clamp. Remove the test equipment, reconnect the vacuum hoses and white (black) single wire connector (EEC IV).
10. On EEC IV equipped vehicles, disconnect the jumper wire. Test the module operation as follows:
    a. Disconnect and plug the vacuum source hose to the ignition timing vacuum switch.
    b. Using an external vacuum source, apply vacuum greater

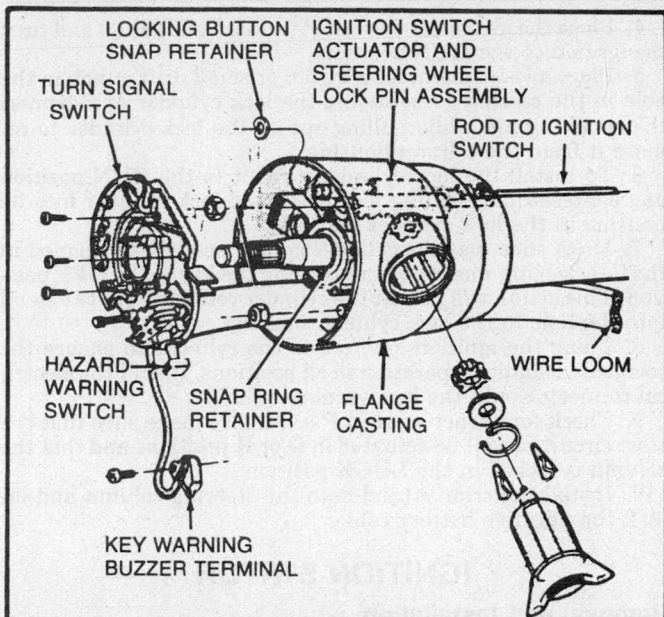

Turnsignal switch and ignition lock cylinder mounting, typical of fixed column

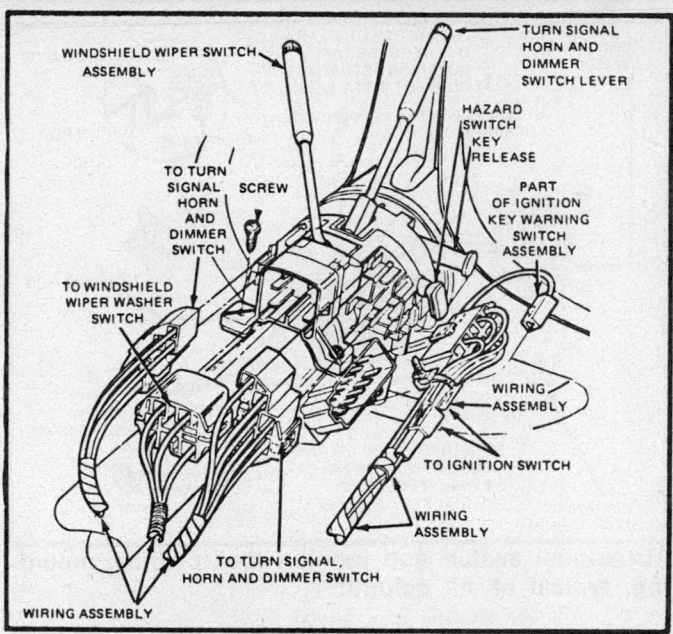

Cluster of switches mounted to steering column

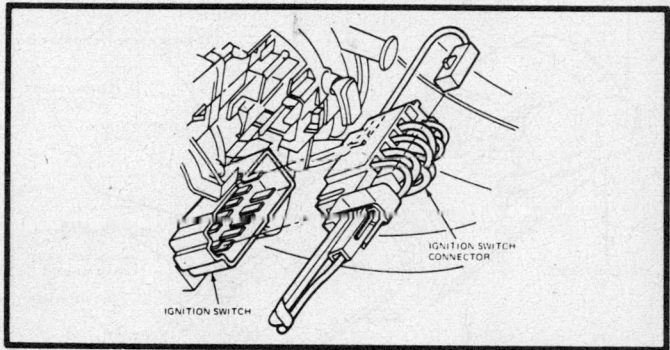

Blade type ignition switch, spade type similar

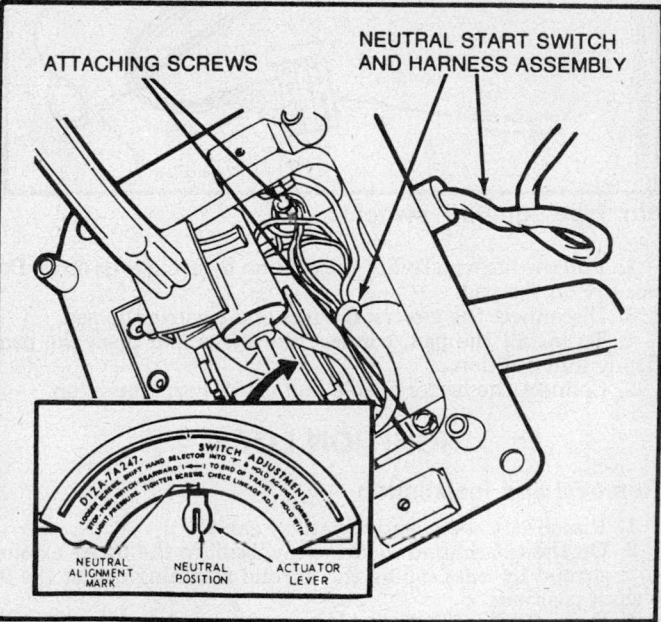

Adjustment of neutral start switch mounted in console

than 12 in. Hg to the switch and compare the ignition timing with the requirements below:

    4 cylinder – per specifications less 32–40
    6 cylinder – per specifications less 21–27
    8 cylinder – per specifications less 16–20

DISTRIBUTORLESS IGNITION

The ignition timing is set at the factory and is not adjustable. If the timing is out of adjustment, the DIS system will have to be checked for proper operation.

Electrical Controls

STEERING WHEEL

Removal and Installation

CAUTION

On vehicles equipped with air bag systems, extreme caution must be used to prevent accidental deployment of the air bag. Battery cables should be disconnected and sharp blows to the steering wheel should be avoided.

---

1. Disconnect the negative battery cable.
2. If the vehicle is equipped with a horn ring, remove it by rotating it counterclockwise. If equipped with a steering wheel crash pad, remove the retaining screws from the underside of the steering wheel and then remove the crash pad. Disconnect the horn wires. If equipped with speed control disconnect the wires from the inside of the steering wheel center.
3. Remove and discard the steering wheel nut, install a steering wheel puller on the end of the shaft and remove the steering wheel.
4. Installation is the reverse of the removal procedure. Be sure that the front wheels are positioned straight ahead before lining up the marks on the steering wheel and column. Use a new locknut.

HORN SWITCH

Removal and Installation

1. Disconnect the negative battery cable.

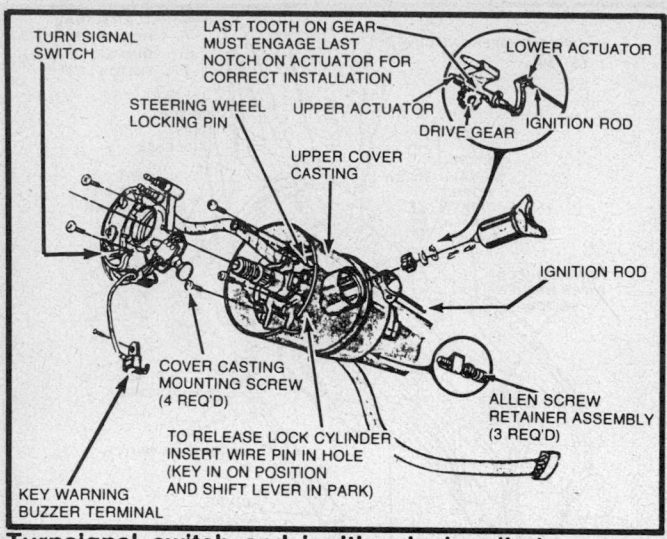

Turnsignal switch and ignition lock cylinder mounting, typical of tilt column

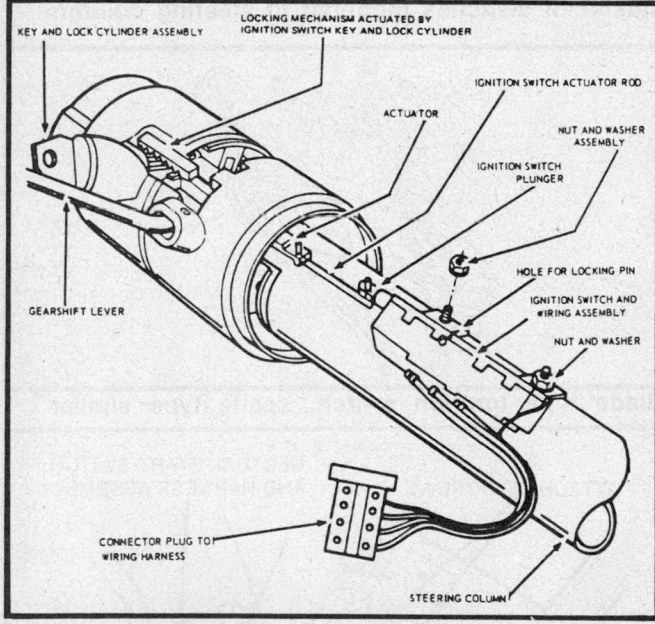

Pin type ignition switch

2. Pull the horn pad off of the column by using even force. Do not pry on the pad.

3. Disconnect the electrical wires and remove the pad.

4. To install the pad, connect the wires and push the pad firmly into position.

5. Connect the battery cable and check horn operation.

IGNITION LOCK

Removal and Installation

1. Disconnect the negative battery cable.

2. On the tilt column models only, remove the upper extension shroud by unsnapping the shroud retaining clip at the 9 o'clock position.

3. Remove the trim shroud halves by removing the attaching screws. Remove the electrical connector from the key warning switch.

4. Place the gear shift lever in **P** (column shift only) and turn the ignition to the **RUN** position.

5. Place a ⅛ in. diameter wire pin or small drift punch in the hole in the casting surrounding the lock cylinder and depress the retaining pin while pulling out on the lock cylinder to remove it from the column housing.

6. To install the lock cylinder, turn it to the **RUN** position and depress the retaining pin. Insert the lock cylinder into its housing in the lock cylinder casting.

7. Make sure that the cylinder is fully seated and aligned in the interlocking washer before turning the key to the **OFF** position. This action will permit the cylinder retaining pin to extend into the hole in the lock cylinder housing.

8. Using the ignition key, rotate the cylinder to ensure the correct mechanical operation in all positions. Install the electrical connector onto the key warning switch.

9. Check for proper start in **P** or **N**. Also make sure that the start circuit cannot be actuated in **D** or **R** positions and that the column is locked in the **LOCK** position.

10. Install the trim shroud onto the steering column and install the negative battery cable.

IGNITION SWITCH

Removal and Installation

1. Disconnect the negative battery cable.

2. Remove the upper shroud below the steering wheel by unsnapping the retaining clips. On the tilt column, it will be necessary to remove the 5 attaching screws. Remove the upper extension shroud by unsnapping the shroud from the retaining clips at the 9 o'clock position.

3. Disconnect the electrical connector from the ignition switch.

4. Drill out the bolts holding the switch to the lock cylinder using a ⅛ in. drill bit.

5. Remove the bolts using an Easy-Out® bolt extractor.

6. Disengage the switch from the actuator pin.

7. Adjust the new ignition switch by sliding the carrier to the **ON** position. Insert a small drill bit through the switch housing and into the carrier to restrict movement of the carrier with respect to the switch housing. A new replacement comes with an adjusting pin already installed.

8. Turn the ignition key to the **ON** position.

9. Install the ignition switch on the actuator pin.

10. Install new "break-off head" bolts and tighten them until the heads break off. Tighten bolts evenly.

11. Remove the drill bit or adjusting pin.

12. Connect all electrical connections and the negative battery cable.

13. Start the vehicle and check for proper operation of the switch.

14. Install the steering column shroud.

NEUTRAL SAFETY SWITCH

Models equipped with a column shift lever are not equipped with a neutral start switch. Instead, an ignition lock cylinder to shift lever interlock prevents these models from being started in any gear other than **P** or **N**.

CLUTCH START SWITCH

Removal and Installation

1. Disconnect the negative battery cable. Disconnect wiring connector.

2. Remove retaining pin from clutch pedal.

3. Remove switch bracket attaching screw.

4. Lift switch and bracket assembly upward to disengage tab from pedal support.

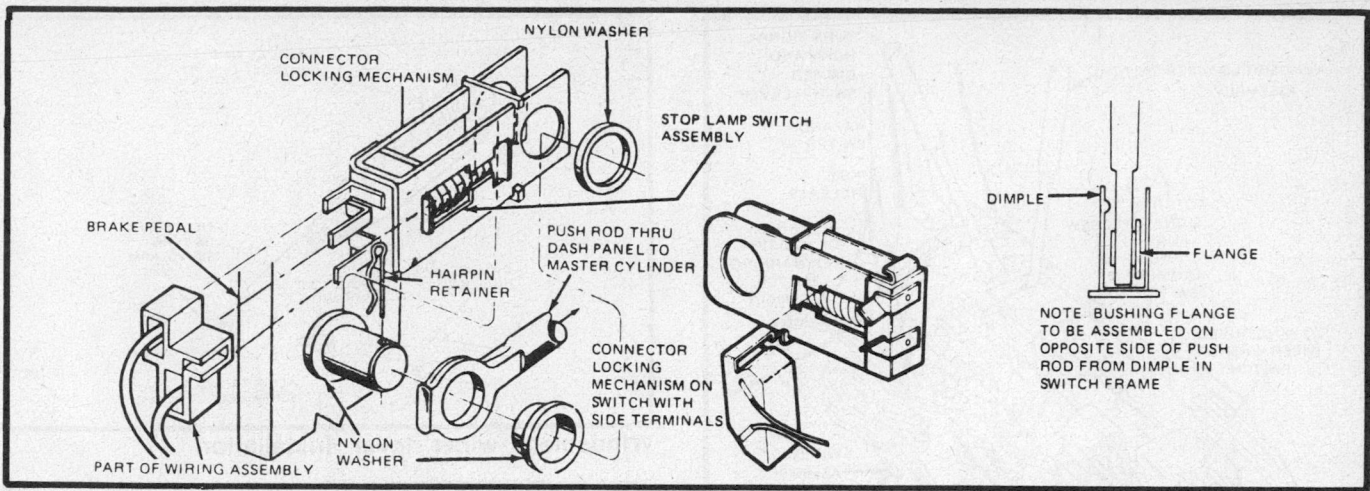

Typical installation of stop lamp switch

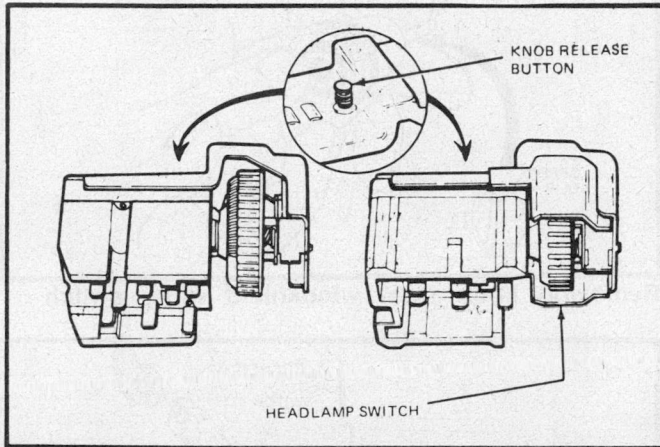

Typical headlamp switch with release button

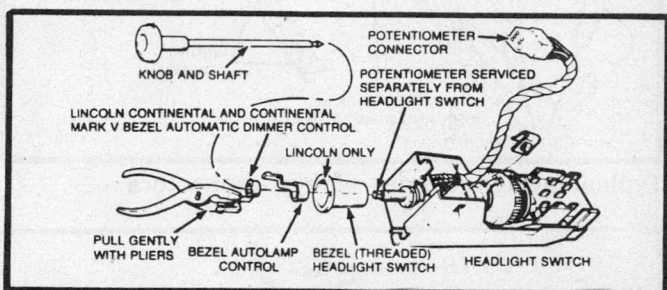

Headlamp switch used with Autolamp system

5. Move the switch outward to disengage actuating rod eyelet from clutch pedal pin and remove switch from vehicle.

NOTE: Always install the switch with the self-adjusting clip about 1.0 in. from the end of the rod. The clutch pedal must be fully up (clutch engaged). Otherwise, the switch may be misadjusted.

6. Place eyelet end of rod onto pivot pin.
7. Swing switch assembly around to line up hole in mounting boss with hole in bracket.
8. Install attaching screw.
9. Replace retaining pin in pivot pin.
10. Connect wiring connector.

STOPLIGHT SWITCH

Removal and Installation

EXCEPT POWER BRAKES

1. Disconnect the negative battery cable. Disconnect the wire harness at the connector from the switch.
2. Remove the hairpin retainer, slide the stoplight switch, the pushrod and the nylon washers and bushings away from the pedal and remove the switch.

NOTE: Since the switch side plate nearest the brake pedal is slotted, it is not necessary to remove the brake

master cylinder pushrod and 1 washer from the brake pedal pin.

3. Position the switch, pushrod, bushing and washers on the brake pedal pin and install the hairpin retainer.
4. Assemble the wire harness connector to the switch and install the wires in the retaining clip.

POWER BRAKES

1. Disconnect the negative battery cable.
2. Disconnect the stoplight switch wire connector from the switch.
3. Loosen the brake booster nuts at the pedal support approximately ¼ in. so booster is free to move eliminating binding during switch removal.
4. Remove the hairpin retainer and outer nylon washer from the pedal pin. Slide the stoplight switch off the brake pedal pin just far enough for the outer arm to clear the pin. Then remove the switch.

NOTE: Since the switch side plate nearest the brake pedal is slotted it is not necessary to remove the brake master cylinder pushrod and 1 spacer washer from the brake pedal pin.

5. Position the new stoplight switch so that it straddles the pushrod, with the slot on the pedal pin and the switch outer frame hole just clearing the pin. Slide the switch upward onto the pin and pushrod. Slide the assembly inboard toward the brake pedal arm.
6. Install the outer nylon washer and the hairpin retainer.
7. Tighten the booster attaching nuts to specification.
8. Connect the stoplight switch wire connector to the switch. Connect the negative battery cable.

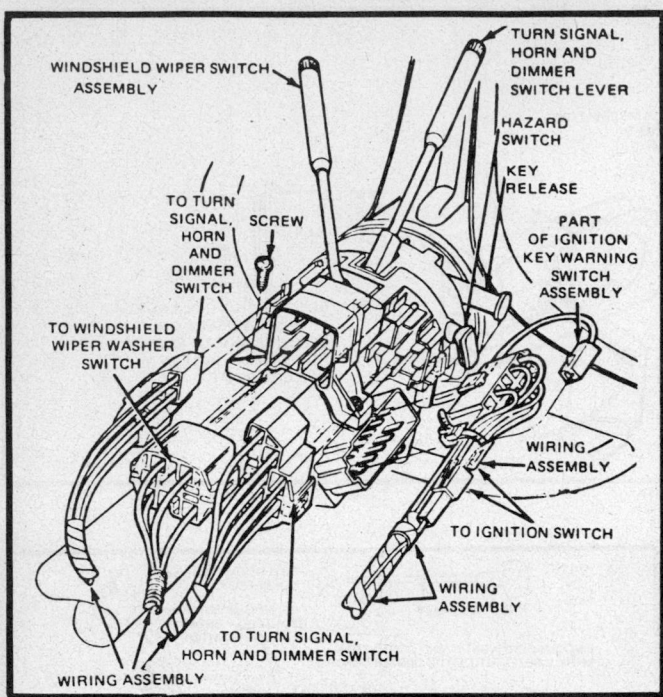

Typical switch cluster wiring connectors

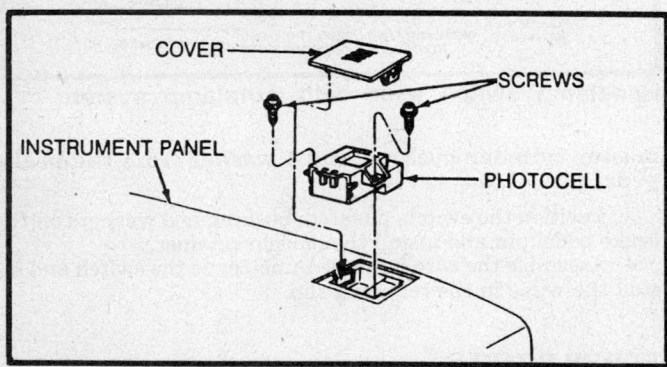

Automatic headlamp dimmer sensor removal 1988–89 Mark VII

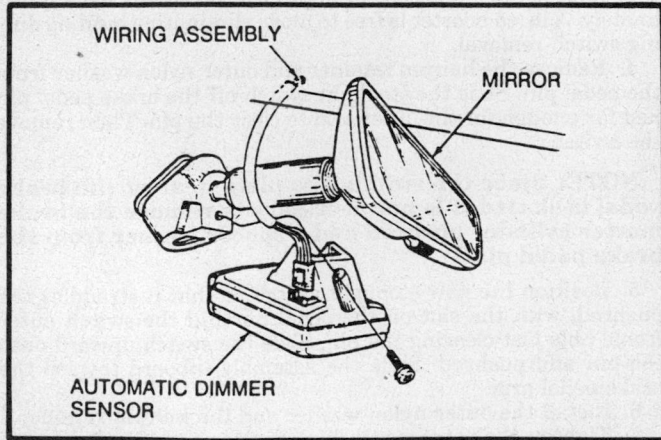

Automatic headlamp dimmer sensor removal Town Car, Cougar, Thunderbird

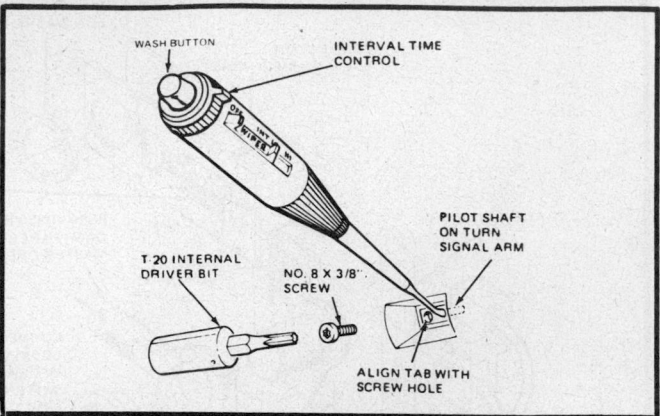

Windshield wiper lever installation

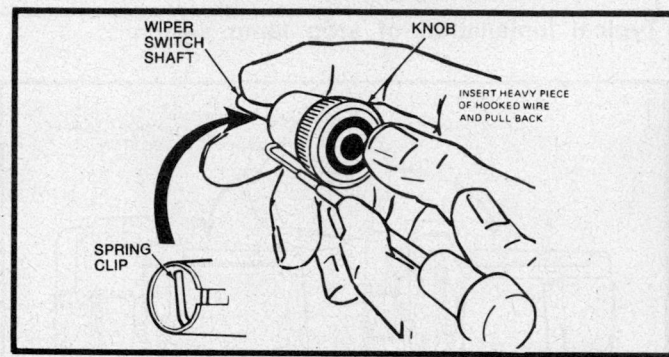

Removing knob from windshield wiper switch

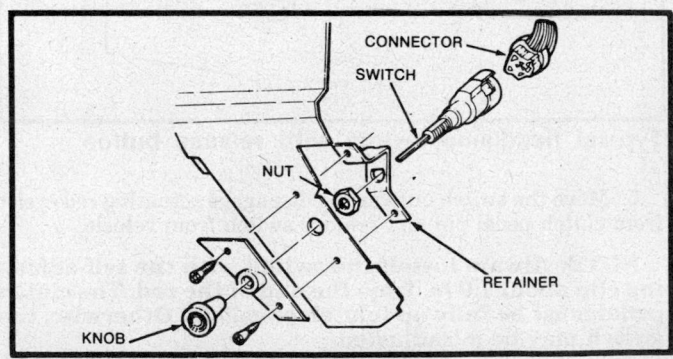

Typical wiper switch installation

NOTE: Stoplight switch wire harness must have sufficient length to travel with switch during full stroke of pedal. If wire length is insufficient, reroute harness or service as required.

9. Check the stoplights for proper operation.

HEADLAMP SWITCH

Removal and Installation

GRAND MARQUIS, CROWN VICTORIA, LTD, MARQUIS, MUSTANG AND CAPRI

1. Disconnect the negative battery cable.
2. Underneath the instrument panel, depress the shaft retaining knob and pull the knob straight out.
3. Unscrew the trim bezel and remove the locknut.
4. Underneath the instrument panel, move the switch toward the front of the vehicle while tilting it downward.

5. Disconnect the wiring from the switch and remove the switch from the vehicle.

6. Installation is the reverse of removal.

TOWN CAR

1. Disconnect the ground cable from the battery.

2. Remove the headlamp switch knob.

3. Remove the auto dimmer bezel and the autolamp delay bezel, if so equipped.

4. Remove the steering column lower shroud.

5. Remove the lower left instrument panel trim bezel.

6. Remove the 5 screws that retain the headlamp switch mounting bracket to the instrument panel.

7. Carefully pull the switch and bracket from the instrument panel and disconnect the wiring connector(s) from the headlamp switch.

8. Remove the locknut and screw that retain the headlamp switch to the switch bracket.

9. Installation is the reverse order of the removal procedure.

MARK VII, CONTINENTAL, THUNDERBIRD AND COUGAR

1. Disconnect the negative battery cable. Remove the lens assembly attaching screws and then the lens assembly.

2. Remove the screws securing the switch to the instrument panel and pull the switch out from the panel.

3. Disconnect the electrical connector and remove the switch from the vehicle.

4. Installation is the reverse order of the removal procedure.

HEADLAMP DELAY SYSTEM

NOTE: The delay system has an additional feature which is the potentiometer, which can be removed from the headlamp switch. Both the headlamp switch and the potentiometer can be replaced separately.

1. Disconnect the negative battery cable and remove the headlight switch.

2. Remove the headlamp switch shaft and knob.

3. Remove the plastic spacer at the rear of the potentiometer by pushing out with a suitable tool.

4. Remove the strap securing the wiring harness to the switch.

5. Loosen the potentiometer retaining nut, washer and slide it out of the headlamp switch.

6. Installation is the reverse order of the removal procedure.

DIMMER SWITCH

Removal and Installation
COLUMN MOUNTED

1. Disconnect the negative battery cable. Remove the shroud from the steering column.

2. Disconnect the steering column wiring connector plug from the bracket and remove the screws that secure the switch to the column.

3. Installation is the reverse of removal procedure.

AUTOMATIC HEADLAMP DIMMER SENSOR

Vehicles equipped with the automatic headlamp dimmer system use a sensor to control the high—low beam operation. This system can also be operated manually with a conventional dimmer lever on the steering column. On some 1986 vehicles, the sensor is located in the front of the vehicle behind the grille. On late 1986 vehicles and all 1987 vehicles the sensor is located in the vehicle attached to the rear view mirror. The mirror mounted sensor can be removed by taking out the retaining screw and disconnecting the electrical connector. On all 1988–90 Mark VII, Town Car, Grand Marquis and Crown Victoria vehicles the dimmer sensor is located in the front right corner of the instrument panel. This sensor can be removed by taking out the retaining screw and removing the assembly from the dash.

1. Disconnect the negative battery cable.

2. Disconnect wire harness at rear of the sensor-amplifier unit. Do not pull on the cable sheathing as this could damage the leads.

3. Remove the sensor-amplifier and bracket mounting screws and remove the unit from vehicle.

4. Be certain that headlamp system is properly aimed. Look through the front chamber to see that at least 50% of the sensor lens can be seen and is clean.

5. Installation is the reverse of removal procedures.

6. Test unit for proper operation and if necessary, adjust the vertical aiming.

TURN SIGNAL SWITCH

Removal and Installation

TOWN CAR, GRAND MARQUIS AND CROWN VICTORIA

1. Disconnect the negative battery cable. On standard steering columns, remove the upper extension shroud (below the steering wheel) by snapping the shroud from the retaining clip. On tilt columns, remove the trim shroud by removing the 5 self-tapping screws.

2. Use a pulling and twisting motion, while pulling straight out, to remove the turn signal switch lever.

3. Peel back the piece of foam rubber from around the switch.

4. Disconnect the switch electrical connectors.

5. Remove the self-tapping screws which secure the switch to the lock cylinder housing and disengage the switch from the housing.

6. To install, align the switch mounting holes with the corresponding holes in the lock cylinder housing. Install the screws.

7. Stick the foam back into place.

8. Align the key on the turn signal lever with the keyway in the switch and push the lever into place.

9. Install the electrical connectors.

10. Install the trim shrouds.

WINDSHIELD WIPER SWITCH

Removal and Installation

1. Disconnect the negative battery cable.

2. Remove the split steering column cover retaining screws.

3. Separate the halves and remove the wiper switch retaining screws.

4. Disconnect the wire connector and remove the wiper switch.

5. The installation of the wiper switch is the reverse of the removal procedure.

WINDSHIELD WIPER MOTOR

Removal and Installation

GRAND MARQUIS, CROWN VICTORIA, CONTINENTAL AND TOWN CAR

1. Disconnect the negative battery cable.

2. Remove the hood seal. Disconnect the right washer nozzle hose and remove the right wiper arm and blade assembly from the pivot shaft.

3. Remove the windshield wiper motor and linkage cover by removing the 2 attaching screws.

4. Disconnect the linkage drive arm from the motor output arm crankpin by removing the retaining clip.

5. Disconnect the 2 push-on wire connectors from the motor.

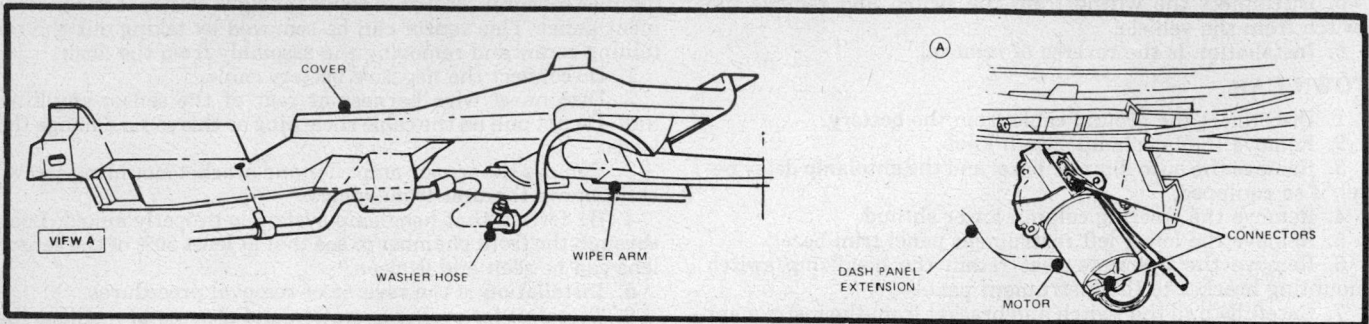

Removal of wiper motor, typical

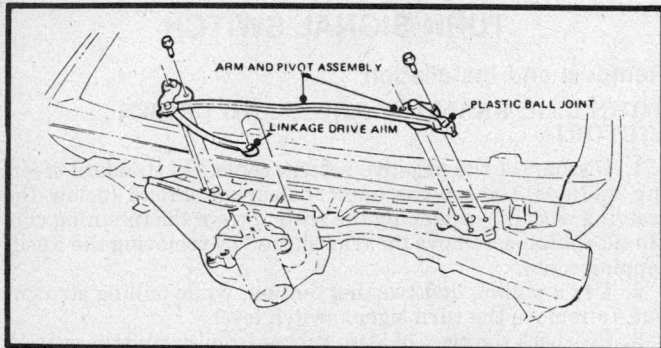

Wiper arm connecting clip and installation pro—cedure

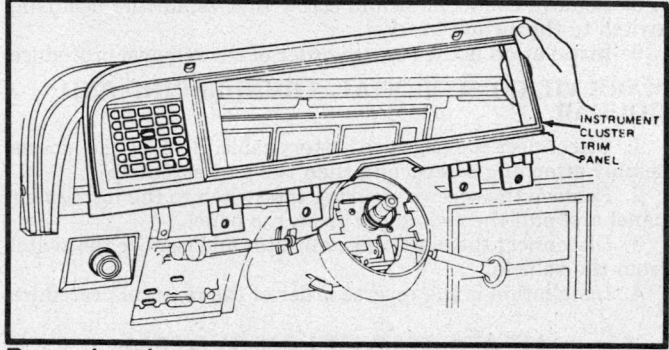

Removing Instrument cluster trim panel, typical

6. Remove the 3 bolts that retain the motor to the dash panel extension and remove the motor.

7. To install, be sure the output arm is in the park position and reverse the removal procedure.

THUNDERBIRD/COUGAR, MUSTANG/CAPRI, LTD/MARQUIS AND MARK VII

1. Disconnect the battery ground cable.
2. Remove the right and left wiper blade assemblies.
3. Remove the grille on the top of the cowl.
4. Disconnect the linkage drive arm from the motor crankpin after removing the clip.
5. Disconnect the wiper motor electrical connector and remove the 3 attaching screws from the motor. Pull the motor from the opening.
6. Be sure the motor crank arm is in the park position and reverse the removal procedure to install.

WINDSHIELD WIPER LINKAGE

Removal and Installation

1. Disconnect the negative battery cable.
2. Remove the wiper motor and disconnect the linkage.
3. The pivot shafts are retained to the body with screws and, on certain models, can individually be removed. On other models, the complete left and right pivot shaft and linkage must be removed as a unit.
4. Installation is the reverse of the removal procedure.

Instrument Cluster

Refer to "Chilton's Electronic Instrumentation Service Manual" for additional coverage..

STANDARD CLUSTER

During the removal and installation procedures, slight varia-

tions may be required from the general outline, to facilitate the removal and installation of the instrument panel and cluster components, due to slight production changes from year to model.

Removal and Installation

GRAND MARQUIS, CROWN VICTORIA, TOWN CAR, LTD AND MARQUIS

1. Disconnect the negative battery cable.
2. Remove the lower steering column cover.
3. Remove the instrument cluster trim cover. Remove the bottom half of the steering column shroud.
4. Reach behind the cluster and disconnect the cluster electrical feed plug and the speedometer cable.
5. Unsnap and remove the steering column shroud cover, if not previously done. Disconnect the transmission indicator cable from the tab in the shroud retainer.
6. Remove the attaching screw for the transmission indicator cable bracket to steering column. disconnect the cable loop from the pin on the steering column.
7. Remove the cluster retaining screws and remove the cluster assembly.
8. The installation is the reverse of the removal procedure.

MUSTANG AND CAPRI

1. Disconnect the negative battery cable.
2. Remove the upper retaining screws from the instrument cluster trim cover and remove the trim cover.
3. Remove 4 screws retaining instrument cluster to the instrument panel on Mustang SVO, disconnect turbo boost pressure hose at the shake brace.
4. Pull the cluster away from the instrument panel and reach behind the instrument cluster to disconnect the speedometer cable by pressing on the flat surface of the plastic connector (quick disconnect).
5. Pull the cluster further away from the instrument panel and disconnect the cluster printed circuit connectors from their receptacles in the cluster backplate.

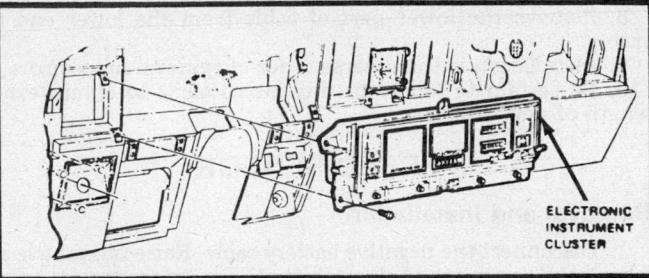

Removing electronic instrument cluster, Thunderbird/Cougar Illustrated

6. Remove cluster.
7. Installation is the reverse order of the removal procedure.

THUNDEREBIRD AND COUGAR

1. Disconnect the negative battery cable.
2. Disconnect the speedometer cable (standard cluster).
3. Remove the instrument panel trim cover and steering column lower shroud.
4. Remove the attaching screw from the transmission indicator quadrant cable bracket to the steering column. Disconnect the cable loop from the pin on the steering column.
5. Remove the cluster retaining screws (standard cluster).
6. Pull the cluster away from the instrument panel and disconnect the speedometer cable.
7. Disconnect the electrical connections from the cluster. Disconnect the ground wire.
8. Remove the cluster from the instrument panel.
9. Reverse the removal procedure to install.

ELECTRONIC CLUSTER

During the removal and installation procedures, slight variations may be required from the general outline, to facilitate the removal and installation of the instrument panel and cluster components, due to slight production changes from year to model.

Removal and Installation

THUNDEREBIRD AND COUGAR

1. Disconnect the negative battery cable.
2. Disconnect the speedometer cable connector.
3. Remove the instrument panel trim cover and steering column lower shroud.
4. Remove the cluster retaining screws.
5. Remove the attaching screw from the transmission indicator quadrant cable bracket to the steering column. Disconnect the cable loop from the pin on the steering column.
6. Pull the cluster away from the instrument panel.
7. Disconnect the electrical connections from the cluster. Disconnect the ground wire.
8. Remove the cluster from the instrument panel.
9. Reverse the removal procedure to install.

TOWN CAR

1. Disconnect the negative battery cable.
2. Remove the steering column cover and lower instrument panel trim cover. Remove the keyboard trim panel and trim panel on left of column.
3. Remove the 10 retaining instrument cluster trim cover screws and remove trim cover.
4. Remove the screws retaining the instrument cluster to the instrument panel and pull cluster forward. Reach behind the cluster, disconnect both feed plugs and ground wire from their receptacles in the cluster back plate.
5. Disconnect the speedometer cable by pressing on the flat

surface of the plastic connector (quick disconnect).
6. Remove the attaching screw from the transmission indicator cable bracket to the steering column. Detach the cable loop from the pin on the shift cane lever of the steering column.
7. Remove the plastic clamp from around steering column. Remove the cluster.
8. Installation is the reverse order of the removal procedure.

MARK VII

1. Disconnect the negative battery cable. Remove the screws retaining instrument finish panel and rotate top of panel toward steering wheel. Disconnect electrical and air sensor connectors at right hand portion of finish panel. Remove panel.
2. Remove 6 screws retaining instrument panel pad and rotate pad toward steering wheel and remove.
3. Remove 4 screws retaining instrument cluster to instrument panel and remove.
4. Disconnect electrical connector at lower left rear corner of cluster.
5. Installation is the reverse order of the removal procedure.

CONTINENTAL

1. Disconnect the negative battery cable. Remove the steering column shroud.
2. Remove left and right instrument panel mouldings. Mouldings are held in with retaining clips.
3. Remove the 2 center moulding retaining screws and remove moulding above climate control head.
4. Remove the ash tray.
5. Remove the 2 remaining screws and take out the center moulding.
6. Remove the screws retaining the instrument cluster finish panel and remove the panel.
7. Disconnect the transmission indicator cable at the steering column.

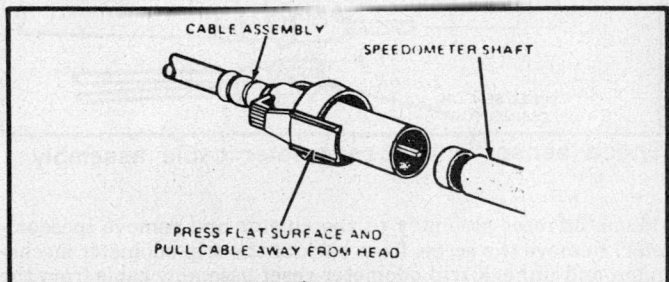

Speedometer cable quick connect

8. Remove the 4 screws retaining the cluster to the instrument panel and disconnect the electrical connector at the lower left corner of the cluster.
9. Remove the instrument cluster from the vehicle.
10. Installation is the reverse order of the removal procedure.

SPEEDOMETER

Removal and Installation

EXCEPT ELECTRONIC CLUSTER

1. Disconnect the negative battery cable.
2. Remove instrument cluster.
3. Disconnect speedometer cable by pressing flat surface and pulling cable away from head (quick connect).
4. Remove screws which attach the lens and mask to the cluster and remove lens and mask.
5. Remove 2 screws attaching speedometer head to cluster and remove speedometer.
6. On Lincoln and Mark VII, remove 2 screws holding trip

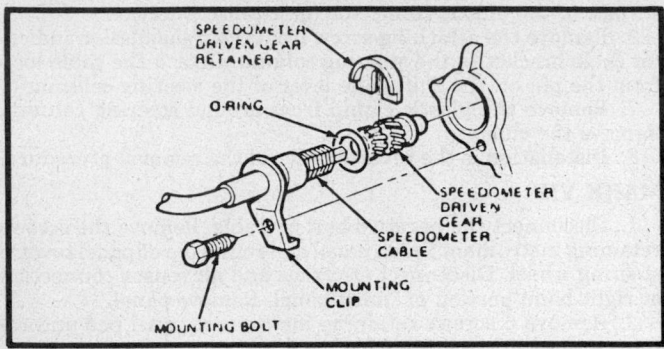

Speedometer cable-to-transmission mounting

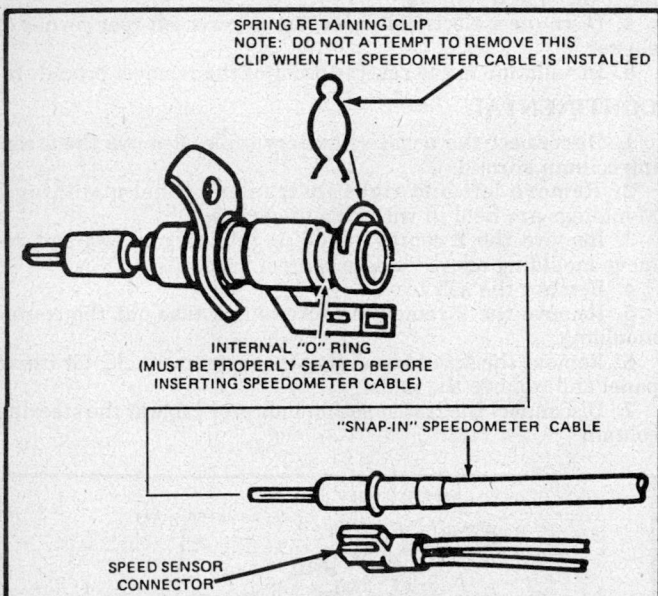

Speed sensor and speedometer cable assembly

odometer reset assembly to the cluster and remove speedometer. Remove the screw from back of the trip odometer mechanism and unhook trip odometer reset assembly cable from the slot in the trip odometer.

7. Installation is the reverse order of removal procedure.

ELECTRONIC

The electronic instrument speedometer, on vehicles equipped, is removed with the electronic instrument cluster. The speedometer is an integral part of the cluster assembly.

SPEEDOMETER CABLE

Removal and Installation

1. Disconnect the negative battery cable.
2. Remove clip at accelerator bracket stud.
3. Remove screws attaching cluster to instrument panel. Pull cluster rearward to gain access to cable.
4. Disconnect speedometer cable (quick disconnect) from speedometer head.
5. Pull speedometer cable out of the upper end of casing.
6. If cable is broken, raise vehicle and support it safely, remove the cable casing at the transmission.
7. Remove the cable and driven gear from the transmission, remove driven gear retainer and remove driven gear and core from cable.

8. Remove the lower part of cable from the lower end of casing.
9. Installation is the reverse order of removal procedures.
10. Be certain to follow cutting instructions to obtain exact length of new cable.

SPEED SENSOR

Removal and Installation

1. Disconnect the negative battery cable. Raise the vehicle on a hoist and remove the bolt retaining the speed sensor mounting clip to the transmission.
2. Remove the sensor and driven gear from the transmission.
3. Disconnect the electrical connector and speedometer cable from the speed sensor.
4. Disconnect the speedometer cable by pulling it out of the speed sensor.

NOTE: Do not attempt to remove the spring retainer clip with the speedometer cable in the sensor.

5. Remove the driven gear retainer and remove the driven gear from the sensor.
6. Position the driven gear to the speed sensor and install the gear retainer.
7. Connect the electrical connector.
8. Insure that the internal O-ring is properly seated in the sensor housing Snap the speedometer cable into the sensor housing.
9. Insert the sensor assembly into the transmission housing and install the retaining bolt and lower the vehicle.

Electrical Circuit Protectors

FUSIBLE LINKS

Fusible links are used to protect the main wiring harness and selected branches from complete burn-out, should a short circuit or electrical overload occur.

CIRCUIT BREAKERS

Circuit breakers are used on certain electrical components requiring high amperage, such as the headlamp circuit, electrical seats and/or windows to name a few. The advantage of the circuit breaker is its ability to open and close the electrical circuit as the load demands, rather than the necessity of a part replacement, should the circuit be opened with another protective device in line.

A list of some of the circuit breakers used, follows:

Headlight and High Beam—one 22 amp circuit breaker incorporated in the lighting switch.

Front and Rear Marker, Side Parking, Rear and License Lamps—
one 15 amp circuit breaker incorporated in the lighting switch.

Windshield Wiper Circuit and Rear Window—one 4.5 amp circuit breaker located in the windshield wiper switch.

Power WindowsCF33—there are 2–20 amp circuit breakers located in the starter relay and the fuse block. On the 1986 Continental and Mark VII there is a 30 amp circuit breaker used inplace of the 20 amp breaker.

Power Seats and Power Door Locks—a 20 amp circuit breaker located in the fuse block is used on all models except, LTD, Marquis, Crown Victoria, Grand Marquis. These models use a 30 amp circuit breaker, which is also located in the fuse block.

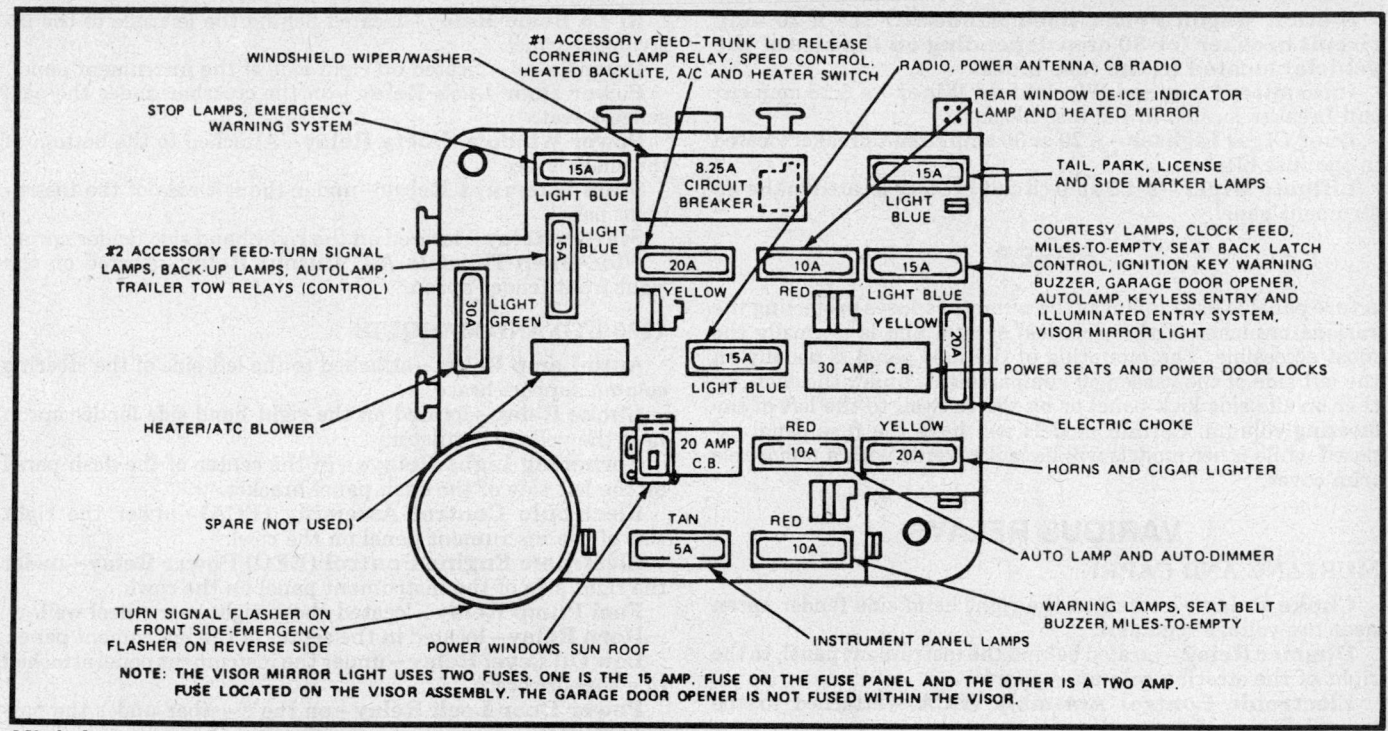

Mini fuse panel, typical of Lincoln Continental

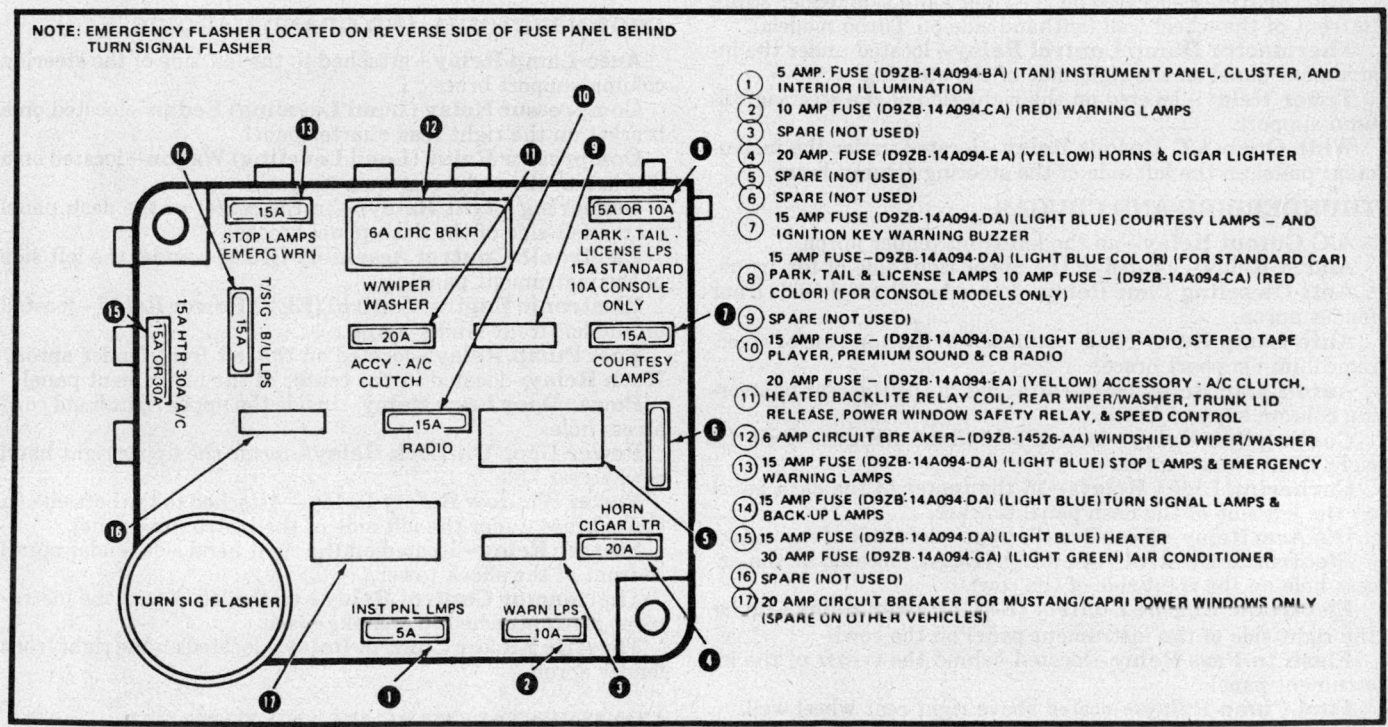

Fuse panel, typical of Thunderbird and Cougar

Station Wagon Power Back Window CF33—a 20 amp circuit breaker (or 30 amp depending on the size of the vehicle) located in the fuse block.

Intermitent 2-speed Windshield Wiper—a 8.25 amp circuit breaker located in the fuse block.

Door Cigar Lighter—A 20 or 30 amp circuit breaker located in the fuse block.

Liftgate Wiper—a 4.5 amp circuit breaker located in the instrument panel.

FUSES

A fuse panel is used to house the numerous fuses protecting the various branches of the electrical system and is normally the most accessible. The mounting of the fuse panel is usually on the left side of the passenger compartment, under the dash, either on the side kick panel or on the firewall to the left of the steering column. Certain models will have the fuse panel exposed while other models will have it covered with a removable trim cover.

VARIOUS RELAYS

MUSTANG AND CAPRI

Choke Relay—located on the right hand side fender apron near the voltage regulator.

Dimmer Relay—located behind the instrument panel, to the right of the steering column support.

Electronic Control Assembly (ECA)—attached to the lower left side of the cowl.

Electronic Engine Control (EEC) Power Relay—attached to the lower right side cowl near the electronic control assembly.

Fuel Pump Relay—located under the driver's seat.

Fuel Relays—at the center of the instrument panel behind the dash panel.

Horn Relay—located on right side of the instrument panel.

Low Oil Level Relay—located in the center of the dash panel.

Starter Relay—located on the right hand side fender apron in front of the wheel well (lefthand side on Turbo models).

Thermactor Dump Control Relay—located under the instrument panel on the right side of the steering.

Timer Relay—located on the right side of the steering column support.

Wide Open A/C Cutout Relay—located under the instrument panel on the left side of the steering column brace.

THUNDERBIRD AND COUGAR

A/C Cutout Relay—on the left front fender apron.

Alarm Relay—located in the upper right side of the trunk.

Anti-Dieseling Time Relay—located on the right side front fender apron.

Auto-Lamp Relay No.1—attached to the top rear of steering column support brace.

Auto-Lamp Relay No.2—attached to the top rear of steering column support brace.

Cooling Fan Relay—located behind the strut tower on the right front fender apron.

Cornering Light Relays—in the center of the dash panel on the left side of the dash panel bracket.

Dis-Arm Relay—located in the upper right side of the trunk.

Electronic Control Assembly (ECA)—located at the access hole on the right side of the cowl.

Electronic Engine Control (EEC) Power Relay—under the right side of the instrument panel on the cowl.

Flash to Pass Relay—located behind the center of the instrument panel.

Fuel Pump Relay—located above right rear wheel well.

Headlight Dimmer Relay—attached to the top rear of steering column support brace.

Hi-Lo Beam Relay—located behind the left side of the instrument panel.

Horn Relay—located on right side of the instrument panel.

Power Door Lock Relay—on the crossbar under the passengers seat.

Power Window Safety Relay—Attached to the bottom of the shake brace.

Start Interrupt Relay—under the left side of the instrument panel.

Starter Relay—located on the right hand side fender apron.

Wide-Open-Throttle A/C Cutout Relay—located on the right front fender apron.

1986 LTD AND MARQUIS

Auto-Lamp Relay—attached to the left side of the steering column support brace.

Choke Relay—located on the right hand side fender apron near the voltage regulator.

Cornering Light Relays—in the center of the dash panel on the left side of the dash panel bracket.

Electronic Control Assembly (ECA)—under the right side of the instrument panel on the cowl.

Electronic Engine Control (EEC) Power Relay—under the right side of the instrument panel on the cowl.

Fuel Pump Relay—located above right rear wheel well.

Horn Relay—located in the center of the instrument panel.

Low Oil Level Relay—under the instrument panel attached to a support brace.

Power Door Lock Relay—on the crossbar under the passengers seat.

Power Door Unlock Relay—on the crossbar under the passengers seat.

Power Window Safety Relay—Attached to the bottom of a shake brace under the left side of the instrument panel.

Starter Relay—located on the right front fender apron in front of the shock tower.

Wide-Open Throttle Cutout Switch—attached to the carburetor. On some vehicles, it is located on the right front fender well.

CROWN VICTORIA AND GRAND MARQUIS

Auto-Lamp Relay—attached to the left side of the steering column support brace.

Compressor Relay (Load Leveling) Sedan—located on a bracket on the right rear quarter panel.

Compressor Relay (Load Leveling) Wagon—located on a bracket on the right rear quarter panel.

Cornering Light Relays—in the center of the dash panel on the left side of the dash panel bracket.

Electronic Control Assembly (ECA)—under the left side of the instrument panel.

Electronic Engine Control (EEC) Power Relay—located on the left front fender apron.

Fuel Pump Relay—located on the left front fender apron.

Horn Relay—located in the center of the instrument panel.

Power Door Lock Relay—inside the upper right hand cowl access hole.

Power Door Un-Lock Relay—inside the upper right hand cowl access hole.

Power Window Safety Relay—Attached to the bottom of a shake brace under the left side of the instrument panel.

Starter Relay—located on the right hand side fender apron in front of the shock tower.

Thermactor Control Relay—on the left side of the instrument panel attached to a shake brace.

Throttle Kicker Control Relay—located on the right front fender apron.

CONTINENTAL, MARK VII AND TOWN CAR

A/C Cut-Out Relay—located on the left front fender apron.

VIEW SHOWING CORRECTLY ADJUSTED DUMP VALVE

DUMP VALVE

PAD ON BRAKE PEDAL

.050" DUMP VALVE BLACK HOUSING MUST CLEAR WHITE PLASTIC PAD ON BRAKE PEDAL WITH BRAKE PEDAL PULLED TO REARMOST POSITION

Dump valve adjustment

Air Suspension Relay (Load Leveling)—located on the left front fender apron.

Alarm Relay—located under the right side of the package tray in the trunk.

Anti-Theft Starter Interrupt Relay—located under the instrument panel on the left side support brace.

Auto-Lamp Relay—attached to the left side of the steering column support brace.

Cooling Fan Relay—located on the right front fender apron.

Cornering Light Relays—in the center of the dash panel on the left side of the dash panel bracket.

Defrost Switch/Relay—located in the center of the instrument panel.

Disarm Relay—located under the right side of the package tray in the trunk.

Electronic Control Assembly (ECA)—located on the right side of the cowl.

Electronic Engine Control (EEC) Relay—located on the right side of the cowl.

Flash to Pass Relay—attached to the instrument panel brace.

Fuel Pump Relay—located on the left hand deck-lid hinge support.

Heated Seat Relays—located under the driver's or the passenger's seat.

Hi-Lo Beam Relay—attached to the instrument panel brace (above the fuse block on the 1985–87 Continental).

Horn Relay—located in the center of the instrument panel.

Interior Light Relay—in the center of the dash panel on the left side of the dash panel bracket.

Inverter Relay—located under the right side of the package tray in the trunk.

Power Antenna Relay—located in the right side of the trunk.

Power Mirror Relays—are located in the left side of the trunk.

Power Window Safety Relay—Attached to the bottom of a shake brace under the left side of the instrument panel.

Starter Relay—located on the left hand side fender apron.

TURN SIGNAL AND HAZARD FLASHERS

The turn signal and hazard flashers are located in the fuse box.

Speed Control

Refer to "Chilton's Chassis Electronics Service Manual" for additional coverage.

ACTUATOR CABLE

Linkage Adjustment

1. If equipped with a carburetor, set stroke on hot idle condition with the throttle positioner solenoid disengaged.
2. Remove the speed control cable retaining clip.
3. Push speed control cable through adjuster until a slight tension is felt.
4. Insert the cable retaining clip and snap into place.

VACUUM DUMP VALVE

Adjustment

The vacuum dump valve is movable in its mounting bracket. It should be adjusted so that it is closed (no vacuum leaks) when the brake pedal is in its normal release position (not depressed) and open when the pedal is depressed. Use a hand vacuum pump to make this adjustment.

COOLING AND HEATING SYSTEMS

WATER PUMP

Removal and Installation

1. Drain the cooling system.
2. Disconnect the negative battery cable.
3. On vehicles with power steering, remove the drive belt.
4. If the vehicle is equipped with air conditioning, remove the idler pulley bracket and air conditioner drive belt. On supercharged engines, relieve the tension from the automatic tension adjuster and remove the belt.
5. On engines with a thermactor pump, remove the belt.
6. Disconnect the lower radiator hose and heater hose from the water pump.
7. Remove the retaining screws and position the fan shroud rearward.
8. Remove the fan and spacer from the engine and if the vehicle is equipped with a fan shroud, remove the fan and shroud from the engine as an assembly.
9. On 4 cylinder engines, remove the cam belt outer cover.
10. On vehicles equipped with water pump mounted alterna-

tors, loosen alternator mounting bolts, remove the alternator belt and remove the alternator adjusting arm bracket from the water pump.

11. Loosen bypass hose at water pump, if equipped.
12. Remove water pump retaining screws and remove pump from engine. On 3.8L engines, the 2 bolts through the thermostat housing must also be removed; they retain the lower portion of the pump housing.
13. Clean any gasket material from the pump mounting surface.
14. Remove the heater hose fitting from the old pump and install it on the new pump.
15. Coat both sides of the new gasket with a water-resistant sealer, then install the pump reversing the procedure.

Electric Cooling Fan

System Operation

The electric cooling fan system on 2.3L equipped Thunderbird

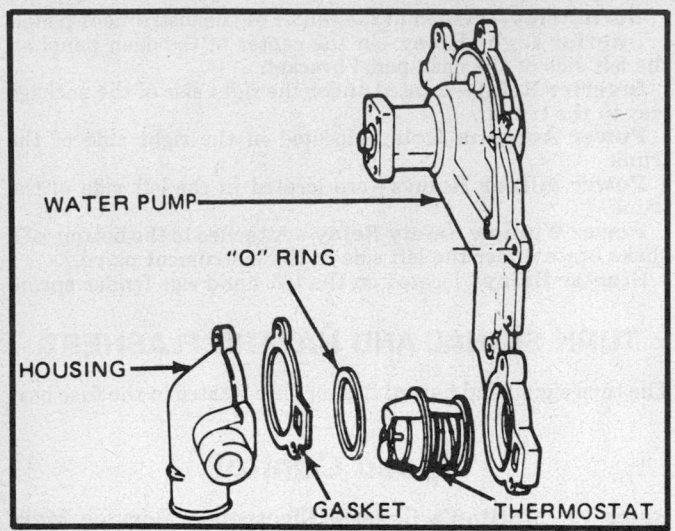

Water pump and thermostat installation, V6 engine

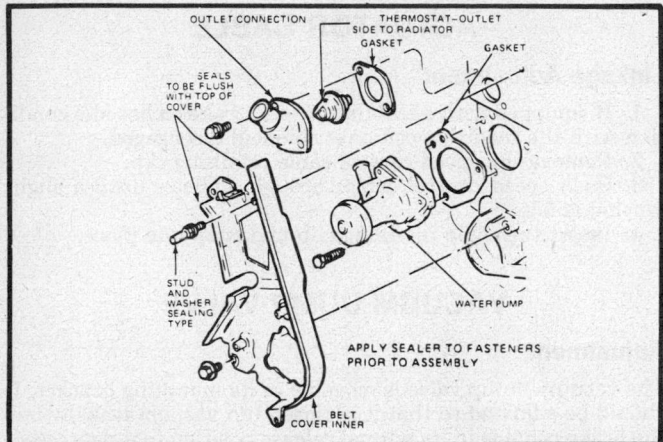

Water pump, thermostat, and inner timing belt cover on 2300 cc engine

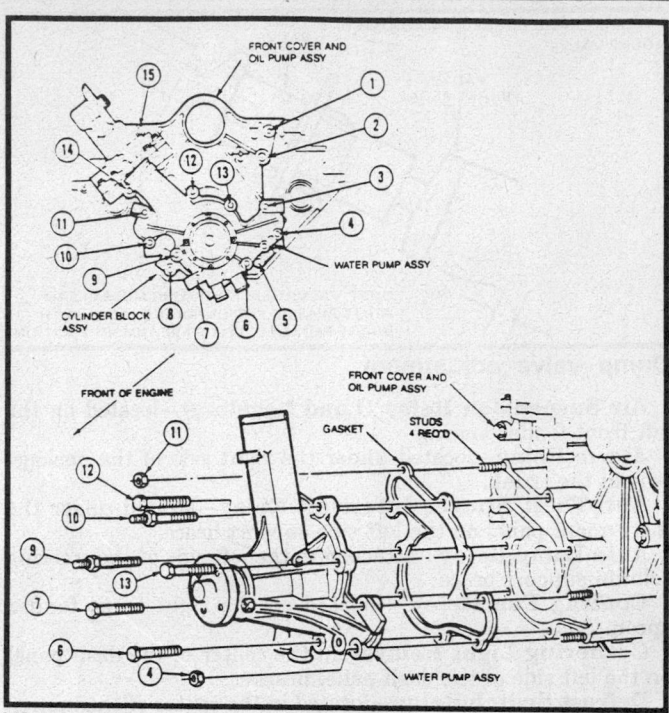

Water pump mounting—3.8L SC engine

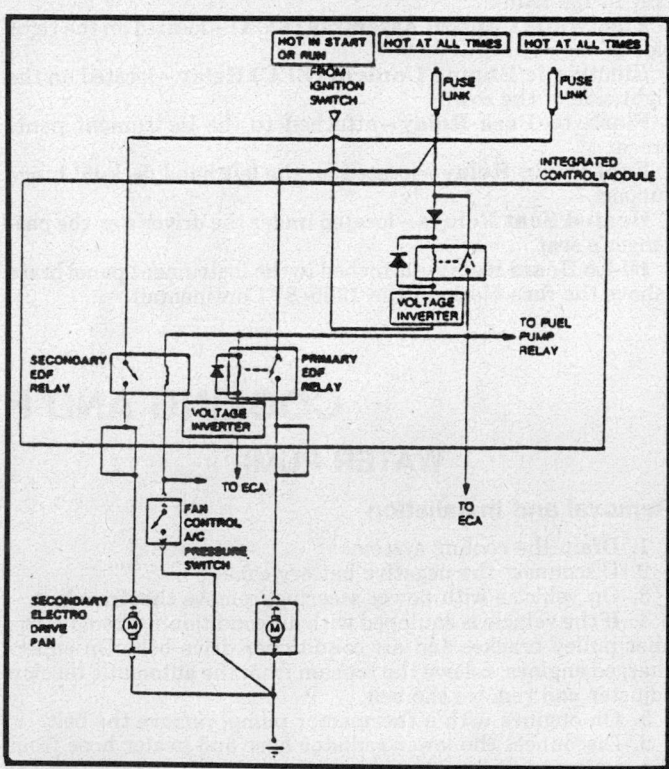

Cooling fan wiring schematic—Thunderbird

and Mustang, is designed to provide engine cooling whenever the A/C is turned on or when the coolant temperature exceeds 221°F. This is accomplished with a cooling fan controller, the controller consists of 2 relays mounted a printed circuit board. One relay powers the cooling fan and the other powers the A/C compressor coil, solid state circuitry controls the timing for the relays. The cooling fan controller is located under the left side of the instrument panel near the steering column.

When the engine coolant temperature reaches 221°F the cooling fan temperature switch (located in the heater hose tube) will close to complete the ground circuit to the to the fan relay coil in the controller. This will activate the fan which will operate until the coolant temperature is decreased to approximately 201°F. During A/C operation, the A/C clutch cycling pressure switch controls the evaporater temperature by controlling the compressor operation. The pressure switch will cause the fan relay to operate first, then the A/C relay will operate if voltage is available at the fan motor terminal. The A/C compressor will cycle with the pressure switch.

Removal and Installation

1. Disconnect the negative battery cable and remove the fan wiring harness from the routing clip.
2. Disconnect the wiring harness from the fan motor connec-

tor and pull up on the single lock finger to separate the connectors.
3. Remove the 4 mounting bracket attaching screws and remove the fan assembly from the vehicle.
4. Remove the retaining clip from the end of the motor shaft and remove the fan.

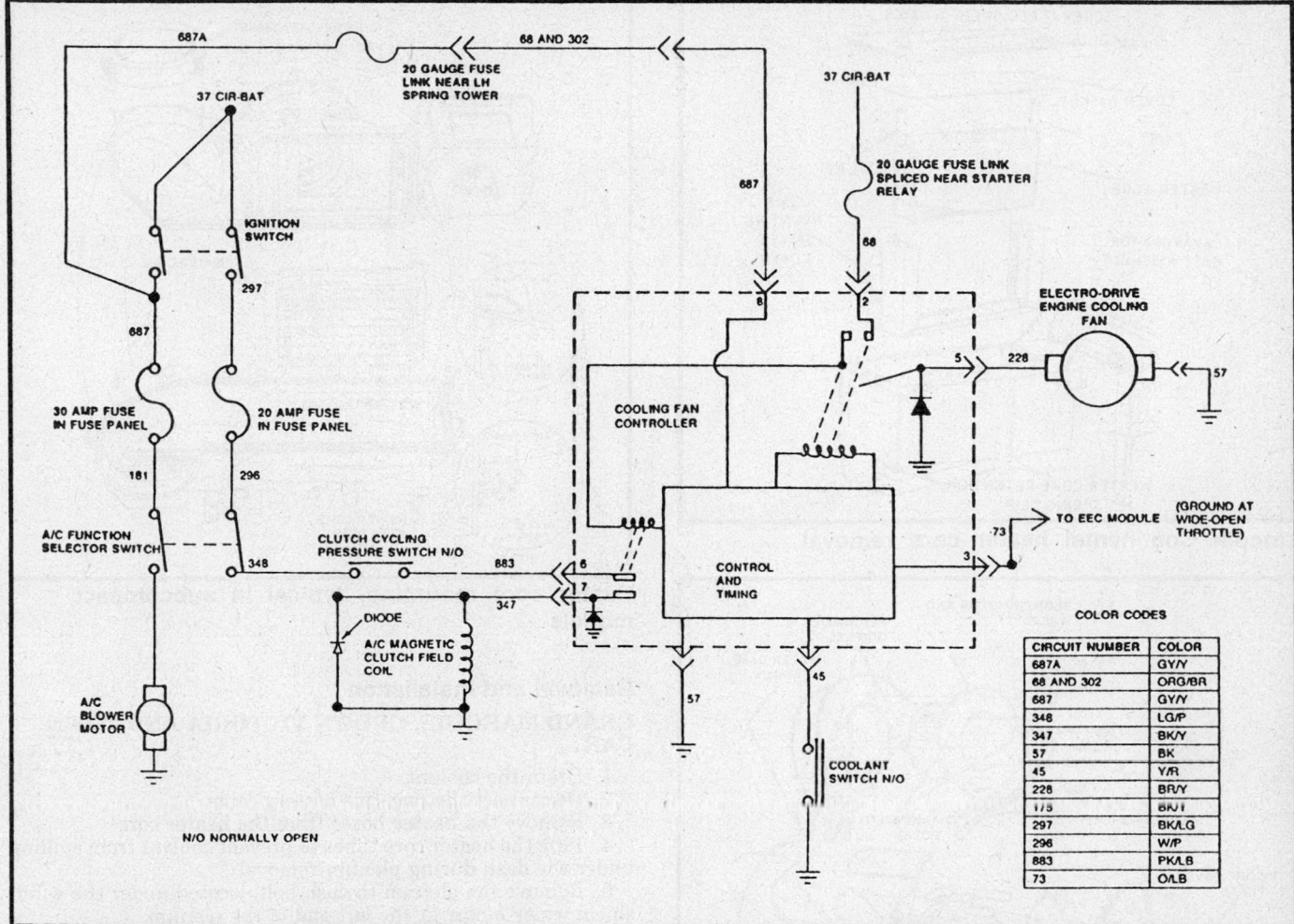

Cooling fan wiring schematic — Mustang

5. Remove the nuts attaching the fan motor to the mounting bracket.

NOTE: After the retaining clip has been removed there may be a small burr left on the shaft, this burr must be removed in order to remove the fan off of the motor shaft.

6. Position the fan motor on the mounting bracket and torque the attaching nuts to 70–95 inch lbs.

7. Install the fan and retaining clip on the motor shaft and position the fan assembly in the vehicle with the mounting bracket attaching screws.

8. Connect the motor wiring connector to the wiring harness and be sure that the lock finger on the connector snaps firmly into place.

9. Connect the negative battery cable and check the fan for proper operation.

BLOWER MOTOR

Removal and Installation

GRAND MARQUIS, CROWN VICTORIA AND TOWN CAR

1. Disconnect the negative battery cable.

2. Disconnect the blower motor lead connector from the wiring harness connector.

3. Remove the blower motor cooling tube from the blower motor.

4. Remove the 4 retaining screws.

5. Turn the motor and wheel assembly slightly to the right so that the bottom edge of the mounting plate follows the contour of the wheel well splash panel. Lift up on the blower and remove it from the blower housing.

6. Installation is the reverse of removal.

CONTINENTAL, MARK VII, THUNDERBIRD, COUGAR, LTD, MARQUIS, 1986 MUSTANG AND CAPRI

1. Disconnect the negative battery cable.

2. Remove the air inlet duct and blower housing assembly from the vehicle.

3. Remove the 4 retaining screws.

4. Turn the motor and wheel assembly slightly to the right so that the bottom edge of the mounting plate follows the contour of the wheel well splash panel. Lift up on the blower and remove it from the blower housing.

5. Installation is the reverse of removal.

1987–90 MUSTANG

1. Disconnect the negative battery cable. Loosen glove com-

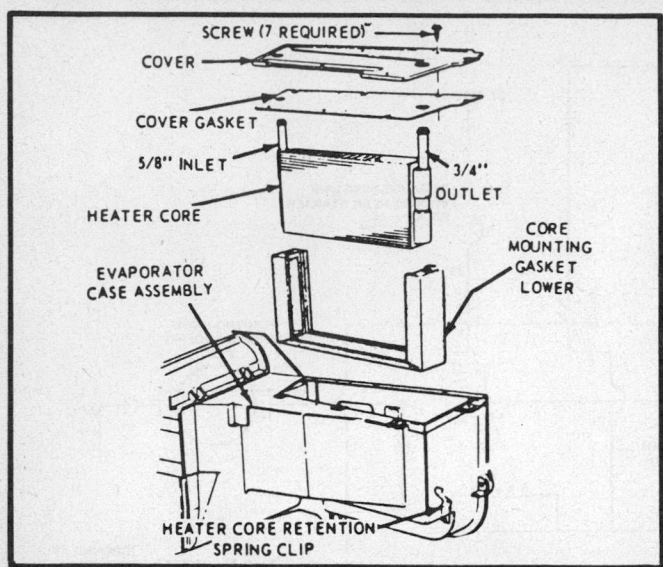

Lincoln Continental heater core removal

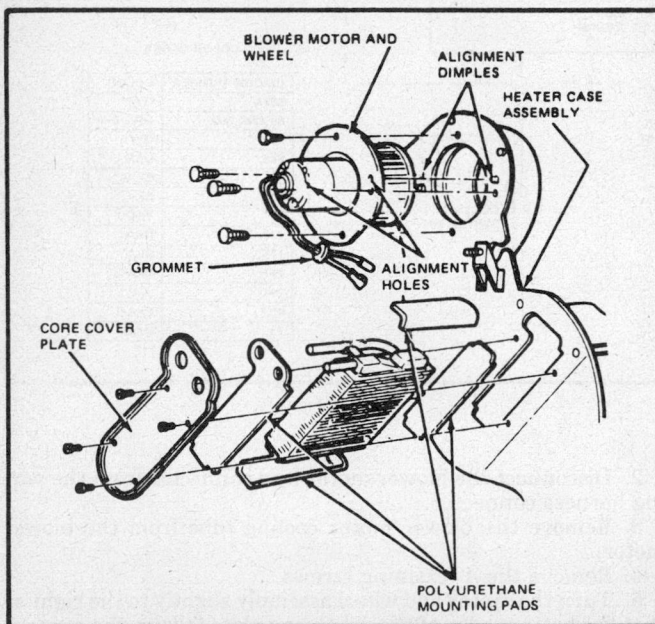

Heater blower and core installation in Cougar, LTD II and Thunderbird — typical

partment assembly by squeezing the sides together to disengage the retainer tabs.

2. Let the glove compartment and door hang down in front of instrument panel and remove blower motor cooling hose.

3. Disconnect electrical wiring harness. Remove 4 screws attaching motor to housing. Pull motor and wheel out of housing.

4. Installation is the reverse of the removal procedure.

HEATER CORE WITHOUT AIR CONDITIONING

Refer to "Chilton's Auto Heating and Air Conditioning Manual" for additional coverage.

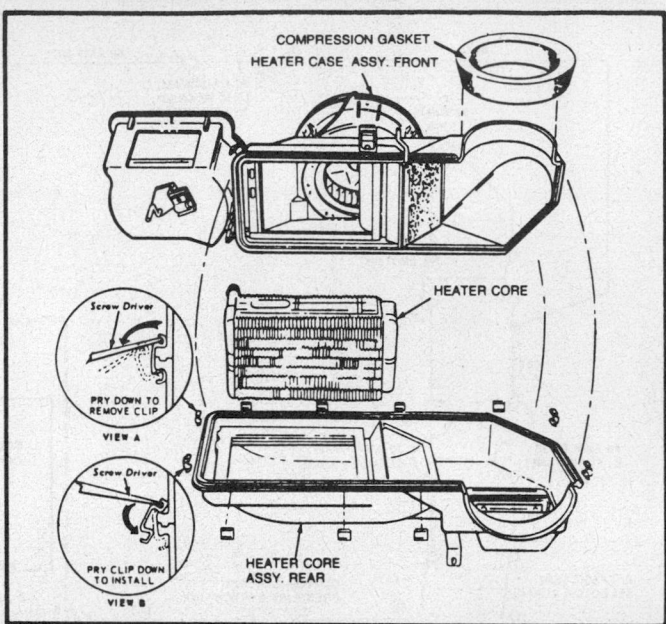

Heater core mounting, typical in subcompact models

Removal and Installation

GRAND MARQUIS, CROWN VICTORIA AND TOWN CAR

1. Drain the coolant.
2. Disconnect the negative battery cable.
3. Remove the heater hoses from the heater core.
4. Plug the heater core tubes to prevent coolant from spilling under the dash during plenum removal.
5. Remove the plenum to dash bolt, located under the windshield wiper motor at the left end of the plenum.
6. Remove the retaining nut from the heater case (engine side).
7. Disconnect the vacuum supply hose from the vacuum fitting and push the grommet and hose into the passenger compartment.
8. Remove the glove box assembly.
9. Loosen the right door sillplate and remove the right side cowl trim panel.
10. Remove the lower right instrument panel to side cowl bolt.
11. Remove the instrument panel pad.
12. Remove the temperature control cable from the top of the plenum. Then, disconnect the temperature control cable from the blend door crank arm.
13. Remove the push clip attaching the center register duct bracket to the plenum and rotate the bracket up to the right.
14. Disconnect the vacuum jumper harness at the multiple vacuum connector near the floor air distribution duct.
15. Disconnect the white vacuum hose from the outside air door vacuum motor.
16. Remove the 2 screws attaching the seat side of the floor air distribution duct to the plenum.

NOTE: **It may be necessary to remove the 2 screws attaching the lower panel door vacuum motor to the mounting bracket to gain access to the floor air distribution duct screw.**

17. Remove the plastic pushpin fastener from the floor air distribution duct and remove the duct.
18. Remove the remaining plenum retaining nuts from the lower flange of the plenum.

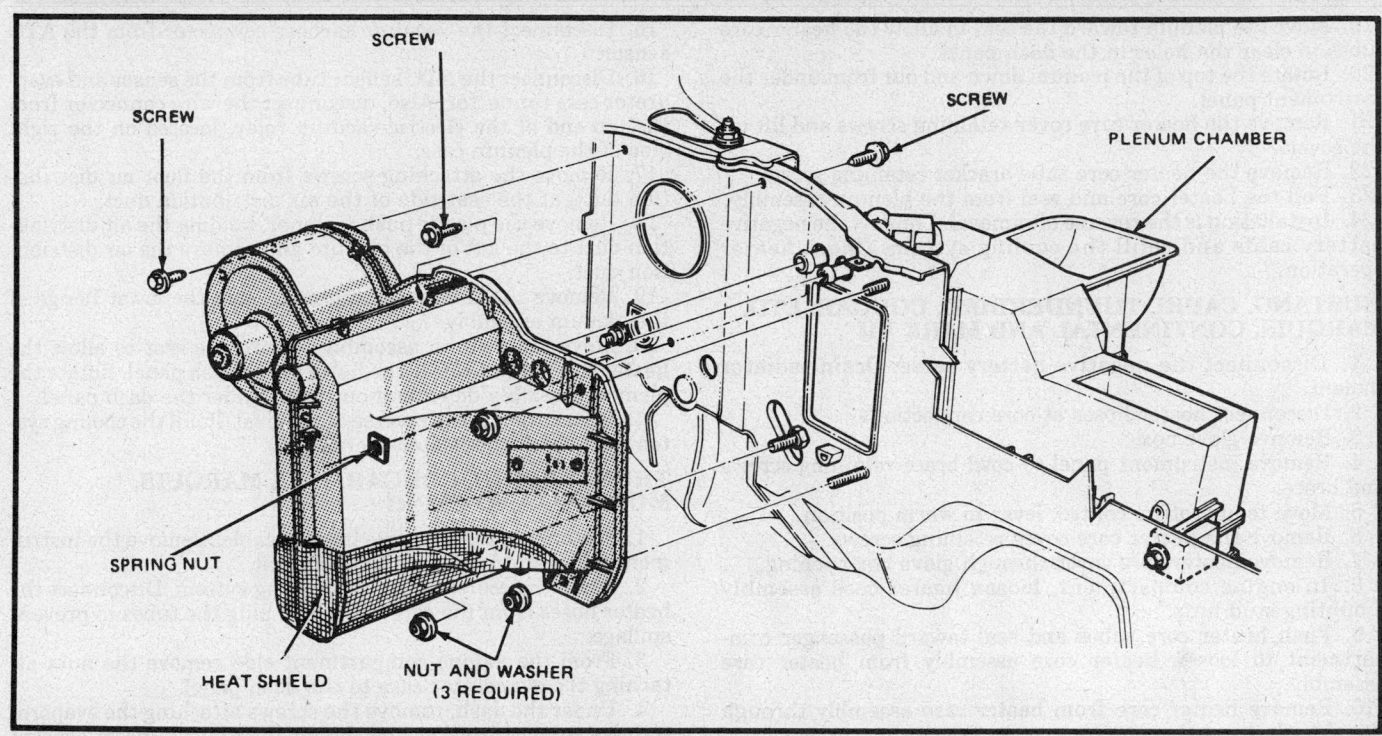

Heater core housing removal, typical of Lincoln

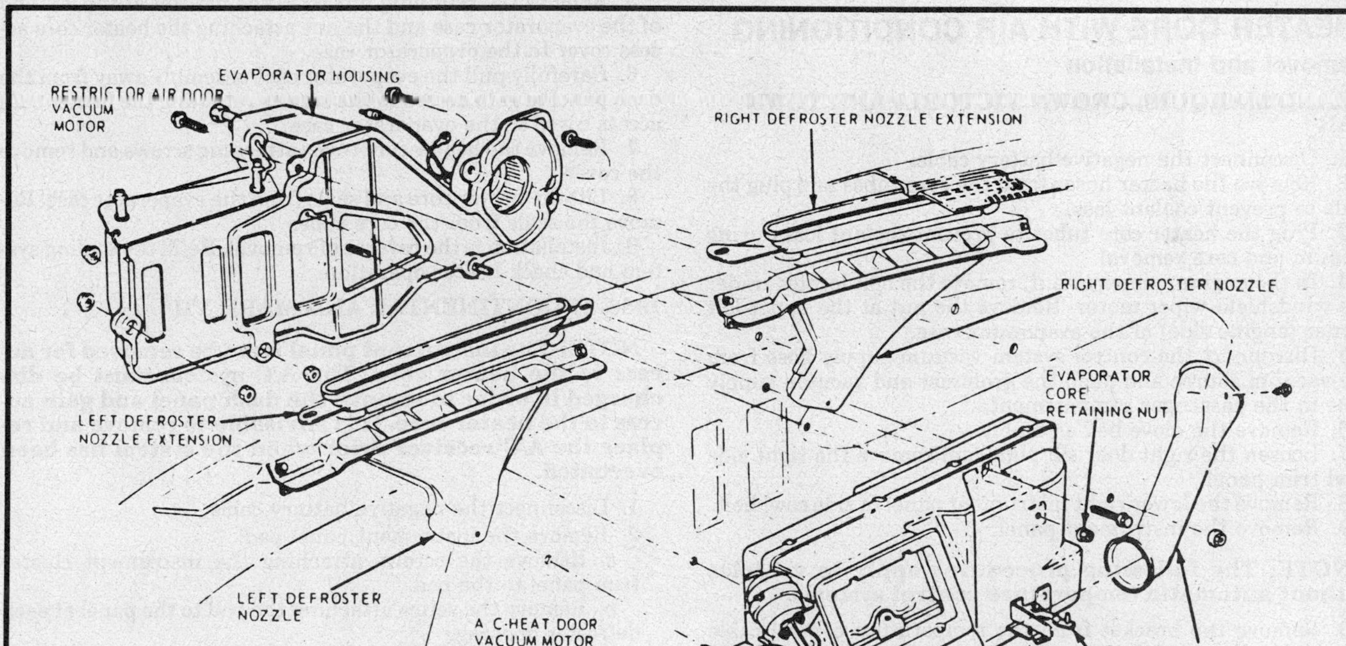

Exploded view of a typical heater/air conditioner assembly used in full sized vehicles

19. Move the plenum toward the seat to allow the heater core tubes to clear the holes in the dash panel.

20. Rotate the top of the plenum down and out from under the instrument panel.

21. Remove the heater core cover retaining screws and lift off the cover.

22. Remove the heater core tube bracket retaining screw.

23. Pull the heater core and seal from the plenum assembly.

24. Installation is the reverse of removal. Connect the negative battery cable and refill the cooling system. Check heater operation.

MUSTANG, CAPRI, THUNDERBIRD, COUGAR, LTD, MARQUIS, CONTINENTAL AND MARK VII

1. Disconnect the negative battery cable. Drain radiator coolant.

2. Disconnect heater hoses at core connections.

3. Remove glove box.

4. Remove instrument panel to cowl brace retaining screws and brace.

5. Move temperature control lever to warm position.

6. Remove the heater core cover retaining screws.

7. Remove heater core cover through glove box opening.

8. In engine compartment, loosen heater case assembly mounting stud nuts.

9. Push heater core tubes and seal toward passenger compartment to loosen heater core assembly from heater case assembly.

10. Remove heater core from heater case assembly through the glove box opening.

11. Reverse procedure for installation.

HEATER CORE WITH AIR CONDITIONING

Removal and Installation

GRAND MARQUIS, CROWN VICTORIA AND TOWN CAR

1. Disconnect the negative battery cable.

2. Remove the heater hoses from the core tubes and plug the ends to prevent coolant loss.

3. Plug the heater core tubes to prevent coolant loss during plenum and core removal.

4. In the engine compartment, remove the bolt located under the windshield wiper motor. Remove the nut at the upper left corner (engine side) of the evaporator case.

5. Disconnect the control system vacuum supply hose from the vacuum source and push the grommet and vacuum supply hose in the passenger compartment.

6. Remove the glove box assembly.

7. Loosen the right door sill plate and remove the right side cowl trim panel.

8. Remove the lower right instrument panel to side cowl bolt.

9. Remove the instrument panel.

NOTE: The following procedures apply to vehicles without automatic temperature control systems.

10. Remove the bracket from the temperature control cable housing at the top of the plenum assembly. Disconnect the temperature control cable from the blend door crank arm.

11. Remove the push clip attaching the center register duct bracket to the plenum and rotate the bracket up to the right.

12. Disconnect the vacuum jumper harness at the multiple vacuum connector near the floor air distribution duct.

13. Disconnect the white vacuum hose from the outside recirculating door vacuum motor.

NOTE: The following procedures apply to vehicles with automatic temperature controls.

14. Disconnect the temperature control cable from the ATC sensor.

15. Disconnect the vacuum harness connector from the ATC sensor.

16. Disconnect the ATC sensor tube from the sensor and evaporator case connector. Also, disconnect the wire connector from the top end of the electric-vacuum relay, located on the right side of the plenum case.

17. Remove the attaching screws from the floor air distribution duct, at the seat side of the air distribution duct.

18. Remove the plastic push fastener, holding the air distribution duct to the left of the plenum and remove the air distribution duct.

19. Remove the final retaining nuts from the lower flange of the plenum assembly.

20. Move the plenum assembly toward the seat to allow the heater core tubes to clear the holes in the dash panel. Rotate the plenum assembly down and out from under the dash panel.

21. Installation is the reverse of removal. Refill the cooling system and check the heater operation.

THUNDERBIRD, COUGAR, LTD, MARQUIS, MUSTANG AND CAPRI

1. Disconnect the negative battery cable. Remove the instrument panel and lay it on the front seat.

2. Drain the coolant from the cooling system. Disconnect the heater hoses from the core tubes and plug the tubes to prevent spillage.

3. From the engine compartment side remove the nuts attaching the evaporator case to the dash panel.

4. Under the dash, remove the screws attaching the evaporator case support bracket and the air inlet duct support bracket to the cowl top panel.

5. Remove the retaining nut from the bracket at the left end of the evaporator case and the nut attaching the heater core access cover to the evaporator case.

6. Carefully pull the evaporator case assembly away from the dash panel to gain access to the screws retaining the heater core access cover to the evaporator case.

7. Remove the heater core cover attaching screws and remove the cover.

8. Lift the heater core and seals from the evaporator case. Remove the seals from the core tubes.

9. Installation is the reverse of removal. Refill the cooling system and check heater operation.

1986–87 CONTINENTAL AND MARK VII

NOTE: The instrument panel must be removed for access to the heater core. The A/C system must be discharged in order to remove the dash panel and gain access to the heater core. It is advisable to remove and replace the A/C receiver drier when the system has been evacuated.

1. Disconnect the negative battery cable.

2. Remove the instrument panel pad:
   a. Remove the screws attaching the instrument cluster trim panel to the pad.
   b. Remove the screw attaching the pad to the panel at each defroster opening.
   c. Remove the screws attaching the edge of the pad to the panel.

3. Remove the steering column opening cover.

4. Remove the nut and bracket holding the steering column to the instrument panel and lay the column across the seat.

5. Remove the instrument panel to brake pedal support screw at the column opening.

6. Remove the screws attaching the lower brace to the panel below the radio and below the glove compartment.

7. Disconnect the temperature cable from the door and case bracket.

8. Unplug the 7 port vacuum hose connectors at the evaporator case.

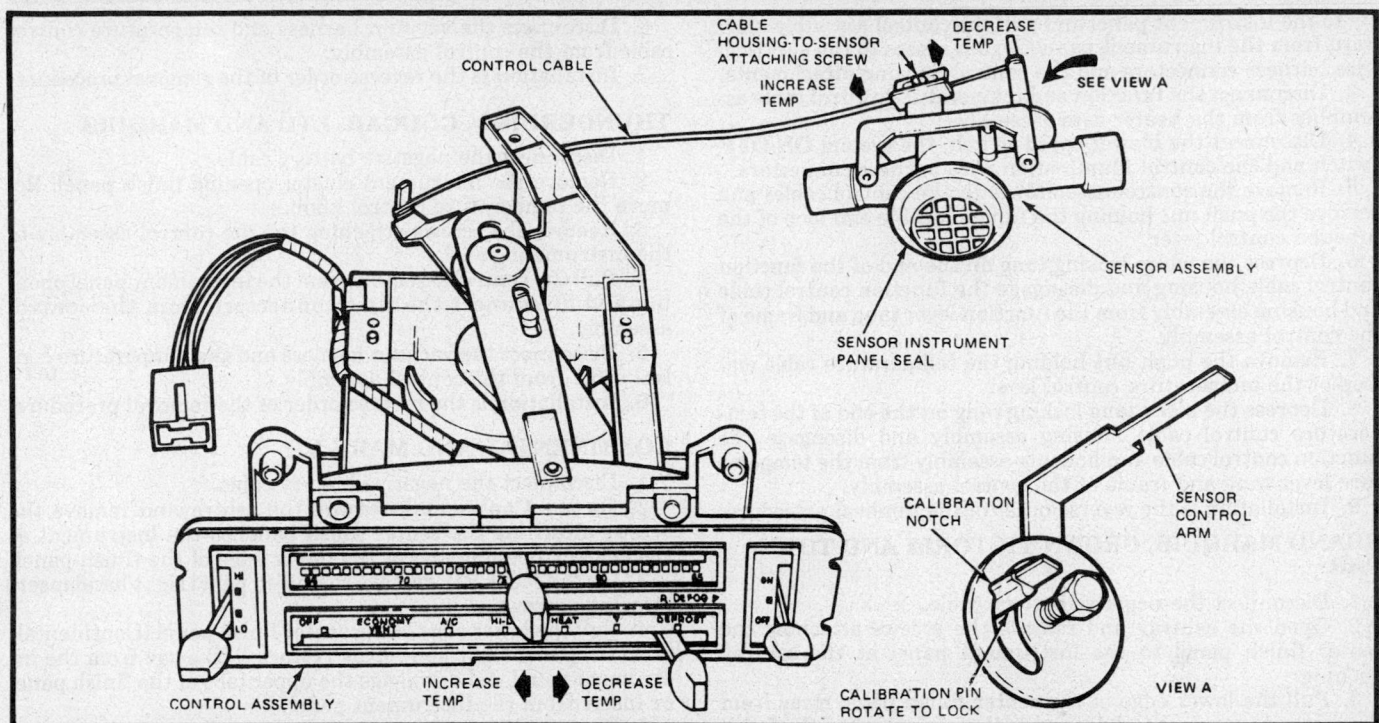

Heater/air conditioner control unit with the automatic temperature control system

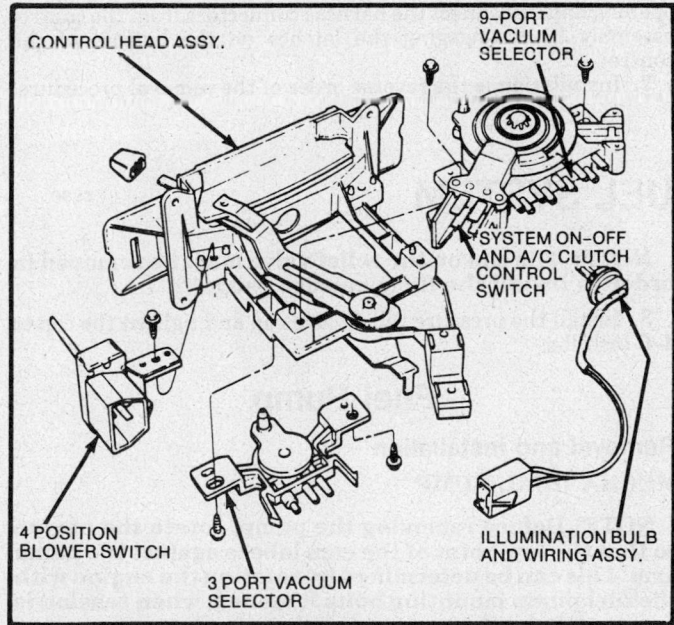

Typical heater/air conditioner control unit

9. Disconnect the resistor wire connector and the blower motor feed wire.

10. Remove the screws attaching the top of the panel to the cowl and support the panel while removing the screws.

11. Remove 1 screw at each end attaching the panel to the cowl panels.

12. Move the panel rearward and disconnect the speedometer cable and any wires preventing the panel from laying flat on the seat.

13. Drain the coolant and disconnect the heater hoses from the heater core, plug the heater core tubes.

14. Remove the nuts retaining the evaporator case to the firewall in the engine compartment.

15. Remove the case support bracket screws and air inlet duct support bracket.

16. Remove the nut retaining the bracket to the dash panel at the left side of the evaporator case and the nut retaining the bracket below the case to dash panel.

17. Pull the case assembly away from the panel to get to the screws retaining the heater core cover to the case.

18. Remove the cover screws and cover, lift the heater core and seals out of the case assembly.

19. Installation is the reverse order of the removal procedure.

CONTROL ASSEMBLY

The AC and/or heater control assembly is mounted to the instrument panel and is surrounded by a trim or finish panel. In most control assembly removal procedures, the instrument cluster trim panel must be removed to expose the control assembly retaining screws. In other vehicle model applications, a separate trim cover is used which may incorporate the radio and ash receiver.

The blower switch is part of the control assembly and can be replaced after the control assembly is removed from the instrument panel.

Either vacuum lines and/or connecting cables are used to control the air flow and temperature settings. These controlling links must be disconnected to remove the control assembly from the instrument panel.

Removal and Installation
MUSTANG AND CAPRI

1. Disconnect the negative battery cable. Remove the attaching screws securing the top edge of the instrument cluster bezel and remove the instrument cluster bezel for access to the control assembly.

2. Remove the attaching screws securing the control assem-

bly to the instrument panel and pull the control assembly rearward from the instrument panel to gain access to the electrical wire harness connectors and the control housing attachments.

3. Disconnect the function and temperature control cable assemblies from the heater case assembly.

4. Disconnect the blower speed switch, the system **ON/OFF** switch and the control illumination wire harness connectors.

5. Remove the control assembly with the control cables and remove the push nut holding the function cable end loop of the function control lever.

6. Depress the white locking tang on the end of the function control cable housing and disengage the function control cable and housing assembly from the function lever tang and frame of the control assembly.

7. Remove the push nut holding the temperature cable end loop of the temperature control lever.

8. Depress the black tang locking tang on the end of the temperature control cable housing assembly and disengage the function control cable and housing assembly from the temperature lever tang and frame of the control assembly.

9. Installation is the reverse order of the removal procedure.

GRAND MARQUIS, CROWN VICTORIA AND TOWN CAR

1. Disconnect the negative battery cable.

2. Open the ashtray and remove the screws attaching the center finish panel to the instrument panel at the ashtray opening.

3. Pull the lower edge of the center finish panel away from the instrument panel and disengage the upper tabs of the finish panel from the instrument panel.

4. Remove the attaching screws holding the control assembly to the instrument panel.

5. Pull the control assembly away from the instrument panel opening and disconnect the wire connectors from the control assembly.

6. Disconnect the vacuum harness and temperature control cable from the control assembly.

7. Installation is the reverse order of the removal procedure.

THUNDERBIRD, COUGAR, LTD AND MARQUIS

1. Disconnect the negative battery cable.

2. Remove the instrument cluster opening finish panel. Remove the temperature control knob.

3. Remove the screws attaching the the control assembly to the instrument panel.

4. Pull the control assembly from the instrument panel opening and disconnect the wire connectors from the control assembly.

5. Disconnect the vacuum harness and the temperature control cable from the control assembly.

6. Installation is the reverse order of the removal procedure.

CONTINENTAL AND MARK VII

1. Disconnect the negative battery cable.

2. On the Continental, remove the ashtray and remove the screws attaching the center finish panel to the instrument at the ashtray opening and at the upper edge of the finish panel.

3. On the Mark VII, remove the finish panel right hand insert attaching screws.

4. Pull the lower edge of the center finish panel (Continental) or finish panel right hand insert (Mark VII) away from the instrument panel and disengage the upper tabs of the finish panel or insert from the instrument panel.

5. Remove the attaching screws holding the control assembly to the instrument panel.

6. Slide the control assembly out from the instrument panel opening and disconnect the harness connectors from the control assembly by disengaging the latches on the bottom of the control.

7. Installation is the reverse order of the removal procedure.

CARBURETED FUEL SYSTEM

FUEL SYSTEM SERVICE PRECAUTION

When working with the fuel system certain precautions should be taken;

1. Always work in a well ventilated area

2. Keep a dry chemical (Class B) fire extinguisher near the work area

3. Always disconnect the negative battery cable

4. Do not make any repairs to the fuel system until all the necessary steps for repair have been reviewed

NOTE: Most Ford vehicles are equipped with an inertia switch that shuts off the fuel pump should the vehicle be hit in the rear. This switch works as a circuit breaker and can be reset. It is normally located in the trunk and there is usually a sticker marking its location. It should be checked first when a fuel supply problem is evident.

FUEL SYSTEM PRESSURE RELIEF

Procedure

1. If the fuel charging assembly is mounted to the engine, remove the fuel tank cap. Using fuel pressure gauge T80L–9974–A, install it to the relief valve and release the pressure from the system by opening the pressure relief valve.

NOTE: The cap on the relief valve must be removed in order to install the fuel pressure gauge.

3. Install the pressure relief valve cap and tighten the cap to 4–6 inch lbs.

Fuel Pump

Removal and Installation

MECHANICAL PUMP

NOTE: Before removing the pump, rotate the engine so that the low point of the cam lobe is against the pump arm. This can be determined by rotating the engine with the fuel pump mounting bolts loosened; when tension is removed from the arm, proceed.

1. Disconnect the negative battery cable. Remove the inlet and outlet lines from the pump.

2. Remove the fuel pump retaining bolts and remove the pump gasket.

3. Clean all gasket material from the pump mounting surface on the engine and apply a coat of oil-resistant sealer to the new gasket.

4. Position pump on the engine and install retaining screws.

5. Reinstall lines, start engine and check for leaks.

NOTE: If resistance is felt while positioning the fuel pump on the block, the camshaft eccentric is in the high position. To ease installation, connect a remote engine

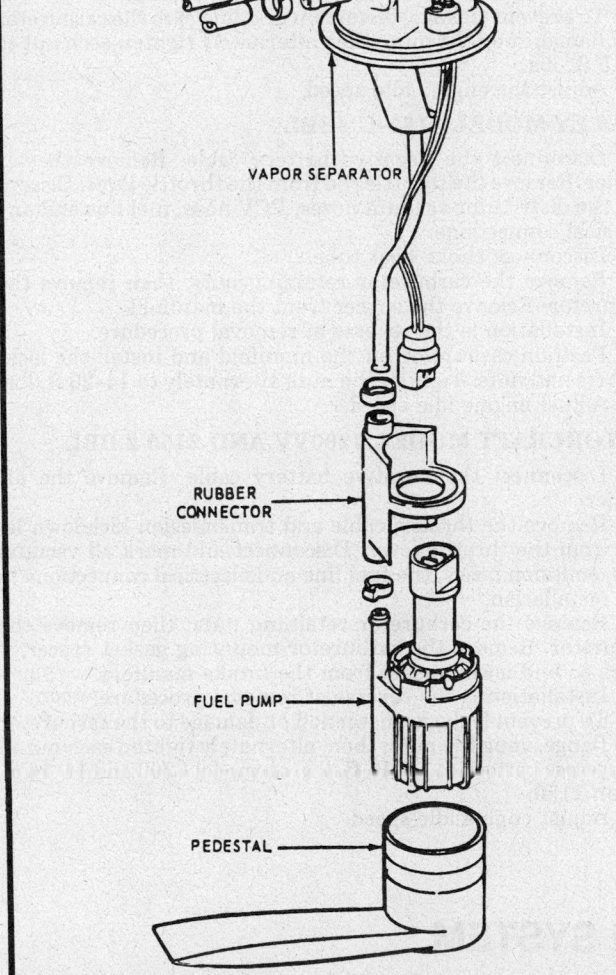

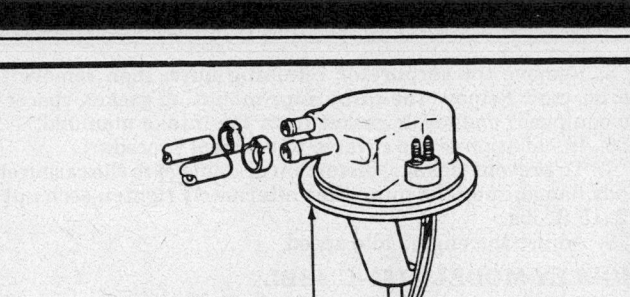

VAPOR SEPARATOR

RUBBER CONNECTOR

FUEL PUMP

PEDESTAL

Tank mounted electric fuel pump, typical

starter switch to the engine and tap the remote switch until resistance fades.

ELECTRIC PUMP

1. Disconnect the negative battery cable.
2. Relieve the fuel system pressure.
3. Raise and safely support the rear of the vehicle.
4. Disconnect the electrical connectors. Disconnect the inlet and outlet fuel lines.
5. Bend down the retaining tab and remove the pump from the mounting bracket ring.
7. Install in reverse order, make sure the pump is indexed correctly in the mounting bracket insulator.

Carburetor

IDLE SPEED

Adjustment

EXCEPT 7200VV

NOTE: If equipped with automatic overdrive transmission, see idle speed adjustment section following.

1. Place the transmission in **P**. Apply the emergency brake and block the wheels.
2. Bring the engine to normal operating temperature. Turn off all accessories and connect a tachometer.
3. Disconnect and plug the vacuum hose at the EGR valve. Place the fast idle adjustment on the specified step of the fast idle cam, (Check the underhood sticker). Check/adjust fast idle rpm to specification. Increase the engine speed momentarily, place fast idle adjustment on the specified step and recheck fast idle rpm. Remove plug and reconnect EGR vacuum hose.
4. Place A/C-heat selector in the **OFF** position. Place transmission in specified position. Check/adjust curb idle rpm, if adjustment is required, loosen TSP/dashpot mounting bracket hold down screw. Adjust the rpm by turning the curb idle adjustment screw and retighten the mounting bracket holddown screw.
5. To set the throttle kicker speed, set the transmission in **N** or **P**, bring the engine to normal operating temperature and turn off all accessories. Place the A/C-heat selector in the **ON** position and disconnect electrical leads to the A/C electromagnetic clutch.
6. Increase the engine speed momentarily. Place the transmission selector in the specified position.
7. Check/Adjust kicker on rpm, if adjustment is required set speed with dashpot adjustment. Reconnect electrical leads to A/C electromagnetic clutch.

7200VV CARBURETOR

1. Place the transmission in **N** or **P**. Apply the emergency brake and block the wheels. Bring the engine to normal operating temperature. Disconnect the vacuum hose at the EGR valve and plug.
2. Place the fast idle adjustment on the second step of the fast idle cam. Check/Adjust fast idle rpm to specification. Rev engine momentarily and recheck. Remove plug from EGR vacuum hose and reconnect.
3. Place A/C selector to the **OFF** position. Disconnect and plug the vacuum hose at the throttle kicker and place the transmission in the specified position (Check the underhood sticker). If adjustment is required, turn the curb idle speed screw. Put the transmission in **N**, increase the engine speed momentarily and recheck.
4. Apply a slight pressure on top of the nylon nut located on the accelerator pump to take up the linkage clearance. Turn the nut on the accelerator pump rod clockwise until a clearance of 0.010–0.005 in. is obtained between the top of the accelerator pump and the pump lever.
5. Turn the accelerator pump rod 1 turn counterclockwise to set the lever lash preload. Remove the plug from the throttle kicker vacuum hose and reconnect.
6. Disconnect and plug the vacuum hose at the VOTM (Vacuum Operated Throttle Modulator) kicker. Connect an external vacuum source providing a minimum of 4.88 in. Hg. to the VOTM kicker. With the transmission in the specified position, check/adjust the VOTM kicker speed.
7. If adjustment is required, turn the saddle bracket adjusting screw. Remove external vacuum source and reconnect VOTM kicker hose.

AUTOMATIC OVERDRIVE EQUIPPED

If the vehicle is equipped with Ford's automatic overdrive trans-

Idle Speed Change	Turns on Linkage Lever Screw
Less than 50 rpm	No change
500-100 rpm increase	1½ turns out
50-100 rpm increase	1½ turns in
100-150 rpm increase	2½ turns out
100-150 rpm decrease	2½ turns in

mission and the idle speed is adjusted by more than 50 rpm, the adjustment screw on the linkage lever at the carburetor must also be adjusted.

VEHICLES EQUIPPED WITH EEC-IV

Curb idle speed (rpm) is controlled by the EEC-IV processor and the idle speed control device. If the control system is operating properly, these speeds are self compensating and cannot be changed by traditional adjustment techniques.

Removal and Installation

MODEL YFA 1661 1 BBL

1. Disconnect the negative battery cable. Remove the air cleaner.
2. Remove the throttle cable or rod from the throttle lever. Disconnect the vacuum lines, fuel filter tube and the electrical connections for the throttle control and Wide Open Throttle-A/C cut-off switch, if equipped.
3. Disconnect electric choke wire at connector.
4. Remove carburetor retaining nuts; then remove carburetor. Remove carburetor mounting gasket, spacer if equipped and lower gasket from the intake manifold.
5. Installation is the reverse of removal procedure.
6. To prevent leakage, distortion or damage to the carburetor body flange, snug the nuts; then alternately tighten each nut to 14-13 ft. lbs.
7. Check and adjust the engine idle speeds.

MODEL YFA 1661 1 BBL FEEDBACK

1. Disconnect the negative battery cable. Remove the air cleaner.
2. Remove the throttle cable or rod from the throttle lever. Disconnect the appropriate vacuum lines and fuel line at the fuel filter.
3. Disconnect the electric choke, feedback solenoid, DC idle speed control motor and throttle position sensor wires.
4. Disconnect the fuel bowl vent hose from the air horn.

5. Remove the carburetor retaining nuts; then remove the carburetor. Remove the carburetor mounting gasket, spacer (if so equipped) and lower gasket from the intake manifold.
6. Installation is the reverse of removal procedure.
7. To prevent leakage, distortion or damage to the carburetor body flange, snug the nuts; then alternately tighten each nut to 12-15 ft. lbs.
8. Adjust the engine idle speed.

HOLLEY MODEL 4180-C 4BBL

1. Disconnect the negative battery cable. Remove the air cleaner. Remove the throttle rod from the throttle lever. Disconnect the distributor vacuum hoses, PCV hose, fuel line and any electrical connections.
2. Disconnect choke heat tube.
3. Remove the carburetor retaining nuts, then remove the carburetor. Remove the spacer from the manifold.
4. Installation is the reverse of removal procedure.
5. Position carburetor on the manifold and install the lockwashers and nuts. Tighten the nuts alternately to 14-20 ft. lbs.
6. Adjust engine idle speed.

MOTORCRAFT MODEL 7200VV AND 2150 2 BBL

1. Disconnect the negative battery cable. Remove the air cleaner.
2. Remove the throttle cable and transmission kickdown levers from the throttle lever. Disconnect and mark all vacuum lines, emission hoses, the fuel line and electrical connections to ease installation.
3. Remove the carburetor retaining nuts; then remove the carburetor. Remove the carburetor mounting gasket spacer, if equipped and lower gasket from the intake manifold.
4. Installation is the reverse of removal procedure.
5. To prevent leakage, distortion or damage to the carburetor body flange, snug the nuts; then, alternately tighten each nut in a crisscross pattern to 12-15 ft. lbs. on model 7200 and 14-16 ft. lbs. on 2150.
6. Adjust engine idle speed.

FUEL INJECTION SYSTEM

Refer to "Chilton's Electronic Engine Controls Manual" for additional coverage.

Description

CENTRAL FUEL INJECTION

The CFI system is a single point, pulse time modulated injection system. Fuel is metered into the air intake stream according to engine demands by 2 solenoid injection valves mounted in a throttle body on the intake manifold.

ELECTRONIC FUEL INJECTION

The EFI system is a multi-point, pulse time, speed density, fuel injection system. Fuel is metered into the intake air stream in accordance with engine demand through 4 injectors mounted on tuned intake manifold.

EFI TURBO

This system is a multi-point, pulse time, mass airflow, fuel injection system. Fuel is metered into the intake air stream through 4 injectors mounted on a tuned intake manifold. A blow-through turbocharger system is utilized to reduce fuel delivery time, increase turbine energy available and eliminate compressor throttling.

SEFI

The Sequential Electronic Fuel Injection (SEFI)system is a multi-point, pulse time, speed density control system. Fuel is metered into each port in sequence with the engine firing order through 8 injectors mounted on a tuned intake manifold.

FUEL SYSTEM SERVICE PRECAUTION

When working with the fuel system certain precautions should be taken;
1. Always work in a well ventilated area
2. Keep a dry chemical (Class B) fire extinguisher near the work area
3. Always disconnect the negative battery cable
4. Do not make any repairs to the fuel system until all the necessary steps for repair have been reviewed

NOTE: Most Ford vehicles are equipped with an inertia switch that shuts off the fuel pump should the vehicle be hit in the rear. This switch works as a circuit breaker and can be reset. It is normally located in the trunk and there is usually a sticker marking its location. It should be checked first when a fuel supply problem is evident.

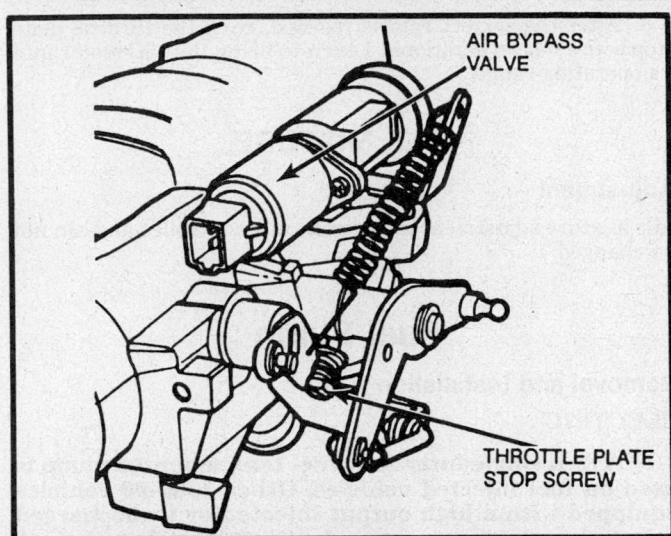

Idle speed adjusting screw 3.8L

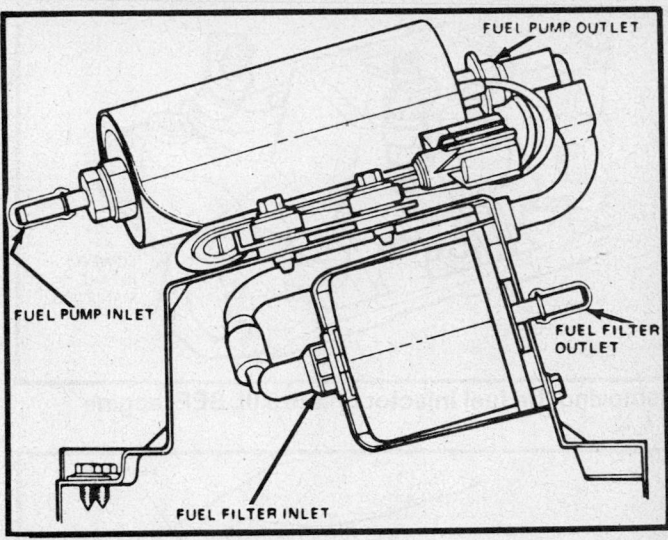

View of the in-line fuel pump

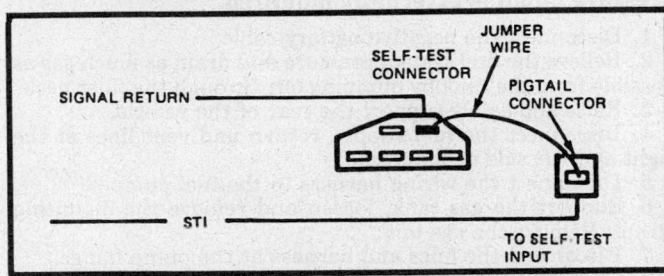

Installing the jumper wire on the 3.8L CFI system

FUEL SYSTEM PRESSURE RELIEF

Procedure

1. If the fuel charging assembly is mounted to the engine, remove the fuel tank cap. Using fuel pressure gauge T80L–9974–A, install it to the relief valve and release the pressure from the system by opening the pressure relief valve.

NOTE: **The cap on the relief valve must be removed in order to install the fuel pressure gauge.**

3. Install the pressure relief valve cap and tighten the cap to 4–6 inch lbs.

IDLE SPEED

NOTE: **Curb idle speed (rpm) is controlled by the EEC-IV processor, on vehicles so equipped and the idle speed control device. If the control system is operating properly, these speeds are self compensating and cannot be changed by traditional adjustment techniques.**

Adjustment

2.3L AND 3.8L ENGINES WITH CFI

1. Remove the air cleaner.
2. Locate the self-test connector and self-test input connector in the engine compartment.
3. Connect a jumper wire between the self-test input connector and the signal return pin (the top right terminal) on the self-test connector.
4. Place the ignition key in the **RUN** position and be careful not to start the engine. Wait approximately 10–15 seconds until

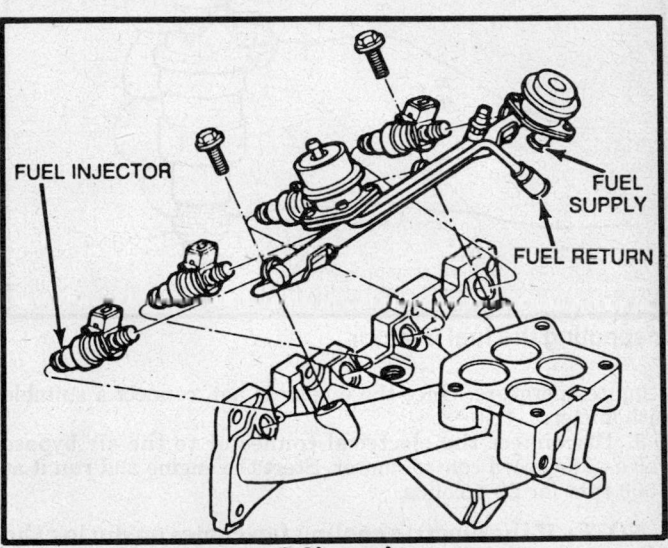

Fuel rail and injectors 2.3L engine

the ISC plunger is fully retracted. Turn the ignition key to the off position and wait an additional 10–15 seconds.
5. Remove the jumper wire from the diagnostic connector and disconnect the electrical connector from the ISC motor. Now perform the throttle stop adjustment as follows:
   a. Remove the CFI assembly from the vehicle.
   b. Use a small punch or equivalent to punch through and remove the aluminum plug which covers the throttle stop adjusting screw.
   c. Remove the throttle stop screw and install a new one.
6. Reinstall the CFI assembly on the vehicle, start engine and allow to stabilize. Check and adjust the idle speed, to specification, by turning the throttle stop screw. Cover throttle stop screw hole with a new cover.
7. Shut off the engine and reconnect the electrical connector to the ISC motor. Remove all test equipment and reinstall the air cleaner assembly.

2.3L OHC/TURBO WITH EFI

1. Apply the parking brake and block the drive wheels. Place the transmission in **N**.
2. Start the engine and let it run until it reaches normal oper-

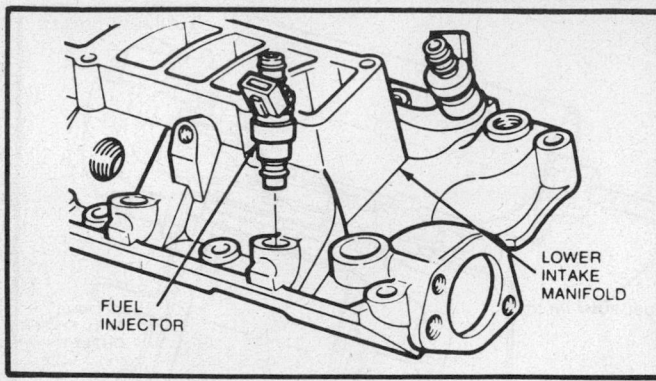

Removing the fuel injector on the 5.0L SEFI engine

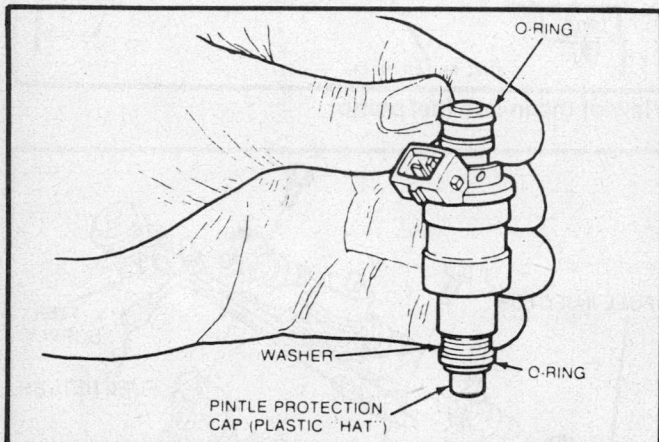

Inspecting the fuel injector

ating temperature. Once the engine is hot, connect a suitable tachometer.

3. Disconnect the electrical connector to the air bypass valve—idle speed control motor. Start the engine and run it at 1500 rpm for 20 seconds.

NOTE: If the electric cooling fan comes on during the idle speed adjusting procedures, wait for the fan to turn off before proceeding.

4. Let the engine return to idle and check the base idle speed.

5. The idle speed should be 700–800 rpm. If adjustment is necessary, turn the throttle stop adjusting screw to reach the specified rpm.

6. Shut the engine off and reconnect the power lead to the idle speed control air bypass valve. Disconnect all test equipment.

5.0L ENGINES WITH EFI

1. Apply the parking brake, block the drive wheels and place the vehicle in **N**.

2. Start the engine and let it run until it reaches normal operating temperature, then turn the engine off. Connect a tachometer to the engine.

3. Turn off all accessories and place the transmission in **P** (automatic transmission) or **N** (manual transmission).

4. Run the engine at 1800 rpm for at least 30 seconds.

5. Place the transmission in **D** (automatic) or **N** (manual). Check the idle speed.

6. Check the Vehicle Emission Information label for the correct idle speed specifications.

7. If the idle speed is not within specifications adjust it by turning the throttle plate stop screw.

8. After the correct rpm is reached, turn the throttle plate stop screw out an additional 1 turn to bring the ISC motor into its operating range.

IDLE MIXTURE

Adjustment

Idle mixture adjustment is electronically controlled and can not be changed.

Fuel Pump

Removal and Installation

ELECTRIC

NOTE: A single internally fuel tank mounted pump is used on fuel injected vehicles. Other 1985–90 vehicles equipped with a high output injected or turbocharged injected engine are equipped with 2 electric pumps. A low-pressure pump is mounted in the tank and a high pressure pump is externally mounted.

1. Disconnect the negative battery cable.

2. Relieve the fuel system pressure and drain as much gas as possible from the tank by pumping out through the filler neck.

3. Raise and safely support the rear of the vehicle.

4. Disconnect the fuel supply, return and vent lines at the right and left side of the frame.

5. Disconnect the wiring harness to the fuel pump.

6. Support the gas tank, loosen and remove the mounting straps. Remove the gas tank.

7. Disconnect the lines and harness at the pump flange.

8. Clean the outside of the mounting flange and retaining ring. Turn the fuel pump lock ring counterclockwise and remove.

9. Remove the fuel pump.

10. Clean the mounting surfaces. Put a light coat of grease on the mounting sufaces and on the new sealing ring. Install the new fuel pump.

11. Installation is in the reverse order of removal. If single high pressure pump system, fill the tank with at least 10 gals. of gas. Turn the ignition key **ON** for 3 seconds. Repeat 6 or 7 times until the fuel system is pressurized. Check for any fitting leaks. Start the engine and check for leaks.

FUEL INJECTOR

Removal and Installation

EFI

1. Disconnect the negative battery cable. Remove the fuel cap from the fuel tank.

2. Relieve the fuel system pressure.

3. Remove the upper intake manifold.

4. Remove the electrical connectors to the fuel injectors and remove the bolts retaining the fuel rail.

5. Remove the fuel rail, with the injectors attached, from the engine.

6. To ease removal of the injector assembly, use a slight back and forth rocking motion to pull the injectors from the engine.

7. Replace the injector O-rings (2 per injector). Inspect the injector plastic hat (covers the injector pintle) and washer for signs of deterioration. Replace as necessary. If the plastic hat is missing, look for it in the intake manifold.

8. Installation is the reverse order of the removal procedure.

9. Install the fuel cap on the fuel tank. Connect the negative battery cable.

10. Add engine coolant if required. Turn the ignition key on and off several times without starting the engine to check for fuel leaks. Check all connections at the fuel rail and all push connections.

NOTE: **The fuel system is normally pressurized to 39 psi.**

11. Start the engine and let it reach normal operating temperature. Check for coolant and fuel leaks

CFI

1. Disconnect the negative battery cable.
2. Relieve the fuel system pressure.
3. Remove the air cleaner inlet from te throttle body.
4. Disconnect the electrical leads from the injectors.
5. Remove the 2 retaining screws from each injector and carefully remove the injector.
6. Install the injector in reverse order, make sure that the O-rings are properly seated.

TURBOCHARGER SYSTEM

For more information on turbochargers, refer to "Chilton's Electronic Engine Controls Manual"

TURBOCHARGER UNIT

Removal and Installation

NOTE: **The turbocharger is serviced by replacement only.**

1. Remove negative cable from the battery.
2. Drain the coolant from the radiator. Loosen upper and lower clamps securing hoses to intercooler.
3. Disconnect aspirator hoses at intercooler and loosen nut securing bracket to engine. Remove intercooler by first lifting and then pulling out.
4. Remove the hex head bolts retaining the throttle body discharge tube to the turbocharger. Also, loosen upper clamp on inlet hose.
5. Identify and disconnect vacuum hose tubes.
0. Disconnect PCV tube from the turbocharger air inlet elbow.
7. Remove throttle body discharge tube and hose as an assembly.
8. Disconnect electrical ground wire from turbocharger air inlet elbow.
9. Remove turbocharger oil supply line.
10. Disconnect oxygen sensor connector at turbocharger.
11. Raise and safely support the vehicle.
12. Disconnect exhaust pipe by removing the exhaust pipe to turbocharger bolts.
13. Remove the bolts from oil return line located below the turbocharger. Do not kink or damage line as it is removed.
14. Remove the lower turbocharger bracket to block bolt.
15. Lower the vehicle.
16. Remove the front lower turbocharger retaining bolt.
17. Simultaneously, remove the remaining nuts as turbocharger is slid off studs.
18. Remove turbocharger assembly from vehicle.
19. Position a new turbocharger gasket on mounting studs. Be sure the bead faces outward.
20. Install the turbocharger assembly on the mounting studs.
21. Install turbocharger bracket on the 2 lower studs. Start the lower retaining nuts followed by the upper retaining nuts.
22. Raise and safely support the vehicle.
23. Install lower bracket to block bolt and tighten to 28–40 ft. lbs. (38–54 Nm).
24. Install a new oil return line gasket. Bolt oil return line to turbocharger. Tighten bolts to 12–21 ft. lbs. (19–29 Nm).
25. Install exhaust pipe. Tighten retaining nuts to 25–35 ft. lbs. (34–47 Nm).
26. Lower vehicle.
27. Using 4 new nuts, tighten the turbocharger to exhaust manifold nuts to 28–40 ft. lbs. (38–54 Nm).
28. Install air inlet tube to turbocharger inlet elbow. Tighten

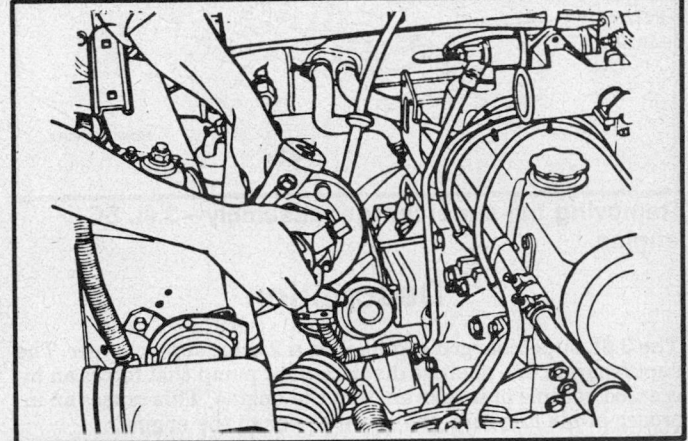

Turbocharger removal

bolts to 15–22 ft. lbs. (20–30 Nm). Tighten hose clamp to 15–22 inch lbs. (1.7–2.5 Nm).
29. Install PCV tube fitting and tighten clamp to 15–22 inch lbs. (1.7–2.5 Nm).
30. Connect all vacuum lines.
31. Connect oxygen sensor.
32. Connect electrical ground wire to air inlet elbow.
33. Install turbocharger oil supply line. Tighten fitting to 9–16 ft. lbs. (12–22 Nm).
34. Install air intake tube and clamp between turbocharger outlet and air intake throttle body. Tighten clamp to 15–20 ft. lbs. (20–27 Nm).
35. Connect ground cable to battery.
36. Start engine and check for leaks.

WASTEGATE ACTUATOR

Removal and Installation

1. Disconnect the negative battery cable. Disconnect hoses from actuator diaphragm and remove turbocharger.
2. Remove clip attaching actuator rod to wastegate arm.
3. Remove the bolts attaching the actuator diaphragm assembly to compressor housing.
4. Install 2 bolts attaching actuator diaphragm assembly to compressor housing. Tighten bolts to 145–165 inch lbs. (16–19 Nm).
5. Unscrew actuator rod end until it just fits over the pin on the wastegate arm, with wastegate arm held closed (full forward).
6. Install clip attaching actuator rod to wastegate arm and apply Loctite® to threads, or crimp the threads on rod.
7. Connect the hoses to the actuator diaphragm.

SUPERCHARGER SYSTEM

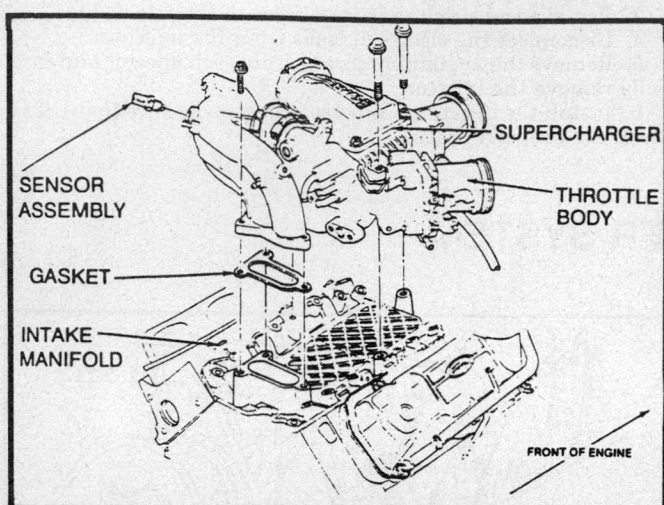

Removing the supercharger assembly—3.8L SC engine

Description

The 3.8L supercharged engine uses a 2 rotor supercharger. The supercharger is a positive displacement pump that forces an increased volume of intake air into the engine. This causes an increase in air pressure and more power to the engine.

The supercharger is serviceable only by replacement. Disassembly of the supercharger unit may void any manufacturers warranty.

SUPERCHARGER UNIT

Removal and Installation

1. Disconnect the negative battery cable. Drain the cooling system. Relieve the fuel system pressure.
2. Remove the air cleaner assembly, including air intake duct and heater tube.
3. Disconnect the accelerator cable at the throttle body and disconnect the speed control cable, if equipped.
4. Disconnect the T.V. cable at the throttle body. Remove the accelerator cable bracket and place it to the side.
5. Disconnect the thermactor hose at the check valve. Disconnect the flexible fuel lines over the valve covers and at the fuel injector rail.
6. Disconnect the upper radiator hose and the coolant bypass hose, at the manifold.
7. Disconnect the heater tube at the intake manifold and remove the tube support bracket, with the fuel lines attached and set it aside.
8. Disconnect vacuum lines at the fuel rail and the supercharger. Disconnect and tag all of the electrical connectors.
9. Remove the air conditioning compressor support bracket. Disconnect the PCV hose from the supercharger and the valve cover.
10. Remove the bolts that retain the supercharger-to-intercooler tube and disconnect the supercharger-to-lower intake manifold inlet tube.

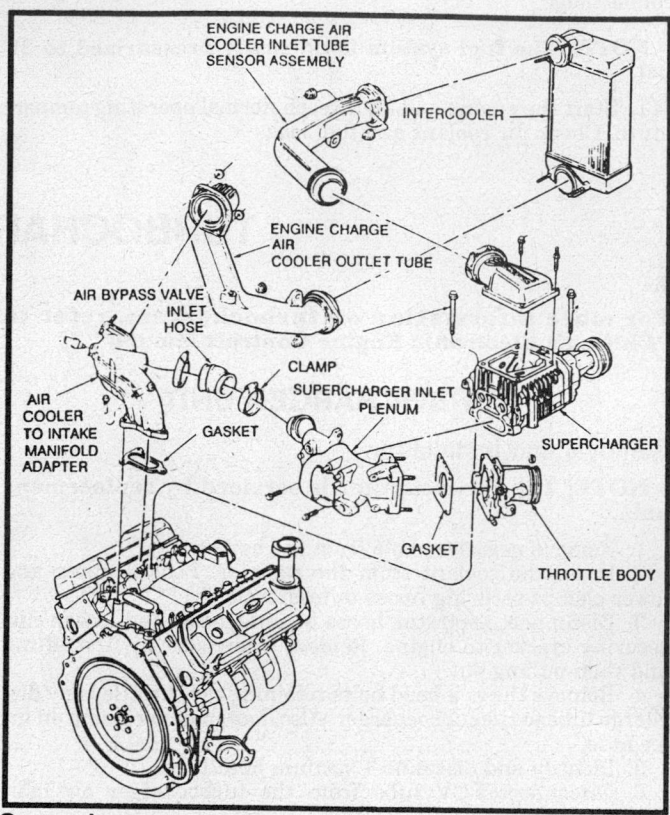

Supercharger system components—3.8L SC engine

11. Relieve the accessory drive belt tension and remove the supercharger drive belt from the super charger pulley.
12. Remove the supercharger retaining bolts and remove the supercharger from the lower intake manifold.
13. Remove the fuel rail assembly from the lower intake manifold. Remove the heater water outlet hose.
14. Install the fuel injectors and fuel rail assembly. Install a new supercharger-to-intake manifold gasket and install the supercharger in position.
15. Install the mounting bolts, tighten the bolts on the supercharger first, to 52–70 ft. lbs. Tighten the air inlet-to-lower manifold bolts to 20–28 ft. lbs.
16. Install the air conditioning compressor bracket. Reconnect all of the electrical connectors and vacuum hoses.
17. Connect the heater tube to the heater elbow. Reconnect the supercharger-to-intercooler tube.
18. Install the heater tube support bracket. Connect the coolant bypass hose and the upper radiator hose.
19. Reconnect the fuel lines to the fuel rail assembly. Connect the flexible fuel lines over the valve covers.
20. Install the accelerator cable bracket. Reconnect the accelerator cable and the T.V. cable.
21. Fill the cooling system to the correct level with the correct coolant and run the engine to normal operating temperature.
22. Bleed the cooling system. Check for leaks.

EMISSION CONTROL SYSTEMS

Refer to "Chilton's Emission Diagnosis and Service Manual" for additional coverage.

Resetting Warning Lamps

These vehicles have an CHECK ENGINE lamp that will light when there is a fault in the engine control system. This light can not be reset without diagnosing the fault in the system. When the system has been diagnosed and the problem corrected, the light will go out.

SERVICE LAMP

1986–89 COUGAR/THUNDERBIRD

The SERVICE light will light after 5000–7500 miles depending on engine operation. To reset the interval light, depress both the TRIP and TRIP RESET buttons on the instrument cluster. The light will go out and 3 beeps will be heard.

EMISSION CONTROLS APPLICATION

PASSENGER CAR — 50 STATES/CANADA

Engine	Vehicle Application	Catalyst(s) Type	Catalyst(s) Location	Fuel System Type, Mfg	Electronic Eng Ctrl	EGR System	Thermactor System	Ignition System	Idle Speed Control
2.3L OHC	Mustang/Capri LTD/Marquis	TWC & COC	DBUB	YFA-1V FBC, Carter	EEC-IV	BVT	MTA	TFI-IV	DCM
2.3L OHC Turbo	SVO Mustang Thunderbird/Cougar Merkur	TWC	UB	EFI	EEC-IV	Ported	None	TFI-IV	BPA
3.8L 50 States	Thunderbird/Cougar LTD/Marquis Mustang/Capri (Canada)	(2) TWC COC	TB UB	CFI	EEC-IV	ELEC	MTA	TFI-IV	DCM
3.8L Canada	Thunderbird/Cougar LTD/Marquis	COC	UB	2150A-2V NFB, Ford	None	IBP	CT	DS-II	TSP/DP
5.0L	Thunderbird/Cougar Cont/Mark VII	(2) TWC COC	TB UB	SEFI	EEC-IV	ELEC	MTA	TFI-IV	BPA
5.0L	Ford/Mercury Lincoln	(2) TWC (2) COC	TB UB	SEFI	EEC-IV	ELEC	MTA	TFI-IV	BPA
5.0L HO	Mustang/Capri Mark VII	(2) TWC (2) COC	TB UB	SEFI	EEC-IV	ELEC	MTA	TFI IV	BPA
5.8L	Ford/Mercury (Police) Canada Trailer Tow	(2) TWC & COC	DBUB	7200-VV FBC, Ford	MCU	IBP	MTA	UIC	TSP

ABBREVIATIONS:

OHC = Overhead Cam
HSC = High Swirl Combustion
HO = High Output
COC = Conventional Oxidation Catalyst
TWC = Three-Way Catalyst
TB = Toe Board
UB = Underbody
UE = Under Engine
DBUB = Dual Brick Underbody
MFG = Manufacturer
FBC = Feedback Carburetor
NFB = Non-Feedback Carburetor
EFI = Electronic Fuel Injection

ELEC = Electronic Valve
SEFI = Sequential EFI
CFI = Central Fuel Injection
EEC-IV = Electronic Engine Control (System-IV)
MCU = Microprocessor Control Unit
EGR = Exhaust Gas Recirculation
EVP = EGR Valve Position
EVR = EGR Valve Regulator
EGRC = EGR Control
EGRV = EGR Vent
PFE = Pressure Feedback Electronic
BP = Backpressure

IBP = Integral Backpressure
CT = Conventional Thermactor
PA = Pulse Air
MTA = Managed Thermactor Air
DS-II = Duraspark II
TFI = Thick Film Ignition
UIC = Universal Ignition Control
M/V = Mechanical Vacuum
BPA = Bypass Air
DCM = D. C. Motor
TSP = Throttle Solenoid Positioner
DP = Dashpot

ENGINE

NOTE: Disconnecting the negative battery cable on some vehicles may interfere with the functions of the on board computer systems and may require the computer to undergo a relearning process, once the negative battery cable is reconnected.

Engine Assembly

Removal and Installation

2.3L ENGINE

1. Raise the hood and secure it in the vertical position.

2. Drain coolant from the radiator and the oil from the crankcase.
3. On non-turbocharged engines, remove air cleaner and exhaust manifold shroud. On the turbocharged engine, disconnect the zip tube from the turbocharger inlet. Remove the ground strap on the turbocharger inlet elbow.
4. Disconnect the negative battery cable.
5. Remove the radiator upper and lower hoses.
6. Remove the radiator and fan. On vehicles equipped with an electric cooling fan, disconnect power lead to fan motor, then remove fan and shroud assembly.
7. Disconnect the heater hose from the water pump and car-

buretor choke fitting.

8. Disconnect the wires from the alternator and starter. Disconnect the accelerator cable from the carburetor or throttle body (EFI). On a vehicle with air conditioning, remove the compressor from the mounting bracket and position it out of the way, leaving the refrigerant lines attached.

9. Disconnect the flexible fuel line at the fuel pump line or at the fuel rail (EFI) and plug the fuel line.

10. Disconnect the coil primary wire at the coil. Disconnect the oil pressure and the water temperature sending unit wires from the sending units.

11. Remove the starter.

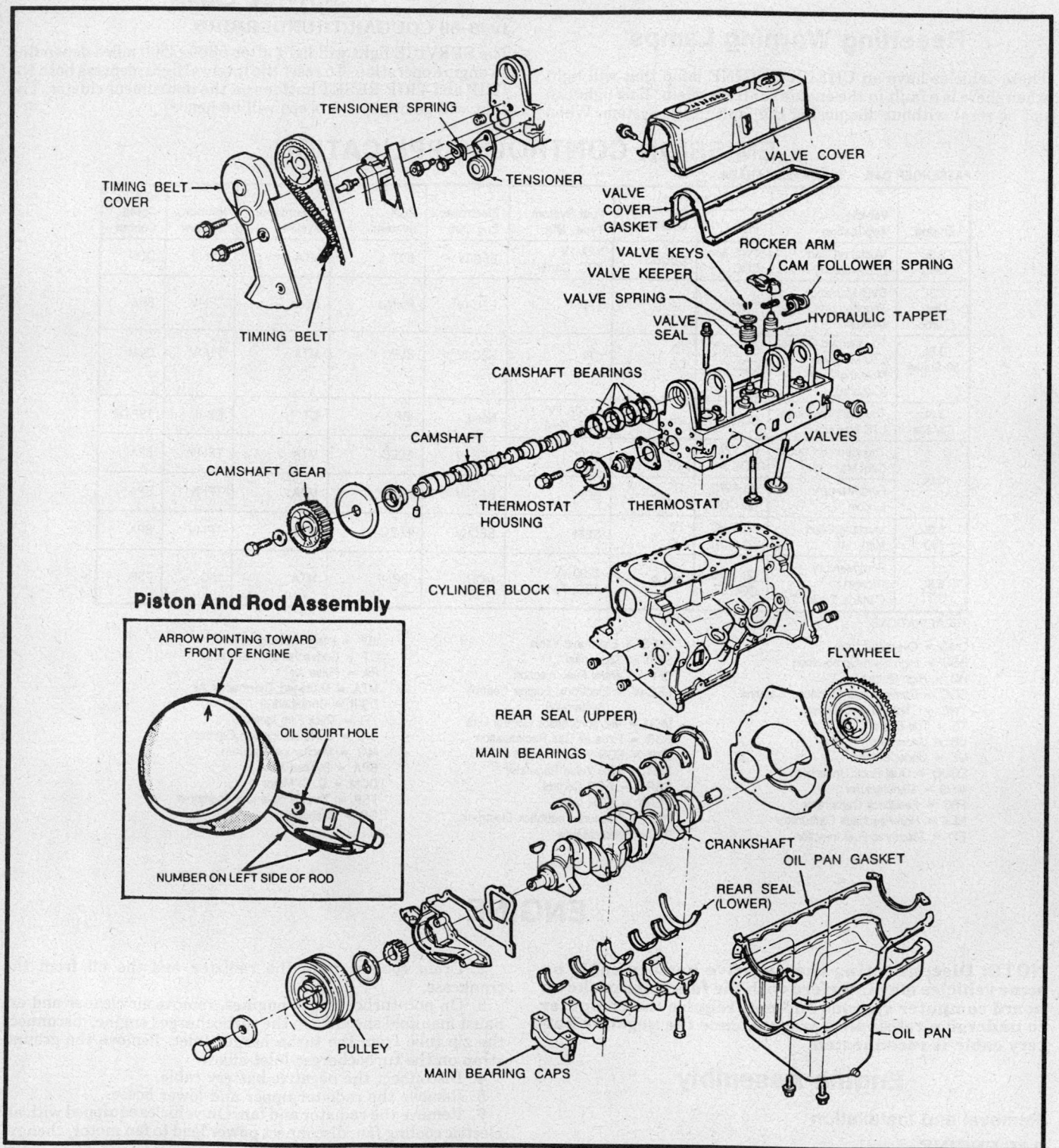

Ford 2.3L 4 cyl-140 cu. in. engine—exploded view

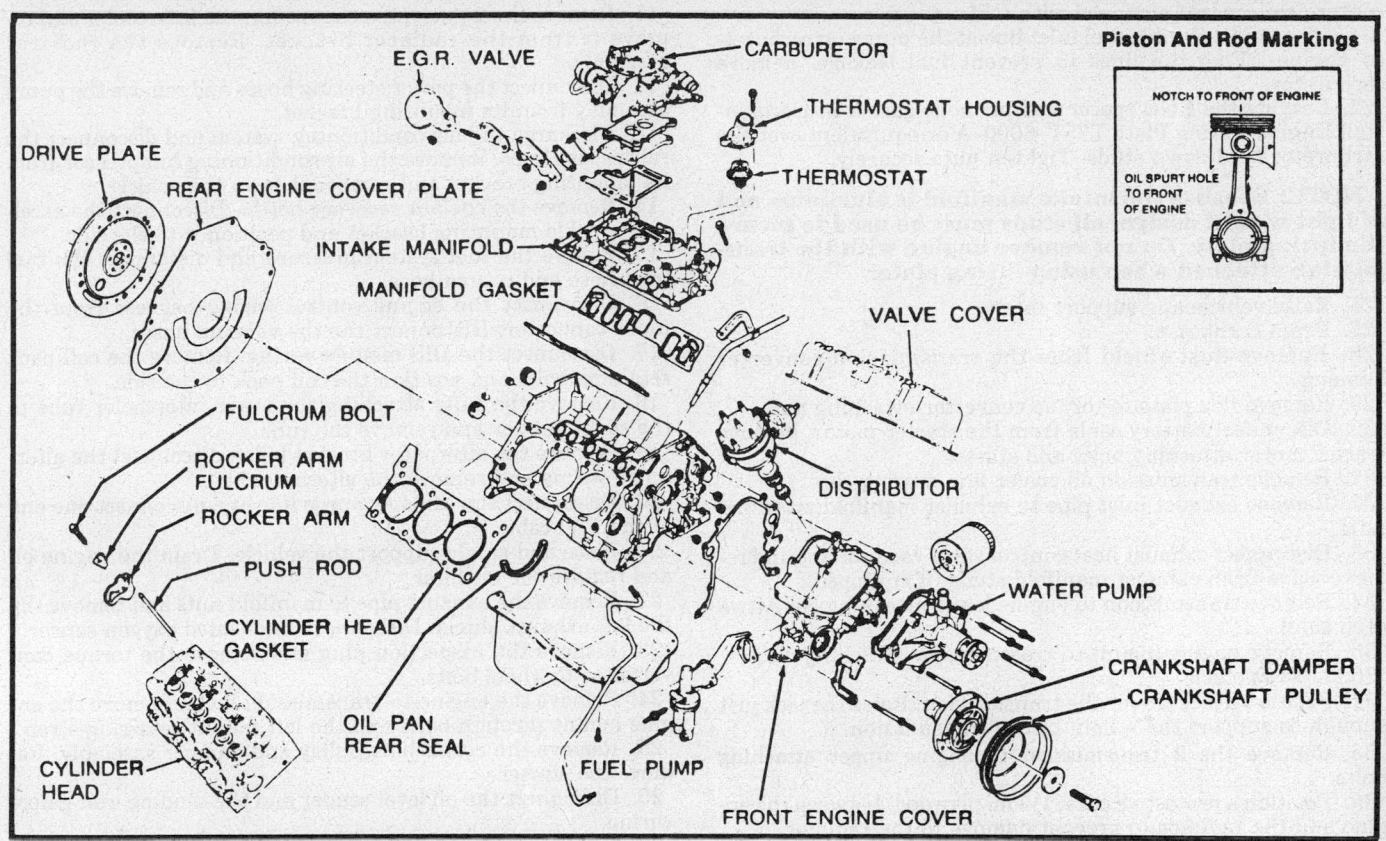

Piston And Rod Markings

NOTCH TO FRONT OF ENGINE

OIL SPURT HOLE TO FRONT OF ENGINE

E.G.R. VALVE · CARBURETOR · THERMOSTAT HOUSING · THERMOSTAT · DRIVE PLATE · REAR ENGINE COVER PLATE · INTAKE MANIFOLD · MANIFOLD GASKET · VALVE COVER · FULCRUM BOLT · ROCKER ARM FULCRUM · ROCKER ARM · PUSH ROD · CYLINDER HEAD GASKET · DISTRIBUTOR · WATER PUMP · CRANKSHAFT DAMPER · CRANKSHAFT PULLEY · CYLINDER HEAD · OIL PAN REAR SEAL · FUEL PUMP · FRONT ENGINE COVER

Ford 3.8L V6-230 cu. In. engine—exploded view

12. Raise and safely support the vehicle. Remove the flywheel or converter housing upper attaching bolts.

13. Disconnect the muffler inlet pipe at the exhaust manifold or turbocharger outlet.

14. Disconnect the engine right and left mounts at the No. 2 crossmember pedestals.

15. Remove the flywheel or converter housing. On a vehicle with a manual transmission, remove the flywheel housing lower attaching bolts.

16. On a vehicle with automatic transmission, disconnect the converter from the flywheel. Disconnect transmission oil cooler lines, if attached to engine at pan rail. Remove the converter housing lower attaching bolts.

17. Lower the vehicle. Support the transmission and flywheel or converter housing with a jack.

18. Attach the engine lifting hooks to the existing lifting brackets. Carefully lift the engine out of the engine compartment. Install the engine on a work stand.

19. Installation is the reverse of removal procedure.

3.8L ENGINE EXCEPT SUPERCHARGED

1. Relieve the fuel system pressure. Drain engine cooling system.

2. Disconnect the negative battery cable.

3. If equipped with an underhood lamp, disconnect the wiring connector.

4. Mark position of the hood hinges and remove the hood.

5. Remove air cleaner assembly including the air intake duct and heat tube.

6. Remove fan shroud attaching screws. Remove the fan/clutch assembly attaching bolts.

7. Remove fan/clutch assembly and shroud.

8. Loosen accessory drive belt idler. Remove the drive belt and the water pump pulley.

9. Disconnect radiator upper and lower hoses at radiator.

10. Disconnect thermactor hose from the downstream air tube check valve, if equipped with CFI.

11. Remove downstream air tube bracket attaching bolt at the rear of the right cylinder head.

12. Remove coil secondary wire from the coil.

13. If equipped with power steering, remove the pump mounting bracket attaching bolts. Leaving the hoses connected, place the pump and bracket assembly aside in a position to prevent the fluid from leaking out.

14. If equipped with air conditioning, remove the mounting bracket attaching bolts. Leaving hoses connected, secure the compressor to the right shock tower.

15. Remove alternator mounting bolts and set alternator aside.

16. Disconnect heater hoses from heater tube and water pump.

17. If equipped with speed control, disconnect the cable at the carburetor or fuel charging assembly.

18. Disconnect necessary vacuum hoses.

19. Remove screw attaching engine ground strap to dash panel.

20. Disconnect transmission linkage at the carburetor or fuel charging assembly.

21. Disconnect accelerator cable at the carburetor and remove cable routing bracket attaching bolts from the intake manifold (two places).

22. Disconnect necessary electrical connectors.

23. Disconnect fuel line and PCV hose at the carburetor, if equipped. Disconnect flexible fuel lines from steel lines over the

rocker arm cover if equipped with CFI.

24. Disconnect flexible fuel inlet line at the pump on carbureted engines. Plug the lines to prevent fuel leakage. Remove carburetor.

25. Leaving the EGR spacer and phenolic gasket in place, install Engine Lifting Plate T75T-6000-A or equivalent over the carburetor hold-down studs. Tighten nuts securely.

NOTE: Because the intake manifold is aluminum and of light weight design, all studs must be used to secure the lifting plate. Do not remove engine with the transmission attached when using lifting plate.

26. Raise vehicle and support safely.
27. Drain crankcase.
28. Remove dust shield from the transmission converter housing.
29. Remove flex plate to torque converter attaching nuts.
30. Disconnect battery cable from the starter motor. Remove starter motor attaching bolts and starter.
31. Remove transmission oil cooler line routing clip.
32. Remove exhaust inlet pipe to exhaust manifold attaching nuts.
33. Disconnect exhaust heat control valve vacuum line and remove valve from exhaust manifold studs (if equipped).
34. Remove transmission to engine lower attaching bolts (two each side).
35. Remove engine mount to crossmember attaching nuts.
36. Lower vehicle.
37. Position a jack under the transmission. Raise the jack just enough to support the weight of the transmission.
38. Remove the 2 transmission to engine upper attaching bolts.
39. Position a protective cover (¼ in. plywood) between the engine and the radiator to prevent damage to the radiator.
40. Raise the engine slightly and carefully pull it away from the transmission. Carefully lift the engine out of the engine compartment (avoid bending or damaging the rear cover plate or other components). Install engine on a work stand.
41. Installation is the reverse of removal procedure.
42. Install engine mount to crossmember attaching nuts and tighten to 70–90 ft. lbs. (95–122 Nm).
43. Install flex plate to torque converter attaching nuts and tighten to 20–30 ft. lbs. (28–40 Nm).
44. Install exhaust inlet pipe to exhaust manifold attaching nuts. Tighten nuts to 16–24 ft. lbs. (21–32 Nm).
45. Position starter motor, install attaching bolts and tighten to 15–20 ft. lbs. (20–27 Nm).
46. Install the fuel charging assembly and tighten hold-down nuts to 12–15 ft. lbs. (16–20 Nm).

3.8L SUPERCHARGED ENGINE

1. Relieve the fuel system pressure. Drain the cooling system.
2. Disconnect the negative battery cable.
3. Disconnect the wirirng for the underhood light. Mark the location of the hood hinges, for proper alignment during installation.
4. Remove the wiper module and left hand cowl vent screen.
5. Disconnect the alternator wiring.
6. Remove the upper intercooler tube at the supercharger and cooler assemblies. Remove the retaining bolt from the cooler tube at the power steering bracket and remove the tube.
7. Remove the upper radiator shield. Release the tension from the accessory drive belt and the supercharger drive belt, remove the belts.
8. Remove the air cleaner-to-throttle body tube assembly.
9. Disconnect the electric cooling fan and remove the assembly. Remove the radiator shroud and fan assembly.
10. Remove the upper radiator hose and disconnect the transmission cooler lines, if equipped with automatic transmission. Disconnect the lower radiator and heater hoses.

11. Remove the 2 push pins that retain the intercooler and remove it from the radiator bracket. Remove the radiator assembly.
12. Disconnect the power steering hoses and remove the pump assembly from its mounting bracket.
13. Discharge the air conditioning system and disconnect the refrigerant lines. Remove the air conditioning compressor from its mounting bracket and remove it from the vehicle.
14. Remove the coolant recovery bottle. Disconnect the accelerator cable mounting bracket and position it to the side.
15. Relieve the fuel system pressure and disconnect the fuel inlet hose and return hose.
16. Disconnect the engine control wiring harness from the multi-connector. Disconnect the the vacuum hoses.
17. Disconnect the DIS module wiring. Remove the coil pack retaining bolts and position the coil pack to the side.
18. Remove the nuts attaching the lower intercooler tube to the supercharger and remove the tube. .
19. Remove the alternator bracket bolts, disconnect the alternator wiring and remove the alternator.
20. Disconnect the canister purge line and disconnect one end of the T.V. cable.
21. Raise and safely support the vehicle. Drain the engine oil and remove the oil filter.
22. Remove the exhaust pipe to manifold nuts and remove the the left exhaust shield. Disconnect the heated oxygen sensor.
23. Remove the inspection plug and remove the torque converter-to-flywheel bolts.
24. Remove the engine-to-transmission bolts. Remove the engine mount through bolts and the left mount retaining strap.
25. Remove the crankshaft pulley and damper assembly. Remove the starter.
26. Disconnect the oil level sender and the sending unit gauge wiring.
27. Lower the vehicle. Position a suitable jack under the transmission and install a suitable engine lifting device.
28. Remove the engine from the vehicle.

To install:

29. With an suitable lifting device installed, install the engine into the engine compartment.
30. Install 2 of the engine-to-transmission bolts and remove the lifting device.
31. Connect the oil pressure switch and level indicator. Install the remaining engine-to-transmission bolts, tighten to 40–50 ft. lbs.
32. Install the torque converter-to-flywheel bolts and tighten to 20–34 ft. lbs. Install the inspection cover. Install the starter.
33. Install the engine mount through bolts and retaining strap, tighten the bolts to 35–50 ft. lbs.
34. Install the oxygen sensor, exhaust pipe-to-manifold and heat shield. Install the crankshaft pulley and damper, tighten the bolt to 93–121 ft. lbs.
35. Install the oil filter and lower the vehicle. Connect the throttle cable bracket and all vacuum lines. Connect the canister purge line.
36. Install the alternator, power steering pump and brackets. Reconnect the power steering lines. Install the air conditioning compressor and lines.
37. Install the radiator and intercooler assemblies. Install the radiator shields and fan assembly.
38. Reconnect the radiator and heater hoses. Connect the intercooler tubes and the transmission oil cooler lines.
39. Install the ignition coil pack and reconnect the engine control harness.
40. Reconnect the fuel lines. Install the accessory and supercharger drive belts and adjust the tension. Install the remaining components.
41. Install the wiper module and cowl vent. Install the hood, aligning the marks during disassembly.
42. Connect the negative battery cable. Refill the cooling system and the engine crankcase to the proper levels. Check the

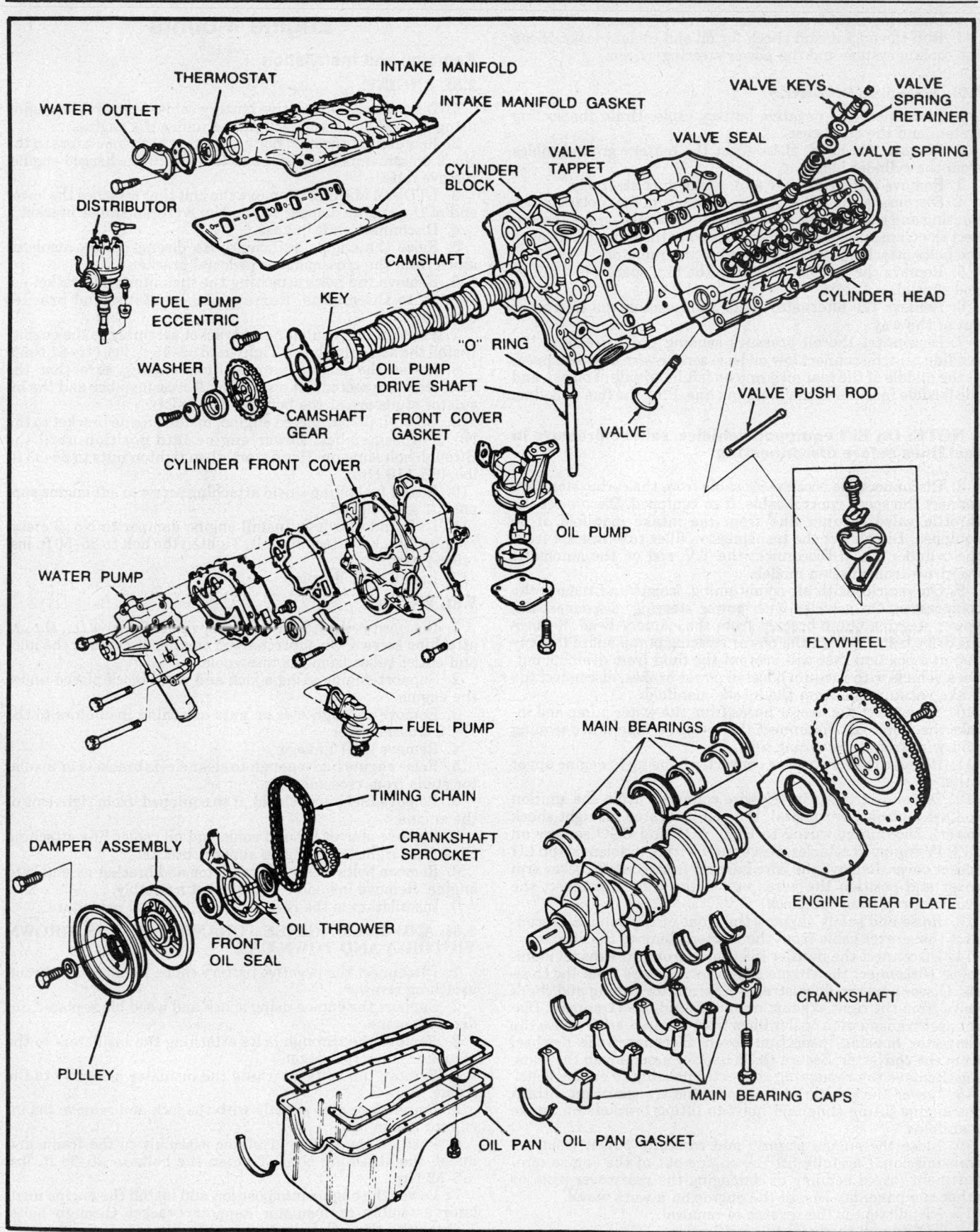

Ford V8 engines — exploded view

power steering fluid level. Recharge the A/C system.

43. Run the engine and check for oil and coolant leaks. Bleed the cooling system and the power steering system.

5.0L AND 5.8L ENGINES

1. Disconnect the negative battery cable. Drain the cooling system and the crankcase.

2. Remove the hood. Disconnect the battery ground cables from the cylinder block.

3. Remove the air cleaner and intake duct assembly.

4. Disconnect the radiator upper hose from the coolant outlet housing and the radiator lower hose at the water pump. Disconnect the transmission oil cooler lines from the radiator. Remove the bolts attaching the fan shroud to the radiator.

5. Remove the radiator. Remove the fan, spacer, belt pulley and shroud.

6. Remove the alternator bolts and position the alternator out of the way.

7. Disconnect the oil pressure sending unit wire from the sending unit, disconnect low oil level sensor wire, if so equipped, at the middle of the rear oil sump on left hand side of oil pan and the flexible fuel line at the fuel tank line. Plug the fuel tank line.

NOTE: On EFI equipped vehicles, relieve pressure in fuel lines before disconnecting.

8. Disconnect the accelerator cable from the carburetor. Disconnect the speed control cable, if so equipped. Disconnect the throttle valve vacuum line from the intake manifold, if so equipped. Disconnect the transmission filler tube bracket from the cylinder block. Disconnect the T.V. rod on the automatic overdrive transmission models.

9. On vehicles with air conditioning, isolate and remove the compressor. On vehicles with power steering, disconnect the power steering pump bracket from the cylinder head. Remove the drive belt. Position the power steering pump out of the way and in a position that will prevent the fluid from draining out. On a vehicle with vacuum boosted power brakes, disconnect the brake vacuum line from the intake manifold.

10. Disconnect the heater hoses from the water pump and intake the manifold. Disconnect the coolant temperature sending unit wire from the sending unit.

11. Remove the flywheel or converter housing to engine upper bolts.

12. Disconnect the primary wire connector from the ignition coil, (except on Continental, the coil is located on right shock tower). Disconnect wiring to ECT, ACT and EGO sensors on EEC IV equipped vehicles. Disconnect wiring to solenoids on LH rocker cover. Remove the wire harness from the left rocker arm cover and position the wires out of the way. Disconnect the ground strap from the block.

13. Raise and safely support the front of the vehicle. Disconnect the starter cable from the starter. Remove the starter.

14. Disconnect the muffler inlet pipes from the exhaust manifolds. Disconnect the engine support insulators from the chassis. Disconnect the downstream Thermactor tubing and check valve from the right exhaust manifold stud, if so equipped. Disconnect transmission cooler lines from retainer and remove the converter housing inspection cover. Disconnect the flywheel from the converter. Secure the converter assembly in the housing. Remove the remaining converter housing to engine bolts.

15. Lower the vehicle and support the transmission. Attach the engine lifting sling and hoist to lifting brackets on intake manifolds.

16. Raise the engine slightly and carefully pull it from the transmission. Carefully lift the engine out of the engine compartment (avoid bending or damaging the rear cover plate or other components). Install the engine on a work stand.

17. Installation is the reverse of removal.

18. Tighten all the bolts to specifications.

Engine Mounts

Removal and Installation

2.3L ENGINE

1. Disconnect the negative battery cable. Support the engine using a wood block and jack placed under the engine.

2. Remove the through bolts attaching both insulators to the No. 2 crossmember pedestal bracket. On turbocharged engine, remove nuts.

3. LTD and Marquis: Remove the bolt that attaches the lower end of the engine damper to the No. 2 crossmember bracket.

4. Disconnect shift linkage.

5. Raise the engine sufficiently to disengage the insulator studs from the crossmember pedestal bracket.

6. Remove the bolts attaching the insulator and bracket assembly to the engine. Remove the insulator and bracket assembly.

7. Position the insulator and bracket assembly to the engine. Install the attaching bolts. Tighten to 33–45 ft. lbs. (45–61 Nm).

8. Lower the engine into position making sure that the insulators are seated flat on the No. 2 crossmember and the insulator studs are at the bottom of the slots.

9. On 2.3L turbocharged engine, install engine bracket to the No. 2 crossmember. Lower engine into position until the through bolts line up. Hand start, then tighten nuts to 65–85 ft. lbs. (88–119 Nm).

10. Install fuel pump shield attaching screw to left engine support, if so equipped.

11. LTD and Marquis: Install engine damper to No. 2 crossmember bracket attaching bolt. Tighten the bolt to 35–50 ft. lbs. (40–64 Nm).

12. Install shift linkage.

3.8L ENGINE

1. Disconnect the negative battery cable. Remove fan shroud attaching screws. On supercharged engine, disconnect the inlet and outlet tubes from the intercooler.

2. Support engine using a jack and wood block placed under the engine.

3. Remove through bolt or nuts attaching insulators to the No. 2 crossmember.

4. Remove shift linkage.

5. Raise engine high enough to clear clevis brackets or insulator studs from crossmember.

6. Remove fuel pump shield, if so equipped, from right side of the engine.

7. Remove starter ground cable and oil cooler line attaching clips from right hand engine support bracket.

8. Remove bolts attaching insulator and bracket assembly to engine. Remove insulator and bracket assembly.

9. Installation is the reverse of the removal procedure.

5.0L AND 5.8L ENGINES – GRAND MARQUIS, CROWN VICTORIA AND TOWN CAR

1. Disconnect the negative battery cable. Remove fan shroud attaching screw.

2. Support the engine using a jack and wood block placed under the engine.

3. Remove the through bolts attaching the insulators to the insulator support bracket.

4. Remove the bolts attaching the insulator assembly to the frame.

5. Raise the engine slightly with the jack and remove the insulator assembly.

6. Position the engine insulator assembly to the frame and install the attaching bolts. Tighten the bolts to 26–38 ft. lbs. (35–52 Nm).

7. Lower the engine into position and install the engine insulator assembly to insulator support bracket through bolts. Tighten the through bolts to 33–46 ft. lbs. (45–62 Nm).

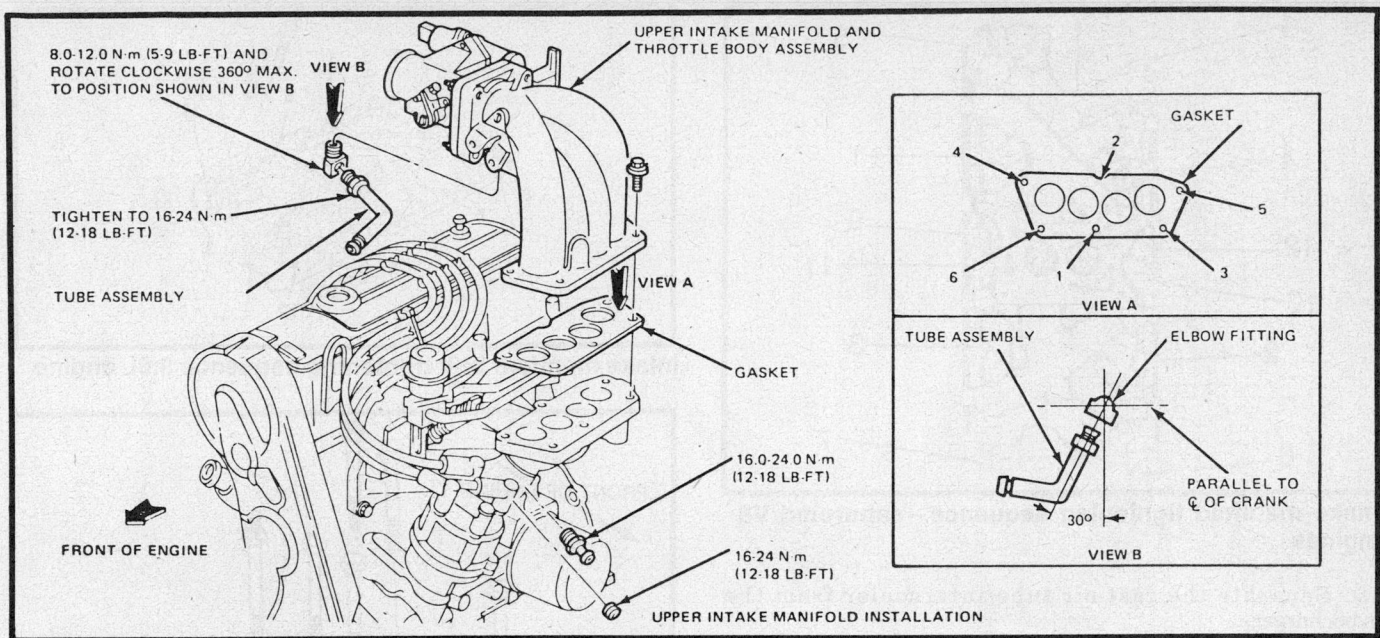

Intake manifold Installation 2.3L engines

8. Install fan shroud attaching screws and tighten to 24–48 inch lbs. (3–5 Nm).

5.0L ENGINE—MUSTANG, CAPRI, COUGAR, THUNDERBIRD, CONTINENTAL AND MARK VII

1. Disconnect the negative battery cable. Remove fan shroud attaching screws.
2. Support the engine using a jack and wood block placed under the engine.
3. Remove the nuts attaching insulators to the No. 2 crossmember.
4. Disconnect shift linkage.
5. Raise the engine sufficiently with the jack to disengage the insulator studs from the crossmember.
6. Remove the engine insulator and bracket assembly to cylinder block attaching bolts. Remove the engine insulator assembly.
7. Position the insulator assembly on the engine and install the attaching bolts. Tighten the bolts to 35–60 ft. lbs. (48–81 Nm).
8. Lower the engine into position making sure that the insulators are seated flat on the No. 2 crossmember and the insulator studs are at the bottom of the slots.
9. Install the insulator to the No. 2 crossmember and start the nut assemblies on the insulator studs and tighten to specification.
10. Install the fan shroud attaching screws and tighten to 24–48 inch lbs. (3–5 Nm).
11. Connect shift linkage.

Intake Manifold

Removal and Installation

2.3L ENGINE

Carbureted

1. Disconnect the negative battery cable. Drain the cooling system and remove the air cleaner.
2. Disconnect the accelerator cable.
3. Disconnect and label the vacuum hoses at the carburetor.
4. Remove the engine oil dipstick.

5. Disconnect the heat tube at the EGR valve.
6. Disconnect and plug the fuel line at the carburetor.
7. Remove the bolt attaching the dipstick to the manifold.
8. Remove the PCV valve from the manifold.
9. Remove the distributor cap screws and the distributor cap.
10. Remove the intake manifold attaching bolts and remove the manifold.
11. Clean all dirt and gasket material from the surfaces on the cylinder head and intake manifold.
12. Position a new gasket and the manifold on the studs. Torque the bolts and nuts to the specified torque in 2 stages.
13. Connect the crankcase ventilation hose to the manifold. Connect the heater hoses to the choke cover and manifold, if equipped.
14. Replace the heat tube, accelerator cable and dipstick assembly.
15. Connect the distributor vacuum lines to the manifold.
16. Connect the fuel line to the carburetor.
17. Install the air cleaner assembly. Fill the cooling system, if drained and check for leaks.

Fuel Injected

1. Disconnect the negative battery cable. Disconnect and label the electrical connectors at:
   a. the air bypass valve
   b. the throttle positioning sensor
   c. injector wiring harness
   d. knock sensor
   e. fan temperature sensor and coolant temperature sensor
2. Disconnect the upper intake manifold vacuum fitting connections by disconnecting the vacuum line fitting at the cast air tube. Disconnect the rear vacuum line at the dash panel tree. Remove the vacuum line to the EGR valve and the vacuum line to the fuel pressure regulator. Label all lines for reinstallation identification.
3. Disconnect the throttle linkage. Unbolt the accelerator cable from the bracket and position the cable out of the way.
4. Remove the bolts that attach the cast air tube/intercooler assembly to the turbocharger.
5. Remove the nuts that attach the air throttle body to the fuel charging assembly.

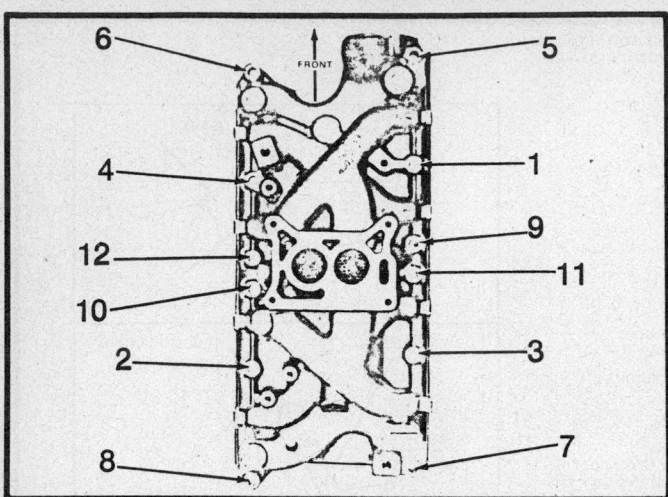

Intake manifold tightening sequence—cabureted V8 engines

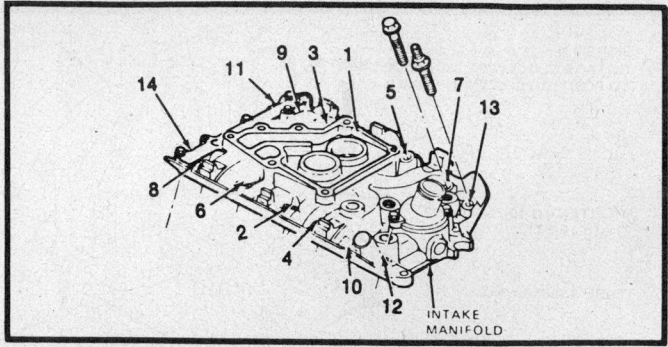

Intake manifold bolt tightening sequence 3.8L engine

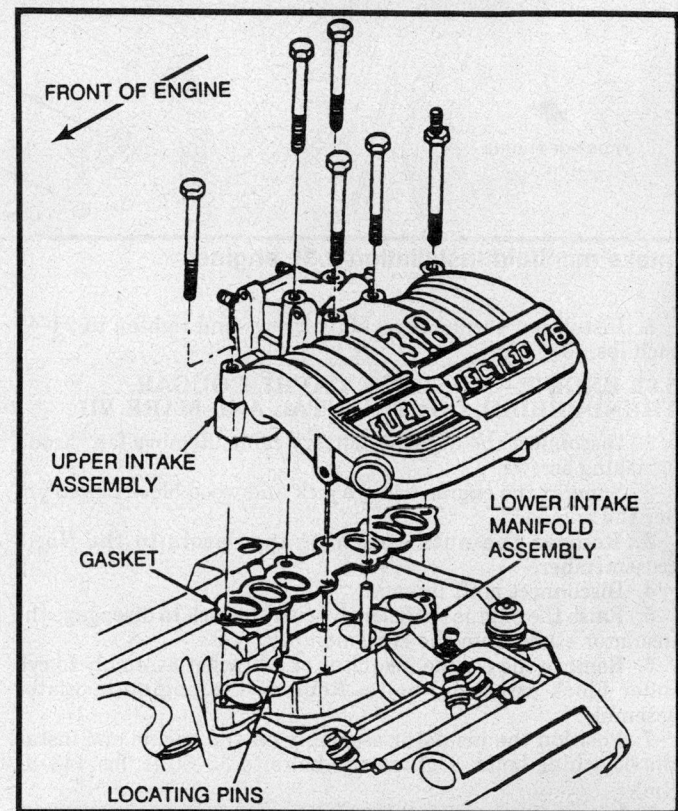

Upper intake manifold mounting 3.8L EFI engine

6. Separate the cast air tube/intercooler from the turbocharger.

7. Remove and discard the mounting gasket between the cast tube and the turbocharger. Remove the throttle body and cast tube.

8. Disconnect the PCV system hose from the fitting on the underside of the upper intake manifold.

9. Disconnect the water bypass hose at the lower intake manifold.

10. Loosen the EGR flange nut and disconnect the EGR tube.

11. Remove the fuel injector wiring harness bracket retaining nuts and the bracket after separating the dipstick bracket.

12. Remove the upper intake manifold retaining bolts and or studs and remove the upper intake manifold assembly.

13. Relieve the fuel system pressure and disconnect the push-connect fuel supply line.

14. Disconnect the fuel return line from the fuel supply manifold.

15. Disconnect the electrical connectors from the fuel injectors and move the harness aside.

16. Remove the fuel supply manifold retaining bolts and remove the manifold carefully. Injectors can be removed at this time by exerting a slight twisting/pulling motion.

17. Remove the bottom and the top retaining bolts from the lower manifold. Remove the manifold.

18. Clean and inspect all mounting surfaces of the fuel charge manifolds and cylinder head.

19. Clean and oil all stud threads. Install a new mounting gasket over the studs.

20. Install the lower manifold to the cylinder head with lift bracket in position. Install the 4 upper manifold nuts fingertight. Install the 4 remaining nuts and tighten all nuts to 12–15 ft. lbs. in the proper torque sequence.

21. Install the remaining components in the reverse order of removal. Fuel supply manifold bolts are tighten to 12–15 ft. lbs. Upper manifold mounting bolts 15–22 ft. lbs. Dipstick and injector wiring harness bolts 15–22 ft. lbs. Cast air tube to turbocharger 14–21 ft. lbs. Air throttle body mounting 12–15 ft. lbs.

3.8L, 5.0L AND 5.8L ENGINES WITH CARBURETOR AND CFI

1. Disconnect the negative battery cable. Drain the cooling system, disconnect the upper radiator hose from the thermostat housing and the bypass hose from the manifold.

2. On all engines, remove the air cleaner and intake duct.

3. Disconnect the high tension lead and wires from the coil. Disconnect the engine wiring loom and position out of the way.

4. Disconnect the spark plug wires at the plugs by twisting and pulling on the molded plug cap only. Remove the distributor cap and wires as an assembly. Disconnect the vacuum hose(s) from the distributor. Disconnect the temperature sending unit wire.

5. Mark the position of the rotor and distributor body in relation to the manifold, remove the distributor hold down bolt and remove the distributor.

6. Remove the thermactor by pass valve and air supply hoses, if equipped.

7. Remove all vacuum lines from the manifold.

NOTE: On CFI equipped engines, discharge the fuel pressure before disconnecting the fuel lines.

8. Disconnect the fuel line and vacuum hoses at the carburetor. Disconnect the accelerator linkage and downshift linkage, if so equipped and position out of the way.

9. Disconnect the crankcase vent hose at the rocker cover.

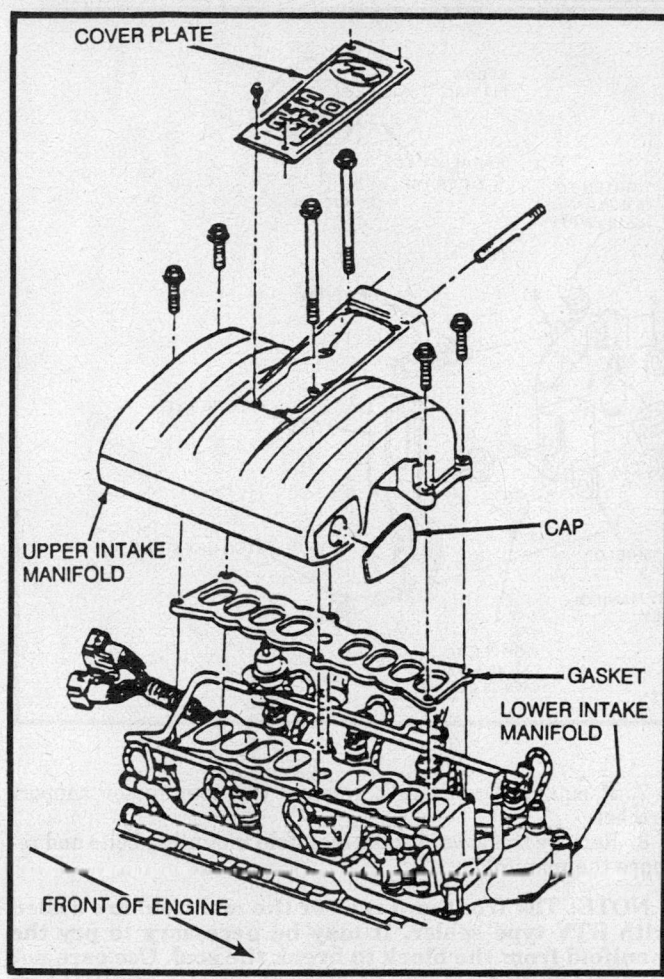

Upper intake manifold mountign 5.0L EFI engine

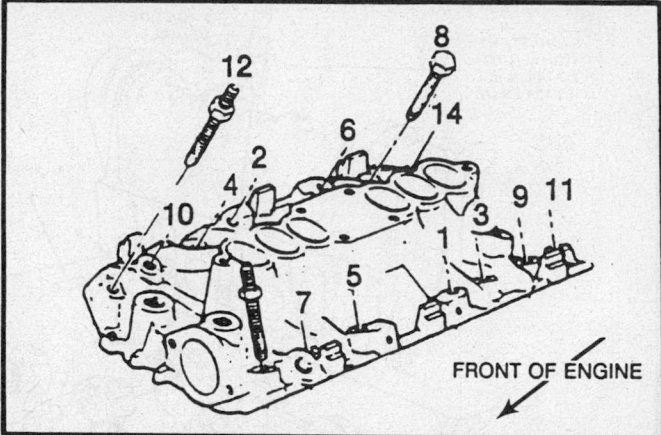

Lower intake manifold tightening sequence 3.8L EFI

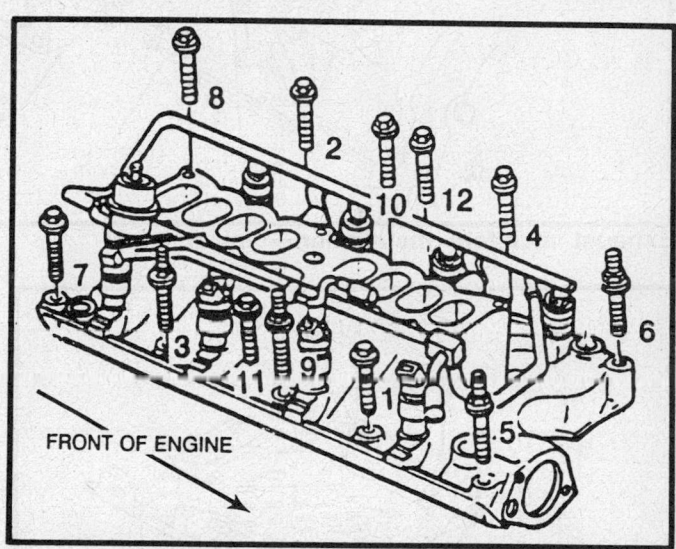

Lower intake manifold tightening sequence 5.0L EFI

10. If equipped with A/C, remove the compressor mounting brackets from the manifold and position the compressor out of the way. Do not disconnect any A/C hoses. Also, remove the coil.

11. Remove the intake manifold and carburetor as an assembly. Be careful not to damage any gasket sealing surfaces.

12. Clean the mating surfaces of the manifold, block and heads. Apply a ⅛ in. bead of silicone sealer to the engine block to cylinder head mating surfaces.

13. Position the new end seals into place on the block, pressing the locating tabs into place. Position new manifold gaskets into place on the heads and apply a ⅛ in. bead of silicone sealer to the end seal to manifold gasket joints.

NOTE: The 3.8L engine uses RTV sealant instead of end seals. Be sure to apply an even bead of sealant when installing the manifold.

14. Carefully lower the manifold into place. After it is positioned, check the seal area to be sure the seals are properly positioned. If they are not, remove the manifold and reposition the seals.

15. Torque the manifold to specification and in sequence in 3 stages. The rest of installation is the reverse of removal. After installation, run the engine to operating temperature and retorque the manifold bolts.

3.8L AND 5.0L ENGINES WITH EFI—EXCEPT 3.8L SUPERCHARGED
Upper Intake Manifold

1. Disconnect the negative battery cable.

2. Relieve the fuel system pressure.

3. Disconnect the electrical connectors at the air bypass valve, throttle position sensor and EGR position sensor.

4. Disconnect the throttle linkage at the throttle ball and the transmission linkage from the throttle body. Remove the 2 bolts securing the cable bracket to the intake manifold and position out of the way.

5. Disconnect and tag the upper intake manifold vacuum lines. Disconnect the vacuum line to the EGR valve and the fuel pressure regulator.

6. Disconnect the vacuum connection to the canister purge line.

7. Remove the PCV vent closure tube at the throttle body and disconnect the hose at the rear of the manifold.

8. Remove the EGR coolant lines from the fittings on the EGR spacer.

9. Remove the 6 upper intake manifold retaining bolts. Remove the manifold and the throttle body as an assembly.

10. To install, clean and inspect the mounting surfaces.

11. Install the upper manifold and throttle body assembly and install the 6 mounting bolts. Torque the mounting bolts to 12-18 ft. lbs.

12. Reconnect all vacuum lines and electrical connections.

13. Connect the throttle linkage and bracket to the manifold.

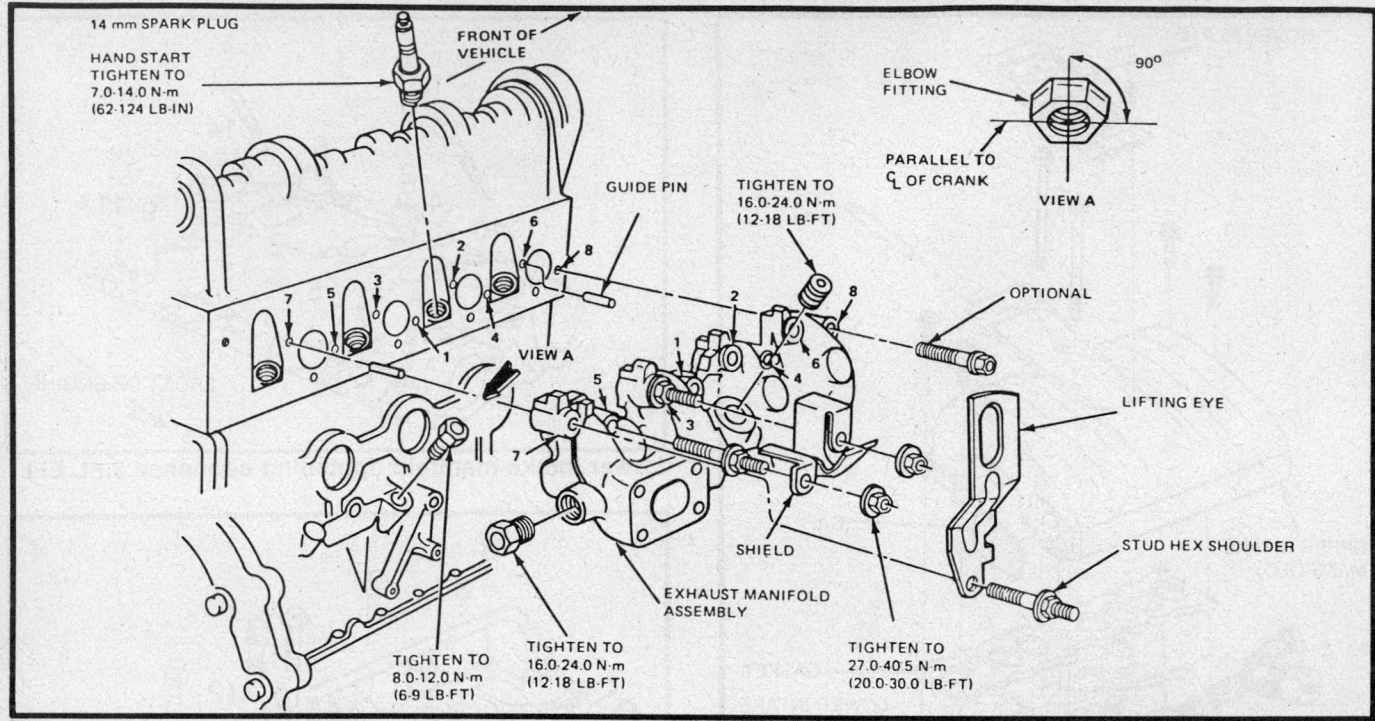

14 mm SPARK PLUG

HAND START
TIGHTEN TO
7.0-14.0 N·m
(62-124 LB·IN)

FRONT OF
VEHICLE

ELBOW
FITTING

90°

PARALLEL TO
CL OF CRANK

VIEW A

GUIDE PIN

TIGHTEN TO
16.0-24.0 N·m
(12-18 LB·FT)

OPTIONAL

LIFTING EYE

VIEW A

STUD HEX SHOULDER

SHIELD

EXHAUST MANIFOLD
ASSEMBLY

TIGHTEN TO
8.0-12.0 N·m
(6-9 LB·FT)

TIGHTEN TO
16.0-24.0 N·m
(12-18 LB·FT)

TIGHTEN TO
27.0-40.5 N·m
(20.0-30.0 LB·FT)

Exhaust manifold installation—typical 4 cyl

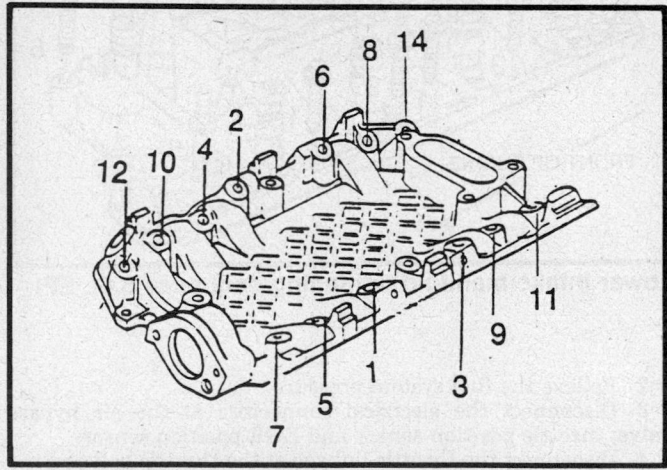

Intake manifold torque sequence—3.8L SC engine

Lower Intake Manifold

1. Disconnect the negative battery cable and relieve fuel system pressure.
2. Remove the upper intake manifold.
3. Disconnect the crossover fuel line from the fuel rail assembly. Remove the injector electrical harness connector.
4. Remove the 4 fuel rail retaining bolts. Remove the fuel rail and the injectors as an assembly.

NOTE: To remove the fuel injectors from the manifold, use a back and forth twisting motion while pulling upward.

5. Disconnect the coolant bypass hose at the manifold. Disconnect the upper radiator hose at the thermostat housing.
6. Remove the heater tube, elbow and attaching bracket from the manifold. Lay the heater tube and bracket aside.

7. If equipped with A/C, remove the compressor support bracket.
8. Remove the lower intake manifold mounting bolts and remove the manifold.

NOTE: The front and rear of the manifold are sealed with RTV type sealer. It may be necessary to pry the manifold from the block to break the seal. Use care not to damage the machined surface of the manifold or engine.

9. To install, clean all mating surfaces. Use new gaskets, apply a continuous 1/8 in. bead of RTV silicone sealer or equivalent at each corner where the cylinder and manifold meet. Apply a 1/16 bead of RTV sealer or equivalent along the outer edge of the gaskets.
10. Carefully lower the intake manifold into position. Check the outer edge of the manifold to make sure that the gaskets stayed in place.
11. Install the manifold bolts and tighten in sequence to 23–25 ft. lbs.

NOTE: On 3.8L engines torque the manifold in 3 steps: first to 8 ft. lbs., then to 15 ft. lbs. and finally to 24 ft. lbs.

12. Install the coolant lines and hoses. Install the fuel rail assembly and the heater tube. If equipped with A/C, install the A/C compressor support bracket.
13. Install the upper intake manifold and throttle body assembly. Connect all electrical leads. Reconnect the fuel lines and the vacuum lines.
14. Check the coolant level and fill. Run the engine and check for fluid leaks.

3.8L SUPERCHARGED ENGINE

1. Disconnect the negative battery cable.
2. Relieve the fuel system pressure.
3. Remove the supercharger assembly.
4. Remove the thermostat housing and the thermostat.
5. Remove the temperature sending unit.
6. Remove the heater elbow and the vacuum hoses.

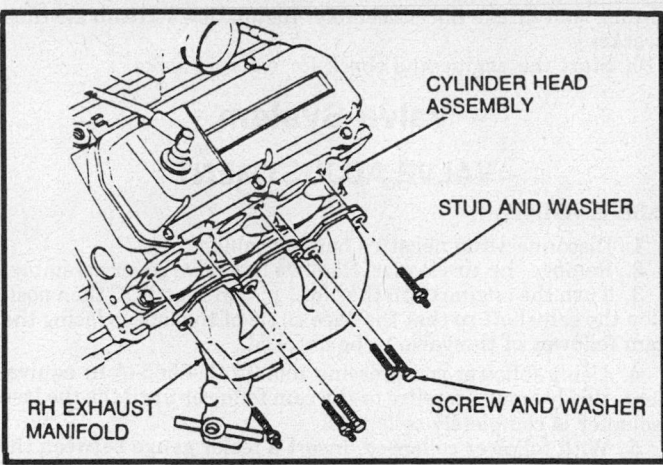

3.8L exhaust manifold mounting

Labels: CYLINDER HEAD ASSEMBLY, STUD AND WASHER, SCREW AND WASHER, RH EXHAUST MANIFOLD

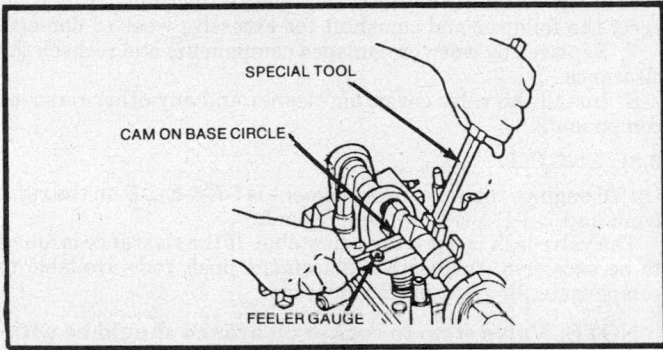

Hydraulic valve lash check

Labels: SPECIAL TOOL, CAM ON BASE CIRCLE, FEELER GAUGE

7. Remove the intake manifold retaining bolts and remove the manifold. If the manifold will not pull off easily, pry up on the edge to break the seal.

8. Clean all gasket mating surfaces. Check for nicked or burred edges on the sealing surfaces.

9. To install the intake manifold, lightly oil all attaching bolts and studs.

10. Apply a dab of gasket and trim adhesive or equivalent, to the cylinder head mating surfaces and install new intake manifold gaskets.

11. Apply a thin bead of silicone sealant to the points where the block and the cylinder head meet.

12. Install new intake manifold seal end gaskets. Lower the intake manifold into position on the block.

13. Install the retaining bolts and tighten in numerical sequence to the correct torque.

14. Install the temperature sending unit, thermostat and housing.

15. Install the heater elbow and the vacuum hoses.

16. Install the supercharger assembly. Run the engine to normal operating temperature and check for leaks.

Exhaust Manifold

Removal and Installation

2.3L ENIGNE

1. Disconnect the negative battery cable.
2. Disconnect the exhaust header pipe at the manifold.
3. Remove the heat shield. Remove the turbocharger, if equipped.
4. Disconnect any brackets from the manifold. Remove the manifold retaining bolts and remove the manifold.

5. Clean and check all gasket surfaces.
6. Installation is the reverse of the removal procedure.

3.8L ENGINE

Left Side

1. Disconnect the negative battery cable. Remove oil level dipstick tube support bracket.
2. Disconnect EGO sensor at the wiring connector, if equipped.
3. Disconnect wires from spark plugs.
4. Raise and safely support the vehicle.
5. Remove manifold to exhaust pipe attaching nuts.
6. Disconnect exhaust heat control valve vacuum line, if equipped.
7. Lower vehicle.
8. Remove exhaust manifold attaching bolts and manifold.
9. If a new exhaust manifold is being installed, remove EGO sensor, if equipped and exhaust heat control valve, if equipped.
10. Installation is the reverse of removal procedure.
11. If equipped with an EGO sensor, coat the threads with high temperature anti-seize compound. Install the sensor into the exhaust manifold and tighten to 27–33 ft. lbs. (37–45 Nm).
12. Install remaining manifold attaching bolts and tighten to 15–22 ft. lbs. (20–30 Nm).

Right Side

1. Disconnect the negative battery cable. Remove air cleaner assembly and heat tube.
2. Disconnect thermactor hose from the downstream air tube check valve, if equipped with CFI.
3. Remove EGO sensor at the wiring connector, if equipped.
4. Disconnect coil secondary wire from the coil and the wires from the spark plugs.
5. Remove spark plugs. Remove outer heat shroud.
6. Raise and safely support the vehicle.
7. Remove transmission dipstick tube.
8. Remove thermactor downstream air tube. Use an EGR clamp cutter and crimping tool to cut the tube clamp at the underbody catalyst, if equipped with CFI.
9. Remove manifold to exhaust pipe attaching nuts.
10. Lower the vehicle.
11. Remove exhaust manifold attaching bolts. Remove manifold and inner heat shroud as an assembly.
12. Installation is the reverse of removal procedures.
13. Install manifold attaching bolts and tighten to 15–25 ft. lbs. (20–30 Nm).
14. Connect exhaust pipe to the manifold and tighten the attaching nuts to 16–24 ft. lbs. (21–32 Nm).

5.0L AND 5.8L ENGINES

1. Disconnect the negative battery cable. On a right exhaust manifold, remove the air cleaner and intake duct assembly and downstream air tube bracket (except Crown Victoria, Grand Marquis, Town Car, Mark VII and Continental).2. Disconnect the automatic choke heat tubes. On left exhaust manifolds, remove the oil dipstick and tube assembly, air cleaner and inlet duct assembly (Crown Victoria, Grand Marquis, Town Car, Mark VII and Continental).
3. Remove speed control bracke try, if so equipped.
4. Disconnect the exhaust manifold from the muffler inlet pipe. Remove the attaching nuts and then remove the spark plug wires and spark plugs. Disconnect the exhaust gas oxygen (EGO) sensor if equipped.
5. Remove the attaching bolts and washers and remove the exhaust manifold.
6. Clean the mating surfaces of the exhaust manifold and cylinder head. Clean the mounting flange of the exhaust manifold and muffler inlet pipe.
7. Position the exhaust manifold on the cylinder head and install the attaching bolts and washers. Working from the center to the ends, tighten the bolts to specifications. Install the spark

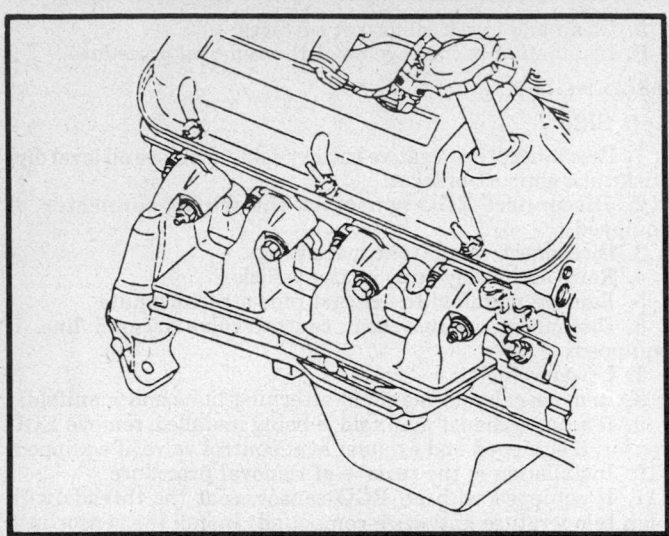

5.0L and 5.8L exhaust manifold mounting

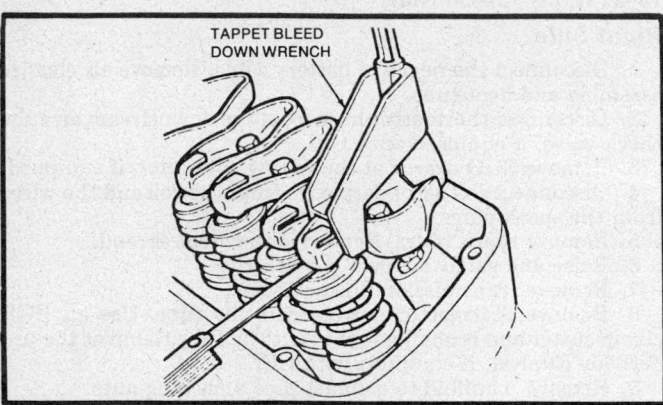

Checking valve clearance

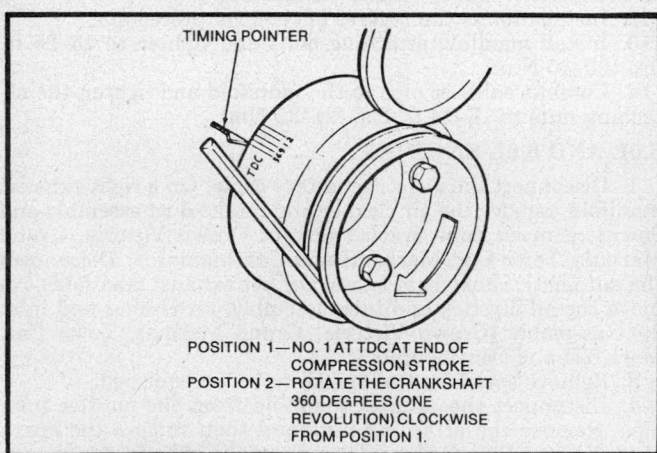

POSITION 1—NO. 1 AT TDC AT END OF
COMPRESSION STROKE.
POSITION 2—ROTATE THE CRANKSHAFT
360 DEGREES (ONE
REVOLUTION) CLOCKWISE
FROM POSITION 1.

Position of crankshaft for checking and adjusting valve clearance

plugs and spark plug wires. Connect the exhaust gas oxygen sensor (EGO) if equipped.

8. Position the muffler inlet pipe to the manifold. Install the tighten the attaching nuts to specification.

9. Install the automatic choke heat tubes. Install the air

cleaner and intake duct assembly. Install downstream air tube bracket.

10. Start the engine and check for exhaust leaks.

Valve System

VALVE ADJUSTMENT

2.3L ENGINE

1. Disconnect the negative battery cable.
2. Remove the air cleaner. Remove the valve cover assembly.
3. Turn the engine until the No. 1 piston is at TDC then position the camshaft so that the base circle of the lobe is facing the cam follower of the valve to be checked.
4. Using follower compressing tool T745–6565–A or equivalent, slowly apply pressure to the cam follower until the the lash adjuster is completely collapsed.
5. With follower collapsed, insert a feeler gauge between the base circle of the camshaft and follower. The clearance should not be more than 0.040–0.050 in.
6. If the clearance is excessive, remove the camshaft and inspect the follower and camshaft for excessive wear or damage.
7. Replace any worn or damaged components and recheck the clearance.
8. Install the valve cover, air cleaner and any other removed components.

3.8L ENGINE

On V6 engines the valve arrangement is I-E-I-E-I-E on the right bank and E-I-E-I-E-I on the left bank.

The valve lash is not truly adjustable. If the clearance is found to be excessive, there are replacement push rods available to compensate for some excess clearance.

NOTE: Valve stem to rocker clearance should be within specification with the tappet completely collapsed.

1. Disconnect the negative battery cable.
2. Remove the valve cover assembly on the side to be checked.
3. Turn the engine until the No. 1 piston is at TDC after the compression stroke.
4. The following valves can be checked with the engine in this position:
   a. No. 1 intake – No. 1 exhaust
   b. No. 3 intake – No. 2 exhaust
   c. No. 6 intake – No. 4 exhaust
5. Rotate the engine 360 degrees and check the following valves:
   a. No. 2 intake – No. 3 exhaust
   b. No. 4 intake – No. 5 exhaust
   c. No. 5 intake – No. 6 exhaust
6. Check each of the lifters by placing the hydraulic lifter compressing tool on the rocker arm and slowly applying pressure to the tappet, until the tappet bottoms.
7. Hold the tappet in this position and check the clearance between the rocker arm and the and the valve stem tip. Clearance should not exceed ⅜ in.
8. Repeat this operation for each valve to be checked.
9. If the clearance is greater than specification, replace the pushrod with a longer one.

5.0L AND 5.8L ENGINES

On V8 engines the valve arrangement is I-E-I-E-I-E-I-E on the right bank and E-I-E-I-E-I-E-I on the left bank.

The valve lash is not truly adjustable. If the clearance is found to be excessive, there are replacement pushrods available to compensate for some excess clearance.

NOTE: Valve stem to rocker clearance should be within specification with the tappet completely collapsed.

1. Disconnect the negative battery cable.

2. Remove the valve cover assembly on the side to be checked.

3. Turn the engine until the No. 1 piston is at TDC after the compression stroke.

4. The following valves can be checked with the engine in this position:

    a. No. 1 intake—No. 1 exhaust

    b. No. 4 intake—No. 3 exhaust

    c. No. 8 intake—No. 7 exhaust

5. Rotate the engine 180 degrees and check the following valves:

    a. No. 3 intake—No. 2 exhaust

    b. No. 7 intake—No. 6 exhaust

6. Rotate the engine 270 degrees and check the following valves:

    a. No. 2 intake—No. 4 exhaust

    b. No. 5 intake—No. 5 exhaust

    c. No. 6 intake—No. 8 exhaust

6. Check each of the lifters by placing the hydraulic lifter compressing tool on the rocker arm and slowly applying pressure to the tappet, until the tappet bottoms.

7. Hold the tappet in this position and check the clearance between the rocker arm and the and the valve stem tip. Clearance should not exceed ⅜ in.

8. Repeat this operation for each valve to be checked.

9. If the clearance is greater than specification, replace the pushrod with a longer one.

VALVE LIFTERS

Removal and Installation

3.8L ENGINE

NOTE: Before replacing a tappet for noisy operation, be sure the noise is not caused by improper valve to rocker arm clearance or by worn rocker arms or pushrods.

1. Disconnect the negative battery cable. Disconnect secondary ignition wires at the spark plugs.

2. Remove plug wire routing clips from the studs on the rocker arm cover attaching bolts. Lay the plug wires, with the routing clips toward the front of the engine.

3. Remove intake manifold.

4. Remove rocker arm covers.

5. Sufficiently loosen each rocker arm fulcrum attaching bolt to allow the rocker arm to be lifted off the pushrod and rotate to 1 side.

6. Remove pushrods. The location of each pushrod should be identified. When the engine is assembled each rod should be installed in its original position.

7. Remove the lifters using a magnet. The location of each tappet should be identified. When the engine is assembled, each tappet should be installed in its original position.

8. Installation is the reverse of removal procedure.

9. For each valve rotate the crankshaft until the tappet rests on the heel (base circle) of the camshaft lobe. Position rocker arm over the pushrods. Install fulcrums and tighten fulcrum attaching bolt to 7–15 Nm (62–132 inch lb.).

10. Final tightening fulcrum bolts to 25–35 Nm (19–25 ft. lbs.). For final tightening, the camshaft may be in any position.

NOTE: If the lifters are stuck in the bores due to excessive varnish or gum deposits, it may be necessary to use a plier type tool or a claw type tool to aid removal. When using a remover tool, rotate the tappet back and forth to loosen it from the gum or varnish that may have formed on the tappet.

Fulcrums must be fully seated in cylinder head and pushrods must be seated in rocker arm sockets prior to final tightening.

5.0L AND 5.8L ENGINES

1. Disconnect the negative battery cable. Remove the intake manifold and related parts.

2. Remove the crankcase ventilation hoses, PCV valve and elbows from the valve rocker arm covers.

3. Remove the valve rocker arm covers. Loosen the valve rocker arm fulcrum bolts and rotate the rocker arms to the side.

4. Remove the valve pushrods and identify them so that they can be installed in their original position.

5. Using a magnet, remove the lifters and place them in a rack so that they can be installed in their original bores.

NOTE: 1987–90 5.0L engines are equipped with roller type hydraulic lifters.

6. Lifters and bores are to be lubricated with engine oil, classification SF, before installation. Installation is the reverse of the removal procedure.

VALVE ROCKER ARM

Removal and Installation

2.3L ENGINE

1. Disconnect the negative battery cable. Remove the valve rocker arm cover and associated parts as required.

2. Rotate the camshaft so that the base circle of the cam is facing the cam follower of the cylinder to be worked on.

3. Using valve spring compressor, collapse the lash adjuster and/or depress the valve spring if necessary and slide the cam follower over the lash adjuster and out.

4. Lift the hydraulic lash adjuster.

5. Place the hydraulic lash adjuster in position in the bore.

6. Using valve spring compressor, collapse the lash adjuster as necessary to position the cam follower over the lash adjuster and the valve stem. It may also be necessary to compress the valve spring.

7. Before rotating the camshaft to the next position, be sure the lash adjuster just installed is fully compressed and released.

8. Clean the gasket surfaces of the valve cover and cylinder head adhesive. Allow to dry past the "wet" stage and then install gasket in valve cover. Coat cylinder head contact surfaces with the same adhesive, allowing the adhesive to dry past the "wet" stage. Install the valve cover and gasket, making sure locating tabs are properly positioned in slots in cover.

9. Install 8 screws and tighten to 62–97 inch lbs. (7–11 Nm).

3.8L, 5.0L AND 5.8L ENGINES

1. Disconnect the negative battery cable.

2. On the right side, disconnect the automatic choke heat chamber air inlet hose. Remove the air cleaner and duct.

3. On the 3.8L and 5.0L engines remove the automatic choke heat tube. Remove the PCV fresh air tube from the rocker cover and disconnect the EGR vacuum amplifier hoses.

4. Remove the thermactor bypass valve and air supply hoses. Disconnect the spark plug wires.

5. On the left side, remove the wiring harness from the clips. Remove the rocker arm cover.

6. On the 3.8L supercharged engine remove the supercharger-to-intercooler tube.

7. Remove the rocker arm stud nut or bolt. fulcrum seat and rocker arm.

8. Lubricate all parts with heavy SE oil before installation. When installing, rotate the crankshaft until the lifter is on the base of the cam circle (low point, no lift) and assemble the rocker arm. Torque the nut or bolt to 17–23 ft. lbs., 19–25 ft. lbs. on 3.8L supercharged engine.

NOTE: Some later engines are using RTV sealant instead of valve cover gaskets. Always apply an even ⅛ in. bead of sealant along the channel of the valve cover after cleaning.

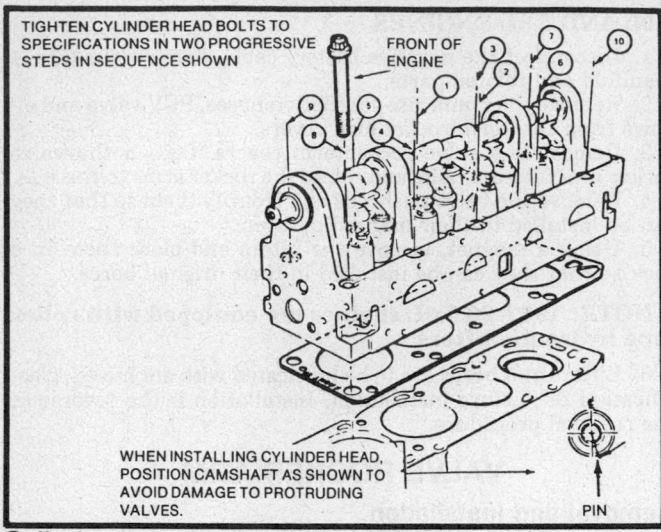

TIGHTEN CYLINDER HEAD BOLTS TO SPECIFICATIONS IN TWO PROGRESSIVE STEPS IN SEQUENCE SHOWN

FRONT OF ENGINE

WHEN INSTALLING CYLINDER HEAD, POSITION CAMSHAFT AS SHOWN TO AVOID DAMAGE TO PROTRUDING VALVES.

PIN

Cylinder head installation – 4cyl

Cylinder Head

Removal and Installation

2.3L ENGINE

1. Disconnect the negative battery cable. Drain the cooling system.
2. Remove the air cleaner and the valve rocker cover. On turbocharged vehicles remove the inlet tube between the turbocharger and the throttle body.
3. Remove the intake and exhaust manifolds. The intake manifold, installed valves and sensors (if equipped) and carburetor can be removed as an assembly.
4. Remove the camshaft drive belt cover.
5. Loosen the drive belt tensioner and remove the drive belt.
6. Remove the water outlet from the cylinder head.
7. Remove the cylinder head bolts evenly and remove the cylinder head.
8. Position a new cylinder head gasket on the block. Rotate the camshaft so that the locating pin is at the 5 o'clock position, to avoid valve damage.
9. Position the cylinder head on the block. Install the bolts finger tight and torque in sequence to specifications in 2 stages.

NOTE: If difficulty in positioning the head on the block is encountered, guide pins may be fabricated by cutting the heads off 2 extra cylinder head bolts.

10. Set the crankshaft at TDC and be sure that the camshaft drive gear and distributor are positioned correctly.
11. Install the camshaft drive belt and release the tensioner. Rotate the crankshaft 2 full turns clockwise (facing the engine) to remove all slack from the belt. The timing marks should again be aligned. Tighten the tensioner lockbolt and pivot bolts.
12. Install the camshaft drive belt cover.
13. Apply sealer to the water outlet and new gasket and install.
14. Install the intake and exhaust manifolds.
15. Adjust the valve clearance.
16. Install a new valve cover gasket and install the valve cover.
17. Install the air cleaner and crankcase ventilation hose. On turbo models install the inlet tube between the turbo charger and the throttle body.
18. Refill the cooling system. Run the engine and check for leaks.

3.8L ENGINE EXCEPT SUPERCHARGED

1. Drain the cooling system.
2. Disconnect the negative battery cable.
3. Remove air cleaner assembly including the air intake duct and heat tube.
4. Loosen accessory drive belt idler. Remove drive belt.
5. If the left cylinder head is being removed, perform the following:
   a. Remove oil fill cap.
   b. If equipped with power steering, remove pump mounting brackets attaching bolts. Leaving the hoses connected, place the pump/bracket assembly aside in a position to prevent the fluid from leaking out.
   c. If equipped with air conditioning, remove the mounting bracket attaching bolts. Leaving hoses connected, position compressor aside.
6. If right cylinder head is being removed, perform the following:
   a. Disconnect thermactor air control valve or bypass valve hose assembly at the air pump.
   b. Disconnect thermactor air control valve or bypass valve hose assembly at the air pump.
   c. Disconnect thermactor tube support bracket from the rear of the cylinder head.
   d. Remove accessory drive idler.
   e. Remove alternator.
   f. Remove thermactor pump pulley. Remove thermactor pump.
   g. Remove alternator bracket.

NOTE: If equipped with tripminder, the fuel supply tube (fuel pump to sensor) must be disconnected to gain access to the alternator bracket upper attaching bolt.

   h. Remove PCV valve.
7. Remove intake manifold.
8. Remove valve rocker arm cover attaching screws.
9. Remove exhaust manifold(s).
10. Loosen rocker arm fulcrum attaching bolts enough to allow the rocker arm to be lifted off the pushrod and rotated to 1 side.
11. Remove pushrods. Identify the position of each rod. The rods should be installed in their original position during assembly.
12. Remove cylinder head attaching bolts and discard.
13. Remove cylinder head(s).

NOTE: Lightly oil all bolt and stud bolt threads before installation except those specifying special sealant.

14. Clean all mating surfaces.
15. Position new head gasket(s) on the cylinder block using the dowels for alignment.
16. Position cylinder head(s) on block.
17. Install new cylinder head bolts (8 each side). Apply a thin coating of Pipe Sealant to the threads of the short cylinder head bolts (nearest to the exhaust manifold). Do not apply sealant to the long bolts.

NOTE: Always use new cylinder head bolts to assure a leak-tight assembly. Torque retention with used bolts can vary, which may result in coolant or compression leakage at the cylinder head mating surface area.

18. Tighten the new cylinder head attaching bolts in sequence as follows:
   a. 37 ft. lbs. (50 Nm)
   b. 45 ft. lbs. (60 Nm)
   c. 52 ft. lbs. (70 Nm)
   d. 59 ft. lbs. (80 Nm)
   e. Back-off the attaching bolts 2–3 turns.

19. After backing off the head bolts 2–3 turns, retorque in 4 steps and in sequence as follows:
   a. 37 ft. lbs. (50 Nm)
   b. 45 ft. lbs. (60 Nm)
   c. 52 ft. lbs. (70 Nm)
   d. 59 ft. lbs. (80 Nm)

NOTE: When cylinder head attaching bolts have been tightened using multi-step torque procedure, it is not necessary to retighten the bolts after extended engine operation.

20. Install the pushrods, in their original position.
21. For each valve rotate the crankshaft until the tappet rests on the heel (base circle) of the camshaft lobe, before tightening the fulcrum attaching bolts.
22. Position rocker arm over the pushrods, install fulcrums and tighten fulcrum attaching bolts to 61–132 inch lbs. (7–15 Nm).

NOTE: Fulcrums must be fully seated in cylinder head and pushrods must be seated in rocker arm sockets prior to final tightening.

23. Lubricate all rocker arm assemblies with heavy engine oil.

NOTE: If the original valve train components are being installed, a valve clearance check is not required. If a component has been replaced, perform a valve clearance check.

24. Install the exhaust manifold(s).
25. Position cover and new gasket on the cylinder head and install attaching bolts. Note the location of spark plug wire routing clip stud bolts. Tighten attaching bolts to 80–106 inch lbs. (9–12 Nm).
26. Install the intake manifold.
27. Install the spark plugs, if removed.
28. Connect the secondary wires to the spark plugs.
29. If the left cylinder head is being installed, perform the following:
   a. Install the oil filler cap.
   b. If equipped with air conditioning, install the compressor mounting and support brackets.
   c. If equipped with power steering, install the pump mounting and support brackets.
30. If the right cylinder head is being installed, perform the following:
   a. Install PCV valve.
   b. Install the alternator bracket. Tighten attaching nuts to 30–40 ft. lbs. (40–55 Nm).
   c. If equipped with a tripminder, connect fuel supply line (fuel pump to sensor). Tighten the fitting securely.
   d. Install the thermactor pump and pump pulley.
   e. Install the alternator.
   f. Install the accessory drive belt idler pulley.
   g. Install the thermactor air control valve or air bypass valve hose. Tighten the clamps securely to the air pump assembly.
31. Install the accessory drive belt and tighten to specification. Attach the thermactor tube(s) support bracket to the rear of the cylinder head. Tighten attaching bolts to 30–40 ft. lbs. (40–55 Nm).
32. Connect cable to the battery negative terminal.
33. Fill cooling system with the specified coolant.
34. Start engine and check for coolant, fuel and oil leaks.
35. Check and, if necessary, adjust the curb idle speed.
36. Install the air cleaner assembly including the air intake duct and heat tube.

3.8L SUPERCHARGED ENGINE

1. Drain the cooling system and disconnect the negative battery cable.

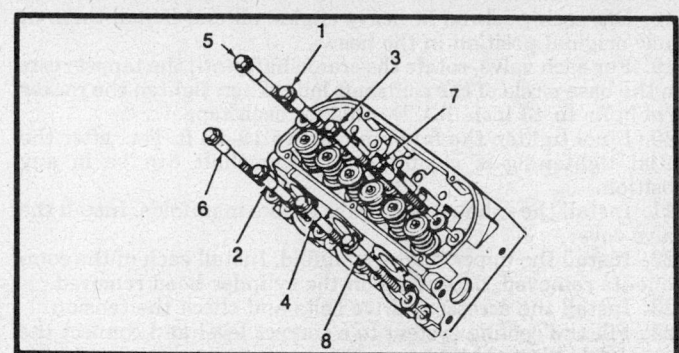
Cylinder head bolt torque sequence—V6 engine

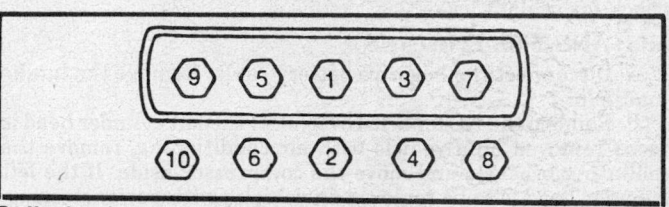
Cylinder head bolt torque sequence—V8 engines

2. Remove the air cleaner assembly, air intake duct.
3. Remove the accessory and supercharger drive belts.
4. If the left cylinder head is being removed, remove the following components:
   a. Oil filler cap
   b. Power steering pump front bracket mounting bolts
   c. Alternator assembly and main belt tensioner
   d. Power steering pump/alternator bracket mounting bolts, lay pump and bracket aside
5. When removing the power steering pump and bracket, leave the hoses attached.
6. If the right cylinder head is being removed, remove the following components:
   a. Thermactor tube support bracket
   b. Air conditioner compressor drive belt and main drive belt
   c. Thermactor pump pulley and thermactor
   d. Air conditioning compressor, lay it aside
   e. PCV valve
7. When removing the air conditioning compressor, leave the refrigerant lines attached.
8. Remove the upper intake manifold assembly. Remove the valve cover.
9. Remove the lower intake manifold and remove the exhaust manifold.
10. Loosen the rocker arm fulcrum attaching bolts enough to allow the rocker arm to be lifted off the pushrod an turn the rocker arms to the side.
11. Remove the pushrods, noting the position of each for installation.
12. Remove the head bolts and throw them away, new bolts must be used for reassembly.
13. Remove the head and discard the gasket. Check all head surfaces for warping or signs of water leakage.
14. Clean all gasket mating surfaces for assembly.
15. Position new cylinder head bolts on the cylinder block using dowel pins to keep them properly lined up.
16. Position the heads on the block. Apply a thin coating of pipe sealant with Teflon® or equivalent to the threads of the short cylinder head bolts (the bolts nearest to the exhaust manifold). Do not apply sealant to the long bolts, instead, dip them in clean oil.
17. Tighten the cylinder head bolts to the correct specification and in the correct sequence.

18. Dip each pushrod in heavy engine oil and install them in their original position in the heads.

19. For each valve, rotate the crankshaft until the tappet rests on the base circle of the camshaft lobe. Then tighten the rocker arm bolts to 43 inch. lbs. Do this for each tappet.

20. Final tighten the fulcrum bolts to 19–25 ft. lbs., after the intial tightening is complete. The camshaft can be in any position.

21. Install the exhaust and lower intake manifolds. Install the valve cover.

22. Install the upper intake manifold. Install each of the components removed, depending on the cylinder head removed.

23. Install the accessory drive belts and check the tension.

24. Fill the cooling system to e correct level and connect the negative battery cable.

25. Run the engine to normal operating temperature and check for coolant leaks.

5.0L AND 5.8L ENGINES

1. Disconnect the negative battery cable. Remove the intake manifold.

2. Remove the rocker arm cover(s). If the left cylinder head is to be removed on a vehicle with air conditioning, remove the mounting brackets and move the compressor aside. If the left cylinder head is to be removed on vehicles with power steering, disconnect the power steering pump bracket from the left cylinder head and remove the drive belt from the pump pulley. Position the power steering pump out of the way and in a position that will prevent the oil from draining out. Remove thermactor crossover tube from the rear of cylinder heads.

3. If the right cylinder head is to be removed, remove the alternator mounting bracket bolts and spacer from the right cylinder head assembly.

4. Disconnect the exhaust manifold(s) from the muffler inlet pipe(s).

5. Loosen the rocker arm fulcrum bolts so that the rocker arms can be rotated to the side. Remove the push rods in sequence so that they may be installed in their original positions. Remove the exhaust valve stem caps.

6. Remove the cylinder head attaching bolts and lift the cylinder head off the block. If required, remove the exhaust manifolds to gain access to the lower attaching bolts. Remove and discard the cylinder head gasket.

7. Clean all of the gasket mating surfaces. If the cylinder head was removed for a cylinder head gasket replacement, check the flatness of the cylinder head and block gasket surfaces.

8. Position the new cylinder head gasket over the cylinder dowels on the block. Position the cylinder head on the block and install the attaching bolts.

9. The cylinder head bolts are tightened in 3 progressive steps. Tighten all the bolts in sequence to specifications. When the cylinder head bolts have been tightened to specification, it is not necessary to retorque the bolts after extended operation. However, the bolts may be checked and retightened, if desired. If removed, install the exhaust manifolds and tighten the attaching bolts to specification.

10. Install the pushrods, making sure that they are in their original positions in the cylinder head.

11. Install the exhaust valve stem caps.

12. Install the rocker arms. If all original components are being installed, a valve clearance adjustment is not necessary. If any valve train components are replaced, perform a valve clearance adjustment.

13. Connect the exhaust manifold(s) at the muffler inlet pipe(s). Tighten nuts to specification.

14. If the right cylinder head was removed, install the alternator attaching bracket on the right cylinder head assembly. Install the alternator. Adjust the drive belt tension to specifications.

15. Clean the valve rocker arm cover(s). Position the valve rocker cover gasket in each cover, making sure that the tabs en-gage the notches in the cover, making sure that the tabs engage the notches in the cover. Install valve rocker arm cover(s). The valve rocker cover is tightened in 2 steps. Tighten the bolts to specifications. After the engine reaches operating temperature, retighten bolts to the same specifications.

16. Install the A/C compressor, if equipped. Install the power steering drive belt and power steering pump bracket. Install the bracket attaching bolts. Adjust the drive belt to specifications. Install the thermactor crossover tube at rear of cylinder heads.

17. Install the intake manifolds.

Camshaft

Removal and Installation

2.3L ENGINE

NOTE: The camshaft can be replaced with the cylinder head still mounted on the engine in the vehicle, or with the cylinder head removed from the vehicle.

1. Disconnect the negative battery cable. Drain the cooling system. Remove the air cleaner assembly. On turbocharged engines, remove the intercooler to throttle body tube and the intercooler inlet tube. Remove the intercooler mounting bolts and remove the intercooler.

2. Label and remove all wires, electrical harnesses, vacuum lines and cables that will interfere with valve cover removal.

3. On fuel injected engines, relieve the fuel system pressure.

4. Remove the alternator and mounting brackets as an assembly and position to the side.

5. Remove the upper and lower radiator hoses. Remove the fan, motor and mounting shroud as an assembly.

6. Remove the valve cover.

7. Set the engine at No. 1 cylinder TDC on the compression stroke. Remove the timing belt.

8. Raise and safely support the front of the vehicle. Remove the right and left engine mount through bolts and joint to bracket retaining bolts.

9. Place a block of wood on a floor jack and raise the engine, carefully, as high as it will go. Place blocks of wood between the engine mounts. Lower the engine and lower the vehicle to the ground.

10. Remove the rocker arms.

11. Remove the camshaft drive gear attaching bolt and washer and remove the gear and belt guide plate.

12. The camshaft is removed through the front of the cylinder head after removing the front cam bearing seal. Use a new seal during assembly.

13. Reverse the removal procedure to install the camshaft and cylinder head (if removed).

NOTE: After any procedure requiring removal of the rocker arms, each lash adjuster must be fully collapsed after assembly, then released. This must be done before the camshaft is turned.

3.8L, 5.0L AND 5.8L ENGINES

1. Disconnect the negative battery cable. Remove the intake manifold.

2. Remove the cylinder front cover, timing chain and sprockets.

3. Remove the grille and radiator. On vehicles with air conditioning, remove the condenser retaining bolts and position it out of the way. Do not disconnect refrigerant lines.

4. Remove the rocker arm covers.

5. Remove the pushrods and lifters and keep them in order so that they can be installed in their original positions.

6. Remove the camshaft thrust plate and washer, if so equipped. Remove the camshaft from the front of the engine.

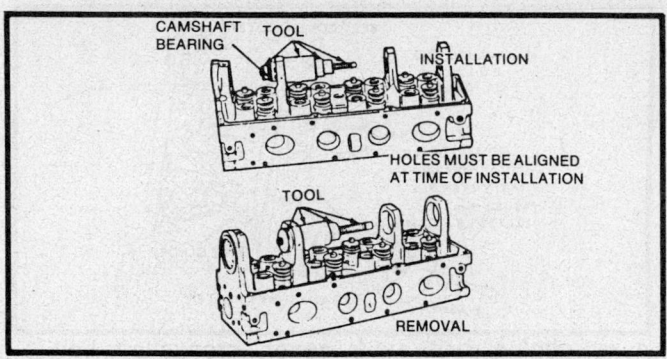

2.3L camshaft bearing removal and installation

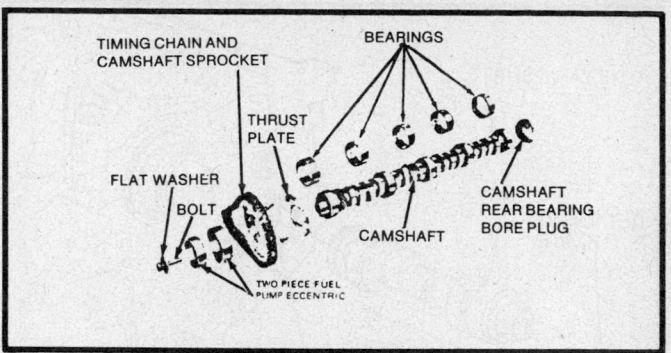

3.8L camshaft and bearing assembly

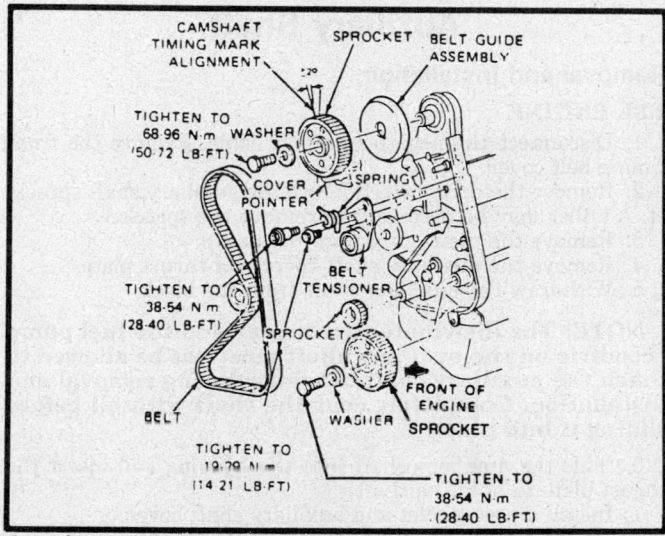

4 cyl camshaft drive train

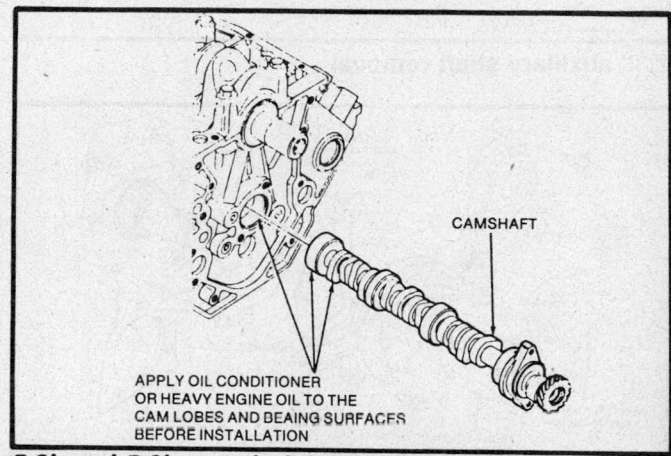

5.0L and 5.8L camshaft installation

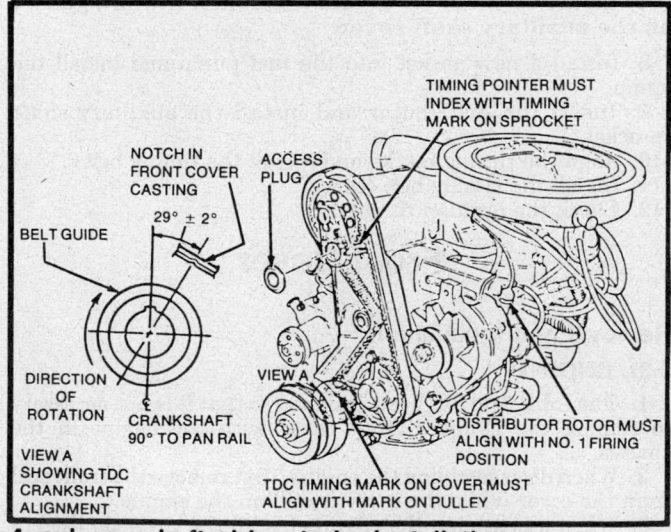

4 cyl camshaft drive train installation

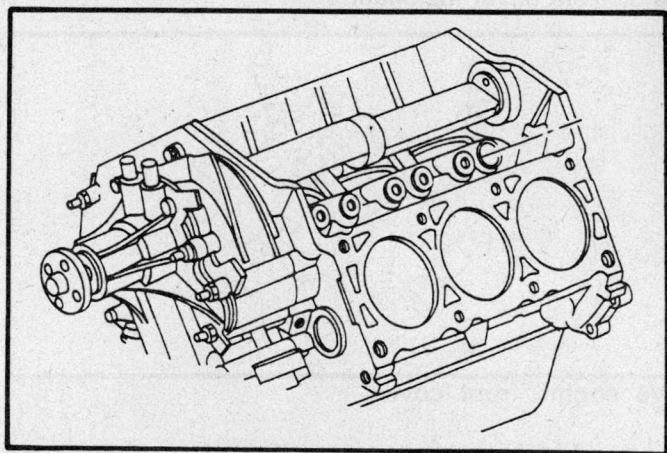

1988 balance shaft location — 3.8L engine

Balance Shaft

Removal and Installation

1988 3.8L ENGINE

1. Disconnect the negative battery cable.
2. Remove the radiator and shroud. If equipped with A/C, remove the condenser and place it aside. Do not disconnect the refrigerant lines.
3. Remove the intake manifold assembly.
4. Remove the cylinder front cover assembly.
5. Remove the camshaft timing sprocket and the timing chain. Remove the balance shaft drive gear from the camshaft

Use care not to damage camshaft lobes or journals while removing the cam from the engine.

7. Before installing the camshaft, coat the lobes with engine assembly lubricant, the journals and valve parts with heavy oil.

8. Reverse the procedure to install.

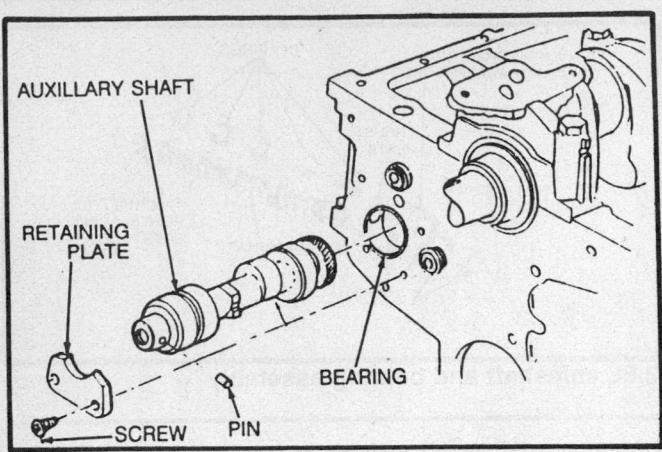

2.3L auxillary shaft removal

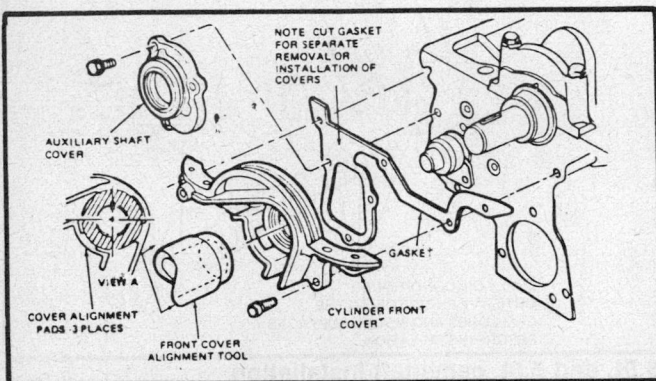

2.3L front cover installation

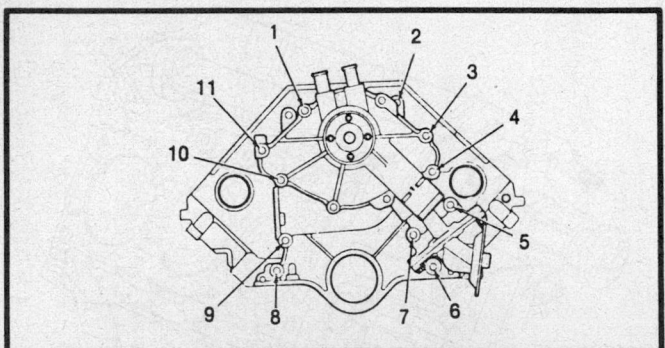

V6 engine front cover

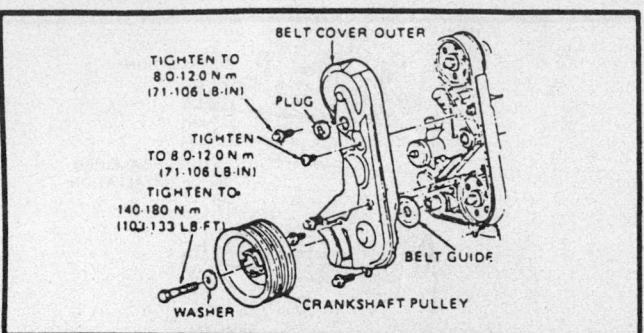

4 cyl timing belt outer cover, crankshaft belt guide and pulley Installation

Auxiliary Shaft

Removal and Installation

2.3L ENGINE

1. Disconnect the negative battery cable. Remove the front timing belt cover.
2. Remove the drive belt. Remove the auxiliary shaft sprocket. A puller may be necessary to remove the sprocket.
3. Remove the distributor and fuel pump.
4. Remove the auxiliary shaft cover and thrust plate.
5. Withdraw the auxiliary shaft from the block.

NOTE: The distributor drive gear and the fuel pump eccentric on the auxiliary shaft must not be allowed to touch the auxiliary shaft bearings during removal and installation. Completely coat the shaft with oil before sliding it into place.

6. Slide the auxiliary shaft into the housing and insert the thrust plate to hold the shaft.
7. Install a new gasket and auxiliary shaft cover.

NOTE: The auxiliary shaft cover and cylinder front cover share a common gasket. Cut off the old gasket around the cylinder cover and use half of the new gasket on the auxiliary shaft cover.

8. Install a new gasket into the fuel pump and install the pump.
9. Insert the distributor and install the auxiliary shaft sprocket.
10. Align the timing marks and install the timing belt.
11. Install the timing belt cover.
12. Check the ignition timing.

Front Cover

Removal and Installation

2.3L ENGINE

1. The front seal has been designed so that it is not necessary to remove the cylinder front cover with the engine in the chassis.
2. When disassembling the engine, first remove the front seal from the cover while the cover is still on the engine.
3. When assembling the engine, install the cover on the engine without the seal and then use tool to press the seal into place. This will avoid damage to the seal.
4. Before finally adjusting the cover into position and tightening the attaching bolts, use tool to position the cover in relation to the crankshaft. Tighten the bolts to 8–12 Nm (6–9 ft. lbs.) with this tool in place. This will assure that the timing belt does not interfere with the front cover when operating.

end. Mark the relationship of the balance shaft with the driven gear.

6. Remove the balance shaft gear from the end of the balance shaft. Remove the balance shaft thrust plate and remove the shaft.
7. To install, lubricate the bearing lobes of the balance shaft with assembly lubricant and install the balance shaft into the block. Install the shaft thrust plate and the driven gear.
8. Install the balance shaft drive gear, aligning the keyway, on the end of the camshaft.
9. Install the timing belt and gear, the front cover assembly and the intake manifold. Install the radiator and A/C condenser. Install the grill.
10. Fill all fluids and run the engine to check for leaks. Correct all fluid levels, as necessary.

3.8L, 5.0L AND 5.8L ENGINES

1. Drain cooling system.
2. Disconnect the negative battery cable.
3. Remove air cleaner assembly and air intake duct. On supercharged engines remove the intercooler intake and outlet tubes.
4. Remove fan/clutch assembly and shroud.
5. Loosen accessory drive belt idler. Remove drive belt and water pump pulley.
6. If equipped with power steering, remove pump mounting brackets attaching bolts. Leaving the hoses connected, place the pump/bracket assembly aside in a position to prevent the fluid from leaking out.
7. If equipped with air conditioning, remove compressor front support bracket. Leave compressor in place.
8. Disconnect hoses at water pump.
9. Disconnect radiator upper hose at thermostat housing.
10. Disconnect coil wire from distributor cap and remove cap with the secondary wires attached. Remove distributor assembly.
11. If equipped with tripminder, remove the fuel flow meter support bracket (the fuel lines will support the flow meter).
12. Raise vehicle and safely support.
13. Remove crankshaft damper using puller.
14. Remove fuel pump to carburetor fuel line to fuel pump, (2150–2V only).
15. Remove oil filter.
16. Disconnect radiator lower hose at the water pump.
17. On the 3.8L engine, remove the oil pan. On all other engines, it is not necessary to remove the oil pan, however, the oil pan should be covered to prevent debris from entering..

NOTE: On the 3.8L engines, the front cover cannot be removed without removing the oil pan.

18. Lower vehicle.
19. Remove front cover attaching bolts. It is not necessary to remove water pump.

NOTE: Do not overlook the cover attaching bolt located behind the oil filter adapter. The front cover will break if pried upon when all attaching bolts are not removed.

20. Remove ignition timing indicator.
21. Remove front cover and water pump as an assembly.

NOTE: On the 3.8L engine, the front cover contains the oil pump and intermediate shaft. If a new front cover is to be installed, remove the water pump, oil pump, oil filter adapter and intermediate shaft from the old front cover.

22. Installation is the reverse of the removal procedure. Lubricate crankshaft front oil seal with clean engine oil. Tighten all bolts to specifications.

Front Cover Oil Seal

Removal and Installation

EXCEPT 2.3L ENGINE

1. Disconnect the negative battery cable.
2. Remove the fan shroud assembly. Remove the cooling fan and pulley.
3. Remove the accessory drive belts.
4. Remove the crankshaft pulley, install puller on crankshaft damper and remove the damper.
5. Place front cover seal remover T70P–6B070–B or equivalent on to the front cover plate over the front seal. Tighten the 2 through bolts to force the puller under the seal flange. Alter-

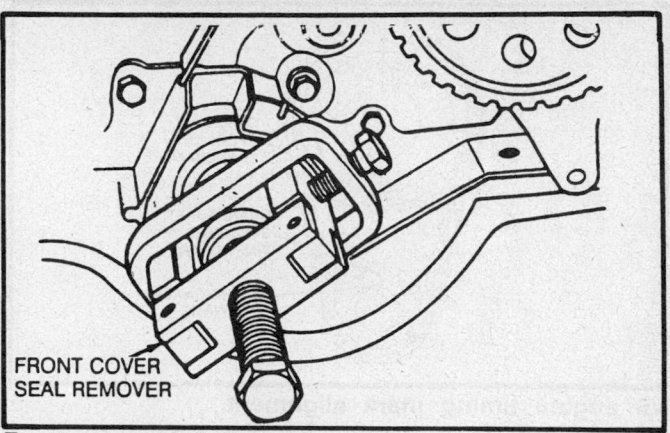

FRONT COVER
SEAL REMOVER

Front cover seal removal

nately tighten the puller bolts 1 turn at a time to remove the seal.
6. To install, use a new oil seal and coat with oil. Install the seal into tool T70P–6B070–A or equivalent. Install the tool on the front of the crankshaft and tighten adjuster screw to force the seal into the front cover.
7. Coat the outside of the seal and install the damper and pulley to the crankshaft.
8. Install the cooling fan and pulley. Install the accessory drive belts and adjust the belt tension. Attach the fan shroud to the radiator and run the engine to check for leaks.

2.3L ENGINE

1. Disconnect the negative battery cable. Remove the front timing belt cover.
2. Relieve the tension on the timing belt and remove it.
3. Remove the crankshaft sprocket using tool T74P–6306–A crankshaft sprocket remover or equivalent.
4. Using front seal removing tool T74P–6700–B or equivalent, place the jaws of the tool on the thin edge of the seal and remove the seal.
5. To install, lubricate the outer edge of the seal with light grease. Using front seal installer T74P–6150–A, place the seal on the tool and install the seal/tool into place.
6. Install the crankshaft sprocket and install the timing belt on to the timing gear.
7. Install the front cover. Run the engine and check for leaks.

Timing Chain and Gears

Removal and Installation

EXCEPT 2.3L ENGINE

1. Drain cooling system, remove air cleaner and disconnect the negative battery cable.
2. Disconnect the radiator hoses and remove the radiator.
3. Disconnect heater hose at water pump. Slide water pump by pass hose clamp toward the pump.
4. Loosen alternator mounting bolts at the alternator. Remove the alternator support bolt at the water pump. Remove thermactor (air) pump on all engines equipped. If equipped with power steering or air conditioning. unbolt the component, remove the belt and lay the pump aside with the lines attached. On supercharged models, disconnect the supercharger inlet and outlet tubes.
5. Remove the fan, spacer, pulley and drive belt.
6. Drain the crankcase.
7. Remove pulley from crankshaft pulley adapter. Remove cap screw and washer from front end of crankshaft. Remove crankshaft pulley adapter with a puller.

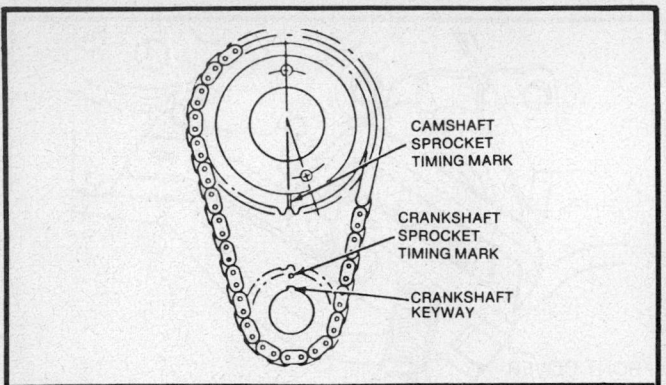

V6 engine timing mark alignment

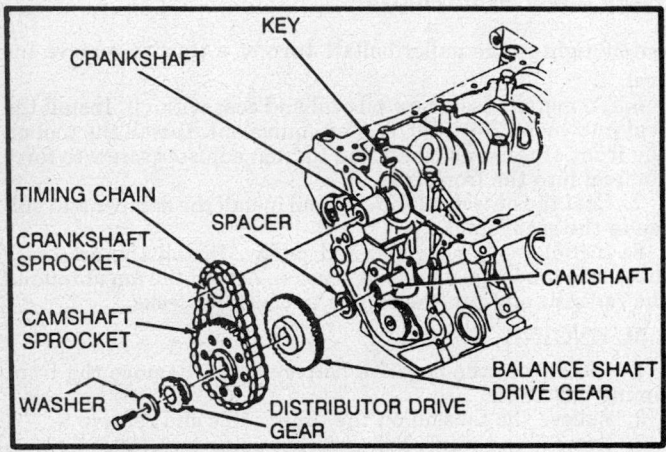

1988–89 3.8L Timing chain and gears

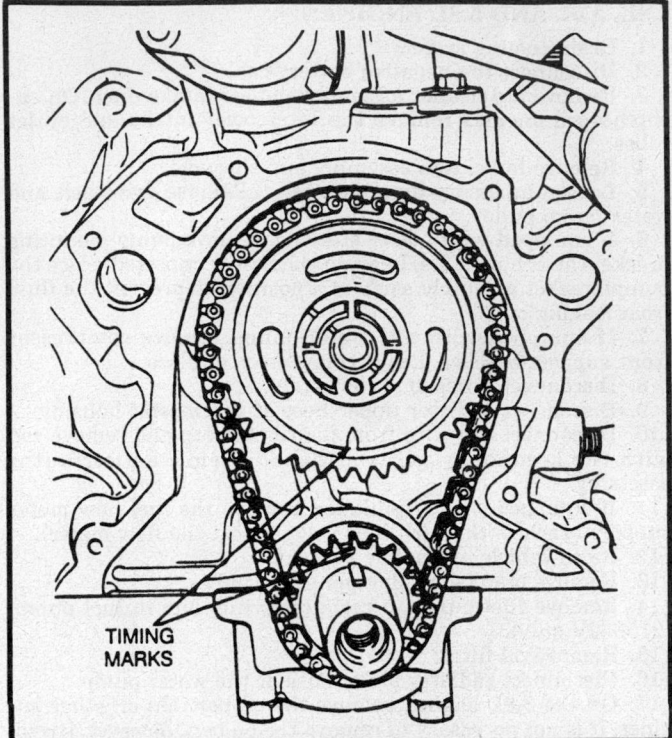

5.0L and 5.8L timing mark alignment

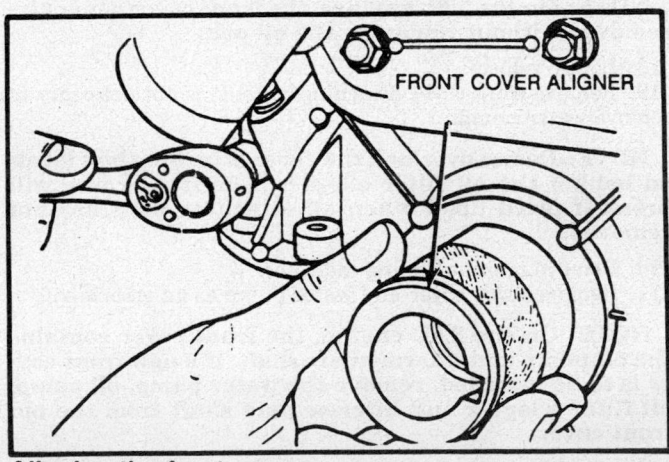

Aligning the front cover

8. On models equipped with fuel injection, relieve the fuel system pressure. Disconnect fuel pump outlet line at the pump. Remove fuel pump retaining bolts and lay the pump to the side. Remove the engine oil dipstick. Remove the distributor on 3.8L engines.

NOTE: On the 3.8L engine, it is necessary to drop the oil pan before the front cover cam be removed.

9. Remove the front cover attaching bolts. On the 3.8L engine, remove the water pump and front cover as an assembly.
10. Remove the crankshaft oil slinger if so equipped. On 1986–87 3.8L engines, remove the camshaft thrust button and spring.

NOTE: 1988 3.8L engines are equipped with an internal balance shaft. The balance shaft is driven off of the camshaft, by a gear positioned behind the camshaft timing sprocket. When removing the timing chain and sprockets, care should be taken to keep this gear in its proper position.

11. Check the timing chain deflection.
12. Crank engine until the timing sprocket timing marks are aligned at their closest together position.
13. Remove crankshaft sprocket cap screw, washers and fuel pump eccentric. Slide both sprockets and chain forward and off as an assembly.
14. Position sprockets and chain on the camshaft and crankshaft with both of the timing marks aligned at their closest together position. Install the fuel pump eccentric, washers and sprocket attaching bolt. Torque the sprocket attaching bolt to 40–45 ft. lbs.
15. Install the crankshaft front oil slinger.

NOTE: When replacing the front cover on the 1986–1987 3.8L engine, RTV sealer is used. Apply an even 1/8 in. bead on the cover mating surface. 1988–90 3.8L engines use a gasket.

16. Clean all gasket mating surfaces and install a new front cover seal.
17. Coat a new cover gasket with sealer and position it on the block.

NOTE: On all engines, trim away the exposed portion of the oil pan gasket flush with the cylinder block. Cut and position the required portion of a new gasket to the oil pan, applying sealer to both sides of it. On 3.8L engines, after installing the cylinder front cover, install the oil pan using a new gasket.

18. Install front cover, using a crankshaft to cover alignment

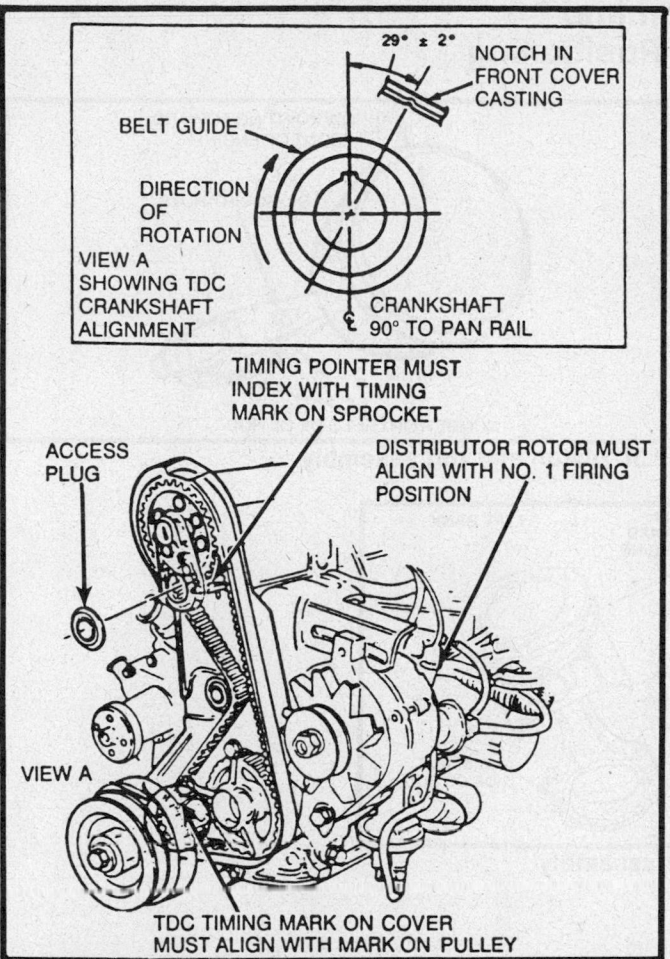

2.3L timing belt alignment check

tool. Coat the threads of the attaching bolts with sealer. Torque attaching bolts to 12–15 ft. lbs.

19. Install the fuel pump, connect fuel pump outlet tube.

20. Install the crankshaft pulley adapter and torque attaching bolt. Install crankshaft pulley.

21. Install the water pump pulley, drive belt, spacer and fan.

22. Install the alternator support bolt at the water pump. Tighten the alternator mounting bolts. Adjust drive belt tension. Install Thermactor pump if so equipped.

23. Install radiator and connect all coolant and heater hoses. Connect battery cables.

24. Refill cooling system and the crankcase.

25. Start engine and operate at fast idle.

26. Check for leaks, install air cleaner. Adjust ignition timing and make all final adjustments.

Timing Belt and Tensioner

Adjustment Check

2.3L ENGINE

Should the camshaft drive belt jump timing by a tooth or 2, the engine could still run; but very poorly. To visually check for correct timing of the crankshaft, auxiliary shaft and the camshaft follow this procedure:

There is an access plug provided in the cam drive belt cover so that the camshaft timing can be checked without removing the drive belt cover. Remove the access plug, turn the crankshaft until the timing mark on the crankshaft damper indicates TDC and observe that the timing mark on the camshaft drive sprocket is aligned with the pointer on the inner belt cover. Also, the rotor of the distributor must align with the No. 1 cylinder firing position.

Removal And Installation

2.3L ENGINE

1. Disconnect the negative battery cable. Set the engine with the No. 1 cylinder at TDC. The crankshaft and camshaft timing marks should align with their respective pointers and the distributor rotor should point to the No. 1 plug tower.

2. Loosen the adjustment bolts on the alternator and accessories and remove the drive belts. To provide clearance for removing the camshaft belt, remove the fan and pulley.

3. Remove the timing belt front cover.

4. Remove the distributor cap from the distributor and position it out of the way.

5. Loosen the belt tensioner adjustment and pivot bolts. Lever the tensioner away from the belt and retighten the adjustment bolt to hold it away.

6. Remove the crankshaft bolt and pulley. Remove the belt guide behind the pulley.

7. Remove the timing belt by sliding it off the camshaft pulley and off of the engine.

8. Install the new belt over the crankshaft pulley first, then in an counterclockwise direction install it over the auxiliary shaft sprocket and the camshaft sprocket. Adjust the belt fore and aft so that it is centered on the sprockets.

9. Loosen the tensioner adjustment bolt, allowing it to spring back against the belt.

10. Rotate the crankshaft 2 complete turns in the normal rotation direction to remove any belt slack. Turn the crankshaft until the timing check marks are lined up. If the timing has slipped, remove the belt and repeat the procedure.

11. Tighten the tensioner adjustment bolt to 14–21 ft. lbs. and the pivot bolt to 28–40 ft. lbs.

12. Replace the belt guide and crankshaft pulley, distributor cap, belt outer cover, fan and pulley, drive belts and accessories. Adjust the accessory drive belt tension. Start the engine and check the ignition timing.

NOTE: Never turn the crankshaft in the opposite direction of normal rotation. Backward rotation of the crankshaft may cause the timing belt to slip and alter the timing.

Rings/Piston and Connecting Rod Positioning

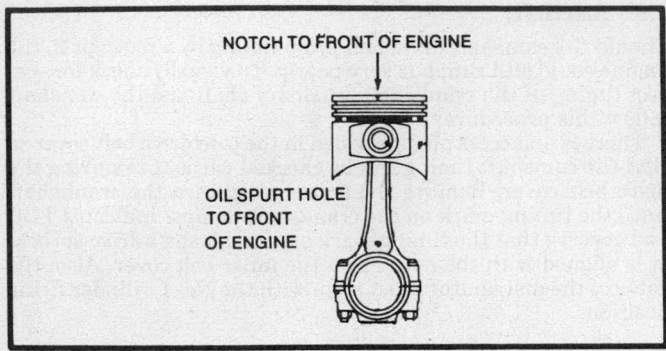

3.8L piston and rod assembly

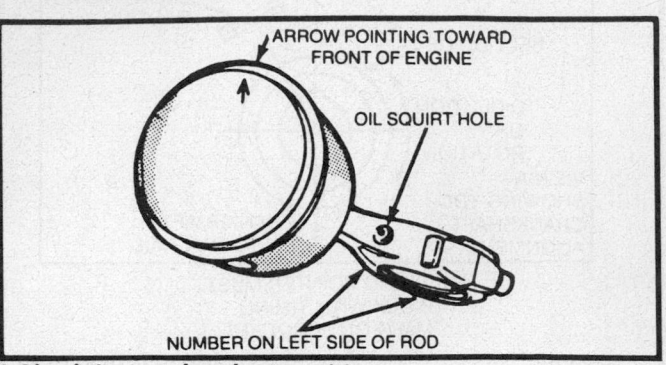

2.3L piston and rod assembly

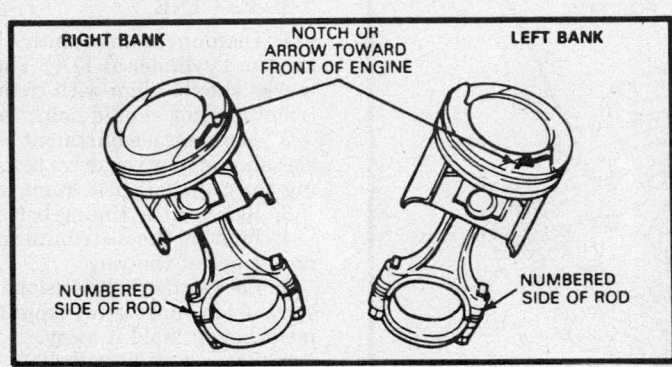

5.0L and 5.8L piston and rod assembly

ENGINE LUBRICATION SYSTEM

Oil Pan

Removal and Installation

2.3L ENGINE

1. Disconnect the negative battery cable.
2. Remove the fan shroud or fan shroud and electric fan assembly.
3. Raise and safely support the vehicle. Drain the crankcase.
4. Remove the right and left engine support bolts and nuts.
5. Using a jack with a piece of wood between the raising point and jack contact points, raise the engine as high as it will go. Place blocks of wood between the mounts and chassis brackets. Lower the engine. Remove shake brace.
6. Remove the sway bar retaining bolts and lower the sway bar.
7. Remove the starter motor.
8. Remove steering gear retaining bolts and lower the gear.
9. Remove the oil pan retaining bolts. Pivot the oil pan forward over the crossmember and remove.
10. Install new oil pan gasket and end seals.
11. Position the oil pan to the cylinder block and install retaining bolts and tighten to 20 inch lbs..
12. Reposition the steering gear and install bolts and nuts.
13. Install starter.
14. Raise the engine enough to remove the wood blocks, lower the engine. Install shake brace.

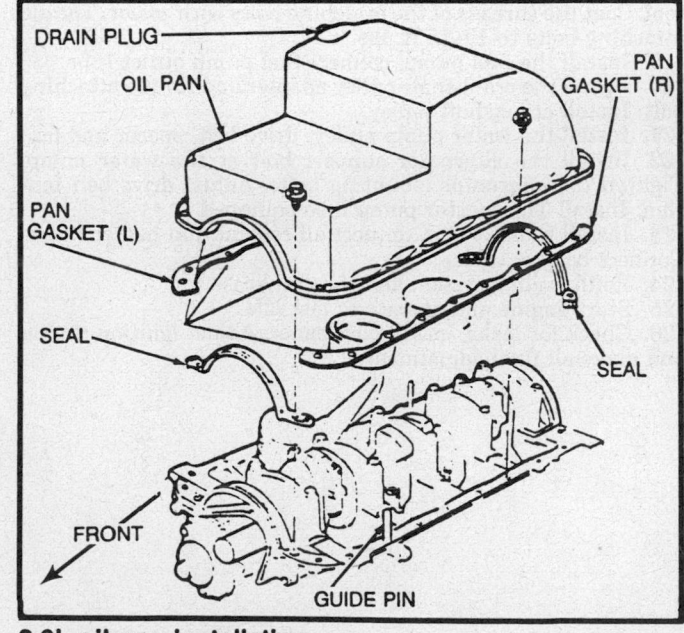

2.3L oil pan installation

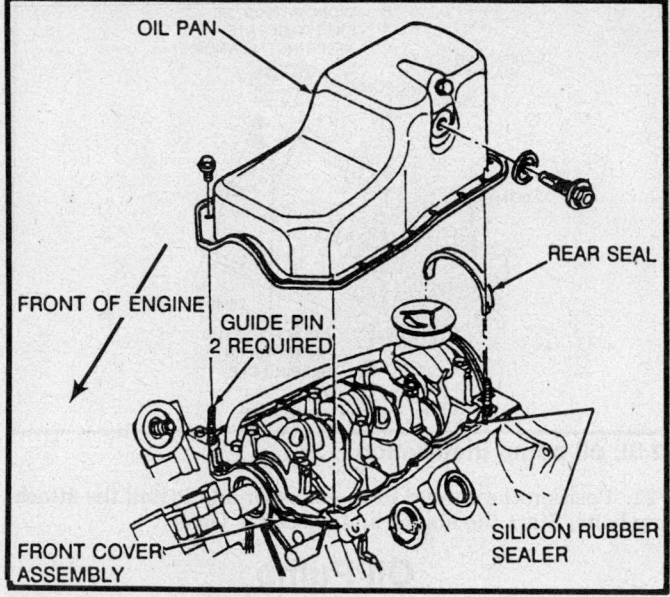

3.8L oil pan installation

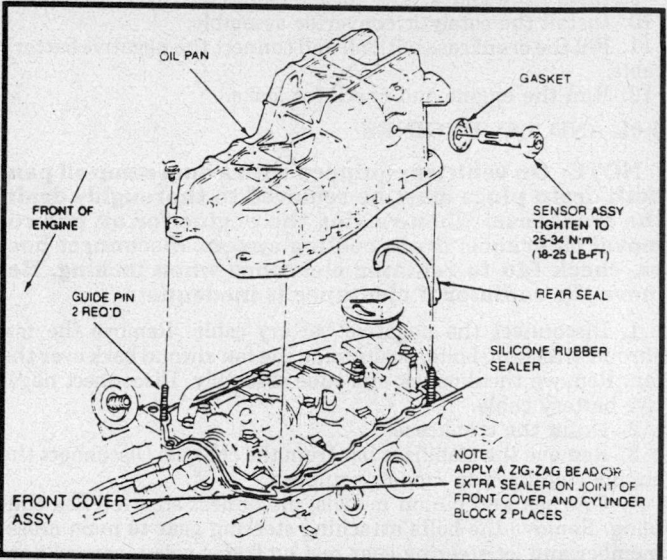

Removing the oil pan—3.8L SC engine

15. Install the right and left engine mount bolts and nuts, tighten to 33–45 ft. lbs..
16. Install the sway bar.
17. Install the fan shroud.
18. Fill the crankcase with oil.
19. Connect battery cable, run engine and check for leaks.

1985–87 3.8L ENGINE

1. Disconnect the negative battery cable.
2. Remove the air cleaner assembly including the air intake duct.
3. Remove the fan shroud attaching bolts and position the shroud back over the fan.
4. Remove the oil level dipstick.
5. Remove the screws attaching the vacuum solenoids to the dash panel. Lay the solenoids to the dash panel. Lay the solenoids on the engine without disconnecting the vacuum hoses or electrical connectors.
6. Raise and safely support the vehicle. Remove the exhaust manifold to exhaust pipe attaching nuts.
7. Drain the crankcase.
8. Remove the oil filter.
9. Remove the bolts attaching the shift linkage bracket to the transmission bell housing. Remove the starter motor for more clearance if necessary.
10. Disconnect the transmission cooler lines at the radiator. Remove power steering hose retaining clamp from frame.
11. Remove the converter cover.
12. On models equipped with rack and pinion steering, proceed with the following appropriate steps:
13. Remove the engine damper to No. 2 crossmember bracket attaching bolt. The damper must be disconnected from the crossmember.
14. Disconnect steering flex coupling. Remove the 2 bolts attaching the steering gear to main crossmember and let the steering gear rest on the frame away from oil pan.
15. Remove the front engine insulator attaching nut and washer.
16. Raise the engine 2–3 in. and insert wood blocks between the engine mounts and the vehicle frame.

NOTE: On some vehicles equipped with rack and pinion steering it may be necessary to raise the engine as much as 5 in. to provide adequate pan to crossmember

clearance. Watch the clearance between the transmission dipstick tube and the thermactor downstream air tube. If the tubes contact before adequate pan to crossmember clearance is provided, lower the engine and remove the transmission dipstick tube and the downstream air tube.

17. Remove the oil pan attaching bolts. Work the oil pan loose and remove.
18. On vehicles with limited clearance, lower the oil pan onto the crossmember. Remove the oil pickup tube attaching nut. Lower the pick up tube/screen assembly into the pan and remove the oil pan through the front of the vehicle.
19. Remove the oil pan seal from the main bearing cap and discard.
20. Clean the gasket surfaces on the cylinder block, oil pan and oil pick-up tube.
21. Apply ⅛ in. bead of RTV sealer to all gasket mating surfaces of the oil pan and the engine front cover.
22. Install the oil pan. Torque the pan bolts to 80–106 inch. lbs.

NOTE: On models with limited clearance place the oil pick-up tube/screen assembly in the oil pan.

23. The balance of installation is the reverse of the removal procedure.
24. Fill the crankcase to the correct level with the oil.
25. Start the engine and check the fluid levels in the transmission.
26. Check for engine oil and transmission fluid leaks.

1988–90 3.8L ENGINE

1. Disconnect the negative battery cable.
2. Raise and safely support the vehicle. Drain the oil and remove the oil filter.
3. Remove the catalytic converter assembly from the exhaust manifold.
4. Remove the starter and remove the torque converter cover.
5. Remove the oil pan retaining bolts and remove the oil pan.
6. Clean all gasket mating surfaces.
7. Using a new gasket, apply a ⅛ in. bead of sealer to all gasket mating surfaces.
8. Install oil pan and tighten the retaining bolts to 80–106 inch lbs.

9. Install the starter and torque converter cover.
10. Install the catalytic converter assembly.
11. Fill the crankcase with oil and connect the negative battery cable.
12. Run the engine and check for leaks.

5.0L AND 5.8L ENGINES

NOTE: On vehicles equipped with a dual sump oil pan, both drain plugs must be removed to thoroughly drain the crankcase. When raising the engine for oil pan removal clearance; drain cooling system, disconnect hoses, check fan to radiator clearance when jacking. Remove the radiator if clearance is inadequate.

1. Disconnect the negative battery cable. Remove the fan shroud attaching bolts, positioning the fan shroud back over the fan. Remove the dipstick and tube assembly. Disconnect negative battery cable.
2. Drain the crankcase.
3. Remove the stabilizer bar from the chassis. Disconnect the engine stabilizer on models equipped.
4. On rack and pinion models, disconnect steering flex coupling. Remove the bolts attaching steering gear to main crossmember and let steering gear rest on frame away from oil pan. Disconnect power steering hose retaining clamp from frame. Remove the starter motor.
5. Remove the idler arm bracket retaining bolts (if equipped) and pull the linkage down and out of the way.
6. Disconnect and plug the fuel line from the gas tank at the fuel pump. 7. Disconnect and lower the exhaust pipe/converter assemblies if they will interfere with pan removal/installation. Raise the engine and place 2 wood blocks between the engine mounts and the vehicle frame. Remove converter inspection cover.

NOTE: On fuel injected engines, relieve the fuel system pressure.

8. Remove the K braces (4 bolts).
9. Remove the oil pan attaching bolts and lower oil pan to the frame.
10. Remove oil pump attaching bolts and the inset tube attaching nut from the No. 3 main bearing cap stud and lower the oil pump into the oil pan.
11. Remove the oil pan, rotating the crankshaft as necessary to clear the counterweights.
12. Clean the gasket mounting surfaces thoroughly. Coat the surfaces on the block and pan with sealer. Position the pan side gaskets on the engine block. Install the rear main cap seal with the tabs over the pan side gaskets.
13. Position oil pump and inlet tube into the oil pan. Slide the oil pan into position under the engine. With the oil pump intermediate shaft in position in the oil pump, position the oil pump to the cylinder block and the inlet tube to the stud on the No. 3 main bearing cap attaching bolt. Install the attaching bolts and tighten to specification. Position the oil pan on the engine and install the attaching bolts. Tighten the bolts (working from the center toward the ends) 9–11 ft. lbs. for $^{5}/_{16}$ in. bolts and 7–9 ft. lbs. for ¼ in. bolts.
14. Position the steering gear to the main crossmember. Install the 2 attaching bolts and tighten to specification. Connect the steering flex coupling to the steering gear.
15. Position the rear K braces and install the 4 attaching bolts.
16. Raise the engine and remove the wood blocks.
17. Install the stabilizer bar.
18. Lower the engine and install the engine mount attaching bolts. Tighten to 33–46 ft. lbs. Install the torque converter inspection cover.
19. Install the oil dipstick, tube assembly and fill crankcase with the specified engine oil. Install the idler arm.
20. Connect the transmission oil cooler lines. Connect the battery cable.

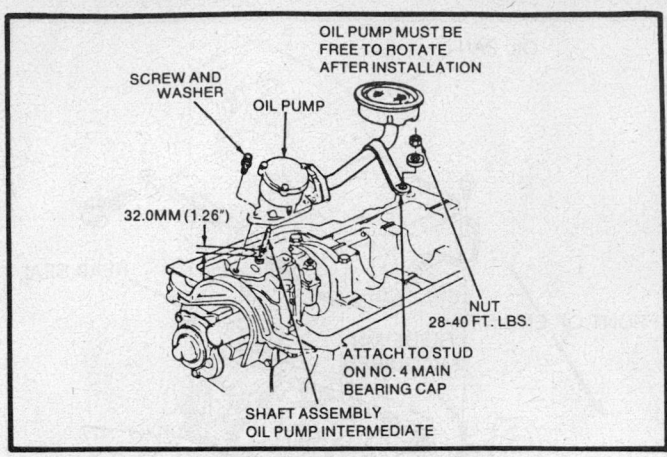

2.3L oil pump installation

21. Position the shroud to the radiator and install the attaching bolts. Start the engine and check for leaks.

Oil Pump

Removal and Installation

EXCEPT 3.8L ENGINE

1. Disconnect the negative battery cable. Remove the oil pan.
2. Remove the oil pump inlet tube and screen assembly.
3. Remove the oil pump attaching bolts and gasket. Remove the oil pump intermediate shaft.
4. To install, prime the oil pump by filling the inlet and outlet ports with engine oil and rotating the shaft of pump to distribute the oil.
5. Position the intermediate drive shaft into the distributor socket.
6. Position a new gasket on the pump body and insert the intermediate drive shaft into pump body.
7. Install the pump and intermediate shaft as an assembly.

NOTE: Do not force the pump if it does not seat. The drive shaft may be misaligned with the distributor shaft. To align, rotate the intermediate drive shaft into a new position.

8. Install and torque the oil pump attaching screws to 12–15 ft. lbs. on the 2.3L engine, 20–25 ft. lbs. on 5.0L and 5.8L engines.
9. Install oil pan.

3.8L ENGINE

NOTE: The oil pump is mounted in the front cover assembly. Oil pan removal is necessary for pick-up tube/screen replacement or service only.

1. Disconnect the negative battery cable. Raise and safely support the vehicle.
2. Remove the oil filter.
3. Remove the cover/filter mount assembly. On supercharged engines, remove the oil cooler assembly.
4. Lift the pump gears from their mounting pocket in the front cover.
5. Clean all gasket mounting surfaces.
6. Inspect the mounting pocket for wear. If excessive wear is present, complete timing cover assembly replacement is necessary.
7. Inspect the cover/filter mount gasket to timing cover surface for flatness. Place a straight edge across the flat and check clearance with a feeler gauge. If the measured clearance exceeds 0.004 in., replace the cover/filter mount.

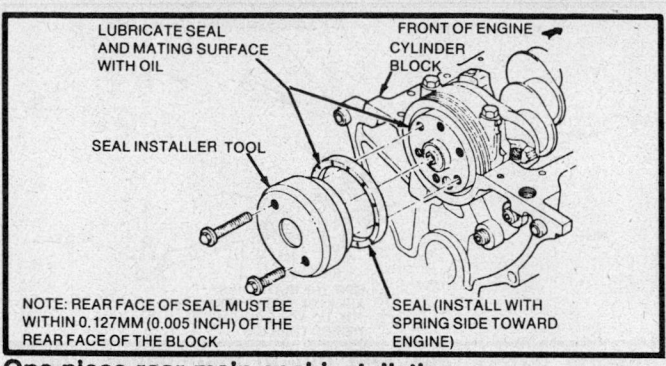

LUBRICATE SEAL AND MATING SURFACE WITH OIL

FRONT OF ENGINE

CYLINDER BLOCK

SEAL INSTALLER TOOL

NOTE: REAR FACE OF SEAL MUST BE WITHIN 0.127MM (0.005 INCH) OF THE REAR FACE OF THE BLOCK

SEAL (INSTALL WITH SPRING SIDE TOWARD ENGINE)

One piece rear main seal installation

8. Replace the pump gears if wear is excessive.
9. Remove the plug from the end of the pressure relief valve passage using a small drill and slide hammer. Use caution when drilling.
10. Remove the spring and valve from the bore. Clean all dirt, gum and metal chips from the bore and valve. Inspect all parts for wear. Replace as necessary.

NOTE: It is necessary to prime the oil pump after it has been disassembled to prevent it from failing on initial startup. this can be done by lightly packing the oil pump gear cavity with petroleum jelly before final assembly.

11. Install the valve and spring after lubricating them with engine oil. Install cover/filter mount using a new mounting gasket. Tighten the mounting bolts to 18–22 ft. lbs. Install the oil filter, add necessary oil for correct level.

Rear Main Oil Seal

Removal and Installation
SPLIT SEAL

1. Disconnect the negative battery cable. Remove the oil pan.
2. Loosen all the main bearing caps, allowing the crankshaft to lower slightly.

NOTE: The crankshaft should not be allowed to drop more than $\frac{1}{32}$ in.

3. Remove the rear main bearing cap and remove the seal from the cap and block.

NOTE: Be very careful not to scratch the sealing surface. Remove the oil seal retaining pin from the cap, if equipped. It is not used with the replacement seal.

4. Carefully clean the seal grooves in the cap and block with solvent.
5. Soak the new seal halves in clean engine oil.
6. Install the upper half of the seal in the block with the undercut side of the seal toward the front of the engine. Slide the seal around the crankshaft journal until ⅜ in. protrudes beyond the base of the block.
7. Tighten all the main bearing caps (except the rear main) to specifications.
8. Install the lower seal into the rear cap, with the undercut side facing the front of the engine. Allow ⅜ in. of the seal to protrude above the surface, at the opposite end from the block seal.
9. Squeeze a $\frac{1}{16}$ in. bead of silicone sealant onto the outer center edges of the bearing cap.
10. Install the rear cap and torque to specifications.
11. Install the oil pump and pan. Fill the crankcase with oil, start the engine and check for leaks.

SINGLE SEAL

1. Disconnect the negative battery cable. Remove the transmission and on manual transmission equipped vehicles, remove the clutch and flywheel.
2. Punch 2 holes in the crankshaft rear oil seal on opposite sides of the crankshaft, just above the bearing cap to cylinder block split line. Install a sheet metal screw in each of the holes or use a small slide hammer and pry the crankshaft rear main oil seal from the block.

NOTE: Use extreme caution not to scratch the crankshaft oil seal surface.

3. Clean the oil seal recess in the cylinder block and main bearing cap.
4. Coat the seal and all of the seal mounting surfaces with oil and install the seal in the recess, driving it in place with an oil seal installation tool T82L–6701–A or equivalent.
5. Install the flywheel, clutch and transmission in the reverse order of removal.

FRONT SUSPENSION AND STEERING

For front suspension component removal and installation procedures, refer to the unit repair section. For steering wheel removal and installation, refer to electrical controls section.

Manual Steering Gear

Removal and Installation

1. Disconnect the negative battery cable.
2. Remove the bolt retaining the flex coupling to the input shaft.
3. Leave the ignition key in the **ON** position and raise the vehicle.
4. Remove the tie rod end studs from the spindle arms.
5. Support the steering gear and remove the nuts, insulator washers and bolts retaining the gear to the No. 2 crossmember. Remove the steering gear.

6. Insert the input shaft into the flexible coupling aligning the flats. Position the steering gear to the No. 2 crossmember and tighten the bolts to 90–100 ft. lbs. (122–135 Nm).
7. Connect the tie rod ends and tighten nuts to 41–47 ft. lbs. (55–63 Nm), install new cotter pins and bend the ends to the side.
8. Lower the vehicle and install the bolt retaining the flexible coupling to the input shaft. Tighten the bolt to 20–37 ft. lbs. (28–50 Nm).
9. Check the toe and reset if necessary.

Adjustment

The manual rack and pinion gear provides 2 means of service adjustment. The gear must be removed from the vehicle to perform both adjustments.

SUPPORT YOKE-TO-RACK

1. Mount the steering gear on a bench mounted holding fix-

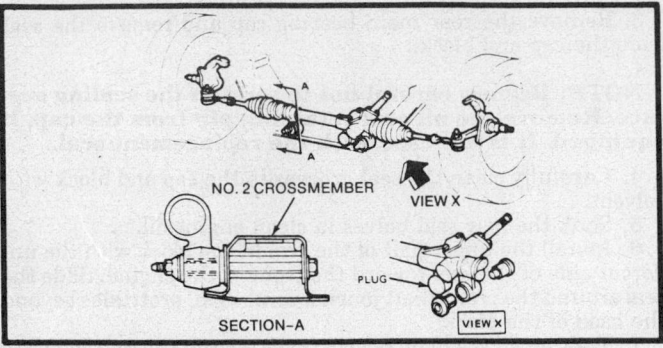

Typical rack and pinion steering gear and link

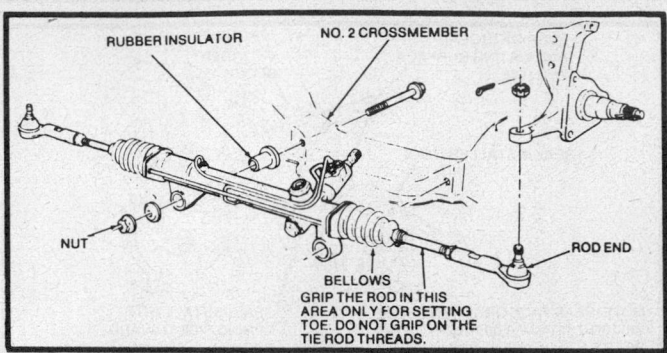

Integral power rack and pinion installation, Ford unit illustrated, TRW unit similar

ture, tool T57L-500-B or equivalent. Rotate the pinion to set gear on center.

2. Remove yoke cover, gasket, shims and yoke spring. Clean cover and housing flange areas thoroughly. Reinstall cover, omitting the gasket, shims and the spring.

3. Tighten the bolts lightly until the cover just touches the yoke. Measure the gap between the cover and the housing flange. With the gasket, add selected shims to give a combined pack thickness 0.005–0.006 in. (0.13–0.15mm) greater than the measured gap.

4. Tighten cover bolts to 15–21 ft. lbs. (21–29 Nm).

PINION BEARING PRELOAD

1. Mount the steering gear on a bench mounted holding fixture, tool T57L-500-B or equivalent. Loosen the bolts of the yoke cover to relieve spring pressure on the rack.

2. Remove pinion cover and gasket. Remove the spacer and shims. Install a new gasket.

3. Fit shims between the upper bearing and the spacer until the top of the spacer is flush with the gasket. Check with a straight edge using light pressure.

4. Add an 0.0025 in. (0.06mm) shim to the pack in order to preload the bearings. The spacer must be assembled next to the pinion cover.

5. Remove oil seal from cover using centering tool T81P-3504-Y or equivalent. Tighten bolts to 15–21 ft. lbs. (21–29 Nm). Install pinion shaft oil seal.

Power Steering Gear

Removal and Installation
INTEGRAL

1. Disconnect the negative battery cable. Remove the stone shield. Tag the fluid lines and disconnect them from the steering gear. Plug the lines and ports in the gear to prevent entry of dirt.

2. Remove the clamp bolts that hold the flexible coupling to the steering gear.

3. Raise the vehicle and remove the sector shaft attaching nut. Remove the pitman arm with a special pulling tool.

4. Support the steering gear and remove the attaching bolts.

5. Work the gear free of the flex coupling. Remove the gear and flex coupling.

6. Installation is the reverse of the removal procedure. Fill with fluid and bleed the system.

RACK AND PINION

Removal and Installation
EXCEPT CONTINENTAL AND MARK VII

1. Disconnect the negative battery cable.

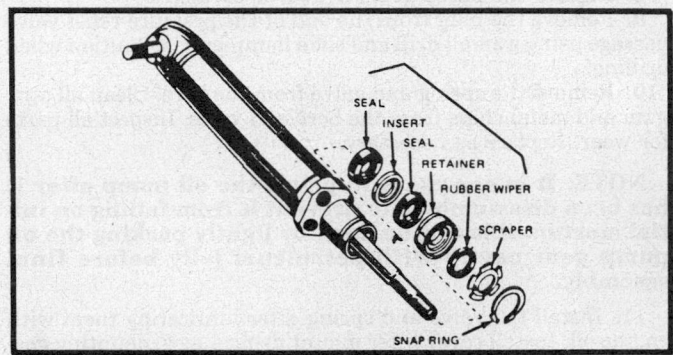

Power cylinder and seal assembly

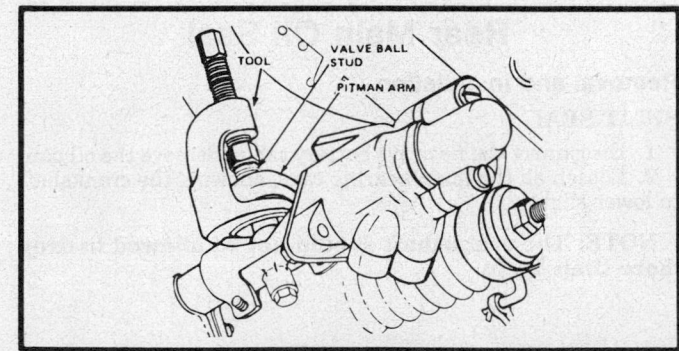

Removing control valve ball stud from the control valve

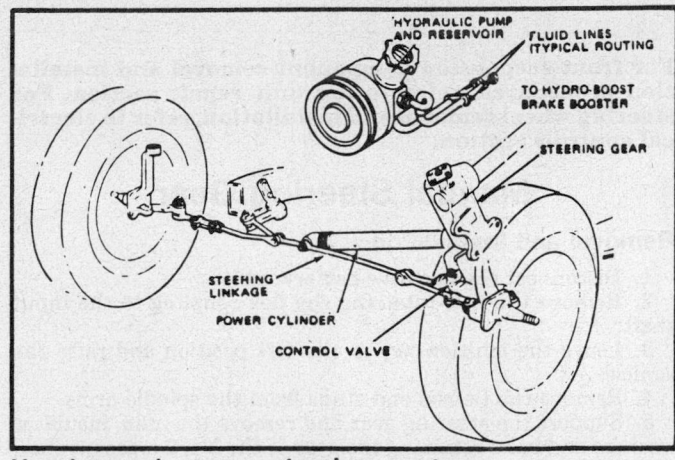

Non-integral power steering system

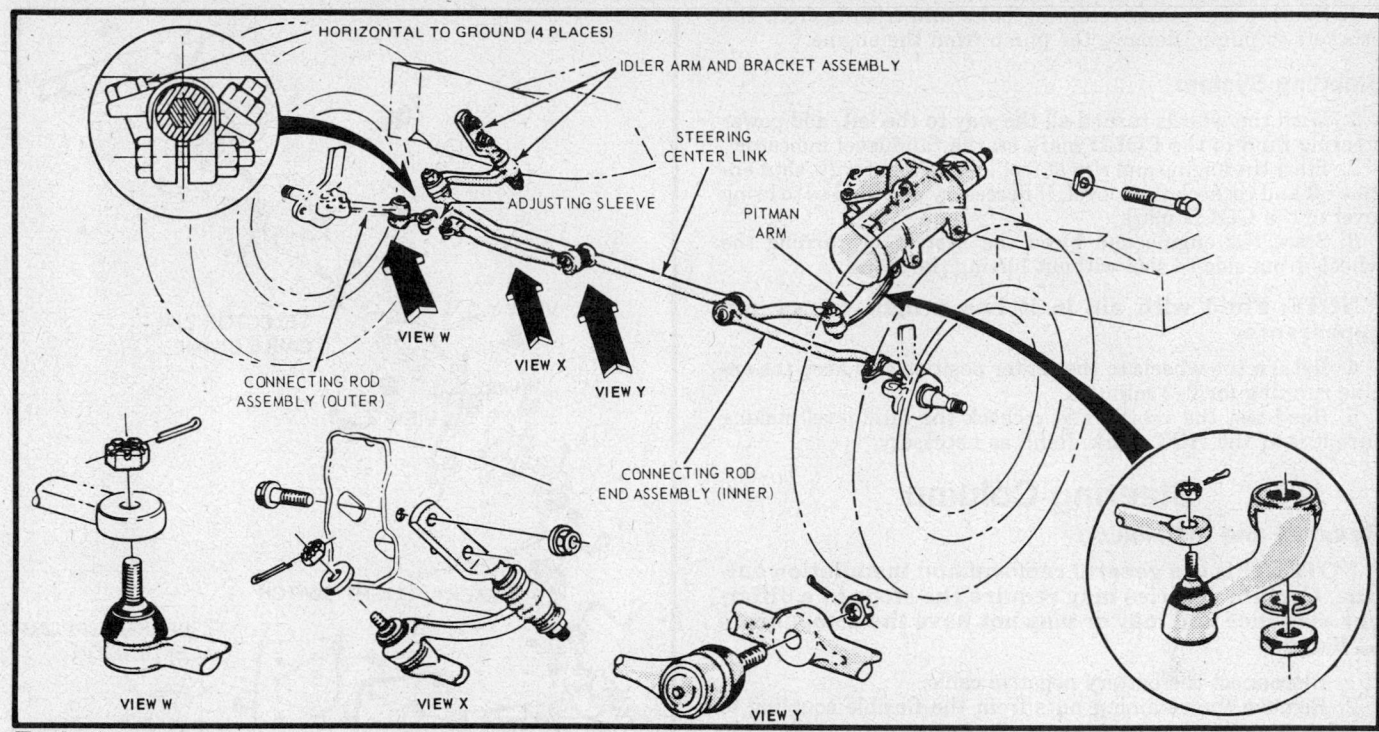

HORIZONTAL TO GROUND (4 PLACES)
IDLER ARM AND BRACKET ASSEMBLY
STEERING CENTER LINK
ADJUSTING SLEEVE
PITMAN ARM
VIEW W
VIEW X
VIEW Y
CONNECTING ROD ASSEMBLY (OUTER)
CONNECTING ROD END ASSEMBLY (INNER)
VIEW W
VIEW X
VIEW Y

Typical manual or power steering linkage and gear assembly

2. Remove the bolt retaining the flexible coupling to the steering input shaft.

3. Place the ignition key in the **ON** position and raise the vehicle and support safely.

4. Remove the 2 tie rod end retaining nuts and cotter pins. Separate the tie rod stud from the spindle arms with the use of a separator tool.

5. Support the rack and pinion and remove the retaining nuts, washers and bolts from the rack and pinion to the crossmember.

6. Lower the gear assembly slightly to gain access to the pressure and return line fittings. Disconnect the fittings and plug the openings to prevent the entry of dirt.

7. Remove the rack and pinion gear assembly from the vehicle.

8. The installation of the rack and pinion assembly is the reverse of the removal procedure. Fill with fluid and bleed the system.

CONTINENTAL AND MARK VII

1. Turn **OFF** the air suspension switch, which is located in the trunk of the vehicle.

2. Disconnect the negative battery cable and turn the ignition switch to the **RUN** position.

3. Raise and support the vehicle safely and position a drain pan under the power steering lines in order to catch the fluid when the lines are removed.

4. Remove the bolt retaining the flexible coupling to the intake shaft.

5. Remove the 2 tie rod end retaining cotter pins and nuts. Separate the studs from the spindle arms, using ball joint spindle press T57P-3006-B or equivalent.

6. Remove the 2 nuts, insulator washers and bolts retaining the steering gear to the No. 2 crossmember.

7. Remove the front rubber insulators and move the gear assembly forward so as to be able to remove the rear rubber insulators.

8. Position the gear to allow access to the hydraulic lines and disconnect the lines.

9. Pull the left hand side of the steering gear forward to clear the mounting spike and allow it to drop as far as possible without forcing it. Rotate the top of the gear assembly forward to clear the engine oil filter and remove the steering gear.

10. Installation is the reverse order of the removal procedure. Be sure to install a new rubber insulators and also new plastic seals on the hydraulic line fittings. Torque the lines to 10–15 ft. lbs. (14–20 Nm).

11. Refill the system with power steering fluid and bleed the system.

Power Steering Pump

Removal and Installation

1. Disconnect the negative battery cable. Disconnect the return and pressure lines from the power steering pump and allow to drain into a container. When the system is drained of fluid, plug the openings to avoid entry of dirt into the system. On supercharged models, remove the supercharger drive belt and the inlet tube.

NOTE: The Ford model CII power steering pump has a fiberglass nylon reservoir, incorporating a pump pressure fitting that allows the pump pressure line to swivel. This is normal and does not indicate a loose fitting. Do not remove the base fitting from the pump reservoir.

2. Loosen the drive belt tensioning nuts or bolts to facilitate the removal of the belt.

NOTE: On the fixed pump system, the alternator must be loosened to remove the pump drive belt.

3. On the fixed pump system, the pump pulley must be removed from the pump shaft with a puller tool, before the pump can be removed from the brackets.

NOTE: Do not hammer on the end of the pump shaft. Internal pump damage can be done.

4. Remove the pump retaining bolts and/or nuts from the brackets to pump. Remove the pump from the engine.

Bleeding System

1. With the wheels turned all the way to the left, add power steering fluid to the **COLD** mark on the fluid level indicator.
2. Start the engine and run at fast idle momentarily, shut engine off and recheck fluid level. If necessary add fluid to to bring level to the **COLD** mark.
3. Start the engine and bleed the system by turning the wheels from side to side without hitting the stops.

NOTE: Fluid with air in it has a light tan or red appearance.

4. Return the wheels to the center position and keep the engine running for 2–3 minutes.
5. Road test the vehicle and recheck the fluid level making sure it is at the **HOT** mark. Refill as necessary.

Steering Column

Removal and Installation

NOTE: This is a general removal and installation outline. Certain vehicles may require the steps in a different sequence and may or may not have the components as listed.

1. Disconnect the battery negative cable.
2. Remove the retaining nuts from the flexible coupling to the flange on the steering input shaft. Separate the safety strap and bolt assembly from the flexible coupling and disconnect the transmission shift rod from the control shift lever.
3. Remove the steering wheel assembly and the steering column trim shrouds.
4. Remove the steering column cover and hood release mechanism.
5. Disconnect all electrical connections to the steering column switches.

NOTE: To gain access to various nuts and bolts, the instrument cluster may have to be removed on certain models.

6. Loosen the nuts holding the column to the brake pedal support, allowing the column to be lowered enough to gain access to the shift quadrant indicator cable.

NOTE: Do not lower the column to the point where excessive weight is on the cable or plastic lever. Damage can result.

7. Disconnect the shift quadrant indicator cable from the cleat on the shift indicator lever. Remove the cable from the steering column tube.
8. Remove the screws holding the dust shield boot to the dash panel.
9. Remove the attaching bolts holding the column to the brake pedal support and lower the column to clear the mounting bolts.
10. Pull the column out so that the U-joint assembly will pass through the clearance hole in the dash panel.
11. With the column assembly out of the vehicle, the shift lever grommet should be replaced before installing the unit back into the vehicle.
12. Install the steering column assembly into the dash opening so that the U-joint and lower shift cane clears the opening.
13. Align the 4 bolts on the brake pedal support with the mounting holes on the column collar and bracket. Attach the nuts loosely and allow the column to hang with a clearance between the column and the instrument panel.
14. Loosely assemble the shift selector cable clamp to the steering column outer tube.

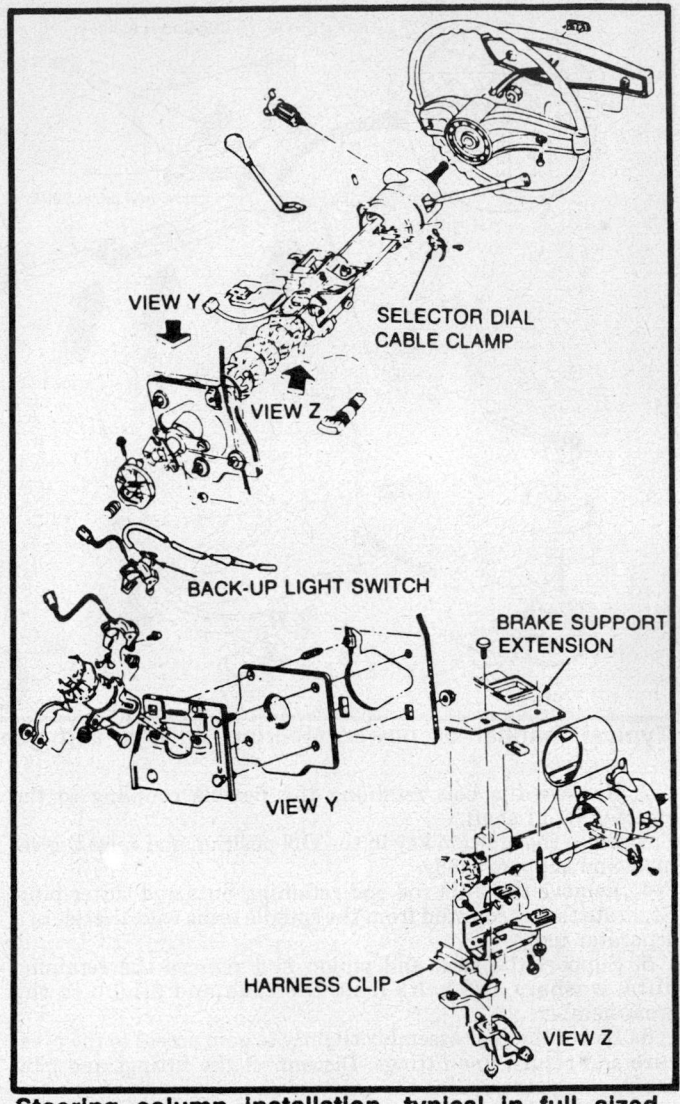

Steering column installation, typical in full sized car models except Lincoln

15. Attach the cable to the shift lever cleat.
16. Tighten the nuts that hold the column to the brake pedal support. torque to 20–37 ft. lbs.
17. Move the shift selector to the **D** position against the drive stop on the insert plate. Rotate the indicator bracket back and forth until the pointer in the instrument cluster points to the center of the letter **D**. Tighten the adjusting nut on the bracket.
18. Connect the electrical connectors to the wiring harness.
19. Engage the safety strap and bolt assembly to the flange on the steering gear input shaft. Tighten the nuts to a torque of 20–37 ft. lbs.

NOTE: The safety strap must be properly positioned to prevent metal to metal contact after tightening the nuts. The flexible coupling must not be distorted when the nuts are tightened. The flexible coupling must have a ⅛ in. coupling insulator flatness.

20. Connect the shift rod to the shift lever. Adjust the linkage as follows:
    a. Raise the vehicle so that the transmission shift rod adjustment nut can be loosened and the transmission shift lever is in the **D** position.

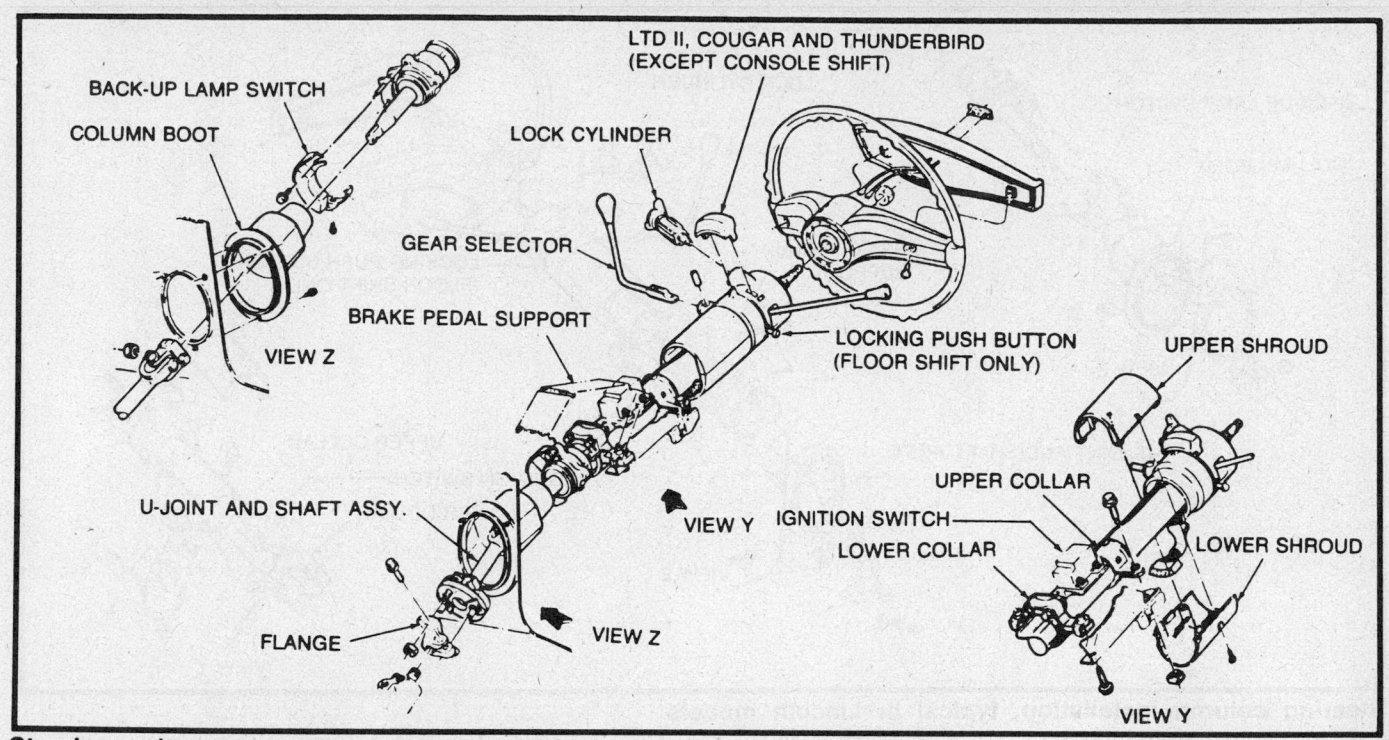

BACK-UP LAMP SWITCH

COLUMN BOOT

LTD II, COUGAR AND THUNDERBIRD
(EXCEPT CONSOLE SHIFT)

LOCK CYLINDER

GEAR SELECTOR

BRAKE PEDAL SUPPORT

VIEW Z

LOCKING PUSH BUTTON
(FLOOR SHIFT ONLY)

UPPER SHROUD

U-JOINT AND SHAFT ASSY.

VIEW Y

UPPER COLLAR

IGNITION SWITCH

LOWER COLLAR

LOWER SHROUD

FLANGE

VIEW Z

VIEW Y

Steering column mounting, typical in Cougar, LTD II and Thunderbird

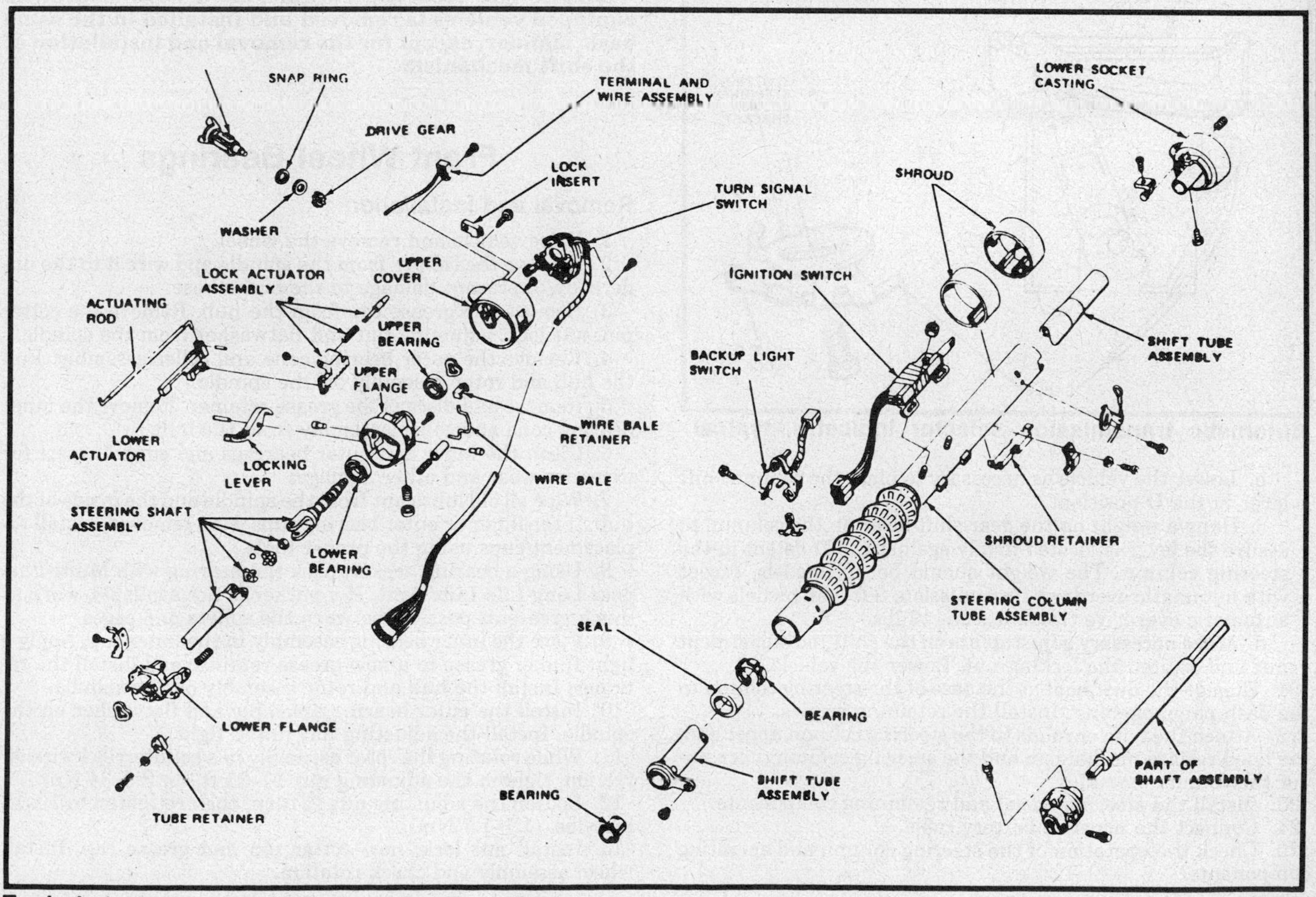

SNAP RING

DRIVE GEAR

WASHER

TERMINAL AND
WIRE ASSEMBLY

LOCK
INSERT

TURN SIGNAL
SWITCH

SHROUD

LOWER SOCKET
CASTING

LOCK ACTUATOR
ASSEMBLY

UPPER
COVER

ACTUATING
ROD

UPPER
BEARING

UPPER
FLANGE

IGNITION SWITCH

BACKUP LIGHT
SWITCH

SHIFT TUBE
ASSEMBLY

LOWER
ACTUATOR

LOCKING
LEVER

WIRE BALE
RETAINER

WIRE BALE

STEERING SHAFT
ASSEMBLY

LOWER
BEARING

SHROUD RETAINER

STEERING COLUMN
TUBE ASSEMBLY

LOWER FLANGE

SEAL

BEARING

PART OF
SHAFT ASSEMBLY

BEARING

SHIFT TUBE
ASSEMBLY

TUBE RETAINER

Exploded view of typical tilt steering column

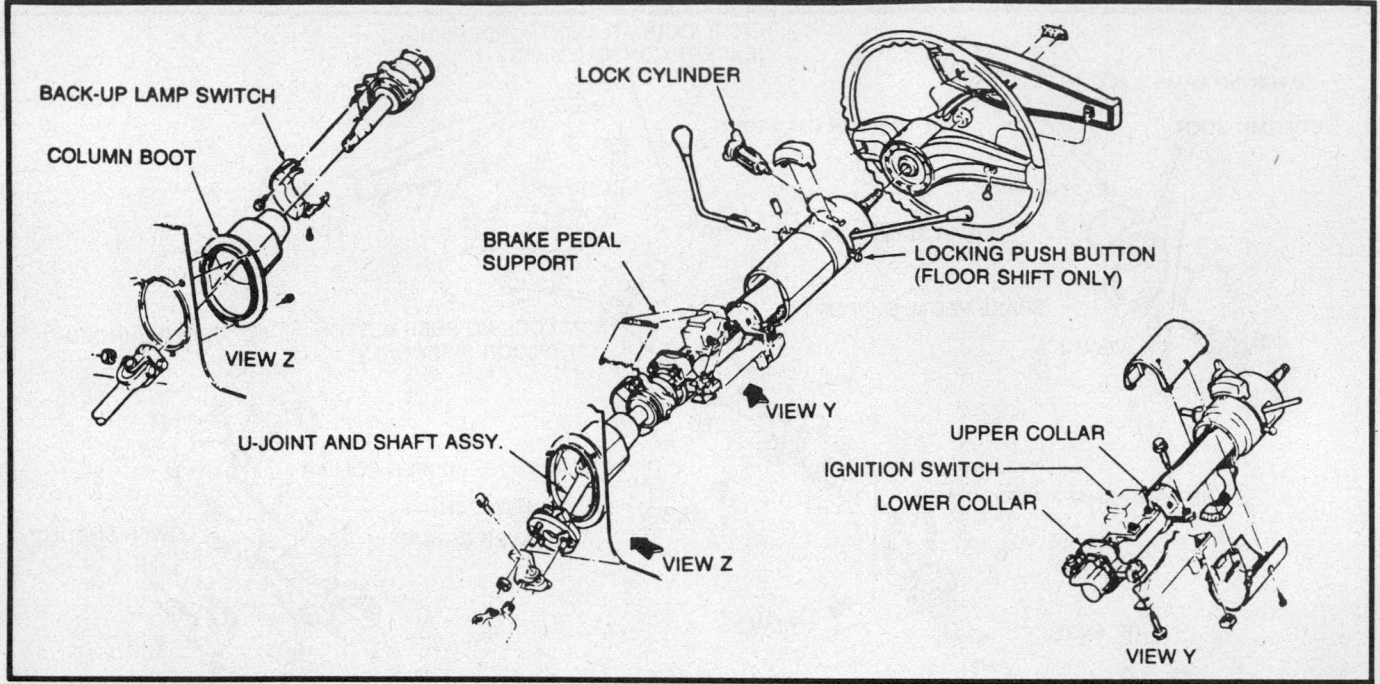

Steering column installation, typical in Lincoln models

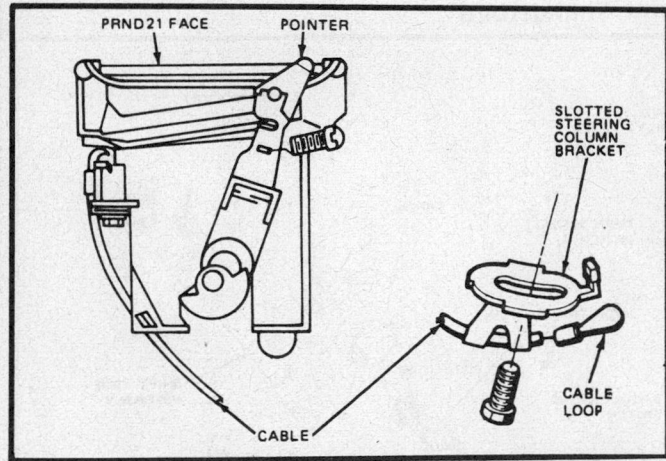

Automatic transmission selector indicator, typical

b. Lower the vehicle as necessary to place the column shift lever in the **D** position.

c. Hang a weight on the gear shift lever on the column, to assure the lever is located firmly against the **D** detent in the steering column. The weight should be: all models, except with automatic overdrive transmission, 8 lbs; all models with automatic overdrive transmission, 12 lbs.

d. Make necessary adjustments on the shift rod adjustment nut and tighten the locking nut. Lower the vehicle.

21. Engage the dust boot at the base of the steering column to the dash panel opening. Install the retaining screws.

22. Attach the trim shrouds to the steering column upper end, the hood release mechanism and the steering column cover under the column assembly.

23. Install the steering wheel and remaining components.

24. Connect the negative battery cable.

25. Check the operation of the steering column and operating components.

NOTE: The steering column used with floorshift equipped vehicles is removed and installed in the same basic manner, except for the removal and installation of the shift mechanism.

Front Wheel Bearings

Removal and Installation

1. Raise vehicle and remove the wheel.

2. Remove the caliper from the spindle and wire it to the underbody to prevent damage to the brake hose.

3. Remove the grease cap from the hub. Remove the cotter pin, nut lock, adjusting nut and flatwasher from the spindle.

4. Remove the outer bearing cone and roller assembly. Pull the hub and rotor assembly off the spindle.

5. Remove and discard the grease retainer. Remove the inner bearing cone and roller assembly from the hub.

6. Clean the inner and outer bearings and cups. Inspect for excessive wear and other damage.

7. Wipe all old lubricant from the spindle and the inside of the hub. If the inner or outer bearing cups were removed, install replacement cups using the proper tools.

8. Using a bearing packer, pack the bearing with Multi-Purpose Long-Life Lubricant. If a packer is not available, work as much grease as possible between the rollers and cages.

9. Place the inner bearing assembly in the inner cup. Apply a light film of grease to a new grease retainer and install the retainer. Install the hub and rotor assembly on the spindle.

10. Install the outer bearing assembly and flatwasher on the spindle. Install the adjusting nut finger tight.

11. While rotating the rotor assembly in a counterclockwise direction, tighten the adjusting nut 17–25 ft. lb. (23–34 Nm).

12. Loosen the adjusting nut ½ turn, then retighten to 10–12 inch lbs. (1.1–1.7 Nm).

13. Install nut lock, new cotter pin and grease cap. Install wheel assembly and check rotation.

BRAKES

For brake service, drum and rotor specifications, refer to the unit repair section

Master Cylinder

Removal and Installation

NOTE: On vehicles equipped with the anti-lock braking system, it is necessary to relieve the brake system pressure before performing any type of service. The pressure can be relieved by, placing the key in the OFF position and pumping the brake pedal at least 20 times or until increased pedal effort is felt.

1. Disconnect the negative battery cable.
2. Remove the brake tubes from the primary and secondary outlet ports of the master cylinder and pressure control valves.
3. Remove the nuts attaching master cylinder to the brake booster assembly. Disconnect brake warning lamp connector.
4. Slide the master cylinder forward and upward from vehicle.
5. Installation is the reverse of the removal procedure. Fill master cylinder to **MAX** line on side of reservoir with heavy duty brake fluid. Bleed brake system.

Proportioning Valve

Removal And Installation

1. Disconnect the brake warning lamp switch wire harness connector from the warning lamp switch.
2. Disconnect the front brake system inlet tube and rear system inlet tube from the brake control valve assembly.
3. Disconnect the left and right front brake outlet tubes from the brake control valve assembly.
4. Disconnect the rear system outlet tube from the brake control valve assembly.
5. Remove the screw that retains the brake control valve assembly on the frame. Remove the assembly from the vehicle.

NOTE: The brake control valve assembly is serviced only as an assembly.

6. Position the brake valve assembly on the frame. Install the mounting screw for frame mounting and tighten to 7–11 ft. lbs.
7. Install the inlet and outlet tubes in the reverse order of the removal procedure and torque tube nuts to 10–18 ft. lbs.
8. Connect the brake warning lamp switch wiring harness connector to the brake warning lamp switch. Verify the connection by turning the ignition switch to the **ON** position; lamp must go on. Also confirm that the locking fingers on the connector are locked into the switch.
9. Bleed the brake system and centralize the the pressure differential valve by:
   a. Turn the ignition switch to the **ON** or **ACC** position.
   b. Depress the brake pedal and the piston will center itself, causing the brake warning lamp to go out (if it was illuminated).
   c. Turn the ignition switch to the **OFF** position.
   d. Before driving the vehicle, check the operation of the brakes and be sure that a firm pedal is obtained.

NOTE: During the brake system bleeding operation on vehicles equipped with a metering valve, the metering valve bleeder rod must be pushed in (pressure bleeding).

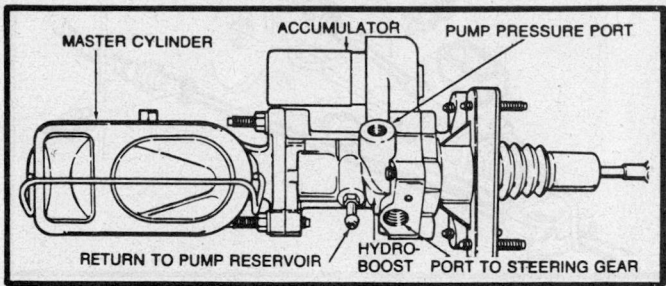
Hydro-boost brake unit

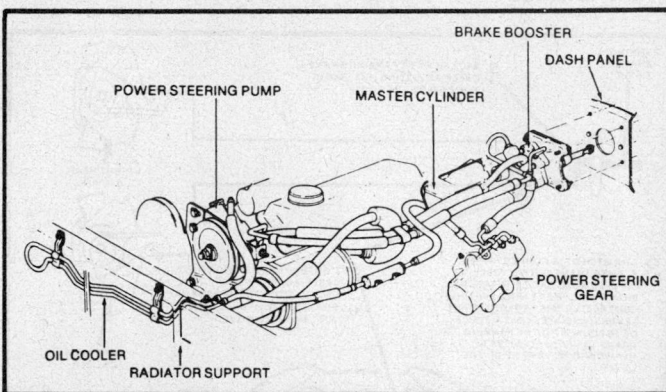
Typical hydro-boost brake system

Bleeding System

NOTE: When any part of the hydraulic system has been disconnected for service, air may enter the system causing a spongy pedal action or brake system failure. Bleed the system, after it has been opened, to ensure that all air is expelled.

1. Bleed the master cylinder before any wheel cylinders or calipers.
2. Loosen the upper secondary outlet fitting. Push the brake pedal down through full travel. Close the outlet fitting, then return the pedal to the full released position.
3. Wait 5 seconds, then repeat operation until air bubbles cease to appear. Loosen the upper primary outlet fitting and repeat Step 2.
4. Continue to bleed the system, rear wheel cylinders first.
5. Place a suitable box wrench on the bleeder fitting and attach a rubber drain tube to fitting. Submerge free end of tube in a container partially filled with clean brake fluid, loosen bleeder fitting and repeat Step 2 and 3.
6. Refill master cylinder after each wheel cylinder or caliper is bled and install master cylinder cover and gasket.

Power Brake Booster

Removal and Installation

1. Disconnect the negative battery cable. Working inside the vehicle below the instrument panel, disconnect booster valve operating rod from the brake pedal assembly. To do this, disconnect the stop light switch wires at the connector. Remove the hairpin retainer and nylon washer from the pedal pin. Slide the switch off just enough for the outer arm to clear the pin. Remove the switch.2. Slide the boost push rod, bushing and inner nylon washer off the pedal pin.

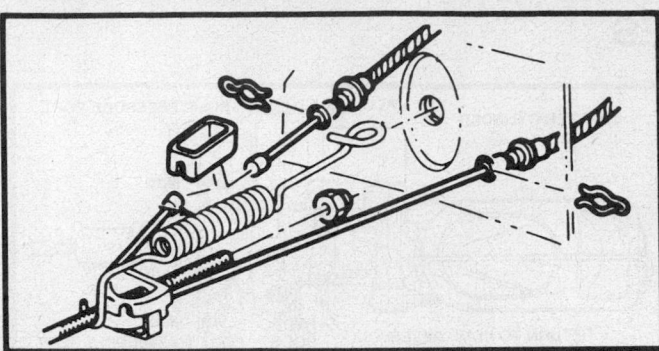

Parking brake cable equalizer used with rear drum brakes

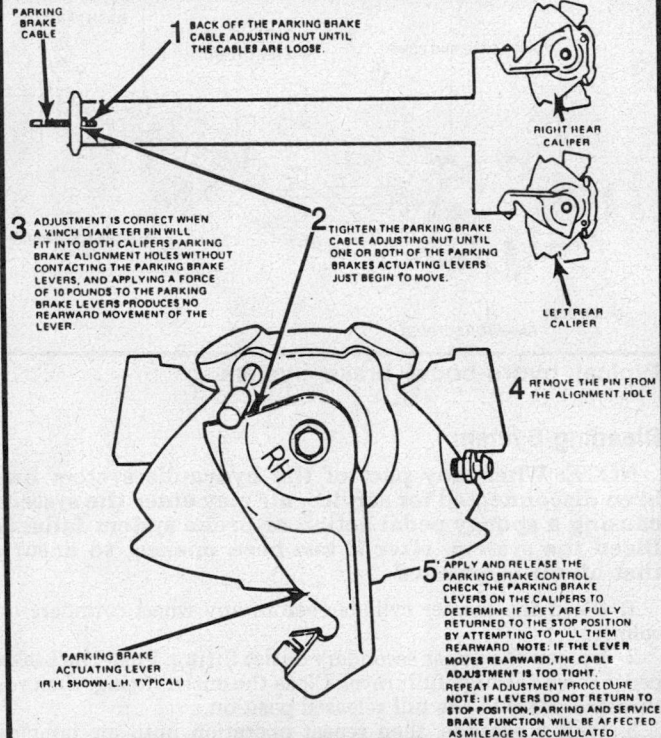

Parking brake adjustment with rear disc brakes

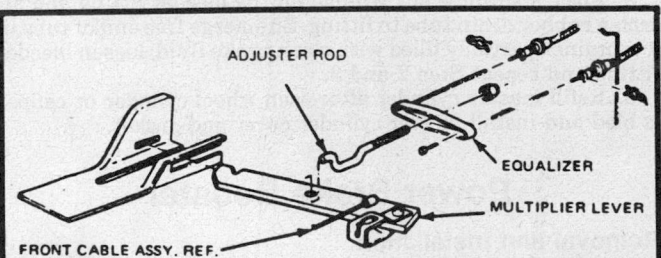

Parking brake cable equalizer used with rear disc brakes

3. Remove the air cleaner for working clearance if necessary.

4. On vehicles equipped with the 2.3L engine, disconnect the accelerator cable at the carburetor.

5. Remove the securing screw from the accelerator shaft bracket and remove the cable from the bracket. Remove the 2 screws attaching the bracket to the manifold; rotate the bracket toward the engine.

6. Disconnect the brake lines at the master cylinder outlet fittings.

7. Disconnect manifold vacuum hose from the booster unit. On cars equipped with speed control, remove the left cowl screen in the engine compartment. Remove the 3 nuts retaining the speed control servo to the firewall and move the servo out of the way.

8. Remove the 4 bracket to firewall attaching bolts.

9. Remove the booster and bracket assembly from the firewall, sliding the valve operating rod out from the engine side.

10. Install the booster assembly and the master cylinder. Reconnect the fluid lines. Reconnect the brake pedal arm to the booster. Bleed the brakes after installation is complete.

HYDRO-BOOST UNIT

Removal and Installation

1. Disconnect the negative battery cable. Open the hood and remove the nuts attaching the master cylinder to the brake booster.

2. Remove the master cylinder from the hydro-boost accumulator.

3. Set the master cylinder aside without disturbing the hydraulic lines.

4. Disconnect the pressure, steering and return lines from the accumulator.

5. Plug the lines and ports.

6. Working below the instrument panel, disconnect the hydro-boost pushrod from the brake pedal. To do this, disconnect the stoplight switch at the connector. Remove the hairpin retainer. Slide the stoplight switch from the brake pedal pin far enough to clear the switch outer pin hole. Remove the switch from the pin.

7. Loosen the hydro-boost attaching nuts and remove the pushrod, washers and bushing from the brake pedal pin.

8. Remove the accumulator.

9. Installation is the reverse of removal. Leave the hydro-boost mounting nuts loose until the pushrod and stoplight switch are connected to the brake pedal. After installation, remove the coil wire from the distributor. Fill the power steering reservoir and while cranking the engine, pump the brake pedal. Do not move the steering wheel until all the air has been pumped out of the system.

10. Check the power steering fluid level, install the coil wire, start the engine and pump the brakes while steering from lock to lock. Check for leaks.

Parking Brake

Adjustments

NOTE: If a new cable is installed, prestretch it by applying and releasing it 5 times before making any adjustments.

REAR DRUM BRAKES

In most cases, a rear brake shoe adjustment will provide satisfactory parking brake action. However, if parking brake cables are excessively loose after releasing the handbrake, proceed as follows:

1. Raise and safely support the vehicle. Fully release the parking brake.

2. Loosen locknut on equalizer rod under the car. Then loosen the nut in front of the equalizer, several turns.

3. Turn the locknut forward against the equalizer until the cables are tight enough so that the rear wheels cannot be turned by hand. Then, back off the adjustment until the rear wheels turn freely.

4. When cables are properly adjusted, tighten both nuts against the equalizer.

5. Apply and release the brake and feel for freeness of rear wheels.

REAR DISC BRAKES

NOTE: Parking brake adjustment is critical on 4 wheel disc brake equipped vehicles. If a caliper has been overhauled or pads changed, be sure to pump pedal lightly approximately 30 times, before adjusting parking brake.

1. Raise and safely support the vehicle. Fully release the parking brake.

2. Locate the adjusting nut beneath the vehicle on the driver's side. While observing the parking brake actuating levers on the rear calipers, tighten the adjusting nut until the levers just begin to move.

3. Apply and release parking brake control. Check the parking brake levers on the calipers to determine if they are fully returned to the stop position by attempting to pull them rearward.

4. If lever does not contact caliper lever stop, the cable adjustment is to tight. Repeat adjustment procedure.

CLUTCH AND TRANSMISSION

Refer to "Chilton's Professional Transmission Service Manual" for additional coverage.

Clutch Linkage

NOTE: All vehicles have self-adjusting clutches. No adjustments are necessary.

HYDRAULIC CLUTCH SYSTEM

Bleeding

1. Clean all dirt and grease from the cap to make sure that no foreign subtances enter the system.

2. Remove the cap and diaphragm and fill the reservoir to the top with the approved DOT 3 brake fluid. Fully loosen the bleed screw which is in the slave cylinder body next to the inlet connection.

3. At this point bubbles of air will appear at the bleed screw outlet. When the slave cylinder is full and a steady stream of fluid comes out of the slave cylinder bleeder, tighten the bleed screw.

4. Assemble the diaphragm and cap to the reservoir, fluid in the reservoir should be level with the step. Exert a light load of about 20 lbs. to the slave cylinder piston by pushing the release lever towards the cylinder and loosen the bleed screw. Maintain a constant light load, fluid and any air that is left will be expelled through the bleed port. Tighten the bleed screw when a steady flow of fluid and no air is being expelled.

5. Fill the reservoir fluid level back to normal capacity and if necessary, repeat Step 4.

6. Exert a light load to the release lever, but do not open the bleeder screw as the piston in the slave cylinder will move slowly down the bore. Repeat this operation 2-3 times, the fluid movement will force any air left in the system into the reservoir. The hydraulic system should now be fully bled.

7. Check the the operation of the clutch hydraulic system and repeat this procedure if necesary. Check the push rod travel at the slave cylinder to insure the minimum travel 0.57 in.

Clutch

Removal and Installation

1. Disconnect the negative battery cable. Lift the clutch pedal to its uppermost position to disengage the pawl and quadrant. Push quadrant forward, unhook cable from quadrant and allow quadrant to slowly swing rearward.

2. Raise and safely support the vehicle and remove the dust shield.

Hydraulic clutch components

Self-adjusting clutch mechanism

3. Disconnect cable from the release lever. Remove the retaining clip and remove the clutch cable from the flywheel housing. On turbocharged engines, remove the clutch slave cylinder.

4. Remove starter and bolts that secure engine rear plate to front lower part of flywheel housing.

5. Remove the transmission, then the flywheel housing.

6. Remove clutch release lever from housing by pulling it through the window in housing until retainer spring is disengaged from pivot. Remove release bearing from release lever.

7. Loosen the pressure plate cover attaching bolts evenly to release spring tension gradually and avoid distorting cover. If same pressure plate and cover are to be installed, mark cover and flywheel so that pressure plate can be installed in its original position.

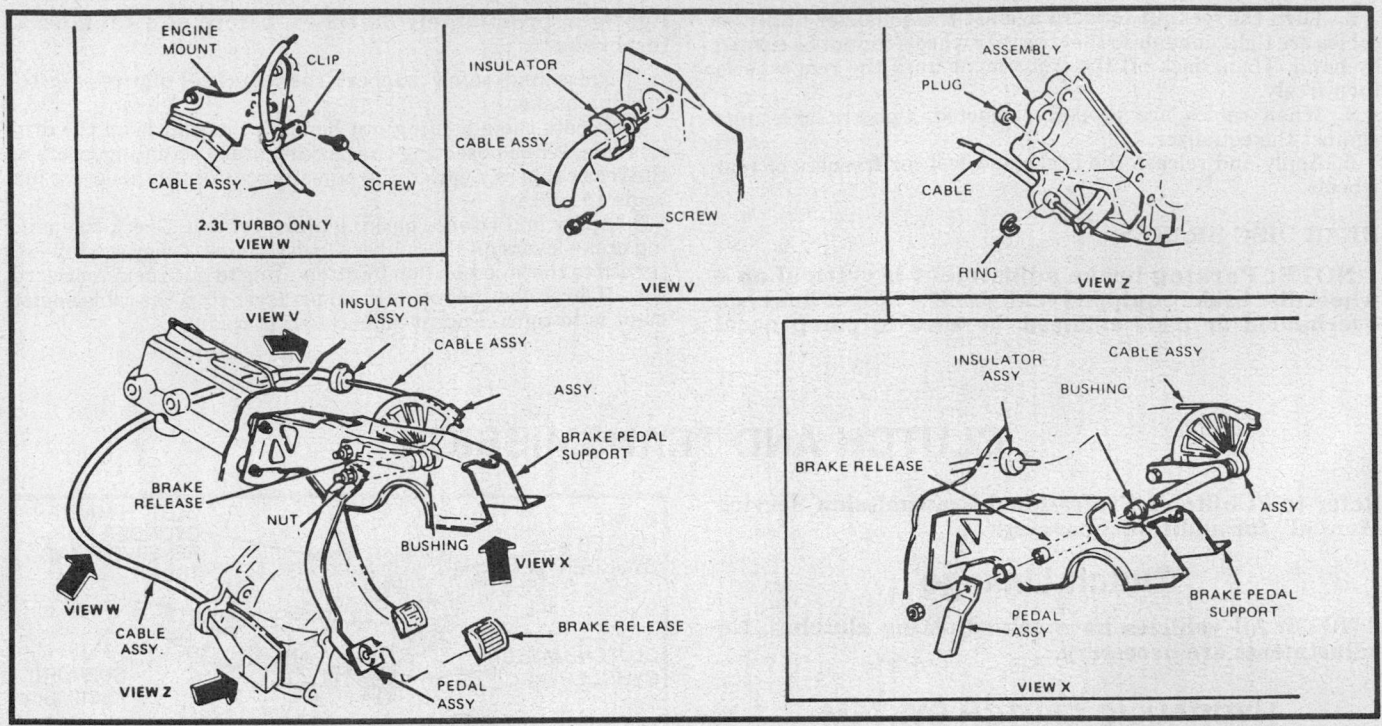

Clutch pedal installation with self-adjusting clutch mechanism

8. Installation is the reverse of the removal procedure. Align clutch disc using proper alignment tool inserted in pilot bearing. Tighten bolts to specifications.

Manual Transmission

Removal and Installation

NOTE: This is a general removal and installation outline. Certain vehicles may require the steps in a different sequence and may or may not have the components as listed.

1. Disconnect the negative battery cable. Disconnect and remove the starter, if the clutch is to be removed. Remove the shift boot retainer and shifter lever.

2. On 4 speed transmission: working under the hood, remove the upper clutch housing to engine bolts.

3. Raise and safely support the vehicle.

4. Matchmark the driveshaft and axle flange for reassembly. Disconnect the driveshaft at the rear universal joint and remove the driveshaft. Plug the extension housing.

5. Disconnect the speedometer cable at the transmission extension. Disconnect the seat belt sensor wires and the back-up lamp switch wires. Remove the clutch lever boot and cable on Mustang and Capri.

6. Disconnect the gear shift rods from the transmission shift levers. If the vehicle is equipped with a 4 speed, remove the bolts that secure the shift control bracket to extension housing. Support the engine with a jack.

7. Remove the bolt holding the extension housing to the rear support and remove the muffler inlet pipe bracket to housing bolt.

8. Remove the rear support bracket insulator nuts from the underside of the crossmember. Remove the crossmember.

9. Place a jack under the rear of the engine oil pan. Raise or lower the engine slightly as necessary to provide access to the bolts.

10. Remove transmission to flywheel housing bolts.

11. Slide the transmission back and out of the car. It may be necessary to slide the catalytic converter bracket forward to provide clearance on some models.

12. To remove the clutch, remove release lever retracting spring. Disconnect pedal at the equalizer bar, of the clutch cable from the housing, as applicable.

13. Remove the bolts that secure engine rear plate to front lower part of bellhousing.

14. Remove the bolts that attach bellhousing to cylinder block and remove the housing and release lever as a unit. Remove the clutch release lever by pulling it through the window in the housing until the retainer spring disengages from the pivot.

15. Loosen the pressure plate cover attaching bolts evenly to release spring pressure. Mark cover and flywheel to facilitate reassembly in same position.

16. Remove 6 attaching bolts while holding pressure plate cover. Remove pressure plate and clutch disc.

─────────────── **CAUTION** ───────────────

Do not depress the clutch pedal while the transmission is removed.

17. Before installing the clutch, clean the flywheel surface. Inspect the flywheel and pressure plate for wear, scoring, or burn marks (blue color). Light scoring and wear may be cleaned up with emery paper; heavy wear may require refacing of the flywheel or replacement of the damaged parts.

18. Attach the clutch disc and pressure plate assembly to the flywheel. The 3 dowel pins on the flywheel, if so equipped, must be properly aligned. Damaged pins must be replaced. Avoid touching the clutch plate surface. Tighten the bolts finger tight.

19. Align the clutch disc with the pilot bushing. Torque cover bolts to 12–24 ft. lbs. with the 4 cylinder, 12–20 ft. lbs. for all others.

20. Lightly lubricate the release lever in the flywheel housing and install the dust shield.

21. Apply very little lubricant on the release bearing retainer journal. Fill the groove in the release bearing hub with grease. Clean all excess grease from the inside bore of the hub to pre-

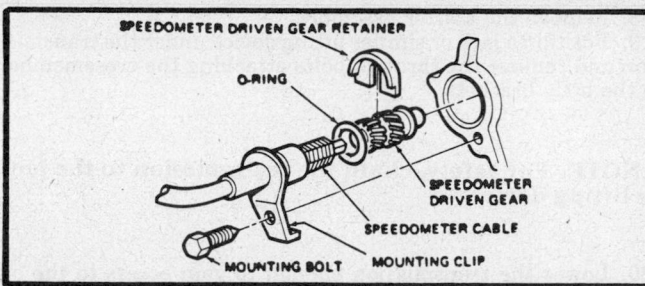

Typical attachment of speedometer driven gear to transmission

vent clutch disc contamination. Attach the release bearing and hub on the release lever.

22. Make sure the flywheel housing and engine block are clean. Any missing damaged mounting dowels must be replaced. Install the flywheel housing and torque the attaching bolts to 38–61 ft. lbs. on all V8 engines and 28–38 ft. lbs. on the 2.3L engines. Install the dust cover and torque the bolts to 17–20 ft. lbs.

23. Connect the release rod or cable and the retracting spring. Connect the pedal to equalizer rod at the equalizer bar.

24. After moving the transmission back just far enough for the pilot shaft to clear the clutch housing, move it upward and into position on the flywheel housing. It may be necessary to put the transmission in gear and rotate the output shaft to align the input shaft and clutch splines.

25. Move the transmission forward and into place against the flywheel housing and install the transmission attaching bolts finger-tight.

26. Tighten the transmission bolts to 37–42 ft. lbs. on all cars.

27. Install the crossmember and torque the mounting bolts to 20–30 ft. lbs. Slowly lower the engine onto the crossmember.

20. Torque the rear mount to 00–50 ft. lbs.

29. Connect gear shift rods and the speedometer cable. Install the starter and dust ring.

30. Remove the plug from the extension housing and install the driveshaft, aligning the marks made previously.

31. Refill transmission to proper level. On floorshift models, install the boot retainer and shift lever.

Automatic Transmission

Removal and Installation

EXCEPT C5 TRANSMISSION

NOTE: This is a general removal and installation outline. Certain model vehicles may require the steps in a different sequence and may or may not have the components as listed.

1. Disconnect the negative battery cable. Raise the vehicle and support safely.

2. Drain the fluid from the transmission by removing all oil pan bolts except the 2 at the front. Loosen the 2 at the front and drop the oil pan at the rear to allow the fluid to drain into a container. When drained, reinstall a few of the bolts to hold the pan in place.

3. Remove the converter bottom cover and remove the converter drain plug, if equipped to allow the converter to drain. After the converter has drained, reinstall the drain plug and tighten. Remove the converter to adapter plate bolts by turning the converter to expose the bolts.

NOTE: Crank the engine over with a wrench on the crankshaft pulley attaching bolt.

4. Matchmark and disconnect the driveshaft assembly.

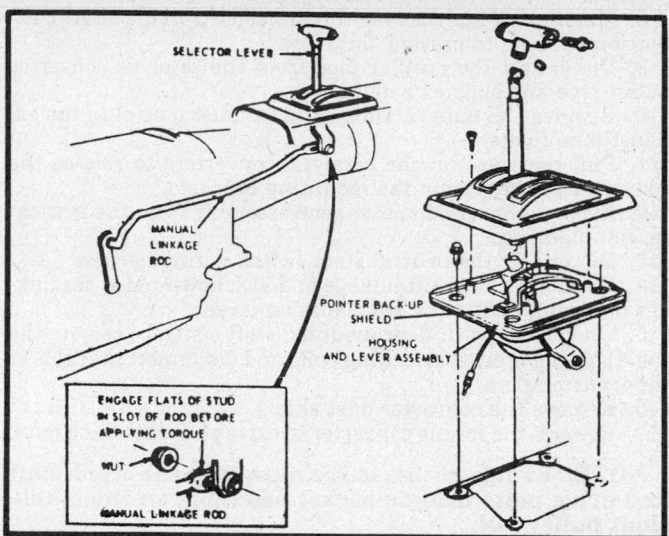

Adjustment of shift linkage when equipped with console

NOTE: Fluid will leak from the extension housing unless a cap is installed over the output shaft and in the extension housing.

5. Remove the speedometer cable from the extension housing.

6. Disconnect the manual control shift rod and the downshift rod from the transmission control levers.

7. Remove the starter cable and remove the starter.

8. Remove the electrical wires and vacuum lines, as required from the transmission assembly. Remove the bellcrank bracket, if equipped from the converter housing.

9. Place a support under the transmission and slightly raise it. It may be necessary to raise the engine hood and loosen the fan shroud.

10. Remove the rear crossmember and engine rear support. Disconnect the necessary exhaust components.

11. Lower the transmission to expose the oil cooler line fittings. Disconnect the lines from the transmission.

12. Support the engine and remove the dipstick tube and all the bell housing retaining bolts except for the top 2.

13. Chain the transmission to the jack or support unit for safety.

14. Remove the 2 top bolts from the converter housing and move the transmission rearward and down from under the vehicle. Hold the converter in place to avoid having it drop from the transmission.

15. The installation of the transmission assembly is the reverse of the removal procedure.

16. Fill the unit with correct fluid to its proper level, start the engine and check the transmission for leakage.

C-5 TRANSMISSION

1. Open the hood and protect the fenders with covers.

2. Disconnect the negative battery cable.

3. On Cougar with 3.8L engine, remove the air cleaner assembly.

4. Remove the fan shroud retaining bolts and position the shroud back over the fan.

5. Loosen the clamp and disconnect the thermactor air injector hose at the catalytic converter check valve on Cougar with 3.8L engine.

6. On Cougar with 3.8L engine, remove the top bell housing to engine bolts from the engine compartment.

7. Raise the vehicle and support safely. Drain the oil pan.

8. Matchmark and remove the driveshaft. Plug the rear extension opening to prevent fluid loss.

9. Disconnect the muffler pipe from the catalytic converter outlet pipe and support safely.

10. Remove the nuts retaining the exhaust pipe(s) to the exhaust manifold(s).

11. Pull rearward on the catalytic converters to release the converter hangers from the mounting brackets.

12. Remove the speedometer gear assembly from the rear extension housing.

13. Disconnect the neutral start switch wiring harness.

14. Disconnect the shift linkage and kick down rod at the linkage bellcrank and at the transmission lever.

15. On vehicles with floor mounted shift controls, remove the cable routing bracket attaching bolts and disconnect the cable at the transmission.

16. Remove the converter dust shield.

17. Remove the torque converter to drive plate attaching nuts.

NOTE: To gain access to the nuts, turn the crankshaft and drive plate using a socket assembly on the crankshaft pulley nut.

18. Remove the starter assembly.

19. Position a jack or similar lifting device under the transmission and remove the through bolts attaching the crossmember to the body brackets.

NOTE: For safety, chain the transmission to the jack or lifting device.

20. Lower the transmission enough to gain access to the oil cooler lines and disconnect.

21. Remove the remaining bell housing to engine bolts and pull the transmission rearward to disengage the converter studs from the drive plate.

22. Carefully lower the transmission from under the vehicle, being careful not to drop the converter assembly.

23. Installation is the reverse of the removal procedure.

24. Fill the transmission with the correct fluid (Ford type H) and start the engine. Check for fluid leakage. Correct the fluid level as necessary.

DRIVESHAFT

Removal and Installation

1. Raise and safely support the vehicle. Matchmark the rear driveshaft yoke and the companion flange so that the parts may be reassembled in the same way to maintain balance.

2. Remove the U-bolts and straps or coupling flange nuts and bolts at the rear of the driveshaft and tape the loose bearing caps to the spider.

3. Allow the rear of the driveshaft to drop down slightly. Pull the driveshaft and slip yoke out of the transmission extension housing.

4. Plug the transmission to prevent fluid leakage.

5. To install, lubricate the yoke splines and install the yoke into the transmission extension housing, aligning the splines. Be careful not to bottom the slip yoke hard against the transmission seal.

6. Rotate the pinion flange as necessary to align the matchmarks made earlier. New bolts should be used and torque the attaching bolts to 70–95 ft. lbs.

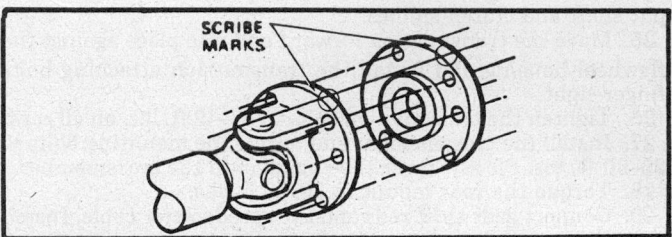

Matching driveshaft to pinion shaft flanges by the scribed marks

Universal Joint

Removal and Installation

Refer to the unit repair section for overhaul procedures.

REAR AXLE AND REAR SUSPENSION

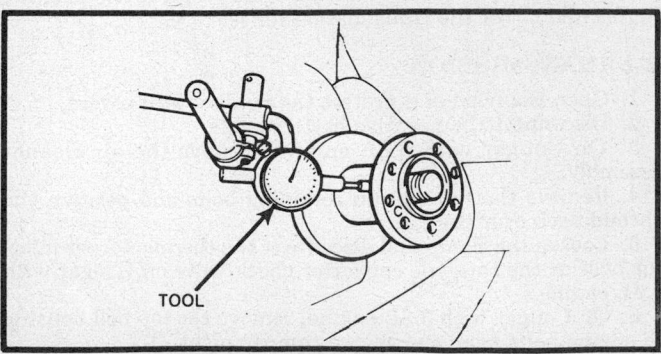

Checking companion flange radial runout typical

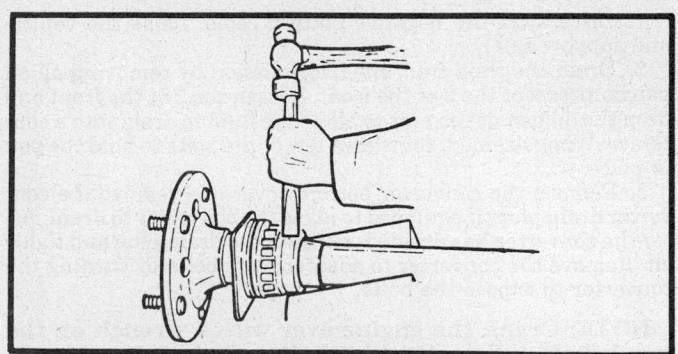

Scoring axle shaft bearing retainer prior to removal

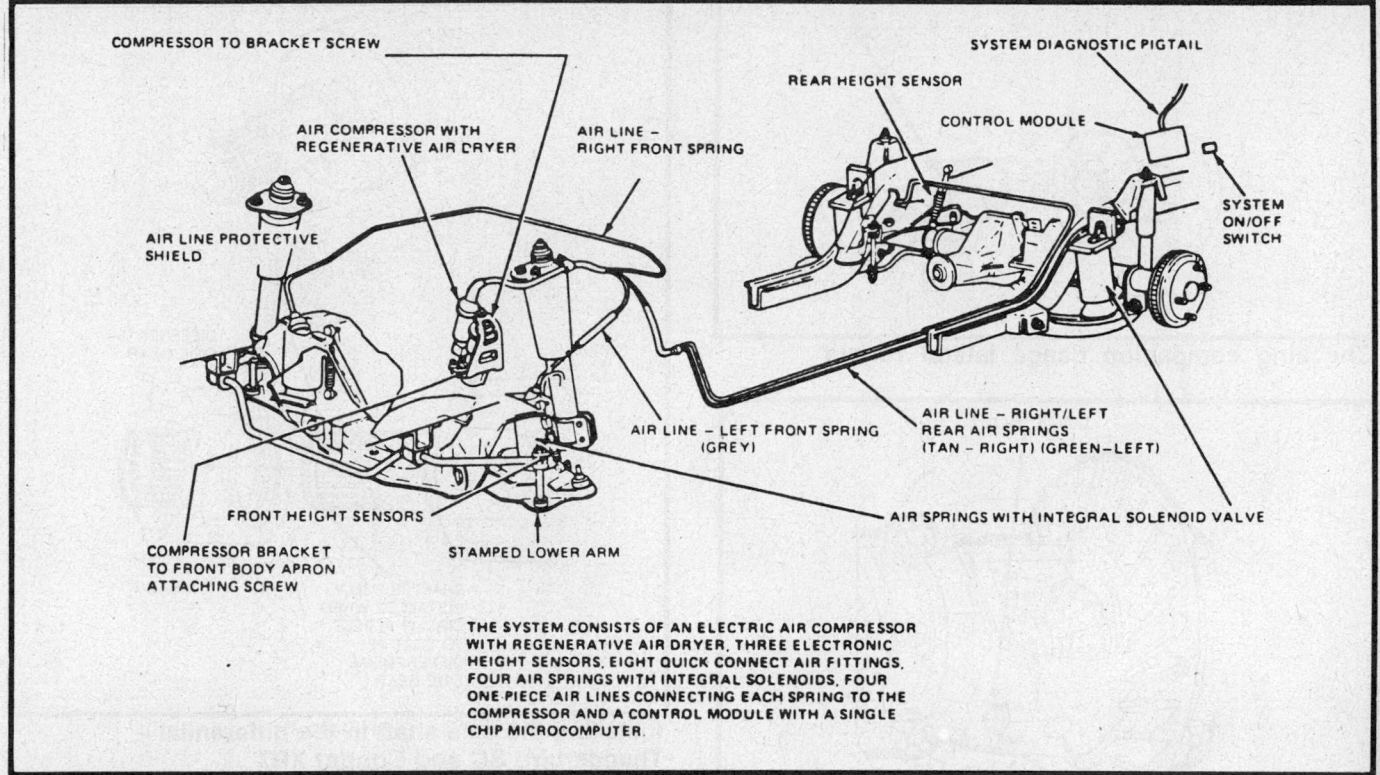

COMPRESSOR TO BRACKET SCREW

SYSTEM DIAGNOSTIC PIGTAIL

REAR HEIGHT SENSOR

CONTROL MODULE

AIR COMPRESSOR WITH REGENERATIVE AIR DRYER

AIR LINE — RIGHT FRONT SPRING

SYSTEM ON/OFF SWITCH

AIR LINE PROTECTIVE SHIELD

AIR LINE — LEFT FRONT SPRING (GREY)

AIR LINE — RIGHT/LEFT REAR AIR SPRINGS (TAN — RIGHT) (GREEN — LEFT)

FRONT HEIGHT SENSORS

STAMPED LOWER ARM

AIR SPRINGS WITH INTEGRAL SOLENOID VALVE

COMPRESSOR BRACKET TO FRONT BODY APRON ATTACHING SCREW

THE SYSTEM CONSISTS OF AN ELECTRIC AIR COMPRESSOR WITH REGENERATIVE AIR DRYER, THREE ELECTRONIC HEIGHT SENSORS, EIGHT QUICK CONNECT AIR FITTINGS, FOUR AIR SPRINGS WITH INTEGRAL SOLENOIDS, FOUR ONE-PIECE AIR LINES CONNECTING EACH SPRING TO THE COMPRESSOR AND A CONTROL MODULE WITH A SINGLE CHIP MICROCOMPUTER.

Air spring suspension system

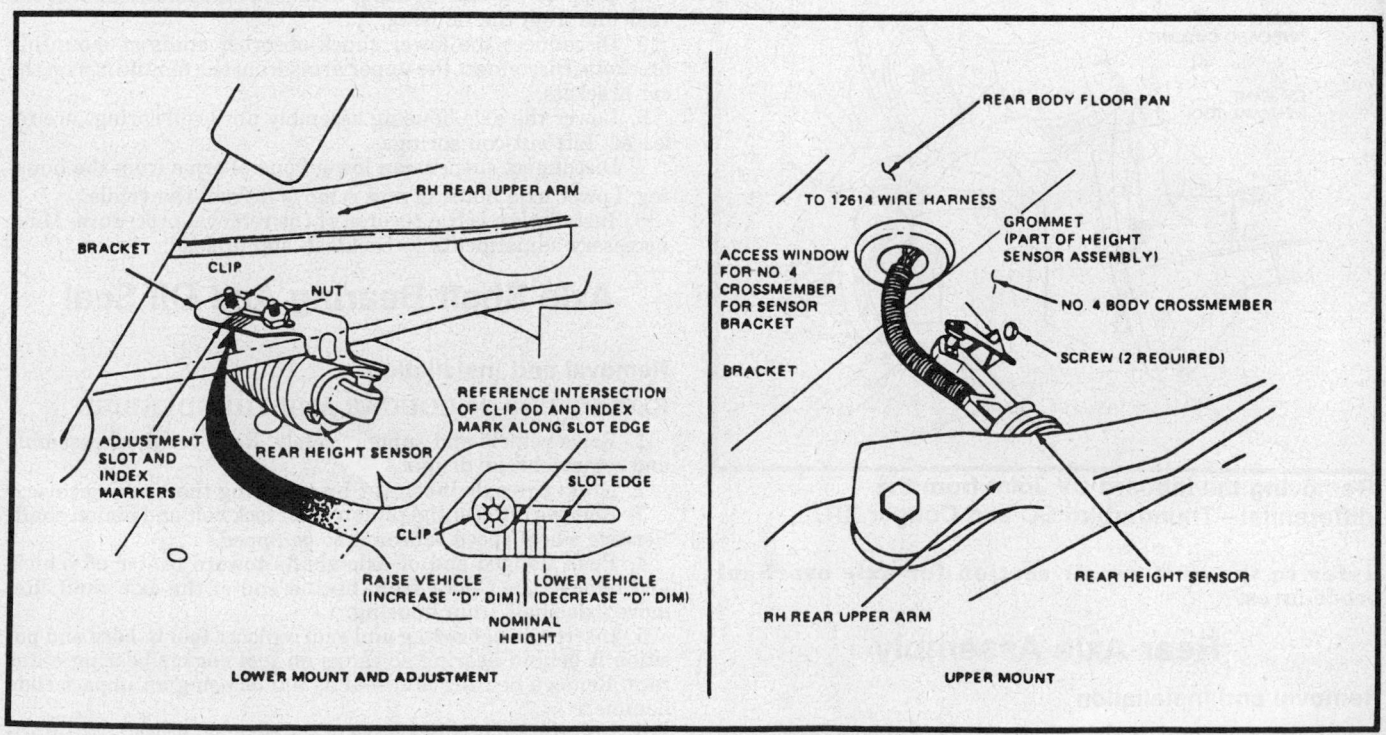

RH REAR UPPER ARM

BRACKET

CLIP

NUT

REFERENCE INTERSECTION OF CLIP OD AND INDEX MARK ALONG SLOT EDGE

ADJUSTMENT SLOT AND INDEX MARKERS

REAR HEIGHT SENSOR

SLOT EDGE

CLIP

RAISE VEHICLE (INCREASE "D" DIM)

LOWER VEHICLE (DECREASE "D" DIM)

NOMINAL HEIGHT

LOWER MOUNT AND ADJUSTMENT

REAR BODY FLOOR PAN

TO 12614 WIRE HARNESS

GROMMET (PART OF HEIGHT SENSOR ASSEMBLY)

ACCESS WINDOW FOR NO. 4 CROSSMEMBER FOR SENSOR BRACKET

NO. 4 BODY CROSSMEMBER

BRACKET

SCREW (2 REQUIRED)

REAR HEIGHT SENSOR

RH REAR UPPER ARM

UPPER MOUNT

Rear suspension ride height adjustment

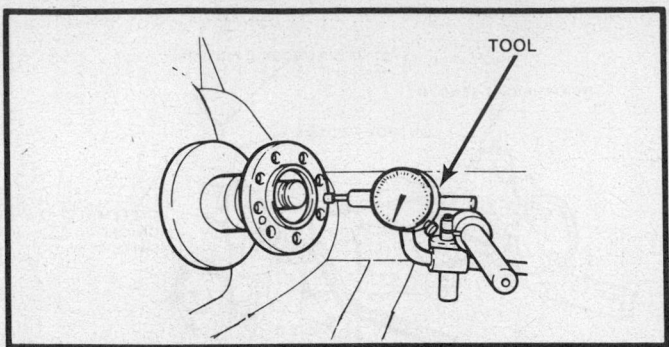

Checking companion flange lateral runout

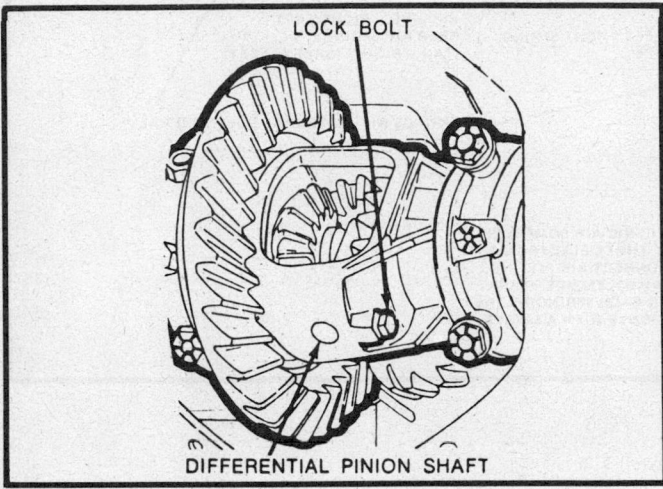

Removing the differential pinion shaft lockbolt

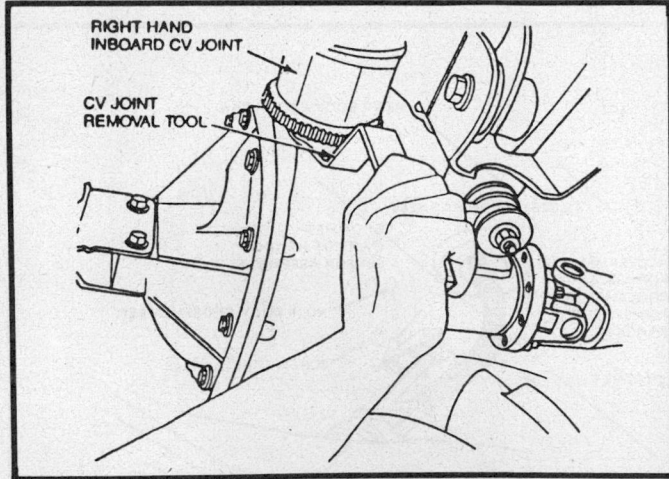

Removing the inboard CV joint from the differential—Thunderbird SC and Cougar XR7

Refer to the unit repair section for axle overhaul procedures.

Rear Axle Assembly

Removal and Installation

1. Raise and support the vehicle safely. Remove the wheels and brake drums.

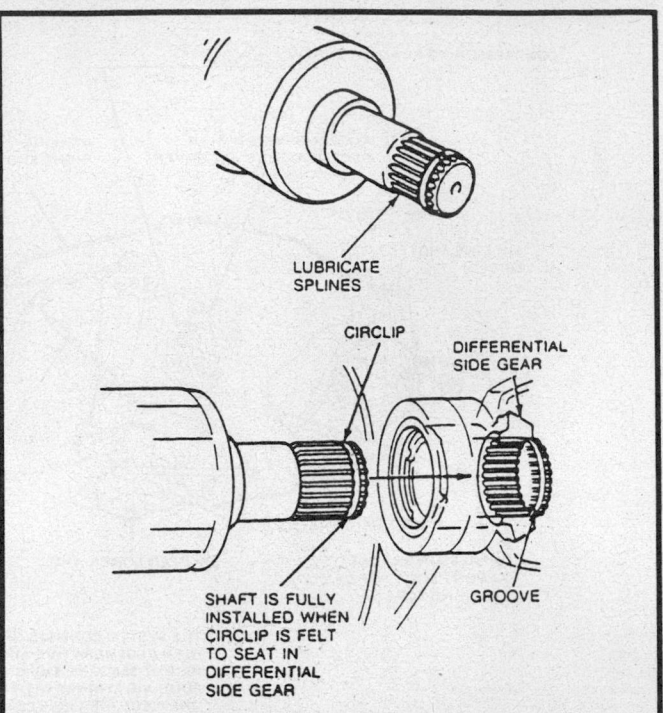

Installing the axle shaft in the differential—Thunderbird SC and Cougar XR7

2. Position the brake junction block and lines out of the way. Disconnect the electrical connectors from the brake calipers on vehicles equipped with ABS.
3. Mark the driveshaft yoke and companion flange. Disconnect the driveshaft at the companion flange.
4. Support the axle housing with jack stands. Disconnect the vent line from the housing.
5. Disconnect the lower shock absorber studs at mounting brackets. Disconnect the upper arms from the mountings on the ear brackets.
6. Lower the axle housing assembly until coil springs are released. Lift out coil springs.
7. Disconnect suspension lower control arms from the housing. Lower axle housing and remove it from the vehile.
8. Installation is the reverse of the removal procedure. Make necessary adjustments to backlash and preload.

Axle Shaft Bearing And Oil Seal

Removal and Installation
EXCEPT 1989-90 COUGAR AND THUNDERBIRD

1. Raise vehicle and support safely. Remove wheel assembly and remove brake drums.
2. Drain the axle lubricant by removing the housing cover.
3. Remove differential pinion shaft lock bolt and pinion shaft. Remove wheel speed sensor if so equipped.
4. Push flanged end of axle shafts toward center of vehicle and remove the C-lock from button end of the axle shaft. Remove axle shaft from housing.
5. Insert wheel bearing and seal replacer tool in bore and position it behind bearing so tangs on tool engage bearing outer race. Remove bearing and seal as a unit using an impact slide hammer.
6. Installation is the reverse of the removal procedure. Lubricate new bearing with rear axle lubricant.

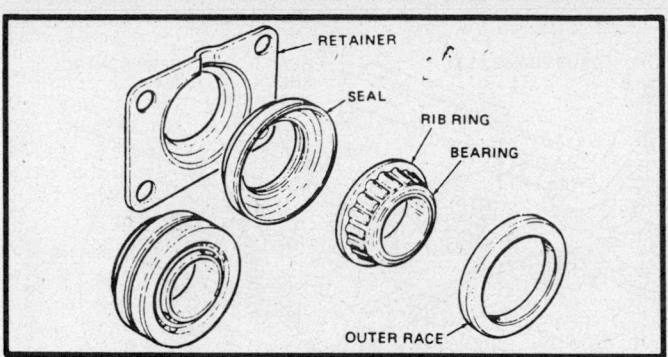

Tapered bearing and retainer-removable carrier axle

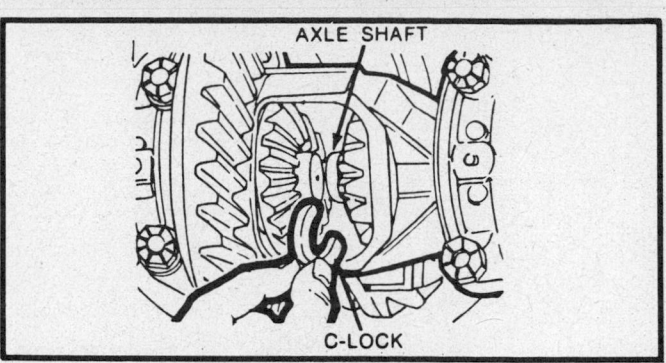

Removing the axle shaft "C" locks

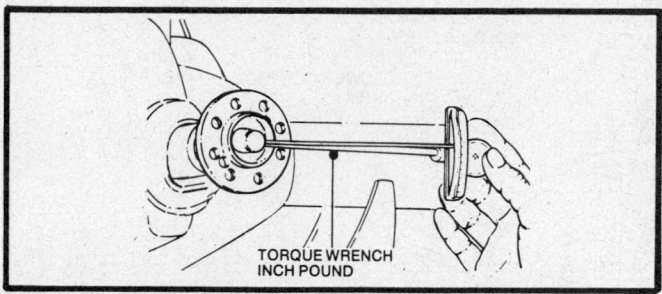

Checking pinion bearing preload

Rear Halfshaft

Removal and Installation

1989-90 COUGAR AND THUNDERBIRD

NOTE: Before removing the rear halfshafts, new inboard CV joint stub shaft circlips and 2 new differential oil seals must be used for assembly.

1. Remove the right side wheel cover and wheel lug nuts.
2. Raise and safely support the vehicle, supporting it by the frame.
3. On vehicles with anti-lock brakes, remove the anti-lock sensor bolts and remove the sensors.
4. Pull back on the parking brake cable release lever and on the cable, this will release the tension. Remove the cable from the caliper.
5. Remove the upper and lower caliper retaining bolts and re-move the caliper. Support the caliper out of the way with a wire, do not support the caliper with the brake lines.
6. Remove the brake rotor. Remove the upper control arm nut and bolt and wire the upper control arm, up and out of the way.
7. Using a paint marker, mark the position of the lower control arm in relation to the knuckle with the arms in the relaxed position.

NOTE: Failure to mark this relationship will cause axle bind up and incorrect ride height, causing tire wear and misalignment.

8. Remove the lower control arm to knuckle bolt. Remove the right halfshaft (inboard CV joint) from the differential housing using halfshaft remover tool T89-3514-A or equivalent.
9. Remove the halfshaft and knuckle assembly from the vehicle. Insert a plug of some sort into the differential housing to prevent fluid loss.
10. Install new circlips on the halfshaft, by sliding it into the groove on the slined end of the shaft.
11. Remove the plug from the differential housing. Lightly lubricate the stub shaft splines and carefully align the splines on the shaft with the splines in the differential.
12. Push the knuckle inward to seat the circlip in the differential side gear groove. Use care not to damage the seal.
13. Install the lower control arm bolt and nut, tighten to 118-148 ft. lbs.
14. Install the upper arm retaining bolt and tighten to 118-148 ft. bs.
15. Install the brake rotor. Install the brake caliper and tighten the retaining bolts to 80-100 ft. lbs.
16. Install the parking brake cable and the anti-lock sensor.
17. Install the tire and wheel assembly. Some vehicles have unidirectional tires, note the direction before installation.

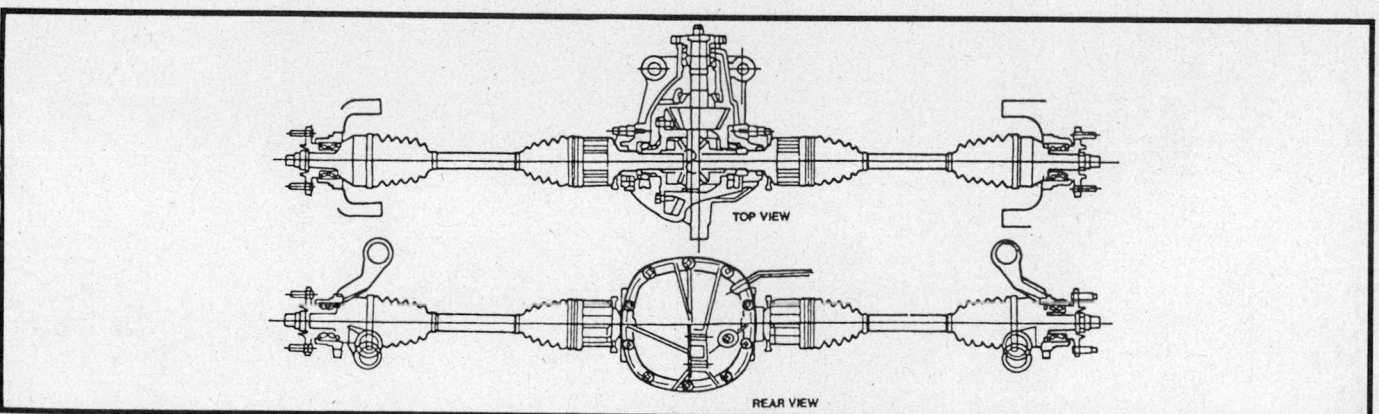

Wheel runout measurement

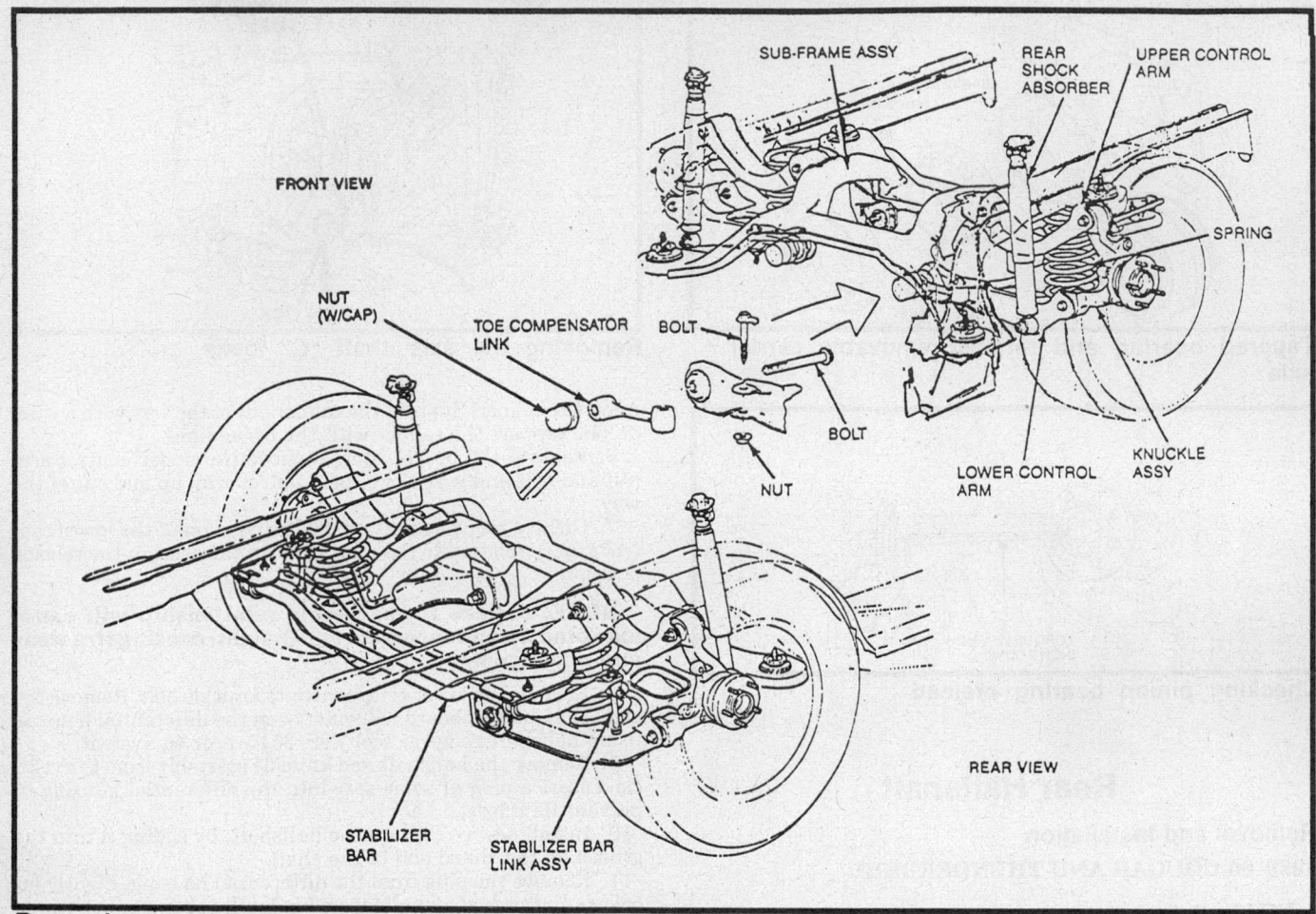

Rear axle assembly and related components

YEAR IDENTIFICATION

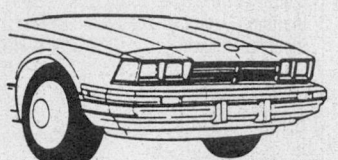
1986-88 Century

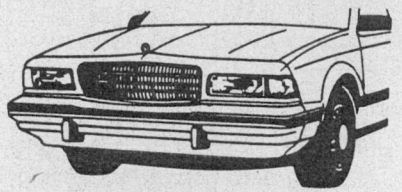
1989–90 Century

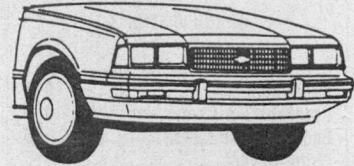
1986-89 Celebrity

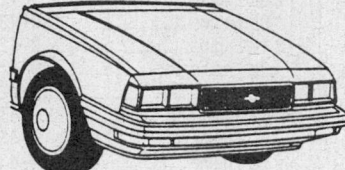
1986-89 Celebrity Eurosport

1985-86 Cutlass Ciera

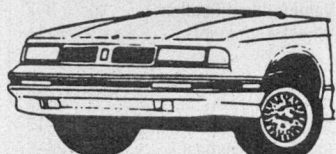
1987–90 Cutlass Ciera/GT

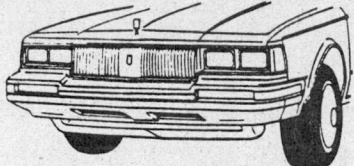
1986–88 Cutlass Cruiser

1989–90 Cutlass Cruiser

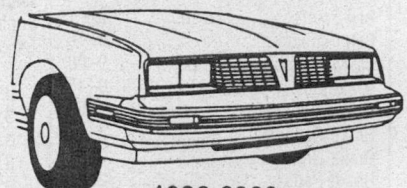
1986 6000

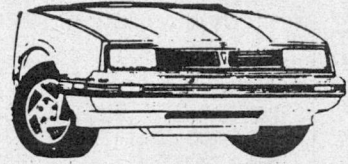
1987-88 6000 SE/LE

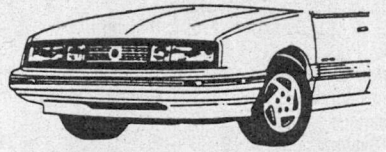
1989–90 6000 SE/LE

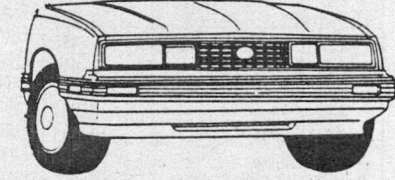
1986-89 6000 STE

VEHICLE IDENTIFICATION CHART

It is important for servicing and ordering parts to be certain of the vehicle and engine identification. The VIN (vehicle identification number) is a 17 digit number visible through the windshield on the driver's side of the dash and contains the vehicle and engine identification codes. The tenth digit indicates model year and the eighth digit indicates engine code. It can be interpreted as follows:

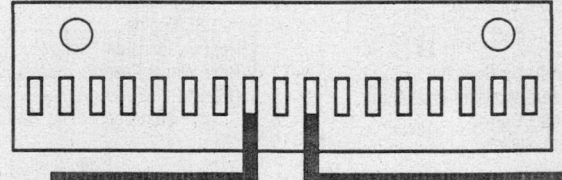

Engine Code						Model Year	
Mode	Cu. In.	Liters	Cyl.	Fuel Sys.	Eng. Mfg.	Code	Year
R	151	2.5	4	TBI	Pontiac	G	1986
X	173	2.8	6	2 bbl	Chevrolet	H	1987
W	173	2.8	6	MFI	Chevrolet	J	1988
T	192	3.1	6	MFI	Chevrolet	K	1989
N	204	3.3	6	SFI	Buick	L	1990
3	231	3.8	6	SFI	Buick		
B	231	3.8	6	SFI	Buick		

ENGINE IDENTIFICATION

Year	Model	Engine Displacement Cu. In. (liter)	Engine Series Identification (VIN)	No. of Cylinders	Engine Type
1986	Celebrity	151 (2.5)	R	4	TBI
	Celebrity	173 (2.8)	X	6	2 bbl
	Celebrity	173 (2.8) HO	W	6	MFI
	Century	151 (2.5)	R	4	TBI
	Century	173 (2.8)	X	6	2 bbl
	Century	231 (3.8)	3	6	SFI
	Cutlass Ciera	151 (2.5)	R	4	TBI
	Cutlass Ciera	173 (2.8) ①	X	6	2 bbl
	Cutlass Ciera	173 (2.8)	W	6	MFI
	Cutlass Ciera	231 (3.8)	3	6	SFI
	Cutlass Ciera	231 (3.8)	B	6	SFI
	6000	151 (2.5)	R	4	TBI
	6000	173 (2.8)	X	6	2 bbl
	6000	173 (2.8)	W	6	MFI
1987	Celebrity	151 (2.5)	R	4	TBI
	Celebrity	173 (2.8)	W	6	MFI
	Century	151 (2.5)	R	4	TBI
	Century	173 (2.8)	W	6	MFI
	Century	231 (3.8)	3	6	SFI
	Cutlass Ciera	151 (2.5)	R	4	TBI
	Cutlass Ciera	173 (2.8)	W	6	MFI
	Cutlass Ciera	231 (3.8) HO	3	6	SFI
	6000	151 (2.5)	R	4	TBI
	6000	173 (2.8)	W	6	MFI
1988	Celebrity	151 (2.5)	R	4	TBI
	Celebrity	173 (2.8)	W	6	MFI
	Century	151 (2.5)	R	4	TBI
	Century	173 (2.8)	W	6	MFI
	Century	231 (3.8)	3	6	SFI
	Cutlass Ciera	151 (2.5)	R	4	TBI
	Cutlass Ciera	173 (2.8)	W	6	MFI
	Cutlass Ciera	231 (3.8)	3	6	SFI
	6000	151 (2.5)	R	4	TBI
	6000	173 (2.8)	W	6	MFI
1989-90	Celebrity	151 (2.5)	R	4	TBI
	Celebrity	173 (2.8)	W	6	MFI
	Century	151 (2.5)	R	4	TBI
	Century	173 (2.8)	W	6	MFI
	Century	204 (3.3)	N	6	MFI
	Cutlass Ciera	151 (2.5)	R	4	TBI
	Cutlass Ciera	173 (2.8)	W	6	MFI
	Cutlass Ciera	204 (3.3)	N	6	MFI
	6000	151 (2.5)	R	4	TBI
	6000	173 (2.8)	W	6	MFI

GENERAL MOTORS—"A" BODY
CENTURY • CELEBRITY • CUTLASS CIERA • 6000—FWD

ENGINE IDENTIFICATION

Year	Model	Engine Displacement Cu. In. (liter)	Engine Series Identification (VIN)	No. of Cylinders	Engine Type
1989-90	6000	192 (3.1)	T	6	MFI

TBI Throttle Body Injection
MFI Multiport Fuel Injection
SFI Sequential Fuel Injection

bbl Carburetor barrels
HO High output
① Canada only

GENERAL ENGINE SPECIFICATIONS

Year	VIN	No. Cylinder Displacement cu. in. (liter)	Fuel System Type	Net Horsepower @ rpm	Net Torque @ rpm (ft. lbs.)	Bore × Stroke (in.)	Compression Ratio	Oil Pressure @ rpm
1986	R	4-151 (2.5)	TBI	92 @ 4000	134 @ 2800	4.000 × 3.000	8.3:1	37.5 @ 2000
	X	6-173 (2.8)	2 bbl	112 @ 4800	145 @ 2100	3.500 × 3.000	8.5:1	50-65 @ 1200
	W	6-173 (2.8)	MFI	130 @ 4800	155 @ 3600	3.503 × 2.992	8.9:1	50-65 @ 1200
	3	6-231 (3.8)	SFI	150 @ 4400	200 @ 2000	3.800 × 3.400	8.0:1	37 @ 2400
	B	6-231 (3.8)	SFI	150 @ 4400	200 @ 2000	3.800 × 3.400	8.0:1	37 @ 2400
1987	R	4-151 (2.5)	TBI	92 @ 4000	134 @ 2800	4.000 × 3.000	8.3:1	37.5 @ 2000
	W	6-173 (2.8)	MFI	130 @ 4800	155 @ 3600	3.503 × 2.992	8.9:1	50-65 @ 1200
	3	6-231 (3.8)	SFI	150 @ 4400	200 @ 2000	3.800 × 3.400	8.0:1	37 @ 2400
1988	R	4-151 (2.5)	TBI	92 @ 4000	134 @ 2800	4.000 × 3.000	8.3:1	37.5 @ 2000
	W	6-173 (2.8)	MFI	130 @ 4800	155 @ 3600	3.503 × 2.992	8.9:1	50-65 @ 1200
	3	6-231 (3.8)	SFI	150 @ 4400	200 @ 2000	3.800 × 3.400	8.0:1	37 @ 2400
1989-90	R	4-151 (2.5)	TBI	92 @ 4000	134 @ 2800	4.000 × 3.000	8.3:1	37.5 @ 2000
	W	6-173 (2.8)	MFI	130 @ 4800	155 @ 3600	3.503 × 2.992	8.9:1	50-65 @ 1200
	T	6-192 (3.1)	MPFI	120 @ 4200	175 @ 2200	3.503 × 3.312	8.8:1	50-65 @ 2400
	N	6-204 (3.3)	SFI	160 @ 5200	185 @ 2000	3.700 × 3.160	9.0:1	45 @ 2000

TBI Throttle Body Injection
MFI Multi-port Fuel Injection
SFI Sequential Multi-port Fuel Injection
HO High output

GASOLINE ENGINE TUNE-UP SPECIFICATIONS
Refer to Section 34 for all spark plug recommendations

Year	VIN	No. Cylinder Displacement cu. in. (liter)	Spark Plugs Gap (in.)	Ignition Timing (deg.) MT	Ignition Timing (deg.) AT	Compression Pressure (psi)	Fuel Pump (psi)	Idle Speed (rpm) MT	Idle Speed (rpm) AT	Valve Clearance In.	Valve Clearance Ex.
1986	R	4-151 (2.5)	.060	①	①	NA	6.0-7.0	①	①	Hyd.	Hyd.
	X	6-173 (2.8)	.045	①	①	NA	6.0-7.0	①	①	Hyd.	Hyd.
	W	6-173 (2.8)	.045	①	①	NA	40.0-46.0	①	①	Hyd.	Hyd.
	3	6-231 (3.8)	.080	①	①	NA	34.0-40.0	①	①	Hyd.	Hyd.
	B	6-231 (3.8)	.045	①	①	NA	34.0-40.0	①	①	Hyd.	Hyd.
1987	R	4-151 (2.5)	.060	①	①	NA	6.0-7.0	①	①	Hyd.	Hyd.
	W	6-173 (2.8)	.045	①	①	NA	40.0-46.0	①	①	Hyd.	Hyd.
	3	6-231 (3.8)	.080	①	①	NA	34.0-40.0	①	①	Hyd.	Hyd.
1988	R	4-151 (2.5)	.060	①	①	NA	6.0-7.0	①	①	Hyd.	Hyd.
	W	6-173 (2.8)	.045	①	①	NA	40.0-46.0	①	①	Hyd.	Hyd.

GASOLINE ENGINE TUNE-UP SPECIFICATIONS
Refer to Section 34 for all spark plug recommendations

Year	VIN	No. Cylinder Displacement cu. in. (liter)	Spark Plugs Gap (in.)	Ignition Timing (deg.) MT	AT	Compression Pressure (psi)	Fuel Pump (psi)	Idle Speed (rpm) MT	AT	Valve Clearance In.	Ex.
1988	3	6-231 (3.8)	.080	①	①	NA	34.0–40.0	①	①	Hyd.	Hyd.
1989	R	4-151 (2.5)	.060	①	①	NA	6.0–7.0	①	①	Hyd.	Hyd.
	W	6-173 (2.8)	.045	①	①	NA	40.0–46.0	①	①	Hyd.	Hyd.
	T	6-192 (3.1)	.045	①	①	NA	34.0–47.0	①	①	Hyd.	Hyd.
	N	6-204 (3.3)	.060	①	①	NA	37.0–43.0	①	①	Hyd.	Hyd.
1990		SEE UNDERHOOD SPECIFICATIONS STICKER									

① Refer to underhood specifications sticker

FIRING ORDERS

NOTE: To avoid confusion, always replace spark plug wires one at a time.

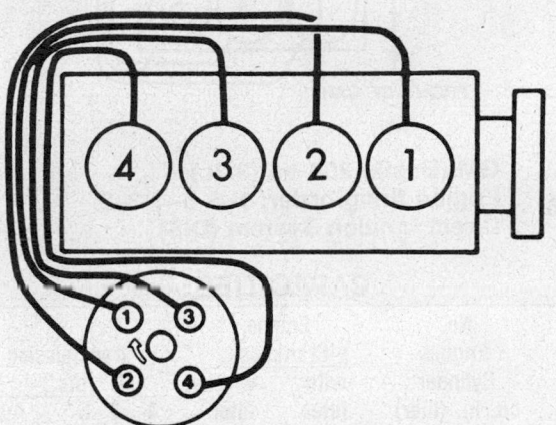

GM (Pontiac) 151–4
Engine firing order: 1–3–4–2
Distributor rotation: clockwise

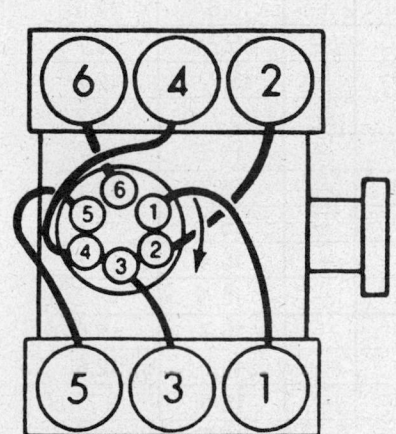

GM (Chevrolet) 173 V6 (2.8 L)
Engine firing order: 1–2–3–4–5–6
Distributor rotation: clockwise

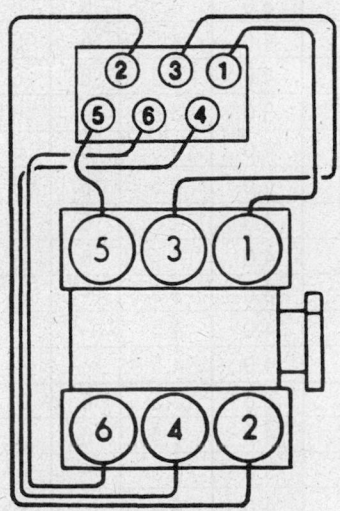

GM (CPC) 173 V6 (2.8L)
Engine firing order: 1–2–3–4–5–6

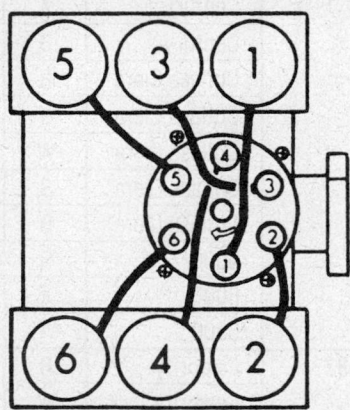

GM (Buick) 181 V6 (3.0L)
GM (Buick) 231 V6 (3.8L)
Engine firing order: 1–6–5–4–3–2
Distributor rotation: clockwise

FIRING ORDERS

NOTE: To avoid confusion, replace spark plug wires one at a time.

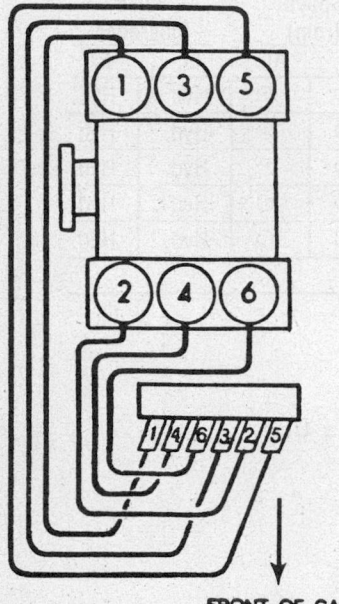

GM (Chevrolet) 192 V6 (3.1L)
Engine firing order: 1–2–3–4–5–6
Direct Ignition System (DIS)

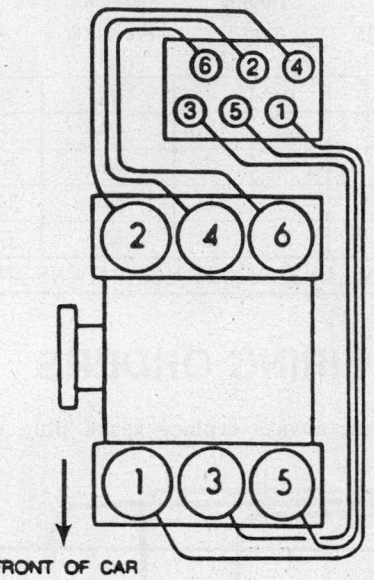

GM (Buick) 204 V6 (3.3L)
Engine firing order: 1–6–5–4–3–2
Direct Ignition System (DIS)

CAPACITIES

Year	Model	VIN	No. Engine Cylinder cu. in. (liter)	Engine Crankcase with filter	Engine Crankcase without filter	Transmission (pts.) 4	Transmission (pts.) 5	Transmission (pts.) Auto.	Drive Axle (pts.)	Fuel Tank (gals.)	Cool Sys. (qts.)
1986	Celebrity	R	151 (2.5)	3.0	3.5	6	—	④	—	15.7 ③	9.6
	Celebrity	X	173 (2.8)	4.0	4.5	6	—	④	—	15.7 ③	12.6
	Celebrity	W	173 (2.8)	4.0	4.5	6	—	④	—	15.7 ③	12.6
	Century	R	151 (2.5)	3.0	3.5	6	6	8 ①	—	16.6 ⑤	9.7
	Century	X	173 (2.8)	4.0	4.5	6	6	8 ①	—	16.6 ⑤	11.8
	Century	3	231 (3.8)	4.0	4.5	6	6	8 ①	—	16.6 ⑤	12.6
	Cutlass Ciera	R	151 (2.5)	3.0	3.5	6	6	④	—	15.7 ⑤	9.7
	Cutlass Ciera	X	173 (2.8)	4.0	4.5	6	6	④	—	15.7 ⑤	12.7
	Cutlass Ciera	W	173 (2.8)	4.0	4.5	6	6	④	—	15.7 ⑤	12.7
	Cutlass Ciera	3	231 (3.8)	4.0	4.5	6	6	④	—	15.7	12.7
	Cutlass Ciera	B	231 (3.8)	4.0	4.5	6	6	④	—	15.7	12.7
	6000	R	151 (2.5)	3.0	3.5	—	—	④	—	15.7	9.7
	6000	X	173 (2.8)	4.0	4.5	—	—	④	—	16.4	12.7
	6000	W	173 (2.8)	4.0	4.5	—	—	④	—	16.4	12.7
1987	Celebrity	R	151 (2.5)	3.0	3.5	6	—	④	—	15.7	9.6
	Celebrity	W	173 (2.8)	4.0	4.5	6	—	④	—	15.7	12.6
	Century	R	151 (2.5)	3.0	3.5	—	—	8 ①	—	15.5	9.7 ②
	Century	W	173 (2.8)	4.0	4.0	—	—	④	—	15.5	12.5
	Century	3	231 (3.8)	4.0	4.5	—	—	8 ①	—	15.5	12.6
	Cutlass Ciera	R	151 (2.5)	3.0	3.5	6	6	④	—	15.7	12.0

CAPACITIES

Year	Model	VIN	No. Engine Cylinder cu. in. (liter)	Engine Crankcase with filter	Engine Crankcase without filter	Transmission (pts.) 4	5	Auto.	Drive Axle (pts.)	Fuel Tank (gals.)	Cool Sys. (qts.)
1987	Cutlass Ciera	W	173 (2.8)	4.0	4.5	6	6	④	—	15.7	13.5
	Cutlass Ciera	3	231 (3.8)	4.0	4.5	6	6	④	—	15.7	12.7
	6000	R	151 (2.5)	3.0	3.5	—	4	④	—	15.7	9.7 ②
	6000	W	173 (2.8)	4.0	4.5	—	4	④	—	16.4	12.9
1988	Celebrity	R	151 (2.5)	3.0	3.5	—	4	④	—	15.7	9.7 ②
	Celebrity	W	173 (2.8)	4.0	4.0	—	4	④	—	15.7	13.5
	Century	R	151 (2.5)	3.0	3.5	—	—	④	—	15.7	9.7 ②
	Century	W	173 (2.8)	4.0	4.5	—	—	④	—	15.7	13.5
	Century	3	231 (3.8)	4.0	4.5	—	—	④	—	15.7	12.7
	Cutlass Ciera	R	151 (2.5)	3.0	3.5	6	6	④	—	15.7	12.0
	Cutlass Ciera	W	173 (2.8)	4.0	4.5	6	6	④	—	15.7	13.5
	Cutlass Ciera	3	231 (3.8)	4.0	4.5	6	6	④	—	15.7	12.7
	6000	R	151 (2.5)	4.0	4.5	—	—	④	—	15.7	9.7 ②
	6000	W	173 (2.8)	4.0	4.5	—	—	④	—	15.7	13.5
1989-90	Celebrity	R	151 (2.5)	4.0	4.5	—	—	④	—	15.7	9.7
	Celebrity	W	173 (2.8)	4.0	4.5	—	—	④	—	15.7	13.2
	Century	R	151 (2.5)	4.0	4.5	—	—	④	—	15.7	9.7
	Century	W	173 (2.8)	4.0	4.5	—	—	④	—	15.7	13.2
	Century	N	204 (3.3)	4.0	4.5	—	—	④	—	15.7	15.7
	Cutlass Ciera	R	151 (2.5)	4.0	4.5	—	—	④	—	15.7	9.7
	Cutlass Ciera	W	173 (2.8)	4.0	4.5	—	—	④	—	15.7	13.2
	Cutlass Ciera	N	204 (3.3)	4.0	4.5	—	—	④	—	15.7	12.7
	6000	R	151 (2.5)	4.0	4.5	—	—	④	—	15.7	9.7
	6000	W	173 (2.8)	4.0	4.5	—	—	④	—	15.7	13.2
	6000	T	192 (3.1)	4.0	4.5	—	—	④	—	15.7	12.6

① Overhaul—12 pts. ⑤ Wagon—15.7 gals.
② Heavy Duty—12 qts.
③ 2.8L Code X—16.4 gals.

④ 125C—8 pts.
　Overhaul—12 pts.
　440—T4—13 pts.
　Overhaul—20 pts.

CAMSHAFT SPECIFICATIONS

All measurements given in inches.

Year	VIN	No. Cylinder Displacement cu. in. (liter)	Journal Diameter 1	2	3	4	5	Lobe Lift In.	Ex.	Bearing Clearance	Camshaft End Play
1986	R	4-151 (2.5)	1.869	1.869	1.869	—	—	0.232	0.232	0.0007–0.0027	0.0015–0.0050
	X	6-173 (2.8)	1.869	1.869	1.869	1.869	—	0.263	0.273	0.0010–0.0040	—
	W	6-173 (2.8)	1.869	1.869	1.869	1.869	—	0.263	0.273	0.0010–0.0040	—
	3	6-231 (3.8)	1.786	1.786	1.786	1.786	1.786	0.397	0.397	①	—
	B	6-231 (3.8)	1.786	1.786	1.786	1.786	1.786	0.397	0.397	①	—

CAMSHAFT SPECIFICATIONS
All measurements given in inches.

Year	VIN	No. Cylinder Displacement cu. in. (liter)	Journal Diameter					Lobe Lift		Bearing Clearance	Camshaft End Play
			1	2	3	4	5	In.	Ex.		
1987	R	4-151 (2.5)	1.869	1.869	1.869	—	—	0.232	0.232	0.0007–0.0027	0.0015–0.0050
	W	6-173 (2.8)	1.869	1.869	1.869	1.869	—	0.263	0.273	0.0010–0.0040	—
	3	6-231 (3.8)	1.786	1.786	1.786	1.786	1.786	0.397	0.397	①	—
1988	R	4-151 (2.5)	1.869	1.869	1.869	—	—	0.232	0.232	0.0007–0.0027	0.0015–0.0050
	W	6-173 (2.8)	1.8678–1.8815	1.8678–1.8815	1.8678–1.8815	1.8678–1.8815	—	0.262	0.273	0.0010–0.0040	—
	3	6-231 (3.8)	1.785–1.786	1.785–1.786	1.785–1.786	1.785–1.786	1.785–1.786	0.245	0.245	0.0005–0.0035	—
1989-90	R	4-151 (2.5)	1.869	1.869	1.869	—	—	0.232	0.232	0.0007–0.0027	0.0015–0.0050
	W	6-173 (2.8)	1.8678–1.8815	1.8678–1.8815	1.8678–1.8815	1.8678–1.8815	—	0.262	0.273	0.0010–0.0040	—
	T	6-192 (3.1)	1.8678–1.8815	1.8678–1.8815	1.8678–1.8815	1.8678–1.8815	—	0.263	0.273	0.0010–0.0040	—
	N	6-204 (3.3)	1.7850–1.7860	1.7850–1.7860	1.7850–1.7860	1.7850–1.7860	—	0.250	0.255	0.0005–0.0035	—

NA—Not available
① No. 1—0.0005–0.0025
No. 2-5—0.0005–0.0035

CRANKSHAFT AND CONNECTING ROD SPECIFICATIONS
All measurements are given in inches.

Year	VIN	No. Cylinder Displacement cu. in. (liter)	Crankshaft				Connecting Rod		
			Main Brg. Journal Dia.	Main Brg. Oil Clearance	Shaft End-play	Thrust on No.	Journal Diameter	Oil Clearance	Side Clearance
1986	R	4-151 (2.5)	2.2995–2.3005	0.0005–0.0022	0.0035–0.0085	5	1.9995–2.0005	0.0005–0.0026	0.006–0.022
	X	6-173 (2.8)	2.4397–2.4946	0.0017–0.0030	0.0020–0.0067	3	1.9984–1.9994	0.0014–0.0036	0.006–0.017
	W	6-173 (2.8)	2.4397–2.4946	0.0017–0.0030	0.0020–0.0067	3	1.9984–1.9994	0.0014–0.0036	0.006–0.017
	3	6-231 (3.8)	2.4995	0.0003–0.0018	0.003–0.011	2	2.2487–2.2495	0.0005–0.0026	0.006–0.023
	B	6-231 (3.8)	2.4995	0.0003–0.0018	0.003–0.011	2	2.2487–2.2487	0.0005–0.0026	0.006–0.023
1987	R	4-151 (2.5)	2.2995–2.3005	0.0005–0.0022	0.0035–0.0085	5	1.9995–2.0005	0.0005–0.0026	0.006–0.022
	W	6-173 (2.8)	2.6473–2.6483	0.0016–0.0033	0.002–0.008	3	1.9983–1.9993	0.0013–0.0026	0.006–0.017
	3	6-231 (3.8)	2.4995	0.0003–0.0018	0.003–0.011	2	2.2487–2.2495	0.0005–0.0026	0.004–0.015
1988	R	4-151 (2.5)	2.3000	0.0005–0.0022	0.0035–0.0085	5	1.9995–2.0005	0.0005–0.0026	0.006–0.022

CRANKSHAFT AND CONNECTING ROD SPECIFICATIONS

All measurements are given in inches.

Year	VIN	No. Cylinder Displacement cu. in. (liter)	Crankshaft Main Brg. Journal Dia.	Crankshaft Main Brg. Oil Clearance	Crankshaft Shaft End-play	Thrust on No.	Connecting Rod Journal Diameter	Connecting Rod Oil Clearance	Connecting Rod Side Clearance
1988	W	6-173 (2.8)	2.6473–2.6483	0.0016–0.0033	0.002–0.008	3	1.9983–1.9993	0.0013–0.0026	0.006–0.017
	3	6-231 (3.8)	2.4988–2.4998	0.0003–0.0018	0.003–0.011	2	2.2487–2.2495	0.0005–0.0026	0.006–0.023
1989-90	R	4-151 (2.5)	2.3000	0.0005–0.0022	0.0035–0.0085	5	1.9995–2.0005	0.0005–0.0026	0.006–0.022
	W	6-173 (2.8)	2.6473–2.6483	0.0016–0.0033	0.002–0.008	3	1.9983–1.9993	0.0013–0.0026	0.006–0.017
	T	6-192 (3.1)	2.6473–2.6483	0.0012–0.0027	0.002–0.008	3	1.9983–1.9994	0.0013–0.0031	0.014–0.027
	N	6-204 (3.3)	2.4988–2.4998	0.0003–0.0018	0.003–0.011	3	2.2487–2.2499	0.0003–0.0026	0.003–0.015

VALVE SPECIFICATIONS

Year	VIN	No. Cylinder Displacement cu. in. (liter)	Seat Angle (deg.)	Face Angle (deg.)	Spring Test Pressure (lbs.)	Spring Installed Height (In.)	Stem-to-Guide Clearance (in.) Intake	Stem-to-Guide Clearance (in.) Exhaust	Stem Diameter (in.) Intake	Stem Diameter (in.) Exhaust
1986	R	4-151 (2.5)	46	45	176 @ 1.260	1.690	0.0010–0.0027	0.0010–0.0027	0.3420–0.3430	0.3420–0.3430
	X	6-173 (2.8)	46	45	155 @ 1.160	1.610	0.0010–0.0027	0.0010–0.0027	0.3410–0.3416	0.3410–0.3416
	W	6-173 (2.8)	46	45	155 @ 1.160	1.610	0.0010–0.0027	0.0010–0.0027	0.3410–0.3416	0.3410–0.3416
	3	6-231 (3.8)	45	45	220 @ 1.340	1.727	0.0015–0.0032	0.3405–0.3032	0.3405–0.3412	0.3405–0.3412
	B	6-231 (3.8)	45	45	220 @ 1.340	1.727	0.0015–0.0032	0.0015–0.0032	0.3405–0.3412	0.3405–0.3412
1987	R	4-151 (2.5)	46	45	176 @ 1.254	1.690	0.0010–0.0027	0.0010–0.0032	0.3410–0.3140	0.3410–0.313
	W	6-173 (2.8)	46	45	215 @ 1.291	1.727	0.0015–0.0027	0.0015–0.0027	0.3412–0.3416	0.3412–0.3416
	3	6-231 (3.8)	45	45	195 @ 1.340	1.727	0.0015–0.0032	0.0015–0.0032	0.3405–0.3412	0.3405–0.3412
1988	R	4-151 (2.5)	46	46	176 @ 1.254	1.440	—	—	0.3130–0.3140	0.3120–0.3130
	W	6-173 (2.8)	46	45	215 @ 1.291	1.727	0.0010–0.0027	0.0010–0.0027	0.3412–0.3416	0.3412–0.3416
	3	6-231 (3.8)	45	45	195 @ 1.340	1.727	0.0015–0.0035	0.0015–0.0032	0.3405–0.3412	0.3405–0.3412
1989-90	R	4-151 (2.5)	46	46	176 @ 1.254	1.440	—	—	0.3130–0.3140	0.3120–0.3130
	W	6-173 (2.8)	46	45	215 @ 1.291	1.727	0.0010–0.0027	0.0010–0.0027	0.3412–0.3416	0.3412–0.3416
	T	6-192 (3.1)	46	45	215 @ 1.291	1.575	0.0010–0.0027	0.0010–0.0027	—	—

VALVE SPECIFICATIONS

Year	VIN	No. Cylinder Displacement cu. in. (liter)	Seat Angle (deg.)	Face Angle (deg.)	Spring Test Pressure (lbs.)	Spring Installed Height (in.)	Stem-to-Guide Clearance (in.)		Stem Diameter (in.)	
							Intake	Exhaust	Intake	Exhaust
1989-90	N	6-204 (3.3)	46	45	215 @ 1.291	1.701	0.0010–0.0027	0.0010–0.0027	—	—

PISTON AND RING SPECIFICATIONS

All measurements are given in inches.

Year	VIN	No. Cylinder Displacement cu. in. (liter)	Piston Clearance	Ring Gap			Ring Side Clearance		
				Top Compression	Bottom Compression	Oil Control	Top Compression	Bottom Compression	Oil Control
1986	R	4-151 (2.5)	0.0014–0.0022 ①	0.010–0.020	0.010–0.020	0.020–0.060	0.002–0.003	0.001–0.003	0.015–0.055
	X	6-173 (2.8)	0.0017–0.0027	0.010–0.020	0.010–0.020	0.020–0.055	0.0012–0.0028	0.0016–0.0037	0.008
	W	6-173 (2.8)	0.0017–0.0027	0.010–0.020	0.010–0.020	0.020–0.055	0.0012–0.0028	0.0016–0.0037	0.008
	3	6-231 (3.8)	0.001–0.002	0.013–0.023	0.013–0.023	0.015–0.035	0.003–0.005	0.003–0.005	0.0035
	B	6-231 (3.8)	0.001–0.002	0.013–0.023	0.013–0.023	0.015–0.035	0.003–0.005	0.003–0.005	0.0035
1987	R	4-151 (2.5)	0.0014–0.0022 ①	0.010–0.020	0.010–0.020	0.020–0.060	0.002–0.003	0.001–0.003	0.015–0.055
	W	6-173 (2.8)	0.0020–0.0028	0.010–0.020	0.010–0.020	0.020–0.055	0.001–0.003	0.001–0.003	0.005–0.008
	3	6-231 (3.8)	0.001–0.002	0.013–0.023	0.013–0.023	0.015–0.035	0.003–0.005	0.003–0.005	0.0035
1988	R	4-151 (2.5)	0.0014–0.0022 ①	0.010–0.020	0.010–0.020	0.020–0.060	0.002–0.003	0.001–0.003	0.015–0.055
	W	6-173 (2.8)	0.0020–0.0028	0.010–0.020	0.010–0.020	0.020–0.055	0.001–0.003	0.001–0.003	0.005–0.008
	3	6-231 (3.8)	0.001–0.002	0.013–0.023	0.013–0.023	0.015–0.035	0.003–0.005	0.003–0.005	0.0035
1989-90	R	4-151 (2.5)	0.0014–0.0022 ①	0.010–0.020	0.010–0.020	0.020–0.060	0.002–0.003	0.001–0.003	0.015–0.055
	W	6-173 (2.8)	0.0020–0.0028	0.010–0.020	0.010–0.020	0.020–0.055	0.001–0.003	0.001–0.003	0.005–0.008
	T	6-192 (3.1)	0.0022–0.0028	0.010–0.020	0.010–0.020	0.010–0.050	0.002–0.004	0.002–0.004	0.008 ②
	N	6-204 (3.3)	0.0004–0.0022	0.010–0.025	0.010–0.025	0.010–0.040	0.0013–0.0031	0.0013–0.0031	0.0011–0.0081

① Measured 1/8 in. down from piston top
② Maximum clearance

TORQUE SPECIFICATIONS
All readings in ft. lbs.

Year	VIN	No. Cylinder Displacement cu. in. (liter)	Cylinder Head Bolts	Main Bearing Bolts	Rod Bearing Bolts	Crankshaft Pulley Bolts	Flywheel Bolts	Manifold Intake	Manifold Exhaust	Spark Plugs
1986	R	4-151 (2.5)	92	70	32	200	44	29	①	15
	X	6-173 (2.8)	65–90	68	37	75	50	23	25	7–15
	W	6-173 (2.8)	65–90	68	37	75	50	23	25	7–15
	3	6-231 (3.8)	①	100	45	200	60	32	37	20
	B	6-231 (3.8)	①	100	45	200	60	32	37	20
1987	R	4-151 (2.5)	①	70	32	162	②	25	①	15
	W	6-173 (2.8)	①	68	37	75	③	25	15–23	10–25
	3	6-231 (3.8)	①	100	45	219	60	32	37	20
1988	R	4-151 (2.5)	①	70	32	162	②	25	①	15
	W	6-173 (2.8)	①	68	37	75	③	25	15–23	10–25
	3	6-231 (3.8)	①	100	45	219	60	32	37	20
1989–90	R	4-151 (2.5)	①	70	32	162	②	25	①	15
	W	6-173 (2.8)	①	68	37	75	③	25	15–23	10–25
	T	6-192 (3.1)	33	63–83	34–40	66–85	③	25	15–23	10–25
	N	6-204 (3.3)	35	90	20	219	61 ④	88	30	20

NA Not Available
① Refer to sequence and torque procedyre in text
② Manual transmission—69 ft. lbs.
　Automatic transmission—55 ft. lbs.
③ Manual transmission—52 ft. lbs.
　Automatic transmission—46 ft. lbs.
④ Apply P/N 1052624
⑤ Rotate wrench an additional quarter turn

WHEEL ALIGNMENT

Year	Model	Caster Range (deg.)	Caster Preferred Setting (deg.)	Camber Range (deg.)	Camber Preferred Setting (deg.)	Toe-in (in.)	Steering Axis Inclination (deg.)
1986	Celebrity, Century, Cutlass Ciera, 6000	1P–3P	2P	1/2N–1/2P	0	3/32N–3/32P	NA
1987	Celebrity, Century, Cutlass Ciera, 6000	1P–3P	2P	1/2N–1/2P	0	3/32N–3/32P	NA
1988	Celebrity, Century, Cutlass Ciera, 6000	1P–3P	2P	1/2N–1/2P	0	3/32N–3/32P	NA
1989–90	Celebrity, Century, Cutlass Ciera, 6000	1P–3P	2P	1/2N–1/2P	0	3/32N–3/32P	NA

NA Not available
N Negative
P Positive

ELECTRICAL

NOTE: Disconnecting the negative battery cable on some vehicles may interfere with the functions of the on board computer systems and may require the computer to undergo a relearning process, once the negative battery cable is reconnected.

For testing and overhaul procedures on starters, alternators and voltage regulators, refer to the Unit Repair section.

Charging System

ALTERNATOR

Removal and Installation

1. Disconnect the negative battery cable.
2. Remove the 2 terminal plug and battery lead on the back of the alternator.
3. Loosen the alternator mounting bolts and pivot bolt.
4. Remove the alternator belt and and through bolt.
5. Remove the alternator from the engine.
6. Installation is the reverse of the removal procedure. Adjust the alternator belt to specification.

VOLTAGE REGULATOR

Removal and Installation

The voltage regulator is a solid state unit mounted inside the alternator. No adjustment can be performed on the voltage regulator. Should the regulator require service, the alternator must be disassembled.

BELT TENSION

Adjustment

V-BELT

1. Place the tension gauge midway between the accessory pulleys. Install the gauge on the longest belt span possible. If the belt is notched on the inner surface, place the middle finger of the tensioner gauge into 1 of the notches.
2. To adjust, loosen the accessory adjusting and pivot bolts. Move the accessory inward or outward to obtain the correct tension listed in the specification chart, then tighten the adjusting bolt and pivot bolt.

SERPENTINE BELT

A single serpentine belt is used to drive all engine accessories. The belt tension is maintained by a spring loaded tensioner. The belt tensioner has the ability to control the belt tension over a broad range of belt lengths. However, there are limits to which the tensioner can compensate for varying lengths. If the belt tension is below the minimum specifications, replace the belt tensioner.

Check the serpentine belt tension with tool J-23600B or equivalent in the following manner:

1. Start the engine and run until operating temperature is reached.
2. Shut the engine **OFF** and place the tension gauge midway between the pulleys. Install the gauge on the longest belt span possible. If the belt is notched on the inner surface, place the middle finger of the tensioner gauge into 1 of the notches. Correct belt tension readings should be approximately 40 lbs. (4 cylinder engine) and 70 lbs. (6 cylinder engine).

Starting System

STARTER

Removal and Installation

1. Disconnect the negative battery cable at the battery.
2. If necessary, remove the engine side strut bolt and uper radiator panel bracket.
3. On 3.3L and 3.8L engines, discharge the air conditioning system.
4. Raise and support the vehicle safely.
5. Remove the cooling fan lower retaining bolts and disconnect the electrical connection at the fan, as required.

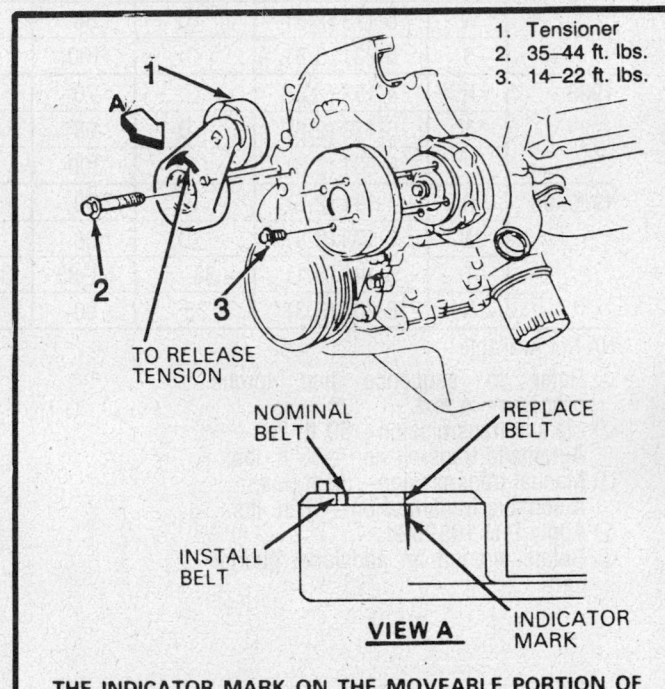

1. Tensioner
2. 35–44 ft. lbs.
3. 14–22 ft. lbs.

TO RELEASE TENSION

NOMINAL BELT — REPLACE BELT
INSTALL BELT — INDICATOR MARK
VIEW A

THE INDICATOR MARK ON THE MOVEABLE PORTION OF THE TENSIONER MUST BE WITHIN THE LIMITS OF THE SLOTTED AREA ON THE STATIONARY PORTION OF THE TENSIONER. ANY READING OUTSIDE THESE LIMITS INDICATES EITHER A DEFECTIVE BELT OR TENSIONER.

Belt tensioner, 6–173 engine shown

	5/16" WIDE	3/8" & 13/32" WIDE	7/16" WIDE
NEW BELT	350 N Max. 80 Lbs. Max.	620 N Max. 140 Lbs. Max.	750 N Max. 165 Lbs. Max.
USED BELT	200 N Min. 50 Lbs. Min.	300 N Min. 70 Lbs. Min.	400 N Min. 90 Lbs. Min.

Typical belt tensions

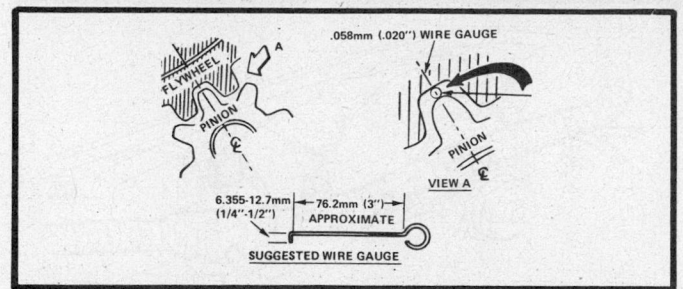

.058mm (.020") WIRE GAUGE

FLYWHEEL
PINION

6.355-12.7mm
(1/4"-1/2")

PINION

VIEW A

76.2mm (3")
APPROXIMATE

SUGGESTED WIRE GAUGE

If excessive starter noise is encountered during cranking, check the starter pinion-to-flywheel clearance as shown.

6. Lower the vehicle.

7. Remove the cooling fan upper.

8. Remove the spark plug wires and oil indicator tube, as required.

9. Raise and support the vehicle safely.

10. Remove the exhaust manifold flange bolts, manifold bolts and manifold, as required.

11. Remove the air conditioning manifold retaining bolt from the air conditioning compressor and remove the air conditioning line retaining bolt, as required.

12. Remove the electrical wiring from the starter motor.

13. Remove the flywheel inspection cover.

14. Remove the starter mounting bolts and starter motor. Remove the shims, if used.

15. Installation is the reverse of the removal procedure.

Ignition System

DISTRIBUTOR

Removal and Installation

2.5L ENGINE

TIMING NOT DISTURBED

1. Disconnect the negative battery cable. Raise and support the vehicle safely.

2. Remove the 2 rear cradle attaching bolts. Lower the cradle enough to allow access to the distributor.

3. Remove the brake line support to floor pan attaching screws.

4. Remove the coil wire from the distributor and remove the distributor cap.

5. Scribe marks indicating the position of the rotor to the distributor housing and housing to block.

6. Loosen the distributor clamp screw and position the clamp aside. Remove the distributor from the engine. The drive gear on the distributor shaft is helical, and the shaft will rotate slightly as the distributor is removed. Note and mark the position of the rotor at this second position.

NOTE: Do not crank the engine with the distributor removed.

To install:

7. Rotate the distributor shaft until the rotor aligns with the second mark you made (when the shaft stopped moving). Lubricate the drive gear with clean engine oil and install the distributor into position. As the distributor is installed, the rotor should move to the mark you made first, indicating rotor position before the distributor was removed. This will ensure proper timing. If the marks do not align properly, remove the distributor and try again.

8. Complete installation by reversing the removal procedure.

TIMING DISTURBED

If the engine was cranked while the distributor was removed, proceed as followed:

1. Remove the No. 1 spark plug.

2. Place your thumb over the spark plug hole. Crank the engine slowly until compression is felt.

3. Align the timing mark on the crankshaft pulley with the **0** mark on the timing scale attached to the front of the engine.

4. Turn the distributor shaft until the rotor points between the No. 1 and No. 3 spark plug towers on the cap. Install the distributor into the engine.

5. Install the distributor cap, spark plug wires, coil wire and ignition feed wire.

6. Check and adjust engine timing.

EXCEPT 2.5L ENGINE

TIMING NOT DISTURBED

1. Disconnect the negative battery cable.

2. Disconnect the battery feed wire, tachometer lead and coil connector from the distributor cap. Remove the distributor cap.

3. Remove the distributor clamp screw and hold-down clamp.

4. Scribe marks indicating the position of the rotor to the distributor housing and housing to block.

5. Remove the distributor from the engine. The drive gear on the distributor shaft is helical, and the shaft will rotate slightly as the distributor is removed. Note and mark the position of the rotor at this second position.

NOTE: Do not crank the engine with the distributor removed.

To install:

6. Rotate the distributor shaft until the rotor aligns with the second mark you made (when the shaft stopped moving). Lubricate the drive gear with clean engine oil and install the distributor into position. As the distributor is installed, the rotor should move to the mark you made first, indicating rotor position before the distributor was removed. This will ensure proper timing. If the marks do not align properly, remove the distributor and try again.

7. Complete installation by reversing the removal procedure.

TIMING DISTURBED

If the engine was cranked while the distributor was removed, proceed as followed:

1. Remove the No. 1 spark plug.

2. Place your thumb over the spark plug hole. Crank the engine slowly until compression is felt.

3. Align the timing mark on the crankshaft pulley with the **0** mark on the timing scale attached to the front of the engine.

4. Turn the distributor shaft until the rotor points between the No. 1 and No. 6 spark plug towers on the cap. Install the distributor into the engine.

5. Install the distributor cap and spark plug wires.

6. Check and adjust engine timing.

IGNITION TIMING

Adjustment

NOTE: Always refer to the underhood Vehicle Emission Control Information Label located in the engine compartment before adjusting timing. If the label differs from the following procedures, follow the information on the underhood label.

Some engines are equipped with a magnetic timing probe hole which is used solely with special electronic timing equipments.

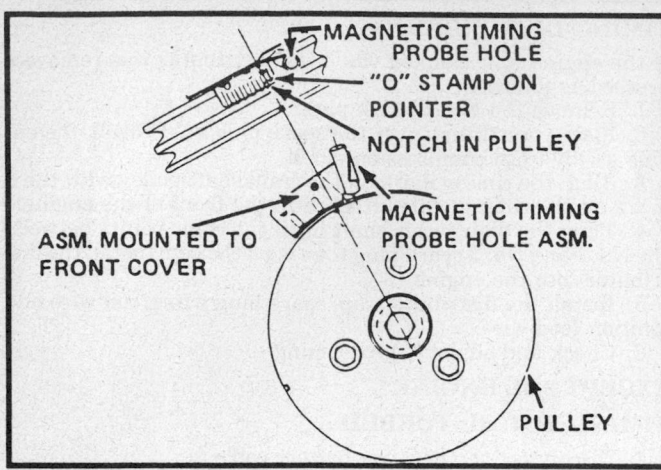

Magnetic timing probe hole—typical

CELEBRITY AND 6000

1986

1. Shift the transaxle into **P** for automatic transaxle, or **N** for manual transaxle. Apply the parking brake and block the drive wheels.

2. Connect a timing light to the No. 1 spark plug wire. Do not pierce the spark plug wire to connect the timing light.

3. Start the engine and run until operating temperature is reached.

NOTE: On vehicles equipped with Electronic Spark Timing (EST), it will be necessary to disconnect the EST connector at the distributor. This causes the engine to operate in the bypass timing mode.

4. Aim the timing light at the degree scale. If the reading differs from specification, adjustment is necessary.

5. Loosen the distributor holddown clamp and rotate the distributor until the desired ignition timing is achieved. Then, tighten the holddown clamp and recheck the timing.

6. Turn the engine **OFF** and remove the timing light.

CUTLASS CIERA

1986 With 2.5L Engine

The timing procedure used is referred too as an averaging method. The averaging method involves the use of both the No. 1 and No. 4 spark plug wires to trigger the timing light.

1. Shift the transaxle into **P** for automatic transaxle, or **N** for manual transaxle. Apply the parking brake and block the drive wheels.

2. Connect a timing light to the No. 1 spark plug wire. Do not pierce the spark plug wire to connect the timing light.

3. Start the engine and run until operating temperature is reached.

4. With the air cleaner installed, all accessories **OFF** and cooling fan not running, verify that the check engine light is not **ON**.

5. Locate the Assembly Line Connector Link (ALCL) on the lower edge of the instrument panel, right side of the steering column. Ground the diagnostic test terminal **A** to **B**. The check engine light will come **ON**.

6. Record the position of the timing mark.

7. Repeat Step 5 but use No 4 spark plug lead. Take the total of the 2 recorded timing marks and divide by 2 to come up with the average timing.

Example:

No. 1 cylinder 4° + No. 4 cylinder 8° = 12°

12° ÷ 2 = 6° Average Timing

8. If the timing is not within specification, subtracting the av-

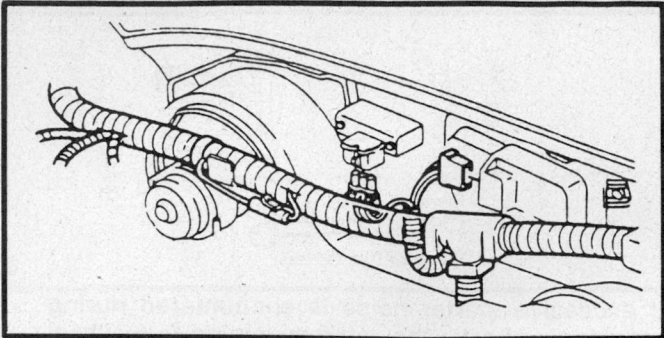

Set timing connector location

erage timing from the timing specifications will determine the amount of timing change on No. 1 cylinder.

Example:

Spec. Time of 8° − Avg. Time 10° = −2° of timing

9. Remove the ground from the ALCL connector. Disconnect the ECM harness from the positive battery pigtail for 10 seconds with the key in the **OFF** position.

2.8L Engine

1. Shift the transaxle into **P** for automatic transaxle, or **N** for manual transaxle. Apply the parking brake and block the drive wheels.

2. Connect a timing light to the No. 1 spark plug wire. Do not pierce the spark plug wire to connect the timing light.

3. Start the engine and run until operating temperature is reached. Verify the check engine light is not **ON**.

4. Locate the set timing or EST bypass line connector in the engine compartment near the blower motor housing along the cowl.

5. Disconnect the set timing connector.

6. Aim the timing light at the degree scale. If the reading differs from specification, adjustment is necessary.

7. Loosen the distributor holddown clamp and rotate the distributor until the desired ignition timing is achieved. Then, tighten the holddown clamp and recheck the timing.

8. Reconnect the set timing connector. Turn the ignition **OFF** and remove the PMP/ECM fuse from the fuse block for 10 seconds to cancel any stored codes.

9. Remove the timing light.

3.0L and 3.8L Engines

1. Shift the transaxle into **P** for automatic transaxle, or **N** for manual transaxle. Apply the parking brake and block the drive wheels.

2. Connect a timing light to the No. 1 spark plug wire. Do not pierce the spark plug wire to connect the timing light.

3. Start the engine and run until operating temperature is reached.

4. With the engine at operating temperature, verify that the check engine light is not **ON**.

5. Locate the Assembly Line Connector Link (ALCL) on the lower edge of the instrument panel, right side of the steering column. Ground the diagnostic test terminal **A** to **B**. The check engine light will come **ON**.

6. Aim the timing light at the degree scale. If the reading differs from specification, adjustment is necessary.

7. Loosen the distributor holddown clamp and rotate the distributor until the desired ignition timing is achieved. Then, tighten the holddown clamp and recheck the timing.

8. Remove the ground from the ALCL connector. Turn the ignition **OFF** and remove the timing light.

CENTURY

1986 Except 2.5L Engine

1. Shift the transaxle into **P** for automatic transaxle, or **N** for

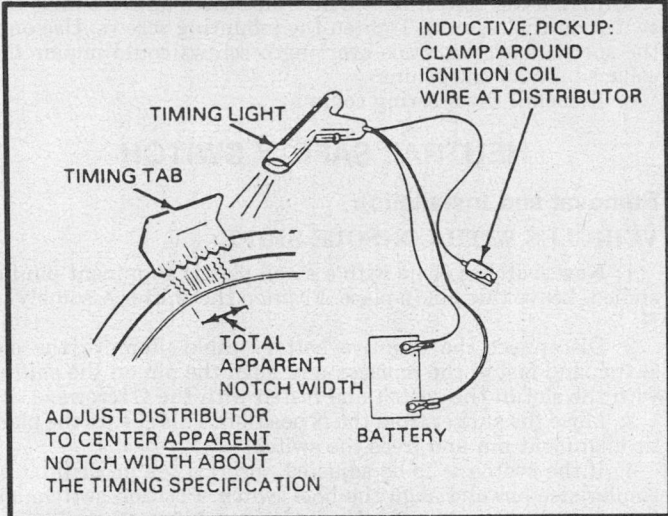

TIMING LIGHT

TIMING TAB

INDUCTIVE PICKUP: CLAMP AROUND IGNITION COIL WIRE AT DISTRIBUTOR

TOTAL APPARENT NOTCH WIDTH

BATTERY

ADJUST DISTRIBUTOR TO CENTER <u>APPARENT</u> NOTCH WIDTH ABOUT THE TIMING SPECIFICATION

Timing tab—2.5L engine

manual transaxle. Apply the parking brake and block the drive wheels.

2. Connect a timing light to the No. 1 spark plug wire. Do not pierce the spark plug wire to connect the timing light.

3. Start the engine and run until operating temperature is reached.

4. Aim the timing light at the degree scale. If the reading differs from specification, adjustment is necessary.

5. Loosen the distributor holddown clamp and rotate the distributor until the desired ignition timing is achieved. Then, tighten the holddown clamp and recheck the timing.

6. Turn the ignition **OFF** and remove the timing light.

2.5L Engine

The timing procedure used is referred too as an averaging method. The averaging method involves the use of a double notched crankshaft pulley. When timing the engine, the coil wire instead of the No. 1 plug wire is used. The notch for the No. 1 cylinder is scribed acrosss all 3 edges of the double sheave pulley. The other notch 180 degrees away from the No. 1 cylinder notch.

To correctly time the engine, use the following procedure:

1. Shift the transaxle into **P** for automatic transaxle, or **N** for manual transaxle. Apply the parking brake and block the drive wheels.

2. Clamp a timing light inductive pick-up around the high tension coil wire. Loosen the distributor clamp nut slightly.

3. On vehicles equipped with Electronic Spark Timing (EST), disconnect the 4 terminal EST connector. This cause the engine to operate in the bypass mode.

4. Start the engine and run until operating temperature is reached.

5. Aim the timing light at the timing tab.

NOTE: A slight juggling of the pulley notch may appear due to the fact that each cylinder firing is displayed.

6. Rotate the distributor in the direction of advance or retard as necessary to center the total apparent notch width about the correct timing specification. This insures that the average cylinder timing is as close to the specification as possible.

7. After adjustment is completed, shut the engine **OFF**. Tighten the distributor clamp nut, being carefull not to disturbed the distributor position. Recheck the timing.

8. Reconnect the distributor 4 terminal EST connector.

9. Shut the engine **OFF**. Remove the ECM No. 1 fuse for 10 seconds to clear any trouble codes.

1987–90 ALL VEHICLES

All 1987–90 vehicles are equipped with a Distributorless Ignition System; also referred to as Direct Ignition System (DIS). The system consists of a coil pack, ignition module, crankshaft reluctor ring, magnetic sensor and an Electronic Control Module (ECM). Timing advance and retard are accomplished through the ECM with Electronic Spark Timing (EST) and Electronic Spark Control (ESC). No adjustment is possible.

Electrical Controls

STEERING WHEEL

Removal and Installation

NOTE: When installing the steering wheel, always make sure that the turn signal lever is in the neutral position.

1. Disconnect the negative battery cable. Remove the trim retaining screws from behind the wheel. On steering wheels with a center cap, pull off the cap.

2. Lift the trim off and pull the horn wires from the turn signal cancelling cam.

3. Remove the retainer and the steering wheel nut.

4. Mark the wheel-to-shaft relationship and then remove the wheel with a puller.

5. Install the wheel on the shaft, aligning the previously made marks. Tighten the nut to 30 ft. lbs.

6. Insert the horn wires into the cancelling cam.

7. Install the center trim and reconnect the battery cable.

HORN SWITCH

Removal and Installation

STANDARD STEERING WHEEL

1. Disconnect the negative battery cable.

2. Remove the screws attaching the horn pad assembly from the underside of the steering wheel. Lift the horn pad from the steering wheel.

3. Disconnect the horn contact terminal from the pad. If the contact terminal comes out of or is removed from the turn signal cancelling cam tower, it can be reinstalled by pushing it into the tower and rotating the steering wheel clockwise to lock it into position.

4. Installation is the reverse of the removal procedure. Connect the negative battery cable.

SPORT STEERING WHEEL

1. Disconnect the negative battery cable.

2. Remove the center ornament from the steering wheel.

3. Remove the steering wheel nut and retainer.

4. Remove the horn switch and insulator assembly.

5. Remove the switch retainer screw and separate the switch from the insulator.

6. Installation is the reverse of the removal procedure. Connect the negative battery cable.

IGNITION LOCK

Removal and Installation

1. Disconnect the negative battery cable. Place the lock in the **RUN** position. Remove the steering wheel.

2. Remove the lock plate, turn signal switch and buzzer switch.

3. Remove the screw and lock cylinder.

NOTE: If the screw is dropped on removal, it could fall into the column, requiring complete disassembly to retrieve the screw.

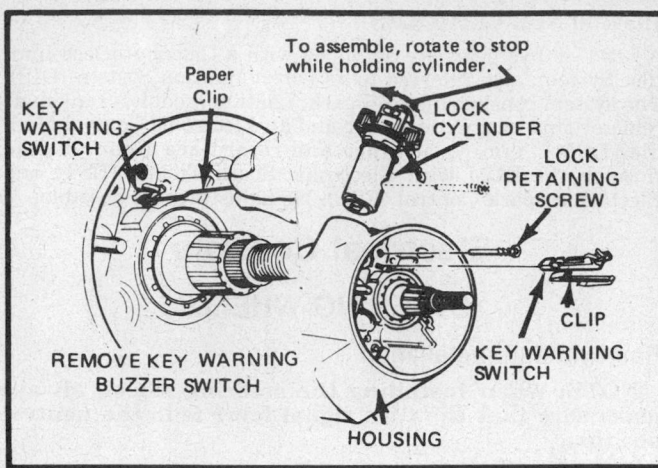

Mounting of the ignition lock cylinder assembly removal of the key warning switch is shown in the inset

4. Rotate the cylinder clockwise to align cylinder key with the keyway in the housing.
5. Push the lock all the way in.
6. Install the screw. Tighten the screw to 14 inch lbs. for adjustable columns and 25 inch lbs. for standard columns.

IGNITION SWITCH

Removal and Installation

The switch is located inside the channel section of the brake pedal support and is completely inaccessible without first lowering the steering column. The switch is actuated by a rod and rack assembly. A gear on the end of the lock cylinder engages the toothed upper end of the rod.

1. Disconnect the negative battery cable. Lower the steering column; be sure to properly support it.
2. Put the ignition switch in the **OFF–UNLOCKED** position. With the cylinder removed, the rod is in the **LOCK** position when it is in the next to the uppermost detent. **OFF–UNLOCKED** position is 2 detents from the top.
3. Remove the 2 switch screws and remove the switch assembly.
4. Before installing, place the new switch in **OFF–UNLOCKED** position and make sure the lock cylinder and actuating rod are in **OFF–UNLOCKED** (third detent from the top) position.

5. Install the activating rod into the switch and assemble the switch on the column. Tighten the mounting screws. Use only the specified screws since overlength screws could impair the collapsibility of the column.
6. Reinstall the steering column.

NEUTRAL SAFETY SWITCH

Removal and Installation
VEHICLES WITH CONSOLE SHIFT

1. New switches come with a small plastic alignment pin installed. Leave this pin in place. Position the shifter assembly in **N**.
2. Disconnect the negative battery cable. Remove the old switch and install the replacement, align the pin on the shifter with the slot in the switch and fasten with the 2 screws.
3. Move the shifter from the **N** position. This shears the plastic alignment pin and frees the switch.
4. If the switch is to be adjusted, insert a $\frac{3}{32}$ in. drill bit or similar size pin and align the hole switch. Position switch, adjust as necessary. Remove the pin before shifting from **N**.

VEHICLES WITH COLUMN SHIFT

1. Disconnect the negative battery cable. Remove wire connectors from the combination back-up and neutral safety switch.
2. Remove 2 screws attaching the switch to the steering column.
3. Installation is the reverse of the removal procedure. To adjust a new switch:
   a. Position the shift lever in **N**.
   b. Loosen the attaching screws. Install a 0.090 in. gauge pin into the outer hole in the switch cover.
   c. Rotate the switch until the pin goes into the alignment hole in the inner plastic slide.
   d. Tighten the switch to column attaching screws and remove the gauge pin. Torque the screws to 20 inch lbs. maximum.
   e. Make sure that the engine starts only in the **P** and **N** positions.

Adjustment

1. After the switch is installed, move the housing towards the **L** gear position.
2. Shift the gear selector into the **P** position.
3. The main housing and the housing back should ratchet. This will provide proper switch adjustment.
4. Repeat if necessary.

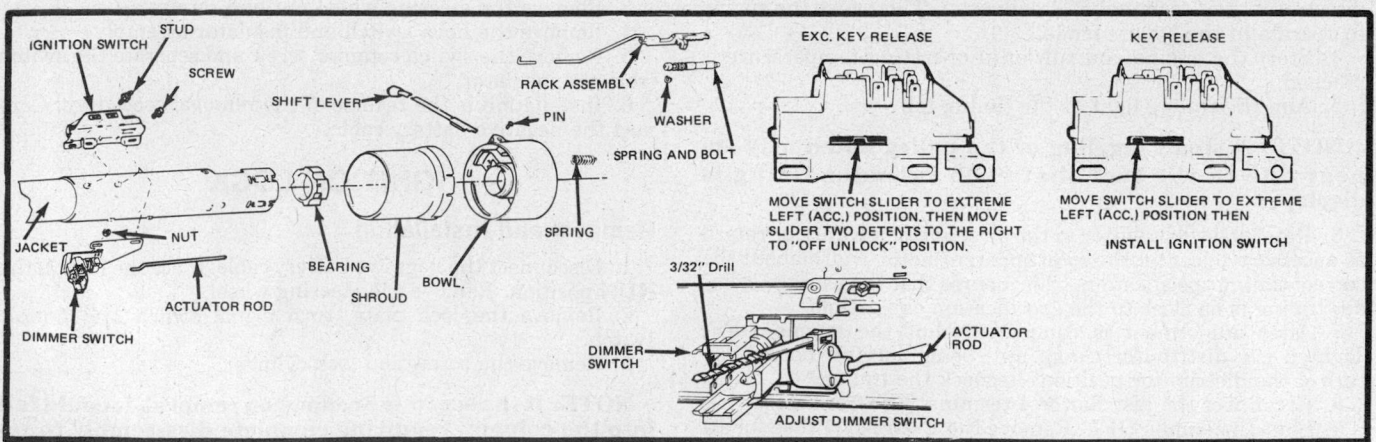

Installation of the ignition switch

CLUTCH START SWITCH

Adjustment

1. Lift the clutch pedal to its uppermost position. Check the operation of the pawl and the quadrant. Make sure that the pawl disengages from the quadrant when the pedal is pulled to this position.
2. Check the quadrant for free rotation in both directions.
3. Depress the clutch pedal slowly several times to set the pawl into mesh with the quadrant teeth.

Removal and Installation

1. Disconnect the negative battery cable. Support the clutch pedal against the bumper stop in order to release the pawl from the quadrant. Disconnect the clutch cable from the release lever at the transaxle assembly.

CAUTION

Be careful to prevent the cable from snapping towards the rear of the vehicle possibly causing bodily injury. The quadrant in the adjusting mechanism can also be damaged by allowing the cable to snap rearward.

2. From inside the vehicle, disconnect the clutch cable from the quadrant. Lift the locking pawl away from the quadrant. Slide the cable away from the pedal along the right side of the quadrant.
3. Remove the neutral start switch from the pedal. Remove the pedal pivot nut, bolt and clutch pedal from the mounting bracket.
4. Note the position of the adjusting mechanism, the pawl and quadrant springs. Remove the E-ring.
5. Inspect the components for tooth damage and replace any components found to be defective.
6. Installation is the reverse of the removal procedure. Check the clutch operation and adjust by lifting the clutch pedal up to allow the mechanism to adjust the cable length. Depress the pedal slowly several times to set the pawl into mesh with the quadrant teeth.

STOPLIGHT SWITCH

Adjustment

1. The switch is mounted on the brake pedal bracket.
2. To adjust, depress the pedal and push the switch through the circular retaining clip until it contacts the brake pedal, then pull the pedal up against the internal pedal stop. This places the switch in the correct position within the clip.

Removal and Installation

1. Disconnect the negative battery cable. Disconnect the electrical connector to the switch.
2. Remove the switch from the brake pedal bracket.
3. Install the new switch into the bracket.
4. Connect the electrical connector.
5. Adjust the switch.

HEADLAMP SWITCH

Removal and Installation
CELEBRITY

1. Disconnect the negative battery cable.
2. Remove the headlamp switch knob.
3. Remove the instrument panel trim pad.
4. Unbolt the switch mounting plate from the instrument panel carrier.
5. Disconnect the wiring from the switch.
6. Remove the switch.
7. Installation is the reverse of the removal procedure.

6000

1. Disconnect the negative battery cable.
2. Remove the steering column trim cover and headlight rod and knob by reaching behind the instrument panel and depressing the lock tab.
3. Remove the left instrument panel trim plate.
4. Unbolt and remove the switch and bracket assembly from the instrument panel.
5. Loosen the bezel and remove the switch from the bracket.
6. Installation is the reverse of the removal procedure.

CUTLASS CIERA

1. Disconnect the negative battery cable.
2. Remove the left side instrument panel trim pad.
3. Unbolt the switch from the instrument panel.
4. Pull the switch rearward and remove it.
5. Installation is the reverse of the removal procedure.

CENTURY

1. Disconnect the negative battery cable.
2. Remove the instrument panel trim plate.
3. Remove the left side instrument panel switch trim panel by removing the three screws and gently rocking the panel out.
4. Remove the 3 screws and pull the switch straight out.
5. Installation is the reverse of the removal procedure.

DIMMER SWITCH

Removal and Installation

1. Disconnect the negative battery cable.
2. Remove the steering wheel. Remove the trim cover.
3. Remove the turn signal switch assembly.
4. Remove the ignition switch stud and screw. Remove the ignition switch.
5. Remove the dimmer switch actuator rod by sliding it from the switch assembly.
6. Remove the dimmer switch bolts and remove the dimmer switch.
7. Installation is the reverse of the removal procedure.
8. Adjust the dimmer switch by depressing the switch slightly and inserting a $3/32$ in. drill bit into the adjusting hole. Push the switch up to remove any play and tighten the dimmer switch adjusting screw.

TURN SIGNAL SWITCH

Removal and Installation

1. Disconnect the negative battery cable. Remove the steering wheel and trim cover.
2. Loosen the cover screws. Pry the cover upward and remove it from the shaft.
3. Position the U-shaped lock plate compressing tool on the end of the steering shaft and compress the lockplate by turning the shaft nut clockwise. Pry the wire snapring out of the shaft groove.
4. Remove the tool and lift the lock plate off the shaft.
5. Slip the cancelling cam, upper bearing preload spring, and thrust washer off the shaft.
6. Remove the turn signal lever. Push the flasher knob in and unscrew it. Remove the button retaining screw and remove the button, spring and knob.
7. Pull the switch connector out the mast jacket and tape the upper part to facilitate switch removal. Attach a long piece of wire to the turn signal switch connector. When installing the turn signal switch, feed this wire through the column first, and then use this wire to pull the switch connector into position. On vehicle equipped with tilt wheel, place the turn signal and shifter housing in **LOW** position and remove the harness cover.
8. Remove the 3 switch mounting screws. Remove the switch

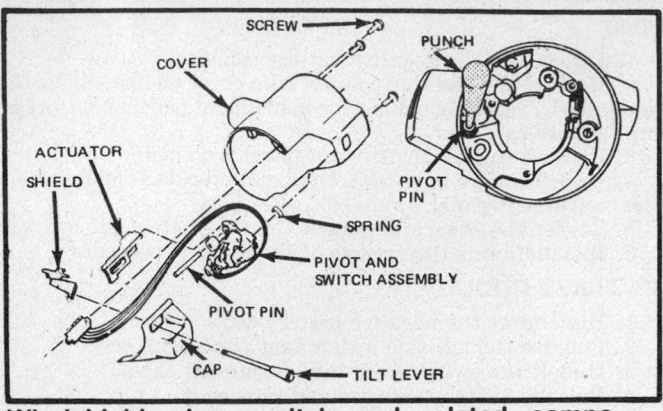

Windshield wiper switch and related components—models with tilt wheel

by pulling it straight up while guiding the wiring harness cover through the column.

9. Install the replacement switch by working the connector and cover down through the housing and under the bracket. On vehicle equipped with tilt wheel, the connector is worked down through the housing, under the bracket, and then the cover is installed on the harness.

10. Install the switch mounting screws and the connector on the mast jacket bracket. Install the column-to-dash trim plate.

11. Install the flasher knob and the turn signal lever.

12. With the turn signal lever in neutral and the flasher knob out, slide the thrust washer, upper bearing preload spring, and cancelling cam onto the shaft.

13. Position the lock plate on the shaft and press it down until a new snapring can be inserted in the shaft groove. Always use a new snapring when assembling.

14. Install the cover and the steering wheel.

WINDSHIELD WIPER SWITCH

Removal and Installation

1. Disconnect the negative battery cable.

2. Remove the steering wheel and turn signal switch. It may be necessary to first remove the column mounting nuts and remove the 4 bracket-to-mast jacket screws, then separate the bracket from the mast jacket to allow the connector clip on the ignition switch to be pulled out of the column assembly.

3. Tag and disconnect the washer/wiper switch lower connector.

4. Remove the screws attaching the column housing to the mast jacket. Be sure to note the position of the dimmer switch actuator rod for reassembly in the same position. Remove the column housing and switch as an assembly.

NOTE: Certain Tilt and Travel columns are equipped with a removable plastic cover on the column housing. This provides access to the wiper switch without removing the entire column housing.

5. Turn upside down and use a drift to remove the pivot pin from the washer/wiper switch. Remove the switch.

6. Place the switch into position in the housing. Install the pivot pin.

7. Position the housing onto the mast jacket and attach by installing the screws. Install the dimmer switch actuator rod in the same position as noted when removed. Check switch operation.

8. Reconnect lower end of the switch assembly.

9. Install remaining components in reverse order of the removal procedure.

WINDSHIELD WIPER MOTOR

Removal and Installation

1. Disconnect the negative battery cable.
2. Remove the air intake grille.
3. Loosen the wiper linkage to drive arm attaching nuts.
4. Remove the transmission link from the drive arm.
5. Disconnect the wiring and hoses from the motor.
6. Unbolt and remove the motor.
7. Installation is the reverse of the removal procedure.

WIPER LINKAGE/TRANSMISSION

Removal and Installation

1. Disconnect the negative battery cable. Remove the wiper arm and blade assemblies.

2. Loosen, but do not remove, the drive link-to-crank arm attaching nuts.

3. Remove the air intake grille and the cowl vent screen.

4. Disconnect the motor drive link(s) from the motor crank arm.

5. Remove the transmission-to-body attaching screws.

6. Remove the wiper transmission(s).

7. Installation is the reverse of the removal procedure. When installing the transmission, position the assembly into the plenum chamber through the upper shroud panel openings.

Instrument Cluster

Refer to "Chilton's Electronic Instrumentation Service Manual" for additional coverage.

Removal and Installation

CELEBRITY

1. Disconnect the negative battery cable.
2. Remove instrument panel hush panel.
3. Remove vent control housing, as required.
4. On non-air conditioning vehicles, remove steering column trim cover screws and lower cover with vent cables attached. On air conditioning vehicles, remove trim cover attaching screws and remove cover.
5. Remove instrument cluster trim pad.
6. Remove ash tray, retainer and fuse block, disconnect wires as necessary.
7. Remove headlamp switch knob and instrument panel trim plate. Disconnect electrical connectors of any accessory switches in trim plate.
8. Remove cluster assembly and disconnect speedometer cable, **PRNDL** and cluster electrical connectors.
9. Installation is the reverse of the removal procedure.

6000

1. Disconnect the negative battery cable.
2. Remove the center and left hand lower instrument panel trim plate.
3. Remove the screws holding the instrument cluster to the instrument panel carrier.
4. Remove the instrument cluster lens to gain access to the speedometer head and gauges.
5. Remove right-hand and left-hand hush panels, steering column trim cover and disconnect parking brake cable and vent cables, if so equipped.
6. Remove steering column retaining bolts and drop steering column.
7. Disconnect temperature control cable, inner to outer A/C wire harness and inner to outer A/C vacuum harness, if so equipped.
8. Disconnect chassis harness behind left lower instrument

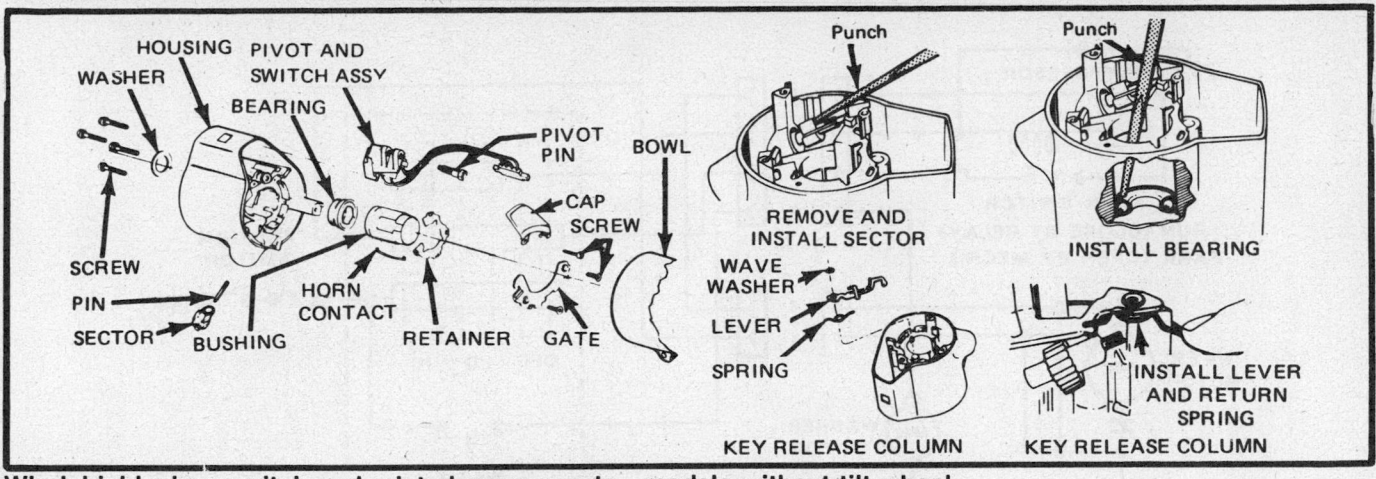

Windshield wiper switch and related components—models without tilt wheel

panel and ECM connectors behind glove box. Disconnect instrument panel harness at cowl.

9. Remove center instrument panel trim plate and remove radio if so equipped.

10. Disconnect neutral switch and brake light switch.

11. Remove upper instrument panel retaining screws.

12. Remove lower instrument panel retaining screws, nuts and bolts.

13. Pull instrument panel assembly out far enough to disconnect ignition switch, headlight dimmer switch and turn signal switch. Disconnect all other accessory wiring and vacuum lines necessary to remove instrument panel assembly.

14. Remove instrument panel assembly with wiring harness.

15. Installation is the reverse of the removal procedure.

CUTLASS CIERA

1. Disconnect the negative battery cable. Remove left instrument panel trim pad.

2. Remove instrument panel cluster trim cover.

3. Disconnect speedometer cable at transmission or cruise control transducer if equipped.

4. Remove steering column trim cover.

5. Disconnect shift indicator clip from steering column shift bowl.

6. Remove 4 screws attaching cluster assembly to instrument panel.

7. Pull assembly out far enough to reach behind cluster and disconnect speedometer cable.

8. Remove cluster assembly.

9. Installation is the reverse of the removal procedure.

CENTURY

1. Disconnect the negative battery cable.

2. Disconnect the speedometer cable and pull it through the firewall.

3. Remove the left side hush panel retaining screws and nut.

4. Remove the right side hush panel retaining screws and nut.

5. Remove the shift indicator cable clip.

6. Remove the steering column trim plate.

7. Put the gear selector in **L**. Remove the retaining screws and gently pull out the instrument panel trim plate.

8. Disconnect the parking brake cable at the lever by pushing it forward and sliding it out of its slot.

9. Unbolt and lower the steering column.

10. Remove the gauge cluster retaining screws and pulling the cluster out far enough to disconnect any wires, then pull the cluster out.

11. Installation is the reverse of the removal procedure.

	SWITCH MODE	MIST	OFF	PULSE	LO	HI	WASH
	TERMINAL #						
PULSE	1	●	●	●	●	●	●
	2	B(+)	—	B(+)	B(+)	—	B(+)
	3	B(+)	B(+)	—	B(+)	—	B(+)
	4	●	●	●	●	●	●
	5	—	—	—	—	B(+)	—
	6	B(+)✳	B(+)✳	B(+)✳	B(+)✳	B(+)✳	B(+)✳
STANDARD	1	⊠	●	⊠	●	●	●
	2	⊠	—	⊠	B(+)	B(+)	B(+)
	3	⊠	B(+)	⊠	B(+)	—	B(+)
	4	⊠	●	⊠	●	●	●
	5	⊠	—	⊠	—	B(+)	—
	6	⊠	—	⊠	—	—	B(+)

NOTE

All voltage readings taken with respect to vehicle ground.

● = Continuity between terminals 1 and 4

To use Wiper/Washer Switch Check chart, probe terminals 1 thru 6 with digital voltmeter and wiper switch in various positions.

✳Voltage might be slightly less than source (B+) voltage.

Windshield wiper/washer switch check

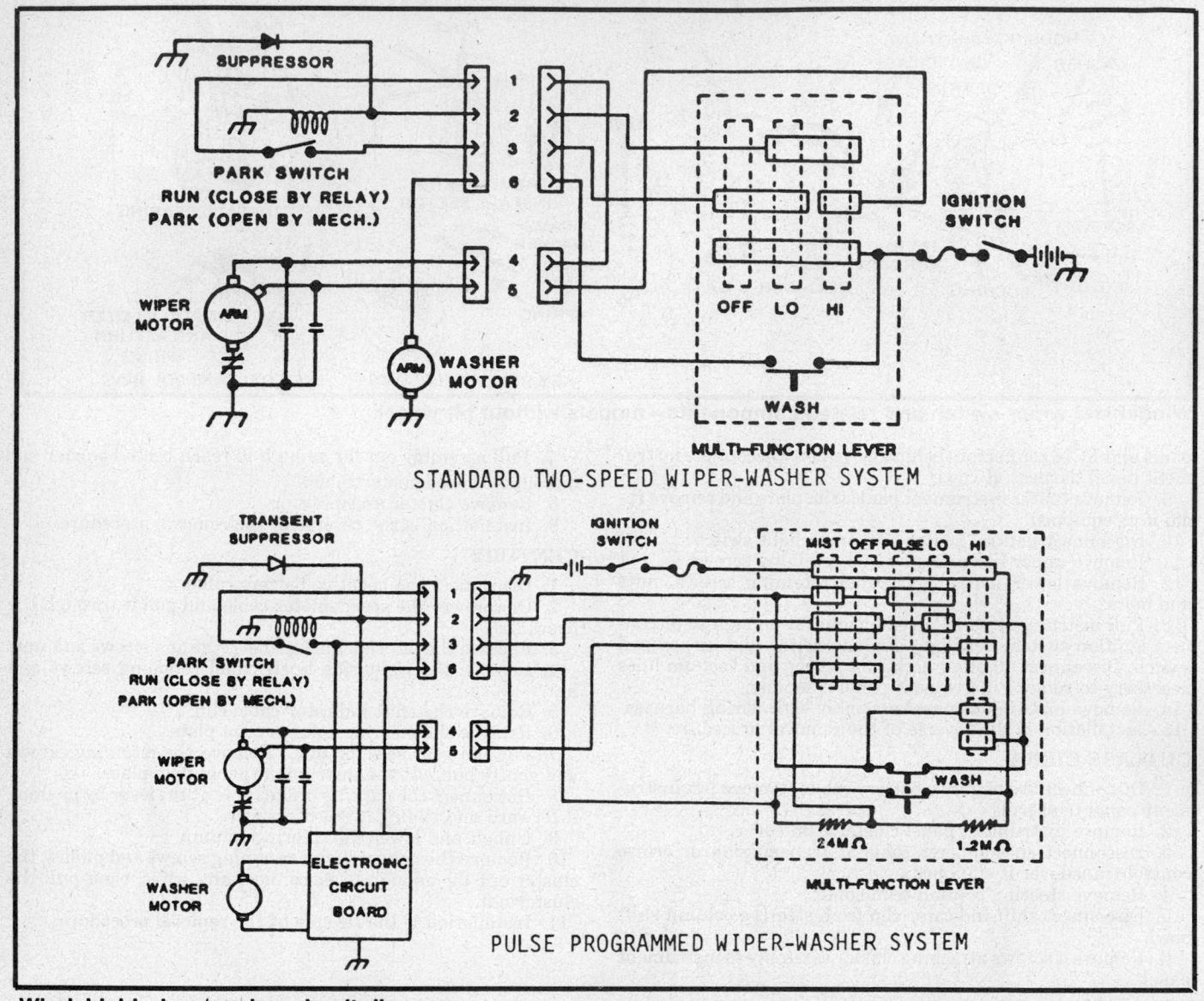

Windshield wiper/washer circuit diagrams

SPEEDOMETER

Removal and Installation

CELEBRITY

1. Disconnect the negative battery cable.
2. Remove the cluster trim panel.
3. Remove the cluster lens screws. Remove the cluster lens.
4. Remove the speedometer to cluster attaching screws. Remove the speedometer from the instrument cluster.
5. Disconnect the speedometer cable and remove the speedometer assembly.
6. Installation is the reverse of the removal procedure.

6000

1. Disconnect the negative battery cable.
2. Remove the center and left lower trim plates.
3. Remove the screws holding the instrument cluster assembly to the dash assembly. Remove the instrument cluster.
4. Remove the instrument cluster lens screws. Remove the instrument cluster lens.
5. Remove the screws holding the speedometer to the instru-

ment cluster. Remove the speedometer.
6. Disconnect the speedometer cable from the rear of the speedometer.
7. Installation is the reverse of the removal procedure.

CUTLASS CIERA

1. Disconnect the negative battery cable.
2. Remove the instrument cluster assembly.
3. Remove the vehicle speed sensor screw from the rear of the speedometer. Remove the vehicle speed sensor if equipped.
4. Remove the speedometer lens screws and remove the speedometer lens. Remove the bezel.
5. Remove the screw that hold the speedometer to the instrument cluster.
6. Remove the speedometer head by pulling forward. Disconnect the speedometer cable by prying gently on the retainer and pulling the speedometer cable out of the speedometer head.
7. Installation is the reverse of the removal procedure.

CENTURY

1. Disconnect the negative battery cable.
2. Remove the left hand trim plate.

3. Remove the instrument cluster housing screws. Remove the instrument cluster. If the vehicle is equipped with tilt-wheel steering, working room can be gained by removing the tilt-wheel cover.

4. Remove the speedometer lens screws and remove the speedometer lens.

5. Disconnect the speedometer cable by pushing in on the retaining clip and pulling back on the cable.

6. Remove the screws holding the speedometer to the instrument and remove the speedometer assembly.

7. Installation is the reverse of the removal procedure.

SPEEDOMETER CABLE

Removal and Installation

1. Disconnect the negative battery cable.
2. Remove the steering column trim plate.
3. Remove the speedometer cable casing from the head of the speedometer.
4. Remove the cable from the transaxle assembly.
5. Install the new cable making sure that the bend radius does not exceed 6 in.
6. Installation is the reverse of the removal procedure.

Electrical Circuit Protectors

FUSIBLE LINKS

There are several locations where fusible links can be found. They are located ahead of the left hand front shock tower, near the positive battery connection or at the starter solenoid near the front of the engine.

CIRCUIT BREAKERS

Circuit breakers are used along with the fusible links to protect the various components of the electrical system, such as headlights, the windshield wipers and electric windows. The circuit breakers are located either in the switch or mounted on or near the lower lip of the instrument panel, to the right or left of the steering column.

FUSE PANEL

The fuse panel is located on the left side of the vehicle. It is under the instrument panel assembly. In order to gain access to the fuse panel, it may be necessary to first remove the under dash padding.

COMPUTER

The electronic module is located on the right side of the vehicle. It is positioned under the instrument panel. In order to gain access to the electronic control module, it will be necessary to first remove the trim panel.

CONVENIENCE CENTER AND VARIOUS RELAYS

The convenience center is a swing down unit located on the underside of the instrument panel near the fuse panel. It provides a central location for various relays, hazard flasher units and buzzers. All units are easily replaced with plug-in modules.

VARIOUS RELAYS, SWITCHES AND SENSORS

CELEBRITY, CIERA, 6000

A/C Compressor Relay—is located on the upper right corner of the engine cowl.

A/C Delay Relay—is located in the upper right corner of the engine cowl.

A/C Heater Blower Relay—is located on the plenum, on the right side of the firewall.

A/C High Pressure Cut-Out Switch—is located on the left side of the compressor.

A/C Temperature Cut-Out Switch—is located on the top of the engine near the fuel filter.

Altitude Advance Relay—is located on the left inner fender, in front of the shock tower.

Assembly Line Diagnostic Link—is located on the bottom of the instrument oanel, near the steering column.

Charging System Relay—is located behind the instrument panel, near the fuse block.

"Check Engine" Light Driver—is taped to the instrument panel harness behind the glove box.

Choke Relay (Non EFI)—is located on the convenience center.

Constant Run Relay—is located on the left inner fender wheel well.

Coolant Fan In-Line Fuse—is located in the engine compartment in front of the left front shock tower.

Coolant Fan Low-Speed Relay—is located on the left inner fender wheel well, on a bracket on the 4 cylinder engines and on the fender panel in front of the left front shock tower on the V6 models.

Coolant Fan Relay—is located on the left front wheel well on the bracket on the 4 cylinder engine and on the fender panel ahead of the left front shock tower on the V6 engine.

Coolant Fan Switch—is located in front of the engine below the left side valve cover on the 4 cylinder engine and on the top of the V6 engine in front of the distributor.

Coolant Temperature Sensor—is located on the left center side of the 4 cylinder engines and on the top of the V6 engine in front of the distributor.

Coolant Temperature Switch—is located on the top of the engine near the fuel filter.

Cruise Control Module—is located behind the instrument panel, above the accelerator pedal.

Defogger Timer Relay—is located behind the instrument panel, under the instrument cluster.

Diagnostic Dwell Meter Connector—is located near the upper right side of the engine cowl.

Early Fuel Evaporation Heater Relay—is located on the upper right side of the engine cowl.

Electronic Control Module (ECM)—is located behind the right side of the instrument panel.

Electronic Level Control Relay—is located on the frame behind the left rear wheel well.

Fuel Pump Relay—is located on the upper right side of the engine cowl.

Headlight-Key-Seat Buzzer—is located on the convenience center.

Heater Blower Resistors—is located on the right plenum.

High Mount Stop Light Relays—are located on the left rear wheel well, in the trunk.

Horn Relay—is located on the convenience center.

Knock Sensor—is located on the top left side of the engine, below the front of the oxygen sensor.

Low Brake Vacuum Relay—is taped to the instrument panel above the fuse block.

Low Brake Vacuum Switch—is located on top of the brake booster unit.

Oxygen Sensor—is located in the exhaust manifold. the left front shock tower.

Rear Wiper Relay—is located in the top center of the tailgate.

Speed Sensor—is located on the top right side of the transaxle.

Starter Interrupt Relay—is located above the ashtray, taped to the instrument panel harness.

Throttle Kicker Relay—is located on the front of the engine compartment, at the right side of the radiator support.

Throttle Position Sensor—is located on the throttle body.

CENTURY

A/C Coolant Fan Relay (2.5L)—is located on the right side of the firewall.

Assembly Line Diagnostic Link—is located in the center of the instrument panel, underneath the steering column.

Blower Relay—is located on the right side of the firewall.

Convenience Center (1986–87)—is located behind the right side of the instrument panel, behind the glove box.

Coolant Fan Delay Relay (SFI)—is located in front of the left front shock tower, on a bracket.

Coolant Fan Relay—is located in front of the left front shock tower.

Coolant Fan Switch (SFI)—is located on the top right hand side of the engine and to the left of the generator.

Coolant Fan Switch (2.5L)—is located on the top of the engine, near the distributor.

Coolant Temperature Fan Switch (2.5L)—is located on the left front side of the engine, below the valve cover.

Coolant Temperature Sensor (V6)—is located on the top of the engine above the water pump.

Coolant Temperature Sensor (2.5L)—is located on the left side of the engine below the water cooolant outlet.

Early Fuel Evaporation Heater—is located on top of the engine.

Early Fuel Evaporation Heater Switch—is located on top of the engine, near the distributor.

EGR Solenoid Valve—is located on a bracket, above the left side of the valve cover.

Electronic Control Module—is located under the right side of the instrument panel, behind the glove box.

Electronic Level Control Height Sensor—is located on the frame under the rear of the vehicle.

Electronic Spark Timing Distributor (V6)—is located on the top right side of the engine.

Electronic Spark Timing Distributor (2.5L)—is located on the top left rear side of the engine.

Fuel Pump Relay (2.5L)—is located in the relay bracket on the right side of the firewall.

High Speed Coolant Fan Relay—is located on the left front side of the engine.

Horn Relay—is located under the instrument panel, in the convenience center.

Low Speed Coolant Fan Relay—is located near the battery, on the left side of the radiator shroud.

Oxygen Sensor—is located in the exhaust manifold.

Power Steering Cut-Out Switch—is located on the bottom of the steering rack.

Power Steering Pressure Switch—is located on the left side of the engine above the transaxle.

Rear Wiper Relay—is located in the top center of the tailgate.

Starter Interrupt Relay—is taped to the instrument panel harness, above the right side ashtray.

Throttle Kicker Relay—is located in the left front side of the engine compartment.

Vehicle Speed Sensor—is connected to the rear center of the instrument cluster.

Vehicle Speed Sensor Buffer—is located under the left side of the instrument panel, behind the instrument cluster.

Wiper/Washer Motor Module—is located on the left side of the firewall.

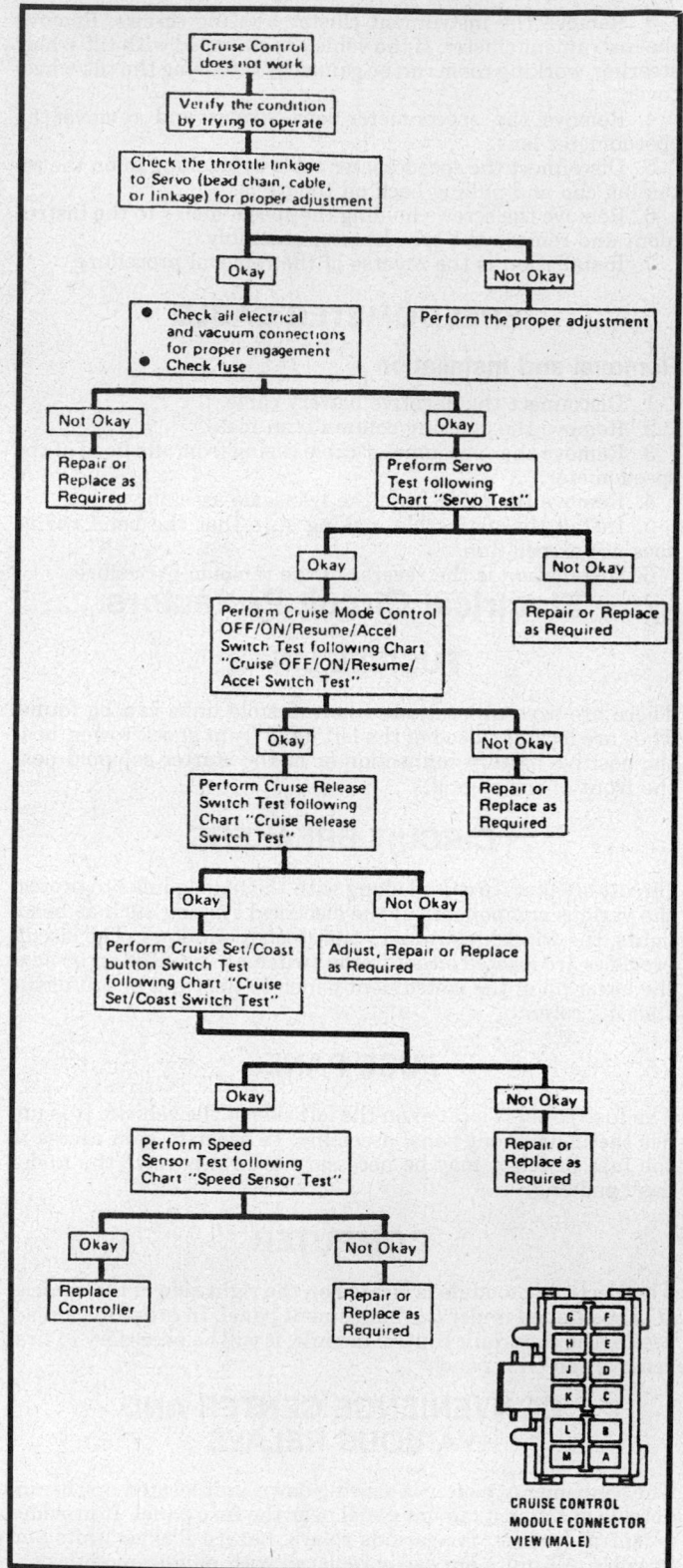

Cruise Control Diagnosis

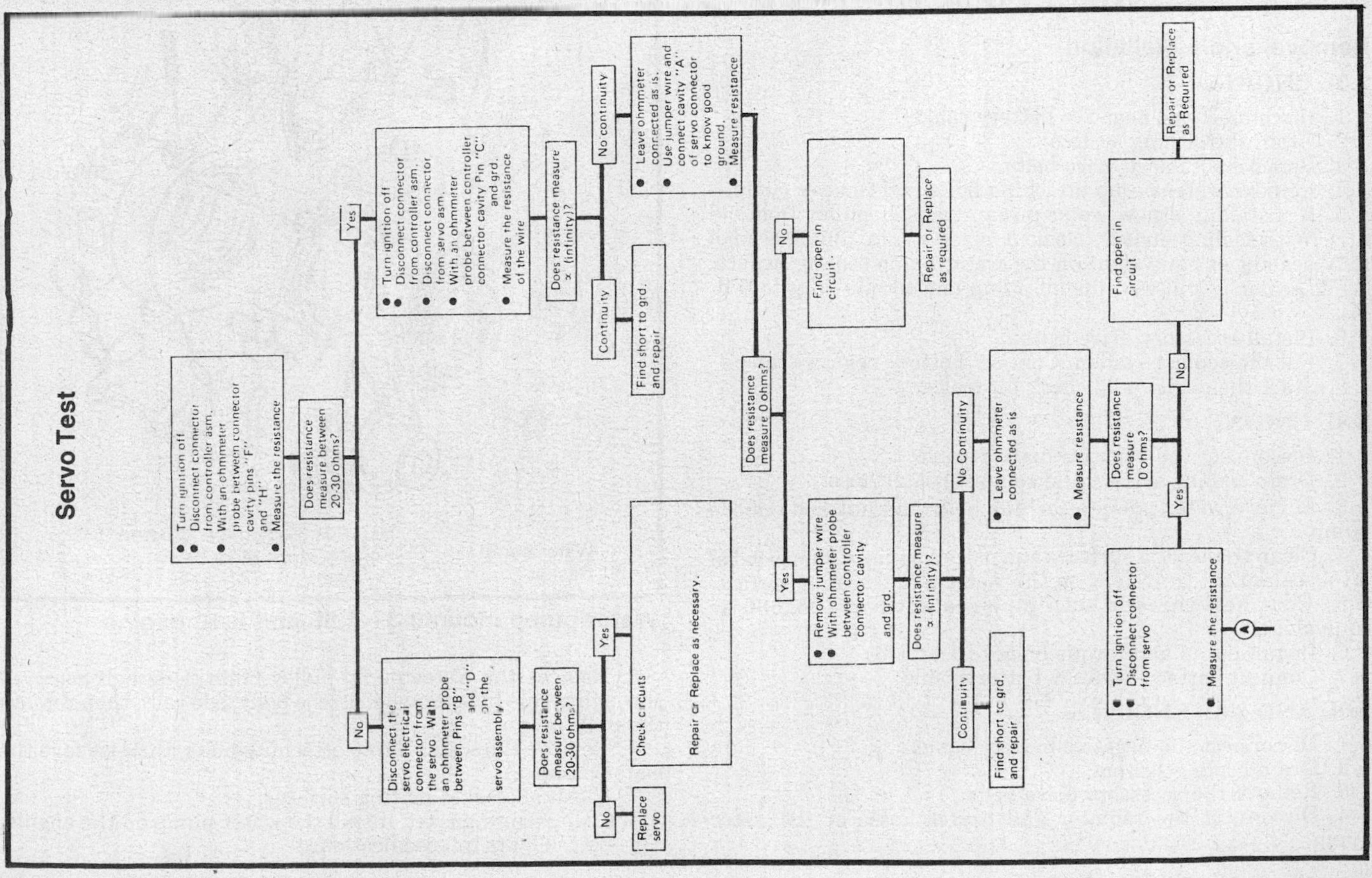

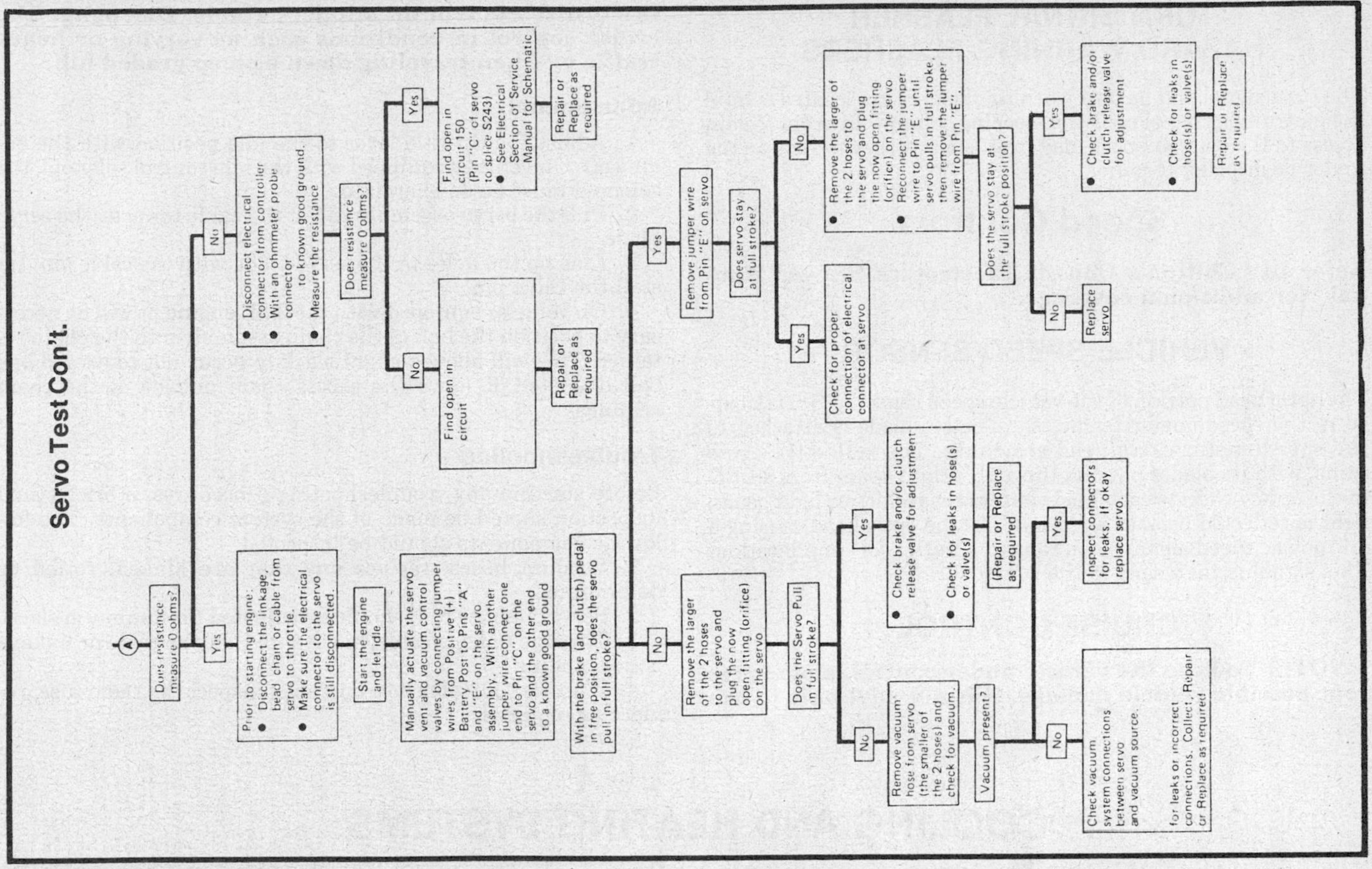

Servo Test Con't.

Ⓐ

Does resistance measure 0 ohms?

- No →
  - Disconnect electrical connector from controller
  - With an ohmmeter probe connector to known good ground
  - Measure the resistance

  Does resistance measure 0 ohms?
  - Yes → Find open in circuit 150 (Pin "C" of servo to splice S243) • See Electrical Section of Service Manual for Schematic → Repair or Replace as required
  - No → Find open in circuit → Repair or Replace as required

- Yes →
  Prior to starting engine:
  - Disconnect the linkage, bead chain or cable from servo to throttle.
  - Make sure the electrical connector to the servo is still disconnected.

  Start the engine and let idle.

  Manually actuate the servo vent and vacuum control valves by connecting jumper wires from Positive (+) Battery Post to Pins "A" and "E" on the servo assembly. With another jumper wire connect one end to Pin "C" on the servo and the other end to a known good ground.

  With the brake (and clutch) pedal in free position, does the servo pull in full stroke?
  - Yes → **Remove jumper wire from Pin "E" on servo.** **Does servo stay at full stroke?**
    - No → Remove the larger of the 2 hoses to the servo and plug the now open fitting (orifice) on the servo • Reconnect the jumper wire to Pin "E" until servo pulls in full stroke, then remove the jumper wire from Pin "E". **Does the servo stay at the full stroke position?**
      - Yes → Check brake and/or clutch release valve for adjustment • Check for leaks in hose(s) or valve(s) → Repair or Replace as required
      - No → Replace servo
    - Yes → Check for proper connection of electrical connector at servo
  - No → Remove the larger of the 2 hoses to the servo and plug the now open fitting (orifice) on the servo. **Does the Servo Pull in full stroke?**
    - Yes → • Check brake and/or clutch release valve for adjustment • Check for leaks in hose(s) or valve(s) → (Repair or Replace as required) → Inspect connectors for leaks. If okay replace servo.
    - No → Remove vacuum hose from servo (the smaller of the 2 hoses) and check for vacuum. **Vacuum present?**
      - Yes →
      - No → Check vacuum system connections between servo and vacuum source. for leaks or incorrect connections. Collect, Repair or Replace as required.

Servo Test

- Turn ignition off
- Disconnect connector from controller asm.
- With an ohmmeter probe between connector cavity pins "F" and "H".
- Measure the resistance

Does resistance measure between 20-30 ohms?
- Yes →
  - Turn ignition off
  - Disconnect connector from controller asm.
  - Disconnect connector from servo asm.
  - With an ohmmeter probe between controller connector cavity Pin "C" and grd.
  - Measure the resistance of the wire

  Does resistance measure ∞ (infinity)?
  - No continuity → Leave ohmmeter connected as is. Use jumper wire and connect cavity "A" at servo connector to know good ground. Measure resistance → No → Find open in circuit → Repair or Replace as required
  - Continuity → Find short to grd. and repair

  Does resistance measure 0 ohms?
  - No → Leave ohmmeter connected as is → Measure resistance → Repair or Replace as Required
  - Yes → Turn ignition off. Disconnect connector from servo. Measure the resistance Ⓐ → Find open in circuit → **Does resistance measure 0 ohms?**
    - Yes →
    - No →

  • Remove jumper wire • With ohmmeter probe between controller connector cavity and grd. **Does resistance measure ∞ (infinity)?**
  - No Continuity →
  - Continuity → Find short to grd. and repair

- No → Disconnect the servo electrical connector from the servo. With an ohmmeter probe between Pins "B" and "D" on the servo assembly. **Does resistance measure between 20-30 ohms?**
  - Yes → Check circuits. Repair or Replace as necessary.
  - No → Replace servo

TURN SIGNAL FLASHER
HAZARD WARNING FLASHERS

The turn signal and hazard warning flashers are located behind the instrument panel near the steering column. In order to gain access to the component it may first be necessary to remove the under dash padding panel.

Speed Controls

Refer to "Chilton's Chassis Electronics Service Manual" for additional coverage.

VEHICLE SPEED SENSOR

The optic head portion of the vehicle speed sensor (VSS) is located in the speedometer frame. A reflective blade is attached to the speedometer cable/head assembly. The reflective blade spins, with its blades passing through a light beam from a LED in the optic head. As each blade enters the reflective light beam, light is reflected back to a photocell in the optic head causing a low power speed signal to be sent to a buffer for amplification. This signal is then sent to the controller.

CRUISE CONTROL

NOTE: To keep the vehicle under control, and to prevent possible vehicle damage, it is not advisable to use the cruise control on slippery roads. Disengage the cruise control in conditions such as varying or heavy traffic or when traveling down a steep graded hill.

Adjustments

1. Adjust the throttle lever to the idle position with the engine off. On vehicles equipped with the idle control solenoid, the solenoid must be de-energized.
2. Pull the servo assembly end of the cable towards the servo blade.
3. Line up the holes in the servo blade with the cable pin. Install the cable pin.
4. On vehicles equipped with the 2.8L engine, it will be necessary to position the ball of the chain assembly into the chain retainer. This will allow a slight slack to occur not to exceed one ball diameter. Remove the excess chain outside of the chain retainer.

Troubleshooting

Before starting any troubleshooting procedures, a brief visual inspection should be made of the system components. The following components should be inspected:

1. Vacuum hoses; replace any that are kinked, rotted or deteriorated.
2. Servo chain or rod; should be adjusted for minimum slack.
3. Throttle linkage/cable; make sure that the cable or linkage is not binding.
4. If cruise control is non-operable, inspect the radio fuse, replace as required.

COOLING AND HEATING SYSTEMS

Water Pump

Removal and Installation

2.5L ENGINE

1. Disconnect the negative battery cable.
2. Drain the cooling system.
3. Remove accessory drive belts.
4. Remove water pump attaching bolts and remove pump.
5. If installing a new water pump, transfer pulley from old unit. With sealing surfaces cleaned, place a ⅛ in. (3mm) bead of RTV sealant or equivalent on the water pump sealing surface. While sealer is still wet, install pump and torque bolts to 6 ft. lbs.
6. Install accessory drive belts.
7. Fill the cooling system. Connect battery negative cable.
8. Start the engine and check for leaks.

2.8L ENGINE

1. Disconnect the negative battery cable.
2. Drain cooling system and remove heater hose.
3. Remove water pump attaching bolts and nut and remove pump.
4. Clean the sealing surfaces and place a ³⁄₃₂ in. (2mm) bead of RTV sealant or equivalent on the water pump sealing surface.
5. Coat bolt threads with pipe sealant No. 1052080 or equivalent.
6. Install pump and torque bolts to 10 ft. lbs.
7. Connect battery negative battery cable.

3.0L AND 3.8L ENGINES

1. Disconnect the negative battery cable.
2. Drain cooling system.
3. Remove the accessory drive belts.
4. Disconnect the radiator and heater hoses at the water pump.

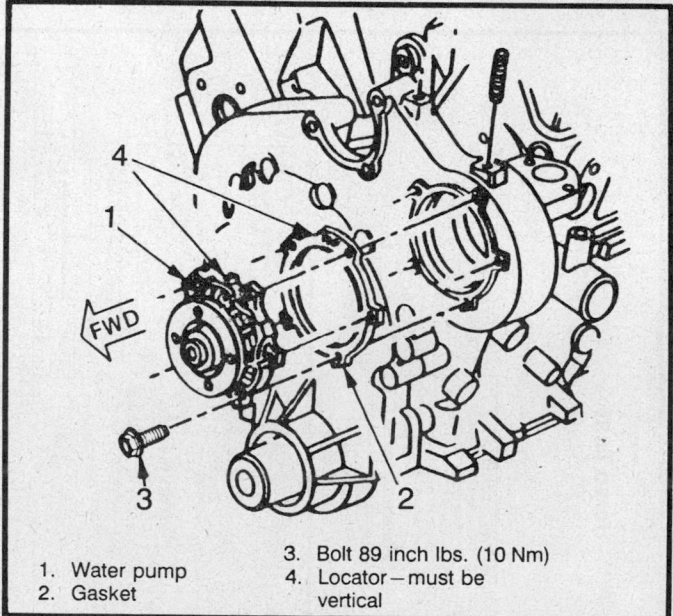

1. Water pump
2. Gasket
3. Bolt 89 inch lbs. (10 Nm)
4. Locator—must be vertical

Water pump mounting—2.8L and 3.1L engine

5. Remove the water pump pulley bolts (long bolt removed through access hole provided in the body side rail), then remove the pulley.
6. Remove the water pump attaching bolts, then remove the water pump.
7. Clean all gasket mating surfaces.
8. Using a new gasket, install the water pump on the engine. Torque the bolts to specifications.

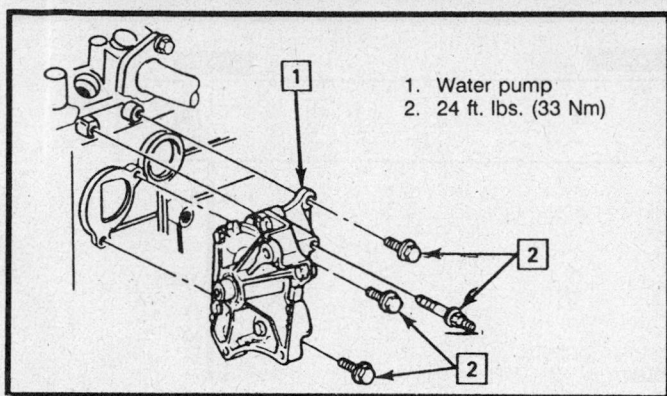

Water pump mounting—2.5L engine

1. Water pump
2. 24 ft. lbs. (33 Nm)

9. Install the water pump pulley, then torque the bolts to specifications.

10. The remainder of the installation is the reverse of removal.

3.1L ENGINE

1. Disconnect the negative battery cable.
2. Drain cooling system.
3. Remove the serpentine belt.
4. Remove the heater hose and radiator hose.
5. Remove the water pump cover attaching bolts and remove the cover.

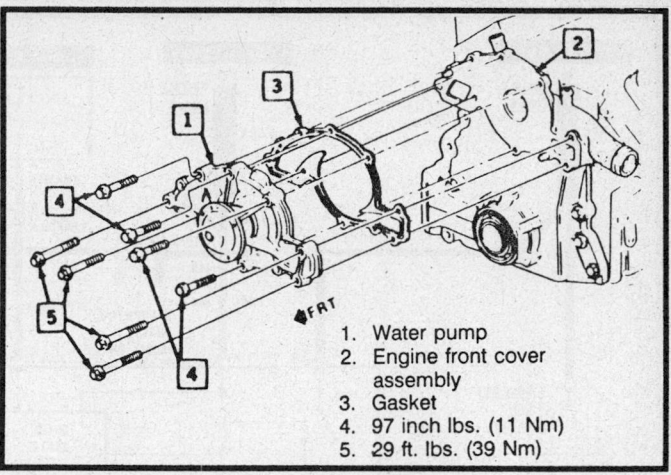

Water pump mounting—3.3L engine

1. Water pump
2. Engine front cover assembly
3. Gasket
4. 97 inch lbs. (11 Nm)
5. 29 ft. lbs. (39 Nm)

6. Remove the water pump attaching bolts and remove the water pump.

To install:

7. Position the water pump on the engine and install the attaching bolts. Torque bolts to 89 inch lbs. (10 Nm).

8. Install the water pump cover and attaching bolts.

9. Complete installation by reversing the removal procedure.

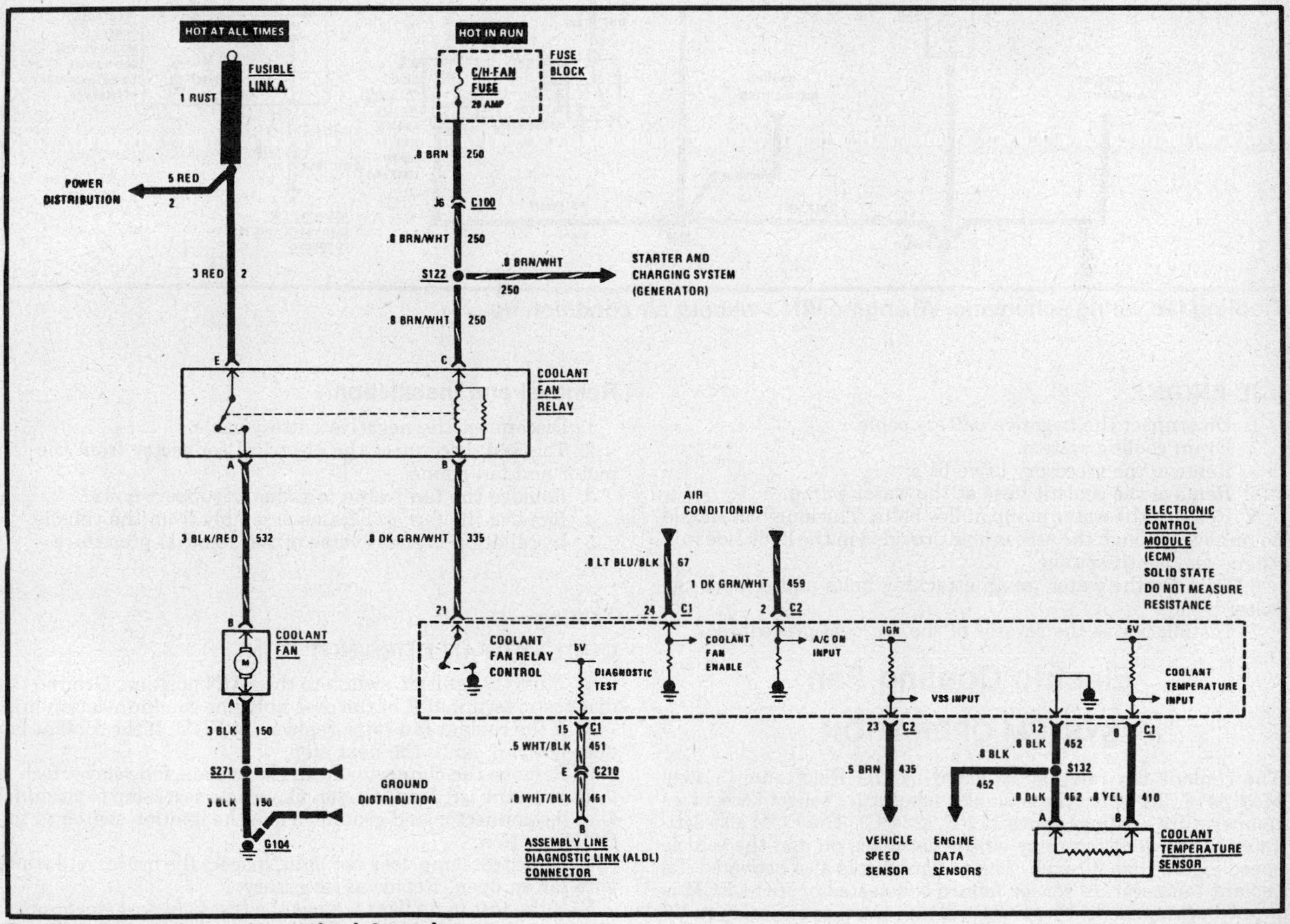

Cooling fan wiring schematic, L4 engine

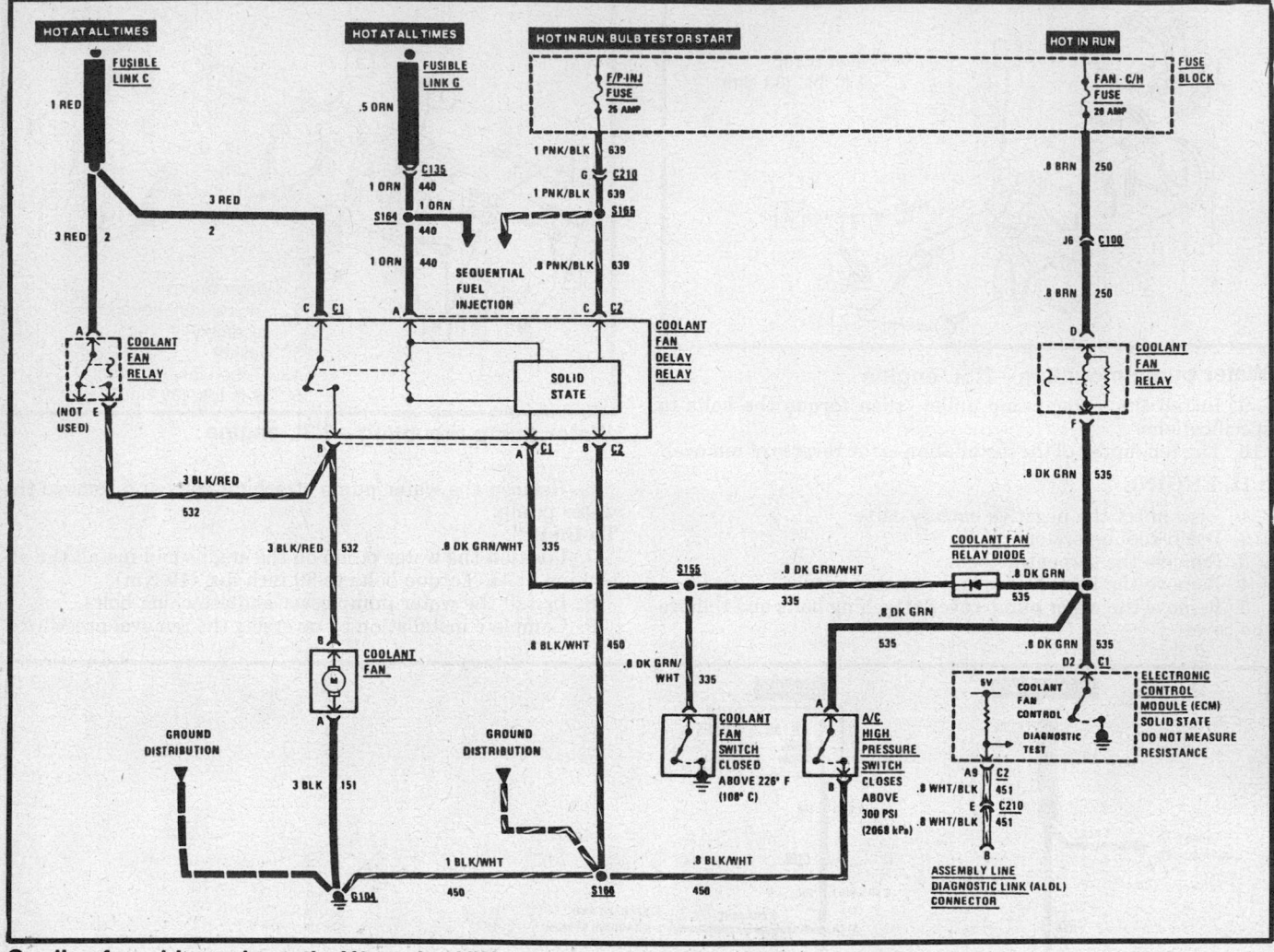

Cooling fan wiring schematic, V6 engine VIN 3 without air conditioning

3.3L ENGINE

1. Disconnect the negative battery cable.
2. Drain cooling system.
3. Remove the accessory drive belt.
4. Remove the coolant hose at the water pump.
5. Remove the water pump pulley bolts. The long bolt should be remove through the access hole provided in the body side rail. Then, remove the pulley.
6. Remove the water pump attaching bolts and remove the water pump.
7. Installation is the reverse of the removal procedure.

Electric Cooling Fan

SYSTEM OPERATION

The coolant fan relay is activated by the Electronic Control Module (ECM) when the coolant temperature sensor recognizes temperature readings above 112°F. (234°C). The ECM also activates the coolant fan relay when the A/C is on and the vehicle speed is less than 40 mph. The coolant fan is also activated if a coolant temperature sensor failure is detected or if the ECM is in the back up mode. The ECM will also activate the relay on V6 engines when the A/C pressure exceeds 233 psi.

Removal and Installation

1. Disconnect the negative battery cable.
2. Tag and disconnect the electrical connector from the fan motor and fan frame.
3. Remove the fan frame to radiator support bolts.
4. Remove the fan and frame assembly from the vehicle.
5. Installation is the reverse of the removal procedure.

Testing

COOLANT FAN DOES NOT RUN

1. Turn the ignition switch to the **RUN** position. Ground the diagnostic terminal **B** of the assembly line communication link.
2. If the coolant fan runs, replace the ECM. If the coolant fan does not run, go to the next step.
3. Remove the connector from the coolant fan relay which is located on the left front fender. Connect a test lamp to terminal **C** of the connector and ground. Turn the ignition switch to the **RUN** position.
4. If the test lamp does not light, inspect the brown and white wire for an open. Repair as necessary.
5. If the test lamp lights, move the test light from terminal **C** to terminal **E** of the coolant fan relay connector.

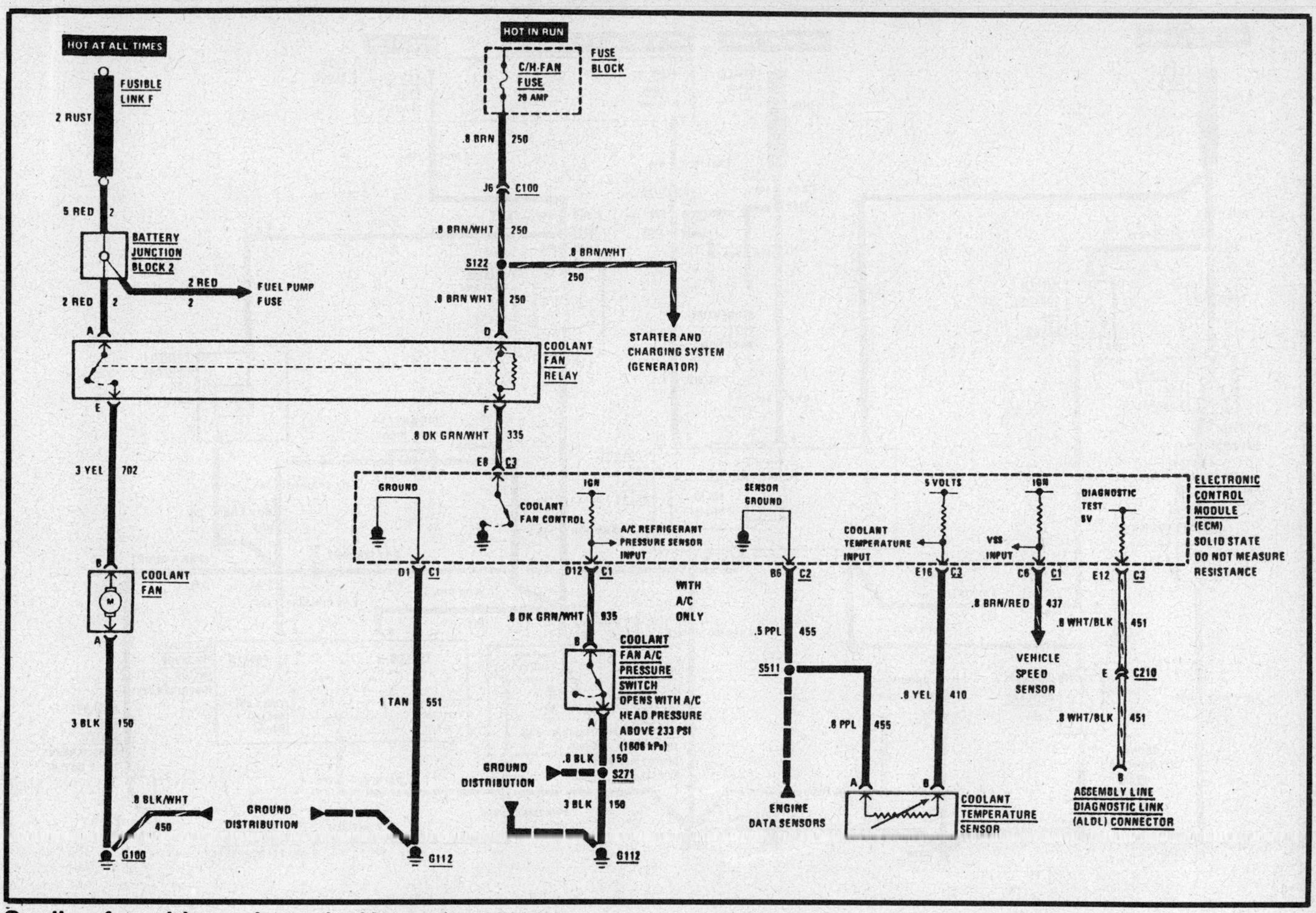

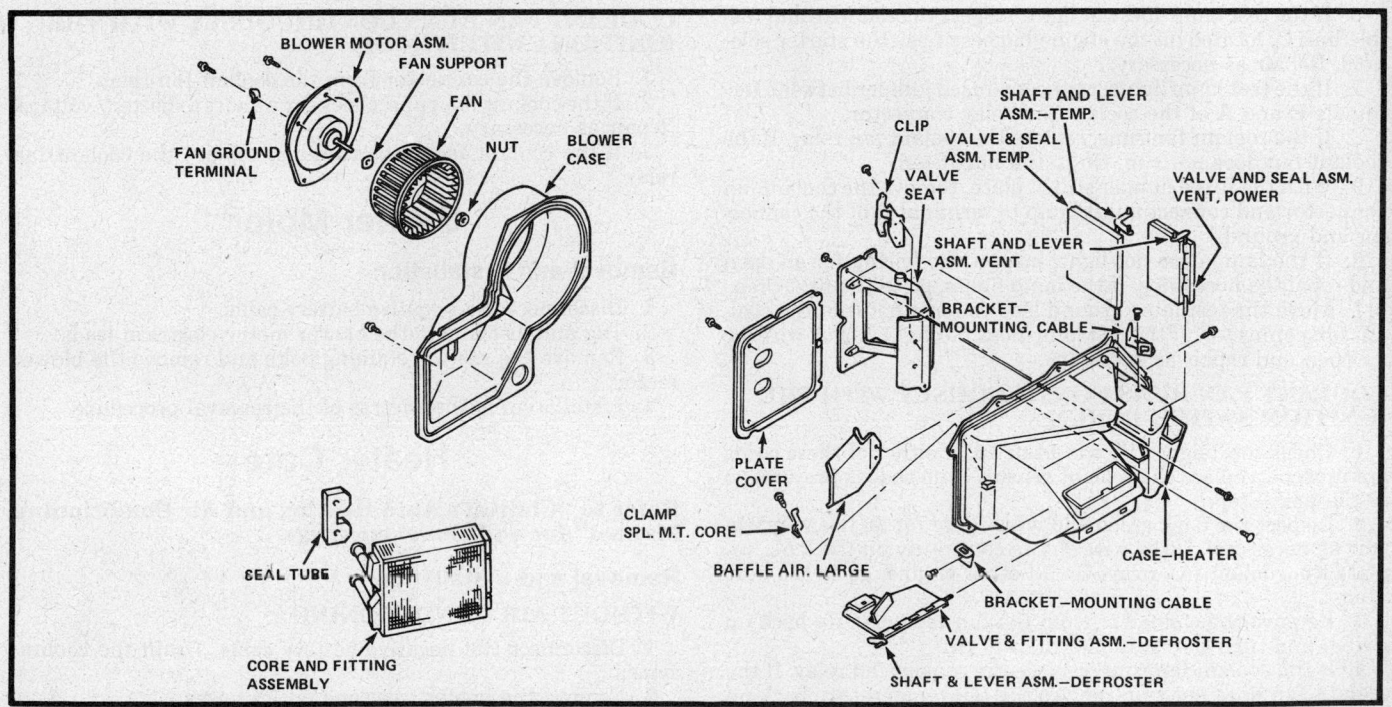

Cooling fan wiring schematic, V6 engine VIN W

Heater core, blower motor, and related components—typical

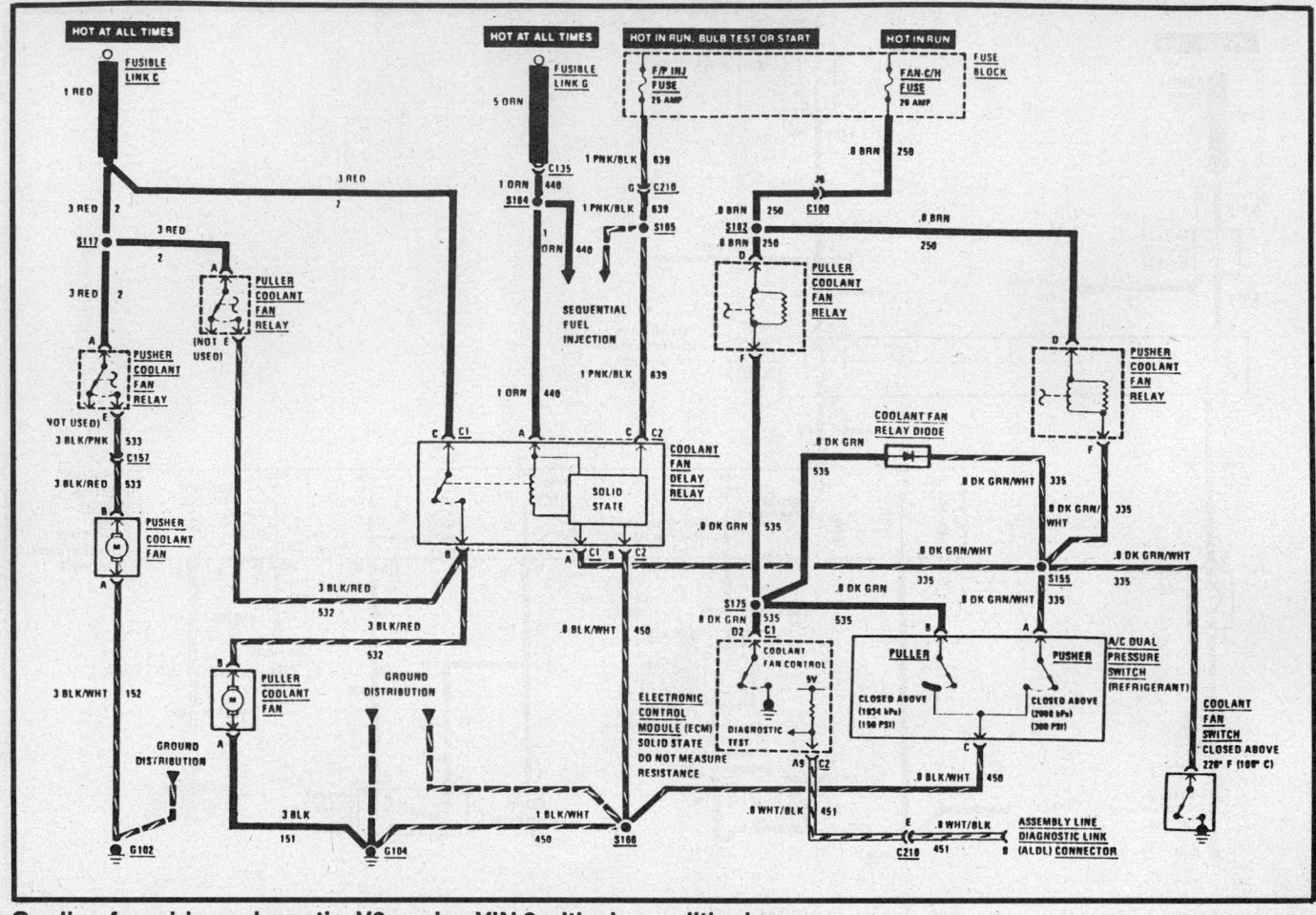

Cooling fan wiring schematic, V6 engine VIN 3 with air conditioning

6. If the test lamp does not light, inspect the red wire and fusible link C, located on the engine harness near the starter solenoid. Repair as necessary.

7. If the test lamp lights, connect a fused jumper between terminals **E** and **A** of the coolant fan relay connector.

8. If the coolant fan runs, replace the coolant fan relay. If the coolant fan does not run. Go to the next Step.

9. With the fused jumper still in place, remove the coolant fan connector and connect a test lamp to terminal **B** of the connector and ground.

10. If the lamp does not light, inspect the wiring for an open and repair as necessary. If the lamp lights, go to the next Step.

11. Move the test lamp ground lead to terminal **A** of the coolant fan connector. If the test lamp does not light, check wire for an open and repair as necessary.

COOLANT FAN RUNS CONTINUOUSLY WITH THE IGNITION SWITCH IN RUN

1. Check for diagnostic code 14 or 15. If either of these codes are present, replace the coolant sensor. If no code is present, go to the next Step.

2. Inspect the dark green and white wire for an open and repair as necessary. If the wire shows continuity on the 2.5L, replace the coolant fan relay. On all other engine, go to the next Step.

3. Remove the connector from the fan temperature back up switch and turn the ignition switch to run.

4. If the coolant fan runs, replace the coolant fan relay. If the coolant fan does not run, replace the fan temperature back up switch located between the coolant fan relay and the ECM.

COOLANT FAN RUNS CONTINUOUSLY WITH THE IGNITION SWITCH IN OFF

1. Remove the connector from the coolant fan relay.

2. If the coolant fan runs, check for a short to battery voltage. Repair as necessary.

3. If the coolant fan stops running, replace the coolant fan relay.

Blower Motor

Removal and Installation

1. Disconnect the negative battery cable.

2. Tag and disconnect the blower motor electrical leads.

3. Remove the motor retaining bolts and remove the blower motor.

4. Installation is the reverse of the removal procedure.

Heater Core

Refer to "Chilton's Auto Heating and Air Conditioning Manual" for additional coverage.

Removal and Installation

WITHOUT AIR CONDITIONING

1. Disconnect the negative battery cable. Drain the cooling system.

2. Remove the heater inlet and outlet hoses.

3. Remove the radio noise suppression strap.

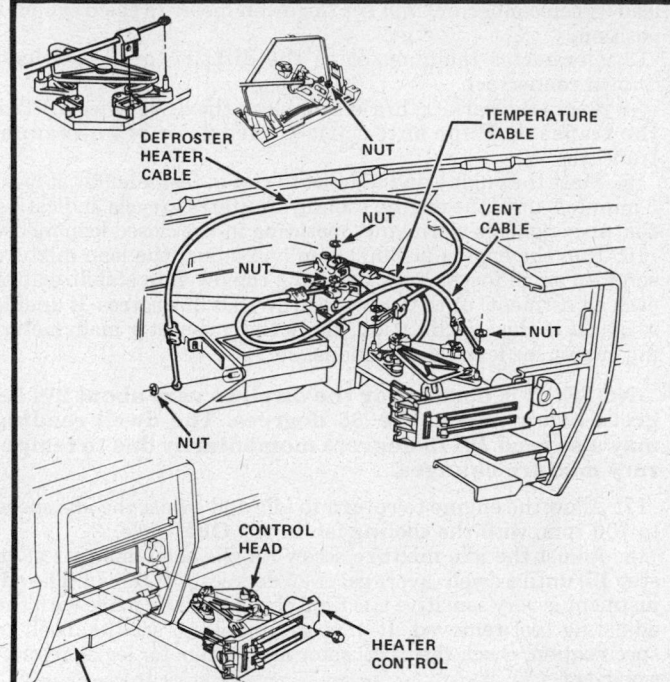

Mounting and cable routing of the horizontal-style heater A/C control unit

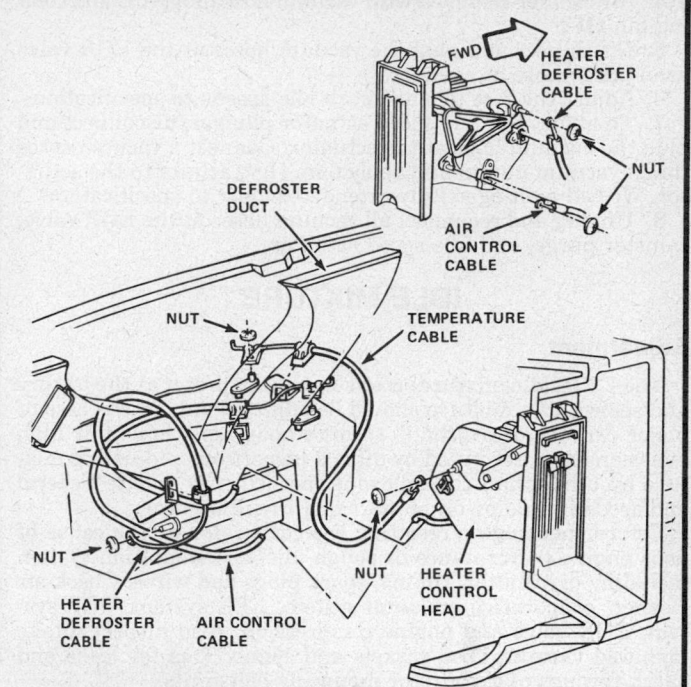

Mounting and cable routing of the vertical-style heater A/C control unit

4. Remove the core cover retaining screws. Remove the cover.
5. Remove the core.
6. Installation is the reverse of the removal procedure.

WITH AIR CONDITIONING

1. Disconnect the negative battery cable. Drain the cooling system.
2. Disconnect the heater hoses at the heater core.
3. Remove the heater duct and the lower side covers.
4. Remove the lower heater outlet.
5. Remove the housing cover-to-air valve housing clips.
6. Remove the housing cover bolts. Remove the housing cover.
7. Remove the core retaining straps. Remove the core tubing retainers. Lift out the heater core.

8. Installation is the reverse of the removal procedure.

TEMPERATURE CONTROL BLOWER SWITCH

Removal and Installation

1. Disconnect the negative battery cable.
2. Remove the necessary trim panels in order to gain access to the control head retaining screws.
3. Remove the control head retaining screws. Pull out and disconnect the cables, vacuum lines and electrical connections from the control head.
4. Remove the control head assembly.
5. Installation is the reverse of the removal procedure.

CARBURETED FUEL SYSTEM

Fuel Pump

Removal and Installation

1. Disconnect the negative battery cable. Raise and support the vehicle safely.
2. Remove the shields and the oil filter, as required.
3. Disconnect the hoses from the pump.
4. Loosen the fuel line at the carburetor and disconnect the line from the pump.
5. Remove the attaching bolts and the pump.
6. Installation is the reverse of the removal procedure. Tighten the attaching bolts evenly and alternately. Check for leakage after the engine is started.

Carburetor

IDLE SPEED

Adjustment

The E2SE carburetor use a vacuum operated idle speed actuator (throttle kicker) that is mounted on the carburetor. A vacuum solenoid controls the vacuum applied to the idle speed actuator. The vacuum solenoid can be energized either by the ECM or the fast idle relay (mounted on the front core support).

1. Apply the parking brake and block the drive wheels.
2. Connect a tachometer to the engine.
3. Start the engine and run to normal operating temperature (closed loop).

4. Air cleaner removed with vacuum hose plug, A/C and cooling fan **OFF**.

5. Disconnect and plug the vacuum hoses at the EGR valve asnd purge hose at canister.

6. Adjust the fast idle and curb idle speeds to specification.

7. To adjust the idle speed actuator plunger, disconnect and plug the vacuum hose at the actuator. Connect a vacuum sorce (hand vacuum pump) and apply 6 in. Hg. vacuum to the actuator. With the plunger fully extended, adjust to specification.

8. Unplug and reconnect all vacuum hoses at the EGR valve, canister purge, and idle speed actuator.

IDLE MIXTURE

Adjustment

The E2SE idle mixture screws have been preset at the factory and sealed. Idle mixture should be adjusted only in the case of major carburetor overhaul, throttle body replacement or high emissions as determined by official inspections. Adjusting mixture by other than the following method may violate Federal and/or California or other state or Provincial laws.

Before checking or resetting the carburetor as the cause of poor engine performance or rough idle, check ignition system including distributor, timing, spark plugs and wires. Check air cleaner, evaporative emission system, EFE system, PCV system, EGR valve and engine compression. Also inspect intake manifold vacuum hose gaskets and connections for leaks and check torques of carburetor mounting bolts/nuts.

1. Disconnect the negative battery cable. Remove the carburetor.

2. Remove the idle mixture screw plugs, then lightly seal the screws.

3. Back out the screws 1½ turns.

4. Remove the idle air bleed screw plug from the air horn. Lightly seat the air bleed screws, then back it out 5 turns.

5. Remove the vent stack and screen assembly in order to gain access to the lean mixture screw. Lightly seat the lean mixture screw, then back it out 2½ turns.

6. Reinstall the carburetor on the engine, but do not install the air cleaner and gasket.

7. Disconnect the bowl vent line at the carburetor.

8. Disconnect the plug and vacuum hose at the tee in the bowl vent line (if so equipped).

9. Disconnect the canister purge and EGR line at the carburetor, then plug the carburetor fitting.

10. Remove the thermal vacuum switch (for the secondary vacuum break) from the air cleaner.

11. Disconnect the vacuum hose which connects the thermal vacuum switch to the thermostatic air cleaner sensor, then cap the open port of the thermal vacuum switch.

12. Connect a dwell meter to the mixture control solenoid test lead (green connector) and set the dwell meter to the 6 cylinder position.

13. Connect a tachometer to the distributor TACH lead (brown connector).

14. Apply the parking brake and block the drive wheels. Place the transaxle **P** for automatic transaxle or **N** for manual transaxle.

15. Start the engine and allow it to run at fast idle (for at least 3 minutes) until the engine cooling fan starts to cycle, indicating that the engine is warm and operating in the closed loop mode.

16. Run the engine at 3000 rpm and adjust the lean mixture screw in small increments (allowing the dwell to stabilize after each adjustment) until the average dwell is 35 degrees. If unable to adjust to this specification, check the carburetor main metering circuit for leaks, restrictions, etc.

NOTE: **It is normal for the dwell to vary about 2½ degrees below and above 35 degrees. The dwell reading may also read 10–15 degrees momentarily due to temporary mixture changes.**

17. Allow the engine to return to idle and adjust the idle speed to 700 rpm, with the cooling fan in the **OFF** cycle.

18. Adjust the idle mixture screw (in the same manner as in step 16) until a dwell (average) of 25 degrees is obtained. The adjustment is very sensitive the final check must be made with the adjusting tool removed. If you are unable to set the dwell to specification, check the carburetor idle system for leaks, restrictions, etc.

19. Raise the engine rpm to 3000 and make sure that the dwell stabilizes and averages 35 degrees at this rpm. Repeat Steps 16–19, if required.

20. Remove the tachometer and dwell meter, reattach the hoses as they were originally and reinstall the items previously removed.

21. Set the idle speed to the figure given on the underhood emissions label.

Removal and Installation

1. Disconnect the negative battery cable. Remove the air cleaner and gasket.

2. Tag and disconnect any electrical connectors. Disconnect the vacuum lines and the fuel supply pipe.

3. Disconnect the accelerator linkage.

4. Disconnect the downshift cable if the vehicle is equipped with automatic transaxle.

5. If the vehicle is equipped with cruise control, disconnect the cruise control linkage.

6. Remove the carburetor attaching bolts. Remove the carburetor. Remove the early fuel evaporation assembly, if equipped.

7. Installation is the reverse of the removal procedure. Start the engine and check for leaks.

FUEL INJECTION SYSTEM

Refer to "Chilton's Electronic Engine Controls Manual" for additional coverage.

Description

THROTTLE BODY INJECTION (TBI)

The Model 300 throttle body injection is used on all 2.5L engines. The throttle body injection resembles a carburetor in appearance, but does away with much of the carburetor's complexity. The throttle body injection system is centrally located on the intake manifold.

The throttle body injection system is completely controlled by the ECM, which monitors engine temperature, throttle position, vehicle speed and several other engines related conditions then updates the injector opening times in relation to the information given by these sensors.

The throttle body is also equipped with an idle air control motor. The idle air control motor operates pintle valve at the side of the throttle body. The idle air control motor also compensates for accessory loads changing engine friction during break-in. The idle air control motor is controlled by the ECM.

The throttle body injection system is made primarily of aluminum and simple in construction. It contains an electrically operated solenoid, a pressure regulator and an idle air control valve. A fuel return fitting, fuel inlet and throttle position sensor are also included in the throttle body injection system.

PORT FUEL INJECTION (PFI)

The port fuel injection system is used on all V6 engines. This system utilizes an injection system where the injectors turn on at every crankshaft revolution. The intake manifold function, like that of a diesel, is used to only let air into the engine. The fuel is injected by separate injectors that are mounted over the intake valve. A fuel rail is attached to the top of the intake manifold and supplies fuel to all injectors. The ECM controls the injector on time so that the correct amount of fuel is metered depending on driving conditions.

The air cleaner is remotely mounted. It is connected to the intake manifold by a flexible air duct. Also mounted between the air cleaner and the intake plenum, are the mass flow sensor and the throttle body. The throttle body design is very simple as it handles only air. It also utilizes an integral idle air control to govern the idle speed and a throttle position sensor.

IDLE SPEED

Adjustment
THROTTLE BODY INJECTION (TBI)

NOTE: This procedure should be performed only when the throttle body parts have been replaced.

1. Remove the air cleaner and gasket.
2. Plug the vacuum port on the TBI marked THERMAC.
3. If the vehicle is equipped with a tamper resistant plug covering the throttle stop screw, the TBI unit must be removed from the engine.
4. Reinstall the throttle body on the engine. Remove the throttle valve cable from the throttle control bracket to allow access to the throttle stop screw.
5. Connect a tachometer to the engine.
6. Start the engine and run it to normal operating temperature.
7. Install tool J-33047 or equivalent into the idle air passage of the throttle body. Be sure that the tool is fully seated and that no air leaks exist.
8. Place the transaxle P for automatic transaxle or N for manual transaxle. Using a No. 20 Torx bit, turn the minimum air screw until the engine rpm is within specification.
9. Stop the engine and remove the special tool.
10. Install the cable on the throttle body.
11. Use RTV sealant to cover the throttle stop screw.

PORT FUEL INJECTION (PFI)

1. Using an awl, pierce the idle stop screw plug (located on the side of the throttle body) and remove it by prying it from the housing.
2. Using a jumper wire, ground the diagnostic lead of the IAC motor.
3. Turn the ignition ON. Do not start the engine. After 30 seconds, disconnect the IAC electrical connector. Remove the diagnostic lead ground lead and start the engine. Allow the system to go to closed loop.
4. Adjust the idle set screw to 550 rpm for the A/T (in D) or 650 rpm for the M/T (N).
5. Turn the ignition OFF and reconnect the IAC motor lead.
6. Using a voltmeter, adjust the TPS to 0.55 ± 0.1 volt and secure the TPS.
7. Recheck the setting, then start the engine and check for proper idle operation.
8. Seal the idle stop screw with silicone sealer.

IDLE MIXTURE

Adjustment

Idle mixture on both the Throttle Body Injection (TBI) and the Port Fuel Injection (PFI) systems is controlled by the ECM.

The ECM monitors information from several sensors to determine how much fuel to give the engine. The fuel is delivered under one of several conditions called "Modes." All modes are controlled by the ECM.

FUEL SYSTEM PRESSURE RELIEF

Procedure
THROTTLE BODY INJECTION (TBI)

1. On a cold engine, remove the fuse marked "Fuel Pump" from the fuse block in the passenger compartment.
2. Crank the engine, engine will start and run until the fuel supply remaining in the fuel lines is exhausted. When the engine stops, engage the starter again for 3.0 seconds to assure dissipation of any remaining pressure.
3. With the ignition OFF, replace the fuel pump fuse.

MULTI-PORT FUEL INJECTION (MPFI)

1. Disconnect the negative battery cable to avoid possible fuel discharge if an accidental attempt is made to start the engine.
2. Loosen the fuel filler cap to relieve the tank pressure.
3. Connect fuel gauge J34730-1 or equavalent to fuel valve. Wrap a shop towel around the fitting while connecting gauge to avoid spillage.
4. Install bleed hose into an approved container and open valve to relieve system pressure.

Fuel Pump

The fuel pump used on all vehicles equipped with fuel injection system is attached to the fuel sending unit located inside the fuel tank.

Removal and Installation

1. Relive the fuel system pressure.
2. Disconnect the negative battery cable.
3. Raise and support the vehicle safely. Drain the fuel tank.
4. Disconnect wiring from the tank.
5. Remove the ground wire retaining screw from under the body.
6. Disconnect all hoses from the tank.
7. Support the tank on a jack and remove the retaining strap nuts.
8. Lower the tank and remove it from the vehicle.
9. Remove the fuel gauge/pump retaining ring using a spanner wrench such as tool J-24187 or equivalent.
10. Remove the gauge unit and the pump.
11. Installation is the reverse of the removal procedure. Always replace the O-ring under the gauge/pump retaining ring.

FUEL INJECTOR

All fuel injectors are serviced as a complete assembly only. Since it is an electrical component, it should not be immersed in any type of cleaner.

NOTE: Always support the fuel rail to avoid damaging other components while removing the injectors.

Removal and Installation
THROTTLE BODY INJECTION

1. Relieve fuel system pressure. Disconnect the negative battery cable to avoid possible fuel discharge if an accidental attempt is made to start the engine.
2. Remove the air cleaner assembly.
3. Squeeze the 2 tabs on the injector electrical connector together and pull straight upward.
4. Remove the fuel meter cover retaining screws. The 2 front

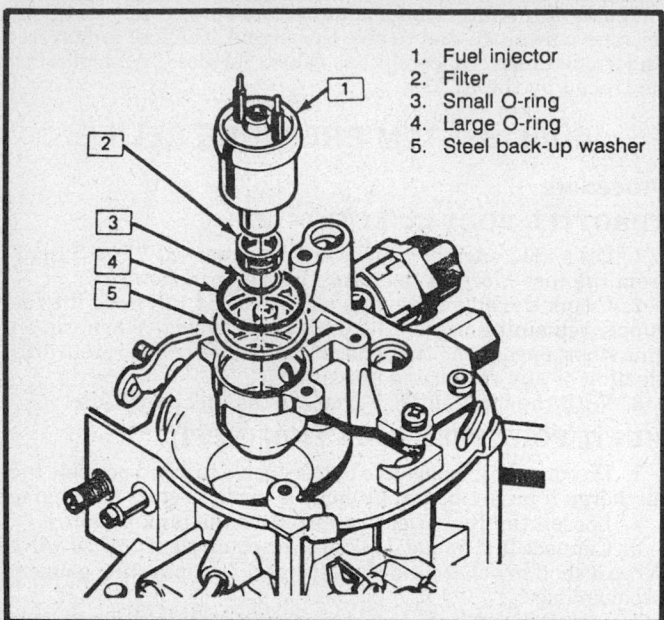

1. Fuel injector
2. Filter
3. Small O-ring
4. Large O-ring
5. Steel back-up washer

Fuel injector components

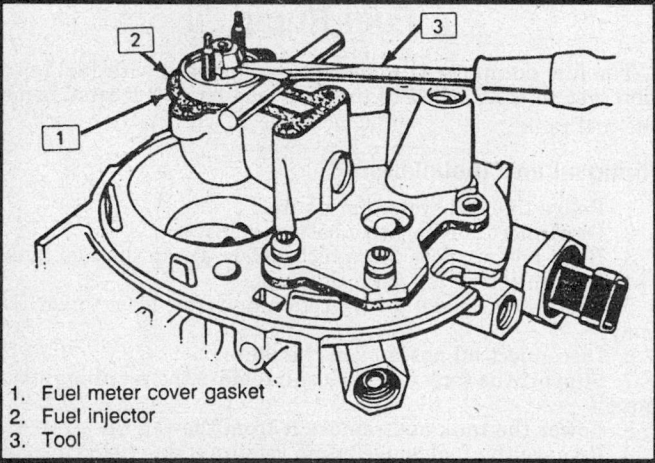

1. Fuel meter cover gasket
2. Fuel injector
3. Tool

Removing the injector—TBI

retaining screws are shorter than the 3 rear retaining screws. Remove the fuel meter cover.

5. With the fuel meter cover gasket in place, use a prying tool and carefully lift the injector until it is free from the fuel meter body.

6. Remove the small O-ring from the injector nozzle end.

Carefully rotate the injector fuel filter back and forth, and remove the filter from the base of the injector.

7. Remove and discard the fuel meter cover gasket. Remove the large O-ring and steel back-up washer from the top counterbore of the fuel meter body injector cavity.

To install:

8. Install the fuel injector nozzle filter on the nozzle end of the fuel injector, with the larger end of the filter facing the injector, so that the filter covers raised rib at the base of the injector.

9. Lubricate the new small O-ring with automatic transmission fluid and push the O-ring on the nozzle end of the injector until it presses against the injector fuel filter.

10. Install the steel backup washer in the top counterbore of the fuel meter body injector cavity.

11. Lubricate the new large O-ring with automatic transmission fluid and install it directly over the backup washer. Be sure the O-ring is seated properly in the cavity and is flush with the top of the fuel meter body casting surface.

12. Install the injector into the cavity, aligning the raised lug on the injector base with cast-in notch in the fuel meter body cavity. Push down on the injector until it is fully seated in the cavity. The electrical terminals of the injector will be approximately parallel to the throttle shaft.

13. Install a new dust seal into the recess on the fuel meter body.

14. Install a new fuel outlet passage gasket on the fuel meter cover and a new cover gasket on the fuel meter body.

15. Install the fuel meter cover, making sure the pressure regulator dust seal and cover gaskets are in place; then, apply a thread locking compound to the threads on the fuel meter cover attaching screws. Install the fuel meter cover attaching screws and lockwashers and torque to 28 inch lbs. (3 Nm). The 2 short screws go to the front of the injector.

MULTI–PORT FUEL INJECTION

1. Relieve fuel system pressure. Disconnect the negative battery cable to avoid possible fuel discharge if an accidental attempt is made to start the engine.

2. Remove the intake manifold plenum.

3. Remove the fuel rail.

4. Remove the injector retaining clips and remove the injectors.

5. Remove the injector O-ring seals from both ends of the injector and discard.

To install:

6. Lubricate the new injector seals with clean engine oil, and install on the injectors.

7. Install new injector retaining clips on the injectors. Position the open end of the clip facing the injector electrical connector.

8. Install the injectors into the fuel rail assembly. Push in far enough to engage the retainer clip with the machined slots on the injector socket.

9. Install the fuel rail assembly and intake manifold plenum.

10. Complete installation by reversing the removal procedure.

EMISSION CONTROL SYSTEM

Refer to "Chilton's Emission Diagnosis and Service Manual" for additional coverage.

1986-90

Catalytic converter
Early fuel evaporation (EFE)
Exhaust gas recirculation (EGR)
Positive crankcase ventilation (PCV)
Thermostatic air cleaner (THERMAC)
Pulse air injection reaction (PAIR)
Electronic spark timing (EST)
Evaporative emission control system (EECS)
Electronic control module (ECM)

Oxygen sensor
Mixture control solenoid (MCS)
Vacuum regulator valve (VRV)
Exhaust pressure regulator valve (EPRV)
Response vacuum reducer (VMV)
Idle air bleed valve
Crankcase depression regulator valve (diesel only)
Transmission converter clutch (TCC)
Shift light control (manual transmissions only)
Electric cooling fan control
A/C wide open throttle control (WOT)
Electronic spark control (ESC)

CLEARING TROUBLE CODES

Procedure

When the electronic control module finds a problem, the "CHECK ENGINE"/"SERVICE ENGINE SOON" light will come on and a trouble code will be recorded in the electronic control module memory. If the problem is not constant, the light will go out after approximately 10 seconds.

NOTE: **Disconnecting the negative battery cable on some vehicles may interfere with the functions of the on board computer systems and may require the computer to undergo a relearning process, once the negative battery cable is reconnected.**

Engine Assembly

Removal and Installation

2.5L ENGINE

With Manual Transaxle

1. Relieve the fuel system pressure. Disconnect the negative battery cable.
2. Scribe reference marks at the hood supports and remove the hood. Install covers on both fenders.
3. Raise and support the vehicle safely. Remove front mount-to-cradle nuts.
4. Remove forward exhaust pipe.
5. Remove starter assembly.
6. Remove flywheel inspection cover.
7. Lower the vehicle.
8. Remove the air cleaner assembly.
9. Remove all bellhousing retaining bolts.
10. Remove forward torque reaction rod from engine and core support.
11. If equipped with air conditioning, remove the air conditioning belt and compressor and position to the side.
12. Remove emission hoses at canister.
13. Remove power steering hose, if equipped.
14. Remove vacuum hoses and electrical connectors at solenoid.
15. Remove heater blower motor.
16. Disconnect throttle cable.
17. Drain cooling system.
18. Disconnect heater hose.
19. Disconnect engine harness at bulkhead connector.
20. Install an engine lift support tool and partially hoist the engine. Remove heater hose at intake manifold and disconnect fuel line.
21. Completely remove the engine from the vehicle.
To install:
22. Partially lower the engine into the vehicle. Connect the heater hose and fuel line.
23. Lower the engine completely and install the 4 upper bell housing retaining bolts.
24. Raise and support the vehicle safely.
25. Install the 2 lower bell housing retaining bolts.
26. Install the front mount-to-cradle nuts.
27. Install the starter assembly and flywheel inspection cover.
28. Install the exhaust pipe and lower the vehicle.
29. Complete installation by reversing the removal procedure.
30. After the engine has been completely installed. Fill the cooling system, connect the negative battery cable, start the engine and check for leaks.

With Automatic Transaxle

1. Relieve the fuel system pressure. Disconnect the negative battery cable.

ENGINE

The trouble code will stay in the electronic control module memory until the battery voltage to the module is discontinued. Disconnecting the battery pigtail harness from the positive battery terminal for 10 seconds with the ignition **OFF**, will clear all stored trouble codes.

NOTE: **To prevent damage to the electronic control module, the key must be OFF when disconnecting or reconnecting the power to the module.**

2. Scribe reference marks at the hood supports and remove the hood. Install covers on both fenders.
3. Drain the cooling system. Remove the air cleaner assembly and preheat tube.
4. Disconnect engine harness connector.
5. Disconnect all external vacuum hose connections.
6. Remove throttle and transaxle linkage at EFI assembly and intake manifold.
7. Remove upper radiator hose.
8. If equipped with air conditioning, remove the air conditioning compressor from mounting brackets and set aside. Do not discharge the air conditioning system.
9. Remove front engine strut assembly.
10. Disconnect heater hoses.
11. Raise the vehicle and support it safely. Remove transaxle to engine bolts leaving the upper 2 bolts in place.
12. Remove front mount-to-cradle nuts.
13. Remove forward exhaust pipe.
14. Remove flywheel inspection cover and remove starter motor.
15. Remove torque converter to flywheel bolts.
16. Remove power steering pump and bracket with hoses attached and set aside.
17. Remove lower radiator hose.
18. Remove the 2 rear transaxle support bracket bolts.
19. Remove fuel supply line at fuel filter.
20. Using a floor jack and a block of wood placed under the transaxle, raise engine and transaxle until engine front mount studs clear cradle.
21. Connect engine lift equipment and put tension on engine.
22. Remove the 2 remaining transaxle bolts.
23. Slide engine forward and remove from the vehicle.
To install:
24. Position the engine inside the vehicle aligning with the transaxle bell housing.
25. With the engine supported by the lifting tool, install the 2 upper bell housing bolts. Do not lower the engine while the jack is supporting the transaxle.
26. Remove the transaxle support jack and lower the engine onto the engine mounts. Remove the engine lift tool.
27. Raise the vehicle and install the front mount-to-chassis nuts.
28. Complete installation by reversing the removal procedure. After the engine has been completely installed. Fill the cooling system, connect the negative battery cable, start the engine and check for leaks.

2.8L AND 3.1L ENGINES

1. On vehicles equipped with fuel injection, relieve the fuel system pressure.
2. Disconnect the negative battery cable. Scribe reference marks at the hood supports and remove the hood. Install covers on both fenders.
3. On carbureted equipped vehicles, remove the air cleaner assembly.
4. On fuel injected equipped vehicles, remove the airflow tube at the air cleaner and throttle valve.
5. Drain the cooling system.
6. Disconnect vacuum hoses to all non-engine mounted components.

7. Disconnect the accelerator linkage and T.V. cable. Disconnect the cruise control cable, if equipped.

8. Disconnect the engine harness connector from the ECM and pull the connector through the front of dash. Disconnect the engine harness from the junction block at the dash panel.

9. Remove the engine strut bracket from the radiator support and position aside, as required.

10. Disconnect the radiator hoses from radiator and heater hoses from engine. Disconnect and plug the transaxle cooler lines.

11. On fuel injected equipped vehicles, remove the serpentine belt cover and belt.

12. On vehicles with the air conditioning compressor mounted on the upper portion of the engine, remove the AIR pump and bracket. Then, remove the air conditioning compressor from the mounting bracket and position aside.

13. If equipped, remove power steering pump from engine and set it aside.

14. Disconnect and plug the fuel lines.

15. Disconnect the EGR at the exhaust, as required.

16. Raise and support the vehicle safely.

17. On vehicles with the air conditioning compressor mounted on the lower portion of the engine, remove the air conditioning compressor from the engine. Do not discharge the air conditioning system.

18. Remove the engine front mount-to-cradle and mount-to-engine bracket retaining nuts, as required.

19. Disconnect and tag all electrical wiring at the starter. Remove the starter retaining bolts and remove the starter.

20. On vehicles equipped with automatic transaxle, remove the transaxle inspection cover and disconnect the torque converter from the flex plate.

21. On carbureted equipped vehicles, remove the crankshaft lower pulley and remove all belts.

22. Disconnect the exhaust pipe.

23. Remove the 1 transaxle-to-engine bolt from the back side of the engine.

24. Disconnect the power steering cut-off switch, if equipped.

25. Lower the vehicle.

26. Remove the exhaust crossover pipe.

27. Remove the remaining transaxle-to-engine bolts.

28. Support the transaxle by positioning a floor jack and a block of wood under the transaxle. Install an engine lift tool and remove the engine from the vehicle.

To install:

29. Position the engine in the vehicle while aligning the transaxle. Install the transaxle-to-engine bolts. Torque the attaching bolts to 55 ft. lbs. (75 Nm).

30. Position the front engine mount studs in the cradle and engine bracket.

31. Remove the engine lift tool. Raise and support the vehicle safely.

32. Install the engine mount retaining nuts.

33. Complete installation by reversing the removal procedure. After the engine has been completely installed. Fill the cooling system, connect the negative battery cable, start the engine and check for leaks.

3.0L AND 3.8L ENGINES

1. Disconnect the negative battery cable. Scribe reference marks at the hood supports and remove the hood. Install covers on both fenders.

2. Remove the air cleaner assembly and drain the cooling system.

3. Disconnect vacuum hoses to all non-engine mounted components.

4. Disconnect the detent cable and accelerator linkage.

5. Disconnect the engine electrical harness and ground strap.

6. Disconnect the heater hoses from the engine and radiator

hoses from the radiator. Disconnect the transaxle cooler lines, if equipped.

7. Remove the power steering pump and bracket assembly.

8. Raise and support the vehicle safely.

9. Disconnect the exhaust pipe from the manifold.

10. Disconnect the fuel lines.

11. Remove the engine front mount to cradle retaining nuts.

12. Disconnect and tag all electrical wiring at the starter. Remove the starter retaining bolts and remove the starter.

13. On vehicles equipped with automatic transaxle, remove the flex plate cover and disconnect the flex plate from the torque converter.

14. Remove the retaining bolts from the transaxle rear support bracket.

15. Lower the vehicle and place a support under the transaxle rear extension.

16. Remove the engine strut bracket from the radiator support and position aside.

17. Remove the transaxle-to-engine retaining bolts.

18. If equipped with air conditioning, remove the air conditioning compressor from the mounting bracket and lay aside.

19. Install an engine lift tool and remove the engine from the vehicle.

To install:

20. Position the engine in the vehicle and align the engine front mount studs. Align the transaxle and install the transaxle-to-engine retaining bolts.

21. Remove the engine lift tool.

22. Install the air conditioning compressor on the mounting bracket, as required.

23. Raise the vehicle. Install the retaining bolts to the transaxle rear support bracket.

24. Complete installation by reversing the removal procedure. After the engine has been completely installed. Fill the cooling system, connect the negative battery cable, start the engine and check for leaks.

3.3L ENGINE

1. Disconnect the negative battery cable. Scribe reference marks at the hood supports and remove the hood. Install covers on both fenders.

2. Relieve the fuel system pressure.

3. Disconnect the negative battery cable.

4. Drain the cooling system. Disconnect the radiator and heater hoses. Disconnect and plug the transaxle cooler lines.

5. Remove the upper engine strut and engine cooling fan.

6. Remove the intake duct from the throttle body. Disconnect vacuum hosing to all non-engine mounted components. Disconnect all electrical connections.

7. Remove the cable bracket and cables from the throttle body.

8. Remove the serpentine belt. Remove the power steering pump and locate to the side.

9. Remove the upper transaxle to engine retaining bolts.

10. Raise and support the vehicle safely.

11. Remove the air conditioning compressor and locate to the side.

12. Remove the engine mount to frame nuts, flywheel dust cover and flywheel to converter bolts.

13. Remove the lower engine to transaxle bolts. 1 bolt is located behind the transaxle case and engine block.

14. Lower the vehicle. Install an engine lift tool and remove the engine from the vehicle.

15. Installation is the reverse of the removal procedure. After the engine has been completely installed. Fill the cooling system, connect the negative battery cable, start the engine and check for leaks.

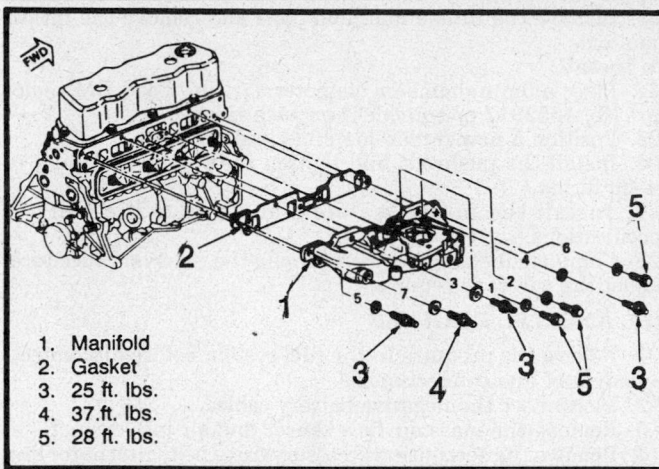

1. Manifold
2. Gasket
3. 25 ft. lbs.
4. 37 ft. lbs.
5. 28 ft. lbs.

1986 intake manifold torque sequence – 2.5L engine

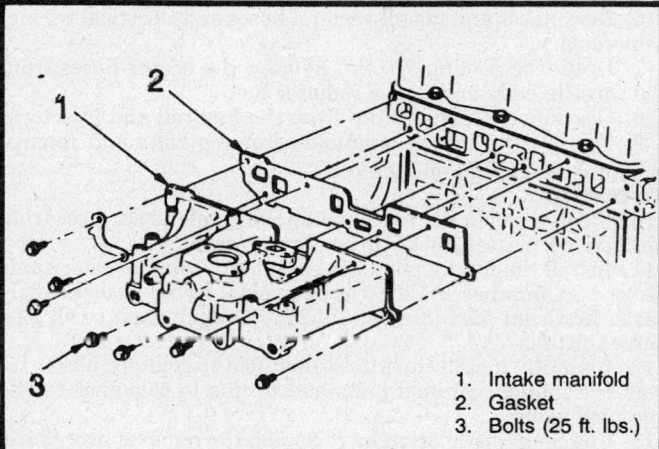

1. Intake manifold
2. Gasket
3. Bolts (25 ft. lbs.)

1987–90 intake manifold assembly – 2.5L engine

Engine Mounts

Removal and Installation

1. Disconnect the negative battery cable.
2. Raise and support the vehicle safely.
3. Using a suitable tool, support the engine and remove the engine mounting bracket nuts.
4. Raise the engine slightly until the engine mount is free from the vehicle chassis.
5. Remove the nuts holding the engine mount to the frame.
6. Remove the engine mounts and discard.
7. Installation is the reverse of the removal procedure.

Intake Manifold

Removal and Installation

2.5L ENGINE

1. Relieve the pressure in the fuel system before disconnecting any fuel line connections.
2. Disconnect the negative battery cable.
3. Remove the air cleaner and the PCV valve.
4. Drain the cooling system into a clean container.
5. Disconnect the fuel and vacuum lines and the electrical connections.
6. Disconnect the throttle linkage at the EFI unit. Disconnect the transaxle downshift linkage and cruise control linkage.

7. Remove the bell crank and the throttle linkage. Position to the side for clearance.
8. Remove the heater hose at the intake manifold.
9. Remove the pulse air check valve bracket from the manifold, as required.
10. Remove the manifold attaching bolts and remove the manifold.

To install:

11. Clean the cylinder head and intake manifold surfaces from any foreign matter, nicks or heavy scratches.
12. Install the intake manifold with a new gasket and tighten the retaining bolts in sequence to the specified torque value.
13. Complete installation by reversing the removal procedure.

2.8L ENGINE
WITH CARBURETOR

1. Disconnect the negative battery cable. Remove the rocker covers.
2. Drain the cooling system.
3. If equipped, remove the AIR pump and bracket.
4. Remove the distributor cap. Mark the position of the ignition rotor in relation to the distributor body, and remove the distributor. Do not crank the engine with the distributor removed.
5. Remove the heater and radiator hoses from the intake manifold.
6. Remove the power brake vacuum hose.
7. Disconnect and label the vacuum hoses. Remove the EFE pipe from the rear of the manifold.
8. Remove the carburetor linkage. Disconnect and plug the fuel line.
9. Remove the manifold retaining bolts and nuts.
10. Remove the intake manifold. Remove and discard the gaskets, and scrape off the old silicone seal from the front and rear ridges.

To install:

NOTE: The gaskets are marked for right and left side installation; do not interchange them.

11. Clean the sealing surface of the engine block and apply a $^3/_{16}$ in. bead of silicone sealer to each ridge.
12. Install the new gaskets onto the heads. The gaskets will have to be cut slightly to fit past the center pushrods. Do not cut any more material than necessary. Hold the gaskets in place by extending the ridge bead of sealer ¼ in. onto the gasket ends.
13. Install the intake manifold. The area between the ridges

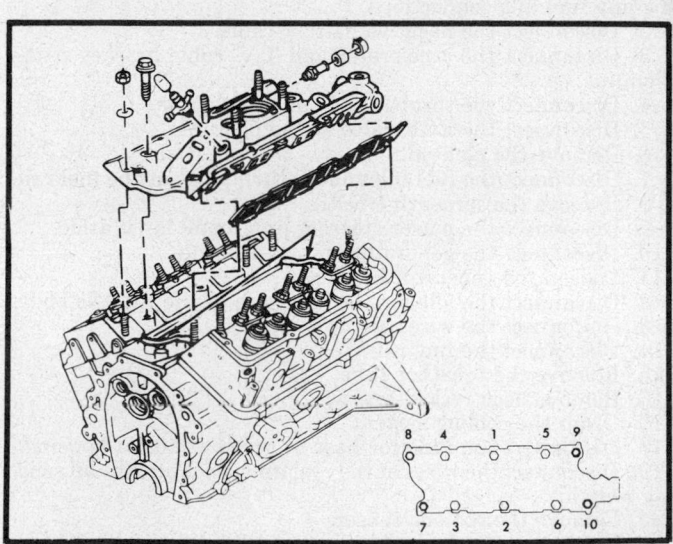

1986 intake manifold torque sequence – 2.8L engine

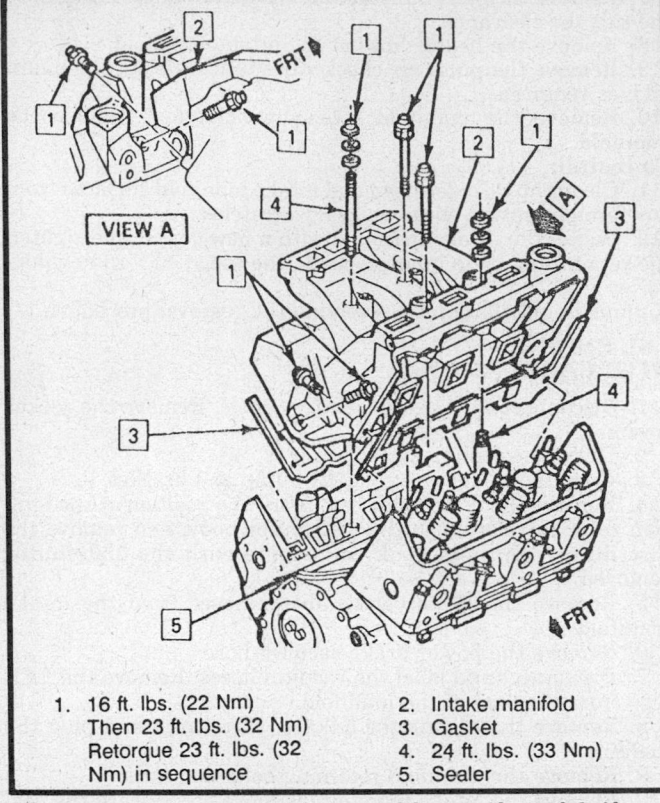

1. 16 ft. lbs. (22 Nm) Then 23 ft. lbs. (32 Nm) Retorque 23 ft. lbs. (32 Nm) in sequence	2. Intake manifold 3. Gasket 4. 24 ft. lbs. (33 Nm) 5. Sealer

1987–90 Intake manifold assembly—2.8L and 3.1L engine

and the manifold should be completely sealed.

14. Install the retaining bolts and nuts, and tighten in sequence to 23 ft. lbs. Do not overtighten; the manifold is made from aluminum, and can be warped or cracked with excessive force.

15. Complete installation by reversing the removal procedure. Adjust the valve and ignition timing, as required.

2.8L AND 3.1L ENGINES WITH MFI

1. Relieve the pressure in the fuel system before disconnecting any fuel line connections.
2. Disconnect the negative battery cable.
3. Disconnect the accelerator and T.V. cable bracket at the plenum.
4. Disconnect the throttle body at the plenum.
5. Disconnect the EGR valve at the plenum.
6. Remove the plenum.
7. Disconnect the fuel inlet and return pipes at the fuel rail.
8. Remove the serpentine belt.
9. Disconnect the power steering pump and lay it aside.
10. Disconnect the generator and lay it aside.
11. Loosen the generator bracket.
12. Disconnect the idle air vacuum hose at the throttle body.
13. Disconnect the wires at the injectors.
14. Disconnect the fuel rail.
15. Remove the breather tube.
16. Remove both rocker covers.
17. Drain the cooling system.
18. Disconnect the radiator hose at the thermostat housing.
19. Disconnect the wires at the coolant sensor and the oil sending switch.
20. Remove the coolant sensor.
21. Disconnect the bypass hose at the fill neck and head.
22. Loosen the rocker arms and remove the pushrods.

23. Remove the intake manifold bolts and remove the intake manifold.

To install:

24. Place a 5mm diameter diameter ($^3/_{16}$ in.) bead GM sealer part No. 1052917 or equvalent on each ridge.
25. Position a new intake manifold gasket.
26. Install the pushrods and tighten the rocker arm nuts to 14–20 ft. lbs.
27. Install the intake manifold and torque the bolts to specifications.
28. Complete installation by reversing the removal procedure. Adjust the valve, as required.

3.0L AND 3.8L ENGINES

1. Relieve the pressure in the fuel system before disconnecting any fuel line connections.
2. Disconnect the negative battery cable.
3. Remove the mass air flow sensor and air intake duct.
4. Remove the serpentine accessory drive belt, alternator and bracket.
5. Remove the ignition coil module, T.V. cable, throttle cable and cruise control cable.
6. Disconnect and tag all vacuum hoses and electrical wiring, as necessary.
7. Drain the cooling system. Remove the heater hoses from the throttle body and upper radiator hose.
8. Disconnect the fuel lines from the fuel rail and injectors.
9. Remove the intake manifold retaining bolts and remove the intake manifold and gasket.

To install:

10. Clean the cylinder head and intake manifold surfaces from any foreign matter, nicks or heavy scratches.
11. Install the intake manifold gasket and rubber seals. Apply sealer part number 1050026 or equivalent to the gasket. Apply sealer/lubricant part number 1052080 or equivalent to all pipe thread fitting.
12. Carefully install the intake manifold to cylinder block. Install the intake manifold bolts and torque in sequence to the specified value.
13. Complete installation by reversing the removal procedure.

3.3L ENGINE

1. Relieve the pressure in the fuel system before disconnecting any fuel line connections.
2. Disconnect the negative battery cable.
3. Drain the cooling system.
4. Remove the serpentine belt, alternator and braces and power steering pump braces.
5. Remove the coolant bypass hose, heater pipe and upper radiator hose.

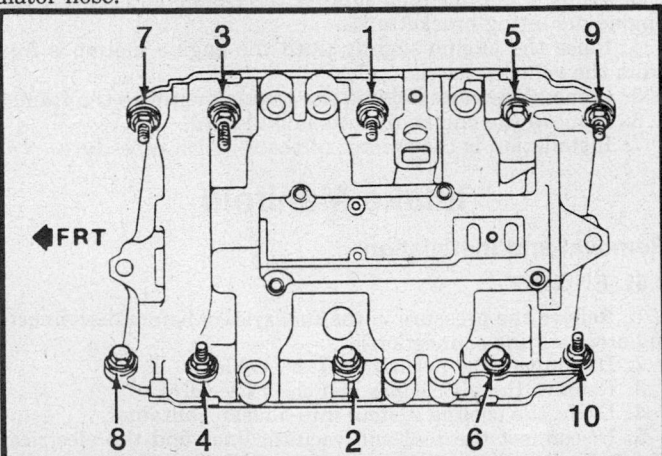

1987–90 intake manifold torque sequence—3.0L, 3.3L and 3.8L engines

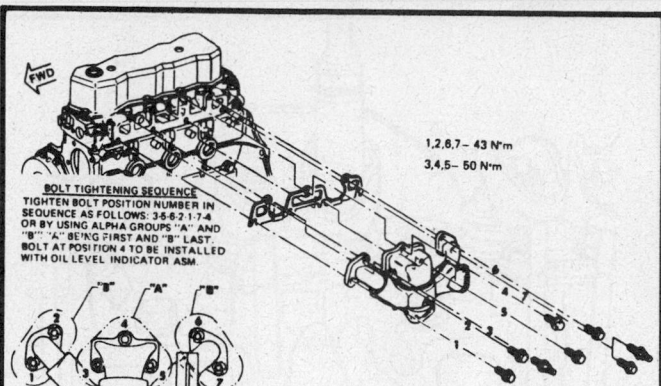

1986–90 exhaust manifold assembly—2.5L engine

6. Remove the air inlet duct, throttle cable bracket and cables.

7. Disconnect and tag all vacuum hoses and electrical connectors, as necessary.

8. Remove the fuel rail, vapor canister purge line and heater hose from the throttle body.

9. Remove the intake manifold retaining bolts and intake manifold.

To install:

10. Clean the cylinder head and intake manifold surfaces from any foreign matter, nicks or heavy scratches.

11. Apply sealer part number 12345336 or equivalent to the ends of the manifold seals. Clean the intake manifold bolts and bolt holes. Apply thread lock compound part number 1052624 or equivalent to the intake manifold bolt threads before assembly.

12. Install the new gasket and intake manifold. Tighten the intake manifold bolts twice to 88 inch lbs. (10 Nm) in the proper sequence.

13. Complete installation by reversing the removal procedure.

Exhaust Manifold

Removal and Installation

2.5L ENGINE

1. Disconnect the negative battery cable. Remove the air cleaner and the EFI preheat tube.

2. Remove the manifold strut bolts from the radiator support panel and the cylinder head.

3. Remove the A/C compressor bracket to one side. Do not disconnect any of the refrigerant lines.

4. If necessary, remove the dipstick tube attaching bolt, and the engine mount bracket from the cylinder head.

5. Raise the vehicle and support safely. Disconnect the exhaust pipe from the manifold.

6. Remove the manifold attaching bolts and remove the manifold.

7. Install the exhaust manifold and gasket to the cylinder head. Torque all bolts in sequence to the specified torque value.

8. Complete installation by reversing the removal procedure.

2.8L AND 3.1L ENGINES

Left Side

1. Disconnect the negative battery cable.

2. On carbureted equipped vehicles, remove the air cleaner and the carburetor heat stove pipe.

3. Remove the air supply plumbing from the exhaust manifold, as required.

4. Remove the coolant recovery bottle, if necessary.

5. Remove the serpentine belt cover and belt, as required.

6. Remove the air conditioning compressor and lay aside, if necessary.

7. Remove the right side torque strut, air conditioning and torque strut mounting bracket, as required.

8. On fuel injected equipped vehicles, remove the heat shield.

9. Remove the exhaust crossover pipe at the manifold.

10. Remove the exhaust manifold retaining bolts and manifold.

11. Installation is the reverse of the removal procedure.

Right Side

1. Disconnect the negative battery cable.

2. On carbureted equipped vehicles, remove the air cleaner and AIR bracket at the exhaust flange.

3. Raise and support the vehicle safely.

4. Disconnect the exhaust pipe and lower the vehicle.

5. On fuel injected equipped vehicles, remove the air cleaner assembly, breather, mass air flow sensor and heatshield.

6. Remove the crossover at the manifold.

7. Remove the accelerator and T.V. cables and brackets, as required.

8. Remove the exhaust manifold retaining bolts and remove the manifold.

9. Installation is the reverse of the removal procedure.

3.0L AND 3.8L ENGINES

Left Side

1. Disconnect the battery ground.

2. Unbolt and remove the crossover pipe.

3. Remove the upper engine support strut.

4. Unbolt and remove the manifold.

5. Installation is the reverse of the removal procedure.

Right Side

1. Disconnect the negative battery cable.

2. Remove the pinch bolt at the steering gear intermediate shaft and separate the intermediate shaft from the stub shaft.

NOTE: Failure to disconnect the intermediate shaft from the rack and pinion stub shaft can result in damage to the steering gear and/or intermediate shaft. This damage can cause loss of steering control which could result in a vehicle crash with possible bodily injury.

3. Raise and support the vehicle safely.

4. Remove the exhaust pipe from the manifold.

5. Lower the vehicle.

6. Remove the upper engine support strut.

7. Place a floor jack under the front crossmember and take up the weight of the vehicle.

8. Remove the 2 front body mount bolts along with their cushions and retainers.

9. Remove the cushions from the bolts and thread the bolts and their retainers a minimum of 3 turns into the cradle cage nuts so that the bolts serve to hold the cradle and prevent movement.

10. Lower the floor jack so that the crossmember contacts the body mount bolt retainers. Check for any hose or wire interference problems.

11. Remove the alternator, disconnect the power steering pump and remove its bracket.

12. Disconnect the manifold from the crossover pipe.

13. Remove the exhaust manifold retaining bolts and remove the manifold.

14. Installation is the reverse of the removal procedure.

3.3L ENGINE

Left Side

1. Disconnect the negative battery cable.

2. Remove the air cleaner inlet ducting. Remove the spark plug wires.

3. Remove the 2 bolts attaching the exhaust crossover pipe to the manifold.

4. Remove the engine lift hook, manifold heat shield and oil level indicator.

5. Remove the exhaust manifold retaining bolts and remove the manifold.

6. Installation is the reverse of the removal procedure.

RIGHT SIDE

1. Disconnect the negative battery cable.

2. Remove the spark plug wires, oxygen sensor connector, throttle cable bracket and cables.

3. Remove the brake booster hose from the manifold.

4. Remove the 2 bolts attaching the exhaust crossover pipe to the manifold.

5. Remove the exhaust pipe to manifold bolts, engine lift hook and transaxle oil level indicator tube.

6. Remove the manifold heat shield. Remove the exhaust manifold retaining bolts and remove the manifold.

7. Installation is the reverse of the removal procedure.

Valve System

Adjustment
EXCEPT 2.8L ENGINE

Hydraulic valve lifters keep all parts of the valve train in constant contact and adjust automatically to maintain zero lash under all conditions.

2.8L ENGINE

Anytime the valve train has been disturbed, the valve lash must be readjusted.

1. Crank the engine until the timing mark on the damper lines up with the **0** mark on the timing scale. Both valves in the No. 1 cylinder should be closed. If the valves are moving as the timing marks align, the engine is in the No. 4 firing position. Turn the crankshaft one more revolution. With the engine in the No. 1 firing position, adjust the following valves: exhaust—1, 2, 3 and intake—1, 5, 6.

2. Back out the adjusting nut until lash is felt at the pushrod. Then, turn in the adjusting nut until all lash is removed. This can be determine by rotating the pushrod while turning the adjusting nut. When all lash has been removed, turn the adjusting nut in 1½ additional turns to center the lifter plunger.

3. Rotate the crankshaft one full revolution, until the timing mark on the damper lines up with the **0** mark on the timing scale once again. This is the No. 4 firing position. Adjust the following valves: exhaust—4, 5, 6 and intake—2, 3, 4.

VALVE LIFTERS

Removal and Installation
2.5L ENGINE

1. Disconnect the negative battery cable.

2. Remove the intake manifold and pushrod cover.

3. Loosen the rocker arms and rotate to clear the pushrods.

4. Remove the pushrods, retainer and guide.

5. Remove the lifters. Keep all components separated so they may be reinstalled in the same location.

To install:

6. Lubricate the lifters with engine oil and install the lifters in their bore.

7. Install the guides, retainers and pushrods.

8. With the lifter on the base circle of the camshaft, tighten the rocker arm bolts to 24 ft. lbs. (32 Nm).

9. Complete installation by reversing the removal procedure.

EXCEPT 2.5L ENGINE

1. Disconnect the negative battery cable.

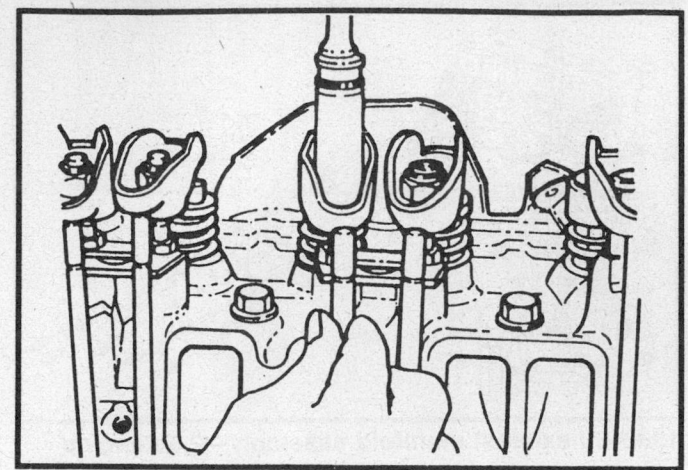

Adjusting valve lash—2.8L engine

2. Drain the cooling system.

3. Remove the valve cover and the intake manifold.

4. If the engine is equipped with individual rocker arms, loosen the rocker arm adjusting nut and rotate the arm so as to clear the pushrod.

5. If the engine is equipped with a rocker shaft assembly, remove the rocker shaft retaining bolts/nuts and remove the shaft assembly.

NOTE: Be sure to keep all valve train parts in order so they may be reinstalled in their original locations and with the same mating surfaces as when removed.

6. Remove the pushrods and valve lifters using tool J3049 or equivalent.

7. Installation is the reverse of the removal procedure. Lubricate the bearing surfaces with Molykote® or its equivalent. Adjust the valves, as required.

VALVE ROCKER SHAFT/ARM ASSEMBLY

Removal and Installation
2.5L ENGINE

1. Relieve pressure in the fuel system before disconnecting any fuel lines.

2. Disconnect the negative battery cable.

3. Remove the valve cover.

4. If only the pushrod is being removed, loosen the rocker arm bolt and swing the rocker arm aside.

5. Remove the rocker arm nut and ball.

6. Lift the rocker arm off the stud, keeping rocker arms in order for installation.

7. Installation is the reverse of the removal procedure.

2.8L AND 3.1L ENGINES

1. Relieve pressure in the fuel system before disconnecting any fuel lines.

2. Disconnect the negative battery cable. Remove the valve covers.

3. Remove the rocker arm nuts, pivot balls, rocker arms and pushrods. Keep all components separated so they may be reinstalled in the same location.

NOTE: The intake and exhaust pushrods are of different lengths.

To install:

4. Install the pushrods in their original location. Be sure they are seated in the lifter.

5. Coat the bearing surfaces of the rocker arms and pivots balls with Molykote of equivalent.

6. On engine equipped with adjustable lifters, install the rocker arms and pivot balls. Loosely retain with the rocker arms nuts until the valve lash is eliminated.

7. On engine equipped with non-adjustable lifters, install the pushrods. Make sure the lower ends of the pushrods are in the lifter seats. Install the rocker arm nuts and torque the nuts to 14–20 ft. lbs. (20–27 Nm).

8. Complete installation by reversing the removal procedure.

9. Adjust valve lash, as required.

3.0L AND 3.8L ENGINES

1. Relieve pressure in the fuel system before disconnecting any fuel lines.

2. Disconnect the negative battery cable. Remove the valve covers.

3. Remove the rocker arm shaft(s). Place the shaft on a clean surface.

4. Remove the nylon rocker arm retainers. A pair of slip joint pliers is good for this.

5. Slide the rocker arms off the shaft and inspect them for wear or damage. Keep them in order.

NOTE: If it become necessary to replace 1 or more rocker arms, it must be noted that all service rocker arms are stamped R for right and L for left. Be sure the rocker arms are installed on the rocker arm shaft in the correct sequence.

6. Installation is the reverse of the removal procedure.

3.3L ENGINE

1. Relieve pressure in the fuel system before disconnecting any fuel lines. Disconnect the negative battery cable.

2. Remove the valve covers.

3. Remove the rocker arm bolts, pivots, and rocker arms assembly. Keep all components separated so they may be reinstalled in the same location.

4. Installation is the reverse of the removal procedure.

Cylinder Head

Removal and Installation

2.5L ENGINE

1. Relieve the pressure in the fuel system before disconnecting any fuel line connections.

2. Disconnect the negative battery cable.

3. Drain the cooling system. Remove the air cleaner and the oil level indicator tube.

4. Disconnect the throttle linkage and fuel lines.

5. Disconnect the oxygen sensor connector. Remove the intake and exhaust manifolds.

6. Remove the alternator bracket to cylinder head bolts, as required.

7. If equipped with air conditioning, remove the A/C compressor bracket bolts and position the compressor aside. Do not disconnect any of the refrigerant lines.

8. Disconnect and tag all vacuum and electrical connections from the cylinder head.

9. Disconnect the radiator hoses and engine strut rod bolt from the upper support.

10. Remove the power steering pump bracket, if top mounted.

11. Remove the rocker arm cover, rocker arms, and pushrods.

12. Remove the cylinder head bolts and remove the cylinder head from the engine.

To install:

13. Clean the cylinder head and block from any foreign matter, nicks or heavy scratches. Clean the cylinder head bolt threads and threads in the cylinder block.

14. Position the new cylinder head gasket over the dowel pins.

15. Carefully guide the cylinder head into place. Coat the cylinder head bolts with sealing compound and install finger tight.

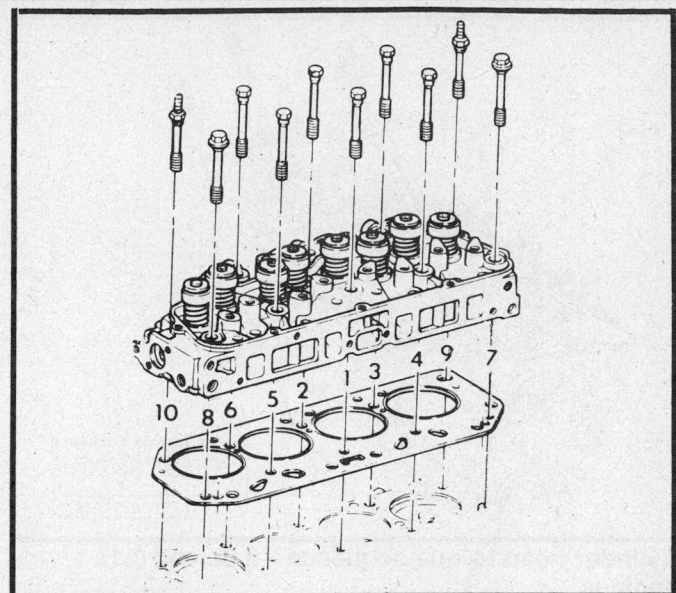

Cylinder head torque sequence—2.5L engine

16. On 1986 vehicles, tighten the bolts in sequence, in 3 equal steps to the specified torque.

17. On 1987 and later vehicles, torque the cylinder head bolts as follows:

   a. Torque the cylinder head bolts gradually to 25 ft.lbs in the proper sequence.

   b. Torque all bolts except No. 9 in sequence again to 22 ft. lbs. Torque No. 9 to 29 ft. lbs.

   c. Repeat sequence. Turn all bolts, except No. 9, 120 degrees (2 flats). Turn No. 9 a quarter turn (90 degrees).

18. Complete installation by reversing the removal procedure.

2.8L AND 3.1L ENGINES

Left Side

1. If the vehicle is equipped with fuel injection, relieve the pressure in the fuel system before disconnecting any fuel line connections.

2. Disconnect the negative battery cable. Raise the vehicle and support it safely.

3. Drain the cylinder block and lower the vehicle.

4. Remove the oil level indicator tube, rocker arm cover, intake manifold and plenum, as required.

5. Remove the exhaust crossover, generator bracket, AIR pump and brackets.

6. Disconnect and tag all electrical wiring and vacuum hoses that may interfere with the removal of the left cylinder head.

7. Loosen the rocker arm until the pushrods can be removed. Remove the pushrods. Keep the pushrods in the same order as removed.

8. Remove the cylinder head bolts. Remove the cylinder head. Do not pry on the head to loosen it.

To install:

9. Clean the cylinder head and block from any foreign matter, nicks or heavy scratches. Clean the cylinder head bolt threads and threads in the cylinder block.

10. Position the new cylinder head gasket over the dowel pins with the words "This Side Up" facing upwards. Carefully guide the cylinder head into place. On 1986 vehicles, coat the cylinder head bolts with sealing compound and tighten them in sequence to the proper specifications. Install the pushrods and loosely retain with the rocker arms. Make sure the lower ends of the pushrods are in the lifter seats.

11. On 1987–90 vehicles, install the pushrods. Make sure the lower ends of the pushrods are in the lifter seats. Install the

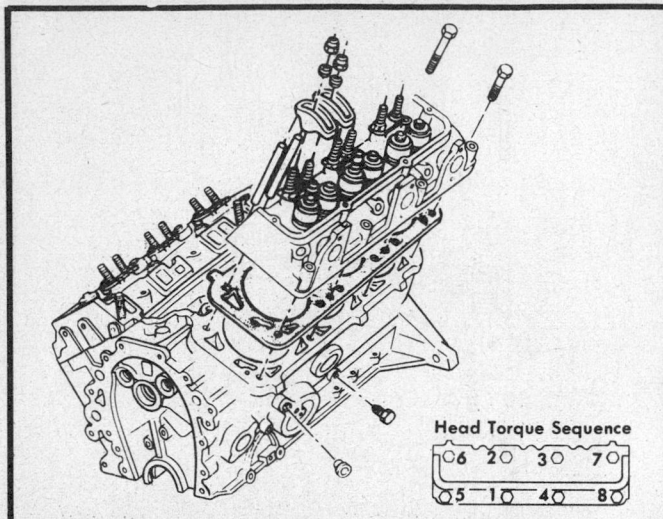

Cylinder head torque sequence — 2.8L and 3.1L engines

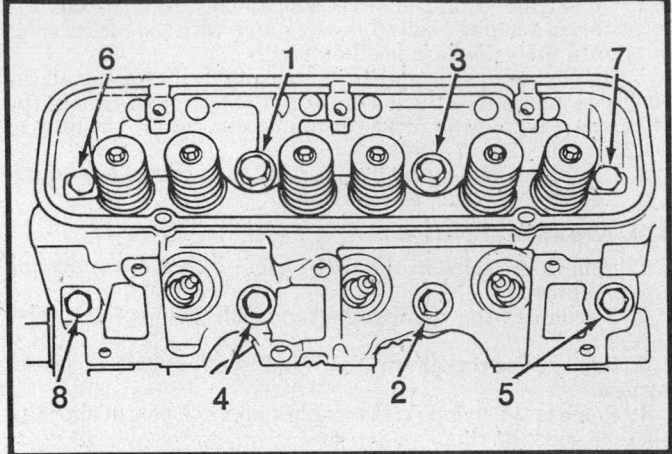

Cylinder head torque sequence — 3.0L, 3.3L and 3.8L engines

rocker arm nuts and torque the nuts to 14–20 ft. lbs. (20–27 Nm).

12. Install the intake manifold.

13. Complete installation by reversing the removal procedure.

14. Adjust the valve lash, as required.

Right Side

1. If the vehicle is equipped with fuel injection, relieve the pressure in the fuel system before disconnecting any fuel line connections.

2. Disconnect the negative battery cable. Raise the vehicle and support it safely.

3. Drain the cylinder block and lower the vehicle.

4. If equipped, removes the cruise control servo bracket, the air management valve and hose, and the intake manifold.

5. Remove the exhaust pipe at crossover, crossover and heat shield, as required.

6. Disconnect and tag all electrical wiring and vacuum hoses that may interfere with the removal of the right cylinder head.

8. Remove the rocker cover. Loosen the rocker arm nuts and remove the pushrods. Keep the pushrods in the order in which they were removed.

9. Remove the cylinder head bolts. Remove the cylinder head. Do not pry on the head to loosen it.

To install:

10. Clean the cylinder head and block from any foreign matter, nicks or heavy scratches. Clean the cylinder head bolt threads and threads in the cylinder block.

11. Position the new cylinder head gasket over the dowel pins with the words "This Side Up" facing upwards. Carefully guide the cylinder head into place. On 1986 vehicles, coat the cylinder head bolts with sealing compound and tighten them in sequence to the proper specifications. Install the pushrods and loosely retain with the rocker arms. Make sure the lower ends of the pushrods are in the lifter seats.

12. On 1987–90 vehicles, install the pushrods. Make sure the lower ends of the pushrods are in the lifter seats. Install the rocker arm nuts and torque the nuts to 14–20 ft. lbs. (20–27 Nm).

13. Install the intake manifold.

14. Complete installation by reversing the removal procedure.

15. Adjust the valve lash, as required.

3.0L AND 3.8L ENGINES

1. Relieve the pressure in the fuel system before disconnecting any fuel line connections.

2. Disconnect the negative battery cable. Raise the vehicle and support it safely.

3. Drain the cylinder block and lower the vehicle.

4. Remove the accessory drive belt(s).

5. Remove the alternator, A.I.R. pump, oil indicator and power steering pump, as required. Position to the side.

6. Remove the throttle cable. Remove the cruise control cable, if equipped.

7. Disconnect the fuel lines and fuel rail, as required.

8. Remove the heater hoses and radiator hoses.

9. Disconnect and tag all vacuum and electrical wiring.

10. Remove the radiator and cooling fan, if necessary.

11. Remove the intake manifold and valve cover.

12. Remove the exhaust manifold(s).

13. Remove the rocker arm assembly and pushrods.

14. Remove the cylinder head bolts and remove the cylinder head.

To install:

15. Clean the cylinder head and block from any foreign matter, nicks or heavy scratches. Clean the cylinder head bolt threads and threads in the cylinder block.

16. Position the new cylinder head gasket on the block.

NOTE: When using steel gaskets, use sealer part number 1050026 or equivalent on the gaskets.

17. Carefully guide the cylinder head into place. Coat the cylinder head bolts with sealing compound and install. Gradually tighten the cylinder head bolts 3 times around in the proper sequence to specifications.

18. Install the exhaust manifold.

19. Install the pushrods, rocker arm assembly and intake manifold.

20. Complete installation by reversing the removal procedure.

3.3L ENGINE

1. Relieve the pressure in the fuel system before disconnecting any fuel line connections.

2. Disconnect the negative battery cable. Raise the vehicle and support it safely.

3. Drain the cylinder block and lower the vehicle.

4. Remove the intake manifold and exhaust manifold.

5. Remove the valve cover.

6. Remove the ignition module and coils as a unit.

7. Disconnect and tag all electrical wiring and vacuum hoses, as necessary.

8. If equipped with air conditioning, remove the air conditioning compressor and position to the side.

9. Remove the alternator and power steering pump and position to the side. Remove the belt tensioner assembly.

10. Remove the rocker arm assembly, guide plate and pushrods.

11. Remove the cylinder head bolts and remove the cylinder head.

To install:

12. Clean the cylinder head and block from any foreign matter, nicks or heavy scratches. Clean the cylinder head bolt threads and threads in the cylinder block.

13. Position the new cylinder head gasket on the block.

14. Carefully guide the cylinder head into place. Coat the cylinder head bolts with sealing compound. Gradually tighten the cylinder head bolts 3 times around in the proper sequence to specifications.

15. Install the pushrods, guide plate and rocker arm assembly. Tighten the rocker arm pivot bolts to 28 ft. lbs. (38 Nm).

16. Complete installation by reversing the removal procedure.

Camshaft

Removal and Installation

2.5L ENGINE

1. Relieve the pressure in the fuel system before disconnecting any fuel line connections.

2. Disconnect the negative battery cable.

3. Remove the engine from the vehicle and support on a suitable engine stand.

4. Remove the rocker cover, rocker arms, and pushrods.

5. Remove the distributor, spark plugs, and fuel pump.

6. Remove the pushrod cover and gasket. Remove the lifters.

7. Remove the alternator, the alternator lower bracket and the front engine mount bracket assembly.

8. Remove the oil pump driveshaft and gear assembly.

9. Remove the crankshaft hub and timing gear cover.

10. Remove the 2 camshaft thrust plate screws by working through the holes in the gear.

11. Remove the camshaft and gear assembly by pulling it through the front of the block. Take care not to damage the bearings.

12. If replacement of the camshaft gear is necessary, use the following procedure:

   a. Remove the camshaft gear using an arbor press and adapter.

   b. Position the thrust plate to avoid damage by interference with the Woodruff key as the gear is removed.

   c. When assembling the gear onto the camshaft, support the camshaft at the back of the front journal in the arbor press using press plate adapters.

   d. Press the gear on the shaft until it bottoms against the spacer ring.

   e. Measure the end clearance of the thrust plate. End clearance should be 0.0015–0.0050 in.

   f. If clearance is less than 0.0015, replace the spacer ring.

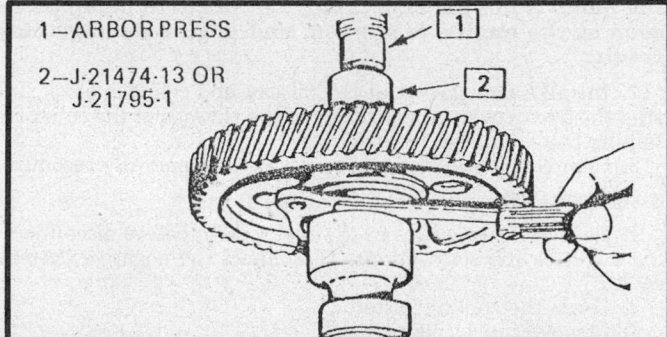

1—ARBOR PRESS

2—J-21474-13 OR J-21795-1

Camshaft timing gear/thrust plate end clearance— 2.5L engine

g. If clearance is more than 0.0050, replace the thrust plate.

To install:

13. Lubricate the camshaft journals with a high quality engine oil supplement and carefully install the camshaft and gear into the cylinder block.

14. Rotate the camshaft and crankshaft so that the timing marks on the gear theeth line up. The engine is now in No. 4 cylinder firing position.

15. Install the camshaft thrust plate to block screw. Torque the screw to 90 inch lbs. (10 Nm).

16. Complete installation by reversing the removal procedure.

2.8L, 3.1L AND 3.3L ENGINES

1. Relieve the pressure in the fuel system before disconnecting any fuel line connections.

2. Disconnect the negative battery cable.

3. Remove the engine from the vehicle and support on a suitable engine stand.

4. Remove the intake manifold, valve cover, rocker arms, pushrods and valve lifters.

5. Remove the crankshaft balancer and front cover.

6. Remove the timing chain and sprockets.

7. Carefully remove the camshaft. Avoid marring the camshaft bearing surfaces.

To install:

8. Coat the camshaft with lubricant part number 1052365 or equivalent and install the camshaft.

9. Install the timing chain and sprocket.

10. Install the camshaft thrust button and front cover.

11. Complete installation by reversing the removal procedure.

12. Adjust the valves, as required.

3.0L AND 3.8L ENGINES

1. Relieve the pressure in the fuel system before disconnecting any fuel line connections.

2. Disconnect the negative battery cable.

3. Remove the engine from the vehicle and support on a suitable engine stand.

4. Remove the intake manifold.

5. Remove the rocker arm covers.

6. Remove the rocker arm assemblies, pushrods and lifters.

7. Remove the timing chain cover.

NOTE: Align the timing marks of the camshaft and crankshaft sprockets to avoid burring the camshaft journals by the crankshaft.

8. Remove the timing chain, camshaft sensor magnet assembly and sprockets.

To install:

9. Coat the camshaft with lubricant part number 1052365 or equivalent and install the camshaft.

10. Install the timing chain, camshaft sensor magnet assembly and sprockets.

11. Install the camshaft thrust button and front cover.

12. Complete installation by reversing the removal procedure.

Timing Case Cover/Oil Seal

Removal and Installation

2.5L ENGINE

1. Relieve the pressure in the fuel system before disconnecting any fuel line connections.

2. Disconnect the negative battery cable.

3. Remove the inner fender splash shield. Remove the crankshaft hub.

4. Remove the alternator lower bracket and the front engine mounts.

5. Using a floor jack, raise the engine.

6. Remove the engine mount mounting bracket-to-cylinder

block bolts. Remove the bracket and mount as an assembly.

7. Remove the oil pan-to-front cover screws and front cover-to-block screws.

8. Pull the cover slightly forward, just enough to allow cutting of the oil pan front seal flush with the block on both sides.

9. Remove the front cover and attached portion of the pan seal.

10. Clean the gasket surfaces thoroughly.

To install:

11. Cut the tabs from the new oil pan front seal.

12. Install the seal on the front cover pressing the tips into the holes provided.

13. Coat the new gasket with sealer and position it on the front cover.

14. Apply a ⅛ in. bead of silicone sealer to the joint formed at the oil pan and stock.

15. Align the front cover seal with a centering tool and install the front cover. Tighten the screws. Install the hub.

2.8L ENGINE

1986-87

1. Relieve the pressure in the fuel system before disconnecting any fuel line connections.

2. Disconnect the negative battery cable.

3. Remove the water pump.

4. Remove the compressor without disconnecting any A/C lines and lay it aside.

5. Remove harmonic balancer, using a suitable puller.

NOTE: The outer ring (weight) of the harmonic balancer is bonded to the hub with rubber. The balancer must be removed with a puller which acts on the inner hub only. Pulling on the outer portion of the balancer will break the rubber bond or destroy the tuning of the torsional damper.

6. Disconnect the lower radiator hose and heater hose.

7. Remove timing gear cover attaching screws, and cover and gasket.

8. After removing the timing cover, pry oil seal out of front of cover. Lubricate the seal lip and install new lip seal with lip (open side of seal) facing toward the cylinder block. Carefully drive or press seal into place.

To install:

9. Clean all the gasket mounting surfaces on the front cover and block. Apply a continuous ³⁄₂₂ in. bead of sealer (GM part No. 1052357 or equivalent) to front cover sealing surface and around coolant passage ports and central bolt holes.

10. Apply a bead of silicone sealer to the oil pan-to-cylinder block joint.

11. Install a centering tool in the crankshaft snout hole in the front cover and install the cover.

12. Install the front cover bolts finger tight, remove the centering tool and tighten the cover bolts.

13. Complete installation by reversing the removal procedure.

2.8L AND 3.1L ENGINES

1988-90

1. Relieve the pressure in the fuel system before disconnecting any fuel line connections. Disconnect the negative battery cable.

2. Drain the cooling system.

3. Remove the tensioner and serpentine belt.

4. Remove the alternator and power steering pump. Locate and support these accessories to the side.

5. Raise and support the vehicle safely.

6. Remove the inner splash shield. Remove the torsion damper using tool J–24420–B or equivalent.

7. Remove the flywheel cover at the transaxle and starter.

8. Remove the serpentine belt idler pulley.

9. Drain the engine oil. Remove the oil pan and lower front cover bolts.

10. Lower the vehicle.

11. Remove the radiator hose at the water pump. Remove the heater hose at fill pipe.

12. Remove the bypass hose and overflow hoses. Remove the canister purge hose.

13. Remove the upper front cover retaining bolts and remove the front cover.

14. After removing the timing cover, pry oil seal out of front of cover. Lubricate the seal lip and install new lip seal with lip (open side of seal) facing toward the cylinder block. Carefully drive or press seal into place.

To install:

15. Clean the mating surfaces of the front cover and cylinder block.

16. Install a new gasket. Make sure not to damage the sealing surfaces. Apply sealer part number 1052080 or equivalent to the sealing surface of the front cover.

17. Position the front cover on the engine block and install the upper cover bolt.

18. Raise and support the vehicle safely. Install the oil pan and lower cover bolts.

19. Complete installation by reversing the removal procedure.

3.0L AND 3.8L ENGINES

1. Relieve the pressure in the fuel system before disconnecting any fuel line connections. Disconnect the negative battery cable.

2. Disconnect the lower radiator hose and the heater hose at the water pump.

3. Remove the 2 nuts from the front engine mount at the cradle and raise the engine using a suitable lifting device.

4. Remove the water pump pulley and all drive belts.

5. Remove the alternator and brackets.

6. Remove the distributor.

NOTE: If the timing chain and sprockets are not going to be disturbed, note the position of the distributor rotor for reinstallation in the same position.

7. Remove the balancer bolt and washer, and using a puller, remove the balancer.

8. Remove the cover-to-block bolts. Remove the 2 oil pan-to-cover bolts.

9. Remove the cover and gasket.

10. After removing the timing cover, pry oil seal out of front of cover. Lubricate the seal lip and install new lip seal with lip (open side of seal) facing toward the cylinder block. Carefully drive or press seal into place.

To install:

11. Clean the mating surfaces of the front cover and cylinder block.

NOTE: Remove the oil pump cover and pack the space around the oil pump gears completely full of petroleum jelly. There must be no air space left inside the pump. If the pump is not packed, it may not begin to pump oil as soon as the engine is started, and engine damage may result.

12. Install a new gasket at the oil pan and cylinder block. Install the front cover. Apply sealer to the threads of the cover retaining bolts and secure the cover.

13. Complete installation by reversing the removal procedure.

3.3L ENGINE

1. Relieve the pressure in the fuel system before disconnecting any fuel line connections. Disconnect the negative battery cable.

2. Drain the cooling system.

3. Remove the serpentine belt.

4. Remove the heater pipes. Remove the coolant bypass hose and lower radiator hose from cover.

5. Raise and support the vehicle safely.

6. Remove the inner splash shield.

7. Remove the crankshaft balancer.

8. Disconnect all electrical connectors at the camshaft sensor, crankshaft sensor and oil pressure sender.

9. Remove the oil pan to front cover retaining bolts, front cover retaining bolts and remove the front cover.

10. After removing the timing cover, pry oil seal out of front of cover. Lubricate the seal lip and install new lip seal with lip (open side of seal) facing toward the cylinder block. Carefully drive or press seal into place.

To install:

11. Clean the mating surfaces of the front cover and cylinder block.

12. Install a new gasket on the cylinder block. Install the front cover. Apply sealer to the threads of the cover retaining bolts and secure the cover. Tighten the bolts to 22 ft. lbs. (30 Nm).

13. Install the oil pan to front cover bolts. Tighten the bolts to 88 inch lbs. (10 Nm).

14. Reconnect all electrical connectors. Adjust the crankshaft sensor using tool J-37087 or equivalent.

15. Complete installation by reversing the removal procedure.

Timing Gears and Chain

Removal and Installation

2.5L ENGINE

NOTE: The camshaft gear is press fitted on the camshaft. If replacement of the camshaft gear is necessary, the engine must be removed from the vehicle and the camshaft and gear removed from the engine.

1. Relieve the pressure in the fuel system before disconnecting any fuel line connections.

2. Disconnect the negative battery cable.

3. Remove the engine from the vehicle.

4. Remove the camshaft and gear assembly from the engine block.

5. Using an arbor press and adapter, remove the gear from the camshaft. Position the thrust plate to avoid damage by interference with the Wooddruff key as the gear is removed.

To install:

6. Support the camshaft at the back of the front journal in the arbor press using press plate adapters.

7. Position the spacer ring thrust plate over the end of the shaft and woodruff key in keyway.

8. Press the gear on the shaft with the bottom against the spacer ring. Measure the end clearance at the thrust plate. Clearance should be within 0.0015–0.0050 in. (0.0381–1.270mm).

9. If the clearance is less than 0.0015 in. (0.0381mm), replace the spacer ring.

10. If more than 0.0050 in. (1.270mm), make certain the gear is seated properly against the spacer. If the clearance is still excessive, replace the thrust plate.

11. Measure the backlash at position outside the 2 retainer plate access holes and at 2 other areas 90 degrees from these holes. If the backlash is not within specifications, replace the camshaft and crankshaft gears.

12. Lubricate the camshaft journals with a high quality engine oil supplement. Install the camshaft and gear into the engine block.

13. Rotate the camshaft and crankshaft so that the timing marks on the gear teeth line up. The engine is now in No. 4 cylinder firing position.

14. Install the camshaft thrust plate to block screws and tighten to 90 inch lbs. (10 Nm).

15. Complete installation by reversing the removal procedure.

2.8L AND 3.1L ENGINES

1. Relieve the pressure in the fuel system before disconnect-

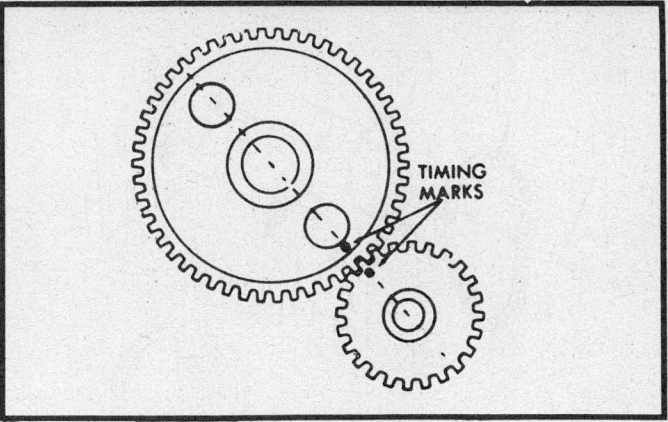

Timing gear alignment—2.5L engine

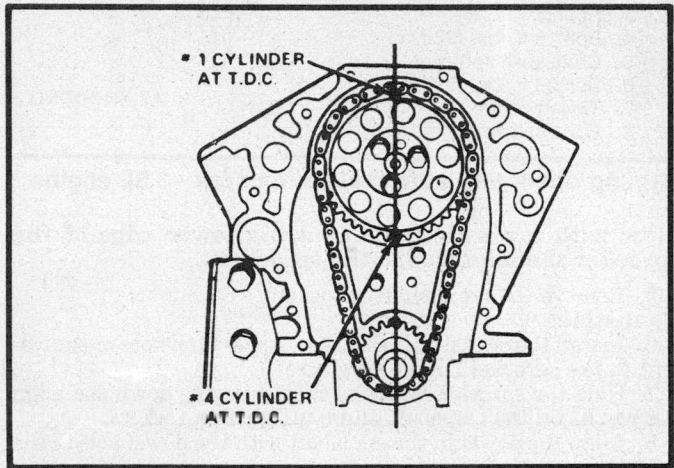

Timing gear alignment—2.8L and 3.1L engine

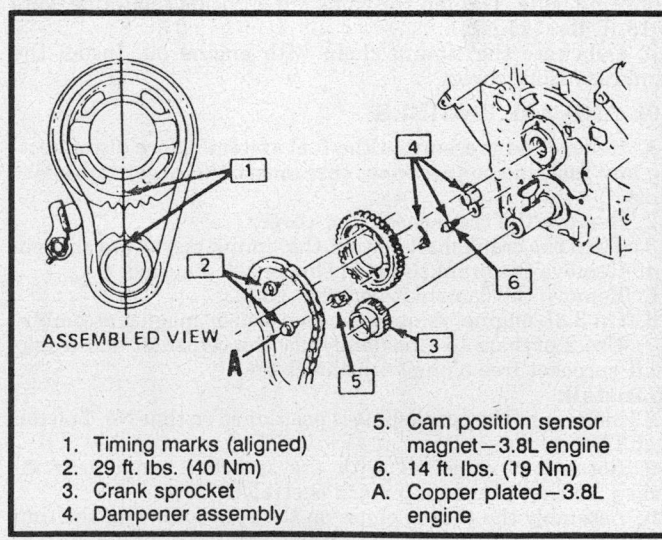

1. Timing marks (aligned)
2. 29 ft. lbs. (40 Nm)
3. Crank sprocket
4. Dampener assembly
5. Cam position sensor magnet—3.8L engine
6. 14 ft. lbs. (19 Nm)
A. Copper plated—3.8L engine

Timing chain and sprockets—3.0L and 3.8L engines

ing any fuel line connections. Disconnect the negative battery cable.

2. Remove the crankcase front cover.

3. Place the No. 1 piston at TDC with the marks on the camshaft and crankshat sprockets aligned.

4. Remove the camshaft sprocket and chain.

NOTE: If the sprocket does not come off easily, a light

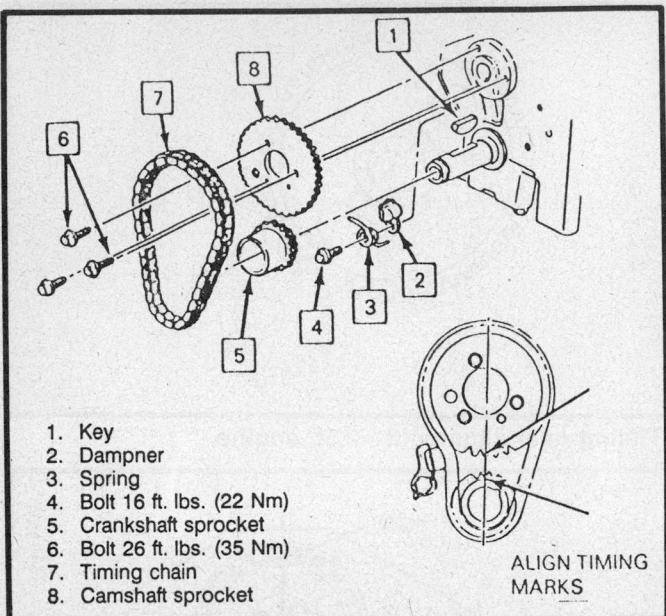

1. Key
2. Dampner
3. Spring
4. Bolt 16 ft. lbs. (22 Nm)
5. Crankshaft sprocket
6. Bolt 26 ft. lbs. (35 Nm)
7. Timing chain
8. Camshaft sprocket

ALIGN TIMING MARKS

Timing chain and sprockets alignment—3.3L engine

blow with a plastic mallet on the lower edge of the sprocket should dislodge the sprocket.

5. Remove the crankshaft sprocket.

To install:

6. Install the crankshaft sprocket. Apply Molykote or equivalent to the sprocket thrust surgface.

7. Hold the sprocket with the chain hanging down and align the marks on the camshaft and crankshaft sprockets.

8. Align the dowel in the camshaft with the dowel hole in the camshaft sprocket.

9. Draw the camshaft sprocket onto the camshaft using the mounting bolts. Tighten the camshaft sprocket mounting bolts to 18 ft. lbs. (25 Nm).

10. Lubricate the timing chain with engine oil. Install the crankcase front cover.

3.0L AND 3.8L ENGINES

1. Relieve the pressure in the fuel system before disconnecting any fuel line connections. Disconnect the negative battery cable.

2. Remove the crankcase front cover.

3. Turn the crankshaft so that the timing marks are aligned.

4. Remove the crankshaft oil slinger, as required.

5. Remove the camshaft sprocket bolts.

6. On 3.8L engine, remove the cam sensor magnet assembly.

7. Use 2 prybars to alternately pry the camshaft and crankshaft sprocket free along with the chain.

To install:

8. Make sure the crankshaft is positioned so that No. 1 piston is at TDC.

9. Rotate the camshaft with the sprocket temporarily installed, so that the timing mark is straight down.

10. Assembly the timing chain on the sprockets with the timing marks aligned. Install the timing chain and sprocket.

11. On 3.8L engine, install the cam sensor magnet assembly.

12. Install the oil slinger with the large part of the cone toward the front of the engine, as required.

13. Install the camshaft sprocket bolt, thrust botton and spring.

14. Install the timing chain dampener and engine front cover.

3.3L ENGINE

1. Relieve the pressure in the fuel system before disconnect-

Rings/Pistons/Connecting Rod Positioning

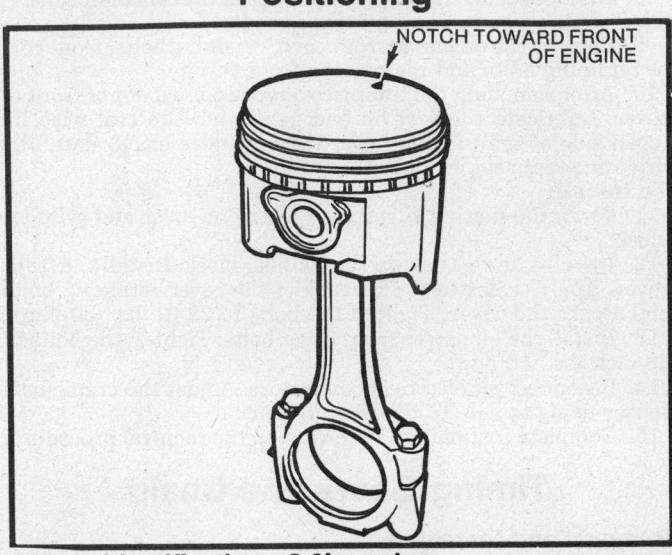

NOTCH TOWARD FRONT OF ENGINE

Piston identification—2.8L engine

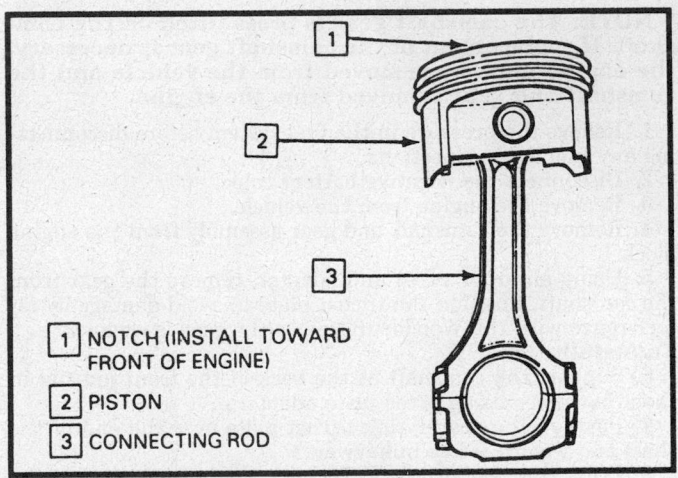

1 NOTCH (INSTALL TOWARD FRONT OF ENGINE)
2 PISTON
3 CONNECTING ROD

Piston identification—3.3L engine

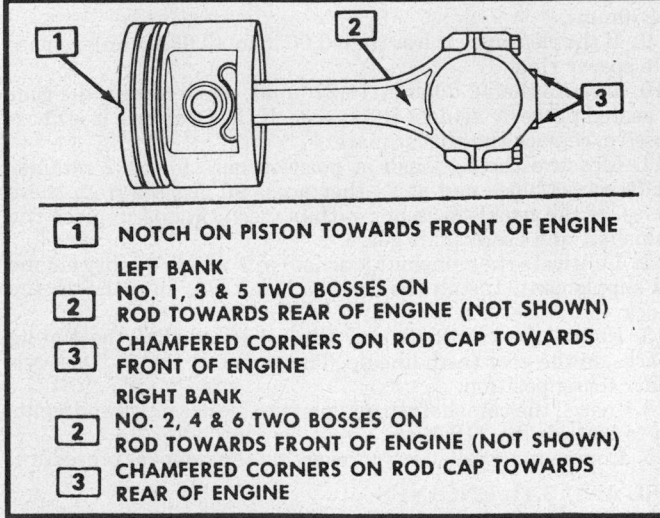

1 NOTCH ON PISTON TOWARDS FRONT OF ENGINE

LEFT BANK

2 NO. 1, 3 & 5 TWO BOSSES ON ROD TOWARDS REAR OF ENGINE (NOT SHOWN)

3 CHAMFERED CORNERS ON ROD CAP TOWARDS FRONT OF ENGINE

RIGHT BANK

2 NO. 2, 4 & 6 TWO BOSSES ON ROD TOWARDS FRONT OF ENGINE (NOT SHOWN)

3 CHAMFERED CORNERS ON ROD CAP TOWARDS REAR OF ENGINE

Piston identification—3.0L and 3.8L engines

ing any fuel line connections. Disconnect the negative battery cable.

2. Remove the crankcase front cover and camshaft thrust bearing.

3. Turn the crankshaft so that the timing marks are aligned.

4. Remove the timing chain dampner and camshaft sprocket bolts.

5. Remove the camshaft sprocket and chain. Remove the crankshaft sprocket.

To install:

6. Make sure the crankshaft is positioned so that No. 1 piston is at TDC.

7. Rotate the camshaft with the sprocket temporarily installed, so that the timing mark is straight down.

8. Assembly the timing chain on the sprockets with the timing marks aligned. Install the timing chain and sprocket.

9. Install the camshaft sprocket bolts. Torque the bolts to 27 ft. lbs. (37 Nm).

10. Install the timing chain dampener and engine front cover.

ENGINE LUBRICATION SYSTEM

Oil Pan

Removal and Installation

2.5L ENGINE

1. Disconnect the negative battery cable. Raise and support the vehicle safely. Drain the oil.

2. Remove cradle to front engine mount nuts.

3. Disconnect exhaust pipe at manifold and at rear transaxle mount.

4. Disconnect starter and remove flywheel housing inspection cover.

5. Remove upper generator bracket. Remove the splash shield, if equipped, in order to gain working clearance.

6. Install suitable engine support equipment and raise engine.

7. Remove lower generator bracket and engine support bracket.

8. Remove oil pan retaining bolts and remove oil pan.

To install:

9. Thoroughly clean all gasket sealing surfaces.

10. Install rear oil pan gasket in rear main bearing cap and apply a small quantity of sealer in depressions where pan gasket engages into block.

11. Install front oil pan gasket on timing gear cover pressing tips into holes provided in cover.

12. Install side gaskets on oil pan using grease as a retainer.

13. Apply a 1/8 in. by 1/4 in. long bead of sealer at split lines of front and side gaskets.

14. Install oil pan. Bolts into timing gear cover should be installed last. They are installed at an angle and holes line up after rest of pan bolts are snugged up.

15. Complete installation by reversing the removal procedure. Fill crankcase with oil, run engine and check for leaks.

2.8L AND 3.1L ENGINES

1. Disconnect the battery ground.

2. On vehicles equipped with serpentine belt, remove the serpentine belt cover, belt and tensioner.

3. If necessary, support the engine with tool J–28467–A or equivalent, using an extra support leg.

4. Raise and safely support the vehicle.

5. Drain the oil.

6. Remove the right tire and wheel assembly. Remove the splash shield.

7. Remove the steering gear pinch bolt, as required.

8. Remove the transaxle mount retaining nuts and engine to frame mount retaining nuts, as required.

9. Remove the front engine horse collar bracket from the block, as required.

10. Remove the bellhousing cover and remove the starter.

11. Possition a jackstand under the frame front center crossmember.

12. Loosen, but do not remove the rear frame bolts.

13. Remove the front frame bolts and lower the front frame.

14. Remove the oil pan retaining bolts and remove the oil pan.

15. Installation is the reverse of the removal procedure.

NOTE: The oil pan on some vehicles may not require a gasket. If a gasket is not required, the oil pan is installed using RTV gasket material. Make sure that the sealing surfaces are free of old RTV material. Use a 1/8 in. bead of RTV material on the pan sealing flange. Torque the pan bolts to 8–10 ft. lbs.

3.0L AND 3.8L ENGINE

1. Disconnect the battery ground cable.

2. Raise and safely support the vehicle.

3. Drain the oil.

4. Remove the bellhousing cover.

5. Unbolt and remove the oil pan.

6. Installation is the reverse of removal. RTV gasket material is used in place of a gasket. Make sure that the sealing surfaces are free of all old RTV material. Use a 1/8 in. bead of RTV material on the oil pan sealing flange. Torque the pan bolts to 10–14 ft. lbs.

3.3L ENGINE

1. Disconnect the negative battery cable.

2. Raise and support the vehicle safely.

3. Drain the engine oil.

4. Remove the transaxle converter cover and starter motor.

5. Remove the oil filter, oil pan retaining bolts and oil pan assembly.

To install:

6. Clean the oil pan and cylinder block mating surfaces.

7. Install a new oil pan gasket to the oil pan flange.

8. Install the oil pan and torque the retaining bolts 8–10 ft. lbs.

9. Complete installation by reversing the removal procedure.

Oil Pump

Removal and Installation

2.5L ENGINE

1. Disconnect the negative battery cable.

2. Raise and support the vehicle safely.

3. Drain the engine oil and remove the oil pan.

4. Remove the 2 flange mounting bolts and nut from the main bearing cap bolt.

5. Remove the pump and screen as an assembly.

To install:

6. Remove the 4 cover attaching screws and cover from the oil pump assembly.

7. Pack the space around the oil pump gears completely full of petroleum jelly. There must be no air space left inside the pump. If the pump is not packed, it may not begin to pump oil as soon as the engine is started, and engine damage may result.

8. Align the oil pump shaft to match with the oil pump drive shaft tang, then install the oil pump to the block positioning the

flange over the oil pump driveshaft lower bushing. Do not use any gasket. Torque the bolts to 20 ft. lbs. (30 Nm).

9. Install the oil pan using a new gasket and seals.
10. Complete installation by reversing the removal procedure.

2.8L AND 3.1L ENGINES

1. Disconnect the negative battery cable.
2. Raise and support the vehicle safely.
3. Drain the engine oil and remove the oil pan.
4. Remove the pump to rear main bearing cap bolt and remove the pump and extension shaft.

To install:

5. Remove the 4 cover attaching screws and cover from the oil pump assembly.
6. Pack the space around the oil pump gears completely full of petroleum jelly. There must be no air space left inside the pump. If the pump is not packed, it may not begin to pump oil as soon as the engine is started, and engine damage may result.
7. Assemble the pump and extension shaft with retainer to rear main bearing cap, aligning the top end of the extension shaft with the lower end of the distributor drive gear.
8. Install the pump to the rear bearing cap bolt and torque to specifications. Install the oil pan.
9. Complete installation by reversing the removal procedure.

3.0L, 3.3L AND 3.8L ENGINES

1. Disconnect the negative battery cable.
2. Raise and support the vehicle safely.
3. Drain the engine oil.
4. Remove the oil filter.
5. Unbolt the oil pump cover from the timing chain cover.
6. Slide out the oil pump gears. Remove the oil pressure relief valve cap, spring and valve. Do not attempt to remove the oil filter bypass valve and spring. Clean all parts thoroughly in solvent and check for wear.

To install:

7. Lubricate and install the pressure relief valve and spring in the bore of the oil pump cover.
8. Install the relief valve spring retaining cap and gasket.
9. Install the oil pump drive and driven gears. Pack the gear pockets full of petroleum jelly.
10. Install the oil pump cover. Alternately tighten the cover screws.
11. Complete installation by reversing the removal procedure.

Rear Main Oil Seal

Removal and Installation

2.5L ENGINE

1. Disconnect the negative battery cable.

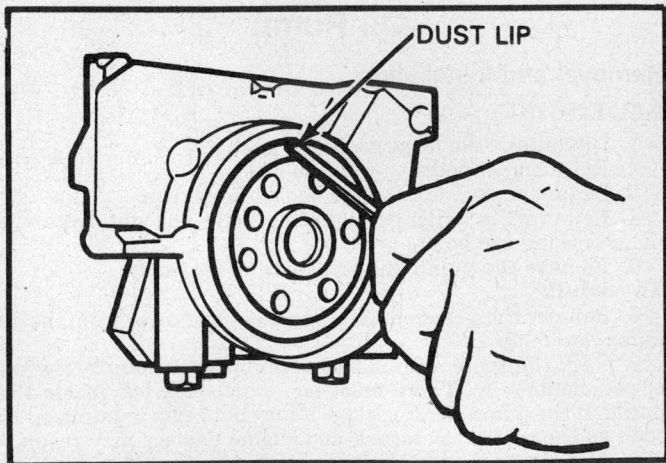

Remove rear main seal—2.8L and 3.1L engines

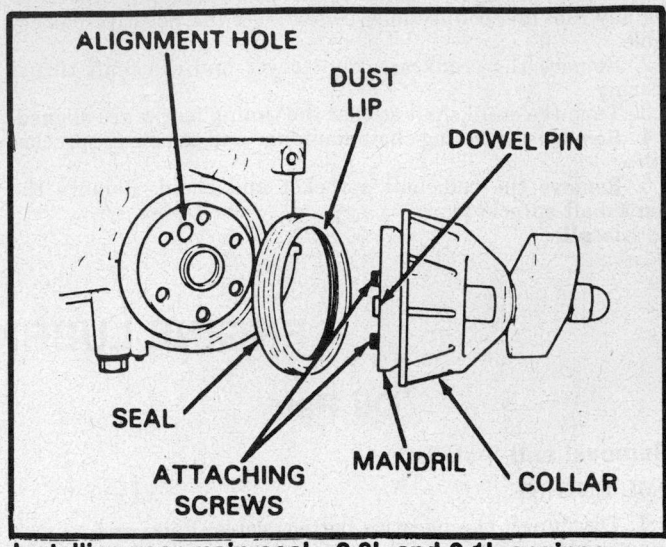

Installing rear main seal—2.8L and 3.1L engines

2. Support the engine. Remove the transaxle and flywheel.
3. Being careful not to scratch the crankshaft, pry out the old seal with an suitable pry tool.
4. Coat the new seal with clean engine oil, and install it by hand (or use seal installer tool J–34924) onto the crankshaft. The seal backing must be flush with the block opening.
5. Install all other parts in reverse of removal.

2.8 AND 3.1L ENGINES

1. Disconnect the negative battery cable.
2. Support the engine with tool J–28467–A or equivalent.
3. Remove the transaxle and flywheel.
4. Carefully remove the old seal by inserting a prying tool through the dust lip at an angle. Pry out the old seal with an suitable pry tool.
5. Coat the new seal with clean engine oil, and install it using seal installer tool J–34686 or equivalent.
6. Complete installation by reversing the removal procedure.

3.0L, 3.3 AND 3.8L ENGINES

1. Disconnect the negative battery cable.
2. Raise and support the vehicle safely.
3. Drain the engine oil and remove the oil pan.
4. Remove the rear main bearing cap. Remove the oil seal from the bearing cap.

To install:

5. Insert a packing tool J–21526–2 or equivalent against one end of the seal in the cylinder block. Pack the old seal in until it

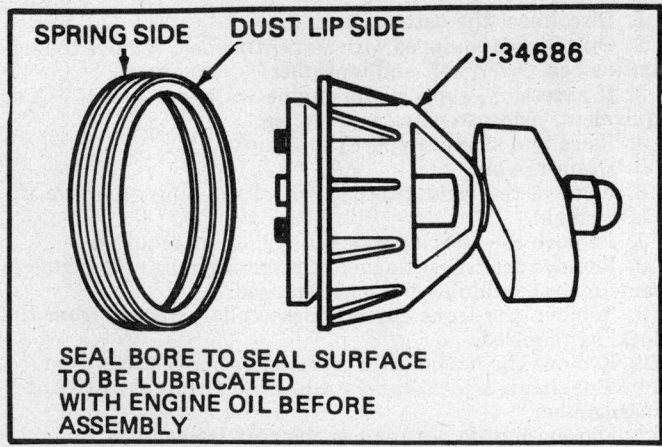

Rear main seal and tool—2.8L and 3.1L engines

is tight. Pack the other end of seal in the same manner.

6. Measure the amount the seal was driven up into the block on one side and add approximately $\frac{1}{16}$ (2mm). With a single edge razor blade, cut this amount off of the old lower seal. The bearing cap can be used as a holding fixture.

7. Install the packing guide tool J–21526–1 or equivalent onto the cylinder block.

8. Using the packing tool, work the short pieces of the seal into the guide tool and pack into the cylinder block until the tool hits the built in stop. Repeat this step on the other side. A small amount of oil on the pieces of seal may be helpful when packing into the cylinder block.

9. Remove the guide tool.

10. Install a new rope seal in the bearing cap and install the cap. Torque the retaining bolts to specifications.

11. Complete installation by reversing the removal procedure.

FRONT SUSPENSION AND STEERING

For front suspension component removal and installation procedures, refer to unit repair section. For steering wheel removal and installation, refer to electrical control section.

Steering Rack and Pinion

Removal and Installation

1. Disconnect the negative battery cable. Raise and safely support vehicle. Allow the front suspension to hang freely. Disconnect the power steering hoses from the gear, where equipped.

2. Move the intermediate shaft seal upward and remove the intermediate shaft-to-stub shaft pinch bolt.

3. Remove both front wheels.

4. Remove the cotter pins and nut from both tie rod ends. Disconnect the tie rod ends from the steering knuckles.

5. Remove the air management system pipe bracket bolt from the crossmember.

6. Support the engine cradle with a floor jack. Remove the 2 rear cradle mount bolts and, using a jack, lower the rear of the engine cradle about 4–5 in.

NOTE: Do not lower the engine cradle too far or damage to surrounding components will result.

7. Remove the rack and pinion heat shield.

8. Remove the 2 rack and pinion mount bolts.

9. Remove the rack and pinion assembly through the left wheel opening.

10. Installation is the reverse of removal. Torque the mount bolts to 70 ft. lbs.; the tie rod end nuts to 30 ft. lbs.; the pinch bolt to 45 ft. lbs.

Power Steering Pump

Removal and Installation

2.5L ENGINE

1. Disconnect the negative battery cable. Raise and support the vehicle safely.

2. Remove the pump drive belt and siphon the fluid from the pump reservoir.

3. Disconnect the hydraulic lines from the pump.

4. Remove the radiator hose clamp bolt.

5. Remove the upper and lower bolts and nuts from the front pump bracket.

6. Remove the pump and bracket from the engine.

7. Installation is the reverse of the removal procedure. Be sure to adjust the drive belt tension and bleed the hydraulic system.

EXCEPT 2.5L ENGINE

1. Disconnect the negative battery cable at the battery. Remove air cleaner if necessary.

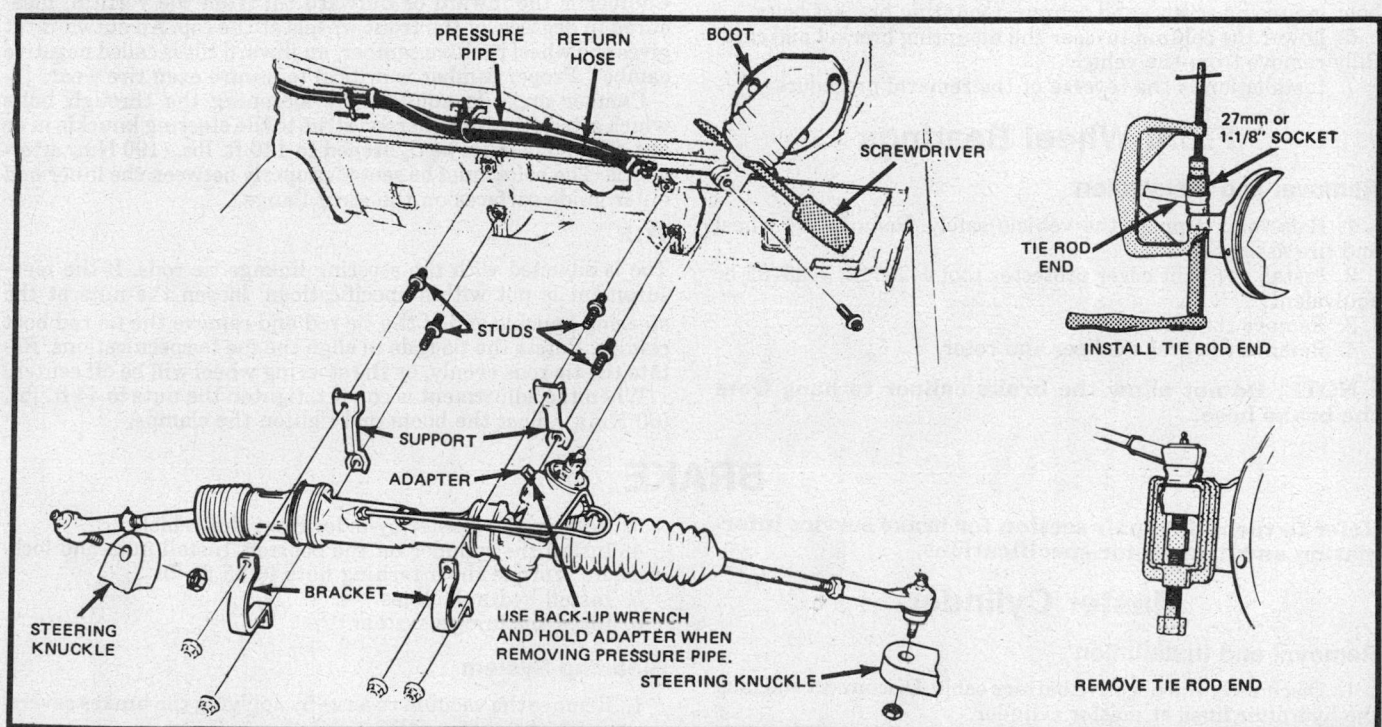

Steering rack and related components, 1985–89

2. Disconnect the blower motor wiring and remove the blower motor.

3. Remove the coolant hose from the water pump.

4. Siphon the fluid out of the pump reservoir, then disconnect the lines from the pump.

5. Remove the pump drive belt.

6. Remove the 1 nut which attaches the rear pump bracket to the engine bracket.

7. Remove the 2 front pump bracket-to-engine bolts, then remove the pump and bracket assembly.

8. Installation is the reverse of the removal procedure. Be sure to adjust the drive belt tension and bleed the hydraulic system.

Steering Column

NOTE: Once the steering column is removed from the vehicle, the column is extremely susceptible to damage. Dropping the column assembly on its end could collapse the steering shaft or loosen the plastic injections which maintain column rigidity. Leaning on the column assembly could cause the jacket to bend or deform. Any of the above damage could impair the column's collapsible design. If it is necessary to remove the steering wheel, use a standard wheel puller. Under no condition should the end of the shaft be hammered upon, as hammering could loosen the plastic injection which maintains column rigidity.

Removal and Installation

1. Disconnect the negative battery cable.

2. If column repairs are to be made, remove the steering wheel.

3. Remove the nuts and bolts attaching the flexible coupling to the bottom of the steering column. Remove the safety strap and bolt if equipped.

4. Remove the steering column trim shrouds and column covers.

5. Disconnect all wiring harness connectors. Remove the dust boot mounting screws and column mounting bracket bolts.

6. Lower the column to clear the mounting bracket and carefully remove from the vehicle.

7. Installation is the reverse of the removal procedure.

Front Wheel Bearings

Removal and Installation

1. Raise and support the vehicle safely. Remove the wheel and tire assembly.

2. Install the boot cover protector tool J–28712, J–33162 or equivalent.

3. Remove the hub nut.

4. Remove the brake caliper and rotor.

NOTE: Do not allow the brake caliper to hang from the brake hose.

5. Remove the 3 hub and bearing attaching bolts. If the old bearing is to be reused, matchmark the bolts and holes.

6. Using a puller tool J–28733 or the equivalent, remove the bearing. If corrosion is present, make sure the bearing is loose in the knuckle before using the puller.

7. Clean the mating surfaces of all dirt and corrosion. Check the knuckle bore and knuckle seal for damage. If a new bearing is to be installed, remove the old knuckle seal and install a new one.

To install:

8. Grease the lips of the new seal before installation; install with a seal driver.

9. Push the bearing onto the halfshaft. Install a new washer and hub nut.

10. Tighten the new hub nut on the halfshaft until the bearing is seated. If the rotor and hub start to rotate as the hub nut is tightened, insert a long bolt through the cut out in the hub assembly to prevent rotation. Do not apply full torque to the hub nut at this time-just seat the bearing.

11. Install the brake shield and the bearing retaining bolts. Tighten the bolts evenly.

12. Install the caliper and rotor. Install the caliper bolts and tighten to 21–35 ft. lbs.

13. Install the wheel and tire assembly. Lower the vehicle. Tighten the hub nut to 185 ft. lbs.

Torque Procedure

The front wheel bearings are sealed, non-adjustable units which require no periodic attention. They are bolted to the steering knuckle by means of an integral flange.

Front Wheel Alignment

Procedure

CASTER

Caster is not adjustable.

CAMBER

Camber is the inward or outward tilt from the vertical, measured in degrees, of the front wheels at the top. An outward tilt gives the wheel positive camber, an inward tilt is called negative camber. Proper camber is critical to assure even tire wear.

Camber angle is adjusted by loosening the through bolts which attach the MacPherson strut to the steering knuckle in or out. The bolts must be tightened to 140 ft. lbs. (190 Nm) afterwards. The bolts must be seated properly between the inner and outer guide surfaces on the strut flange.

TOE

Toe is adjusted with the steering linkage tie rods. If the measurement is not within specifications, loosen the nuts at the steering knuckle end of the tie rod and remove the tie rod boot clamps. Rotate the tie rods to align the toe to specifications. Rotate the tie rods evenly, or the steering wheel will be off center.

When the adjustment is correct, tighten the nuts to 44 ft. lbs. (60 Nm). Adjust the boots and tighten the clamps.

BRAKE

Refer to the unit repair section for brake service information and drum/rotor specifications.

Master Cylinder

Removal and Installation

1. Disconnect the negative battery cable. Disconnect and plug the hydraulic lines at master cylinder.

2. Remove the master cylinder retaining nuts and lockwashers.

3. Remove the master cylinder from the vehicle.

4. Install the cylinder on the booster. Install nuts and lockwashers. Torque the attaching nuts to 25 ft. lbs.

5. Install hydraulic lines.

6. Bleed the brakes system.

Bleeding System

1. Remove the vacuum reserve by applying the brakes several times with the engine **OFF**.

2. Fill the master cylinder to within ¼ in. of the reservoir rim

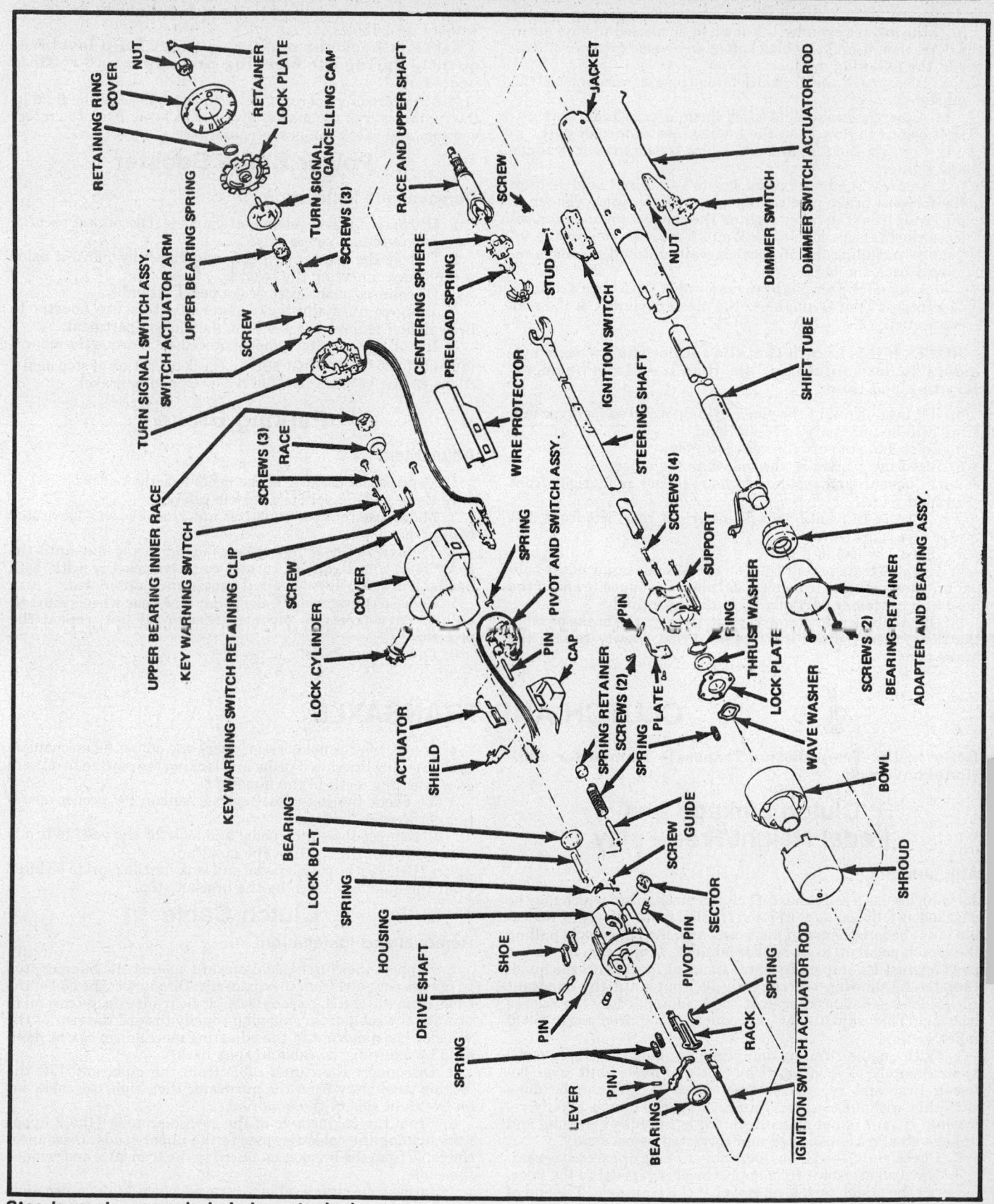

Steering column exploded view—typical

and keep it at least ½ full of fluid during the bleeding operation.

3. If the master cylinder is known or suspected to have air in the bore, then it must be bled before any wheel cylinder of caliper in the following manner:

    a. Disconnect the forward brake pipe connection at the master cylinder.

    b. Allow the brake fluid to fill the master cylinder bore until it begins to flow from the foward pipe connector port.

    c. Connect the forward brake pipe to the master cylinder and tighten.

    d. Depress the brake pedal slowly 1 time and hold. Loosen the forward brake pipe connection at the master cylinder to purge air from the bore. Tighten the connection and then release the brake pedal slowly. Wait 15 seconds. Repeat the sequence, including the 15 seconds wait, until all the air is removed from the bore.

    e. After all the air has been removed at the forward connection, repeat Step **D** and bleed the master cylinder at the rear connection.

NOTE: If it is known that the calipers and wheels cylinders do not contain any air, then it will not be necessary to bleed them.

4. If it is known that the wheel cylinders and calipers contain air, it will be necessary to bleed them.

5. Raise and support the vehicle safely.

6. Bleed the system in the following sequence:

    a. Conventional system—right rear, left rear, right front and left front.

    b. Except conventional system—right rear, left front, left rear and right front.

7. Bleed 1 wheel at a time.

8. Install a transparent tube on the bleeder screw of the caliper or wheel cylinder to be bled and place the opposite end of the hose in a container partially fill with brake fluid.

9. Open the bleeder screw ¾ turn. Depress the brake pedal to the floor, then tighten the bleeder screw. Slowly release the brake pedal.

10. Repeat the bleeding operation until clear brake fluid flows without air bubbles.

NOTE: Check the master cylinder fluid level frequently during the bleeding procedure and refill if necessary.

11. After bleeding operation is completed, discard the fluid in the container. Fill the master cylinder to ¼ in. from the reservoir rim and check the brake operation.

Power Brake Booster

Removal and Installation

1. Disconnect the negative battery cable. Disconnect vacuum hose from vacuum check valve.

2. Unbolt the master cylinder and carefully move it aside without disconnecting the hydraulic lines.

3. Disconnect pushrod at brake pedal assembly.

4. Remove nuts and lockwashers that secure booster to firewall and remove booster from engine compartment.

5. Install by reversing removal procedure. Torque the mounting nuts to 25 ft. lbs. Make sure to check operation of stop lights. Allow engine vacuum to build before applying brakes.

Parking Brake

Adjustment

1. Depress the parking brake pedal exactly 3 clicks.

2. Raise and support the vehicle safely.

3. Make sure that the equalizer nut groove is well lubricated with grease.

4. Tighten the parking brake cable adjusting nut until the right rear wheel can be turned counterclockwise with both hands, but locks when clockwise rotation is attempted.

5. Release the parking brake pedal. The rear wheels must be able to turn freely in either direction; if not, repeat the procedure.

6. Lower the vehicle.

CLUTCH AND TRANSAXLE

Refer to the Transmission/Transaxle Manual for additional coverage.

Clutch Linkage and Pedal Height/Free—play

Adjustments

All vehicles use a self-adjusting clutch mechanism which may be checked as follows. As the clutch friction material wears, the cable must be lengthened. This is accomplished by simply pulling the clutch pedal up to its rubber bumper. This action forces the pawl against its stop and rotates it out of mesh with the quadrant teeth, allowing the cable to play out until the quadrant spring load is balanced against the load applied by the release bearing. This adjustment procedure is required every 5000 miles or less.

1. With engine running and brake on, hold the clutch pedal approximately ½ in. from floor mat and move shift lever between first and reverse several times. If this can be done smoothly without clashing into reverse, the clutch is fully releasing. If shift is not smooth, clutch is not fully releasing and linkage should be inspected and corrected as necessary.

2. Check clutch pedal bushings for sticking or excessive wear.

3. Have an assistant fully apply the clutch pedal to the floor. Observe the clutch fork level travel at the transaxle. The end of the clutch fork lever should have a total travel of approximately 1.5–1.7 in.

4. If fork lever is not correct, check the adjusting mechanism by depressing the clutch pedal and looking for pawl to firmly engage with the teeth in the quadrant.

5. To check the self-adjusting mechanism for proper operation, proceed as follows:

    a. Depress the clutch pedal and look for the pawl to firmly engage with the teeth in the quadrant.

    b. Release the clutch pedal and look for the pawl to be lifted off the quadrant teeth by the bracket stop.

Clutch Cable

Removal and Installation

1. Support the clutch pedal upward against the bumper stop to release the pawl from the quadrant. Disconnect the end of the cable from the clutch release lever at the transaxle. Be careful to prevent the cable from snapping rapidly toward the rear of the vehicle. The quadrant in the adjusting mechanism can be damaged by allowing the cable to snap back.

2. Disconnect the clutch cable from the quadrant. Lift the locking pawl away from the quadrant, then slide the cable out on the right side of the quadrant.

3. From the engine side of the cowl disconnect the 2 upper nuts holding the cable retainer to the upper studs. Disconnect the cable from the bracket mounted to the transaxle and remove the cable.

4. Inspect the clutch cable for frayed wires, kinks, worn ends and excessive friction. If any of these conditions exist, replace the cable.

To install:

5. With the gasket in position on the 2 upper studs, position a new cable with the retaining flange against the bracket.

6. Attach the end of the cable to the quadrant, being sure to route the cable underneath the pawl.

7. Attach the two upper nuts to the retainer mounting studs, and torque to specifications.

8. Attach the cable to the bracket mounted to the transaxle.

9. Support the clutch pedal upward against the bumper stop to release the pawl from the quadrant. Attach the outer end of the cable to the clutch release lever. Be sure not to yank on the cable, since overloading the cable could damage the quadrant.

10. Check clutch operation and adjust by lifting the clutch pedal up to allow the mechanism to adjust the cable length. Depress the pedal slowly several times to set the pawl into mesh with the quadrant teeth.

Clutch Master and Slave Cylinder

NOTE: The clutch hydraulic system is serviced as a complete unit, it has been bled of air and filled with fluid.

Removal and Installation

1. Disconnect the negative battery cable.
2. Remove the hush panel from inside the vehicle.
3. Remove the clutch master cylinder retaining nuts at the front of the dash.
4. Remove the slave cylinder retaining nuts at the transaxle.
5. Remove the hydraulic system as a unit from the vehicle.
6. Install the slave cylinder to the transmission support bracket aligning the push rod into the pocket on the clutch fork outer lever. Tighten the retaining nuts evenly to prevent damage to the slave cylinder. Torque the nuts to 40 ft. lbs.

NOTE: Do not remove the plastic pushrod retainer from the slave cylinder. The straps will break on the first clutch pedal application.

7. Position the clutch master cylinder to the front of the dash. Torque the nuts evenly to 20 ft. lbs.

8. Remove the pedal restrictor from the pushrod. Lube the pushrod bushing on the clutch pedal. Connect the pushrod to the clutch pedal and install the retaining clip.

9. If equipped with cruise control, check the switch adjustment at the clutch pedal bracket.

NOTE: When adjusting the cruise control switch, do not exert an upward force on the clutch pedal pad of more than 20 lbs. or damage to the master cylinder pushrod retaining ring may result.

10. Install the hush panel.
11. Press the clutch pedal down several times. This will break the plastic retaining straps on the slave cylinder push rod. Do not remove the plastic button on the end of the pushrod.
12. Connect the negative battery cable.

Clutch

Removal and Installation

1. Disconnect the negative battery cable.
2. Disconnect the clutch cable from the transaxle.
3. On 1987–90 vehicles, remove the hush panel from inside

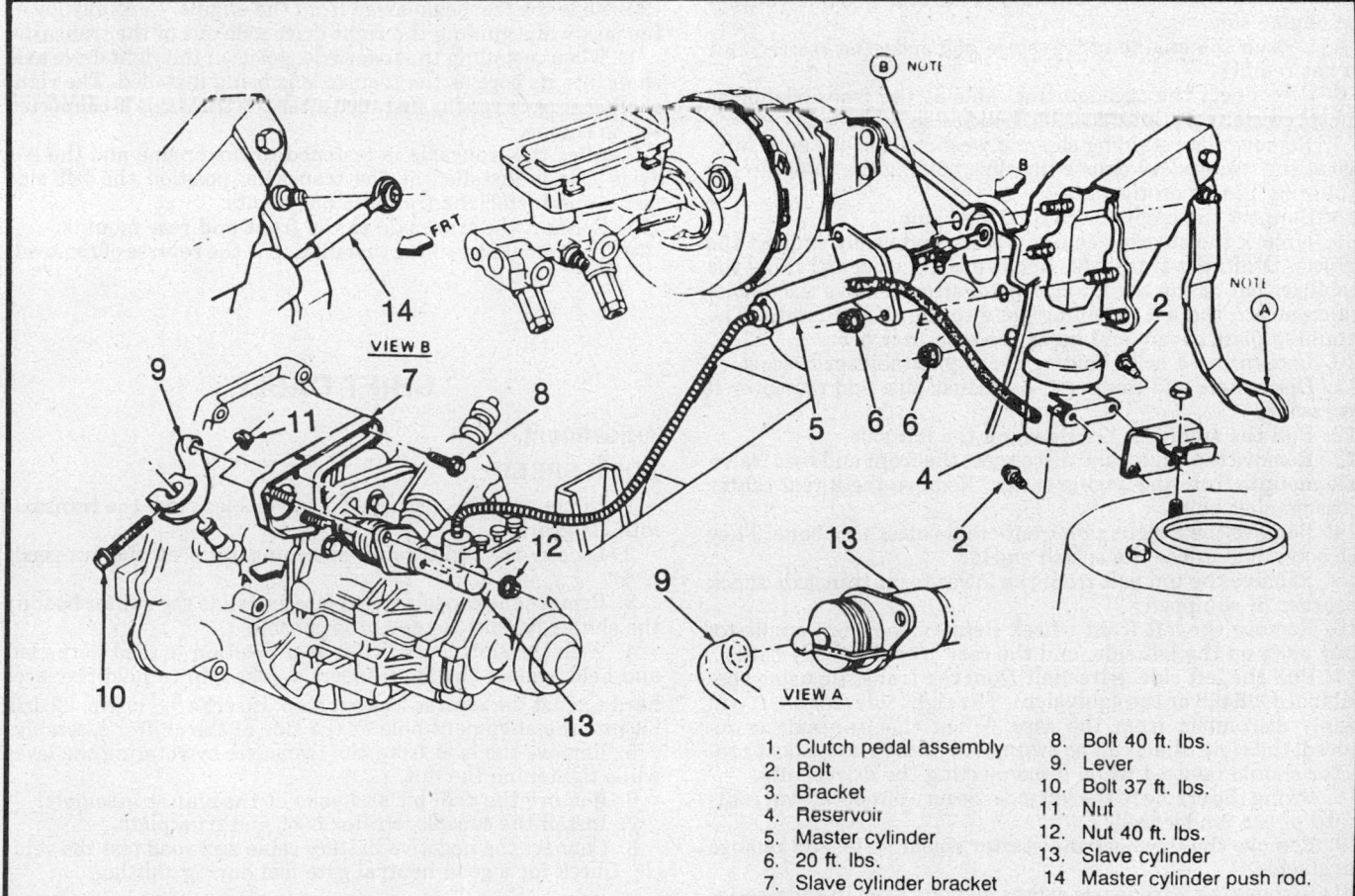

1. Clutch pedal assembly	8. Bolt 40 ft. lbs.
2. Bolt	9. Lever
3. Bracket	10. Bolt 37 ft. lbs.
4. Reservoir	11. Nut
5. Master cylinder	12. Nut 40 ft. lbs.
6. 20 ft. lbs.	13. Slave cylinder
7. Slave cylinder bracket	14. Master cylinder push rod

Clutch hydraulic system

the vehicle and disconnect the clutch master cylinder pushrod from the clutch pedal.

4. Remove the transaxle assembly.

5. Mark the relationship between the pressure plate and flywheel.

6. Evenly and carefully loosen the pressure plate bolts until the spring pressure is relieved.

7. Support the pressure plate and remove the pressure plate retaining bolts. Remove the pressure plate and disc.

NOTE: Do not disassemble the pressure plate and disc assembly. If the unit is defective, replace as an assembly.

8. Clean and lubricate all parts as required.

9. Installation is the reverse of the removal procedure. Note that the disc is installed with the damper springs offset towards the transaxle. Most discs are marked FLYWHEEL SIDE. If the old pressure plate is to be reused, align the marks made previously.

Manual Transaxle

Removal and Installation

FOUR SPEED

1. Disconnect the negative battery cable.

2. Remove the 2 transaxle strut bracket bolts on the left side of the engine compartment, if equipped.

3. As required, on vehicles euipped with a V6 engine, disconnect the fuel lines and fuel line clamps at the clutch cable bracket.

4. Remove the top 4 engine-to-transaxle bolts, and the one at the rear near the firewall. The one at the rear is installed from the engine side.

5. Loosen the engine-to-transaxle bolt near the starter, but do not remove.

6. Disconnect the speedometer cable at the transaxle, or at the speed control transducer on vehicles so equipped.

7. Remove the retaining clip and washer from the shift linkage at the transaxle. Remove the clips holding the cables to the mounting bosses on the case.

8. Support the engine with a lifting chain.

9. Unlock the steering column. Raise and safely support the vehicle. Drain the transaxle. Remove the 2 nuts attaching the stabilizer bar to the left lower control arm. Remove the 4 bolts which attach the left retaining plate to the engine cradle. The retaining plate covers and holds the stabilizer bar.

10. Loosen the 4 bolts holding the right stabilizer bracket.

11. Disconnect and remove the exhaust pipe and crossover if necessary.

12. Pull the stabilizer bar down on the left side.

13. Remove the 4 nuts and disconnect the front and rear transaxle mounts from the engine cradle. Remove the 2 rear center crossmember bolts.

14. Remove the 3 right side front cradle attaching bolts. They are accessible under the splash shield.

15. Remove the top bolt from the lower front transaxle shock absorber, if equipped.

16. Remove the left front wheel. Remove the front cradle-to-body bolts on the left side, and the rear cradle-to-body bolts.

17. Pull the left side driveshaft from the transaxle using special tool J–28468 or the equivalent. The right side axle shaft will simply disconnect from the case. When the transaxle is removed, the right shaft can be swung out of the way. A boot protector should be used when disconnecting the driveshafts.

18. Swing the cradle to the left side. Secure out of the way, outboard of the fender well.

19. Remove the flywheel and starter shield bolts, and remove the shields.

20. Remove the 2 transaxle extension bolts from the engine-to-transaxle bracket, if equipped.

21. Place a jack under the transaxle case. Remove the last en-gine-to-transaxle bolt. Pull the transaxle to the left, away from the engine, then down and out from under the vehicle.

22. Installation is the reverse of removal. Position the right axle shaft into its bore as the transaxle is being installed. When the transaxle is bolted to the engine, swing the cradle into position and install the cradle-to-body bolts immediately. Be sure to guide the left axle shaft into place as the cradle is moved back into position.

FIVE SPEED

1. Disconnect the negative battery cable.

2. Remove the air cleaner and air intake duct assembly.

3. Remove the sound insulator from inside the car.

4. Remove the clutch master cylinder pushrod from the clutch pedal.

5. Remove the clutch slave cylinder from the transaxle.

6. Disconnect the exhaust crossover pipe.

7. Disconnect the shift cables at the transaxle.

8. Install the engine support fixture J–28467.

9. Remove the top engine to transaxle bolts.

10. Raise and safely support the vehicle.

11. Install the drive axle boot seal protectors with special tool J–34754.

12. Remove the left front wheel and tire.

13. Remove the Left side frame and disconnect the rear transaxle mount from the bracket.

14. Drain the transaxle.

15. Disengage the drive axles from the transaxle.

16. Remove the clutch housing cover bolts.

17. Disconnect the speedometer cable.

18. Attach a jack to the transaxle case.

19. Remove the remaining transaxle to engine bolts.

20. Slide the transaxle away from the engine. Carefully lower the jack while guiding the right drive axle out of the transaxle.

21. When installing the transaxle, position the right drive axle shaft into its bore as the transaxle is being installed. The right shaft cannot be readily installed after the transaxle is connected to the engine.

22. After the transaxle is fastened to the engine and the left drive axle is installed at the transaxle, position the left side frame and install the frame to body bolts.

23. Connect the transaxle to the front and rear mounts.

24. The remainder of the installation is the reverse of removal.

SHIFT CABLE

Adjustment

FOUR SPEED

1. Disconnect the negative battery cable. Place the transaxle into 1st gear.

2. Loosen the shift cable attaching nuts at the transaxle lever.

3. Remove the console trim plate and slide the shifter boot up the shifter handle. Remove the console.

4. With the shift lever in 1st gear position (pulled to the left and held against the stop) insert a yoke clip to hold the lever hard against the reverse lockout stop. Insert a $5/32$ or No. 22 drill bit into the alignment hole at the side of the shifter assembly.

5. Remove the lash from the transaxle by rotating the lever while tightening the nut.

6. Remove the drill bit and yoke at the shifter assembly.

7. Install the console, shifter boot and trim plate.

8. Connect the negative battery cable and road test the vehicle. Check for a good neutral gate feel during shifting.

NOTE: It may be necessary to fine tune the adjustment after road testing.

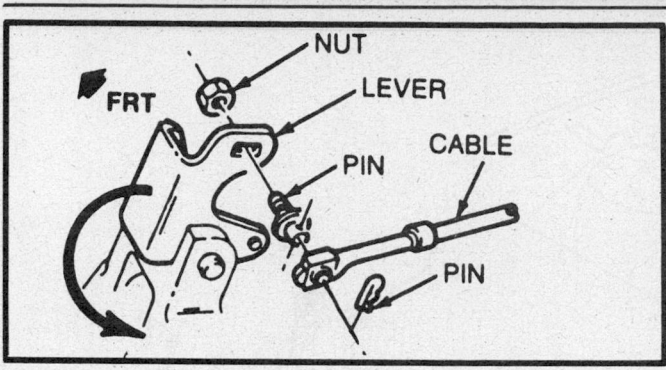

Removing lash from the transaxle—rotate in direction shown

Automatic Transaxle

Removal and Installation

THM 125C

NOTE: By September 1, 1991, Hydra-matic will have changed the name designation of the THM 125C automatic transaxle. The new name designation for this transaxle will be Hydra-matic 3T40. Transaxles built between 1989 and 1990 will serve as transitional years in which a dual system, made up of the old designation and the new designation will be in effect.

1. Disconnect the negative battery cable.
2. Remove the air cleaner.
3. Unbolt the detent cable attaching bracket at the transaxles.
4. Pull up on the detent cable cover at the transaxle until the cable is exposed. Disconnect the cable from the rod.
5. Remove the 2 transaxle strut bracket bolts at the transaxle, if equipped.
6. Remove all the engine-to-transaxle bolts except the one near the starter. The one nearest the firewall is installed from the engine side of the vehicle.
7. Loosen, but do not remove the engine-to-transaxle bolt near the starter.
8. Disconnect the speedometer cable at the upper and lower coupling. On vehicles equipped with cruise control, remove the speedometer cable at the transducer.
9. Remove the retaining clip and washer from the shift linkage at the transaxle. Remove the 2 shift linkage at the transaxle. Remove the 2 shift linkage bracket bolts.
10. Disconnect and plug the cooler lines at the transaxle.
11. Install an engine holding fixture. Raise the engine enough to take its weight off the mounts.
12. Unlock the steering column. Raise and safely support the vehicle.
13. Remove the 2 nuts holding the anti-sway bar to the left lower control arm (driver's side).
14. Remove the 4 bolts attaching the covering plate over the stabilizer bar to the engine cradle on the left side of vehicle.
15. Loosen but do not remove the 4 bolts holding the stabilizer bar bracket to the right side of the engine cradle. Pull the bar downward.
16. Disconnect the front and rear transaxle mounts at the engine cradle.
17. Remove the 2 rear center crossmember bolts.
18. Remove the 3 right (passenger) side front engine cradle attaching bolts. The nuts are accessible under the splash shield next to the frame rail.
19. On vehicles equipped with V6 engine, remove the top bolt from the lower front transaxle shock absorber, as required.
20. Remove the left side front and rear cradle-to-body bolts.
21. Remove the left front wheel. Attach an axle shaft removing

tool J–28468 or equivalent to a slide hammer. Place the tool behind the axle shaft cones and pull the cones out away from the transaxle. Remove the right shaft in the same manner. Set the shafts out of the way. Plug the openings in the transaxle to prevent fluid leakage and the entry of dirt.
22. Swing the partial engine cradle to the left (driver) side and wire it out of the way outboard of the fender well.
23. Remove the 4 torque converter and starter shield bolts. Remove the 2 transaxle extension bolts from the engine-to-transaxle bracket.
24. Attach a transaxle jack to the case.
25. Use a felt pen to matchmark the torque converter and flywheel. Remove the 3 torque converter-to-flywheel bolts.
26. Remove the transaxle-to-engine bolt near the starter. Remove the transaxle by sliding it to the left, away from the engine.
27. Installation is the reverse of the removal procedure. As the transaxle is installed, slide the right axle shaft into the case. Install the cradle-to-body bolts before the stabilizer bar is installed. To aid in stabilizer bar installation, a pry hole has been provided in the engine cradle.

THM 440–T4

NOTE: By September 1, 1991, Hydra-matic will have changed the name designation of the THM 440–T4 automatic transaxle. The new name designation for this transaxle will be Hydra-matic 4T60. Transaxles built between 1989 and 1990 will serve as transitional years in which a dual system, made up of the old designation and the new designation will be in effect.

1. Disconnect the negative battery cable.
2. Remove the air cleaner and disconnect the T.V. cable at the throttle body.
3. Disconnect the shift linkage at the transaxle.
4. Install the engine support fixture tool J–28467 or equivalent.
5. Disconnect all electrical connectors.
6. Remove the 3 bolts from the transaxle to the engine.
7. Disconnect the vacuum line at the modulator.
8. Raise and safely support the vehicle.
9. Remove the left front wheel and tire assembly.
10. Remove the left side ball joint from the steering knuckle.
11. Disconnect the brake line bracket at the strut.

NOTE: A drive axle seal protector tool J–34754 should be modified and installed on any drive axle prior to service procedures on or near the drive axle. Failure to do so could result in seal damage or joint failure.

12. Remove the drive axles from the transaxle.

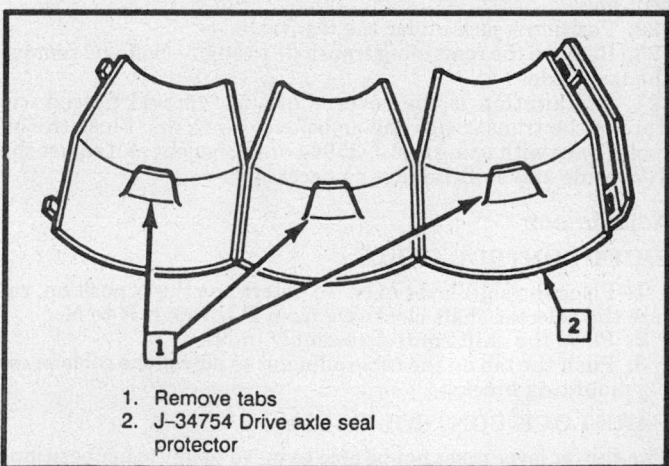

1. Remove tabs
2. J–34754 Drive axle seal protector

Modifying seal protector tool J–34754

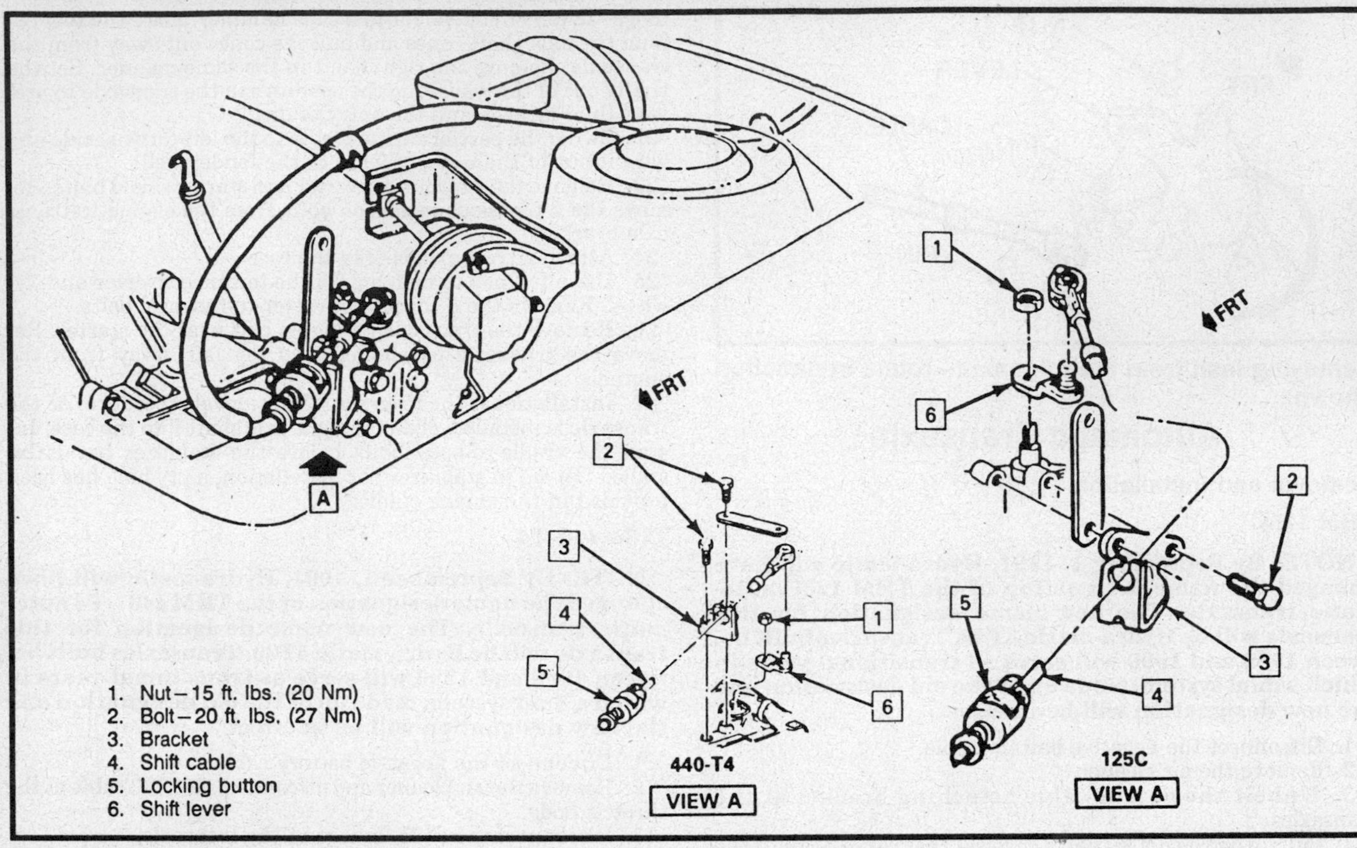

1. Nut – 15 ft. lbs. (20 Nm)
2. Bolt – 20 ft. lbs. (27 Nm)
3. Bracket
4. Shift cable
5. Locking button
6. Shift lever

440-T4

VIEW A

125C

VIEW A

Shift control assembly – typical

13. Disconnect the pinch bolt at the intermediate steering shaft. Failure to do so could cause damage to the steering gear.
14. Remove the frame to stabilizer bolts.
15. Remove the stabilizer bolts at the control arm.
16. Remove the left front frame assembly.
17. Disconnect the speedometer cable or wire connector from the transaxle.
18. Remove the extension housing to engine block support bracket.
19. Disconnect the cooler pipes.
20. Remove the converter cover, and converter to flywheel bolts.
21. Remove all of the remaining transaxle to engine bolts except one.
22. Position a jack under the transaxle.
23. Remove the remaining transaxle to engine bolt and remove the transaxle.
24. Installation is the reverse of the removal procedure. Torque the transaxle to engine bolts to 55 ft. lbs. Flush the oil cooler lines with using tool J-35944 or equivalent and adjust the T.V. cable and shift linkage as necessary.

Adjustment

SHIFT CONTROL CABLE

1. Place the shift lever in **N**. To determine the **N** position, rotate the selector shaft clockwise from **P** through **R** to **N**.
2. Place the shift control assembly in **N**.
3. Push the tab on the cable adjuster to adjust the cable in cable mounting bracket.

PARK/LOCK CONTROL CABLE

The shifter lever must not be able to move to any other positions with the shift lever in **P** and the key in the **LOCK** position. Also, with the key in the **RUN** position and the shift lever in **N**, make sure you cannot turn the key to the **LOCK** position. If these conditions cannot be met, adjustment is necessary.

1. If the key cannot be removed in the **P** position, snap the connector lock button to the **UP** position.
2. Move the cable connector nose rearward until the key can be removed from the ignition.
3. Pusn the snap lock button down.

NEUTRAL START AND BACK-UP LAMP SWITCH

1. Place the shift shaft in **N**.
2. Align the flats on te shift shaft with the switch.

1. Lock button
2. Inhibitor
3. Cable – column end fitting

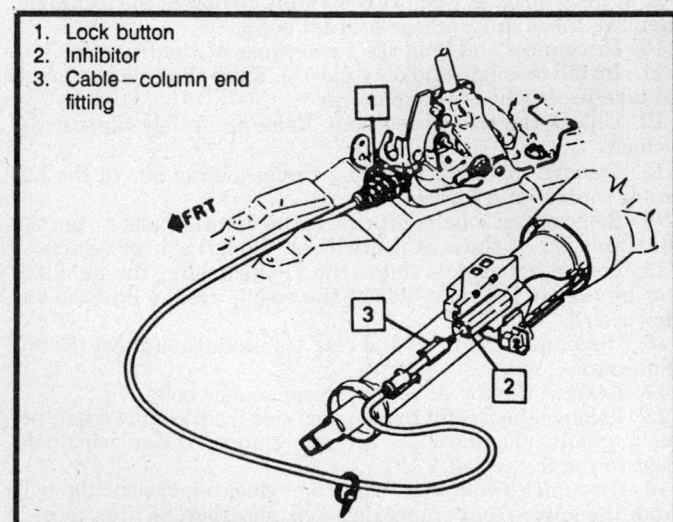

Park lock cable – typical

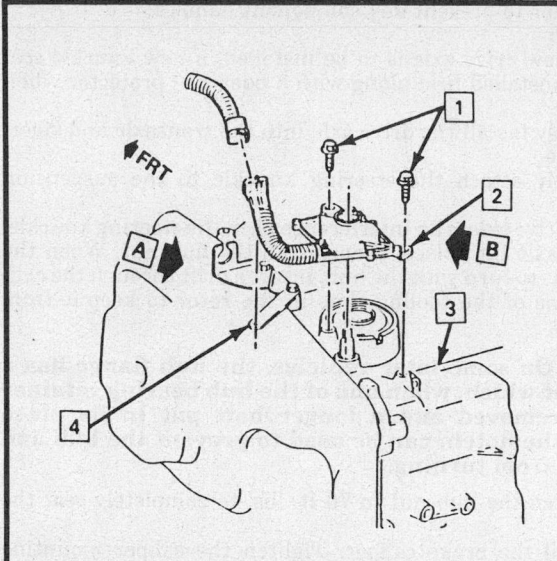

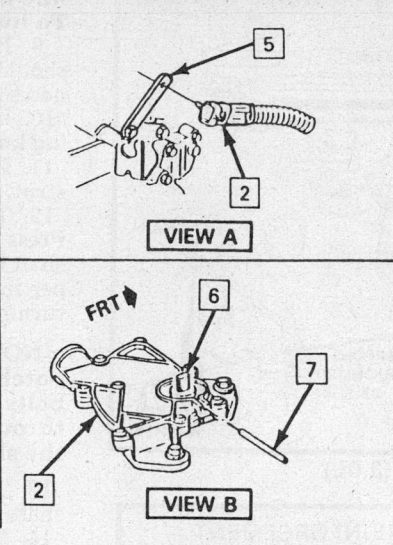

VIEW A

VIEW B

1. Bolt — 21 ft. lbs. (28 Nm)
2. Switch assembly
3. Transaxle
4. Bracket (125C)
5. Bracket (440-T4)
6. Trans. shaft
7. ³/₃₂ inch. drill bit or 2.34 dia. gage pin

Park/neutral start and back-up switch

3. Assembly the mounting bolts-to-case, loosely.
4. Insert a $\frac{3}{32}$ drill bit or 2.34 diameter gauge pin in the service adjustment hole and rotate the switch until the pin drops in to a depth of $\frac{9}{64}$ (9mm).
5. Tighten the mounting bolts.

T.V. CABLE

1. With the engine **OFF**, depress and hold down the readjust tab at the T.V. cable adjuster.
2. Move the cable conduit until it stops against the fitting. Release the readjustment tab.
3. Rotate the throttle lever by hand to its full travel position. The slider must ratchet toward the lever when the lever is rotated to its full travel.

NOTE: Check that the cable moves freely. The cable may appear to function properly with the engine OFF and COLD. Recheck after the engine is HOT.

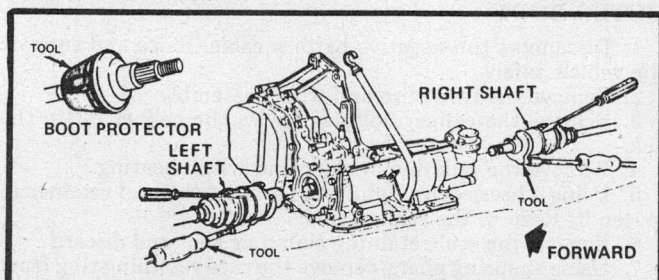

Special tools used for the removal of the axle driveshafts

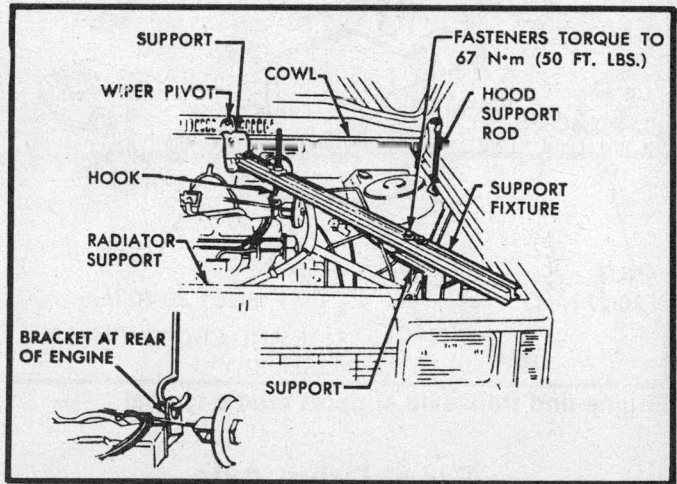

Engine support fixture arrangement—151 (2.5L) engine

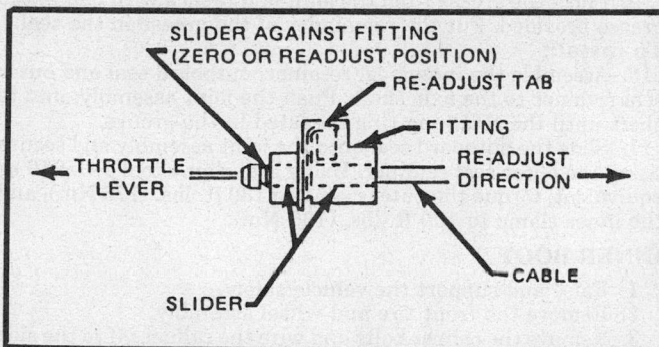

T.V. cable adjuster

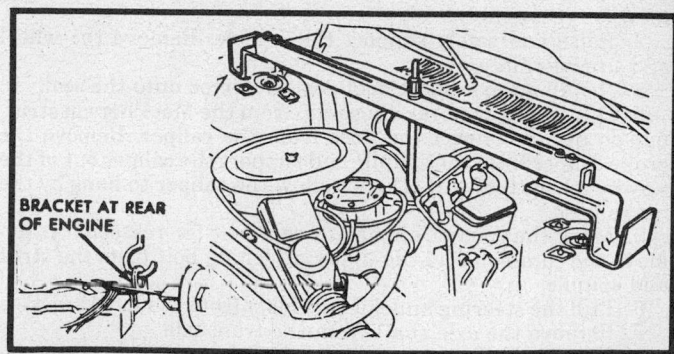

Engine support fixture arrangement—173 (2.8L) engine

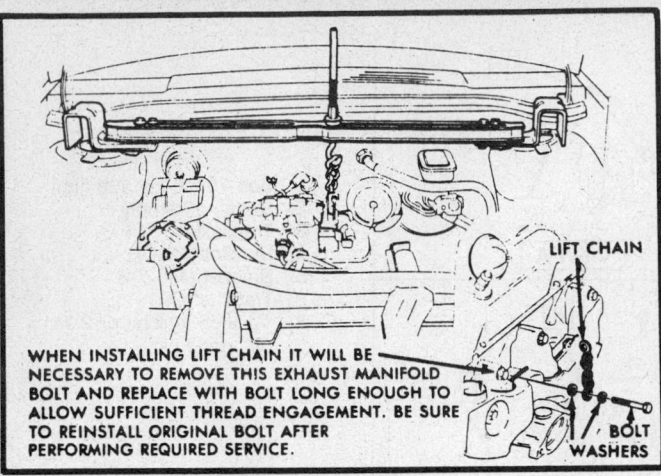

WHEN INSTALLING LIFT CHAIN IT WILL BE NECESSARY TO REMOVE THIS EXHAUST MANIFOLD BOLT AND REPLACE WITH BOLT LONG ENOUGH TO ALLOW SUFFICIENT THREAD ENGAGEMENT. BE SURE TO REINSTALL ORIGINAL BOLT AFTER PERFORMING REQUIRED SERVICE.

LIFT CHAIN

BOLT WASHERS

Engine support fixture—6–181 (3.0L)

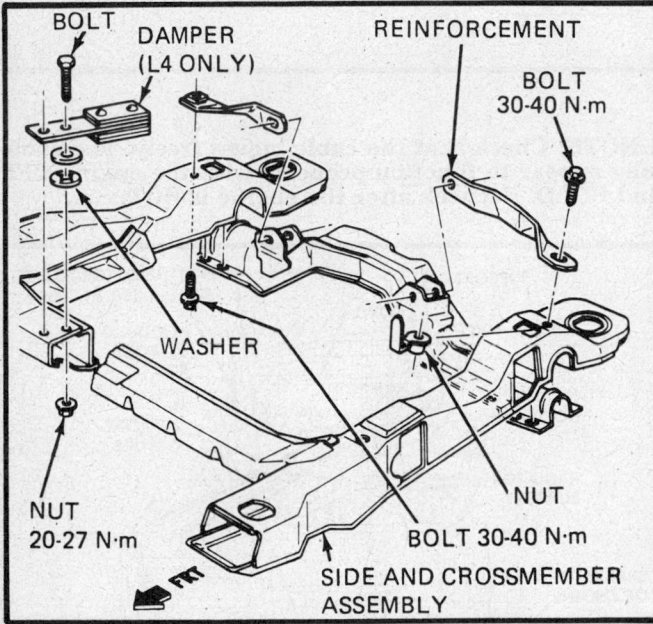

BOLT

DAMPER (L4 ONLY)

REINFORCEMENT

BOLT 30-40 N·m

WASHER

NUT 20-27 N·m

NUT

BOLT 30-40 N·m

SIDE AND CROSSMEMBER ASSEMBLY

Engine and transaxle support cradle-typical

Front Drive Axle

Removal and Installation

1. Remove the hub nut and discard. A new hub nut must be used for reassembly.
2. Raise and safely support the vehicle. Remove the wheel and tire assembly.
3. Install an axle shaft boot seal protector onto the seal.
4. Disconnect the brake hose clip from the MacPherson strut, but do not disconnect the hose from the caliper. Remove the brake caliper from the spindle and support the caliper out of the way by a length of wire. Do not allow the caliper to hang by the brake hose.
5. Mark the camber alignment cam bolt for reassembly. Remove the cam bolt and the upper attaching bolt from the strut and spindle.
6. Pull the steering knuckle assembly from the strut bracket.
7. Remove the axle shaft from the transaxle.
8. Using spindle remover tool J–28733 or the equivalent, remove the axle shaft from the hub and bearing assembly. Do not allow the axle shaft to hang free, if necessary, support using

wire in order to prevent any component damage.

To install:

9. If a new drive axle is to be installed, a new knuckle seal should be installed first along with a boot seal protector when necessary.
10. Loosely install the drive axle into the transaxle and steering knuckle.
11. Loosely attach the steering knuckle to the suspension strut.
12. The drive axle is an interference fit in the steering knuckle. Press the axle into place, then install the hub nut. When the shaft begins to turn with the hub, insert a drift through the caliper into one of the cooling slots in the rotor to keep it from turning.

NOTE: **On some later vehicles, the hub flange has a notch in it which, when one of the hub bearing retainer bolts is removed and a longer bolt put in its place through the notch, can be used to prevent the hub and the shaft from turning.**

13. Tighten the hub nut to 70 ft. lbs. to completely seat the shaft.
14. Install the brake caliper. Tighten the caliper mounting bolts to 30 ft. lbs.
15. Load the hub assembly by lowering it onto a jackstand. Align the camber cam bolt marks made during removal, install the bolt and tighten to 140 ft. lbs. Tighten the upper nut to the same torque valve.
16. Install the axle shaft all the way into the transaxle using a suitable tool inserted into the groove provided on the inner retainer. Tap the tool until the shaft seats in the transaxle. Remove the boot seal protector.
17. Connect the brake hose clip the the strut. Install the tire and wheel, lower the vehicle and tighten the hub nut to 192 ft. lbs.

Boot

Removal and Installation

OUTER BOOT

1. Disconnect the negative battery cable. Raise and support the vehicle safely.
2. Remove the front tire and wheel assembly.
3. Remove the caliper bolts and wire the caliper off to the side.
4. Remove the hub nut, washer and wheel bearing.
5. Using a brass drift, lightly tap around the seal retainer to loosen it. Remove the seal retainer.
6. Remove the seal retaining clamp or ring and discard.
7. Using snapring pliers, remove the race retaining ring from the axle shaft.
8. Pull the outer joint assembly and the outboard seal away from the axle shaft.
9. Flush the grease from the joint and repack with half of the grease provided. Put the remainder of the grease in the seal.

To install:

10. Assemble the inner seal retainer, outboard seal and outer seal retainer to the axle shaft. Push the joint assembly onto te shaft until the retaining ring is seated in the groove.
11. Slide the outboard seal onto the joint assembly and secure using the outer seal retainer. Using seal clamp tool J–35910 or equivalent, torque the outer clamp to 130 ft. lbs. (176 Nm), and the inner clamp to 100 ft. lbs. (136 Nm).

INNER BOOT

1. Raise and support the vehicle safely.
2. Remove the front tire and wheel assembly.
3. Remove the caliper bolts and wire the caliper off to the side of the vehicle.
4. Remove the hub nut, washer and wheel bearing.

5. Remove the front drive axle. Place in a suitable holding fixture being careful not place undue pressure on the axle shaft.

6. Remove the joint assembly retaining ring. Remove the joint assembly.

7. Remove the race retaining ring and remove the seal retainer.

8. Remove the inner seal retaining clamp. Remove the inner joint seal.

9. Flush the grease from the joint and repack with half of the grease provided. Put the remainder of the grease in the seal.

To install:

10. Assemble the inner seal retainer, outboard seal and outer seal retainer to the axle shaft. Push the joint assembly onto te shaft until the retaining ring is seated in the groove.

11. Slide the outboard seal onto the joint assembly and secure using the outer seal retainer. Using seal clamp tool J–35910 or equivalent, torque the outer clamp to 130 ft. lbs. (176 Nm), and the inner clamp to 100 ft. lbs. (136 Nm).

REAR AXLE AND REAR SUSPENSION

Refer to unit repair section for axle overhaul procedure and rear suspension services.

Rear Axle Assembly

Removal and Installation

1. Raise and support the vehicle safely.

NOTE: If removing the rear axle on a twin post hoist, the axle assembly must be supported securely otherwise when certain fasteners are removed the axle assembly could slip from the hoist.

2. Remove the rear wheels. Remove the rear brake drums. Disconnect the parking brake from the rear axle.

3. Remove the brake brackets from the vehicle frame.

4. Remove the rear shock absorbers. Remove the track bar.

5. Disconnect the rear brake hoses.

6. Lower the axle assembly and remove the coil springs and insulators.

7. Remove the hub attaching bolts. Remove the hub and bearing assembly.

8. Remove the control arm bracket attaching bolts. Remove the control arms. Lower the axle from the vehicle.

9. Installation is the reverse of the removal procedure. Bleed the brake system and adjust the parking brake, as required.

1—POSITION LEG OF UPPER COIL ON SPRINGS PARALLEL TO AXLE ASM. & TOWARDS SIDE OF VEHICLE WITHIN LIMITS SHOWN.

2—UNDERBODY

3—INSULATOR

4—SPRING

5—AXLE ASM.

6—LOWER SPRING INSULATOR

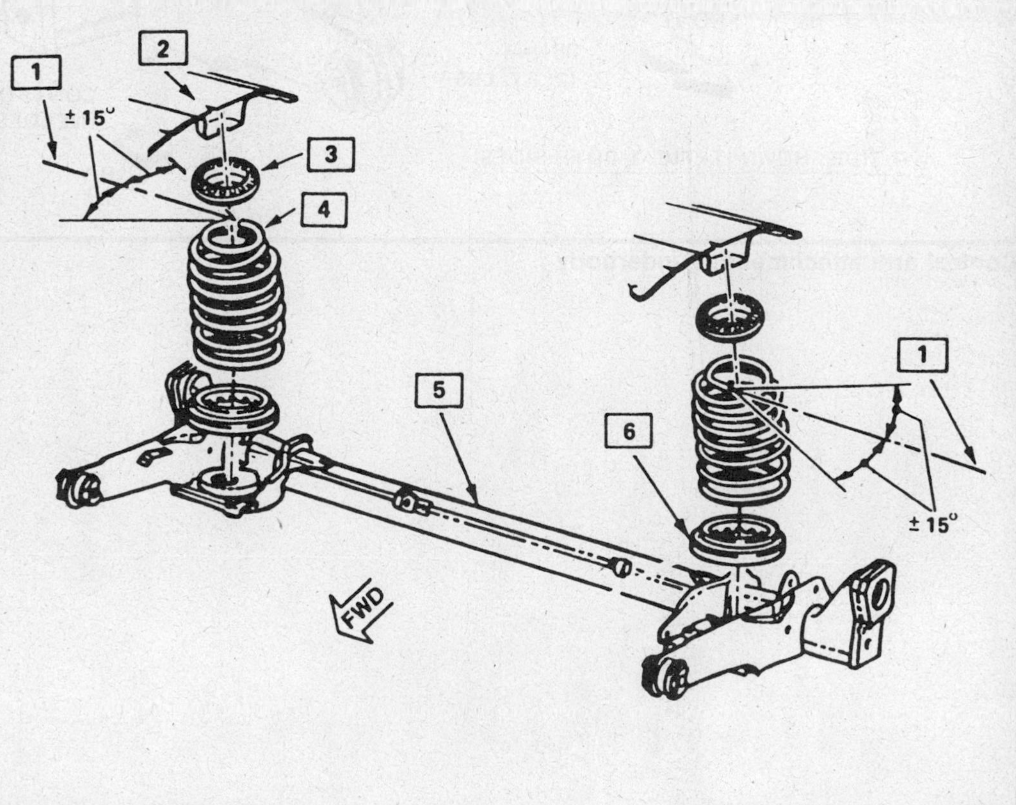

Rear axle assembly—exploded view

Rear Wheel Hub and Bearing Assembly

Removal and Installation

A single unit hub and bearing assembly is bolted to both ends of the rear axle assembly. The hub and bearing assembly is a sealed unit which requires no maintenance. The unit must be replaced as an assembly and cannot be disassembled or adjusted.

1. Disconnect the negative battery cable.
2. Raise and support the vehicle safely.
3. Remove the wheel and tire assembly. Remove the brake drum.
4. Remove the 4 hub and bearing assembly to rear axle attaching bolts and remove the hub and bearing assembly from the axle.
5. Installation is the reverse of the removal procedure.

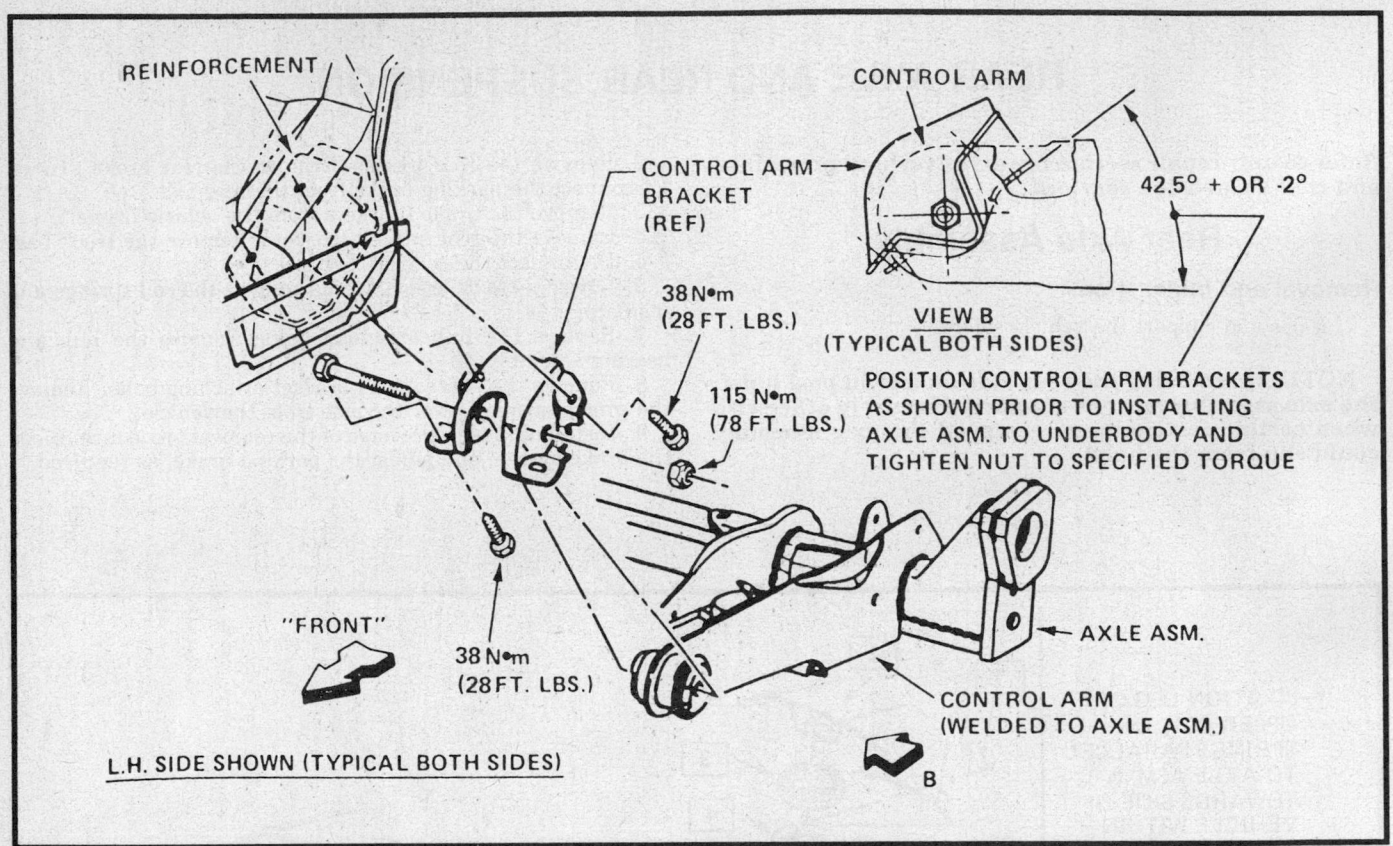

REINFORCEMENT

CONTROL ARM

CONTROL ARM
BRACKET
(REF)

42.5° + OR -2°

38 N•m
(28 FT. LBS.)

115 N•m
(78 FT. LBS.)

VIEW B
(TYPICAL BOTH SIDES)

POSITION CONTROL ARM BRACKETS
AS SHOWN PRIOR TO INSTALLING
AXLE ASM. TO UNDERBODY AND
TIGHTEN NUT TO SPECIFIED TORQUE

AXLE ASM.

CONTROL ARM
(WELDED TO AXLE ASM.)

"FRONT"

38 N•m
(28 FT. LBS.)

B

L.H. SIDE SHOWN (TYPICAL BOTH SIDES)

Control arm attachment at underbody

YEAR IDENTIFICATION

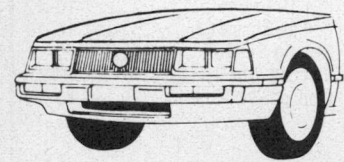

1986 Electra and Park Avenue

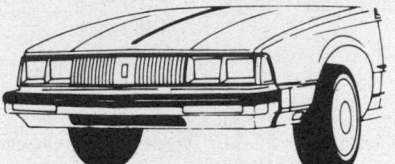

1986 Ninety Eight Regency Brougham

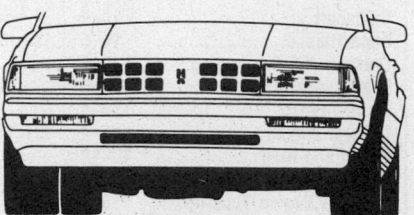

1989–90 Oldsmobile Touring Sedan

1987–90 Deville and Fleetwood

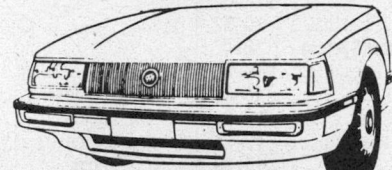

1987–90 Electra and Park Avenue

1987–90 Ninety Eight Regency Brougham

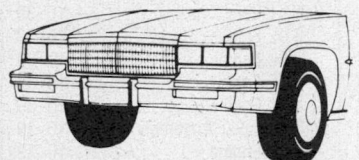

1986 Deville and Fleetwood

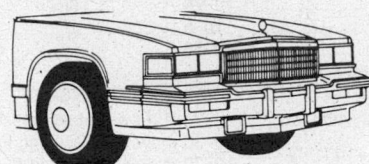

Cadillac Touring Sedan

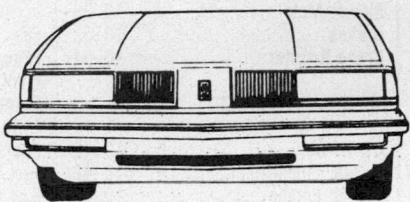

1987–90 Delta 88 and Royale

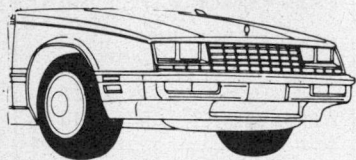

1988–90 LeSabre T–Type

1986 LeSabre Limited

1987–90 Bonneville SE/LE

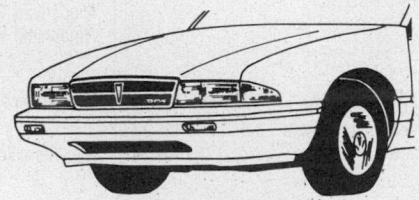

1987–90 LeSabre

1987–90 Bonneville SSE

VEHICLE IDENTIFICATION

It is important for servicing and ordering parts to be certain of the vehicle and engine identification. The VIN (vehicle identification number) is a 17 digit number visible through the windshield on the driver's side of the dash and contains the vehicle and engine identification codes. The tenth digit indicates model year and the eigth digit indicates engine code. It can be interpreted as follows:

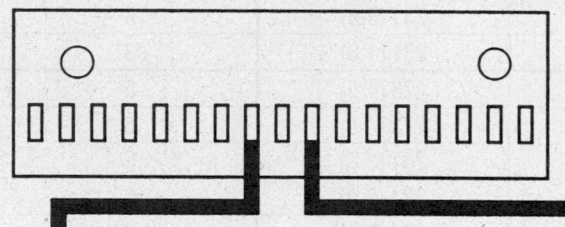

Engine Code						Model Year	
Code	Cu. In.	Liters	Cyl.	Fuel Sys.	Eng. Mfg.	Code	Year
L	181	3.0	6	MFI	Buick	F	1985
3	231	3.8	6	SFI	Buick	G	1986
B	231	3.8	6	SFI	Buick	H	1987
C	231	3.8	6	SFI	Buick	J	1988
T	263	4.3	6	Diesel	Oldsmobile	K	1988
8	250	4.1	8	DFI	Cadillac	L	1989
5	273	4.5	8	DFI	Cadillac	M	1990

ENGINE IDENTIFICATION

Year	Model	Engine Displacement cu. in. (liter)	Engine Series Identification (VIN)	No. of Cylinders	Engine Type
1986	DeVille	250 (4.1)	8	6	OHV
	Fleetwood	250 (4.1)	8	6	OHV
	Electra	231 (3.8)	3	6	OHV
	Electra	231 (3.8)	B	6	OHV
	Park Avenue	231 (3.8)	3	6	OHV
	Park Avenue	231 (3.8)	B	6	OHV
	LeSabre	181 (3.0)	L	6	OHV
	LeSabre	231 (3.8)	3	6	OHV
	LeSabre	231 (3.8)	B	6	OHV
	Ninety Eight	231 (3.8)	3	6	OHV
	Ninety Eight	231 (3.8)	B	6	OHV
	Delta 88	181 (3.0)	L	6	OHV
	Delta 88	231 (3.8)	3	6	OHV
	Delta 88	231 (3.8)	B	6	OHV
1987	DeVille	250 (4.1)	8	8	OHV
	Fleetwood	250 (4.1)	8	8	OHV
	Electra	231 (3.8)	3	6	OHV
	Park Avenue	231 (3.8)	3	6	OHV
	LeSabre	231 (3.8)	3	6	OHV
	LeSabre	231 (3.8)	B	6	OHV
	Ninety Eight	231 (3.8)	3	6	OHV
	Delta 88	231 (3.8)	3	6	OHV

ENGINE IDENTIFICATION

Year	Model	Engine Displacement cu. in. (liter)	Engine Series Identification (VIN)	No. of Cylinders	Engine Type
1987	Delta 88	231 (3.8)	B	6	OHV
	Bonneville	231 (3.8)	3	6	OHV
1988	DeVille	273 (4.5)	5	8	OHV
	Fleetwood	273 (4.5)	5	8	OHV
	Electra	231 (3.8)	C	6	OHV
	Park Avenue	231 (3.8)	C	6	OHV
	LeSabre	231 (3.8)	3	6	OHV
	Ninety Eight	231 (3.8)	C	6	OHV
	Delta 88	231 (3.8)	3	6	OHV
	Bonneville	231 (3.8)	3	6	OHV
	Bonneville	231 (3.8)	C, 3	6	OHV
1989-90	DeVille	273 (4.5)	5	8	OHV
	Fleetwood	273 (4.5)	5	8	OHV
	Electra	231 (3.8)	C	6	OHV
	Park Avenue	231 (3.8)	C	6	OHV
	LeSabre	231 (3.8)	C	6	OHV
	Ninety Eight	231 (3.8)	C	6	OHV
	Delta 88	231 (3.8)	C	6	OHV
	Bonneville	231 (3.8)	C	6	OHV

OHV—Overhead valve

GENERAL ENGINE SPECIFICATIONS

Year	VIN	No. Cylinder Displacement cu. in. (liter)	Fuel System Type	Net Horsepower @ rpm	Net Torque @ rpm (ft.lbs.)	Bore × Stroke (in.)	Compression Ratio	Oil Pressure @ rpm
1986	L	6-181 (3.0)	MFI	125 @ 4900	150 @ 2400	3.800 × 2.660	9.0:1	37 @ 2400
	3	6-231 (3.8)	SFI	150 @ 4400	200 @ 2000	3.800 × 3.400	8.5:1	37 @ 2000
	B	6-231 (3.8)	SFI	140 @ 4400	200 @ 2000	3.800 × 3.400	8.5:1	37 @ 2000
	8	8-250 (4.1)	DFI	130 @ 4200	200 @ 2000	3.465 × 3.307	8.5:1	30 @ 2000
1987	3	6-231 (3.8)	SFI	150 @ 4400	200 @ 2000	3.800 × 3.400	8.5:1	37 @ 2000
	B	6-231 (3.8)	SFI	150 @ 4400	200 @ 2000	3.800 × 3.400	8.5:1	37 @ 2400
	8	8-250 (4.1)	DFI	130 @ 4200	200 @ 2000	3.465 × 3.307	9.0:1	30 @ 2000
1988	3	6-231 (3.8)	SFI	150 @ 4400	200 @ 2000	3.800 × 3.400	8.5:1	37 @ 2000
	C	6-231 (3.8)	SFI	165 @ 5200	210 @ 2000	3.800 × 3.400	8.5:1	37 @ 2400
	5	8-273 (4.5)	DFI	155 @ 4000	240 @ 2800	3.622 × 3.307	9.0:1	37 @ 1500
1989-90	C	6-231 (3.8)	SFI	165 @ 5200	210 @ 2000	3.800 × 3.400	8.5:1	37 @ 2400
	5	8-273 (4.5)	DFI	155 @ 4000	240 @ 2800	3.622 × 3.307	9.0:1	37 @ 1500

SFI Sequential Fuel Injection
DFI Digital Fuel Injection

GASOLINE ENGINE TUNE-UP SPECIFICATIONS
Refer to Section 34 for all spark plug recommendations

Year	VIN	No. Cylinder Displacement cu. in. (liter)	Spark Plugs Gap (in.)	Ignition Timing (deg.) MT	AT	Compression Pressure (psi)	Fuel Pump (psi)	Idle Speed (rpm) MT	AT	Valve Clearance In.	Ex.
1986	L	6-181 (3.0)	.045	—	①	NA	34-44	—	①	Hyd.	Hyd.
	3	6-231 (3.8)	.080	①	①	NA	28-36	①	①	Hyd.	Hyd.
	B	6-231 (3.8)	.080	①	①	NA	28-36	①	①	Hyd.	Hyd.
	8	6-250 (4.1)	.060	①	①	NA	40	①	①	Hyd.	Hyd.
1987	3	6-231 (3.8)	.080	①	①	NA	28-36	①	①	Hyd.	Hyd.
	B	6-231 (3.8)	.080	—	①	NA	26-36	—	①	Hyd.	Hyd.
	8	6-250 (4.1)	.060	①	①	NA	40	①	①	Hyd.	Hyd.
1988	3	6-231 (3.8)	.080	①	①	NA	27-36	①	①	Hyd.	Hyd.
	C	6-231 (3.8)	.060	①	①	NA	27-36	①	①	Hyd.	Hyd.
	5	8-273 (4.5)	.060	①	①	NA	11.6	①	①	Hyd.	Hyd.
1989	C	6-231 (3.8)	.060	①	①	NA	27-36	①	①	Hyd.	Hyd.
	5	8-273 (4.5)	.060	①	①	NA	11.6	①	①	Hyd.	Hyd.
1990		SEE UNDERHOOD SPECIFICATIONS STICKER									

NOTE: The underhood specifications sticker often reflects tune-up specification changes made in production. Sticker figures must be used if they disagree with those in this chart. Part numbers in this chart are not recommendations by Chilton for any product by brand name

NA Not available

Hyd. Hydraulic

① These vehicles are equipped with computerized emissions systems which have no distributor vacuum advance unit. The idle speed and ignition timing are controlled by the emissions computer.

FIRING ORDER

NOTE: To avoid confusion, replace the spark plugs and wires one at a time.

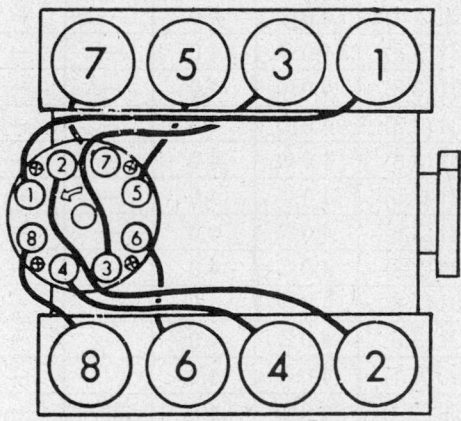

Cadillac 250 cu. in. (4.1L) and 273 cu. in. (4.5L) V8 engines
Firing order: 1–8–4–3–6–5–7–2
Distributor rotation: counterclockwise

FIRING ORDER

NOTE: To avoid confusion, replace the spark plugs and wires one at a time.

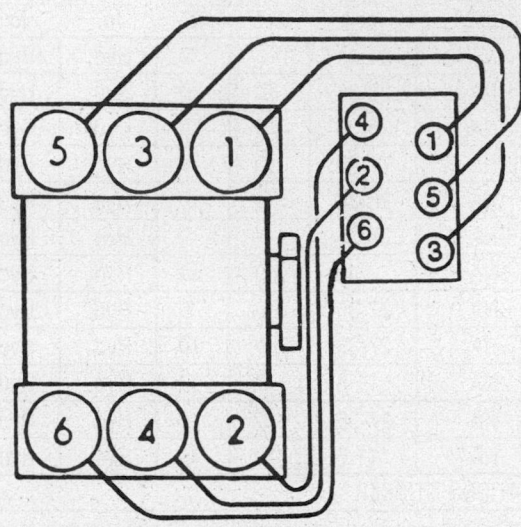

Buick 231 cu. in. (3.8L VIN 3 & B) V6
Firing order: 1–6–5–4–3–2
C³I ignition system

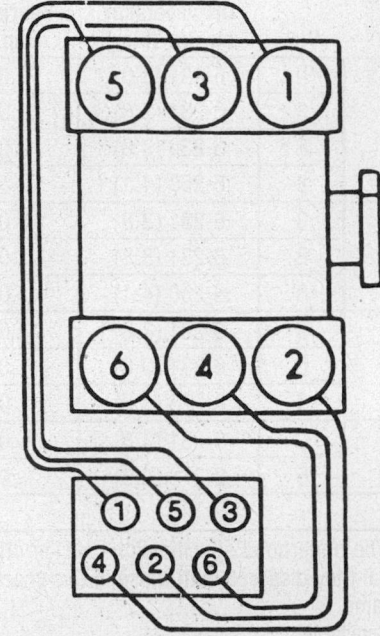

Buick 231 cu. in. (3.8L-VIN 3) V6 engine
Firing order: 1–6–5–4–3–2
C³I ignition system

CAPACITIES

Year	Model	VIN	No. Cylinder Displacement cu. in. (liter)	Engine Crankcase		Transmission (pts.)			Drive Axle (pts.)	Fuel Tank (gal.)	Cooling System (qts.)
				with Filter	without Filter	4-Spd	5-Spd	Auto			
1986	DeVille	8	8-250 (4.1)	4.0 ①	4.0	—	—	13.0	—	18	13.2
	Fleetwood	8	8-250 (4.1)	4.0 ①	4.0	—	—	13.0	—	18	13.2
	Electra	3	6-231 (3.8)	4.0 ①	4.0	—	—	13.0	—	18	13.2
	Electra	B	6-231 (3.8)	4.0 ①	4.0	—	—	13.0	—	18	13.2
	Park Avenue	B	6-231 (3.8)	4.0 ①	4.0	—	—	13.0	—	18	13.2
	Park Avenue	B	6-231 (3.8)	4.0 ①	4.0	—	—	13.0	—	18	13.2
	LeSabre	L	6-181 (3.0)	4.0 ①	4.0	—	—	13.0	—	18	12.2
	LeSabre	3	6-231 (3.8)	4.0 ①	4.0	—	—	13.0	—	18	12.6
	LeSabre	B	6-231 (3.8)	4.0 ①	4.0	—	—	13.0	—	18	12.6
	Ninety Eight	3	6-231 (3.8)	4.0 ①	4.0	—	—	13.0	—	18	12.6
	Ninety Eight	B	6-231 (3.8)	4.0 ①	4.0	—	—	13.0	—	18	12.6
1987	DeVille	8	8-250 (4.1)	4.0 ①	4.0	—	—	13.0	—	18	13.2 ②
	Fleetwood	8	8-250 (4.1)	4.0 ①	4.0	—	—	13.0	—	18	13.2 ②
	Electra	3	8-231 (3.8)	4.0 ①	4.0	—	—	13.0	—	18	13.3
	Park Avenue	3	8-231 (3.8)	4.0 ①	4.0	—	—	13.0	—	18	13.3
	LeSabre	B	8-231 (3.8)	4.0 ①	4.0	—	—	13.0	—	18	13.0
	LeSabre	3	8-231 (3.8)	4.0 ①	4.0	—	—	13.0	—	18	13.0

CAPACITIES

Year	Model	VIN	No. Cylinder Displacement cu. in. (liter)	Engine Crankcase with Filter	Engine Crankcase without Filter	Transmission (pts.) 4-Spd	Transmission (pts.) 5-Spd	Transmission (pts.) Auto	Drive Axle (pts.)	Fuel Tank (gal.)	Cooling System (qts.)
1987	Ninety Eight	3	8-231 (3.8)	4.0 ①	4.0	—	—	13.0	—	18	13.3
	Delta 88	B	8-231 (3.8)	4.0 ①	4.0	—	—	13.0	—	18	13.3
	Delta 88	3	8-231 (3.8)	4.0 ①	4.0	—	—	13.0	—	18	13.3
	Bonneville	3	8-231 (3.8)	4.0 ①	4.0	—	—	13.0	—	18	13.3
1988	DeVille	5	8-273 (4.5)	5.5	5.0	—	—	13.0	—	18	13.0 ②
	Fleetwood	5	8-273 (4.5)	5.5	5.0	—	—	13.0	—	18	13.0 ②
	Electra	C	6-231 (3.8)	4.0 ①	4.0	—	—	13.0	—	18	13.0
	Park Avenue	C	6-231 (3.8)	4.0 ①	4.0	—	—	13.0	—	18	13.0
	LeSabre	3	6-231 (3.8)	4.0 ①	4.0	—	—	13.0	—	18	13.0
	Ninety Eight	C	6-231 (3.8)	4.0 ①	4.0	—	—	13.0	—	18	12.50
	Delta 88 Royale	3	6-231 (3.8)	4.0 ①	4.0	—	—	13.0	—	18	13.25
	Bonneville	C, 3	6-231 (3.8)	4.0 ①	4.0	—	—	13.0	—	18	13.0
	Bonneville	C	6-231 (3.8)	4.0 ①	4.0	—	—	13.0	—	18	13.0
1989–90	DeVille	5	8-273 (4.5)	5.5	5.0	—	—	13.0	—	18	13.0 ②
	Fleetwood	5	8-273 (4.5)	5.5	5.0	—	—	13.0	—	18	13.0 ②
	Electra	C	6-231 (3.8)	4.0 ①	4.0	—	—	13.0	—	18	13.0
	Park Avenue	C	6-231 (3.8)	4.0 ①	4.0	—	—	13.0	—	18	13.0
	LeSabre	C	6-231 (3.8)	4.0 ①	4.0	—	—	13.0	—	18	13.0
	Ninety Eight	C	6-231 (3.8)	4.0 ①	4.0	—	—	13.0	—	18	12.50
	Delta 88 Royale	C	6-231 (3.8)	4.0 ①	4.0	—	—	13.0	—	18	13.25
	Bonneville	C	6-231 (3.8)	4.0 ①	4.0	—	—	13.0	—	18	13.0

① Additional oil may be necessary to bring the level to full

② Use a coolant solution specifically designed for use in aluminum engines. Be sure that the coolant used meets GM spec. No. 1825M or is labeled for use in aluminum engines

CAMSHAFT SPECIFICATIONS

All measurements given in inches.

Year	VIN	No. Cylinder Displacement cu. in. (liter)	Journal Diameter 1	Journal Diameter 2	Journal Diameter 3	Journal Diameter 4	Journal Diameter 5	Lobe Lift In.	Lobe Lift Ex.	Bearing Clearance	Camshaft End Play
1986	L	6-181 (3.0)	1.780–1.787	1.780–1.787	1.780–1.787	1.780–1.787	—	0.368	0.384	①	NA
	3	6-231 (3.8)	1.785	1.786	1.786	1.786	—	0.368	0.384	①	NA
	B	6-231 (3.8)	1.785	1.786	1.786	1.786	—	0.392	0.392	①	NA
	8	8-250 (4.1)	2.035–2.036	2.015–2.016	1.995–1.996	1.975–1.976	1.955–1.956	0.384	0.396	0.0018–0.0037	NA
1987	3	6-231 (3.8)	1.785	1.786	1.786	1.786	—	0.368	0.384	①	NA
	B	6-231 (3.8)	1.780–1.787	1.780–1.787	1.780–1.787	1.780–1.787	—	0.392	0.392	①	NA
	8	8-250 (4.1)	2.035–2.036	2.015–2.016	1.995–1.996	1.975–1.976	1.955–1.956	0.384	0.396	0.0018–0.0037	NA

CAMSHAFT SPECIFICATIONS

All measurements given in inches.

Year	VIN	No. Cylinder Displacement cu. in. (liter)	Journal Diameter 1	2	3	4	5	Lobe Lift In.	Ex.	Bearing Clearance	Camshaft End Play
1988	3	6-231 (3.8)	1.785	1.786	1.786	1.786	—	0.245	0.245	①	NA
	C	6-231 (3.8)	1.785	1.786	1.786	1.786	—	0.272	0.272	①	NA
	5	8-273 (4.5)	2.035–2.036	2.015–2.016	1.995–1.996	1.975–1.976	1.955–1.956	0.384	0.396	0.0018–0.0037	NA
1989–90	C	6-231 (3.8)	1.785	1.786	1.786	1.786	—	0.253	0.255	.0005–.0035	NA
	5	8-273 (4.5)	2.035–2.036	2.015–2.016	1.995–1.996	1.975–1.976	1.955–1.956	0.384	0.396	0.0018–0.0037	NA

NA Not available   ① No. 1:0.0005–0.0025   No. 2–5: 0.0005–0.0035

CRANKSHAFT AND CONNECTING ROD SPECIFICATIONS

All measurements are given in inches.

Year	VIN	No. Cylinder Displacement cu. in. (liter)	Crankshaft Main Brg. Journal Dia.	Main Brg. Oil Clearance	Shaft End-play	Thrust on No.	Connecting Rod Journal Diameter	Oil Clearance	Side Clearance
1986	L	6–181 (3.0)	2.4995	0.0003–0.0018	0.003–0.011	2	2.2487–2.2495	0.0005–0.0026	0.006–0.023
	3	6–231 (3.8)	2.4990–2.5000	0.0003–0.0018	0.0030–0.0110	2	2.2487–2.2499	0.0003–0.0028	0.003–0.015
	B	6–231 (3.8)	2.4990–2.5000	0.0003–0.0018	0.0030–0.0110	2	2.2487–2.2499	0.0003–0.0028	0.003–0.015
	8	8–250 (4.1)	2.6400	0.0004–0.0027	0.0010–0.0070	3	1.9291	0.0005–0.0028	0.008–0.020
1987	B	6–231 (3.8)	2.4995	0.0003–0.0018	0.003–0.011	2	2.2487–2.2495	0.0005–0.0026	0.006–0.023
	3	6–231 (3.8)	2.4995	0.0003–0.0018	0.0030–0.0110	2	2.2487–2.2499	0.0003–0.0028	0.003–0.015
	8	8–250 (4.1)	2.6354–2.6364	0.0004–0.0027	0.0010–0.0070	3	1.9291	0.0005–0.0028	0.008–0.020
1988	3	6–231 (3.8)	2.4988–2.4998	0.0003–0.0018	0.0030–0.0110	2	2.2487–2.2495	0.0003–0.0028	0.003–0.015
	C	6–231 (3.8)	2.4988–2.4998	0.0003–0.0018	0.0030–0.0110	2	2.2487–2.2495	0.0003–0.0028	0.003–0.015
	5	8–273 (4.5)	2.6354–2.6364	0.0004–0.0027	0.0010–0.0070	3	1.9291	0.0005–0.0028	0.008–0.020
1989–90	C	6–231 (3.8)	2.4988–2.4998	0.0003–0.0018	0.0030–0.0110	2	2.2487–2.2495	0.0003–0.0028	0.003–0.015
	5	8–273 (4.5)	2.6354–2.6364	0.0004–0.0027	0.0010–0.0070	3	1.9291	0.0005–0.0028	0.008–0.020

VALVE SPECIFICATIONS

Year	VIN	No. Cylinder Displacement cu. in. (liter)	Seat Angle (deg.)	Face Angle (deg.)	Spring Test Pressure (lbs.)	Spring Installed Height (in.)	Stem-to-Guide Clearance (in.)		Stem Diameter (in.)	
							Intake	Exhaust	Intake	Exhaust
1986	L	6-181 (3.0)	45	45	220 @ 1.340	1.727	0.0015–0.0035	0.0015–0.0032	0.3401–0.3412	0.3405–0.3412
	3	6-231 (3.8)	46	45	90	1.727	0.0015–0.0035	0.0015–0.0032	0.3401–0.3412	0.3405–0.3412
	B	6-231 (3.8)	45	45	105	1.727	0.0015–0.0035	0.0015–0.0032	0.3401–0.3412	0.3405–0.3412
	8	8-250 (4.1)	45	44	185	1.730	0.0010–0.0030	0.0010–0.0030	0.3413–0.3420	0.3411–0.3418
1987	3	6-231 (3.8)	46	45	90	1.727	0.0015–0.0035	0.0015–0.0032	0.3401–0.3412	0.3405–0.3412
	B	6-231 (3.8)	45	45	185 @ 1.340	1.727	0.0015–0.0035	0.0015–0.0032	0.3401–0.3412	0.3405–0.3412
	8	8-250 (4.1)	45	44	185	1.730	0.0010–0.0030	0.0010–0.0030	0.3413–0.3420	0.3411–0.3418
1988	3	6-231 (3.8)	46	45	90	1.727	0.0015–0.0035	0.0015–0.0032	0.3401–0.3412	0.3405–0.3412
	C	6-231 (3.8)	45	45	105	1.730	0.0015–0.0035	0.0015–0.0032	0.3401–0.3412	0.3405–0.3412
	5	6-273 (4.5)	45	44	185	1.730	0.0010–0.0030	0.0010–0.0030	0.3413–0.3420	0.3411–0.3418
1989–90	C	6-231 (3.8)	45	45	105	1.730	0.0015–0.0035	0.0015–0.0032	0.3401–0.3412	0.3405–0.3412
	5	6-273 (4.5)	45	44	185	1.730	0.0010–0.0030	0.0010–0.0030	0.3413–0.3420	0.3411–0.3418

TORQUE SPECIFICATIONS

All readings in ft. lbs.

Year	VIN	No. Cylinder Displacement cu. in. (liter)	Cylinder Head Bolts	Main Bearing Bolts	Rod Bearing Bolts	Crankshaft Pulley Bolts	Flywheel Bolts	Manifold		Spark Plugs
								Intake	Exhaust	
1986	L	6-181 (3.0)	①	100	40	200	60	32	37	20
	3	6-231 (3.8)	60⑤	100	40	200	60	32	37	20
	B	6-231 (3.8)	60⑤	100	40	200	60	32	25	20
	8	8-250 (4.1)	90③	85	22	18	63	41	18	11
1987	3	6-231 (3.8)	60⑤	100	40	219	60	32	37	20
	B	6-231 (3.8)	①	100	45	219	60	32	37	20
	8	8-250 (4.1)	90③	85	22	18	63	41	18	11
1988	3	6-231 (3.8)	60⑤	100	40	219	60	80⑥	37	20
	C	6-231 (3.8)	60⑤	100	40	219	60	80⑥	37	20
	5	8-273 (4.5)	90③	85	22	18	63	41	18	11
1989–90	C	6-231 (3.8)	60⑤	90	43	219	61	88	41	20
	5	8-273 (4.5)	90③	85	22	18	63	41	18	11

① All exc. bolt No. 5, 6, 11, 12, 13, 14: 142 ft.lbs.
  Bolt No. 5, 6, 11, 12, 13, 14: 59 ft.lbs.
③ See text for proper tightening sequence
⑤ 3 step procedure: should you reach 60 ft. lbs. at any time in Step 2 or Step 3, stop tightening. Do not complete the balance of the 90 degree turn of this bolt
  Step 1: 25 ft. lbs.   Step 2: 90 degrees   Step 3: 90 degrees
⑥ Inch lbs.

PISTON AND RING SPECIFICATIONS

All measurements are given in inches.

Year	VIN	No. Cylinder Displacement cu. in. (liter)	Piston Clearance	Ring Gap			Ring Side Clearance		
				Top Compression	Bottom Compression	Oil Control	Top Compression	Bottom Compression	Oil Control
1986	3	6-231 (3.8)	0.0008–0.0020	0.010–0.020	0.010–0.020	0.015–0.055	0.0030–0.0050	0.0030–0.0050	0.0035 Max.
	L	6-181 (3.0)	②	0.010–0.020	0.010–0.022	0.015–0.055	0.0030–0.0050	0.0030–0.0050	0.0035– Max.
	B	6-231 (3.8)	0.0008–0.0020	0.010–0.020	0.010–0.020	0.015–0.055	0.0030–0.0050	0.0030–0.0050	0.0035 Max.
	8	8-250 (4.1)	0.0010–0.0018	0.023–0.025	0.023–0.025	0.010–0.050	0.0016–0.0037	0.0016–0.0037	None (side sealing)
1987	3	6-231 (3.8)	0.0008–0.0020	0.010–0.020	0.010–0.020	0.015–0.055	0.0030–0.0050	0.0030–0.0050	0.0035 Max.
	B	6-231 (3.8)	②	0.010–0.020	0.010–0.022	0.015–0.055	0.0030–0.0050	0.0030–0.0050	0.0035– Max.
	8	8-250 (4.1)	0.0010–0.0018	0.023–0.025	0.023–0.025	0.010–0.050	0.0016–0.0037	0.0016–0.0037	None (side sealing)
1988	3	6-231 (3.8)	0.0004–0.0022	0.010–0.020	0.010–0.022	0.015–0.055	0.0010–0.0030	0.0010–0.0030	0.0005–0.0065
	C	6-231 (3.8)	①	0.010–0.025	0.010–0.025	0.015–0.055	0.0013–0.0031	0.0013–0.0031	0.0011–0.0081
	5	6-273 (3.8)	0.0010–0.0018	0.023–0.025	0.023–0.025	0.010–0.050	0.0016–0.0037	0.0016–0.0037	None (side sealing)
1989–90	C	6-231 (3.8)	①	0.010–0.025	0.010–0.025	0.015–0.055	0.0013–0.0031	0.0013–0.0031	0.0011–0.0081
	5	6-273 (3.8)	0.0010–0.0018	0.023–0.025	0.023–0.025	0.010–0.050	0.0016–0.0037	0.0016–0.0037	None (side sealing)

① Skirt top: 0.0007–0.0027
Skirt bottom: 0.0010–0.0045

② Top Land—.046–.05 in.
Skirt Top—.0008–.0020 in.

Skirt Bottom—.0013–.0035 in.

WHEEL ALIGNMENT

Year	Model	Caster		Camber		Toe-in (in.)	Steering Axis Inclination (deg.)
		Range (deg.)	Preferred Setting (deg.)	Range (deg.)	Preferred Setting (deg.)		
1986	DeVille	1½P–3½P	2½P	5/16N–1¼P	½	3/32 ①	—
	Fleetwood	1½P–3½P	2½P	5/16N–1¼P	½	3/32 ①	—
	Electra	2P–3P	2½P	②	½P	7/32 ①	—
	Park Ave.	2P–3P	2½P	②	½P	7/32 ①	—
	LeSabre	2P–3P	2½P	②	②	0	—
	Ninety Eight	2P–3P	2½P	②	②	3/32 ①	—
	Delta 88	2P–3P	2½P	②	②	0	12 13/16P
1987	DeVille	1½P–3½P	2½P	5/16N–1¼P	½	3/32P ①	—
	Fleetwood	1½P–3½P	2½P	5/16N–1¼P	½	3/32P ①	—
	Electra	2P–3P	2½P	②	½P	3/32P ①	—
	Park Ave.	2P–3P	2½P	②	½P	3/32P ①	—

WHEEL ALIGNMENT

Year	Model	Caster Range (deg.)	Caster Preferred Setting (deg.)	Camber Range (deg.)	Camber Preferred Setting (deg.)	Toe-in (in.)	Steering Axis Inclination (deg.)
1987	LeSabre	2P–3P	2½P	5/16N–11/16P	3/16P	0	—
	Ninety Eight	2P–3P	2½P	②	②	3/32P①	—
	Delta 88	2P–3P	2½P	5/16N–11/16P	3/16P	0	12 13/16P
	Bonneville	2P–3P	2½P	5/16N–11/16P	3/16P	0	—
1988	DeVille	2½P–3½P	3P	1N–0	½N	0	—
	Fleetwood	2½P–3½P	3P	1N–0	½N	0	—
	Electra	2P–3P	2½P	⅓N–⅔P	⅕P	0	—
	Park Ave.	2P–3P	2½P	⅓N–⅔P	⅕P	0	—
	LeSabre	2P–3P	2½P	5/16N–11/16P	3/16P	0	—
	Ninety Eight	2P–3P	2½P	⅓N–⅔P	⅕P	0	—
	Delta 88	2P–3P	2½P	5/16N–11/16P	3/16P	0	12 13/16P
	Bonneville	2P–3P	2½P	5/16N–11/16P	3/16P	0	—
1989–90	DeVille	2½P–3½P	3P	②	②	0	—
	Fleetwood	2½P–3½P	3P	②	②	0	—
	Electra	2½P–3½P	3P	5/16N–11/16P	3/16P	0	—
	Park Ave.	2½P–3½P	3P	5/16N–11/16P	3/16P	0	—
	LeSabre	2½P–3½P	3P	5/16N–11/16P	3/16P	0	—
	Ninety Eight	2½P–3½P	3P	5/16N–11/16P	3/16P	0	—
	Delta 88	2½P–3½P	3P	5/16N–11/16P	3/16P	0	—
	Bonneville	2½P–3½P	3P	5/16N–11/16P	3/16P	0	—

① In or out pref: 0
N Negative
P Positive

② Left wheel
   Min.—1N
   Pref.—½N
   Max.—0

Right wheel
   Min.—0
   Pref.—½P
   Max.—1P

ELECTRICAL

NOTE: Disconnecting the negative battery cable on some vehicles may interfere with the functions of the on board computer systems and may require the computer to undergo a relearning process, once the negative battery cable is reconnected.

For testing and overhaul procedures on starters, alternators and voltage regulators, refer to the Unit Repair Section.

Charging System
ALTERNATOR
Removal and Installation

1. Disconnect the negative terminal from the battery.
2. Label and disconnect the electrical connectors from the back of the alternator.
3. Remove the brace at the back of the alternator (if equipped).
4. Loosen the belt tensioner and rotate it counterclockwise to remove the serpentine drive belt.
5. While supporting the alternator, remove the mounting bolts and the alternator.
6. To install, reverse the removal procedures. If not equipped with a serpentine drive belt, adjust the drive belt to have ¼–½ in. play midway along the longest free span of the belt. If a serpentine drive belt is used, tighten the tensioner pulley.

VOLTAGE REGULATOR
Removal and Installation

An alternator with an integral voltage regulator is standard equipment. There are no adjustments possible with this unit.

To replace the voltage regulator, the alternator must be removed and disassembled.

BELT TENSION
Adjustment

A single (serpentine) belt is used to drive all engine mounted accessories. Drive belt tension is maintained by a spring loaded tensioner. A belt squeak when the engine is started or stopped is normal and has no effect on belt durability. The drive belt tensioner can control belt tension over a broad range belt lengths; however, there are limits to the tensioner's ability to compensate.

1. Inspect tensioner markings to see if the belt is within operating lengths. Replace belt if the belt is excessively worn or is outside of the tensioner's operating range.
2. Run engine with no accessories on until the engine is warmed up. Turn the engine **OFF** read belt tension with tool J-23600–B belt tension gauge or equivalent placed halfway between the alternator and the A/C compressor. For non-A/C applications read tension between the power steering pump and crankshaft pulley. Remove tool.

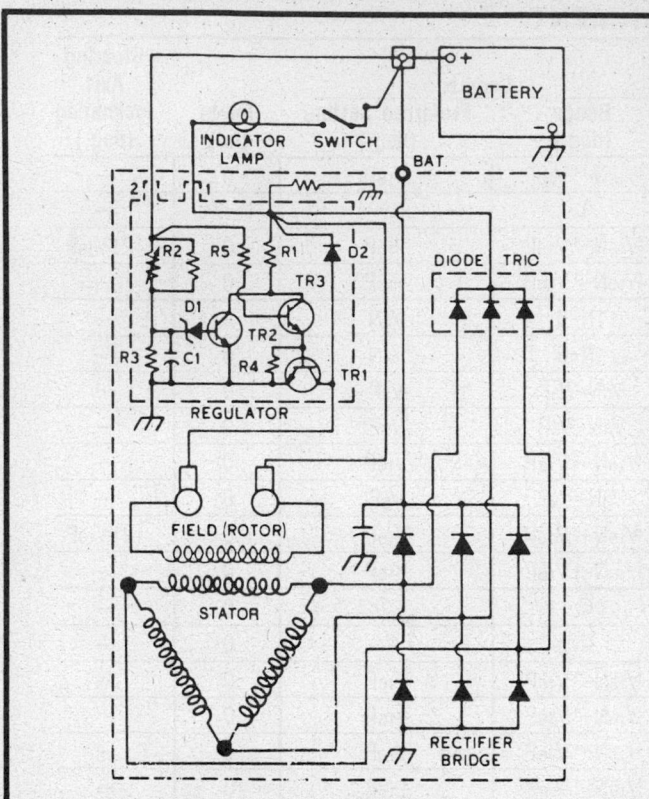

Alternator regulator in charging circuit

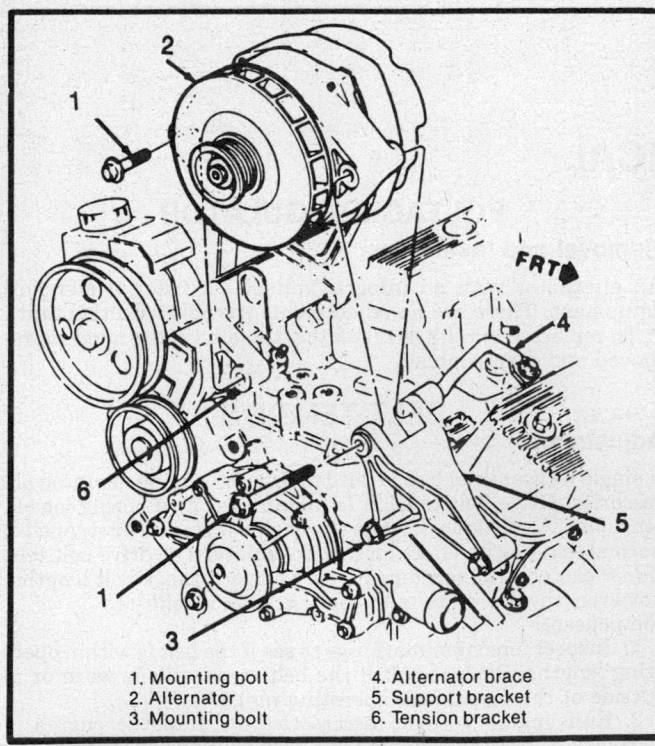

1. Mounting bolt
2. Alternator
3. Mounting bolt
4. Alternator brace
5. Support bracket
6. Tension bracket

Alternator mounting and related components

3. Start the engine (with accessories off) and allow the system to stabilize for 15 seconds. Turn the engine off. Using an 18mm box end wrench, apply clockwise force (tighten) to the tensioner

pulley bolt. Release the force and immediately take a tension reading without disturbing belt tensioner position.

4. Using the same wrench, apply a counterclockwise force to the tensioner pulley bolt and raise the pulley to the **install** position. Slowly lower the pulley to the **at rest** position and take a tension reading without disturbing the belt tensioner position.

5. Average the three readings. If the average of the 3 readings is lower than the tension specified and the belt is within the tensioner's operating range, replace the belt tensioner. The drive belt tension should be 110 lbs. (4.1L and 4.5L) or never below 67 lbs. (3.0L and 3.8L). If the belt tensioner is adjusted beyond it movable limit, replace the serpentine drive belt.

Starting System

STARTER

Removal and Installation

1. Disconnect the negative terminal from the battery.
2. Raise and support the vehicle safely.

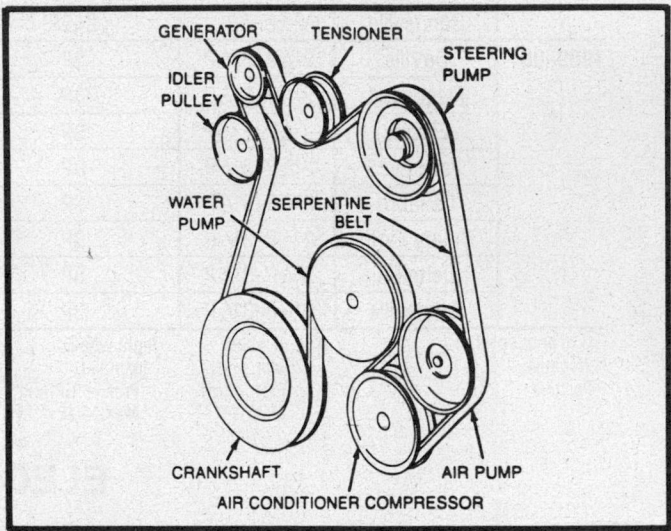

View of the serpentine drive belt routing—4.1L and 4.5L engines

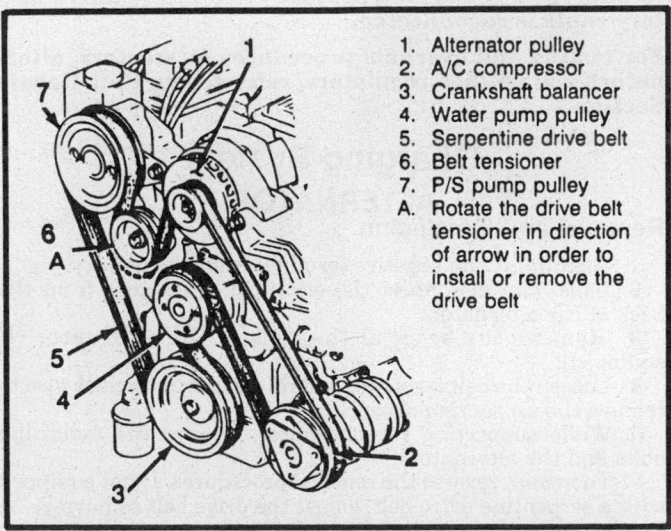

1. Alternator pulley
2. A/C compressor
3. Crankshaft balancer
4. Water pump pulley
5. Serpentine drive belt
6. Belt tensioner
7. P/S pump pulley
A. Rotate the drive belt tensioner in direction of arrow in order to install or remove the drive belt

View of the serpentine drive belt routing—3.0L and 3.8L engine

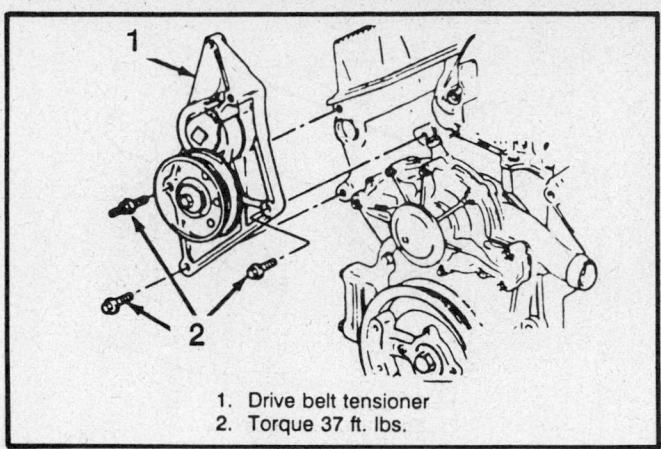

1. Drive belt tensioner
2. Torque 37 ft. lbs.

Serpentine belt tensioner—3.0L and 3.8L engines

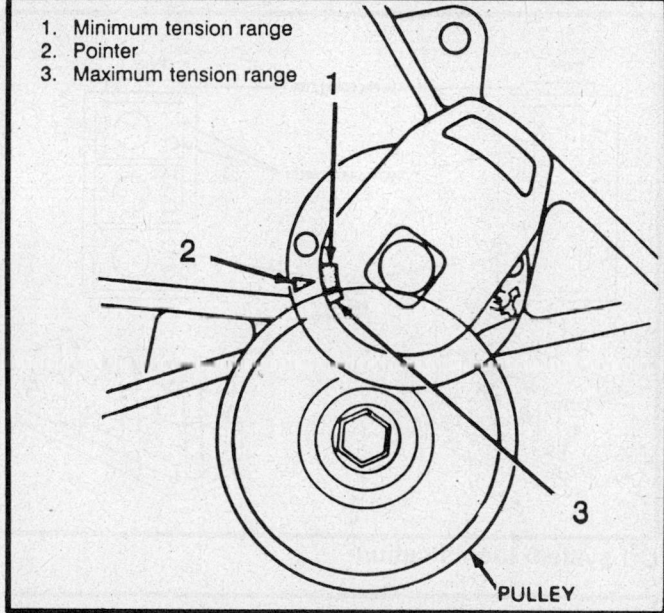

1. Minimum tension range
2. Pointer
3. Maximum tension range

PULLEY

Belt tensioner range—3.0L and 3.8L engine

3. If equipped, remove the splash shields and/or braces which may be in the way.

4. Label and disconnect the electrical connectors from the starter.

NOTE: On some models it may be necessary to remove the crossover pipe to complete this procedure.

5. Remove the starter-to-engine bolts and the starter.

NOTE: Note the location of any shims so that they may be replaced in the same positions upon installation.

6. To install, reverse the removal procedures; be sure to install the shims. Check the starter operation.

Ignition System

The 4.1L and 4.5L engines are equipped with High Energy Ignition (HEI) system, utilizing Electronic Spark Timing (EST). The EST distributor uses no mechanical or vacuum advance and is easily identified by the absence of a vacuum advance and the presence of a 4-terminal connector.

All other engines are equipped with Computer Controlled Coil Ignition (C^3I), which eliminates the distributor. The 3.0L with C^3I is slightly different than the 3.8L engine. It is not a sequentially injected engine, therefore a discrete camshaft signal is not necessary. The ECM provides multiport injection from processing the crankshaft signal only.

The C^3I system consists of the coil pack, ignition module, various hall effect sensors, interrupter rings and electronic control module (ECM). There are 3 types of C^3I systems used. Type 1 coils have 3 plug wires on each side of the coil assembly; Type 2 coils have all 6 wires connected on one side of the coil. All components are serviced as complete assemblies, although individual coils are available for Type 2 coil packs. The third system, know as Type 3 or fast start is similar in appearance to Type 1. In fact the coil packs are interchangeable; however, the module is electronically different and the harness connector plugs are not compatible. There are differences in the harness, the crankshaft sensor and the harmonic balancer. When troubleshooting or replacing components, it is important to determine which C^3I system is installed on the engine. Since the ECM controls the ignition timing, no timing adjustments are necessary or possible.

DISTRIBUTOR

Removal and Installation
ENGINE NOT DISTURBED

1. Disconnect the negative terminal from the battery.
2. Label and disconnect all wires leading from the distributor cap.
3. Remove the distributor cap by turning the 4 latches counterclockwise. Lift off the distributor cap and carefully move it aside.
4. Disconnect the 4 terminal ECM connector harness from the distributor, if not already done.
5. Remove the distributor hold down nut and clamp.

NOTE: On the 4.1L and 4.5L engines, use distributor hold-down clamp bolt tool No. J–29791 or equivalent to loosen the hold-down nut and clamp.

6. Using a piece of chalk or paint, mark the rotor-to-distributor body and the distributor body-to-engine positions. Pull the distributor upward until the rotor just stops turning (counterclockwise); note the position of the rotor once again. Remove the distributor.

NOTE: Do not crank the engine with the distributor removed.

7. On certain engines, a thrust washer is used between the distributor drive gear and the crankcase. This washer may stick to the bottom of the distributor when it is removed. Always make sure that this washer is at the bottom of the distributor bore before installation. On Digital Fuel Injection (DFI) systems, the malfunction trouble codes must be cleared after removal or adjustment of the distributor. This is accomplished by removing battery voltage to terminal **R** of the distributor for 10 seconds.

8. To install the distributor, rotate the distributor shaft until the rotor aligns with the second mark (when the shaft stopped moving). Lubricate the drive gear with clean engine oil and install the distributor into the engine. As the distributor is installed, the rotor should rotate to the first alignment mark; this will ensure proper timing. If the marks do not align properly, remove the distributor and reset; be sure to install the thrust washer (if equipped).

9. Install the clamp and hold-down nut. Tighten the nut until the distributor can just be moved with a little effort.

10. Connect all wires and hoses. Install the distributor cap. Check and/or adjust the ignition timing.

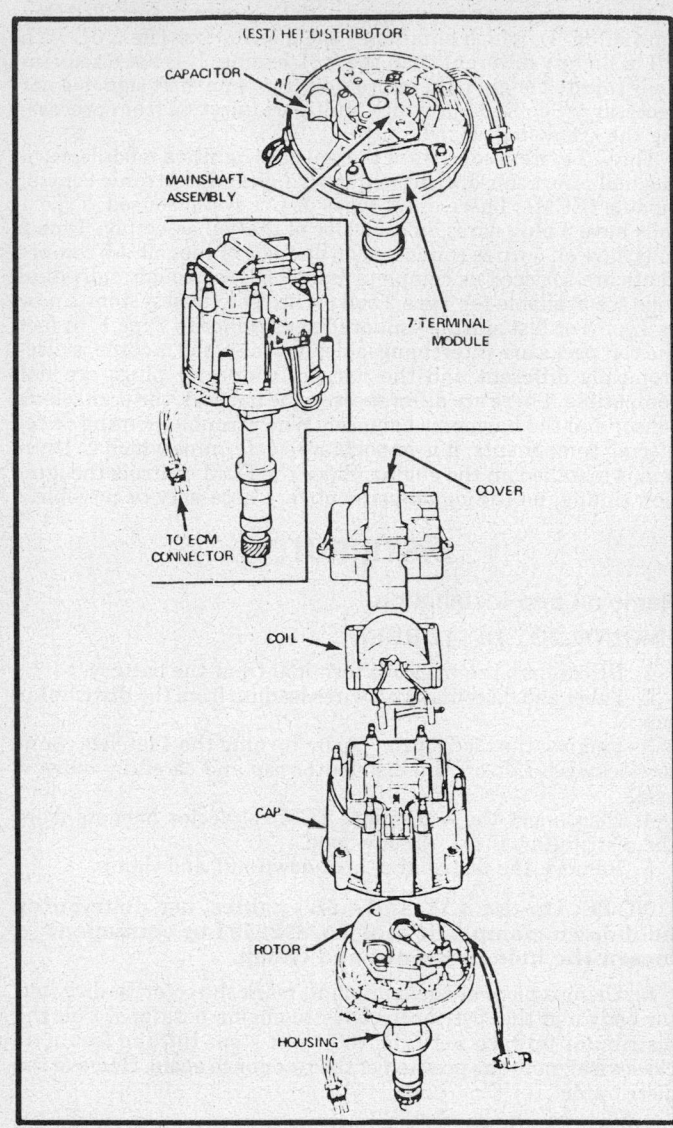

Exploded view of the HEI distributor

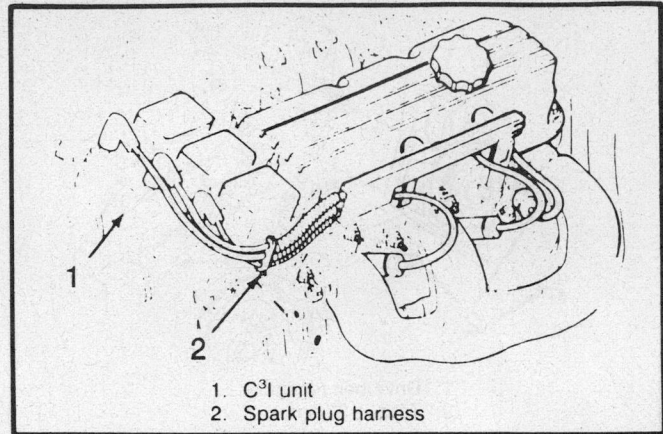

1. C³I unit
2. Spark plug harness

C³I ignition system (engine C 3800)

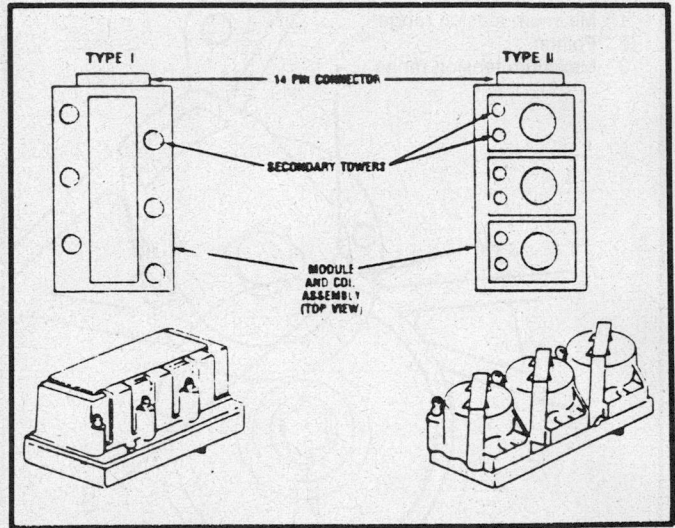

C³I system identification

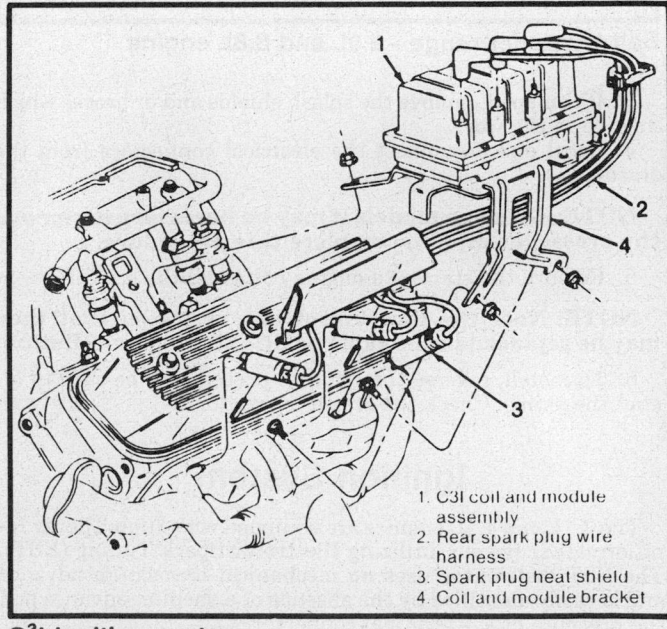

1. C3I coil and module assembly
2. Rear spark plug wire harness
3. Spark plug heat shield
4. Coil and module bracket

C³I ignition system

ENGINE DISTURBED

If the engine has been disturbed (cranked) after the distributor was removed, perform the following installation procedure:

1. Remove the No. 1 spark plug.
2. Rotate the crankshaft until No. 1 piston is at the TDC of its compression stroke.

NOTE: The compression stroke can be determined by placing a thumb over the hole while an assistant slowly cranks the engine. Crank until compression is felt at the hole and continue cranking slowly until the timing mark on the crankshaft pulley aligns with the 0 degrees timing mark located on the timing chain cover.

3. Position the distributor in the block but do not, at this time, allow it to engage with the drive gear.

4. Rotate the distributor shaft until the rotor points between No. 1 and No. 8 spark plug towers (V8) or No. 1 and No. 6 (V6) and lower the distributor to engage the camshaft.

NOTE: It may be necessary to turn the rotor a small amount in either direction in order to achieve this engagement. The rotor will rotate slightly as the distribu-

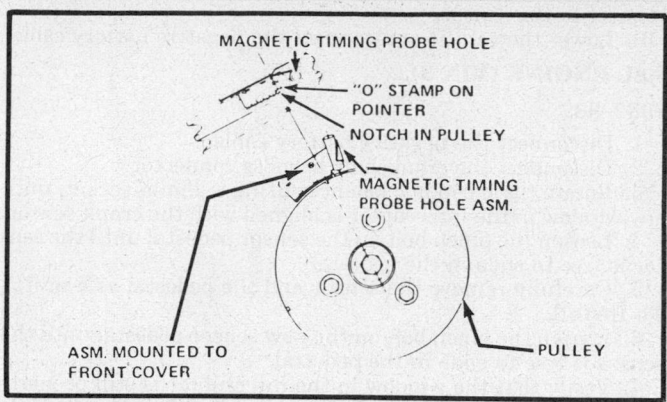

View of the special magnetic timing hole—4.1L and 4.5L engines

Crankshaft and camshaft location—3.8L engine

tor gear engages. If installed correctly, the rotor should point toward the No. 1 spark plug terminal in the distributor cap.

5. Press down firmly on the distributor housing. This will ensure that the distributor shaft engages the oil pump shaft, thereby allowing the distributor to fully contact the engine block.

6. Install the hold-down clamp and tighten the nut until it is snug (not tight).

7. Install the distributor cap, making sure that the rotor points to No. 1 terminal in the cap.

8. Attach all wires and hoses.

9. Start the engine. Check and/or adjust the ignition timing. Torque the distributor hold-down nut to 20 ft. lbs.

IGNITION TIMING

Adjustment

NOTE: The 4.1L and 4.5L engines incorporate a magnetic timing probe hole for use with special electronic timing equipment. Consult the manufacturer's instructions before using this system. The following procedure is for use with the HEI-EST distributor. For placement of sensors on the C³I systems, see the underhood sticker and follow the procedure given.

1. Connect a timing light to the No. 1 spark plug wire according to the light manufacturer's instructions; do not pierce the spark plug wire to connect the timing light.

2. Follow the instructions on the emission control label located in the engine compartment.

3. If equipped with an Electronic Spark Timing (EST) distributor, disconnect the 4-wire terminal plug from the distributor. Some models may require grounding the diagnostic connector **ALCL** located under the left side of the dash.

4. Start the engine and allow it to run at idle speed.

5. Aim the timing light at the degree scale just over the harmonic balancer.

6. Adjust the timing by loosening the hold-down clamp and rotate the distributor until the desired ignition advance is achieved. When the correct timing marks are aligned, tighten the clamp.

NOTE: On the 4.1L and 4.5L engines, use the distributor wrench tool No. J-29791 or equivalent to loosen the hold-down nut.

7. Adjust the timing, replace and tighten the hold-down clamp. To advance the timing, rotate the distributor opposite the normal direction of rotor rotation. Retard the timing by rotating the distributor in the normal direction of rotor rotation.

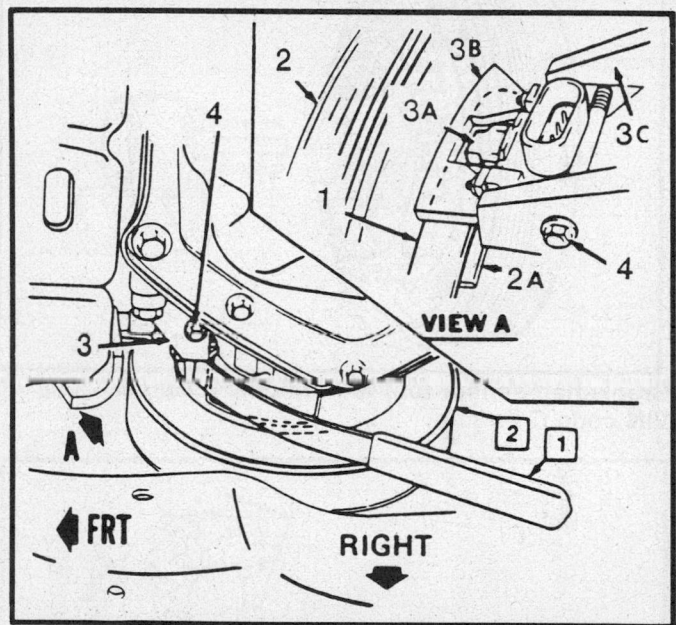

Crankshaft sensor adjustment—1987-88 with 3.8L VIN code 3 engine

NOTE: On Digital Fuel Injection (DFI) system, the malfunction trouble codes must be cleared after removal or adjustment of the distributor. This is accomplished by removing battery voltage to terminal R of the distributor for 10 seconds.

The 3.0 and the 3.8L engines use a Computer Controlled Coil Ignition (C³I) system. The system does not use a distributor; instead, it uses a coil pack, an ignition module, a crankshaft sensor and a camshaft sensor; no adjustment is necessary.

CRANKSHAFT SENSOR

Removal and Installation

3.0L AND 3.8L ENGINES

1986

1. Disconnect the negative battery cable.
2. Disconnect the sensor 4 terminal connector.
3. Raise the vehicle and support safely.
4. Remove the harmonic balancer, where necessary.

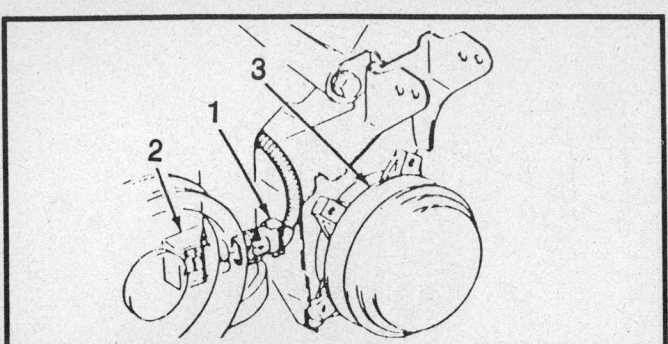

Combination sensor—3.0L engine

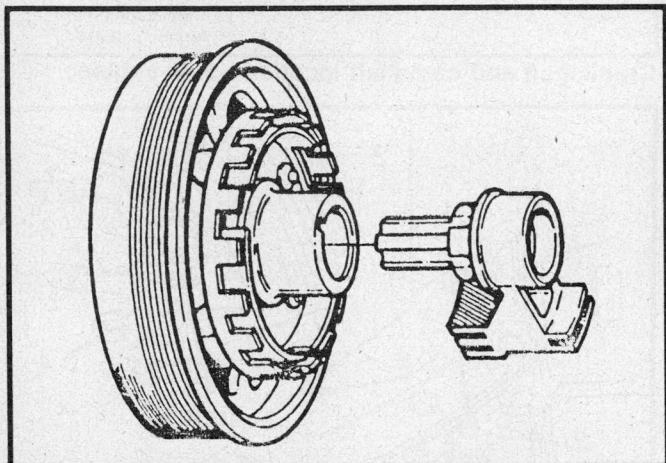

Crankshaft sensor tool to harmonic balancer—3.8L VIN code C engine

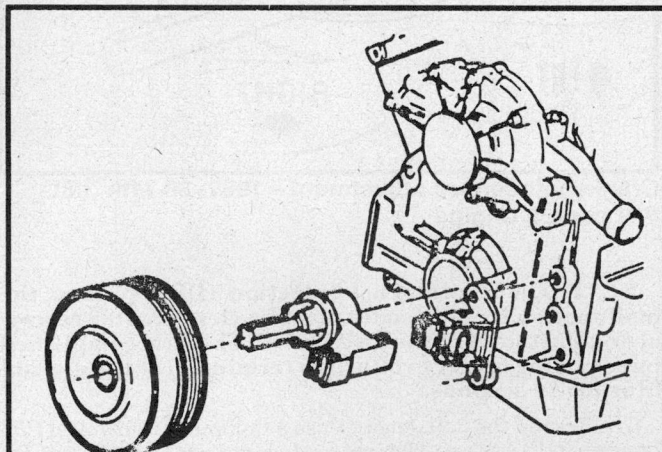

Crankshaft sensor tool to crankshaft—3.8L VIN code C engine

5. Remove the sensor assembly.

To install:

6. Install the sensor assembly.

7. Install the harmonic balancer.

8. Adjust the sensor for equal distance on each side of the disc. There should be approximately 0.30 in. clearance between the disc and the sensor. The disc should be checked at 3 locations at approximately 120 degrees apart. The sensor pinch bolt should be torqued to to 30 in. lbs.

9. Route the 4 terminal connector to its original location and connect to the sensor.

10. Lower the vehicle and connect the negative battery cable.

3.8L ENGINE (VIN 3)

1987–88

1. Disconnect the negative battery cable.

2. Disconnect the crankshaft harness connector.

3. Rotate the harmonic balancer using a 28mm socket, until any window in the interrupter is aligned with the crank sensor.

4. Loosen the pinch bolt on the sensor pedestal until the sensor is free to slide in the pedestal.

5. Carefully remove the sensor and the pedestal as a unit.

To install:

6. Loosen the pinch bolt on the new sensor pedestal until the sensor is free to slide in the pedestal.

7. Verify that the window in the interrupter is still properly positioned and install the sensor and pedestal as a unit while making sure that the interrupter ring is aligned with the proper slot.

8. Install the pedestal to the engine and torque the bolts to 22 ft. lbs.

3.8L ENGINE (VIN C)

1988–90

1. Disconnect the negative battery cable.

2. Remove the serpentine drive belt.

3. Raise the vehicle and support it safely.

4. Remove the right front tire.

5. Remove the inner fender access panel.

6. Using a 28mm socket, remove the crankshaft balancer bolt and balancer.

7. Disconnect the sensor electrical connector.

8. Remove the sensor and pedestal from the block face.

9. Remove the sensor from the pedestal.

To install:

10. Loosely install the crankshaft sensor on the pedestal.

11. Position the sensor with the pedestal attached on special tool J–37089.

12. Position the special tool on the crankshaft.

13. Install the bolts to hold the pedestal to the block face and torque to 14–28 ft. lbs.

14. Torque the pedestal pinch bolt to 30–35 ft. lbs.

15. Remove special tool J–37089.

16. Place special tool J–37089 on the harmonic balencer and turn. If any vane of the harmonic balancer touches the tool, replace the balencer assembly.

17. Install the balancer on the crankshaft.

18. Torque the crankshaft bolt to 200–239 ft. lbs.

19. Install the inner fender access panel.

20. Install the wheel and torque the lug nuts to 100 ft. lbs.

21. Lower the vehicle and install the serpentine belt.

22. Connect the battery cable.

Adjustment

3.8L ENGINE (VIN 3)

1987–88

1. Rotate harmonic balancer, using a 28mm socket and pull handle, until the interrupter ring(s) full the sensor slot(s) and edge of interrupter window is aligned with edge of the deflector on the pedestal.

2. Insert adjustment tool J–36179 or equivalent into the gap between sensor and interrupter on each side of interrupter ring. If gauge will not slide past sensor on either side of interrupter ring, the sensor is out of adjustment or interrupter ring is bent. This clearance should be checked at 3 positions around the outer interrupter ring approximately 120 degrees apart. If found out of adjustment, the sensor should be removed and inspected for potential damage.

3. Loosen the pinch bolt on sensor pedestal and insert adjust-

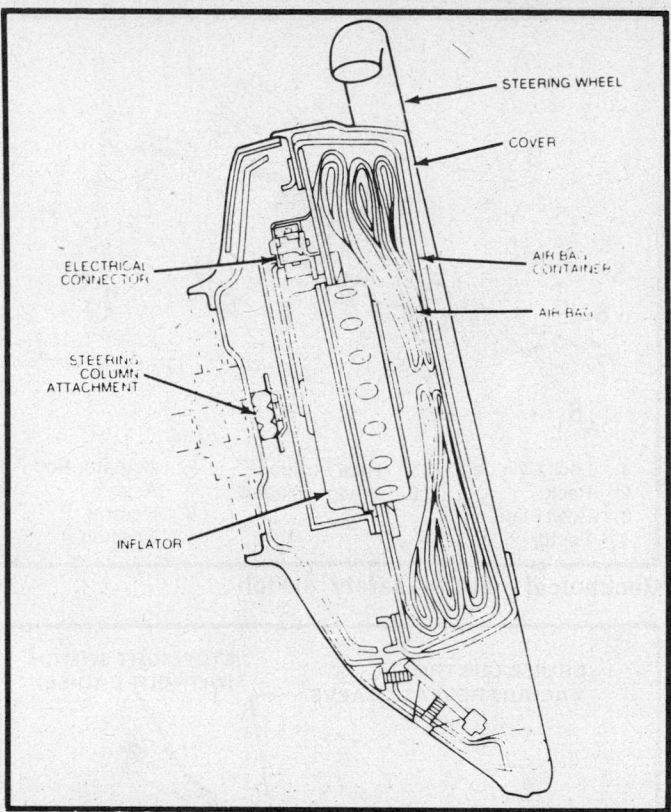

Inflatable restraint steering wheel

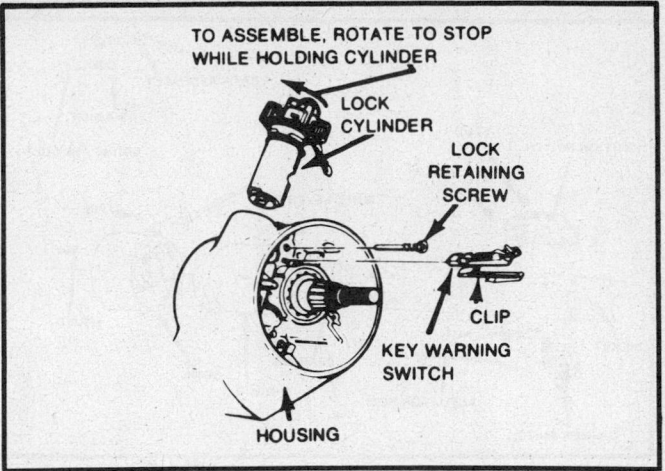

Ignition lock cylinder

ment tool J–38179 or equivalent into the gap between sensor and interrupter on each side of interrupter ring.

4. Slide the sensor into contact against gauge and interrupter ring.

5. Torque sensor retaining pinch bolt to 30 inch lbs. while maintaining light pressure on the sensor against gauge and interrupter ring. Re-check at 3 locations approximately 120 degrees apart. If interrupter ring contacts sensor at any point during harmonic balancer rotation, the interrupter ring has excessive runout and must be replaced.

CAMSHAFT SENSOR

Removal and Installation

On the 3.8L engine the crankshaft sensor is mounted at the harmonic balencer and the camshaft sensor at the camshaft gear.

On the 3.0L engine the cranksaft and camshaft sensors are combined into one dual sensor called a combination sensor which is mounted at the harmonic balancer. For the 3.0L engine, refer to the crankshaft sensor procedure above.

1. Disconnect negative battery cable.
2. Remove sensor electrical connection.
3. Remove the camshaft sensor attaching bolt and remove the sensor.

To install:

4. Reposition the camshaft sensor and install the electrical connector.
5. Torque the sensor attaching bolt to 75 in. lbs.
6. Connect the battery cable.

Electrical Controls

STEERING WHEEL

Removal and Installation

1. Disconnect the negative battery terminal from the battery.

2. If equipped with a horn button, pry the button from the center of the steering wheel. If equipped with center pad, remove the screws from the rear of the steering wheel. If equipped with an air bag module, remove the screws from the rear of the steering wheel.

CAUTION

When removing the air bag module, place it on a flat surface with the air bag facing upwards. If this is not done, the air module could inflate prematurely causing bodily harm.

3. Disconnect the horn electrical connector from the steering wheel assembly.
4. Remove the steering wheel-to-steering column nut.
5. Using a scratch awl, matchmark the steering wheel-to-shaft relationship.
6. Using the steering wheel puller tool, press the steering wheel from the steering column.
7. To install, align the matchmarks and the reverse the removal procedures. Torque the steering wheel-to-steering column nut to 30 ft. lbs.

IGNITION LOCK

Removal and Installation

1986–87

1. Disconnect the negative battery cable and remove the turn signal switch assembly.
2. Position the ignition switch in the **RUN** position.
3. Remove the buzzer switch, the lock cylinder-to-steering column screw and the lock cylinder.

NOTE: If the screw is dropped on removal, it could fall into the column, requiring complete disassembly to retrieve the screw.

4. To install the lock cylinder, rotate the cylinder clockwise to align cylinder key with the keyway in the housing.
5. Push the lock all the way in.
6. Install the lock cylinder-to-steering column screw. Torque the lock cylinder-to-steering column screw to 14 inch lbs. (tilt columns) and 25 inch lbs. (standard).

1988–90

1. Disconnect the negative battery cable and remove the turn signal switch assembly.
2. Remove the key from the lock cylinder. Remove the buzzer switch and clip.
3. Reinsert the key into the lock cylinder and turn it to the **LOCK** position.

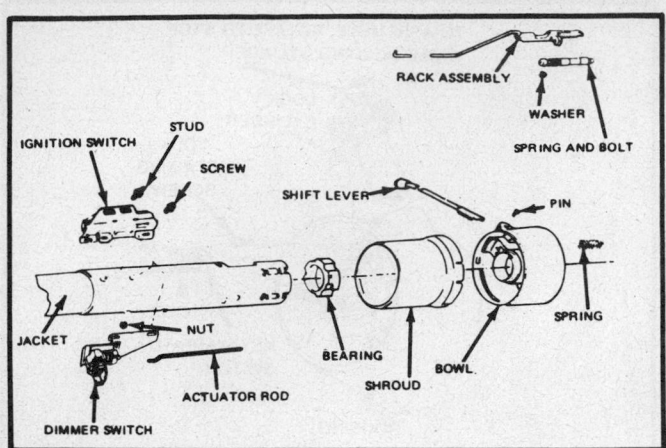

Ignition switch

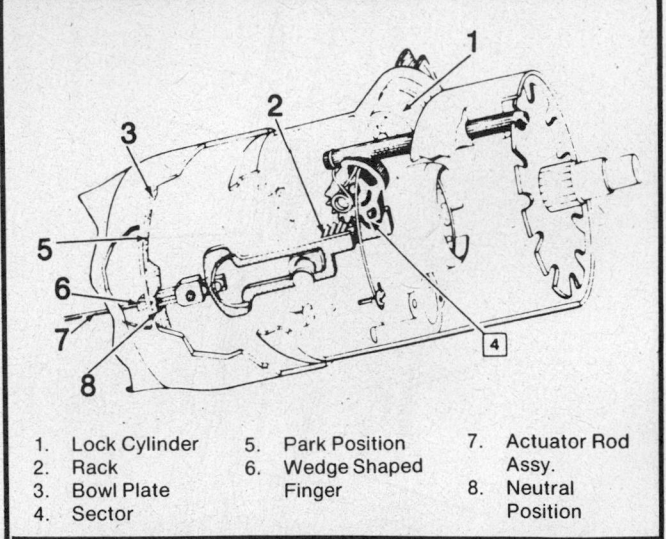

1. Lock Cylinder	5. Park Position	7. Actuator Rod Assy.	
2. Rack	6. Wedge Shaped Finger		
3. Bowl Plate		8. Neutral Position	
4. Sector			

Mechanical neutral safety switch

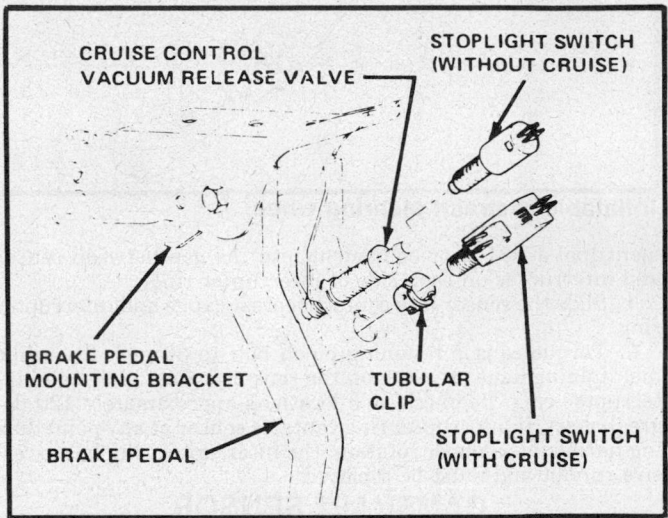

Stoplight switch—typical

4. Remove the cylinder lock-to-steering column screw and the lock set.

5. To install the cylinder lock and torque the lock-to-steering column screw to 22 inch lbs.

6. Position the key in the **RUN** position and reverse the removal procedures. Torque the turn signal switch-to-steering column screws to 30 inch lbs. and the turn signal lever screw to 20 inch lbs.

IGNITION SWITCH

Removal and Installation

The switch is located inside the channel section of the brake pedal support and is completely inaccessible without first lowering the steering column. The switch is actuated by a rod and rack assembly. A gear on the end of the lock cylinder engages the toothed upper end of the rod.

1. Disconnect the negative battary cable and lower the steering column; be sure to properly support it.

2. Position the switch in the **OFF-UNLOCKED** position. With the cylinder removed, the rod is in **LOCK** when it is in the next to the uppermost detent; **OFF-UNLOCKED** is 2 detents from the top. Remove the 2 switch screws and the switch assembly.

4. To install, position the new switch in **OFF-UNLOCKED** position; make sure the lock cylinder and actuating rod are in **OFF-UNLOCKED** (third detent from the top) position.

5. Install the activating rod into the switch and assemble the switch on the column. Tighten the mounting screws.

NOTE: Use only the specified screws since overlength screws could impair the collapsibility of the column.

6. To complete the installation, reverse the removal procedures.

MECHANICAL NEUTRAL START SYSTEM

A mechanical block system is used, rather than an electrical neutral start system. The system only allows the block cylinder to rotate to the start position when the shift lever is in **N** or **P** detent.

STOPLIGHT SWITCH

Removal and Installation

1. Disconnect the negative terminal from the battery. Remove the underdash trim panel, if equipped.

2. Loosen the tubular clip from the stoplight switch assembly.

3. Disconnect the electrical connector from the rear of the switch assembly.

4. Remove the stoplight switch from the vehicle.

5. To install, reverse the removal procedures.

Adjustment

The stoplight switch is located on a bracket at the top of the brake pedal.

1. Install the switch into the tubular clip until the switch assembly seats itself on the tubular clip.

2. Pull the brake pedal rearward against the pedal stop.

3. The switch will be moved in the tubular clip which will adjust itself properly.

NOTE: Certain 1986–88 vehicles may light up the brake warning light for no apparent reason. After careful inspection of the braking system and no reason is found, the cause may be found in the parking brake mechanism. A small rubber stop may have been lost from the braking mechanism. This allows the brake switch to be compressed, grounding it and causing the

brake warning light to operate. If this problem is found, replace the rubber stop with part number 25527682 and install a new switch assembly in the mechanism.

HEADLAMP SWITCH

Removal and Installation

1. Disconnect negative terminal from the battery. Remove the steering column lower cover or the instrument panel trim plate covering the headlamp switch, if equipped with a rocker-type headlamp switch.

2. Disconnect the electrical harness retainer below headlight switch assembly. On Buick, the switch connector is integral with the instrument panel; simply pull the switch outward to disconnect it.

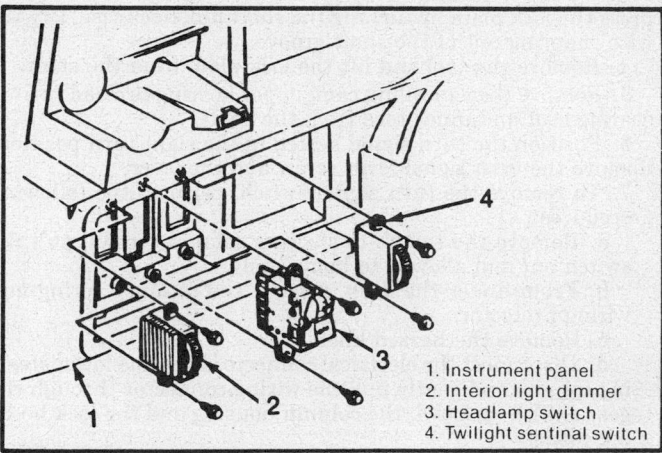

1. Instrument panel
2. Interior light dimmer
3. Headlamp switch
4. Twilight sentinal switch

Light switch assembly

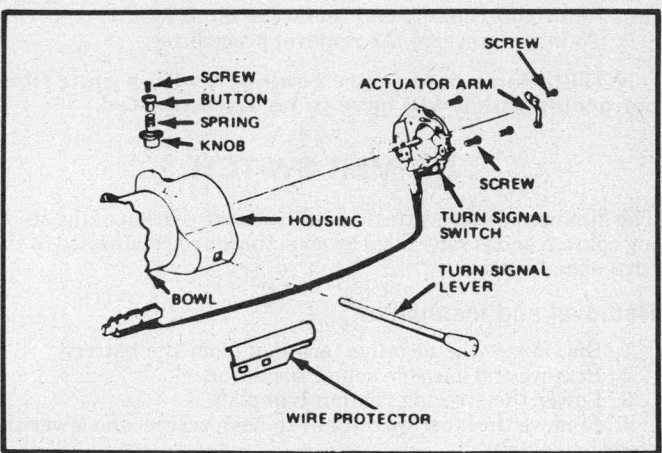

Turn signal switch

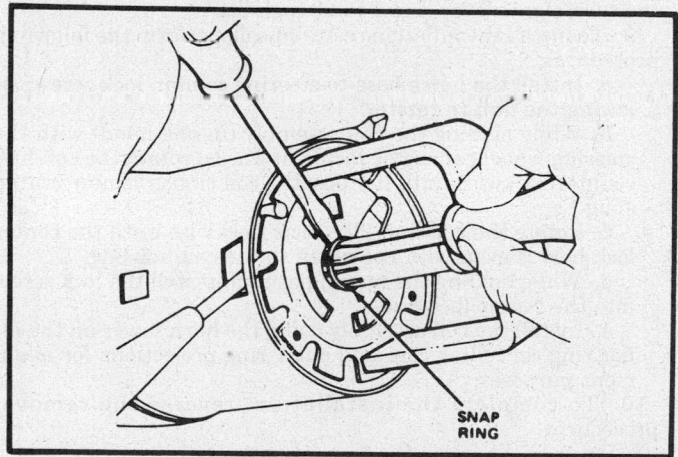

Depress the lockplate and remove the snapring

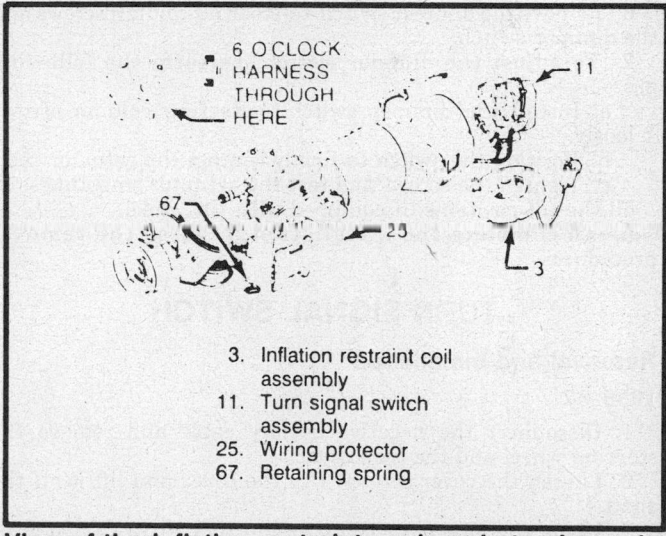

3. Inflation restraint coil assembly
11. Turn signal switch assembly
25. Wiring protector
67. Retaining spring

View of the inflation restraint equipped steering column

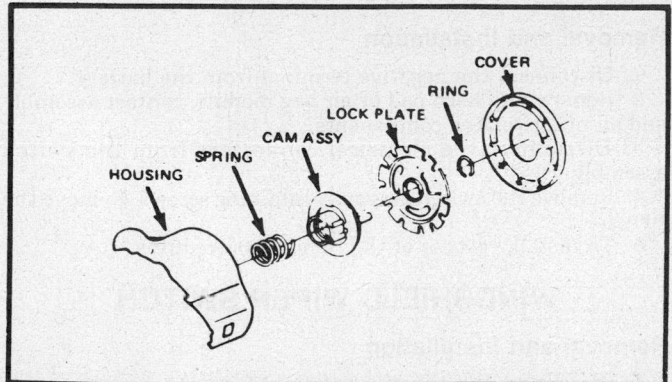

Remove these parts for access to the turn signal switch

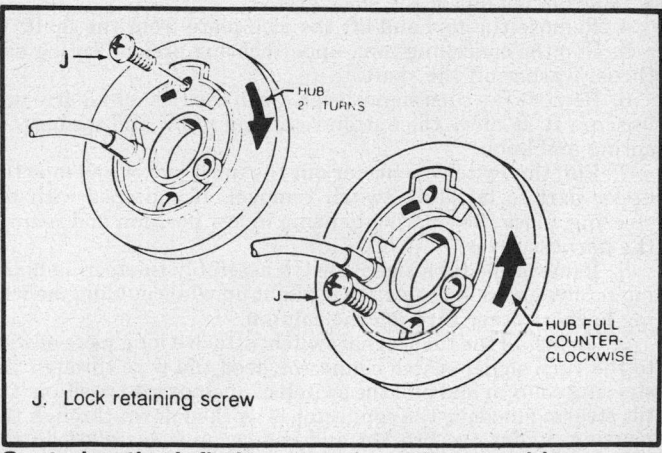

J. Lock retaining screw

Centering the inflation restraint coil assembly

3. On knob-type switches, depress spring loaded release button on top of headlight switch and remove switch, knob and rod assembly (switch **ON**).

4. Remove screw with ground wire at bottom of switch housing and any other mounting screws.

5. Pull assembly down and rearward, disconnect wiring harness connectors, bulb(s) and remove assembly.

6. To install, reverse the removal procedures.

NOTE:. Some models are equipped with a optic fiber connector which will have to be disconnected.

DIMMER SWITCH

The dimmer switch is attached to the lower portion of the steering column and is controlled by an actuator rod connected to the turn signal lever.

Removal and Installation

1. Disconnect the negative terminal from the battery.
2. Remove the left side sound insulator.
3. Lower the steering column trimplate.
4. Remove the steering column-to-dash screws and lower the steering column.
5. Disconnect the electrical connector from the dimmer switch.
6. Remove the dimmer switch-to-steering column screws and the dimmer switch.
7. To adjust the dimmer switch, perform the following procedures:
   a. Install the dimmer switch-to-steering column screws loosly.
   b. Position the switch to firmly contact the actuator rod.
   c. Tighten the screws and test the actuator smoothness in all the tilt positions (if equipped with tilt wheel).
8. To complete the installation, reverse the removal procedures.

TURN SIGNAL SWITCH

Removal and Installation

1986–87

1. Disconnect the negative battery cable and remove the steering wheel and the trim cover.
2. Loosen the cover screws. Pry the cover and lift it off the shaft.
3. Using the lock plate compression tool No. J–23653–A or equivalent, position it on the end of the steering shaft and compress the lock plate by turning the shaft nut clockwise. Pry the wire snap-ring out of the shaft groove.
4. Remove the tool and lift the lock plate from the shaft.
5. Slip the cancelling cam, upper bearing preload spring and thrust washer off the shaft.
6. Remove the turn signal lever. Push the flasher knob in and unscrew it. Remove the button retaining screw and the button, spring and knob.
7. Pull the switch connector out the mast jacket and tape the upper part to facilitate switch removal. If equipped with tilt steering, place the steering housing in low position and remove the harness cover.
8. Remove the turn signal switch assembly-to-steering housing screws and pull the switch straight up while guiding the wiring harness cover through the column.
9. To install the turn signal switch, attach a long piece of wire to the turn signal switch connector, feed the wire through the steering column and pull the switch connector into position. On tilt steering models, the connector is worked down through the housing, under the bracket and the cover is installed on the harness.

10. To complete the installation, reverse the removal procedures. Check the operation of the components.

1988–90

1. Disconnect the nergative battery cable and remove the steering wheel and the shroud.
2. Remove the inflation restraint (air bag module) coil assembly-to-steering shaft lock screw (home boss) and retaining ring. Remove the coil assembly from the shaft and allow it to hang freely.
3. Using the lock plate compression tool No. J–23653–A or equivalent, position it on the end of the steering shaft and compress the lock plate by turning the shaft nut clockwise. Pry the wire snapring out of the shaft groove.
4. Remove the tool and lift the lock plate from the shaft.
5. Remove the cancelling cam, upper bearing preload spring, bearing seat and inner race from the shaft.
6. Position the turn signal switch in the right turn position. Remove the turn signal lever screw and the lever.
7. To remove the turn signal switch, perform the following procedures:
   a. Remove the switch-to-steering column screws, pull the switch out and allow it to hang freely.
   b. From under the dash, remove the retainer spring and wiring protector.
   c. Remove the hazard knob.
   d. Disconnect the electrical connector from the lower steering column and gently pull the wiring connector through the gear shift lever bowl, the column housing and the lock housing cover.
8. To install, reverse the removal procedures. Torque the turn signal switch-to-steering column screws to 30 inch lbs. and the turn signal lever screw to 20 inch lbs.
9. To install the inflation restraint coil, perform the following procedures:
   a. Install the home boss-to-steering column lock screw, allowing the hub to rotate.
   b. While holding the coil assembly (in one hand) with the steering wheel connector facing upwards, rotate the coil hub counterclockwise until it stops; the coil ribbon is now wound snug.
   c. Rotate the coil hub 2½ turns clockwise until the center lock hole is even with the notch in the coil housing.
   d. While holding the hub in position, install the lock screw into the center lock hole.
   e. Install the coil assembly using the horn tower on the inner ring cancelling cam and outer ring projections for alignment purposes.
10. To complete the installation, reverse the removal procedures.

HORN SWITCH

Removal and Installation

1. Disconnect the negative terminal from the battery.
2. Remove the horn pad or air bag module, contact assembly and all other related components.
3. Disconnect the electrical connectors from the switch assembly.
4. Remove the switch assembly retaining screws. Remove the switch.
5. To install, reverse of the removal procedures.

WINDSHIELD WIPER SWITCH

Removal and Installation

1. Disconnect the negative terminal from the battery.
2. Remove the steering wheel, the cover and the lock plate assembly.

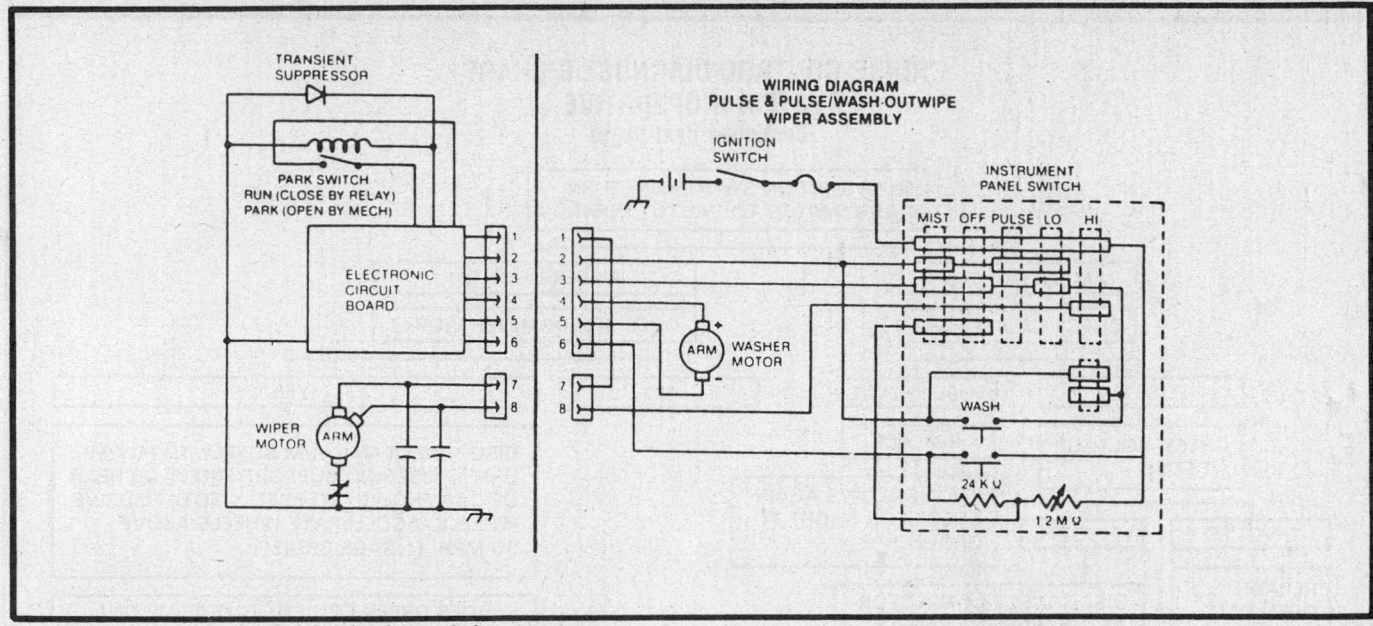

Schematic of the windshield wiper delay system

3. Remove the turn signal actuator arm, the lever and the hazard flasher button.

4. Remove the turn signal switch screws, the lower steering column trim panel and the steering column bracket bolts.

5. Disconnect the the turn signal switch and the wiper switch connectors.

6. Pull the turn signal switch rearward 6 or 8 inches, remove the key buzzer switch and cylinder lock.

7. Remove and pull the steering column housing rearward. Remove the housing cover screw.

8. Remove the wiper switch pivot and the switch.

9. To install, reverse the removal procedure.

WINDSHIELD WIPER MOTOR

Removal and Installation

1. Disconnect the negative battery cable and remove the wiper arms, the cowl screen or grille.

2. Disconnect the washer hose under the screen.

3. Loosen the linkage drive link-to-crankarm attaching nuts and the link from the arm.

4. Disconnect the wiring and washer hoses.

5. Remove the 3 motor-to-chassis screws, guide the crankarm through the hole in the dash and remove the motor.

6. To install, reverse the removal procedures.

DELAY WIPER CONTROLS

The wiper delay is controlled from the multi-function switch and can be varied from 0–25 seconds between wiper sweeps. The electronic circuit board is located inside the wiper motor cover. The circuit board must be replaced as an assembly.

WINDSHIELD WIPER LINKAGE

Removal and Installation

1. Disconnect the negative terminal from the battery.

2. Remove the arm blades, lower reveal moulding and the cowl vent screen.

3. Disengage the link retainer between the drive link and the crank arm.

4. Remove the transmission to body attaching bolts.

5. Remove the transmission and linkage as an assembly.

6. To install, reverse the removal procedures.

Instrument Cluster

Refer to "Chilton's Electronic Instrumentation Service Manual"

Removal and Installation

STANDARD

1. Disconnect the negative terminal from the battery.

2. Remove the left sound insulator. Lower the steering column (if necessary) in order to gain working clearance.

3. If equipped with quartz clusters, removal of the steering column trim cover may be required in order to remove the shift indicator clip.

4. Remove the instrument panel trim in order to gain access to the instrument panel retaining bolts. Remove the instrument panel retaining bolts.

5. Pull the instrument panel forward. Label and disconnect all the electrical connectors.

6. Remove the instrument panel assembly from the vehicle.

7. To install, reverse the removal procedures. Be sure the shift indicator is properly aligned.

DIGITAL

1. Disconnect the negative terminal from the battery. Remove the defroster grille.

2. Remove the instrument panel top cover-to-instrument panel screws.

3. If equipped with a twilight sentinel, pop up the photocell retainer and turn the photocell counterclockwise in the retainer and pull it down-and-out.

4. Slide the instrument panel top cover out far enough to disconnect the aspirator hose, electrical connector to the in-car sensor and the electrical connector to the electro-luminescent inverter.

5. Remove the instrument panel top cover from the instrument panel. If equipped with quartz electronic speedometer clusters, remove the steering column trim cover, so the shift indicator can be removed.

6. Remove the instrument cluster-to-instrument panel carri-

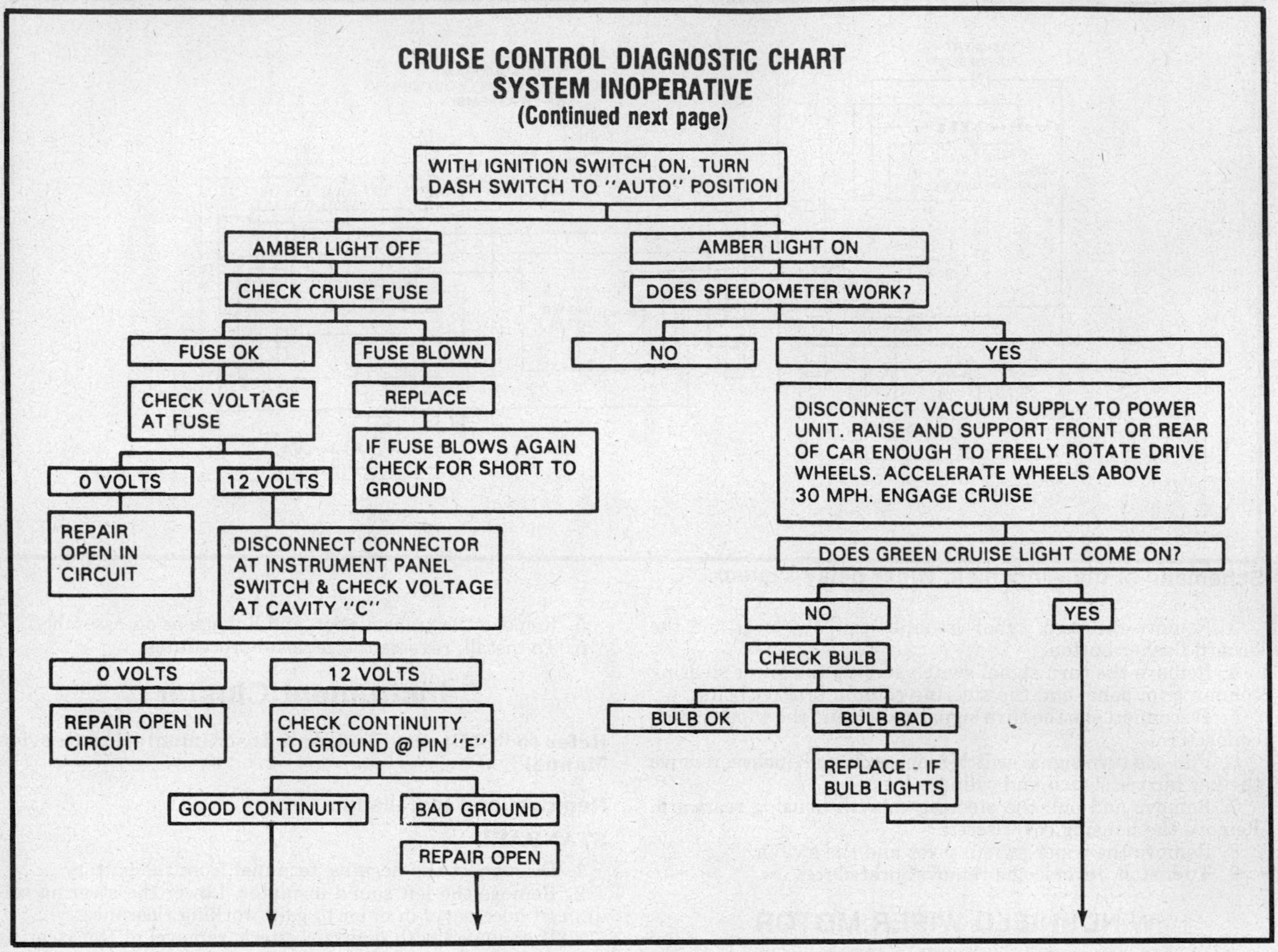

CRUISE CONTROL DIAGNOSTIC CHART
SYSTEM INOPERATIVE
(Continued next page)

WITH IGNITION SWITCH ON, TURN DASH SWITCH TO "AUTO" POSITION

AMBER LIGHT OFF

CHECK CRUISE FUSE

FUSE OK

CHECK VOLTAGE AT FUSE

0 VOLTS | 12 VOLTS

REPAIR OPEN IN CIRCUIT

DISCONNECT CONNECTOR AT INSTRUMENT PANEL SWITCH & CHECK VOLTAGE AT CAVITY "C"

0 VOLTS | 12 VOLTS

REPAIR OPEN IN CIRCUIT

CHECK CONTINUITY TO GROUND @ PIN "E"

GOOD CONTINUITY | BAD GROUND

REPAIR OPEN

FUSE BLOWN

REPLACE

IF FUSE BLOWS AGAIN CHECK FOR SHORT TO GROUND

AMBER LIGHT ON

DOES SPEEDOMETER WORK?

NO | YES

DISCONNECT VACUUM SUPPLY TO POWER UNIT. RAISE AND SUPPORT FRONT OR REAR OF CAR ENOUGH TO FREELY ROTATE DRIVE WHEELS. ACCELERATE WHEELS ABOVE 30 MPH. ENGAGE CRUISE

DOES GREEN CRUISE LIGHT COME ON?

NO | YES

CHECK BULB

BULB OK | BULB BAD

REPLACE - IF BULB LIGHTS

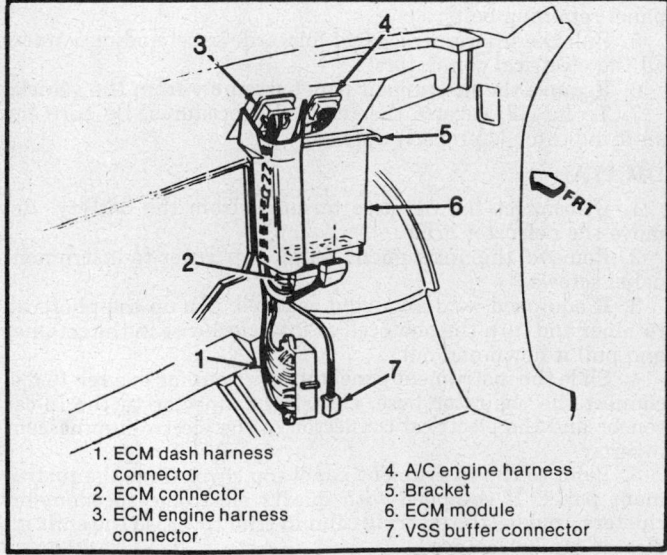

1. ECM dash harness connector
2. ECM connector
3. ECM engine harness connector
4. A/C engine harness
5. Bracket
6. ECM module
7. VSS buffer connector

Typical electronic control module (ECM) mounting

er screws. Pull the cluster housing assembly straight out; this will separate the electrical connectors from the cluster.

NOTE: It may be helpful to tilt the wheel all the way down and pull the gear select lever to low, when removing the cluster.

7. To install, reverse the removal procedures.

SPEEDOMETER

Removal and Installation

1. Disconnect the negative terminal from the battery. Remove the instrument cluster (left side) trim plate.
2. Remove the 4 screws holding the lenses to the cluster assembly and remove the lenses. On tilt columns, remove the tilt lever.
3. Remove the speedometer retaining screws.
4. If equipped with a mechanical speedometer, pull the assembly forward in order to disconnect the speedometer cable and electrical connectors. To gain slack it may be necessary to disconnect the cable at the cruise control transducer or the transaxle.
5. If equipped with an electronic speedometer, remove Vehicle Speed Sensor (VSS) and the electrical connector.
6. Remove the speedometer assembly from the vehicle.
7. To install, reverse the removal procedures.

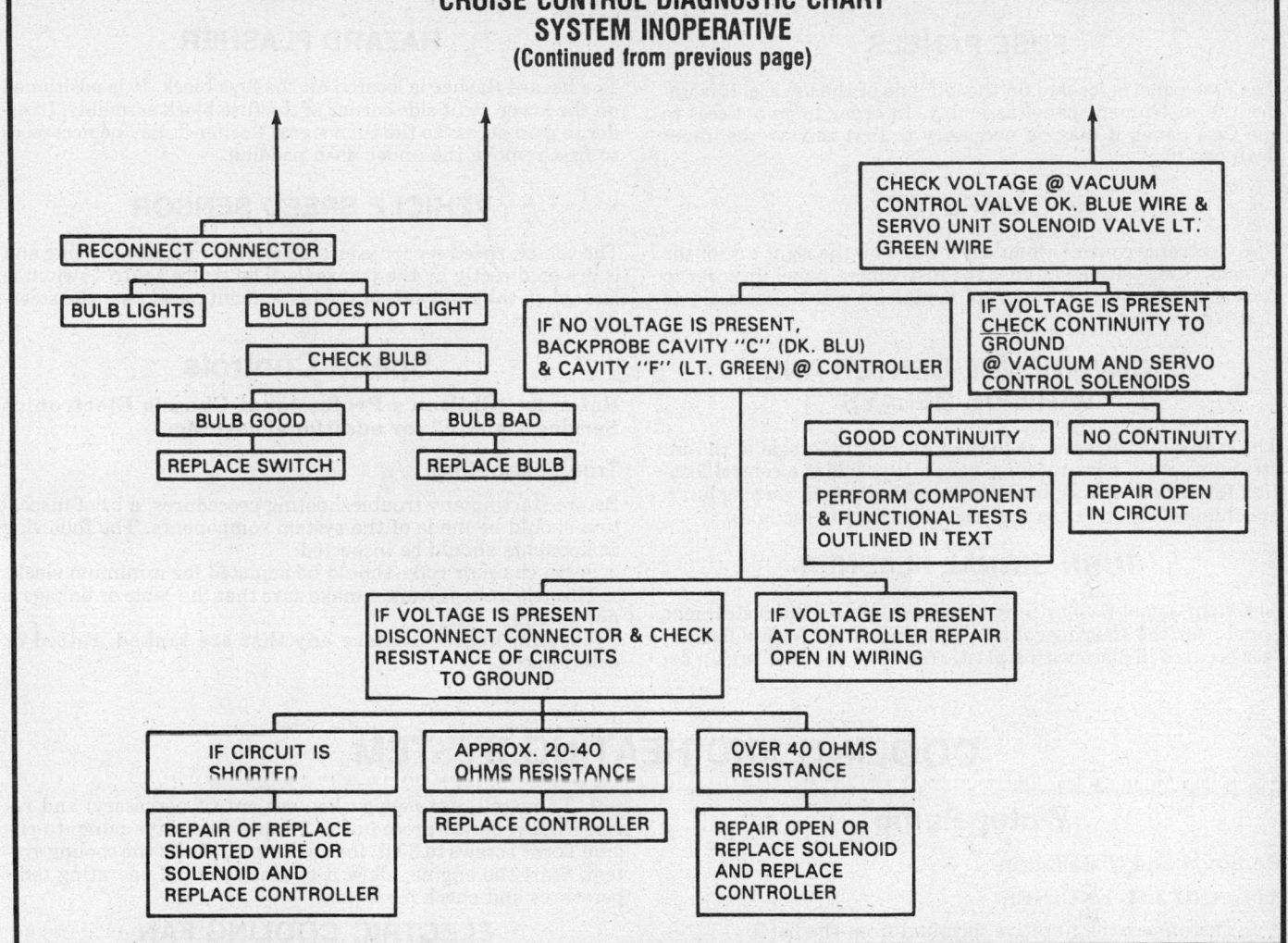

CRUISE CONTROL DIAGNOSTIC CHART
SYSTEM INOPERATIVE
(Continued from previous page)

Speedometer Cable

Removal and Installation

1. Disconnect the negative terminal from the battery.
2. Remove the retaining screws from the instrument cluster trim plate, instrument cluster lens and the transaxle shift indicator assembly. Remove the lens and retainers.
3. Remove the temperature indicator and the fuel gauge.
4. Remove the speedometer assembly-to-housing screws. Pull the speedometer forward and disconnect the screw holding the vehicle speed sensor.
5. Remove the speedometer cable and the speedometer.
6. To install, reverse the removal procedures.

Electrical Circuit Protectors

FUSIBLE LINKS

Fusible links are sections of wire, with special insulation, designed to melt under electrical overload. Replacements are simply spliced into the wire. There may be as many as 5 of these in the engine compartment wiring harness. These are:
1. Horn relay to the fuse panel circuit
2. Charging circuit from the starter solenoid to the horn relay

3. Starter solenoid to the ammeter circuit
4. Horn relay to the rear window defroster circuit, if equipped

The fusible links are all 2 wire gauges smaller than the wires they protect.

NOTE: Most models have fusible links at these locations.

Replacement

1. Find and repair the cause of the electrical overload.
2. Disconnect the negative terminal from the battery.
3. Disconnect the fusible link from the junction block or starter solenoid.
4. Cut the harness directly behind the connector in order to remove the damaged fusible link.
5. Strip the harness wire approximately ½ in.
6. Connect the new fusible link to the harness wire using a crimp on the connector. Solder the connection, if necessary, using resin core solder.
7. Tape all exposed wire using electrical tape.
8. Connect the fusible link to the junction block or starter solenoid and reconnect the negative battery cable.

CIRCUIT BREAKERS

Circuit breakers are incorporated in the wiring of the following systems; headlight switch, horn wiring, power/memory seats and the Delco-Bose radio systems.

FUSE PANELS

The fuse panel is located on the left side of the vehicle. It is under the instrument panel assembly. In order to gain access to the fuse panel, it may be necessary to first remove the under dash padding.

COMPUTER

The electronic control module is located on the right side of the vehicle. It is positioned under the instrument panel. In order to gain access to electronic control module, it will be necessary to first remove the trim panel.

CONVENIENCE CENTER AND VARIOUS RELAYS

The convenience center is located on the underside of the instrument panel near the fuse panel. It provides a central location for various relays, hazard flasher units and warning buzzers/chimes. All units are replaced with plug-in modules.

TURN SIGNAL FLASHER

The turn signal flasher unit is located behind the instrument panel near the steering column, along with the hazard flasher. It is secured in place with a plastic retainer. In order to gain access to components, it may first be necessary to remove certain under dash padding.

HAZARD FLASHER

The hazard flasher is located on the fuse block. It is positioned on the lower right side corner of the fuse block assembly. In order to gain access to the turn signal flasher it may be necessary to first remove the under dash padding.

VEHICLE SPEED SENSOR

The vehicle speed sensor is located on the transaxle housing and is driven directly by the transaxle. The cruise control switch is located on the right side of the instrument panel near the steering column.

Speed Controls

Refer to "Chilton's Professional Chassis Electronics Service Manual" for additional coverage.

Troubleshooting

Before starting any troubleshooting procedures, a brief inspection should be made of the system components. The following components should be inspected:
Servo chain or rod—should be adjusted for minimum slack.
Throttle linkage/cable—make sure that the cable or linkage is not binding.
Vacuum hoses—replace any that are kinked, rotted or deteriorated.

COOLING AND HEATING SYSTEM

Water Pump

Removal and Installation

3.0L AND 3.8L ENGINES

1. Disconnect the negative terminal from the battery.
2. Drain the cooling system.
3. Remove the serpentine drive belt.
4. Remove the coolant hoses from the water pump.
5. Remove the water pump pulley bolts and the pulley; the long bolt can be removed through the access hole in the body side rail.
6. Remove the water pump-to-engine bolts and the pump.
7. Clean the gasket mounting surfaces. Inspect the parts for damage and/or wear; replace the parts, if necessary.
8. To install, use a new gasket, sealant (if necessary) and reverse the removal procedures. Torque the water pump-to-engine bolts to 29 ft. lbs. (long) and 97 inch lbs. (short). Refill and bleed the cooling system.

4.1L AND 4.5L ENGINES

1. Disconnect the negative terminal from the battery.
2. Drain the cooling system.
3. If equipped with air conditioning, remove the accumulator from its bracket, move the bracket and accumulator aside without discharging the A/C system.
4. Remove the right cross-car brace.
5. Remove the accessory drive belt.
6. Remove the water pump pulley-to-water pump bolts and the pulley.
7. Remove the water pump-to-engine bolts and the water pump.
8. Using a gasket scraper, clean the gasket mounting surfaces.

9. To install, use new gasket, sealant (if necessary) and reverse the removal procedures. Torque the water pump-to-engine Torx® screws to 30 ft. lbs., bolts to 30. Refill the cooling system. Start the engine, allow it to reach normal operating temperatures and check for leaks.

ELECTRIC COOLING FAN

Testing

1. Disconnect the electrical connector from the cooling fan.

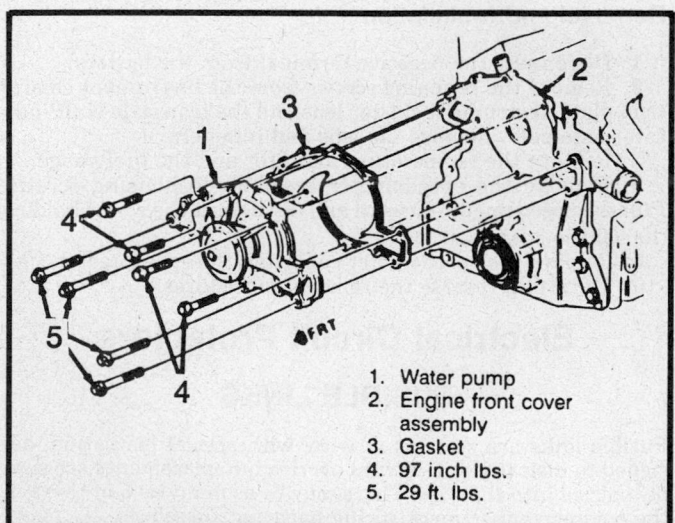

1. Water pump
2. Engine front cover assembly
3. Gasket
4. 97 inch lbs.
5. 29 ft. lbs.

Exploded view of the water pump—3.0L and 3.8L engines

2. Using an ammeter and jumper wires, connect the fan motor in series with the battery and ammeter. With the fan running, check the ammeter reading, it should be 3.4–5.0 amps; if not, replace the motor.

3. Reconnect the fan's electrical connector. Start the engine, allow it to reach temperatures above 194°F and confirm that the fan runs. If the fan doesn't run, replace the temperature switch.

Removal and Installation

NOTE: The Electric Cooling Fan relay, on all models except Cadillac, is located at the front of the engine compartment in a bracket on the left side. On Cadillac, the electric cooling fan relay is located on the left side of the engine compartment, near the Electronic Level Control (ELC) compressor.

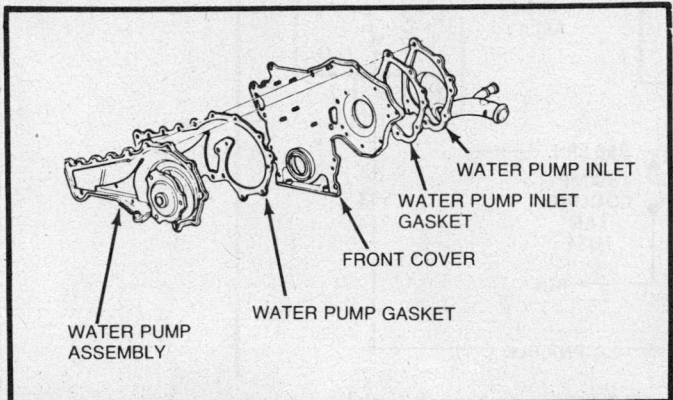

Exploded view of the water pump—4.1L and 4.5L engines

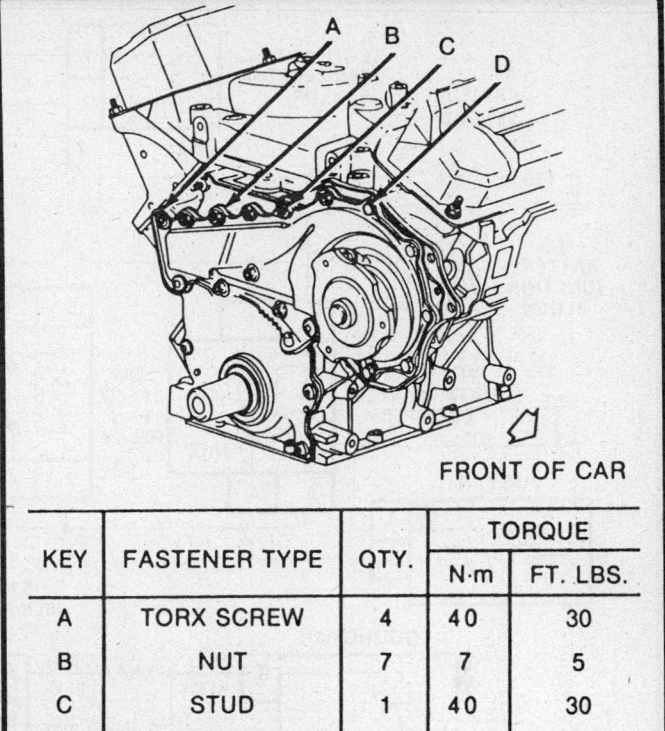

FRONT OF CAR

KEY	FASTENER TYPE	QTY.	TORQUE	
			N·m	FT. LBS.
A	TORX SCREW	4	40	30
B	NUT	7	7	5
C	STUD	1	40	30
D	HEX SCREW	7	7	5

Water pump torque specifications—4.1L and 4.5L engines

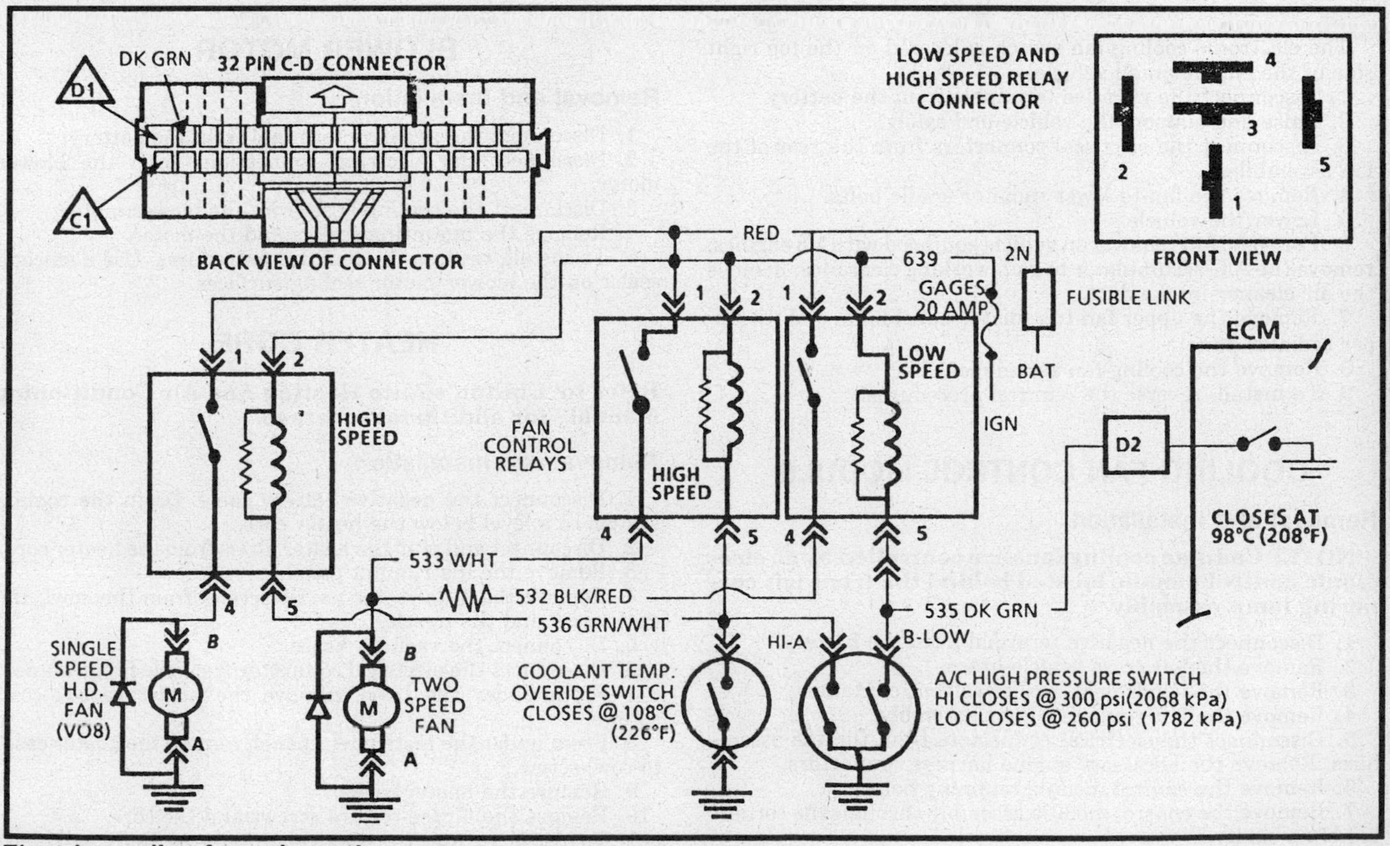

Electric cooling fan schematic—1986–87 3.0L and 3.8L engine

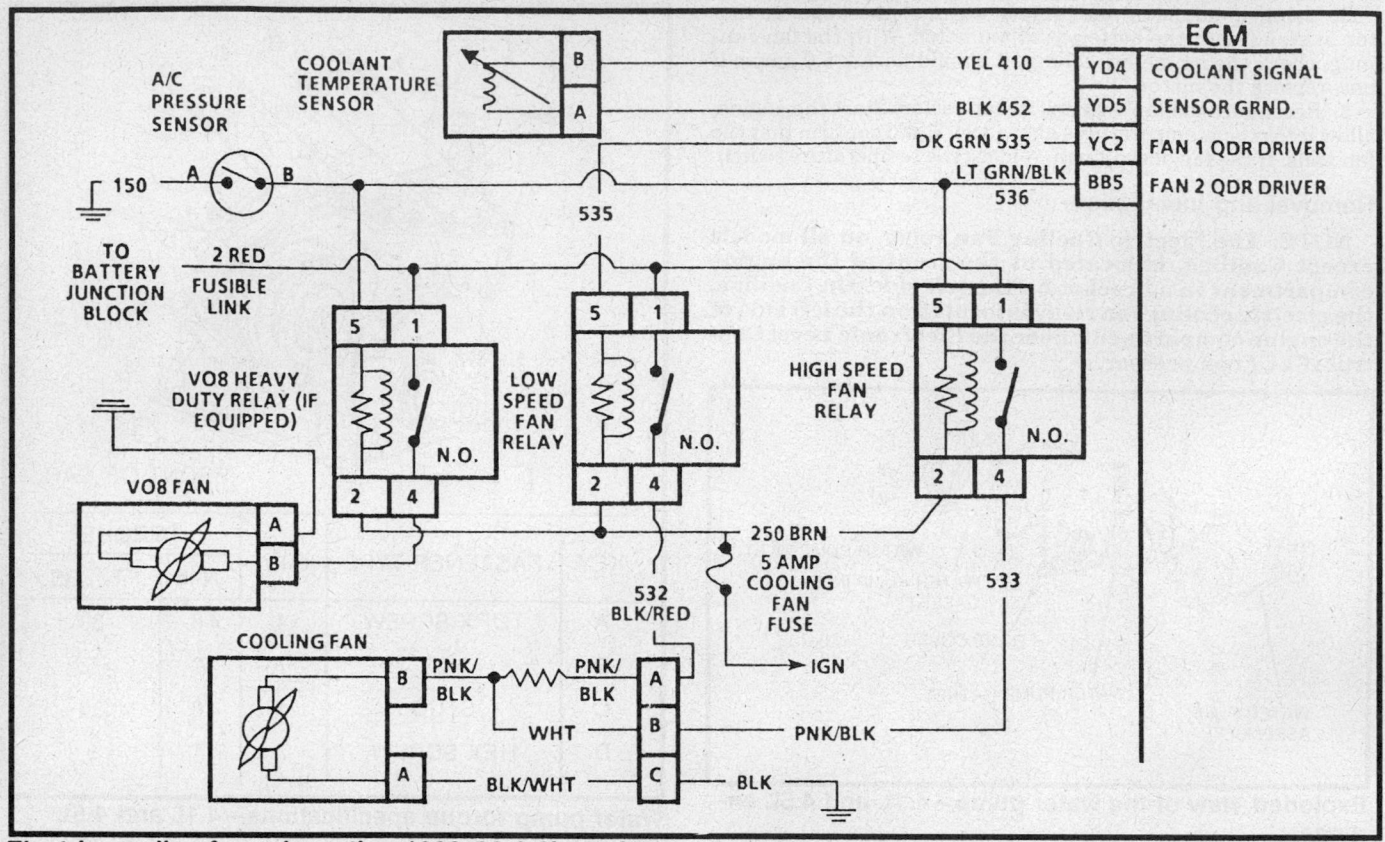

Electric cooling fan schematic—1988–90 3.8L engine

The electronic cooling fan switch is located on the top right side of the engine on all vehicles.

1. Disconnect the negative terminals from the battery.
2. Raise and support the vehicle and safely.
3. Disconnect the electrical connectors from the rear of the fan assemblies.
4. Remove the fan-to-lower radiator cradle bolts.
5. Lower the vehicle.
6. For right fan removal on vehicle equipped with V8 engines, remove the A/C accumulator to gain working clearance. Remove the air cleaner intake duct.
7. Remove the upper fan-to-radiator panel bolts and the upper radiator panel.
8. Remove the cooling fan assemblies.
9. To install, reverse the removal procedures.

COOLING FAN CONTROL MODULE

Removal and Installation

NOTE: Cadillac cooling fans are controlled by an electronic control module located behind the front left cornering lamp assembly.

1. Disconnect the negative terminal from the battery.
2. Remove the left cross vehicle brace.
3. Remove the windshield washer solvent container.
4. Remove the left cornering lamp assembly.
5. Disconnect the electrical connectors from the fan assemblies. Remove the necessary engine harness connectors.
6. Remove the control module retaining bolts.
7. Remove the control module assembly through the cornering lamp cavity.
8. To install, reverse the removal procedures.

BLOWER MOTOR

Removal and Installation

1. Disconnect the negative terminal from the battery.
2. Disconnect the electrical connections from the blower motor.
3. Disconnect the cooling hose from the blower motor.
4. Remove the mounting screws and the motor.
5. To install, reverse the removal procedures. Use a silicone sealer on the blower motor sealing surfaces.

HEATER CORE

Refer to "Chilton's Auto Heating And Air Conditioning Manual" for additional coverage.

Removal and Installation

1. Disconnect the negative battery cable. Drain the cooling system to a level below the heater core.
2. Disconnect and plug the heater hoses from the heater core.
3. Remove the instrument panel.
4. Remove the 4 defroster nozzle screws from the cowl, the case screw and the nozzle.
5. Disconnect the vacuum hoses.
6. Disconnect the electrical connector from the programmer.
7. From under the hood, remove the heater case-to-cowl screws.
8. From under the instrument panel, remove the heater case-to-cowl screw.
9. Remove the heater case.
10. Remove the 4 case-to-core screws and the core.
11. To install, reverse the removal procedures. Refill and bleed the cooling system.

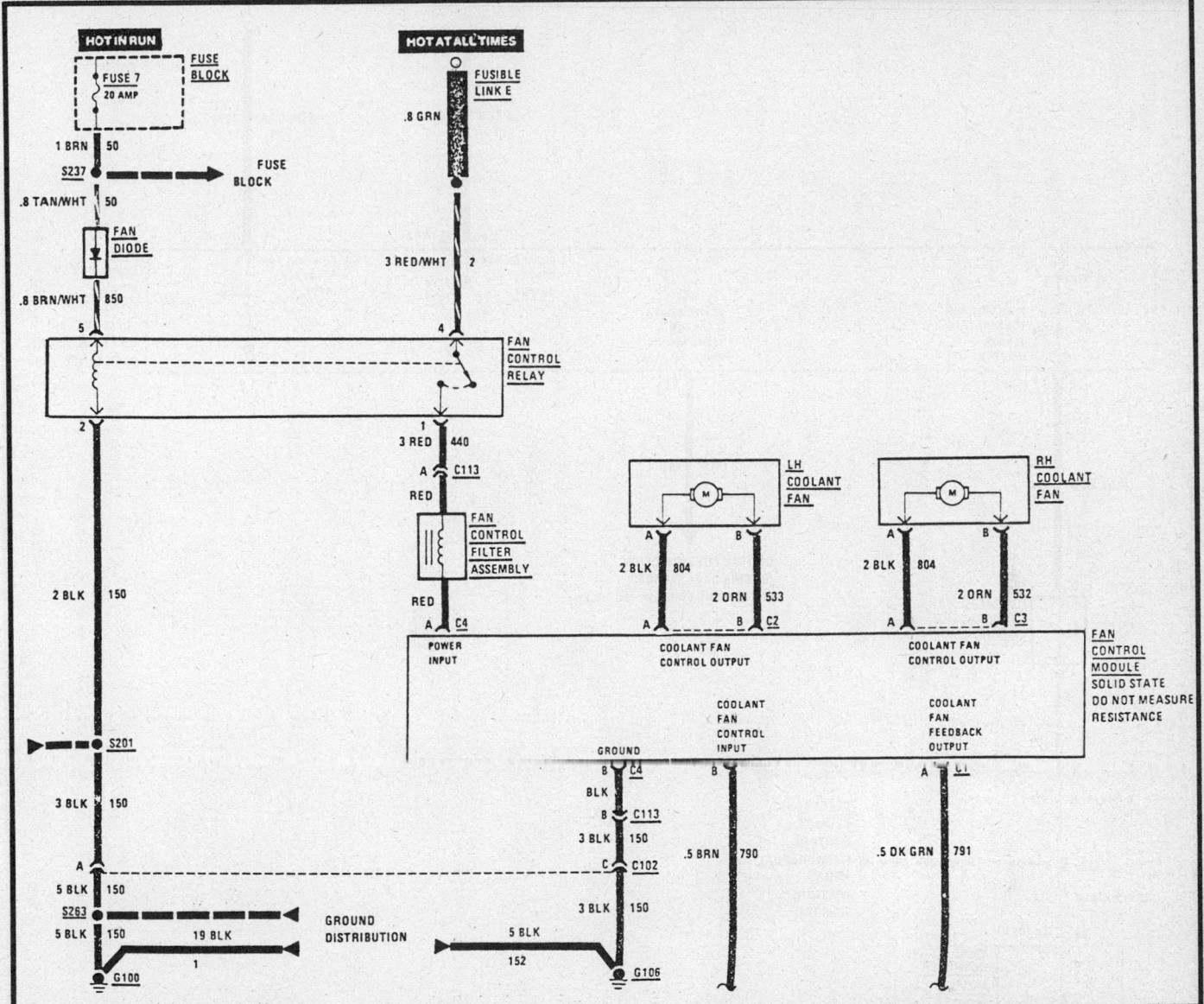

Electric cooling fan schematic—4.1L engine

Temperature Control/Blower Switch

Removal and Installation

1. Disconnect the negative terminal from the battery.
2. Remove the necessary trim panels in order to gain access to the control head retaining screws.

3. Remove the control head retaining screws. Pull out and disconnect the cables, electrical connections and vacuum lines from the rear of the control head.
4. Remove the control head assembly form the vehicle.
5. To install, reverse the removal procedures.

FUEL INJECTION

Refer to "Chilton's Electronic Engine Control Manual" for additional coverage.

Description

DIGITAL FUEL INJECTION

The Digital Fuel Injection (DFI) system is a throttle body fuel injection system, in which 2 solenoid actuated fuel injectors are mounted in the throttle body and inject fuel into the intake manifold. The DFI system controls the air/fuel mixture for combustion by monitoring selected engine operating conditions and electronically metering fuel requirements to meet those conditions.

The system consists of the following subsystems; the fuel delivery system, air induction system, engine sensors, electronic control unit (ECU), electronic spark timing (EST), idle speed control system (ISC), exhaust gas recirculation system (EGR) a

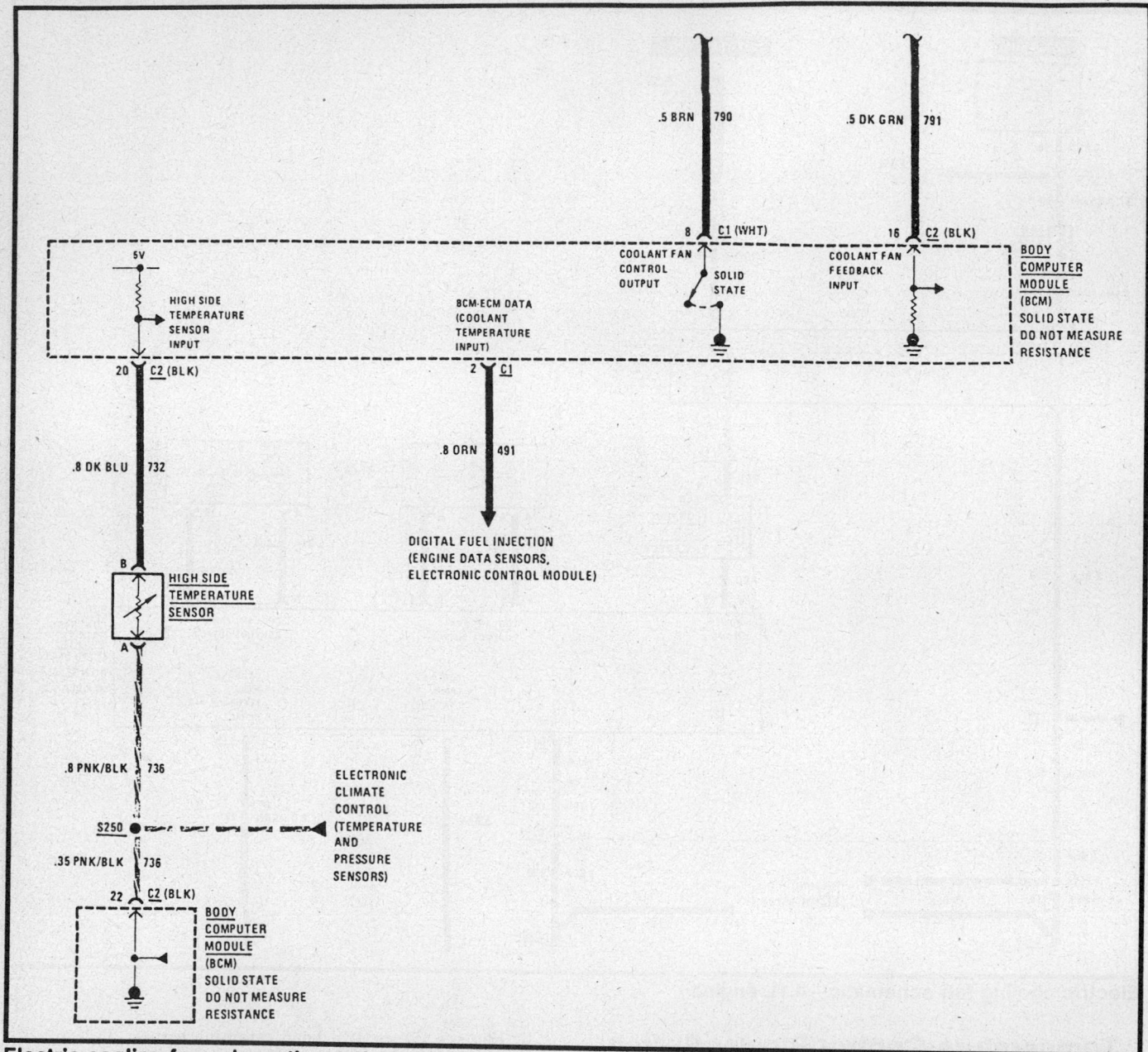

Electric cooling fan schematic – 4.1L engine (cont.)

charcoal canister, oxygen sensors and diagnostic readout systems.

PORT FUEL INJECTION

The Port Fuel Injection (PFI)system or Sequential Fuel Injection (SFI) has an injector installed near each intake valve inlet port. Each injector opens independently of each other, once every 2 revolutions of the crankshaft and prior to the opening of the intake valve for the cylinder to be fired. The Electronic Control Modules (ECM) is in complete control of both system during all phases of engine operation.

IDLE SPEED

Adjustment

DIGITAL FUEL INJECTION SYSTEM

NOTE: The engine idle speed is controlled by the elec-

tronic control module. Idle adjustment is only necessary when the idle speed control motor or the throttle body has been replaced. Before adjusting the idle speed, record, diagnosis, repair and clear all trouble codes in the ECM memory.

1. Remove the air cleaner assembly. Connect a suitable tachometer and timing light. Start the engine and allow it to reach normal operating temperatures.
2. Turn all the accessories off. Check and adjust the ignition timing.
3. Place the steering wheel in the center position and the transmission selector in the **P** position.
4. To retract the idle speed control motor (ISC) plunger, unlock the ISC motor connector but do not disconnect the motor. Open the throttle and hold it at approximately 1500 rpm.
5. Close the throttle switch by depressing the ISC plunger.

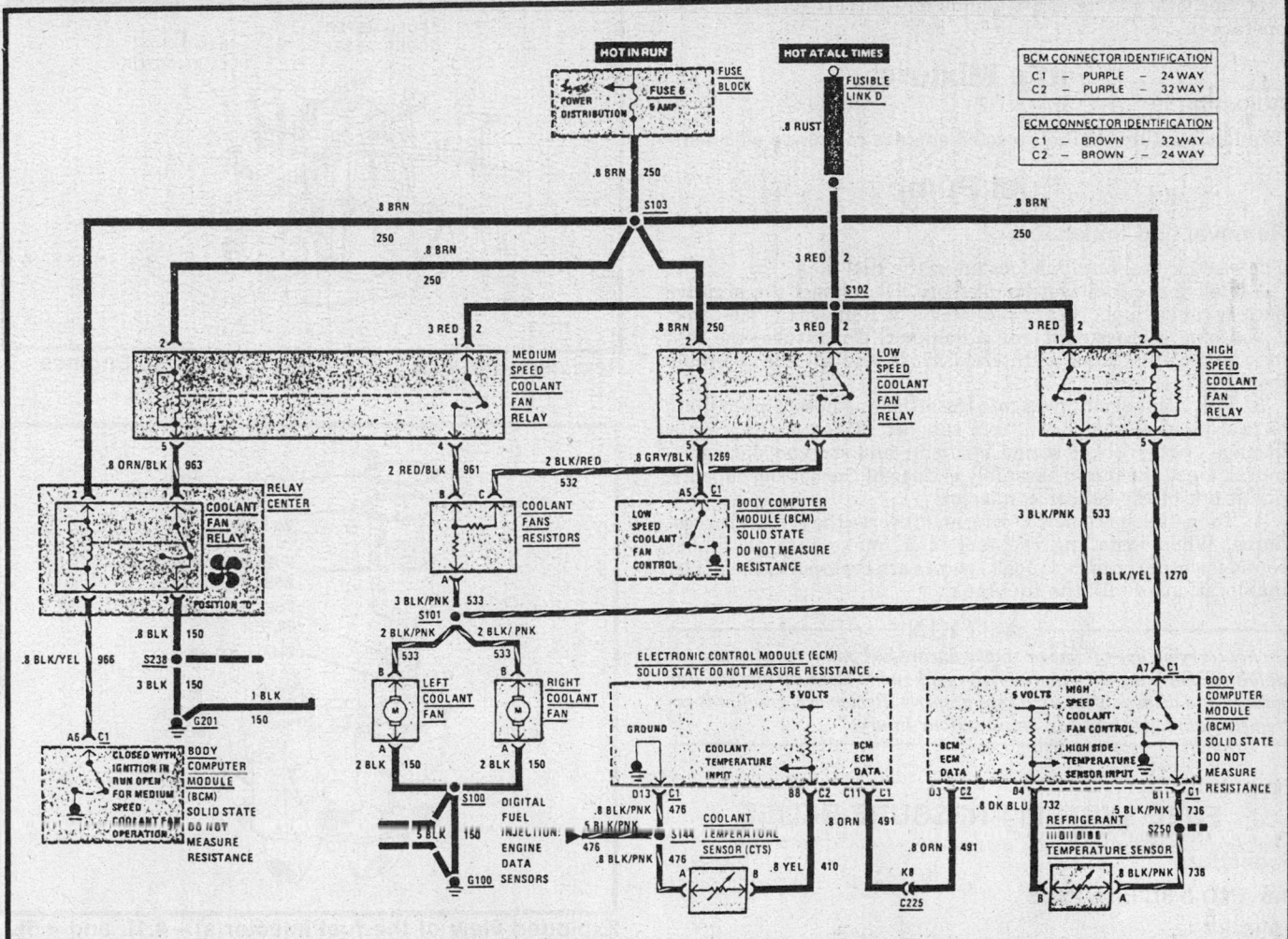

Electric cooling fan schematic – 4.5L engine

When the plunger is fully retracted, continue to hold the throttle open and the throttle switch closed, while disconnecting the ISC motor.

6. Return the throttle to idle; be sure not to power the ISC motor in the fully retracted position for more than 4 seconds or damage to the electronic control module may occur.

7. The ISC plunger should now be retracted. If the plunger still contacts the throttle lever, turn the plunger in so it is not touching. With the ISC plunger fully retracted and not touching the throttle lever, the idle speed should be 450 rpm.

8. Check the throttle position sensor adjustment. With the ISC motor fully retracted and the throttle against the stop screw. Turn the ISC plunger adjustment screw to obtain a 0.160 in. gap between the throttle lever and the plunger.

9. Shut the engine **OFF**, disconnect all the test equipment and reconnect all harness connectors. Turn the ignition off for a least 10 seconds. Start the engine and check the ISC motor for proper operation.

NOTE: This procedure may have recorded intermittent trouble codes in the DFI computer. After all the connections have been made and the system is restored to normal operations, these codes must be cleared.

10. To clear the ECM codes, perform the following porcedures:
   a. Turn the key to the **ON** position.

b. Then simultaneously press the **OFF** and **HI** buttons in the climate control panel until E.O.O appears in the readout.

11. To clear the Body Computer Module (BCM), depress the **OFF** and **LO** buttons simultaneously until F.O.O appears.

PORT FUEL INJECTION

NOTE: This adjustment should be performed only when the throttle body parts have been replaced. Engine must be at normal operating temperatures before making an adjustment.

1. With a scratch awl or equivalent, piece the idle stop screw plug and apply leverage to remove it.

2. Ground the ALDL diagnostic test lead and turn ignition switch **ON** position, without starting engine for at least 30 seconds.

3. After 30 seconds, disconnect the Idle Air Control (IAC) electrical connector.

4. Remove ground wire from diagnostic lead. Firmly set the parking brake and block the front drive wheels.

5. Start the engine and place the transaxle in D. Using the minimum idle stop set screw and adjust the idle speed to 450–550 rpm.

6. Turn ignition switch **OFF** and reconnect connector at IAC motor.

7. Adjust throttle position sensor to 0.36–0.44V.

8. Recheck setting, start engine and inspect for proper idle operation.

Idle Mixture

Adjustment

The idle mixture on fuel injected engines cannot be adjusted.

Fuel Pump

Removal and Installation

The electric fuel pump is located in the fuel tank.

1. Relive the fuel system pressure. Disconnect the negative battery cable. Support ther vehicle safely. Remove the fuel tank.
2. Using a brass drift and a hammer, drive (turn) the cam lock ring-to-fuel tank counterclockwise and lift the assembly from the fuel tank.
3. Pull the fuel pump up into the attaching hose while pulling outward away from the bottom support. Take care to prevent damage to the rubber sound insulator and strainer during removal. Once the pump assembly is clear of the bottom support, pull it out of the rubber connector.
4. To install, use a new O-ring and reverse the removal procedures. When installing the fuel tank, make sure all rubber sound isolators or anti-squeak spacers are replaced in their original locations. Refill the fuel tank.

--- CAUTION ---

Do not carry an open flame or smoke during fuel pump removal and installation. Have a good supply of rags on hand to clean up any gasoline spillage and dispose of all used rags properly. Remember, gasoline is extremely flammable and can cause serious injury.

FUEL SYSTEM PRESSURE RELIEF

Procedure

3.0 AND 3.8L ENGINES

1986–87

1. From the fuse panel, remove the fuel pump fuse.
2. Start the engine and allow it run until it uses all the fuel.
3. Replace the fuse.
4. Disconnect the negative battery cable.

3.8L ENGINE

1988–90

1. Disconnect the negative battery cable.
2. Loosen the fuel filler cap to relieve the tank vapor pressure.
3. Connect fuel pressure gauge J–34730–1 or equivalent to the fuel pressure connection. Wrap a shop towel around the fitting while connecting the gauge to avoid spillage.
4. Install a bleed hose into a container and open the valve to bleed the system pressure. The system is now safe for servicing.

4.1L ENGINE

If the engine has been operated, allow a few minutes for it to bleed-down.

4.5L ENGINE

1. Disconnect the negative battery cable.
2. Loosen the fuel filler cap to relieve the tank vapor pressure.
3. Connect fuel pressure gauge J–34730–1 or equivalent to the fuel pressure connection. Wrap a shop towel around the fitting while connecting the gauge to avoid spillage.
4. Install a bleed hose into a container and open the valve to bleed the system pressure. The system is now safe for servicing.

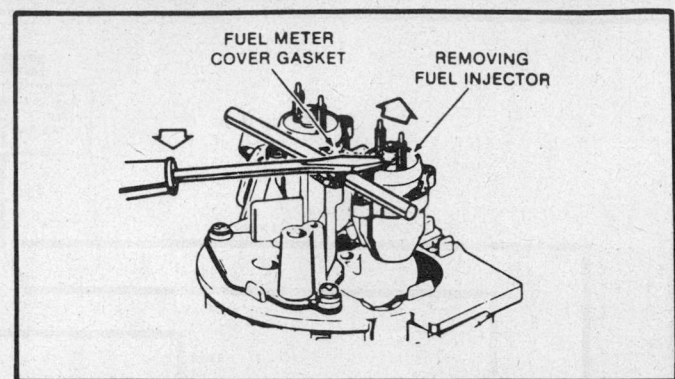

Removing the fuel injector—4.1L and 4.5L Engines

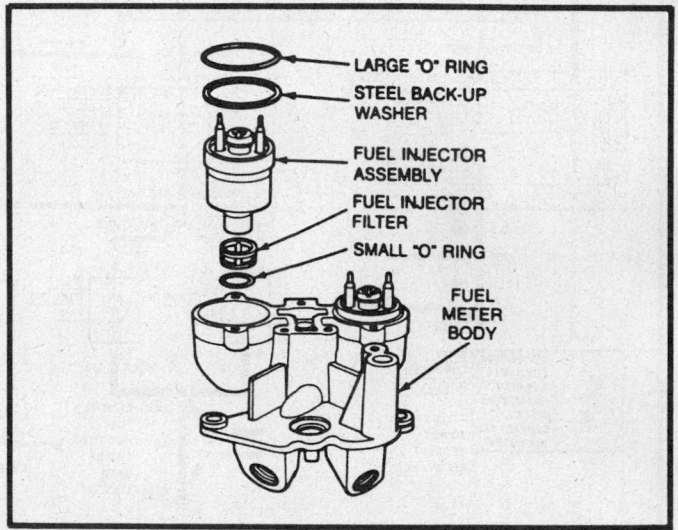

Exploded view of the fuel injector(s)—4.1L and 4.5L engines

FUEL INJECTOR

Removal and Installation

3.0L AND 3.8L ENGINES

1. Properly relieve the fuel system pressure. Remove the air cleaner assembly. Disconnect the negative battery cable.
2. Label and disconnect the fuel injector electrical connectors.
3. Remove the fuel rail retaining bolts. Remove the fuel rail.
4. Separate the injector from the fuel rail.
5. To install, use new O-rings and reverse the removal procedures. Start the engine and check for leaks.

4.1L AND 4.5L ENGINES

NOTE: Care must be taken when removing injectors to prevent damage to the electrical connector pins on the injector and the nozzle. The injectors are serviced as a complete assembly only. Injectors are an electrical component and should not be immersed in any type of cleaner.

1. On the 4.1L engine, if the engine was recently operated, allow the fuel pressure to bleed down. On the 4.5L engine properly release the fuel system pressure.
2. Disconnect the negative battery cable. Remove the air cleaner.

3. Disconnect the electrical connector from the fuel injector(s) by squeezing the 2 tabs together and pulling it straight up.

4. Remove the fuel meter cover-to-throttle body screws and the cover; be sure to note the position of the 4 short screws. Allow the gasket to remain in place to prevent damage to the casting housing.

5. Using a small pry bar and a ¼ in. rod, pry the fuel injector(s) from the throttle body; discard the O-rings.

6. To install, use new O-rings (lubricate with Dexron® II automatic transmission fluid) and reverse the removal procedures. When installing the injectors, simply push them into the sockets. Start the engine and check for leaks.

EMISSION CONTROL SYSTEMS

3.0L ENGINE

Oxygen sensor
Coolant temperature sensor
Throttle position sensor
Vehicle speed sensor
Air temperature sensor
EGR valve
EGR vacuum control solenoid
Electronic control module
Mass air flow sensor
Electronic spark control system
Prom
Calpak
Fuel injectors
Fuel rail
Throttle body assembly
Idle air control valve
Vapor canister
Canister purge solenoid
Computer controlled coil ignition system (C^3I)
ESC knock sensor
ESC module
Torque converter clutch
PCV system
Catalytic converter

3.8L ENGINE

Positive crankcase ventilation
Evaporative emission control
Early fuel evaporation system
Catalytic converter
Exhaust gas recirculation
Computer command control
Deceleration valve
Air injection reactor
Controlled combustion system
Transmission converter clutch
Electronic spark Control
Electronic Spark Timing
Thermostatic air cleaner
Fuel injectors
Idle air meter
Cooling fan relay
Manifold air temperature sensor
Knock sensor—3.8L (231 CID) V6
Mass air flow system—3.8L (231 CID) V6

NOTE: Emissions equipment listed above is not used on every engine application.

4.1L AND 4.5L ENGINE

Positive crankcase ventilation
Evaporative emission control
Exhaust gas recirculation

Air injection reactor
Thermostatic air cleaner
Viscous converter clutch

EMISSIONS INDICATOR

Clearing Codes

The dash mounted "Service Soon" and "Service Now" lights are used to indicated to the mechanic or owner of a malfunction that the computer has detected in the vehicle's operation. The malfunctions can be related to the operating sensors or the electronic control module (ECM). The service light will go out automatically if the trouble is cleared or intermittent.

The ECM, however will automatically store the trouble code until the diagnostic system is "Cleared".

On all models, except Cadillac, this is accomplished by removing battery voltage to the ECM for 30 seconds.

To prevent ECM damage, the key must be **OFF** when disconnecting or reconnecting power to the ECM.

To disconnect battery voltage to the ECM, on all models except Cadillac, perform one of the following:
1. Remove the ECM fuse from the fuse panel.
2. Remove the DOM pigtail.
3. Disconnect the battery cable.

NOTE: Disconnecting the battery cable should only be done as a last resort as it will also clear the digital radio, digital clock, trip odometer etc.

To clear the ECM codes on Cadillacs:
1. Turn the key to the **ON** position.
2. Then simultaneously press the **OFF** and **HI** buttons in the climate control panel until E.O.O appears in the readout.
3. To clear the Body Computer Module BCM on Cadillacs, perform the following procedure:
   a. Depress the **OFF** and **LO** buttons simultaneously until "F.O.O" appears.

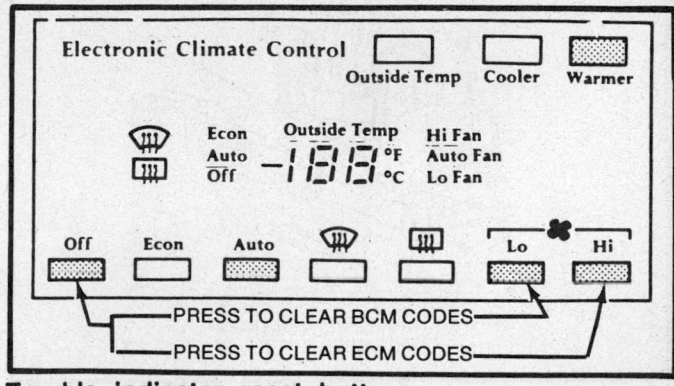

Trouble indicator reset buttons

ENGINE

NOTE: Disconnecting the negative battery cable on some vehicles may interfere with the functions of the on board computer systems and may require the computer to undergo a relearning process, once the negative battery cable is reconnected.

Engine Assembly

Removal and Installation

3.0L AND 3.8L ENGINES

1. Disconnect the negative terminal from the battery. Using a scribing tool, matchmark the hood hinges and remove the hood.
2. Label and disconnect the air flow sensor wiring. Depressurize the fuel system.
3. Remove the air intake duct. Remove the throttle cable and bracket from the throttle body. Place a clean drain pan under the radiator, open the drain cock and drain the cooling system.
4. Raise and support the vehicle safely.
5. Remove the exhaust pipe-to-exhaust manifold bolts and separate the exhaust pipe.
6. Remove the engine mount bolts.
7. If equipped with a driveline vibration absorber, remove the bolts and disconnect the absorber.
8. Label and disconnect the electrical connectors from the starter. Remove the starter-to-engine bolts and the starter.
9. If equipped with air conditioning, disconnect the compressor and position it out of the way; Do not disconnect the refrigerant lines.
10. Place a catch pan under the power steering gear, disconnect the hydraulic lines, drain the fluid and wire the hoses out of the way.
11. Remove the lower transaxle-to-engine bolts.

NOTE: One bolt is situated between the transaxle case and the engine block; it is installed in the opposite direction of the other bolts.

12. Remove the flywheel cover. Matchmark the flexplate-to-torque converter relationship to insure proper alignment upon installation. Remove the flexplate-to-torque converter bolts.
13. Remove the engine support bracket-to-transaxle bolts and the bracket. Lower the vehicle.
14. Using a vertical engine hoist, attach it to the engine and support the weight.
15. Remove the radiator and heater hoses from the engine; position them out of the way.
16. Remove hoses from the vacuum modulator and canister purge lines.
17. Disconnect the engine electrical wiring harness(es) and tie it (them) out of way.

18. Remove the upper transaxle-to-engine bolts.
19. Using the proper engine removal equippment, carefully remove the engine from the vehicle.
20. To install, reverse the removal procedures. Refill the cooling system. Start the engine, allow it to reach normal operating temperatures and check for leaks.

4.1L AND 4.5L V8 ENGINES

1. Disconnect the negative terminal from the battery. Place a clean drain pan under the radiator, open the drain cock and drain the cooling system.
2. Remove the air cleaner. Using a scribing tool, matchmark the hood to the support brackets and remove the hood.
3. If equipped with air conditioning, perform the following procedures:
   a. Remove the hose strap from the right-strut tower.
   b. Remove the accumulator from its bracket and position it out of the way.
   c. Remove the canister hoses from the accumulator bracket.
   d. Remove the accumulator bracket from the wheel house.
4. Remove the cooling fans, the accessory drive belt, the radiator and heater hoses.
5. Label and disconnect the electrical connectors from the following items:
   a. Oil pressure switch
   b. Coolant temperature sensor
   c. Distributor
   d. EGR solenoid
   e. Engine temperature switch
6. Label and disconnect the cables from the following items:
   a. Accelerator

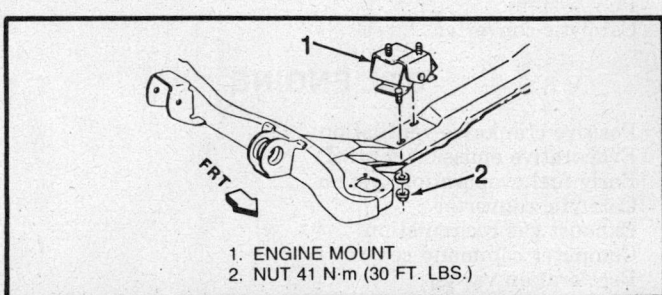

1. ENGINE MOUNT
2. NUT 41 N·m (30 FT. LBS.)

View of the right side engine mount—3.0L and 3.8L engine

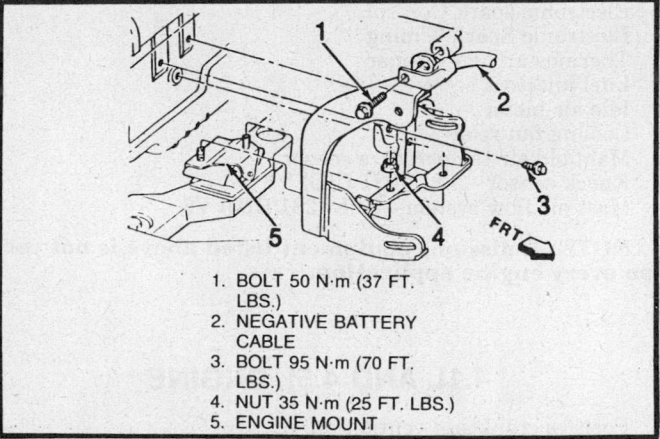

1. BOLT 50 N·m (37 FT. LBS.)
2. NEGATIVE BATTERY CABLE
3. BOLT 95 N·m (70 FT. LBS.)
4. NUT 35 N·m (25 FT. LBS.)
5. ENGINE MOUNT

View of the left side engine mount—3.0L and 3.8L engine

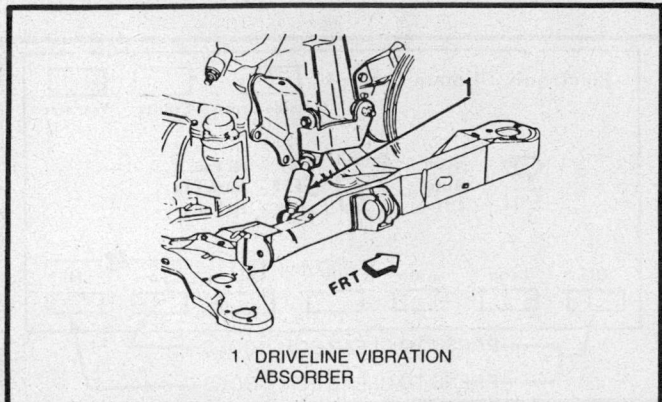

1. DRIVELINE VIBRATION ABSORBER

Typical driveline vibration absorber

b. Cruise control linkage

c. Transaxle throttle valve (TV) cable

7. If equipped with cruise control, remove the diaphragm (with the bracket) and move it aside.

8. Remove the vacuum supply hose and the exhaust crossover pipe.

9. Disconnect the oil cooler lines from the oil filter adapter, the oil line cooler bracket from the transaxle and position them aside.

10. Remove the air cleaner mounting bracket.

11. Using a catch pan or a shop rag, carefully bleed the fuel pressure from the Schrader valve. Disconnect the fuel lines from the throttle body. Remove the fuel line bracket from the transaxle and secure the fuel lines out of the way.

NOTE: When bleeding the fuel system, be sure to have a container or rags on hand to catch excess fuel. Take precautions to avoid the risk of fire.

12. Remove the small vacuum line from the brake booster.

13. Label and disconnect the AIR solenoid electrical and hose connections. Remove the AIR valves with the bracket.

14. Label and disconnect the electrical connectors from the following:

a. Idle Speed Control (ISC) motor

b. Throttle Position Switch (TPS)

c. Fuel injectors

d. Manifold Air Temperature (MAT) sensor

e. Oxygen sensor

f. Electric Fuel Evaporator (EFE) grid

g. Alternator bracket

15. Remove the power steering pump hose strap from the stud-headed bolt in front of the right cylinder head and the stud-headed bolt.

16. Remove the AIR pipe clip located near the No. 2 spark plug.

17. Remove the power steering pump and belt tensioner (with bracket); wire them out of the way.

18. Raise and support the vehicle safely.

19. Label and disconnect the electrical connectors from the starter and the ground wire from the cylinder block.

20. Remove the 2 flywheel covers. Remove the starter-to-engine bolts and the starter. Matchmark the flywheel-to-torque converter location. Remove the 3 flywheel-to-torque converter bolts and slide the converter back into the bell housing.

21. If equipped with air conditioning, perform the following procedures:

a. Remove the compressor lower dust shield.

b. Remove the right front wheel/tire assembly and outer wheelhouse plastic shield.

c. Remove the compressor-to-bracket bolts and lower the compressor from the engine; do not disconnect the refrigerant lines.

22. Remove the lower radiator hose.

23. From the lower right front of the engine and cradle, remove the driveline vibration dampener (with brackets) and the engine-to-transaxle bracket bolts. Pull the alternator wire (with plastic cover), down and out of the way.

24. Remove the exhaust pipe-to-manifold bolts (with springs) and the AIR pipe-to-converter bracket from the exhaust manifold stud.

NOTE: Be careful not to lose the springs when detaching the exhaust pipe.

25. Remove the lower right side bell housing-to-engine bolt. Lower the vehicle.

26. Using a vertical engine hoist, attach it to the engine and support it.

27. Remove the upper bell housing-to-engine bolts and left front engine mount bracket-to-engine bolts. Remove the engine from the vehicle.

28. To install, reverse the removal procedures. Refill the cooling system. Start the engine, allow it to reach normal operating temperatures and check for leaks.

Engine Mounts

Removal and Installation

3.0L AND 3.8L ENGINES

1. Disconnect the negative terminal from the battery.

2. Raise and support the vehicle.

3. Remove the engine through mount bolt. Using a vertical lifting device, attach it to the engine and raise the engine.

4. Remove the engine mount bolts and the mount.

5. To install, reverse the removal procedures.

NOTE: If a vibration or a shudder should occur on acceleration from 1–10 mph on a 1986 Delta 88 (without a Hydro-Mount engine mount), the right rear engine mount and brackets should be loosened to relieve any stress situation in this area that may have been introduced at the time of assembly. If movement occurs when loosened, the mount and brackets should be retightened and the car road tested to see if the vibration still exists. If it does, installation of a Hydro-Mount engine mount is necessary. This repair does not apply to vehicles built after June 1, 1986. Vehicles built after that date were assembled with Hydro-Mount engine mount.

4.1L and 4.5L ENGINES

Right

1. Open the hood, disconnect the negative terminal from the battery and brace from the engine bracket to the engine.

2. Remove the 2 nuts securing the engine bracket to the mount.

3. Raise the vehicle and support it safely.

4. Support the vehicle with stands at each front frame horn.

5. Remove the 2 nuts on the engine mount securing to the frame.

6. Remove the 2 nuts securing the transaxle mount to the mount.

7. Remove the 2 nuts securing the transaxle mount to the frame bracket.

8. Raise the engine using engine support tool No. J–28467 or its equivalent.

9. Raise the engine until the bracket is free from the engine mount. Remove the stud and the 2 bolts that secure the bracket to the block. Remove the mount and bracket by pulling forward.

10. Remove the transaxle mounting bracket from the transaxle.

11. Remove the mount assembly.

To install:

12. Position the engine mount and bracket, in place between the transaxle and frame and secure the bracket to the transaxle with the 2 bolts and tighten to 34 ft. lbs.

13. While lowering the engine, guide the motor mount into location and install the engine mount to frame and transaxle mount to frame bracket with the 2 nuts each, and tighten to 22 ft. lbs.

14. Install the 2 nuts to the engine mount studs and the 2 nuts to transaxle mount studs and tighten to 22 ft. lbs.

15. Remove the brace from the engine bracket to engine.

16. Remove the stands and lower ther hoist.

LEFT

1. Raise the vehicle and support it safely.

2. Support the vehicle with stands at each front frame horn.

3. Remove the 1 nut securing the mount to the transaxle bracket and 2 nuts securing the mount to the frame.

4. Lift the engine using engine support tool No. J–28467 or its equivalent.

5. Remove the 3 bolts securing the bracket to the transaxle.

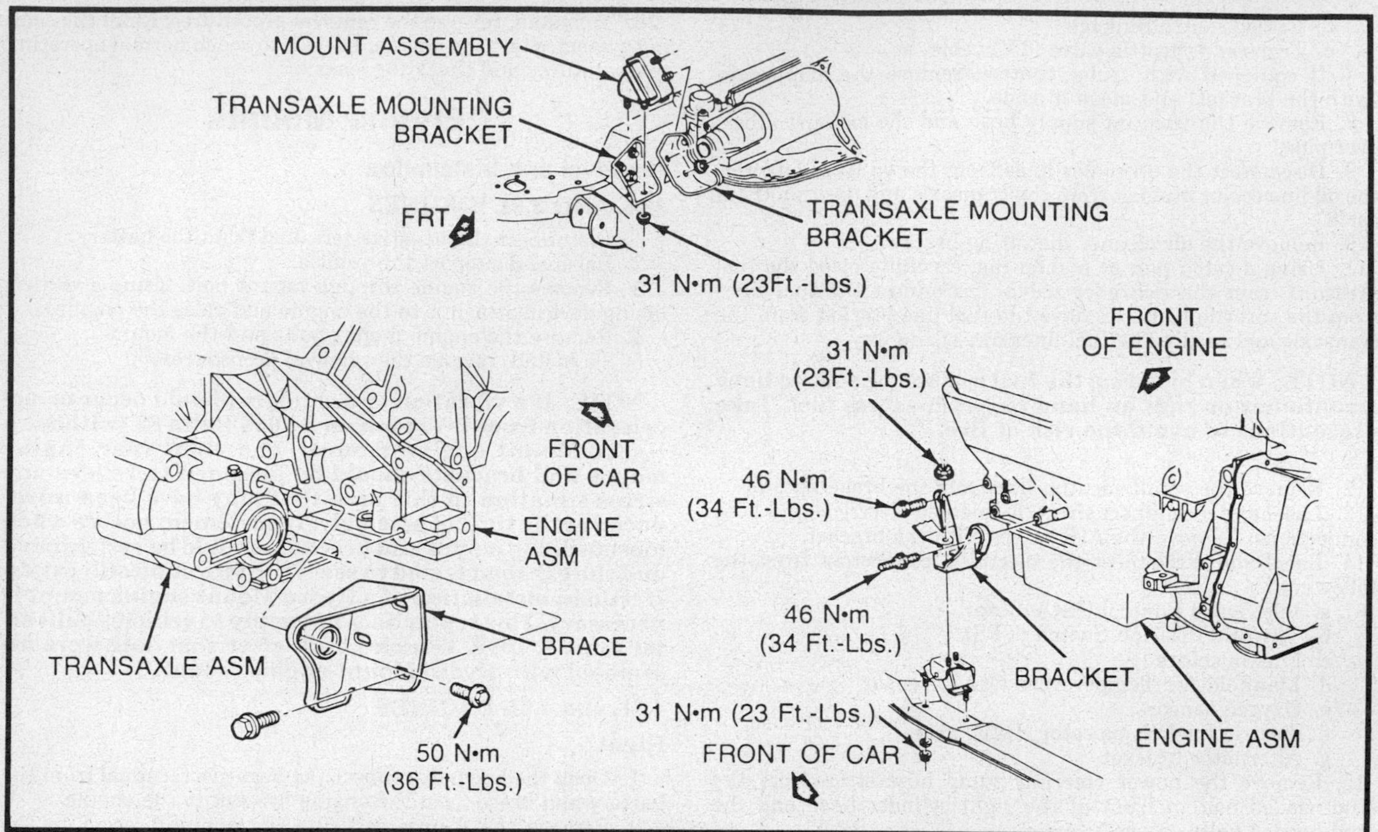

MOUNT ASSEMBLY

TRANSAXLE MOUNTING BRACKET

FRT

TRANSAXLE MOUNTING BRACKET

31 N•m (23Ft.-Lbs.)

FRONT OF ENGINE

31 N•m (23Ft.-Lbs.)

46 N•m (34 Ft.-Lbs.)

46 N•m (34 Ft.-Lbs.)

31 N•m (23 Ft.-Lbs.)

FRONT OF CAR

FRONT OF CAR

ENGINE ASM

TRANSAXLE ASM

BRACE

50 N•m (36 Ft.-Lbs.)

BRACKET

ENGINE ASM

Views of the right-side engine, brace and transaxle mounts—4.1L and 4.5L engines

TRANSAXLE MOUNTING BRACKET

31 N•m (23 FT-LBS)

A

B

TRANSAXLE MOUNTING BRACKET

FRT

31 N•m (23 FT-LBS)

FRAME ASM

52 N•m (38 FT-LBS)

FRT

GUIDE — OIL COOLER PIPES

FRT

52 N•m (38 FT-LBS)   VIEW A

VIEW B

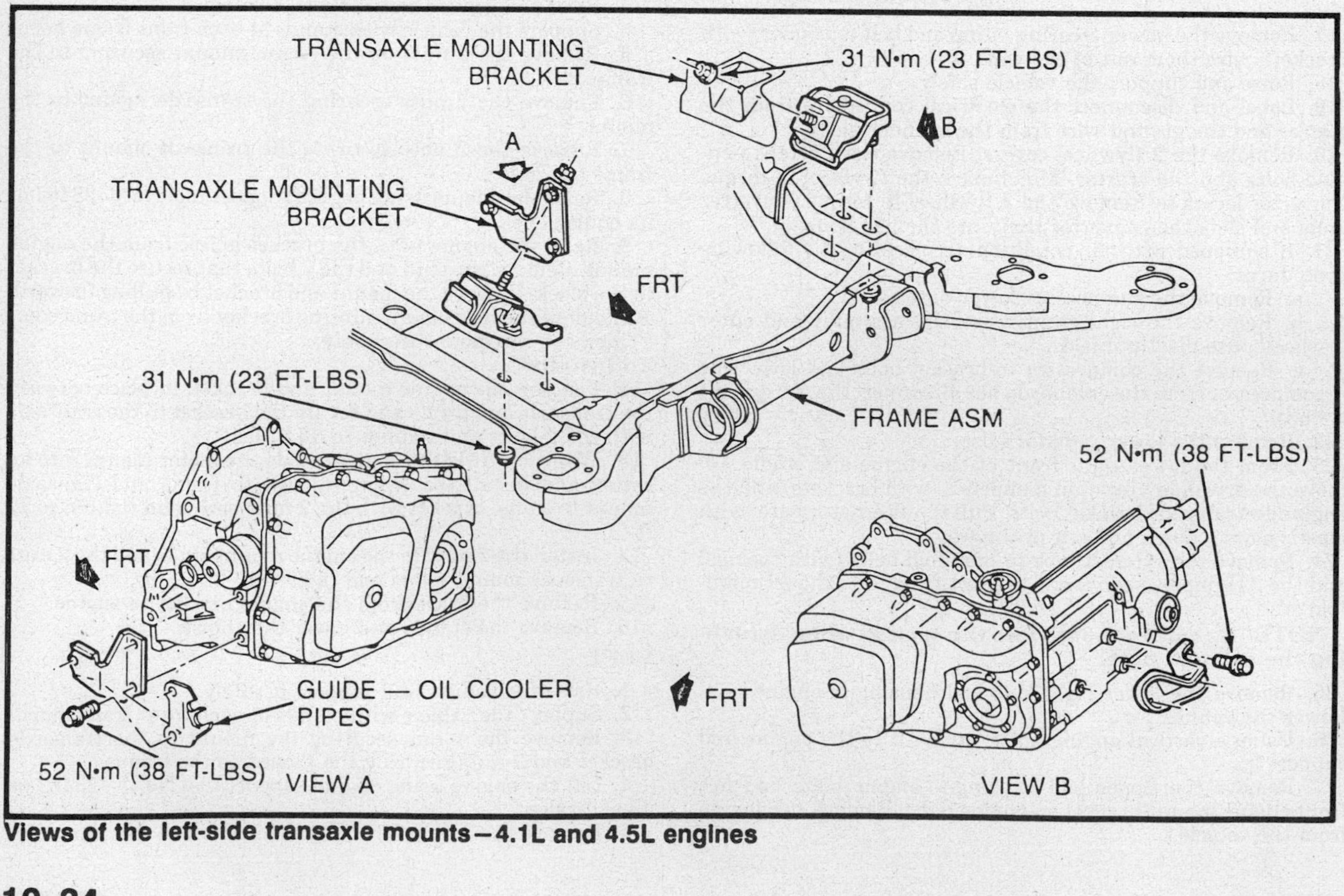

Views of the left-side transaxle mounts—4.1L and 4.5L engines

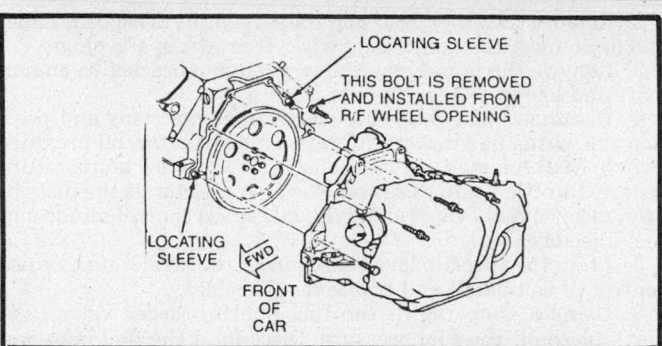

Exploded view of the transaxle-to-engine assembly— 4.1L and 4.5L engines

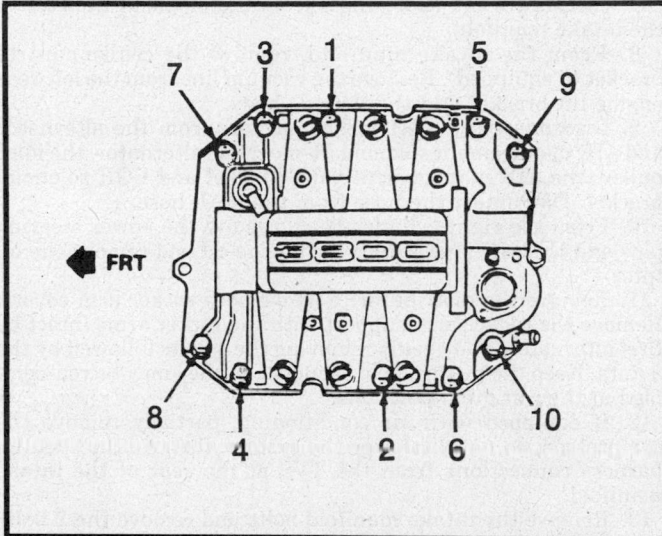

View of intake manifold bolt torquing sequence— 1988–90 3.8L engine

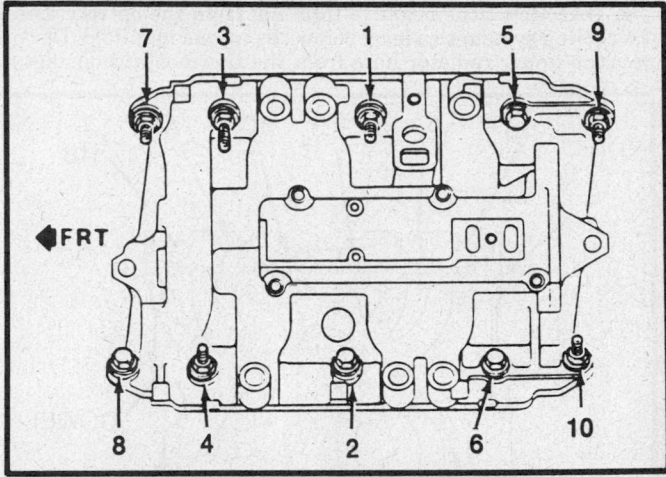

View of intake manifold bolt torquing sequence— 1986–87 3.0L and 3.8L engine

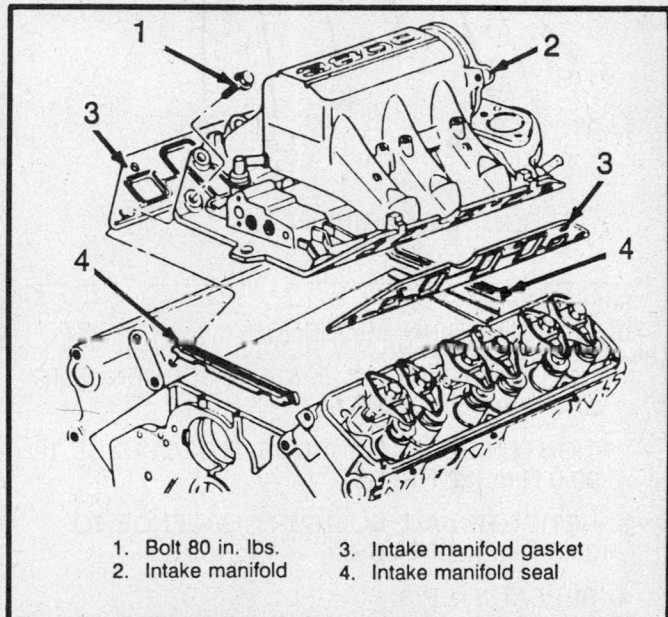

1. Bolt 80 in. lbs.
2. Intake manifold
3. Intake manifold gasket
4. Intake manifold seal

Intake manifold and gaskets—1988–90 3.8L engine

6. Raise the engine assembly until the brackets are free.

7. Remove the mount and bracket by pulling it upward.

To install:

8. Position the engine mount and bracket, in place between the transaxle and frame and tighten the 3 bracket to 41 ft. lbs. and nuts to 22 ft lbs.

9. Lower the transaxle onto the mount until it is seated.

10. Install the 1 nut securing the mount to the bracket and tighten to 22 ft. lbs.

Intake Manifold

Removal and Installaion

3.0L AND 3.8L ENGINES

1. Relieve the fuel system pressure.

2. Disconnect the negative terminal from the battery. Place a clean drain pan under the radiator, open the draincock and drain the cooling system.

3. Remove the serpentine drive belt, the alternator and the bracket.

4. Remove the power steering pump, the braces and move it aside; do not disconnect the pressure lines.

5. Remove the coolant bypass hose, the heater pipe and the upper radiator hose from the intake manifold.

6. Remove the vacuum hoses and disconnect the electrical connectors from the intake manifold.

7. Remove the EGR pipe, the EGR valve and the adapter from the throttle body.

8. Remove the throttle body coolant pipe, the throttle body and the throttle body adapter.

9. Disconnect the rear spark plug wires. Remove the intake manifold-to-engine bolts and the manifold.

10. Clean the gasket mounting surfaces.

11. To install, use new gaskets, sealant number 12345336 or equivalent (on the ends of the manifold seals) and reverse the removal procedures. Torque the intake manifold (in sequence) to 37 ft. lbs. (1986–87) or TWICE to 88 inch lbs. (1988–90 VIN code C). Refill the cooling system. Start the engine, allow it to reach normal operating temperatures and check for leaks.

4.1L AND 4.5L ENGINES

NOTE: Some vehicles equipped with the 4.1L and 4.5L engines have been experiencing oil leakage at the intake manifold to block seal, due to a split intake manifold seal. When repairing this leak, replace the old seal with a new silicone seal (part number 3634619) The new seal is easily identified by its gray color.

1. Disconnect the negative terminal from the battery. Drain the cooling system to a level below the intake manifold. Disconnect the upper radiator hose from the thermostat housing.

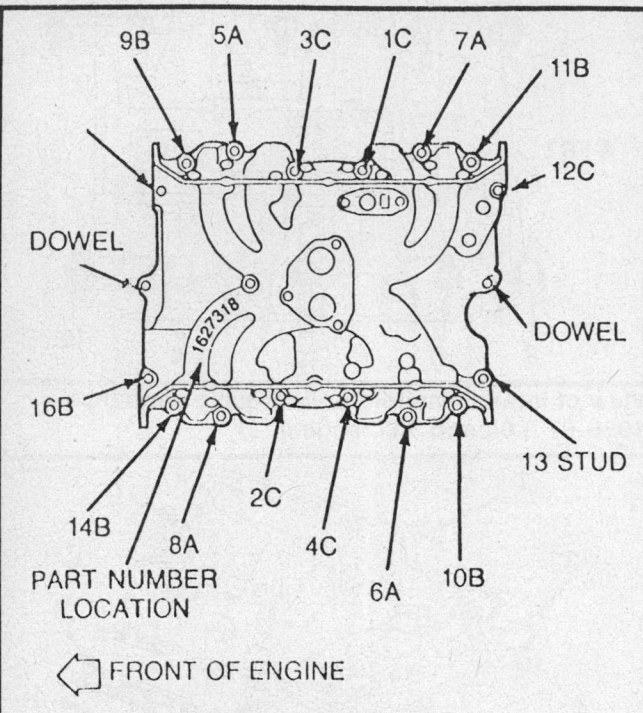

BOLT TIGHTENING SEQUENCE

1. TIGHTEN BOLTS 1, 2, 3, & 4 IN SEQUENCE TO 20.0 N·m (15 FT-LBS).

2. TIGHTEN BOLTS 5 THRU 16 IN SEQUENCE TO 30.0 N·m (22 FT-LBS).

3. RETIGHTEN ALL BOLTS IN SEQUENCE TO 30.0 N·m (22 FT-LBS).

4. REPEAT STEP 3.

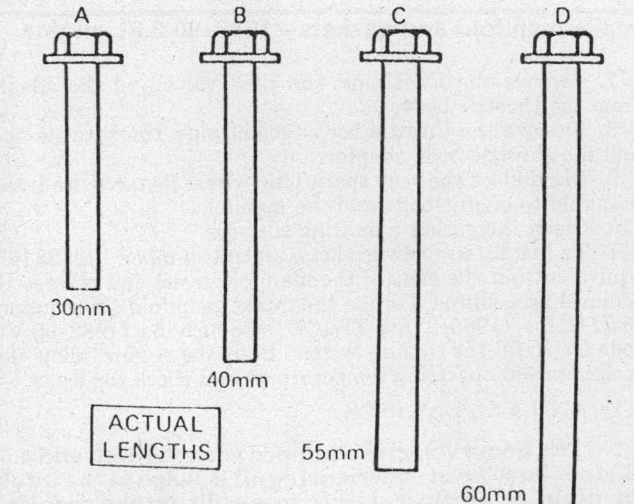

Intake manifold bolt size and torque sequence — 1986–87 4.1L engine

2. Remove the air cleaner and the serpentine drive belt. Label and disconnect the spark plug wires from the spark plugs.

3. Remove the upper power steering pump bracket-to-engine bolts and loosen the lower nuts.

4. Disconnect the following electrical connections and position the wiring harness out of the way: distributor, oil pressure switch, EGR solenoid, coolant sensor, mass airflow temperature sensor, throttle position sensor, 4-way connector at the distributor, electric fuel evaporator grid, idle speed control motor and fuel injectors.

5. From the throttle lever, disconnect the accelerator, cruise control (if equipped) and transaxle TV cables.

6. Using a shop rag at the fuel line Schraeder valve (test port), bleed off the fuel pressure. Disconnect the fuel inlet and return lines from the throttle body. From the transaxle, remove the fuel line brackets and move the lines aside; disconnect the modulator vacuum line.

7. Disconnect the heater hose from the nipple at the rear of the intake manifold.

8. From the intake manifold, remove the cruise control bracket (if equipped). Remove the vacuum line from the left rear engine lift bracket and the throttle body.

9. Disconnect the electrical connectors from the alternator and AIR management solenoid. Remove the alternator, the idler pulley, the AIR management valve/bracket and EGR solenoid/bracket. Disconnect the hose from the MAP hose.

10. From the right cylinder head, remove the power steering pipe and the AIR pipe. Drain the engine oil and remove the oil filter.

11. Remove the distributor. Remove both rocker arm covers. Remove the rocker arm support with the rocker arms intact by first alternately and evenly removing the 4 bolts followed by the 5 nuts. Keep the pushrods in sequence so they may be reassembled in their original positions.

12. If equipped with air conditioning, partially remove the compressor; do not discharge the system. Remove the vacuum harness connections from the TVS at the rear of the intake manifold.

13. Remove the intake manifold bolts and remove the 2 bolts securing the lower thermostat housing to the front cover. Remove the engine lift brackets or bend them out of the way.

14. Remove the intake manifold and lower the thermostat housing as an assembly by lifting it straight up off of the dowels.

15. Clean the gasket mounting surfaces.

16. To install, use new gaskets, apply RTV sealant No. 1052366 to the 4 corners where the end seals meet and reverse the removal procedures.

17. On 1986–88 engines torque the intake manifold-to-engine bolts, as follows:
  a. Torque the No. 1–4 bolts (in sequence) to 15 ft. lbs.
  b. Torque the No. 5–16 bolts (in sequence) to 22 ft. lbs.
  c. Retorque all bolts (in sequence) to 22 ft. lbs.
  d. Recheck all bolts (in sequence) to 22 ft. lbs.

18. On 1989–90 engines torque the intake manifold-to-engine bolts, as follows:
  a. Torque the No. 1–4 bolts (in sequence) to 8 ft. lbs.
  b. Torque the No. 5–16 bolts (in sequence) to 8 ft. lbs.
  c. Retorque all bolts (in sequence) to 12 ft. lbs.
  d. Recheck all bolts (in sequence) to 12 ft. lbs.

19. To complete the installation, use new gaskets and reverse the removal procedures. Refill the cooling system. Start the engine allow it to reach normal operating temperatures and check for leaks.

Exhaust Manifold

Removal and Installation

3.0L AND 3.8L ENGINES

Left Side

1. Disconnect the negative terminal from the battery.

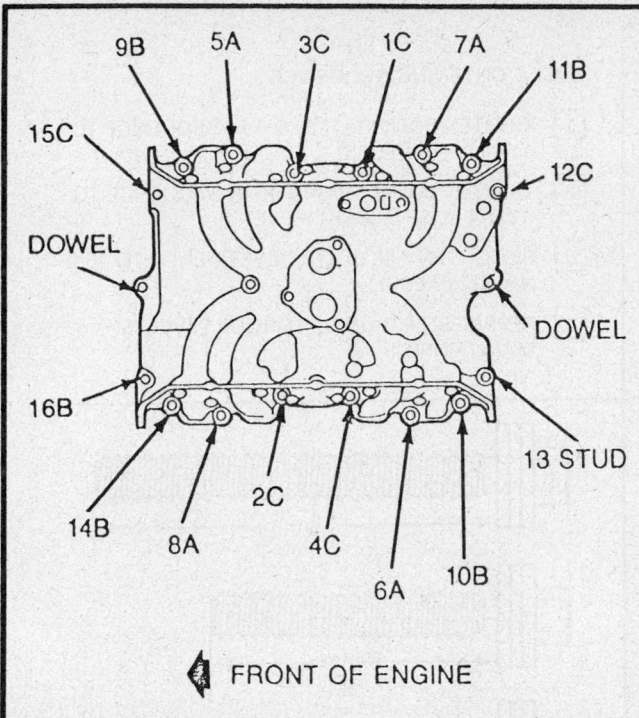

FRONT OF ENGINE

BOLT TIGHTENING SEQUENCE

1. TIGHTEN BOLTS 1, 2, 3, & 4 IN SEQUENCE TO 20.0 N•m (15 FT-LBS).

2. TIGHTEN BOLTS 5 THRU 16 IN SEQUENCE TO 30.0 N•m (22 FT-LBS).

3. RETIGHTEN ALL BOLTS IN SEQUENCE TO 30.0 N•m (22 FT-LBS).

4. REPEAT STEP 3.

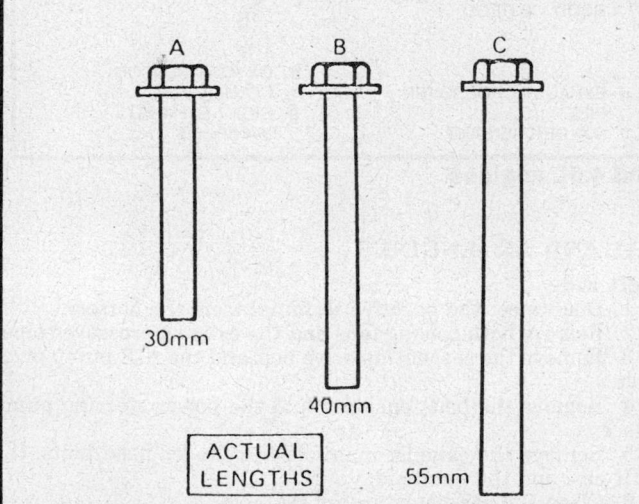

ACTUAL LENGTHS

Intake manifold bolt size and torque sequence—1988 4.5L engine

2. If necessary, remove the mass air flow sensor, air intake duct and crankcase ventilation pipe.

3. Remove the exhaust crossover pipe-to-exhaust manifold bolts.

4. Label and disconnect the spark plug wires.

5. Remove the exhaust manifold-to-cylinder head bolts and the manifold.

6. If necessary, remove the oil dipstick tube to provide access to the manifold bolts.

7. Using a putty knife, clean the gasket mounting surfaces.

8. To install, use a new gasket and reverse the removal procedures. Torque the exhaust manifold-to-cylinder head bolts to 37 ft. lbs. and the exhaust crossover pipe-to-manifold bolts to 22 ft. lbs. Start the engine and check for exhaust leaks.

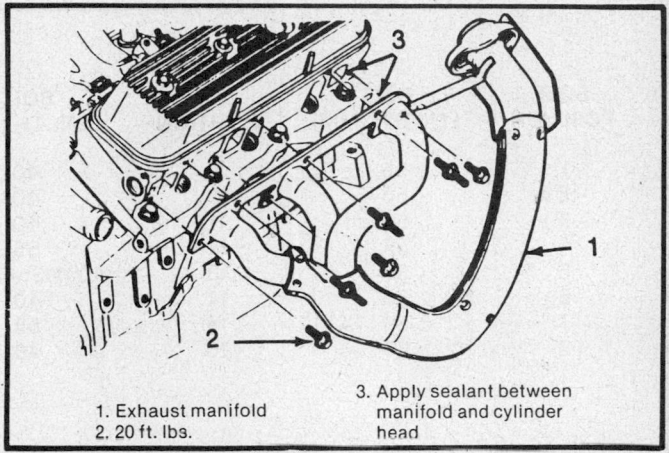

1. Exhaust manifold
2. 20 ft. lbs.
3. Apply sealant between manifold and cylinder head

Left exhaust manifold mounting—1986–88 3.0L and 3.8L (VIN code B,3) engines

Right Side

1. Disconnect the negative terminal from the battery.

2. If necessary, disconnect the mass air flow sensor, air intake duct, the crankcase ventilation pipe and the IAC connector from the throttle body.

3. Label and disconnect the wires from the spark plugs. Disconnect the oxygen sensor lead.

4. If equipped, disconnect the heater inlet pipe from the manifold studs.

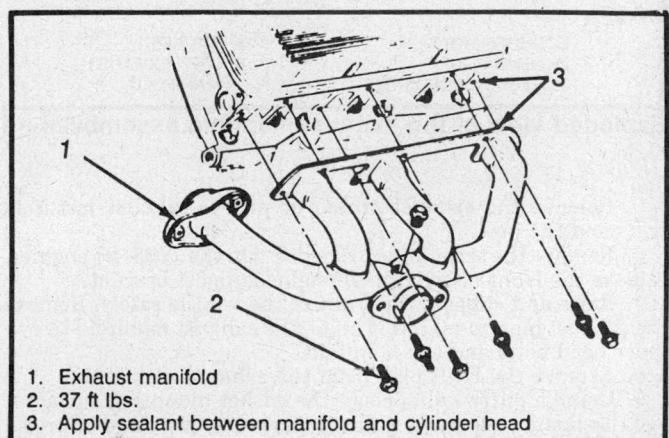

1. Exhaust manifold
2. 37 ft lbs.
3. Apply sealant between manifold and cylinder head

Right exhaust manifold mounting—1986–88 3.0L and 3.8L (VIN code B,3) engines

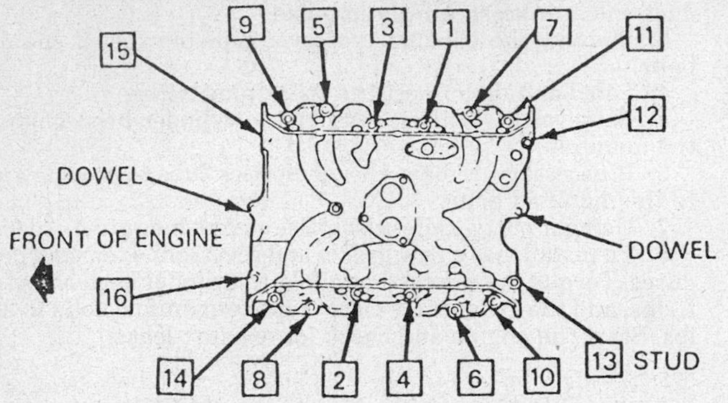

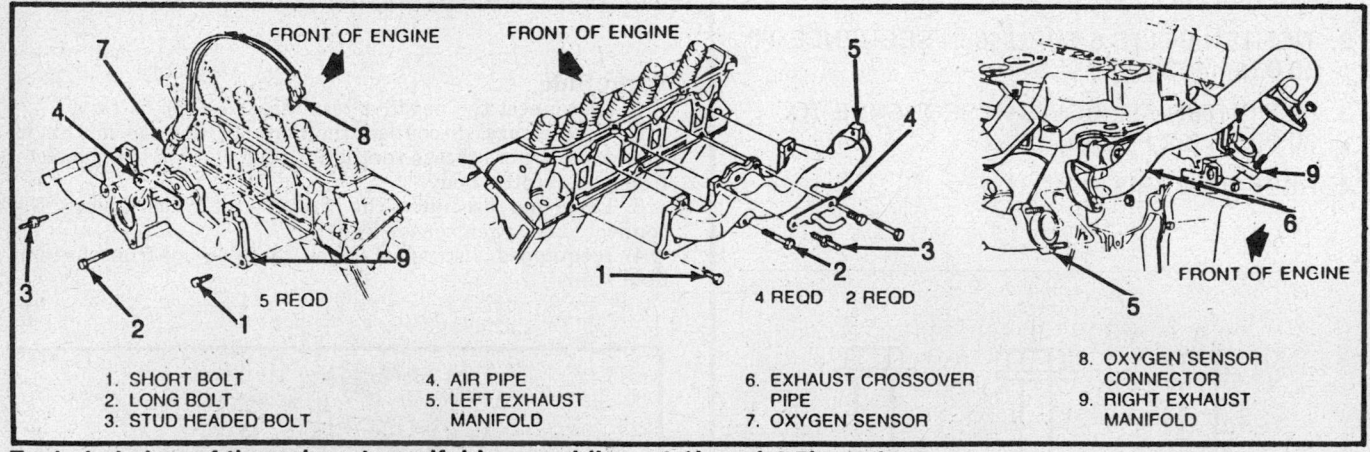

BOLT TIGHTENING SEQUENCE

1. TIGHTEN BOLTS 1, 2, 3, & 4 IN SEQUENCE TO 12.0 N·m (8 FT·LBS).

2. TIGHTEN BOLTS 5 THRU 16 IN SEQUENCE TO 12.0 N·m (8 FT·LBS).

3. RETIGHTEN ALL BOLTS IN SEQUENCE TO 16.0 N·m (12 FT·LBS).

4. REPEAT STEP 3 UNTIL TORQUE LEVEL IS MAINTAINED.

BOLT POSITION	BOLT LENGTH (MM)	BOLT POSITION	BOLT LENGTH (MM)
1	55	9	40
2	55	10	40
3	55	11	40
4	55	12	55
5	30	13	40 W/Studhead
6	30	14	40
7	30	15	55
8	30	16	40

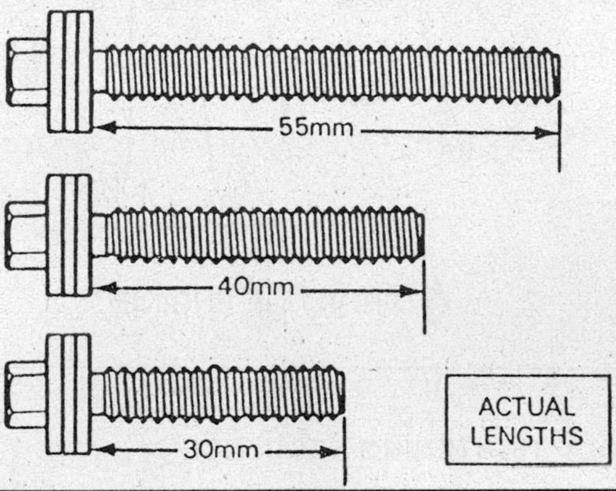

ACTUAL LENGTHS

Intake manifold bolt size and torque sequence—1989–90 4.5L engine

1. SHORT BOLT
2. LONG BOLT
3. STUD HEADED BOLT
4. AIR PIPE
5. LEFT EXHAUST MANIFOLD
6. EXHAUST CROSSOVER PIPE
7. OXYGEN SENSOR
8. OXYGEN SENSOR CONNECTOR
9. RIGHT EXHAUST MANIFOLD

Exploded view of the exhaust manifold assemblies—4.1L and 4.5L engines

5. Remove the exhaust crossover pipe-to-exhaust manifold bolts and the pipe.

6. Remove the serpentine drive belt. On the 1985–87 engines, remove the front alternator-to-engine support bracket.

7. Raise and support the front of the vehicle safely. Remove the exhaust pipe-to-manifold bolts, the exhaust manifold-to-cylinder head bolts and the manifold.

8. Remove the EGR pipe from the exhaust manifold.

9. Using a putty knife, clean the gasket mounting surfaces.

10. To install, use a new gasket and reverse the removal procedures. Torque the exhaust manifold-to-cylinder head bolts to 37 ft. lbs.on engine codes L, 3, B. and 41 ft. lbs. for engine code C. Start the engine and check for exhaust leaks.

4.1L AND 4.5L ENGINES
Left Side

1. Disconnect the negative terminal from the battery.

2. Remove both cooling fans and the exhaust crossover pipe.

3. Remove the serpentine drive belt and the AIR pump pivot bolt.

4. Remove the belt tensioner and the power steering pump brace.

5. Remove the exhaust manifold-to-cylinder head bolts, the AIR pipe and the manifold.

6. Clean the gasket mounting surfaces.

7. To install, use new gaskets and reverse the removal procedures. Torque the exhaust manifold-to-engine bolts to 18 ft. lbs.

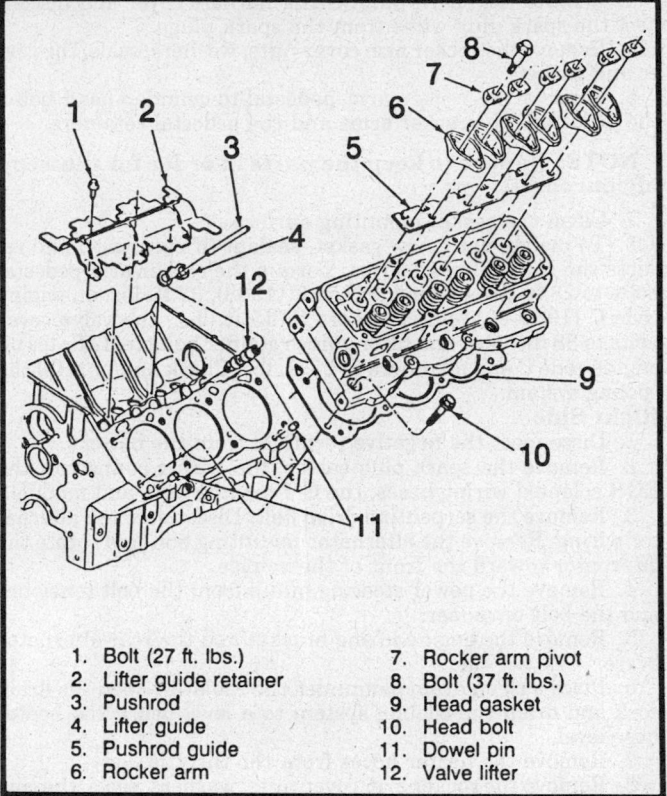

1. 24 ft. lbs.
2. Lifter guide retainer
3. Lifter guide
4. Lifter
5. Pushrod
6. Head gasket
7. Pedestal retainer
8. Rocket arm
9. Pedestal
10. Double ended bolt— 45 ft. lbs.
11. Bolt—45 ft. lbs.

Exploded view of the rocker arm assembly—1986–88 3.8L VIN code 3 engine

1. Bolt (27 ft. lbs.)
2. Lifter guide retainer
3. Pushrod
4. Lifter guide
5. Pushrod guide
6. Rocker arm
7. Rocker arm pivot
8. Bolt (37 ft. lbs.)
9. Head gasket
10. Head bolt
11. Dowel pin
12. Valve lifter

Exploded view of the rocker arm assembly—1988–90 VIN code C engine

Start the engine and check for exhaust leaks.

Right Side

1. Disconnect the negative battery cable. Remove the air cleaner.
2. Remove the exhaust crossover pipe. Disconnect the oxygen and coolant temperature sensors.
3. Remove the catalytic converter-to-AIR pipe clip bolt.
4. Remove the 2 front manifold-to-cylinder head bolts. Raise and support the vehicle safely.
5. Disconnect the converter air pipe bracket from the stud and remove the converter-to-manifold exhaust pipe.
6. Remove the remaining exhaust manifold-to-cylinder head bolts, the AIR pipe and the manifold.
7. Clean the gasket mounting surfaces.
8. To install, use new gaskets and reverse the removal procedures. Torque the intake manifold-to-engine bolts to 18 ft. lbs. Start the engine and check for exhaust leaks.

Valve Systems

All engines use hydraulic lifters. Valve systems with hydraulic lifters operate with zero clearance in the valve train. The rocker arms are non-adjustable. The lifter will compensate if there is slack in the system; if there is excessive play, the entire system should be checked.

If the valve guides are found to be worn past allowable limits, they will have to be either replaced or rebored and valves with oversize stem installed.

VALVE ARRANGEMENT

3.0L AND 3.8L ENGINES

Right Side—E-I-I-E-I-E (front-to-rear)
Left Side—E-I-E-I-I-E (front-to-rear)

4.1L AND 4.5L ENGINES

Right Side—I-E-I-E-E-I-E-I (front-to-rear)

Left Side—I-E-I-E-E-I-E-I (front-to-rear)

VALVE LIFTERS

Removal and Installation

3.0L AND 3.8L ENGINES

1. Remove the intake manifold.
2. Remove the rocker arm cover and discard the old gasket.
3. Remove the rocker arm assemblies.
4. Remove the push rods. Using a valve lifter removal tool, remove the valve lifters.
5. Clean the gasket mounting surfaces.
6. To install, lubricate the lifters with clean engine oil, use new gaskets and reverse the removal procedures.

4.1L AND 4.5L ENGINES

1. Remove the intake manifold.
2. Remove the valve guide retainer on the 4.5L engine.
3. Remove the valve lifter and the valve lifter guides (4.5L engine) and retain the valve lifters in order so that they may be installed in their original position.
4. Installation is the reverse of removal.

VALVE ROCKER ARMS

Removal and Installation

3.0L AND 3.8L ENGINES

Left Side

1. Disconnect the negative terminal from the battery.
2. If equipped, remove the upper engine support strut and bracket.
3. Remove the PCV valve and pipe.

4. Remove the spark plug wiring harness cover and disconnect the spark plug wires from the spark plugs.

5. Remove the rocker arm cover nuts, washers, seals, the cover and gasket.

6. Remove the rocker arm pedestal-to-cylinder head bolts, the pedestals, the rocker arms and the pedestal retainers.

NOTE: Be sure to keep the parts in order for reassembly purposes.

7. Clean the gasket mounting surfaces.

8. To install, use a new gasket, sealant (if necessary) and reverse the removal procedures. Torque the rocker arm pedestal bolts to 28 ft. lbs. on engine code C (1988), 37 ft. lbs. on engine code C (1989–90) and all others to 45 ft. lbs., the valve cover bolts to 88 inch lbs. and lifter guide retainer bolts to 27 ft. lbs on engine code C and all others to 25 ft. lbs. Check and/or refill the cooling system.

Right Side

1. Disconnect the negative terminal from the battery.

2. Remove the spark plug cables, the wiring connector, the EGR solenoid wiring/hoses, the C³I module nuts and module.

3. Remove the serpentine drive belt. Disconnect the alternator wiring. Remove the alternator mounting bolt and rotate the alternator toward the front of the vehicle.

4. Remove the power steering pump from the belt tensioner and the belt tensioner.

5. Remove the engine lifting bracket and the rear alternator brace.

6. Place a clean drain pan under the radiator, open the drain cock and drain the cooling system to a level below the heater hose level.

7. Remove the heater hoses from the throttle body.

8. Remove the rocker arm cover nuts, washers, seals, the cover and gasket (discard the gasket).

9. Remove the rocker arm pedestal-to-cylinder head bolts, the pedestals, the rocker arms and the pedestal retainers.

NOTE: Be sure to keep the parts in order for reassembly purposes.

10. Clean the gasket mounting surfaces.

11. To install, use a new gasket, sealant (if necessary) and reverse the removal procedures. Torque the rocker arm pedestal bolts to 28 ft. lbs. on engine code C (1988), 37 ft. lbs. on engine code C (1989–90) and all others to 45 ft. lbs., the valve cover bolts to 88 inch lbs. and lifter guide retainer bolts to 27 ft. lbs on engine code C and all others to 25 ft. lbs. Check and/or refill the cooling system.

4.1L AND 4.5L ENGINES

Left Side

1. Disconnect the negative terminal from the battery. Remove the air cleaner, the PCV valve, the throttle return spring and the serpentine drive belt.

2. Loosen the lower power steering pump bracket nuts.

3. Remove the power steering pump, the belt tensioner, the bracket-to-engine bolts and the bracket. Move the power steering pump assembly toward the front of the vehicle; DO NOT disconnect the pressure hoses.

4. Remove the left side spark plug wires and conduit.

5. Remove the rocker arm cover-to-cylinder screws, the cover and the gasket/seals (discard them).

6. Remove the rocker arm pivot-to-rocker arm support bolts, the pivots and the rocker arms.

7. If necessary, remove the rocker arm support-to cylinder head nuts/bolts and the support.

8. Clean the gasket mounting surfaces. Inspect the parts for wear and/or damage and replace the parts (if necessary).

9. To install, lubricate the parts with clean engine oil, use a new gasket (coat both sides with RTV sealant), install RTV sealant between the intake manifold-to-cylinder head mating surfaces and reverse the removal procedures. Torque the rocker

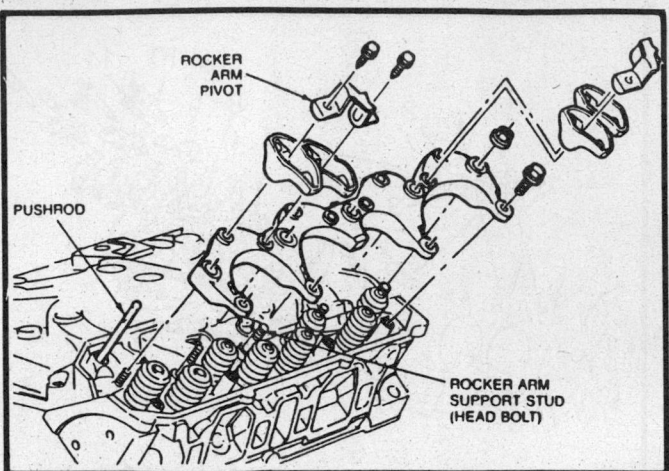

Exploded view of the rocker arm assembly—4.1L and 4.5L engines

arm support-to-cylinder head nuts to 37 ft. lbs., the rocker arm support-to-cylinder head bolts to 7 ft. lbs., the rocker arm pivots-to-rocker arm support bolts to 22 ft. lbs. and the rocker arm cover-to-cylinder head screws to 8 ft. lbs. Check and/or refill the crankcase. Start the engine and check for leaks.

Right Side

1. Disconnect the negative terminal from the battery. Remove the air cleaner and the AIR management valve with bracket (move the assembly aside).

2. From the throttle body, remove the Manifold Absolute Pressure (MAP) hose.

3. Remove the right side spark plug wires and conduit.

4. Remove the fuel vapor canister pipe bracket from the valve cover stud.

5. Drain the cooling system to a level below the thermostat housing. Remove the heater hose from the thermostat housing and move it aside.

6. Remove the brake booster vacuum hose from the intake manifold.

7. Remove the rocker arm cover-to-cylinder screws, the cover and the gasket/seals (discard them).

8. Remove the rocker arm pivot-to-rocker arm support bolts, the pivots and the rocker arms.

9. If necessary, remove the rocker arm support-to cylinder head nuts/bolts and the support.

10. Clean the gasket mounting surfaces. Inspect the parts for wear and/or damage and replace the parts (if necessary).

11. To install, lubricate the parts with clean engine oil, use a new gasket (coat both sides with RTV sealant), install RTV sealant between the intake manifold-to-cylinder head mating surfaces and reverse the removal procedures. Torque the rocker arm support-to-cylinder head nuts to 37 ft. lbs., the rocker arm support-to-cylinder head bolts to 7 ft. lbs., the rocker arm pivots-to-rocker arm support bolts to 22 ft. lbs. and the rocker arm cover-to-cylinder head screws to 8 ft. lbs. Check and/or refill the crankcase. Start the engine and check for leaks.

Cylinder Head

Removal and Installation

3.0L AND 3.8L ENGINES

1. Drain the cooling system and disconnect the negative battery cable.

2. Depressurize the fuel system.

3. Disconnect Mass Air Flow sensor wiring and air intake duct.

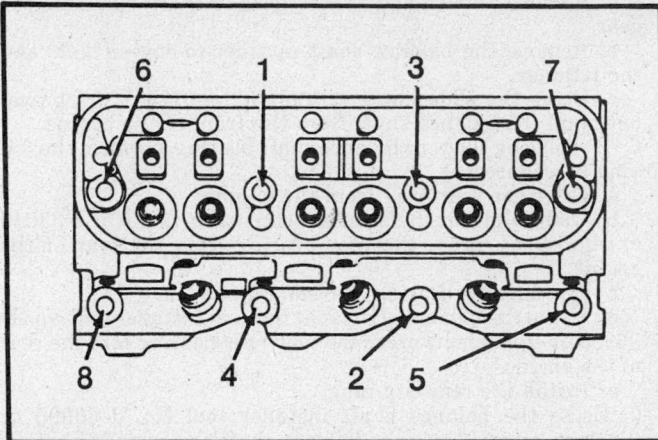

Cylinder head bolt torque sequence—3.0 and 3.8L engine

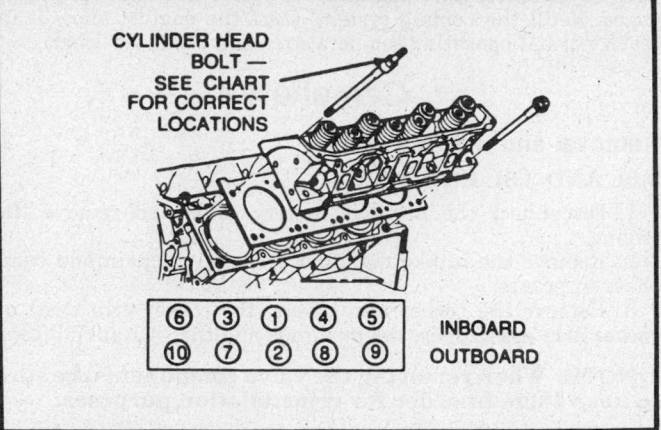

View of the cylinder head bolt torquing sequence—4.1L and 4.5L engines

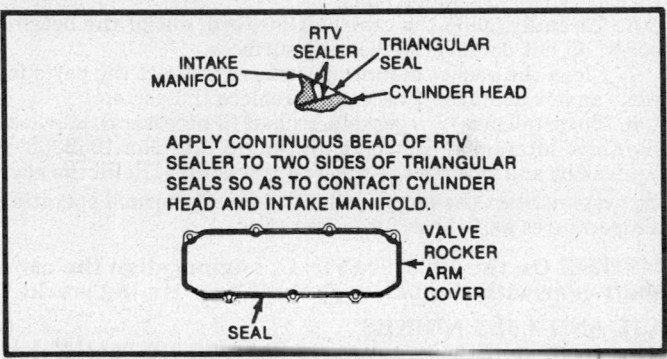

View of the RTV sealant installation—4.1L and 4.5L engines

4. Remove T.V. and accelerator cables, cruise control cable if so equipped on engine codes L, B, 3.
5. Remove crankcase ventilation pipe on engine codes L, B, 3.
6. Remove all hoses, vacumm lines and wiring to gain access.
7. Remove fuel rail.
8. Remove the intake manifold.
9. Remove from front (left) cylinder head the C³I unit, spark plug wires, alternator bracket and one A/C compressor bracket bolt on engine code C (3.8L).
10. Remove from rear (right) cylinder head the power steering pump, belt tensioner assembly and fuel line heat shield on engine code C (3.8L).
11. Disconnect the exhaust crossover pipe.
12. Remove the exhaust manifolds.
13. Remove the valve covers, rocker arms, guide plates and pushrods. Keep all parts in order so they may be reassembled in their original locations.
14. Loosen the cylinder head bolts in reverse of the torque sequence, then remove the bolts and lift off the cylinder head.
15. Clean all gasket mating surfaces and the cylinder head bolt holes in the block.
16. Installation is the reverse of removal, replace all gaskets and seals. Apply sealant number 1052080 or equivalent to the cylinder head bolts.
17. Torque the head bolts as follows on 1986–88 engines:
   a. Torque the cylinder head bolts in the sequence shown to 25 ft. lbs.
   b. Tighten each cylinder head bolt ¼ turn (90 degrees) in sequence.
   c. Tighten each cylinder head bolt an additional ¼ turn in sequence.

NOTE: Should you reach 60 ft. lbs. of torque at any time in Steps 17 and 18, stop tightening the bolt at this point. Do not complete the balance of the 90 degree turn. Failure to follow the given procedure will cause head gasket failure and possible engine damage.

18. Torque the head bolts as follows for 1989–90 engines:
   a. Torque the cylinder head bolts in the sequence shown to 35 ft. lbs.
   b. Tighten each cylinder head bolt 130 degrees in sequence.
   c. Tighten each bolt 30 degrees in sequence.
19. Apply sealant no. 1052624 to the pedestal bolts and torque the rocker arm pedestal bolts to 28 ft. lbs. on engine code C (1988), 37 ft. lbs. on engine code C (1989–90) and all others to 44 ft. lbs. the valve cover bolts 88 in. lbs. and lifter guide retainer bolts to 27 ft. lbs on engine code C all others to 25 ft. lbs.
20. Check oil and coolant level, road test and check for leaks.

4.1L AND 4.5L ENGINES
Left Side
1. Remove the intake manifold.
2. Remove both cooling fans.
3. Disconnect the exhaust manifold crossover pipe, the exhaust pipe-to-exhaust manifold bolts, the exhaust manifold-to-cylinder head bolts and the exhaust manifold.
4. Remove the cylinder head-to-engine bolts and the cylinder head.
5. Clean the gasket mounting surfaces.
6. To install, use new gaskets, apply clean engine oil to the cylinder head bolt threads and reverse the removal procedures. Torque the cylinder head bolts (in sequence) using 3 steps: 1st to 38 ft. lbs., 2nd to 68 ft. lbs. and 3rd to 90 ft. lbs. (bolts No. 1, 3 and 4).
7. To complete the installation, reverse the removal procedures. Refill the cooling system, start the engine, allow it to reach normal operating temperatures and check for leaks.
Right Side
1. Remove the intake manifold.
2. Disconnect the exhaust manifold crossover pipe, the exhaust pipe-to-exhaust manifold bolts, the exhaust manifold-to-cylinder head bolts and the exhaust manifold.
3. Remove the cylinder head-to-engine bolts and the cylinder head.
4. Clean the gasket mounting surfaces.
5. To install, use new gaskets, apply clean engine oil to the cylinder head bolt threads and reverse the removal procedures. Torque the cylinder head bolts (in sequence) using 3 steps: 1st to 38 ft. lbs., 2nd to 68 ft. lbs. and 3rd to 90 ft. lbs. (bolts No. 1, 3 and 4).

6. To complete the installation, reverse the removal procedures. Refill the cooling system, start the engine, allow it to reach normal operating temperatures and check for leaks.

Camshaft

Removal and Installation

3.0L AND 3.8L ENGINES

1. Disconnect the negative battery cable and remove the engine.
2. Remove the intake manifold, the timing chain and camshaft sprockets.
3. Remove the rocker arm covers, the rocker arm shaft or rocker arm assemblies, the pushrods and the hydraulic lifters.

NOTE: When removing the valve components, be sure to keep them in order for reinstallation purposes.

4. On the 1988–90 (VIN C) engine, remove the camshaft gear from the camshaft.
5. On the 1986–90 (VIN 3) engine, remove the camshaft thrust bearing-to-engine bolts.
6. Carefully, slide the camshaft forward, out of the bearing bores; do not damage the bearing surfaces.
7. Clean the gasket mounting surfaces. Inspect the parts for wear and/or damage; if necessary, replace the parts.
8. To install, use new gaskets, sealant (if necessary), lubricate the valve lifters and camshaft with multi-lube No. 1052365 or equivalent and reverse the removal procedures. Refill the cooling system. Start the engine, allow it to reach normal operating temperatures and check for leaks.

NOTE: On the 1988–90 (VIN C) engine, align the camshaft gear with the balancer shaft gear timing marks.

4.1L AND 4.5L ENGINES

To perform this procedure, the engine must be removed from the vehicle.

1. Remove the intake manifold and the timing chain.
2. Remove the valve lifters.

NOTE: When removing the valve components, be sure to keep the parts in order for reinstallation purposes.

3. Carefully slide the camshaft out from the front of the engine; be sure not to damage the camshaft bearings.
4. Clean the gasket mounting surfaces. Inspect the parts for wear and/or damage; if necessary, replace the parts.
5. To install, lubricate the camshaft with engine oil, use new gaskets, sealant (if necessary) and reverse the removal procedures. Torque the camshaft sprocket-to-camshaft screws to 37 ft. lbs.

NOTE: If a new camshaft is to be installed, new lifters and a distributor drive gear must also be installed.

6. To complete the installation, reverse the removal procedures. Refill the cooling system. Start the engine, allow it to reach normal operating temperatures and check for leaks.

Balance Shaft

Removal and Installation

3.8L ENGINE (VIN C)

1. Remove the engine and secure it to a workstand.
2. Remove the flywheel-to-crankshaft bolts and the flywheel.
3. Remove the timing chain cover-to-engine bolts and the cover.
4. Remove the camshaft sprocket-to-camshaft gear bolts, the sprocket, the timing chain and the gear.
5. To remove the balance shaft, perform the following procedures:

a. Remove the balance shaft gear-to-shaft bolt and the gear.
b. Remove the balance shaft retainer-to-engine bolts and the retainer.
c. Using the slide hammer tool No. J–6125–B or equivalent, pull the balance shaft from the front of the engine.
6. If replacing the rear balance shaft bearing, perform the following procedures:
a. Drive the rear plug from the engine.
b. Using the camshaft remover/installer tool No. J–33049 or equivalent, press the rear bearing from the rear of the engine.
c. Dip the new bearing in clean engine oil.
d. Using the balance shaft rear bearing installer tool No. J–36995 or equivalent, press the new rear bearing into the rear of the engine.
e. Install the rear cup plug.
7. Using the balance shaft installer tool No. J–36996 or equivalent, screw it into the balance shaft and install the shaft into the engine; remove the installer tool.
8. Clean the gasket mounting surfaces. Inspect the parts for wear and/or damage; replace the parts, if necessary.
9. Install the balance shaft retainer. Torque the balance shaft retainer-to-engine bolts to 27 ft. lbs.
10. Align the balance shaft gear with the camshaft gear timing marks. Install the balance shaft gear onto the balance shaft. Torque the balance gear-to-balance shaft bolt to 14 ft. lbs, then using a torque angle meter tool, rotate another 35 degrees.
11. To complete the installation, use new gaskets, sealant (if necessary) and reverse the removal procedures. Torque the flywheel-to-crankshaft bolts to 61 ft. lbs. Refill the cooling system. Start the engine, allow it reach normal operating temperatures and check for leaks.

Front Cover and Oil Seal

Removal and Installation

3.0L and 3.8L ENGINES

Cover Removed

1. Disconnect the negative terminal from the battery.
2. PLace a clean drain pan under the radiator, open the drain cock and drain the engine coolant. Remove the lower radiator hose and the coolant bypass hose from the front cover. Remove the heater pipes.
3. Remove the front engine cradle mount bolts. Using a vertical lifting device, secure it to the engine and raise it slightly.
4. Remove the serpentine drive belt and the water pump pulley.

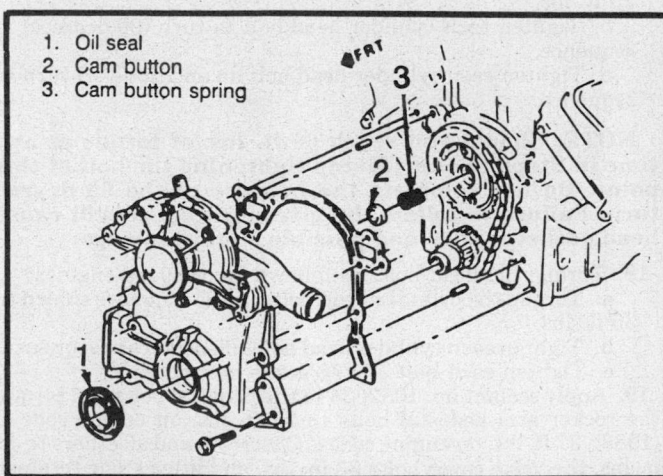

1. Oil seal
2. Cam button
3. Cam button spring

Exploded view of the front cover assembly—3.0L and 3.8L engines

5. Label and disconnect the alternator wiring. Remove the alternator and the alternator bracket.

6. On the 1988–90 engines, remove the inner splash shield.

7. Remove the crankshaft balancer bolt/washer and the balancer.

8. Disconnect the electrical connectors from the crankshaft sensor, the camshaft sensor and the oil pressure switch.

9. Remove the oil pan-to-front cover bolts, the front cover-to-engine bolts and the front cover. Using a small pry bar, remove the oil seal and discard it.

10. To replace the front oil seal, perform the following procedures:

   a. Using a small pry bar, pry the oil seal from the front cover; be careful not to damage the sealing surfaces.

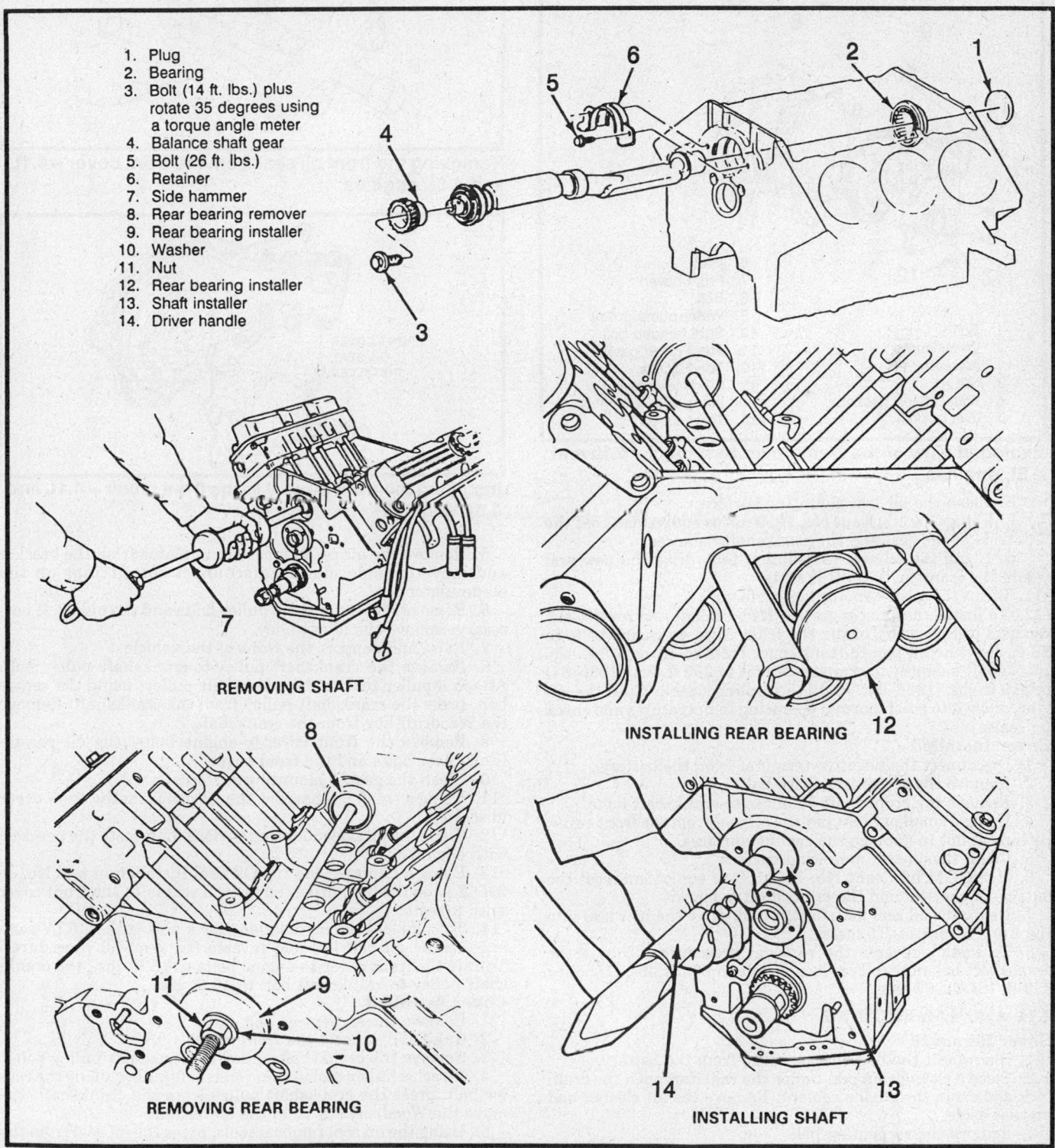

1. Plug
2. Bearing
3. Bolt (14 ft. lbs.) plus rotate 35 degrees using a torque angle meter
4. Balance shaft gear
5. Bolt (26 ft. lbs.)
6. Retainer
7. Side hammer
8. Rear bearing remover
9. Rear bearing installer
10. Washer
11. Nut
12. Rear bearing installer
13. Shaft installer
14. Driver handle

REMOVING SHAFT

INSTALLING REAR BEARING

REMOVING REAR BEARING

INSTALLING SHAFT

Balance shaft removal and installation—3.8L (VIN code C) engines

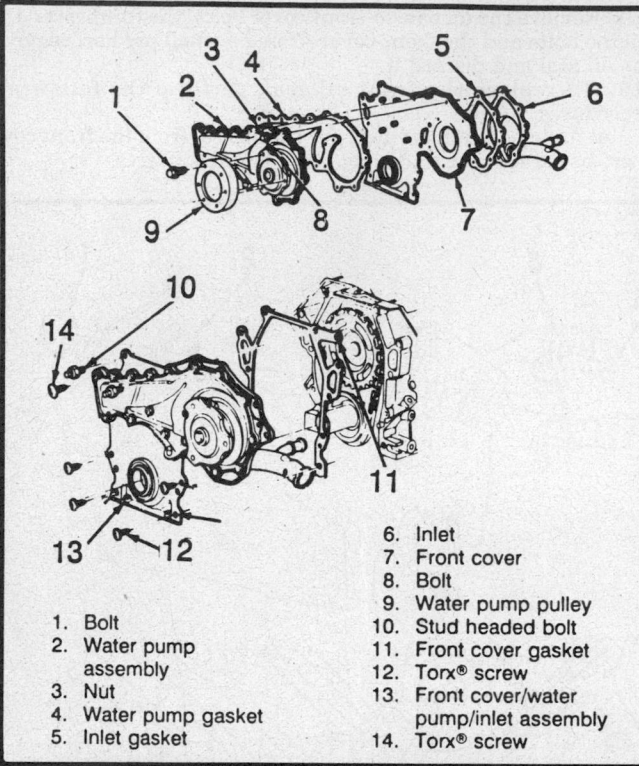

1. Bolt
2. Water pump assembly
3. Nut
4. Water pump gasket
5. Inlet gasket
6. Inlet
7. Front cover
8. Bolt
9. Water pump pulley
10. Stud headed bolt
11. Front cover gasket
12. Torx® screw
13. Front cover/water pump/inlet assembly
14. Torx® screw

Exploded view of the front cover assembly—4.1L and 4.5L engines

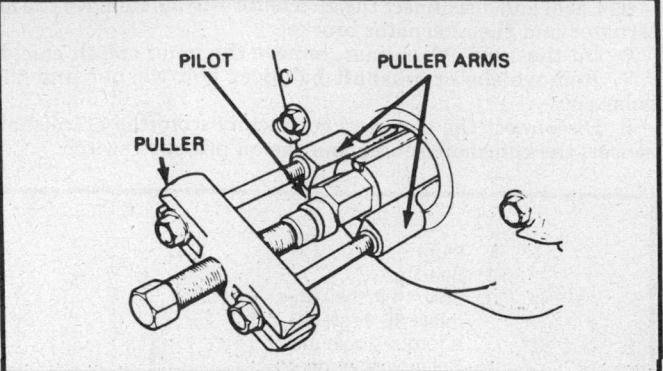

Removing the front oil seal from the front cover—4.1L and 4.5L engines

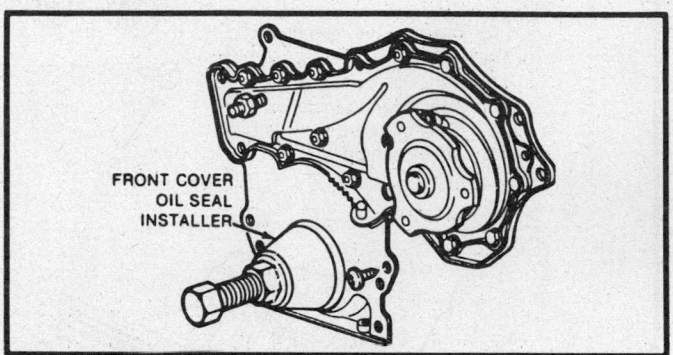

Installing the front oil seal to the front cover—4.1L and 4.5L engines

b. Clean the oil seal mounting surface.
c. Using GM lubricant No. 1050169 or equivalent, coat the outside of the seal and the crankshaft balancer.
d. Using the oil seal installation tool, drive the new seal into the front cover until it seats.
11. Clean the gasket mounting surfaces.
12. To install, use a new gasket, RTV sealant and reverse the removal procedures. Torque the front cover-to-engine bolts to 22 ft. lbs., the oil pan-to-front cover bolts to 88 inch lbs., the crankshaft balancer-to-crankshaft bolt to 200 ft. lbs. (1986–87) or 219 ft. lbs. (1988–90). Refill the cooling system. Start the engine, allow it to reach normal operating temperatures and check for leaks.

Cover Installed
1. Disconnect the negative terminal from the battery.
2. Remove the serpentine drive belt.
3. Remove the crankshaft balancer-to-crankshaft bolts.
4. Using a small pry bar, pry the oil seal from the front cover; be careful not to damage the sealing surfaces.
5. Clean the oil seal mounting surface.
6. Using GM lubricant No. 1050169 or equivalent, coat the outside of the seal and the crankshaft balancer.
7. Using the oil seal installation tool, drive the new seal into the front cover until it seats.
8. To install, reverse the removal procedures. Torque the crankshaft balancer-to-crankshaft bolt to 200 ft. lbs. (1986) or 219 ft. lbs. (1987–90).

4.1L AND 4.5L ENGINES
Cover Removed
1. Disconnect the negative terminal from the battery.
2. Place a clean drain pan under the radiator, open the drain cock and drain the engine coolant. Remove the air cleaner and move it aside.
3. Remove the serpentine belt.
4. Label and disconnect the alternator wiring. Remove the alternator and the alternator bracket.

5. Remove the air conditioner accumulator from the bracket and move it aside; do not disconnect the fittings on the accumulator.
6. Remove the water pump pulley bolts and the pulley. If necessary, remove the idler pulley.
7. Raise and support the front of the vehicle.
8. Remove the crankshaft pulley-to-crankshaft pulley bolt. Attach a puller tool to the crankshaft pulley; using the center bolt, press the crankshaft pulley from the crankshaft. Remove the Woodruff key from the crankshaft.
9. Remove the front cover-to-engine bolts, the oil pan-to-front cover bolts and the front cover.
10. Clean the gasket mounting surfaces.
11. Using a small pry bar, pry the oil seal from the front cover (discard it).
12. Clean the oil seal mounting surface. Lubricate the new seal with engine oil.
13. Using a hammer and the Oil Seal Installation tool No. J–29662 or equivalent, drive the new oil seal in to the front cover until it seats.
14. To complete the installation, use a new gasket, RTV sealant (on the oil pan lip) and reverse the removal procedures. Torque the front cover-to-engine bolts to 15 ft. lbs., the crankshaft pulley-to-crankshaft bolt to 18 ft. lbs.

Cover Installed
1. Remove the serpentine belt.
2. Raise and support the front of the vehicle.
3. Remove the crankshaft pulley-to-crankshaft pulley bolt.
4. Attach a puller tool to the crankshaft pulley; using the center bolt, press the crankshaft pulley from the crankshaft. Remove the Woodruff key from the crankshaft.
5. Using the oil seal removal tools, press the oil seal from the front cover.
6. Clean the oil seal mounting surface.

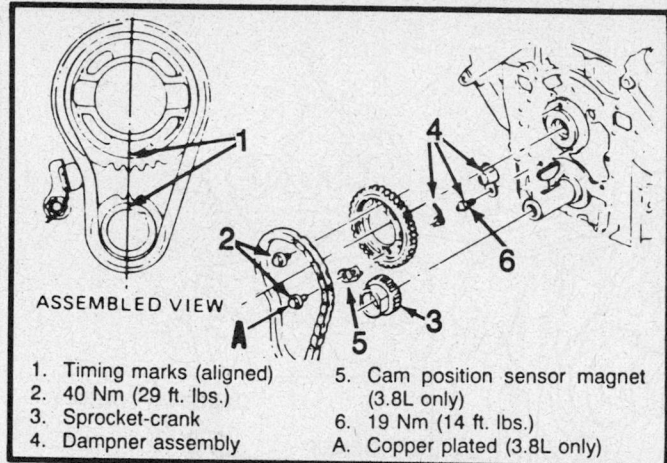

1. Timing marks (aligned)
2. 40 Nm (29 ft. lbs.)
3. Sprocket-crank
4. Dampner assembly
5. Cam position sensor magnet (3.8L only)
6. 19 Nm (14 ft. lbs.)
A. Copper plated (3.8L only)

Exploded view of the timing chain and sprockets—3.0L and 3.8L (VIN code 3) engines

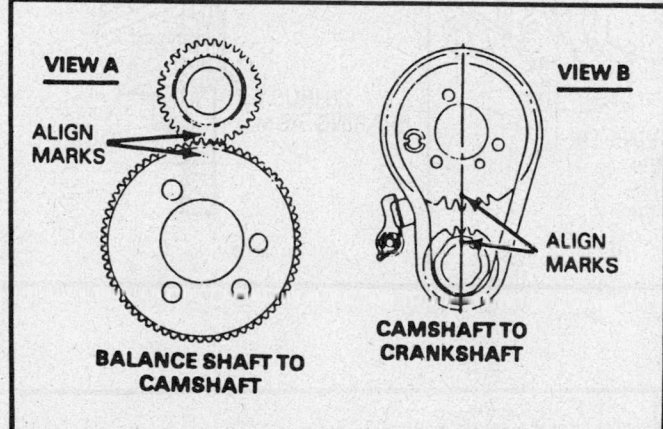

View of the timing chain/sprockets and balancer shaft alignment—3.8L (VIN C) engine

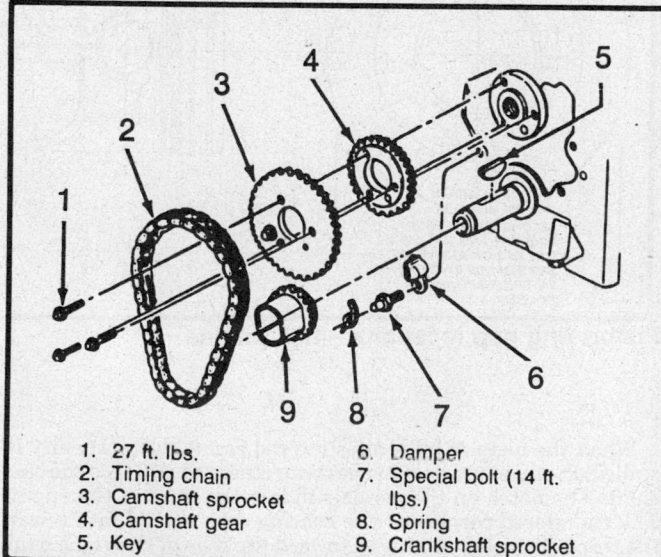

1. 27 ft. lbs.
2. Timing chain
3. Camshaft sprocket
4. Camshaft gear
5. Key
6. Damper
7. Special bolt (14 ft. lbs.)
8. Spring
9. Crankshaft sprocket

Exploded view of the timing chain, sprockets and balancer shaft sprocket—3.8L (VIN C) engine

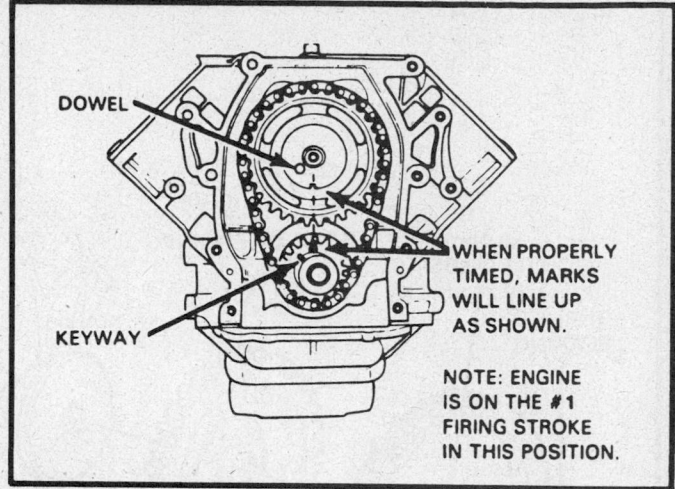

Timing chain sprocket alignment—4.1L engine

7. Lubricate the new seal with engine oil.
8. Using a hammer and the Oil Seal Installation tool No. J–29662 or equivalent, drive the new oil seal in to the front cover until it seats.
9. To complete the installation, reverse the removal procedures. Torque the crankshaft pulley-to-crankshaft bolt to 18 ft. lbs.

Timing Chain and Sprocket

Removal and Installation

3.0L AND 3.8L ENGINES

1. Remove the front cover.
2. Remove the button and spring from the center of the camshaft. Align the marks of the timing sprockets as they must be close together.
4. Remove the camshaft sprocket bolts, the sprocket and the timing chain.
5. Remove the crankshaft sprocket and the Woodruff key (be sure not to lose the key).
6. Clean the gasket mounting surfaces. Inspect the parts for wear and/or damage; if necessary, replace the parts.
7. To install the timing chain and sprockets, perform the following procedures:
   a. Assemble the timing chain on the camshaft sprocket and crankshaft sprockets.
   b. Align the O-marks on the sprockets; they must face each other.
   c. Slide the assembly onto the camshaft and crankshaft. Install the camshaft sprocket-to-camshaft bolts. Torque the camshaft sprocket-to-camshaft sprocket bolts to 20 ft. lbs. (1986) or 28 ft. lbs. (1987–90).

NOTE: On the 1988–90 (VIN C) engine, align the camshaft sprocket mark with the balancer shaft sprocket mark.

8. Using petroleum jelly, pack the oil pump.
9. To complete the installation, use new gaskets, sealant (if necessary) and reverse the removal procedures. Refill the cooling system. Start the engine, allow it to reach normal operating temperatures and check for leaks.

4.1L AND 4.5L ENGINES

1. Remove the front cover.

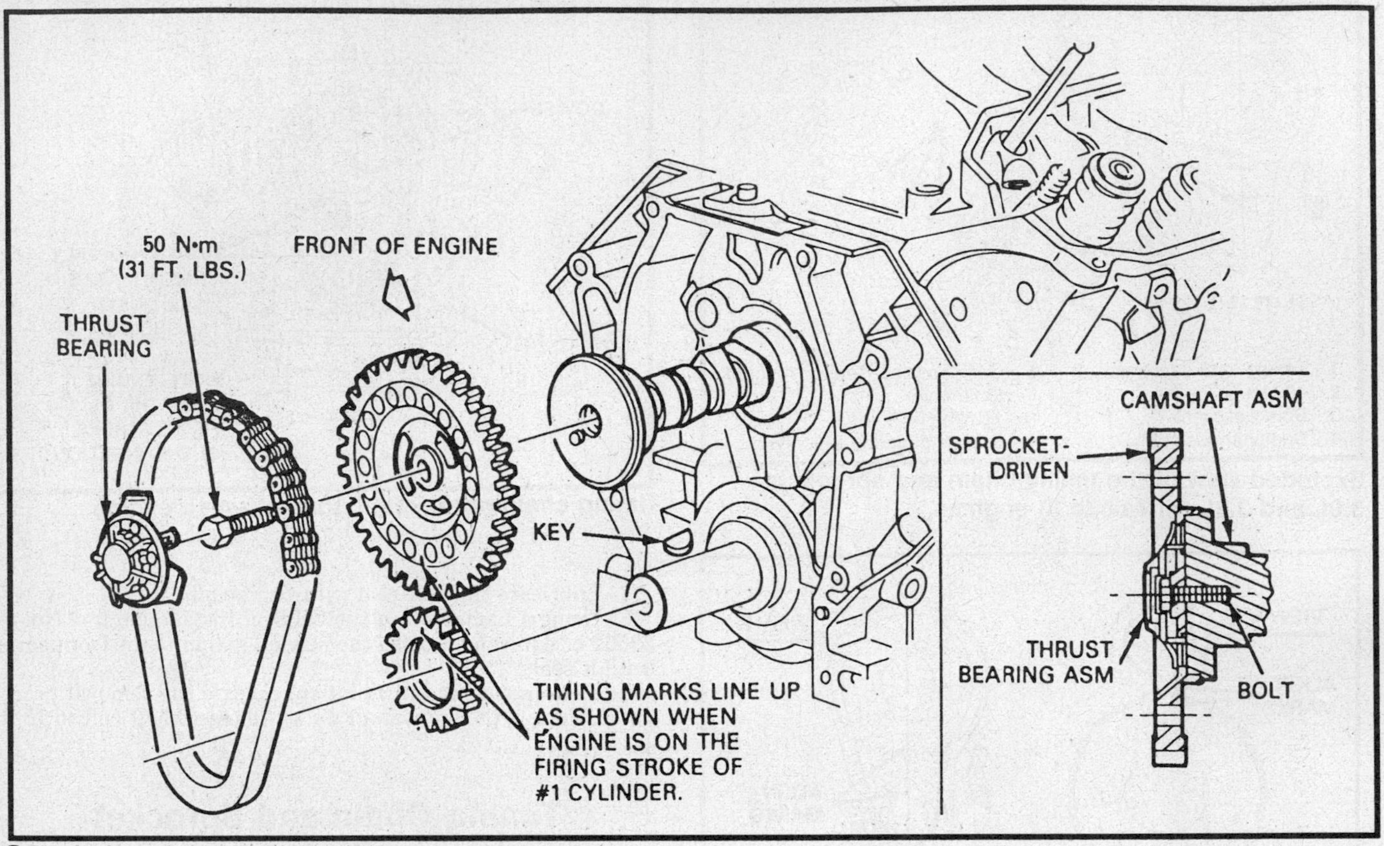

50 N•m (31 FT. LBS.)   FRONT OF ENGINE

THRUST BEARING

KEY

TIMING MARKS LINE UP AS SHOWN WHEN ENGINE IS ON THE FIRING STROKE OF #1 CYLINDER.

CAMSHAFT ASM
SPROCKET-DRIVEN
THRUST BEARING ASM   BOLT

Camshaft and timing chain alignment—4.5L engine

2. Remove the oil slinger from the crankshaft. Rotate the engine to align the sprocket timing marks; the No. cylinder will be on the TDC of its compression stroke.

3. From the camshaft, remove the camshaft thrust button (replace it) and the camshaft sprocket-to-camshaft screw. Slide the camshaft sprocket, the crankshaft sprocket and timing chain from the engine as an assembly.

4. Clean the gasket mounting surfaces. Inspect the parts for wear and/or damage; if necessary, replace the parts.

5. To install the timing chain and sprockets, perform the following procedures:

   a. Assemble the timing chain on the camshaft sprocket and crankshaft sprockets.

   b. Align the timing marks on the sprockets; they must face each other.

   c. Align the dowel pin in the camshaft with the index hole in the sprocket.

   d. Slide the assembly onto the camshaft and crankshaft. Install the camshaft sprocket-to-camshaft bolts. Torque the camshaft sprocket-to-camshaft sprocket bolt to 37 ft. lbs. (4.1L engine) and 31 ft. lbs. (4.5L engine).

6. To complete the installation, use new gaskets, sealant (if necessary) and reverse the removal procedures. Refill the cooling system. Start the engine, allow it to reach normal operating temperatures and check for leaks.

Rings, Pistons and Connecting Rod

Positioning

All compression rings are marked with a dimple, a letter **T**, a letter **O** or the word **TOP** to identify the side of the ring which must face toward the top of the piston.

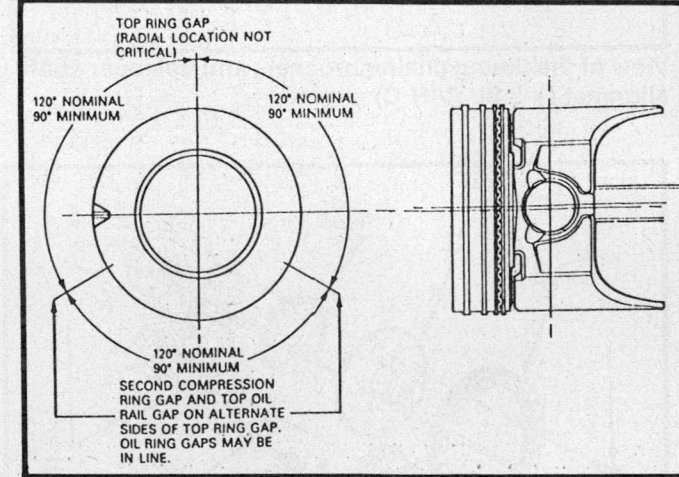

Piston ring gap locations—4.5L engine

When the piston and connecting rod assembly is properly installed, the oil spurt hole in the connecting rod will face the camshaft. The notch on the piston will face the front of the engine. The chamfered corners of the bearing caps should face toward the front of the left bank and toward the rear of the right bank. The boss on the connecting rod should face toward the front of the engine for the right bank and to the rear of the engine on the left bank.

Rings Piston And Connecting Rod Positioning

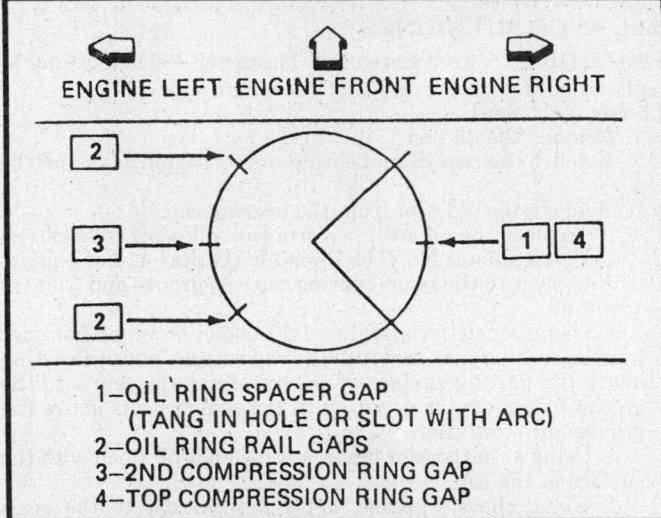

Piston ring gap locations—3.0L and 3.8L engines

1—OIL RING SPACER GAP
(TANG IN HOLE OR SLOT WITH ARC)
2—OIL RING RAIL GAPS
3—2ND COMPRESSION RING GAP
4—TOP COMPRESSION RING GAP

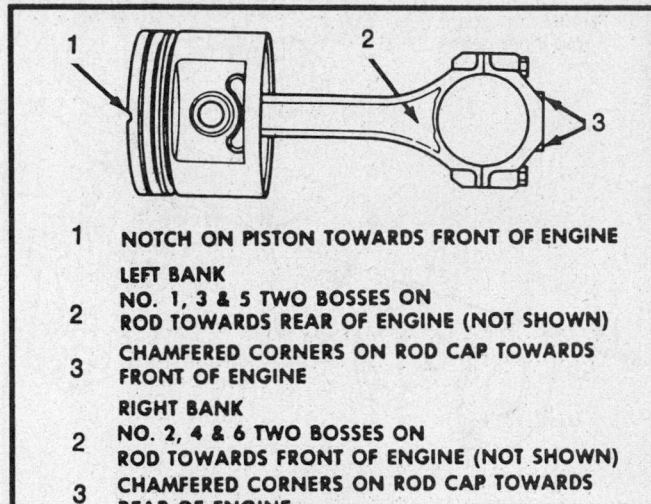

1 NOTCH ON PISTON TOWARDS FRONT OF ENGINE

LEFT BANK
2 NO. 1, 3 & 5 TWO BOSSES ON ROD TOWARDS REAR OF ENGINE (NOT SHOWN)
3 CHAMFERED CORNERS ON ROD CAP TOWARDS FRONT OF ENGINE

RIGHT BANK
2 NO. 2, 4 & 6 TWO BOSSES ON ROD TOWARDS FRONT OF ENGINE (NOT SHOWN)
3 CHAMFERED CORNERS ON ROD CAP TOWARDS REAR OF ENGINE

Piston and connecting rod positioning

ENGINE LUBRICATION SYSTEM

Oil Pan

Removal and Installation

3.0L AND 3.8L ENGINES

1. Disconnect the negative terminal from the battery.
2. Raise and support the vehicle safely. Drain the crankcase.
3. Remove the flywheel cover.
4. On the 1987–90 engines, remove the oil filter and the starter motor.
5. Remove the oil pan-to-engine bolts and the oil pan.
6. Clean the gasket mounting surfaces.
7. To install, use new gaskets, sealant and reverse the removal procedures. Torque the oil pan-to-engine bolts to 88 inch lbs., (124 in lbs. on code C engines). Refill the crankcase. Start the engine and check for leaks.

4.1 AND 4.5L ENGINES

1. Disconnect the negative terminal from the battery. Raise and support the front of the vehicle.
2. Drain the crankcase and remove the oil filter. Remove the flywheel inspection cover and the support struts.
3. Disconnect the front exhaust pipe at the exhaust manifolds and remove the bolt at the catalytic converter bracket. Lower the exhaust pipe.
4. Remove the oil pan-to-engine bolts and the oil pan.

NOTE: If the pan is difficult to remove, lightly tap the edges with a plastic hammer.

5. Clean the gasket mounting surfaces.
6. To install, use a new gasket, sealant and reverse the removal procedures. Torque the oil pan-to-engine bolts to 11 ft. lbs. Refill the crankcase. Start the engine and check for leaks.

Oil Pump

Removal and Installation

3.0L AND 3.8L ENGINES

The oil pump, located at the bottom of the front cover, is an integral part of the front cover; the crankshaft passes through it.

1. Remove the front cover.
2. Clean the gasket mounting surfaces.
3. To inspect the pump gears, perform the following procedures:
   a. Remove the oil pump cover-to-front cover screws and the cover.

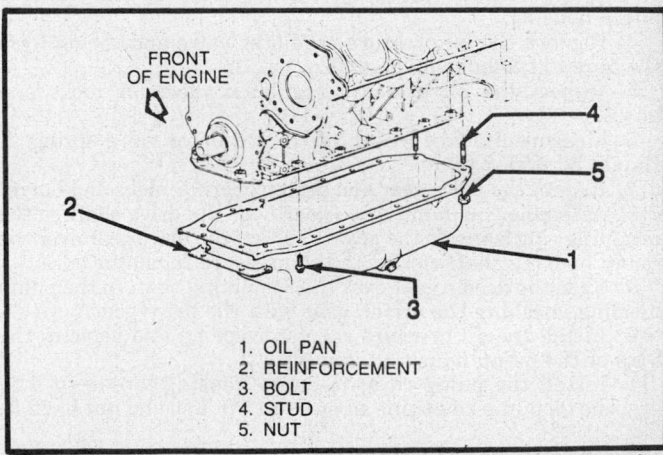

1. OIL PAN
2. REINFORCEMENT
3. BOLT
4. STUD
5. NUT

Exploded view of the oil pan assembly—4.1L and 4.5L engines

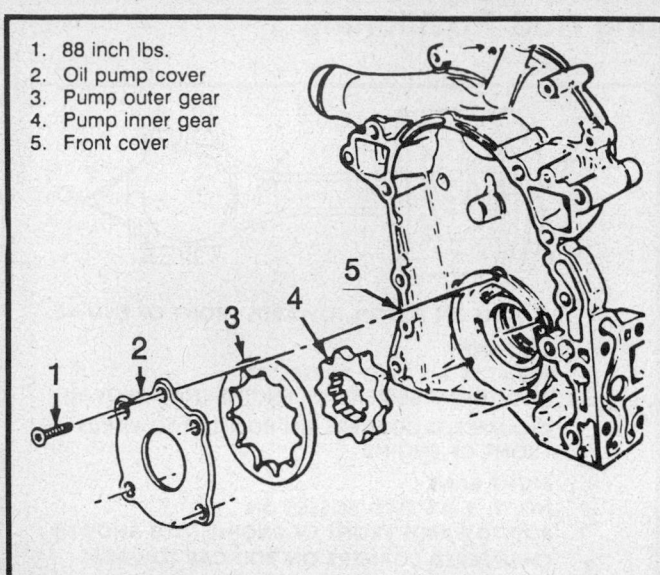

1. 88 inch lbs.
2. Oil pump cover
3. Pump outer gear
4. Pump inner gear
5. Front cover

Exploded view of the oil pump assembly—3.0L and 3.8L engines

  b. Remove the inner and outer pump gears.
  c. Using solvent, clean the gears.
  d. Inspect the gears for wear and/or damage; if necessary, replace the parts.
  e. Using petroleum jelly, pack the pump and reinstall the parts. Torque the oil pump cover-to-front cover screws to 88 inch lbs.

NOTE: Unless the pump is primed, it won't produce oil pressure when the engine is started.

  4. To complete the installation, use new gaskets, sealant (if necessary) and reverse the removal procedures. Check and/or refill the crankcase. Replace the oil filter. Start the engine and check for leaks.

4.1L AND 4.5L ENGINES

  1. Remove the oil pan.
  2. Remove the oil pump-to-engine screws/nut and the oil pump from the engine.
  3. To disassemble, remove the oil pump cover-to-housing screws, slide the drive shaft, drive gear and driven gear from the pump housing.
  4. Remove the oil pressure regulator valve and spring from the bore in the housing assembly.
  5. Inspect the oil pressure regulator valve for nicks and burrs.
  6. Measure the free length of the regulator valve spring. It should be 2.57–2.69 in.
  7. Inspect the drive gear and driven gear for nicks and burrs.
  8. Assemble the pump drive gear over the drive shaft so the retaining ring is inside the gear. Position the drive gear over the pump housing shaft closest to the pressure regulator bore.
  9. Slide the driven gear over the remaining shaft in the pump housing, meshing the driven gear with the drive gear.
  10. Install the oil pressure regulator spring and valve in the bore of the pump housing assembly.
  11. Install the pump cover-to-pump housing screws to 5 ft. lbs., the oil pump-to-engine screws to 15 ft. lbs. and nut to 22 ft. lbs.
  12. To complete the installation, use new gaskets and reverse the removal procedures. Refill the crankcase. Start the engine and check for leaks.

Rear Main Oil Seal

Removal and Installation

3.0L AND 3.8L ENGINES
Braided fabric rope seals are used. The upper seal half cannot be replaced without removing the crankshaft.
Lower Half-Seal
  1. Remove the oil pan.
  2. Remove the rear main bearing cap-to-engine bolts and the cap.
  3. Remove the old seal from the bearing cap.
  4. To replace the oil seal, perform the following procedures:
    a. Using sealant No. GM 1052621, Loctite® 414 or equivalent, apply it to the main bearing cap seal groove and wait for 1 minute.
    b. Using a new rope seal and a wooden dowel or hammer handle, roll the new seal into the cap so both ends projecting above the parting surface of the cap; force the seal into the groove by rubbing it down, until the seal projects above the groove not more than $\frac{1}{16}$ in.
    c. Using a sharp razor blade, cut the ends off flush with the surface of the cap.
    d. Using chassis grease, apply a thin coat to the seals surface.
  5. To install the neoprene sealing strips (side seals), perform the following procedures:
    a. Using light oil or kerosene, soak the strips for 5 minutes.

NOTE: The neoprene composition seals will swell up once exposed to the oil and heat. It is normal for the seals to leak for a short time, until they become properly seated. The seals must not be cut to fit.

    b. Place the sealing strips in the grooves on the sides of the bearing cap.
  6. Using sealer No. GM 1052621 or equivalent, apply it to the main bearing cap mating surface; do not apply sealer to the bolt holes.
  7. To install, reverse the removal procedures. Torque the main bearing cap-to-engine bolts to 100 ft. lbs. (3.0L and 3.8L code B, 3), 90 ft. lbs (3.8L code C). Refill the crankcase. The engine must be operated at low rpm when first started, after a new seal is installed.
Upper Half-Seal
Engine removal is not necessary if the following time saver procedure is followed.
  1. Remove the oil pan.
  2. Remove the rear main bearing cap-to-engine bolts and the cap.
  3. Using the seal packing tool No. J–21526–1 or equivalent, insert it against each side of the upper seal and drive the seal until it is tight.
  4. Measure the amount the seal was driven into the engine and add about $\frac{1}{16}$ in. Using a razor blade, cut that amount off the old lower seal.
  5. Using the seal packing tool No. J–21526–1 or equivalent, work the short packing pieces into the cylinder block; a small amount of oil on the seal will help the installation.
  6. Repeat this process on the other side.
  7. Install the lower bearing cap.
  8. To complete the installation, reverse the removal procedures. Torque the main bearing cap-to-engine bolts to 100 ft. lbs. (3.0L and 3.8L code B, 3), 90 ft. lbs (3.8L code C). Refill the crankcase. The engine must be operated at low rpm when first started, after a new seal is installed.
4.1L AND 4.5L ENGINES
  1. Remove the transaxle.
  2. Remove the flywheel-to-crankshaft bolts and the flywheel.
  3. Using a shop rag, clean around the seal area.
  4. Using the rear main oil seal removal tool No. J–26868 or

equivalent, pry the oil seal from the rear of the engine.

5. Lubricate the new seal lips with wheel bearing grease and position it on crankshaft with the spring side facing the inside of the engine.

6. Using the rear main oil seal installing tool No. J–34604 or equivalent, press the seal into the engine block until it is flush.

7. To complete the installation, reverse the removal procedures. Start the engine and check for leaks.

Connecting and Main Bearings

Replacement

Note the locations of main bearings. Upper bearings are grooved for distribution of oil to the connecting rods, while the lower mains are plain.

Engine bearings are of the precision insert type. They are available for service in standard and various undersizes. Upper and lower bearing inserts may be different. Be careful to align the oil holes; do not obstruct any oil passages. Bearing inserts must not be shimmed. Do not touch the bearing surface of the insert with bare fingers. Skin oil and acids will etch the bearing surface.

NOTE: Bearing failure, other than normal wear, must be investigated carefully. Inspect the crankshaft, connecting rods and the bearing bores. Avoid damage to the crankshaft journals during removal and installation.

FRONT SUSPENSION AND STEERING

For front suspension component removal and installation procedures, refer to unit repair section. For steering wheel removal and installation, refer to electrical control section.

Power Steering Rack

Removal and Installation

1. Raise and support the front of the vehicle safely. Allow the front suspension to hang freely. Disconnect the pressure lines from the steering gear and drain the excess fluid into a container; be sure to plug the openings.

2. Move the intermediate shaft cover upward and remove the intermediate shaft-to-stub shaft pinch bolt.

3. Remove both front wheel assemblies.

4. Remove the cotter pins and nut from both tie rod ends. Disconnect the tie rod ends from the steering knuckles.

5. Remove the line retainer.

6. Remove the outlet and pressure hose.

7. Remove the rack/pinion assembly-to-chassis bolts.

8. Loosen the front engine cradle mounting bolts and the lower the rear of the cradle about 3 in. (76mm) onto jackstands.

D not lower the rear of the engine cradle too far.

9. Remove the rack and pinion assembly.

10. To install, reverse the removal procedures. Tighten the rack mounting bolts to 50 ft. lbs. (68 Nm). Tighten the tie rod end nut to 35–52 ft. lbs. (50–70 Nm). Refill the power steering pump reservoir. Bleed the power steering system and check for leaks. Check and/or adjust the front wheel alignment.

Adjustment

NOTE: For the following adjustments, the power steering gear should be removed from the vehicle and positioned it in a vise.

THRUST BEARING PRELOAD

1. Using a punch and a hammer, loosen the power steering gear stub shaft lock nut and remove the locknut.

2. Using a spanner wrench tool, tighten the stub shaft adjuster plug until the thrust bearing is firmly bottomed; 20 ft. lbs.

3. Place alignment marks on the adjuster plug and the housing.

4. Using a ruler, measure back (counterclockwise) ½ in. and place a second mark.

5. Using the Spanner Wrench tool No. J–7624 or equivalent, turn the adjuster plug counterclockwise until it aligns with the second mark.

6. While holding the adjuster plug stationary, to maintain the alignment, tighten the adjuster plug lock nut.

OVER-CENTER ADJUSTMENT—PITMAN SHAFT

1. Using a pitman arm puller tool No. J–29107 or equivalent, press the pitman arm from the power steering gear.

2. Align the flat on the stub shaft parallel with the side cover.

3. From the rear of the power steering gear, align the pitman arm block tooth with the center of the over-center preload adjuster.

4. Loosen the pitman arm adjuster locknut. Back off the pitman arm preload adjuster until it stops and rotate it inward 1 full turn.

5. Using an inch lb. torque wrench and socket on the stub, record the torque reading (pressure required to move the shaft).

6. Using the torque reading, add 6–10 inch lbs. to it; tighten the preload adjuster to acquire the new calculated reading.

7. After the new torque reading is achieved, maintain the preload adjuster from turning and torque the preload adjuster lock nut to 20 ft. lbs.

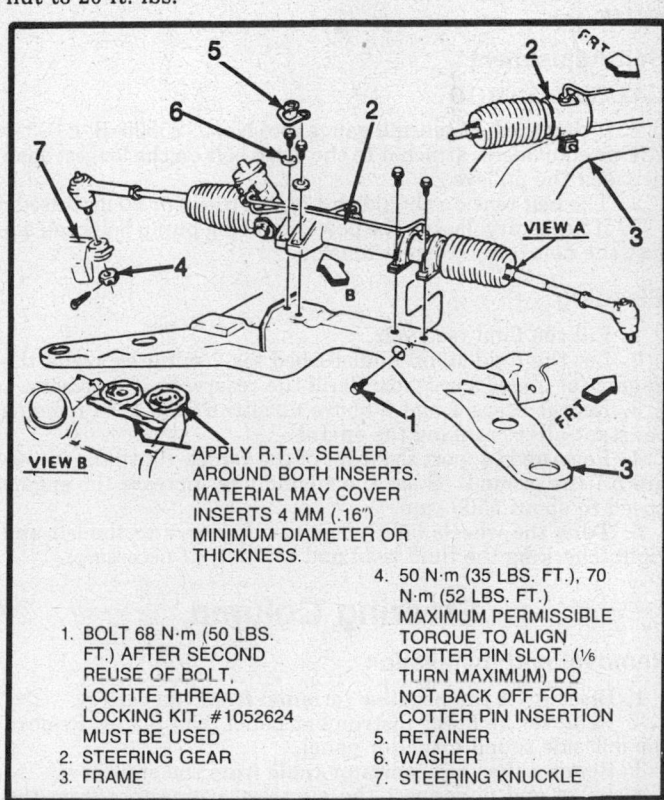

APPLY R.T.V. SEALER AROUND BOTH INSERTS. MATERIAL MAY COVER INSERTS 4 MM (.16") MINIMUM DIAMETER OR THICKNESS.

1. BOLT 68 N·m (50 LBS. FT.) AFTER SECOND REUSE OF BOLT, LOCTITE THREAD LOCKING KIT, #1052624 MUST BE USED
2. STEERING GEAR
3. FRAME
4. 50 N·m (35 LBS. FT.), 70 N·m (52 LBS. FT.) MAXIMUM PERMISSIBLE TORQUE TO ALIGN COTTER PIN SLOT. (⅙ TURN MAXIMUM) DO NOT BACK OFF FOR COTTER PIN INSERTION
5. RETAINER
6. WASHER
7. STEERING KNUCKLE

Rack and pinion assembly

8. Install the power steering gear into the vehicle. Torque the pitman arm-to-power steering gear nut to 185 ft. lbs. Refill the power steering pump reservoir. Bleed the power steering system.

Power Steering Pump

Removal and Installation

3.0L AND 3.8L ENGINES

1. Disconnect the negative battery cable.
2. Remove the air cleaner assembly on the 3.0L engine.
3. Remove the drive belt and then the alternator itself.
4. Raise the vehicle and support it safely.
5. Disconnect and plug the pressure and return lines at the pump.
6. Remove the rear pump adjustment bracket-to-pump nut. Lower the vehicle. 7. Remove the alternator adjustment bracket and support brace.
8. Remove the rear pump adjustment bracket and then remove the pump assembly.
9. Remove the front pump adjustment bracket and then remove the pulley.
10. Installation is in the reverse order of removal. Adjust the drive belts and bleed the power steering system.

4.1L AND 4.5L ENGINES

1. Disconnect the negative terminal from the battery.
2. Remove the serpentine drive belt and the power steering pump pulley.
3. Disconnect and plug the high pressure and feed lines from the pump.
4. Remove the power steering pump-to-bracket bolts and the pump.
5. To install, reverse the removal procedures. Torque the power steering pump-to-bracket bolts to 30 ft. lbs. Refill the power steering pump reservoir. Bleed the power steering system.

Belt Adjustment

GAUGE METHOD

1. Using the belt tension gauge tool No. J–23600–B, BT–33–73F or equivalent, attach it to the drive belt on the longest span between the pulleys.
2. The belt tension should be 170 lbs. (new) or 90 lbs. (used).
3. If necessary, loosen the power steering pump bolts and adjust the belt to the correct tension.

Bleeding

1. Fill the fluid reservoir.
2. Let the fluid stand undisturbed for 2 minutes, crank the engine for about 2 seconds. Refill the reservoir, if necessary.
3. Repeat Steps 1 and 2 above until the fluid level remains constant after cranking the engine.
4. Raise and support the front of the vehicle (until the wheels are off the ground). Start the engine and increase the engine speed to about 1500 rpm.
5. Turn the wheels lightly against the stops to the left and right, checking the fluid level and refilling (if necessary).

Steering Column

Removal and Installation

1. Disconnect the negative terminal from the battery.
2. Remove the lower instrument panel trim plates. Remove the left side sound insulator panel.
3. Remove the shift indicator cable from the shift bowl.
4. Label and disconnect the electrical connectors from the steering column.

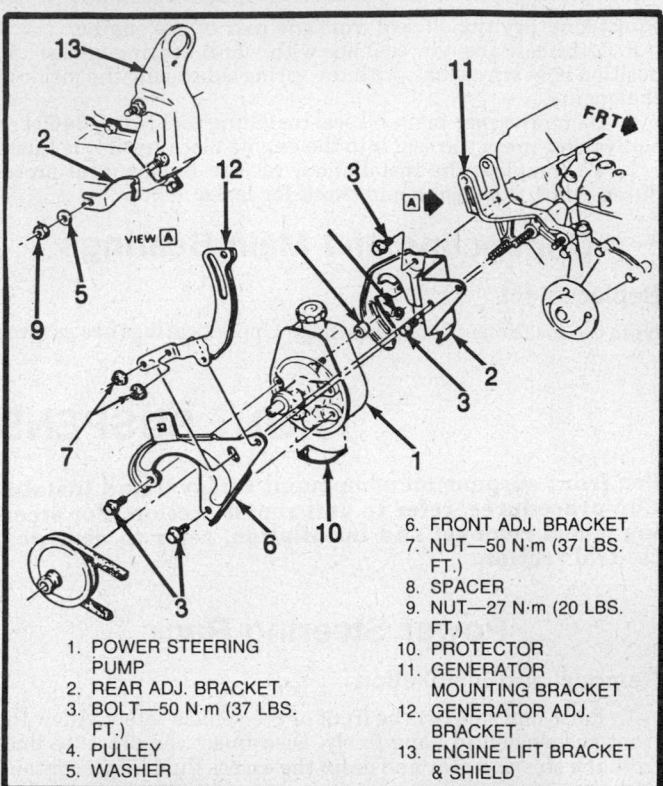

1. POWER STEERING PUMP
2. REAR ADJ. BRACKET
3. BOLT—50 N·m (37 LBS. FT.)
4. PULLEY
5. WASHER
6. FRONT ADJ. BRACKET
7. NUT—50 N·m (37 LBS. FT.)
8. SPACER
9. NUT—27 N·m (20 LBS. FT.)
10. PROTECTOR
11. GENERATOR MOUNTING BRACKET
12. GENERATOR ADJ. BRACKET
13. ENGINE LIFT BRACKET & SHIELD

Exploded view of the power steering pump assembly—3.0L and 3.8L engines

5. Remove the steering column-to-dash bolts.
6. Remove the steering shaft-to-intermediate shaft bolt.
7. Remove the steering column from the vehicle.
8. To install, reverse of the removal procedures. Inspect the steering column operations.

Front Wheel Bearing

Removal and Installation

NOTE: Use caution during halfshaft removal, damage to the tri-pots may occur if the halfshaft is overextended.

1. Remove the hub nut.
2. Raise and support the vehicle safely. Remove the wheel assembly.
3. Install a halfshaft boot seal protector tool onto the boot.
4. Disconnect the brake hose clip from the MacPherson strut; do not disconnect the hose from the caliper. Remove the brake caliper from the spindle and support the caliper on a length of wire; DO NOT allow the caliper to hang by the brake hose.
5. Using a scratch awl, mark the camber alignment cam bolt for reassembly. Remove the cam bolt and the upper attaching bolt from the strut and spindle.
6. Pull the steering knuckle assembly from the strut bracket.
7. Using the spindle removal tool No. J–28733 or equivalent, remove the halfshaft from the hub/bearing assembly.
8. Press the bearing from the hub assembly and install a new bearing.
9. Loosely install the halfshaft into the transaxle and steering knuckle.
10. Loosely attach the steering knuckle-to-strut bolts.
11. Press the halfshaft into place and install the hub nut. When the shaft begins to turn with the hub, insert a drift through the caliper into one of the cooling slots in the rotor to

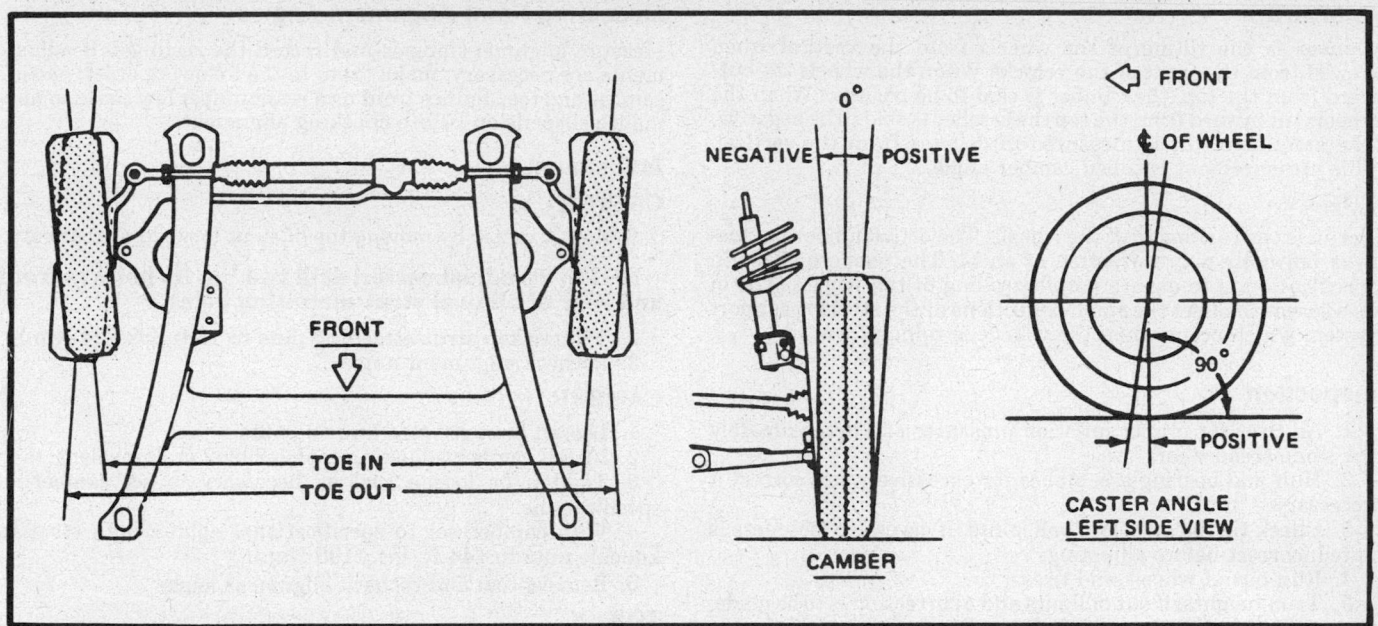

Caster, camber, toe

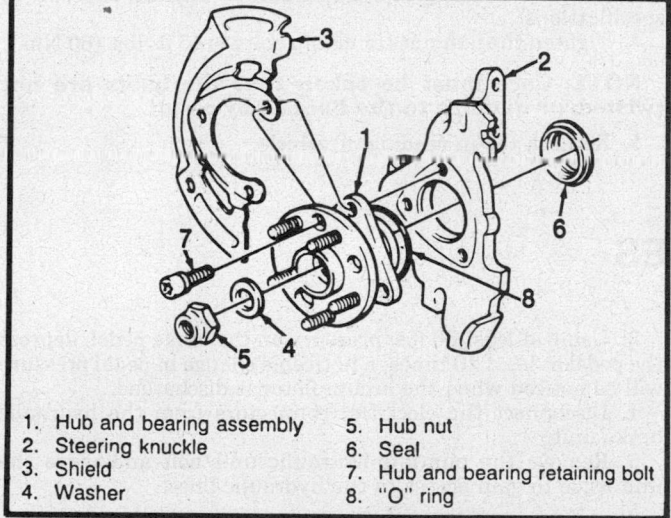

1. Hub and bearing assembly
2. Steering knuckle
3. Shield
4. Washer
5. Hub nut
6. Seal
7. Hub and bearing retaining bolt
8. "O" ring

Hub and bearing assembly—Exploded view

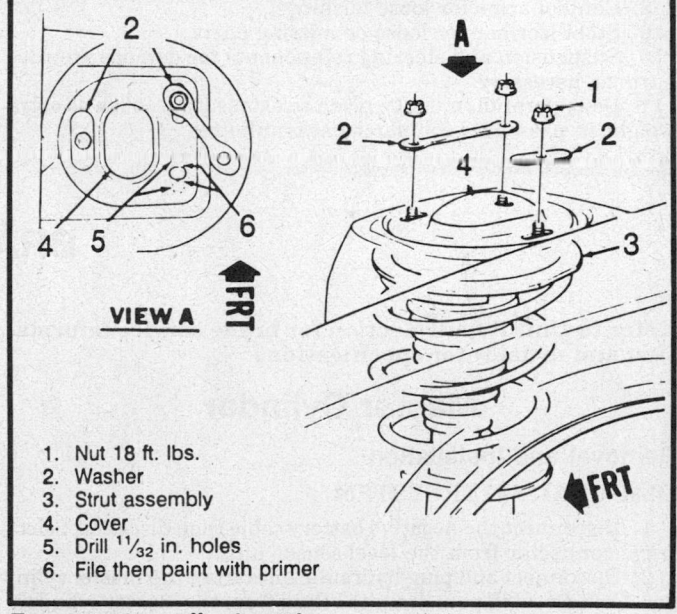

1. Nut 18 ft. lbs.
2. Washer
3. Strut assembly
4. Cover
5. Drill $^{11}/_{32}$ in. holes
6. File then paint with primer

Front caster adjustment

keep it from turning. Insert a long bolt in the hub flange to prevent the shaft from turning. Torque the hub nut to 70 ft. lbs. to completely seat the shaft.

12. Torque the caliper-to-steering knuckle bolts to 38 ft. lbs.

13. Load the hub assembly by lowering it onto a jackstand. Align the camber cam bolt marks made during removal, install the bolt and torque to 140 ft. lbs. Tighten the upper nut to the same value.

14. Install the halfshaft all the way into the transaxle using a small prybar inserted into the groove provided on the inner retainer. Tap the prybar until the shaft seats in the transaxle. Remove the boot seal protector.

15. Connect the brake hose clip to the strut. Install the wheel assembly, lower the vehicle and torque the hub nut 185 ft. lbs.

Torque Procedure

All vehicles covered in this section utilize a permanently sealed and lubricated front wheel bearing assembly.

If the halfshaft or wheel bearing have been replaced, the wheel bearing must be retorqued.

1. Lower the vehicle to rest the wheel on the ground.

2. Torque the hub nut to 180 ft. lbs. and complete the assembly procedures; no other adjustments are necessary or possible.

Front Wheel Alignment

CASTER

Caster is the tilting of the steering axis either forward or backward from the vertical, when viewed from the side of the vehicle. A backward tilt is said to be positive and a forward tilt is said to be negative.

CAMBER

Camber is the tilting of the wheels from the vertical when viewed from the front of the vehicle. When the wheels tilt outward from the top, the camber is said to be positive. When the wheels tilt inward from the top the camber is said to be negative. The amount of tilt is measured in degrees from the vertical. This measurement is called camber angle.

TOE-IN

Toe-in is the turning in of the wheels. The actual amount of toe-in is normally only a fraction of an in. The purpose of toe-in specification is to ensure parallel rolling of the wheels. Toe-in also serves to offset the small deflections of the steering support system which occur when the vehicle is rolling forward.

Inspection

1. All tires for proper inflation pressures and approximately the same tread wear.
2. Hub and bearing assemblies for excessive wear; correct if necessary.
3. Check tie rod ends and ball joints. If excessive looseness is noted, correct before adjusting.
4. Run-out of wheels and tires.
5. Trim heights; if out of limits and a correction is to be made, the correction must be made before adjusting caster, camber or toe-in.
6. Rack and pinion looseness at frame.
7. Strut dampeners for proper operation.
8. Control arms for loose bushings.
9. Stabilizer bar for loose or missing parts.
10. Suspension and steering components for damage. Replace parts as necessary.
11. Consideration must be given to excess loads, such as extra weight in passenger compartment/trunk area.

Measuring Front Alignment Angles

Measure alignment angles and record the readings. If adjustments are necessary, make them in the following order; caster, camber and toe. Jounce front and rear bumper few times to normalize suspension before checking alignment.

Adjustment

CASTER

1. Adjust caster by moving top of strut forward or rearward.

NOTE: To adjust caster, drill two $^{11}\!/_{32}$ in. holes at front and rear of all oval strut mounting holes.

2. Tighten top strut attaching nuts to 18 ft. lbs. (24 Nm.).
3. Recheck alignment angle

CAMBER

1. Loosen both strut to knuckle nuts.
2. Install camber adjusting tool J–29862 or equivalent.
3. Tighten or loosen tool as necessary to set camber to specifications.
4. With camber set to specifications, tighten both strut to knuckle nuts to 144 ft. lbs. (195 Nm.).
5. Remove tool and recheck alignment angle.

TOE

1. Obtain toe-in reading of vehicle.
2. Loosen the jam nuts on the tie rod.
3. Rotate the tie rod adjuster to adjust the toe to specifications.
4. Tighten the jam nuts or clamp bolts to 45 ft. lbs. (60 Nm.).

NOTE: Care must be taken that the boots are not twisted, or damage to the boots may result.

5. Recheck toe-in reading of vehicle.

BRAKES

Refer to Unit Repair Section for brake service information and drum/rotor specifications

Master Cylinder

Removal and Installation

DIAGONAL SPLIT SYSTEM

1. Disconnect the negative battery cable then disconnect electrical connector from the level sensor unit.
2. Disconnect and plug hydraulic lines from the master cylinder. Using a catch pan, drain the fluid from the master cylinder.
3. If not equipped with a power brake booster, perform the following procedures:
    a. Remove the pushrod from the brake pedal.
    b. Remove the master cylinder-to-cowl nuts and the master cylinder.
4. Remove the power brake booster then the master cylinder-to-power brake booster nuts and the master cylinder.
5. To install, reverse the removal procedures. Refill the master cylinder with clean brake fluid. Bleed the brake system.

ANTI-LOCK SYSTEM

NOTE: The hydraulic accumulator is under pressure and must be depressurized before attempting to dismantle the system.

1. Disconnect the negative terminal from the battery.
2. Firmly apply the parking brake.

3. Using at least 50 lbs. pressure on the brake pedal, depress the pedal at least 20 times; a noticable change in pedal pressure will be noticed when the accumulator is discharged.
4. Disconnect the electrical connectors from the hydraulic brake unit.
5. Remove the pump-to-hydraulic unit bolt and move the unit aside to gain access to the hydraulic lines.

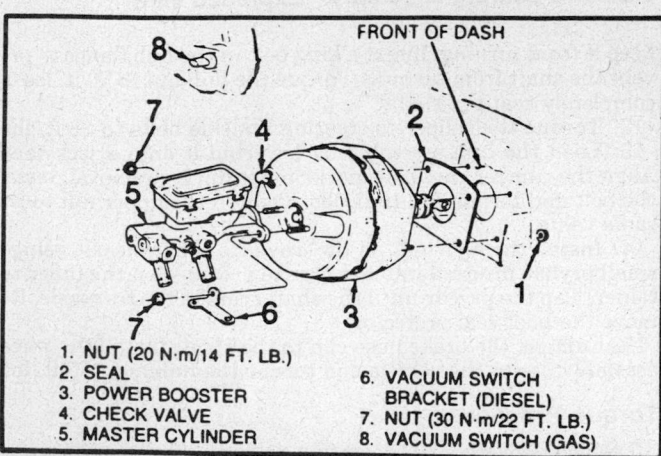

1. NUT (20 N·m/14 FT. LB.)
2. SEAL
3. POWER BOOSTER
4. CHECK VALVE
5. MASTER CYLINDER
6. VACUUM SWITCH BRACKET (DIESEL)
7. NUT (30 N·m/22 FT. LB.)
8. VACUUM SWITCH (GAS)

Typical master cylinder and power booster mounting

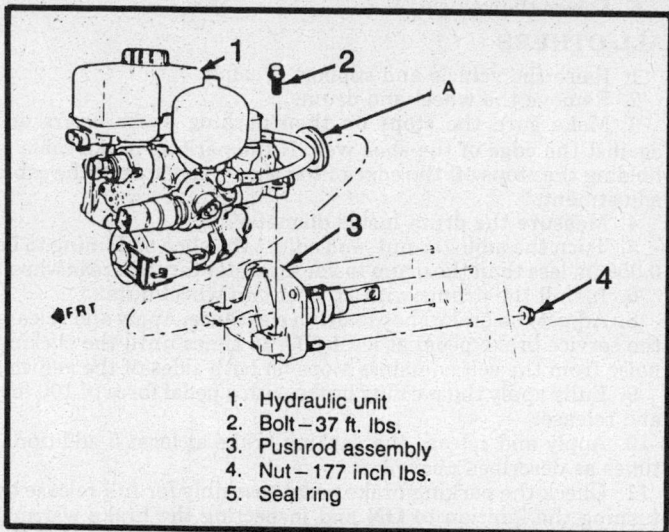

1. Hydraulic unit
2. Bolt—37 ft. lbs.
3. Pushrod assembly
4. Nut—177 inch lbs.
5. Seal ring

View of the anti-lock hydraulic brake unit

6. Using a back-up wrench, disconnect the hydraulic lines from the hydraulic unit.
7. From under the dash, disconnect the pushrod from the brake pedal.
8. Move the dust boot forward, past the pushrod hex and unscrew the 2 pushrod halves.
9. Remove the hydraulic unit-to-pushrod bracket bolts and separate the hydraulic unit from the pushrod bracket; half of the pushrod will remain locked in the hydraulic unit.
10. Disassemble the master cylinder from the hydraulic unit.
11. To install, assemble the master cylinder to the hydraulic unit and reverse the removal procedures. Torque the hydraulic unit-to-pushrod bracket bolts to 37 ft. lbs. Bleed the brake system.

Bleeding Procedure

DIAGONAL SPLIT SYSTEM

1. Check and/or refill the master cylinder reservoir.
2. If the master cylinder has air in it, perform the following procedures:

   a. Loosen the front brake line at the master cylinder and allow the fluid to flow from the port. When no air is present, retighten the brake line.

   b. Slowly, depress the brake pedal (once) and hold it. Loosen the brake line from the master cylinder to purge the port, retighten the brake line and slowly, release the brake pedal. Wait 15 seconds and repeat this procedure. Repeat this procedure until all air has been removed from the master cylinder.

   c. Loosen the rear brake line at the master cylinder and allow the fluid to flow from the port. When no air is present, retighten the brake line.

   d. Slowly, depress the brake pedal (once) and hold it. Loosen the brake line from the master cylinder to purge the port, retighten the brake line and slowly, release the brake pedal. Wait 15 seconds and repeat this procedure. Repeat this procedure until all air has been removed from the master cylinder.

3. Using a transparent vinyl tube, connect it to the right rear wheel cylinder bleeder valve and insert the other end in a beaker ½ full of clean brake fluid.
4. Slowly, depress the brake pedal and hold it, open the bleeder valve and purge the cylinder. Tighten the bleeder screw and slowly release the brake pedal; wait for 15 seconds and repeat this procedure.

NOTE: To bleed a wheel cylinder or caliper, repeat the sequence at least 10 times.

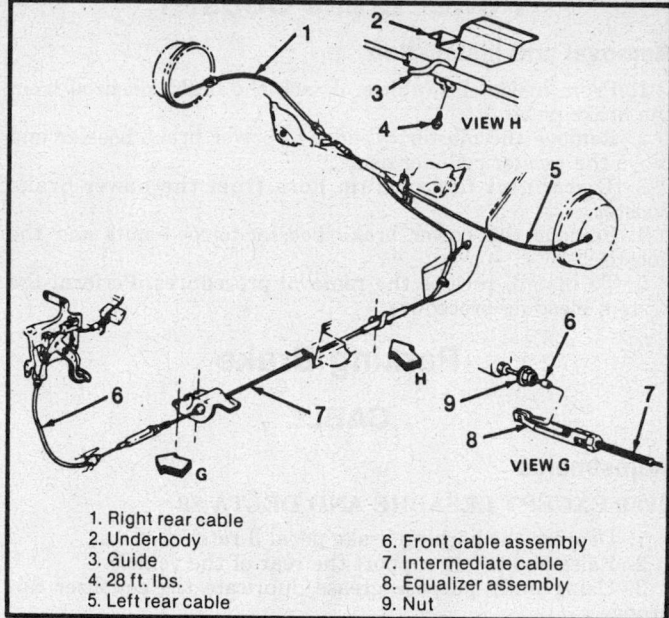

1. Right rear cable
2. Underbody
3. Guide
4. 28 ft. lbs.
5. Left rear cable
6. Front cable assembly
7. Intermediate cable
8. Equalizer assembly
9. Nut

Parking brake cable assembly

5. The bleeding sequence is right rear, left front, left rear and right front.
6. After bleeding, inspect the pedal for sponginess and the brake warning light for unbalanced pressure; if either of the conditions exist, repeat the bleeding procedure.

ANTI-LOCK SYSTEM

Front Brakes

1. Check and/or refill the master cylinder reservoir.
2. Using a transparent vinyl tube, connect it to the right rear wheel cylinder bleeder valve and insert the other end in a beaker ½ full of clean brake fluid.
3. Slowly, depress the brake pedal and hold it, open the bleeder valve and purge the cylinder. Tighten the bleeder screw and slowly release the brake pedal; wait for 15 seconds and repeat this procedure.

NOTE: To bleed a wheel cylinder or caliper, repeat the sequence at least 10 times.

4. The bleeding sequence is either front caliper.
5. After bleeding, inspect the pedal for sponginess and the brake warning light for unbalanced pressure; if either of the conditions exist, repeat the bleeding procedure.

Rear Brakes

1. Check and/or refill the master cylinder reservoir.
2. Turn the ignition switch **ON** and allow the system to charge.

NOTE: The pump will turn off when the system is charged.

3. Using a transparent vinyl tube, connect it to a rear wheel bleeder valve and insert the other end in a beaker ½ full of clean brake fluid.
4. Open the bleeder valve and slightly depress the brake pedal for at least 10 seconds or until air is removed from the brake system.
5. Repeat the bleeding procedure for the other rear wheel.
6. After bleeding, inspect the pedal for sponginess and the brake warning light for unbalanced pressure; if either of the conditions exist, repeat the bleeding procedure.

Power Brake Booster

Removal and Installation

1. From inside the vehicle, detach the brake pushrod from the brake pedal.
2. Remove the master cylinder-to-power brake booster and move the master cylinder aside.
3. Disconnect the vacuum hose from the power brake booster.
4. Remove the power brake booster-to-cowl nuts and the booster.
5. To install, reverse the removal procedures. Perform the system bleeding procedure.

Parking Brake

CABLE

Adjustments

1986 EXCEPT LESABRE AND DELTA 88

1. Depress the parking brake pedal 3 ratchet clicks.
2. Raise and safely support the rear of the vehicle.
3. Using multi-purpose grease, lubricate the equalizer nut groove.
4. Tighten the adjusting nut until the right rear wheel can just be turned rearward with both hands but is locked when forward rotation is attempted.
5. With the mechanisms totally disengaged, both rear wheels should turn freely in either direction with no brake drag.

NOTE: Do not adjust the parking brake cable to tight for brake drag may result.

6. Lower the vehicle.

ALL OTHERS

1. Raise the vehicle and support it safely.
2. Remove the wheel and drums.
3. Make sure the stops on then parking brake levers are against the edge of the shoe web. If the parking brake cable is holding the stops off the edge of the shoe webb, loosen the cable adjustment.
4. Measure the drum inside diameter.
5. Turn the adjuster nut, and adjust the shoe and lining to be 0.050 in. less than the drum inside diameter for each rear wheel.
6. Install the drums with at least two wheel nuts.
8. Adjust the brake shoe to drum clearance. Apply and release the service brake pedal at least 30 – 35 times until the clicking noise from the self adjusters stops on both sides of the vehicle.
9. Fully apply the parking brake with a pedal force of 100 lbs. and release.
10. Apply and release the parking brake at least 5 additional times as described above.
11. Check the parking brake pedal assembly for full release by turning the ignition to **ON** and inspecting the brake warning lamp. The lamp should be off. If the brake lamp is on and the parking brake appears to be fully released, operate the pedal release lever and pull downward on the front parking brake cable to remove the slack from the assembly.
12. Remove the drums.
13. Adjust the parking brake cable until a 1/8 in. drill ca be inserted into the space between the shoe web and the parking brake lever. Satisfactory adjustment is achieved when a 1/8 in. drill will will fit into the notch but a 1/4 in. drill will not.
14. Install the brake drums and wheels.
15. Lower the vehicle and check the operation of the parking brake.

TRANSAXLE

Automatic Transaxle

Removal and Installation

3.0L AND 3.8L ENGINES

1. Disconnect the negative terminal from the battery. Disconnect the wire connector at the mass air flow sensor.
2. Remove the air intake duct and the mass air flow sensor as an assembly.
3. Disconnect the cruise control assembly and the the shift control linkage.
4. Label and disconnect the following:
   a. Park/Neutral switch
   b. Torque converter clutch
   c. Vehicle speed sensor
   d. Vacuum modulator hose at the modulator
5. Remove the 3 top transaxle-to-engine block bolts and install an engine support fixture.
6. Raise the vehicle and support it safely. Remove both front wheels and turn the steering wheel to the full left position.
7. Remove the right front ball joint nut and separate the control arm from the steering knuckle.
8. Remove the right halfshaft.

NOTE: Be careful not to allow the drive axle splines to contact any portion of the lip seal.

9. Using a medium pry bar, remove the left halfshaft; be careful not to damage the pan. Install drive axle boot seal protectors.
10. Remove 3 bolts at the transaxle and 3 nuts at the cradle member. Remove the left front transaxle mount.

11. Remove the right front mount-to-cradle nuts. Remove the left rear transaxle mount-to-transaxle bolts.
12. Remove the right rear transaxle mount. Remove the engine support bracket-to-transaxle case bolts.
13. Remove the flywheel cover, matchmark the flywheel-to-torque converter and remove the flywheel-to-converter bolts.

NOTE: Be sure to matchmark the flywheel-to-converter relationship for proper alignment upon reassembly.

14. Remove the rear cradle member-to-front cradle dog leg.
15. Remove the front left cradle-to-body bolt and the front cradle dog leg-to-right cradle member bolts.
16. Install a transaxle support fixture into position.
17. Remove the cradle assembly by swinging it aside and supporting it with jackstand.
18. Disconnect and plug the oil cooler lines at the transaxle.

NOTE: One bolt is located between the transaxle and the engine block; it is installed in the opposite direction.

19. Remove the remaining lower transaxle-to-engine bolts and lower the transaxle from the vehicle.
20. To install, reverse the removal procedures. Check the fluid level and all adjustments.

4.1L AND 4.5L ENGINES

1. Disconnect the negative terminal from the battery. Remove the air cleaner and the TV cable.

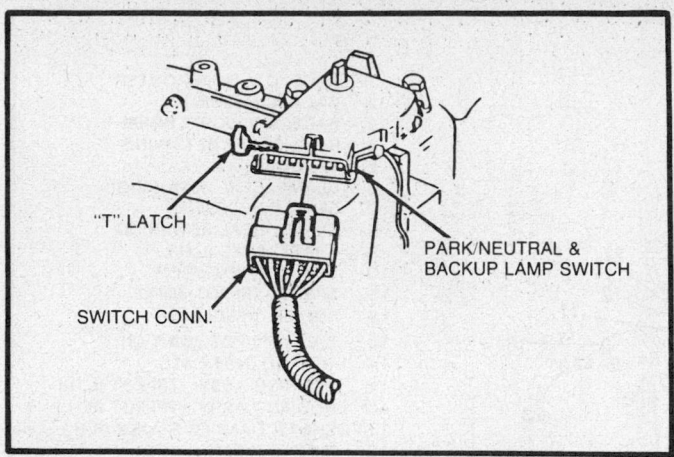

T-latch connector

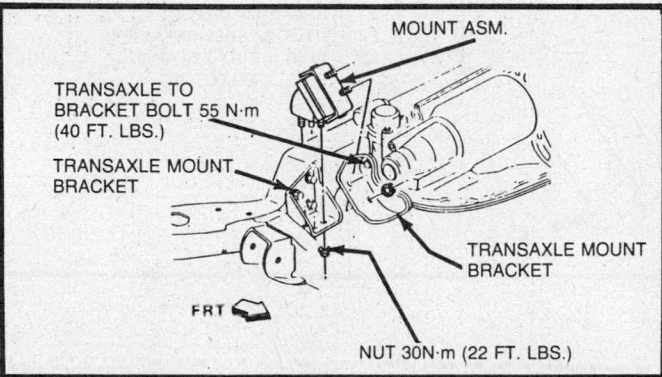

Exploded view of the right transaxle mount—3.8L engine—all others are similar

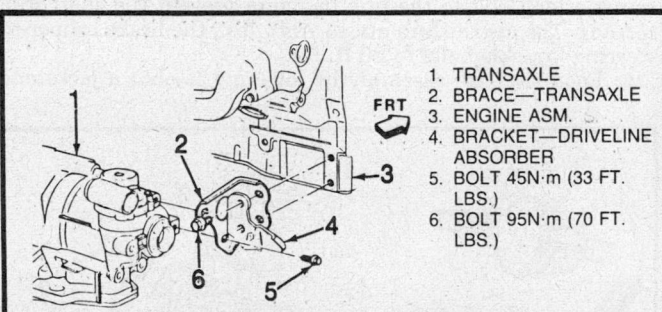

1. TRANSAXLE
2. BRACE—TRANSAXLE
3. ENGINE ASM.
4. BRACKET—DRIVELINE ABSORBER
5. BOLT 45N·m (33 FT. LBS.)
6. BOLT 95N·m (70 FT. LBS.)

Exploded view of the transaxle brace and brackets—3.8L engine—all others are similar

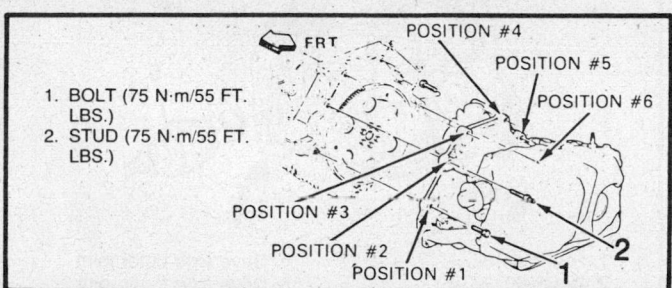

1. BOLT (75 N·m/55 FT. LBS.)
2. STUD (75 N·m/55 FT. LBS.)

Exploded view of the transaxle-to-engine assembly; remove No. 6 bolt last—4.1L and 4.5L engines

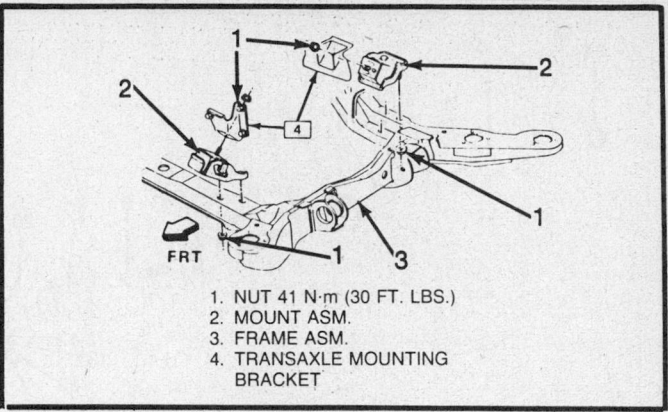

1. NUT 41 N·m (30 FT. LBS.)
2. MOUNT ASM.
3. FRAME ASM.
4. TRANSAXLE MOUNTING BRACKET

Exploded view of the left transaxle mounts—3.8L engine—all others are similar

2. Disconnect the shift linkage from the transaxle. Using an engine support fixture tool, connect it to and support the engine.

3. Label and disconnect the electrical connectors from the following items:
   a. Converter clutch
   b. Vehicle speed sensor
   c. Vacuum line at the modulator

4. Remove the upper bell housing-to-engine bolts and studs.

5. Raise and support the vehicle safely. Remove both front wheels.

6. From the left side of the vehicle, disconnect the lower ball joint from steering knuckle. Remove both drive axles from the transaxle.

7. Remove the stabilizer bar-to-left control arm bolt.

8. Remove the left front cradle assembly.

9. Remove the extension housing-to-engine support bracket.

10. Disconnect and plug the oil cooler lines at the transaxle case.

11. Remove the right and left transaxle mount attachments.

12. Remove the flywheel splash shield. Matchmark the torque converter-to-flyheel and remove the converter-to-flywheel bolts.

13. Remove the lower bellhousing bolts except the lower rear on (No. 6).

14. Using a floor jack, position it under the transaxle and remove the last bell housing bolt.

NOTE: To reach the last bell housing bolt, use a 3 in. socket wrench extension through the right wheel arch opening.

15. Remove the transaxle assembly.

16. To install, reverse the removal procedures. Check the fluid level and all adjustments.

SHIFT INDICATOR

Removal and Installation

1. Disconnect the negative terminal from the battery.
2. Remove the instrument cluster trim plate.
3. Remove the shift indicator clip. and the indicator.
4. To install, reverse the removal procedures. Inspect the indicator operation.

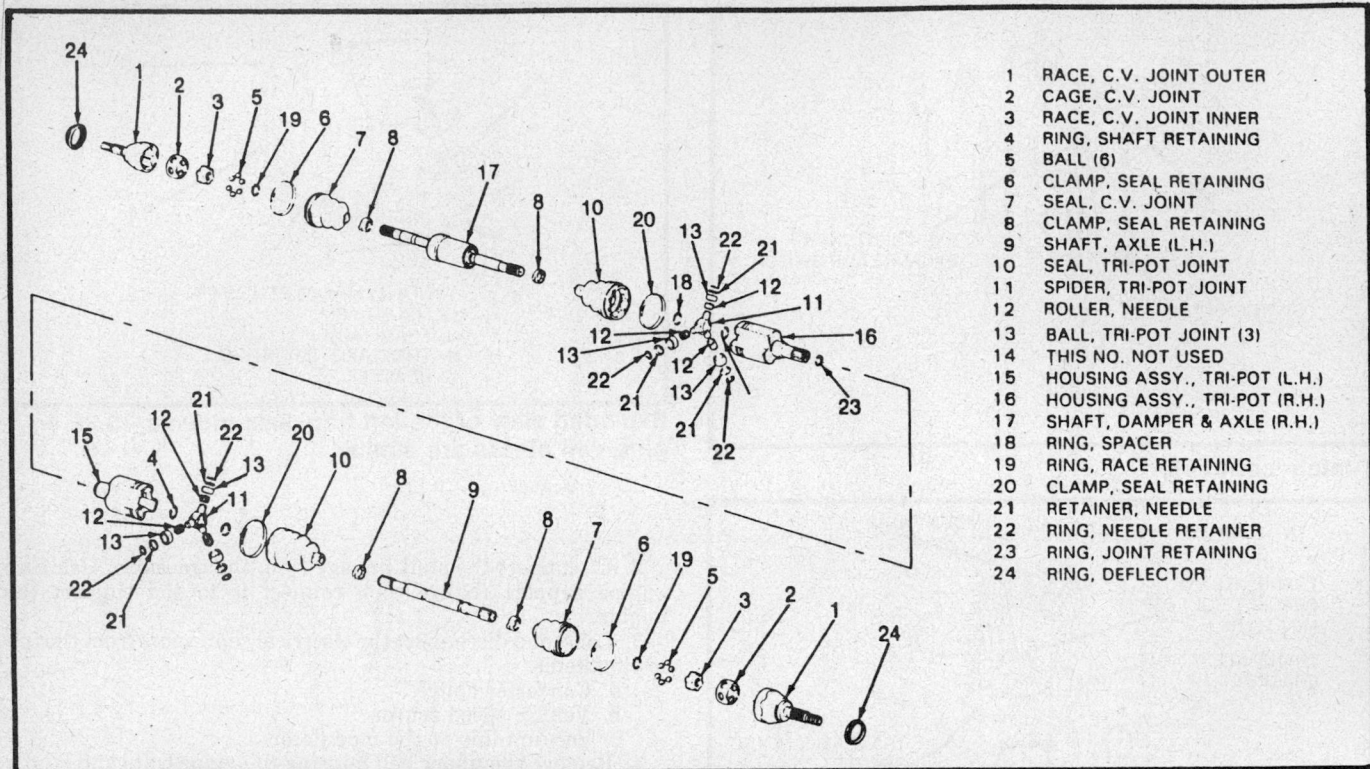

1	RACE, C.V. JOINT OUTER
2	CAGE, C.V. JOINT
3	RACE, C.V. JOINT INNER
4	RING, SHAFT RETAINING
5	BALL (6)
6	CLAMP, SEAL RETAINING
7	SEAL, C.V. JOINT
8	CLAMP, SEAL RETAINING
9	SHAFT, AXLE (L.H.)
10	SEAL, TRI-POT JOINT
11	SPIDER, TRI-POT JOINT
12	ROLLER, NEEDLE
13	BALL, TRI-POT JOINT (3)
14	THIS NO. NOT USED
15	HOUSING ASSY., TRI-POT (L.H.)
16	HOUSING ASSY., TRI-POT (R.H.)
17	SHAFT, DAMPER & AXLE (R.H.)
18	RING, SPACER
19	RING, RACE RETAINING
20	CLAMP, SEAL RETAINING
21	RETAINER, NEEDLE
22	RING, NEEDLE RETAINER
23	RING, JOINT RETAINING
24	RING, DEFLECTOR

Exploded view of the halfshaft assemblies

HALFSHAFTS

Front Drive Axle

HALFSHAFT

Removal and Installation

1986–88

NOTE: Use care when removing the drive axle. Tri-pots can be damaged if the drive axle is overextended.

1. Remove the hub nut.
2. Raise and support the front of the vehicle. Remove the wheel assembly.
3. Using the axle shaft boot seal protector tool No. J–28712 or equivalent, install it onto the seal.
4. Disconnect the brake hose clip from the MacPherson strut, do not disconnect the hose from the caliper. Remove the brake caliper from the spindle and hang the caliper out of the way, using a length of wire; do not allow the caliper to hang by the brake hose.
5. Mark the camber alignment cam bolt for reassembly. Remove the cam bolt and the upper strut-to-steering knuckle bolt.
6. Pull the steering knuckle assembly from the strut bracket.
7. Using spindle removal tool No. J–28733 or equivalent, remove the halfshaft from the hub/bearing assembly.
8. If a new halfshaft is to be installed, a new steering knuckle seal should be installed first.
9. Loosely install the halfshaft into the transaxle and steering knuckle.
10. Loosely attach the steering knuckle-to-strut bolts.
11. The halfshaft is an interference fit in the steering knuckle. Press the axle into place and install the hub nut. When the shaft begins to turn with the hub, insert a drift through the caliper

into one of the cooling slots in the rotor to keep it from turning. Insert a long bolt in the hub flange to prevent the shaft from turning. Torque the hub nut to 70 ft. lbs., the brake caliper-to-steering knuckle bolts to 30 ft. lbs.

12. Load the hub assembly by lowering it onto a jackstand.

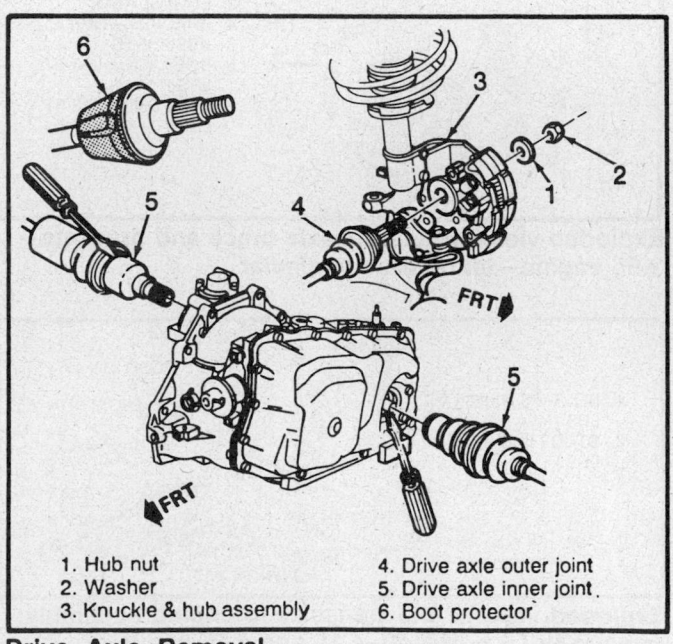

1. Hub nut	4. Drive axle outer joint
2. Washer	5. Drive axle inner joint
3. Knuckle & hub assembly	6. Boot protector

Drive Axle Removal

Align the camber cam bolt marks made during removal, install the bolt and tighten to 140 ft. lbs. Tighten the upper nut to the same value.

13. Install the halfshaft all the way into the transaxle, using a small prybar inserted into the groove provided on the inner retainer. Tap the pry bar until the shaft seats in the transaxle. Remove the boot seal protector.

14. Connect the brake hose clip to the strut. Install the wheel assembly and lower the vehicle. Torque the hub nut to 185 ft. lbs.

1989–90

NOTE: Use care when removing the drive axle. Tripots can be damaged if the drive axle is overextended.

1. Raise and safely support the front of the vehicle. Remove the wheel and tire assembly.

2. Use an axle shaft boot seal protector tool and install it onto the seal.

3. Insert drift into rotor and caliper to prevent rotor from turning.

4. Remove hub nut and washer using a hub nut socket tool.

5. Remove the lower ball joint cotter pin and nut and loosen the joint using J–29330 ball joint separator tool. If removing the right axle, turn the wheel to the left, if removing the left axle turn the wheel to the right.

6. With a pry bar between the suspension support and the lower control arm, separate the joint.

7. Pull out on the lower knuckle area and with a plastic or rubber mallet strike the end of the axle shaft to disengage the axle from the hub and bearing. The shaft nut can be partially installed to protect the threads.

8. Separate the hub and bearing assembly from the drive axle and move the strut and knuckle assembly rearward. Remove the inner joint from the transaxle using tool J–2468 or J–33008, or from the intermediate shaft, if so equipped.

To install:

9. Seat the driveaxle into the transaxle by placing the screwdriver into the groove on the joint housing and tapping until seated.

10. Verify the drive axle is seated into the transaxle by grasping on the housing and pulling outboard. Do not pull on the drive axle shaft.

11. Install the drive axle into the hub and bearing assembly.

12. Install the lower ball joint to the knuckle. Tighten the nut to 41 ft. lbs. minimum and to 50 ft. lbs. maximum to install the cotter pin.

13. Install the cotter pin.

14. Install the washer and new shaft nut.

15. Insert drift into rotor and caliper to prevent rotor from turning.

16. Torque the shaft nut to 185 ft. lbs.

17. Remove the boot protector.

18. Install the wheel and lower the vehicle.

Boots

Removal and Installation
INNER BOOT (INBOARD)

1. Remove the halfshaft.

2. Remove the joint assembly retaining ring and the joint assembly.

3. Remove the bearing race retaining ring and the seal retainer.

4. Remove the inner seal retainer clamp and the inner joint seal.

5. To install, pack the joint with grease and reverse the removal procedures.

OUTER BOOT (OUTBOARD)

1. Remove the halfshaft.

2. Using a brass drift, lightly tap around the seal retainer to loosen it. Remove the seal retainer.

3. Remove the seal retainer clamp and discard.

4. Using snap-ring pliers, remove the race retaining ring from the axle shaft.

5. Pull the outer joint assembly and the outboard seal away from the halfshaft.

6. To install, pack the joint with grease and reverse the removal procedures.

CV-Joints

For CV-joint overhaul procedures, please refer to the Unit Repair Section.

REAR AXLE AND REAR SUSPENSION

Refer to the unit repair section for rear suspension services and axle overhaul procedures

Rear Wheel Hub/Bearing Assembly

A single unit hub and bearing assembly is bolted to both ends of the rear axle assembly. These take the place of "rear axles" used on rear wheel drive vehicles. The hub and bearing assembly is a sealed unit which requires no maintenance. The unit must be replaced as an assembly and cannot be disassembled or adjusted.

NOTE: Certain vehicles incorporate Torx® bolts which hold the bearing and hub assembly to the vehicle and also supports the brake assembly. Upon removal of these bolts, be sure to support the brake assembly with a wire so it does not hang by the brake cable lines.

Removal and Installation

1. Raise and support the vehicle safely.
2. Remove the wheel/tire assembly and the brake drum.

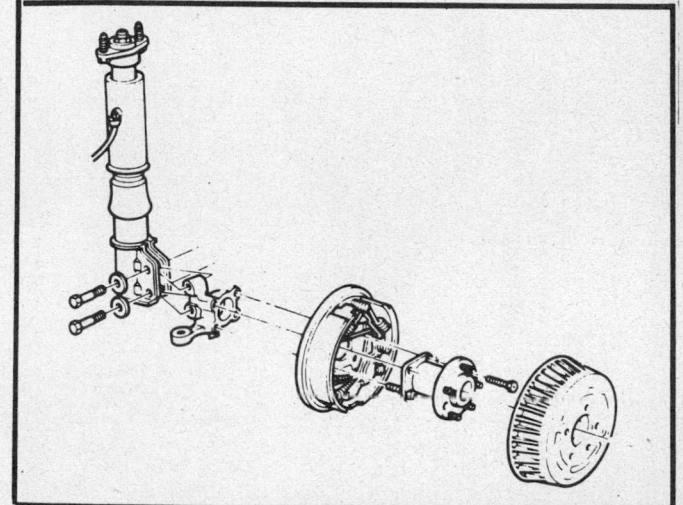

Rear hub and bearing assembly—exploded view

NOTE: Do not hammer on the brake drum as damage to the bearing could result.

3. Remove the hub/bearing assembly-to-knuckle bolts and remove the hub/bearing assembly.

NOTE: The bolts which attach the hub/bearing assembly also support the brake assembly. When removing these bolts, support the brake assembly with a wire or other means; do not allow the brake line support the brake assembly.

4. To install, reverse the removal procedures. Torque the hub/bearing assembly-to-rear knuckle Torx® bolts to 52 ft. lbs.

Adjustments

There is no necessary adjustment to the rear wheel bearing and hub assembly.

Rear Wheel Alignment

Preliminary Adjustments

NOTE: Be sure the vehicle has a full tank of gas.

1. In the trunk, place a 200 lb. minimum weight.
2. Turn the ignition switch **ON**; this will activate the Electronic Leveling Control **ELC** compressor.

3. When the **Car is Leveling** light turns **ON**, turn the ignition switch **OFF** and remove the 200 lb. weight.
4. After waiting 30 seconds (time for the ELC system to exhaust), roll the vehicle forward/backward several complete wheel rotations (to eliminate the camber change effects).
5. Bounce the bumper (up and down) to normalize the springs position.

NOTE: When bouncing the vehicle, gradually reduce the applied force and allow the vehicle to come to rest.

Alignment

CAMBER

1. Loosen the rear strut-to-knuckle nuts.
2. Using the Camber Adjusting tool No. J–29862 or equivalent, install it onto the strut.
3. Adjust the rear wheel camber to ± 0.5 degrees.
4. Torque the strut-to-knuckle nuts to 144 ft. lbs. and recheck the camber.

TOE

1. Loosen the tie rod end-to-tie rod locknut.
2. Adjust the toe to ± 1 degree (0.05 in.), by turning the inner rod.
3. Torque the tie rod end-to-tie rod lock nut to 48 ft. lbs.

YEAR IDENTIFICATION

1989–90 Tornado

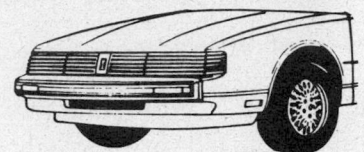

1986–88 Toronado

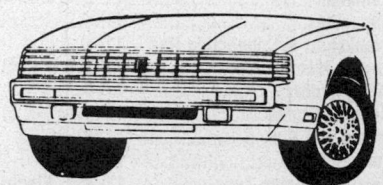

1987–90 Trofeo

1988–90 Oldsmobile Touring Sedan

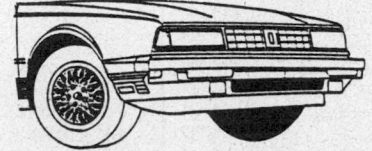

1986–90 Eldorado

1986–90 Seville

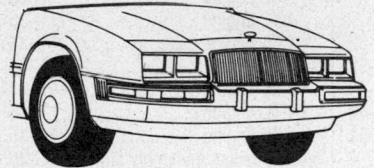

1986-87 Riviera

1988–90 Riviera

1987–90 Allante

1988–90 Reatta

VEHICLE IDENTIFICATION CHART

It is important for servicing and ordering parts to be certain of the vehicle and engine identification. The VIN (vehicle identification number) is a 17 digit number visible through the windshield on the driver's side of the dash and contains the vehicle and engine identification codes. The tenth digit indicates model year and the eighth digit indicates engine code. It can be interpreted as follows:

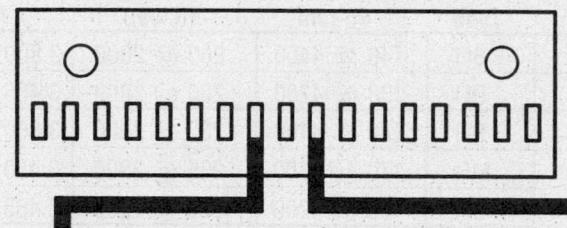

Engine Code

Code	Cu. In.	Liters	Cyl.	Fuel Sys.	Eng. Mfg.
3	231	3.8	6	SFI	Buick
C	231	3.8	6	SFI	Buick
8	250	4.1	8	DFI	Cadillac
7	250	4.1	8	MFI	Cadillac
5	273	4.5	8	DFI	Cadillac

Model Year

Code	Year
G	1986
H	1987
J	1988
K	1989
L	1990

DFI Digital Fuel Injection
SFI Sequential Fuel Injection
MFI Multi-Port Fuel Injection

ENGINE IDENTIFICATION

Year	Model	Engine Displacement cu. In. (liter)	Engine Series Identification (VIN)	No. of Cylinders	Engine Type
1986	Eldorado	250 (4.1)	8	8	OHV
	Riviera	231 (3.8)	3	6	OHV
	Seville	250 (4.1)	8	8	OHV
	Toronado	231 (3.8)	3	6	OHV
1987	Allante	250 (4.1)	7	8	OHV
	Eldorado	250 (4.1)	8	8	OHV
	Riviera	231 (3.8)	3	6	OHV
	Seville	250 (4.1)	8	8	OHV
	Toronado	231 (3.8)	3	6	OHV
1988	Allante	250 (4.1)	7	8	OHV
	Eldorado	273 (4.5)	5	8	OHV
	Reatta	231 (3.8)	C	6	OHV
	Riviera	231 (3.8)	C	6	OHV
	Seville	273 (4.5)	5	8	OHV
	Toronado	231 (3.8)	C	6	OHV
1989-90	Allante	273 (4.5)	5	8	OHV
	Eldorado	273 (4.5)	5	8	OHV
	Reatta	231 (3.8)	C	6	OHV
	Riviera	231 (3.8)	C	6	OHV
	Seville	273 (4.5)	5	8	OHV
	Toronado	231 (3.8)	C	6	OHV

OHV Overhead valves

GENERAL ENGINE SPECIFICATIONS

Year	VIN	No. Cylinder Displacement cu. in. (liter)	Fuel System Type	Net Horsepower @ rpm	Net Torque @ rpm (ft.lbs.)	Bore × Stroke (in.)	Compression Ratio	Oil Pressure @ rpm
1986	3	6-231 (3.8)	SFI	140 @ 4400	200 @ 2000	3.800 × 3.400	8.5:1	37 @ 2400
	8	8-250 (4.1)	DFI	130 @ 4200	200 @ 2200	3.465 × 3.307	9.0:1	40 @ 1500
1987	3	6-231 (3.8)	SFI	140 @ 4400	200 @ 2000	3.800 × 3.400	8.5:1	37 @ 2400
	7	8-250 (4.1)	MFI	170 @ 4300	235 @ 3200	3.460 × 3.310	8.5:1	37 @ 1500
	8	8-250 (4.1)	DFI	130 @ 4200	200 @ 2200	3.465 × 3.310	9.0:1	37 @ 1500
1988	5	8-273 (4.5)	DFI	155 @ 4200	240 @ 2800	3.620 × 3.310	9.0:1	37 @ 1500
	7	8-250 (4.1)	MFI	170 @ 4300	235 @ 3200	3.460 × 3.310	8.5:1	37 @ 1500
	C	6-231 (3.8)	SFI	165 @ 5200	210 @ 2000	3.800 × 4.060	8.5:1	37 @ 2400
1989-90	5	8-273 (4.5)	DFI	155 @ 4200	240 @ 2800	3.620 × 3.310	9.0:1	37 @ 1500
	C	8-231 (3.8)	SFI	165 @ 5200	210 @ 2000	3.800 × 4.060	8.5:1	37 @ 2400

NOTE: Horsepower and torque are SAE net figures. They are measured at the rear of the transmission with all accessories installed and operating. Since the figures vary when a given engine is installed in different models, some are representative, rather than exact.
PFI Port Fuel Injection
SFI Sequential Fuel Injection
DFI Digital Fuel Injection
MFI Multiport Fuel Injection
NA Not available

GASOLINE ENGINE TUNE-UP SPECIFICATIONS
Refer to Section 34 for all spark plug recommendations

Year	VIN	No. Cylinder Displacement cu. in. (liter)	Spark Plugs Gap (in.)	Ignition Timing (deg.) MT	AT	Compression Pressure (psi)	Fuel Pump (psi)	Idle Speed (rpm) MT	AT	Valve Clearance In.	Ex.
1986	3	6-231 (3.8)	0.045	—	①	100	38	—	500	Hyd.	Hyd.
	8	8-250 (4.1)	0.060	—	10B②	140	9–12	—	①	Hyd.	Hyd.
1987	3	6-231 (3.8)	0.045	—	①	100	38	—	500	Hyd.	Hyd.
	8	8-250 (4.1)	0.060	—	10B②	140	9–12	—	①	Hyd.	Hyd.
	7	8-250 (4.1)	0.060	—	①	140–165	65–95	—	①	Hyd.	Hyd.
1988	C	6-231 (3.8)	0.060	—	①	—	27–36	—	①	Hyd.	Hyd.
	5	8-273 (4.5)	0.060	—	①	140–165	46.5	—	①	Hyd.	Hyd.
	7	8-250 (4.1)	0.060	—	①	140–165	65–95	—	①	Hyd.	Hyd.
1989	C	6-231 (3.8)	0.060	—	①	—	27–36	—	①	Hyd.	Hyd.
	5	8-273 (4.5)	0.060	—	①	140–165	46.5	—	①	Hyd.	Hyd.
1990		SEE UNDERHOOD SPECIFICATIONS STICKER									

NOTE: Check the underhood emission control sticker for correct timing procedure. Some engines require grounding 2 connector or disconnecting a distributor plug to set base timing. Use the sticker specifications if different from above.
B Before Top Dead Center
① Controlled by ECM
② 800 rpm in Park

FIRING ORDERS

NOTE: To avoid confusion, always replace spark plug wires one at a time.

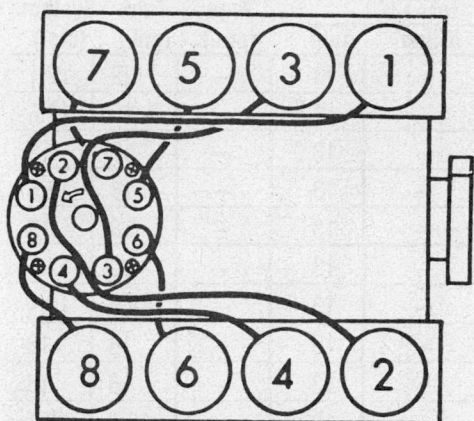

GM 4.1L and 4.5L engines
Engine firing order: 1-8-4-3-6-5-7-2
Distributor rotation: counterclockwise

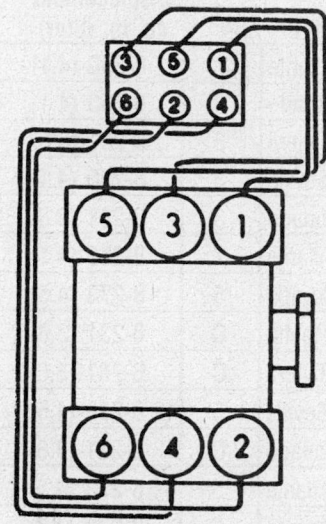

GM Buick 231 (3.8L) V6 Code 3
Firing order with the C³I Ignition System

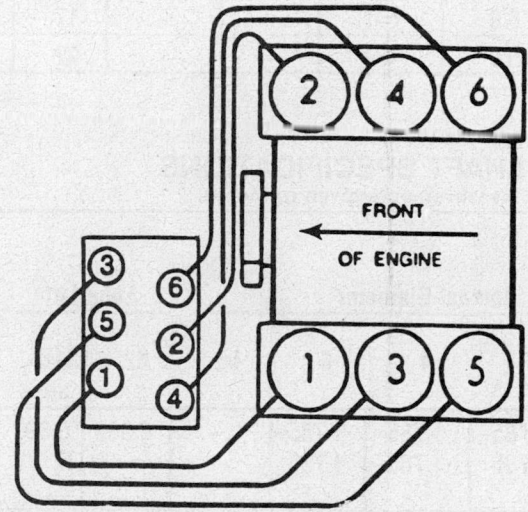

GM Buick 231 (3.8L) Code C
Firing order with the C³I Ignition System

CAPACITIES

Year	Model	VIN	No. Cylinder Displacement cu. in. (liter)	Engine Crankcase with Filter	Engine Crankcase without Filter	Transmission (pts.) 4-Spd	Transmission (pts.) 5-Spd	Transmission (pts.) Auto.	Drive Axle (pts.)	Fuel Tank (gal.)	Cooling System (qts.)
1986	Eldorado	8	8-250 (4.1)	5.0	4.0	—	—	13	—	18	12
	Riviera	3	6-231 (3.8)	4.5	4.0	—	—	13	—	18	12
	Seville	8	8-250 (4.1)	5.5	4.0	—	—	13	—	18	13
	Toronado	3	6-231 (3.8)	4.5	4.0	—	—	13	—	18	12

CAPACITIES

Year	Model	VIN	No. Cylinder Displacement cu. In. (liter)	Engine Crankcase with Filter	Engine Crankcase without Filter	Transmission (pts.) 4-Spd	Transmission (pts.) 5-Spd	Transmission (pts.) Auto.	Drive Axle (pts.)	Fuel Tank (gal.)	Cooling System (qts.)
1987	Allante	7	8-250 (4.1)	6.0	5.0	—	—	13	—	22	12.1
	Eldorado	8	8-250 (4.1)	6.0	5.0	—	—	13	—	18	12.6
	Riviera	3	6-231 (3.8)	5.0	4.0	—	—	13	—	18	13
	Seville	8	8-250 (4.1)	6.0	5.0	—	—	13	—	18	12.6
	Toronado	3	6-231 (3.8)	5.0	4.0	—	—	13	—	18	13
1988	Allante	7	8-250 (4.1)	6.0	5.0	—	—	13	—	22	12.1
	Eldorado	5	8-273 (4.5)	6.0	5.0	—	—	13	—	18.8	12.1
	Reatta	C	8-231 (3.8)	5.0	4.0	—	—	13	—	18	13
	Riviera	C	6-231 (3.8)	5.0	4.0	—	—	13	—	18	13
	Seville	5	8-273 (4.5)	6.0	5.0	—	—	13	—	18.8	12.1
	Toronado	C	6-231 (3.8)	5.0	4.0	—	—	13	—	18	13
1989-90	Allante	5	8-273 (4.5)	6.0	5.0	—	—	17	—	22	12
	Eldorado	5	8-273 (4.5)	6.0	5.0	—	—	17	—	18.8	12
	Reatta	C	8-231 (3.8)	5.0	4.0	—	—	17	—	18.2	10
	Riviera	C	6-231 (3.8)	5.0	4.0	—	—	17	—	18.2	12
	Seville	5	8-273 (4.5)	6.0	5.0	—	—	17	—	18.8	12
	Toronado	C	6-231 (3.8)	5.0	4.0	—	—	22	—	18.8	12

CAMSHAFT SPECIFICATIONS
All measurements given in inches.

Year	VIN	No. Cylinder Displacement cu. In. (li000021	Journal Diameter 2	Journal Diameter 3	Journal Diameter 4	Journal Diameter 5	In.	Lobe Lift Ex.	Lobe Lift Clearance	Bearing End Play	Camshaft
1986	3	6-231 (3.8)	1.785–1.786	1.785–1.786	1.785–1.786	1.785–1.786	—	0.397	0.397	0.0005–0.0035 ①	NA
	8	8-250 (4.1)	NA	NA	NA	NA	NA	0.384	0.396	0.0020–0.0040	NA
1987	3	6-231 (3.8)	1.785–1.786	1.785–1.786	1.785–1.786	1.785–1.786	—	0.245	0.245	0.0005–0.0035 ①	NA
	8	8-250 (4.1)	NA	NA	NA	NA	NA	0.384	0.396	0.0018–0.0037	NA
	7	8-250 (4.1)	NA	NA	NA	NA	NA	0.384	0.396	0.0018–0.0037	NA
1988	C	6-231 (3.8)	1.785–1.786	1.785–1.786	1.785–1.786	1.785–1.786	—	0.253	0.255	0.0005–0.0035	NA
	7	8-250 (4.1)	NA	NA	NA	NA	NA	0.384	0.396	0.0018–0.0037	NA

CAMSHAFT SPECIFICATIONS
All measurements given in inches.

Year	VIN	No. Cylinder Displacement cu. in. (liter)	Journal Diameter 1	2	3	4	5	Lobe Lift In.	Ex.	Bearing Clearance	Camshaft End Play
1988	5	8-273 (4.5)	NA	NA	NA	NA	NA	0.384	0.396	0.0018–0.0037	NA
1989-90	C	6-231 (3.8)	1.785–1.786	1.786–1.786	1.786–1.786	1.786–1.786	—	0.253	0.255	0.0005–0.0035	NA
	5	8-273 (4.5)	NA	NA	NA	NA	NA	0.384	0.396	0.0018–0.0037	NA

NA Not available
① Journal No. 1—0.0005-0.0025 in.

CRANKSHAFT AND CONNECTING ROD SPECIFICATIONS
All measurements are given in inches.

Year	VIN	No. Cylinder Displacement cu. in. (liter)	Crankshaft Main Brg. Journal Dia.	Main Brg. Oil Clearance	Shaft End-play	Thrust on No.	Connecting Rod Journal Diameter	Oil Clearance	Side Clearance
1986	3	6-231 (3.8)	2.4995	0.0003–0.0018	0.003–0.011	2	2.2487–2.2495	0.0009–0.0026	0.003–0.015
	8	8-250 (4.1)	2.6374–2.6384	0.0016–0.0039 ①	0.0010–0.0070	3	1.929	0.0005–0.0028	0.008–0.020
1987	3	6-231 (3.8)	2.4995	0.0003–0.0018	0.003–0.011	2	2.2487–2.2495	0.0003–0.0028	0.003–0.015
	7	8-250 (4.1)	2.6374–2.6384	0.0016–0.0039 ①	0.0010–0.0070	3	1.929	0.0005–0.0028	0.008–0.020
	8	8-250 (4.1)	2.6374–2.6384	0.0016–0.0039 ①	0.0010–0.0070	3	1.929	0.0005–0.0028	0.008–0.020
1988	C	6-231 (3.8)	2.4998–2.4998	0.0003–0.0018	0.003–0.011	2	2.2487–2.2495	0.0003–0.0028	0.003–0.015
	7	8-250 (4.1)	2.6374–2.6384	0.0016–0.0039 ①	0.0010–0.0070	3	1.929	0.0005–0.0028	0.008–0.020
	5	8-273 (4.5)	2.6374–2.6384	0.0016–0.0039 ①	0.0010–0.0070	3	1.929	0.0005–0.0028	0.008–0.020
1989-90	C	6-231 (3.8)	2.4998–2.4998	0.0003–0.0018	0.003–0.011	2	2.2487–2.2495	0.0003–0.0028	0.003–0.015
	5	8-273 (4.5)	2.6374–2.6384	0.0016–0.0039 ①	0.0010–0.0070	3	1.929	0.0005–0.0028	0.008–0.020

① No. 4—0.0008–0.0031

VALVE SPECIFICATIONS

Year	VIN	No. Cylinder Displacement cu. in. (liter)	Seat Angle (deg.)	Face Angle (deg.)	Spring Test Pressure (lbs.)	Spring Installed Height (in.)	Stem-to-Guide Clearance (in.) Intake	Stem-to-Guide Clearance (in.) Exhaust	Stem Diameter (in.) Intake	Stem Diameter (in.) Exhaust
1986	3	6-231 (3.8)	45	45	185 @ 1.34	$1^{25}/_{32}$	0.0015–0.0035	0.0015–0.0032	0.3401–0.3412	0.3405–0.3412
	8	8-250 (4.1)	45	44	182 @ 1.28	$1^{25}/_{32}$	0.0010–0.0030	0.0010–0.0030	0.3420–0.3413	0.3411–0.3418
1987	3	6-231 (3.8)	46	45	90 @ 1.727	$1^{23}/_{32}$	0.0015–0.0035	0.0015–0.0032	0.3401–0.3412	0.3405–0.3412
	7	8-250 (4.1)	45	44	99 @ 1.730	$1^{23}/_{32}$	0.0010–0.0030	0.0010–0.0030	0.3413–0.3420	0.3411–0.3418
	8	8-250 (4.1)	45	44	99 @ 1.730	$1^{23}/_{32}$	0.0010–0.0030	0.0010–0.0030	0.3413–0.3420	0.3411–0.3418
1988	C	6-231 (3.8)	45	45	105 @ 1.730	$1^{23}/_{32}$	0.0015–0.0035	0.0015–0.0032	0.3401–0.3412	0.3405–0.3412
	7	8-250 (4.1)	45	44	99 @ 1.730	$1^{23}/_{32}$	0.0010–0.0030	0.0010–0.0030	0.3413–0.3420	0.3411–0.3418
	5	8-273 (4.5)	45	44	99 @ 1.730	$1^{23}/_{32}$	0.0010–0.0030	0.0010–0.0030	0.3413–0.3420	0.3411–0.3418
1989-90	C	6-231 (3.8)	45	45	105 @ 1.730	$1^{23}/_{32}$	0.0015–0.0035	0.0015–0.0032	0.3401–0.3412	0.3405–0.3412
	5	8-273 (4.5)	45	44	99 @ 1.730	$1^{23}/_{32}$	0.0010–0.0030	0.0010–0.0030	0.3413–0.3420	0.3411–0.3418

PISTON AND RING SPECIFICATIONS
All measurments are given in inches.

Year	VIN	No. Cylinder Displacement cu. in. (liter)	Piston Clearance	Ring Gap Top Compression	Ring Gap Bottom Compression	Ring Gap Oil Control	Ring Side Clearance Top Compression	Ring Side Clearance Bottom Compression	Ring Side Clearance Oil Control
1986	3	6-231 (3.8)	0.0013–0.0035 ④	0.013–0.023	0.013–0.023	0.015–0.035	0.0030–0.0050–	0.0030–0.0050–	0.0035
	8	8-250 (4.1)	0.0010–0.0018 ①	0.015–0.025	0.015–0.025	0.010–0.050	0.0020–0.0040	0.0020–0.0040	None ②
1987	3	6-231 (3.8)	0.0004–0.0022	0.010–0.020	0.010–0.022	0.015–0.055	0.0010–0.0030	0.0010–0.0030	0.0005 0.0065
	7	8-250 (4.1)	0.0010–0.0018	0.015–0.024	0.015–0.024	0.010–0.050	0.0016–0.0037	0.0016–0.0037	None ②
	8	8-250 (4.1)	0.0010–0.0018	0.015–0.024	0.015–0.024	0.010–0.050	0.0016–0.0037	0.0016–0.0037	None ②
1988	C	6-231 (3.8)	⑤	0.010–0.025	0.010–0.025	0.015–0.055	0.0013–0.0031	0.0013–0.0031	0.0011–0.0081

PISTON AND RING SPECIFICATIONS

All measurments are given in inches.

Year	VIN	No. Cylinder Displacement cu. in. (liter)	Piston Clearance	Ring Gap Top Compression	Ring Gap Bottom Compression	Ring Gap Oil Control	Ring Side Clearance Top Compression	Ring Side Clearance Bottom Compression	Ring Side Clearance Oil Control
1988	7	8-250 (4.1)	0.0010–0.0018	0.015–0.024	0.015–0.024	0.010–0.050	0.0016–0.0037	0.0016–0.0037	None ②
	5	8-273 (4.5)	0.0010–0.0018	0.015–0.024	0.015–0.024	0.010–0.050	0.0016–0.0037	0.0016–0.0037	None ②
1989-90	C	6-231 (3.8)	⑤	0.010–0.025	0.010–0.025	0.015–0.055	0.0013–0.0031	0.0013–0.0031	0.0011–0.0081
	5	8-273 (4.5)	0.0010–0.0018	0.015–0.024	0.015–0.024	0.010–0.050	0.0016–0.0037	0.0016–0.0037	None ②

① Measured at top of skirt
② Side sealing
③ Not used
④ Measured at bottom of piston skirt
⑤ Skirt top–0.0007–0.0027
Skirt bottom–0.0010–0.0045

TORQUE SPECIFICATIONS

All readings in ft. lbs.

Year	VIN	No. Cylinder Displacement cu. in. (liter)	Cylinder Head Bolts	Main Bearing Bolts	Rod Bearing Bolts	Crankshaft Pulley Bolts	Flywheel Bolts	Manifold Intake	Manifold Exhaust	Spark Plugs
1986	3	6-231 (3.8)	②	100	40	200	60	32	37	20
	8	8-250 (4.1)	②	85	22	18	37	22	18	11
1987	3	6-231 (3.8)	60②	100	40	219	60	32	37	20
	7	8-250 (4.1)	90②	85	22	18	37	22②	18	11
	8	8-250 (4.1)	90②	85	22	18	37	22②	18	11
1988	C	6-231 (3.8)	60②	100	40	219	60	88①	37	20
	7	8-250 (4.1)	90②	85	22	18	37	22②	18	11
	5	8-273 (4.5)	90②	85	22	18	70	22②	18	11
1989-90	C	6-231 (3.8)	60②	100	40	219	60	88①	37	20
	5	8-273 (4.5)	90②	85	22	18	70	12②	18	11

① Inch lbs.
② See text

WHEEL ALIGNMENT

Year	Model		Caster Range (deg.)	Caster Preferred Setting (deg.)	Camber Range (deg.)	Camber Preferred Setting (deg.)	Toe-in (in.)	Steering Axis Inclination (deg.)
1986	Eldorado	Front	1½P-3½P	2½P	½N-½P	0	⅕P-⅗N	—
		Rear	—	—	—	—	0-⅖①	—
	Riviera	Front	1½P-3½N	2½P	½N-½P	0	⅒P-⅒N	—
		Rear	—	—	—	—	0-⅖①	—

WHEEL ALIGNMENT

Year	Model		Caster Range (deg.)	Caster Preferred Setting (deg.)	Camber Range (deg.)	Camber Preferred Setting (deg.)	Toe-in (in.)	Steering Axis Inclination (deg.)
1986	Seville	Front	$1\frac{1}{2}P$-$3\frac{1}{2}P$	$2\frac{1}{2}P$	$\frac{1}{2}N$-$\frac{1}{2}P$	0	$\frac{1}{5}P$-$\frac{3}{5}N$	—
		Rear	—	—	—	—	0-$\frac{2}{5}$①	—
	Toronado	Front	$1\frac{1}{2}P$-$3\frac{1}{2}P$	$2\frac{1}{2}P$	$\frac{1}{2}N$-$\frac{1}{2}P$	0	$\frac{1}{10}P$-$\frac{1}{10}N$	—
		Rear	—	—	—	—	0-$\frac{2}{5}$①	—
1987	Allante	Front	$2P$-$3P$	$2\frac{1}{2}P$	$\frac{1}{2}N$-$\frac{1}{2}P$	0	$\frac{1}{10}P$-$\frac{1}{10}N$	—
		Rear	—	—	—	—	0-$\frac{1}{5}P$①	—
	Eldorado	Front	$2P$-$3P$	$2\frac{1}{2}P$	$\frac{1}{2}N$-$\frac{1}{2}P$	0	$\frac{1}{10}P$-$\frac{1}{10}N$	—
		Rear	—	—	—	—	0-$\frac{1}{5}P$①	—
	Riviera	Front	$1\frac{3}{10}P$-$3\frac{3}{10}N$	$2\frac{3}{10}P$	$\frac{4}{5}P$-$\frac{4}{5}P$	0	$\frac{1}{10}P$-$\frac{1}{10}N$	—
		Rear	—	—	$1N$-$\frac{2}{5}P$	$\frac{7}{10}N$	0-$\frac{1}{5}N$①	—
	Seville	Front	$2P$-$3P$	$2\frac{1}{2}P$	$\frac{1}{2}N$-$\frac{1}{2}P$	0	$\frac{1}{10}P$-$\frac{1}{10}N$	—
		Rear	—	—	—	—	0-$\frac{1}{5}P$①	—
	Toronado	Front	$1\frac{1}{2}P$-$3\frac{1}{2}N$	$2\frac{1}{2}P$	$\frac{4}{5}N$-$\frac{4}{5}P$	0	$\frac{1}{10}P$-$\frac{1}{10}N$	—
		Rear	—	—	$1N$-$\frac{2}{5}P$	$\frac{7}{10}N$	0-$\frac{1}{5}N$①	—
1988	Allante	Front	$2\frac{3}{10}P$-$3\frac{3}{10}N$	$2\frac{4}{5}P$	$\frac{4}{5}N$-$\frac{4}{5}P$	0	0-$\frac{1}{5}N$	—
		Rear	—	—	—	—	0-$\frac{1}{5}P$①	—
	Eldorado	Front	$1\frac{3}{10}P$-$3\frac{3}{10}N$	$2\frac{3}{10}P$	$\frac{4}{5}N$-$\frac{4}{5}P$	0	$\frac{1}{10}P$-$\frac{1}{10}N$	—
		Rear	—	—	—	—	0-$\frac{1}{5}P$①	—
	Reatta	Front	$1\frac{4}{5}P$-$3\frac{4}{5}P$	$2\frac{4}{5}P$	$\frac{1}{2}N$-$\frac{1}{2}P$	0	$\frac{1}{5}N$-$\frac{1}{5}P$	—
		Rear	—	—	—	—	0-$\frac{1}{5}P$①	—
	Riviera	Front	$1\frac{3}{10}P$-$3\frac{3}{10}N$	$2\frac{3}{10}P$	$\frac{4}{5}N$-$\frac{4}{5}P$	0	$\frac{1}{10}P$-$\frac{1}{10}N$	—
		Rear	—	—	—	—	0-$\frac{1}{5}P$①	—
	Seville	Front	$1\frac{3}{10}P$-$3\frac{3}{10}N$	$2\frac{3}{10}P$	$\frac{4}{5}N$-$\frac{4}{5}P$	0	$\frac{1}{10}P$-$\frac{1}{10}N$	—
		Rear	—	—	—	—	0-$\frac{1}{5}P$①	—
	Toronado	Front	$1\frac{3}{10}P$-$3\frac{3}{10}N$	$2\frac{3}{10}P$	$\frac{4}{5}N$-$\frac{4}{5}P$	0	$\frac{1}{10}P$-$\frac{1}{10}N$	—
		Rear	—	—	—	—	0-$\frac{1}{5}P$①	—
1989-90	Allante	Front	$2\frac{3}{10}P$-$3\frac{3}{10}N$	$2\frac{4}{5}P$	$\frac{4}{5}N$-$\frac{4}{5}P$	0	0-$\frac{1}{5}N$	—
		Rear	—	—	—	—	0-$\frac{1}{5}P$①	—
	Eldorado	Front	$1\frac{3}{10}P$-$3\frac{3}{10}N$	$2\frac{3}{10}P$	$\frac{4}{5}N$-$\frac{4}{5}P$	0	$\frac{1}{10}P$-$\frac{1}{10}N$	—
		Rear	—	—	—	—	0-$\frac{1}{5}P$①	—
	Reatta	Front	$1\frac{4}{5}P$-$3\frac{4}{5}P$	$2\frac{4}{5}P$	$\frac{4}{5}N$-$\frac{4}{5}P$	0	$\frac{1}{5}N$-$\frac{1}{5}P$	—
		Rear	—	—	—	—	0-$\frac{1}{5}P$①	—
	Riviera	Front	$1\frac{3}{10}P$-$3\frac{3}{10}N$	$2\frac{3}{10}P$	$\frac{4}{5}N$-$\frac{4}{5}P$	0	$\frac{1}{10}P$-$\frac{1}{10}N$	—
		Rear	—	—	—	—	0-$\frac{1}{5}P$①	—
	Seville	Front	$1\frac{3}{10}P$-$3\frac{3}{10}N$	$2\frac{3}{10}P$	$\frac{4}{5}N$-$\frac{4}{5}P$	0	$\frac{1}{10}P$-$\frac{1}{10}N$	—
		Rear	—	—	—	—	0-$\frac{1}{5}P$①	—
	Toronado	Front	$1\frac{3}{10}P$-$3\frac{3}{10}N$	$2\frac{3}{10}P$	$\frac{4}{5}N$-$\frac{4}{5}P$	0	$\frac{1}{10}P$-$\frac{1}{10}N$	—
		Rear	—	—	—	—	0-$\frac{1}{5}P$①	—

P Positive
N Negative
① Degrees

ELECTRICAL

NOTE: Disconnecting the negative battery cable on some vehicles may interfere with the functions of the on board computer systems and may require the computer to undergo a relearning process, once the negative battery cable is reconnected.

For testing and overhaul procedures on starters, alternators and voltage regulators, refer to the Unit Repair Section.

Charging System

ALTERNATORS

Removal and Installation

1. Disconnect the negative battery cable.
2. Label and disconnect the electrical connectors from the back of the alternator.
3. Release the tension from the drive belt and remove the belt from the alternator pulley. Do not remove the belt from any other pulleys.
4. Remove the alternator-to-bracket bolts and the alternator from the vehicle.
5. To install, reverse the removal procedures.

NOTE: If equipped with air conditioning, it may be necessary to remove the compressor retaining bracket.

VOLTAGE REGULATOR

Removal and Installation

An alternator with an integral voltage regulator is standard equipment. There are no adjustments possible with this unit.

To replace the voltage regulator, the alternator must be removed and disassembled.

BELT TENSION

NOTE: Most engines are equipped with a serpentine, self adjusting drive belt; no adjustment is necessary.

Adjustment

Using the belt tension gauge tool, adjust the alternator belt if the tension is below 300N, as indicated on the gauge. If the belt is used, the correct belt tension is 600N, as indicated on the gauge. If the belt is new, the correct tension is 900N, as indicated on the gauge.

Starting System

STARTER

Removal and Installation

NOTE: On some engines, it may be necessary to move the fuel lines out of the way. Remove the fuel lines from the retaining clamp and loosen the regulator.

1. Relieve the fuel pressure. Disconnect the negative battery cable.
2. Raise and safely support the vehicle.
3. If equipped with a starter splash shield, remove it.
4. Disconnect and label the wires from the solenoid.
5. Remove the starter-to-engine bolts and the starter.
6. To install, reverse the removal procedures.

NOTE: If starter shims were removed, be sure to replace them in their original location to assure proper drive pinion-to-flywheel engagement.

Ignition System

DISTRIBUTOR

The Electronic Spark Timing (EST) distributor uses no mechanical or vacuum advance and is easily identified by the absence of a vacuum advance and the presence of a four terminal connector.

Another type of ignition system is the Computer Controlled Coil Ignition (C^3I) system. The C^3I system does not use a distributor; instead, it uses a coil pack, an ignition module, a crankshaft sensor and a camshaft sensor. The following procedure is for the HEI distributor.

Removal and Installation

TIMING NOT DISTURBED

1. Disconnect the negative battery cable.
2. Remove the distributor cap and electrical harness connector from the distributor.
3. Using a piece of chalk, matchmark the rotor to the distributor body and the distributor body to the block.
4. Remove the hold-down clamp and lift the distributor from the engine until the rotor stops turning. Mark the position of the rotor again and remove the distributor.

To install:

5. Insert the distributor into the engine, making sure the tip of the rotor is aligned with the alignment marks on the distributor housing and the engine.
6. Make sure the oil pump intermediate driveshaft is properly seated in the oil pump.
7. Install the distributor lock but do not tighten.
8. Reconnect the electrical harness connector(s) to the distributor, then, install distributor cap.
9. Start the engine and allow it to reach normal operating temperatures. Check and/or adjust the timing.

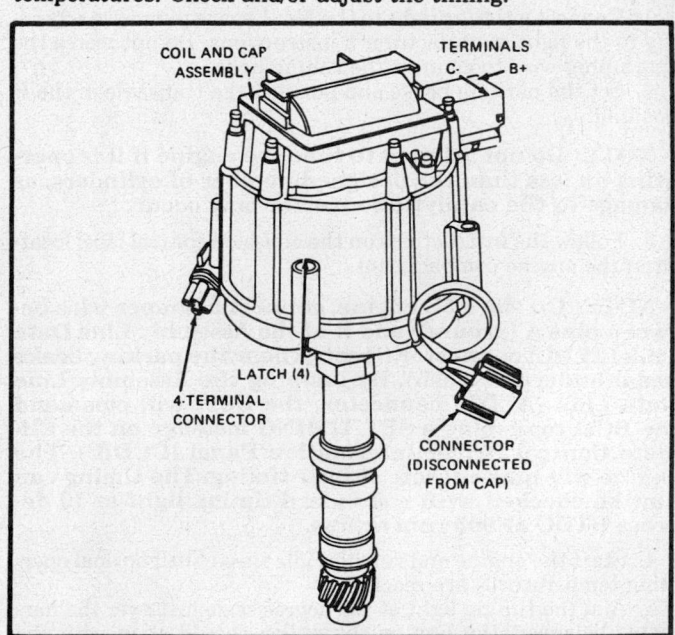

View of a typical EST distributor—V6

TIMING DISTURBED

1. Disconnect the negative battery cable.
2. Remove the distributor cap and the electrical harness connector from the distributor.
3. Using a piece of chalk, matchmark the rotor to the distributor body and the distributor body to the block.
4. Remove the hold-down clamp and lift the distributor from the engine until the rotor stops turning. Mark the position of the rotor again and remove the distributor.

To install:

5. Remove the No. 1 spark plug and place a finger over the hole. Using a wrench on the crankshaft pulley bolt, slowly turn the engine until compression is felt.
6. Align the timing marks so the No. 1 cylinder is on TDC of the compression stroke.
7. Position the distributor in the engine with the rotor at No. 1 firing position. Make sure the oil pump intermediate driveshaft is properly seated in the oil pump.
8. Install the distributor retainer and lock bolt, tighten the lock bolt.
9. Reconnect the electrical harness connector(s) to the distributor and install distributor cap.
10. Start the engine and allow it to reach normal operating temperatures. Check and/or adjust the timing.

IGNITION TIMING

Adjustment

NOTE: Always consult the underhood sticker before adjusting timing. If the underhood sticker differs from the following procedures, follow the sticker.

3.8L ENGINE

The 3.8L (Code 3 and C) engines are equipped with a C³I ignition system which do not incorporate a distributor. There is no initial timing except replacement of sensors.

4.1L AND 4.5L ENGINES

NOTE: The engine incorporates a magnetic timing probe hole for use with special electronic timing equipment. The following procedure is for use with the HEI—EST distributor.

1. Connect a timing light to the No. 1 spark plug wire according to the light manufacturer's instructions. Do not pierce the spark plug wire to connect the timing light.
2. Set the parking brake and position the transaxle in the **P** position.

NOTE: Do not attempt to time the engine if it is operating on less than the designed number of cylinders, as damage to the catalytic converter may occur.

3. Follow the instructions on the emission control label located in the engine compartment.

NOTE: On the 4.5L engine, connect a jumper wire between pins A (ground) and B of the Assembly Line Data Link (ALDL) connector (located near the parking brake pedal under the dash). By jumping the Assembly Line Data Link (ALDL) connector, the ECM will command the BCM to display a SET TIMING message on the Climate Control Driver Information Panel (CCDIC). The engine will now operate at base timing. The timing can now be checked with a standard timing light at 10 degrees BTDC at 900 rpm or less.

4. Start the engine and run it at idle speed until normal operating temperatures are reached.
5. Aim the timing light at the degree scale just over the harmonic balancer; the line on the pulley should align with the mark on the timing plate.

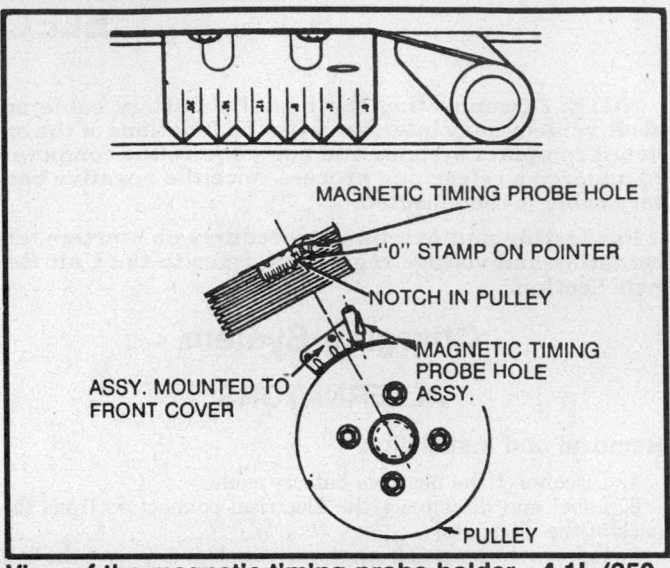

View of the magnetic timing probe holder—4.1L (250 cu. in.) and 4.5L (273 cu. in.) V8 engines

6. If necessary to adjust the timing, use the distributor wrench tool, to loosen the hold-down clamp, then, rotate the distributor until the desired ignition advance is achieved. When the correct timing is set, torque the hold-down clamp nut/bolt to 20 ft. lbs.

NOTE: To advance the timing, rotate the distributor opposite the normal direction of rotor rotation. Retard the timing by rotating the distributor in the normal direction of rotor rotation.

Electrical Controls

STEERING WHEEL

Removal and Installation

ALLANTE, ELDORADO AND SEVILLE

1. Disconnect the negative battery cable.
2. For the Allante, pry the horn trim pad from the steering wheel. For the Eldorado and Seville, remove the steering wheel-to-horn pad screws (located behind the steering wheel) and the horn trim pad. Remove the horn contact wire, ground connector and cruise control wiring connector.
3. Remove the telescope locking lever assembly-to-adjuster screws. Unscrew and remove the telescoping adjuster from the steering shaft.
4. Remove the telescoping lever assembly. Scribe an alignment mark on the steering wheel hub-in-line with the slash mark on the steering shaft.
5. Remove the steering wheel-to-steering shaft locknut. Using the steering wheel puller, press the steering wheel from the steering shaft.

NOTE: When removing the steering wheel, be sure to remove the cruise control wire from it.

To install:

6. Feed the cruise control wire through the steering wheel, align the matchmark and reverse the removal procedures. Torque the steering wheel-to-steering shaft to 35 ft. lbs.

NOTE: For ease of installation, fully extend the steering shaft and install the lock plate compressor screw

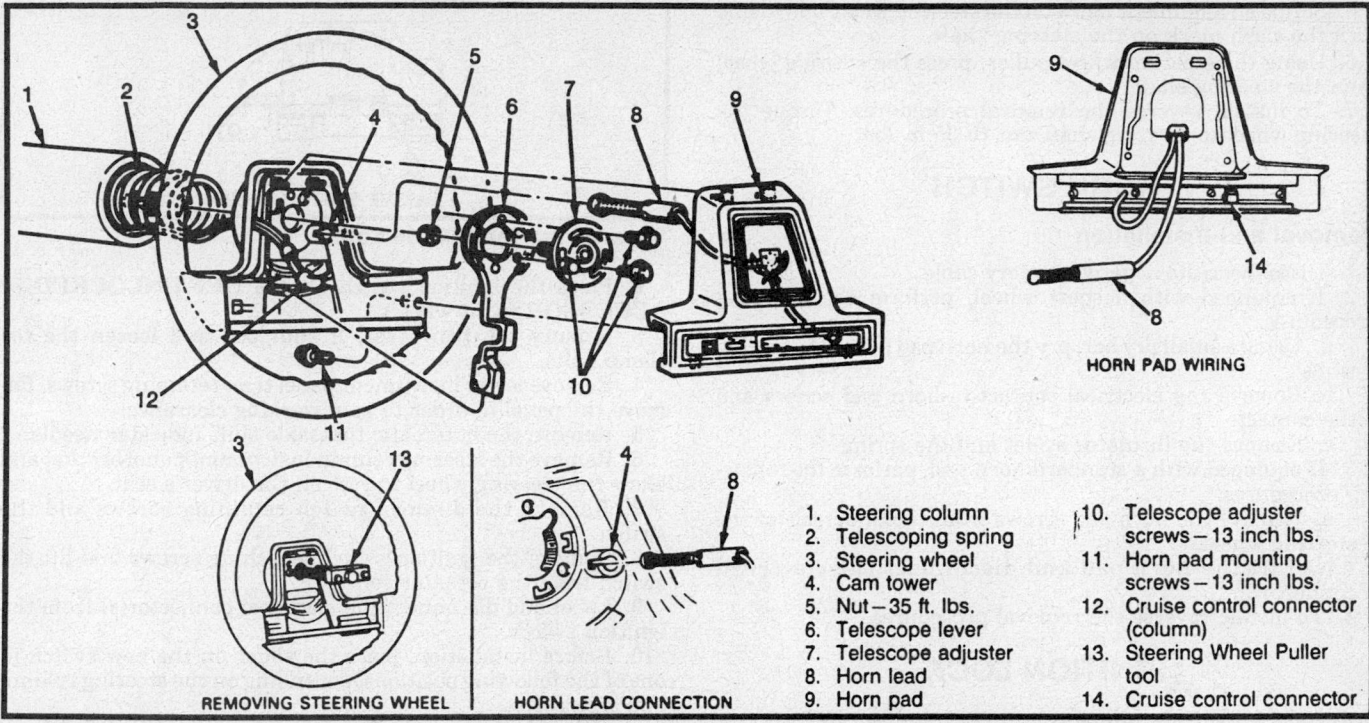

1. Steering column	10. Telescope adjuster screws—13 inch lbs.
2. Telescoping spring	11. Horn pad mounting screws—13 inch lbs.
3. Steering wheel	12. Cruise control connector (column)
4. Cam tower	13. Steering Wheel Puller tool
5. Nut—35 ft. lbs.	14. Cruise control connector
6. Telescope lever	
7. Telescope adjuster	
8. Horn lead	
9. Horn pad	

Exploded view of the steering wheel assembly—Eldorado and Seville—Allante is similar

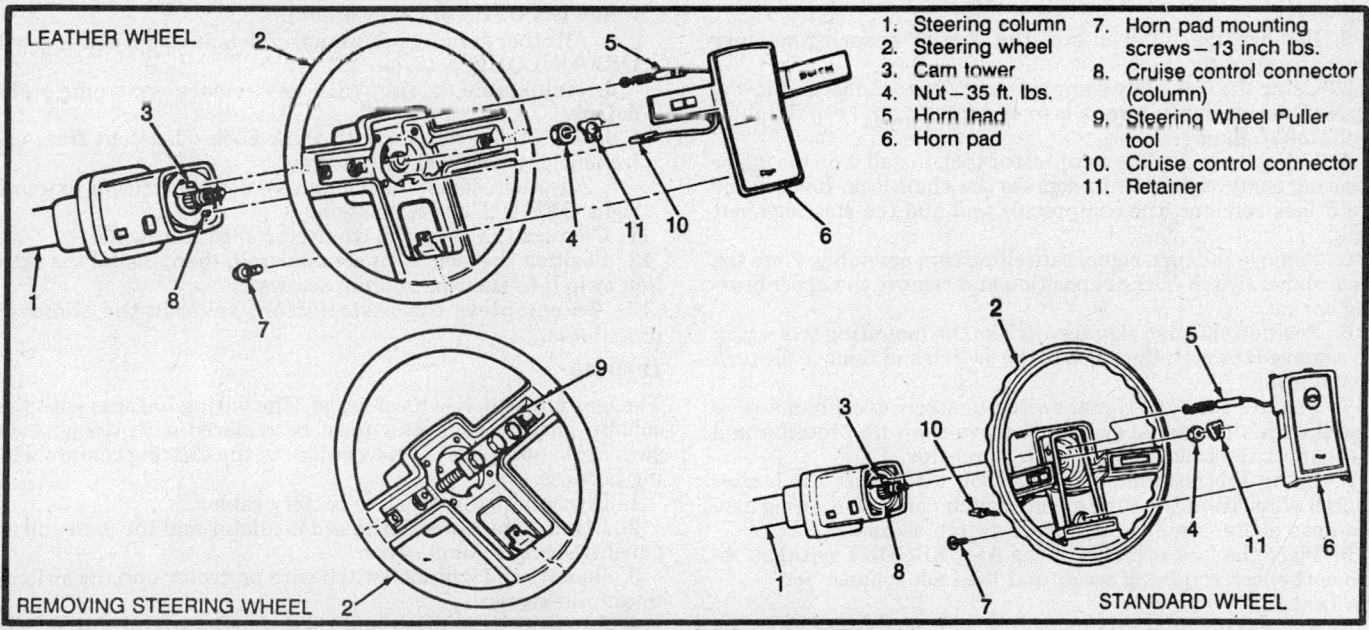

1. Steering column	7. Horn pad mounting screws—13 inch lbs.
2. Steering wheel	8. Cruise control connector (column)
3. Cam tower	9. Steering Wheel Puller tool
4. Nut—35 ft. lbs.	10. Cruise control connector
5. Horn lead	11. Retainer
6. Horn pad	

Exploded view of the steering wheel assembly—Reatta, Riviera and Toronado

tool, hand tight; this will keep the shaft extended when installing the steering wheel. Feed the cruise control wire through the wheel.

7. Remove the tool and place the telescoping lever in the 5 O'clock position.

8. Thread the telescope adjuster assembly finger tight onto the shaft. Install the screws into the telescoping adjuster lever.

9. Move the adjuster lever all the way to the right. The steering wheel should move freely in and out. Move the adjuster lever to the left. The steering wheel should be locked in place with the telescope lever approximately ¼ in. from the left side of the

shroud opening. The lever must not contact the shroud in the full locked position. Loosen and adjust the lever as required.

REATTA, RIVIERA AND TORONADO

1. Disconnect the negative battery cable.

2. Remove the steering wheel-to-horn pad screws (located behind the steering wheel) and lift the pad from the steering wheel.

3. If the steering wheel is equipped with control buttons, disconnect the electrical connector(s).

4. Remove the steering wheel-to-shaft retainer, if equipped and nut.

5. Scribe an alignment mark on the steering wheel hub in line with the slash mark on the steering shaft.

6. Using the steering wheel puller, press the steering wheel from the steering shaft.

7. To install, reverse the removal procedures. Torque the steering wheel-to-steering shaft nut to 35 ft. lbs.

HORN SWITCH

Removal and Installation

1. Disconnect the negative battery cable.

2. If equipped with a sport wheel, perform the following procedures:

    a. Using a small pry bar, pry the horn pad from the steering wheel.

    b. Remove the electrical contact-to-horn pad screws and the contact.

    c. Remove the insulator eyelet and the spring.

3. If equipped with a standard horn pad, perform the following procedures:

    a. Remove the horn pad screws from the underside of the steering wheel.

    b. Lift the horn pad and disconnect the electrical connector.

4. To install, reverse the removal procedures.

IGNITION LOCK

Removal and Installation

1. Disconnect the negative battery cable. Remove the steering wheel.

2. Remove the bumper and the carrier snapring retainer from the steering shaft.

3. Using the lock plate compressor screw tool, install it in the upper steering shaft, torque it to 40 inch lbs., to keep the shaft from telescoping.

4. Using the lock plate compressor tool, install it on the upper steering shaft, tighten it to depress the shaft lock. Remove the shaft lock retainer, the compressor tool and the steering shaft lock.

5. Remove the turn signal cancelling cam assembly. Place the turn signal switch in the N position and remove the upper bearing spring.

6. Position the turn signal switch so the mounting screws can be removed through the holes in the switch and remove the turn signal lever.

7. Remove the turn signal switch-to-steering column screws and lift the turn signal switch. Remove the wire protector and disconnect the turn signal switch connector.

8. Using the terminal remover tool, disconnect the buzzer switch wires from the turn signal switch connector. Using needle-nose pliers, remove the buzzer switch assembly.

9. Place the lock cylinder in the ACCESSORY position, remove the lock retaining screw and the lock cylinder set.

To install:

10. Reverse the removal procedures. Torque the lock retaining screw to 22 inch lbs., the turn signal switch screws to 59 inch lbs. and the turn signal lever screw to 53 inch lbs.

11. Check the operation of the switches and the steering column.

IGNITION SWITCH

The ignition switch is located on the upper side of the lower steering column.

Removal and Installation

1986–88

1. Disconnect the negative battery cable.

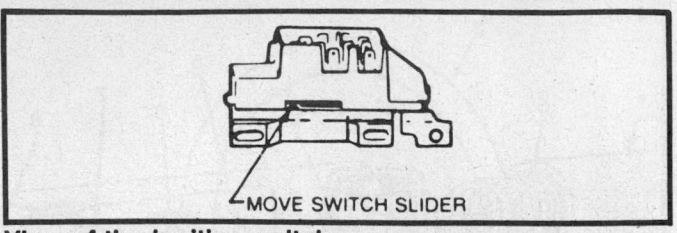

MOVE SWITCH SLIDER

View of the ignition switch

2. Place the ignition switch on the **OFF/UNLOCKED** or **ACCESSORY** (tilt wheel).

3. Remove top pan cover, if equipped and loosen the toe clamp bolts.

4. Remove lower instrument panel trim retaining screws. Remove the panel in order to gain working clearance.

5. Remove the automatic transaxle shift indicator needle.

6. Remove the steering column instrument panel bracket and allow the steering wheel to rest on the driver's seat.

7. Remove the dimmer switch retaining screws and the switch.

8. Remove the ignition switch attaching screws and lift the switch from the actuator rod.

9. Label and disconnect the electrical connector(s) from the ignition switch.

10. Before installation, place the slider on the new switch in one of the following positions, depending on the steering column and accessories:

    a. Standard column with key release—extreme left detent.

    b. Standard column with Park Lock—1 detent from extreme left **OFF/LOCK** position.

    c. All other standard columns—2 detents from extreme left **OFF/UNLOCK** position.

    d. Adjustable column with key release—extreme right detent.

    e. Adjustable column with Park Lock—1 detent from extreme right **OFF/LOCK** position.

    f. All other adjustable columns—2 detents from extreme right **OFF/UNLOCK** position.

11. Connect the electrical connector(s) to the switch.

12. Position the switch on actuator rod, then, install the ignition switch-to-steering column screws.

13. To complete the installation, reverse the removal procedures.

1989–90

The ignition switch is hard-wired. The wiring harness with the column harness connector must be replaced with the ignition switch. Do not splice the new switch to the existing column wiring harness.

1. Disconnect the negative battery cable.

2. Remove the lower left sound insulator and the instrument panel steering column cover.

3. Remove the ignition switch wire protector and the switch-to-column screws.

4. Remove the ignition and turn signal switch column harness connectors from the dash connector.

5. Disconnect the turn signal harness connector from the column harness connector.

6. Remove the ignition switch assembly with the switch, harness and connector.

7. To install, reverse the removal procedures.

NEUTRAL SAFETY/BACK-UP LIGHT SWITCH

Removal and Installation

All neutral safety/back-up light switches come with a small plastic alignment pin installed. Leave this pin in place.

1. Place the shifter assembly in the N position.

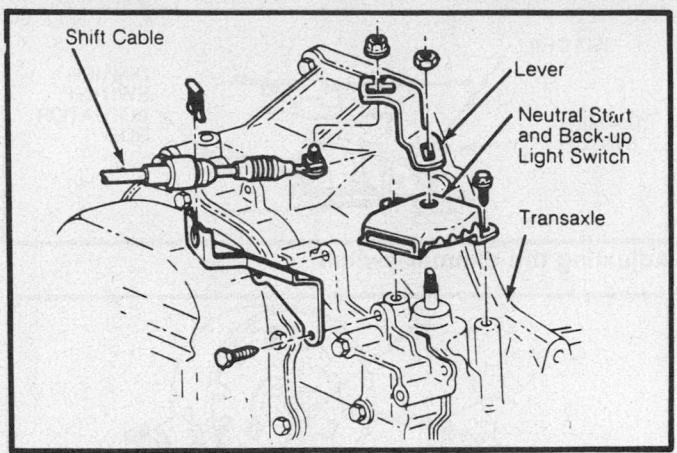

View of the neutral safety/back-up switch

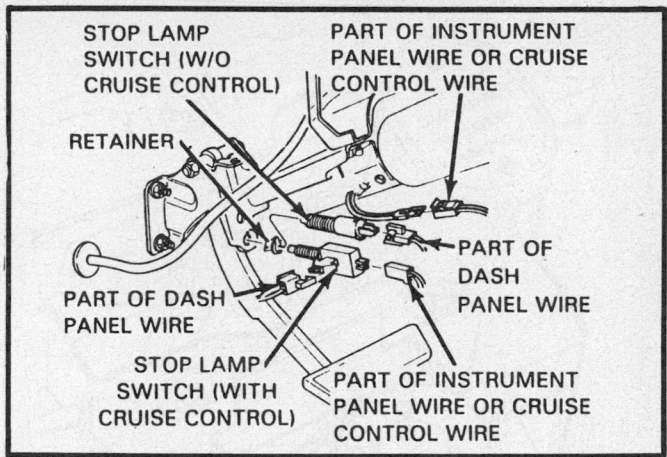

View of the stoplight switch

2. Remove the shifter lever-to-switch nut and the lever.
3. Disconnect the electrical connector from the neutral safety/back-up light switch.
4. Remove the neutral safety/back-up light switch-to-transaxle bolts and the switch from the vehicle.
To install:
5. Position the shifter shaft in the **N** position.

NOTE: If using an old switch or the plastic pin (new switch) is broken, install a ³⁄₃₂ in. pin gauge (drill bit) into the neutral safety/back-up light switch; the switch is locked into its neutral position.

6. Align the flats of the shifter shaft and the neutral safety/back-up light, then, align the switch-to-tang on the transaxle. Torque the switch-to-transaxle bolts to 22 ft. lbs. Remove the pin gauge.
7. To complete installation, reverse the removal procedures. Make sure the engine starts only in the **P** and **N** positions.

STOPLIGHT SWITCH

NOTE: When the brake pedal is in the fully released position, the stoplight switch plunger should be fully depressed against the pedal arm. The switch is adjusted by moving it in or out.

Adjustment

1. Remove the stoplight switch from the brake pedal bracket.
2. Insert the switch into the retainer until the switch body seats on the tube clip.
3. Pull the brake pedal rearward against the internal pedal stop.

NOTE: The switch will be moved in the retainer resulting in proper adjustment.

4. When no further adjustment clicks are heard and the stop lights remain **OFF**, the stop light switch will be properly seated.

Removal and Installation

1. Disconnect the negative battery cable. Remove the underdash hush panel, if equipped.
2. Locate the stoplight switch on the brake pedal bracket.
3. Remove the tubular retaining clip.
4. Remove the stoplight switch electrical connectors.
5. Remove the switch assembly from the vehicle.
6. To install, reverse the removal procedures and perform the adjustment procedures.

HEADLAMP SWITCH

Removal and Installation

1986–88

The headlamp switch is located on a switch pod, located on the left side of the instrument panel.
1. Disconnect the negative battery cable. Remove the instrument panel trim plate.
2. Remove the switch pod screws and pull the switch outward. Disconnect the electrical connectors and remove the switch from the vehicle.
3. To install, reverse the removal procedures. Check the operation of the switch.

1989–90

The headlight switch is located on the left side of the instrument panel.
1. Remove the left trim plate screws and the trim plate, if equipped.
2. Remove the left air vent, if equipped.
3. Remove the headlamp switch screws, pull the switch forward and disconnect the electrical connectors or the fiber optic lead, if equipped.
4. Remove the headlamp switch.
5. To install, reverse the removal procedures.

CONCEALED HEADLAMPS

Manual Operation

REATTA

Each headlamp is equipped with a door actuator. In the event of an actuator failure, the actuator can be manually operated to open the door.
1. Raise the hood.
2. At the headlamp actuator, remove the protective cap.
3. Rotate the actuator knob to manually raise the headlamp door.

TORONADO

The manual headlamp opener is located near the center of the radiator support between the radiator and the grille, in front of the hood latch assembly.
1. From the relay center in the engine compartment, remove the No. 2 fuse.
2. Raise the hood. Remove the manual headlamp knob's protective cover.
3. Rotate the knob clockwise until the headlamp doors open.

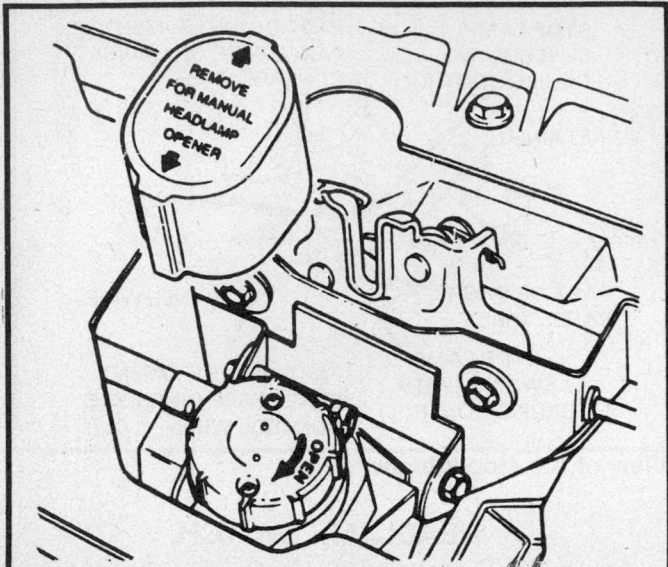

Removing the protective cap from the manual head-light opener—Toronado 1986-88

4. To manually close the headlamp doors, rotate the knob counterclockwise and reverse the removal procedures.

DIMMER SWITCH

The dimmer switch is attached to the lower steering column jacket. It is activated by a rod attached to the turn signal lever.

Removal and Installation

1. Disconnect the negative battery cable.
2. If necessary, remove the lower steering column trim cover.
3. Disconnect the electrical connector from the dimmer switch.
4. Remove the dimmer switch-to-steering column screws and the dimmer switch.
5. To install, position the actuator rod into the dimmer switch hole and reverse the removal procedures. Adjust the dimmer switch by depressing the switch slightly and inserting a $^3/_{32}$ in. drill bit into the adjusting hole. Push the switch up to remove any play and tighten the dimmer switch adjusting screw.

COMBINATION SWITCH

The combination switch is a multi-function switch which consists of the turn signal, headlamp beam, cruise control, windshield washer and wiper switches.

Removal and Installation

1. Disconnect the negative battery cable. Remove the steering wheel.
2. Remove the bumper and the carrier snaping retainer from the steering shaft.
3. Using the lock plate compressor screw tool, install it in the upper steering shaft, torque it to 40 inch lbs., to keep the shaft from telescoping.
4. Using the lock plate compressor tool, install it on the upper steering shaft, tighten it to depress the shaft lock. Remove the shaft lock retainer, the compressor tool and the steering shaft lock.
5. Remove the turn signal cancelling cam assembly. Place the turn signal switch in the **N** position and remove the upper bearing spring.

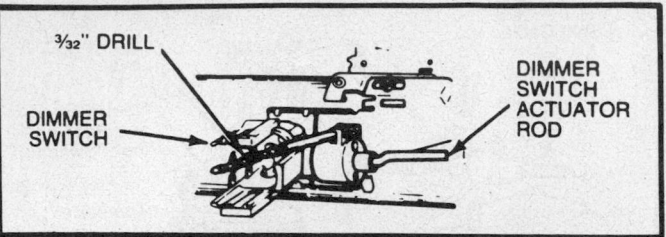

Adjusting the dimmer switch

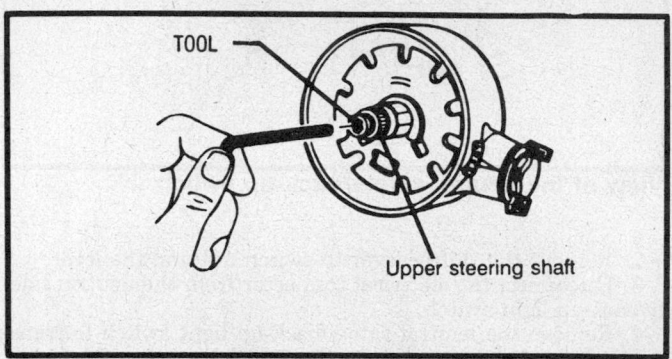

Installing the lock plate compressor screw

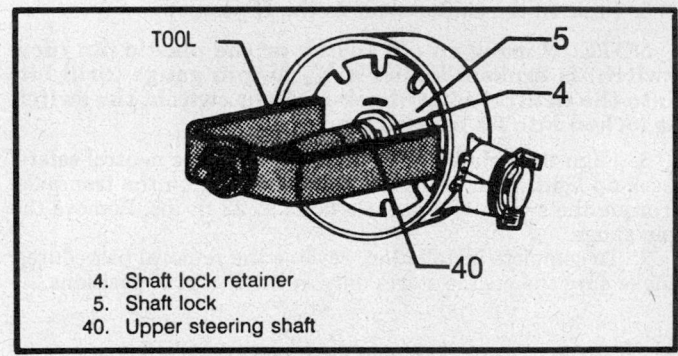

4. Shaft lock retainer
5. Shaft lock
40. Upper steering shaft

Compressing the shaft lock

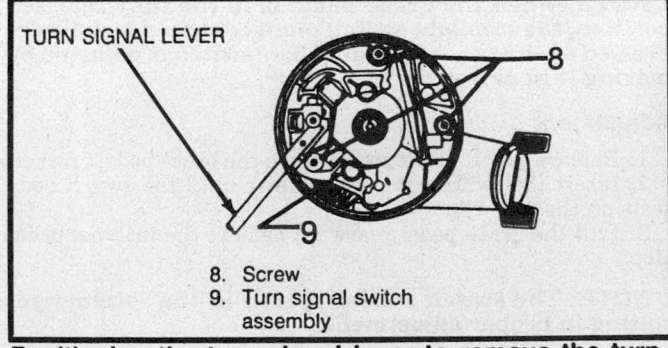

8. Screw
9. Turn signal switch assembly

Positioning the turn signal lever to remove the turn signal switch screws

6. Position the turn signal switch so the mounting screws can be removed through the holes in the switch and remove the turn signal lever.
7. Remove the turn signal switch-to-steering column screws and lift the turn signal switch. Remove the wire protector and disconnect the turn signal switch connector.
8. Using the terminal remover tool, disconnect the buzzer switch wires from the turn signal switch connector. Using needle-nose pliers, remove the buzzer switch assembly.

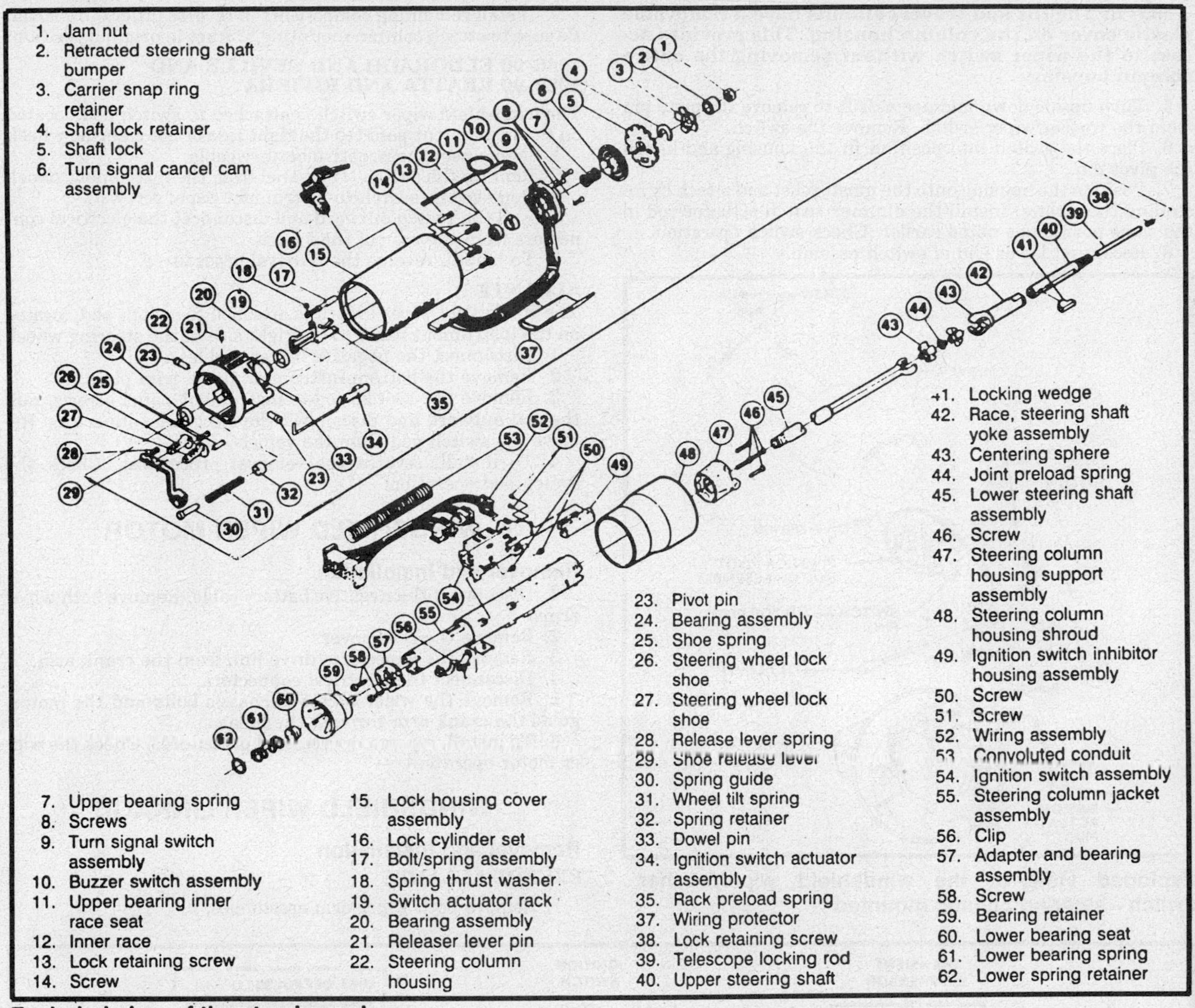

1. Jam nut
2. Retracted steering shaft bumper
3. Carrier snap ring retainer
4. Shaft lock retainer
5. Shaft lock
6. Turn signal cancel cam assembly
7. Upper bearing spring
8. Screws
9. Turn signal switch assembly
10. Buzzer switch assembly
11. Upper bearing inner race seat
12. Inner race
13. Lock retaining screw
14. Screw
15. Lock housing cover assembly
16. Lock cylinder set
17. Bolt/spring assembly
18. Spring thrust washer
19. Switch actuator rack
20. Bearing assembly
21. Releaser lever pin
22. Steering column housing
23. Pivot pin
24. Bearing assembly
25. Shoe spring
26. Steering wheel lock shoe
27. Steering wheel lock shoe
28. Release lever spring
29. Shoe release lever
30. Spring guide
31. Wheel tilt spring
32. Spring retainer
33. Dowel pin
34. Ignition switch actuator assembly
35. Rack preload spring
37. Wiring protector
38. Lock retaining screw
39. Telescope locking rod
40. Upper steering shaft
41. Locking wedge
42. Race, steering shaft yoke assembly
43. Centering sphere
44. Joint preload spring
45. Lower steering shaft assembly
46. Screw
47. Steering column housing support assembly
48. Steering column housing shroud
49. Ignition switch inhibitor housing assembly
50. Screw
51. Screw
52. Wiring assembly
53. Convoluted conduit
54. Ignition switch assembly
55. Steering column jacket assembly
56. Clip
57. Adapter and bearing assembly
58. Screw
59. Bearing retainer
60. Lower bearing seat
61. Lower bearing spring
62. Lower spring retainer

Exploded view of the steering column

TAN/BLACK
(LOCATION 10)
TAB
LIGHT GREEN
(LOCATION 9)
TURN SIGNAL
SWITCH CONNECTOR

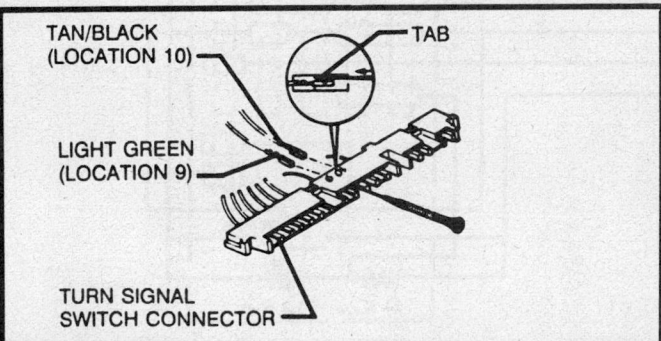

Separating the buzzer switch wires from the turn signal electrical connector.

9. Place the lock cylinder in the **ACCESSORY** position, remove the lock retaining screw and the lock cylinder set.

10. Lifting the turn signal switch assembly, gently pull the wires through the steering column shroud.

11. To install, reverse the removal procedures. Torque the:
Lock retaining screw to 22 inch lbs.
Turn signal switch screws to 59 inch lbs.
Turn signal lever screw to 53 inch lbs.

WINDSHIELD WIPER SWITCH

Removal and Installation

1986–87 RIVIERA AND 1986–90 TORONADO

1. Disconnect the negative battery cable. Remove the steering wheel.

2. It may be necessary to loosen both column mounting nuts and remove the bracket-to-mast jacket screws. Separate the bracket from the mast jacket to allow the connector clip on the ignition switch to be pulled out of the column assembly.

3. Disconnect the washer/wiper switch lower connector.

4. Remove the screws attaching the column housing to the mast jacket. Be sure to note the position of the dimmer switch actuator rod for reassembly in the same position. Remove the column housing and switch as an assembly.

NOTE: The tilt and travel columns have a removable plastic cover on the column housing. This provides access to the wiper switch without removing the entire column housing.

5. Turn upside down and use a drift to remove the pivot pin from the washer/wiper switch. Remove the switch.

6. Place the switch into position in the housing and install the pivot pin.

7. Position the housing onto the mast jacket and attach by installing the screws. Install the dimmer switch actuator rod in the same position as noted earlier. Check switch operation.

8. Reconnect lower end of switch assembly.

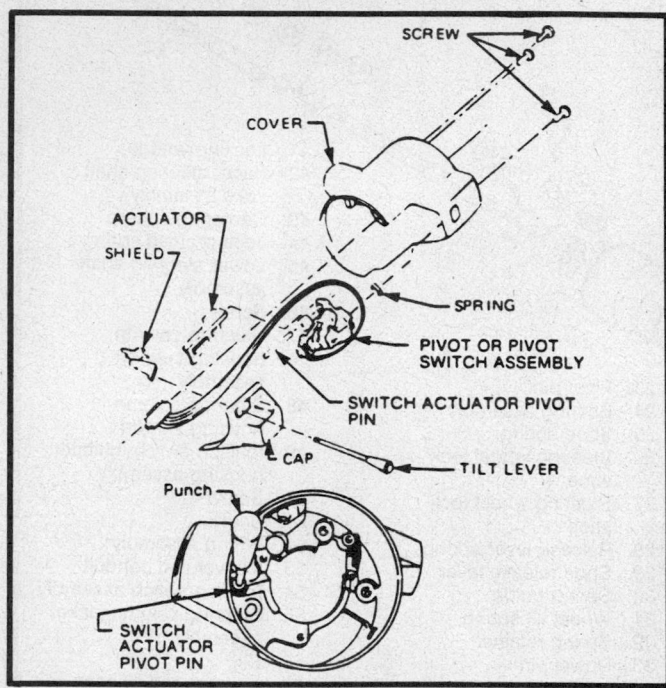

Exploded view of the windshield wiper/washer switch—steering column mounted

9. Install remaining components in reverse order of removal. Be sure to attach column mounting bracket in original position.

1986–90 ELDORADO AND SEVILLE AND 1988–90 REATTA AND RIVIERA

The windshield wiper switch is attached to switch pod, located on the instrument panel to the right side of the steering wheel.

1. Disconnect the negative battery cable.
2. Remove the switch trim panel from the instrument panel.
3. Remove the switch-to-instrument panel screws.
4. Pull the switch outward and disconnect the electrical connectors from the rear of the switch.
5. To install, reverse the removal procedures.

ALLANTE

The windshield wiper switch is attached to switch pod, located on the instrument panel to the right side of the steering wheel.

1. Disconnect the negative battery cable.
2. Remove the bottom instrument panel trim plate.
3. Remove the switch pod-to-instrument panel screws, pull the pod outward and disconnect the electrical connectors. Remove the switch pod from the vehicle.
4. To install, reverse the removal procedures. Check the switch pod operation.

WINDSHIELD WIPER MOTOR

Removal and Installation

1. Disconnect the negative battery cable. Remove both wiper arms.
2. Remove the cowl cover.
3. Remove the wiper arm drive link from the crank arm.
4. Disconnect the electrical connectors.
5. Remove the wiper motor-to-chassis bolts and the motor; guide the crank arm through the hole.
6. To install, reverse the removal procedures. Check the wiper motor operation.

WINDSHIELD WIPER LINKAGE

Removal and Installation
EXCEPT ALLANTE

1. Remove both wiper arm assemblies.

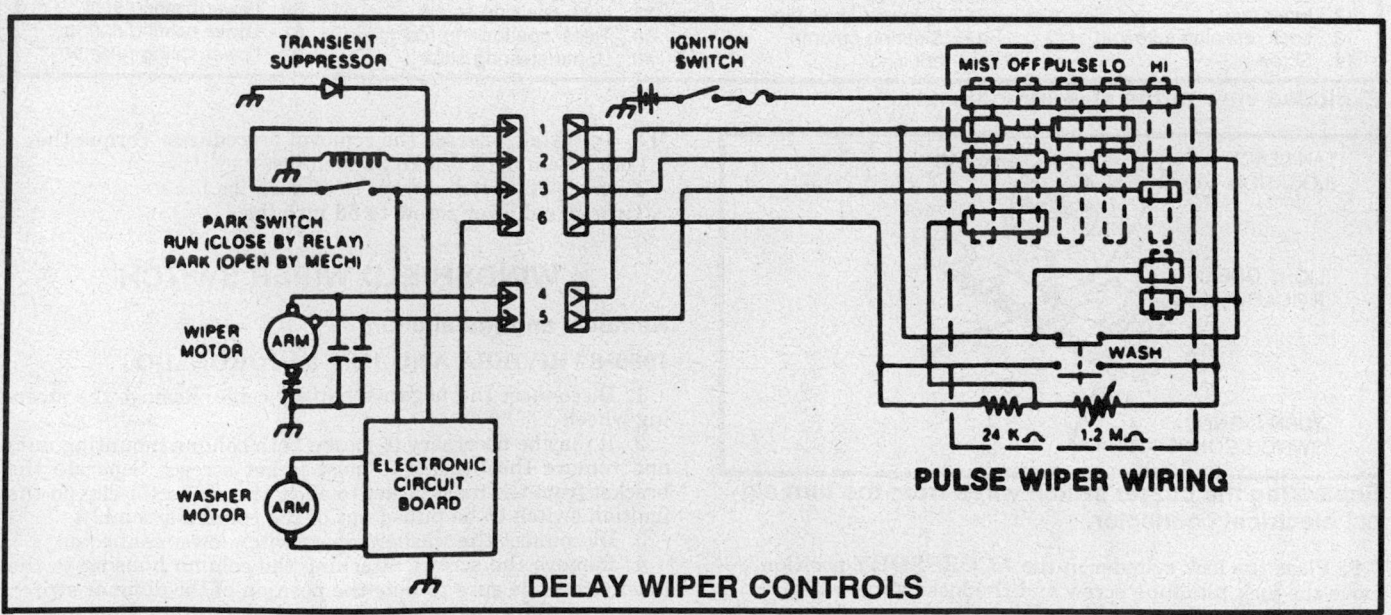

DELAY WIPER CONTROLS

PULSE WIPER WIRING

Schematic of the delay wiper system

NOTE: On some models, it may be necessary to remove the front cowl panel(s) and screen.

2. Remove the motor crank arm-to-transmission drive link nut and the transmission drive link.

3. Remove the transmission-to-cowl screws.

NOTE: If necessary, drill out the motor support bracket spot welds. Bend the bracket in order to gain working clearance.

4. Remove the linkage and transmission assembly by sliding it through the plenum chamber opening or under the left side dash panel extension.

5. To install, reverse the removal procedures. Torque the transmission drive link-to-motor crank arm to 6 ft. lbs. Adjust the wiper arm/blade assembly.

ALLANTE

1. Raise the hood. Raise the both wiper arms from the glass, move the locking latch outward and remove the wiper arm.

2. Remove the lower windshield reveal molding and the cowl vent screen.

3. Using a small pry bar, place it between the drive link and the crank arm and pry (twist) the drive link from the crank arm.

4. From the left side, remove the transmission-to-body screws.

5. From the right side, remove the support-to-body screws.

6. Guide the transmission/linkage assembly through the plenum chamber opening.

7. To install, reverse the removal procedures. Adjust the wiper arm/blade assembly. Check the operation of the wiper assembly.

Instrument Cluster

Refer to "Chilton's Electronic Instrumentation Service Manual" for additional coverage.

Removal and Installation

ALLANTE

1. Disconnect the negative battery cable.

2. Remove the left and right switch pod trim plates.

3. Remove the cluster trim plate.

4. Remove the cluster assembly-to-dash screws, pull the cluster forward and disconnect the electrical connectors.

5. Remove the clutser assembly from the vehicle.

6. To install, reverse the removal procedures.

REATTA AND RIVIERA WITH DIGITAL CLUSTER

1. Disconnect the negative battery cable.

2. Remove the center, left and right trim covers.

3. Remove the instrument cluster-to-dash screws, then, pull the cluster straight out of the housing.

4. To install, reverse of removal procedures.

SEVILLE AND ELDORADO

1. Disconnect the negative battery cable. Remove the screws located along the top and remove the instrument panel trim plate.

2. Remove the mounting screws and the filter lens.

3. Remove the warning light lens screws and the lens. Remove the trip odometer reset button.

4. Remove the instrument panel cluster screws. Pull the cluster off the electrical connections and remove it. Using a pair of pliers, hold the retaining tabs at either end of the cluster board and remove the board.

5. To install the cluster, align it with the electrical connectors, push it into the instrument panel and reverse the removal procedures.

TORONADO

1. Disconnect the negative battery cable.

2. Remove the steering column trim cover. Lower the steering column.

3. Remove the instrument panel trim plate.

4. Remove the cluster-to-instrument panel screws.

5. Pull the cluster rearward and remove it.

6. To install, reverse the removal procedures.

SPEEDOMETER

Removal and Installation

The vehicles are equipped with a digital instrument cluster. All instruments are serviced by replacing the cluster.

Electrical Circuit Protectors

FUSIBLE LINKS

The fusible links are located near the starter solenoid, they are attached to the lower ends of the main supply wires. The fusible links serve as additional circuit protection in the event of an electrical overload. In order to gain access to the fusible links, it may be necessary to raise the vehicle first.

CIRCUIT BREAKERS

A circuit breaker is an electrical switch which breaks the circuit during an electrical overload. The circuit breaker will remain open until the short or overload condition in the circuit is corrected.

The circuit breakers are located on the left side of the vehicle. They are under the instrument panel. In order to gain access to the circuit breakers, it may be first necessary to remove the under dash padding.

FUSE PANELS

EXCEPT ALLANTE

The fuse panel is located on the right underside of the instrument panel, usually near the glove box. There is usually another panel at the front of the vehicle, under the hood.

ALLANTE

The fuse panel is located in the center of the console, concealed by the ashtry.

COMPUTERS

ELECTRONIC CONTROL MODULE

The Electronic Control Module (ECM) is located on the right side of the vehicle and is positioned behind the kick panel. In order to gain access to the electronic control module, it will first be necessary to remove the control panel.

1987–90 BODY CONTROL MODULE

The Body Control Module (BCM) is located behind the center of the instrument panel. On the Eldorado, Seville and Toronado, it is located behind the center of the instrument panel; in order to gain access to the body control module, it is necessary to remove the instrument panel compartment. On the Reatta/Riviera, it is located behind the glove box. On the Allante, it is located behind the instrument pod at the right side of the instrument panel.

1987–90 CENTRAL POWER SUPPLY

The central power supply provides operating power to the electronic system and is attached to the brake pedal support, located under the dash near the steering wheel.

CONVENIENCE CENTER AND VARIOUS RELAYS

1986

The convenience center is located on the underside of the instrument panel near the fuse block. It provides a central location for various relays, hazard flasher units and warning chimes. All units are replaced with plug in modules.

1987–90
Except Allante

The relay center, which incorporates various relays, is located behind the glove box.

Allante

The various relays are scattered through out the vehicle, located mainly behind the instrument panel and glove box. There are a few located under the hood.

TURN SIGNAL FLASHER

The turn signal flasher unit is located behind the instrument panel near the steering column. In order to gain access to the components, it may be necessary to remove certain under dash padding.

NOTE: On the Eldorado and Seville (1987–88), a turn signal/hazard control module is used to control the signal and hazard light operations.

HAZARD WARNING FLASHER

1986 RIVIERA, 1986 ELDORADO AND SEVILLE AND 1986–90 TORONADO—The hazard flasher is located on the fuse panel.

1987–90 REATTA AND RIVIERA—The hazard flasher is located behind the left side of the instrument panel.

1987–90 ALLANTE, ELDORADO AND SEVILLE—A turn signal/hazard control module, instead of a hazard flasher, is used to control the hazard operation.

VEHICLE SPEED SENSOR

On some models, the vehicle speed sensor is located on the back of the instrument cluster; on other models, it is mounted directly to the transaxle. It provides signals to the cruise control module which indicate vehicle speed.

Speed Controls

Refer to "Chilton's Chassis Electronics Service Manual" for additional coverage.

The location of the cruise control switch varies with the model and the year. One may be located on the right side of the instrument panel near the steering column; another may be part of the combination switch, mounted on the steering column and another may be installed on the horn pad.

A vacuum release switch and an electrical disconnect switch are mounted on the upper brake pedal bracket. The vacuum switch vents the servo vacuum to the atmosphere when the pedal is depressed. The electrical switch disengages the system electronically when the brake pedal is depressed.

Adjustment
CABLE

1. Retract the ISC motor by selecting ECM override ESO3 "ISC Motor". Press the "Cooler" button on the CCDIC. The ISC will slowly retract to a fully retracted position (about 20 seconds).
2. Once the ISC has fully retracted, make sure the throttle lever is resting on the minimum idle speed screw.
3. Make sure the ISC plunger is not touching the throttle lever; if it is, adjust (turn in) the plunger so it is not.
4. Select the servo blade hole based on minimum cable slack.

SWITCH

The switch is located at the top of the brake pedal bracket.
1. Install the switch retainer.
2. Depress the brake pedal.
3. Push the switch through the retainer and listen for clicks.
4. Pull the brake pedal fully rearward against the pedal stop until the clicks can no longer be heard.
5. Depress the brake pedal and repeat the last step to make sure no brakes can be heard.

Troubleshooting

1. Cruise system surges—inspect the vacuum servo and the throttle linkage for free and smooth operation. Inspect the vacuum hoses for leaks, restrictions or pinches.
2. High or Low cruise set speed—inspect the vacuum hoses for leaks, restrictions or proper routing. Inspect the servo for excessive slack. If no problem is found, replace the ECM.
3. Excessive loss of cruise on hills—inspect the vacuum hoses for leaks, restrictions or proper routing. Inspect the check valve for proper operation.
4. Tap (up or down) control inoperative—the ECM may be faulty.

COOLING AND HEATING SYSTEMS

Water Pump

Removal and Installation
3.8L ENGINE

1. Disconnect the negative battery cable.
2. Position a drain pan under the radiator, open the drain cock and drain the cooling system.
3. Disconnect the hoses from the water pump.
4. Remove the drive belt(s).
5. Remove the water pump pulley bolts and the pulley.

NOTE: The long bolt is removed through the access hole provided in the body side rail.

6. Remove the water pump-to-engine bolts and the pump.
To install:
7. Clean the gasket mounting surfaces.
8. Using a new gasket and sealant, if necessary, reverse the removal procedures. Torque the water pump-to-engine long bolts to 22 ft. lbs. (1986–87) or 29 ft. lbs. (1988–90) and the short bolts to 97 inch lbs.
9. Refill the cooling system. Start the engine, allow it to reach

1. Water pump
2. Engine front cover assembly
3. Gasket
4. 97 inch lbs.
5. 29 ft. lbs.

Exploded view of the water pump—3.8L engine

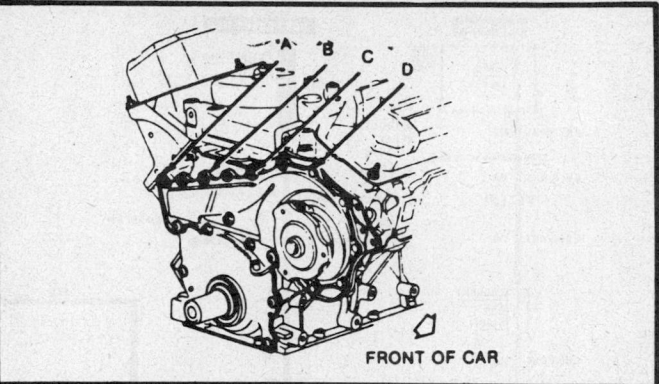

Locations for fasteners on the 4.1L V8 water pump. A fasteners are Torx® screws; B fasteners are nuts; C fasteners are studs; and D fasteners are hex screws. Torque A and C to 30 ft. lbs.; B and D to 5 ft. lbs.

normal operating temperatures and check for leaks. Adjust the drive belt(s) to correct tension.

NOTE: Because the radiator is made of aluminum and plastic, make sure the antifreeze solution is approved for use in cooling systems with a high aluminum content. GM recommends the use of a supplement/sealant part number 3634621, or equivalent, specifically designed for use in aluminum engines to protect the engine from damage.

4.1L AND 4.5L ENGINES

1. Disconnect the negative battery cable.
2. Position a drain pan under the radiator, open the drain cock and drain the cooling system.
3. Remove the air filter assembly. Disconnect and remove the coolant recovery tank.
4. Disconnect and remove the cross brace.
5. While applying tension to the drive belt, to hold the water pump pulley from moving, remove the water pulley bolts.
6. Remove the drive belt and the water pump pulley.
7. Remove the water pump-to-engine bolts and the pump.

To install:
8. Clean the gasket mounting surfaces.
9. Using a new gasket and sealant, if necessary, reverse the removal procedures. Torque the:
Pulley-to-water pump bolts to 25 ft. lbs.
Water pump-to-engine Torx® bolts 5 ft. lbs.
Water pump-to-engine stud nuts to 30 ft. lbs.
Remaining fasteners to 5 ft. lbs.

NOTE: Because the engines use an aluminum block and the radiator is made of aluminum, make sure the antifreeze solution is approved for use in cooling systems with a high aluminum content. GM recommends the use of a supplement/sealant part number 3634621, or equivalent, specifically designed for use in aluminum engines to protect the engine from damage.

Electric Cooling Fan

Removal and Installation
ALLANTE

1. Disconnect the negative battery cable.
2. Remove the air cleaner duct and the air conditioning hose bracket, if necessary.
3. Remove the fan-to-radiator screws.
4. Disconnect the electrical connector from the fan.
5. Remove the fan assembly from the vehicle.

6. To install, reverse the removal procedures.

ELDORADO AND SEVILLE

1. Disconnect the negative battery cable.
2. Remove the radiator cover panel.
3. Remove the fan control module and bracket.
4. Remove the grille.
5. Disconnect the electrical connector from the fan and remove the fan.
6. To install, reverse the removal procedures.

REATTA AND RIVIERA

1. Disconnect the negative battery cable.
2. Disconnect the electrical harness connector from the fan and the frame.
3. Remove the fan-to-radiator support screws and the fan assembly from the vehicle.
4. To install, reverse the removal procedures.

TORONADO

1. Disconnect the negative battery cable.
2. Remove the front splash shield.
3. Remove the engine mount bracket.
4. Disconnect the electrical connector from the fan.
5. Remove the fan-to-radiator screws and the fan assembly from the vehicle.
6. To install, reverse the removal procedures.

Radiator Fan Switch

Removal and Installation

1. Disconnect the negative battery cable.
2. Disconnect the fresh air cleaner duct in order to gain working clearance.
3. Remove the air conditioning hose bracket to gain access to the fan assembly.
4. Disconnect the electrical connector from the fan motor.
5. Remove the cooling fan-to-radiator bolts and the fan assembly from the vehicle.
6. To install, reverse the removal procedures. Torque the fan-to-radiator bolts to 9 ft. lbs.

Testing
COOLING FAN

1. Disconnect the electrical connector from the fan motor.
2. Using a jumper wire, connect the fan's A terminal to ground.
3. Uisng a jumper wire, connect one end to the positive bat-

Schematic of the cooling fan system—Allante

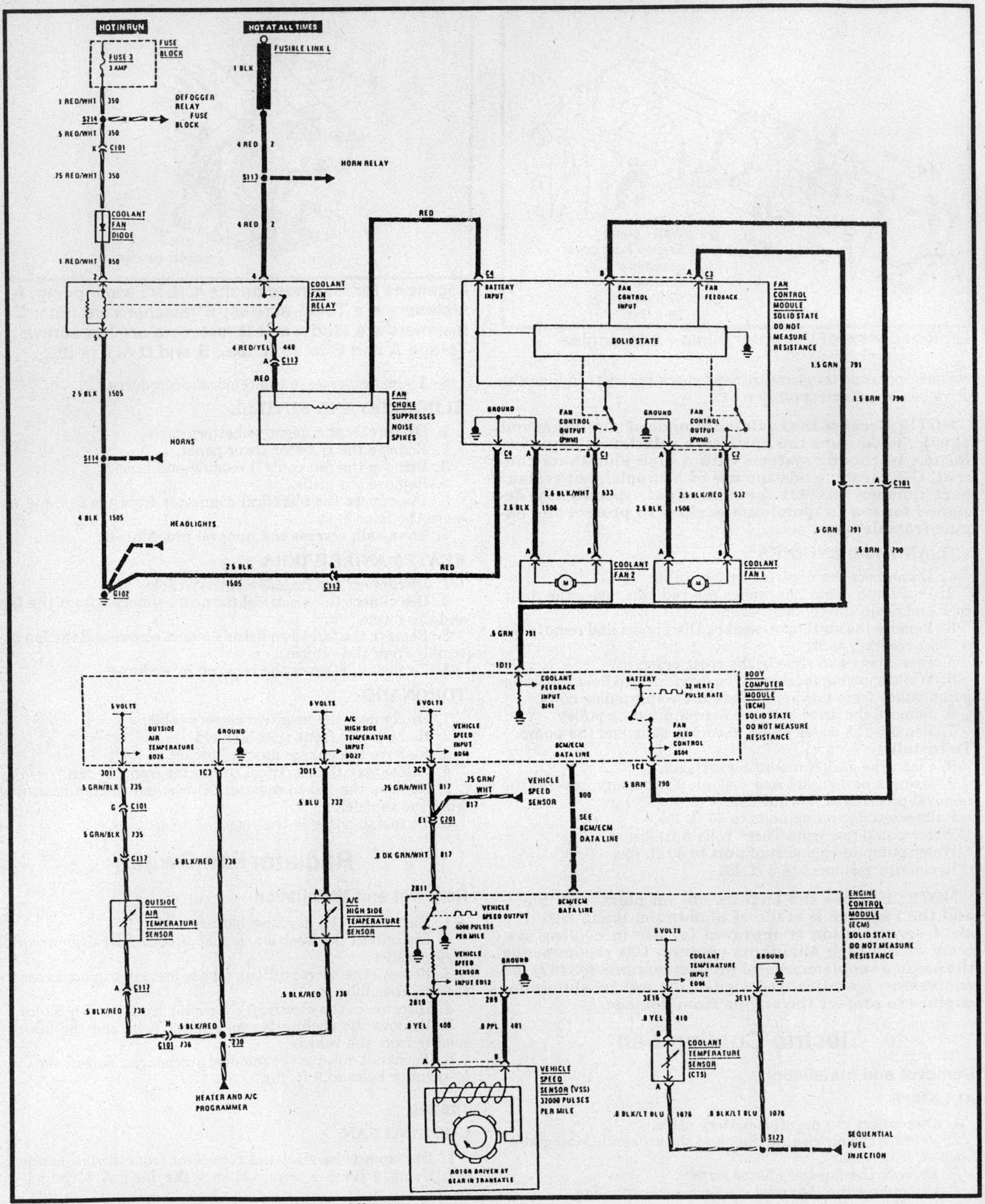

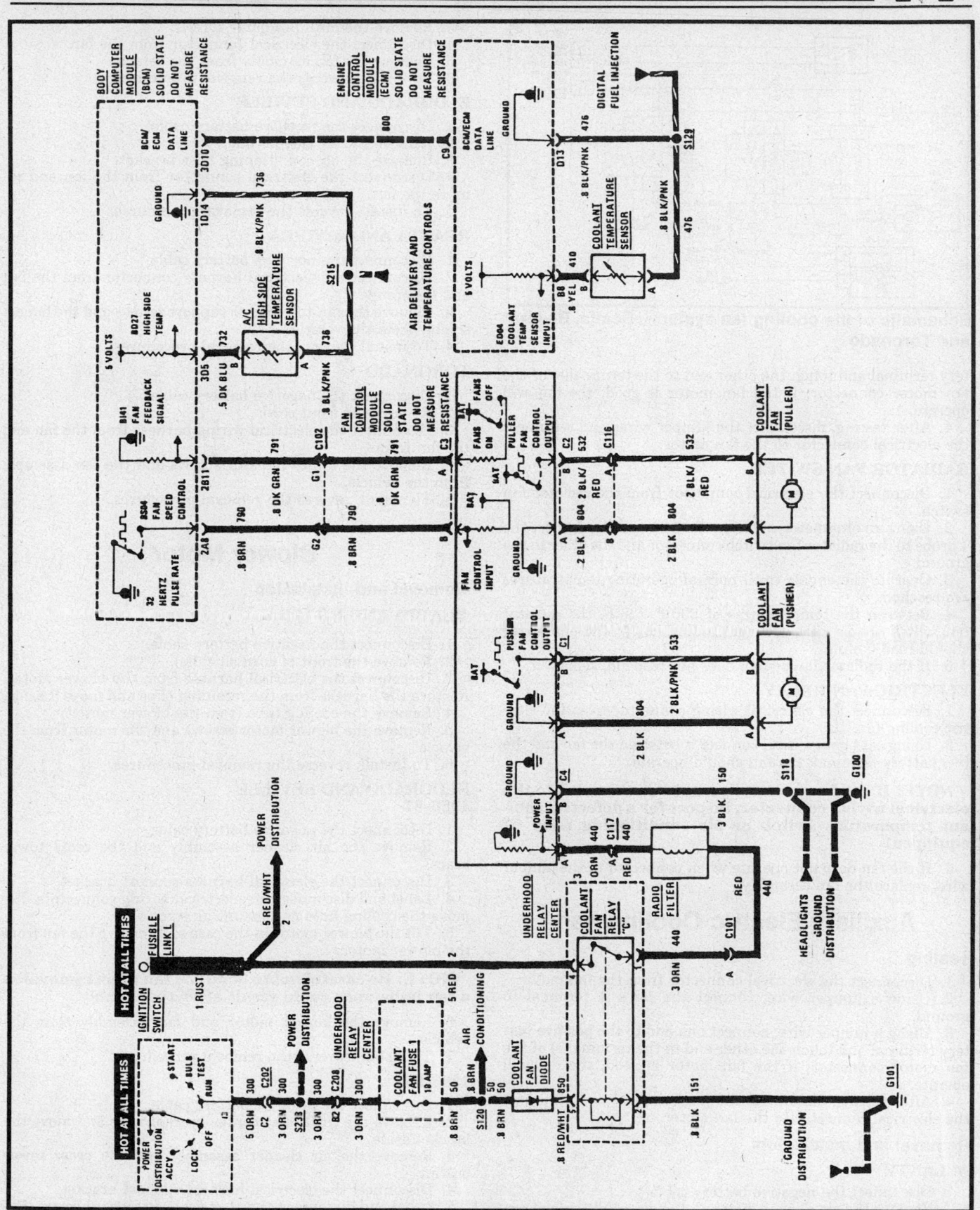

Schematic of the cooling fan system—Eldorado and Seville

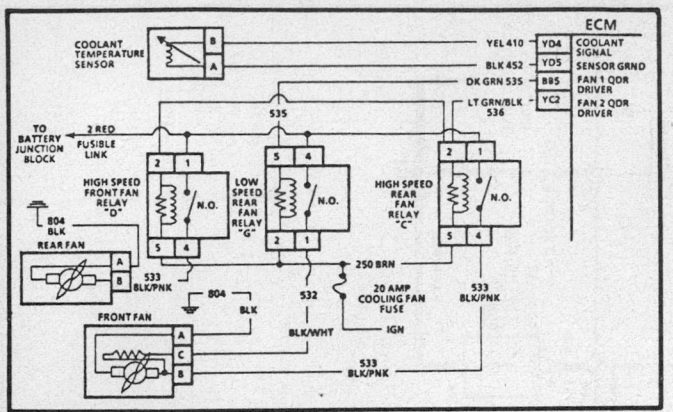

Schematic of the cooling fan system—Reatta, Riviera and Toronado

tery terminal and touch the other end to the terminal(s) of the fan motor connector; if the fan motor is good, the fan will operate.

4. After testing, disconnect the jumper wires and reconnect the electrical connector to the fan motor.

RADIATOR FAN SWITCH

1. Disconnect the electrical connector from the radiator fan switch.
2. Using an ohmmeter, set it on the 1 ohm scale, connect the 1 probe to the radiator fan switch connector and the other to the ground.
3. Operate the engine until normal operating temperatures are reached.
4. Between the temperatures of 230°F–238°F, the radiator fan switch should turn **ON** (grounding itself); the ohmmeter should read 0 ohm.
5. If the radiator fan switch does not respond, replace it.

ELECTRIC FAN RELAY

1. Disconnect the electrical wiring connector from the electric cooling fan.
2. Using a 14 gauge wire, connect it between the fan and the (+) battery terminal; the fan should operate.

NOTE: If the fan does not run while connected to the electrical wiring connector, inspect for a defective coolant temperature switch or air conditioning relay (if equipped).

3. If the fan does not operate when connected to the jumper wire, replace the fan assembly.

Auxiliary Electric Cooling Fan

Testing

1. Disconnect the electrical connector from the fan motor.
2. Using a jumper wire, connect the fan's **A** terminal to ground.
3. Uisng a jumper wire, connect one end to the positive battery terminal and touch the other end to the terminal(s) of the fan motor connector; if the fan motor is good, the fan will operate.
4. After testing, disconnect the jumper wires and reconnect the electrical connector to the fan motor.

Removal and Installation
ALLANTE

1. Disconnect the negative battery cable.
2. Remove the air cleaner duct and the air conditioning hose bracket, if necessary.

3. Remove the fan-to-radiator screws.
4. Disconnect the electrical connector from the fan.
5. Remove the fan assembly from the vehicle.
6. To install, reverse the removal procedures.

ELDORADO AND SEVILLE

1. Disconnect the negative battery cable.
2. Remove the air cleaner duct.
3. Remove the air conditioning hose bracket.
4. Disconnect the electrical connector from the fan and remove the fan.
5. To install, reverse the removal procedures.

REATTA AND RIVIERA

1. Disconnect the negative battery cable.
2. Disconnect the electrical harness connector from the fan and the frame.
3. Remove the fan-to-radiator support screws and the fan assembly from the vehicle.
4. To install, reverse the removal procedures.

TORONADO

1. Disconnect the negative battery cable.
2. Remove the front cowl.
3. Disconnect the electrical wiring harness from the fan and the fan frame.
4. Remove the fan-to-radiator screws and the fan assembly from the vehicle.
5. To install, reverse the removal procedures.

Blower Motor

Removal and Installation
REATTA AND RIVIERA

1. Disconnect the negative battery cable.
2. Remove the front of cowl shield(s).
3. Disconnect the electrical harness from the blower motor. Remove the harness from the retaining clips and move it aside.
4. Remove the cooling tube from the blower motor.
5. Remove the blower motor screws and the motor from the vehicle.
6. To install, reverse the removal procedures.

ELDORADO AND SEVILLE
1986–87

1. Disconnect the negative battery cable.
2. Remove the air cleaner assembly and the cross tower brace.
3. Disconnect the electrical harness support bracket.
4. Label and disconnect the electrical wiring connectors. Remove the cooling hose and mounting screws.
5. Tilt the blower motor in the case and remove the fan from the blower motor.

NOTE: Be careful not to bend the fan upon removal as a fan imbalance could result after reassembly.

6. Remove the blower motor and fan assembly from the vehicle.
7. To install, reverse the removal procedures.

1988–90

1. Disconnect the negative battery cable.
2. Remove the cowl relay center bracket nuts and move the bracket aside.
3. Remove the air cleaner assembly and the cross tower brace.
4. Disconnect the electrical harness support bracket.
5. Label and disconnect the electrical wiring connectors. Remove the cooling hose and mounting screws.

6. Tilt the blower motor in the case and remove the fan from the blower motor.

NOTE: Be careful not to bend the fan upon removal as a fan imbalance could result after reassembly.

7. Remove the blower motor and fan assembly from the vehicle.
8. To install, reverse the removal procedures.

TORONADO

1. Disconnect the negative battery cable.
2. Remove the front of the cowl shield.
3. Remove the bulkhead retaining screw and the bulkhead electrical connector.
4. Remove the Electronic Spark Control (ESC) module electrical connector.
5. Remove the ESC module and bracket assembly.
6. Remove the power steering pump bracket support.
7. Remove the coil bracket nuts. Label and disconnect the electrical connector from the coil.
8. Remove the plug wire guides. Remove the coil/bracket assembly and move it aside. Remove the wiring harness conduit.
9. Remove the blower motor cooling tube.
10. Label and disconnect the electrical connectors from the blower motor. Remove the blower motor mounting screws.
11. Remove the blower motor mounting screws and the blower motor.
12. To install, reverse of the removal procedures.

ALLANTE

1. Disconnect the negative battery cable.
2. Remove the cross tower brace.
3. Partially remove the upper intake manifold by performing the following procedures.
   a. Remove both right rear EGR pipe bolts.
   b. Remove the right rear transaxle dipstick bolt.
   c. Remove the right rear bracket bolt.
   d. Remove the right rear lower intake manifold nuts.
   e. Position the upper intake manifold aside.
4. Remove the electrical harness bracket and disconnect the electrical connector.
5. Remove the cooling hose, the mounting screws and the blower motor.
6. To install, reverse the removal procedures.

Heater Core

Refer to "Chilton's Auto Heating and Air Conditioning Manual" for additional coverage.

Removal and Installation

1986–87 TORONADO AND RIVIERA

NOTE: This procedure involves removing the instrument panel assembly.

1. Disconnect the negative battery cable.
2. Drain the cooling system. Remove the heater hoses from the heater core.
3. Remove the instrument panel sound absorbers which cover the underside of the dash area.
4. Loosen and lower the steering column and remove the left hand trim cover.
5. To remove the instrument cluster, perform the following procedures:
   a. Remove the headlight switch.
   b. Remove the windshield wiper switch, the radio and heater/air conditioning control assembly.
   c. Remove all cluster electrical connections and disconnect the speedometer cable.

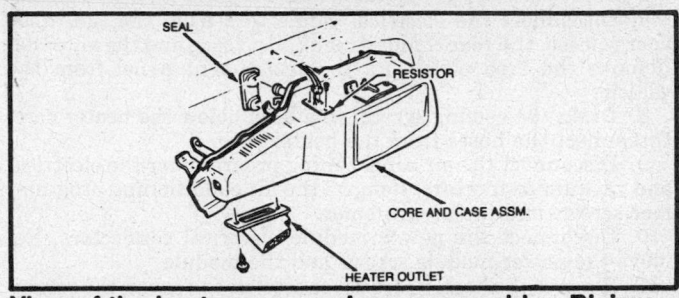

View of the heater case and core assembly—Riviera

   d. Remove the mounting screws and remove the cluster.
6. Remove the front speakers, the manifold-to-heater case screws, the upper/lower instrument panel screws, then, disconnect the brake release cable.
7. Disconnect the instrument panel wiring harness from the dash wiring assembly and the right hand remote control mirror cable from the instrument panel.
8. Disconnect the speedometer cable from its clip and the heater control cable from the heater case.
9. Disconnect all vacuum lines and wiring necessary to remove the instrument panel. If vehicle is equipped with pulse wipers, remove the wiper switch, unlock the connector from the cluster carrier and separate the pulse jumper harness from the connector.
10. Remove the instrument panel and harness assembly.
11. Remove the defroster ducts, disconnect vacuum hoses and temperature cable; remove the blower resistor and the heater assembly nuts.
12. Remove the heater assembly-to-dash screw and clip from inside the vehicle.
13. Remove the heater assembly and the heater core.
14. To install, reverse the removal procedures. Refill the cooling system.

1988–90 REATTA AND RIVIERA

1. Disconnect the negative battery cable.
2. Drain the cooling system.
3. Disconnect the hoses from the heater core.
4. Remove the right side sound insulator and courtesy lamp.
5. Remove the glove box.
6. Disconnect the air conditioning programmer the electrical and vacuum connectors. Remove the air conditioning programmer screws and the programmer.
7. Disconnect the ECM electrical connectors. Remove the ECM and bracket.
8. Disconnect the BCM electrical connectors. Remove the BCM and bracket.
9. Remove the heater core cover screws, the cover, the retaining clip, the heater core screws and the heater core.
10. To install, reverse the removal procedures. Refill the cooling system. Operate the engine until normal operating temperatures are reached and check for leaks. Inspect the operation of the dash controls.

1988–90 TORONADO

1. Disconnect the negative battery cable.
2. Remove the left side sound insulator and courtesy lamp.
3. Remove the right side sound insulator and courtesy lamp.
4. Remove the steering column filler panel screws, the filler panel and the steering column bolts; lower the steering column.
5. Remove the windshield defroster nozzle grille and both deflector housings. Remove the upper instrument panel screws (located under the deflector housings and windshield defroster grille) and bottom instrument panel bolts.
6. Disconnect the bulkhead electrical connector and move the instrument rearward. Remove the aspirator duct.

7. Disconnect the electrical connectors from the fuel filler door release, the rear compartment lid release and the antenna. Remove the fuse panel and the instrument panel from the vehicle.

8. Drain the cooling system to a level below the heater core. Disconnect the hoses from the heater core.

9. Disconnect the air conditioning programmer the electrical and vacuum connectors. Remove the air conditioning programmer screws and the programmer.

10. Disconnect the power module electrical connectors. Remove the power module screws and the module.

11. Remove the heater core cover screws, the cover, the retaining clip, the heater core screws and the heater core.

12. To install, reverse the removal procedures. Refill the cooling system. Operate the engine until normal operating temperatures are reached and check for leaks. Inspect the operation of the dash controls.

ELDORADO AND SEVILLE

1. Disconnect the negative battery cable.
2. Drain the cooling system to a level below the heater core.
3. Remove the glove box screws. Label and disconnect the electrical connectors from the glove box.
4. Remove the glove box assembly from the vehicle.
5. Remove the lower sound insulator to gain working clearance.
6. Remove the air conditioning programmer, the Electronic Control Module (ECM) screws and the ECM.
7. Remove the module assembly heater core cover. Disconnect the hoses from the heater core.
8. Remove the heater core screws and the heater core.
9. To install, reverse the removal procedures. Refill the cooling system.

ALLANTE

1. Disconnect the negative battery cable.
2. Drain the cooling system to a level below the heater core.
3. Remove the glove box screws. Label and disconnect the electrical connectors from the glove box.
4. Remove the glove box assembly from the vehicle.
5. Remove the lower sound insulator to gain working clearance.
6. Remove the radio.
7. Remove the air conditioning programmer, the Electronic Control Module (ECM) screws and the ECM.
8. Remove the module assembly heater core cover. Disconnect the hoses from the heater core.
9. Remove the heater core screws and the heater core.
10. To install, reverse the removal procedures. Refill the cooling system.

AIR MIXTURE VALVE

Adjustment

ALLANTE, ELDORADO AND SEVILLE

1. Remove the glove box.
2. On the temperature control panel, set the temperature for 90°F, allow 1–2 minutes for the programmer arm to travel to it's **MAX HEAT** position.
3. From the programmer output arm, disconnect the threaded rod from the plastic retainer.
4. To check the air mixture valve for free travel, push the valve to the **MAX A/C** position and check for possible binding.

NOTE: Place the pre-load air mixture valve in the MAX HEAT position; pull on the threaded rod to ensure the valve is seating.

5. To avoid influencing the programmer arm or air mixture valve position, carefully snap the threaded rod into the plastic retainer.

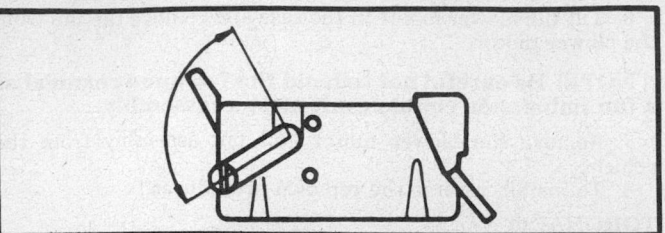

Adjusting the programmer linkage to its maximum heat position

6. Adjust the temperature setting to 60°F, then, check to verify the programmer arm and air mixture valve travel to the **MAX A/C** position.
7. After adjustment, reverse the removal procedures.

TEMPERATURE CONTROL/BLOWER SWITCH

Removal and Installation

1986 TORONADO

1. Disconnect the negative battery cable.
2. Remove the necessary components preventing access to the control unit such as trim panels, radio, etc.
3. Remove the temperature control mounting screws.
4. Pull the control unit forward and disconnect the vacuum lines, if equipped, the control cable(s) and the electrical connectors from the back of the unit.
5. To install, reverse the removal procedures. Check the system for proper operation.

1987–90 TORONADO

This vehicle is equipped with an Electronic Comfort Control which is located above the center console.

1. Disconnect the negative battery cable.
2. To remove the instrument panel trim plate, perform the following procedures:
   a. Remove the trim plate-to-instrument panel screws.
   b. To disengage the clips, pull the trim plate rearward.
   c. Disconnect the electrical connectors from the switches and remove the trim plate.
3. Remove the electronic comfort control assembly-to-instrument panel bracket screws, pull rearward on the assembly and disconnect the electrical connector.
4. To install, reverse the removal procedures. Check the system for proper operation.

REATTA AND RIVIERA

This vehicle is equipped with a Graphic Control Center (GCC) assembly which is an integrated information system. The assembly provides the driver with fingertip control of more information than ever before available. All controls are adjusted directly on the screen.

1. Disconnect the negative battery cable.
2. Remove the center trim-to-instrument trim screws and the trim.
3. Remove the Graphic Control Center (GCC) assembly-to-instrument panel screws and pull the assembly rearward.
4. Disconnect the electrical connectors from the rear of the assembly.
5. To install, reverse the removal procedures. Check the system for proper operation.

ELDORADO, SEVILLE AND ALLANTE

These vehicles are equipped with a Climate Control Driver Information Center (CCDIC) which is located over the center console.

1. Disconnect the negative battery cable.
2. Remove the center trim plate-to-instrument panel screws and the trim plate.
3. Remove the Climate Control Driver Information Center (CCDIC)-to-instrument panel screws and pull the panel rearward.

4. Disconnect the electrical connector(s) from the rear of the panel and remove the panel from the vehicle.
5. To install, reverse the removal procedures. Check the system for proper operation.

FUEL INJECTION SYSTEM

Refer to "Chilton's Electronic Engine Controls Manual" for additional coverage.

Description

DIGITAL FUEL INJECTION (DFI)

The Digital Fuel Injection (DFI) system is a throttle body fuel injection system, in which 2 solenoid actuated fuel injectors are mounted in the throttle body and inject fuel into the intake manifold. The DFI system controls the air/fuel mixture for combustion by monitoring selected engine operating conditions and electronically metering fuel requirements to meet those conditions.

The system consists of the following subsystems; the fuel delivery system, air induction system, engine sensors, electronic control unit (ECU), electronic spark timing (EST), idle speed control system (ISC), exhaust gas recirculation system (EGR), a charcoal canister, oxygen sensors and diagnostic readout systems.

MULTI-PORT FUEL INJECTION (MFI)
AND SEQUENTIAL FUEL INJECTION (SFI)

The Multi-Port Fuel Injection (MFI) or Sequential Fuel Injection (SFI) has an injector installed near each intake valve inlet port. Each injector opens independently of each other, once every 2 revolutions of the crankshaft and prior to the opening of the intake valve for the cylinder to be fired. The Electronic Control Modules (ECM) is in complete control of both system during all phases of engine operation.

IDLE SPEED

Adjustment

NOTE: Idle speed adjustment is not required unless throttle body parts have been replaced, the Throttle Position Sensor (TPS) and/or the Idle Speed Control (ISC) have been adjusted.

Before performing the minimum idle speed adjustment, visually inspect the vacuum hoses for leaks, splits or cuts, the throttle body and intake manifold for vacuum leaks. Vacuum leaks can cause the engine(s) to run at a high rpm.

MULTI-PORT FUEL INJECTION (MFI)

1. Using a scratch awl, pierce and pry the idle speed screw plug from the throttle body; it can be discarded and not replaced.
2. Connect a tachometer to the engine. Set the parking brake, place the transaxle in the **P**, position the steering wheel in the straight ahead position and turn **OFF** the air conditioning and all accessories.
3. Operate the engine until normal operating temperatures are reached.
4. Check and/or adjust the timing.
5. On the Climate Control Driver Information Panel (CCDIC), press the "COOLER" button and wait for at least 20 seconds; this will cause the ISC motor plunger to retract. Once

the motor has retracted, inspect the throttle lever to make sure it is resting on the minimum idle speed screw.
6. If the minimum idle speed it too high, use a T-20 Torx® Driver to adjust the minimum idle speed screw. The minimum idle speed should be 450–550 rpm (0–500 miles) or 450–600 rpm (above 500 miles).
7. After adjustment, disconnect the test equipment and turn the ignition switch **OFF** for 10 seconds.
8. Turn the engine **ON**, check the ISC operation and inspect the ECM and/or BCM readout for stored codes or telltale lights. Perform the diagnostics.
9. Disconnect the negative battery cable for 10 seconds; this will reset the TPS learned value in the ECM.

DIGITAL FUEL INJECTION (DFI)

1. Connect a tachometer to the engine. Set the parking brake, place the transaxle in the **P**, position the steering wheel in the straight ahead position. Turn **OFF** the air conditioning and all accessories. Ground the green test connector located near the alternator.
2. Operate the engine until normal operating temperatures are reached.
3. Check and/or adjust the timing.
4. Remove the air cleaner and plug the THERMAC vacuum tap.
5. To retract plunger of the ISC motor, perform the following procedures.
   a. Disconnect the ISC connector and connect the jumper harness to the ISC.
   b. Connect the jumper wire leading to the ISC terminal C to 12V at the battery or junction block.
   c. Apply finger pressure to the ISC plunger (close the throttle switch). Touch the jumper wire connected to the ISC terminal D to ground until the ISC plunger retracts fully and stops; do not allow the ground wire to be connected for longer than necessary for damage to the ISC motor can result.

NOTE: Never connect a voltage source to the ISC motor terminals A and B as damage to the internal throttle switch contacts will result.

   d. Once the motor has retracted, inspect the throttle lever to make sure it is resting on the minimum idle speed screw.
6. If the minimum idle speed it too high, adjust the minimum idle speed screw. The minimum idle speed should be 375–500 rpm (0–500 miles) or 475–550 rpm (above 500 miles).
7. After adjustment, disconnect the test equipment and turn the ignition switch **OFF** for 10 seconds.
8. Turn the engine **ON**, check the ISC operation and inspect the ECM and/or BCM readout for stored codes or telltale lights. Perform the diagnostics.
9. Disconnect the negative battery cable for 10 seconds; this will reset the TPS learned value in the ECM.

SEQUENTIAL FUEL INJECTION (SFI)

1. Set the parking brake, place the transaxle in the **P**, position the steering wheel in the straight ahead position. Turn **OFF** the air conditioning and all accessories.

8. Start the engine and inspect the idle speed.

IDLE AIR CONTROL VALVE

The idle air control valve controls engine idle speed by bypassing air around the throttle valve. It responds to a number of electronic signals, actually compensating for changes in engine load. It is not adjustable.

IDLE MIXTURE

On these models the air/fuel mixture is controlled by the electronic control module of the Computer Command Control (CCC) system.

NOTE: Idle mixture is adjusted at the factory and should not be attempted.

FUEL SYSTEM PRESSURE RELIEF

Procedure

1. Disconnect the fuel pump electrical connector or remove the fuse labeled "Fuel Pump" from the fuse block.
2. Operate the engine until it stalls. Crank the engine for 3 full seconds to ensure there is no fuel pressure in the system.
3. Disconnect the negative battery cable.

Fuel Pump

— CAUTION —
Do not drain or store fuel in an open container. Serious explosion and fire hazard exists. Empty the contents of the fuel tank into an approved gasoline storage container and take precautions to avoid the risk of fire.

Removal and Installation

1. Relieve the fuel pressure.
2. Disconnect the negative battery cable.
3. Raise and safely support the vehicle.

NOTE: Make sure the rear end is supported securely so in the next step, weight distribution changes will not cause it to become unbalanced.

4. Drain the fuel tank and remove it from the vehicle.
5. Using a hammer and the brass bar, drive the cam locking ring counterclockwise to release it and lift the sending unit from the tank.
6. Pull the fuel pump up into the attaching pipe while pulling it outward, away from the support on the bottom of the tank. Make sure not to damage the rubber insulator and the strainer. When the pump is entirely clear of the bottom support, pull it out of the rubber connector to remove it.
7. Inspect the attaching hose and the rubber sound insulator from the bottom of the pump for signs of deterioration and replace parts, if necessary.
8. To install, use a new O-ring, push the fuel pump into the attaching hose and reverse the removal procedures. Start the engine and check for leaks.

NOTE: When installing the cam locking ring over the assembly, turn it clockwise to lock it.

TIMING SENSORS

The timing sensors are used on the 1988–90 3.8L engines.

Removal and Installation

CRANKSHAFT SENSOR

The crankshaft sensor is attached to the front cover directly behind the crankshaft pulley.

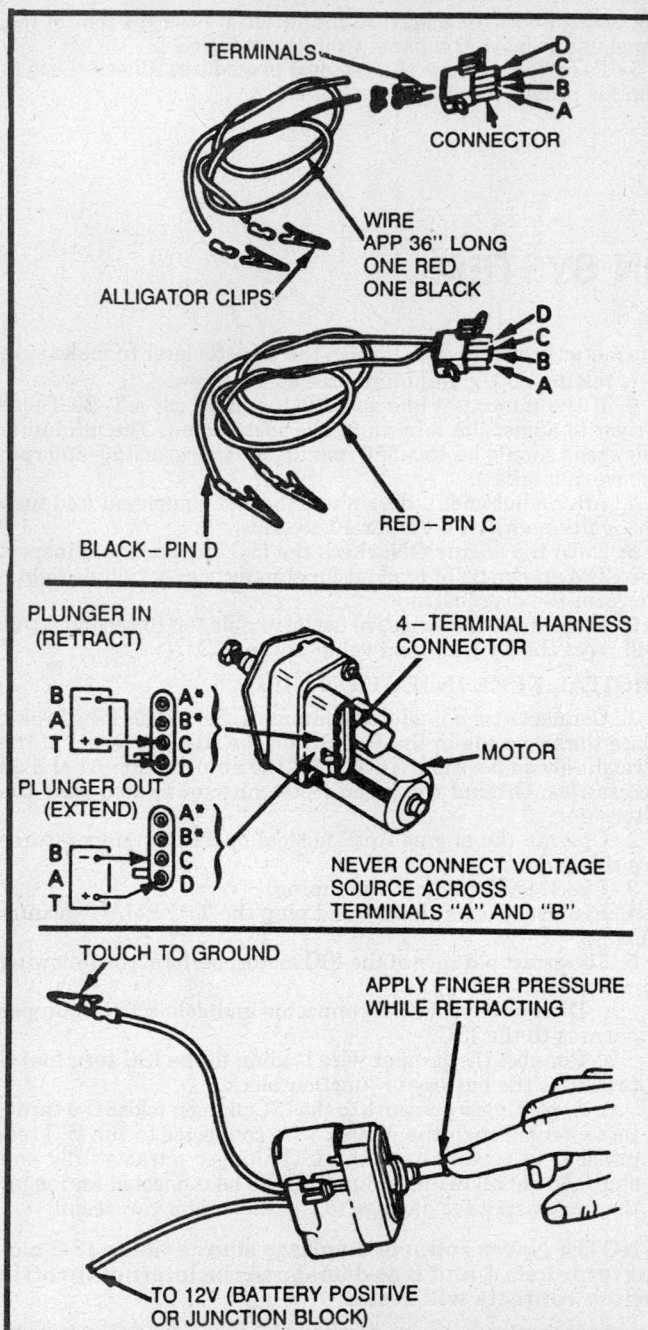

Using a jumper harness to retract/extend the Idle Speed Control (ISC) unit

2. With the ignition switch turned **OFF**, enter ECM outputs mode "EO07" and wait for 30 seconds.
3. Turn the ignition switch **ON** and disconnect the electrical connector from the Idle Air Control (IAC) motor.
4. Operate the engine until normal operating temperatures are reached and enter the ECM diagnostic data "ED11" to read rpm.
5. If necessary, adjust the idle spot screw to 450–550 rpm.
6. Turn the engine **OFF** and reconnect the electrical connector to the IAC motor.
7. To the ECM, enter data "ED01". Loosen the Throttle Position Sensor (TPS) screw(s), adjust the TPS to 350–450MV and retorque the screws.

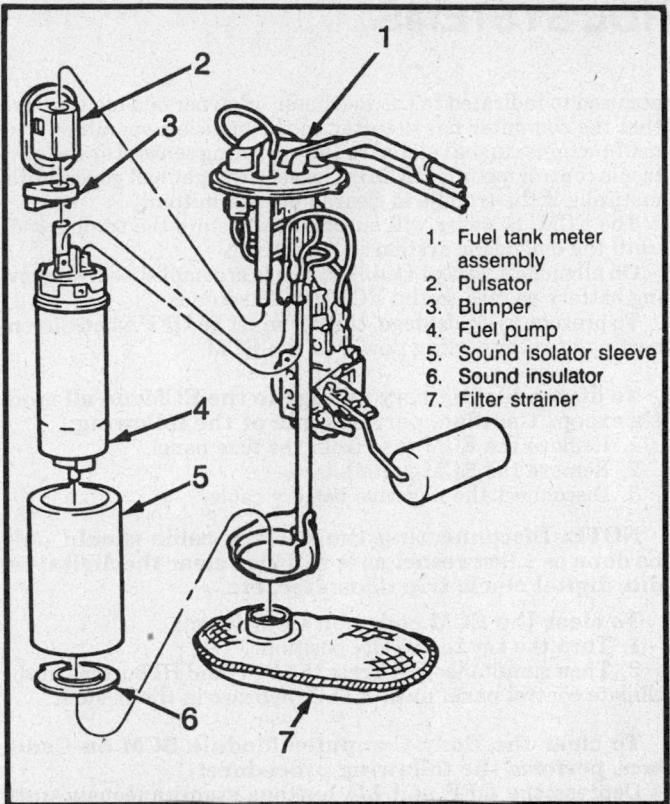

1. Fuel tank meter assembly
2. Pulsator
3. Bumper
4. Fuel pump
5. Sound isolator sleeve
6. Sound insulator
7. Filter strainer

Exploded view of the electric fuel pump/sending unit assembly

1. Disconnect the negative battery cable. Remove the serpentine drive belt.
2. Raise and safely support the vehicle.
3. Remove the right front wheel and the right inner fender access cover.
4. Using a 28mm socket, remove the harmonic balancer-to-crankshaft bolt. Remove the harmonic balancer.
5. Disconnect the electrical connector from the crankshaft sensor.
6. Remove the crankshaft sensor/pedestal assembly-to-engine bolts and the sensor from the pedestal.
To install:
7. Position the sensor on the pedestal. Position the sensor/pedestal assembly on the alignment tool, and the assembly on the crankshaft.
8. Torque the pedestal-to-engine bolts to 14–28 ft. lbs. and the pedestal pinch bolt to 30–35 ft. lbs.
9. Remove the alignment tool.
10. Using the alignment tool, position it on the harmonic balancer and turn it; if any vane of the balancer touches the tool, replace the balancer.
11. Install the balancer. Torque the balancer-to-crankshaft bolt to 200–239 ft. lbs.
12. To complete the installation, reverse the removal procedures.

CAMSHAFT SENSOR
The camshaft sensor is attached to the front cover at the lower left side of the water pump pulley.
1. Disconnect the negative battery cable.
2. Remove the water pump pulley-to-water pump bolts.
3. Remove the serpentine drive belt.
4. Remove the electrical connector from the camshaft sensor.

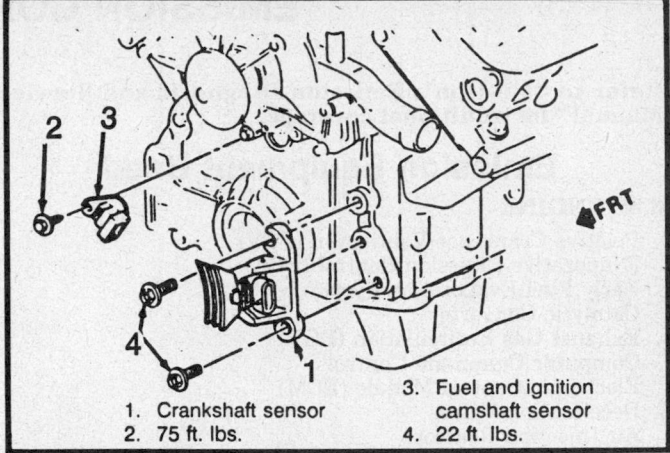

1. Crankshaft sensor
2. 75 ft. lbs.
3. Fuel and ignition camshaft sensor
4. 22 ft. lbs.

Exploded view of the camshaft and crankshaft timing sensors—3.8L C³I engines

5. Remove the sensor-to-engine bolt. Remove the sensor by pulling and twisting it.
6. To install, lubricate the O-ring and reverse the removal procedures. Torque the camshaft sensor-to-engine bolt to 115 inch lbs.

FUEL INJECTOR

Removal and Installation
MULTI PORT FUEL INJECTION (MFI) AND SEQUENTIAL FUEL INJECTION (SFI)
1. Relieve the fuel pressure. Disconnect the negative battery cable.
2. Label and disconnect the fuel injector electrical connectors.
3. Remove the fuel rail retaining bolts. Remove the fuel rail.
4. Separate the injector from the fuel rail.
5. To install, use new O-rings and reverse the removal procedures. Start the engine and check for leaks.

DIGITAL FUEL INJECTION (DFI)

NOTE: Care must be taken when removing injectors to prevent damage to the electrical connector pins on the injector and the nozzle. The injectors are serviced as a complete assembly only. Injectors are an electrical component and should not be immersed in any type of cleaner.

1. If the engine was recently operated, allow the fuel pressure to bleed down.
2. Disconnect the negative battery cable. Remove the air cleaner.
3. Disconnect the electrical connector from the fuel injector(s) by squeezing both tabs together and pulling it straight up.
4. Remove the fuel meter cover-to-throttle body screws and the cover; be sure to note the position of the short screws. Allow the gasket to remain in place to prevent damage to the casting housing.
5. Using a small pry bar and a ¼ in. rod, pry the fuel injector(s) from the throttle body; discard the O-rings.
6. To install, use new O-rings (lubricate with Dexron®II automatic transmission fluid) and reverse the removal procedures. When installing the injectors, simply push them into the sockets. Start the engine and check for leaks.

EMISSION CONTROL SYSTEMS

Refer to "Chilton's Emission Diagnosis and Service Manual" for additional coverage.

Emission Equipment Used

3.8L ENGINE

Positive Crankcase Ventilation (PCV)
Evaporative Emission Control (EEC)
Early Fuel Evaporation System
Catalytic Converter
Exhaust Gas Recirculation (EGR)
Computer Command Control
Electronic Control Module (ECM)
Deceleration Valve
Air Injection Reactor
Controlled Combustion System
Transmission Converter Clutch (TCC)
Electronic Spark Control (ESC)
Electronic Spark Timing
Thermostatic Air Cleaner
Fuel injectors
Idle air meter
Cooling fan relay(s)
Manifold air temperature sensor
Crankshaft sensor
Camshaft sensor
Knock sensor
Mass air flow system

4.1L AND 4.5L ENGINES

Positive Crankcase Ventilation (PCV)
Evaporative Emission Control (EEC)
Early Fuel Evaporation System
Catalytic Converter
Exhaust Gas Recirculation (EGR)
Computer Command Control
Electronic Control Module (ECM)
Deceleration Valve
Air Injection Reactor
Controlled Combustion System
Transmission Converter Clutch (TCC)
Electronic Spark Control (ESC)
Electronic Spark Timing
Thermostatic Air Cleaner
Fuel injectors
Idle air meter
Cooling fan relay(s)
Manifold air temperature sensor

NOTE: Emissions equipment listed above is not used on every engine application.

Resetting Emission Warning Lamps

Procedures
EMISSIONS INDICATOR
Clearing Codes

The dash mounted "Service Soon" and "Service Now" lights are used to indicated to the mechanic or owner of a malfunction that the computer has detected in the vehicle's operation. The malfunctions can be related to the operating sensors or the electronic control module (ECM). The service light will go out automatically if the trouble is cleared or intermittent.

The ECM, however will automatically store the trouble code until the diagnostic system is "Cleared".

On all models, except Cadillac, this is accomplished by removing battery voltage to the ECM for 30 seconds.

To prevent ECM damage, the key must be **OFF** when disconnecting or reconnecting power to the ECM.

To disconnect battery voltage to the ECM, on all models except Cadillac, perform one of the following:
1. Remove the ECM fuse from the fuse panel.
2. Remove the ECM pigtail.
3. Disconnect the negative battery cable.

NOTE: Disconnecting the battery cable should only be done as a last resort as it will also clear the digital radio, digital clock, trip odometer, etc.

To clear the ECM codes on Cadillacs:
1. Turn the key to the ON position.
2. Then simultaneously press the OFF and HI buttons in the climate control panel until E.O.O. appears in the readout.

To clear the Body Computer Module BCM on Cadillacs, perform the following procedure:
Depress the OFF and LO buttons simultaneously until "F.O.O." appears.

ENGINE OIL CHANGE INDICATOR (EOCI)
Eldorado and Seville

The BCM calculates the oil life index based on the inputs and data received from the ECM. When the index drops below 3%, the Driver Information Center (DIC) will display "Change Engine Oil". After an oil change, the index may be reset by displaying the oil life index, depressing and holding the "ENGINE DATA" and "RESET/RECALL" buttons simultaneously until the oil life index shows 100%.

Toronado

Engine oil life is displayed through the engine data as the "Oil Life Index" and as a "Change Oil" message. The "Oil Life Index" display is followed by a number between 0 to 100; this is the percentage of oil life remaining based on driving conditions and mileage driven since the last time the oil life indicator was reset. When the oil life index reaches 0, the "Change Oil" message will appear; indicating the oil should be changed.

After the oil is changed, reset the message. Depress the "ENG DATA" and "GAGES" buttons, on the Instrument Panel Control (IPC), simultaneously, for several seconds. During this period, the "Oil Life Reset" message will be displayed.

NOTE: Continue holding the ENG DATA and GAGES buttons until the "Oil Life Index 100" message appears; this will reset the oil life index.

The "Change Oil" message will remain off until the next oil change is needed.

ENGINE

NOTE: Disconnecting the negative battery cable on some vehicles may interfere with the functions of the on board computer systems and may require the computer to undergo a relearning process, once the negative battery cable is reconnected.

Engine

Removal and Installation

1986–87 TORONADO AND RIVIERA

1. Disconnect the negative battery cable. Matchmark the hood hinges and remove the hood.
2. Position a drain pan under the radiator, open the drain cock and drain the cooling system.
3. Remove the air inlet and radiator hoses.
4. Disconnect the following electrical connectors:
    a. Fuel rail and other injection system connectors
    b. Engine ground wires
    c. Oil pressure sending unit
    d. EGR solenoid
    e. Coolant temperature sending units
    f. Throttle body electrical connections
    g. Crankshaft and camshaft sensors
    h. Alternator
5. Remove the serpentine drive belt. Remove the power steering pump and move it aside; do not disconnect the pressure hoses, if possible.
6. Remove the alternator. Disconnect and remove the heater hoses.
7. Remove the throttle cable bracket and the cruise control cables from the throttle lever.
8. Disconnect both fuel lines.
9. Remove the cooling fan and radiator.
10. Disconnect the exhaust Y-pipe, remove the exhaust manifold on the forward side of the engine. Label and disconnect the vacuum lines between the engine and components mounted on the firewall.
11. Remove the engine-to-transaxle bolts, the vibration damper and bracket from the engine.
12. Remove the ground strap and wiring harness bolts. Remove the engine-to-transaxle bracket. Raise and safely support the vehicle.
13. Remove the air conditioning compressor-to-bracket bolts, move it aside and support it without disturbing the refrigerant hoses. Remove the exhaust pipe.
14. Remove the engine-to-mount nuts. Matchmark the torque converter-to-flywheel and remove the torque converter-to-flywheel bolts.
15. Remove the left front wheel and the remaining engine-to-transaxle bolts. Make sure to remove the bolt that faces in the opposite direction.
16. Remove the engine-to-transaxle bracket and lower the vehicle. Using an engine vertical lifting device, connect it to the engine and lift the engine from the vehicle.

To install:

17. Reverse the removal procedures. Align the torque converter-to-flywheel matchmarks. Torque the:
    Damper pulley-to-crankshaft bolt to 200 ft. lbs.
    Exhaust manifold-to-cylinder head bolts to 37 ft. lbs.
    Transaxle-to-engine bolts to 55 ft. lbs.
    Engine mount-to-engine nuts 70 ft. lbs.
18. Refill the cooling system. Start the engine, allow it to reach normal operating temperatures and check for leaks.

NOTE: When installing the torque converter-to-flywheel, make sure the weld nuts on the converter are flush with the flywheel.

1988–90 TORONADO, RIVIERA AND REATTA

1. Matchmark the hood hinge-to-hood and remove the hood.
2. Relieve the fuel pressure and disconnect the fuel lines from the fuel rail.
3. Disconnect the negative battery cable. Remove the air intake duct.
4. Remove the upper engine strut. From the throttle body, remove the throttle cable bracket and the cables.
5. Raise and safely support the vehicle.
6. Position a drain pan under the radiator, open the drain cock and drain the cooling system.
7. Remove the exhaust pipe from the rear exhaust manifold.
8. Using a vertical lifting device, secure it to the engine and support its weight. Remove the engine mounting bolts.
9. Disconnect the electrical connectors from the starter. Remove the starter-to-engine bolts and the starter.
10. Remove the serpentine drive belt. Remove the air conditioning compressor-to-bracket bolts and move the compressor aside; do not disconnect the pressure hoses.
11. Disconnect and plug the power steering hoses at the steering gear.
12. Remove the lower transaxle-to-engine bolts.

NOTE: One of the lower transaxle bolts is located between the transaxle case and the engine block; it is installed in the opposite direction.

13. Remove the flywheel cover. Matchmark the torque converter-to-flywheel for alignment purposes. Remove the torque converter-to-flywheel bolts and slide the torque converter rearward.
14. Remove the engine support bracket-to-transaxle bolts and the bracket.
15. Lower the vehicle.
16. Disconnect the vacuum hoses from the vacuum modulator and the emission control canister. Disconnect and move aside any electrical harness connectors which may be in the way.
17. Remove the radiator and heater hoses from the engine.
18. Remove the remaining transaxle-to-engine bolts. Lift the engine assembly from the vehicle and attach it to a work stand.
19. To install, reverse the removal procedures. Align the torque converter-to-flywheel matchmarks. Torque the torque converter-to-flywheel bolts to 46 ft. lbs. Refill the cooling system and the power steering reservoir. Start the engine, allow it to reach normal operating temperatures and check for leaks.

ELDORADO AND SEVILLE

1. Disconnect the negative battery cable. Position a drain pan under the radiator, open the drain cock and drain the cooling system.
2. Remove the air cleaner. Matchmark the hood hinge-to-hood and remove the hood.
3. Remove the cooling fan and the accessory drive belt.
4. Remove the upper radiator hose and disconnect the heater hose from the thermostat housing.
5. Disconnect the following electrical connectors, positioning the wires out of the way:
    a. Oil pressure sending unit
    b. Coolant temperature sensor
    c. Distributor
    d. EGR solenoid
    e. Engine temperature switch
    f. Idle speed control
    g. Throttle position sensor
    h. Injector electrical connections
    i. MAT sensor
    j. Oxygen sensor

k. Throttle body base warmer

l. Alternator

m. Ground wires at the alternator mounting bracket

6. Disconnect the accelerator, the cruise control and the transaxle throttle valve cables from the throttle lever.

7. Disconnect the cruise control diaphragm/bracket and move them out of the way.

8. Disconnect the transaxle oil cooler lines from the radiator. Remove the radiator.

9. Disconnect and remove the oil cooler lines from the oil filter adapter.

10. Remove the oil cooler lines-to-transaxle bracket.

11. Remove the air cleaner bracket and the oil filter housing adapter.

12. Disconnect the air injection tubes from the diverter valve.

13. Remove the right front and right rear body braces.

14. Remove the right front heater hose and the coolant reservoir.

15. Remove the Air Injection Reactor (AIR) filter box and bracket. Remove the idler pulley for the accessory drive belt.

16. Remove the power steering line brace from the right cylinder head. Remove the pump and belt tensioner as an assembly and position them forward of the engine.

——————— CAUTION ———————

Make sure to follow carefully the instructions in the next 2 steps. Air conditioning refrigerant has a boiling point of −26°F. Follow fuel pressure release procedures carefully to avoid injury.

17. Discharge the air conditioning system and remove the air conditioning lines from the accumulator and condenser.

18. Position a metal container and a rag so as to catch the fuel and carefully depress the center pin at the Schrader valve on the fuel line until all fuel pressure is exhausted. Disconnect supply and return fuel lines from the throttle body. Remove the fuel line bracket from the transaxle and move the fuel lines aside.

19. Remove the EGR lines and brackets. Remove the vacuum modulator line and the fuel filter; reposition them aside.

20. Raise and safely support the vehicle.

21. Remove the starter heat shield. Label and disconnect the electrical connectors from the starter. Disconnect any ground wires still connected at the block.

22. Disconnect and remove the exhaust crossover pipe. Remove the starter-to-engine bolts and the starter.

23. Remove the torque converter covers. Matchmark the torque converter-to-flywheel and remove the flywheel-to-torque converter bolts.

24. Remove the air conditioning compressor lower dust shield, the right front tire and the outer wheelhouse plastic shield.

25. Remove the right rear transaxle-to-engine mount bolt and the lower engine mounting damper nut.

26. Remove the front engine mount nuts and the right rear transaxle mount nuts.

27. Remove the alternator. Remove the oxygen sensor wires. Remove the heater bypass bracket from the right side of the vehicle.

28. Remove the right side engine brace and lower the vehicle to the ground.

29. Remove the engine-to-transaxle bolts; the bolts are accessible from the top.

30. Run a chain from a lifting crane down to both lift points on top of the engine and ensure it is secure. Lift the engine out of the vehicle.

To install:

31. Situate a floor jack under the transaxle and raise it slightly so it will align with the engine. Lower the engine into the engine compartment, being careful not to damage accessories that are still in position. Change the engine and transaxle angles as necessary to get good alignment and then engage the dowels that are on the engine block with the corresponding holes in the transaxle.

32. Install the upper transaxle-to-engine bolts. Lower the engine, directing it squarely onto its mounts. Remove the lifting equipment.

33. To complete the installation, reverse the removal procedures. Make sure to replenish all fluids with the required type and quantity. Recharge the air conditioning system charged. Operate the engine until normal operating temperatures are reached and check for leaks.

ALLANTE

1. Disconnect the negative battery cable. Position a drain pan under the radiator, open the drain cock and drain the cooling system.

2. Remove the air cleaner. Matchmark the hood hinge-to-hood and remove the hood.

3. Remove the cooling fans and the accessory drive belt.

4. Remove the upper intake manifold. Remove the upper radiator hose and disconnect the heater hose from the thermostat housing.

5. Disconnect the following electrical connectors, positioning the wires out of the way:

a. Oil pressure sending unit

b. Coolant temperature sensor

c. Distributor

d. EGR solenoid

e. Engine temperature switch

f. Idle speed control

g. Throttle position sensor

h. Injector electrical connections

i. MAT sensor

j. Oxygen sensor

k. Throttle body base warmer

l. Alternator

m. Ground wires at the alternator mounting bracket

6. Disconnect the accelerator, the cruise control and the transaxle throttle valve cables from the throttle lever.

7. Disconnect the cruise control diaphragm/bracket and move them aside.

8. Disconnect the transaxle oil cooler lines from the radiator. Remove the radiator.

9. Disconnect and remove the oil cooler lines from the oil filter adapter.

10. Remove the oil cooler lines-to-transaxle bracket.

11. Remove the air cleaner bracket and the oil filter adapter.

12. Disconnect the air injection tubes from the diverter valve.

13. Remove the cross brace.

14. Remove the right front heater hose and the coolant reservoir.

15. Remove the Air Injection Reactor (AIR) filter and bracket.

16. Remove the power steering line brace from the right cylinder head. Remove the pump and belt tensioner as an assembly and position them forward of the engine.

——————— CAUTION ———————

Make sure to follow carefully the instructions in the next 2 steps. Air conditioning refrigerant has a boiling point of −26°F. Follow fuel pressure release procedures carefully to avoid injury.

17. Discharge the air conditioning system and remove the air conditioning lines from the accumulator and condenser.

18. Position a metal container and a rag so as to catch the fuel and carefully depress the center pin at the Schrader valve on the fuel line until all fuel pressure is exhausted. Disconnect supply and return fuel lines from the fuel rail. Remove the fuel line bracket from the transaxle and move the fuel lines aside.

19. Raise and safely support the vehicle.

20. Label and disconnect the electrical connectors from the starter. Disconnect any ground wires still connected at the block.

21. Disconnect the oxygen level sensor wire and the remove the oxygen sensors.

22. Disconnect and remove the exhaust Y-pipe. Remove the starter-to-engine bolts and the starter.

23. Remove the torque converter covers. Matchmark the torque converter-to-flywheel and remove the flywheel-to-torque converter bolts.

24. Remove the air conditioning compressor lower dust shield, the right front tire and the outer wheelhouse plastic shield.

25. Remove the right rear transaxle-to-engine mount bolt, the front engine mount nuts and the right rear transaxle mount bolts.

26. Remove the alternator. Remove the oxygen sensor wires. Remove the heater bypass bracket from the right side of the vehicle.

27. Remove the right side engine brace and lower the vehicle to the ground.

28. Remove the engine-to-transaxle bolts; the bolts are accessible from the top.

29. Run a chain from a lifting crane down to both lift points on top of the engine and ensure it is secure. Lift the engine out of the vehicle.

To install:

30. Situate a floor jack under the transaxle and raise it slightly so it will align with the engine. Lower the engine into the engine compartment, being careful not to damage accessories that are still in position. Change the engine and transaxle angles as necessary to get good alignment; engage the dowels that are on the engine block with the corresponding holes in the transaxle.

31. Install the upper transaxle-to-engine bolts. Lower the engine, directing it squarely onto its mounts. Remove the lifting equipment.

32. To complete the installation, reverse the removal procedures. Make sure to replenish all fluids with the required type and quantity. Recharge the air conditioning system charged. Operate the engine until normal operating temperatures are reached and check for leaks.

Engine Mounts

Removal and Installation

EXCEPT ALLANTE, ELDORADO AND SEVILLE

1. Disconnect the negative battery cable.
2. Raise and safely support the vehicle.
3. Remove the engine through mount bolt. Raise and support the engine properly.
4. Remove the engine mount retaining bolts. Remove the engine mount.
5. To install, reverse the removal procedures.

ALLANTE, ELDORADO AND SEVILLE
Right Side

1. Disconnect the negative battery cable.
2. Remove the brace from the engine bracket to engine.
3. Remove the engine bracket-to-mount nuts.
4. Raise and safely support the vehicle.
5. Remove the nuts securing the engine mount to the frame. Remove the nuts securing the transaxle mount to the frame bracket.
6. Using the engine support tool, raise the engine.
7. Raise the engine slowly until the bracket is free from the engine and transaxle mount. Remove the bracket-to-block stud and bolts. Remove the mount and bracket by pulling forward.
8. Remove the transaxle mounting bracket from the transaxle. Remove the mount assembly.
9. To install, reverse the removal procedures.

Left Side

1. Disconnect the negative battery cable. Remove the air cleaner assembly.
2. Remove the serpentine belt and discharge the air conditioning system.

3. Install the engine support tool.
4. Remove the lower center exhaust manifold nut and top nut of the engine damper.
5. Raise and safely support the vehicle.
6. Remove the right side engine compartment splash shield and air conditioning splash shield.
7. Remove the engine damper. Remove both air conditioning compressor brackets. Remove the air conditioning compressor.
8. Remove the water pipe bracket bolt.
9. Remove the engine mount bracket bolts from the engine block and cradle. Remove the engine mount and bracket through the right hand wheel well.
10. To install, reverse the removal procedures.

Intake Manifold

Removal and Installation

3.8L ENGINE

1986–87

1. Relieve the fuel pressure.
2. Disconnect the negative battery cable. Drain the cooling system. Remove the air intake duct and mass airflow sensor.
3. Remove the serpentine drive belt, alternator and alternator bracket.
4. Remove the ignition module and associated wiring. Disconnect wiring and vacuum lines that will interfere with removal of the manifold.
5. Disconnect and remove the throttle, cruise control and transaxle valve cables from the throttle body.
6. Remove the upper radiator hose. Disconnect the heater hoses at the throttle body.
7. Disconnect the electrical connections for the injectors.
8. Remove the fuel rail bolts and the fuel rail. Replace all O-rings on injectors that are to be reused.
9. Label and remove the spark plug wires.
10. Remove the intake manifold bolts, the manifold and gasket.

To install:

11. Clean all mating surfaces.
12. Using new gaskets and sealant (GM part number 1050026, for a steel gasket), reverse the removal procedures. Pipe thread fittings must be sealed with a sealer and lubricant such as GM part number 1052080. Torque the intake manifold-to-engine bolts to 37 ft. lbs. (in sequence).
13. To complete the installation, reverse the removal procedures. Replenish all fluids. Start the engine, operate it until normal temperatures are reached and check for leaks.

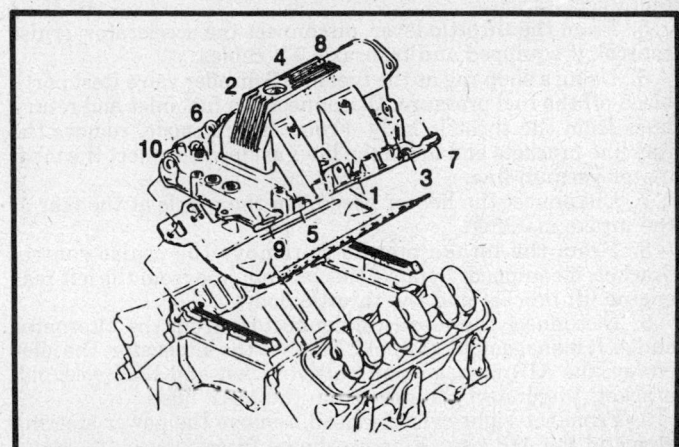

Intake manifold bolt torquing sequence—V6 engine with fuel injection

1988–90

1. Relieve the fuel pressure.
2. Disconnect the negative battery cable. Place a clean drain pan under the radiator, open the drain cock and drain the cooling system.
3. Remove the serpentine drive belt, the alternator and the bracket.
4. Remove the power steering pump, the braces and move it aside; do not disconnect the pressure lines.
5. Remove the coolant bypass hose, the heater pipe and the upper radiator hose from the intake manifold.
6. Remove the vacuum hoses and disconnect the electrical connectors from the intake manifold.
7. Remove the EGR pipe, the EGR valve and the adapter from the throttle body.
8. Remove the throttle body coolant pipe, the throttle body and the throttle body adapter.
9. Disconnect the rear spark plug wires. Remove the intake manifold-to-engine bolts and the manifold.

To install:

10. Clean the gasket mounting surfaces.
11. Using new gaskets and sealant number 12345336 or equivalent (on the ends of the manifold seals), reverse the removal procedures. Torque the intake manifold, in sequence, to 88 inch lbs. (1988) or 12 ft. lbs. (1989–90). Refill the cooling system. Start the engine, allow it to reach normal operating temperatures and check for leaks.

4.1L AND 4.5L ENGINES

NOTE: Some vehicles equipped with the 4.1L and 4.5L engines have been experiencing oil leakage at the intake manifold to block seal, due to a split intake manifold seal. When repairing this leak, replace the old seal with a new silicone seal (part number 3634619). The new seal is easily identified by its gray color.

1. Disconnect the negative battery cable. Drain the cooling system to a level below the intake manifold. Disconnect the upper radiator hose from the thermostat housing.
2. Remove the air cleaner and the drive belt. Label and disconnect the spark plug wires from the spark plugs.
3. Remove the upper power steering pump bracket-to-engine bolts and loosen the lower nuts.
4. Disconnect the following electrical connections and position the wiring harness out of the way: distributor, oil pressure switch, EGR solenoid, coolant sensor, mass airflow temperature sensor, throttle position sensor, 4-way connector at the distributor, electric fuel evaporator grid, idle speed control motor and fuel injectors.
5. From the throttle lever, disconnect the accelerator, cruise control, if equipped and transaxle TV cables.
6. Using a shop rag at the fuel line Schrader valve (test port), bleed off the fuel pressure. Disconnect the fuel inlet and return lines from the throttle body. From the transaxle, remove the fuel line brackets and move the lines aside; disconnect the modulator vacuum line.
7. Disconnect the heater hose from the nipple at the rear of the intake manifold.
8. From the intake manifold, remove the cruise control bracket, if equipped. Remove the vacuum line from the left rear engine lift bracket and the throttle body.
9. Disconnect the electrical connectors from the alternator and AIR management solenoid. Remove the alternator, the idler pulley, the AIR management valve/bracket and EGR solenoid/bracket. Disconnect the hose from the MAP hose.
10. From the right cylinder head, remove the power steering pipe and the AIR pipe. Remove the oil filter.
11. Remove the distributor. Remove both rocker arm covers. Remove the rocker arm support with the rocker arms intact by first alternately and evenly removing the bolts followed by the

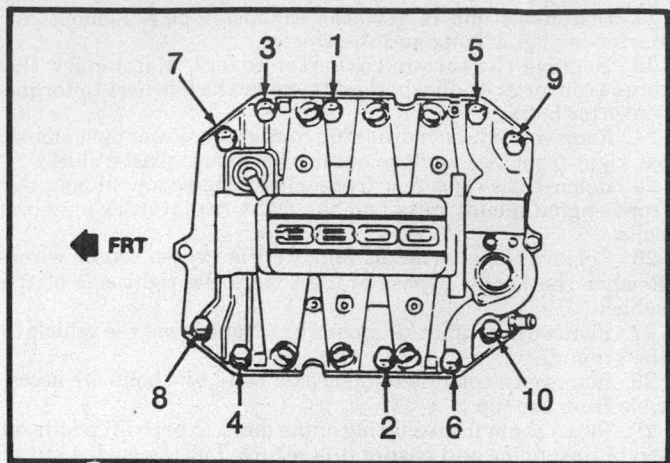

Intake manifold bolt torquing sequence—1988–90 3.8L

nuts. Keep the pushrods in sequence so they may be reassembled in their original positions.

12. If equipped with air conditioning, partially remove the compressor; do not discharge the system. Remove the vacuum harness connections from the TVS at the rear of the intake manifold.
13. Remove the intake manifold bolts and remove both bolts securing the lower thermostat housing to the front cover. Remove the engine lift brackets or bend them out of the way.
14. Remove the intake manifold and lower the thermostat housing as an assembly by lifting it straight up off of the dowels.

To install:

15. Clean the gasket mounting surfaces.
16. Using new gaskets, apply RTV sealant to the 4 corners where the end seals meet and reverse the removal procedures.
17. To torque the intake manifold-to-engine bolts, perform the following procedures:
  a. Torque the No. 1–4 bolts (in sequence) to 15 ft. lbs (1988) or 8 ft. lbs. (1989–90).
  b. Torque the No. 5–16 bolts (in sequence) to 22 ft. lbs. (1988) or 8 ft. lbs. (1989–90).
  c. Retorque all bolts (in sequence) to 22 ft. lbs. (1988) or 12 ft. lbs. (1989–90).
  d. Recheck all bolts (in sequence) to 22 ft. lbs. (1988) or 12 ft. lbs. (1989–90).
18. To complete the installation, use new gaskets and reverse the removal procedures. Refill the cooling system. Start the engine, allow it to reach normal operating temperatures and check for leaks.

Exhaust Manifold

Removal and Installation

3.8L ENGINE

Left Side

1. Disconnect the negative battery cable.
2. If necessary, remove the mass air flow sensor, air intake duct and crankcase ventilation pipe.
3. Remove the exhaust crossover pipe-to-exhaust manifold bolts.
4. Label and disconnect the spark plug wires.
5. Remove the exhaust manifold-to-cylinder head bolts and the manifold.
6. If necessary, remove the oil dipstick tube to provide access to the manifold bolts.

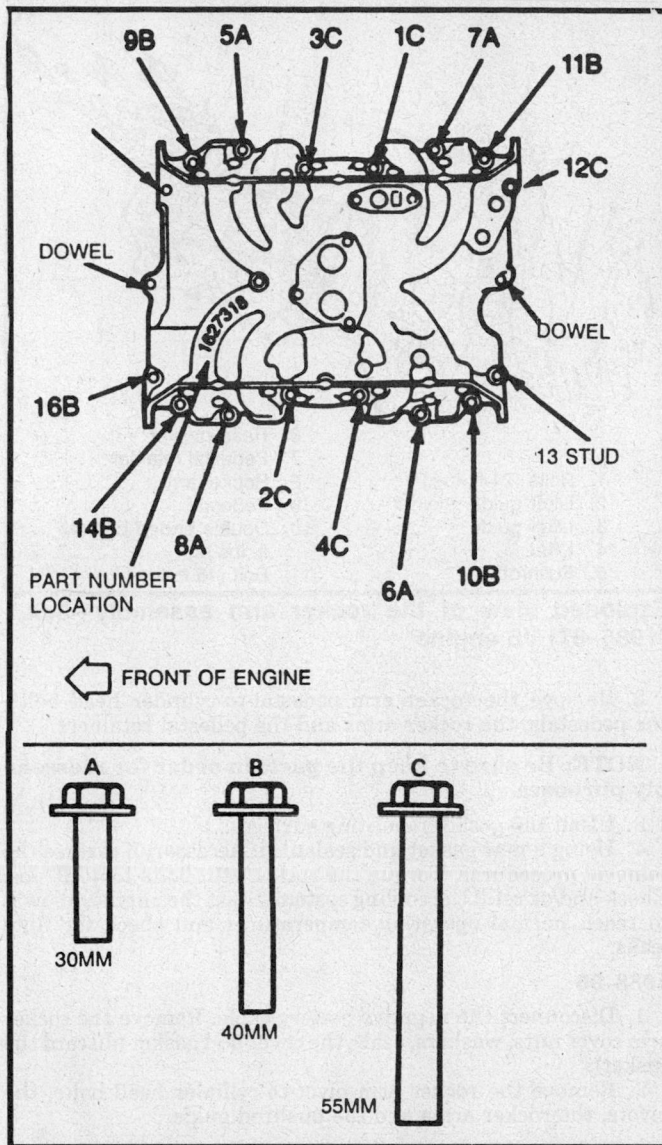

DOWEL

1627318

PART NUMBER
LOCATION

DOWEL

13 STUD

FRONT OF ENGINE

A — 30MM

B — 40MM

C — 55MM

Intake manifold bolt torquing sequence—1986–88 4.1L and 1988–90 4.5L engines

To install:

7. Clean the gasket mounting surfaces.

8. Using a new gasket, reverse the removal procedures. Torque the exhaust manifold-to-cylinder head bolts to 37 ft. lbs. and the exhaust crossover pipe-to-manifold bolts to 22 ft. lbs.

9. Start the engine and check for exhaust leaks.

Right Side

1. Disconnect the negative battery cable.

2. If necessary, disconnect the mass air flow sensor, air intake duct, the crankcase ventilation pipe and the IAC connector from the throttle body.

3. Label and disconnect the wires from the spark plugs. Disconnect the oxygen sensor lead.

4. If equipped, disconnect the heater inlet pipe from the manifold studs.

5. Remove the exhaust crossover pipe-to-exhaust manifold bolts and the pipe.

6. Remove the serpentine drive belt. On the 1986–87, remove the front alternator-to-engine support bracket.

7. Raise and safely support the vehicle. Remove the exhaust pipe-to-manifold bolts, the exhaust manifold-to-cylinder head bolts and the manifold.

8. Remove the EGR pipe from the exhaust manifold.

To install:

9. Clean the gasket mounting surfaces.

10. Using a new gasket, reverse the removal procedures. Torque the exhaust manifold-to-cylinder head bolts to 37 ft. lbs. and the exhaust crossover pipe-to-manifold bolts to 22 ft. lbs.

11. Start the engine and check for exhaust leaks.

4.1L AND 4.5L ENGINES

Left Side

1. Disconnect the negative battery cable, the oxygen sensor wire and the spark plug wires.

2. Remove both cooling fans.

3. Remove the serpentine drive belt and the AIR pipe from the air pump.

4. Remove the belt tensioner and the power steering pump brace.

5. Raise and safely support the vehicle.

6. Remove the exhaust Y-pipe and the air conditioning-to-manifold brace.

7. Remove the exhaust manifold-to-cylinder head bolts, the AIR pipe and the manifold.

To install:

8. Clean the gasket mounting surfaces.

9. Using new gaskets, reverse the removal procedures. Torque the exhaust manifold-to-engine bolts to 18 ft. lbs. Start the engine and check for exhaust leaks.

Right Side

1. Disconnect the negative battery cable. Remove the air cleaner.

2. Remove the EGR pipe from the manifold.

3. Raise and safely support the vehicle.

4. Disconnect the Y-pipe from the manifold.

5. From the front of the manifold, remove the engine mount brace.

6. Disconnect the oxygen sensor wire.

7. Remove the exhaust manifold-to-cylinder head bolts and the manifold.

To install:

8. Clean the gasket mounting surfaces.

9. Using new gaskets, reverse the removal procedures. Torque the exhaust manifold-to-engine bolts to 18 ft. lbs. Start the engine and check for exhaust leaks.

Valve System

VALVE ADJUSTMENT

All engines use hydraulic lifters which are non-adjustable. Hydraulic valve lifters keep all parts of the valve train in constant contact and adjust automatically to maintain 0 lash under all conditions.

3.8L ENGINE

E–I–E–I–I–E (left side, front-to-rear)
E–I–I–E–I–E (right side, front-to-rear)

4.1L AND 4.5L ENGINES

I–E–I–E–E–I–E–I (both sides, front-to-rear)

VALVE LIFTERS

Removal and Installation

1. Disconnect the negative battery cable. Remove the intake manifold.

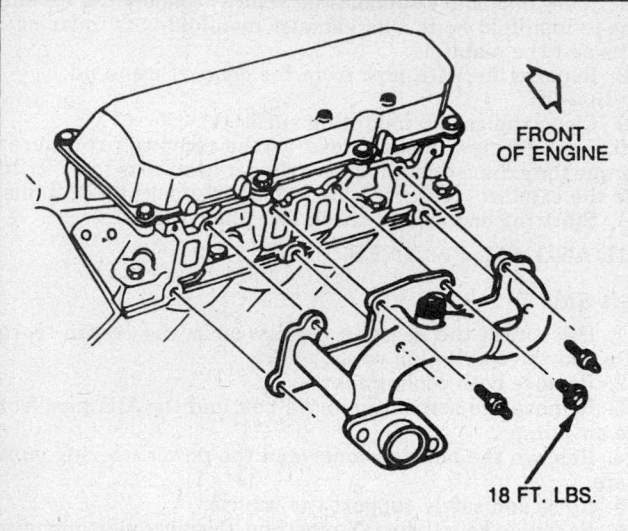

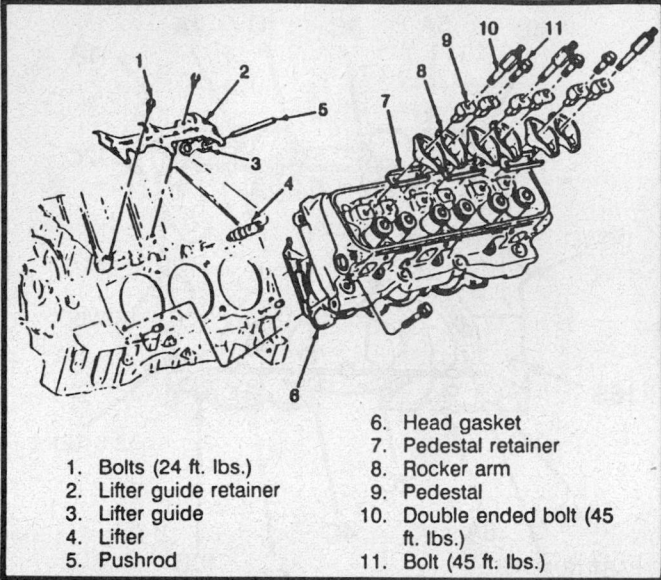

1. Bolts (24 ft. lbs.)
2. Lifter guide retainer
3. Lifter guide
4. Lifter
5. Pushrod
6. Head gasket
7. Pedestal retainer
8. Rocker arm
9. Pedestal
10. Double ended bolt (45 ft. lbs.)
11. Bolt (45 ft. lbs.)

Exploded view of the rocker arm assembly—3.8L (1986–87) V6 engine

2. Remove the rocker arm pedestal-to-cylinder head bolts, the pedestals, the rocker arms and the pedestal retainers.

NOTE: **Be sure to keep the parts in order for reassembly purposes.**

3. Clean the gasket mounting surfaces.
4. Using a new gasket and sealant (if necessary), reverse the removal procedures. Torque the rocker arm bolts to 45 ft. lbs. Check and/or refill the cooling system. Start the engine, allow it to reach normal operating temperatures and check for fluid leaks.

1988–90

1. Disconnect the negative battery cable. Remove the rocker arm cover nuts, washers, seals, the cover and gasket (discard the gasket).
2. Remove the rocker arm pivot-to-cylinder head bolts, the pivots, the rocker arms and the pushrod guide.

NOTE: **Be sure to keep the parts in order for reassembly purposes.**

3. Clean the gasket mounting surfaces.
4. Using a new gasket and sealant (if necessary), reverse the removal procedures. Torque the rocker arm bolts to 28 ft. lbs. Check and/or refill the cooling system. Check and/or refill the cooling and lubrication systems. Start the engine, allow it to reach normal operating temperatures and check for leaks.

4.1L AND 4.5L ENGINES

1. Disconnect the negative battery cable. Remove the rocker arm cover.
2. Remove the rocker arm support-to-cylinder head bosses bolts.
3. Remove the rocker arm support-to-cylinder head stud nuts.

NOTE: **This method of removal is preferred as the pivot assemblies may be damaged if the pivot bolt torque is not removed evenly against the valve spring tension.**

4. Place the rocker arm support in a vise and remove the rocker arm pivot-to-rocker arm support bolts.
To install:
5. Lubricate all parts with axle lube part number 1052271 or

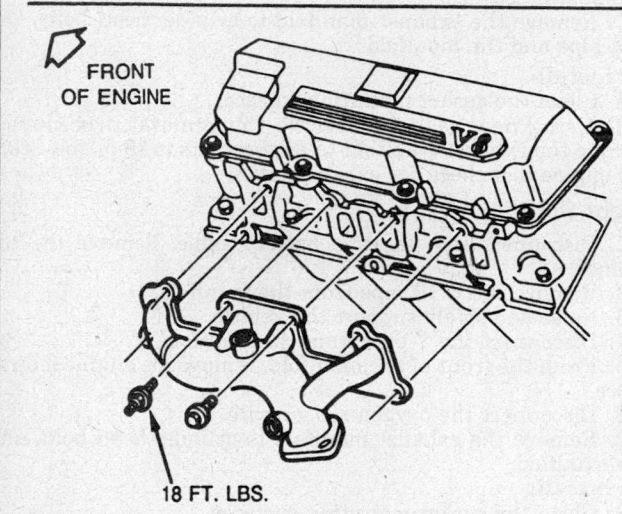

Exploded view of the exhaust manifolds—4.1L and 4.5L engines

2. Remove the rocker arm cover and discard the old gasket.
3. Remove the rocker arm assemblies.
4. Remove the pushrods. Using the valve lifter removal tool, remove the valve lifters.
To install:
5. Clean the gasket mounting surfaces.
6. Lubricate the lifters with clean engine oil, use new gaskets and/or sealant and reverse the removal procedures.

VALVE ROCKER SHAFT/ARM ASSEMBLY

Removal and Installation

3.8L ENGINE

The 3.8L engine uses individual rocker arm and pedestal assemblies.

1986–87

1. Disconnect the negative battery cable. Remove the rocker arm cover nuts, washers, seals, the cover and gasket (discard the gasket).

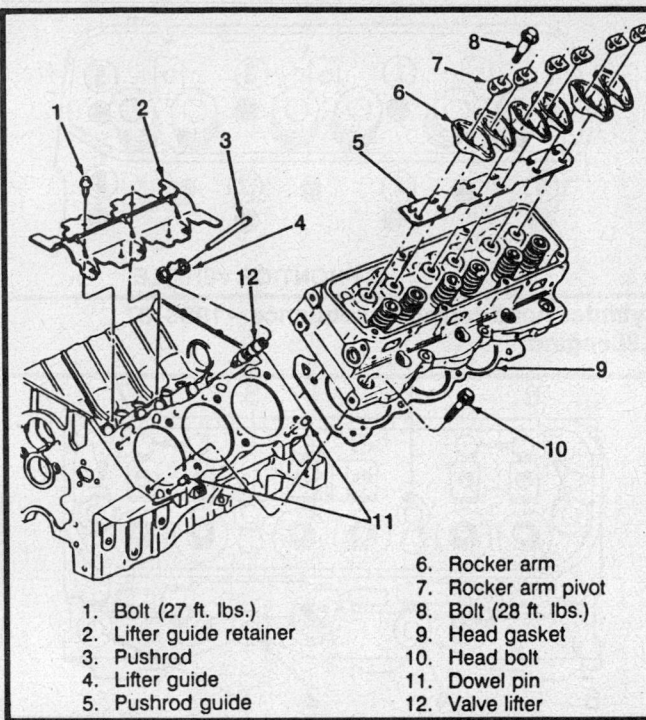

1. Bolt (27 ft. lbs.)	6. Rocker arm
2. Lifter guide retainer	7. Rocker arm pivot
3. Pushrod	8. Bolt (28 ft. lbs.)
4. Lifter guide	9. Head gasket
5. Pushrod guide	10. Head bolt
	11. Dowel pin
	12. Valve lifter

Exploded view of the rocker arm assembly—1988–90 3.8L engine

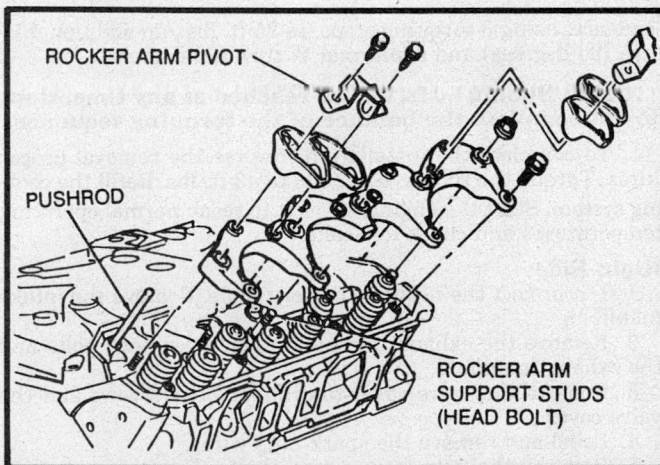

Exploded view of the rocker arm assembly—1986–88 4.1L and 1988–90 4.5L engines

equivalent and reverse the removal procedures. Torque the rocker arm pivot-to-rocker arm support bolts to 22 ft. lbs.

NOTE: The pivot bolts are self-tapping.

6. Position the pushrod into the seat of each rocker arm and loosely install the retaining nuts.

7. Recheck the pushrods for being seated correctly. Tighten the nuts alternately and evenly, checking the position of the pushrods while tightening.

8. When the nuts have been seated and the pushrods are correct. Torque the rocker arm support-to-cylinder head nuts to 37 ft. lbs. and the bolts to 7 ft. lbs.

9. To complete the installation, reverse the removal procedures. Start the engine and check for leaks.

CHECKING VALVE TIMING

Procedure

3.8L ENGINE

1. Disconnect the negative battery cable. Remove the front cover.

2. Remove the button and spring from the center of the camshaft.

3. Rotate the crankshaft to align the marks of the timing sprockets; they must be close together.

4. If the timing is not correct, remove the camshaft sprocket bolts, the sprocket and the timing chain.

To install:

5. Clean the gasket mounting surfaces. Inspect the parts for wear and/or damage; if necessary, replace the parts.

6. To install the timing chain and sprockets, perform the following procedures:

    a. Assemble the timing chain on the camshaft sprocket and crankshaft sprockets.

    b. Align the 0 marks on the sprockets; they must face each other.

    c. Slide the assembly onto the camshaft and crankshaft. Install the camshaft sprocket-to-camshaft bolts. Torque the camshaft sprocket-to-camshaft sprocket bolts to 20 ft. lbs. (1986) or 28 ft. lbs. (1987–90).

NOTE: On the 1988–90 (VIN C) engine, align the camshaft sprocket mark with the balancer shaft sprocket mark.

7. To complete the installation, use new gaskets, sealant (if necessary) and reverse the removal procedures. Refill the cooling system. Start the engine, allow it to reach normal operating temperatures and check for leaks.

4.1L AND 4.5L ENGINES

1. Disconnect the negative battery cable. Remove the front cover-to-engine screws and the cover with the water pump and lower thermostat housing as an assembly.

2. Remove the oil slinger from the crankshaft.

3. Rotate the crankshaft to align the timing marks on the camshaft and crankshaft; they must be aligned and facing each other.

4. If the timing marks are not aligned, rotate the crankshaft and align the timing marks to TDC.

5. Remove the camshaft sprocket-to-camshaft screw, the camshaft and crankshaft sprockets with the chain attached.

To install:

6. Reverse the removal procedures. After installing the timing chain over the camshaft sprocket rotate the crankshaft until the crankshaft sprocket timing mark is positioned straight up.

7. Install the cam sprocket and timing chain over the crankshaft so the timing marks are aligned.

8. Hold the camshaft sprocket in position against the end of the camshaft and press the sprocket on the camshaft by hand. Make sure the camshaft index pin is align with the sprocket index hole.

9. If necessary, keep the engine from rotating while torquing the camshaft sprocket screw to 37 ft. lbs.

NOTE: Engine timing has been set so the No. 1 cylinder is in the TDC firing position. If the distributor was removed make sure the rotor is positioned on the No. 1 cylinder firing position.

10. Install the oil slinger on the crankshaft with the smaller end of the slinger against the crankshaft sprocket. Install the engine front cover.

11. To complete the installation, reverse the removal procedures.

Cylinder Head

Removal and Installation

1986–87 3.8L ENGINE

1. Disconnect the negative battery cable. Remove the air cleaner.
2. Place a drain pan under the radiator, open the drain cock and drain the cooling system.
3. If equipped with air conditioning, remove the compressor from the mounting bracket and position it aside; do not disconnect any lines. Disconnect the AIR hose at the check valve.
4. Remove the intake manifold-to-engine bolts and the manifold.
5. If removing the right cylinder head, loosen the alternator belt, disconnect the electrical connectors and remove the alternator.
6. If removing the left cylinder head, remove the dipstick, power steering pump and air pump, if equipped.
7. Disconnect and label the plug wires.
8. Disconnect the exhaust manifold-to-cylinder head bolts and the manifold.
9. Remove the rocker arm cover and the rocker shaft assembly; lift out the pushrods. Be extremely careful to avoid getting dirt in the valve lifters. Keep the pushrods in order; they must be returned to their original positions.
10. Remove the cylinder head bolts, the cylinder head and gasket.
To install:
11. Clean the gasket mounting surfaces.
12. Reverse the removal procedures. Torque the cylinder head-to-engine bolts in the following manner:
    a. Use a heavy duty thread sealer on the head bolts.
    b. Torque the head bolts to 25 ft. lbs. in the proper sequence.

NOTE: Should 60 ft. lbs. be reached at any time in the next 2 steps, stop; do not complete the balance of the 90 degree turn.

    c. Tighten each bolt ¼ turn (90 degrees) in sequence.
    d. Tighten each bolt an additional ¼ turn (90 degrees) in sequence.
13. To complete the installation, reverse the removal procedures. Refill the cooling system. Operate the engine until normal operating temperatures are reached and check for leaks.

1988–90 3.8L ENGINE

Left Side
1. Disconnect the negative battery cable. Remove the intake manifold.
2. Remove the exhaust manifold-to-cylinder head bolts and the exhaust manifold.
3. Remove the valve cover-to-cylinder head screws and the valve cover.
4. Label and remove the spark plug wires. Remove the C³I unit-to-cylinder head bolts and the unit.
5. Remove the serpentine drive belt, the alternator-to-bracket bolts, the alternator, the alternator bracket-to-engine bolts and the bracket.
6. If equipped with air conditioning, remove the compressor-to-bracket bolts and move it aside; do not disconnect the refrigerant lines.
7. Remove the rocker arm assemblies, the guide plate and the pushrods; keep them in order for reinstallation purposes.
8. Remove the cylinder head bolts and the cylinder head.
To install:
9. Clean and inspect the gasket mounting surfaces.
10. Using new gaskets, apply sealant part number 1052080 or equivalent, on the cylinder head bolt threads and reverse the removal procedures. Torque the cylinder head-to-engine bolts, in

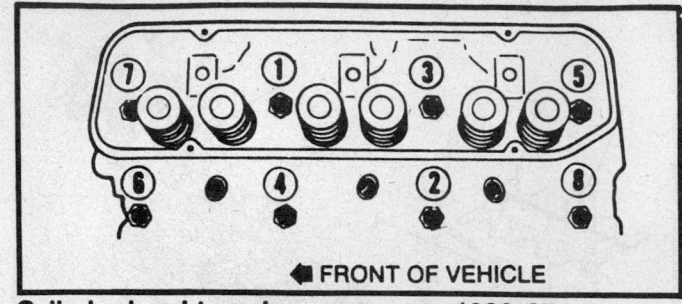

Cylinder head torquing sequence—1986–87 3.8L engine

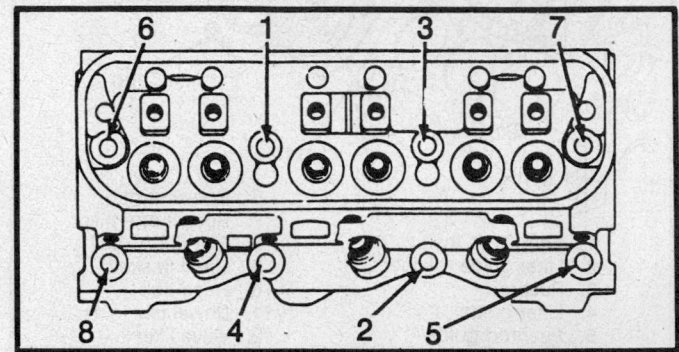

Cylinder head torquing sequence—1988–90 3.8L engine

sequence, using 3 torquing steps, to 25 ft. lbs., an additional ¼ turn (90 degrees) and additional ¼ turn (90 degrees).

NOTE: Should 60 ft. lbs. be reached at any time, stop; do not complete the balance of the torquing sequence.

11. To complete the installation, reverse the removal procedures. Torque the rocker arm bolts to 43 ft. lbs. Refill the cooling system. Start the engine, allow it to reach normal operating temperatures and check for leaks.

Right Side
1. Disconnect the negative battery cable. Remove the intake manifold.
2. Remove the exhaust manifold-to-cylinder head bolts and the exhaust manifold.
3. Remove the valve cover-to-cylinder head screws and the valve cover.
4. Label and remove the spark plug wires.
5. Remove the serpentine drive belt, the power steering pump-to-bracket bolts, the belt tensioner assembly and the fuel line heat shield.
6. Remove the rocker arm assemblies, the guide plate and the pushrods; keep them in order for reinstallation purposes.
7. Remove the cylinder head bolts and the cylinder head.
To install:
8. Clean and inspect the gasket mounting surfaces.
9. Using new gaskets, apply sealant part number 1052080 or equivalent, on the cylinder head bolt threads and reverse the removal procedures. Torque the cylinder head-to-engine bolts, in sequence, using 3 torquing steps, to 25 ft. lbs., an additional ¼ turn (90 degrees) and additional ¼ turn (90 degrees).

NOTE: Should 60 ft. lbs. be reached at any time, stop; do not complete the balance of the torquing sequence.

10. To complete the installation, reverse the removal procedures. Torque the rocker arm bolts to 43 ft. lbs. Refill the cooling system. Start the engine, allow it to reach normal operating temperatures and check for leaks.

4.1L ENGINE

1. Disconnect the negative battery cable. Drain the engine coolant.
2. Remove the intake and exhaust manifolds.
3. Disconnect all electrical and ground connections from the cylinder head.
4. When removing the left cylinder head, partially remove the power steering pump.
5. When removing the right cylinder head, remove the alternator and the heater hose from the rear of the head.
6. Remove the air pump, if equipped.
7. Remove bolts holding the rocker arm cover to the heads and remove the cover.
8. Remove nuts holding the rocker arm support to cylinder head, the support and rocker arm assemblies. Store these assemblies so they may be reinstalled in their correct locations.
9. Remove the pushrods and store them with their respective rocker arm assemblies.
10. Remove the cylinder head bolts.
11. Lift the cylinder head off of the block.

NOTE: Install cylinder liner holders to prevent loss of the bottom seal.

12. Remove all gasket material from the cylinder head and block mating surfaces.

To install:

13. Reverse the removal procedures.
14. When torquing the head bolts, use the 3 step method. Torque the bolts to ⅓ of the total torque listed in the sequence shown. Once this is done, repeat the same procedure, this time torquing all the bolts to ⅔ of the total listed torque. Finally torque the bolts to the recommended torque of 90 ft. lbs. Refill the cooling system. Operate the engine until normal operating temperatures are reached and check for leaks.

4.5L ENGINE
Left Side

1. Disconnect the negative battery cable.
2. Drain the cooling system.
3. Remove the rocker arm covers.
4. Remove the intake manifold-to-engine bolts and intake manifold.
5. Disconnect the exhaust manifold crossover pipe, the exhaust pipe-to-exhaust manifold bolts, the exhaust manifold-to-cylinder head bolts and the exhaust manifold.
6. Remove the engine lifting bracket and the dipstick tube.
7. Remove the AIR bracket-to-engine bolts and move the bracket aside.
8. Remove the cylinder head-to-engine bolts and the cylinder head.

To install:

9. Clean the gasket mounting surfaces.
10. Using new gaskets, sealant, if necessary, apply GM lubricant part number 1052356 or equivalent, to the cylinder head bolt threads and reverse the removal procedures. Torque the cylinder head bolts (in sequence) using 3 steps: 1st to 38 ft. lbs., 2nd to 68 ft. lbs. and 3rd to 90 ft. lbs. (bolts No. 1, 3 and 4).
11. To complete the installation, reverse the removal procedures. Refill the cooling system. Start the engine, allow it to reach normal operating temperatures and check for leaks.

Right Side

1. Remove negative battery cable.
2. Drain the cooling system.
3. Remove the rocker arm covers.
4. Remove the intake manifold-to-engine bolts and intake manifold.
5. Disconnect the exhaust manifold crossover pipe, the exhaust pipe-to-exhaust manifold bolts, the exhaust manifold-to-cylinder head bolts and the exhaust manifold.

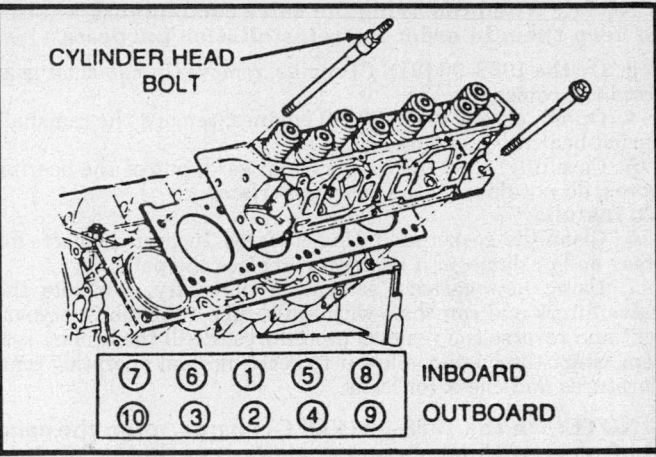

Cylinder head torquing sequence—1986–87 4.1L engine

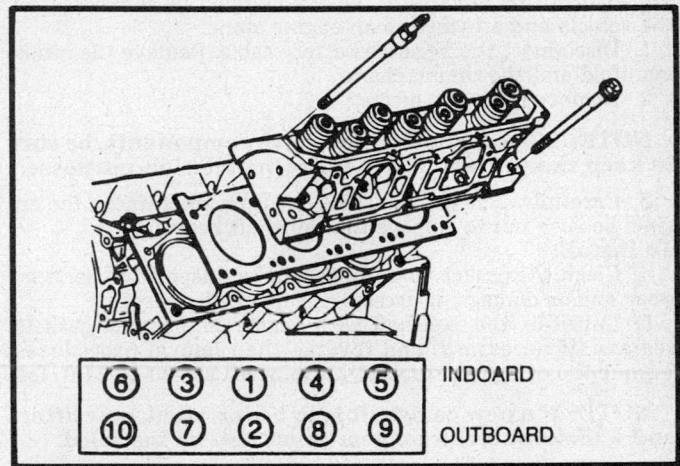

Cylinder head torquing sequence—1988 4.1L and 1988–90 4.5L engines

6. Remove the engine lifting bracket.
7. Remove the AIR bracket-to-engine bolts and move the bracket aside.
8. Remove the cylinder head-to-engine bolts and the cylinder head.

To install:

9. Clean the gasket mounting surfaces.
10. Using new gaskets, sealant, if necessary, apply GM lubricant part number 1052356 or equivalent, to the cylinder head bolt threads and reverse the removal procedures. Torque the cylinder head bolts, in sequence, using 3 steps: 1st to 38 ft. lbs., 2nd to 68 ft. lbs. and 3rd to 90 ft. lbs. (bolts No. 1, 3 and 4).
11. To complete the installation, reverse the removal procedures. Refill the cooling system. Start the engine, allow it to reach normal operating temperatures and check for leaks.

Camshaft

Removal and Installation
3.8L ENGINE

1. Disconnect the negative battery cable. Remove the intake manifold, the timing chain and camshaft sprockets.
2. Remove the rocker arm covers, the rocker arm shaft or rocker arm assemblies, the pushrods and the hydraulic lifters.

NOTE: When removing the valve components, be sure to keep them in order for reinstallation purposes.

3. On the 1988–90 (VIN C) engine, remove the camshaft gear from the camshaft.

4. On all, except the 1988–90 engines, remove the camshaft thrust bearing-to-engine bolts.

5. Carefully, slide the camshaft forward, out of the bearing bores; do not damage the bearing surfaces.

To install:

6. Clean the gasket mounting surfaces. Inspect the parts for wear and/or damage; if necessary, replace the parts.

7. Using new gaskets, sealant, if necessary, lubricate the valve lifters and camshaft with multi-lube 1052365 or equivalent and reverse the removal procedures. Refill the cooling system. Start the engine, allow it to reach normal operating temperatures and check for leaks.

NOTE: On the 1988–90 (VIN C) engine, align the camshaft gear with the balancer shaft gear timing marks.

4.1L AND 4.5L ENGINES

To perform this procedure, the engine must be removed from the vehicle and attached to an engine stand.

1. Disconnect the negative battery cable. Remove the intake manifold and the timing chain.

2. Remove the valve lifters.

NOTE: When removing the valve components, be sure to keep the parts in order for reinstallation purposes.

3. Carefully slide the camshaft out from the front of the engine; be sure not to damage the camshaft bearings.

To install:

4. Clean the gasket mounting surfaces. Inspect the parts for wear and/or damage; if necessary, replace the parts.

5. Lubricate the camshaft with engine oil, use new gaskets, sealant (if necessary) and reverse the removal procedures. Torque the camshaft sprocket-to-camshaft screws to 37 ft. lbs.

NOTE: If a new camshaft is to be installed, new lifters and a distributor drive gear must also be installed.

6. To complete the installation, reverse the removal procedures. Refill the cooling system. Start the engine, allow it to reach normal operating temperatures and check for leaks.

Balance Shaft

Removal and Installation

1988–90 3.8L ENGINE

1. Disconnect the negative battery cable. Remove the engine and secure it to a workstand.

2. Remove the flywheel-to-crankshaft bolts and the flywheel.

3. Remove the timing chain cover-to-engine bolts and the cover.

4. Remove the camshaft sprocket-to-camshaft gear bolts, the sprocket, the timing chain and the gear.

5. To remove the balance shaft, perform the following procedures:

   a. Remove the balance shaft gear-to-shaft bolt and the gear.

   b. Remove the balance shaft retainer-to-engine bolts and the retainer.

   c. Using the slide hammer tool, pull the balance shaft from the front of the engine.

6. If replacing the rear balance shaft bearing, perform the following procedures:

   a. Drive the rear plug from the engine.

   b. Using the camshaft remover/installer tool, press the rear bearing from the rear of the engine.

   c. Dip the new bearing in clean engine oil.

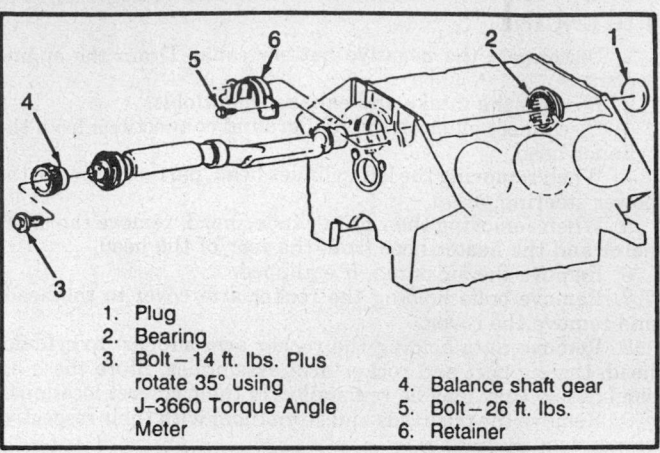

1. Plug
2. Bearing
3. Bolt—14 ft. lbs. Plus rotate 35° using J-3660 Torque Angle Meter
4. Balance shaft gear
5. Bolt—26 ft. lbs.
6. Retainer

Exploded view of the balance shaft assembly—1988–90 3.8L (Code C) engine

   d. Using the balance shaft rear bearing installer tool, press the new rear bearing into the rear of the engine.

   e. Install the rear cup plug.

To install:

7. Using the balance shaft installer tool, screw it into the balance shaft and install the shaft into the engine; remove the installer tool.

8. Clean the gasket mounting surfaces. Inspect the parts for wear and/or damage; replace the parts, if necessary.

9. Install the balance shaft retainer. Torque the balance shaft retainer-to-engine bolts to 27 ft. lbs.

10. Align the balance shaft gear with the camshaft gear timing marks. Install the balance shaft gear onto the balance shaft. Torque the balance gear-to-balance shaft bolt to 45 ft. lbs.

11. To complete the installation, use new gaskets, sealant (if necessary) and reverse the removal procedures. Torque the flywheel-to-crankshaft bolts to 60 ft. lbs. Refill the cooling system. Start the engine, allow it reach normal operating temperatures and check for leaks.

Timing Case Cover/Oil Seal

Removal and Installation

3.8L ENGINE
Cover Removed

1. Disconnect the negative battery cable.

2. Place a clean drain pan under the radiator, open the drain cock and drain the engine coolant. Remove the lower radiator hose and the coolant bypass hose from the timing case cover. Remove the heater pipes.

3. Remove the front engine cradle mount bolts. Using a vertical lifting device, secure it to the engine and raise it slightly.

4. Remove the serpentine drive belt and the water pump pulley.

5. Label and disconnect the alternator wiring. Remove the alternator and the alternator bracket.

6. On the 1988–90, remove the inner splash shield.

7. Remove the crankshaft balancer bolt/washer and the balancer.

8. Disconnect the electrical connectors from the crankshaft sensor, the camshaft sensor and the oil pressure switch.

9. Remove the oil pan-to-timing case cover bolts, the timing case cover-to-engine bolts and the cover. Using a small pry bar, remove the oil seal and discard it.

10. To replace the timing case oil seal, perform the following procedures:

   a. Using a small pry bar, pry the oil seal from the timing case cover; be careful not to damage the sealing surfaces.

b. Clean the oil seal mounting surface.

c. Using GM lubricant part number 1050169 or equivalent, coat the outside of the seal and the crankshaft balancer.

d. Using the oil seal installation tool, drive the new seal into the timing case cover until it seats.

To install:

11. Clean the gasket mounting surfaces.

12. Using a new gasket and sealant part number 1052080 or equivalent, reverse the removal procedures. Torque the:

Timing case cover-to-engine bolts to 22 ft. lbs.

Oil pan-to-timing case cover bolts to 88 inch lbs.

Crankshaft balancer-to-crankshaft bolt to 200 ft. lbs. (1986–87) or 219 ft. lbs. (1988–90)

13. Refill the cooling system. Start the engine, allow it to reach normal operating temperatures and check for leaks.

Cover Installed

1. Disconnect the negative battery cable.

2. Remove the drive belt.

3. Remove the crankshaft balancer-to-crankshaft bolts.

4. Using a small pry bar, pry the oil seal from the timing case cover; be careful not to damage the sealing surfaces.

To install:

5. Clean the oil seal mounting surface.

6. Using GM lubricant part number 1050169 or equivalent, coat the outside of the seal and the crankshaft balancer.

7. Using the oil seal installation tool, drive the new seal into the timing case cover until it seats.

8. To complete the installation, reverse the removal procedures. Torque the crankshaft balancer-to-crankshaft bolt to 200 ft. lbs. (1986–87) or 219 ft. lbs. (1988–90).

4.1L AND 4.5L ENGINES
Cover Removed

1. Disconnect the negative battery cable.

2. Place a clean drain pan under the radiator, open the drain cock and drain the engine coolant. Remove the air cleaner and move it aside.

3. Remove the serpentine belt.

4. Label and disconnect the alternator wiring. Remove the alternator and the alternator bracket.

5. Remove the air conditioner accumulator from the bracket and move it aside; do not disconnect the fittings on the accumulator.

6. Remove the water pump pulley bolts and the pulley. If necessary, remove the idler pulley.

7. Raise and safely support the vehicle.

8. Remove the crankshaft pulley-to-crankshaft pulley bolt. Using a wheel puller, attach it to the crankshaft pulley; using the center bolt, press the crankshaft pulley from the crankshaft. Remove the woodruff key from the crankshaft.

9. Remove the timing case cover-to-engine bolts, the oil pan-to-timing case cover bolts and the cover.

10. Clean the gasket mounting surfaces.

11. Using a small pry bar, pry the oil seal from the timing case cover (discard it).

To install:

12. Clean the oil seal mounting surface. Lubricate the new seal with engine oil.

13. Using a hammer and the oil seal installation tool, drive the new oil seal in to the timing case cover until it seats.

14. To complete the installation, use a new gasket, RTV sealant (on the oil pan lip) and reverse the removal procedures. Torque the timing case cover-to-engine bolts to 15 ft. lbs. and the crankshaft pulley-to-crankshaft bolt to 18 ft. lbs.

Cover Installed

1. Disconnect the negative battery cable. Remove the crankshaft pulley.

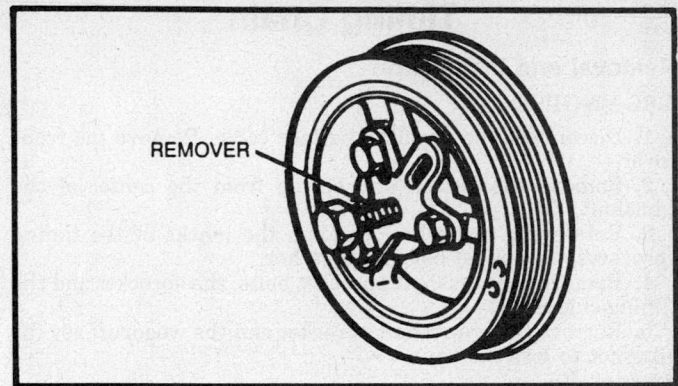

Using the Wheel Puller tool to remove the damper pulley—4.1L and 4.5L engines

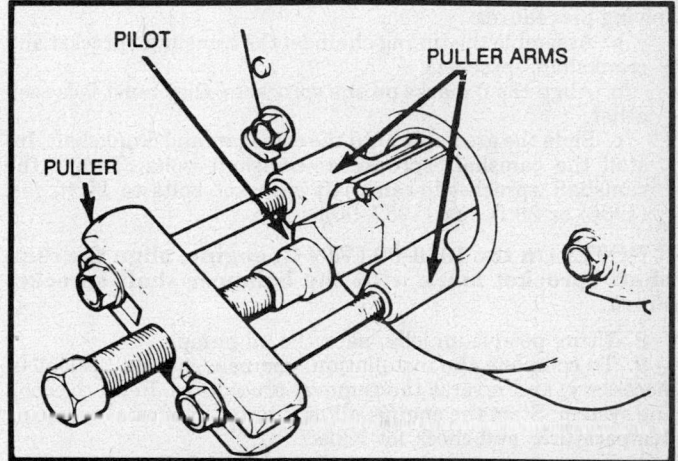

Removing the front oil seal—4.1L and 4.5L engines

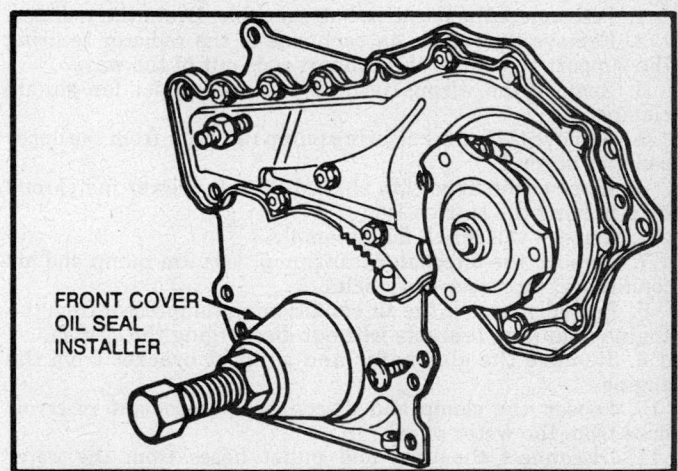

Installing the front oil seal—4.1L and 4.5L engines

2. Using the oil seal removal tools, press the oil seal from the timing case cover.

3. Clean the oil seal mounting surface.

4. Lubricate the new seal with engine oil.

5. Using a hammer and the oil seal installation tool, drive the new oil seal in to the timing case cover until it seats.

6. To complete the installation, reverse the removal procedures. Torque the crankshaft pulley-to-crankshaft bolt to 18 ft. lbs.

Timing Chain

Removal and Installation

3.8L ENGINE

1. Disconnect the negative battery cable. Remove the front cover.
2. Remove the button and spring from the center of the camshaft.
3. Rotate the crankshaft to align the marks of the timing sprockets; they must be close together.
4. Remove the camshaft sprocket bolts, the sprocket and the timing chain.
5. Remove the crankshaft sprocket and the woodruff key (be sure not to lose the key).

To install:

6. Clean the gasket mounting surfaces. Inspect the parts for wear and/or damage; if necessary, replace the parts.
7. To install the timing chain and sprockets, perform the following procedures:

   a. Assemble the timing chain on the camshaft sprocket and crankshaft sprockets.

   b. Align the 0 marks on the sprockets; they must face each other.

   c. Slide the assembly onto the camshaft and crankshaft. Install the camshaft sprocket-to-camshaft bolts. Torque the camshaft sprocket-to-camshaft sprocket bolts to 20 ft. lbs. (1986) or 28 ft. lbs. (1987–90).

NOTE: On the 1988–90 (VIN C) engine, align the camshaft sprocket mark with the balancer shaft sprocket mark.

8. Using petroleum jelly, pack the oil pump.
9. To complete the installation, use new gaskets, sealant (if necessary) and reverse the removal procedures. Refill the cooling system. Start the engine, allow it to reach normal operating temperatures and check for leaks.

4.1L AND 4.5L ENGINE

1. Disconnect the negative battery cable. Drain the radiator.
2. Remove the screws on each side of the radiator securing the support rod. Move the support rods out of the way.
3. Remove the wiring harness from the upper fan shroud clamps.
4. Remove the power steering pump reservoir from the upper radiator shroud.
5. Remove the upper fan shroud from the lower fan shroud by removing the staples.
6. Remove the clutch fan assembly.
7. Remove the alternator, air pump, vacuum pump and air condition compressor drive belts.
8. Partially remove the air conditioning compressor from the engine mounting brackets without discharging the system.
9. Remove the alternator and support bracket from the engine.
10. Loosen the clamp and disconnect the coolant reservoir hose from the water pump.
11. Disconnect the inlet and outlet hoses from the water pump.
12. Drain the crankcase by either removing the crankcase plugs (one on each side) or by elevating the rear wheels. This will prevent coolant from draining into the oil pan as the front cover is removed.
13. Remove the water pump and crankcase pulleys.
14. Remove the air conditioning bracket from the water pump.
15. Remove the timing mark tab from the front cover.
16. Remove the crankcase pulley to hub bolts and separate the pulley from the hub.
17. Remove the plug from the end of the crankshaft. Install a puller and remove the hub.

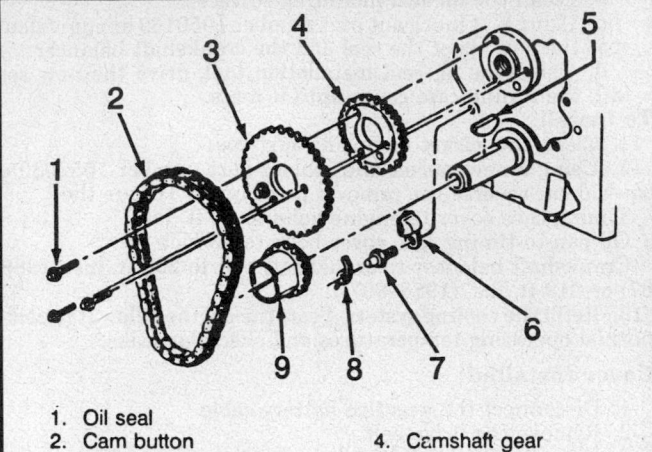

1. Oil seal
2. Cam button
3. Cam button spring

AC:
1. 27 ft. lbs.
2. Timing chain
3. Camshaft sprocket

4. Camshaft gear
5. Key
6. Damper
7. Bolt – 14 ft. lbs.
8. Spring
9. Crankshaft sprocket

Exploded view of the timing chain assembly—1988–90 3.8L (Code C) engine—other 3.8L engines are similar

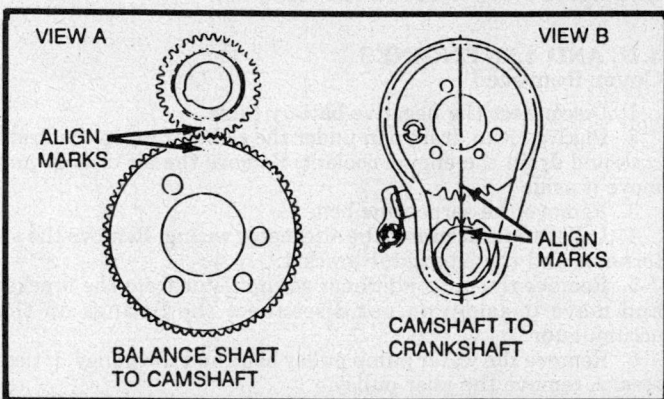

View of the timing sprocket alignment—3.8L engine—the balance shaft gear alignment is used on the 1988–90 3.8L (Code C) engine ONLY

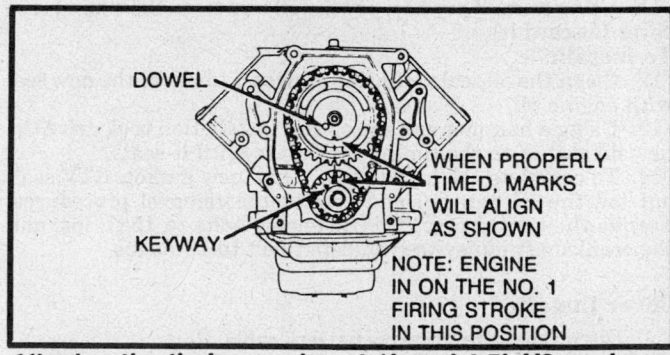

Aligning the timing marks—4.1L and 4.5L V8 engines

18. Remove the remaining front cover-to-engine screws and the cover with the water pump and lower thermostat housing as an assembly.

19. Remove the oil slinger from the crankshaft. Rotate the crankshaft and align the timing marks to TDC.

20. Remove the camshaft sprocket-to-camshaft screw, the camshaft and crankshaft sprockets with the chain attached.

To install:

21. Reverse the removal procedures. After installing the timing chain over the camshaft sprocket rotate the crankshaft until the crankshaft sprocket timing mark is positioned straight up.

22. Install the cam sprocket and timing chain over the crankshaft so the timing marks are aligned.

23. Hold the camshaft sprocket in position against the end of the camshaft and press the sprocket on the camshaft by hand. Make sure the camshaft index pin is align with the sprocket index hole.

24. If necessary, keep the engine from rotating while torquing the camshaft sprocket screw to 37 ft. lbs.

NOTE: Engine timing has been set so the No. 1 cylinder is in the TDC firing position. If the distributor was removed, make sure the rotor is positioned on the No. 1 cylinder firing position.

25. Install the oil slinger on the crankshaft with the smaller end of the slinger against the crankshaft sprocket. Install the engine front cover.

26. To complete the installation, reverse the removal procedures.

Rings/Piston/Connecting Rod Positioning

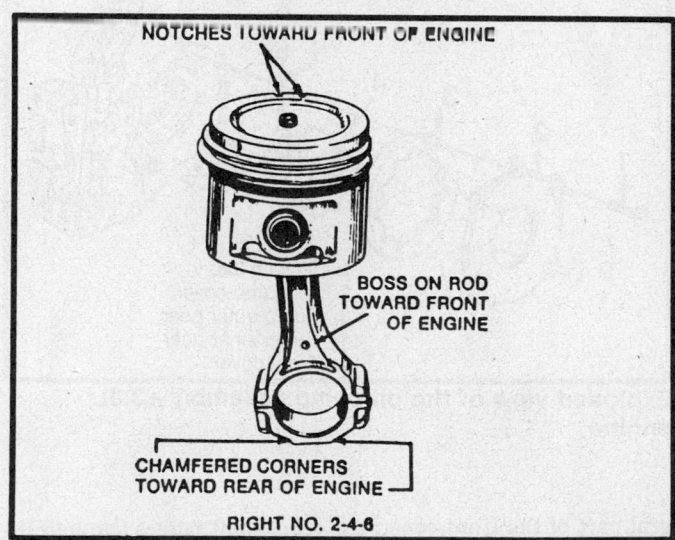

View of the right bank piston and rod positioning—3.8L engine

All compression rings are marked with a dimple, a letter **T** or the word **TOP** to identify the side of the ring which must face toward the top of the piston.

When the piston and connecting rod assembly is properly installed, the oil spurt hole in the connecting rod will face the camshaft. The notch on the piston will face the front of the engine. The chamfered corners of the bearing caps should face toward the front of the left bank and toward the rear of the right bank. The boss on the connecting rod should face toward the front of the engine for the right bank and to the rear of the engine on the left bank.

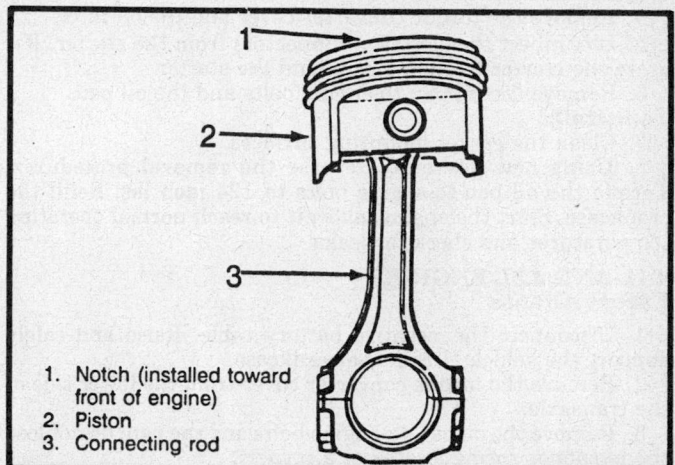

1. Notch (installed toward front of engine)
2. Piston
3. Connecting rod

View of the piston assembly using 1 notch on the piston and the oil hole on the side of the connecting rod—4.1L and 4.5L engines

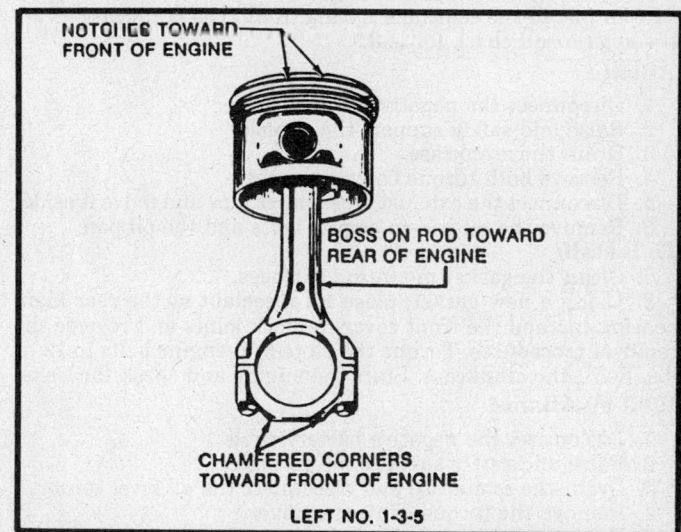

View of the left bank piston and rod positioning—3.8L engine

LUBRICATION SYSTEM

Oil Pan

Removal and Installation

3.8L ENGINE

1. Disconnect the negative battery cable.
2. Raise and safely support the vehicle.
3. Drain the crankcase.
4. Remove the torque converter cover and the oil filter.
5. Disconnect the electrical connectors from the starter. Remove the starter-to-engine bolts and the starter.
6. Remove the oil pan-to-engine bolts and the oil pan.

To install:

7. Clean the gasket mounting surfaces.
8. Using new gasket(s), reverse the removal procedures. Torque the oil pan-to-engine bolts to 124 inch lbs. Refill the crankcase. Start the engine, allow it to reach normal operating temperatures and check for leaks.

4.1L AND 4.5L ENGINES
Except Allante

1. Disconnect the negative battery cable. Raise and safely support the vehicle. Drain the crankcase.
2. Remove the torque converter cover from the lower side of the transaxle.
3. Remove the oil pan-to-engine bolts and the pan; do not lose the tensioner spring located at a corner.

To install:

4. Clean the gasket mounting surfaces.
5. Using new gaskets and sealant, reverse the removal procedures. Torque the oil pan-to-engine bolts to 88 inch lbs. Make sure to install the tensioner spring. Refill the crankcase. Start the engine and check for leaks.

Allante

1. Disconnect the negative battery cable.
2. Raise and safely support the vehicle.
3. Drain the crankcase.
4. Remove both torque converter covers.
5. Disconnect the exhaust crossunder pipe and move it aside.
6. Remove the oil pan-to-engine bolts and the oil pan.

To install:

7. Clean the gasket mounting surfaces.
8. Using a new gasket, place RTV sealant at the rear main bearing cap and the front cover-to-block joints and reverse the removal procedures. Torque the oil pan-to-engine bolts to 12 ft. lbs. Refill the crankcase. Start the engine and check for leaks.

1987–90 Allante

1. Disconnect the negative battery cable.
2. Raise and safely support the vehicle.
3. Drain the crankcase and disconnect the oil level sensor.
4. Remove the torque converter cover.
5. Remove the exhaust Y-pipe.
6. Remove the oil pan-to-engine bolts/nuts and the oil pan.

To install:

7. Clean the gasket mounting surfaces.
8. Using a new gasket, place RTV sealant at the rear main bearing cap and the front cover-to-block joints and reverse the removal procedures. Torque the oil pan-to-engine bolts to 12 ft. lbs. Refill the crankcase. Start the engine and check for leaks.

Oil Pump

Removal and Installation

3.8L ENGINE

The oil pump, located in the bottom of the front cover, is an inte-

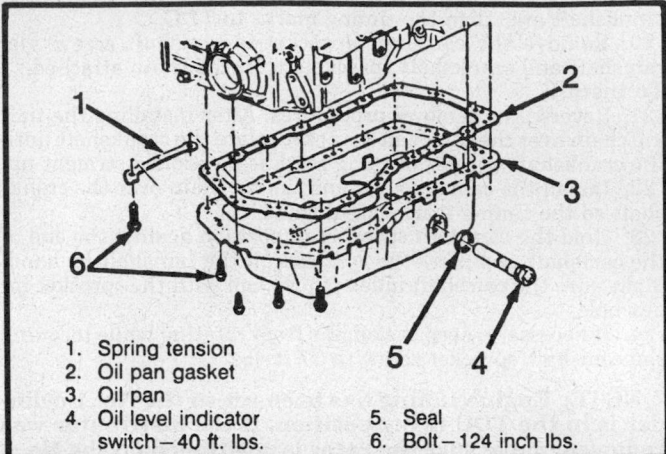

1. Spring tension
2. Oil pan gasket
3. Oil pan
4. Oil level indicator switch—40 ft. lbs.
5. Seal
6. Bolt—124 inch lbs.

Exploded view of the oil pan assembly—1988–90 3.8L (Code C) engines

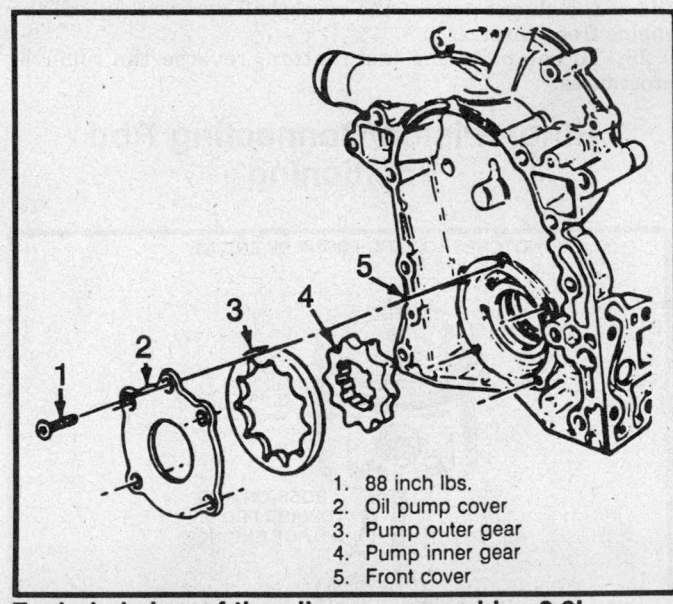

1. 88 inch lbs.
2. Oil pump cover
3. Pump outer gear
4. Pump inner gear
5. Front cover

Exploded view of the oil pump assembly—3.8L engine

gral part of the front cover; the crankshaft passes through it.

1. Disconnect the negative battery cable. Remove the front cover.
2. Clean the gasket mounting surfaces.
3. To inspect the pump gears, perform the following procedures:

a. Remove the oil pump cover-to-front cover screws and the cover.

b. Remove the inner and outer pump gears.

c. Using solvent, clean the gears.

d. Inspect the gears for wear and/or damage; if necessary, replace the parts.

To install:

4. Using petroleum jelly, pack the pump and reinstall the parts. Torque the oil pump cover-to-front cover screws to 88 inch lbs.

NOTE: Unless the pump is properly primed this way, it won't produce any oil pressure when the engine is started.

5. To complete the installation, use new gaskets, sealant, if necessary and reverse the removal procedures. Check and/or refill the crankcase. Replace the oil filter. Start the engine and check for leaks.

4.1L AND 4.5L ENGINES

1. Disconnect the negative battery cable. Remove the oil pan.
2. Remove the oil pump-to-engine screws/nut and the oil pump from the engine.
3. To disassemble, remove the oil pump cover-to-housing screws, slide the driveshaft, drive gear and driven gear from the pump housing.
4. Remove the oil pressure regulator valve and spring from the bore in the housing assembly.
5. Inspect the oil pressure regulator valve for nicks and burrs.
6. Measure the free length of the regulator valve spring. It should be 2.57–2.69 in.
7. Inspect the drive gear and driven gear for nicks and burrs.
8. Assemble the pump drive gear over the driveshaft so the retaining ring is inside the gear. Position the drive gear over the pump housing shaft closest to the pressure regulator bore.
9. Slide the driven gear over the remaining shaft in the pump housing, meshing the driven gear with the drive gear.
10. Install the oil pressure regulator spring and valve in the bore of the pump housing assembly.
11. Install the pump cover-to-pump housing screws to 5 ft. lbs., the oil pump-to-engine screws to 15 ft. lbs. and nut to 22 ft. lbs.
12. To complete the installation, use new gaskets and reverse the removal procedures. Refill the crankcase. Start the engine and check for leaks.

Inspection

1. If foreign matter is present, determine it's source.
2. Check the pump cover and housing for cracks, scoring and/or damage; if necessary, replace the housing(s).
3. Inspect the idler gear shaft for looseness in the housing; if necessary, replace the pump or timing chain, depending on the model.
4. Inspect the pressure regulator valve for scoring or sticking; if burrs are present, remove them with an oil stone.
5. Inspect the pressure regulator valve spring for loss of tension or distortion; if necessary, replace it.
6. Inspect the suction pipe for looseness, if pressed into the housing, and the screen for broken wire mesh; if necessary, replace them.
7. Inspect the gears for chipping, galling and/or wear; if necessary, replace them.
8. Inspect the driveshaft and driveshaft extension for looseness and/or wear; if necessary, replace them.

Rear Main Oil Seal

Removal and Installation

ELDORADO AND SEVILLE

NOTE: To perform this procedure, use a seal removal tool and a seal installer tool.

1. Disconnect the negative battery cable. Remove the transaxle.
2. Unbolt and remove the flexplate from the rear end of the crankshaft.
3. Using a seal removal tool, remove the old seal. Throughly clean the seal bore of any leftover seal material with a clean rag.

To install:

4. Lubricate the lip of the new seal with wheel bearing grease. Position it over the crankshaft and into the seal bore with the spring facing inside the engine.
5. Using a seal installer tool, press the seal into place. The seal must be square (this is the purpose of the installer) and flush with the block to 1mm indented.
6. To complete the installation, reverse the removal procedures. Torque the flexplate-to-crankshaft bolts to 37 ft. lbs. Refill the crankshaft. Operate the engine and check for leaks.

ALLANTE

1. Disconnect the negative battery cable. Remove the transaxle.
2. Remove the flywheel-to-crankshaft bolts and the flywheel.
3. Using a shop rag, clean around the seal area.
4. Using the rear main oil seal removal tool, pry the oil seal from the rear of the engine.
5. Lubricate the new seal lips with wheel bearing grease and position it on crankshaft with the spring side facing the inside of the engine.
6. Using the rear main oil seal installing tool, press the seal into the engine block until it is flush.
7. To complete the installation, reverse the removal procedures. Start the engine and check for leaks.

REATTA, RIVIERA AND TORONADO

Braided fabric rope seals are used. The upper seal half cannot be replaced without removing the crankshaft.

Lower Half-Seal

1. Disconnect the negative battery cable. Remove the oil pan.
2. Remove the rear main bearing cap-to-engine bolts and the cap.
3. Remove the old seal from the bearing cap.

To install:

4. To replace the oil seal, perform the following procedures.
   a. Using sealant GM part number 1052621, Loctite® 414 or equivalent, apply it to the main bearing cap seal groove and wait for 1 minute.
   b. Using a new rope seal and a wooden dowel or hammer handle, roll the new seal into the cap so both ends projecting above the parting surface of the cap; force the seal into the groove by rubbing it down, until the seal projects above the groove not more than $\frac{1}{16}$ in.
   c. Using a sharp razor blade, cut the ends off flush with the surface of the cap.
   d. Using chassis grease, apply a thin coat to the seals surface.
5. To install the neoprene sealing strips (side seals), perform the following procedures:
   a. Using light oil or kerosene, soak the strips for 5 minutes.

NOTE: The neoprene composition seals will swell up once exposed to the oil and heat. It is normal for the seals to leak for a short time, until they become properly seated. The seals must not be cut to fit.

   b. Place the sealing strips in the grooves on the sides of the bearing cap.
6. Using sealer GM part number 1052621 or equivalent, apply it to the main bearing cap mating surface; do not apply sealer to the bolt holes.
7. To complete the installation, reverse the removal procedures. Torque the main bearing cap-to-engine bolts to 100 ft. lbs. Refill the crankcase. The engine must be operated at low rpm when first started, after a new seal is installed.

Upper Half-Seal

Engine removal is not necessary if the following Time Saver procedure is followed.

1. Disconnect the negative battery cable. Remove the oil pan.

2. Remove the rear main bearing cap-to-engine bolts and the cap.

To install:

3. Using the seal packing tool, insert it against each side of the upper seal and drive the seal until it is tight.

4. Measure the amount the seal was driven into the engine and add about $\frac{1}{16}$ in. Using a razor blade, cut that amount off the old lower seal.

5. Using the seal packing tool, work the short packing pieces into the cylinder block; a small amount of oil on the seal will help the installation.

6. Repeat this process on the other side.

7. Install the lower bearing cap.

8. To complete the installation, reverse the removal procedures. Torque the main bearing cap-to-engine bolts to 100 ft. lbs. Refill the crankcase. The engine must be operated at low rpm when first started, after a new seal is installed.

Oil Pump Cover and Gears

Removal and Installation

3.8L ENGINE

1. Disconnect the negative battery cable.

2. Raise and safely support the vehicle. Remove the oil filter.

3. Remove the oil pump cover-to-timing chain cover bolts, the oil pump cover assembly, drive gear and the driven gear.

4. Remove the oil pump pressure relief valve cap, spring and relief valve.

To install:

5. Clean all the parts in solvent and blow them dry with compressed air.

6. Reverse the removal procedures. Make sure to lubricate all the relief valve parts with clean engine oil. After reassembling the gears into the pump housing, thoroughly pack all the voids between gears and the housing with petroleum jelly to ensure that the pump will prime itself.

NOTE: Failure to pack the oil pump with petroleum jelly before reassembling the pump and starting the engine could cause engine damage, due to lack of oil pressure.

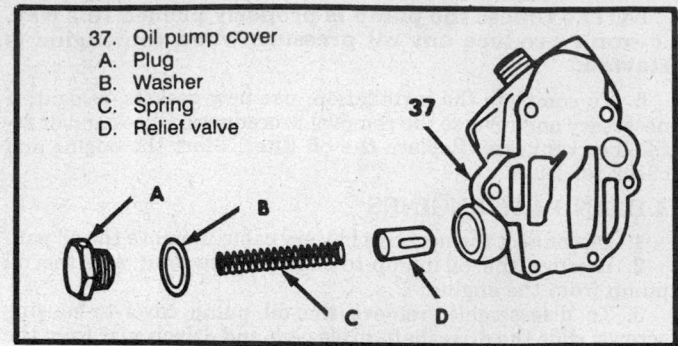

37. Oil pump cover
A. Plug
B. Washer
C. Spring
D. Relief valve

Exploded view of the oil pump cover—3.8L engine

7. To complete the installation, use new gaskets and reverse the removal procedures. Torque the pressure regulator valve cap to 35 ft. lbs. and the pump cover bolts, alternately, in several stages, to 12 ft. lbs.

8. Refill the oil pan. Operate the engine and check for leaks.

Connecting Rod and Main Bearing

Replacement

Note the locations of main bearings. Upper bearings are grooved for distribution of oil to the connecting rods, while the lower mains are plain. Thrust is taken by thrust bearing located at center (No. 2) bearing cap.

Engine bearings are of the precision insert type. They are available for service in standard and various undersizes. Upper and lower bearing inserts may be different. Be careful to align the oil holes; do not obstruct any oil passages. Bearing inserts must not be shimmed. Do not touch the bearing surface of the insert with bare fingers. Skin oil and acids will etch the bearing surface.

NOTE: Bearing failure, other than normal wear, must be investigated carefully. Inspect the crankshaft, connecting rods and the bearing bores. Avoid damage to the crankshaft journals during removal and installation.

FRONT SUSPENSION AND STEERING

For front suspension component removal and installation procedures, refer to unit repair section.

For steering wheel removal and installation, refer to electrical control section.

Steering Rack and Pinion

Adjustment

1. Disconnect the negative battery cable. Loosen the adjuster plug locknut.

2. Turn the adjuster plug clockwise until it bottoms and back it off 50–70 degrees.

3. Check the pinion torque; it should be 16 inch lbs.

4. While holding the adjuster plug, torque the locknut to 50 ft. lbs.

Removal and Installation

1. Disconnect the negative battery cable.

2. Raise and safely support the vehicle.

3. Remove both front tire and wheel assemblies.

4. Remove the intermediate shaft lower pinch bolt.

5. Remove the tie rod ends from the steering knuckles.

6. Remove the line retainer. Disconnect and plug the return and pressure hose from the steering rack and pinion.

7. Label and disconnect the electrical connection at the idle speed power steering switch.

8. Remove the rack and pinion assembly retaining bolts. Remove the rack and pinion assembly.

To install:

9. Reverse the removal procedures. Torque the:

Rack and pinion attaching bolts to 50 ft. lbs.

Tie rod end nuts to 7.5 ft. lbs., plus, an additional ⅓ turn

Tie rod-to-steering knuckle the nut to 33 ft. lbs.

Intermediate shaft coupling bolt to 30 ft. lbs.

NOTE: After tightening the castellated nut, align the nut slot to cotter pin hole by tightening only; do not loosen.

10. Bleed the power steering system and check for leaks.

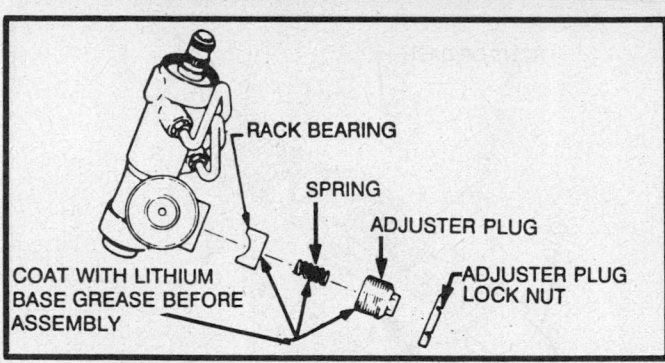

RACK BEARING

SPRING

ADJUSTER PLUG

COAT WITH LITHIUM BASE GREASE BEFORE ASSEMBLY

ADJUSTER PLUG LOCK NUT

Exploded view of the power steering rack adjustment assembly

Power Steering Pump

Removal and Installation

3.8L ENGINE

1. Disconnect the negative battery cable.
2. Remove the serpentine drive belt, the alternator bolts and the alternator.
3. Raise and safely support the vehicle.
4. Disconnect and plug the pressure and return lines from the pump.
5. Remove the rear pump adjustment bracket-to-pump nut.
6. Remove the alternator adjustment bracket and support brace.
7. Remove the rear pump adjustment bracket and the pump assembly.
8. Remove the front pump adjustment bracket and the pulley.
9. To install, reverse the removal procedures. Refill the power steering pump reservoir. Bleed the power steering system.

4.1L AND 4.5L ENGINES

1. Disconnect the negative battery cable.
2. Remove the serpentine drive belt, the power steering pump pulley.
3. Disconnect and plug the high pressure and feed lines from the pump.
4. Remove the power steering pump-to-bracket bolts and the pump.
5. To install, reverse the removal procedures. Torque the power steering pump-to-bracket bolts to 30 ft. lbs. Refill the power steering pump reservoir. Bleed the power steering system.

Belt Adjustment

DEFLECTION METHOD

1. Disconnect the negative battery cable. Loosen the power steering pump adjusting bolt.
2. Move the pump until the drive belt deflection is ⅜–½ in. on the longest span between the pulleys.
3. Retorque the power steering pump bolts.

GAUGE METHOD

1. Disconnect the negative battery cable. Using the belt tension gauge tool, attach it to the drive belt on the longest span between the pulleys.
2. The belt tension should be 170 lbs. (new) or 90 lbs. (used).
3. If necessary, loosen the power steering pump bolts and adjust the belt to the correct tension.

Bleeding System

1. Fill the fluid reservoir.

2. Let the fluid stand undisturbed for 2 minutes, crank the engine for about 2 seconds. Refill the reservoir, if necessary.
3. Repeat above steps until the fluid level remains constant after cranking the engine.
4. Raise and safely support the vehicle (until the wheels are off the ground). Start the engine and increase the engine speed to about 1500 rpm.
5. Turn the wheels lightly against the stops to the left and right, checking the fluid level and refilling (if necessary).

Steering Column

Removal and Installation

1. Disconnect the negative battery cable.
2. Remove the left side sound absorber from the dash area.
3. Remove the steering column trim cover.
4. Label and disconnect the electrical connectors from the steering column. Remove the wiring harness protector.
5. Remove the park lock cable from the ignition switch, if equipped.
6. Remove the lower column mounting bolts.

NOTE: On the Toronado, remove the pinch bolt.

7. If equipped with a column shifter, disconnect the shift linkage at the column.
8. Remove the upper steering column-to-instrument panel bolts and the column assembly from the vehicle.

To install:

9. Reverse the removal procedures. Loosely install the upper steering column bolts and torque the lower column bolts to 20 ft. lbs.

NOTE: Failure to install the upper bolts first may result in a cracked lower bearing casting.

10. To complete the installation, reverse the removal procedures and check the operation of the steering column.

Front Wheel Hub and Bearings

NOTE: The bearings are preadjusted and require no lubrication, maintenance or adjustment. There are darkened areas on the bearing assembly which are from a heat treating process.

Removal and Installation

1. Raise and safely support the vehicle.
2. Place jackstands under the cradle and lower the vehicle slightly so the weight of the vehicle rests on the jackstands and not on the control arms.
3. Remove the wheel assembly.
4. Insert a drift punch into the rotor and remove the hub nut/washer.
5. Remove the brake caliper, support and the rotor.
6. Using the front hub spindle remover tool, separate the halfshaft from the hub.
7. Remove the hub/bearing assembly-to-steering knuckle bolts and the hub/bearing assembly.

To install:

8. If replacing the seal, drive the seal towards the engine. Cut the seal off the halfshaft; be careful not to damage the drive axle boot.

NOTE: If the speed sensor bracket is removed or loosened from the steering knuckle, the speed sensor gap must be adjusted. If the speed sensor is removed from the bracket, speed sensor wax must be applied to the sensor before it is reinstalled in the bracket. Failure to apply the wax will permit corrosion and may result in sensor failure.

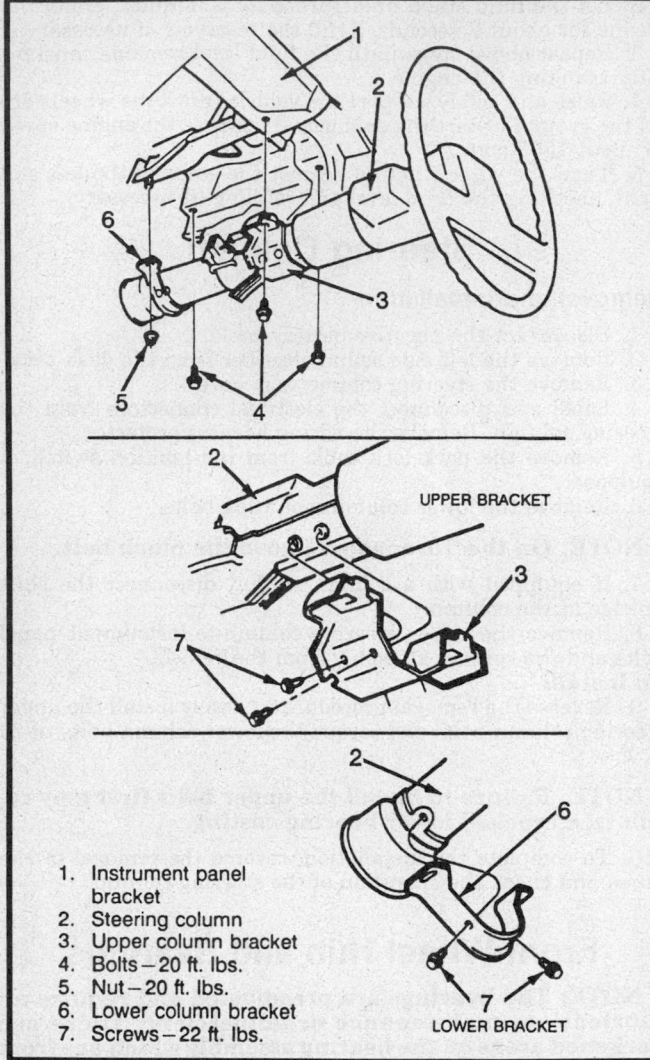

1. Instrument panel bracket
2. Steering column
3. Upper column bracket
4. Bolts—20 ft. lbs.
5. Nut—20 ft. lbs.
6. Lower column bracket
7. Screws—22 ft. lbs.

View of the steering column assembly

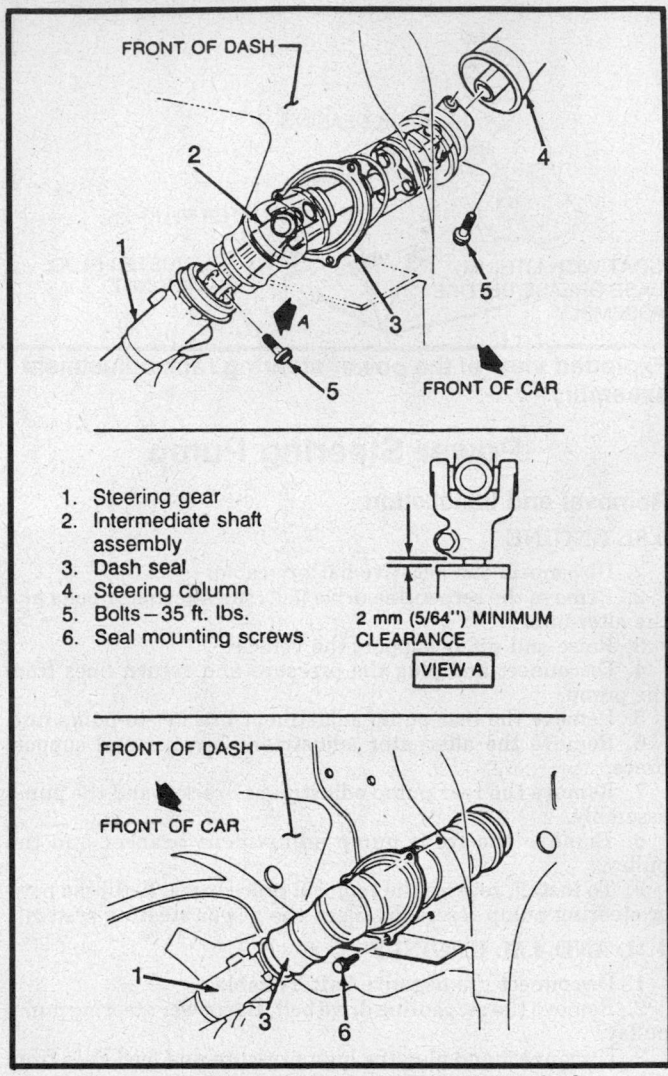

1. Steering gear
2. Intermediate shaft assembly
3. Dash seal
4. Steering column
5. Bolts—35 ft. lbs.
6. Seal mounting screws

2 mm (5/64") MINIMUM CLEARANCE

VIEW A

View of the steering column intermediate shaft assembly

9. To install the new grease seal, lubricate the with wheel bearing grease and using the hub seal installer tool, install the seal.

10. To complete the installation, reverse the removal procedures. Torque the:
Hub/bearing assembly-to-steering knuckle bolts to 70 ft. lbs.
Hub nut to 180 ft. lbs.
Wheel nuts to 100 ft. lbs.

Alignment

Procedures

Before adjusting the caster or camber angles, jounce the front of vehicle a couple of times to allow for normal standing height.

To adjust caster, loosen the upper control arm shaft to frame nuts. Add or subtract shims from front to rear or rear to front, as required. To adjust camber, subtract or add an equal amount of shims at both front and rear of the support shaft.

To adjust the toe-in, place the steering gear on the high point by positioning the front wheels in a straight ahead position.

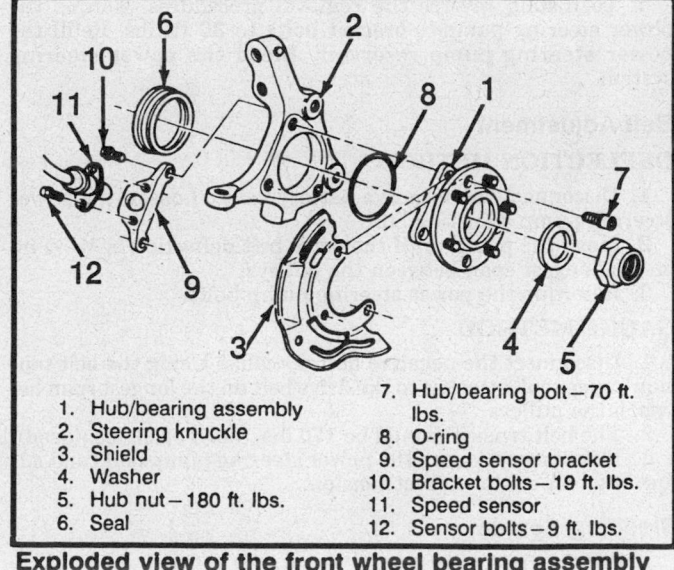

1. Hub/bearing assembly
2. Steering knuckle
3. Shield
4. Washer
5. Hub nut—180 ft. lbs.
6. Seal
7. Hub/bearing bolt—70 ft. lbs.
8. O-ring
9. Speed sensor bracket
10. Bracket bolts—19 ft. lbs.
11. Speed sensor
12. Sensor bolts—9 ft. lbs.

Exploded view of the front wheel bearing assembly

Mark 12 o'clock position on the steering shaft and position the steering wheel for straight ahead driving. Loosen the tie rod clamp bolts and rotate the tie rod adjuster tubes to obtain the proper specifications. Turn both rods the same amount and in the same direction to place the steering wheel and gear in the straight ahead position.

BRAKES

Refer to unit repair section for brake service information and drum/rotor specifications.

Master Cylinder

DIAGONAL SPLIT SYSTEM

Removal and Installation

1. Disconnect the negative battery cable. If equipped with a fluid level sensor switch, disconnect the electrical connector.
2. Disconnect and plug hydraulic lines. Drain the master cylinder.
3. Remove the master cylinder-to-power brake booster nuts and the master cylinder.
4. To install, reverse the removal procedures. Torque the mounting nuts to 26 ft. lbs. Refill the master cylinder and bleed the system.

Bleeding System

This procedure is used to bench bleed the master cylinder.
1. Refill the master cylinder reservoir.
2. Push the plunger several times to force fluid into the piston.
3. Continue pumping the plunger until the fluid is free of the air bubbles.
4. Plug the outlet ports and install the master cylinder.

Anti-Lock Brake System

TEVES SYSTEM

Removal and Installation

NOTE: The hydraulic accumulator is under pressure and must be depressurized before attempting to dismantle the system.

1. Disconnect the negative battery cable.
2. Firmly apply the parking brake.
3. Using at least 50 lbs. pressure on the brake pedal, depress the pedal at least 20 times; a noticable change in pedal pressure will be noticed when the accumulator is discharged.
4. Disconnect the electrical connectors from the hydraulic brake unit.
5. Remove the pump-to-hydraulic unit bolt and move the unit aside to gain access to the hydraulic lines.
6. Using a back-up wrench, disconnect the hydraulic lines from the hydraulic unit.
7. From under the dash, disconnect the pushrod from the brake pedal.
8. Move the dust boot forward, past the pushrod hex and unscrew both pushrod halves.
9. Remove the hydraulic unit-to-pushrod bracket bolts and separate the hydraulic unit from the pushrod bracket; half of the pushrod will remain locked in the hydraulic unit.
10. Disassemble the master cylinder from the hydraulic unit.
11. To install, assemble the master cylinder to the hydraulic unit and reverse the removal procedures. Torque the hydraulic

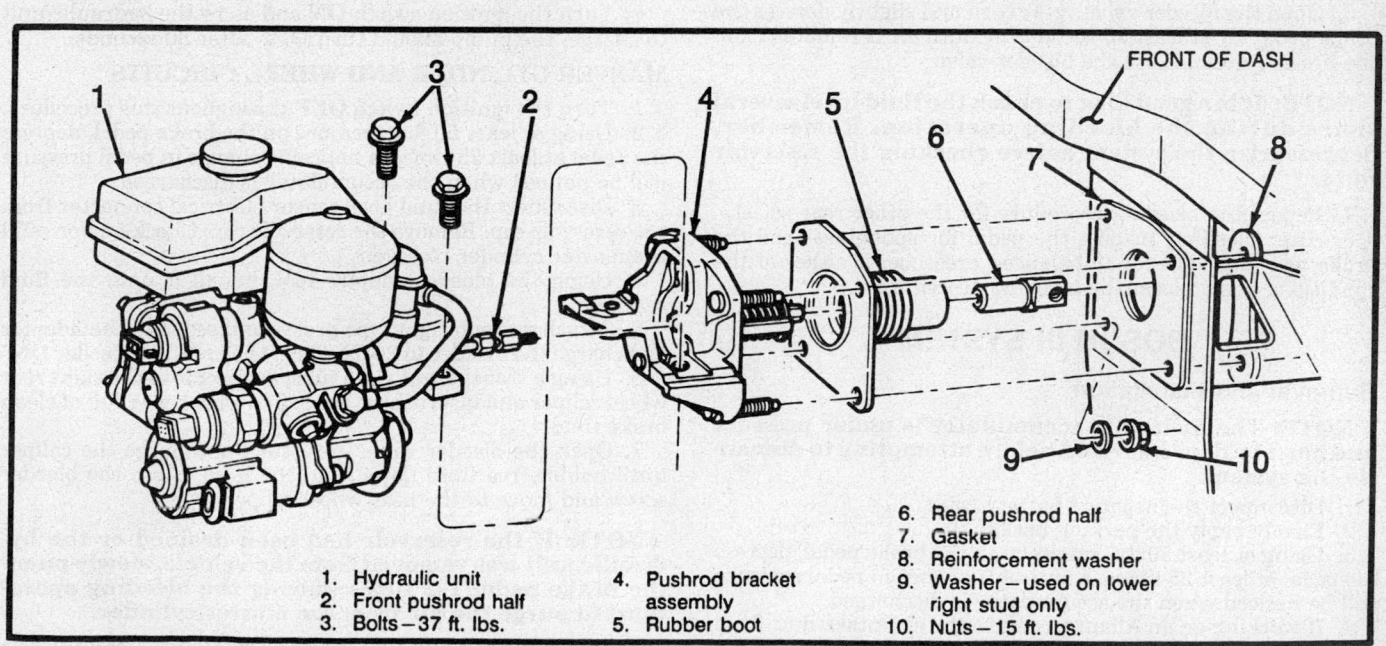

1. Hydraulic unit
2. Front pushrod half
3. Bolts—37 ft. lbs.
4. Pushrod bracket assembly
5. Rubber boot
6. Rear pushrod half
7. Gasket
8. Reinforcement washer
9. Washer—used on lower right stud only
10. Nuts—15 ft. lbs.

Exploded view of the anti-lock brake system hydraulic unit—Teves—all except Allante

unit-to-pushrod bracket bolts to 37 ft. lbs. Bleed the brake system.

Bleeding Procedure

FRONT BRAKES

1. Turn the ignition switch **OFF** throughout this procedure.
2. Using at least 50 lbs. pressure on the brake pedal, depress the pedal at least 25 times; a noticable change in pedal pressure will be noticed when the accumulator is discharged.
3. Remove the reservoir cap. Check and/or refill the master cylinder reservoir.
4. Using the bleeder adapter tool, install it onto the fluid reservoir.
5. Attach a diaphragm type pressure bleeder to the adapter and charge the bleeder to 20 psi.
6. Using a transparent vinyl tube, connect it to either front wheel caliper and insert the other end in a beaker ½ full of clean brake fluid.
7. Open the bleeder valve ½–¾ turn and purge the caliper until bubble free fluid flows from the hose.
8. Tighten the bleeder screw and remove the bleeder equipment.
9. Turn the ignition switch **ON** and allow the pump to charge the accumulator.
10. After bleeding, inspect the pedal for sponginess and the brake warning light for unbalanced pressure; if either of the conditions exist, repeat the bleeding procedure.

REAR BRAKES

1. Turn the ignition switch **OFF**.
2. Using at least 50 lbs. pressure on the brake pedal, depress the pedal at least 25 times; a noticable change in pedal pressure will be noticed when the accumulator is discharged.
3. Check and/or refill the master cylinder reservoir.
4. Turn the ignition switch **ON** and allow the system to charge.

NOTE: The pump will turn OFF when the system is charged.

5. Using a transparent vinyl tube, connect it to a rear wheel bleeder valve and insert the other end in a beaker ½ full of clean brake fluid.
6. Open the bleeder valve ½–¾ turn and slightly depress the brake pedal for at least 10 seconds or until air is removed from the brake system. Close the bleeder valve.

NOTE: It is a good idea to check the fluid level several times during the bleeding operation. Remember, depressurize the system before checking the reservoir fluid.

7. Repeat the bleeding procedure for the other rear wheel.
8. After bleeding, inspect the pedal for sponginess and the brake warning light for unbalanced pressure; if either of the conditions exist, repeat the bleeding procedure.

BOSCH III SYSTEM

Removal and Installation

NOTE: The hydraulic accumulator is under pressure and must be depressurized before attempting to dismantle the system.

1. Disconnect the negative battery cable.
2. Firmly apply the parking brake.
3. Using at least 50 lbs. pressure on the brake pedal, depress the pedal at least 25 times; a noticable change in pedal pressure will be noticed when the accumulator is discharged.
4. If working on an Allante, remove the air intake duct from the air cleaner and the throttle body.
5. Remove the cross-car brace.

6. Disconnect the electrical connectors from the hydraulic brake unit and the pump motor. Using a siphon, remove as much fluid from the reservoir as possible.
7. Remove the pressure hose fitting (banjo bolt) from the hydraulic unit; be careful not to drop the fitting washers. Disconnect the return hose from the reservoir fitting.
8. Using a back-up wrench, disconnect the hydraulic lines from the hydraulic unit.
9. From under the dash, remove the driver's side sound insulator panel. From the pedal hub pin, remove the pushrod retainer and the foam washer.
10. From the engine compartment, remove the hydraulic unit-to-mounting adapter nuts.
11. Move the hydraulic unit to disengage the pushrod-to-pedal hub pin.
12. Remove the hydraulic unit from the vehicle.
13. To install, reverse the removal procedures. Torque the hydraulic unit-to-mounting bracket nuts to 20 ft. lbs. Refill the reservoir to the **FULL** mark. Turn the ignition **ON** and allow the pump to charge the hydraulic accumulator. Bleed the brake system.

Bleeding Procedure

PUMP AND BOOSTER

1. Turn the ignition switch **OFF**.
2. Using at least 50 lbs. pressure on the brake pedal, depress the pedal at least 25 times; a noticable change in pedal pressure will be noticed when the accumulator is discharged.
3. Check and/or refill the reservoir to the **FULL** mark.
4. Using a transparent vinyl hose, connect it to a pump bleeder screw and insert the other end in a beaker ½ full of clean brake fluid.
5. Loosen the bleeder screw ½–¾ turn. Turn the ignition switch **ON**; the pump should run forcing fluid from the hose. When the fluid becomes bubble-free, turn the ignition switch **OFF**, tighten the bleeder screw.
6. Move the transparent vinyl hose to the hydraulic unit bleeder screw. Loosen the bleeder screw ½–¾ turn. Turn the ignition switch **ON**; the pump should run forcing fluid from the hose. When the fluid becomes bubble-free, turn the ignition switch **OFF**, tighten the bleeder screw.
7. Disconnect the bleeder hose.
8. Turn the ignition switch **ON** and allow the hydraulic unit to charge; the pump should turn **OFF** after 30 seconds.

MASTER CYLINDER AND WHEEL CIRCUITS

1. Turn the ignition switch **OFF** throughout this procedure.
2. Using at least 50 lbs. pressure on the brake pedal, depress the pedal at least 25 times; a noticable change in pedal pressure will be noticed when the accumulator is discharged.
3. Disconnect the fluid level sensor electrical connector from the reservoir cap. Remove the reservoir cap. Check and/or refill the master cylinder reservoir.
4. Using the bleeder adapter tool, install it onto the fluid reservoir.
5. Attach a diaphragm type pressure bleeder to the adapter and charge the bleeder to 20 psi. Turn the pressure bleeder **ON**.
6. Using a transparent vinyl tube, connect it to the right rear wheel caliper and insert the other end in a beaker ½ full of clean brake fluid.
7. Open the bleeder valve ½–¾ turn and purge the caliper until bubble-free fluid flows from the hose. Close the bleeder screw and move to the next wheel caliper.

NOTE: If the reservoir had been drained or the hydraulic unit was removed from the vehicle, slowly pump the brake pedal 1–2 times (during the bleeding operation) to purge the air from the master cylinder.

8. The correct bleeding procedure is: right rear, left front, left rear and right front.

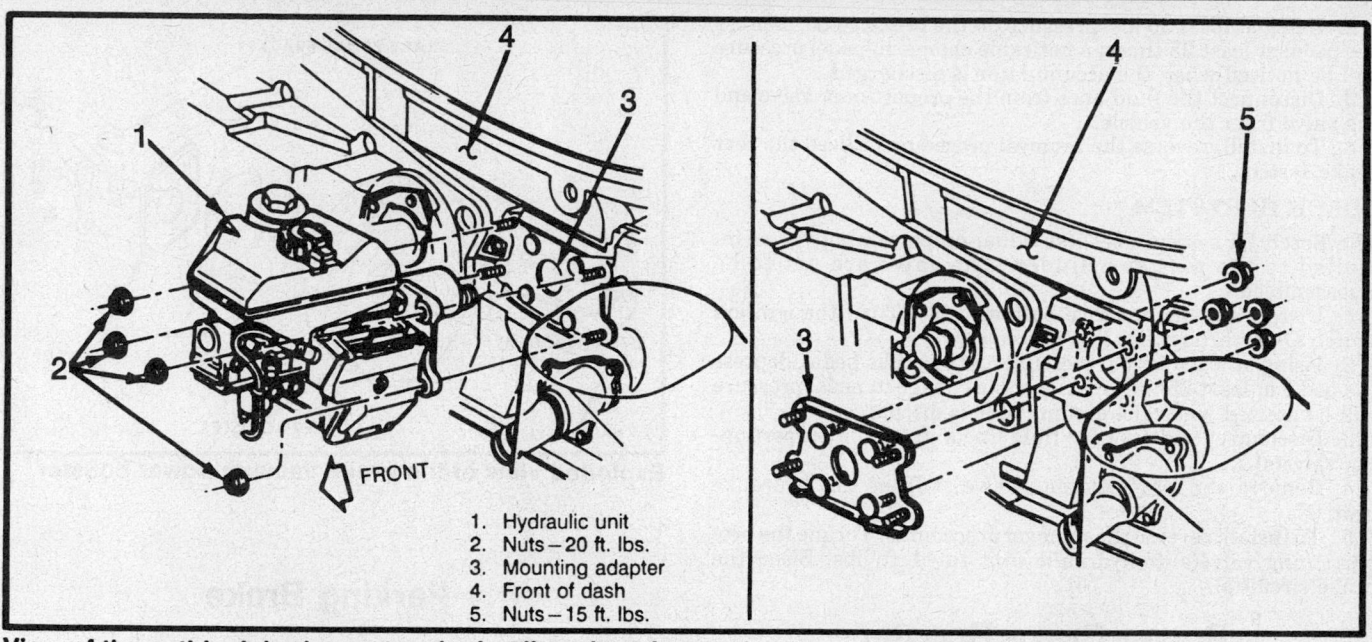

1. Hydraulic unit
2. Nuts—20 ft. lbs.
3. Mounting adapter
4. Front of dash
5. Nuts—15 ft. lbs.

View of the anti-lock brake system hydraulic unit and mounting bracket—Bosch III—Allante

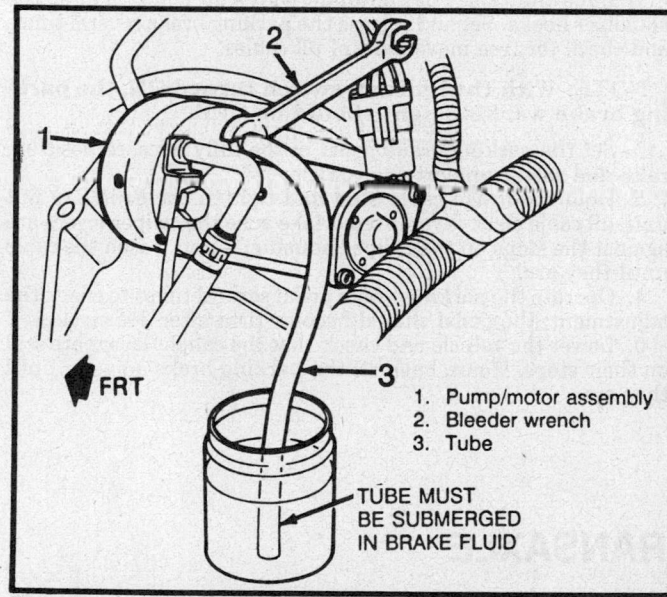

1. Pump/motor assembly
2. Bleeder wrench
3. Tube

TUBE MUST BE SUBMERGED IN BRAKE FLUID

Bleeding the pump/motor assembly—Bosch III—Allante

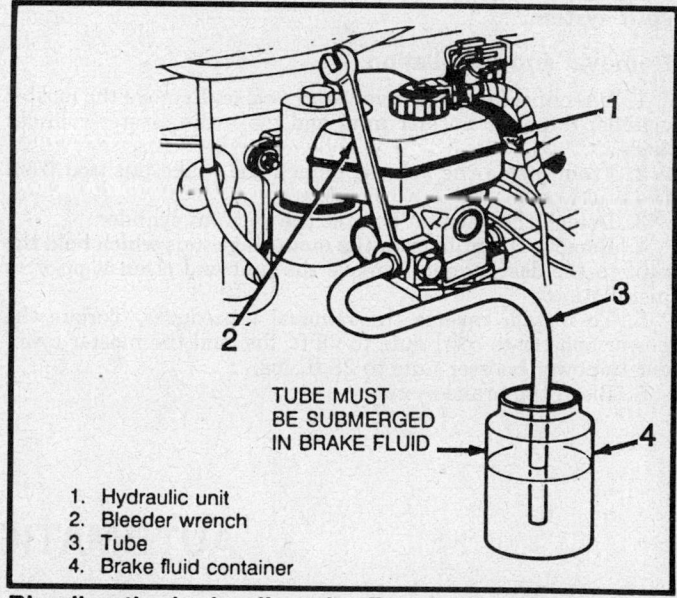

TUBE MUST BE SUBMERGED IN BRAKE FLUID

1. Hydraulic unit
2. Bleeder wrench
3. Tube
4. Brake fluid container

Bleeding the hydraulic unit—Bosch III—Allante

9. After bleeding, remove the bleeding equipment refill the reservoir (using a clean syringe) to the FULL mark. Turn the ignition switch **ON** and allow the pump to charge the accumulator.

Proportioning Valve

DIAGONAL SPLIT SYSTEM

Removal and Installation

NOTE: Individual proportioning valves are installed on the master cylinder outlets.

1. Disconnect the negative battery cable. Disconnect and plug the fluid lines from the proportioning valves.

2. Remove the proportioning valves and O-rings from the master cylinder.

3. To install, use new O-rings and reverse the removal procedures. Torque the proportioning valve-to-master cylinder to 18–30 ft. lbs. Refill the master cylinder reservoir with clean brake fluid. Bleed the brake system.

ANTI-LOCK SYSTEM

Removal and Installation

TEVES SYSTEM

The Teves system uses a single proportioner valve located near the left rear wheel. The valve is not to be disassembled.

1. Disconnect the negative battery cable. Turn the ignition switch **OFF** throughout this procedure.

2. Using at least 50 lbs. pressure on the brake pedal, depress the pedal at least 25 times; a noticable change in pedal pressure will be noticed when the accumulator is discharged.

3. Disconnect the fluid lines from the proportioner valve and the valve from the vehicle.

4. To install, reverse the removal procedures. Bleed the rear brake system.

BOSCH III SYSTEM

The Bosch III system uses individual proportioning valves installed to the master cylinder. The valve are not to be disassembled.

1. Disconnect the negative battery cable. Turn the ignition switch **OFF** throughout this procedure.

2. Using at least 50 lbs. pressure on the brake pedal, depress the pedal at least 25 times; a noticable change in pedal pressure will be noticed when the accumulator is discharged.

3. Disconnect and plug the fluid line(s) from the proportioning valve(s).

4. Remove the proportioning valve(s) from the hydraulic unit.

5. To install, reverse the removal procedures. Torque the proportioning valve(s)-to-hydraulic unit to 11 ft. lbs. Bleed the brake circuit(s).

Power Brake Booster

NOTE: This procedure is used only with the diagonal split system.

Removal and Installation

1. Disconnect the negative battery cable. Remove the master cylinder-to-power booster nuts and move the master cylinder aside.

2. From inside the vehicle, detach the brake pushrod from the brake pedal.

3. Detach the vacuum hose at the vacuum cylinder.

4. Remove the nuts from the mounting studs which hold the unit to the dash panel. Remove the unit and clean it prior to installation.

5. To install, reverse the removal procedures. Torque the power booster-to-cowl nuts to 28 ft. lbs. and the master cylinder-to-power booster nuts to 28 ft. lbs.

6. Bleed the brake system.

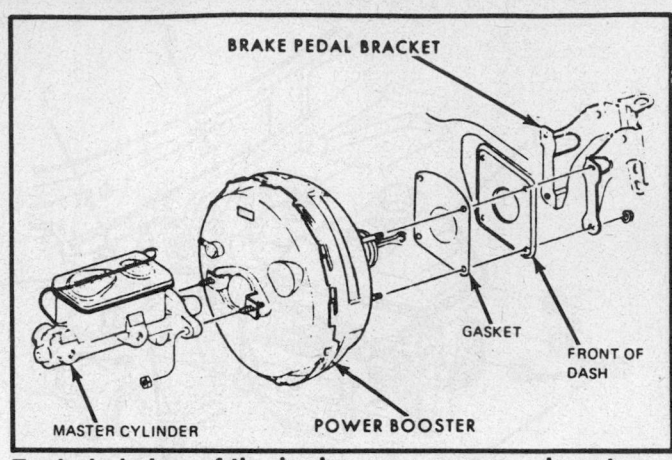

Exploded view of the brake vacuum power booster

Parking Brake

Adjustments

1. Lube the cables at the underbody rub points and at the equalizer hooks. Set and release the parking brake several times and check for free movement of all cables.

NOTE: With the ignition switch turned ON, the parking brake warning light should be OFF.

2. Set the parking brake pedal in the fully released position, raise and safely support the vehicle.

3. Hold the brake cable stud and tighten the equalizer nut until all cable slack is removed. Make sure the caliper levers are against the stops on the caliper housing; if not, loosen the cable until they are.

4. Operate the parking brake pedal several times to check the adjustment; the pedal should become firm after 3½ strokes.

5. Lower the vehicle and check that the caliper levers are still on their stops. If not, back off the parking brake adjuster until they are.

AUTOMATIC TRANSAXLE

Refer to "Chilton's Transmission Service Manual" for additional coverage.

Removal and Installation

1986–87 RIVIERA AND TORONADO

NOTE: To perform this procedure, an engine support tool and a drive axle remover tool are necessary.

1. Disconnect the negative battery cable. Install the engine support fixture.

2. Disconnect the vacuum line from the modulator; electrical connections involved with the transaxle; transaxle valve cable at the throttle body and at the transaxle; the cruise control servo.

3. Disconnect the shift selector bracket and cable from the transaxle. Disconnect the neutral start switch.

4. Remove the top transaxle mounting bolts.

5. Remove the bolts that fasten the wiring harness to the transaxle. Remove the driveline dampener bracket.

6. Raise and safely support the vehicle.

7. Disconnect and drain the transaxle oil cooler lines at the transaxle.

8. Remove the torque converter cover. Scribe the relationship between the flexplate and the converter so the same relationship may be established on reinstallation for balance. Remove the converter-to-flexplate bolts, turning the crankshaft, as necessary.

9. Remove the left side transaxle mounting bolts. Remove the engine mounting nuts.

10. Disconnect the sway bar links. Disconnect the left side ball joint from the knuckle.

11. Disconnect the left side driveshaft from the transaxle using a special tool J–33008 or equivalent.

12. Disconnect the left side of the frame by removing the bolts.

13. Position a floor jack under the transaxle and support it securely.

14. Remove both remaining engine-to-transaxle bolts.

NOTE: One of the bolts is located between the transaxle case and the block, it is installed in the direction opposite to the others.

15. Remove the engine-to-transaxle bracket.
16. Remove the right drive axle from the transaxle and hang it securely.
17. Remove the transaxle.

To install:

18. Slide the transaxle into position, install the lower engine-to-transaxle bolts and torque to 55 ft. lbs.
19. Install the engine-to-transaxle bracket. Install the left side frame assembly bolts.
20. Install the engine mounting nuts. Install the left side transaxle mounting bolts.
21. To complete the installation, reverse the removal procedures. Torque the transaxle mounting bolts to 55 ft. lbs. and the converter-to-flexplate bolts to 46 ft. lbs.
22. Make sure the scribe marks are aligned.

1988–90 REATTA, RIVIERA AND TORONADO

1. Disconnect the negative battery cable. Remove the air intake duct.
2. Disconnect the throttle valve (T.V.) cable from the transaxle and the throttle body. Disconnect the cruise control servo and cable.
3. Remove the exhaust pipe crossover.
4. Disconnect the shift control linkage lever from from the manual shaft and the mounting bracket from the transaxle.
5. Disconnect the electrical harness connectors from the neutral start/backup light switch, the torque converter clutch (TCC) and the vehicle speed sensor (VSS).
6. From the vacuum modulator, disconnect the hose.
7. Remove the upper transaxle-to-engine bolts.
8. Using the engine support fixture tool, attach it to the engine, turn the wing nuts to relieve the tension on the engine cradle and mounts.
9. Turn the steering wheel to the **FULL LEFT** position.
10. Raise and safely support the vehicle. Remove both from wheel assemblies.
11. Using the drive axle seal protector tool, install one on each halfshaft. Remove both front ball joint-to-steering knuckle nuts and separate the control arms from the steering knuckles.
12. Using a medium pry bar, pry the halfshaft from the transaxle and support it on a wire; do not remove the halfshaft from the steering knuckle.

NOTE: When removing the halfshaft, be careful not to damage the seal lips.

13. Remove the right rear transaxle-to-frame nuts, the left rear transaxle mount-to-transaxle bolts and the right rear transaxle mount.
14. From the left control arm, remove the stabilizer shaft.
15. Remove the flywheel cover bolts and the cover.
16. Matchmark the torque converter-to-flywheel bolts for reinstallation purposes. Remove the torque converter-to-flywheel bolts and push the torque converter back into the transaxle.
17. Remove the partial frame-to-main frame bolts, the partial frame-to-body bolts and the partial frame.
18. Disconnect and plug the oil cooler tubes from the transaxle.
19. Remove the lower transaxle-to-engine bolts.

NOTE: One bolt is located between the engine and the transaxle case and is positioned in the opposite direction.

20. Lower the transaxle from the vehicle; be careful not to damage the hoses, lines and wiring.
21. To install, reverse the removal procedures. Align the torque converter-to-flywheel matchmarks and torque the bolts

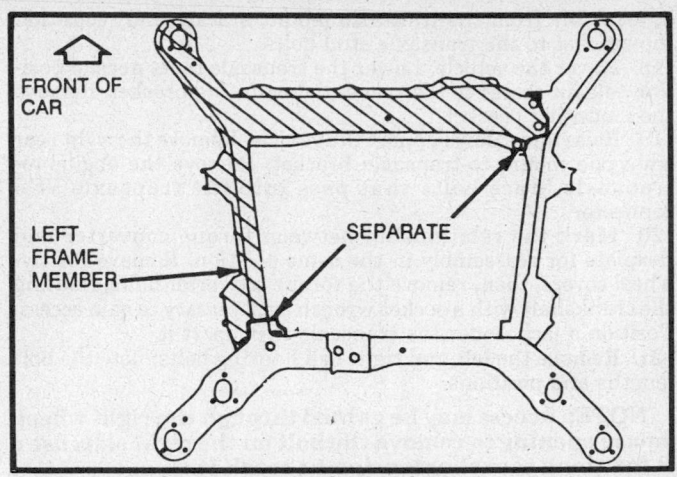

View of the frame separation points

to 46 ft. lbs. Check and/or adjust the T.V. and shift control cables. Check and/or refill the transaxle fluid. Road test the vehicle and check for leaks.

NOTE: When installing the halfshafts, be careful not to damage the oil seals.

ELDORADO, SEVILLE AND ALLANTE

1. Disconnect the negative battery cable. Remove the air cleaner assembly. Disconnect the transaxle throttle valve cable.
2. Remove the cruise control servo and bracket assembly. Disconnect the electrical connectors going to the distributor, oil pressure sending unit and transaxle.
3. Remove the bracket for the engine oil cooler lines.
4. Remove the shift linkage bracket from the transaxle and the manual shift lever from the manual shift shaft; leave the cable attached to the lever and bracket.
5. Remove the fuel line bracket and disconnect the neutral safety switch connector.
6. Remove the vacuum modulator.
7. Remove the throttle valve cable support bracket and engine oil cooler line bracket. Remove the bell housing bolts except the left and right side bolts; note the bolt lengths and positions.
8. Remove the air injection reactor crossover pipe fitting and reposition the pipe. Remove the radiator hose bracket and transaxle mount-to-bracket nuts.
9. Install an engine support fixture, noting the positions of the hooks.
10. Raise and safely support the vehicle.
11. Remove both front wheels, the right and left stabilizer link bolts. Remove the ball joint cotter pins and nuts, and press the ball joints from the steering knuckles.
12. Remove the air conditioner splash shield and the mount cover for the forwardmost cradle insulator.
13. Remove the hose connections from the ends of the air injection reactor pipes. Remove the vacuum hoses and the wire loom from the clips at the front of the cradle.
14. Remove the engine mount and dampener-to-cradle attachments. Remove the transaxle mount-to-cradle attachments. Remove the wire loom clip from the transaxle mount bracket and lower the vehicle.
15. Using both left side support hooks on the engine support fixture to raise the transaxle 2 inches from its normal position. Raise and safely support the vehicle.
16. Remove the right front and left rear transaxle-to-cradle bolts and the left stabilizer mount bolts. Remove the foremost cradle mount insulator bolt and the left cradle member, separate the right front corner first.
17. Remove the air injection reactor management valve/brack-

et assembly from the transaxle mount bracket and reposition the bracket to the transaxle stud bolts.

18. Lower the vehicle. Lower the transaxle to its normal position to gain access to the transaxle mounting bracket. Remove the mounting bracket.

19. Raise and safely support the vehicle. Remove the right rear transaxle mount-to-transaxle bracket. Remove the engine-to-transaxle brace bolts that pass into the transaxle VSS connector.

20. Mark the relationship between torque converter and flexplate for reassembly in the same position. Remove the flywheel covers, then, remove the torque converter bolts, rotating the crankshaft with a socket wrench as necessary to gain access. Position a jack under the transaxle to support it.

21. Remove the left and right bell housing bolts; note the bolt lengths and positions.

NOTE: Access may be gained through the right wheelhouse opening to remove the bolt on the right side; use a 3 foot long socket extension to reach it.

22. Disconnect the oil cooler lines at the transaxle, drain them and plug the openings. Then, install drive axle boot seal protectors and disconnect the driveshafts at the transaxle. Suspend the drive axles out of the way and remove the transaxle.

To install:

23. Reverse the removal procedures placing the bolts in their original positions. Torque the bell housing bolts to 55 ft. lbs.

24. Turn the converter until it is aligned with the flexplate as originally installed. Install the converter-to-flexplate bolts and torque to 46 ft. lbs. Install the splash shield under the converter. Unplug and reconnect the oil cooler lines to the transaxle case. Torque the fittings to 15 ft. lbs.

25. To complete the installation, reverse the removal procedures, observing the following torque figures:

Forward most insulator mount bolt—74 ft. lbs.
Cradle-to-cradle mounting bolts—74 ft. lbs.
Upper transaxle mount bracket stud bolts—74 ft. lbs.
Side transaxle mount bracket stud bolts—50 ft. lbs.
Left or rear transaxle mount nuts—35 ft. lbs.
Engine mount-to-cradle attachments—35 ft. lbs.
Right rear mount bracket-to-transaxle bolts—50 ft. lbs.
Right rear mount bracket nuts—35 ft. lbs.
Stabilizer mount bolts—38 ft. lbs.
Ball joint nuts—81 ft. lbs.
Shift cable bracket-to-transaxle bolts—18 ft. lbs.
Lug nuts—100 ft. lbs.

26. Adjust the transaxle valve cable and the shift linkage. Refill the transaxle to the proper level. Operate the engine until normal operating temperatures are reached. Adjust the level until it is correct.

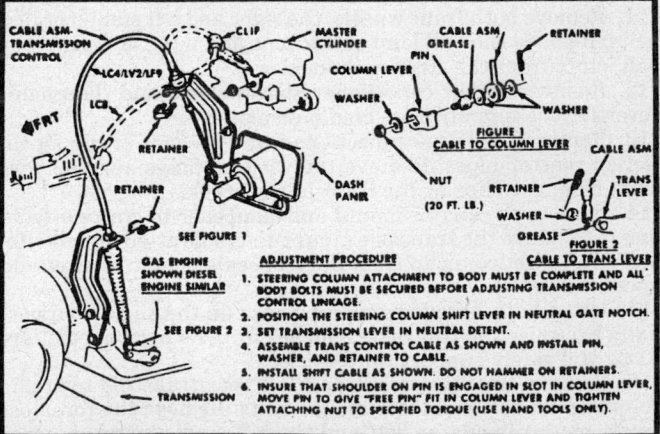

View of the shift control adjustment—1986–87 Riviera and Toronado

Adjustment

SHIFT LINKAGE
Except 440-T4 Transaxle

1. Move the shift lever to the **N** position.
2. Place the transaxle lever in the **N** detent.
3. Attach the shift cable to the pin and tighten the retaining nut.

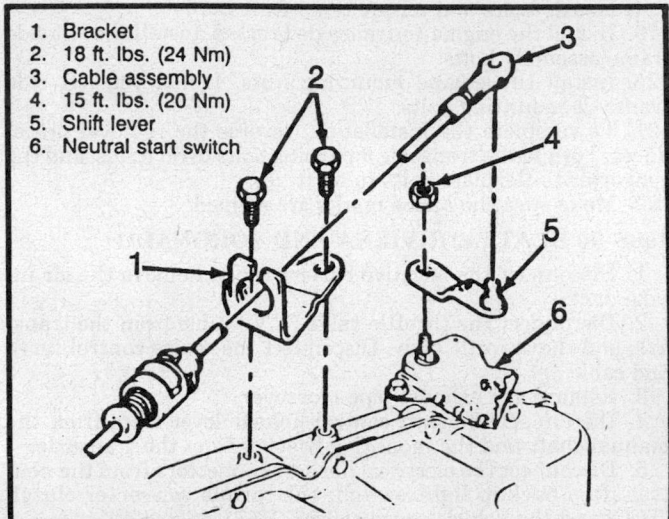

1. Bracket
2. 18 ft. lbs. (24 Nm)
3. Cable assembly
4. 15 ft. lbs. (20 Nm)
5. Shift lever
6. Neutral start switch

Exploded view of the shift control cable—440-T4 transaxle

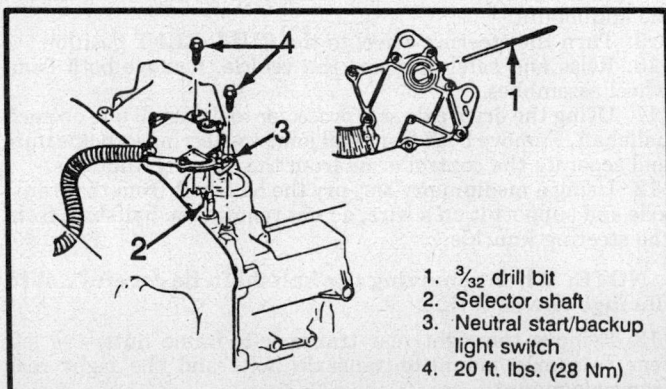

1. ³⁄₃₂ drill bit
2. Selector shaft
3. Neutral start/backup light switch
4. 20 ft. lbs. (28 Nm)

Adjusting the neutral start/backup light switch

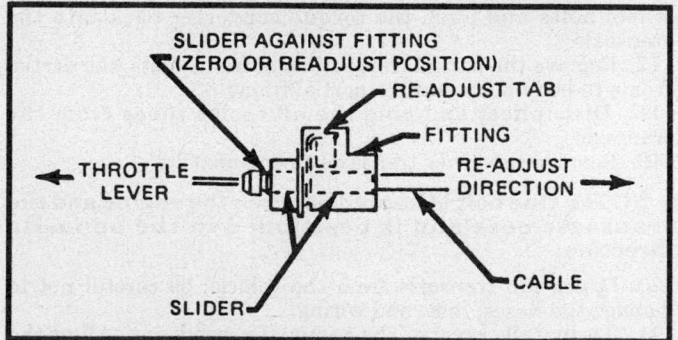

View of the T.V. cable adjuster

4. Assemble the bushing and the retainer at the shift cable; tighten the attaching nut.

440-T4 Transaxle

1. Move the shift lever to the **N** position.
2. Place the transaxle lever in the **N** detent.

NOTE: The N detent can be found by rotating the selector shaft clockwise from P through R to N.

3. Push the cable adjuster tab to adjust the cable in the cable mounting bracket.

NEUTRAL START/BACKUP LIGHT SWITCH

1. Position the transaxle control shifter assembly into the **N** notch in the detent plate.
2. Loosen the neutral start/backup light switch-to-transaxle screws, rotate the switch to align the service adjustment slots and insert a $3/32$ in. gauge pin or drill bit into the slots.
3. Torque the switch-to-transaxle screws to 20 ft. lbs. (28 Nm) and remove the pin gauge or drill bit.

T.V. CABLE

1. With the engine stopped, depress the accelerator pedal fully and have an assistant check the throttle body for wide open throttle.

NOTE: If the throttle body cannot achieve full throttle, repair the accelerator system.

2. At the engine end of the TV cable, depress and hold down the metal readjust tab, move the slider until it stops against the fitting and release the readjustment tab.
3. Rotate the throttle lever, by hand, to it's full travel position.
4. The slider must move, ratchet, toward the lever when the lever is rotated to it's full travel position.

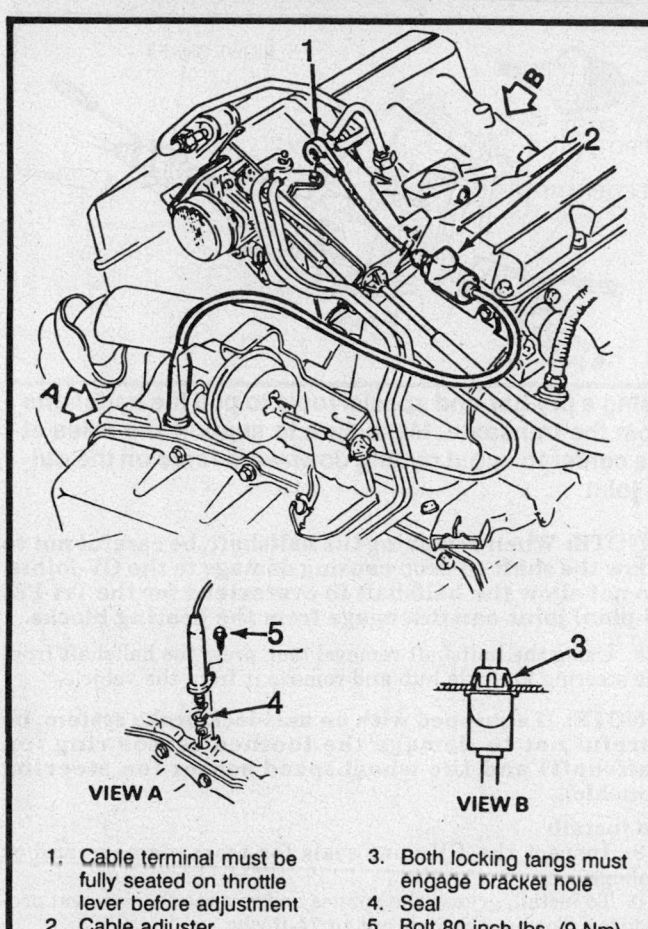

1. Cable terminal must be fully seated on throttle lever before adjustment
2. Cable adjuster
3. Both locking tangs must engage bracket hole
4. Seal
5. Bolt 80 inch lbs. (9 Nm)

View of the T.V. cable assembly

HALFSHAFTS

The halfshafts consist of an inner and outer constant velocity joint. The right halfshaft is equipped with a torsional damper mounted in the center. The inner constant velocity (CV) joint has complete flexibility, plus inward and outward movement. The outer constant velocity (CV) joint has complete flexibility but doesn't allow for inward and outward movement.

Halfshaft

Removal and Installation
LEFT SIDE
1986–87
Riviera and Toronado

NOTE: Secure a halfshaft spindle remover set tool. Also, if the vehicle uses silicone boot seals, halfshaft boot seal protectors must be installed before the halfshaft is disconnected. If the vehicle uses thermoplastic seals, these are not required. They are needed with the silicone seals because, without them, the joint

may turn to too sharp an angle, causing the seal to be damaged in a way that is not readily detectible. These are identified by GM tool J–28712 or equivalent (for the outer seal), and tool J–33162 or equivalent (for the inner seal).

1. Remove the hub nut and washer from the halfshaft. Raise and safely support the vehicle. Remove the left wheel.

NOTE: If the vehicle has silicone seals, install the protectors.

3. Remove the brake caliper, the caliper support and the rotor.
4. Remove the steering knuckle-to-strut bolts and pull the knuckle out of the strut bracket.
5. Using the special tool, pull the halfshaft from the transaxle.

NOTE: Support the shaft at the center so there will be no downward force on the outer joint.

6. Using a spindle removal tool, remove the halfshaft from the hub/bearing assembly and the vehicle. Do not remove the boot seal protector unless complete disassembly is necessary.

To install:

7. Loosely position the halfshaft into the steering knuckle and transaxle.

8. Place the the steering knuckle into position in the strut bracket and install the bolts. Torque to 144 ft. lbs.

9. To complete the installion, reverse the removal procedures.

NOTE: If the vehicle uses a prevailing torque hub nut, use a new nut, torque it to specifications, making sure the threads are undamaged, free of oil and grease. Otherwise, the halfshaft may not be retained safely.

10. Install a new prevailing torque hub nut and washer and torque it to 74 ft. lbs. Remove the object used to hold the rotor stationary.

11. Seat the halfshaft into the transaxle with a prybar resting against the groove provided on the inner retainer. Tap the prybar lightly to seat the snapring and lock the halfshaft into the transaxle. Verify that the snapring has been seated by grasping the housing (not the shaft) and pulling it outboard. If the shaft is locked, it will not pull free.

12. Torque the lug nuts to 100 ft. lbs.

Eldorado and Seville

NOTE: To perform this procedure, use a special puller tool and a new prevailing torque nut from the halfshaft.

1. Remove the hub nut and washer. Raise and safely support the vehicle.

2. Remove the wheel/tire assembly.

3. Remove the brake caliper and rotor.

4. Disconnect the stabilizer bar from the control arm, the tie rod end from the steering knuckle and the lower ball joint stud from the steering knuckle. Use a pry bar and a wood block (to protect the case), pry the halfshaft from the transaxle case.

5. Using the puller tool, force the halfshaft from the hub and remove the halfshaft from the vehicle. Inspect the boot seals for damage and replace (if necessary).

To install:

6. Position the halfshaft ends into the steering knuckle and transaxle without fully seating them.

7. Reconnect the lower ball joint-to-steering knuckle and torque the nut 37 ft. lbs. Reconnect the stabilizer bar-to-lower control arm and the tie rod end-to-steering knuckle.

8. Using new bolts, reinstall the brake caliper.

9. Install a washer and new prevailing torque nut; torque the nut to 74 ft. lbs. Insert a prybar into a slot in the brake caliper to prevent the halfshaft from turning when torquing the nut.

10. Position a prybar into the CV-joint housing groove, tap it with a hammer until the halfshaft is seated in the transaxle. Grab the halfshaft housing (not the halfshaft) and pull it outward to make sure the halfshaft is properly seated.

11. To complete the installation, reverse the removal procedures. Torque the hub nut to 183 ft. lbs.

1988–90 All Vehicles

1. Remove the hub nut and washer.

2. Raise and safely support the vehicle. Remove the front wheel.

3. Remove the brake caliper and rotor.

4. Remove the stabilizer link from the control arm.

5. Remove the tie rod end-to-steering knuckle cotter pin and nut. Using a ball joint removal tool, separate the tie rod end from the steering knuckle.

6. Remove the lower ball joint-to-steering knuckle cotter pin and nut. Using a ball joint removal tool, separate the lower ball joint from the steering knuckle.

7. Using a pry bar and a wooden block, pry the halfshaft from the steering knuckle and supsend it on a wire.

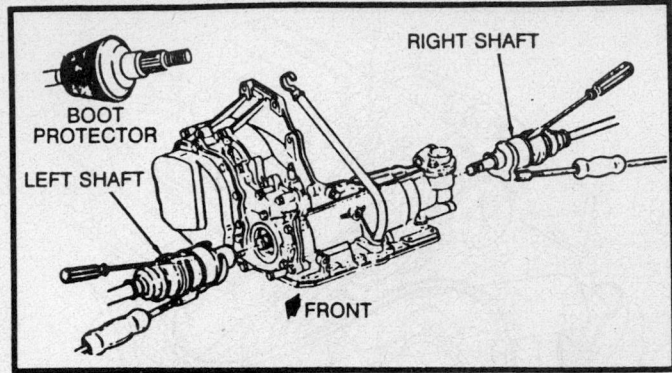

Using a pry bar and special tools to pull the halfshafts from the transaxle. Make sure to support the axles at the center to avoid putting downward force on the outer joint

NOTE: When removing the halfshaft, be careful not to allow the shaft to drop causing damage to the CV-joints. Do not allow the halfshaft to overextend for the Tri-Pot (S-plan) joint can disengage from the bearing blocks.

8. Using the halfshaft removal tool, press the halfshaft from the steering knuckle hub and remove it from the vehicle.

NOTE: If equipped with an anti-lock brake system, be careful not to damage the toothed sensor ring (on halfshaft) and the wheel speed sensor (on steering knuckle).

To install:

9. Inspect the CV-joint seals for tears, damage and/or leakage.

10. To install, grease the splines and reverse the removal procedures. Torque the hub nut to 74 ft. lbs.

NOTE: To keep the halfshaft from turning, place a small drift pin in one of the rotor's slots.

11. Using a small pry bar, place it in the halfshaft CV-joint groove and tap the halfshaft into the transaxle until the snapring seats. Lower the vehicle. Torque the hub nut to 183 ft. lbs.

RIGHT SIDE
1986–87

Riviera and Toronado

NOTE: Secure a halfshaft spindle remover set tool. Also, if the vehicle uses silicone boot seals, halfshaft boot seal protectors must be installed before the halfshaft is disconnected. If the vehicle uses thermoplastic seals, these are not required. They are needed with the silicone seals because, without them, the joint may turn to too sharp an angle, causing the seal to be damaged in a way that is not readily detectible. These are identified by GM tool No. J–28712 or equivalent (for the outer seal), and tool No. J–33162 or equivalent (for the inner seal).

1. Remove the hub nut and washer from the halfshaft. Raise and safely support the vehicle. Remove the right wheel.

NOTE: If the vehicle has silicone seals, install the protectors described in the note above.

3. Remove the brake caliper, the caliper support and the rotor.

4. Remove the steering knuckle-to-strut bolts and pull the knuckle out of the strut bracket.

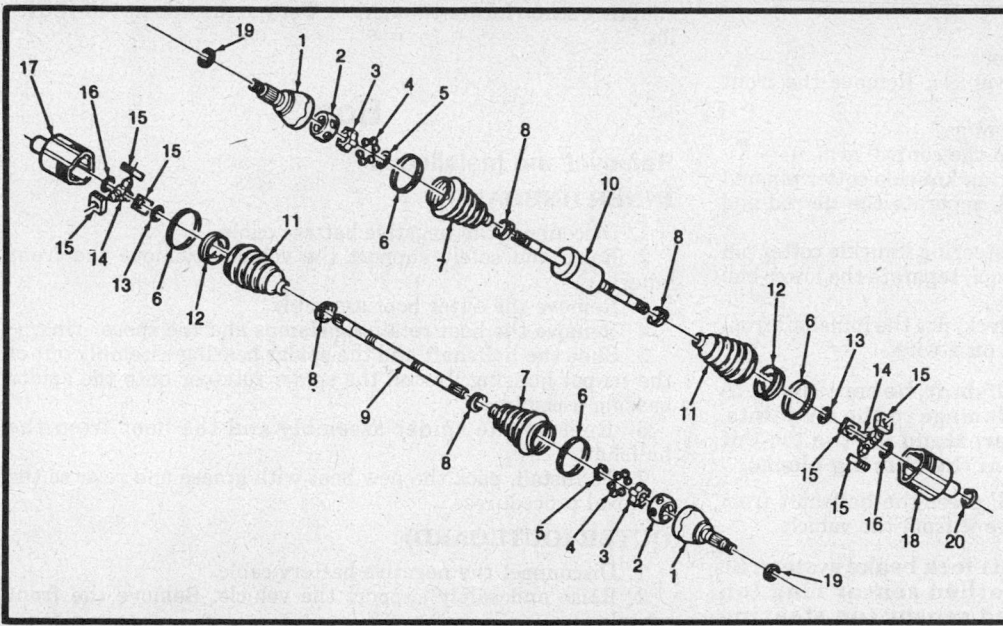

1. CV-joint outer race
2. CV-joint cage
3. CV-joint inner race
4. Balls
5. Race retaining ring
6. Seal retaining clamp
7. CV-joint seal
8. Seal retaining clamp
9. Left side halfshaft
10. Right side damper shaft assy.
11. Tri-Pot (S-plan) joint assy.
12. Trilobal Tri-Pot bushing
13. Spacer ring
14. Tri-Pot (S-plan) joint spider
15. Bearing block assy.
16. Shaft retaining ring
17. Left side Tri-Pot (S-plan) housing
18. Right side Tri-Pot (S-plan) housing
19. Deflector ring
20. Joint retaining ring

Exploded view of the halfshaft assemblies—Tri-Pot (S-plan)—1988–90

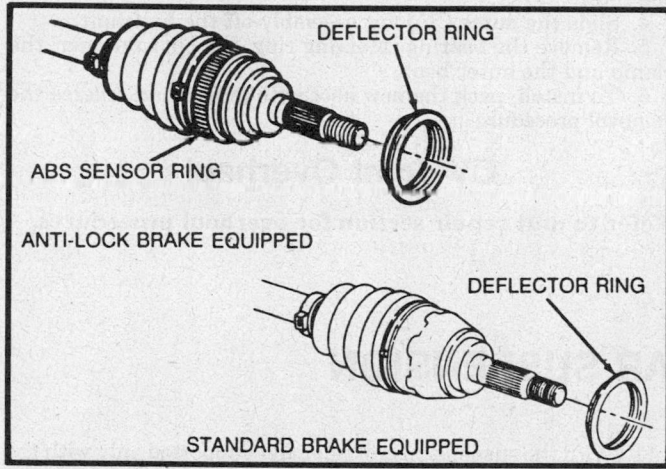

DEFLECTOR RING
ABS SENSOR RING
ANTI-LOCK BRAKE EQUIPPED

DEFLECTOR RING
STANDARD BRAKE EQUIPPED

View of the 2 types of outer CV-joint assemblies and deflector rings—1988–90

5. Using the special tool, pull the halfshaft from the transaxle.

NOTE: Support the shaft at the center so there will be no downward force on the outer joint.

6. Using the spindle removal tool, remove the halfshaft from the hub/bearing assembly and the vehicle. Do not remove the boot seal protector unless complete disassembly is necessary.
To install:
7. Loosely position the halfshaft into the steering knuckle and transaxle.
8. Place the the steering knuckle into position in the strut bracket and install the bolts. Torque to 144 ft. lbs.
9. To complete the installion, reverse the removal procedures.

NOTE: If the vehicle uses a prevailing torque hub nut, use a new nut, torque it to specifications, making sure the threads are undamaged, free of oil and grease. Otherwise, the halfshaft may not be retained safely.

10. Install a new prevailing torque hub nut and washer and torque them to 74 ft. lbs. Remove the object used to hold the rotor stationary.
11. Seat the halfshaft into the transaxle with a prybar resting against the groove provided on the inner retainer. Tap the prybar lightly to seat the snapring and lock the halfshaft into the transaxle. Verify that the snapring has been seated by grasping the housing (NOT the shaft itself) and pulling it outboard. If the shaft is locked, it will not pull free.
12. Torque the lugnuts to 100 ft. lbs.

Eldorado and Seville

NOTE: To perform this procedure, use a special puller tool and a new prevailing torque nut from the halfshaft.

1. Remove the hub nut and washer. Raise and safely support the vehicle.
2. Remove the wheel/tire assembly.
3. Remove the brake caliper and rotor.
4. Disconnect the stabilizer bar from the control arm, the tie rod end from the steering knuckle and the lower ball joint stud from the steering knuckle. Use a pry bar and a wood block (to protect the case), pry the halfshaft from the transaxle case.
5. Using the puller tool, force the halfshaft from the hub and remove the halfshaft from the vehicle. Inspect the boot seals for damage and replace (if necessary).
To install:
6. Position the halfshaft ends into the steering knuckle and transaxle without fully seating them.
7. Reconnect the lower ball joint-to-steering knuckle and torque the nut 37 ft. lbs. Reconnect the stabilizer bar-to-lower control arm and the tie rod end-to-steering knuckle.
8. Using new bolts, reinstall the brake caliper.
9. Install a washer and new prevailing torque nut; torque the nut to 74 ft. lbs. Insert a prybar into a slot in the brake caliper to prevent the halfshaft from turning when torquing the nut.
10. Position a prybar into the CV-joint housing groove, tap it with a hammer until the halfshaft is seated in the transaxle. Grab the halfshaft housing (not the halfshaft) and pull it outward to make sure the halfshaft is properly seated.
11. To complete the installation, reverse the removal procedures. Torque the hub nut to 183 ft. lbs.

1988–90 All Vehicles

1. Remove the hub nut and washer.
2. Raise and safely support the vehicle. Remove the front wheel assembly.
3. Remove the brake caliper and rotor.
4. Remove the stabilizer link from the control arm.
5. Remove the tie rod end-to-steering knuckle cotter pin and nut. Using a ball joint removal tool, separate the tie rod end from the steering knuckle.
6. Remove the lower ball joint-to-steering knuckle cotter pin and nut. Using a ball joint removal tool, separate the lower ball joint from the steering knuckle.
7. Using a pry bar and a wooden block, pry the halfshaft from the steering knuckle and suspend it on a wire.

NOTE: When removing the halfshaft, be careful not to allow the shaft to drop causing damage to the CV-joints. Do not allow the halfshaft to overextend for the Tri-Pot (S-plan) joint can disengage from the bearing blocks.

8. Using a halfshaft removal tool, press the halfshaft from the steering knuckle hub and remove it from the vehicle.

NOTE: If equipped with an anti-lock brake system, be careful not to damage the toothed sensor ring (on halfshaft) and the wheel speed sensor (on steering knuckle).

To install:
9. Inspect the CV-joint seals for tears, damage and/or leakage.
10. To install, grease the splines and reverse the removal procedures. Torque the hub nut to 74 ft. lbs.

NOTE: To keep the halfshaft from turning, place a small drift pin in one of the rotor's slots.

11. Using a small pry bar, place it in the halfshaft CV-joint groove and tap the halfshaft into the transaxle until the snapring seats. Lower the vehicle. Torque the hub nut to 183 ft. lbs.

Boot

Removal and Installation
INNER (INBOARD)

1. Disconnect the negative battery cable.
2. Raise and safely support the vehicle. Remove the front wheels.
3. Remove the outer boot assembly.
4. Remove the boot retaining clamps and the spacer ring.
5. Slide the halfshaft and the spider bearing assembly out of the tri-pot housing. Install the spider retainer onto the spider bearing assembly.
6. Remove the spider assembly and the boot from the halfshaft.
7. To install, pack the new boot with grease and reverse the removal procedures.

OUTER (OUTBOARD)

1. Disconnect the negative battery cable.
2. Raise and safely support the vehicle. Remove the front wheels.
3. Remove the brake caliper and support on a wire. Remove the rotor.
4. Slide the outer CV-joint assembly off the halfshaft.
5. Remove the bearing retaining ring, the boot retainer, the clamp and the outer boot.
6. To install, pack the new boot with grease and reverse the removal procedures.

CV-Joint Overhaul

Refer to unit repair section for overhaul procedures.

REAR AXLE AND REAR SUSPENSION

Refer to the unit repair section for axle overhaul procedures and rear suspension services.

Rear Axle Assembly

Removal and Installation

1. Disconnect the negative battery cable. Raise and safely support the vehicle. Remove the wheel assemblies.
2. Remove the brake calipers and position out of the way using a length of wire.
3. Remove the necessary suspension components in order to gain access to the Electronic Level Control (ELC) unit.
4. Label and disconnect the electrical connections from the height sensor and compressor.
5. Remove the air intake filter from the underbody.
6. Remove the parking brake cable from the equalizer and reposition the intermediate cable away from the crossmember assembly.
7. If equipped with a brake crossover tube, remove the retaining bolts and disconnect the crossover tube.
8. Remove the right rear crossover retaining bolt.
9. Support the rear crossmember assembly using jackstands of a suitable length.
10. Remove the crossmember forward arm bolts, upper mounting bolts and lower insulators.

11. With the suspension crossmember supported only with the jackstands, slowly raise the vehicle away from the crossmember assembly.

NOTE: When raising the vehicle, note the position of the hoses, pipes and brake calipers in order to prevent damage during the removal procedure.

12. To install, reverse the removal procedures.

MacPherson Strut

Removal and Installation

1. Raise and safely support the rear of the vehicle on jackstands, positioned under the outboard end of the control arm to slightly compress the spring.
2. Remove the wheel assembly. Install 2 lug nuts to retain the rotor.

NOTE: If equipped with Electronic Load Control (ELC), disconnect the air lines before removing shocks. Purge the new shocks of air before installing (on all models) by repeatedly extending and compressing them. On ALC equipped models, the shocks should be fully extended before installing air lines.

3. If equipped, remove the stabilizer bar-to-strut bolt. Remove and support the caliper on a wire.

NOTE: Before removing the left strut, disconnect the ELC height sensor link.

4. Remove the knuckle pinch bolt from the outboard end of the control arm; do not remove it.

5. Remove the upper strut-to-body nut, retainer and the upper insulator. Slowly remove the jackstand to relieve the spring pressure. Compress the strut (by hand).

6. Using a plastic hammer, gently tap the shock out of it's retainer. Remove the lower insulator and the strut from the vehicle.

To install:

7. Seat the strut in the knuckle with the tang on the strut bottom (in the knuckle slot) and reverse the removal procedures. Torque the:

Knuckle pinch bolt to 40 ft. lbs.
Upper strut-to-suspension support nut to 65 ft. lbs.
Knuckle-to-control arm nut/bolt to 59 ft. lbs.
Stabilizer shaft bolt to 43 ft. lbs. (if equipped)

8. Follow any special instructions in the air strut package.

Transverse Rear Spring

Removal and Installation

1. Raise and safely support the rear of the vehicle with jackstands placed under the frame. Remove the tire and wheel from the side the spring will be drawn from.

2. If working on the left side and the vehicle is equipped with an Electronic Level Control, disconnect the ELC height sensor link.

3. If equipped with a stabilizer bar, disconnect the mounting bolt from the strut.

4. Reinstall 2 wheel nuts opposite each other to hold the rotor onto the hub/bearing assembly.

5. Remove and suspend the brake caliper on a wire.

6. Loosen but do not remove the knuckle pivot bolt on the outboard end of the control arm.

7. Remove the strut rod cap, mounting nut, retainer and upper insulator. Compress the strut by hand and remove the lower insulator.

8. If equipped with anti-lock brakes, disconnect the wheel speed sensor.

9. Remove the inner control arm nuts. Support the knuckle and control arm with a floorjack and remove the inner control arm bolts. Remove the control arm, knuckle, strut, hub/bearing and rotor as an assembly.

10. Using a jackstand, capable of supporting the entire weight of the vehicle, suspend the outer end of the spring securely.

— **CAUTION** —

Make sure the jackstand is squarely positioned under the spring so the stand will not shift or personal injury could result.

11. Gradually and cautiously lower the vehicle until it's weight compresses the spring so there is no weight on the spring retainer. Remove the retainer mounting bolts, the retainer and the lower insulator from that side of the vehicle. Raise the vehicle slowly until the jackstand is free of downward pressure from the spring and remove it.

12. Draw the spring out of the rear suspension. Remove the upper spring insulators as necessary.

To install:

13. Replace any insulators that required replacement. Upper/outboard insulators must be installed so the molded arrow points toward the vehicle centerline. Torque the center and outboard insulator nuts to 21 ft. lbs.

14. Position the spring into the crossmember. Make sure the

1. Underbody assembly
2. Suspension support insulators
3. Upper strut mounting nut
4. Strut mount insulators
5. Strut
6. Knuckle
7. Hub/bearing assembly
8. Control arm
9. Spring retainer
10. Spring insulators
11. Single leaf spring
12. Stabilizer Shaft
13. Suspension support
14. Trim height adjustment spacer

Exploded view of the rear suspension system

outboard and center insulator locating bands are centered on the insulators.

15. Using a jackstand, support the outer end of the spring securely.

— **CAUTION** —

Make sure the jackstand is squarely positioned under the spring so the stand will not shift or personal injury could result.

16. Carefully and gradually lower the vehicle until it's weight will permit easy installation of the spring retainer.

17. Install the lower insulator and spring retainer and torque the bolts to 21 ft. lbs. Raise the vehicle carefully and when the spring is clear, remove the jackstand.

18. Position the assembled control arm, knuckle, strut, hub/bearing and rotor assembly into the crossmember assembly. Install the inner control arm bolts and nuts just hand tight.

19. If equipped with an anti-lock brakes, reconnect the wheel speed sensor.

20. Install the lower strut insulator and position the strut rod into the suspension support assembly.

21. Install the upper strut insulator, retainer and nut. Torque the upper strut nut to 65 ft. lbs., the knuckle pivot bolt to 59 ft. lbs. and the inner control arm bolts to 66 ft. lbs.

22. Install the strut rod cap. Install the stabilizer mounting bolt (if equipped) and torque this bolt to 43 ft. lbs.

23. Remove both wheel nuts retaining the brake rotor. Install the remaining parts in reverse of the removal procedure. Check and/or adjust the rear end alignment.

Rear Wheel Bearings

Removal and Installation

1. Raise and safely support the vehicle.

2. Remove the wheel assembly.

3. Remove the caliper and suspend it with a wire; do not disconnect the brake line.

4. If equipped with rotor retainers, remove and discard them. Remove the rotor.

5. Remove the hub/bearing assembly-to-knuckle bolts and the assembly from the vehicle.

NOTE: The hub/bearing assembly is to replaced as an assembly; no overhaul procedure is available.

6. To install, reverse the removal procedures. Torque the hub/bearing assembly bolts to 52 ft. lbs. and the caliper-to-caliper bracket bolts to 83 ft. lbs.

Adjustment

No adjustment procedures are available for the hub/bearing assembly.

Rear Wheel Alignment

Procedure

1. Before inspecting the rear wheel alignment, perform the following procedures:
    a. Be sure the vehicle is properly loaded.
    b. If equipped with an Electronic Level Control (ELC) compressor, turn the ignition switch **ON**.
    c. When the **CAR IS LEVELING** light turns **ON**, turn the ignition switch **OFF** and remove the weight from the trunk.
    d. Pause for 30 seconds; the system is venting.
    e. Push the vehicle forward or backward several complete wheel rotations; this will eliminate the effects of camber change.
2. Bounce the rear of the vehicle, several times to normalize the springs and allow it to come to rest.

NOTE: Toe adjustments are made at the lower control arm inner bushing bolts.

3. Loosen the front and rear inner control arm mounting bolts. Using a pry bar, pry between the rear control arm bolt-to-support assembly.

NOTE: Move the control arm outward to increase the toe-in or inward to increase the toe-out.

4. Torque the inside rear control arm bolt to 66 ft. lbs. and the inside front control arm mounting bolt to 66 ft. lbs. Recheck the setting.

RIDE HEIGHT

Adjustment

1. Lift the front bumper 1½ in., let go and allow it to settle; repeat this procedure 3 times.
2. Measure the left front rocker panel-to-ground level and the right front rocker panel-to-ground level dimensions.
3. Push downward on the front bumper 1½ in., let go and allow it to settle; repeat this procedure 3 times.
4. Measure the left front rocker panel-to-ground level and the right front rocker panel-to-ground level dimensions.

NOTE: The true heights are the average of both measurements

5. Lift the rear bumper 1½ in., let go and allow it to settle; repeat this procedure 3 times.
6. Measure the left rear rocker panel-to-ground level and the right rear rocker panel-to-ground level dimensions.
7. Push downward on the rear bumper 1½ in., let go and allow it to settle; repeat this procedure 3 times.
8. Measure the left rear rocker panel-to-ground level and the right rear rocker panel-to-ground level dimensions.

NOTE: The true heights are the average of both measurements.

9. Adjustment is made by repair or replacement of damaged or worn parts.

YEAR IDENTIFICATION

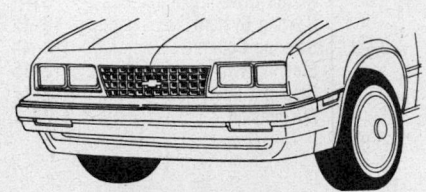

1986–87 Cavalier

1988–90 Cavalier

1988–90 Cavalier Z24

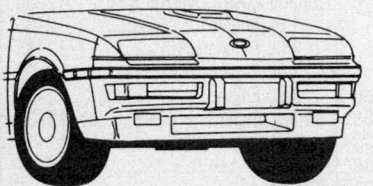

1986–90 Skyhawk SE

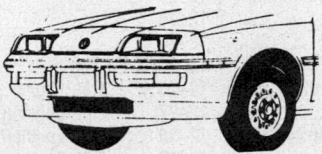

1986–90 Skyhawk Sedan

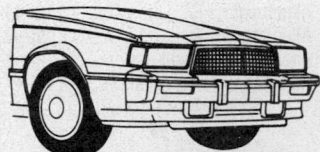

1986-88 Cimarron

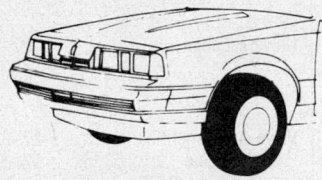

1986–88 Firenza GT

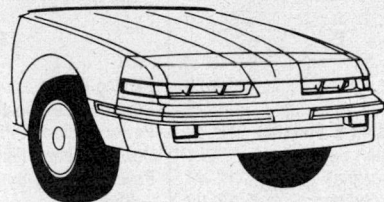

1986–90 Sunbird GT

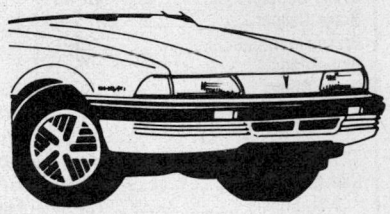

1988–90 Sunbird LE

VEHICLE IDENTIFICATION

It is important for servicing and ordering parts to be certain of the vehicle and engine identification. The VIN (vehicle identification number) is a 17 digit number visible through the windshield on the driver's side of the dash and contains the vehicle and engine identification codes. The tenth digit indicates model year, and the eighth digit indicates engine code. It can be interpreted as follows:

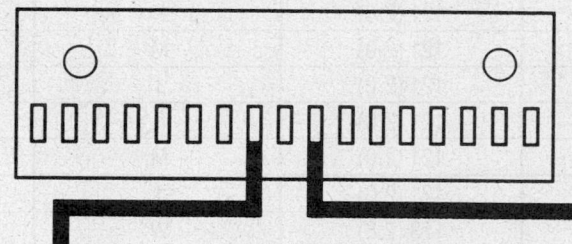

Engine Code

Code	Cu. In.	Liters	Cyl.	Fuel Sys.	Eng. Mfg.
0	111 (OHC)	1.8	4	TBI	Pontiac
J	111 (OHC)	1.8	4	MFI Turbo	Pontiac
P	121 (OHV)	2.0	4	TBI	Chevrolet
M	121 (OHC)	2.0	4	MFI Turbo	①
1	121 (OHV)	2.0	4	TBI HO	Chevrolet
K	121 (OHC)	2.0	4	TBI	①
W	173	2.8	V6	MFI	Chevrolet

Model Year

Code	Year
G	1986
H	1987
J	1988
K	1989
L	1990

OHV Overhead Valve engine
OHC Overhead Cam engine
TBI Throttle Body Injection
MFI Multi-Port Fuel Injection

① Chevrolet-Pontiac-GM of Canada

ENGINE IDENTIFICATION

Year	Model	Engine Displacement cu. in. (liter)	Engine Series Identification (VIN)	No. of Cylinders	Engine Type
1986	Cavalier	121 (2.0)	P	4	OHV
	Cavalier	173 (2.8)	W	6	OHV
	Cimarron	121 (2.0)	P	4	OHV
	Cimarron	173 (2.8)	W	6	OHV
	Firenza	111 (1.8)	0	4	OHC
	Firenza	121 (2.0)	P	4	OHV
	Firenza	173 (2.8)	W	6	OHV
	Sunbird	111 (1.8)	0	4	OHC
	Sunbird	111 (1.8)	J	4	OHC—Turbo
	Skyhawk	111 (1.8)	0	4	OHC
	Skyhawk	111 (1.8)	J	4	OHC—Turbo
	Skyhawk	121 (2.0)	P	4	OHV
1987	Cavalier	121 (2.0)	1	4	OHV
	Cavalier	173 (2.8)	W	6	OHV
	Cimarron	121 (2.0)	1	4	OHV
	Cimarron	173 (2.8)	W	6	OHV
	Firenza	121 (2.0)	1	4	OHV
	Firenza	121 (2.0)	K	4	OHC
	Firenza	173 (2.8)	W	6	OHV

ENGINE IDENTIFICATION

Year	Model	Engine Displacement cu. in. (liter)	Engine Series Identification (VIN)	No. of Cylinders	Engine Type
1987	Sunbird	121 (2.0)	K	4	OHC
	Sunbird	121 (2.0)	M	4	OHC—Turbo
	Skyhawk	121 (2.0)	1	4	OHV
	Skyhawk	121 (2.0)	K	4	OHC
	Skyhawk	121 (2.0)	M	4	OHC—Turbo
1988	Cavalier	121 (2.0)	1	4	OHV
	Cavalier	173 (2.8)	W	6	OHV
	Cimarron	173 (2.8)	W	6	OHV
	Firenza	121 (2.0)	1	4	OHV
	Firenza	121 (2.0)	K	4	OHC
	Sunbird	121 (2.0)	K	4	OHC
	Sunbird	121 (2.0)	M	4	OHC—Turbo
	Skyhawk	121 (2.0)	K	4	OHC
1989-90	Cavalier	121 (2.0)	1	4	OHV
	Cavalier	173 (2.8)	W	6	OHV
	Sunbird	121 (2.0)	K	4	OHC
	Sunbird	121 (2.0)	M	4	OHC—Turbo
	Skyhawk	121 (2.0)	1	4	OHV

OHV—Overhead valve
OHC—Overhead cam
OHC—Turbo—Overhead cam with turbocharger

GENERAL ENGINE SPECIFICATIONS

Year	VIN	No. Cylinder Displacement cu. in. (liter)	Fuel System Type	Net Horsepower @ rpm	Net Torque @ rpm (ft. lbs.)	Bore × Stroke (in.)	Com-pression Ratio	Oil Pressure @ rpm
1986	O	4-111 (1.8)	TBI	84 @ 5200	102 @ 2800	3.34 × 3.13	8.8:1	45 @ 2400
	J	4-111 (1.8)	MFI Turbo	150 @ 5600	150 @ 2800	3.34 × 3.13	8.0:1	65 @ 2500
	P	4-121 (2.0)	TBI	86 @ 4900	100 @ 3000	3.50 × 3.15	9.3:1	68 @ 1200
	W	6-173 (2.8)	MFI	120 @ 4800	155 @ 3600	3.50 × 2.99	8.9:1	50 @ 2400
1987	M	4-121 (2.0)	MFI Turbo	160 @ 5600	160 @ 2800	3.38 × 3.38	8.0:1	65 @ 2500
	1	4-121 (2.0)	TBI (HO)	90 @ 5600	108 @ 3200	3.50 × 3.15	9.0:1	63–77 @ 1200
	K	4-121 (2.0)	TBI	102 @ 5200	130 @ 2800	3.38 × 3.38	8.8:1	45 @ 2000
	W	6-173 (2.8)	MFI	120 @ 4800	155 @ 3600	3.50 × 2.99	8.9:1	50 @ 2400
1988	M	4-121 (2.0)	MFI Turbo	160 @ 5600	160 @ 2800	3.38 × 3.38	8.0:1	65 @ 2500
	1	4-121 (2.0)	TBI (HO)	90 @ 5600	108 @ 3200	3.50 × 3.15	9.0:1	63–77 @ 1200
	K	4-121 (2.0)	TBI	102 @ 5200	130 @ 2800	3.38 × 3.38	8.8:1	45 @ 2000
	W	6-173 (2.8)	MFI	120 @ 4800	155 @ 3600	3.50 × 2.99	8.9:1	50 @ 2400
1989-90	M	4-121 (2.0)	MFI Turbo	160 @ 5600	160 @ 2800	3.38 × 3.38	8.0:1	65 @ 2500
	1	4-121 (2.0)	TBI (HO)	90 @ 5600	108 @ 3200	3.50 × 3.15	9.0:1	63–77 @ 1200

GENERAL ENGINE SPECIFICATIONS

Year	VIN	No. Cylinder Displacement cu. in. (liter)	Fuel System Type	Net Horsepower @ rpm	Net Torque @ rpm (ft. lbs.)	Bore × Stroke (in.)	Compression Ratio	Oil Pressure @ rpm
1989-90	K	4-121 (2.0)	TBI	102 @ 5200	130 @ 2800	3.38 × 3.38	8.8:1	45 @ 2000
	W	6-173 (2.8)	MFI	120 @ 4800	155 @ 3600	3.50 × 2.99	8.9:1	50 @ 2400

GASOLINE ENGINE TUNE-UP SPECIFICATIONS

Year	VIN	No. Cylinder Displacement cu. in. (liter)	Spark Plugs Gap (in.)	Ignition Timing (deg.) MT	Ignition Timing (deg.) AT	Compression Pressure (psi)	Fuel Pump (psi)	Idle Speed (rpm) MT	Idle Speed (rpm) AT	Valve Clearance In.	Valve Clearance Ex.
1986	0	4-111 (1.8)	0.060	8B	8B	NA	9–13	②	②	Hyd.	Hyd.
	J	4-111 (1.8)	0.035	②	②	NA	26–32	②	②	Hyd.	Hyd.
	P	4-121 (2.0)	0.035	②	②	NA	12	②	②	Hyd.	Hyd.
	W	6-173 (2.8)	0.045	②	②	NA	30–37	②	②	Hyd.	Hyd.
1987	M	4-121 (2.0)	0.060	②	②	NA	25–30	②	②	Hyd.	Hyd.
	1	4-121 (2.0)	0.035	②	②	NA	10–12	②	②	Hyd.	Hyd.
	K	4-121 (2.0)	0.060	②	②	NA	10	②	②	Hyd.	Hyd.
	W	6-173 (2.8)	0.045	②	②	NA	30–37	②	②	Hyd.	Hyd.
1988	M	4-121 (2.0)	0.060	②	②	NA	25–30	②	②	Hyd.	Hyd.
	1	4-121 (2.0)	0.035	②	②	NA	10–12	②	②	Hyd.	Hyd.
	K	4-121 (2.0)	0.060	②	①	NA	10	②	②	Hyd.	Hyd.
	W	6-173 (2.8)	0.045	②	②	NA	30–37	②	②	Hyd.	Hyd.
1989	M	4-121 (2.0)	0.060	②	②	NA	25–30	②	②	Hyd.	Hyd.
	1	4-121 (2.0)	0.035	②	②	NA	10–12	②	②	Hyd.	Hyd.
	K	4-121 (2.0)	0.060	②	②	NA	10	②	②	Hyd.	Hyd.
	W	6-173 (2.8)	0.045	②	②	NA	30–37	②	②	Hyd.	Hyd.
1990			SEE UNDERHOOD SPECIFICATIONS STICKER								

NOTE: The underhood specifications sticker often reflects tune-up specifications changes made in production. Sticker figures must be used if they disagree with those in this chart.

Part numbers in this chart are not recommendations by Chilton for any product by brand name

B Before top dead center

NA Not available at time of publication

① Not used

② See underhood specifications sticker

FIRING ORDERS

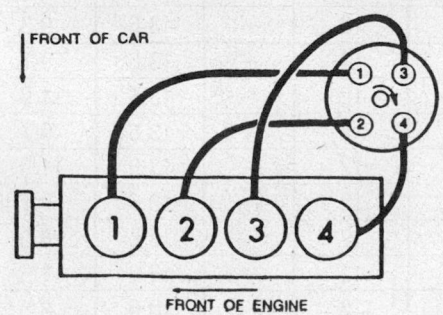

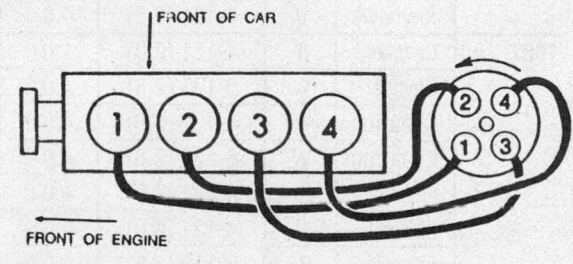

111 cu. in. (1.8L) OHC
Engine firing order: 1–3–4–2
Distributor rotation: counterclockwise

FIRING ORDERS

NOTE: To avoid confusion, always replace spark plug wires one at a time.

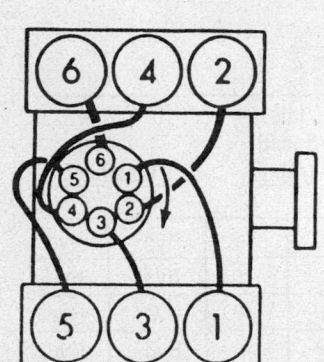

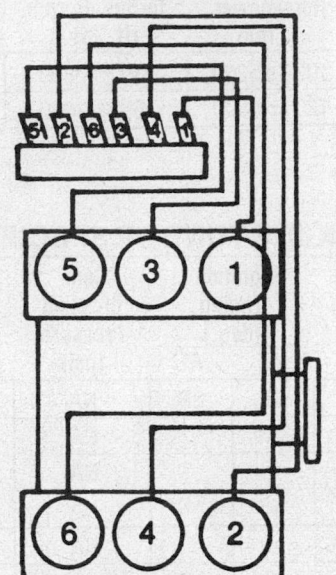

173 cu. in. (2.8L)
Engine firing order: 1–2–3–4–5–6
Distributor roatation: clockwise

173 cu. In. 2.8L V6
Firing order: 1–2–3–4–5–6

121 cu. in. (2.0L)
Firing order: 1–3–4–2

CAPACITIES

Year	Model	VIN	No. Cylinder Displacement cu. in. (liter)	Engine Crankcase with Filter	Engine Crankcase without Filter	Transmission (pts.) 4-Spd	5-Spd	Auto ②	Drive Axle (pts.)	Fuel Tank (gal.)	Cooling System (qts.)
1986	Cavalier	P	4-121 (2.0)	4.0 ①	4.0	6	4	12	—	13.6	9.3
	Cavalier	W	6-173 (2.8)	4.0 ①	4.0	6	4	12	—	13.6	11.0
	Cimarron	P	4-121 (2.0)	4.0 ①	4.0	—	4	12	—	14.0	9.3
	Cimarron	W	6-173 (2.8)	4.0 ①	4.0	—	4	12	—	14.0	11.0
	Firenza	0	4-111 (1.8)	4.0 ①	4.0	6	6	12	—	13.6	7.9
	Firenza	P	4-121 (2.0)	4.0 ①	4.0	6	6	12	—	13.6	9.3
	Firenza	W	6-173 (2.8)	4.0 ①	4.0	6	6	12	—	13.6	11.0
	Sunbird	0	4-111 (1.8)	4.0 ①	4.0	6	4	12	—	13.6	7.9
	Sunbird	J	4-111 (1.8)	4.0 ①	4.0	6	4	12	—	13.6	7.8
	Skyhawk	0	4-111 (1.8)	4.0 ①	4.0	6	6	12	—	13.6	7.9
	Skyhawk	J	4-111 (1.8)	4.0 ①	4.0	6	6	12	—	13.6	7.8
	Skyhawk	P	4-121 (2.0)	4.0 ①	4.0	6	6	12	—	13.6	9.3
1987	Cavalier	1	4-121 (2.0)	4.0 ①	4.0	6	4	12	—	13.6	9.7
	Cavalier	W	6-173 (2.8)	4.0 ①	4.0	6	4	12	—	13.6	11.0
	Cimarron	1	4-121 (2.0)	4.0 ①	4.0	—	4	12	—	13.6	9.7
	Cimarron	W	6-173 (2.8)	4.0 ①	4.0	—	4	12	—	13.6	11.0
	Firenza	1	4-121 (2.0)	4.0 ①	4.0	—	6	12	—	13.6	9.7
	Firenza	K	4-121 (2.0)	4.0 ①	4.0	—	6	12	—	13.6	8.5
	Firenza	W	6-173 (2.8)	4.0 ①	4.0	—	6	12	—	13.6	11.0
	Sunbird	K	4-121 (2.0)	4.0 ①	4.0	—	4	12	—	13.6	8.5
	Sunbird	M	4-121 (2.0)	4.0 ①	4.0	—	4	12	—	13.6	8.5

CAPACITIES

Year	Model	VIN	No. Cylinder Displacement cu. in. (liter)	Engine Crankcase with Filter	Engine Crankcase without Filter	Transmission (pts.) 4-Spd	Transmission (pts.) 5-Spd	Transmission (pts.) Auto ②	Drive Axle (pts.)	Fuel Tank (gal.)	Cooling System (qts.)
1987	Skyhawk	1	4-121 (2.0)	4.0 ①	4.0	—	6	12	—	13.6	9.7
	Skyhawk	K	4-121 (2.0)	4.0 ①	4.0	—	6	12	—	13.6	8.5
	Skyhawk	M	4-121 (2.0)	4.0 ①	4.0	—	6	12	—	13.6	8.5
1988	Cavalier	1	4-121 (2.0)	4.0 ①	4.0	6	4	12	—	13.6	9.7
	Cavalier	W	6-173 (2.8)	4.0 ①	4.0	6	4	12	—	13.6	11.0
	Cimarron	W	6-173 (2.8)	4.0 ①	4.0	—	4	12	—	13.6	11.0
	Firenza	1	4-121 (2.0)	4.0 ①	4.0	—	6	12	—	13.6	9.7
	Firenza	K	4-121 (2.0)	4.0 ①	4.0	—	6	12	—	13.6	8.5
	Sunbird	K	4-121 (2.0)	4.0 ①	4.0	—	4	12	—	13.6	8.5
	Sunbird	M	4-121 (2.0)	4.0 ①	4.0	—	4	12	—	13.6	8.5
	Skyhawk	K	4-121 (2.0)	4.0 ①	4.0	—	6	12	—	13.6	8.5
1989-90	Cavalier	1	4-121 (2.0)	4.0 ①	4.0	—	4	12	—	13.6	9.7
	Cavalier	W	6-173 (2.8)	4.0 ①	4.0	—	4	12	—	13.6	11.0
	Sunbird	K	4-121 (2.0)	4.0 ①	4.0	—	4	12	—	13.6	8.5
	Sunbird	M	4-121 (2.0)	4.0 ①	4.0	—	4	12	—	13.6	8.5
	Skyhawk	1	4-121 (2.0)	4.0 ①	4.0	—	6	12	—	13.6	9.7

① When changing the oil filter, additional oil will be needed
② Overhaul capacity, refill capacity is approximately 8 pts.

CAMSHAFT SPECIFICATIONS
All measurements given in inches.

Year	VIN	No. Cylinder Displacement cu. in. (liter)	Journal Diameter 1	Journal Diameter 2	Journal Diameter 3	Journal Diameter 4	Journal Diameter 5	Lobe Lift In.	Lobe Lift Ex.	Bearing Clearance	Camshaft End Play
1986	0	4-111 (1.8)	1.6714–1.6720	1.6812–1.6816	1.6911–1.6917	1.7009–1.7015	1.7108–1.7114	0.2409	0.2409	NA	0.0160–0.0640
	J	4-111 (1.8)	1.6174–1.6720	1.6812–1.6816	1.6911–1.6917	1.7009–1.7015	1.7108–1.7114	0.2409	0.2409	NA	0.0160–0.0640
	P	4-121 (2.0)	1.8677–1.8696	1.8677–1.8696	1.8677–1.8696	1.8677–1.8696	1.8677–1.8696	0.2600	0.2600	0.0010–0.0039	NA
	W	6-173 (2.8)	1.8678–1.8815	1.8678–1.8815	1.8678–1.8815	1.8678–1.8815	1.8678–1.8815	0.2626	0.2732	NA	NA
1987	M	4-121 (2.0)	1.6714–1.6720	1.6812–1.6816	1.6911–1.6917	1.7009–1.7015	1.7108–1.7114	0.2409	0.2409	0.0008	0.0160–0.0640
	1	4-121 (2.0)	1.8670–1.8690	1.8670–1.8690	1.8670–1.8690	1.8670–1.8690	1.8670–1.8690	0.2600	0.2600	0.0010–0.0040	NA
	K	4-121 (2.0)	1.6714–1.6720	1.6812–1.6816	1.6911–1.6917	1.7009–1.7015	1.7108–1.7114	0.2409	0.2409	0.0008	0.0160–0.0640
	W	6-173 (2.8)	1.8678–1.8815	1.8678–1.8815	1.8678–1.8815	1.8678–1.8815	1.8678–1.8815	0.2626	0.2732	NA	NA
1988	M	4-121 (2.0)	1.6714–1.6720	1.6812–1.6816	1.6911–1.6917	1.7009–1.7015	1.7108–1.7114	0.2409	0.2409	0.0008	0.0160–0.0640
	1	4-121 (2.0)	1.8670–1.8690	1.8670–1.8690	1.8670–1.8690	1.8670–1.8690	1.8670–1.8690	0.2600	0.2600	0.0010–0.0040	NA
	K	4-121 (2.0)	1.6714–1.6720	1.6812–1.6816	1.6911–1.6917	1.7009–1.7015	1.7108–1.7114	0.2409	0.2409	0.0008	0.0160–0.0640

CAMSHAFT SPECIFICATIONS
All measurements given in inches.

Year	VIN	No. Cylinder Displacement cu. in. (liter)	Journal Diameter					Lobe Lift		Bearing Clearance	Camshaft End Play
			1	2	3	4	5	In.	Ex.		
1988	W	6-173 (2.8)	1.8678–1.8815	1.8678–1.8815	1.8678–1.8815	1.8678–1.8815	1.8678–1.8815	0.2626	0.2732	NA	NA
1989-90	M	4-121 (2.0)	1.6714–1.6720	1.6812–1.6816	1.6911–1.6917	1.7009–1.7015	1.7108–1.7114	0.2409	0.2409	0.0008	0.0160–0.0640
	1	4-121 (2.0)	1.8670–1.8690	1.8670–1.8690	1.8670–1.8690	1.8670–1.8690	1.8670–1.8690	0.2600	0.2600	0.0010–0.0040	NA
	K	4-121 (2.0)	1.6714–1.6720	1.6812–1.6816	1.6911–1.6917	1.7009–1.7015	1.7108–1.7114	0.2409	0.2409	0.0008	0.0160–0.0640
	W	6-173 (2.8)	1.8678–1.8815	1.8678–1.8815	1.8678–1.8815	1.8678–1.8815	1.8678–1.8815	0.2626	0.2732	NA	NA

NA Not available

CRANKSHAFT AND CONNECTING ROD SPECIFICATIONS
All measurements are given in inches.

Year	VIN	No. Cylinder Displacement cu. in. (liter)	Crankshaft				Connecting Rod		
			Main Brg. Journal Dia.	Main Brg. Oil Clearance	Shaft End-play	Thrust on No.	Journal Diameter	Oil Clearance	Side Clearance
1986	0	4-111 (1.8)	①	0.0006–0.0016	0.0027–0.0118	3	1.9278–1.9286	0.0007–0.0024	0.0027–0.0095
	J	4-111 (1.8)	①	0.0006–0.0016	0.0027–0.0118	3	1.9278–1.9286	0.0007–0.0024	0.0027–0.0095
	P	4-121 (2.0)	2.4944–2.4955 ②	0.0006–0.0018 ③	0.0019–0.0071	4	1.9983–1.9993	0.0009–0.0031	0.0039–0.0240
	W	6-173 (2.8)	2.6473–2.6482	0.0016–0.0033	0.0024–0.0083	3	1.9983–1.9994	0.0014–0.0037	0.0063–0.0173
1987	M	4-121 (2.0)	①	0.0006–0.0016	0.0030–0.0120	3	1.9278–1.9286	0.0007–0.0024	0.0027–0.0095
	1	4-121 (2.0)	2.4945–2.4954	0.0006–0.0019	0.0020–0.0080	4	1.9983–1.9994	0.0010–0.0031	0.0040–0.0150
	K	4-121 (2.0)	①	0.0006–0.0016	0.0030–0.0120	3	1.9278–1.9286	0.0007–0.0024	0.0027–0.0095
	W	6-173 (2.8)	2.6473–2.6482	0.0016–0.0033	0.0024–0.0083	3	1.9983–1.9994	0.0014–0.0037	0.0063–0.0173
1988	M	4-121 (2.0)	①	0.0006–0.0016	0.0030–0.0120	3	1.9278–1.9286	0.0007–0.0024	0.0027–0.0095
	1	4-121 (2.0)	2.4945–2.4954	0.0006–0.0019	0.0020–0.0080	4	1.9983–1.9994	0.0010–0.0031	0.0040–0.0150
	K	4-121 (2.0)	①	0.0006–0.0016	0.0030–0.0120	3	1.9278–1.9286	0.0007–0.0024	0.0027–0.0095
	W	6-173 (2.8)	2.6473–2.6482	0.0016–0.0033	0.0024–0.0083	3	1.9983–1.9994	0.0014–0.0037	0.0063–0.0173
1989-90	M	4-121 (2.0)	①	0.0006–0.0016	0.0030–0.0120	3	1.9278–1.9286	0.0007–0.0024	0.0027–0.0095
	1	4-121 (2.0)	2.4945–2.4954	0.0006–0.0019	0.0020–0.0080	4	1.9983–1.9994	0.0010–0.0031	0.0040–0.0150

CRANKSHAFT AND CONNECTING ROD SPECIFICATIONS

All measurements are given in inches.

Year	VIN	No. Cylinder Displacement cu. in. (liter)	Main Brg. Journal Dia.	Crankshaft Main Brg. Oil Clearance	Shaft End-play	Thrust on No.	Connecting Rod Journal Diameter	Oil Clearance	Side Clearance
1989-90	K	4-121 (2.0)	①	0.0016–0.0016	0.0030–0.0120	3	1.9278–1.9286	0.0007–0.0024	0.0027–0.0095
	W	6-173 (2.8)	2.6473–2.6482	0.0016–0.0033	0.0024–0.0083	3	1.9983–1.9994	0.0014–0.0037	0.0063–0.0173

① Bearings are identified by color:
Brown 2.2830–2.2832; ② No. 5: 2.4936–2.4946
Green 2.2827–2.2830 ③ No. 5: 0.0014–0.0027

VALVE SPECIFICATIONS

Year	VIN	No. Cylinder Displacement cu. in. (liter)	Seat Angle (deg.)	Face Angle (deg.)	Spring Test Pressure (lbs.)	Spring Installed Height (in.)	Stem-to-Guide Clearance (in.) Intake	Exhaust	Stem Diameter (in.) Intake	Exhaust
1986	O	4-111 (1.8)	46	46	NA	NA	0.0006–0.0016	0.0012–0.0024	NA	NA
	J	4-111 (1.8)	46	46	NA	NA	0.0006–0.0016	0.0012–0.0024	NA	NA
	P	4-121 (2.0)	46	45	183 @ 1.33	1.60	0.0011–0.0026	0.0014–0.0031	0.3139–0.3144	0.3129–0.3136
	W	6-173 (2.8)	46	45	195 @ 1.18	1.57	0.0010–0.0027	0.0010–0.0027	NA	NA
1987	M	4-121 (2.0)	45	46	NA	NA	0.0006–0.0020	0.0010–0.0024	NA	NA
	1	4-121 (2.0)	46	45	183 @ 1.33	1.60	0.0011–0.0026	0.0014–0.0030	0.0490–0.0560	0.0630–0.0750
	K	4-121 (2.0)	45	46	NA	NA	0.0006–0.0020	0.0010–0.0024	NA	NA
	W	6-173 (2.8)	46	45	195 @ 1.18	1.57	0.0010–0.0027	0.0010–0.0027	0.0610–0.0730	0.0670–0.0790
1988	M	4-121 (2.0)	45	46	NA	NA	0.0006–0.0020	0.0010–0.0024	NA	NA
	1	4-121 (2.0)	46	45	183 @ 1.33	1.60	0.0011–0.0026	0.0014–0.0030	0.0490–0.0560	0.0630–0.0750
	K	4-121 (2.0)	45	46	NA	NA	0.0006–0.0020	0.0010–0.0024	NA	NA
	W	6-173 (2.8)	46	45	195 @ 1.18	1.57	0.0010–0.0027	0.0010–0.0027	0.0610–0.0730	0.0670–0.0790
1989-90	M	4-121 (2.0)	45	46	NA	NA	0.0006–0.0020	0.0010–0.0024	NA	NA
	1	4-121 (2.0)	46	45	183 @ 1.33	1.60	0.0011–0.0026	0.0014–0.0030	0.0490–0.0560	0.0630–0.0750
	K	4-121 (2.0)	45	46	NA	NA	0.0006–0.0020	0.0010–0.0024	NA	NA
	W	6-173 (2.8)	46	45	195 @ 1.18	1.57	0.0010–0.0027	0.0010–0.0027	0.0610–0.0730	0.0670–0.0790

PISTON AND RING SPECIFICATIONS

All measurements are given in inches.

Year	VIN	No. Cylinder Displacement cu. in. (liter)	Piston Clearance	Ring Gap			Ring Side Clearance		
				Top Compression	Bottom Compression	Oil Control	Top Compression	Bottom Compression	Oil Control
1986	O	4-111 (1.8)	0.0008	0.0010–0.0020	0.0010–0.0020	0.0010–0.0020	0.0020–0.0030	0.0010–0.0024	Snug
	J	4-111 (1.8)	①	0.0010–0.0020	0.0010–0.0020	0.0010–0.0020	0.0020–0.0030	0.0010–0.0024	Snug
	P	4-121 (2.0)	0.0008–0.0018	0.0098–0.0197	0.0098–0.0197	Snug	0.0012–0.0027	0.0012–0.0027	0.0078
	W	6-173 (2.8)	0.0007–0.0017	0.0098–0.0197	0.0098–0.0197	0.020–0.055	0.0012–0.0027	0.0016–0.0037	0.0078 Max
1987	M	4-121 (2.0)	0.0012–0.0020	0.012–0.020	0.012–0.020	0.016–0.055	0.0020–0.0030	0.0010–0.0024	—
	1	4-121 (2.0)	0.0098–0.0220	0.0100–0.0200	0.0100–0.0200	0.010–0.050	0.0010–0.0030	0.0010–0.0030	0.0006–0.0090
	K	4-121 (2.0)	0.0004–0.0012	0.012–0.020	0.012–0.020	0.016–0.055	0.0020–0.0030	0.0010–0.0024	—
	W	6-173 (2.8)	0.0007–0.0017	0.0098–0.0197	0.0098–0.0197	0.020–0.055	0.0012–0.0027	0.0016–0.0037	0.0078 Max
1988	M	4-121 (2.0)	0.0012–0.0020	0.012–0.020	0.012–0.020	0.016–0.055	0.0020–0.0030	0.0010–0.0024	—
	1	4-121 (2.0)	0.0098–0.0220	0.0100–0.0200	0.0100–0.0200	0.010–0.050	0.0010–0.0030	0.0010–0.0030	0.0006–0.0090
	K	4-121 (2.0)	0.0004–0.0012	0.012–0.020	0.012–0.020	0.016–0.055	0.0020–0.0030	0.0010–0.0024	—
	W	6-173 (2.8)	0.0022–0.0035	0.010–0.020	0.010–0.020	0.010–0.050	0.002–0.0035	0.002–0.0035	0.0080 Max
1989–90	M	4-121 (2.0)	0.0012–0.0020	0.012–0.020	0.012–0.020	0.016–0.055	0.0020–0.0030	0.0010–0.0024	—
	1	4-121 (2.0)	0.0098–0.0220	0.0100–0.0200	0.0100–0.0200	0.010–0.050	0.0010–0.0030	0.0010–0.0030	0.0006–0.0090
	K	4-121 (2.0)	0.0004–0.0012	0.012–0.020	0.012–0.020	0.016–0.055	0.0020–0.0030	0.0010–0.0024	—
	W	6-173 (2.8)	0.0022–0.0035	0.010–0.020	0.010–0.020	0.010–0.050	0.002–0.0035	0.002–0.0035	0.0080 Max

① 0.0004–0.0012

TORQUE SPECIFICATIONS

All readings in ft. lbs.

Year	VIN	No. Cylinder Displacement cu. in. (liter)	Cylinder Head Bolts	Main Bearing Bolts	Rod Bearing Bolts	Crankshaft Pulley Bolts	Flywheel Bolts	Manifold		Spark Plugs
								Intake	Exhaust	
1986	O	4-111 (1.8)	①	57	39	115 ⑪	45	25	16	15
	J	4-111 (1.8)	①	57	39	115 ⑪	45	25	16	15
	P	4-121 (2.0)	65–75	63–77	34–40	68–84 ⑩	45–63 ②	18–25	20–30	15
	W	6-173 (2.8)	70	68	37	75	45	23	16	15
1987	M	4-121 (2.0)	③	44 ④	26 ⑤	20 ⑥	48 ⑦	16	16	15
	1	4-121 (2.0)	⑧	63–77	34–43	68–89	63 ②	15–22	6–13	15

TORQUE SPECIFICATIONS
All readings in ft. lbs.

Year	VIN	No. Cylinder Displacement cu. in. (liter)	Cylinder Head Bolts	Main Bearing Bolts	Rod Bearing Bolts	Crankshaft Pulley Bolts	Flywheel Bolts	Manifold Intake	Manifold Exhaust	Spark Plugs
1987	K	4-121 (2.0)	③	44 ④	26 ⑤	20 ⑥	48 ⑦	16	16	15
	W	6-173 (2.8)	33 ⑨	63–83	34–45	66–84	45	18	14–22	15
1988	M	4-121 (2.0)	③	44 ④	26 ⑤	20 ⑥	48 ⑦	16	16	15
	1	4-121 (2.0)	⑧	63–77	34–43	68–89	63 ②	15–22	6–13	15
	K	4-121 (2.0)	③	44 ④	26 ⑤	20 ⑥	48 ⑦	16	16	15
	W	6-173 (2.8)	33 ⑨	63–83	34–45	66–84	45	18	14–22	15
1989–90	M	4-121 (2.0)	③	44 ④	26 ⑤	20 ⑥	48 ⑦	16	16	15
	1	4-121 (2.0)	⑧	63–77	34–43	68–89	63 ②	15–22	6–13	15
	K	4-121 (2.0)	③	44 ④	26 ⑤	20 ⑥	48 ⑦	16	16	15
	W	6-173 (2.8)	33 ⑨	63–83	34–45	66–84	45	18	14–22	15

CAUTION: Verify the correct original equipment engine is in the vehicle by referring to the VIN engine code before torquing any bolts.

① Torque bolts to 18 ft.lb., then turn each bolt 60 degrees, in sequence, 3 times for a 180 degree rotation, then run the engine to normal operating temperature and turn each bolt, in sequence, an additional 30–50 degrees

② Auto. Trans.—45–59

③ Step 1—18 ft. lbs.
Step 2—Tighten additional 180 degrees in 3 steps of 60 degrees each
Step 3—Warm engine—tighten bolts additional 30–50 degree turn

④ Plus additional 45–50 degree turn

⑤ Plus additional 45 degree turn

⑥ Crankshaft pulley to sprocket bolts

⑦ Plus additional 30 degree turn

⑧ Long bolts—73–83 ft. lbs.
Short bolts—62–70 ft. lbs.

⑨ Coat thread with sealer an additional 90 degree turn

⑩ Crankshaft pulley center

⑪ Crankshaft sprocket retaining bolts

WHEEL ALIGNMENT

Year	Model	Caster Range (deg.)	Caster Preferred Setting (deg.)	Camber Range (deg.)	Camber Preferred Setting (deg.)	Toe-in (in.)	Steering Axis Inclination (deg.)
1986	Cavalier	NA	NA	$3/16$P–$1^3/16$P	$^{13}/_{16}$P	$1/4$–0 ①	$13^1/_2$
	Sunbird	NA	NA	$3/16$P–$1^3/16$P	$^{13}/_{16}$P	$1/4$–0 ①	$13^1/_2$
	Firenza	NA	NA	$3/16$P–$1^3/16$P	$^{13}/_{16}$P	$1/4$–0 ①	$13^1/_2$
	Skyhawk	NA	NA	$3/16$P–$1^3/16$P	$^{13}/_{16}$P	$1/4$–0 ①	$13^1/_2$
	Cimarron	NA	NA	$3/16$P–$1^3/16$P	$^{13}/_{16}$P	$1/4$–0 ①	$13^1/_2$
1987	Cavalier	NA	NA	$3/16$P–$1^3/16$P	$^{13}/_{16}$P	0 ③	$13^1/_2$
	Sunbird	NA	NA	$3/16$P–$1^3/16$P	$^{13}/_{16}$P	0 ③	$13^1/_2$
	Firenza	NA	NA	$3/16$P–$1^3/16$P	$^{13}/_{16}$P	0 ③	$13^1/_2$
	Skyhawk	NA	NA	$3/16$P–$1^3/16$P	$^{13}/_{16}$P	0 ③	$13^1/_2$
	Cimarron	NA	NA	$3/16$P–$1^3/16$P	$^{13}/_{16}$P	0 ③	$13^1/_2$
1988	Cavalier	NA	NA	$3/16$P–$1^3/16$P ②	$^{13}/_{16}$P ②	0	$13^1/_2$
	Sunbird	NA	NA	$3/16$P–$1^3/16$P	$^{13}/_{16}$P	0	$13^1/_2$
	Firenza	NA	NA	$3/16$P–$1^3/16$P	$^{13}/_{16}$P	0	$13^1/_2$
	Skyhawk	NA	NA	$3/16$P–$1^3/16$P	$^{13}/_{16}$P	0	$13^1/_2$
	Cimarron	NA	NA	$3/16$P–$1^3/16$P	$^{13}/_{16}$P	0	$13^1/_2$

WHEEL ALIGNMENT

Year	Model	Caster Range (deg.)	Caster Preferred Setting (deg.)	Camber Range (deg.)	Camber Preferred Setting (deg.)	Toe-in (in.)	Steering Axis Inclination (deg.)
1989–90	Cavalier	NA	NA	$^3/_{16}$P–1$^3/_{16}$P ②	$^{13}/_{16}$P ②	0	13$^1/_2$
	Sunbird	NA	NA	$^3/_{16}$P–1$^3/_{16}$P	$^{13}/_{16}$P	0	13$^1/_2$
	Skyhawk	NA	NA	$^3/_{16}$P–1$^3/_{16}$P	$^{13}/_{16}$P	0	13$^1/_2$

NA Not adjustable
① Preferred setting—$^1/_8$ degree out
② Z-24; 1N–1P. Preferred setting is 0 camber
③ If vehicle is equipped with P215-60R14 tires setting is $^1/_8$ degree out

ELECTRICAL

NOTE: **Disconnecting the negative battery cable on some vehicles may interfere with the functions of the on board computer systems and may require the computer to undergo a relearning process, once the negative battery cable is reconnected.**

For testing and overhaul procedures on starters, alternators and voltage regulators, refer to the Unit Repair section.

Charging System

ALTERNATOR

Removal and Installation

1. Disconnect the negative battery cable.
2. Disconnect the 2 terminal plug and battery lead from the rear of the alternator.
3. If equipped with V-belts, loosen the alternator adjusting bolt and remove the the belt. If equipped with a serpentine belt, loosen the belt tensioner and remove the belt.
4. Remove the alternator mounting bolts and remove the alternator from the engine.
5. To install, position the alternator on the engine and install the mounting bolts.
6. Install and tension the drive belt. Tighten the mounting and adjusting bolts.
7. Connect the alternator wiring and negative battery cable.

VOLTAGE REGULATOR

All vehicles are equipped with an internal voltage regulator. Removal and installation requires alternator disassembly.

BELT TENSION

Gauge Method

V-BELTS

Using belt tension gauge J-23600 or equivalent, adjust the alternator belt if the tension is below 300N, as indicated on the gauge. If the old belt is used, the correct belt tension is 350N, as indicated on the gauge. If the belt is new, the correct tension is 600N, as indicated on the gauge.

SERPENTINE BELTS

Serpentine belts are tensioned by loosening and rotating the belt tensioner. The correct belt tension is indicated on the indicator mark of the belt tensioner. If the indicator mark is not within specification, replace the belt or the tensioner.

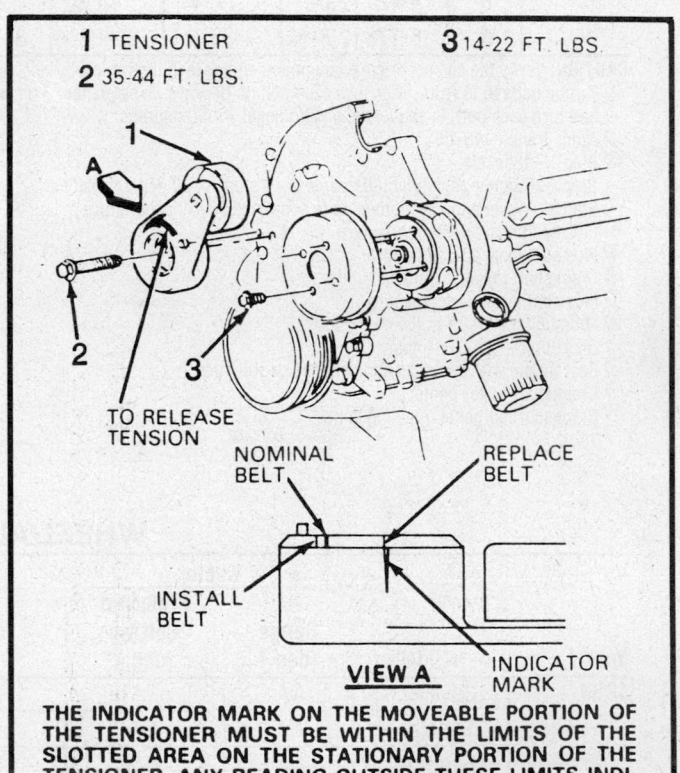

THE INDICATOR MARK ON THE MOVEABLE PORTION OF THE TENSIONER MUST BE WITHIN THE LIMITS OF THE SLOTTED AREA ON THE STATIONARY PORTION OF THE TENSIONER. ANY READING OUTSIDE THESE LIMITS INDICATES EITHER A DEFECTIVE BELT OR TENSIONER.

Tensioner assembly 2.8L engine

NOTE: **To remove or install the belt, push (rotate) the tensioner. Care should be taken to avoid twisting or bending the tensioner when applying torque.**

Starting System

STARTER

Removal and Installation

2.0L AND 2.8L OHV ENGINES

1. Disconnect the negative battery cable. Raise and support the vehicle safely.
2. Disconnect and tag the solenoid wires and battery cable at the starter.

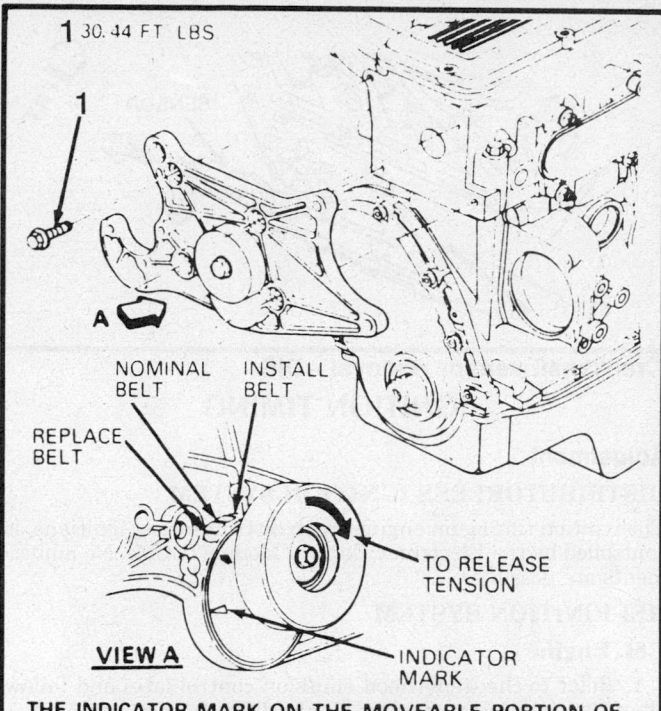

Tensioner assembly 2.0L engine

THE INDICATOR MARK ON THE MOVEABLE PORTION OF THE TENSIONER MUST BE WITHIN THE LIMITS OF THE SLOTTED AREA ON THE STATIONARY PORTION OF THE TENSIONER. ANY READING OUTSIDE THESE LIMITS INDICATES EITHER A DEFECTIVE BELT OR TENSIONER.

3. Remove the rear starter motor support bracket. Remove the air conditioning compressor support rod, if equipped.

4. Support the starter motor and remove the 2 starter-to-engine bolts.

5. Remove the starter motor. Note the location and number of any shims.

To install:

6. Install the starter motor, placing any amount of shims removed in the original location.

7. Tighten the mounting bolts to 25–35 ft. lbs.

8. Install the support bracket and air conditioning compressor rod, if removed.

9. Connect the starter wiring.

10. Connect the negative battery cable and check the starter operation.

1.8L AND 2.0L OHC ENGINES

1. Disconnect the negative battery cable.

2. Remove the air cleaner assembly.

3. Remove the lower starter motor mounting bolt.

4. Remove the rear starter motor brace.

5. Disconnect and tag the wiring at the starter.

6. Remove the upper starter motor mounting bolt.

7. Raise and support the vehicle safely.

8. On vehicles equipped with an automatic transaxle, disconnect the speedometer cable.

9. Push the shifter cable up and guide the starter, armature end first, down between the stabilizer bar and the engine.

To install:

10. Install the starter motor from under the vehicle, armature end first.

11. On vehicles equipped with an automatic transaxle, connect the speedometer cable.

12. Install the upper and lower mounting bolts. Connect the wiring.

13. Install the rear starter motor brace. Install the air cleaner assembly.

14. Connect the negative battery cable and check the starter motor operation.

Ignition System

DISTRIBUTOR

Removal and Installation

2.0L AND 2.8L OHV ENGINES

Timing Not Disturbed

1. Disconnect the negative battery cable.

2. Tag and disconnect all wires leading from the distributor cap.

3. Remove the air cleaner housing.

4. Remove the distributor cap.

5. Disconnect the AIR pipe-to-exhaust manifold hose at the air management valve.

6. Unscrew the rear engine lift bracket bolt and nut, lift it off the stud and position the entire assembly out of the way to facilitate better access to the distributor.

7. Mark the position of the distributor, relative to the engine block and scribe a mark on the distributor body indicating the initial position of the rotor.

8. Remove the hold-down nut and clamp from the base of the distributor. Remove the distributor from the engine. The drive gear on the distributor shaft is helical and the shaft will rotate slightly as the distributor is removed. Note and mark the position of the rotor at this second position.

9. To install the distributor, rotate the shaft until the rotor aligns with the second mark made. Lubricate the drive gear with clean engine oil and install the distributor into the engine. As the distributor is installed, the rotor should rotate to the first mark made. This will ensure proper ignition timing. If the marks do not align properly, remove the distributor and repeat the procedure.

10. Install the clamp and hold-down nut.

11. The remainder of the installation is the reverse of the removal procedure.

12. Start the engine and check the ignition timing when finished.

Timing Disturbed

1. Remove the No. 1 cylinder spark plug.

2. Place a finger over the spark plug hole while rotating the engine slowly by hand, until compression is felt.

3. Align the timing mark on the crankshaft pulley with the **0** degree mark on the timing scale on the front of the engine. This places the engine at TDC of the compression stroke for No. 1 cylinder.

4. Rotate the distributor shaft until the rotor points to the No. 1 spark plug tower on the distributor cap.

5. Install the distributor in the engine. Be sure to align the distributor-to-engine matchmarks.

6. Install the hold down clamp and bolt. Start and run the engine.

7. Check and adjust the ignition timing.

1.8L AND 2.0L OHC ENGINES

Timing Not Disturbed

1. Disconnect the negative battery cable.

2. Tag the spark plug wires and remove the wires and ignition coil from the distributor.

3. Disconnect the wiring from the distributor.

4. Remove the 2 distributor hold-down nuts.

5. Remove the distributor.

6. Installation is the reverse of removal. Torque the hold-down nuts to 13 ft. lbs. Check and/or adjust the ignition timing when finished.

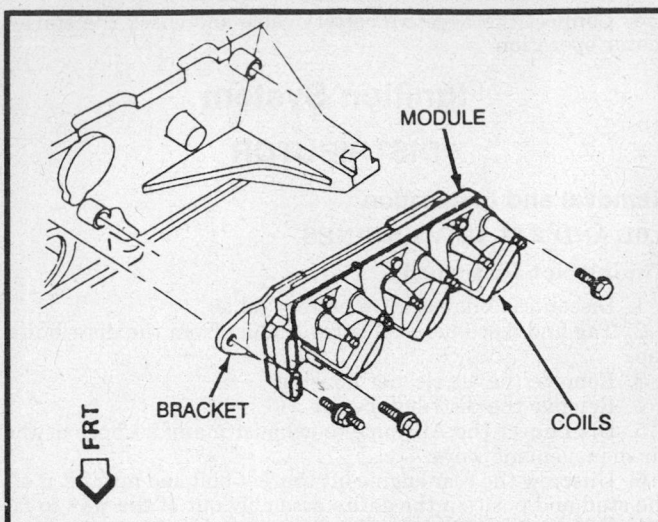

Ignition coil pack—DIS

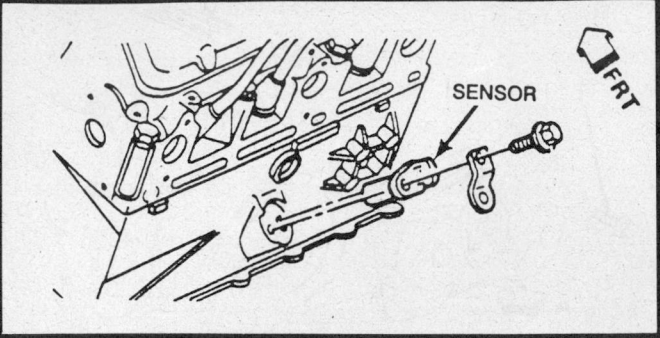

Crankshaft sensor removal—DIS

IGNITION TIMING

Adjustment

DISTRIBUTORLESS IGNITION SYSTEM

The ignition timing on engines with distributorless ignitions, is controlled by the Electronic Control Module (ECM). No adjustments are possible.

HEI IGNITION SYSTEM

1.8L Engine

1. Refer to the underhood emission control label and follow all of the timing instructions if they differ from below.
2. Warm the engine to normal operating temperature.
3. Place the transmission in **N** or **P**. Apply the parking brake and block wheels.
4. Air conditioning, cooling fan and choke must be **OFF**. Do not remove the air cleaner, except as noted.
5. Ground the ALCL connector under the dash by installing a jumper wire between the **A** and **B** terminals. The **CHECK ENGINE** light should begin flashing.
6. Connect an inductive timing light to the No.1 spark plug wire lead and record timing.
7. Connect an inductive timing light to the No.4 spark plug wire lead and record timing.
8. Add the 2 timing numbers and divide by 2 to obtain "average timing".

NOTE: For example: No. 1 timing = 4 degrees and No. 4 timing = 8 degrees; 4 + 8 = 12 ÷ 2 = 6 degrees average timing. If a change is necessary, subtract the average timing from the timing specification to determine the amount of timing change to No. 1 cylinder. For example: if the timing specification is 8 degrees and the average timing is 6 degrees, advance the No. 1 cylinder 2 degrees to set the timing.

9. To correct the timing, loosen the distributor hold down clamp, adjust the distributor and retighten the hold down bolt.
10. Once the timing is properly set, remove the jumper wire from the ALCL connector.
11. If necessary to clear the ECM memory, disconnect the ECM harness from the positive battery pigtail for 10 seconds with the key in the **OFF** position.

2.0L and 2.8L Engines

1. Refer to the underhood emission control label and follow all of the timing instructions if they differ from below.
2. Warm the engine to normal operating temperature.
3. Place the transmission in **N** or **P**. Apply parking brake and block the wheels.
4. Air conditioning, cooling fan and choke must be **OFF**. Do not remove the air cleaner, except as noted.
5. Connect an inductive timing light to the coil lead. Peel back the protective covering on the coil lead to make a good connection.

Timing Disturbed

1. Remove the No. 1 cylinder spark plug.
2. Place a finger over the spark plug hole while rotating the engine slowly by hand, until compression is felt.
3. Align the timing mark on the crankshaft pulley with the **0** degree mark on the timing scale on the front of the engine. This places the engine at TDC of the compression stroke for No. 1 cylinder.
4. Rotate the distributor shaft until the rotor points to the No. 1 spark plug tower on the distributor cap.
5. Install the distributor in the engine. Be sure to align the distributor-to-engine matchmarks.
6. Install the hold down clamp and bolt. Start and run the engine.
7. Check and adjust the ignition timing.

DISTRIBUTORLESS IGNITION SYSTEM (DIS)

Removal and Installation

COIL PACK

1. Disconnect the negative battery cable.
2. Disconnect the electrical wires from the coil pack.
3. Mark the location of the spark plug wires on the coil pack and remove the wires.
4. Remove the coil pack mounting bolts and remove the assembly from the block.

To install:

NOTE: With the coil pack removed, the coils can each be removed and the ignition module can be removed as well.

5. Install the coil pack on the block.
6. Reconnect the plug wires to their original location.
7. Connect the coil pack wiring.
8. Connect the negative battery cable.

CRANKSHAFT SENSOR

1. Disconnect the negative battery cable.
2. Disconnect the sensor harness plug.
3. Remove the sensor-to-block bolt and remove the sensor from the engine.
4. To install the sensor, position the sensor in the block and install the sensor bolt. Torque the sensor bolt to 71 inch lbs.
5. Reconnect the sensor harness plug.

NOTE: On engine codes P, 1 and W disconnect the single wire HEI bypass connector (tan/black wire) usually near the distributor on 4 cylinder engines and near the left shock tower on 6 cylinder engines. This will cause the engine to operate in the bypass timing mode, do this instead of grounding the test terminal.

6. Ground the ALCL connector under the dash by installing a jumper wire between the **A** and **B** terminals. The **CHECK ENGINE** light should begin flashing.

7. Using the timing light, check the position of the timing mark.

8. Optimum timing of all cylinders is achieved when the apparent notch width is centered with the timing mark.

NOTE: A notch for the No.1 cylinder is scribed across all 3 edges of the double groove pulley. Another notch is scribed 180 degrees away only across the center edge of the pulley. Since the coil high tension lead is triggering the timing light, timing for all cylinders is shown, causing a slight jiggling of the timing notch and an apparent increase in the width of the timing notch.

9. To correct the timing, loosen the distributor hold down clamp, adjust the distributor and retighten the hold down bolt.

10. Once the timing is properly set, remove the jumper wire from the ALCL connector.

11. If necessary to clear the ECM memory, disconnect the ECM harness from the positive battery pigtail for 10 seconds with the key in the **OFF** position.

Electrical Controls

STEERING WHEEL

Removal and Installation
SPORT WHEEL

1. Disconnect the negative battery cable.
2. Remove the center horn cap from the steering wheel.
3. Remove the retainer.
4. Remove the shaft nut.
5. Matchmark the wheel hub and shaft before removal of the wheel.
6. Install a steering wheel puller and remove the steering wheel.

To install:

7. Position the spring, eyelet and insulator into the tower on the column.
8. Align the matchmarks and install the steering wheel onto the shaft. Install the retaining nut and tighten to 30 ft. lbs.
9. Install the retainer and center cap. Connect the negative battery cable.

STANDARD WHEEL

1. Disconnect the negative battery cable.
2. Pull the pad from the wheel. The horn lead is attached to the pad at one end; the other end of the pad has a wire with a spade connector. The horn lead is disconnected by pushing and turning; the spade connector is unplugged.

NOTE: If equipped with cruise control, unplug the connectors from the pad.

3. Remove the retainer under the pad.
4. Remove the steering shaft nut.
5. Matchmark the steering wheel to the steering shaft.
6. Remove the steering wheel using a steering wheel puller.

To install:

7. Install the wheel on the shaft, aligning the matchmarks. Install the shaft nut and tighten to 30 ft. lbs.
8. Install the retainer.

9. Plug in the spade connector. Push and turn the horn lead to connect.
10. Install the horn pad. Connect the negative battery cable.

HORN SWITCH

Removal and Installation
STANDARD STEERING WHEEL

1. Disconnect the negative battery cable.
2. Remove the screws attaching the horn pad assembly from the underside of the steering wheel. Lift the horn pad from the steering wheel.
3. Disconnect the horn contact terminal from the pad. If the contact terminal comes out of, or is removed from the turn signal cancelling cam tower, it can be re-installed by pushing it into the tower and rotating the steering wheel clockwise to lock it into position.
4. Installation is the reverse of removal. Connect the negative battery cable.

SPORT STEERING WHEEL

1. Disconnect the negative battery cable.
2. Pull up on the center ornament assembly and remove it from the steering wheel.
3. Remove the steering wheel nut and retainer nut.
4. Remove the horn switch and insulator assembly.
5. Remove the 3 screws and separate the switch from the insulator.
6. Installation is the reverse of the removal. Install the negative battery cable.

IGNITION LOCK

Removal and Installation
STANDARD STEERING COLUMN

1. Remove the steering wheel.
2. Turn the ignition key to the **RUN** position.
3. Remove the lock plate, turn signal or combination switch and the key warning buzzer switch. The warning buzzer switch is pulled out with small tool.
4. Remove the lock cylinder retaining screw and lock cylinder.

NOTE: If the retaining screw is dropped during removal, it could fall into the column, requiring complete column disassembly to retrieve the screw.

5. Rotate the cylinder clockwise to align the cylinder key with the keyway in the housing.
6. Push the lock all the way in.
7. Install the screw. Tighten to 15 inch lbs.
8. The remainder of the installation is the reverse of the removal. Turn the lock to **RUN** position and push the key warning buzzer switch into place.

TILT STEERING COLUMN

1. Disconnect the negative battery cable. Remove the steering wheel.
2. Remove the rubber sleeve bumper from the steering shaft.
3. Using an appropriate tool, remove the plastic retainer.
4. Using a spring compressor, compress the upper steering shaft spring and remove the C-ring. Release the steering shaft lockplate, the horn contact carrier and the upper steering shaft preload spring.
5. Remove the 4 screws which hold the upper mounting bracket and then remove the bracket.
6. Slide the harness connector out of the bracket on the steering column. Tape the upper part of the harness and connector.
7. Disconnect the hazard button and position the shift bowl, on automatic transmission equipped vehicles in the **PARK** posi-

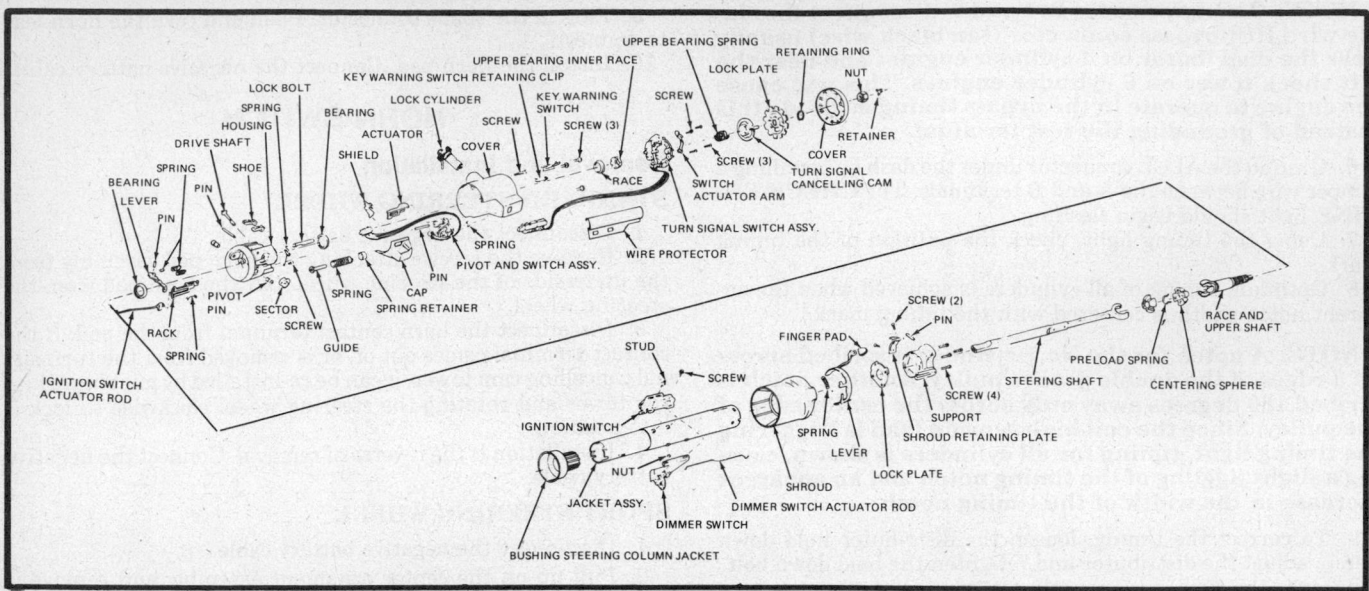

Key release tilt wheel steering column

tion. Remove the turn signal lever from the column.

8. If the vehicle is equipped with cruise control, remove the harness protector from the harness. Attach a piece of wire to the switch harness connector. Before removing the turn signal lever, loop a piece of wire and insert it into the turn signal lever opening. Use the wire to pull the cruise control harness out through the opening. Pull the rest of the harness up through and out of the column. Remove the guide wire from the connector and secure the wire to the column. Remove the turn signal lever.

9. Pull the turn signal switch up until the end connector is within the shift bowl. Remove the hazard flasher lever. Allow the switch to hang.

10. Place the ignition key in the **RUN** position.

11. Depress the center of the lock cylinder retaining tab with a suitable tool and then remove the lock cylinder.

12. Installation is the reverse of the removal procedure.

IGNITION SWITCH

Removal and Installation

The switch is located inside the channel section of the brake pedal support and is completely inaccessible without first lowering the steering column. The switch is actuated by a rod and rack assembly. A gear on the end of the lock cylinder engages the toothed upper end of the rod.

1. Lower the steering column; be sure to properly support it.

2. Put the switch in the **OFF-UNLOCKED** position. With the cylinder removed, the rod is in **OFF-UNLOCKED** position when it is in the next to the uppermost detent.

3. Remove the 2 switch screws and remove the switch assembly.

4. Before installing, place the new switch in **OFF-UN-LOCKED** position and make sure the lock cylinder and actuating rod are in **OFF-UNLOCKED** position (second detent from the top).

5. Install the activating rod into the switch and assemble the switch on the column. Tighten the mounting screws. Use only the specified screws, since overlength screws could impair the effectiveness of the column to collapse.

6. Install the steering column.

NEUTRAL SAFETY/REVERSE LIGHT SWITCH

Removal and Installation

The neutral safety/reverse light switch is located on top of the transaxle.

1. Disconnect the negative battery cable.

2. Disconnect the shift linkage at the transaxle.

3. Disconnect the electrical connector from the switch.

4. Remove the switch mounting bolts and remove the switch from the transaxle.

5. To install the switch, place the shift shaft in the **N** detent.

6. Align the flats on the shift shaft with the flats on the switch and slide the switch into position.

7. Install the mounting bolts and tighten to 22 ft. lbs.

8. Connect the shift linkage and the negative battery cable.

Adjustment

1. Place the shift lever in the **N** detent.

2. Loosen the switch attaching bolts.

3. Rotate the switch on the shift shaft to align the service adjustment hole with the carrier tang.

4. Insert an $3/32$ in. drill bit or piece of wire into the hole.

5. Tighten the mounting bolts to 22 ft. lbs and remove the gauge wire.

6. Make sure that the vehicle will only start in **N** or **P**, if the vehicle will start in other gears, readjust it.

CLUTCH START SWITCH

The clutch start switch is used on cars equipped with a manual transaxle. The switch prevents the engine from starting unless the clutch pedal is depressed.

Removal and Installation

1. Disconnect the negative battery cable.

2. Unbolt the switch from the clutch pedal assembly and disconnect the wiring.

3. Install the new switch in reverse order of removal.

STOPLIGHT SWITCH

Removal and Installation

The stoplight, cruise control and cruise control vacuum switch are all located on the brake pedal mounting bracket and are adjusted in an identical manner.

1. Remove the wiring from switch and remove the switch.
2. To install, insert the retaining tubular clip in bracket on the pedal assembly.
3. With the pedal depressed, insert the switch into the tubular clip until the switch body seats on clip.

NOTE: Audible clicks can be heard as threaded portion of switch is pushed through the clip toward the brake pedal. Vacuum release valve and stoplight switch are self-adjusting.

4. Connect the wiring for the switch.

HEADLIGHT SWITCH

Removal and Installation

CAVALIER, SUNBIRD AND CIMARRON

1. Disconnect the negative battery cable.
2. Pull the knob out fully. Remove the knob from rod by depressing the retaining clip from the underside of the knob.
3. Remove the trimplate.
4. Remove the switch by removing nut, rotating the switch 180 degrees, then tilting forward and pulling it out. Disconnect the wire harness.
5. Installation is the reverse of the removal procedure.

SKYHAWK AND FIRENZA

1. Disconnect the negative battery cable.
2. Remove the left side trim cover.
3. Remove the screws attaching the headlight switch to the instrument panel.
4. Pull the switch rearward in order to remove it from the vehicle.
5. Installation is the reverse of the removal procedure.

DIMMER SWITCH

Removal and Installation

1. Disconnect the negative battery cable. Remove the steering wheel. Remove the trim cover.
2. Remove the turn signal switch assembly.
3. Remove the ignition switch stud and screw. Remove the ignition switch.
4. Remove the dimmer switch actuator rod by sliding it from the switch assembly.
5. Remove the dimmer switch bolts and remove the dimmer switch.
6. Installation is the reverse of the removal procedure.
7. Adjust the dimmer switch by depressing the switch slightly and inserting a $\frac{3}{32}$ in. drill bit into the adjusting hole. Push the switch up to remove any play and tighten the dimmer switch adjusting screw.

TURN SIGNAL SWITCH

Removal and Installation

NOTE: Before removing the turn signal switch, be sure the lever is in the OFF or CENTER position.

1. Disconnect the negative battery cable. Remove the steering wheel. Remove the trim cover.
2. Pry the cover from the steering column.
3. Position a U-shaped lockplate compressing tool on the end

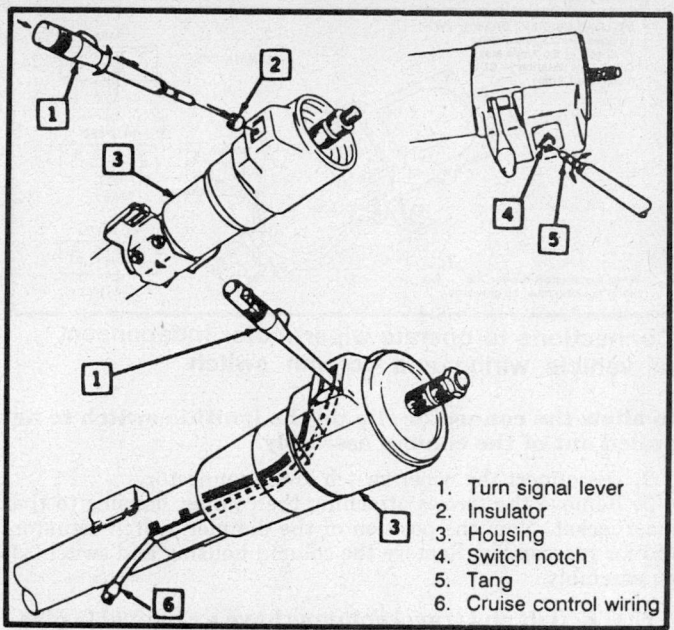

1. Turn signal lever
2. Insulator
3. Housing
4. Switch notch
5. Tang
6. Cruise control wiring

Removing the multi-function lever

of the steering shaft nut clockwise. Pry the wire snapring on the shaft groove off.

4. Remove the tool and lift the lockplate off the shaft.
5. Slip the cancelling cam, upper bearing preload spring and thrust washer off the shaft.
6. Remove the turn signal lever. Remove the hazard flasher button retaining screw and remove the button, spring and knob.
7. Pull the switch connector out of the mast jacket and tape the upper part to facilitate switch removal. Attach a long piece of wire to the turn signal switch connector. When installing the turn signal switch, feed this wire through the column first and then use this wire to pull the switch connector into position. On tilt wheels, place the turn signal and shifter housing in **LOW** position and remove the harness cover.
8. Remove the 3 switch mounting screws. Remove the switch by pulling it straight up while guiding the wire harness cover through the column.

To install:

9. Install the replacement switch by working the connector and cover down through the housing and under the bracket. On tilt vehicles equipped with tilt steering, the connector is worked down through the housing, under the bracket and then the cover is installed on the harness.
10. Install the switch mounting screws and the connector on the mast jacket bracket. Install the column-to-dash trim plate.
11. Install the flasher knob and turn the signal lever.
12. With the turn signal lever in middle position and the flasher knob out, slide the thrust washer, upper bearing preload spring and cancelling cam onto the shaft.
13. Position the lock plate on the shaft and press it down until a new snapring can be inserted in the shaft groove. Always use a new snapring when assembling.
14. Install the cover and steering wheel. Connect the negative battery cable.

WINDSHIELD WIPER SWITCH

Removal and Installation

1. Disconnect the negative battery cable. Remove the steering wheel and turn signal switch.

NOTE: It may be necessary to loosen the 2 column mounting nuts and remove the 4 bracket-to-mast jacket

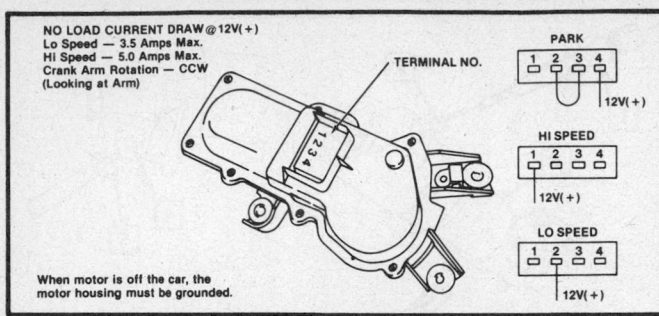

NO LOAD CURRENT DRAW @ 12V(+)
Lo Speed — 3.5 Amps Max.
Hi Speed — 5.0 Amps Max.
Crank Arm Rotation — CCW
(Looking at Arm)

TERMINAL NO.

PARK
1 2 3 4
12V(+)

HI SPEED
1 2 3 4
12V(+)

LO SPEED
1 2 3 4
12V(+)

When motor is off the car, the
motor housing must be grounded.

Connections to operate wiper motor independent
of vehicle wiring and column switch

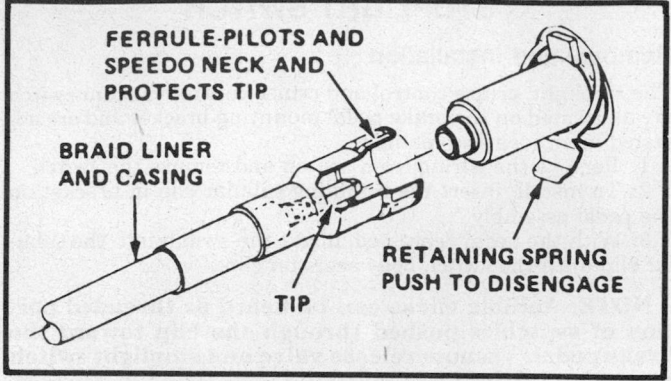

FERRULE-PILOTS AND
SPEEDO NECK AND
PROTECTS TIP

BRAID LINER
AND CASING

TIP

RETAINING SPRING
PUSH TO DISENGAGE

Speedometer cable attachment at cluster

to allow the connector clip on the ignition switch to be pulled out of the column assembly.

2. Disconnect the wiper switch lower connector.
3. Remove the screws attaching the column housing to the mast jacket. Note the position of the dimmer switch actuator rod for reassembly. Remove the column housing and switch as an assembly.

NOTE: Tilt and travel columns have a removable plastic cover on the column housing. This provides access to the wiper switch without removing the entire column housing.

4. Turn the switch upside down and use a drift to remove the pivot pin from the switch. Remove the switch.
To install:
5. Place the switch into the housing and install the pivot pin.
6. Position and attach the housing onto the mast jacket by installing the screws.
7. Install the dimmer switch actuator rod in the same position as noted earlier. Check the switch operation.
8. Reconnect lower switch wiring.
9. Install the remaining components in reverse order of removal. Be sure to attach column mounting bracket in the original position.

WIPER MOTOR

Removal and Installation

1. Disconnect the negative battery cable. Loosen (but do not remove) the drive link-to-crank arm attaching nuts to detach the drive link from the motor crank arm.
2. Tag and disconnect all electrical leads from the wiper motor.
3. Unscrew the mounting bolts, rotate the motor up and outward and remove it.
4. Guide the crank arm through the opening in the body and then tighten the mounting bolts to 4–6 ft. lbs.
5. Install the drive link to the crank arm with the motor in the park position.
6. Installation is the reverse of the removal procedure.

WIPER LINKAGE

Removal and Installation

1. Remove the wiper arms.
2. Remove the shroud top vent grille.
3. Loosen (but do not remove) the drive link-to-crank arm attaching nuts.
4. Unscrew the linkage-to-cowl panel retaining screws and remove the linkage.
5. Installation is the reverse of the removal procedure.

Instrument Cluster

Refer to "Chiltons Electronic Instrumentation Service Manual" for additional coverage.

Removal and Installation
CAVALIER, CIMARRON AND SUNBIRD

1. Disconnect the negative battery cable.
2. Remove the speedometer cluster trimplate.
3. Remove the speedometer cluster attaching screws.
4. Lower the steering column. Pull the cluster away from the instrument panel and disconnect the speedometer cable.
5. Disconnect the vehicle speed sensor connector from the cluster. Disconnect all other electrical connectors as required.
6. Remove the cluster housing from the vehicle.
7. Installation is the reverse of the removal procedure.

SKYHAWK AND FIRENZA

1. Disconnect the negative battery cable.
2. Remove the steering column trim cover. Remove the left and right hand trim cover.
3. Remove the cluster trim cover.
4. Remove the screws attaching the lens and bezel to the cluster carrier.
5. Lower the steering wheel column by removing the 2 upper steering column attaching bolts.
6. Remove the screws attaching the cluster housing to the cluster carrier. Pull the cluster out slightly from the instrument panel and disconnect the speedometer cable. Disconnect all others connectors.
7. Remove the cluster housing from the vehicle.
8. Installation is the reverse of the removal procedure.

NOTE: On some 1987–88 Firenza vehicles, equipped with manual control air conditioning, may exhibit metallic rattle or buzzing noise coming from the center of the instrument panel. Under certain road or engine load conditions, with the air conditioning on, the metal defroster valve in the air conditioning module assembly may vibrate against the case causing the noise. The noise may be heard in all modes except defrost.

SPEEDOMETER

Removal and Installation

1. Disconnect the negative battery cable.
2. Remove instrument panel from vehicle.
3. Remove speedometer cluster from instrument panel.
4. Remove cluster lens and face plate.
5. Remove screws securing speedometer to cluster assembly and remove speedometer.
6. Installation is the reverse of the removal procedure.

MEMORY CHIP REPLACEMENT

After speedometer/cluster removal, if the speedometer is to be replaced, the speedometer/cluster memory chip should be removed from the old cluster assembly and placed in the new one. It can be removed using a non-volatile chip remover/replacer set.

SPEEDOMETER CABLE

Removal and Installation

1. Disconnect the negative battery cable.
2. Reach behind the instrument cluster and push the speedometer cable casing toward the speedometer while depressing the retaining spring on the back of the instrument cluster case.3. Once the retaining spring has released, hold it in while pulling outward on the casing to disconnect the casing from the speedometer.

NOTE: Removal of the steering column trim plate and/or the speedometer cluster may provide better access to the cable.

4. Remove the cable casing sealing plug from the dash panel. Then, pull the casing down from behind the dash and remove the cable.
5. If the cable is broken and cannot be entirely removed from the top, support the vehicle securely and then unscrew the cable casing connector at the transaxle. Pull the bottom part of the cable out and then screw the connector back onto the transaxle.
6. Lubricate the new cable and reverse the removal procedures.

Electrical Circuit Protectors

FUSIBLE LIKS

Fusible links are used to prevent major wire harness damage in the event of short circuit or an overload condition in the wiring circuits which are normally not fused, due to carrying high amperage loads or because of their locations within the wiring harness. Each fusible link is of a fixed value for a specific electrical load and should a link fail, the cause of failure must be determined and repaired prior to installing a new fusible link of the same value.

CIRCUIT BREAKERS

Circuit breakers are used along with the fusible links to protect the various components of the electrical system, such as headlights, the windshield wipers and electric windows. The circuit breakers are located either in the switch or mounted on or near the lower lip of the instrument panel, to the right or left of the steering column.

FUSE PANELS

The fuse panel is located on the left side of the vehicle. It is under the instrument panel assembly. In order to gain access to the fuse panel, it may be necessary to first remove the under dash padding.

COMPUTERS

ELECTRONIC CONTROL MODULE

The Electronic Control Module (ECM) is located on the right side of the vehicle. It is positioned in front of the right hand kick panel. In order to gain access to the assembly, remove the trim panel.

CONVENIENCE CENTER AND VARIOUS RELAYS

The convenience center is located on the underside of the instrument panel near the fuse panel. It provides a central location for various relays, hazard flasher units and buzzers. All units are easily replaced with plug-in modules.

TURN SIGNAL FLASHER

The turn signal flasher is located directly under the steering column of the vehicle. It is secured in place by means of a plastic retainer. In order to gain access to the component, it may be necessary to remove the underdash padding panel.

HAZARD FLASHER

The hazard flasher is located in the fuse block. It is positioned on the lower right hand corner of the fuse block assembly. In order to gain access to the turn signal flasher, it may be necessary to first remove the under dash padding.

ELECTRICAL SPEED SENSOR

The optic head portion of the Vehicle Speed Sensor (VSS) is located in the speedometer frame. A reflective blade is attached to the speedometer cable head assembly. The reflective blade spins, with its blade passing through a light beam, light is reflected back to a photocell in the optic head causing a low power speed signal to be sent to a buffer for amplification. This signal is then sent to the controller.

SPEED CONTROL

Refer to "Chiltons Chassis Electronics Service Manual" for additional coverage.

Adjustment

RELEASE SWITCH AND VALVE

1. Depress the brake pedal and insert the vacuum release valve into the retainer until a click is heard indicating that the valve switch is seated.
2. Allow the brake pedal to travel rearward to the positive stop.
3. The valve switch will be moved through the retainer into the proper position.

NOTE: Audible clicks can be heard as threaded portion of switch is pushed through the clip toward the brake pedal. Vacuum release valve and stoplight switch are self-adjusting.

SERVO LINKAGE

1. Install the cable into the engine bracket. Route the cable assembly to the servo bracket.
2. Pull the servo end of the cable towards the servo assembly without moving the throttle lever.
3. Line up the pin in the end of the cable with 1 of the holes in the servo assembly tab.
4. Insert the cable pin into 1 of the 6 holes in the servo bracket. Install the retainer.

NOTE: Do not stretch the cable to make a certain connection as this will prevent the engine from returning to idle. Use the next closest hole.

COOLING AND HEATING SYSTEM

Water Pump

Removal and Installation

1.8L AND 2.0L OHC ENGINE

1. Disconnect the negative battery cable.
2. Drain the cooling system.
3. Remove the engine timing belt.
4. Remove the timing belt rear protective covers.
5. Remove the hose from the water pump.
6. Remove the water pump retaining bolts. Remove the pump and the sealing ring from the vehicle.
7. Installation is the reverse of removal. Torque water pump bolts to 18 ft. lbs.

2.0L OHV ENGINE

1. Disconnect the negative battery cable.
2. Drain the cooling system.
3. Remove all accessory drive belts.
4. Remove the alternator.
5. Unscrew the water pump pulley mounting bolts and then pull off the pulley.
6. Remove the mounting bolts and remove the water pump.
7. Place a ⅛ in. bead of RTV sealant on the water pump sealing surface. While the sealer is still wet, install the pump and tighten the bolts to 15–22 ft. lbs.
8. Installation of the remaining components is in the reverse order of removal.

2.8L ENGINE

1. Disconnect the negative battery cable.
2. Drain the cooling system.
3. Remove drive belts or serpentine belt.
4. Remove water pump pulley.
5. Remove water pump retaining bolts and remove the water pump.
6. To install reverse the removal procedures. Torque the water pump mounting bolts to 6–9 ft. lbs.

Electric Cooling Fan

The coolant fan relay is activated by the Electronic Control Module (ECM) when the coolant temperature sensor recognizes temperature readings above 230°F (108°C) on 2.0L engine and 223°F (106°C) on all other engines. The coolant fan is also activated if a coolant temperature sensor failure is detected code 14 or 15 or if the ECM is in the back up mode. The ECM will also activate the cooling fan relay on 2.8L engine when the air conditioning pressure exceeds 200 psi. and on 1.8L and 2.0L engines when air conditioning is turned on and low pressure switch is closed.

NOTE: The ECM controls the cooling fan by grounding CKT 335 green/yellow wire. Once the ECM turns the fan relay on, it will keep fan on for a minimum of 30 seconds, or until vehicle speed exceeds 70 mph on the 2.8L engine.

Testing

NOTE: If the fan does not run while connected to the electrical wiring connector, inspect for a defective coolant temperature switch or air conditioning relay (if equipped). Always check body wiring for frayed or loose connections.

1. Disconnect the electrical wiring connector from the electric cooling fan.
2. Using a 14 gauge jumper wire, connect it between the fan and the positive battery terminal; the fan should run.

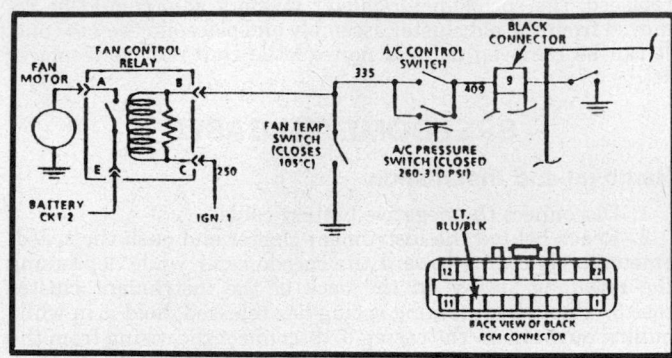
Cooling fan control circuit—1.8L engine code 0

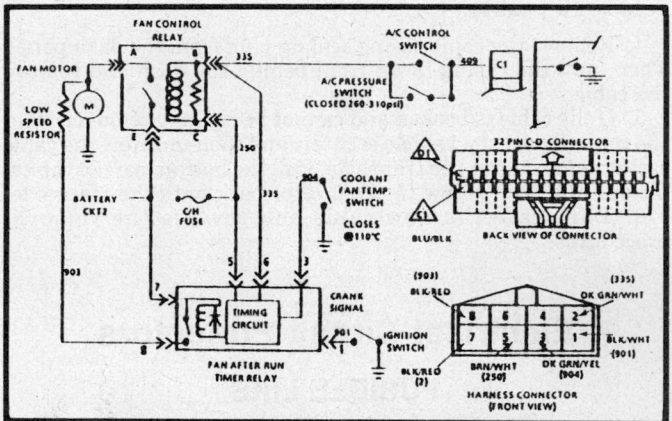
Cooling fan control circuit—1.8L engine code J

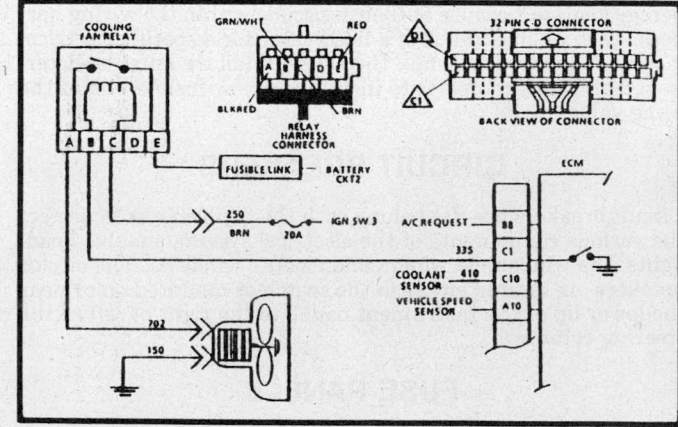
Cooling fan control circuit—2.0L engine code P

3. If the fan does not run when connected to the jumper wire, replace the fan assembly.

FAN AND MOTOR ASSEMBLY

Removal and Installation

1. Disconnect the negative battery cable.
2. Tag and disconnect the wiring harness from the fan frame and motor assembly.

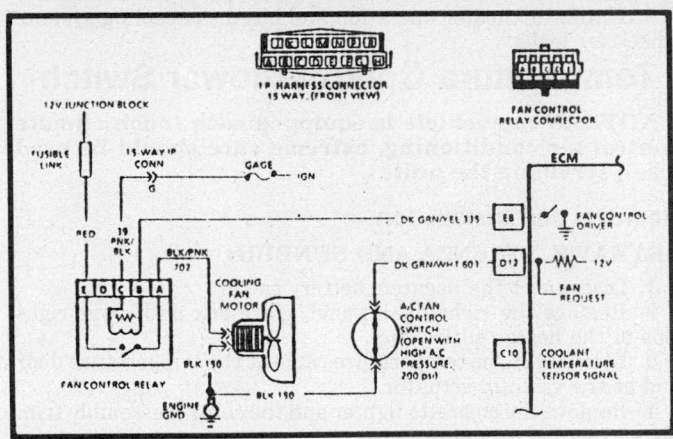

Cooling fan control circuit—2.8L engine code W

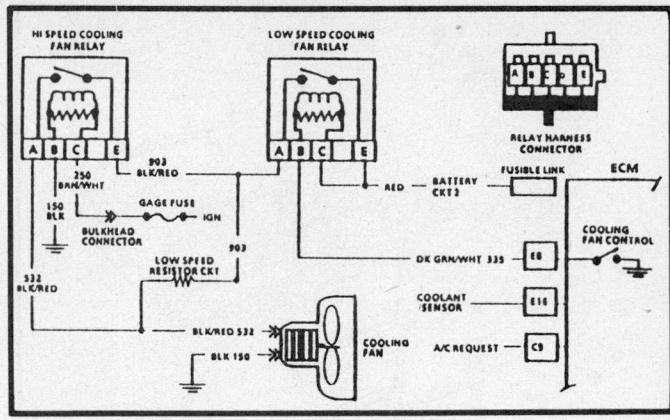

Cooling fan control circuit—2.0L engine code M

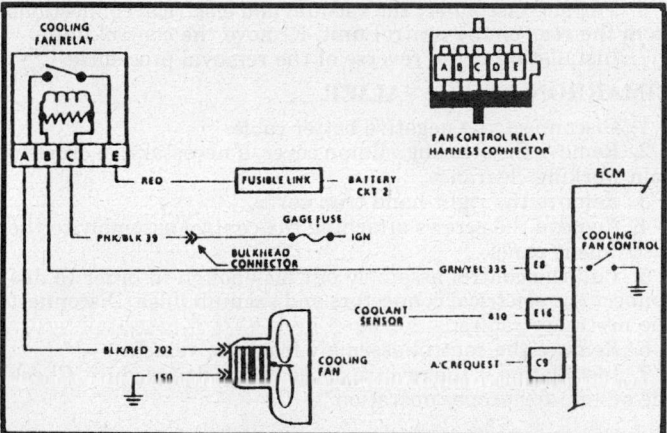

Cooling fan control circuit—2.0L engine code 1

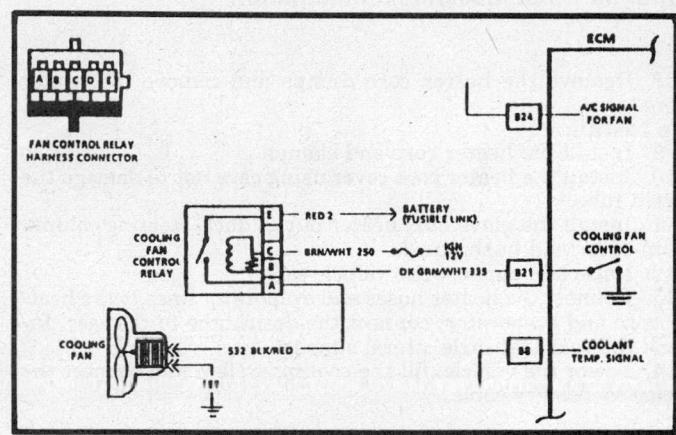

Cooling fan control circuit—2.0L engine code K

3. Remove the fan assembly retaining bolts. Remove the fan and motor assembly from the vehicle.

4. Installation is the reverse of the removal procedure.

Blower Motor

Removal and Installation

1. Disconnect the negative battery cable.

2. Disconnect the electrical connections at the blower motor and blower resistor.

3. Remove the plastic water shield from the right side of the cowl.

4. Remove the blower motor retaining screws and remove the blower motor and cage.

5. Hold the blower motor cage and remove retaining nut from the blower motor shaft.

6. Remove the blower motor and cage.

To install:

7. Install the cage on the new motor.

8. Check that the retaining nut is on tight, the motor rotates and the fan cage is not interferring with the motor.

9. Install the motor in the heater assembly, connect the wiring and check the motor operation in all speeds.

Heater Core

Refer to "Chilton's Auto Heating and Air Conditioning Manual" for additional coverage.

Removal and Installation

WITHOUT AIR CONDITIONING

1. Disconnect the negative battery cable and drain the cooling system.

2. Remove the heater hoses at the heater core.

3. Remove the heater outlet deflector.

4. Remove the heater core cover retaining screws. Remove the heater core cover.

5. Remove the heater core retaining straps and remove the heater core.

6. Install the new heater core and retaining straps.

7. Install the heater oulet deflector and heater core cover.

8. Connect the heater hoses to the core.

9. Fill and bleed the cooling system when finished. Check for leaks and the heater operation.

WITH AIR CONDITIONING

1. Disconnect the negative battery cable and drain the cooling system.

2. Raise and safely support the front of the vehicle.

3. Disconnect the drain tube from the heater case.

4. Remove the rear lateral transaxle support.

5. Remove the heater hoses and evaporator lines from the heater core and evaporator.

6. Lower the vehicle. Remove the right and left hush panels, steering column trim cover, heater outlet duct and glove box.

7. Remove the heater core cover. Pull the cover straight to the rear so it does not damage the drain tube.

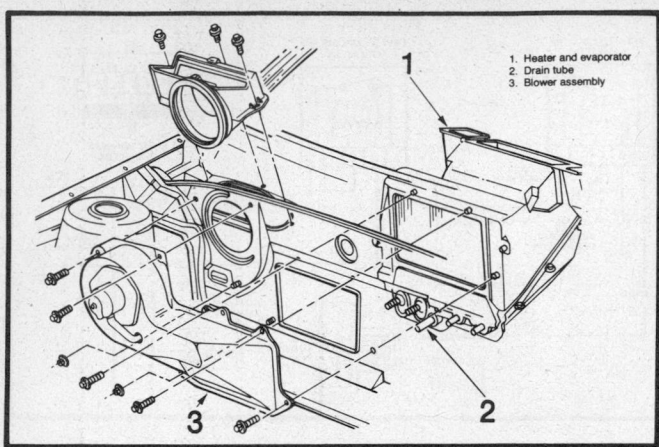

1. Heater and evaporator
2. Drain tube
3. Blower assembly

Heater evaporator assembly, blower assembly and air inlet assembly installation

8. Remove the heater core clamps and remove the heater core.
To install:
9. Install the heater core and clamps.
10. Install the heater core cover using care not to damage the drain tube.
11. Install the glove box, heater outlet duct, steering column trim cover and hush panels.
12. Raise and support the vehicle safely.
13. Connect the heater hoses and evaporator lines to the heater core and evaporator, connect the drain tube to the case. Install the rear transaxle lateral support.
14. Lower the vehicle, fill the cooling system and connect the negative battery cable.

15. Check the heater operation and bleed the cooling system. Check for leaks.

Temperature Control/Blower Switch

NOTE: If the vehicle is equipped with touch climate control air conditioning, extreme care should be used when servicing the unit.

Removal and Installation
SKYHAWK, FIRENZA AND SUNBIRD

1. Disconnect the negative battery cable.
2. Remove the right hush panel, glove box and lower right side of the heater outlet duct.
3. Disconnect the temperature cable at the temperature door and at the vacuum actuator.
4. Remove the cigarette lighter and the control assembly trim plate.
5. Remove the control panel screws. Remove the control panel from the dashboard.
6. Tag and disconnect the vacuum and electrical connections from the rear or the control unit. Remove the control unit.
7. Installation is the reverse of the removal procedure.

CIMARRON AND CAVALIER

1. Disconnect the negative batter cable.
2. Remove the steering column cover, if necessary, in order to gain working clearance.
3. Remove the right hand trim cover.
4. Remove the screws attaching the control assembly to the instrument panel.
5. Pull the control assembly out far enough in order to disconnect the electrical connectors and vacuum lines. Disconnect the necessary cables.
6. Remove the control assembly from the vehicle.
7. Installation is the reverse of the removal procedure. Check the system for proper operation.

FUEL INJECTION SYSTEM

Refer to "Chilton's Electronic Engine Controls Manual" for additional coverage.
NOTE: When working with the fuel system certain precautions should be taken; always work in a well ventilated area, keep a dry chemical (Class B) fire extinguisher near the work area. Always disconnect the negative battery cable and do not make any repairs to the fuel system until all the necessary steps for repair have been reviewed.

Description

THROTTLE BODY INJECTION

The TBI unit is computer controlled and supplies the correct amount of fuel during all engine operating conditions. In the TBI system, a single fuel injector mounted at the top of the throttle body, sprays fuel through the throttle valve and into the intake manifold. The activating signal for the injector originates with the electronic control module (ECM), which monitors engine temperature, throttle position, vehicle speed and several other engine-related conditions. A fuel pressure regulator inside the throttle body maintains fuel pressure at 9–13 psi and routes unused fuel back to the fuel tank through a fuel return line.

MULTI-PORT INJECTION

The injectors are mounted on a fuel rail and are activated by a signal from the electronic control module (ECM). The injector is a solenoid operated valve which remains open depending on the width of the electronic pulses (length of the signal) from the ECM; the longer the open time, the more fuel is injected. In this manner, the air/fuel mixture can be precisely controlled for maximum performance with minimum emissions. A pressure regulator maintains 28–36 psi in the fuel line to the injectors and the excess fuel is fed back to the tank.

IDLE SPEED AND MIXTURE

Adjustment
THROTTLE BODY INJECTION

The idle speed on fuel injected engines is controlled by the Electronic Control Module (ECM) and the idle stop screw is sealed at the factory to prevent adjustment. No adjustments are necessary, however, if testing and diagnosis show that the idle speed needs adjustment, the plug is removable.

1. Remove the air cleaner and plug the thermactor vacuum port.
2. Remove the T.V. cable from the throttle control bracket.
3. Set the parking brake and block the drive wheels.
4. Using a punch, mark the location of the center of the throttle housing casting over the minimum idle stop screw plug.
5. Drill a $5/32$ in. hole through the throttle body casting in this location. Drill through to the plug.
6. Using a small punch, in the drilled hole, drive out the plug.
7. Connect a tachometer to the engine. Disconnect the IAC motor plug.
8. Start the engine and put the transaxle in **P**, allow the idle to stabilize.

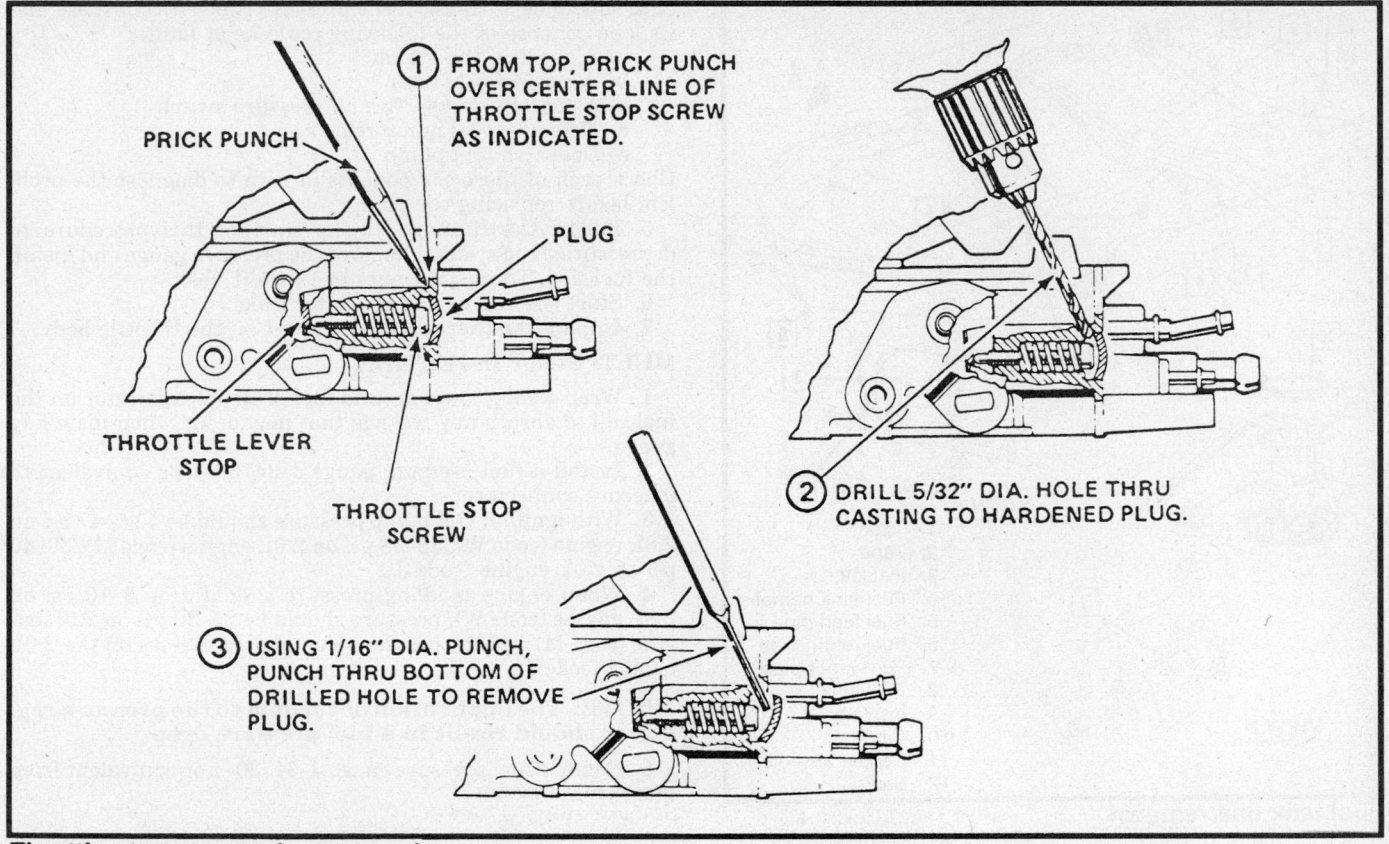

PRICK PUNCH

① FROM TOP, PRICK PUNCH OVER CENTER LINE OF THROTTLE STOP SCREW AS INDICATED.

PLUG

THROTTLE LEVER STOP

THROTTLE STOP SCREW

② DRILL 5/32" DIA. HOLE THRU CASTING TO HARDENED PLUG.

③ USING 1/16" DIA. PUNCH, PUNCH THRU BOTTOM OF DRILLED HOLE TO REMOVE PLUG.

Throttle stop screw plug removal

9. Install tool J–33047 or equivalent, into the idle air passage of the throttle body.

10. Using a No. 20 Torx® bit, turn the throttle stop screw until the engine rpm is 750–800 rpm for the 1.8L engine and 2.0L engine.

11. Reinstall the T.V. cable on the throttle bracket. Stop the engine and remove the tools.

12. Reconnect the IAC motor connector.

13. Seal the hole in the throttle body with silicone sealant. Install the air cleaner.

MULTI-PORT INJECTION

The throttle stop screw, used in regulating the minimum idle speed, is adjusted at the factory and is not necessary to change during normal operation. This adjustment should be performed only when the throttle body has been replaced.

1. Remove air cleaner and have engine reach normal operating temperature.

2. Using a awl, pierce the idle stop screw plug and apply leverage to remove it.

3. With IAC valve connected, ground diagnostic test terminal.

4. Turn **ON** ignition, do not start engine. Wait at least 30 seconds.

5. With ignition **ON**, disconnect IAC electrical connector.

6. Remove ground from diagnostic test terminal and start engine. Allow engine to go to closed loop.

7. Adjust idle stop screw to:
   a. 550 rpm in **D** (automatic transaxle)
   b. 650 rpm in **N** (manual transaxle)

8. Turn ignition **OFF** and reconnect connector at IAC valve.

9. Do not adjust TPS unless setting is outside of 0.235–0.750 limits.

10. Start engine and inspect for proper idle operation.

Idle Mixture Adjustment

All fuel control functions are controlled by the Electronic Control Module (ECM). No adjustments are necessary.

FUEL SYSTEM PRESSURE RELIEF

Procedure

1. Release the fuel vapor pressure in the fuel tank by removing the fuel tank cap and reinstalling it.

2. With the engine running, remove the connector of the fuel pump relay and wait until the engine stops.

3. Once the engine is stopped, crank it a few times with the starter for about 3 seconds with the relay disconnected.

4. If the fuel pressure can't be released in the above manner because the engine failed to run, disconnect the negative battery cable, cover the union bolt of the fuel line with an absorbent cloth and loosen the union bolt slowly to release the fuel pressure gradually.

Fuel Pump

Removal and Installation

The electric fuel pump is located in the fuel tank.

1. Relieve the fuel system pressure.

2. Disconnect the battery ground.

3. Raise and support the vehicle safely.

4. Remove the fuel filler cap.

5. Drain the fuel tank. Due to a restrictor in the fuel filler neck, a siphon cannot be used to drain the tank. Disconnect the fuel feed hose from the chassis feed pipe at the rear of the vehicle. Connect a length of hose to the feed line and into a container. Apply voltage to the pump at the pump test lead, terminal **G**

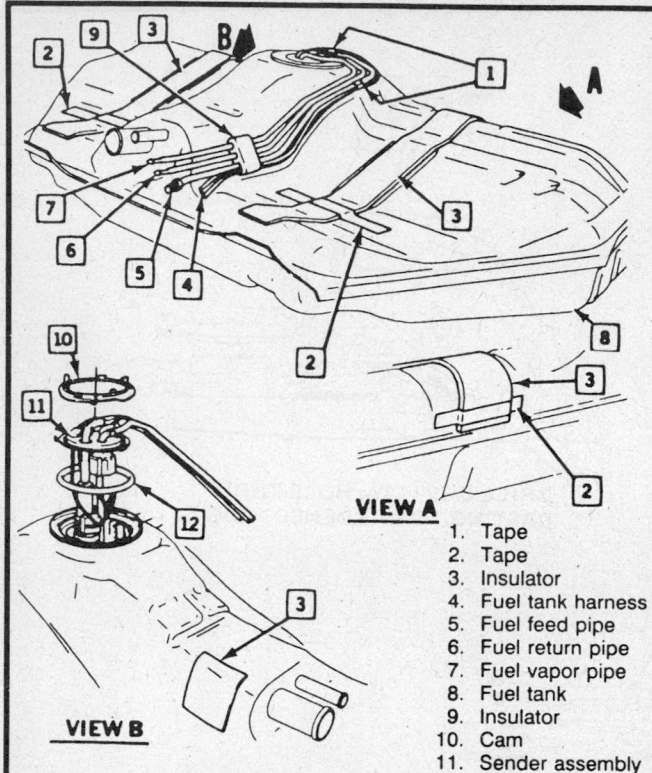

1. Tape
2. Tape
3. Insulator
4. Fuel tank harness
5. Fuel feed pipe
6. Fuel return pipe
7. Fuel vapor pipe
8. Fuel tank
9. Insulator
10. Cam
11. Sender assembly
12. Seal

Fuel tank unit removal

on the ALCL (Assembly Line Communication Link) and run the pump until the tank is empty. Do not run the pump after the tank is empty, as this will damage the pump.

6. Disconnect the wiring from the tank.
7. Disconnect the filler neck hose and the vent hose.
8. Remove the fuel tank strap rear support bolts and lower the tank on a jack, just enough to disconnect the fuel feed line, return and vapor lines from the fuel meter.
9. Remove the tank.
10. Remove the fuel meter/pump assembly by turning the cam lockring counterclockwise. Lift the assembly from the tank and remove the pump from the meter.
11. Pull the pump up onto the attaching hose while pulling outward from the bottom support. Take care not to damage the rubber insulator and strainer. After the pump is clear of the bottom support pull it out of the rubber connector.
12. Installation is the reverse of removal. Use a new O-ring on the tank cam lockring.

Pressure Testing

THROTTLE BODY INJECTION

NOTE: Before performing any tests, do the following to prevent personal injury: Remove the fuel pump fuse from the fuse panel in the passenger compartment. Start the engine and run it until all fuel in the system is used. Crank the engine for an additional 3 seconds to relieve any residual pressure. Turn the ignition to OFF and replace the fuse.

1. Remove the air cleaner and plug the thermal vacuum port on the throttle body unit.
2. Remove the steel fuel line from between the throttle body unit and the fuel filter.
3. Install a fuel pressure gauge with at least a 15 psi capacity between the throttle body and the filter.
4. Start the engine and observe the pressure reading. Pres-

sure should be 9–13 psi. If the pressure is not within these limits, one or more of the following could be at fault:
  a. A short in the system
  b. A clogged fuel filter
  c. A shorted or defective oil pressure switch
  d. Defective fuel pump relay
  e. Defective fuel pump
Check each of these components in turn to diagnose the problem before replacing the pump.

5. Follow the cautions at the start of this procedure to depressurize the system. Remove the pressure gauge and install the fuel line. Torque the nuts to 19–25 ft. lbs.
6. Start the engine and check for leaks.
7. Unplug the thermal vacuum port on the throttle body.

MULTI PORT INJECTION

1. Wrap a shop towel around fuel pressure connector on the fuel rail to absorb any leakage that may occur when installing gauge.
2. Install a fuel pressure gauge J–34730–1 or equivalent to pressure connector.
3. With ignition **ON** pump pressure should be 40.5–47 psi on 2.8L engine (code W), 35–38 psi on 2.0L engine (code M), 30–40 psi on 2.0L engine (code J).
4. When engine is idling pressure should drop 3–10 psi on 2.8L engine (code W), pressure should be 25–30 psi on 2.0L engine (code M) and the pressure should drop 3–6 psi on the 2.0L engine (code J).

NOTE: The application of vacuum to the pressure regulator should result in a fuel pressure drop.

5. Remove fuel pressure gauge J–34730–1 or equivalent from pressure connector.

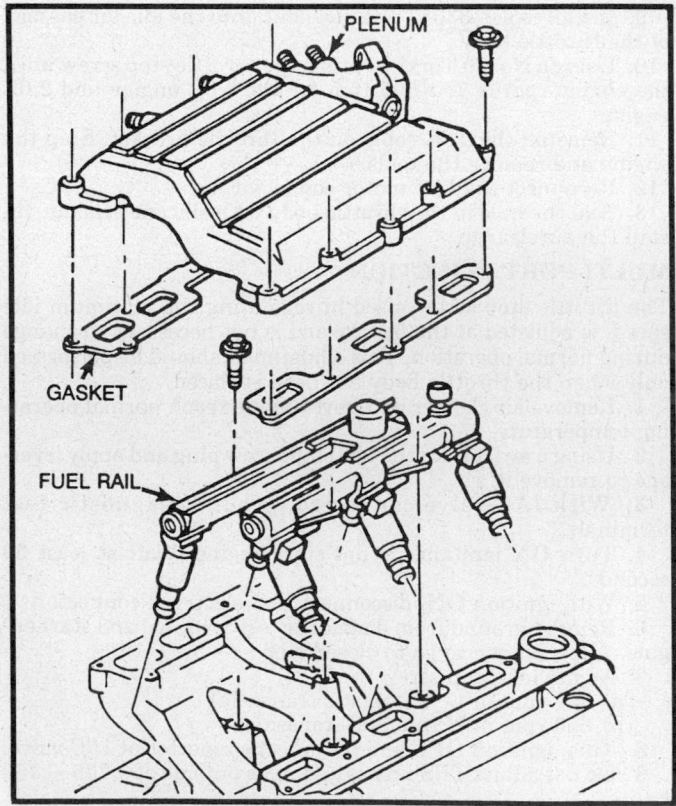

Removing the plenum and fuel rail—2.8L

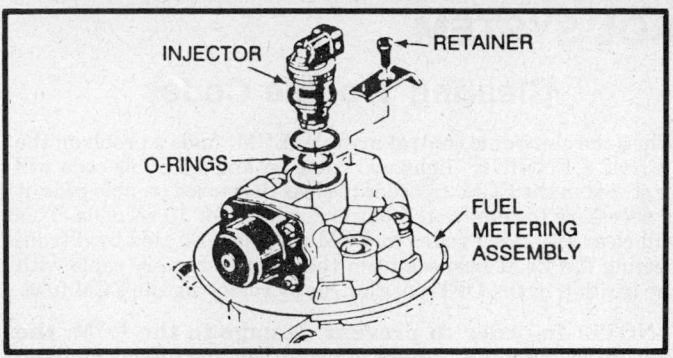

Removing the fuel injector—TBI

FUEL INJECTOR

NOTE: Use care in removing injector to prevent damage to the electrical pins on top of the injector. The fuel injectors are an electrical component. Do not immerse in any type of cleaner.

Removal and Installation

THROTTLE BODY INJECTION

1. Relieve the fuel pump pressure.
2. Disconnect the negative battery cable.
3. Remove the TBI cover and gasket.

4. Disconnect the electrical connector to fuel injector.
5. Remove the injector retainer.
6. Using a fulcrum, place a suitable tool under the ridge opposite the connector end and carefully pry injector out.
7. To install, reverse the removal procedures. Be sure the electrical connector end, on the injector is facing in the direction to the cut-out in the fuel meter body for the wire grommet to fit properly.

NOTE: Remove the upper and lower O-rings from injector body and in fuel injector cavity and replace with new O-rings before installing injector.

MULTI PORT INJECTION

NOTE: The fuel rail is removed as an assembly, then the injectors can be removed.

1. Disconnect the negative battery cable. Relieve the fuel system pressure.
2. Tag and disconnect the fuel injection electrical connections.
3. Remove the upper intake manifold plenum asssmbly. Remove the necessary components in order to gain access to the fuel rail retaining bolts.
4. Remove the fuel rail retaining bolts. Remove the fuel rail assembly.
5. Separate the fuel injector from the fuel rail.
6. Installation is the reverse of the removal procedure. Replace the O-rings when installing the injectors.

TURBOCHARGER SYSTEM

Description

The turbocharger is basically an air compressor or air pump. It consists of a turbine or hot wheel, a shaft, a compressor or cold wheel, a turbine housing, a compressor housing and a center housing which contains bearings, a turbine seal assembly and a compressor seal assembly.

TURBOCHARGER UNIT

Removal and Installation

1. Disconnect the negative battery cable.
2. Raise and safely support the vehicle.
3. Remove the Lower fan retaining screws.
4. Disconnect the exhaust pipe at the turbocharger.
5. Remove air conditioning rear support bracket.
6. Remove the turbocharger support bracket from the engine.
7. Disconnect the oil drain and water return pipes at turbo.
8. Lower the vehicle and remove coolant recovery pipe.
9. Remove induction tube, coolant fan and oxygen sensor.
10. Disconnect the oil and water feed pipes.
11. Remove the air intake duct and vacuum hose at the actuator.
12. Remove the exhaust manifold retaining nuts, remove the turbocharger and manifold as an assembly.
13. Remove the turbocharger from exhaust manifold.
To install:
14. Install the turbocharger to the exhaust manifold and torque the bolts to 18 ft. lbs.

15. Install a new manifold gasket and install the manifold in position on the block. Tighten the bolts to 16 ft. lbs.

NOTE: Before installing a new gasket on the 1.8L MFI Turbo engine, check for the location of the stamped part number on the surface. This gasket should be installed with this number toward the manifold. The gasket appears to be the same in either direction but it is not. Installing the gasket backwards will result in a leak.

16. Install the air intake duct and the vacuum hose actuator.
17. Install the induction tube and O_2 sensor. Install the coolant recovery tube.
18. Raise and safely support the vehicle. Connect the oil drain and water return pipe to the turbocharger.
19. Install the turbocharger support bracket. Connect the exhaust pipe to the turbocharger and install the rear air conditioning support bracket.
20. Install the lower fan retaining screws. Lower the vehicle and connect the negative battery cable. Check all fluid levels.

TURBOCHARGER WASTEGATE UNIT

Removal and Installation

1. Disconnect the negative battery cable. Remove the induction tube.
2. Remove the clip attaching the wastegate linkage to the actuator rod.
3. Disconnect the vacuum hose. Remove the wastegate mounting bolts and remove the wastegate actuator.
4. Installation is the reverse of the removal procedure.

EMISSION CONTROL SYSTEM

COMPONENTS

Positive Crankcase Ventilation (PCV)
Exhaust Gas Recirculation (EGR)
Electronic Control Module (ECM)
Throttle Position Sensor(TPS)
Electronic Spark Control (ESC)
Electronic Spark Timing (EST)
Evaporative Emission Control System (EECS)
Coolant sensor
Oxygen sensor
Air Injection Control System (A.I.R)
Pulsair system
Catalytic Converter

Clearing Trouble Codes

When the electronic control module (ECM) finds a problem, the "CHECK ENGINE" light will come on and a trouble code will be stored in the ECM. In order to clear the stored trouble code, it is necessary to remove the battery voltage for 10 seconds. This will clear all stored codes in ECM memory. Do this by disconnecting the ECM harness from the positive battery cable with the ignition in the **OFF** position, or by removing the ECM fuse.

NOTE: In order to prevent damage to the ECM, the key must be OFF when connecting or disconnecting power to the ECM.

ENGINE

Engine Assembly

NOTE: Disconnecting the negative battery cable on some vehicles may interfere with the functions of the on board computer systems and may require the computer to undergo a relearning process, once the negative battery cable is reconnected.

Removal and Installation

2.0L ENGINE (CODES P AND 1)

NOTE: Special tool J–24420 crankshaft pulley hub remover is required. The engine is removed from the top of vehicle.

1. Disconnect the negative battery cable and relieve the fuel system pressure.
2. Drain the cooling system.
3. Remove the air cleaner.
4. Disconnect the accelerator and T.V. cables.
5. Disconnect the ECM harness at engine.
6. Disconnect the necessary vacuum hoses.
7. Disconnect all of the cooling hoses at engine.
8. Remove the exhaust heat shield.
9. If equipped with air conditioning, remove the adjustment bolt at motor mount.
10. Disconnect engine wiring harness at bulkhead.
11. Remove the windshield washer bottle.
12. Remove the alternator and power steering belt.
13. Disconnect the fuel hoses.
14. Raise and safely support the vehicle. If equipped with air conditioning, remove the air conditioning brace.
15. Remove inner fender splash shield.
16. If equipped with air conditioning, remove the air conditioning compressor.
17. Remove flywheel splash shield.
18. Disconnect and the tag starter wires.
19. Disconnect the front starter brace.
20. Remove the starter.
21. Remove the torque converter bolts.
22. Remove the crankshaft pulley and hub using tool J–24420 or equivalent.
23. Remove the oil filter.
24. Disconnect the engine-to-transaxle bracket.
25. Disconnect the right rear mount.
26. Disconnect exhaust at manifold and at center hanger.
27. Disconnect the T.V. and shift cable.
28. Remove the lower bellhousing bolts.
29. Lower the vehicle.
30. Remove the right front motor mount nuts.
31. Remove alternator and adjusting brace.
32. Disconnect the master cylinder and push it aside.
33. Install a suitable lifting device.
34. Remove the right front motor mount bracket.
35. Remove upper bellhousing bolts.
36. Remove the power steering pump while lifting engine.
37. Carefully remove the engine from the vehicle.
To install:
38. Install the engine mount alignment bolt no. M6X1X65 to ensure proper power train alignment.
39. Slowly lower the engine into the vehicle, leaving the lifting device attached.
40. Install the transaxle bracket. Install the mount to the side frame and secure with new bolts.
41. With the engine weight not on the mounts, tighten the transaxle bolts to 48–63 ft. lbs.
42. Tighten the right front mount nuts.
43. Lower the engine weight onto the mounts. Remove the lifting device. Raise and support the vehicle safely.
44. Installation of the remaining components is in the reverse order of removal. Check the powertrain alignment bolt; if excessive force is required to remove the bolt, loosen the transaxle bolts and realign the powertrain.

1.8L ENGINE (VIN CODES O AND J) AND 2.0L ENGINE (VIN CODES K AND M)

NOTE: This procedure requires the use of a special powertrain alignment bolt no. M6X1X65. The engine is removed from the bottom of the vehicle.

1. Disconnect the negative battery cable and relieve fuel pressure.
2. Drain the cooling system.
3. Remove the air cleaner assembly.
4. Disconnect the engine electrical harness at bulkhead.
5. Disconnect the electrical connector at brake cylinder.
6. Remove the throttle cable from bracket and EFI assembly.
7. Remove and tag the vacuum hoses from EFI assembly.
8. Remove the power steering high pressure hose at cut-off switch.
9. Remove and tag the vacuum hoses at map sensor and canister.
10. Disconnect the air conditioning relay cluster switches.
11. Remove the power steering return hose at pump.
12. Disconnect the ECM wire connections, feed the harness through bulkhead and lay harness over engine.
13. Remove the upper and lower radiator hoses from engine.
14. Remove the electrical connections from the temperature switch at thermostat housing.

15. Raise and support the vehicle safely.
16. Disconnect the transaxle shift cable at transmission.
17. Remove the speedometer cable at transaxle and bracket.
18. Disconnect the exhaust pipe at the exhaust manifold.
19. Remove the exhaust pipe from converter.
20. Remove the heater hoses from heater core.
21. Remove fuel lines at the flex hoses.
22. Remove the transaxle cooler lines at flex hoses.
23. Remove the left and right front wheels.
24. Remove the right hand spoiler section and splash shield.
25. Remove the right and left brake calipers and support with wire.
26. Remove right and left tie rod ends.
27. Disconnect the electrical connections at air conditioning compressor.
28. Remove the air conditioning compressor and mounting brackets, support the air conditioning compressor by wiring it in a wheel opening.
29. Remove the front suspension support attachment bolts (6 bolts each side).
30. Lower the vehicle.
31. Support the front of vehicle by placing 2 short stands under core support.
32. Position a front post hoist to the rear of cowl.
33. Position a 4 × 4 × 6 timber on the front post hoist.
34. Raise the vehicle enough to remove stands.
35. Position a 4-wheel dolly under engine and transaxle assembly.
36. Position three 4 × 4 × 12 blocks under the engine and transaxle assembly only, letting support rails hang free.
37. Lower the vehicle onto 4-wheel dolly slightly.
38. Remove the rear transaxle mount attachment bolts.
39. Remove the left front engine mount attachment bolts.
40. Remove the 2 engine support to body attachment bolts behind right hand inner axle U-joint.
41. Remove 1 attaching bolt and nut from right hand chassis side rail to engine mount bracket.
42. Remove 6 strut attachment nuts.
43. Raise the vehicle, letting the engine, transaxle and suspension rest on the 4-wheel dolly.
To install:
44. Position the engine and transaxle assembly in chassis.
45. Install transaxle and left front mounts to side rail bolts loosely.
46. Install M6X1X65 alignment bolt in left front mount to prevent powertrain misalignment.
47. Torque transaxle mount bolts to 42 ft. lbs. and left front mount bolts to 18 ft. lbs.
48. Install right rear mount to body bolts and torque to 38 ft. lbs.
49. Install right rear mount to chassis side rail bolt and nut torque to 38 ft. lbs.
50. Place a lifting device under the control arms. Raise them into position and install retaining nuts.
51. Raise and support the vehicle safely.
52. Using suitable lifting equipment, raise the control arms and attach tie rod ends.
53. Complete the installation by installing the remaining components in reverse order.

2.8L ENGINE

NOTE: Always release the fuel pressure before starting repair. The engine is removed from the top of the vehicle.

1. Disconnect the negative battery cable. Drain the cooling system and remove the air cleaner assembly. Mark the bolt location and remove the hood.
2. Remove the air flow sensor. Remove the exhaust crossover heat shield and remove the crossover pipe.
3. Remove the serpentine belt tensioner and belt.

4. Remove the power steering pump mounting bracket. Disconnect the heater pipe at the power steering pump mounting bracket.
5. Disconnect the radiator hoses from the engine.
6. Disconnect the accelerator and throttle valve cable at the throttle valve.
7. Remove the alternator. Tag and disconnect the wiring harness at the engine.
8. Relieve the fuel pressure and disconnect the fuel hose. Disconnect the coolant bypass and the overflow hoses at the engine.
9. Tag and remove the vacuum hoses to the engine.
10. Raise the vehicle and support it safely.
11. Remove the inner fender splash shield. Remove the harmonic balancer.
12. Remove the flywheel cover. Remove the starter bolts. Tag and disconnect the electrical connections to the starter. Remove the starter.
13. Disconnect the wires at the oil sending unit.
14. Remove the air conditioning compressor and related brackets.
15. Disconnect the exhaust pipe at the rear of the exhaust manifold.
16. Remove the flex plate-to-torque converter bolts.
17. Remove the transaxle-to-engine bolts. Remove the engine-to-rear mount frame nuts.
18. Disconnect the shift cable bracket at the transaxle. Remove the lower bell housing bolts.
19. Lower the vehicle and disconnect the heater hoses at the engine.

NOTE: It may be necessary to remove the engine hood. Using an awl, scribe marks around the hood hinges to help aid correct hood alignment upon installation.

20. Install a suitable engine lifting device. While supporting the engine and transaxle, remove the upper bell housing bolts.
21. Remove the front mounting bolts.
22. Remove the master cylinder from the booster.
23. Remove the engine assembly from the vehicle.
To install:
24. Install the engine in position in the vehicle.
25. Install the upper transaxle-to-engine bolts.
26. Raise and safely support the vehicle.
27. Install the lower transaxle-to-engine bolts.
28. Reconnect the shift cable bracket to the transaxle.
29. Install the engine mounts, tightening the front mount-to-frame bolts to 61 ft. lbs. and the engine mount to bracket bolts to 50 ft. lbs.
30. Install the flywheel to converter bolts.
31. Reconnect the exhaust pipe and install the air conditioning compressor. Install the flywheel cover.
32. Reconnect the coolant hoses and the fuel lines.
33. Install the wiring harness at the engine and install the alternator.
34. Lower the vehicle and install the accessory drive belt.
35. Refill all of the fluids and connect the negative battery cable.
36. Install the hood. Install the air cleaner assembly.
37. Road test the vehicle.

Engine Mounts

Removal and Installation

FRONT

1. Disconnect the negative battery cable.
2. Raise the vehicle and support safely.
3. Using a suitable fixture, support the engine and remove the engine mount nuts.
4. Remove the inner fender shield.
5. Remove the engine mount bolts. The manufacturer recom-

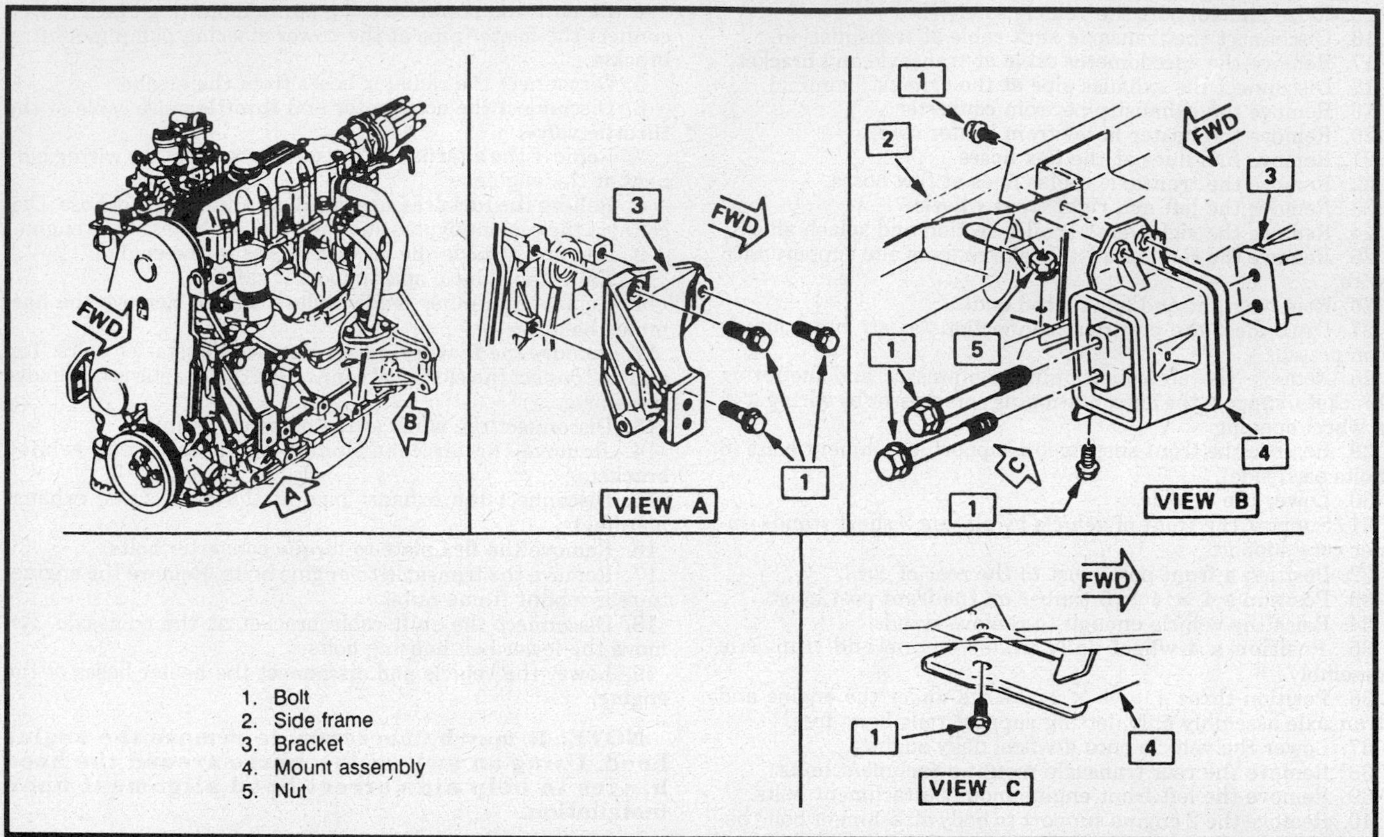

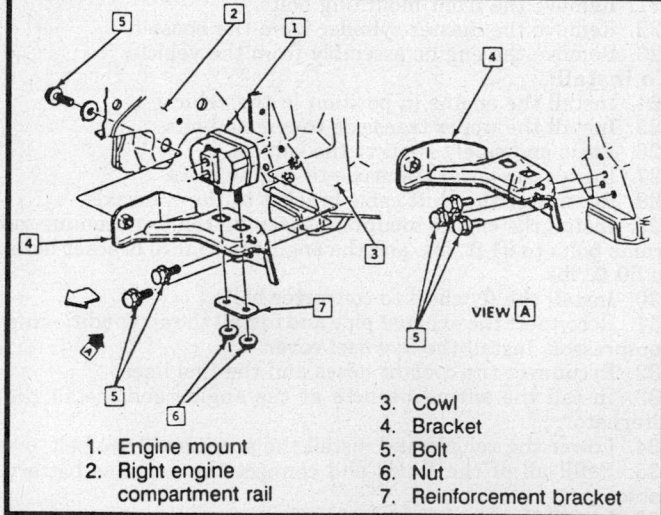

1. Bolt
2. Side frame
3. Bracket
4. Mount assembly
5. Nut

Front engine mount removal

1. Engine mount
2. Right engine compartment rail
3. Cowl
4. Bracket
5. Bolt
6. Nut
7. Reinforcement bracket

Rear engine mount removal

mends discarding the engine mount bolts and replacing with new bolts. Note the location and length of each bolt for reassembly.

6. Remove the engine mount.
7. Installation is the reverse of the removal procedure.

REAR

1. Disconnect the negative battery cable.
2. Raise the vehicle and support safely.
3. If equipped with manual transaxle, remove the oil filter in order to gain working clearance.

4. Using a suitable fixture, support the engine and remove the engine mounting nuts.
5. Remove the engine mounting bolts. Remove the engine mount.
6. Installation is the reverse of the removal procedure.

NOTE: On some 1987 Sunbirds, engine codes K and M, fatigue fracture of the rear engine mount may occur. The ignition coil and bracket are mounted to the rear engine mount. If the mount fractures, the coil may become unsupported.

Intake Manifold

Removal and Installation

1.8L AND 2.0L ENGINES

1. Release the fuel pressure. Disconnect the negative battery terminal from the battery.
2. Remove induction tube and hoses.
3. Disconnect and tag wiring to throttle body, fuel injectors, MAP sensor and wastegate if so equipped.
4. Disconnect and tag PCV hose and vacuum hoses on the throttle body.
5. Remove the throttle cable and the cruise control cable if so equipped.
6. Remove wiring to the ignition coil and remove the manifold support bracket.
7. Remove the rear bolt from alternator bracket, power steering adjusting bracket and front alternator adjusting bracket.
8. Remove the fuel lines to the fuel rail and regulator outlet.
9. Remove the retaining nuts and washers and intake manifold.

To install:

10. Use a new gasket on the manifold surface and mount the manifold in position.

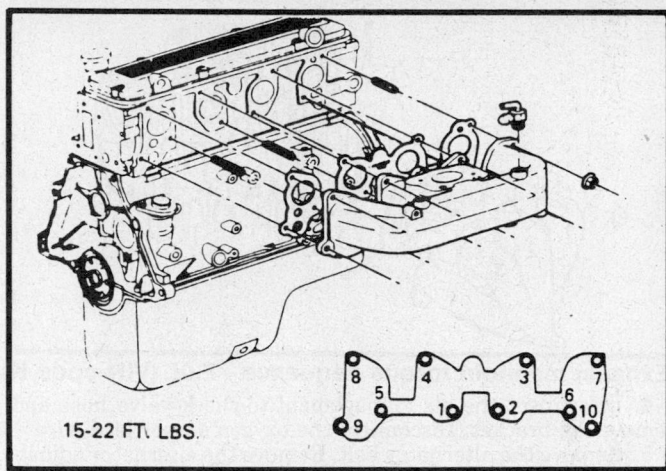

Intake manifold installation—2.0L engine code 1

15-22 FT. LBS.

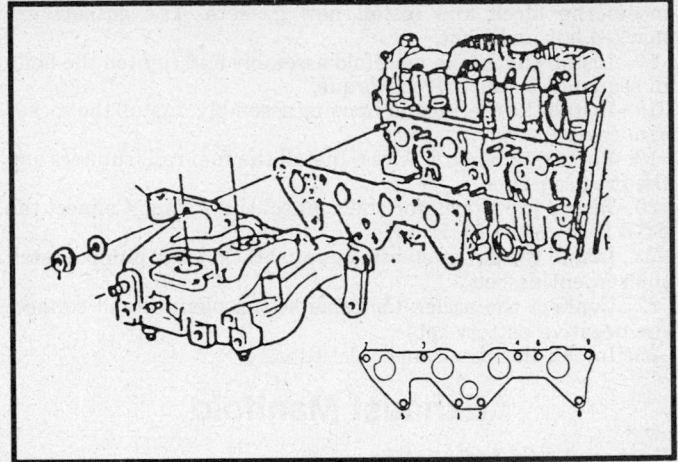

Intake manifold torque sequence—2.0L (VIN code K)

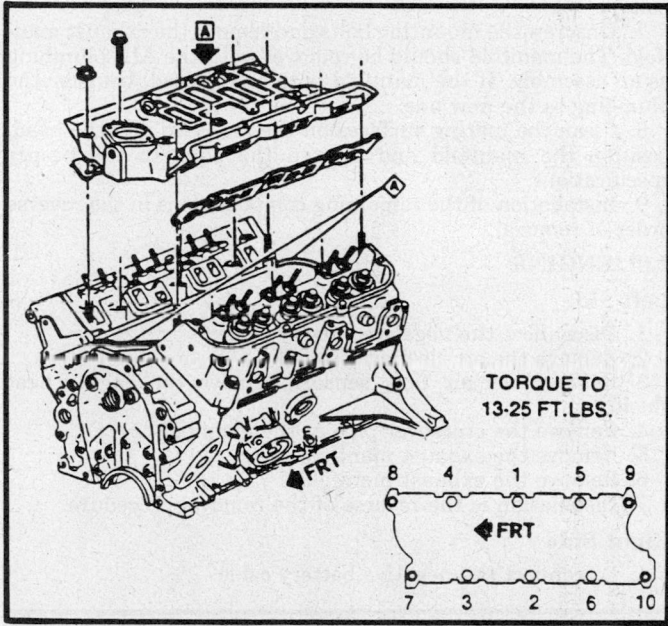

Intake manifold tightening sequence—V6 engine

TORQUE TO 13-25 FT. LBS.

FRT

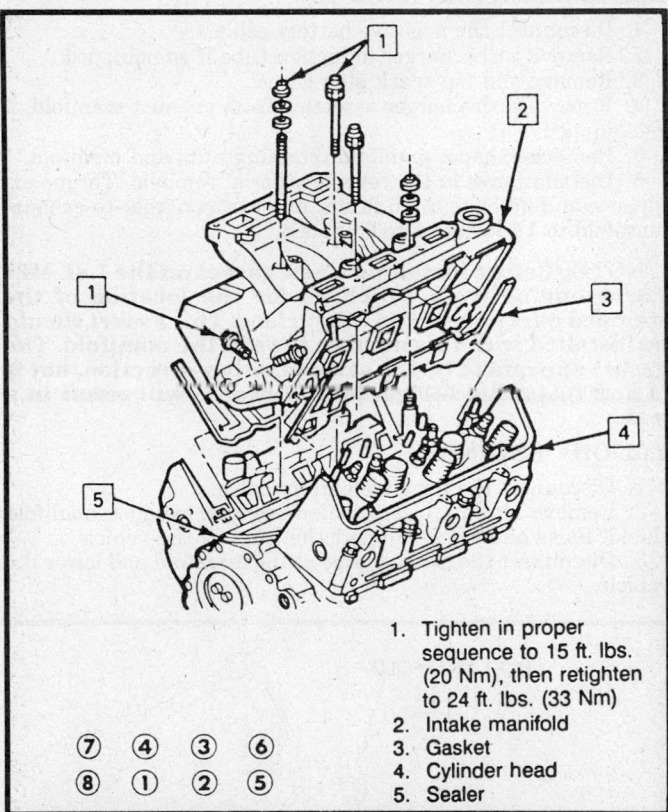

1. Tighten in proper sequence to 15 ft. lbs. (20 Nm), then retighten to 24 ft. lbs. (33 Nm)
2. Intake manifold
3. Gasket
4. Cylinder head
5. Sealer

Intake manifold installation—1987–90 2.8L

11. Tighten the bolts to the correct torque and in sequence.
12. Reconnect the fuel lines. Install the bolt for the power steering adjusting bracekt and the alternator.
13. Connect the ignition coil wiring and connect the vacuum hoses.
14. Connect the induction tube and hoses.
15. Reconnect all of the electrical wiring and the battery cable.

2.8L ENGINE

1. Disconnect the negative battery cable and relieve fuel pressure. Remove the air cleaner inlet tube.
2. Disconnect the accelerator cable bracket at the plenum.
3. Disconnect the throttle body and the EGR pipe from the EGR valve. Remove the plenum assembly.
4. Disconnect the fuel line along the fuel rail.
5. Disconnect the serpentine drive belt. Remove the power steering pump mounting bracket.
6. Remove the heater pipe at the power steering pump bracket.
7. Tag and disconnect the wiring at the alternator, remove the alternator.
8. Disconnect the wires from the cold start injector assembly. Remove the injector assembly from the intake manifold.

9. Disconnect the idle air vacuum hose at the throttle body. Disconnect the wires at the injectors.
10. Remove the fuel rail, breather tube and the fuel runners from the engine.
11. Tag and disconnect the coil wires.
12. Remove the rocker arm covers. Drain the cooling system, disconnect the radiator hose at the thermostat housing. Disconnect the heater hose from the thermostat housing and the thermostat wiring.
13. Mark and remove the distributor, if equipped.
14. Remove the thermostat assembly housing.
15. Remove the intake manifold bolts and remove the intake manifold from the engine.
To install:
16. Apply a bead of sealant to the points where the manifold

meets the block and install new gaskets. The gaskets are marked left and right.

17. Install the intake manifold assembly and tighten the bolts in sequence to the correct torque.

18. Install the thermostat housing assembly. Install the rocker arm covers.

19. Reconnect the coil wires. Install the fuel rail, runners and the breather tube.

20. Install the alternator and connect the wiring. Connect the EGR tube to the EGR valve.

21. Install the power steering pump bracket and pump. Install the serpentine belt.

22. Connect the acclerator cable at the plenum and connect the negative battery cable.

23. Install the air cleaner inlet tube.

Exhaust Manifold

Removal and Installation

1.8L AND 2.0L OHC ENGINES

1. Disconnect the negative battery cable.
2. Remove turbocharger induction tube if so equipped.
3. Remove and tag spark plug wires.
4. Remove turbocharger assembly from exhaust manifold, if so equipped.
5. Remove exhaust manifold retaining nuts and manifold.
6. Installation is in the reverse order of removal. Torque exhaust manifold bolts to 16 ft. lbs. and turbocharger-to-exhaust manifold to 18 ft. lbs. if so equipped.

NOTE: **Before installing a new gasket on the 1.8L MFI Turbo engine (code J), check for the location of the stamped part number on the surface. This gasket should be installed with this number toward the manifold. The gasket appears to be the same in either direction, but it is not. Installing the gasket backwards will result in a leak.**

2.0L OHV ENGINE

1. Disconnect the negative battery cable.
2. Remove the air cleaner. Remove the exhaust manifold shield. Raise and safely support the front of the vehicle.
3. Disconnect the exhaust pipe at the manifold and lower the vehicle.

Exhaust manifold torque sequence—2.0L (VIN code K)

4. Disconnect the air management-to-check valve hose and remove the bracket. Disconnect the oxygen sensor lead wire.
5. Remove the alternator belt. Remove the alternator adjusting bolts, loosen the pivot bolt and pivot the alternator upward.
6. Remove the alternator brace and the AIR pipes bracket bolt.
7. Unscrew the mounting bolts and remove the exhaust manifold. The manifold should be removed with the AIR plumbing as an assembly. If the manifold is to be replaced, transfer the plumbing to the new one.
8. Clean the mating surfaces on the manifold and the head, position the manifold and tighten the bolts to the proper specifications.
9. Installation of the remaining components is in the reverse order of removal.

2.8L ENGINE

Left Side

1. Disconnect the negative battery cable.
2. Remove the air cleaner assembly.
3. Remove the air flow sensor. Remove the engine heat shield.
4. Remove the crossover pipe at the manifold.
5. Remove the exhaust manifold bolts.
6. Remove the exhaust manifold.
7. Installation is the reverse of the removal procedure.

Right Side

1. Disconnect the negative battery cable.

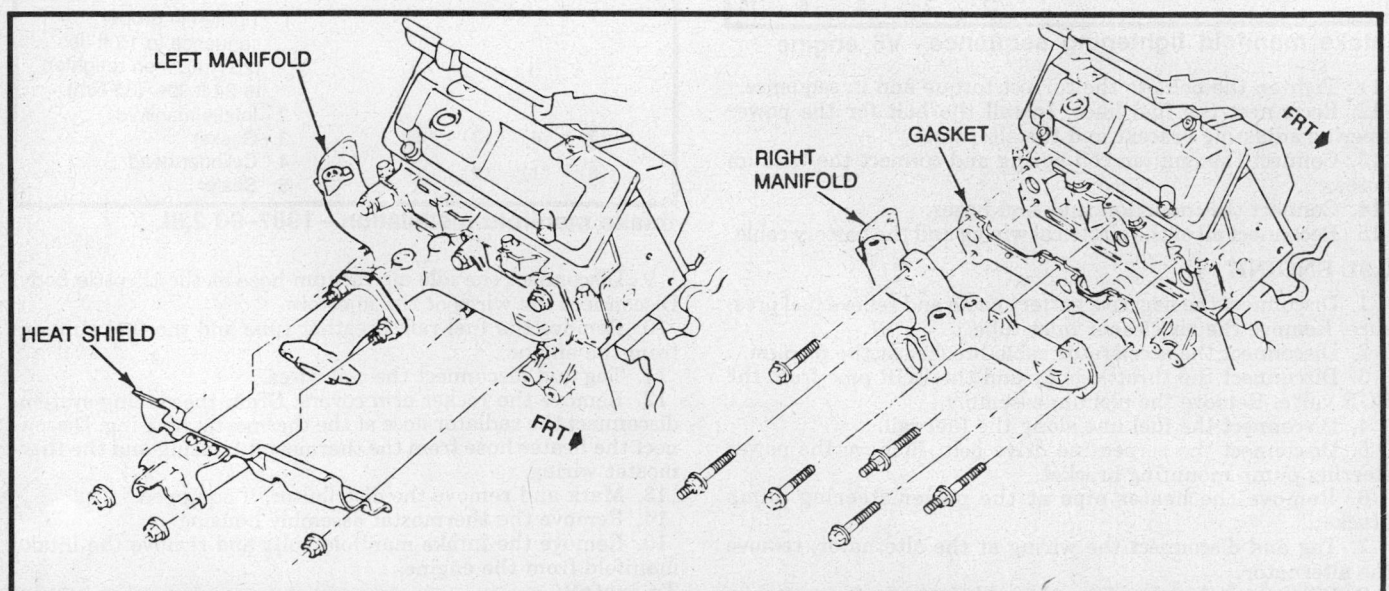

Exhaust manifold installation—2.8L

2. Remove the air cleaner assembly.

3. Remove the air flow sensor. Remove the engine heat shield.

4. Disconnect the crossover pipe at the manifold.

5. Disconnect the accelerator and throttle valve cable at the throttle lever and the plenum. Move aside to gain working clearance.

6. Disconnect the power steering line at the power steering pump.

7. Remove the EGR valve assembly.

8. Raise the vehicle and support safely.

9. Disconnect the exhaust pipe at the exhaust manifold.

10. Lower the vehicle.

11. Remove the manifold bolts. Remove the exhaust manifold.

12. Installation is the reverse of the removal procedure.

Valve System

Valve Adjustment

Hydralic valve lifters used in the 2.0 and 2.8L engines (1987–90), with aluminun heads, are not adjustable. If noise is present in the valve system of these engines, check the torque on the rocker arm nuts. The correct torque should be 11–18 ft. lbs. for the 2.0L engine and 14–20 ft. lbs. for the 2.8L engine. No other adjustment is necessary for these engines. If noise is still present, check the condition of the camshaft, lifters, rocker arms, pushrods and valves and replace as necessary.

On all 1986 engines, valve adjustment should only be done if the valve system has been overhauled or if noise is present. Adjust the valves according to the procedures below.

1.8L AND 2.0L OHC ENGINES

The valve train on the OHC 4 cylinder engine is automatically adjusted by the hydraulic rocker arm and valve lash compensators.

2.0L OHV ENGINE

1. Rotate the engine until the mark on the crankshaft pulley lines up with the **0** mark on the timing tab. Remove the rocker cover.

2. Determine that the engine is in the No. 1 firing position. While rotating the engine, check the No. 1 rocker arm as the mark on the crankshaft pulley comes near the **0** mark. If the valves are not moving, the engine is in the No. 1 firing position. If the valves are moving, rotate the engine 1 complete revolution.

3. The following valves may be adjusted with the engine in the No. 1 firing position:
Exhaust — 1 and 3
Intake — 1 and 2

4. To adjust the valves, loosen the adjusting nut until lash is felt at the pushrod. Turn the adjusting nut clockwise until all lash is removed. With all lash removed, turn the nut in another 1½ turns.

5. Rotate the engine 1 complete revolution. Line up the crankshaft pulley with the **0** mark. This is the No. 4 firing position. Adjustment the following valves:
Exhaust — 2 and 4
Intake — 3 and 4

6. Install the rocker arm covers. Start the engine, check the timing and idle speed.

2.8L ENGINE

1. Rotate the engine until the timing mark on the harmonic balancer lines up with the **0** mark on the timing tab. Remove the rocker covers.

2. To determine that the engine is in the No. 1 firing position, while rotating the engine, place a finger on the No. 1 rocker arms as the timing mark nears the **0** mark. If the valves are not moving, the engine is in the No. 1 firing position.

3. With the engine in the No. 1 firing position, the following valves may be adjusted:

Intake — 1, 5, 6
Exhaust — 1, 2, 3

4. To adjust the valves, back the adjusting nut out until lash is felt at the pushrod. Turn the adjusting in just until all lash is removed.

5. When all lash has been removed, turn the adjusting nut in 1½ additional turns.

6. Rotate the engine 1 complete revolution until the timing tab **0** mark and balancer mark are aligned. The engine is now in the No. 4 firing position. With the engine is in this position, adjust following valves:
Intake — 2, 3, 4
Exhaust — 4, 5, 6

7. Install the rocker arm covers. Start the engine, check idle speed and timing.

VALVE LIFTERS

Removal and Installation

1. Disconnect the negative battery cable.

2. On the 2.8L engine, remove the intake manifold.

3. Remove the rocker arm cover.

4. Loosen the rocker arm holding nut and move the rocker arm to the side.

5. Remove the pushrod.

6. Using a suitable tool, remove the valve lifter.

7. Installation is the reverse of removal procedure. Fill lifter assembly with engine oil and lubricate the bottom of the valve lifter with Molykote® or its equivalent prior to installation.

8. Adjust valves as previously outlined.

VALVE ROCKER AND ROCKER ARM COVER ASSEMBLY

Removal and Installation

1.8L AND 2.0L OHC ENGINES

1. Disconnect the negative battery cable. Remove camshaft carrier cover.

2. Hold the valves in place with compressed air, using air adapter J–22794 or equivalent in spark plug hole.

3. Compress the valve springs with special tool J–33302–25 or equivalent.

4. Remove the rocker arms. Keep the rocker arms in order for reassembly.

5. To install, reverse the removal procedures using new gasket.

2.0L OHV ENGINE

1. Disconnect the negative battery cable. Remove the air cleaner. Remove the rocker cover.

2. Remove the rocker arm nut and ball. Lift the rocker arm off the stud and the pushrods from the engine. Always keep the valve system parts in order.
To install:

3. Coat the rocker arm balls with Molykote®, or equivalent.

4. Install the pushrods in the order removed, making sure that they seat properly in the lifter.

5. Install the rocker arms, balls and nuts in the order removed and adjust the valve lash.

NOTE: The valve system on 1987–90 engine is not adjustable. The correct rocker arm torque is 11–18 ft. lbs.

6. Installation of the remaining components is in the reverse order of removal.

2.8L ENGINE

Left Side

1. Disconnect the negative battery cable. Disconnect the bracket tube at the rocker cover.

2. Remove the spark plug wire cover. Drain the cooling system and remove the heater hose at the filler neck.

3. Remove the rocker arm cover bolts and remove the rocker cover.

4. Remove the rocker arm nuts and remove the rocker arms. Note the order of removal for installation.

5. Install the rocker arms in the correct order. Adjust valve lash.

NOTE: The valve system on 1987–90 engine is not adjustable. The correct rocker arm torque is 14–20 ft. lbs.

6. The remainder of the installation is the reverse of the removal.

Right Side

1. Disconnect the negative battery cable. Disconnect the brake booster vacuum line at the bracket.
2. Disconnect the cable bracket at the plenum.
3. Disconnect the vacuum line bracket at the cable bracket.
4. Disconnect the lines at the alternator brace stud.
5. Remove the rear alternator brace.
6. Remove the serpentine belt.
7. Remove the alternator and support it out of the way.
8. Remove the PCV valve.
9. Loosen the alternator bracket.
10. Remove the spark plug wires. Remove the rocker cover bolts and remove the rocker cover.
11. Remove the rocker arm nuts and remove the rocker arms. Note the order of removal for installation.
12. Install the rocker arms in the correct order. Adjust valve lash.

NOTE: The valve system on 1987–90 engine is not adjustable. The correct rocker arm torque is 14–20 ft. lbs.

13. The remainder of the installation is the reverse of the removal.

Cylinder Head

Removal and Installation

2.0L OHV ENGINES

NOTE: The engine must be cold before removing the cylinder head. Always release the fuel pressure before starting repair.

1. Disconnect the negative battery cable.
2. Drain the cooling system.
3. Remove the air cleaner. Raise and safely support the vehicle.
4. Remove the exhaust shield. Disconnect the exhaust pipe.
5. Remove the heater hose from the intake manifold. Lower the vehicle.
6. Unscrew the mounting bolts and remove the engine lift bracket (includes air management).
7. Remove the distributor. Disconnect the vacuum manifold at the alternator bracket.
8. Tag and disconnect the remaining vacuum lines at the intake manifold and thermostat.
9. Remove the air management pipe at the exhaust check valve.
10. Disconnect the accelerator linkage at the TBI unit and remove the linkage bracket.
11. Tag and disconnect all necessary wires. Remove the upper radiator hose at the thermostat.
12. Remove the bolt attaching the dipstick tube and hot water bracket.
13. Remove the idler pulley. Remove the AIR unit and power steering pump drive belts.
14. Remove the AIR bracket-to-intake manifold bolt. If equipped with power steering, remove the air pump pulley, the

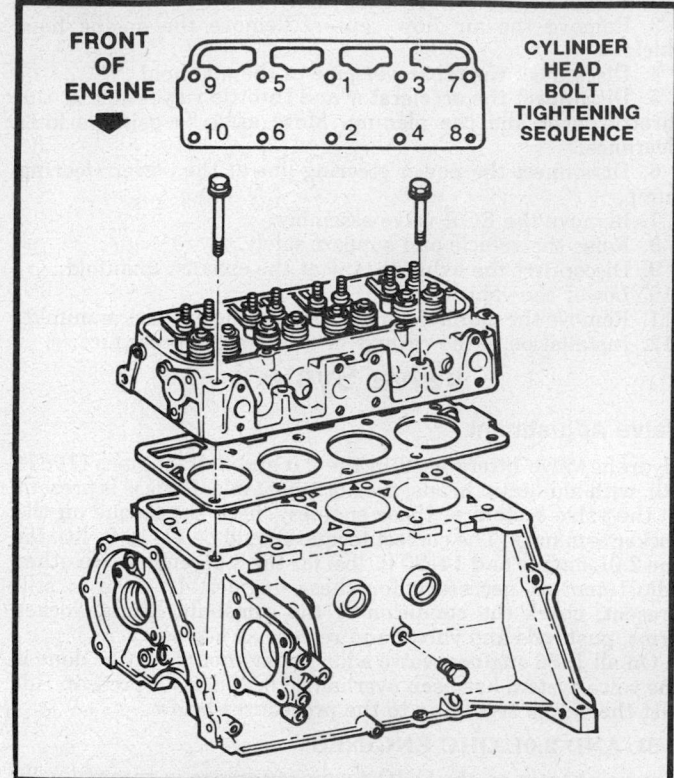

Cylinder head installation—OHV engine code P

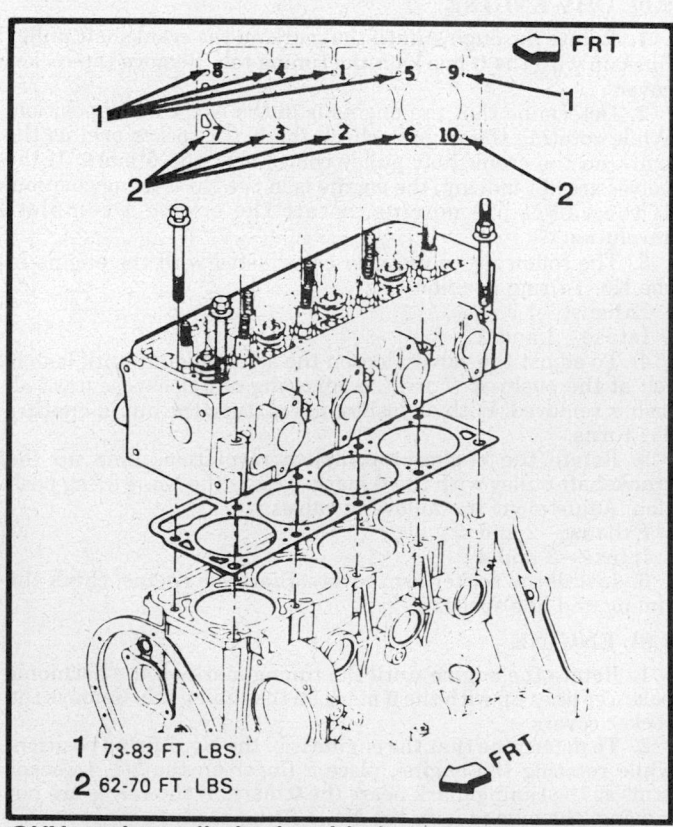

1 73-83 FT. LBS.
2 62-70 FT. LBS.

OHV engine cylinder head bolt torque sequence engine code 1

AIR through bolt and the power steering adjusting bracket.

15. Loosen the AIR mounting bracket lower bolt so that the bracket will rotate.

16. Disconnect and plug the fuel line at the TBI unit.

17. Remove the alternator. Remove the alternator brace from the head and remove the upper mounting bracket.

18. Remove the cylinder head cover. Remove the rocker arms and pushrods keeping all parts in order for correct installation.

19. Remove the cylinder head bolts. Remove the cylinder head with the TBI unit, intake and exhaust manifolds still attached.

To install:

20. The gasket surfaces on both the head and the block must be clean of any foreign matter and free of any nicks or heavy scratches. Bolt threads in the block and the bolts must be clean.

21. Place a new cylinder head gasket in position over the dowel pins on the block. Carefully guide the cylinder head into position.

22. Coat the cylinder bolts with sealing compound and install them finger tight.

23. Using a torque wrench, gradually tighten the bolts in the sequence to the correct torque.

24. Reinstall the AIR unit and pipes. Install the power steering pump and brackets.

25. Reconnect the fuel lines and the hoses. Connect the exhaust pipe to the manifold.

26. Install the valve cover and connect the linkage at the TBI unit or the carburetor.

27. Install the distributor and connect the vacuum lines.

28. Install the air cleaner and fill all the fluids.

29. Run the engine and check for leaks.

1.8L AND 2.0L OHC ENGINES

NOTE: Cylinder head gasket replacement is necessary if camshaft carrier/cylinder head bolts are loosened. The head bolts should always be loosened when cold. New head bolts should be used every time camshaft carrier/cylinder head or gasket are replaced.

1. Disconnect the negative battery cable. Remove the air cleaner and relieve fuel pressure.

2. Drain the cooling system.

3. Remove the alternator and pivot bracket at the camshaft carrier housing.

4. Disconnect the power steering pump and bracket, lay it to one side.

5. Disconnect the ignition coil electrical connections and remove coil.

6. Disconnect the spark plug wires and distributor cap, remove the distributor.

7. Remove the throttle cable from the bracket at intake manifold.

8. Disconnect the throttle cable, downshift cable and T.V. cable from the EFI assembly.

9. Disconnect the ECM connectors from the EFI assembly.

10. Remove the vacuum brake hose at filter.

11. Disconnect the inlet and return fuel lines at flex joints.

12. Remove the water pump bypass hose at the intake manifold and water pump.

13. Disconnect the ECM harness connectors at intake manifold.

14. Disconnect the heater hose from intake manifold.

15. Disconnect the exhaust pipe at exhaust manifold.

NOTE: On engine code M, remove the exhaust manifold to turbo connection and O₂ sensor connection.

16. Disconnect the breather hose at camshaft carrier.

17. Remove the upper radiator hose.

18. Disconnect the engine electrical harness and wires from thermostat housing.

19. Remove the timing cover.

20. Remove the timing probe holder.

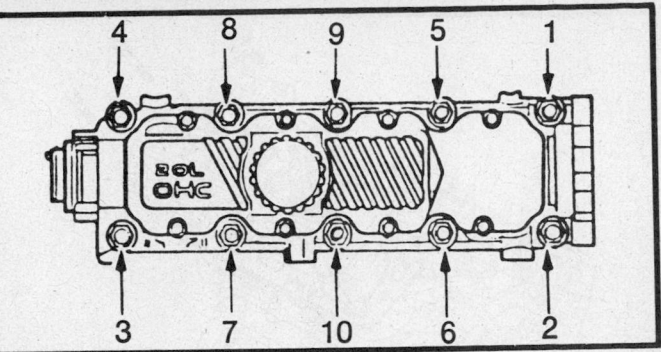

Camshaft carrier/cylinder head bolt loosening sequence

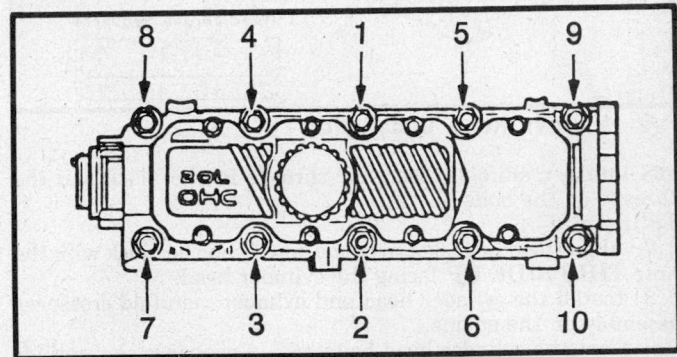

Camshaft carrier/cylinder head bolt torque sequence

21. Loosen the water pump retaining bolts and remove timing belt.

22. Loosen the camshaft carrier and cylinder head attaching bolts a little at a time in sequence shown.

23. Remove the camshaft carrier assembly.

24. Remove the cylinder head, intake manifold and exhaust manifold as an assembly.

To install:

25. Install a new cylinder head gasket in position on the block.

26. Apply a continuous bead of gasket maker to the cam carrier cover.

27. Install the cylinder head in position and tighten the bolts in sequence to the correct torque.

28. Install the camshaft carrier and tighten the bolts in sequence and to the correct torque.

29. Install the timing belt.

30. Reconnect the electrical harness and the breather hose at the camshaft carrier.

31. Connect the exhaust pipe at the manifold and attach the heater hose to the intake manifold.

32. Connect the brake hose at the filter. Connect the throttle and T.V. cable.

33. Refill the cooling system and connect the negative battery cable.

34. Run the engine and check for leaks.

2.8L ENGINE

Left Side

1. Drain the cooling system. Remove the rocker cover.

2. Remove the intake manifold. Disconnect the exhaust crossover at the right exhaust manifold.

3. Disconnect the oil level indicator tube bracket.

4. Loosen the rocker arms nuts enough to remove the pushrods.

5. Starting with the outer bolts, remove the cylinder head bolts. Remove the cylinder head with the exhaust manifold.

6. Clean and inspect the surfaces of the cylinder head, block

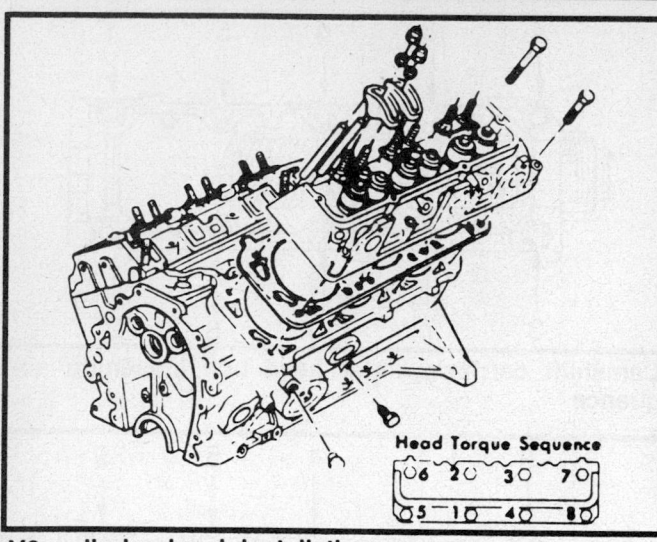

V6 cylinder head installation

and intake manifold. Clean the threads in the block and the threads on the bolts.

To install:

7. Align the new gasket over the dowels on the block with the note **THIS SIDE UP** facing the cylinder head.

8. Install the cylinder head and exhaust manifold crossover assembly on the engine.

9. Coat the cylinder head bolts with a proper sealer and install the bolts hand tight.

10. Following the correct sequence, torque the bolts to the correct specifications.

11. Install the pushrods in the same order that they were removed in. Adjust the valve lash.

NOTE: The valve system on 1987–90 engine is not adjustable. The correct rocker arm torque is 14–20 ft. lbs.

12. Install the intake manifold using a new gasket and following the correct sequence, torque the bolts to the correct specification.

13. The remainder of the installation is the reverse of the removal.

Right Side

1. Disconnect the negative battery cable. Drain the cooling system.

2. Raise and safely support the vehicle. Disconnect the exhaust manifold from the exhaust pipe.

3. Lower the vehicle. Disconnect the exhaust manifold from the cylinder head and remove the manifold.

4. Remove the rocker cover. Remove the intake manifold.

5. Loosen the rocker arms enough so that the pushrods can be removed. Note the position of the pushrods for assembly.

6. Starting with the outer bolts, remove the cylinder head bolts and remove the cylinder head.

7. Inspect and clean the surfaces of the cylinder head, engine block and intake manifold.

8. Clean the threads in the engine block and the threads on the cylinder head bolts.

To install:

9. Align the new gasket on the dowels on the engine block with the note **THIS SIDE UP** facing the cylinder head.

10. Install the cylinder head on the engine. Coat the head bolts with a proper sealer. Install and tighten the bolts hand tight.

11. Using the correct sequence, torque the bolts to the correct specifications.

12. Install the pushrods in the same order as they were removed. Adjust the valve lash.

NOTE: The valve system on 1987–90 2.8L engine is not adjustable. The correct rocker arm torque is 14–20 ft. lbs.

13. Install the intake manifold using a new gasket. Following the correct sequence, torque the bolts to the proper specification.

14. The remainder of the installation is the reverse of the removal.

Camshaft

Removal and Installation

2.0L OHV ENGINE

1. Remove the engine assembly.

2. Remove the intake manifold.

3. Remove the cylinder head cover, pivot the rocker arms to the sides and remove the pushrods, keeping them in order. Remove the valve lifters, keeping them in order.

4. Remove the front cover.

5. Remove the distributor.

6. Remove the fuel pump and its pushrod.

7. Remove the timing chain and sprocket.

8. Carefully pull the camshaft from the block, being sure that the camshaft lobes do not contact the bearings.

To install:

9. Lubricate the camshaft journals with clean engine oil. Lubricate the lobes with Molykote® or the equivalent. Install the camshaft into the engine, being extremely careful not to contact the bearings with the cam lobes.

10. Install the timing chain and sprocket. Install the fuel pump and pushrod. Install the timing cover. Install the distributor.

11. Install the valve lifters. If a new camshaft has been installed, new lifters should be used to ensure durability of the cam lobes.

12. Install the pushrods and rocker arms and the intake manifold.

13. Install the engine assembly. Adjust the valve lash after installing the engine.

14. Install the cylinder head cover.

1.8L AND 2.0L OHC ENGINES

1. Disconnect the negative battery cable. Remove the camshaft carrier cover.

2. Hold the valves in place with compressed air, using an air adapter J–22794 or equivalent in the spark plug hole. Compress the valve springs with a special tool J–33302–25 and remove rocker arms. Keep rocker arms in order for reassembly.

3. Remove the timing belt front cover.

4. Remove the timing belt.

5. Remove the camshaft sprocket.

6. Mark and remove the distributor.

7. Remove the camshaft thrust plate from rear of camshaft carrier.

8. Slide the camshaft rearward and remove it from the carrier.

To install:

9. Install a new camshaft carrier front oil seal using tool J–33085 or equivalent.

10. Place the camshaft in the carrier.

NOTE: Take care not to damage the carrier front oil seal when installing the camshaft.

11. Install the camshaft thrust plate retaining bolts. Torque bolts to 70 inch lbs.

12. Check the camshaft endplay, which should be within 0.016–0.064 in.

13. Install the distributor.

14. Install the camshaft sprocket.

15. Install the timing belt.

16. Install the timing belt front cover.

17. Using an air adapter J–22794 or equivalent, in the spark plug hole to hold the valve closed and install valve train compressing fixture J–33302. Compress valve springs and replace rocker arms.

18. Install the camshaft carrier cover.

2.8L ENGINE

1. Disconnect the negative battery cable. Remove the engine assembly from the vehicle.

2. Remove the intake manifold.

3. Remove the rocker arm covers. Remove the rocker arm nuts, balls, rocker arms and pushrods.

NOTE: Always keep valve train parts in order for correct installation.

4. Remove the upper front cover bolts. Remove the lower cover bolts and the front cover.

5. Remove the camshaft sprocket bolts, camshaft sprocket and timing chain.

6. Remove the camshaft by carefully sliding it out the front of the engine. Measure the camshaft bearing journals using a micrometer and replace the camshaft if the journals exceed 0.0009 in. (0.025mm) out of round.

7. Installation is the reverse of removal. When installing a new camshaft, lubricate the camshaft lobes with GM E.O.S. or equivalent.

Camshaft Carrier

Removal and Installation

1.8L AND 2.0L OHC ENGINES

NOTE: Whenever the camshaft carrier bolts are loosened, it is necessary to remove the cylinder head and replace the cylinder head gasket.

1. Disconnect the negative battery cable. Disconnect the crankcase ventilation hose from the camshaft carrier.

2. Mark and remove the distributor.

3. Remove the camshaft sprocket.

4. Loosen the camshaft carrier and cylinder head attaching bolts a little at a time in sequence.

NOTE: Camshaft carrier and cylinder head bolts should be loosened in sequence and only when the engine is cold.

5. Remove the camshaft carrier.

6. Remove the camshaft thrust plate from the rear of the camshaft carrier.

7. Slide the camshaft rearward and remove it from the carrier.

8. Remove the carrier front oil seal.

To install:

9. Install a new carrier front oil seal using tool J–33085.

10. Place the camshaft in the carrier.

NOTE: Take care not to damage the carrier front oil seal when installing the camshaft.

11. Install the camshaft thrust plate and the retaining bolts. Torque the bolts to 70 inch lbs.

12. Check the camshaft endplay which should be within 0.016–0.064 in. (0.04–0.16mm).

13. Clean the sealing surfaces on cylinder head and carrier. Apply a continuous 3mm bead of RTV sealer.

14. Install the camshaft carrier on the cylinder head.

15. Install the camshaft carrier and cylinder head attaching bolts.

16. Torque the bolts a little at a time in the proper sequence, as cylinder head, to 18 ft. lbs. Turn each bolt 60 degrees clockwise

in the proper sequence for 3 times until a 180 degrees rotation is obtained, or equivalent to ½ turn.

17. Install the camshaft sprocket.

18. Install the distributor.

19. Connect the positive crankcase ventilation hose to the camshaft carrier.

NOTE: After remainder of installation is completed, start engine and let it run until the thermostat opens. Torque all cylinder head bolts an additional 30–50 degrees in the proper sequence.

Timing Case Cover

Removal and Installation

2.0L OHV ENGINE

NOTE: The following procedure requires the use of a front cover centering tool J–35468 and crankshaft puller J–24420.

1. Disconnect the negative battery cable. Remove the engine accessory drive belts.

2. Although not absolutely necessary, removal of the right front inner fender splash shield will facilitate access to the front cover.

3. Remove the center bolt from the crankshaft pulley and retaining bolts, remove the pulley. Using a puller J–24420 or equivalent remove hub from the crankshaft.

4. Remove the alternator lower bracket.

5. Remove the oil pan-to-front cover bolts.

6. Remove the front cover-to-block bolts and remove the front cover. If the front cover is difficult to remove, use a rubber mallet to loosen it.

To install:

7. The surfaces of the block and front cover must be clean and free of oil. Apply a ⅛ in. bead of RTV sealant to the cover. The sealant must be wet to the touch when the bolts are torqued down.

NOTE: When applying RTV sealant to the front cover, be sure to keep it out of the bolt holes. When installing hub or pulley note position of key on crankshaft.

8. Position the front cover on the block using a centering tool J–35468 and tighten the screws.

9. Installation of the remaining components is in the reverse order of removal.

1.8L OHC ENGINE

1. Disconnect the negative battery cable.

2. Remove the alternator pivot bolts and power steering belt.

3. Disconnect the canister purge hose.

4. Remove the upper timing belt cover retaining bolts.

5. Raise the vehicle and support safely.

6. Remove the right front wheel assembly and remove the splash shield.

7. Remove the lower timing belt cover retaining bolts.

8. Remove the timing belt cover.

9. To install reverse removal procedures.

2.0L OHC ENGINE

1. Disconnect the negative battery cable.

2. Remove the tensioner and bolt.

3. Remove the serpentine belt.

4. Unsnap the upper and lower cover. Remove the cover.

5. To install reverse the removal procedures.

2.8L ENGINE

1. Disconnect the negative battery cable.

2. Drain the cooling system and remove the coolant recovery tank from the vehicle.

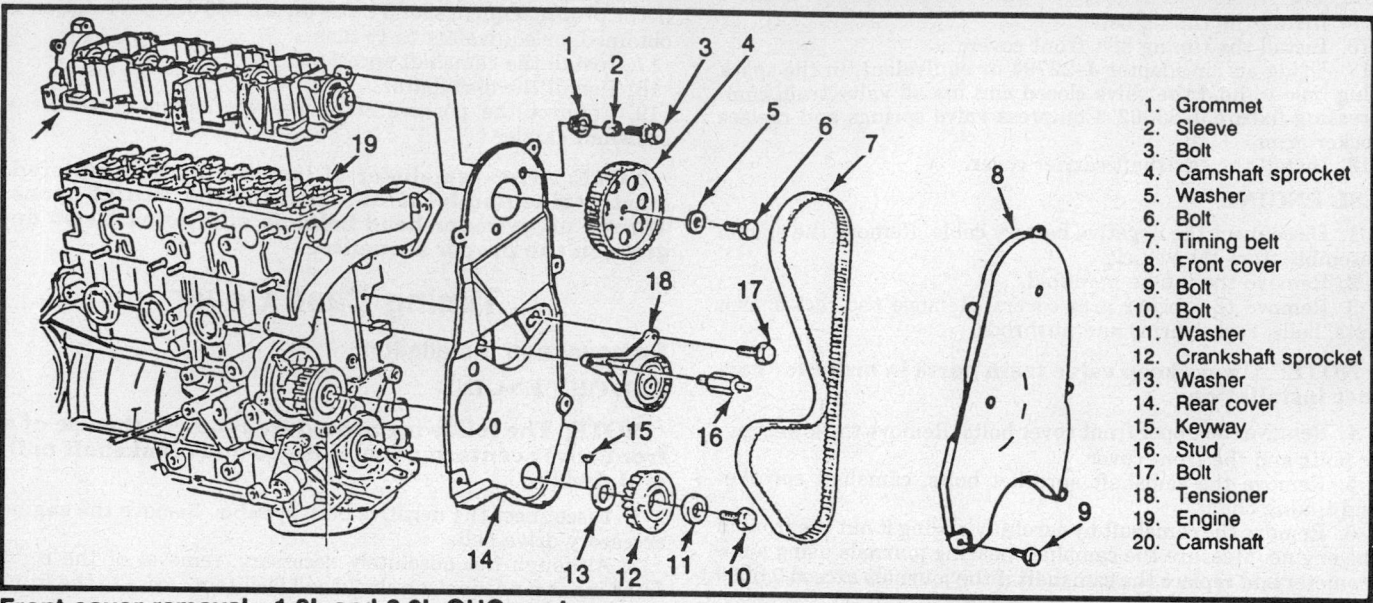

1. Grommet
2. Sleeve
3. Bolt
4. Camshaft sprocket
5. Washer
6. Bolt
7. Timing belt
8. Front cover
9. Bolt
10. Bolt
11. Washer
12. Crankshaft sprocket
13. Washer
14. Rear cover
15. Keyway
16. Stud
17. Bolt
18. Tensioner
19. Engine
20. Camshaft

Front cover removal—1.8L and 2.0L OHC engines

3. Disconnect the MAP sensor and EGR sensor solenoids.
4. Remove the serpentine belt and adjusting pulley.
5. Tag and disconnect the heater hose at the power steering bracket.
6. Tag and disconnect the alternator wiring and remove the alternator.
7. Raise the vehicle and support it safely.
8. Remove the inner fender splash shield.
9. Remove the harmonic balancer with tool J-24420 or equivalent puller.
10. Remove the oil pan-to-block bolts and remove the oil pan. Remove the lower cover bolts.
11. Lower the vehicle and disconnect the radiator hoses at the water pump.
12. Remove the heater hose from the thermostat housing.
13. Disconnect the overflow hoses and the canister purge hose.
14. Remove the front cover.

To install:

15. Apply a bead of sealer to the front cover surface.
16. Install a new front cover gasket and front oil seal.
17. Install the front cover and tighten to 20–28 ft. lbs.

18. Raise and safely support the vehicle. Install the oil pan and the lower front cover bolts.
19. Install the crankshaft balancer.
20. Install the inner splash shield and lower the vehicle.
21. Install the radiator hoses and the power steering pump.
22. Install the alternator and the accessory drive belt.
23. Refill the fluids and connect the negative battery cable.

OIL SEAL REPLACEMENT

OHV ENGINE

1. The oil seal can be replaced with the front cover either on or off the engine.
2. If the cover is on the engine, remove the crankshaft pulley and hub first.
3. Pry out the seal using a suitable tool, being careful not to distort the seal mating surfaces.
4. Install the new seal so that the open, or helical side, is towards the engine.
5. Press it into place with a seal driver.
6. Install the hub and pulley, if removed.

OHC ENGINE

1. Remove the crankshaft sprocket.
2. Remove the crankshaft key and rear thrust washer.
3. Using a suitable prybar, pry out the front oil seal.
4. Place the protective sleeve of special tool set J33083 (seal installer) or equivalent, onto the crankshaft.
5. Lubricate the lip of the new seal. Using special tool J33083, install the seal.
6. Remove the protective sleeve.
7. Install the rear thrust washer and key on the crankshaft.
8. Install the crankshaft sprocket.

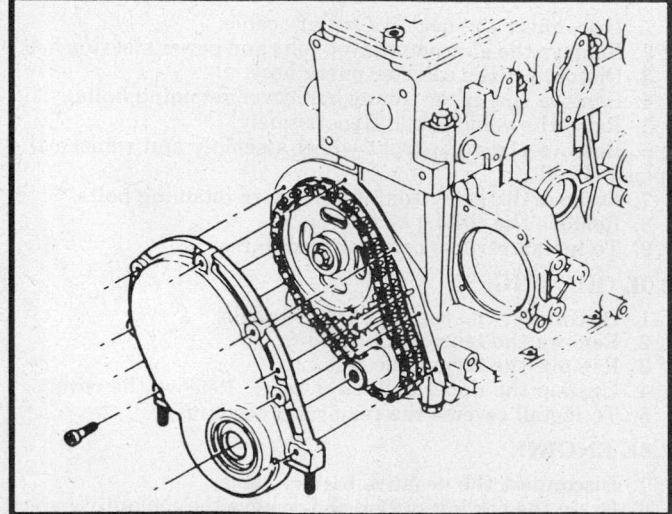

Front cover removal—2.0L OHV engine

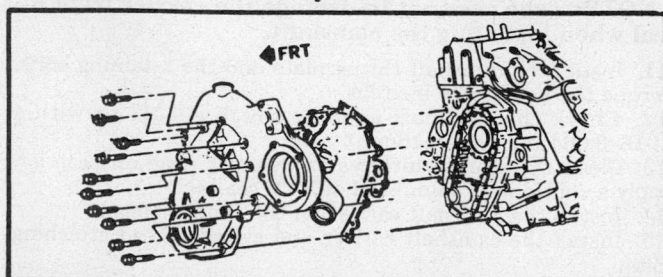

Front cover assembly—2.8L engine

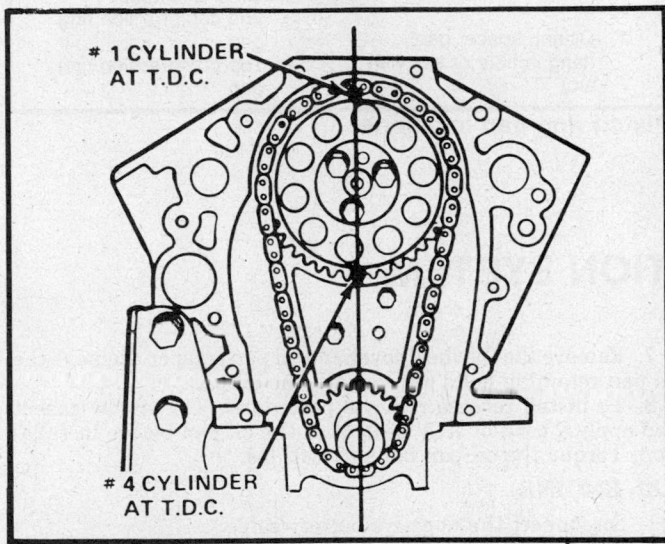

Timing mark OHV—4 cylinder

Timing marks—V6 engine

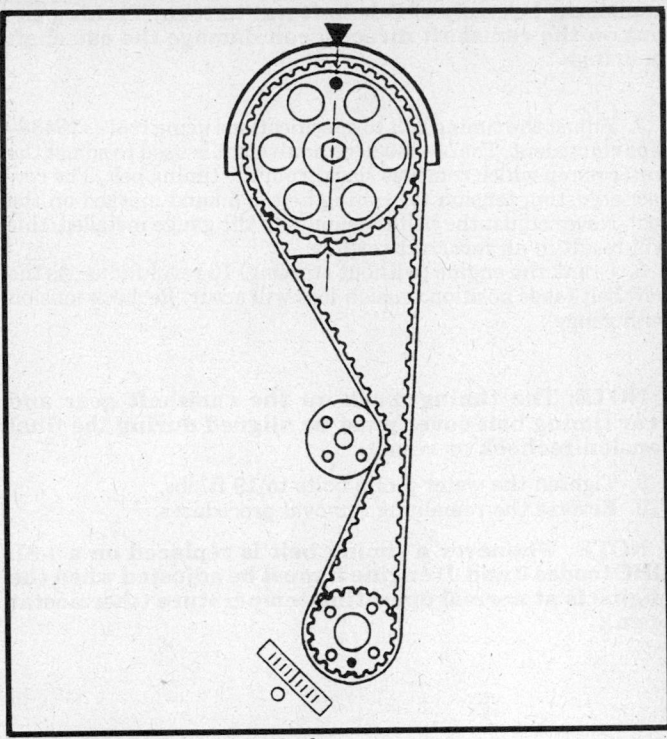

OHC timing belt installation

Timing Chain and Sprockets

Removal and Installation

2.0L OHV ENGINE

1. Disconnect the negative battery cable. Remove the front cover.
2. Place the No. 1 piston at **TDC** of the compression stroke so that the marks on the camshaft and crankshaft sprockets are in alignment.
3. Loosen the timing chain tensioner nut as far as possible, without actually removing it.
4. Remove the camshaft sprocket bolts and remove the sprocket and chain together. If the sprocket does not slide from the camshaft easily, a light blow with a soft tool at the lower edge of the sprocket will loosen it.
5. Use a gear puller J-2288-8-20 or equivalent and remove the crankshaft sprocket.

To install:

6. Press the new crankshaft sprocket back onto the crankshaft.
7. Install the timing chain over the camshaft sprocket and around the crankshaft sprocket. Make sure that the marks on the 2 sprockets are in alignment. Lubricate the thrust surface with Molykote®, or equivalent.
8. Align the dowel in the camshaft with the dowel hole in the sprocket and install the sprocket onto the camshaft. Use the

mounting bolts to draw the sprocket onto the camshaft and tighten them to 27–33 ft. lbs.
9. Lubricate the timing chain with clean engine oil. Tighten the chain tensioner.
10. Installation of the remaining components is in the reverse order of the removal procedure.

2.8L ENGINE

1. Disconnect the negative battery cable.
2. Remove the front cover.
3. Position the No. 1 piston at **TDC** with the marks on the crankshaft and camshaft sprockets aligned.
4. Remove the camshaft sprocket bolts.
5. Remove the camshaft sprocket and chain from the front of the engine.

NOTE: If the sprocket does not move freely from the camshaft, a light blow using a plastic tool on the lower edge of the sprocket should dislodge it.

6. Installation is the reverse of removal. Draw the camshaft sprocket onto the camshaft using the mounting bolts. Lubricate the timing chain with engine oil prior to installation.

Timing Belt and Tensioner

Removal and Installation

1.8L AND 2.0L OHC ENGINES

1. Disconnect the negative battery cable.
2. Remove the timing belt cover.
3. Remove the crankshaft pulley.
4. Drain the radiator and remove the coolant reservoir.
5. Loosen the water pump bolts and remove timing belt.

To install:

6. Install the new timing belt and crankshaft pulley.

NOTE: Check if the mark on the camshaft sprocket lines up with mark on the rear timing belt cover. The timing mark on the crankshaft pulley should line up at 10 degrees BTDC on the indicator scale. Do not turn

camshaft. Use only crankshaft nut to turn. Turning the nut on the camshaft directly can damage the camshaft bearings.

7. Adjust the timing belt to specifications using tool J-26486-A or equivalent. Tool J-33039 or equivalent is used to adjust the water pump which removes slack from the timing belt. The correct adjusting tension for timing belt is a band marked on the tool. Never adjust the belt tension with the gauge installed, this will result in an incorrect reading.

8. Crank the engine (without starting) 10 revolutions. As the new belt takes position tension loss will occur. Recheck tension with gauge.

NOTE: The timing mark on the camshaft gear and rear timing belt cover must be aligned during the final tension recheck or resset.

9. Tighten the water pump bolts to 19 ft. lbs.
10. Reverse the remaining removal procedures.

NOTE: Whenever a timing belt is replaced on a 1.8L OHC (codes 0 and J) engine it must be adjusted when the engine is at normal operating temperature (thermostat open).

Rings/Piston/Connecting Rod Positioning

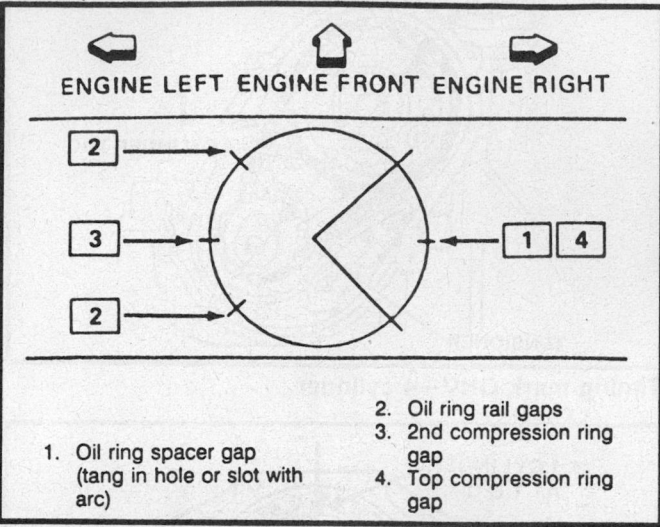

ENGINE LEFT   ENGINE FRONT   ENGINE RIGHT

1. Oil ring spacer gap (tang in hole or slot with arc)
2. Oil ring rail gaps
3. 2nd compression ring gap
4. Top compression ring gap

Piston ring gap locations

ENGINE LUBRICATION SYSTEM

Oil Pan

Removal and Installation

2.0L OHV ENGINE

1. Disconnect the negative battery cable.
2. Raise and safely support the vehicle. Drain the crankcase.
3. Remove the air conditioning brace, if equipped.
4. Remove the exhaust shield and disconnect the exhaust pipe at the manifold.
5. Remove the starter motor and position it out of the way.
6. Remove the flywheel cover. Remove the oil pan retaining bolts and remove the oil pan.

To install:

NOTE: Prior to oil pan installation, check that the sealing surfaces on the pan, cylinder block and front cover are clean and free of oil. If installing the old oil pan, be sure that all old RTV has been removed.

7. Apply a ⅛ in. bead of RTV sealant to the oil pan sealing surface. Use a new oil pan rear seal and install the pan in place. Tighten the bolts to 9–13 ft. lbs.
8. Install the flywheel cover and the starter.
9. Connect the exhaust pipe at the manifold.
10. Install the exhaust shield and install the air conditioning brace.
11. Connect the negative battery cable and run the vehicle to normal operating temperature. Check for leaks.

1.8L AND 2.0L OHC ENGINES

1. Disconnect the negative battery cable.
2. Raise and safely support the vehicle.
3. Remove the right front wheel assembly.
4. Remove the front splash shield.
5. Drain the crankcase.
6. Remove the exhaust pipe from the manifold, on turbocharged vehicles, remove exhaust pipe from wastegate.

7. Remove the flywheel cover and oil pan scraper. Remove the oil pan retaining bolts and remove the oil pan.
8. To install reverse removal procedures. Use a new gasket and apply a bead of RTV sealant to the oil pan before installation. Torque the oil pan bolts to 4 ft. lbs.

2.8L ENGINE

1. Disconnect the negative battery cable.
2. Remove the serpentine belt and the tensioner.
3. Support the engine with tool J-28467 or equivalent.
4. Raise and safely support the vehicle. Drain the engine oil.
5. Remove the right tire and wheel assembly. Remove the right inner fender splash shield.
6. Remove the steering gear pinch bolt. Remove the transaxle mount retaining bolts.
7. Remove the engine-to-cradle mounting nuts. Remove the front engine collar bracket from the block.
8. Remove the starter shield and the flywheel cover. Remove the starter.
9. Loosen, but DO NOT remove the rear engine cradle bolts.
10. Remove the front cradle bolts. Remove the oil pan retaining bolts and nuts. Remove the oil pan.

To install:

11. Clean the gasket mating surfaces.
12. Install a new gasket on the oil pan. Apply silicon sealer to the portion of the pan that contacts the rear of the block.
13. Install the oil pan, nuts and retaining bolts. Tighten to 13–18 ft. lbs.
14. Install the front cradle bolts and tighten the rear cradle bolts. Install the starter and splash shield. Install the flywheel shield.
15. Attach the collar bracket to the block, install the engine-to-cradle nuts. Install the transaxle mount nuts.
16. Install the steering pinch bolt. Install the right inner fender splash shield and tire assembly. Lower the vehicle.
17. Remove the engine support tool. Install the serpentine belt and tensioner.

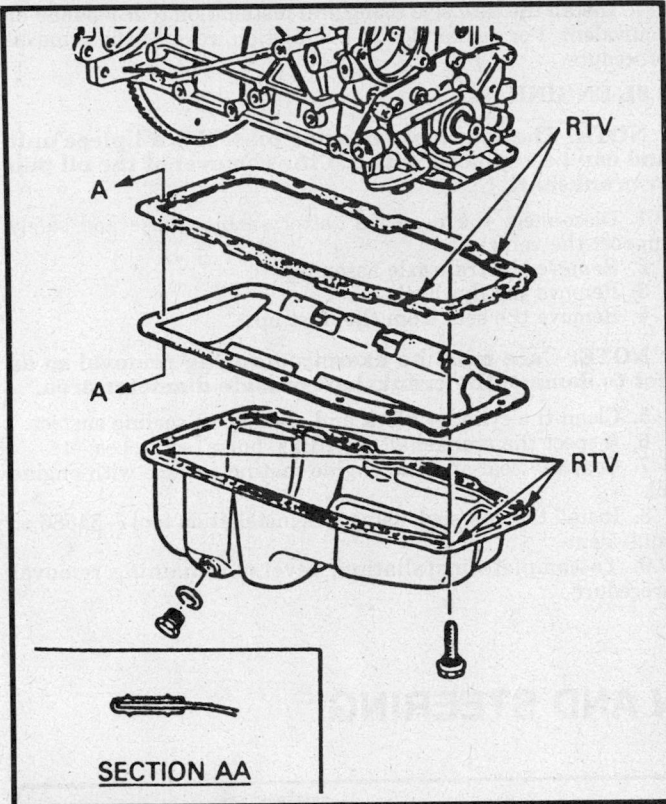

SECTION AA

Oil pan installation—1.8L and 2.0L engines

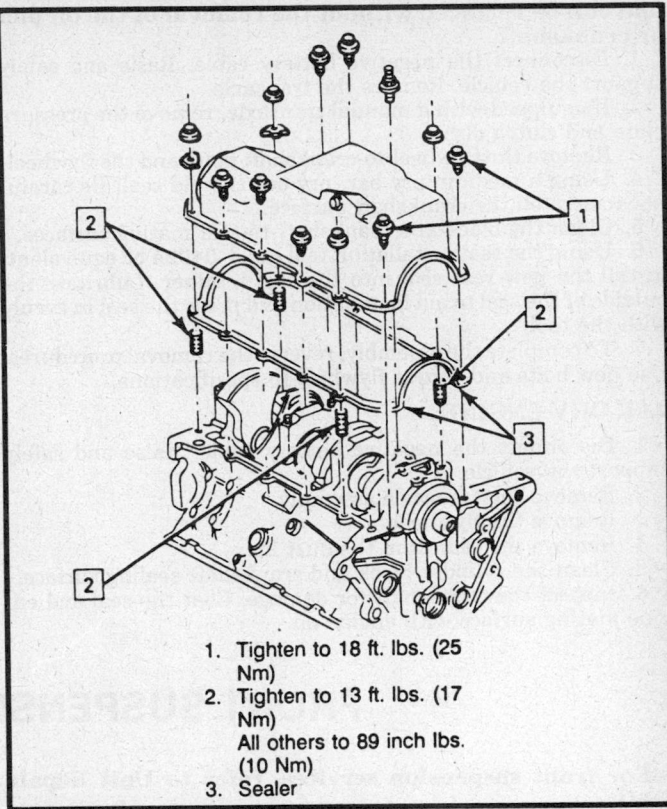

1. Tighten to 18 ft. lbs. (25 Nm)
2. Tighten to 13 ft. lbs. (17 Nm)
   All others to 89 inch lbs. (10 Nm)
3. Sealer

Oil pan installation—2.8L engine

18. Fill the crankcase to the correct level. Connect the negative battery cable. Run the engine to normal operating temperature and check for leaks.

Oil Pump

Removal and Installation

1.8L AND 2.0L OHC ENGINES

1. Disconnect the negative battery cable. Remove the crankshaft sprocket.
2. Remove the timing belt rear cover.
3. Disconnect the connector at oil pressure switch.
4. Raise and safely support the vehicle. Drain the engine oil and remove the oil pan.
5. Remove the oil filter.
6. Unbolt and remove the oil pick-up tube.
7. Unbolt and remove the oil pump.
8. Installation is the reverse of removal. Use new gaskets in all instances. Torque the oil pump bolts to 5 ft. lbs. Torque the oil pan bolts to 4 ft. lbs. and the oil pick-up tube bolts to 5 ft. lbs.

2.0L OHV ENGINE

1. Disconnect the negative battery cable.
2. Raise and safely support the vehicle. Drain the engine oil and remove the engine oil pan.
3. Remove the pump attaching bolts and carefully lower the pump.
4. Install in reverse order. To ensure immediate oil pressure on start-up, the oil pump gear cavity should be packed with petroleum jelly. Installation torque is 26–35 ft. lbs. on the oil pump mounting bolts.

2.8L ENGINE

1. Disconnect the negative battery cable.

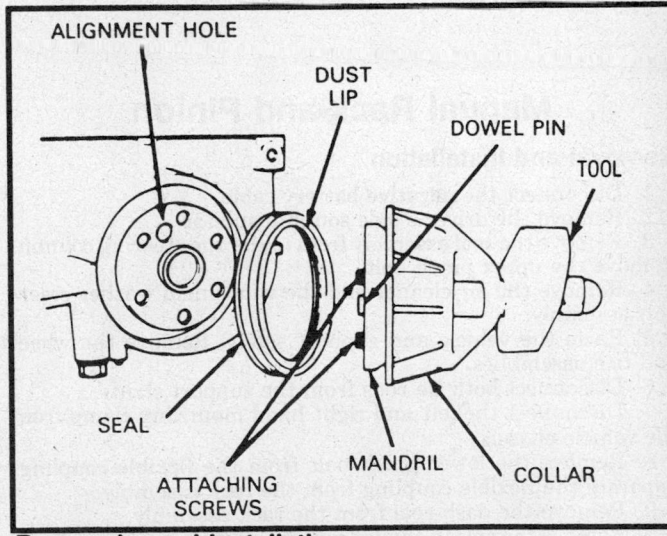

Rear main seal installation

2. Raise and safely support the vehicle. Drain the engine oil and remove the oil pan.
3. Remove the rear main bearing cap.
4. Remove the oil pump and extension shaft.
5. Installation is the reverse of the removal procedure.

Rear Main Oil Seal

Removal and Installation

1.8L AND 2.0L OHC ENGINES

NOTE: The rear main bearing oil seal is a 1 piece unit

and can be replaced without the removal of the oil pan or crankshaft.

1. Disconnect the negative battery cable. Rasie and safely support the vehicle. Remove the transaxle.
2. If equipped with a manual transaxle, remove the pressure plate and clutch disc.
3. Remove the flywheel-to-crankshaft bolts and the flywheel.
4. Using a medium pry bar, pry out the old seal; Be careful not to scratch the crankshaft surface.
5. Clean the block and crankshaft-to-seal mating surfaces.
6. Using the seal installation tool no. J–34924 or equivalent, install the new rear seal into the seal retainer. Lubricate the outside of the seal to aid installation and press the seal in evenly with the tool.
7. To complete the assembly, reverse the removal procedures. Use new bolts and torque flywheel to specifications.

2.0L OHV ENGINE

1. Disconnect the negative battery cable. Raise and safely support the vehicle.
2. Remove the transaxle assembly.
3. Remove the flywheel.
4. Remove the seal from the dust lip.
5. Clean the cylinder block and crankshaft sealing surface.
6. Inspect the crankshaft for damage. Coat the seal and engine mating surface with engine oil.

7. Install the new seal using seal installation tool J–34686 or equivalent. For remainder of installation, reverse the removal procedure.

2.8L ENGINE

NOTE: The rear main bearing oil seal is a 1 piece unit and can be replaced without the removal of the oil pan or crankshaft.

1. Disconnect the negative battery cable. Raise and safely support the vehicle.
2. Remove the transaxle assembly.
3. Remove the flywheel.
4. Remove the seal from the dust lip.

NOTE: Care must be exercised during removal so as not to damage the crankshaft outside diameter area.

5. Clean the cylinder block and crankshaft sealing surface.
6. Inspect the crankshaft for nicks, burrs, scratches, etc.
7. Coat the seal and the engine mating surface with engine oil.
8. Install the new seal, using seal installation tool J–34686 or equivalent.
9. To complete installation, reverse remaining removal procedure.

FRONT SUSPENSION AND STEERING

For front suspension services, refer to Unit Repair section.
For steering wheel removal and installation, refer to Electrical Controls.

Manual Rack and Pinion

Removal and Installation

1. Disconnect the negative battery cable.
2. Remove the driver's side sound insulator.
3. Remove the seal assembly from under the steering column. Remove the upper pinch bolt.
4. Remove the air cleaner and the windshield washer reservoir assembly.
5. Raise the vehicle and support safely. Remove the wheel and tire assemblies.
6. Disconnect both tie rods from the support struts.
7. Disconnect the left and right hand mounting clamp from the vehicle chassis.
8. Remove the lower pinch bolt from the flexible coupling. Separate the flexible coupling from the rack assembly.
9. Remove the dash seal from the rack assembly.
10. Remove the splash shield from the driver's side inner fender if equipped.
11. Slide the rack and pinion assembly through the driver's side fender opening.

To install:

12. Install the rack and pinion into position in the vehicle.
13. Install the splash shield into the drivers side fender opening.
14. Lower the vehicle slightly and install the dash seal. Connect the flexible coupling and install the lower pinch bolt.
15. Connect the mounting clamps and connect the tie rods.
16. Install the wheel and tire assemblies.
17. Install the air cleaner and washer fluid reservoir.
18. Install the drivers side sound insulator and connect the negative battery cable.

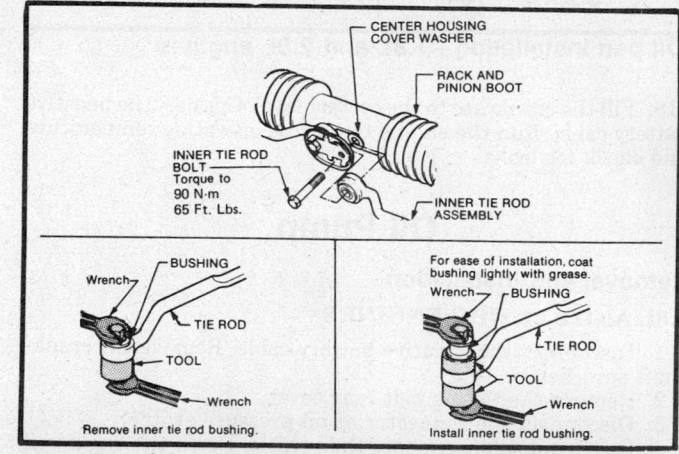

Inner tie rod and pivot bushing, removal and installation

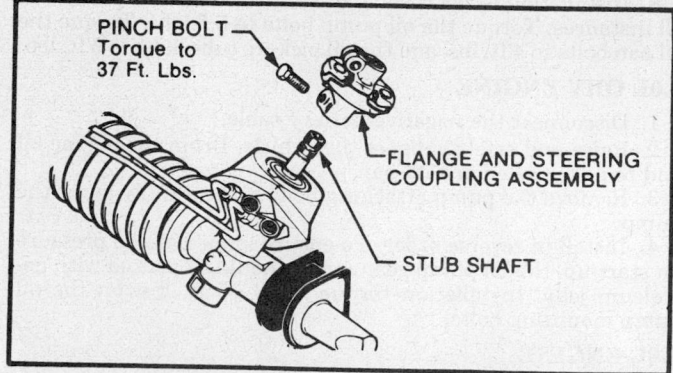

Steering coupling removal and installation

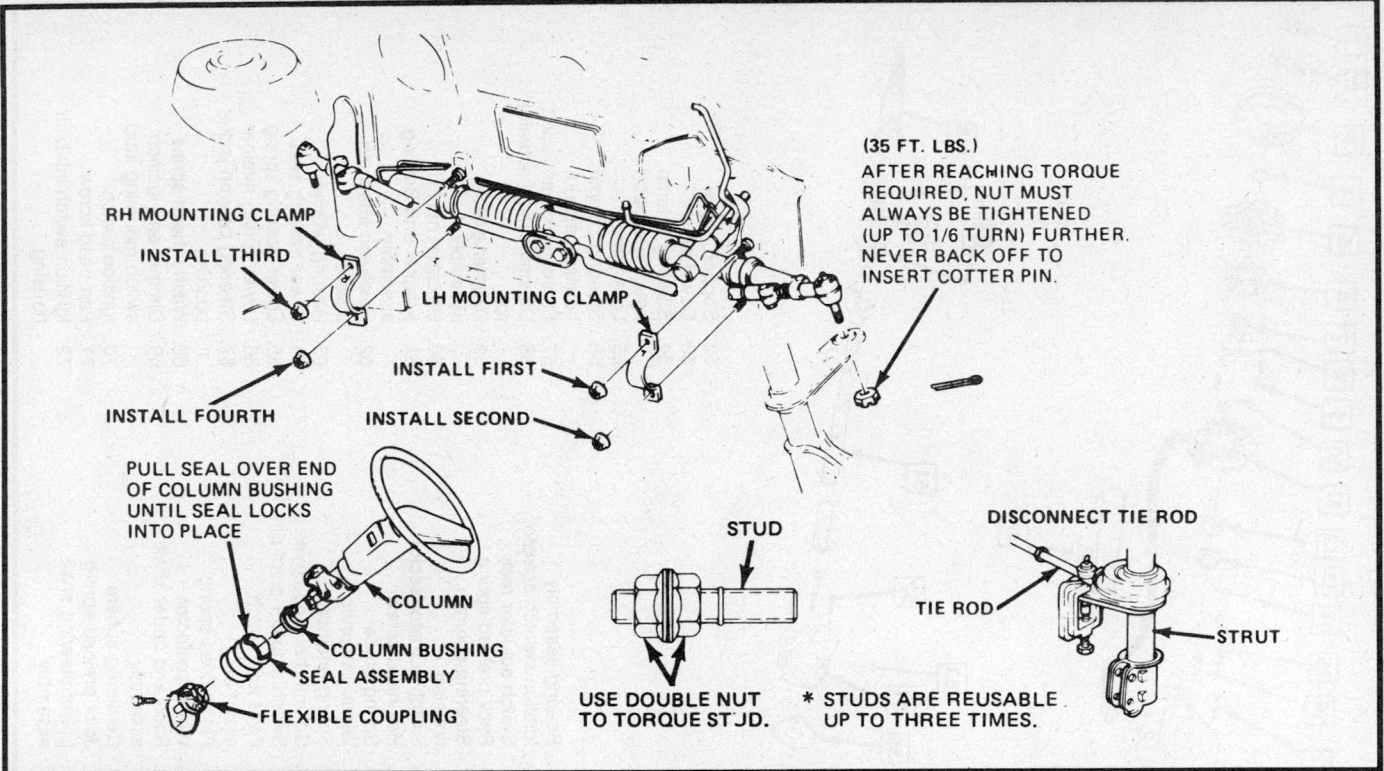

RH MOUNTING CLAMP

INSTALL THIRD

LH MOUNTING CLAMP

INSTALL FIRST

INSTALL FOURTH

INSTALL SECOND

PULL SEAL OVER END
OF COLUMN BUSHING
UNTIL SEAL LOCKS
INTO PLACE

COLUMN

COLUMN BUSHING

SEAL ASSEMBLY

FLEXIBLE COUPLING

(35 FT. LBS.)
AFTER REACHING TORQUE
REQUIRED, NUT MUST
ALWAYS BE TIGHTENED
(UP TO 1/6 TURN) FURTHER.
NEVER BACK OFF TO
INSERT COTTER PIN.

STUD

USE DOUBLE NUT
TO TORQUE STUD.

* STUDS ARE REUSABLE
UP TO THREE TIMES.

DISCONNECT TIE ROD

TIE ROD

STRUT

Power rack and pinion unit mounting

1. TURN FORCING SCREW UNTIL AXLE
SPLINES ARE JUST LOOSE

Removing drive axle from hub and bearing assembly

Power Rack and Pinion

Removal and Installation

1. Disconnect the negative battery cable. Remove the air cleaner.
2. Raise and safely support the vehicle.
3. Remove both front wheel assemblies.
4. Remove the intermediate shaft lower pinch bolt at the steering gear. Remove the intermediate shaft from the stub shaft.
5. Disconnect the electrical lead at the power steering idle switch.
6. Separate the tie rod ends from the knuckle assembly. Remove the rear sub-frame mounting bolts and lower the rear of the sub-frame approximately 4 in.

7. Remove the steering rack heat shield. Disconnect the pressure lines at the steering gear.
8. Remove the rack and pinion mounting bolts, remove the rack and pinion through the left wheel opening.

To install:

9. Install the rack and pinion through the left wheel opening. Tighten the mounting bolts to 59 ft. lbs. Connect the pressure lines, tighten the fittings to 20 ft. lbs.
10. Install the rack heat shield, tighten the retaining bolts to 53 inch lbs. Attach the tie rod ends to the steering knuckle.
11. Connect the electrical lead to the power steering idle switch. Attach the intermediate shaft to the stub shaft, tighten the pinch bolt to 35 ft. lbs.
12. Install both wheel assemblies. Lower the vehicle.
13. Install the air cleaner. Connect the negative battery cable. Fill and bleed the power steering system.

Power Steering Pump

Removal and Installation

NOTE: When power steering pump is being replaced, pump pulley will have to be transfered as necessary.

1. Disconnect the negative battery cable. Remove the necessary components to gain access to the power steering pump.
2. Loosen the adjusting bolt and remove the drive belt.
3. Remove the pump to bracket bolts and remove the adjusting bolt.
4. Remove the high pressure fitting from the pump.
5. Disconnect the reservoir to pump hose from the pump.
6. Remove the pump.
7. Installation is in the reverse order of removal. Adjust the belt tension and bleed the system.

Bleeding the System

1. Raise the front of the vehicle and support safely.
2. With the wheels turned all the way to the left, add power

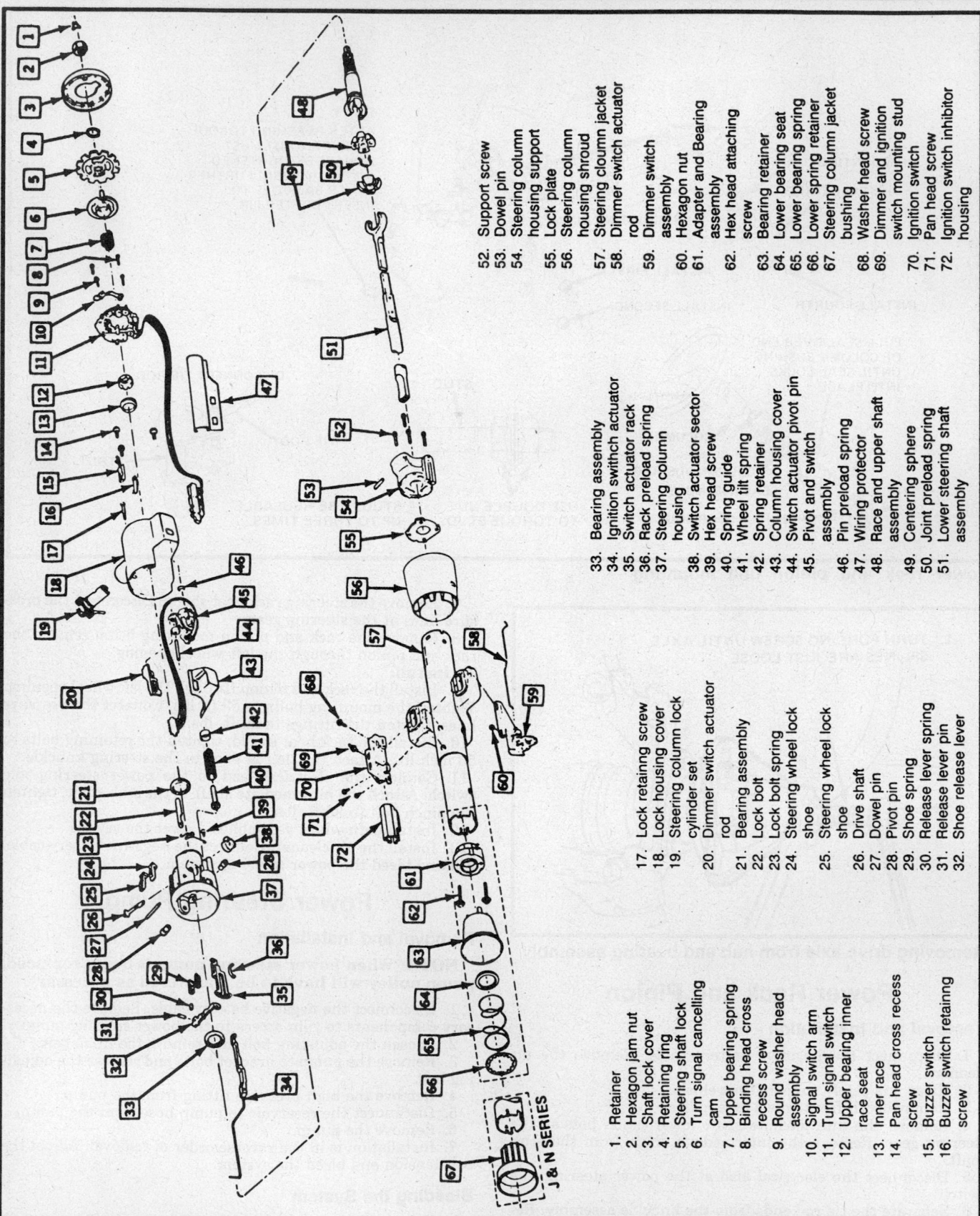

1. Retainer
2. Hexagon jam nut
3. Shaft lock cover
4. Retaining ring
5. Steering shaft lock
6. Turn signal cancelling cam
7. Upper bearing spring
8. Binding head cross recess screw
9. Round washer head assembly
10. Signal switch arm
11. Turn signal switch
12. Upper bearing inner race seat
13. Inner race
14. Pan head cross recess screw
15. Buzzer switch
16. Buzzer switch retainng screw
17. Lock retaining screw
18. Lock housing cover
19. Steering column lock cylinder set
20. Dimmer switch actuator rod
21. Bearing assembly
22. Lock bolt
23. Lock bolt spring
24. Steering wheel lock shoe
25. Steering wheel lock shoe
26. Drive shaft
27. Dowel pin
28. Pivot pin
29. Shoe spring
30. Release lever spring
31. Release lever pin
32. Shoe release lever
33. Bearing assembly
34. Ignition switch actuator
35. Switch actuator rack
36. Rack preload spring
37. Steering column housing
38. Switch actuator sector
39. Hex head screw
40. Spring guide
41. Wheel tilt spring
42. Spring retainer
43. Column housing cover
44. Switch actuator pivot pin
45. Pivot and switch assembly
46. Pin preload spring
47. Wiring protector
48. Race and upper shaft assembly
49. Centering sphere
50. Joint preload spring
51. Lower steering shaft assembly
52. Support screw
53. Dowel pin
54. Steering column housing support
55. Lock plate
56. Steering column housing shroud
57. Steering cloumn jacket
58. Dimmer switch actuator rod
59. Dimmer switch assembly
60. Hexagon nut
61. Adapter and Bearing assembly
62. Hex head attaching screw
63. Bearing retainer
64. Lower bearing seat
65. Lower bearing spring
66. Lower spring retainer
67. Steering column jacket bushing
68. Washer head screw
69. Dimmer and ignition switch mounting stud
70. Ignition switch
71. Pan head screw
72. Ignition switch inhibitor housing

J & N SERIES

Tilt stering column components

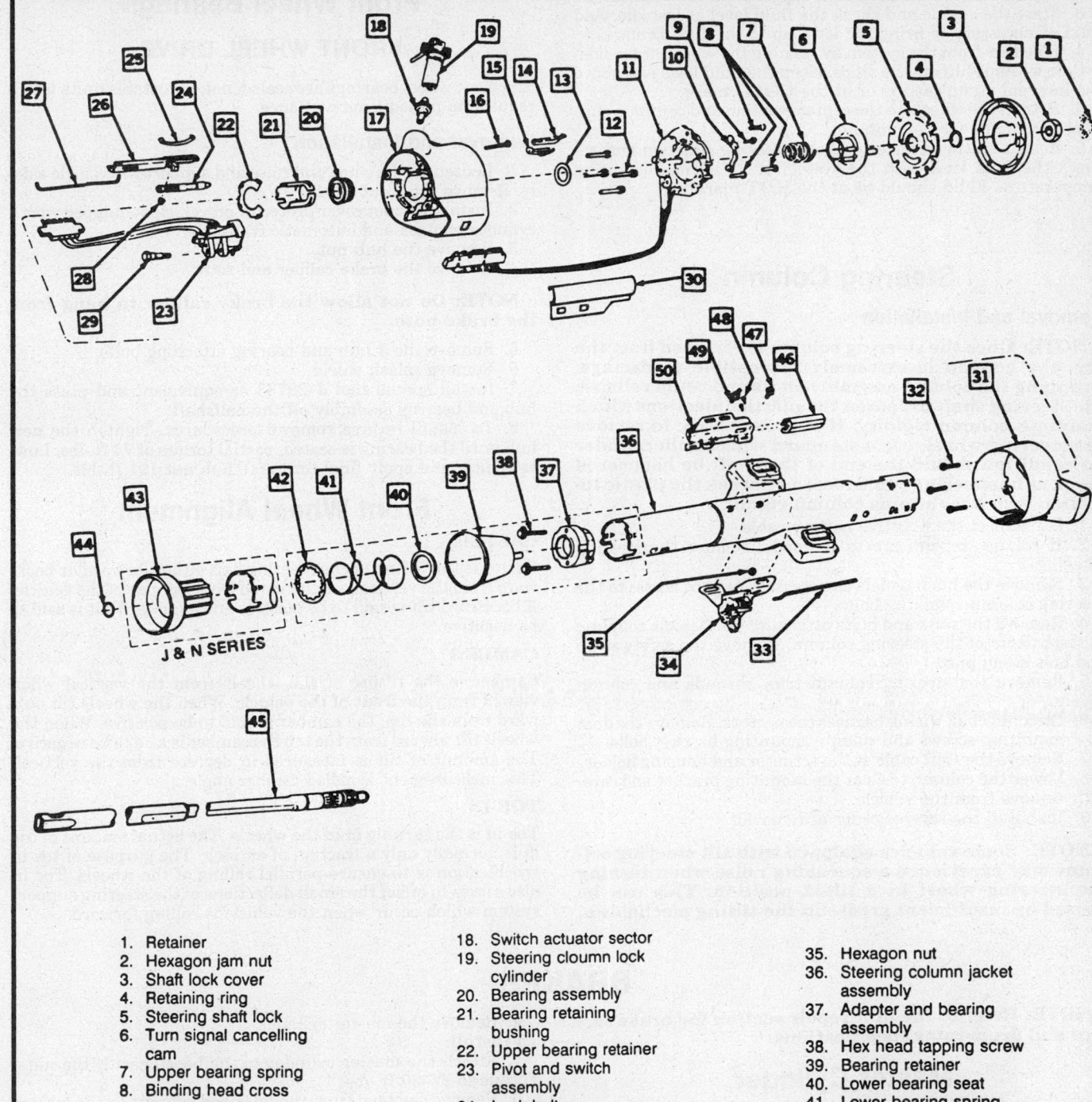

J & N SERIES

1. Retainer
2. Hexagon jam nut
3. Shaft lock cover
4. Retaining ring
5. Steering shaft lock
6. Turn signal cancelling cam
7. Upper bearing spring
8. Binding head cross recess screw
9. Round washer head assembly
10. Signal switch arm
11. Turn signal switch
12. Hex head tapping screw
13. Thrust washer
14. Buzzer switch assembly
15. Buzzer switch retaining clip
16. Lock retaining screw
17. Steering column housing

18. Switch actuator sector
19. Steering cloumn lock cylinder
20. Bearing assembly
21. Bearing retaining bushing
22. Upper bearing retainer
23. Pivot and switch assembly
24. Lock bolt
25. Rack preload spring
26. Switch actuator rack
27. Switch actuator rod
28. Spring thrust washer
29. Switch actuator pivot pin
30. Wiring protector
31. Floor shift bowl
32. Cross rocess screw
33. Dimmer switch actuator rod
34. Dimmer switch assembly

35. Hexagon nut
36. Steering column jacket assembly
37. Adapter and bearing assembly
38. Hex head tapping screw
39. Bearing retainer
40. Lower bearing seat
41. Lower bearing spring
42. Lower spring retainer
43. Steering column jacket bushing
44. Retaining ring
45. Steering shaft assembly
46. Ignition switch housing assembly
47. Washer head screw
48. Pan head screw
49. Dimmer and ignition switch mounting stud
50. Ignition switch assembly

Standard steering column components

steering fluid to the **COLD** mark on the fluid level indicator.

3. Start the engine and check the fluid level at fast idle. Add fluid, if necessary to bring the level up to the **COLD** mark.

4. Bleed air from the system by turning the wheels from side-to-side without hitting the stops. Keep the fluid level just above the internal pump casting or at the **COLD** mark.

5. Return the wheels to the center position and continue running the engine for 2–3 minutes.

6. Road test the vehicle to check steering function and re-check the fluid level with the system at its normal operating temperature. Fluid should be at the **HOT** mark.

Steering Column

Removal and Installation

NOTE: Once the steering column is removed from the car, the column is extremely susceptible to damage. Dropping the column assembly on its end could collapse the steering shaft or loosen the plastic injections which maintain column rigidity. If it is necessary to remove the steering wheel, use a standard wheel puller. Under no condition should the end of the shaft be hammered upon, as hammering could loosen or break the plastic injection which maintains column rigidity.

1. Disconnect the negative battery cable.

2. If column repairs are to be made, remove the steering wheel.

3. Remove the hush panels as necessary to gain access to the steering column retaining bolts.

4. Remove the nuts and bolts attaching the flexible coupling to the bottom of the steering column. Remove the safety strap and bolt if equipped.

5. Remove the steering column trim shrouds and column covers.

6. Disconnect all wiring harness connectors. Remove the dust boot mounting screws and column mounting bracket bolts.

7. Remove the shift cable at the actuator and housing holder.

8. Lower the column to clear the mounting bracket and carefully remove from the vehicle.

9. Install in the reverse order of removal.

NOTE: Some vehicles equipped with tilt steering columns may experience a squeaking noise when turning the steering wheel in a tilted position. This can be caused by insufficient grease in the tilting mechanism.

Front Wheel Bearings

FRONT WHEEL DRIVE

The front wheel bearings are sealed, non-adjustable units which require no periodic maintenance.

Removal and Installation

1. Loosen the hub nut and raise and support the vehicle safely. Remove the front wheel.

2. Install the boot cover protector on vehicles equipped with 4 cylinder engines and automatic transaxle.

3. Remove the hub nut.

4. Remove the brake caliper and rotor.

NOTE: Do not allow the brake caliper to hang from the brake hose.

5. Remove the 3 hub and bearing attaching bolts.

6. Remove splash shield.

7. Install special tool J–28733 or equivalent and press the hub and bearing assembly off the halfshaft.

8. To install reverse removal procedures. Tighten the new hub until the bearing is seated, partial torque of 74 ft. lbs. Lower vehicle and apply final torque to hub nut 191 ft. lbs.

Front Wheel Alignment

CASTER

Caster is the tilting of the steering axis either forward or backward from the vertical, when viewed from the side of the vehicle. A backward tilt is said to be positive and a forward tilt is said to be negative.

CAMBER

Camber is the tilting of the wheels from the vertical when viewed from the front of the vehicle. When the wheels tilt outward from the top, the camber is said to be positive. When the wheels tilt inward from the top the camber is said to be negative. The amount of tilt is measured in degrees from the vertical. This measurement is called camber angle.

TOE-IN

Toe-in is the turning in of the wheels. The actual amount of toe in is normally only a fraction of an inch. The purpose of toe in specification is to ensure parallel rolling of the wheels. Toe in also serves to offset the small deflections of the steering support system which occur when the vehicle is rolling forward.

BRAKES

NOTE: Refer to the unit repair section for brake service and drum/rotor specifications.

Master Cylinder

Removal and Installation

1. Disconnect the negative battery cable. Disconnect the electrical connector from the master cylinder.

2. Place a container under the master cylinder to catch the brake fluid. Disconnect the brake tubes from the master cylinder; use a flare nut wrench or equivalent. Plug the ends of the tubes.

NOTE: Brake fluid is harmful to paint. Wipe up any spilled fluid immediately and flush the area with clear water.

3. Remove the 2 nuts attaching the master cylinder to the booster or firewall.

4. Remove the master cylinder.

To install:

5. Attach the master cylinder to the booster with the nuts. Torque to 22–30 ft. lbs.

6. Remove the tape from the lines and connect to the master cylinder. Torque to 10–15 ft. lbs. Connect the electrical lead.

7. Bleed the brakes.

NOTE: When installing a master cylinder that mounts on an angle, attempts to bleed the system (with the cylinder installed) can allow air to enter the system. To remove air, it is necesary to raise the rear of the vehicle until the master cylinder bore is level.

Bleeding System

On diagonally split brake systems, start the manual bleeding procedure with the right-rear, then the left-front, the left-rear and the right-front.

1. Clean the bleeder screw at each wheel.
2. Attach a small rubber hose to the bleed screw and place the end in a clear container of fresh brake fluid.
3. Fill the master cylinder with fresh brake fluid. The master cylinder reservoir should be checked and topped often during the bleeding procedure.
4. Have an assistant slowly pump the brake pedal and hold the pressure.
5. Open the bleeder screw about ¼ turn. The pedal should fall to the floor as air and fluid are pushed out. Close the bleeder screw while the assistant holds the pedal to the floor, then slowly release the pedal and wait 15 seconds. Repeat the process until no more air bubbles are forced from the system when the brake pedal is applied. It may be necessary to repeat this 10 or more times to get all of the air from the system.
6. Repeat this procedure on the remaining wheel cylinders and calipers.

NOTE: Remember to wait 15 seconds between each bleeding and do not pump the pedal rapidly. Rapid pumping of the brake pedal pushes the master cylinder secondary piston down the bore in a manner that makes it difficult to bleed the system.

7. Check the brake pedal for sponginess and the brake warning light for an indication of unbalanced pressure. Repeat the entire bleeding procedure to correct either of these conditions.

Power Brake Booster

Removal and Installation

1. Disconnect the negative battey cable. Remove the master cylinder from the booster. It is not necessary to disconnect the lines from the master cylinder. Move the cylinder aside.
2. Disconnect the vacuum booster pushrod from the brake

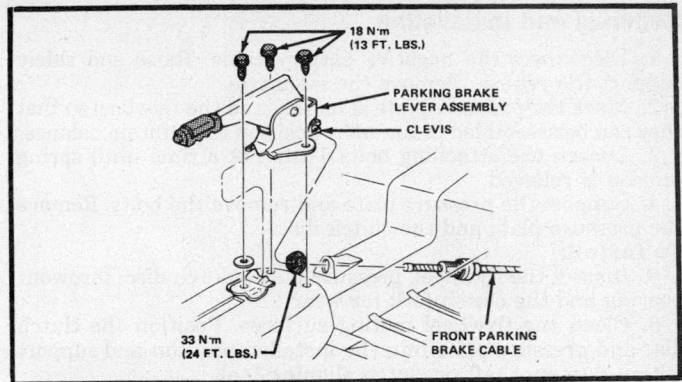

Parking brake lever

pedal inside the vehicle. Remove vacuum hose from check valve.
3. Remove the attaching nuts from inside the vehicle. Remove the booster.
4. Installation is the reverse of the removal procedure.

Parking Brake

Adjustments

1. Raise and support the vehicle with both rear wheels off the ground.
2. Pull the parking brake lever exactly 5 clicks.
3. Loosen the equalizer locknut, then tighten the adjusting nut until the right rear wheel can just be turned backwards using 2 hands, but is locked in the forward rotation.
4. Tighten the locknut. When mechanism is totally disengaged, rear wheels must turn freely in either direction with no brake drag.

CLUTCH AND TRANSAXLE

Clutch Linkage

Adjustments

These vehicles use an hydraulic clutch system which provides automatic clutch adjustment. No adjustment of the clutch linkage or pedal height is required.

Clutch Master/Slave Cylinder

Removal and Installation

NOTE: The clutch hydraulic system is serviced as a complete unit. Individual components of the system are not available separately.

1. Disconnect the negative battery terminal from the battery.
2. Remove the hush panel from the under the dash.

NOTE: On vehicles equipped with the 2.8L engine, remove the air cleaner, mass air flow sensor and air intake duct as an assembly. Disconnect electrical lead at the washer bottle and remove washer bottle from vehicle.

3. Disconnect the master cylinder pushrod from the clutch pedal.
4. Remove the master cylinder-to-cowl brace nuts and remove master cylinder.
5. Remove the slave cylinder retaining nuts at the transaxle and remove slave cylinder. Remove the hydraulic system as a unit from the vehicle.
6. Installation is the reverse of the removal procedure. Bleed the hydraulic system.

NOTE: Do not remove the plastic pushrod retainer from the slave cylinder. The strap will break on the first clutch pedal application.

Bleeding Hydraulic System

1. Clean dirt and grease from the cap to ensure no foreign substances enter the system.
2. Fill reservoir to the top with approved brake fluid only.

NOTE: Brake fluid must be certified to DOT 3 specification.

3. Fully loosen the bleed screw which is in the slave cylinder body.
4. Fluid will now begin to move from the master cylinder, down the tube, to the slave cylinder. The reservoir must be kept full at all times.
5. When the slave cylinder is full, a steady stream of fluid will come from the slave outlet. At this point, tighten bleed screw.
6. Start the engine, push the clutch pedal to the floor and select reverse gear. There should be no grating of gears. If there is the system still contains air.

Clutch Assembly

— CAUTION —

The clutch plate contains asbestos, which has been determined to be a cancer causing agent. Never clean the clutch surfaces with compressed air. Avoid inhaling any dust from any clutch surface.

Removal and Installation

1. Disconnect the negative battery cable. Raise and safely support the vehicle. Remove the transaxle.
2. Mark the pressure plate assembly and the flywheel so that they can be assembled in the same position to maintain balance.
3. Loosen the attaching bolts 1 turn at a time until spring tension is relieved.
4. Support the pressure plate and remove the bolts. Remove the pressure plate and the clutch disc.

To install:

5. Inspect the flywheel, pressure plate, clutch disc, throwout bearing and the clutch fork for wear.
6. Clean the flywheel mating surfaces. Position the clutch disc and pressure plate into the installed position and support with a dummy shaft or clutch aligning tool.

NOTE: Clutch plate must be installed correctly. Clutch plate is marked INSTALL FLYWHEEL SIDE. Always replace clutch and pressure plate as a set.

7. Install the pressure plate-to-flywheel bolts. Tighten them in a criss-cross pattern.
8. Lubricate the outside grooves and the inside recess of the release bearing with high temperature grease. Wipe off any excess. Install the release bearing.
9. Install the transaxle.

Manual Transaxle

Removal and Installation

1. Disconnect the negative battery cable.
2. Install an engine holding bar so that one end is supported on the cowl tray over the wiper motor and the other end rests on the radiator support. Use padding and be careful not to damage the paint or body work with the bar. Attach a lifting hook to the engine lift ring and to the bar and raise the engine enough to take the pressure off the motor mounts.

NOTE: If a lifting bar and hook is not available, a chain hoist can be used, however, during the procedure the vehicle must be raised, at which time the chain hoist must be adjusted to keep tension on the engine/transaxle assembly.

3. Remove the heater hose clamp at the transaxle mount bracket. Disconnect the electrical connector and remove the horn assembly.
4. Remove the transaxle mount attaching bolts. Discard the bolts attaching the mount to the side frame; new bolts must be used at installation.
5. Disconnect the clutch master cylinder pushrod from the clutch pedal and disconnect the clutch slave cylinder from the transaxle support bracket and move it aside.
6. Remove the transaxle mount bracket attaching bolts and nuts.
7. Disconnect the ground cables at the transaxle mounting stud.
8. Remove the 4 upper transaxle-to-engine mounting bolts.
9. Raise the vehicle and support it on stands. Remove the left front wheel.
10. Remove the left front inner splash shield. Remove the transaxle strut and bracket.
11. Remove the clutch housing cover bolts.
12. Disconnect the speedometer cable at the transaxle.
13. Disconnect the stabilizer bar at the left suspension support and control arm.
14. Disconnect the ball joint from the steering knuckle.
15. Remove the left suspension support attaching bolts and remove the support and control arm as an assembly.
16. Install boot protectors and disengage the drive axles at the transaxle. Remove the left side shaft from the transaxle.

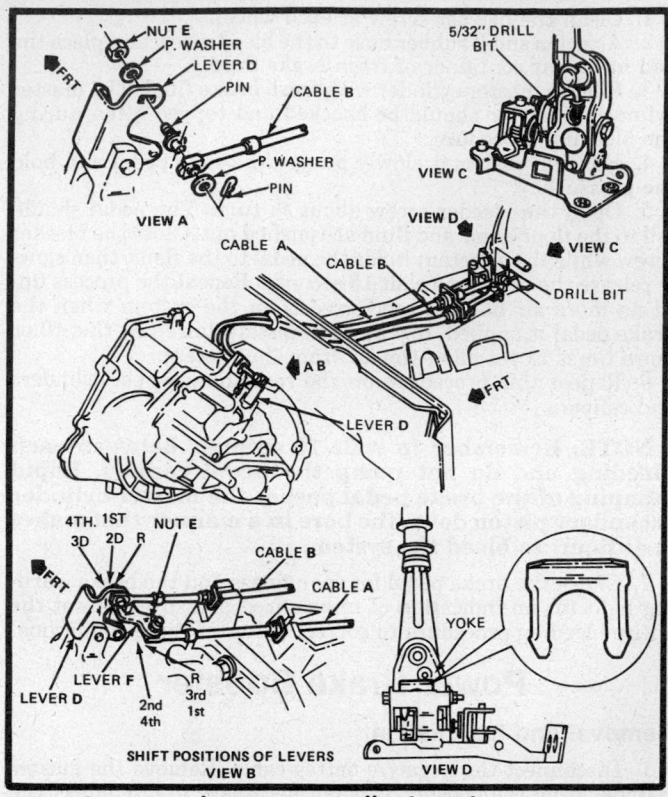

Manual transaxle on car adjustment

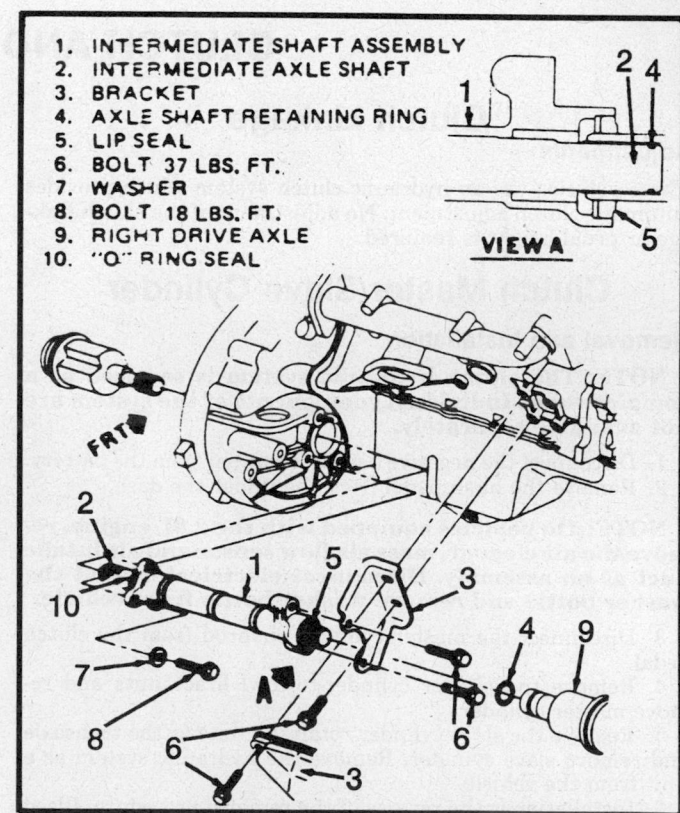

1. INTERMEDIATE SHAFT ASSEMBLY
2. INTERMEDIATE AXLE SHAFT
3. BRACKET
4. AXLE SHAFT RETAINING RING
5. LIP SEAL
6. BOLT 37 LBS. FT.
7. WASHER
8. BOLT 18 LBS. FT.
9. RIGHT DRIVE AXLE
10. "O" RING SEAL

Intermediate shaft assembly—2.8L engine

17. Position a jack under the transaxle case, remove the lower 2 transaxle-to-engine mounting bolts and remove the transaxle by sliding it towards the driver's side, away from the engine. Carefully lower the jack, guiding the right shaft out the transaxle.

To install:

18. Raise the transaxle into position and guide the right drive axle into its bore as the transaxle is being raised. The right drive axle can not be readily installed after the transaxle is connected to the engine.

19. Installation of the remaining components is in the reverse order of removal with the following notes:

   a. Tighten the transaxle-to-engine mounting bolts to 55 ft. lbs.

   b. Tighten the suspension support-to-body attaching bolts to 75 ft. lbs. and the clutch housing cover bolts to 10 ft. lbs.

   c. Using new bolts, install and tighten the transaxle mount-to-side frame to 40 ft. lbs.

   d. When installing the bolts attaching the mount-to-transaxle bracket, check the alignment bolt at the engine mount. If excessive effort is required to remove the alignment bolt, realign the powertrain components and tighten the bolts to 40 ft. lbs. and remove the alignment bolt.

Shift Cable Adjustment

1. Disconnect the negative battery terminal from the battery.
2. Shift the transaxle into 1st gear.
3. Loosen shift cable attaching nuts **E** at transaxle lever **D** and **F**.
4. Remove the console trim plate and slide the shifter boot up the shifter handle. Remove the console.
5. With the shift lever in 1st gear position (pulled to left and held against stop), insert a yoke clip to hold the lever hard against the reverse lockout stop. Install a $5/32$ in. or No. 22 drill bit into the alignment hole at the side of shifter assembly.
6. Remove lash from the transaxle by rotating lever **D** in direction of arrow (do not force lever) while tightening the nut **E**.
7. Tighten the nut **E** on the lever **F**.
8. Remove the drill bit and yoke clip at the shifter assembly.
9. Install the console, shifter boot and trim plate.
10. Connect the battery cable and roadtest the vehicle, check for a good neutral gate feel during shifting.

Automatic Transaxle

NOTE: By September 1, 1991, Hydra-matic will have changed the name designation of the THM 125C automatic transaxle. The new name designation for this transaxle will be Hydra-matic 3T40. Transaxles built between 1989 and 1990 will serve as transitional years in which a dual system, made up of the old designation and the new designation will be in effect.

Removal and Installation

1. Disconnect the negative terminal from the battery. Remove the air cleaner, bracket, mass air flow (MAF) sensor and air tube as an assembly.
2. Disconnect the exhaust crossover from the right side manifold and remove the left side exhaust manifold, then, raise and support the manifold/crossover assembly.
3. Disconnect the T.V. cable from the throttle lever and the transaxle.
4. Remove the vent hose and the shift cable from the transaxle.

5. Remove the fluid level indicator and the filler tube.
6. Using the engine support fixture tool no. J–28467 or equivalent and the adapter tool no. J–35953 or equivalent, install them on the engine.
7. Remove the wiring harness-to-transaxle nut.
8. Label and disconnect the wires for the speed sensor, TCC connector and the neutral safety/back up light switch.
9. Remove the upper transaxle-to-engine bolts.
10. Remove the transaxle-to-mount through bolt, the transaxle mount bracket and the mount.
11. Raise and safely support the vehicle.
12. Remove the front wheel assemblies.
13. Disconnect the shift cable bracket from the transaxle.
14. Remove the left side splash shield.
15. Using a modified drive axle seal protector tool no. J–34754 or equivalent, install one on each drive axle to protect the seal from damage and the joint from possible failure.
16. Using care not to damage the halfshaft boots, disconnect the halfshafts from the transaxle.
17. Remove the torsional and lateral strut from the transaxle. Remove the left side stabilizer link pin bolt.
18. Remove the left frame support bolts and move it out of the way.
19. Disconnect the speedometer wire from the transaxle.
20. Remove the transaxle converter cover and matchmark the converter to the flywheel for assembly.
21. Disconnect and plug the transaxle cooler pipes.
22. Remove the transaxle-to-engine support.
23. Using a transmission jack, position and secure it to the transaxle and remove the remaining transaxle-to-engine bolts.
24. Make sure that the torque converter does not fall out and remove the transaxle from the vehicle.

NOTE: The transaxle cooler and lines should be flushed any time the transaxle is removed for overhaul, or to replace the pump, case or converter.

To install:

25. Put a small amount of grease on the pilot hub of the converter and make sure that the converter is properly engaged with the pump.
26. Raise the transaxle to the engine while guiding the right-side halfshaft into the transaxle.
27. Install the lower transaxle mounting bolts, tighten to 55 ft. lbs. and remove the jack.
28. Align the converter with the marks made previously on the flywheel and install the bolts hand tight.
29. Torque the converter bolts to 46 ft. lbs.; retorque the first bolt after the others.
30. Install the starter assembly. Install the left side halfshaft.
31. Install the converter cover, oil cooler lines and cover. Install the sub-frame assembly. Install the lower engine mount retaining bolts and the transaxle mount nuts.
32. Install the right and left ball joints. Install the power steering rack, heat shield and cooler lines to the frame.
33. Install the right and left inner fender splash shields. Install the tire assemblies.
34. Lower the vehicle. Connect all electrical leads. Install the upper transaxle mount bolts, tighten to 55 ft. lbs.
35. Attach the crossover pipe to the exhaust manifold. Connect the EGR tube to the crossover.
36. Connect the T.V. cable and the shift cable. Install the air cleaner and inlet tube.
37. Remove the engine support tool. Connect the negative battery cable.

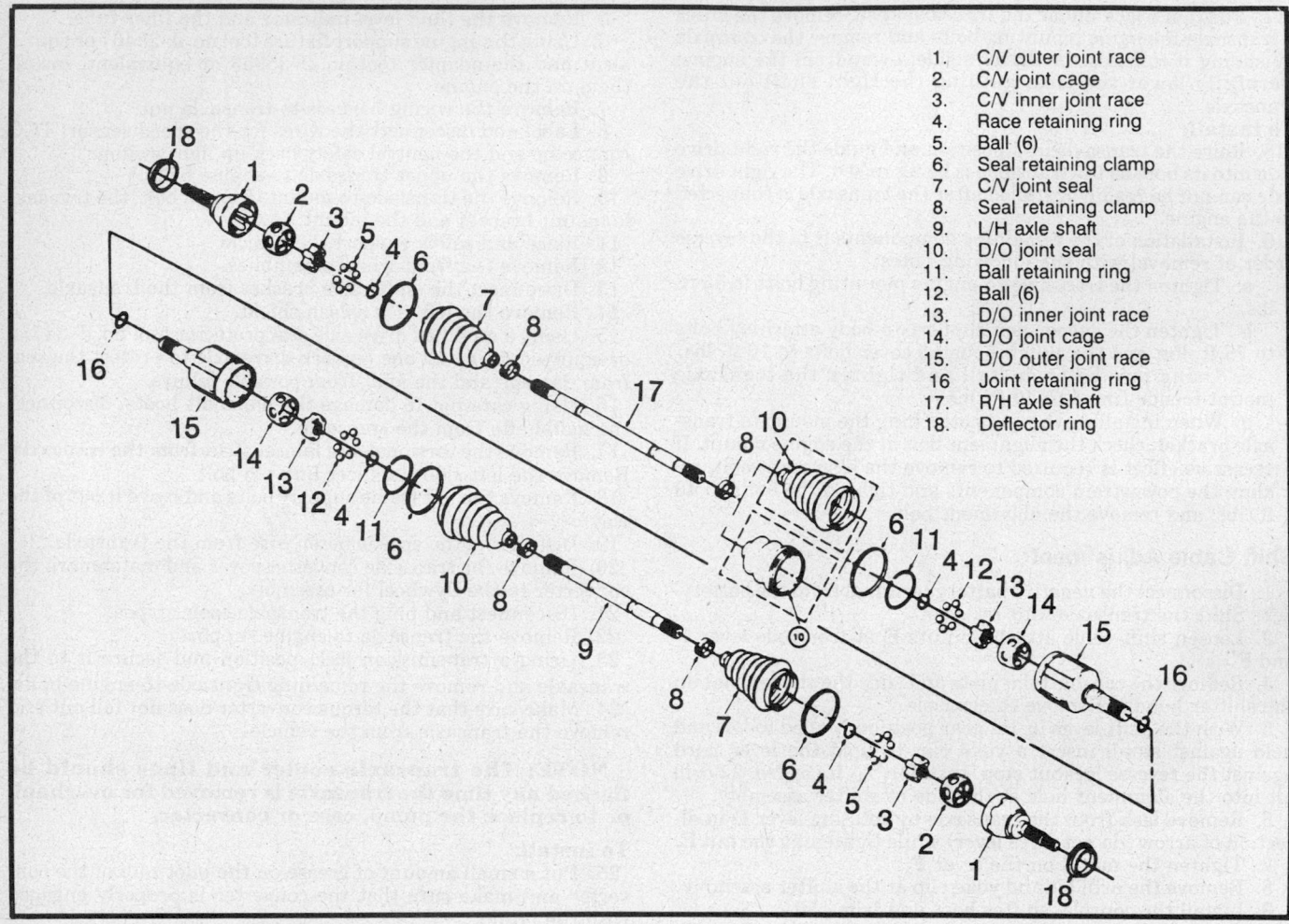

1. C/V outer joint race
2. C/V joint cage
3. C/V inner joint race
4. Race retaining ring
5. Ball (6)
6. Seal retaining clamp
7. C/V joint seal
8. Seal retaining clamp
9. L/H axle shaft
10. D/O joint seal
11. Ball retaining ring
12. Ball (6)
13. D/O inner joint race
14. D/O joint cage
15. D/O outer joint race
16 Joint retaining ring
17. R/H axle shaft
18. Deflector ring

Drive axle—double offset design

HALFSHAFTS

FRONT DRIVE AXLE

Removal and Installation

NOTE: On vehicles equipped with tri-pot joints, care must be exercised not to allow joints to become overextended. Overextending the joint could result in separation of internal components.

1. Raise and safely support the vehicle. Do not support under lower control arms.
2. Remove the wheel and tire assemblies.
3. Remove the hub nut and washer.
4. Remove the caliper bolts and support caliper. Do not let the caliper hang by the brake hose.
5. Remove the rotor and lower ball joint nut.
6. Remove the stabilizer bolt from lower control arm.

NOTE: Install the drive axle seal boot protectors J–34754 or equivalent on the outer drive seal.

7. Install J–28733 or equivalent and press the drive axle in and away from the hub. The drive axle should only be pressed in until the press fit between the drive axle and hub is loose.
8. Separate and remove the lower ball joint from the steering knuckle.

9. Install J–28468 or equivalent and slide hammer assembly. Remove the drive axle.

To install:

10. To install the drive axle, start the splines of the drive axle into the transaxle and push drive axle inward until it snaps into place.
11. Verify that the drive axle is seated into the transaxle by grasping on the housing and pulling outboard.
12. Torque the new axle shaft nut to 74 ft. lbs. Lower the vehicle and apply a final torque to the axle shaft nut of 191 ft. lbs.
13. The remainder of the installation is the reverse of the removal procedure.

NOTE: On some vehicles equipped with the 2.8L engine and a manual transaxle, an intermediate shaft assembly is used. The intermediate shaft is removed similar to the regular drive axle.

Boot

Removal and Installation
OUTER

1. Remove the drive axle assembly.
2. Remove the steel deflector ring by using brass drift to tap it

off. If the rubber ring is used, slide it off.

3. Cut the seal retaining clamps and lift the boot up to gain access to retaining ring.

4. Using snapring pliers J–8059 or equivalent, spread the retaining ring inside the outer CV-joint and remove joint from shaft.

5. Slide the boot off shaft.

To install:

6. Clean the splines of the shaft and the CV-joint with solvent and repack the joint. Install a new retaining ring inside the joint.

NOTE: When repacking CV-joint, make sure to add grease to axle boot.

7. Install the inner boot clamp, boot, outer boot clamp on shaft.

8. Push the joint assembly onto the shaft until the ring is seated on the shaft.

9. Slide the boot and 2 clamps onto the joint and install the clamps on both the inner and outer part of the boot. Install deflector ring.

10. Install the drive axle assembly.

INNER

1. Remove the drive axle assembly.

2. Cut the seal retaining clamps and lift the boot up to gain access to retaining ring for spider assembly.

3. Using snapring pliers J–8059 or equivalent, remove the retaining ring from shaft and remove the spider assembly. Slide the old boot off axle shaft.

To install:

4. Clean the splines of the shaft and the CV-joint with solvent and repack the joint.

NOTE: When repacking CV-joint, make sure to add grease to axle boot.

5. Install the inner boot clamp, boot, outer boot clamp on shaft.

6. Push the tri-pot assembly onto the shaft until the retaining ring is seated on the shaft.

7. Slide the boot and 2 clamps onto the joint and install the clamps on both the inner and outer part of the boot.

8. Install the drive axle assembly.

NOTE: Be sure the spacer ring is seated in groove on axle at reassembly.

CV-Joint

Refer to the Unit Repair section for overhaul procedures.

REAR AXLE AND REAR SUSPENSION

For axle overhaul procedures and suspension services, refer to Unit Repair section.

For suspension services, refer to Unit Repair section.

Rear Axle Assembly

Removal and Installation

1. Raise and safely support the rear of the vehicle.

2. If equipped, remove the stabilizer bar from the axle assembly.

3. Remove the wheel and tire assemblies.

NOTE: Do not hammer on the brake drum as damage to the wheel bearing may result.

4. Remove the lower shock absorber-to-axle assembly nuts/bolts and separate the shock absorbers from the rear axle assembly.

5. Disconnect the parking brake cable from the rear axle assembly.

6. Disconnect the brake lines from the rear axle assembly.

7. Lower the rear axle assembly, then remove the coil springs and the insulators.

8. Remove the rear axle assembly-to-chassis bolts and lower the axle assembly.

9. Installation is the reverse of removal.

Rear Wheel Bearing and Oil Seal

Removal and Installation

1. Raise and safely support the rear of the vehicle.

2. Remove the wheel and tire assembly.

3. Remove the brake drum.

NOTE: Do not hammer on the brake drum during removal or damage to the assembly could result.

4. Remove the 4 hub/bearing assembly-to-rear axle assembly nuts/bolts and the hub/bearing assembly from the axle.

NOTE: The top-rear attaching bolt will not clear the brake shoe when removing the hub and bearing assembly. Partially remove the hub prior to removing this bolt.

5. Installation is the reverse of the removal procedure.

Rear Wheel Bearings

Adjustment

The rear wheel bearing assembly is non-adjustable and is serviced by replacement only.

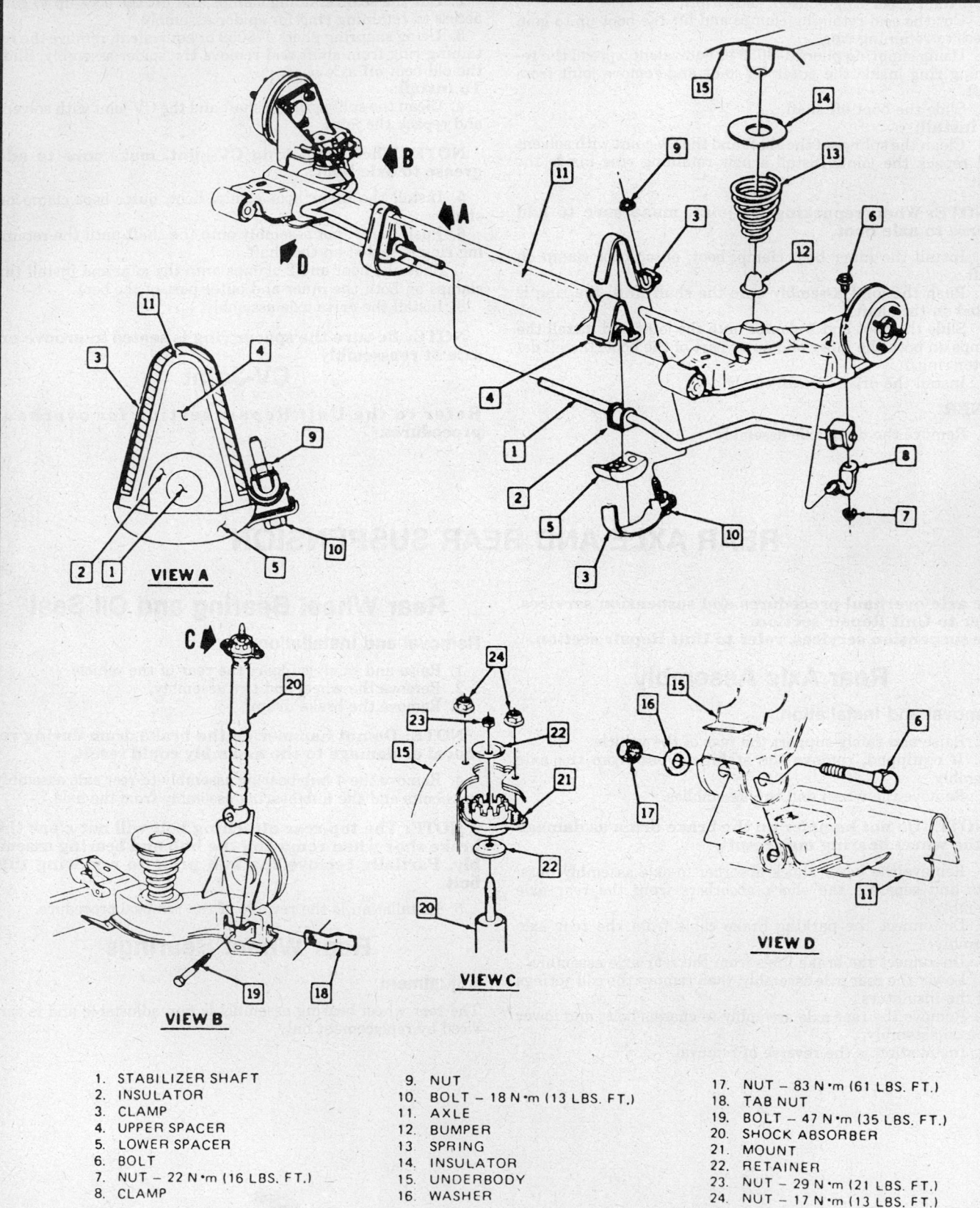

VIEW A

VIEW B

VIEW C

VIEW D

1. STABILIZER SHAFT
2. INSULATOR
3. CLAMP
4. UPPER SPACER
5. LOWER SPACER
6. BOLT
7. NUT — 22 N·m (16 LBS. FT.)
8. CLAMP

9. NUT
10. BOLT — 18 N·m (13 LBS. FT.)
11. AXLE
12. BUMPER
13. SPRING
14. INSULATOR
15. UNDERBODY
16. WASHER

17. NUT — 83 N·m (61 LBS. FT.)
18. TAB NUT
19. BOLT — 47 N·m (35 LBS. FT.)
20. SHOCK ABSORBER
21. MOUNT
22. RETAINER
23. NUT — 29 N·m (21 LBS. FT.)
24. NUT — 17 N·m (13 LBS. FT.)

Rear axle assembly

YEAR IDENTIFICATION

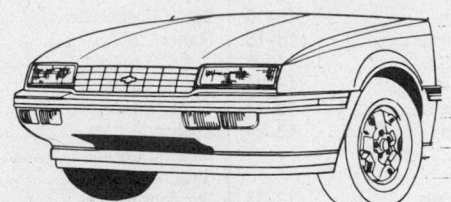

1987–88 Beretta and Corsica

1989–90 Beretta and Corsica

VEHICLE IDENTIFICATION

It is important for servicing and ordering parts to be certain of the vehicle and engine identification. The VIN (vehicle identification number) is a 17 digit number visible through the windshield on the driver's side of the dash and contains the vehicle and engine identification codes. The tenth digit indicates model year, and the eighth digit indicates engine code. It can be interpreted as follows:

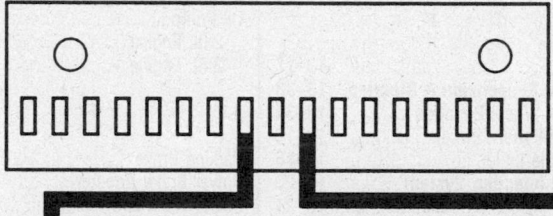

Engine Code						Model Year	
Code	Cu. In.	Liters	Cyl.	Fuel Sys.	Eng. Mfg.	Code	Year
1	121	2.0	4	TBI	Chevrolet	H	1987
W	173	2.8	V6	MPI	Chevrolet	J	1988
						K	1989
						L	1990

ENGINE IDENTIFICATION

Year	Model	Engine Displacement cu. in. (liter)	Engine Series Identification (VIN)	No. of Cylinders	Engine Type
1987	Beretta	121 (2.0)	1	4	OHV
	Beretta	173 (2.8)	W	6	OHV
	Corsica	121 (2.0)	1	4	OHV
	Corsica	173 (2.8)	W	6	OHV
1988	Beretta	121 (2.0)	1	4	OHV
	Beretta	173 (2.8)	W	6	OHV
	Corsica	121 (2.0)	1	4	OHV
	Corsica	173 (2.8)	W	6	OHV
1989-90	Beretta	121 (2.0)	1	4	OHV
	Beretta	173 (2.8)	W	6	OHV
	Corsica	121 (2.0)	1	4	OHV
	Corsica	173 (2.8)	W	6	OHV

OHV Overhead Valves

GENERAL ENGINE SPECIFICATIONS

Year	VIN	No. Cylinder Displacement cu. in. (liter)	Fuel System Type	Net Horsepower @ rpm	Net Torque @ rpm (ft.lbs.)	Bore × Stroke (in.)	Compression Ratio	Oil Pressure @ rpm
1987	1	4-121 (2.0)	TBI	90 @ 5600	108 @ 3200	3.500 × 3.150	9.0:1	63-77 @ 1200
	W	6-173 (2.8)	MPI	125 @ 4500	160 @ 3600	3.500 × 2.990	8.9:1	50-65 @ 1200
1988	1	4-121 (2.0)	TBI	90 @ 5600	108 @ 3200	3.500 × 3.150	9.0:1	63-77 @ 1200
	W	6-173 (2.8)	MPI	125 @ 4500	160 @ 3600	3.500 × 2.990	8.9:1	50-65 @ 1200
1989-90	1	4-121 (2.0)	TBI	90 @ 5600	108 @ 3200	3.500 × 3.150	9.0:1	63-77 @ 1200
	W	6-173 (2.8)	MPI	125 @ 4500	160 @ 3600	3.500 × 2.990	8.9:1	50-65 @ 1200

MPI Multi-Port Fuel Injection
TBI Throttle Body Injection

GASOLINE ENGINE TUNE-UP SPECIFICATIONS
Refer to Section 34 for all spark plug recommendations

Year	VIN	No. Cylinder Displacement cu. in. (liter)	Spark Plugs Gap (in.)	Ignition Timing (deg.) MT	Ignition Timing (deg.) AT	Compression Pressure (psi)	Fuel Pump (psi)	Idle Speed (rpm) MT	Idle Speed (rpm) AT	Valve Clearance In.	Valve Clearance Ex.
1987	1	4-121 (2.0)	0.035	①	①	②	10-12	①	①	Hyd.	Hyd.
	W	6-173 (2.8)	0.045	①	①	②	10-12	①	①	Hyd.	Hyd.
1988	1	4-121 (2.0)	0.035	①	①	②	10-12	①	①	Hyd.	Hyd.
	W	6-173 (2.8)	0.045	①	①	②	10-12	①	①	Hyd.	Hyd.
1989	1	4-121 (2.0)	0.035	①	①	②	10-12	①	①	Hyd.	Hyd.
	W	6-173 (2.8)	0.045	①	①	②	10-12	①	①	Hyd.	Hyd.
1990		SEE UNDERHOOD SPEICIFCATIONS STICKER									

① Ignition timing and idle speed is controlled by the electronic control module. No adjustments are possible

② When analyzing compression test results, look for uniformity among cylinders rather than specific pressures

FIRING ORDERS

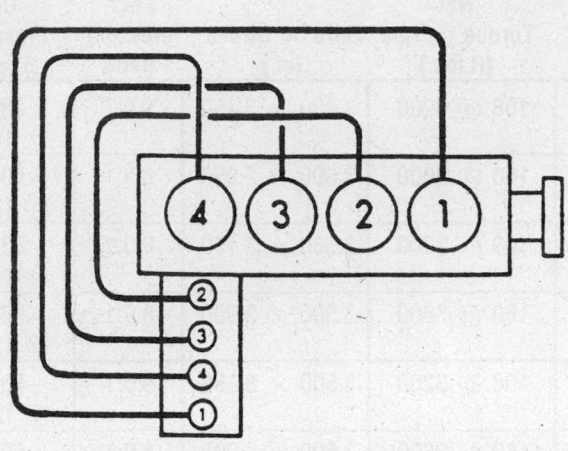

121 cu. in. 2.0L 4 cyl
Firing order: 1–3–4–2

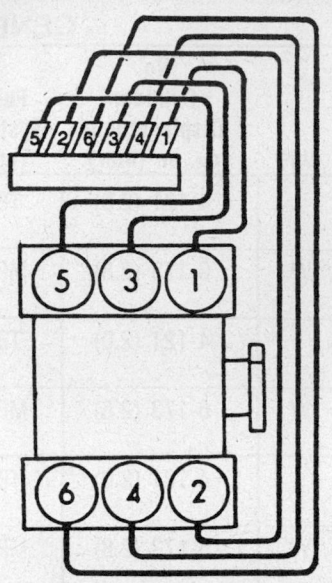

173 cu. in. 2.8L V6
Firing order: 1–2–3–4–5–6

CAPACITIES

Year	Model	VIN	No. Cylinder Displacement cu. in. (liter)	Engine Crankcase with Filter	Engine Crankcase without Filter	Transmission (pts.) 4-Spd	Transmission (pts.) 5-Spd	Transmission (pts.) Auto.	Drive Axle (pts.)	Fuel Tank (gal.)	Cooling System (qts.)
1987	Beretta	1	4-121 (2.0)	4.5	4.0	NA	5.4①	8.0②	NA	13.6	8.8
		W	6-173 (2.8)	4.5	4.0	NA	5.4①	8.0②	NA	13.6	11.4
	Corsica	1	4-121 (2.0)	4.5	4.0	NA	5.4①	8.0②	NA	13.6	8.8
		W	6-173 (2.8)	4.5	4.0	NA	5.4①	8.0②	NA	13.6	11.4
1988	Beretta	1	4-121 (2.0)	4.0	4.0	NA	5.4①	8.0②	NA	14	9.6③
		W	6-173 (2.8)	4.0	4.0	NA	5.4①	8.0②	NA	14	11④
	Corsica	1	4-121 (2.0)	4.0	4.0	NA	5.4①	8.0②	NA	14	9.6③
		W	6-173 (2.8)	4.0	4.0	NA	5.4①	8.0②	NA	14	11④
1989-90	Beretta	1	4-121 (2.0)	4.0	4.0	NA	4.0	8.0	NA	14	14.1⑤
		W	6-173 (2.8)	4.0	4.0	NA	4.0	8.0	NA	14	⑥
	Corsica	1	4-121 (2.0)	4.0	4.0	NA	4.0	8.0	NA	14	14.1⑤
		W	6-173 (2.8)	4.0	4.0	NA	4.0	8.0	NA	14	⑥

NA Not applicable
① 5 speed (Getrag)—4 pts.
② This figure is for drain and refill. After a complete overhaul, use 16.0 pts. If the torque converter is replaced, use 18.0 pts.
③ With air conditioning—9.8 qts.
④ With air conditioning—11.1 qts.
⑤ Without air conditioning—13.1 qts.
⑥ Automatic transaxle
    With air conditioning—16.6 qts.
    Without air conditioning—16.7 qts.
    Manual transaxle
    With air conditioning—16.1 qts.
    Without air conditioning—16.2 qts.

CAMSHAFT SPECIFICATIONS
All measurements given in inches.

Year	VIN	No. Cylinder Displacement cu. in. (liter)	Journal Diameter 1	2	3	4	5	Lobe Lift In.	Ex.	Bearing Clearance	Camshaft End Play
1987	1	4-121 (2.0)	1.867–1.869	1.867–1.869	1.867–1.869	1.867–1.869	1.867–1.869	0.260	0.260	0.001–0.004	NA
	W	6-173 (2.8)	1.867–1.881	1.867–1.881	1.867–1.881	1.867–1.881	— —	0.262	0.273	0.001–0.004	NA
1988	1	4-121 (2.0)	1.867–1.869	1.867–1.869	1.867–1.869	1.867–1.869	1.867–1.869	0.260	0.260	0.001–0.004	NA
	W	6-173 (2.8)	1.867–1.881	1.867–1.881	1.867–1.881	1.867–1.881	— —	0.262	0.273	0.001–0.004	NA
1989-90	1	4-121 (2.0)	1.867–1.869	1.867–1.869	1.867–1.869	1.867–1.869	1.867–1.869	0.260	0.260	0.001–0.004	NA
	W	6-173 (2.8)	1.867–1.881	1.867–1.881	1.867–1.881	1.867–1.881	— —	0.262	0.273	0.001–0.004	NA

NA Not available

CRANKSHAFT AND CONNECTING ROD SPECIFICATIONS
All measurements are given in inches.

Year	VIN	No. Cylinder Displacement cu. in. (liter)	Crankshaft Main Brg. Journal Dia.	Main Brg. Oil Clearance	Shaft End-play	Thrust on No.	Connecting Rod Journal Diameter	Oil Clearance	Side Clearance
1987	1	4-121 (2.0)	2.4945–2.4954	0.0006–0.0019	0.002–0.008	1	1.9983–1.9994	0.001–0.003	0.004–0.015
	W	6-173 (2.8)	2.6473–2.6483	0.0016–0.0033	0.0024–0.0083	4	1.9983–1.9993	0.001–0.003	0.006–0.017
1988	1	4-121 (2.0)	2.4945–2.4954	0.0006–0.0019	0.002–0.008	1	1.9983–1.9994	0.001–0.003	0.004–0.015
	W	6-173 (2.8)	2.6473–2.6483	0.0016–0.0033	0.0024–0.0083	4	1.9983–1.9993	0.001–0.003	0.006–0.017
1989-90	1	4-121 (2.0)	2.4945–2.4954	0.0006–0.0019	0.002–0.008	1	1.9983–1.9994	0.001–0.003	0.004–0.015
	W	6-173 (2.8)	2.6473–2.6483	0.0016–0.0033	0.0024–0.0083	4	1.9983–1.9993	0.001–0.003	0.006–0.017

VALVE SPECIFICATIONS

Year	VIN	No. Cylinder Displacement cu. in. (liter)	Seat Angle (deg.)	Face Angle (deg.)	Spring Test Pressure (lbs.)	Spring Installed Height (in.)	Stem-to-Guide Clearance (in.) Intake	Exhaust	Stem Diameter (in.) Intake	Exhaust
1987	1	4-121 (2.0)	46	45	73-81 @ 1.6	1.60①	0.0011–0.0023	0.0014–0.0028	NA	NA
	W	6-173 (2.8)	46	45	90 @ 1.7	1.70①	0.0010–0.0027	0.0010–0.0027	NA	NA
1988	1	4-121 (2.0)	46	45	73-81 @ 1.6	1.60①	0.0011–0.0023	0.0014–0.0028	NA	NA

VALVE SPECIFICATIONS

Year	VIN	No. Cylinder Displacement cu. in. (liter)	Seat Angle (deg.)	Face Angle (deg.)	Spring Test Pressure (lbs.)	Spring Installed Height (in.)	Stem-to-Guide Clearance (in.) Intake	Stem-to-Guide Clearance (in.) Exhaust	Stem Diameter (in.) Intake	Stem Diameter (in.) Exhaust
	W	6-173 (2.8)	46	45	90 @ 1.7	1.70①	0.0010–0.0027	0.0010–0.0027	NA	NA
1989-90	1	4-121 (2.0)	46	45	73-81 @ 1.6	1.60①	0.0011–0.0023	0.0014–0.0028	NA	NA
	W	6-173 (2.8)	46	45	90 @ 1.7	1.70①	0.0010–0.0027	0.0010–0.0027	NA	NA

NA Not available
① With valve closed

PISTON AND RING SPECIFICATIONS
All measurments are given in inches.

Year	VIN	No. Cylinder Displacement cu. in. (liter)	Piston Clearance	Ring Gap Top Compression	Ring Gap Bottom Compression	Ring Gap Oil Control	Ring Side Clearance Top Compression	Ring Side Clearance Bottom Compression	Ring Side Clearance Oil Control
1987	1	4-121 (2.0)	0.0010–0.0022	0.010–0.020	0.010–0.020	0.010–0.050	0.001–0.003	0.001–0.003	0.0080
	W	6-173 (2.8)	0.0020–0.0030	0.010–0.020	0.010–0.020	0.020–0.055	0.001–0.003	0.001–0.003	0.0080
1988	1	4-121 (2.0)	0.0010–0.0022	0.010–0.020	0.010–0.020	0.010–0.050	0.001–0.003	0.001–0.003	0.0080
	W	6-173 (2.8)	0.0020–0.0030	0.010–0.020	0.010–0.020	0.020–0.055	0.001–0.003	0.001–0.003	0.0080
1989-90	1	4-121 (2.0)	0.0010–0.0022	0.010–0.020	0.010–0.020	0.010–0.050	0.001–0.003	0.001–0.003	0.0080
	W	6-173 (2.8)	0.0020–0.0030	0.010–0.020	0.010–0.020	0.020–0.055	0.001–0.003	0.001–0.003	0.0080

TORQUE SPECIFICATIONS
All readings in ft. lbs.

Year	VIN	No. Cylinder Displacement cu. in. (liter)	Cylinder Head Bolts	Main Bearing Bolts	Rod Bearing Bolts	Crankshaft Pulley Bolts	Flywheel Bolts	Manifold Intake	Manifold Exhaust	Spark Plugs
1987	1	4-121 (2.0)	62-70 ①	63-77	34-43	66-89	45-59②	15-22	6-13	20
	W	6-173 (2.8)	③	63-83	34-44	67-85	45-59②	18	15-23	20
1988	1	4-121 (2.0)	62-70 ①	63-77	34-43	66-89	45-59②	15-22	6-13	20
	W	6-173 (2.8)	③	63-83	34-44	67-85	45-59②	18	15-23	20
1989-90	1	4-121 (2.0)	62-70 ①	63-77	34-43	66-89	45-59②	15-22	6-13	20
	W	6-173 (2.8)	③	63-83	34-44	67-85	45-59②	18	15-23	20

① Specification is for the shorter bolts. Torque the longer bolts to 73-83 ft. lbs.

② Specification is for automatic trans-axle. Torque the manual transaxle bolts to 47-63 ft. lbs.

③ Cylinder head bolts should first be torqued to 33 ft.lbs. Then tighten the bolts by rotating the torque wrench an additional 90 degrees

WHEEL ALIGNMENT

Year	Model		Caster Range (deg.)	Caster Preferred Setting (deg.)	Camber Range (deg.)	Camber Preferred Setting (deg.)	Toe-in (in.)	Steerig Axis Inclination (deg.)
1987	Beretta	Front	$7/10$P-$2\ 7/10$P	$1\ 7/10$P①	$3/10$P-$1\ 3/10$P	$8/10$P	$1/16$N-$1/16$P	—
		Rear	—	—	0-$1\ 3/10$P	$1/10$P	$1/8$P	—
	Corsica	Front	$7/10$P-$2\ 7/10$P	$1\ 7/10$P①	$3/10$P-$1\ 3/10$P	$4/5$P	$1/16$N-$1/16$P	—
		Rear	—	—	$3/10$P-$1\ 2/10$P	$1/4$P	$1/8$P	—
1988	Beretta	Front	$7/10$P-$2\ 7/10$P	$1\ 7/10$P①	$3/10$P-$1\ 3/10$P	$8/10$P	$1/16$N-$1/16$P	—
		Rear	—	—	0-$1\ 3/10$P	$1/10$P	$1/8$P	—
	Corsica	Front	$7/10$P-$2\ 7/10$P	$1\ 7/10$P①	$3/10$P-$1\ 3/10$P	$4/5$P	$1/16$N-$1/16$P	—
		Rear	—	—	$3/10$P-$1\ 2/10$P	$1/4$P	$1/8$P	—
1989-90	Beretta	Front	$2/5$P-$1\ 9/10$P	$1\ 2/10$P	0-$1\ 2/10$P	$6/10$P	0	—
		Rear	—	—	$9/10$N-$4/10$P	$1/4$P	$5/16$P	—
	Corsica	Front	$2/5$P-$1\ 9/10$P	$1\ 2/10$P	0-$1\ 2/10$P	$6/10$P	0	—
		Rear	—	—	$8/10$N-$3/10$P	$1/4$P	$1/4$P	—

① Not adjustable

ELECTRICAL

NOTE: Disconnecting the negative battery cable on some vehicles may interfere with the functions of the on board computer systems and may require the computer to undergo a relearning process, once the negative battery cable is reconnected.

For testing and overhaul procedures on starters, alternators and voltage regulators, refer to the Unit Repair Section.

Charging System

ALTERNATOR

Removal and Installation

1. Disconnect the negative battery terminal.
2. Label and disconnect the electrical connectors from the back of the alternator.
3. Loosen the alternator mounting bolts.
4. Remove the serpentine drive belt.
5. Remove the alternator-to-bracket bolts and the alternator.
6. To install, reverse the removal procedures.

VOLTAGE REGULATOR

An alternator with an integral voltage regulator is standard equipment. There are no adjustments possible with this unit. Should the voltage regulator require repair, the alternator must be disassembled.

BELT TENSION

A single (serpentine) belt is used to drive all engine mounted

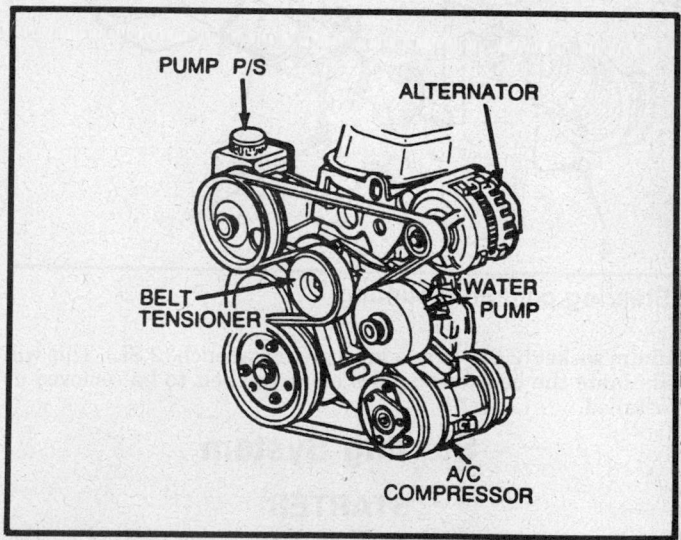

View of the drive belt routing—2.0L engine

components. Drive belt tension is maintained by a spring loaded tensioner.

NOTE: The drive belt tensioner can control belt tension over a wide range of belt lengths; however, there are limits to the tensioner's ability to compensate for various belt lengths. Installing the wrong size belt and using the tensioner outside its operating range can result in poor tension control and/or damage to the tensioner, belt and driven components.

Removal and Installation

To remove or install the drive belt, rotate the tensioner with a

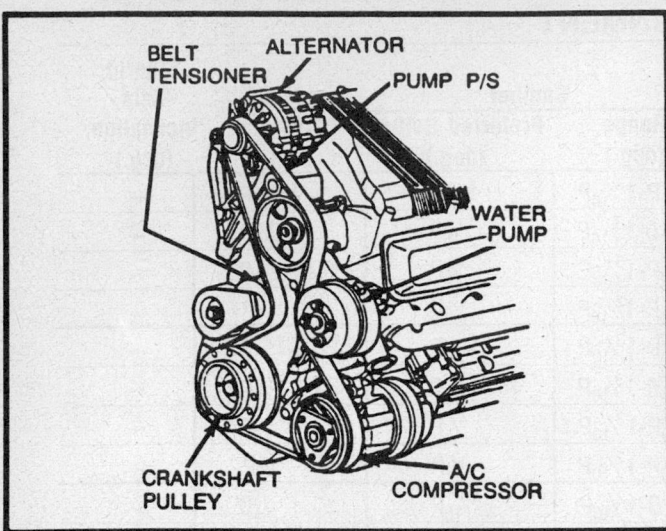

View of the drive belt routing—2.8L engine

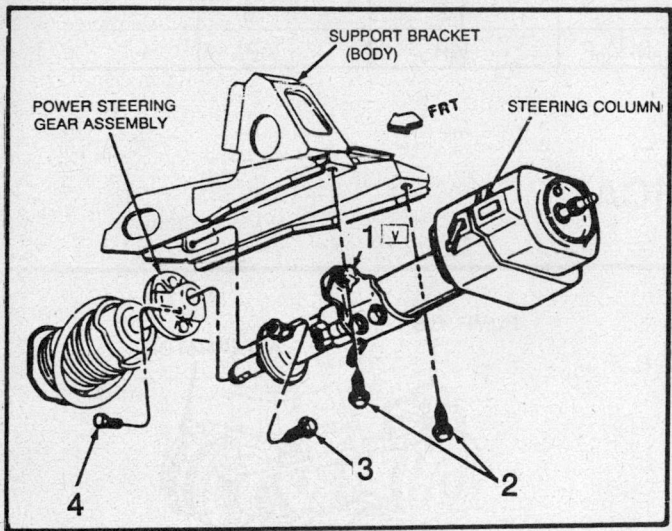

Steering column mounting

15mm socket (2.0L) or a ¾ in. open end wrench (2.8L). This will eliminate the belt tension and allow the belt to be removed or installed.

Starting System

STARTER

Removal and Installation

1. Disconnect the negative battery terminal.
2. Raise and safely support the vehicle.
3. Label and disconnect the electrical connectors from the starter.
4. On the 2.0L engine, remove the rear starter motor support bracket and air conditioning compressor support rod.
5. Remove the starter-to-engine bolts and the starter.
6. To install, reverse the removal procedures; reinstall any shims that were removed. Torque the starter-to-engine bolts to 32 ft. lbs. (43 Nm).

Ignition System

All engines use a distributorless ignition. Distributorless igni-

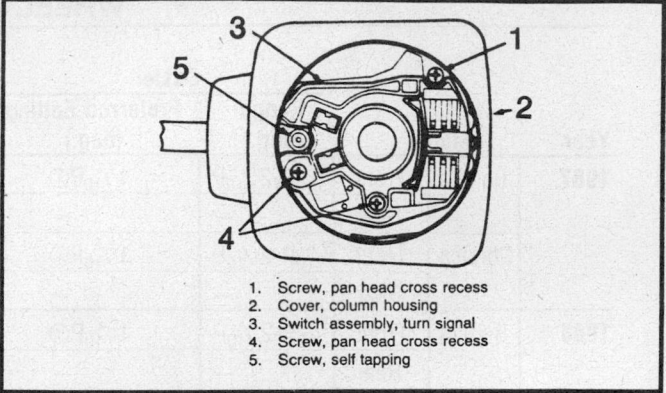

1. Screw, pan head cross recess
2. Cover, column housing
3. Switch assembly, turn signal
4. Screw, pan head cross recess
5. Screw, self tapping

Turn signal switch mounting

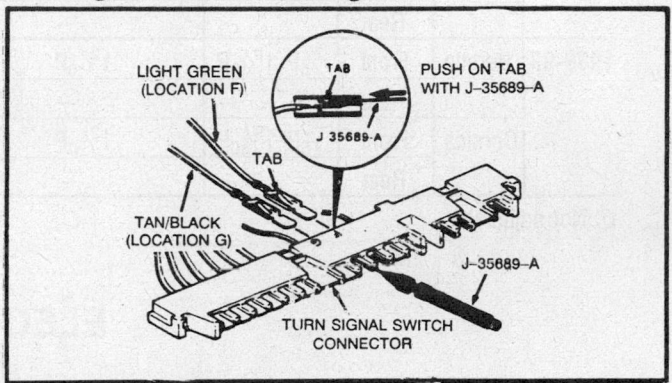

Removing terminals from turn signal switch connector

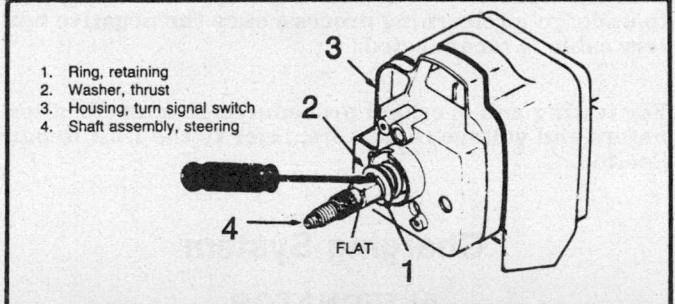

1. Ring, retaining
2. Washer, thrust
3. Housing, turn signal switch
4. Shaft assembly, steering

Removing turn signal switch housing

tion systems use a waste spark method of spark distribution. Each cylinder is paired with its comparison cylinder in the firing order. This places 1 cylinder on the compression stroke with the comparison cylinder on the exhaust stroke. The cylinder that is on the exhaust stroke uses very little spark allowing most of the spark to go to the cylinder on the compression stroke. This process reverses when the cylinder roles reverse. There are 2 coils for the 2.0L engine and 3 coils for the 2.8L engine. The Direct Ignition System (DIS) is used on both engines.

Since no distributor is used, the timing references are gathered from the engine sensors.

IGNITION TIMING

Adjustment

Ignition timing is controlled by the Electronic Control Module (ECM). No adjustments are possible.

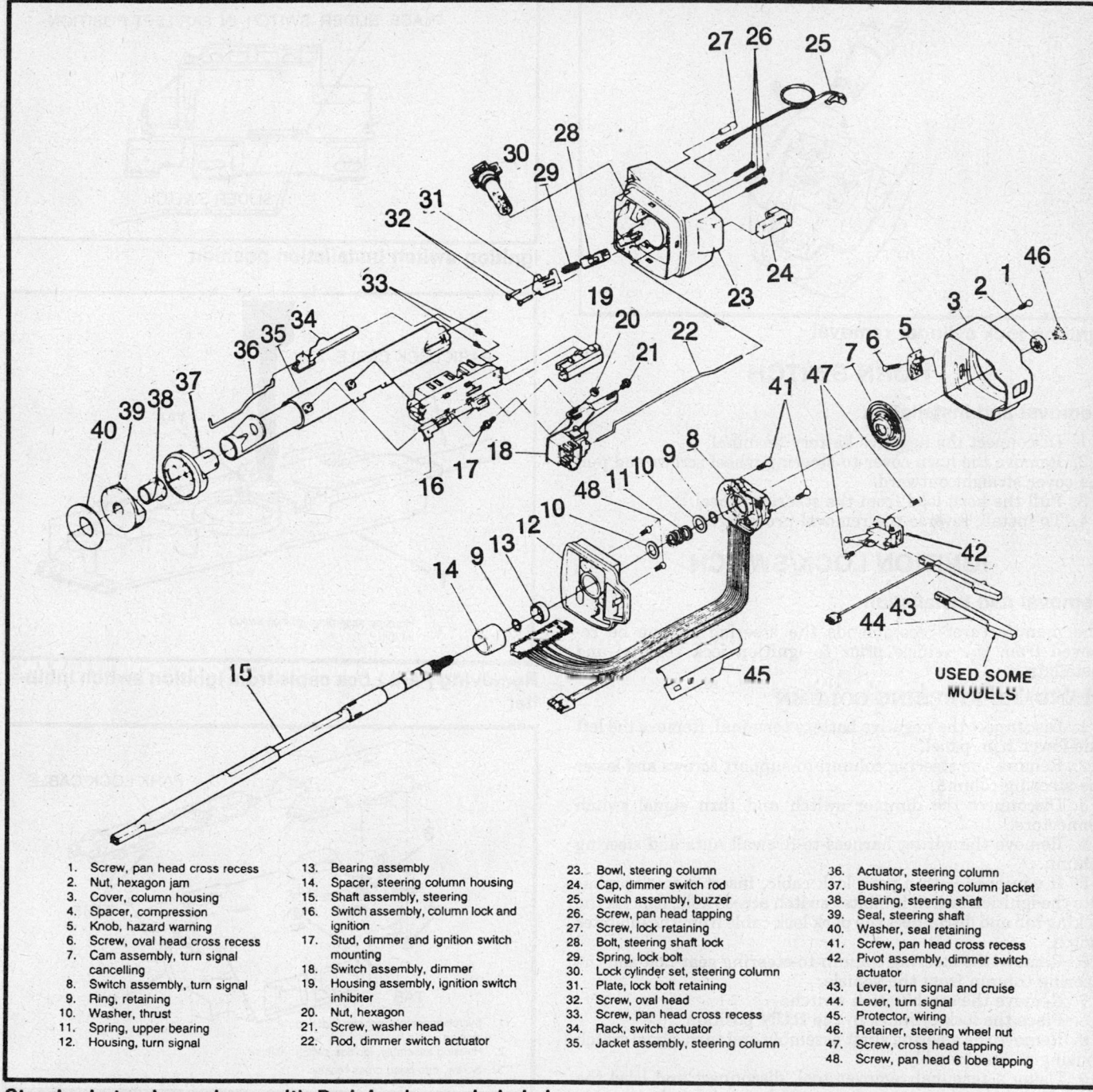

1. Screw, pan head cross recess	13. Bearing assembly	23. Bowl, steering column	36. Actuator, steering column
2. Nut, hexagon jam	14. Spacer, steering column housing	24. Cap, dimmer switch rod	37. Bushing, steering column jacket
3. Cover, column housing	15. Shaft assembly, steering	25. Switch assembly, buzzer	38. Bearing, steering shaft
4. Spacer, compression	16. Switch assembly, column lock and	26. Screw, pan head tapping	39. Seal, steering shaft
5. Knob, hazard warning	ignition	27. Screw, lock retaining	40. Washer, seal retaining
6. Screw, oval head cross recess	17. Stud, dimmer and ignition switch	28. Bolt, steering shaft lock	41. Screw, pan head cross recess
7. Cam assembly, turn signal	mounting	29. Spring, lock bolt	42. Pivot assembly, dimmer switch
cancelling	18. Switch assembly, dimmer	30. Lock cylinder set, steering column	actuator
8. Switch assembly, turn signal	19. Housing assembly, ignition switch	31. Plate, lock bolt retaining	43. Lever, turn signal and cruise
9. Ring, retaining	inhibiter	32. Screw, oval head	44. Lever, turn signal
10. Washer, thrust	20. Nut, hexagon	33. Screw, pan head cross recess	45. Protector, wiring
11. Spring, upper bearing	21. Screw, washer head	34. Rack, switch actuator	46. Retainer, steering wheel nut
12. Housing, turn signal	22. Rod, dimmer switch actuator	35. Jacket assembly, steering column	47. Screw, cross head tapping
			48. Screw, pan head 6 lobe tapping

Standard steering column with Park Lock—exploded view

Electrical Controls

STEERING WHEEL

Removal and Installation

1. Disconnect the negative battery terminal. Turn the steering wheel so the wheels are in the straight ahead position.

2. From the rear of the steering wheel, remove the horn cover-to-steering wheel screws. Disconnect the horn electrical connector from the steering wheel.

3. Remove the steering wheel-to-column retainer, nut, washer (if equipped) and damper assembly.

4. Using a marking tool, mark the steering wheel alignment with the steering shaft for realignment purposes.

5. Using a steering wheel puller, press the steering wheel from the steering column.

6. To install, reverse the removal procedures. Torque the steering wheel nut to 30 ft. lbs.

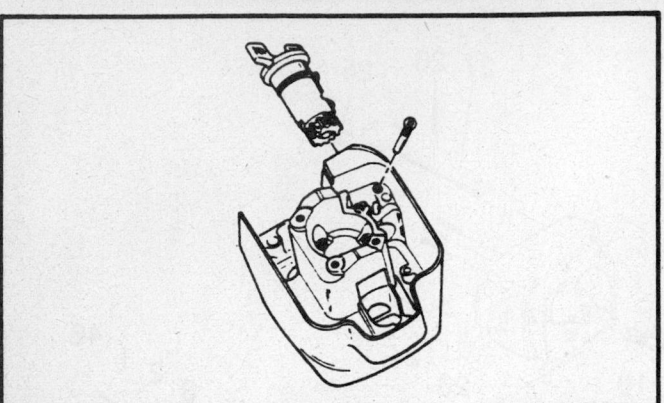

Ignition lock cylinder removal

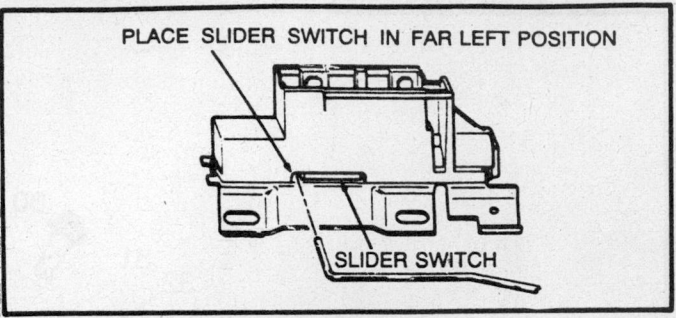

PLACE SLIDER SWITCH IN FAR LEFT POSITION

SLIDER SWITCH

Ignition switch installation position

HORN SWITCH

Removal and Installation

1. Disconnect the negative battery terminal.
2. Remove the horn cover-to-steering wheel screws and pull the cover straight outward.
3. Pull the horn lead from the steering wheel.
4. To install, reverse the removal procedures.

IGNITION LOCK/SWITCH

Removal and Installation

The manufacturer recommends the steering column be removed from the vehicle prior to ignition lock removal and installation.

STANDARD STEERING COLUMN

1. Disconnect the negative battery terminal. Remove the left side lower trim panel.
2. Remove the steering column-to-support screws and lower the steering column.
3. Disconnect the dimmer switch and turn signal switch connectors.
4. Remove the wiring harness-to-firewall nuts and steering column.
5. If equipped with a park lock cable, insert a small prybar into the ignition switch inhibiter switch access hole, depress the locking tab and disconnect the park lock cable from the inhibiter switch.
6. Remove the steering column-to-steering gear bolt and the steering column from the vehicle.
7. Remove the combination switch.
8. Place the lock cylinder in the **RUN** position.
9. Remove the steering shaft assembly and turn signal switch housing as an assembly.
10. Using a terminal remover tool, disconnect and label the wires F and G on the connector at the buzzer switch assembly from the turn signal switch electrical harness connector.
11. Place the lock cylinder in the **RUN** position and remove the buzzer switch.
12. Place the lock cylinder in the **ACCESSORY** position. Remove the lock cylinder retaining screw and the lock cylinder.
13. Remove the dimmer switch nut/bolt, the dimmer switch and actuator rod.
14. Remove the dimmer switch mounting stud (the mounting nut was mounted to it).
15. Remove the ignition switch-to-steering column screws and the ignition switch.
16. Remove the lock bolt screws and the lock bolt.
17. Remove the switch actuator rack and ignition switch.
18. Remove the steering shaft lock and spring.

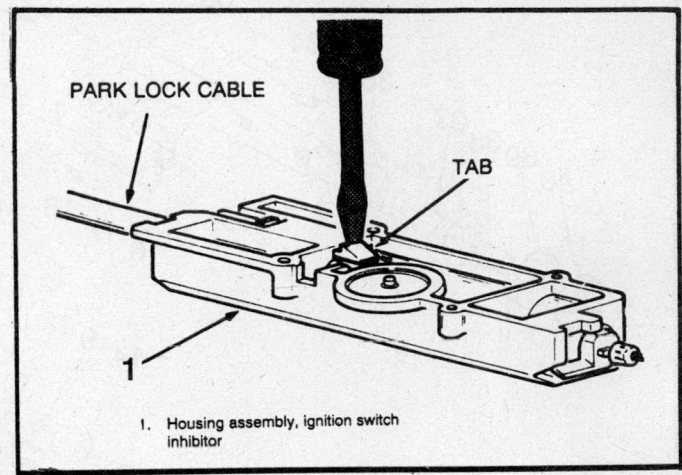

PARK LOCK CABLE

TAB

1. Housing assembly, ignition switch inhibitor

Removing Park Lock cable from ignition switch inhibiter

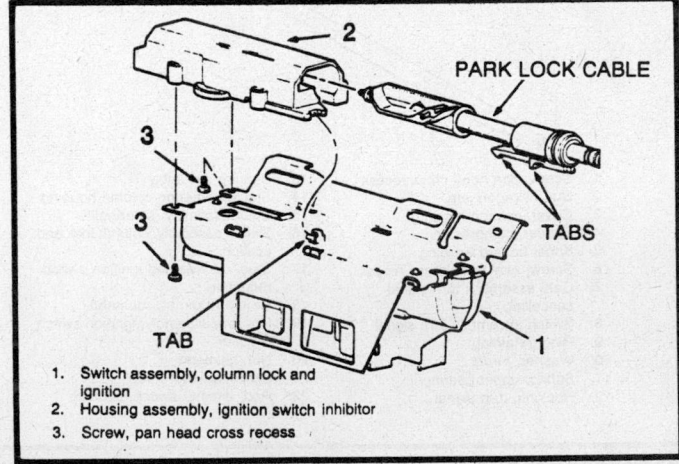

2

PARK LOCK CABLE

3

3

TABS

TAB

1

1. Switch assembly, column lock and ignition
2. Housing assembly, ignition switch inhibitor
3. Screw, pan head cross recess

Park Lock cable installation

To install:

19. To install the lock bolt, lubricate it with lithium grease and install the lock bolt, spring and retaining plate.
20. Lubricate the teeth on the switch actuator rack. Install the rack and the ignition switch through the opening in the steering bolt until it rests on the retaining plate.
21. Install the steering column lock cylinder set by holding the barrel of the lock cylinder, insert the key and turn it to the **ACCESSORY** position.
22. Install the lock set in the steering column while holding the rack against the lock plate.
23. Install the lock retaining screw and torque the screw to 27

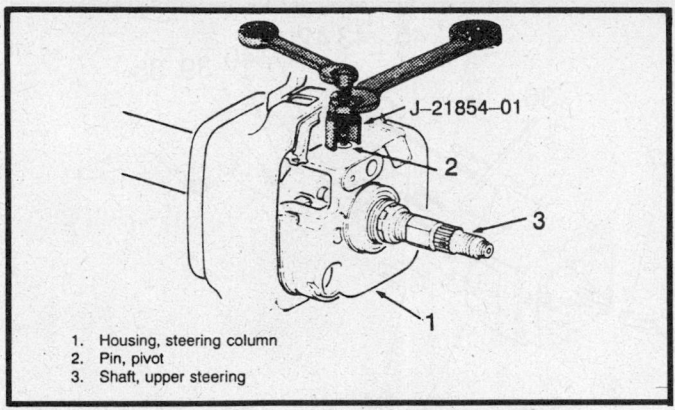

1. Housing, steering column
2. Pin, pivot
3. Shaft, upper steering

Removing pivot pins from tilt steering column

inch lbs. Insert the key in the lock cylinder and turn the lock cylinder to the **START** position and the rack will extend.

24. Center the slotted holes on the ignition switch mounting plate and install the ignition switch mounting screw and nut.

25. Install the dimmer switch and actuator rod into the center slot on the switch mounting plate. Torque the dimmer switch stud to 35 inch lbs.

26. Install the buzzer switch and turn the lock cylinder to the **RUN** position. Push the switch in until it is bottomed out with the plastic tab that covers the lock retaining screw.

27. Install the steering shaft and turn signal housing as an assembly.

28. Install the turn signal switch. Torque the turn signal switch housing screws to 88 inch lbs., the turn signal switch screws to 35 inch lbs. and the steering wheel locknut to 30 ft. lbs.

29. To complete the installation, reverse the removal procedures.

TILT STEERING COLUMN

1. Disconnect the negative battery terminal. Tilt the column up as far as it will go and remove the left side lower trim panel.

2. Remove the steering column-to-support screws and lower the steering column.

3. Disconnect the dimmer switch and turn signal switch connectors.

4. Remove the wiring harness-to-firewall nuts and steering column.

5. If equipped with a park lock cable, insert a small prybar into the ignition switch inhibiter switch access hole, depress the locking tab and disconnect the park lock cable from the inhibiter switch.

6. Remove the steering column-to-steering gear bolt and the steering column from the vehicle.

7. Remove the combination switch.

8. Using a flat type pry blade, position it in the square opening of the spring retainer, push downward (to the left) to release the spring retainer. Remove the wheel tilt spring.

9. Remove the spring retainer, the tilt spring and the tilt spring guide.

10. Remove the shoe pin retaining cap. Using a pivot pin removal tool, remove both pivot pins.

11. Place the lock cylinder in the **RUN** position.

12. Pull the shoe release lever and release the steering column housing.

13. Remove the column housing, the steering shaft assembly and turn signal switch housing as an assembly.

14. Using a terminal remover tool, disconnect and label the wires F and G on the connector at the buzzer switch assembly from the turn signal switch electrical harness connector.

15. Place the lock cylinder in the **RUN** position and remove the buzzer switch.

16. Place the lock cylinder in the **ACCESSORY** position. Remove the lock cylinder retaining screw and the lock cylinder.

17. Remove the dimmer switch nut/bolt, the dimmer switch and actuator rod.

18. Remove the dimmer switch mounting stud (the mounting nut was mounted to it).

19. Remove the ignition switch-to-steering column screws and the ignition switch.

20. Remove the lock bolt screws and the lock bolt.

21. Remove the switch actuator rack and ignition switch.

22. Remove the steering shaft lock and spring.

To install:

23. Reverse the removal procedures.

24. To install the lock bolt, lubricate it with lithium grease and install the lock bolt, spring and retaining plate.

25. Lubricate the teeth on the switch actuator rack. Install the rack and the ignition switch through the opening in the steering bolt until it rests on the retaining plate.

26. Install the steering column lock cylinder set by holding the barrel of the lock cylinder, insert the key and turn the key to the **ACCESSORY** position.

27. Install the lock set in the steering column while holding the rack against the lock plate.

28. Install the lock retaining screw and torque the screw to 27 inch lbs. Insert the key in the lock cylinder. Turn the lock cylinder to the **START** position and the rack will extend.

29. Center the slotted holes on the ignition switch mounting plate. Install the ignition switch mounting screw and nut.

30. Install the dimmer switch and actuator rod into the center slot on the switch mounting plate. Torque the dimmer switch stud to 35 inch lbs.

31. Install the buzzer switch and turn the lock cylinder to the **RUN** position. Push the switch in until it is bottomed out with the plastic tab that covers the lock retaining screw.

32. Install the steering shaft and turn signal housing as an assembly.

33. Install the turn signal switch. Torque the turn signal switch housing screws to 88 inch lbs., the turn signal switch screws to 35 inch lbs. and the steering wheel locknut to 30 ft. lbs.

34. To complete the installation, reverse the removal procedures.

NEUTRAL SAFETY SWITCH

The neutral safety switch is a part of the park/neutral and back-up light switch and is located on top of the transaxle.

Removal and Installation

1. Disconnect the negative battery cable and the electrical connector from the switch.

2. Remove the switch-to-transaxle screws and the switch.

To install:

3. Place the transaxle's shift control lever in the **N** notch in the detent plate.

4. Position the switch onto the transaxle and install the screws loosely.

5. Rotate the switch on the shifter assembly to align the service adjustment hole with the carrier tang hole.

6. Using a 3/32 in. drill bit or gauge pin, insert it into the service adjustment hole to a depth of 3/8 in. (9mm).

7. Tighten the switch-to-transaxle screws and remove the drill bit or gauge pin.

8. To complete the installation, reverse the removal procedures. Start the engine and check the switch operation.

CLUTCH START SWITCH

Adjustment

1. Remove the lower, left trim panel and locate the switch on

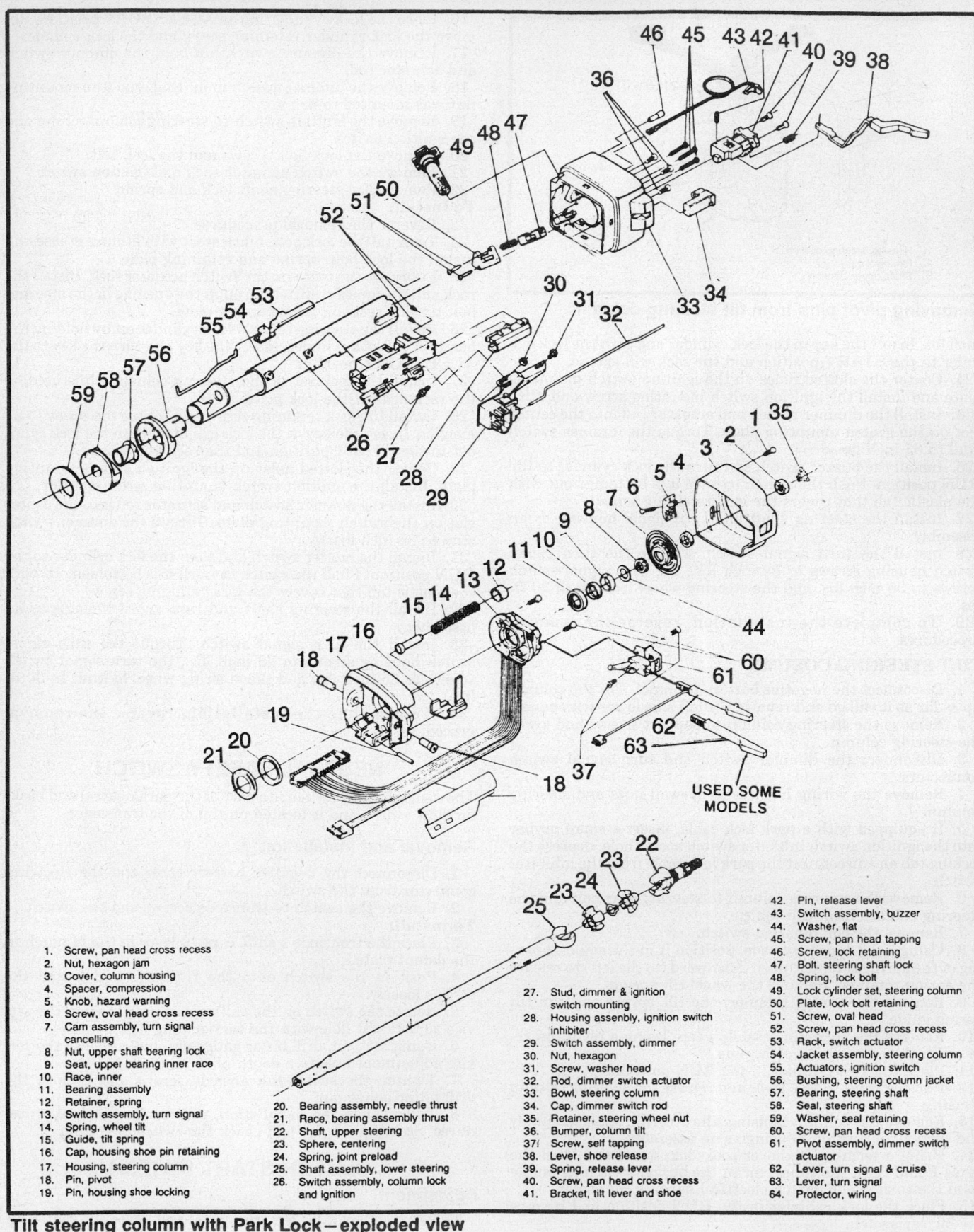

1. Screw, pan head cross recess
2. Nut, hexagon jam
3. Cover, column housing
4. Spacer, compression
5. Knob, hazard warning
6. Screw, oval head cross recess
7. Cam assembly, turn signal cancelling
8. Nut, upper shaft bearing lock
9. Seat, upper bearing inner race
10. Race, inner
11. Bearing assembly
12. Retainer, spring
13. Switch assembly, turn signal
14. Spring, wheel tilt
15. Guide, tilt spring
16. Cap, housing shoe pin retaining
17. Housing, steering column
18. Pin, pivot
19. Pin, housing shoe locking
20. Bearing assembly, needle thrust
21. Race, bearing assembly thrust
22. Shaft, upper steering
23. Sphere, centering
24. Spring, joint preload
25. Shaft assembly, lower steering
26. Switch assembly, column lock and ignition

27. Stud, dimmer & ignition switch mounting
28. Housing assembly, ignition switch inhibiter
29. Switch assembly, dimmer
30. Nut, hexagon
31. Screw, washer head
32. Rod, dimmer switch actuator
33. Bowl, steering column
34. Cap, dimmer switch rod
35. Retainer, steering wheel nut
36. Bumper, column tilt
37. Screw, self tapping
38. Lever, shoe release
39. Spring, release lever
40. Screw, pan head cross recess
41. Bracket, tilt lever and shoe

42. Pin, release lever
43. Switch assembly, buzzer
44. Washer, flat
45. Screw, pan head tapping
46. Screw, lock retaining
47. Bolt, steering shaft lock
48. Spring, lock bolt
49. Lock cylinder set, steering column
50. Plate, lock bolt retaining
51. Screw, oval head
52. Screw, pan head cross recess
53. Rack, switch actuator
54. Jacket assembly, steering column
55. Actuators, ignition switch
56. Bushing, steering column jacket
57. Bearing, steering shaft
58. Seal, steering shaft
59. Washer, seal retaining
60. Screw, pan head cross recess
61. Pivot assembly, dimmer switch actuator
62. Lever, turn signal & cruise
63. Lever, turn signal
64. Protector, wiring

USED SOME MODELS

Tilt steering column with Park Lock—exploded view

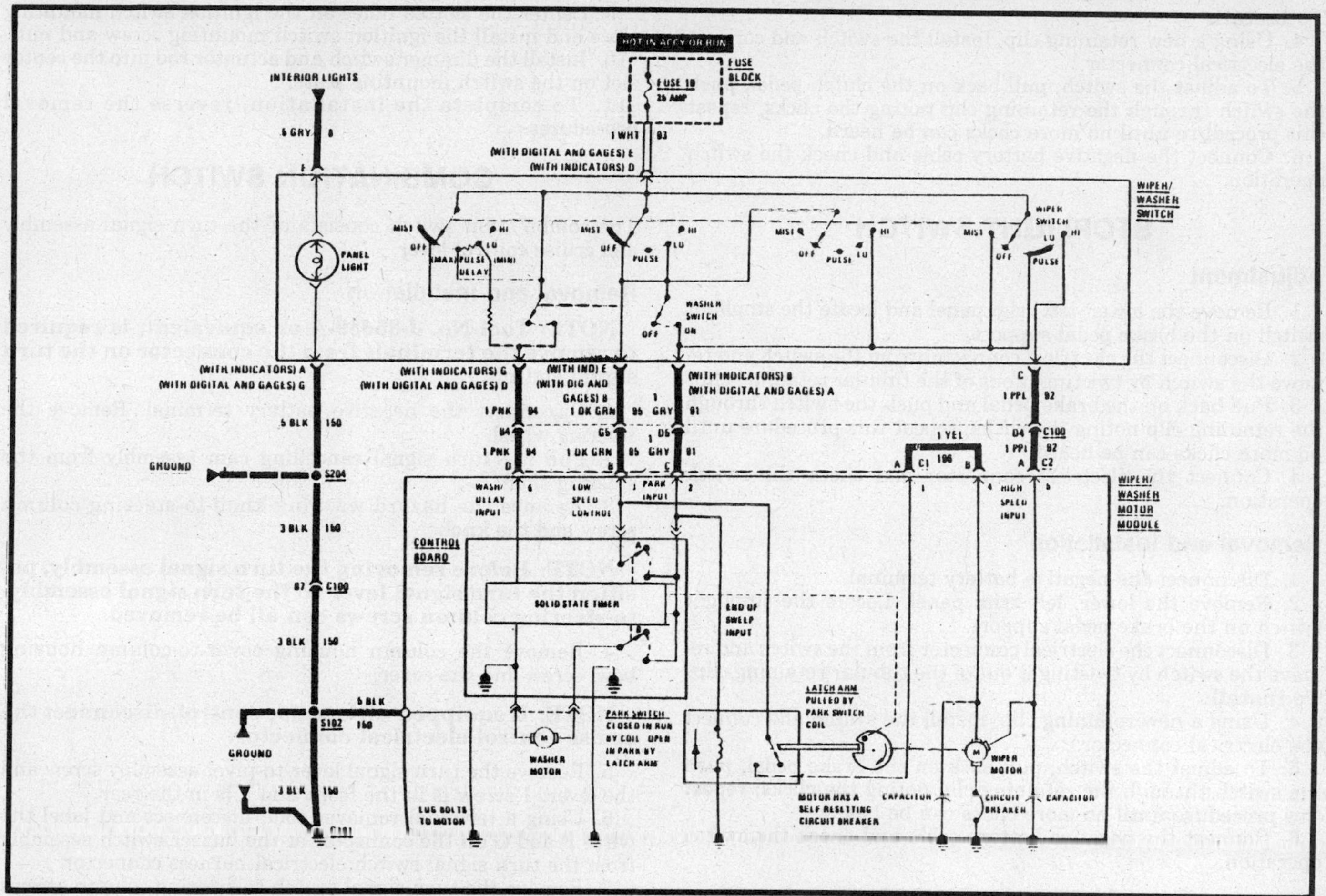

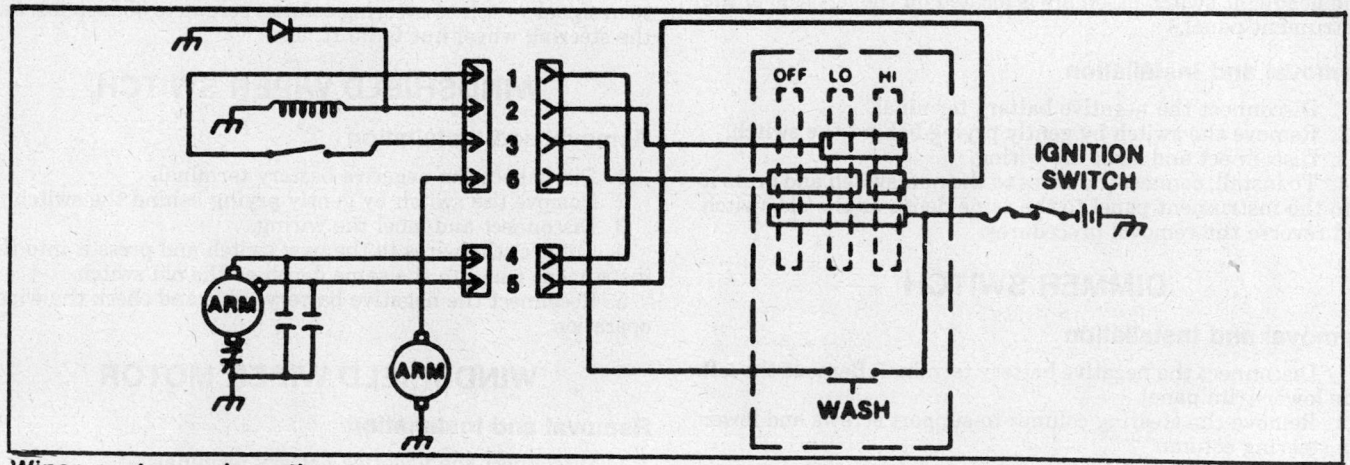

Delay wiper schematic

Wiper system schematic

the clutch pedal support.

2. Disconnect the electrical connector from the switch and remove the switch by twisting it out of the tubular retaining clip.

3. Pull back on the clutch pedal and push the switch through the retaining clip noting the clicks; repeat this procedure until no more clicks can be heard.

4. Connect the electrical connector and check the switch operation.

Removal and Installation

1. Disconnect the negative battery terminal.

2. Remove the lower, left trim panel. Locate the switch on the clutch pedal support.

3. Disconnect the electrical connector from the switch and remove the switch by twisting it out of the tubular retaining clip.

To install:

4. Using a new retaining clip, install the switch and connect the electrical connector.

5. To adjust the switch, pull back on the clutch pedal, push the switch through the retaining clip noting the clicks; repeat this procedure until no more clicks can be heard.

6. Connect the negative battery cable and check the switch operation.

STOPLIGHT SWITCH

Adjustment

1. Remove the lower, left trim panel and locate the stoplight switch on the brake pedal support.

2. Disconnect the electrical connector from the switch and remove the switch by twisting it out of the tubular retaining clip.

3. Pull back on the brake pedal and push the switch through the retaining clip noting the clicks; repeat this procedure until no more clicks can be heard.

4. Connect the electrical connector and check the switch operation.

Removal and Installation

1. Disconnect the negative battery terminal.

2. Remove the lower, left trim panel. Locate the stoplight switch on the brake pedal support.

3. Disconnect the electrical connector from the switch and remove the switch by twisting it out of the tubular retaining clip.

To install:

4. Using a new retaining clip, install the switch and connect the electrical connector.

5. To adjust the switch, pull back on the brake pedal, push the switch through the retaining clip noting the clicks; repeat this procedure until no more clicks can be heard.

6. Connect the negative battery cable and check the switch operation.

HEADLAMP SWITCH

The headlight switch assembly is located on the left side of the instrument panel.

Removal and Installation

1. Disconnect the negative battery terminal.

2. Remove the switch by gently prying behind the switch.

3. Disconnect and label the wiring.

4. To install, connect the wires to the new switch and press it into the instrument panel to the same depth as the old switch and reverse the removal procedures.

DIMMER SWITCH

Removal and Installation

1. Disconnect the negative battery terminal. Remove the left side lower trim panel.

2. Remove the steering column-to-support screws and lower the steering column.

3. Disconnect the dimmer switch and turn signal switch connectors.

4. Remove the wiring harness-to-firewall nuts and steering column.

5. Remove the dimmer switch nut/bolt, the dimmer switch and actuator rod.

6. Remove the switch actuator rack and ignition switch.

To install:

7. Torque the dimmer switch stud to 35 inch lbs.

8. Lubricate the teeth on the switch actuator rack. Install the rack and the ignition switch through the opening in the steering bolt until it rests on the retaining plate.

9. Center the slotted holes on the ignition switch mounting plate and install the ignition switch mounting screw and nut.

10. Install the dimmer switch and actuator rod into the center slot on the switch mounting plate.

11. To complete the installation, reverse the removal procedures.

COMBINATION SWITCH

The combination switch consists of the turn signal assembly and cruise control lever.

Removal and Installation

NOTE: **Tool No. J-35689-A or equivalent, is required to remove the terminals from the connector on the turn signal switch.**

1. Disconnect the negative battery terminal. Remove the steering wheel.

2. Pull the turn signal cancelling cam assembly from the steering shaft.

3. Remove the hazard warning knob-to-steering column screw and the knob.

NOTE: **Before removing the turn signal assembly, position the turn signal lever so the turn signal assembly-to-steering column screws can all be removed.**

4. Remove the column housing cover-to-column housing bowl screw and the cover.

NOTE: **If equipped with cruise control, disconnect the cruise control electrical connector.**

5. Remove the turn signal lever-to-pivot assembly screw and the lever; 1 screw is in the front and 1 is in the rear.

6. Using a terminal remover tool, disconnect and label the wires F and G on the connector at the buzzer switch assembly from the turn signal switch electrical harness connector.

7. Remove the turn signal switch-to-steering column screws and the switch.

8. To install, reverse the removal procedures. Torque the turn signal switch-to-steering column screws to 35 inch lbs. and the steering wheel nut to 30 ft. lbs.

WINDSHIELD WIPER SWITCH

Removal and Installation

1. Disconnect the negative battery terminal.

2. Remove the switch by gently prying behind the switch.

3. Disconnect and label the wiring.

4. Connect the wires to the new switch and press it into the instrument panel to the same depth as the old switch.

5. Reconnect the negative battery cable and check the wiper operation.

WINDSHIELD WIPER MOTOR

Removal and Installation

1. Disconnect the negative battery terminal.

2. Remove the left side wiper arm.

3. Disconnect the wiper motor drive link from the crank arm.

4. Disconnect the electrical connectors and washer hoses.

5. Remove the wiper motor-to-chassis bolts and the wiper motor by guiding the crank arm through the hole.

6. To install, reverse the removal procedures.

DELAY WIPER CONTROLS

Electronic logic circuits on a pulse wiper system's printed circuit board establish all timing and washer commands. When the

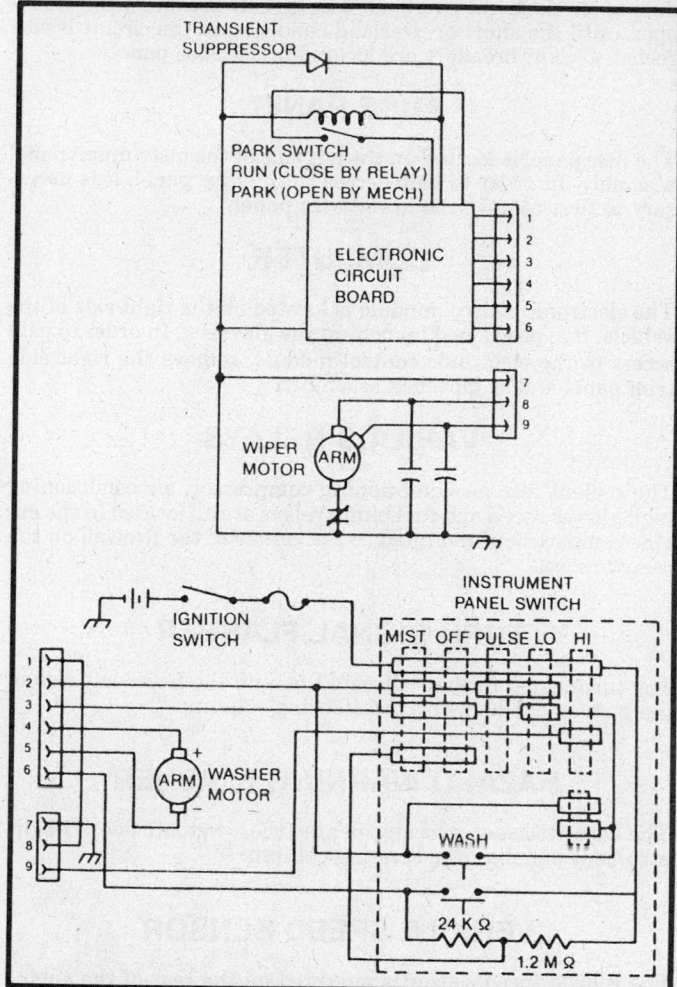

Schematic of the delay windshield wiper system

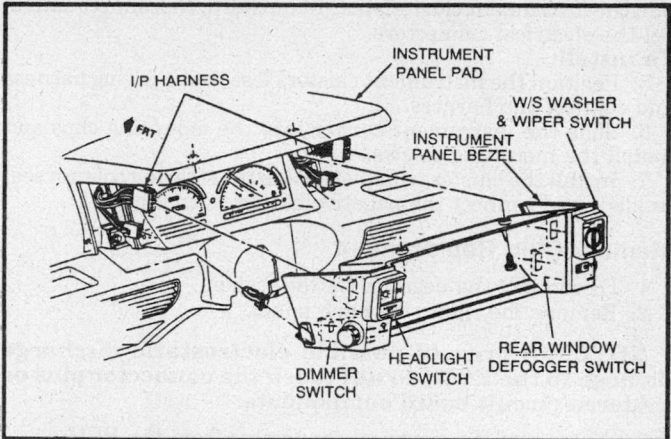

Instrument cluster mounting—Corsica shown, Beretta similar

WASH switch is depressed for less than 1 second, the washer sprays only during the wiper arm outwipe and pulsates operation for 2½ seconds. Then, the wiper dry wipes for nearly 6 seconds before shutting off.

If the WASH switch is depressed for more than 1 second, a demand wash is performed for as long as the switch is depressed. The wash action is followed by 6 seconds of dry wipes before shut-off. With the control switch positioned on the LO or HI speeds, the respective brush circuit is completed to the +12V source and the wiper motor runs at that particular speed setting.

Moving the switch to the PULSE mode operates the wiper motor intermittently and the delay can be varied by moving the switch back and forth in the delay mode. An instantaneous wipe can be obtained by moving the switch to the MIST position. If the switch is depressed continually, a continuous wiping action will be performed.

WINDSHIELD WIPER LINKAGE

Removal and Installation

1. Raise the hood and remove both wiper arm and blade assemblies.
2. Loosen, but do not remove, the drive link-to-motor crank arm nuts.
3. Remove the air inlet panel.

4. Disconnect the drive links from the motor crank arm.
5. Remove the wiper linkage-to-chassis bolts.
6. Remove the linkage assembly through the access hole in the upper shroud panel.
7. To install, reverse the removal procedures. Torque the drive link-to-motor crank arm nut to 64 inch lbs.

Instrument Cluster

Refer to "Chilton's Electronic Instrumentation Service Manual" for additional coverage.

Removal and Installation

1. Disconnect the negative battery terminal.
2. Remove the screw from the upper, center instrument cluster trim plate.
3. Slide the steering column seal out and remove the trim plate by pulling it straight outward.
4. Remove both upper instrument cluster-to-dash screws and pull the instrument cluster straight outward. Disconnect and label the electrical connectors.

To install:

5. Position the instrument cluster close to the wiring harness and connect the harness.
6. Slide the instrument cluster into the mounting clips and install the mounting screws.
7. Install the cluster trim plate, slide the steering column seal in place and connect the negative battery terminal.

SPEEDOMETER

Removal and Installation

The speedometer and gauge cluster is replaced as an assembly only.

NOTE: Whenever working on any electronic equipment, make sure to have a clean, static free environment in which to work. Always cover the work surface with a mat that is grounded and static free. Static electricity from walking across the floor or sliding across a car seat is enough to damage any equipment.

1. Disconnect the negative battery terminal.
2. Remove the screw from the upper, center instrument cluster trim plate.
3. Slide the steering column seal out and remove the trim plate by pulling it straight outward.
4. Remove both upper instrument cluster-to-dash screws and

pull the instrument cluster straight outward. Disconnect and label the electrical connectors.

To install:

5. Position the instrument cluster close to the wiring harness and connect the harness.

6. Slide the instrument cluster into the mounting clips and install the mounting screws.

7. Install the cluster trim plate, slide the steering column seal in place and connect the negative battery terminal.

Memory Chip Replacement

1. Disconnect the negative battery cable.
2. Remove the right side hush panel.

NOTE: To prevent possible electrostatic discharge damage to the ECM, do not touch the connector pins or soldered circuit board components.

3. Disconnect the electrical connectors from the ECM.
4. Remove the ECM-to-bracket nuts and the ECM.
5. Remove the ECM access cover screws and the cover.
6. Using a PROM removal tool, engage 1 end of the PROM carrier with the hooked end of the tool, press on the vertical bar end of the tool and rock the engaged end of the PROM carrier up as far as possible.
7. Engage the opposite end of the PROM, in the same manner, and rock this end up as far as possible. Repeat this procedure until the PROM is removed from the ECM.

To install:

8. Align the small notch on the PROM carrier with the PROM socket, press the PROM carrier until it is firmly seated in the socket.
9. To complete the installation, reverse the removal procedures.
10. To check if the PROM is seated and working correctly, perform the following procedures:

    a. Turn the ignition switch **ON**.

    b. Groung the diagnostic test connector in the ALDL connector.

    c. Allow code 12 to flash 4 times to verify that no codes are present; this indicates that the PROM is properly installed.

    d. If trouble code 51 occurs or the "service engine soon light" stays **ON** constantly with no codes, the PROM is not fully seated or is defective.

VEHICLE SPEED SENSOR

The vehicle speed sensor is located on the upper, right rear side of the automatic transaxle or the upper, left rear side of the manual transaxle. If sends speed information to the ECM, which, uses the information for engine operation and also, controls the speedometer operation.

1. Disconnect the negative battery cable.
2. Disconnect the electrical connector from the vehicle speed sensor.
3. Remove the vehicle speed sensor-to-transaxle screws and the sensor.
4. To install, use a new O-ring seal and reverse the removal procedures.

Electrical Circuit Protectors

FUSIBLE LINKS

Fusible links are sections of wire, with special insulation, designed to melt under electrical overload. Replacements are simply spliced into the wire. There may be as many as seven of these in the engine compartment wiring harnesses.

CIRCUIT BREAKERS

A circuit breaker is an electrical switch which breaks the circuit during an electrical overload. The circuit breaker will remain open until the short or overload condition in the circuit is corrected. Circuit breakers are located in the fuse panel.

FUSE PANEL

The fuse panel is located on the left side of the instrument panel assembly. In order to gain access to the fuse panel, it is necessary to first remove the lower trim panel.

COMPUTER

The electronic control module is located on the right side of the vehicle. It is positioned up behind the glovebox. In order to gain access to the electronic control module, remove the right side trim panel and/or glovebox assembly.

VARIOUS RELAYS

The coolant fan, air conditioning compressor, air conditioning high blower speed and fuel pump relays are all located in the engine compartment mounted to the center of the firewall on the relay bracket.

TURN SIGNAL FLASHER

The turn signal flasher is located behind the lower left side of the instrument panel on the steering column.

HAZARD WARNING FLASHER

The hazard flasher is located behind the lower left side of the instrument panel on the steering column.

VEHICLE SPEED SENSOR

The vehicle speed sensor is mounted on the rear of the engine near the oil filter.

Speed Controls

Refer to "Chilton's Chassis Electronics Service Manual" for additional coverage.

RELEASE SWITCHES

Adjustment

BRAKE PEDAL RELEASE SWITCH

The brake pedal release switch is located at the top of the brake pedal, directly above the brake pedal switch.

1. Remove the lower steering column cover.
2. Pull the brake pedal release switch from the mounting bracket.
3. Depress the brake pedal and insert the brake pedal release switch into the tubular retainer bracket until it seats on the retainer.

NOTE: Note that clicks can be heard as the threaded portion of the valve passes through the retainer toward the brake pedal.

4. Pull the brake pedal rearward against the pedal stop until audible clicks can no longer be heard.
5. Release the brake pedal and again, pull the pedal rearward to make sure no more clicks can be heard.
6. Reinstall the lower steering column panel.

CLUTCH PEDAL RELEASE SWITCH

The clutch pedal release switch is located at the top of the clutch pedal.

1. Remove the lower steering column cover.
2. Pull the clutch pedal release switch from the mounting bracket.
3. Depress the clutch pedal and insert the clutch pedal release switch into the tubular retainer bracket until it seats on the retainer.

NOTE: Note that clicks can be heard as the threaded portion of the valve passes through the retainer toward the clutch pedal.

4. Pull the clutch pedal rearward against the pedal stop until audible clicks can no longer be heard.
5. Release the clutch pedal and again, pull the pedal rearward to make sure no more clicks can be heard.
6. Reinstall the lower steering column panel.

CRUISE CONTROL CABLE

Troubleshooting

1. Start the engine and turn **ON** the speed control main switch.
2. Drive the vehicle above 25 mph.
3. Engage the speed control and check the following functions: set, disengage, coast and resume.

Adjustment

1. With the servo cable installed on the brackets, place the cable over the stud on the servo lever so the stud engages the slot in the cable end.
2. Connect the cable to the throttle lever and release the lever.
3. Pull the servo end of the cable towards the servo as far as possible without moving the throttle.
4. Attach the cable to the servo in the closest alignment holes without moving the throttle.

NOTE: Do not stretch the cable to attach it to the servo. This will not allow the engine to return to idle.

5. The cable is now adjusted properly.

COOLING AND HEATING SYSTEMS

Water Pump

Removal and Installation

1. Disconnect the negative battery terminal.
2. Remove the serpentine drive belt.
3. On the 2.0L engine, remove the alternator and bracket with wires attached and position it out of the way.
4. Remove the water pump pulley bolts and remove the pulley.
5. Remove the water pump-to-engine bolts and the pump.

To install:

6. Clean the gasket mounting surfaces.
7. Using new gaskets and sealant (if necessary), reverse the removal procedures. Torque the water pump-to-engine bolts to 14–22 ft. lbs. on the 2.0L engine or to 6–9 ft. lbs. on the 2.8L engine.
8. Refill and bleed the cooling system.
9. To complete the installation, reverse the removal procedures. Start the engine, allow it to reach normal operating temperatures and check for leaks.

Electric Cooling Fan

SYSTEM OPERATION

The electric cooling fans are controlled by the Electronic Control Module (ECM). The coolant temperature sensor in the engine sends a signal to the ECM when the engine coolant temperature reaches 223°F. The ECM grounds the cooling fan relay which turns **ON** the fan. The cooling fan will also turn **ON** if the air conditioning pressure switch detects a pressure more than 200 psi and the vehicle speed is less than 70 mph. If the cooling fan is turned **ON** by the ECM for any reason, the fan will cycle for no less than 30 seconds.

Removal and Installation

1. Disconnect the negative battery terminal.
2. Disconnect the electrical wiring harness from the cooling fan frame.

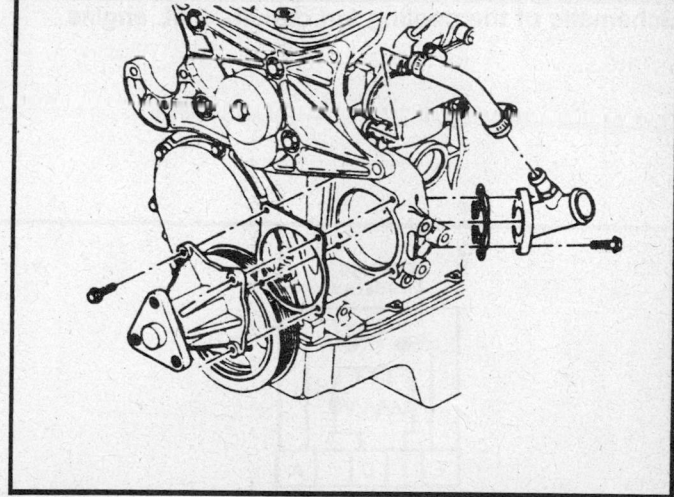

Exploded view of the water pump—2.0L engine

3. Remove the fan assembly from the radiator support.
4. To install, reverse the removal procedures. Torque the fan assembly-to-radiator support bolts to 7 ft. lbs.

Testing

COOLANT TEMPERATURE SWITCH

The coolant temperature switch is located at the left side of the engine on the coolant outlet (2.0L engine) or on the top, left side of the engine (2.8L engine).

1. Drain the cooling system to a level below the coolant temperature switch.
2. Disconnect the electrical connector and remove the switch.
3. Using an ohmmeter, connect it's leads to the switch and submerge the tip of the switch in a container of water.
4. Heat the water to at least 230°F (108°C); the switch should close and cause the ohmmeter to show conductivity.
5. Allow the switch to cool to at least 220°F (101°C); the

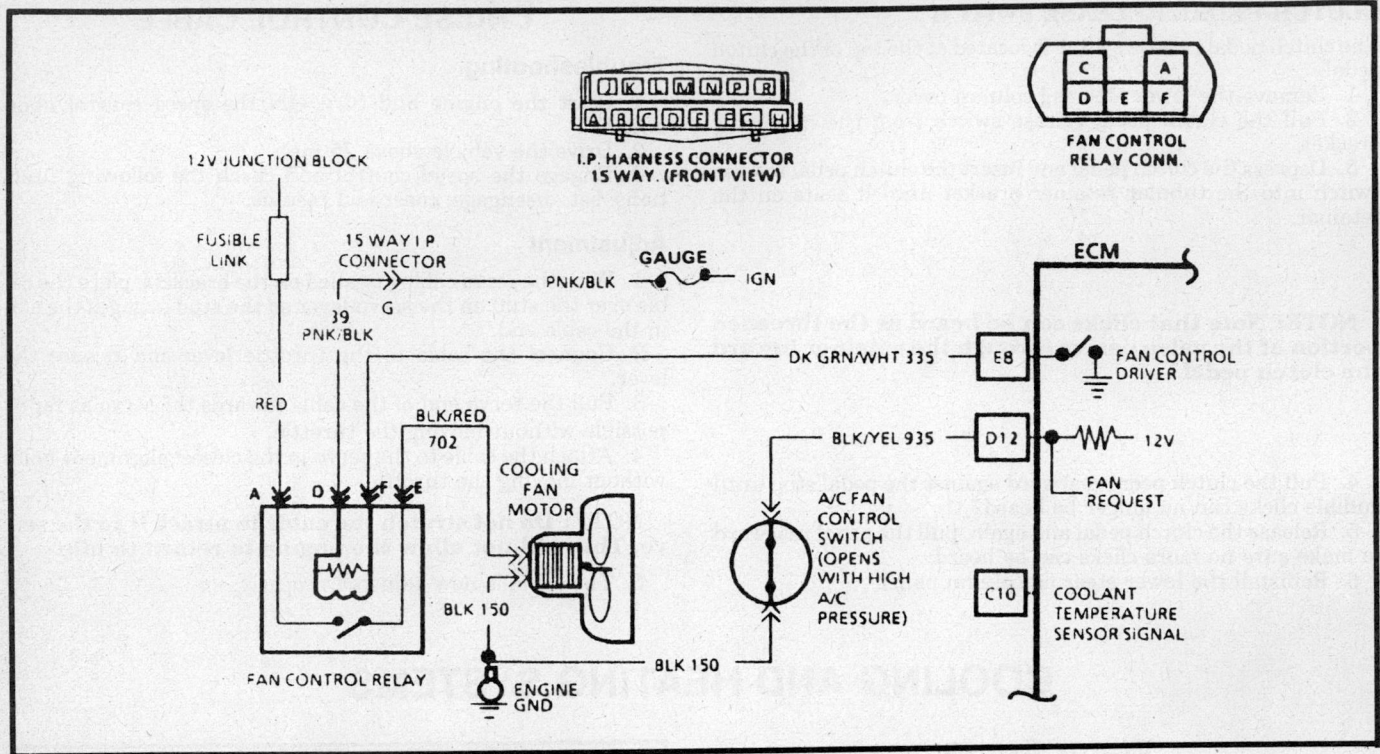

Schematic of the cooling fan circuit—2.8L engine

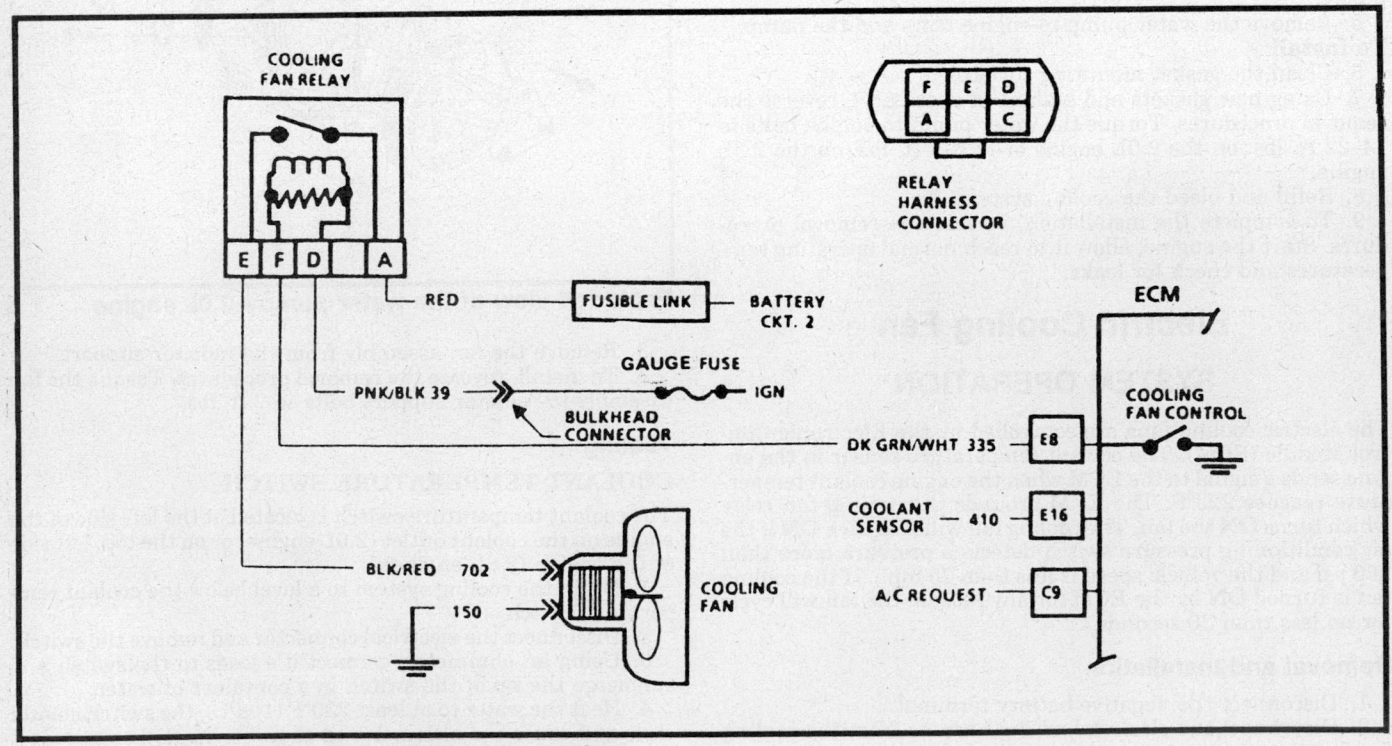

Schematic of the cooling fan circuit—2.0L engine

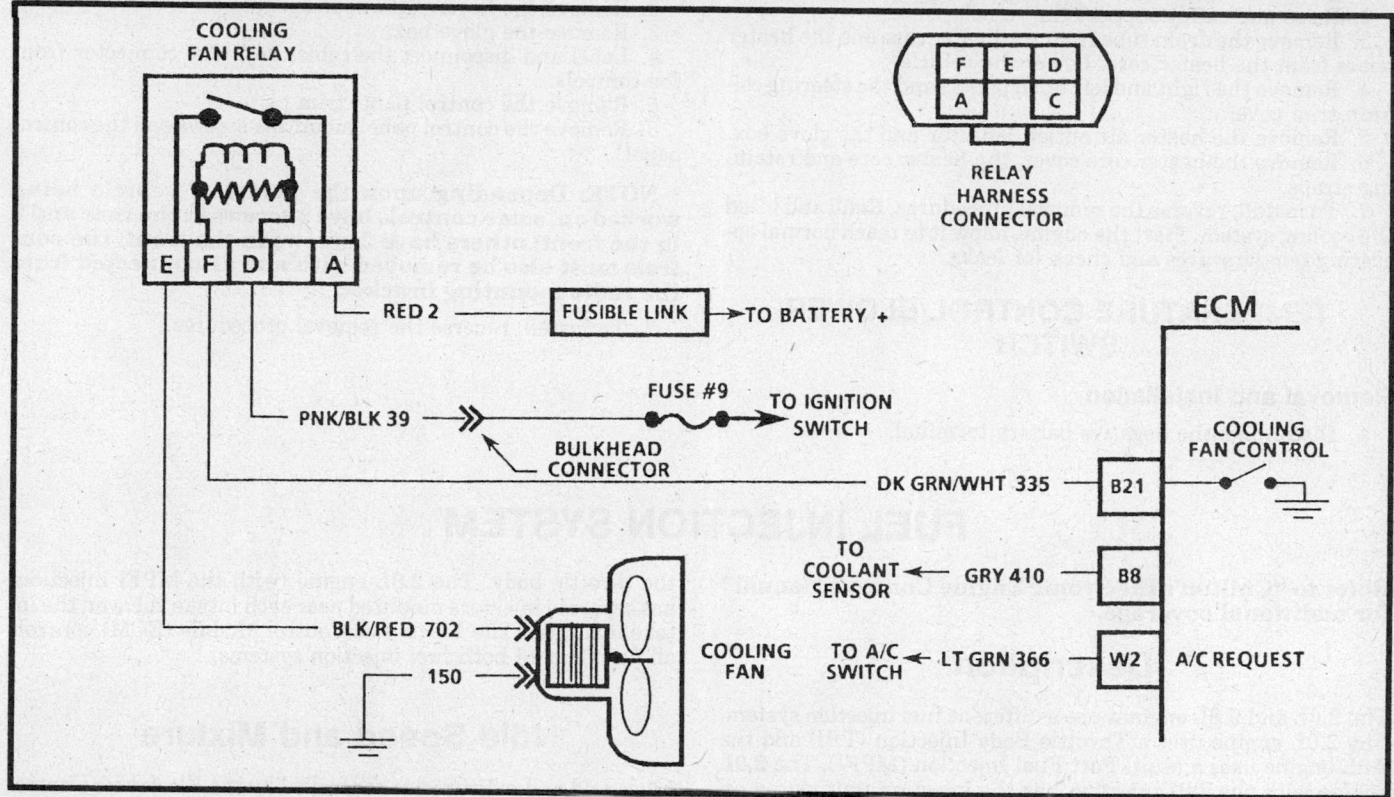

Schematic of the cooling fan system

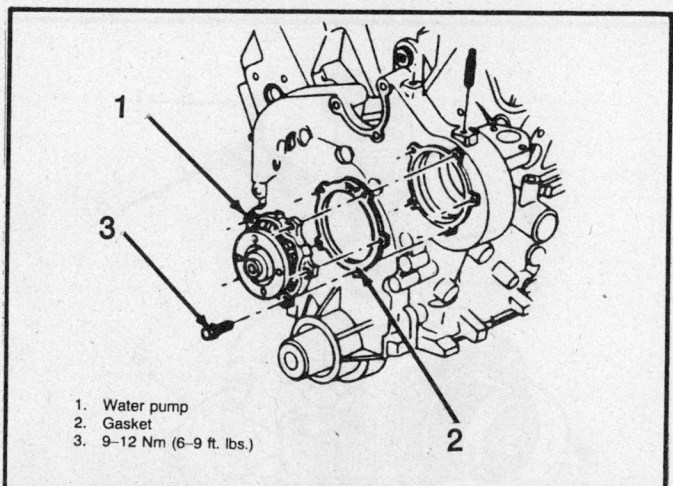

Exploded view of the water pump assembly—2.8L engine

1. Water pump
2. Gasket
3. 9–12 Nm (6–9 ft. lbs.)

switch should open and cause the ohmmeter to show no conductivity.

6. If the switch does respond accordingly, replace it.

COOLANT FAN PRESSURE SWITCH

If equipped with air conditioning, the coolant fan pressure switch is located on the refrigerant line at the front, right side of the engine compartment.

When the air conditioning switch is turned **ON** and the low pressure switch is **CLOSED**, the cooling fan will turn **ON**.

ELECTRIC FAN RELAY

The electric fan relay is located at the center, front of the dash on the relay block.

The ECM reads the sensor information and sends an electrical impulse to the relay's primary circuit causing the cooling fan to turn **ON**.

Blower Motor

Removal and Installation

1. Disconnect the negative battery terminal.
2. Disconnect the electrical connections from the blower motor and resistor.
3. Remove the plastic water shield from the right side of the cowl.
4. Remove the blower motor-to-chassis screws and the blower motor.
5. Remove the cage retaining nut and the cage.

To install:

6. Install the cage on the new blower motor with the opening facing away from the motor.
7. To complete the installation, reverse the removal procedures.

Heater Core

Refer to "Chilton's Auto Heating and Air Conditioning Manual" for additional coverage.

Removal and Installation

The heater core assembly is located under the dash.

1. Disconnect the negative battery terminal. Drain the cooling system.

2. Raise and safely support the vehicle.

3. Remove the drain tube from the heater case and the heater hoses from the heater core. Lower the vehicle.

4. Remove the right and left hush panels and the steering column trim cover.

5. Remove the heater air outlet deflector and the glove box.

6. Remove the heater core cover, the heater core and retaining straps.

7. To install, reverse the removal procedures. Refill and bleed the cooling system. Start the engine, allow it to reach normal operating temperatures and check for leaks.

TEMPERATURE CONTROL/BLOWER SWITCH

Removal and Installation

1. Disconnect the negative battery terminal.

2. Remove the lower-right sound insulator.

3. Remove the glove box.

4. Label and disconnect the cables and wire connector from the controls.

5. Remove the control panel trim plate.

6. Remove the control panel mounting screws and the control panel.

NOTE: Depending upon the model of vehicle being worked on, some controls have 2 screws in the rear and 2 in the front; others have 2 screws in the front, the controls must also be removed with and disconnected from the radio mounting bracket.

7. To install, reverse the removal procedures.

FUEL INJECTION SYSTEM

Refer to "Chilton's Electronic Engine Controls Manual" for additional coverage.

Description

The 2.0L and 2.8L engines use a different fuel injection system. The 2.0L engine uses a Throttle Body Injection (TBI) and the 2.8L engine uses a Multi Port Fuel Injection (MPFI). The 2.0L engine with the TBI injection has the injection unit placed on the throttle body. The 2.8L engine (with the MPFI injection) has separate injectors mounted near each intake valve on the intake manifold. The Electronic Control Module (ECM) controls all functions of both fuel injection systems.

Idle Speed and Mixture

Idle speed and mixture are controlled by the Electronic Control Module (ECM). No adjustments are possible.

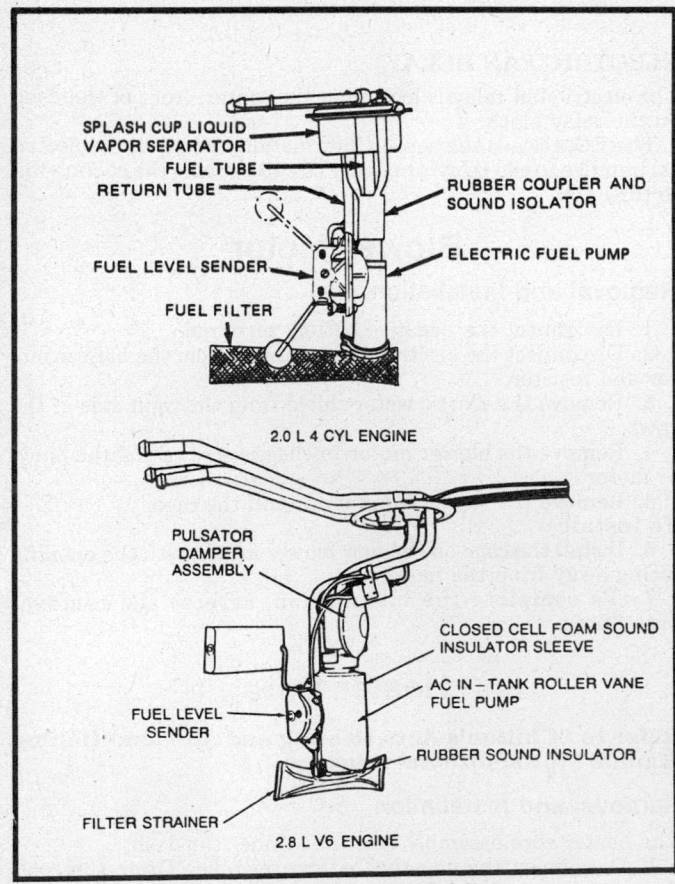

Fuel pump and sending unit assemblies

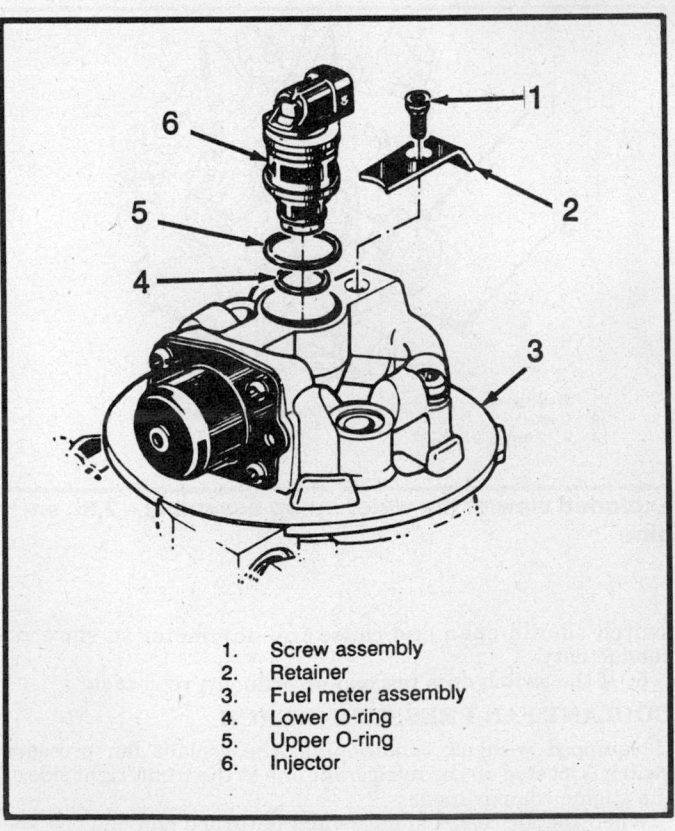

1. Screw assembly
2. Retainer
3. Fuel meter assembly
4. Lower O-ring
5. Upper O-ring
6. Injector

Exploded view of the fuel injector—2.0L engine

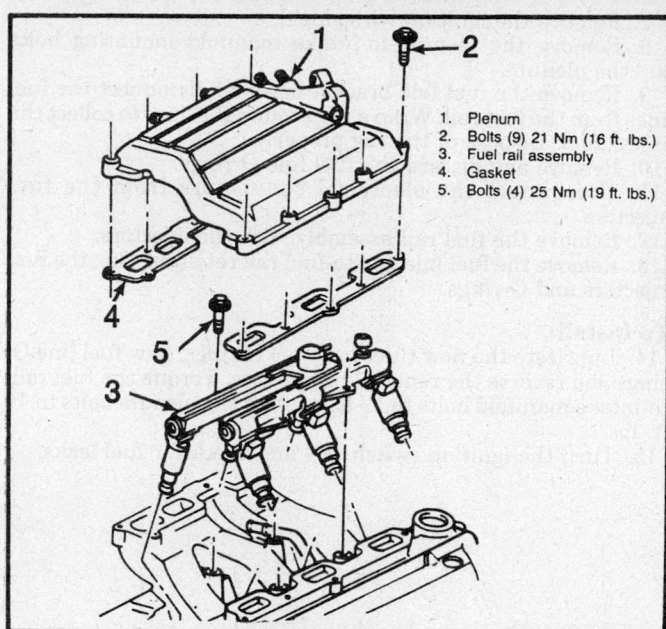

1. Plenum
2. Bolts (9) 21 Nm (16 ft. lbs.)
3. Fuel rail assembly
4. Gasket
5. Bolts (4) 25 Nm (19 ft. lbs.)

Fuel rail mounting—2.8L engine

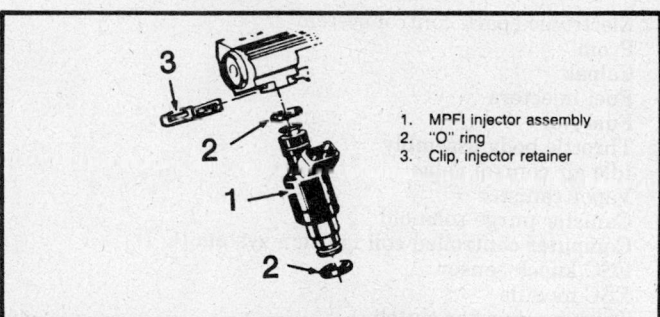

1. MPFI injector assembly
2. "O" ring
3. Clip, injector retainer

Fuel injector mounting to fuel rail

FUEL SYSTEM PRESSURE RELIEF

Procedure

NOTE: Make sure the engine is cold before disconnecting any portion of the fuel system.

THROTTLE BODY INJECTION

1. Disconnect the negative battery terminal. Using a shop rag, wrap it around the fuel line fitting.
2. Open the fuel line and absorb any excess fuel remaining in the line.
3. To install, use a new O-ring and reverse the removal procedures.

MULTI PORT FUEL INJECTION

1. Disconnect the negative battery terminal. Using a fuel gauge tool, connect it to the fuel pressure connector.

NOTE: Be sure to wrap a shop cloth around the fuel line fitting when connecting the fuel gauge tool to the fuel pressure connector.

2. Place the bleeder hose and shop cloth in an approved fuel container. Open the pressure valve to bleed the fuel pressure from the system.
3. After the fuel pressure is bled, retighten the fuel pressure valve.

Fuel Pump

CAUTION

The fuel system pressure must be relieved before attempting any service procedures. Use caution to avoid the risk of fire by disposing of any fuel and fuel soaked rags properly.

Removal and Installation

The fuel pump is located in the fuel tank. Removal and installation procedures require the fuel tank to be removed from the vehicle.
1. Relieve the fuel pressure.
2. Disconnect the negative battery terminal.
3. Using a siphon hose and pump, drain the fuel from the fuel tank.
4. Raise and safely support the vehicle.
5. Support the fuel tank and disconnect the retaining straps.
6. Lower the tank some. Disconnect the sending unit wire, the hoses and the ground strap. Remove the fuel tank from the vehicle.
7. Using a locking cam tool, remove the sending unit retaining cam from the fuel tank.
8. Remove the sending unit and the O-ring gasket (discard it) from the fuel tank.
9. To install, use a new O-ring gasket and reverse the removal procedures; be sure to reinstall the anti-squeak pieces on top of the fuel tank. Torque the retaining straps to 26 ft. lbs. Refill the fuel tank, start the engine and check for leaks.

CRANKSHAFT TIMING SENSORS

The crankshaft timing sensor is located in the engine block, directly below the direct ignition system module (ignition coils) on the 2.0L engine or on the opposite side of the engine from the direct ignition system module (ignition coils) on the 2.8L engine.

The sensor reads the slots of the reluctor wheel, mounted on the crankshaft, to created an induced voltage pulse for the direct ignition system (DIS). Based on the crankshaft sensor pulses, the DIS module sends reference signals to the ECM. The ECM activates the fuel injector(s) based on the every other reference pulse.

Removal and Installation

1. Disconnect the electrical connector from the crankshaft sensor.
2. Remove the sensor-to-engine bolt and the sensor.
3. If necessary, replace the O-ring on the sensor.
4. To install, lubricate the O-ring with engine oil and reverse the removal procedures. Torque the sensor-to-engine bolt to 71 inch lbs. (8.7 Nm)

FUEL INJECTOR

Removal and Installation

2.0L ENGINE

The fuel injector is serviced as a complete unit, only. Since it is an electrical unit, handle it with care and do not immerse it any kind solvent or cleaner.
1. Disconnect the negative battery terminal. Relieve the pressure in the fuel system.
2. From the throttle body, remove the bonnet and the gasket.
3. Disconnect the electrical connector from the fuel injector.
4. Remove the fuel injector-to-throttle body retainer screw and the retainer.
5. Using a small pry bar and a fulcrum, place the blade under

the ridge opposite the electrical connector and carefully pry the injector from the throttle body.

6. Remove and discard the O-rings from the fuel injector.

7. Inspect the injector for dirt and contamination. If replacing the injector, be sure to use an identical part.

8. To install, lubricate the new O-rings with Dexron®II fluid, install the O-rings on the fuel injector and reverse the removal procedures. Torque the fuel injector-to-throttle body retainer screw to 27 inch lbs. Turn the ignition switch ON and check for leaks.

2.8L ENGINE

1. Relieve the pressure in the fuel system.
2. Disconnect the negative battery terminal.
3. Label and disconnect the vacuum lines from the plenum.
4. Remove the EGR valve from the plenum.
5. Remove the throttle body-to-plenum bolts and the throttle body.
6. Remove the throttle cable bracket bolts.

7. Remove the ignition wire shield.
8. Remove the plenum-to-intake manifold mounting bolts and the plenum.
9. Remove the fuel line bracket bolt and disconnect the fuel lines from the fuel rail. Wrap a rag around the lines to collect the excess fuel. Dispose of the rag properly.
10. Remove and discard the fuel line O-rings.
11. Disconnect the electrical connectors from the fuel injectors.
12. Remove the fuel rail assembly with the injectors.
13. Remove the fuel injector-to-fuel rail retaining clip, the fuel injectors and O-rings.

To install:

14. Lubricate the new (fuel injector) O-rings, new fuel line O-rings and reverse the removal procedures. Torque the fuel rail-to-intake manifold bolts to 19 ft. lbs. and the plenum bolts to 16 ft. lbs.
15. Turn the ignition switch ON and check for fuel leaks.

EMISSION CONTROL SYSTEMS

Refer to "Chilton's Emission Diagnosis and Service Manual" for additional coverage.

Emission Equipment Used

2.0L ENGINE

Electronic control module (ECM)
Oxygen sensor
Coolant temperature sensor (CTS)
Throttle position sensor (TPS)
Vehicle speed sensor (VSS)
Manifold absolute pressure (MAP) sensor
Idle air control (IAC)
Electronic spark timing (EST)
Prom
Manifold air temperature sensor (MAT)
Torque converter clutch (TCC)
Throttle body injection (TBI) assembly
Charcoal canister
Exhaust gas recirculation (EGR) valve
Positive crankcase ventilation (PCV) system
Thermostatic air cleaner (TAC)
Catalytic converter

2.8L ENGINE

Oxygen sensor
Coolant temperature sensor
Throttle position sensor
Vehicle speed sensor
Air temperature sensor
EGR valve
EGR vacuum control solenoid
Electronic control module
Mass air flow sensor

Electronic spark control system
Prom
Calpak
Fuel injectors
Fuel rail
Throttle body assembly
Idle air control valve
Vapor canister
Canister purge solenoid
Computer controlled coil ignition system (C³I)
ESC knock sensor
ESC module
Torque converter clutch
PCV system
Catalytic converter

Resetting Emission Warning Lamps

Procedure

When the ECM finds a problem, the "Check Engine/Service Engine Soon" light will turn ON and a trouble code will be recorded in the ECM memory. If the problem is intermittent, the "Check Engine/Service Engine Soon" light turn OFF after 10 seconds, when the fault goes away. However, the trouble code will stay in the ECM memory until the battery voltage to the ECM is removed. Removing the battery voltage for 10 seconds will clear all stored trouble codes. This is done by disconnecting the ECM harness from the positive battery pigtail for 10 seconds with the ignition OFF or by disconnecting the ECM fuse, designated ECM or ECM/BAT, from the fuse holder.

NOTE: To prevent ECM damage, the ignition switch must be OFF when disconnecting or reconnecting power to ECM (for example battery cable, ECM pigtail, ECM fuse, jumper cables, etc.).

ENGINE MECHANICAL

NOTE: Disconnecting the negative battery cable on some vehicles may interfere with the functions of the on board computer systems and may require the computer to undergo a relearning process, once the negative battery cable is reconnected.

Engine

Removal and Installation

2.0L ENGINE

1. Relieve the fuel pressure. Disconnect the battery terminals (negative terminal first). Remove the battery from the vehicle.
2. Position a clean drain pan under the radiator, open the drain cock and drain the cooling system. Remove the air intake hose.
3. From the throttle body, disconnect the T.V. and accelerator cables. Disconnect the ECM electrical harness connector from the engine.
4. Remove all vacuum hoses (not a part of the engine assembly), the upper/lower radiator hoses and the heater hoses from the engine.
5. Remove the heat shield from the exhaust manifold. Disconnect and label the engine wiring harness from the firewall.
6. Disconnect the windshield washer hoses and the bottle. Rotate the tensioner pulley (to reduce the belt tension) and remove the serpentine drive belt.
7. Disconnect and plug the fuel hoses. Raise and safely support the vehicle.
8. Remove the right side inner fender splash shield.
9. Remove the air conditioning compressor-to-bracket bolts and move it aside (so it will not interfere with the engine removal); do not disconnect the refrigerant lines.
10. Remove the flywheel splash shield. Label and disconnect electrical wires from the starter.
11. Remove the front starter brace, the starter-to-engine bolts and the starter.
12. If equipped with an automatic transaxle, remove the torque converter-to-flywheel bolts and push the converter back into the transaxle.
13. Remove the crankshaft pulley-to-crankshaft bolt. Using a crankshaft pulley hub remover tool, press the pulley from the crankshaft.
14. Remove the oil filter. Remove the engine-to-transaxle support bracket.
15. Disconnect the right rear engine mount.
16. Remove the exhaust pipe-to-exhaust manifold bolts, the exhaust pipe from the center hanger and loosen the muffler hanger.
17. Remove the T.V. and shift cable bracket. Remove both lower engine-to-transaxle bolts.
18. Lower the vehicle. From the intake manifold, remove the T.V. and accelerator cable bracket.
19. Remove the right front engine mount nuts. Disconnect the electrical connectors. Remove the alternator-to-bracket bolts and the alternator.
20. Remove the master cylinder-to-booster nuts, move the master cylinder and support it out of the way; do not disconnect the brake lines.
21. Using a vertical lifting device, install to the engine and lift it slightly.
22. Remove the right front engine mount bracket. Remove the remaining engine-to-transaxle bolts.
23. Remove the power steering pump-to-engine bolts and move it aside; do not disconnect the high pressure hoses.

24. Carefully lift and remove the engine from the vehicle.
To install:
25. Reverse the removal procedures. Install the power steering pump while lowering the engine into the vehicle.
26. To insure proper engine alignment, loosely install the engine mounts and raise the engine slightly.
27. Torque the engine-to-engine mount bolts to 40 ft. lbs., the engine-to-engine mount nuts to 20 ft. lbs. and the engine-to-transaxle bolts to 55 ft. lbs.
28. Refill the cooling system. Start the engine, allow it to reach normal operating temperatures and check for leaks.

2.8L ENGINE

1. Relieve the fuel pressure. Disconnect the battery terminals (the negative terminal first). Remove the battery from the vehicle.
2. Remove the air cleaner, the air inlet hose and the mass air flow sensor.
3. Position a clean drain pan under the radiator, open the drain cock and drain the cooling system. Remove the exhaust manifold crossover assembly bolts and separate the assembly from the exhaust manifolds.
4. Remove the serpentine belt tensioner and the drive belt. Remove the power steering pump-to-bracket bolts and support the pump out of the way.
5. Disconnect the radiator hose from the engine.
6. Disconnect the T.V. and accelerator cables from the throttle valve bracket on the plenum.
7. Disconnect the electrical connectors. Remove the alternator-to-bracket bolts and the alternator. Label and disconnect the electrical wiring harness from the engine.
8. Disconnect and plug the fuel hoses. Remove the coolant overflow and bypass hoses from the engine.
9. From the charcoal canister, disconnect the purge hose. Label and disconnect all the necessary vacuum hoses.
10. Using a engine holding fixture tool, support the engine.
11. Raise and safely support the vehicle.
12. Remove the right inner fender splash shield. Remove the crankshaft pulley-to-crankshaft bolt. Using a wheel puller, press the crankshaft pulley from the crankshaft.
13. Remove the flywheel cover. Label and disconnect the starter wires. Remove the starter-to-engine bolts and the starter.
14. Disconnect the wires from the oil pressure sending unit.
15. Remove the air conditioning compressor-to-bracket bolts and the bracket-to-engine bolts. Support the compressor so it will not interfere with the engine; do not disconnect the refrigerant lines.
16. Disconnect the exhaust pipe from the rear of the exhaust manifold.
17. If equipped with an automatic transaxle, remove the torque converter-to-flywheel bolts and push the converter into the transaxle.
18. Remove the front and rear engine mount bolts along with the mount brackets.
19. Remove the intermediate shaft bracket from the engine.
20. Disconnect the shifter cable from the transaxle.
21. Remove the lower engine-to-transaxle bolts and lower the vehicle.
22. Disconnect the heater hoses from the engine.
23. Using an vertical engine lift, install it to the engine and lift it slightly. Remove the engine holding fixture. Using a floor jack, support the transaxle.
24. Remove the upper engine-to-transaxle bolts. Remove the front engine mount bolts and transaxle mounting bracket.
25. Remove the engine from the vehicle.
To install:
26. Reverse the removal procedures.

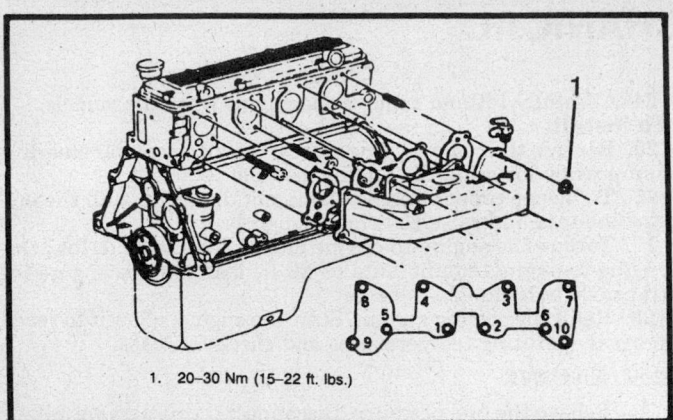

1. 20–30 Nm (15–22 ft. lbs.)

Intake manifold bolt torque sequence—2.0L 4 cyl engine

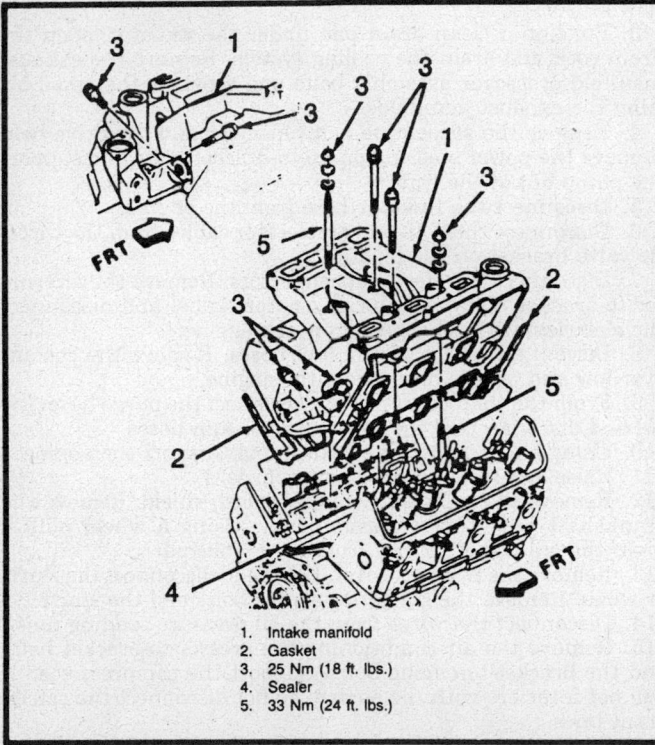

1. Intake manifold
2. Gasket
3. 25 Nm (18 ft. lbs.)
4. Sealer
5. 33 Nm (24 ft. lbs.)

Intake manifold installation—2.8L V6 engine

27. To insure proper engine alignment, loosely install the engine mounts and raise the engine slightly. Torque the engine mounting bolts to 65 ft. lbs., the engine-to-transaxle bolts to 55 ft. lbs.

28. Refill the cooling system. Start the engine, allow it to reach normal operating temperatures and check for leaks.

Engine Mounts

Removal and Installation

FRONT

1. Disconnect the negative battery terminal.
2. Remove the upper mount-to-body bracket bolts.
3. Raise and safely support the vehicle.

4. Using an engine holding fixture tool, support the engine.
5. Remove the left side inner fender shield.
6. Remove the lower engine mount-to-body bracket bolt.
7. Raise the engine (slightly) and remove the engine mount through bolt.
8. Remove the lower engine mount-to-engine bracket bolt and the mount.
9. To install, reverse the removal procedures. Torque the engine mount through bolt to 66–81 ft. lbs. and the engine mount-to-bracket bolts to 55–66 ft. lbs.

REAR

1. Disconnect the negative battery terminal.
2. Raise and safely support the vehicle.
3. Using an engine holding fixture tool, support the engine.
4. Remove the engine mount nuts/bolts and the engine mount.
5. To install, reverse the removal procedures. Torque the mounting bolts to 44–56 ft. lbs. and nuts to 14–20 ft. lbs.

Intake Manifold

Removal and Installation

2.0L ENGINE

1. Disconnect the negative battery terminal. Relieve the fuel pressure. Remove the TBI cover.
2. Drain the cooling system. Label and disconnect the vacuum lines and electrical connectors from the intake manifold.
3. Disconnect and plug the fuel line.
4. Disconnect the TBI linkage. Remove the throttle body-to-intake manifold bolts and the throttle body.
5. Remove the serpentine drive belt. Remove the power steering pump-to-bracket bolts and support the pump out of the way; do not disconnect the pressure hoses.
6. Raise and safely support the vehicle.
7. Disconnect the T.V. cable, accelerator cable and brackets.
8. Remove the heater hose from the bottom of the intake manifold. Lower the vehicle.
9. Remove the intake manifold-to-cylinder head nuts/bolts and the manifold.

To install:

10. Clean the gasket mounting surfaces.
11. Using new gaskets, reverse the removal procedures. Torque the intake manifold-to-cylinder heads bolts, in the proper sequence to 15–22 ft. lbs.
12. Refill the cooling system. Start the engine, allow it to reach normal operating temperatures and check for leaks.

2.8L ENGINE

1. Disconnect the negative battery terminal. Relieve the fuel pressure. Drain the cooling system.
2. Disconnect the T.V. and accelerator cables from the plenum.
3. Remove the throttle body-to-plenum bolts and the throttle body. Remove the EGR valve.
4. Remove the plenum-to-intake manifold bolts and the plenum. Disconnect and plug the fuel lines and return pipes at the fuel rail.
5. Remove the serpentine drive belt. Remove the power steering pump-to-bracket bolts and support the pump out of the way; do not disconnect the pressure hoses.
6. Remove the alternator-to-bracket bolts and support the alternator out of the way.
7. Loosen the alternator bracket. From the throttle body, disconnect the idle air vacuum hose.
8. Label and disconnect the electrical connectors from the fuel injectors. Remove the fuel rail.
9. Remove the breather tube. Disconnect the runners.
10. Remove both rocker arm cover-to-cylinder head bolts and

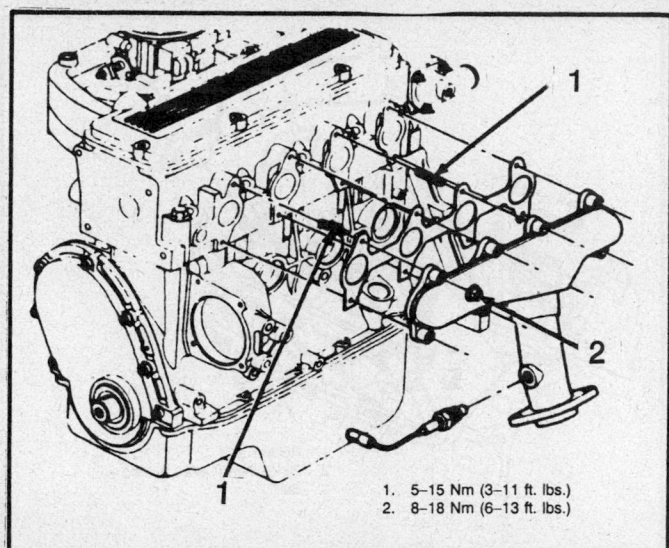

1. 5–15 Nm (3–11 ft. lbs.)
2. 8–18 Nm (6–13 ft. lbs.)

Exhaust manifold installation—2.0L 4 cyl engine

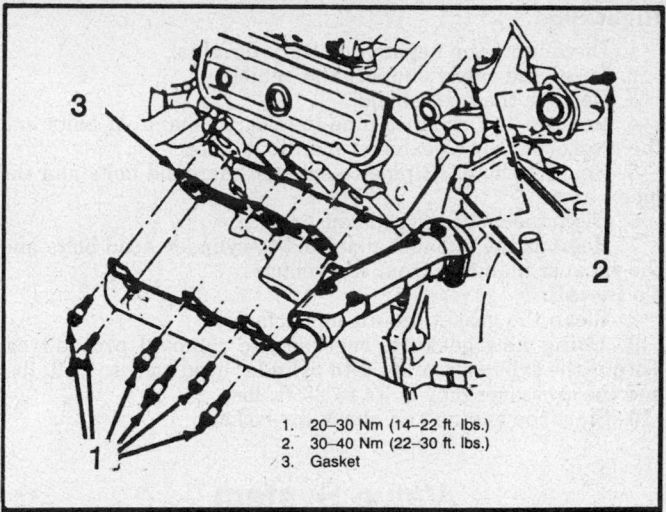

1. 20–30 Nm (14–22 ft. lbs.)
2. 30–40 Nm (22–30 ft. lbs.)
3. Gasket

Left side exhaust manifold installation—2.8L V6 engine

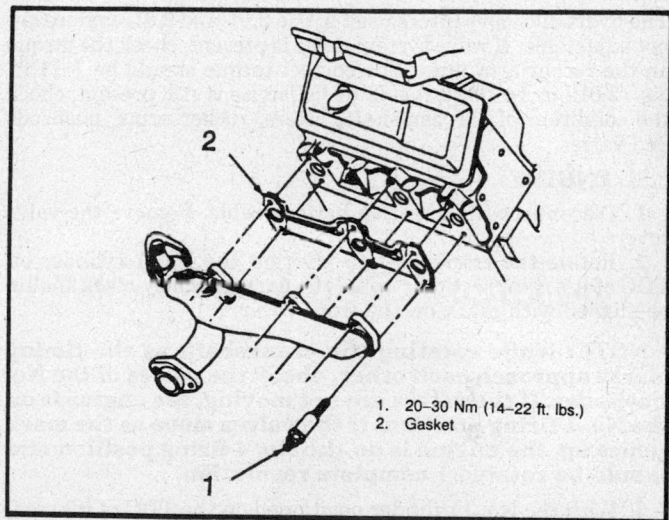

1. 20–30 Nm (14–22 ft. lbs.)
2. Gasket

Right side exhaust manifold installation—2.8L V6 engine

the covers. Remove the radiator hose from the thermostat housing.

11. Label and disconnect the electrical connectors from the coolant temperature sensor and oil pressure sending unit. Remove the coolant sensor.

12. Remove the bypass hose from the filler neck and cylinder head.

13. Remove the intake manifold-to-cylinder head bolts and the manifold.

14. Loosen the rocker arm nuts, turn them 90 degrees and remove the pushrods; be sure to keep the components in order for installation purposes.

To install:

15. Clean all gasket mounting surfaces.

16. Using new gaskets, place a 3/16 in. bead of RTV sealant on the ridges of the manifold and reverse the removal procedures.

17. Torque the intake manifold-to-cylinder head bolts, following the torquing sequence, to 24 ft. lbs. and the nuts to 18 ft. lbs.

18. Refill the cooling system. Start the engine, allow it to reach normal operating temperatures and check for leaks.

Exhaust Manifold

Removal and Installation

2.0L ENGINE

1. Disconnect the negative battery terminal.
2. Disconnect the oxygen sensor wire.
3. Remove the serpentine belt.
4. Remove the alternator-to-bracket bolts and position the alternator, with the wires attached, out of the way.
5. Raise and safely support the vehicle.
6. Disconnect the exhaust pipe-to-exhaust manifold bolts and lower the vehicle.
7. Remove the exhaust manifold-to-cylinder head bolts.
8. Remove the exhaust manifold from the exhaust pipe flange and the manifold from the vehicle.

To install:

9. Clean the gasket mounting surfaces.
10. Using new gaskets, reverse the removal procedures. Torque the exhaust manifold-to-cylinder head nuts to 3–11 ft. lbs. and bolts to 6–13 ft. lbs.
11. Start the engine and check for leaks.

2.8L ENGINE
Left Side

1. Disconnect the negative battery terminal. Drain the cooling system.
2. Remove the air cleaner, air inlet hose and the mass air flow sensor.
3. Remove the coolant bypass pipe. Remove the manifold heat shield.
4. Disconnect the exhaust manifold crossover assembly at the right manifold.
5. Remove the exhaust manifold-to-cylinder head attaching bolts.
6. From the right manifold, remove the exhaust manifold with the crossover assembly.

To install:

7. Clean the gasket mounting surfaces.
8. Using new gaskets, reverse the removal procedures. Torque the exhaust manifold-to-cylinder head bolts to 19 ft. lbs. and the crossover bolts to 25 ft. lbs.
9. Start the engine and check for exhaust leaks.

Right Side

1. Disconnect the negative battery terminal.
2. Raise and safely support the vehicle.
3. Remove the heat shield.
4. Remove the exhaust pipe-to-exhaust manifold bolts and the crossover pipe-to-exhaust manifold bolts.
5. Remove the EGR pipe-to-exhaust manifold bolts and the pipe.
6. Disconnect the oxygen sensor wire.
7. Remove the exhaust manifold-to-cylinder head bolts and the exhaust manifold from the vehicle.

To install:

8. Clean the gasket mounting surfaces.
9. Using new gaskets, reverse the removal procedures. Torque the exhaust manifold-to-cylinder head bolts to 19 ft. lbs. and the crossover pipe bolts to 25 ft. lbs.
10. Start the engine and check for leaks.

Valve System

VALVE ADJUSTMENT

The hydraulic valve lifters used in the 2.0L and 2.8L engines are not adjustable. If valve system noise is present, check the torque on the rocker arm nuts. The correct torque should be 7–11 ft. lbs. (2.0L) or 14–20 ft. lbs. (2.8L). If noise is still present, check the condition of the camshaft, lifters, rocker arms, pushrods and valves.

2.8L ENGINE

1. Disconnect the negative battery cable. Remove the valve covers.
2. Rotate the crankshaft to position the No. 1 cylinder on TDC of it's compression stroke; the damper pulley mark should be aligned with mark on the front cover.

NOTE: While rotating the crankshaft, as the timing marks approach each other, check the valves of the No. 1 cylinder. If the valves are not moving, the engine is on the No. 1 firing position. If the valves move as the mark comes up, the engine is on the No. 4 firing position and should be rotated 1 complete revolution.

3. With the No. 1 cylinder positioned on the TDC of it's compression, adjust the:
   a. Exhaust valves of cylinders No. 1, 2 and 3
   b. Intake valves of cylinders No. 1, 5 and 6
4. Adjust the valve by performing the following procedures:
   a. Back off the adjusting nut until lash is felt at the pushrod.
   b. Turn the adjusting nut until all lash is removed; this is determined by rotating the pushrod while turning the adjusting nut.
   c. When the lash is removed, turn the nut an additional 1½ turns.
5. Rotate the crankshaft 1 complete revolution and realign the timing marks.
6. With the No. 4 cylinder positioned on the TDC of it's compression, adjust the exhaust valves of cylinders No. 4, 5 and 6 and the intake valves of cylinders No. 2, 3 and 4.
7. Adjust the valve by performing the following procedures:
   a. Back off the adjusting nut until lash is felt at the pushrod.
   b. Turn the adjusting nut until all lash is removed; this is determined by rotating the pushrod while turning the adjusting nut.
   c. When the lash is removed, turn the nut an additional 1½ turns.
8. Reinstall the removed parts. Start the engine and check it's operation.

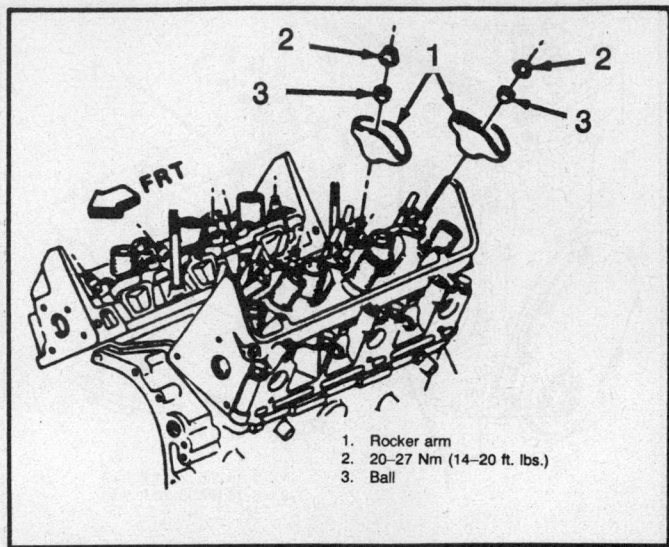

1. Rocker arm
2. 20–27 Nm (14–20 ft. lbs.)
3. Ball

Rocker arm installation—2.8L V6 engine

VALVE LIFTERS

Removal and Installation

2.0L ENGINE

1. Disconnect the negative battery terminal. Remove the rocker arm cover.
2. Loosen the rocker arms nuts enough to move the rocker arms aside and remove the pushrods.
3. Using a valve lifter remover tool, remove the lifters from the engine.

To install:

4. Using Molykote® or equivalent, coat the base of the new lifters. Using a valve lifter remover tool, install the lifters into the engine.
5. To complete the installation, reverse the removal procedures. Torque the rocker arm nuts to 7–11 ft. lbs. and the rocker arm cover bolts to 8 ft. lbs.

2.8L ENGINE

1. Disconnect the negative battery terminal.
2. Drain the cooling system.
3. Remove the rocker arm covers and intake manifold.
4. Loosen the rocker arms nuts enough to move the rocker arms aside and remove the pushrods.
5. Remove the lifters from the engine.

To install:

6. Using Molykote® or equivalent, coat the base of the new lifters and install them into the engine.
7. To complete the installation, position the pushrods and the rocker arms correctly into their original positions. Torque the rocker arm nuts to 18 ft. lbs. and the intake manifold-to-cylinder head bolts to 20 ft. lbs.

VALVE ROCKER ARMS

Removal and Installation

2.0L ENGINE

1. Disconnect the negative battery terminal. Remove the air hose from the TBI unit and the air cleaner.
2. Remove the intake manifold-to-rocker cover hose.
3. Remove the rocker arm cover bolts and the cover.
4. Remove the rocker arm nuts and the rocker arms.

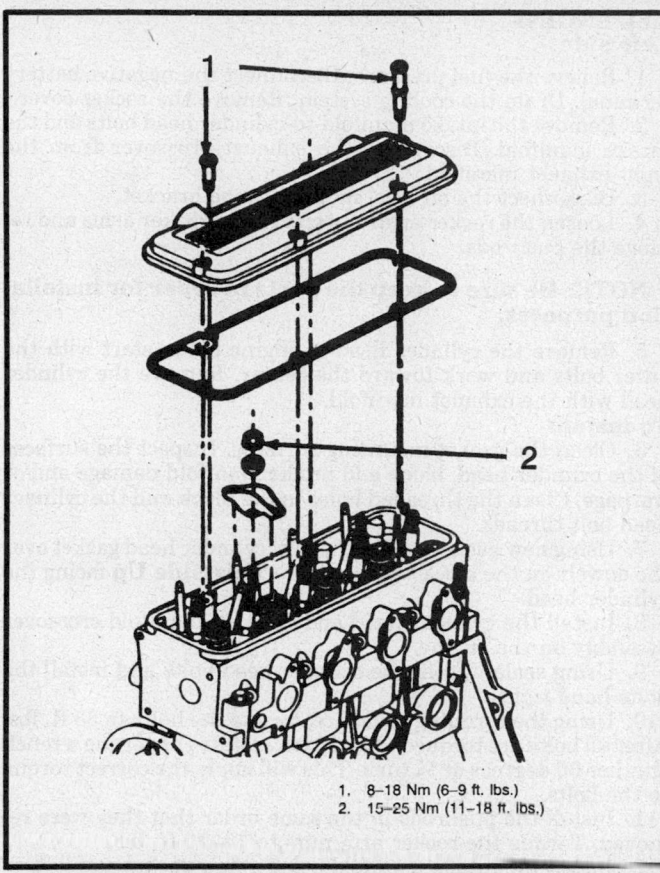

1. 8–18 Nm (6–9 ft. lbs.)
2. 15–25 Nm (11–18 ft. lbs.)

Rocker arm and cover installation — 2.0L 4 cyl engine

NOTE: Be sure to keep the components in order for installation purposes.

To install:
5. Using new gaskets and sealant, if necessary, reverse the removal procedures. Torque the rocker arm nuts to 7–11 ft. lbs.
6. To complete the installation, reverse the removal procedures.

2.8L ENGINE

Left Side

1. Disconnect the negative battery terminal. Disconnect the bracket tube from the rocker cover.
2. Remove the spark plug wire cover. Drain the cooling system and remove the heater hose from the filler neck.
3. Remove the rocker arm cover-to-cylinder head bolts and the rocker cover.

NOTE: If the rocker arm cover will not lift off the cylinder head easily, strike the end with the palm of the hand or a rubber mallet.

4. Remove the rocker arm nuts and the rocker arms; be sure to keep the components in order for installation purposes.
To install:
5. Clean the gasket mounting surfaces.
6. Using new gaskets and sealant, reverse the removal procedures.
7. Torque the rocker arm nuts to 14–20 ft. lbs.
8. Start the engine and check for leaks.

Right Side

1. Disconnect the negative battery terminal. Disconnect the brake booster vacuum line from the bracket.

2. Disconnect the cable bracket from the plenum.
3. Disconnect the vacuum line bracket from the cable bracket.
4. Disconnect the lines from the alternator brace stud.
5. Remove the rear alternator brace and the serpentine drive belt.
6. Remove the alternator and support it out of the way.
7. Remove the PCV valve.
8. Loosen the alternator bracket.
9. Disconnect the spark plug wires from the spark plugs. Remove the rocker cover-to-cylinder head bolts and the rocker cover.

NOTE: If the rocker arm cover will not lift off the cylinder head easily, strike the end with the palm of the hand or a rubber mallet.

10. Remove the rocker arm nuts and the rocker arms; be sure to keep the components in order for installation purposes.
To install:
11. Clean the gasket mounting surfaces.
12. Using new gaskets and sealant, reverse the removal procedures.
13. Torque the rocker arm nuts to 14–20 ft. lbs.

CHECKING VALVE TIMING

Procedure

1. Disconnect the negative battery terminal. Remove the timing case cover.
2. Rotate the crankshaft to until the marks on the crankshaft and camshaft sprockets are directly aligned; if not, loosen the timing chain tensioner.
3. Align the tabs on the tensioner with the marks on the camshaft and crankshaft sprockets and tighten the tensioner.
4. To complete the installation, reverse the removal procedures.

Cylinder Head

Removal and Installation

2.0L ENGINE

1. Relieve the fuel pressure. Disconnect the negative battery terminal.
2. Drain the cooling system. Remove the TBI cover.
3. Raise and safely support the vehicle.
4. Disconnect the exhaust pipe-to-exhaust manifold bolts and separate the exhaust pipe from the manifold.
5. Lower the vehicle. Disconnect the heater hose from the intake manifold.
6. Disconnect the T.V. and accelerator cable bracket.
7. Label and disconnect the vacuum hoses from the intake manifold and thermostat.
8. Disconnect the accelerator linkage from the TBI unit.
9. Label and disconnect the electrical wiring from the engine.
10. Disconnect the upper radiator hose from the thermostat. Remove the serpentine belt.
11. Remove the power steering pump-to-bracket bolts and support the pump out of the way; do not disconnect the high pressure hoses from the pump.
12. Disconnect and plug the fuel lines. Remove the alternator-to-bracket bolts and the alternator. Position it out of the way (with electrical connectors attached).
13. Remove the alternator rear brace.
14. Remove the rocker arm cover-to-cylinder head bolts and the cover. Remove the rocker arm bolts, the rocker arms and pushrods; be sure to keep valve train components in the order that they were removed.
15. Starting with the outer bolts, remove the cylinder head-to-engine bolts.

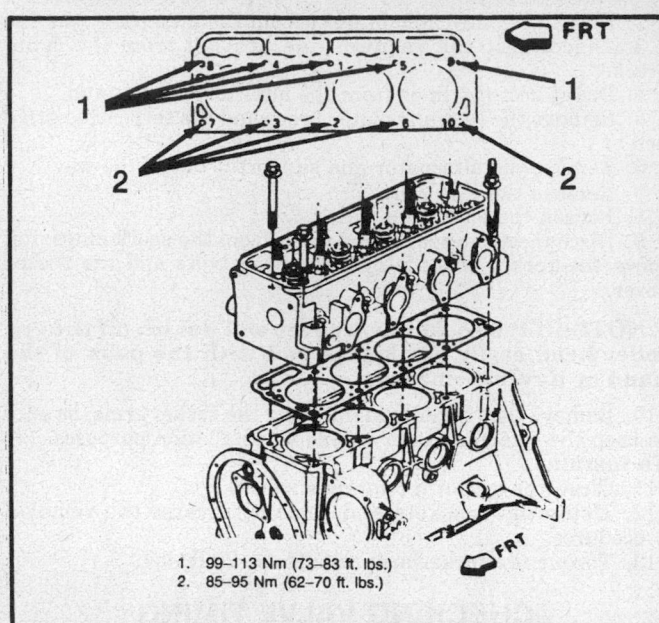

1. 99–113 Nm (73–83 ft. lbs.)
2. 85–95 Nm (62–70 ft. lbs.)

Cylinder head bolt torque sequence—2.0L 4 cyl engine

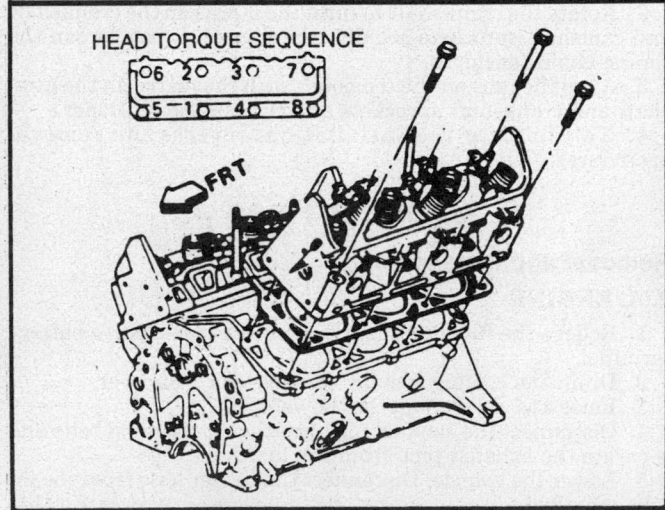

HEAD TORQUE SEQUENCE

Cylinder head bolt torque sequence—2.8L V6 engine

To install:

16. Clean and inspect the gasket mounting surfaces. Make sure the threads on the cylinder head bolts and in the block are clean.

17. Using sealant, coat both sides of the new head gasket and install the gasket on the dowel pins on the block.

18. Install the cylinder head and tighten the head bolts hand tight.

19. Following the torquing sequence, torque the head bolts (in 3 steps) to 73–83 ft. lbs. (intake side) and 62–70 ft. lbs. (exhaust side).

20. Install the pushrods and rocker arms in the same order they were removed. Torque the rocker arm nuts to 7–11 ft. lbs.

21. To complete the installation, reverse the removal procedures. Refill the cooling system. Start the engine, allow it to reach normal operating temperatures and check for leaks.

2.8L ENGINE
Left Side

1. Relieve the fuel pressure. Disconnect the negative battery terminal. Drain the cooling system. Remove the rocker cover.

2. Remove the intake manifold-to-cylinder head bolts and the intake manifold. Disconnect the exhaust crossover from the right exhaust manifold.

3. Disconnect the oil level indicator tube bracket.

4. Loosen the rocker arms nuts, turn the rocker arms and remove the pushrods.

NOTE: Be sure to keep the parts in order for installation purposes.

5. Remove the cylinder head-to-engine bolts; start with the outer bolts and work toward the center. Remove the cylinder head with the exhaust manifold.

To install:

6. Clean the gasket mounting surfaces. Inspect the surfaces of the cylinder head, block and intake manifold damage and/or warpage. Clean the threaded holes in the block and the cylinder head bolt threads.

7. Using new gaskets, align the new cylinder head gasket over the dowels on the block with the note **This Side Up** facing the cylinder head.

8. Install the cylinder head and exhaust manifold crossover assembly on the engine.

9. Using sealant, coat the cylinder head bolts and install the bolts hand tight.

10. Using the torquing sequence, torque the bolts to 33 ft. lbs. After all bolts are torqued to 33 ft. lbs., rotate the torque wrench another 90 degrees or ¼ turn. This will apply the correct torque to the bolts.

11. Install the pushrods in the same order that they were removed. Torque the rocker arm nuts to 14–20 ft. lbs.

12. Install the intake manifold using a new gasket and following the correct sequence, torque the bolts to the correct specification.

13. To complete the installation, reverse the removal procedures. Refill the cooling system. Operate the engine until normal operating temperatures are reached and check for leaks.

Right Side

1. Relieve the fuel pressure. Disconnect the negative battery terminal. Drain the cooling system.

2. Raise and safely support the vehicle. Remove the exhaust manifold-to-exhaust pipe bolts and separate the pipe from the manifold.

3. Lower the vehicle. Remove the exhaust manifold-to-cylinder head bolts and the manifold.

4. Remove the rocker arm cover. Remove the intake manifold-to-cylinder head bolts and the intake manifold.

5. Loosen the rocker arms nuts, turn the rocker arms and remove the pushrods.

NOTE: Be sure to keep the components in order for reassembly purposes.

6. Remove the cylinder head-to-engine bolts (starting with the outer bolts and working toward the center) and the cylinder head.

To install:

7. Clean the gasket mounting surfaces. Inspect the parts for damage and/or warpage; if necessary, machine or replace the parts.

8. Clean the engine block's threaded holes and the cylinder head bolt threads.

9. Using new gaskets, reverse the removal procedures. Using sealant, coat the cylinder head bolts and install the bolts hand tight.

10. Using the torquing sequence, torque the bolts to 33 ft. lbs. After all bolts are torqued to 33 ft. lbs., rotate the torque wrench

another 90 degrees or ¼ turn; this will apply the correct torque to the bolts.

11. Install the pushrods in the same order as they were removed. Torque the rocker arm nuts to 14–20 ft. lbs.

12. Follow the torquing sequence, use a new gasket and install the intake manifold.

13. To complete the installation, reverse the removal procedures. Refill the cooling system. Start the engine, allow it to reach normal operating temperatures and check for leaks.

Camshaft

Removal and Installation

2.0L ENGINE

1. Relieve the fuel pressure. Disconnect the negative battery terminal. Remove the engine and attach it to an engine stand.

2. Remove the timing chain and sprocket from the engine.

3. Drain the engine oil and remove the oil filter.

4. Remove the rocker cover. Loosen the rocker arms and turn the rocker arms 90 degrees. Remove the pushrods and lifters; note the position of the valve train components for reassembly purposes.

5. Remove the oil pump drive.

6. Remove the camshaft thrust plate-to-engine bolts and carefully pull the camshaft from the engine.

NOTE: Use care when removing and installing the camshaft; do not damage the camshaft bearings or the bearing surfaces on the camshaft.

To install:

7. Clean gasket mounting surfaces.

8. Lubricate the lobes of the new camshaft and insert the camshaft into the engine.

NOTE: If a new camshaft is being used replace all of the lifters. Used lifters can only be used on the camshaft that they were originally installed with; provided they are installed in the exact same position they were removed.

9. Align the marks on the camshaft and crankshaft sprockets Install the timing chain and sprocket.

10. To complete the installation, use new gaskets and reverse the removal procedures. Torque the rocker arm nuts to 11–18 ft. lbs.

2.8L ENGINE

1. Relieve the fuel pressure. Disconnect the negative battery terminal. Remove the engine and attach it to an engine stand.

2. Remove the intake manifold, the timing chain and sprockets.

NOTE: Be sure to the valve train components in order for reassembly purposes.

3. Remove the valve lifters.

4. Carefully pull the camshaft from the front of the engine.

NOTE: The camshaft journals are all the same size. Use extreme care when removing or installing the camshaft not to damage the camshaft bearings or the bearing journals of the camshaft.

To install:

5. Clean gasket mounting surfaces.

6. If installing a new camshaft, lubricate the camshaft lobes and insert the camshaft in the engine.

NOTE: If a new camshaft is being used, replace all of the lifters. Used lifters can only be used on the camshaft that they were originally installed with; provided they are installed in the exact same position they were removed.

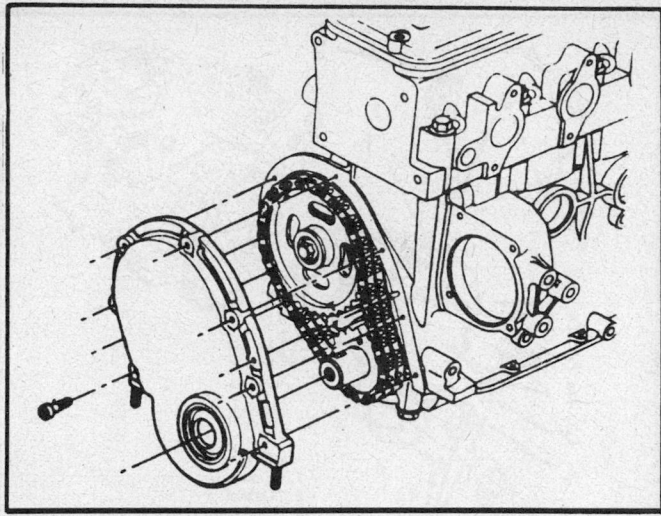

Front cover installation—2.0L 4 cyl engine

7. Align the camshaft and crankshaft sprocket marks. Install the timing chain and sprocket.

8. Install the front cover and valve train components. Torque the rocker arm nuts to 14–20 ft. lbs.

9. To complete the installation, reverse the removal procedures. Start the engine, allow it to reach normal operating temperatures and check for leaks.

Timing Case Cover

Removal and Installation

2.0L ENGINE

1. Disconnect the negative battery terminal.

2. Raise and safely support the vehicle.

3. Drain the engine oil and remove the oil pan.

4. Lower the vehicle.

5. Remove the serpentine belt and the belt tensioner.

6. Remove the crankshaft pulley retaining bolt. Using a crankshaft pulley puller tool, remove the crankshaft pulley.

7. Remove the timing case cover bolts. Tap the cover with a rubber mallet and remove the cover.

To install:

8. Clean gasket mounting surfaces.

9. Using new gaskets, install the timing case cover over the dowels on the block and reverse the removal procedures. Torque the timing case cover-to-engine bolts to 6–9 ft. lbs.

10. Using a crankshaft pulley installer tool, press the pulley onto the crankshaft. Torque the crankshaft pulley bolt to 66–88 ft. lbs.

11. To complete the installation, reverse the removal procedures. Start the engine and check for leaks.

2.8L ENGINE

1. Disconnect the negative battery terminal. Drain the cooling system.

2. Remove the serpentine belt and the belt tensioner.

3. Remove the alternator-to-bracket bolts and with the wires attached to the alternator, position it out of the way.

4. Remove the power steering pump-to-bracket bolts and support it out of the way; do not disconnect the pressure hoses.

5. Raise and safely support the vehicle.

6. Remove the right side inner fender splash shield and the flywheel dust cover.

7. Using a crankshaft pulley puller tool, remove the crankshaft damper.

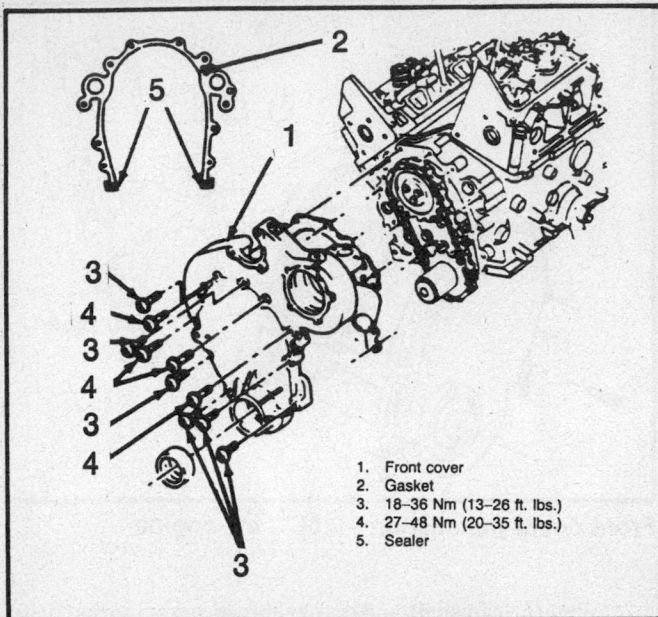

1. Front cover
2. Gasket
3. 18–36 Nm (13–26 ft. lbs.)
4. 27–48 Nm (20–35 ft. lbs.)
5. Sealer

Front cover installation—2.8L V6 engine

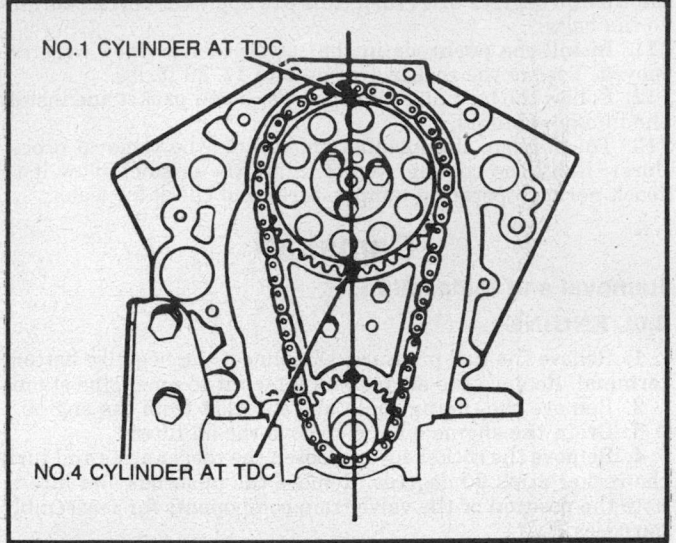

Timing chain and sprockets installation—2.8L V6 engine

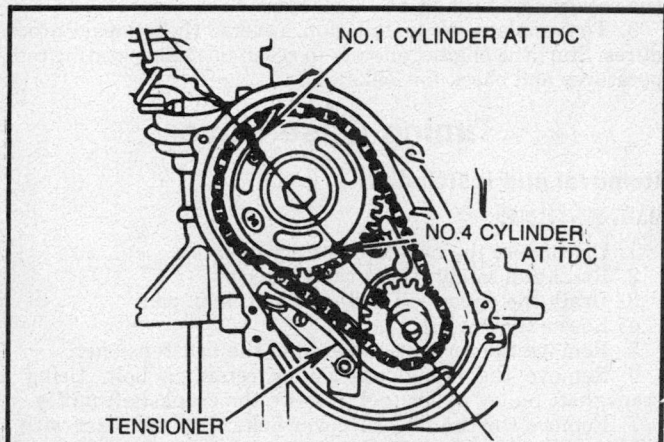

Timing chain and sprockets installation—2.0L 4 cyl engine

8. Label and disconnect the starter wires and remove the starter.

9. Loosen the front 5 oil pan bolts (on both sides) enough to lower the oil pan ½ in.

10. Lower the vehicle. Disconnect the radiator hose from the water pump.

11. Disconnect the heater coolant hose from the cooling system filler pipe.

12. Remove the bypass and overflow hoses.

13. Remove the water pump pulley. Disconnect the canister purge hose.

14. Remove the spark plug wire shield from the water pump.

15. Remove the upper timing case cover-to-engine bolts and the timing case cover.

To install:

16. Clean gasket mounting surfaces.

17. Using silicone sealant and a new gasket, apply a thin bead to the front cover mating surface, install the timing case cover on the engine. Apply silicone sealant to the sections of the oil pan rails that were lowered and install the mounting bolts.

18. Using a crankshaft pulley installer tool, press the damper pulley onto the crankshaft.

19. To complete the installation, reverse the removal procedures. Start the engine and check for oil leaks.

Timing Case Oil Seal

Removal and Installation

2.0L ENGINE

1. Disconnect the negative battery terminal. Remove the serpentine belt.

2. Raise and safely support the vehicle. Remove the right front wheel and tire assembly.

3. Remove the inner fender splash shield.

4. Remove the crankshaft pulley bolt.

5. Using a crankshaft pulley puller tool, remove the crankshaft pulley.

6. Using a small pry bar, pry the oil seal from the front cover.

NOTE: Use care not to damage the seal seat or the crankshaft while removing or installing the seal. Inspect the sealing surface of the crankshaft for grooves or other wear.

To install:

7. Using an oil seal centering tool, drive the new seal into the cover with the lip facing towards the engine.

8. Install a crankshaft pulley installer tool, onto the crankshaft pulley and press the pulley onto the crankshaft.

9. To complete the installation, reverse the removal procedures. Torque the pulley bolt to 66–88 ft. lbs.

2.8L ENGINE

1. Disconnect the negative battery terminal. Remove the serpentine belt.

2. Raise and safely support the vehicle. Remove the right side inner fender splash shield.

3. Remove the damper retaining bolt.

4. Using a crankshaft pulley puller tool, press the damper pulley from the crankshaft.

5. Using a small pry bar, pry out the seal in the front cover.

NOTE: Use care not to damage the seal seat or the crankshaft while removing or installing the seal. Inspect the crankshaft seal surface for signs of grooves or wear.

To install:

6. Using a seal installer tool, drive the new seal in the cover with the lip facing towards the engine.

7. Using a crankshaft pulley installer tool, press the crankshaft pulley onto the crankshaft. Torque the damper bolt to 67–85 ft. lbs.

8. To complete the installation, reverse the removal procedures.

Timing Sprockets and Chain

Removal and Installation

2.0L ENGINE

1. Disconnect the negative battery terminal. Remove the timing case cover.

2. Rotate the crankshaft to until the marks on the crankshaft and camshaft sprockets are aligned.

3. Remove the timing chain tensioner upper bolt.

4. Loosen the timing chain tensioner nut as far as possible but do not remove the nut.

5. Remove the timing chain and camshaft sprocket.

6. Using a gear puller, remove the crankshaft sprocket.

To install:

7. Before installing the camshaft sprocket, lubricate the thrust side with Molykote® or equivalent. Using a sprocket installer tool, install the crankshaft sprocket.

8. Align the camshaft sprocket mark with the crankshaft sprocket marks. Install the timing chain and camshaft sprocket.

9. Press the camshaft sprocket onto the camshaft, using the camshaft sprocket bolt. Torque the camshaft sprocket bolt to 66–88 ft. lbs.

10. Align the tabs on the tensioner with the marks on the camshaft and crankshaft sprockets and tighten the tensioner.

11. To complete the installation, reverse the removal procedures.

2.8L ENGINE

1. Disconnect the negative battery terminal. Remove the front cover.

2. Rotate the crankshaft to position the No. 1 piston at TDC with the crankshaft and camshaft sprockets aligned.

NOTE: When the camshaft and crankshaft marks are aligned, the No. 4 piston is on the TDC of its compression stroke.

3. Remove the camshaft sprocket bolts, the sprocket and the timing chain.

4. Remove the crankshaft sprocket.

To install:

5. Before installing the sprocket(s), apply Molykote® or equivalent, to the thrust face of the sprocket(s).

6. Install the sprocket on the crankshaft.

7. Hold the camshaft sprocket with the chain hanging down. Align the marks on the camshaft and crankshaft sprockets.

8. Align the dowel in the camshaft with the sprocket. Install the sprocket and timing chain using a camshaft bolt to pull the sprocket into position.

9. Torque the camshaft bolts to 15–20 ft. lbs.

10. Lubricate the new timing chain with clean engine oil.

11. To complete the installation, reverse the removal procedures. Start the engine and check for leaks.

Piston, Rings and Rod Positioning

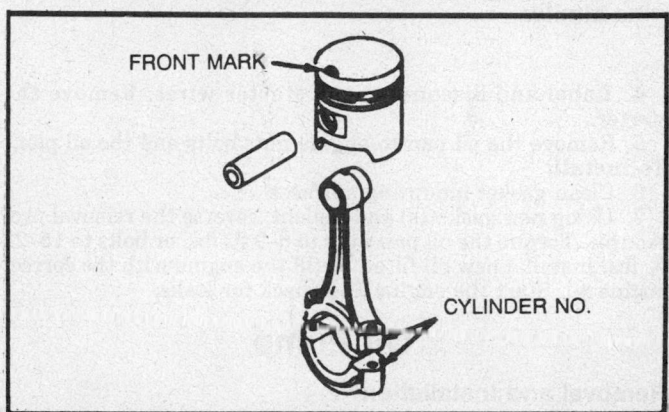

Piston and connecting rod position—2.0L 4 cyl and 2.8L V6 engines

LUBRICATION SYSTEM

Oil Pan

Removal and Installation

2.0L ENGINE

1. Disconnect the negative battery terminal. Remove the exhaust pipe shield.

2. Raise and safely support the vehicle. Drain the engine oil.

3. Disconnect the air conditioning brace from the starter and the air conditioning bracket.

4. Disconnect the starter brace from the block. Label and disconnect the starter wires. Remove the starter.

5. Remove the flywheel dust cover.

6. Remove the right support bolts and lower the support for clearance to remove the oil pan. If equipped with an automatic transaxle, remove the oil filter and extension.

7. Remove the oil pan-to-engine bolts and the oil pan.

To install:

8. Clean gasket mounting surfaces.

9. Using new gaskets and sealant, reverse the removal procedures. Torque the oil pan-to-engine bolts to 6 ft. lbs.

NOTE: Place a small bead of RTV sealant on the oil pan-to-engine block sealing surface. Apply a thin layer of RTV sealant on the ends of the oil pan rear seal.

10. To complete the installation, reverse the removal procedures. Install a new oil filter. Refill the engine with the clean engine oil. Start the engine and check for leaks.

2.8L ENGINE

1. Disconnect the negative battery terminal.

2. Raise and safely support the vehicle. Drain the engine oil.

3. Remove the flywheel dust cover.

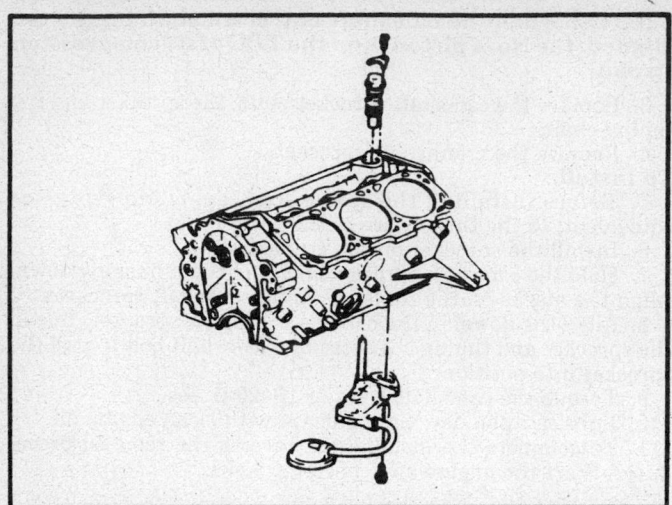

Oil pump installation—2.8L V6 engine—2.0L 4 cyl engine similar

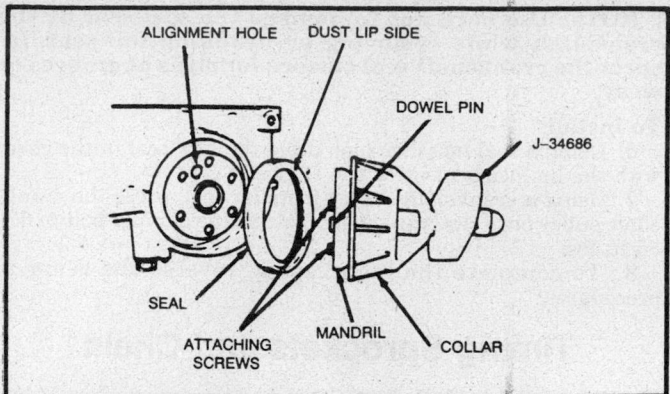

Rear main bearing oil seal installation—2.0L 4 cyl and 2.8L V6 engines

4. Label and disconnect the starter wires. Remove the starter.

5. Remove the oil pan-to-engine nuts/bolts and the oil pan.

To install:

6. Clean gasket mounting surfaces.

7. Using new gasket(s) and sealant, reverse the removal procedures. Torque the oil pan nuts to 6–9 ft. lbs. or bolts to 15–22 ft. lbs. Install a new oil filter. Refill the engine with the correct engine oil. Start the engine and check for leaks.

Oil Pump

Removal and Installation

1. Disconnect the negative battery terminal. Raise and safely support the vehicle. Drain the engine oil.

2. Remove the oil pan-to-engine bolts and the oil pan.

3. Remove the oil pump-to-rear main bearing cap bolt, the oil pump and extension shaft.

To install:

4. Using new gaskets and sealant, reverse the removal procedures. Torque the oil pump-to-bearing cap bolt to 25–38 ft. lbs. and the upper oil pump drive bolt to 14–22 ft. lbs. on the 2.0L engine or to 25–38 ft. lbs. on the 2.8L engine

5. Refill the engine with clean engine oil. Start the engine and check for oil pressure and leaks.

Inspection

1. If foreign matter is present, determine it's source.

2. Check the pump cover and housing for cracks, scoring and/or damage; if necessary, replace the housing(s).

3. Inspect the idler gear shaft for looseness in the housing; if necessary, replace the pump or timing chain, depending on the model.

4. Inspect the pressure regulator valve for scoring or sticking; if burrs are present, remove them with an oil stone.

5. Inspect the pressure regulator valve spring for loss of tension or distortion; if necessary, replace it.

6. Inspect the suction pipe for looseness, if pressed into the housing, and the screen for broken wire mesh; if necessary, replace them.

7. Inspect the gears for chipping, galling and/or wear; if necessary, replace them.

8. Inspect the driveshaft and driveshaft extension for looseness and/or wear; if necessary, replace them.

Rear Main Oil Seal

Removal and Installation

NOTE: This procedure should only be performed if tool No. J-34686 or equivalent, is available. This is a special tool designed for this application.

1. Disconnect the negative battery terminal. Remove the transaxle.

2. If equipped with a manual transaxle, matchmark and remove the clutch assembly/flywheel assembly. If equipped with an automatic transaxle, remove the flywheel.

3. Using a small pry bar, pry the rear main seal from the engine.

NOTE: Use care when removing or installing the seal to avoid damage to the crankshaft sealing surface. If equipped with a manual transaxle, inspect the condition of the clutch to insure that the clutch was not damaged by oil loss from the rear main seal.

To install:

4. To install the rear main oil seal, perform the following procedures:

    a. Lubricate the seal bore and seal surface with engine oil.

    b. Using a seal installation tool, press the new rear oil seal into the engine. The seal must fit squarely against the back of the tool.

    c. Align the dowel pin of the tool with the dowel pin in the crankshaft and tighten the attaching screws on the tool to 2–5 ft. lbs.

    d. Tighten the T-handle of the tool to push the seal into the seal bore.

    e. Loosen the T-handle. Remove the attaching screws and tool.

    f. Check the seal to make sure it is seated squarely in the bore.

5. To complete the installation, reverse the removal procedures. Torque the flywheel-to-crankshaft bolts to 45–59 ft. lbs. for automatic transaxles or to 47–63 ft. lbs. for manual transaxles.

6. Start the engine and check for leaks.

Connecting Rod and Main Bearings

Replacement

Engine bearings are of the precision insert type. They are available for service in standard and various undersizes. Upper and lower bearing inserts may be different. Be careful to align holes.

Do not obstruct any oil passages. Bearing inserts must not be shimmed. Do not touch the bearing surface of the insert with bare fingers. Skin oil and acids will etch the bearing surface.

NOTE: Bearing failure, other than normal wear, must be investigated carefully. Inspect the crankshaft, con- necting rods and the bearing bores. Avoid damage to the crankshaft journals during removal and installation.

—— **CAUTION** ——
Use care when handling the pistons. Worn piston rings are sharp and may cause injury.

FRONT SUSPENSION AND STEERING

For front suspension component removal and installation procedures, refer to unit repair section.

For steering wheel removal and installation, refer to electrical control section.

Power Steering Rack and Pinion

Adjustment

1. Disconnect the negative battery terminal. Raise and safely support the vehicle.
2. With the front tires off the ground, loosen the locknut on the bottom of the steering rack.
3. Turn the adjuster plug clockwise until it bottoms out in the housing.
4. Turn the adjuster plug in the opposite direction 50–70 degrees.
5. While holding the adjuster plug, torque the locknut to 50 ft. lbs.

NOTE: If the adjuster plug is not held, damage to the pinion teeth on the steering rack may occur.

C. Check to make sure the steering wheel returns to center.

Removal and Installation

1. Disconnect the negative battery terminal. From inside the vehicle, remove the left side lower sound insulator.
2. Remove the upper steering shaft-to-steering rack coupling pinch bolt.
3. Place a drain pan under the steering gear and disconnect the pressure lines from the steering gear.
4. Raise and safely support the vehicle.
5. Remove both front wheel and tire assemblies.
6. Using a ball joint remover, disconnect the tie rod ends from the steering knuckles.
7. Lower the vehicle.
8. Remove both steering gear-to-chassis clamps.
9. Slide the steering gear forward and remove the lower steering shaft-to-steering rack coupling pinch bolt.
10. From the firewall, disconnect the coupling and seal from the steering gear.
11. Raise and safely support the vehicle.
12. Through the left wheel opening, remove the steering gear with the tie rods.
To install:
13. Reverse the removal procedures.
14. Torque the steering gear-to-chassis clamp bolts to 28 ft. lbs., the tie rod nut to 44 ft. lbs. and the fluid lines to 18 ft. lbs.
15. Refill power steering pump reservoir and bleed the power steering system.

Power Steering Pump

Removal and Installation

1. Disconnect the negative battery terminal.
2. Remove the pressure and return hoses from the pump and drain the system into a suitable container.
3. Cap the fittings at the pump.

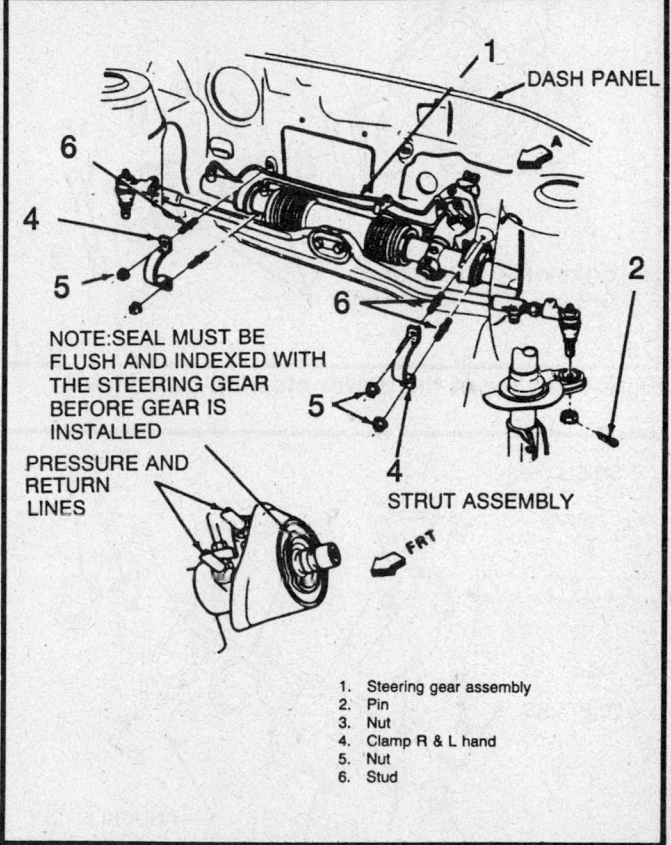

NOTE: SEAL MUST BE FLUSH AND INDEXED WITH THE STEERING GEAR BEFORE GEAR IS INSTALLED

PRESSURE AND RETURN LINES

DASH PANEL

STRUT ASSEMBLY

FRT

1. Steering gear assembly
2. Pin
3. Nut
4. Clamp R & L hand
5. Nut
6. Stud

Power steering gear mounting

4. Remove the serpentine belt.
5. Locate the pump attaching bolts through the pulley and remove the bolts.
6. Remove the pump assembly.
7. To install, reverse the removal. Torque the power steering pump bolts to 20 ft. lbs. Refill power steering pump reservoir and bleed the system.

Bleeding System

NOTE: Automatic transmission fluid is not compatible with the seals and hoses of the power steering system. Under no circumstances should automatic transmission be used in place of power steering fluid in this system.

1. With the engine turned **OFF**, turn the wheels all the way to the left.
2. Fill the reservoir with power steering fluid until the level is at the **COLD** mark on the reservoir.
3. Start and operate the engine at fast idle for 15 seconds. Turn the engine **OFF**.
4. Recheck the fluid level and fill it to the **COLD** mark.

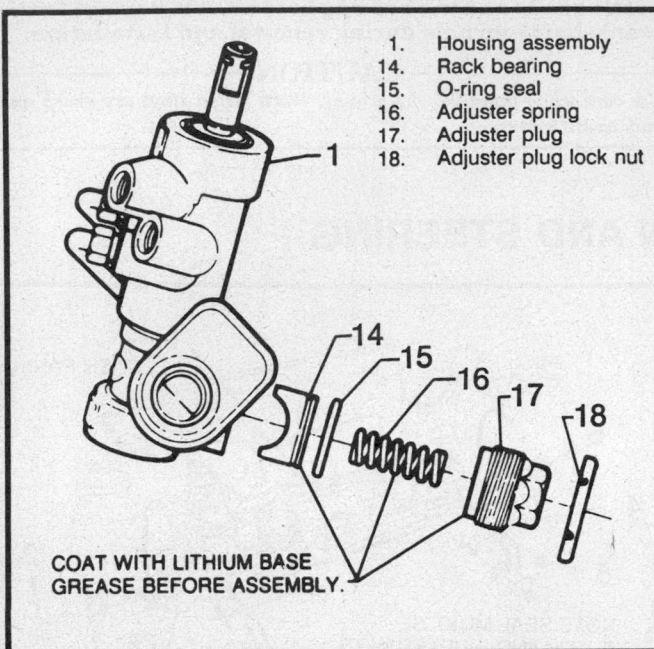

1. Housing assembly
14. Rack bearing
15. O-ring seal
16. Adjuster spring
17. Adjuster plug
18. Adjuster plug lock nut

COAT WITH LITHIUM BASE GREASE BEFORE ASSEMBLY.

Exploded view of the power steering gear pinion

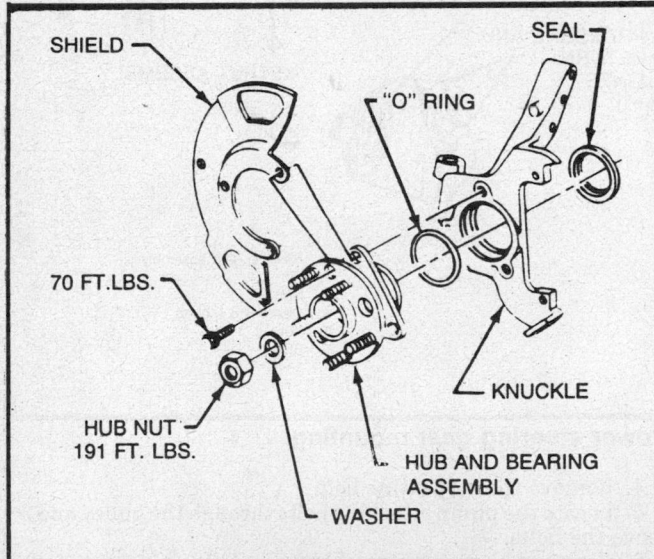

SHIELD
SEAL
"O" RING
70 FT. LBS.
HUB NUT 191 FT. LBS.
KNUCKLE
HUB AND BEARING ASSEMBLY
WASHER

Hub, knuckle and bearing—exploded view

5. Start the engine and bleed the system by turning the wheels in both directions slowly to the stops.
6. Stop the engine and check the fluid. Fluid that still has air in it will be a light tan color.
7. Repeat this procedure until all air is removed from the system.

Steering Column

Removal and Installation

1. Disconnect the negative battery terminal. Remove the left side lower trim panel.
2. Remove the upper steering column mounting bolts. Lower the steering column onto the seat.

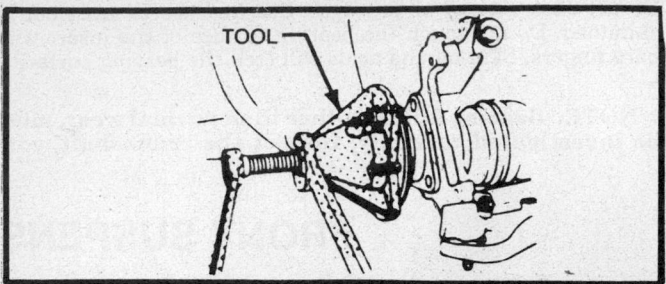

TOOL

Removing halfshaft from steering knuckle bearing

3. Disconnect the dimmer switch and turn signal switch eletrical connectors.
4. Remove the wiring harness-to-firewall/steering column nuts.

NOTE: If the vehicle is equipped with a park lock, the park lock cable must be disconnected by pressing the locking tab at the ignition switch inhibiter before removing the column from the vehicle.

5. Remove both lower steering column-to-steering rack bolts and the steering column from the vehicle.
To install:
6. Push the convoluted seal over the rag joint.
7. Connect the electrical connectors. Insert the steering column into the rag coupling. Raise the column and loosely assembly the capsule bolts.
8. Install and torque the lower shackle bolt to 29 ft. lbs. (40 Nm).
9. Torque the capsule bolts to 20 ft. lbs. (27 Nm).
10. To complete the installation, reverse the removal procedures.

Front Wheel Drive Hub Knuckle and Bearing

Removal and Installation

The hub and bearing are replaced as an assembly only.
1. With the vehicle weight on the tires, loosen the hub nut.
2. Raise and safely support the vehicle. Remove the wheel and tire assembly.
3. Install a boot cover over the outer CV joint boot.
4. Remove the hub nut. Remove the brake caliper and support it out of the way (on a wire); do not allow the caliper to hang on the brake line.
5. Remove the hub and bearing mounting bolts.
6. Remove the brake rotor splash shield.
7. Using a hub puller tool, press the hub and bearing from the halfshaft.
8. Disconnect the stabilizer link from the lower control arm.
9. Using a ball joint remover, separate the ball joint from the steering knuckle.
10. Remove the halfshaft from the knuckle and support it out of the way.
11. Using a brass drift, remove the inner knuckle seal.
To install:
12. Clean and inspect the steering knuckle bore and the bearing mating surfaces.
13. Install a new O-ring between the bearing and knuckle assembly.
14. Install the hub/bearing assembly and torque the nuts to 90 ft. lbs.
15. Using a seal driver tool, install it into the steering knuckle; be sure to lubricate the new seal and the bearing with a high temperature wheel bearing grease.
16. Reconnect the lower ball joint.

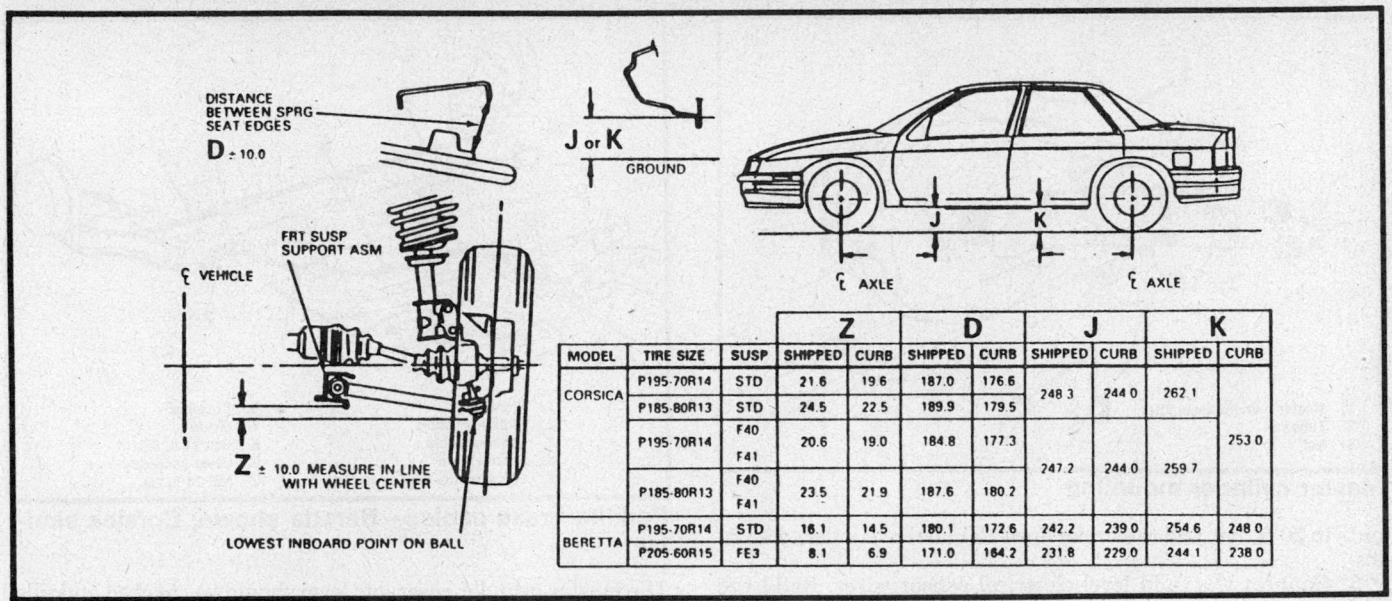

View of the ride height adjustment

MODEL	TIRE SIZE	SUSP	Z SHIPPED	Z CURB	D SHIPPED	D CURB	J SHIPPED	J CURB	K SHIPPED	K CURB
CORSICA	P195-70R14	STD	21.6	19.6	187.0	176.6	248.3	244.0	262.1	
	P185-80R13	STD	24.5	22.5	189.9	179.5				
	P195-70R14	F40 F41	20.6	19.0	184.8	177.3	247.2	244.0	259.7	253.0
	P185-80R13	F40 F41	23.5	21.9	187.6	180.2				
BERETTA	P195-70R14	STD	16.1	14.5	180.1	172.6	242.2	239.0	254.6	248.0
	P205-60R15	FE3	8.1	6.9	171.0	164.2	231.8	229.0	244.1	238.0

17. Install the hub, bearing nut and washer on the halfshaft. Torque the nut to 71 ft. lbs.

18. Install the brake rotor, caliper and the wheel/tire assembly.

19. Lower the vehicle and torque the hub nut to 191 ft. lbs.

Front Wheel Alignment

NOTE: Refer to the specifications listed at the vehicle section.

Adjustment

CASTER AND CAMBER

Caster and camber are preset at the factory and are not adjustable. Toe can be adjusted by loosening the clamps on the outer tie rods and rotating the tie rods to obtain the proper specification. Torque the tie rod clamp to 33 ft. lbs.

RIDE HEIGHT

To perform these adjustments, the vehicle must be on a flat level surface, have coolant filled to the maximum capacity, have a full tank of fuel and the tire pressure to full vehicle capacity.

The true heights are the average of the high and low measurements.

Front

The front ride height adjustment consists of the Z and J dimensions.

1. Lift the front bumper approximately 1½ in. (38mm) and allow the vehicle to settle; repeat this procedure at least 3 times.

2. Measure and record the Z and J dimensions.

NOTE: The Z measurement is the distance from the bottom of the front suspension support assembly to the bottom of the lower ball joint. The J measurement is the distance from the bottom of the front rocker panel to the ground.

3. Push the front bumper downward approximately 1½ in. (38mm) and allow it to rebound; perform this procedure at least 3 times.

4. Measure and record the Z and J dimensions. The true dimensions are the average of the high and low readings.

Rear

The rear ride height adjustment consists of the D and K dimensions.

1. Lift the rear bumper approximately 1½ in. (38mm) and allow the vehicle to settle; repeat this procedure at least 3 times.

2. Measure and record the D and K dimensions.

NOTE: The D measurement is the distance between the spring seat edges. The K measurement is the distance from the bottom of the rear rocker panel to the ground.

3. Push the rear bumper downward approximately 1½ in. (38mm) and allow it to rebound; perform this procedure at least 3 times.

4. Measure and record the D and K dimensions. The true dimensions are the average of the high and low readings.

BRAKES

Refer to unit repair section for brake service information and drum/rotor specifications.

Master Cylinder

Removal and Installation

1. Disconnect the negative battery terminal and the electrical connector from the fluid level sensor.

2. Disconnect and plug the 4 brake lines on the master cylinder.

3. Remove the master cylinder-to-power booster nuts and the master cylinder with the reservoir attached.

To install:

4. Bench bleed the new master cylinder and reverse the removal procedures. Torque the master cylinder-to-power booster

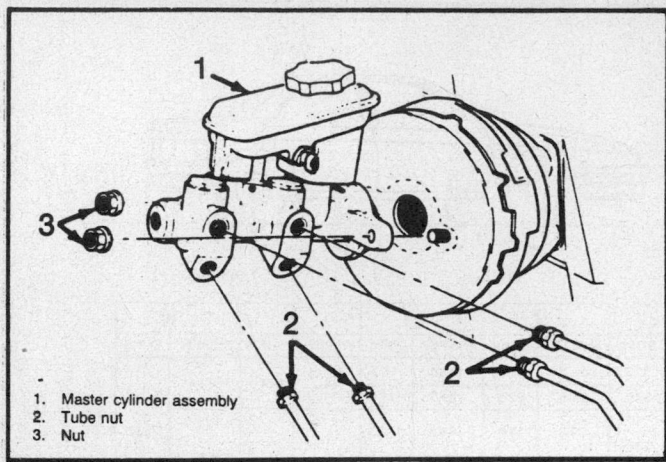

1. Master cylinder assembly
2. Tube nut
3. Nut

Master cylinder mounting

nuts to 20 ft. lbs. and the brake lines-to-master cylinder to 13 ft. lbs.

5. Connect the fluid level electrical sensor wires. Refill the reservoir with an approved DOT 3 brake fluid and bleed the brake system.

Bleeding System

This procedure is used to bench bleed the master cylinder.
1. Refill the master cylinder reservoir.
2. Push the plunger several times to force fluid into the piston.
3. Continue pumping the plunger until the fluid is free of the air bubbles.
4. Plug the outlet ports and install the master cylinder.

Power Brake Booster

Removal and Installation

1. Disconnect the negative battery terminal. Remove the master cylinder.

NOTE: Place the master cylinder in an upright position to prevent fluid loss.

2. Remove the lower-left trim panel inside the vehicle and disconnect the brake pedal-to-booster pushrod from the brake pedal.
3. Disconnect the vacuum line from the booster.
4. Remove the brake booster mounting nuts and the booster.
To install:
5. Reverse the removal procedures. Torque the master cylinder-to-power booster to 20 ft. lbs. and the power booster mounting nuts to 20 ft. lbs.
6. Bleed the brake system.

Bleeding System

1. Clean the bleeder screw at each wheel.
2. Attach a small rubber hose to the bleed screw and place the end in a clear container of fresh brake fluid.
3. Fill the master cylinder reservoir with fresh brake fluid.

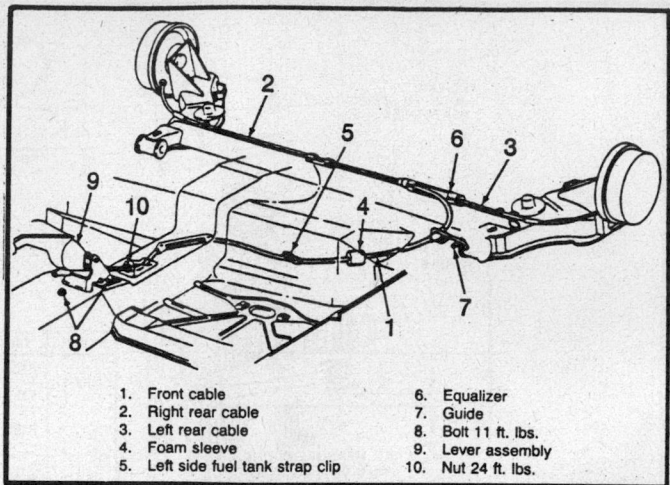

1. Front cable
2. Right rear cable
3. Left rear cable
4. Foam sleeve
5. Left side fuel tank strap clip
6. Equalizer
7. Guide
8. Bolt 11 ft. lbs.
9. Lever assembly
10. Nut 24 ft. lbs.

Parking brake cables—Beretta shown, Corsica similar

The master cylinder reservoir level should be checked and filled often during the bleeding procedure.

4. Have an assistant slowly pump the brake pedal and hold the pressure.
5. Open the bleeder screw about 1/4 turn. The pedal should fall to the floor as air and fluid are pushed out. Close the bleeder screw while the assistant holds the pedal to the floor. Slowly release the pedal and wait 15 seconds. Repeat the process until no more air bubbles are forced from the system when the brake pedal is applied. It may be necessary to repeat this 10 or more times to get all of the air from the system.
6. Repeat this procedure on the remaining wheel cylinders and calipers. Make sure the master cylinder does not run out of brake fluid.

NOTE: Remember to wait 15 seconds between each bleeding and do not pump the pedal rapidly. Rapid pumping of the brake pedal pushes the master cylinder secondary piston down the bore in a manner that makes it difficult to bleed the system.

7. Check the brake pedal for sponginess and the brake warning light for an indication of unbalanced pressure. Repeat the entire bleeding procedure to correct either of these conditions. Check the fluid level when finished.

Parking Brake

Adjustment

1. Apply and release the parking brake lever (10 clicks) at least 6 times. Apply the parking brake lever 4 clicks.
2. Raise and safely support the vehicle.
3. Locate the access hole in the backing plate and adjust the parking brake cable until a 1/8 in. drill bit can be inserted between the the brake shoe webbing and the parking brake lever.
4. Check to make sure a 1/4 in. drill bit will not fit in the same position.
5. Release the parking brake and check to see if both wheels turn freely by hand.
6. Lower the vehicle.

CLUTCH AND TRANSAXLE

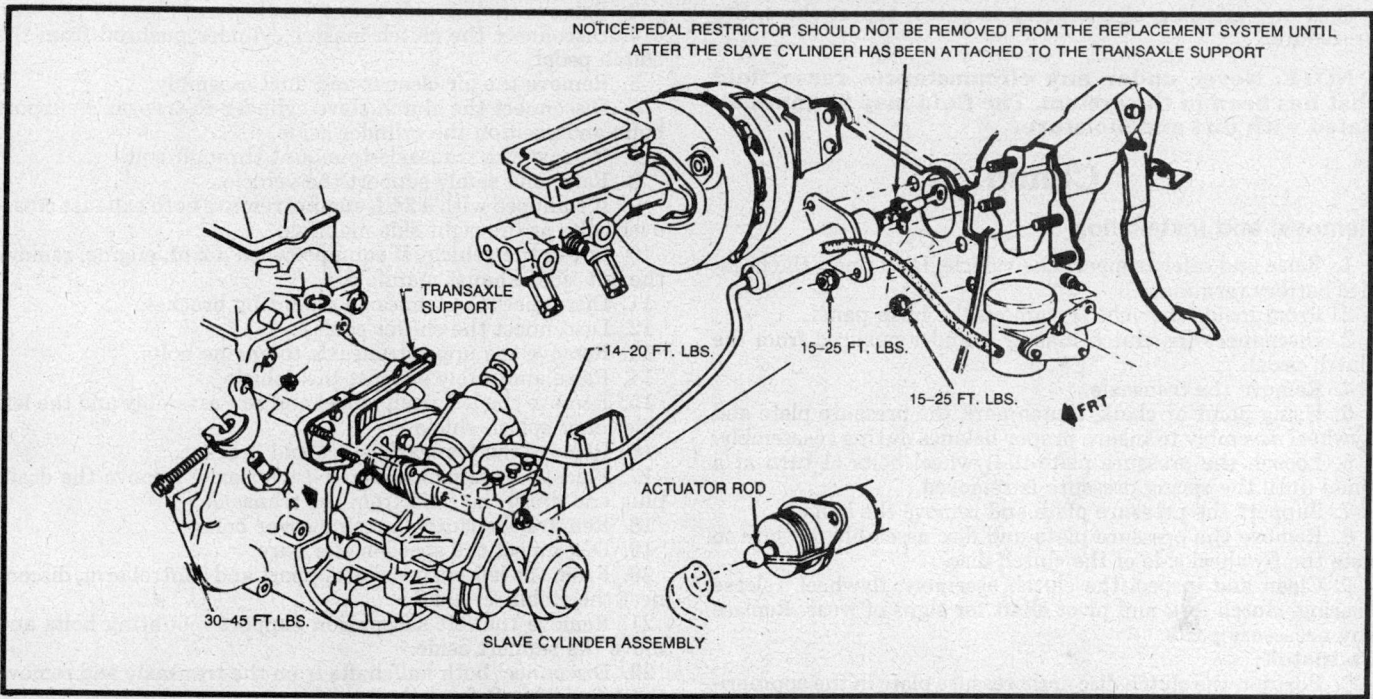

NOTICE:PEDAL RESTRICTOR SHOULD NOT BE REMOVED FROM THE REPLACEMENT SYSTEM UNTIL AFTER THE SLAVE CYLINDER HAS BEEN ATTACHED TO THE TRANSAXLE SUPPORT

TRANSAXLE SUPPORT

*14–20 FT. LBS.

15–25 FT. LBS.

15–25 FT. LBS.

FRT

ACTUATOR ROD

30–45 FT.LBS.

SLAVE CYLINDER ASSEMBLY

Clutch master and slave cylinder installation

Refer to "Chilton's Transmission Service Manual" for additional coverage.

Clutch Master and Slave Cylinder

A hydraulic clutch mechanism is used on all clutch equipped vehicles. This mechanism uses a clutch master cylinder with a remote reservoir and a slave cylinder connected to the master cylinder. Whenever the system is disconnected for repair or replacement, the clutch system must be bled to insure proper operation.

Removal and Installation

The clutch master and slave cylinders are removed from the vehicle as an assembly. After installation the clutch hydraulic system must be bled.
1. Disconnect the negative battery terminal.
2. From inside the vehicle, remove the hush panel.

NOTE: If equipped with a 2.8L engine, remove the air cleaner, the mass air flow sensor and the air intake duct as an assembly.

3. Disconnect the clutch master cylinder pushrod from the clutch master cylinder.
4. From the front of the dash, remove the trim cover.
5. Remove the clutch master cylinder-to-clutch pedal bracket nuts and the remote reservoir-to-chassis screws.
6. Remove the slave cylinder-to-transaxle nuts and the slave cylinder.
7. Remove the hydraulic system (as a unit) from the vehicle.
To install:
8. Install the slave cylinder-to-transaxle support, align the pushrod to the clutch fork outer lever pocket. Torque the slave cylinder-to-transaxle support nuts to 14–20 ft. lbs.

NOTE: If installing a new clutch hydraulic system, do not break the pushrod plastic retainer; the straps will break on the first pedal application.

9. Install the master cylinder-to-clutch pedal bracket. Torque the nuts evenly (to prevent damaging the master cylinder) to 15–20 ft. lbs. and reverse the removal procedures. Remove the pedal restrictor from the pushrod. Lubricate the pushrod bushing on the clutch pedal; if the bushing is cracked or worn, replace it.
10. If equipped with cruise control, check the switch adjustment at the clutch pedal bracket.

NOTE: When adjusting the cruise control switch, do not exert more than 20 lbs. of upward force on the clutch pedal pad for damage to the master cylinder pushrod retaining rod can result.

11. Depress the clutch pedal several times to break the plastic retaining straps; do not remove the plastic button from the end of the pushrod.
12. To complete the installation, reverse the removal procedures. If necessary, bleed the clutch hydraulic system.

System Bleeding

1. Remove any dirt or grease around the reservoir cap so dirt cannot enter the system.
2. Fill the reservoir with an approved DOT 3 brake fluid.
3. Loosen, but do not remove, the bleeder screw on the slave cylinder.
4. Fluid will now flow from the master cylinder to the slave cylinder.

NOTE: It is important that the reservoir remain filled throughout the procedure.

5. Air bubbles should now appear at the bleeder screw.
6. Continue this procedure until a steady stream of fluid without any air bubbles is present.
7. Tighten the bleeder screw. Check the fluid level in the reservoir and refill to the proper mark.
8. The system is now fully bled. Check the clutch operation

by starting the engine, pushing the clutch pedal to the floor and placing the transmission in reverse.

9. If any grinding of the gears is noted, repeat the entire procedure.

NOTE: Never under any circumstances reuse fluid that has been in the system. The fluid may be contaminated with dirt and moisture.

Clutch

Removal and Installation

1. Raise and safely support the vehicle. Disconnect the negative battery terminal.

2. From inside the vehicle, remove the hush panel.

3. Disconnect the clutch master cylinder pushrod from the clutch pedal.

4. Remove the transaxle.

5. Using paint or chalk, matchmark the pressure plate and flywheel assembly to insure proper balance during reassembly.

6. Loosen the pressure plate-to-flywheel bolts (1 turn at a time) until the spring pressure is removed.

7. Support the pressure plate and remove the bolts.

8. Remove the pressure plate and disc assembly; be sure to note the flywheel side of the clutch disc.

9. Clean and inspect the clutch assembly, flywheel, release bearing, clutch fork and pivot shaft for signs of wear. Replace any necessary parts.
To install:

10. Position the clutch disc and pressure plate in the appropriate position, support the assembly with an alignment tool.

NOTE: Make sure the clutch disc is facing the same direction it was when removed. If the same pressure plate is being reused, align the marks made during the removal, install the pressure plate retaining bolts. Tighten them gradually and evenly.

11. Remove the alignment tool and torque the pressure plate-to-flywheel bolts to 15 ft. lbs. Lightly lubricate the clutch fork ends. Fill the recess ends of the release bearing with grease. Lubricate the input shaft with a light coat of grease.

12. To complete the installation, reverse the removal procedures.

NOTE: The clutch lever must not be moved towards the flywheel until the transaxle is bolted to the engine. Damage to the transaxle, release bearing and clutch fork could occur if this is not followed.

13. Bleed the clutch system and check the clutch operation when finished.

Pedal Height/Free-Play Adjustment

Push the clutch pedal all the way to the floor; the distance of travel should be 7.4 in.

Manual Transaxle

Removal and Installation

NOTE: Before performing any maintenance that requires the removal of the slave cylinder, transaxle or clutch housing, the clutch master cylinder pushrod must first be disconnected from the clutch pedal. Failure to disconnect the pushrod will result in permanent damage to the slave cylinder if the clutch pedal is depressed with the slave cylinder disconnected.

MUNCIE

1. Disconnect the negative battery terminal.

2. Using an engine support fixture tool and an adapter, in-

stall them on the engine and raise the engine enough to take the engine weight off of the engine mounts.

3. Remove the left side sound insulator.

4. Disconnect the clutch master cylinder pushrod from the clutch pedal.

5. Remove the air cleaner and duct assembly.

6. Disconnect the clutch slave cylinder-to-transaxle support bolts and position the cylinder aside.

7. Remove the transaxle-to-mount through bolt.

8. Raise and safely support the vehicle.

9. If equipped with a 2.8L engine, remove both exhaust crossover bolts at the right side manifold.

10. Lower the vehicle. If equipped with a 2.8L engine, remove the left side exhaust manifold.

11. Disconnect the transaxle mounting bracket.

12. Disconnect the shifter cables.

13. Remove the upper transaxle-to-engine bolts.

14. Raise and safely support the vehicle.

15. Remove the left front wheel and tire assembly and the left side inner splash shield.

16. Remove the transaxle strut and bracket.

17. Place a drain pan under the transaxle, remove the drain plug and drain the fluid from the transaxle.

18. Remove the clutch housing cover bolts.

19. Disconnect the speedometer wire.

20. From the left suspension support and control arm, disconnect the stabilizer shaft.

21. Remove the left suspension support mounting bolts and move the support aside.

22. Disconnect both halfshafts from the transaxle and remove the left halfshaft from the vehicle.

23. Using a transmission jack, attach it to and support the transaxle.

24. Remove the remaining transaxle-to-engine bolts.

25. Slide the transaxle away from the engine, lower it and remove the right side halfshaft.
To install:

26. Reverse the removal procedures. When installing, guide the right side halfshaft into the transaxle while it is being installed in the vehicle.

27. Torque the transaxle-to-engine bolts to 60 ft. lbs., the transaxle mount-to-body bolt to 80 ft. lbs., the transaxle strut bolts 50 ft. lbs., the slave cylinder-to-transaxle nuts to 14–20 ft. lbs. and the shifter cable-to-transaxle nuts to 90 inch lbs.

28. Refill the transaxle and check for leaks.

NOTE: The clutch lever must not be moved towards the flywheel until the transaxle is bolted to the engine. Damage to the transaxle, release bearing and clutch fork could occur if this is not followed.

ISUZU

1. Disconnect the negative battery terminal.

2. Using an engine support fixture tool and an adapter, install them on the engine and raise the engine enough to take the engine weight off of the engine mounts.

3. Remove the left side sound insulator.

4. Disconnect the clutch master cylinder pushrod from the clutch pedal.

5. Disconnect the clutch slave cylinder-to-transaxle support bolts and position the cylinder aside.

6. Remove the wiring harness from the transaxle mount bracket and the shift wire electrical connector.

7. Remove the transaxle-to-mount bolts and the transaxle mount bracket-to-chassis nuts/bolts.

8. Disconnect the shift cables and remove the retaining clamp from the transaxle. Remove the ground cables from the transaxle mounting studs.

9. Raise and safely support the vehicle.

10. Remove the left front wheel and tire assembly and the left side inner splash shield.

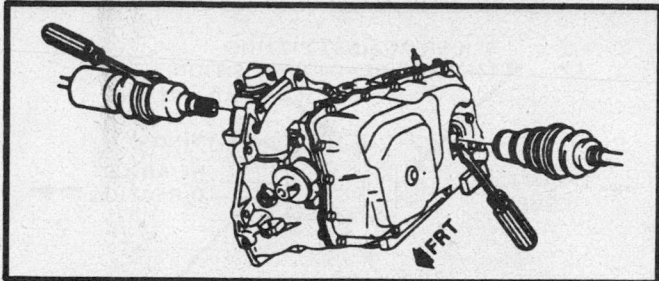

Removing halfshafts from transaxle

11. Remove the transaxle front strut and bracket.
12. Remove the clutch housing cover bolts. Disconnect the speedometer wire connector.
13. From the left suspension support and control arm, disconnect the stabilizer shaft.
14. Remove the left suspension support mounting bolts and move the support aside.
15. Disconnect both halfshafts from the transaxle and remove the left halfshaft from the vehicle.
16. Place a drain pan under the transaxle, remove the drain plug and drain the fluid from the transaxle.
17. Using a transmission jack, attach it to and support the transaxle.
18. Remove the transaxle-to-engine bolts.
19. Slide the transaxle away from the engine, lower it and remove the right side halfshaft.

To install:
20. Reverse the removal procedures. When installing, guide the right side halfshaft into the transaxle while it is being installed in the vehicle. Torque the transaxle-to-engine bolts to 60 ft. lbs., the transaxle mount-to-body bolt to 80 ft. lbs., the transaxle strut bolts 50 ft. lbs., the slave cylinder-to-transaxle nuts to 14–20 ft. lbs. and the shifter cable-to-transaxle nuts to 90 inch lbs.
21. Refill the transaxle and check for leaks.

NOTE: The clutch lever must not be moved towards the flywheel until the transaxle is bolted to the engine. Damage to the transaxle, release bearing and clutch fork could occur if this is not followed.

Adjustment

No adjustments are possible on the manual transaxle shifting cables or linkage. If the transaxle is not engaging completely, check for stretched cables or broken shifter components or a faulty transaxle.

Automatic Transaxle

NOTE: By September 1, 1991, Hydra-matic will have changed the name designation of the THM 125C automatic transaxle. The new name designation for this transaxle will be Hydra-matic 3T40. Transaxles built between 1989 and 1990 will serve as transitional years in which a dual system, made up of the old designation and the new designation will be in effect.

Removal and Installation
2.0L ENGINE

1. Disconnect the negative battery terminal. Remove the air cleaner and air intake assembly.
2. Disconnect the T.V. cable from the throttle lever and the transaxle.
3. Remove the fluid level indicator and the filler tube.
4. Using an engine support fixture tool and an adapter, install them onto the engine.

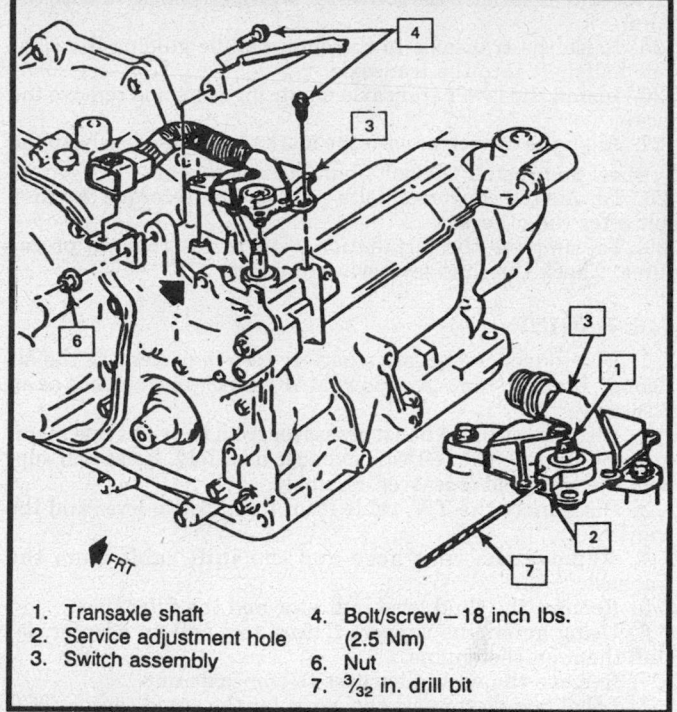

1. Transaxle shaft	4. Bolt/screw—18 inch lbs. (2.5 Nm)
2. Service adjustment hole	6. Nut
3. Switch assembly	7. ³⁄₃₂ in. drill bit

Adjusting the park/neutral and back-up light switch

5. Remove the wiring harness-to-transaxle nut.
6. Label and disconnect the electrical connectors for the speed sensor, TCC connector and the neutral safety/backup light switch.
7. Disconnect the shift linkage from the transaxle.
8. Remove the upper transaxle-to-engine bolts, the transaxle mount and bracket assembly.
9. Disconnect the rubber hose that runs from the transaxle to the vent pipe.
10. Raise and safely support the vehicle.
11. Remove the front wheels and tire assemblies.
12. Disconnect the shift linkage and bracket from the transaxle.
13. Remove the left side splash shield.
14. Using a modified drive axle seal protector tool, install 1 on each drive axle to protect the seal from damage and the joint from possible failure.
15. Using care not to damage the halfshaft boots, disconnect the halfshafts from the transaxle.
16. Remove the transaxle strut. Remove the left side stabilizer link pin bolt and bushing clamp nuts from the support.
17. Remove the left frame support bolts and move it out of the way.
18. Disconnect the speedometer wire from the transaxle.
19. Remove the transaxle converter cover and matchmark the torque converter-to-flywheel for reassembly.
20. Disconnect and plug the transaxle cooler pipes.
21. Remove the transaxle-to-engine support.
22. Using a transmission jack, position and secure the jack to the transaxle. Remove the remaining transaxle-to-engine bolts.
23. Making sure the torque converter does not fall out, remove the transaxle from the vehicle.

NOTE: The transaxle cooler and lines should be flushed any time the transaxle is removed for overhaul or replacing the pump, case or converter.

To install:
24. Put a small amount of grease on the pilot hub of the con-

verter and make sure the converter is properly engaged with the pump.

25. Raise the transaxle to the engine while guiding the right side halfshaft into the transaxle.

26. Install the lower transaxle mounting bolts and remove the jack.

27. Align the converter with the marks made previously on the flywheel and install the bolts hand tight.

28. Torque the converter bolts to 46 ft. lbs.; retorque the first bolt after the others.

29. To complete the installation, reverse the removal procedures. Check the fluid level when finished.

2.8L ENGINE

1. Disconnect the negative battery terminal. Remove the air cleaner, bracket, Mass Air Flow (MAF) sensor and air tube as an assembly.

2. Disconnect the exhaust crossover from the right side manifold and remove the left side exhaust manifold. Raise and support the manifold/crossover assembly.

3. Disconnect the T.V. cable from the throttle lever and the transaxle.

4. Remove the vent hose and the shift cable from the transaxle.

5. Remove the fluid level indicator and the filler tube.

6. Using an engine support fixture tool and an adapter, install them on the engine.

7. Remove the wiring harness-to-transaxle nut.

8. Label and disconnect the wires for the speed sensor, TCC connector and the neutral safety/backup light switch.

9. Remove the upper transaxle-to-engine bolts.

10. Remove the transaxle-to-mount through bolt, the transaxle mount bracket and the mount.

11. Raise and safely support the vehicle.

12. Remove the front wheel and tire assemblies.

13. Disconnect the shift cable bracket from the transaxle.

14. Remove the left side splash shield.

15. Using a modified drive axle seal protector tool, install 1 on each drive axle to protect the seal from damage and the joint from possible failure.

16. Using care not to damage the halfshaft boots, disconnect the halfshafts from the transaxle.

17. Remove the torsional and lateral strut from the transaxle. Remove the left side stabilizer link pin bolt.

18. Remove the left frame support bolts and move it out of the way.

19. Disconnect the speedometer wire from the transaxle.

20. Remove the transaxle converter cover and matchmark the converter-to-flywheel for assembly.

21. Disconnect and plug the transaxle cooler pipes.

22. Remove the transaxle-to-engine support.

23. Using a transmission jack, position and secure it to the transaxle. Remove the remaining transaxle-to-engine bolts.

24. Make sure the torque converter does not fall out and remove the transaxle from the vehicle.

NOTE: The transaxle cooler and lines should be flushed any time the transaxle is removed for overhaul, to replace the pump, case or converter.

To install:

25. Put a small amount of grease on the pilot hub of the converter and make sure the converter is properly engaged with the pump.

26. Raise the transaxle to the engine while guiding the right side halfshaft into the transaxle.

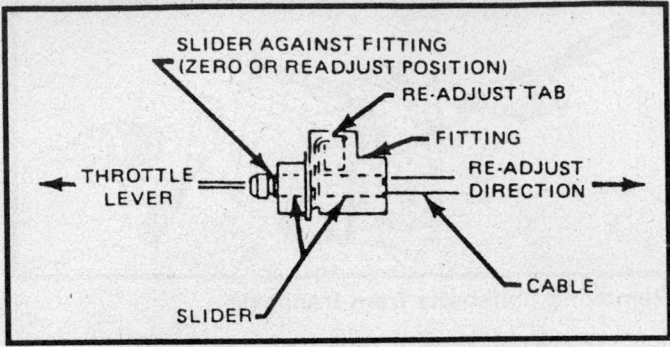

View of the throttle valve (T.V.) cable adjuster

27. Install the lower transaxle mounting bolts and remove the jack.

28. Align the converter with the marks made previously on the flywheel and install the bolts hand tight.

29. Torque the converter bolts to 46 ft. lbs.; retorque the first bolt after the others.

30. To complete the installation, reverse the removal procedures. Check the fluid level when finished.

Adjustment

SHIFT CONTROL CABLE

1. Loosen the cable-to-transaxle shift lever nut so the cable is free.

2. Position the gear shift selector and the transaxle shift lever into the **N** position.

3. While holding transaxle's shift lever out of the **P** position, torque the shift cable-to-shift lever nut to 11 ft. lbs. (15 Nm) for floor shift or 15 ft. lbs. (20 Nm) for column shift.

THROTTLE VALVE (T.V.)

1. Turn the engine **OFF**.

2. At the end of the T.V. cable (engine side), depress and hold down the cable's metal readjustment tab.

3. Move the slider until it stops against the fitting and release the readjustment tab.

4. Rotate the throttle lever (by hand) to it's full travel position; the T.V. slider should move (ratchet) toward the lever when the lever. Release the T.V.

5. After adjustment, make sure the cable moves freely and road test the vehicle.

NOTE: Even if the cable appears to function properly when the engine is cold or stopped, recheck it after the engine is hot.

PARK/NEUTRAL AND BACK-UP LIGHT SWITCH

The switch assembly is located on top of the transaxle.

1. Place the transaxle's shift control lever in the **N** notch in the detent plate.

2. Loosen the switch-to-transaxle screws.

3. Rotate the switch on the shifter assembly to align the service adjustment hole with the carrier tang hole.

4. Using a $\frac{3}{32}$ in. drill bit or gauge pin, insert it into the service adjustment hole to a depth of $\frac{3}{8}$ in. (9mm).

5. Tighten the switch-to-transaxle screws and remove the drill bit or gauge pin.

HALFSHAFTS

Halfshaft

Removal and Installation

If equipped with an automatic transaxle, the inner joint on the right side halfshaft uses a male spline that locks into the transaxle gears. The left side halfshaft uses a female spline that is installed over the stub shaft on the transaxle.

An intermediate shaft is installed between the transaxle and the right halfshaft.

EXCEPT INTERMEDIATE SHAFT

1. With the weight of the vehicle on the tires, loosen the hub nut.
2. Raise and safely support the vehicle.
3. Remove the hub nut.
4. Install boot protectors on the boots.
5. Remove the brake caliper with the line attached and support it (on a wire) out of the way; do not allow the caliper to hang from the line.
6. Remove the brake rotor and caliper mounting bracket.
7. Remove the strut to steering knuckle bolts. Pull the steering knuckle out of the strut bracket.
8. Using a halfshaft removal tool and an extention, remove the halfshafts from the transaxle and support them safely.
9. Using a spindle remover tool, remove the halfshaft from the hub and bearing.

To install:

10. Loosely place the halfshaft on the transaxle and in the hub and bearing.
11. Properly position the steering knuckle to the strut bracket and install the bolt. Torque the bolts to 133 ft. lbs.
12. Install the brake rotor, caliper bracket and caliper. Place a holding device in the rotor to prevent it from turning.
13. Install the hub nut and washer. Torque the nut to 71 ft. lbs.
14. Seat the halfshafts into the transaxle using a prybar on the groove on the inner retainer.
15. Verify that the shafts are seated by grasping the CV joint and pulling outwards; do not grasp the shaft. If the snap ring is seated, the halfshaft will remain in place.
16. To complete the installation, reverse the removal procedures. When the vehicle is lowered with the weight on the wheels, final torque the hub nut to 191 ft. lbs.

INTERMEDIATE SHAFT

1. Raise and safely support the vehicle. Remove the front right wheel and tire assembly.
2. Drain the transaxle.
3. Using a modified seal protector, place it over the outer seal.
4. Remove the stabilizer bar from the right control arm.
5. Remove the right ball joint-to-steering knuckle cotter pin and nut. Using a ball joint remover tool, separate the ball joint from the steering knuckle.
6. Pull the steering knuckle outward and separate the halfshaft from the intermediate shaft.
7. Remove the intermediate shaft housing-to-bracket bolts and the lower bracket-to-engine bolt. Loosen the upper bracket-to-engine bolt and swing the bracket out of the way.
8. Remove the intermediate shaft housing-to-transaxle bolts, disengage the housing from the transaxle and remove the intermediate shaft assembly.

To install:

9. Lubricate the intermediate shaft splines with grease and reverse the removal procedures. Torque the intermediate shaft housing-to-transaxle bolts to 18 ft. lbs. (25 Nm), the intermediate shaft housing-to-bracket bolts to 37 ft. lbs. (50 Nm) and the bracket-to-engine bolts to 37 ft. lbs. (50 Nm).

1. Intermediate shaft assembly
2. Intermediate axle shaft
3. Bracket
4. Axle shaft retaining ring
5. Lip seal
6. Bolt—37 ft. lbs. (50 Nm)
7. Washer
8. Bolt—18 ft. lbs.
9. Right drive axle
10. O-ring seal

Exploded view of the intermediate shaft assembly

10. To complete the installation reverse the removal procedures. Refill the transaxle.

Boot

Removal and Installation

INNER

1. Remove the halfshaft.
2. Remove the CV joint housing-to-transaxle bolts.
3. Cut the seal retaining clamps and remove the old boot from the shaft.
4. Using a pair of snapring pliers, remove the retaining ring from the shaft and remove the spider assembly.

To install:

5. Using solvent, clean the splines of the shaft and repack the joint.
6. Install the inner boot clamp first and the new boot second.
7. Push the CV joint assembly onto the shaft until the retaining ring is seated on the shaft.
8. Slide the boot onto the joint. Install both the inner and outer clamps.
9. To complete the installation, reverse the removal procedures.

OUTER

1. Remove the halfshaft from the vehicle.
2. Cut off the boot retaining clamps and discard them. Remove the old boot.
3. If equipped with a deflector ring, use a brass drift and carefully tap it off.
4. Using a pair of snapring pliers, spread the retaining ring

inside the outer CV joint and tap the joint off the halfshaft.

To install:

5. Using solvent, clean the splines of the halfshaft and the CV joint and repack the joint. Install a new retaining ring inside the joint.

6. Install the inner boot clamp first, the new boot second.

7. Push the joint assembly onto the halfshaft until the ring is seated on the shaft.

8. Slide the boot onto the joint and install the clamps on both the inner and outer part of the boot.

9. To complete the installation, reverse the removal procedures.

Universal Joints

Refer to the unit repair section for overhaul procedures.

REAR SUSPENSION

Refer to the unit repair section for rear suspension services.

Rear Wheel Bearing

Removal and Installation

The rear wheel hub and bearing are replaced as an assembly only.

1. Raise and safely support the vehicle.
2. Remove the wheel and tire assembly and the brake drum.
3. Remove the hub/bearing assembly-to-rear axle nuts/bolts.

NOTE: The top mounting bolt will not clear the brake shoe when removing the hub and bearing. The hub and bearing must be partially removed while the top bolt is being turned out.

To install:

4. To install, insert and turn the top bolt in while installing the hub and bearing. Install the other bolts.

5. Torque the hub/bearing assembly-to-rear axle nuts/bolts to 38 ft. lbs.

6. Install the brake drum and wheel and tire assembly.

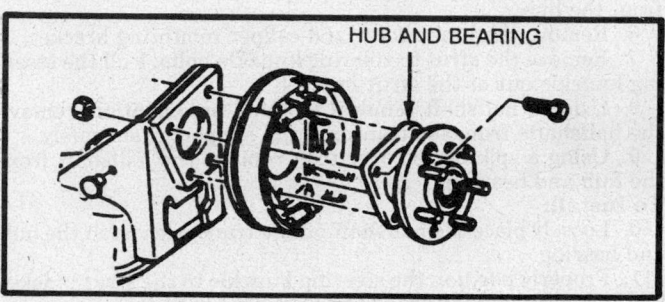

Rear wheel hub and bearing mounting

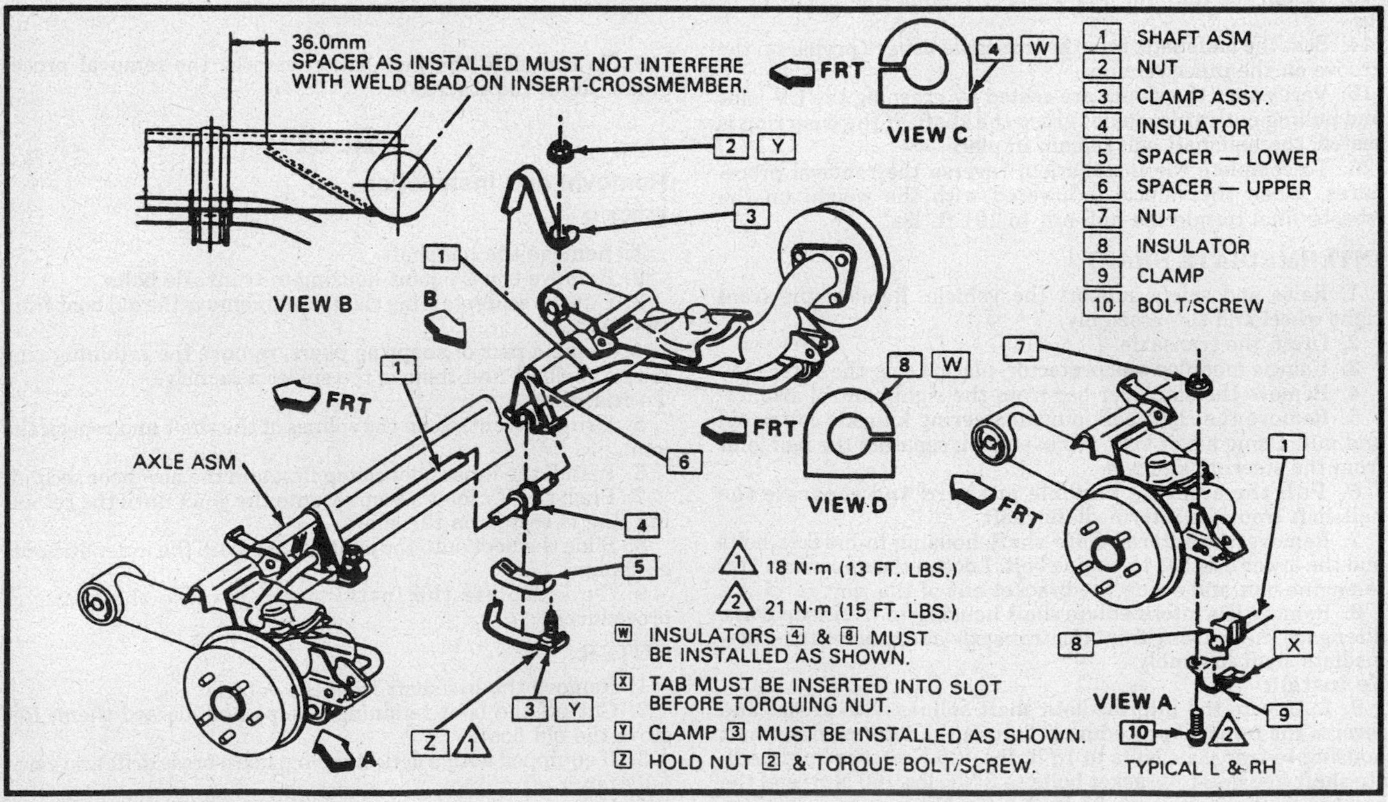

Stabilizer assembly—Beretta

1	SHAFT ASM
2	NUT
3	CLAMP ASSY.
4	INSULATOR
5	SPACER — LOWER
6	SPACER — UPPER
7	NUT
8	INSULATOR
9	CLAMP
10	BOLT/SCREW

36.0mm
SPACER AS INSTALLED MUST NOT INTERFERE WITH WELD BEAD ON INSERT-CROSSMEMBER.

VIEW C
VIEW B
VIEW D
VIEW A
AXLE ASM
FRT
TYPICAL L & RH

⚠1 18 N·m (13 FT. LBS.)

⚠2 21 N·m (15 FT. LBS.)

W INSULATORS 4 & 8 MUST BE INSTALLED AS SHOWN.

X TAB MUST BE INSERTED INTO SLOT BEFORE TORQUING NUT.

Y CLAMP 3 MUST BE INSTALLED AS SHOWN.

Z HOLD NUT 2 & TORQUE BOLT/SCREW.

YEAR IDENTIFICATION

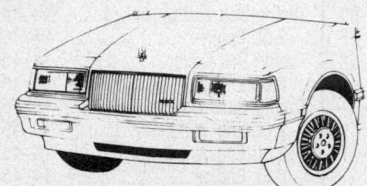

1987–90 Skylark

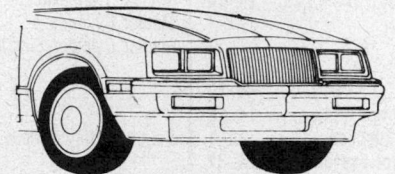

1986–87 Somerset

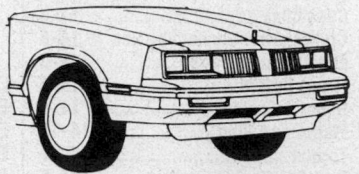

1986 Calais

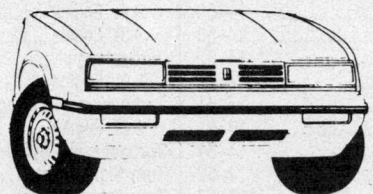

1987 Calais GT

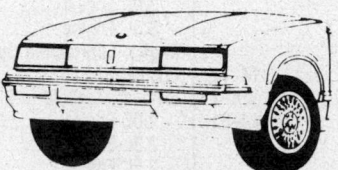

1986 Calais GT

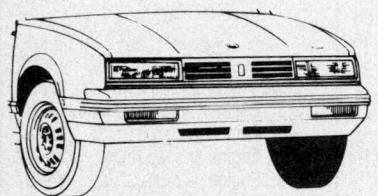

1987 Calais

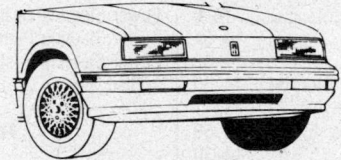

1988–89 Calais International, 1990 Calais

1986 Grand Am

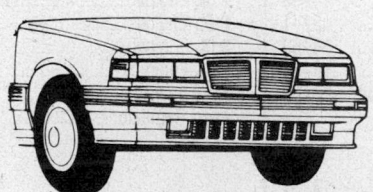

1986-87 Grand Am SE

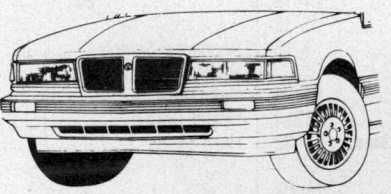

1987–90 Grand Am SE/LE

VEHICLE IDENTIFICATION

It is important for servicing and ordering parts to be certain of the vehicle and engine identification. The VIN (vehicle identification number) is a 17 digit number visible through the windshield on the driver's side of the dash and contains the vehicle and engine identification codes. The tenth digit indicates model year, and the eighth digit indicates engine code. It can be interpreted as follows:

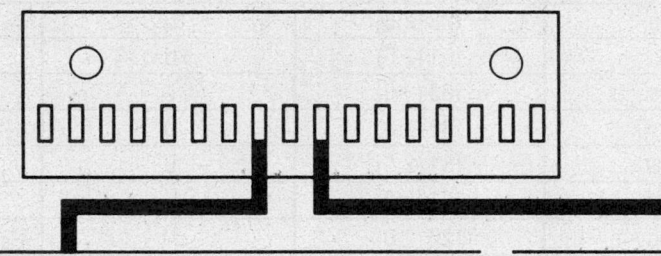

Engine Code							Model Year	
Code	Cu. In.	Liters	Cyl.	Fuel Sys.	Eng. Mfg.		Code	Year
K	122	2.0	4	MPI	Pontiac		G	1986
M	122	2.0	4	MPI	Pontiac		H	1987
A	138	2.3	4	MPI	Oldsmobile		J	1988
D	138	2.3	4	MFI	Oldsmobile		K	1989
U	151	2.5	4	TBI	Pontiac		L	1990
L	181	3.0	6	MFI	Buick			
N	204	3.3	6	MFI	Buick			

TBI Throttle Body Injection
MFI Multi-port Fuel Injection

ENGINE IDENTIFICATION

Year	Model	Engine Displacement cu. in. (liter)	Engine Series Identification (VIN)	No. of Cylinders	Engine Type
1986	Grand Am	151 (2.5)	U	4	OHV
	Grand Am	181 (3.0)	L	6	OHV
	Calais	151 (2.5)	U	4	OHV
	Calais	181 (3.0)	L	6	OHV
	Somerset	151 (2.5)	U	4	OHV
	Somerset	181 (3.0)	L	6	OHV
	Skylark	151 (2.5)	U	4	OHV
	Skylark	181 (3.0)	L	6	OHV
1987	Grand Am	122 (2.0)	K	4	OHC
	Grand Am	122 (2.0)	M	4	OHC Turbo
	Grand Am	151 (2.5)	U	4	OHV
	Grand Am	181 (3.0)	L	6	OHV
	Calais	151 (2.5)	U	4	OHV
	Calais	183 (3.0)	L	6	OHV
	Somerset	151 (2.5)	U	4	OHV
	Somerset	181 (3.0)	L	6	OHV
	Skylark	151 (2.5)	U	4	OHV
	Skylark	181 (3.0)	L	6	OHV
1988	Grand Am	122 (2.0)	K	4	OHC
	Grand Am	122 (2.0)	M	4	OHC Turbo
	Grand Am	188 (2.3)	D	4	DOHC
	Grand Am	151 (2.5)	U	4	OHV

ENGINE IDENTIFICATION

Year	Model	Engine Displacement cu. in. (liter)	Engine Series Identification (VIN)	No. of Cylinders	Engine Type
1988	Calais	138 (2.3)	D	4	DOHC
	Calais	151 (2.5)	U	4	OHV
	Calais	183 (3:0)	L	6	OHV
	Skylark	138 (2.3)	D	4	DOHC
	Skylark	151 (2.5)	U	4	OHV
	Skylark	181 (3.0)	L	6	OHV
1989-90	Grand Am	122 (2.0)	M	4	OHC Turbo
	Grand Am	138 (2.3)	D	4	DOHC
	Grand Am	138 (2.3)	A	4	DOHC
	Grand Am	151 (2.5)	U	4	OHV
	Calais	138 (2.3)	D	4	DOHC
	Calais	138 (2.3)	A	4	DOHC
	Calais	151 (2.5)	U	4	OHV
	Calais	204 (3.3)	N	6	OHV
	Skylark	138 (2.3)	D	4	DOHC
	Skylark	151 (2.5)	U	4	OHV
	Skylark	204 (3.3)	N	6	OHV

OHV—Overhead valve
OHC—Overhead cam
OHC—Turbo—Overhead cam with turbocharger
DOHC—Double overhead cam

GENERAL ENGINE SPECIFICATIONS

Year	VIN	No. Cylinder Displacement cu. in. (liter)	Fuel System Type	Net Horsepower @ rpm	Net Torque @ rpm (ft. lbs.)	Bore × Stroke (in.)	Compression Ratio	Oil Pressure @ rpm
1986	U	4-151 (2.5)	TBI	92 @ 4400	134 @ 2800	4.00 × 3.00	9.0:1	37 @ 2000
	L	6-181 (3.0)	MFI	125 @ 4900	150 @ 2400	3.80 × 2.70	9.0:1	37 @ 2400
1987	K	4-122 (2.0)	MFI	NA	NA	3.40 × 3.40	8.8:1	NA
	M	4-122 (2.0)	MFI ①	167 @ 4500	175 @ 4000	3.40 × 3.40	8.0:1	NA
	D	4-138 (2.3)	MFI	150 @ 4500	150 @ 2400	3.62 × 3.35	9.5:1	25 @ 2000
	U	4-151 (2.5)	TBI	92 @ 4400	132 @ 2800	4.00 × 3.00	9.0:1	37 @ 2000
	L	6-181 (3.0)	MFI	125 @ 4900	150 @ 2400	3.80 × 2.70	9.0:1	37 @ 2400
1988	K	4-122 (2.0)	MFI	NA	NA	3.40 × 3.40	8.8:1	NA
	M	4-122 (2.0)	MFI ①	167 @ 4500	175 @ 4000	3.40 × 3.40	8.0:1	NA
	D	4-138 (2.3)	MFI	150 @ 5200	160 @ 4000	3.62 × 3.35	9.5:1	25 @ 2000
	U	4-151 (2.5)	TBI	98 @ 4300	135 @ 3200	4.00 × 3.00	9.0:1	37 @ 2000
	L	6-181 (3.0)	MFI	125 @ 4900	150 @ 2400	3.80 × 2.70	9.0:1	37 @ 2400
1989-90	M	4-122 (2.0)	MFI ①	167 @ 4500	175 @ 4000	3.40 × 3.40	8.0:1	65 @ 2500
	A	4-138 (2.3)	MFI	180 @ 6200	160 @ 5200	3.62 × 3.35	10.0:1	NA
	D	4-138 (2.3)	MFI	160 @ 6200	155 @ 5200	3.62 × 3.35	9.5:1	25 @ 2000
	U	4-151 (2.5)	TBI	110 @ 5200	135 @ 3200	4.00 × 3.00	9.0:1	37 @ 2000
	N	6-204 (3.3)	MFI	160 @ 5200	185 @ 3200	3.70 × 3.16	9.0:1	45 @ 2000

TBI Throttle Body Injection
MFI Multi-port Fuel Injection
① Turbo

TUNE-UP SPECIFICATIONS
Refer to Section 34 for all spark plug recommendations

Year	VIN	No. Cylinder Displacement cu. in. (liter)	Spark Plugs Gap (in.)	Ignition Timing (deg.) MT	Ignition Timing (deg.) AT	Compression Pressure (psi)	Fuel Pump (psi)	Idle Speed (rpm) MT	Idle Speed (rpm) AT	Valve Clearance In.	Valve Clearance Ex.
1986	U	4-151 (2.5)	0.060	8B	8B	100	12	①	①	Hyd.	Hyd.
	L	6-181 (3.0)	0.040	15B	15B	100	34–44	①	①	Hyd.	Hyd.
1987	K	4-122 (2.0) ④	0.035	8B	8B	100	—	①	①	Hyd.	Hyd.
	M	4-122 (2.0) ②	0.035	8B	8B	100	—	①	①	Hyd.	Hyd.
	D	4-138 (2.3)	0.035	—	—	—	34–44	—	—	Hyd.	Hyd.
	U	4-151 (2.5)	0.060	8B	8B	100	12	①	①	Hyd.	Hyd.
	L	6-181 (3.0)	0.040	15B	15B	100	34–44	①	①	Hyd.	Hyd.
1988	K	4-122 (2.0) ④	0.035	8B	8B	100	—	①	①	Hyd.	Hyd.
	M	4-122 (2.0) ②	0.035	8B	8B	100	—	①	①	Hyd.	Hyd.
	D	4-138 (2.3)	0.035	—	—	—	34–44	—	—	Hyd.	Hyd.
	U	4-151 (2.5)	0.060	—	—	100	9–13	①	①	Hyd.	Hyd.
	L	6-181 (3.0)	0.045	③	③	100	34–44	①	①	Hyd.	Hyd.
1989	M	4-122 (2.0) ②	0.035	8B	8B	100	—	①	①	Hyd.	Hyd.
	A	4-138 (2.3)	0.035	—	—	100	—	34–44	①	Hyd.	Hyd.
	D	4-138 (2.3)	0.035	—	—	—	34–44	—	—	Hyd.	Hyd.
	U	4-151 (2.5)	0.060	—	—	100	9–13	①	①	Hyd.	Hyd.
	N	6-204 (3.3)	0.060	—	—	100	36–43	①	①	Hyd.	Hyd.
1990		SEE UNDERHOOD SPECIFICATIONS STICKER									

NOTE: The Underhood Specifications sticker often reflects tune-up specification changes made in production. Sticker figures must be used if they disagree with those in this chart.
B Before Top Dead Center
Hyd—Hydraulic valve lifters
① See Underhood Specifications sticker
② Turbocharged
③ No timing adjustment required with C³I ignition
④ Non-Turbocharged

CAPACITIES

Year	Model	VIN	No. Cylinder Displacement cu. in. (liter)	Engine Crankcase with Filter	Engine Crankcase without Filter	Transmission (pts.) 4-Spd	Transmission (pts.) 5-Spd	Transmission (pts.) Auto	Drive Axle (pts.)	Fuel Tank (gal.)	Cooling System (qts.)
1986	Grand Am	U	151 (2.5)	3.5	3.0	—	5.4	11.7	—	13.6	7.9 ①
	Grand Am	L	181 (3.0)	4.5	4.0	—	—	18.0	—	13.6	10.3
	Calais	U	151 (2.5)	3.5	3.0	—	5.4	11.7	—	13.6	7.9 ①
	Calais	L	181 (3.0)	4.5	4.0	—	—	18.0	—	13.6	10.3
	Somerset	U	151 (2.5)	3.5	3.0	—	5.4	11.7	—	13.6	7.9 ①
	Somerset	L	181 (3.0)	4.5	4.0	—	—	18.0	—	13.6	10.3
	Skylark	U	151 (2.5)	3.5	3.0	—	5.4	11.7	—	13.6	7.9 ①
	Skylark	L	181 (3.0)	4.5	4.0	—	—	18.0	—	13.6	10.3
1987	Grand Am	K	122 (2.0)	4.0	3.8	—	6.0	11.0	—	13.6	7.8 ①
	Grand Am	M	122 (2.0)	4.0	3.8	—	6.0	11.0	—	13.6	7.8 ①
	Grand Am	U	151 (2.5)	3.5	3.0	—	5.4	11.7	—	13.6	7.9
	Grand Am	L	181 (3.0)	4.5	4.0	—	—	18.0	—	13.6	10.3
	Calais	U	151 (2.5)	3.5	3.0	—	5.4	11.7	—	13.6	7.9 ①
	Calais	L	183 (3.0)	4.5	4.0	—	—	18.0	—	13.6	10.3

CAPACITIES

Year	Model	VIN	No. Cylinder Displacement cu. in. (liter)	Engine Crankcase with Filter	Engine Crankcase without Filter	Transmission (pts.) 4-Spd	Transmission (pts.) 5-Spd	Transmission (pts.) Auto	Drive Axle (pts.)	Fuel Tank (gal.)	Cooling System (qts.)
1987	Somerset	U	151 (2.5)	3.5	3.0	—	5.4	11.7	—	13.6	7.9 ①
	Somerset	L	181 (3.0)	4.5	4.0	—	—	18.0	—	13.6	10.3
	Skylark	U	151 (2.5)	3.5	3.0	—	5.4	11.7	—	13.6	7.9 ①
	Skylark	L	181 (3.0)	4.5	4.0	—	—	18.0	—	13.6	10.3
1988	Grand Am	K	122 (2.0)	4.5	4.0	—	6.0 ②	8.0 ③	—	13.6	8.0
	Grand Am	M	122 (2.0)	4.5	4.0	—	6.0 ②	8.0 ③	—	13.6	8.0
	Grand Am	D	138 (2.3)	4.5	4.0	—	6.0 ②	8.0 ③	—	13.6	7.6
	Grand Am	U	151 (2.5)	4.5	4.0	—	6.0 ②	8.0 ③	—	13.6	7.8
	Calais	D	138 (2.3)	4.5	4.0	—	6.0 ②	8.0 ③	—	13.6	7.6
	Calais	U	151 (2.5)	4.5	4.0	—	6.0	8.0 ③	—	13.6	7.8
	Calais	L	181 (3.0)	4.5	4.0	—	6.0 ②	8.0 ③	—	13.6	10.3
	Skylark	D	138 (2.3)	4.5	4.0	—	6.0 ②	8.0 ③	—	13.6	7.6
	Skylark	U	151 (2.5)	4.5	4.0	—	6.0 ②	8.0 ③	—	13.6	7.8
	Skylark	L	181 (3.0)	4.5	4.0	—	6.0 ②	8.0 ③	—	13.6	7.8
1989-90	Grand Am	K	122 (2.0)	4.5	4.0	—	6.0 ②	8.0 ③	—	13.6	8.0
	Grand Am	M	122 (2.0)	4.5	4.0	—	6.0 ②	8.0 ③	—	13.6	8.0
	Grand Am	A	138 (2.3)	4.5	4.0	—	6.0 ②	8.0 ③	—	13.6	8.0
	Grand Am	D	138 (2.3)	4.5	4.0	—	6.0 ②	8.0 ③	—	13.6	7.6
	Grand Am	U	151 (2.5)	4.5	4.0	—	6.0 ②	8.0 ③	—	13.6	7.8
	Calais	A	138 (2.3)	4.5	4.0	—	6.0 ②	8.0 ③	—	13.6	7.6
	Calais	D	138 (2.3)	4.5	4.0	—	6.0 ②	8.0 ③	—	13.6	7.8
	Calais	U	151 (2.5)	4.5	4.0	—	6.0	8.0 ③	—	13.6	7.6
	Calais	N	204 (3.3)	4.5	4.0	—	6.0 ②	8.0 ③	—	13.6	7.6
	Skylark	D	138 (2.3)	4.5	4.0	—	6.0 ②	8.0 ③	—	13.6	7.6
	Skylark	U	151 (2.5)	4.5	4.0	—	6.0 ②	8.0 ③	—	13.6	7.8
	Skylark	N	204 (3.3)	4.5	4.0	—	6.0 ②	8.0 ③	—	13.6	10.3

① With air conditioning
② Manual 5 speed MK7 or MT2—5.4 pts.
③ Manual 5 speed MG1 or MG2—4.4 pts.

FIRING ORDERS

NOTE: To avoid confusion, always replace spark plug wires one at a time.

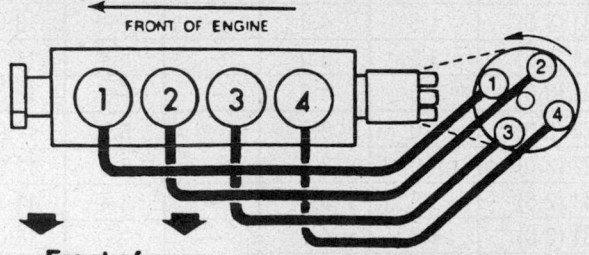

FRONT OF ENGINE

Front of car

GM (PONTIAC) 122 2.0L
Engine firing order:1–3–4–2
Distributor rotation:counterclockwise

FIRING ORDERS

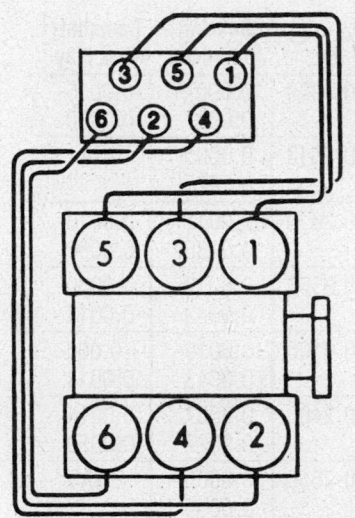

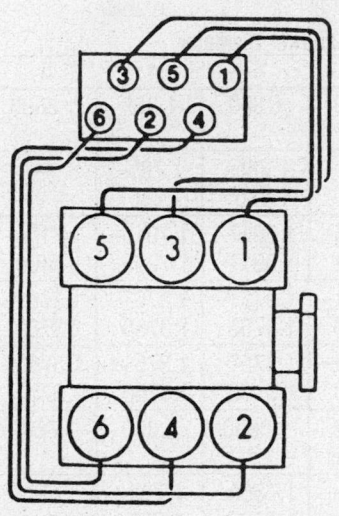

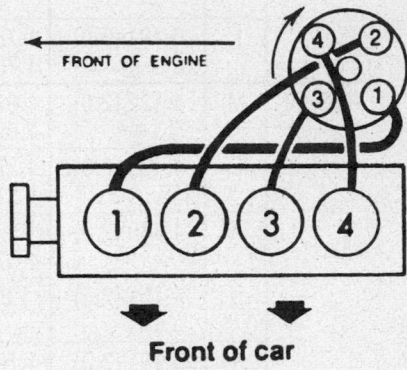

FRONT OF ENGINE

Front of car

GM (Buick) 181 V6 (3.0L)
Engine firing order: 1–6–5–4–3–2

GM (Buick and Oldsmobile)
204 V6 (3.3L)
Engine firing order: 1–6–5–4–3–2

GM (PONTIAC) 151 2.5L
Engine firing order:1–3–4–2
Distributor rotation:clockwise

CAMSHAFT SPECIFICATIONS
All measurements given in inches.

Year	VIN	No. Cylinder Displacement cu. in. (liter)	Journal Diameter					Lobe Lift		Bearing Clearance	Camshaft End Play
			1	2	3	4	5	In.	Ex.		
1986	U	4-151 (2.5)	1.8690	1.869	1.8690	1.869	1.8690	0.3980	0.3980	0.0007–0.0027	0.0015–0.0050
	L	6-181 (3.0)	1.7850–1.7860	1.785–1.786	1.7850–1.7860	1.785–1.786	—	0.3580	0.3840	0.0005–0.0025	NA
1987	M	4-122 (2.0)	1.6720–1.6714	1.6816–1.6812	1.6917–1.6911	1.7015–1.7009	1.7114–1.7108	0.2409	—	0.0008	0.0016–0.0064
	K	4-122 (2.0)	1.6712–1.6706	1.6818–1.6812	1.6917–1.6911	1.7015–1.7009	1.7106–1.7100	0.2625	0.2625	0.0011–0.0035	0.0016–0.0064
	D	4-138 (2.3)	1.3751–1.3760	1.3751–1.3760	1.3751–1.3760	1.3751–1.3760	1.3751–1.3760	0.3400	0.3500	0.0019–0.0043	0.006–0.0014
	U	4-151 (2.5)	1.8690	1.8690	1.8690	1.869	1.8690	0.3980	0.3980	0.0007–0.0027	0.0015–0.0050
	L	6-181 (3.0)	1.7850–1.7860	1.785–1.786	1.7850–1.7860	1.785–1.786	—	0.3580	0.3840	0.0005–0.0025	NA
1988	M	4-122 (2.0)	1.6720–1.6714	1.6816–1.6812	1.6917–1.6911	1.7015–1.7009	1.7114–1.7108	0.2409	—	0.0008	0.0016–0.0064
	K	4-122 (2.0)	1.6712–1.6706	1.6818–1.6812	1.6917–1.6911	1.7015–1.7009	1.7106–1.7100	0.2625	0.2625	0.0011–0.0035	0.0016–0.0064
	D	4-138 (2.3)	1.3751–1.3760	1.3751–1.3760	1.3751–1.3760	1.3751–1.3760	1.3751–1.3760	0.3400	0.3500	0.0019–0.0043	0.0060–0.0014

CAMSHAFT SPECIFICATIONS

All measurements given in inches.

Year	VIN	No. Cylinder Displacement cu. in. (liter)	Journal Diameter					Lobe Lift		Bearing Clearance	Camshaft End Play
			1	2	3	4	5	In.	Ex.		
1988	U	4-151 (2.5)	1.8690	1.869	1.869	1.869	1.8690	0.3980	0.3980	0.0007–0.0027	0.0015–0.0050
	L	6-181 (3.0)	1.7850–1.7860	1.785–1.786	1.785–1.786	1.785–1.786	—	0.3580	0.3840	0.0005–0.0025	NA
1989-90	M	4-122 (2.0)	1.6712–1.6706	1.6818–1.6812	1.6917–1.6911	1.7015–1.7009	1.7106–1.7100	0.2625	0.2625	0.0011–0.0035	0.0016–0.0064
	D	4-138 (2.3)	1.3751–1.3760	1.3751–1.3760	1.3751–1.3760	1.3751–1.3760	1.3751–1.3760	0.3400	0.3500	0.0019–0.0043	0.0060–0.0014
	A	4-138 (2.3)	1.5728–1.5720	1.3751–1.3760	1.3751–1.3760	1.3751–1.3760	1.3751–1.3760	0.4100	0.4100	0.0019–0.0043	0.006–0.0014
	U	4-151 (2.5)	1.8690	1.869	1.8690	1.869	1.8690	0.2480	0.2480	0.0007 0.0027	0.0014 0.0050
	N	6-204 (3.3)	1.7850–1.7860	1.785–1.786	1.7850–1.7860	1.785–1.786	—	0.2500	0.2550	0.0005–0.0035	NA

NA Not available

CRANKSHAFT AND CONNECTING ROD SPECIFICATIONS

All measurements are given in inches.

Year	VIN	No. Cylinder Displacement cu. in. (liter)	Crankshaft				Connecting Rod		
			Main Brg. Journal Dia.	Main Brg. Oil Clearance	Shaft End-play	Thrust on No.	Journal Diameter	Oil Clearance	Side Clearance
1986	U	4-151 (2.5)	2.3000	0.0005–0.0022	0.0035–0.0085	5	2.0000	0.0005–0.0022	0.0060–0.0220
	L	6-181 (3.0)	2.4995	0.0003–0.0018	0.0030–0.0150	2	2.4870	0.0005–0.0026	0.0030–0.0150
1987	K	4-122 (2.0)	2.2830–2.2833	0.0006–0.0016	0.0003–0.0012	3	1.9278–1.9286	0.0007–0.0024	0.0027–0.0095
	M	4-122 (2.0)	2.2830–2.2833 ①	0.0006–0.0016	0.0003–0.0012	3	1.9278–1.9286	0.0007–0.0024	0.0027–0.0095
	D	4-138 (2.3)	2.0470–2.0474	0.0005–0.0020	0.0034–0.0095	3	1.8887–1.8897	0.0005–0.0025	0.0059–0.0177
	U	4-151 (2.5)	2.3000	0.0005–0.0022	0.0035–0.0085	5	2.000	0.0005–0.0022	0.006–0.022
	L	6-181 (3.0)	2.4995	0.0003–0.0018	0.0030–0.0085	2	2.487	0.0005–0.0026	0.0030–0.0150
1988	K	4-122 (2.0)	2.2830–2.2833	0.0006–0.0016	0.0003–0.0012	3	1.9278–1.9286	0.0007–0.0024	0.0027–0.0095
	M	4-122 (2.0)	2.2830–2.2833	0.0006–0.0016	0.0003–0.0012	3	1.9278–1.9286	0.0007–0.0024	0.0027–0.0095
	D	4-138 (2.3)	2.0470–2.0474	0.0005–0.0020	0.0034–0.0095	3	1.8887–1.8897	0.0005–0.0025	0.0059–0.0177
	U	4-151 (2.5)	2.3000	0.0005–0.0022	0.0035–0.0085	5	2.000	0.0005–0.0022	0.0060–0.0220
	L	6-181 (3.0)	2.4988–2.4998	0.0003–0.0018	0.0030–0.0011	2	2.4870	0.0003	0.0030–0.0150

CRANKSHAFT AND CONNECTING ROD SPECIFICATIONS

All measurements are given in inches.

Year	VIN	No. Cylinder Displacement cu. in. (liter)	Crankshaft				Connecting Rod		
			Main Brg. Journal Dia.	Main Brg. Oil Clearance	Shaft End-play	Thrust on No.	Journal Diameter	Oil Clearance	Side Clearance
1989-90	M	4-122 (2.0)	2.2830– 2.2833	0.0006– 0.0016	0.0003– 0.0012	3	1.9279– 1.9287	0.0007– 0.0024	0.0027– 0.0095
	A	4-138 (2.3)	2.0470– 2.0480	0.0005– 0.0023	0.0034– 0.0095	3	1.8887– 1.8897	0.0005– 0.0020	0.0059– 0.0177
	D	4-138 (2.3)	2.0470– 2.0480	0.0005– 0.0023	0.0034– 0.0095	3	1.8887– 1.8897	0.0005– 0.0020	0.0059– 0.0177
	U	4-151 (2.5)	2.3000	0.0005– 0.0020	0.0006– 0.0110	5	2.0000	0.0005– 0.0030	0.0060– 0.0240
	N	6-204 (3.3)	2.4988– 2.4998	0.0003– 0.0018	0.0030– 0.0011	2	2.2490– 2.2500	0.0003– 0.0026	0.0030– 0.0150

① Brown; Green—2.2827–2.2830

VALVE SPECIFICATIONS

Year	VIN	No. Cylinder Displacement cu. in. (liter)	Seat Angle (deg.)	Face Angle (deg.)	Spring Test Pressure (lbs.)	Spring Installed Height (in.)	Stem-to-Guide Clearance (in.)		Stem Diameter (in.)	
							Intake	Exhaust	Intake	Exhaust
1986	U	4-151 (2.5)	46	45	82	1.66	0.0010– 0.0027	0.0010– 0.0027	0.3130– 0.3140	0.3120– 0.3130
	L	0-101 (3.0)	45	45	220	1.34	0.0015– 0.0035	0.0015– 0.0032	0.3401– 0.3412	0.3405– 0.3412
1987	K	4-122 (2.0)	45	46	—	—	0.0006– 0.0020	0.0010– 0.0024	—	—
	M	4-122 (2.0)	45	46	—	—	0.0006– 0.0020	0.0010– 0.0024	—	—
	D	4-138 (2.3)	45	①	64–70	1.42– 1.44	0.0009– 0.0027	0.0015– 0.0032	0.2751– 0.2744	0.2754– 0.2739
	U	4-151 (2.5)	46	45	75	1.44	—	—	0.3130– 0.3140	0.3120– 0.3130
	L	6-181 (3.0)	45	45	90	1.73	0.0015– 0.0035	0.0015– 0.0032	0.3401– 0.3412	0.3405– 0.3412
1988	K	4-122 (2.0)	45	46	—	—	0.0006– 0.0020	0.0010– 0.0024	—	—
	M	4-122 (2.0)	45	46	—	—	0.0006– 0.0020	0.0010– 0.0024	0.2751– 0.2744	0.2754– 0.2739
	D	4-138 (2.3)	45	①	64–70	1.42– 1.44	0.0009– 0.0027	0.0015– 0.0032	0.2751– 0.2744	0.2754– 0.2739
	U	4-151 (2.5)	46	45	71–78	1.44	—	—	0.3130– 0.3140	0.3120– 0.3130
	L	6-181 (3.0)	46	45	90	1.73	0.0015– 0.0035	0.0015– 0.0032	0.3401– 0.3412	0.3405– 0.3412
1989-90	M	4-122 (2.0)	45	46	74–82	1.48	0.0006– 0.0017	0.0010– 0.0024	0.2760– 0.2755	0.2753– 0.2747
	A	4-138 (2.3)	45	①	64–70	1.42– 1.44	0.0009– 0.0027	0.0015– 0.0032	0.2751– 0.2744	0.2740– 0.2747
	D	4-138 (2.3)	45	①	64–70	1.42– 1.44	0.0009– 0.0027	0.0015– 0.0032	0.2751– 0.2744	0.2740– 0.2747

VALVE SPECIFICATIONS

Year	VIN	No. Cylinder Displacement cu. in. (liter)	Seat Angle (deg.)	Face Angle (deg.)	Spring Test Pressure (lbs.)	Spring Installed Height (in.)	Stem-to-Guide Clearance (in.)		Stem Diameter (in.)	
							Intake	Exhaust	Intake	Exhaust
1989-90	U	4-151 (2.5)	46	45	75	1.68	0.0010–0.0026	0.0013–0.0041	0.3130–0.3140	0.3120–0.3130
	N	6-204 (3.3)	45	45	76–84	1.69–1.75	0.0015–0.0035	0.0015–0.0032	0.3401–0.3412	0.3405–0.3412

① 44 degrees intake face angle
44.5 degrees exhaust face angle

PISTON AND RING SPECIFICATIONS

All measurements are given in inches.

Year	VIN	No. Cylinder Displacement cu. in. (liter)	Piston Clearance	Ring Gap			Ring Side Clearance		
				Top Compression	Bottom Compression	Oil Control	Top Compression	Bottom Compression	Oil Control
1986	U	4-151 (2.5)	0.0014–0.0022 ①	0.010–0.020	0.010–0.020	0.020–0.060	0.002–0.003	0.001–0.003	0.015–0.055
	L	6-181 (3.0)	0.0008–0.0020 ②	0.010–0.020	0.010–0.020	0.015–0.055	0.003–0.005	0.003–0.005	0.0035
1987	K	4-122 (2.0)	0.0040–0.0012	0.012–0.020	0.012–0.020	0.016–0.055	0.002–0.003	0.001–0.003	—
	M	4-122 (2.0)	0.0012–0.0020	0.012–0.020	0.012–0.020	0.016–0.055	0.002–0.003	0.001–0.003	—
	D	4-138 (2.3)	0.0007–0.0020	0.016–0.025	0.016–0.025	0.016–0.055	0.002–0.004	0.0016–0.0031	
	U	4-151 (2.5)	0.0014–0.0022 ①	0.010–0.020	0.010–0.020	0.020–0.060	0.002–0.003	0.001–0.003	0.015–0.055
	L	6-181 (3.0)	0.0008–0.0020 ②	0.010–0.020	0.010–0.020	0.015–0.055	0.003–0.005	0.003–0.005	0.0035
1988	K	4-122 (2.0)	0.0040–0.0012	0.012–0.020	0.012–0.020	0.016–0.055	0.002–0.003	0.001–0.003	—
	M	4-122 (2.0)	0.0012–0.0020	0.012–0.020	0.012–0.020	0.016–0.055	0.002–0.003	0.001–0.003	—
	D	4-138 (2.3)	0.0007–0.0020	0.016–0.025	0.016–0.025	0.016–0.055	0.002–0.004	0.0016–0.0031	—
	U	4-151 (2.5)	0.0014–0.0022 ①	0.010–0.020	0.010–0.020	0.020–0.060	0.002–0.003	0.001–0.003	0.015–0.055
	L	6-181 (3.0)	0.0010–0.0045 ②	0.010–0.020	0.010–0.022	0.015–0.055	0.001–0.003	0.001–0.003	0.0005–0.0065
1989-90	M	4-122 (2.0)	0.0012–0.0020	0.010–0.020	0.012–0.020	0.016–0.055	0.002–0.004	0.002–0.003	—
	A	4-138 (2.3)	0.0007–0.0020	0.014–0.024	0.016–0.026	0.016–0.055	0.002–0.004	0.0016–0.0031	—
	D	4-138 (2.3)	0.0007–0.0020	0.014–0.024	0.016–0.026	0.016–0.055	0.002–0.004	0.0016–0.0031	—

PISTON AND RING SPECIFICATIONS

All measurements are given in inches.

Year	VIN	No. Cylinder Displacement cu. in. (liter)	Piston Clearance	Ring Gap			Ring Side Clearance		
				Top Compression	Bottom Compression	Oil Control	Top Compression	Bottom Compression	Oil Control
1989-90	U	4-151 (2.5)	0.0014–0.0022 ①	0.010–0.020	0.010–0.020	0.020–0.060	0.002–0.003	0.001–0.003	0.015–0.055
	N	6-204 (3.3)	0.0004–0.0022 ②	0.010–0.025	0.010–0.025	0.010–0.040	0.001–0.003	0.001–0.003	0.001–0.008

① Measured 1.8 in. from piston top
② Measured at top of piston skirt

TORQUE SPECIFICATIONS

All readings in ft. lbs.

Year	VIN	No. Cylinder Displacement cu. in. (liter)	Cylinder Head Bolts	Main Bearing Bolts	Rod Bearing Bolts	Crankshaft Pulley Bolts	Flywheel Bolts	Manifold Intake	Manifold Exhaust	Spark Plugs
1986	U	4-151 (2.5)	⑭	70	32	162	44	37 ①	32 ⑥	15
	L	6-181 (3.0)	⑫	100	45	200	60	32	37	20
1987	K	4-122 (2.0)	②	44 ③	26 ④	20	48 ⑦	16	16	15
	M	4-122 (2.0)	②	44 ③	20 ④	20	48 ⑦	16	16	15
	D	4-138 (2.3)	⑧	15 ⑨	15 ⑩	74 ⑨	46	18 ⑪	27	15–18
	U	4-151 (2.5)	⑭	70	32	162	44	37 ①	32 ⑥	15
	L	6-181 (3.0)	⑫	100	45	219	60	32	37	20
1988	K	4-122 (2.0)	②	44 ③	26 ④	20	48 ⑦	16	16	15
	M	4-122 (2.0)	②	44 ③	26 ④	20	48 ⑦	16	16	15
	D	4-138 (2.3)	⑧	15 ⑨	15 ⑩	74 ⑨	46	40 ⑪	27	15–18
	U	4-151 (2.5)	⑮	70	32	162	55 ④	32	32 ⑥	15–18
	L	6-181 (3.0)	⑫	100	45	219	60	32	37	20
1989-90	M	4-122 (2.0)	②	44 ③	26 ④	20	48 ⑦	16	16	15
	A	4-138 (2.3)	⑧	15 ⑨	15 ⑩	74 ⑨	①	18 ⑪	27	15–18
	D	4-138 (2.3)	⑧	15 ⑨	15 ⑩	74 ⑨	①	18 ⑪	27	15–18
	U	4-151 (2.5)	⑮	70	32	162	55 ④	32	32 ⑥	15–18
	N	6-204 (3.3)	⑯	90	20	219	61	7	30	20

① Flywheel to crankshaft to 22 ft. lbs. plus 45° turn flywheel to converter 46 ft. lbs.
② Step 1: 18 ft. lbs.
Step 2: Tighten additional 180 degrees in 3 steps of 60 degrees each
Step 3: Warm engine—tighten bolts additional 30–50 degree turn
③ Plus additional 45–50 degree turn
④ Plus additional 45 degrees turn
⑤ Not used
⑥ Bolts 3–5—to 37 ft. lbs.
⑦ Plus 30 degree turn
⑧ Short bolts—26 ft. lbs. plus 80 degree turn
Long bolts—26 ft. lbs. plus 90 degree turn
⑨ Plus 90 degree turn

⑩ Plus 75 degree turn
⑪ Brace-to-manifold stud nut—18 ft. lbs. VIN D
Brace-to-block stud nut—40 ft. lbs.
Brace-to-manifold—40 ft. lbs.
⑫ Should you reach 60 ft. lbs. at any time, do not complete Steps 2 and 3
Step 1—Tighten bolts 25 ft. lbs. in sequence
Step 2—Tighten each bolt 1/4 turn in sequence
Step 3—Tighten each bolt an additional 1/4 turn in sequence
⑬ Not used

⑭ Torque head bolts in sequence to 18 ft. lbs. Repeat sequence bringing torque to 22 ft. lbs. on all bolts except No. 9, torque to 29 ft. lbs. Repeat sequence. Turn all bolts 120 degrees (2 flats). Torque No. 9 1/4 turn
⑮ Torque all head bolts in sequence to 18 ft. lbs. Repeat sequence bringing torque to 26 ft. lbs. on all bolts except No. 9, torque to 18 ft. lbs. Repeat sequence turning all bolts 90 degrees
⑯ Torque head bolts in sequence to 35 ft. lbs. Turn all bolts 30° in sequence. Turn the center 4 bolts an additional 30° in sequence.

WHEEL ALIGNMENT

Year	Model	Caster Range (deg.)	Caster Preferred Setting (deg.)	Camber Range (deg.)	Camber Preferred Setting (deg.)	Toe-in (in.)	Steering Axis Inclination (deg.)
1986	Somerset	23/34P-2 23/32P	1 23/32P	1/4P-1 7/16P	27/32P	0	13 1/2
	Calais	11/16P-2 11/16P	1 11/16P	7/32N-1 13/32P	13/16P	1/16N	13 1/2
	Grand Am	11/16P-2 11/16P	1 11/16P	7/32N-1 13/32P	13/16P	1/16N	13 1/2
1987	Skylark	23/34P-2 23/32P	1 23/32P	1/4P-1 7/16P	27/32P	0	13 1/2
	Somerset	23/34P-2 23/32P	1 23/32P	1/4P-1 7/16P	27/32P	0	13 1/2
	Calais	11/16P-2 11/16P	1 11/16P	7/32N-1 13/32P	13/16P	1/16N	13 1/2
	Grand Am	11/16P-2 11/16P	1 11/16P	7/32N-1 13/32P	13/16P	1/16N	13 1/2
1988	Skylark	13/16N-4 3/16P	1 11/16P	3/16N-1 13/16P	13/16	0	13 1/2
	Calais	13/16N-4 3/16P	1 11/16P	3/16N-1 13/16P	13/16	0	13 1/2
	Grand Am	13/16N-4 3/16P	1 11/16P	3/16N-1 13/16P	13/16	0	13 1/2
1989-90	Skylark	11/16P-2 11/16	1 11/16P	1/8P-1 1/2P	13/16	0	13 1/2
	Calais	11/16P-2 11/16	1 11/16P	1/8P-1 1/2	13/16	0	13 1/2
	Grand Am	11/16P-2 11/16	1 11/16P	1/8P-1 1/2	13/16	0	13 1/2

ELECTRICAL

NOTE: Disconnecting the negative battery cable on some vehicles may interfere with the functions of the on board computer systems and may require the computer to undergo a relearning process, once the negative battery cable is reconnected.

For testing and overhaul procedures on starters, alternators and voltage regulators, refer to the Unit Repair section.

Charging System

ALTERNATOR

Removal and Installation

EXCEPT 2.3L ENGINE

1. Disconnect the negative battery terminal from the battery.
2. Remove the 2-terminal plug and the battery lead from the back of the alternator assembly.
3. Loosen the adjusting bolts and remove the alternator belt. On engines with a serpentine belt, loosen the serpentine belt tensioner and rotate it counterclockwise to remove the drive belt.
4. Remove the alternator retaining bolts and lift the alternator assembly from the vehicle.
5. Continue the installation in the reverse order of the removal procedure. Check and/or adjust the drive belt tension. Tighten the serpentine belt tensioner pulley if so equipped.

2.3L ENGINE

1. Disconnect negative battery cable.
2. Remove serpentine belt. Loosen tensioner pulley bolt and rotate tensioner counterclockwise.

NOTE: When rotating the serpentine belt tensioner, use a 13mm wrench or equivalent that is at least 24 in. long.

3. Disconnect the vacuum lines at front of engine and remove vacuum harness retaining bracket.
4. Disconnect and tag electrical connections from injector harness and alternator.
5. Remove 2 rear alternator mounting bolts.
6. Remove front alternator bolt and engine harness clip.
7. Remove alternator out between the engine lifting eyelet and the air conditioning compressor and condenser hose.

NOTE: Extreme care must be taken during removal and installation not to damage the air conditioning compressor and condenser hose.

8. Continue the installation in the reverse order of the removal procedure.

VOLTAGE REGULATOR

Removal and Installation

The voltage regulator is incorporated within the alternator assembly. There is no adjustment procedure. Should the regulator require service, the alternator must be disassembled.

BELT TENSION

Adjustment

GAUGE METHOD

EXCEPT 2.5L ENGINE

A single serpentine belt is used to drive engine mounted accessories. Drive belt tension is maintained by a spring loaded tensioner. The drive belt tensioner can control belt tension over a broad range belt lengths; however, there are limits to the tensioner's ability to compensate.

1. Disconnect the negative battery cable.
2. Inspect tensioner markings to see if the belt is within operating lengths. Replace belt if the belt is excessively worn or is outside of the tensioner's operating range.

NOTE: On early production some serpentine belts were slightly short. This will position the tensioner adjustment outside of its marked range. There is no need to replace any parts since normal function is not affected.

3. Run the engine until operating temperature is reached. Be sure all accessories are **OFF**. Read the belt tension using a belt tension gauge tool placed halfway between the alternator and the air conditioning compressor. For non air conditioning applications read, tension between the power steering pump and crankshaft pulley. Remove the tool.

4. Using an 18mm box end wrench, apply clockwise force tighten to the tensioner pulley bolt. Release the force and immediately take a tension reading without disturbing belt tensioner position.

5. Using the same wrench, apply a counterclockwise force to the tensioner pulley bolt and raise the pulley to the install position. Slowly lower the pulley to the at rest position and take a tension reading without disturbing the belt tensioner position.

6. Repeat Steps 4 and 5, 3 times and average the readings. If the average of the 3 readings is lower than 50 lbs. on the 2.0L engine and 2.3L engine, 79 lbs. on the 3.0L engine and 65 lbs. on the 3.3L engine the belt is within the tensioner's operating range, replace the belt tensioner.

2.5L ENGINE

1. Disconnect the negative battery cable.
2. Loosen the alternator mounting bolts.
3. Using a standard belt tension gauge, install it onto the center longest span of the drive belt.
4. Using a medium pry bar, apply pressure to the center of the alternator, not against either end frame. When the drive belt tension is 90–100 lbs. for a used belt or 165–175 lbs. for a new belt, tighten the alternator mounting bolts.

Starting System

STARTER

Removal and Installation

EXCEPT 2.3L ENGINE

1. Disconnect the negative battery terminal from the battery.
2. Raise and support the vehicle safely. Disconnect the electrical wiring from the starter.
3. Remove the dust cover bolts and pull the dust cover back to gain access to the front starter bolt.
4. Remove the front starter bolt.
5. Remove the rear support bracket.
6. Pull the rear dust cover back to gain access to the rear starter bolt and remove the rear bolt.
7. Push the dust cover back into place and pull the starter assembly back and out.

NOTE: Be sure to note any shims during removal so they may be installed in their original location.

8. Continue the installation in the reverse order of the removal procedure. Torque the starter-to-engine bolts to 31 ft. lbs. on the 2.0L, 2.3L and 2.5L engines and 35 ft. lbs. on the 3.0L and 3.3L engines.

2.3L ENGINE

1. Disconnect the negative battery cable.
2. Remove air cleaner to throttle body duct.
3. Remove and tag electrical connectors from TPS, IAC and MAP sensor.
4. Remove vacuum harness assembly from intake and position aside.
5. Remove coolant fan shroud retaining bolts and remove shroud including MAP sensor.

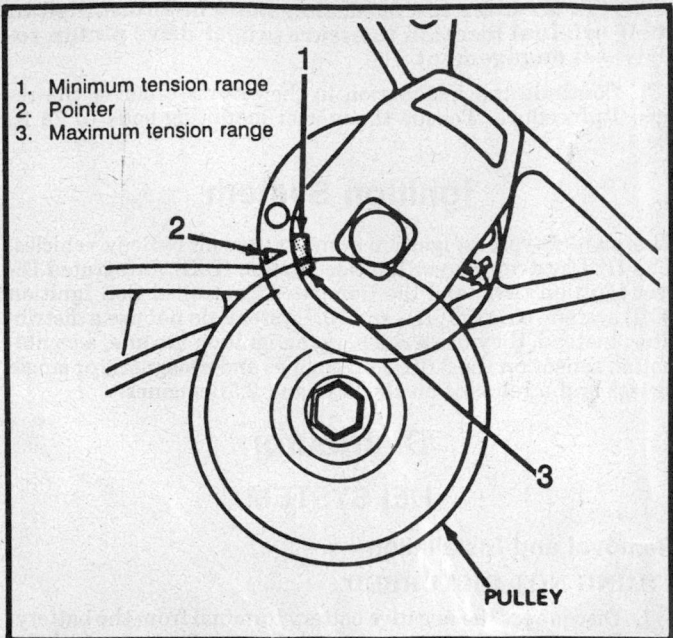

1. Minimum tension range
2. Pointer
3. Maximum tension range

PULLEY

Tensioner operating range

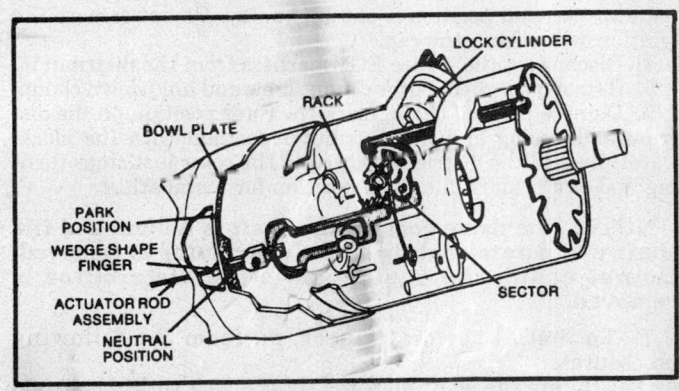

LOCK CYLINDER
RACK
BOWL PLATE
PARK POSITION
WEDGE SHAPE FINGER
ACTUATOR ROD ASSEMBLY
NEUTRAL POSITION
SECTOR

Mechanical neutral start system – typical

6. Remove upper radiator support.
7. Disconnect and tag electrical connector from coolant fan.
8. Lift the fan assembly out of the 2 lower insulators. Rotate the bracket so the 2 lower bracket legs point upward. Move the fan assembly toward the left driver's side until the fan overlaps the radiator tank to core seam by approximately 1 in. Remove the fan assembly up, out the top.

NOTE: Because of low clearance, special care must be taken not to damage the lock tang on the TPS with the fan bracket

9. Remove harness retaining clip from engine mount bracket stud and starter mounting bolts.
10. Tilt rear of starter towards the radiator, pull the starter out and rotate solenoid towards the radiator to gain access to the electrical connections.

NOTE: Take care not to damage the crank sensor mounted directly to the rear of the starter.

11. Disconnect electrical connections at solenoid.
12. Move starter to the left driver's side of the vehicle and remove out the top.

NOTE: If shims are used, they must be reinstalled in their original location to assure proper drive pinion-to-flywheel engagement.

13. Continue the installation in the reverse order of the removal procedure. Torque the starter mounting bolts to 74 ft. lbs.

Ignition System

There are 4 types of ignition systems used on N-Body vehicles. The HEI system, Direct Ignition System (DIS), Integrated Direct Ignition (IDI) and the Computer Controlled Coil Ignition (C^3I) system. The C^3I, IDI and DIS systems do not use a distributor; instead, they use a coil pack, an ignition module, a combination sensor on the 3.0L, 3.3L engines and a magnetic or single sensor and a reluctor on the 2.3L and 2.5L engines.

Distributor

HEI SYSTEM

Removal and Installation

TIMING NOT DISTURBED

1. Disconnect the negative battery terminal from the battery.
2. Disconnect the ignition switch battery feed wire and the tachometer lead, if equipped from the distributor cap.
3. Release the coil connectors from the cap. Remove the distributor cap and position it out of the way. Do not remove the ignition wires from the cap.
4. Disconnect the 4-wire ECM harness from the distributor.
5. Remove the distributor clamp screw and hold down clamp.
6. Using a piece of chalk, mark the rotor position on the distributor housing and the distributor position with the block. Carefully pull the distributor up until the rotor just stops turning and again mark the rotor position for installation.

NOTE: The drive gear on the shaft is helical and the shaft will rotate slightly as the distributor is removed. Do not crank the engine while the distributor is removed.

7. To install the distributor, perform the following procedures:
   a. Rotate the shaft until the rotor aligns with the second mark.
   b. Using clean engine oil, lubricate the drive gear and install the distributor into the engine.
   c. When installing the distributor, turn the rotor to the first mark made during removal; this ensures proper timing.

NOTE: If the marks do not align properly, remove the distributor and reinstall again.

8. Continue the installation in the reverse order of the removal procedure. Install the clamp hold down and nut. Start the engine and check the ignition timing.

TIMING DISTURBED

If the engine was accidently cranked while the distributor was removed, use the following procedure for installation. The engine must be set on TDC of the compression stroke to obtain the proper spark timing.

1. Remove the No. 1 spark plug.
2. Place finger over the No. 1 spark plug hole and crank the engine slowly until compression is felt.
3. Align the timing mark on the damper pulley with the **0** degree mark on the engine timing plate.
4. To install the distributor, perform the following procedures:
   a. Rotate the shaft until the rotor aligns with the second mark.

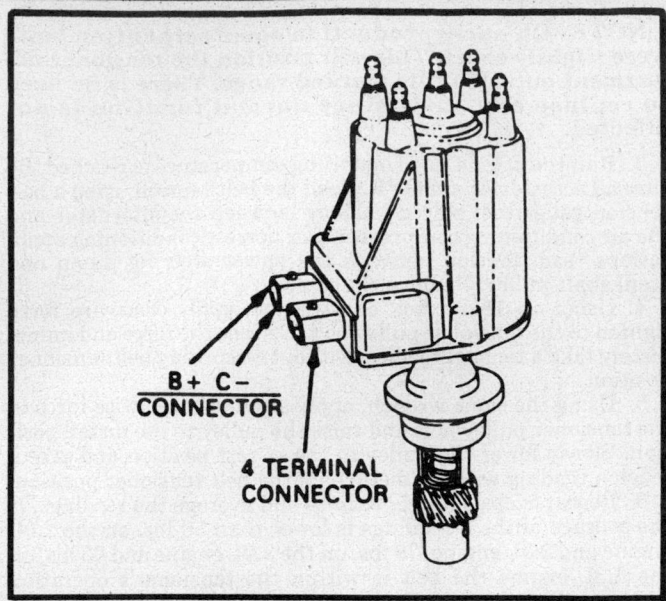

View of the HEI/EST distributor—2.5L engine

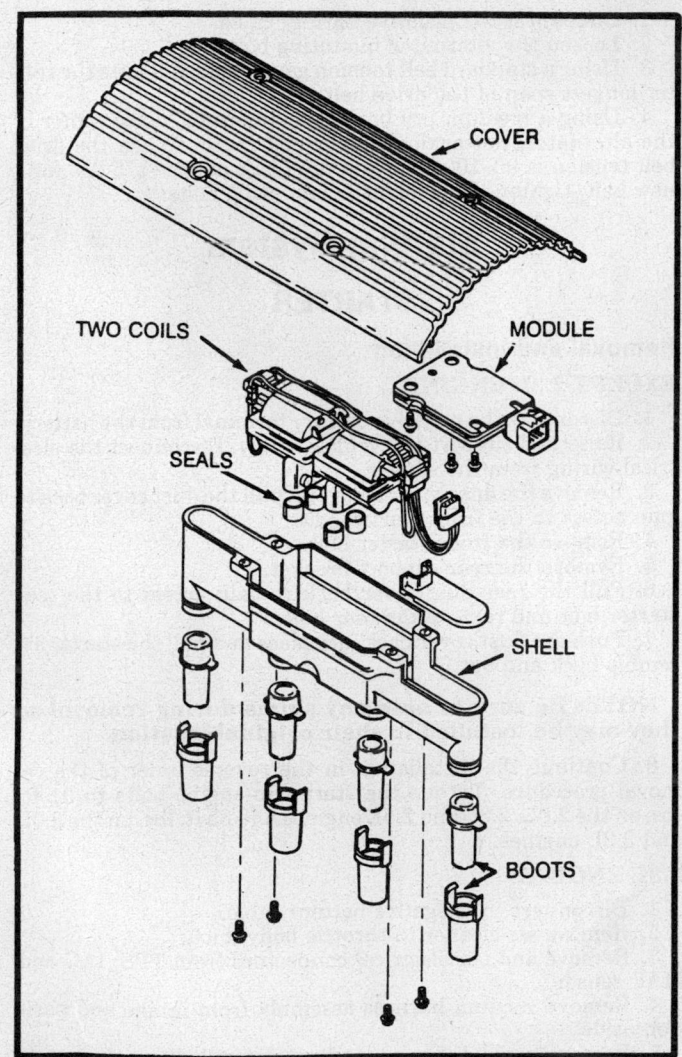

Integrated Direct Ignition

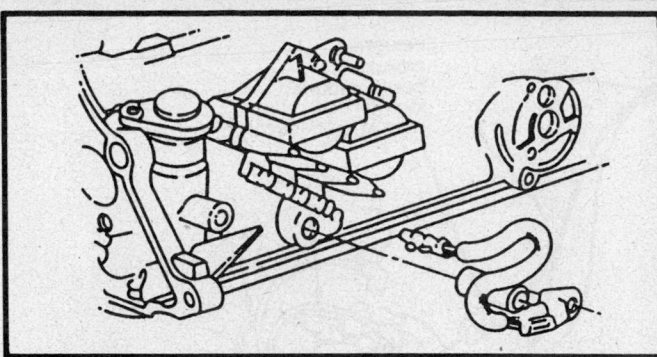

Direct Ignition system

b. Using clean engine oil, lubricate the drive gear and install the distributor into the engine.

c. When installing the distributor, turn the rotor to the first mark made during removal; this ensures proper timing.

NOTE: If the marks do not align properly, remove the distributor and reinstall again.

5. Continue the installation in the reverse order of the removal procedure. Install the clamp hold down nut. Start the engine. Check and/or adjust the ignition timing.

IGNITION TIMING

Adjustment

2.0L ENGINE

1. Refer to the underhood emission control label and follow all of the timing instructions if they differ from below.

2. Warm engine to normal operating temperature.

3. Place transaxle in **N** or **P**. Apply parking brake and block wheels.

4. The air conditioning, cooling fan and choke must be off. Do not remove air cleaner, unless required.

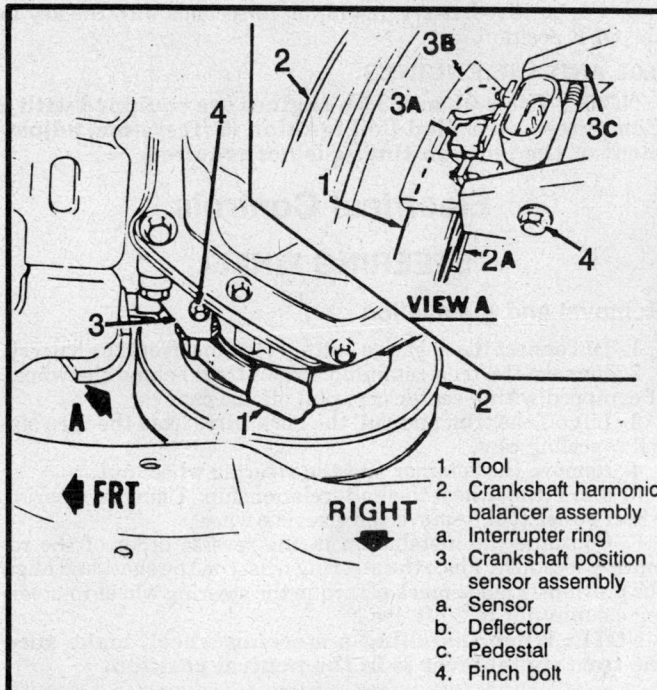

VIEW A

1. Tool
2. Crankshaft harmonic balancer assembly
   a. Interrupter ring
3. Crankshaft position sensor assembly
   a. Sensor
   b. Deflector
   c. Pedestal
4. Pinch bolt

Crankshaft sensor adjustment

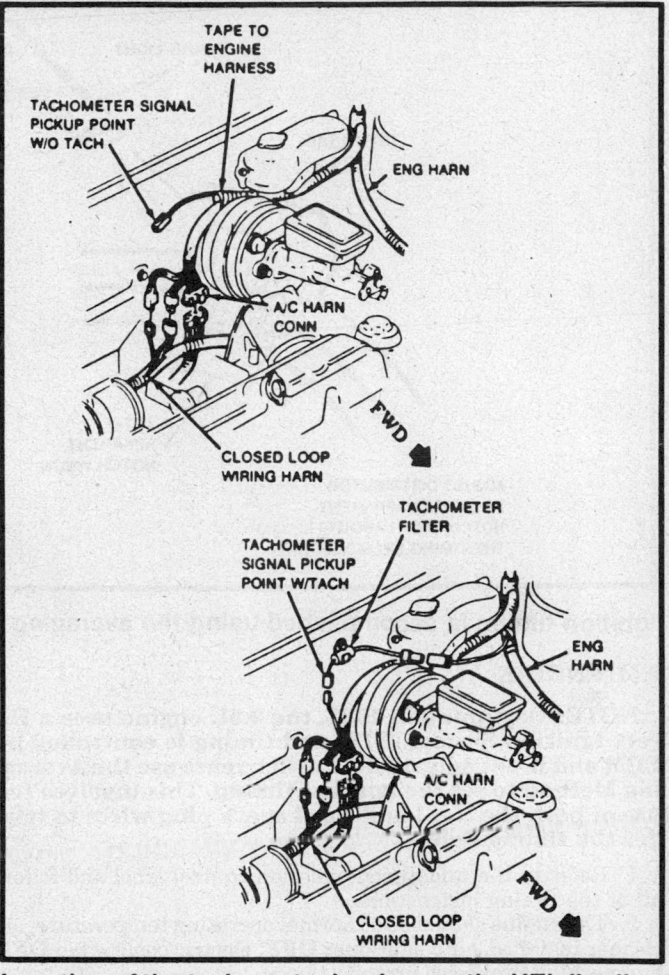

Location of the tachometer hookup on the HEI distributor—2.5L engine

5. Connect inductive timing light to coil lead. Peel back the protective covering on the coil lead to make good connection.

6. Ground the ALCL connector under the dash by installing a jumper wire between the **A** and **B** terminals. The check engine light should begin flashing.

7. Using the timing light, check the position of the timing mark.

8. Optimum timing of all cylinders is achieved when the apparent notch width is centered with the timing mark.

NOTE: A notch for the No. 1 cylinder is scribed across all 3 edges of the double groove pulley. Another notch is scribed 180 degrees away only across the center edge of the pulley. Since the coil high tension lead is triggering the timing light, timing for all 4 cylinders is shown, causing a slight jiggling of the timing notch and an apparent increase in the width of the timing notch.

9. To correct the timing, loosen the distributor hold down clamp, adjust the distributor and retighten the hold down bolt.

10. Once the timing is properly set, remove the jumper wire from the ALCL connector.

11. If necessary to clear the ECM memory, disconnect the ECM harness from the positive battery pigtail for 10 seconds with the key in the **OFF** position.

2.3L ENGINE

This engine is equipped with Integrated Direct Ignition (IDI) adjustment of the ignition timing is not required.

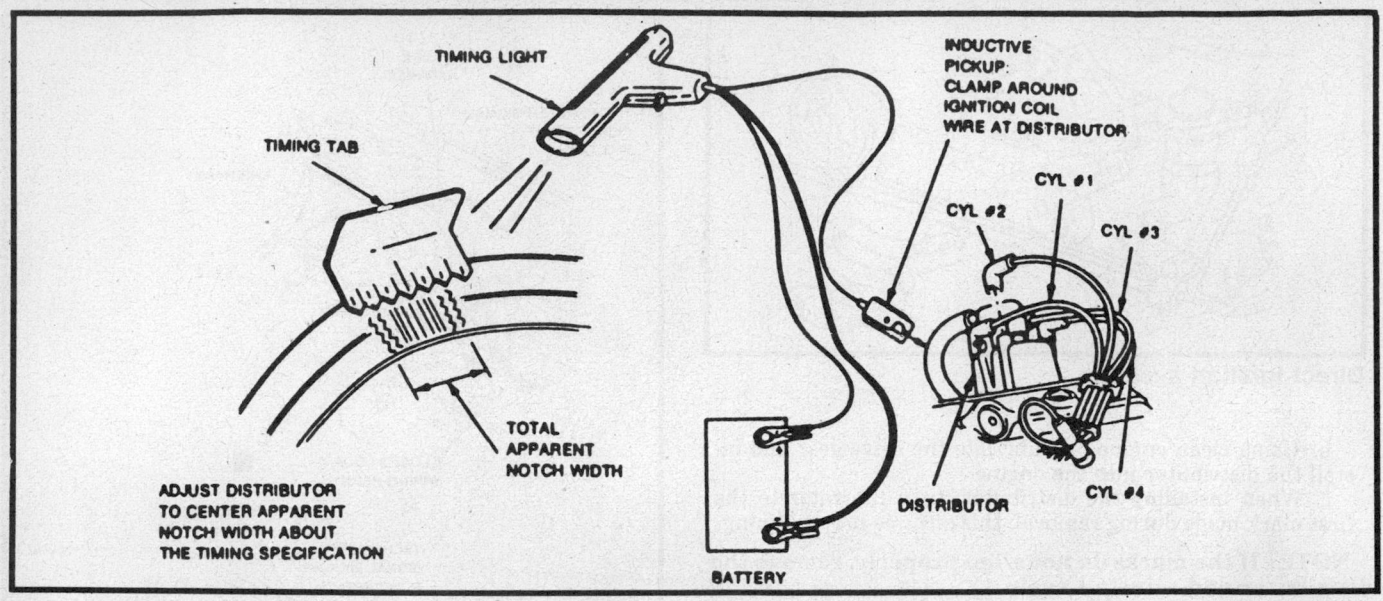

Ignition timing is accomplished using the averaging method—2.5L engine

2.5L ENGINE

NOTE: Beginning in 1987, the 2.5L engine uses a Direct Ignition System (DIS) and timing is controlled by ECM and is not adjustable. Earlier years use the Averaging Method to set the ignition timing. This involves the use of both the No. 1 and No. 4 spark plug wires to trigger the timing light.

1. Refer to the underhood emission control label and follow all of the timing instructions.
2. The engine should be at normal operating temperature, air cleaner installed, air conditioner **OFF**, electric cooling fan **OFF** and parking brake set firmly.
3. Place the automatic transaxle in **P** or the manual transaxle in **N**.

NOTE: The engines are equipped with a magnetic probe timing light receptacle, located at 9.5 degrees ATDC. Do not use a normal timing light with this receptacle.

4. Using an inductive timing light, connect it to the No. 1 plug wire and make sure the check engine light is not on.
5. Ground the ALCL connector under the dash by installing a jumper wire between the **A** and **B** terminals. The check engine light should begin flashing.
6. Using the timing light, check and record the position of the timing mark.
7. Repeat Step 4, but connect the timing light inductive pickup to the No. 4 spark plug wire. Take the total of the 2 recorded timing marks and divide by 2 to arrive at an average timing position.

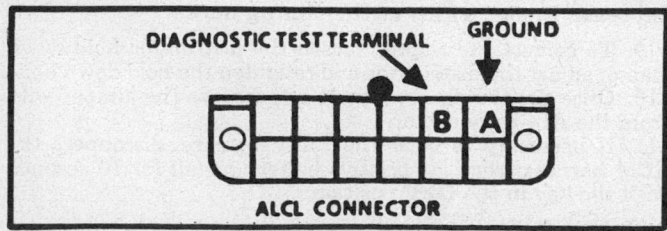

To read stored trouble codes, connect terminals A and B together with a jumper wire—2.5L engine

NOTE: For example: No. 1 timing = 4 degrees and No. 4 timing = 8 degrees; 4 + 8 = 12 ÷ 2 = 6 degrees average timing. If a change is necessary, subtract the average timing from the timing specification to determine the amount of timing change to No. 1 cylinder. For example: if the timing spec is 8 degrees and the average timing is 6 degrees, advance the No. 1 cylinder 2 degrees to set the timing.

8. To correct the timing, loosen the distributor hold down clamp, adjust the distributor and retighten the hold down bolt.
9. Once the timing is properly set, remove the jumper wire from the ALCL connector.
10. To clear the ECM memory, disconnect the ECM harness from the positive battery pigtail for 10 seconds with the key in the **OFF** position.

3.0L AND 3.3L ENGINES

NOTE: The 3.0L and 3.3L engines are equipped with a Computer Controlled Coil Ignition (C³I) system, adjustment of the ignition timing is not required.

Electrical Controls

STEERING WHEEL

Removal and Installation

1. Disconnect the negative battery terminal from the battery.
2. Remove the trim retaining screws from behind the wheel. If equipped with a center cap, pull off the cap.
3. Lift off the trim and pull the horn wires from the turn signal canceling cam.
4. Remove the retainer and the steering wheel nut.
5. Mark the wheel-to-shaft relationship. Using a steering wheel puller tool, remove the steering wheel.
6. Continue the installation in the reverse order of the removal procedure. Place the steering wheel on the shaft and align the previously made marks. Torque the steering wheel-to-steering column nut to 30 ft. lbs.

NOTE: When installing a steering wheel, make sure the turn signal lever is in the neutral position.

7. Insert the horn wires into the canceling cam, install the center trim and reconnect the battery terminal.

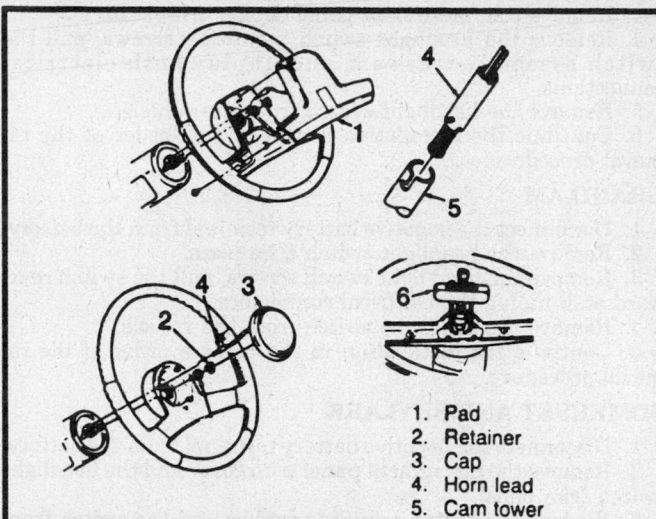

1. Pad
2. Retainer
3. Cap
4. Horn lead
5. Cam tower

Removing the steering wheel

HORN SWITCH

Removal and Installation

STANDARD STEERING WHEEL

1. Disconnect the negative battery terminal from the battery.
2. Remove the screws attaching the horn pad assembly from the backside of the steering wheel. Lift the horn pad from the steering wheel.
3. Disconnect the horn contact terminal from the pad. If the contact terminal comes out or is removed from the turn signal cancelling cam tower, it can be reinstalled by pushing it into the tower and rotating the steering wheel clockwise to lock it into position.
4. Continue the installation in the reverse order of the removal procedure.

SPORT STEERING WHEEL

1. Disconnect the negative battery terminal from the battery.
2. Using a small pry bar, pry the center ornament from the steering wheel.
3. Remove the steering wheel nut and retainer.
4. Remove the horn switch and insulator assembly.
5. Remove the switch retainer screw and separate the switch from the insulator.
6. Continue the installation in the reverse order of the removal procedure.

IGNITION LOCK

Removal and Installation

1. Disconnect the negative battery cable. Position the ignition lock cylinder in the **RUN** position.
2. Remove the steering wheel. Remove the lock plate, turn signal switch and the buzzer switch.
3. Remove the lock cylinder retaining screw. Remove the lock cylinder.
4. To install, rotate the lock cylinder clockwise to align the cylinder key with the keyway in the lock housing.
5. Push the lock all the way in. Install the screw.
6. Install the screw and tighten to 14 inch lbs. on adjustable columns or 25 inch lbs. on standard columns.

IGNITION SWITCH

Removal and Installation

The ignition switch is located on the upper side of the lower steering column area and is completely inaccessible without

← MOVE SWITCH SLIDER TO EXTREME RIGHT POSITION

View of the ignition switch

first lowering the steering column. The switch is actuated by a rod and rack assembly. A gear on the end of the lock cylinder engages the toothed upper end of the rod.

1. Disconnect the negative battery cable.
2. Remove the left instrument panel insulator.
3. Remove the left instrument panel trim pad and the steering column trim collar.
4. Remove the steering column upper support bracket bolts and remove the support bracket.
5. Carefully lower the steering column; be sure to properly support it.
6. Disconnect the wiring from the ignition switch.
7. Remove the ignition switch-to-steering column screws and the ignition switch assembly from the steering column.
8. Before installing, place the slider on the new switch in one of the following positions, depending on the steering column and accessories:
   a. Standard column with key release — extreme left detent.
   b. Standard column with **PARK/LOCK** — 1 detent from extreme left.
   c. All other standard columns — 2 detents from extreme left.
   d. Adjustable column with key release — extreme right detent.
   e. Adjustable column with **PARK/LOCK** — 1 detent from extreme right.
   f. All other adjustable columns — 2 detents from extreme right.
9. Install the activating rod into the switch and assembly the switch to the column. Tighten the mounting screws. Do not use oversize screws as they could impair the collapsibility of the column.
10. Continue the installation in the reverse order of the removal procedure.

NEUTRAL SAFETY SWITCH

Adjustment

FLOOR SHIFT AUTOMATIC TRANSAXLE

1. Place shifter assembly in the N position.
2. Loosen switch mounting screws.
3. Rotate switch on shifter assembly to align service adjustment hole with carrier tang hole.
4. Insert a $\frac{3}{32}$ in. diameter gauge pin or drill bit to a depth of $\frac{5}{8}$ in. into the service adjustment hole.
5. Torque attaching screws to 22 ft. lbs. and remove gauge pin.
6. Verify that engine will only start in **P** or **N**.

COLUMN SHIFT AUTOMATIC TRANSAXLE

All column shift automatic transaxle models use the mechanical neutral safety system. This system has a mechanical block which prevents cranking the engine when the shift lever is in any position except **P** or **N**. The mechanical block is a wedge-shaped finger added to the ignition switch actuator rod. The finger will pass through the bowl plate only when the shift lever is in **P** or **N**. This prevents turning the ignition lock cylinder to the

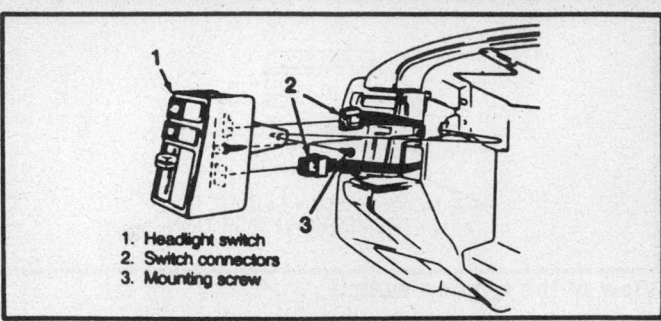

1. Headlight switch
2. Switch connectors
3. Mounting screw

Removing the headlight switch assembly

START position when the transaxle is in a drive range. When the shift lever is in either **P** or **N**, the finger passes through the bowl plate notches, allowing the lock cylinder to turn to the **START** position.

CLUTCH START SWITCH

Removal and Installation

1. Disconnect the negative battery terminal from the battery.
2. Remove the under dash lower hush panel, if equipped.
3. Remove the electrical connections from the switch.
4. Remove the clutch switch retaining screws and carefully remove the switch from the clutch pedal.
5. Continue the installation in the reverse order of the removal procedure. Be sure to check the proper engagement of the switch once installation has been completed.

STOPLIGHT SWITCH

NOTE: When the brake pedal is in the fully released position, the stoplight switch plunger should be fully depressed against the pedal arm.

Adjustment

The stoplight switch is mounted on the brake pedal bracket directly below the brake cruise release valve.
1. Depress the brake pedal and push the switch through the circular retaining clip until it contacts the brake pedal.
2. Pull the pedal rearward, up against the internal pedal stop. This places the switch in the correct position within the clip.
3. Check the light operation.

Removal and Installation

1. Disconnect the negative battery cable.
2. Remove the under dash lower hush panel, if equipped.
3. Disconnect the stoplight switch electrical connector.
4. Remove the switch from the bracket.
5. Make sure that the tubular clip is in the brake pedal mounting bracket.
6. Depress the brake pedal and insert the switch into the tubular clip until it seats on the clip; a click will be heard.
7. Pull the brake pedal fully rearward, against the pedal stop, until the clicking sounds can no longer be heard; the switch is adjusting itself in the bracket.
8. Release the brake pedal, pull the pedal rearward again to assure that the adjustment is complete.

HEADLAMP SWITCH

Removal and Installation
CALAIS

1. Disconnect the negative battery terminal from the battery.
2. Remove the lower steering column collar.

3. Remove the instrument panel cluster trim plate.
4. Remove the headlight switch mounting screws, pull the switch assembly rearward and unplug both electrical connections.
5. Remove the headlight switch from the vehicle.
6. Continue the installation in the reverse order of the removal procedure.

GRAND AM

1. Disconnect the negative battery terminal from the battery.
2. Remove the headlight switch trim plate.
3. Remove the head light switch screws, pull the switch rearward and unplug the electrical connectors.
4. Remove the headlight switch from the vehicle.
5. Continue the installation in the reverse order of the removal procedure.

SOMERSET AND SKYLARK

1. Disconnect the negative battery terminal from the battery.
2. Remove the instrument panel trim cover and the headlight switch trim panel.
3. Remove the switch retaining screws and the switch from the vehicle.
4. Continue the installation in the reverse order of the removal procedure.

DIMMER SWITCH

The dimmer switch is mounted on the steering column and is a part of the combination switch.

Removal and Installation

1. Disconnect the negative battery terminal from the battery.
2. Remove the steering wheel and the trim cover.
3. Remove the turn signal switch assembly.
4. Remove the ignition switch stud and the screw. Remove the ignition switch.
5. Remove the dimmer switch actuator rod by sliding it from the switch assembly.
6. Remove the dimmer switch screws and the dimmer switch.
7. Continue the installation in the reverse order of the removal procedure. To adjust the dimmer switch, depress it slightly, insert a $3/32$ in. dia. drill bit into the adjusting hole, push the switch up to remove any play and tighten the adjusting screw.

COMBINATION SWITCH

Removal and Installation

NOTE: The combination switch provides for control of the headlight beams, turn signals, cruise control if so equipped and windshield washer/wiper.

1. Disconnect the negative battery cable.
2. Remove the steering wheel.
3. Loosen the cover screws and remove the cover.
4. Position the U-shaped lock plate compressor on the end of the steering shaft and compress the lock plate by turning the shaft nut clockwise. Pry the wire snapring out of the shaft groove.
5. Remove the tool and lift the lock plate off the shaft.
6. Slip the canceling cam, upper bearing preload spring and thrust washer off the shaft.
7. Remove the turn signal lever. Push the flasher knob in and unscrew it. Remove the button retaining screw, the button, spring and knob.
8. Pull the switch connector out the mast jacket and tape the upper part to aid the switch removal. Attach a long piece of wire to the turn signal switch connector. When installing the turn signal switch, feed this wire through the column first, use the wire to pull the switch connector into position. If equipped with a tilt steering column, position the turn signal and shifter housing in low position, remove the harness cover.

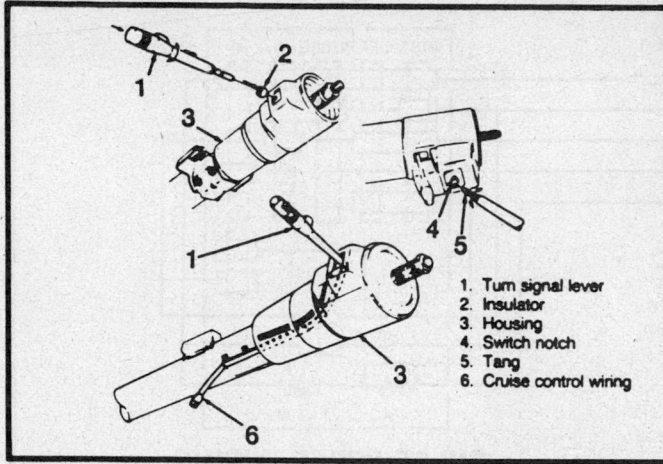

1. Turn signal lever
2. Insulator
3. Housing
4. Switch notch
5. Tang
6. Cruise control wiring

Replacing the combination switch

9. Remove the 3 switch mounting screws and the switch by pulling it straight up while guiding the wiring harness connector through the column.

10. Install the replacement switch by working the connector and cover down through the housing, under the bracket. On tilt columns, the connector is worked down through the housing and under the remove the cover.

11. Install the switch mounting screws and the connector on the mast jacket bracket. Install the column-to-dash trim plate.

12. Install the flasher knob and the turn signal lever.

13. With the turn signal lever in neutral and the flasher knob pulled out, slide the thrust washer, upper bearing preload spring and canceling cam onto the shaft.

14. Position the lock plate on the shaft and press it down until a new snapring can be inserted in the shaft groove. Always use a new snapring when assembling.

15. Continue the installation in the reverse order of the removal procedure.

WINDSHIELD WIPER SWITCH

Removal and Installation

CALAIS

1. Disconnect the negative battery cable.
2. Remove lower filler panel.
3. Remove the cluster trim plate screws. Remove the wiper switch mounting screws.
4. Pull the wiper switch rearward and unplug the electrical connectors.
5. Continue the installation in the reverse order of the removal procedure.

GRAND AM

1. Disconnect the negative battery cable.
2. Remove the wiper switch trim plate.
3. Remove the wiper switch retaining screws. Pull the switch assembly rearward and unplug the electrical connectors.
4. Remove the wiper switch from the vehicle.
5. Continue the installation in the reverse order of the removal procedure.

SOMERSET AND SKYLARK

1. Disconnect the negative battery cable.
2. Remove the instrument panel trim cover.
3. Remove the wiper switch trim panel.
4. Remove the switch retaining screws.
5. Pull the switch assembly rearward and unplug the electrical connectors.
6. Continue the installation in the reverse order of the removal procedure.

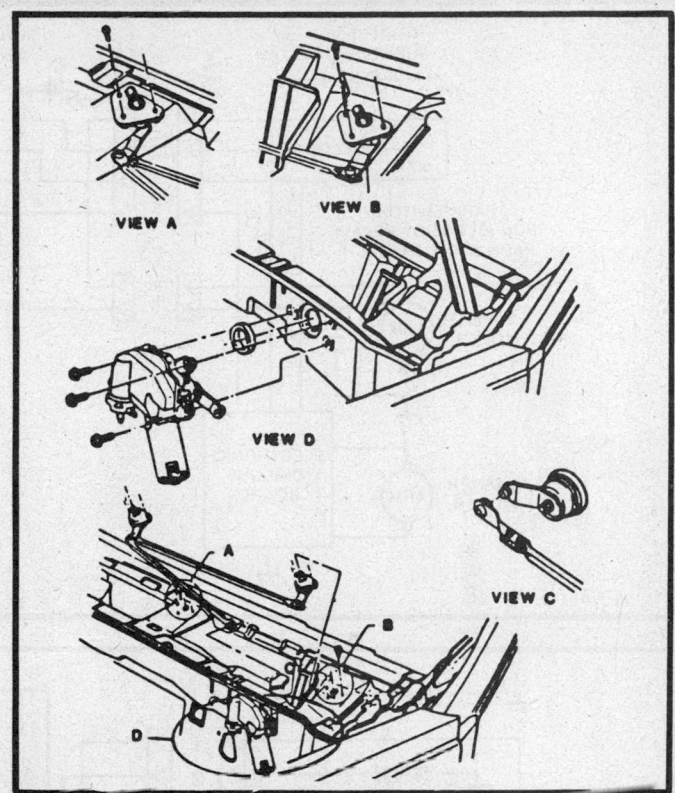

VIEW A VIEW B VIEW D VIEW C

A B D

Removing the windshield wiper motor

WINDSHIELD WIPER MOTOR

Removal and Installation

1. Disconnect the negative battery terminal from the battery.
2. Remove the wiper arm assemblies.
3. Loosen, but do not remove, the drive link-to-motor crank arm nuts.
4. Remove the air inlet screw panel and the drive link from the motor crank arm.
5. Disconnect the electrical connectors from the motor.
6. Remove the wiper motor retaining bolts and the wiper motor and linkage by guiding it through the access hole in the upper shroud panel.
7. Continue the installation in the reverse order of the removal procedure.

WINDSHIELD WIPER LINKAGE

Removal and Installation

1. Disconnect the negative battery cable.
2. Remove the wiper arms and blades. Remove the cowl screen or grille.
3. Raise the hood.
4. Working under the hood, disconnect the motor wiring. Reach through the cowl opening and loosen, but do not remove the transmission drive link-to-motor crank arm nuts. Disconnect the drive link from the crank arm.
5. Remove the motor-to-cowl screws and the motor, guiding the crank arm through the hole.

NOTE: Before assembling the crank arm to the transmission drive link, position the motor in the park position.

6. Continue the installation in the reverse order of the removal procedure.

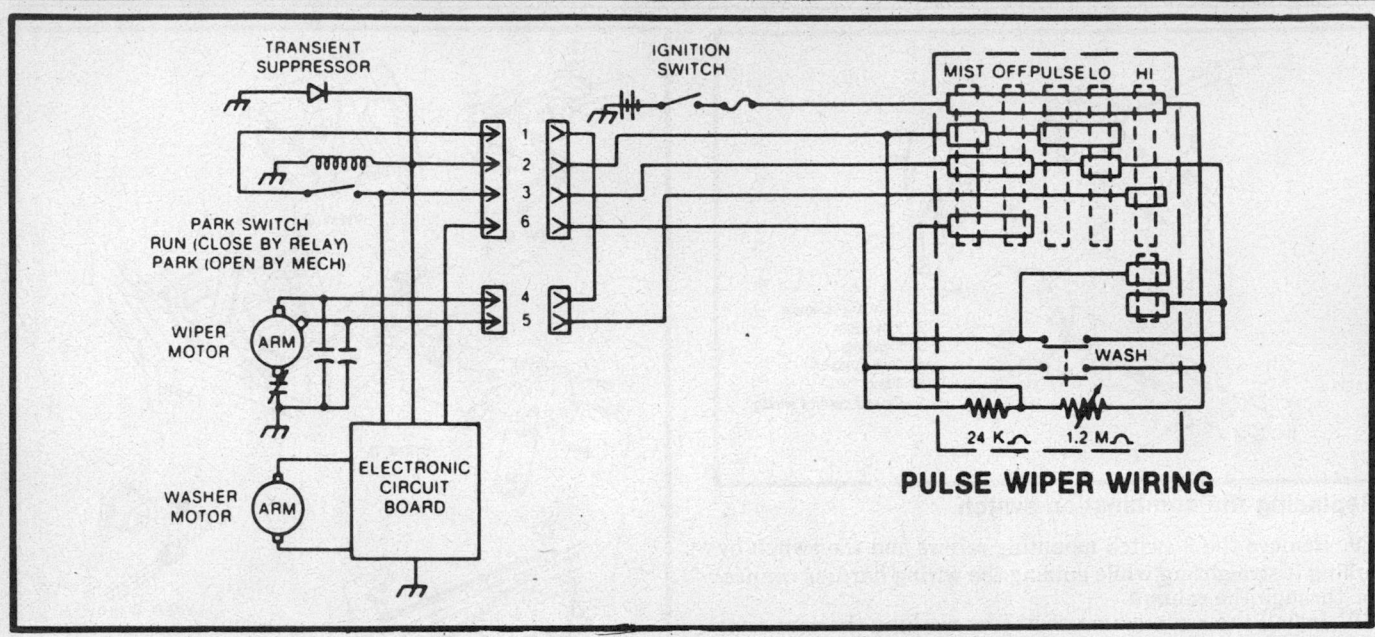

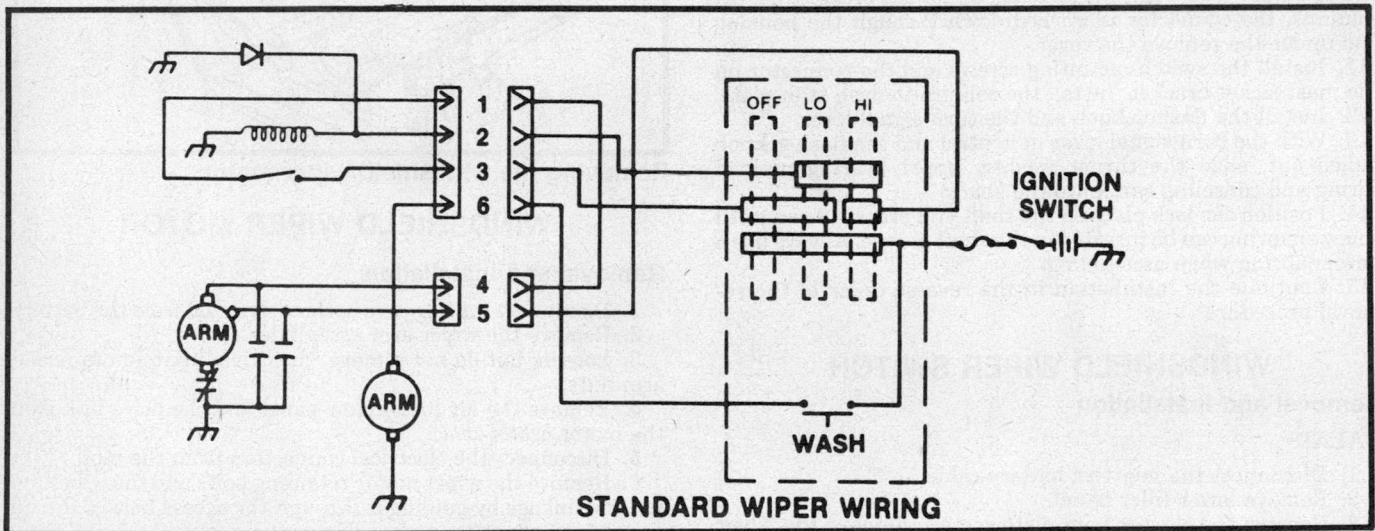

Wiper/washer circuit electrical schematic

Instrument Cluster

Refer to "Chilton's Electronic Instrumentation Service Manual" for additional coverage.

Removal and Installation

CALAIS

1. Disconnect the negative battery terminal from the battery.
2. Remove the steering column collar and the steering column opening filler screws.
3. Remove the cluster trim plate screws and the trim plate.
4. Remove the steering column support bolt and lower the steering column.
5. Remove the cluster-to-instrument panel pad screws and the cluster by pulling it rearward.
6. Continue the installation in the reverse order of the removal procedure.

GRAND AM, SOMERSET AND SKYLARK

1. Disconnect the negative battery terminal from the battery.

2. Remove the cluster lower trim plate.
3. Lower the steering column.
4. Remove the upper cluster trim plate.
5. Remove the cluster retaining screws and the cluster, by pulling it rearward.
6. Continue the installation in the reverse the removal procedure.

SPEEDOMETER

The speedometer is a speed indicator assembly which is incorporates both a season odometer and a trip odometer.

The odometers are driven by a stepper motor. The odometer discs are geared so that as any 1 disc finishes a complete revolution, the next disc to the left is turned $1/10$ of a revolution.

The speedometer is completely electric and therefore input to the speedometer is relayed by the vehicle speed sensor, located on the transaxle. The speedometer is serviced only as a part of the instrument cluster assembly.

Removal and Installation

VEHICLE SPEED SENSOR

1. Disconnect the negative battery cable.
2. Raise the vehicle and support it safely.
3. Remove the vehicle sensor electrical lead from the transaxle.
4. Remove the sensor retaining clip and remove the vehicle sensor and O-ring.
5. Complete the installation in the reverse order of the removal procedure.
6. Prior to installation, lubricate the new O-ring with transmission fluid.

Electrical Circuit Protectors

FUSIBLE LINKS

Fusible links are used to prevent major wire harness damage in the event of a short circuit or an overload condition in the wiring circuits which are normally not fused, due to carrying high amperage loads or because of their locations within the wiring harness. Each fusible link is of a fixed value for a specific electrical load and should a link fail, the cause of the failure must be determined and repaired prior to installing a new fusible link of the same value.

The N-Body vehicles have 5 fusible links. Four are at the starter and 1 is located behind the battery. They protect the starting and charging circuits, lighting, cooling fan and Electronic Control Module (ECM).

To replace a fusible link, cut off the burned link beyond the original splice. Replace the link with a new one of the same rating. If the splice has 2 wires, 2 repair links are required, 1 for each wire. Connect the new fusible link to the wire, crimp or solder securely.

NOTE: Use only replacements of the same electrical capacity as the original link. Replacements of a different electrical value will not provide adequate system protection and could lead to ECM damage.

CIRCUIT BREAKERS

The headlights are protected by a circuit breaker in the headlamp switch. If the circuit breaker trips, the headlights will either flash on and off or stay off altogether. The circuit breaker resets automatically after the overload is removed. There are also 2 circuit breakers in the fuse box, 1 for the power windows and the other for all power accessories.

The windshield wipers are also protected by a circuit breaker. If the motor overheats, the circuit breaker will trip, remaining off until the motor cools or the overload is removed.

FUSE PANEL

The fuse panel is located on the left-side of the vehicle. It is under the instrument panel assembly. In order to gain access to the fuse panel, it may be necessary to remove the under dash padding.

The amperage of each fuse and the circuit it protects are marked on the fusebox or the fusebox cover. In addition, the amperage of the fuse is marked on the plastic fuse body so that it faces out when installed. Replacing a fuse with one of a higher amperage rating is not recommended and could cause electrical damage. A suspected blown fuse can easily be pulled out and inspected; the clear plastic body gives full view of the element to blade construction for visual inspection.

NOTE: On some vehicles, whenever a battery cable is disconnected or 12 volt power is lost, the Delco-Loc® ra- dio will be inoperative when 12 volts is reapplied. LOC will appear on the graphic display. Turn ignition and radio ON, press the mute button on the steering wheel control to reactivate the radio.

CONVENIENCE CENTER

The convenience center, on some vehicles, is a swing down unit that is located on the underside of the instrument panel. This component provides a central location and easy access to buzzers, relays and flasher units.

ELECTRONIC CONTROL MODULE (ECM)

The electronic control module is located on the right side of the vehicle, underneath the dash pad. To gain access to this component, remove the right dash pad trim panel or glovebox assembly.

VARIOUS RELAYS

Various relays are attached to the convenience center, which provides a central location. All units are easily replaced with plug-in modules.

TURN SIGNAL FLASHER

The turn signal flasher is located behind the instrument panel, on the left hand side of the steering column. Replacement is accomplished by unplugging the old flasher and inserting a new one.

HAZARD WARNING FLASHER

The hazard flasher is located forward of the console. Replacement is accomplished by unplugging the old flasher and inserting a new one.

ELECTRICAL SPEED SENSOR

The optic head portion of the electrical speed sensor is located in the speedometer frame. A reflective blade spins with its blades passing through a light beam from a LED in the optic head. As each blade enters the reflective light beam, light is reflected back to a photocell in the optic head causing a low power speed signal to be sent to a buffer for amplification. This signal is then sent to the controller.

Speed Controls

Refer to "Chilton's Chassis Electronics Service Manual" for additional coverage.

Adjustment

1. Adjust the throttle lever to the idle position with the engine off.

NOTE: On models equipped with the idle control solenoid, the solenoid must be de-energized.

2. Pull the servo assembly end of the cable towards the servo blade.
3. Align the holes in the servo blade with the cable pin. Install the cable pin.

Troubleshooting

Before starting any troubleshooting procedures, a brief visual inspection should be made of the system components. The following components should be inspected:

1. Vacuum hoses—replace any that are kinked, rotted or deteriorated.

2. Servo chain or rod—make sure that the cable or linkage is not binding.

3. Throttle linkage/cable—make sure that the cable or linkage is not binding.

4. If cruise control in non-operable—inspect the radio fuse, replace as required.

COOLING AND HEATING SYSTEMS

Water Pump

Removal and Installation

2.0L ENGINE

1. Disconnect negative battery cable.
2. Drain cooling system.
3. Remove timing belt.
4. Remove water pump retaining bolts, water pump and seal ring.
5. Continue the installation in the order of the reverse removal procedure. Torque water pump bolts to 18 ft. lbs.

2.3L ENGINE

1. Disconnect the negative battery cable and oxygen sensor connector.
2. Drain coolant. Remove heater hose from thermostat housing for more complete coolant drain.
3. Remove upper and lower exhaust manifold heat shields.
4. Remove exhaust manifold brace to manifold bolt.
5. Break loose the manifold to exhaust pipe spring loaded bolts using a 13mm box wrench.
6. Raise and support vehicle.
7. Remove the manifold to exhaust pipe bolts out of the exhaust pipe flange by using a $^7/_{32}$ in. (5.5mm) socket and rotate clockwise, as if tightening a bolt with right hand threads or removing a bolt with left hand threads. It is necessary to relieve the spring pressure from 1 bolt prior to removing the second bolt. If the spring pressure is not relieved it will cause the exhaust pipe to twist and bind up the bolt as it is removed. Relieve the spring pressure as follows:
   a. Thread 1 bolt out 4 turns.
   b. Move to the other bolt and turn it all the way out of the exhaust pipe flange.
   c. Return to the first bolt and rotate it the rest of the way out of the exhaust pipe flange.
8. Pull down and back on the exhaust pipe to disengage it from the exhaust manifold bolts.

9. Remove radiator outlet pipe from oil pan and transaxle. Leave the lower radiator hose attached and pull down on the outlet pipe to remove it from the water pump.
10. Lower vehicle.
11. Remove exhaust manifold, seals and gaskets.
12. Remove water pump cover to block bolts and water pump assembly to timing chain housing nuts.

NOTE: On early production engines, it may be necessary to loosen and reposition the rear engine mount, mount-to-engine block bracket to gain clearance.

13. Remove water pump and cover assembly.
14. Continue the installation in the reverse order of the removal procedure. Start all bolts hand tight. Torque bolts/nuts to specifications in order.
   a. Pump assembly to chain housing nuts—19 ft. lbs.
   b. Pump cover to pump assembly—106 inch lbs.
   c. Cover to block—19 inch lbs.
   d. Radiator outlet pipe assembly to cover—125 inch lbs.
15. Refill cooling system, start engine and check for leaks.

2.5L, 3.0L AND 3.3L ENGINES
NOTE: Special pulley removal and installation tools are required to remove and install the water pump pulley on the 2.5L engine.

1. Disconnect the negative battery terminal from the battery.
2. Position a drain pan under the radiator, open the drain cock and drain the cooling system.
3. Remove the drive belts.
4. Remove the fan, pulley and radiator shroud, as required to gain working clearance and access to the water pump bolts.
5. Remove the radiator and heater hoses from the water pump.
6. Remove the water pump-to-engine bolts.
NOTE: On the 3.0L and 3.3L engines, the long bolt is removed through the access hole that is provided in the body side rail.

7. Remove the water pump from the vehicle.

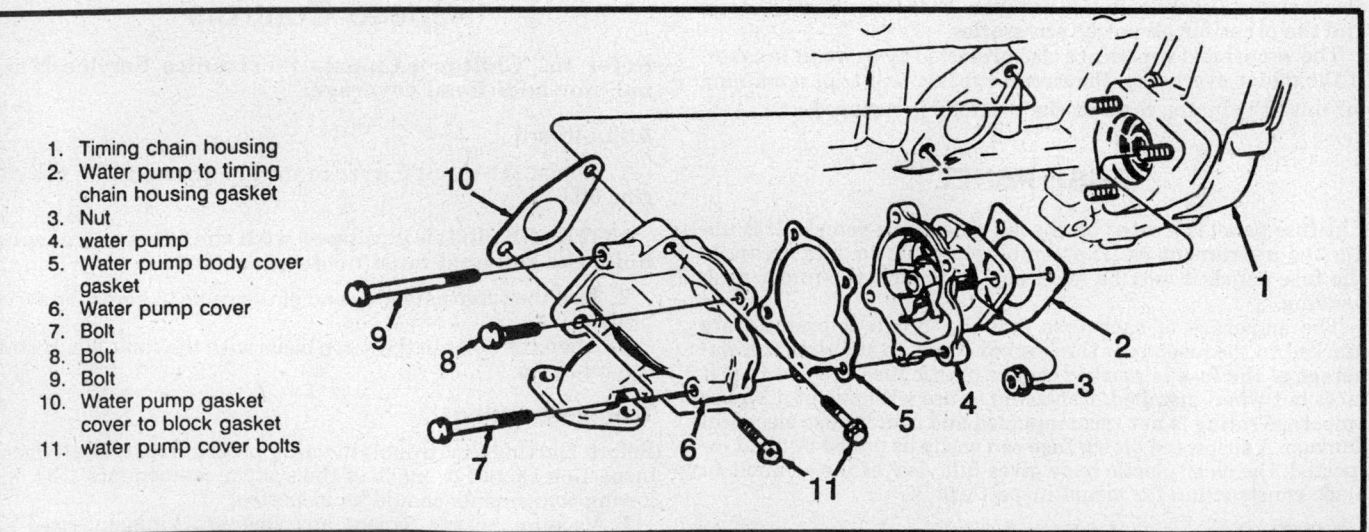

1. Timing chain housing
2. Water pump to timing chain housing gasket
3. Nut
4. water pump
5. Water pump body cover gasket
6. Water pump cover
7. Bolt
8. Bolt
9. Bolt
10. Water pump gasket cover to block gasket
11. water pump cover bolts

Water pump installation—2.3L Quad 4

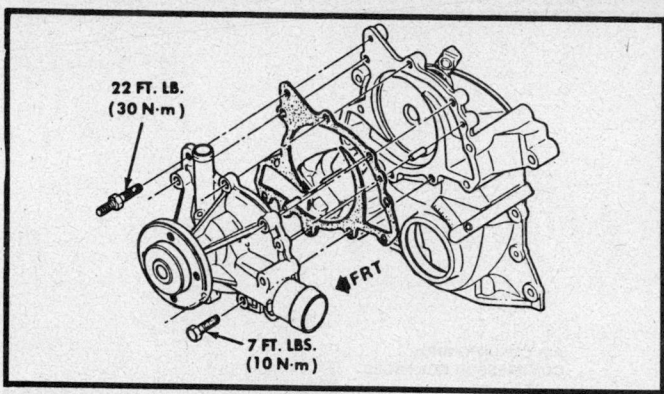

Exploded view of the water pump assembly—3.0L and 3.3L engines

NOTE: On the 2.5L engine, remove the water pump pulley and transfer it to the replacement assembly; using a pulley removal tool and a pulley installation tool.

8. Using a gasket scraper, clean the gasket mounting surfaces.

9. Continue the installation in the reverse of removal procedure.

10. Clean all gasket mating surfaces and place a ⅛ in. bead of RTV sealant on all sealing surfaces.

11. Water pump mounting bolts must also be coated with RTV sealer to avoid coolant leaks.

12. Torque the water pump mounting bolts as follows:
2.5L engine—25 ft. lbs.
3.0L engine—97 inch lbs.
3.3L engine—84 inch lbs.

13. Refill the cooling system.

14. Start the engine, allow it to reach normal operating temperature and check for leaks.

Electric Cooling Fan

Testing

NOTE: If the fan does not run while connected to the electrical wiring connector, inspect for a defective coolant temperature switch or air conditioning relay, if equipped. Always check body wiring for frayed or loose connections.

1. Disconnect the electrical wiring connector from the electric cooling fan.

2. Using a 14 gauge jumper wire, connect it between the fan and the positive battery terminal; the fan should run.

3. If the fan does not run when connected to the jumper wire, replace the fan assembly.

Removal and Installation

1. Disconnect the negative battery cable.

2. Disconnect electrical harness from fan motor and fan frame.

3. Remove fan frame to radiator support attaching bolts.

4. Remove fan and frame as an assembly.

5. Remove cooling fan from frame.

6. Continue the installation in the reverse order of the removal procedures.

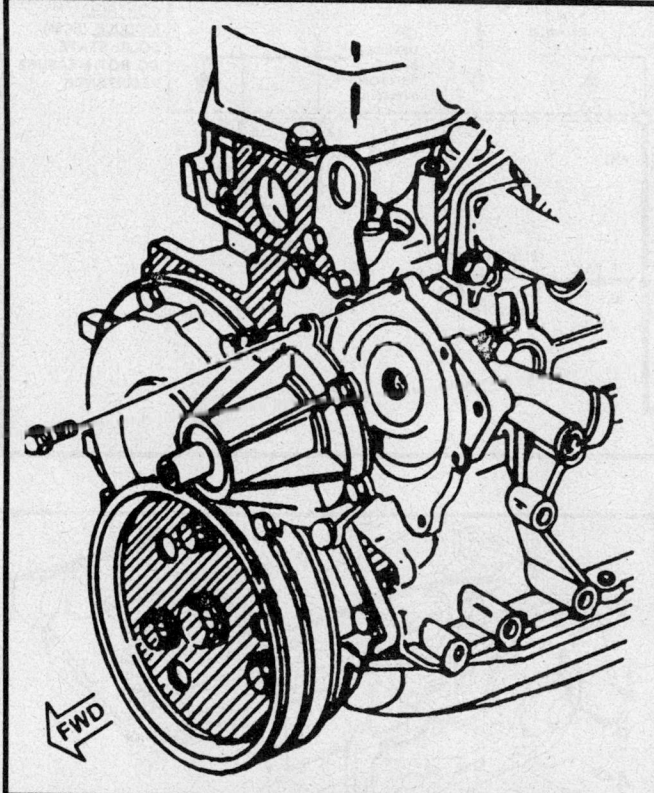

View of the water pump mounting—2.5L engine

RADIATOR FAN SWITCH

On the 3.0L and 3.3L engines, the radiator fan switch is located on the top right hand end of the engine. On the 4 cylinder engine, the radiator fan switch is located on the upper left hand front of the engine.

Testing

1. Disconnect the electrical connector from the radiator fan switch.

2. Using an ohmmeter, set on the 1 ohm scale, connect the 1 probe to the radiator fan switch connector and the other to ground.

3. Operate the engine until normal operating temperature are reached.

4. Between the temperature of 230–238°F, the radiator fan switch should turn ON grounding itself; the ohmmeter should read 0.

5. If the radiator fan switch does not respond, replace it.

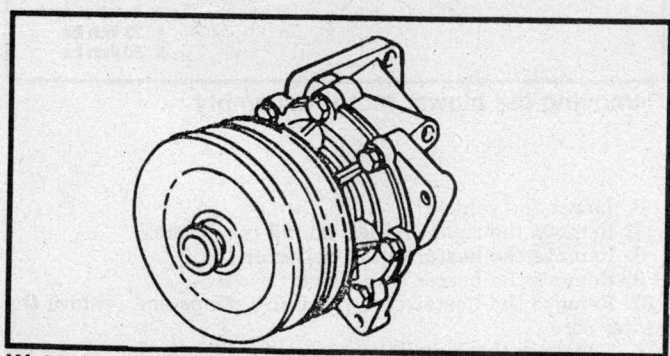

Water pump and pulley assembly—2.5L engine

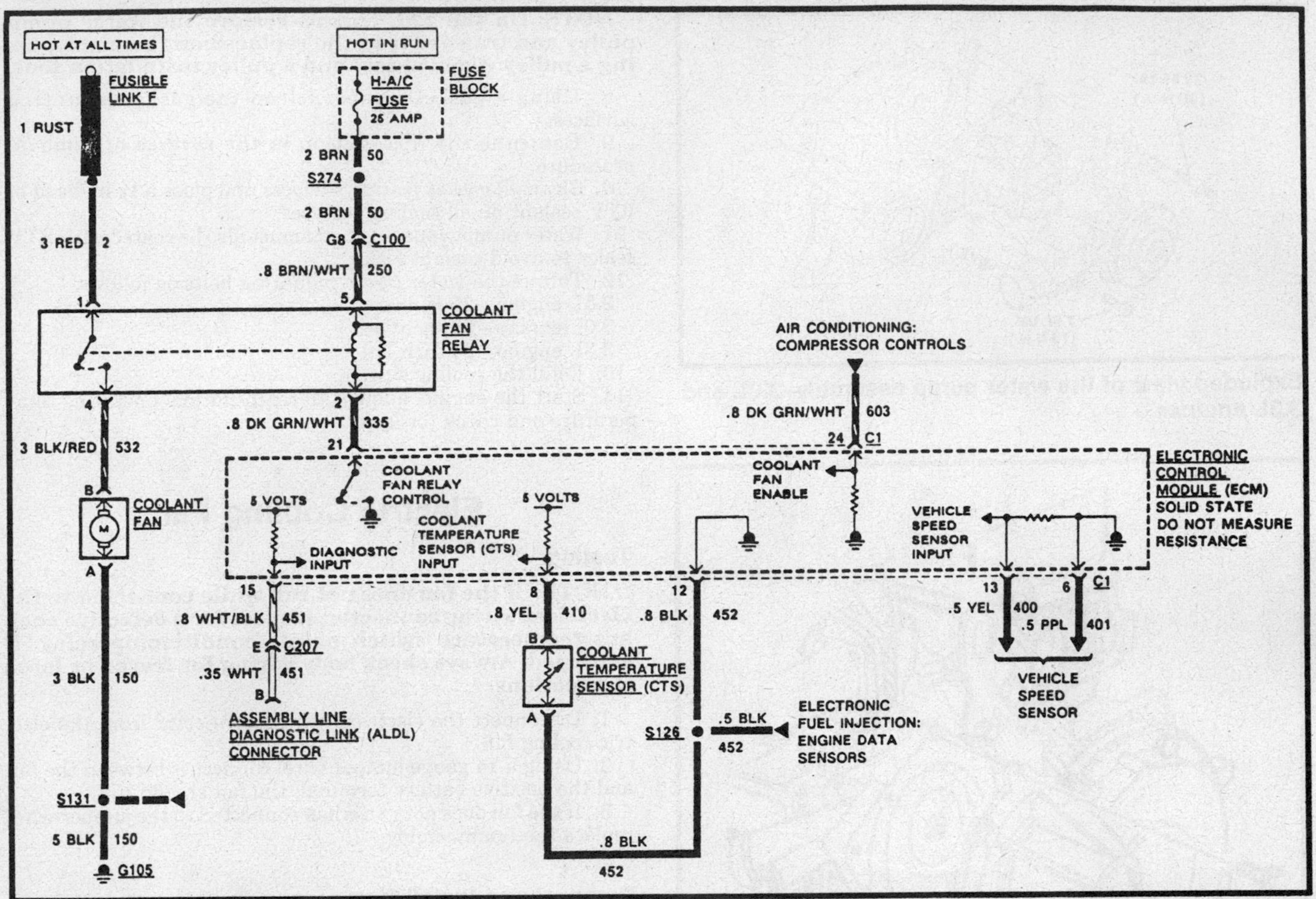

Cooling fan schematic—2.5L

Blower Motor

Removal and Installation

1. Disconnect negative battery terminal from the battery.
2. If equipped with a 3.0L or 3.3L engine, remove the serpentine drive belt and the 2 power steering pump-to-bracket bolts, move the pump aside.
3. Remove the blower motor screws.
4. Disconnect wiring connector.
5. Slide blower motor assembly forward enough to remove nut retaining fan.
6. Slide fan out of housing.
7. Remove the blower motor.
8. If necessary, remove the fan from the blower motor.
9. Continue the installation in the reverse order of the removal procedure.

Heater Core

Refer to "Chilton's Auto Heating and Air Conditioning Manual" for additional coverage.

Removal and Installation

1. Disconnect negative battery terminal from the battery.
2. Place a clean drain pan under the radiator, open the drain cock and drain cooling system.
3. Remove the console extensions and the console ducts.
4. Raise and support the the vehicle safely.
5. Disconnect the hoses from the heater case and drain.

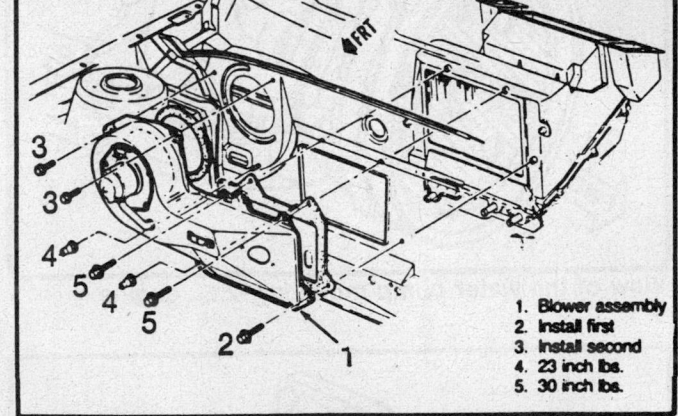

Removing the blower motor assembly

6. Lower the vehicle.
7. Remove the right and left sound insulators.
8. Remove the heater outlet deflector.
9. Remove the heater core cover.
10. Remove the heater core retaining straps and remove the heater core.
11. Continue the installation in the reverse order of the removal procedure. Refill the cooling system.

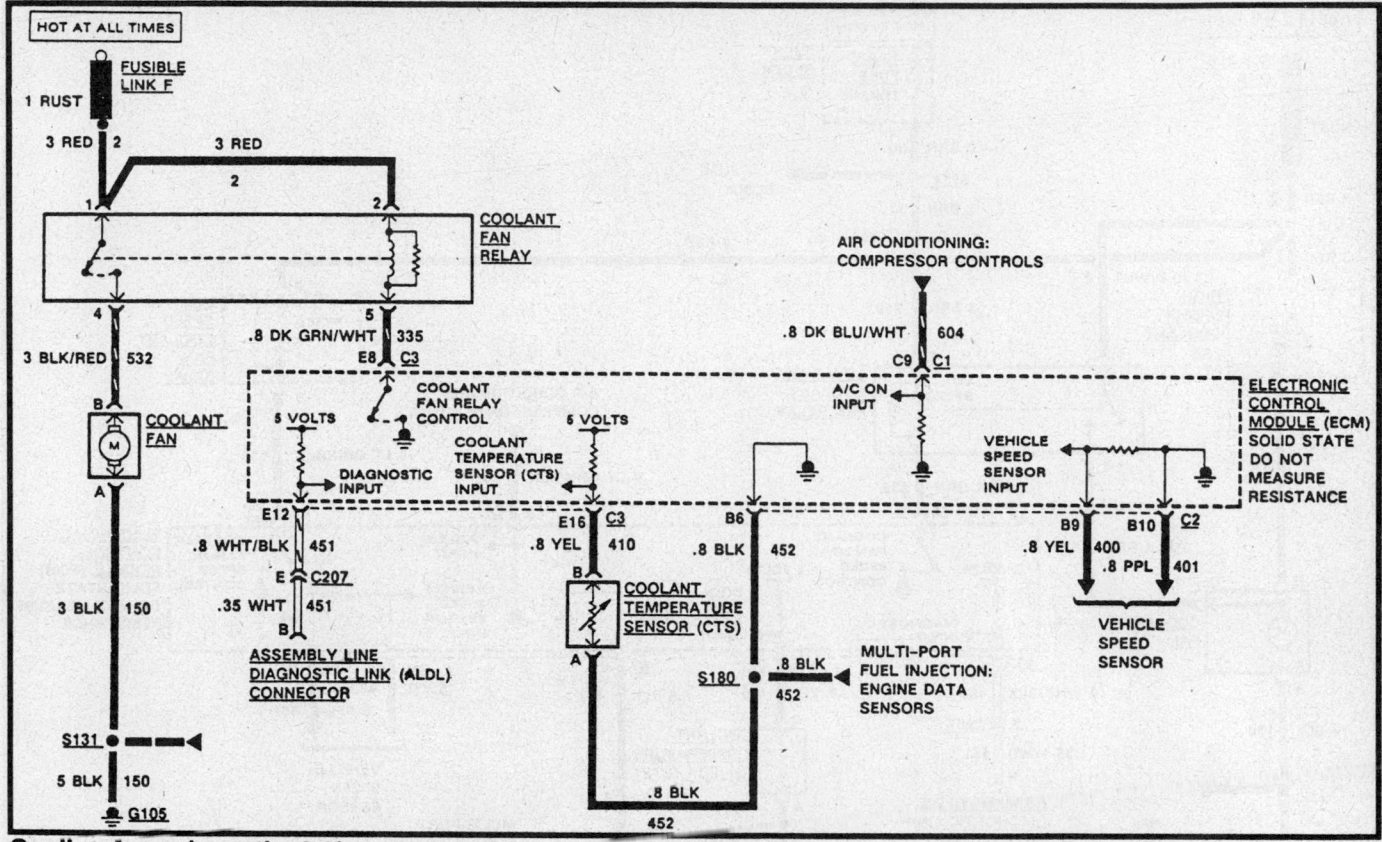

Cooling fan schematic–2.0L

Temperature Control/Blower Switch

Removal and Installation

CALAIS

1. Disconnect the negative battery terminal from the battery.
2. Remove the lower steering column trim and collar. Remove the center trim and the instrument panel compartment insert.
3. Remove the right instrument panel trim and the lower instrument panel trim.
4. Remove the control assembly retaining screws and pull the assembly forward.
5. Disconnect the temperature cable at the control head. Disconnect all vacuum and electrical connections from the control assembly. Remove the control head from the vehicle.
6. Continue the installation in the reverse order of the removal procedure.

GRAND AM

1. Disconnect the negative battery terminal.
2. Remove the radio trim plate and the right hush panel.
3. Remove the console extension.
4. Remove the control assembly retaining screws. Pull the control assembly out far enough to disconnect all electrical, vacuum and cable connections.
5. Remove the control assembly from the vehicle.
6. Continue the installation in the reverse order of the removal procedure.

SOMERSET AND SKYLARK

1. Disconnect the negative battery terminal.
2. Remove the temperature control trim plate.
3. Remove the temperature control retaining screws and pull the control assembly forward.
4. Disconnect the control cable, all electrical and vacuum connections from the control assembly.
5. Remove the control assembly from the vehicle.
6. Continue the installation in the reverse order of the removal procedure.

FUEL INJECTION SYSTEM

Refer to "Chilton's Electronic Engine Controls Manual" for additional coverage.

Description And Type

THROTTLE BODY INJECTION (TBI)

With throttle body injection TBI, model 300 1986 or 700 1987– 90, an injection unit is placed on the intake manifold where the carburetor is normally mounted. The TBI unit is computer controlled and supplies the correct amount of fuel during all engine operating conditions. In the TBI system, a single fuel injector mounted at the top of the throttle body, sprays fuel through the throttle valve and into the intake manifold. The activating signal for the injector originates with the electronic control module

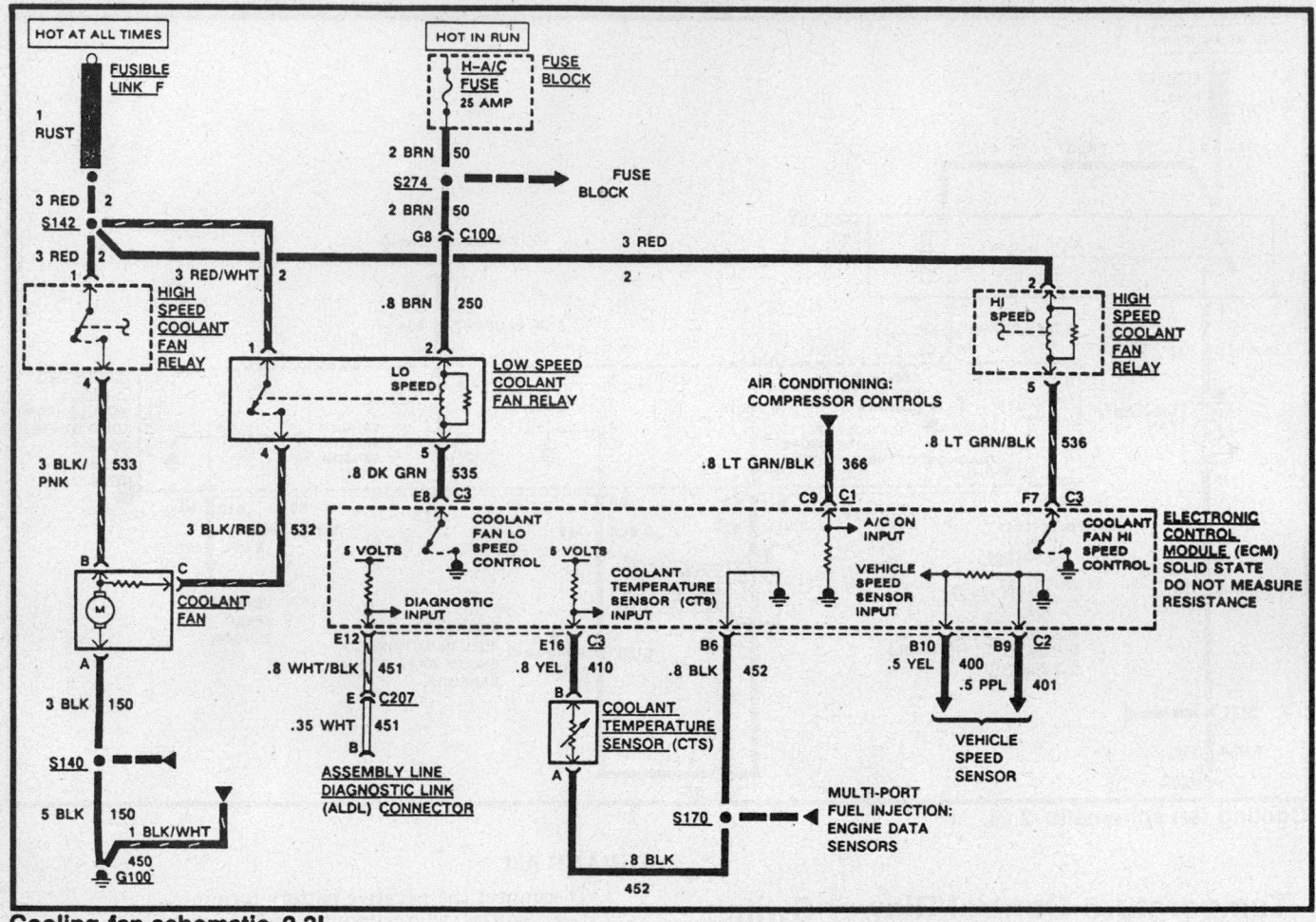

Cooling fan schematic—2.3L

ECM, which monitors engine temperature, throttle position, vehicle speed and several other engine related conditions. A fuel pressure regulator inside the throttle body maintains fuel pressure at 9–13 psi and routes unused fuel back to the fuel tank through a fuel return line.

MULTI-PORT FUEL INJECTION (MFI)

This system uses Bosch fuel injectors, one at each intake port. The injectors are mounted on a fuel rail and are activated by a signal from the electronic control module ECM. The injector is a solenoid operated valve which remains Open depending on the width of the electronic pulses (length of the signal) from the ECM; the longer the open time, the more fuel is injected. In this manner, the air/fuel mixture can be precisely controlled for maximum performance with minimum emissions. A pressure regulator maintains 28–36 psi in the fuel line to the injectors and the excess fuel is fed back to the tank.

IDLE SPEED

Adjustment

The idle speed and mixture are electronically controlled by the Electronic Control Module (ECM). All adjustments are preset at the factory. The only time the idle speed should need adjustment is when the throttle body assembly has been replaced. The throttle stop screw, used in regulating the minimum idle speed, is adjusted at the factory and is not necessary to perform. This adjustment should be performed only when the throttle body has been replaced

2.5L ENGINE WITH 300 TBI

NOTE: The following procedures require the use a tachometer, GM tool J–33047, BT–8207 or equivalent, Torx® bit No. 20, silicone sealant, a 5/32 in. drill bit, a prick punch and a 1/16 in. pin punch.

1. Remove the air cleaner and the gasket. Be sure to plug the thermac vacuum port air cleaner vacuum line-to-throttle body on the throttle body.
2. Remove the throttle valve cable from the throttle control bracket to provide access to the minimum air adjustment screw.
3. Using the manufacturer's instructions, connect a tachometer to the engine.
4. Remove the electrical connector from the idle air control IAC valve, located on the throttle body.
5. If necessary to remove the throttle stop screw cover, perform the following procedures:
   a. Using a prick punch, mark the housing at the top over the center line of the throttle stop screw.
   b. Using a 5/32 in. drill bit, drill a hole on an angle, through the casting to the hardened cover.
   c. Using a 1/16 in. pin punch, place it through the hole and drive out the cover to expose the throttle stop screw.
6. Place the transmission in **P** for automatic transaxles or **N** for manual transaxles, start the engine and allow the idle speed to stabilize.
7. Using the GM tool No. J–33047, BT–8207 or equivalent, install it into the idle air passage of the throttle body; be sure that the tool is fully seated in the opening and no air leaks exist.
8. Using a Torx® bit No. 20, turn the throttle stop screw until

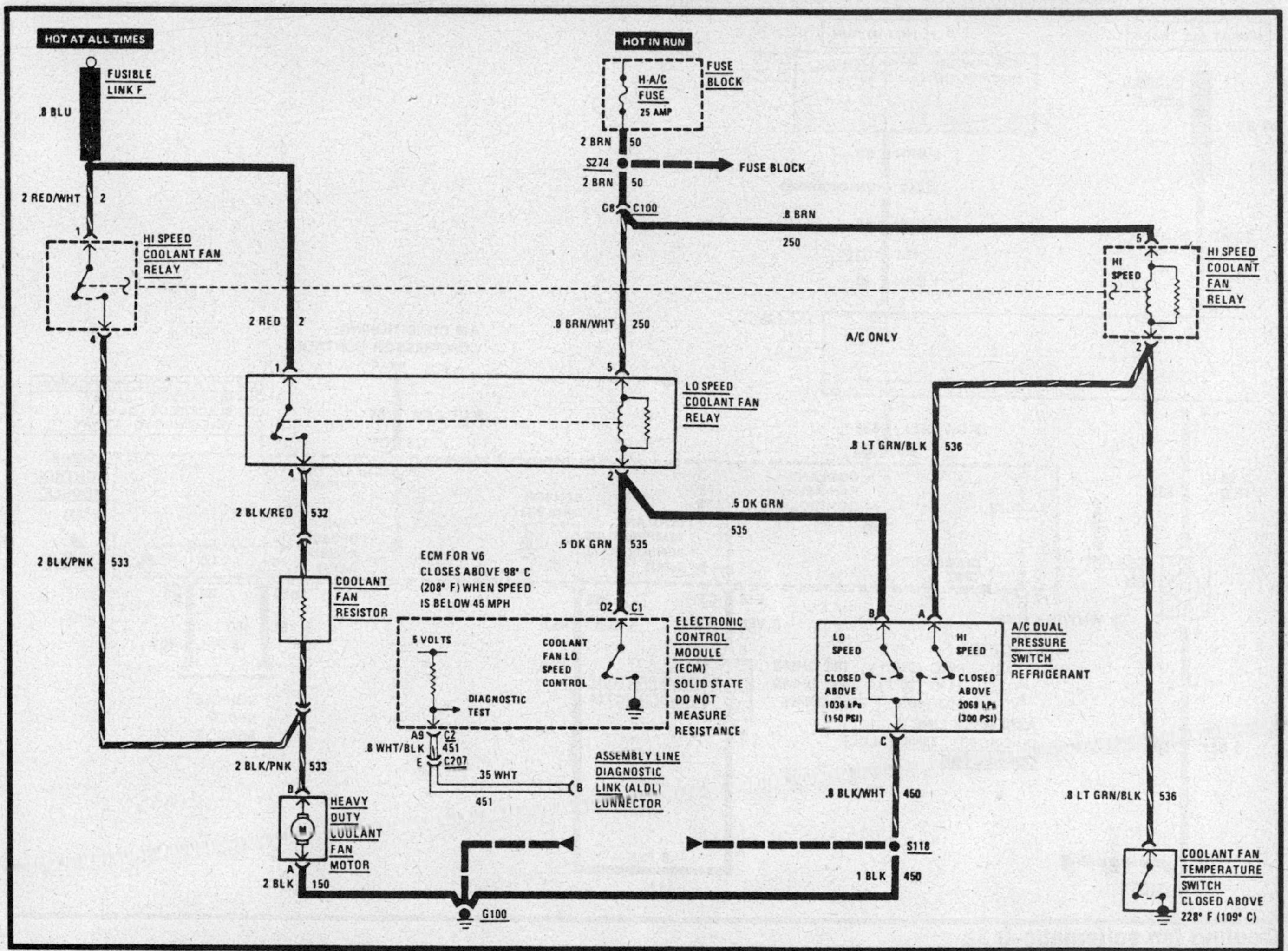

HOT AT ALL TIMES

FUSIBLE LINK F

.8 BLU

2 RED/WHT 2

HI SPEED COOLANT FAN RELAY

2 RED 2

2 BLK/PNK 533

2 BLK/RED 532

COOLANT FAN RESISTOR

ECM FOR V6 CLOSES ABOVE 98° C (208° F) WHEN SPEED IS BELOW 45 MPH

5 VOLTS

COOLANT FAN LO SPEED CONTROL

DIAGNOSTIC TEST

ELECTRONIC CONTROL MODULE (ECM) SOLID STATE DO NOT MEASURE RESISTANCE

A9 C2 451

C207

E

.8 WHT/BLK

.35 WHT

451

ASSEMBLY LINE DIAGNOSTIC LINK (ALDL) CONNECTOR

2 BLK/PNK 533

B

HEAVY DUTY COOLANT FAN MOTOR

M

A

2 BLK 150

G100

HOT IN RUN

FUSE BLOCK

H-A/C FUSE 25 AMP

2 BRN 50

S274

2 BRN 50

G8 C100

.8 BRN 250

.8 BRN/WHT 250

5

LO SPEED COOLANT FAN RELAY

5 DK GRN 535

.5 DK GRN 535

D2 C1

A/C ONLY

HI SPEED COOLANT FAN RELAY

5

2

.8 LT GRN/BLK 536

.5 DK GRN 535

B A

LO SPEED HI SPEED

CLOSED ABOVE 1036 kPa (150 PSI)

CLOSED ABOVE 2068 kPa (300 PSI)

A/C DUAL PRESSURE SWITCH REFRIGERANT

C

.8 BLK/WHT 450

S118

1 BLK 450

.8 LT GRN/BLK 536

COOLANT FAN TEMPERATURE SWITCH CLOSED ABOVE 228° F (109° C)

Cooling fan schematic—3.0L

the engine speed is 475–525 rpm for automatic transaxles in **P** or **N**) or 750–800 rpm for manual transaxles in **N**).

9. With the idle speed adjusted, stop the engine, remove the tool No. J–33047, BT–8207 or equivalent, from the throttle body.

10. Reconnect the idle air control (IAC) electrical connector.

11. Using silicone sealant, cover the throttle stop screw.

12. Reinstall the gasket and the air cleaner assembly.

2.5L ENGINE WITH 700 TBI

NOTE: The following procedures require the use a tachometer, GM Torx® Bit No. 20, silicone sealant, a 5/32 in. drill bit, a prick punch and a 1/16 in. pin punch.

The throttle stop screw, used in regulating the minimum idle speed, is adjusted at the factory and is not necessary to perform. This adjustment should be performed only when the throttle body has been replaced.

1. Remove the air cleaner and gasket.

2. Using a awl, pierce the idle stop screw plug and apply leverage to remove it.

3. Connect a tachometer to the engine.

4. With the idle air control valve (IAC) connected, ground the **A** terminal of the Assembly Line Communications Link (ALCL) connector.

5. Turn the ignition switch **ON** do not start the engine and wait 45 seconds.

NOTE: When the ignition is turned ON, the IAC valve will extend and seat itself in the throttle body.

6. Disconnect the electrical harness connector from the IAC valve.

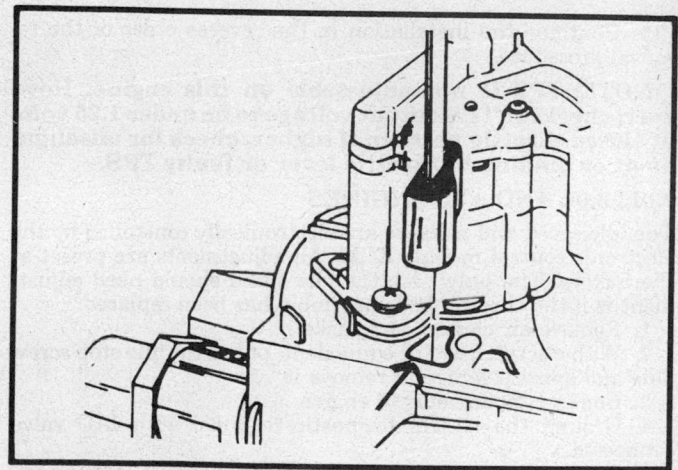

Installing tool No. J-33047 into the idle air passage— model 300 TBI

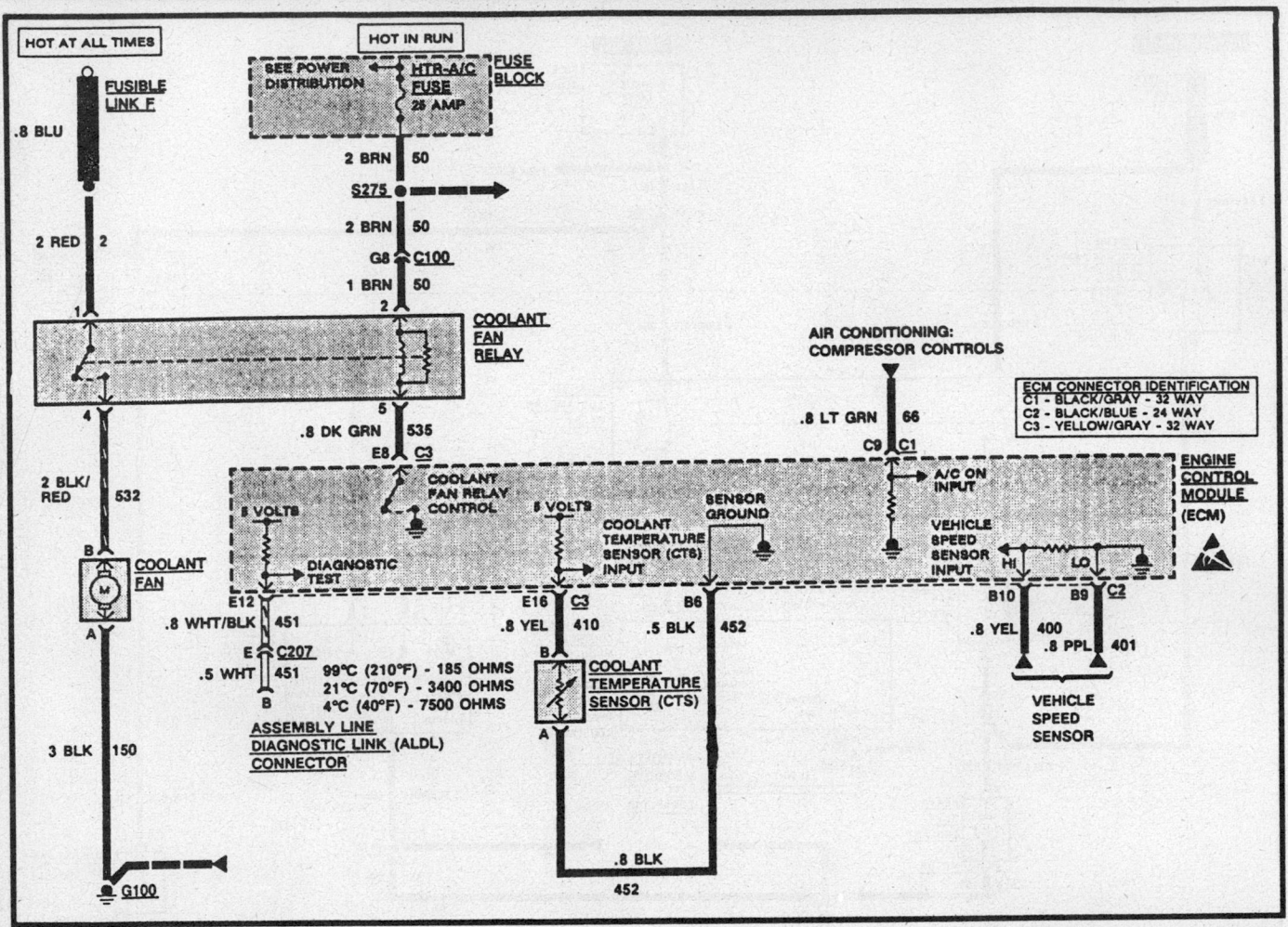

Cooling fan schematic—3.3L

7. Remove the ground from the diagnostic terminal and start the engine. Place the transaxle in **NEUTRAL** and allow the engine to stabilize.

8. Adjust the idle stop screw to obtain 575–625 rpm.

9. When the adjustment is complete, turn the ignition switch **OFF** and reconnect the IAC electrical connector.

10. Using silicone sealant, cover the minimum air adjustment screw.

11. Continue the installation in the reverse order of the removal procedure.

NOTE: TPS is non-adjustable on this engine. However, check for TPS output voltage to be under 1.25 volts at closed throttle postion. If higher, check for misalignment or binding in throttle lever or faulty TPS.

2.0L, 3.0L AND 3.3L ENGINES

The idle speed and mixture are electronically controlled by the electronic control module ECM. All adjustments are preset at the factory. The only time the idle speed should need adjustment is if the throttle body assembly has been replaced.

1. Remove air cleaner and gasket.

2. With a scratch awl or equivalent, pierce the idle stop screw plug and apply leverage to remove it.

3. Connect tachometer to engine.

4. Ground the ALDL diagnostic terminal with IAC valve connected.

5. Turn ignition switch to **ON** position, without starting engine for at least 45 seconds. This allows IAC valve pintle to extend and seat in throttle body.

6. Disconnect the idle air control (IAC) electrical connector.

7. Remove ground wire from diagnostic terminal. Firmly set the parking brake.

8. Start the engine and place the transaxle in **N**. Allow engine rpm to stabilize. Using the minimum idle stop set screw and adjust to 550–650 rpm on the 2.0L engine and 450–550 rpm on the 3.0L engine.

NOTE: On 2.0L engine the TPS is non-adjustable. However, check for TPS output voltage to be under 1.25 volts at closed throttle position. If higher, check for misalignment or binding in throttle lever or faulty TPS. On 3.0L engine and 3.3L engines place transaxle in D and block drive wheels. After adjusting minimum idle speed check and adjust TPS to 0.50–0.60 volts.

9. Turn ignition switch **OFF** and reconnect connector at IAC valve.

10. Use silicone sealant to cover minimum air adjustment screw.

11. Install air cleaner and gasket.

12. Check and clear any trouble codes. Start engine and inspect for proper idle operation.

2.3L ENGINE

The throttle plate stop screw or minimum air rate adjustment should not be considered the minimum idle speed, as on other fuel injected engines. Low internal friction resulted in a calibrated minimum air rate which is too low to allow most engines to idle. The adjustment is preset at the factory and no further adjustment should be necessary.

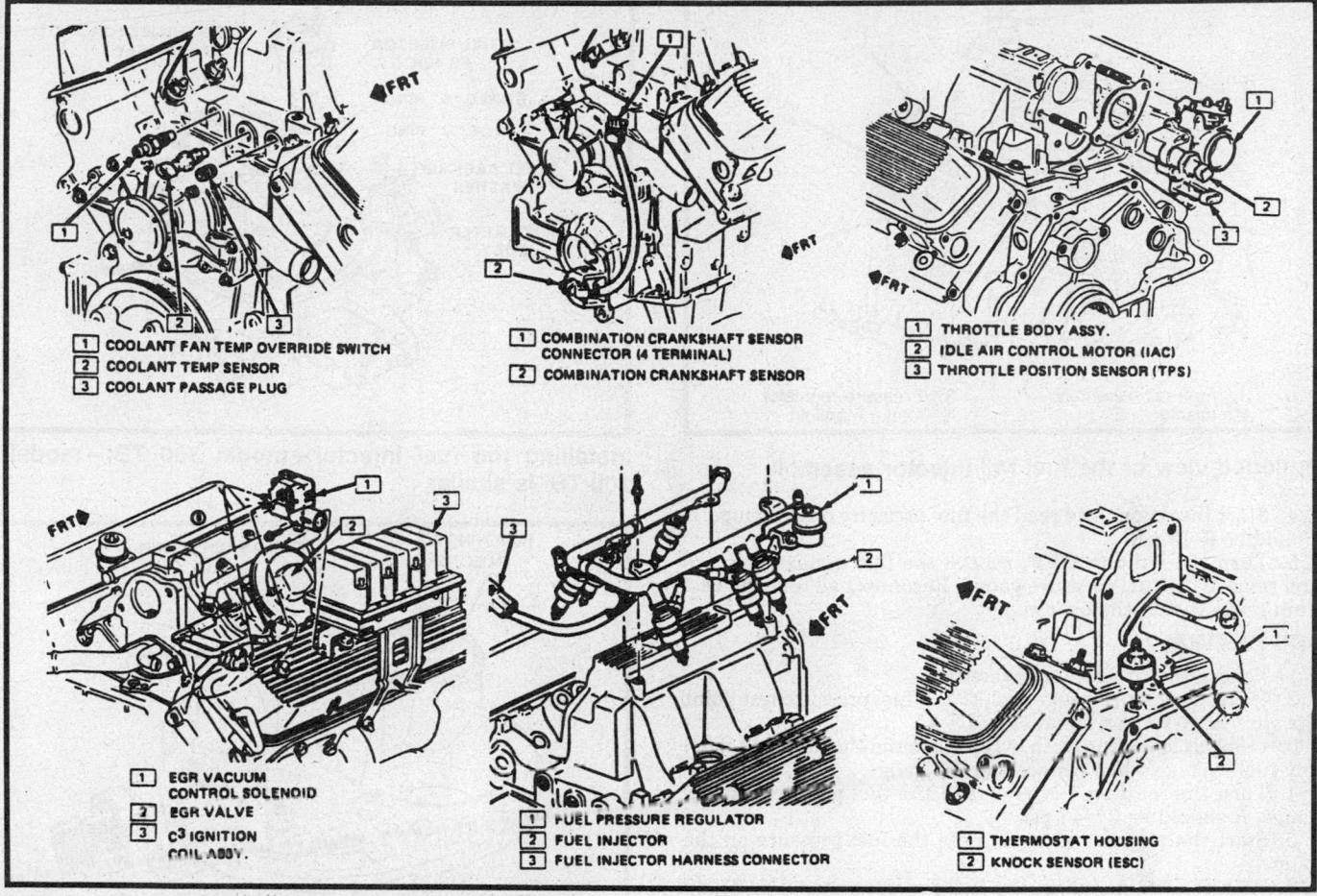

1. COOLANT FAN TEMP OVERRIDE SWITCH
2. COOLANT TEMP SENSOR
3. COOLANT PASSAGE PLUG

1. COMBINATION CRANKSHAFT SENSOR CONNECTOR (4 TERMINAL)
2. COMBINATION CRANKSHAFT SENSOR

1. THROTTLE BODY ASSY.
2. IDLE AIR CONTROL MOTOR (IAC)
3. THROTTLE POSITION SENSOR (TPS)

1. EGR VACUUM CONTROL SOLENOID
2. EGR VALVE
3. C³ IGNITION COIL ASSY.

1. FUEL PRESSURE REGULATOR
2. FUEL INJECTOR
3. FUEL INJECTOR HARNESS CONNECTOR

1. THERMOSTAT HOUSING
2. KNOCK SENSOR (ESC)

Multi-port fuel injection components—3.0L engine

FUEL SYSTEM PRESSURE RELIEF

Procedure

2.3L AND 2.5L ENGINES

1. From the fuse block in the passenger compartment, remove the fuse marked fuel pump or disconnect the harness connector at the tank.
2. Start the engine and allow it to idle until it stalls.
3. Crank the engine for an additional 3 seconds to make sure all of the fuel pressure is exhausted from the fuel lines.
4. Turn the ignition switch **OFF** and reinstall the fuel pump fuse.

2.0L, 3.0L AND 3.3L ENGINES

1. Using a fuel pressure gauge tool connect it to the fuel pressure valve.

NOTE: Wrap a clean shop towel around the fitting while making connections to catch any fuel spray.

2. Install a bleed hose onto the gauge assembly and place the end in a suitable container.
3. Open the pressure gauge valve and bleed the fuel pressure from the system.
4. Close the pressure gauge bleed screw.

Fuel Pump

The fuel pump is located in the fuel tank. The fuel tank must be removed to replace the pump.

--- CAUTION ---
Do not drain or store fuel in an open container. Serious explosion and fire hazard exists. Empty the contents of the fuel tank into an approved gasoline storage container and take precautions to avoid the risk of fire.

Removal and Installation

1. Relieve the fuel system pressure.
2. Disconnect the negative battery terminal from the battery.
3. Raise and support the vehicle safely. Drain the fuel tank.
4. Remove the fuel tank by supporting it and disconnecting the 2 retaining straps. Lower the tank enough to disconnect the sending unit wires, hoses and ground strap if equipped.
5. Lower the fuel tank from the vehicle and remove the sending unit.

NOTE: The sending unit is retained by a cam lock ring. The fuel pump is attached to the tank sending unit.

6. Continue the installation in the reverse order of the removal procedure. Use new O-rings and anti-squeak pieces on top of the tank. Tighten the retaining straps.

Pressure Testing

TBI SYSTEM

1. Relieve the fuel system pressure.
2. Remove the air cleaner and plug the thermac vacuum port on the throttle body.
3. Connect a pressure gauge tool, install it on the throttle body side of the fuel filter at the rear of the vehicle near the fuel tank.

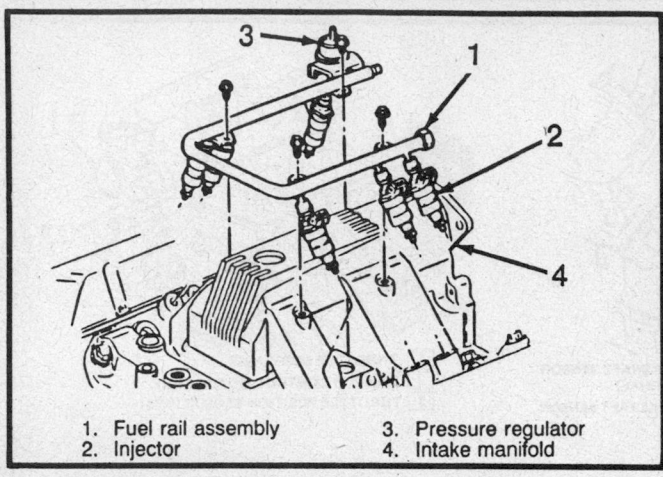

1. Fuel rail assembly
2. Injector
3. Pressure regulator
4. Intake manifold

Exploded view of the fuel rail/injector assembly

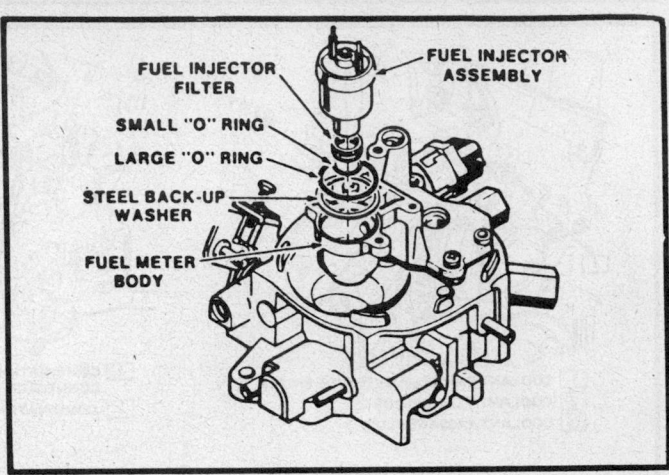

Installing the fuel injector—model 300 TBI—model 700 TBI is similar

4. Start the engine and read the fuel pressure on the gauge, it should be 9–13 psi.

5. Turn the ignition **OFF**, relieve the fuel system pressure and remove the fuel pressure gauge. Reconnect all fuel and vacuum lines. Install the air cleaner.

MFI SYSTEM

1. Relieve the fuel system pressure.
2. Using a pressure gauge tool, to the fuel pressure test point the shrader fitting on the fuel rail.
3. Using a clean shop cloth, wrap it around the fitting to catch any fuel leakage when connecting the gauge.
4. Turn the ignition **ON** and read the fuel pressure on the gauge, it should be 37–43 psi.
5. Start the engine and again note the fuel pressure on the gauge.
6. With the engine idling, the fuel pressure should be 33–40 psi. This idle pressure will vary somewhat depending on barometric pressure, but in any case it should be lower.
7. Relieve the fuel system pressure and disconnect the gauge.

Fuel Filter

Removal and Installation

An inline fuel filter is used on all engines. It is located on a frame crossmember near the rear of the vehicle.
1. Relieve the fuel system pressure.
2. Raise and support the the vehicle safely.
3. Using a backup wrench, remove the fuel line fittings from the fuel filter.
4. Remove the fuel filter-to-crossmember screws and the filter from the vehicle.
5. Continue the installation in the reverse order of the removal procedure. Use a new fuel filter and O-rings. Torque the fuel line-to-filter connectors to 22 ft. lbs.

FUEL INJECTOR

NOTE: When removing the injectors, be careful not to damage the electrical connector pins, on top of the injector, the injector fuel filter and the nozzle. The fuel injector is serviced as a complete assembly only. It is an electrical component and should not be immersed in any kind of cleaner.

Removal and Installation
EXCEPT 2.5L ENGINE

1. Relieve the fuel system pressure.

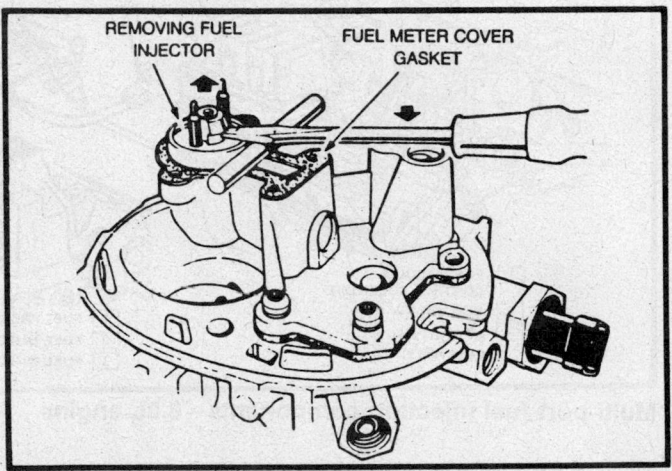

Removing the fuel injector—model 300 TBI—model 700 TBI is similar

2. Disconnect the negative battery terminal from the battery.
3. Disconnect the fuel line from the fuel rail.
4. Remove the fuel rail-to-intake manifold bolts and the fuel rail assembly from the intake manifold.

NOTE: When removing the fuel rail, the fuel injectors will pull straight out of the intake manifold.

5. Remove the fuel injector-to-fuel rail retaining clips and the injectors from the fuel rail.
6. Continue the installation in the reverse order of the removal procedure. Use new O-rings on the fuel injectors.

2.5L ENGINE—MODEL 300 TBI

1. Relieve the fuel system pressure.
2. Remove the air cleaner. Disconnect the negative battery terminal from the battery.
3. At the injector connector, squeeze the 2 tabs together and pull it straight up.
4. Remove the fuel meter cover and leave the cover gasket in place.
5. Using a small pry bar, carefully lift the injector until it is free from the fuel meter body.
6. Remove the small O-ring from the nozzle end of the injector. Carefully rotate the injector's fuel filter back and forth to remove it from the base of the injector.
7. Discard the fuel meter cover gasket.

8. Remove the large O-ring and backup washer from the top of the counterbore of the fuel meter body injector cavity.

9. Prior to installation, lubricate the O-rings with automatic transmission fluid, then firmly push into the fuel injector cavity. Continue the installation the in the reverse order of the removal procedure. Start the engine and check for fuel leaks.

2.5L ENGINE—MODEL 700 TBI

1. Relieve the fuel system pressure.
2. Remove the air cleaner. Disconnect the negative battery terminal from the battery.
3. Disconnect the electrical connector from the fuel injector.
4. Remove the injector retainer-to-throttle body screw and the retainer.

5. Using a small pry bar and a fulcrum, carefully lift the injector until it is free from the fuel meter body.
6. Remove the O-rings form the nozzle end of the injector.
7. Inspect the fuel injector filter for dirt and/or contamination.
8. Prior to installation, lubricate the O-rings with automatic transmission fluid and place them on the fuel injector.
9. Continue the installation in the reverse order of the removal procedure. Push the fuel injector straight into the fuel meter body, apply thread locking compound on the fuel injector retainer screw and install. Start the engine and check for fuel leaks.

TURBOCHARGER SYSTEM

Refer to "Chilton's Electronic Engine Controls Manual" for additional coverage.

Turbocharger Unit

Removal and Installation

1. Disconnect the negative battery cable.
2. Raise vehicle and support it safely.
3. Drain the engine coolant.
4. Remove the fan retaining screws.
5. Disconnect exhaust pipe.
6. Remove the air conditioning compressor rear support bracket.
7. Remove turbocharger support bracket to engine.
8. Disconnect and plug the oil drain pipe at turbocharger.
9. Disconnect water return pipe at turbocharger.
10. Lower vehicle and remove coolant recovery pipe.
11. Remove induction turbo, coolant fan, oxygen sensor.
12. Disconnect oil and water feed pipe.
13. Remove air intake duct and vacuum hose at actuator.
14. Remove the exhaust manifold retaining nuts and remove turbocharger and manifold as an assembly.
15. Remove turbocharger from exhaust manifold.
16. Continue the installation in the reverse order of the removal procedure. Torque the exhaust manifold bolts to 16 ft. lbs. and turbocharger to exhaust manifold to 18 ft. lbs.

TURBOCHARGER WASTEGATE UNIT

Removal and Installation

1. Disconnect the negative battery cable.
2. Remove air induction tube.
3. Disconnect actuator rod to wastegate clip.
4. Disconnect vacuum hose.
5. Remove retaining screws from actuator to turbo.
6. Remove actuator assembly.
7. Continue the installation in the reverse removal order of the removal procedure.

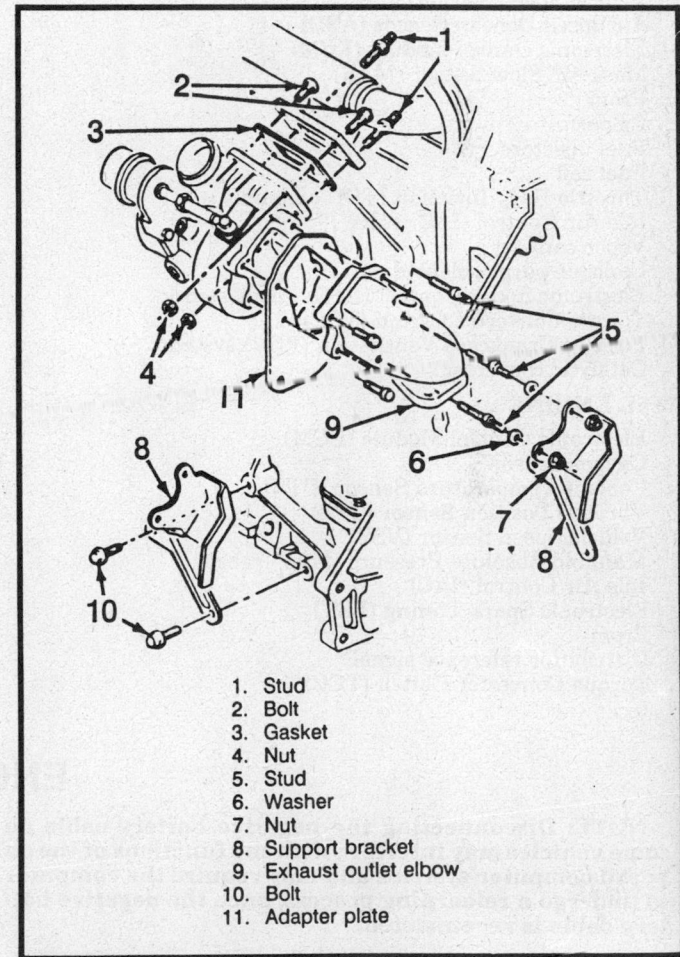

1. Stud
2. Bolt
3. Gasket
4. Nut
5. Stud
6. Washer
7. Nut
8. Support bracket
9. Exhaust outlet elbow
10. Bolt
11. Adapter plate

Turbocharger mounting 2.0L

EMISSION CONTROL SYSTEMS

Refer to "Chilton's Emission Diagnosis and Service Manual" for additional coverage.

2.0L, 3.0L AND 3.3L ENGINES

Oxygen sensor
Coolant Temperature Sensor (CTS)
Throttle Position Sensor (TPS)
Vehicle Speed Sensor (VSS)

Air Temperature Sensor (ATS)
Exhaust Gas Recirculation (EGR) valve
Exhaust Gas Recirculation (EGR) vacuum control solenoid
Electronic control module (ECM)
Mass Air Flow Sensor (MAS)
Electronic Spark Control (ESC) system
Prom

Calpak
Fuel injectors
Fuel rail
Throttle Body Injection (TBI) assembly
Idle Air Control (IAC) valve
Vapor canister
Canister purge solenoid
Computer Controlled Coil Ignition (C³I) system
Electronic Spark Control (ESC) knock sensor
Electronic Spark Control (ESC) module
Torque Converter Clutch (TCC)
Positive Crankcase Ventilation (PCV) system
Catalytic converter

2.3L ENGINE

Oxygen sensor
Coolant Temperature Sensor (CTS)
Throttle Position Sensor (TPS)
Vehicle Speed Sensor (VSS)
Air Speed Density Sensor (ASD)
Electronic control module (ECM)
Mass Air Flow Sensor (MAS)
Prom
Calpak
Fuel injectors
Fuel rail
Throttle Body Injection (TBI) assembly
Idle Air Control (IAC) valve
Vapor canister
Canister purge solenoid
Electronic Spark Control (ESC) knock sensor
Torque Converter Clutch (TCC)
Positive Crankcase Ventilation (PCV) system
Catalytic converter

2.5L ENGINE

Electronic Control Module (ECM)
Oxygen sensor
Coolant Temperature Sensor (CTS)
Throttle Position Sensor (TPS)
Vehicle Speed Sensor (VSS)
Manifold Absolute Pressure (MAP) sensor
Idle Air Control (IAC)
Electronic Spark Timing (EST)
Prom
Distributor reference signal
Torque Converter Clutch (TCC)

Throttle Body Injection (TBI) assembly
Charcoal canister
Exhaust Gas Recirculation (EGR) valve
Positive Crankcase Ventilation (PCV) system
Thermostatic Air Cleaner (TAC)
Catalytic converter
Direct Ignition System (DIS)

Resetting Emission Warning Lamps

NOTE: The following procedure is necessary to clear the trouble codes which are stored in the ECM.

Procedure

1. Make sure the ignition switch is turned **OFF**.
2. Disconnect the negative battery terminal, the ECM pigtail or the ECM fuse for 10 seconds.

NOTE: If the negative battery terminal is disconnected, loss of the digital units will occur, such as: clock and radio.

3. Reconnect the disconnected electrical connector.

Engine Oil Life Index

Vehicles equipped with an Engine Oil Life Index (EOLI), will display a **CHANGE ENGINE OIL** light indicating when the engine oil should be changed. The change engine oil interval is determined by the Engine Oil life Index (EOLI) and will usually fall at or between the 2 recommended alternative intervals of 3,000 and 7,500 miles or 1 year. Under severe driving conditions, it is suggested the engine oil be change on a more frequently basis. The Engine Oil life Index (EOLI) is incorporated as a part of the Driver Information System Display assembly.

Procedure

The Oil Life Index should be reset after each oil change.
1. Press the **RESET** and **OIL** buttons simultaneously for at least 5 seconds when the light is illuminated on the Oil Life Index display. The Driver Information System Display assembly will reset the oil life Index to 100 percent.

NOTE: To prevent accidental reset, the Oil Life Index is stored in a non-volatile memory chip and will not reset by disconnecting the battery or fuse.

ENGINE

NOTE: Disconnecting the negative battery cable on some vehicles may interfere with the functions of the on board computer systems and may require the computer to undergo a relearning process, once the negative battery cable is reconnected.

Engine Assembly

Removal and Installation
2.0L, 2.3L AND 2.5L ENGINES

NOTE: The following procedure is for removing the engine and transaxle as an assembly. This assembly is removed from the bottom of the vehicle.

1. Relieve the fuel system pressure.
2. Disconnect both battery terminals from the battery.
3. Drain cooling system.
4. Remove the air cleaner assembly.
5. Disconnect the electronic control module connections and

feed harness through the bulkhead. Lay the harness across the engine.
6. Disconnect the engine wiring harness after tagging all connectors and lay it across the engine.
7. Label and disconnect the heater hoses, the radiator hoses and the vacuum lines.
8. If equipped with air condition, remove the compressor from the engine and lay it aside; do not disconnect the refrigerant lines.
9. If equipped with power steering, remove the power steering pump from its mount and lay it aside. Remove the power steering pump bracket from the engine.
10. Remove the front transaxle strut.
11. If equipped with a manual transaxle, disconnect the clutch and transaxle linkage. Remove the throttle cable from the TBI unit.
12. If equipped with an automatic transaxle, disconnect the transaxle cooler lines, shifter linkage, downshift cable and throttle cable from the TBI unit.
13. Disconnect the redundant ground and multi-relay bracket.

14. Raise and support the vehicle safely.

15. Remove the front wheels. Remove the calipers and wire them up out of the way. Do not allow the calipers to hang by the brake hoses.

16. Remove the brake rotors.

17. Remove the knuckle-to-strut bolts.

18. Disconnect the exhaust pipe-to-manifold bolts and move it aside.

19. Remove the 4 body-to-cradle bolts at the lower control arms. Loosen the remaining 8 body-to-cradle bolts at their ends. Remove a bolt at each cradle side, leaving 1 bolt per corner.

20. Support the vehicle with safety stands, under the radiator frame support.

21. Position a jack to the rear of the body pan with a 4 × 4 in. × 6 ft. timber spanning the vehicle.

22. Raise the vehicle just enough to remove the safety stands.

23. Position a dolly under the engine/transaxle assembly with three 4 × 4 in. blocks for additional support.

24. Lower the vehicle slightly, allowing the engine/transaxle assembly to rest on the dolly.

25. Remove the engine mount bolts and the right front bracket. Remove the remaining cradle-to-body bolts.

26. Raise vehicle leaving engine, transaxle and suspension on dolly.

27. Continue the installation in the reverse order of the removal procedure. Refill the cooling system. Start the engine and check for leaks.

3.0L ENGINE

NOTE: The engine is removed from the top of the vehicle.

1. Relieve the fuel system pressure.

2. Disconnect the battery terminal from the battery.

3. Using an awl, scribe marks around the hood hinges and remove the hood.

4. Raise and support the vehicle safely. Position a clean drain pan under the radiator, open the drain cock and drain the cooling system.

5. Remove the starter and torque converter cover.

6. Remove the torque converter-to-flywheel bolts. Matchmark the torque converter to the flywheel for reassembly.

7. Remove the serpentine drive belt. If equipped with air conditioning, remove the compressor from the engine and position it aside; do not disconnect any refrigerant lines.

8. Disconnect the heater hoses and the lower radiator hose from the engine.

9. Remove the front motor mount bolts and the right inner fender splash shield.

10. Remove the transaxle-to-engine mount bolt located between the transaxle and the cylinder block.

11. Remove the 2 right rear motor mount bolts.

12. Disconnect the exhaust pipe from the exhaust manifold flange.

13. Lower the vehicle.

14. Label and disconnect the alternator wiring and the alternator.

15. If equipped with power steering, remove the power steering pump and the fluid lines.

16. Disconnect the mass air flow sensor and the air intake duct. Disconnect the top radiator hose.

17. Disconnect the electric fan wiring and remove the fan assembly. Remove the radiator.

18. Install an vertical lifting device to the engine and support the engine, remove the left upper transaxle mount.

19. If necessary, disconnect and remove the master cylinder.

20. Disconnect and remove the fuel lines from the fuel rail.

21. Disconnect the throttle, the T.V. and the cruise control cables.

22. Remove the remaining engine-to-transaxle bolts. Lift the engine from the vehicle using the lifting device.

23. Continue the installation in the reverse order of the removal procedure. Refill the cooling system. Start the engine and check for fluid leaks.

3.3L ENGINE

1. Relieve the fuel system pressure.

2. Disconnect the battery terminal from the battery.

3. Using an awl, scribe marks around the hood hinges and remove the hood.

4. Raise and support the vehicle safely. Position a clean drain pan under the radiator, open the drain cock and drain the cooling system.

5. Remove the radiator and heater hoses.

6. Remove the cooling fan.

7. Remove the vacuum hoses from the power brake booster and evaporative canister unit.

8. Remove the cable bracket and cables from the throttle body.

9. Remove the serpentine drive belt and remove the power steering pump. Position the power steering pump to the side.

10. Disconnect all electrical connections from the engine.

11. Remove the upper transaxle-to-engine bolts.

12. Raise the vehicle and support it safely.

13. Remove the air conditioning compressor and position it to the side. Do not discharge the system.

14. Remove the rear engine mount-to-bracket bolts.

15. Remove the flywheel dust cover and remove the flywheel-to-convertor bolts.

16. Using an awl, scribe marks in relationship to convertor-to-flywheel, for assembly purposes.

17. Remove the engine-to-transaxle bolts.

NOTE: There is a single bolt located between the transaxle case and the engine block and is installed in the opposite direction.

18. Lower the vehicle.

19. Remove the front engine mount-to-bracket bolts.

20. Lift the engine from the vehicle using the lifting device.

21. Continue the installation in the reverse order of the removal procedure. Torque the following:

Convertor-to-flywheel bolts in 2 steps—46 ft. lbs. (63 Nm).

Flywheel cover-to-transaxle—46 inch lbs. (6 Nm). Refill the cooling system. Start the engine and check for fluid leaks.

Engine Mounts

Removal and Installation

1. Disconnect the negative battery terminal from the battery.

2. Using an engine support fixture, locate it in the center of the cowl and properly fasten it to the engine before the mounts are removed; support the engine.

3. Raise and support the vehicle safely.

4. Remove the engine mount-to-chassis bolts.

5. Remove the mount-to-engine bracket nuts and the engine mounts from the vehicle.

6. Continue the installation in the reverse order of the removal procedure.

Intake manifold

Removal and Installation

2.0L ENGINE

1. Relieve the fuel system pressure. Disconnect the negative battery cable.

2. Remove induction tube and hoses.

3. Disconnect and tag wiring to throttle body, fuel injectors, MAP sensor and wastegate.

4. Disconnect and tag PCV hose and vacuum hoses on throttle body.

5. Remove throttle cable and cruise control cable if so equipped.

6. Remove the fuel return line from the throttle cable support bracket.

7. Remove wiring to ignition coil and remove manifold support bracket.

8. Remove the vacuum hoses fromt the rear of the manifold.

9. Remove the transmission fill tube bracket.

10. Remove the manifold support bracket.

11. Remove the heater tube support bracket on the lower side of the manifold.

12. Disconnect wires from the injectors.

13. Drain and remove the coolant recovery tank.

14. Remove the serpentine drive belt.

15. Remove rear bolt from alternator bracket, the power steering adjusting bracket and front alternator adjusting bracket.

16. Remove the alternator.

17. Remove fuel lines to fuel rail and regulator outlet.

18. Remove retaining nuts and washers and remove the intake manifold.

19. Continue the installation in the reverse order of the removal procedure. Use a new gasket. Torque the intake manifold retaining nuts to 18 ft. lbs. (24 Nm).

NOTE: The rear adjusting bracket must be the last part secured to prevent distorting the accessory drive system. This will prevent the belt from coming off.

2.3L ENGINE

1. Disconnect the negative battery cable.

2. Remove the coolant fan shroud, vacuum hose and electrical connector from the MAP sensor.

3. Disconnect the throttle body to air cleaner duct.

4. Remove the throttle cable bracket.

5. Remove the power brake vacuum hose, including the retaining bracket to power steering bracket and position it to the side.

6. Remove the throttle body from the intake manifold with electrical harness, coolant hoses, vacuum hoses and throttle cable attached. Position these components aside.

7. Remove the oil/air separator bolts and hoses. Leave the hoses attached to the separator, disconnect from the oil fill, chain housing and the intake manifold. Remove as an assembly.

8. Remove the oil fill cap and oil level indicator stick.

9. Pull the oil tube fill upward to unseat from block and remove.

10. Disconnect the injector harness connector.

11. Remove the fill tube out top, rotating as necessary to gain clearance for the oil/air separator nipple between the intake tubes and fuel rail electrical harness.

12. Remove the intake manifold support bracket bolts and nut. Remove the intake manifold retaining nuts and bolts.

13. Remove the intake manifold.

NOTE: Intake manifold mounting hole closest to chain housing is slotted for additional clearance.

14. Install the intake manifold and gasket. Tightening the intake manifold bolts/nuts in sequence and to 18 ft. lbs. (25 Nm). Tighten intake manifold brace and retainers hand tight. Tighten to specifications in the following sequence:
   a. Nut to stud bolt—18 ft. lbs. (25 Nm).
   b. Bolt to intake manifold—40 ft. lbs. (55 Nm).
   c. Bolt to cylinder block—40 ft. lbs. (55 Nm).

15. Lubricate a new oil fill tube ring seal with engine oil and install tube down between No. 1 and 2 intake tubes. Rotate as necessary to gain clearance for oil/air separator nipple on fill tube.

16. Locate the oil fill tube in its cylinder block opening. Align the fill tube so it is approximately in its installed position. Place the palm of your hand over the oil fill opening and press straight down to seat fill tube and seal into cylinder block.

17. Install oil/air separator assembly, it may be necessary to

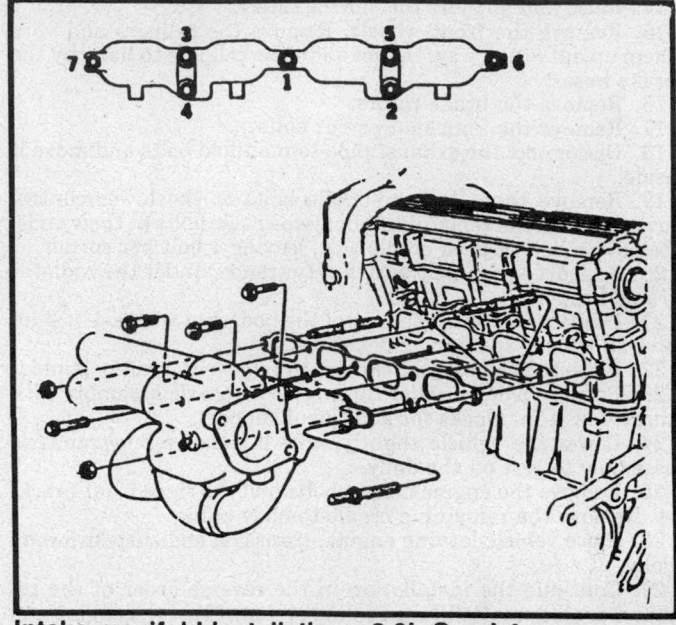

Intake manifold installation—2.3L Quad 4

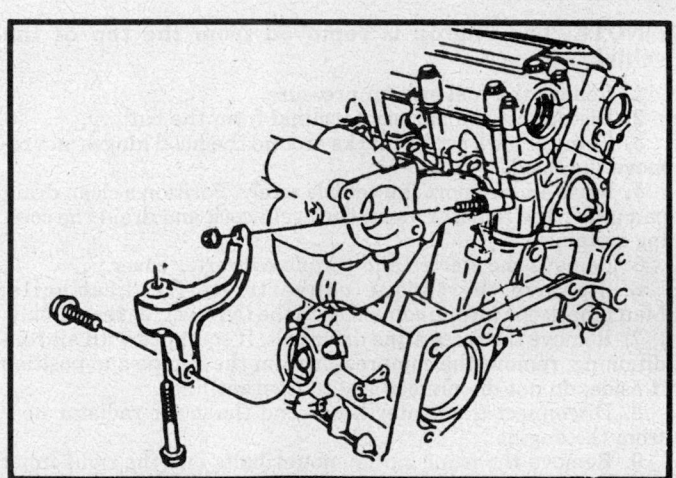

Intake manifold brace—2.3L Quad 4

lubricate the hoses for ease of assembly.

18. Install throttle body to intake manifold using a new gasket.

19. Reverse the remaining removal procedures. Torque intake manifold to the following:
   Brace-to-block—40 ft. lbs. (55 Nm).
   Brace-to-manifold—40 ft. lbs. (55 Nm).
   Brace-to- manifold stud 18 ft. lbs. (25 Nm).

Intake manifold-to-cylinder head bolts in sequence—18 ft. lbs. (25 Nm).

2.5L ENGINE

1. Relieve the system fuel pressure.

2. Disconnect the negative battery terminal from the battery.

3. Remove the air cleaner, PCV valve and hose.

4. Position a drain pan under the radiator, open the drain cock and drain the cooling system.

5. Label and remove the vacuum lines. Disconnect the fuel lines from the TBI unit.

6. Label and disconnect the electrical wiring and throttle linkage from the TBI.

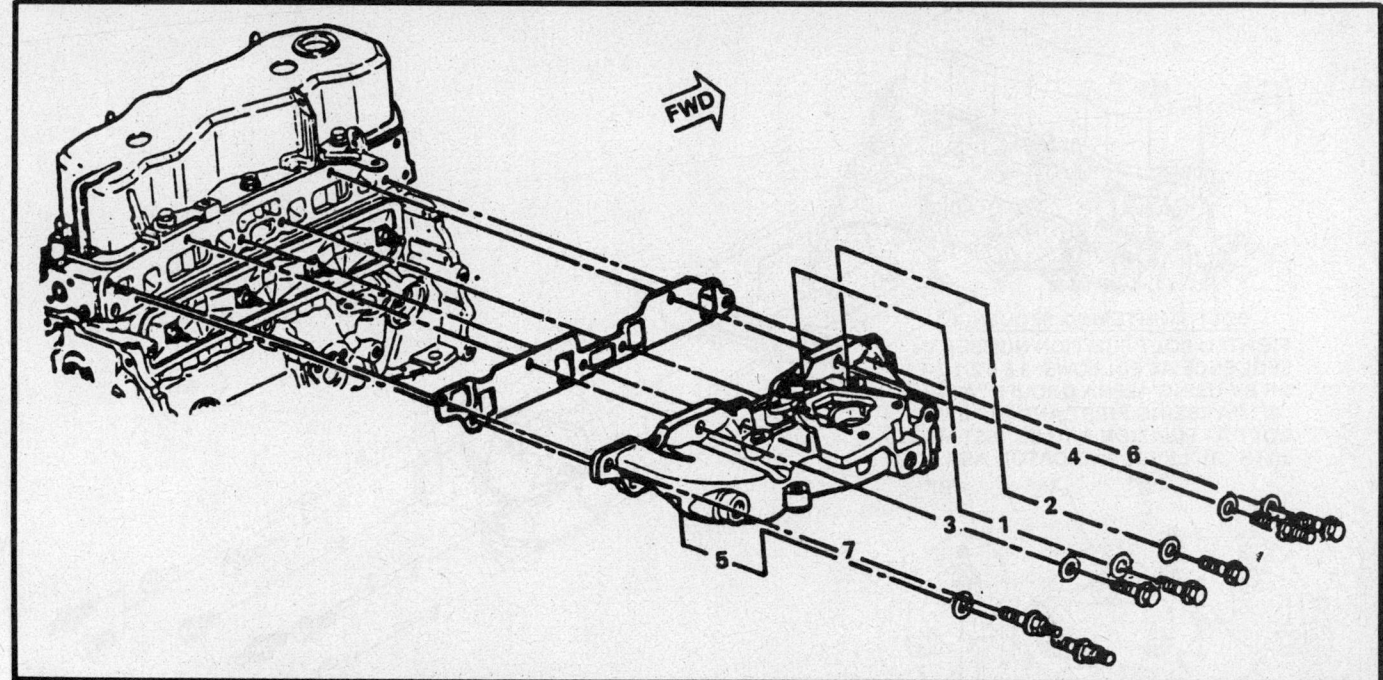

FWD

Intake manifold bolt torque sequence 2.5L

7. If equipped, disconnect the transaxle downshift linkage and the cruise control linkage.

8. Disconnect the throttle linkage and bell crank; position the assembly to the side for clearance.

9. Disconnect the heater hoses. If equipped with power steering, disconnect and remove the upper power steering pump bracket.

10. Remove the ignition coil.

11. Remove the intake manifold-to-cylinder head bolts and the intake manifold.

12. Using a gasket scraper, clean the gasket mounting surfaces.

13. Continue the installation in the reverse order of the removal procedure. Use new gaskets and sealant. Torque the intake manifold-to-engine bolts in sequence to 25 ft. lbs. (34 Nm).

3.0L AND 3.3L ENGINES

1. Relieve the fuel system pressure.

2. Disconnect the negative battery terminal from the battery.

3. Disconnect the mass air flow sensor and remove the air intake duct.

4. Remove the serpentine drive belt, alternator and bracket.

5. Remove the C^{3}I ignition module and bracket.

6. Label and remove all the necessary vacuum and electrical wiring connectors.

7. Remove the throttle, cruise control and T.V. cables from the throttle body assembly.

8. Position a drain pan under the radiator, open the drain cock and drain the cooling system. Disconnect the heater hoses from the throttle body.

9. Remove the upper radiator hose from the intake manifold.

10. Remove the fuel lines, the fuel rail and the fuel injectors. Remove the spark plug wires.

11. Remove the intake manifold-to-engine bolts and the intake manifold.

12. Using a gasket scraper, clean the gasket mounting surfaces.

13. Continue the installation in the reverse order of the removal procedure. Use new gaskets and sealant. Torque intake manifold-to-cylinder head bolts in sequence to 32 ft. lbs. (43 Nm).

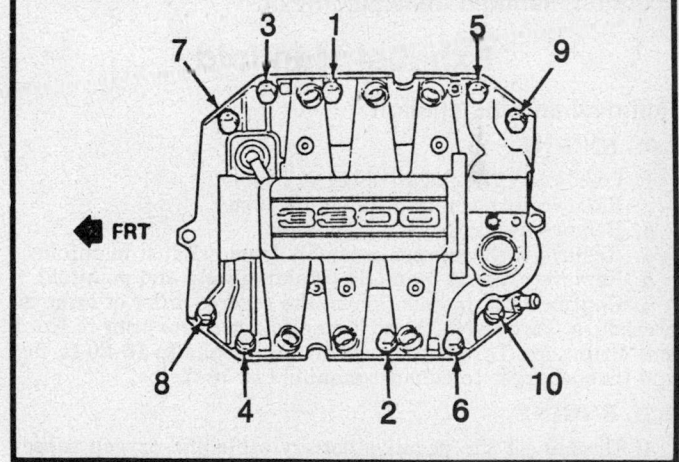

FRT

Intake manifold bolt tightening sequence 3.3L engine

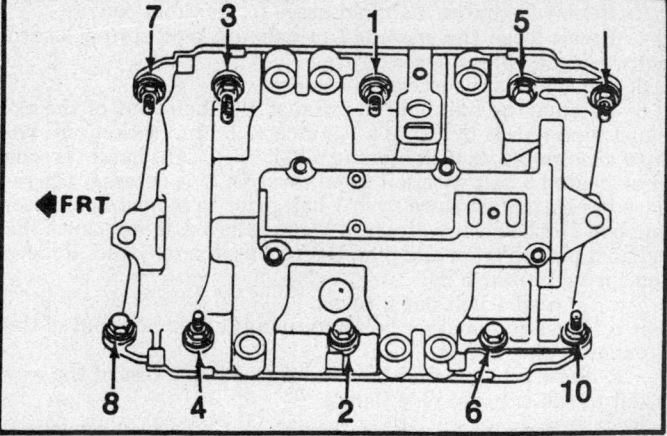

FRT

Intake manifold torque sequence—3.0L engine

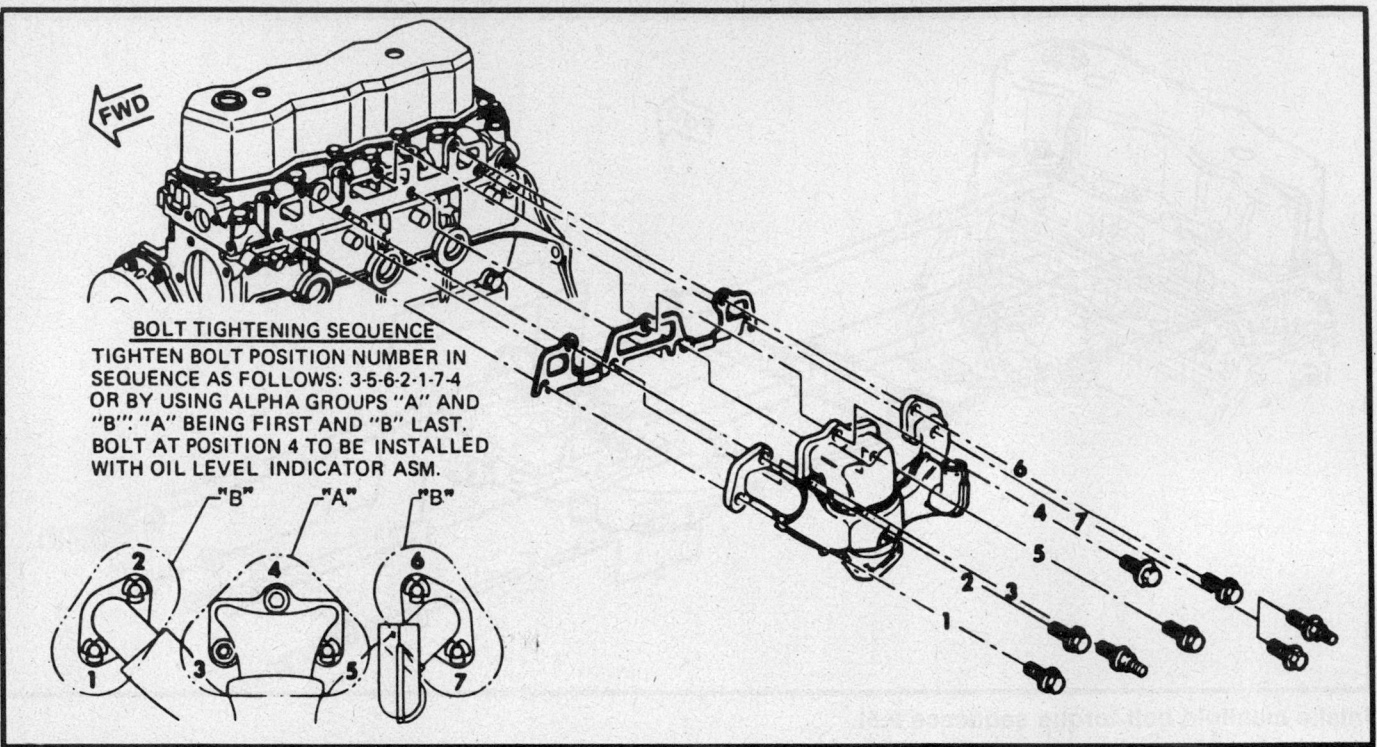

BOLT TIGHTENING SEQUENCE
TIGHTEN BOLT POSITION NUMBER IN SEQUENCE AS FOLLOWS: 3-5-6-2-1-7-4 OR BY USING ALPHA GROUPS "A" AND "B": "A" BEING FIRST AND "B" LAST. BOLT AT POSITION 4 TO BE INSTALLED WITH OIL LEVEL INDICATOR ASM.

Exhaust manifold installation 2.0L

Exhaust Manifold

Removal and Installation

2.0L ENGINE

1. Disconnect the negative battery cable.
2. Remove turbocharger induction tube.
3. Remove and tag spark plug wires.
4. Remove turbocharger assembly from exhaust manifold.
5. Remove exhaust manifold retaining nuts and manifold.
6. Continue the installation in the reverse order of removal procedure. Torque No. 2 and 3 manifold runners prior to No. 1 and 4 runners. Torque exhaust manifold bolts to 16–20 ft. lbs. and turbocharger to exhaust manifold to 18 ft. lbs.

2.3L ENGINE

1. Disconnect the negative battery cable and oxygen sensor connector.
2. Remove upper and lower exhaust manifold heat shields.
3. Remove exhaust manifold brace to manifold bolt.
4. Break loose the manifold to exhaust pipe spring loaded bolts using a 13mm box wrench.
5. Raise and support vehicle safely.
6. Remove the manifold to exhaust pipe bolts out of the exhaust pipe flange by using a $\frac{7}{32}$ inch (5.5 mm) socket and **rotate clockwise** as if tightening a bolt with right hand threads or removing a bolt with left hand threads. It is necessary to relieve the spring pressure from 1 bolt prior to removing the second bolt. If the spring pressure is not relieved, it will cause the exhaust pipe to twist and bind the bolt as it is removed. Relieve the spring pressure by:
   a. Thread 1 bolt out 4 turns.
   b. Move to the other bolt and turn it all the way out of the exhaust pipe flange.
   c. Return to the first bolt and rotate it the rest of the way out of the exhaust pipe flange.
7. Pull down and back on the exhaust pipe to disengage it from the exhaust manifold bolts.

8. Lower vehicle.
9. Remove exhaust manifold to cylinder head retaining nuts and remove exhaust manifold.
10. Continue the installation in the reverse order of removal.

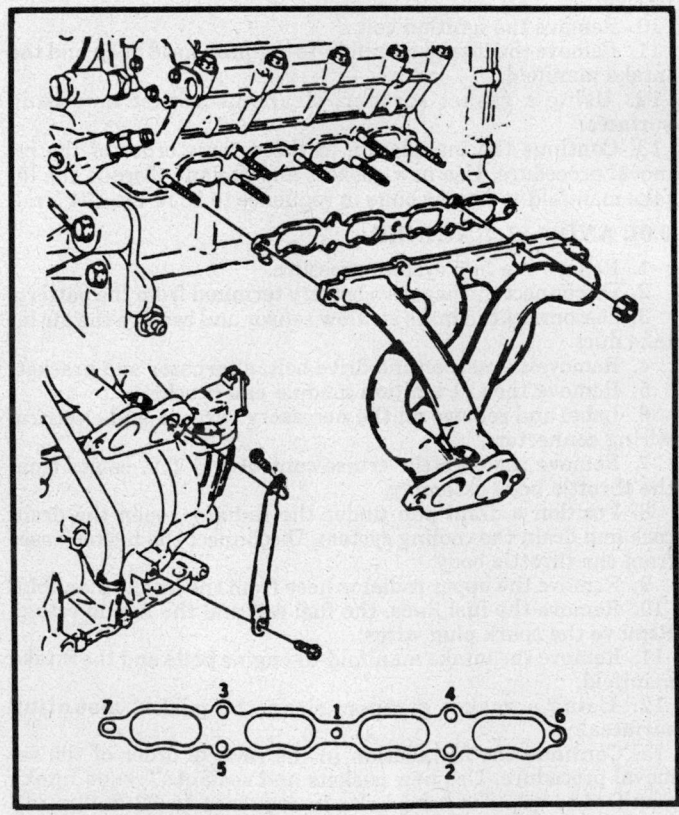

Exhaust manifold installation—2.3L Quad 4

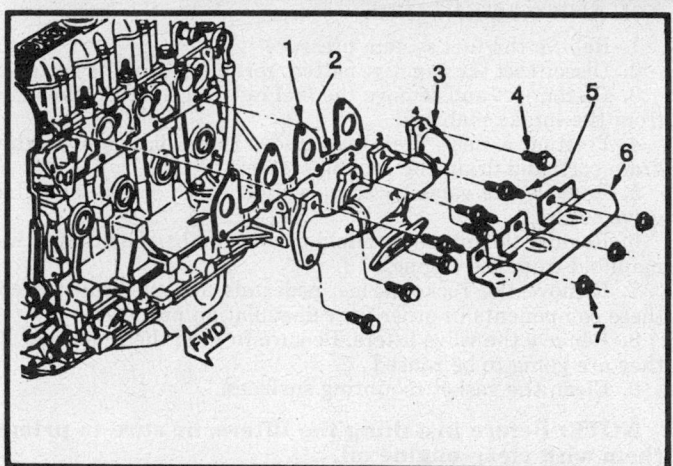

Exhaust manifold torque sequence—2.5L engine

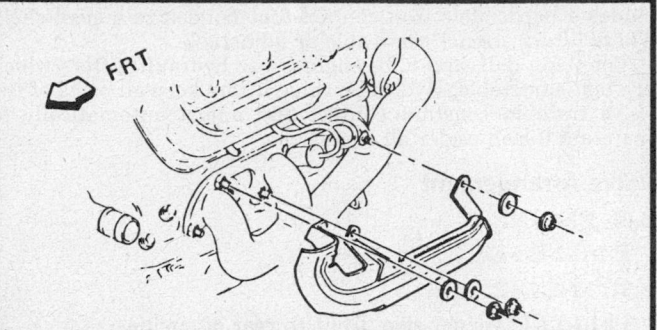

View of the left exhaust manifold assembly—3.0L engine

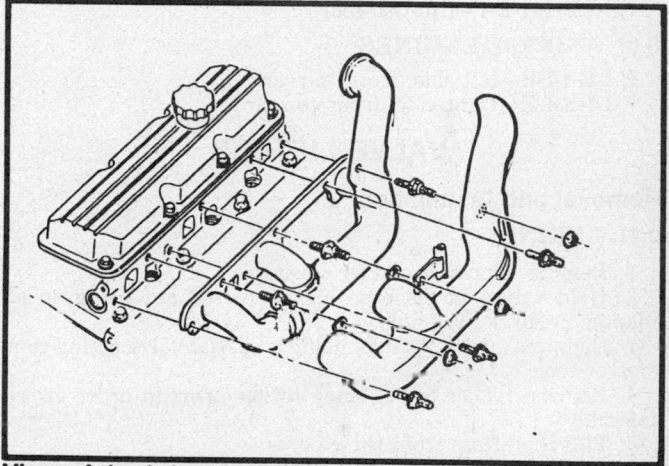

View of the left exhaust manifold assembly—3.3L engine

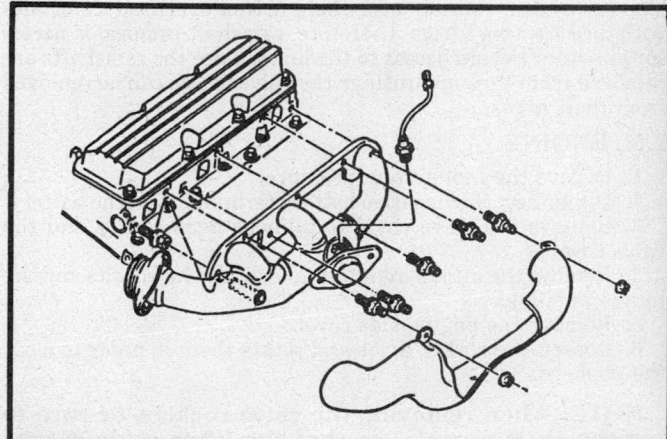

View of the right exhaust manifold assembly—3.3L engine

In sequence torque exhaust manifold bolts to head 27 ft. lbs., manifold to exhaust pipe 22 ft. lbs. and manifold to brace 19 ft. lbs.

NOTE: Turn bolts in evenly to avoid cocking the exhaust pipe and binding the bolts. Turn bolts in until fully seated.

2.5L ENGINE

1. Disconnect the negative battery terminal from the battery.
2. Remove the air cleaner.
3. Remove the alternator top engine mount and position the unit to one side.
4. Disconnect the oxygen sensor connector.
5. Raise and support the vehicle safely.
6. Disconnect the exhaust pipe-to-exhaust manifold bolts and lower the exhaust pipe.
7. Lower the vehicle.
8. Remove the exhaust manifold-to-cylinder head retaining bolts and lift the exhaust manifold from the engine.
9. Using a gasket scraper, clean the gasket mounting surfaces.
10. Continue the installation in the reverse order of the removal procedure. Use new gaskets. Torque the exhaust manifold-to-cylinder head bolts in sequence to 32 ft. lbs. (43 Nm).

3.0L AND 3.3L ENGINES—LEFT SIDE FRONT

1. Disconnect the negative battery cable.
2. Disconnect air cleaner mounting bolts.
3. Remove the bolts attaching the exhaust crossover pipe to the manifold.
4. Tag and disconnect the spark plug wires.
5. Remove engine cooling fan.
6. Remove the mounting bolts and remove the manifold.

NOTE: The oil dipstick tube may have to be removed to provide access to the manifold bolts.

7. Continue the installation in the reverse order of removal procedure. Apply sealer between manifold and cylinder head.

3.0L AND 3.3L ENGINES—RIGHT SIDE REAR

1. Disconnect the negative battery cable.
2. Remove the 2 bolts attaching exhaust pipe to manifold.
3. Disconnect oxygen sensor wire.
4. Disconnect and tag spark plug wires.
5. Remove 2 nuts retaining crossover pipe to manifold.
6. Remove serpentine belt.
7. Remove power steering pump.
8. Remove heater hose from tube, heat shield and C³I bracket nuts.
9. Remove the bolts attaching manifold to cylinder head
10. Continue the installation in the reverse order of the removal procedure. Apply sealer between manifold and cylinder head.

Valve System

VALVE ADJUSTMENT

The 2.0L engine valve lash compensators are located in the top of the cylinder head which maintain 0 lash. On the 2.3L direct acting hydraulic valve lifters are used. The valve lifter body includes a hardenable iron contact foot bonded to a steel shell. These lifters are not servicable or adjustable.

The 2.5L, 3.0L and 3.3L engines use hydraulic lifters which are non-adjustable. Hydraulic valve lifters keep all parts of the valve train in constant contact and adjust automatically to maintain 0 lash under all conditions.

Valve Arrangement

2.0L ENGINE

E-I-E-I-E-I-E-I

2.3L ENGINE

I/I-I/I-I/I-I/I — right-side, front to rear of engine
E/E-E/E-E/E-E/E — left-side, front to rear of engine

2.5L ENGINE

I-E-I-E-E-I-E-I — front-to-rear

3.0L AND 3.3L ENGINES

E-I-E-I-I-E — left-side, front-to-rear
E-I-I-E-I-E — right-side, front-to-rear

VALVE LIFTERS

Removal and Installation

2.0L ENGINE

1. Remove camshaft carrier cover.
2. Hold valves in place with compressed air, using an air adapter in spark plug hole.
3. Compress valve springs using a special valve spring compressor tool.
4. Remove rocker arms. Keep rocker arms in order for reassembly.
5. Pull the lifters from their bores.
6. Installation is the reverse order of the removal procedure.

2.3L ENGINE

The valve train consists of 2 chain driven overhead camshafts with direct acting lifters, therefore, camshaft removal is necessary in order to gain access to the lifers. Once the camshafts are removed from their mountings the valve lifters can be removed from their bores.

2.5L ENGINE

1. Relieve the fuel system pressure.
2. Disconnect the negative battery terminal from the battery.
3. Remove the valve cover-to-cylinder head screws and the valve cover.
4. Remove the intake manifold-to-cylinder head bolts and the intake manifold.
5. Remove the engine side cover.
6. Loosen the rocker arms and rotate them in order to clear the pushrods.

NOTE: When removing the valve rockers, be sure to remove them in pairs so that the lifter guide can be removed.

7. Remove the pushrods, retainer and guide from each cylinder.
8. Remove the valve lifters; be sure to keep them in order if they are going to be reused.
9. Clean the gasket mounting surfaces.

NOTE: Before installing the lifters, be sure to prime them with clean engine oil.

10. Continue the installation in the reverse order of the removal procedure. Use new gaskets and sealant if necessary. Start the engine, allow it to reach normal operating temperature and check for leaks.

3.0L AND 3.3L ENGINES

1. Relieve the fuel system pressure.
2. Disconnect the negative battery terminal from the battery.
3. Disconnect and remove the fuel rail and the throttle body from the intake manifold.
4. Position a clean drain pan under the radiator, open the drain cock and drain the cooling system.
5. Remove the valve cover-to-cylinder head screws and the valve covers.
6. Remove the intake manifold-to-cylinder head bolts and the manifold from the engine.
7. Remove the rocker arms, pedestals and pushrods; keep these components in order for reinstallation purposes.
8. Remove the valve lifters. Be sure to keep them in order if they are going to be reused.
9. Clean the gasket mounting surfaces.

NOTE: Before installing the lifters, be sure to prime them with clean engine oil.

10. Continue the installation in the reverse order of the removal procedure. Use new gaskets and sealant if necessary. Refill the cooling system. Start the engine, allow it to reach normal operating temperature and check for leaks.

VALVE ROCKER ASSEMBLY

Removal and Installation

2.0L ENGINE

1. Relieve the fuel system pressure.
2. Disconnect the negative battery cable.
3. Remove camshaft carrier cover.
4. Hold valves in place with compressed air, using an air adapter in spark plug hole.
5. Compress valve springs with special valve spring compressing tool.
6. Remove rocker arms. Keep rocker arms in order for reassembly.
7. Continue the installation in the reverse order of the removal procedure.

2.3L ENGINE

The valve train consists of 2 chain driven overhead camshafts with direct acting lifters.

2.5L ENGINE

1. Relieve the fuel system pressure.
2. Disconnect the negative battery terminal from the battery.
3. Label and disconnect all electrical wiring connectors and the vacuum hoses which inhibit the valve cover removal.
4. Remove the valve cover-to-cylinder head bolts and lift off the valve cover.
5. Remove the rocker arm bolts and balls, lift off the rocker arms.

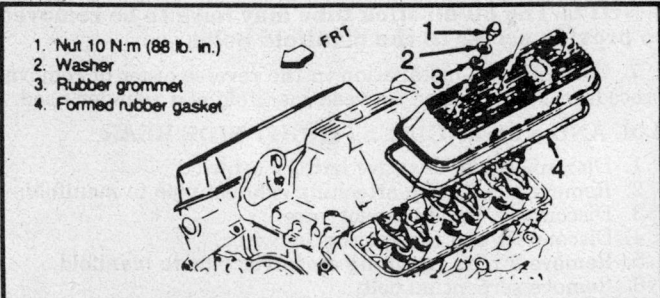

1. Nut 10 N·m (88 lb. in.)
2. Washer
3. Rubber grommet
4. Formed rubber gasket

View of the rocker arm cover and gasket assembly — 3.0L and 3.3L engines

NOTE: If only the pushrods are being replaced, simply loosen the rocker arm bolt and swing them aside. Keep all removed components in order so they may be assembled in their original locations.

6. Clean the gasket mounting surfaces. Inspect and/or replace any damaged parts.

7. Install the pushrods, making sure they seat properly in the lifters.

8. Install the rocker arms, balls and nuts. Tighten the rocker arm nuts until all lash is eliminated.

9. Continue the installation in the reverse order of the removal procedure. Use new gaskets and sealant if necessary.

3.0L ENGINE – LEFT FRONT COVER

1. Relieve the fuel system pressure.

2. Disconnect the negative battery terminal from the battery.

3. In order to gain access to the valve cover retaining bolts, disconnect all electrical components, disconnect and plug any vacuum hoses which may be in the way.

4. Remove the valve cover-to-cylinder head screws and the valve cover.

5. Remove the rocker arm pedestal-to-cylinder head bolts, the rocker arm and pedestal assembly.

6. Clean the gasket mounting surfaces.

NOTE: Be sure to coat new components with clean engine oil before installation.

7. Continue the installation in the reverse order of the removal procedure. Use new gaskets and sealant if necessary. Torque rocker arm pedestal bolts to 45 ft. lbs. (60 Nm).

3.0L ENGINE – RIGHT REAR COVER

1. Relieve the fuel system pressure.

2. Disconnect the negative battery terminal.

3. Remove the C^3I ignition coil module. Remove the spark plug wires, electrical connectors, EGR solenoid wiring and vacuum hoses.

4. Remove the serpentine belt, alternator wiring and the rear alternator bracket-to-engine bolt. Rotate the alternator toward the front of the vehicle.

5. Remove the power steering pump from the belt tensioner and the tensioner assembly.

6. Remove the engine lift bracket and the rear alternator brace.

7. Drain the radiator below the heater hose level. Remove the throttle body heater hoses.

8. Remove the valve cover-to-cylinder head screws and the valve cover from the engine.

9. Remove the rocker arm pedestal-to-cylinder head bolts and remove the rocker arm and pedestal assembly.

10. Clean the gasket mounting surfaces.

NOTE: Be sure to coat new components with clean engine oil before installation.

11. Continue the installation in the reverse order of the removal procedure. Use new gaskets and sealant if necessary. Torque rocker arm pedestal bolts to 45 ft. lbs. (60 Nm).

12. Refill the cooling system. Start the engine, allow it to reach normal operating temperature and check for leaks.

3.3L ENGINE – LEFT FRONT COVER

1. Relieve the fuel system pressure.

2. Disconnect the negative battery terminal from the battery.

3. In order to gain access to the valve cover retaining bolts, disconnect all electrical components, disconnect and plug any vacuum hoses which may be in the way.

4. Remove the serpentine drive belt.

5. Remove the alternator brace bolt and remove the alternator belt.

6. Remove the spark plug wire harness.

7. Remove the valve cover-to-cylinder head screws and the valve cover.

8. Remove the rocker arm pedestal-to-cylinder head bolts, the rocker arm and pedestal assembly.

9. Clean the gasket mounting surfaces.

NOTE: Be sure to coat new components with clean engine oil before installation.

10. Continue the installation in the reverse order of the removal procedure. Use new gaskets and sealant if necessary. Torque the pedestal bolts to 28 ft. lbs. (38 Nm).

3.3L ENGINE – RIGHT REAR COVER

1. Relieve the fuel system pressure.

2. Disconnect the negative battery terminal.

3. Remove the serpentine drive belt.

4. Loosen the power steering pump bolts and slide the pump forward.

5. Remove the power steering braces.

6. Remove the spark plug wires from the spark plugs.

7. Remove the valve cover-to-cylinder head screws and the valve cover from the engine.

8. Remove the rocker arm pedestal-to-cylinder head bolts, remove the rocker arm and pedestal assembly.

9. Clean the gasket mounting surfaces.

NOTE: Be sure to coat new components with clean engine oil before installation.

10. Continue the installation in the reverse order of the removal procedure. Use new gaskets and sealant if necessary. Torque the pedestal bolts to 28 ft. lbs. (38 Nm).

11. Refill the cooling system. Start the engine, allow it to reach normal operating temperature and check for leaks.

Cylinder Head

Removal and Installation

2.0L ENGINE

NOTE: Cylinder head gasket replacement is necessary if camshaft carrier/cylinder head bolts are loosened. The head bolts should always be loosen when cold. New head blots should be used every time camshaft carrier/cylinder head or gasket are replaced.

1. Relieve the fuel system pressure. Remove induction tube.

2. Drain coolant and remove negative battery cable.

3. Remove alternator and bracket.

4. Remove ignition coil.

5. Remove distributor and wiring, after marking distributor housing to block and rotor position to housing. Tag spark plug wires and all electrical connections.

6. Disconnect all cables from throttle body.

7. Disconnect and tag all electrical connections TBI and intake manifold.

8. Remove hoses from vacuum brake, fuel inlet and return lines. Remove heater hoses.

9. Remove intake manifold and water pump.

10. Remove breather from camshaft carrier.

11. Remove upper radiator support.

12. Remove exhaust manifold to turbocharger connection and oxygen sensor connection.

13. Disconnect and tag wiring at engine harness and thermostat housing.

14. Remove timing belt.

15. Loosen camshaft carrier/cylinder head bolts gradually in sequence.

16. Remove camshaft carrier, rocker arms and valve lash compensators.

17. Remove cylinder head and exhaust manifold as an assembly.

To install;

18. Use new gasket. Apply a continuous 3mm bead of anerobic

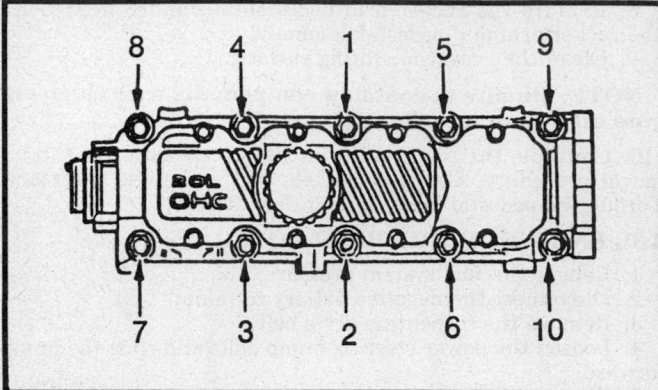

Camshaft carrier and cylinder head bolt torque sequence 2.0L

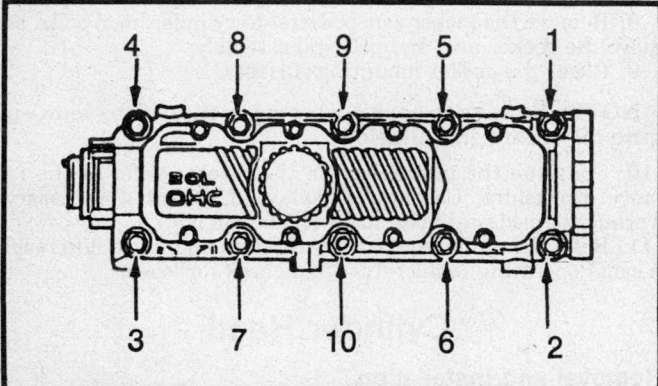

Camshaft carrier and cylinder head bolt loosening sequence 2.0L

sealer to sealing surface of camshaft carrier. Always replace camshaft carrier/cylinder head retaining bolts.
19. Torque head bolts in 4 steps in sequence:
Step 1, Torque all bolts in sequence—18 ft. lbs. (25 Nm).
Step 2, Tighten all bolts an additional 60 degrees.
Step 3, Tighten all bolts in sequence—120 degrees.
Step 4, Tighten all bolts in sequence—180 degrees.
20. Install the rear cover and timing belt.
21. Connect all wiring to the engine harness and thermostat housing.
22. Install the exhaust manifold to turbo connection and the oxygen sensor connection.
23. Install the upper radiator support.
24. Install the breather on the camshaft carrier.
25. Install the intake manifold and water pump.
26. Connect all hoses to the vacuum brake, fuel inlet and return lines. Install the heater hoses.
27. Connect all electrical connections to the TBI and intake manifold.
28. Connect all cables to the throttle body.
29. Position the distributor in place in relationship to the marks made during removal. Connect the spark plug wires and all electrical connections.
30. Install the ignition coil.
31. Install the alternator and bracket.
32. Fill radiator with coolant. Connect the negative battery cable.
33. Start the engine, allow to reach operation temperature and check for leaks.

2.3L ENGINE
1. Relieve the fuel system pressure. Remove negative battery cable and drain cooling system.

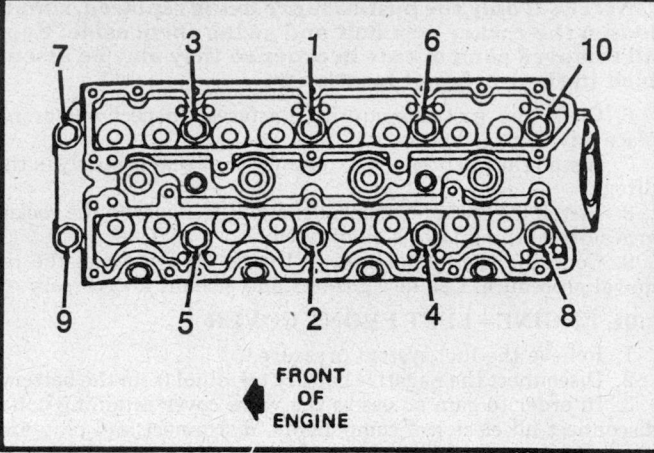

FRONT OF ENGINE

Cylinder head bolt torque sequence—2.3L Quad 4

2. Disconnect heater inlet and throttle body heater hoses from water outlet. Disconnect upper radiator hose from water outlet.
3. Remove exhaust manifold.
4. Remove intake and exhaust camshaft housings.
5. Remove oil cap and dipstick. Pull oil fill tube upward to unseat from block.
6. Disconnect and tag injector harness electrical connector.
7. Disconnect throttle body to air cleaner duct. Remove throttle cable and bracket an position aside.
8. Remove throttle body from intake manifold with electrical harness, hoses, cable attached and position aside.
9. Disconnect and tag MAP sensor vacuum hose from intake manifold.
10. Remove intake manifold bracket to block bolt.
11. Disconnect and tag 2 coolant sensor connections.
12. Remove cylinder head to block bolts.

NOTE: When removing cylinder head to block bolts follow reverse of tighten sequence.

13. Remove cylinder head and gasket.

NOTE: Clean all gasket surfaces with plastic or wood scraper. Do not use any sealing material.

To install;
14. Install the cylinder head gasket to the cylinder block and carefully position the cylinder head in place.
15. Coat the head bolt threads with clean engine oil and allow the oil to drain off before installing.
16. Torque the cylinder head bolts in sequence in 2 steps as follows:
Step 1, in sequence, torque the long and short cylinder head to block bolts—26 ft. lbs. (35 Nm).
Step 2, in sequence, tighten the short bolts—80 degree turn and the long bolts—90 degree turn.
17. Install the intake manifold bracket-to-block bracket bolt and bracket.
18. Connect the MAP sensor vacuum hose to the intake manifold.
19. Install the throttle body on the intake manifold with electrical harness, hoses and cable attached.
20. Connect the throttle body-to-air cleaner duct. Install the throttle cable and bracket.
21. Connect the injector harness electrical connector.
22. Connect the 2 coolant sensor connections.
23. Install the oil cap and dipstick. Install the oil fill tube into the block.
24. Install the exhaust and intake camshaft housings.
25. Install the exhaust manifold.
26. Connect the heater inlet and throttle body heater hoses to

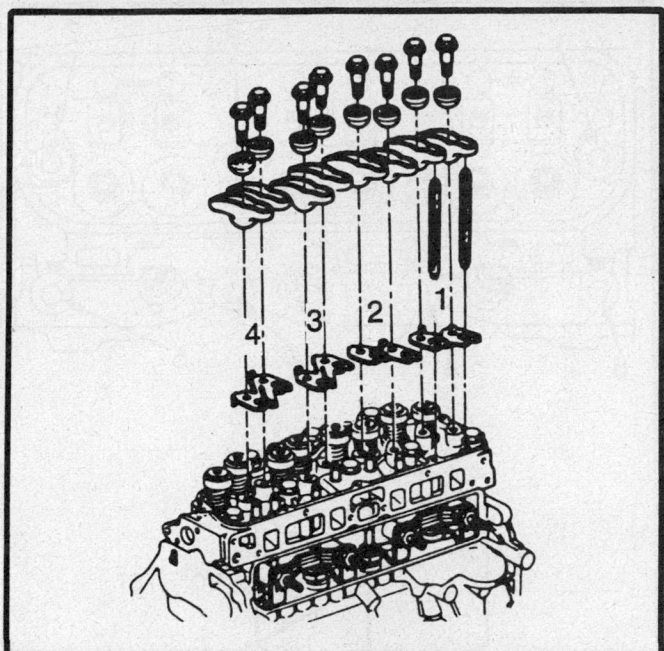

Exploded view of the valve rocker assembly—2.5L engine

NUMBERS SHOWN DESIGNATE BOLT POSITIONS AND BOLT TIGHTENING SEQUENCE.

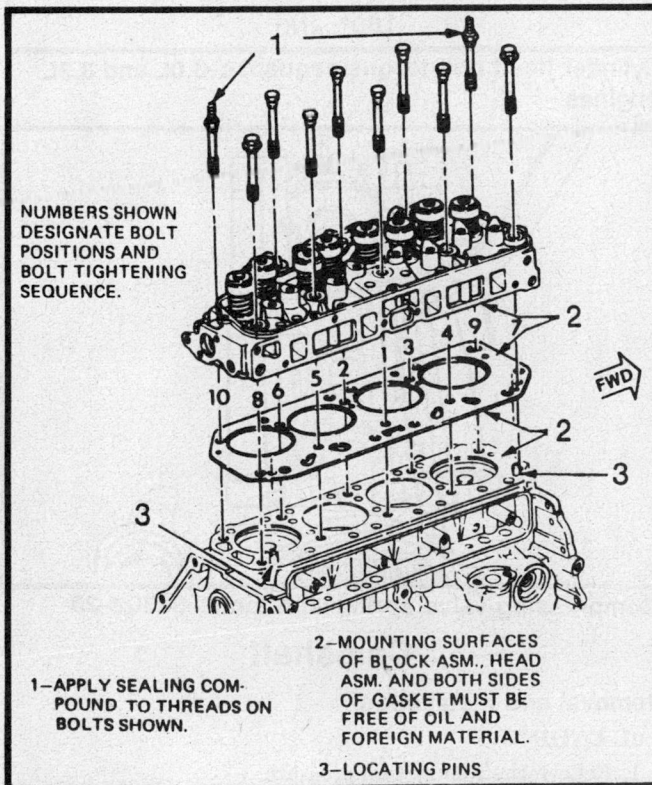

1—APPLY SEALING COMPOUND TO THREADS ON BOLTS SHOWN.

2—MOUNTING SURFACES OF BLOCK ASM., HEAD ASM. AND BOTH SIDES OF GASKET MUST BE FREE OF OIL AND FOREIGN MATERIAL.

3—LOCATING PINS

Cylinder head bolt torque sequence—2.5L engine

the water outlet. Connect the upper radiator hose to the water outlet.

27. Fill the cooling system and connect the negative battery cable.

28. Start the engine, allow it to reach operating temperature and check for leaks.

2.5L ENGINE

1. Relieve the fuel system pressure.
2. Disconnect the negative battery terminal from the battery.
3. Position a drain pan under the radiator, open the drain cock and drain the cooling system. Remove the dipstick tube.
4. Remove the air cleaner assembly.
5. Raise the vehicle and support it safely. Disconnect the exhaust pipe-to-manifold bolts and separate the exhaust pipe from the manifold.
6. Lower the vehicle.
7. Label and disconnect the electrical wiring and throttle linkage from the TBI assembly.
8. Remove the heater hose from the intake manifold.
9. Remove the ignition coil. Label and disconnect the electrical wiring connectors from the intake manifold and the cylinder head. Remove the alternator.
10. If equipped with air conditioning, remove the compressor and lay it aside; do not disconnect the refrigerant lines.
11. If equipped with power steering, remove the upper bracket from the power steering pump.
12. Remove the radiator hoses from the engine.
13. Remove the rocker arm covers, rocker arms and pushrods.
14. Remove the cylinder head-to-engine bolts and lift the cylinder head from the engine.
15. Clean the gasket mating surfaces.

To install;

16. Position a new head gasket over the dowel pins in the cylinder block.
17. Carefully place the cylinder head on the cylinder block over the dowel pins.
18. Install the cylinder head bolts and torque using the following procedures:

   a. On 1986–87 vehicles, torque head bolts in sequence in stages to 18. ft. lbs. Repeat sequence, bringing torque to 22 ft. lbs. on all bolts except No. 9, which is torqued to 29 ft. lbs. Repeat sequence; turn all bolts 120 degrees 2 flats. Torque No. 9 an additional ¼ turn.

   b. 1988–90 vehicles, torque all head bolts in sequence gradually to 18 ft. lbs. Repeat sequence, bringing torque to 26 ft. lbs. on all bolts except No. 9 which is torqued to 18 ft. lbs. Repeat sequence, turning all bolts 90 degrees.

19. On all model years, tightening sequence and bolt location is the same, torque specification and method differ slighty. Bolts No. 1 and No. 9 must be installed as illustrated.
20. Install the pushrods, rocker arms and cover.
21. Install the radiator hoses.
22. Install the power steering pump and upper bracket.
23. If equipped with air condition, install the air conditioning compressor.
24. Install the ignition coil and connect the electrical wiring connectors to the intake manifold and the cylinder head.
25. Install the alternator.
26. Install the heater hose to the intake manifold.
27. Connect the electrical wiring and throttle linkage to the TBI assembly.
28. Raise the vehicle and support is safely.
29. Install the exhaust pipe-to-manifold bolts and connect the exhaust pipe to the manifold.
30. Install the air cleaner assembly.
31. Refill the cooling system.
32. Connect the negative battery cable. Start the engine and allow it to reach operating temperature. Check for leaks.

3.0L AND 3.3L ENGINES

1. Relieve the fuel system pressure.
2. Disconnect the negative battery terminal from the battery.
3. Remove the mass air flow sensor and the air intake duct.
4. Remove the C³I ignition module and wiring.
5. Remove the serpentine drive belt, the alternator and bracket.

6. Label and remove all necessary vacuum lines and electrical connections.

7. Remove the fuel lines, the fuel rail and the spark plug wires.

8. Position a drain pan under the radiator, open the drain cock and drain the cooling system. Remove the heater/radiator hoses from the throttle body and intake manifold. Remove the cooling fan and the radiator.

9. Remove the intake manifold-to-engine bolts and the manifold from the engine.

10. Remove the valve covers. Remove the rocker arms, the pedestals and pushrods.

NOTE: When removing the valve parts, be sure to keep the parts in order, so they may be assembled in their original locations.

11. Remove the left exhaust manifold-to-engine bolts and the manifold from the engine.

12. If equipped with power steering, remove the power steering pump. Remove the dipstick and dipstick tube.

13. Remove the left cylinder head-to-engine bolts in reverse of the torque sequence and lift the left cylinder head from the engine.

14. Raise and support the vehicle safely. Remove the right exhaust manifold-to-engine bolts.

15. Remove the right cylinder head-to-engine bolts in reverse of the torque sequence and lift the right cylinder head from the engine.

16. Clean the gasket mounting surfaces.

To install;

17. Position a new head gasket on the cylinder block dowel pins.

18. Carefully place the cylinder head on the cylinder block.

19. Install the cylinder head-to-engine bolts.

20. Torque the cylinder head bolts in in sequence to the following procedure.

On the 3.0L engine:
Step 1, tighten all bolts in sequence—25 ft. lbs. (34 Nm).
Step 2, in sequence tighten all bolts a ¼ turn.
Step 3, in sequence tighten all bolts an additional ¼ turn.

NOTE: If 60 ft. lbs. of torque is reached at any time, do not complete the additional angle torque.

On the 3.3L engine:
Step 1, tighten all bolts in sequence—35 ft. lbs. (47 Nm).
Step 2, in sequence tighten all bolts 130 degrees.
Step 3, rotate the center 4 bolts an additional 30 degrees in sequence.

21. Install the intake manifold and mounting bolts. Torque the bolts in sequence and to specifications.

22. Raise and support the vehicle safely. Install the exhaust manifold-to-engine bolts.

23. Lower the vehicle.

24. If equipped with power steering, install the power steering pump. Install the dipstick and dipstick tube.

25 Install new valve cover gaskets and install the valve covers.

26. Install the rocker arms, pedestals and bolts. Tighten pedestal bolts to 43 ft. lbs. (58 Nm) for the 3.0L engine and 28 ft. lbs. (38 Nm) for the 3.3L engine.

27. Install the intake manifold-to-engine bolts and the manifold to the engine.

28. Install the heater and radiator hoses to the throttle body and intake manifold.

29. Install the cooling fan and the radiator.

30. Install the fuel lines, the fuel rail and the spark plug wires.

31. Install all vacuum lines and electrical connections.

32. Install the serpentine drive belt, the alternator and bracket.

33. Install the C³I ignition module and wiring.

34. Install the mass air flow sensor and the air intake duct.

35. Connect the negative battery cable. Start the engine and allow it to reach operating temperature. Check for leaks.

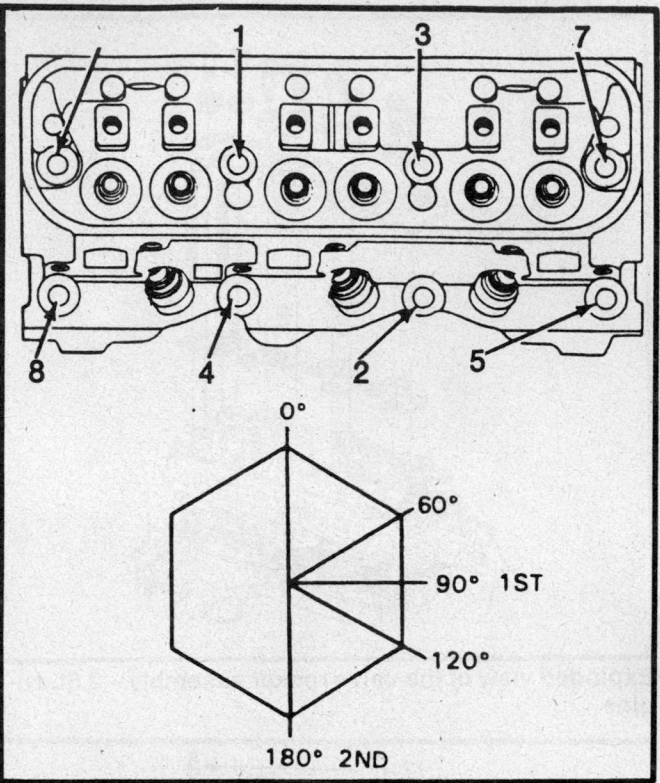

Cylinder head bolt torque sequence—3.0L and 3.3L engines

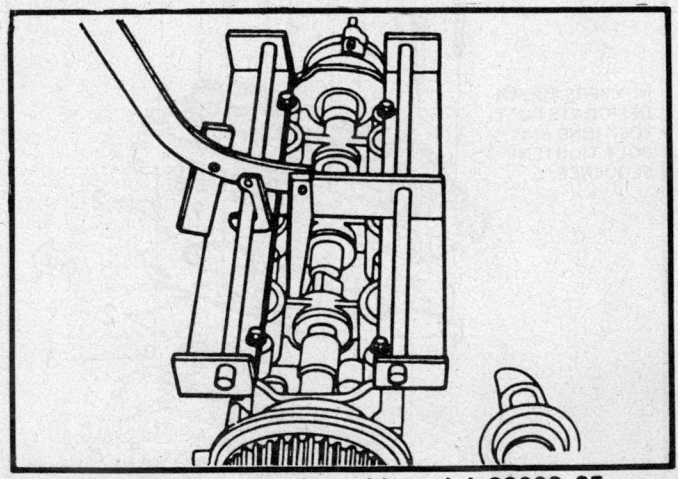

Compressing valve spring with tool J–33302–25

Camshaft

Removal and Installation

2.0L ENGINE

1. Relieve the fuel system pressure.

2. Disconnect the negative battery cable.

3. Remove camshaft carrier cover.

4. Hold valves in place with compressed air, using an air adapter in spark plug hole.

5. Compress valve springs with special valve spring compressing tool.

6. Remove rocker arms. Keep rocker arms in order for reassembly. Remove camshaft sprocket.

7. Using a piece of chalk, mark the rotor position on the distributor housing and the distributor position with the block. Carefully pull the distributor up until the rotor just stops turning and again mark the rotor position for installation. Remove the distributor.

8. Remove camshaft thrust plate from rear of carrier.

9. Remove camshaft by sliding it to the rear.

10. Continue the installation in the reverse of the removal procedure. Use new gaskets and sealant if necessary. Torque the rear thrust plate to 70 inch lbs. and camshaft sprocket retaining bolts to 34 ft. lbs.

2.3L ENGINE—INTAKE CAMSHAFT

NOTE: Any time the camshaft housing to cylinder head bolts are loosened or removed, the camshaft housing to cylinder head gasket must be replaced.

1. Relieve the fuel system pressure. Disconnect the negative battery cable.

2. Remove ignition coil and module assembly electrical connections mark or tag if necessary.

3. Remove 4 ignition coil and module assembly to camshaft housing bolts and remove assembly by pulling straight up. Use a special spark plug boot wire remover tool to remove connector assemblys if stuck to the spark plugs.

4. Remove the idle speed power steering pressure switch connector.

5. Loosen 3 power steering pump pivot bolts and remove drive belt.

6. Disconnect the 2 rear power steering pump bracket to transaxle bolts.

7. Remove the front power steering pump bracket to cylinder block bolt.

8. Disconnect the power steering pump assembly and position aside.

9. Using special tools remove power steering pump drive pulley from intake camshaft.

10. Remove oil/air separator bolts and hoses. Leave the hoses attached to the separator, disconnect from the oil fill, chain housing and intake manifold. Remove as an assembly.

11. Remove vacuum line from fuel pressure regulator and fuel injector harness connector.

12. Disconnect fuel line retaining clamp from bracket on top of intake camshaft housing.

13. Remove fuel rail to camshaft housing retaining bolts.

14. Remove fuel rail from cylinder head. Cover injector openings in cylinder head and cover injector nozzles. Leave fuel lines attached and position fuel rail aside.

15. Disconnect timing chain and housing but do not remove from the engine.

16. Remove intake camshaft housing cover to camshaft housing retaining bolts.

17. Remove intake camshaft housing to cylinder head retaining bolts. Use the reverse of the tightening procedure when loosening camshaft housing to cylinder head retaining bolts. Leave 2 bolts loosely in place to hold the camshaft housing while separating camshaft cover from housing.

18. Push the cover off the housing by threading 4 of the housing to head retaining bolts into the tapped holes in the cam housing cover. Tighten the bolts in evenly so the cover does not bind on the dowel pins.

19. Remove the 2 loosely installed camshaft housing to head bolts and remove cover, discard gaskets.

20. Note the position of the chain sprocket dowel pin for reassembly. Remove camshaft being careful not to damage the camshaft oil seal from camshaft or journals.

21. Remove intake camshaft oil seal from camshaft and discard seal. This seal must be replaced any time the housing and cover are separated.

NOTE: If the camshaft is being replaced, the lifters

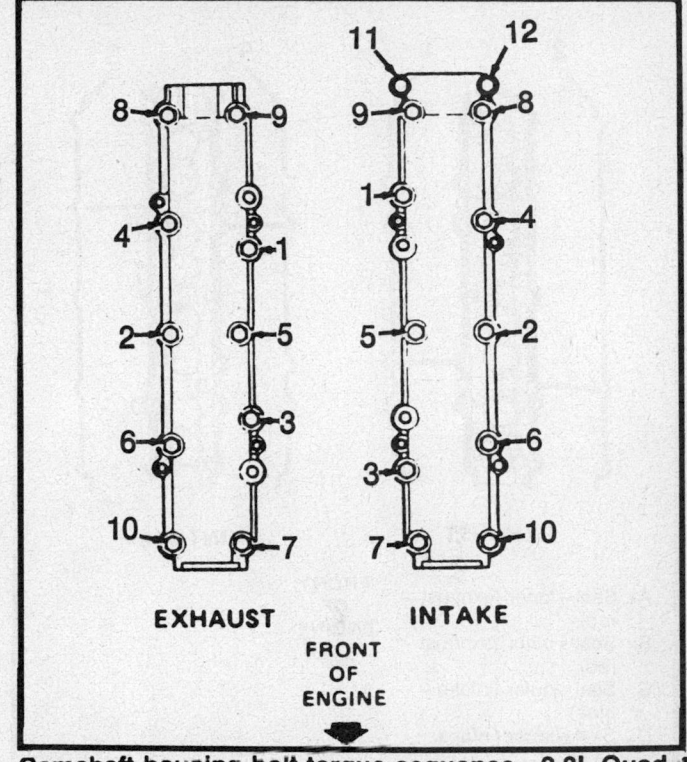

EXHAUST   INTAKE

FRONT OF ENGINE

Camshaft housing bolt torque sequence—2.3l Quad 4

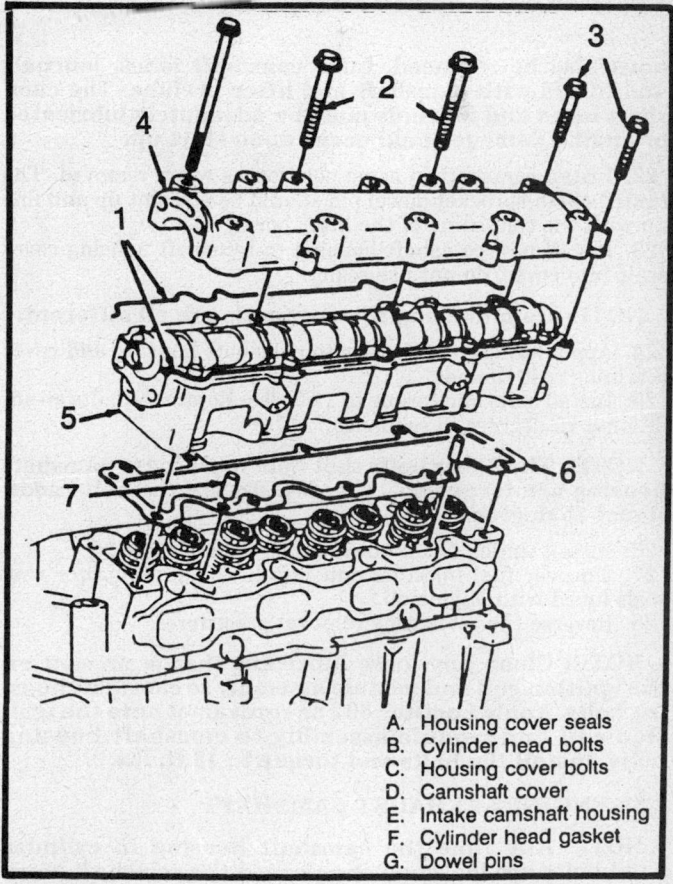

A. Housing cover seals
B. Cylinder head bolts
C. Housing cover bolts
D. Camshaft cover
E. Intake camshaft housing
F. Cylinder head gasket
G. Dowel pins

Camshaft housing assembly—2.3L Quad 4

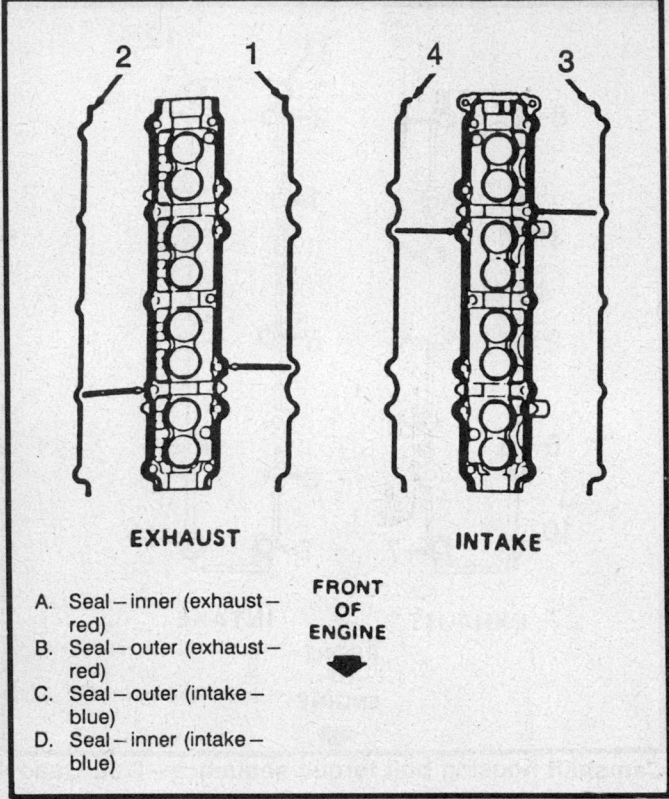

EXHAUST   **INTAKE**

FRONT
OF
ENGINE

A. Seal—inner (exhaust—red)
B. Seal—outer (exhaust—red)
C. Seal—outer (intake—blue)
D. Seal—inner (intake—blue)

Camshaft cover seals—2.3L Quad 4

must also be replaced. Lube camshaft lobes, journals and lifters with camshaft and lifter prelube. The camshaft lobes and journals must be adequately lubricated or engine damage could occur upon start up.

22. Install camshaft in same position as when removed. The timing chain sprocket dowel pin should be straight up and line up with the centerline of the lifter bores.
23. Install new camshaft housing to camshaft housing cover seals into cover, do not use sealer.

NOTE: Cam housing to cover seals are all different.

24. Apply locking type sealer to camshaft housing and cover retaining bolt threads.
25. Install bolts and torque to 11 ft. lbs. Rotate the bolts an additional 75 degrees in sequence.

NOTE: The 2 rear bolts that hold fuel pipe to camshaft housing are torque to 11 ft. lbs. Rotate the bolts additional 25 degrees.

26. Install timing chain housing and timing chain.
27. Uncover fuel injectors and install new fuel injector ring seals lubed with engine oil.
28. Reverse the remaining removal procedures.

NOTE: Clean any loose lubricant that is present on the ignition coil and module assembly to camshaft housing bolts. Apply Loctite® 592 or equivalent onto the ignition coil and module assembly to camshaft housing bolts. Install the bolts and torque to 13 ft. lbs.

2.3L ENGINE—EXHAUST CAMSHAFT

NOTE: Any time the camshaft housing to cylinder head bolts are loosened or removed the camshaft housing to cylinder head gasket must be replaced.

1. Relieve the fuel system pressure. Disconnect the negative battery cable.
2. Remove electrical connection from ignition coil and module assembly.
3. Remove 4 ignition coil and module assembly to camshaft housing bolts and remove assembly by pulling straight up. Use a special tool to remove connector assembly if stuck to the spark plugs.
4. Remove electrical connection from oil pressure switch.
5. Remove transaxle fluid level indicator tube assembly from exhaust camshaft cover and position aside.
6. Remove exhaust camshaft cover and gasket.
7. Disconnect timing chain and housing, but do not remove from the engine.
8. Remove exhaust camshaft housing to cylinder head bolts. Use the reverse of the tightening procedure when loosening camshaft housing while separating camshaft cover from housing.
9. Push the cover off the housing by threading 4 of the housing to head retaining bolts into the tapped holes in the camshaft cover. Tighten the bolts in evenly so the cover does not bind on the dowel pins.
10. Remove the 2 loosely installed camshaft housing to cylinder head bolts and remove cover, discard gaskets.
11. Loosely reinstall 1 camshaft housing to cylinder head bolt to retain the housing during camshaft and lifter removal.
12. Note the position of the chain sprocket dowel pin for reassembly. Remove camshaft being careful not to damage the camshaft or journals

NOTE. If the camshaft is being replaced, the lifters must also be replaced. Lube camshaft lobe, journals and lifters with camshaft and lifter prelube. The camshaft lobes and journals must be adequately lubricated or engine damage could occur upon start up.

13. Install camshaft in same position as when removed. The timing chain sprocket dowel pin should be straight up and line up with the centerline of the lifter bores.
14. Install new camshaft housing to camshaft housing cover seals into cover, no sealer is needed.

NOTE. Cam housing to cover seals are all different.

15. Apply locking type sealer to camshaft housing and cover retaining bolt threads.
16. Install camshaft housing cover to camshaft housing.
17. Install bolts and torque in sequence to 11 ft. lbs. Then rotate the bolts 75 degrees in sequence.
18. Install timing chain housing and timing chain.
19. Install exhaust camshaft housing cover and new gasket and torque to 10 ft. lbs.
20. Reverse the remaining removal procedures.

NOTE: Clean any loose lubricant that is present on the ignition coil and module assembly to camshaft housing bolts. Apply Loctite® 592 or equivalent onto the ignition coil and module assembly to camshaft housing bolts. Install the bolts and torque to 13 ft. lbs.

2.5L ENGINE

NOTE: Relieve the fuel system pressure before disconnecting any fuel lines.

1. Remove the engine from the vehicle. Secure the engine to a holding fixture.
2. Remove the rocker cover, rocker arms and pushrods.
3. Remove the distributor, the spark plug wires and the spark plugs.
4. Remove the pushrod cover, the gasket and the lifters.
5. Remove the alternator, alternator lower bracket and the front engine mount bracket assembly.
6. Remove the oil pump driveshaft and gear assembly.
7. Remove the crankshaft pulley and front cover.

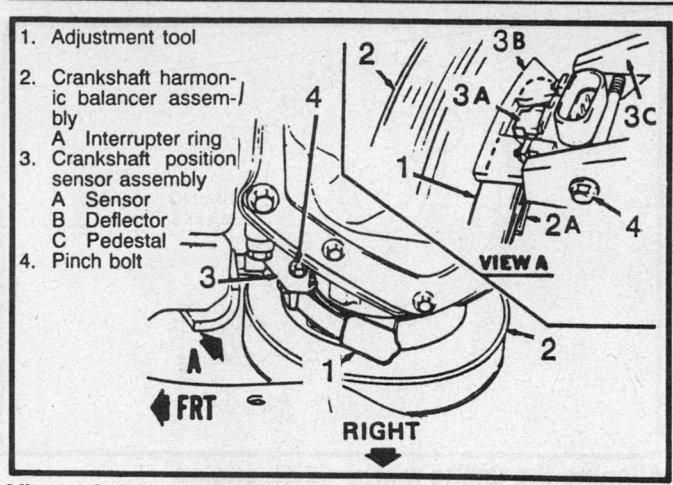

1. Adjustment tool
2. Crankshaft harmon-
   ic balancer assem-
   bly
   A Interrupter ring
3. Crankshaft position
   sensor assembly
   A Sensor
   B Deflector
   C Pedestal
4. Pinch bolt

View of the combination (camshaft/crankshaft) sensor—V6 engine

8. Remove the 2 camshaft thrust plate screws by working through the holes in the gear.
9. Remove the camshaft and gear assembly by pulling it through the front of the block. Take care not to damage the bearings while removing the camshaft.
10. Clean the gasket mounting surfaces. Inspect the parts for wear, scoring and/or damage; if necessary, replace the damaged parts.

NOTE: Coat the camshaft with a liberal amount of clean engine oil supplement before installing

11. Continue the installation in the reverse order of the removal procedure. Use new gaskets and sealant if necessary. Torque the crankshaft pulley-to-crankshaft bolt to 102 ft. lbs. for 1986–90 vehicles and the camshaft thrust plate-to-engine bolts to 90 inch lbs. and the front cover-to-engine bolts to 90 inch lbs.

3.0L AND 3.3L ENGINES

NOTE: Relieve the fuel system pressure before disconnecting any fuel lines.

1. Remove the engine from the vehicle.
2. Remove the intake manifold-to-engine bolts and the manifold.
3. Remove the valve covers, rocker arm assemblies, pushrods and lifters. Keep all parts in order for reassembly.
4. Remove the crankshaft balancer from the crankshaft.
5. Remove the front cover-to-engine bolts and the front cover.
6. Rotate the crankshaft to align the timing marks on the timing sprockets.
7. Remove the camshaft sprocket-to-camshaft bolts and remove the camshaft sprocket and the timing chain.
8. Remove the camshaft retainer bolts and slide the camshaft forward out of the engine block. Take care not to damage the bearings while removing the camshaft.
9. Clean the gasket mounting surfaces. Inspect the parts for wear, scoring and/or damage; if necessary, replace the damaged parts.

NOTE: Coat the camshaft with a liberal amount of clean engine oil prior to installation.

10. Continue the installation in the reverse order of the removal procedure. Use new gaskets and sealant if necessary. Torque the following:
   Camshaft sprocket-to-camshaft bolts
   3.0L engine—19 ft. lbs.

3.3L engine—26 ft. lbs.
Front cover-to-engine bolts
   3.0L engine—22 ft. lbs.
   3.3L engine—22 ft. lbs.
Crankshaft pulley bolt
   3.0L engine—200–225 ft. lbs.
   3.3L engine—219 ft. lbs.
Oil pan-to-front cover bolts
   3.0L engine—88 inch lbs.
   3.3L engine—124 inch lbs.
Water pump pulley bolts
   3.0L engine—97 inch lbs.
   3.3L engine—142 inch lbs.

11. Refill the cooling system. Start the engine, allow the engine to reach normal operating temperature and check for leaks.

Timing Case/Front Cover

Removal and Installation

2.0L ENGINE

1. Disconnect negative battery cable.
2. Remove tensioner and bolt.
3. Remove serpentine belt.
4. Unsnap upper and lower cover.
5. Continue the installation in the reverse order of the removal procedure

2.3L ENGINE

1. Disconnect the negative battery terminal from the battery. Remove coolant recovery reservoir.
2. Remove the serpentine drive belt.

NOTE: To avoid personal injury when rotating the serpentine belt tensioner, use a 13mm wrench that is at least 24 in. long.

3. Remove upper cover fasteners.
4. Raise vehicle and support it safely.
5. Remove right front wheel assembly.
6. Remove right lower splash shield.
7. Remove crankshaft balancer assembly.
8. Remove lower cover fasteners and lower vehicle.
9. Remove the front cover.
10. Continue the installation in the reverse order of the removal procedure. Torque retaining bolt and washer for balancer assembly to 74 ft. lbs.

NOTE: The automatic transaxle crankshaft balancer must not be installed on a manual transaxle engine

2.5L ENGINE

1. Disconnect the negative battery cable.

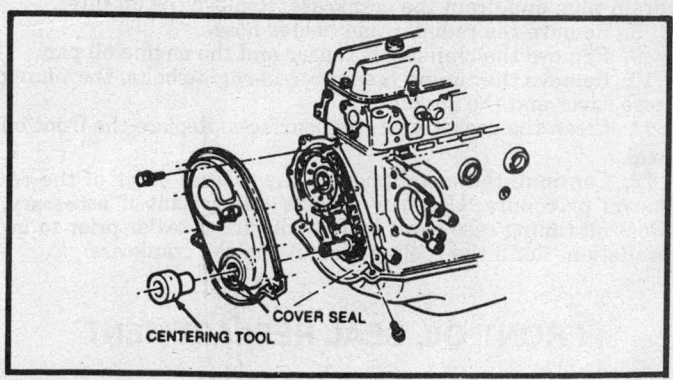

Timing case cover installation; a centering tool can aid in positioning—2.5L engine

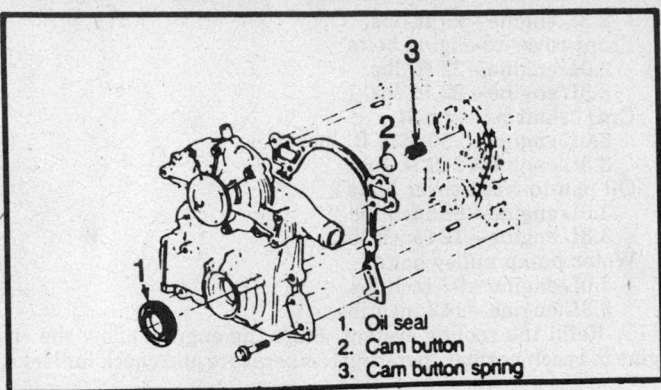

1. Oil seal
2. Cam button
3. Cam button spring

Timing case cover installation; a centering tool can aid in positioning—3.0L and 3.3L engines

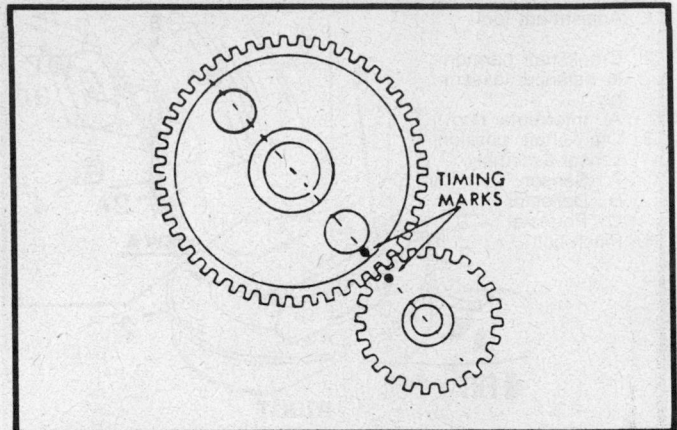

TIMING MARKS

Aligning the timing marks—2.5L engine

2. Raise the vehicle and support it safely. Remove the inner fender splash shield.

3. Remove the fan pulley and the crankshaft pulley hub.

4. Remove the timing case cover-to-engine bolts and the timing case cover.

5. Clean the gasket mounting surfaces.

6. Using RTV sealant, apply a ⅜ in. wide by ³⁄₁₆ in. thick bead to the oil pan/timing case cover.

7. Using RTV sealant, apply a ¼ in. wide by ⅛ in. thick bead to the timing case cover at the engine block mating surfaces.

8. Using a oil seal installation tool, install a new front oil seal.

NOTE: A centering tool which fits over the crankshaft seal and is used to correctly position the timing case cover during installation.

9. Partially tighten the 2 opposing timing case cover screws and tighten the remaining cover screws and remove the centering tool from the timing case cover.

10. Continue the installation in the reverse order of the removal procedure.

3.0L AND 3.3L ENGINES

1. Disconnect the negative battery cable.

2. Position a drain pan under the radiator, open the drain cock and drain the cooling system.

3. Loosen, but do not remove, the water pump pulley bolts. Remove the serpentine drive belt and the pulley.

4. Remove the water pump-to-engine bolts and the water pump.

5. Raise and support the vehicle safely. Remove the right front wheel assembly and the right inner fender splash shield.

6. Remove the crankshaft harmonic balancer.

7. Place an oil drain pan under the crankcase, remove the drain plug and drain the crankcase. Remove the oil filter.

8. Remove the radiator and heater hoses.

9. Remove the crankshaft sensor and the engine oil pan.

10. Remove the timing case cover-to-engine bolts, the timing case cover and the gasket.

11. Clean the gasket mounting surfaces. Replace the front oil seal.

12. Continue the installation in the reverse order of the removal procedure. Use new gaskets and sealant if necessary. Coat all timing case cover bolts with thread sealer prior to installation. Refill the cooling system and the crankcase.

FRONT OIL SEAL REPLACEMENT

1. Disconnect the negative battery cable.
2. Remove the front cover.
3. Using a small pry bar, pry out the old oil seal.

NOTE: Use care to avoid damage to seal bore or seal contact surfaces.

4. Be sure to clean the oil seal mounting surface.

5. Use the appropriate installation tool and drive the oil seal into the front cover.

6. Lubricate balancer and seal lip with clean engine oil.

7. Continue the install reverse of the removal procedure. Use new gaskets and sealant if necessary.

Timing Gears

Removal and Installation

2.5L ENGINE

NOTE: If the camshaft gear is to be replaced, the engine must be removed from the vehicle. The crankshaft gear may be replaced with the engine in the vehicle.

1. Disconnect the negative battery terminal from the battery.

2. Raise and support the vehicle safely.

3. Remove the inner fender splash shield.

4. Remove the accessory drive belts. Remove the crankshaft pulley-to-crankshaft pulley bolt and slide the pulley from the crankshaft.

5. If replacing the camshaft gear, perform the following procedures:

   a. Remove the engine from the vehicle and secure it onto a suitable holding fixture.

   b. Remove the camshaft from the engine.

   c. Using an arbor press, press the camshaft gear from the camshaft.

   d. To install the camshaft gear onto the camshaft, press the gear onto the shaft until a thrust clearance of 0.0015–0.0050 in. exists.

6. If removing the crankshaft gear, perform the following procedures:

   a. Remove the front cover-to-engine bolts.

   b. Remove the retaining bolt and slide the crankshaft gear forward off the crankshaft.

7. Clean the gasket mounting surfaces. Inspect the parts for damage and/or wear; if necessary, replace the damaged parts.

8. Continue the installation in the reverse order of the removal procedure. Align the timing marks, use new gaskets and sealant on the timing cover. Torque the crankshaft pulley-to-crankshaft bolt to 162 ft. lbs. for the 1986–90 and the camshaft thrust plate-to-engine bolts to 90 inch lbs. and the front cover-to-engine bolts to 90 inch lbs.

Timing Chain and Sprockets

Removal and Installation

2.3L ENGINE

NOTE: Prior to removing the timing chain, review the entire procedure.

1. Disconnect the negative battery cable.
2. Remove front engine cover and crankshaft oil slinger.
3. Rotate the crankshaft clockwise, as viewed from front of engine/normal rotation until the camshaft sprockets' timing dowel pin holes line up with the holes in the timing chain housing. The mark on the crankshaft sprocket should line up with the mark on the cylinder block. The crankshaft sprocket keyway should point upwards and line up with the centerline of the cylinder bores. This is the timed position.
4. Remove 3 timing chain guides.
5. Raise vehicle and support in safely.
6. Gently pry off timing chain tensioner spring retainer and remove spring.

NOTE: Two styles of tensioner are used. One with a spring post, early production and 1 without a spring post, late production. Both styles are identical in operation and are interchangeable.

7. Remove timing chain tensioner shoe retainer.
8. Make sure all the slack in the timing chain is above the tensioner assembly; remove the chain tensioner shoe. The timing chain must be disengaged from the wear grooves in the tensioner shoe in order to remove the shoe. Slide a prybar under the timing chain while pulling shoe outward.
9. If difficulty is encountered removing chain tensioner shoe, proceed as follows:
   a. Lower the vehicle.
   b. Hold the intake camshaft sprocket with a holding tool and remove the sprocket bolt and washer.
   c. Remove the washer from the bolt and re-thread the bolt back into the camshaft by hand, the bolt provides a surface to push against.
   d. Remove intake camshaft sprocket using a 3-jaw puller in the 3 relief holes in the sprocket. Do not attempt to pry the sprocket off the camshaft or damage to the sprocket or chain housing could occur. Remove tensioner assembly retaining bolts and tensioner.

— CAUTION —

Tensioner piston is spring loaded and could fly out causing personal injury.

10. Remove chain housing to block stud (timing chain tensioner shoe pivot).
11. Remove timing chain

NOTE: Failure to follow this procedure could result in severe engine damage.

12. Tighten intake camshaft sprocket retaining bolt and washer, to specification while holding sprocket with tool J–36013 if removed.
13. Install a special tool through holes in camshaft sprockets into holes in timing chain housing, this positions the camshafts for correct timing.
14. If the camshafts are out of position and must be rotated more than ⅛ turn in order to install the alignment dowel pins:
   a. The crankshaft must be rotated 90 degrees clockwise off of TDC in order to give the valves adequate clearance to open.
   b. Once the camshafts are in position and the dowels installed, rotate the crankshaft counterclockwise back to top dead center. Do not rotate the crankshaft clockwise to TDC, valve or piston damage could occur.
15. Install timing chain over exhaust camshaft sprocket, around idler sprocket and around crankshaft sprocket.
16. Remove the alignment dowel pin from the intake camshaft. Using a dowel pin remover tool rotate the intake camshaft sprocket counterclockwise enough to slide the timing chain over the intake camshaft sprocket. Release the camshaft sprocket wrench. The length of chain between the 2 camshaft sprockets will tighten. If properly timed, the intake camshaft alignment dowel pin should slide in easily. If the dowel pin does not fully index, the camshafts are not timed correctly and the procedure must be repeated.
17. Leave the alignment dowel pins installed.
18. With slack removed from chain between intake camshaft sprocket and crankshaft sprocket, the timing marks on the crankshaft and the cylinder block should be aligned. If marks are not aligned, move the chain 1 tooth forward or rearward, remove slack and recheck marks.
19. Tighten chain housing to block stud (timing chain tensioner shoe pivot). Stud is installed under the timing chain. Tighten to 19 ft. lbs.
20. Reload timing chain tensioner assembly to its zero position as follows:
   a. Assemble restraint cylinder, spring and nylon plug into plunger. Index slot in restraint cylinder with peg in plunger. While rotating the restraint cylinder clockwise, push the restraint cylinder into the plunger until it bottoms. Keep rotating the restraint cylinder clockwise but allow the spring to push it out of the plunger. The pin in the plunger will lock the restraint in the loaded position.
   b. Install tool J–36589 or equivalent onto plunger assembly.
   c. Install plunger assembly into tensioner body with the long end toward the crankshaft when installed.
21. Install tensioner assembly to chain housing. Recheck plunger assembly installation. It is correctly installed when the long end is toward the crankshaft.
22. Install and tighten timing chain tensioner bolts and tighten to 10 ft. lbs.
23. Install tensioner shoe and tensioner shoe retainer.
24. Remove special tool J–36589 and squeeze plunger assembly into tensioner body to unload the plunger assembly.
25. Lower vehicle enough to reach and remove the alignment dowel pins. Rotate crankshaft clockwise 2 full rotations. Align crankshaft timing mark with mark on cylinder block and reinstall alignment dowel pins. Alignment dowel pins will slide in easily if engine is timed correctly.

NOTE: If the engine is not correctly timed, severe engine damage could occur.

26. Install 3 timing chain guides and crankshaft oil slinger.
27. Install engine front cover.
28. Start engine and check for oil leaks.

3.0L AND 3.3L ENGINES

1. Disconnect the negative battery cable.
2. Position a drain pan under the radiator, open the drain cock and drain the cooling system. Disconnect the cooling hose from the water pump.
3. Raise and support the vehicle safely.
4. Remove the inner fender splash shield.
5. Remove the serpentine drive belt.
6. Remove the crankshaft pulley-to-crankshaft bolt and slide the pulley from the crankshaft.
7. Remove the front cover-to-engine bolts and the cover.
8. Rotate the crankshaft to align the timing marks on the sprockets.
9. Remove the camshaft sprocket-to-camshaft bolts, remove the camshaft sprocket and chain.
10. Remove the crankshaft sprocket by sliding it forward.
11. Clean the gasket mounting surfaces. Inspect the timing chain and the sprockets for damage and/or wear; if necessary, replace the damaged components.

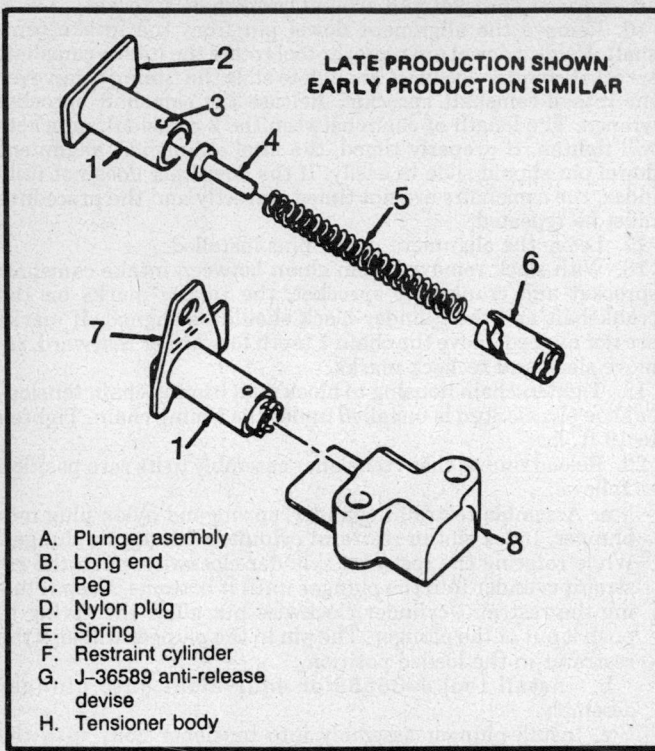

LATE PRODUCTION SHOWN
EARLY PRODUCTION SIMILAR

A. Plunger asembly
B. Long end
C. Peg
D. Nylon plug
E. Spring
F. Restraint cylinder
G. J–36589 anti-release devise
H. Tensioner body

Timing chain tensioner—2.3L Quad 4

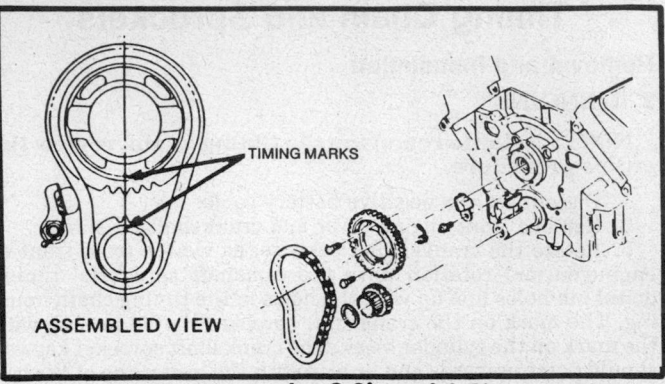

TIMING MARKS

ASSEMBLED VIEW

Aligning the timing marks—3.0L and 3.3L engines

12. Continue the installation in the reverse order of the removal procedure. Use a new gasket and sealant. Make sure the timing marks are aligned on the sprockets.

13. Torque the following:
   Camshaft sprocket-to-camshaft bolts—19 ft. lbs.
   Front cover-to-engine bolts—22 ft. lbs.
   Crankshaft pulley bolt—200–225 ft. lbs.
   Oil pan-to-front cover bolts—88 inch lbs.
   Water pump pulley bolts—97 inch lbs.

14. Refill the cooling system. Start the engine, allow the engine to reach normal operating temperature and check for leaks.

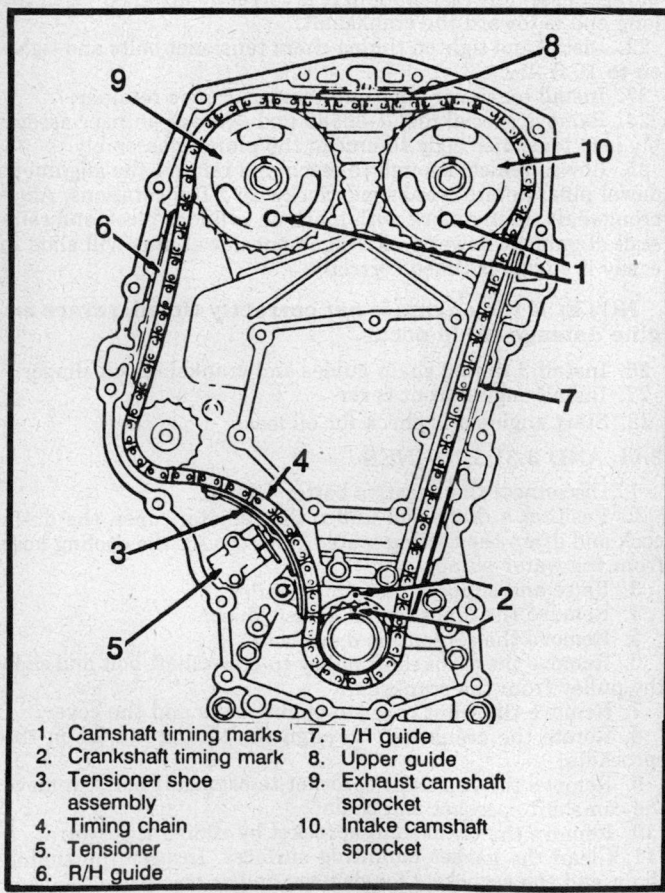

1.	Camshaft timing marks	7.	L/H guide
2.	Crankshaft timing mark	8.	Upper guide
3.	Tensioner shoe assembly	9.	Exhaust camshaft sprocket
4.	Timing chain	10.	Intake camshaft sprocket
5.	Tensioner		
6.	R/H guide		

Timing chain installation—2.3L Quad 4

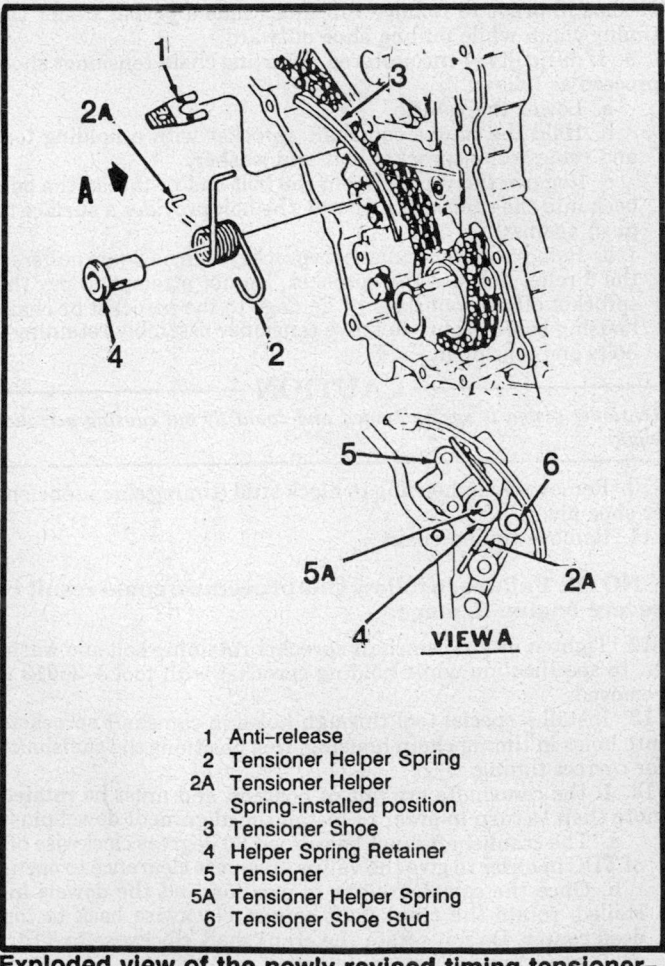

VIEW A

1	Anti–release
2	Tensioner Helper Spring
2A	Tensioner Helper Spring-installed position
3	Tensioner Shoe
4	Helper Spring Retainer
5	Tensioner
5A	Tensioner Helper Spring
6	Tensioner Shoe Stud

Exploded view of the newly revised timing tensioner—1987–88 2.3L engine

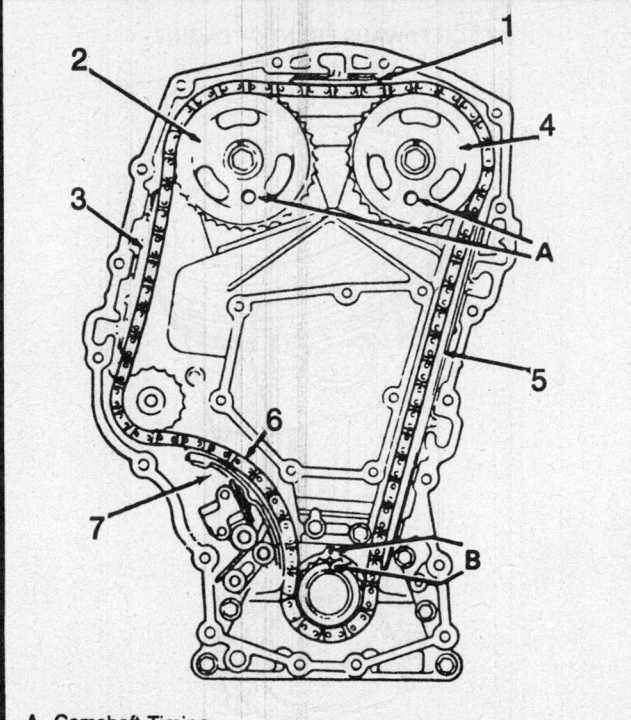

A Camshaft Timing-
   Alignment Pin Locations
B Crankshaft Gear-Timing
   Marks
1 Upper Timing Chain
   Guide
2 Exhaust Camshaft
   Sprocket
3 Intake Camshaft
   Sprocket
4 L.H. Timing Chain Guide
5 Timing Chain
6 Timing Chain Tensioner
   Shoe Assembly
7 Timing Chain Tensioner

Newly revised timing tensioner and chain, installed position–2.3L engine

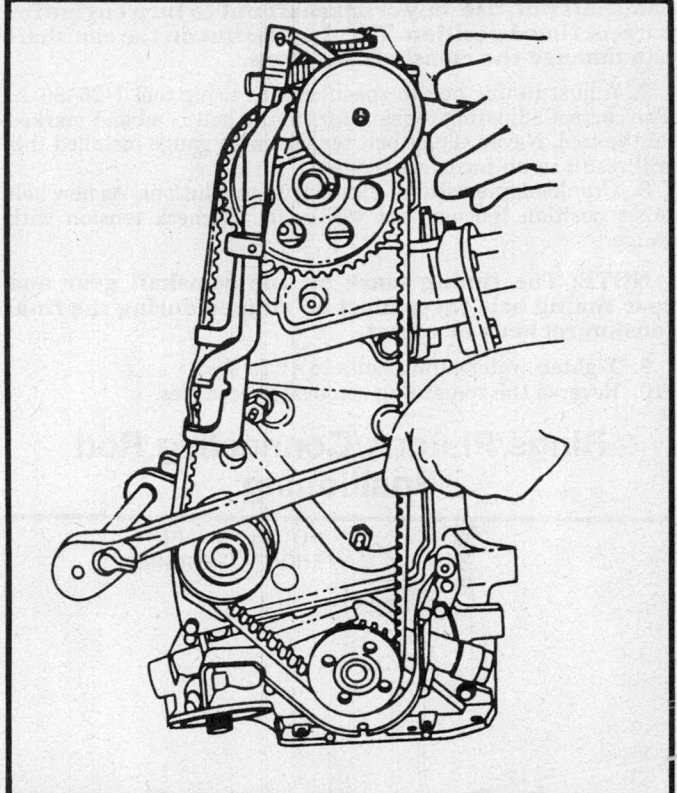

Timing belt adjustment 2.0L

NOTE: The new shoe has an integral lock to retain the shoe to the new stud.

7. Install the tensioner helper spring on the post of the timing chain tensioner.
8. Push the plastic retainer sleeve on to the helper spring post on the tensioner to retain the helper spring.
9. Remove the anti-release from the tensioner and squeeze the plunger assembly into the tensioner body to unload the plunger.
10. Inspect the tensioner shoe helper spring for the correct position.
11. Position the camshaft and crankshaft in correct timing positions.
12. Install the new timing chain and related components supplied in the kit. Use new gaskets.

Timing Belt and Tensioner

Removal and Installation

2.0L ENGINE

1. Disconnect negative battery cable.
2. Remove timing belt cover.
3. Remove crankshaft pulley.
4. Drain radiator and remove coolant reservoir.
5. Loosen water pump bolts and remove timing belt.
6. Install new timing belt and crankshaft pulley.

INCREASING TIMING CHAIN TENSION SERVICE BULLETIN

2.3L ENGINE

Some 1987–88 vehicles equipped with the 2.3L engine may exhibit a light knocking and/or rattle noise noticeable from the timing chain housing and water pump area. This noise is most prevalent at or slightly above idle speed with the engine at normal operating temperature. This noise is usually caused by low timing chain tension. A service kit is available to increase the timing chain tension and thereby reduce the noise. The kit includes the following:
Timing chain
Timing chain tensioner shoe
Timing chain tensioner shoe stud
Timing chain tensioner helper
Timing chain tensioner helper spring
Helper spring retainer sleeve
Timing chain housing cover gasket

Removal and Installation

1. Disconnect the negative battery cable.
2. Remove front engine cover and crankshaft oil slinger.
3. Remove the timing chain and chain tensioner.
4. Install the new timing chain tensioner shoe stud. Torque the retainer bolt–19 ft. lbs. (26 Nm).
5. Install the new timing chain tensioner to chain housing. Torque retainer bolts to 10 ft. lbs. (14 Nm).
6. Install the new timing chain shoe-to-shoe stud.

NOTE: Check if the mark on the camshaft sprocket lines up with mark on the rear timing belt cover. The timing mark on the crankshaft pulley should line up at 10 degrees BTDC on the indicator scale. Do not turn the

camshaft nut, use only crankshaft nut to turn engine for correct timed position. Turning the nut on the camshaft can damage the camshaft bearings.

7. Adjust timing belt to specifications using tool J–26486–A. The correct adjusting tension for timing belt is a band marked on the tool. Never adjust belt tension with gauge installed this will result in an incorrect reading.

8. Crank engine without starting 10 revolutions. As new belt takes position tension loss will occur. Recheck tension with gauge.

NOTE: The timing mark on the camshaft gear and rear timing belt cover must be aligned during the final tension recheck or reset.

9. Tighten water pump bolts to 18 ft. lbs.

10. Reverse the remaining removal procedures.

Rings/Pistons/Connecting Rod Positioning

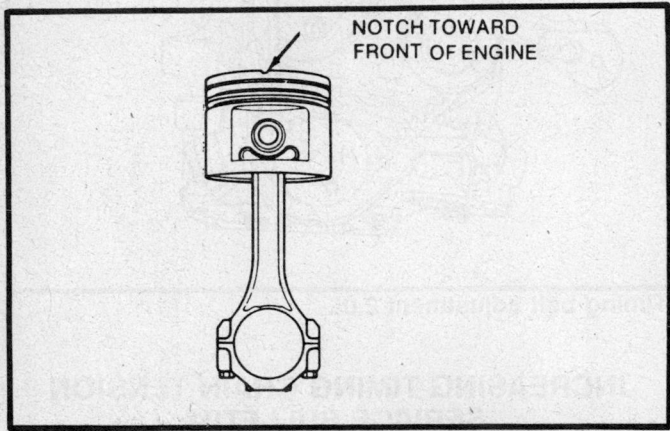

Piston Identification–3.0L and 3.3L engines

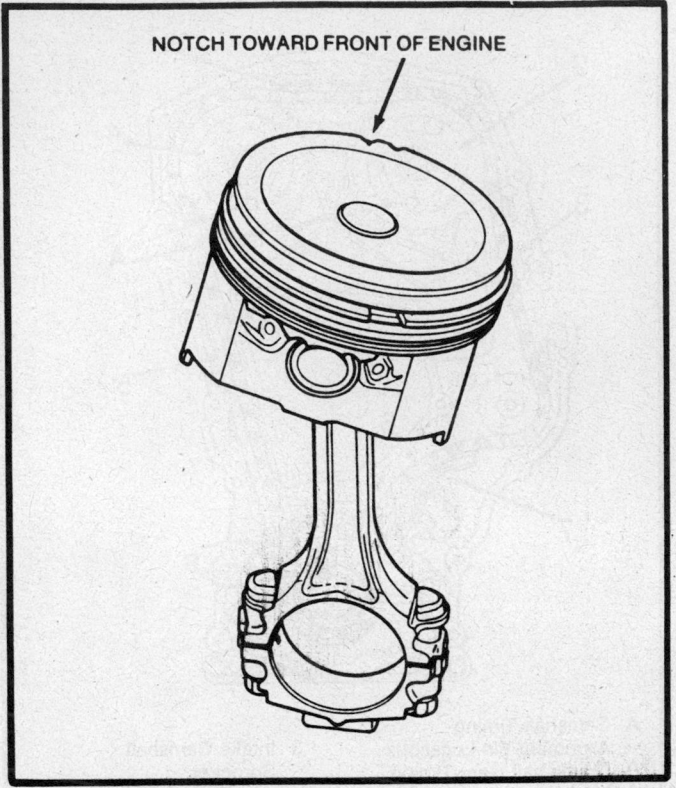

Piston Identification – 2.5L engine

ENGINE LUBRICATION

Oil Pan

Removal and Installaion

2.0L ENGINE

1. Disconnect the negative battery cable.
2. Raise and support the vehicle safely.
3. Remove the right front wheel assembly.
4. Remove the front splash shield.
5. Drain the crankcase.
6. Remove the exhaust pipe from the turbocharger wastegate.
7. Remove the flywheel cover bolts.
8. Remove the oil pan retaining bolts.
9. Remove the oil pan, gasket and oil pan scraper.
10. Continue the installation in the reverse order of the removal procedure. Use a new gasket and sealant. Torque oil pan bolts to 4 ft. lbs.

2.3L ENGINE

1. Disconnect the negative battery cable.
2. Raise and support the vehicle safely.
2. Remove the flywheel inspection cover.
3. Remove the splash shield-to-suspension support bolt.
4. Remove the radiator outlet pipe-to-oil pan bolt.

5. Remove the transaxle-to-oil pan nut and stud using a 7mm socket.
6. Gently pry the spacer out from between oil pan and transaxle.
7. Remove the oil pan bolts. Remove the oil pan from the engine.
8. Continue the installation in the reverse order of the removal procedures. Torque vertical retaining bolts **A** and **C**, looking straight up at installed oil pan – 106 inch lbs. Torque the horizontal retaining bolts **B** – 17 ft. lbs.

NOTE: The crankshaft may have to be rotated to gain clearance.

2.5L ENGINE

NOTE: If the vehicle is equipped with a manual transaxle, it is necessary to remove the engine before the oil pan can be remove from its mounting.

1. Disconnect the negative battery cable.
2. Raise and support the vehicle safely. Drain the engine oil.
3. Disconnect the exhaust pipe and hangers from the exhaust manifold, allow it to swing out of the way.
4. Disconnect electrical connectors from the starter. Remove the starter-to-engine bolts, the starter and the flywheel housing inspection cover from the engine.

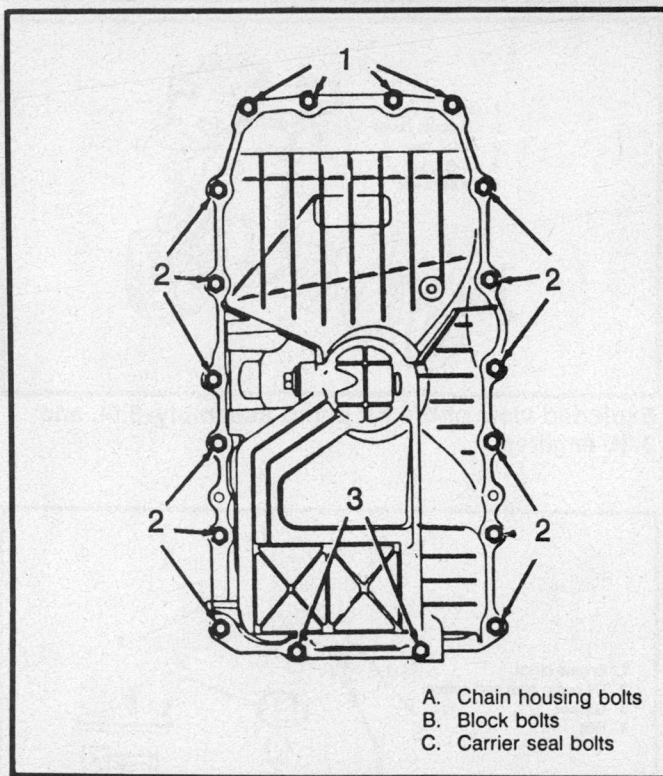

A. Chain housing bolts
B. Block bolts
C. Carrier seal bolts

Oil pan installation—2.3L Quad 4

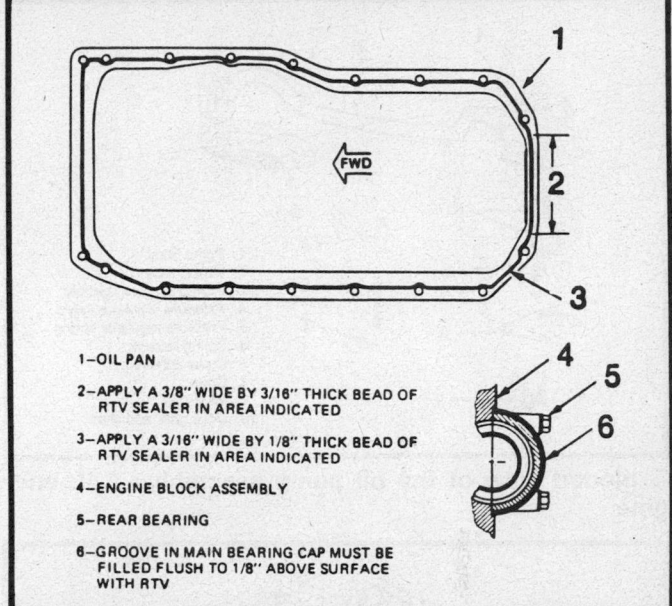

1—OIL PAN
2—APPLY A 3/8" WIDE BY 3/16" THICK BEAD OF RTV SEALER IN AREA INDICATED
3—APPLY A 3/16" WIDE BY 1/8" THICK BEAD OF RTV SEALER IN AREA INDICATED
4—ENGINE BLOCK ASSEMBLY
5—REAR BEARING
6—GROOVE IN MAIN BEARING CAP MUST BE FILLED FLUSH TO 1/8" ABOVE SURFACE WITH RTV

Applying sealant to the oil pan—2.5L engine

5. Remove the oil pan-to-engine bolts and the oil pan.
6. Using a gasket scraper, clean the gasket mounting surfaces.
7. Apply a small amount of sealant at the rear bearing depressions where the oil pan engages the block.
8. Apply a small amount of sealant at the front timing gear cover at the block mating surfaces.
9. Apply a ⅛ × ¼ in. long bead of sealant along the flange of the oil pan; be sure to keep the sealant inside of the bolt holes.
10. Continue the installaion in the reverse order of the removal procedure. Torque the oil pan-to-engine bolts—20 ft. lbs. Refill the crankcase with oil, start the engine, allow it to reach normal operating temperature and check for leaks.

NOTE: The bolts into the front cover should be installed last; they are installed at an angle and the holes line up after the rest of the pan bolts are snugged up.

3.0L AND 3.3L ENGINES

1. Disconnect the negative battery cable.
2. Raise and support the vehicle safely.
3. Position an oil drain pan under the engine, remove the drain plug and drain the engine oil.
4. Remove the flywheel cover.
5. Remove the starter.
6. Remove the oil filter.
7. Remove the oil pan-to-engine bolts and the oil pan tensioner spring, located behind the oil filter adapter.
8. Remove the oil pan from the engine.
9. Clean the gasket mounting surfaces.
10. Continue the installation in the reverse order of the removal procedure. Use sealant if necessary and a new gasket. Torque the oil pan-to-engine bolts—88 inch lbs. for the 3.0L engine and 124 inch lbs. for the 3.3L engine. Refill the crankcase, operate the engine to normal operating temperature and check for leaks.

Oil Pump

Removal and Installation

2.0L ENGINE

1. Disconnect negative battery cable.
2. Remove crankshaft sprocket.
3. Remove rear timing belt cover.
4. Disconnect and tag oil pressure electrical connection.
5. Raise and support the vehicle safely.
6. Drain the engine oil.
7. Remove oil pan and oil filter.
8. Remove oil pump and pickup tube.
9. Remove front oil seal from housing.
10. Continue the installation in the reverse order of the removal procedure. Torque oil pump to 5 ft. lbs. and use a new ring for pickup tube.

2.3L ENGINE

1. Disconnect the negative battery cable.
2. Raise and support the vehicle safely.
3. Remove the retaining bolts and the oil pan.
4. Remove the oil pump assembly retainers, bolts and nut.
5. Remove the oil pump assembly and shims if so equipped.

NOTE: Oil pump drive gear backlash must be checked when any of the following components are replaced: oil pump assembly, oil pump drive gear, crankshaft and cylinder block.

6. Continue the installation in the reverse order of the removal procedure. Torque oil pump to block bolts—33 ft.lbs.

2.5L ENGINE

NOTE: In 1987, a force balancer assembly is used on some engines. In 1988–90, a force balancer assembly is used on all engines. The force balancer includes a Gerotor type oil pump. The oil pump drives off the back side of one of the balance shafts. On these engines with Gerotor type oil pump, the oil filter is serviced through an opening in the oil pan. The following procedure is for gear type oil pump, which is driven off the camshaft. It is not necessary to remove the balancer assembly when

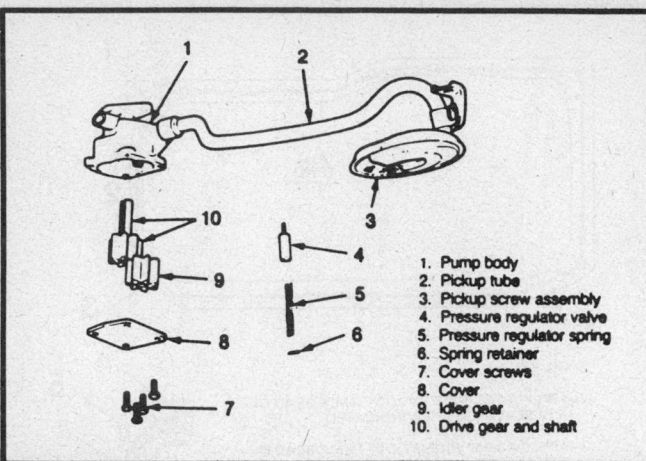

1. Pump body
2. Pickup tube
3. Pickup screw assembly
4. Pressure regulator valve
5. Pressure regulator spring
6. Spring retainer
7. Cover screws
8. Cover
9. Idler gear
10. Drive gear and shaft

Exploded view of the oil pump assembly—2.5L engine

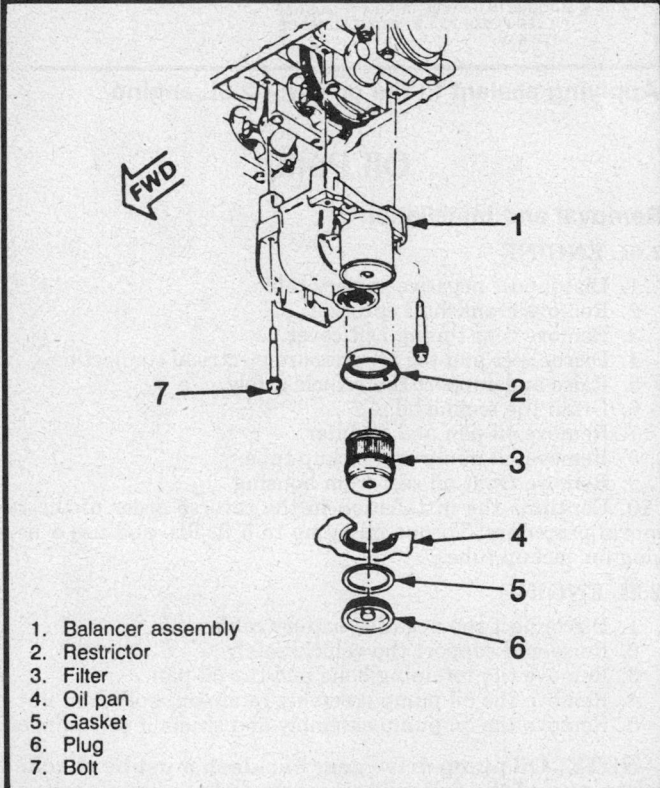

1. Balancer assembly
2. Restrictor
3. Filter
4. Oil pan
5. Gasket
6. Plug
7. Bolt

Force balancer assembly 2.5L

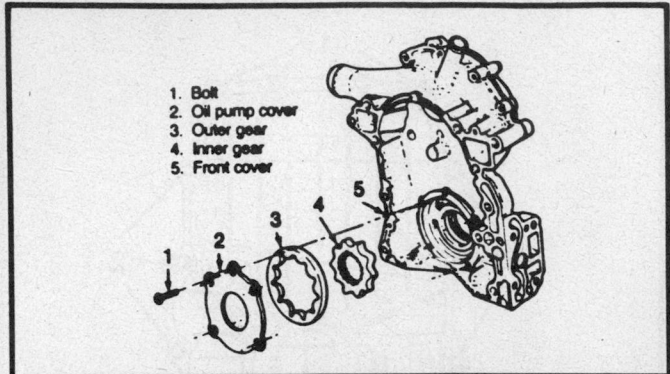

1. Bolt
2. Oil pump cover
3. Outer gear
4. Inner gear
5. Front cover

Exploded view of the oil pump assembly—3.0L and 3.3L engines

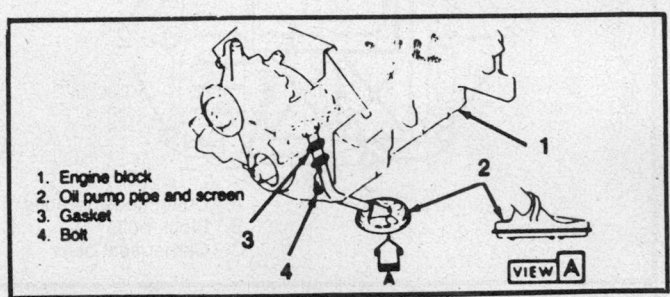

1. Engine block
2. Oil pump pipe and screen
3. Gasket
4. Bolt

VIEW A

View of the oil pump and screen assembly—3.0L and 3.3L engines

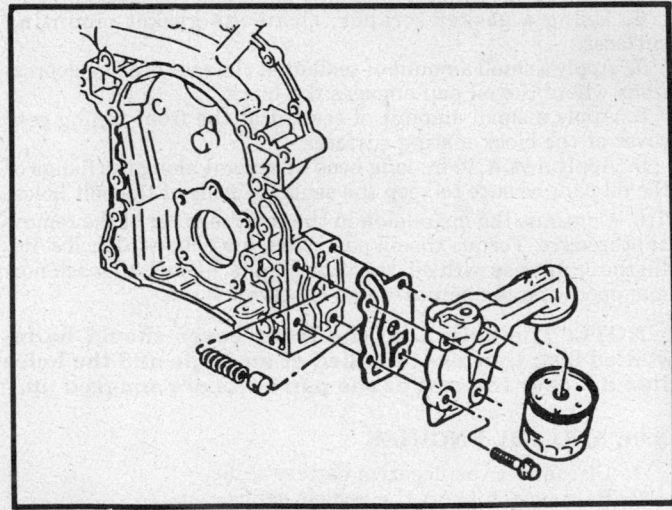

Oil filter and adapter assembly—3.3L engine

servicing the pump or presure regulator. However should the balancer be removed, it must be rebalanced.

1. Disconnect the negative battery cable.
2. Raise and support the vehicle safely.
3. Remove the oil pan-to-engine bolts and the oil pan.
4. Remove the oil pump-to-engine bolts.
5. Remove the oil pump, pipe and screen as an assembly.
6. Continue the installation in the reverse order of the removal procedure. Torque the oil pump-to-engine bolts to 22 ft. lbs., the oil pan-to-engine bolts to 20 ft. lbs.
7. Refill the crankcase with new oil. Start the engine, allow it to reach normal operating temperature and check for leaks.

3.0L AND 3.3L ENGINES

1. Disconnect the negative battery cable.
2. Remove the front cover.
3. Raise the vehicle and support it safely.
4. Drain the engine oil. Lower the vehicle.
5. Remove the oil filter adapter, the pressure regulator valve and the valve spring.
6. Remove the oil pump cover-to-oil pump screws and the cover.
7 Remove the oil pump gears.
8. Using a gasket scraper, clean the gasket mounting surfaces. Using solvent, clean all of the parts. Inspect the parts for wear, scoring and/or damage.

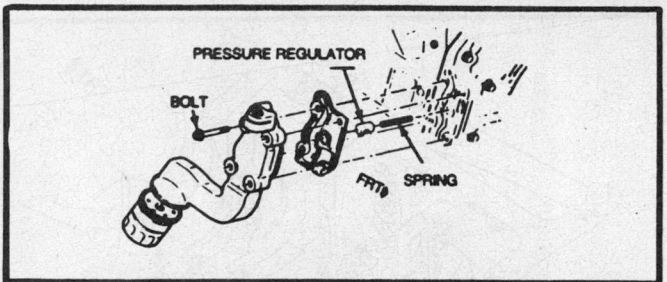

Exploded view of the oil filter adapter—3.0L engine

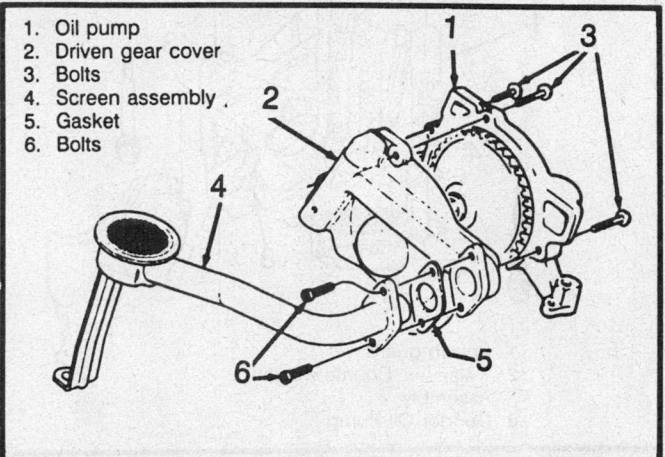

1. Oil pump
2. Driven gear cover
3. Bolts
4. Screen assembly
5. Gasket
6. Bolts

Oil pump assembly—2.3L Quad 4

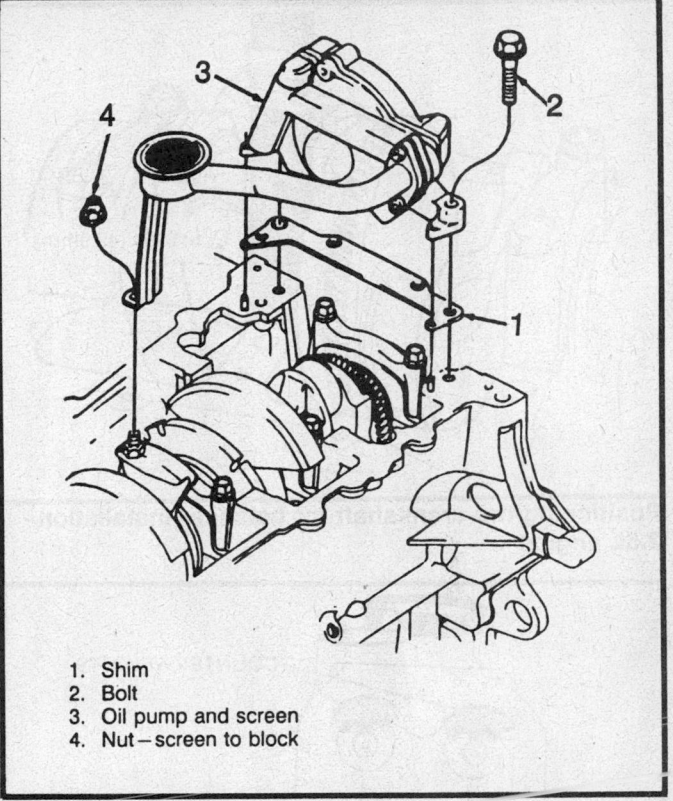

1. Shim
2. Bolt
3. Oil pump and screen
4. Nut—screen to block

Oil pump installation

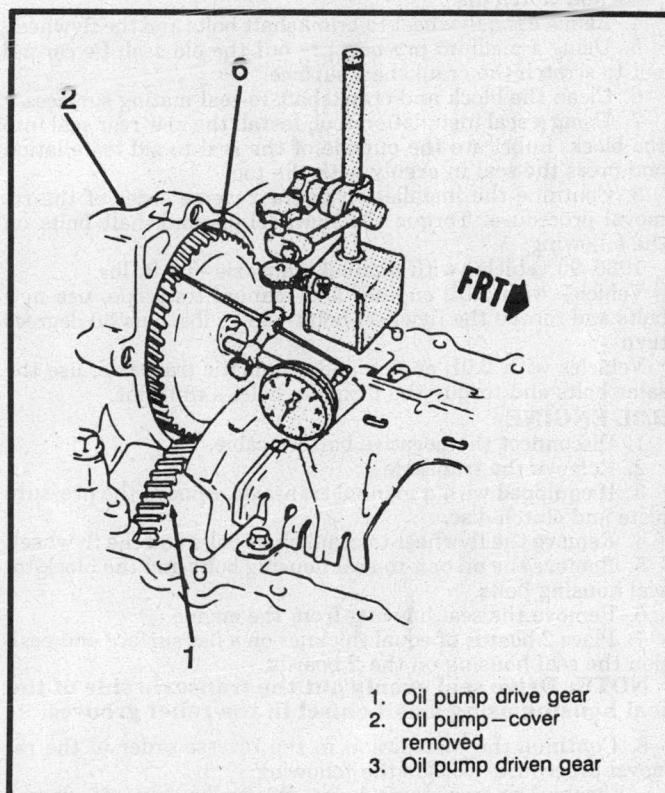

1. Oil pump drive gear
2. Oil pump—cover removed
3. Oil pump driven gear

Measuring oil pump driven gear backlash

9. To assemble, perform the following procedures:
   a. Using engine oil, lubricate the oil pump gears.
   b. Using petroleum jelly, pack the pump cavity.
   c. Install the oil pump cover-to-oil pump and torque the screws to 97 inch lbs.
10. Continue the installation in the reverse order of the removal procedure. Torque the oil filter adapter-to-engine bolts to 30 ft. lbs. for the 3.0L and 24 ft. lbs., for the 3.3L engine.

OIL PUMP DRIVE GEAR BACKLASH

Adjustment
2.3L ENGINE

1. With oil pump assembly off engine, remove 3 retaining bolts and separate the driven gear cover and screen assembly from the oil pump.
2. Install the oil pump on the block using the original shims. Tighten the bolts to 33 ft. lbs.
3. Install the dial indicator assembly to measure backlash between oil pump to drive gear.
4. Record oil pump drive to driven gear backlash correct backlash clearance is 0.010–0.014. When taking measurement crankshaft cannot move.
5. Remove shims to decrease clearance and add shims to increase clearance.
6. When proper clearance is reached rotate crankshaft ½ turn and recheck clearance.
7. Remove oil pump from block reinstall driven gear cover and screen assembly to pump and tighten to 106 inch lbs.
8. Reinstall the pump assembly on block. Torque oil pump-to-block bolts 33 ft.lbs.

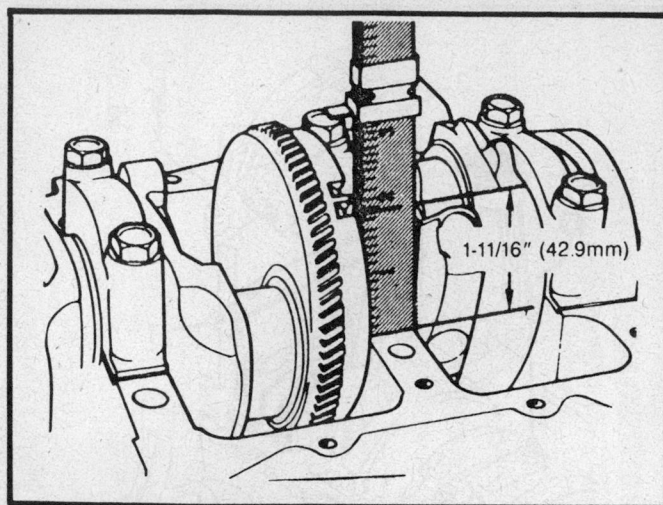

Positioning the crankshaft for balancer installation— 2.5L engine

Balancer counterwieght positions—2.5L engine

FORCE BALANCER

Removal and Installation

2.5L ENGINE

1. Disconnect the negative battery cable.
2. Raise and support the vehicle safely.
3. Remove the oil pan.
4. Remove the balancer retaining bolts and remove the balancer from the engine.

To install,

5. Turn the crankshaft to top center, No. 1 cylinder on compression stroke TDC.
6. Measure the distance from the engine block to the first cut of the double notch on the reluctor ring. This dimension should be 1 $\frac{11}{16}$ in. (42.8mm).
7. Mount the balancer with the counterweights parallel and pointing away from the crankshaft.
8. Install the retaining bolts and tighten as follows:
   Short bolts—9 ft. lbs. (12 Nm) plus 75 degree turn
   Long bolts—9 ft. lbs. (12 Nm) plus 90 degree turn
9. Install the oil pan and retaining bolts. Torque the oil pan bolts—20 ft. lbs. (27 Nm).

Rear Main Oil Seal

Removal and Installation

2.0L and 2.5L ENGINES

1. Disconnect the negative battery cable.
2. Remove the transaxle.

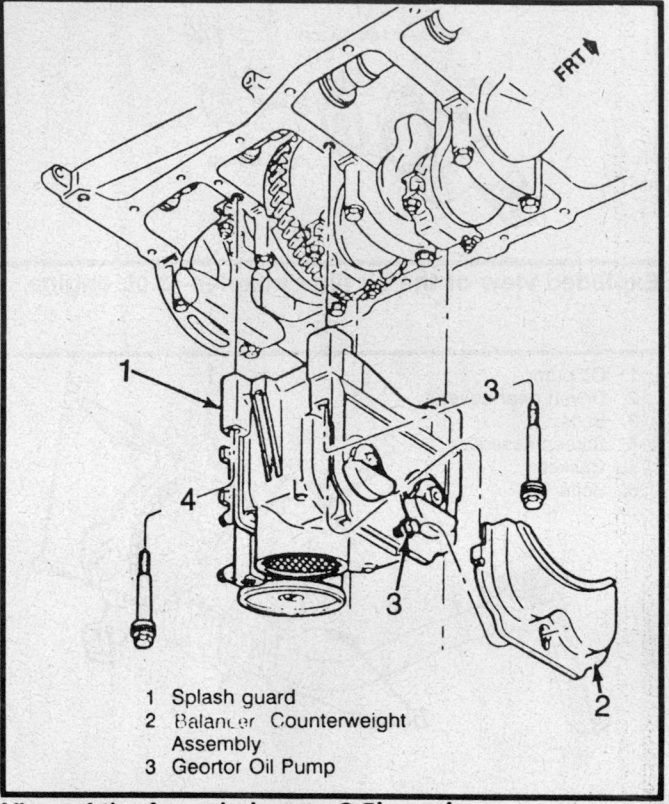

1 Splash guard
2 Balancer Counterweight Assembly
3 Geortor Oil Pump

View of the force balancer—2.5L engine

3. If equipped with a manual transaxle, remove the pressure plate and clutch disc.
4. Remove the flywheel-to-crankshaft bolts and the flywheel.
5. Using a medium pry bar, pry out the old seal; Be careful not to scratch the crankshaft surface.
6. Clean the block and crankshaft-to-seal mating surfaces.
7. Using a seal installation tool, install the new rear seal into the block. Lubricate the outside of the seal to aid installation and press the seal in evenly with the tool.
8. Continue the installation in the reverse order of the removal procedure. Torque the flywheel-to-crankshaft bolts on the following:
   1986–90 vehicles with manual transaxle—69 ft. lbs.
   Vehicles with 2.0L engines and manual transaxle, use new bolts and torque the flywheel bolts—48 ft. lbs. plus 30 degrees turn.
   Vehicles with 2.0L engine and automatic transaxle, use the same bolts and torque the flexplate bolts—48 ft. lbs.

2.3L ENGINE

1. Disconnect the negative battery cable.
2. Remove the transaxle.
3. If equipped with a manual transaxle, remove the pressure plate and clutch disc.
4. Remove the flywheel-to-crankshaft bolts and the flywheel.
5. Remove the oil pan-to-seal housing bolts and the block-to-seal housing bolts.
6. Remove the seal housing from the engine.
7. Place 2 boards of equal thickness on a flat surface and position the seal housing on the 2 boards.

NOTE: Drive seal evenly out the transaxle side of the seal housing using small chisel in the relief grooves.

8. Continue the installation in the reverse order of the removal procedure. Torque the following:
   Flywheel-to-crankshaft bolts—22 ft. lbs. plus 45 degree turn
   Flywheel-to-converter bolts—46 ft. lbs.

3.0L AND 3.3L ENGINES

The rear main oil seal is a 2-piece, rope type and is located to the rear of the main bearing.

1. Raise and support the vehicle safely.
2. Position a oil drain pan under the engine, remove the drain plug and drain the oil. Remove the oil pan-to-engine bolts and the oil pan.
3. Remove the rear main bearing cap-to-engine bolts and the bearing cap from the engine.
4. Remove the old seal from the bearing cap.

NOTE: If a new rope seal is used, the crankshaft must be removed to avoid this procedure, part of the original seal can be used in the following manner.

5. Using a seal packing tool, insert it against one end of the seal in the cylinder block. Pack the old seal into the groove until it is packed tight, repeat the procedure on the other end of the seal.
6. Measure the amount the seal was driven up and add approximately $\frac{1}{16}$ in. Cut this length from the old seal removed from the lower bearing cap, repeat for the other side.

NOTE: When cutting the seal into short lengths, use a double edge blade and the lower bearing cap as a holding fixture.

7. Using a seal packer guide, install it onto the cylinder block.
8. Using the packing tool, work the short pieces into the guide tool and pack into the cylinder block until the tool hits the built-in stop.

NOTE: It may help to use oil on the short seal pieces when packing into the block.

9. Repeat Steps 7 and 8 for the other side.
10. Remove the guide tool.
11. Install a new rope seal into the lower bearing cap.
12. Install the lower main bearing cap and torque the bolts as folllows:
Main bearing caps:
    3.0L engine—100 ft. lbs. (135 Nm)
    3.3L engine—90 ft. lbs. (122 Nm)
13. Continue the installation in the reverse order of the removal procedure. Torque the oil pan-to-engine bolts to 88 inch lbs. for the 3.0L engine and 124 inch lbs. for the 3.3L engine. Refill the crankcase. Start the engine, allow it to reach normal operating temperature and check for leaks.

Connecting and Main Bearings

Replacement

CONNECTING ROD BEARINGS

Connecting rod bearings consist of 2 halves or shells which are interchangeable in the rod and cap. When the shells are placed into position, the ends extend slightly beyond the rod and cap surfaces, so when the rod bolts are torqued, the shells will be clamped tightly in place to insure positive seating. To prevent turning, a tang holds the shells in place.

NOTE: The ends of the bearing shells must never be filed flush with the mating surface of the rod and cap. Under no circumstances should the rod end or cap be

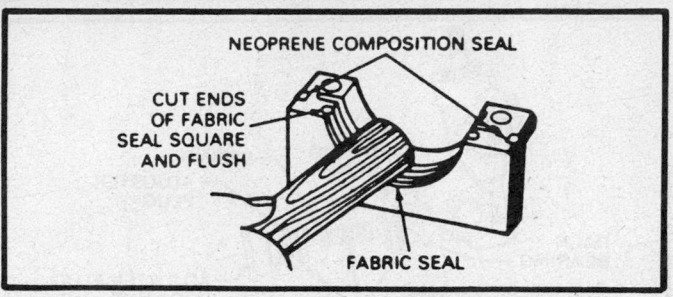

Installing the rear main bearing cap oil seal–3.0L and 3.3L engines

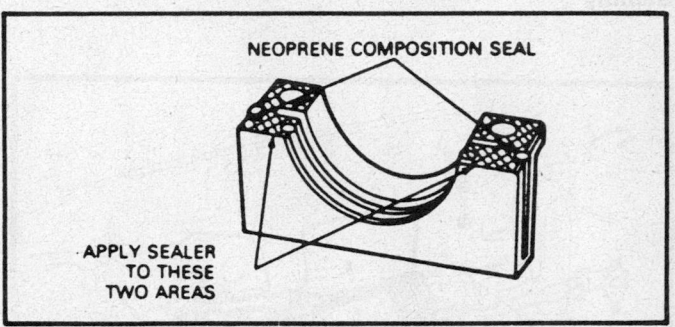

Applying sealant to the bearing cap–3.0L and 3.3L engines

filed to adjust the bearing clearance, nor should shims of any kind be used.

If a rod bearing becomes noisy or is worn so that its clearance on the crank journal is excessive, a new bearing of the correct undersize must be selected and installed since there is no provision for adjustment.

Inspect the rod bearings while the rod assemblies are out of the engine. If the shells are scored or show flaking, they should be replaced. If they are in good shape, check for proper clearance on the crank journal. Any scoring or ridges on the crank journal means the crankshaft must be replaced or reground and fitted with an undersize bearing.

MAIN BEARINGS

Like connecting rod big end bearings, the crankshaft main bearings are shell type inserts that do not utilize shims and cannot be adjusted. The bearings are available in various standard and undersizes. If the main bearing clearance is found to be excessive, a new bearing both upper and lower halves is required.

NOTE: Factory undersized crankshafts are marked, sometimes with a 9 and/or a large spot of green paint; the bearing caps also will have the paint on each side of the undersized journal.

Generally, the lower half of the bearing shell except the No. 1 bearing, shows greater wear and fatigue. If the lower half only shows the effects of normal wear, no heavy scoring or discoloration, it can usually be assumed that the upper half is also in good shape; conversely, if the lower half is heavily worn or damaged, both halves should be replaced.

FRONT SUSPENSION AND STEERING

For front suspension component removal and installation procedures, refer to unit repair section.

For steering wheel removal and installation, refer to electrical control section.

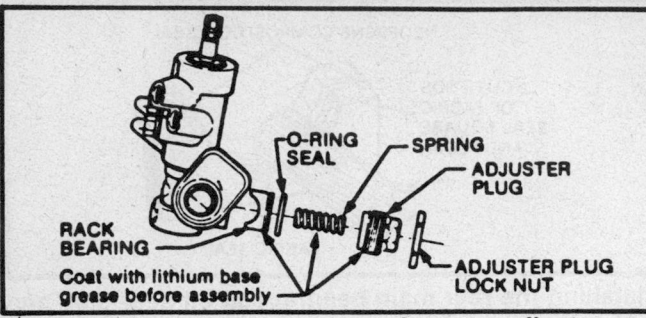

Exploded view of the power steering gear adjuster assembly

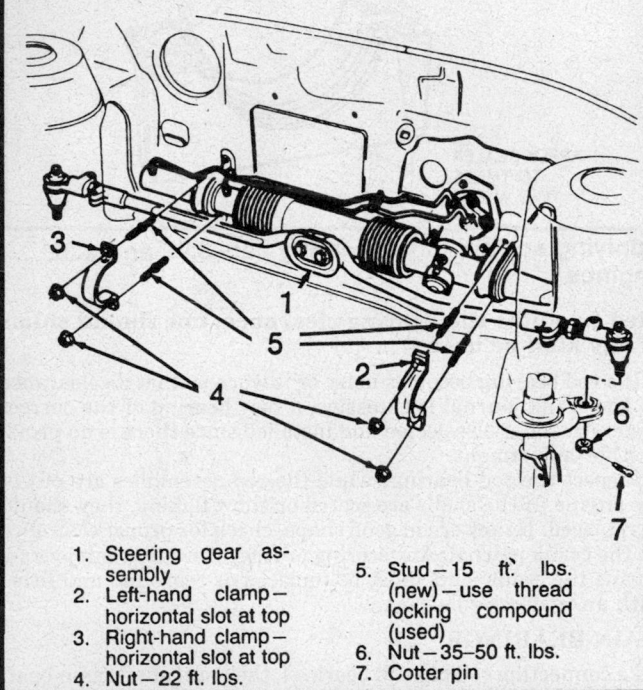

1. Steering gear assembly
2. Left-hand clamp—horizontal slot at top
3. Right-hand clamp—horizontal slot at top
4. Nut — 22 ft. lbs.
5. Stud — 15 ft. lbs. (new) — use thread locking compound (used)
6. Nut — 35–50 ft. lbs.
7. Cotter pin

Exploded view of the power steering rack and pinion

Power Steering Rack

Adjustment

1. Raise and support the vehicle safely.
2. Make sure that the steering wheel is centered.
3. Loosen the adjuster plug locknut.
4. Turn the adjuster plug counterclockwise until it is loose in the housing.
5. With the rack centered, turn the adjuster plug clockwise until it bottoms, back it off 50–70 degrees.
6. While holding the adjuster plug stationary, torque the adjuster plug locknut to 50 ft. lbs.

Removal and Installation

1. Remove the left side sound insulator.
2. Disconnect the upper pinch bolt on the steering coupling assembly.
3. Disconnect the clamp nuts.
4. Raise and support the vehicle safely.
5. Remove the clamp nut.

6. Remove both front wheel assemblies.
7. Remove the tie rod end-to-steering knuckle cotter pin and castle nut. Using a puller tool, disconnect the tie rod ends from the steering knuckles.
8. Lower the vehicle.
9. Disconnect the fluid line retainer.
10. Disconnect and plug the pressure tubes from the power steering rack.
11. Move the steering rack forward and remove the lower pinch bolt on the coupling assembly.
12. Disconnect the coupling from the steering rack.
13. Remove the rack and pinion assembly with the dash seal through the left wheel opening.

NOTE: If the studs were removed with the mounting clamps, reinstall the studs into the cowl and torque to specifications. If the stud has been reused for the 2nd time, use thread Loctite® to secure the threads.

14. Continue the installation in the reverse order of the removal procedure. Use new cotter pins. Torque the power steering rack-to-chassis clamp nuts to 28 ft. lbs., the tie rod end-to-steering knuckle nut to 35–50 ft. lbs. and the steering coupling-to-power steering unit pinch bolt to 29 ft. lbs. Refill the power steering pump reservoir and bleed the system.

Power Steering Pump

Removal and Installation

2.3L ENGINE

1. Disconnect the negative battery cable.
2. Remove pressure and return lines at pump.
3. Disconnect rear bracket to pump bolts.
4. Remove drive belt and position aside.
5. Remove rear bracket to transaxle bolts.
6. Remove front bracket to engine bolt.
7. Remove pump with bracket as an assembly.
8. Continue the installation in the reverse order of the removal procedure. Transfer pulley and bracket as necessary. Torque bracket to pump bolts to 19 ft. lbs.

2.5L ENGINE

1. Disconnect the negative battery cable.
2. Remove the drive belt.
3. Disconnect and plug the pressure tubes from the power steering pump.
4. Remove the front adjustment bracket-to-rear adjustment bracket bolt.
5. Remove the front adjustment bracket-to-engine bolt and spacer.
6. Remove the pump with the front adjustment bracket.
7. If installing a new pump, transfer the pulley and front adjustment bracket to the new pump.
8. Continue the installation in the reverse order of the removal procedure. Torque the pump-to-bracket bolts to 20 ft. lbs. and the front adjustment bracket-to-rear adjustment bracket bolts to 38 ft. lbs. Adjust the drive belt tension. Refill the pump reservoir with power steering fluid. Bleed the air from the power steering system.

2.0L, 3.0L AND 3.3L ENGINES

1. Disconnect the negative battery cable.
2. Remove the serpentine drive belt.
3. Remove the power steering pump-to-engine bolts.
4. Pull the pump forward and disconnect the pressure tubes.
5. Remove the pump and transfer the pulley as necessary.
6. Continue the installation in the reverse order of the removal procedure. Install and adjust the drive belt. Torque the pump-to-bracket bolts to 20 ft. lbs.
7. Refill the pump reservoir with power steering fluid. Bleed the air from the power steering system.

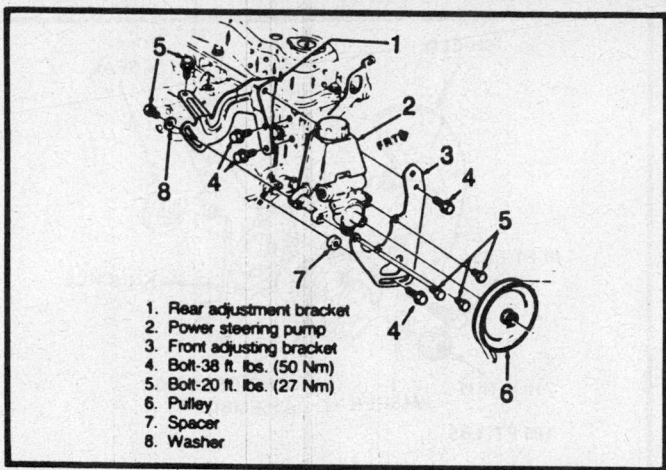

1. Rear adjustment bracket
2. Power steering pump
3. Front adjusting bracket
4. Bolt-38 ft. lbs. (50 Nm)
5. Bolt-20 ft. lbs. (27 Nm)
6. Pulley
7. Spacer
8. Washer

Exploded view of the power steering pump assembly—2.5L engine

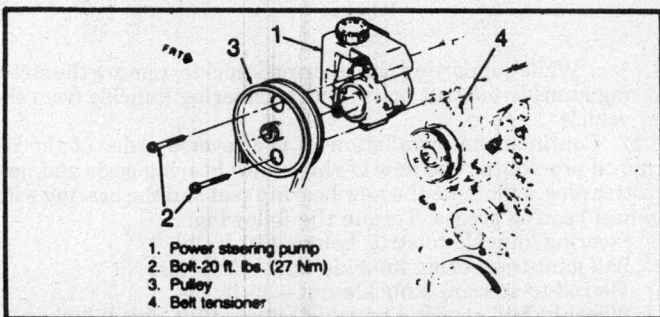

1. Power steering pump
2. Bolt-20 ft. lbs. (27 Nm)
3. Pulley
4. Belt tensioner

View of the power steering pump assembly—3.0L engine

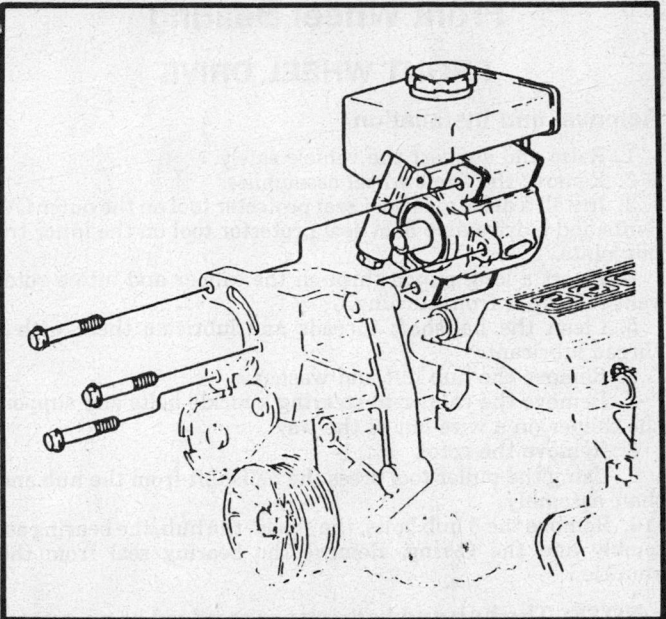

Power steering pump mounting–3.3L engine

Bleeding System

If the power steering hydraulic system has been serviced, an accurate fluid level reading cannot be obtained unless air is bled from the system.

1. With the vehicle raised and safely supported add power steering fluid to the **COLD** mark on the fluid level indicator.
2. Start the engine and check the fluid level at fast idle. Add fluid, if necessary to bring the level up to the **COLD** mark.
3. Bleed air from the system by turning the wheels from side-to-side without hitting the stops. Keep the fluid level just above the internal pump casting or at the **COLD** mark. Fluid with air in it has a light tan or red appearance.
4. Return the wheels to the center position and continue running the engine for 2–3 minutes.
5. Lower vehicle and road test to check steering function and recheck the fluid level with the system at its normal operating temperature. Fluid should be at the **HOT** mark.

Steering Column

Removal and Installation

1. Disconnect the negative battery cable.
2. If column repairs are to be made, remove the steering wheel.
3. Remove the steering column-to-intermediate shaft coupling pinch bolt. Remove the safety strap and bolt if equipped.
4. Remove the steering column trim shrouds and column covers.
5. Disconnect all wiring harness connectors. Remove the dust boot mounting screws and steering column-to-dash bracket bolts.
6. Lower the column to clear the mounting bracket and carefully remove from the vehicle.
7. Continue the installation in the reverse order of the removal procedure. Torque the steering column-to-dash bolts to 20 ft. lbs. and the steering column-to-intermediate shaft coupling pinch bolt to 29 ft. lbs.

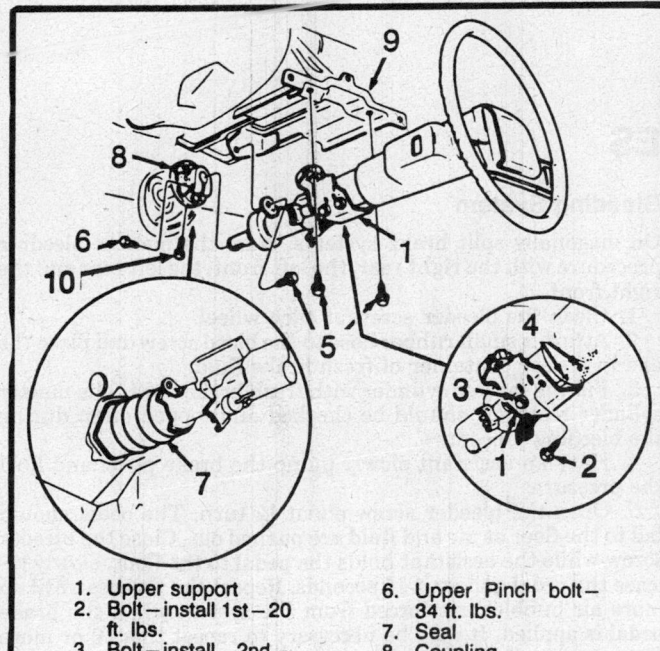

1. Upper support
2. Bolt—install 1st—20 ft. lbs.
3. Bolt—install 2nd—20 ft. lbs.
4. Bolt—install last—20 ft. lbs.
5. Bolt—20 ft. lbs.
6. Upper Pinch bolt—34 ft. lbs.
7. Seal
8. Coupling
9. Instrument Panel Bracket
10. Lower Pinch bolt—29 ft. lbs.

Replacing the steering column

Front Wheel Bearing

FRONT WHEEL DRIVE

Removal and Installation

1. Raise and support the vehicle safely.
2. Remove the front wheel assemblies.
3. Install a drive axle boot seal protector tool on the outer CV-joints and a drive axle boot seal protector tool on the inner tripot joints.
4. Insert a long punch through the caliper and into a rotor vent to keep it from turning.
5. Clean the halfshaft threads and lubricate them with a thread lubricant.
6. Remove the hub nut and washer.
7. Remove the caliper-to-steering knuckle bolts and support the caliper on a wire out of the way.
8. Remove the rotor.
9. Using the puller tool press the halfshaft from the hub and shaft assembly.
10. Remove the 3 hub bolts, the shield, the hub, the bearing assembly and the O-ring. Remove the bearing seal from the knuckle.

NOTE: The hub and bearing are serviced as an assembly only.

11. To remove the steering knuckle, perform the following procedures:
    a. At the ball joint-to-steering knuckle and the tie-rod-to-steering knuckle intersections, remove the cotter pins and nuts.
    b. Using a ball joint removal tool, separate the ball joint and the tie-rod end from the steering knuckle.

NOTE: Before removing the steering knuckle from the strut, be sure to scribe alignment marks between them, so the installation can be easily performed.

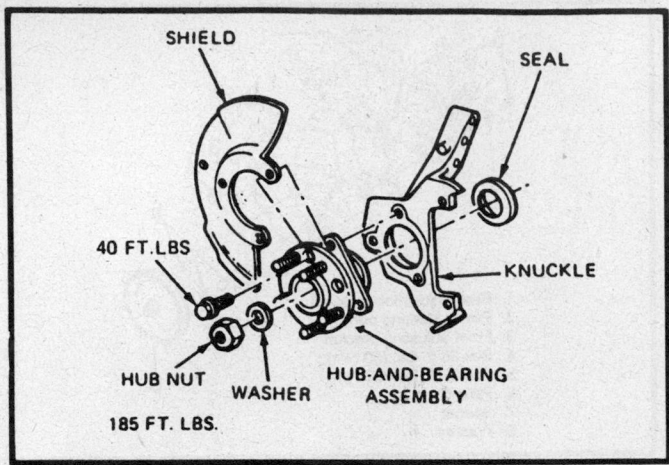

Exploded view of the front hub and bearing assembly

c. While supporting the steering knuckle, remove the steering knuckle-to-strut bolts and the steering knuckle from the vehicle.
12. Continue the installation in the reverse order of the removal procedure. Use new O-rings, new bearing seals and new cotter pins. Lubricate the new bearing seal and the bearing with wheel bearing grease. Torque the following:
    Steering knuckle-to-strut bolts—140 ft. lbs.
    Ball joint-to-steering knuckle nut—55 ft. lbs.
    Tie-rod-to-steering knuckle nut—35 ft. lbs.
    Wheel hub-to-steering knuckle bolts—40 ft. lbs. (55 Nm)
    Caliper-to-steering knuckle bolts—28 ft. lbs. (38 Nm)
    Halfshaft-to-hub nut—185 ft. lbs. (260 Nm). Check and/or adjust the front end alignment.

BRAKES

Refer to unit repair section for brake service information and drum/rotor specifications.

Master Cylinder

Removal and Installation

1. Disconnect the negative battery cable.
2. Disconnect the electrical connector from the warning switch.
3. Disconnect and plug the hydraulic lines to prevent the entry of dirt into the system.
4. Remove the master cylinder-to-power booster retaining nuts and remove the master cylinder from the power booster.
5. Drain and discard the brake fluid from the master cylinder.

NOTE: Exercise caution when handling the brake fluid as it will damage the painted surfaces.

6. Continue the installation in the reverse order of the removal procedure.
7. Torque the master cylinder-to-power booster nuts to 22–30 ft. lbs.
8. Refill the master cylinder reservoir with clean brake fluid. Bleed the brake system.

Bleeding System

On diagonally split brake systems, start the manual bleeding procedure with the right rear, the left front, the left rear and the right front.
1. Clean the bleeder screw at each wheel.
2. Attach a small rubber hose to the bleed screw and place the end in a clear container of fresh brake fluid.
3. Fill the master cylinder with fresh brake fluid. The master cylinder reservoir should be checked and topped often during the bleeding procedure.
4. Have an assistant slowly pump the brake pedal and hold the pressure.
5. Open the bleeder screw about ¼ turn. The pedal should fall to the floor as air and fluid are pushed out. Close the bleeder screw while the assistant holds the pedal to the floor, slowly release the pedal and wait 15 seconds. Repeat the process until no more air bubbles are forced from the system when the brake pedal is applied. It may be necessary to repeat this 10 or more times to get all of the air from the system.
6. Repeat this procedure on the remaining wheel cylinders and calipers.

NOTE: Remember to wait 15 seconds between each bleeding and do not pump the pedal rapidly. Rapid pumping of the brake pedal pushes the master cylinder

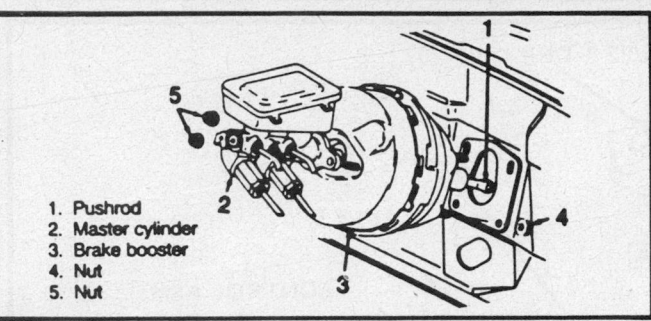

1. Pushrod
2. Master cylinder
3. Brake booster
4. Nut
5. Nut

View of the master cylinder and power brake booster assembly

secondary piston down the bore in a manner that makes it difficult to bleed the system.

7. Check the brake pedal for sponginess and the brake warning light for an indication of unbalanced pressure. Repeat the entire bleeding procedure to correct either of these conditions.

Power Brake Booster

Removal and Installation

1. Disconnect the negative battery cable.
2. Working inside the vehicle, detach the brake pushrod from the brake pedal.
3. Disconnect the hydraulic lines from the master cylinder and the vacuum line from the power booster.
4. Remove the power booster-to-cowl nuts and the booster/master cylinder assembly. Continue disassembly to separate the booster and master cylinder on the bench.
5. Continue the installation in the reverse order of the removal procedure.

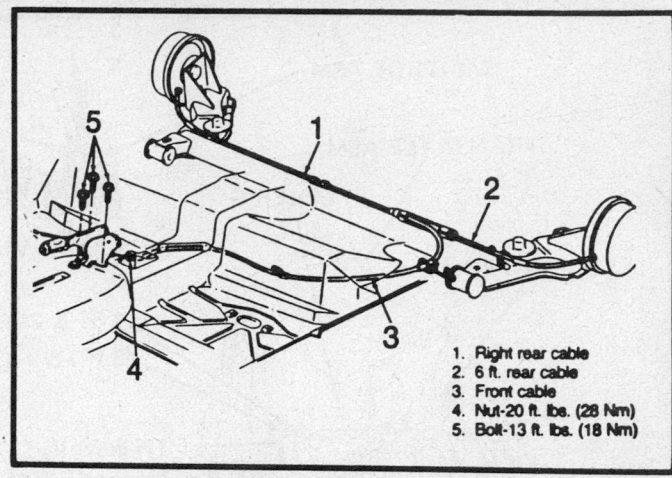

1. Right rear cable
2. 6 ft. rear cable
3. Front cable
4. Nut-20 ft. lbs. (28 Nm)
5. Bolt-13 ft. lbs. (18 Nm)

View of the parking brake cable routing

6. Torque the master cylinder-to-power booster nuts—28 ft. lbs. Bleed the brake system.

Parking Brake

Adjustment

1. Depress the parking brake pedal exactly 5 ratchet clicks.
2. Raise and support the vehicle safely.
3. Check that the equalizer nut groove is liberally lubricated with chassis lube. Tighten the adjusting nut until the right rear wheel can just be turned to the rear with both hands but is locked when forward rotation is attempted.
4. With the mechanism totally disengaged, both rear wheels should turn freely in either direction with no brake drag. Do not adjust the parking brake so tightly as to cause brake drag.

CLUTCH AND TRANSAXLE

Refer to "Chilton's Transmission Service Manual" for additional coverage.

Hydraulic Clutch

Adjustments

These vehicles use a hydraulic system which provides automatic clutch adjustment, no adjustment of the clutch linkage or pedal height is required.

Clutch

─────── **CAUTION** ───────

The clutch plate contains asbestos, which has been determined to be a cancer causing agent. Never clean the clutch surfaces with compressed air! Avoid inhaling any dust from any clutch surface! When cleaning clutch disc surfaces, use a commercially available clutch cleaning fluid.

Removal and Installation

1. Disconnect the negative battery cable.
2. Remove the transaxle.
3. Mark the pressure plate assembly and the flywheel so that they may be assembled in their original position. They are balanced as an assembly at the factory.
4. Loosen the attaching bolts 1 turn at a time until all spring tension is released.
5. Support the pressure plate and remove the bolts and remove the pressure plate, clutch disc, throwout bearing and the

clutch fork and pivot shaft assembly. Replace any parts found to be defective.

6. Inspect the flywheel, pressure plate, clutch disc, throwout bearing and the clutch fork and pivot shaft for signs of wear and replace the parts as necessary.

7. Using a stiff bristle brush, not wire bristles, clean the pressure plate and flywheel mating surfaces. Position the clutch disc and pressure plate into the installed position and support with a

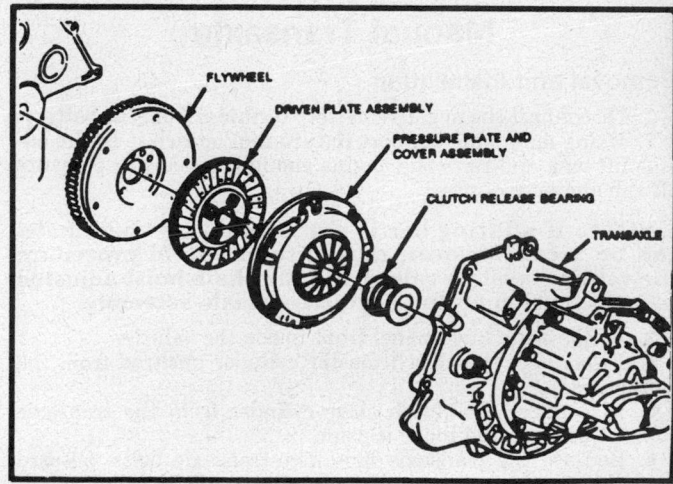

FLYWHEEL
DRIVEN PLATE ASSEMBLY
PRESSURE PLATE AND COVER ASSEMBLY
CLUTCH RELEASE BEARING
TRANSAXLE

Exploded view of the clutch assembly—MTX

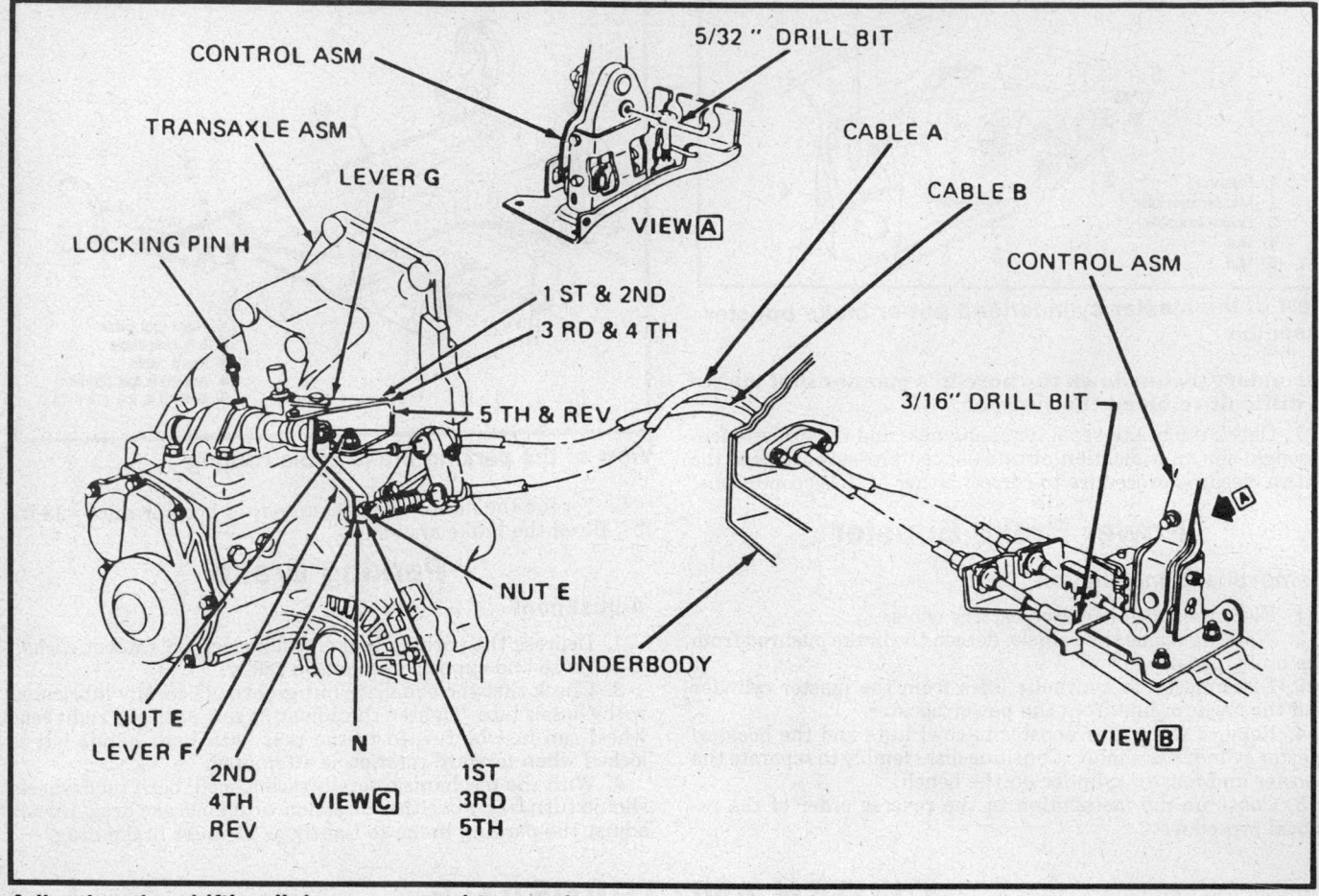

CONTROL ASM

TRANSAXLE ASM

LEVER G

LOCKING PIN H

5/32" DRILL BIT

CABLE A

CABLE B

CONTROL ASM

1 ST & 2ND

3 RD & 4 TH

5 TH & REV

VIEW A

3/16" DRILL BIT

NUT E

UNDERBODY

VIEW B

NUT E
LEVER F

2ND
4TH
REV

N

VIEW C

1ST
3RD
5TH

Adjusting the shifting linkage—manual transaxle

clutch alignment tool. The clutch plate is assembled with the damper springs offset toward the transaxle.

8. Install the pressure plate-to-flywheel bolts and tighten gradually in a criss cross pattern to 15 ft. lbs. (20 Nm).

9. Lubricate the outside grooves and the inside recess of the release bearing with high temperature grease. Wipe off the excess and install the bearing.

10. Continue the installation in the reverse order of the removal procedure.

Manual Transaxle

Removal and Installation

1. Disconnect the negative battery terminal from the battery.

2. Using an engine support fixture tool, attach it to the engine lift ring and raise the engine enough to take the pressure off the engine mounts.

NOTE: If a lifting bar is not available, a chain hoist can be used. However, during the removal procedure the vehicle must be raised and the chain hoist adjusted to keep tension on the engine/transaxle assembly.

3. Remove the hush panel from inside the vehicle.

4. Disconnect the clutch master cylinder pushrod from the clutch pedal.

5. Disconnect the clutch slave cylinder from the transaxle support bracket and move it aside.

6. Remove the transaxle mount-to-transaxle bolts. Discard the bolts attaching the mount to the side frame. New bolts must be used upon installation.

7. Remove the transaxle mount bracket attaching bolts and nuts.

8. Disconnect the shift cables and retaining clips from the transaxle. Disconnect the ground cables from the transaxle mounting stud.

9. Remove the air management valve-to-chassis bolts to gain clearance to remove the upper right transaxle-to-engine bolt.

10. Raise and support the vehicle safely. Remove the left front wheel assembly.

11. Remove the left front inner splash shield. Remove the transaxle strut and bracket.

12. Remove the clutch housing cover bolts.

13. Disconnect the speedometer cable or sensor from the transaxle.

14. Disconnect the stabilizer bar from the left suspension support and control arm.

15. Disconnect the ball joint-to-steering knuckle nut and separate the ball joint from the steering knuckle.

16. Remove the left suspension support attaching bolts, the support and control arm as an assembly.

17. Using boot protectors, install them and disengage the halfshafts from the transaxle. Remove the left side shaft from the transaxle.

18. Using a transmission jack, position it under and secure it to the transaxle case. Remove the transaxle-to-engine mounting bolts.

19. Remove the transaxle by sliding it toward the driver's side, away from the engine. Carefully lower the jack, guiding the right shaft out of the transaxle. Place the transaxle on a work bench.

20. Continue the installation in the reverse of the removal pro-

cedure. When installing the transaxle, be sure to guide the right halfshaft into its bore as the transaxle is being raised.

NOTE: The right halfshaft cannot be readily installed after the transaxle is connected to the engine.

21. Torque the following:
Transaxle-to-engine bolts—55 ft. lbs.
Suspension support-to-chassis bolts—75 ft. lbs.
Clutch housing cover bolts to 10 ft. lbs.
Using new bolts, install and torque the transaxle mount-to-side frame—35 ft. lbs. Adjust the shift linkage cables.

NOTE: When installing the mount-to-transaxle bracket bolts, check the alignment bolt at the engine mount.

Linkage Adjustment

1. Disconnect the negative battery terminal from the battery.
2. Shift the transaxle into 3rd gear.
3. On top of the transaxle, remove the lock pin **H** and reinstall the tapered end down; this will lock the transaxle in 3rd gear.
4. Loosen the shift cable nuts **E** at the transaxle levers **G** and **F**.
5. Remove the trim plate from the console and slide the shifter boot up the shifter handle and remove the console.
6. Using a $5/32$ in. or No. 22 drill bit, install it into the alignment hole at the side of the shifter assembly.
7. Using a $3/16$ in. drill bit, install it into the select lever hole and the slot in the shifter plate.
8. Tighten the **E** nuts at the **G** and **F** levers and remove the drill bits from the alignment holes. Remove the lockpin **H** and reinstall it with the tapered end up.
9. Continue the installation in the reverse order of the removal procedure. Road test the vehicle.

NOTE: When shifting, there should be a good neutral gate feel.

Automatic Transaxle

Removal and Installation

1. Disconnect the negative battery cable.
2. Remove the air cleaner assembly. If equipped with a 3.0L engine or 3.3L engine, remove the mass air flow sensor and air intake duct.
3. Disconnect the throttle valve T.V. cable from the throttle lever and the transaxle.
4. If equipped with a 2.3L engine, remove the power steering and position it to the side.
5. Remove the transaxle dipstick and tube from the engine.
6. Install an engine support tool. Insert a $1/4 \times 2$ in. bolt in the hole at the front right motor mount to maintain the driveline alignment.
7. Remove the wiring harness-to-transaxle nut. Disconnect the wiring connectors from the speed sensor, TCC connector, Neutral safety switch and backup lamp switch.

NOTE: When servicing requires that the T-latch type wiring connector be disconnected from the switch, care must be taken to ensure proper reassembly of both the connector and the T-latch. Failure to do so may result in intermittent loss of switch functions.

8. Remove the shift linkage from the transaxle.
9. Remove the top 2 transaxle-to-engine bolts and the upper left transaxle mount along with the bracket assembly.
10. Remove the rubber hose from the transaxle vent pipe. Remove the remaining upper engine-to-transaxle bolts.
11. Raise and support the vehicle safely. Remove both front wheel/tire assemblies.
12. If equipped with a 2.3L engine remove both lower ball joints and stablalizer shafts links.

13. Position an oil drain pan under the transaxle, remove the drain plug and drain the transaxle fluid.
14. Remove the shift linkage and bracket from the transaxle.
15. Using a drive axle boot seal protector, install it on the inner seals.

NOTE: Some vehicles may use a gray silicone boot on the inboard axle joint. Use boot protector tool on these boots. All other boots are made from a black thermo plastic material and do not require the use of a boot seal protector.

16. Remove both ball joints-to-control arms nuts and separate the ball joints from the control arms.
17. Remove both halfshafts and support them with a cord or wire.
18. Remove the transaxle mounting strut.
19. Remove the left stabilizer bar link pin bolt, left frame bushing clamp nuts and left frame support assembly.

NOTE: Before disconnecting, be sure to matchmark the flexplate and torque converter for installation purposes.

20. Remove the transaxle converter cover. Remove the torque converter-to-flexplate bolts.
21. Disconnect and plug the transaxle oil cooler lines.
22. Remove the transaxle-to-engine support bracket and install the transaxle removal jack.
23. Remove the remaining transaxle-to-engine retaining bolts and the transaxle from the vehicle.
24. Continue the installation in the reverse order of the removal procedures. Torque the torque converter-to-flex plate bolts to 46 ft. lbs. Refill the transaxle with the proper grade and type automatic transaxle fluid.

T.V Cable Adjustment

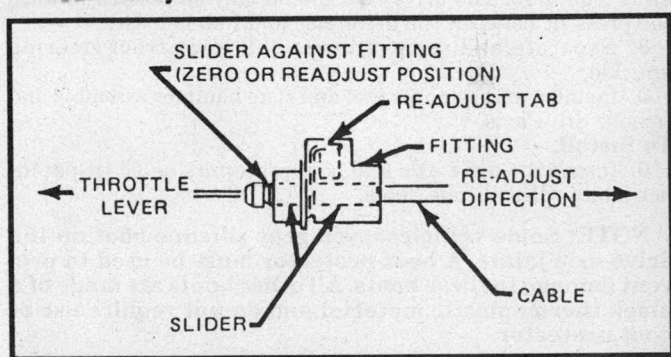

T.V. cable adjuster—with slider

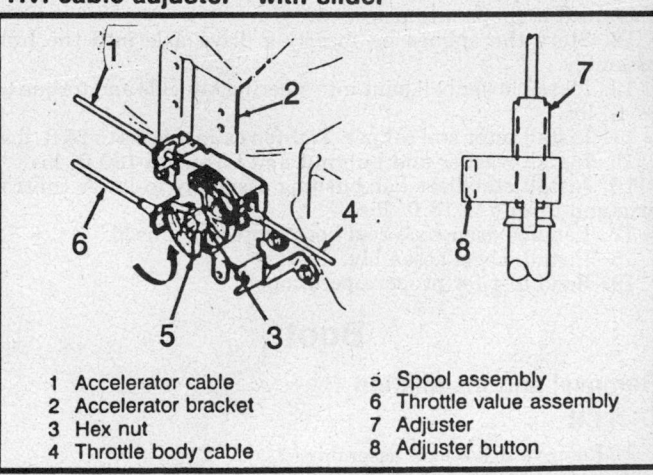

1 Accelerator cable		5 Spool assembly	
2 Accelerator bracket		6 Throttle value assembly	
3 Hex nut		7 Adjuster	
4 Throttle body cable		8 Adjuster button	

T.V. cable adjuster—without slider

EXCEPT 2.3L ENGINE

1. Disconnect the negative battery cable.
2. Depress and hold down the adjustment tap at the T.V. cable adjuster.
3. Release throttle lever by hand to is full travel position, or on the 2.5L engine press the accelerator pedal to the full travel position.
4. The slider must move toward the lever when the lever is rotated to the full travel position, or on the 2.5L engine when the accelerator pedal is pressed to the full travel position.

5. Inspect the cable for free movement. The cable may appear to function properly with the engine stopped an cold. Recheck the cable after the engine is warm. Road test the vehicle.

2.3L ENGINE

1. Disconnect the negative battery cable.
2. Rotate the T.V. cable adjuster body at the transaxle 90 degrees and pull the cable conduit out until the slider mechanism contacts the stop.
3. Rotate the adjuster body back to the original position.
4. Using a torque wrench, rotate the T.V. cable adjuster until 75 inch lbs. (8.5 Nm) is reached. Road test the vehicle.

HALFSHAFTS

Front Drive Axle

Removal and Installation

NOTE: On vehicles equipped with tri-pot joints, care must be exercised not to allow joints to become overextended. Overextending the joint could result in separation of internal components.

1. Raise vehicle and support it safely the under body lift points. Do not support under lower control arms.
2. Remove wheel assemblies.
3. Remove hub nut and washer.
4. Remove caliper bolts and support caliper. Do not let the caliper hang by brake hose.
5. Remove rotor and lower ball joint nut.
6. Remove stabilizer bolt from lower control arm.
7. Install a drive axle pressing tool and press drive axle in and away from hub. The drive axle should only be pressed in until the press fit between the drive axle and hub is loose.
8. Separate and remove lower ball joint from steering knuckle.
9. Install a axle remover tool and slide hammer assembly and remove drive axle.

To install,

10. Install the drive axle seal boot protectors on all tri-pot inner joints with silicone boots.

NOTE: Some vehicles use a gray silicone boot on the drive axle joints. A boot protector must be used to prevent damage to these boots. All other boots are made of a black thermoplastic material and do not require use of boot protector.

11. Start splines of drive axle into transaxle and push drive axle until it snaps into place.
12. Start the splines by inserting drive axle into the hub assembly.
13. Install lower ball joint into steering knuckle and torque to 37 ft. lbs.
14. Install rotor and caliper. Tighten caliper bolts to 28 ft. lbs.
15. Install washer and hub nut and torque to 180 ft. lbs.
16. Install stabilizer bar bushing assembly to lower control arm and torque to 13 ft. lbs.
17. Remove drive axle seal boot protector if used.
18. Install wheel assembly.
19. Road test for proper operation.

Boot

Removal and Installation

OUTER

1. Remove drive axle assembly.
2. Remove steel deflector ring by using brass drift to tap it off. If rubber ring is used, slide it off.

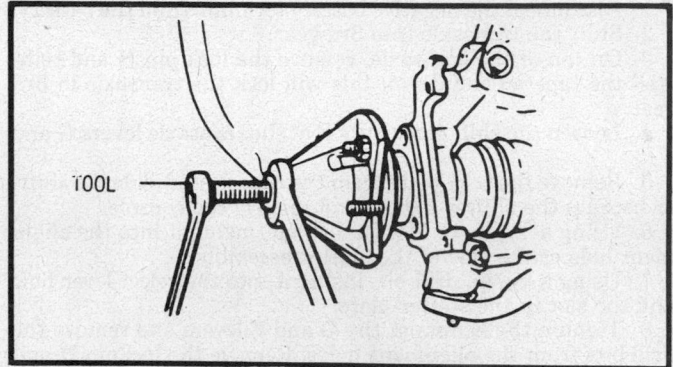

Pressing the halfshaft from the steering knuckle

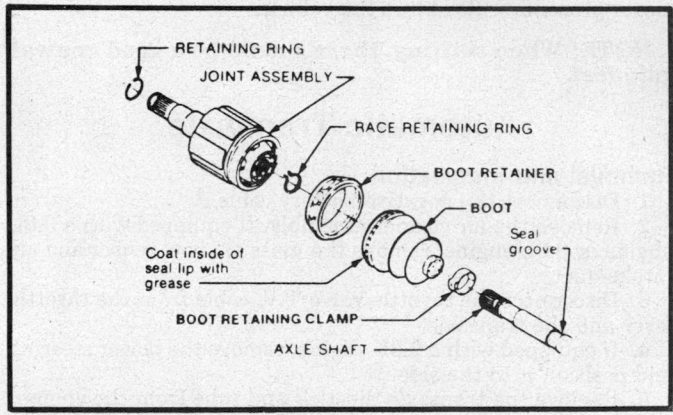

Exploded view of the halfshaft tri-pot joint—inner boot assembly

3. Cut seal retaining clamps and lift boot up to gain access to retaining ring.
4. Using snapring pliers, spread the retaining ring inside the outer CV-joint and remove joint from shaft.
5. Slide boot off shaft.
6. Clean the splines of the shaft and the CV-joint with solvent and repack the joint. Install a new retaining ring inside the joint.

NOTE: When repacking CV-joint make sure to add grease to axle boot.

7. Install the inner boot clamp, boot, outer boot clamp on shaft.
8. Push the joint assembly onto the shaft until the ring is seated on the shaft.
9. Slide the boot and 2 clamps onto the joint and install the clamps on both the inner and outer part of the boot.
10. Install drive axle assembly.

INNER

1. Remove drive axle assembly and place in a suitable holding fixture. Do not allow over extention of the joint.
2. Cut seal retaining clamps and lift boot up to gain access to retaining ring for spider assembly.
3. Using snapring pliers remove the retaining ring from shaft and remove the spider assembly. Slide old boot off axle shaft.
4. Clean the splines of the shaft and the CV-joint with solvent and repack the joint.

NOTE: When repacking CV-joint make sure to add grease to axle boot.

5. Install the inner boot clamp, boot, outer boot clamp on shaft.
6. Push the tri-pot assembly onto the shaft until the retaining ring is seated on the shaft.
7. Slide the boot and 2 clamps onto the joint and install the clamps on both the inner and outer part of the boot.
8. Install drive axle assembly.

NOTE: Be sure spacer ring is seated in groove on axle at reassembly.

CV-Joint

Refer to unit repair section for overhaul procedures.

REAR AXLE AND REAR SUSPENSION

Rear Axle Assembly

Removal and Installation

1. Raise and support the vehicle safely under the control arms.
2. If equipped, remove the stabilizer bar from the axle assembly.
3. Remove the wheel assemblies.

NOTE: Do not hammer on the brake drum as damage to the wheel bearing may result.

4. Remove the lower shock absorber-to-axle assembly nuts/bolts and separate the shock absorbers from the rear axle assembly.
5. Disconnect the parking brake cable from the rear axle assembly.
6. Disconnect the brake lines from the rear axle assembly; be sure that the assembly is not suspended by the brake lines.
7. Lower the rear axle assembly and remove the coil spring wheel hub assembly to the new rear axle assembly. Torque the following:
Hub/bearing assembly-to-rear axle assembly nuts and bolts — 39 ft. lbs.
Rear axle assembly-to-body nuts and bolts — 67 ft. lbs.
Lower shock absorber-to-axle assembly nngs and the insulators.
8. Remove the rear axle assembly-to-chassis bolts and lower the axle assembly.
9. If replacing the rear axle assembly, remove the wheel hub-to-axle assembly bolts, the hub, the bearing and the backing plate assembly. Install theut and bolt — 35 ft. lbs.

Rear Wheel Bearing and Oil Seal

Removal and Installation

1. Raise and support the vehicle safely.

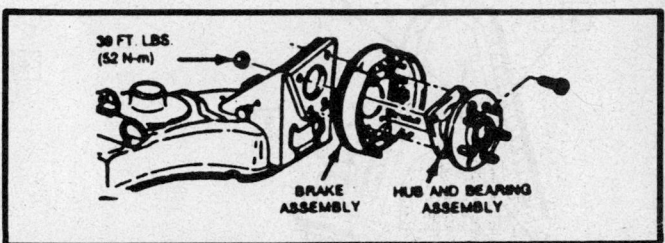

Removing the rear axle hub/bearing assembly

2. Remove the wheel assembly.
3. Remove the brake drum.

NOTE: Do not hammer on the brake drum during removal or damage to the assembly could result.

4. Remove the 4 hub/bearing assembly-to-rear axle assembly nuts/bolts and the hub/bearing assembly from the axle.

NOTE: The top rear attaching bolt will not clear the brake shoe when removing the hub and bearing assembly. Partially remove the hub prior to removing this bolt.

5. Continue the installation in the reverse order of the removal procedure. Torque the hub/bearing assembly-to-rear axle assembly nuts/bolts to 39 ft. lbs.

Rear Wheel Bearings

Adjustment

The rear wheel bearing assembly is non-adjustable and is serviced by replacement only.

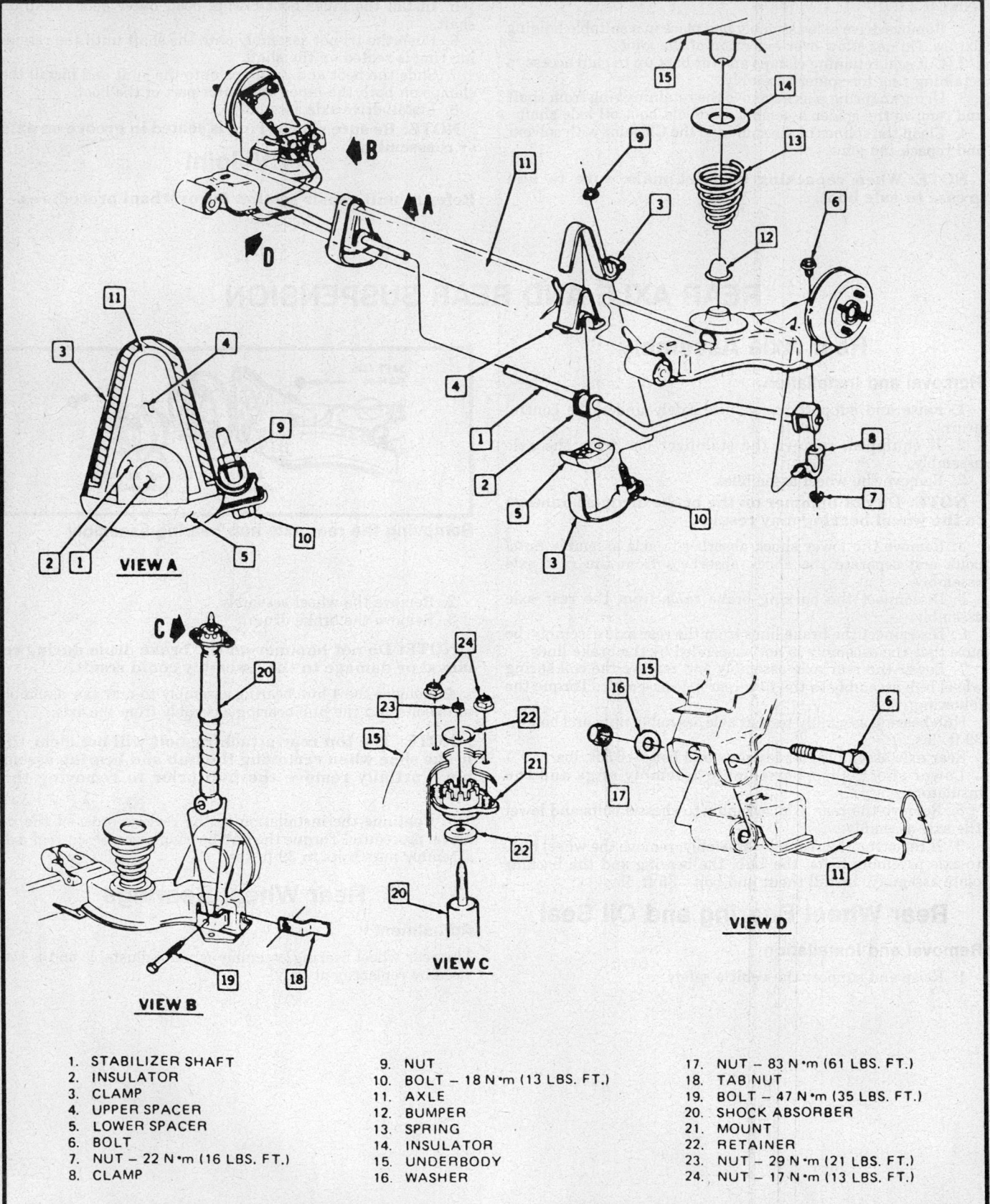

VIEW A

VIEW B

VIEW C

VIEW D

1. STABILIZER SHAFT	9. NUT	17. NUT – 83 N•m (61 LBS. FT.)
2. INSULATOR	10. BOLT – 18 N•m (13 LBS. FT.)	18. TAB NUT
3. CLAMP	11. AXLE	19. BOLT – 47 N•m (35 LBS. FT.)
4. UPPER SPACER	12. BUMPER	20. SHOCK ABSORBER
5. LOWER SPACER	13. SPRING	21. MOUNT
6. BOLT	14. INSULATOR	22. RETAINER
7. NUT – 22 N•m (16 LBS. FT.)	15. UNDERBODY	23. NUT – 29 N•m (21 LBS. FT.)
8. CLAMP	16. WASHER	24. NUT – 17 N•m (13 LBS. FT.)

14-64 Rear suspension and related components

YEAR IDENTIFICATION

1988-90 Regal

1988-90 Grand Prix

1988-90 Cutlass Supreme

1988-90 Grand Prix SE

1990 Lumina

VEHICLE IDENTIFICATION

It is important for servicing and ordering parts to be certain of the vehicle and engine identification. The VIN (vehicle identification number) is a 17 digit number visible through the windshield on the driver's side of the dash and contains the vehicle and engine identification codes. The tenth digit indicates model year and the eighth digit indicates engine code. It can be interpreted as follows:

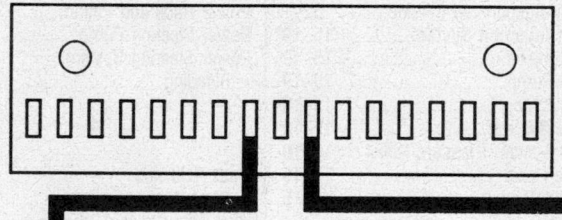

	Engine Code						Model Year	
Code	Cu. In.	Liters	Cyl.	Fuel Sys.	Eng. Mfg.		Code	Year
R	151	2.5	L4	TBI	Pontiac		J	1988
W	173	2.8	V6	MFI	Chevrolet		K	1989
T	192	3.1	V6	MFI	Chevrolet		L	1990

ENGINE IDENTIFICATION

Year	Model	Engine Displacement cu. in. (liter)	Engine Series Identification (VIN)	No. of Cylinders	Engine Type
1988	Grand Prix	173 (2.8)	W	6	OHV
	Supreme	173 (2.8)	W	6	OHV
	Regal	173 (2.8)	W	6	OHV
1989-90	Grand Prix	173 (2.8)	W	6	OHV
	Grand Prix	192 (3.1)	T	6	OHV

ENGINE IDENTIFICATION

Year	Model	Engine Displacement cu. in. (liter)	Engine Series Identification (VIN)	No. of Cylinders	Engine Type
1989–90	Supreme	173 (2.8)	W	6	OHV
	Supreme	192 (3.1)	T	6	OHV
	Regal	173 (2.8)	W	6	OHV
	Regal	192 (3.1)	T	6	OHV
	Lumina	151 (2.5)	R	4	OHV
	Lumina	192 (3.1)	T	6	OHV

OHV Over Head Valve

GENERAL ENGINE SPECIFICATIONS

Year	VIN	No. Cylinder Displacement cu. in. (liter)	Fuel System Type	Net Horsepower @ rpm	Net Torque @ rpm (ft.lbs.)	Bore × Stroke (in.)	Compression Ratio	Oil Pressure @ rpm
1988	W	6-173 (2.8)	MFI	125 @ 4500	160 @ 3600	3.500 × 2.990	8.9:1	15 @ 1100
1989-90	R	4-151 (2.5)	TBI	98 @ 4500	134 @ 2800	4.000 × 3.000	8.3:1	26 @ 800
	W	6-173 (2.8)	MFI	125 @ 4500	160 @ 3600	3.500 × 2.990	8.9:1	15 @ 1100
	T	6-192 (3.1)	MFI	140 @ 4500	185 @ 3600	3.500 × 3.310	8.8:1	15 @ 1100

GASOLINE ENGINE TUNE-UP SPECIFICATIONS
Refer to Section 34 for all spark plug recommendations

Year	VIN	No. Cylinder Displacement cu. in. (liter)	Spark Plugs Gap (in.)	Ignition Timing (deg.) MT	AT	Compression Pressure (psi)	Fuel Pump (psi)	Idle Speed (rpm) MT	AT	Valve Clearance In.	Ex.
1988	W	6-173 (2.8)	.045	①	①	②	40–47	①	①	Hyd.	Hyd.
1989	R	4-151 (2.5)	.060	①	①	②	26–32	①	①	Hyd.	Hyd.
	W	6-173 (2.8)	.045	①	①	②	40–47	①	①	Hyd.	Hyd.
	T	6-192 (3.1)	.455	①	①	②	40–47	①	①	Hyd.	Hyd.
1990		SEE UNDERHOOD SPECIFICATION STICKER									

① Ignition timing and idle speed are controlled by the Electronic Control Module. No adjustment is necessary

② Look for uniformity between cylinders rather than pressure. Lowest reading not less than 70% of the highest. No reading less than 100 psi

FIRING ORDERS

NOTE: To avoid confusion, always replace spark plug wires one at a time.

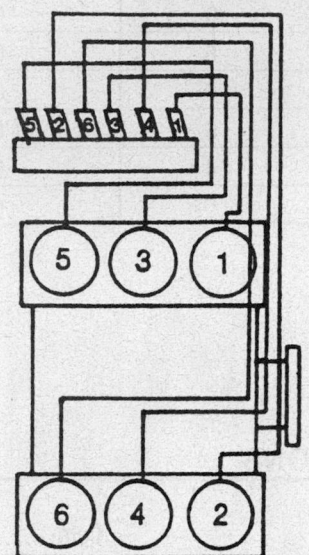

2.8L and 3.1L (173 and 192 cu. in.)
Firing order: 1-2-3-4-5-6

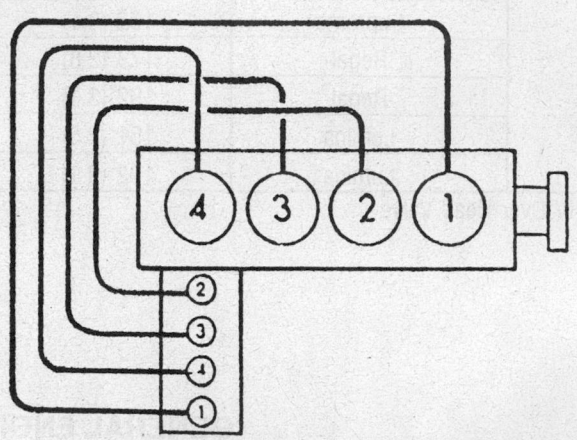

2.5L engine (151 cu. in.) Firing order: 1-3-4-2

CAPACITIES

Year	Model	VIN	No. Cylinder Displacement cu. in. (liter)	Engine Crankcase with Filter	Engine Crankcase without Filter	Transmission (pts.) 4-Spd	Transmission (pts.) 5-Spd	Transmission (pts.) Auto.	Drive Axle (pts.)	Fuel Tank (gal.)	Cooling System (qts.)
1988	Grand Prix	W	6-173 (2.8)	4.0	3.8	—	5	16①	—	16	②
	Cutlass Supreme	W	6-173 (2.8)	4.0	3.8	—	5	16①	—	16	②
	Regal	W	6-173 (2.8)	4.0	3.8	—	—	16①	—	16	②
1989-90	Grand Prix	W	6-173 (2.8)	4.0	3.8	—	5	12③	—	16	12.6
	Grand Prix	T	6-192 (3.1)	4.0	3.8	—	5	12③	—	16	12.6
	Cutlass Supreme	W	6-173 (2.8)	4.0	3.8	—	5	12③	—	16	12.6
	Cutlass Supreme	T	6-192 (3.1)	4.0	3.8	—	5	12③	—	16	12.6
	Regal	W	6-173 (2.8)	4.0	3.8	—	—	12③	—	16	12.6
	Regal	T	6-173 (3.1)	4.0	3.8	—	—	12③	—	16	12.6
	Lumina	R	4-151 (2.5)	4.0	3.8	—	—	12③	—	16	12.6
	Lumina	T	6-192 (3.1)	4.0	3.8	—	—	12③	—	16	12.6

① Drain and refill only.
   Complete overhaul—22 pts.

② Without air conditioning—12.3 qts.
   With air conditioning—12.6 qts.

③ Drain and refill only.
   Complete overhaul—16 pts.

CAMSHAFT SPECIFICATIONS
All measurements given in inches.

Year	VIN	No. Cylinder Displacement cu. in. (liter)	Journal Diameter 1	2	3	4	5	Lobe Lift In.	Ex.	Bearing Clearance	Camshaft End Play
1988	W	6-173 (2.8)	1.867–1.881	1.867–1.881	1.867–1.881	1.867–1.881	—	0.262	0.273	.001–.004	—
1989-90	R	4-151 (2.5)	1.869	1.869	1.869	—	—	0.248	0.248	.001–.003	0.0014–0.0050
	W	6-173 (2.8)	1.867–1.881	1.867–1.881	1.867–1.881	1.867–1.881	—	0.262	0.273	.001–.004	—
	T	6-192 (3.1)	1.867–1.881	1.867–1.881	1.867–1.881	1.867–1.881	—	0.262	0.273	.001–.004	—

CRANKSHAFT AND CONNECTING ROD SPECIFICATIONS
All measurements are given in inches.

Year	VIN	No. Cylinder Displacement cu. in. (liter)	Crankshaft Main Brg. Journal Dia.	Main Brg. Oil Clearance	Shaft End-play	Thrust on No.	Connecting Rod Journal Diameter	Oil Clearance	Side Clearance
1988	W	6-173 (2.8)	2.6473–2.6483	0.0016–0.0032	0.0024–0.0083	3	1.9994–1.9983	0.0013–0.0026	0.006–0.017
1989-90	R	4-151 (2.5)	2.3000	0.0005–0.0220	0.0005–0.0180	5	2.0000–	0.0005–0.0030	0.006–0.024
	W	6-173 (28)	2.6473–2.6483	0.0012–0.0027	0.0024–0.0083	3	1.9994–1.9983	0.0014–0.0036	0.014–0.027
	T	6-192 (3.1)	2.6473–2.6483	0.0024–0.0027	0.0012–0.0083	3	1.9994–1.9983	0.0014–0.0036	0.014–0.027

VALVE SPECIFICATIONS

Year	VIN	No. Cylinder Displacement cu. in. (liter)	Seat Angle (deg.)	Face Angle (deg.)	Spring Test Pressure (lbs.)	Spring Installed Height (in.)	Stem-to-Guide Clearance (in.) Intake	Exhaust	Stem Diameter (in.) Intake	Exhaust
1988	W	6-173 (2.8)	46	45	90 @ 1.70①	1.70	0.0010–0.0027	0.0010–0.0027	NA	NA
1989-90	R	4-151 (2.5)	46	45	75 @ 1.68①	1.68	0.0010–0.0026	0.0013–0.0041	NA	NA
	W	6-173 (2.8)	46	45	90 @ 1.70①	1.57	0.0010–0.0027	0.0010–0.0027	NA	NA
	T	6-192 (3.1)	46	45	90 @ 1.70①	1.57	0.0010–0.0027	0.0010–0.0027	NA	NA

① Valve closed

GENERAL MOTORS—"W" BODY
REGAL (1988–90) • LUMINA • CUTLASS (1988–90) • GRAND PRIX (1988–90)—FWD

PISTON AND RING SPECIFICATIONS
All measurments are given in inches.

Year	VIN	No. Cylinder Displacement cu. in. (liter)	Piston Clearance	Ring Gap			Ring Side Clearance		
				Top Compression	Bottom Compression	Oil Control	Top Compression	Bottom Compression	Oil Control
1988	W	6-173 (2.8)	0.0020–0.0030	0.016–0.020	0.010–0.020	0.020–0.055	0.001–0.003	0.001–0.003	0.008
1989-90	R	4-151 (2.5)	0.0020–0.0022	0.010–0.020	0.010–0.020	0.020–0.060	0.002–0.003	0.001–0.003	0.015–0.055
	W	6-173 (2.8)	0.0009–0.0022	0.001–0.020	0.001–0.020	0.001–0.003	0.002–0.003	0.002–0.003	0.008
	T	6-192 (3.1)	0.0009–0.0022	0.001–0.020	0.001–0.020	0.001–0.003	0.002–0.003	0.002–0.003	0.008

TORQUE SPECIFICATIONS
All readings in ft. lbs.

Year	VIN	No. Cylinder Displacement cu. in. (liter)	Cylinder Head Bolts	Main Bearing Bolts	Rod Bearing Bolts	Crankshaft Pulley Bolts	Flywheel Bolts	Manifold		Spark Plugs
								Intake	Exhaust	
1988	W	6-173 (2.8)	①	72	40	77	46	4	19	18
1989-90	R	4-151 (2.5)	②	65	29	162	55	25	③	18
	W	6-173 (2.8)	①	70	37	76	46	④	18	18
	T	6-192 (3.1)	①	70	37	76	46	④	18	18

① Torque in 2 steps:
  1st step   33 ft. lbs.
  2nd step — Turn an additional 90 degrees (¼) turn
② Torque in 3 steps:
  1st step   18 ft. lbs.
  2nd step   26 ft. lbs.
  3rd step   Turn an additional 90 degrees (¼) turn
③ Torque in 2 steps:
  1st step   15 ft. lbs.
  2nd step   24 ft. lbs.
④ Torque inner bolts to 37 ft. lbs. and outer bolts 26 ft. lbs.

WHEEL ALIGNMENT

Year	Model	Caster		Camber		Toe-in (in.)	Steering Axis Inclination (deg.)
		Range (deg.)	Preferred Setting (deg.)	Range (deg.)	Preferred Setting (deg.)		
1988	Cutlass Supreme	1½P-2½P	2P	$\frac{3}{16}$P–1$\frac{3}{16}$P	$\frac{11}{16}$P	$\frac{3}{32}$N–$\frac{3}{32}$P	NA
	Grand Prix	1½P-2½P	2P	$\frac{3}{16}$P–1$\frac{3}{16}$P	$\frac{11}{16}$P	$\frac{3}{32}$N–$\frac{3}{32}$P	NA
	Regal	1½P-2½P	2P	$\frac{3}{16}$P–1$\frac{3}{16}$P	$\frac{11}{16}$P	$\frac{3}{32}$N–$\frac{3}{32}$P	NA
1989-90	Cutlass Supreme	1$\frac{5}{16}$P-2$\frac{5}{16}$P	1$\frac{13}{16}$P	$\frac{3}{16}$P–1$\frac{3}{16}$P	$\frac{11}{16}$P	$\frac{3}{32}$N–$\frac{3}{32}$P	NA
	Grand Prix	1$\frac{5}{16}$P-2$\frac{5}{16}$P	1$\frac{13}{16}$P	$\frac{3}{16}$P–1$\frac{3}{16}$P	$\frac{11}{16}$P	$\frac{3}{32}$N–$\frac{3}{32}$P	NA
	Regal	1½P-2½P	2P	$\frac{3}{16}$P–1$\frac{3}{16}$P	$\frac{11}{16}$P	$\frac{3}{32}$N–$\frac{3}{32}$P	NA
	Lumina	1½P-2½P	2P	$\frac{3}{16}$P–1$\frac{3}{8}$P	$\frac{11}{16}$P	$\frac{3}{32}$N–$\frac{3}{32}$P	NA

NA Not adjustable

ELECTRICAL

NOTE: Disconnecting the negative battery cable on some vehicles may interfere with the functions of the on board computer systems and may require the computer to undergo a relearning process, once the negative battery cable is reconnected.

For testing and overhaul procedures on starters, alternators and voltage regulators, refer to the Unit Repair section.

Charging System

ALTERNATOR

Removal and Installation

1. Disconnect the negative battery cable.
2. Disconnect the electrical connectors at the rear of the alternator.
3. Remove the accessory drive belt.
4. Remove the mounting bolts and remove the alternator from the vehicle.
5. Install the alternator, tighten the upper mounting bolt to 18 ft. lbs. (25 Nm) and the lower bolt to 37 ft. lbs. (49 Nm).
6. Attach the electrical connector. Install the accessory drive belt.
7. Connect the negative battery cable.

VOLTAGE REGULATOR

Removal and Installation

The voltage regulator is located inside the alternator assembly and is not removable without first disassembling the alternator.

Belt Tension Adjustment

A single serpentine belt is used to drive all engine mounted components. Drive belt tension is maintained by a spring loaded tensioner.

NOTE: The drive belt tensioner can control the belt tension over a wide range of belt lengths; however, there are limits to the tensioners ability to compensate for various belt lengths. Installing the wrong size belt and using the tensioner outside of its operating range can result in poor tension control and damage to the tensioner, drive belt and driven components.

To remove the accessory drive belt, use a ¾ in. open end wrench and relieve the tension from the belt. This will allow the belt to be removed.

Starting System

STARTER

Removal and Installation

1. Disconnect the negative battery cable.
2. Raise and safely support the vehicle.
3. Tag and disconnect the wires from the starter.
4. Remove the starter motor cover and the 2 bolts retaining the starter.
5. Remove the starter and any shims.
6. Install the starter, install shims in their original location.
7. Attach the starter cover and the wiring.
8. Lower the vehicle. Connect the negative battery cable.

Ignition System

All engines use a distributorless ignition. Distributorless ignition systems use a "Waste-Spark" method of spark distribution. Each cylinder is paired with its opposing cylinder in the firing order. This makes one cylinder that is on the compression stroke fire with the opposing cylinder that is on the exhaust stroke. The cylinder that is on the exhaust stroke uses very little spark allowing most of the spark to go to the cylinder on the compression stroke. This process reverses when the cylinder roles reverse. There are 3 coils for the Direct Ignition System (DIS), when used with the V6 engine and 2 coils for the system, when used with the 2.5L engine.

Removal and Installation

1. Disconnect the negative battery cable.
2. Remove the air cleaner.
3. Raise and safely support the vehicle.
4. Note positions of spark plug wires and remove.
5. Remove the DIS assembly from the vehicle.
6. Install the DIS assembly and tighten the bolts to 18 ft.lb. (25 Nm).
7. Install the spark plug wires and electrical connectors.

NOTE: The DIS assembly has to be removed to get to the crankshaft sensor.

IGNITION TIMING

Ignition timing is controlled by the Electronic Control Module (ECM). No adjustment is possible.

Electrical Controls

STEERING WHEEL

Removal and Installation

1. Disconnect the negative battery cable.
2. Push down and turn the horn pad and remove retainer.
3. Disconnect the horn electrical lead from the canceling cam tower.
4. Turn the ignition switch to the ON position.
5. Scribe an alignment mark on the steering wheel hub in line with the slash mark on the steering shaft.
6. Loosen the steering shaft nut and install a steering wheel puller. Remove the steering wheel.
7. Align the matchmarks on the wheel hub and shaft and install the steering wheel. Tighten the steering shaft nut to 30 ft. lbs. (41 Nm).
8. Connect the horn electrical lead and install the horn pad.
9. Connect the negative battery cable.

HORN SWITCH

Removal and Installation

1. Disconnect the negative battery cable.
2. Push down and turn the horn pad and retainer.
3. Disconnect the horn electrical lead from the canceling cam tower.
4. Connect the electrical lead and press the horn pad into place.

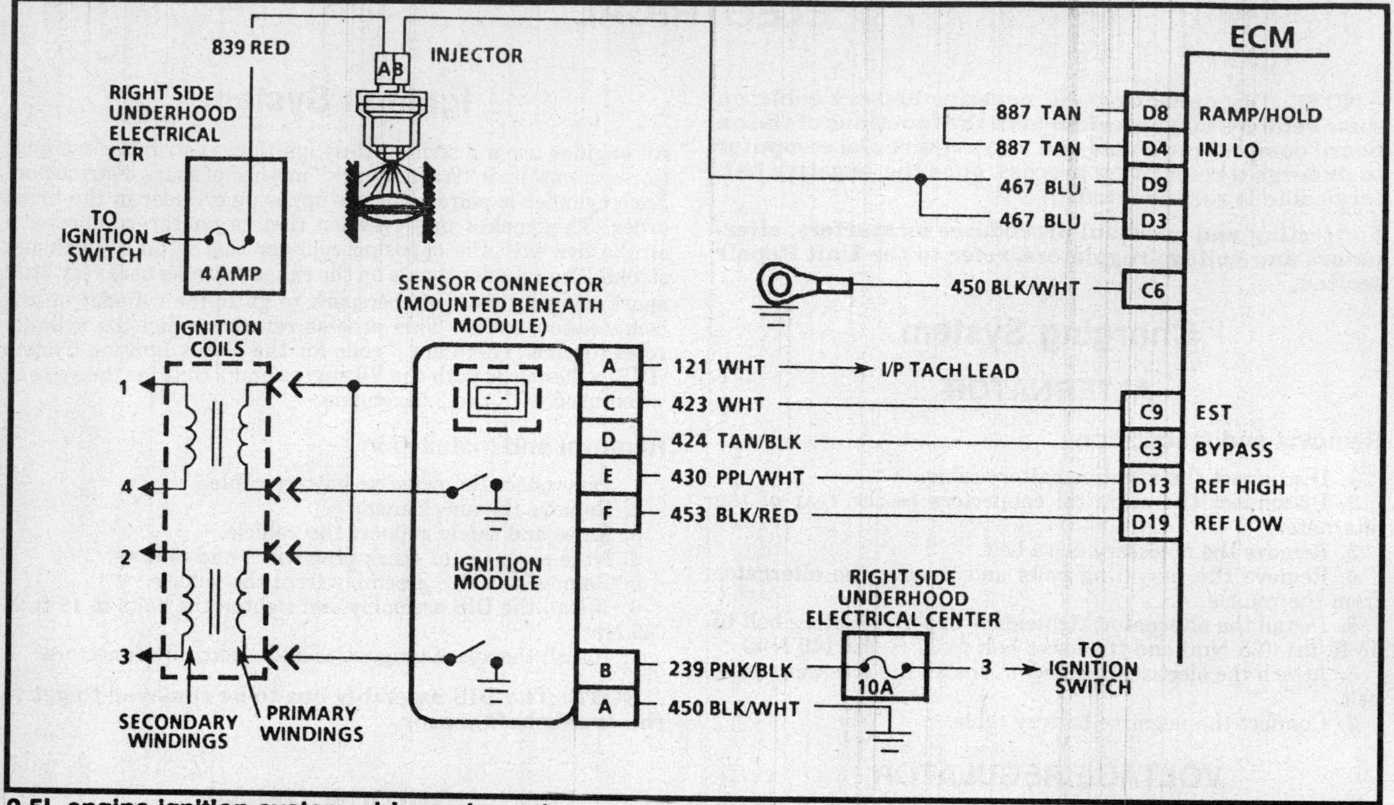

839 RED

INJECTOR

A B

ECM

RIGHT SIDE UNDERHOOD ELECTRICAL CTR

TO IGNITION SWITCH

4 AMP

887 TAN — D8 — RAMP/HOLD
887 TAN — D4 — INJ LO
467 BLU — D9
467 BLU — D3

450 BLK/WHT — C6

SENSOR CONNECTOR (MOUNTED BENEATH MODULE)

IGNITION COILS

1
4
2
3

SECONDARY WINDINGS   PRIMARY WINDINGS

IGNITION MODULE

A — 121 WHT → I/P TACH LEAD
C — 423 WHT → C9 — EST
D — 424 TAN/BLK → C3 — BYPASS
E — 430 PPL/WHT → D13 — REF HIGH
F — 453 BLK/RED → D19 — REF LOW

RIGHT SIDE UNDERHOOD ELECTRICAL CENTER

B — 239 PNK/BLK — 10A — 3 → TO IGNITION SWITCH
A — 450 BLK/WHT

2.5L engine ignition system wiring schematic

BULKHEAD CONN

MINI HARNESS IS LOCATED AT RT. FRT. FENDER BEHIND RELAY CENTER

ECM

FUEL PANEL
10A
ECM/IGN FUSE
C2

439 PNK/BLK — B10 — IGNITION

10A — 639 BLK/PNK — A

INJ. 2, 4, 6

F — 467 LT BLU — D9

10A
IGN 1
RT. SIDE ELECTRICAL CENTER

BLK MINI HARNESS CONN.

10A — 839 PNK/BLK — K

INJ. 1, 3, 5

BLK MINI HARNESS CONN

E — 468 LT GRN — D3

INJECTOR DRIVER

450 BLK/WHT — D4
551 TAN/WHT — D10

INJECTOR DRIVER GROUNDS

COIL ASSEMBLIES

IGN 1 — 10A

1
4
3
6
5
2

SECONDARY   PRIMARY WINDING

DIRECT IGNITION SYSTEM MODULE

B+ — B — 239 PNK/BLK
GND — A — 450 BLK/WHT

SIGNAL
A
B
C

SHIELD

YEL
PPL

A
B

CRANK SENSOR

CRANKSHAFT

A
B
C
D
E
F

424 TAN/BLK — C3 — BYPASS
423 WHT — C9 — EST

121 WHT → TACH SIGNAL

430 PPL/WHT — D13 — REFERENCE
453 BLK/RED — D19 — GROUND

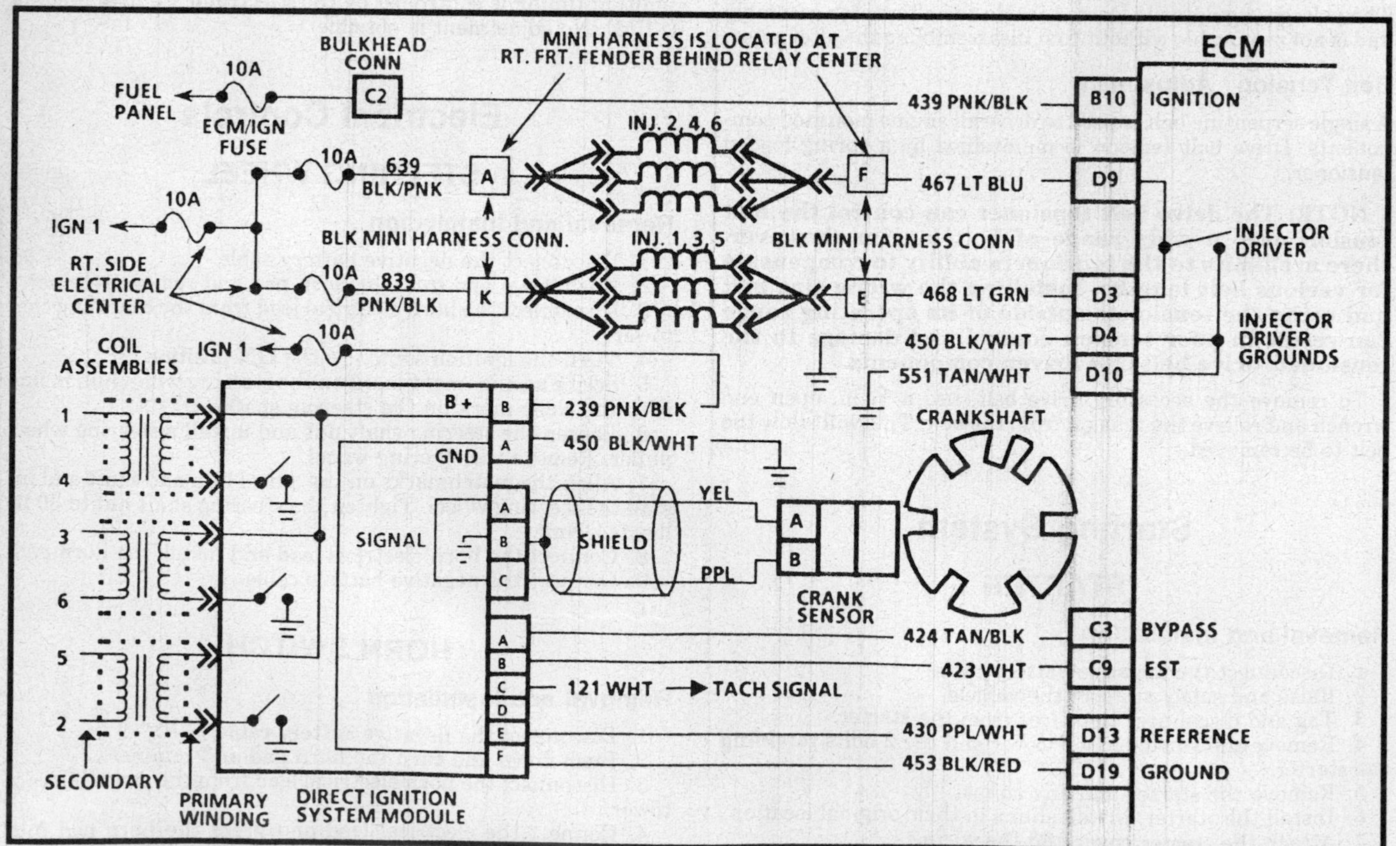

2.8L and 3.1L engines ignition system wiring schematic

IGNITION LOCK

Removal and Installation

STANDARD COLUMN

1. Disconnect the negative terminal from the battery. Remove the left side lower trim panel.
2. Remove the steering column-to-support screws and lower the steering column.
3. Disconnect the dimmer switch and turn signal switch connectors.
4. Remove the wiring harness-to-firewall nuts.
5. Remove the steering column-to-steering gear bolt and the steering column from the vehicle.
6. Remove the combination switch.
7. Place the lock cylinder in the **RUN** position.
8. Remove the steering shaft assembly and turn signal switch housing as an assembly.
9. Using the terminal remover tool J–35689–A or equivalent, disconnect and label the wires **F** and **G** on the connector at the buzzer switch assembly from the turn signal switch electrical harness connector.
10. With the lock cylinder in the **RUN** position, remove the buzzer switch.
11. Place the lock cylinder in the **ACC** position, remove the lock cylinder retaining screw and the lock cylinder.
12. Remove the dimmer switch nut/bolt, the dimmer switch and actuator rod.
13. Remove the dimmer switch mounting stud (the mounting nut was mounted to it).
14. Remove the ignition switch-to-steering column screws and the ignition switch.
15. Remove the lock bolt screws and the lock bolt.
16. Remove the switch actuator rack and ignition switch.
17. Remove the steering shaft lock and spring.

To install:

18. To install the lock bolt, lubricate it with lithium grease and install the lock bolt, spring and retaining plate.
19. Lubricate the teeth on the switch actuator rack, install the rack and the ignition switch through the opening in the steering bolt until it rests on the retaining plate.
20. Install the steering column lock cylinder set by holding the barrel of the lock cylinder, inserting the key and turning the key to the **ACC** position.
21. Install the lock set in the steering column while holding the rack against the lock plate.
22. Install the lock retaining screw. Insert the key in the lock cylinder and turn the lock cylinder to the **START** position and the rack will extend.
23. Center the slotted holes on the ignition switch mounting plate and install the ignition switch mounting screw and nut.
24. Install the dimmer switch and actuator rod into the center slot on the switch mounting plate.
25. Install the buzzer switch and turn the lock cylinder to the **RUN** position. Push the switch in until it is bottomed out with the plastic tab that covers the lock retaining screw.
26. Install the steering shaft and turn signal housing as an assembly.
27. Install the turn signal switch. Install the steering wheel to the column, torque the steering shaft nut to 30 ft. lbs. (41 Nm).
28. Install the steering column in the vehicle. Connect all electrical leads. Install the lower trim panels.
29. Connect the negative battery cable.

TILT COLUMN

1. Disconnect the negative terminal from the battery. Tilt the column up as far as it will go and remove the left side lower trim panel.
2. Remove the steering column-to-support screws and lower the steering column.

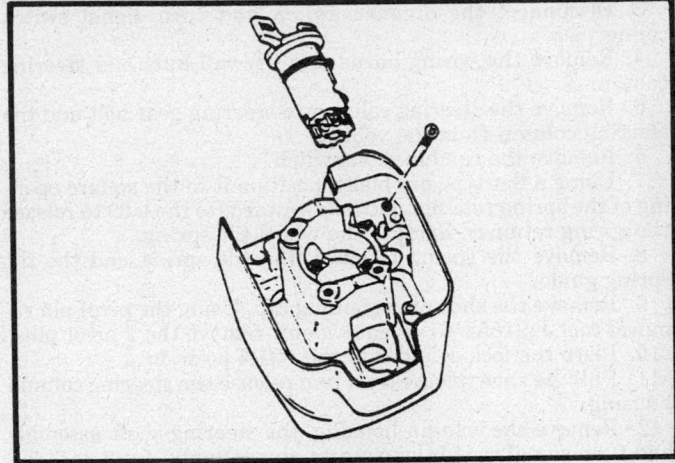
Removing the ignition lock cylinder

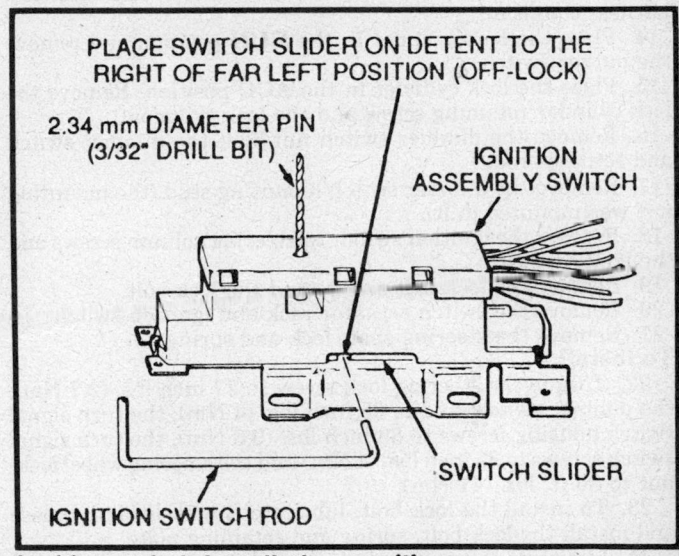

PLACE SWITCH SLIDER ON DETENT TO THE RIGHT OF FAR LEFT POSITION (OFF-LOCK)

2.34 mm DIAMETER PIN (3/32" DRILL BIT)

IGNITION ASSEMBLY SWITCH

SWITCH SLIDER

IGNITION SWITCH ROD

Ignition switch Installation position

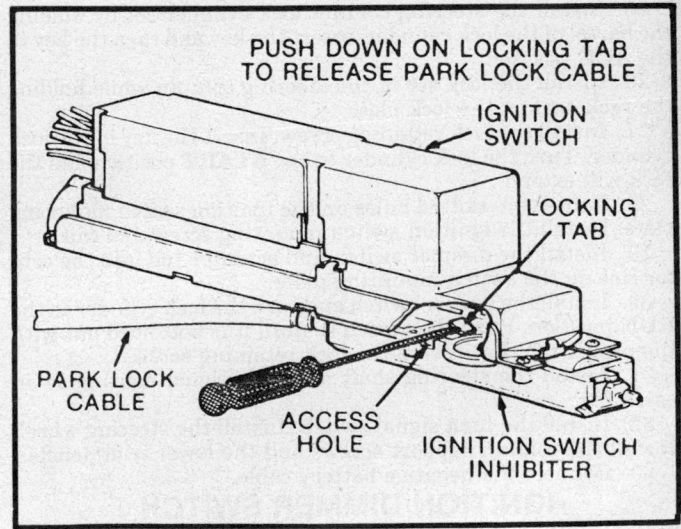

PUSH DOWN ON LOCKING TAB TO RELEASE PARK LOCK CABLE

IGNITION SWITCH

LOCKING TAB

PARK LOCK CABLE

ACCESS HOLE

IGNITION SWITCH INHIBITER

Park lock cable removal

3. Disconnect the dimmer switch and turn signal switch connectors.

4. Remove the wiring harness-to-firewall nuts and steering column.

5. Remove the steering column-to-steering gear bolt and the steering column from the vehicle.

6. Remove the combination switch.

7. Using a flat type pry blade, position it in the square opening of the spring retainer, push downward (to the left) to release the spring retainer. Remove the wheel tilt spring.

8. Remove the spring retainer, the tilt spring and the tilt spring guide.

9. Remove the shoe pin retaining cap. Using the pivot pin removal tool J–21854–01 or equivalent, remove the 2 pivot pins.

10. Place the lock cylinder in the **RUN** position.

11. Pull the shoe release lever and release the steering column housing.

12. Remove the column housing, the steering shaft assembly and turn signal switch housing as an assembly.

13. Using the terminal remover tool J–35689–A or equivalent, disconnect and label the wires **F** and **G** on the connector at the buzzer switch assembly from the turn signal switch electrical harness connector.

14. Place the lock cylinder in the **RUN** position and remove the buzzer switch.

15. Place the lock cylinder in the **ACC** position. Remove the lock cylinder retaining screw and the lock cylinder.

16. Remove the dimmer switch nut/bolt, the dimmer switch and actuator rod.

17. Remove the dimmer switch mounting stud (the mounting nut was mounted to it).

18. Remove the ignition switch-to-steering column screws and the ignition switch.

19. Remove the lock bolt screws and the lock bolt.

20. Remove the switch actuator rack and ignition switch.

21. Remove the steering shaft lock and spring.

To install:

22. Torque the steering lock screw to 27 inch lbs. (2.7 Nm), the dimmer switch stud to 35 inch lbs. (4 Nm), the turn signal switch housing screws to 88 inch lbs. (9.8 Nm), the turn signal switch screws to 35 inch lbs. (4 Nm) and the steering wheel lock-nut to 30 ft. lbs. (41 Nm).

23. To install the lock bolt, lubricate it with lithium grease and install the lock bolt, spring and retaining plate.

24. Lubricate the teeth on the switch actuator rack. Install the rack and the ignition switch through the opening in the steering bolt until it rests on the retaining plate.

25. Install the steering column lock cylinder set by holding the barrel of the lock cylinder, insert the key and turn the key to the **ACC** position.

26. Install the lock set in the steering column while holding the rack against the lock plate.

27. Install the lock retaining screw. Insert the key in the lock cylinder. Turn the lock cylinder to the **START** position and the rack will extend.

28. Center the slotted holes on the ignition switch mounting plate. Install the ignition switch mounting screw and nut.

29. Install the dimmer switch and actuator rod into the center slot on the switch mounting plate.

30. Install the buzzer switch and turn the lock cylinder to the **RUN** position. Push the switch in until it is bottomed out with the plastic tab that covers the lock retaining screw.

31. Install the steering shaft and turn signal housing as an assembly.

32. Install the turn signal switch. Install the steering wheel. Install the column support screws and the lower trim panels.

33. Connect the negative battery cable.

IGNITION/DIMMER SWITCH

Removal and Installation

1. Disconnect the negative battery cable.

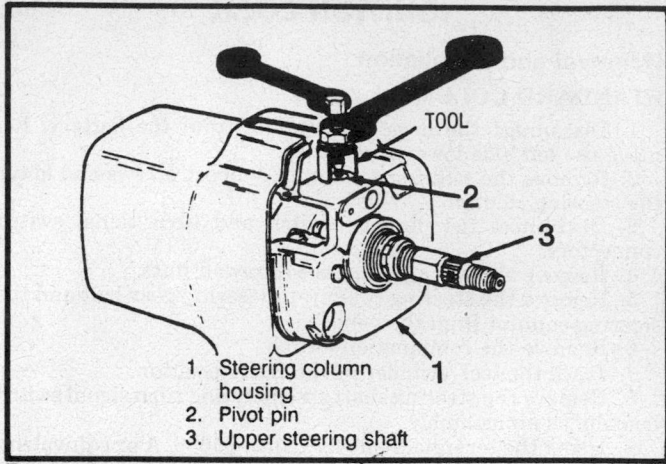

1. Steering column housing
2. Pivot pin
3. Upper steering shaft

Removing the pivot pin

2. Place the gear shifter in **P** and the lock cylinder in the **OFF-LOCK** position.

3. Remove the steering column.

4. Remove the turn signal, dimmer and pulse switch electrical connectors.

5. Remove the bowl shield.

6. Remove the switch components in order of dimmer switch nut, upper mounting stud, lower mounting stud and switch from the switch actuator rod.

To install:

7. Place the switch slider in the far left position and move back one detent to the right of the **OFF-LOCK** position.

8. Insert a $^3/_{32}$ in. drill bit into the adjustment hole on the switch slider during installation.

9. Install the switch and rod.

10. Install the switch jacket and bowl with the lower mounting stud. Tighten the stud to 36 inch lbs. (4 Nm).

11. Remove the adjustment tool.

12. Install the dimmer switch actuator rod with the tab first, through the hole in the instrument panel bracket and into the switch rod cap.

13. Install the dimmer switch and adjust using a $^3/_{32}$ in. drill bit into the hole in the top. Remove all excess lash. Do not tighten at this time.

14. After adjustment has been made, tighten the dimmer switch nut and mounting stud to 36 inch lbs. (4 Nm). Remove the adjusting tool.

15. Install the column jacket, bowl and shield.

16. Connect the turn signal, pulse and dimmer switch electrical connectors.

17. Connect the negative battery cable.

NEUTRAL SAFETY SWITCH

Removal and Installation

1. Place the selector lever in the **N** detent. Disconnect the negative battery cable.

2. Remove the air cleaner, as required.

3. Raise and safely support the vehicle.

4. Remove the switch harness.

5. Lower the vehicle.

6. Remove the vacuum lines and electrical connectors from the cruise control servo, if equipped.

7. Remove the shift lever, cruise control servo and switch. Do not disconnect the lever from the cable.

8. Align the notch on the inner sleeve of the switch with the notch on the switch body.

9. Install the switch and tighten the bolts to 18 ft. lbs. (24 Nm).

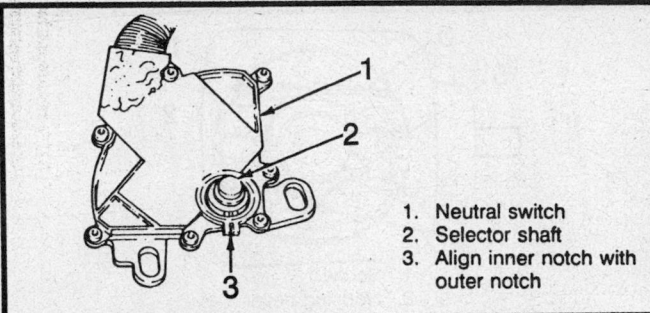

1. Neutral switch
2. Selector shaft
3. Align inner notch with outer notch

Neutral safety switch

10. Install the shift lever and tighten the nut to 15 ft. lbs. (20 Nm).

11. Raise and safely support the vehicle, connect the switch harness and lower the vehicle.

12. Install the cruise control servo, vacuum lines and electrical connectors, if equipped.

13. Install the air cleaner, as required and connect the negative battery cable.

CLUTCH START SWITCH

Removal and Installation

1. Disconnect the negative terminal from the battery.

2. Remove the lower left trim panel. Locate the switch on the clutch pedal support.

3. Disconnect the electrical connector from the switch and remove the switch by twisting it out of the tubular retaining clip.

4. Using a new retaining clip, install the switch and connect the electrical connector.

5. To adjust the switch, pull back on the clutch pedal, push the switch through the retaining clip noting the clicks; repeat this procedure until no more clicks can be heard.

6. Connect the negative battery cable and check the switch operation.

STOPLIGHT SWITCH

Removal and Installation

1. Disconnect the negative battery cable.

2. Remove the lower left trim panel. Locate the stoplight switch on the brake pedal support.

3. Disconnect the plug on the switch and remove the switch by twisting it out of the tubular retaining clip. If the vehicle is equipped with cruise control, unplug the vacuum line from the cruise control cut-off switch.

4. Install the new switch using a new retaining clip and connect the wire.

5. Adjust the switch by pulling back on the brake pedal noting the clicks as the switch is pushed through the retaining clip.

6. Repeat the procedure until no clicks can be heard.

7. Connect the negative battery cable and check the switch operation.

HEADLAMP SWITCH

Removal and Installation

CUTLASS SUPREME, REGAL AND LUMINA

1. Disconnect the negative battery cable.

2. Remove the 4 instrument cluster trim plate retaining screws and plate. Remove the air outlet trim plate.

3. Remove the 2 screws retaining the switch and remove the switch from the instrument panel.

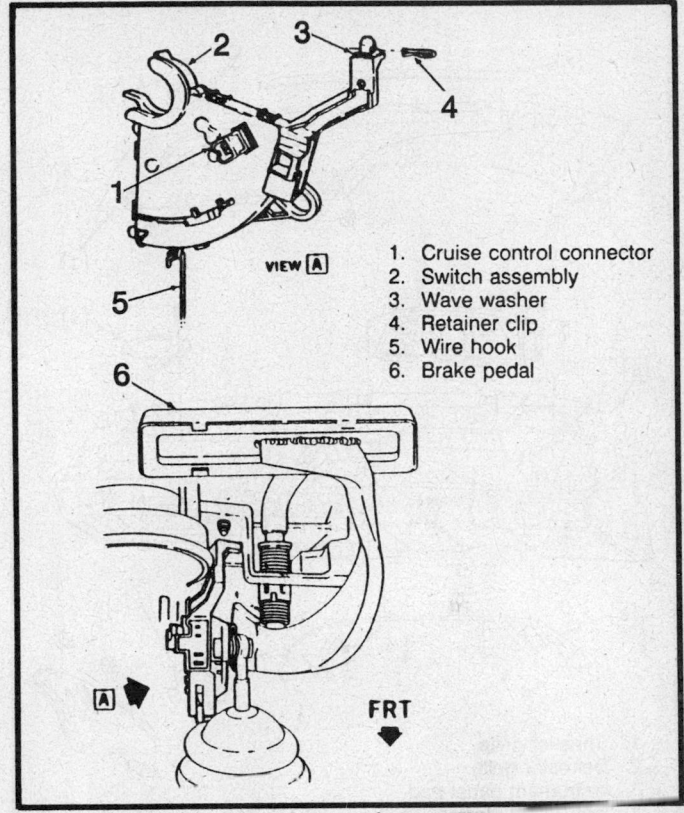

1. Cruise control connector
2. Switch assembly
3. Wave washer
4. Retainer clip
5. Wire hook
6. Brake pedal

VIEW Ⓐ

Stop light switch location and mounting

4. Disconnect the electrical connector from the switch and remove the switch.

5. To install the switch, connect the electrical connector and install the switch in the instrument panel.

6. Install the air outlet and cluster trim plates.

7. Connect the negative battery cable.

GRAND PRIX

1. Disconnect the negative battery cable.

2. Remove the screw retaining the headlight switch to the instrument panel.

3. Pull the top of the switch out to release the lower retaining clips and remove it from the instrument panel.

4. Disconnect the electrical connector and remove the switch from the vehicle.

5. To install the switch, connect the electrical connector and install the switch in the instrument panel.

6. Connect the negative battery cable.

TURN SIGNAL/COMBINATION SWITCH

Removal and Installation

NOTE: Tool J–35689–A or equivalent, is required to remove the terminals from the connector on the turn signal switch.

1. Disconnect the negative battery cable. Remove the steering wheel.

2. Pull the turn signal canceling cam assembly from the steering shaft.

3. Remove the hazard warning knob-to-steering column screw and the knob.

NOTE: Before removing the turn signal assembly, position the turn signal lever so the turn signal assembly to steering column screws can all be removed.

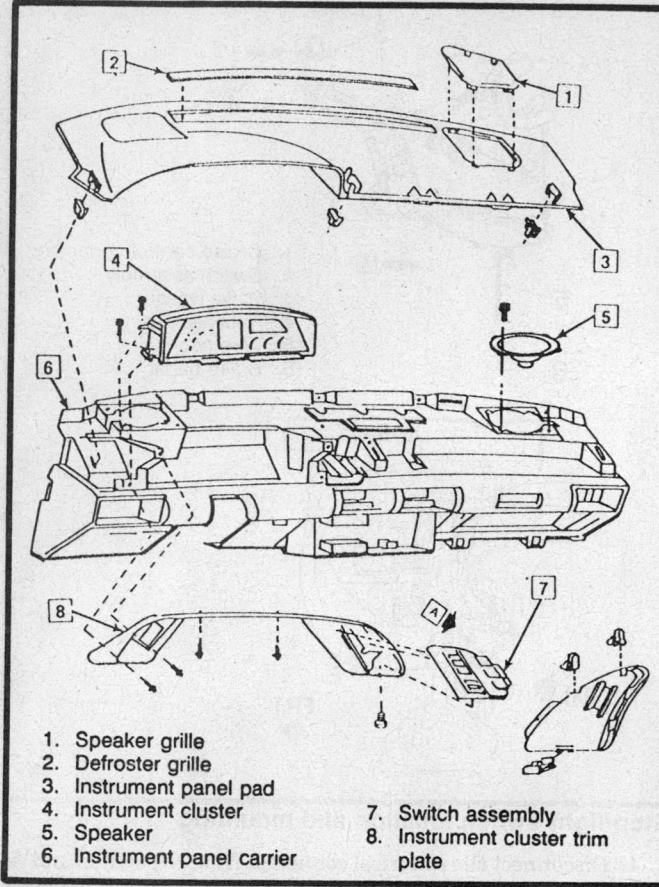

1. Speaker grille
2. Defroster grille
3. Instrument panel pad
4. Instrument cluster
5. Speaker
6. Instrument panel carrier
7. Switch assembly
8. Instrument cluster trim plate

Removing headlamp switch–Grand Prix

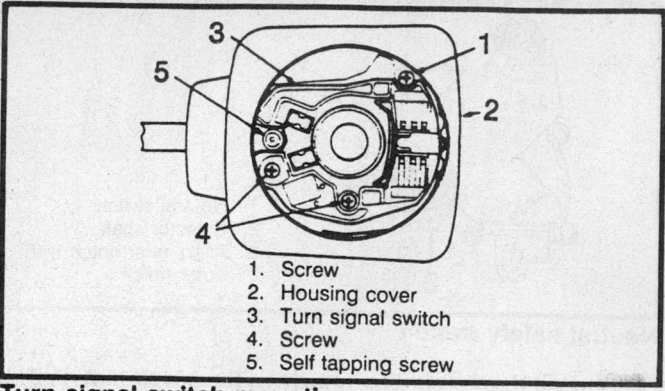

1. Screw
2. Housing cover
3. Turn signal switch
4. Screw
5. Self tapping screw

Turn signal switch mounting

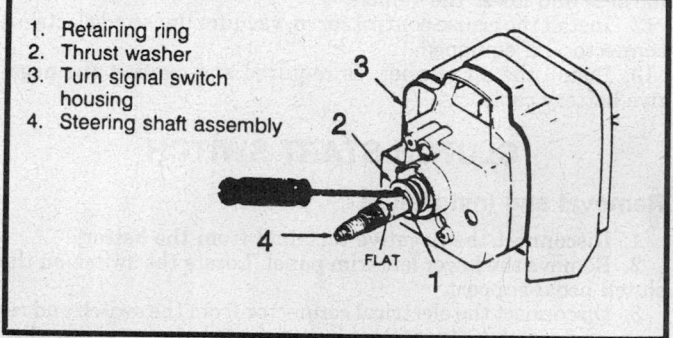

1. Retaining ring
2. Thrust washer
3. Turn signal switch housing
4. Steering shaft assembly

Removing the turn signal switch housing

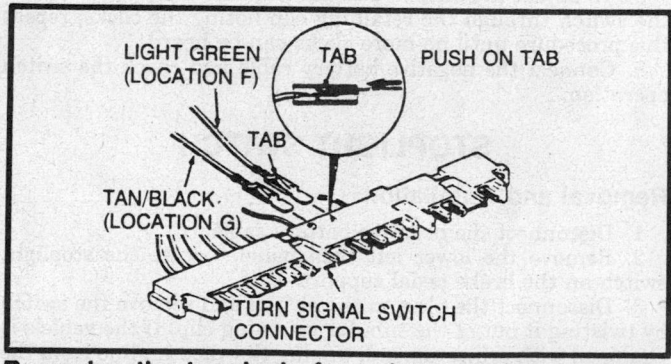

Removing the terminals from the turn signal switch connector

4. Remove the column housing cover-to-column housing bowl screw and the cover.

NOTE: If equipped with cruise control, disconnect the cruise control electrical connector.

5. Remove the turn signal lever-to-pivot assembly screw and the lever; 1 screw is in the front and the other screw is in the rear.

6. Remove the wiring protector from the opening in the instrument panel bracket and separate from the wires.

7. Using the terminal remover tool J–35689–A or equivalent, disconnect and label the wires **F** and **G** on the connector at the buzzer switch assembly from the turn signal switch electrical harness connector.

8. Remove the turn signal switch-to-steering column screws and the switch.

9. Install the turn signal switch to the steering column, torque the turn signal switch-to-steering column screws to 35 inch lbs. (4 Nm).

10. Install the electrical connectors and install the turn signal lever to the pivot assembly. Install the hazard flasher knob. Install the canceling cam.

11. Install the wiring protector and connect the wiring harness.

12. Install the steering wheel. Connect the negative battery cable.

WINDSHIELD WIPER SWITCH

Removal and Installation

The windshield wiper switch is mounted on the right side of the instrument cluster, on Grand Prix. On 1988 Cutlass Supreme, Regal and 1990 Lumina, it is located on the left side of the instrument cluster in combination with the headlamp switch. On 1989/90 Cutlass Supreme and Regal, the switch is located on the turn signal/combination switch.

1. Disconnect the negative battery cable.
2. Remove the screw retaining the switch panel to the instrument panel.
3. Remove the switch from the instrument panel by pulling the bottom out and releasing the top retaining clips.
4. Disconnect the electrical connector from the switch and remove it from the vehicle.
5. To install the switch, connect the electrical leads and push the switch into position.
6. Install the retaining screw. Connect the negative battery cable.

WINDSHIELD WIPER MOTOR

Removal and Installation

1. Disconnect the negative battery cable.
2. Remove the washer hose, cap and retaining nut from each wiper arm. Remove the wiper arms from the vehicle.
3. Remove the screws retaining the cowl cover. Lower the hood partially and remove the cowl cover. Remove the air inlet panel and underhood lamp switch, if so equipped.
4. Disconnect the wiring harness connectors at the wiper motor and the washer hose at the firewall.
5. Remove the 3 screws from the bellcrank housing and lower the wiper transmission.
6. If the motor is inoperative, rotate the crank arm to the inner wipe position. Engage a pliers against the top edge of the crank arm and the crank arm nut as a pivot point. Move the crank arm to the correct position.
7. Remove the wiper module assembly from the vehicle. To remove the wiper motor from the module assembly, remove the 3 screw retaining the motor and remove the motor. To remove the linkage, remove the screws retaining the linkage to the module.
8. To install, attach the motor to the module assembly and install the module assembly in the vehicle.
9. Attach the bellcrank to module assembly and install the cowl cover, air inlet panel.
10. Attach the electrical connectors to the motor and attach the washer hose to the firewall. Install the wiper arms, nuts and caps. Attach the washer hoses to the wiper arms.
11. Connect the negative battery cable.

DELAY WIPER CONTROLS

Operation

These vehicles use an optional pulse wipe system. The wipe positions include **PULSE, LOW, HIGH, MIST** and **OFF**. With the wiper switch in the **PULSE** position, the voltage is supplied to the wiper motor module and current flows on 2 paths. The first is through the park relay coil to ground. The second is through the control board, closed park relay contacts and the wiper motor to ground. When the wiper motor runs, it signals the control board at the end of each sweep. When a sweep is completed, the control board interrupts power to the wiper motor and waits a period of time before allowing current to flow to the wiper motor for another sweep. The pulse delay switch controls the amount of time between sweeps.

WINDSHIELD WIPER LINKAGE

Removal and Installation

1. Disconnect the negative battery cable.
2. Remove the windshield wiper motor.
3. Remove the 2 linkage socket screws and the socket from the link ball.
4. Remove the bellcrank mounting screws and linkage from the module.

NOTE: The wiper motor must be put into the inner wiper position.

5. Position the crank arm in the inner wiper position.
6. Using a suitable tool, align the hole in the motor with the hole in the bellcrank. Tighten the socket screws to the crank arm ball.
7. Install the wiper motor with body seals and linkage.
8. Install the wiper arms and blades. Connect the negative battery cable.

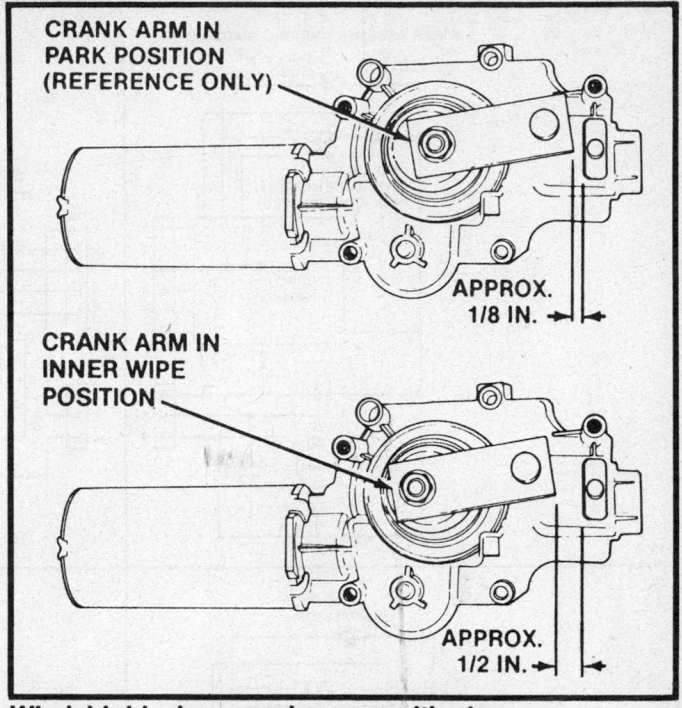

CRANK ARM IN PARK POSITION (REFERENCE ONLY)

APPROX. 1/8 IN.

CRANK ARM IN INNER WIPE POSITION

APPROX. 1/2 IN.

Windshield wiper crank arm positioning

Instrument Cluster

Refer to the "Chilton's Electronic Instrumentation Service Manual" for additional coverage.

NOTE: When handling any electronic part that has an ESD (electrostatic discharge) sticker: do not open package until ready to install, avoid touching electrical terminals of the part, ground the package to a known good ground on the vehicle and always touch a good ground before handling the part, especially after sliding across the seat.

Removal and Installation

CUTLASS SUPREME

1. Disconnect the negative battery cable.
2. Remove the 5 screws retaining the cluster trim plate. Pull the bottom of the trim plate out and remove it from the vehicle.
3. Open the glove box and remove the lower storage compartment. Remove the 2 screws in the glove box opening.
4. Remove the defroster grille and remove the 2 screws inside the opening. Remove the 2 screws at the side of the instrument cluster.
5. Lift up on the upper panel pad and remove the pad. Remove the screws retaining the instrument cluster and remove the cluster from the instrument panel. Disconnect the electrical connectors.
6. Install the cluster to the instrument panel. Connect the electrical leads.
7. Install the upper panel pad. Install the defroster grille and the glove box compartment.
8. Install the cluster trim panel. Connect the negative battery cable.

GRAND PRIX

1. Disconnect the negative battery cable.
2. Remove the wiper and headlight switch assemblies.
3. Remove the 2 screws in each of the switch openings and re-

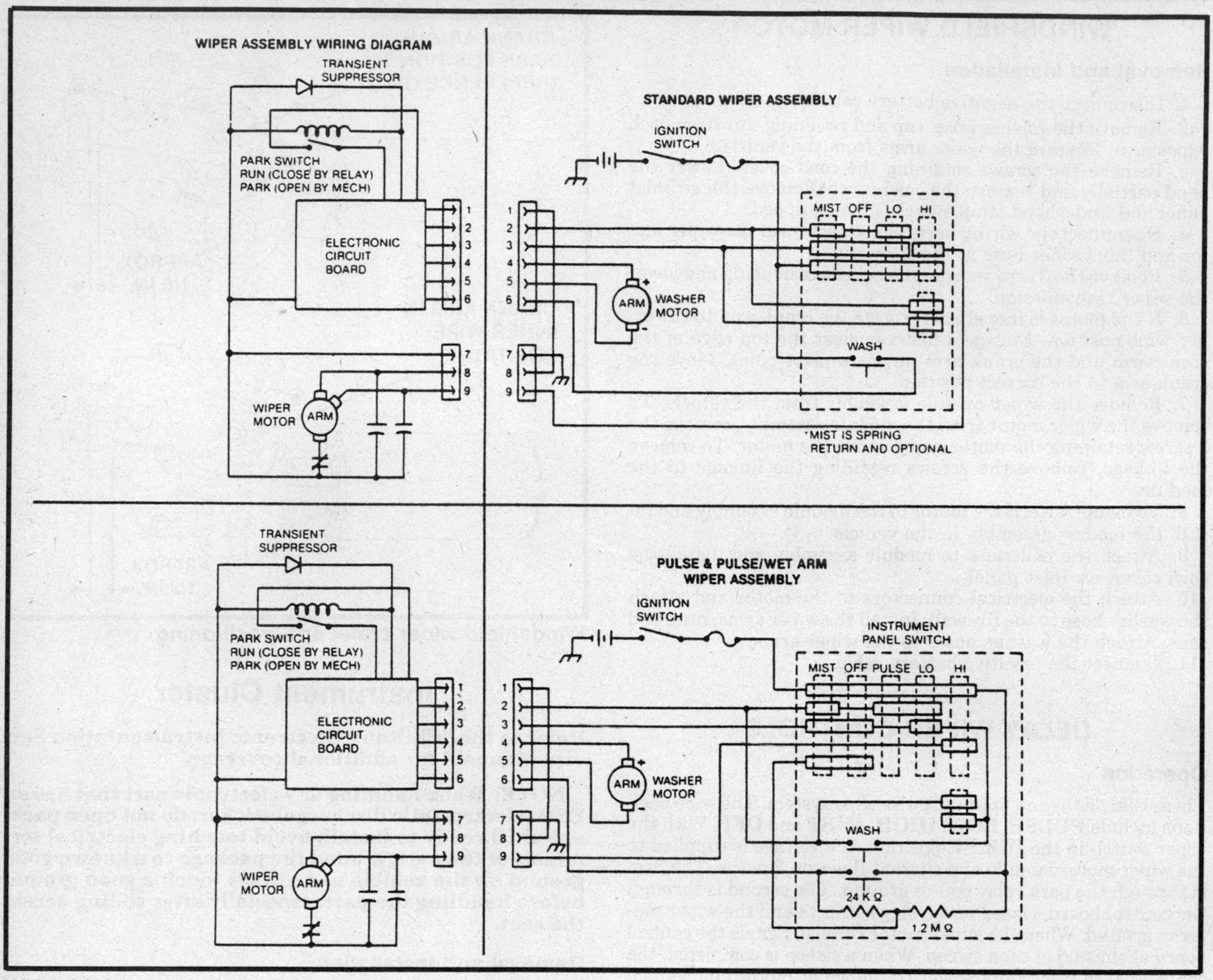

WIPER ASSEMBLY WIRING DIAGRAM

TRANSIENT SUPPRESSOR

PARK SWITCH
RUN (CLOSE BY RELAY)
PARK (OPEN BY MECH)

ELECTRONIC CIRCUIT BOARD

1
2
3
4
5
6

7
8
9

WIPER MOTOR
ARM

STANDARD WIPER ASSEMBLY

IGNITION SWITCH

ARM WASHER MOTOR

MIST OFF LO HI

WASH

*MIST IS SPRING RETURN AND OPTIONAL

TRANSIENT SUPPRESSOR

PARK SWITCH
RUN (CLOSE BY RELAY)
PARK (OPEN BY MECH)

ELECTRONIC CIRCUIT BOARD

1
2
3
4
5
6

7
8
9

WIPER MOTOR
ARM

PULSE & PULSE/WET ARM WIPER ASSEMBLY

IGNITION SWITCH

ARM WASHER MOTOR

INSTRUMENT PANEL SWITCH

MIST OFF PULSE LO HI

WASH

24 K Ω
1.2 M Ω

Windshield wiper wiring schematics

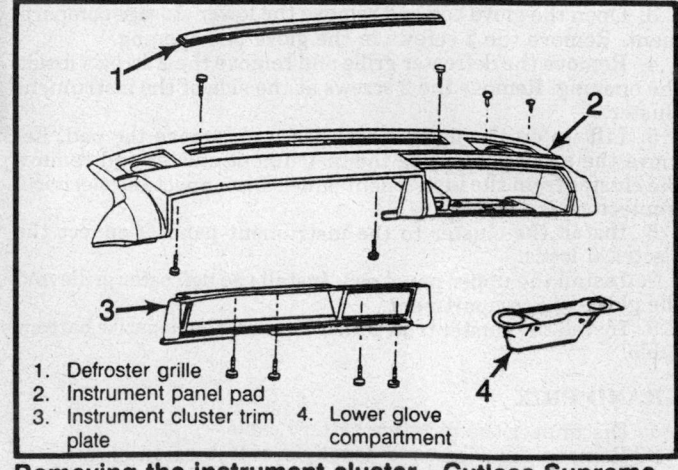

1. Defroster grille
2. Instrument panel pad
3. Instrument cluster trim plate
4. Lower glove compartment

Removing the instrument cluster—Cutlass Supreme

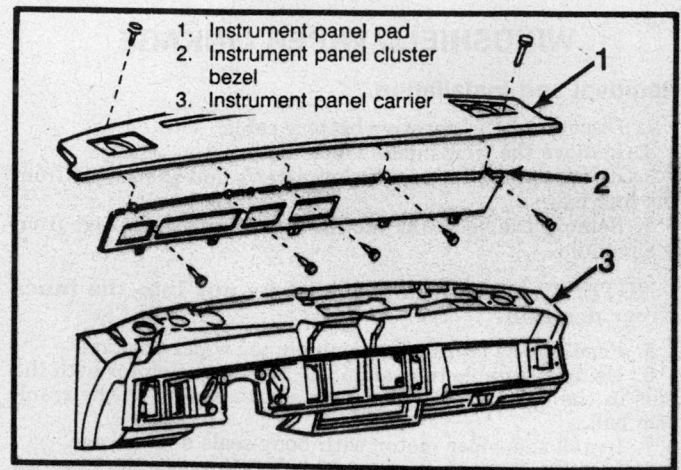

1. Instrument panel pad
2. Instrument panel cluster bezel
3. Instrument panel carrier

Removing the instrument cluster—Regal

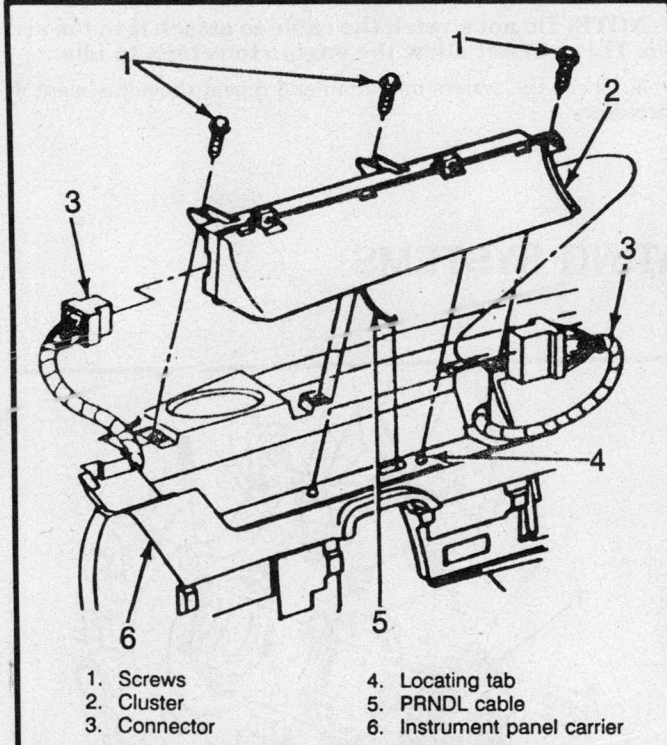

CLUSTER

FRT

INSTRUMENT PANEL

Removing the instrument cluster — Grand Prix

1. Screws
2. Cluster
3. Connector
4. Locating tab
5. PRNDL cable
6. Instrument panel carrier

Removing the instrument cluster—Lumina

move the 2 screws from the top of the cluster trim plate. Remove the cluster trim plate.

4. Remove the glove box and remove the screw above the glove box opening.

5. Lift the front of the instrument panel pad and pull it back to release it from the instrument panel. Remove it from the vehicle.

6. Remove the 4 screws retaining the instrument cluster and pull the cluster forward. Disconnect the electrical connectors and remove the cluster from the vehicle.

7. Install the cluster to the instrument panel. Connect the electrical leads.

8. Install the upper panel pad. Install the glove box.

9. Install the cluster trim panel.

10. Connect the negative battery cable.

LUMINA

1. Disconnect the negative battery cable.

2. Disconnect the daytime running lamp sensor, if so equipped.

3. Remove the screws under the edge of the instrument panel pad.

4. Remove the instrument panel pad by lifting the front edge and pull rearward to release then lift up and out.

5. Remove the cluster retaining screws and disconnect the wiring harnesses.

6. Disconnect the PRNDL cable from the steering column. Remove the instrument cluster assembly.

7. Install the instrument cluster.

8. Install the instrument panel pad.

SPEEDOMETER

The speedometer and gauges are serviced as a unit. Removal of the instrument cluster is necessary in order to gain access to the circuit board that controls the gauges.

SPEEDOMETER DRIVE/GOVERNOR

The speedometer drive is located in the transaxle housing. This unit is a solid state unit with no speedometer cable.

Removal and Installation

1. Disconnect the negative battery cable.

2. Remove the electrical connector from the speedo drive assembly.

3. Remove the drive retaining screws and drive unit.

4. Install the drive unit with a new O-ring and torque the screws to 8 ft. lbs. (11 Nm).

Electrical Circuit Protectors

FUSIBLE LINKS

Fusible links are sections of wire, with special insulation, designed to melt under electrical overload. Replacements are simply spliced into the wire. The wires are located at the starter solenoid terminal and the right side electrical center in the engine compartment.

CIRCUIT BREAKERS

A circuit breaker is an electrical switch which breaks the circuit during an electrical overload. The circuit breaker will remain open until the short or overload condition in the circuit is corrected. Circuit breakers are located in the fuse panel and component center located behind the instrument panel.

FUSE PANEL

The fuse panel is located on the left side of the instrument panel in Regal, Cutlass Supreme and Lumina. It is located on the right side of the instrument panel in the Grand Prix. In order to gain access to the fuse panel, it may be necessary to first remove the lower trim panel.

COMPUTER

The Electronic Control Module (ECM) is located on the right front wheel well at the front of the strut tower.

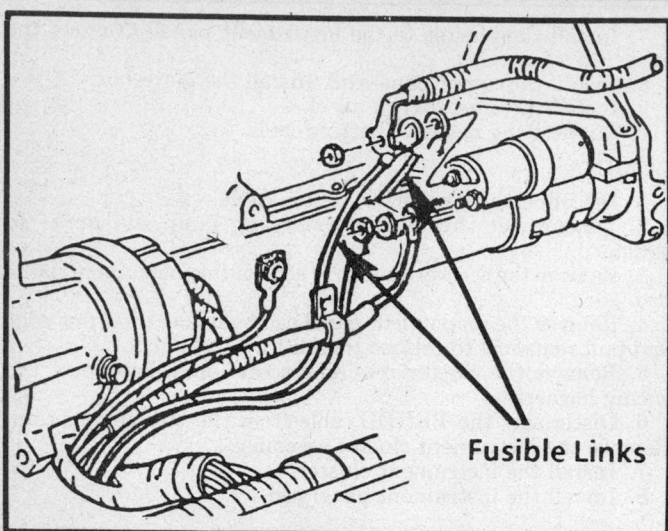

Fusible link location

VARIOUS RELAYS

The coolant fan, A/C compressor, are located in the engine compartment mounted to the right side of the firewall on the relay bracket. The high and low blower relays are located in the component center located behind the instrument panel on the left side. The power door lock relay is located on the left side behind the instrument panel.

TURN SIGNAL/HAZARD FLASHER

The hazard flasher is located in the component center behind the instrument panel. The turn signal flasher is located behind the lower left side of the instrument panel on the steering column support.

VEHICLE SPEED SENSOR

The vehicle speed sensor is mounted on the right rear of transaxle near the oil filter.

Speed Controls

Refer to "Chilton's Professional Chassis Electronics Service Manual" for additional coverage.

Adjustment

1. With the servo cable installed on the brackets, place the cable over the stud on the servo lever so the stud engages the slot in the cable end.
2. Connect the cable to the throttle lever and release the lever.
3. Pull the servo end of the cable towards the servo as far as possible without moving the throttle.
4. Attach the cable to the servo in the closest alignment holes without moving the throttle.

NOTE: Do not stretch the cable to attach it to the servo. This will not allow the engine to return to idle.

5. Check the system operation and repeat the adjustment as necessary.

COOLING AND HEATING SYSTEMS

Water Pump

Removal and Installation
2.5L ENGINE
1. Disconnect the negative battery cable.
2. Remove the alternator.
3. Remove the conponent center heat shield.
4. Partially drain the engine coolant.
5. Remove the water pump retaining bolts, water pump and pulley.
6. Clean gasket mating surfaces.
7. Install the pulley, water pump with a new gasket and tighten the retaining bolts to 24 ft. lbs. (33 Nm).
8. Install the component center heat shield and alternator.
9. Refill the cooling system and connect the negative battery cable. Check for coolant leaks.

2.8L AND 3.1L ENGINES
1. Disconnect the negative battery cable.
2. Drain the cooling system.
3. Remove the accessory drive belt.
4. Remove the radiator.
5. Remove the water pump pulley.
6. Remove the water pump mounting bolts and remove the water pump.
7. Clean the gasket mating surfaces.
8. Install the water pump to the engine and tighten the mounting bolts to 89 inch lbs. (10 Nm).

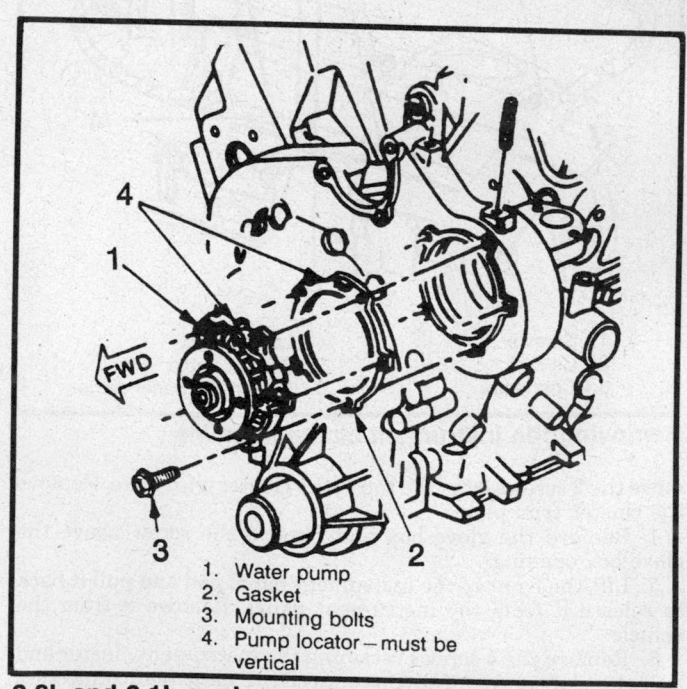

1. Water pump
2. Gasket
3. Mounting bolts
4. Pump locator—must be vertical

2.8L and 3.1L engines water pump mounting

1. Water pump
2. 24 ft. lbs. (33 Nm)

2.5L engine water pump mounting

9. Attach the water pump pulley. Install the accessory drive belt.
10. Fill the cooling system and connect the negative battery cable.

Electric Cooling Fan

SYSTEM OPERATION

The electric cooling fans are controlled by the electronic control module. The coolant temperature sensor in the engine sends a signal to the ECM when the engine coolant temperature reaches 223°F (205°C). The ECM grounds the cooling fan relay which turns the fan **ON**. The cooling fan will also turn **ON** if the A/C pressure switch detects a pressure more than 200 psi and the vehicle speed is less than 70 mph (113 Km/h). If the cooling fan is turned **ON** by the ECM for any reason, the fan will cycle for no less than 30 seconds.

Removal and Installation

1. Disconnect the negative battery cable.
2. Disconnect the electrical wiring harness from the cooling fan frame.
3. Remove the fan assembly from the radiator support.
4. Install the fan assembly to the radiator support. Torque the fan assembly-to-radiator support bolts to 7 ft. lbs. (9.5 Nm).
5. Attach the wiring harness and connect the negative battery cable.

COOLING FAN RELAY

The cooling fan relay is located in the right side electrical center on the inner fender. The heavy duty relay goes into the far left socket and the standard duty relay goes in the center socket.

Blower Motor

Removal and Installation

1. Disconnect the negative terminal from the battery.
2. Disconnect the electrical connections from the blower motor and resistor.

3. Remove the plastic water shield from the right side of the cowl.
4. Remove the blower motor-to-chassis screws and the blower motor.
5. Remove the cage retaining nut and the cage. On some 1989 models, the cage has to be removed by pulling straight off the shaft or by cutting slots in the shaft sleeve with a hot knife in 3 places. Start the cuts from the cage dome and continue to cut through the plastic material to the end of the shaft.
6. Install the cage on the new blower motor with the opening facing away from the motor.
7. Install the blower motor and screws. Connect the electrical leads to the motor and resistor.
8. Install the water shield to the cowl. Connect the negative battery cable.

Heater Core

Refer to "Chilton's Auto Heating and Air Conditioning Manual" for additional coverage.

Removal and Installation

1. Disconnect the negative battery cable.
2. Drain the cooling system.
3. Remove the upper firewall weatherstrip. Remove the upper cowl.
4. Remove the heater hoses from the core.
5. Inside the vehicle, remove the sound insulator panel. Remove the rear seat duct adapter.
6. Remove the heater duct. Remove the heater core cover and remove the heater core.
7. Install the heater core and cover. Install the rear seat duct adapter.
8. Install the sound insulator.
9. Attach the heater hoses to the core. Install the upper cowl and the weatherstrip.
10. Fill the cooling system and check for leaks. Connect the negative battery cable.

TEMPERATURE CONTROL BLOWER SWITCH

Removal and Installation

1. Disconnect the negative battery cable.
2. Remove the lower left instrument panel trim pad.
3. Remove the control panel trim.
4. Remove the screws on the left of the assembly and pull the assembly out.
5. Disconnect the electrical leads and remove the control panel.
6. To install, connect the electrical leads and install the panel.
7. Install the lower panel pad and connect the negative battery cable.

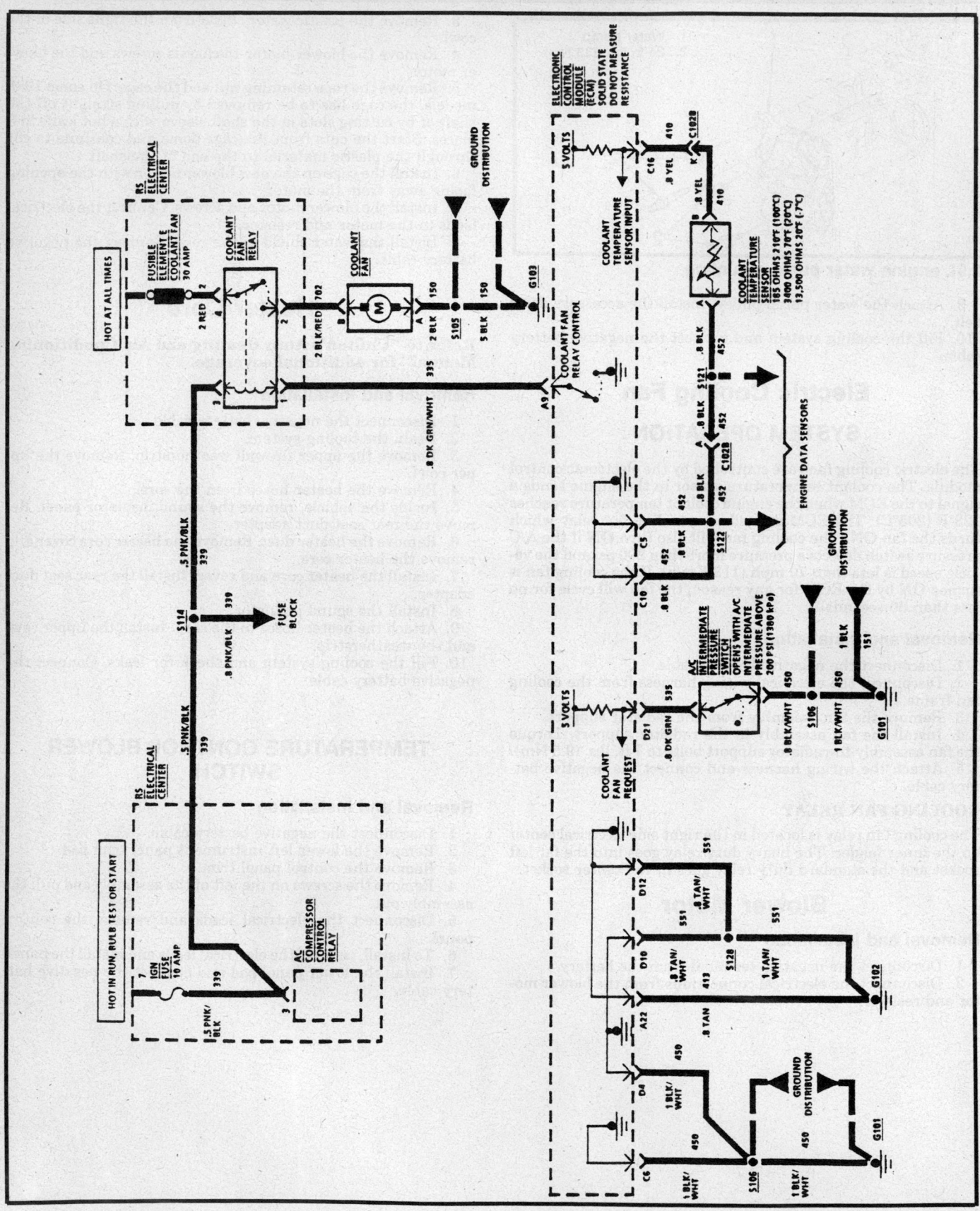

Coolant fan circuit

FUEL INJECTION SYSTEM

Refer to "Chilton's Electronic Engine Controls Manual" for additional coverage.

Description

The Throttle Body Injection (TBI) and Multi-port Fuel Injection (MFI) systems uses an electric fuel pump mounted in the tank. The throttle body assembly is placed on the intake manifold where the carburetor is normally mounted. A single fuel injector supplies the engine with fuel. The 2.8L and 3.1L MFI system is incorporated into the intake manifold and air intake plenum. Each cylinder has its own fuel injector. Both are computer controlled systems that supply the correct amount of fuel during all engine operating conditions.

IDLE SPEED

Idle speed and mixture are controlled by the ECM. No adjustments are possible.

FUEL SYSTEM PRESSURE RELIEF

Procedure

NOTE: When working with the fuel system certain precautions should be taken; always work in a well ventilated area, keep a dry chemical (Class B) fire extinguisher near the work area. Always disconnect the negative battery cable and do not make any repairs to the fuel system until all the necessary steps for repair have been reviewed.

2.5L ENGINE

1. Remove the fuel filler cap.
2. Remove the fuel pump fuse from the fuse block located in the passenger compartment.
3. Start the engine and run until the engine stops due to the lack of fuel.
4. Crank the engine for 3 seconds to ensure all pressure is relieved.
5. Make sure the negative battery cable is disconnected.

2.8L AND 3.1L ENGINES

1. Connect fuel pressure gauge J–34730–1, or equivalent to the fuel pressure connection.
2. Wrap a shop cloth around the fitting while connecting the gauge to catch any leaking fuel.
3. Install the bleed hose into an approved container and open the valve. Connect the negative battery cable.
4. When the repair to the fuel system is complete check all of the fittings for leaks.

Fuel Pump

Removal and Installation

The fuel pump is an integral part of the fuel level sensor assembly, located in the fuel tank.
1. Disconnect the negative battery cable.
2. Drain all fuel from the fuel tank.
3. Raise and safely support the vehicle. Support the fuel tank and remove the retaining straps.
4. Lower the fuel tank slightly and disconnect the fuel lines, hoses and the sending unit electrical connectors.
5. Remove the tank from the vehicle.
6. Remove the sending unit retaining cam using tool J–24187 or equivalent and remove the sending unit assembly from the tank.

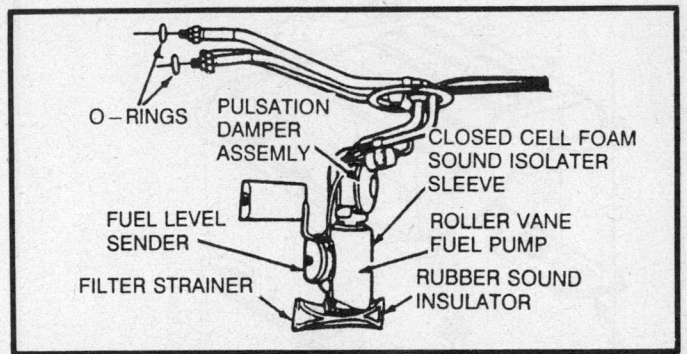

Fuel pump and sending unit assembly

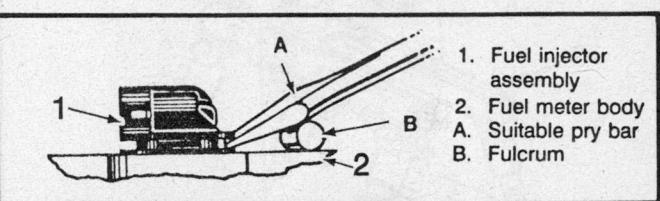

1. Fuel injector assembly
2. Fuel meter body
A. Suitable pry bar
B. Fulcrum

2.5L engine fuel injector removal

7. Use a new O-ring and install the sending unit assembly into the tank.
8. Raise the tank into position and attach all fuel lines, hoses and electrical connectors to the tank.
9. Install the retaining straps. Tighten the tank retaining strap bolts to 26 ft. lbs. (34 Nm).
10. Lower the vehicle and refill the tank. Connect the negative battery cable.

FUEL INJECTORS

Removal and Installation
2.5L ENGINE

1. Disconnect the negative battery cable and release fuel pressure.
2. Remove the air intake duct and disconnect the electrical connector to the fuel injector.
3. Remove the injector screw and retainer.
4. Using a fulcrum, place a suitable pry bar under the ridge opposite the connector end and carefully pry the injector out of the cavity.
5. Remove the upper and lower O-rings from the injector and cavity.
6. Inspect the injector and fuel lines for dirt and contamination. If excess contamination is present, the fuel system will have to be flushed.

NOTE: Make sure the replacement injector is an identical part. The injectors from other model 700 systems may fit, but are calibrated for different flow rates. Check the part on the side of the throttle body.

7. Lubricate the new upper and lower O-rings with automatic transmission fluid and place them on the injector. Make sure the upper O-ring is in the groove and the lower one is flush against the filter.
8. Install the injector into the cavity by pushing straight into the fuel injector cavity.
9. Install the injector retainer and coat the screw with thread locking compound. Tighten the attaching screw to 27 inch lbs. (3.0 Nm).

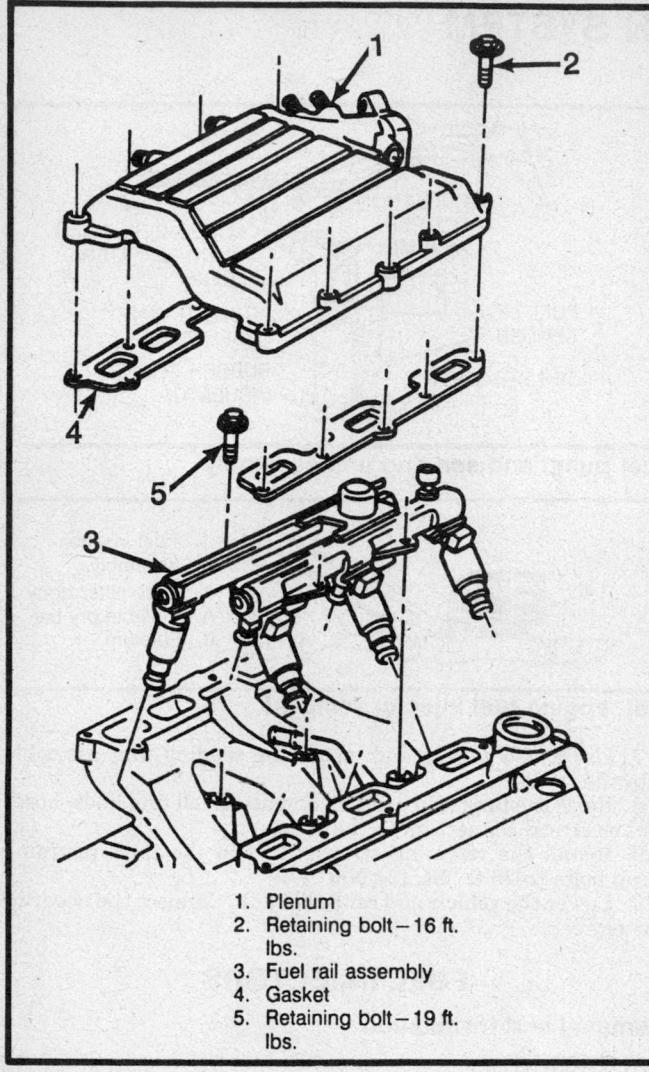

1. Plenum
2. Retaining bolt – 16 ft. lbs.
3. Fuel rail assembly
4. Gasket
5. Retaining bolt – 19 ft. lbs.

Removing the plenum and fuel rail

10. Connect the injector electrical connector and negative battery cable.

2.8L AND 3.1L ENGINES

1. Relieve the pressure in the fuel system.

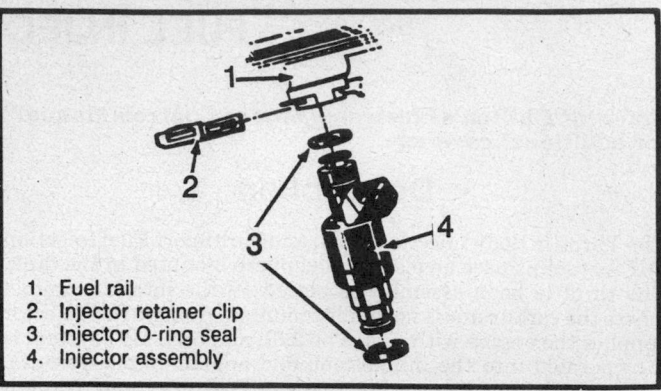

1. Fuel rail
2. Injector retainer clip
3. Injector O-ring seal
4. Injector assembly

2.8L and 3.1L engines fuel injector

2. Disconnect the negative terminal from the battery. Remove the air inlet tube.

3. Label and disconnect the vacuum lines from the plenum.

4. Remove the EGR valve from the plenum.

5. Remove the 2 throttle body-to-plenum bolts and the throttle body.

6. Remove the throttle cable bracket bolts.

7. Remove the ignition wire shield.

8. Remove the plenum-to-intake manifold mounting bolts and the plenum.

9. Remove the fuel line bracket bolt and disconnect the fuel lines from the fuel rail. Wrap a rag around the lines to collect the excess fuel. Dispose of the rag properly.

10. Remove and discard the fuel line O-rings.

11. Disconnect the electrical connectors from the fuel injectors.

12. Remove the fuel rail assembly with the injectors.

13. Remove the fuel injector-to-fuel rail retaining clip, the fuel injectors and O-rings.

To install:

14. Lubricate the new (fuel injector) O-rings and install the fuel rail assembly. Torque the fuel rail-to-intake manifold bolts to 19 ft. lbs. (26 Nm).

15. Connect the fuel lines to the fuel rail. Attach the electrical connectors to the injectors.

16. Install the plenum to manifold bolts and tighten and the plenum bolts to 16 ft. lbs. (22 Nm).

17. Install the throttle body to the plenum. Install the EGR valve. Reconnect all vacuum and electrical leads. Install the air inlet tube.

18. Connect the negative battery cable.

EMISSION CONTROL SYSTEMS

2.5L ENGINE

Oxygen sensor
Coolant temperature sensor
Throttle position sensor
Vehicle speed sensor
EGR valve
EGR vacuum control solenoid
Electronic control module
Electronic spark control system
Prom
Calpak
Fuel injector

Throttle body assembly
Idle air control valve
Vapor canister
Canister purge solenoid
Direct Ignition System (DIS)
Torque converter clutch
PCV system
Catalytic converter

2.8L AND 3.1L ENGINES

Oxygen sensor
Coolant temperature sensor

Throttle position sensor
Vehicle speed sensor
Air temperature sensor
EGR valve
EGR vacuum control solenoid
Electronic control module
Mass air flow sensor
Electronic spark control system
Prom
Calpak
Fuel injectors
Fuel rail
Throttle body assembly
Idle air control valve
Vapor canister
Canister purge solenoid
Direct Ignition System (DIS)
ESC knock sensor
ESC module
Torque converter clutch
PCV system

Resetting Warning Lamps

Procedure

When the ECM finds a problem, the "Check Engine/Service Engine Soon" light will turn **ON** and a trouble code will be recorded in the ECM memory. If the problem is intermittent, the "Check Engine/Service Engine Soon" light turn **OFF** after 10 seconds, when the fault goes away. However, the trouble code will stay in the ECM memory until the battery voltage to the ECM is removed. Removing the battery voltage for 10 seconds will clear all stored trouble codes. This is done by disconnecting the ECM harness from the positive battery pigtail for 10 seconds with the ignition **OFF** or by disconnecting the ECM fuse, designated ECM or ECM/BAT, from the fuse holder.

NOTE: To prevent ECM damage, the ignition switch must be OFF when disconnecting or reconnecting power to ECM (for example battery cable, ECM pigtail, ECM fuse, jumper cables, etc.).

ENGINE MECHANICAL

NOTE: Disconnecting the negative battery cable on some vehicles may interfere with the functions of the on board computer systems and may require the computer to undergo a relearning process, once the negative battery cable is reconnected.

Engine Assembly

Removal and Installation

1. Disconnect the battery cables. Matchmark the hood and the hood hinges, remove the hood.
2. Disconnect and remove the air inlet tube from the throttle body and the air cleaner.
3. Disconnect the throttle cable, T.V. linkage, cruise control cable and all other electrical wiring from the engine.
4. Relieve the fuel system pressure and remove the fuel lines from the fuel rails.
5. Relieve the serpentine belt tension and remove the belt.
6. Drain the cooling system and remove the radiator and heater hoses.
7. Remove the A/C compressor mounting bolts and remove the compressor, Do not disconnect the refrigerant lines. Lay the compressor to the side.
8. Remove the power steering pump mounting bolts and lay the pump aside.
9. Disconnect the brake booster vacuum line.
10. Raise and safely support the vehicle. Remove the flywheel cover and remove the starter.
11. Remove the torque converter bolts. Remove the transaxle bracket.
12. Remove the front engine retaining nuts. Remove the exhaust pipe at the crossover.
13. Lower the vehicle. Remove the engine torque struts.
14. Remove the coolant recovery bottle. Remove the left crossover pipe-to-manifold clamp.
15. Pull the engine forward and support it. Disconnect the bulkhead connector.
16. Remove the right crossover pipe-to-manifold clamp. Remove the engine support and allow the engine to return to its normal position.

17. Support the transaxle and remove the transaxle-to-engine bolts.
18. Attach a suitable lifting device and remove the engine assembly.

To install:

19. Install the engine, align it with the transaxle housing and insert the transaxle-to-engine bolts. Tighten the transaxle and torque converter bolts to 55 ft. lbs. (75 Nm)
20. Remove the lifting device. Install the left and right crossover pipe clamps.
21. Attach the bulkhead connector. Install the coolant recovery bottle and the engine torque struts.
22. Raise and safely support the vehicle. Attach the crossover pipe.
23. Install the front engine mount nuts and tighten to 63 ft. lbs. (86 Nm).
24. Attach the transaxle bracket and install the torque converter bolts. Install the flywheel cover.
25. Install the starter. Install the A/C compressor and lower the vehicle.
26. Attach the heater and radiator hoses. Install the power steering pump.
27. Install the accessory drive belt. Connect the fuel lines to the fuel rail. Connect any electrical wiring that was disconnected.
28. Connect the throttle cable, T.V. linkage and the cruise control cable.
29. Attach the air inlet tube. Align the matchmarks on the hood and hinges and install the hood.
30. Connect the negative battery cable. Fill the cooling system.

Engine Mounts

Removal and Installation

2.5L ENGINE

1. Disconnect the negative battery cable.
2. Raise and safely support the vehicle
3. Remove the engine-to-chassis nuts.
4. Disconnect the engine torque struts.
5. Install an engine support fixture J–28467–A or equivalent.

6. Remove the upper mount-to-engine bracket nuts and remove the mount.

7. Install the mount and mount-to-engine bracket. Tighten the nuts to 32 ft. lbs. (43 Nm).

8. Install and tighten the torque strut nuts to 32 ft. lbs. (43 Nm).

9. Lower the vehicle and remove the engine support fixture.

2.8L AND 3.1L ENGINES

1. Disconnect the negative battery cable. Raise and safely support the vehicle.

2. Remove the engine mount retaining nuts from below the cradle mounting bracket.

3. Raise the engine slightly to provide clearance and remove the engine mount-to-bracket nuts.

4. Remove the engine mount.

5. Install the mount in position and tighten the mount-to-bracket nuts to 32 ft. lbs. (43 Nm). Lower the engine into position.

6. Install the mounting bracket-to-cradle nuts and tighten to 63 ft. lbs. (86 Nm).

7. Lower the vehicle and connect the negative battery cable.

Intake Manifold

Removal and Installation

2.5L ENGINE

1. Disconnect the negative battery cable.

2. Remove the air cleaner assembly.

3. Remove the PCV valve and hose at the throttle body assembly.

4. Drain the engine coolant at the radiator.

5. Release the fuel pressure and remove the fuel lines from the throttle body.

6. Remove the vacuum lines and brake booster hose from the throttle body.

7. Remove all linkage and wiring from the TBI assembly.

8. Rotate the engine forward.

9. Remove the heater hose.

10. Remove the seven intake manifold retaining bolts and the manifold.

To install:

11. Clean all gasket surfaces on the cylinder head and intake manifold.

12. Install the intake manifold with a new gasket.

13. Install all the retaining bolts and washers hand tight.

14. Tighten the bolts in proper sequence to 25 ft.lbs. (34 Nm).

15. Rotate the engine to the original position.

16. Install all heater hoses, vacuum hoses, throttle linkages and wiring.

17. Install the fuel lines.

18. Refill the engine coolant.

19. Install the PCV valve and hose to the TBI assembly.

20. Install the air cleaner assembly and connect the negative battery cable. Check for leaks.

2.8L AND 3.1L ENGINES

1. Disconnect the negative battery cable. Drain the cooling system.

2. Disconnect the T.V. and accelerator cables from the plenum.

3. Remove the throttle body-to-plenum bolts and the throttle body. Remove the EGR valve.

4. Remove the plenum-to-intake manifold bolts and the plenum. Disconnect and plug the fuel lines and return pipes at the fuel rail.

5. Remove the serpentine drive belt. Remove the power steering pump-to-bracket bolts and support the pump out of the way; Do not disconnect the pressure hoses.

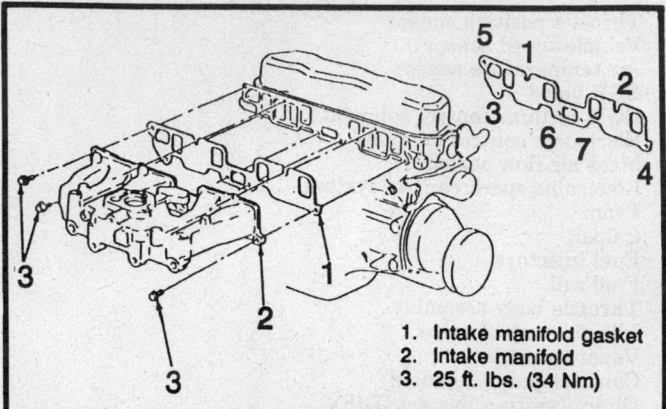

2.5L engine intake manifold mounting and torque procedure

1. Intake manifold gasket
2. Intake manifold
3. 25 ft. lbs. (34 Nm)

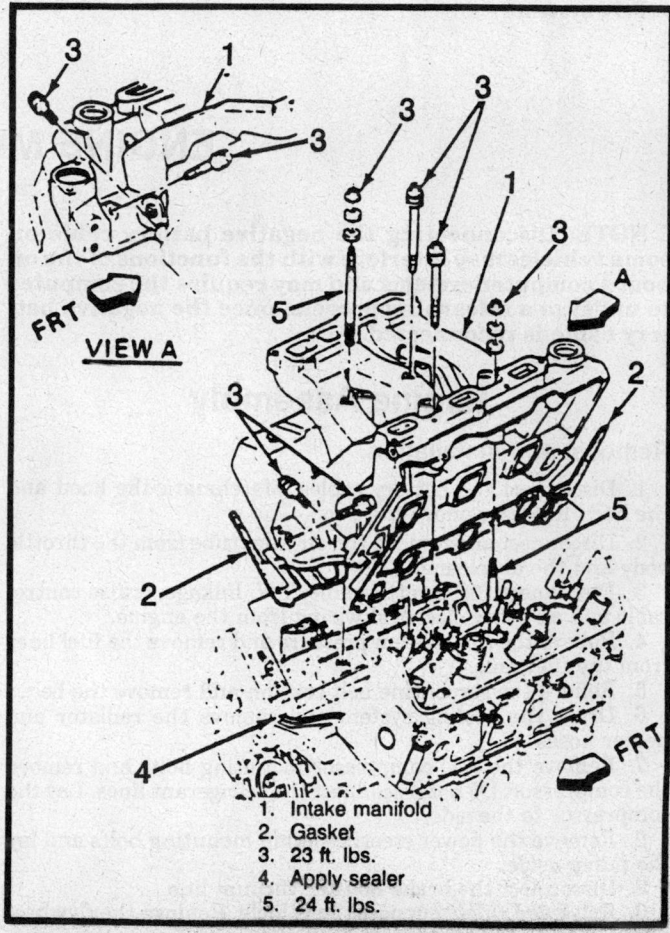

2.8L and 3.1L engines intake manifold mounting and torque procedure

1. Intake manifold
2. Gasket
3. 23 ft. lbs.
4. Apply sealer
5. 24 ft. lbs.

6. Remove the alternator-to-bracket bolts and support the alternator out of the way.

7. Loosen the alternator bracket. From the throttle body, disconnect the idle air vacuum hose.

8. Label and disconnect the electrical connectors from the fuel injectors. Remove the fuel rail.

9. Remove the breather tube. Disconnect the runners.

10. Remove both rocker arm cover-to-cylinder head bolts and

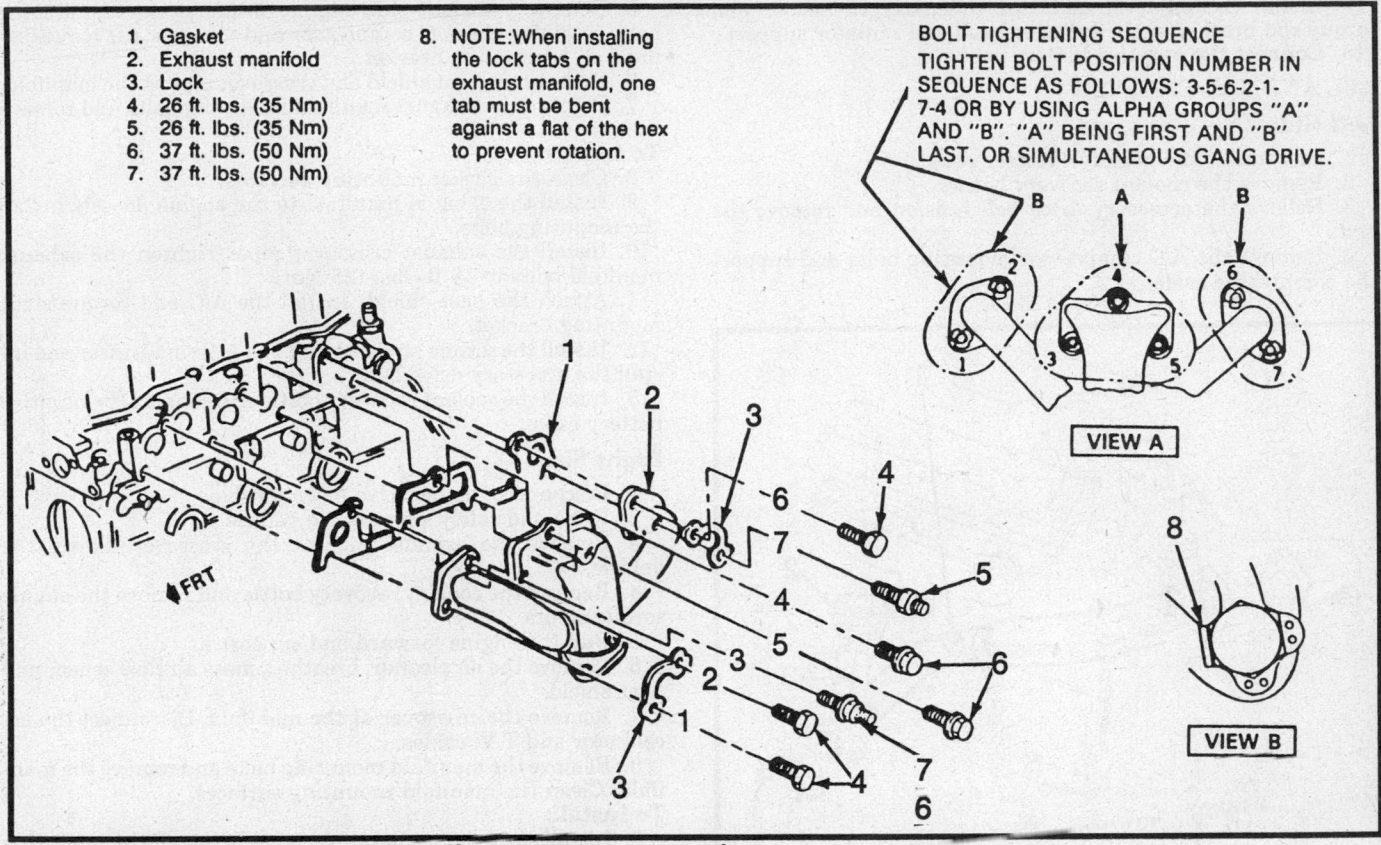

1. Gasket
2. Exhaust manifold
3. Lock
4. 26 ft. lbs. (35 Nm)
5. 26 ft. lbs. (35 Nm)
6. 37 ft. lbs. (50 Nm)
7. 37 ft. lbs. (50 Nm)
8. NOTE:When installing the lock tabs on the exhaust manifold, one tab must be bent against a flat of the hex to prevent rotation.

BOLT TIGHTENING SEQUENCE
TIGHTEN BOLT POSITION NUMBER IN SEQUENCE AS FOLLOWS: 3-5-6-2-1-7-4 OR BY USING ALPHA GROUPS "A" AND "B". "A" BEING FIRST AND "B" LAST. OR SIMULTANEOUS GANG DRIVE.

VIEW A

VIEW B

2.5L engine exhaust manifold mounting and torque procedure

the covers. Remove the radiator hose from the thermostat housing.

11. Label and disconnect the electrical connectors from the coolant temperature sensor and oil pressure sending unit. Remove the coolant sensor.

12. Remove the bypass hose from the filler neck and cylinder head.

13. Remove the intake manifold-to-cylinder head bolts and the manifold.

14. Loosen the rocker arm nuts, turn them 90 degrees and remove the pushrods; be sure to keep the components in order for installation purposes.

15. Clean all of the gasket mounting surfaces.

To install:

16. Place a bead of RTV sealer or equivalent on each ridge where the intake manifold and block meet. Install the intake manifold gasket in place on the block.

17. Install the pushrods and reposition the rocker arms, tighten the rocker arm nuts to 18 ft. lbs. (25 Nm).

18. Mount the intake manifold on the engine and tighten the bolts to 23 ft. lbs. (29 Nm).

19. Connect the heater inlet pipe to the manifold. Install and connect the coolant sensor.

20. Attach the radiator hoses. Connect the wire at the oil sending switch.

21. Install the rocker covers, tighten the retaining bolts to 90 inch lbs. (10 Nm).

22. Install the runners, breather tube, fuel rail and connect the wires at the fuel injectors.

23. Install the alternator bracket and the alternator. Install the power steering pump.

24. Connect the fuel lines to the fuel rail. Install the EGR valve.

25. Install the plenum and mount the throttle body to the plenum.

26. Connect the accelerator cable and the T.V. cable.

27. Fill the cooling system. Connect the negative battery cable.

28. Run the engine until it reaches normal operating temperature and check for coolant and oil leaks.

Exhaust Manifold

Removal and Installation

2.5L ENGINE

1. Disconnect the negative battery cable.

2. Remove the torque strut bolts at the radiator panel and cylinder head.

3. Remove the oxygen sensor and the oil level indicator tube.

4. Raise and safely support the vehicle.

5. Remove the exhaust pipe from the manifold and lower the vehicle.

6. Bend rocking tabs away from the bolts and remove the retaining bolts and washers.

7. Remove the exhaust manifold and gasket.

To install:

8. Clean the sealing surfaces of the cylinder head and manifold.

9. Lubricate the bolt threads with anti-seize compound and install the exhaust manifold with a new gasket.

10. Tighten the bolts in sequence.

11. Bend the locking tabs against the bolts.

12. Raise and support the vehicle safely.

13. Install the exhaust pipe to the manifold and lower the vehicle.

14. Install the oil level indicator tube, oxygen sensor and torque rod bracket at the cylinder head and radiator support.

15. Connect the negative battery cable.

2.8L AND 3.1L ENGINES

Left Side

1. Disconnect the negative battery cable.

2. Remove the coolant recovery bottle.

3. Relieve the accessory drive belt tension and remove the belt.

4. Remove the A/C compressor mounting bolts and support the compressor aside.

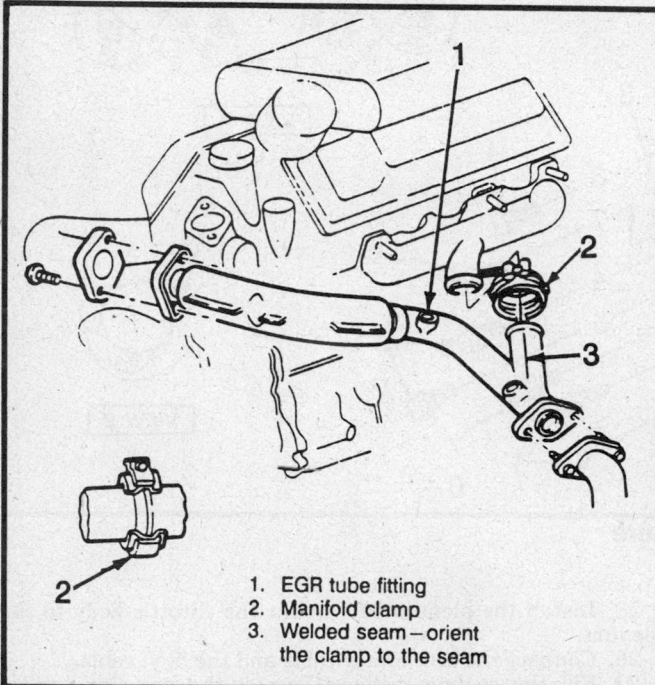

1. EGR tube fitting
2. Manifold clamp
3. Welded seam – orient the clamp to the seam

2.8L and 3.1L engines exhaust manifold crossover mounting

5. Remove the right side engine torque strut. Remove the bolts retaining the A/C compressor and torque strut mounting bracket, remove the bracket.

6. Remove the heat shield and crossover pipe at the manifold.

7. Remove the exhaust manifold mounting bolts and remove the manifold.

To install:

8. Clean the gasket mounting surfaces.

9. Install the exhaust manifold to the engine, loosely install the mounting bolts.

10. Install the exhaust crossover pipe. Tighten the exhaust manifold bolts to 18 ft. lbs. (25 Nm)

11. Attach the heat shield. Install the A/C and torque strut mounting bracket.

12. Install the torque strut. Mount the A/C compressor and install the accessory drive belt.

13. Install the coolant recovery bottle and connect the negative battery cable.

Right Side

1. Disconnect the negative battery cable.

2. Raise and safely support the vehicle.

3. Remove the exhaust pipe at the crossover. Lower the vehicle.

4. Remove the coolant recovery bottle and remove the engine torque struts.

5. Pull the engine forward and support it.

6. Remove the air cleaner, breather, mass air flow sensor and heat shield.

7. Remove the crossover at the manifold. Disconnect the accelerator and T.V. cables.

8. Remove the manifold mounting bolts and remove the manifold. Clean the manifold mounting surfaces.

To install:

9. Install the exhaust manifold, loosely install the mounting bolts.

10. Attach the crossover at the manifold. Tighten the manifold mounting bolts to 18 ft. lbs. (25 Nm).

11. Connect the accelerator and T.V. cables.

12. Attach the air cleaner, breather and mass air flow sensor.

13. Remove the engine support and allow the engine to roll back into position.

14. Install the coolant recovery bottle and the engine torque struts.

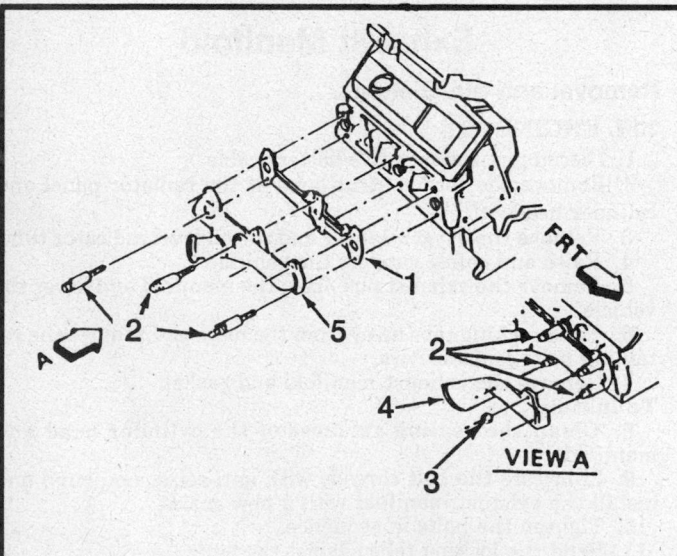

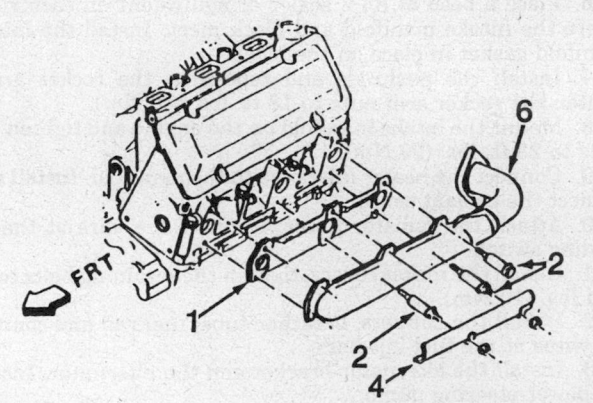

1. Gasket
2. 18 ft. lbs.
3. 90 inch lbs.
4. Heat shield
5. Right exhaust manifold
6. Left exhaust manifold

2.8L and 3.1L engines exhaust manifold mounting

15. Raise and safely support the vehicle. Install the exhaust pipe to the crossover.

16. Lower the vehicle. Connect the negative battery cable.

Valve System

Valve Adjustment

Hydraulic valve lifters are used, which are not adjustable. If valve system noise is present, check the torque on the rocker arm nuts. It should be 14–20 ft. lbs. (19–27 Nm). If the noise is still present check the condition of the the valve train components.

Valve Lifters

Removal and Installation

2.5L ENGINE

1. Disconnect the negative battery cable.
2. Remove the rocker arm cover.
3. Remove the intake manifold.
4. Remove the pushrod cover.
5. Loosen the rocker arms and move to the side.
6. Mark and remove the pushrods, retainer and lifter guides.
7. Mark and remove the lifters.

NOTE: Mark each valve component location for reassembly.

8. Lubricate all bearing surfaces and lifters with engine oil and install the lifters.
9. Install the lifter guides, retainers and pushrods.
10. Position the rocker arms over the pushrods and tighten the rocker arm nuts to 24 ft. lbs. (32 Nm) with the lifter at the base circle of the camshaft.
11. Install the pushrod cover, intake manifold and rocker arm cover.
12. Connect the negative battery cable.

2.8L AND 3.1L ENGINES

1. Disconnect the negative terminal from the battery.
2. Drain the cooling system.
3. Remove the rocker arm covers and intake manifold.
4. Loosen the rocker arms nuts enough to move the rocker arms to one side and remove the pushrods.
5. Remove the lifters from the engine.
6. Using Molykote® or equivalent, coat the base of the new lifters and install them into the engine.
7. Position the pushrods and the rocker arms correctly into their original positions. Torque the rocker arm nuts to 18 ft. lbs. (25 Nm).
8. Install the intake manifold and tighten the intake manifold-to-cylinder head bolts to specification.
9. Install the rocker cover. Connect the negative battery cable.
10. Fill the cooling system.

Valve Rocker Assembly

Removal and Installation

2.5L ENGINE

1. Disconnect the negative battery cable.
2. Remove the rocker arm cover.
3. Remove the rocker arm bolt and ball.
4. Remove the rocker arm and guide.

NOTE: Mark all valve components so they are reinstalled in their original location.

5. If removed, install the pushrod through the cylinder head and into the lifter seat.

6. Install the guide, rocker arm, ball and bolt. Tighten the rocker arm bolts to 24 ft. lbs. (32 Nm).
7. Install the rocker arm cover.

2.8L AND 3.1L ENGINES

Left Side

1. Disconnect the negative battery cable. Disconnect the bracket tube from the rocker cover.
2. Remove the spark plug wire cover. Drain the cooling system and remove the heater hose from the filler neck.
3. Remove the rocker arm cover-to-cylinder head bolts and the rocker cover.

NOTE: If the rocker arm cover will not lift off the cylinder head easily, strike the end with the palm of the hand or a rubber mallet.

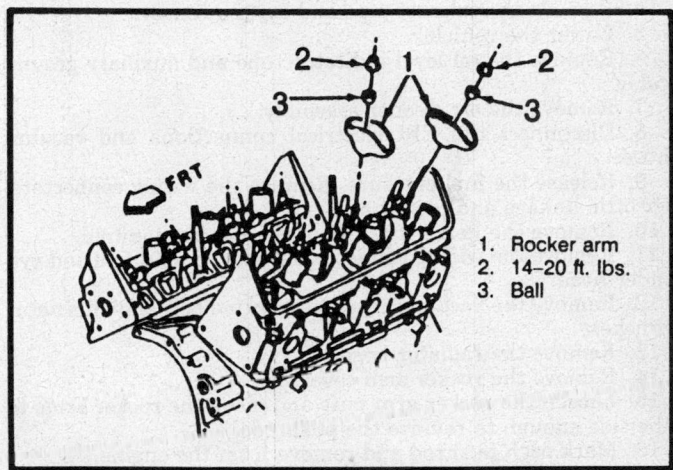

1. Rocker arm
2. 14–20 ft. lbs.
3. Ball

2.8L and 3.1L engines rocker arm positioning

4. Remove the rocker arm nuts and remove the rocker arms, keep the components in order for installation purposes.
5. Clean the gasket mounting surfaces.
6. To install, use new rocker cover gaskets apply a bead of sealant, GM 1052917 or equivalent, to the rocker cover and install it.
7. Install the spark plug wire cover and attach the heater hose to the filler neck. Fill the cooling system.
8. Torque the rocker arm nuts to 14–20 ft. lbs. (19–27 Nm).

Right Side

1. Disconnect the negative battery cable. Disconnect the brake booster vacuum line from the bracket.
2. Disconnect the cable bracket from the plenum.
3. Disconnect the vacuum line bracket from the cable bracket.
4. Disconnect the lines from the alternator brace stud.
5. Remove the rear alternator brace and the serpentine drive belt.
6. Remove the alternator and support it out of the way.
7. Remove the PCV valve.
8. Loosen the alternator bracket.
9. Disconnect the spark plug wires from the spark plugs. Remove the rocker cover-to-cylinder head bolts and the rocker cover.

NOTE: If the rocker arm cover will not lift off the cylinder head easily, strike the end with the palm of the hand or a rubber mallet.

10. Remove the rocker arm nuts and the rocker arms; be sure to keep the components in order for installation purposes.

To install:

11. Clean the gasket mounting surfaces.

12. To install, use new rocker cover gaskets apply a bead of sealant, GM 1052917 or equivalent, to the rocker cover and install it.

13. Install the spark plug wire cover and attach the heater hose to the filler neck. Fill the cooling system.

14. Tighten the rocker arm nuts to 14–20 ft. lbs. (19–27 Nm).

Cylinder Head

Removal and Installation

2.5L ENGINE

1. Disconnect the negative battery cable.
2. Drain the cooling system.
3. Raise and safely support the vehicle.
4. Remove the exhaust pipe and oxygen sensor.
5. Lower the vehicle.
6. Remove the oil level indicator tube and auxiliary ground cable.
7. Remove the air cleaner assembly.
8. Disconnect the EFI electrical connections and vacuum hoses.
9. Release the fuel pressure. Remove the wiring connectors, throttle linkage and fuel lines.
10. Remove the heater hose from the intake manifold.
11. Remove the wiring connectors from the manifold and cylinder head.
12. Remove the vacuum hoses, serpentine belt and alternator bracket.
13. Remove the radiator hoses.
14. Remove the rocker arm cover.
15. Loosen the rocker arm nuts and move the rocker arms to the side enough to remove the pushrods.
16. Mark each pushrod and remove from the engine.

NOTE: Mark each valve component to ensure that they are replaced in the same location as removed.

17. Remove the cylinder head bolts.
18. Tap the sides of the cylinder head with a plastic hammer to dislodge the gasket. Remove the cylinder head with the intake and exhaust manifold still attached.
19. If the cylinder head has to be serviced or replaced, remove the intake manifold, exhaust manifold and remaining hardware.

To install:

20. Before installing, clean the gasket surfaces of the head and block.
21. Check the cylinder head for warpage using a straight edge.
22. Match up the old head gasket with the new one to ensure the holes are exact. Install a new gasket over the dowel pins in the cylinder block.
23. Install the cylinder head in place over the dowel pins.
24. Coat the cylinder head bolt threads with sealing compound and install finger tight.
25. Tighten the cylinder head bolts gradually in the sequence.
26. Install the pushrods, rocker arms and nuts (or bolts) in the same location as removed. Tighten the nuts (or bolts) to 24 ft. lbs. (32 Nm).
27. Install the rocker arm cover.
28. Install the radiator hoses, alternator bracket and serpentine belt.
29. Connect all intake manifold and cylinder head wiring.
30. Install the vacuum hoses and heater hose at manifold.
31. Install the wiring, throttle linkage and fuel lines to the throttle body assembly.
32. Install the oil level indicator tube-to-exhaust manifold.
33. Install the air cleaner assembly and refill the cooling system.

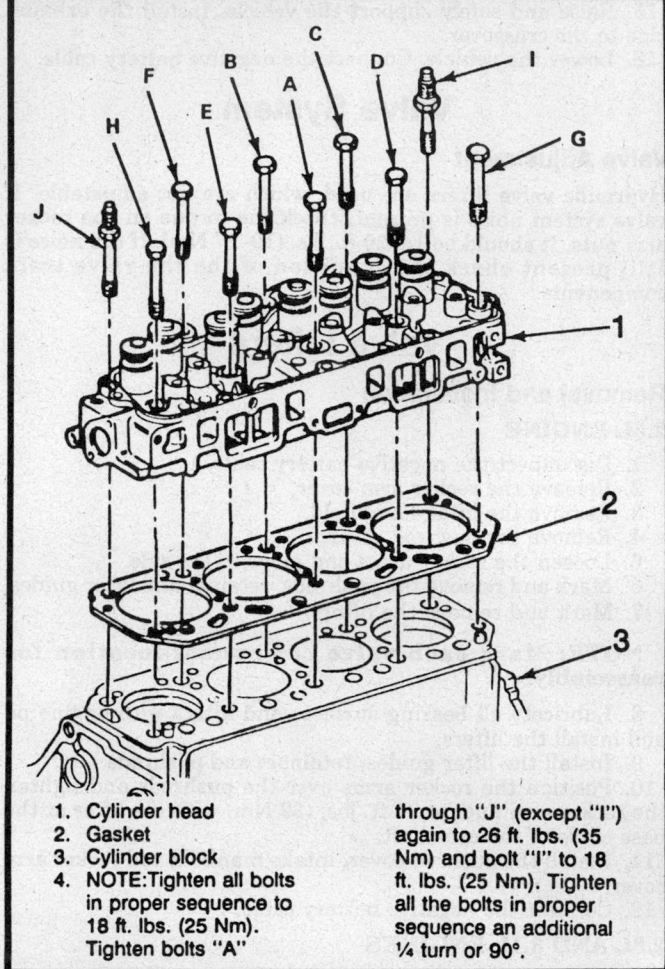

1. Cylinder head
2. Gasket
3. Cylinder block
4. NOTE: Tighten all bolts in proper sequence to 18 ft. lbs. (25 Nm). Tighten bolts "A" through "J" (except "I") again to 26 ft. lbs. (35 Nm) and bolt "I" to 18 ft. lbs. (25 Nm). Tighten all the bolts in proper sequence an additional ¼ turn or 90°.

2.5L engine cylinder head torque procedure

34. Raise and safely support the vehicle.
35. Install the exhaust pipe and oxygen sensor.
36. Lower the vehicle and connect the negative battery cable.
37. Start the engine and check for leaks.

2.8L AND 3.1L ENGINES

Left Side

1. Drain the cooling system. Remove the rocker cover.
2. Remove the intake manifold-to-cylinder head bolts and the intake manifold. Disconnect the exhaust crossover from the right exhaust manifold.
3. Disconnect the oil level indicator tube bracket.
4. Loosen the rocker arms nuts, turn the rocker arms and remove the pushrods.

NOTE: Be sure to keep the parts in order for installation purposes.

5. Remove the cylinder head-to-engine bolts; start with the outer bolts and work toward the center. Remove the cylinder head with the exhaust manifold as an assembly.

To install:

6. Clean the gasket mounting surfaces. Inspect the surfaces of the cylinder head, block and intake manifold for damage and/or warpage. Clean the threaded holes in the block and the cylinder head bolt threads.
7. Use new gaskets, align the new cylinder head gasket over the dowels on the block with the note **THIS SIDE UP** facing the cylinder head.

8. Install the cylinder head and exhaust manifold crossover assembly on the engine.

9. Using GM sealant 1052080 or equivalent, coat the cylinder head bolts and install the bolts hand tight.

10. Using the correct sequence, torque the bolts to 33 ft. lbs. (45 Nm). After all bolts are torqued to 33 ft. lbs. (45 Nm), rotate the torque wrench another 90 degrees or ¼ turn. This will apply the correct torque to the bolts.

11. Install the pushrods in the same order that they were removed. Torque the rocker arm nuts to 14–20 ft. lbs. (19–27 Nm).

12. Install the intake manifold using a new gasket and following the correct sequence, torque the bolts to the correct specification.

13. Install the oil level indicator tube and install the rocker cover. Install the air inlet tube.

14. Connect the negative battery cable. Refill the cooling system. Start the engine and check for leaks.

Right Side

1. Disconnect the negative battery cable. Drain the cooling system.

2. Raise and safely support the vehicle. Remove the exhaust manifold-to-exhaust pipe bolts and separate the pipe from the manifold.

3. Lower the vehicle. Remove the exhaust manifold-to-cylinder head bolts and the manifold.

4. Remove the rocker arm cover. Remove the intake manifold-to-cylinder head bolts and the intake manifold.

5. Loosen the rocker arms nuts, turn the rocker arms and remove the pushrods.

NOTE: Be sure to keep the components in order for reassembly purposes.

6. Remove the cylinder head-to-engine bolts (starting with the outer bolts and working toward the center) and the cylinder head.

To install:

7. Clean the gasket mounting surfaces. Inspect the parts for damage and/or warpage.

8. Clean the engine block's threaded holes and the cylinder head bolt threads.

9. To install, use new gaskets and reverse the removal procedures. Using GM sealant 1052080 or equivalent, coat the cylinder head bolts and install the bolts hand tight.

10. Place the cylinder head gasket on the engine block dowels with the note **THIS SIDE UP** facing the cylinder head.

11. Using the torquing sequence, torque the bolts to 33 ft. lbs. (45 Nm). After all bolts are torqued to 33 ft. lbs. (45 Nm), rotate the torque wrench another 90 degrees or ¼ turn. This will apply the correct torque to the bolts.

12. Install the pushrods in the same order as they were removed. Torque the rocker arm nuts to 14–20 ft. lbs. (19–27 Nm).

13. Follow the torquing sequence, use a new gasket and install the intake manifold.

14. Install the oil level indicator tube and install the rocker cover. Install the air inlet tube.

15. Refill the cooling system. Start the engine, allow it to reach normal operating temperatures and check for leaks.

Camshaft

Removal and Installation

2.5L ENGINE

NOTE: For the removal of the camshaft, the engine assembly must be removed from the vehicle.

1. Disconnect the negative battery cable.

2. Remove the engine assembly from the vehicle.

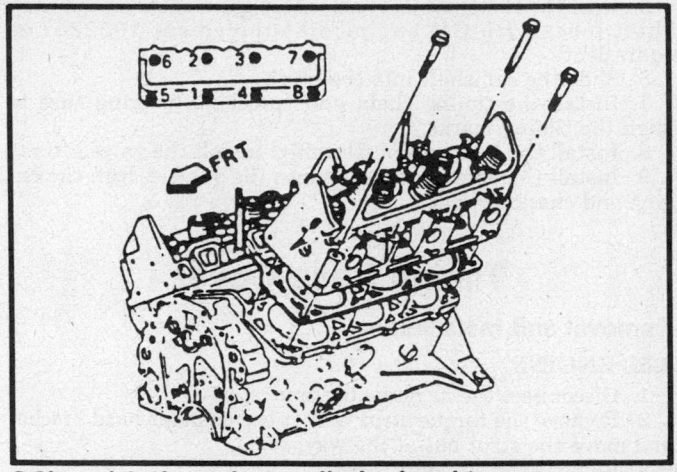

2.8L and 3.1L engines cylinder head torque sequence

3. Remove the rocker arm cover and pushrods.

4. Remove the pushrod cover and valve lifters.

5. Remove the serpentine belt, crankshaft pulleys and vibration dampener.

6. Remove the front cover.

7. Remove the camshaft thrust plate screws.

NOTE: The camshaft journals are the same diameter. Care must be taken when removing the camshaft to avoid damage to the cam bearings.

8. Carefully slide the camshaft and gear through the front of the block.

9. To remove the camshaft gear, use a arbor press and adapter.

10. Old and new camshafts should be cleaned with solvent and compressed air before being installed.

To install:

11. Install the camshaft gear onto the camshaft with an arbor press.

12. Measure the end clearance with a feeler gauge between the cam journal and thrust plate. The measurement should be between 0.0015 in. – 0.0050. in. If the measurement is less than 0.0015, replace the spacer ring. If the measurement is more than 0.0050, replace the thrust plate.

NOTE: Always apply assembly lube (GM E.O.S 1052367 or equivalent) to the cam journals and lobes. If this procedures is not done, cam damage may result.

13. Carefully install the camshaft into the engine block by rotating and pushing forward until seated.

14. Install the thrust plate screws and torque to 89 inch lbs. (10 Nm).

15. Install the front cover, vibration dampener and serpentine belt.

16. Install the valve lifter and pushrod cover.

17. Install the pushrods and rocker arm cover.

18. Install the engine into the vehicle.

19. Refill all necessary fluids.

20. Start the engine and check for leaks.

2.8L AND 3.1L ENGINES

NOTE: For the removal of the camshaft the engine assembly must be removed from the vehicle.

1. Remove the engine assembly from the vehicle.

2. Remove the rocker covers and remove the valve lifters.

3. Remove the front cover assembly, timing chain and sprockets.

4. Remove the camshaft by sliding it from the block.

5. Coat the camshaft journals with engine oil. Coat the camshaft lobes with GM engine oil supplement 1052367 or equivalent.

6. Slide the camshaft into the block.

7. Install the timing chain and sprockets, making sure to align the timing marks.

8. Install the front cover assembly. Install the valve lifters.

9. Install the engine assembly into the vehicle. Run the engine and check for leaks.

Timing Case Cover

Removal and Installation

2.5L ENGINE

1. Disconnect the negative battery cable.

2. Remove the torque strut bolt at the cylinder head bracket and move the strut out of the way.

3. Remove the serpentine belt.

4. Install the engine support fixture tool J–28467–A and J–36462.

5. Raise and safely support the vehicle.

6. Remove the right front tire assembly.

7. Disconnect the right lower ball joint from the knuckle.

8. Remove the two right hand frame attaching bolts.

9. Loosen the two left hand frame attaching bolts, but do not remove.

10. Lower the vehicle.

11. Lower the engine on the right hand side. Raise and safely support the vehicle.

12. Remove the engine vibration dampener using a dampener puller.

13. Remove the timing cover retaining bolts and cover.

To install:

14. Clean all gasket mating surfaces with solvent and a gasket scraper.

15. Apply a ⅜ in. wide by ³/₁₆ in. thick bead of RTV sealer to the joint at the oil pan and timing cover.

16. Apply a ¼ in. wide by ⅛ in. thick bead of RTV sealer to the timing cover at the block mating surface.

17. Install a new timing cover oil seal using a timing cover seal installer tool J–34995 or equivalent.

18. Install the cover onto the block and install the retaining bolts loosely.

19. Install the timing cover seal installer tool J–34995 to align the timing cover.

20. Tighten the opposing bolts to hold the cover in place.

21. Torque the bolts in sequence and to the proper specification. Remove the timing cover oil seal installer tool.

22. Install the crankshaft vibration dampener and torque the bolt to 162 ft.lb. (220 Nm).

23. Lower the vehicle.

24. Raise the engine to its proper position using the support fixture.

25. Raise and safely support the vehicle.

26. Raise the frame and install the removed frame bolts. Torque the bolts to 103 ft. lbs. (140 Nm).

27. Install the right ball joint and tighten the nut.

28. Install the right front tire, torque the lug nuts to 100 ft. lbs. (136 Nm) and lower the vehicle.

29. Remove the engine support fixture.

30. Install the torque strut and bolt to the cylinder head bracket.

31. Install the serpentine belt, connect the negative battery cable and check for oil leaks.

2.8L AND 3.1L ENGINES

1. Disconnect the negative terminal from the battery. Drain the cooling system.

2. Remove the serpentine belt and the belt tensioner.

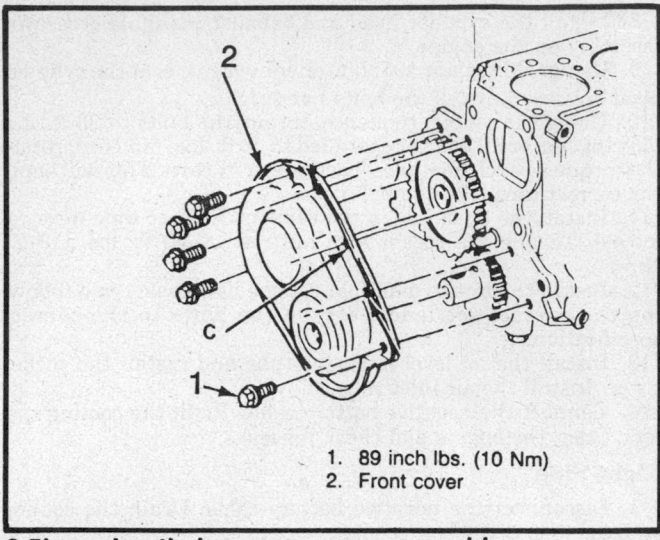

1. 89 inch lbs. (10 Nm)
2. Front cover

2.5L engine timing case cover assembly

3. Remove the alternator-to-bracket bolts and remove the alternator, with the wires attached, support it out of the way.

4. Remove the power steering pump-to-bracket bolts and support it out of the way. Do not disconnect the pressure hoses.

5. Raise and safely support the vehicle.

6. Remove the right side inner fender splash shield. Remove the flywheel dust cover.

7. Using a crankshaft pulley puller tool. Remove the crankshaft damper.

8. Label and disconnect the starter wires, remove the starter.

9. Drain the engine oil and remove the oil pan. Remove the lower front cover bolts.

10. Lower the vehicle. Disconnect the radiator hose from the water pump.

11. Disconnect the heater coolant hose from the cooling system filler pipe.

12. Remove the bypass and overflow hoses.

13. Remove the water pump pulley. Disconnect the canister purge hose.

14. Remove the spark plug wire shield from the water pump.

15. Remove the upper front cover-to-engine bolts and remove the front cover.

16. Clean front cover mounting surfaces.

To install:

17. Apply a thin bead of silicone sealant on the front cover mating surface and using a new gasket, install the front cover on the engine with the top bolts to hold it in place.

18. Raise and safely support the vehicle.

19. Install the oil pan. Install the lower front cover bolts, tighten all of the front cover bolts to 26–35 ft. lbs. (35–48 Nm).

20. Install the serpentine belt and idler pulley. Install the damper on the engine using tool J–29113 or equivalent. Install the starter.

21. Install the inner fender splash shield. Lower the vehicle.

22. Attach the radiator hose too the water pump and attach the heater hoses.

23. Install the power steering pump and the alternator.

24. Attach the spark plug wire shield. Fill the cooling system.

25. Connect the negative battery cable. Check for coolant and oil leaks.

Timing Case Cover Oil Seal

Removal and Installation

1. Disconnect the negative terminal from the battery. Remove the serpentine belt.

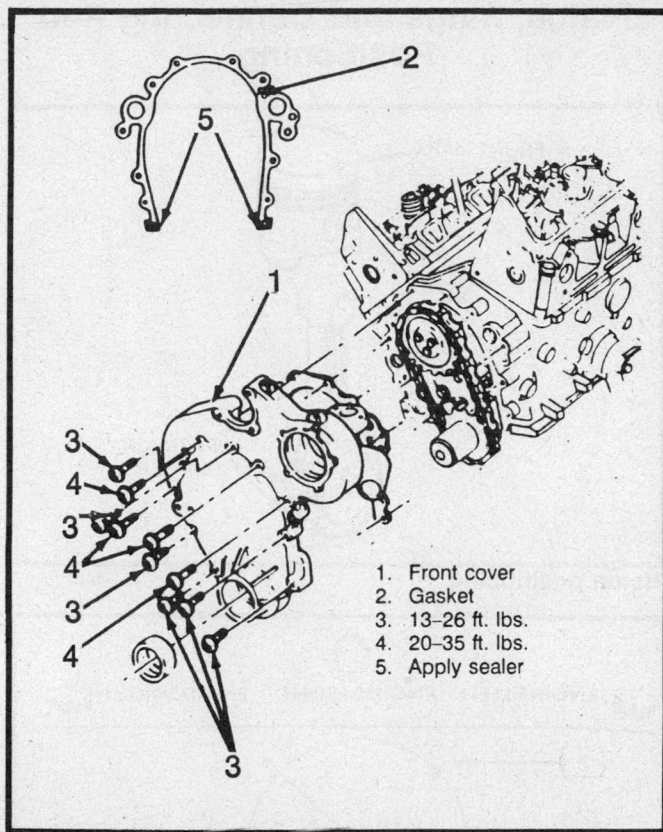

1. Front cover
2. Gasket
3. 13–26 ft. lbs.
4. 20–35 ft. lbs.
5. Apply sealer

2.8L and 3.1L engines timing case cover assembly

2. Raise and safely support the vehicle. Remove the right side inner fender splash shield.

3. Remove the damper retaining bolt.

4. Using a crankshaft pulley puller tool, press the damper pulley from the crankshaft.

5. Using a small pry bar, pry out the seal in the front cover.

NOTE: Use care not to damage the seal seat or the crankshaft while removing or installing the seal. Inspect the crankshaft seal surface for signs of wear.

6. Coat the new seal with oil. Using a seal installer tool, drive the new seal in the cover with the lip facing towards the engine.

7. Using a crankshaft pulley installer tool, press the crankshaft pulley onto the crankshaft. Torque the damper bolt for the 2.8L and 3.1L to 67–85 ft. lbs. (90–115 Nm) and 162 ft. lbs. (220 Nm) for the 2.5L.

8. Install the inner fender splash shield. Lower the vehicle.

9. Install the serpentine belt. Connect the negative battery cable. Run the engine to normal operating temperature and check for leaks.

Timing Gears

Removal and Installation

2.5L ENGINE

1. Disconnect the negative battery cable.
2. Remove the engine from the vehicle.
3. Remove the damper, front cover and camshaft. Align the timing marks on the crank and cam gears.
4. To remove the camshaft gear, use a arbor press and adapter. Position the thrust plate to avoid damage to the woodruff key as the gear is removed.
5. Remove the crankshaft gear with a suitable pry bar.

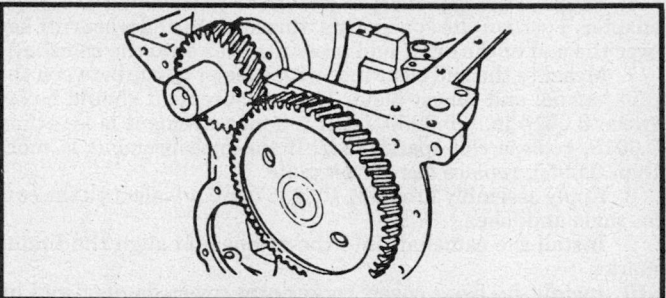

2.5L engine timing mark alignment

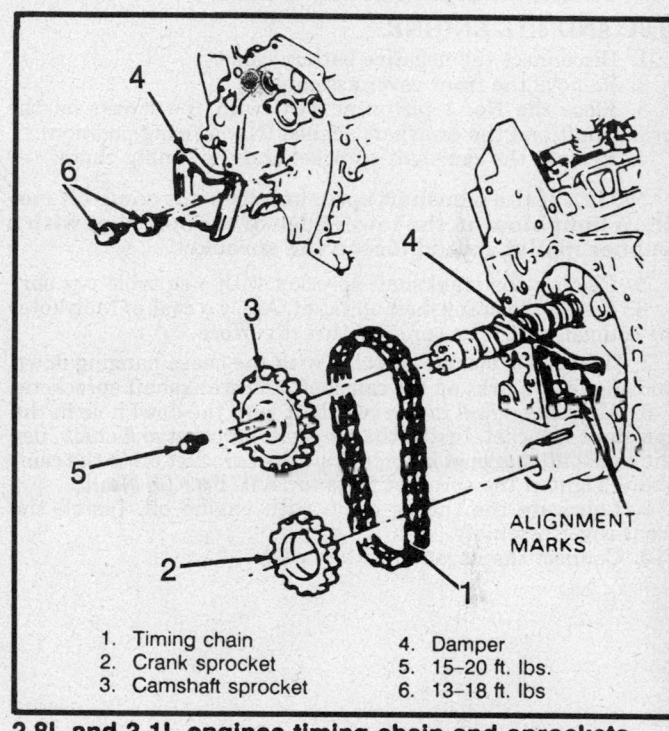

1. Timing chain
2. Crank sprocket
3. Camshaft sprocket
4. Damper
5. 15–20 ft. lbs.
6. 13–18 ft. lbs

2.8L and 3.1L engines timing chain and sprockets

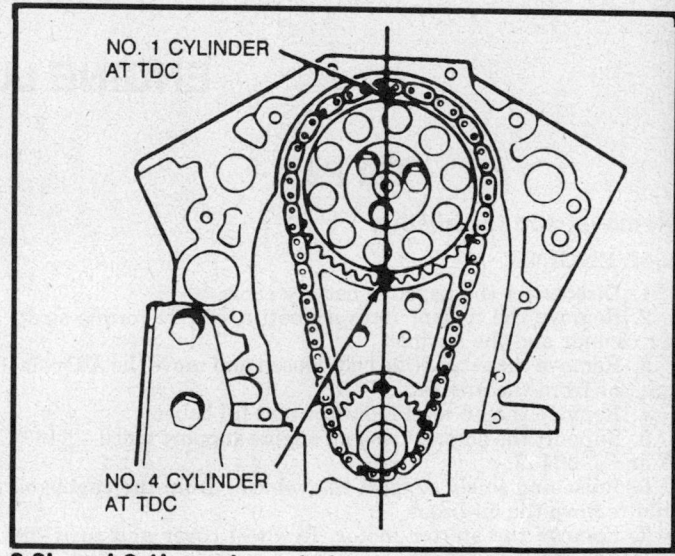

NO. 1 CYLINDER AT TDC

NO. 4 CYLINDER AT TDC

2.8L and 3.1L engines timing mark alignment

6. Support the camshaft in the arbor press using the press adapter. Position the spacer ring, thrust plate and woodruff key over the end of the shaft and press the gear onto the camshaft.

7. Measure the end clearance with a feeler gauge between the cam journal and thrust plate. The measurement should be between 0.0015 in. – 0.0050. in. If the measurement is less than 0.0015, replace the spacer ring. If the measurement is more than 0.0050, replace the thrust plate.

8. Apply assembly lube GM 1052367 or equivalent to the cam journals and lobes.

9. Install the camshaft into the engine and align the timing marks.

10. Install the front cover, rocker arm cover, damper and install the engine into the engine into the vehicle.

11. Connect the negative battery cable.

2.8L AND 3.1L ENGINE

1. Disconnect the negative battery cable.
2. Remove the front cover assembly.
3. Place the No. 1 piston at TDC with the marks on the crankshaft and the camshaft aligned (No. 4 firing position).
4. Remove the camshaft sprocket and the timing chain.

NOTE: If the camshaft sprocket does not come off easily, a light blow on the lower edge of the sprocket with a rubber mallet should loosen the sprocket.

5. Remove the crankshaft sprocket with a suitable pry bar.
6. Install the crankshaft sprocket. Apply a coat of Molykote® or equivalent, to the sprocket thrust surface.
7. Hold the camshaft sprocket with the chain hanging down and align the marks on the camshaft and crankshaft sprockets.
8. Align the dowel in the camshaft with the dowl hole in the camshaft sprocket. Install the camshaft sprocket and chain, use the camshaft sprocket bolts to draw the sprocket on to the camshaft. Tighten the sprocket bolts to 18 ft. lbs. (25 Nm).
9. Lubricate the timing chain with engine oil. Install the front cover assembly.
10. Connect the negative battery cable.

Piston, Rings and Connecting Rod Positioning

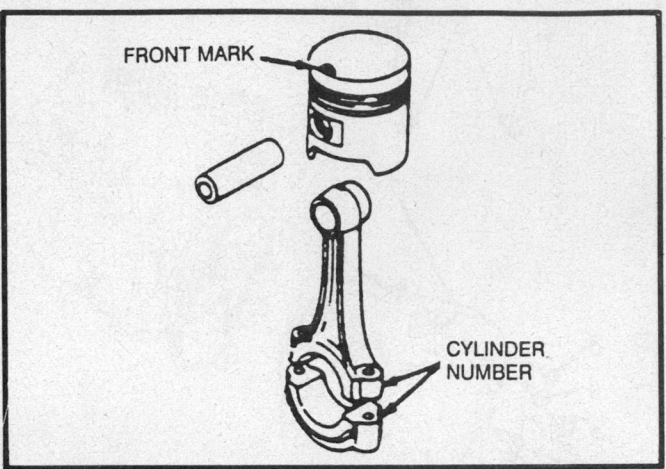

Piston positioning

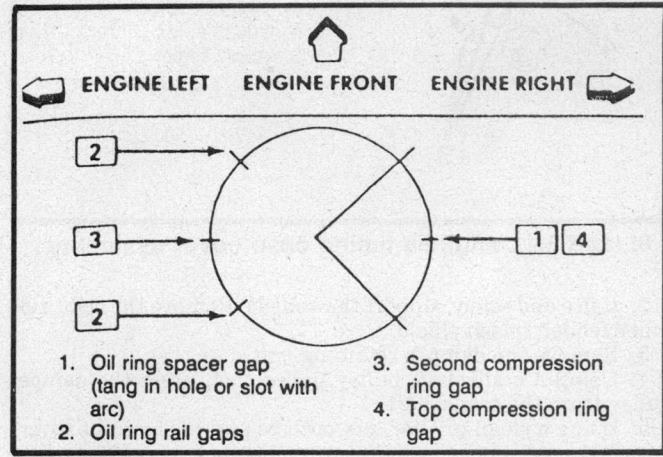

1. Oil ring spacer gap (tang in hole or slot with arc)
2. Oil ring rail gaps
3. Second compression ring gap
4. Top compression ring gap

Piston ring end gap positioning

ENGINE LUBRICATION

Oil Pan

Removal and Installation

2.5L ENGINE

1. Disconnect the negative battery cable.
2. Remove the coolant recovery bottle, engine torque strut, air cleaner and the air inlet.
3. Remove the serpentine belt, loosen and move the A/C compressor from the bracket.
4. Remove the oil level indicator and fill tube.
5. Support the engine using an engine support tool J–28467–A and J–36462.
6. Raise and safely support the vehicle, drain the engine oil and remove the oil filter.
7. Remove the starter motor, flywheel cover and turn the front wheels to full right.

8. Remove the engine wiring harness retainers under the oil pan on the right and left sides.
9. Remove the right engine splash shield, front engine mount bracket bolts and nuts.
10. Remove the transaxle mount nuts.
11. Using the engine support fixture tool J–28467–A and J–36462, raise the engine about 2 inches.
12. Remove the front engine mount, bracket and loosen the frame bolts.
13. Remove the oil pan retaining bolts and oil pan.

To install:

14. Clean all gasket surfaces and apply RTV sealer to the oil pan and engine surfaces.
15. Install the oil pan and retaining bolts and tighten to 89 inch lbs. (10 Nm).
16. Install the frame bolts and tighten to 103 ft. lbs. (140 Nm).

17. Install the engine mount, bracket, lower the engine into position and install the transaxle mount nuts.

18. Install the engine mount nuts and bracket bolts.

19. Install the engine splash shield, wiring harness to the oil pan, flywheel cover and the starter motor.

20. Lower the vehicle and remove the engine support fixtures.

21. Install the oil level indicator and tube assembly.

22. Reinstall the A/C compressor to its original location and serpentine belt.

23. Install the air inlet, air cleaner, torque strut and coolant recovery bottle.

24. Connect the negative battery cable and fill the engine with oil.

2.8L AND 3.1L ENGINES

1. Disconnect the negative battery cable.
2. Remove the serpentine belt and the tensioner.
3. Support the engine with tool J–28467 or equivalent.
4. Raise and safely support the vehicle. Drain the engine oil.
5. Remove the right tire and wheel assembly. Remove the right inner fender splash shield.
6. Remove the steering gear pinch bolt. Remove the transaxle mount retaining bolts.
7. Remove the engine-to-cradle mounting nuts. Remove the front engine collar bracket from the block.
8. Remove the starter shield and the flywheel cover. Remove the starter.
9. Loosen, but do not remove the rear engine cradle bolts.
10. Remove the front cradle bolts. Remove the oil pan retaining bolts and nuts. Remove the oil pan.

To install:

11. Clean the gasket mating surfaces.
12. Install a new gasket on the oil pan. Apply silicon sealer to the portion of the pan that contacts the rear of the block.
13. Install the oil pan, nuts and retaining bolts. Tighten to 13–18 ft. lbs. (18–25 Nm).
14. Install the front cradle bolts and tighten the rear cradle bolts. Install the starter and splash shield. Install the flywheel shield.
15. Attach the collar bracket to the block, install the engine-to-cradle nuts. Install the transaxle mount nuts.
16. Install the steering pinch bolt. Install the right inner fender splash shield and tire assembly. Lower the vehicle.
17. Remove the engine support tool. Install the serpentine belt and tensioner.
18. Fill the crankcase to the correct level. Connect the negative battery cable. Run the engine to normal operating temperature and check for leaks.

Force Balancer Assembly

Removal and Installation

2.5L ENGINE

1. Disconnect the negative battery cable. Raise and support the vehicle safely. Drain the crankcase and remove the oil filter.
2. Remove the oil pan retaining bolts. Remove the oil pan. Remove the restrictor, oil pump cover, oil pump gears and pressure regulator valve.
3. Clean all sludge, oil and varnish from the pump assembly with carburetor cleaner.
4. Lubricate all parts with engine oil and pack all pump cavities with petroleum jelly for pump priming.
5. Install the pump gears, pump cover and pressure regulator. Torque the pump cover bolts to 7 ft. lbs. (10 Nm).
6. Install the plug and pin and make sure the pin is properly seated.
7. Clean and install the oil pump inlet screen, oil pan and new filter. Torque the oil pan bolts to 20 ft. lbs. (27 Nm).
8. Refill the crankcase with engine oil. Start the engine and check for oil pressure and leaks.

Force balancer counterweight positioning

Force balancer alignment

Oil Pump

Removal and Installation

NOTE: On the 2.5L engine, the force balancer assembly does not have to be removed to service the oil pump or pressure regulator assemblies.

1. Raise and safely support the vehicle.
2. Drain the engine oil.
3. Remove the oil pan.
4. Remove the oil pump retaining bolts, remove the oil pump and pump driveshaft.
5. Install the oil pump and pump driveshaft. Tighten the oil pump mounting bolts to 30 ft. lbs. (41 Nm) for the 2.8L and 3.1L and to 89 inch lbs. (10 Nm) for the 2.5L.
6. Install the oil pan. Lower the vehicle.
7. Fill the crankcase to the correct level with oil. Run the vehicle and check for leaks.

Rear Main Bearing Oil Seal

Removal and Installation

NOTE: The 2.5L, 2.8L and 3.1L engines use a round rear oil seal that requires removal of the transaxle and flywheel.

1. Support the engine with tool J–28467 or equivalent. Raise and safely support the vehicle.
2. Remove the transaxle assembly. Remove the flywheel.
3. Using a small pry bar or equivalent, insert it through the dust lip at an angle and pry the old seal from the block.

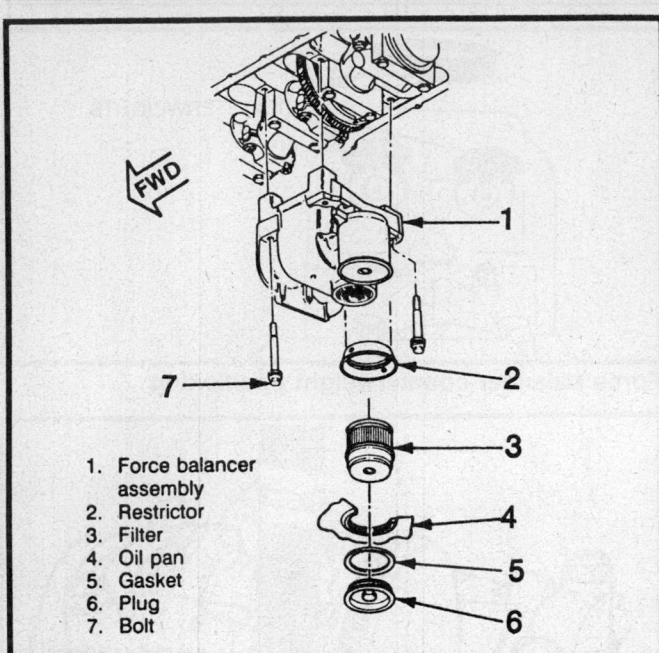

1. Force balancer assembly
2. Restrictor
3. Filter
4. Oil pan
5. Gasket
6. Plug
7. Bolt

2.5L engine oil pump/force balancer assembly

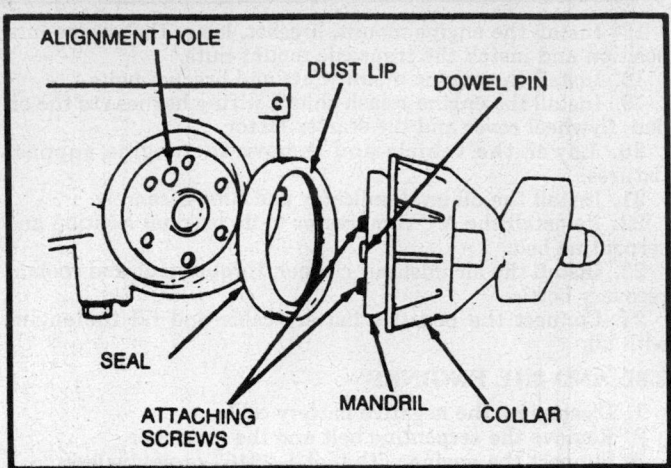

Rear main seal replacement

4. Inspect the seal bore and the crankshaft end for any damage.
5. Coat the inside lip of the seal with engine oil and install it on the seal installation tool J–34686 or equivalent.
6. Align the dowel pin of the tool with the dowel pin of the crankshaft. Install the tool on the crankshaft and turn the wing nut until the tool and seal are fully seated on the crankshaft.
7. Loosen the wing nut and remove the tool. Check the seal to make sure it is properly seated.
8. Install the flywheel and the transaxle.
9. Remove the engine support tool. Run the engine and check for leaks.

Connecting Rod and Main Bearings

Removal and Installation

NOTE: The connecting rod and main bearings are designed to have a slight projection above the rod and cap faces to insure a positive contact. The bearings can be replaced without removing the rod and piston assemblies from the engine.

1. Disconnect the negative battery cable.
2. Raise and safely support the vehicle.
3. Drain the engine oil and remove the oil pan.
4. With the connecting rod journal at the bottom of the travel, mark each bearing cap with the cylinder number on the machined surfaces of the connecting rod and cap for identification when installing, then remove the rod nuts and caps.
5. Inspect journals for roughness and wear. Use fine grit polishing cloth saturated with engine oil to remove burrs.
6. Install new bearings and check clearances. Torque the bearing caps to specification.
7. Install the oil pan and fill with engine oil.

FRONT SUSPENSION AND STEERING

For front suspension component removal and installation procedures, refer to the Unit Repair section.

For steering wheel removal and installation, refer to the electrical control section.

Power Rack and Pinion

Adjustment

1. Disconnect the negative battery cable.
2. Loosen the adjuster plug locknut and turn clockwise until it bottoms in the housing, then back off 50 to 70 degrees (one flat).
3. Raise and safely support the vehicle. Center the steering wheel.
4. Tighten the locknut to the adjuster plug. Tighten to 50 ft. lbs. (70 Nm) while holding the adjuster plug stationary. Make sure the steering does not bind. Connect the negative battery cable.

Removal and Installation

1. Disconnect the negative battery cable. Remove the air cleaner.
2. Raise and safely support the vehicle.
3. Remove both front wheel assemblies.
4. Remove the intermediate shaft lower pinch bolt at the steering gear. Remove the intermediate shaft from the stub shaft.
5. Disconnect the electrical lead at the power steering idle switch.
6. Separate the tie rod ends from the knuckle assembly. Remove the rear sub-frame mounting bolts and lower the rear of the sub-frame approximately 4 in.
7. Remove the steering rack heat shield. Disconnect the pressure lines at the steering gear.
8. Remove the rack and pinion mounting bolts, remove the rack and pinion through the left wheel opening.
To install:
9. Install the rack and pinion through the left wheel opening. Tighten the mounting bolts to 59 ft. lbs. (81 Nm). Connect the pressure lines, tighten the fittings to 20 ft. lbs. (27 Nm).

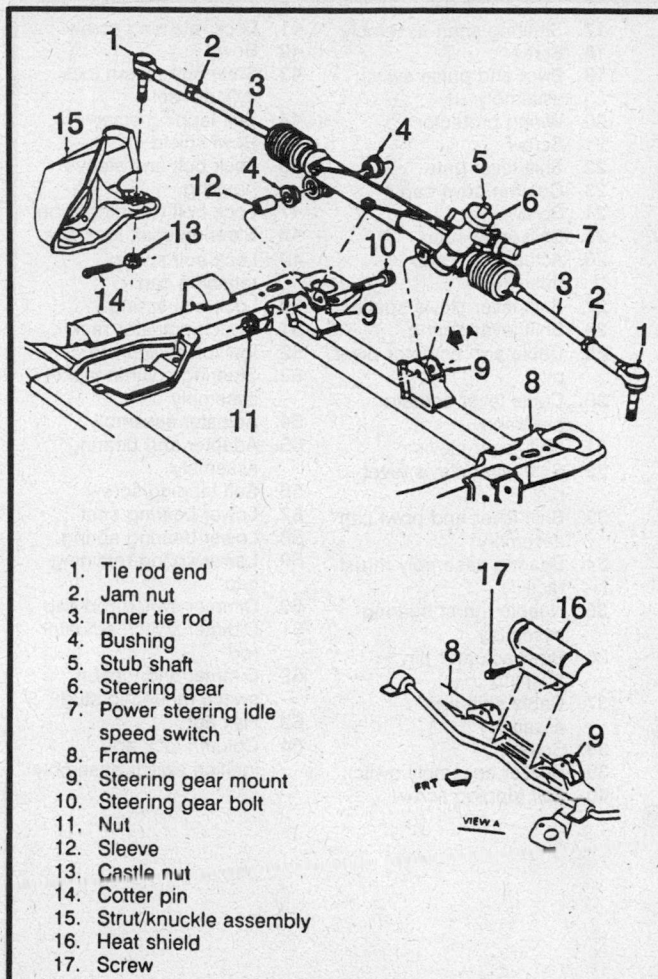

1. Tie rod end
2. Jam nut
3. Inner tie rod
4. Bushing
5. Stub shaft
6. Steering gear
7. Power steering idle speed switch
8. Frame
9. Steering gear mount
10. Steering gear bolt
11. Nut
12. Sleeve
13. Castle nut
14. Cotter pin
15. Strut/knuckle assembly
16. Heat shield
17. Screw

Steering gear and mounting

10. Install the rack heat shield, tighten the retaining bolts to 53 inch lbs. (6 Nm). Attach the tie rod ends to the steering knuckle.
11. Connect the electrical lead to the power steering idle switch. Attach the intermediate shaft to the stub shaft, tighten the pinch bolt to 35 ft. lbs. (48 Nm).
12. Install both wheel assemblies, tighten lug nuts to 100 ft. lbs. (136 Nm) and lower the vehicle.
13. Install the air cleaner. Connect the negative battery cable. Fill and bleed the power steering system.

Power Steering Pump

Removal and Installation

2.5L ENGINE

1. Disconnect the negative battery cable.
2. Raise and safely support the vehicle.
3. Remove the pressure and return hoses from the pump and drain the fluid.
4. Lower the vehicle, remove the ECM heat shield and serpentine belt.
5. Remove the pump mounting bolts and pump.
6. Install the pump and tighten the bolts to 20 ft. lbs. (27 Nm).
7. Install the serpentine belt, ECM heat shield and raise and safely support the vehicle.

8. Install the inlet and outlet hoses and lower the vehicle.
9. Refill the pump with power steering fluid and bleed the system. Connect the negative battery cable.

2.8L AND 3.1L ENGINES

1. Disconnect the negative terminal from the battery.
2. Remove the pressure and return hoses from the pump and drain the system into a suitable container.
3. Cap the fittings at the pump.
4. Remove the serpentine belt.
5. Locate the pump attaching bolts through the pulley and remove the bolts.
6. Remove the pump assembly.
7. Install the pump and torque the mounting bolts to 18 ft. lbs. (25 Nm).
8. Reconnect the hoses to the pump and install the serpentine belt.
9. Refill the power steering pump reservoir and bleed the system. Connect the negative battery cable.

Bleeding the System

NOTE: Automatic transmission fluid is not compatible with the seals and hoses of the power steering system. Under no circumstances should automatic transmission be used in place of power steering fluid in this system.

1. With the engine turned **OFF**, turn the wheels all the way to the left.
2. Fill the reservoir with power steering fluid until the level is at the cold mark on the reservoir.
3. Start and run the engine at fast idle for 15 seconds. Turn the engine **OFF**.
4. Recheck the fluid level and fill it to the cold mark.
5. Start the engine and bleed the system by turning the wheels in both directions slowly to the stops.
6. Stop the engine and check the fluid. Fluid that still has air in it will be a light tan color.
7. Repeat this procedure until all of the air is removed from the system.

Steering Column

Removal and Installation

1. Disconnect the negative battery cable.
2. Remove the lower left hand trim panel below the steering column.
3. Push the top of the intermediate shaft seal down for access to the intermediate shaft seal coupling.
4. Remove the intermediate shaft coupling pinch bolt.
5. Disconnect the shift indicator cable end and casing from the column.

NOTE: If the vehicle is equipped with park lock, disconnect the park lock cable from the column.

6. Disconnect the shift cable from the ball stud on the shift lever.
7. Remove the lower column bolts first and then remove the upper bolts. Lower the column to the seat.
8. Disconnect the electrical connectors and remove the column from the vehicle.

To install:

9. Install the column into the vehicle and loosely install the column bolts. Install the intermediate shaft pinch bolt and tighten it to 35 ft. lbs. (48 Nm).
10. Connect the electrical connector and all the shift cables. Connect the park lock cable, if equipped.
11. Tighten the steering column mounting bolts to 18 ft. lbs. (25 Nm).

1. Hex nut
2. Spacer and cancelling cam
3. Retaining ring
4. Thrust washer
5. Upper bearing spring
6. Thrust washer
7. Screw
8. Column housing cover
9. Hazard warning
10. Screw
11. Turn signal switch assembly
12. Screw
13. Steering column housing
14. Bearing assembly
15. Steering clumn housing assembly
16. Steering column housing spacer
17. Steering shaft assembly
18. Screw
19. Pivot and pulse switch assembly
20. Wiring protector
21. Screw
22. Shift lever gate
23. Column bowl cap
24. Screw
25. Shift lever seal
26. Actuator pin cap bushing
27. Shfit lever clevis spacer
28. Shift lever spring
29. Cable arm actuator pivot pin
30. Cable lever actuator assembly
31. Shift lever clevis
32. Shift lever clevis pivot pin
33. Shift lever and bowl cap assembly
34. Bearing assembly thrust race
35. Needle thrust bearing assembly
36. Bowl actuator pin bushing
37. Cable shift arm assembly
38. Screw
39. Buzzer assembly switch
40. Self tapping screw
41. Lock retaining screw
42. Bowl
43. Steering column lock cylinder set
44. Self tapping screw
45. Bowl shield
46. Lock bolt and sleeve housing
47. Lock bolt retaining tube
48. Steering shaft lock bolt
49. Lock bolt spring retaining cap
50. Lock bolt spring
51. Switch actuator rack
52. Ignition switch rod
53. Steering column jacket assembly
54. Adjuster assembly
55. Adapter and bearing assembly
56. Self tapping screw
57. Lower bearing seat
58. Lower bearing spring
59. Lower spring retaining cap
60. Dimmer switch rod cap
61. Dimmer switch actuator rod
62. Dimmer and igntion switch mounting stud
63. Hex nut
64. Column lock and ignition switch assembly

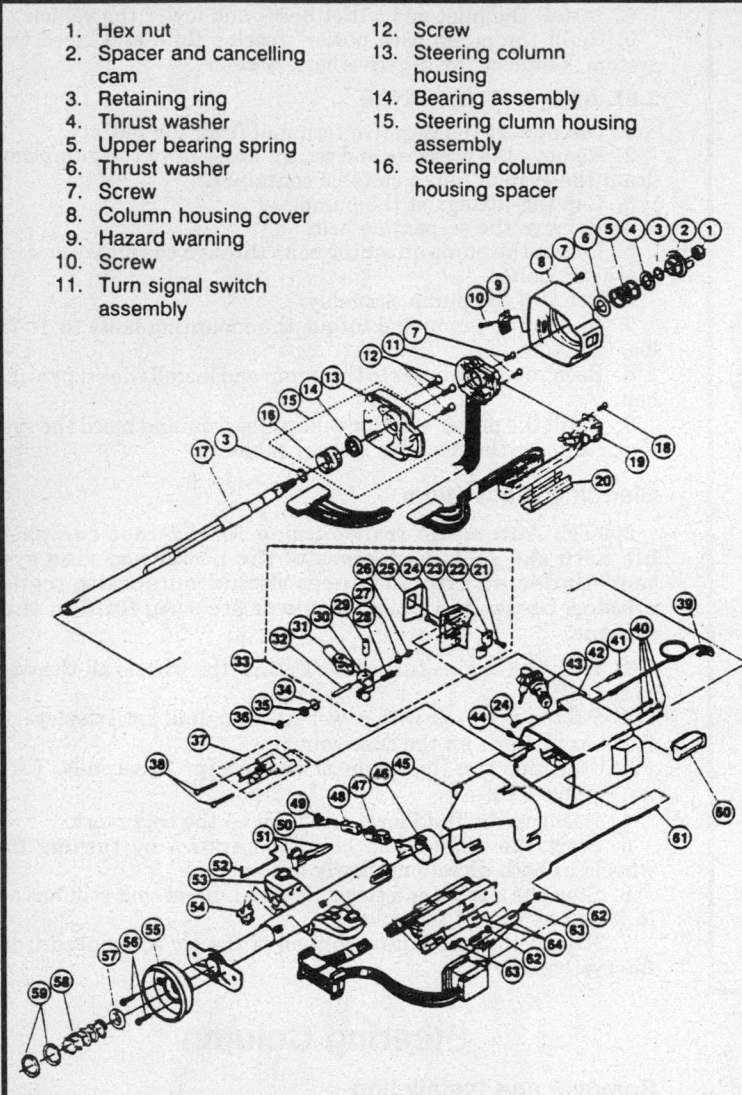

Standard steering column — exploded view

12. Reposition the intermediate shaft seal and install the trim panel.
13. Connect the negative battery cable.

Front Wheel Drive Hub, Knuckle and Bearings

Removal and Installation

The hub and bearing are replaced as an assembly only.
1. With the vehicle weight on the tires, loosen the hub nut a complete turn.
2. Raise and support the vehicle. Remove the wheel and tire assembly.
3. Install a boot cover over the outer CV joint boot.
4. Remove the hub nut. Remove the brake caliper and support it out of the way. Do not allow the caliper to hang on the brake line. Remove the rotor.
5. Remove the hub and bearing mounting bolts.
6. Remove the brake rotor splash shield and ABS sensor, if so equipped.

7. Install the hub puller tool J–28733 or equivalent and press the hub and bearing from the halfshaft.
8. Disconnect the stabalizer link from the lower control arm.
9. Using a ball joint puller tool and separate the ball joint from the steering knuckle.
10. Remove the halfshaft from the knuckle and support it out of the way.
11. Using a brass drift, remove the inner knuckle seal.
To install:
12. Clean and inspect the steering knuckle bore and the bearing mating surfaces.
13. Install a new O-ring between the bearing and knuckle assembly.
14. Install the hub and bearing assembly and torque the nuts to 52 ft. lbs. (70 Nm).
15. Using a seal driver tool, install it into the steering knuckle; be sure to lubricate the new seal and the bearing with a high temperature wheel bearing grease.
16. Reconnect the lower ball joint.
17. Install the hub, bearing nut and washer on the halfshaft, torque the nut to 71 ft. lbs. (95 Nm).

1. Hex nut
2. Cancelling cam assembly
3. Pan head screw
4. Column housing cover
5. Hazard warning knob
6. Screw
7. Turn signal switch
8. Upper shaft bearing lock nut
9. Flat washer
10. Inner race seat
11. Inner race
12. Bearing assembly
13. Steering column housing
14. Steering column housing assembly
15. Pivot pin
16. Spring retainer
17. Thrust washer
18. Needle thrust bearing assembly
19. Thrust bearing race assembly
20. Wheel tilt spring
21. Upper steering shaft
22. Tilt spring guide
23. Centering sphere
24. Joint preload spring
25. Lower steering shaft assembly
26. Steering shaft assembly
27. Self tapping screw
28. Pivot and pulse switch assembly
29. Wiring protector
30. Self tapping screw
31. Buzzer switch assembly
32. Housing shoe retainer cap
33. Pan head self tapping screw
34. Lock retaining screw
35. Steering column lock cylinder
36. Steering column bowl
37. Self tapping screw
38. Bowl shield
39. Lock bolt and sleeve housing
40. Lock bolt retainer tube
41. Steering shaft lock bolt
42. Lock bolt spring.
43. Lock bolt spring retainer cap
44. Switch actuator rack
45. Ignition switch rod
46. Steering column jacket assembly
47. Adapter and bearing assembly
48. Self tapping screw
49. Lower bearing seat
50. Lower bearing spring
51. Lower spring retainer
52. Tilt lever and bracket assembly
53. Column tilt bumper
54. Dimmer switch rod cap
55. Dimmer switch actuator rod
56. Hex nut
57. Dimmer and ignition switch mounting stud
58. Ignition switch assembly

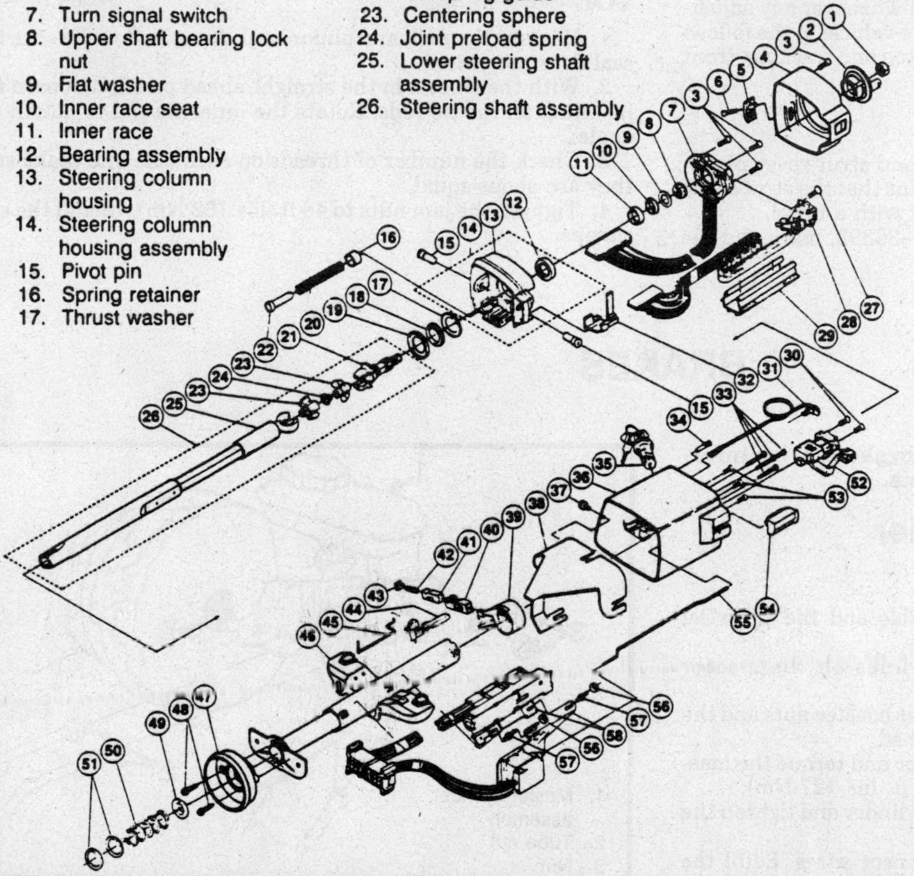

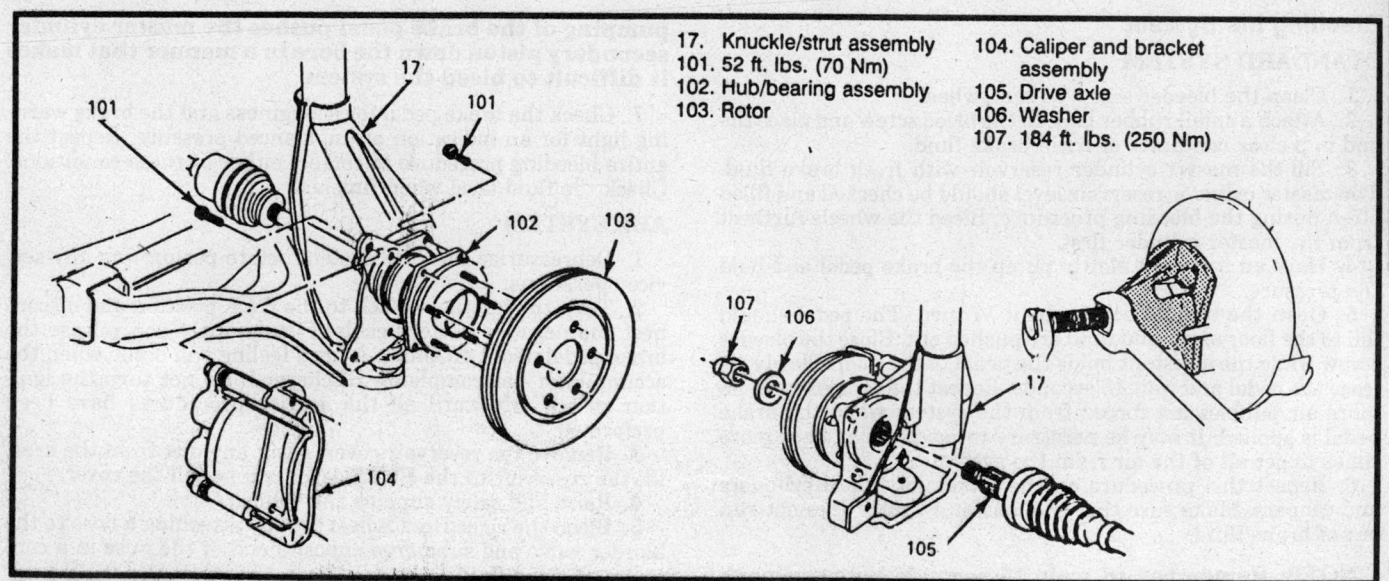

Tilt steering column—exploded view

17. Knuckle/strut assembly
101. 52 ft. lbs. (70 Nm)
102. Hub/bearing assembly
103. Rotor
104. Caliper and bracket assembly
105. Drive axle
106. Washer
107. 184 ft. lbs. (250 Nm)

Front knuckle, bearing and hub assembly

18. Install the brake rotor, caliper and ABS sensor, if so equipped. Install the wheel and tire.

19. Lower the vehicle and torque the hub nut to 184 ft. lbs. (250 Nm).

Front Wheel Alignment

A 4 wheel alignment should be performed whenever any adjustments are made to the front end. Align the vehicle in the following order; rear wheel camber, rear wheel toe and tracking, front wheel camber and toe.

CAMBER

1. Remove the strut cover plate nuts and strut cover plate.
2. Lift the front of the vehicle to the point that the strut studs clear the strut tower and cover the strut with a towel.
3. Using a strut alignment template J–36892, mark and file the 3 holes to the specified amount. Do not exceed 0.2 in. (5mm).
4. Paint the exposed metal with primer and body paint.
5. Lower the vehicle and guide the strut studs into the slotted holes.
6. Install the strut cover plate, nuts and set camber to specifications. Tighten the strut nuts to 17 ft. lbs. (24 Nm).

TOE

1. Remove the rack and pinion seal clamp and make sure the seal does not twist.
2. With the wheels in the straight ahead position, loosen the jam nuts on the tie rods. Rotate the inner tie rod to obtain toe angle.
3. Check the number of threads on each side and make sure they are about equal.
4. Tighten the jam nuts to 46 ft. lbs. (62 Nm). Install the seal clamps.

BRAKES

Refer to the unit repair section for brake service information and drum/rotor specifications.

Master Cylinder

Removal and Installation

1. Disconnect the negative battery cable and the electrical connector from the fluid level sensor.
2. Disconnect and plug the brake lines on the master cylinder.
3. Remove the master cylinder-to-power booster nuts and the master cylinder with the reservoir attached.
4. Install the master cylinder-to-booster and torque the master cylinder-to-power booster nuts to 20 ft. lbs. (27 Nm).
5. Connect the brake lines-to-master cylinder and tighten the fittings to 13 ft. lbs. (17 Nm).
6. Connect the fluid level electrical sensor wires. Refill the reservoir with an approved DOT 3 brake fluid and bleed the brake system.

Bleeding the System

STANDARD SYSTEM

1. Clean the bleeder screw at each wheel.
2. Attach a small rubber hose to the bleed screw and place the end in a clear container of fresh brake fluid.
3. Fill the master cylinder reservoir with fresh brake fluid. The master cylinder reservoir level should be checked and filled often during the bleeding procedure. Bleed the wheels furthest from the master cylinder first.
4. Have an assistant slowly pump the brake pedal and hold the pressure.
5. Open the bleeder screw about ¼ turn. The pedal should fall to the floor as air and fluid are pushed out. Close the bleeder screw while the assistant holds the pedal to the floor. Slowly release the pedal and wait 15 seconds. Repeat the process until no more air bubbles are forced from the system when the brake pedal is applied. It may be necessary to repeat this ten or more times to get all of the air from the system.
6. Repeat this procedure on the remaining wheel cylinders and calipers. Make sure that the master cylinder does not run out of brake fluid.

NOTE: Remember to wait 15 seconds between each bleeding and do not pump the pedal rapidly. Rapid

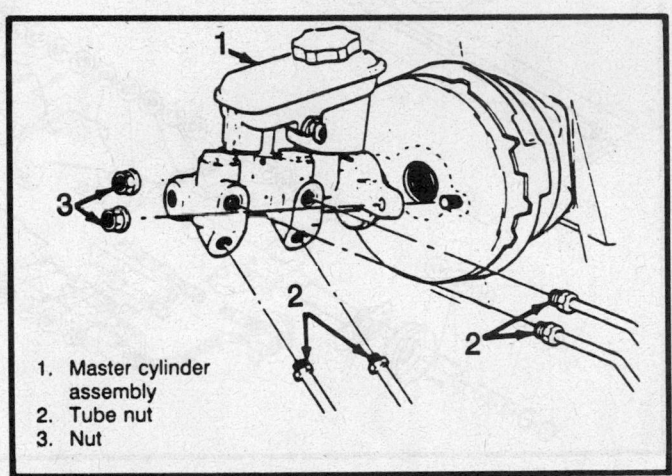

1. Master cylinder assembly
2. Tube nut
3. Nut

Master cylinder mounting

pumping of the brake pedal pushes the master cylinder secondary piston down the bore in a manner that makes it difficult to bleed the system.

7. Check the brake pedal for sponginess and the brake warning light for an indication of unbalanced pressure. Repeat the entire bleeding procedure to correct either of these conditions. Check the fluid level when finished.

ABS SYSTEM

1. Depressurize the ABS system before performing any service operations.
2. Turn the ignition switch to the OFF position and disconnect the negative battery cable. Firmly apply and release the brake pedal about 40 times. A hard feeling will occur when the accumulator has completely discharged. Do not turn the ignition switch ON until all the service procedures have been performed.
3. Remove the reservoir cover, clean any dirt from the area, fill the reservoir to the FULL level and install the cover.
4. Raise and safely support the vehicle.
5. Bleed the right front wheel first by attaching a hose to the bleeder valve and submerge opposite end of the hose in a container of clean fluid.
6. Open the bleeder valve, have an assistant slowly depress

the brake pedal and tap on the caliper with a rubber hammer to free tapped air.

7. Close the valve, check and add new fluid as necessary. Repeat procedures until the pedal feels firm and no bubbles are observed in the bleeder hose. Repeat procedures for left wheel. Connect the negative battery cable.

8. Turn the ignition switch **ON** and allow the pump motor to run. Shut the ignition **OFF** if the pump runs for more than 60 seconds. Check for leaks if the pump runs for more than 60 seconds.

9. Bleed the right rear wheel by attaching hose, open the bleeder valve, turn the ignition switch **ON** and slowly depress the brake part way until the fluid begins to flow from the bleeder. Hold for 15 seconds. Do NOT fully depress the brake pedal. Close the valve and release the pedal.

10. Fill the reservoir with brake fluid and repeat procedures for left rear wheel.

Power Brake Booster

Removal and Installation

1. Disconnect the negative battery cable and remove the left side under dash panel.

2. Remove the booster grommet bolt and remove the grommet.

3. Remove the pushrod from the brake pedal. Remove the master cylinder from the booster.

4. Using tool J–2280501 or equivalent, unlock the booster from the mounting flange by turning it counterclockwise. Remove the booster from the vehicle.

5. Install the booster to the mounting flange. Install the pushrod to the brake pedal.

6. Install the master cylinder to the booster. Install the booster grommet and bolt.

7. Install the trim panel.

Parking Brake

NOTE: Parking brake adjustment is critical on 4 wheel disc brake systems.

Adjustment

1. Depress the service brake pedal 3 times.
2. Fully apply and release the parking brake 3 times.
3. Raise and safely support the vehicle. Remove the rear wheel assemblies. Install 2 lug nuts on each rear hub to retain the rotors.
4. The parking brake levers on both calipers should be against the lever stops on the caliper housings. If the levers are not against the stops, check for binding in the rear cables and loosen the cables at the adjuster until both of the levers are against their stops.
5. Tighten the parking brake cable at the adjusters until the levers just start to move off the stop.

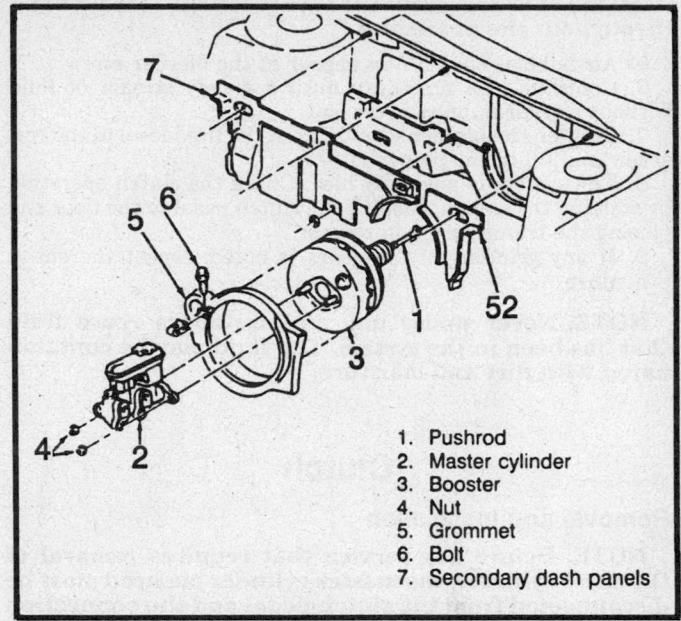

1. Pushrod
2. Master cylinder
3. Booster
4. Nut
5. Grommet
6. Bolt
7. Secondary dash panels

Power brake booster mounting

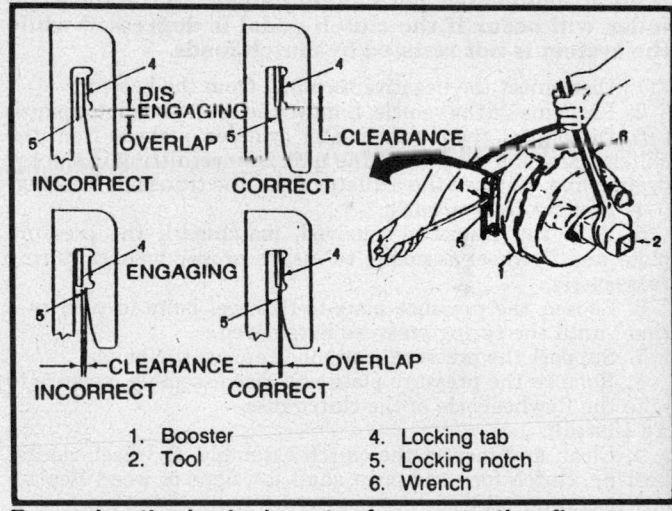

1. Booster
2. Tool
4. Locking tab
5. Locking notch
6. Wrench

Removing the brake booster from mounting flange

6. Operate the parking brake several times to check the adjustment. A firm pedal should be reached with 2 strokes of the pedal. The rear wheels should not move forward when the brake is applied.

7. Install the wheels and tires. Lower the vehicle.

CLUTCH AND TRANSAXLE

Hydraulic Clutch Linkage

Adjustment

No adjustments are possible on the manual transaxle shifting cables or linkage. If the transaxle is not engaging completely, check for stretched cables, broken shifter components, worn clutch or a faulty transaxle.

Bleeding

1. Remove any dirt or grease around the reservoir cap so that dirt cannot enter the system.
2. Fill the reservoir with an approved DOT 3 brake fluid.
3. Loosen, but do not remove, the bleeder screw on the slave cylinder.
4. Fluid will now flow from the master cylinder to the slave cylinder.

NOTE: It is important that the reservoir remain filled throughout the procedure.

5. Air bubbles should now appear at the bleeder screw.
6. Continue this procedure until a steady stream of fluid without any air bubbles is present.
7. Tighten the bleeder screw. Check the fluid level in the reservoir and fill to the proper mark.
8. The system is now fully bled. Check the clutch operation by starting the engine, pushing the clutch pedal to the floor and placing the transmission in reverse.
9. If any grinding of the gears is noted, repeat the entire procedure.

NOTE: Never under any circumstances reuse fluid that has been in the system. The fluid may be contaminated with dirt and moisture.

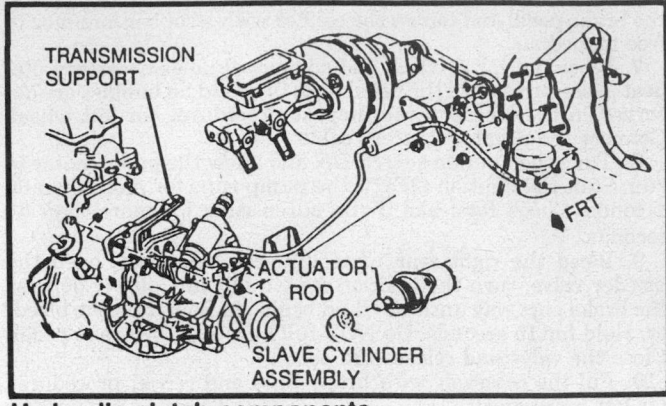

Hydraulic clutch components

Clutch

Removal and Installation

NOTE: Before any service that requires removal of the slave cylinder, the master cylinder pushrod must be disconnected from the clutch pedal and the connection in the hydraulic lines must be separated using J–36221. If not disconnected, permanent damage to the slave cylinder will occur if the clutch pedal is depressed while the system is not resisted by clutch loads.

1. Disconnect the negative terminal from the battery.
2. From inside the vehicle, remove the sound insulator panel.
3. Disconnect the clutch master cylinder pushrod from the clutch pedal and disconnect the quik connect fitting in the hydraulic line. Remove the actuator from the transaxle housing.
4. Remove the transaxle.
5. With the transaxle removed, matchmark the pressure plate and flywheel assembly to insure proper balance during reassembly.
6. Loosen the pressure plate-to-flywheel bolts (a turn at a time) until the spring pressure is removed.
7. Support the pressure plate and remove the bolts.
8. Remove the pressure plate and disc assembly; be sure to note the flywheel side of the clutch disc.

To install:
9. Clean and inspect the clutch assembly, flywheel, release bearing, clutch fork and pivot shaft for signs of wear. Replace any necessary parts.
10. Position the clutch disc and pressure plate in the appropriate position, support the assembly with alignment tool No. J–29074, J–35822 or equivalent.

NOTE: Make sure the clutch disc is facing the same direction it was removed. If the same pressure plate is being reused, align the marks made during removal and install, install the pressure plate retaining bolts and tighten them gradually and evenly.

11. Remove the alignment tool and torque the pressure plate-to-flywheel bolts to 15 ft. lbs. (21 Nm). Lightly lubricate the clutch fork ends. Fill the recess ends of the release bearing with grease. Lubricate the input shaft with a light coat of grease.
12. Install the transaxle assembly. Install the clutch master cylinder pushrod and install the sound insulator panel.

NOTE: The clutch lever must not be moved towards the flywheel until the transaxle is bolted to the engine. Damage to the transaxle, release bearing and clutch fork could occur if this is not followed.

13. Connect the negative battery cable. Bleed the clutch system and check the clutch operation.

Manual Transaxle

Removal and Installation

NOTE: Before performing any maintenance that requires the removal of the slave cylinder, transaxle or clutch housing, the clutch master cylinder pushrod must first be disconnected from the clutch pedal. Failure to disconnect the pushrod will result in permanent damage to the slave cylinder if the clutch pedal is depressed with the slave cylinder disconnected.

1. Disconnect the negative battery cable.
2. Install the engine support tool J–28467 or equivalent.
3. Remove the air cleaner housing and intake tube. Disconnect the clutch slave cylinder from the transaxle.
4. Disconnect the electrical connection at the speed sensor assembly. Disconnect the clutch and shift cables from the transaxle.
5. Remove the exhaust crossover pipe at the left manifold and remove the EGR tube from the crossover.
6. Loosen the crossover-to-right exhaust manifold clamp and move the crossover pipe to gain access to the transaxle bolts (V6 engine).
7. Remove the 2 upper transaxle mounting bolts and remove the 2 upper mounting studs. Leave 1 bottom bolt and stud attached.
8. Disconnect the electrical connection at the backup lamp switch. Raise and safely support the vehicle.
9. Drain the transaxle fluid. Remove the clutch housing cover. Remove both front tire assemblies.
10. Remove the inner fender splash shields from both side of the vehicle. Disconnect the power steering lines from the frame.
11. Remove the rack and pinion heat shield and remove the rack and pinion from the frame.
12. Disconnect the right and left ball joints. Remove the upper transaxle mount retaining bolts. Remove the lower engine mount retaining nuts.
13. Remove the sub-frame retaining bolts and remove the sub-frame from the vehicle. Remove the starter and support it aside.
14. Remove the right and left drive axles from the transaxle. Support the axles to the frame with wire to prevent damage to the CV-joints. Support the transaxle and remove the remaining bolt and stud. Remove the transaxle from the vehicle.

To install:
15. Align the transaxle with the engine and install. Install the lower transaxle-to-engine mounting bolt and stud, tightening to 55 ft. lbs. (75 Nm).
16. Install the starter assembly. Install the left and right drive axles.
17. Install the sub-frame and retaining bolts. Install the lower engine mount retaining nuts.
18. Install the upper transaxle retaining bolts, tightening to 55

ft. lbs. (75 Nm). Install the right and left ball joints to the steering knuckles.

19. Install the rack and pinion, heat shield and lines to the frame. Install the right and left inner fender splash shields.

20. Install the clutch housing cover, tighten the screws to 115 inch lbs. (13 Nm). Lower the vehicle.

21. Attach the crossover pipe to the manifolds and attach the EGR pipe to the crossover.

22. Attach the shift and clutch cables to the transaxle. Connect all of the electrical connectors. Install the air cleaner housing and tube. Remove the engine support tool.

23. Fill the transaxle with fluid. Connect the negative battery cable.

Automatic Transaxle

NOTE: By September 1, 1991, Hydra-matic will have changed the name designations of the THM 125C and THM 440-R4 automatic transaxle. The new name designation for these transaxles will be Hydra-matic 3T40 and 4T60. Transaxles built between 1989 and 1990 will serve as transitional years in which a dual system, made up of the old designation and the new designation will be in effect.

Removal and Installation

1. Disconnect the negative battery cable. Remove the air cleaner, bracket, MAF (mass air flow) sensor and air tube as an assembly.

2. Disconnect the exhaust crossover from the right side manifold and remove the left side exhaust manifold, then, raise and support the manifold/crossover assembly on V6 engines.

3. Disconnect the T.V. cable from the throttle lever and the transaxle.

4. Remove the vent hose and the shift cable from the transaxle.

5. Remove the fluid level indicator and the filler tube.

6. Using a engine support fixture tool J-28467 or equivalent and the adapter tool J-35953 or equivalent, install them on the engine.

7. Remove the wiring harness-to-transaxle nut.

8. Label and disconnect the wires for the speed sensor, TCC connector and the neutral safety/backup light switch.

9. Remove the upper transaxle-to-engine bolts.

10. Remove the transaxle-to-mount through bolt, the transaxle mount bracket and the mount.

11. Raise and safely support the vehicle.

12. Remove the front wheel assemblies.

13. Disconnect the shift cable bracket from the transaxle.

14. Remove the left side splash shield.

15. Using a modified drive axle seal protector tool J-34754 or equivalent, install one on each drive axle to protect the seal from damage and the joint from possible failure. Support the axles to the body to prevent CV-joint damage.

16. Using care not to damage the halfshaft boots, disconnect the halfshafts from the transaxle.

17. Remove the torsional and lateral strut from the transaxle. Remove the left side stabilizer link pin bolt.

18. Remove the left frame support bolts and move it out of the way.

19. Disconnect the speedometer wire from the transaxle.

20. Remove the transaxle converter cover and matchmark the converter to the flywheel for assembly.

21. Disconnect and plug the transaxle cooler pipes.

22. Remove the transaxle-to-engine support.

23. Using a transmission jack, position and secure it to the transaxle and remove the remaining transaxle-to-engine bolts.

24. Make sure that the torque converter does not fall out and remove the transaxle from the vehicle.

NOTE: The transaxle cooler and lines should be flushed any time the transaxle is removed for overhaul, or to replace the pump, case or converter.

To install:

25. Put a small amount of grease on the pilot hub of the converter and make sure that the converter is properly engaged with the pump.

26. Raise the transaxle to the engine while guiding the right side halfshaft into the transaxle.

27. Install the lower transaxle mounting bolts, tighten to 55 ft. lbs. (75 Nm) and remove the jack.

28. Align the converter with the marks made previously on the flywheel and install the bolts hand tight.

29. Torque the converter bolts to 46 ft. lbs. (61 Nm). Retorque the first bolt after the others.

30. Install the starter assembly. Install the left side halfshaft.

31. Install the converter cover, oil cooler lines and cover. Install the sub-frame assembly. Install the lower engine mount retaining bolts and the transaxle mount nuts.

32. Install the right and left ball joints. Install the power steering rack, heat shield and cooler lines to the frame.

33. Install the right and left inner fender splash shields. Install the tire assemblies.

34. Lower the vehicle. Connect all electrical leads. Install the upper transaxle mount bolts, tighten to 55 ft. lbs. (75 Nm).

35. Attach the crossover pipe to the exhaust manifold. Connect the EGR tube to the crossover.

36. Connect the T.V. cable and the shift cable. Install the air cleaner and inlet tube.

37. Remove the engine support tool. Connect the negative battery cable.

HALFSHAFTS

Drive Axle

Removal and Installation

On vehicles equipped with an automatic transaxle, the left drive axle uses a female spline which installs over a stub shaft protruding from the transaxle. The right drive axle uses a male and interlocks with the transaxle gears using barrel type snaprings. On models equipped with a manual transaxle, the left drive axle uses a male spline locking into the gear assembly. The right drive axle uses a female spline that installs into the intermediate axle shaft.

1. With the weight of the vehicle on the tires, loosen the hub nut.

2. Raise and safely support the vehicle.

3. Remove the hub nut.

4. Install boot protectors on the boots.

5. Remove the brake caliper with the line attached and safely support it out of the way; do not allow the caliper to hang from the line.

6. Remove the brake rotor and caliper mounting bracket.

7. Remove the strut-to-steering knuckle bolts. Pull the steering knuckle out of the strut bracket.

8. Using a halfshaft removal tool J-33008 or equivalent and

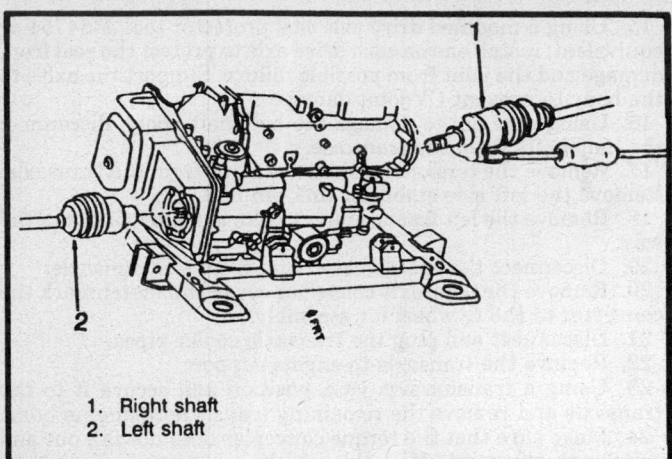

1. Right shaft
2. Left shaft

Removing the halfshafts

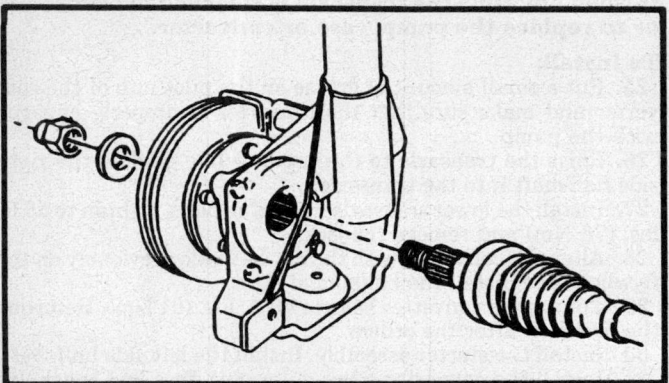

Removing the halfshaft from the hub/knuckle assembly

the extention tool J–29794 or equivalent, remove the halfshafts from the transaxle and support them safely.

9. Using a spindle remover tool J–28733 or equivalent, remove the halfshaft from the hub and bearing.

10. Loosely place the halfshaft on the transaxle and in the hub and bearing.

11. Properly position the steering knuckle to the strut bracket and install the bolt. Torque the bolts to 133 ft. lbs. (178 Nm).

12. Install the brake rotor, caliper bracket and caliper. Place a holding device in the rotor to prevent it from turning.

13. Install the hub nut and washer. Torque the nut to 71 ft. lbs. (95 Nm).

14. Seat the halfshafts into the transaxle.

15. Verify that the shafts are seated by grasping the CV-joint and pulling outwards. Do not grasp the shaft. If the snapring is seated, the halfshaft will remain in place.

16. Remove the boot protectors and lower the vehicle.

17. When the vehicle is lowered with the weight on the wheels, final torque the hub nut to 184 ft. lbs. (250 Nm).

Boot

Removal and Installation

INNER

1. Remove the halfshaft.

2. Remove the CV-joint housing-to-transaxle bolts.

3. Cut the seal retaining clamps and remove the old boot from the shaft.

4. Using a pair of snapring pliers, remove the retaining ring from the shaft and remove the spider assembly.

5. Using solvent, clean the splines of the shaft and repack the joint.

6. Install the inner boot clamp first and the new boot second.

7. Push the CV-joint assembly onto the shaft until the retaining ring is seated on the shaft.

8. Slide the boot onto the joint. Install both the inner and outer clamps.

9. To complete the installation, reverse the removal procedures.

1. 37 Ft. Lbs.
2. 18 Ft. Lbs.
3. Intermediate drive shaft bracket
4. Intermediate drive shaft
5. Transaxle assembly
6. Knuckle and strut

Removing the intermediate drive shaft—manual transmission equipped vehicles

OUTER

1. Remove the halfshaft from the vehicle.
2. Cut off the boot retaining clamps and discard them. Remove the old boot.
3. If equipped with a deflector ring, use a brass drift and carefully tap it off.
4. Using a pair of snapring pliers, spread the retaining ring inside the outer CV-joint and tap the joint off the halfshaft.
5. Using solvent, clean the splines of the halfshaft and the CV-joint and repack the joint. Install a new retaining ring inside the joint.

6. Install the inner boot clamp first, the new boot second.
7. Push the joint assembly onto the halfshaft until the ring is seated on the shaft.
8. Slide the boot onto the joint and install the clamps on both the inner and outer part of the boot.
9. To complete the installation, reverse the removal procedures.

CV-Joints

Refer to the Unit Repair Section.

REAR AXLE AND REAR SUSPENSION

Refer to the unit repair section for axle overhaul procedures and rear suspension service.

Rear Wheel Bearing

Removal and Installation

The rear wheel bearing and hub are non-serviceable. The bearing and hub are replaced as an assembly.

1. Raise and safely support the vehicle.
2. Remove the wheel assembly.
3. Remove the brake caliper and support it aside.
4. Remove the brake rotor.
5. Remove the hub/bearing assembly mounting bolts and remove the assembly from the knuckle.
6. Install the hub/bearing assembly to the knuckle and tighten the mounting bolts to 48 ft. lbs. (65 Nm).

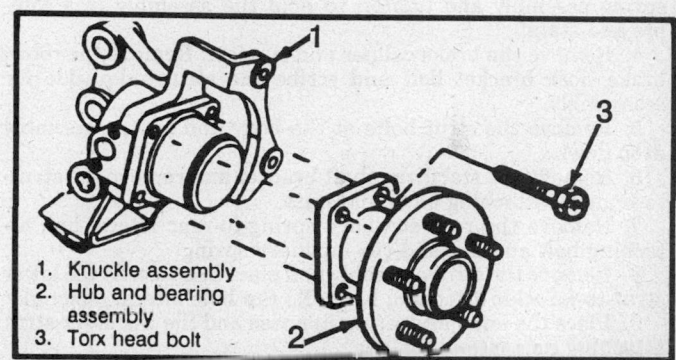

1. Knuckle assembly
2. Hub and bearing assembly
3. Torx head bolt

Rear hub and bearing assembly

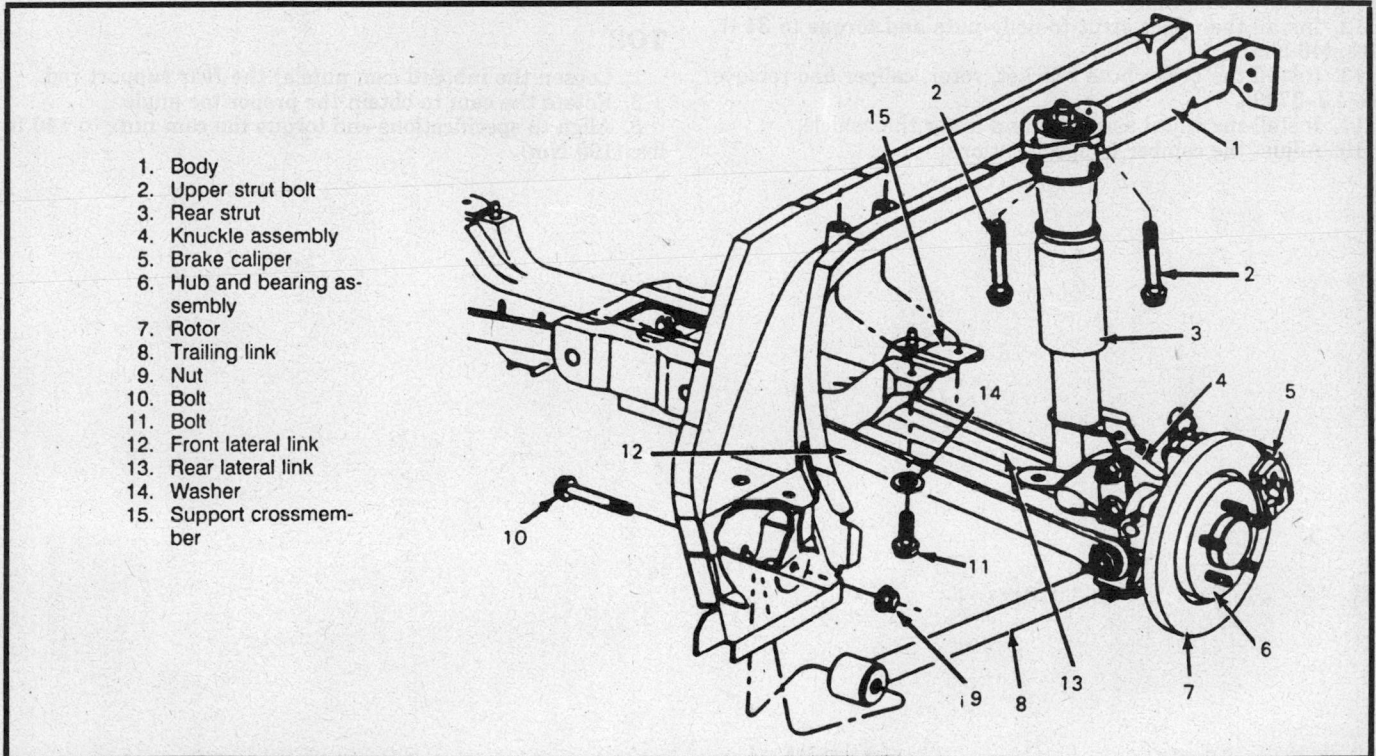

1. Body
2. Upper strut bolt
3. Rear strut
4. Knuckle assembly
5. Brake caliper
6. Hub and bearing assembly
7. Rotor
8. Trailing link
9. Nut
10. Bolt
11. Bolt
12. Front lateral link
13. Rear lateral link
14. Washer
15. Support crossmember

Rear suspension components

7. Install the brake rotor and attach the brake caliper.

8. Install the wheel and lower the vehicle.

Rear Wheel Alignment

A rear wheel alignment should be performed whenever any adjustments are made to the front end. Align the vehicle in the following order; rear wheel camber, rear wheel toe and tracking, front wheel camber and toe.

CAMBER

1. Raise and safely support the vehicle and remove the rear wheel assembly.

2. Support the suspension under the rear knuckle and hub with a jackstand.

3. Thread tool J–37098 or equivalent into the auxiliary spring assembly and tighten to hold the assembly in a compressed state.

4. Remove the brake caliper and support. Remove the rotor, brake hose bracket bolt and scribe the strut-to-knuckle for reassembly.

5. Remove the strut bolts at the body and let the assembly drop down.

6. Remove the stabilizer shaft bracket and remove the strut-to-knuckle attaching bolts and nuts.

7. Remove the rear auxiliary spring-to-rear lateral link attaching bolt and nut and the auxiliary spring.

8. Remove the strut assembly and place in a vise. At the lower strut-to-knuckle attaching hole, file the hole lateral (oblong).

9. Place the auxiliary spring in a vise and file the lower strut attaching hole lateral (oblong).

10. Place the stabilizer bracket in a vise and file the lower stabilizer bracket-to-strut attaching hole lateral (oblong).

11. Install the strut assembly-to-knuckle, auxiliary spring-to-rear lateral link and stabilizer shaft bracket. Do not tighten the strut bolts at this time.

12. Install the upper strut-to-body nuts and torque to 34 ft. lbs. (46 Nm).

13. Install the brake hose bracket, rotor, caliper and remove tool J–37098.

14. Install the wheel assembly and lower the vehicle.

15. Adjust the camber to specifications.

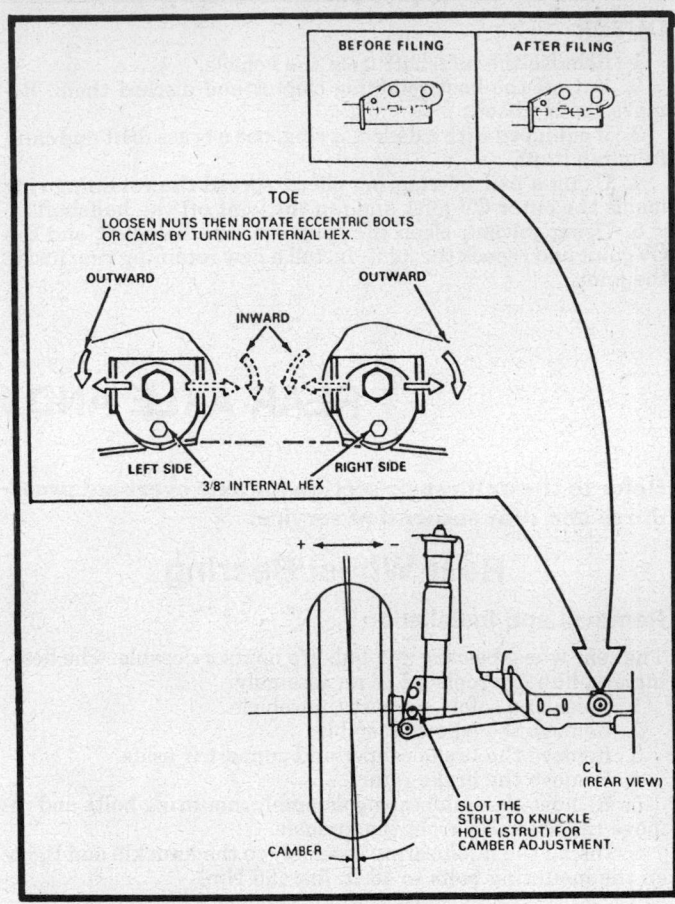

Rear wheel alignment procedures

TOE

1. Loosen the inboard cam nuts at the rear support rod.

2. Rotate the cam to obtain the proper toe angle.

3. Align to specifications and torque the cam nuts to 140 ft. lbs. (190 Nm).

YEAR IDENTIFICATION

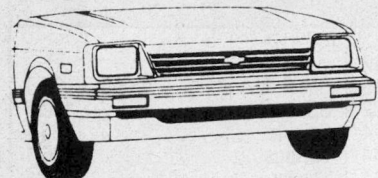

1985-86 Sprint

1987-88 Sprint Turbo

1987-88 Sprint Metro

1989–90 Metro

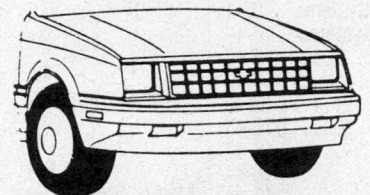

1985-86 Spectrum

1987-88 Spectrum

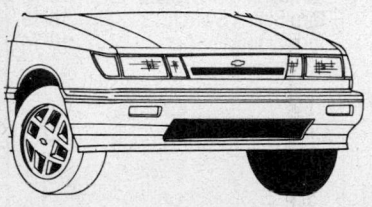

1987-88 Spectrum Turbo

1989–90 Spectrum

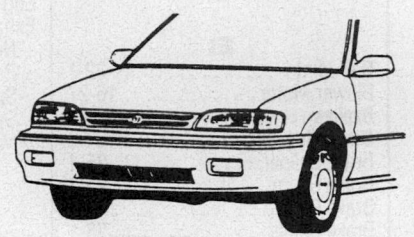

1989–90 Prizm

ENGINE IDENTIFICATION

Year	Model	Engine Displacement cu. in. (liter)	Engine Series Identification (VIN)	No. of Cylinders	Engine Type
1986	Sprint	3-61 (1.0)	5	3	SOHC
	Spectrum	4-90 (1.5)	7	4	SOHC
	Nova	4-97 (1.6)	4	4	SOHC
1987	Sprint	3-61 (1.0)	5	3	SOHC
	Sprint	3-61 (1.0)	2	3	SOHC
	Spectrum	4-90 (1.5)	7	4	SOHC
	Spectrum	4-90 (1.5)	9	4	SOHC
	Nova	4-97 (1.6)	4	4	SOHC
1988	Sprint/Firefly	3-61 (1.0)	5	3	SOHC
	Sprint/Firefly	3-61 (1.0)	2	3	SOHC
	Spectrum	4-90 (1.5)	7	4	SOHC
	Spectrum	4-90 (1.5)	9	4	SOHC
	Nova	4-97 (1.6)	4	4	SOHC
	Nova	4-97 (1.6)	5	4	DOHC
1989-90	Metro	3-61 (1.0)	6	3	SOHC
	Spectrum	4-90 (1.0)	7	4	SOHC
	Prizm	4-97 (1.6)	6	4	DOHC

SOHC Single overhead cam engine
DOHC Dual overhead cam engine

VEHICLE IDENTIFICATION

It is important for servicing and ordering parts to be certain of the vehicle and engine identification. The VIN (vehicle identification number) is a 17 digit number visible through the windshield on the driver's side of the dash and contains the vehicle and engine identification codes. The tenth digit indicates model year and the eighth digit indicates engine code. It can be interpreted as follows:

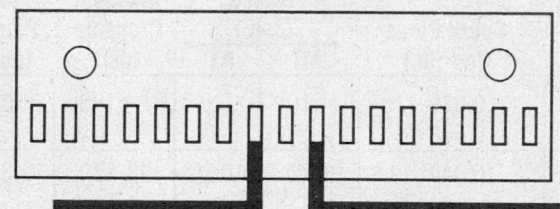

Engine Code							Model Year	
Code	Cu. In.	Liters	Cyl.	Fuel Sys.	Eng. Mfg.		Code	Year
4	97	1.6	4	2 bbl	Toyota		G	1986
5①	97	1.6	4	EFI	Toyota		H	1987
6①	97	1.6	4	EFI	Toyota		J	1988
7	90	1.5	4	2 bbl	Isuzu		K	1989
9	90	1.5	4	Turbo	Isuzu		L	1990
5	61	1.0	3	2 bbl	Suzuki			
2	61	1.0	3	Turbo	Suzuki			
6	61	1.0	3	TBI	Suzuki			

① Twincam

GENERAL ENGINE SPECIFICATIONS

Year	VIN	No. Cylinder Displacement cu. in. (liter)	Fuel System Type	Net Horsepower @ rpm	Net Torque @ rpm (ft.lbs.)	Bore × Stroke (in.)	Compression Ratio	Oil Pressure @ rpm
1986	5	3-61 (1.0)	2 bbl	48 @ 5100	57 @ 3200	2.91 × 3.03	9.5:1	48
	7	4-90 (1.5)	2 bbl	70 @ 5400	87 @ 3400	3.03 × 3.11	9.6:1	49 @ 5200
	4	4-97 (1.6)	2 bbl	74 @ 4800	85 @ 2800	3.19 × 3.03	9.0:1	34 @ 2000
1987	5	3-61 (1.0)	2 bbl	48 @ 5100	77 @ 3200	2.91 × 3.03	9.5:1	48
	5①	3-61 (1.0)	2 bbl	46 @ 4700	78 @ 3200	2.91 × 3.03	9.8:1	48
	2	3-61 (1.0)	EFI	70 @ 5500	107 @ 3500	2.91 × 3.03	8.3:1	48
	7	4-90 (1.5)	2 bbl	70 @ 5400	87 @ 3400	3.03 × 3.11	8.2:1	49 @ 5200
	9	4-90 (1.5)	Turbo	110 @ 5400	120 @ 3400	3.03 × 3.11	8.0:1	49 @ 5200
	4	4-97 (1.6)	2 bbl	74 @ 5200	85 @ 2800	3.19 × 3.03	9:0:1	34 @ 2000
1988	5	3-61 (1.0)	2 bbl	48 @ 5100	77 @ 3200	2.91 × 3.03	9.5:1	48
	5	3-61 (1.0)	2 bbl	46 @ 4700	78 @ 3200	2.91 × 3.03	9.8:1	48
	2	3-61 (1.0)	EFI	70 @ 5500	107 @ 3500	2.91 × 3.03	8.3:1	48
	7	4-90 (1.5)	2 bbl	70 @ 5400	87 @ 3400	3.03 × 3.11	9.6:1	49 @ 5200
	9	4-90 (1.5)	Turbo	110 @ 5400	120 @ 3400	3.03 × 3.11	8.0:1	49 @ 5200
	4	4-97 (1.6)	2 bbl	74 @ 5200	85 @ 2800	3.19 × 3.03	9.0:1	34 @ 2000
	5	4-97 (1.6)	EFI	110 @ 6600	98 @ 4800	3.19 × 3.03	9.4:1	56 @ 3000
1989-90	6②	3-61 (1.0)	EFI	55 @ 5700	58 @ 3300	2.91 × 3.03	9.5:1	39 @ 4000
	6	3-61 (1.0)	EFI	49 @ 4700	58 @ 3300	2.91 × 3.03	9.5:1	39 @ 4000
	7	4-90 (1.5)	2 bbl	70 @ 5400	87 @ 3400	3.03 × 3.11	9.6:1	49 @ 5200
	6	4-97 (1.6)	MFI	102 @ 5800	101 @ 4800	3.19 × 3.03	9.5:1	56 @ 3000

① ER model   ② LSI model

GASOLINE ENGINE TUNE-UP SPECIFICATIONS
Refer to Section 34 for all spark plug recommendations

Year	VIN	No. Cylinder Displacement cu. in. (liter)	Spark Plugs Gap (in.)	Ignition Timing (deg.) MT	Ignition Timing (deg.) AT	Compression Pressure (psi)	Fuel Pump (psi)	Idle Speed (rpm) MT	Idle Speed (rpm) AT	Valve Clearance In.	Valve Clearance Ex.
1986	5	3-61 (1.0)	0.039–0.043	10	6	199	3.5	750	850	0.006	0.008
	7	4-90 (1.5)	0.040	15①	10③	128-179	3.8–4.7	700	950	0.006	0.010
	4	4-97 (1.6)	0.043	0	0	160	2.5–3.5	650	750	0.008	0.012
1987	5	3-61 (1.0)	0.039–0.043	10	6	199	4.0	750⑧	850	0.006	0.008
	2	3-61 (1.0)	0.039–0.043	12	—	199	25–33	750	—	0.006	0.008
	7	4-90 (1.5)	0.040	15①	10③	128-179	3.8–4.7	700	950	0.006	0.010
	9	4-90 (1.5)	0.040	15②	NA	128-179	28.4⑤	950	NA	0.006	0.010
	4	4-97 (1.6)	0.043	0	0	160	2.5–3.5	650	800	0.008	0.012
1988	5	3-61 (1.0)	0.039–0.043	10	6	199	4.0	750⑧	850	0.006	0.008
	2	3-61 (1.0)	0.039–0.043	12	—	199	2.5–3.3	750	—	0.006	0.008
	7	4-90 (1.5)	0.040 0.043	15①	10③	128-179	3.8–4.7	700	950	0.006	0.010
	9	4-90 (1.5)	0.040	15②	NA	128-179	2.8④	950	NA	0.006	0.010
	4	4-97 (1.6)	0.043	0	0	128-178	3.5	650	750	0.008	0.012
	5	4-97 (1.6)	0.043		10B④	142-179	NA	800	800	⑥	⑦
1989	6	3-61 (1.0)	0.039–0.043	⑨	⑨	199	26	750	850	Hyd.	Hyd.
	7	4-90 (1.5)	0.040	15①	10③	128-179	3.8–4.7	750	1000	0.006	0.010
	6	4-97 (1.6)	0.031	10B	10B	142-191	NA	700	700	0.006–0.010	0.008–0.012
1990					SEE UNDERHOOD SPECIFICATIONS STICKER							

NOTE—The underhood specifications sticker often reflects tune-up specification changes made in production. Sticker figures must be used if they disagree with those in this chart.

NA Not available

① @ 750 rpm
② @ 950 rpm
③ @ 1000 rpm
④ Use jumper wire to short circuit both terminals of the check engine connector located need the wiper motor. When the jumper wire is removed and the transaxle is in Neutral, the ignition timing should be more than 16 degrees BTDC (manual) or 12 degrees BTDC (automatic)

⑤ @ 900 rpm with pressure regulator connected
⑥ Cold—0.006-0.010 in. Hot—0.008-0.012 in.
⑦ Cold—0.008-0.012 in. Hot—0.010-0.014 in.
⑧ ER model—700 rpm
⑨ See underhood sticker

FIRING ORDERS

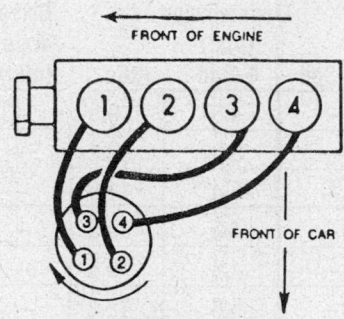

1.6L 4A-GE (Isuzu)
16-valve, twincam engine
Firing order: 1–3–4–2

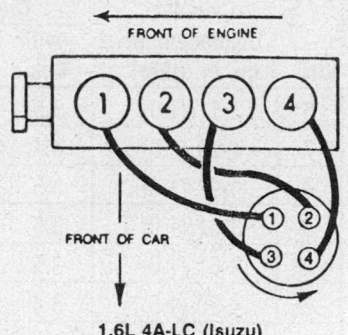

1.6L 4A-LC (Isuzu)
8-valve engine
Firing order: 1–3–4–2

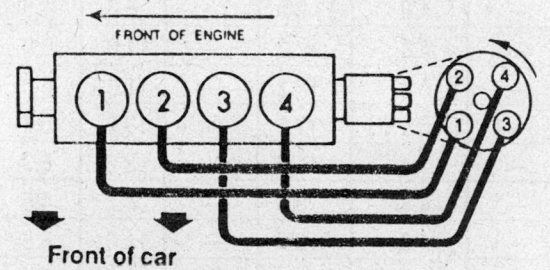

GM (Isuzu) 4–90 (1.5L)
Engine firing order: 1–3–4–2
Distributor rotation: counterclockwise—Spectrum

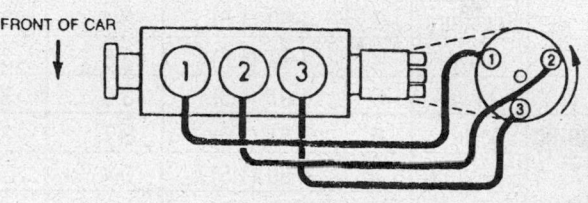

GM (Suzuki) 61 cu. in. (1.0L)
Engine firing order: 1–3–2
Distributor rotation: counterclockwise—Sprint and Metro

WHEEL ALIGNMENT

Year	Model	Caster		Camber		Toe-in (in.)	Steering Axis Inclination (deg.)
		Range (deg.)	Preferred Setting (deg.)	Range (deg.)	Preferred Setting (deg.)		
1986	Sprint	—	$3^3/_{16}$P	—	1	$^1/_{16}$	$12^3/_{16}$
	Spectrum	$1^3/_4$P–$2^3/_4$P	$2^1/_4$P	$^7/_{16}$N–$1^1/_{16}$P	$^{11}/_{32}$P	$0 +^1/_{16}$	①②
	Nova	$1^3/_4$P–$2^3/_4$P	$^5/_6$P	$^3/_4$N–$^1/_4$P	$^1/_4$P	$0 +0.078$	—
1987	Sprint	—	$3^3/_{16}$	—	$^1/_4$	0	$12^3/_{16}$
	Spectrum	$1^3/_4$P–$2^3/_4$P	$2^1/_4$P	$^7/_{16}$N–$1^1/_{16}$P	$^{11}/_{32}$P	$0 +^1/_{16}$	①②
	Nova	$^1/_8$–$1^1/_2$P	$^7/_8$	$^1/_4$N–$^3/_4$P	$^1/_2$N	0.04–0.08	—
1988	Sprint	—	$3^3/_{16}$	—	$^1/_4$	0	$12^3/_{16}$
	Spectrum	$1^3/_4$P–$2^3/_4$P	$2^1/_4$P	$^7/_{16}$N–$1^1/_{16}$P	$^{11}/_{32}$P	$0 +^1/_{16}$	①②
	Nova	$^1/_8$–$1^2/_3$P	$^9/_{10}$P	$^3/_4$N–$^1/_4$P	$^1/_4$N	0–0.078	—
	Nova Twincam	1N–$1^1/_2$P	$^1/_4$P	$^3/_4$N–$^1/_4$P	$^1/_4$N	0–0.078	—
1989-90	Metro	1P–5P	3P	1N–1P	0	0	$25^{11}/_{16}$
	Spectrum	$1^3/_4$–$2^3/_4$P	$2^1/_4$P	$^{11}/_{16}$N–$1^5/_{16}$P	$^5/_{16}$	0	16
	Prizm	$^{11}/_{16}$P–$2^3/_{16}$P③	$1^7/_{16}$P	$^9/_6$N–$1^5/_{16}$P	$^3/_{16}$	$^3/_{64}$	NA
	Prizm	$^9/_{16}$P–$2^2/_8$P④	$1^5/_{16}$	$^1/_2$N–1P	$^1/_4$	$^3/_{64}$	NA

① Inside—37°40' full lock ③ Manual transaxle
② Outside—32°30' full lock ④ Automatic transaxle

GENERAL MOTORS—GEO
NOVA • PRIZM • SPECTRUM • SPRINT • METRO • FIREFLY

CAPACITIES

Year	Model	VIN	No. Cylinder Displacement cu. in. (liter)	Engine Crankcase with Filter	Engine Crankcase without Filter	Transmission (pts.) 4-Spd	Transmission (pts.) 5-Spd	Transmission (pts.) Auto.	Drive Axle (pts.)	Fuel Tank (gal.)	Cooling System (qts.)
1986	Sprint	5	3-61 (1.0)	3.5	3.5	—	4.8	9.5	—	8.3	4.5
	Spectrum	7	4-90 (1.5)	3.4	3.0	—	5.8	12.2	—	11.0	6.8
	Nova	4	4-97 (1.6)	3.5	3.2	—	5.4	11.6	—	13.2	6.3
1987	Sprint	5	3-61 (1.0)	3.5	3.5	—	4.8	9.5	—	8.3	4.5
	Sprint	2	3-61 (1.0)	3.5	3.5	—	4.8	9.5	—	8.3	4.5
	Spectrum	7	4-90 (1.5)	3.4	3.0	—	5.8	12.2	—	11.0	7.5
	Spectrum	9	4-90 (1.5)	3.4	3.0	—	5.8	12.2	—	11.0	7.5
	Nova	4	4-97 (1.6)	3.5	3.2	—	5.4	11.6	—	13.2	6.3
1988	Sprint	5	3-61 (1.0)	3.5	3.5	—	4.8	9.5	—	8.3	4.5
	Sprint	2	3-61 (1.0)	3.5	3.5	—	4.8	9.5	—	8.3	4.5
	Spectrum	7	4-90 (1.5)	3.4	3.0	—	5.8	12.2	—	11.0	6.8
	Spectrum	9	4-90 (1.5)	3.4	3.0	—	5.8	12.2	—	11.0	6.8
	Nova	4	4-97 (1.6)	3.5	3.2	—	5.4	11.6	—	13.2	6.4
	Nova	5	4-97 (1.6)	3.9	3.6	—	5.4	16.6	—	13.2	6.3
1989-90	Metro	6	3-61 (1.0)	3.7	3.7	—	4.8	9.6	—	8.7	4.5
	Spectrum	7	4-90 (1.5)	3.4	3.0	—	4.0	13.8	—	11.0	6.8
	Prizm	6	4-97 (1.6)	3.4	3.2	—	5.8	11.6	—	13.0	6.3

CRANKSHAFT AND CONNECTING ROD SPECIFICATIONS
All measurements are given in inches.

Year	VIN	No. Cylinder Displacement cu. in. (liter)	Crankshaft Main Brg. Journal Dia.	Crankshaft Main Brg. Oil Clearance	Crankshaft Shaft End-play	Crankshaft Thrust on No.	Connecting Rod Journal Diameter	Connecting Rod Oil Clearance	Connecting Rod Side Clearance
1986	5	3-61 (1.0)	①	0.0012	0.0083	3	1.6532	0.0015	0.0058
	7	4-90 (1.5)	1.8865–1.8873	0.0008–0.0020	0.0024–0.0095	2	1.5720–1.5726	0.0010–0.0023	0.0079–0.0138
	4	4-97 (1.6)	1.8892–1.8898	0.0006–0.0019 ③	0.0008–0.0073	3	1.5742–1.5748	0.0008–0.0020	0.0059–0.0089
1987	2	3-61 (1.0)	①	0.0012	0.0044–0.0122	3	1.6532	0.0012–0.0190	NA
	5	3-61 (1.0)	①	0.0012	0.0044–0.0122	3	1.6532	0.0012–0.0190	NA
	7	4-90 (1.5)	1.8865–1.8873	0.0008–0.0020	0.0024–0.0095	2	1.5720–1.5726	0.0010–0.0023	0.0079–0.0138
	9	4-90 (1.5)	1.8865–1.8873	0.0008–0.0020	0.0024–0.0095	2	1.5720–1.5726	0.0010–0.0023	0.0079–0.0138
	4	4-97 (1.6)	1.8892–1.8898	0.0006–0.0019 ③	0.0008–0.0073	3	1.5742–1.5748	0.0008–0.0020	0.0059–0.0089
1988	2	3-61 (1.0)	①	0.0012	0.0044–0.0122	3	1.6532	0.0012–0.0190	NA

CRANKSHAFT AND CONNECTING ROD SPECIFICATIONS
All measurements are given in inches.

Year	VIN	No. Cylinder Displacement cu. in. (liter)	Crankshaft Main Brg. Journal Dia.	Crankshaft Main Brg. Oil Clearance	Crankshaft Shaft End-play	Crankshaft Thrust on No.	Connecting Rod Journal Diameter	Connecting Rod Oil Clearance	Connecting Rod Side Clearance
	5	3-61 (1.0)	①	0.0012	0.0044–0.0122	3	1.6532	0.0012–0.0190	0.0039–0.780
	7	4-90 (1.5)	1.8865–1.8873	0.0008–0.0020	0.0024–0.0095	2	1.5720–1.5726	0.0010–0.0023	0.0079–0.0138
	9	4-90 (1.5)	1.8865–1.8873	0.0008–0.0020	0.0024–0.0095	2	1.5720–1.5726	0.0010–0.0023	0.0079–0.0138
1989-90	6	3-61 (1.0)	①	0.0012	0.0080–0.0073	3	1.6529–1.6535	0.0012–0.019	NA
	7	4-90 (1.5)	1.8865–1.8873	0.0008–0.0020	0.0024–0.0095	3	1.5526	0.0009–0.0229	0.0079–0.0138
	6	4-97 (1.6)	1.8865–1.8873	0.0006–0.0013	0.0008–0.0073	3	1.5420–1.5748	0.0008–0.0020	0.0059–0.0098

NA Not available
① Bearing cap stamped
No. 1 – 1.7710-1.7712   No. 3 – 1.7712-17714   ② Maximum clearance – 0.0031
No. 2 – 1.7714-1.7716   No. 4 – 1.7710-1.7712   ③ Maximum clearance – 0.0039

CAMSHAFT SPECIFICATIONS
All measurements given in inches.

Year	VIN	No. Cylinder Displacement cu. in. (liter)	Journal Diameter 1	Journal Diameter 2	Journal Diameter 3	Journal Diameter 4	Journal Diameter 5	Lobe Lift In.	Lobe Lift Ex.	Bearing Clearance	Camshaft End Play
1986	5	3-61 (1.0)	1.7372–1.7381	1.7451–1.7460	1.7530–1.7539	1.7609–1.7618	—	1.512	1.512	0.0029	—
	7	4-90 (1.5)	1.0210–1.0220	1.0210–1.0220	1.0210–1.0220	1.0210–1.0220	1.0210–1.0220	1.426	1.426	0.0024–0.0044	0.0039–0.0071
	4	4-97 (1.6)	1.1015–1.1022	1.1015–1.1022	1.1015–1.1022	1.1015–1.1022	—	1.541 ①	1.541 ①	0.0015–0.0029	0.0031–0.0071
1987	2	3-61 (1.0)	1.7372–1.7381	1.7451–1.7460	1.7530–1.7539	1.7609–1.7618	—	1.512	1.512	0.0029	—
	5	3-61 (1.0)	1.7372–1.7381	1.7451–1.7460	1.7530–1.7539	1.7609–1.7618	—	1.512	1.512	0.0029	—
	7	4-90 (1.5)	1.0210–1.0220	1.0210–1.0220	1.0210–1.0220	1.0210–1.0220	1.021–1.022	1.426	1.426	0.0024–0.0044	0.0039–0.0071
	9	4-90 (1.5)	1.021–1.0220	1.0210–1.0220	1.0210–1.0220	1.0210–1.0220	1.021–1.022	1.426	1.426	0.0024–0.0044	0.0039–0.0071
	4	4-97 (1.6)	1.1015–1.1022	1.1015–1.1022	1.1015–1.1022	1.1015–1.1022	—	1.541 ①	1.541 ①	0.0015–0.0029	0.0031–0.0071
1988	2	3-61 (1.0)	1.7372–1.7381	1.7451–1.7460	1.7530–1.7539	1.7609–1.7618	—	1.512	1.512	0.0029	—
	5	3-61 (1.0)	1.7372–1.7381	1.7451–1.7460	1.7530–1.7539	1.7609–1.7618	—	1.512	1.512	0.0029	—
	7	4-90 (1.5)	1.0210–1.0220	1.0210–1.0220	1.0210–1.0220	1.0210–1.0220	1.021–1.022	1.426	1.426	0.0024–0.0044	0.0039–0.0071

CAMSHAFT SPECIFICATIONS
All measurements given in inches.

Year	VIN	No. Cylinder Displacement cu. in. (liter)	Journal Diameter 1	2	3	4	5	Lobe Lift In.	Ex.	Bearing Clearance	Camshaft End Play
1988	9	4-90 (1.5)	1.0210–1.0220	1.0210–1.0220	1.0210–1.0220	1.0210–1.0220	1.021–1.0220	1.426	1.426	0.0024–0.0044	0.0039–0.0071
	4	4-97 (1.6)	1.1015–1.1022	1.1015–1.1022	1.1015–1.1022	1.1015–1.1022	—	1.541 ①	1.541– ①	0.0015–0.0029	0.0031–0.0071
	4	4-97 (1.6)	1.1015–1.1022	1.1015–1.1022	1.1015–1.1022	1.1015–1.1022	—	1.541 ①	1.541– ①	0.0015–0.0029	0.0031–0.0071
	5	4-97 (1.6)	1.0610–1.0616	1.0610–1.0616	1.0610–1.0616	1.0610–1.0616	1.061–1.062	1.399–1.400	1.399–1.400	0.0014–0.0028	0.0031–0.0075
1989-90	6	3-61 (1.0)	1.0220–1.0228	1.1795–1.1803	1.1795–1.1803	—	—	1.560–2.566	1.560–2.566	0.008–0.0024	—
	7	4-90 (1.5)	1.0210–1.0220	1.0210–1.0220	1.0210–1.0220	1.0210–1.022	1.021–1.022	1.426	1.426	0.0024–0.0044	0.00394–0.0071
	6	4-97 (1.6)	0.9822	0.9035	0.9035	0.9035	—	1.370	1.359	0.0014–0.0028	0.0043

① Minimum lobe height

VALVE SPECIFICATIONS

Year	VIN	No. Cylinder Displacement cu. in. (liter)	Seat Angle (deg.)	Face Angle (deg.)	Spring Test Pressure (lbs.)	Spring Installed Height (in.)	Stem-to-Guide Clearance (in.) Intake	Exhaust	Stem Diameter (in.) Intake	Exhaust
1986	5	3-61 (1.0)	45	45	60	1.63	0.0014	0.0020	0.2745	0.2740
	7	4-90 (1.5)	45	45	47 @ 1.57	1.57	0.0009–0.0022	0.0012–0.0025	0.2740–0.2750	0.2740–0.2744
	4	4-97 (1.6)	45	44.5	46.3	1.52	0.0010–0.0024	0.0012–0.0026	0.2744–0.2750	0.2742–0.2748
1987	2	3-61 (1.0)	45	45	60	1.63	0.0014	0.0020	0.2745	0.2740
	5	3-61 (1.0)	45	45	60	1.63	0.0014	0.0020	0.2745	0.2740
	7	4-90 (1.5)	45	45	47 @ 1.57	1.57	0.0009–0.0022	0.0012–0.0025	0.2740–0.2750	0.2740–0.2744
	9	4-90 (1.5)	45	45	47 @ 1.57	1.57	0.0009–0.0022	0.0012–0.0025	0.2740–0.2750	0.2740–0.2744
	4	4-97 (1.6)	45	44.5	46.3	1.52	0.0010–0.0024	0.0012–0.0026	0.2744–0.2750	0.2742–0.2748
1988	2	3-61 (1.0)	45	45	60	1.63	0.0014	0.0020	0.2745	0.2740
	5	3-61 (1.0)	45	45	60	1.63	0.0014	0.0020	0.2745	0.2740
	7	4-90 (1.5)	45	45	47 @ 1.57	1.57	0.0009–0.0022	0.0012–0.0025	0.2745–0.2750	0.2740–0.2744
	9	4-90 (1.5)	45	45	47 @ 1.57	1.57	0.0009–0.0022	0.0012–0.0025	0.2745–0.2750	0.2740–0.2744
	5	4-97 (1.6)	45	44.5	32.2	1.366	0.0010–0.0024	0.0012–0.0026	0.2350–0.2356	0.2348–0.2354
	4	4-97 (1.6)	45	44.5	46.3	1.52	0.0010–0.0024	0.0012–0.0026	0.2744–0.2750	0.2742–0.2748

VALVE SPECIFICATIONS

Year	VIN	No. Cylinder Displacement cu. in. (liter)	Seat Angle (deg.)	Face Angle (deg.)	Spring Test Pressure (lbs.)	Spring Installed Height (in.)	Stem-to-Guide Clearance (in.) Intake	Stem-to-Guide Clearance (in.) Exhaust	Stem Diameter (in.) Intake	Stem Diameter (in.) Exhaust
1989-90	6	3-61 (1.0)	45	45	44 @ 1.28	—	0.0008–0.0021	0.0014–0.0024	0.2148–0.2151	0.2146–0.2151
	7	4-90 (1.5)	45	45	47 @ 1.57	1.57	0.0009–0.0022	0.0118–0.0025	0.2740–0.2750	0.2740–0.27440
	6	4-97 (1.6)	45	45.5	32.2	1.36	0.0031	0.0039	0.2350–0.2356	0.2348–0.2354

PISTON AND RING SPECIFICATIONS
All measurments are given in inches.

Year	VIN	No. Cylinder Displacement cu. in. (liter)	Piston Clearance	Ring Gap Top Compression	Ring Gap Bottom Compression	Ring Gap Oil Control	Ring Side Clearance Top Compression	Ring Side Clearance Bottom Compression	Ring Side Clearance Oil Control
1986	5	3-61 (1.0)	0.0008–0.0015	0.0079–0.0129	0.0079–0.0137	0.0079–0.0275	0.0012–0.0027	0.0008–0.0023	—
	7	4-90 (1.5)	0.0011–0.0019	0.0098–0.0138	—	0.0039–0.0236	0.0010–0.0026	—	—
	4	4-97 (1.6)	0.0035–0.0043	0.0098–0.0185	0.0059–0.0165	0.0118–0.0402	0.0016–0.0031	0.0012–0.0028	Snug
1987	5	3-61 (1.0)	0.0008–0.0015	0.0079–0.0129	0.0079–0.0137	0.0079–0.0275	0.0012–0.0027	0.0008–0.0023	—
	2	3-61 (1.0)①	0.0008–0.0015	0.0079–0.0119	0.0079–0.0119	0.0079–0.0237	0.0012–0.0030	0.0008–0.0023	—
	5	3-61 (1.0)	0.0008–0.0015	0.0079–0.0157	②	0.0079–0.0275	0.0012–0.0027	—	—
	7	4-90 (1.5)	0.0011–0.0019	0.0098–0.0138	②	0.0039–0.0236	0.0010–0.0026	—	—
	9	4-90 (1.5)	0.0011–0.0019	0.0106–0.0153	0.0098–0.0145	0.0039–0.0236	0.0010–0.0026	0.0008–0.0024	Snug
	4	4-97 (1.6)	0.0035–0.0043	0.0098–0.0185	0.0059–0.0165	0.1180–0.4020	0.0160–0.0031	0.0012–0.0028	—
1988	5	3-61 (1.0)	0.0008–0.0015	0.0079–0.0129	0.0079–0.0137	0.0079–0.0275	0.0012–0.0027	0.0008–0.0023	—
	2	3-61 (1.0)	0.0008–0.0015	0.0079–0.0119	0.0079–0.0119	0.0079–0.0237	0.0012–0.0030	0.0008–0.0023	—
	5	3-61 (1.0)①	0.0008–0.0015	0.0079–0.0157	②	0.0079–0.0275	0.0012–0.0027	—	—
	7	4-90 (1.5)	0.0011–0.0019	0.0098–0.0138	②	0.0039–0.0236	0.0010–0.0026	—	—
	9	4-90 (1.5)	0.0011–0.0019	0.0106–0.0153	0.0098–0.0145	0.0039–0.0236	0.0010–0.0026	0.0008–0.0024	—
	4	4-97 (1.6)	0.0035–0.0043	0.0098–0.0185	0.0059–0.0165	0.1180–0.4020	0.0160–0.0031	0.0012–0.0028	Snug
	5	4-97 (1.6)	0.0039–0.0047	0.0098–0.0138	0.0078–0.0118	0.0059–0.0031	0.0016–0.0031	0.0012–0.0028	Snug

PISTON AND RING SPECIFICATIONS
All measurments are given in inches.

Year	VIN	No. Cylinder Displacement cu. in. (liter)	Piston Clearance	Ring Gap			Ring Side Clearance		
				Top Compression	Bottom Compression	Oil Control	Top Compression	Bottom Compression	Oil Control
1989-90	6	3-61 (1.0)	0.0008–0.0015	0.0079–0.0129	0.0079–0.0137	0.0079–0.0275	0.0012–0.0027	0.0008–0.0023	—
	7	4-90 (1.5)	0.0011–0.3500	0.2500–0.3500	—	—	0.0009–0.0026		
	6	4-97 (1.6)	0.1124–0.0031	0.0098–0.0138	0.0059–0.0118	0.0039–0.0236	0.0016–0.0031	0.0012–0.0028	—

① ER model
② ER model has only one compression ring

TORQUE SPECIFICATIONS
All readings in ft. lbs.

Year	VIN	No. Cylinder Displacement cu. in. (liter)	Cylinder Head Bolts	Main Bearing Bolts	Rod Bearing Bolts	Crankshaft Pulley Bolts	Flywheel Bolts	Manifold		Spark Plugs
								Intake	Exhaust	
1986	5	3-61 (1.0)	48	38	25	50	44	17	17	20
	7	4-90 (1.5)	②	65	25	108	22①	17	17	18
	4	4-97 (1.6)	40-47	40-47	34-39	80-94	55-61	15-21	15-21	20
1987	2	3-61 (1.0)	48	38	25	50	44	17	17	20
	5	3-61 (1.0)	48	38	25	50	44	17	17	20
	7	4-90 (1.5)	②	65	25	108	22①	17	17	18
	9	4-90 (1.5)	②	65	25	108	22①	17	17	18
	4	4-97 (1.6)	43	43	29	80-94	55-61	15-21	15-21	20
1988	2	3-61 (1.0)	48	38	25	50	44	17	17	20
	5	3-61 (1.0)	48	38	25	50	44	17	17	20
	7	4-90 (1.5)	②	65	25	108	22①	17	17	18
	9	4-90 (1.5)	②	65	25	108	22①	17	17	18
	4	4-97 (1.6)	43	43	29	87	58	20	18	13
	5	4-97 (1.6)	③	44	36	101	58	20	18	13
1989-90	6	3-61 (1.0)	54	40	26	8	45	17	17	18
	7	4-90 (1.5)	②	65	25	108	22①	17	17	18
	6	4-97 (1.6)	44	44	36	87	58[4]	14	18	20

① Tighten an additional 45 degrees after torquing
② 1st step—29 ft. lbs.; 2nd step—58 ft. lbs.
③ 1st—Torque in sequence to 22 ft. lbs.
2nd—Torque in sequence another ¼ turn
3rd—Torque in sequence another ¼ turn

ELECTRICAL

NOTE: Disconnecting the negative battery cable on some vehicles may interfere with the functions of the on board computer systems and may require the computer to undergo a relearning process, once the negative battery cable is reconnected.

For testing and overhaul procedures on starters, alternators and voltage regulators, refer to the Unit Repair Section.

Charging System

ALTERNATOR

Removal and Installation

NOVA AND PRIZM

1. Disconnect the negative terminal from the battery.
2. Label and disconnect each alternator wiring connector.
3. Loosen the alternator adjusting lockbolt (located in the slotted bar at the bottom of the unit) and the hinge nut/bolt, located at the top of the unit. Turn the adjusting bolt to shift the alternator toward the block; remove the drive belt.
4. Remove the adjusting bolt, the hinge nut/bolt and the alternator.
5. To install, reverse the removal procedures.
NOTE: The drive belt serrations run along the length of the belt. Make sure serrations align with indentations on the pulleys; all serrations must ride inside the pulley surface.

SPECTRUM

1. Disconnect the negative battery terminal from the battery.

NOTE: Failure to disconnect the negative cable may result in injury from the positive battery lead at the alternator and may short the alternator and regulator during the removal process.

2. Disconnect and label the 2 terminal plug and the battery leads from the rear of the alternator.
3. Loosen the mounting bolts. Push the alternator inwards and slip the drive belt off the pulley.
4. Remove the mounting bolts and remove the alternator.
5. To install, place the alternator in its brackets and install the mounting bolts. Do not tighten them yet.
6. Slip the belt back over the pulley. Pull outwards on the unit and adjust the belt tension. Tighten the mounting and adjusting bolts.
7. Install the electrical leads and the negative battery cable.

SPRINT AND METRO

1. Disconnect the negative battery cable.
2. Disconnect the wiring connectors from the back of the alternator.
3. Remove the adjusting arm mounting bolt, the lower pivot bolt and the drive belt.
4. Remove the alternator.
5. To install, reverse the removal procedures. Adjust the drive belt to have $\frac{1}{4}$–$\frac{3}{8}$ in. play on the longest run of the drive belt.

Voltage Regulator

Removal and Installation

NOVA AND PRIZM

1. Disconnect the negative terminal from the battery.
2. Remove the nut and terminal insulator.

3. Remove the 3 nuts and the end cover.
4. Remove the 5 screws, brush holder and IC regulator.
5. To install, reverse the removal procedures.

SPECTRUM, SPRINT AND METRO

A solid state regulator is mounted within the alternator. All regulator components are enclosed in a solid mold. The regulator is non-adjustable and requires no maintenance.

Starting System

STARTER

Removal and Installation

NOVA AND PRIZM

1. Disconnect the negative terminal from the battery.
2. Disconnect the electrical connectors from the starter terminals.
3. Remove the transaxle cable and bracket from the transaxle.
4. Remove the starter-to-engine bolts and the starter from the vehicle.
5. To install, reverse the removal procedures. Torque the starter-to-engine bolts to 29 ft. lbs.

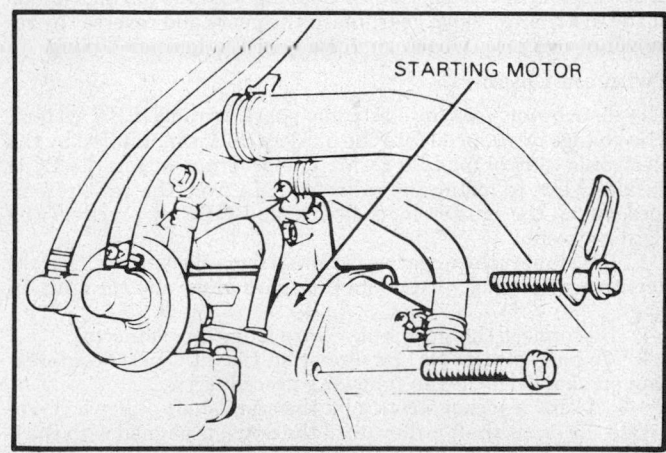

Starter motor mounting—Sprint and Metro

SPECTRUM

1. Disconnect the negative battery terminal from the battery.
2. Disconnect the ignition switch lead wire and the battery cable from the starter motor terminal.
3. Remove the 2 mounting bolts from the starter and remove the starter.
4. To install, reverse the removal procedures.

SPRINT AND METRO

1. Disconnect the negative battery cable.
2. Disconnect the ignition switch wire and the battery cable from the starter.
3. Remove the 2 engine-to-starter mounting bolts and remove the starter.
4. To install, reverse the removal procedures.

Ignition System

DISTRIBUTOR

Removal and Installation

NOVA AND PRIZM

Except Twincam Engine

The distributor uses vacuum and centrifugal advances for spark timing control. The voltage introduced into the pickup coil turns the ignition module **ON** and **OFF**. The ignition module turns the ignition coil **ON** and **OFF** creating high voltage for the spark plugs.

1. Disconnect the negative terminal from the battery.
2. Remove the No. 1 spark plug. Place your finger in the spark plug hole and rotate the crankshaft (clockwise) until you feel air being forced from the cylinder; this is the TDC of the No. 1 cylinder compression stroke. Align the crankshaft pulley notch with the **0** degrees mark on the timing plate.
3. Disconnect the distributor wire from the connector.
4. Disconnect the hoses and the vacuum advance unit.
5. Disconnect the distributor cap and move it aside.
6. Using a piece of chalk, make alignment marks of the distributor housing-to-engine block and the rotor-to-distributor housing.
7. Remove the distributor hold-down bolt(s) and the distributor from the engine; the rotor must be rotated slightly to remove the distributor.
8. To install, use a new O-ring on the distributor housing, lubricate the drive gear teeth with engine oil, align the protrusion at the bottom of the distributor housing with the pin on the side of the distributor drive gear, mesh the gears and reverse the removal procedures. Check and/or adjust the ignition timing.

Twincam Engine

The distributor uses an electronic spark advance ESA system. The voltage introduced into the pick-up coils is monitored by the electronic control module ECM. The program within the ECM decides when to, using the collected data from the various sensors, turns the igniter module **ON** and **OFF** at precisely the right moment.

1. Disconnect the negative terminal from the battery. Disconnect the spark plug wires from the spark plugs and the ignition coil.
2. Disconnect the distributor wire from the connector.
3. To position the No. 1 cylinder on the TDC of its compression stroke, perform the following procedures:
   a. Using a socket wrench on the crankshaft pulley bolt, rotate the crankshaft pulley until the notch is aligned with the **0** degree mark on the timing plate.
   b. Remove the oil filler cap and look for the cavity in the camshaft; if it is not visible, rotate the crankshaft pulley one complete revolution.

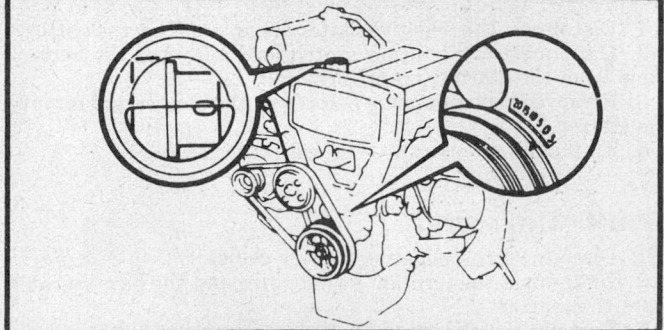

Aligning the crankshaft pulley and the camshaft cavity-twincam engine — Nova and Prizm

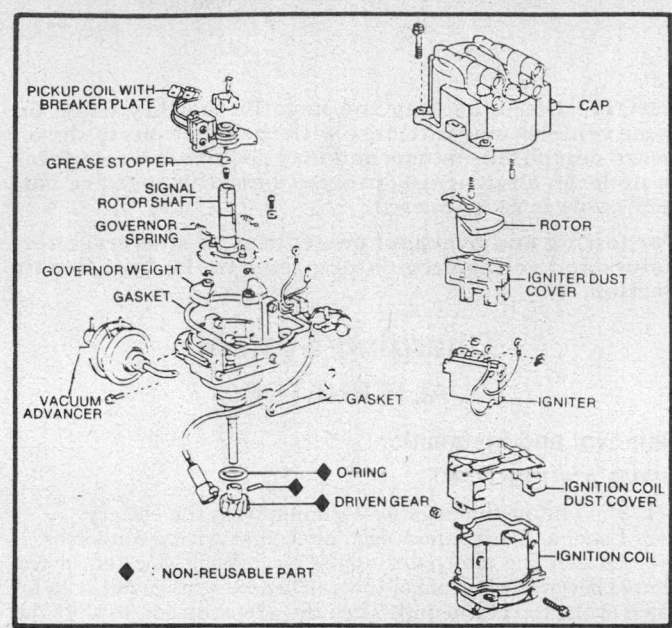

Exploded view of the distributor — except twincam engine — Nova

Aligning the distributor drive shaft with the housing- twincam engine — Nova and Prizm

4. Remove the distributor-to-engine hold-down bolts and the distributor from the engine.
5. Remove the distributor from the engine and the O-ring from the distributor; discard the O-ring.
6. To install the distributor, use a new O-ring and perform the following procedures:
   a. Turn the distributor to align the drive shaft drilled mark with housing cavity.
   b. Align the center of the distributor flange with the center of the cylinder head bolt hole, then, install the distributor.
   c. Install the hold-down bolt and torque it to 14 ft. lbs.
7. To complete the installation, reverse the removal procedures. Check and/or adjust the ignition timing.

NOTE: When performing the ignition timing procedures, never allow the ignition coil terminal to touch ground for it could result in damage to the ignition coil and/or igniter.

SPECTRUM

Timing Not Disturbed

1. Disconnect the negative battery terminal from the battery.
2. Remove the distributor cap.
3. Mark and remove all electrical leads and vacuum lines connected to the distributor assembly.

4. Mark the relationship of the rotor to the distributor housing and the distributor housing to the engine.

5. Remove the hold-down bolt, clamp and distributor.

6. To install, reverse the removal procedures and check the timing.

Timing Disturbed

If the engine was cranked while the distributor was removed, you will have to place the engine on TDC of the compression stroke to obtain the proper ignition timing.

1. Remove the No. 1 spark plug.

2. Place your thumb over the spark plug hole. Crank the engine slowly until compression is felt. It will be easier if you have someone rotate the engine by hand, using a wrench on the crankshaft pulley.

3. Align the timing mark on the crankshaft pulley with the **0** degrees mark on the timing scale attached to the front of the engine. This places the engine at TDC of the compression stroke.

4. Turn the distributor shaft until the rotor points to the No. 1 spark plug tower on the cap.

5. Install the distributor into the engine. Be sure to align the distributor-to-engine block mark made earlier.

6. To complete the installation, reverse the removal procedures and check the timing.

SPRINT AND METRO

1. Disconnect the negative battery cable.

2. Disconnect the wiring harness at the distributor and the vacuum line at the distributor vacuum unit.

3. Remove the distributor cap.

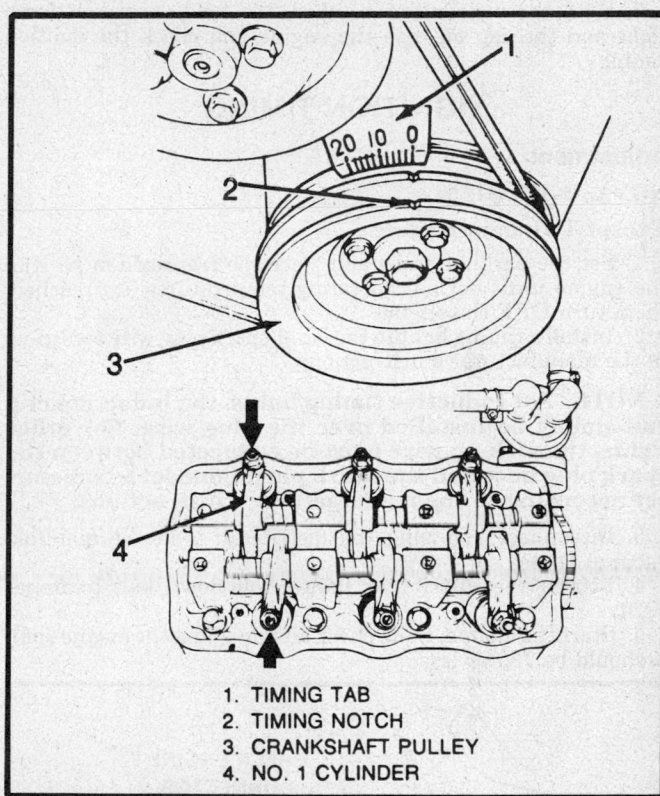

1. TIMING TAB
2. TIMING NOTCH
3. CRANKSHAFT PULLEY
4. NO. 1 CYLINDER

Timing notch and zero mark—Sprint and Metro

Exploded view of the distributor—Spectrum

TIMING MARK

View of the timing marks—Spectrum

NOTE: Mark the distributor body in reference to where the rotor is pointing. Mark the distributor hold down bracket and cylinder head for a reinstallation location point.

4. Remove the hold down bolt and the distributor from the cylinder head. Do not rotate the engine after the distributor has been removed.

5. To install, aligning all of the reference marks and install the distributor into the off-set slot in the camshaft.

6. With the distributor installed, the hold down bolt hand tight and the cap on, run the engine and check the ignition timing.

IGNITION TIMING

Adjustment

NOVA AND PRIZM

Except Twincam Engine

1. Set the parking brake and place the transaxle in **N**. Run the engine until normal operating temperatures are reached, then, turn **OFF** the engine.

2. Install a timing light to the No. 1 spark plug wire according to the manufacturer's instructions.

NOTE: For inductive timing lights, the induction clip can simply be installed over the plug wire. For other lights, the pick-up wire must be connected between the spark plug boot and the spark plug. Connect a tachometer according to the manufacturer's instructions.

3. Disconnect and plug the distributor-to-intake manifold vacuum hoses.

4. Loosen the distributor flange hold-down bolt to finger tight.

5. Start the engine, then, check and/or adjust the engine rpm; it should be 750 or less.

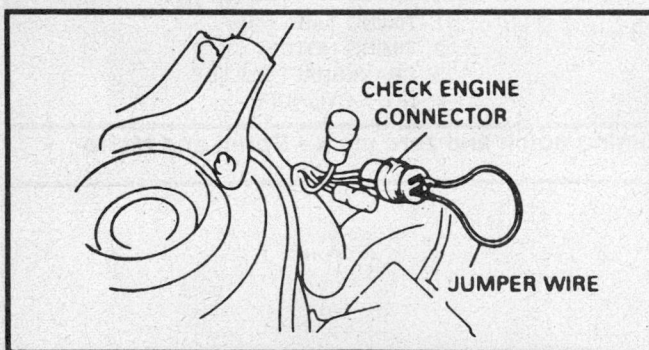

Using a jumper wire to short the check engine connector-twincam engine—Nova and Prizm

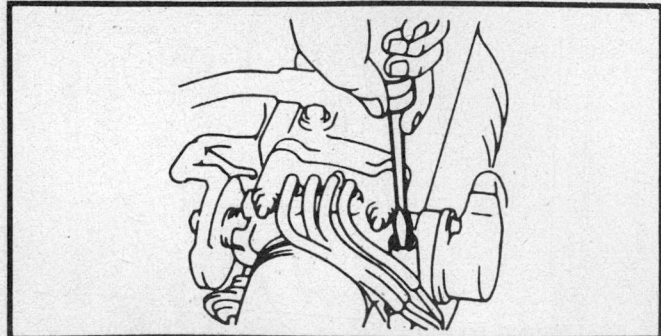

Adjusting the idle speed screw-twincam engine—Nova and Prizm

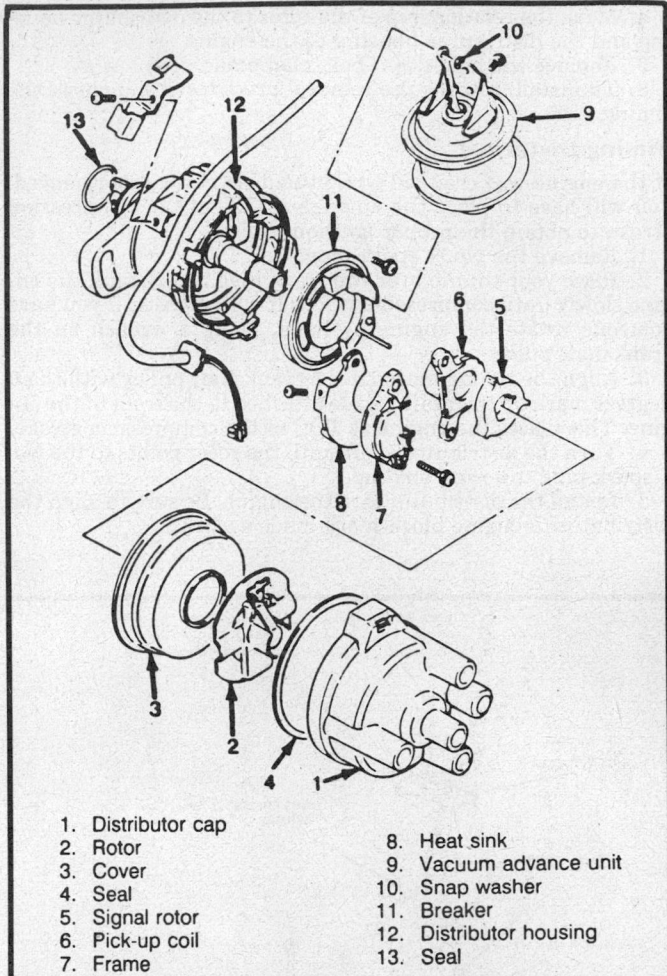

1. Distributor cap	8. Heat sink
2. Rotor	9. Vacuum advance unit
3. Cover	10. Snap washer
4. Seal	11. Breaker
5. Signal rotor	12. Distributor housing
6. Pick-up coil	13. Seal
7. Frame	

Exploded view of the distributor—Sprint and Metro

6. Aim the timing light at the scale on the timing cover near the front pulley; the timing should be 0 degrees BTDC. If the timing is not correct, turn the distributor slightly to correct it. Once the reading is correct, tighten the hold-down bolt and recheck the timing.

7. Stop the engine, remove the timing light, then, unplug and reconnect the distributor vacuum hoses.

Twincam Engine

Nova

1. Firmly apply the parking brake and place the transaxle in the **N** detent.

2. Run the engine until normal operating temperatures are reached, then, stop the engine.

3. Using a jumper wire, connect it to the check engine connector located near the wiper motor.

4. Using a timing light, connect it to the No. 1 spark plug wire. Loosen the distributor hold-down bolt until it is finger tight.

5. Start the engine, then, check and/or adjust the idle speed; it should be 800 rpm.

6. Aim the timing light at the timing cover plate near the crankshaft pulley; the notch on the crankshaft pulley should align the 10 degrees BTDC timing mark on the timing plate.

7. To adjust the engine timing, turn the distributor slightly to align the marks, then, tighten the hold-down bolt and recheck the timing.

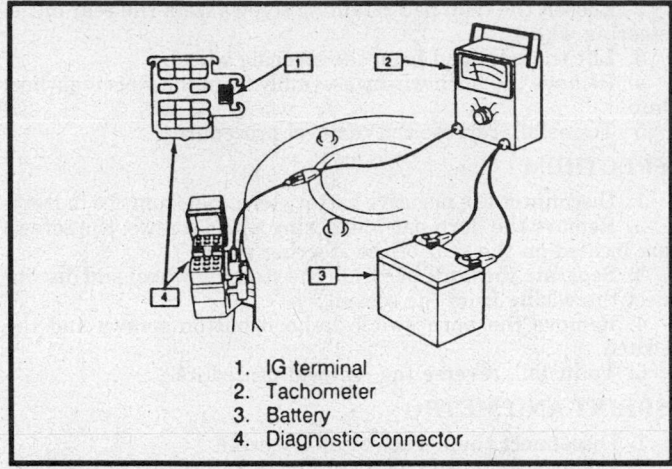

1. IG terminal
2. Tachometer
3. Battery
4. Diagnostic connector

Tachometer connections—Prizm

8. When the adjustment is correct, remove the jumper wire from the check engine connector and recheck the timing marks. The timing should now be more than 16 degrees BTDC (manual transaxle) or more than 12 degrees BTDC (automatic transaxle).

Prizm

1. Firmly apply the parking brake and place the transaxle in the **N** detent.
2. Connect a tachometer to the battery and the diagnostic connector. Do not ground the tachometer terminal.
3. Run the engine until normal operating temperatures are reached, then, stop the engine.
4. Remove the diagnostic connector cap and insert a jumper wire between terminals **E1** and **T**.
5. Using a timing light, connect it to the No. 1 spark plug wire. Loosen the distributor hold-down bolt until it is finger tight.
6. Start the engine, then, check and/or adjust the idle speed; it should be 700 rpm.
7. Aim the timing light at the timing cover plate near the crankshaft pulley; the notch on the crankshaft pulley should align with the specified timing mark on the timing plate. Use the timing specification noted on the underhood sticker.
8. To adjust the engine timing, turn the distributor slightly to align the marks, then, tighten the hold-down bolt and recheck the timing.
9. When the adjustment is correct, remove the jumper wire from diagnostic connector and install the cap.
10. Disconnect the ACV conncector.
11. Recheck the timing marks. The timing should now be 10 degrees BTDC.
12. Reconnect the ACV connector.
13. Disconnect the timing light.

SPECTRUM

1. Set the parking brake and block the wheels.
2. Place the manual transmission in **N** or the automatic transmission in the **P** detent.
3. Allow the engine to reach normal operating temperature. Make sure that the choke valve is open. Turn off all of the accessories.
4. If equipped with power steering, place the front wheels in a straight line.
5. Disconnect and plug the distributor vacuum line, the canister purge line, the EGR vacuum line and the ITC valve vacuum line at the intake manifold.
6. Connect a timing light to the No. 1 spark plug wire and a tachometer to the tachometer filter connector on the coil, tachometer filter is mounted near distributor hold down bolt.

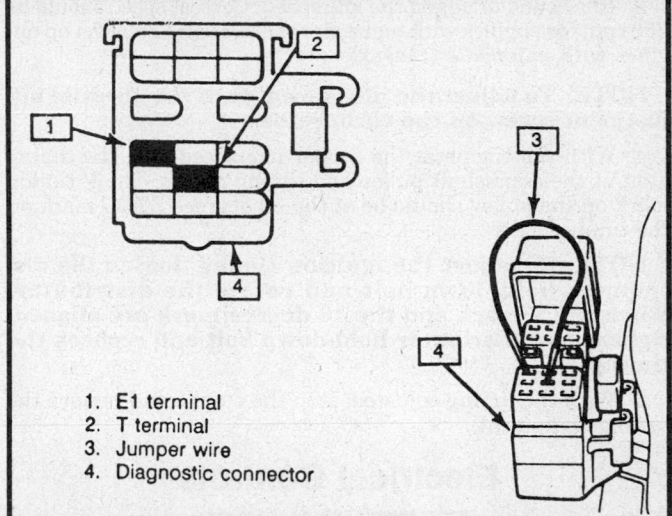

1. E1 terminal
2. T terminal
3. Jumper wire
4. Diagnostic connector

Diagnostic connector with jumper wire—Prizm

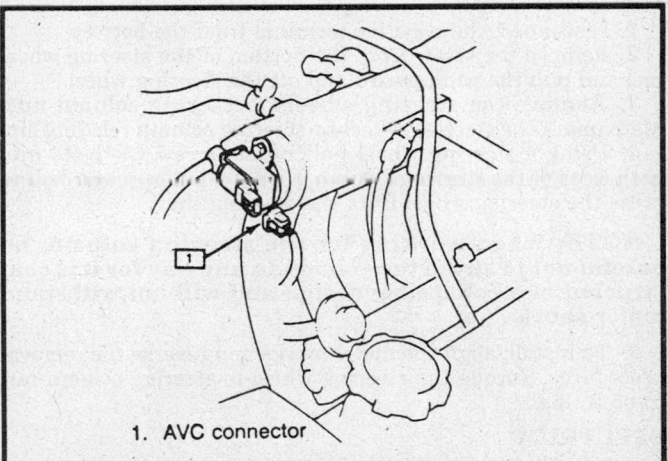

1. AVC connector

Removing the AVC connector—Prizm

NOTE: Check the idle speed and adjust as needed.

7. Loosen the distributor flange bolt.
8. Using the timing light, align the notch on the crankshaft pulley with the mark on the timing cover by turning the distributor.

NOTE: Adjust the timing to 15 degrees BTDC at 750 rpm (manual transaxle) or 10 degrees BTDC at 1000 rpm (automatic transaxle).

9. After the timing marks have been aligned, tighten the distributor flange bolt, then reinstall all vacuum lines.

SPRINT AND METRO

Before setting timing , make sure that the headlights, heater fan, engine cooling fan and any other electrical equipment is turned **OFF**. If any current drawing systems are operating, the idle up system will operate and cause the idle speed to be higher than normal.

1. Connect a tachometer to the negative terminal of the ignition coil. Connect a timing light to the No. 1 spark plug wire. Refer to the underhood sticker.
2. Start and run the engine until it reaches normal operating temperature.

3. Check and/or adjust the idle speed. Correct speed should be 750 rpm for engines with manual transaxles and 850 rpm on engines with automatic transaxles.

NOTE: To adjust the idle speed, turn the throttle adjustment screw on the carburetor.

4. With the engine at the proper idle speed, aim the timing light at the crankshaft pulley and timing marks. The **V** timing mark on the pulley should be at the 10 degrees BTDC mark on the timing plate.

NOTE: To adjust the ignition timing, loosen the distributor hold down bolt and rotate the distributor. When the V mark and the 10 degree mark are aligned, tighten the distributor hold-down bolt and recheck the timing.

5. With the timing adjusted, stop the engine and remove the testing equipment.

Electrical Controls
STEERING WHEEL

Removal and Installation
NOVA AND PRIZM

1. Disconnect the negative terminal from the battery.
2. Remove the screw from the bottom of the steering wheel pad and pull the pad upward and off the steering wheel.
3. Remove the steering wheel-to-steering column nut. Matchmark the steering wheel-to-steering column relationship.
4. Using a steering wheel puller tool, screw the bolts into both sides of the steering column, turn the puller center bolt to press the steering wheel from the steering shaft.

NOTE: When working on the steering column, be careful not to strike the column in any way for it is constructed of a collapsible design and will not withstand major shock.

5. To install, align the matchmarks and reverse the removal procedures. Torque the steering wheel-to-steering column nut to 25 ft. lbs.

SPECTRUM

1. Disconnect the negative battery terminal from the battery.
2. Using a suitable tool, remove the shroud screws from the rear-side of the steering wheel (Type 1) or pry the shroud from the steering wheel (Type 2).
3. Disconnect the horn connector and remove the shroud.
4. Remove the nut/washer retaining the steering wheel to the steering shaft.
5. Using a steering wheel puller, remove the steering wheel.
6. To install, reverse the removal procedures.

SPRINT AND METRO

1. Disconnect the negative battery cable.
2. Loosen the pad screws and remove the the pad.
3. Remove the steering wheel nut.
4. Scribe a matchmark line on the steering wheel and the shaft.
5. Using a steering wheel puller, pull the steering wheel from the steering shaft.
6. To install, reverse the removal procedures. Torque the steering wheel nut to 19–29 ft. lbs.

HORN SWITCH

Removal and Installation
NOVA AND PRIZM

1. Disconnect the negative terminal from the battery.

2. Loosen the trim pad retaining screws from the rear of the steering wheel.
3. Lift the trim pad from the steering wheel.
4. Remove the horn wiring assembly from the steering wheel hub.
5. To install, reverse the removal procedure.

SPECTRUM

1. Disconnect the negative battery terminal from the battery.
2. Remove the horn bar-to-steering wheel screws; the screws are located on the rear of the steering wheel.
3. Separate the horn bar from the steering wheel and disconnect the wiring from the socket.
4. Remove the horn switch-to-horn button screws and the switch.
5. To install, reverse the removal procedure.

SPRINT AND METRO

1. Disconnect the negative battery cable.
2. Remove the horn pad by pulling it outwards.
3. Replace the necessary components and install the horn pad.
4. Connect the negative battery cable.

IGNITION LOCK AND SWITCH

Removal and Installation
NOVA AND PRIZM

1. Disconnect the negative battery cable. Remove the combination switch.
2. If equipped with a tilt steering column, perform the following procedures:
   a. Remove the tension springs and grommets, the tilt lever (the bolt has left-hand threads), the adjusting nut/washer.
   b. Pull out the lock bolt, then, remove the upper and lower column supports.
3. From the lower steering column, disconnect the ignition switch electrical connector.
4. Remove the retainer-to-upper bracket screws and the retainer from the upper bracket.
5. Using snapring pliers, remove the snapring from the upper bracket.
6. Insert the key into the ignition switch and release the steering lock.
7. Using a hammer and a pin punch, drive the tapered bolt from the upper bracket.
8. Remove the upper bracket-to-steering column tube bolts and the upper bracket.
9. To install, release the steering lock and install the upper bracket-to steering column bolts (tighten the bolts finger tight). Torque the upper bracket-to-steering column bolts to 14 ft. lbs.
10. If installing the tilt steering mechanism, perform the following procedures:
   a. Apply grease to the bushings and the O-rings, then, install the lower support-to-tube.
   b. Using multi-purpose grease, apply it to the tilt bracket-to-steering column mating surfaces, then, install the upper support and lock bolt.

NOTE: If there is any play in the adjusting support, snug-up the adjusting nut.

   c. Install the tilt lever. Move the lever to loosen the bracket-to-column bolt, adjust the column height and move the lever to lock the column position; if the lever is out of position, reposition the adjusting nut.
   d. Install the tilt lever retaining screw (left-hand thread) and torque it. Install the tension springs and grommets.
11. To complete the installation, reverse the removal procedures.

SPECTRUM

1. Disconnect the negative battery cable. Remove the combination switch.

2. Insert the key into the ignition and place the key in the **ON** position (the lock bar must be pulled all the way in).

3. Remove the snapring and rubber cushion from the steering shaft.

4. Disconnect the switch wires at the connectors.

5. Remove the 2 screws retaining the ignition/starter switch and remove the switch.

6. To install, reverse the removal procedures.

SPRINT AND METRO

1. Disconnect the negative battery cable. Remove the steering column.

2. Place the column on a bench.

3. Using a sharp point center punch and a hammer, remove the steering lock mounting bolts.

4. Turn the ignition key to **ACC** or **ON** positions and remove the lock assembly from the steering column.

5. To install, reverse the removal procedures. After installing the lock, turn the key to **LOCK** position and pull out the key. Turn the steering shaft to make sure the shaft is locked. Install new mounting bolts to the lock housing, tighten until the bolt heads break off. Torque the lower bracket bolts to 8–12 ft. lbs.; the upper bracket bolts to 10 ft. lbs. and the steering shaft bolt to 15–22 ft. lbs.

NEUTRAL SAFETY SWITCH

Removal and Installation

NOVA AND PRIZM

1. Disconnect the negative battery cable.

2. Disconnect the electrical connector at the switch.

3. Raise the vehicle and support it safely.

4. Remove the switch retaining bolts and remove the switch.

5. Installation is the reverse of removal. Align the groove and neutral basic line. Hold the switch in position and tighten the bolts to 48 inch lbs.

6. Check and make sure the engine starts in only the **P** and **N** detents.

SPECTRUM

1. Disconnect the negative battery cable.

2. Disconnect the electrical connector for the switch at the left fender.

3. Raise the vehicle and support it safely.

4. Remove the switch retaining bolts and remove the switch.

5. Installation is the reverse of removal. Add transaxle fluid as necessary.

6. Check and make sure the engine starts in only the **P** and **N** detents.

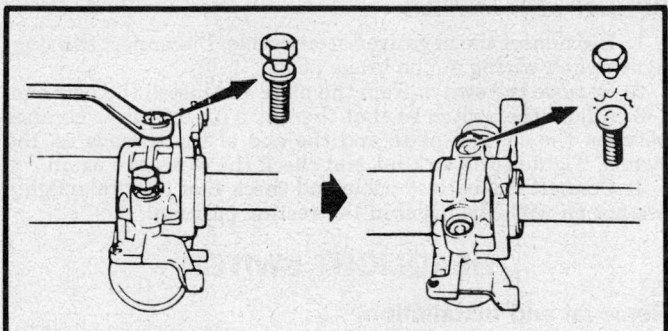

Tighten the ignition switch mounting bolts until the heads break off – Sprint and Metro

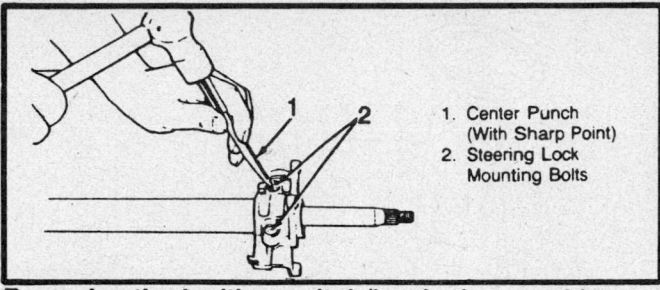

1. Center Punch (With Sharp Point)
2. Steering Lock Mounting Bolts

Removing the ignition switch/key lock assembly – Sprint and Metro

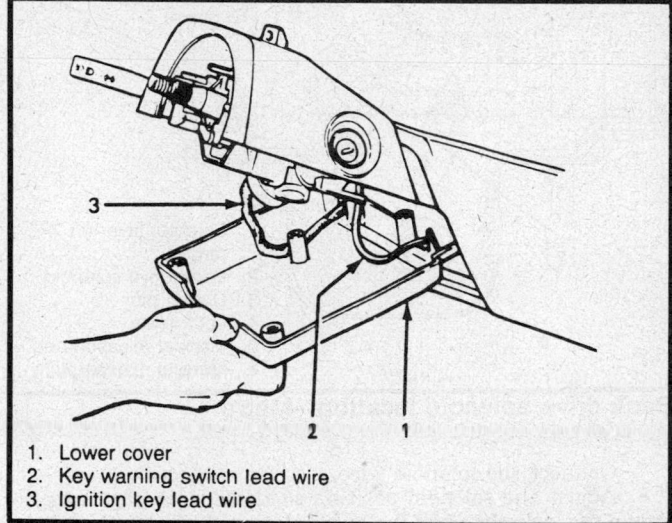

1. Lower cover
2. Key warning switch lead wire
3. Ignition key lead wire

Lower steering column cover – Sprint and Metro

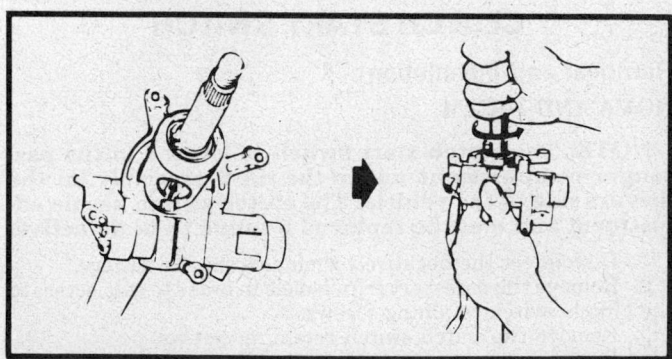

Align the slot in the steering shaft with the tab on the switch to install – Sprint and Metro

SPRINT AND METRO

These vehicles use a back drive system (solenoid) to keep the selector lever always in the **P** detent position when starting the engine with the ignition key.

1. Disconnect the negative battery cable.

2. Remove the solenoid to housing attaching screws.

3. Disconnect the solenoid wire and remove the solenoid.

To install:

4. Shift the selector lever to the **P** range.

5. Apply grease to the upper and lower edges of the lock plate before installing the back drive solenoid.

6. Position the solenoid to the housing and install the retaining screws hand tight.

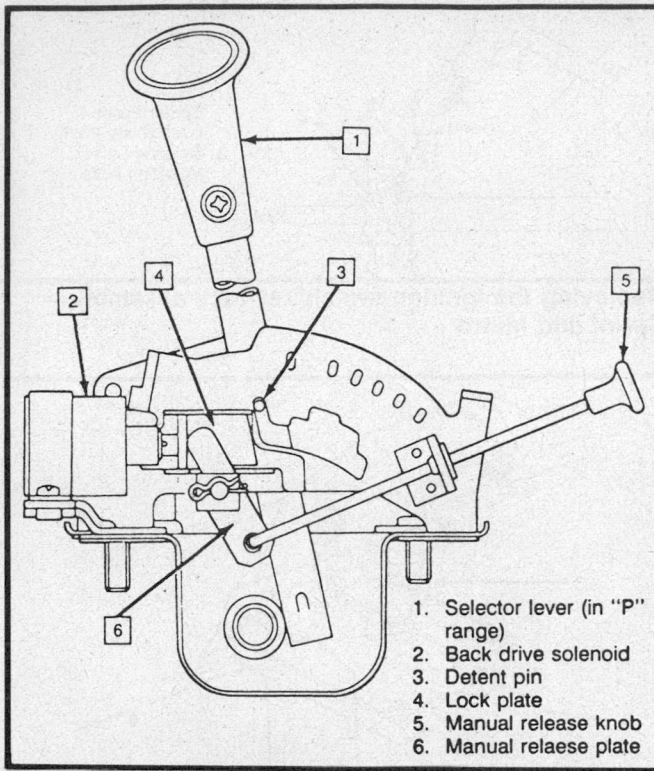

1. Selector lever (in "P" range)
2. Back drive solenoid
3. Detent pin
4. Lock plate
5. Manual release knob
6. Manual relaese plate

Back drive solenoid location—Metro

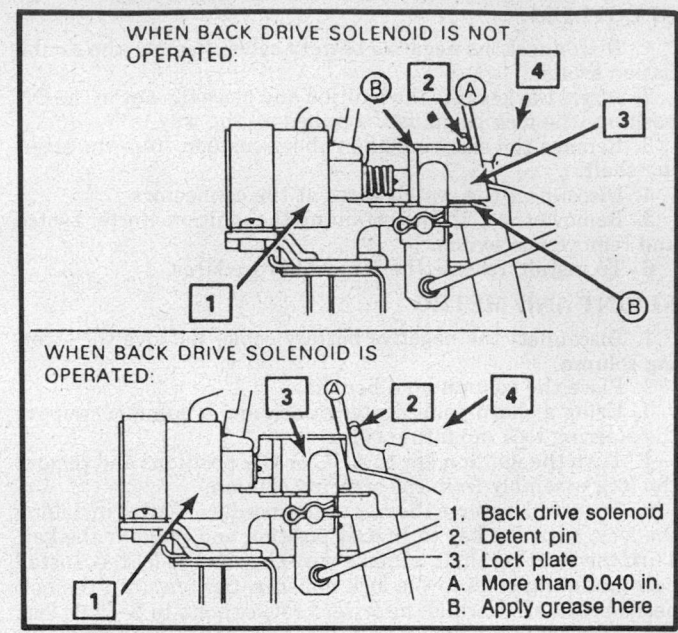

1. Back drive solenoid
2. Detent pin
3. Lock plate
A. More than 0.040 in.
B. Apply grease here

Lock plate position—Metro

7. Connect the solenoid wire.
8. Adjust the solenoid position so there is no clearance between the lock plate and the guide plate and tighten the retaining screws.

CLUTCH START SWITCH

Removal and Installation

NOVA AND PRIZM

NOTE: The clutch start switch is located in the passenger compartment under the dash assembly on the drivers side of the vehicle. The clutch switch has no adjustment and must be replaced if found to be defective.

1. Disconnect the negative terminal from the battery.
2. Remove the necessary trim panels in order to gain access to the clutch switch retaining screws.
3. Remove the clutch switch retaining screws.
4. Pull the switch down from its retainer and disconnect the electrical connections.
5. To install, reverse the removal procedures.

SPECTRUM

1. Disconnect the negative battery terminal from the battery.
2. Disconnect the electrical connector from the switch.
3. Remove the clutch start switch-to-brake pedal stop bracket screw and the switch from the clutch pedal.
4. To install, reverse the removal procedures

SPRINT AND METRO

1. Disconnect the negative battery terminal from the battery.
2. Disconnect the electrical connector from the switch.
3. Loosen the locknut then uncrew the clutch start switch from the clutch pedal.
4. To install, reverse the removal procedures

STOP LIGHT SWITCH

Removal and Installation

NOVA AND PRIZM

The stoplight switch is attached to a bracket at the top of the brake pedal.

1. Disconnect the negative battery cable. Remove the lower instrument panel cover.
2. Disconnect the electrical connector from the stoplight switch.
3. Remove the stoplight switch-to-bracket nut and the switch.
4. To install, reverse the removal procedures. Adjust the switch so the stoplights turn with slight movement of the brake pedal.

SPECTRUM

1. Disconnect the negative battery cable. Remove stop light switch locknut.
2. Remove switch by pulling straight out of pedal assembly.
3. To install push switch straight in, push the brake pedal by turning the stop light switch, so that free play in the brake pedal is eliminated, then tighten the stop light switch locknut.

SPRINT AND METRO

1. Disconnect the negative battery cable. Disconnect the stoplight switch wiring at the brake pedal.
2. Remove the switch from the plate and install the new one.
3. Adjust the switch so that there is 0.02–0.04 in. clearance between the contact plate and the end of the threads on the switch. Tighten the locknut and check the clearance again.
4. Connect the battery cable and check that the brake lights are not on with the pedal in the resting position.

HEADLIGHT SWITCH

Removal and Installation

NOVA AND PRIZM

The headlight switch is located on the left-side of the combination switch which attached to the steering column.

1. Disconnect the negative battery cable. Remove the combination switch screws and the switch assembly.

2. Trace the headlight/dimmer switch wiring harness to the multi-connector. Using a scratch awl, push in the multi-connector lock levers and pull wires from the connector.

3. To install, reverse the removal procedures. Check the operation of the headlight/dimmer switch.

SPECTRUM

The headlight control switch is a 3 position, push type switch which is located at the left side of the instrument panel. The dimmer/passing light switch is a part of and actuated by the turn signal switch.

1. Disconnect the negative battery cable. Remove the instrument cluster bezel retaining screw and the bezel.

2. Disconnect the headlight and the windshield wiper control switch electrical connectors.

3. Place the bezel on a bench and remove the 2 nuts securing the headlight control switch.

4. Remove the headlight control switch.

5. To install, reverse the removal procedures.

SPRINT AND METRO

1. Disconnect the negative battery cable.
2. Remove the steering column trim panel.
3. Lower the steering column.
4. Remove the cluster bezel and the bezel.
5. Disconnect the headlight switch connector.
6. Remove the headlight switch.
7. To install, reverse the removal procedures.

COMBINATION SWITCH

Removal and Installation
NOVA AND PRIZM

1. Disconnect the negative battery cable. Remove the steering wheel.

2. Remove the lower instrument finish panel, air duct and column lower cover.

3. From the base of the steering column shroud, disconnect the ignition switch and turn signal electrical connector.

4. Remove the combination switch-to-steering column screws and the combination switch with the upper column cover.

5. To install, reverse the removal procedures.

Spectrum

1. Disconnect the negative battery terminal from the battery.

2. Remove the horn shroud, steering wheel nut/washer and steering wheel assembly.

3. Remove the steering cowl attaching screw and steering cowl.

4. Disconnect the combination/starter switch connector.

5. Remove the turn signal/dimmer switch attaching screw and switch.

6. To install, reverse the removal procedures.

TURN SIGNAL/DIMMER SWITCH ASSEMBLY

Removal and Installation
SPRINT AND METRO

1. Disconnect the negative battery cable. Remove the steering wheel.

2. Remove the upper and lower steering column covers.

3. Disconnect the turn signal/dimmer switch assembly electrical connector.

4. Remove the screws and the turn signal/dimmer switch assembly from the steering column.

5. To install, reverse the removal procedures.

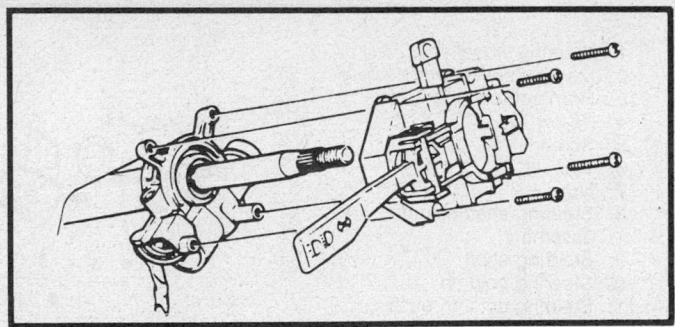

Turn signal/dimmer switch mounting—Sprint and Metro

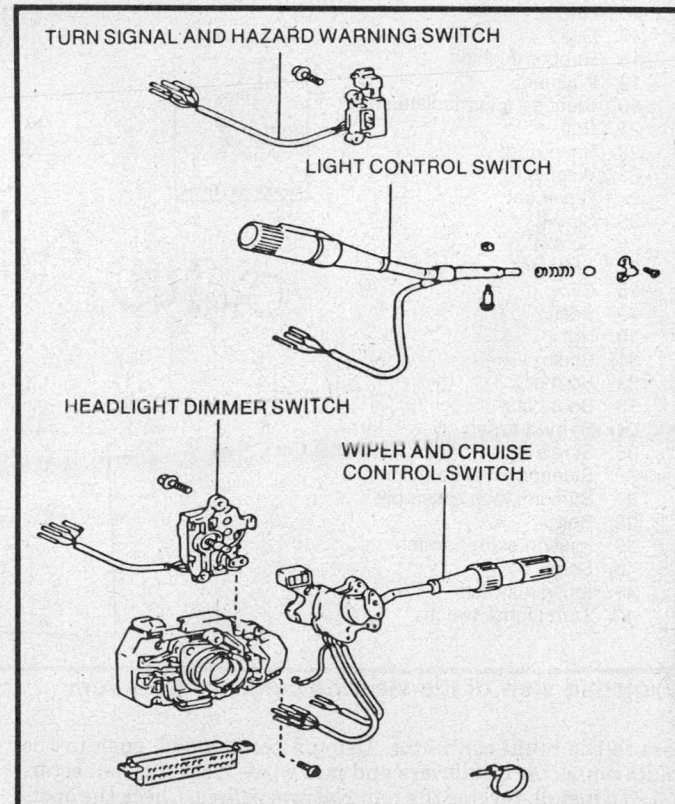

Exploded view of combination switch—Nova and Prizm

NOTE: When installing, be careful that the lead wires do not get caught by the lower cover.

WINDSHIELD WIPER SWITCH

Removal and Installation
NOVA AND PRIZM
Front

The front wiper switch is located on the right-side of the combination switch attached to the steering column.

1. Disconnect the negative battery cable. Remove the wiper/cruise control assembly switch-to-combination switch screws and the switch assembly.

2. Trace the wiper/cruise control assembly switch wiring har-

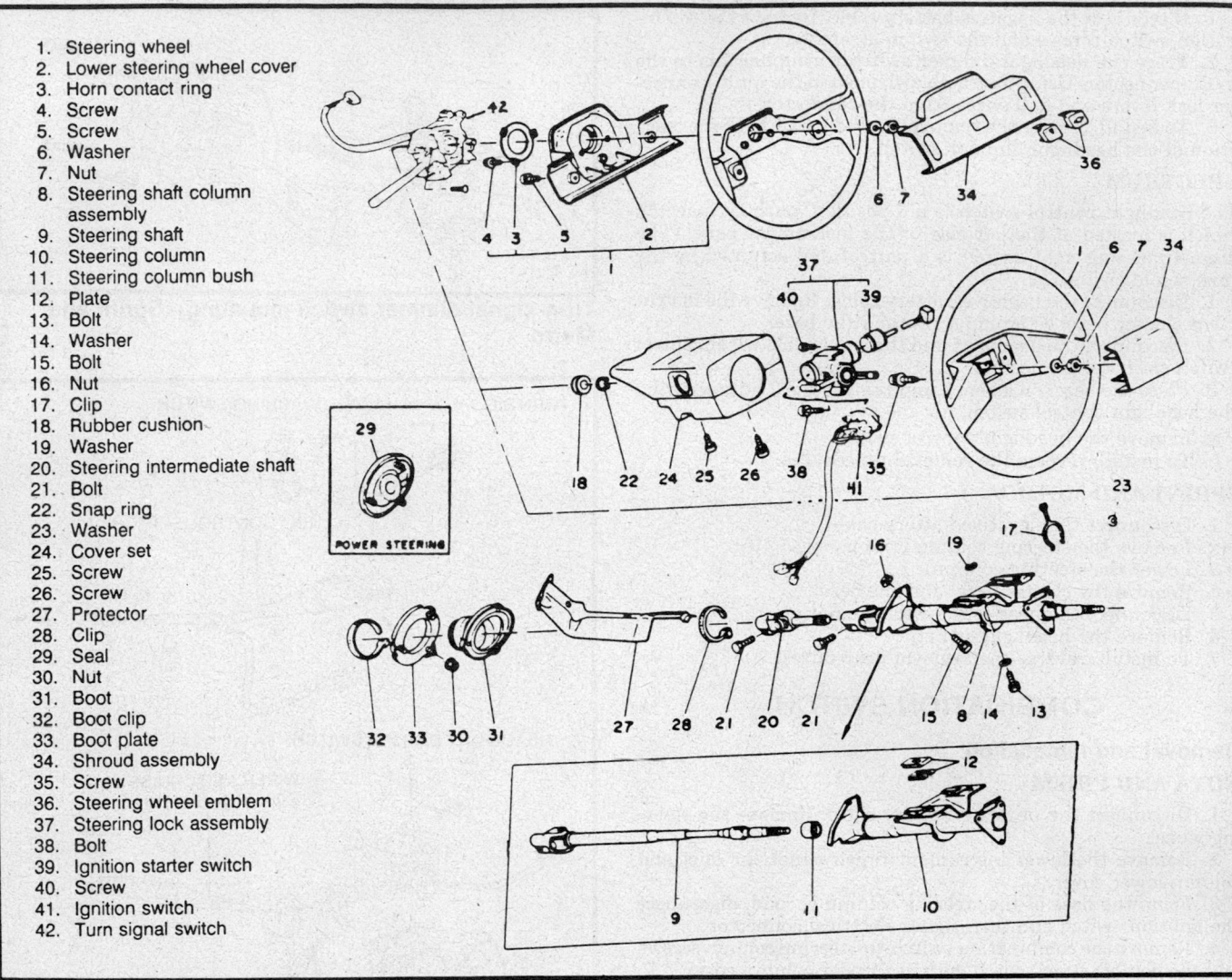

1. Steering wheel
2. Lower steering wheel cover
3. Horn contact ring
4. Screw
5. Screw
6. Washer
7. Nut
8. Steering shaft column assembly
9. Steering shaft
10. Steering column
11. Steering column bush
12. Plate
13. Bolt
14. Washer
15. Bolt
16. Nut
17. Clip
18. Rubber cushion
19. Washer
20. Steering intermediate shaft
21. Bolt
22. Snap ring
23. Washer
24. Cover set
25. Screw
26. Screw
27. Protector
28. Clip
29. Seal
30. Nut
31. Boot
32. Boot clip
33. Boot plate
34. Shroud assembly
35. Screw
36. Steering wheel emblem
37. Steering lock assembly
38. Bolt
39. Ignition starter switch
40. Screw
41. Ignition switch
42. Turn signal switch

POWER STEERING

Exploded view of the steering column—Spectrum

ness to the multi-connector. Using a scratch awl, push in the multi-connector lock levers and pull wires from the connector.

3. To install, reverse the removal procedures. Check the operation of the windshield wiper switch and the cruise control system.

Rear

1. Disconnect the negative terminal from the battery.
2. On the Nova, use a small pry bar and pry the rear wiper switch from the front of the instrument panel.
3. On the Prizm, remove the trim bezel.
4. Disconnect the electrical connector from the rear wiper switch.
5. To install, reverse the removal procedures. Check the operation of the rear wiper switch.

SPECTRUM

Front

1. Disconnect the negative battery cable. Remove the the instrument cluster bezel.
2. Remove the wiper switch electrical connector, attaching nuts and bracket.
3. Remove the wiper switch.
4. To install, reverse the removal procedures.

Rear

1. Disconnect the negative battery cable. Using a small tool, pry the switch panel from the dash.
2. Pull the switch out and disconnect the electrical connector.
3. To install, reverse the removal procedures.

SPRINT AND METRO

1. Disconnect the negative battery cable.
2. Remove the steering column trim panel.
3. Lower the steering column.
4. Remove the cluster bezel and the bezel.
5. Disconnect the wiper switch connector.
6. Remove the wiper switch.
7. To install, reverse the removal procedures.

WINDSHIELD WIPER MOTOR

Removal and Installation

NOVA AND PRIZM

Front

1. Disconnect the negative terminal from the battery.

2. From the engine compartment, disconnect the electrical connector from the windshield wiper motor.

3. Remove the wiper motor-to-chassis screws.

4. Disconnect the wiper motor from the windshield wiper crank arm; be careful not to bend the linkage.

5. To install, reverse the removal procedures. Check the operation of the front windshield wiper motor.

Rear

The rear wiper motor is located in the rear hatch.

1. Disconnect the negative terminal from the battery.

2. Remove the rear wiper arm-to-wiper motor nut and wiper arm.

3. From inside the rear hatch, remove the rear wiper cover, then, disconnect the electrical connector from the rear wiper motor.

4. Remove the wiper motor-to-hatch screws and the wiper motor from the hatch.

5. To install, reverse the removal procedures. Check the operation of the rear wiper motor.

SPECTRUM

Front

1. Disconnect the negative battery terminal from the battery.

2. Remove the locknuts retaining the wiper arms and the wiper arms.

3. Remove the cowl cover, wiper motor cover and the electrical connector.

4. Disconnect the drive arm from the wiper link.

5. Remove the mounting bolts and the wiper motor.

6. To install, reverse the removal procedures.

Rear

1. Disconnect the negative battery terminal from the battery.

2. Remove the trim pad and the wiper arm assemblies.

3. Remove the mounting bolts and the motor assembly.

4. Disconnect the electrical connector.

5. To install, reverse the removal procedures.

SPRINT AND METRO

Front

1. Disconnect the negative battery cable.

2. Disconnect the crank arm from the wiper motor.

3. Disconnect the electrical connector from the wiper motor.

4. Remove the wiper motor from the vehicle.

5. To install, reverse the removal procedures.

Rear

1. Disconnect the negative battery cable.

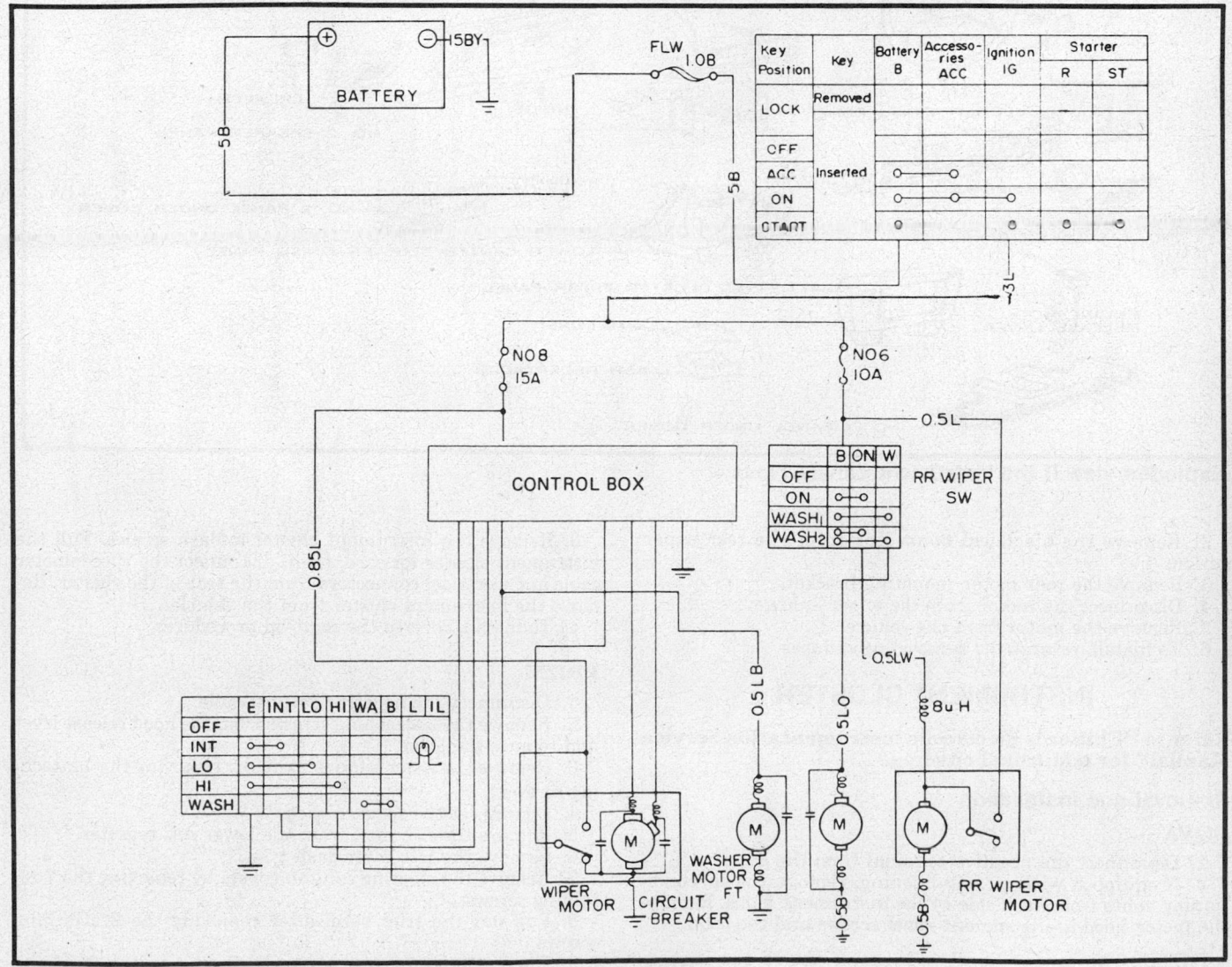

Schematic of the windshield wiper control system— Spectrum

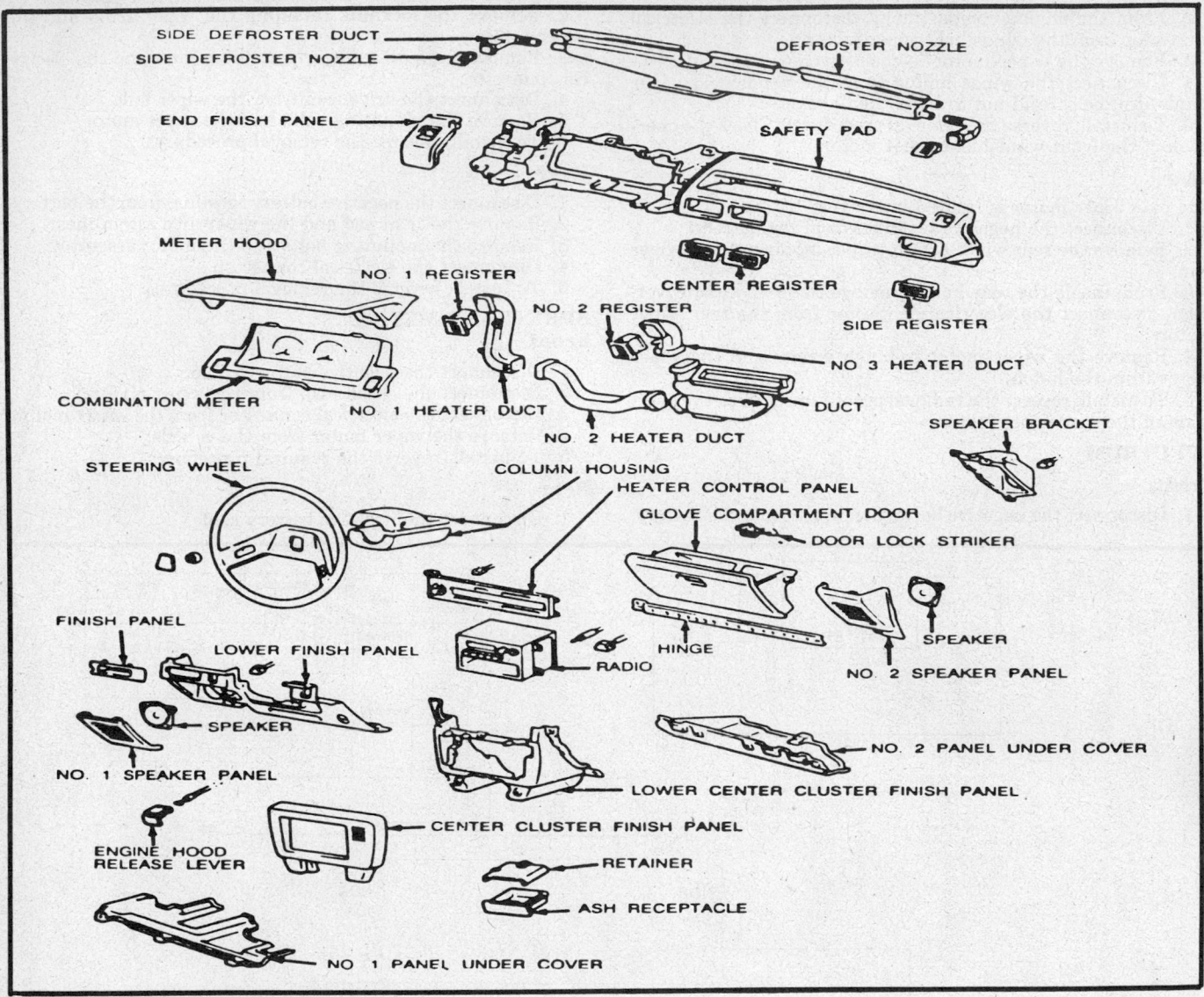

Exploded view if the instrument panel—Nova

2. Remove the electrical connector from the rear wiper motor.

3. Remove the rear motor mounting bracket.

4. Disconnect the motor from the wiper linkage.

5. Remove the motor from the vehicle.

6. To install, reverse the removal procedures.

INSTRUMENT CLUSTER

Refer to "Chilton's Electronic Instrumentation Service Manual" for additional coverage

Removal and Installation

NOVA

1. Disconnect the negative terminal from the battery.

2. If equipped with air conditioning, remove the air conditioning vents from each side of the instrument panel. Remove the meter hood-to-instrument panel screws and the hood.

NOTE: The meter hood is located above the instrument cluster.

3. Remove the instrument cluster-to-dash screws. Pull the instrument cluster forward, then, disconnect the speedometer cable and electrical connectors from the rear of the cluster. Remove the instrument cluster from the vehicle.

4. To install, reverse the removal procedures.

PRIZM

1. Disconnect the negative battery cable.

2. Remove the 2 attaching screws from the hood release lever and remove the lever.

3. Remove the lower left dash trim by removing the 4 attaching screws.

4. Disconnect the speaker wire.

5. Remove the A/C duct from the lower A/C regester.

6. Remove the left lower dash trim.

7. Remove the steering column covers by removing the 7 retaining screws.

8. Pull out the trim bezel after removing the 2 attaching screws.

9. Disconnect the cruise control/defogger switch from the electrical connector.

10. Disconnect any electrical connections from the trim bezel and remove the trim bezel.

11. Remove the 4 attaching screws from the cluster bezel.

12. Disconnect the electrical connectors from the hazard flasher and dimmer switches.

13. Remove the cluster bezel.

14. Remove the 4 attaching screws from the cluster.

15. Disconnect the speedometer cable and electrical connections from the cluster.

16. Remove the cluster from the vehicle.

17. Installation is the reverse of removal.

SPECTRUM

1. Disconnect the negative battery terminal from the battery.

2. Remove the instrument cluster bezel retaining screws and bezel.

3. Disconnect the windshield wiper and lighting switch connectors.

4. Remove the instrument cluster retaining screws and pull out the assembly.

5. Remove the trip reset knob and the assembly glass.

6. Remove the buzzer, sockets and bulbs.

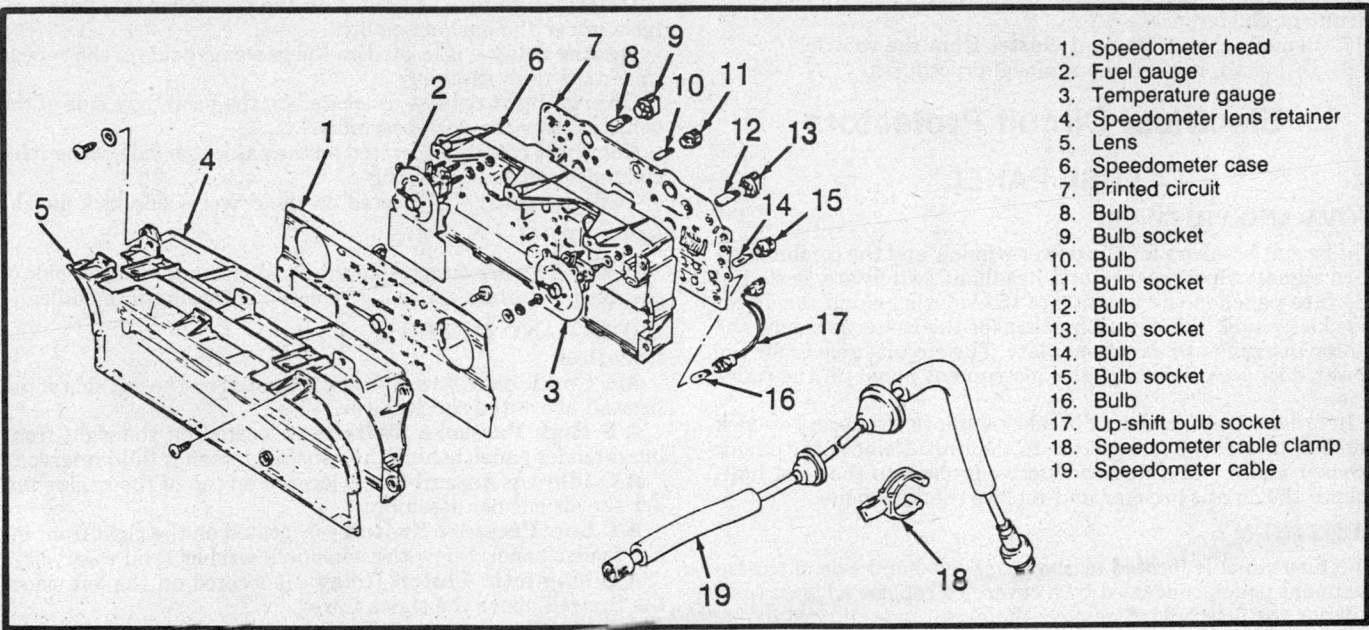

1. Speedometer head
2. Fuel gauge
3. Temperature gauge
4. Speedometer lens retainer
5. Lens
6. Speedometer case
7. Printed circuit
8. Bulb
9. Bulb socket
10. Bulb
11. Bulb socket
12. Bulb
13. Bulb socket
14. Bulb
15. Bulb socket
16. Bulb
17. Up-shift bulb socket
18. Speedometer cable clamp
19. Speedometer cable

Exploded view of the instrument cluster without tachometer—Sprint and Metro

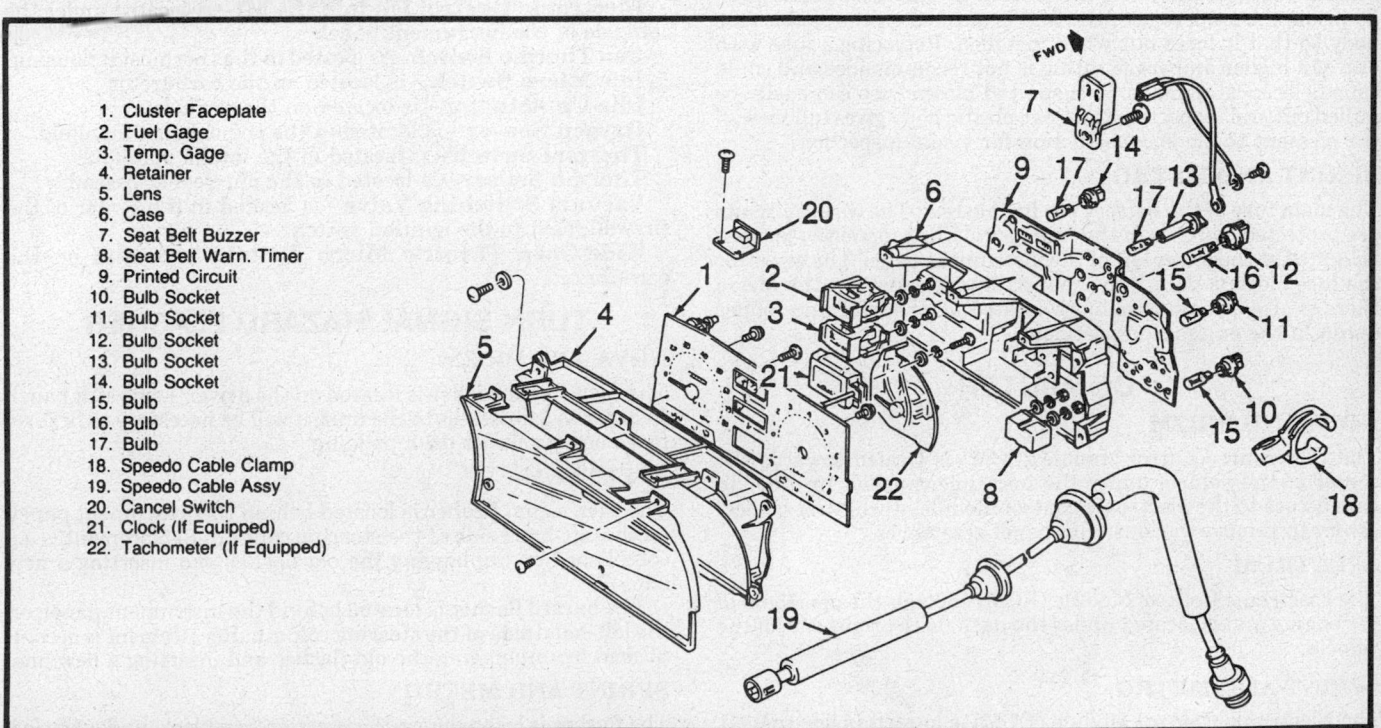

1. Cluster Faceplate
2. Fuel Gage
3. Temp. Gage
4. Retainer
5. Lens
6. Case
7. Seat Belt Buzzer
8. Seat Belt Warn. Timer
9. Printed Circuit
10. Bulb Socket
11. Bulb Socket
12. Bulb Socket
13. Bulb Socket
14. Bulb Socket
15. Bulb
16. Bulb
17. Bulb
18. Speedo Cable Clamp
19. Speedo Cable Assy
20. Cancel Switch
21. Clock (If Equipped)
22. Tachometer (If Equipped)

Exploded view of the instrument cluster with tachometer—Sprint and Metro

7. Remove the speedometer assembly, fuel and temperature gauge.

8. Remove the tachometer, if so equipped.

9. To install, reverse the removal procedures.

SPRINT AND METRO

1. Disconnect the negative battery cable.

2. Remove the steering column trim panel.

3. Lower the steering column.

4. Remove the cluster lens and the cluster mounting screws.

5. Disconnect the speedometer cable at the transaxle and at the instrument cluster.

6. Disconnect and mark the electrical connectors at the instrument cluster.

7. Remove the instrument cluster from the vehicle.

8. To install, reverse the removal procedures.

Electrical Circuit Protectors

FUSE PANEL

NOVA AND PRIZM

The circuit breakers for the power window and the combination turn signal/ wiper washer and headlight switch are located in the fuse panel on the left-side of the vehicle behind the driver side kick panel. The circuit breaker for the heater is behind the center instrument panel trim plate. The circuit breaker for the power door lock is behind the instrument panel on the right-side.

In order to reset a circuit breaker, remove the necessary kick panel(s) in order to gain access to the unit. Remove the circuit breaker and insert a non-conductive probe into the reset hole. Install the circuit breaker and replace the kick panel.

SPECTRUM

The fuse panel is located at the lower left-hand side of the instrument panel, concealed by a cover. To replace a blown fuse, pull out the fuse holder, remove the blown fuse and install one of the same amperage.

Each fuse is marked on the fusebox or the fusebox cover. In addition, the amperage of the fuse is marked on the plastic fuse body so that it faces out when installed. Replacing a fuse with one of a higher amperage rating is not recommended and could cause electrical damage. A suspected blown fuse can easily be pulled out and inspected; the clear plastic body gives full view of the element to blade construction for visual inspection.

SPRINT AND METRO

The main fuse at the battery is a fusible link. The wiring circuits are protected by fuses in the fuse block. The junction/fuse block is located at the lower left of the instrument panel. The cover for the fuse block is built into the instrument panel. On the Metro there is also a main fuse block located on the left hand fender apron in the engine compartment.

COMPUTER

NOVA AND PRIZM

The Electronic Control Module (ECM) is located towards the center of the vehicle under the instrument panel. In order to gain access to the electronic control module, it will first be necessary to remove various trim panel assemblies.

SPECTRUM

The Electronic Control Module (ECM) controls the operation of the engine and is located under the dash on the right side of the vehicle.

SPRINT AND METRO

The Electronic Control Module (ECM) is located inside the left hand instrument panel.

VARIOUS RELAYS

NOVA AND PRIZM

Location

Starter relay— is located at the front left side of the engine compartment.

Air conditioning relay— is located at the front left side of the engine compartment.

Fan— is located at the front left side of the engine compartment.

Main engine relays— are located at the front left side of the engine compartment.

Defogger relay— is located on the passenger side of the vehicle under the dash assembly.

Heater relay— is located on the passenger side of the vehicle under the dash assembly.

Charge light relay— is located on the passenger side of the vehicle under the dash assembly.

Seat belt relay— is located on the passenger side of the vehicle under the dash assembly.

Tailight relay— is located on the driver's side kick panel.

SPECTRUM

Various relays are attached to the brackets under the left-side of the dash. All units are easily replaced with plug-in modules.

SPRINT AND METRO
Location

A/C Condenser Fan Relay—is located on the left side of the firewall above the shock tower.

A/C High Pressure Switch—is located on the right front inner fender panel. behind the winshield washer fluid reservoir.

A/C Idle-Up Assembly—is located on top of the engine under the air cleaner assembly.

A/C Low Pressure Switch—is located on the right front inner fender panel, below the winshield washer fluid reservoir.

A/C Magnetic Clutch Relay—is located on the left sideof the firewall above the shock tower.

Coolant Temperature Switch—is located on the top of the engine, on the coolant intake pipe.

Electronic Control Module (ECM)—is located under the left side of the instrument panel.

Fan Thermo Switch—is located in the thermostat housing.

Idle Micro Switch—is located on the carburetor.

Idle-Up Actuator—is located on the carburetor.

Oxygen Sensor—is located in the the exhaust manifold.

Thermal Switch—is located in the intake manifold.

Thermo Sensor—is located in the air cleaner assembly.

Vacuum Switching Valve—is located in the center of the firewall, next to the ignition switch.

Wide-Open Throttle Micro Switch—is located on the carburetor.

TURN SIGNAL/HAZARD FLASHER

NOVA AND PRIZM

The turn signal flasher is located on the driver's-side kick panel. In order to gain access to the unit, it will be necessary to first remove certain under dash padding.

SPECTRUM

The turn signal flasher is located behind the instrument panel, on the left-hand side of the steering column. Replacement is accomplished by unplugging the old flasher and inserting a new one.

The hazard flasher is located behind the instrument panel, on the left-hand side of the steering column. Replacement is accomplished by unplugging the old flasher and inserting a new one.

SPRINT AND METRO

The flasher is located near the junction/fuseblock, under the left hand side of the instrument panel.

ELECTRICAL SPEED SENSOR

NOVA AND PRIZM

The cruise control system is controlled by a computer located under the instrument panel on the passenger-side of the vehicle. The speed sensor is located within the computer. In order to gain access to the unit, it will first be necessary to remove the right-side kick panel.

SPECTRUM

The speed sensor is attached to the transmission at the speedometer cable location. It utilizes a magnetic reel switch which opens and closes 4 times per revolution of the speedometer cable.

Speed Controls

Refer to Chilton's Electronic Chassis Service Manual for additional coverage.

CONTROL (MAIN) SWITCH

TESTING

NOVA

1. Connect the positive lead from the battery to terminal 2.
2. Check that there is continuity between terminals 2 and 6 with the main switch turned ON.
3. Check that there is no continuity between terminals 2 and 6 with the main switch turned OFF.
4. Replace the switch if continuity is not as specified.

PRIZM

1. Connect a lead from the battery positive terminal to terminal 4.
2. Connect a lead from the battery negative terminal to terminal 5.
3. Using a voltmeter, check that there is continuity between terminals 3 and 4 of the cruise control module connector with the cruise control switch at CRUISE.
4. Check that there is no continuity between terminals 3 and 4 of the cruise control module connector with the cruise control switch turned OFF.
5. Replace the switch if continuity is not as specified.

BRAKE SWITCH

Adjustments

SPECTRUM

When the brake pedal is fully released, the pushrod should serve as the brake pedal stopper. Adjust the brake pedal height.

CLUTCH SWITCH

Adjustment

SPECTRUM

Adjust the clutch switch by rotating it inward until the threaded portion bottoms out on the bracket face, then, tighten the locknut firmly.

SERVO CABLE

Adjustment

SPECTRUM

1. Position and hold the accelerator pedal so that the engine runs at its normal idling speed.
2. Using a cable clamp and a self locking hex nut, lightly secure the cable casing to the bracket.
3. Being careful not to pull the throttle off the idle position, adjust the cable casing so that there is light tension on the cable.
4. Tighten the cable clamp.

SPRINT AND METRO

1. Position the accelerator pedal so that the engine runs at normal idling speed. Hold the accelerator pedal in this position.
2. Lightly secure the cable casing to the bracket using the cable clamp and self locking nut.
3. Adjust the cable casing so that there is a light tension on the servo cable, but make sure not to pull the throttle off the idle setting.
4. Tighten the clamp securely.

Troubleshooting

SPECTRUM

Before starting any troubleshooting procedures, a brief visual inspection should be made of the system components. The following components should be inspected:
1. For the system to operate, the vehicle must be moving at least 30 mph.
2. Servo cable—make sure that the cable is not binding.
3. Throttle linkage—make sure that the linkage is not binding.
4. If cruise control is non-operable, inspect the following items:
   a. A blown fuse, replace as required.
   b. Insufficent ground.
   c. Control mode SET/COAST switch inoperative.
   d. Defective or improperly adjusted brake and/or clutch switch.
   e. Defective speed sensor.
   f. Defective electronic speed module.

COOLING AND HEATING SYSTEMS

Water Pump

Removal and Installation

NOVA AND PRIZM

1. Disconnect the negative battery cable.
2. Drain the cooling system.
2. Loosen the water pump pulley-to-water pump bolts. If equipped with power steering, remove the power steering pump drive belt.
3. Loosen the alternator adjusting and mounting bolts, move the alternator to relieve the belt tension, then, remove the alternator/water pump drive belt.
4. Remove the water pump pulley-to-water pump bolts and the pulley.
5. Remove the water pump inlet-to-engine bolts (from the side of the block), the inlet pipe-to-water pump nuts and the inlet pipe (discard the O-ring).
6. Remove the dipstick tube bracket bolt and the dipstick tube; be sure to plug the hole in the block with a clean rag.
7. For the non-twincam engine, remove the upper timing belt front cover. For the twincam engine, remove the upper and middle timing belt front covers.

8. Remove the water pump-to-engine bolts and the water pump from the engine; discard the water pump-to-engine O-ring.

9. Using the proper tool, clean the gasket mounting surfaces.

10. To install the water pump, use a new O-ring and reverse the removal procedures. Torque the water pump-to-engine bolts to 11 ft. lbs.

11. When installing the oil dipstick tube, use a new O-ring and coat it with engine oil.

12. To complete the installation, use a new O-ring and reverse the removal procedures. Refill the cooling system. Start the engine, allow it to reach normal operating temperatures and check for leaks.

SPECTRUM

1. Disconnect the negative battery cable and drain the cooling system.

2. Loosen the power steering pump adjustment bolts and remove the belt.

3. Remove the timing belt.

4. Remove the tension pulley and spring.

5. Remove the water pump mounting bolts, the water pump and gasket. Clean the mounting surfaces of all gasket material.

6. To install, reverse the removal procedures. Torque the water pump to 17 ft. lbs. and the tension pulley to 30 ft. lbs.

SPRINT AND METRO

1. Disconnect the negative battery cable.

2. Drain the cooling system.

3. Remove the water pump belt and pulley.

4. Remove the crankshaft pulley, the timing belt outside cover, the timing belt and the tensioner.

5. Remove the mounting bolts and the water pump.

6. Clean the gasket mating surfaces.

7. To install, use a new gasket/sealer and reverse the removal procedures. Torque the water pump bolts to 7.5–9 ft. lbs. Adjust the water pump belt deflection to ¼–⅜ in. between the water pump and the crankshaft pulleys.

ELECTRIC COOLING FAN

Testing

NOVA AND PRIZM

1. Disconnect the electrical connector from the cooling fan.

2. Using an ammeter and jumper wires, connect the fan motor in series with the battery and ammeter. With the fan running, check the ammeter reading, it should be 3.4–5.0A; if not, replace the motor.

3. Reconnect the fan's electrical connector. Start the engine, allow it to reach temperatures above 194°F and confirm that the fan runs. If the fan doesn't run, replace the temperature switch.

SPECTRUM

1. Disconnect the electrical wiring connector from the electric cooling fan.

2. Using a 14 gauge wire, connect it between the fan and the positive terminal; the fan should run.

NOTE: If the fan does not run while connected to the electrical wiring connector, inspect for a defective coolant temperature switch or A/C relay (if equipped).

3. If the fan does not run when connected to the jumper wire, replace the fan assembly.

Removal and Installation

ALL VEHICLES

1. Disconnect the negative terminal from the battery.

2. Label and disconnect the electrical connector from the cooling fan motor.

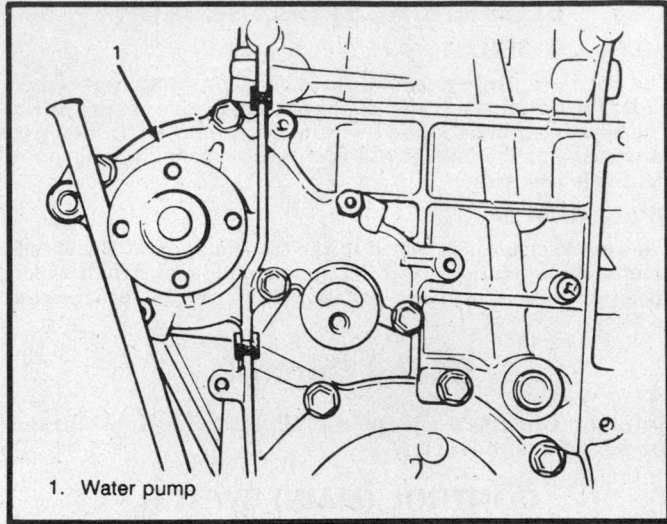

1. Water pump

Water pump mounting—Sprint and Metro

3. Remove the fan shroud-to-radiator frame bolts and the fan/shroud assembly from the vehicle.

4. Remove the fan blade-to-motor nut, fan blade and washer.

5. Remove the fan-to-shroud bolts and the fan motor from the shroud.

6. Test the fan motor and replace it (if necessary).

7. To install, reverse the removal procedures and check the fan operation.

RADIATOR FAN SWITCH

Testing

SPRINT AND METRO

1. Drain the cooling system and remove the thermo switch from the thermostat neck.

2. Connect an ohmmeter to the thermo switch.

3. Place the threads of the switch in water while heating the water gradually.

4. Check if there is continuity when the temperature of the water rises to 201°F–208°F. There should be no continuity when the temperature falls down to 192°F–199°F. Replace the switch if necessary.

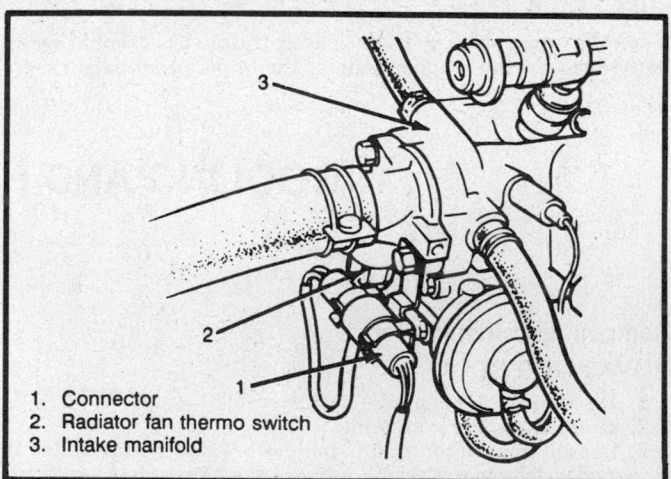

1. Connector
2. Radiator fan thermo switch
3. Intake manifold

Radiator fan thermo switch location—Sprint and Metro

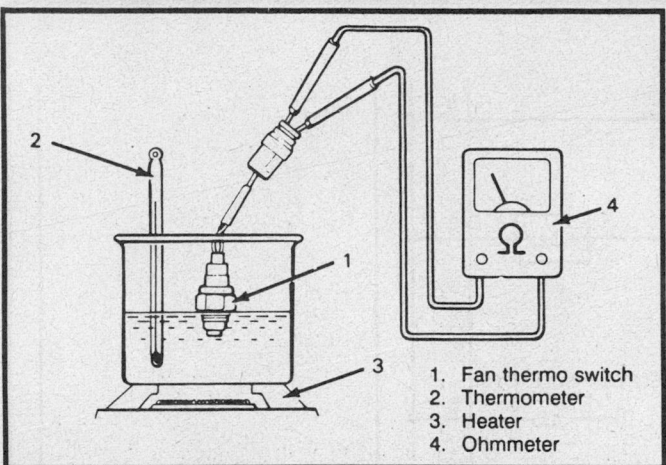

1. Fan thermo switch
2. Thermometer
3. Heater
4. Ohmmeter

Testing the radiator fan thermo switch—Sprint and Metro

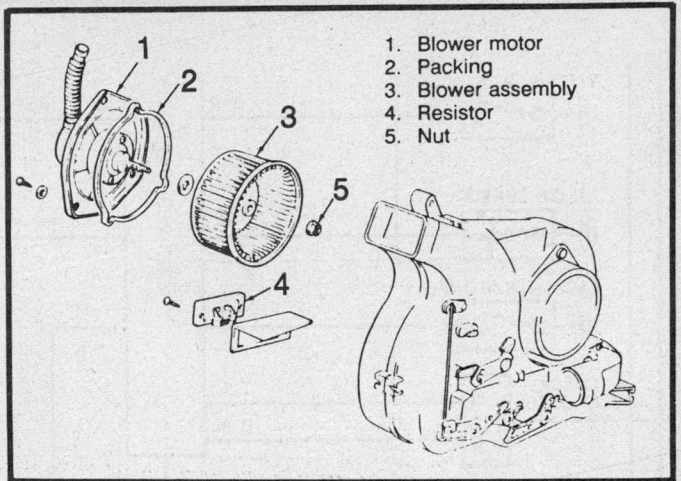

1. Blower motor
2. Packing
3. Blower assembly
4. Resistor
5. Nut

Blower motor mounting—Sprint and Metro

ELECTRIC FAN RELAYS

Testing

SPRINT AND METRO

NOTE: The radiator fan relay should be checked with the engine cold. This will prevent the fan from suddenly turning on while disconnecting or connecting the wiring.

To test the electric fan relay with the engine cold, disconnect the wiring to the temperature or pressure switch. Jump the two wires together and check that the fan is operating. If the fan operates, the relay is working.

Blower Motor

Removal and Installation

NOVA

The heater blower motor is located inside the vehicle, behind the glove box
1. Disconnect the negative battery cable. Remove the 3 heater assembly retainer-to-chassis screws.
2. Remove the glove box-to-chassis screws and the glove box.
3. Remove the duct-to-blower/heater assemblies screws and the duct; the duct is located between the blower and heater assemblies.
4. Disconnect the blower motor wiring connector and the air source selector control cable from the blower assembly case.
5. Remove the blower assembly-to-heater case nuts/bolt and blower assembly.
6. Separate the blower motor from the blower assembly.
7. To install, reverse the removal procedures and test the motor.

PRIZM

The blower motor is located underneath the instrument panel at the far right side of the vehicle. It is accessible from below the instrument panel.
1. Disconnect the negative battery cable.
2. Disconnect the rubber air duct between the motor and the heater assembly.
3. Disconnect the electrical connector from the motor.
4. Remove the 3 screws retaining the motor and remove the motor.
5. Installation is the reverse of removal.

SPECTRUM

1. Disconnect the negative battery cable. Disconnect the blower motor electrical connector at the motor case.
2. If equipped with A/C, remove the rubber hose from the blower case.
3. Rotate the blower motor case counterclockwise and remove the blower motor assembly.
4. To install, reverse the removal procedures.

SPRINT AND METRO

1. Disconnect the negative battery cable.
2. Disconnect the defroster hose on the steering column side.
3. Disconnect the blower motor electrical connector.
4. Remove the 3 mounting screws and the blower motor.
5. To install, reverse the removal procedures.

Heater Core

Refer to "Chilton's Auto Heating and Air Conditioning Manual" for additional coverage.

Removal and Installation

NOVA

1. Disconnect the negative battery cable. Drain the cooling system.
2. In the engine compartment, disconnect the heater hoses from the heater unit.
3. From inside the vehicle (under the dash), remove the lower heater unit case-to-heater case clips and remove the lower case.
4. Using a medium prybar, separate and remove the lower portion of the case from the heater case.
5. Remove the heater core from the heater case.
6. Inspect the heater hoses for cracking and deterioration, then, the heater core for leakage and corrosion; replace the items, if necessary.
7. To install, reverse the removal procedures. Refill the cooling system. Start the engine, allow it to reach normal operating temperatures and check for leaks. Turn the heater controls to **MAX HEAT** and check the heater operation.

PRIZM

The heater case and core are located directly behind the center console. The access the case and core, the entire console must be removed as well as most of the instrument panel assembly.
1. Disconnect the negative battery cable. Remove the steering wheel.
2. Remove the trim bezel from the instrument panel.

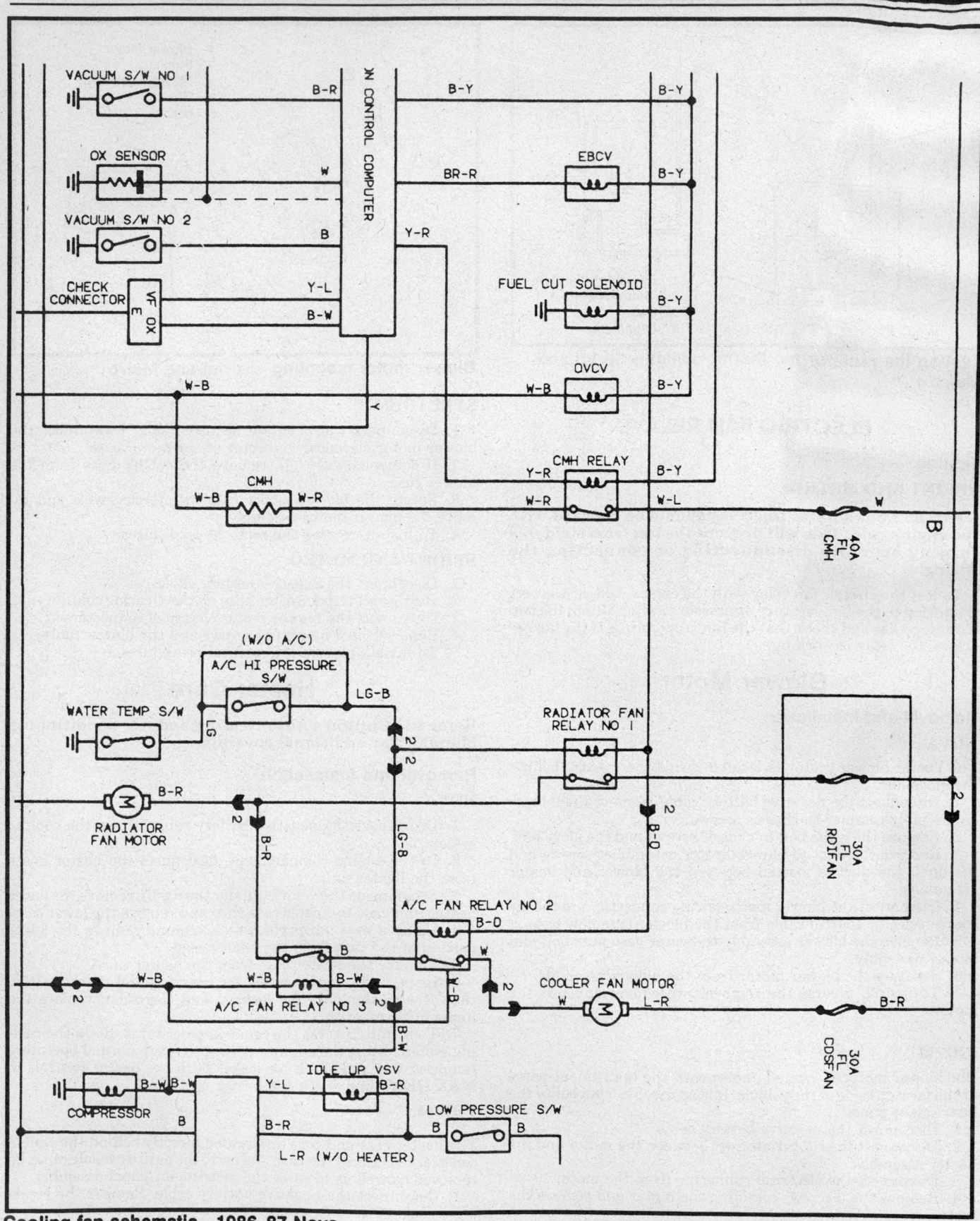

Cooling fan schematic—1986–87 Nova

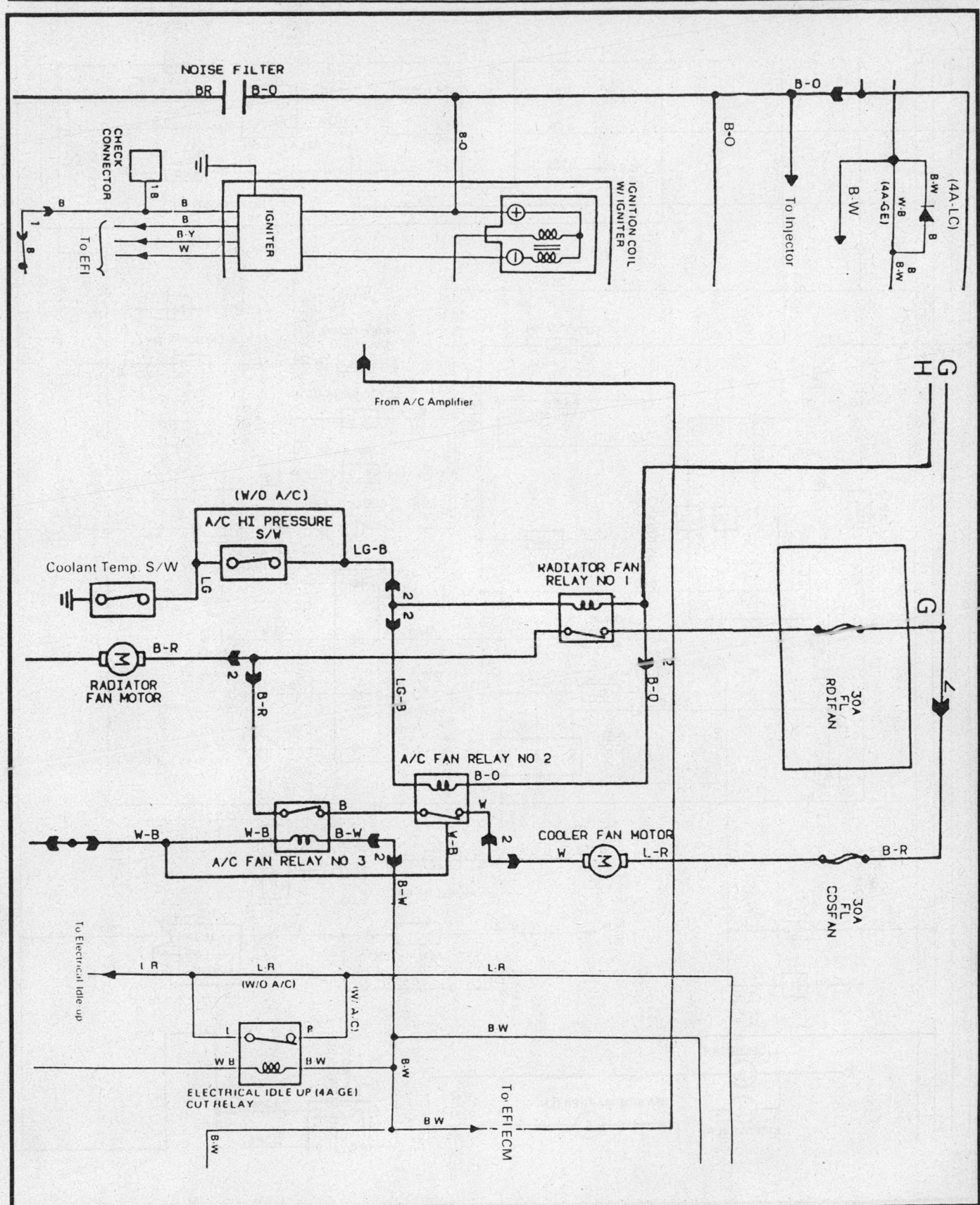

Cooling fan schematic—1988 Nova

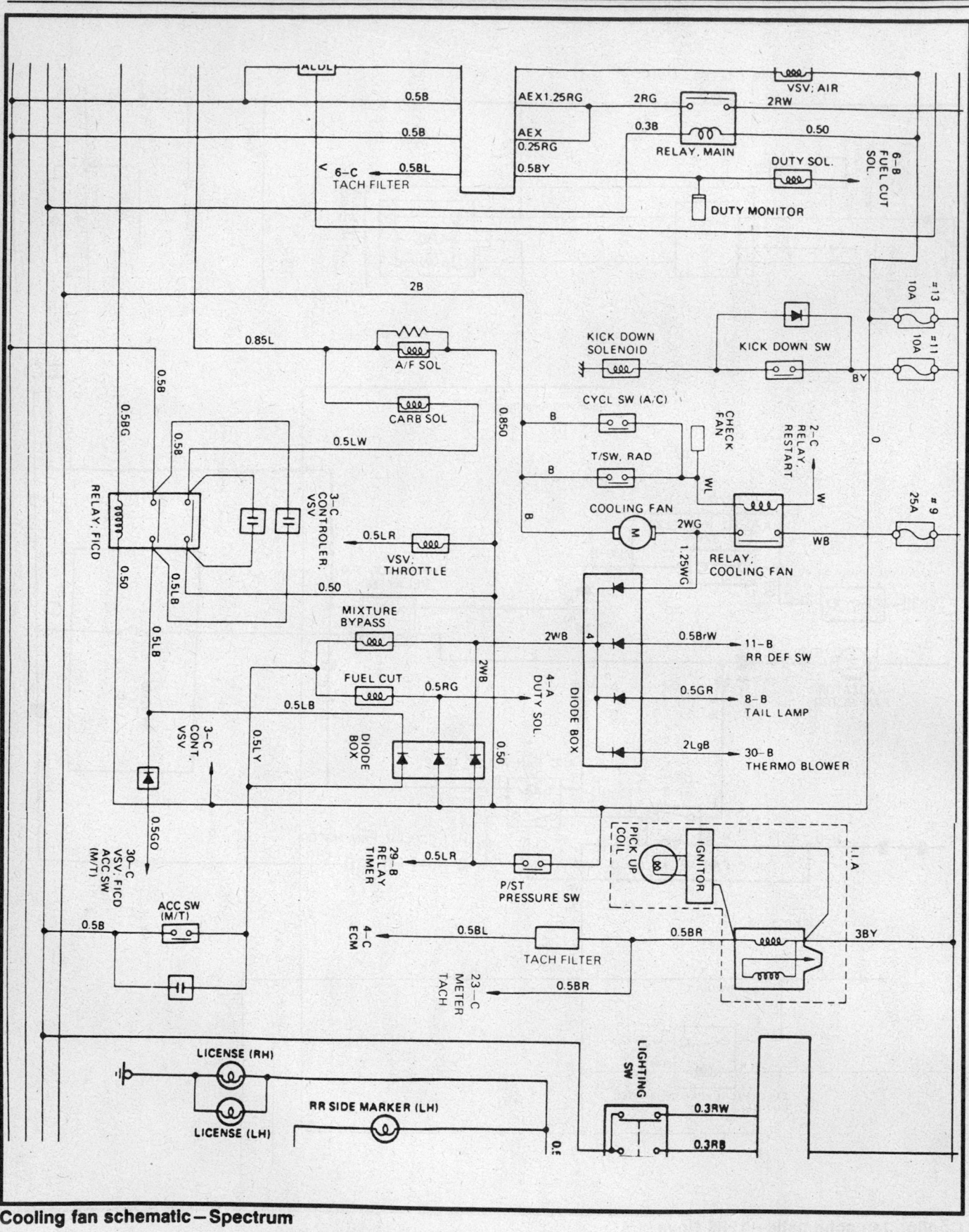

Cooling fan schematic—Spectrum

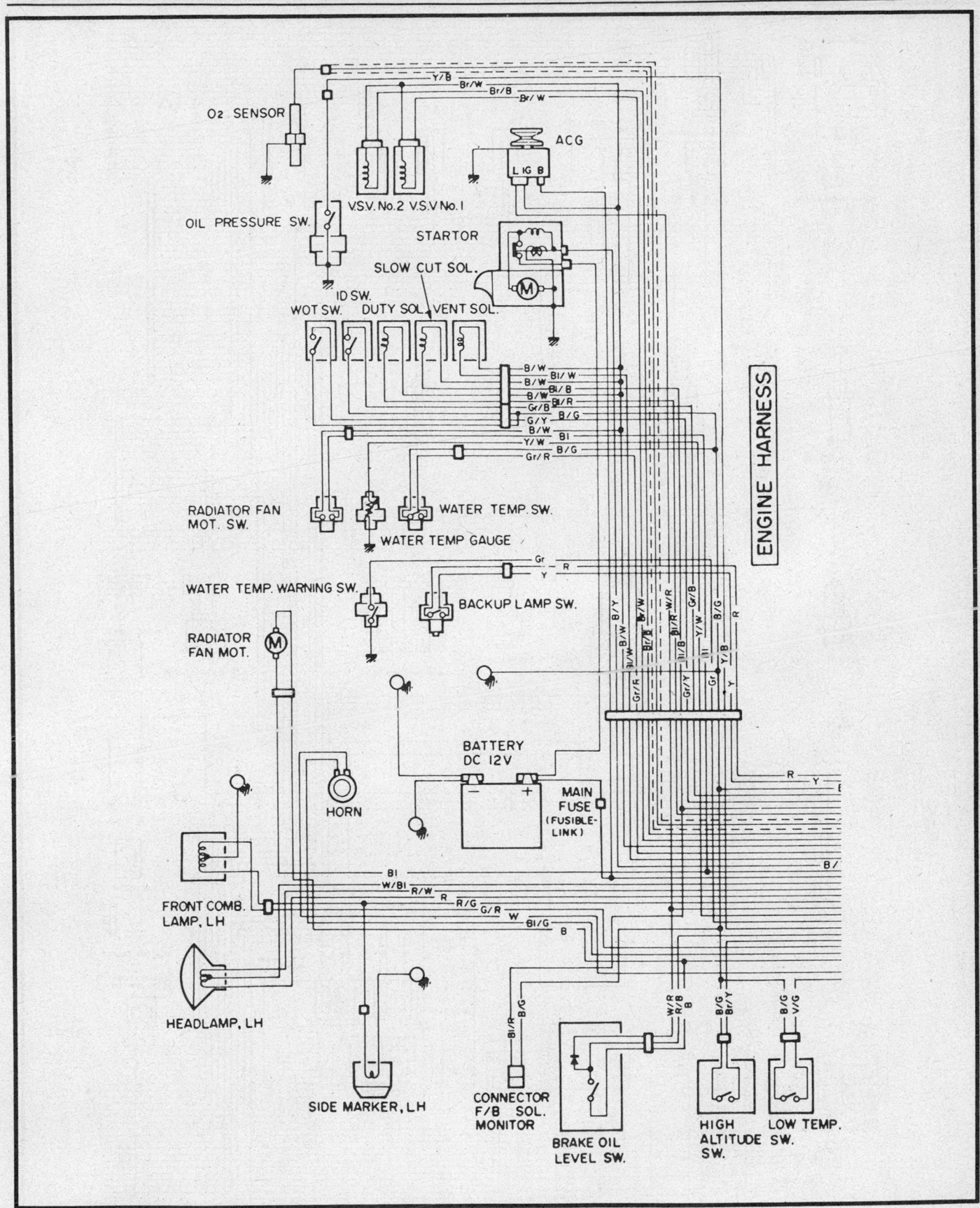

Cooling fan schematic—Sprint

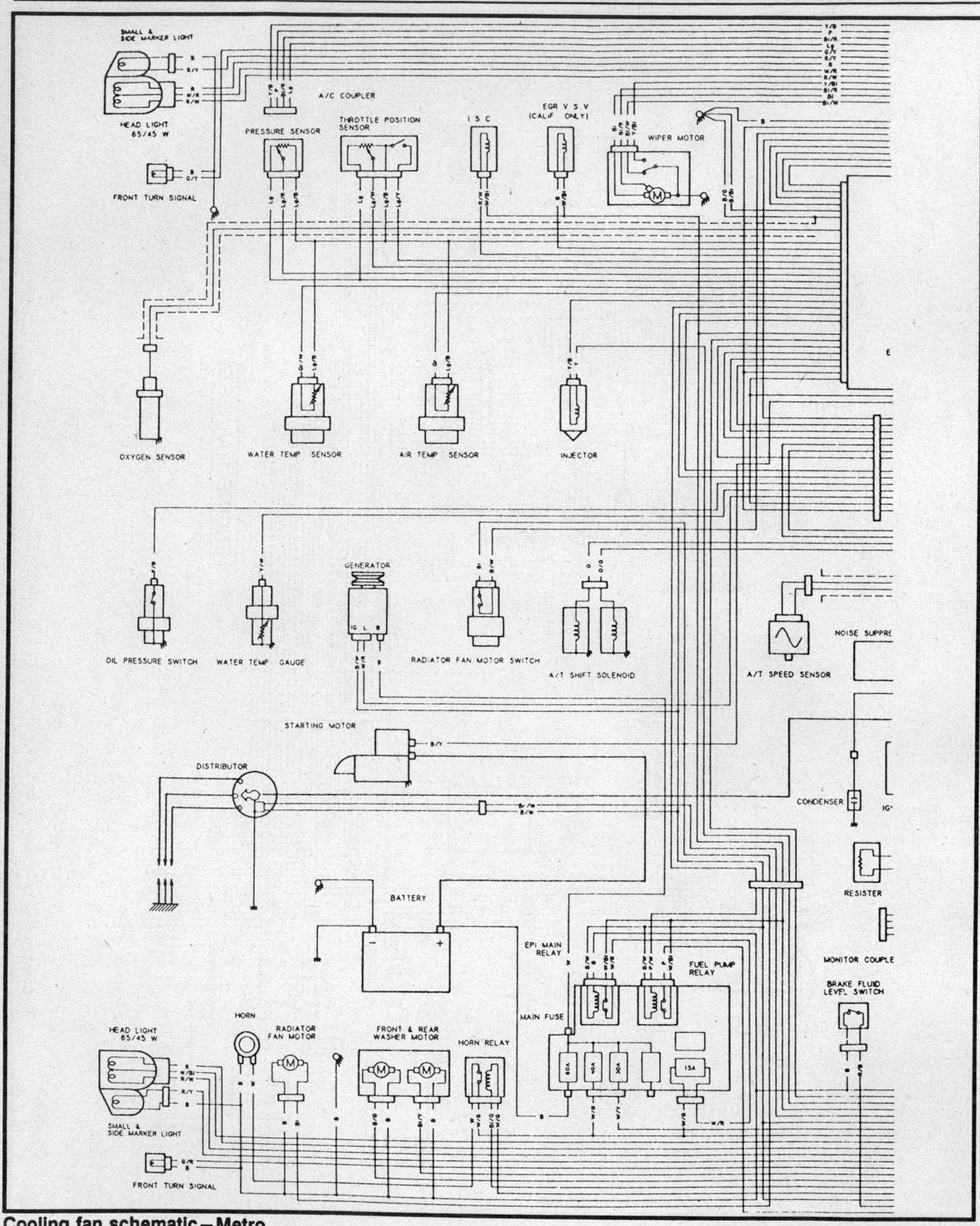

Cooling fan schematic—Metro

3. Remove the cup holder from the console.

4. Remove the radio.

5. Remove the instrument panel assembly, cluster assembly, center console and all console trim, lower dash trim, side window air deflectors, and all instrument panel wiring harnesses.

6. Drain the coolant from the cooling system.

7. Disconnect all cables and ducts from the heater case.

8. Disconnect the blower switch harness and the heater control assembly.

9. Disconnect the 2 center console support braces.

10. Remove all mounting bolts, nuts and clips from the heater and air distribution cases.

11. Remove the heater and air distribution cases.

12. Remove the screws and clips from the case, separate the case halves, and remove the core from the case.

13. Installation is the reverse of removal. Fill the cooling system.

SPECTRUM

1. Disconnect the negative battery cable. Disconnect the heater hoses in the engine compartment.

2. At the lower part of the heater unit case, remove the 6 retaining clips.

3. Using a small pry bar, pry open the lower part of the case and remove it.

4. Remove the core assembly insulator and the core assembly.

5. To install, reverse the removal procedures.

SPRINT AND METRO

1. Disconnect the negative battery cable. Drain the cooling system.

2. Disconnect the 2 water hoses from the radiator at the heater unit.

3. Remove the glove box from the upper instrument panel.

4. Remove the defroster hoses from the heater case.

5. Disconnect the electrical connectors from the blower motor and the heater resistor.

6. Disconnect the 3 control cables from the heater case side levers.

7. Pull out the center vent louver.

8. Disconnect both side vent ducts from the center duct vent.

9. Remove the center duct vent and the ashtray's upper plate.

10. Remove the instrument member stay and the heater assembly mounting nuts.

11. Loosen the three heater case top mounting bolts through the glove box opening.

12. Raise the dash panel and remove the heater control assembly.

13. Separate the heater case into 2 sections by removing the clips.

14. Pull the heater core from the heater unit.

15. To install, reverse the removal procedures. Refill the cooling system. Start the engine, bring it to normal operating temperature and check for leaks.

TEMPERATURE CONTROL/BLOWER SWITCH

Removal and Installation

NOVA AND PRIZM

1. Disconnect the negative terminal from the battery.

2. Remove the instrument panel center cluster assembly.

3. Pull the instrument cluster assembly out enough to disconnect the electrical connectors from the rear of the unit.

4. Remove the temperature control/blower switch from the vehicle.

5. To install, reverse the removal procedures. Check the system operation.

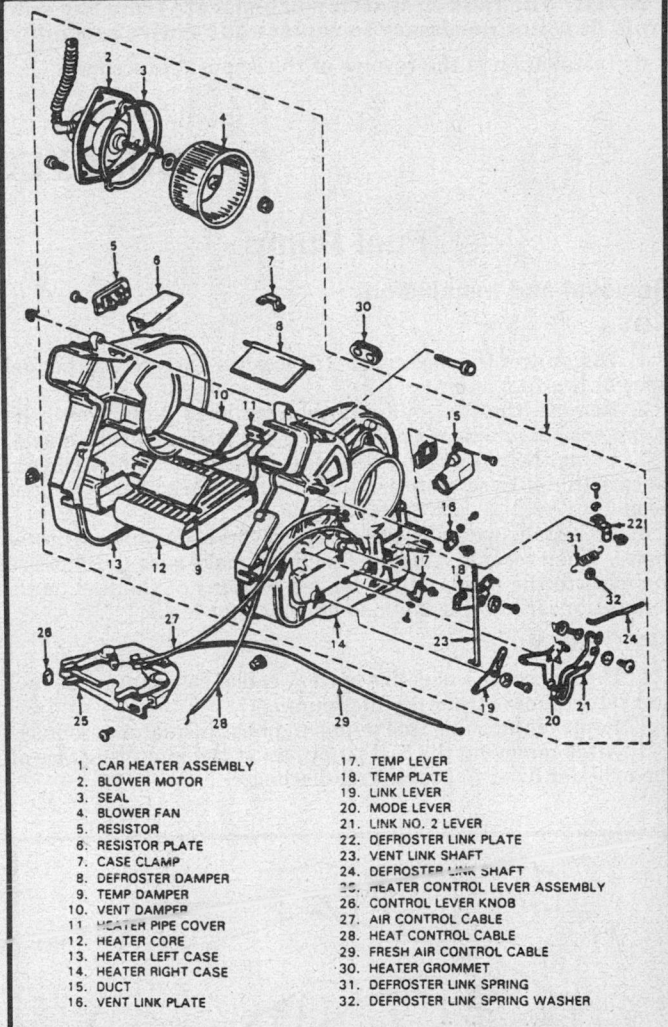

1. CAR HEATER ASSEMBLY	17. TEMP LEVER
2. BLOWER MOTOR	18. TEMP PLATE
3. SEAL	19. LINK LEVER
4. BLOWER FAN	20. MODE LEVER
5. RESISTOR	21. LINK NO. 2 LEVER
6. RESISTOR PLATE	22. DEFROSTER LINK PLATE
7. CASE CLAMP	23. VENT LINK SHAFT
8. DEFROSTER DAMPER	24. DEFROSTER LINK SHAFT
9. TEMP DAMPER	25. HEATER CONTROL LEVER ASSEMBLY
10. VENT DAMPER	26. CONTROL LEVER KNOB
11. HEATER PIPE COVER	27. AIR CONTROL CABLE
12. HEATER CORE	28. HEAT CONTROL CABLE
13. HEATER LEFT CASE	29. FRESH AIR CONTROL CABLE
14. HEATER RIGHT CASE	30. HEATER GROMMET
15. DUCT	31. DEFROSTER LINK SPRING
16. VENT LINK PLATE	32. DEFROSTER LINK SPRING WASHER

Exploded view of the heater assembly—Sprint and Metro

SPECTRUM

1. Disconnect the negative battery terminal from the battery.

2. Remove the control knobs from the control lever assembly.

3. Remove the control lever assembly lens. Disconnect the illumination bulb.

4. From the blower/heater assembly, disconnect the control cables.

5. Remove the control lever assembly-to-dash screws. Pull the assembly out and disconnect the electrical and control cable connections.

6. Remove the blower, the A/C and the heater switches.

7. To install, reverse the removal procedures. Adjust the control cables and check the operation.

SPRINT AND METRO

1. Disconnect the negative battery cable. Pull out the control lever knobs to remove.

2. Remove the trim panel from in front of the control levers.

3. Remove the upper glove box panel.

4. Remove the control assembly mounting screws and slide the controls out enough to disconnect the cables and wiring.

5. Replace the necessary components.

NOTE: The blower switch will separate from the controls. It is not necessary to replace the entire assembly.

6. Installation is the reverse of the removal procedure.

7. When installing, clamp the blower switch wire to the control assembly.

8. Make sure that the levers have full travel in both directions during installation. Adjust if necessary.

CARBURETED FUEL SYSTEM

Fuel Pump

Removal and Installation

NOVA

1. Disconnect the negative battery cable. Disconnect the fuel lines at the fuel pump.

2. Remove the fuel pump-to-cylinder head bolts, then, the pump, gasket and heat shield, noting the position of the shield.

3. Using the proper tool, clean the gasket mounting surfaces; be careful not to scratch the aluminum surface of the cylinder head.

4. To install, use a new gasket and reverse the removal procedures. When reconnecting the fuel lines, make sure the clips are installed to the inside of the bulged sections of the fuel pump connections. Start the engine and check for leaks.

SPECTRUM

1. Disconnect the negative battery cable. Disconnect the fuel and return hoses from the fuel pump.

2. Remove the bolts, fuel pump and heat insulator assembly.

3. After removing the fuel pump, cover the mounting face of the cylinder head to prevent oil discharge.

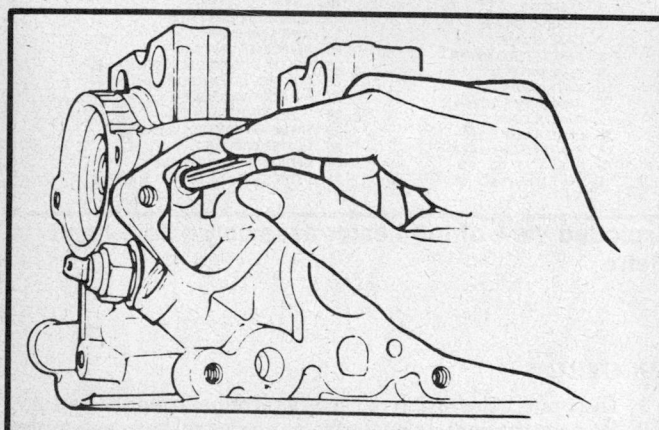

Installing the fuel pump push rod in the cylinder head—Sprint

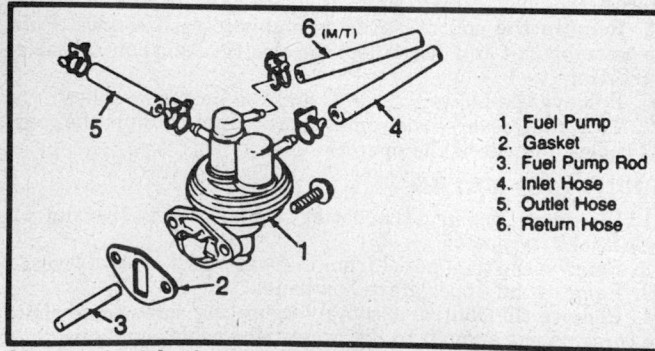

1. Fuel Pump
2. Gasket
3. Fuel Pump Rod
4. Inlet Hose
5. Outlet Hose
6. Return Hose

Mechanical fuel pump assembly—Sprint

4. To install, reverse the removal procedures. Replace the heat insulator assembly.

SPRINT

1. Remove and replace the fuel tank cap, this procedure releases the pressure within the fuel system.

2. Disconnect the negative battery cable.

3. Remove the air cleaner from the carburetor.

4. Remove the fuel inlet, outlet and return hoses from the fuel pump.

5. Remove the fuel pump mounting bolts, the pump and the pump rod from the cylinder head.

6. To install, lubricate the pump rod, use a new gasket and reverse the removal procedures.

Carburetor

Removal and Installation

NOVA

1. Disconnect the negative battery cable. To remove the air cleaner, perform the following procedures.

   a. Disconnect the air intake hose.

   b. Label and disconnect the emission control hoses from the air cleaner.

   c. Remove the wing nut, mounting bolts and the air cleaner from the carburetor.

2. Disconnect the accelerator cable from the carburetor. If equipped with an automatic transaxle, disconnect the transaxle throttle linkage from the carburetor.

3. Disconnect the wiring connector form the carburetor solenoid valve(s).

4. Label and disconnect the emission control hoses from the carburetor. Disconnect and drain the fuel inlet hose. Disconnect the evaporative emissions canister hose.

5. Remove the cold mixture heater wire clamp and the EGR vacuum control bracket.

6. Remove the carburetor-to-intake manifold nuts, the carburetor and gasket from the intake manifold. Using a clean shop, seal off the intake manifold opening.

7. Using the proper tool, clean the gasket mounting surfaces of the carburetor and manifold.

8. To install, use a new gasket and reverse the removal procedures. Install and adjust the throttle and transaxle linkages to the carburetor. Start the engine and check for fuel leaks.

SPECTRUM

1. Disconnect the negative battery terminal from the battery.

2. Remove the air cleaner.

3. Disconnect the harness connector and hoses.

4. Remove the accelerator cable from the carburetor.

5. Remove the bolts securing the carburetor to the intake manifold. Remove the carburetor and place a cover over the intake manifold.

6. To install, reverse the removal procedures and torque carburetor fixing bolts to 7.2 ft. lbs. then start the engine and check for leaks.

SPRINT

1. Remove and replace the fuel tank cap, this procedure releases the pressure within the fuel system.

2. Disconnect the negative battery cable.

3. Disconnect the warm air, the cold air, the second air, the vacuum and the EGR modulator hoses from the air cleaner case.

4. Remove the air cleaner case from the carburetor.

5. Disconnect the accelerator cable and the electrical wiring from the carburetor.

6. Remove the emission control and the fuel hoses from the carburetor.

7. Disconnect the No. 1 and No. 2 choke hoses from the carburetor.

8. Remove the mounting bolts and the carburetor from the intake manifold.

9. To install, use new gaskets and reverse the removal procedures. Torque the carburetor mounting bolts to 18 ft. lbs.

IDLE SPEED

Adjustment

NOVA

Except Twincam Engine

1. Turn off all of the accessories, firmly set the parking brake and position the transaxle in **N**.

2. Check and/or adjust the ignition timing.

3. Start the engine and allow it to reach normal operating temperatures; make sure the choke is in the wide open position.

4. Inspect the fuel level sight glass on the carburetor to make sure the fuel is at the correct level.

5. At the distributor, locate the service engine connector; remove the rubber cap from it. Using a tachometer, connect the positive terminal to the service connector.

NOTE: When using a tachometer, consult the manufacturer's information to be sure it is compatible with the system.

6. Adjust the idle speed screw to 650 rpm (manual transaxles), 750 rpm (automatic transaxles).

SPECTRUM

Non-Turbocharged Engine

1. Set the parking brake and block the wheels.

2. Place the manual transmission in **N** or the automatic transaxle in **P**. Check the float level. Establish a normal operating temperature and make sure that the choke plate is open.

3. Turn off all of the accessories and wait until the cooling fan is not operating.

4. If equipped with power steering, place the wheels in the straight forward position. Remove the air filter.

5. Disconnect and plug the distributor vacuum line, canister purge line, EGR vacuum line and ITC valve vacuum line.

6. Connect a tachometer to the coil tachometer connector and a timing light to the No. 1 spark plug wire. Check the timing and idle speed.

7. If the idle speed needs adjusting, turn the idle speed adjusting screw.

8. If equipped with A/C, adjust the system to **MAX/COLD** and place the blower on **HIGH** position. Set the fast idle speed by turning the adjust bolt of the Fast Idle Control Diaphragm to 850 rpm (automatic transaxle) or 980 rpm (manual transaxle).

9. When adjustment is completed, turn the engine off, remove the test equipment, install the air filter and vacuum lines.

SPRINT AND METRO

Check and/or adjust the accelerator cable free-play, ignition timing, valve lash and the emission control wiring and hoses. Make sure that the headlights, heater fan, engine cooling fan and any other electrical equipment is turned **OFF**. If any current drawing system is operating, the idle up system will operate and cause the idle speed to be higher than normal.

1. Connect a tachometer to the primary negative terminal of the ignition coil and refer to the underhood sticker.

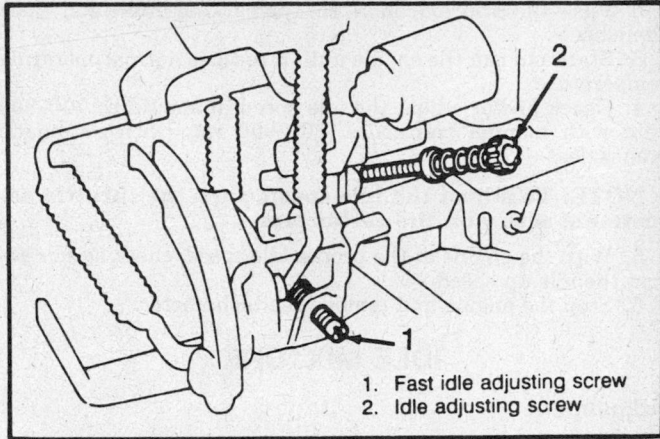

1. Fast idle adjusting screw
2. Idle adjusting screw

View of the carburetor's idle and fast idle adjusting screws—Nova

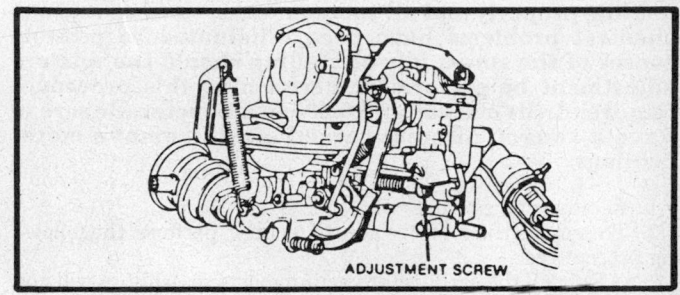

ADJUSTMENT SCREW

Idle speed adjustment screw location—Spectrum

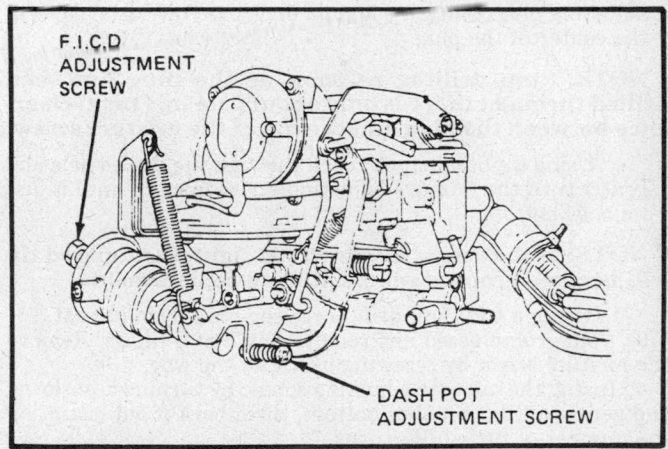

F.I.C.D ADJUSTMENT SCREW

DASH POT ADJUSTMENT SCREW

Fast idle control device adjustment screw location—Spectrum

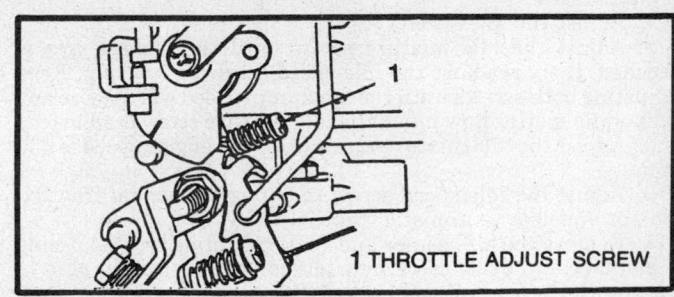

1 THROTTLE ADJUST SCREW

Idle speed adjustment screw—Sprint

2. Place the transaxle in **N**, set the parking brake and block the wheels.

3. Start and run the engine until it reaches normal operating temperature.

4. Check and/or adjust the idle speed, it should be 700–800 rpm with manual transaxles, 800–900 rpm with automatic transaxles.

NOTE: To adjust the idle speed, turn the throttle adjustment screw on the carburetor.

5. With the engine at the proper idle speed, check and/or adjust the idle up speed.

6. Stop the engine and remove the tachometer.

IDLE MIXTURE

Adjustment

NOVA

NOTE: Idle mixture does not require adjustment as a matter of routine maintenance. Only if the engine will not idle properly and all vacuum leaks, tune-up and mechanical problems have been eliminated as possible causes of the rough idle or stalling should the mixture adjustment be performed. Performing this procedure requires drills of 0.256 and 0.295 in. diameter. Be sure to have a source of compressed air to remove metal drillings.

1. Remove the carburetor.

2. To remove the mixture adjusting plug, perform the following procedures:

   a. Plug all the carburetor vacuum ports so drillings will not be able to enter them.

   b. Using a center punch, mark the center of the mixture adjusting plug. Using a 0.256 in. drill, carefully drill a hole in the center of the plug.

NOTE: Stop drilling as soon as the plug has been drilled through; there is only about 0.04 in. (1mm) clearance between the plug and the top of the mixture screw.

   c. Using a suitable tool, reach through the drilled hole and gently turn the mixture adjusting screw inward, until it just touches bottom.

NOTE: If the screw is turned too tight, the tapered tip will become grooved, necessitating replacement.

   d. Using a 0.295 in. drill, force the plug from its seat.

3. Using compressed air, remove any metal filings. Remove the mixture screw by screwing it out all the way.

4. Install the mixture adjusting screw, by turning it in slowly and gently until it touches bottom, then, back it out (counting the number of turns) 3¼ turns.

5. Reinstall the carburetor, then, reconnect the vacuum hoses and air cleaner.

6. Start the engine and allow it to reach normal operating temperatures.

7. Adjust the idle speed.

8. Adjust the idle mixture screw until the highest rpm is reached, then, readjust the idle speed screw to 700 rpm. Keep adjusting both screws until the maximum speed will not rise any higher, no matter how much the idle mixture screw is adjusted.

9. Adjust the idle mixture screw until the engine speed is 650 rpm.

10. Adjust the idle speed screw to 650 rpm (manual transaxles), or 750 rpm (automatic transaxles).

11. Remove the air cleaner and EGR mounting bracket. Using a hammer and drift, tap a new idle mixture adjusting plug in place with the tapered end inward. Reinstall the air cleaner and EGR vacuum modulator bracket.

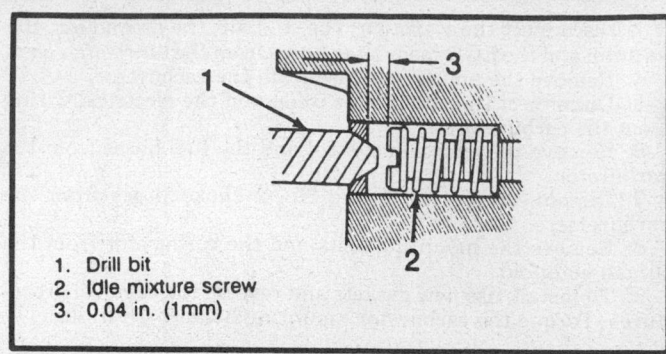

1. Drill bit
2. Idle mixture screw
3. 0.04 in. (1mm)

Drilling the mixture adjusting screw plug from the carburetor base—Nova

SPECTRUM

NOTE: The idle mixture screw is adjusted and sealed at the factory and no service adjustment is required. However, if the necessity of adjustment arises for some reason, adjustment of the idle mxture screw is a possible by removing the plug but it must be replugged again after adjustment is completed.

1. Remove the carburetor from the engine.

2. Using a center punch, make a punch mark on the idle mixture sealing plug. Drill a hole through the plug, insert a threaded screw and pull the plug from the throttle body. The width of the plug is about 0.39 in. (10 mm).

NOTE: If the idle mixture screw is damaged from the drilling process, replace the screw.

3. Lightly seat the idle mixture screw, then back out 3 turns (manual transaxle) or 2 turns (automatic transaxle). Do not overtighten the idle mixture screw.

4. Reinstall the carburetor and the air cleaner.

5. Adjust the idle speed.

6. Using a dwell meter, connect the positive lead to the duty monitor and the negative lead to ground. Place the meter dial on the 4 cylinder scale. Turn the idle mixture screw until the dwell meter reads 45 degrees (4 cylinder scale).

7. Turn A/C on **MAX/COLD** and blower on **HIGH** then adjust the bolt on the FICD and set the fast idle to 850 rpm (MT) or 980 (AT), if so equipped then stop the engine and remove the test equipment.

8. Drive a new idle mixture plug into the throttle body, flush with the throttle body apply Locktite No.262 or its equivalent to the plug.

9. Recheck all adjustments and road test.

SPRINT AND METRO

The carburetor is adjusted at the factory and no further adjustment should be necessary. However, if the engine performance

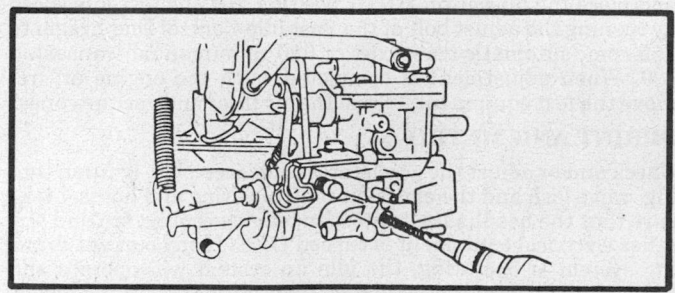

Drilling the mixture adjusting screw plug from the carburetor base—Spectrum

is poor, the emission test fails, or the carburetor has been replaced or overhauled, an idle mixture adjustment is necessary. Before adjusting the idle mixture, check the timing/idle speed and the valve lash. Make sure that all electrical accessories are turned **OFF**.

1. Remove the carburetor from the intake manifold.
2. Using an $^{11}/_{64}$ in. bit, drill through the idle mixture screw housing, in line with the retaining pin. Use a punch to drive the pin from the housing.
3. Install the carburetor to the intake manifold by reversing the removal procedures.
4. Place the transaxle in **N**, set the parking brake and block the wheels.
5. Start the engine and bring it to normal operating temperatures.
6. Disconnect the duty cycle check connector, located near the water reservoir tank. Connect the positive terminal of a dwell meter to the blue/red wire and the negative terminal to the black/green wire.
7. Set the dwell meter to the 6 cylinder position, make sure that the indicator moves.
8. Check and/or adjust the idle speed.

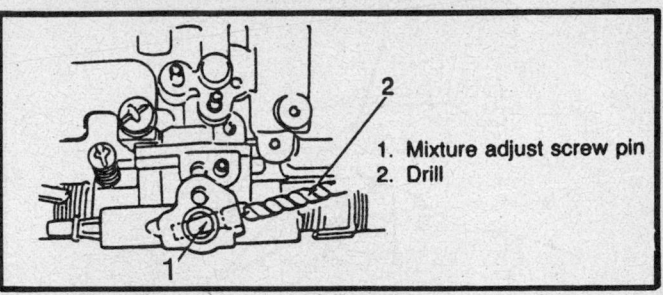

1. Mixture adjust screw pin
2. Drill

Removing the carburetor idle mixture pin—Sprint

9. Operate the engine at idle speed and adjust the idle mixture screw, allow the engine to stabilize between adjustments. Adjust the dwell to 21–27 degrees; recheck the idle speed and adjust, if necessary.
10. After completing the adjustment, stop the engine, disconnect the dwell meter and connect the duty cycle check connector to the coupler.
11. Install a new idle mixture adjust screw pin in the throttle housing, drive it in place.

FUEL INJECTION SYSTEM

Refer to "Chilton's Electronic Engine Controls Manual" for additional coverage.

IDLE SPEED

ADJUSTMENT

NOVA AND PRIZM

1. Make sure the ignition timing is correct.
2. Using a jumper wire, connect it to the check engine connector located near the wiper motor.
3. Start the engine, then, check and/or adjust the idle speed; it should be 800 rpm.
4. When the adjustment is correct, remove the jumper wire from the check engine connector and recheck the timing marks.

SPECTRUM

1. Set the parking brake.
2. Block the front wheels.
3. Place the select lever in **N**.
4. Make the idling speed adjustment with the engine at normal operating temperature, with **A/C OFF** and front wheels facing straight ahead.

NOTE: All electrical equipment (lights, rear defogger, heater, etc.) should be turned off.

5. Make sure check engine light is not on.
6. Ground test terminal (ALDL connector).
7. Increase engine speed over 2000 rpm to reset the position of idle air control valve.
8. Set idle adjust screw to 950 rpm.
9. Remove test terminal ground and clear ECM trouble code.

SPRINT

1. With a tachometer attached, run the engine until it reaches normal operating temperature.
2. Turn off all electrical loads such as lights, A/C etc.
3. Turn the idle speed adjusting screw until the idle speed is at 700–800 rpm.

FUEL SYSTEM PRESSURE RELIEF

Procedure

NOVA AND PRIZM

Twincam Engine

NOTE: Make sure the engine is cold before disconnecting any portion of the fuel system.

1. Disconnect the negative battery cable.
2. Using a shop rag, wrap it around the fuel line fitting.
3. Open the fuel line and absorb any excess fuel remaining in the line.
4. When replacing the be sure to install a new O-ring.

SPECTRUM

1. Remove the fuel pump fuse from the fuse block or disconnect the harness connector at the tank.
2. Start the engine. It should run and then stall when the fuel in the lines is exhausted. When the engine stops, crank the starter for about 3 seconds to make sure all pressure in the fuel lines is released.

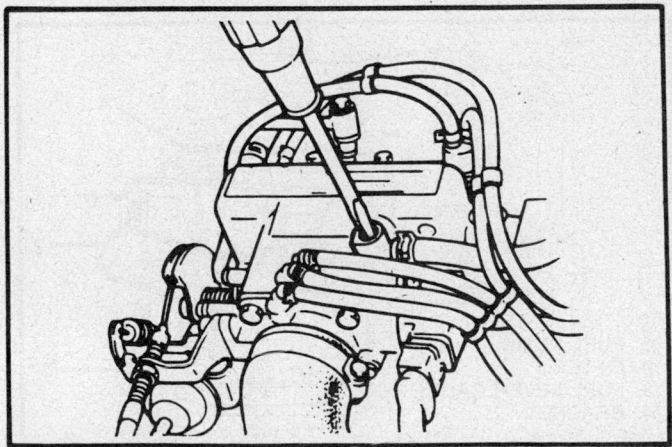

Idle speed adjustment screw—Sprint

1. FUEL PUMP RELAY OR MAIN RELAY
2. FUEL PUMP RELAY LEAD WIRE
   (PINK, PINK/WHITE, WHITE/BLUE, WHITE/BLUE)
3. RIGHT FRONT SUSPENSION STRUT

Fuel pump relay wire identification—Sprint and Metro

3. Disconnect the negative battery cable.
4. Install the fuel pump fuse after repair is made and reconnect the battery cable.

SPRINT AND METRO

1. Release the fuel vapor pressure in the fuel tank by removing the fuel tank cap then reinstalling it.
2. With the engine running, remove the connector of the fuel pump relay and wait until the engine stops itself.

NOTE: The main relay and fuel pump relay are identical. Which one to connect to the fuel lead wire is not specified. Identify the fuel pump relay by the color of the lead wire. The fuel pump relay lead wire is pink, pink/white, white/blue, white/blue.

3. Once the engine is stopped, crank it a few times with the starter for about 3 seconds each time (with the relay connector disconnected).
4. If the fuel pressure can't be released in the above manner because the engine failed to run in Step 2, disconnect the negative battery cable, cover the union bolt of the high fuel pressure line with an appropriate rag and loosen the union bolt slowly to release the fuel pressure gradually.

Fuel Pump

Removal and Installation
NOVA AND PRIZM

1. Release the fuel system pressure.
2. Disconnect the negative terminal from the battery.
3. Raise and support the vehicle safely. Drain the fuel from the fuel tank. Remove the fuel tank-to-chassis straps and lower the tank slightly. Disconnect the electrical connector and the fuel line from the fuel tube.
4. Remove the fuel pump bracket-to-fuel tank bolts and the bracket.
5. Remove the electrical connectors from the fuel pump, the fuel pump from the bracket and the fuel hose.
6. From the bottom of the fuel pump, remove the rubber cushion, the clip and pull out the filter.
7. To install, use a new bracket-to-fuel tank gasket and reverse the removal procedures. Refill the fuel tank.

SPECTRUM

1. Relieve fuel pressure then disconnect negative battery cable.

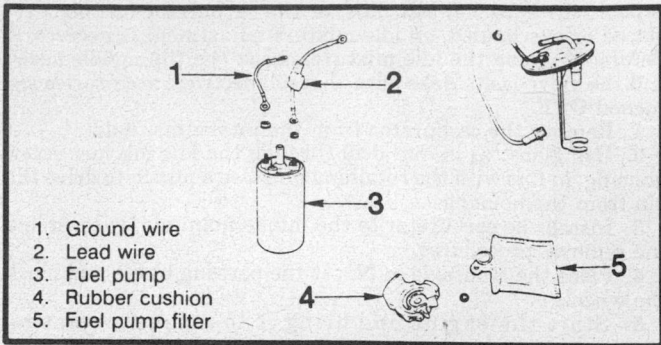

1. Ground wire
2. Lead wire
3. Fuel pump
4. Rubber cushion
5. Fuel pump filter

Electric fuel pump components—Spectrum

2. Raise and support the vehicle safely. Drain fuel tank.
3. Remove all gas line hose connections and fuel pump ground wire.
4. Remove filler neck hose and clamp.
5. Remove breather hose and clamp.
6. Disconnect fuel tank hose to evaporator pipe.
7. Remove fuel tank mounting bolts and lower tank from vehicle. At this point remove hose from pump to fuel fiter.
8. Remove fuel pump bracket plate and fuel pump as an assembly.
9. Remove pump bracket, rubber cushion and fuel pump filter.
10. To install, reverse the removal procedures. Be careful, to push the lower side of the fuel pump, together with the rubber cushion, into the fuel pump bracket.

SPRINT AND METRO

NOTE: The fuel tank must be lowered to gain access to the fuel pump which is located in the fuel tank.

1. Relieve the fuel system pressure.
2. Disconnect the negative battery cable.
3. Remove the rear seat cushion and disconnect the fuel gauge and fuel pump lead wires.
4. Raise and support the vehicle safely.
5. Drain the fuel tank by pumping or siphoning the fuel out through the fuel feed line (tank to fuel filter line).
6. Remove the tank from the vehicle.
7. Remove the fuel pump and fuel level gauge bracket from the fuel tank.
8. Remove the fuel pump from the fuel tank.
9. Installation is the reverse of removal. Clean the fuel filter in the tank.

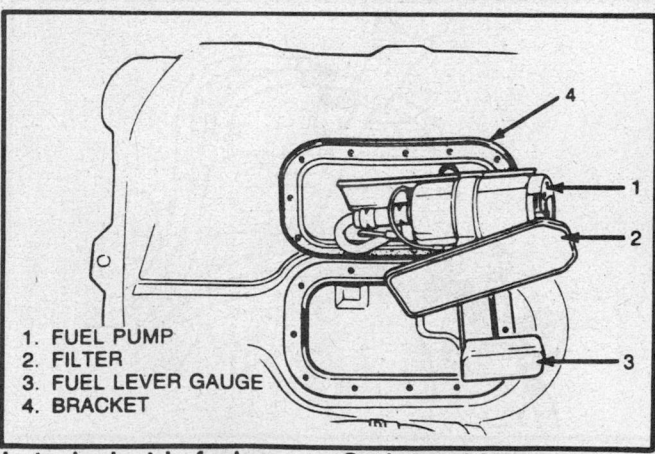

1. FUEL PUMP
2. FILTER
3. FUEL LEVER GAUGE
4. BRACKET

In tank electric fuel pump—Sprint and Metro

FUEL INJECTOR

Removal and Installation

NOVA AND PRIZM

1. Disconnect the negative terminal from the battery. Relieve the pressure in the fuel system.
2. Disconnect the electrical connectors from the fuel injectors.
3. Remove the fuel injector-to-engine bolts and pull the fuel injector assembly from the block.
4. Separate the fuel injector from the fuel line and discard the O-rings.
5. To install, use new O-rings (lubricate the O-rings with engine oil or gasoline) and reverse the removal procedures.
6. Turn the ignition switch **ON** and check for fuel leaks. Start the engine and check the operation.

SPRINT

1. Relieve the fuel system pressure.
2. Disconnect the negative battery cable.
3. Remove the intake air hose between the throttle body and intercooler.
4. Disconnect the accelerator cable.
5. Disconnect the PCV and fuel return hoses from the delivery pipe.
6. Disconnect the throttle position sensor wiring coupler.
7. Disconnect the fuel injector wiring harness.
8. Remove the cold start valve from the delivery pipe.
9. Disconnect the fuel pressure regulator vacuum hose.
10. Disconnect the fuel feed hose from the delivery pipe.
11. Remove the fuel pressure regulator from the delivery pipe.
12. Remove the delivery pipe from the engine with the fuel injectors attached.
13. Remove the fuel injector(s) from the delivery pipe.
14. To install, replace the O-ring on any injector removed from the delivery pipe.
15. Lightly coat the new O-ring with engine oil when installing.

NOTE: After the injectors are installed in the fuel delivery pipe, make sure that they rotate freely in the pipe before installation.

16. Check the insulator in the engine and replace, if necessary.
17. Install the delivery pipe and injector assembly in the engine.
18. Continue the installation in the reverse of the removal procedure.
19. When finished, run the engine and check for fuel leaks.

METRO

1. Relieve the fuel system pressure.
2. Disconnect the negative battery cable.
3. Remove the air cleaner assembly.
4. Remove the injector cover and upper insulator.
5. Disconnect the electrical connector and remove the injector.

To install:

6. Apply a thin coat of transmission fluid or gasoline to the new upper and lower O-rings and install them on the injectors.
7. Install a new lower injector insulator into the injector cavity.
8. Push the injector straight into the fuel injection cavity. Do not twist.
9. Install a new upper insulator and the injection cover.

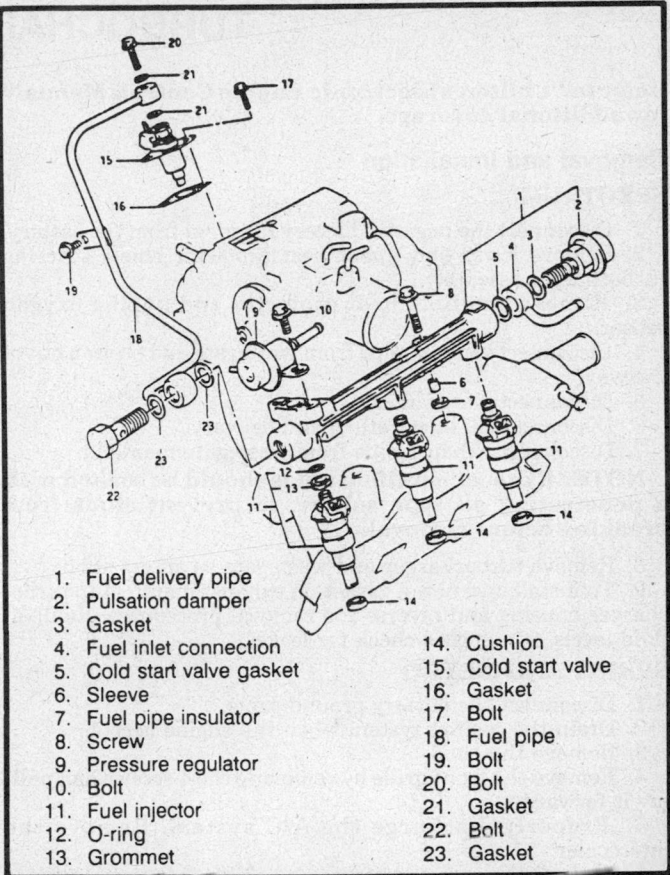

1. Fuel delivery pipe
2. Pulsation damper
3. Gasket
4. Fuel inlet connection
5. Cold start valve gasket
6. Sleeve
7. Fuel pipe insulator
8. Screw
9. Pressure regulator
10. Bolt
11. Fuel injector
12. O-ring
13. Grommet
14. Cushion
15. Cold start valve
16. Gasket
17. Bolt
18. Fuel pipe
19. Bolt
20. Bolt
21. Gasket
22. Bolt
23. Gasket

Fuel rail and injector mounting, turbocharged engine—Sprint

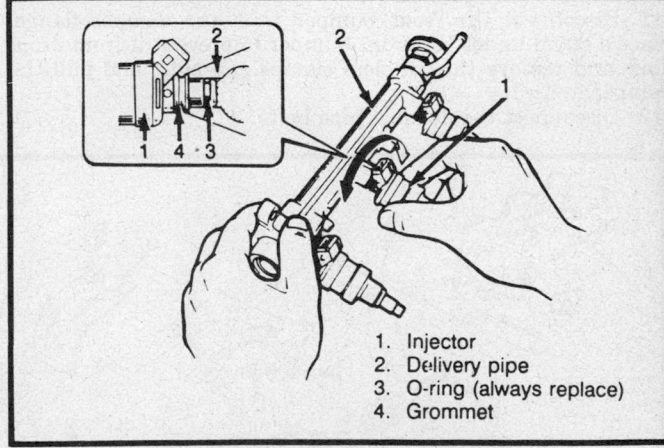

1. Injector
2. Delivery pipe
3. O-ring (always replace)
4. Grommet

Injector must rotate freely in the fuel rail, turbocharged engine—Sprint

10. Install the injector cover screws to 31 in. lbs.
11. Connect the electrical connector to the injector, facing it lug side upward on clamp subwire securely.
12. Connect the negative battery cable.

TURBOCHARGER SYSTEM

Refer to "Chilton's Electronic Engine Controls Manual" for additional coverage.

Removal and Installation

SPECTRUM

1. Disconnect the negative battery terminal from the battery.
2. Remove lower and upper heat protector shield covering turbocharger assembly.
3. Remove manifold heat protecter and unplug oxygen sensor.
4. Disconnect vacuum pipe from wastegate and positon out of the way.
5. Disconnect water lines.
6. Disconnect oil lines return and delivery.
7. Disconnect exhaust pipe from wastegate manifold.

NOTE: Exhaust manifold studs should be soaked with a penetrating oil type solvent to prevent studs from breaking before removal.

8. Remove turbocharger and wastegate as an assembly.
9. To install, use new a gasket on exhaust manifold to turbocharger housing and reverse the removal procedures. Refill all fluid levels, run engine check for leaks.

SPRINT AND METRO

1. Disconnect the battery ground cable.
2. Drain the cooling system when the engine is cool.
3. Remove the hood.
4. Remove the front grille by removing the 4 screws and pulling it forward.
5. Properly discharge the A/C system. Remove the intercooler.
6. Remove the radiator hoses.
7. Disconnect the radiator fan motor coupler.
8. Disconnect the front upper member.
9. Remove the A/C condensor, if so equipped.
10. Remove the radiator.
11. Disconnect the front bumper from the damper flange. Place a stand under the front bumper to prevent it from dropping, and remove the couplers clamps and bolts and pull the bumper foward.
12. Disconnect the exhaust pipe bolts.

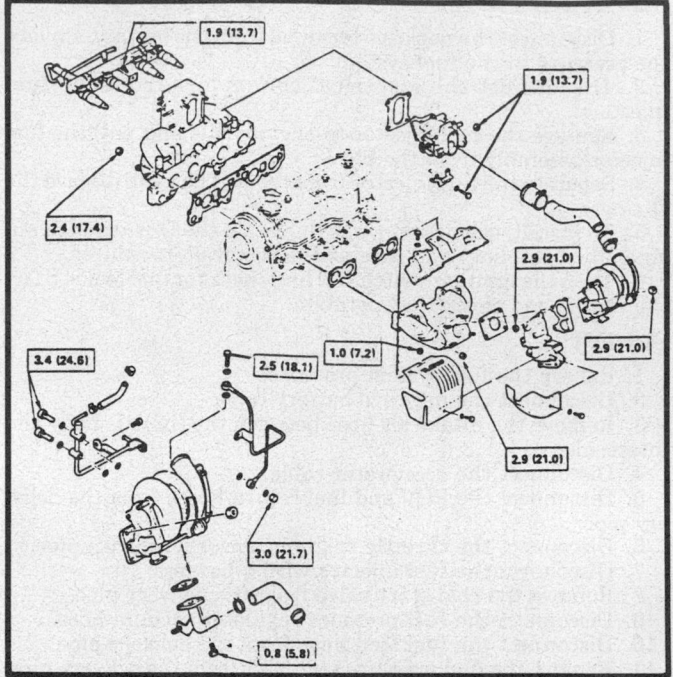

Turbocharger assembly torque specifications, Kg. M (ft. lbs.) – Spectrum

13. Remove the A/C compressor, if so equipped.
14. Remove the turbocharger cover.
15. Unclamp the oxygen sensor wire.
16. Remove the turbocharger side cover.
17. Lower the exhaust pipe support bracket bolt.
18. Remove the upper exhaust pipe together with the lower exhaust pipe.
19. Disconnect the air outlet pipe.
20. Disconnect the air inlet hose clamp bolt on the cylinder head.

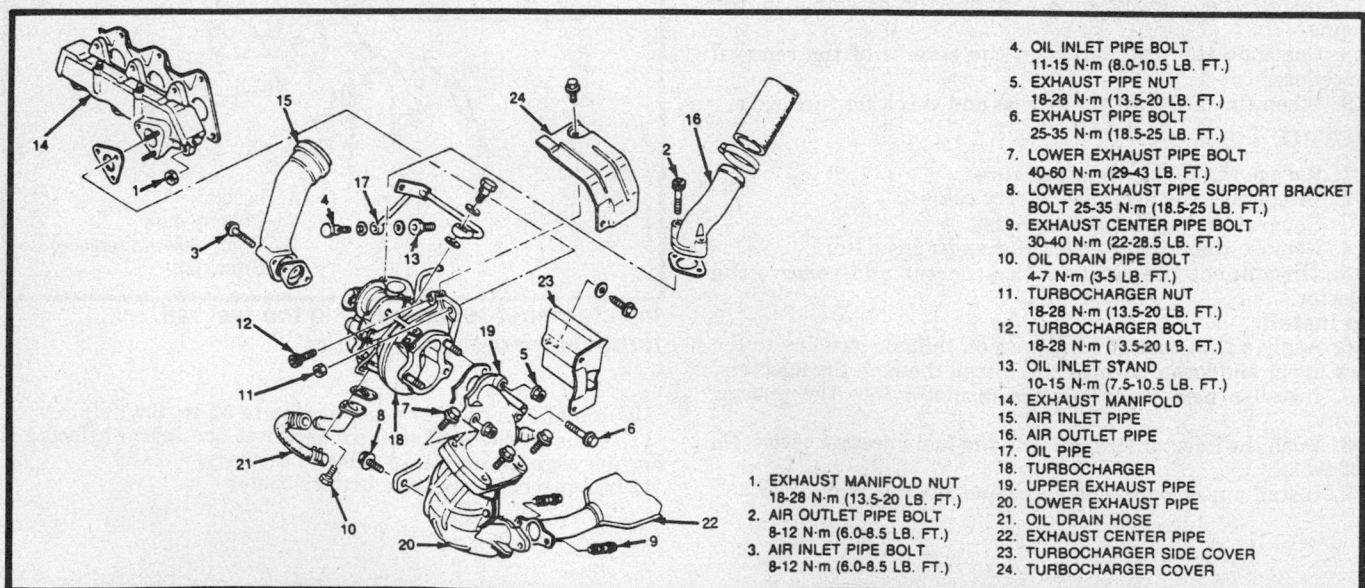

4. OIL INLET PIPE BOLT
11-15 N·m (8.0-10.5 LB. FT.)
5. EXHAUST PIPE NUT
18-28 N·m (13.5-20 LB. FT.)
6. EXHAUST PIPE BOLT
25-35 N·m (18.5-25 LB. FT.)
7. LOWER EXHAUST PIPE BOLT
40-60 N·m (29-43 LB. FT.)
8. LOWER EXHAUST PIPE SUPPORT BRACKET
BOLT 25-35 N·m (18.5-25 LB. FT.)
9. EXHAUST CENTER PIPE BOLT
30-40 N·m (22-28.5 LB. FT.)
10. OIL DRAIN PIPE BOLT
4-7 N·m (3-5 LB. FT.)
11. TURBOCHARGER NUT
18-28 N·m (13.5-20 LB. FT.)
12. TURBOCHARGER BOLT
18-28 N·m (3.5-20 L B. FT.)
13. OIL INLET STAND
10-15 N·m (7.5-10.5 LB. FT.)
14. EXHAUST MANIFOLD
15. AIR INLET PIPE
16. AIR OUTLET PIPE
17. OIL PIPE
18. TURBOCHARGER
19. UPPER EXHAUST PIPE
20. LOWER EXHAUST PIPE
21. OIL DRAIN HOSE
22. EXHAUST CENTER PIPE
23. TURBOCHARGER SIDE COVER
24. TURBOCHARGER COVER

1. EXHAUST MANIFOLD NUT
18-28 N·m (13.5-20 LB. FT.)
2. AIR OUTLET PIPE BOLT
8-12 N·m (6.0-8.5 LB. FT.)
3. AIR INLET PIPE BOLT
8-12 N·m (6.0-8.5 LB. FT.)

Turbocharger assembly – Sprint

21. Disconnect the air inlet pipe.
22. Disconnect the air inlet pipe from the cylinder block.
23. Disconnect the oil drain hose.
24. Disconnect the water pipe cylinder head clamp bolt.
25. Disconnect the water hoses.
26. Remove the turbocharger from the engine.
27. Installation is the reverse of removal. Always use new gaskets during installation. Recharge A/C system.

TURBOCHARGER WASTEGATE UNIT

Removal and Installation

SPECTRUM

1. Disconnect the negative battery terminal from the battery.

2. Remove lower and upper heat protector shield covering turbocharger assembly.
3. Remove manifold heat protecter and unplug O_2 sensor.
4. Disconnect vacuum pipe from wastegate and position out of the way.
5. Remove nuts holding wastegate to turbocharger assembly.
6. To install, use new a gasket on wastegate to turbocharger housing and reverse the removal procedures.

SPRINT

The turbocharger wastegate is not replacable as a separate unit. If the wastegate needs replacing, the complete turbocharger assembly must be replaced.

EMISSION CONTROL SYSTEMS

EQUIPMENT USED

NOVA EXCEPT TWIMCAM
Positive Crankcase Ventilation (PCV)
Fuel Evaporative Emission Control System (EVAP)
Throttle Positioner (TP)
Exhaust Gas Recirculation System (EGR)
Air Suction System (AS)
Carburetor feedback system
Three Way and Oxidation Catalyst System (TWC-OC)
High Altitude Compensation System (HAC)
Automatic Hot Air Intake System (HAI)
Hot Idle Compensation System (HIC)
Automatic choke system
Choke Breaker System (CB)
Choke opener system
Auxiliary Acceleration Pump (AAP)
Deceleration fuel cut system
Heat Control Valve
Cold Mixture Heater System (CMH)

NOVA TWINCAM
Positive Crankcase Ventilation (PCV)
Throttle Positioner (TP)
Exhaust Gas Recirculation (EGR)
3-Way and Oxidation Catalst (TWO-OC)
Air Suction (AS)
High Altitude Compensation (HAC)
Hot Idle Compenstaion (HIC)
Automatic choke
Choke Breaker (CB)
Choke opener
Auxiliary Accelerator Pump (AAP)
Heat control valve
Deceleration fuel cutoff
Cold Mixture Heater (CMH)
Fuel evaporator control
Carburetor feedback system

PRIZM
Electronic Control Module (ECM)
Oxygen sensor
Coolant temperature sensor
Throttle switch
Manifold Air Temperature sensor (MAT)
Manifold Absolute Pressure sensor (MAP)
Crank angle sensor
Vehicle speed sensor
Engine start signal
A/C signal
Vacuum switching valve
EGR system

Ignition system
Evaporative Emission Control System (EECS)
Positive crankcase ventilitation system

SPECTRUM
Electronic Control Module (ECM)
Oxygen Sensor
Coolant Temperature Sensor (CTS)
Throttle Position Sensor (TPS)
Vehicle Speed Sensor (VSS)
Early fuel evaporation system
Programmable Read Only Memmory (PROM)
High altitude emission control solenoid valve
High Altitude emission control altitude sensing switch
Clutch switch
Inlet air temperature switch
Transaxle switch
Mixture control valve
Thermal vacuum valve
Charcoal canister
Exhaust Gas Recirculation (EGR) valve
Positive Crankcase Ventilation (PCV) system
Thermostatic Air Cleaner (TAC)
Three way catalytic converter

SPRINT
Positive crankcase ventilitation system
Computer controlled emission control system
Thermostatically controlled air cleaner(1986)
Intake air temperature control system(1987–89)
Hot idle compensator (non-turbo only)
Idle-up system
Bowl ventilation system (non-turbo only)
Three-way catalyst
Fuel cut system
Exhaust gas recirculation system
Electronic Control Module (ECM)
Coolant temperature sensor
Surge tank
Vacuum switching valve
Oxygen sensor
Throttle position sensor
Air flow meter (turbo only)
Electronic fuel injector (turbo only)
Turbocharger intercooler
Knock sensor (turbo only)

METRO
Electronic Control Module (ECM)
Oxygen sensor
Coolant temoerature sensor
Throttle switch (M/T models)

Throttle position sensor (A/T models)
Manifold air temperature sensor
Manifold absolute pressure sensor
Ignition signal
Crank angle sensor
Vehicle speed sensor
EGR system
CPU (Central Processing Unit) of the ECM
Evaporative Emission Control System (EECS)
Positive crankcase ventilitation system

Resetting Warning Lights

SPECTRUM

NOTE: The following procedure is necessary to clear the trouble codes which are stored in the ECM.

Procedure

1. Make sure the ignition switch is turned **OFF**.
2. Disconnect the negative battery terminal, the ECM pigtail or the ECM fuse for 10 seconds.
3. Reconnect the electrical connector.

ENGINE

NOTE: Disconnecting the negative battery cable on some vehicles may interfere with the functions of the on board computer systems and may require the computer to undergo a relearning process, once the negative battery cable is reconnected.

Engine Assembly

Removal and Installation

NOVA

Except Twincam Engine

1. Disconnect the negative terminal from the battery. Drain the cooling system.
2. Properly discharge the A/C system.
3. Using a scratch awl, scribe the hood hinge-to-hood outline, then, using an assistant remove the hood.
4. Remove the air cleaner assembly and associated ducting.
5. From the radiator, remove the upper coolant hose and the overflow hose. Disconnect the coolant hose from the coolant pipe at the rear of the cylinder head and the coolant hose from the thermostat housing.
6. Disconnect the fuel hoses from the fuel pump.
7. Remove the drive belt from the alternator, the power steering pump if equipped and the A/C compressor if equipped. If equipped with power steering, remove the power steering pump-to-engine bolts and move the pump aside, do not disconnect the pressure hoses. If equipped with air conditioning, remove the compressor-to-engine bolts and move it aside; do not disconnect the pressure hoses.
8. Label and disconnect the electrical connectors that will interfere with the engine removal.
9. Label and disconnect the vacuum hoses running between the engine and firewall or fender well mounted accessories.
10. Label and disconnect the electrical connectors from the transaxle.
11. Disconnect the speedometer cable from the transaxle.
12. Raise and support the vehicle safely. Drain the engine oil and the transaxle fluid.
13. Disconnect the exhaust pipe-to-exhaust manifold bolts and separate the exhaust pipe from the manifold.
14. Disconnect the air hose from the catalytic converter, if so equipped.
15. If equipped with an automatic transaxle, disconnect and plug the oil cooler tubes from the radiator.
16. Remove the under covers from both sides of the vehicle.
17. Disconnect the cable and the bracket from the transaxle.
18. Disconnect the steering knuckles from the lower control arms.
19. Disconnect the halfshafts from the transaxle.
20. Remove the flywheel cover. If equipped with an automatic transaxle, mark the torque converter-to-flexplate, then, remove the torque converter-to-flexplate bolts and move the torque converter back into the transaxle.
21. Disconnect the front and rear engine mounts from the center member.
22. Lower the vehicle.
23. Remove the radiator-to-chassis bolts and the radiator (with the fans) from the vehicle.
24. Using a overhead lift, attach it to and support the engine.
25. Remove the through bolt from right-side engine mount, then, the left-side transaxle mount bolt and the mount.
26. Remove the engine/transaxle assembly from the vehicle. Remove the transaxle-to-engine bolts and separate the transaxle from the engine, then, secure the engine to a work stand.
27. To install, reverse the removal procedures. Refill the cooling system, the transaxle and the engine with clean fluid. Start the engine, allow it to reach normal operating temperatures and check for leaks.

If equipped with an automatic transaxle, torque the torque converter-to-flexplate bolts to 58 ft. lbs.

Torque the halfshaft-to-transaxle bolts to 27 ft. lbs.
Torque the engine-to-crossmember mount bolts to 29 ft. lbs.
Torque the exhaust pipe-to-exhaust manifold to 46 ft. lbs.
Torque the power steering pump-to-bracket bolt to 29 ft. lbs.
Torque the power steering adjusting bolt to 32 ft. lbs.

TWINCAM ENGINE

1. Disconnect the negative terminal from the battery.
2. roperly relieve the fuel system pressure.
3. Drain the cooling system.
4. Using a scratch awl, scribe the hood hinge-to-hood outline, then, using an assistant remove the hood.
5. Remove the air cleaner assembly, the coolant tank reservoir and the PVC hose.
6. Disconnect the heater hoses from the water inlet housing and the fuel hose from the fuel filter.
7. If equipped with a manual transaxle, remove the clutch slave cylinder-to-transaxle bolts and the slave cylinder, then, move the cylinder aside.
8. Disconnect the vacuum hose from the charcoal canister.
9. Disconnect the speedometer cable from the transaxle and the accelerator cable from the throttle body.
10. If equipped with cruise control, perform the following procedures:
    a. Remove the cables from the throttle body.
    b. Disconnect the vacuum hose from the actuator.
    c. Remove the actuator cover bolts and the cover.
    d. Disconnect the actuator connector, then, remove the actuator.
11. Remove the ignition coil.
12. To remove the main wiring harness, perform the following procedures:
    a. Remove the right side of the cowl panel and disconnect the No. 4 junction block connectors.

b. Remove the ECM cover and disconnect the ECM connectors, then, pull the main wiring harness into the engine compartment.

13. Disconnect the No. 2 junction block connectors and the ground strap terminals.

14. Disconnect the windshield washer change valve connector, the battery cable from the starter, the cruise control vacuum pump and switch connectors.

15. Disconnect the vacuum hose from the power brake booster.

16. If equipped with air conditioning, perform the following procedures:
   a. Remove the vane pump pulley nut.
   b. Loosen the idler pulley adjusting and pulley nuts.
   c. Remove the compressor-to-bracket bolts, then, move the compressor aside and secure it.
   d. Disconnect the oil pressure connector.
   e. Remove the compressor bracket bolts, the vane pump bolts, then, move the vane pump and bracket aside and suspend it.

17. Raise and support the vehicle safely. Drain the engine crankcase and transaxle fluid. on jackstands.

18. Remove the splash shields.

19. If equipped with an automatic transaxle, disconnect and plug the oil cooler from the radiator.

20. Remove the exhaust pipe-to-exhaust manifold bolts and separate the pipe from the manifold. Disconnect the oxygen sensor connector.

21. Remove the flywheel housing cover.

22. Remove the front and rear engine mounts from the center member, then, the center member.

23. Disconnect the right-side control arm from the steering knuckle and halfshafts from the transaxle.

24. Lower the vehicle.

25. Using a vertical hoist, secure the engine to it and support the engine; secure the engine wiring and hoses to the lift chain.

26. Remove the right-side engine mount, then, the left-side engine mount from the transaxle bracket.

NOTE: When lifting the engine be careful not to damage the throttle position sensor or the power steering gear housing.

27. Lift the engine/transaxle assembly from the vehicle.

28. To separate the transaxle from the engine, perform the following procedures:
   a. Remove the radiator fan temperature switch connector and the start injector time switch connector.
   b. Disconnect the vacuum hoses from the BVSV's.
   c. Remove the No. 1 and 2 hoses from the water bypass pipes.
   d. Disconnect the electrical connector from the back-up switch, the water temperature sensor and the water temperature switch.
   e. If equipped with an automatic transaxle, disconnect the neutral start switch connector and the transaxle solenoid connector, then, remove the torque converter-to-flexplate bolts; be sure to push the torque converter back into the transaxle.
   f. Remove the starter, the transaxle-to-engine bolts and the transaxle.

29. To install, reverse the removal procedures. Refill the cooling system, the engine crankcase and transaxle. Start the engine, allow it to reach normal operating temperatures and check for leaks.

Torque the torque converter-to-flexplate bolts to 20 ft. lbs.

Torque the starter-to-engine bolts to 29 ft. lbs.

Torque the halfshaft-to-transaxle nuts to 27 ft. lbs.

Torque the right-side control arm-to-steering knuckle nuts/bolts to 47 ft. lbs.

Torque the cross member-to-chassis bolts to 29 ft. lbs.

Torque the engine mounts-to-cross member bolts to 35 ft. lbs.

Torque the exhaust pipe to-exhaust manifold nuts to 46 ft. lbs.

PRIZM

1. Scribe matchmarks around the hood hinges and then remove the hood. Remove the engine undercovers.

2. Properly relieve the fuel system pressure.

3. Remove the air cleaner along with its hose.

4. Remove the coolant reservoir tank. Remove the radiator and cooling fan.

5. Disconnect the accelerator and throttle cables at the carburetor on models with automatic transmissions.

6. Disconnect the No. 2 junction block, the graound strap connector and the ground strap. Disconnect the vacuum hoses at the brake booster, power steering pump, A/C compressor and EBCV.

7. Disconnect the fuel lines at the fuel pump. Disconnect the heater hoses at the water inlet housing.

8. Disconnect the power steering pump and lay it aside with the hydraulic lines still attached. Do the same with the A/C compressor.

9. Disconnect the speedometer cable. On vehicles with a manual transmission, remove the clutch release cylinder and position it out of the way with the hydraulic lines still attached.

10. Disconnect the shift control cables and then raise and support the vehicle safely. Drain the engine coolant and oil. Drain the gear oil from the transaxle.

11. Remove the 2 nuts from the flange and then disconnect the exhaust pipe at the manifold. Disconnect the halfshafts at the transaxle.

12. Remove the 2 hole covers and then remove the front, center and rear engine mounts from the center member. Remove the 5 bolts and insulators and remove the center member.

13. Attach an engine hoist chain to the lifting brackets on the engine and then remove the 3 bolts and mounting stay. Remove the bolt, 2 nuts and the through bolt and pull out the right side engine mount. Remove the 2 bolts and the left mounting stay. Remove the 3 bolts and disconnect the left engine mount bracket from the transaxle. Lift the engine/transaxle assembly out of the vehicle.

14. Installation is in the reverse order of removal. Please note the following:
   a. Tighten the right engine mount insulator bolt to 47 ft. lbs. (64 Nm); tighten the nut to 38 ft. lbs. (52 Nm). Align the insulator with the bracket on the body and tighten the bolt to 64 ft. lbs. (87 Nm).
   b. Align the left engine mount insulator bracket with the transaxle bracket and tighten the bolt to 35 ft. lbs. (48 Nm).
   c. Install the right mounting stay and tighten the 3 bolts to 31 ft. lbs. (42 Nm). Install the left stay and tighten the 2 bolts to 15 ft. lbs. (21 Nm).
   d. Install the engine center member and tighten the 5 bolts to 45 ft. lbs. (61 Nm).
   e. Install the front and rear engine mounts and bolts. Align the bolts holes in the brackets with the center member and tighten the front mount bolts to 35 ft. lbs. (48 Nm); tighten the center and rear mounts to 38 ft. lbs. (52 Nm). Install the 2 hole covers and tighten the rear mounting bolt to 58 ft. lbs. (78 Nm).

SPECTRUM

1. Remove the hood, relieve the fuel system presseure and disconnect the negative battery cable.

2. Drain the cooling system.

3. Remove the air cleaner and the throttle cable at the carburetor.

4. Disconnect the heater hoses at the intake manifold, the coolant hose at the thermostat housing and the thermostat housing at the cylinder head.

5. On turbochraged models, remove the throttle cable, fuel lines, connectors at carburetor also remove turbocharger vacuum, oil and water lines.

6. Remove the distributor from the cylinder head.

7. Disconnect the oxygen sensor electrical connector.

8. Support the engine using a vertical lift and remove the right motor mount.

9. Disconnect the necessary electrical connectors and vacuum hoses.

10. Disconnect the flex hose at the exhaust manifold and the lower radiator hose at the block.

11. Remove the upper A/C compressor bolt and remove the belt.

12. Disconnect the power steering bracket at the block and remove the belt.

13. Disconnect the fuel lines from the fuel pump and the electrical connectors from under the carburetor.

14. Remove the upper starter bolt. Raise and support the vehicle safely.

15. Drain the oil from the crankcase and remove the oil filter.

16. Disconnect the oil temperature switch connector.

17. Disconnect the exhaust pipe bracket at the block and the exhaust pipe at the manifold.

18. Remove the A/C compressor and move to one side. Do not disconnect the A/C refrigerant lines. Remove the alternator wires.

19. Remove the flywheel cover and the converter bolts, then install a flywheel holding tool J–35271 or equivalent.

20. Disconnect the starter wires and remove the starter.

21. Remove the front right wheel and inner splash shield.

22. Lower the engine by lowering the crossmember enough to gain access to the crankshaft pulley bolts, then remove the pulley.

23. Raise the engine and crossmember. Remove the engine support.

24. Lower the vehicle and support the transmission.

25. Remove the transaxle to engine bolts. Remove the engine.

26. To install, reverse the removal procedures, adjust the drive belts and refill the fluids.

SPRINT AND METRO

1. Properly relieve the fuel system pressure. Remove the battery cables.

2. Remove the hood, battery, battery tray, air cleaner and the outside air duct.

3. Drain the cooling system.

4. Disconnect and tag the radiator, heater and vacuum hoses from the engine.

5. Disconnect the cooling fan wiring.

6. Remove the cooling fan, shroud and radiator as an assembly.

7. Remove the fuel hoses from the fuel pump.

8. Remove the brake booster hose from the intake manifold, accelerator cable from the carburetor and speed control cable from the transaxle.

9. Remove the clutch cable and bracket from the transaxle.

10. Disconnect and tag the necessary wiring from the engine and transaxle.

11. Remove the A/C compressor adjusting bolt and drive belt splash shield.

12. Raise and support the vehicle safely. Drain the engine oil and the transaxle fluid.

13. Disconnect the exhaust pipe from the exhaust manifold.

14. Remove the A/C pivot bolt, the drive belt and the mounting bracket.

15. Disconnect the gearshift control shaft and extension rod at the transaxle.

16. Disconnect the ball joints.

17. Remove the axle shafts from the transaxle.

18. Remove the engine torque rods and the transaxle mount nut.

19. Lower the vehicle.

20. Remove the engine side mount and the mount nuts.

21. Connect a vertical hoist to the engine, then lift the engine and transaxle assembly from the vehicle.

22. To install, reverse the removal procedures. Refill the engine, the transaxle and the cooling system.

Engine Mounts

Removal and Installation

NOVA AND PRIZM

1. Disconnect the negative terminal from the battery.

2. Raise and support the vehicle safely.

3. Using an engine support fixture tool No. J-28467 or equivalent, attach it to the engine and support it.

4. Remove the center member hole covers, loosen the engine center mount and lower the vehicle.

5. Remove the two bolts/nuts from the front, rear and right-side engine mounts.

6. Lower the vehicle.

7. From the left-side engine mount, remove the 2 bolts (manual transaxle) or 3 bolts (automatic transaxle).

8. Remove the through bolts from the engine mounts. Raise the engine in order to relieve engine weight from the mount. Remove the mounts from the vehicle.

9. To install, reverse the removal procedures. Torque the engine-to-cross member bolts to 35 ft. lbs. and the engine mount through bolts to 58 ft. lbs.

SPECTRUM

1. Disconnect the negative battery terminal from the battery.

2. Raise and support the vehicle safely.

3. Support the engine.

4. Remove the through nuts and bolts from engine mounts.

5. Remove the 4 bolts attaching the beam and remove beam.

6. Remove the front and or rear engine mounting rubbers.

NOTE:Install new bolts for mounts and torque engine mounting nut and bolts to 60 ft. lbs.

7. To install, reverse the removal procedures.

SPRINT AND METRO

Front

1. Disconnect the negative battery cable.

2. Remove the motor mount nut.

3. Raise the and support the vehicle safely. Support the engine.

4. Remove the mount and frame bracket. Separate and remove the mount from the bracket.

5. Installation is the reverse of the removal procedure.

Rear

1. Disconnect the negative battery cable.

2. Raise and support the vehicle safely.

3. Remove the motor mount to body bracket nut.

4. Support the engine.

5. Remove the mount and frame bracket. Separate and remove the mount from the bracket.

6. Installation is the reverse of the removal procedure.

Intake Manifold

Removal and Installation

NOVA

Twincam Engine

1. Disconnect the negative terminal from the battery. Remove the air cleaner assembly.

2. Drain the cooling system. Remove the upper radiator hose.

3. Disconnect the accelerator and throttle valve cable from the throttle body.

4. Label and disconnect the necessary vacuum hoses. Disconnect the brake vacuum hose from the intake manifold.

5. Relieve the fuel pressure, then, disconnect and remove the fuel delivery pipe with the fuel injectors.

6. Raise and support the vehicle safely.

7. Disconnect the temperature sensor connector from the water outlet housing. Remove the water outlet housing-to-engine bolts with the No. 1 by pass pipe.

8. Remove the intake manifold bracket, the intake manifold-to-engine bolts, the intake manifold (with the air control valve) and gaskets from the cylinder head.

9. Using the proper tool, clean the gasket mounting surfaces. Inspect the intake manifold and air control valve for damage and/or warpage; maximum warpage for both is 0.002 in., if the warpage is greater, replace the intake manifold or air control valve.

10. To install, use new gaskets and reverse the removal procedures. Torque the intake manifold-to-cylinder head bolts to 20 ft. lbs., the intake manifold bracket-to-engine bolts to 20 ft. lbs. and the fuel delivery pipe-to-engine bolts to 13 ft. lbs. Start the engine and check for leaks.

PRIZM

1. Disconnect the battery negative cable. Relieve the fuel system pressure.

2. Drain coolant.

3. Remove the air cleaner assembly.

4. Disconnect the throttle cable and accelerator cable from bracket (automatic transaxle).

5. Disconnect all necessary vacuum hoses.

6. Disconnect the throttle position sensor, cold start injector, injector connectors, the air control valve and vacuum sensor.

7. Disconnect the cold start injector pipe.

8. Disconnect the water hose from air valve.

9. Raise and suitably support the vehicle.

10. Remove the intake manifold bracket.

11. Lower vehicle.

12. Remove the 7 bolts, 2 nuts, ground cable, intake manifold, and gasket.

13. Measure the intake manifold with a straight edge and a feeler gage at the cylinder head mating surface. If warpage exceeds 0.008 in. (0.2 mm), replace the intake manifold.

To install:

14. Install the new gasket, intake manifold, 7 bolts, 2 nuts, and ground cable connector.

15. Raise and suitably support the vehicle.

16. Install the intake manifold bracket.

17. Lower vehicle.

18. Tighten the intake manifold bolts to 14 ft. lbs. (19 Nm).

19. Connect the water hose to the air valve.

20. Connect the cold-start injector pipe.

21. Connect the throttle position sensor, the cold start injector, the air control valve and the vacuum sensor.

22. Connect all the vacuum hoses.

23. Connect the throttle and accelerator cables to bracket (automatic transaxle).

24. Refill coolant.

25. Install the air cleaner assembly.

26. Connect the battery negative (-) cable.

SPECTRUM

Non-Turbocharged Engine

1. Disconnect the negative battery terminal from the battery. Drain the cooling system.

2. Remove the bolt securing the alternator adjusting plate to the engine.

3. Disconnect and label all of the hoses attached to the air cleaner and remove the air cleaner.

4. Disconnect the air inlet temperature switch wiring connector.

5. Disconnect and label the hoses, electrical connectors, and control cable attached to the carburetor.

6. If equipped with A/C, disconnect the FIDC vacuum hose, the pressure tank control valve hose, the distributor 3-way connector hose and the VSV wiring connector.

7. Remove the carburetor attaching bolts (located beneath the intake manifold), then remove the carburetor and the EFE heater.

8. At the intake manifold, remove the PCV hose, the water bypass hose, the heater hoses, the EGR valve/canister hose, the distributor vacuum advance hose and the ground wires.

9. Disconnect the thermometer unit switch wiring connector.

10. Remove the intake manifold attaching nuts/bolts and the intake manifold.

11. Clean the sealing surfaces of the intake manifold and cylinder head.

12. To install, use new gaskets and reverse the removal procedures. Torque the intake manifold to 17 ft. lbs.; then adjust the engine control cable and the alternator belt tension. Refill the engine with coolant and check for leaks.

Turbocharged Engine

1. Relieve the fuel system pressure. Disconnect the negative battery terminal from the battery.

2. Remove pressure regulator and oil seperator.

3. Disconnect vacuum line from VSV and remove vacuum switching valve from bracket.

4. Remove oil seperator/VSV bracket and hanger as an assembly.

5. Remove throttle valve assembly and engine harness assembly (mark or tag harness connections if necessary).

6. Remove idle air control valve, relief valve and MAP sensor.

7. Disconnect vacuum line from back pressure transducer and unclip transducer from hold down bracket.

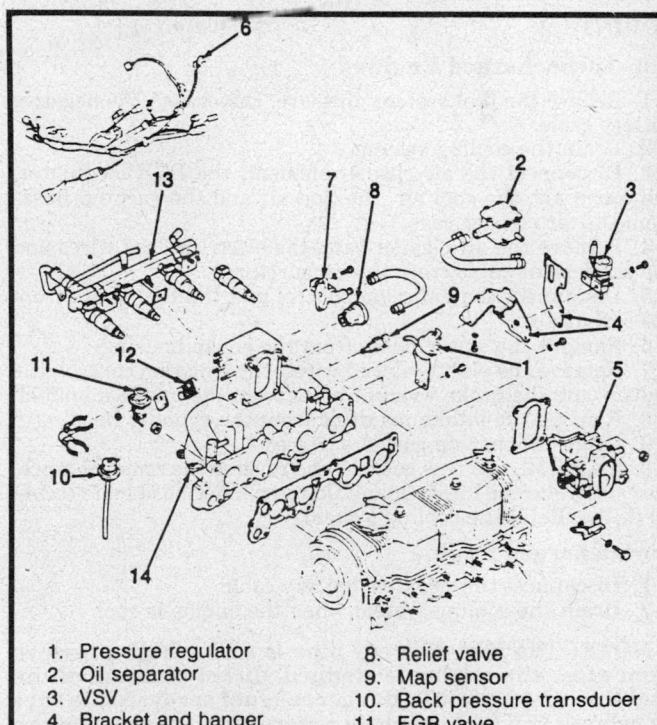

1. Pressure regulator	8. Relief valve
2. Oil separator	9. Map sensor
3. VSV	10. Back pressure transducer
4. Bracket and hanger	11. EGR valve
5. Throttle valve assembly	12. Adaptor
6. Engine harness assembly	13. Fuel injector with pipe
7. Idle air control valve	14. Intake manifold

Intake manifold turbocharged model — Spectrum

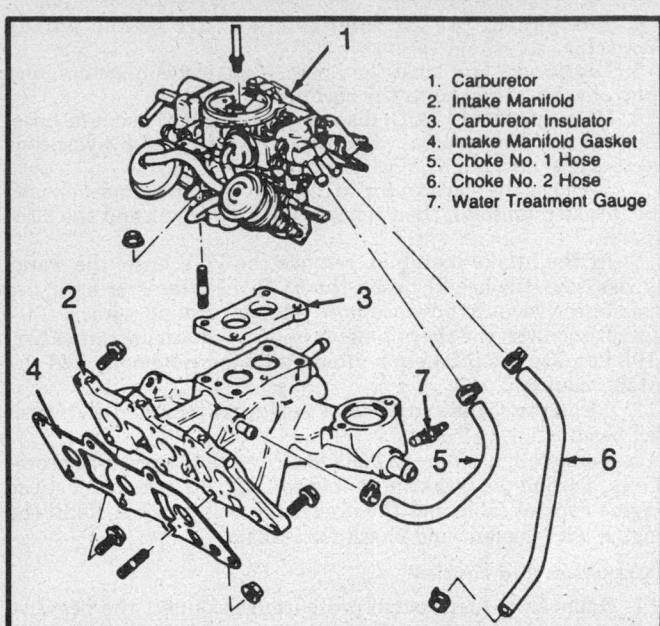

1. Carburetor
2. Intake Manifold
3. Carburetor Insulator
4. Intake Manifold Gasket
5. Choke No. 1 Hose
6. Choke No. 2 Hose
7. Water Treatment Gauge

Exploded view of the intake manifold and carburetor assembly—Sprint

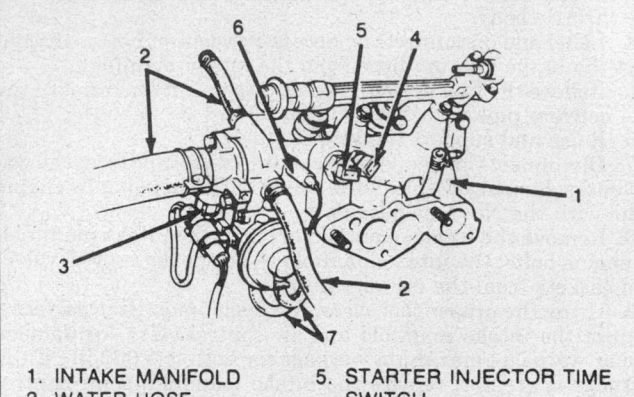

1. INTAKE MANIFOLD
2. WATER HOSE
3. RADIATOR FAN SWITCH
4. WATER TEMPERATURE SENSOR
5. STARTER INJECTOR TIME SWITCH
6. WATER TEMPERATURE GAUGE
7. EGR VALVE VACUUM HOSE

Intake manifold assembly—Sprint with turbocharged engines

8. Remove EGR valve and adaptor plate.
9. Remove fuel injectors and fuel pipe connected to rail as one unit and postion out of way then remove intake manifold with common chamber
10. To install, use new gaskets and reverse the removal procedures. Torque the intake manifold to 17 ft. lbs. Start and run engine check for leaks.

SPRINT

Non-Turbocharged Engine

1. Relieve the fuel system pressure. Disconnect the negative battery cable.
2. Drain the cooling system.
3. Disconnect the air cleaner element, the EGR modulator, the warm air, the cool air, the 2nd air and the vacuum hoses from the air cleaner case.
4. Remove the air cleaner case, the electrical lead wires and the accelerator cable from the carburetor.
5. Disconnect the emission control and the fuel hoses from the carburetor.
6. Remove the water hoses from the choke housing.
7. Remove the electrical lead wires, the emission control, the coolant and the brake vacuum hoses from the intake manifold.
8. Remove the intake manifold from the cylinder head.
9. Clean the mating gasket surfaces.
10. To install, use new gaskets and reverse the removal procedures. Torque the intake manifold-to-cylinder head bolts to 14–20 ft. lbs. Refill the cooling system.

Turbocharged Engine

1. Disconnect the negative battery cable.
2. Drain the cooling system when the engine is cool.

NOTE: The fuel delivery pipe is under high pressure even after the engine is stopped, direct removal of the fuel line may result in dangerous fuel spray. Make sure to release the fuel pressure according to the procedure outlined under Fuel System in this section.

3. Remove the surge tank together with the throttle body.
4. Disconnect the fuel injector couplers.
5. Disconnect the fuel hoses from the delivery pipe.

6. Remove the delivery pipe together with the injectors.
7. Disconnect the water temperature gauge wire (yellow/white).
8. Disconnect the starter injector time switch coupler (brown).
9. Disconnect the water temperature sensor coupler (green).
10. Disconnect the radiator fan switch coupler.
11. Disconnect the water hoses and the EGR vacuum hoses.
12. Remove the intake manifold retaining bolts then remove the manifold fropm the vehicle.
13. Installation is the reverse of removal, with the following precautions:
    a. Use a new intake manifold gasket.
    b. If an injector was removed from the delivery pipe a new O-ring should be used.
    c. Torque the intake manifold retaining bolts to 17 ft. lbs.
    d. After the ignition is turned on check for fuel leaks.

METRO

1. Relieve the fuel system pressure.
2. Disconnect the negative battery cable.
3. Drain the cooling system.
4. Remove the air cleaner assembly.
5. Disconnect the following wires:
    a. Vacuum switching valve for EGR valve
    b. Water temperature sensor
    c. Idle speed control solenoid valve
    d. Ground wires from the intake manifold
    e. Fuel injector
    f. Throttle switch or throttle position sensor
    g. Water temperature gauge
6. Disconnect the fuel return and feed hoses from the throttle body.
7. Disconnect the water hoses from the throttle body and the intake manifold.
8. Disconnect the following hoses:
    a. Canister purge hose from the intake manifold
    b. Canister hose from its pipe
    c. Pressure sensor hose from the intake manifold
    d. Brake booster hose from the intake manifold
9. Disconnect the PCV hose from the cylinder head cover.
10. Disconnect the accelerator cable from the throttle body.
11. Disconnect any other lines and cables as necessary.
12. Remove the intake manifold with the throttle body from the cylinder head.

To install:

13. Install the intake manifold to the cylinder head, using a new gasket, install the clamps and tighten the intake manifold retaining bolts to 17 ft. lbs.

14. Reinstall all vacuum and water hoses.

15. Install the fuel feed and return hoses.

16. Install all electrical lead wires.

17. Install the accelerator cable to the throttle body.

18. Install the air cleaner assembly.

19. Fill the cooling system and reconnect the negative battery cable.

Exhaust Manifold

Removal and Installation

NOVA AND PRIZM

Twincam Engine

1. Disconnect the negative terminal from the battery.

2. Remove the exhaust manifold heat shield.

3. Raise and support the vehicle safely.

4. Remove the exhaust pipe-to-exhaust manifold nuts and separate the pipe from the manifold. Remove the exhaust manifold bracket from the exhaust manifold, the exhaust manifold-to-engine bolts, the exhaust manifold and gasket (discard the gasket) from the cylinder head.

5. Using the proper tool, clean the gasket mounting surfaces. Inspect the exhaust manifold for damage and/or warpage; maximum warpage is 0.012 in., if the warpage is greater, replace the exhaust manifold.

6. To install, use a new gasket and reverse the removal procedures. Torque the exhaust manifold-to-cylinder head bolts to 18 ft. lbs. Start the engine and check for leaks.

SPECTRUM

1. Disconnect the negative battery terminal from the battery and the oxygen sensor wiring connector.

2. Disconnect the Thermostatic Air Cleaner (TAC) flex hose. Disconnect the vacuum and oil lines on turbocharged engines.

3. Remove the hot air cover and raise the vehicle.

4. Disconnect the vacuum and oil lines on turbocharged engines

5. Disconnect the exhaust pipe from the exhaust manifold and lower the vehicle.

6. Remove the nuts and bolts securing the exhaust manifold to the cylinder head. Clean the gasket mounting surfaces.

7. To install, use new gaskets and reverse the removal procedures. Torque the exhaust manifold to 17 ft. lbs. or 21 ft. lbs. turbocharged model then start the engine and check for leak

SPRINT AND METRO

Non-Turbocharged Engine

1. Disconnect the negative battery cable.

2. Raise and support the vehicle safely.

3. Remove the exhaust pipe at the exhaust manifold.

4. Remove the lower heat shield bolt and the 2nd air pipe at the exhaust manifold.

5. If equipped, remove the A/C drive belt and the lower adjusting bracket.

6. Lower the vehicle.

7. Remove the spark plug and the oxygen sensor wires.

8. Remove the hot air shroud from the exhaust manifold.

9. Remove the 2nd air valve hoses, the valve and the pipe from the exhaust manifold.

10. Remove the mounting bolts and the exhaust manifold.

11. Clean the gasket mating surfaces.

12. To install, use a new gasket and reverse the removal procedures. Torque the exhaust manifold fasteners to 14–20 ft. lbs. and the exhaust pipe to 30–43 ft. lbs.

Turbocharged Engine

1. Remove the turbocharger assembly.

2. Remove the exhaust manifold.

3. Installation is the reverse of removal. Install a new gasket.

Combination Manifold

Removal and Installation

NOVA AND PRIZM

Except Twincam Engine

1. Disconnect the negative terminal from the battery.

2. Remove the air cleaner assembly. Label and disconnect the vacuum hoses.

3. Disconnect the throttle valve and the accelerator cables from the carburetor. Label and disconnect the electrical connectors from the carburetor.

4. Disconnect the fuel line from the fuel pump and drain the excess fuel into a metal container.

5. Disconnect or remove any emission control hardware that may be the way. Remove the carburetor-to-combination manifold nuts and the carburetor from the combination manifold; discard the gasket.

6. Remove the Early Fuel Evaporation (EFE) gasket. Remove the vacuum line, the dashpot bracket and the carburetor heat shield.

7. Raise and support the vehicle safely. Remove the exhaust pipe-to-combination manifold bolts, the exhaust bracket from the engine and the air hose from the catalytic converter pipe.

8. Lower the vehicle.

9. Disconnect the brake vacuum hose from the combination manifold. Remove the accelerator and throttle cable brackets.

10. Working from the center outward, remove the combination manifold-to-cylinder head nuts in several stages so tension is gradually released.

11. Remove the combination manifold from the cylinder head.

12. Using the proper tool, clean the gasket mounting surfaces. Inspect the manifold for damage and/or warpage.

13. To install, use new gaskets and reverse the removal procedures. Torque the combination manifold-to-cylinder head bolts to 18 ft. lbs. Start the engine and check for leaks.

Valve System

VALVE

Adjustment

NOVA AND PRIZM

Except Twincam Engine

1. Operate the engine until normal operating temperatures are reached, then, turn the engine **OFF**. Remove the air cleaner and the valve cover.

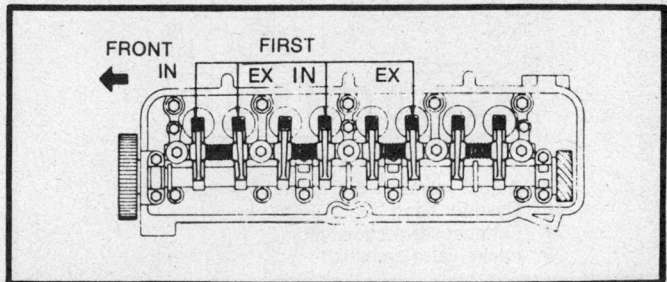

Valve adjustment sequence-step 1 except twincam engine—Nova

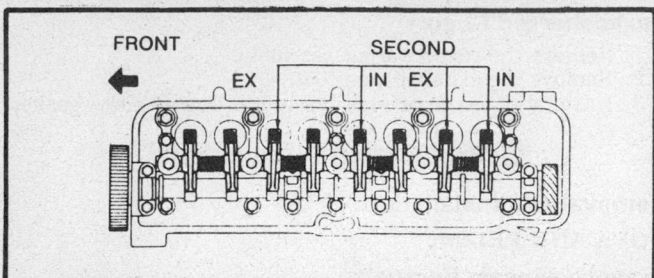

Valve adjustment sequence-step 2 except twincam engine—Nova

NOTE: If clearances are being set because parts have been disassembled, adjust the valves COLD, then, reset them with the engine HOT.

2. Using a socket wrench on the crankshaft pulley bolt, turn the crankshaft until the No. 1 cylinder is positioned to the TDC of its compression stroke; the rocker arms of the No. 1 cylinder should be loose.

NOTE: The notch on the crankshaft pulley should align with the 0 degrees mark on the timing plate.

3. Using a 0.008 in. feeler gauge, adjust the intake valve clearance of cylinder No. 1 and 2. Using a 0.012 in. feeler gauge, adjust the exhaust valve clearance of cylinders No. 1 and 3.

4. To adjust each valve, perform the following procedures:

a. Loosen the rocker arm adjusting nut; it may be necessary to back-off the adjusting screw.

b. Slide the feeler gauge between the rocker arm and valve tip. The surfaces will just touch, giving a very slight pull on the gauge.

c. Using a screwdriver (to turn the rocker arm screw) and a wrench (to hold the rocker arm lock nut), adjust the valve clearance, then, tighten the rocker arm lock nut.

d. Recheck the clearance and readjust (if necessary).

5. Rotate the crankshaft one complete revolution (360 degrees), then, realign the crankshaft pulley notch with the 0 degrees mark on the timing plate.

6. Using a 0.008 in. feeler gauge, adjust the intake valve clearance of cylinder No. 3 and 4. Using a 0.012 in. feeler gauge, adjust the exhaust valve clearance of cylinders No. 2 and 4.

7. To install, use a new gasket, sealant (if necessary) and reverse the removal procedures. Install the air cleaner. Adjust the engine timing and idle speed.

Twincam Engine

1. With the engine COLD, remove the valve covers.

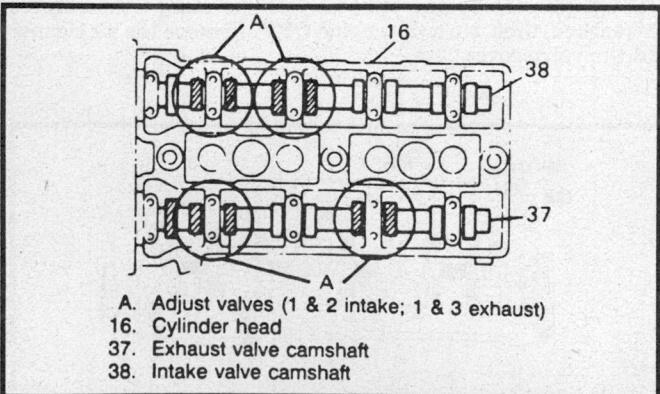

A. Adjust valves (1 & 2 intake; 1 & 3 exhaust)
16. Cylinder head
37. Exhaust valve camshaft
38. Intake valve camshaft

Measuring the valve clearance-step 1-twincam engine—Nova

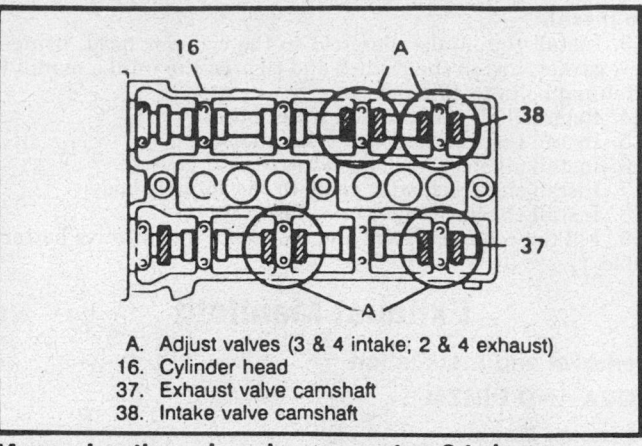

A. Adjust valves (3 & 4 intake; 2 & 4 exhaust)
16. Cylinder head
37. Exhaust valve camshaft
38. Intake valve camshaft

Measuring the valve clearance-step 2-twincam engine—Nova

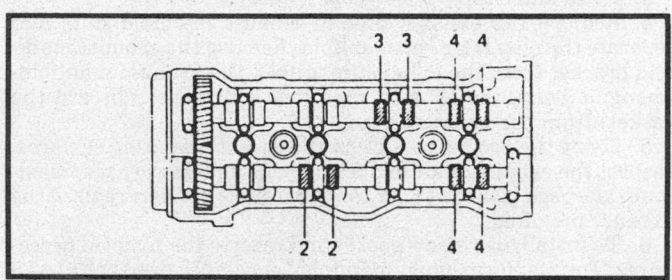

Adjust these valves FIRST—Prizm

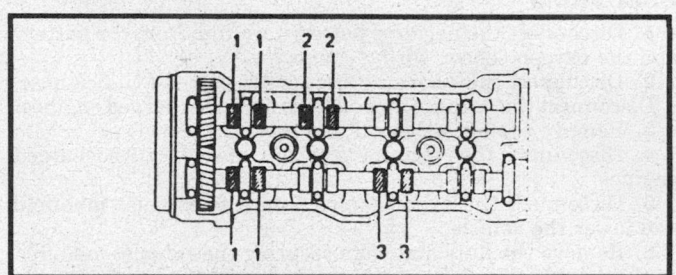

Adjust these valves SECOND—Prizm

2. To inspect the valve clearances, perform the following procedures:

a. Using a socket wrench on the crankshaft pulley, rotate the crankshaft until the No. 1 cylinder is positioned to the TDC of its compression stroke; the valve lifters of the No. 1 cylinder should be loose.

NOTE: The crankshaft pulley notch will align with the 0 degrees mark on the timing plate.

b. Using a feeler gauge, measure and record (valves not within specifications) the intake valve-to-lifter clearances of cylinders No. 1 and 2; the exhaust valve-to-lifter clearances of cylinders No. 1 and 3.

c. Rotate the crankshaft one complete revolution (360 degrees) and realign the crankshaft pulley notch with the 0 degrees mark on the timing plate; the valve lifters of the No. 4 cylinder should be loose.

d. Using a feeler gauge, measure and record (valves not within specifications) the intake valve-to-lifter clearances of cylinders No. 3 and 4; the exhaust valve-to-lifter clearances of cylinders No. 2 and 4.

Installed Shim Thickness (mm)

Measured Clearance (mm)	2.500	2.525	2.550	2.575	2.600	2.620	2.625	2.640	2.650	2.660	2.675	2.680	2.700	2.720	2.725	2.740	2.750	2.775	2.780	2.800	2.820	2.825	2.840	2.860	2.875	2.900	2.920	2.925	2.940	2.960	2.975	2.980	3.000	3.020	3.025	3.040	3.050	3.060	3.075	3.080	3.100	3.120	3.140	3.150	3.175	3.180	3.200	3.225	3.250	3.275	3.300

The measured-clearance rows (0.000–0.009 through 1.001–1.025) and the full matrix of shim numbers are not individually transcribed here.

AVAILABLE SHIMS

Shim No.	Thickness	Shim No.	Thickness
02	2.500 (0.0984)	20	2.950 (0.1161)
04	2.550 (0.1004)	22	3.000 (0.1181)
06	2.600 (0.1024)	24	3.050 (0.1201)
08	2.650 (0.1043)	26	3.100 (0.1220)
10	2.700 (0.1063)	28	3.150 (0.1240)
12	2.750 (0.1083)	30	3.200 (0.1260)
14	2.800 (0.1102)	32	3.250 (0.1280)
16	2.850 (0.1122)	34	3.300 (0.1299)
18	2.900 (0.1142)		

Intake valve clearance (cold):
0.15 − 0.25 mm (0.006 − 0.010 in.)

Example: A 2.800 mm shim is installed and the measured clearance is 0.450 mm. Replace the 2.800 mm shim with shim No. 24 (3.050 mm).

Intake valve shim size chart—Nova twincam engine and Prizm

Installed Shim Thickness (mm) — column headers: 2.500, 2.525, 2.550, 2.575, 2.600, 2.620, 2.625, 2.640, 2.650, 2.660, 2.675, 2.680, 2.700, 2.720, 2.725, 2.740, 2.750, 2.760, 2.775, 2.780, 2.800, 2.820, 2.825, 2.840, 2.860, 2.875, 2.900, 2.920, 2.925, 2.940, 2.950, 2.960, 2.975, 3.000, 3.020, 3.025, 3.040, 3.050, 3.060, 3.075, 3.080, 3.100, 3.120, 3.125, 3.140, 3.160, 3.175, 3.180, 3.200, 3.225, 3.250, 3.275, 3.300

Measured Clearance (mm) — row ranges:

- 0.000 – 0.009
- 0.010 – 0.025
- 0.026 – 0.040
- 0.041 – 0.050
- 0.051 – 0.070
- 0.071 – 0.090
- 0.091 – 0.100
- 0.101 – 0.120
- 0.121 – 0.140
- 0.141 – 0.150
- 0.151 – 0.170
- 0.171 – 0.190
- 0.191 – 0.199
- 0.200 – 0.300
- 0.301 – 0.320
- 0.321 – 0.325
- 0.326 – 0.340
- 0.341 – 0.350
- 0.351 – 0.370
- 0.371 – 0.375
- 0.376 – 0.390
- 0.391 – 0.400
- 0.401 – 0.420
- 0.421 – 0.425
- 0.426 – 0.440
- 0.441 – 0.450
- 0.451 – 0.470
- 0.471 – 0.475
- 0.476 – 0.490
- 0.491 – 0.500
- 0.501 – 0.520
- 0.521 – 0.525
- 0.526 – 0.540
- 0.541 – 0.550
- 0.551 – 0.570
- 0.571 – 0.575
- 0.576 – 0.590
- 0.591 – 0.600
- 0.601 – 0.620
- 0.621 – 0.625
- 0.626 – 0.640
- 0.641 – 0.650
- 0.651 – 0.670
- 0.671 – 0.675
- 0.676 – 0.690
- 0.691 – 0.700
- 0.701 – 0.720
- 0.721 – 0.725
- 0.726 – 0.740
- 0.741 – 0.750
- 0.751 – 0.770
- 0.771 – 0.775
- 0.776 – 0.790
- 0.791 – 0.800
- 0.801 – 0.820
- 0.821 – 0.825
- 0.826 – 0.840
- 0.841 – 0.850
- 0.851 – 0.870
- 0.871 – 0.875
- 0.876 – 0.890
- 0.891 – 0.900
- 0.901 – 0.925
- 0.926 – 0.950
- 0.951 – 0.975
- 0.976 – 1.000
- 1.001 – 1.025
- 1.026 – 1.050
- 1.051 – 1.075

(The chart body is a matrix giving the replacement shim number for each combination of measured clearance and installed shim thickness.)

AVAILABLE SHIMS — mm (in.)

Shim No.	Thickness	Shim No.	Thickness
02	2.500 (0.0984)	20	2.950 (0.1161)
04	2.550 (0.1004)	22	3.000 (0.1181)
06	2.600 (0.1024)	24	3.050 (0.1201)
08	2.650 (0.1043)	26	3.100 (0.1220)
10	2.700 (0.1063)	28	3.150 (0.1240)
12	2.750 (0.1083)	30	3.200 (0.1260)
14	2.800 (0.1102)	32	3.250 (0.1280)
16	2.850 (0.1122)	34	3.300 (0.1299)
18	2.900 (0.1142)		

Exhaust valve clearance (cold):
0.20 – 0.30 mm (0.008 – 0.012 in.)

Example: A 2.800 mm shim is installed and the measured clearance is 0.450 mm. Replace the 2.800 mm shim with shim No. 22 (3.000 mm).

Exhaust valve shim size chart, twincam engine—Nova and Prizm

3. Rotate the crankshaft pulley until the cam lobe (valve being worked on) is positioned in the upward direction.

4. Using the valve clearance adjustment tool set No. J–37141 or equivalent, press the valve lifter downward, then, secure it in downward position (using another tool) and remove the first tool.

5. Using a prybar or a magnetic finger, remove the adjusting shim.

6. To select the correct valve shim(s), perform the following procedures:

    a. Using a micrometer, measure the thickness of the old shim.

    b. Using the valve clearance measurement (already acquired), subtract 0.008 in. (intake valve) or 0.010 in. (exhaust valve) from it; the new calculation is the difference between the old shim and the new shim.

    c. Using the difference (just calculated), add it to the old shim thickness, then, select (from the chart) a new shim with the thickness closest to the new calculation.

7. Install the new shim and remove the hold-down tool.

8. After all valves have met specifications, use new gaskets, sealant (if necessary) and reverse the removal procedures. Adjust the engine timing and idle speed.

SPECTRUM

1. Remove the cylinder head cover.

2. Rotate the engine until the notched line on the crankshaft pulley aligns with the **0** degree mark on the timing gear case. The position of the No. 1 piston should be at TDC of the compression stroke.

3. Set the intake valve to 0.006 in. (cold) for No. 1 and 2 cylinders; exhaust valves to 0.010 in. (cold) for No. 1 and 3 cylinders.

4. When piston in No. 4 cylinder is at TDC on compression stroke set the intake valves to 0.006 in. (cold) for No. 3 and 4 cylinders; exhaust valves to 0.010 in. (cold) for No. 2 and 4 cylinders.

5. After the adjustment has been completed, replace the head cover.

SPRINT AND METRO

1. Remove the air cleaner, (carbureted engine). Remove the rocker cover.

2. Rotate the crankshaft clockwise and align the **V** mark on the crankshaft pulley with the **0** mark on the timing tab.

3. Remove the distributor cap and make sure that the rotor is facing the fuel pump. If not, rotate the crankshaft 360 degrees.

4. Check and/or adjust the valves of the No. 1 cylinder.

NOTE: On a COLD engine, adjust the valves to 0.006 in. (intake) and 0.008 in. (exhaust). On a HOT engine, adjust the valves to 0.010 in. (intake) and 0.012 in. (exhaust).

5. After adjusting the valves of the No. 1 cylinder, rotate the crankshaft pulley 240 degrees (the **V** mark should align with the lower left oil pump mounting bolt, when facing the crankshaft pulley) and adjust the valves of the No. 3 cylinder.

6. After adjusting the valves of the No. 3 cylinder, rotate the crankshaft pulley 240 degrees (the **V** mark should align with the lower right oil pump mounting bolt, when facing the crankshaft pulley) and adjust the valves of the No. 2 cylinder.

7. After the valves have been adjusted, install the removed items by reversing the removal procedures. Torque the valve adjustment locknuts to 11–13 ft. lbs.

VALVE LIFTERS

Removal and Installation
NOVA EXCEPT TWINCAM ENGINE

1. Disconnect the negative terminal from the battery. Drain the cooling system.

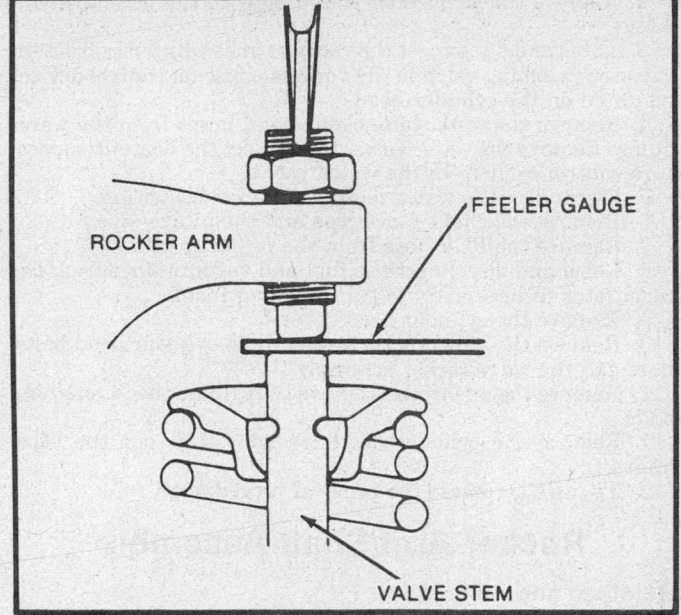

Valve lash adjustment—Spectrum

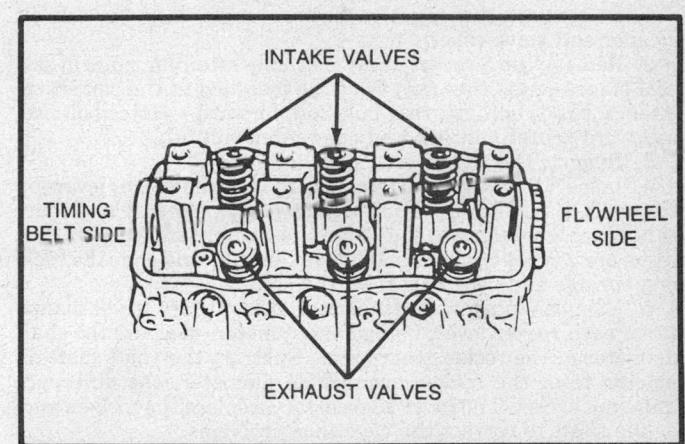

Valve identification in cylinder head—Sprint and Metro

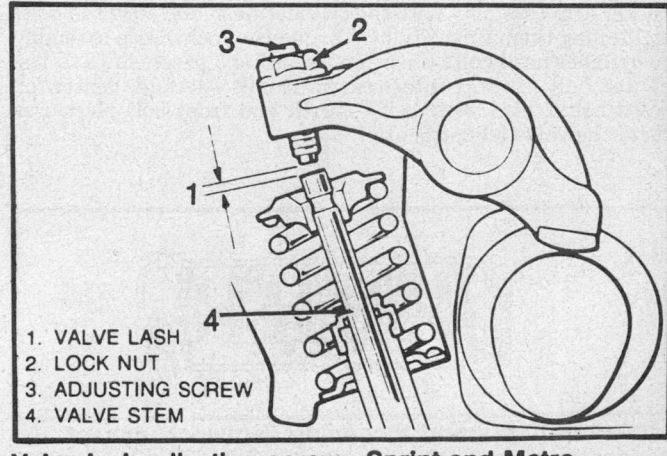

1. VALVE LASH
2. LOCK NUT
3. ADJUSTING SCREW
4. VALVE STEM

Valve lash adjusting screw—Sprint and Metro

2. Remove the air cleaner assembly with the accompanying hoses.

3. Label and disconnect the vacuum lines which run from the vacuum switching valve to the various emission control devices mounted on the cylinder head.

4. Remove the water hose clamps and hoses from the water pump. Remove the water valve. Disconnect the heater temperature control cable from the water valve.

5. Disconnect the water temperature sender wiring.

6. Remove the choke stove pipe and the intake pipe.

7. Remove the PCV hose from the intake manifold.

8. Label and disconnect the fuel and vacuum lines from the carburetor (if necessary) to gain working room.

9. Remove the cylinder head cover.

10. Remove the valve rocker assembly-to-cylinder head bolts/nuts and the valve rocker assembly.

11. Remove the pushrods. Remove the cylinder head retaining bolts.

12. Remove the cylinder head assembly. Lift out the valve lifters.

13. To install, reverse the removal procedures.

Rocker Arm/Shaft Assembly

Removal and Installation

NOVA AND PRIZM

Except Twincam Engine

1. Disconnect the negative battery cable. Remove the air cleaner and valve cover.

2. Remove the 5 rocker shaft assembly retaining bolts in several stages—note that they Must be loosened in the correct sequence: Front bolt 1st, rear bolt 2nd, forward—center bolt 3rd, rearward-center bolt 4th and the center bolt 5th.

3. Remove the rocker arm/shaft assembly.

4. Inspect for wear by attempting to rock the rocker levers on the shaft. If negligible motion is felt, wear is acceptable. If there is noticeable wear, note the order of assembly and the fact that there are 2 types of rockers. Remove the bolts and slide the rockers, springs and pedestals from the shaft.

5. Using an internal dial indicator, measure the inside diameter of each rocker lever; using a micrometer, measure the shaft diameter at the rocker wear areas. Subtract the shaft shaft diameter from the rocker arm inside diameter; the difference must not exceed 0.0024 in. If necessary, replace the rockers and/or the shaft to correct the clearance problems.

6. Assemble the pedestals, rockers, springs and bolts in reverse order of disassembly. Using clean engine oil, lubricate wear surfaces thoroughly. Install the rocker arm shaft with the oil holes facing downward.

7. Loosen the valve adjusting screw locknuts. Install the rocker arm assembly onto the cylinder head and start the bolts, tightening them finger tight. Torque the rocker arm assembly-to-cylinder head bolts (in sequence) using 3 passes to 18 ft. lbs.: center bolt—first, center/rearward bolt—second, center/forward bolt—third, rear bolt—fourth and front bolt—last. Perform the valve adjustment.

8. To complete the installation, use new gasket(s), sealant (if necessary) and reverse the removal procedures.

SPECTRUM

1. Disconnect the negative battery terminal from the battery. Remove the PCV hoses.

2. Remove the spark plug wires from the mounting clip.

3. Remove the ground wire from the right rear side of the head cover.

4. Support the engine and remove the right side engine mounting rubber, bolts and plate.

5. Remove the mounting bracket on the timing cover.

6. Remove the 4 bolts holding the timing cover and the 2 bolts holding the cylinder head cover.

7. Loosen the timing cover and remove the cylinder head cover.

NOTE: If the cylinder head cover sticks, strike the end of the cover with a rubber mallet.

8. Remove the rocker arm bracket bolts in sequence (work from both ends equally, toward the middle).

9. Remove the rocker arm shafts and then the rocker arms from the shafts.

10. Using the proper tool, clean the sealing surfaces of the cover and the cylinder head.

11. To install, apply sealer to the sealing surfaces and reverse the removal procedures.

NOTE: The rocker arm shafts are different from each other, make sure they are installed in the same position that they were removed. Install the rocker arms with the identification marks toward the front of the engine. Apply sealant to the bracket and cylinder head mating surfaces of the front and rear rocker brackets.

12. To complete the installation, mount the rocker assemblies securely to the dowel pins on the cylinder head. Torque the rocker arm bolts to 16 ft. lbs. Start the engine and check for leaks.

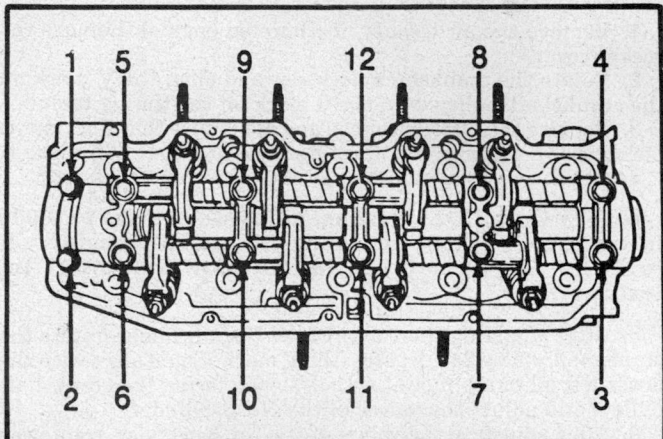

Rocker arm/shaft removal sequence—Spectrum

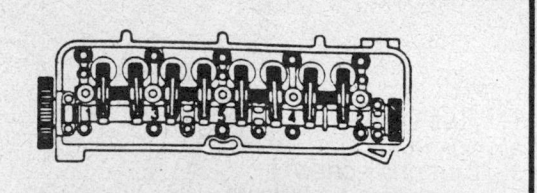

Rocker arm support loosening sequence, except twincam engine—Nova

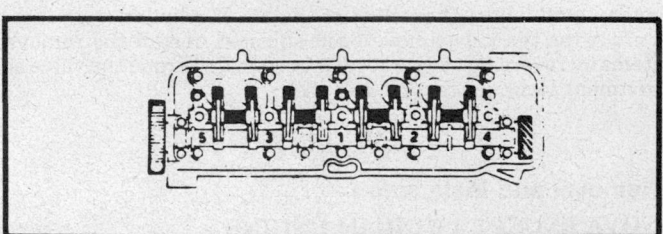

Rocker arm support torquing sequence except twincam engine—Nova

SPRINT AND METRO

1. Disconnect the negative battery cable.
2. Remove the air cleaner and the cylinder head cover.
3. Remove the distributor cap, then mark the position of the rotor and the distributor housing with the cylinder head. Remove the distributor and the case from the cylinder head.
4. Loosen the rocker arm valve adjusters, turn back the adjusting screws so that the rocker arms move freely.
5. Remove the rocker arm shaft retaining screws and pull out the shafts. Remove the rocker arms and springs from the cylinder head.

NOTE: Make a note of the differences between the rocker arm shafts. The intake shaft's stepped end is 0.55 in., which faces the camshaft pulley; the exhaust shaft's stepped end is 0.59 in., which faces the distributor.

6. To install, use new gaskets and reverse the removal procedures. Torque the rocker arm shaft screws to 7–9 ft. lbs. Adjust the valve clearances. Check and/or adjust the ignition timing.

Cylinder Head

Removal and Installation

NOVA

Except Twincam Engine

1. Disconnect the negative terminal from the battery.
2. Drain the engine coolant into a clean container, opening both the radiator and cylinder block drain cocks.
3. Remove the air cleaner. Label and disconnect all vacuum hoses.
4. Raise and support the vehicle safely. Drain the engine oil. Remove the exhaust pipe-to-exhaust manifold nuts and separate the exhaust pipe from the manifold. Remove the exhaust pipe bracket from the engine. Remove the hose from the catalytic converter pipe.
5. If equipped with power steering, loosen the power steering pump pivot bolt. Lower the vehicle.
6. Disconnect the accelerator and throttle cables from the carburetor and cable bracket.
7. Disconnect electrical harness from the cowl, the oxygen sensor and the distributor.
8. Disconnect the fuel hoses from the fuel pump.

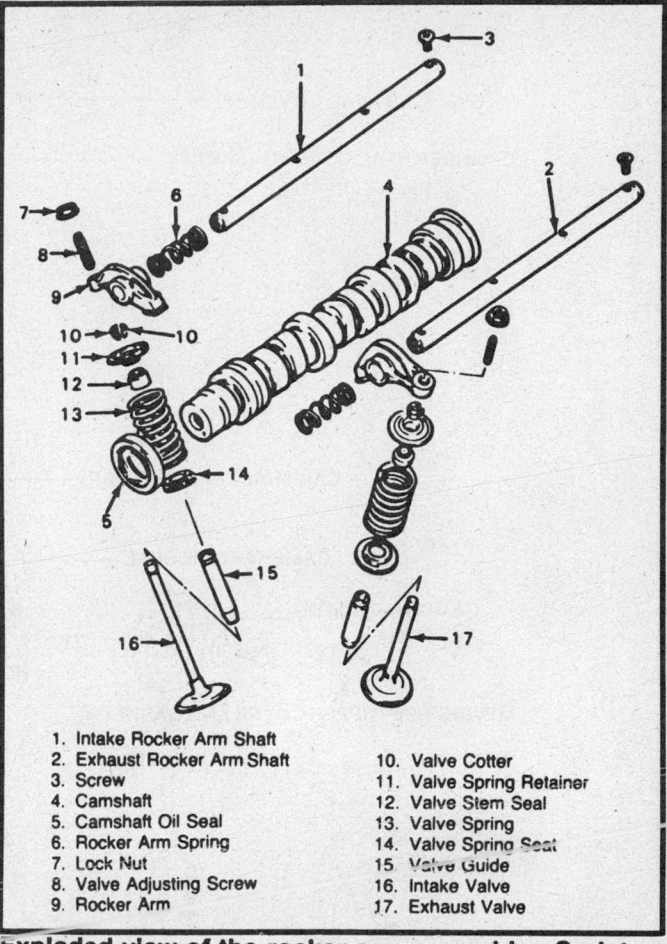

1. Intake Rocker Arm Shaft
2. Exhaust Rocker Arm Shaft
3. Screw
4. Camshaft
5. Camshaft Oil Seal
6. Rocker Arm Spring
7. Lock Nut
8. Valve Adjusting Screw
9. Rocker Arm
10. Valve Cotter
11. Valve Spring Retainer
12. Valve Stem Seal
13. Valve Spring
14. Valve Spring Seat
15. Valve Guide
16. Intake Valve
17. Exhaust Valve

Exploded view of the rocker arm assembly—Sprint and Metro

9. Disconnect the upper radiator hose from the water outlet, then, remove the water outlet from the cylinder head. Remove the heater hose.
10. If equipped with power steering, remove the adjusting bracket from the engine.
11. Remove the PCV valve and the wiring harness that passes over the valve cover.
12. Label and disconnect the spark plug wires, the electrical connector and the vacuum hoses from the distributor.
13. Remove the upper timing belt cover-to-cylinder head bolts and the cover.
14. Remove the cylinder head cover-to-cylinder head bolts, the cover and the gasket.
15. Remove the alternator drive belt. Remove the water pump pulley-to-water pump bolts and the pulley.
16. Using socket wrench on the crankshaft pulley bolt, rotate the crankshaft to position the No. 1 cylinder on the **TDC** of its compression stroke; the crankshaft pulley notch is aligned with the **0** degrees mark on the timing plate and the No. 1 cylinder rocker arms are loose.
17. Remove the distributor-to-cylinder head hold-down bolts and the distributor.
18. Matchmark the timing belt and sprocket for reassembly in the same position; mark an arrow on the timing belt for rotation direction.
19. Loosen the idler pulley bolt. Move it so as to release the timing belt tension and snug the idler pulley bolt. Remove the timing belt; avoid twisting or bending it.
20. Loosen the head bolts (in sequence), in 3 stages, then, re-

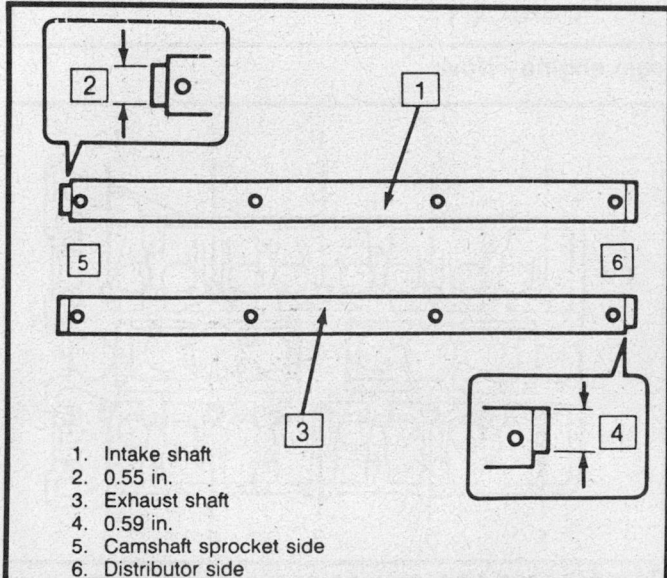

1. Intake shaft
2. 0.55 in.
3. Exhaust shaft
4. 0.59 in.
5. Camshaft sprocket side
6. Distributor side

Identifying rocker arm shafts—Sprint and Metro

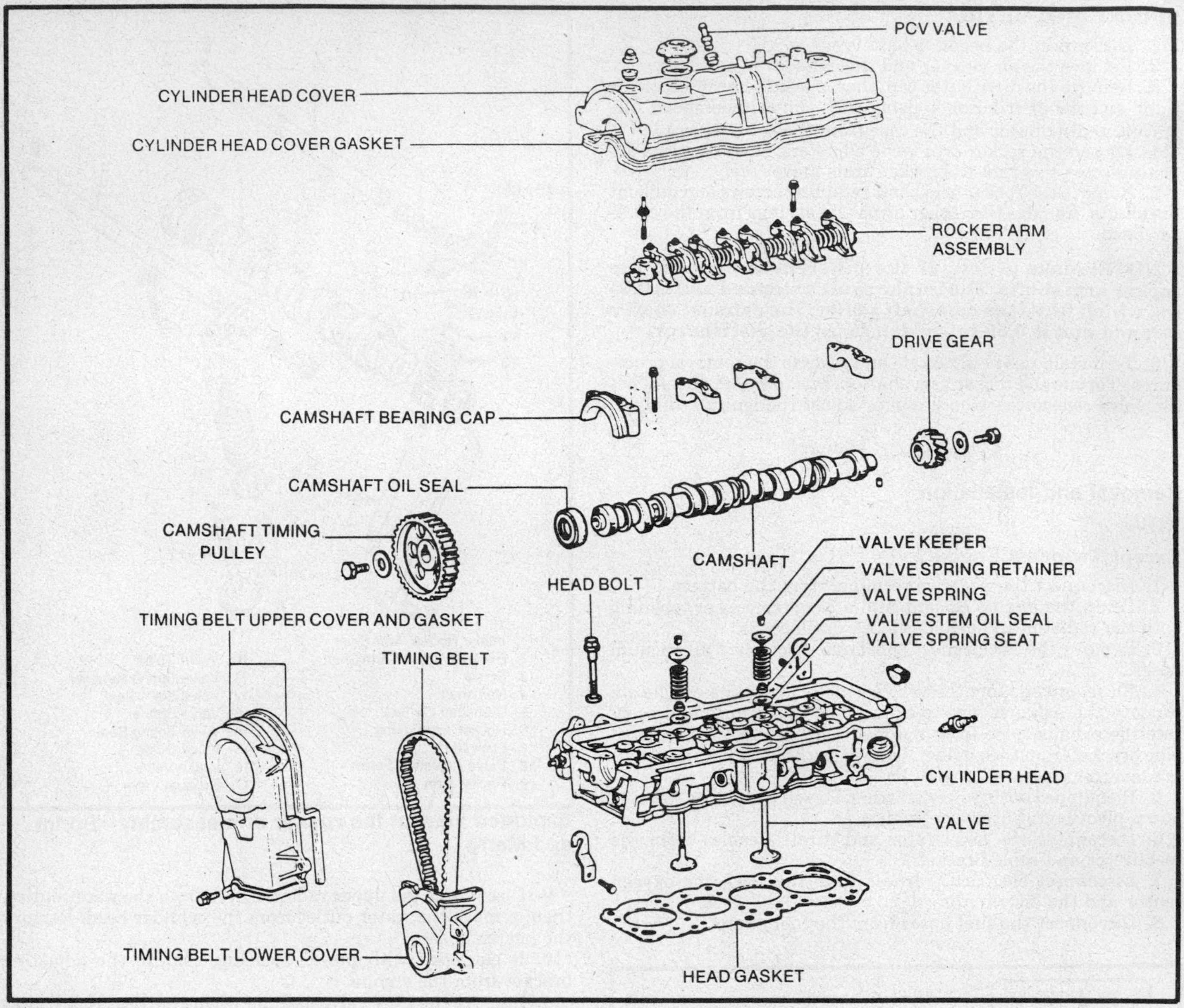

PCV VALVE

CYLINDER HEAD COVER

CYLINDER HEAD COVER GASKET

ROCKER ARM ASSEMBLY

DRIVE GEAR

CAMSHAFT BEARING CAP

CAMSHAFT OIL SEAL

CAMSHAFT TIMING PULLEY

VALVE KEEPER
VALVE SPRING RETAINER
VALVE SPRING
VALVE STEM OIL SEAL
VALVE SPRING SEAT

HEAD BOLT

CAMSHAFT

TIMING BELT UPPER COVER AND GASKET

TIMING BELT

CYLINDER HEAD

VALVE

TIMING BELT LOWER COVER

HEAD GASKET

Exploded view of the cylinder head assembly except twincam engine—Nova

move them. Lift the head directly off the block. If it is necessary to pry the head off the block, use a bar between the head and the projection provided on top of the block.

NOTE: Do not pry except at the projection provided. Be careful not to damage the block or cylinder head sealing surface.

21. Using the proper tool, clean the gasket mounting surfaces. Using wire brush, clean the cylinder head chambers.
22. To install, use new gaskets, sealant (if necessary) and reverse the removal procedures.

NOTE: When installing the cylinder head gasket, position the side with the sealer facing upwards.

23. Torque the cylinder head-to-engine bolts (in sequence), using 3 passes, to 43 ft. lbs., the camshaft sprocket-to-camshaft bolt to 34 ft. lbs. and the timing belt idler bolt to 27 ft. lbs.
24. Rotate the crankshaft through two complete revolutions and check the timing belt tension; the tension should be 0.024–0.28 in.

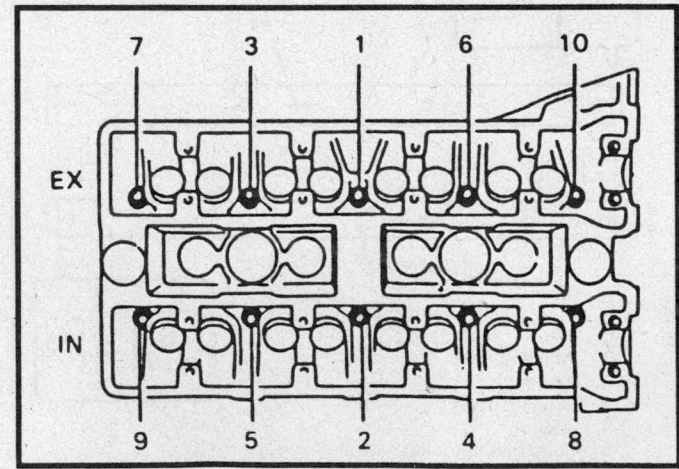

Cylinder head bolt torquing sequence, twincam engine—Nova

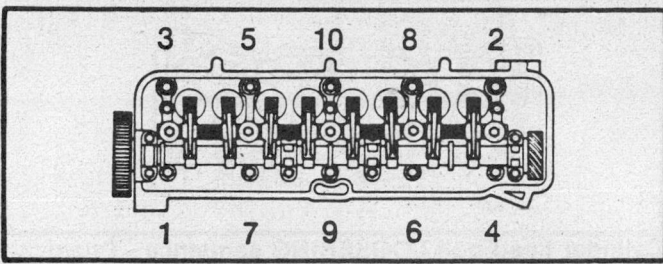

Cylinder head bolt loosening sequence except twincam engine—Nova

25. Adjust the valves with the engine **COLD**. Operate the engine until normal operating temperatures are reached and check for leaks. Readjust the valves with the engine **HOT**. Set the ignition timing.

Twincam Engine

1. Disconnect the negative terminal from the battery. Relieve the fuel system pressure.
2. Drain the engine coolant. Remove the air cleaner assembly.
3. Disconnect the throttle cable and the cruise control cable from the throttle linkage. Remove the ignition coil.
4. From the rear of the cylinder head, remove the heater hose. Remove the vacuum hoses from the throttle body. Remove the water outlet hose from cylinder head and the radiator.
5. If equipped with cruise control, remove the actuator and the bracket assembly.
6. Remove the hoses from the PCV valve and the power brake booster.
7. Remove the pressure regulator, the EGR valve (with lines) and the cold start injector hose.
8. Disconnect and remove the No. 1 fuel line.
9. From the auxiliary air valve, remove the No. 1 and No. 2 water by-pass hoses.
10. Remove the vacuum pipe and the cylinder head rear cover.
11. Label and disconnect the electrical harness connectors. Remove the distributor-to-cylinder hold-down bolt and the distributor.
12. Remove the exhaust manifold-to-cylinder head bolts and separate the exhaust manifold from the cylinder head.
13. Remove the fuel delivery pipe-to-engine bolts and the delivery pipe with the injectors; do not drop the fuel injectors.
14. Remove the intake manifold bracket, the intake manifold-to-cylinder head bolts (in sequence), the intake manifold and the intake air control valve.
15. If equipped with power steering, remove the drive belt. Remove the alternator drive belt and the cylinder head covers.
16. Remove the water outlet with the No. 1 by pass pipe and drive belt adjusting bar assembly.
17. To position the No. 1 cylinder on the **TDC** of its compression stroke, perform the following procedures:
    a. Remove the spark plugs.
    b. Using a socket wrench on the crankshaft pulley, rotate the crankshaft to align the notch in the crankshaft pulley with the idler pulley bolt.
    c. The valve lifters of the No. 1 cylinder should be loose; if not, rotate the crankshaft one complete revolution.
18. Remove the right side engine mount, the right-side engine mount bracket, then, the upper and middle timing belt covers.
19. Using chalk or paint, place match marks on the timing belt and the timing belt pulleys, then, remove the timing belt from the timing belt pulleys.

NOTE: When removing the timing belt, be sure to support it so the meshing with the timing belt pulleys does not change. Do not allow it to come in contact with oil or water.

20. While securing the camshafts, remove each camshaft pulley-to-camshaft bolt, washer and pulley. Remove the inner timing belt cover.
21. Remove the camshaft bearing cap-to-cylinder head bolts, the caps (keep them in order) and the camshafts (keep them in order).
22. Using the cylinder head bolt removal sequence, remove the cylinder head bolts and lift the cylinder head from the engine.
23. Using the proper tool, clean the gasket mounting surfaces. Using a wire brush, clean the carbon from the cylinder head cavities. Inspect the cylinder head for damage and/or warpage.

NOTE: When cleaning the cylinder head, be careful, for the cylinder head is made of aluminum which is a soft material.

To install:
24. To install the cylinder head, use a new gasket (make sure it is installed in the correct direction), lubricate the bolt threads in engine oil and reverse the removal procedures.

NOTE: The intake-side bolts are 3.45 in. long and the exhaust-side bolts are 4.25 in. long.

25. To torque the cylinder head-to-engine bolts, perform the following procedures:
    a. Torque the cylinder head-to-engine bolts (in sequence) to 22 ft. lbs.
    b. Using paint, place a paint mark on the cylinder head bolts.
    c. Torque the bolts (in sequence) ¼ turn (90 degrees).
    d. Retorque the bolts (in sequence) another ¼ turn (90 degrees).
26. To install the camshafts, apply RTV sealant to the camshaft oil seal bearing cap-to-cylinder head surfaces, lightly coat the seal lip with multi-purpose grease, then, install the new oil seals and camshafts. Torque the camshaft bearing cap-to-cylinder head bolts to 9 ft. lbs.

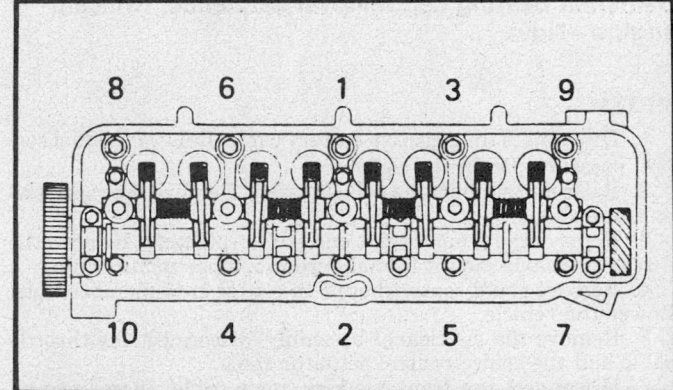

Cylinder head bolt torquing sequence except twincam engine—Nova

27. Install the camshaft pulleys-to-camshaft bolts to 34 ft. lbs. Align the timing belt marks with the camshaft pulley marks and install the timing belt onto the camshaft pulleys.
28. Using a wrench on the timing belt pulley, rotate the crankshaft 2 complete revolutions and check the timing belt alignment points.
29. To complete the installation, use new O-rings, new gaskets, sealant (if necessary) and reverse the removal procedures. Torque the intake manifold-to-cylinder head bolts to 20 ft. lbs., the exhaust manifold-to-cylinder head bolts to 18 ft. lbs. Refill the cooling system. Start the engine, allow it to reach normal operating temperatures and check for leaks. Check and/or adjust the ignition timing.

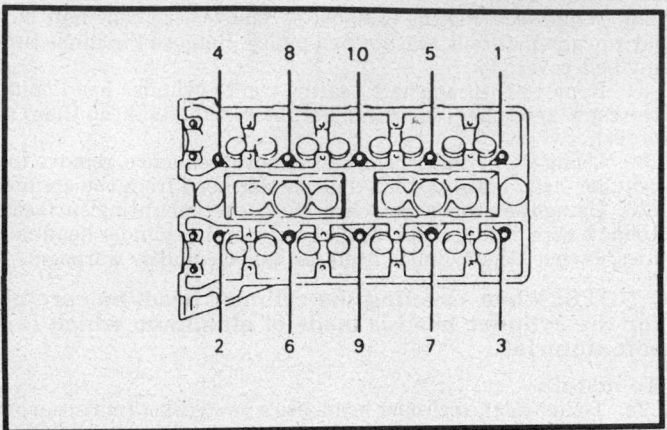

Cylinder head bolt loosening sequence, twincam engine—Nova

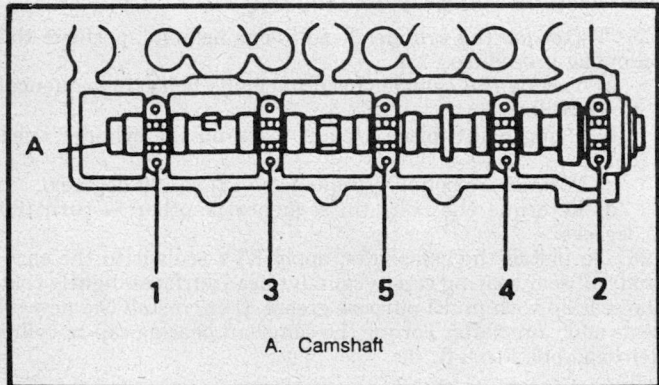

A. Camshaft

Camshaft bearing cap removal sequence, twincam engine—Nova

PRIZM

1. Disconnect the negative battery cable. Relieve the fuel system pressure. Drain the coolant.

2. Raise and support the vehicle safely. Remove the right lower stone shield.

3. Remove the 2 mount nut and stud protectors. Remove the 2 rear transaxle mount to main crossmember mount nuts.

4. Remove the 2 center mount to center crossmember nuts. Lower the vehicle.

5. Remove the air cleaner assembly, disconnect the throttle cable and the cruise control actuator cable.

6. Disconnect the transaxle kick down cable. Disconnect all necessary electrical connections and vacuum lines.

7. Disconnect the fuel inlet line. Disconnect the cold start injector pipe. Remove the fuel rail. Disconnect the coolant and heater hoses.

8. Remove the water outlet and inlet housings. Disconnect the spark plug wires and remove the PCV valve.

9. Remove the cylinder head cover. Loosen the air conditioning compressor, power steering pump, and generator brackets as applicable.

10. Remove the accessory drive belts. Remove the air conditioning idler pulley. Disconnect the electrical connections at cruise control actuator and remove the cruise control actuator and bracket.

11. Remove windshield washer reservoir. Support the engine with a J 28467–A support fixture or its equivalent.

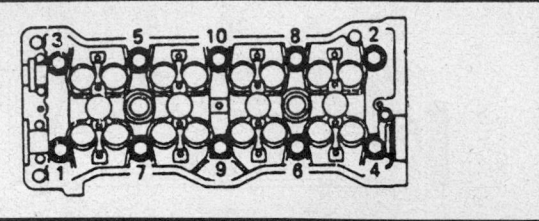

Cylinder head bolt LOOSENING sequence—Prizm

12. Remove the right engine mount through bolt. Raise the engine and properly support it.

13. Remove the water pump pulley. Lower the engine. Disconnect the engine wiring harness from upper timing belt cover.

14. Raise and suitably support the vehicle. Remove the cylinder head-to-cylinder block bracket.

15. Remove the exhaust manifold support bracket. Disconnect the exhaust pipe from exhaust manifold.

16. Remove the upper and center timing belt cover. Remove the right engine mount bracket. Remove the distributor.

17. Set the number 1 cylinder at TDC on its compression stroke. Turn the crankshaft pulley and align its groove with the 0 mark of the timing belt cover.

18. Check that the camshaft gear hole is aligned with the exhaust camshaft cap mark. Remove the plug from the lower timing belt cover.

20. Place alignment marks on the camshaft timing gear and belt.

21. Loosen the idler pulley mount bolt and push the idler pulley toward the left as far as it will go, then tighten it temporarily.

22. Remove the timing belt from the camshaft timing gear after marking its position in relation to the camshaft timing gear.

23. Hold the timing belt with a cloth.

NOTE: Support the belt so the meshing of the crankshaft timing gear and timing belt does not shift. Be careful not to drop anything inside the timing belt cover. Do not allow the belt to come in contact with oil, water, or dust.

24. Remove the cylinder head bolts in the proper sequence using a 10mm, 12 point deep well socket.

NOTE: Head warping or cracking could result from incorrect removal.

25. Remove the cylinder head with intake and exhaust manifolds. If the head is difficult to lift off, carefully pry with a bar between the cylinder head and a cylinder block projection.

NOTE: Be careful not to damage the cylinder head and block mating surface. Lift the cylinder head from the dowels on the cylinder block and place it on wooden blocks on a bench.

26. Remove the intake and exhaust manifolds.

27. Remove as necessary the camshafts, the valve lifters and shims, the spark plug tubes, the valves using a J 8062 spring compressor and a J 37979–A adapter, the valve stem oil seals, and the half circle plug.

To install

28. Install the half circle plug to the cylinder head. Apply GM No.1052751 or equivalent sealant to the plug.

29. Install the valves. Install the new oil seals on the valves using a J 38232 seal installer.

NOTE: The intake valve oil seal is brown and the exhaust valve oil seal is black.

30. Install the spring seat, spring, and spring retainer on the cylinder head. Using a J 8062 spring compressor and a J 37979–A adapter, compress the valve springs and place the 2 keepers

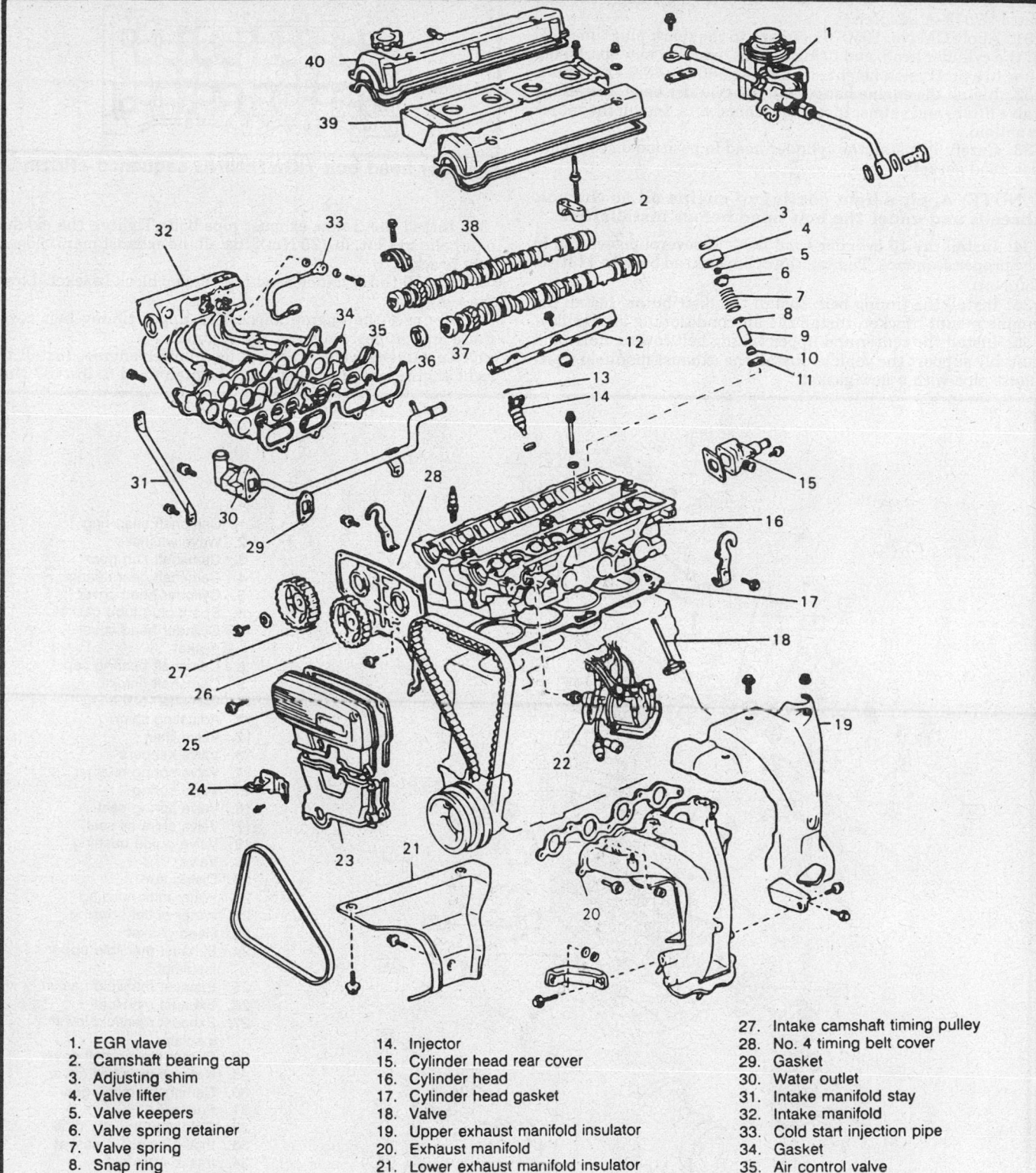

1. EGR vlave
2. Camshaft bearing cap
3. Adjusting shim
4. Valve lifter
5. Valve keepers
6. Valve spring retainer
7. Valve spring
8. Snap ring
9. Valve guide bushing
10. Valve stem oil seal
11. Valve spring seal
12. Delivery pipe
13. O-Ring
14. Injector
15. Cylinder head rear cover
16. Cylinder head
17. Cylinder head gasket
18. Valve
19. Upper exhaust manifold insulator
20. Exhaust manifold
21. Lower exhaust manifold insulator
22. Distributor
23. No. 2 timing belt cover
24. Engine mounting bracket
25. No. 3 timing belt cover
26. Exhaust camshaft timing pulley
27. Intake camshaft timing pulley
28. No. 4 timing belt cover
29. Gasket
30. Water outlet
31. Intake manifold stay
32. Intake manifold
33. Cold start injection pipe
34. Gasket
35. Air control valve
36. Gasket
37. Exhaust valve camshaft
38. Intake valve camshaft
39. Cylinder head center cover
40. Cylinder head cover

Exploded view of the cylinder head assembly, twincam engine–Nova

around valve stem. Remove the J 8062 spring compressor and the J 37979–A adapter.

31. Apply GM No. 1052751 sealant to the spark plug tube hole of the cylinder head, and using a press, install a new spark plug tube to a protrusion height of 1.835 – 1.866 in. (46.6 – 47.4mm).

32. Install the engine hangers to the cylinder head. Install the valve lifters and shims. Install the camshafts. Install the intake manifold.

33. Carefully install the cylinder head in position on the cylinder head gasket.

NOTE: Apply a light coating of engine oil on the bolt threads and under the bolt head before installation.

34. Install the 10 cylinder head bolts in several passes and in the proper sequence. Tighten the cylinder head bolts to 44 ft. lb. (60 Nm).

35. Install the timing belt. Install the distributor. Install the engine mount bracket. Install the air conditioning idler pulley.

36. Install the center and upper timing belt covers. Raise and suitably support the vehicle. Install the exhaust manifold to exhaust pipe with a new gasket.

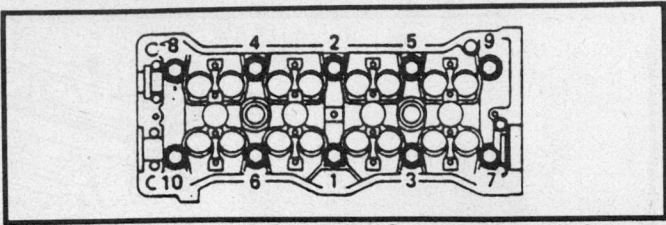

Cylinder head bolt TIGHTENING sequence—Prizm

37. Install the 2 new exhaust pipe bolts. Tighten the exhaust pipe bolts to 18 ft. lb. (25 Nm). Install the exhaust manifold support bracket.

38. Install the cylinder head-to-cylinder block bracket. Lower the vehicle.

39. Connect the engine harness to upper timing belt cover. Raise and properly support the engine.

40. Install the water pump pulley. Lower engine. Install the right engine mount through bolt. Tighten to 64 ft. lbs. (87 Nm).

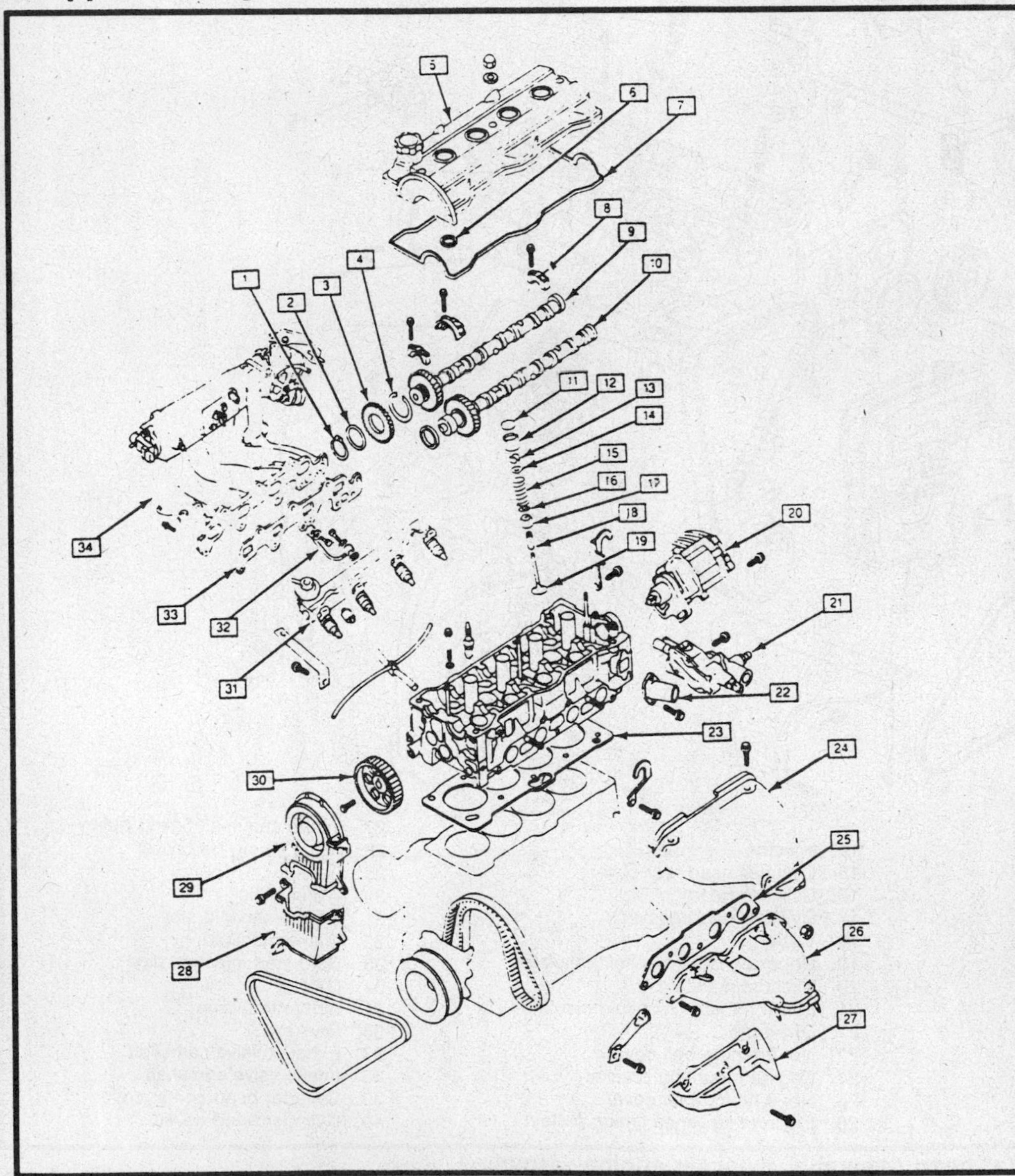

1. Camshaft snap ring
2. Wave washer
3. Camshaft sub gear
4. Camshaft gear spring
5. Cylinder head cover
6. Spark plug tube gasket
7. Cylinder head cover gasket
8. Camshaft bearing cap
9. Camshaft (intake)
10. Camshaft (exhaust)
11. Adjusting shim
12. Valve lifter
13. Valve keepers
14. Valve spring retainer
15. Valve spring
16. Valve spring seat
17. Valve stem oil seal
18. Valve guide bushing
19. Valve
20. Distributor
21. Water inlet housing
22. Water outlet housing
23. Head gasket
24. Exhaust manifold upper insulator
25. Exhaust manifold gasket
26. Exhaust manifold
27. Exhaust manifold lower insulator
28. Center timimg belt cover
29. Upper timing belt cover
30. Camshaft timimn gear
31. Fuel rail
32. Cold start injector pipe
33. Intake manifold gasket
34. Intake manifold

Exploded view of the cylinder head assembly—Prizm

41. Remove the J 28467-A support fixture. Install the windshield washer reservoir.

42. Install the cruise control actuator and bracket and connect the electrical conncetor.

43. Install the accessory drive belts and adjust to the proper tensions as applicable.

44. Install the cylinder head cover. Install the PCV valve and spark plug wires. Install the water inlet and outlet housings.

45. Install the heater hoses and all coolant hoses. Install the fuel rail. Install the cold-start injector pipe.

46. Install the fuel inlet line. Connect all necessary electrical connections and vacuum lines.

47. Install the transaxle kick down cable, connect the cruise control actuator cable and the throttle cable. Install the air cleaner assembly.

48. Raise and suitably support the vehicle. Install the 2 rear mount-to-main crossmember nuts.
Install the 2 center transaxle mount-to-center crossmember nuts.

49. Tighten the rear transaxle mount-to-main crossmember nuts to (45 ft. lbs. (61 Nm). Tighten the center transaxle mount-to-center crossmember nuts to (45 ft. lbs. (61 Nm).

50. Install both mount nut and stud protectors. Install the right lower stone shield.

51. Lower the vehicle. Refill coolant and install the battery negative cable.

SPECTRUM

1. Relieve the fuel system pressure. Disconnect the negative battery terminal from the battery.

2. Drain the cooling system.

3. Remove the air cleaner.

4. Disconnect the flex hose and oxygen sensor at the exhaust manifold.

5. Disconnect the exhaust pipe bracket at the block and the exhaust pipe at the manifold. On turbocharged engine disconnect exhaust pipe at wastegate manifold and disconnect vacumm line for turbocharger control.

6. Disconnect the spark plug wires.

7. Remove the thermostat housing, the distributor, the vacuum advance hoses and the ground cable at the cylinder head.

8. Disconnect the fuel hoses at the fuel pump on non-turbocharged engine.

9. From the carburetor, if so equipped, remove the necessary hoses and the throttle cable.

10. Remove engine harness asembly from fuel injectors and fuel line from fuel injector pipe on turbocharged model.

11. Disconnect the vacuum switching valve electrical connector and the heater hoses.

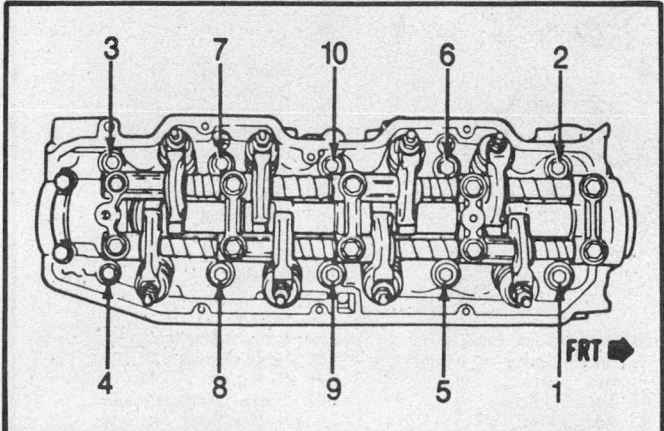

Cylinder head bolt removal sequence — Spectrum

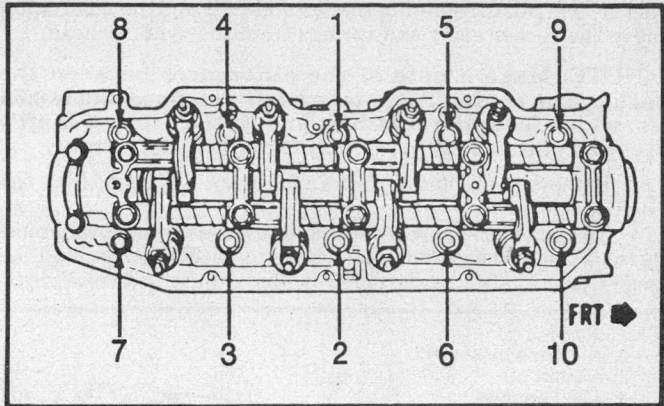

Cylinder head bolt torque sequence — Spectrum

12. Remove the alternator, power steering and A/C adjusting bolts, brackets and drive belts.

13. Support the engine using a vertical hoist. Remove the right hand motor mount and the bracket at the front cover.

14. Rotate the engine to align the timing marks, then remove the timing gear cover.

15. Loosen the tension pulley and remove the timing belt from the camshaft timing pulley.

16. Disconnect the carburetor fuel line at the fuel pump and remove the fuel pump.

17. Disconnect the intake manifold coolant hoses.

18. Remove the cylinder head bolts (remove the bolts from both ends at the same time, working toward the middle) and the cylinder head. Clean all of the mounting surfaces.

19. Compress the valves; then remove the keepers, springs, seals and valves.

20. To install, use new seals and gaskets, apply oil to the bolt threads and torque the head bolts.

NOTE: When torquing the cylinder head bolts, work from the middle toward both ends, alternating from one side to the other. First, torque the bolts to 29 ft. lbs. and then final torque them to 58 ft. lbs.

21. After torquing, adjust the valve clearance and complete the installation procedures, by reversing the removal procedures.

SPRINT AND METRO

1. Disconnect the negative battery cable and relieve the fuel system pressure.

2. Drain the cooling system.

3. Remove the air cleaner and the cylinder head cover.

4. Remove the distributor cap, then mark the position of the rotor and the distributor housing with the cylinder head. Remove the distributor and the case from the cylinder head.

5. Remove the accelerator cable from the carburetor. Remove the emission control and the coolant hoses from the carburetor/intake manifold.

6. Remove the electrical lead connectors from the carburetor/intake manifold and the lead wire from the oxygen sensor.

7. Remove the fuel hoses from the fuel pump and the pump from the cylinder head.

8. Remove the brake vacuum hose from the intake manifold.

9. Remove the crankshaft pulley, the outside cover, the timing belt and the tensioner from the front of the engine.

10. Remove the exhaust and the 2nd air pipes from the exhaust manifold.

11. Remove the exhaust/intake manifolds and the engine side mount from the cylinder head.

12. Loosen the rocker arm valve adjusters, turn back the adjusting screws so that the rocker arms move freely. Remove the

rocker arm shaft retaining screws and pull out the shafts. Remove the rocker arms and springs from the cylinder head.

NOTE: Make a note of the differences between the rocker arm shafts. The intake shaft's stepped end is 0.55 in., which faces the camshaft pulley; the exhaust shaft's stepped end is 0.59 in., which faces the distributor.

13. Remove the mounting bolts and the cylinder head from the engine.

14. To install, use new gaskets and reverse the removal procedures. Torque the cylinder head bolts to 46–50.5 ft. lbs. and the rocker arm shaft screws to 7–9 ft. lbs. Adjust the valve clear-

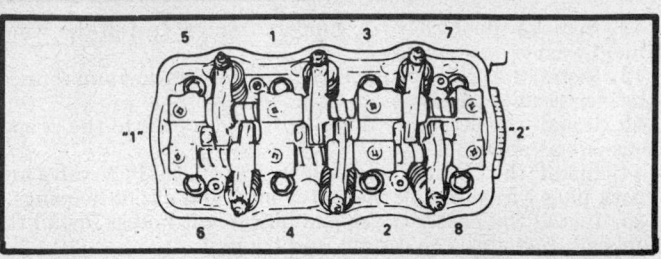

Cylinder head bolt torque sequence—Sprint and Metro

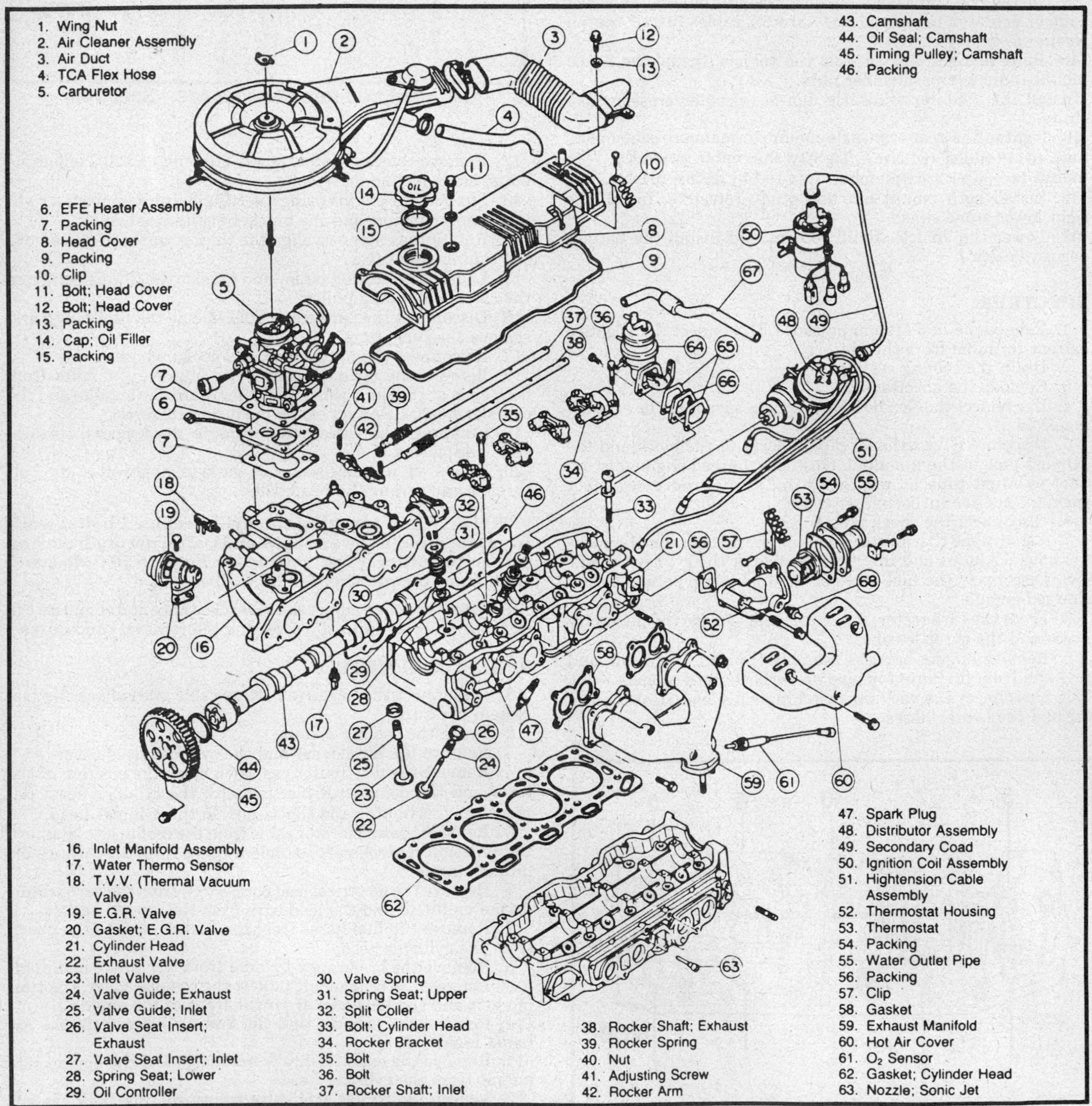

1. Wing Nut
2. Air Cleaner Assembly
3. Air Duct
4. TCA Flex Hose
5. Carburetor

6. EFE Heater Assembly
7. Packing
8. Head Cover
9. Packing
10. Clip
11. Bolt; Head Cover
12. Bolt; Head Cover
13. Packing
14. Cap; Oil Filler
15. Packing

16. Inlet Manifold Assembly
17. Water Thermo Sensor
18. T.V.V. (Thermal Vacuum Valve)
19. E.G.R. Valve
20. Gasket; E.G.R. Valve
21. Cylinder Head
22. Exhaust Valve
23. Inlet Valve
24. Valve Guide; Exhaust
25. Valve Guide; Inlet
26. Valve Seat Insert; Exhaust
27. Valve Seat Insert; Inlet
28. Spring Seat; Lower
29. Oil Controller

30. Valve Spring
31. Spring Seat; Upper
32. Split Coller
33. Bolt; Cylinder Head
34. Rocker Bracket
35. Bolt
36. Bolt
37. Rocker Shaft; Inlet

38. Rocker Shaft; Exhaust
39. Rocker Spring
40. Nut
41. Adjusting Screw
42. Rocker Arm

43. Camshaft
44. Oil Seal; Camshaft
45. Timing Pulley; Camshaft
46. Packing

47. Spark Plug
48. Distributor Assembly
49. Secondary Coad
50. Ignition Coil Assembly
51. Hightension Cable Assembly
52. Thermostat Housing
53. Thermostat
54. Packing
55. Water Outlet Pipe
56. Packing
57. Clip
58. Gasket
59. Exhaust Manifold
60. Hot Air Cover
61. O₂ Sensor
62. Gasket; Cylinder Head
63. Nozzle; Sonic Jet

Exploded view of the top of the engine—Spectrum

ances. Refill the cooling system. Check and/or adjust the ignition timing.

Camshaft

Removal and Installation

NOVA

Except Twincam Engine

1. Remove the upper timing belt front cover and the valve cover; do not remove the timing belt.

2. Disconnect the negative battery cable and the spark plug wires, then, remove the distributor-to-engine hold-down bolt, the distributor and the distributor gear bolt.

3. Disconnect the hoses from the fuel pump, then, remove the fuel pump.

4. Using a socket wrench on the crankshaft pulley bolt, rotate the crankshaft (clockwise) to position the No. 1 cylinder on the TDC of its compression stroke; the rocker arms of the No. 1 cylinder will be loose, if not, rotate the crankshaft one complete revolution.

5. Loosen the rocker arm adjusting nuts and back off the adjusting screw. Remove the rocker shaft-to-cylinder head assembly.

6. Place alignment marks on the timing belt and the timing pulleys; also, mark the direction of timing belt rotation.

7. Loosen the idler pulley bolt and push the pulley as far left as possible, then, retighten the bolt. Remove the timing belt from the camshaft timing pulleys, support it so it will remain in mesh with the crankshaft pulley; be careful not to get oil on the timing belt.

8. Use a large open-end wrench, secure the camshaft (on the flats), then, remove the camshaft pulley-to-camshaft bolt; the camshaft flats are located between the first and second cam lobes. Remove the camshaft pulley.

9. Remove the camshaft bearing cap bolts, the caps and the camshaft; keep the caps in order for reinstallation purposes.

10. Remove the distributor drive gear.

11. Inspect the camshaft for damage and/or wear; if necessary, replace the camshaft.

12. To install, insert the distributor drive gear, plate washer and bolt.

13. Using clean engine oil, coat all bearing surfaces, then, install the camshaft and No. 2, 3 and 4 bearing caps (in their proper positions and direction).

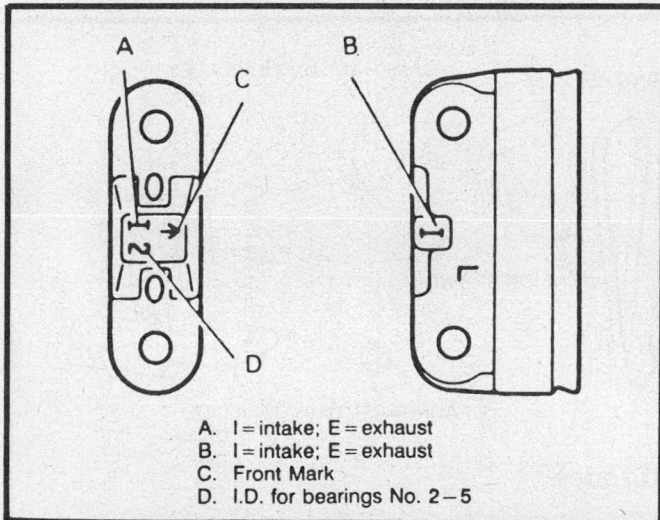

A. I = intake; E = exhaust
B. I = intake; E = exhaust
C. Front Mark
D. I.D. for bearings No. 2–5

View of the camshaft bearing caps, twincam engine— Nova

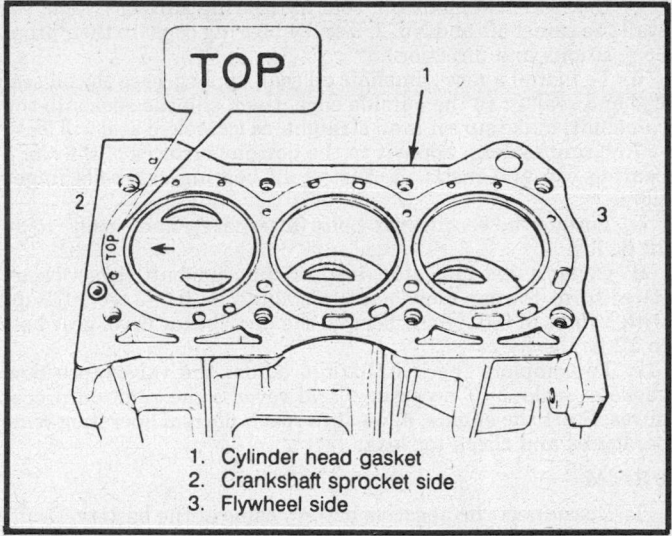

1. Cylinder head gasket
2. Crankshaft sprocket side
3. Flywheel side

Cylinder head gasket installation position—Sprint and Metro

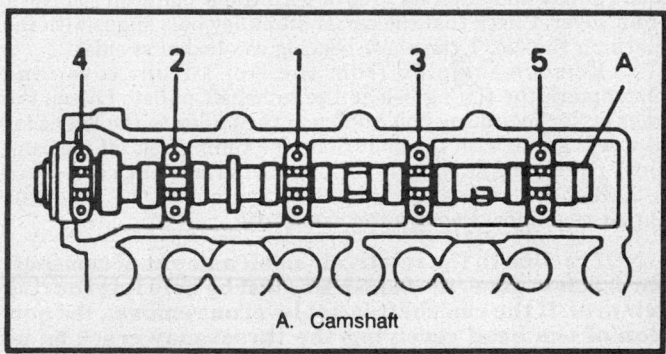

A. Camshaft

Camshaft bearing cap torque sequence, twincam engine—Nova

14. To install a new camshaft oil seal, apply grease the oil seal lips and sealant to the outside edge, then, slip the seal onto the camshaft; make sure it is on straight, as a crooked seal will leak.

15. Using sealant, apply it to the bottom surfaces of the No. 1 bearing cap and install it. Install all bearing cap bolts finger tight.

16. Torque the bearing cap bolts (alternately and evenly) to 8–10 ft. lbs.

17. Using a dial indicator, inspect the camshaft thrust clearance (front-to-rear movement; it should be 0.0031–0.0071 in. with a limit of 0.0098 in. Torque the distributor drive gear bolt to 22 ft. lbs.

18. To complete the installation, adjust the valves, use new gaskets, sealant (if necessary) and reverse the removal procedures. Start the engine, allow it to reach normal operating temperatures and check for leaks.

Twincam Engine

1. Disconnect the negative battery cable.

2. Remove the cylinder head covers and the camshaft pulleys.

3. Loosen and remove the camshaft bearing caps-to-cylinder head bolts in sequence. Remove the camshaft bearing caps and camshafts; be sure to keep the parts in order for reinstallation purposes.

4. Using the proper tool, clean the gasket mounting surfaces. Inspect the camshaft for wear and/or damage, if necessary, replace the camshaft.

5. Using clean engine oil, coat all bearing surfaces, then, install the camshaft and No. 2, 3 and 4 bearing caps (in their proper positions and direction).

6. To install a new camshaft oil seal, apply grease the oil seal lips and sealant to the outside edge, then, slip the seal onto the camshaft; make sure it is on straight, as a crooked seal will leak.

7. Using sealant, apply it to the bottom surfaces of the No. 1 bearing cap and install it. Install all bearing cap bolts finger tight.

8. Torque the bearing cap bolts (alternately and evenly) to 8–10 ft. lbs.

9. Using a dial indicator, inspect the camshaft thrust clearance (front-to-rear movement; it should be 0.0031–0.0075 in. with a limit of 0.0118 in. Torque the distributor drive gear bolt to 22 ft. lbs.

10. To complete the installation, adjust the valves, use new gaskets, sealant (if necessary) and reverse the removal procedures. Start the engine, allow it to reach normal operating temperatures and check for leaks.

PRIZM

1. Disconnect the negative battery cable at the battery. Drain the engine coolant.

2. Remove the spark plugs and the cylinder head cover.

3. Remove the No. 3 and No. 2 front covers. Turn the crankshaft pulley and align its groove with the **0** mark on the No. 1 front cover. Check that the camshaft pulley hole aligns with the mark on the No. 1 camshaft bearing cap (exhaust side).

4. Remove the plug from the No. 1 front cover and matchmark the timing belt to the camshaft pulley. Loosen the idler pulley mounting bolt and push the pulley to the left as far as it will go; tighten the bolt. Slide the timing belt off the camshaft pulley and support it so it won't fall into the case.

5. Remove the camshaft pulley and check the camshaft thrust clearance. Remove the camshafts.

NOTE: Due to the relatively small amount of camshaft thrust clearance, the camshaft must be held level during removal. If the camshaft is not level on removal, the portion of the head receiving the thrust may crack or be damaged.

6. Set the service bolt hole on the intake camshaft gear (the one not attached to the timing pulley!) at the 12 o'clock position so that the Nos. 1 and 3 cylinder camshaft lobed can push their lifters evenly. Loosen the No. 1 bearing caps on each camshaft a little at a time and remove them.

7. Secure the intake camshaft sub-gear to the main gear with a service bolt to eliminate any torsional spring force. Loosen the remaining bearing caps a little at a time, in the proper sequence and remove the intake camshaft. If the camshaft cannot be lifted out straight and level, retighten the bolts in the No. 3 bearing cap and loosen them a little at a time with the gear pulled up.

8. Turn the exhaust camshaft approximately 105 degrees so the knock pin is about 5 minutes before the 6:30 o'clock position. Loosen the remaining bearing caps a little at a time, in the proper sequence and remove the exhaust camshaft. If the camshaft cannot be lifted out straight and level, retighten the bolts in the No. 3 bearing cap and loosen them a little at a time with the gear pulled up.

To install:

9. Position the exhaust camshaft into the cylinder head as it was removed. Position the bearing caps over each journal so that the arrows point forward and then tighten the bolts gradually, in the proper sequence to 9 ft. lbs. (13 Nm).

10. Coat the lip of a new oil seal with MP grease and drive it into the camshaft.

11. Set the knock pin on the exhaust camshaft so it is just above the edge of the cylinder head and engage the intake camshaft gear to the exhaust gear so that the mark on each gear is in alignment. Roll the intake camshaft down onto the bearing journals while engaging the gears with each other.

12. Position the bearing caps over each journal on the intake camshaft so that the arrows point forward and then tighten the bolts gradually, in the proper sequence to 9 ft. lbs. (13 Nm).

13. Remove the service bolt and install the No. 1 intake bearing cap. If it does not fit properly, pry the camshaft gear backwards until it does. Tighten the bolts to 9 ft. lbs. (13 Nm).

14. Rotate the camshafts 1 revolution (360 degrees) from TDC to TDC and check that the marks on the 2 gears are still aligned.

15. Install the camshaft timing pulley making sure that the camshaft knock pins and the matchmarks are in alignment. Lock each camshaft and tighten the pulley bolts to 43 ft. lbs. (59 Nm).

16. Align the matchmarks made during removal and then install the timing belt on the camshaft pulley. Loosen the idler pulley set bolt. Make sure the timing belt meshing at the crankshaft pulley does not shift.

17. Rotate the crankshaft clockwise 2 revolutions from TDC to TDC. Make sure that each pulley aligns with the marks made previously.

18. Tighten the set bolt on the timing belt idler pulley to 27 ft. lbs. (37 Nm). Measure the timing belt deflection at the top span between the 2 camshaft pulleys. It should deflect no more than

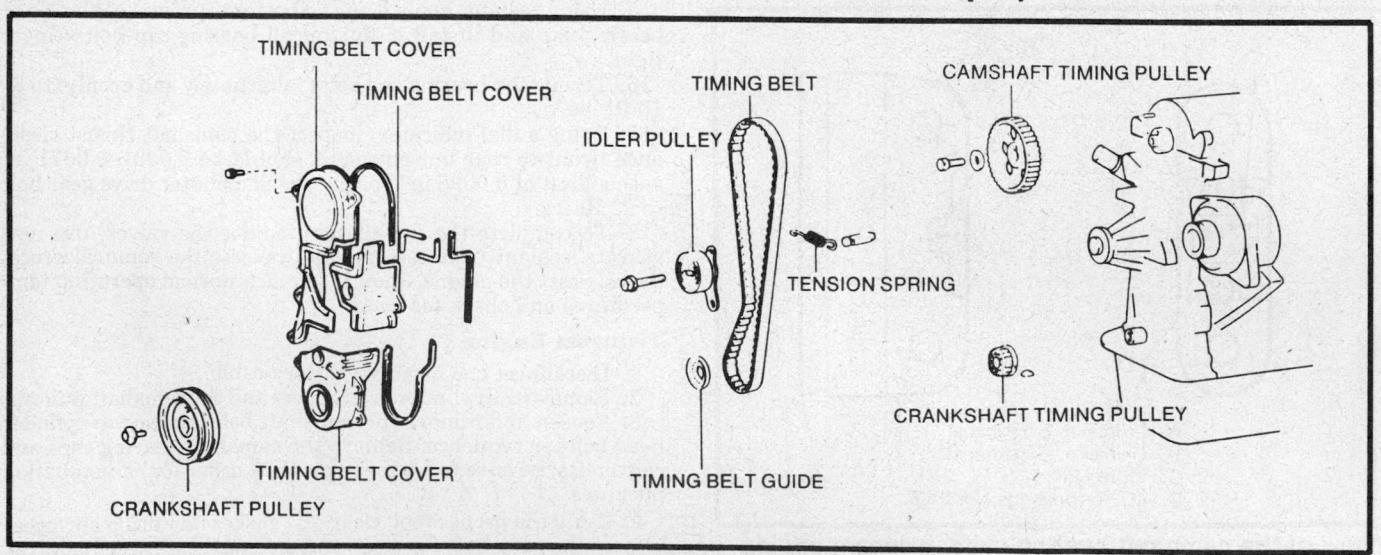

TIMING BELT COVER
TIMING BELT COVER
TIMING BELT
IDLER PULLEY
CAMSHAFT TIMING PULLEY
TENSION SPRING
TIMING BELT COVER
CRANKSHAFT PULLEY
TIMING BELT GUIDE
CRANKSHAFT TIMING PULLEY

Exploded view of the timing belt assembly-except twincam engine–Nova

0.16 in. at 4.4 lbs. of pressure. If deflection is greater, readjust by using the idler pulley.

19. Installation of the remaining components is in the reverse order of removal.

SPECTRUM

1. Disconnect the negative battery terminal from the battery.
2. Align the crankshaft pulley notch with the 0 degree mark on the timing cover.
3. Remove the cylinder head cover.
4. Remove the timing cover.
5. Loosen the camshaft timing gear bolts (Do not rotate the engine).
6. Loosen the timing belt tensioner and remove the timing belt from the camshaft timing gear.
7. Remove the rocker arm shaft/rocker arm assembly.
8. Remove the distributor bolt and the distributor.
9. Remove the camshaft and the camshaft seal.
10. To install, drive a new camshaft seal on the camshaft using the seal installation tool no. J–35268 or equivalent, reverse the removal procedures, adjust the valves and the timing belt.

SPRINT AND METRO

1. Remove the timing belt.
2. Remove the air cleaner, rocker arm cover, distributor and distributor case. Remove the rocker arm shafts and the rocker arms.
3. Remove the fuel pump and fuel pump pushrod from the cylinder head.
4. Using a spanner wrench tool J–34836 to hold the camshaft pulley, remove the camshaft pulley bolt, the pulley, the alignment pin and the inside cover.
5. Carefully slide the camshaft from the rear of the cylinder head.
6. Clean the gasket mounting surfaces. Check for wear and/or damage, replace the parts as necessary.
7. To install, use new gaskets/seals and reverse the removal procedures. Torque the camshaft pulley bolt to 41–46 ft. lbs. Adjust the valve clearances and check the timing.

Timing Belt And Front Covers

Removal and Installation

NOVA EXCEPT TWINCAM ENGINE

This engine uses a 3 piece timing belt cover assembly; any individual cover can be removed by performing one of the following procedures.

Upper

1. Disconnect the negative terminal from the battery.
2. Loosen the water pump pulley bolts and remove the alternator/water pump drive belt. If equipped with power steering, remove the power steering pump drive belt.
3. Remove the water pump pulley bolts and pulley. Drain the cooling system.
4. Disconnect the upper radiator hose from the water pump outlet. Label and disconnect all vacuum hoses that may be in the way.
5. Remove the upper timing belt front cover-to-engine bolts.

NOTE: To remove the lower timing belt cover-to-engine bolts, it may be necessary to raise and support the vehicle, then, remove them from underneath.

6. Remove the upper timing belt front cover and gasket.
7. Using the proper tool, clean the gasket mounting surfaces.
8. To install, use a new gasket, sealant (if necessary) and reverse the removal procedures. Adjust the drive belts. Refill the cooling system. Start the engine, allow it to reach normal operating temperatures and check for leaks.

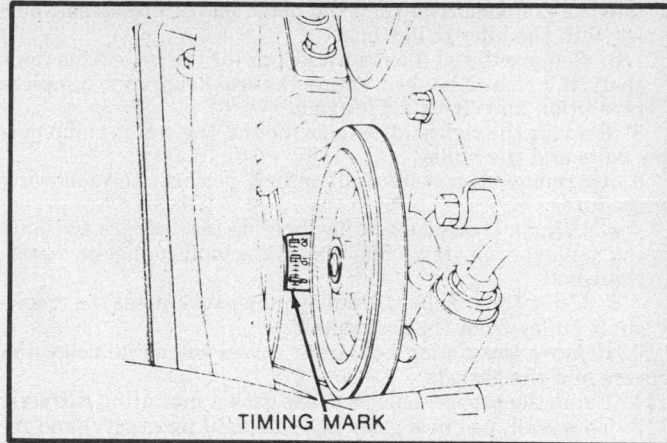

TIMING MARK

Positioning the No. 1 cylinder on TDC—Spectrum

Middle

1. Remove the upper timing belt front cover.
2. If equipped with air conditioning, loosen the idler pulley mounting bolt. Loosen the adjusting nut, then, remove the A/C drive belt, the idler pulley (with adjusting bolt).
3. Remove the alternator bolts and move it aside.
4. Remove the middle timing belt front cover-to-engine bolts, the cover and gasket.
5. Using the proper tool, clean the gasket mounting surfaces.
6. To install, use a new gasket, sealant (if necessary) and reverse the removal procedures. Adjust the drive bolts. Refill the cooling system. Start the engine, allow it to reach normal operating temperatures and check for leaks.

Lower

1. Disconnect the negative terminal from the battery.
2. Loosen the alternator adjusting bolts and remove the drive belt.
3. If equipped with air conditioning, remove the drive belt.
4. Raise and support the vehicle safely.
5. Remove the right-side under cover, the flywheel cover, the crankshaft pulley-to-crankshaft bolt and the crankshaft pulley.
6. Remove the lower timing belt front cover-to-engine bolts, the cover and gasket.
7. Using the proper tool, clean the gasket mounting surfaces.
8. To install, use a new gasket, sealant (if necessary) and reverse the removal procedures. Torque the crankshaft pulley-to-crankshaft bolt to 80–94 ft. lbs. Adjust the drive belt(s).

NOVA WITH TWINCAM ENGINE

This engine uses a 3 piece timing belt front cover assembly of an interlocking design. To removal any portion of the cover, disassembly must start from the top and work to the bottom.

. Disconnect the negative terminal from the battery.

2. Raise and support the vehicle safely, then, remove the right side wheel assembly.
3. Remove the under carriage splash shield and drain the cooling system.
4. Disconnect the accelerator cable, the cruise control cable (if equipped), the cruise control actuator (if equipped) and the ignition coil.
5. Remove the water outlet housing-to-engine bolts and the housing.
6. Remove the drive belt from the power steering pimp (if equipped) and the alternator. Disconnect the spark plug wires from the spark plugs and the spark plugs from the engine.
7. To position the No. 1 cylinder on the TDC of its compression stroke, perform the following procedures:
   a. Using a socket wrench on the crankshaft pulley bolt, ro-

tate the crankshaft to align the notch on the crankshaft pulley with the idler pulley bolt.

b. Remove the oil filler cap and look for the hole in the camshaft; if it cannot be seen, rotate the crankshaft one complete revolution and check for it again.

8. Remove the right-side engine mount, the water pump pulley bolts and the pulley.

9. To remove the crankshaft pulley, perform the following procedures:

a. Using a crankshaft pulley holding tool, secure and hold the pulley while removing the crankshaft pulley-to-crankshaft bolt.

b. Using the crankshaft pulley puller tool, press the crankshaft pulley from the crankshaft.

10. Remove the timing belt front covers-to-engine bolts, the covers and the gaskets.

11. Using the proper tool, clean the gasket mounting surfaces.

12. To install, use new gaskets, sealant (if necessary) and reverse the removal procedures.

13. Using the crankshaft pulley holding tool, secure and hold the pulley while installing the crankshaft pulley-to-crankshaft bolt.

14. To complete the installation, reverse the removal procedures. Adjust the drive belts. Refill the cooling system. Start the engine, allow it to reach normal operating temperatures and check for leaks.

PRIZM

1. Disconnect the negative battery cable. Raise the vehicle and support it safely. Remove the right wheel and undercover. Remove the air cleaner.

2. Remove the 2 mount nut and stud protectors.

3. Remove the 2 rear transaxle mount to main crossmember nuts.

4. Remove the 2 center transaxle mount to center crossmember nuts.

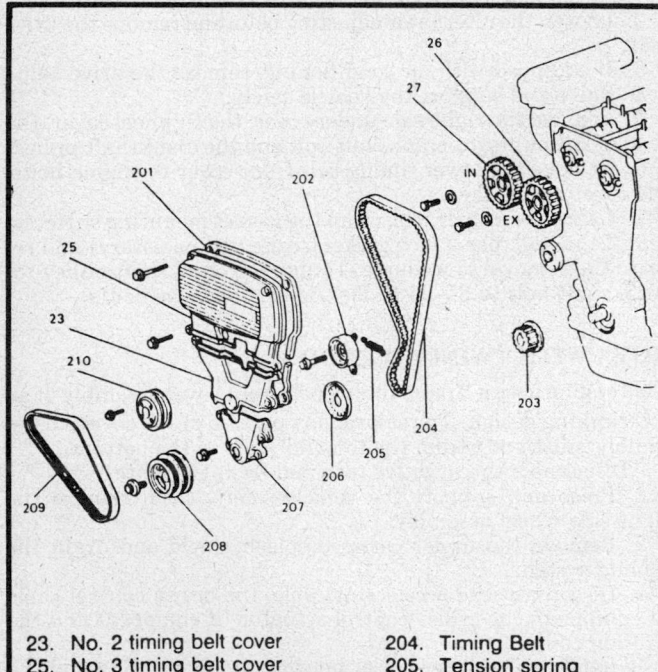

23. No. 2 timing belt cover	204. Timing Belt
25. No. 3 timing belt cover	205. Tension spring
26. Exhaust camshaft timing pulley	206. Timing belt guide
27. Intake camshaft pulley	207. No. 1 timing belt cover
201. Gasket	208. Crankshaft pulley
202. Idler pulley	209. Drive belt
203. Crankshaft timing pulley	210. Water pump pulley

Exploded view of the timing belt assembly, twincam engine—Nova

5. Lower the vehicle.

6. Remove the drive belts. Remove the power steering pump and the A/C compressor (and their brackets!) and position them out of the way. Leave the hydraulic and refrigerant lines connected.

7. Remove the spark plugs and the cylinder head cover. Be sure to scrape off any left-over gasket material. Rotate the crankshaft pulley so that the **0** mark is in alignment with the groove in the No. 1 front cover. Check that the lifters on the No. 1 cylinder are loose; if not, turn the crankshaft 1 complete revolution (360 degrees).

8. Position a floor jack under the engine and remove the right side engine mounting insulator.

9. Remove the water pump and crankshaft pulleys. The crankshaft pulley will require a two-armed puller.

10. Loosen the 9 bolts and remove the Nos. 1, 2 and 3 front covers.

To install:

11. Using the proper tool, clean the gasket mounting surfaces.

12. Use new gaskets, sealant (if necessary) and reverse the removal procedures.

13. Install the crankshaft timing pulley so that the marks on the pulley and the oil pump body are in alignment. Using the crankshaft pulley holding tool, secure and hold the pulley while installing the crankshaft pulley-to-crankshaft bolt.

15. Rotate the crankshaft clockwise 2 revolutions from TDC to TDC. Make sure that each pulley aligns with the marks made previously. If the marks are not in alignment, the valve timing is wrong.

23. Lower the engine.

24. Install the right engine mount through bolt and tighten to 64 ft. lbs.

25. Remove the engine support.

26. The remainder of the installation is the reverse of removal. Tighten the center transaxle mount to center crossmember nuts to 45 ft. lbs. and the rear transaxle mount to main crossmember nuts to 45 ft. lbs.

SPECTRUM

1. Disconnect negative battery cable.

2. Support the engine.

3. Remove the front mount bracket attached to the front cover.

4. Remove front cover.

5. To install, reverse the removal procedures.

Timing Belt and Tensioner

Adjustment

NOVA AND PRIZM

1. Remove the front cover assembly.

2. Using finger pressure on the longest span between pulleys (except twincam) or between the camshaft pulleys (twincam), measure the timing belt deflection; 4.4 lbs. at 0.24–0.28 in. (except twincam) or 0.16 in. (twincam).

3. If adjustment is not correct, loosen the idler pulley bolt and correct the belt tension.

4. To install, the front covers, reverse the removal procedures.

SPECTRUM

1. Remove the front cover.

2. Loosen the timing belt tension pulley bolt.

NOTE: If the belt has been removed or replaced with a new one, perform the following procedures to stretch the belt.

3. Using an Allen wrench, insert it into the hexagonal hole of the tension pulley. Hold the pulley stationary and temporarily tighten the tension pulley-to-engine bolt.

4. Rotate the crankshaft two complete revolutions and align the crankshaft timing pulley groove with the mark on the oil pump.

5. Loosen the tension pulley-to-engine bolt.

6. Using the Allen wrench and a timing belt tension gauge, apply 38 ft. lbs. of tension to the timing belt, hold the pulley stationary and torque the tension pulley-to-engine bolt to 37 ft. lbs.

7. To complete the adjustment, install the front cover.

Removal and Installation
NOVA

1. Remove the front covers.

2. Remove the No. 1 spark plug. Using a socket wrench on the crankshaft pulley bolt, rotate the engine (clockwise) to position the No. 1 cylinder on the TDC of its compression stroke.

NOTE: The TDC of the No. 1 cylinder is located when air is expelled from the cylinder.

3. If reusing the timing belt, mark an arrow showing direction of rotation and matchmark the belt to both pulleys.

4. Loosen the idler pulley mounting bolt and push the idler pulley relieve the belt tension, then, retighten the mounting bolt.

5. Remove the timing belt.

NOTE: Be careful not to bend, twist or turn the belt inside out. Keep grease or water from contacting it. Inspect the belt for cracks, missing teeth or general wear, replace it (if necessary).

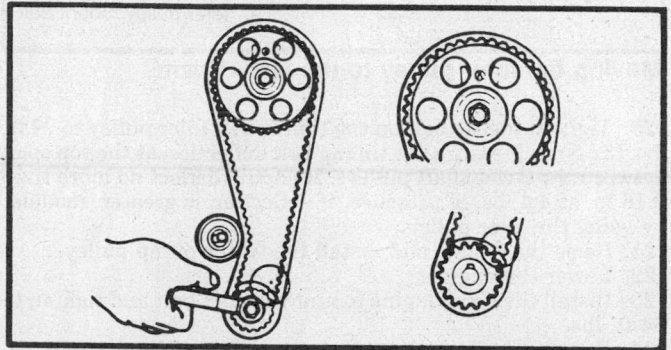

Aligning the valve timing marks except twincam engine—Nova

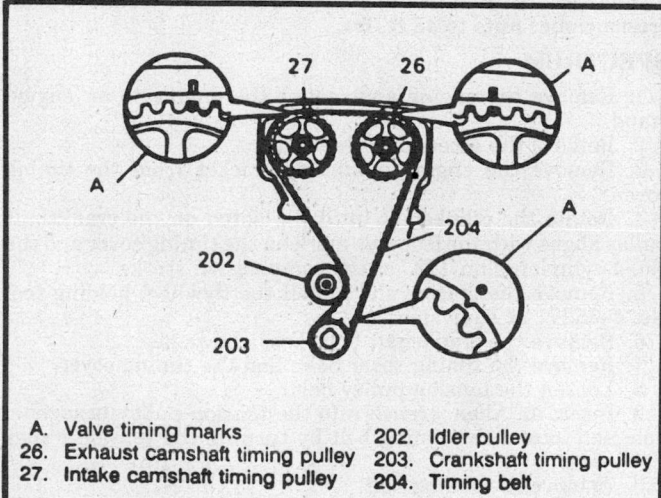

A.	Valve timing marks	202.	Idler pulley
26.	Exhaust camshaft timing pulley	203.	Crankshaft timing pulley
27.	Intake camshaft timing pulley	204.	Timing belt

Aligning the valve timing marks, twincam engine—Nova

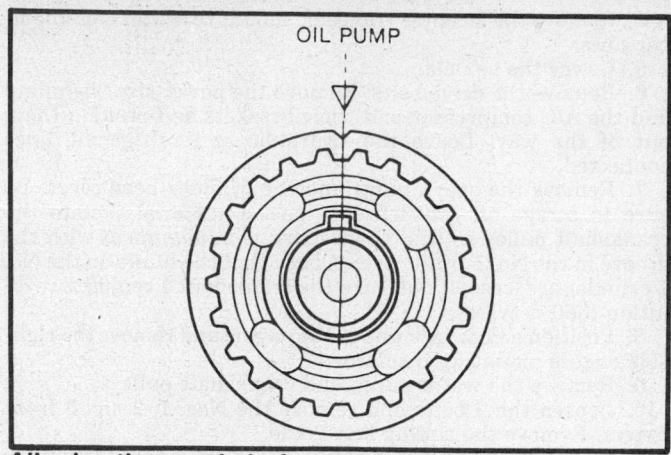

OIL PUMP

Aligning the crankshaft sprocket timing notch with the oil pump mark—Spectrum

6. Install the timing belt by realigning the matchmarks, the belts directional arrow facing clockwise and adjust the timing belt tension. Rotate the crankshaft 2 complete revolutions and recheck the alignment.

7. To complete the installation, reverse the removal procedures. Torque the idler pulley mounting bolt to 27 ft. lbs. Adjust the timing belt tension. Check and/or adjust the timing.

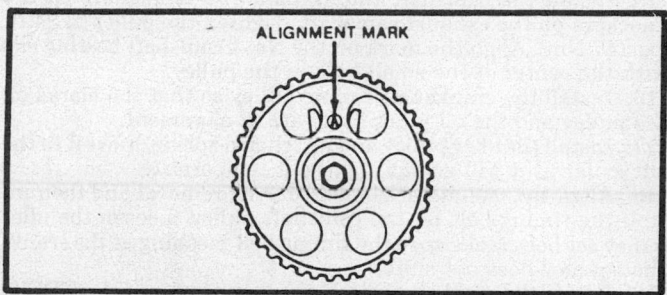

ALIGNMENT MARK

Aligning the camshaft pulley-except twincam engine—Nova

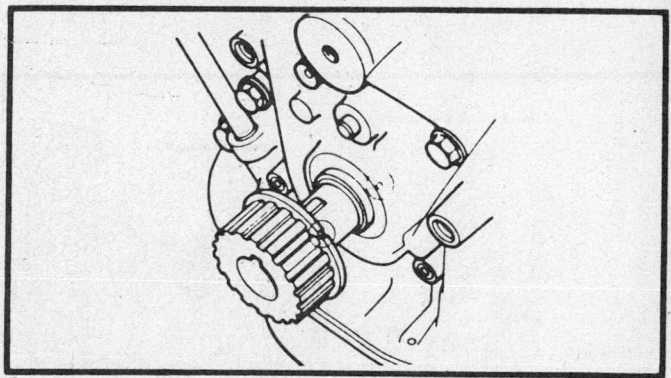

Crankshaft timing pulley alignment—Nova

PRIZM

1. Disconnect the negative battery cable. Raise the vehicle and support it safely. Remove the right wheel and undercover. Remove the air cleaner.

2. Remove the 2 mount nut and stud protectors.

3. Remove the 2 rear transaxle mount to main crossmember nuts.

4. Remove the 2 center transaxle mount to center crossmember nuts.

5. Lower the vehicle.

6. Remove the drive belts. Remove the power steering pump and the A/C compressor and their brackets and position them out of the way. Leave the hydraulic and refrigerant lines connected.

7. Remove the spark plugs and the cylinder head cover. Be sure to scrape off any left-over gasket material. Rotate the crankshaft pulley so that the **0** mark is in alignment with the groove in the No. 1 front cover. Check that the lifters on the No. 1 cylinder are loose; if not, turn the crankshaft 1 complete revolution (360 degrees).

8. Position a floor jack under the engine and remove the right side engine mounting insulator.

9. Remove the water pump and crankshaft pulleys.

10. Loosen the 9 bolts and remove the Nos. 1, 2 and 3 front covers. Remove the timing belt guide.

11. Loosen the bolt on the idler pulley, push it to the left as far as it will go and then retighten it. If reusing the timing belt, draw an arrow on it in the direction of engine revolution (clockwise) and then matchmark the belt to the pulleys as indicated.

12. Remove the timing belt. Remove the idler pulley bolt, the pulley and the tension spring.

13. Remove the crankshaft timing pulley.

14. Lock the camshaft and remove the camshaft timing pulleys.

To install:

15. Install the camshaft timing pulley so it aligns with the knockpin on the exhaust camshaft. Tighten the pulley to 34 ft. lbs. (47 Nm). Align the mark on the No. 1 camshaft bearing cap with the center of the small hole in the pulley.

16. Install the crankshaft timing pulley so that the marks on the pulley and the oil pump body are in alignment.

17. Install the idler pulley and its tension spring, move it to the left as far as it will go and tighten it temporarily.

18. Align the matchmarks made during removal and then install the timing belt on the camshaft pulley. Loosen the idler pulley set bolt. Make sure the timing belt meshing at the crankshaft pulley does not shift.

19. Rotate the crankshaft clockwise 2 revolutions from TDC to TDC. Make sure that each pulley aligns with the marks made previously. If the marks are not in alignment, the valve timing is wrong. Shift the timing belt meshing slightly and then repeat Steps 14–15.

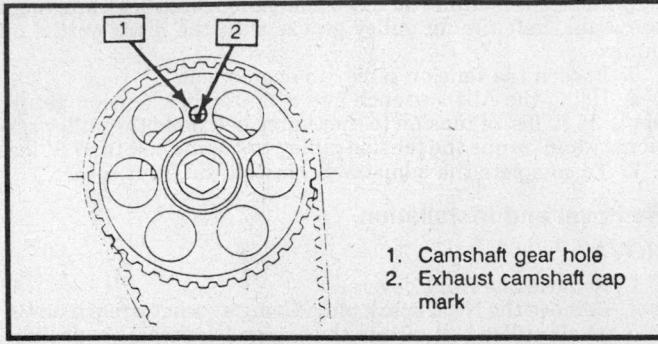

1. Camshaft gear hole
2. Exhaust camshaft cap mark

Aligning the camshaft gear hole and the exhaust camshaft cap mark—Prizm

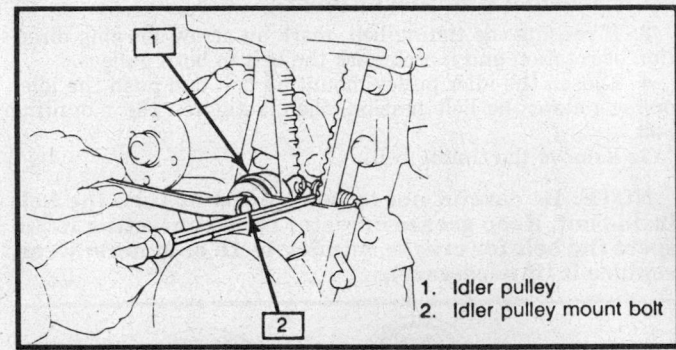

1. Idler pulley
2. Idler pulley mount bolt

Moving the idler pulley to the left—Prizm

20. Tighten the set bolt on the timing belt idler pulley to 27 ft. lbs. (37 Nm). Measure the timing belt deflection at the top span between the 2 camshaft pulleys. It should deflect no more than 0.16 in. at 4.4 lbs. of pressure. If deflection is greater, readjust by using the idler pulley.

21. Raise the engine and install the water pump pulley.

22. Lower the engine.

23. Install the right engine mount through bolt and tighten to 64 ft. lbs.

24. Remove the engine support.

25. The remainder of the installation is the reverse of removal. Tighten the center transaxle mount to center crossmember nuts to 45 ft. lbs. and the rear transaxle mount to main crossmember nuts to 45 ft. lbs.

SPECTRUM

1. Remove the engine and mount the engine to an engine stand.

2. Remove the accessory drive belts.

3. Remove the engine mounting bracket from the timing cover.

4. Rotate the crankshaft until the notch on the crankshaft pulley aligns with the **0** degree mark on the timing cover and the No. 4 cylinder is on TDC of the compression stroke.

5. Remove the starter and install the flywheel holding tool No. J-35271 or equivalent.

6. Remove the crankshaft bolt, boss and pulley.

7. Remove the timing cover bolts and the timing cover.

8. Loosen the tension spring bolt.

9. Insert an Allen wrench into the tension pulley hexagonal hole and loosen the timing belt by turning the tension pulley clockwise.

10. Remove the timing belt.

11. Remove the head cover.

NOTE: Inspect the timing belt for signs of cracking, abnormal wear and hardening. Never expose the belt to

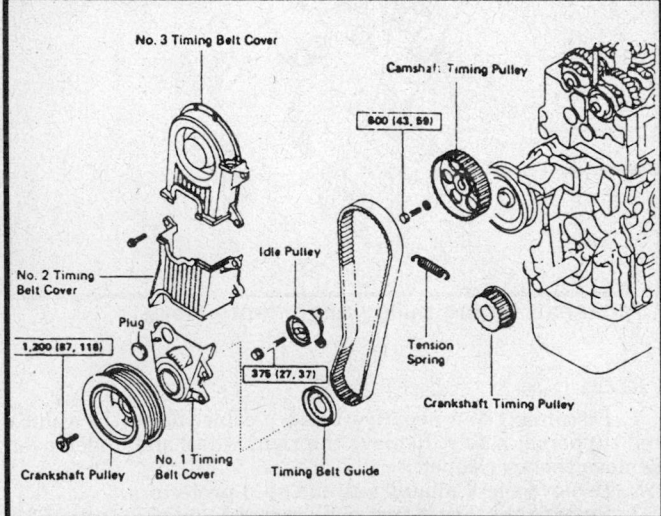

No. 3 Timing Belt Cover

Camshaft Timing Pulley

800 (43, 59)

No. 2 Timing Belt Cover

Idle Pulley

Plug

1,200 (87, 118)

Tension Spring

375 (27, 37)

Crankshaft Timing Pulley

Crankshaft Pulley

No. 1 Timing Belt Cover

Timing Belt Guide

Exploded view of the timing belt assembly—Prizm

oil, sunlight or heat. Avoid excessive bending, twisting or stretching.

To install:

12. Position the Woodruff key on the crankshaft followed by the crankshaft timing gear. Align the groove on the timing gear with the mark on the oil pump.

13. Align the camshaft timing gear mark with the upper surface of the cylinder head and the dowel pin in its uppermost position.

14. Place the timing belt arrow in the direction of the engine rotation and install the timing belt. Tighten the tension pulley bolt.

15. Turn the crankshaft two complete revolutions and realign the crankshaft timing gear groove with the mark on the oil pump.

16. Loosen the tension pulley bolt and apply tension to the belt with an Allen wrench. Torque the pulley bolt to 37 ft. lbs. while holding the pulley stationary.

17. Adjust the valve clearances.

18. To complete the installation, reverse the removal procedures. Torque the crankshaft pulley-to-crankshaft bolt to 109 ft. lbs.

Timing Cover, Belt and Tensioner

Removal and Installation

SPRINT AND METRO

1. Disconnect the negative battery cable.
2. Loosen the water pump pulley bolts and the alternator adjusting bolt.
3. If equipped, remove the A/C compressor adjusting bolt.
4. Raise and support the vehicle safely.
5. Remove the drive belt splash shield, the right fender plug and the drive belts.
6. Remove the crankshaft and the water pump pulleys.
7. Remove the bolts from the bottom of the belt cover.
8. Lower the vehicle.
9. Remove the bolts from the top of the belt cover and the cover.
10. Remove the cylinder head cover and loosen the rocker arm adjusting bolts.
11. Remove the distributor cap.
12. Loosen the tensioner pulley and adjusting stud bolt.
13. Remove the timing belt, the tensioner, the tensioner plate and spring.

To install:

14. Install the tensioner assembly but do not tighten the bolts.
15. Turn the camshaft pulley clockwise and align the mark on the pulley with the **V** mark on the inside cover.
16. Using a 17mm wrench, turn the crankshaft clockwise and align the punch mark on the crankshaft pulley with the arrow mark on the oil pump.
17. With the timing marks aligned, install the timing belt so that there is no belt slack on the right side (facing the engine) of the engine, apply belt tension with the tensioner pulley.
18. Turn the crankshaft 1 rotation clockwise to remove the belt slack. Torque the tensioner stud, first, and then the tensioner bolt to 17–21 ft. lbs.
19. To complete the installation, use new gaskets and reverse the removal procedures. Torque the crankshaft pulley to 7–9 ft. lbs. Adjust the valve clearances.

Timing Sprockets

Removal and Installation

NOVA

Except Twincam Engine

1. Disconnect the negative battery cable.

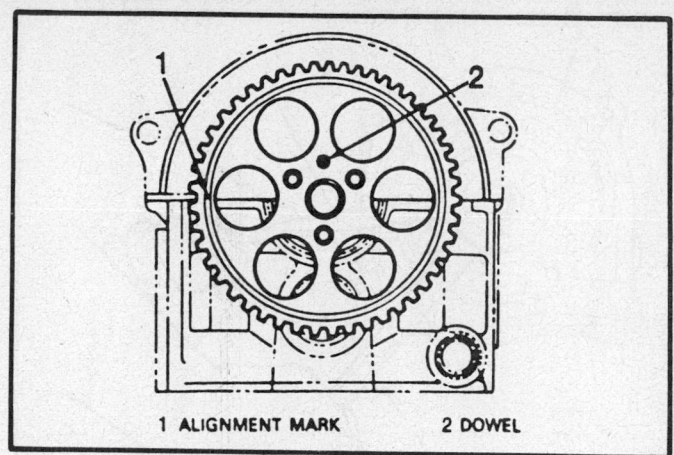

1 ALIGNMENT MARK   2 DOWEL

Aligning the camshaft pulley

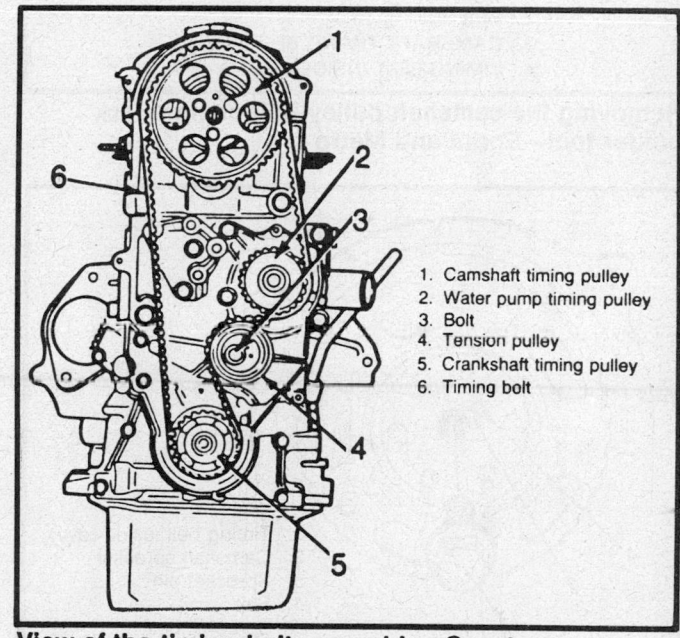

1. Camshaft timing pulley
2. Water pump timing pulley
3. Bolt
4. Tension pulley
5. Crankshaft timing pulley
6. Timing bolt

View of the timing belt assembly — Spectrum

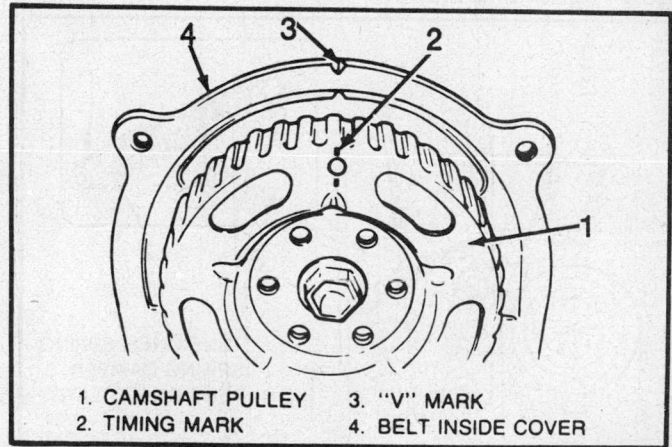

1. CAMSHAFT PULLEY   3. "V" MARK
2. TIMING MARK   4. BELT INSIDE COVER

Camshaft sprocket and inner belt cover timing mark alignment — Sprint and Metro

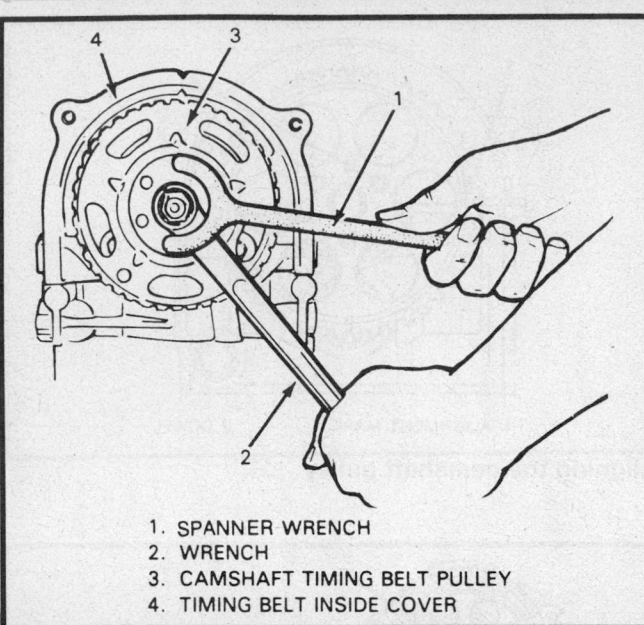

1. SPANNER WRENCH
2. WRENCH
3. CAMSHAFT TIMING BELT PULLEY
4. TIMING BELT INSIDE COVER

Removing the camshaft pulley bolt using a lock holder tool—Sprint and Metro

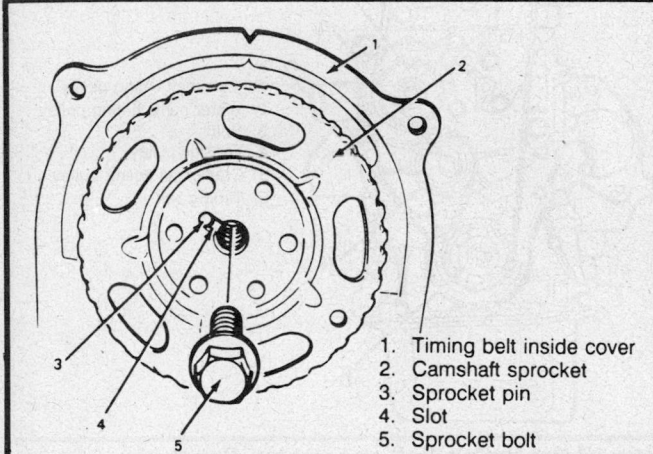

1. Timing belt inside cover
2. Camshaft sprocket
3. Sprocket pin
4. Slot
5. Sprocket bolt

Installing the camshaft sprocket pin and retaining bolt—Sprint and Metro

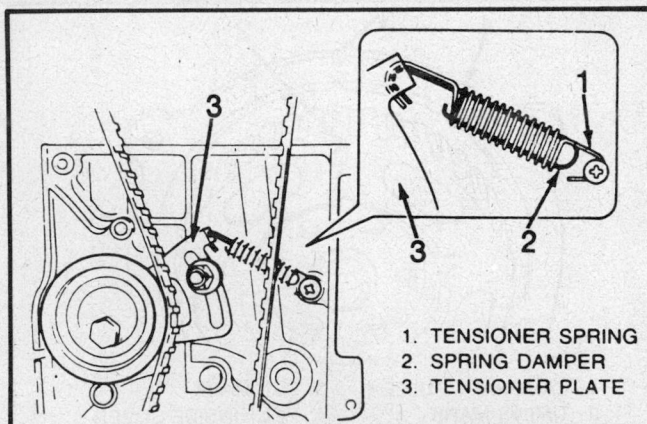

1. TENSIONER SPRING
2. SPRING DAMPER
3. TENSIONER PLATE

Installing tensioner spring and dampner—Sprint and Metro

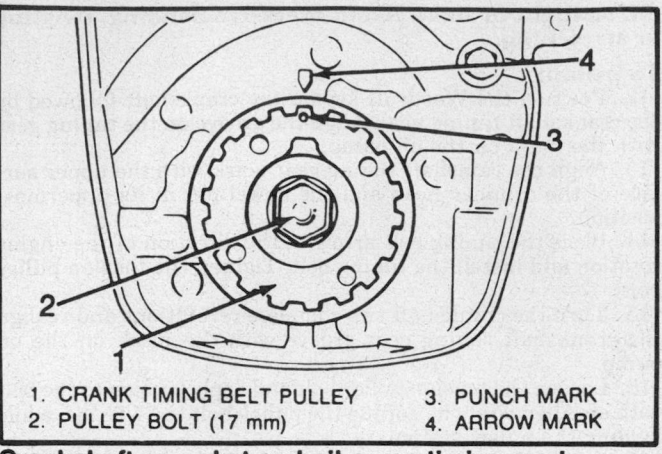

1. CRANK TIMING BELT PULLEY   3. PUNCH MARK
2. PULLEY BOLT (17 mm)   4. ARROW MARK

Crankshaft sprocket and oil pump timing mark alignment—Sprint and Metro

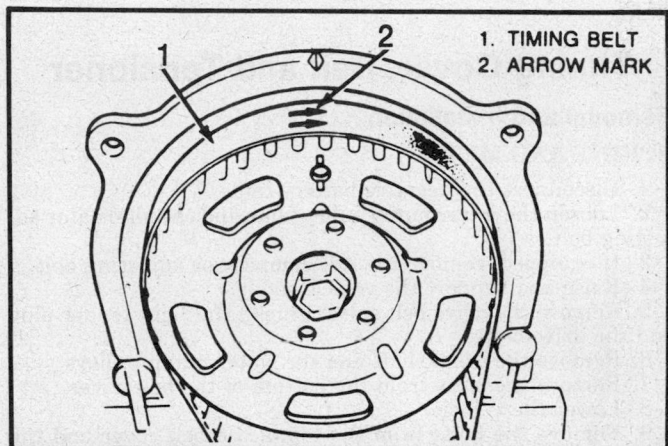

1. TIMING BELT
2. ARROW MARK

Arrow marks on timing belt show direction of rotation—Sprint and Metro

2. Remove the timing belt.
3. To remove the crankshaft timing belt pulley, simply pull it and the key from the crankshaft.
4. To remove the camshaft pulley, perform the following procedures:
    a. Remove the valve cover.
    b. Using an open end wrench, place it on the camshaft flats to secure it.
    c. Using a socket wrench on the camshaft pulley bolt, remove the camshaft pulley bolt and the camshaft pulley.
5. To install the timing belt pulleys, reverse the removal procedures. Torque the camshaft pulley-to-camshaft bolt to 34 ft. lbs.
6. After installing the crankshaft pulley bolt, rotate the crankshaft two complete revolutions and recheck the alignment. Check and/or adjust the timing belt tension. Torque the idler pulley mounting bolt to 27 ft. lbs.
7. To complete the installation, reverse the removal procedures.

Twincam Engine

1. Disconnect the negative battery cable.
2. Remove the timing belt.
3. To remove the crankshaft timing belt pulley, simply pull it and the key from the crankshaft.
4. To remove the camshaft pulleys, perform the following procedures:
    a. Remove both valve covers.

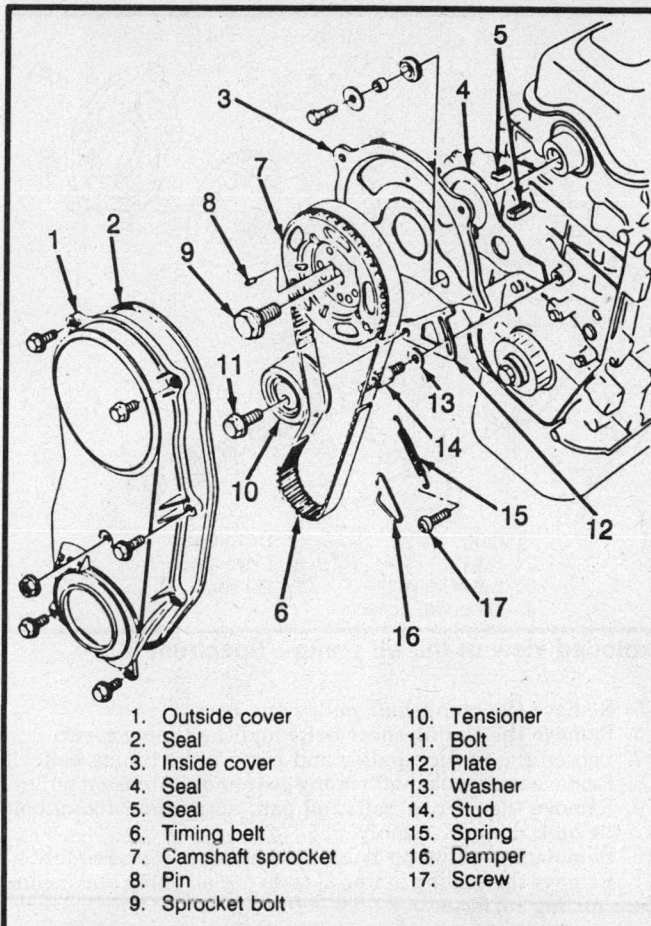

1. Outside cover
2. Seal
3. Inside cover
4. Seal
5. Seal
6. Timing belt
7. Camshaft sprocket
8. Pin
9. Sprocket bolt
10. Tensioner
11. Bolt
12. Plate
13. Washer
14. Stud
15. Spring
16. Damper
17. Screw

Timing belt, tensioner and sprockets-exploded view— Sprint and Metro

b. Secure each camshaft, then, using a socket wrench on the camshaft pulley bolt, remove the camshaft pulley bolt.

c. Using the pulley remover tool No. J-1859-03 or equivalent, press each camshaft pulley from the camshafts.

5. To install the camshaft pulleys, align each with the knock pin and reverse the removal procedures. Torque the camshaft pulley-to-camshaft bolt to 34 ft. lbs.

6. To install the crankshaft timing pulley, simply align it with the keyway and slide it onto the crankshaft.

7. Align the timing belt marks with the pulley marks and install the timing belt.

8. After installing the crankshaft pulley bolt, rotate the crankshaft two complete revolutions and recheck the alignment. Check and/or adjust the timing belt tension. Torque the idler pulley mounting bolt to 27 ft. lbs.

9. To complete the installation, reverse the removal procedures.

SPECTRUM

1. Disconnect the negative battery terminal from the battery.

2. Rotate the crankshaft to place the No. 4 cylinder on the TDC of compression stroke.

3. Remove the front cover-to-mount bracket bolt and the bracket from the vehicle.

4. Remove the front cover-to-engine bolts and the front cover from the engine.

NOTE: Make sure that the camshaft dowel pin is positioned at the top and the mark on the cam sprocket is aligned with the upper cylinder head surface.

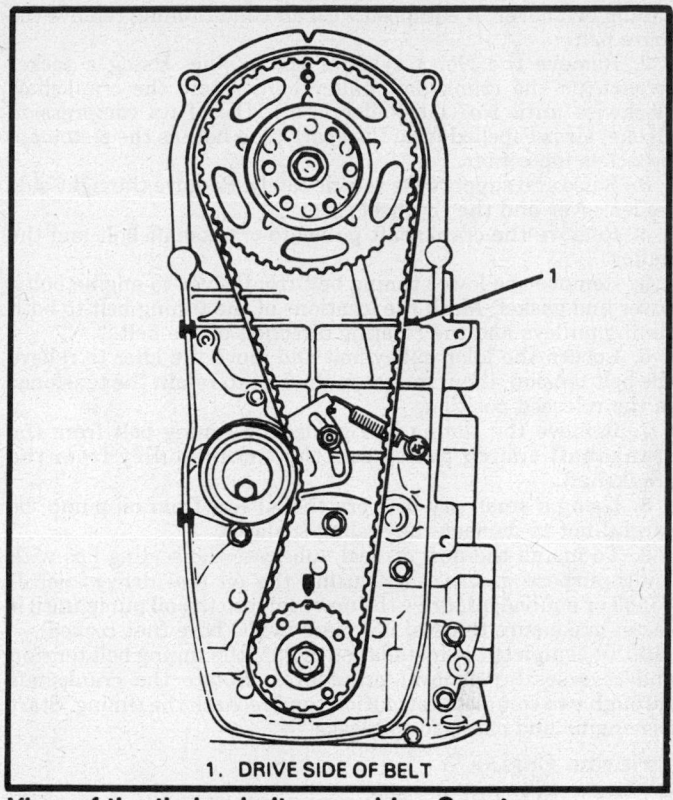

1. DRIVE SIDE OF BELT

View of the timing belt assembly—Spectrum

5. Loosen the timing belt tension pulley-to-engine bolt, then remove the timing belt.

6. Remove the camshaft sprocket-to-camshaft bolts, the camshaft sprocket; allow the timing belt to hang.

7. If the engine has not been disturbed, reverse the removal procedures. Torque the camshaft sprocket-to-camshaft bolt to 7.2 ft. lbs. Adjust the timing belt.

8. To complete the installation, reverse the removal procedures.

Crankshaft Pulley

Removal and Installation
PRIZM

1. Disconnect the negative battery cable.

2. Loosen the A/C compressor, power steering pump, and alternator and set aside. Do not disconnect hoses.

3. Remove the accessory drive belts.

4. Raise and support the vehicle safely.

5. Remove the right front wheel.

6. Remove the right lower stone shield.

7. Remove the crankshaft pulley bolt using a pulley holding tool and remove the pulley using a puller.

8. Installation is the reverse of removal. Tighten the pulley bolt to 87 ft. lbs.

Front Crankshaft Oil Seal

Removal and Installation
NOVA AND PRIZM
Except Twincam Engine

1. Disconnect the negative battery cable. Remove the upper

timing belt cover. If equipped with air conditioning, remove the drive belt.

2. Remove the No. 1 cylinder spark plug. Using a socket wrench on the crankshaft pulley bolt, rotate the crankshaft clockwise until No. 1 cylinder is at TDC of its compression stroke; air is expelled from the spark plug hole as the piston approaches top center.

3. Raise and support the vehicle safely. Remove the right-side under cover and the flywheel cover.

4. Remove the crankshaft pulley-to-crankshaft bolt and the pulley.

5. Remove the lower timing belt front cover-to-engine bolts, cover and gasket. Mark the locations of the timing belt to both timing pulleys and the rotating direction of the belt.

6. Loosen the idler pulley bolt and move the idler to relieve the belt tension, then, retighten the bolt to retain the tensioner in the released position.

7. Remove the timing belt guide, the timing belt from the crankshaft timing pulley and the timing pulley from the crankshaft.

8. Using a small pry bar, pry the oil seal from oil pump; be careful not to damage the sealing surfaces.

9. To install the new oil seal, lubricate the sealing lips with multi-purpose grease, then, using the oil seal driver tool J-35403 or equivalent, drive the new seal into the oil pump until it seats; make sure the seal is square in the bore (not cocked).

10. To complete the installation, adjust the timing belt tension and reverse the removal procedures. Rotate the crankshaft through two complete revolutions and recheck the timing. Start the engine and check for oil leaks.

Twincam Engine

1. Remove the timing belt.

2. Using a small pry bar, pry the oil seal from oil pump; be careful not to damage the sealing surfaces.

3. To install the new oil seal, lubricate the sealing lips with multi-purpose grease, then, using the oil seal driver tool No. J-35403 or equivalent, drive the new seal into the oil pump until it seats; make sure the seal is square in the bore (not cocked).

4. To complete the installation, adjust the timing belt tension and reverse the removal procedures. Rotate the crankshaft through two complete revolutions and recheck the timing. Start the engine and check for oil leaks.

SPECTRUM

1. Remove the engine from the vehicle and position in a suitable holding fixture.

2. Drain the crankcase.

3. Remove the alternator belt and the starter.

4. Install the flywheel holding tool J-35271 or equivalent, to secure the flywheel.

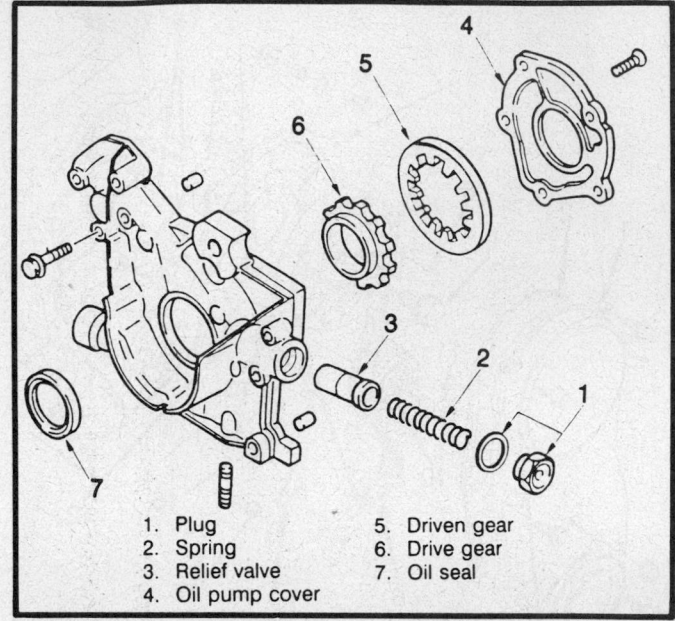

1. Plug
2. Spring
3. Relief valve
4. Oil pump cover
5. Driven gear
6. Drive gear
7. Oil seal

Exploded view of the oil pump—Spectrum

5. Remove the crankshaft pulley and boss.

6. Remove the timing cover bolts and the timing cover.

7. Loosen the tension pulley and remove the timing belt.

8. Remove the crankshaft timing gear and the tension pulley.

9. Remove the oil pan bolts, oil pan, oil strainer fixing bolt and the oil strainer assembly.

10. Remove the oil pump bolts and the oil pump assembly.

11. Remove the sealing material from the oil pump and engine block sealing surfaces.

NOTE: The oil seal is part of the oil pump assembly.

12. With the oil pump removed from the engine, pry the oil seal from the oil pump housing with a small pry bar.

13. To install the new oil seal, drive it into the housing using the seal installing tool J-35269 or equivalent.

14. To install the pump, lubricate the oil pump, use new gaskets, apply sealant to the sealing surfaces and reverse the removal procedures.

Piston and Connecting Rod

Positioning

NOVA AND PRIZM

Note the locations of main bearings. Upper bearings are grooved for distribution of oil to the connecting rods, while the lower

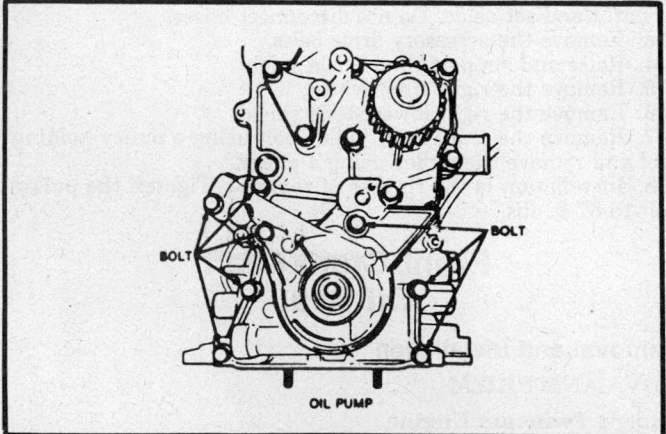

Location of oil pump—Spectrum

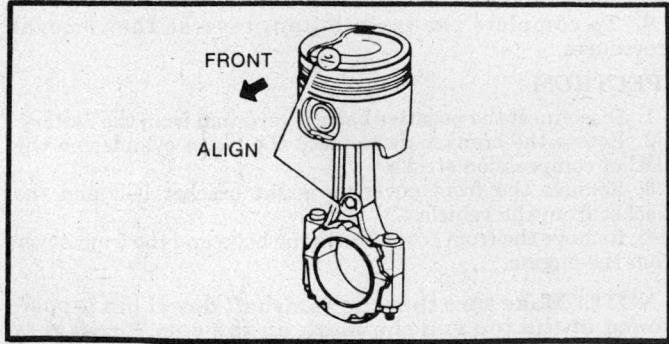

FRONT

ALIGN

Piston alignment marks—Nova and Prizm

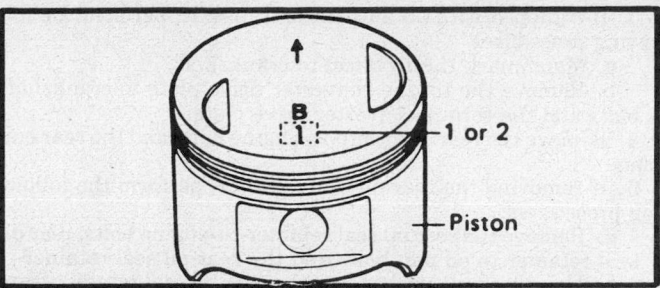

Piston identification—Sprint and Metro

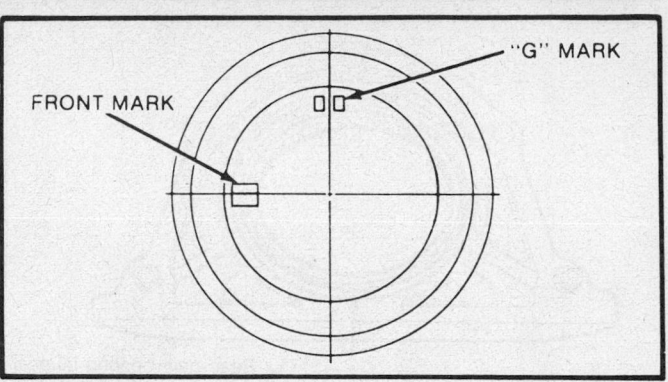

View of the piston directional mark and grade "G" mark—Spectrum

mains are plain. Thrust is taken by washer shaped bearings located on both sides of the center (No. 3) bearing cap, with tabs on the lower washers which fit into notches in the lower cap. Note that both the piston crowns and connecting rods have marks which must face forward when assembling the engine. Note also the sequence of ring installation; in fact the upper outside diameter of the No. 2 compression ring is smaller than the lower O.D., while the No. 1 compression ring has an even, barrel face. Note also the positioning of the oil ring expander and side rail.

SPECTRUM

Install the piston and rod assemblies into the same cylinder bore, facing the same direction from which they were removed. Each piston has a front directional mark stamped on the top surface.

SPRINT AND METRO

There are 2 sizes of pistons available: a No. 1 and a No. 2 (indicating the outside diameter of the piston), the numbers are stamped on top of each piston. An arrow is also stamped on top of each piston, indicating the front of the engine.

A number is stamped at the front right of the engine block, on the cylinder head gasket surface. The number indicates of the pistons sizes, in order, ranging from the front-to-rear cylinders. Install the correct diameter piston (with the arrow facing the front of the engine) and the connecting rod (with the oil hole facing the intake manifold) into the correct cylinder bore.

ENGINE LUBRICATION

Oil Pan

Removal and Installation

NOVA

1. Disconnect the negative terminal from the battery. Raise and support the vehicle safely.
2. Drain the crankcase.
3. Remove the right-side under-cover.
4. Remove the oil pan-to-engine bolts and the oil pan.

NOTE: When removing the oil pan, be careful not to damage the oil pan flange.

5. Using the proper tool, clean the gasket mounting surfaces.
6. To install, use a new gasket, sealant (if necessary) and reverse the removal procedures. Torque the oil pan-to-engine bolts to 4 ft. lbs. Start the engine and check for leaks.

PRIZM

1. Remove the battery negative cable.
2. Raise and suitably support the vehicle.
3. Remove the right and left lower stone shields.
4. Drain the oil.
5. Disconnect the oxygen sensor connector.
6. Disconnect the exhaust pipe from catalytic converter.
7. Disconnect the exhaust pipe from exhaust manifold.
8. Remove the two nuts and 19 bolts from the oil pan.
9. Remove the oil pan.

NOTE: Use caution when removing the oil pan on the oil pump body side since damage to the pump body may occur. Also be careful not to damage the oil pan flange.

10. Remove the 2 bolts, 2 nuts, and the oil strainer/pickup assembly.
11. Remove the oil strainer/pickup assembly gasket.

12. Clean the mating surfaces of the oil pan and cylinder block of all oil residue. Clean both surfaces with a solvent that will not affect the painted surfaces.
To install:
13. Install the oil strainer/pickup assembly and a new gasket with 2 bolts and 2 nuts.
14. Tighten the oil strainer/pickup assembly bolts and nuts to 89 in. lbs. (10 Nm).
15. Apply a continuous bead of GM No. 1050026 sealant to both sides of a new oil pan gasket.
16. Install the oil pan to the cylinder block with 19 bolts and 2 nuts.
17. Tighten the oil pan bolts and nuts to 44 inch lbs. (5 Nm).
18. Install the exhaust pipe to exhaust manifold.
19. Install the exhaust pipe to catalytic convertor.
20. Connect the oxygen sensor connector.
21. Install the right and left lower stone shields.
22. Lower the vehicle.
23. Refill the engine oil.
24. Install the battery negative cable.
25. Start the engine and check for leaks.

SPECTRUM

1. Disconnect the negative battery terminal from the battery.
2. Raise and support the vehicle safely, then drain the crankcase.
3. Disconnect the exhaust pipe bracket from the block and the exhaust pipe at the manifold.
4. Disconnect the right hand tension rod located under the front bumper.
5. Remove the oil pan bolts and oil pan, then clean the sealing surfaces.
6. To install, use a new gasket, apply sealant to the oil pump housing and the rear retainer housing, reverse the removal procedures.

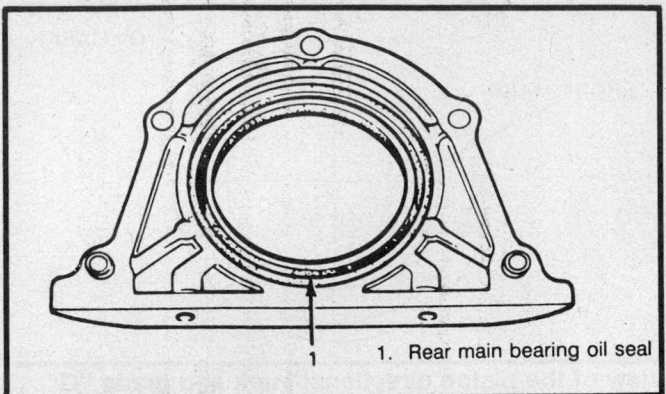

1. Rear main bearing oil seal

Rear main oil seal housing—Sprint and Metro

SPRINT AND METRO

1. Remove the negative battery cable.
2. Raise and support the vehicle safely.
3. Drain the engine oil.
4. Remove the flywheel dust cover.
5. Remove the exhaust pipe at the exhaust manifold.
6. Remove the oil pan bolts, the pan and the oil pump strainer.
7. Clean the gasket mating surfaces.
8. To install, use new gaskets and reverse the removal procedures. Torque the oil pan bolts to 9–12 ft. lbs. Refill the engine oil.

Rear Main Oil Seal

Removal and Installation
NOVA AND PRIZM

1. Remove the transaxle from the vehicle.
2. If equipped with a manual transaxle, perform the following procedures:
    a. Matchmark the pressure plate-to-flywheel.
    b. Remove the pressure plate-to-flywheel bolts and the clutch assembly from the vehicle.
    c. Remove the flywheel-to-crankshaft bolts and the flywheel.

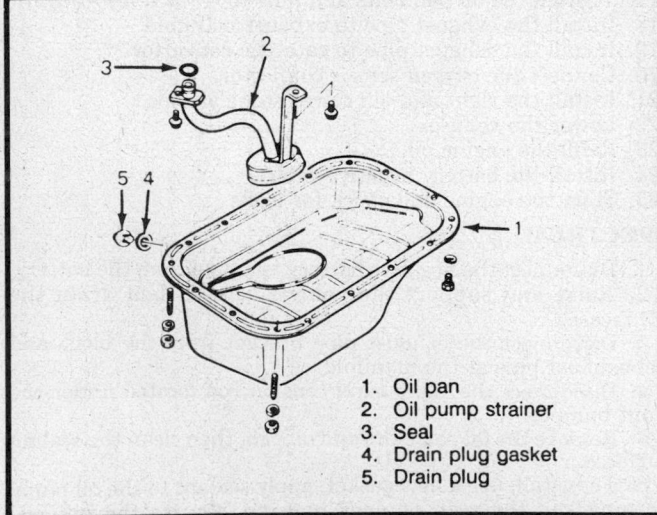

1. Oil pan
2. Oil pump strainer
3. Seal
4. Drain plug gasket
5. Drain plug

Oil pan and strainer mounting—Sprint and Metro

3. If equipped with an automatic transaxle, perform the following procedures:
    a. Matchmark the flywheel-to-crankshaft.
    b. Remove the torque converter drive plate-to-crankshaft bolts and the torque converter drive plate.
4. Remove the rear end plate-to-engine bolts and the rear end plate.
5. If removing the rear oil seal retainer, perform the following procedures:
    a. Remove the rear oil seal retainer-to-engine bolts, rear oil seal retainer to oil pan bolts and the rear oil seal retainer.
    b. Using a small pry bar, pry the rear oil seal retainer from the mating surfaces.
    c. Using a drive punch, drive the oil seal from the rear bearing retainer.
6. To remove the rear oil seal, with the rear oil seal retainer installed, use a small pry bar and pry the seal from the rear oil seal retainer.

NOTE: When removing the rear oil seal, be careful not to damage the seal mounting surface.

7. Clean the oil seal mounting surface.
8. Using multi-purpose grease, lubricate the new seal lips.
9. Using an rear oil seal installation tool J–35388 or equivalent, tap the seal straight into the bore of the retainer.
10. If the rear oil seal retainer was removed from the vehicle, use a new gasket, sealant (if necessary) and reverse the removal procedures; be careful when installing the oil seal over the crankshaft.
11. To complete the installation, reverse the removal procedures. Torque the flywheel-to-crankshaft bolts to 58 ft. lbs. and the torque converter drive plate-to-crankshaft bolts to 61 ft. lbs.

SPECTRUM

1. Remove the transaxle.
2. Remove the oil pan.
3. Remove the pressure plate and clutch (manual transaxle) or torque converter (automatic transaxle), the flywheel bolts and the flywheel from the crankshaft.
4. Remove the rear oil seal retainer and remove the oil seal from the retainer. Clean the sealing surfaces.
5. Using a new oil seal, install the new seal in the oil seal retainer.
6. To install, use new gaskets, apply sealer to the mounting surfaces, apply oil to the seal lips, align the dowel pins of the retainer with the engine block and reverse the removal procedures.

SPRINT AND METRO

1. Remove the transaxle.
2. Raise and support the vehicle safely. Drain the oil and remove the oil pan.
3. Remove the pressure plate, the clutch plate and the flywheel.
4. Remove the mounting bolts and the rear seal housing.
5. Pry the oil seal from the oil seal housing.
6. To install, use new gaskets/seals and reverse the removal procedures. Torque the oil seal housing to 7–9 ft. lbs. and the flywheel to 57–65 ft. lbs.

NOTE: After installing the oil seal housing, trim the gasket flush with the bottom of the case.

Oil Pump

Removal and Installation
NOVA AND PRIZM

1. Raise and support the vehicle safely. Drain the engine oil and remove the oil pan. Remove the timing belt cover assembly.

2. Remove the oil pickup-to-engine brace bolts and the oil pickup.

3. Attach a lifting sling to the engine lift points and securely suspend the engine.

4. Mark the timing belt alignment between the camshaft and the crankshaft pulleys; also, mark the timing belt's direction of rotation. Loosen the idler pulley bolt, relieve the timing belt tension and remove the timing belt from the crankshaft sprocket; keep it engaged with the upper pulley.

5. Remove the crankshaft timing belt pulley and the timing belt idler pulley.

6. Remove the dipstick and dipstick tube.

7. Remove the oil pump-to-engine bolts and the oil pump; it may be necessary to tap lightly on the lower rear surface of the oil pump to loosen it.

8. Using the proper tool, clean the gasket mounting surfaces.

9. To replace the oil pump seal, perform the following procedures:

    a. Using a small pry bar, pry the oil seal from the front of the oil pump; be careful not to damage the seal mounting surface.

    b. Clean the oil seal surface.

    c. Using multi-purpose grease, lubricate the lips of the new oil seal.

    d. Using the oil seal driver tool J–35403 or equivalent, drive the new oil seal into the oil pump until it seats against the seat.

10. Inspect the oil pump for wear and/or damage; if necessary, replace or repair the oil pump.

11. Using petroleum jelly, pack the inside of the oil pump.

12. To install, use new gaskets, sealant (if necessary) and reverse the removal procedures. Engage the oil pump drive (smaller) gear with the crankshaft gear; there are both small and large spline teeth, make sure the teeth correspond properly. Torque the oil pick-up-to-engine bolts to 82 inch lbs. and the oil pump-to-engine bolts to 15 ft. lbs.

13. To complete the installation, reverse the removal procedures. Adjust the valve timing and the drive belt tensions. Refill the crankcase and the cooling system. Start the engine, allow it to reach normal operating temperatures and check for leaks.

SPECTRUM

1. Remove the engine from the vehicle.

2. Remove the alternator belt and the starter.

3. Install the flywheel holding tool J–35271 or equivalent, to secure the flywheel.

4. Remove the crankshaft pulley and boss.

5. Remove the timing cover bolts and the timing cover.

6. Loosen the tension pulley and remove the timing belt.

7. Remove the crankshaft timing gear and the tension pulley.

8. Remove the oil pan bolts, oil pan, oil strainer fixing bolt and the oil strainer assembly.

9. Remove the oil pump bolts and the oil pump assembly.

10. Remove the sealing material from the oil pump and engine block sealing surfaces.

11. To install, lubricate the oil pump, use new gaskets, apply sealant to the sealing surfaces and reverse the removal procedures.

SPRINT AND METRO

1. Remove the timing belt.

2. Raise and support the vehicle safely. Drain the engine oil and remove the oil pan.

3. Use a suitable tool to hold the crankshaft timing belt pulley, remove the crankshaft bolt and pull the timing pulley from the shaft.

4. Remove the alternator mounting bracket and the A/C compressor bracket, if equipped.

5. Remove the alternator adjusting bolt and the upper cover bolt.

6. Remove the oil pump mounting bolts and the oil pump.

7. Pry the crankshaft oil seal from the oil pump.

8. Clean the gasket mounting surfaces. Remove the gear plate from the back of the oil pump and pack the oil pump gears with petroleum jelley.

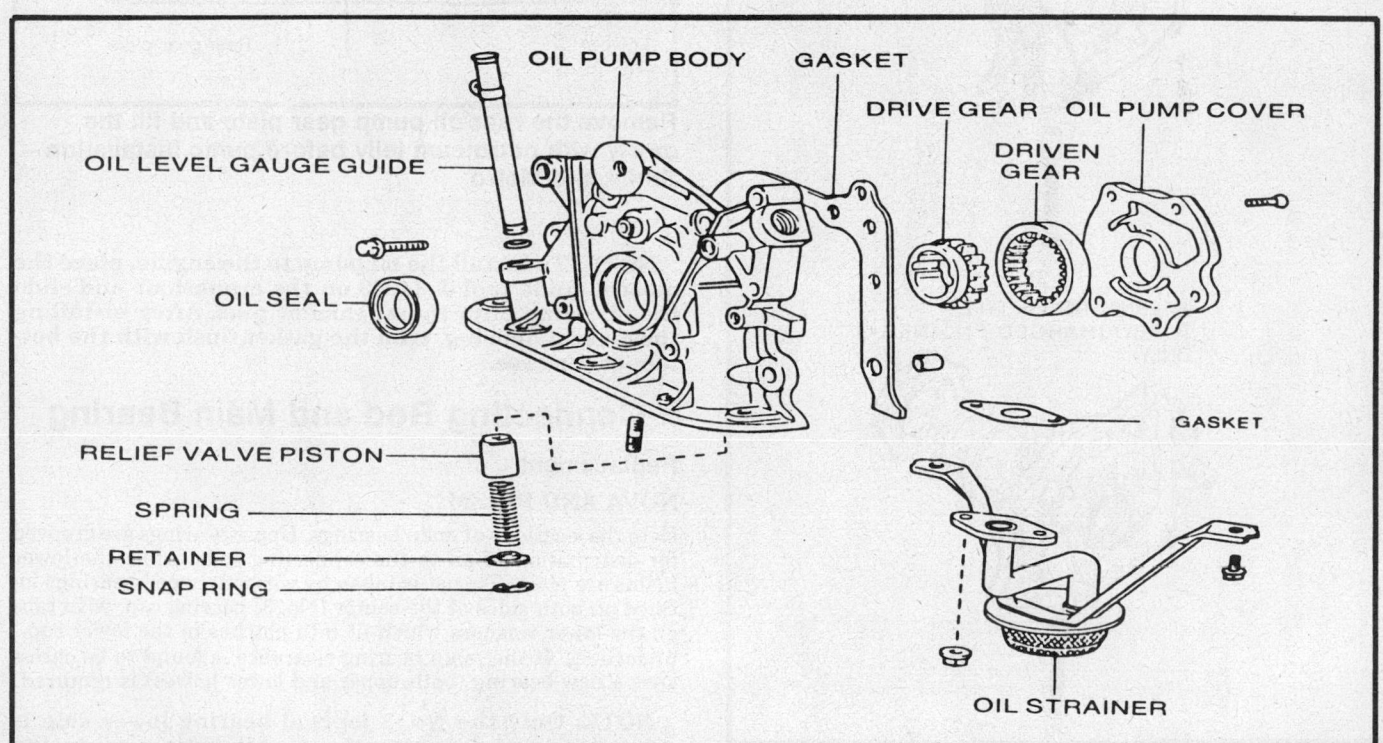

Exploded view of the oil pump—Nova and Prizm

9. To install, use new gaskets/seals and reverse the removal procedures. Torque the oil pump bolts to 7–9 ft. lbs. and the crankshaft timing pulley bolt to 47–54 ft. lbs. Adjust the valve clearances and check the timing.

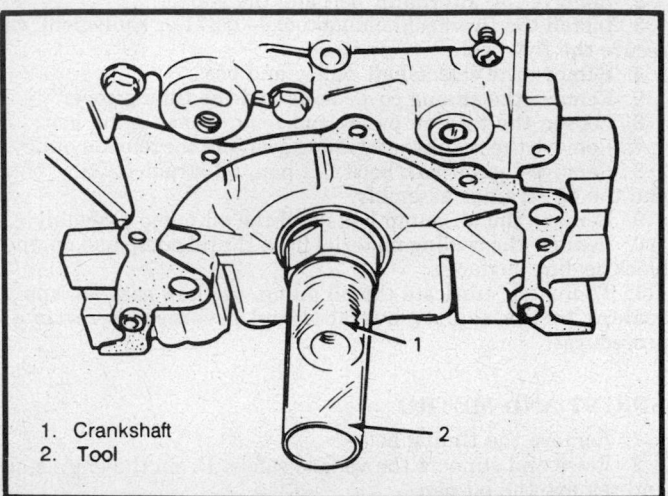

1. Crankshaft
2. Tool

Front seal protector installed on front crankshaft journal—Sprint and Metro

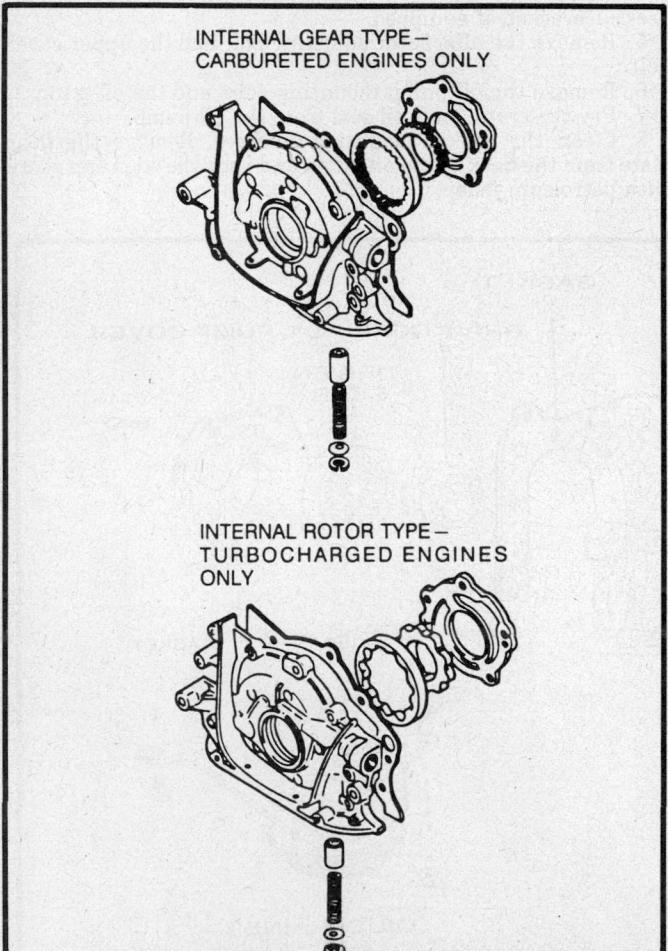

INTERNAL GEAR TYPE—
CARBURETED ENGINES ONLY

INTERNAL ROTOR TYPE—
TURBOCHARGED ENGINES ONLY

Differences in oil pump design for turbo and non turbo engines—Sprint and Metro

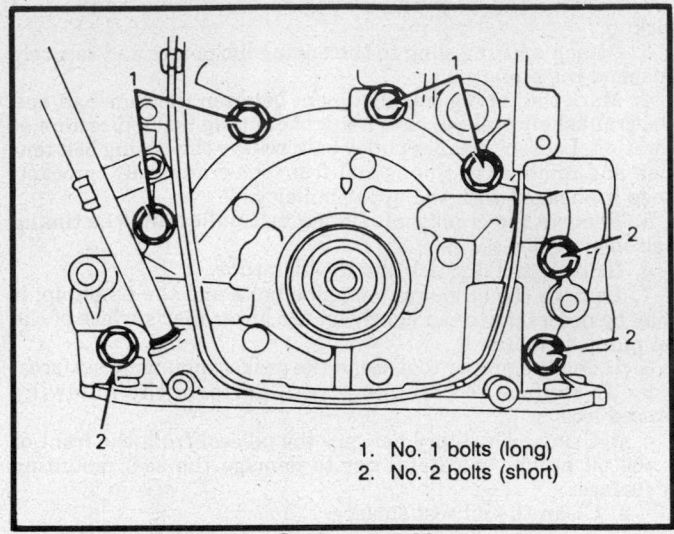

1. No. 1 bolts (long)
2. No. 2 bolts (short)

Oil pump mounting—Sprint and Metro

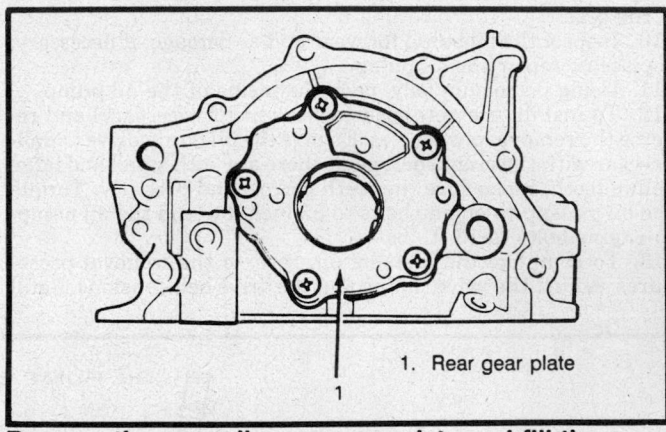

1. Rear gear plate

Remove the rear oil pump gear plate and fill the cavity with petroleum jelly before pump installation—Sprint and Metro

NOTE: To install the oil pump to the engine, place the oil seal guide tool J–34853 on the crankshaft and slide the oil pump onto the alignment pins. After installing the oil seal housing, trim the gasket flush with the bottom of the case.

Connecting Rod and Main Bearing

Replacement

NOVA AND PRIZM

Note the locations of main bearings. Upper bearings are grooved for distribution of oil to the connecting rods, while the lower mains are plain. Thrust is taken by washer shaped bearings located on both sides of the center (No. 3) bearing cap, with tabs on the lower washers which fit into notches in the lower cap. undersizes. If the main bearing clearance is found to be excessive, a new bearing (both upper and lower halves) is required.

NOTE: Only the No. 3 journal bearing lower side is grooveless; pay close attention to this distinction during the installation procedure.

Generally, the lower half of the bearing shell (except the No. 1 bearing) shows greater wear and fatigue. If the lower half only shows the effects of normal wear (no heavy scoring or discoloration), it can usually be assumed that the upper half is also in good shape; conversely, if the lower half is heavily worn or damaged, both halves should be replaced.

SPRINT AND METRO

Engine bearings are of the precision insert type. They are available for in standard and undersizes. Upper and lower bearing inserts may be different. Be careful to align holes. Do not obstruct any oil passages. Bearing inserts must not be shimmed. Do not touch the bearing surface of the insert with bare fingers. Skin oil and acids will etch the bearing surface.

Engine bearings are of the precision insert type. They are available for service in standard and various undersizes. Upper and lower bearing inserts may be different. Be careful to align holes. Do not obstruct any oil passages. Bearing inserts must not be shimmed. Do not touch the bearing surface of the insert with bare fingers. Skin oil and acids will etch the bearing surface.

NOTE: Bearing failure, other than normal wear, must be investigated carefully. Inspect the crankshaft, connecting rods and the bearing bores. Avoid damage to the crankshaft journals during removal and installation.

SPECTRUM

Connecting Rod Bearings

Connecting rod bearings consist of two halves or shells which are interchangeable in the rod and cap. When the shells are placed into position, the ends extend slightly beyond the rod and cap surfaces, so when the rod bolts are torqued, the shells will be clamped tightly in place to insure positive seating and to prevent turning; a tang holds the shells in place. The ends of the bearing shells must never be filed flush with the mating surface of the rod and cap.

If a rod bearing becomes noisy or is worn so that its clearance on the crank journal is excessive, a new bearing of the correct undersize must be selected and installed since there is no provision for adjustment.

NOTE: Under no circumstances should the rod end or cap be filed to adjust the bearing clearance, nor should shims of any kind be used.

Inspect the rod bearings while the rod assemblies are out of the engine. If the shells are scored or show flaking, they should be replaced. If they are in good shape, check for proper clearance on the crank journal. Any scoring or ridges on the crank journal means the crankshaft must be replaced or reground and fitted with an undersize bearing.

NOTE: If the journals are deeply scored or ridged, the crankshaft must be replaced, as regrinding will reduce the durability of the crankshaft.

Main Bearings

Like connecting rod big-end bearings, the crankshaft main bearings are shell-type inserts that do not utilize shims and cannot be adjusted. The bearings are available in various standard and

FRONT SUSPENSION

For front suspension component removal and installation procedures, refer to the Unit Repair Section.

For steering wheel removal and installation, refer to the Electrical Control Section

Manual Steering Gear

Removal and Installation

NOVA AND PRIZM

1. Disconnect the negative battery cable.
2. Remove the intermediate shaft cover.
3. From the steering gear pinion shaft, loosen the upper pinch bolt, then, remove the lower pinch bolt.
4. Loosen the wheel/tire assembly lug nuts.
5. Raise and support the vehicle safely.
6. From the tie rod ends, remove the cotter pins and nuts. Using the ball joint removal tool J–24319–01 or equivalent, press the ball joint from the steering knuckle.
7. Remove the steering gear-to-chassis nuts/bolts and brackets, then, separate the universal joint from the steering gear and slide the steering gear through the access hole.
8. Inspect the steering gear for wear, and/or damage; replace or repair the damaged parts.

NOTE: If the ball joint seal is torn or damaged, replace the ball joint. Make sure the clamps are installed squarely over the rubber insulators so they will not be damaged when the nuts and bolts are torqued.

9. To install, reverse the removal procedures. Torque the steering gear-to-chassis nuts/bolts to 43 ft. lbs., the tie rod end-to-steering knuckle nuts to 36 ft. lbs. and the U-joint pinch clamp bolts to 26 ft. lbs.

NOTE: If new parts have been installed, check and/or adjust the front wheel toe-in and the steering wheel center point.

SPECTRUM

1. Raise and support the vehicle safely.
2. Remove both tie rod ends from the steering knuckles and the left inner tie rod from the rack.
3. Remove the intermediate shaft cover.
4. Loosen the upper pinch bolt and remove the lower pinch bolt at the pinion shaft.
5. Remove the steering gear to body retaining nuts.
6. Remove the rack and pinion assembly.
7. To install, reverse the removal procedures and check the toe-in.

SPRINT AND METRO

1. Remove the tie rod ends from the steering knuckles.
2. Under the dash, remove the steering joint cover.
3. Remove the lower steering shaft-to-steering gear clinch bolt and separate the steering shaft from the steering gear.
4. Remove the steering gear mounting bolts, the brackets and the steering gear case from the vehicle.
5. To install, reverse the removal procedures. Torque the steering gear case bolts to 14–22 ft. lbs.; the steering gear-to-steering shaft bolt to 14–22 ft. lbs. and the tie rod end-to-steering knuckle nut to 22–40 ft. lbs.

Adjustment

NOVA AND PRIZM

NOTE: To perform the adjustment procedure, the steering gear assembly should be removed from the vehicle.

1. Remove the steering gear and place it in a vise.

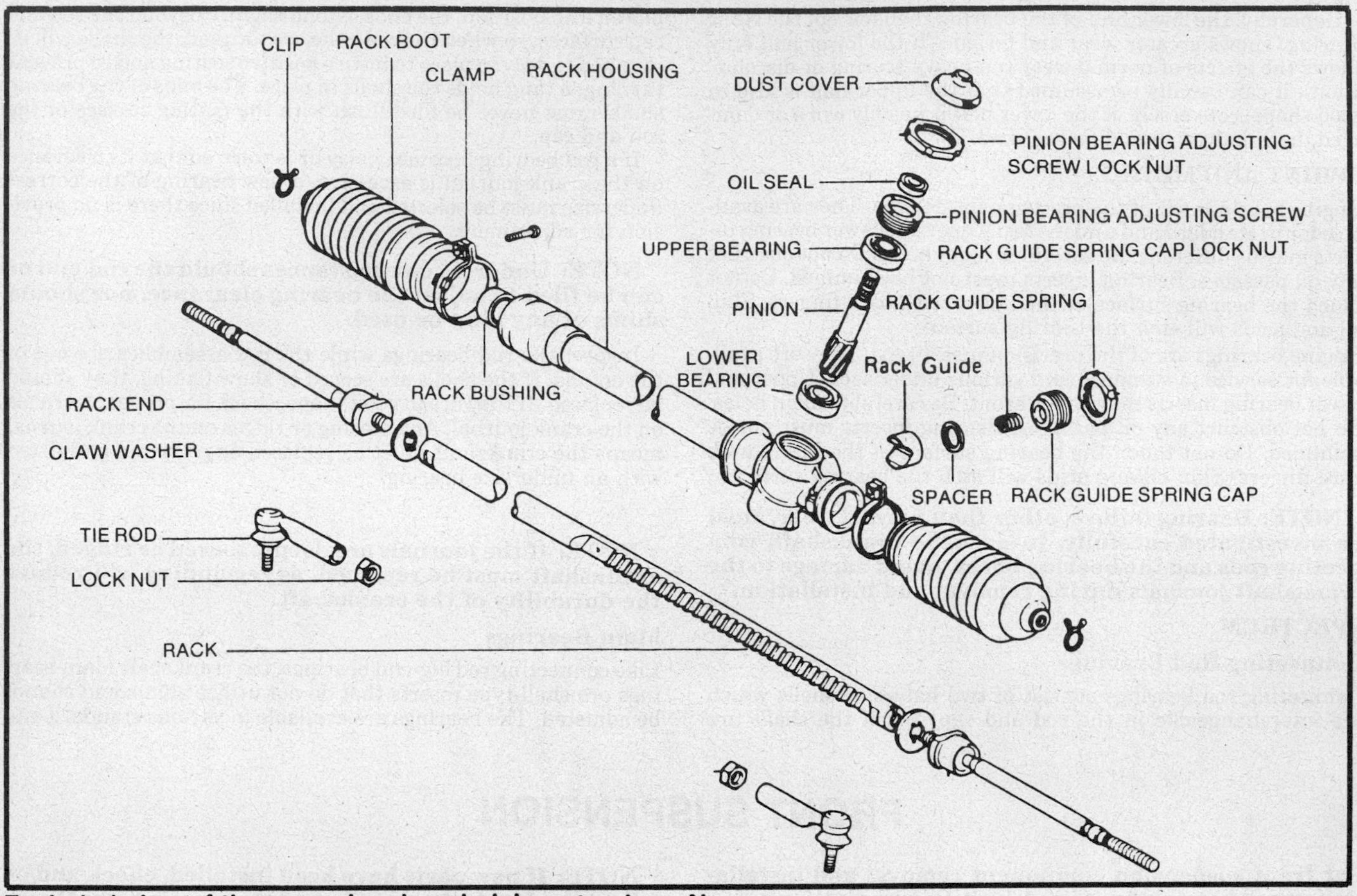

CLIP RACK BOOT
CLAMP RACK HOUSING
DUST COVER
PINION BEARING ADJUSTING SCREW LOCK NUT
OIL SEAL
PINION BEARING ADJUSTING SCREW
UPPER BEARING
RACK GUIDE SPRING CAP LOCK NUT
PINION
RACK GUIDE SPRING
LOWER BEARING Rack Guide
RACK END
CLAW WASHER
RACK BUSHING
SPACER RACK GUIDE SPRING CAP
TIE ROD
LOCK NUT
RACK

Exploded view of the manual rack and pinion steering—Nova

2. To adjust the pinion bearing turning torque, perform the following procedures:

    a. Using the pinion bearing locknut wrench tool No. J–35415 or equivalent, loosen the pinion bearing locknut.

    b. Using a torque wrench, pinion spanner wrench tool No. J–35416 or equivalent, and socket tool No. J–35422 or equivalent, adjust the pinion bearing screw torque to 3.2 inch lbs.

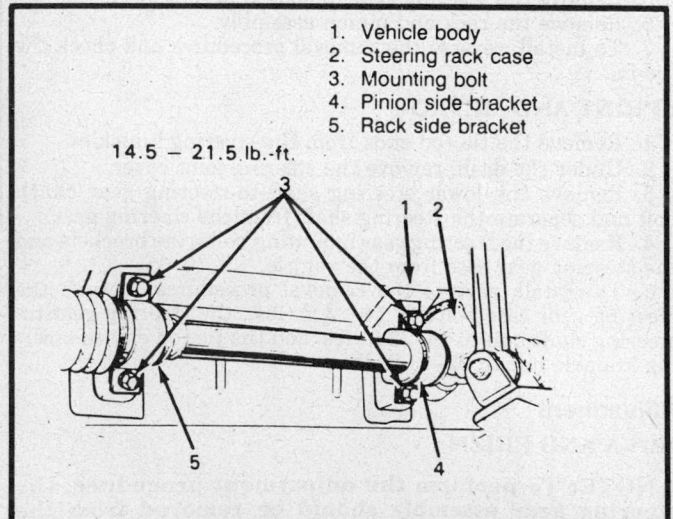

1. Vehicle body
2. Steering rack case
3. Mounting bolt
4. Pinion side bracket
5. Rack side bracket

14.5 — 21.5 lb.-ft.

Rack and pinion steering mounting—Sprint and Metro

    c. Loosen the adjusting screw until the turning torque is 2–2.9 inch lbs.

    d. Using sealant, coat the pinion locknut threads, then, torque the nut to 83 ft. lbs.

    e. Recheck the turning torque, if it is incorrect, repeat this procedure.

3. To adjust the rack guide screw, perform the following procedure:

    a. At the rear of the steering gear, loosen the rack guide spring cap lock nut.

    b. Remove the rack guide adjusting plug.

    c. Install the rack guide adjusting plug and count the number of rotations, then, back-off the plug ½ the number of turns.

    d. Using a socket wrench and socket tool J–35423 or equivalent, hold the rack guide adjusting plug. Using a torque wrench with a lock nut wrench adapter tool J–35692 or equivalent, torque the rack guide lock nut to 18 ft. lbs., then, back-off the nut 25 degrees (use a compass to measure the position in degrees).

    e. Using a torque wrench and socket tool J–35422 or equivalent, check the pinion shaft preload; it should be 6.9–11.3 inch lbs.

NOTE: If the preload is insufficient, retorque the locknut and back it off 12 degrees, then, recheck the preload.

4. Using sealant, coat the lock nut threads and torque the lock nut to 51 ft. lbs.

5. To install the steering gear, reverse the removal procedures.

Power Steering Gear

Removal and Installation

NOVA AND PRIZM

1. Remove the intermediate steering shaft protector. Loosen the upper shaft pinch bolt and remove the lower one.
2. Open the hood and place a drain pan under the steering gear assembly. Clean the area around the inlet and return lines at the steering gear valve.
3. Loosen the wheel lug nuts, then, raise and support the vehicle safely. Remove both front wheel/tire assemblies.
4. Remove the cotter pins and nuts from the tie rod ends. Using the ball joint removal tool J–24319–01 or equivalent, press the tie rod ends from the steering knuckles.
5. Using a floor jack, support the transaxle. Remove the rear center engine mounting member-to-chassis mounting bolts.
6. Remove the rear engine mount-to-mount bracket nut and bolt.
7. Disconnect the pressure and return lines from the steering gear. Remove the steering gear-to-chassis nuts and bolts; raise and lower the rear of the transaxle (as necessary) to gain access to the steering gear-to-chassis nuts and bolts.
8. Remove the steering gear through the access hole.

9. To install, reverse the removal procedures. Torque the steering gear-to-chassis nuts/bolts to 43 ft. lbs., the tie rod end-to-steering knuckle nuts to 36 ft. lbs. and the U-joint pinch clamp bolts to 26 ft. lbs. Add fluid to the pump reservoir and bleed the system.

NOTE: If new parts have been installed, check and/or adjust the front wheel toe-in and the steering wheel center point.

SPECTRUM

1. Raise and support the vehicle safely.
2. Remove both tie rod ends from the steering knuckles and the right inner tie rod from the rack.
3. Place a drain pan under the rack assembly and clean around the pressure lines at the rack valve.
4. Cut the plastic retaining straps at the power steering lines and hose.
5. Remove the power steering pump lines, the rack valve and drain the fluid into the pan.
6. Remove the rack and pinion.
7. To install, reverse the removal procedures, add fluid, bleed the system and check the toe-in.

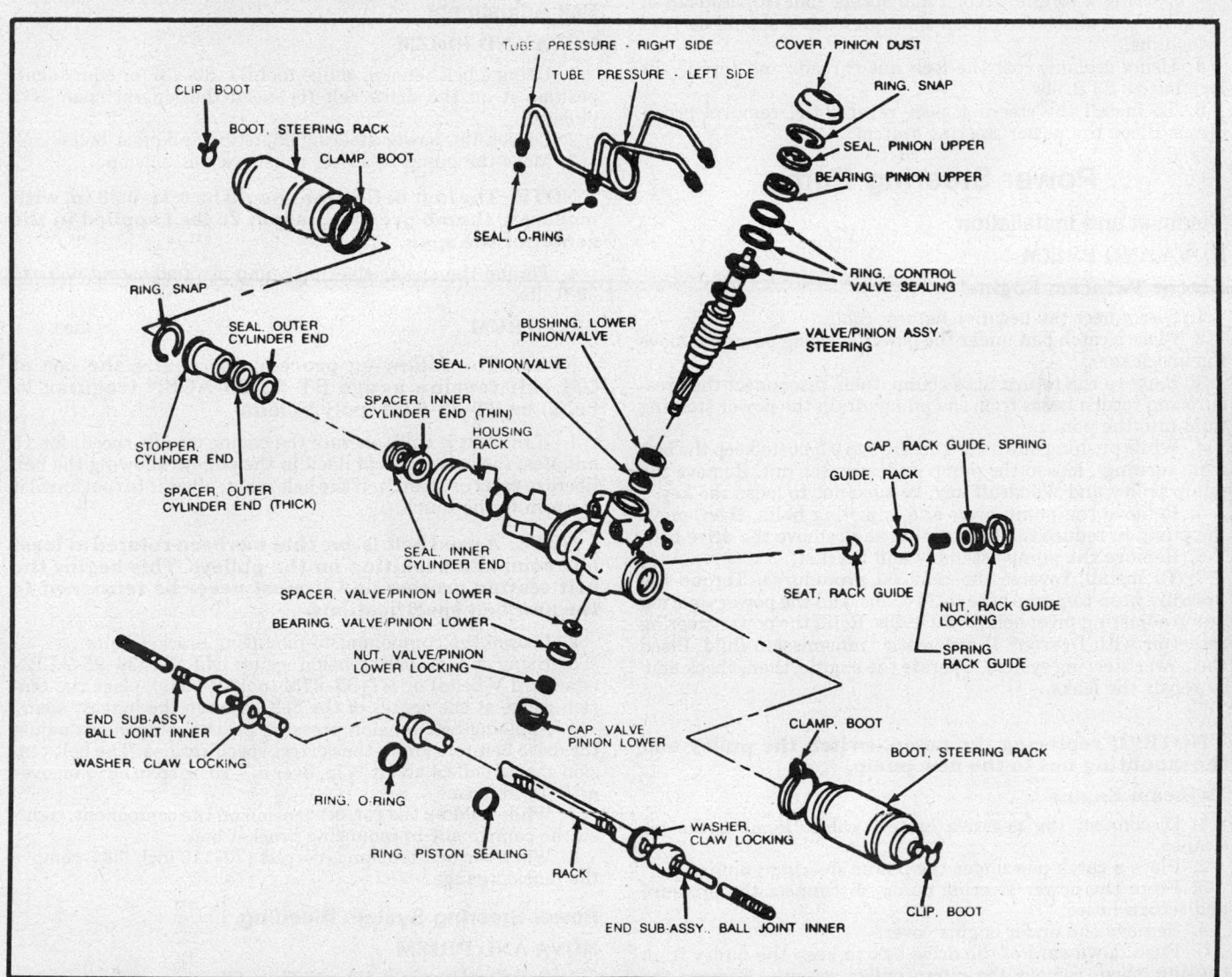

Exploded view of the power rack and pinion steering—Nova

Adjustment

NOVA AND PRIZM

NOTE: To perform the adjustment procedure, the steering gear assembly should be removed from the vehicle.

1. Remove the steering gear and place it in a vise.
2. To adjust the pinion bearing turning torque, perform the following procedures:

   a. Using the socket wrench and socket tool No. J-35428 or equivalent, loosen the pinion bearing lock nut.

   b. Using a socket wrench and socket tool No. J-35428 or equivalent, hold the pinion from turning. Using a torque wrench and socket, torque the lower pinion lock nut to 48 ft. lbs.

3. To adjust the rack guide cap, perform the following procedure:

   a. At the rear of the steering gear, loosen the rack guide spring cap lock nut.

   b. Using a socket wrench and socket tool No. J-35423 or equivalent, torque the rack guide lock nut to 18 ft. lbs., then, back-off the nut 12 degrees (use a compass to measure the position in degrees).

   c. Using a torque wrench and socket tool No. J-35428 or equivalent, check the pinion shaft preload; it should be 7–11 inch lbs.

4. Using sealant, coat the lock nut threads and torque the lock nut to 33 ft. lbs.
5. To install the steering gear, reverse the removal procedures. Bleed the power steering system.

Power Steering Pump

Removal and Installation

NOVA AND PRIZM

Except Twincam Engine

1. Disconnect the negative battery cable.
2. Place a catch pan under the power steering pump. Remove the air cleaner.
3. Remove the return hose clamp, then, disconnect the pressure and return hoses from the pump; drain the power steering fluid into the pan.
4. While pushing downward on the drive belt (to keep the belt from turning), loosen the pump pulley center nut. Remove the pump pulley and Woodruff key; be sure not to loose the key.
5. Remove the pump pivot and adjusting bolts, then, move the pump to reduce the belt tension and remove the drive belt.
6. Remove the pump assembly and bracket.
7. To install, reverse the removal procedures. Torque the pressure hose-to-pump hose to 34 ft. lbs. and the power steering pump adjusting/pivot bolts to 29 ft. lbs. Refill the power steering reservoir with Dexron® II automatic transmission fluid. Bleed the power steering system. Operate the engine, then, check and/or repair the leaks.

NOTE: If replacing the pump, switch the pulley and the mounting nut to the new pump.

Twincam Engine

1. Disconnect the negative battery cable. Remove the air cleaner.
2. Place a catch pan under the power steering pump.
3. From the power steering pump, disconnect the pressure and return hoses.
4. Remove the under engine cover.
5. Push downward of the drive belt to keep the pulley from turning, then, remove the pump pulley set nut. Remove the drive belt.

6. Remove the pump pulley and the Woodruff key; be careful not to loose the key.
7. Remove the upper, lower and pivot bolts.
8. Disconnect the oil pressure switch connector.
9. Remove the power steering pulley, pump-to-bracket bolts and the pump.
10. To install, reverse the removal procedures. Torque the pressure hose-to-pump hose to 33 ft. lbs. and the power steering pump adjusting/pivot bolts to 29 ft. lbs. Refill the power steering reservoir with Dexron® II automatic transmission fluid. Bleed the power steering system. Operate the engine, then, check and/or repair the leaks.

SPECTRUM

1. Disconnect the negative battery cable.
2. Place a drain pan below the pump.
3. Remove the pressure hose clamp, pressure hose and return hose. Drain the fluid from the pump and reservoir.
4. Remove the adjusting bolt, pivot bolt and drive belt.
5. Remove the pump assembly.
6. To install, reverse the removal procedures, tighten the pressure hose to 20 ft. lbs., adjust the drive belt, fill the reservoir and bleed the system.

Belt Adjustment

NOVA AND PRIZM

1. Using a belt tension gauge tool BT-33-73F or equivalent, position it on the drive belt (between the longest span of 2 pulleys).
2. Loosen the power steering adjusting and pivot bolts.
3. Move the pump to adjust the drive belt tension.

NOTE: The belt deflection should be 0.31–0.39 in. with moderate thumb pressure (about 20 lbs.) applied in the center of the span.

4. Torque the power steering pump pivot/adjusting bolts to 29 ft. lbs.

SPECTRUM

NOTE: The following procedures require the use of GM belt tension gauge BT-33-95-ACBN (regular V-belts) or BT-33-97M (poly V-belts).

1. If the belt is cold, operate the engine (at idle speed) for 15 minutes; the belt will seat itself in the pulleys allowing the belt fibers to relax or stretch. If the belt is hot, allow it to cool, until it is warm to the touch.

NOTE: A used belt is one that has been rotated at least one complete evolution on the pulleys. This begins the belt seating process and it must never be tensioned to the new belt specifications.

2. Loosen the component-to-mounting bracket bolts.
3. Using a GM belt tension gauge No. BT-33-95-ACBN (standard V-belts) or BT-33-97M (poly V-belts), place the tension gauge at the center of the belt between the longest span.
4. Applying belt tension pressure on the component, adjust the drive belt tension to the correct specifications. The belt tension should deflect about ¼ in. over a 7–10 in. span or ½ in. over a 13–16 in. span.
5. While holding the correct tension on the component, tighten the component-to-mounting bracket bolt.
6. When the belt tension is correct (70–110 inch lbs.), remove the tension gauge.

Power Steering System Bleeding

NOVA AND PRIZM

1. Raise and support the vehicle safely.
2. The engine must be turned **OFF** and the wheels turned all

the way to the left. Fill the power steering pump reservoir with Dexron®II to the **COLD** mark.

3. Start the engine and allow it to run at fast idle for 30 seconds. Turn the engine **OFF** and recheck the power steering reservoir; if necessary, refill the reservoir to the **COLD** mark.

4. Start the engine and turn the steering wheel from lock-to-lock several times.

5. Repeat the bleeding procedure until all the air is bled from the steering system.

6. After bleeding the system, road test the vehicle to make sure the steering is functioning properly and is free of noise.

SPECTRUM

1. Turn the wheels to the extreme left.
2. With the engine stopped, add power steering fluid to the **MIN** mark on the fluid indicator.
3. Start the engine and run it for 15 seconds at fast idle.
4. Stop the engine, recheck the fluid level and refill to the **MIN** mark.
5. Start the engine and turn the wheels from side to side (3 times).
6. Stop the engine check the fluid level.

NOTE: If air bubbles are still present in the fluid, the procedures must be repeated.

Steering Column

Removal and Installation
NOVA AND PRIZM

1. Disconnect the negative terminal from the battery.
2. Remove the steering wheel.

3. Remove the two set bolts securing the universal joint-to-jack housing and the steering column shaft. Remove the universal joint.

4. Remove the lower instrument panel trim cover. Remove the lower steering column trim cover.

5. Label and disconnect the steering column electrical connectors.

6. Remove the upper steering column cover and the switch assembly.

7. Remove the steering column mounting bolts.

8. Remove the steering column from the vehicle.

9. To install, reverse the removal procedures. Inspect the steering wheel operations.

SPECTRUM

1. Disconnect the negative battery cable.
2. From under the dash, remove the steering column protector nut, clip and protector.
3. Remove the pinch bolt between the intermediate shaft and the steering shaft.
4. Remove the mounting bracket bolts from the lower column.
5. Remove the steering column-to-instrument panel mounting bolts.
6. Remove the electrical connectors and park lock cable at the ignition switch.

NOTE: If equipped with an automatic transaxle, remove the park lock cable bracket.

7. Remove the steering column assembly.
8. To install, reverse the removal procedures. Torque the steering shaft pinch bolts to 19 ft. lbs.

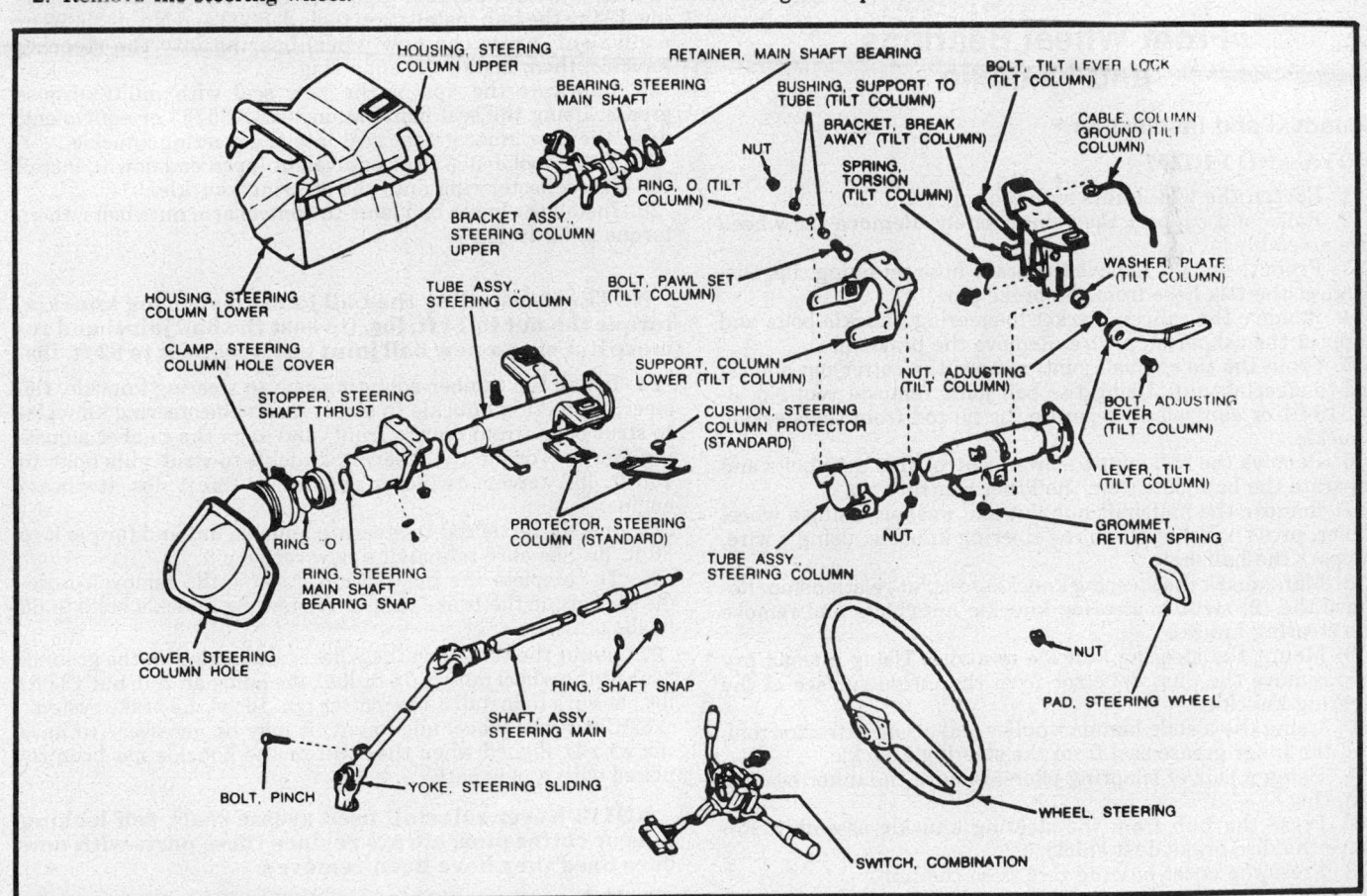

Exploded view of the steering column—Nova

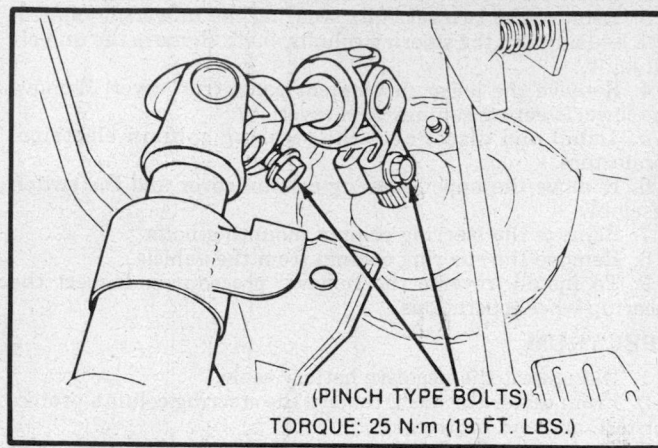

(PINCH TYPE BOLTS)
TORQUE: 25 N·m (19 FT. LBS.)

View of the steering column pinch bolts—Spectrum

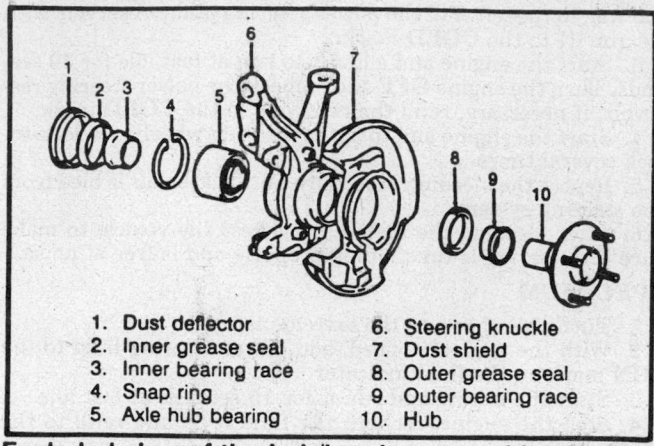

1. Dust deflector	6. Steering knuckle
2. Inner grease seal	7. Dust shield
3. Inner bearing race	8. Outer grease seal
4. Snap ring	9. Outer bearing race
5. Axle hub bearing	10. Hub

Exploded view of the hub/bearing assembly—Nova and Prizm

SPRINT AND METRO

1. Disconnect the negative battery cable. Remove the steering wheel and combination switch.
2. Remove the lower pinch bolt and separate the lower steering column shaft from the steering column. Disconnect and tag the electrical connectors from the steering column.
3. Remove the upper steering column mounting bolts and the column from the dash.
4. To install, reverse the removal procedure. Torque the lower bracket bolts to 8–12 lbs., the upper bracket bolts to 10 ft. lbs. and the steering shaft bolt to 15–22 ft. lbs.

Front Wheel Bearings and Knuckle

Removal and Installation

NOVA AND PRIZM

1. Loosen the wheel nuts and hub nut.
2. Raise and support the vehicle safely. Remove the wheel/tire assembly.
3. From the strut, remove the brake hose retaining clip. Disconnect the flex hose from the brake pipe.
4. Remove the caliper bracket-to-steering knuckle bolts and support the caliper on a wire. Remove the brake disc.
5. From the tie rod ball joint, remove the cotter pin and tie rod-to-steering nut. Using the ball joint removal tool No. J-24319-01 or equivalent, separate the tie rod from the steering knuckle.
6. Remove the ball joint-to-lower control arm nuts/bolts and separate the ball joint from the lower control arm.
7. Remove the halfshaft hub nut and washer. Using a wheel puller, press halfshaft from the steering knuckle; using a wire, support the halfshaft.
8. Matchmark the steering knuckle-to-strut relationship. Remove the (2) strut-to-steering knuckle nuts/bolts and remove the steering knuckle.
9. Mount the steering knuckle in a vise. Using a small pry bar, remove the dust deflector from the inside surface of the steering knuckle.
10. Using the a slide hammer puller and a seal extractor tool, pull the inner grease seal from the steering knuckle.
11. Using a pair of snapring pliers, remove the inner bearing snapring.
12. Press the hub from the steering knuckle assembly. Remove the disc brake dust shield.
13. Press the outer bearing race from the hub.
14. Using a seal removal tool, remove the outer grease seal from the steering knuckle.

15. Drive the bearing assembly from the steering knuckle.
16. Clean and inspect all parts. Replace any parts that appear worn or damaged. Replace all grease seals.
17. Drive the new bearing assembly into the steering knuckle.
18. Using the seal installation tool J-35737-1 or equivalent, lubricate the seal lips with multi-purpose grease and drive the new outer grease seal into the steering knuckle.
19. Apply sealer to the dust shield and install it onto the steering knuckle.
20. Apply multi-purpose grease to the seal lip, seal and bearing. Using the hub installation tools J-8092 and No. J-35399 or equivalent, press the new wheel bearing into the steering knuckle, then, install the snap ring.
21. Lubricate the lips of the new seal with multi-purpose grease. Using the seal installation tool J-35737 or equivalent, drive the new inner grease seal into the steering knuckle.
22. Using tool J-35379 or equivalent (open end down), install the dust deflector ring onto the steering knuckle.
23. Install the lower ball joint-to-control arm nuts/bolts, then, torque to 59 ft. lbs.

NOTE: If installing the ball joint-to-steering knuckle, torque the nut to 14 ft. lbs. (to seat the ball joint) and remove it. Using a new ball joint nut, torque it to 82 ft. lbs.

24. Install the camber adjusting cam to steering knuckle, the steering steering knuckle to strut. Insert the steering knuckle-to-strut bolts (from rear to front) and align the camber adjusting marks. Torque the steering knuckle-to-strut nuts/bolts to 105 ft. lbs. (except twincam engine) or 166 ft. lbs. (twincam engine).
25. Install the tie rod-to-steering knuckle nut and torque it to 36 ft. lbs.; be sure to install a new cotter pin.
26. To complete the installation, reverse the removal procedures. Torque the brake caliper-to-steering knuckle bolts to 65 ft. lbs.
27. Lower the vehicle so the wheels are resting on the ground. Torque the wheel nuts to 76 ft. lbs., the halfshaft hub nut 137 ft. lbs.; be sure to install a new cotter pin. Bleed the brake system.
28. Check the wheel alignment; it may be necessary to have the wheels aligned when the strut or the knuckle has been replaced with a new part.

NOTE: Never reinstall used grease seals, self locking nuts or cotter pins; always replace these parts with new ones once they have been removed.

29. If the cotter pin holes are not aligned, bend the tangs on the cap, slightly to align the holes; Never back off the nut.

SPECTRUM

1. Raise and support the vehicle safely, allowing the wheels to hang.

2. Remove the front wheel assemblies, the hub grease caps and the cotter pins.

3. Install the drive axle boot seal protector tool No. J–28712 or equivalent, on the outer CV-joints and the drive axle boot seal protector tool No. J–34754 or equivalent, on the inner Tri-Pot joints.

NOTE: Clean the halfshaft threads and lubricate them with a thread lubricant.

4. Remove the hub nut and washer.

5. Remove the caliper-to-steering knuckle bolts and support the caliper (on a wire) out of the way.

6. Remove the rotor.

7. Using a slide hammer puller and the puller attachment tool J–34866 or equivalent, pull the hub from the halfshaft.

8. Remove the tie rod-to-steering knuckle cotter pin and the nut. Using the ball joint separator tool J–21687–02 or equivalent, press the tie rod ball joint from the steering knuckle.

9. To remove the steering knuckle from the vehicle, perform the following procedures:

    a. Remove the lower ball joint-to-control arm nuts/bolts.

NOTE: Before separating the steering knuckle from the strut, be sure to scribe matchmarks on each component.

    b. Remove the steering knuckle-to-strut nuts/bolts and the steering knuckle from the vehicle.

10. Using a medium pry bar, pry the grease seals from the steering knuckle. Using a pair of internal snapring pliers, remove the internal snap rings from the steering knuckle.

11. Support the steering knuckle (face down) on an arbor press (on 2 press blocks). Position tool J–35301 or equivalent, on the rear-side of the hub bearing, then, press the bearing from the steering knuckle.

12. Using an arbor press, the wheel puller tool J–35893 or equivalent and a piece of bar stock, press the bearing inner race from the wheel hub.

13. Clean the parts in solvent and blow dry with compressed air.

To Install:

14. Using wheel bearing grease, lubricate the inside of the steering knuckle.

15. Using the internal snapring pliers, install the outer snap ring into the steering knuckle.

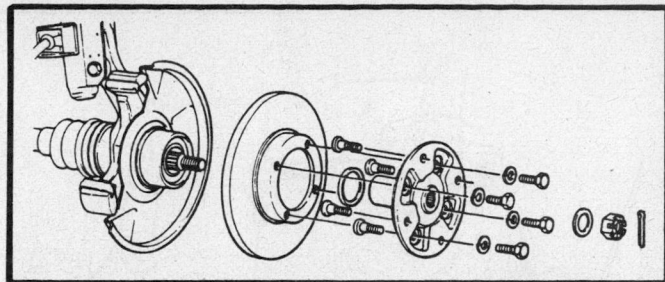

Exploded view of the front wheel hub assembly— Sprint and Metro

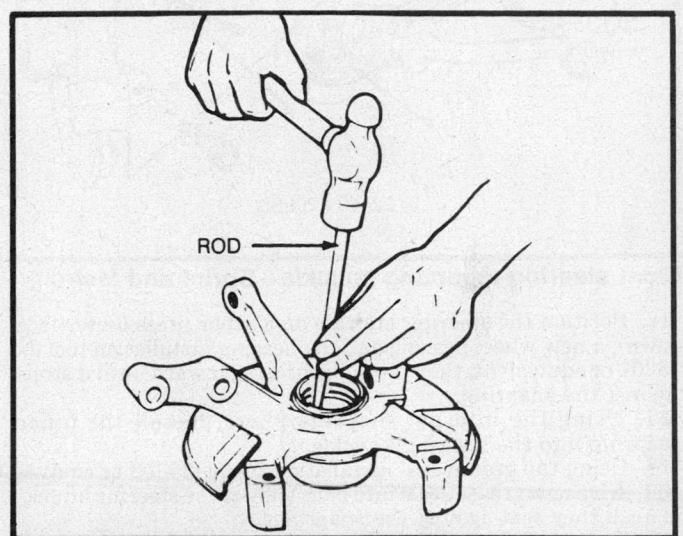

ROD

Removing the outer wheel bearing from the steering knuckle—Sprint and Metro

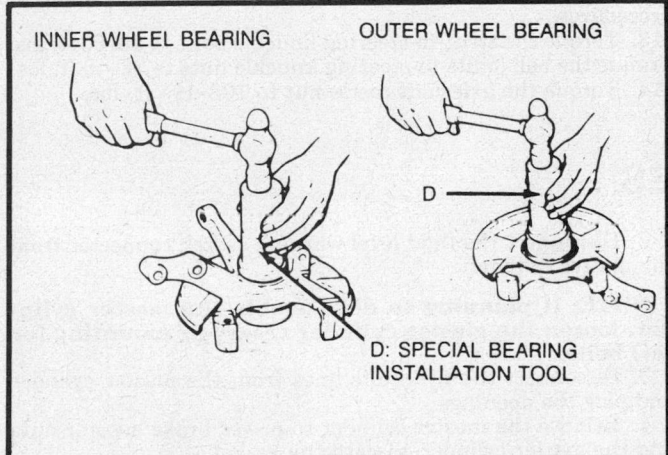

INNER WHEEL BEARING   OUTER WHEEL BEARING

D

D: SPECIAL BEARING INSTALLATION TOOL

Installing inner and outer wheel bearings in the steering knuckle—Sprint and Metro

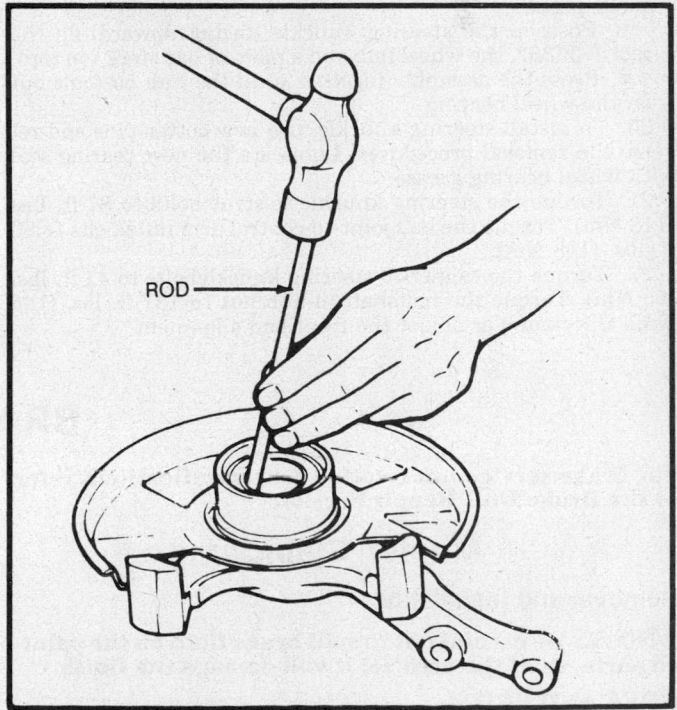

ROD

Remove inner wheel bearing from the steering knuckle—Sprint and Metro

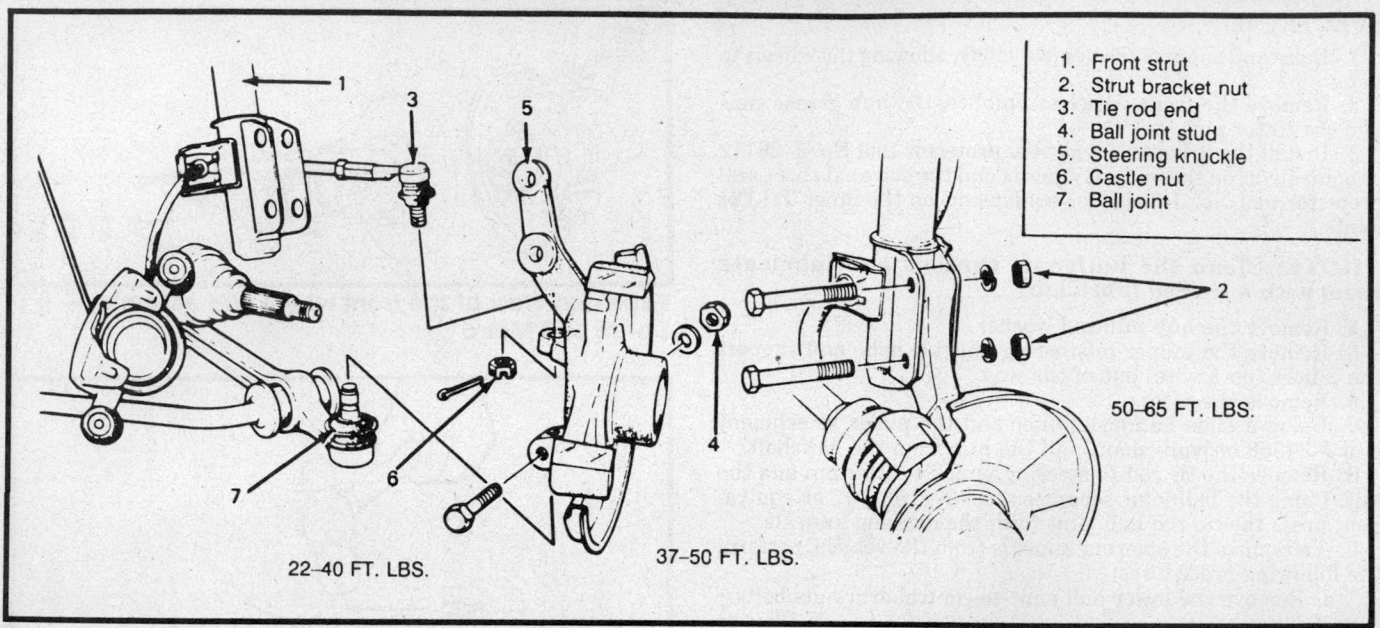

1. Front strut
2. Strut bracket nut
3. Tie rod end
4. Ball joint stud
5. Steering knuckle
6. Castle nut
7. Ball joint

50–65 FT. LBS.

22–40 FT. LBS.

37–50 FT. LBS.

Front steering mounting knuckle—Sprint and Metro

16. Position the steering knuckle on a arbor press (outer face down), a new wheel bearing and the bearing installation tool J–35301 or equivalent, then press the bearing inward until it stops against the snapring.

17. Using the internal snapring pliers, install the inner snapring into the steering knuckle.

18. Using the grease seal installation tool J–35303 or equivalent, drive new grease seals into both ends of the steering knuckle until they seat against the snaprings.

19. To install the hub into the steering knuckle, perform the following procedure:

  a. Position tool J–35302 or equivalent, facing upward on a arbor press.

  b. Position the steering knuckle (facing upward) on the tool J–35302, the wheel hub and a piece of bar stock (on top).

  c. Press the assembly together until the hub bottoms out on the wheel bearing.

20. To install steering knuckle, use new cotter pins and reverse the removal procedures. Lubricate the new bearing seal with wheel bearing grease.

21. Torque the steering knuckle-to-strut bolts to 87 ft. lbs. (118 Nm). Torque the ball joint-to-control arm nuts/bolts to 80 ft. lbs. (108 Nm).

22. Torque the caliper-to-steering knucklebolts to 41 ft. lbs. (55 Nm). Torque the halfshaft-to-hub nut to 137 ft. lbs. (186 Nm). Check and/or adjust the front end alignment.

SPRINT AND METRO

1. Raise and support the vehicle safely. Remove the front wheel asssembly. Remove the hub from the steering knuckle.

2. Remove the tie rod end cotter pin and nut.

3. Using the ball joint removal tool J–21687–02, remove the ball joint from the steering knuckle.

4. Remove the ball stud bolt from the steering knuckle.

5. Remove the strut-to-steering knuckle bolts.

6. Remove the steering knuckle and support the axleshaft.

7. Using a brass drift, drive the inner and outer wheel bearings from the steering knuckle.

8. Remove the spacer and clean the steering knuckle cavity.

9. Lubricate the new bearings and the steering knuckle cavity.

10. Using the installation tool J–34856, drive the new bearings (with the internal seals facing outward) into the steering knuckle.

11. Using the seal installation tool J–34881, drive the new seal into the steering knuckle (grease the seal lip).

12. To complete the installation, reverse the removal procedures.

13. Torque the strut-to-steering knuckle bolts to 50–65 ft. lbs. Torque the ball joints-to-steering knuckle nuts to 22–40 ft. lbs.

14. Torque the axleshaft castle nut to 108–195 ft. lbs.

BRAKES

For brake service information and specifications, refer to the Brake Unit Repair Section

Master Cylinder

Removal and Installation

NOTE: Be careful not to spill brake fluid on the painted surfaces of the vehicle; it will damage the finish.

NOVA AND PRIZM

1. Disconnect the negative battery cable. Using a syringe, remove the brake fluid from the master cylinder.

2. Disconnect the fluid level warning switch connector from the master cylinder.

NOTE: If planning to disassemble the master cylinder, loosen the master cylinder reservoir mounting (or set) bolts.

3. Disconnect the hydraulic lines from the master cylinder and plug the openings.

4. Remove the master cylinder-to-power brake booster nuts and the master cylinder; discard the gasket.

5. To install the master cylinder, use a new gasket, clean out the groove on the lower installation surface, confirm that the **UP** mark on the master cylinder boot is in the correct position

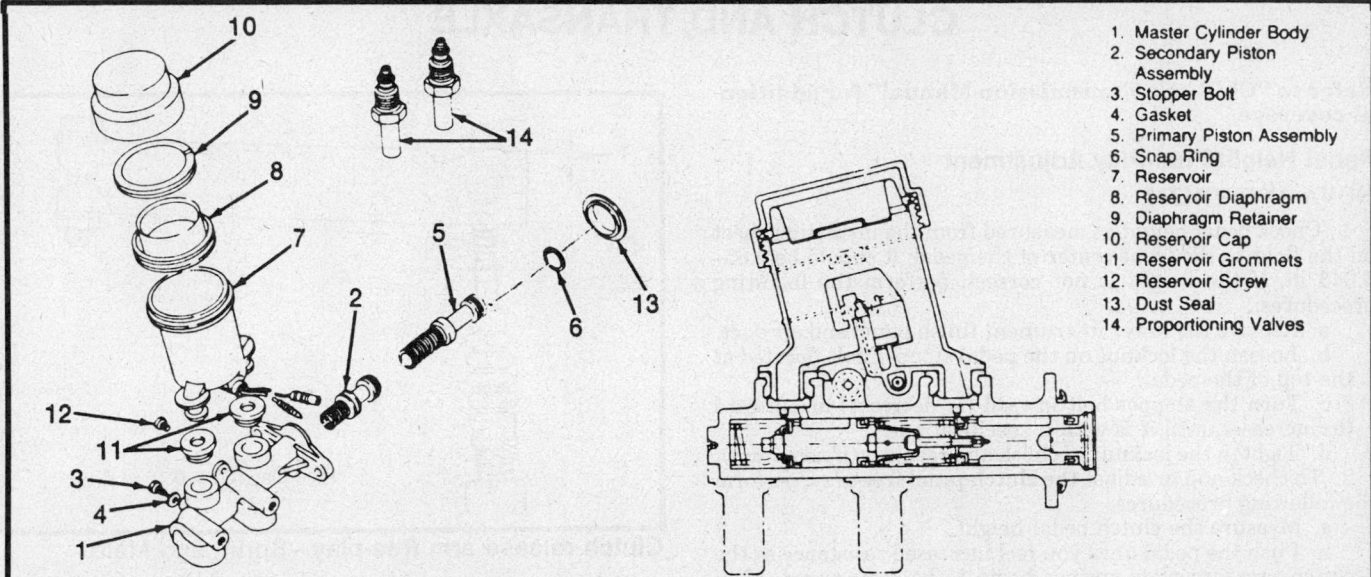

1. Master Cylinder Body
2. Secondary Piston Assembly
3. Stopper Bolt
4. Gasket
5. Primary Piston Assembly
6. Snap Ring
7. Reservoir
8. Reservoir Diaphragm
9. Diaphragm Retainer
10. Reservoir Cap
11. Reservoir Grommets
12. Reservoir Screw
13. Dust Seal
14. Proportioning Valves

Exploded view of the master cylinder assembly—Spectrum

(at the top), adjust the pushrod and reverse the removal procedures.

6. Torque the master cylinder-to-power brake booster nuts to 9 ft. lbs. and the brake lines to 11 ft. lbs.

7. Connect the level warning switch connector. Refill the fluid reservoir and bleed the brake system.

8. Check for fluid leakage and tighten or replace fittings as necessary.

9. Adjust the pedal height and free-play.

SPECTRUM

1. Disconnect the negative battery cable. Remove some brake fluid from the master cylinder with a syringe.

2. Disconnect and cap or tape the openings of the brake tube.

3. Disconnect the brake fluid level warning switch connector.

4. Remove the 2 nuts securing the master cylinder to the power brake booster.

5. Remove the master cylinder from the power brake booster.

6. To install, reverse the removal procedures, add fluid to the reservoir and bleed the brake system.

SPRINT AND METRO

1. Disconnect the negative battery cable. Clean around the reservoir cap and take some of the fluid out with a syringe.

2. Disconnect and plug the brake tubes from the master cylinder.

3. Remove the mounting nuts and washers.

4. Remove the master cylinder.

5. To install, reverse the removal procedures. Torque the mounting bolts to 8–12 ft. lbs. Bleed the brake system.

Power Brake Booster

Removal and Installation
NOVA AND PRIZM

NOTE: To perform this procedure, use a booster push-rod gauge GM part No. J-34873-A or equivalent to set the booster pushrod length.

1. Disconnect the negative battery cable. Remove the master cylinder and the 3-way union from the power brake booster.

2. Pull back the clamp and disconnect the booster vacuum line from the power brake booster.

3. Remove the instrument panel lower finish panel and the air duct.

4. Remove the brake pedal return spring.

5. Locate the clevis rod at the brake pedal (under the dash), then, pull out the clip and remove the clevis pin.

6. Remove the brake booster-to-cowl, the the booster, bracket and gasket.

7. To adjust the power brake booster pushrod, perform the following procedures:

   a. Using the push rod gauge tool J-34873-A or equivalent, set the short-side on the booster.

NOTE: The head of the pin sits near the end of the booster pushrod.

   b. Check the gap between the head of the tool's pin and the pushrod; it should be zero. If necessary, adjust the pushrod by turning it until the pushrod just touches the pin.

8. To install, reverse the removal procedures. Torque the power brake booster-to-chassis nuts to 9 ft. lbs. Bleed the brake system and check for leaks in the system. Adjust the pedal height and free-play.

SPECTRUM

1. Disconnect the negative battery cable.

2. Remove the master cylinder.

3. Remove the vacuum hose from the vacuum servo.

4. Remove the clevis pin from the brake pedal.

5. Remove the 4 nuts from the brake assembly under the dash and remove the power booster from the engine compartment.

6. To install, reverse the removal procedures.

SPRINT AND METRO

1. Disconnect the negative battery cable.

2. Remove the master cylinder.

3. Disconnect the pushrod clevis pin from the brake pedal arm.

4. Disconnect the vacuum hose from the brake booster.

5. Remove the mounting nuts from under the dash and the booster.

6. To install, reverse the removal procedures. Torque the booster-to-cowl nuts to 14–20 ft. lbs. Bleed the brake system, if necessary.

CLUTCH AND TRANSAXLE

Refer to "Chilton's Transmission Manual" for additional coverage.

Pedal Height/Free-Play Adjustment

NOVA AND PRIZM

1. Check pedal height as measured from the insulating sheet on the floor to the front-center of the pedal; it should be 5.65–6.043 in. If the height is not correct, perform the following procedures:
    a. Remove the lower instrument finish panel and air duct.
    b. Loosen the locknut on the pedal stopper bolt (located at the top of the pedal).
    c. Turn the stopper bolt inward (to decrease) or outward (to increase) until it is within specifications.
    d. Tighten the locknut, recheck and readjust (if necessary).
2. To check and/or adjust the clutch pedal free-play, perform the following procedures:
    a. Measure the clutch pedal height.
    b. Push the pedal until you feel increased resistance as the clutch pressure plate springs begin to be compressed. Measure the pedal at this point, then, subtract the smaller figure from the larger one; this is the free-play dimension.

NOTE: The free-play dimension should be 0.20–0.59 in.

    c. If necessary to adjust the free-play, loosen the pushrod locknut, located between the pedal and the clutch master cylinder. Turn the pushrod (clockwise to decrease or counterclockwise to increase) until the dimension is within specifications.
    d. Tighten the locknut, recheck and readjust, if necessary.

Free-Play Adjustment

SPECTRUM

1. Disconnect the negative battery terminal from the battery.

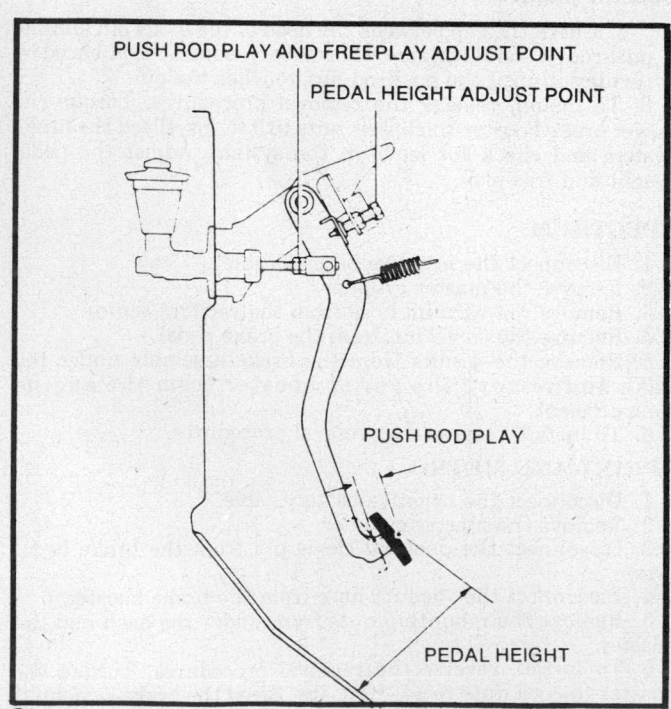

PUSH ROD PLAY AND FREEPLAY ADJUST POINT

PEDAL HEIGHT ADJUST POINT

PUSH ROD PLAY

PEDAL HEIGHT

Clutch pedal adjusting points—Nova and Prizm

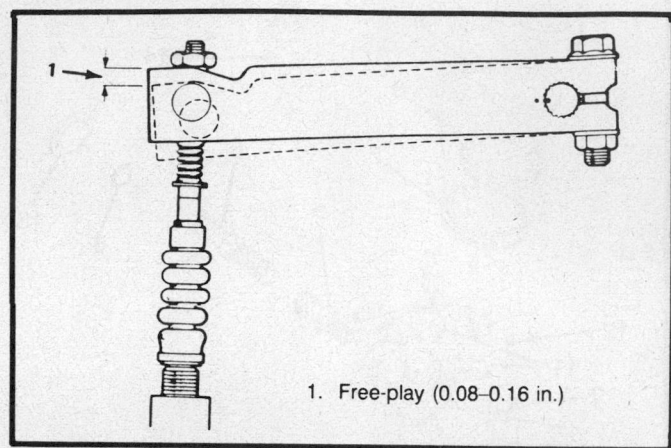

1. Free-play (0.08–0.16 in.)

Clutch release arm free-play—Sprint and Metro

2. Loosen the adjusting nut and pull the cable to the rear until it turns freely.
3. Adjust the cable length by turning the adjusting nut.
4. When the clutch pedal free play travel reaches 0.39–0.79 in. release the cable.
5. When the adjustment has been completed, tighten the locknut.

SPRINT AND METRO

1. At the transaxle, move the clutch release arm to check the free play, it should be 0.08–0.16 in.
2. If necessary, turn the clutch cable joint nut to adjust the cable length.
  The clutch pedal height should be adjusted so that the clutch pedal is the exact same height as the brake pedal. The pedal is adjusted at the stop bolt on the upper end of the pedal pivot.

Clutch Master Cylinder

Removal and Installation

NOVA AND PRIZM

1. Disconnect the negative battery cable.
2. Drain or siphon the fluid from the master cylinder.
3. Remove the lower instrument finish panel and air duct.
4. Remove the pedal return spring, clevis pin and clip.
5. Disconnect the hydraulic line the clutch master cylinder.

NOTE: Do not spill brake fluid on the painted surface of the vehicle.

6. Remove the master cylinder-to-firewall nuts and withdraw the assembly.
7. To install, reverse the removal procedures. Refill the master cylinder reservoir with brake fluid. Bleed the clutch hydraulic system.
8. Operate the clutch pedal and check the system for leaks.
9. Check and/or adjust the clutch pedal height and free-play.

Clutch Slave Cylinder

Removal and Installation

NOVA AND PRIZM

NOTE: Do not spill brake fluid on the painted surface of the vehicle.

1. Disconnect the negative battery cable.

2. Disconnect the hydraulic line from the clutch slave cylinder.

3. Remove the slave cylinder-to-engine bolts and the cylinder.

4. To install, reverse the removal procedures. Refill the clutch master cylinder reservoir with clean brake fluid. Bleed the clutch hydraulic system. Operate the clutch pedal and check for leaks.

Bleeding The Hydraulic System

NOVA AND PRIZM

1. Fill the clutch master cylinder reservoir with brake fluid.

NOTE: Do not spill brake fluid on the painted surface of the vehicle.

2. Fit a vinyl bleeder tube over the bleeder screw at the front of the slave cylinder and place the other end in a clean jar half filled with brake fluid.

3. Have an assistant depress the clutch pedal several times. Loosen the bleeder screw and allow the fluid to flow into the jar.

4. Tighten the screw and have the assistant release the clutch pedal.

5. Repeat bleeding procedure until no air bubbles are present in the fluid.

6. Refill the master cylinder to the specified level, check the system for leaks, then, adjust the clutch pedal height and free-play.

Clutch Cable

Removal and Installation

SPECTRUM

1. Disconnect the negative battery terminal from the battery.

2. Loosen the clutch cable adjusting nuts. Disconnect the cable from the release arm and cable bracket.

3. At the clutch pedal, remove the cable retaining bolt.

4. Disconnect the cable from the front of the dash.

5. Remove the clutch cable from the vehicle.

6. To install, grease the clutch cable pin and reverse the removal procedures.

7. Adjust the clutch cable.

SPRINT AND METRO

1. Disconnect the negative battery cable.

2. Remove the clutch cable joint nut and disconnect the cable from the release arm.

3. Remove the clutch cable bracket mounting nuts and remove the bracket from the cable.

4. Remove the cable retaining bolts at the clutch pedal.

5. Remove the cable from the vehicle.

6. Before installation, apply grease to the hook and pin end of the cable.

7. Connect the cable to the clutch pedal and install the retaining bolts.

8. Install the clutch cable bracket on the cable.

9. Position the bracket on the transaxle and install the mounting bolts.

10. Connect the cable to the release lever and install the joint nut on the cable.

11. Adjust the clutch cable as previously outlined and connect the negative battery cable.

Parking Brake

Adjustment

NOVA AND PRIZM

1. Release the parking brake (all the way). Using 44 lbs. of pulling pressure, slowly pull the lever upward and count the

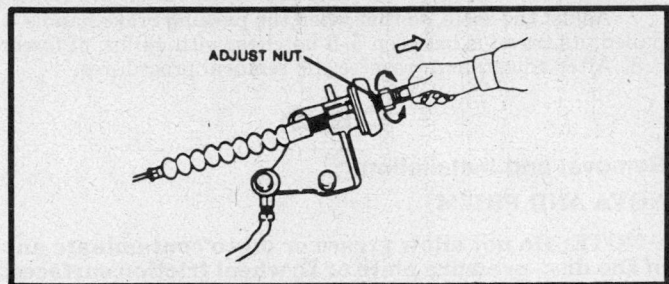

Adjusting the clutch cable — Spectrum

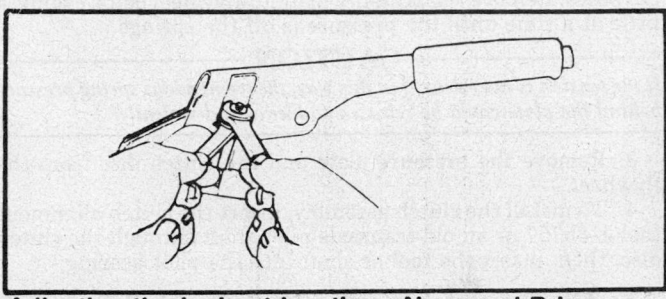

Adjusting the locknut location — Nova and Prizm

number of clicks; 4–7 clicks (except twincam engine) or 5–8 (twincam engine).

2. If the number of clicks is incorrect, adjust the parking brake cable by performing the following procedures:

   a. Remove the console box.

   b. At the rear of the parking brake handle, loosen the cable nut, then, turn the adjusting nut.

3. Secure the adjusting nut position when tighten the locknut. Check the **adjustment and repeat Steps 2 and 3** (if necessary). Tighten the adjusting nut securely and ensure that the adjustment is correct.

SPECTRUM

The parking brake adjustment is normal when the lever moves 7–9 notches at 66 lbs. of force. If it is not within limits, adjust the rear brakes. If this adjustment does not affect the specifications, adjust the parking brake turnbuckle.

SPRINT AND METRO

1. Remove both door seal plates and the seat belt buckle bolts at the floor.

2. Disconnect the shoulder harness bolts at the floor and the interior, bottom trim panels.

3. Raise the rear seat cushion.

4. Pull up the carpet to gain access to the parking brake lever.

5. Loosen the parking brake cable adjusting nuts.

6. Adjust the parking brake cables, so that they work evenly.

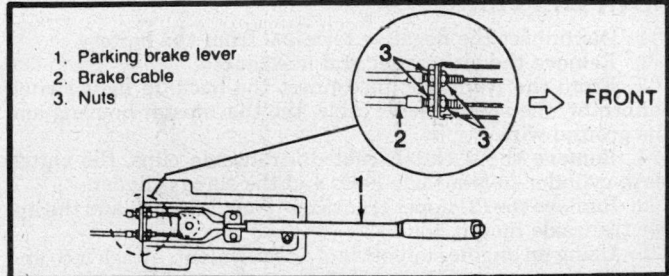

1. Parking brake lever
2. Brake cable
3. Nuts

FRONT

Parking brake cable adjustment — Sprint and Metro

7. Adjust the cable, so that when the parking brake handle is pulled, its travel is between 5–8 notches, with 44 lbs. of force.

8. After adjustment, reverse the removal procedures.

Clutch

Removal and Installation
NOVA AND PRIZM

NOTE: Do not allow grease or oil to contaminate any of the disc, pressure plate or flywheel friction surfaces.

1. Remove the transaxle from the vehicle.

2. Matchmark the pressure plate to flywheel for realignment purposes. Remove the pressure plate-to-flywheel bolts, evenly, a little at a time until the pressure is off the springs.

— CAUTION —

If the tension is not released in this way, the tremendous spring pressure behind the plate could be released suddenly and violently!

3. Remove the pressure plate and the clutch disc from the flywheel.

4. To install the clutch assembly, insert the clutch alignment tool J–35757 or an old transaxle pilot shaft through the clutch disc, then, insert the tool or shaft into the pilot bearing.

NOTE: The clutch disc is installed with the concave side facing the flywheel.

5. Install the pressure plate over the disc with matchmarks aligned and install the bolts. Tighten the bolts alternately and evenly until even pressure is all around. Finally, torque the pressure plate-to-flywheel bolts to 14 ft. lbs. Remove the centering tool or input shaft.

6. To complete the installation, lubricate the release bearing hub and release fork contact points with multi-purpose grease and reverse the removal procedures.

SPECTRUM

1. Remove the transaxle.

2. Install the pilot shaft tool J–35282 or equivalent, into the pilot bearing to support the clutch assembly during the removal procedures.

NOTE: Observe the alignment marks on the clutch and the clutch cover and pressure plate assembly. If the markings are not present, be sure to add them.

3. Loosen the clutch cover and pressure plate assembly retaining bolts evenly (one at a time) until the spring pressure is released.

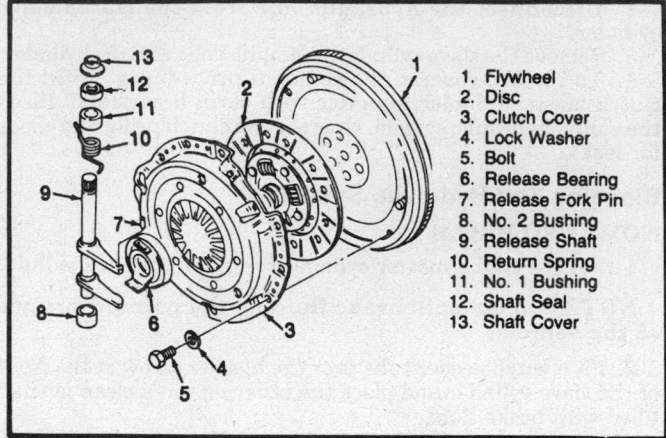

1. Flywheel
2. Disc
3. Clutch Cover
4. Lock Washer
5. Bolt
6. Release Bearing
7. Release Fork Pin
8. No. 2 Bushing
9. Release Shaft
10. Return Spring
11. No. 1 Bushing
12. Shaft Seal
13. Shaft Cover

Exploded view of the clutch assembly—Sprint and Metro

4. Remove the clutch cover and pressure plate assembly and clutch plate.

NOTE: Check the clutch disc, flywheel and pressure plate for wear, damage or heat cracks. Replace all damaged parts.

5. Before installation, lightly lubricate the pilot shaft splines, pilot bearing and pilot release bearing surface with grease.

6. To install, reverse the removal procedures. Torque the clutch cover/pressure plate-to-flywheel bolts evenly to 13 ft. lbs., to avoid distortion.

SPRINT AND METRO

1. Remove the transaxle.

2. Install tool J–34860 into the pilot bearing to support the clutch assembly.

NOTE: Look for the X mark or white painted number on the clutch cover and the X mark on the flywheel. If there are no markings, mark the clutch cover and the flywheel for reassembly purposes.

3. Loosen the clutch cover-to-flywheel bolts, one turn at a time (evenly) until the spring pressure is released.

4. Remove the clutch cover and clutch disc.

5. Inspect the parts for wear, if necessary, replace the parts.

6. To install, reverse the removal procedures. Torque the clutch cover bolts to 14–20 ft. lbs.

MANUAL TRANSAXLE

Removal and Installation
NOVA AND PRIZM

1. Disconnect the negative terminal from the battery.

2. Remove the air cleaner and inlet duct.

3. From the transaxle, disconnect the back-up light switch connector, the speedometer cable, the thermostat housing and the ground wire.

4. Remove the 4 clutch cable-to-transaxle clips, the clutch slave cylinder-to-transaxle bolts and the slave cylinder.

5. Remove the (2) upper transaxle-to-engine bolts and the upper transaxle mount bolt.

6. Using an engine support tool or equivalent, attach it to and support the engine. Raise and support the vehicle safely.

7. Remove the left wheel assembly. From under the vehicle,

remove the left, right and center splash shields. Remove the center beam-to-chassis bolts and the center beam.

8. Remove the flywheel cover-to-engine bolts and the cover.

9. From both sides of the vehicle, disconnect the lower control arms from the steering knuckles.

10. Disconnect both halfshaft from the transaxle.

11. Disconnect the battery cable and ignition switch wire from the starter. Remove the starter-to-engine bolts and the starter.

12. Properly support the transaxle.

13. Remove the transaxle-to-engine bolts and the lower the transaxle from the vehicle.

14. Using the proper tool, clean the gasket mounting surfaces.

15. To install, make sure the input shaft splines align with the clutch disc splines and reverse the removal procedures. Torque the transaxle-to-engine bolts to 47 ft. lbs. (12mm) and to 34 ft.

lbs. (10mm), the halfshaft-to-transaxle nuts to 27 ft. lbs., the crossmember-to-chassis nuts/bolts to 29 ft. lbs. and the left side engine mount bolts to 38 ft. lbs. Check and/or refill the transaxle with fluid.

SPECTRUM

1. Disconnect the negative battery termninal from the battery and the transaxle.
2. Disconnect the wiring connectors, speedometer cable, clutch cable and shift cables from the transaxle.
3. Remove the air cleaner heat tube.
4. Remove the upper transaxle-to-engine bolts.
6. Raise and support the vehicle safely. Drain the oil from the transaxle.7. Remove the left front wheel assembly and splash shield.
8. Disconnect the left tie rod at the steering knuckle and the left tension rod.
9. Disconnect the drive axles and remove the shafts by pulling them straight out from the transaxle (avoid damaging the oil seals).
10. Remove the dust cover at the clutch housing.
11. Using a floor jack, support the transaxle, then remove the transaxle-to-engine retaining bolts.
12. While sliding the transaxle away from the engine, carefully lower the jack, guiding the right axle shaft out of the transaxle.

NOTE: The right axle shaft must be installed into the transaxle when the transaxle is being mated to the engine.

12. To install, reverse the removal procedures.

SPRINT AND METRO

1. Disconnect the negative battery cable and the ground strap at the transaxle.
2. Remove the air cleaner and air pipe.
3. Remove the clutch cable from the clutch release lever.
4. Remove the starter and speedometer cable. Disconnect and tag the electrical wires and wiring harness from the transaxle.
5. Remove the front and rear torque rod bolts at the transaxle.
6. Raise and support the vehicle safely.
7. Drain the transaxle fluid.
8. Remove the exhaust pipe at the exhaust manifold and at the 1st exhaust hanger.
9. Remove the clutch housing lower plate.
10. Disconnect the gear shift control shaft and the extension rod at the transaxle.
11. Remove the left front wheel.
12. Using a pry bar, pry on the inboard joints of the right and left hand axle shafts. This will detach the axle shafts from the snaprings of the differential side gears.
13. On the left side, remove the stabilizer bar mounting bolts and ball joint stud bolt. Push down on the stabilizer bar and remove the ball joint stud from the steering knuckle.
14. Pull the left axle shaft out of the transaxle.
15. Remove the front torque rod.
16. Secure and support the transaxle case with a jack.
17. Remove the transaxle-to-body mounting bolts and the mounts.
18. Remove the transaxle-to-engine mounting bolts.
19. Disconnect the transaxle from the engine by sliding it to the left side and lower the jack.

NOTE: When removing the transaxle, support the right axle shaft, so it does not become damaged.

20. To install, guide the right axle shaft into the transaxle and reverse the removal procedures. Torque the transaxle-to-engine bolts to 35 ft. lbs.
21. Torque the transaxle-to-mount bolts to 34 ft. lbs. Torque the mounting member bolts to 40 ft. lbs.

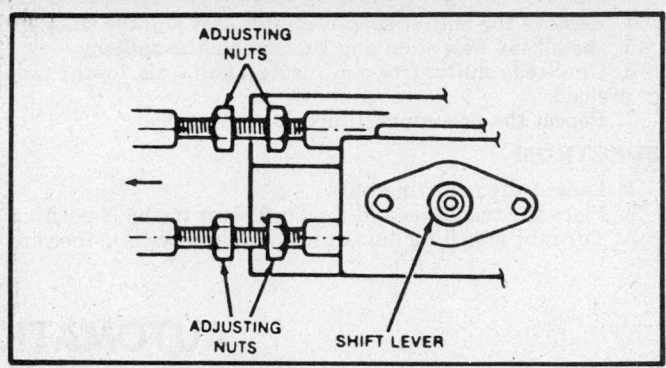

Adjusting the shift linkage of the transaxle— Spectrum

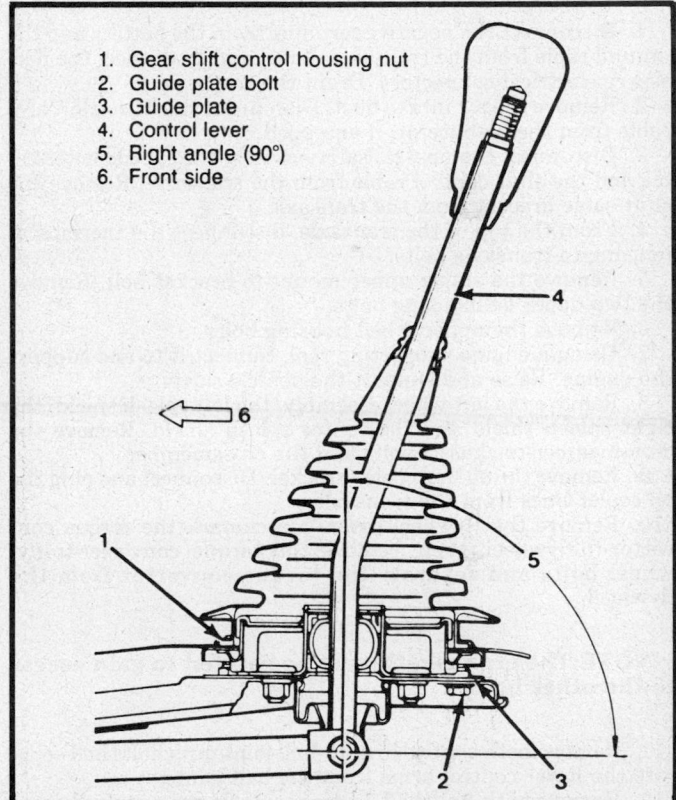

1. Gear shift control housing nut
2. Guide plate bolt
3. Guide plate
4. Control lever
5. Right angle (90°)
6. Front side

Manual transaxle gearshift lever adjustment—Sprint and Metro

22. Torque the stabilizer bar bolts to 30 ft. lbs. Torque the ball joint stud bolt to 44 ft. lbs. Adjust the clutch cable and refill the transaxle.

Linkage Adjustment

NOVA AND PRIZM

Adjustment of shift lever free-play is accomplished through the use of a selective shim installed in the bottom of the lower shift lever seat.

Select a shim of a thickness that allows a preload of 0.1–0.2 lbs. at the top of the lever and install it in the shift lever seat.

To install the shim, perform the following procedures:
1. Disconnect the negative terminal from the battery.
2. Remove the console and the shifter boot.
3. Remove the shifter cover, shift support and cap.

4. Remove the shifter spacer, shifter seat and the shim.
5. Install the new shim and reassemble the shifter.
6. Check the shifter free play, using a pull scale, for the proper preload.
7. Repeat the procedure, if necessary.

SPECTRUM
1. Loosen the adjusting nuts.
2. Place the transaxle and the shift lever in the **N** position.
3. Turn the adjusting nuts until the shift lever is in the vertical position.
4. Tighten the adjusting nuts.

SPRINT AND METRO
1. At the console, loosen the gear shift control housing nuts and the guide plate bolts.
2. Adjust the guide plate, so that the shift lever is centered and at a right angle to the plate.
3. When the guide plate is positioned correctly, torque the guide plate bolts to 7 ft. lbs. and the housing nuts to 4 ft. lbs.

AUTOMATIC TRANSAXLE

Removal and Installation
NOVA AND PRIZM

1. Disconnect the negative terminal from the battery and the ground cable from the transaxle. Label and disconnect the necessary electrical connectors. Drain the transaxle.
2. Remove the air intake duct. Disconnect the Throttle Valve cable from the carburetor, if equipped.
3. Disconnect the neutral safety switch, the speedometer cable and the shift control cable from the transaxle. Remove the shift cable bracket from the transaxle.
4. From the top of the transaxle, disconnect the thermostat housing-to-transaxle bolts.
5. Remove the single upper mount-to-bracket bolt. Remove the two upper bellhousing bolts.
6. Remove the upper 2 bell housing bolts.
7. Using a engine supporting tool, connect it to and support the engine. Raise and support the vehicle safely.
8. Remove the left wheel assembly, the left splash shield, the right splash shield and the center splash shield. Remove the crossmember-to-chassis bolts and the crossmember.
9. Remove the oil line cooler bracket. Disconnect and plug the oil cooler lines from the transaxle.
10. Remove the flywheel cover. Matchmark the torque converter-to-flywheel, then, remove the torque converter-to-flywheel bolts and separate the torque converter from the flywheel.

NOTE: The crankshaft must be rotated to gain access to the other bolts.

11. Remove both control arm-to-ball joint nuts/bolts and separate the lower control arms from the ball joints.
12. Remove both halfshaft-to-transaxle flange nuts and separate the halfshaft from the transaxle; support the halfshaft on a wire.
13. Disconnect the battery cable and ignition wire from the starter. Remove the starter-to-engine bolts and the starter.
14. Remove the lower transaxle-to-engine bolts.
15. Using a wooden block atop a floor jack, support the transaxle.
16. Remove the remaining transaxle-to-engine bolts. Separate the transaxle from the engine and lower it from the vehicle.
To install

17. Align the torque converter-to-flywheel alignment marks and reverse the removal procedures. Torque the transaxle-to-engine bolts to 47 ft. lbs. (12mm bolt) and 34 ft. lbs. (10mm bolt). Torque the left-side engine mount bolts to 38 ft. lbs.
18. Torque the torque converter-to-flywheel bolts to 13 ft. lbs. Torque the halfshaft-to-transaxle nuts/bolts to 27 ft. lbs. Torque the crossmember-to-chassis bolts to 29 ft. lbs.
19. Refill the transaxle with Dexron® II transmission fluid. Start the engine, test drive it and check for leaks.

SPECTRUM
1. Disconnect the negative battery terminal from the battery.
2. Remove the air duct tube from the air cleaner.
3. From the transaxle, disconnect the shift cable, speedometer cable, vacuum diaphragm hose, engine wiring harness clamp and the ground cable.
4. At the left-fender, disconnect the inhibitor switch and the kickdown solenoid wiring connectors.
5. Disconnect the oil cooler lines from the transaxle.
6. Remove the three upper transaxle-to-engine mounting bolts. Raise and support the vehicle safely.
7. Remove both front-wheels and the left-front fender splash shield.
8. Disconnect both tie rod ends at the steering knuckles.
9. Remove both front tension rod brackets and disconnect the rods from the control arms.
10. Disengage the axle shafts from the transaxle.
11. Remove the flywheel dust cover and the converter-to-flywheel attaching bolts.
12. Remove the transaxle rear mount through bolt.
13. Disconnect the starter wiring and the starter. Support the transaxle.
14. Remove the lower transaxle-to-engine mounting bolts and remove the transaxle.
15. To install, reverse the removal procedures. Torque the converter-to-flywheel at 30 ft. lbs., the transaxle-to-engine at 56 ft. lbs., adjust the shift linkage and fill the transaxle with Dexron®II automatic transmission fluid.

SPRINT AND METRO
1. Disconnect the air suction guide from the air cleaner.
2. Disconnect the negative and the positive battery cables.
3. Remove the battery and the battery bracket tray.
4. Remove the negative cable from the transaxle.
5. Disconnect the solenoid wire coupler and the shift lever switch wire couplers.
6. Remove the wiring harness from the transaxle.
7. Remove the speedometer cable from the transaxle.
8. Disconnect the oil pressure control cable from the accelerator cable, and then the accelerator cable from the transaxle.
9. Remove the select cable from the transaxle.
10. Remove the starter motor.
11. Drain the transaxle fluid.
12. Disconnect the oil outlet and inlet hoses from the oil pipes. After disconnecting, plug the 2 oil hoses to prevent fluid in the hoses and oil cooler from draining.
13. Raise the vehicle and support it safely.
14. Remove the exhaust No. 1 pipe.
15. Remove the clutch housing lower plate.
16. Remove the 6 drive plate bolts. To lock the drive plate, engage a screw driver with the drive plate gear through the notch provided at the under side of the transmission case.
17. Remove the left hand front drive axle.
18. Detach the inboard joint of the right hand drive axle from the differential.

19. Disconnect the transaxle mounting member.
20. Securely support the transaxle with a suitable jack for removal.
21. Remove the transaxle left mounting.
22. Remove the bolts fastening the engine and the transaxle.
23. Disconnect the transaxle from the engine by sliding towards the left side, and then, carefully lower the jack.

NOTE: When removing the transaxle assembly from the engine, move it in parallel with the crankshaft and use care so as not to apply excessive force to the drive plate and torque converter. After removing the transaxle assembly, be sure to keep it so that the oil pan is at the bottom. If the transaxle is tilted, fluid in it may flow out.

24. To install the transaxle, reverse the removal procedure noting the following important steps.
25. Before installing the transaxle assembly apply grease around the cup at the center of the torque converter. Then measure the distance between the torque converter flange nut and the transaxle case housing. The distance should be more than 0.85 in. (21.4mm). If the distance is less than 0.85 in. (21.4mm), the torque converter has been installed incorrectly and must be removed and reinstalled correctly.
26. When installing the transaxle, guide the right drive axle into the differential side gear as the transaxle is being raised.
27. After inserting the inboard joints of the right hand and left hand drive axles into the differential side gears, push the inboard joints into the side gears until the snaprings on the drive axles engage the side gears.
28. After connecting the oil pressure control cable to the accelerator cable, check the oil pressure control cable play and adjust if necessary.
29. Install the select cable.
30. Refill the transaxle and check the fluid level.
31. Tighten the following bolts and nuts to specifications.
   a. Drive plate bolts—14 ft. lbs. (19 Nm).
   b. Mounting member bolts—40 ft. lbs. (55 Nm).
   c. Transaxle mounting nuts—33 ft. lbs. (45 Nm).
   d. Transaxle mounting bolts (8mm)—40 ft. lbs. (55 Nm).
   e. Transaxle mounting nuts—40 ft. lbs. (55 Nm).
   f. Stabilizer shaft mounting bolts—31 ft. lbs. (42 Nm).
   g. Ball stud bolt—44 ft. lbs. (60 Nm).
   h. Wheel nuts—40 ft. lbs. (55 Nm).

Throttle Cable Adjustment
NOVA AND PRIZM

1. Depress the accelerator pedal completely and check that the throttle valve opens fully. If the throttle valve does not open fully, adjust the accelerator link
2. Fully depress the accelerator
3. Loosen the adjustment nuts.
4. Adjust the throttle cable housing so that the distance between the end of the boot and the stopper on the cable is correct. The distance must be 0.04 in. (0.1mm).
5. Tighten the adjusting nuts and recheck the adjustment.

Transaxle Shift Control Adjustment
NOVA AND PRIZM

1. Loosen the swivel nut on the lever.
2. Push the manual lever fully towards the right side of the vehicle.
3. Return the lever 2 notches to the **N** position.
4. Set the shift lever in the **N** position.
5. While holding the lever lightly towards the **R** position, tighten the swivel nut.

SPECTRUM

1. Loosen the 2 adjusting nuts at the control rod link and connect the shift cable to the link on the transaxle.

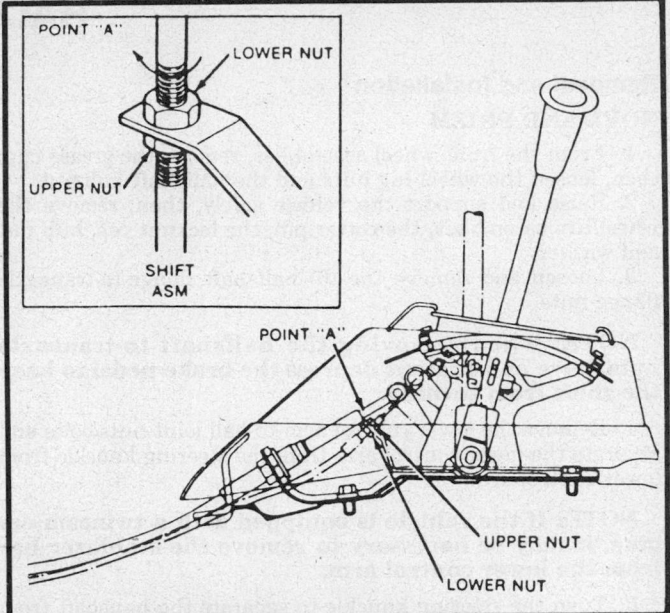

Adjusting the parking lock—Spectrum

2. Shift the transaxle into the **N** detent.
3. Place the shifter lever into the **N** position.
4. Rotate the link assembly clockwise to remove slack in the cable.
5. Tighten the rear adjusting nut until it makes contact with the link. Tighten the front adjusting nut until it makes contact with the link and tighten the adjusting nuts.

Vacuum Modulator

Removal and Installation
SPECTRUM

1. Disconnect the negative battery cable.
2. Disconnect the kickdown solenoid wire connector located at the left fender.
3. Raise the vehicle and suppot it safely.
4. Remove the kickdown solenoid at the transaxle.
5. Remove the vacuum modulator.
6. Installation is the reverse of the removal procedure. If a new modulator is to be installed, adjust the proper vacuum diaphragm rod length.

NEUTRAL START SWITCH

Adjustment
NOVA AND PRIZM

NOTE: If the engine will start with the shift selector in any range other than N or P positions, adjustment is required.

1. Loosen the neutral start switch bolts and set the shift lever in the **N** position.
2. Disconnect the neutral start switch connector.
3. Connect an ohmmeter between the terminals.
4. Adjust the switch to the point where there is continuity between terminals.
5. Connect the neutral switch connector.
6. Torque the switch bolts to 48 inch lbs. (5.4 Nm).
7. Recheck the switch operation.

HALFSHAFT

Removal and Installation

NOVA AND PRIZM

1. From the front wheel assemblies, remove the grease cup, then, loosen the wheel lug nuts and the halfshaft hub nut.
2. Raise and support the vehicle safely, then, remove the wheel/tire assemblies, the cotter pin, the locknut cap, hub nut and washer.
3. Loosen and remove the (6) halfshaft flange-to-transaxle flange nuts

NOTE: When removing the halfshaft-to-transaxle nuts, have an assistant depress the brake pedal to keep the shaft from turning.

4. Remove the lower control arm-to-ball joint nuts/bolts and separate the lower control arm from the steering knuckle from lower control arm.

NOTE: If the vehicle is equipped with a twincam engine, it may be necessary to remove the stabilizer bar from the lower control arm.

5. Turn the steering knuckle to separate the halfshaft from the transaxle.
6. Cover the outboard CV-joint rubber boot with a cloth to prevent damage. Using the wheel puller tool J–25287 or equivalent, press the halfshaft from the steering knuckle and remove the driveshaft.
7. To install the halfshaft, lubricate the splines with multipuprose grease, insert the it into the steering knuckle hub, install the washer and the hub nut, then, tighten the hub nut to draw the halfshaft into the steering knuckle hub until it seats.

NOTE: When torquing the hub nut, have an assistant depress the brake pedal; it may be necessary final torque the hub nut with the vehicle resting on the ground.

8. To complete the installation, reverse the removal procedures. Torque the lower control arm-to-ball joint nuts/bolts to 59 ft. lbs.; the halfshaft-to-transaxle flange nuts to 27 ft. lbs. and the halfshaft-to-steering knuckle hub nut to 137 ft. lbs. Install a new cotter pin.

SPECTRUM

1. Raise and support the vehicle safely, allowing the wheels to hang.
2. Remove the front wheel assemblies, the hub grease caps, the hub nuts and the cotter pins.
3. Install the drive axle boot seal protector tool J–28712 or equivalent, on the outer CV-joints and the drive axle boot seal protector tool J–34754 or equivalent, on the inner Tri-Pot joints.

NOTE: Clean the halfshaft threads and lubricate them with a thread lubricant.

4. Have an assistant depress the brake pedal, then, remove the hub nut and washer.
5. Remove the caliper-to-steering knuckle bolts and support the caliper (on a wire) out of the way.
6. Remove the rotor. Remove the drain plug and drain the oil from the transaxle.
7. Using a slide hammer puller and the puller attachment tool J–34866 or equivalent, pull the hub from the halfshaft.
8. Remove the tie rod-to-steering knuckle cotter pin and the

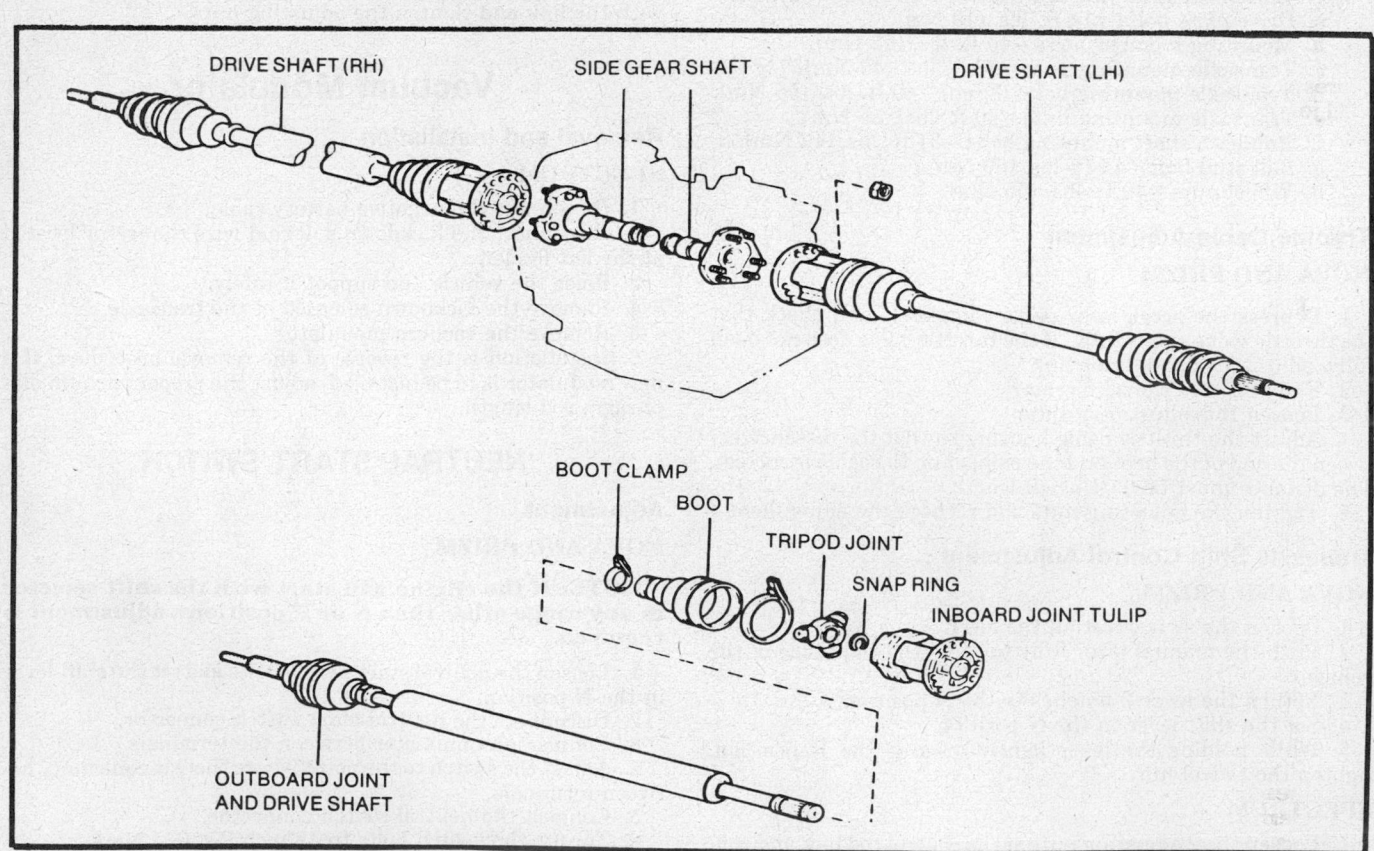

Exploded view of the front drive axle—Nova

nut. Using the ball joint separator tool J–21687–02 or equivalent, press the tie rod ball joint from the steering knuckle.

9. Remove the lower ball joint-to-control arm nuts/bolts.

10. Swing the steering knuckle assembly outward and slide the halfshaft from the steering knuckle.

11. Place a large pry bar between the differential case and the inboard constant velocity joint. Pry the axle shaft from the differential case.

12. Remove the halfshaft assembly.

13. To install, use new cotter pins and reverse the removal procedures. Torque the ball joint-to-control arm nuts/bolts to 80 ft. lbs. (108 Nm), the caliper-to-steering knuckle bolts to 41 ft. lbs. (55 Nm) and the halfshaft-to-hub nut to 137 ft. lbs. (186 Nm). Check and/or adjust the front end alignment.

SPRINT AND METRO

1. Remove the grease cap, the cotter pin and the axle shaft nut from both front wheels.

2. Loosen the wheel nuts.

3. Raise and support the vehicle safely.

4. Remove the front wheels.

5. Drain the transaxle fluid.

6. Using a pry bar, pry on the inboard joints of the right and left hand axle shafts to detach the axle shafts from the snap rings of the differential side gears.

7. Remove the stabilizer bar mounting bolts and the ball joint stud bolt. Pull down on the stabilizer bar and remove the ball joint stud from the steering knuckle.

8. Pull the axle shafts out of the transaxle's side gear, first, and then from the steering knuckles.

NOTE: To prevent the axle shaft boots from becoming damaged, be careful not to bring them into contact with any parts. If any malfunction is found in the either of the joints, replace the joints as an assembly.

9. To install, snap the axle shaft into the transaxle, first, and then into the steering knuckle.

10. To complete the installation, reverse the removal procedures. Torque the stabilizer bar mounting bolts to 30 ft. lbs.; the ball joint stud bolt to 44 ft. lbs. and the axle shaft nut to 144 ft. lbs.

Boot

Removal and Installation

NOVA AND PRIZM

1. Remove the halfshaft.

2. Remove the boot retaining clamps.

3. Remove the inboard joint tulip.

4. Remove the tripod joint snapring and the tripod joint from the halfshaft.

5. Remove the inboard and outboard joint boots.

6. To install, reverse the removal procedures; the inboard joint and clamp is larger than the outboard clamp. Face the beveled side of the tripod axial spline towards the outboard joint.

SPECTRUM

Inner (Inboard)

1. Disconnect the negative battery terminal from the battery.

2. Raise and support the the vehicle safley, the remove the front wheels.

3. Remove the outer boot assembly.

4. Remove the boot retaining clamps and the spacer ring.

5. Slide the axle and the spider bearing assembly out of the tri-pot housing. Install the spider retainer onto the spider bearing assembly.

6. Remove the spider assembly and the boot from the axle.

7. To install, pack the new boot with grease and reverse the removal procedures.

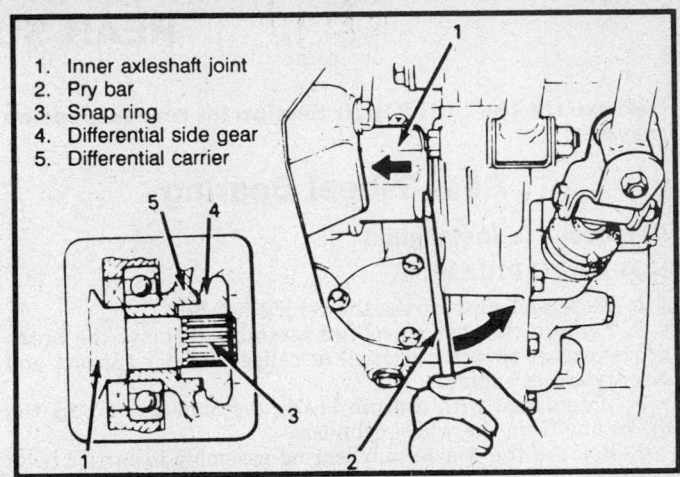

1. Inner axleshaft joint
2. Pry bar
3. Snap ring
4. Differential side gear
5. Differential carrier

Disengaging the axle shaft from the differential side gear snap ring—Sprint and Metro

Outer (Outboard)

1. Disconnect the negative battery terminal from the battery.

2. Raise and support the vehicle safely, then remove the front wheels.

3. Remove the brake caliper and support on a wire, then remove the rotor.

4. Slide the outer CV-joint assembly off the axle shaft.

5. Remove the bearing retaining ring, the boot retainer, the clamp and the outer boot.

6. To install, pack the new boot with grease and reverse the removal procedures.

SPRINT AMD METRO

NOTE: Do not disassemble the wheel side joint (outboard). Replace if found to be defective. Do not disassemble the spider of the differential side joint. If the spider is found to be defective, replace the differential side joint assembly.

1. With the axleshaft removed from the vehicle, remove the boot band from the differential side joint.

2. Remove the housing from the differential side joint.

3. Remove the snapring and spider from the shaft.

4. Remove the inside and outside boots from the shaft.

5. Liberally apply the joint grease to the wheel side joint. Use the black joint grease in the tube included in the wheel side boot set or wheel side joint assembly.

6. Fit the wheel side boot on the shaft. Fill the inside of the boot with the joint grease, approximately 80 grams and fix the boot bands.

7. Fit the differential side boot on the shaft.

8. Liberally apply the joint grease to the differential side joint on the shaft. Use the yellow grease in the tube included in the differential side boot set or differential side joint assembly.

9. Install the spider of the differential side joint on the shaft, facing its chamfered side to the wheel side joint.

10. After installing the spider, fit the snap ring in the groove on the shaft.

11. Fill the inside of the differential side boot with the joint grease, aproximately 130 gram and install the housing. Fix the boot to the housing with a boot band.

12. Correct any distortions or bends in the boots.

13. Install the axleshaft in the vehicle.

Universal Joints

Refer to the the Unit Repair Section for overhaul procedures.

REAR SUSPENSION

Refer to the the Unit Repair Section for rear suspension services.

Rear Wheel Bearing

Removal and Installation

NOVA AND PRIZM

1. Raise and support the the vehicle safely.
2. Remove the rear wheel/tire assembly. Remove the brake drum (except twincam engine) or caliper, caliper support and disc (twincam engine).
3. If equipped with a drum brake, disconnect and plug the brake line from the wheel cylinder.
4. Remove the 4 axle hub/bearing assembly-to-carrier bolts and the hub/bearing assembly and drum brake assembly (except twincam engine) or dust cover (twincam). Remove and discard the O-ring.
5. To disassemble the hub/bearing assembly, perform the following procedures:
   a. Using copper or aluminum, cover the vise jaws, then, insert the hub/bearing assembly into the vise.
   b. Using a socket wrench, remove the hub nut from the hub/bearing assembly.
   c. Using a wheel puller tool, press the bearing case from the axle hub, then, remove the inner race, the inner bearing and the outer bearing.
   d. Using the a wheel puller tool, press the outer bearing inner race from the axle hub.
   e. Remove the seal from the axle hub.
   f. Using an arbor press and a driving tool, install outer bearing inner race onto the bearing outer race and press it from the bearing case.

NOTE: Whenever the wheel bearing assembly is disassembled, it should be replaced with a new one.

6. To install the new wheel bearing, perform the following procedures:
   a. Using multi-purpose, apply it around the bearing outer race.
   b. Using an press and a driver tool, press the new bearing outer race into the bearing case.
   c. Install the new bearings and inner races into the bearing case.
   d. Using multi-purpose grease, lightly coat the new seal. Using a seal installation tool, drive the new seal into the bearing case until it seats.
   e. Using an arbor press and a driver tool, press the bearing case onto the hub. Torque the hub nut to 90 ft. lbs.
   f. Using a chisel and a hammer, stake the hub nut.
7. To install the rear hub/bearing assembly, use a new O-ring and reverse the removal procedures. Torque the hub/bearing assembly-to-axle carrier bolts to 59 ft. lbs.

NOTE: If equipped with drum brakes, reconnect the brake line to the wheel cylinder. Refill the brake master cylinder and bleed the brake system.

SPECTRUM

1. Raise and support the vehicle safely.
2. Remove the rear wheel assemblies.
3. Remove the hub cap, cotter pin, hub nut, washer and outer bearing.
4. Remove the hub.
5. Using a slide hammer puller and attachment, pull the oil seal from the hub. Remove the inner bearing.
6. Using a brass drift and a hammer, drive both bearing races from the hub.
7. Clean, inspect and/or replace all parts.
8. To install, pack the bearings with grease, coat the oil seal lips with grease and reverse the removal procedures. Torque hub nut to 22 ft. lbs.

NOTE: If the cotter pin holes are out of alignment upon reassembly, use a wrench to tighten the nut until the hole in the shaft and a slot of the nut align.

SPRINT AND METRO

1. Raise and support the vehicle safely.
2. Remove the wheel assembly.
3. Remove the dust cap, the cotter pin, the castle nut and the washer.
4. Loosen the adjusting nuts of the parking brake cable.
5. Remove the plug from the rear of the backing plate. Insert a suitable tool through the hole, making contact with the shoe hold down spring, then push the spring to release the parking brake shoe lever.
6. Using a slide hammer tool and a brake drum remover tool, pull the brake drum from the axle shaft.

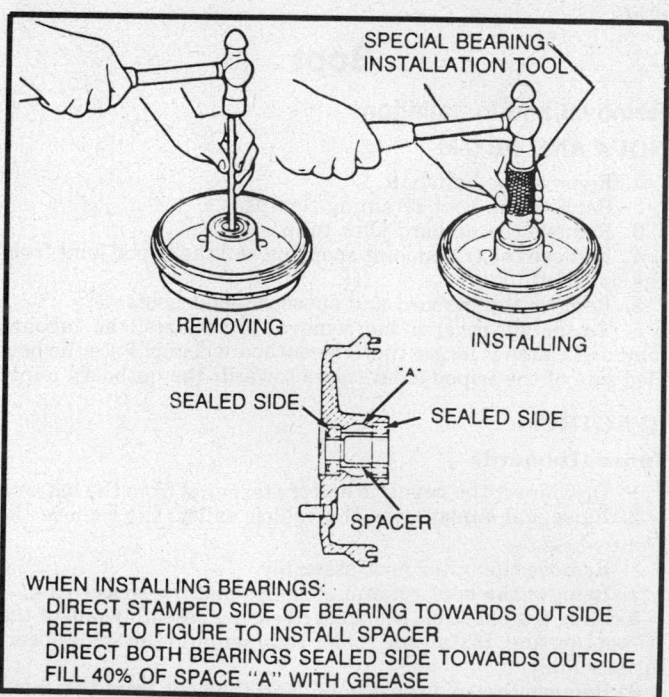

WHEN INSTALLING BEARINGS:
DIRECT STAMPED SIDE OF BEARING TOWARDS OUTSIDE
REFER TO FIGURE TO INSTALL SPACER
DIRECT BOTH BEARINGS SEALED SIDE TOWARDS OUTSIDE
FILL 40% OF SPACE "A" WITH GREASE

Removing and installing rear wheel bearings in drum—Sprint and Metro

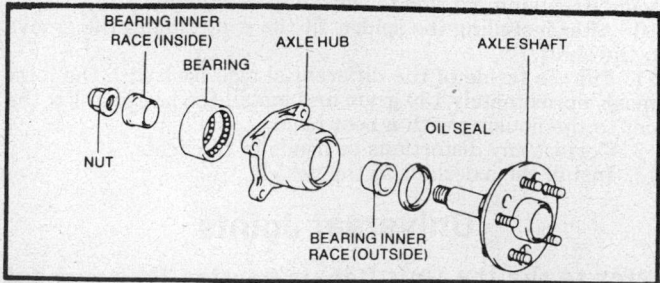

Bearing and oil seal assembly—Nova and Prizm

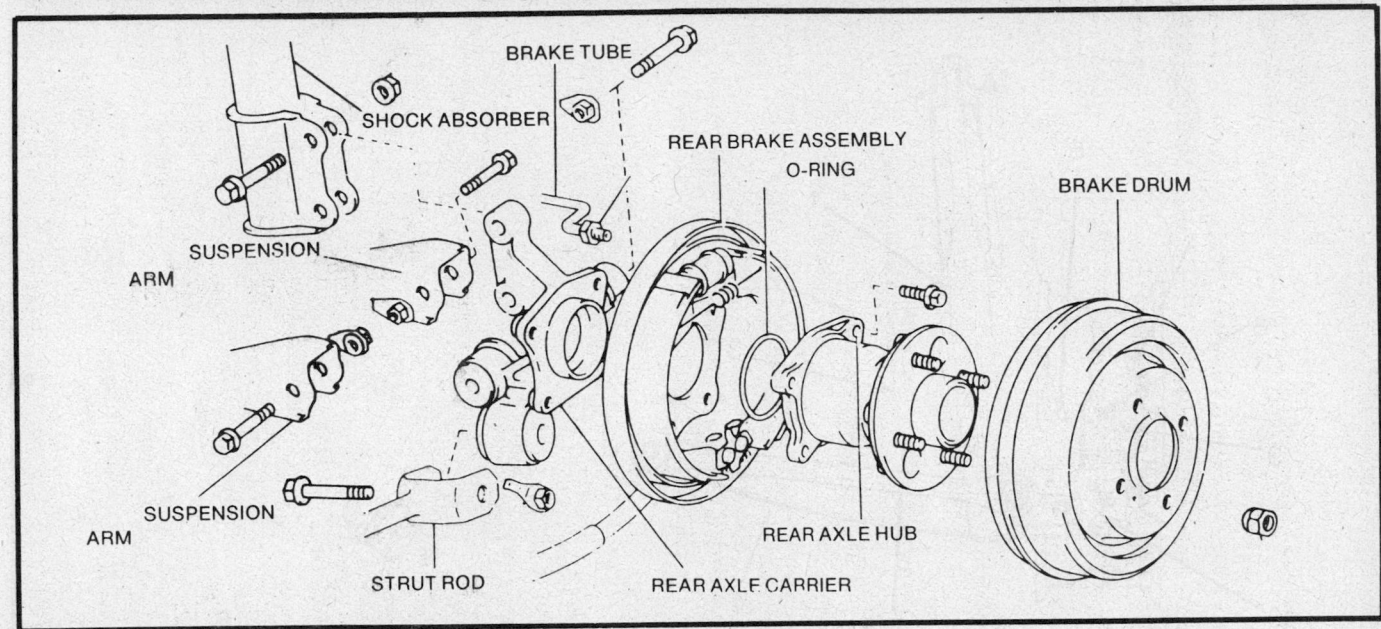

Exploded view of the rear axle hub assembly—Nova and Prizm

7. Using a brass drift and a hammer, drive the rear wheel bearings from the brake drum.

NOTE: When installing the wheel bearings, face the sealed sides (numbered sides) outward. Fill the wheel bearing cavity with bearing grease.

8. Drive the new bearings into the brake drum with the bearing installation tool.

9. To install, use a new seal and reverse the removal procedures. Torque the hub castle nut to 58–86 ft. lbs. Bleed the rear brake system. Operate the brakes 3–5 times to obtain the proper drum-to-shoe clearance. Adjust the parking brake cable.

Rear Wheel Alignment

Procedure
NOVA

1. Check the tires for size, proper inflation and wear.
2. Check the wheel runout; lateral runout should be less than 0.047 in. (1.2mm).
3. Check the rear suspension for looseness.
4. Adjust the toe-in. Left-right error should be less than 0.12 in. (3mm).
5. On a flat surface, move the vehicle forward approximately 10 feet with the front wheels facing forward.
6. Mark the center of each rear tread and measure the distance between the marks of the left and right tires.
7. Move the vehicle forward until the marks on the rear side of the tires comes to the front.
8. Measure the distance between the marks on the front side of the tires. Toe-in should be 0.150 ± 0.16 in. (3.8 ± 4mm).
9. If not within specification, adjust by turning the left and right adjusting nuts an equal amount, but in opposite directions.

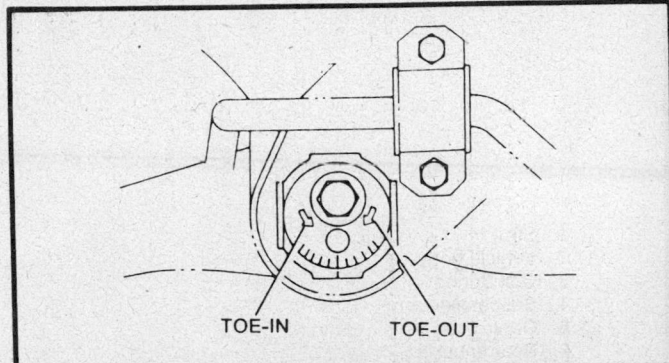

TOE-IN   TOE-OUT

Rear wheel alignment adjusting bolt—Nova

10. The toe-in will change about 0.08 in. (2mm). Torque the nut to 64 ft. lbs. (87 Nm).

SPECTRUM
Rear wheel alignment cannot be adjusted. If out of specification, the cause could be damaged, loose, bent, dented or worn spension parts.

SPRINT AND SPECTRUM
Rear wheel toe is adjusted by the inside control rod bolts. Loosen the right and left control rod inside nuts first and then turn the right and left control rod inside bolts (cam bolts) by the same amount to align the toe to specification.

After adjustment, tighten the right and left inside nuts to the specified torque while holding the control rod inside bolt with another wrench to prevent it from turning.

Caster and camber cannot be adjusted. If caster or camber is out of specification the cause could be damaged, loose, bent, dented or worn spension parts.

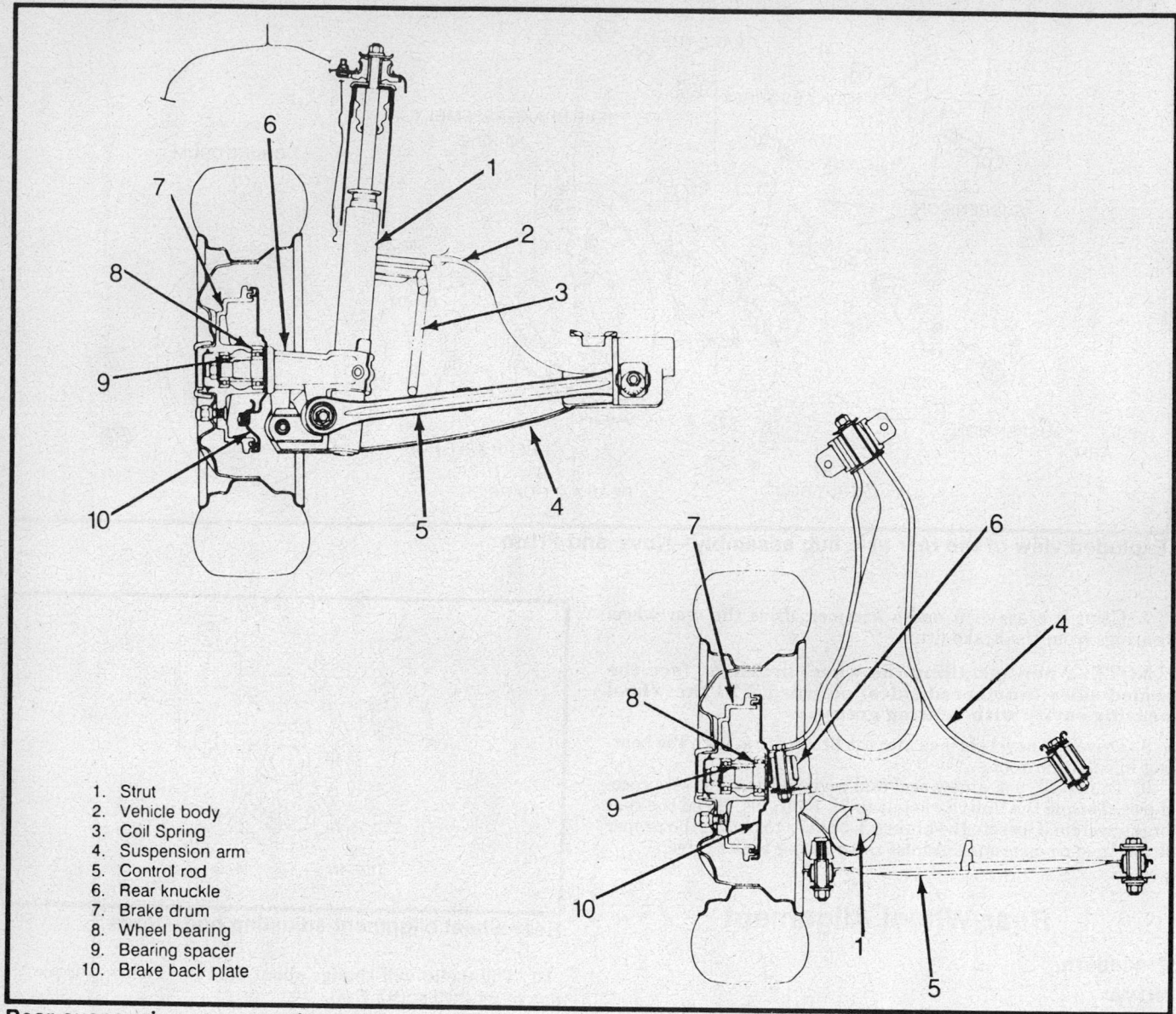

1. Strut
2. Vehicle body
3. Coil Spring
4. Suspension arm
5. Control rod
6. Rear knuckle
7. Brake drum
8. Wheel bearing
9. Bearing spacer
10. Brake back plate

Rear suspension cross section, Metro

YEAR IDENTIFICATION

1988–90 LeMans

VEHICLE IDENTIFICATION

It is important for servicing and ordering parts to be certain of the vehicle and engine identification. The VIN (vehicle identification number) is a 17 digit number visible through the windshield on the driver's side of the dash and contains the vehicle and engine identification codes. The tenth digit indicates model year and the eighth digit indicates engine code. It can be interpreted as follows:

		Engine Code					Model Year	
Code	Cu. In.	Liters	Cyl.	Fuel Sys.	Eng. Mfg.		Code	Year
6	98	1.6	4	TBI	GM		J	1988
K	121	2.0	4	TBI	GM		K	1989
							K	1990

ENGINE IDENTIFICATION

Year	Model	Engine Displacement cu. in. (liter)	Engine Series Identification (VIN)	No. of Cylinders	Engine Type
1988	Lemans	98 (1.6)	6	4	OHC
1989-90	Lemans	98 (1.6)	6	4	OHC
	Lemans	121 (2.0)	K	4	OHC

GENERAL ENGINE SPECIFICATIONS

Year	VIN	No. Cylinder Displacement cu. in. (liter)	Fuel System Type	Net Horsepower @ rpm	Net Torque @ rpm (ft.lbs.)	Bore × Stroke (in.)	Compression Ratio	Oil Pressure @ rpm
1988	6	4-98 (1.6)	TBI	74 @ 5200	88 @ 3400	3.11 × 3.20	8.5:1	55 @ 2000
1989-90	6	4-98 (1.6)	TBI	74 @ 5600	88 @ 3400	3.11 × 3.20	8.5:1	55 @ 2000
	K	4-121 (2.0)	TBI	96 @ 4800	118 @ 3600	3.39 × 3.39	8.8:1	55 @ 2000

GASOLINE ENGINE TUNE-UP SPECIFICATIONS
Refer to Section 34 for all spark plug recommendations

Year	VIN	No. Cylinder Displacement cu. in. (liter)	Spark Plugs Gap (in.)	Ignition Timing (deg.) MT	Ignition Timing (deg.) AT	Compression Pressure (psi)	Fuel Pump (psi)	Idle Speed (rpm) MT	Idle Speed (rpm) AT	Valve Clearance In.	Valve Clearance Ex.
1988	6	4-98 (1.6)	0.06	①	①	②	9–13	①	①	NA	NA
1989	6	4-98 (1.6)	0.06	①	①	②	9–13	①	①	NA	NA
	K	4-121 (2.0)	0.06	①	①	②	9–13	①	①	NA	NA
1990		SEE UNDERHOOD SPECIFICATIONS STICKER									

① See underhood specifications sticker
② Lowest reading not less than 70% of highest. No reading less than 100 psi

FIRING ORDERS

NOTE: To avoid confusion, always replace spark plug wires one at a time.

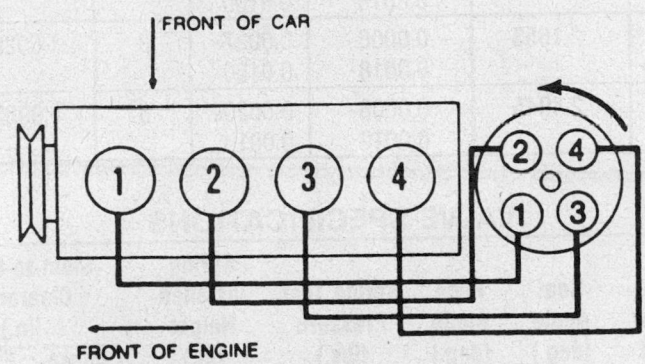

GM (Pontiac) 1.6L and 2.0L engines
Engine firing order: 1–3–4–2
Distributor rotation: counterclockwise

CAPACITIES

Year	Model	VIN	No. Cylinder Displacement cu. in. (liter)	Engine Crankcase with Filter	Engine Crankcase without Filter	Transmission (pts.) 4-Spd	Transmission (pts.) 5-Spd	Transmission (pts.) Auto.	Drive Axle (pts.)	Fuel Tank (gal.)	Cooling System (qts.)
1988	Lemans	6	4-98 (1.6)	4	4	3.5	3.5	8①	—	13.2	8.1
1989-90	Lemans	6	4-98 (1.6)	4	4	3.5	3.5	8①	—	13.0	8.1
	Lemans	K	4-121 (2.0)	4	4	4.0	4.0	8①	—	13.0	8.1

① Overhaul—12 pts.

CAMSHAFT SPECIFICATIONS

All measurements given in inches.

Year	VIN	No. Cylinder Displacement cu. in. (liter)	Journal Diameter 1	2	3	4	5	Lobe Lift In.	Ex.	Bearing Clearance	Camshaft End Play
1988	6	4-98 (1.6)	1.578–1.577	1.588–1.590	1.578–1.597	1.608–1.607	1.618–1.617	0.224	0.245	0.0020–0.0044	0.016–0.064
1989-90	6	4-98 (1.6)	1.578–1.577	1.588–1.590	1.578–1.597	1.608–1.607	1.618–1.617	0.224	0.245	0.0020–0.0044	0.016–0.064
	K	4-121 (2.0)	1.867–1.869	1.867–1.869	1.867–1.869	1.867–1.869	1.867–1.869	0.259	0.259	0.0010–0.0039	0.016–0.064

CRANKSHAFT AND CONNECTING ROD SPECIFICATIONS

All measurements are given in inches.

Year	VIN	No. Cylinder Displacement cu. in. (liter)	Crankshaft Main Brg. Journal Dia.	Main Brg. Oil Clearance	Shaft End-play	Thrust on No.	Connecting Rod Journal Diameter	Oil Clearance	Side Clearance
1988	6	4-98 (1.6)	2.1653	0.0005–0.0018	0.0027–0.0100	3	1.6929	0.0014–0.0031	0.0027–0.0095
1989	6	4-98 (1.6)	2.1653	0.0006–0.0018	0.0027–0.0100	3	1.6929	0.0014–0.0031	0.0027–0.0095
	K	4-121 (2.0)	2.4945	0.0006–0.0019	0.0020–0.0010	3	1.9983	0.0010–0.0031	0.0039–0.0149

VALVE SPECIFICATIONS

Year	VIN	No. Cylinder Displacement cu. in. (liter)	Seat Angle (deg.)	Face Angle (deg.)	Spring Test Pressure (lbs.)	Spring Installed Height (in.)	Stem-to-Guide Clearance (in.) Intake	Exhaust	Stem Diameter (in.) Intake	Exhaust
1988	6	4-98 (1.6)	45	46	62	1.26	0.0006–0.0017	0.0014–0.0025	0.275	0.275
1989-90	6	4-98 (1.6)	45	46	62	1.26	0.0006–0.0017	0.0014–0.0025	0.275	0.275
	K	4-121 (2.0)	45	46	63	1.48	0.0011–0.0026	0.0014–0.0030	0.2753	0.276

PISTON AND RING SPECIFICATIONS

All measurments are given in inches.

Year	VIN	No. Cylinder Displacement cu. in. (liter)	Piston Clearance	Ring Gap Top Compression	Bottom Compression	Oil Control	Ring Side Clearance Top Compression	Bottom Compression	Oil Control
1988	6	4-98 (1.6)	0.0008–0.0016	0.012–0.020	0.012–0.020	0.016–0.055	0.0012–0.0027	0.0012–0.0032	0.0000–0.0050
1989-90	6	4-98 (1.6)	0.0008	0.012–0.020	0.012–0.020	0.016–0.055	0.0012–0.0027	0.0012–0.0032	0.0000–0.0050
	K	4-121 (2.0)	0.0098 0.0022	0.010–0.020	0.010–0.020	0.010–0.050	0.0019–0.0027	0.0019–0.0027	0.0019–0.0032

TORQUE SPECIFICATIONS
All readings in ft. lbs.

Year	VIN	No. Cylinder Displacement cu. in. (liter)	Cylinder Head Bolts	Main Bearing Bolts	Rod Bearing Bolts	Crankshaft Pulley Bolts	Flywheel Bolts	Manifold Intake	Manifold Exhaust	Spark Plugs
1988	6	4-98 (1.6)	18①	36②	18③	40	25④	16	16	18
1989-90	6	4-98 (1.6)	18①	36②	18③	40	25④	16	16	18
	K	4-121 (2.0)	18①	70	38	20	⑤	16	16	18

① Cold—plus 2 turns of 60 degrees each and 1 turn of 30 degrees after warm up (thermostat open)—plus 30–50 degree turn

② Plus a 45–60 degree turn

③ Plus a 30 degree turn

④ Plus a 30–45 degree turn

⑤ Automatic—52 ft. lbs.
Manual—55 ft. lbs.

WHEEL ALIGNMENT

Year	Model		Caster Range (deg.)	Caster Preferred Setting (deg.)	Camber Range (deg.)	Camber Preferred Setting (deg.)	Toe-in (in.)	Steering Axis Inclination (deg.)
1988	Lemans	Front	¾P-2¾P	NA	1¼N-¼P	NA	0	—
		Rear	—	—	1N-0	NA	⅓	—
1989-90	Lemans	Front	¾P-2¾P	NA	1¼N-¼P	NA	0	—
		Rear	—	—	1N-0	NA	⅓	—

P Positive
N Negative

ELECTRICAL

NOTE: Disconnecting the negative battery cable on some vehicles may interfere with the functions of the on board computer systems and may require the computer to undergo a relearning process, once the negative battery cable is reconnected.

For testing and overhaul procedures on starters, alternators and voltage regulators, refer to Unit Repair Section.

Charging System

ALTERNATOR

Removal and Installation

1. Disconnect the negative battery cable.

NOTE: Failure to disconnect the negative cable may result in injury from the positive battery lead at the alternator and may short the alternator and regulator during the removal process.

2. Disconnect and label the electrical terminal plug and the battery lead from the rear of the alternator.

3. Loosen the mounting bolts. Push the alternator inwards and slip the drive belt off the pulley.

4. Remove the mounting bolts and the alternator.

5. Install in the reverse order of removal. Install the electrical leads and the negative battery cable. Adjust the belt tension.

VOLTAGE REGULATOR

A solid state regulator is mounted within the alternator. All regulator components are enclosed in a solid mold. The regulator is non-adjustable and requires no maintenance.

BELT TENSION

Adjustment

NOTE: The following procedure requires the use of a belt tension gauge.

1. If the belt is cold, operate the engine (at idle speed) until it reaches normal operating temperature; the belt will seat itself in the pulleys allowing the belt fibers to relax or stretch. If the belt is hot, allow it to cool, until it is warm to the touch.

NOTE: A used belt is one that has been rotated at least 1 complete revolution on the pulleys. This begins the

1 Alternator
2 Nut
3 Pulley
4 Fan
5 Alternator shaft collar
6 Front housing with bearing
7 Front bearing
8 Rotor
9 Housing screw
10 Ground terminal
11 Rear bearing
12 Regulator
13 Holder
14 Bridge
15 Diode plate
16 Stator
17 Nut
18 Battery terminal
19 Outer insulator
20 Washer
21 Screw
22 Bushing
23 Ring
24 Mounting brace
25 Ground wire connection
26 Screw
27 Bolt
28 Drive belt
29 Nut
30 Bracket washer
31 Bushing (A/C)
32 Bracket
33 Bolt
34 Rear housing with bearing

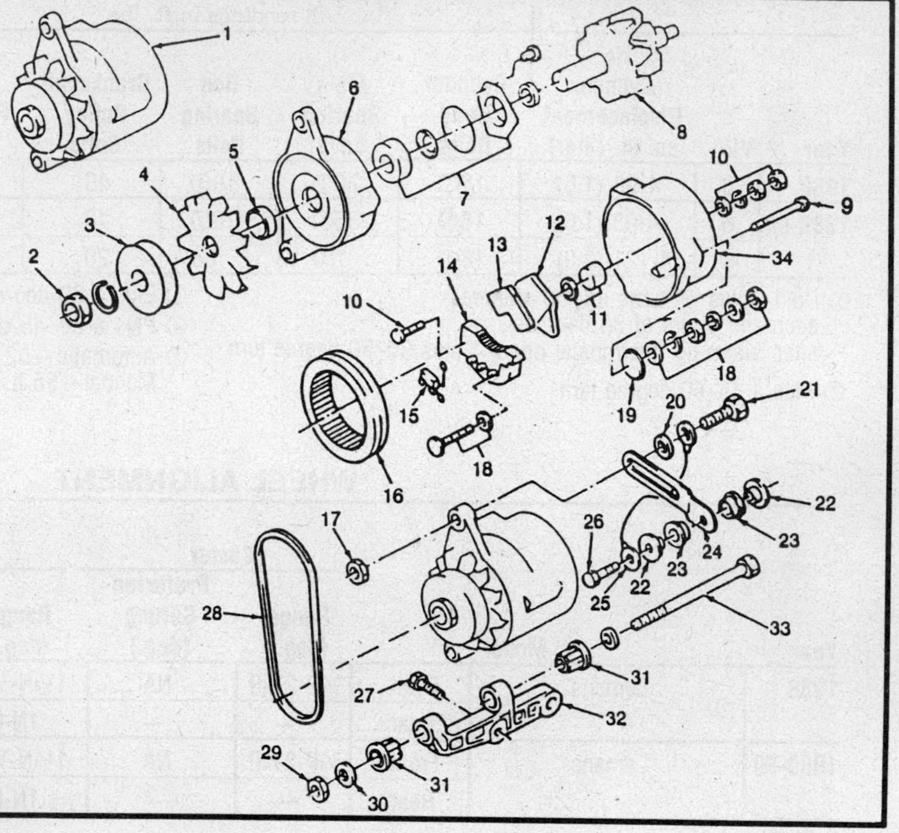

Exploded view of the alternator

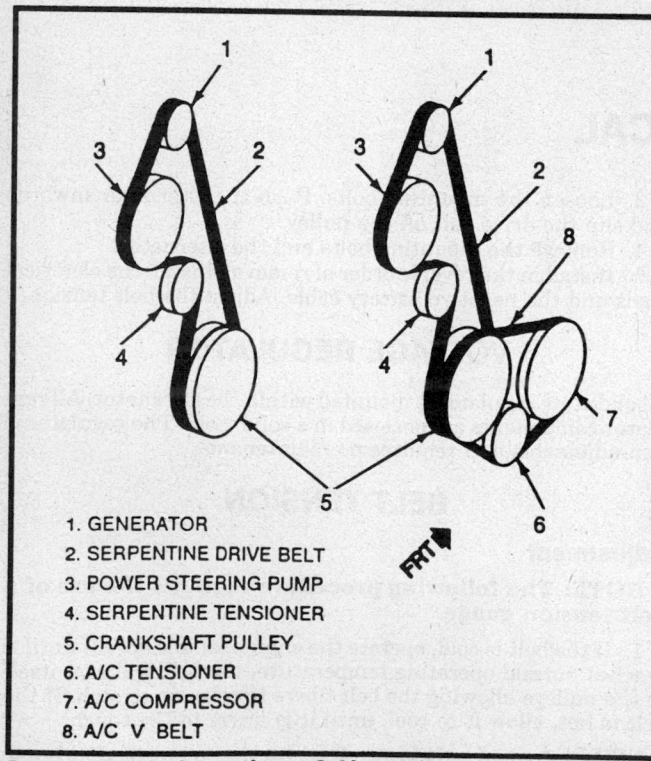

1. GENERATOR
2. SERPENTINE DRIVE BELT
3. POWER STEERING PUMP
4. SERPENTINE TENSIONER
5. CRANKSHAFT PULLEY
6. A/C TENSIONER
7. A/C COMPRESSOR
8. A/C V BELT

Serpentine belt routing—2.0L engine

belt seating process and it must never be tensioned to the new belt specifications.

2. Loosen the alternator mounting bolts.
3. Using a belt tension gauge tool, place the tension gauge at the center of the belt between the pulleys on its longest section.
4. While applying pressure on the component, adjust the drive belt tension to the following:
New belt—155 lbs.
Used belt—80 lbs.
5. While holding tension on the component, tighten the component mounting bolts and remove the tension gauge.

Starting System

STARTER

Removal and Installation

1. Disconnect the negative battery cable.
2. Disconnect the ignition switch lead wire and the battery cable from the starter motor terminal.
3. Remove the starter mounting bolts and the starter.

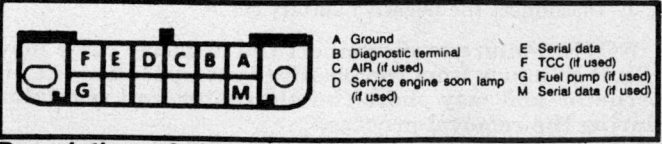

A Ground
B Diagnostic terminal
C AIR (if used)
D Service engine soon lamp (if used)
E Serial data
F TCC (if used)
G Fuel pump (if used)
M Serial data (if used)

Description of the Assembly Line Diagnostic Link (ALDL) connector

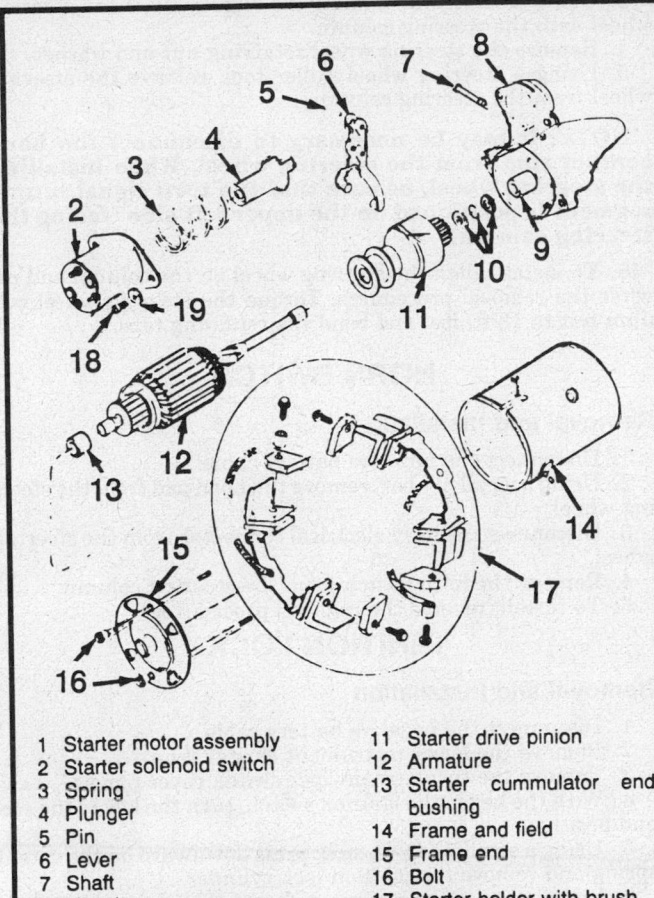

1 Starter motor assembly	11 Starter drive pinion
2 Starter solenoid switch	12 Armature
3 Spring	13 Starter cummulator end bushing
4 Plunger	
5 Pin	14 Frame and field
6 Lever	15 Frame end
7 Shaft	16 Bolt
8 Housing	17 Starter holder with brush
9 Starter drive end bushing	18 Bolt
10 Starter drive pinion bushing	19 Washer

Exploded view of the starter

4. To install, hold the starter in place and install the mounting bolts. Reconnect the battery and ignition leads.

Ignition System

DISTRIBUTOR

Removal and Installation

TIMING NOT DISTURBED

1. Disconnect the negative battery cable.
2. Remove the distributor cap.
3. Mark and remove all electrical leads connected to the distributor assembly.
4. Mark the relationship of the rotor to the distributor housing and the distributor housing to the engine.
5. Remove the hold down bolt, clamp and distributor.
6. To install, align the marks on the distributor housing and the engine. Install all electrical connectors and tighten distributor clamp bolt. Check and adjust the ignition timing as necessary.

TIMING DISTURBED

If the engine was cranked with the distributor removed, it will be necessary to position the engine at TDC on the compression stroke. Follow the procedure listed here. This will enable the proper setting of the ignition timing.
1. Remove the No. 1 spark plug.

2. Place a finger over the spark plug hole. Crank the engine slowly until compression is felt.
3. Align the timing mark on the crankshaft pulley with the **0** degree mark on the timing scale attached to the front of the engine. This places the No. 1 cylinder at the TDC of the compression stroke.
4. Turn the distributor shaft until the rotor points to the No. 1 spark plug tower on the cap.
5. Install the distributor into the engine.
6. Tighten the distributor hold down bolt and reconnect the electrical connections. Check the timing and adjust as necessary.

IGNITION TIMING

Adjustment

1. Make sure the ignition switch is turned **OFF** when connecting electrical equipment to the engine.
2. Using an induction type timing light, connect the pickup lead of the light to the No. 1 spark plug wire.

NOTE: When connecting a timing light to the No. 1 spark plug wire, be sure to use a jumper wire between the spark plug and boot; do not pierce or cut the high tension wire.

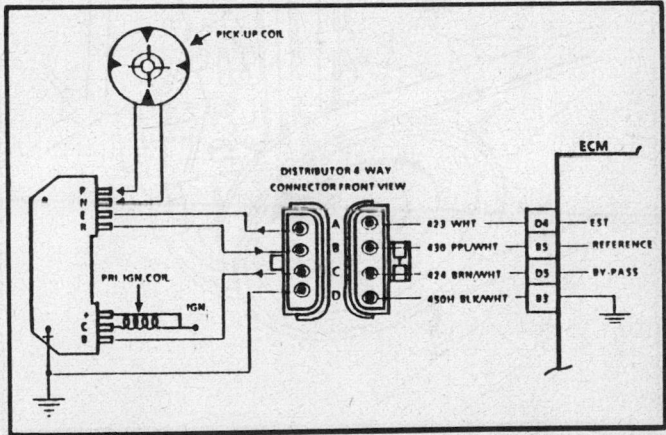

Schematic of the High Energy Ignition (HEI) System with Electronic Spark Timing (EST)

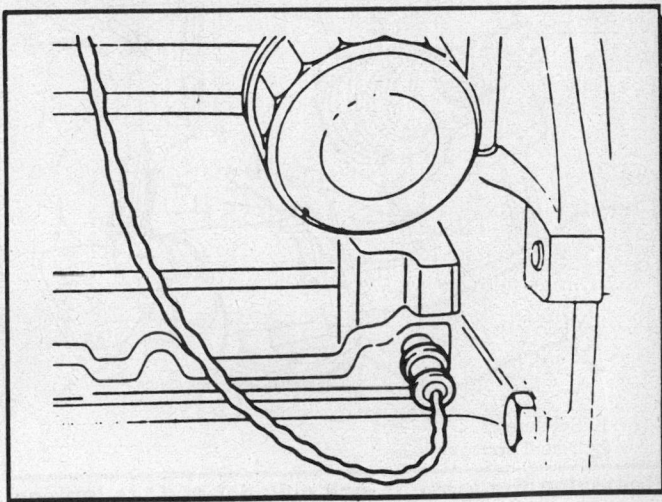

Location of the magnetic timing probe

3. Refer to the Vehicle Emission Information label for the correct specificaton. Start the engine and aim the timing light at the timing mark.

4. The line on the harmonic balancer or crankshaft pulley should align with the mark on the timing plate. If adjustment is necessary, loosen the distributor hold down bolt and rotate the distributor until the timing mark indicates that the correct timing has been reached.

5. Tighten the distributor hold down bolt and recheck the timing, adjust as necessary.

NOTE: If using a magnetic timing probe, install the probe at the lower-left side of the engine. Using the meter and the same procedure as with the timing light, set the timing to 10 degrees BTDC.

Electrical Controls
STEERING WHEEL

Removal and Installation

1. Disconnect the negative battery cable.
2. Remove the horn pad and wires from the steering wheel.

Aligning the timing marks

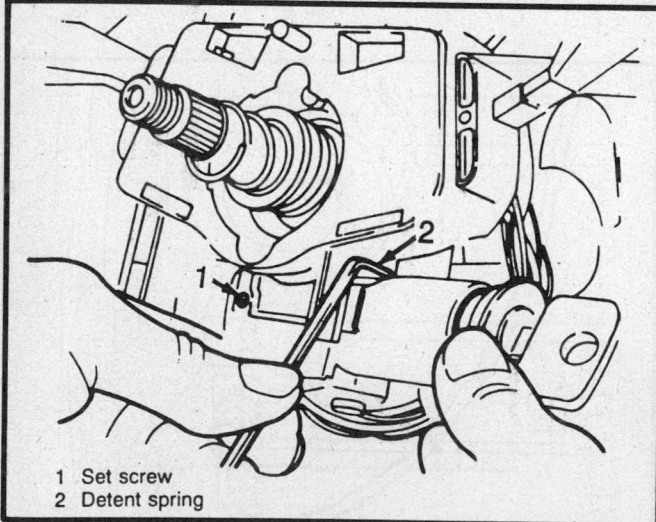

1 Set screw
2 Detent spring

Removing the Ignition lock cylinder and the ignition switch

3. Using a scratch awl, mark the alignment of the steering wheel with the steering column.
4. Remove the steering wheel retaining nut and washer.
5. Using a steering wheel puller tool, remove the steering wheel from the steering column.

NOTE: It may be necessary to disconnect the horn contact ring from the steering wheel. When installing the steering wheel, be sure that the turn signal return segment is positioned on the upper left side (facing the steering column).

6. To install, align the steering wheel on the column and reverse the removal procedures. Torque the steering wheel column nut to 18 ft. lbs. and bend the retaining tabs.

HORN SWITCH

Removal and Installation

1. Disconnect the negative battery cable.
2. Using a small pry bar, remove the horn pad from the steering wheel.
3. Disconnect the horn electrical connector from the steering wheel.
4. Remove the horn switch from the steering column.
5. To install, reverse the removal procedures.

IGNITION LOCK

Removal and Installation

1. Disconnect the negative battery cable.
2. Remove the lower instrument cluster trim.
3. Remove the turn signal/wiper switch cover panels.
4. With the key in the ignition switch, turn the key to the second position.
5. Using a small Allen wrench, press downward on the detent spring and remove the ignition lock cylinder.
6. Installation is the reverse order of the removal position. Place the key in the cylinder and install it into the ignition switch. Install the trim panels and connect the negative battery cable.

IGNITION SWITCH

Removal and Installation

1. Disconnect the negative battery cable.
2. Remove the lower instrument cluster trim.
3. Remove the turn signal/wiper switch cover panels.
4. Disconnect the electrical connector, remove the set screw and remove the ignition switch.
5. Installation is the reverse order of the removal position. Install the ignition switch into place and attach the wiring.
6. Install the set screw. Install the trim panels and connect the negative battery cable.

NEUTRAL SAFETY SWITCH

Removal and Installation

1. Raise the vehicle and support it safely.
2. Disconnect the shift linkage from the transaxle.
3. Disconnect the electrical connector from the switch.
4. Remove the switch to transaxle bolts and the switch from the vehicle.
5. To install, position the shifter shaft in the **N** position.
6. Align the shifter shaft flats with the switch and assemble the mounting bolts loosely.
7. Using a $\frac{3}{32}$ in. pin gauge or drill bit, insert it into the service adjustment hole. Rotate the switch until the gauge drops (the service hole aligns with the carrier tang hole) into a depth of $\frac{9}{64}$ in.

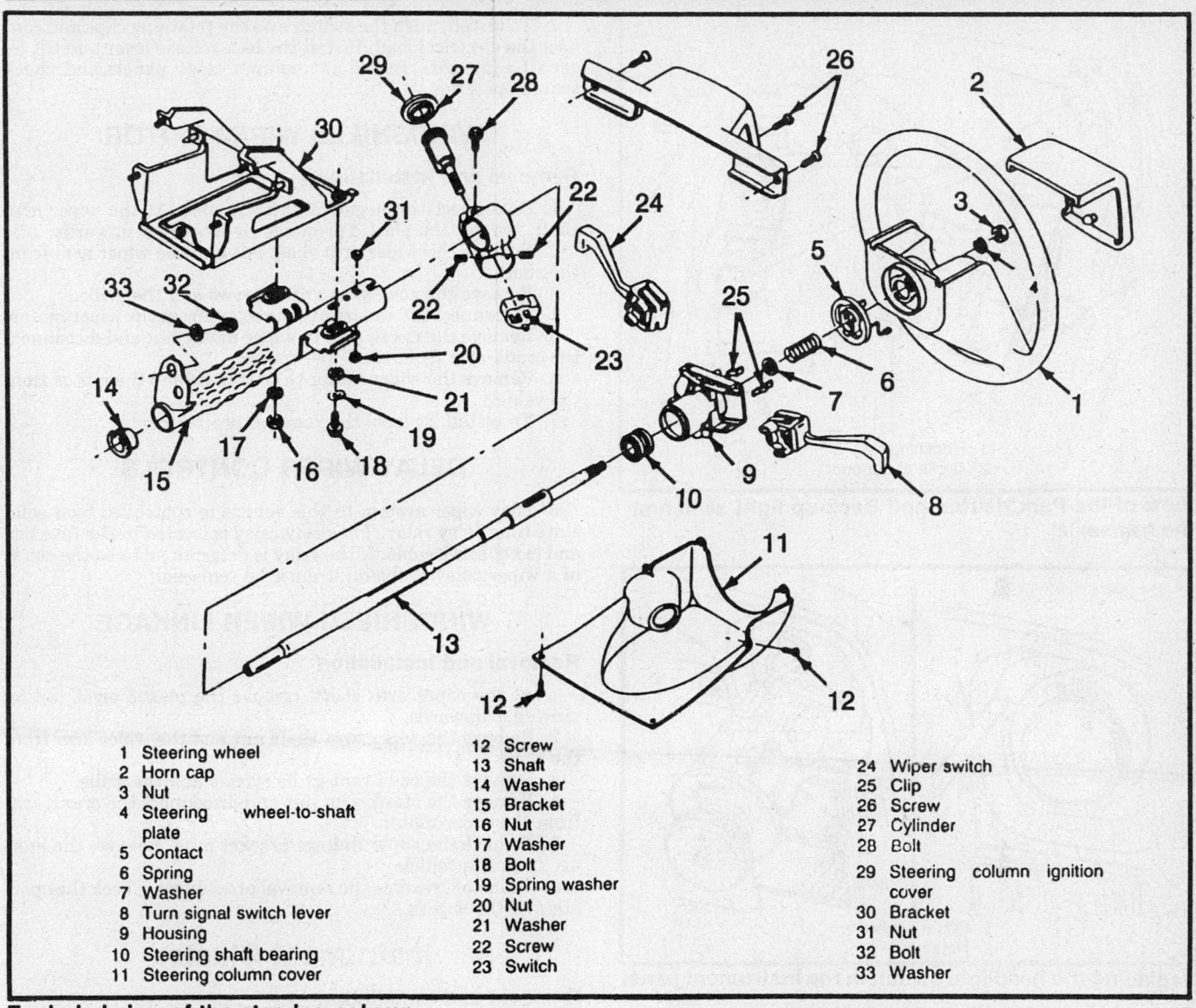

1	Steering wheel	12	Screw			
2	Horn cap	13	Shaft	24	Wiper switch	
3	Nut	14	Washer	25	Clip	
4	Steering wheel-to-shaft plate	15	Bracket	26	Screw	
5	Contact	16	Nut	27	Cylinder	
6	Spring	17	Washer	28	Bolt	
7	Washer	18	Bolt	29	Steering column ignition cover	
8	Turn signal switch lever	19	Spring washer	30	Bracket	
9	Housing	20	Nut	31	Nut	
10	Steering shaft bearing	21	Washer	32	Bolt	
11	Steering column cover	22	Screw	33	Washer	
		23	Switch			

Exploded view of the steering column

8. Torque the switch to transaxle bolts to 22 ft. lbs. and remove the pin gauge.

STOPLIGHT SWITCH

Removal and Installation

1. Disconnect the negative battery cable.
2. Disconnect the electrical connector from the brake light switch (located above the brake pedal).
3. Remove the switch from the tubular clip on the brake pedal mounting bracket.
4. To install and adjust, insert the switch into the clip until the switch body seats on the clip.
5. Pull the brake pedal rearward against the internal pedal stop. The switch will be moved in the tubular clip providing the proper adjustment.

HEADLIGHT SWITCH

Removal and Installation

1. Disconnect the negative battery cable.

2. Using an offset tool, depress the headlight switch retaining clips and pull the switch from the dash.
3. Disconnect the electrical connector from the rear of the switch. Remove the switch from the vehicle.
4. To install, connect the electrical lead and push switch into position in the dash.

COMBINATION SWITCH

The combination switch consists of the turn signal switch and the dimmer switch which is connected to the steering column.

Removal and Installation

1. Disconnect the negative battery cable.
2. Remove the lower instrument panel trim.
3. Remove the upper steering column panel screws from both sides; turn the steering wheel 90 degrees for right and left access.
4. Remove the screws from the lower cover panel and remove the panel.
5. Pull the handle from the lock release lever and unscrew the tilt lever, if equipped.

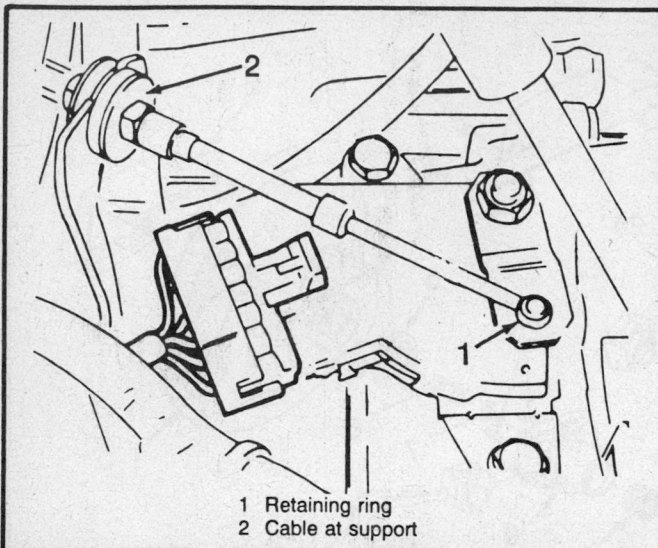

1 Retaining ring
2 Cable at support

View of the Park/Neutral and Back-up light switch at the transaxle

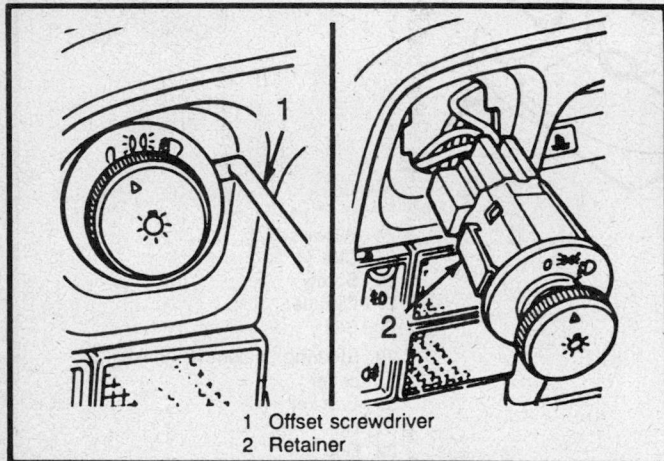

1 Offset screwdriver
2 Retainer

Replacing the headlight switch in the instrument panel

6. Disconnect the electrical connector from the switch housing; push inward on either side of the switch to release it from the retaining clips.

7. To install, push the switch into the retaining clips and connect the electrical lead. Install the lock release lever and tilt lever (if equipped). Install the column cover panels and check switch operation.

WINDSHIELD WIPER SWITCH

Removal and Installation

1. Disconnect the negative battery cable.
2. Remove the lower instrument panel trim.
3. Remove the upper steering column panel screws from both sides; turn the steering wheel 90 degrees for right and left access.
4. Remove the screws from the lower cover panel and remove the panel.
5. Pull the handle from the lock release lever and unscrew the tilt lever if equipped.
6. Disconnect the electrical connector from the switch housing; push inward on either side of the switch to release it from the retaining clips.

7. To install, push the switch into the retaining clips and connect the electrical lead. Install the lock release lever and tilt lever (if equipped). Install the column cover panels and check switch operation.

WINDSHIELD WIPER MOTOR

Removal and Installation

1. Disconnect the negative battery cable. At the wiper arm shaft, remove the plastic pivot cap by moving it upwards.
2. Remove the wiper arm shaft nut and the wiper arm from the shaft.
3. Remove the cowl vent grille screws and the grille.
4. Disconnect the electrical connectors from the wiper motor.
5. Remove the crank arm to wiper motor nut and disconnect the crank arm from the wiper motor.
6. Remove the wiper motor to cowl bolts and the motor from the vehicle.
7. To install, reverse the removal procedures.

DELAY WIPER CONTROLS

The delay wiper system in this vehicle is controlled by a solid state time delay relay. The delay relay is located in the fuse box and is not serviceable. If the relay is determined to be the cause of a wiper delay problem, it must be replaced.

WINDSHIELD WIPER LINKAGE

Removal and Installation

1. At the wiper arm shaft, remove the plastic pivot cap by moving it upwards.
2. Remove the wiper arm shaft nut and the wiper arm from the shaft.
3. Remove the cowl vent grille screws and the grille.
4. Remove the crank arm nut and disconnect the crank arm from the wiper motor.
5. Remove the wiper linkage bracket nuts. Remove the linkage from the vehicle.
6. To install, reverse the removal procedures. Check the operation of the wipers.

Instrument Cluster

Removal and Installation

1. Disconnect the negative battery cable.
2. Remove the instrument cluster trim plate retaining screws and the trim plate.
3. Pull the instrument cluster forward, disconnect the speedometer cable and the electrical connectors from the rear of the instrument cluster.
4. To install, connect the speedometer and the electrical connectors to the instrument cluster. Install the cluster in the dash and install the retaining screws. Check for the proper operation of the speedometer and the gauges.

SPEEDOMETER

Removal and Installation

1. Disconnect the negative battery cable.
2. Remove the instrument panel cluster lens, the face plate and the instrument cluster from the instrument panel.
3. Press the speedometer cable retainer and separate the speedometer cable from the speedometer.
4. Remove the speedometer retaining screws. Remove the speedometer from the cluster.
5. To install, reverse the removal procedures. Check the operaton of the speedometer

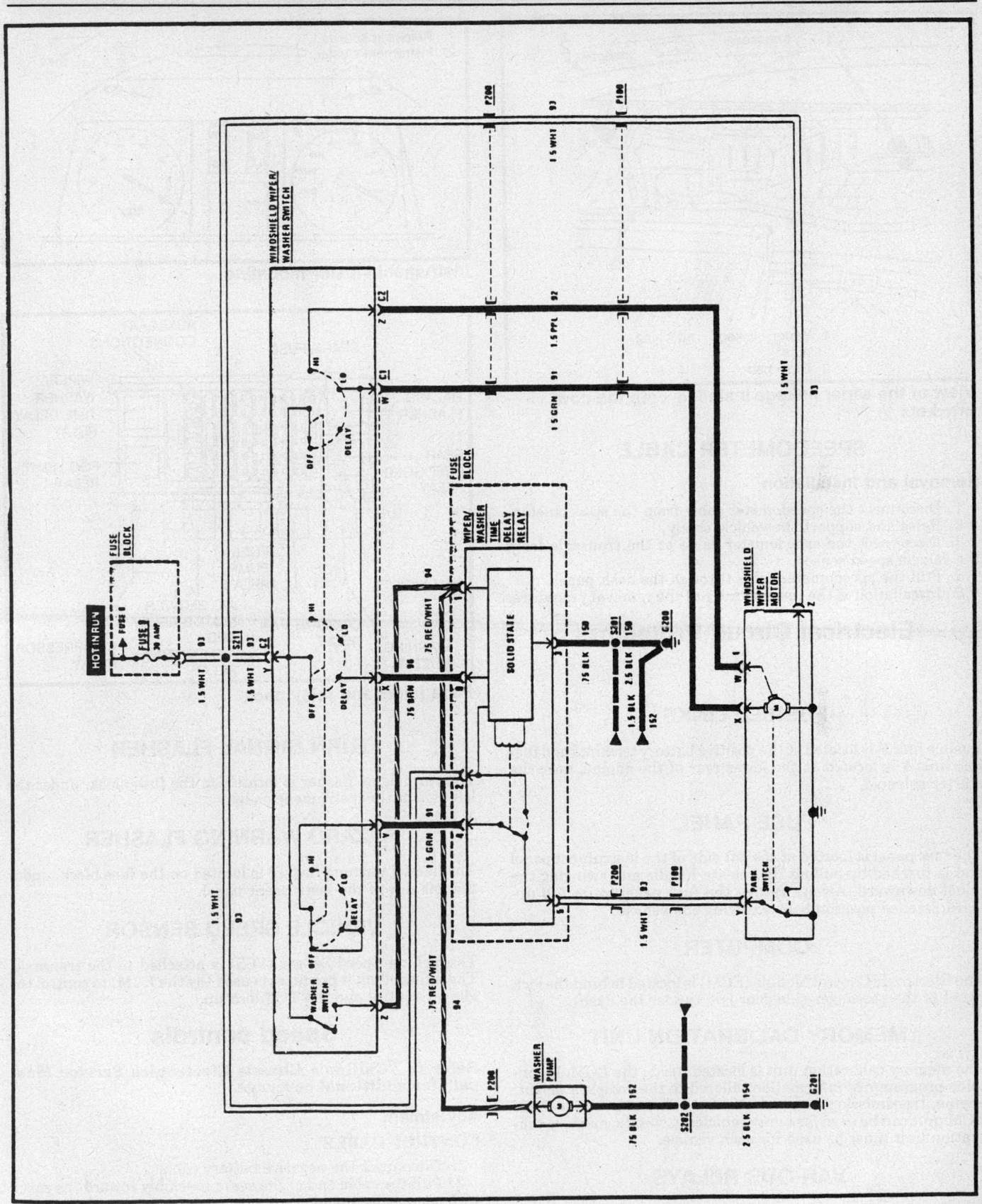

Schematic of the windshield wiper/delay system

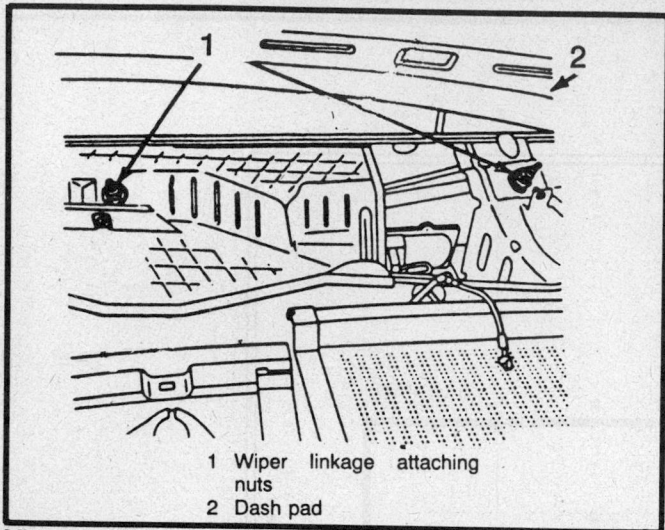

1 Wiper linkage attaching nuts
2 Dash pad

View of the wiper linkage installed onto the cowl brackets

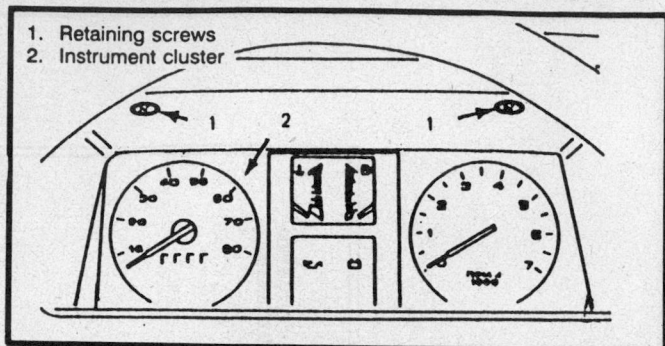

1. Retaining screws
2. Instrument cluster

Instrument cluster mounting

SPEEDOMETER CABLE

Removal and Installation

1. Disconnect the speedometer cable from the speedometer.
2. Raise and support the vehicle safely.
3. Disconnect the speedometer cable at the transaxle from the vehicle speed sensor.
4. Pull the speedometer cable through the dash panel.
5. Installation is the reverse order of the removal procedure.

Electrical Circuit Protectors

FUSIBLE LINKS

Fusible link **B** is located at the positive battery terminal and fusible link **A** is located at the lower rear of the engine, near the starter solenoid.

FUSE PANEL

The fuse panel is located at the left side of the instrument panel and is reached by pulling the release handle and swinging the panel downward. Always return the fuse panel to its full upward, latched position before driving the vehicle.

COMPUTER

The Electronic Control Module (ECM) is located behind the kick panel at the passenger-side door jam (under the dash).

MEMORY CALIBRATION UNIT

The memory calibration unit is located inside the ECM. It contains programmed information tailored to the vehicle's weight, engine, transmission, axle ratio and etc. Even though a single ECM unit can be used for many vehicles, a specific memory calibration unit must be used for each vehicle.

VARIOUS RELAYS

All relays for this vehicle are located on the fuse block, under the left side of the instrument panel.

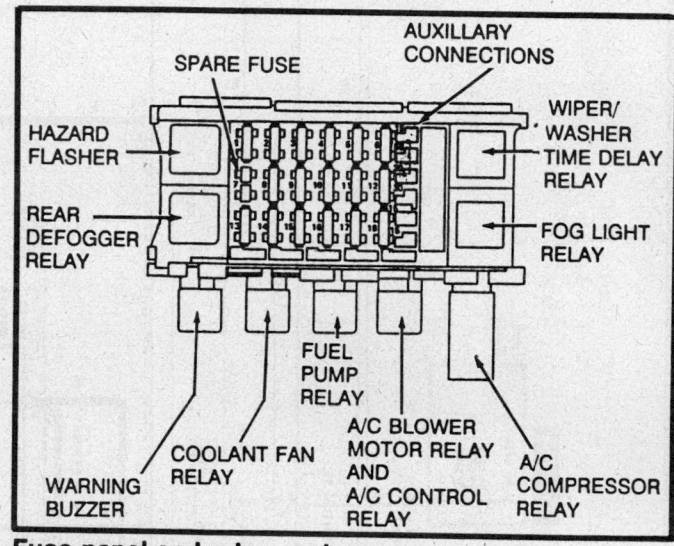

Fuse panel and relay pack

TURN SIGNAL FLASHER

The turn signal flasher is located on the fuse block, under the left side of the instrument panel.

HAZARD WARNING FLASHER

The hazard warning flasher is located on the fuse block, under the left side of the instrument panel.

VEHICLE SPEED SENSOR

The Vehicle Speed Sensor (VSS) is attached to the transaxle. The information it produces is used (by the ECM) to control the idle air control and the TCC lock up.

Speed controls

Refer to "Chilton's Chassis Electronics Service Manual" for additional coverage.

Adjustment
CONTROL CABLE

1. Disconnect the negative battery cable.
2. Pull the cable end of the servo assembly toward the servo without moving the idler pulley cam.
3. If 1 of the 6 holes in the servo assembly tab lines up with the cable pin, connect the pin to the tab with retainer 7.

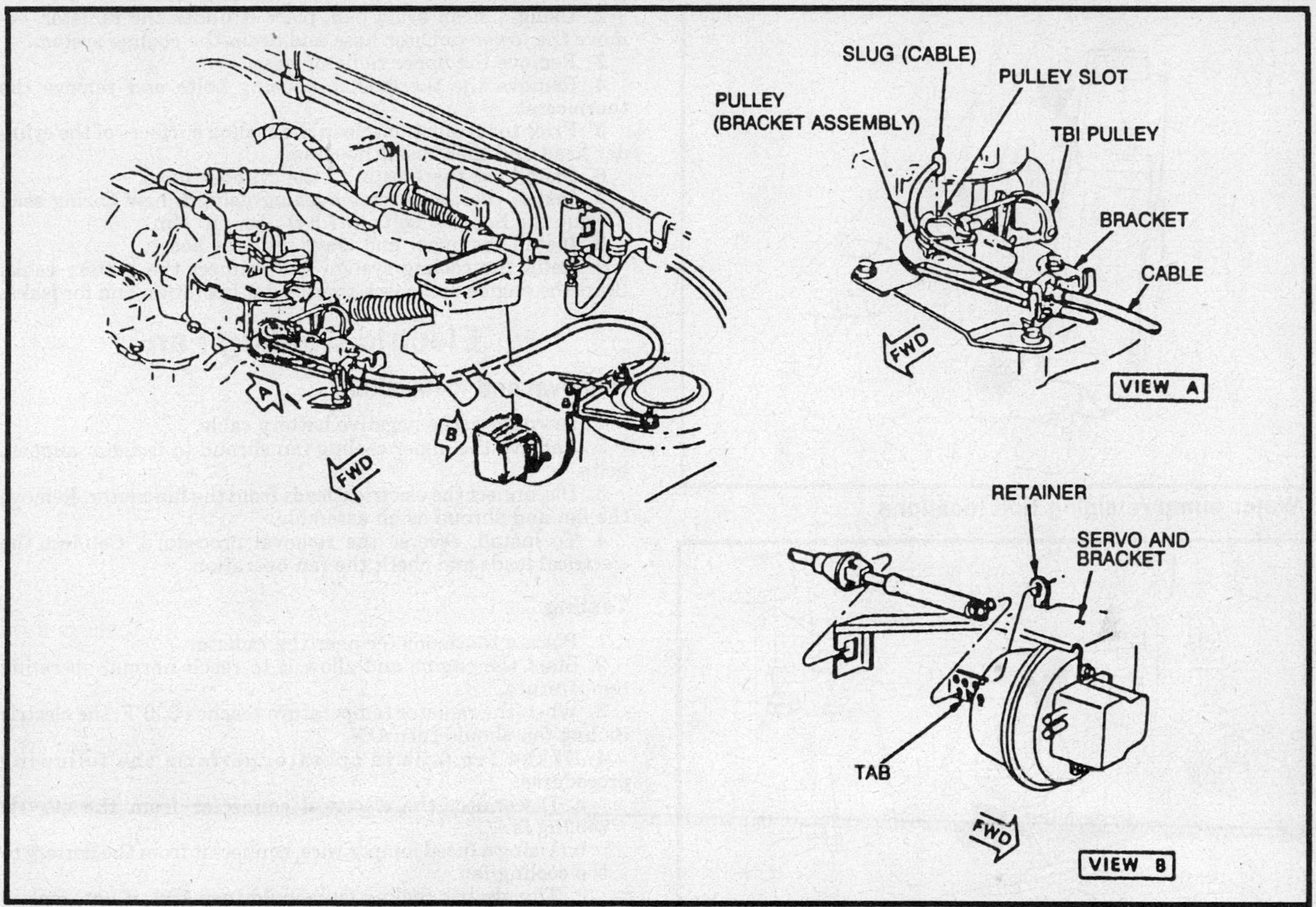

SLUG (CABLE)

PULLEY SLOT

PULLEY (BRACKET ASSEMBLY)

TBI PULLEY

BRACKET

CABLE

FWD

VIEW A

RETAINER

SERVO AND BRACKET

TAB

FWD

VIEW B

Servo and linkage assembly—cruise control

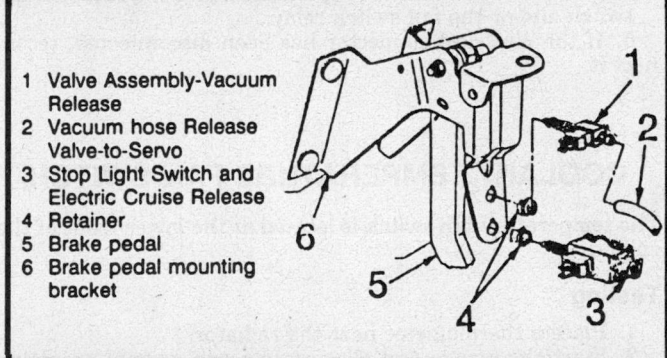

1 Valve Assembly-Vacuum Release
2 Vacuum hose Release Valve-to-Servo
3 Stop Light Switch and Electric Cruise Release
4 Retainer
5 Brake pedal
6 Brake pedal mounting bracket

Vacuum release assembly—cruise control

4. If a tab hole does not line up with the pin, move the cable away from the servo assembly until the next closest tab hole lines up. Connect the pin-to-tab with retainer 7.

NOTE: Do not stretch the cable so as to make a particular tab hole connect to the pin. This could prevent the engine from returning to idle.

5. Connect the battery cable and test operation.

VACUUM RELEASE VALVE

1. Disconnect the negative battery cable.
2. With the brake pedal depressed, insert the valve into the tubular retainer until the valve seats on the retainer.

NOTE: Audible clicks can be heard as the threaded portion of the valve is pushed through the retainer toward the brake pedal.

3. Pull the brake pedal fully rearward against the pedal stop until the audible click sounds can no longer be heard. The valve will be moved in the tubular retainer providing the adjustment.
4. Release the brake pedal and repeat Step 3 to insure that no audible click sounds remain.
5. Connect the battery cable and test operation.

COOLING AND HEATING SYSTEMS

Water Pump

Removal and Installation

1.6L AND 2.0L ENGINES

1. Disconnect the negative battery cable. Drain the cooling system.

2. Remove the front cover, the timing belt and the rear cover.
3. Remove the water pump mounting bolts and the water pump from the engine.
4. Clean the seal mounting surfaces.
5. To install, use a new water pump seal. Coat the sealing surface and the seal ring with grease. Torque the water pump bolts

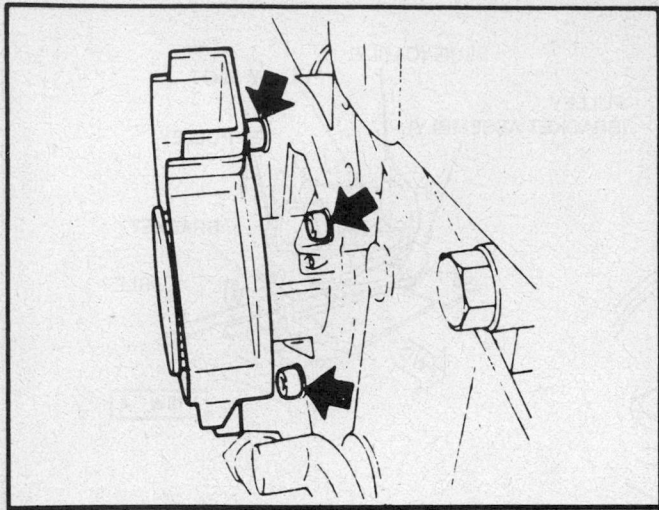

Water pump retaining bolt locations

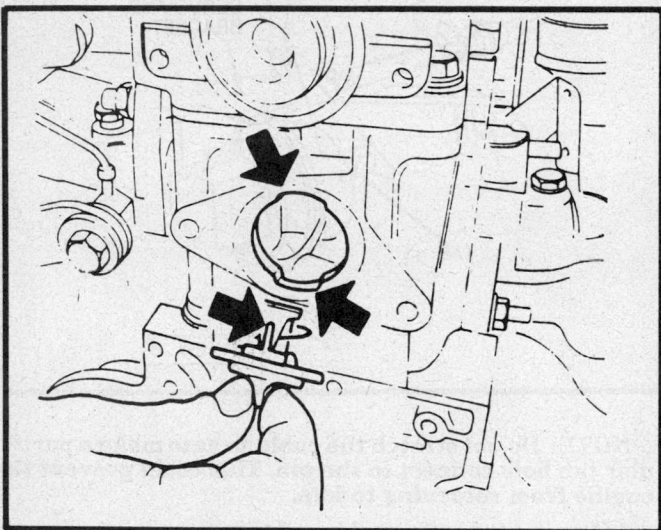

Thermostat positioning

to 71 inch lbs. Refill the cooling system. Start the engine, allow it to reach normal operating temperature and check for leaks, bleed cooling system. Check and adjust the ignition timing if needed.

Thermostat

Removal and Installation

1.6L ENGINE

1. Disconnect the negative battery cable.
2. Using a clean drain pan, place it under the radiator, remove the lower radiator hose and drain the cooling system.
3. Remove the front cover, the timing belt and the rear cover (slip it over the water pump rear cover piece).
4. Remove the water inlet bolts, the water inlet housing and the thermostat.
5. Clean the gasket mounting surfaces.
6. To install, use a new seal and reverse the removal procedures. Torque the thermostat housing bolts to 78 inch lbs. Refill the cooling system and bleed the air from the system.

2.0L ENGINE

1. Disconnect the negative battery cable.

2. Using a clean drain pan, place it under the radiator, remove the lower radiator hose and drain the cooling system.
3. Remove the upper radiator hose.
4. Remove the thermostat housing bolts and remove the thermostat.
5. Prior to installation, clean the sealing surfaces of the cylinder head and thermostat housing.
6. Install the thermostat to the cylinder head.
7. Install the thermostat housing using a new O-ring seal. Torque the housing bolts to 7.5 ft. lbs. (10 Nm).
8. Install the upper and lower radiator hoses.
9. Refill the cooling system and connect the battery cable. Start the engine and check thermostat operation and for leaks.

Electric Cooling Fan

Removal and Installation

1. Disconnect the negative battery cable.
2. Remove the upper cooling fan shroud to radiator support bolts.
3. Disconnect the electrical leads from the fan motor. Remove the fan and shroud as an assembly.
4. To install, reverse the removal procedure. Connect the electrical leads and check the fan operation.

Testing

1. Place a thermometer near the radiator.
2. Start the engine and allow it to reach normal operating temperature.
3. When the radiator temperature reaches 230°F, the electric cooling fan should turn **ON**.
4. If the fan fails to operate, perform the following procedures:
   a. Disconnect the electrical connector from the electric cooling fan.
   b. Using a fused jumper wire, connect it from the battery to the cooling fan.
   c. The electric cooling fan should turn **ON**; if not, replace the fan motor.
   d. If the fan still will not operate, inspect the fuse, the fan switch and/or the fan switch relay.
5. If the electrical connector has been disconnected, reconnect it.

COOLANT TEMPERATURE FAN SWITCH

The temperature fan switch is located at the lower-front of the engine.

Testing

1. Place a thermometer near the radiator.
2. Start the engine and allow it to reach normal operating temperature.
3. When the radiator temperature reaches 230°F, the temperature fan switch should turn the coolant fan **ON**.
4. If the cooling fan fails to operate, disconnect the electrical connector to the fan switch. Place a jumper wire between the terminals of the connector, if the fan runs, replace the temperature fan switch.
5. If the cooling fan still will not operate, inspect the cooling fan, the fuse and the fan switch relay.

NOTE: When checking the fuses, inspect fuse No. 11, without air conditioning or No. 14, with air conditioning.

6. If any electrical connector has been disconnected, reconnect it.

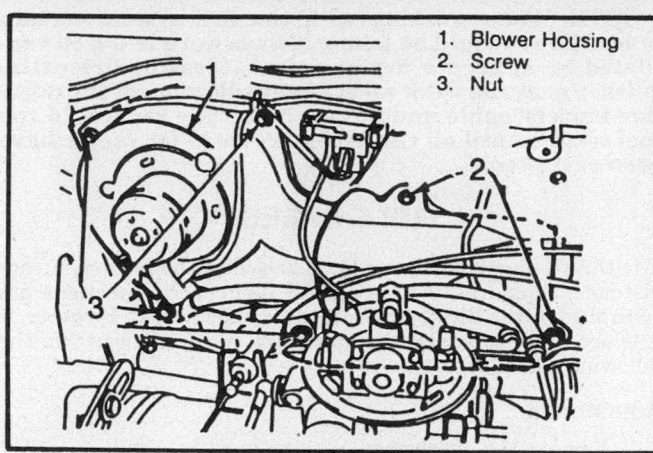

1. Blower Housing
2. Screw
3. Nut

Blower motor mounting

Blower Motor

The heater blower motor is located in the engine compartment, attached to the cowl.

Removal and Installation

1. Disconnect the negative battery cable.
2. Remove the wiper arms.
3. Remove the wind deflector screws and the deflector halves.
4. Remove the right hand windshield washer nozzle from the water deflector.
5. Remove the dash panel seal and clip.
6. Remove the right hand wiper bearing nut.
7. Remove the water deflector.
8. Disconnect the electrical connectors from the blower motor. Remove the heater blower motor retaining screws.
9. Remove the housing, the motor and the housing cover.
10. To install, reverse the removal procedures. Align the motor by first inserting the lower screw, then the upper. Reconnect all electrical leads and check operation.

Heater Core

Refer to "Chilton's Auto Heating and Air Conditioning Manual" for additional coverage.

Removal and Installation

1. Disconnect the negative battery cable.
2. Place a clean drain pan under the radiator, remove the lower coolant hose and drain the cooling system.
3. Using spring clips, close off, label and disconnect the heater hoses from the heater core.
4. Using a pointed plastic tool, remove the package panel from in front of the console.
5. Position the heater control levers to the lowest position on the control unit.
6. Remove the temperature control cable from the air distributor and the actuating lever.
7. From under the glove box, remove the kick panel.
8. Remove the temperature valve linkage from the right side of the air distributor.
9. At the lower right side of the air distributor cover, pull back the carpet to access the screw.
10. Remove the air distributor housing cover screws and the cover.
11. Position the temperature valve to access the upper heater core screws.
12. Remove the heater core housing screws and the heater core.
13. To install, reverse the removal procedures. Refill the cooling system. Start the engine, allow it to reach normal operating temperature and check for leaks.

Temperature Control/Blower Switch

Removal and Installation

1. Disconnect the negative battery cable.
2. If equipped with manual transaxle, remove the gear shift lever boot.
3. Using a pointed plastic tool, remove the package panel from in front of the console.
4. Remove the front floor console shift plate and the front center console.
5. Remove the temperature control cables from the air distributor case.
6. From the under the temperature control unit, remove the control unit retaining screw.
7. Disconnect the electrical connector(s) from the temperature control unit.
8. Remove the temperature control unit from the instrument panel.
9. To install, reverse the removal procedures. Check the operation of the temperature control for ease of operation.

FUEL INJECTION SYSTEM

Refer to "Chilton's Electronic Engine Controls Manual" for additional coverage.

Description

With throttle body injection (TBI), model 700 (1988–90) an injection unit is placed on the intake manifold where the carburetor is normally mounted. The TBI unit is computer controlled and supplies the correct amount of fuel during all engine operating conditions.

In the TBI system, a single fuel injector mounted at the top of the throttle body, sprays fuel through the throttle valve and into the intake manifold. The throttle body resembles a carburetor in appearance but is not as complex; it replaces the carburetors hardware with a single, electrically operated fuel injector.

The injector is actually a solenoid. When activated, a pintle valve is lifted off its seat, allowing the pressurized (10 psi) fuel to spray out. The nozzle of the injector is designed to atomize the fuel for complete air/fuel mixture.

The activating signal for the injector originates with the electronic control module (ECM), which monitors engine temperature, throttle position, vehicle speed and several other engine-related conditions, then continuously updates the injector opening times in relation to the information given by these sensors.

The throttle body is also equipped with an idle air control motor. The idle air control motor operates a pintle valve at the side of the throttle body. When the valve opens it allows air to bypass the throttle, which provides the additional air required to idle at elevated speed when the engine is cold. The idle air control motor also compensates for accessory loads and changing engine friction during break-in. The idle speed control motor is controlled by the ECM.

Fuel pressure for the system is provided by an in-tank fuel pump. The pump is a 2 stage turbine design powered by a DC motor. It is designed for smooth, quiet operation, high flow and fast priming. The design of the fuel inlet reduces the possibility of vapor lock under hot fuel conditions. The pump sends fuel forward through the fuel line to a stainless steel high-flow fuel filter mounted on the engine. From the filter, the fuel moves to the throttle body. The fuel pump inlet is located in a reservoir in the fuel tank which insures a constant supply of fuel to the pump during hard cornering and on steep inclines. The fuel pump is controlled by a fuel pump relay, which in turn receives its signal from the ECM. A fuel pressure regulator inside the throttle body maintains fuel pressure at 10 psi and routes unused fuel back to the fuel tank through a fuel return line. The constant circulation of fuel through the throttle body prevents component overheating and vapor lock.

The electronic control module (ECM), also called a microcomputer, is the controller of the fuel injection system. After receiving inputs from various sensors, the ECM commands the fuel injector, idle air control motor, EST distributor, torque converter clutch (A/T) and other engine actuators to operate in a pre-programmed manner to improve driveability and fuel economy while controlling emissions. The sensing elements update the computer every $^1/_{10}$ second for general information and every 12.5 milli-seconds for critical emissions and driveability information.

The ECM has limited system diagnostic capability. If certain system malfunctions occur, the diagnostic "check engine" light on the instrument panel will illuminate, alerting the driver to the need for service. Since both idle speed and mixture are controlled by the ECM on this system, no adjustments are possible or necessary.

NOTE: When working with the fuel system certain precautions should be taken; always work in a well ventilated area, keep a dry chemical (Class B) fire extinguisher near the work area. Always disconnect the negative battery cable and do not make any repairs to the fuel system until all the necessary steps for repair have been reviewed.

IDLE SPEED

The throttle body is adjusted and sealed at the factory, no adjustment should be performed. All fuel control functions are controlled by the Electronic Control Module (ECM). However, if it is necessary to adjust the minimum idle speed, perform the following procedures.

Adjustment

1. Remove the air cleaner.
2. Using a scratch awl, pierce the idle stop screw plug, apply leverage and remove the plug.
3. Using a tachometer, follow the manufacturer's recommendations and connect it to the engine.
4. Position the transaxle in **P**, for automatic transaxle or **N**, for manual transaxle. Start the engine and allow the rpm to stabilize.
5. Using the special tool BT–8528A or equivalent, position it fully into the idle air passage so that no air leak exists.
6. Using a No. 20 Torx® Bit tool, turn the idle stop screw until the engine speed is 525–575 rpm, for automatic transaxle or 575–625 rpm, for manual transaxle.

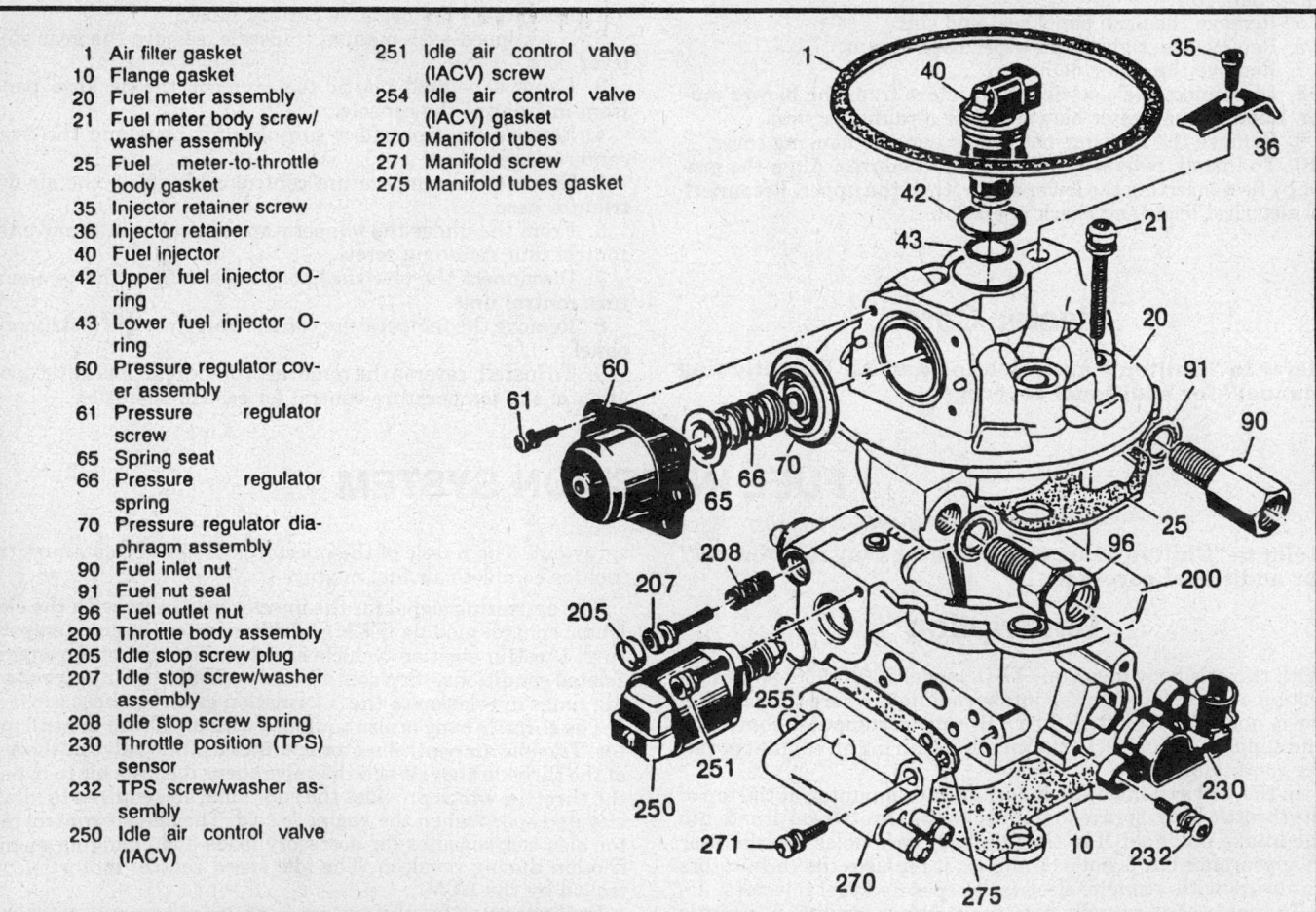

1	Air filter gasket	251	Idle air control valve
10	Flange gasket		(IACV) screw
20	Fuel meter assembly	254	Idle air control valve
21	Fuel meter body screw/		(IACV) gasket
	washer assembly	270	Manifold tubes
25	Fuel meter-to-throttle	271	Manifold screw
	body gasket	275	Manifold tubes gasket
35	Injector retainer screw		
36	Injector retainer		
40	Fuel injector		
42	Upper fuel injector O-ring		
43	Lower fuel injector O-ring		
60	Pressure regulator cover assembly		
61	Pressure regulator screw		
65	Spring seat		
66	Pressure regulator spring		
70	Pressure regulator diaphragm assembly		
90	Fuel inlet nut		
91	Fuel nut seal		
96	Fuel outlet nut		
200	Throttle body assembly		
205	Idle stop screw plug		
207	Idle stop screw/washer assembly		
208	Idle stop screw spring		
230	Throttle position (TPS) sensor		
232	TPS screw/washer assembly		
250	Idle air control valve (IACV)		

Exploded view of the throttle body–Model 700

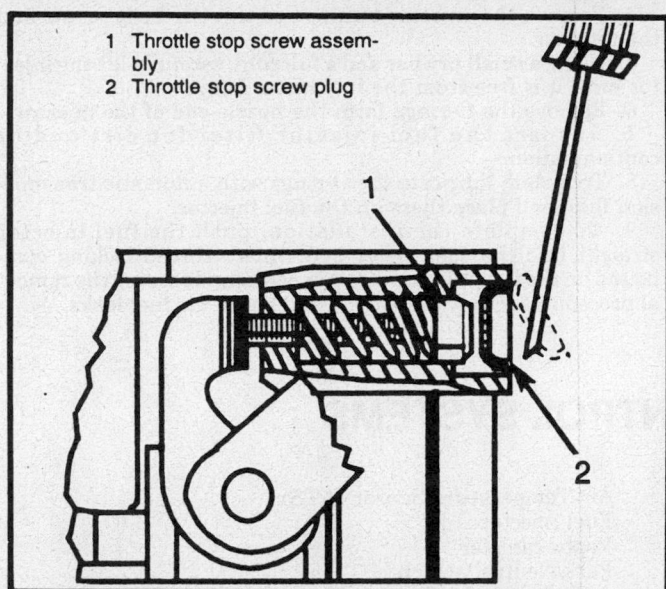

1 Throttle stop screw assembly
2 Throttle stop screw plug

Removing the idle stop screw plug

7. After adjustment, stop the engine, remove the tool No. BT–8528A or equivalent. Using silicone sealant, cover the idle stop screw.

IDLE MIXTURE

Adjustment

The idle mixture is electronically controlled by the Electronic Control Module (ECM), no adjustment is necessary.

FUEL SYSTEM PRESSURE RELIEF

Procedure

Modern fuel injection systems operate under high pressure, this makes it necessary to first relieve the system of pressure before servicing. The pressurized fuel when released may ignite or cause personal injury. The following steps are to be used to relieve the fuel pressure.
1. Remove the fuel punp fuse from the fuse block.
2. Crank the engine and let it run until the remaining fuel in the lines is consumed.
3. Crank engine again to make sure any fuel in the lines has been removed.
4. With the ignition **OFF** replace the fuel pump fuse.
5. Disconnect the negative battery cable.

Fuel Pump

The electric fuel pump is attached to the sending unit and is located in the fuel tank.

Removal and Installation

1. Relieve the fuel system pressure.
2. Disconnect the negative battery cable.
3. Raise the rear seat and remove the floor pan cover.
4. Remove the sending unit to fuel tank bolts and the sending unit from the fuel tank.
5. To install, use new O-rings and reverse the removal procedures.

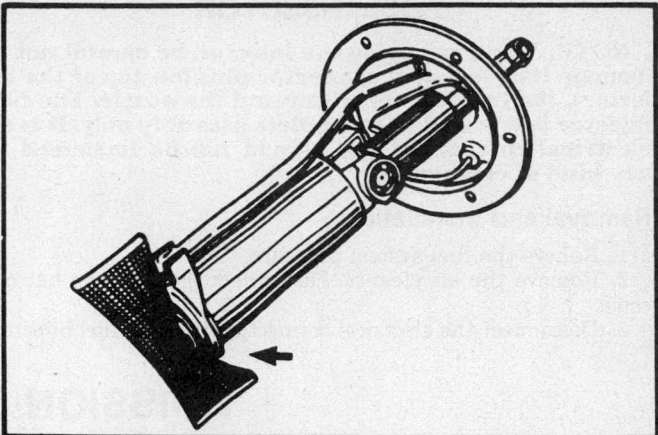

View of the electric fuel pump

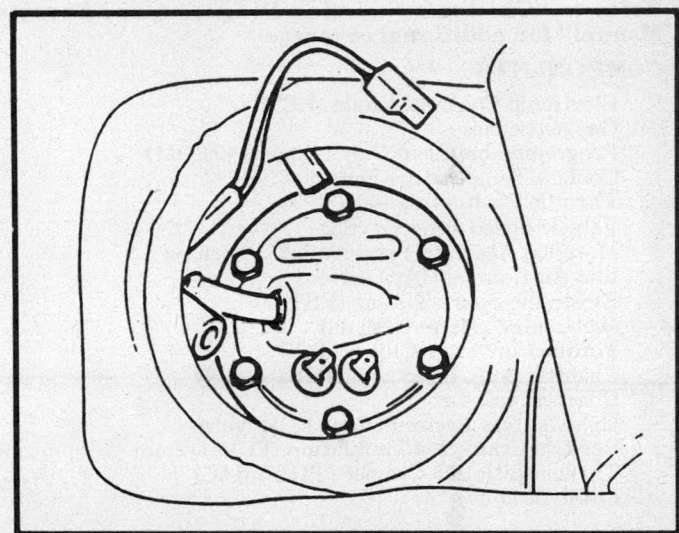

Fuel pump and sender location—under rear seat

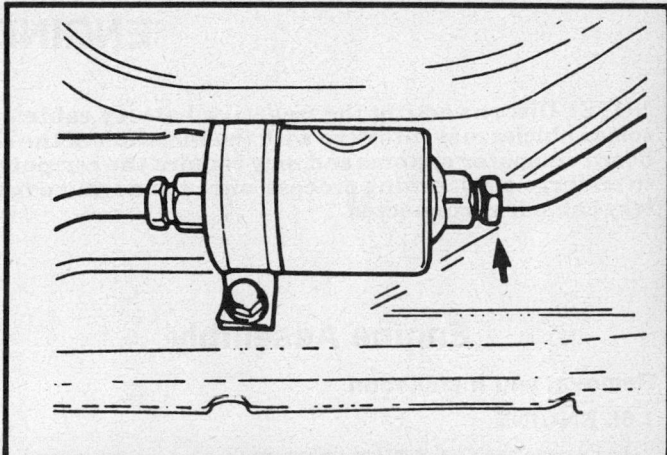

View of the inline fuel filter

FUEL FILTER

The inline fuel filter is located on the rear crossmember of the vehicle. Always use a back-up wrench for removing or installing the fuel line fittings.

FUEL INJECTOR

NOTE: When removing the injector, be careful not to damage the electrical connector pins (on top of the injector), the injector fuel filter and the nozzle. The fuel injector is serviced as a complete assembly only. It is an electrical component and should not be immersed in any kind of cleaner.

Removal and Installation

1. Relieve the fuel system pressure.
2. Remove the air cleaner. Disconnect the negative battery cable.
3. Disconnect the electrical connector from the fuel injector.
4. Remove the injector retainer to throttle body screw and the retainer.
5. Using a small pry bar and a fulcrum, carefully lift the injector until it is free from the fuel meter body.
6. Remove the O-rings form the nozzle end of the injector.
7. Inspect the fuel injector filter for dirt and/or contamination.
8. To install, lubricate the O-rings with automatic transmission fluid and place them on the fuel injector.
9. To complete the installation, push the fuel injector straight into the fuel meter body, place thread locking compound on the fuel injector retainer screw and reverse the removal procedures. Start the engine and check for fuel leaks.

EMISSION CONTROL SYSTEMS

Refer to "Chilton's Emission Diagnosis and Service Manual" for additional coverage.

COMPONENTS

Electronic Control Module (ECM)
Oxygen sensor
Programmable Read Only Memory (PROM)
Coolant Temperature Sensor (CTS)
Throttle Position Sensor (TPS)
Vehicle Speed Sensor (VSS)
Manifold Absolute Pressure (MAP) sensor
Idle Air Control (IAC) valve
Electronic Spark Timing (EST)
Distributor reference signal
Torque Converter Clutch (TCC)
Throttle Body Injection (TBI) assembly
Charcoal canister
Exhaust Gas Recirculation (EGR) valve
Positive Crankcase Ventilation (PCV) system
Thermostatic Air Cleaner (THERMAC)
Catalytic converter
Air Temperature Sensor (ATS)
Fuel injector
Vapor canister
Park/Neutral switch
A/C request signal
Manual transaxle shift light
Canister purge solenoid
Electronic Spark Control (ESC) knock sensor
Electronic Spark Control (ESC) module

Resetting Warning Lamp

Procedure

When the "Service Engine Soon" light turns ON, a trouble code is stored in the ECM memory. If the problem is periodic, the light will turn OFF when the problem goes away. However, the trouble code will stay in the ECM memory until the battery voltage is removed from the ECM.

To erase the ECM memory, turn OFF the ignition switch, then disconnect the battery negative cable, the ECM pigtail or the ECM fuse for 10 seconds.

ENGINE MECHANICAL

NOTE: Disconnecting the negative battery cable on some vehicles may interfere with the functions of the on board computer systems and may require the computer to undergo a relearning process, once the negative battery cable is reconnected.

Engine Assembly

Removal and Installation

1.6L ENGINE

1. Relieve the fuel system pressure.
2. Disconnect the terminals from the battery and chassis ground wire.
3. Position a clean drain pan under the radiator, remove the lower radiator hose and drain the cooling system. Remove the upper radiator hose and the heater hoses.
4. Remove the air cleaner. Detach the cable from the throttle body.
5. Remove the vacuum hoses from the power brake booster, vacuum sensor, intake manifold to vapor canister and throttle valve body to vapor canister.
6. If equipped with automatic transmission, disconnect the throttle body to transaxle cable.
7. Remove the fuel lines from the throttle body. Disconnect and plug the transaxle cooler lines, if equipped.
8. Disconnect the electrical connectors from the distributor, oxygen sensor, oil pressure switch, intake manifold temperature sensor, injector nozzle, IAC, throttle valve. Remove the ground wires from the camshaft housing and the intake manifold, remove the the wiring harness retaining strap.
9. Disconnect the ignition coil plugs and cable, the instrument panel wiring harness multi-connector, the TCC connector, vehicles with automatic transaxle and the neutral safety switch.
10. Raise the vehicle and support it safely.
11. Disconnect the exhaust pipe to intake manifold bolts and disconnect the rear exhaust pipe from the catalytic converter. Remove the exhaust pipe/catalytic converter assembly from the vehicle.
12. Remove the closure plug and the halfshaft from the transaxle.
13. Remove the clutch cover plate and the clutch housing to lower engine block bolts.

14. Lower the vehicle.

15. Using an engine sling, attach it to the engine hooks and support the engine weight.

16. Using the proper equipment, support the transaxle.

17. Remove the front engine mount and the clutch housing to upper engine bolts. Separate the engine from the clutch housing and lift the engine from the vehicle.

To install:

18. Lower the engine into the engine compartment and align it with the clutch housing.

19. Install the upper clutch housing bolts and the front engine mount.

20. Remove transaxle support and engine sling. Torque the engine mount bolts to 29 ft. lbs.

21. Raise the vehicle and support it safely.

22. Install the lower clutch cover bolts and the clutch cover plate.

23. Install the clutch drive shaft.

24. Install the interference suppression capacitor cable to the transmission.

25. Install the exhaust pipe with the catalytic converter.

26. Install the lower radiator hose.

27. Install the neutral safety switch.

28. Vehicles with automatic transaxle, connect the TCC connector.

29. Install the IP harness multiple connector.

30. Lower the vehicle.

31. Connect the fuel lines to the throttle body.

32. Reconnect all the wires and hoses. Refill the cooling system and the engine oil (if drained).

21. Start the engine and check operation.

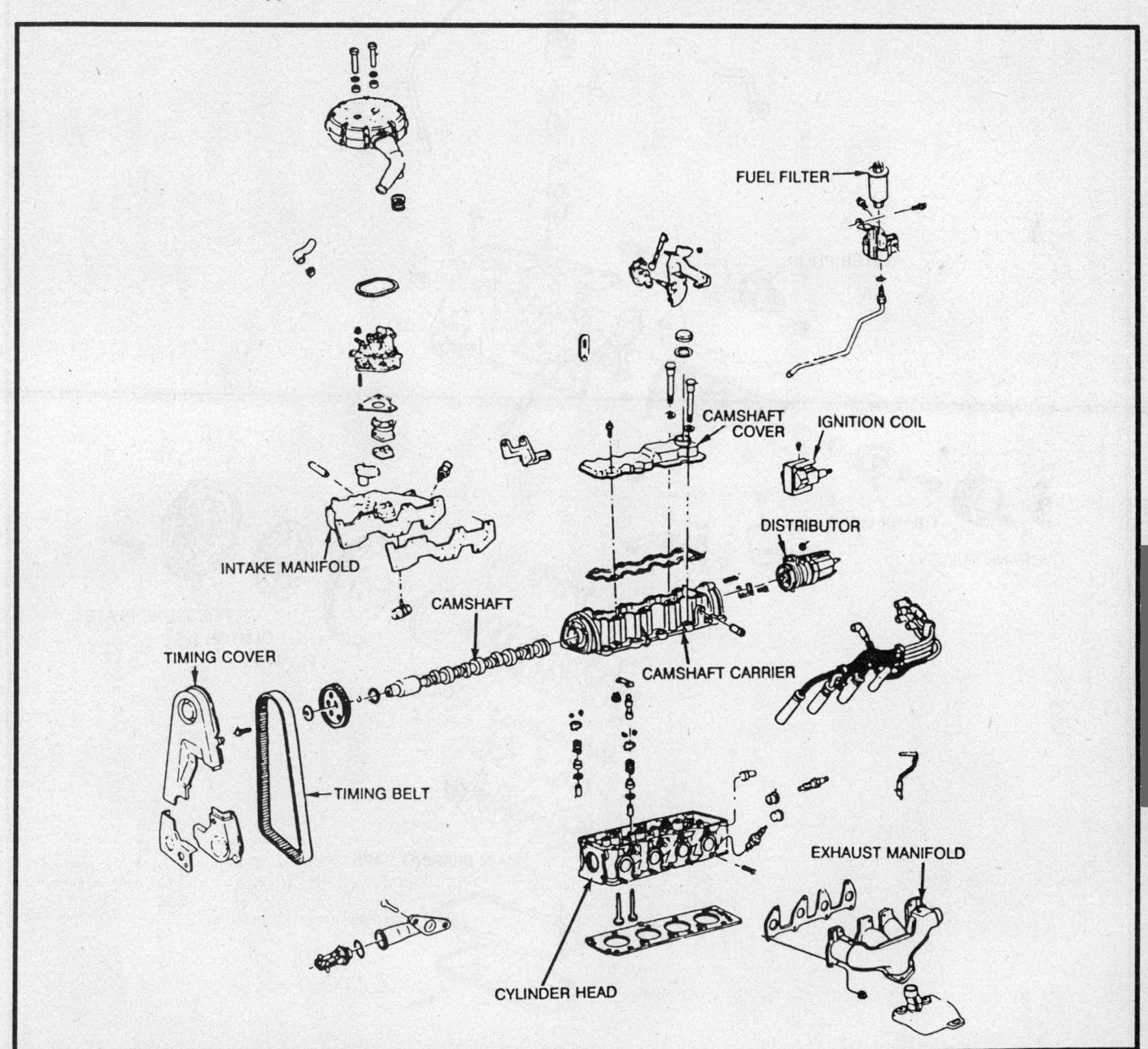

FUEL FILTER

CAMSHAFT COVER

IGNITION COIL

DISTRIBUTOR

INTAKE MANIFOLD

CAMSHAFT

CAMSHAFT CARRIER

TIMING COVER

TIMING BELT

EXHAUST MANIFOLD

CYLINDER HEAD

Exploded view of the upper engine assembly—1.6L engine

2.0L ENGINE

1. Relieve the fuel system pressure.
2. Disconnect the terminals from the battery and chassis ground wire.
3. Position a clean drain pan under the radiator, remove the lower radiator hose and drain the cooling system. Remove the upper radiator hose and the heater hoses.
4. Remove the air cleaner.

5. Remove or disconnect all wires and connectors at the following components;
Engine harness bulk head
Master cylinder
A/C relay cluster switches
Wiper motor
Cooling fan, relay and ground connection
ECM

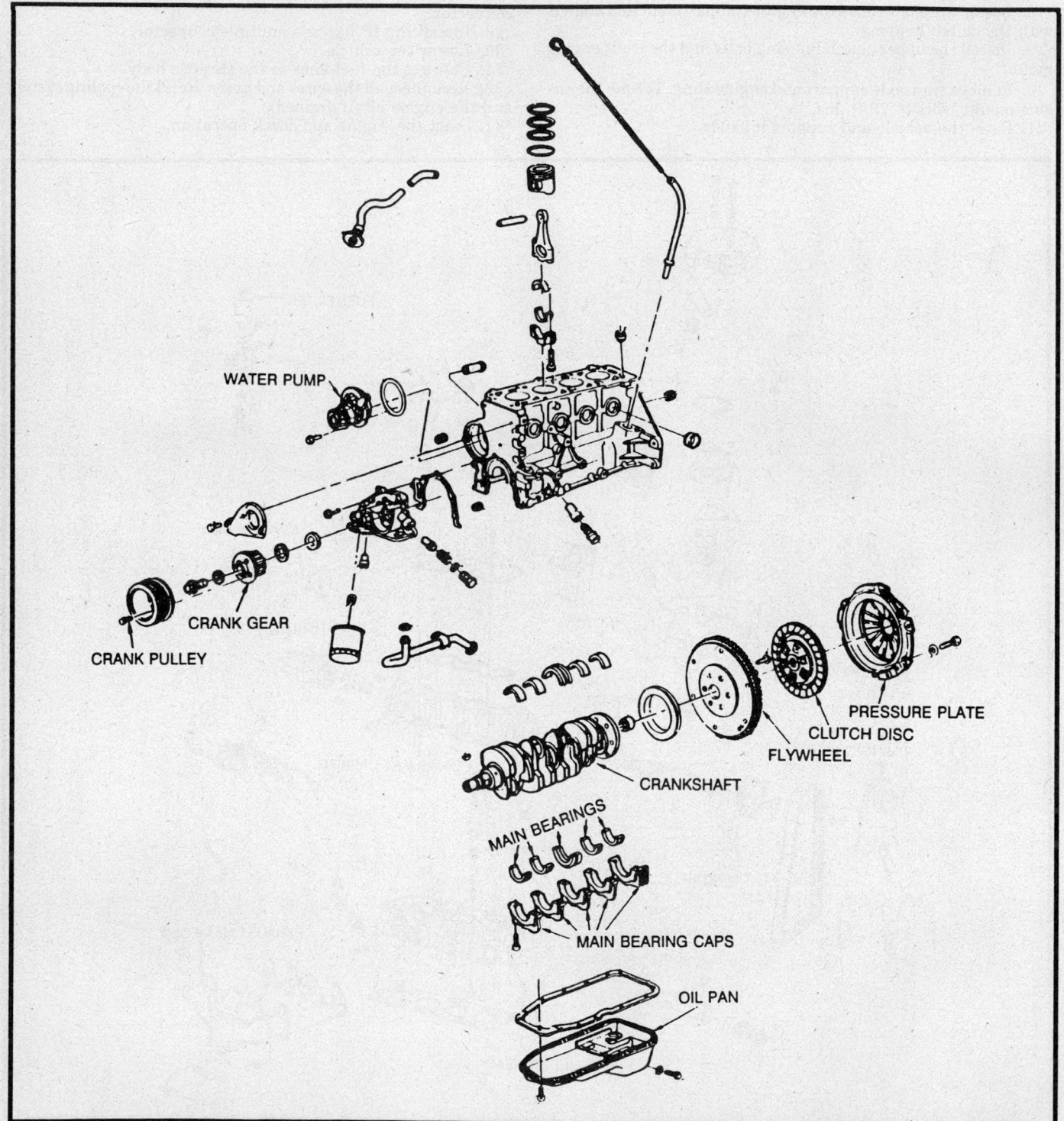

WATER PUMP

CRANK GEAR

CRANK PULLEY

PRESSURE PLATE

CLUTCH DISC

FLYWHEEL

CRANKSHAFT

MAIN BEARINGS

MAIN BEARING CAPS

OIL PAN

Exploded view of the lower engine assembly—1.6L engine

Temperature switch at the thermostat housing.
6. Remove the vacuum hoses from the power brake booster, vacuum sensor, intake manifold to vapor canister and throttle valve body to vapor canister.

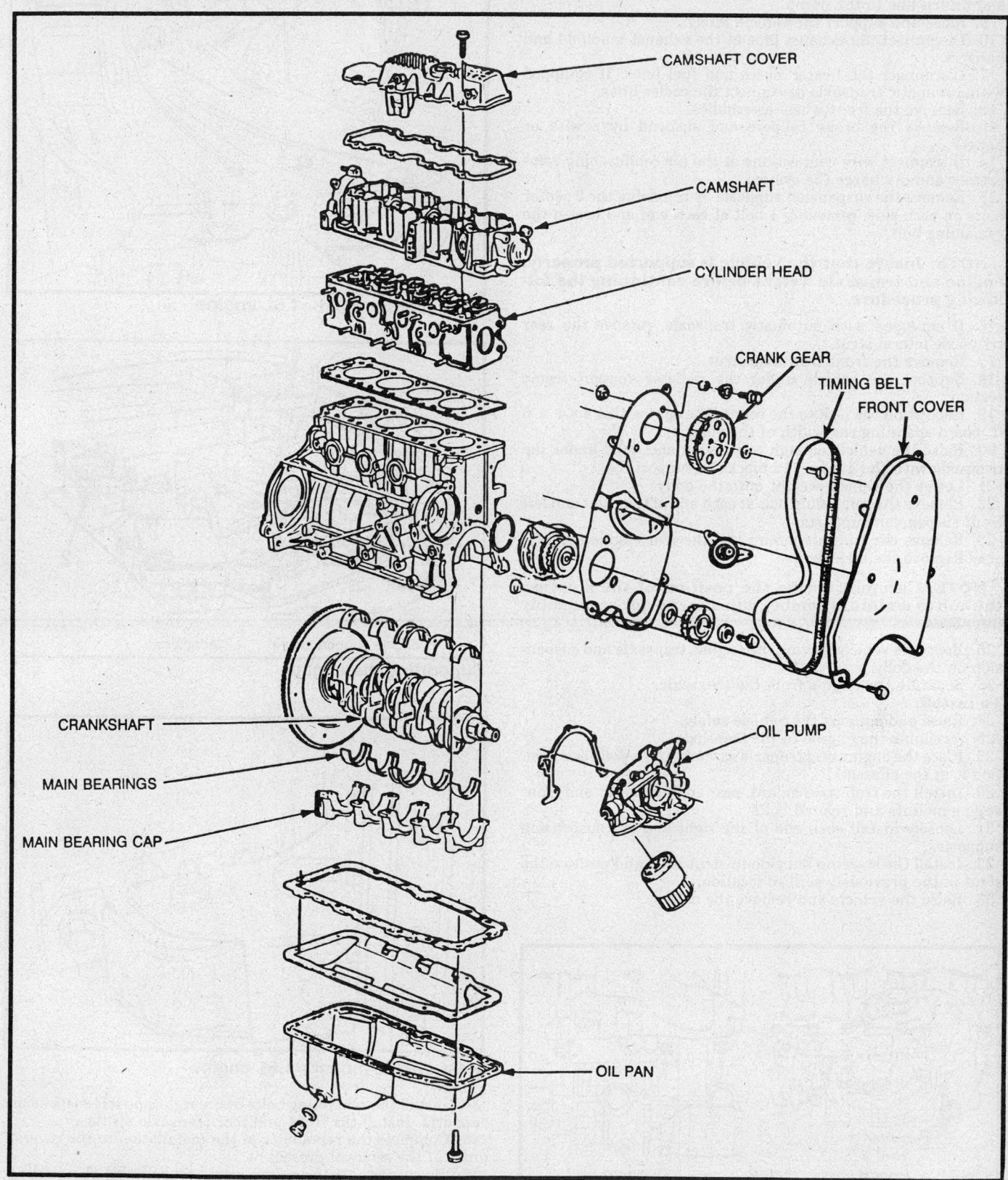

Exploded view of the engine assembly—2.0L engine

7. Disconnect the throttle cable and shift cable.

8. Disconnect the hoses at the power steering cut off switch and return line to the pump.

9. Raise and support the vehicle safely.

10. Disconnect the exhaust pipe at the exhaust manifold and hangers.

11. Disconnect the heater hoses and fuel lines. If equipped with automatic transaxle disconnect the cooler lines.

12. Remove the front wheel assemblies.

13. Remove the brake calipers and suspend by a wire or hanger.

14. Disconnect wire connections at the air conditioning compressor and discharge the system.

15. Remove the suspension supports by removing the 2 center bolts on each side, removing 1 bolt at each end and loosen the remaining bolt.

NOTE: Insure that the vehicle is supported properly, engine and transaxle weight before continuing the following procedure.

16. If equipped with automatic transaxle, remove the rear transaxle lateral strut.

17. Remove the front transaxle strut.

18. Support the vehicle under the radiator support frame section.

19. Reposition the jack to the rear of the cowl with a 4 × 4 × 6 ft. board spanning the width of the vehicle.

20. Raise the vehicle enough to position and dolly under the transaxle with the 4 × 4 × 12 blocks as support.

21. Lower the vehicle weight onto the dolly.

22. Remove the remaining bolt at each end of the right and left front suspension supports.

23. Remove the transaxle mount and the rear engine mount.

24. Remove the strut bolts.

NOTE: Carefully scribe the position of the strut on the hub to maintain camber adjustments for reassembly purposes.

25. Raise the vehicle leaving the engine, transaxle and suspension on the dolly.

26. Separate the engine from the transaxle.

To install:

27. Raise and support the vehicle safely.

28. Assemble the engine to the transaxle.

29. Place the engine and transaxle assembly on a dolly and position it in the chassis.

30. Install the transaxle mount, rear engine mount and front engine mounts and related bolts.

31. Loosely install each end of the right and left suspension supports.

32. Install the steering knuckle-to-strut bolts and position the strut in the previously scribed location.

33. Raise the vehicle and remove the dolly.

Front motor mount—1.6L engine

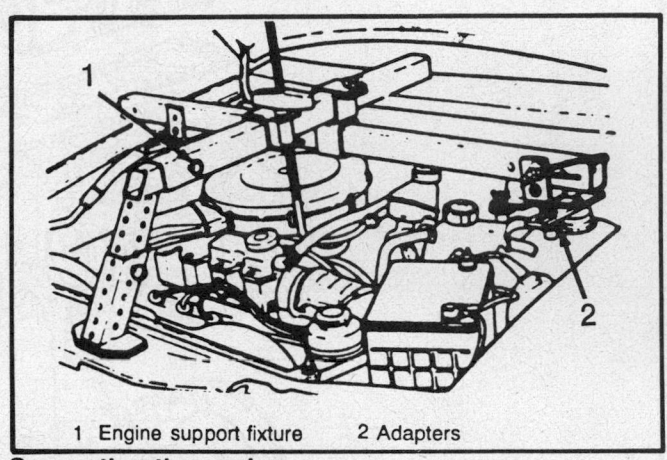

| 1 Engine support fixture | 2 Adapters |

Supporting the engine

Rear engine mount—1.6L engine

34. Install the remaining bolts in the right and left suspension supports. Install the front and rear transaxle struts.

35. Complete the remainder of the installation in the reverse order of the removal procedure.

36. Reconnect all the wires and hoses. Refill the cooling system.

37. Start the engine and check proper operation.

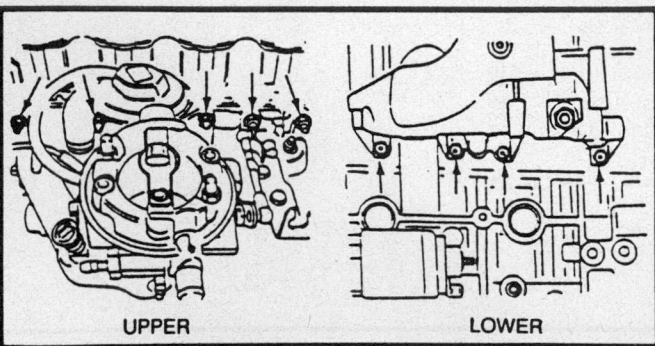

| UPPER | LOWER |

Intake manifold mounting

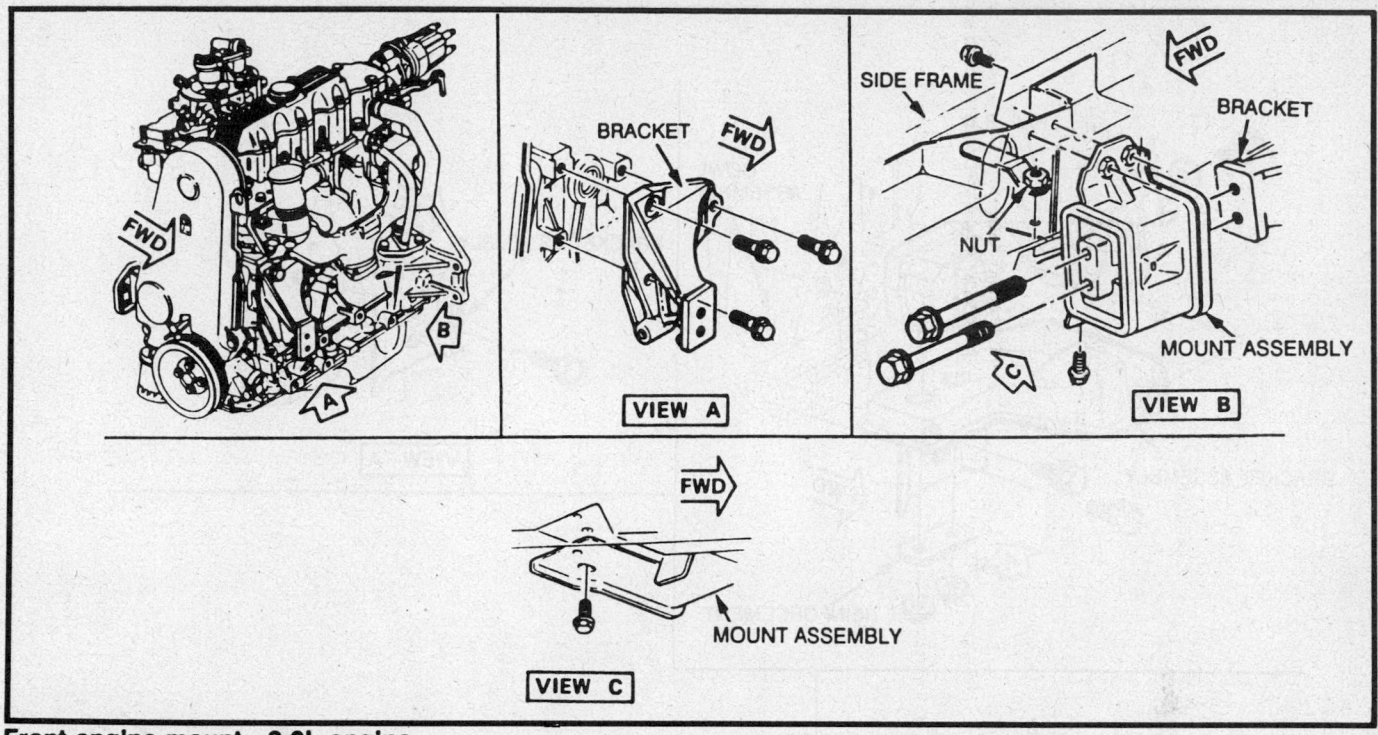

Front engine mount — 2.0L engine

Engine Mount

Removal and Installation

1. Disconnect the negative battery cable.
2. Using an engine support fixture tool, center it on the cowl and attach it to the engine. Raise the engine slightly to take the weight off of the engine mounts.
3. From the front of the engine, remove the engine mount bolts and the mount.
4. Inspect the engine mount for deterioration and replace it, if necessary.
5. To install, reverse the removal procedures. Torque the engine mount to bracket bolts to 29 ft. lbs. and the engine mount to engine bolts to 29 ft. lbs.

Intake Manifold

Removal and Installation

1. Relieve the fuel system pressure.
2. Disconnect the negative battery cable.
3. Position a clean drain pan under the radiator, remove the lower radiator hose and drain the cooling system.
4. Remove the air cleaner. Detach the cable from the throttle body, the intake manifold bracket and the downshift cable.
5. Loosen the alternator and swing it aside.
6. Disconnect the electrical wiring connectors from the throttle body, the intake manifold, the engine wiring harness and the thermostat housing.
7. Remove the intake manifold mounting nuts and washers, remove the manifold from the engine.
8. Clean the gasket mounting surfaces.
9. To install, use a new gasket and reverse the removal procedures. Torque the intake manifold to cylinder head nuts/washers to 16 ft. lbs. Refill the cooling system. Install the air cleaner and the negative battery cable. Start the engine and check for coolant leaks.

Exhaust Manifold

Removal and Installation

1. Disconnect the negative battery cable.
2. Remove the air cleaner. Disconnect the spark plug wires from the spark plugs and the electrical connector at the oxygen sensor. Remove the manifold pre-heater.
3. Remove the exhaust pipe nuts and the exhaust manifold mounting nuts/washers. Remove the exhaust manifold from the engine.
4. Clean the gasket mounting surfaces.
5. To install, use a new gasket and torque the exhaust manifold to cylinder head nuts to 16 ft. lbs. Tighten the exhaust pipe to exhaust manifold nuts to 19 ft. lbs. Attach electrical connector to oxygen sensor and install the pre-heater. Install air cleaner and connect the negative battery cable. Start the engine and check for exhaust leaks.

Valve System

VALVE ADJUSTMENT

The valve train uses hydraulic valve compensators, located in the cylinder head, which eliminate the need for valve lash adjustment.

VALVE LIFTERS/ROCKER ARMS

Removal and Installation

1.6L ENGINE

1. Disconnect the negative battery cable.
2. Remove the camshaft carrier cover bolts and the cover.
3. Remove the spark plugs.

NOTE: When working on a particular cylinder, be sure to rotate the crankshaft until the piston of that cylinder is located on the TDC of its compression stroke.

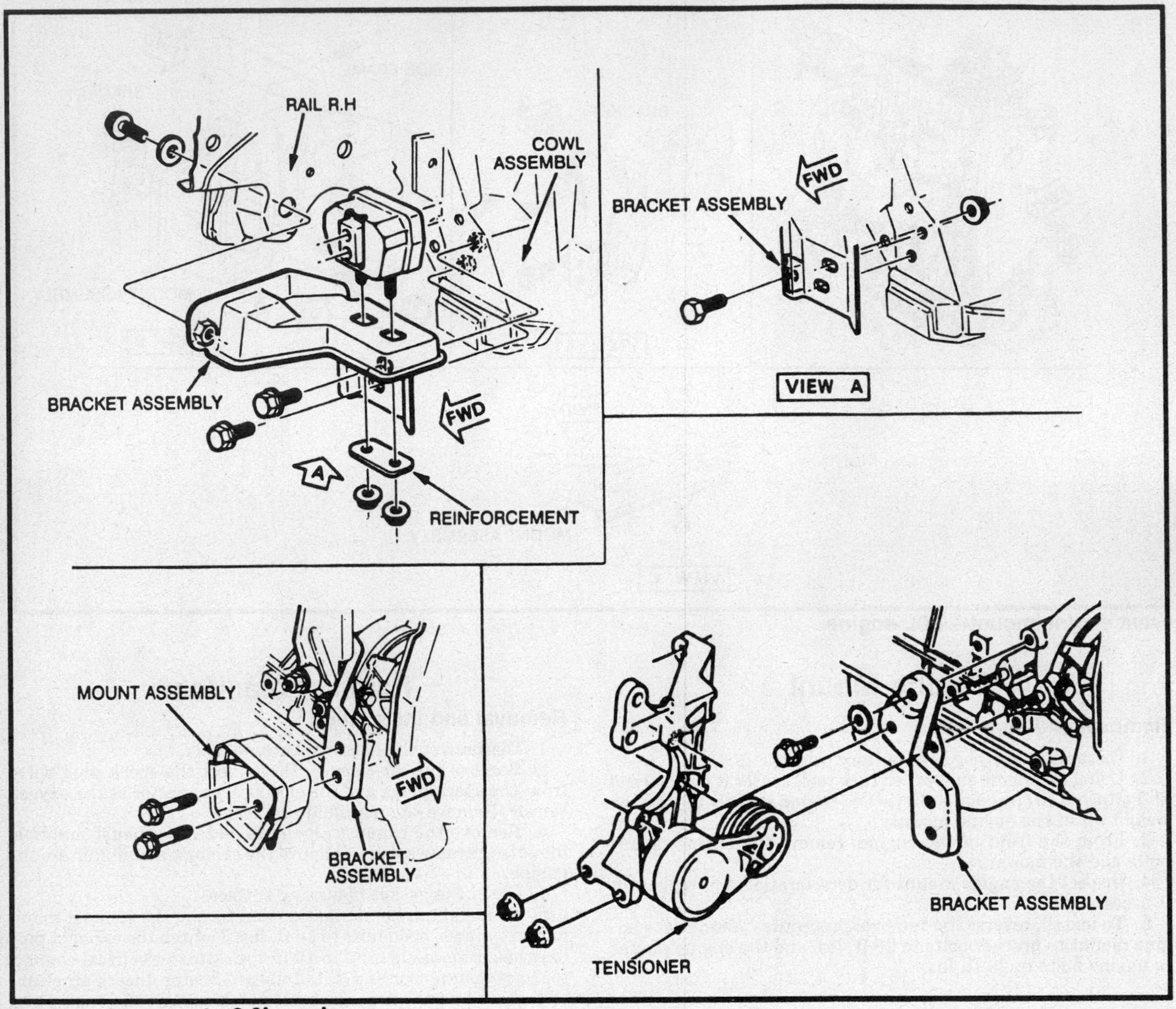

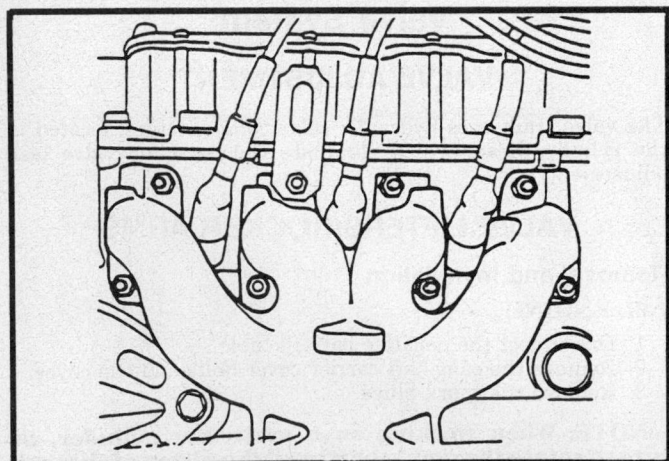

RAIL R.H

COWL ASSEMBLY

BRACKET ASSEMBLY

FWD

VIEW A

BRACKET ASSEMBLY

FWD

A

REINFORCEMENT

MOUNT ASSEMBLY

FWD

BRACKET ASSEMBLY

BRACKET ASSEMBLY

TENSIONER

Rear engine mount—2.0L engine

Exhaust manifold mounting

4. Using a air line adapter tool, install it into the spark plug hole of the cylinder being serviced and apply compressed air.

NOTE: Engine components could move due to compressed air, causing belts and pulleys to rotate with considerable force.

5. Using a valve spring compressor tool, compress the valve springs.

6. Remove the rocker arms and the valve lifters; it is important that all of the valve train parts are kept in the order that they were removed.

7. Inspect and/or replace the worn parts.

8. Clean the gasket mounting surfaces of the camshaft carrier and cover.

9. Installation is the reverse order of the removal procedure. Use a new gasket. Install all parts in their original position. Torque the camshaft carrier cover bolts to 6 ft. lbs. (8 Nm).

2.0L ENGINE

1. Disconnect the negative battery cable.

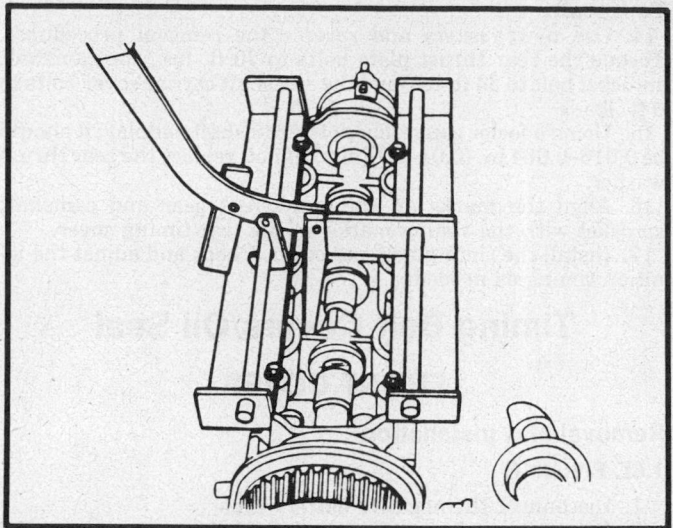

Using the Valve Spring Compressor tool to compress the valve springs

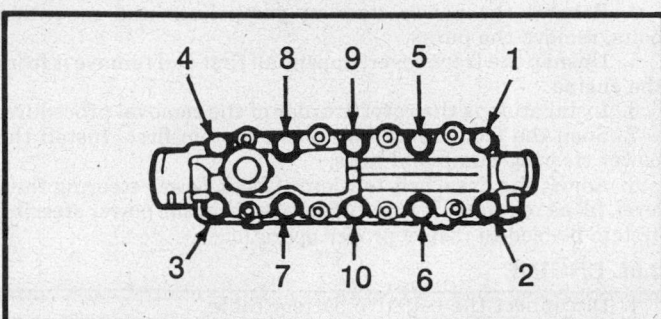

The camshaft carrier/cylinder head bolt removal sequence

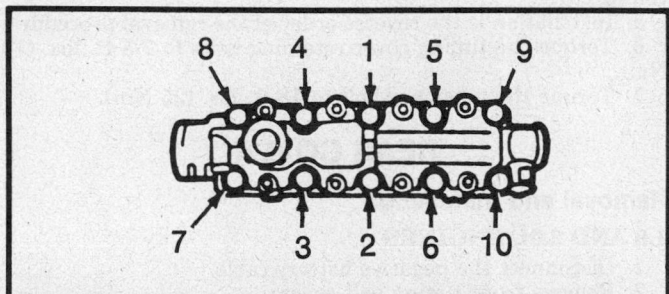

The camshaft carrier/cylinder head bolt torquing sequence

2. Remove the camshaft carrier cover bolts and the cover.

3. Using a valve spring compressor tool, compress the valve springs.

4. Remove the rocker arms and the valve lifters; it is important that all of the valve train parts are kept in the order that they were removed.

5. Inspect and/or replace the worn parts.

6. Clean the gasket mounting surfaces of the camshaft carrier and cover.

7. Installation is the reverse order of the removal procedure. Use a new gasket. Install all parts in their original position. Torque the camshaft carrier cover bolts to 6 ft. lbs. (8 Nm).

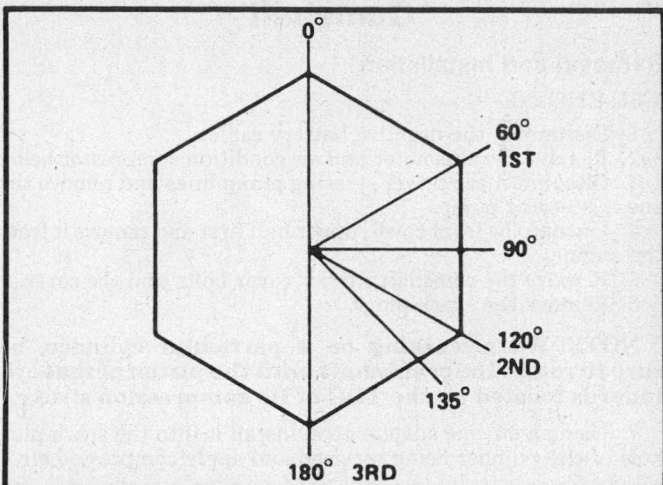

View of the camshaft carrier/cylinder head bolt torque degree chart

Cylinder Head

Removal and Installation

NOTE: Cylinder head gasket replacement is necessary if cylinder head/camshaft carrier bolts are loosened. These bolts should only be loosened when the engine is cold. New cylinder head bolts must be used, because the head bolts are of the stretch bolt design.

1. Relieve the fuel system pressure.

2. Disconnect the negative battery cable.

3. Remove the lower radiator hose and drain the cooling system. Remove the upper radiator hose and the heater hoses.

4. Remove the air cleaner. Detach the throttle cable and remove it from the intake manifold. Remove the downshift cable.

5. Disconnect the electrical wiring connectors from the throttle body, the intake manifold and the oxygen sensor. Disconnect the engine wiring harness at the thermostat housing.

6. Disconnect the exhaust pipe from the exhaust manifold. Remove the alternator bracket and lay the alternator aside.

7. Remove the accessory drive belts, the front covers and the timing belt.

8. Remove the camshaft carrier/cylinder head bolts (in sequence).

9. Remove the camshaft carrier, the rocker arms and the valve lash compensators.

10. Remove the cylinder head with the intake and exhaust manifolds attached.

11. Clean the cylinder head gasket mounting surfaces.

To install:

12. Use a new head gasket, apply a 3mm bead of anerobic sealant to the camshaft carrier sealing surface, use new camshaft carrier/cylinder head bolts and reverse the removal procedures.

13. Torque the camshaft carrier/cylinder head bolts to 18 ft. lbs. (in sequence), then, turn an additional 60 degrees, turn another 60 degrees (to 120 degrees) and finally to 150 degress for the 1.6L engine and 180 degress for the 2.0L engine.

14. Refill the cooling system.

15. Start the engine and allow it to reach normal operating temperature. After operating temperature is reached, torque the camshaft carrier/cylinder head bolts an additional 30–50 degrees. Check for coolant and oil leaks.

16. Check the ignition timing and adjust if necessary.

Camshaft

Removal and Installation

1.6L ENGINE

1. Disconnect the negative battery cable.
2. Remove the alternator and air condition compressor belts.
3. Disconnect the power steering pump lines and remove the power steering pump.
4. Unsnap the front cover, upper half first and remove it from the engine.
5. Remove the camshaft carrier cover bolts and the cover.
6. Remove the spark plugs.

NOTE: When working on a particular cylinder, be sure to rotate the crankshaft until the piston of that cylinder is located on the TDC of its compression stroke.

7. Using a air line adapter tool, install it into the spark plug hole of the cylinder being serviced and apply compressed air.

NOTE: Engine components could move due to compressed air, causing belts and pulleys to rotate with considerable force.

8. Using a valve spring compressor tool, compress the valve springs.
9. Remove the rocker arms and the valve lifters; it is important that all of the valve train parts are kept in the order that they were removed.
10. Hold the camshaft firmly with the proper tool and loosen the camshaft retaining bolt.
11. Using a sprocket remover tool, remove the washer and camshaft sprocket.
12. Remove the distributor.
13. Remove the camshaft thrust plate from the rear carrier.
14. Slide the camshaft out from the rear.
15. Clean the gasket mounting surfaces of the carrier and the cover. Inspect and replace any worn or damaged parts.

To install:

16. Use new gaskets and reverse the removal procedures. Torque the rear thrust plate bolts to 70 ft. lbs., the camshaft sprocket bolt to 34 ft. lbs. and the camshaft carrier cover bolts to 6 ft. lbs.
17. Using a feeler gauge, check the camshaft endplay; it should be 0.016–0.064 in. (0.04–0.16mm), if not, replace the rear thrust washer.
18. Align the marks on the crankshaft gear and camshaft sprocket with the timing marks on the rear timing cover.
19. Install the timing belt and cover. Check and adjust the ignition timing as needed.

2.0L ENGINE

1. Disconnect the negative battery cable.
2. Remove the air cleaner and breather hoses.
3. Remove the camshaft carrier cover bolts and the cover.
4. Remove the serpentine belt.
5. Remove the alternator and bracket from the carrier.
6. Using a valve spring compressor tool, compress the valve springs.
7. Remove the rocker arms and the valve lifters; it is important that all of the valve train parts are kept in the order that they were removed.
8. Hold the camshaft firmly with the proper tool and loosen the camshaft retaining bolt.
9. Using a sprocket remover tool, remove the washer and camshaft sprocket.
10. Remove the distributor.
11. Remove the camshaft thrust plate from the rear carrier.
12. Slide the camshaft out from the rear.
13. Clean the gasket mounting surfaces of the carrier and the cover. Inspect and replace any worn or damaged parts.

To install:

14. Use new gaskets and reverse the removal procedures. Torque the rear thrust plate bolts to 70 ft. lbs., the camshaft sprocket bolt to 34 ft. lbs. and the camshaft carrier cover bolts to 6 ft. lbs.
15. Using a feeler gauge, check the camshaft endplay; it should be 0.016–0.064 in. (0.04–0.16mm), if not, replace the rear thrust washer.
16. Align the marks on the crankshaft gear and camshaft sprocket with the timing marks on the rear timing cover.
17. Install the timing belt and cover. Check and adjust the ignition timing as needed.

Timing Belt Covers/Oil Seal

FRONT COVER

Removal and Installation

1.6L ENGINE

1. Disconnect the negative battery cable.
2. Loosen the alternator mounting bolts and remove the drive belt from the alternator pulley.
3. Loosen the air conditioning compressor mounting bolts and remove the drive belt from the compressor pulley.
4. Remove the power steering pump lines and mounting bolts, remove the pump.
5. Unsnap the front cover, upper half first and remove it from the engine.
6. Installation is the reverse order of the removal procedure.
7. Snap the front cover into place, bottom first. Install the power steering pump and lines.
8. Adjust the drive belt tensions. Check power steering fluid level, fill as required. It is recommended that the power steering system be bled to insure proper operation.

2.0L ENGINE

1. Disconnect the negative battery cable.
2. Loosen the serpentine belt tensioner bolt and allow the tensioner to swing downward.
3. Remove the serpentine belt.
4. Remove the timing cover retaining bolts and remove the timing cover.
5. Installation is the reverse order of the removal procedure.
6. Torque the timing cover retaining bolts to 7.5 ft. lbs. (10 Nm).
7. Torque the tensioner bolt to 18 ft. lbs. (25 Nm).

REAR COVER

Removal and Installation

1.6 AND 2.0L ENGINES

1. Disconnect the negative battery cable.
2. Remove front timing belt cover.
3. Loosen timing belt tensioner and remove timing belt.
4. Remove camshaft sprocket.
5. Remove rear timing cover bolts and remove cover by slipping it around the water pump.
6. To install, slip cover around water pump and install the retaining bolts. Install the camshaft sprocket, tighten to 34 ft. lbs. Slide timing belt over sprocket and adjust tension to specification. Install front cover.

OIL SEAL

1. Disconnect the negative battery cable.
2. Remove the timing belt front cover.
3. Mark the relationship of the timing belt to the crankshaft and camshaft sprockets. Loosen the timing belt tensioner and remove the timing belt.
4. Remove the crankshaft pulley retaining bolt. Remove the

crankshaft sprocket and the rear thrust washer. Remove the rear timing cover mounting screws (4) and remove the cover.

5. Using a small pry bar, pry the front oil seal from the oil pump housing.

6. Using the protective sleeve of the seal installation tool, install it onto the crankshaft.

7. Using a new front oil seal, lubricate the seal lips with engine oil and install it onto the protective sleeve.

8. Using the seal installation tool, install the new oil seal into the oil pump until it seats.

9. To complete the installation, install the rear timing cover, align the marks made prior to removing the timing belt and install the belt. Adjust the tension to specification. Install the crankshaft pulley and sprocket, tighten to 40 ft. lbs.

10. Install the front timing cover and adjust all accessory drive belts to specification. Check ignition timing.

Timing Sprockets and Belt

Removal and Installation
CAMSHAFT SPROCKET

1. Disconnect the negative battery cable.
2. Remove the timing belt front cover.
3. Mark the relationship of the timing belt to the crankshaft and camshaft sprockets. Loosen the timing belt tensioner and remove the timing belt.
4. Remove the camshaft carrier cover to camshaft carrier bolts and remove the cover from the engine.
5. Hold the camshaft in place with an open end wrench and remove the sprocket bolt, washer and sprocket.
6. To install, reverse the removal procedures. Torque the camshaft sprocket bolt to 34 ft. lbs. and the camshaft carrier cover bolts to 6 ft. lbs. Install the timing belt, aligning the marks made prior to removal. Check and adjust the ignition timing as needed.

CRANKSHAFT SPROCKET

1. Disconnect the negative battery cable.
2. Remove the timing belt front cover.
3. Mark the relationship of the timing belt to the crankshaft and camshaft sprockets. Loosen the timing belt tensioner and remove the timing belt.
4. Remove the crankshaft pulley bolt, pulley and thrust washer. Remove the crankshaft sprocket and the Woodruff key.

NOTE: It is recommended to replace the front oil seal when the crankshaft pulley is removed.

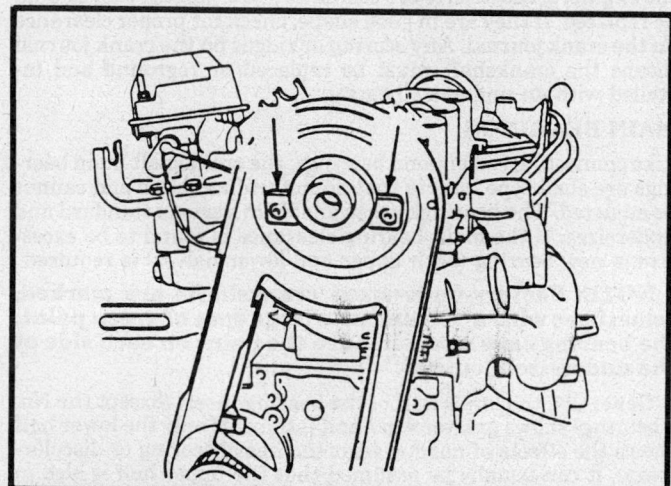

Timing belt cover attachment

5. To install, reverse the removal procedures. Torque the crankshaft pulley bolt to 40 ft. lbs. Install the timing belt, aligning marks made prior to removal. Check and adjust the ignition timing. Adjust the accessory drive belt tensions.

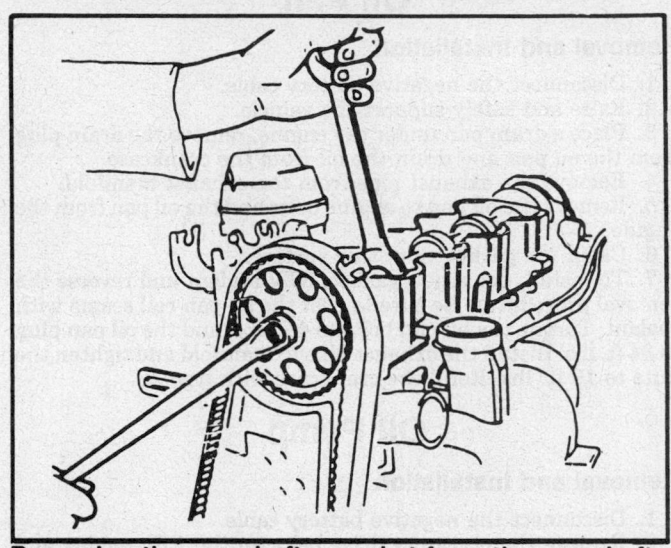

Removing the camshaft sprocket from the camshaft

Pistons, Rings and Rod Positioning

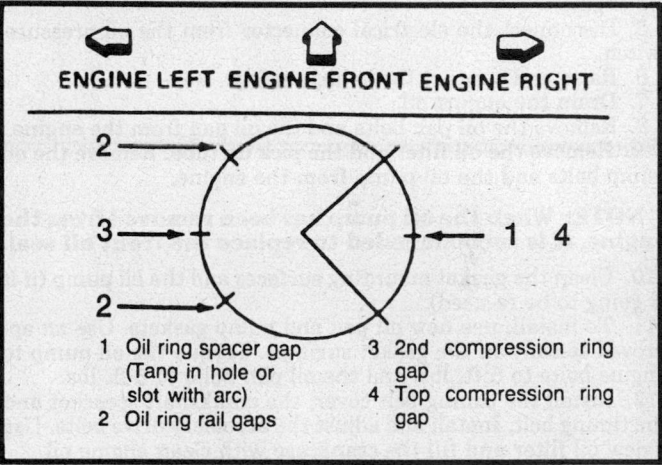

1 Oil ring spacer gap (Tang in hole or slot with arc)
2 Oil ring rail gaps
3 2nd compression ring gap
4 Top compression ring gap

Location of the piston ring gaps

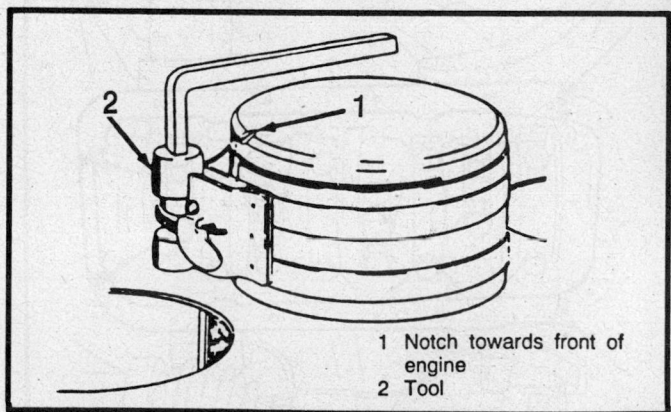

1 Notch towards front of engine
2 Tool

Installing the piston assembly into the engine block

ENGINE LUBRICATION SYSTEM

Oil Pan

Removal and Installation

1. Disconnect the negative battery cable.
2. Raise and safely support the vehicle.
3. Place a drain pan under the engine, remove the drain plug from the oil pan and drain the oil from the crankcase.
4. Remove the exhaust pipe from the exhaust manifold.
5. Remove the oil pan to engine bolts and the oil pan from the engine.
6. Clean the gasket mounting surfaces.
7. To install, use a new gasket, RTV sealant and reverse the removal procedures. Be sure to coat the oil pan rail seams with sealant. Torque the oil pan bolts to 4 ft. lbs. and the oil pan plug to 34 ft. lbs. Install the exhaust pipe to manifold and tighten the nuts to 19 ft. lbs. Refill the crankcase with new oil.

Oil Pump

Removal and Installation

1. Disconnect the negative battery cable.
2. Remove the accessory drive belts on the 1.6L engine and the serpentine belt on the 2.0L engine. Remove the crankshaft pulley assembly.
3. Remove the front timing belt cover and the timing belt.
4. Remove the rear timing belt cover bolts and the cover from the engine.
5. Disconnect the electrical connector from the oil pressure switch.
6. Raise and support the vehicle safely.
7. Drain the engine oil.
8. Remove the oil pan bolts and the oil pan from the engine.
9. Remove the oil filter and the pick up tube. Remove the oil pump bolts and the oil pump from the engine.

NOTE: When the oil pump has been removed from the engine, it is recommended to replace the front oil seal.

10. Clean the gasket mounting surfaces and the oil pump (if it is going to be re-used).
11. To install, use new oil pan and pump gaskets. Use an approved sealant on the gasket surfaces. Torque the oil pump to engine bolts to 5 ft. lbs. and the oil pan bolts to 6 ft. lbs.
12. Install the timing belt cover, the crankshaft sprocket and the timing belt. Install and adjust the accessory drive belts. Use a new oil filter and fill the crankcase with clean engine oil.

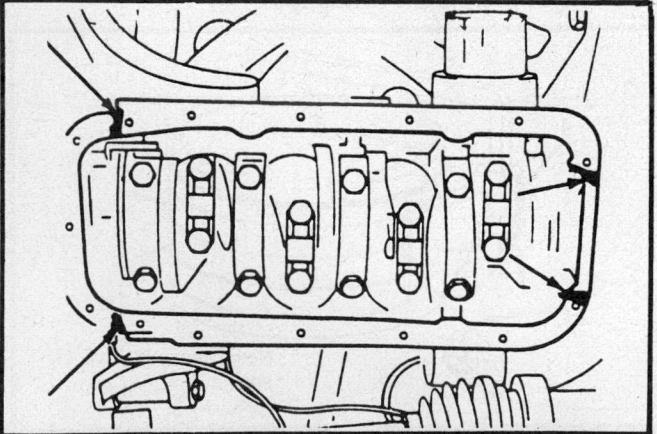

Installing sealant onto the oil pan rail seams

13. Run the engine and check for leaks, also check ignition timing.

Rear Main Oil Seal

Removal and Installation

1. Disconnect the negative battery cable.
2. Raise and support the vehicle safely. Remove the transaxle.
3. If equipped with a manual transaxle, remove the pressure plate/clutch disc assembly. Remove the flywheel bolts.
4. Using a small pry bar, pry the rear main oil seal from its retainer. Clean all gasket mating surfaces thoroughly.
5. Lubricate the new oil seal lips with engine oil. Using the seal installation tool, drive the new rear oil seal into the block until it seats.
6. To complete the installation, reverse the removal procedures. Torque the flywheel bolts to 25 ft. lbs. If equipped with a manual transaxle, turn the flywheel to crankshaft bolts 30–45 degrees beyond the torquing specifications.

Connecting and Main Bearings

Replacement

CONNECTING ROD BEARINGS
Connecting rod bearings consist of 2 halves or bearing inserts which are interchangeable in the rod and cap. When the bearing inserts are placed into position, the ends extend slightly beyond the rod and cap surfaces, so when the rod bolts are torqued, the inserts will be clamped tightly in place to insure positive seating and to prevent turning; a tang holds the inserts in place.

NOTE: The ends of the bearing inserts must never be filed flush with the mating surface of the rod and cap.

If a rod bearing becomes noisy or is worn so that its clearance on the crank journal is excessive, a new bearing of the correct undersize must be selected and installed since there is no provision for adjustment.

NOTE: Under no circumstances should the rod end or cap be filed to adjust the bearing clearance, nor should shims of any kind be used.

Inspect the rod bearings while the rod assemblies are out of the engine. If the inserts are scored or show flaking, they should be replaced. If they are in good shape, check for proper clearance on the crank journal. Any scoring or ridges on the crank journal means the crankshaft must be replaced or reground and installed with an undersize bearing.

MAIN BEARINGS
Like connecting rod big-end bearings, the crankshaft main bearings are shell-type inserts that do not utilize shims and cannot be adjusted. The bearings are available in various standard and undersizes. If the main bearing clearance is found to be excessive, a new bearing (both upper and lower halves) is required.

NOTE: Factory-undersized crankshafts are marked, sometimes with a "9" and/or a large spot of green paint; the bearing caps also will have the paint on each side of the undersized journal.

Generally, the lower half of the bearing insert (except the No. 1 bearing) shows greater wear and fatigue. If only the lower half shows the effects of normal wear (no heavy scoring or discoloration), it can usually be assumed that the upper half is also in good shape; conversely, if the lower half is heavily worn or damaged, both halves should be replaced.

FRONT SUSPENSION AND STEERING

For front suspension component removal and installation procedures, refer to unit repair section.

For steering wheel removal and installation, refer to electrical control section.

Steering Rack And Pinion

Adjustment

1. Raise and support the vehicle safely.
2. Center the steering wheel.
3. Loosen the adjuster plug locknut. Turn the adjuster plug clockwise until it bottoms, then, back it out 50–70 degrees.
4. Inspect the steering pinion torque, it should be 8–20 inch lbs. for manual steering gear and 16 inch lbs. for power steering gear
5. After adjusting the pinion torque, hold the adjuster stationary and torque the adjuster plug locknut to 50 ft. lbs.

Removal and Installation
MANUAL

1. Disconnect the negative battery cable.
2. Position the steering wheel in the straight-ahead position. Remove the steering column to coupling pinch bolt and the pinion shaft to coupling pinch bolt.
3. Remove the air cleaner.
4. Raise and support the vehicle safely.
5. At the center of the manual steering assembly, cut the plate lock in half before attempting to remove the lock plate bolts; do not attempt to reuse the lock plate. Remove both tie rod to steering rack/pinion center bolts.
6. If equipped, remove both steering damper brackets.
7. Remove the steering assembly to chassis bolts and the dash seal from the rack/pinion. Remove the steering assembly through the right-wheel opening.

NOTE: If the studs were removed with the mounting studs, reinstall the studs and retorque. If removed for the 2nd time, reuse the stud with thread locking compound.

7. To install, use new self locking nuts, a new lock plate and reverse the removal procedures. Pay attention to the direction of the notches in the lock plate. Torque the steering rack/pinion to chassis nuts to 28 ft. lbs. and the tie rod to steering rack/pin-

ion bolts to 65 ft. lbs. Adjust the manual steering rack/pinion play.

NOTE: When installing the coupling onto the steering pinion, push it downward and torque the pinion to coupling pinch bolt to 29 ft. lbs. When installing the steering spindle, pull it upward until it stops on the spindle ball bearing and torque the upper pinch bolt to 34 ft. lbs.

POWER

1. Disconnect the negative battery cable.
2. Position the steering wheel in the straight-ahead position. Remove the steering column to coupling pinch bolt and the pinion shaft to coupling pinch bolt.
3. Remove the air cleaner.
4. At the center of the power steering rack/pinion, cut the plate lock in half before attempting to remove the lock plate bolts; do not attempt to reuse the lock plate. Remove both tie rod to steering rack/pinion (center) bolts.
5. Remove the high pressure hoses from the power steering rack/pinion.
6. Remove the steering rack/pinion to chassis bolts and the dash seal from the rack/pinion. Remove the steering rack/pinion through the right-wheel opening.

NOTE: If the studs were removed with the mounting studs, reinstall the studs and retorque. If removed for

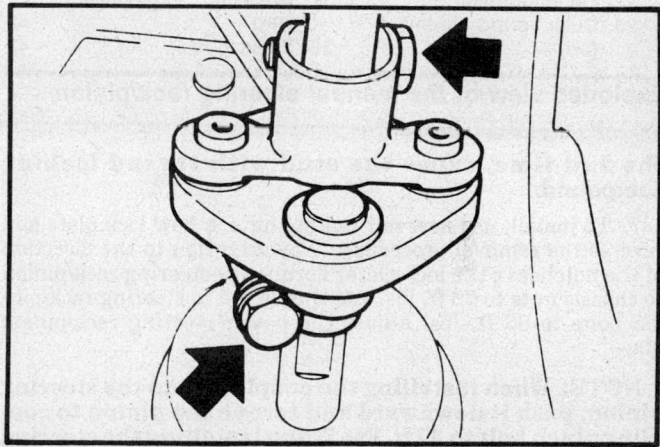
View of the steering column pinch bolts

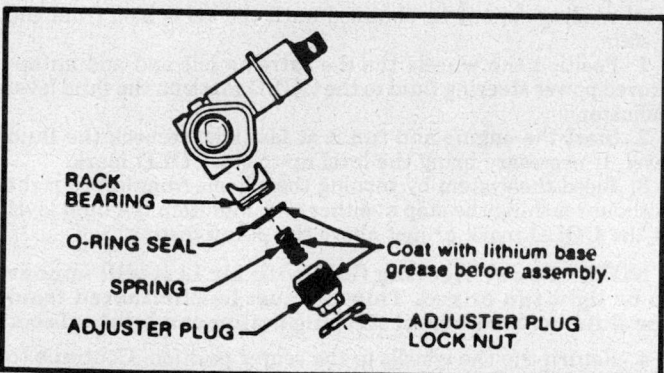
Exploded view of the manual steering gear adjustment assembly

RACK
BEARING
O-RING SEAL
SPRING
ADJUSTER PLUG
Coat with lithium base grease before assembly.
ADJUSTER PLUG
LOCK NUT

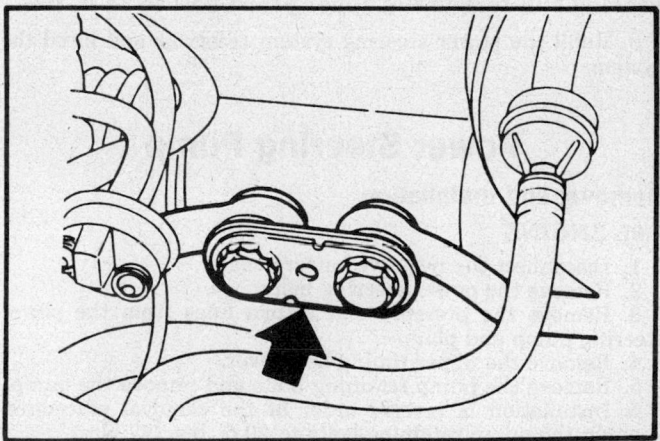
View of the manual steering rack/pinion lock plate

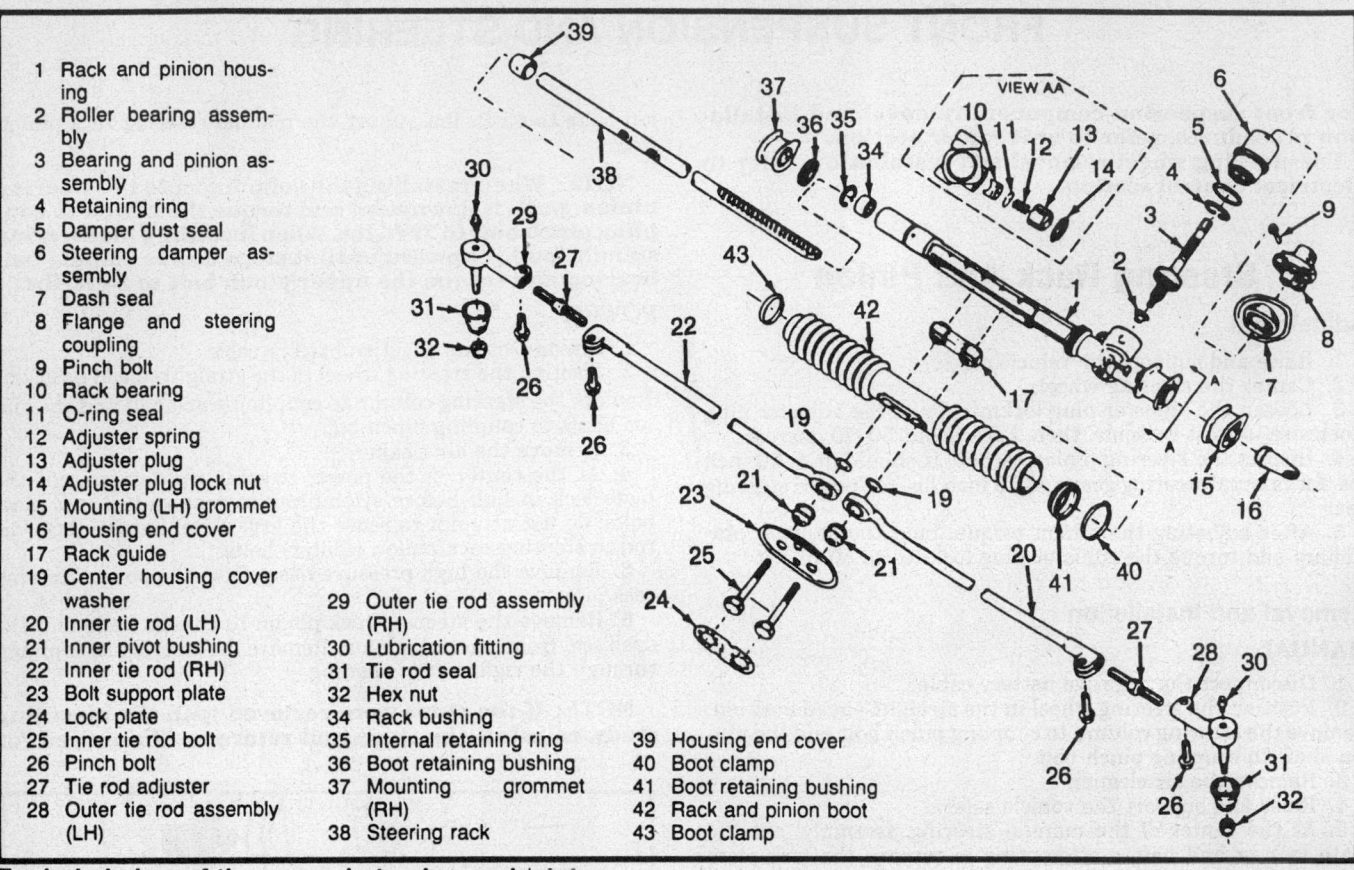

1 Rack and pinion housing
2 Roller bearing assembly
3 Bearing and pinion assembly
4 Retaining ring
5 Damper dust seal
6 Steering damper assembly
7 Dash seal
8 Flange and steering coupling
9 Pinch bolt
10 Rack bearing
11 O-ring seal
12 Adjuster spring
13 Adjuster plug
14 Adjuster plug lock nut
15 Mounting (LH) grommet
16 Housing end cover
17 Rack guide
19 Center housing cover washer
20 Inner tie rod (LH)
21 Inner pivot bushing
22 Inner tie rod (RH)
23 Bolt support plate
24 Lock plate
25 Inner tie rod bolt
26 Pinch bolt
27 Tie rod adjuster
28 Outer tie rod assembly (LH)

29 Outer tie rod assembly (RH)
30 Lubrication fitting
31 Tie rod seal
32 Hex nut
34 Rack bushing
35 Internal retaining ring
36 Boot retaining bushing
37 Mounting grommet (RH)
38 Steering rack

39 Housing end cover
40 Boot clamp
41 Boot retaining bushing
42 Rack and pinion boot
43 Boot clamp

Exploded view of the manual steering rack/pinion

the 2nd time, reuse the stud with thread locking compound.

7. To install, use new self locking nuts, a new lock plate and reverse the removal procedures. Pay attention to the direction of the notches in the lock plate. Torque the steering rack/pinion to chassis nuts to 28 ft. lbs. and the tie rod to steering rack/pinion bolts to 65 ft. lbs. Adjust the power steering rack/pinion play.

NOTE: When installing the coupling onto the steering pinion, push it downward and torque the pinion to coupling pinch bolt to 37 ft. lbs. When installing the steering spindle, pull it upwards until it stops on the spindle ball bearing and torque the upper pinch bolt to 34 ft. lbs.

8. Refill the power steering system reservoir and bleed the system.

Power Steering Pump

Removal and Installation

1.6L ENGINE

1. Disconnect the negative battery cable.
2. Remove the power steering belt.
3. Remove the pressure and return lines from the power steering pump and plug.
4. Remove the upper timing belt cover.
5. Remove the pump retaining bolts and remove the pump.
6. Installation is reverse order of the removal procedure. Tighten the pump retaining bolts to 20 ft. lbs. (27 Nm).
7. Fill the pump with new fluid and bleed the system.

2.0 L ENGINE

1. Disconnect the negative battery cable.
2. Remove the serpentine belt.
3. Remove the pressure and return lines from the power steering pump and plug.
4. Remove the pump retaining bolts which are accessible through the holes of the pulley and remove the pump from the bracket.
5. Installation is reverse order of the removal procedure. Tighten the pump retaining bolts to 18 ft. lbs. (25 Nm).
6. Fill the pump with new fluid and bleed the system.

Bleeding System

If the power steering system has been serviced, an accurate fluid level reading cannot be obtained until the air is bled from the system.

1. Position the wheels the the extreme left and add an approved power steering fluid to the **COLD** mark on the fluid level indicator.
2. Start the engine and run it at fast idle, recheck the fluid level. If necessary bring the level up to the **COLD** mark.
3. Bleed the system by turning the wheels from left to right without reaching the stop at either end. Maintain the fluid level at the **COLD** mark or just above the pump casting.

NOTE: Power steering fluid with air in it will appear to be light tan or red. This air must be eliminated from the fluid before normal steering action can be obtained.

4. Return the the wheels to the center position. Continue to run the engine for 2 or 3 minutes.
5. Road test the vehicle to be sure the steering functions normal and is free of noise.

6. Recheck the fluid level. When the engine has reached normal operating temperature, the level should be at the **HOT** mark. Add fluid if necessary.

7. Check the system for leaks.

Steering Column

Removal and Installation

STANDARD

1. Disconnect the negative battery cable.
2. Remove the upper/lower steering column switch cover panel screws and the panels.

NOTE: When removing the steering column cover panels, it will be necessary to turn the steering 90 degrees in both directions so the screws become visible.

3. From the instrument panel, remove the lower steering column trim.
4. Disconnect the electrical harness connectors from the steering column and ignition lock switches.
5. If equipped with an automatic transmission, disconnect the park lock actuation cable.
6. Unclip the turn signal switch (left side) and the wiper switch (right side).
7. Position the steering wheel in the straight-ahead position.
8. Remove the steering column shaft to steering shaft flange pinch bolt and the steering column to dash bolts.
9. To remove the steering column to instrument panel shear bolts, perform the following procedures:

   a. Using a center punch, center punch the left side shear bolt.

   b. Using an ⅛ in. drill bit, drill a hole through the shear bolt.

   c. Using a bolt extractor tool, drive the extractor tool into the shear bolt and unscrew it.

10. Guide the steering column out of the vehicle.

NOTE: The plastic washer seated loosely on the steering shaft serves to center the steering shaft. It is placed in the steering shaft prior to mounting the assembly and must be removed after the assembly has been completed.

11. To install, center the steering wheel, use a new shear bolt and reverse the removal procedures. Torque the steering column to instrument panel bolt to 16 ft. lbs., the steering column shaft to coupling pinch bolt to 16 ft. lbs., the steering pinion to steering coupling pinch bolt to 16 ft. lbs. and the steering wheel to steering column nut to 18 ft. lbs.

TILT COLUMN

1. Disconnect the negative battery terminal from the battery.
2. From the steering wheel, remove the cover cap with the horn button.
3. Position the steering wheel on the straight-ahead position. Remove the steering wheel nut and washer.
4. Using a steering wheel puller tool, pull the steering wheel from the steering column. do not pound on the steering wheel for damage may occur to the steering column.

NOTE: When removing the steering wheel, make sure the puller hook claws face outwards. If necessary, unclip the contact ring from the steering wheel and replace it with a new one. When installing, make sure the turn signal return segment points to the left. Lubricate the contact finger to contact plate surface.

5. Remove the steering wheel height adjustment lever, the turn signal switch cover screws and both covers.
6. Place the ignition switch (with key) in second position, press detent spring downward and remove the ignition lock cylinder.
7. Disconnect the electrical harness connector from the ignition contact switch, then, remove the headless set screw and the ignition switch. Remove the switch housing screws and push the switch towards the steering wheel.

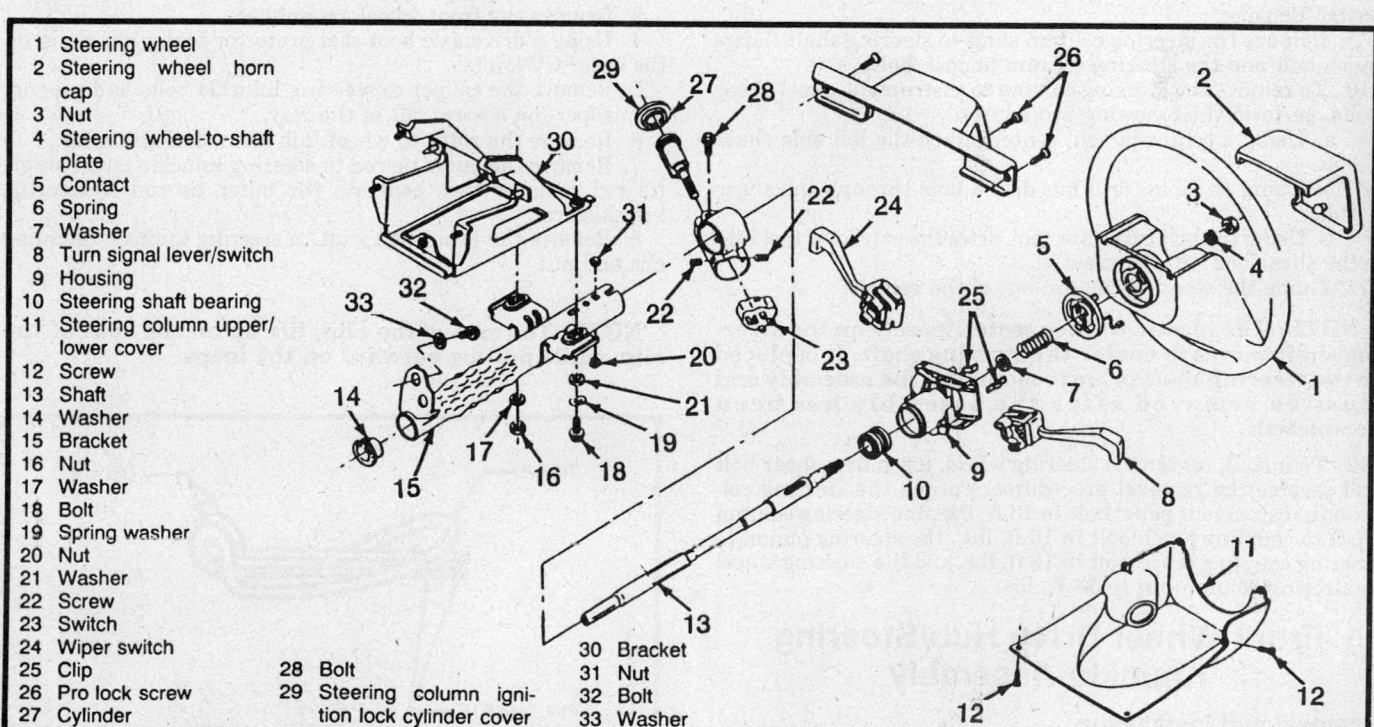

1	Steering wheel
2	Steering wheel horn cap
3	Nut
4	Steering wheel-to-shaft plate
5	Contact
6	Spring
7	Washer
8	Turn signal lever/switch
9	Housing
10	Steering shaft bearing
11	Steering column upper/lower cover
12	Screw
13	Shaft
14	Washer
15	Bracket
16	Nut
17	Washer
18	Bolt
19	Spring washer
20	Nut
21	Washer
22	Screw
23	Switch
24	Wiper switch
25	Clip
26	Pro lock screw
27	Cylinder
28	Bolt
29	Steering column ignition lock cylinder cover
30	Bracket
31	Nut
32	Bolt
33	Washer

Exploded view of the standard steering column

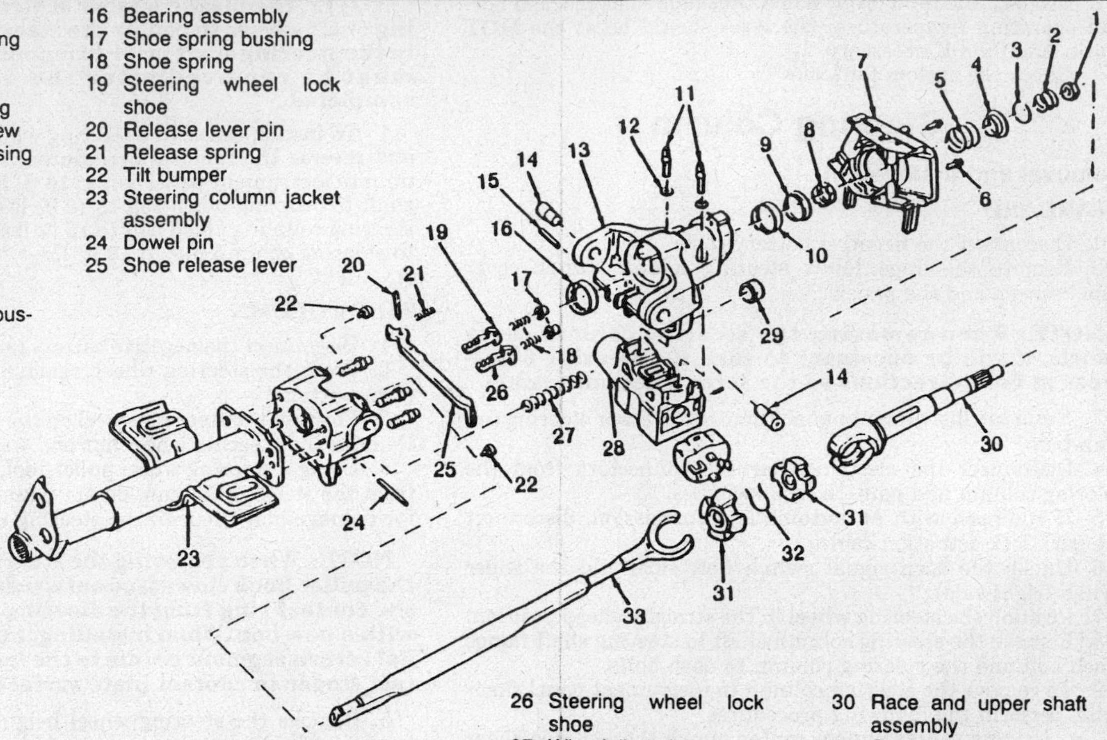

1 Nut
2 Cancelling cam spring
3 Retaining ring
4 Retaining spring
5 Upper bearing spring
6 Washer HD tap screw
7 Signal switch housing assembly
8 Inner race seat
9 Inner race
10 Bearing assembly
11 Shear bolt
12 Shear bolt washer
13 Steering column housing
14 Pivot pin
15 Dowel pin

16 Bearing assembly
17 Shoe spring bushing
18 Shoe spring
19 Steering wheel lock shoe
20 Release lever pin
21 Release spring
22 Tilt bumper
23 Steering column jacket assembly
24 Dowel pin
25 Shoe release lever

26 Steering wheel lock shoe
27 Wheel tilt spring
28 Ignition switch and lock housing
29 Spring retainer

30 Race and upper shaft assembly
31 Centering sphere
32 Joint preload spring
33 Lower steering shaft assembly

Exploded view of the tilt steering column

8. Compress the locking tabs, then, remove the turn signal switch (left side) and the wiper switch (right side) from the switch housing.

9. Remove the steering column shaft to steering shaft flange pinch bolt and the steering column to dash bolts.

10. To remove the steering column to instrument panel shear bolts, perform the following procedures:

    a. Using a center punch, center punch the left side shear bolt.

    b. Using an ⅛ in. drill bit, drill a hole through the shear bolt.

    c. Using the bolt extractor tool, drive the extractor tool into the shear bolt and unscrew it.

11. Guide the steering column out of the vehicle.

NOTE: The plastic washer seated loosely on the steering shaft serves to center the steering shaft. It is placed in the steering shaft prior to mounting the assembly and must be removed after the assembly has been completed.

12. To install, center the steering wheel, use a new shear bolt and reverse the removal procedures. Torque the steering column to instrument panel bolt to 16 ft. lbs., the steering column shaft to coupling pinch bolt to 16 ft. lbs., the steering pinion to steering coupling pinch bolt to 16 ft. lbs. and the steering wheel to steering column nut to 18 ft. lbs.

Front Wheel Drive Hub/Steering Knuckle Assembly

Removal and Installation

1. Loosen the upper strut to body nuts and the wheel lug

nuts. Remove the halfshaft to hub cotter pin, nut and washer.

2. Raise and safely support the vehicle.

3. Remove the front wheel assemblies.

4. Using a drive axle boot seal protector tool, place them on the outer CV-joints.

5. Remove the caliper to steering knuckle bolts and support the caliper (on a wire) out of the way.

6. Remove the rotor to wheel hub screw and the rotor.

7. Remove the outer tie rod to steering knuckle nut. Using a tie rod remover tool, separate the outer tie rod to steering knuckle arm.

8. Remove the lower ball joint to steering knuckle retaining clip and nut.

NOTE: To remove the clip, lift up on the rear of the clip, while pulling outward on the loops.

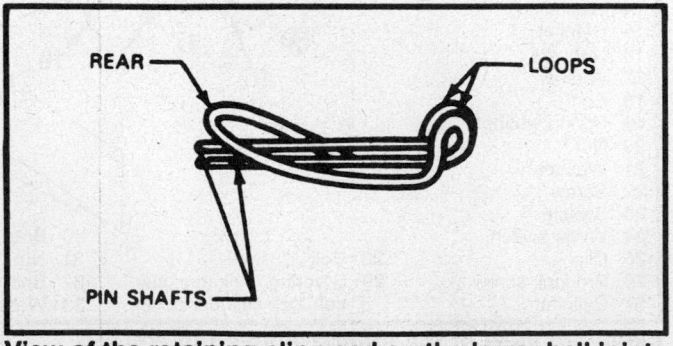

View of the retaining clip used on the lower ball joint

9. Using the ball joint separator tool, separate the lower ball joint from the steering knuckle arm.

10. Using a front wheel hub remover tool, separate the halfshaft from the steering knuckle hub. Using a wire, support the halfshaft.

11. Remove the upper strut to body nuts and washers, then, remove the strut assembly from the vehicle.

12. To install, use a new cotter pin and reverse the removal procedures. Torque the steering knuckle/strut assembly to body

nuts to 22 ft. lbs., the lower ball joint to steering knuckle nut 50 ft. lbs., the tie rod to steering knuckle to 45 ft. lbs.

13. Tighten the disc rotor to hub screw to 3 ft. lbs., the caliper to steering knuckle bolts to 70 ft. lbs. and the halfshaft to hub nut to 74 ft. lbs., back off the nut, retighten to 15 ft. lbs., then, tighten another 90 degrees.

14. Check and/or adjust the front end alignment.

NOTE: When tightening the halfshaft nut, be sure to

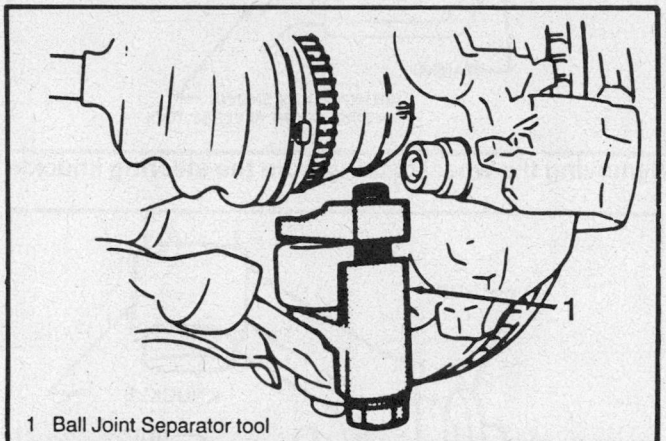

Separating the lower ball joint from the steering knuckle arm

1 Ball Joint Separator tool

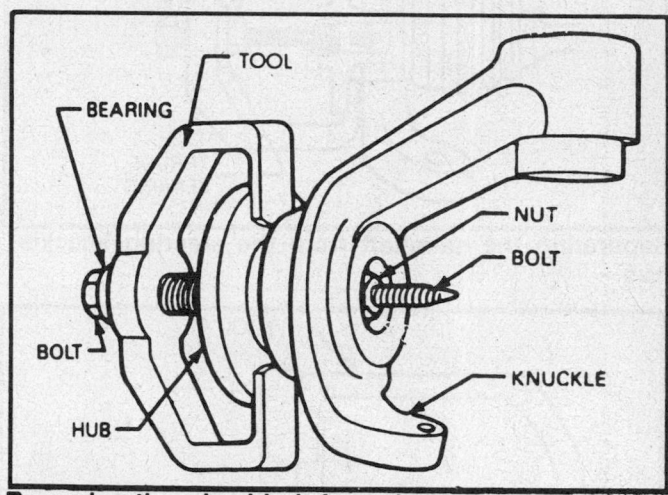

Removing the wheel hub from the steering knuckle

1 Rack and pinion housing
2 Upper pinion bushing
3 Pinion shaft seal
4 Pinion and valve assembly
5 Spool shaft retaining ring
6 Valve body ring
7 Rear assembly stub shaft bearing
8 Stub shaft seal
9 Stub shaft dust seal
10 Retaining ring
11 Dash seal
12 Flange/steering coupling assembly
13 Pinch bolt
14 Rack bearing
15 O-ring seal
16 Adjuster spring
17 Adjuster plug
18 Adjuster plug lock nut
19 Mounting grommet (LH)
20 Housing end cover
21 Pinion bearing assembly
22 Retaining ring
23 Hex lock nut
24 Dust cover
25 Insert/rack guide assembly
26 Center housing cover washer
27 Inner tie rod (LH)
28 Inner pivot bushing
29 Inner tie rod (RH)
30 Inner tie rod plate (RH)
31 Inner tie rod bolt
32 Lock plate
33 Pinch bolt
34 Tie rod adjuster
35 Outer tie rod (LH) assembly
36 Outer tie rod (RH) assembly
37 Lubrication fitting
38 Tie rod seal
39 Hex nut
41 Rod and rack assembly
42 Seal back-up washer
43 Piston rod seal
44 Piston rod guide
45 O-ring seal
46 Rack piston
47 O-ring seal
48 Piston ring
49 Hex nut
50 Cylinder tube assembly
51 Boot clamp
52 Boot retaining bushing
53 Rack and pinion boot
54 Boot retaining bushing
55 Boot clamp
56 Mounting grommet (RH)
57 Cylinder (RT) line assembly
58 Cylinder (LT) line assembly
59 O-ring seal

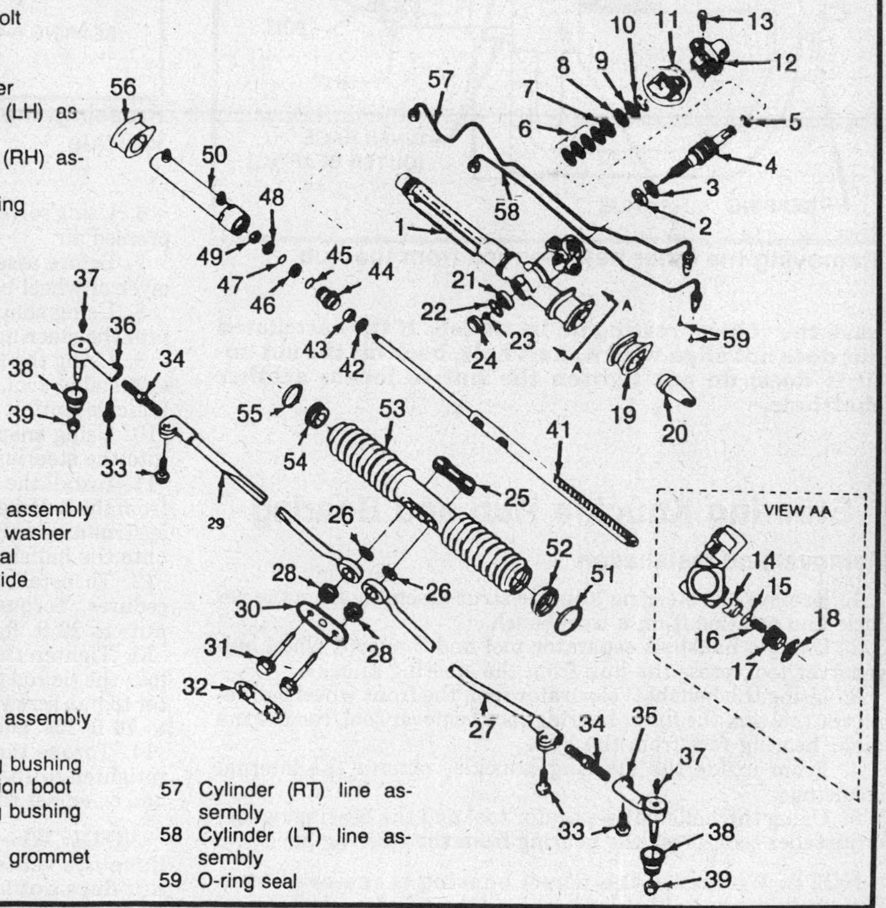

Exploded view of the power steering rack/pinion

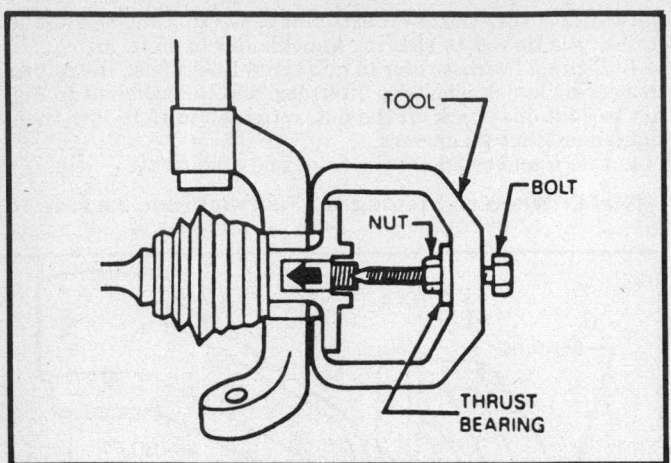

Separating the halfshaft from the steering knuckle hub

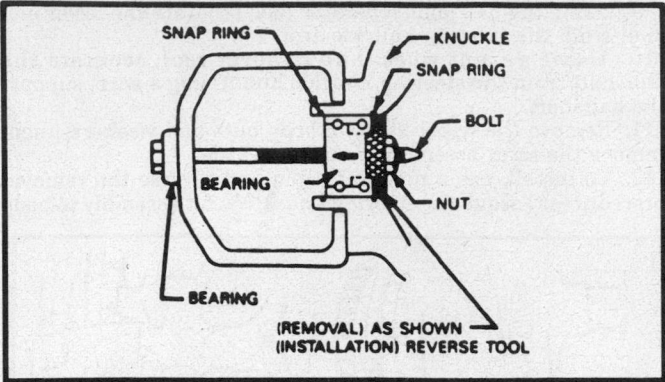

Removing the wheel bearing from the steering knuckle

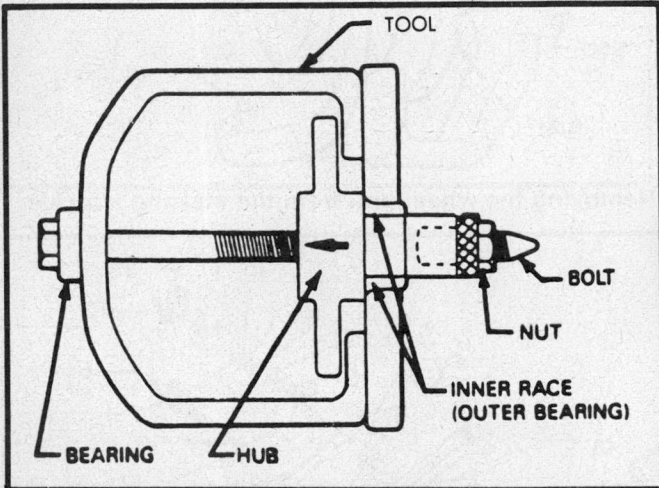

Removing the inner bearing race from the hub

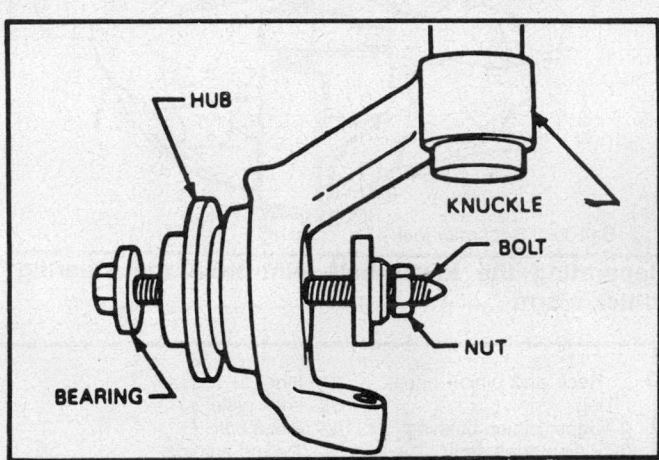

Pressing the new wheel bearing into the steering knuckle

have the vehicle resting on its wheels. If the castellated nut does not align with a shaft hole, back off the nut until it does; do not tighten the nut to locate another shafthole.

Steering Knuckle Hub and Bearing

Removal and Installation

1. Remove the steering knuckle/strut assembly from the vehicle and position it on a workbench.
2. Using a halfshaft separator tool and the front wheel hub remover tool, press the hub from the steering knuckle.
3. Using the halfshaft separator tool, the front wheel hub remover tool and the inner bearing race remover tool, remove the inner bearing race from the hub.
4. From inside the steering knuckle, remove the internal snaprings.
5. Using the halfshaft separator tool and the bearing remover/installer tool, press the bearing from the steering knuckle.

NOTE: Whenever the wheel bearing is removed from the steering knuckle, it must be discarded and replaced with a new one.

6. Using solvent, clean all of the parts and blow dry with compressed air.
7. Before assembling the parts, be sure to coat them with a layer of wheel bearing grease.
8. Using snapring pliers, install the outer internal snapring into the steering knuckle.
9. Using the halfshaft separator tool and the bearing remover/installer tool, press the new wheel bearing into the steering knuckle until it butts against the snapring.
10. Using snapring pliers, install the inner internal snapring into the steering knuckle.
11. Install the strut onto the body. Remove the seal protector from the halfshaft. Install the halfshaft into the steering knuckle/strut assembly. Install the new washer and new halfshaft nut onto the halfshaft.
12. To install, use new cotter pins and reverse the removal procedures. Torque the steering knuckle/strut assembly to body nuts to 22 ft. lbs.
13. Tighten the lower ball joint to steering knuckle nut 50 ft. lbs., the tie rod to steering knuckle nut to 45 ft. lbs., the disc rotor to hub screw to 3 ft. lbs., the caliper to steering knuckle bolts to 70 ft. lbs. and the wheel lug nuts to 65 ft. lbs.
14. Torque the halfshaft to hub nut to 74 ft. lbs., back it off, retighten to 15 ft. lbs., then, tighten another 90 degrees. Check and/or adjust the front end alignment.

NOTE: When tightening the halfshaft nut, be sure to have the vehicle resting on its wheels. If the castellated nut does not align with a shaft hole, back off the nut until it does; do not tighten the nut to locate another shaft hole.

BRAKE SYSTEM

NOTE: Refer to unit repair section for brake service information and drum/rotor specifications.

Master Cylinder

Removal and Installation

1. Disconnect the negative battery cable.
2. Disconnect the electrical connector from the reservoir cap.
3. Disconnect and plug the brake lines from the master cylinder.
4. Remove the master cylinder to power brake booster nuts.
5. Remove the master cylinder from the vehicle.
6. To install, use new self locking nuts and reverse the removal procedures. Torque the master cylinder brake booster nuts to 13 ft. lbs. Refill the master cylinder reservoir with clean brake fluid. Bleed the brake system.

Bleeding System

On diagonally split brake systems, start the manual bleeding procedure with the right rear, then the left front, the left rear and the right front.

1. Clean the bleeder screw at each wheel.
2. Attach a small rubber hose to the bleeder screw and place the other end in a clear container of fresh brake fluid.
3. Refill the master cylinder with fresh brake fluid. The master cylinder reservoir should be checked and topped off often during the bleeding procedure.
4. Have an assistant slowly pump the brake pedal and hold the pressure.
5. Open the bleeder screw about ¼ turn. The pedal should fall to the floor as air and fluid are pushed out. Close the bleeder screw while the assistant holds the pedal to the floor, then, slowly release the pedal and wait 15 seconds. Repeat the process until no more air bubbles are forced from the system when the brake pedal is applied. It may be necessary to repeat this numerous times to get all of the air from the system.
6. Repeat this procedure on the remaining wheel cylinders and calipers.

NOTE: **Remember to wait 15 seconds between each bleeding and do not pump the pedal rapidly. Rapid pumping of the brake pedal pushes the master cylinder secondary piston down the bore in a manner that makes it difficult to bleed the system.**

7. Check the brake pedal for sponginess and the brake warning light for an indication of unbalanced pressure. Repeat the entire bleeding procedure to correct either of these conditions.

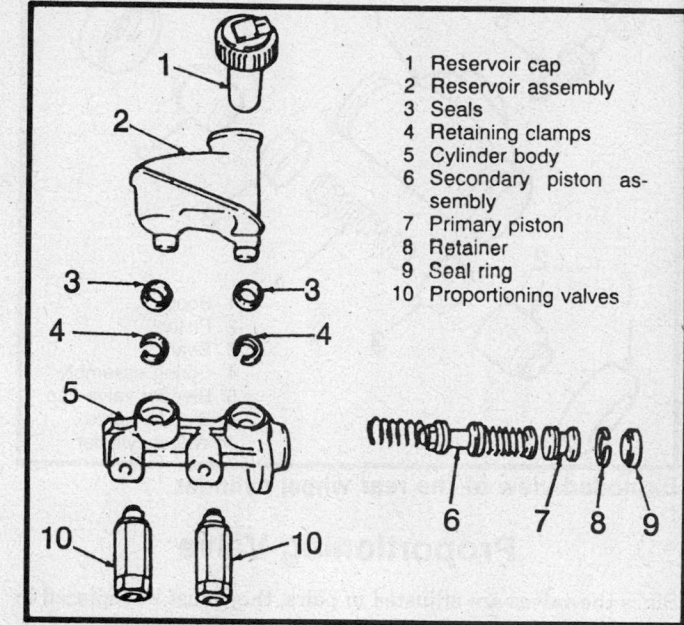

1	Reservoir cap
2	Reservoir assembly
3	Seals
4	Retaining clamps
5	Cylinder body
6	Secondary piston assembly
7	Primary piston
8	Retainer
9	Seal ring
10	Proportioning valves

Exploded view of the master cylinder

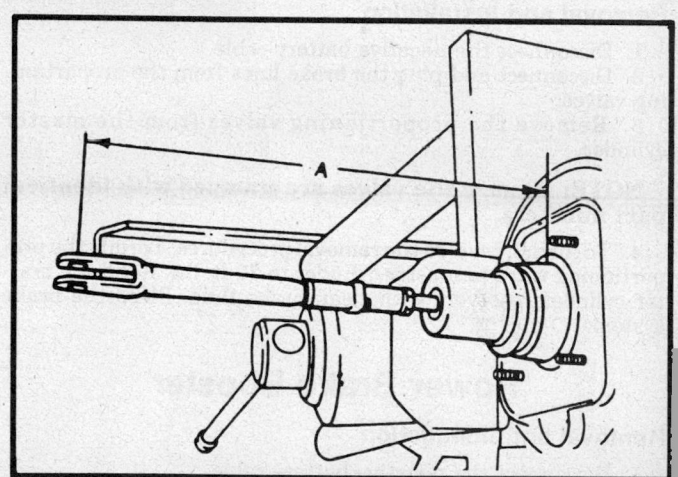

Measuring the push rod length

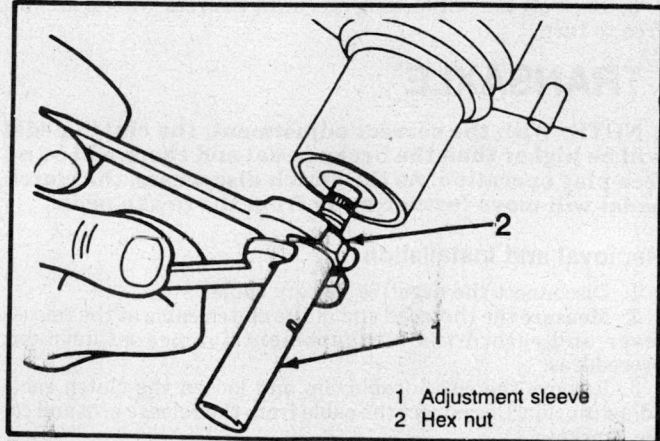

1 Adjustment sleeve
2 Hex nut

Removing the hex nut from the adjusting sleeve

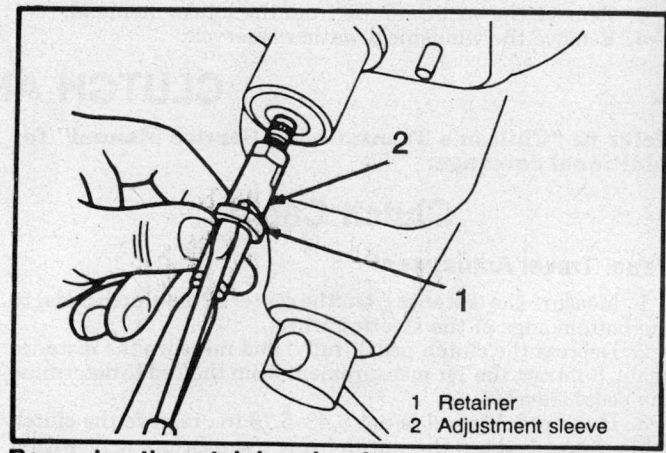

1 Retainer
2 Adjustment sleeve

Removing the retaining ring from the pushrod

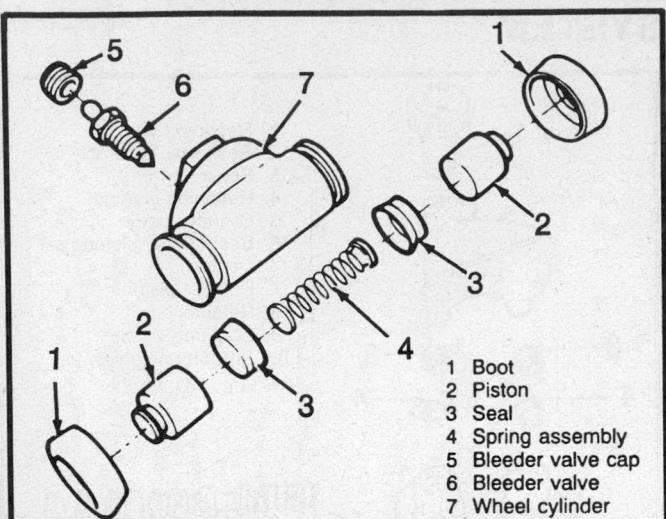

1 Boot
2 Piston
3 Seal
4 Spring assembly
5 Bleeder valve cap
6 Bleeder valve
7 Wheel cylinder

Exploded view of the rear wheel cylinder

Proportioning Valve

Since the valves are adjusted in pairs, they must be replaced in pairs.

Removal and Installation

1. Disconnect the negative battery cable.
2. Disconnect and plug the brake lines from the proportioning valves.
3. Remove the proportioning valves from the master cylinder.

NOTE: Be sure the valves are stamped with identical part numbers.

4. To install, reverse the removal procedures. Torque the proportioning valve to master cylinder to 30 ft. lbs. Refill the master cylinder reservoir with clean brake fluid. Bleed the brake system.

Power Brake Booster

Removal and Installation

1. Disconnect the negative battery cable.
2. Remove the master cylinder from the booster; do not disconnect the brake lines.
3. Remove the vacuum hose from the intake manifold.
4. Remove the windshield washer reservoir.

5. From under the dash, remove the brake light switch and the brake spring.
6. Remove the pushrod to pedal pin retainer and the pin.
7. If not equipped with power steering, remove the brake pedal bracket to dash nuts. If equipped with power steering, remove the lower mounting screw from behind the fluid lines using a flat head socket wrench.
8. To remove the power brake booster and bracket, tilt the brake servo slightly and remove it upwards.
9. From the power brake booster, remove the two-part support bracket and the rubber boot.
10. Remove the pushrod retainer and pushrod, then, unscrew and remove the adjuster sleeve from the piston rod.
11. Unscrew the hex nut.
12. Installation is the reverse order of the removal procedure. Adjust the adjuster sleeve so the distance A is 10.96 in. Torque the two-part bracket to power booster nuts to 16 ft. lbs., the power booster/bracket to dash bolts to 16 ft. lbs., the master cylinder to power booster nuts to 13 ft. lbs. Start the engine and check the brake operation.

Wheel Cylinder

Removal and Installation

1. Raise and safely support the vehicle.
2. Using a piece of chalk, mark the relative position of the wheels to the wheel hub. Remove the wheel/tire assemblies.
3. Remove the brake drum to wheel hub detent screw and the brake drum.
4. Remove the upper return spring and push the brake shoes slightly outward.

NOTE: Note the position of the adjuster assembly and the adjuster actuator to actuator spring.

5. Remove and plug the brake line from the wheel cylinder.
6. Remove the wheel cylinder to backing plate bolt and the wheel cylinder.
7. Installation is the reverse order of the removal procedure. Torque the wheel cylinder to backing plate bolt to 7 ft. lbs. Adjust the rear wheel brakes and the parking brake. Bleed the brake system.

Parking Brake

Adjustment

1. Raise and safely support the vehicle.
2. Release the parking brake.
3. Inspect the parking brake cable for free movement.
4. At the equalizer, adjust the self-locking nut until the wheels are difficult to turn.
5. Back-off the self-locking nut until the rear wheels are just free to turn.

CLUTCH AND TRANSAXLE

Refer to "Chilton's Transmission Service Manual" for additional coverage.

Clutch Cable

Pedal Travel Adjustment

1. Measure the distance from the center of the clutch pedal to the bottom edge of the steering wheel.
2. Depress the clutch pedal (fully) and measure the distance again. Subtract the 1st measurement from the 2nd to determine the pedal travel.
3. If the pedal travel is not 5.43–5.70 in., remove the clutch cable clip and adjust the nut to bring the measurement within specifications.

NOTE: With the correct adjustment, the clutch pedal will be higher than the brake pedal and there will be no free-play operation. As the clutch disc wears, the clutch pedal will move further away from the brake pedal.

Removal and Installation

1. Disconnect the negative battery cable.
2. Measure the threaded end of the clutch cable at the release lever and record the measurement for pre-adjustment procedures.
3. Remove the clutch cable clip and loosen the clutch cable adjusting nut. Disconnect the cable from the release arm and cable bracket.
4. Disconnect the clutch start safety switch.

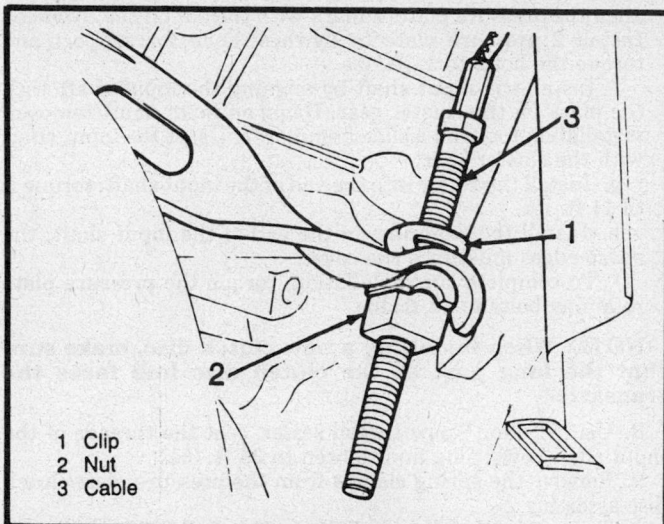

1 Clip
2 Nut
3 Cable

View of the clutch cable adjuster

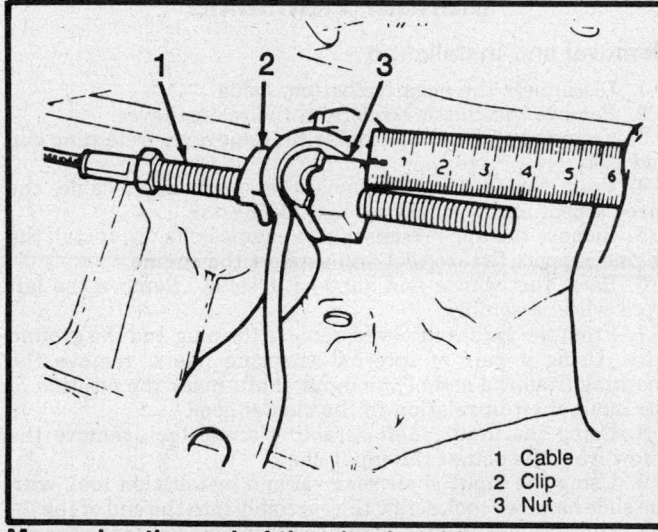

1 Cable
2 Clip
3 Nut

Measuring the end of the clutch cable

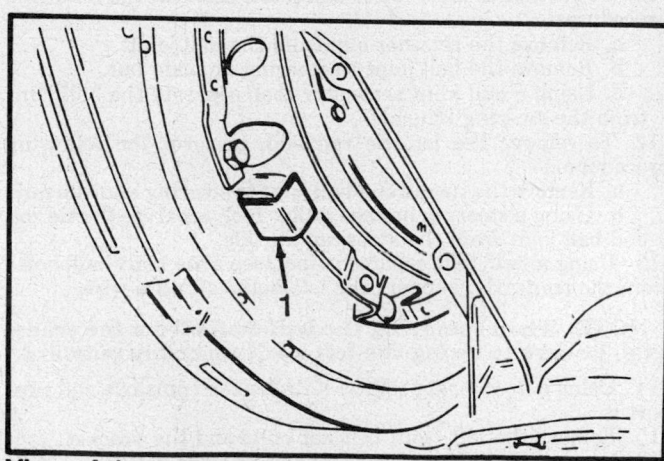

View of the pressure plate spring clamps

5. At the clutch pedal, remove the cable return spring and brace. Remove the clutch pedal retaining nut, spring and shaft. Remove the pedal and pull the cable through the firewall.

6. Disconnect the spring and the cable from the pedal.

7. Remove the clutch cable by pulling it from the engine compartment.

8. To install, coat the clutch pedal shaft with grease and reverse the removal procedures. Adjust the clutch cable to the measurement taken earlier. Adjust the clutch pedal travel.

Clutch

Removal and Installation

It is not necessary to remove the transaxle from this vehicle to replace the clutch assembly.

1. Disconnect the negative battery cable. Remove the clutch cable from the release lever. Raise and safely support the vehicle.

2. From the transaxle cover, remove the plug and the ground wire. Using a pair of internal snapring pliers, remove the snapring from the end of the input shaft; mark the position of the input shaft in relation to the cluster gear.

3. Using a input shaft retaining screw tool, remove the screw from the end of the input shaft.

4. Using the input shaft removal and installation tool, with the slide hammer tool, screw the assembly into the end of the input shaft. Using the slide hammer assembly, disengage the input shaft from the cluster gear.

5. Remove the clutch cover from the bottom of the transaxle and push back the clutch release bearing. Using a set of pressure plate spring clamps tool, rotate the flywheel and install a clamp every 120 degrees.

NOTE: The pressure plate and clutch disc cannot be removed without installing the 3 spring clamps.

6. Remove the pressure plate to flywheel bolts, the pressure plate/clutch disc assembly. Be sure to support the assembly when removing the last bolt.

7. To replace the clutch disc in the assembly, perform the following procedures:

    a. Using a hydraulic press, apply pressure to the pressure plate spring fingers, then, remove the spring clamps.

    b. Reduce the pressure of the press and separate the clutch disc from the pressure plate.

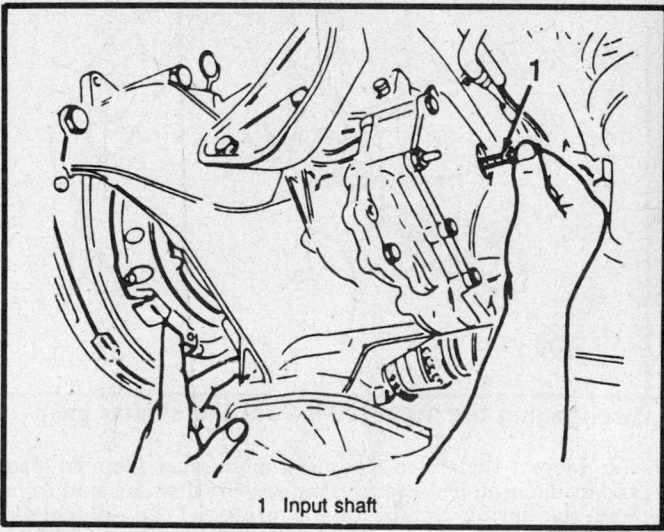

1 Input shaft

Installing the input shaft into the pressure plate/clutch disc assembly

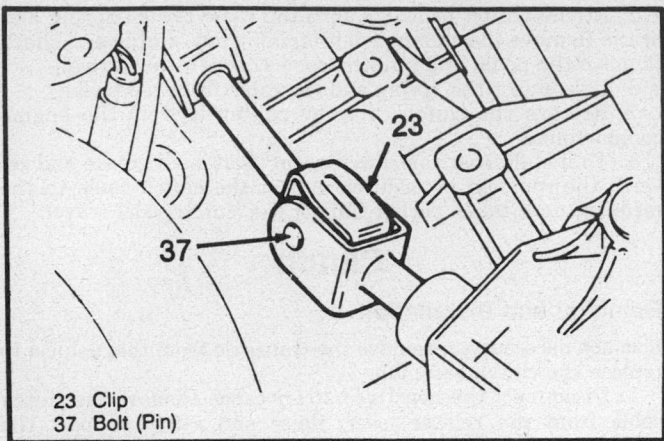

23 Clip
37 Bolt (Pin)

Removing the universal joint clip and bolt

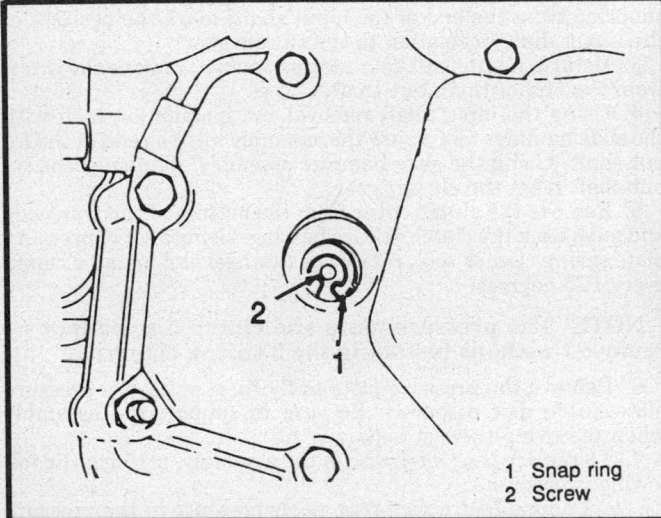

1 Snap ring
2 Screw

View of the input shaft snap ring

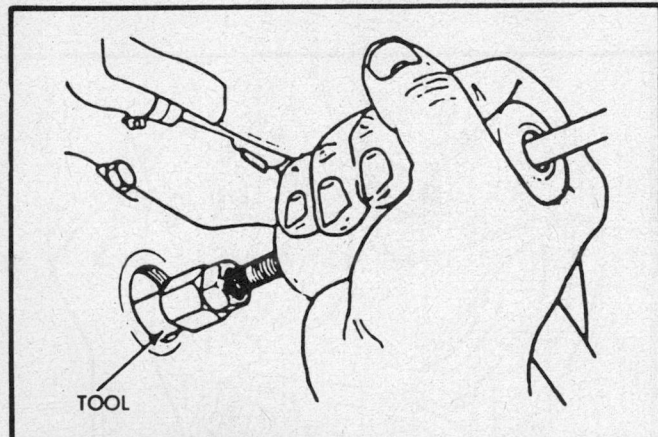

TOOL

Disengaging the input shaft from the cluster gear

c. Inspect the clutch disc and the pressure plate for wear and/or damage, if necessary, replace the disc. Be sure to install the spring clamps to the pressure plate/clutch disc assembly.

d. Using grease, lightly lubricate the clutch disc spline.

e. When installing the pressure plate/clutch disc assembly,

align the pressure plate **V** mark with the dot on the flywheel. Install 2 pressure plate to flywheel bolts for support and torque the bolts to 11 ft. lbs.

f. Install the input shaft by aligning the input shaft with the mark on the cluster gear. Using an input shaft removal/installation tool and a slide hammer tool, seat the input shaft with the cluster gear.

g. Install the screw into the end of the input shaft; torque it to 11 ft. lbs.

h. Install the snapring on the end of the input shaft; the sharp edges must face the cover.

i. To complete the installation, torque the pressure plate retaining bolts to 11 ft. lbs.

NOTE: When installing a new clutch disc, make sure that the long part of the clutch disc hub faces the transaxle.

8. Using Teflon® pipe thread sealer, coat the threads of the input shaft cover plug and tighten to 36 ft. lbs..

9. Remove the spring clamps from the pressure plate/clutch disc assembly.

10. Torque the clutch cover bolts to 62 inch lbs. Install the left tire and wheel assembly, lower the vehicle. Install the clutch cable to the release lever. Check clutch engagement and operation.

Manual Transaxle

Removal and Installation

1. Disconnect the negative battery cable.
2. Remove the clutch cable from the release lever.
3. From the shifter universal joint, remove the retaining clip and bolt.
4. From the transaxle, remove the speedometer cable, the speed sensor and the back-up light connector.
5. Remove the upper transaxle to engine bolts (3). Install the engine support fixture tool and support the engine.
6. Raise the vehicle and support it safely. Remove the left front wheel assembly.
7. From the transaxle cover, remove the plug and the ground wire. Using a pair of internal snapring pliers, remove the snapring from the end of the input shaft; mark the position of the input shaft in relation to the cluster gear.
8. Using the input shaft retaining screw tool, remove the screw from the end of the input shaft.
9. Using the input shaft removal and installation tool, with the slide hammer tool, screw the assembly into the end of the input shaft. Using the slide hammer assembly, disengage the input shaft from the cluster gear.
10. Remove the flywheel cover bolts and the cover.
11. To remove the left lower ball joint, perform the following procedures:
    a. Remove the retainer clip from the ball joint.
    b. Remove the ball joint to steering knuckle nut.
    c. Using a ball joint separator tool, separate the ball joint from the steering knuckle.
12. To remove the left tie rod end, perform the following procedures:
    a. Remove the tie rod end ball joint to steering knuckle nut.
    b. Using a steering linkage puller tool, separate the tie rod end ball joint from the steering knuckle.
13. Using a halfshaft separator tool, separate both halfshafts from the transaxle; support the left halfshaft on a wire.

NOTE: When removing the halfshafts from the transaxle, be sure to swing the left strut assembly outward.

14. Using a floor jack, position it under the transaxle and support it.
15. Remove the left front bracket bolts and the bracket.
16. Remove the left rear bracket to transaxle bolts.
17. Remove the lower transaxle to engine bolts. Move the

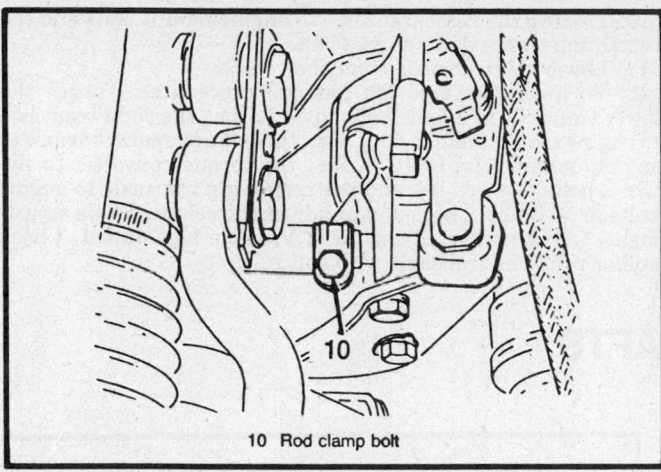

10 Rod clamp bolt

Removing the rod clamp

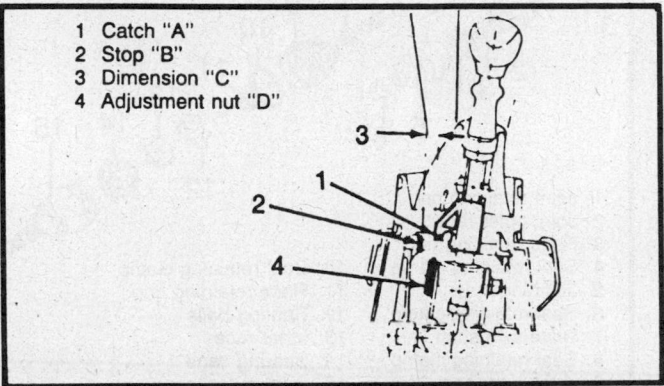

1 Catch "A"
2 Stop "B"
3 Dimension "C"
4 Adjustment nut "D"

Adjusting the shift lever measurements

transaxle away from the engine and downward; guide the right halfshaft from the transaxle, then support it on a wire.

18. Installation is the reverse order of the removal procedure. Guide the halfshafts into the transaxle and torque the lower transaxle to engine bolts—55 ft. lbs., the left rear bracket to transaxle bolts—55 ft. lbs., the left front mount bracket to transaxle bolts—47 ft. lbs., the left front mount bracket to chassis bolts to 55 ft. lbs. and the ball joint to steering knuckle nut—50 ft. lbs.

19. Torque the tie rod end to steering knuckle nut—45 ft. lbs., the input shaft to cluster gear screw—133 inch lbs. and the upper transaxle to engine bolts—55 ft. lbs.

20. Check and/or replenish the transaxle fluid level.

Linkage Adjustment

1. Disconnect the negative battery cable.
2. Position the gear shift lever in the N position.
3. Loosen the shift rod clamp bolt.
4. From the shift lever cover, remove the adjustment hole plug. Turn the shift rod left until a $\frac{3}{16}$ in. gauge pin can be inserted into the adjustment hole into the intermediate shift lever.
5. Remove the boot from the console, then, pull it upward to expose the shift control lever mechanism.
6. With the transaxle in N, place the gear shift lever into the 1st/2nd gear position. With the lever against the stop and the arrow aligned with the notch, torque the rod clamp bolt to 10 ft. lbs., then, turn the bolt another 90–180 degrees.
7. Using a 0.120 in. dia. gauge pin, check the clearance between the A catch and the B stop.
8. Remove the gauge pin and install the plug.

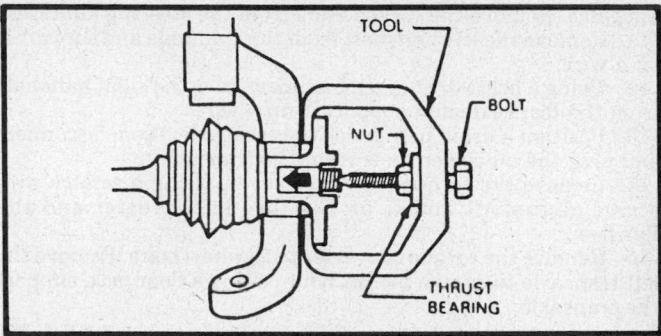

TOOL
BOLT
NUT
THRUST
BEARING

Separating the halfshaft from the wheel hub

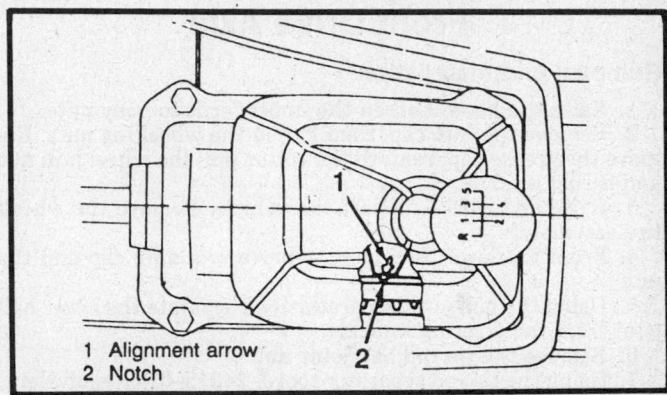

1 Alignment arrow
2 Notch

Aligning the shift lever

9. To further adjust the shift lever, bend back the adjusting nut locking tabs and turn the adjusting nut D until the C dimension is 0.449–0.465 in. Bend up the locking tabs to secure the adjusting nut.

10. To complete the installation, reverse the removal procedures.

Automatic Transaxle

NOTE: By September 1, 1991, Hydra-matic will have changed the name designation of the THM 125C automatic transaxle. The new name designation for this transaxle will be Hydra-matic 3T40. Transaxles built between 1989 and 1990 will serve as transitional years in which a dual system, made up of the old designation and the new designation will be in effect.

Removal and Installation

1. Disconnect the negative battery cable.
2. Remove the air cleaner.
3. Remove the T.V. cable from the transaxle and the throttle body. Remove the cable.
4. Disconnect the shift selector cable from the transaxle lever and the cable bracket; leave the cable attached to the bracket.
5. Disconnect electrical connectors from the speed sensor, the TCC and the park/neutral/back-up light switch.
6. Disconnect the speedometer drive cable from the transaxle.
7. Remove the top transaxle to engine bolts.
8. Using the engine support fixture tool and the adaptor tool, attach it to the engine and support the weight.
9. Raise and safely support the vehicle.
10. Remove both front wheels. Using the ball joint separator tool, separate the ball joints (both sides) from the steering

knuckles. Remove the tie rod ends from the steering knuckles.

11. Remove the left halfshaft from the transaxle and support it on a wire.

12. Using a brass drift and a hammer, drive the right halfshaft from the transaxle and support it on a wire.

13. Position a drain pan under the transaxle, then, disconnect and plug the oil cooler lines from the transaxle.

14. Remove the torque converter cover. Using a scratch awl, scribe alignment marks on the torque converter and the flywheel.

15. Remove the torque converter to flywheel bolts. Remove the left transaxle to engine mount bolts. Using a floor jack, support the transaxle.

16. Remove the right transaxle to engine mount bolts and the remaining transaxle to engine bolts.

17. Lower the transaxle from the vehicle.

18. To install, reverse the removal procedures. Torque the lower transaxle to engine bolts to 54 ft. lbs., the right transaxle to engine mount bolts to 30 ft. lbs., the left and rear transaxle to engine mount bolts to 16 ft. lbs., the torque converter to flywheel bolts to 44 ft. lbs. and the remaining transaxle to engine bolts to 54 ft. lbs. Check and/or adjust the selector cable adjustment. Check and/or adjust the T.V. cable adjustment. Check and/or refill the transaxle with fluid.

HALFSHAFTS

Front Drive Axle

Removal and Installation

1. Raise the hood. Loosen the upper strut to body nuts.

2. Remove the hub cap, then loosen the wheel lug nuts. Remove the grease cap, remove the cotter pin, the wheel hub nut and thrust washer.

3. Raise and safely support the vehicle. Remove the wheel/tire assembly.

4. From the lower ball joint, remove retaining clip and the nut.

5. Using the ball joint separator tool, separate the lower ball joint from the steering knuckle.

6. Remove the tie rod ball joint nut.

7. Using the tie rod separator tool J–24319–01 or equivalent, separate the tie rod from the steering knuckle.

8. Using a halfshaft to hub separator tool, drive the halfshaft from the hub assembly.

9. Position a drain pan under the transaxle. Using a axle shaft to transaxle separator tool and the slide hammer tool, separate and remove the halfshaft from the transaxle.

10. To install, use new retaining clips, cotter pins and reverse the removal procedures. Torque the lower ball joint to steering knuckle nut to 50 ft. lbs., the tie rod to steering knuckle nut to 45 ft. lbs.

11. Lower the vehicle to the floor. Torque the hub to halfshaft nut to 74 ft. lbs., the wheel lug nuts to 65 ft. lbs. and the upper strut to body nuts to 22 ft. lbs. Check and/or refill the transaxle.

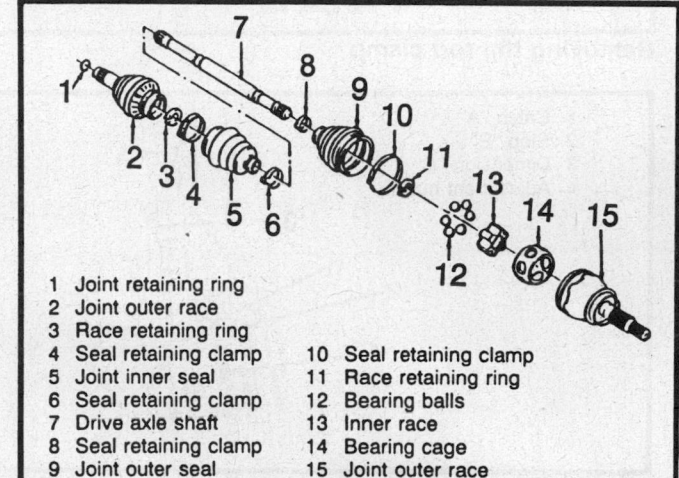

1 Joint retaining ring
2 Joint outer race
3 Race retaining ring
4 Seal retaining clamp
5 Joint inner seal
6 Seal retaining clamp
7 Drive axle shaft
8 Seal retaining clamp
9 Joint outer seal
10 Seal retaining clamp
11 Race retaining ring
12 Bearing balls
13 Inner race
14 Bearing cage
15 Joint outer race

Exploded view of the halfshaft

CV-Joint Overhaul

For all CV-joint overhaul procedures, refer to CV-Joint Overhaul" in the Unit Repair section.

REAR AXLE AND REAR SUSPENSION

Refer to the unit repair section for axle overhaul procedures and rear suspension service.

Rear Axle Assembly

Removal and Installation

1. Raise the vehicle and support it safely.

2. From the underbody, remove the exhaust shield.

3. To remove the parking brake cable, perform the following procedures:

    a. Using a ruler, measure the thread length of the parking brake lever pushrod.

    b. Remove the self-locking nut from the pushrod.

    c. Remove the lock plate and the parking brake cable from the brake cable compensation yoke.

    d. Disconnect the parking brake cable from the guides on the transaxle tunnel and the plastic sleeves from the hook on the fuel tank and move it towards the exhaust muffler.

4. Using a hydraulic jack, position it under a rear axle arm and raise it slightly.

5. At the rear axle bracket, remove the lock clips and disconnect the brake lines from the brake pressure hoses. Remove the brake hoses from the bracket.

6. Remove the shock absorbers and the bolt from the rear axle arm. Lower the hydraulic jack.

7. If necessary to remove the rear spring, perform the following procedure:

    a. Using a pry bar, position it in the shock absorber bracket and press downwards.

    b. Remove the rear spring.

NOTE: The shock absorber and rear spring, for the other side of the vehicle, can be removed in the same order.

8. Center the hydraulic jack under the rear axle to support the axle.

9. Remove the rear axle to chassis bolts, lower the axle and position the parking brake cable over the exhaust muffler.

10. To install, reverse the removal procedures. Torque the shock absorber to rear axle bracket nut/bolt to 52 ft. lbs.

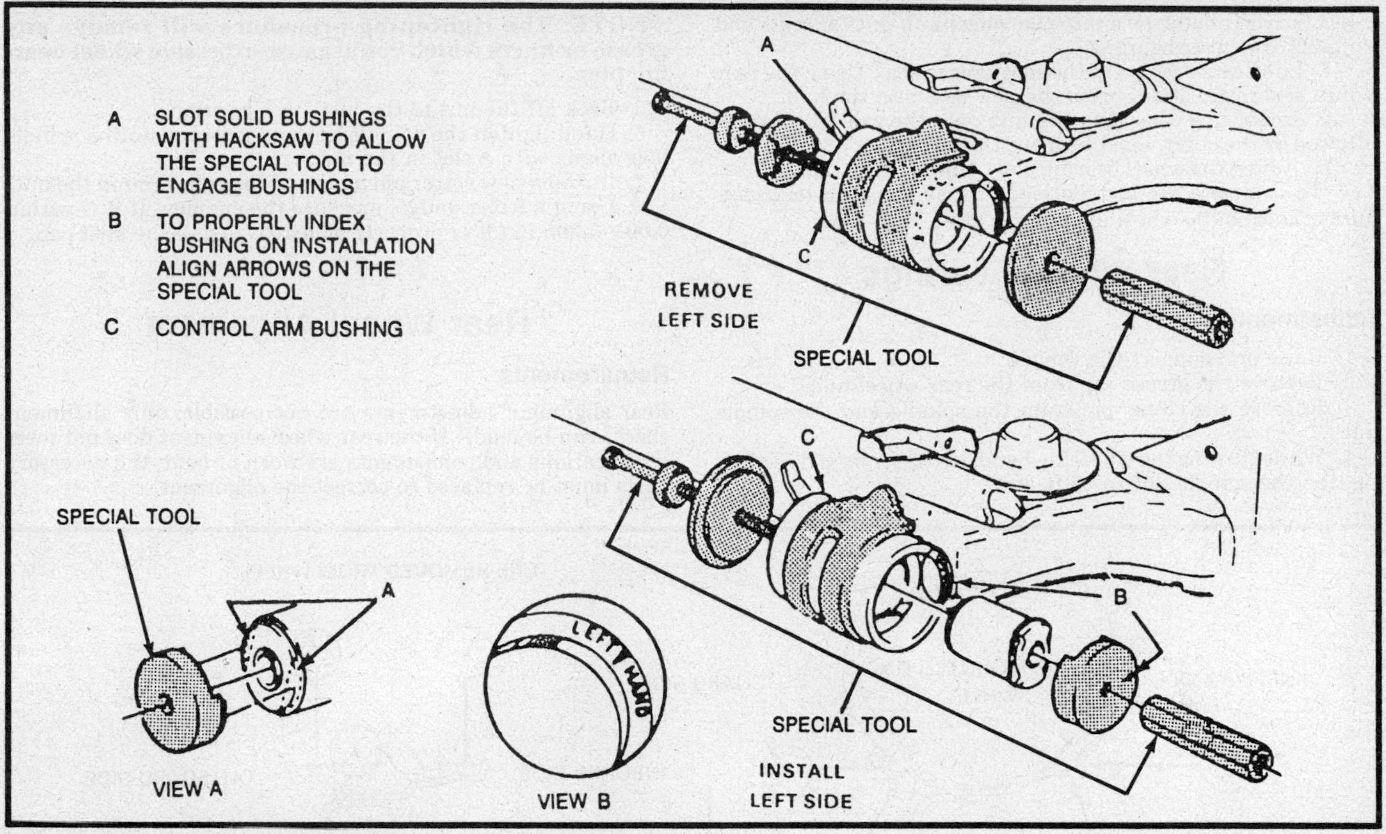

A SLOT SOLID BUSHINGS WITH HACKSAW TO ALLOW THE SPECIAL TOOL TO ENGAGE BUSHINGS

B TO PROPERLY INDEX BUSHING ON INSTALLATION ALIGN ARROWS ON THE SPECIAL TOOL

C CONTROL ARM BUSHING

REMOVE LEFT SIDE

SPECIAL TOOL

SPECIAL TOOL

A

VIEW A

VIEW B

SPECIAL TOOL

INSTALL LEFT SIDE

Rear control arm bushing removal and Installation

11. Reconnect the brake pressure hoses. Adjust the parking brake cable to the dimensions previously measured at the bracket. Adjust the wheel bearing play.

12. Lower the vehicle and torque the wheel lug nuts to 66 ft. lbs. With the vehicle resting at curb height, torque the rear axle to chassis bolts to 70 ft. lbs. Bleed the brake system and adjust the parking brake.

Rear Wheel Bearings

Removal and Installation

1. Raise and safely support the vehicle.
2. Remove the wheel assembly.
3. Remove the brake drum detent screw and the drum.

NOTE: To remove the brake drum, it may be necessary to loosen the parking brake cable and press the parking brake lever inwards (with a pry bar). do not hammer on the brake drum for damage to the bearing may result.

4. Remove the hub/bearing assembly to axle spindle grease cap, cotter pin, hub nut, thrust washer and the outer bearing from the axle spindle.

5. Using a small pry bar, remove the grease seal from the inside of the hub. Remove the inner and outer bearing from the hub.

6. If replacing the wheel bearings, perform the following procedures:

 a. Using a hammer and a drift punch, drive both outer bearing races (in opposite directions) from the wheel hub.

 b. Using cleaning solvent (not gasoline), clean the bearings, races and hub. Using compressed air, blow dry the parts.

 c. Inspect the parts for damage and/or wear. If necessary, replace any defective parts.

 d. Using an arbor press, the rear hub inner and outer bearing race installer tool and the driver handle tool, press the outer bearing, outer race into the wheel hub until it seats.

NOTE: Before installing the wheel bearings, be sure to force wheel bearing grease into the bearing.

 e. Using an arbor press, the rear hub inner and outer bearing race installer tool and the driver handle tool, press the in-

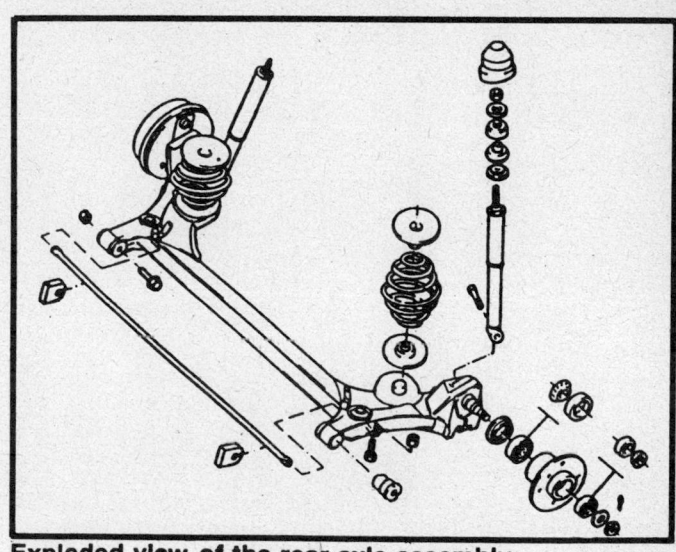

Exploded view of the rear axle assembly

ner bearing, outer race into the wheel hub until it seats and install the inner bearing.

f. Lubricate the lips of the new grease seal. Using the rear hub seal installation, press the new seal into the hub.

g. Install the wheel bearing hub onto the axle spindle, followed by the outer, inner bearing, thrust washer and hub nut.

h. Adjust the wheel bearing play. Adjust the parking brake.

7. To complete the installation, reverse the removal procedures. Torque the wheel lug nuts to 66 ft. lbs.

Rear Wheel Bearings

Adjustment

1. Raise and support the vehicle.
2. Remove the grease cap from the rear wheel hub.
3. Romove the cotter pin from the spindle and the spindle nut.
4. While turning the wheel, by hand, in the forward direction, tighten the spindle nut to 12 ft. lbs.

NOTE: The tightening procedure will remove any grease or burrs which could cause excessive wheel bearing play.

5. Back off the nut to the just loose position.
6. Hand tighten the spindle nut and loosen it until a spindle hole aligns with a slot in the nut.
7. Install a new cotter pin and bend the ends around the nut.
8. Using a feeler gauge, measure the endplay. If it is within 0.001–0.005 in., it is properly adjusted. Install the dust cap.

Rear Wheel Alignment

Requirements

Rear alignment adjustments are not possible; only alignment checks can be made. If the rear wheel alignment does not meet specifications and components are worn or bent, the necessary parts must be replaced to correct the alignment.

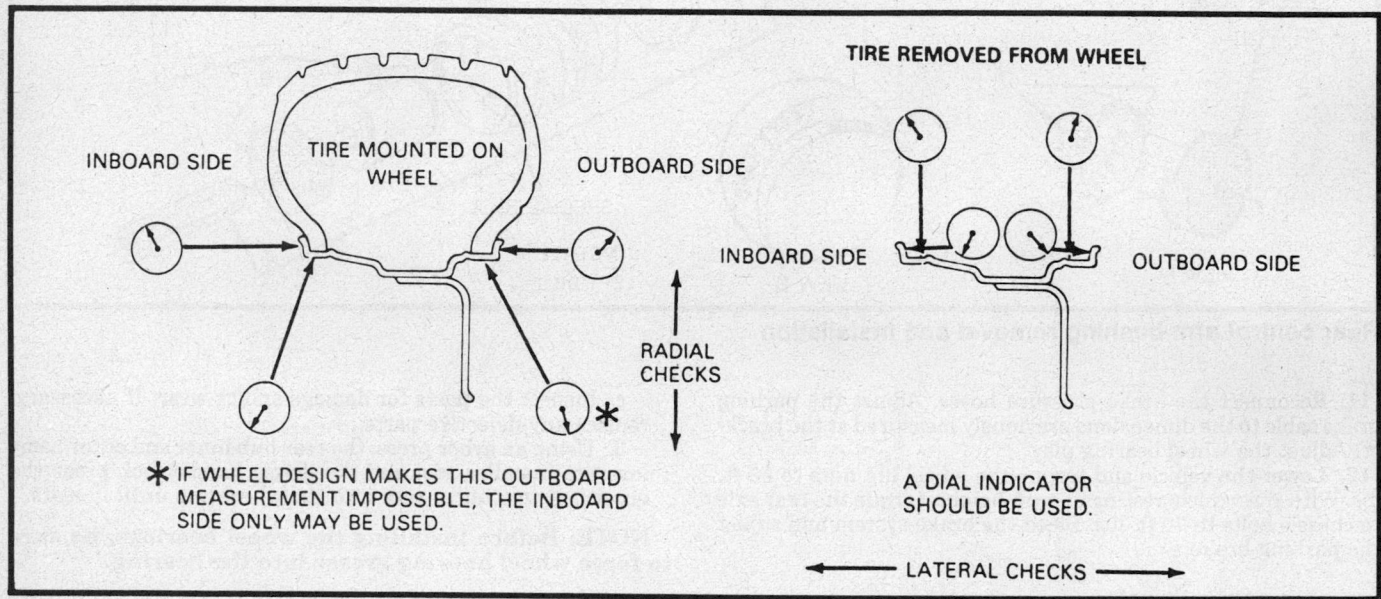

Measuring wheel runnout

YEAR IDENTIFICATION

1986–87 Chevette

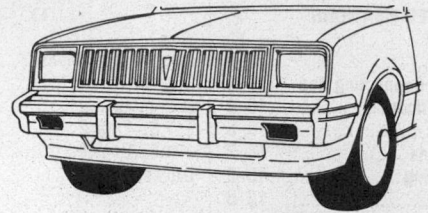

1986–87 Pontiac 1000

VEHICLE IDENTIFICATION CHART

It is important for servicing and ordering parts to be certain of the vehicle and engine identification. The VIN (vehicle identification number) is a 17 digit number visible through the windshield on the driver's side of the dash and contains the vehicle and engine identification codes. The tenth digit indicates model year and the eigth digit indicates engine code. It can be interpreted as follows:

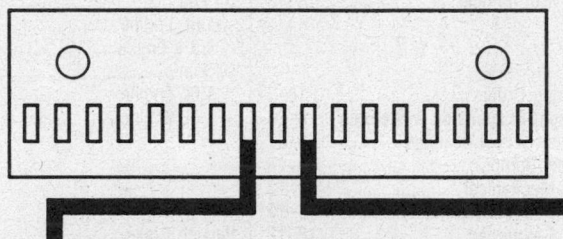

	Engine Code						Model Year	
Code	Cu. In.	Liters	Cyl.	Fuel Sys.	Eng. Mfg.		Code	Year
C	97.6	1.6	4	2 bbl	Chevy		G	1986
D	111	1.8	4	Diesel	Isuzu		H	1987

ENGINE IDENTIFICATION

Year	Model	Engine Displacement cu. in. (liter)	Engine Series Identification (VIN)	No. of Cylinders	Engine Type
1986	Chevette	4-98 (1.6)	C	4	OHC
	Chevette	4-111 (1.8)	D	4	Diesel
	1000	4-98 (1.6)	C	4	OHC
1987	Chevette	4-98 (1.6)	C	4	OHC
	1000	4-98 (1.6)	C	4	OHC

GENERAL ENGINE SPECIFICATIONS

Year	VIN	No. Cylinder Displacement cu. in. (liter)	Fuel System Type	Net Horsepower @ rpm	Net Torque @ rpm (ft.lbs.)	Bore × Stroke (in.)	Compression Ratio	Oil Pressure @ rpm
1986	C	4-98 (1.6)	2 bbl	65 @ 5200	80 @ 2400	3.228 × 2.980	9.0:1	55 @ 2000
	D	4-111 (1.8)	Diesel	51 @ 5000	72 @ 2000	3.310 × 3.230	22.0:1	64 @ 5000
1987	C	4-98 (1.6)	2 bbl	65 @ 5200	80 @ 2400	3.228 × 2.980	9.0:1	55 @ 2000

GASOLINE ENGINE TUNE-UP SPECIFICATIONS
Refer to Section 34 for all spark plug recommendations

Year	VIN	No. Cylinder Displacement cu. in. (liter)	Spark Plugs Gap (in.)	Ignition Timing (deg.) MT	AT	Compression Pressure (psi)	Fuel Pump (psi)	Idle Speed (rpm) MT	AT	Valve Clearance In.	Ex.
1986	C	4-98 (1.6)	.035	8B	8B	—	5.5-6.5	800	700	Hyd.	Hyd.
1987	C	4-98 (1.6)	.035	8B	8B	—	5.5-6.5	800	700	Hyd.	Hyd.

DIESEL ENGINE TUNE-UP SPECIFICATIONS

Year	VIN	No. Engine Displacement cu. in. (liter)	Valve Clearance Intake (in.)	Exhaust (in.)	Intake Valve Opens (deg.)	Injection Pump Setting (deg.)	Injection Nozzle Pressure (psi) New	Used	Idle Speed (rpm)	Cranking Compression Pressure (psi)
1986	D	4-111 (1.8)	.010③	.014③	32	18	1848	1707	625①	441②

① Automatic transmission—725   ② @ 200 rpm   ③ Clearance with engine cold

FIRING ORDER

To avoid confusion, always replace the spark plug wires 1 at a time.

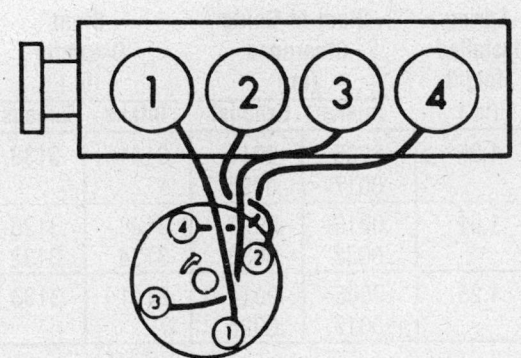

Chevrolet 98 cu. in. (1.6L) 4 cyl.
Engine firing order: 1-3-4-2
Distributor rotation: clockwise

CAPACITIES

Year	Model	VIN	No. Cylinder Displacement cu. in. (liter)	Engine Crankcase with Filter	without Filter	Transmission (pts.) 4-Spd	5-Spd	Auto.	Drive Axle (pts.)	Fuel Tank (gal.)	Cooling System (qts.)
1986	Chevette	C	4-98 (1.6)	4	4	3.5	⑤	6①	1.75	12.5	9②
	Chevette	D	4-111 (1.8)	6	6	—	—	6①	1.75	12.5	9
	1000	C	4-98 (1.6)	4	4	6.0	④	6①	1.75	12.2	9②

CAPACITIES

Year	Model	VIN	No. Cylinder Displacement cu. in. (liter)	Engine Crankcase with Filter	Engine Crankcase without Filter	Transmission (pts.) 4-Spd	Transmission (pts.) 5-Spd	Transmission (pts.) Auto.	Drive Axle (pts.)	Fuel Tank (gal.)	Cooling System (qts.)
1987	Chevette	C	4-98 (1.6)	4	4	3.5	⑤	6①	1.75	12.5	9②
	1000	C	4-98 (1.6)	4	4	6.0	④	6①	1.75	12.2	9②

① Overhaul—10 pts.
② With air conditioning—9.25
④ BW—5.3 pts.
   Isuzu—3.3 pts.
⑤ 69.5mm—3.25 pts.
   77mm—4.0 pts.

CRANKSHAFT AND CONNECTING ROD SPECIFICATIONS
All measurements are given in inches.

Year	VIN	No. Cylinder Displacement cu. in. (liter)	Crankshaft Main Brg. Journal Dia.	Crankshaft Main Brg. Oil Clearance	Crankshaft Shaft End-play	Crankshaft Thrust on No.	Connecting Rod Journal Diameter	Connecting Rod Oil Clearance	Connecting Rod Side Clearance
1986	C	4-98 (1.6)	2.0078–2.0088	①	.004–.008	4	1.809–1.810	.0014–.0031	.004–.012
	D	4-111 (1.8)	2.2010–2.2020	.0015–.0027	.002–.009	3	1.927–1.928	.0016–.0032	NA
1987	C	4-98 (1.6)	2.0078–2.0088	①	.004–.008	4	1.809–1.810	.0014–.0031	.004–.012

① No.5—.0009-.0026
  All others—.0005-.0018

VALVE SPECIFICATIONS

Year	VIN	No. Cylinder Displacement cu. in. (liter)	Seat Angle (deg.)	Face Angle (deg.)	Spring Test Pressure (lbs.)	Spring Installed Height (in.)	Stem-to-Guide Clearance (in.) Intake	Stem-to-Guide Clearance (in.) Exhaust	Stem Diameter (in.) Intake	Stem Diameter (in.) Exhaust
1986	C	4-98 (1.6)	45	46	173	1.25	.0006–.0017	.0014–.0025	.3141	.3133
	D	4-111 (1.8)	45	45	108	1.61	.0015–.0028	.0018–.0030	.3128–.3134	.3126–.3132
1987	C	4-98 (1.6)	45	46	173	1.25	.0006–.0017	.0014–.0025	.3141	.3133

PISTON AND RING SPECIFICATIONS
All measurments are given in inches.

Year	VIN	No. Cylinder Displacement cu. in. (liter)	Piston Clearance	Ring Gap Top Compression	Ring Gap Bottom Compression	Ring Gap Oil Control	Ring Side Clearance Top Compression	Ring Side Clearance Bottom Compression	Ring Side Clearance Oil Control
1986	C	4-98 (1.6)	.0008–.0016	.009–.019	.008–.018	.015–.055	.0012–.0027	.0012–.0032	.0003–.0050
	D	4-111 (1.8)	.0002–.0017	.008–.016	.008–.016	.008–.016	.0035–.0049	.0019–.0033	.0012–.0028
1987	C	4-98 (1.6)	.0008–.0016	.009–.019	.008–.018	.015–.055	.0012–.0027	.0012–.0032	.0003–.0050

TORQUE SPECIFICATIONS
All readings in ft. lbs.

Year	VIN	No. Cylinder Displacement cu. in. (liter)	Cylinder Head Bolts	Main Bearing Bolts	Rod Bearing Bolts	Crankshaft Pulley Bolts	Flywheel Bolts	Manifold Intake	Manifold Exhaust	Spark Plugs
1986	C	4-98 (1.6)	75	50	40	100	50	18	25	22
	D	4-111 (1.8)	②	75	65	110	40	30	①	—
1987	C	4-98 (1.6)	75	50	40	100	50	18	25	22

① Center bolts – 13–18
   End bolts – 19–25

② First tighten to 21–36 ft. lbs. Then retighten to 83–98 (new bolts) or 90–105 (used bolts)

WHEEL ALIGNMENT

Year	Model	Caster Range (deg.)	Caster Preferred Setting (deg.)	Camber Range (deg.)	Camber Preferred Setting (deg.)	Toe-in (in.)	Steering Axis Inclination (deg.)
1986	All	4P-6P	5P	¼P-½P	¼P	¹⁄₁₆P	NA
1987	All	4P-6P	5P	¼P-½P	¼P	¹⁄₁₆P	NA

ELECTRICAL

NOTE: **Disconnecting the negative battery cable on some vehicles may interfere with the functions of the on board computer systems and may require the computer to undergo a relearning process, once the negative battery cable is reconnected.**

For testing and overhaul procedures on starters, alternators and voltage regulators, refer to the Unit repair Section.

Charging System

ALTERNATOR

Removal and Installation

1. Disconnect the negative battery cable.
2. Disconnect the alternator wiring. On vehicles equipped with diesel engine, remove the fan shroud and fresh air duct, then disconnect the oil and vacuum lines at the vacuum pump.
3. Remove the brace bolt and the drive belt.
4. Support the alternator. Remove the mounting bolt and remove the alternator.

NOTE: **On vehicles equipped with diesel engine, the mounting bolts are removed from below the vehicle.**

5. Installation is the reverse of removal. Adjust the alternator belt to the correct specification.

VOLTAGE REGULATOR

The voltage regulator is a solid state unit mounted inside the alternator. The voltage regulator voltage setting cannot be adjusted. Replacement of the voltage regulator requires disassembling of the alternator.

BELT TENSION CHART

	New Belt (lbs.)	Used Belt (lbs.)
Alternator	146	70
Power Steering	146	70
Air Conditioning	168	90

Starting System

STARTER

Removal and Installation

1.6L ENGINE

Without Power Brakes

1. Disconnect the battery negative cable.
2. Remove the air cleaner.
3. Disconnect and plug the fuel line at the carburetor and move it aside.
4. Disconnect and tag the vacuum hoses at the carburetor.
5. Remove the splash shield from the distributor coil and move it aside.

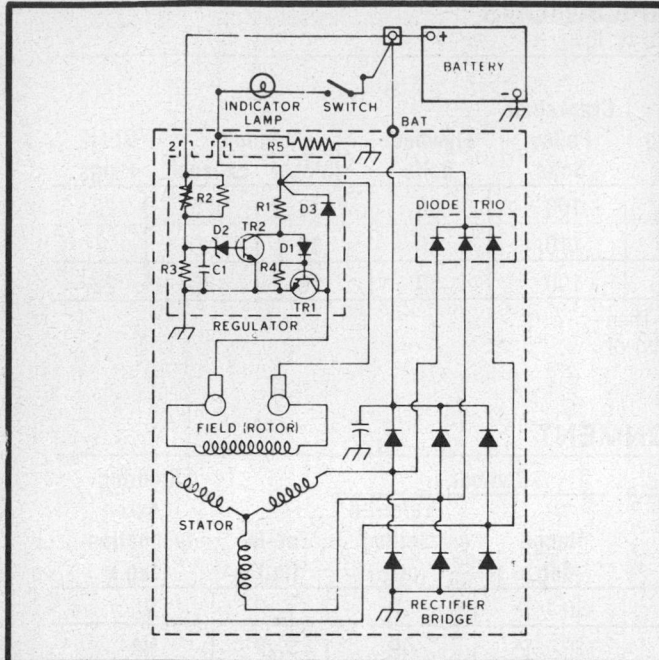

Electrical schematic of Delcotron charging system

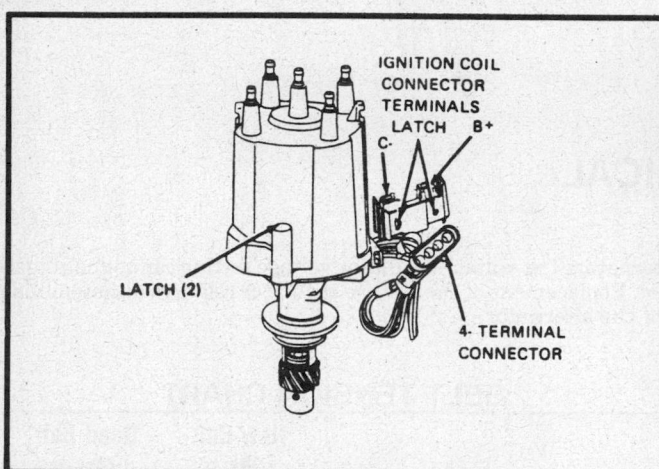

Four terminal connector on EST distributor

6. Using a 6 in. and 12 in. extension with a universal socket, remove the upper starter bolt.

7. Remove the lower starter bolt.

8. Disconnect and tag the starter wiring.

NOTE: The master cylinder mounting nuts can be removed for access to remove the starter. Take care not to bend any of the brakes lines.

9. Installation is the reverse of removal.

With Power Brakes

1. Disconnect the battery ground cable.

2. Remove the air cleaner.

3. Disconnect and plug the fuel line at the carburetor.

4. Remove the splash shield from the distributor coil.

5. Using a 6 in. and 12 in. extension with a universal socket, remove the upper starter bolt.

6. Remove the steering column cover screws and remove the cover.

7. Remove the steering column upper nuts and toe pan screw.

8. Raise and safely support the vehicle. Remove the steering shaft from the steering coupling.

9. Lower the vehicle and move the steering column from inside the vehicle to gain access to the starter.

10. Disconnect and tag the starter wiring.

11. Remove the starter lower bolt and remove the starter.

12. Installation is the reverse of removal.

1.8L ENGINE

1. Disconnect the negative battery cable.

2. Disconnect and tag the starter wiring.

3. Remove the upper mounting nut and the lower mounting bolt.

4. Remove the starter.

5. Installation is the reverse of the removal.

Ignition System

DISTRIBUTOR

Removal and Installation

TIMING NOT DISTURBED

1. Disconnect the negative battery cable.

2. If the vehicle is equipped with air conditioning, disconnect the electrical lead at the air conditioning compressor. Remove the compressor mounting through bolt and 2 adjusting bolts. Remove the compressor upper mounting bracket.

3. Raise and safely support the vehicle. Remove the 2 bolts securing the compressor lower mounting bracket and pull the bracket outward for clearance. Do not disconnect any air conditioning refrigerant lines.

4. Lower the vehicle.

5. Remove the air cleaner.

6. Remove the distributor cap.

7. Remove the ignition coil cover by prying on the flat on the front edge of the cover.

8. Remove the ignition coil mounting bracket bolts.

9. Disconnect the electrical connector with red and brown wires that goes from the ignition coil to the distributor.

10. Remove the fuel pump, gasket and pushrod, noting the direction in which pushrod was installed.

NOTE: The fuel pump pushrod must be installed in exactly the same direction as it was removed.

11. Scribe a mark on the engine in line with the distributor rotor tip. Note the position of the distributor housing in relation to the engine.

12. Remove the distributor hold-down bolt and clamp. Remove the distributor.

13. Complete installation by reversing the removal procedure. Aligning the marks made during removal.

TIMING DISTURBED

1. Remove the No. 1 spark plug and place a finger over the spark plug hole.

2. Manually turn the engine in the normal direction of rotation until compression is felt.

3. Align the timing marks to TDC. Align the marks made during removal and install the distributor.

IGNITION TIMING

Adjustment

NOTE: Refer to and follow all instructions on the Vehicle Emissions Control information label located on the radiator support panel for the latest service procedures or specification changes.

1. Connect a timing light to the number one spark plug. Use a

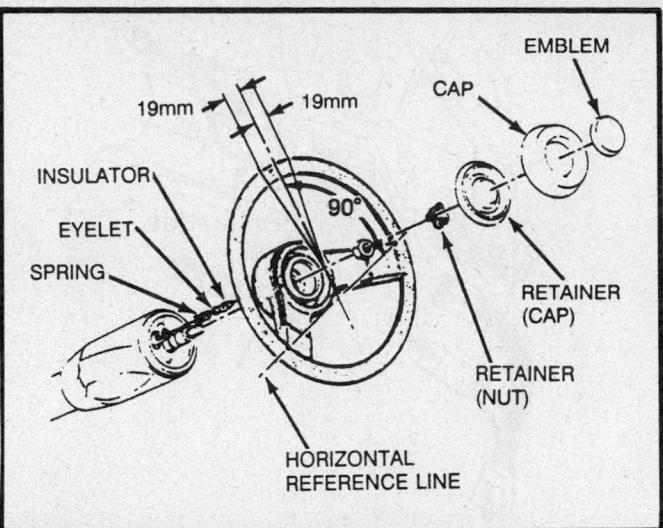

Steering wheel removal and installation

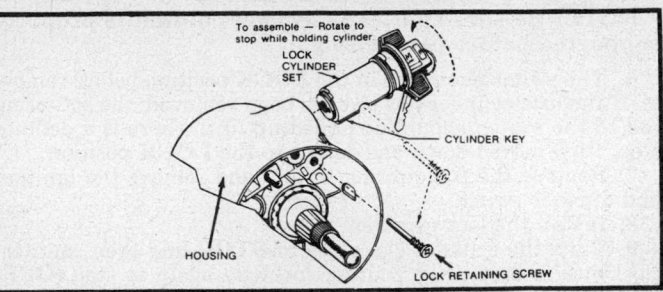

Lock cylinder installation

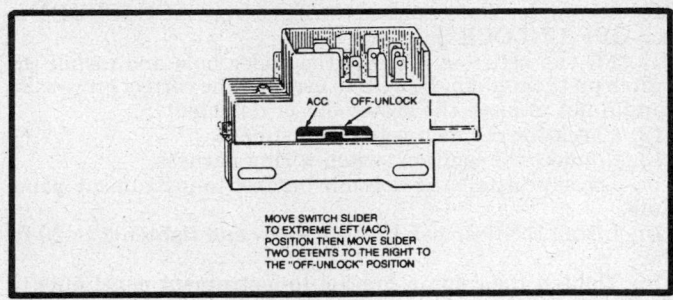

Ignition switch positioning

jumper lead or adapter between the wire and plug, or use a timing light with an inductive type pick-up. Do not pierce the wire or attempt to insert a wire between the boot and the wire.

2. Start and run the engine until it reaches normal operating temperature.

NOTE: On vehicles equipped with Electronic Spark Timing (EST), disconnect the 4 terminal connector at the distributor.

3. Aim the timing light at the timing mark on the balancer or pulley, if the timing marks are not within specifications, loosen the distributor hold-down clamp bolt. Rotate the distributor until the timing marks indicates the correct timing.

4. Tighten the distributor hold-down bolt and recheck the timing.

5. Vehicles equipped with EST, reconnect the 4 terminal connector at the distributor.

6. Turn the engine **OFF**. Disconnect the timing light and reconnect the No. 1 spark wire, if removed.

Electrical Controls

STEERING WHEEL

Removal and Installation

1. Disconnect the negative battery cable.
2. Pull up on the horn cap to remove it. Remove the horn ring-to-steering wheel attaching screws and remove the ring.
3. Remove the wheel nut retainer and the wheel nut.

NOTE: Do not overexpand the retainer.

4. Using a suitable steering wheel puller, remove the steering wheel from its mounting.
To install:
5. Place the turn signal lever in the **N** position and install the steering wheel. Torque the steering wheel nut to 30 ft. lbs. and install the nut retainer. Use caution not to overexpand the nut retainer.
6. Connect the negative battery cable.

HORN SWITCH

Removal and Installation

1. Disconnect the negative battery cable.
2. Pull outward on the horn cap to remove it. Remove the

horn ring-to-steering wheel attaching screws and remove the ring.
3. Installation is the reverse of the removal procedure. Be sure to position the horn ring properly.

IGNITION LOCK

Removal and Installation

The ignition lock is located on the right side of the steering column and should be removed only in the **RUN** position. Removal in any other position will damage the key buzzer switch. The ignition lock cannot be disassembled; if replacement is required, a new cylinder coded to the old key must be installed.

1. Disconnect the negative battery cable. Remove the steering wheel and turn signal switch.
2. Do not remove the buzzer switch or damage to the lock cylinder will result.
3. Place the lock cylinder in the **RUN** position. Remove the securing screw and remove the cylinder.
To install:
4. Hold the cylinder sleeve and rotate knob (key in) clockwise to stop. (This retracts the actuator). Insert the cylinder into the housing bore with the key on the cylinder sleeve aligned with the keyway in the housing. Push the cylinder in until it bottoms and install the retaining screw.
5. Install the turn signal switch and the steering wheel.

IGNITION SWITCH

Removal and Installation

The ignition switch is mounted on top of the mast jacket near the front of the instrument panel. The switch is located inside the channel section of the brake pedal support and is completely inaccessible without first lowering the steering column.

1. Disconnect the negative battery cable.
2. Remove the steering wheel.
3. Move the driver's seat as far back as possible.
4. Remove the floor pan bracket screw.
5. Remove the 2 column bracket-to-instrument panel nuts and lower the column far enough to disconnect the ignition switch wiring harness.

NOTE: Be sure that the steering column is properly supported before proceeding.

6. The switch should be in the **LOCK** position before removal. If the lock cylinder has already been removed, the actuating rod to the switch should be pulled up until there is a definite stop, then moved down one detent to the **LOCK** position.

7. Remove the 2 mounting screws and remove the ignition and dimmer switch.

8. Install the lock cylinder.

9. Turn the cylinder clockwise to **STOP** and then counterclockwise to stop, then counterclockwise again to stop (**OFF-UNLOCK**) position.

10. Place the ignition switch in the **OFF-UNLOCK** position. Move the slider 2 positions to the right from **ACCESSORY** to the **OFF-UNLOCK** position.

11. Fit the actuator rod into the slider hole and install the switch on the column. Be sure to use only the correct screws. Be careful not to move the switch out of its detent.

12. Check the dimmer switch adjustment.

13. Connect the ignition switch wiring harness.

14. Loosely install the column bracket-to-instrument panel nuts.

15. Install the floor pan bracket screw and tighten it to 20 ft. lbs.

16. Tighten the column bracket-to-instrument panel nuts to 22 ft. lbs.

17. Install the steering wheel.

18. Connect the battery negative cable.

GEAR SELECTOR SWITCH

The gear selector switch is located in the console, at the base of the gear selector lever.

Removal and Installation

1. Disconnect the negative battery cable.

2. Remove the console assembly attaching screws and position the console aside.

3. Remove the gear selector switch attaching screws. Disconnect the electrical connector at the switch and remove the switch.

4. Installation is the reverse of the removal procedure.

CLUTCH START SWITCH

The clutch start switch is located on the top of the clutch pedal.

Adjustment

The clutch start switch is self-adjusting and does not require any adjustment.

Removal and Installation

1. Disconnect the negative battery cable. Remove the electrical connection from the switch.

2. Compress the switch retainer and remove the safety switch from the bracket. Rotate the switch slightly so that the actuating shaft retainer can be pulled from the hole of the clutch pedal.

3. Place the new switch in position so that the actuating shaft retainer is in line with the hole of the clutch pedal and then push the switch into the hole of the clutch bracket.

4. Reconnect the electrical connection on the switch and the negative battery cable.

NOTE: The engine should only start with the clutch pedal fully depressed and the ignition switch in the START position.

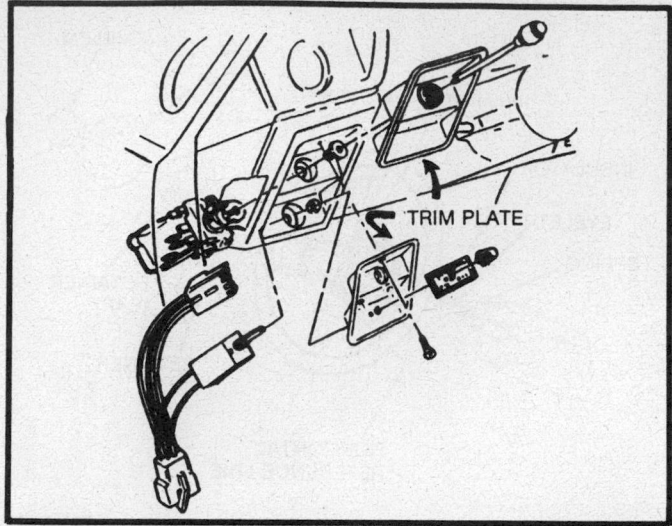
Headlamp switch mounting

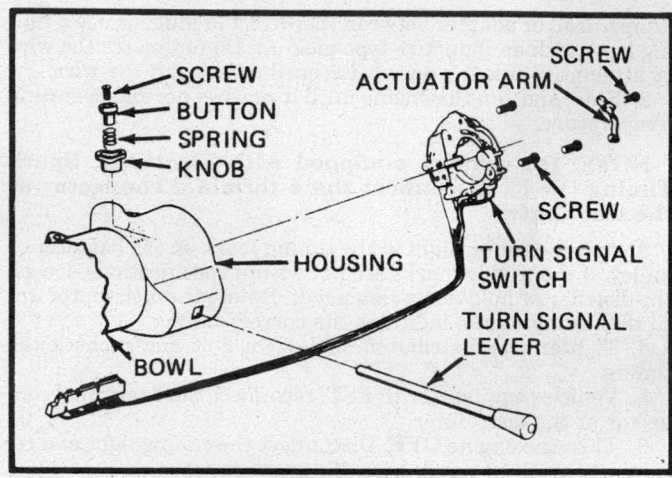
Turn signal switch mounting

STOPLIGHT SWITCH

Removal and Installation

1. Disconnect the negative battery cable. Locate the stoplight switch under the instrument panel on the brake pedal support.

2. Disconnect the wire harness at the switch.

3. Remove the switch from the mounting bracket.

4. Press the new switch into the clip until the shoulder of the switch bottoms out against the clip.

5. Adjust the switch by pulling the brake pedal back to its normal position.

6. Check the operation of the switch. Contact should be made when the brake pedal is depressed 0.53 in. (13.5mm).

HEADLIGHT SWITCH

Removal and Installation

1. Disconnect the negative battery cable.

2. Pull the headlight switch control knob to the **ON** position.

3. Reach up under the instrument panel and depress the switch shaft retainer button while pulling on the switch control shaft knob.

4. Remove the 3 screws and remove the headlight switch trim plate.

5. Remove the light switch ferrule nut from the front of the instrument panel.

6. Disconnect the multi-contact connector from the bottom of the headlight switch.

7. Installation is the reverse of removal.

DIMMER SWITCH

The dimmer switch is incorporated into the ignition switch. Removal and Installation procedures can be found under Ignition Switch.

Adjustment

1. Loosen the dimmer switch attaching screws.
2. Depress the switch slightly to insert a ³⁄₃₂ in. drill. Force the switch up to remove any lash.
3. Tighten the dimmer switch attaching screws.

TURN SIGNAL SWITCH

Removal and Installation

1. Disconnect the negative battery cable. Remove the steering wheel.

2. Position a suitable tool into 1 of the 3 cover slots. Pry up and out on at least 2 slots to free the cover.

3. Press down on the lockplate, but do not relieve the full load of the spring because the ring will rotate and make the removal difficult. Pry the round wire snapring out of the shaft groove and discard it. Lift the lockplate off the end of the shaft.

4. Slide the turn signal canceling cam, upper bearing preload spring and thrust washer off the end of the shaft.

5. Remove the multi-function lever by rotating it clockwise to its stop (**OFF** position), then pull the lever straight out to disengage it.

6. Push the hazard warning knob in and unscrew the knob.

7. Remove the 2 screws, pivot arm and spacer.

8. Wrap the upper part of the connector with tape to prevent snagging the wires during switch removal.

9. Remove the 3 switch mounting screws and pull the switch straight up, guiding the wiring harness through the column housing.

To install:

10. Position the new switch into the housing.

11. Install the 3 switch mounting screws. Replace the spacer and pivot arm. Be sure that the spacer protrudes through the hole in the arm and that the arm finger encloses the turn signal switch frame.

12. Install the hazard warning knob.

13. Make sure that the turn signal switch is in the neutral position and that the hazard warning knob is out. Slide the thrust washer, upper bearing preload spring and the canceling cam into the upper end of the shaft.

14. Place the lockplate and a new snapring onto the end of the shaft. Compress the lockplate as far as possible. Slide the new snapring into the shaft groove and remove the lockplate compressor tool.

15. Install the multi-function lever, guiding the wire harness through the column housing. Align the lever pin with the switch slot. Push on the end of the lever until it is seated securely.

16. Install the steering wheel.

WINDSHIELD WIPER SWITCH

The windshield wiper switch is part of the multi-function switch assembly. The multi-function switch consists of the windshield wiper/washer, headlamp beam selector and directional signal.

Removal and Installation

1. Disconnect the negative battery cable. Remove the steering wheel and turn signal switch. It may be necessary to loosen the 2 steering column mounting nuts and remove the 4 bracket to mast jacket screws, then separate the bracket from the mast jacket to allow the connector clip on the ignition switch to be pulled out of the column assembly.

2. Disconnect the washer/wiper switch lower connector.

3. Remove the screws attaching the column housing to the mast jacket. Be sure to note the position of the dimmer switch actuator rod for reassembly in the same position. Remove the column housing and switch as an assembly.

4. Turn the switch upside down and use a drift to remove the pivot pin from the washer/wiper switch. Remove the switch.

To install:

5. Place a new switch into position in the housing and install the pivot pin.

6. Position the housing onto the mast jacket and attach it by installing the screws. Install the dimmer switch actuator rod in the same position as noted earlier. Check the switch operation.

7. Reconnect lower end of switch assembly.

8. Install remaining components in reverse order of removal. Be sure to attach column mounting bracket in its original position.

WINDSHIELD WIPER MOTOR

Removal and Installation

1. Disconnect the negative battery cable. Working inside the vehicle, reach up under the instrument panel above the steering column and loosen, but do not remove, the transmission drive link-to-motor crank arm attaching nuts.

2. Disconnect the transmission drive link from the wiper rotor crank arm.

3. Raise the hood and disconnect the wiper motor wiring.

4. Remove the 3 motor attaching bolts.

5. Remove the motor while guiding the crank arm through the hole.

6. Align the sealing gasket to the base of the motor and reverse the removal procedure to complete installation.

NOTE: If the wiper motor-to-firewall sealing gasket is damaged during removal, it should be replaced with a new gasket to prevent possible water leaks.

WINDSHIELD WIPER LINKAGE

Removal and Installation

1. Disconnect the negative battery cable. Remove or loosen the instrument panel cover and the instrument panel cluster housing.

2. On vehicles equipped with air conditioning, remove screws and push the left air conditioning duct aside for better access to linkage attaching bolts (left side). Remove the left side air outlet duct, the speedometer cable shield and the instrument panel brace (left side).

3. Working from inside the vehicle, loosen transmission drive link to motor crank arm attaching nuts and disengage drive link.

4. Remove wiper arm and blade assemblies. Remove wiper linkage to dash panel attaching bolts.

5. Move the linkage assembly to the left while rotating the assembly, work it out through instrument panel access hole at right upper center of instrument panel.

To install:

6. Install the assembly through instrument panel access hole and insert serrated shafts through holes in upper dash panel, then install the attaching bolts.

7. Cycle the wiper motor to insure that motor crank arm is in the park position.

8. Attach wiper linkage drive link to wiper motor crank arm.

9. Complete installation by reversing the removal procedure.

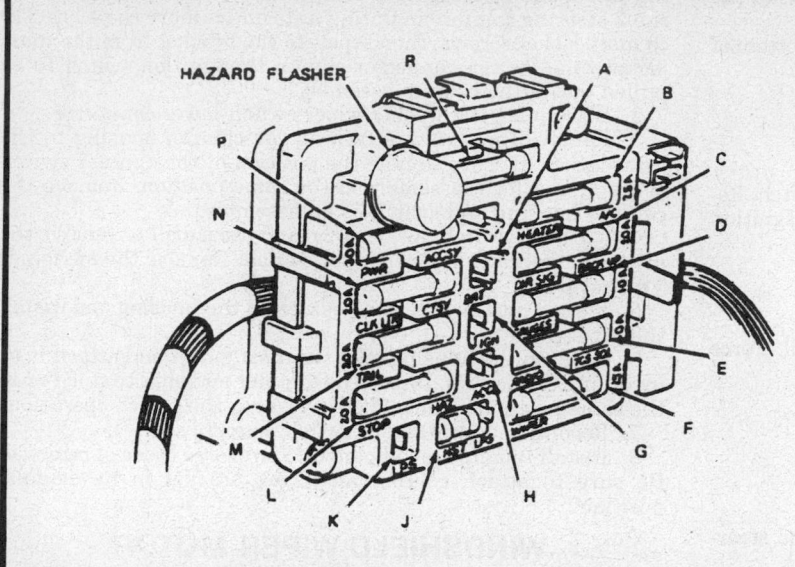

A. Battery receptacle
B. Heater/air conditioner
C. Directional signal/backup lamp
D. Gauges
E. Radio/tcs solenoid
F. Windshield wipers
G. Ignition receptacle
H. Accessory receptacle
I. Hazard flasher
J. Instrument lights
K. Lamp receptacle
L. Stop/hazard warning lamps
M. Tail lamp
N. Clock/lighter/courtesy lamps
P. Power accessory fuse/receptacle
R. Electric choke

Fuse Block and fuse locations

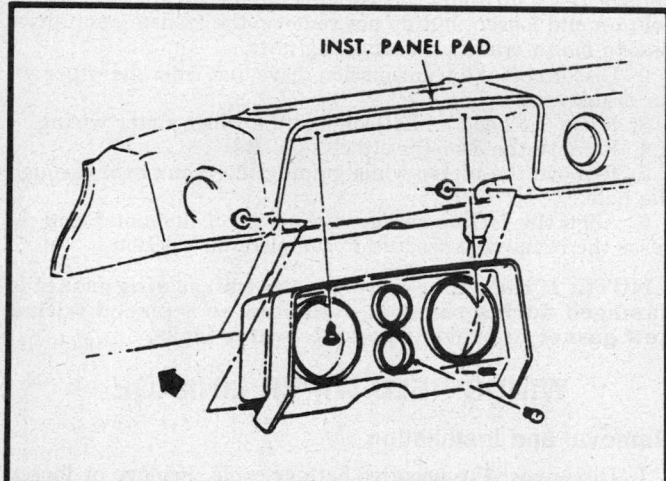

Instrument cluster

Instrument Cluster

Removal and Installation

1. Disconnect the negative battery cable.
2. Remove the clock stem knob, if equipped.
3. Remove the 4 screws and remove the instrument cluster bezel and lens.
4. Remove the 2 nuts securing the instrument cluster to the instrument panel and pull the cluster slightly forward.
5. Disconnect the electrical connector and speedometer cable from the cluster and remove it.
6. Installation is the reverse of removal procedures. Be sure to connect the speedometer cable to the cluster before installation.

SPEEDOMETER

Removal and Installation

1. Disconnect the negative battery cable. Remove the instrument cluster assembly.

2. Remove the speedometer retaining screws from the instrument cluster.
3. Separate the speedometer head from the instrument cluster.
4. Installation is the reverse of the removal procedure.

SPEEDOMETER CABLE

Removal and Installation

1. Disconnect the negative battery cable. Remove the instrument cluster assembly.
2. Pull the core from the speedometer cable housing. If the core is broken in the middle, it will be necessary to disconnect the speedometer cable at the transmission and insert the new core through the top of the housing.
3. Attach the cable housing to the transmission and insert the new core through the top of the housing.
4. Attach the speedometer cable to the rear of the speedometer.
5. Install the instrument cluster assembly and check the speedometer operation.

Electrical Circuit Protectors

FUSIBLE LINKS

Fusible links are provided in all battery feed circuits and other selected circuits. This is a short piece of copper wire approximately 4 in. long in series with the circuit and acts as a fuse. Fusible links are generally located at the starter motor electrical junction.

CIRCUIT BREAKERS

A circuit breaker is an electrical switch which breaks the circuit during an electrical overload. The circuit breaker will remain open until the short or overload condition in the circuit is corrected. Circuit breakers are located in the fuse panel.

FUSE PANEL

The fuse block on some vehicles is a swing-down unit located in the underside of the instrument panel adjacent to the steering column. On other vehicles, the fuse block is located behind the glove box and access is gained through the glove box opening.

ELECTRONIC CONTROL MODULE

The electronic control module is located below the right hand side of the instrument panel.

VARIOUS RELAYS

Location

HORN RELAY—located below the left side of the instrument panel near the fuse box.

A/C BLOWER RELAY—located under the right side of the dash on the A/C module.
REAR WINDOW DEFOGGER RELAY—located behind the left side of the instrument panel.

TURN SIGNAL FLASHER

The turn signal flasher is located above the brake pedal bracket and to the left of the steering column.

HAZARD FLASHER

The hazard flasher is located behind the left side of the instrument panel on the fuse box.

COOLING AND HEATING SYSTEMS

Water Pump

Removal and Installation

1.6L ENGINE

1. Disconnect the battery negative cable. Remove the alternator and air conditioning compressor drive belts.
2. Remove the engine fan, spacer and the pulley.
3. Remove the timing belt front cover by removing the 2 upper bolts, center bolt and 2 lower nuts. Remove the timing belt lower cover retaining nut and remove the cover.
4. Drain the coolant from the engine.
5. Remove the lower radiator hose and the heater hose at the water pump.
6. Turn the crankshaft pulley so that the mark on the pulley is aligned with the **0** mark on the timing scale and that a ⅛ in. drill bit can be inserted through the timing belt upper rear cover and camshaft sprocket.
7. Remove the idler pulley and pull the timing belt off the sprocket. Do not disturb the crankshaft position.
8. Remove the water pump retaining bolts and remove the pump and gasket from the engine.
9. Clean off all the old gasket material from the engine.
To install:
10. With a new gasket in place on the water pump, position the water pump in place on the engine and install the retaining bolts.
11. Install the timing belt onto the cam sprocket.
12. Apply sealer to the idler pulley attaching bolt and install the bolt and the idler pulley. Turn the idler pulley counterclockwise on its mounting bolt to remove the slack in the timing belt.
13. Use a tension gauge to adjust timing belt tension. Check belt tension midway between the tensioner and the cam sprocket on the idler pulley side. Correct belt tension is 70 lbs. Torque the idler pulley mounting bolt to 13–18 ft. lbs.
14. Remove the ⅛ in. drill bit from the upper rear timing belt cover and cam sprocket.
15. Install the lower radiator hose and the heater hose to the water pump.
16. Install the timing belt front covers.
17. Install the water pump pulley, spacer and engine fan.
18. Install the engine drive belt(s).
19. Refill the cooling system.
20. Connect the battery negative cable.
21. Start the engine and check for leaks. Run the engine with the heater on until the thermostat opens, then recheck the coolant level.

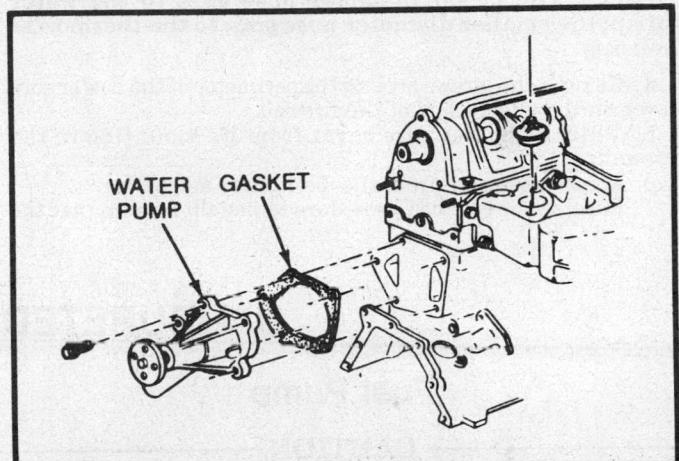

WATER PUMP   GASKET

Water pump mounting—diesel engine

1.8L ENGINE

1. Disconnect the negative battery cable. Drain the cooling system.
2. Remove the fan shroud, fan assembly and the accessory drive belt.
3. Remove the damper pulley retaining bolts and remove the pulley.
4. Remove the upper and lower halves of the front cover and then remove the bypass hose at the pump.
5. Remove the water pump retaining bolts and remove the pump assembly.
6. Installation is in the reverse order of removal.

Blower Motor

Removal and Installation

1. Disconnect the negative battery cable.
2. Disconnect the electrical lead from the blower motor.
3. Scribe a mark to reference the blower motor flange-to-case position.
4. Remove the blower motor-to-case attaching screws and remove the blower motor and wheel as an assembly. Pry the flange gently if the sealer acts as an adhesive.
5. Remove the blower wheel retaining nut and separate the motor and wheel.

6. Reverse the removal procedure to complete installation. Be sure to align the scribe marks made during removal.

NOTE: Assemble the blower wheel to the motor with the open end of the wheel away from the motor. If necessary, replace the sealer at the motor flange.

Heater Core

Refer to "Chilton's Auto Heating and Air Conditioning Manual" for additional coverage.

Removal and Installation

WITHOUT AIR CONDITIONING

1. Disconnect the negative battery cable.
2. Drain the radiator.
3. Disconnect the heater hoses at the heater core tube connections. Use care when removing the hoses as the core tube attachment seams can be easily damaged if too much force is used on them. When the hoses are removed, install plugs in the core tubes to avoid spilling coolant when removing the core.

NOTE: The larger diameter hose goes to the water pump: the smaller diameter hose goes to the thermostat housing.

4. Remove the screws around the perimeter of the heater core cover on the engine side of the firewall.
5. Pull the heater core cover from its mounting in the firewall.
6. Remove the core from the distributor assembly.
7. Reverse the removal procedure to install. Be sure that the core-to-case sealer is intact before replacing the core; use new sealer if necessary. When installation is complete, check for coolant leaks.

WITH AIR CONDITIONING

1. Disconnect the negative battery cable.
2. Disconnect the heater hoses at the core with a drain pan under the vehicle. Plug the hoses to prevent spillage.
3. Remove the air conditioning hose bracket.
4. Removes the heater core case cover and remove the core from the case.
5. Installation is the reverse of removal.

Temperature Control/Blower Switch

Removal and Installation

1. Disconnect the negative battery cable.
2. Remove the 4 screws from the center trim panel, above and below the heater/air conditioning control.
3. Remove the knobs and other necessary hardware from the radio controls, if equipped.
4. Remove the section of instrument panel surrounding the radio and heater controls. On air conditioned equipped vehicles, remove the instrument panel bezel.
5. Remove the 3 heater/air conditioning control to instrument panel screws.
6. Slide the control unit from the dash opening. Do not kink the bowden cables or damage the electrical connectors. When the control unit is out of the dash, disconnect the cables and the electrical connections.
7. Installation is the reverse of the removal procedure.

CARBURETED FUEL SYSTEM

Fuel Pump

CAUTION
Never smoke when working around gasoline! Avoid all sources of sparks or ignition. Remember, gasoline vapors are extremely volatile and can cause serious injury.

Removal and Installation

NOTE: Vehicles equipped with air conditioning requires the removal of the rear compressor bracket for access to the pump.

1. Disconnect the negative battery cable. Raise the vehicle and support it safely.
2. Remove the power steering pump, if equipped.
3. Disconnect the fuel pump inlet and outlet hoses.
4. Remove the fuel pump attaching bolts and remove the pump and gasket.
5. Installation is the reverse of the removal. Start the engine and check for any leaks.

Carburetor

Removal and Installation

1. Disconnect the negative battery cable. Remove air cleaner and gasket.
2. Disconnect the fuel and vacuum lines from the carburetor.
3. Disconnect the accelerator linkage and the electrical connectors.
4. Remove the carburetor attaching nuts and remove the carburetor.

Fuel pump—1.6L engine

5. Remove the Early Fuel Evaporation (EFE) heater and the insulator gasket, if equipped.
6. Be sure the throttle body and intake manifold sealing surfaces are clean.
To install:
7. Install a new EFE heater and an insulator gasket on the manifold, as required.
8. Install the carburetor over the manifold studs.
9. Install the vacuum lines and loosely connect the fuel line.
10. Install and tighten the attaching nuts to 12 ft. lbs.
11. Tighten the fuel inlet nut to 25 ft. lbs.

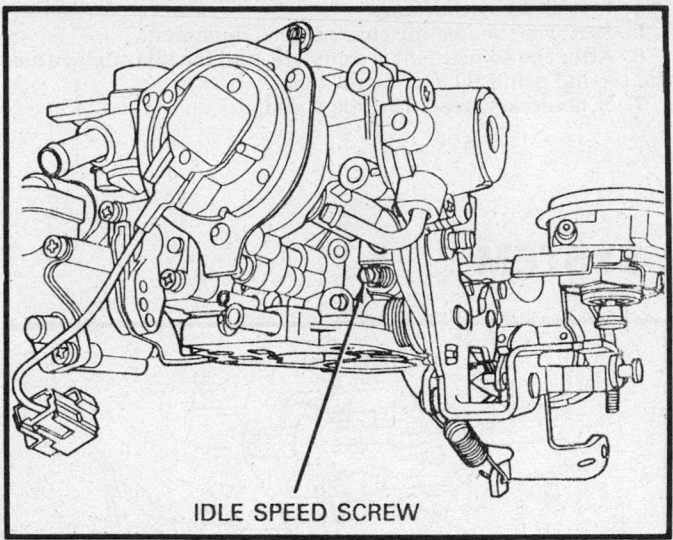

Curb idle speed adjustment

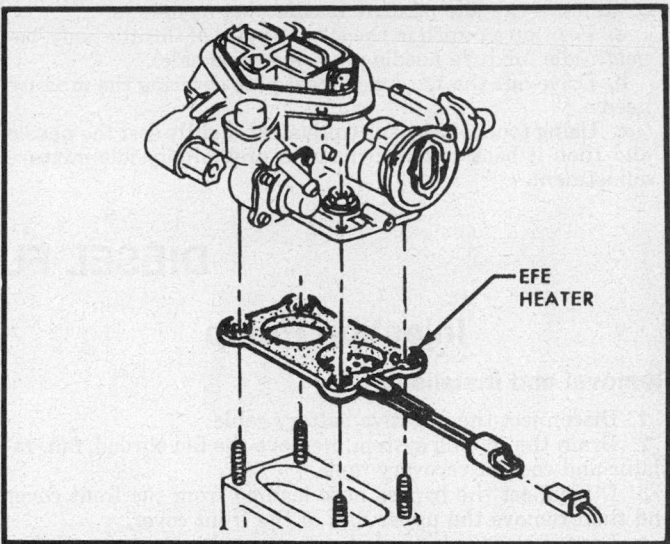

EFE heater and insulator

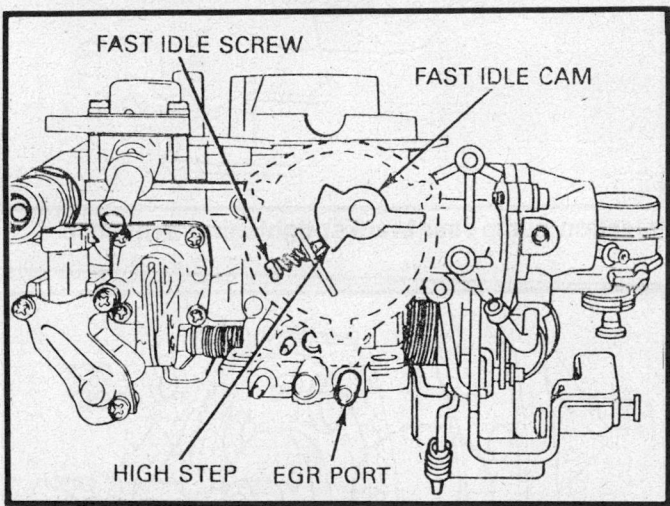

Fast idle speed adjustment

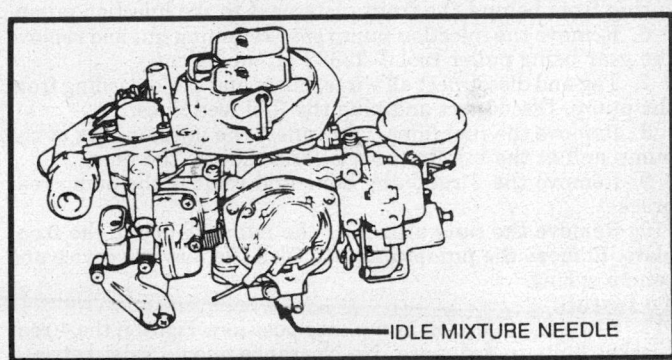

Idle mixture needle location

12. Connect the accelerator linkage and the electrical connectors.
13. Check and adjust the idle speed as required.
14. Install the air cleaner and gasket.

IDLE SPEED

Adjustment

CURB IDLE SPEED

1. Set the parking brake and block the drive wheels.
2. Check the ignition timing and adjust, if necessary. Remove air cleaner assembly.
3. Disconnect the EGR vacuum source at the carburetor and block the port. Disconnect and plug the vacuum hoses for the canister purge tank and the purge control at the canister.
4. Run engine to normal operating temperature, adjust idle speed screw to rpm specified on the vehicle emission control label.
5. Unplug and reconnect all vacuum lines, install air cleaner.

FAST IDLE SPEED

1. Set the parking brake and block the drive wheels.
2. Check the ignition timing and adjust, if necessary. Remove air cleaner assembly.
3. Disconnect the EGR vacuum source at the carburetor and block the port. Disconnect and plug the vacuum hoses for the canister purge tank and the purge control at the canister.
4. Place fast idle screw on highest step of fast idle cam, adjust to rpm specified on vehicle emission control label.
5. Unplug and reconnect all vacuum lines, install air cleaner assembly.

IDLE MIXTURE

Adjustment

NOTE: The idle mixture needle has been preset at the factory and sealed. Do not remove the plug during normal engine maintenance. Idle mixture should be adjusted only in the case of major carburetor overhaul, throttle body replacement or high emissions.

1. Remove the carburetor.
2. Place inverted carburetor on a suitable holding fixture, manifold side up. Use care to avoid damaging linkage tubes and parts protruding from air horn.

3. Remove the idle mixture needle plug as follows:

   a. Position a punch in the locator point of throttle body, beneath idle mixture needle plug (manifold side).

   b. Drive out the hardened steel plug covering the mixture needle.

   c. Using tool J–29030 or equivalent, lightly seat the needle and then it back out 2 turns as a preliminary idle mixture adjustment.

4. Install the carburetor.

5. Perform the idle mixture needle adjustment.

6. After the adjustment is complete, seal the idle mixture needle setting using RTV or equivalent.

7. If necessary, reset the idle speed.

DIESEL FUEL SYSTEM

Injection Pump

Removal and Installation

1. Disconnect the negative battery cable.

2. Drain the cooling system. Remove the fan shroud, fan, radiator and coolant recovery tank.

3. Disconnect the bypass hose leading from the front cover and then remove the upper half of the front cover.

4. Loosen the timing belt tensioner pulley and plate bolts. Slide the tensioner over.

5. Remove the 2 retaining bolts and remove the tension spring from behind the front plate next to the injection pump.

6. Remove the injection pump gear retaining nut and remove the gear using puller tool J–22888 or equivalent.

7. Tag and disconnect all wires, hoses and cables leading from the pump. Disconnect and plug the fuel feed lines.

8. Remove the fuel filter. Disconnect the injector lines at the pump and at the injector nozzles and remove the lines.

9. Remove the 4 retaining bolts and remove the pump rear bracket.

10. Remove the nuts attaching the pump flange to the front plate. Remove the pump complete with the fast idle device and return spring.

To install:

11. Place the injection pump into position. Tighten the 4 rear bracket bolts in sequence. No clearance should exist between the rear bracket and the injection pump bracket.

12. Install the injection pump pulley by aligning it with the key groove. Align the mark on the gear with the mark on the front plate. Then, install the lock bolt (8mm × 1.25). Hold the lock bolt to prevent the pulley from turning and tighten the lock nut to 50–60 ft. lbs. (67–81 Nm).

13. Reconnect all wires, hoses and cables to the pump.

14. Remove the cam cover. Position the No. 1 piston at TDC of the compression stroke and install the fixing plate J–29761 or equivalent into the slot in the rear of the camshaft to prevent it from rotating.

15. Remove the cam gear retaining bolt and, using a suitable puller, remove the gear. Reinstall the gear loosely so that it can be turned smoothly by hand.

16. Hold the timing belt on each side near the lower half of the front cover and move it back and forth until the cogs on the belt engage with those on the lower gears. Slide the belt first over the pump gear and then over the cam gear (the cam gear may have to be turned slightly to properly engage the cogs).

17. Make sure that any slack in the belt is concentrated around the tension pulley and not around or between the 2 upper gears. Depress the tension pulley with a finger and install the tension spring.

18. Partially tighten the tension pulley bolts; first the upper, then the lower. Tighten the cam gear retaining bolt to 45 ft. lbs.

19. Remove the pump gear lock bolt. Remove the fixing plate from the end of the camshaft.

20. Check that the No. 1 piston is still at TDC. Check that the marks on the front plate and the pump gear are still aligned. Check that the fixing plate still fits properly into the rear of the camshaft.

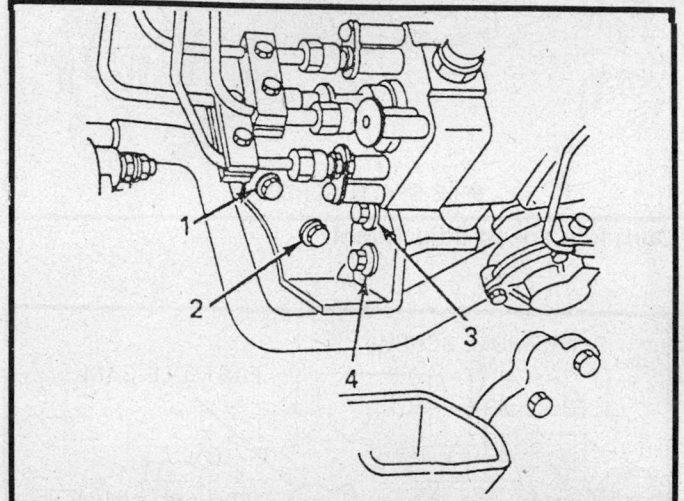

Injection pump rear bracket tightening sequence

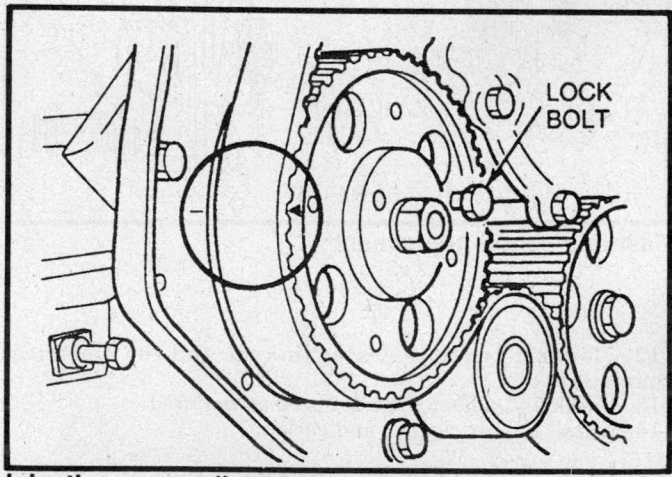

Injection pump alignment mark and lock bolt

NOTE: If Step 20 does not check out correctly, repeat the entire procedure, do not attempt to compensate for any changes by moving the camshaft, pump gear or crankshaft.

21. Loosen the tension pulley and plate bolts. Make sure the belt slack is concentrated around the pulley and then tighten the bolts in the same manner as before. Belt tension should be checked at the mid-point between the cam gear and the pump gear.

22. Installation of the remaining components is in the reverse order of removal.

23. Check the injection timing.

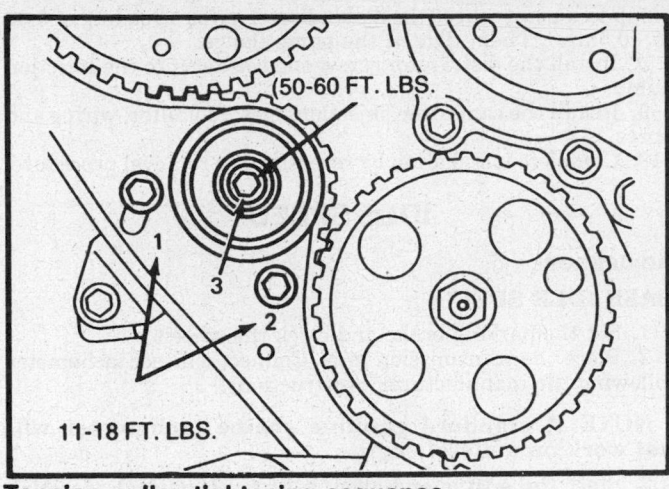

Tension pulley tightening sequence

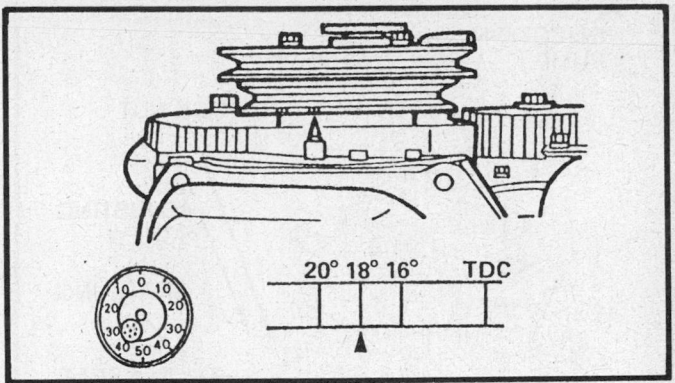

Damper pulley notches

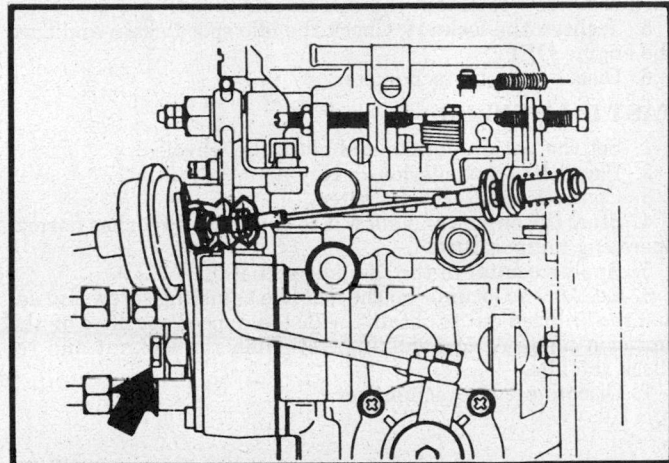

Injection pump distributor screw

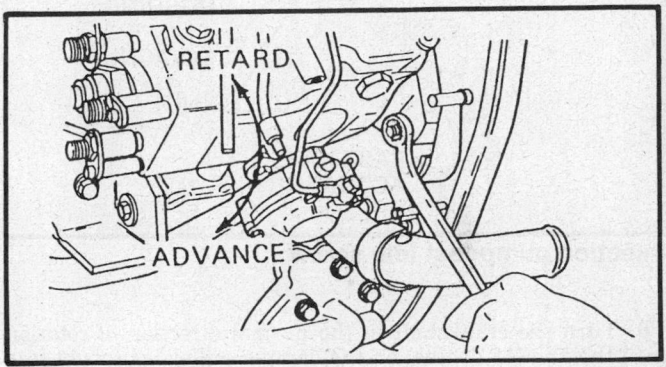

Adjusting the injection pump

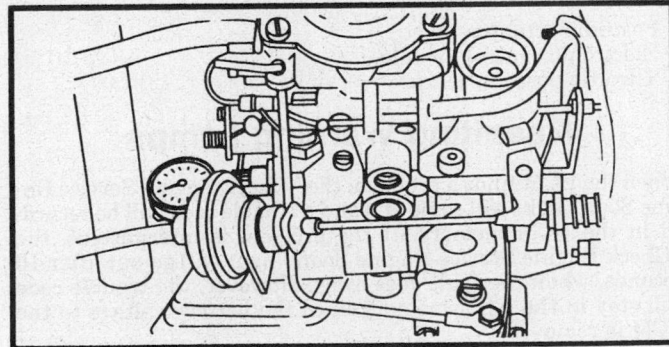

Static timing gauge installation

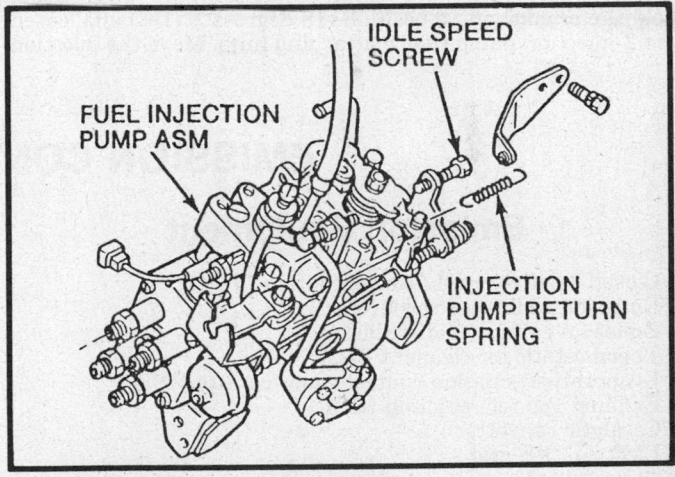

Injection pump base idle screw

INJECTION TIMING

Adjustment

1. Bring No. 1 piston to TDC of the compression stroke. With the upper cover removed, make sure that the timing belt is properly tensioned and the timing marks are aligned.

2. With the cam cover removed, check that the camshaft fixing plate will still fit smoothly into the slot at the rear of the camshaft. Then, remove the fixing plate.

3. Remove the injection lines. Remove the distributor head screw and washer.

4. Install static timing gauge J–29763 or equivalent, and a dial indicator in the distributor head hole. Set the lift approximately 0.04 in. (1mm) from the end of the plunger.

5. Turn the crankshaft until the No. 1 piston is 45–60 degrees BTDC. Then, zero the dial indicator.

NOTE: The damper pulley is provided with notched lines.

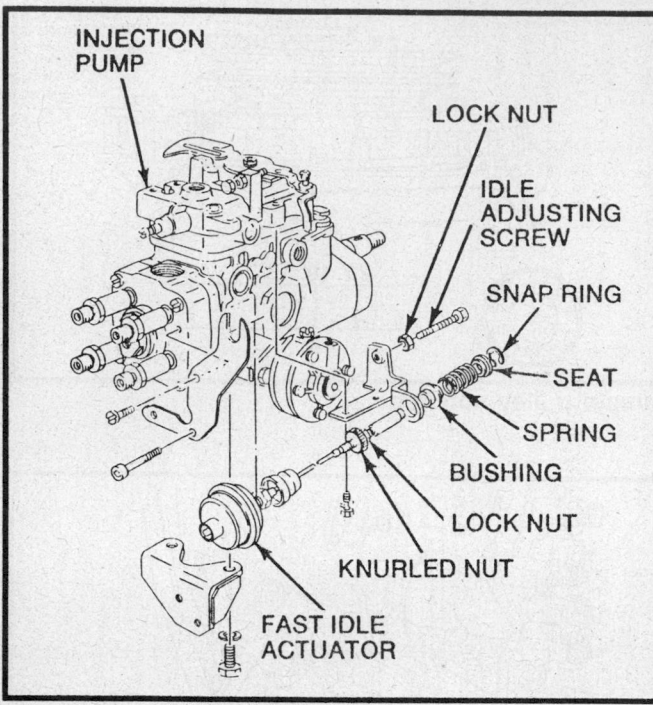

Injection pump fast idle screw

6. Turn the crankshaft in the normal direction of rotation until the line (18 degree) on the damper pulley is brought into alignment with the pointer. Then, read and record the dial indicator reading. Standard reading is 0.02 in. (0.5mm).

7. If the dial indicator reading differs from the specification, hold the crankshaft in position (18 degrees BTDC) and loosen the 2 injection pump flange attaching nuts. Move the injection pump to a point where the dial indicator gives a reading of 0.02 in. (0.5mm). Then, tighten the pump flange.

8. Install the distributor screw and washer into the injection pump.

9. Install the cam cover, injection lines, fuel filter, wiring and hoses.

10. Complete installation by reversing the removal procedure.

IDLE SPEED

Adjustment
BASE IDLE SPEED

1. Set the parking brake and block the wheels.

2. Place the transmission in **N**. Connect a diesel tachometer following the manufacturer's instructions.

NOTE: A standard gasoline engine tachometer will not work on a diesel engine.

3. Start the engine and allow it to reach normal operating temperature.

4. Loosen the locknut on the idle speed adjusting screw and turn the screw to obtain the correct idle speed.

5. Tighten the locknut. Check the idle speed again and turn the engine **OFF**.

6. Disconnect the tachometer.

FAST IDLE SPEED

1. Set the parking brake and block the wheels.

2. Place the transmission in **N**.

3. Connect a diesel tachometer.

4. Start the engine and allow it to run until it reaches normal operating temperature.

5. Apply vacuum to the fast idle actuator.

6. Loosen the locknut on the fast idle adjusting screw and adjust the knurled nut to obtain the fast idle speed specified on the emission label. After adjusting, retighten the locknut and recheck the idle.

7. Disconnect the tachometer.

EMISSION CONTROL SYSTEMS

Emission Equipment

Closed positive crankcase ventilation (PCV)
Emission calibrated carburetor
Emission calibrated distributor
Thermostatic air cleaner (TAC)
Evaporative emission control vapor canister (EEC)
Exhaust gas recirculation (EGR)
Catalytic converter
Electric EFE grid
Electric choke
Pulse air reduction reaction (PAIR)
Deceleration valve
Pulse air shut off valve
Distributor/canister purge thermal vacuum switch (D/CP-TVS)
Vacuum regulator valve
Vacuum break delay valve
Fuel tank pressure control valve
Transmission converter clutch switch (TCC-S)
Transmission converter clutch delay valve (TCC-DV)
Vacuum pump
Low vacuum switch
Vacuum switching valve
Fast idle actuator
Electronic control module
Throttle position sensor

Resetting Warning Lamps

When the ECM finds a problem, the "Check Engine/Service Engine Soon" light will come **ON** and a trouble code will be recorded in the ECM memory. If the problem is intermittent, the "Check Engine/Service Engine Soon" light will go out after 10 seconds, when the fault goes away. However, the trouble code will stay in the ECM memory until the battery voltage to the ECM is removed.

Procedure

Removing battery voltage for 10 seconds will clear all stored trouble codes. Disconnecting the ECM harness from the positive battery pigtail for 10 seconds with the ignition **OFF**, or by disconnecting the ECM fuse, designated ECM or ECM/Bat., from the fuse holder.

NOTE: To prevent ECM damage, the key must be OFF when disconnecting or reconnecting power to ECM (for example battery cable, ECM pigtail, ECM fuse, jumper cables, etc.).

ENGINE

NOTE: Disconnecting the negative battery cable on some vehicles may interfere with the functions of the on board computer systems and may require the computer to undergo a relearning process, once the negative battery cable is reconnected.

Engine Assembly

Removal and Installation

1.6L ENGINE

1. Disconnect the battery cables.
2. Matchmark the hood to the hinges and remove the hood.
3. Remove the battery cable clips from the frame rail.
4. Drain the cooling system. Disconnect the radiator hoses from the engine and the heater hoses at the heater.
5. Tag and disconnect any wires leading from the engine.
6. Remove the radiator upper support and remove the radiator and engine fan.
7. Remove the air cleaner assembly.
8. Disconnect the following items:
   a. Fuel line at the rubber hose along the left frame rail.
   b. Automatic transmission throttle valve linkage.
   c. Accelerator cable.
9. On air conditioned vehicles, remove the compressor from its mount and lay it aside. If equipped with power steering, remove the power steering pump and bracket and lay it aside.
10. Raise and safely support the vehicle.
11. Disconnect the exhaust pipe at the exhaust manifold.
12. Remove the flywheel dust cover on manual transmission vehicles or the torque converter underpan on automatic transmission vehicles.
13. On vehicles equipped with automatic transmission, remove the torque converter-to-flywheel bolts.
14. Remove the converter housing or flywheel housing-to-engine retaining bolts and lower the vehicle.
15. Position a floor jack or other suitable support under the transmission.
16. Remove the safety straps from the front engine mounts and remove the mount nuts.
17. Install the engine lifting apparatus.
18. Remove the engine by pulling it forward to clear the transmission while lifting slowly. Check to make sure that all necessary disconnections have been made and that proper clearance exists with surrounding components.

To install:

19. Install guide pins in the engine block to align with the transmission housing.
20. Install the engine in the vehicle by aligning the engine with the transmission housing.
21. Install the front engine mount nuts and safety straps.
22. Raise and safely support the vehicle.
23. Install the engine-to-transmission housing bolts. Tighten the bolts to 25 ft. lbs.
24. On vehicles equipped with automatic transmission, install the torque converter to the flywheel. Torque the bolts to 35 ft. lbs.
25. Install the flywheel dust cover or torque converter underpan.
26. Install the exhaust pipe to the exhaust manifold and lower the vehicle.
27. Install the air conditioning compressor or the power steering pump, if equipped and adjust drive belt tension.
28. Connect the fuel lines, automatic transmission throttle valve linkage and accelerator cable.
29. Install the air cleaner.
30. Install the engine fan, radiator and radiator upper support.

31. Connect all wires previously disconnected.
32. Connect the radiator and heater hoses and fill the cooling system.
33. Install the battery cable clips along the frame rail.
34. Install the hood.
35. Connect the battery cables, start the engine and check for leaks.

1.8L ENGINE

1. Matchmark the hood to the hinges and remove the hood.
2. Disconnect the negative battery cable first then the positive cable. Remove the battery.
3. Remove the battery cable clips from the frame rail.
4. Drain the cooling system. Disconnect the radiator hoses from the engine and the heater hoses at the heater.
5. Disconnect and tag any wires leading from the engine.
6. Remove the radiator upper support and remove the radiator, engine fan and oil cooler.
7. Remove the air cleaner assembly.
8. Disconnect the following items:
   a. Fuel line at the rubber hose along the left frame rail. Disconnect and plug the fuel lines at the injection pump and position them out of the way.
   b. Accelerator cable.
9. On vehicles equipped with air conditioning, remove the compressor from its mount and lay it aside.
10. Raise and safely support the vehicle.
11. Remove the engine strut (shock-type).
12. Disconnect the exhaust pipe at the exhaust manifold.
13. Remove the flywheel dust cover.
14. Remove the flywheel housing-to-engine retaining bolts and lower the vehicle.
15. Position a floor jack or other suitable support under the transmission.
16. Remove the safety straps from the front engine mounts and remove the mount nuts.
17. Remove the oil filter.
18. Install an appropriate engine lifting apparatus.
19. Remove the engine by pulling forward to clear the transmission while lifting slowly. Check to make sure that all necessary disconnections have been made and that proper clearance exists with surrounding components before removing the engine from the vehicle.

To install:

20. Install the engine lifting apparatus and install guide pins in the engine block.
21. Install the engine in the vehicle by aligning the engine with the flywheel housing.
22. Install the front engine mount nuts and safety straps.
23. Raise and safely support the vehicle.
24. Install the engine-to-flywheel housing bolts. Tighten to 25 ft. lbs.
25. Install the engine strut.
26. Install the exhaust pipe to the exhaust manifold and lower the vehicle.
27. Install the air conditioning compressor and adjust the drive belt tension.
28. Connect the fuel lines and accelerator cable.
29. Install the air cleaner.
30. Install the oil cooler, engine fan, radiator and radiator upper support.
31. Connect all wires previously disconnected.
32. Connect the radiator and heater hoses and fill the cooling system.
33. Install the battery cable clips along the frame rail.
34. Install the hood.
35. Install the battery and connect the battery cables.
36. Start the engine and check for any leaks.

Engine Mounts

Removal and Installation

1.6L ENGINE

Front

1. Disconnect the negative battery cable.
2. Remove the heater assembly and position it on top of the engine.
3. Remove the upper radiator support.
4. Remove the engine mount nuts and retaining wire.
5. Raise the vehicle and support it safely. Using a lifting device, raise the engine.
6. Remove the mount to engine bracket. Remove the engine mount from the vehicle.
7. Installation is the reverse of the removal procedure.

Rear

1. Disconnect the negative battery cable.
2. Raise the vehicle and support it safely.
3. Remove the crossmember to mount bolts and nuts.
4. Raise the transmission and take the weight off of the mount.
5. Remove the mount to transmission retaining bolts.
6. Remove the rear mount from its mounting on the crossmember.
7. Installation is the reverse of the removal procedure.

1.8L ENGINE

Left

1. Disconnect the negative battery cable.
2. Remove the engine mount attaching nut and retaining wire.
3. Raise wire engine. Using tool J–25510 or equivalent, remove the engine mount.
4. Installation is the reverse of the removal procedure.

Right

1. Disconnect the negative battery cable.
2. Raise and support the vehicle safely.
3. Remove the mount attaching bolt from the engine side of mount. Remove the strut from the mount.
4. Lower the vehicle. Remove the seperator and lay aside.
5. Remove the engine mount attaching nut and retaining wire. Using tool J–25510 or equivalent, remove the engine mount.
6. Installation is the reverse of the removal procedure.

Intake Manifold

Removal and Installation

1.6L ENGINE

1. Disconnect the negative battery cable.
2. Drain the cooling system.
3. Remove the air cleaner.
4. Disconnect the upper radiator and heater hoses.
5. Remove the EGR valve.
6. Disconnect all electrical wiring, vacuum hoses and the accelerator linkage from the carburetor.
7. Disconnect the fuel line from the carburetor.
8. Remove the coil.
9. Remove the intake manifold retaining bolts. Remove the intake manifold from the engine.
10. Installation is the reverse of removal. Torque all intake manifold bolts to 15 ft. lbs (20 Nm).

1.8L ENGINE

1. Disconnect the negative battery cable.
2. Disconnect the fresh air hose and the vent hose. Remove the fuel separator.

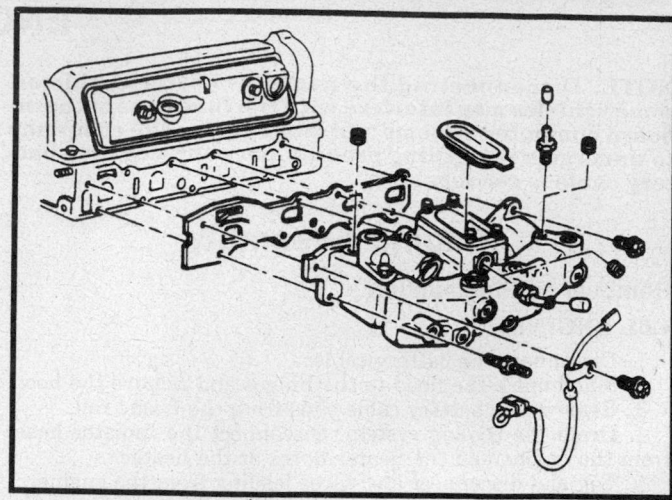

Intake manifold mounting—1.6L engine

3. Tag and disconnect all electrical connectors, the accelerator linkage and the glow plug wires.
4. Disconnect the injector lines at the injection pump and at the injector nozzles. Remove the injector lines and the hold-down clamps.
5. Remove the glow plug line at the cylinder head.
6. If equipped with power steering, remove the drive belt, the idler pulley and the bracket.
7. Remove the upper half of the front cover and the bracket.
8. Remove the intake manifold retaining bolts. Remove the intake manifold from the engine.
9. Position a new gasket over the mounting studs on the cylinder head and install the manifold. Tighten the bolts to 30 ft. lbs.
10. Complete installation by reversing the removal procedure.

Exhaust Manifold

Removal and Installation

1.6L ENGINE

1. Disconnect the negative battery cable.
2. Raise and safely support the vehicle.
3. Disconnect the exhaust pipe from the flange.
4. Lower the vehicle.
5. Remove the carburetor heat tube.
6. Remove the pulse air tubing, if so equipped.
7. Remove the exhaust manifold-to-cylinder head bolts and remove the manifold.
8. Installation is the reverse of removal. Install the 2 upper inner bolts first, to properly position the manifold. Tighten the bolts to the specified torque.

1.8L ENGINE

1. Disconnect the negative battery terminal.
2. Raise and safely support the vehicle.
3. Disconnect the exhaust pipe from the flange.
4. Lower the vehicle.
5. Remove the power steering belt, the flex hose and the power steering pump.
6. Remove the exhaust manifold-to-cylinder head bolts and remove the exhaust manifold from the vehicle.
7. Installation is the reverse of removal. Install the 2 upper inner bolts first, to properly position the manifold. Tighten the bolts to the specified torque.

CYLINDER NO.	1		2		3		4	
VALVES	I	E	I	E	I	E	I	E
STEP. 1	○		○	○			○	
STEP. 2				○	○		○	○

I : INTAKE VALVE
E: EXHAUST VALVE

Valve adjustment sequence—1.8L engine

Depressing the valve spring using the special tool

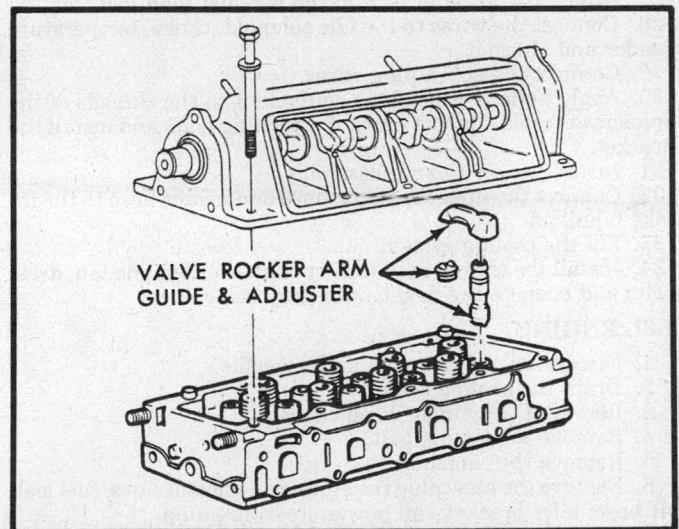

Rocker arm and lash adjuster positioning

Valve System

VALVE ADJUSTMENT

1.6L ENGINE

Adjustment of the hydraulic valve lash adjusters is automatic. No servicing of the lash adjusters is required, except cleanliness should be exercised when handling the valve lash adjusters. Before installation of the valve lash adjusters, fill them with oil and check the lash adjuster oil hole in the cylinder head to make sure that it is unclogged and free of foreign matter.

1.8L ENGINE

NOTE: The rocker arm shaft bracket bolts and nuts should be tightened to 20 ft. lbs. before adjusting the valves.

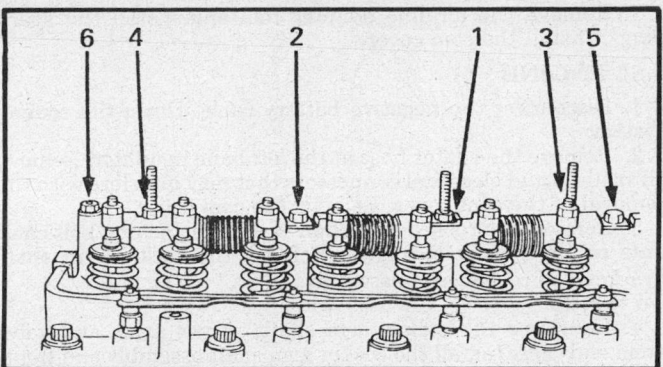

Rocker arm shaft bracket removal and installation torque sequence—1.8L engine

7	3	2	6	10
○	○	○	○	○
○	○	○	○	○
8	4	1	5	9

FRONT

Gas engine cylinder head torque sequence

1. Remove the cylinder head cover retaining bolts and cover.
2. Rotate the crankshaft until the No. 1 piston is at TDC of it's compression stroke.
3. Start with the intake valve on the No. 1 cylinder and insert a feeler gauge of the correct thickness (intake–0.010 in., exhaust–0.014 in.) into the gap between the valve stem cap and the rocker arm. If adjustment is required, loosen the locknut on top of the rocker arm and turn the adjusting screw clockwise to decrease the gap and counterclockwise to increase it. When the correct clearance is reached, tighten the locknut and then recheck the gap. Adjust the remaining 3 valves in this step in the same manner.
4. Rotate the crankshaft 1 complete revolution and adjust the remaining valves accordingly.

VALVE ROCKER SHAFT/ARM ASSEMBLY

Removal and Installation

1.6L ENGINE

1. Disconnect the negative battery cable. Remove the camshaft cover and carburetor from the engine.
2. Using tool J–25477 or equivalent, depress the valve spring and remove the rocker arms. Note the location of all parts so they can be reinstalled in their original location.
3. Remove the spark plugs and install an air line adapter tool J–23590 or equivalent into a spark plug port. Pressurize the cylinder to hold the valves in place.
4. Using tool J–25477 or equivalent, depress the valve spring and remove the rocker guides, valve locks, caps and valve spring. Remove the valve stem oil seal, as required.
To install:
5. Position the valve stem seal over the valve stem and seat against hand. Place the valve spring and cap over the valve stem, compress and install the valve lock.

NOTE: Grease may be used to hold the lock in place while working with the valve spring compressor tool.

6. Install the rocker guides and rocker arms, then remove the compressor tool.

7. Remove the air line adapter tool and install the spark plugs. Install the cam cover.

1.8L ENGINE

1. Disconnect the negative battery cable. Drain the cooling system.
2. Remove the heater hose at the left hand insulator. Remove all vacuum and electrical connectors that may interfere with the removal of the cam cover. Remove the cam cover.
3. Remove the rocker arm shaft bracket attaching bolts and nuts in the proper sequence. Remove the rocker arm shaft bracket and rocker arm assembly.

To install:

4. Lubricate the rocker arm shaft, rocker arms and valve stem end caps. Install the rocker arm shaft assembly and tighten in sequence to 20 ft. lbs. (27 Nm).
5. Adjust the valves, install the cam cover and fill the cooling system.

Cylinder Head

Removal and Installation

1.6L ENGINE

1. Disconnect the negative battery cable.
2. Remove all accessory drive belts.
3. Remove the engine fan, timing belt cover and timing belt.
4. Remove the air cleaner and snorkel assembly.
5. Drain the cooling system and disconnect the upper radiator hose and heater hose at the intake manifold.
6. Remove the accelerator cable support bracket.
7. Disconnect and label the spark plug wires.
8. Disconnect and label the wires from the idle solenoid, choke, temperature sender and alternator.
9. Raise the vehicle and disconnect the exhaust pipe from the exhaust manifold.
10. Remove the dipstick tube bracket-to-manifold attaching bolt.
11. Disconnect the fuel line at the carburetor.
12. Take off the coil cover. Remove the coil bracket bolts and remove the coil.
13. Remove the camshaft cover.
14. Remove the camshaft cover-to-camshaft housing attaching stubs.
15. Remove the rocker arms, rocker arm guides and valve lash adjusters. Keep the parts in order so that they can be installed in their original locations.
16. Remove the camshaft carrier to cylinder head attaching bolts and remove the camshaft carrier. A sharp wedge may be necessary to separate the camshaft carrier from the cylinder head. Be very cautious not to damage the mating surfaces.
17. Remove the manifold and cylinder head as an assembly.

To install:

18. Install a new cylinder head gasket with the words **THIS SIDE UP** facing up over dowel pins in the block. Make sure that the gasket is absolutely clean.
19. Install the manifold and cylinder head assembly.
20. Apply a light, thin continuous bead of sealant to the jointing surfaces of the cylinder head and the camshaft carrier and install the camshaft carrier. Clean any excess sealer from the cylinder head. Apply sealing compound to the camshaft carrier/cylinder head bolts and install the bolts finger-tight. Tighten the bolts a little at a time and in the correct sequence until the final specified torque figure is reached.
21. Install the camshaft cover-to-camshaft housing attaching studs.
22. Install the valve lash adjusters and rocker arm guides. Prelube the rocker arms with engine assembly lubricant and install the rocker arms.
23. Using new gaskets, install the camshaft covers.
24. Install the coil bracket mounting bolt.

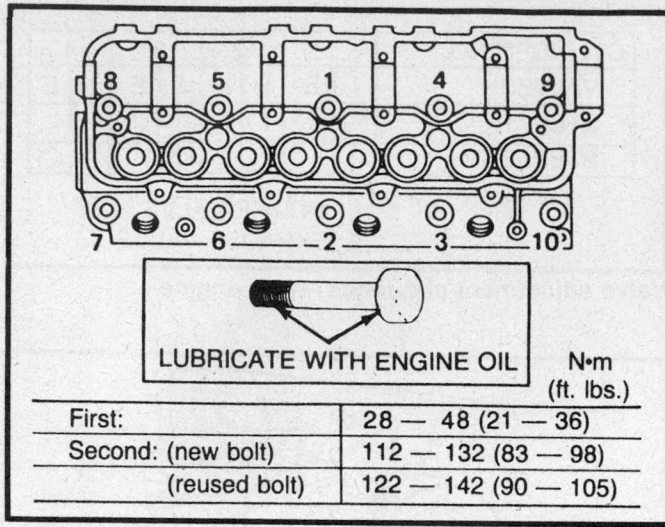

	N•m (ft. lbs.)
First:	28 — 48 (21 — 36)
Second: (new bolt)	112 — 132 (83 — 98)
(reused bolt)	122 — 142 (90 — 105)

LUBRICATE WITH ENGINE OIL

Cylinder head bolt torque sequence—1.8L engine

25. Connect the fuel line to the carburetor.
26. Install the dipstick tube bracket-to-manifold attaching bolt.
27. Attach the exhaust pipe to the exhaust manifold.
28. Connect the wires to the idle solenoid, choke, temperature sender and alternator.
29. Connect the spark plug wires.
30. Apply Teflon® tape or its equivalent to the threads of the accelerator cable support bracket attaching bolts and install the bracket.
31. Install the air cleaner assembly.
32. Connect the upper radiator hose and heater hose to the intake manifold.
33. Fill the cooling system.
34. Install the timing belt, timing belt cover, engine fan, drive belts and connect the negative battery cable.

1.8L ENGINE

1. Disconnect the negative battery cable.
2. Drain the cooling system.
3. Remove the cylinder head cover.
4. Remove the timing belt.
5. Remove the camshaft.
6. Remove the glow plug resistor wire, injector lines, fuel leak off hose, idler bracket and power steering pump.
7. Disconnect the throttle cable at the pump.
8. Disconnect the exhaust pipe at the manifold.
9. Remove the oil feed at the rear of the head and upper radiator hose.
10. Remove the head bolts in the proper sequence. Then, remove the cylinder head with the intake and exhaust manifolds installed.

To install:

11. Place a new gasket over the dowel pins with the word **TOP** facing up.
12. Apply engine oil to the threads and the seating face of the cylinder head bolts, install the cylinder head bolts and tighten them in the proper sequence to the specified torque.
13. Install the camshaft and rocker arm assembly. Loosen the adjusting screws so that the entire rocker arm assembly is held in a free state.
14. Reinstall the timing belt.
15. Connect the upper radiator hose and the oil feed pipe.
16. Connect the exhaust pipe to the manifold.
17. Install the fuel leak-off hose. Connect the injector lines.
18. Connect the glow plug resistor wire.

19. Adjust the valve clearance. Install the cylinder head cover.
20. Refill the cooling system.

Camshaft

Removal and Installation

1.6L ENGINE

NOTE: A special valve spring compressor, tool J–25477 or equivalent is necessary for this procedure. If replacing the camshaft or rocker arms, prelubricate new parts with engine assembly lubricant.

1. Disconnect the negative battery cable.
2. Remove engine accessory drive belts.
3. Remove the engine fan and pulley.
4. Remove the upper and lower front timing belt covers.
5. Loosen the idler pulley and remove the timing belt from the camshaft sprocket.
6. Remove the camshaft sprocket attaching bolt and washer and remove the camshaft sprocket.
7. Remove the camshaft cover. Using the valve spring compressor J–25477 or equivalent, remove the rocker arms and guides. Keep the rocker arms and guides in order so that they can be installed in their original locations.
8. Remove the heater assembly.
9. Remove the camshaft carrier rear cover.
10. Remove the camshaft thrust plate bolts. Slide the camshaft slightly to the rear and remove the thrust plate.
11. Remove the engine mount nuts and wire retainers.
12. Using a floor jack, raise the front of the engine.
13. Remove the camshaft from the camshaft carrier. Heavy pressure will be needed to pull the camshaft and seal forward.

To install:
14. Position the camshaft into the camshaft carrier.
15. Lower the engine on the motor mounts.
16. Install the engine mount nuts and attach the retaining wires.
17. Slide the camshaft slightly to the rear and install the thrust plate. Slide the camshaft forward and install the carrier rear cover.
18. Position and align a new gasket over the end of the camshaft, against the camshaft carrier.
19. Install the heater assembly.
20. Install the valve rocker arms and guides in their original locations using the special valve spring compressor. Install the camshaft covers.
21. Align the dowel in the camshaft sprocket with the hole in the end of the camshaft and install the sprocket.
22. Apply thread locking compound to the sprocket retaining bolt threads and install the bolt and washer. Torque the sprocket retaining bolt to 65–85 ft. lbs.
23. Turn the crankshaft clockwise to bring the No. 1 cylinder to TDC. Make sure that the distributor rotor is in position to fire the No. 1 spark plug. Align the hole in the camshaft sprocket with the hole in the upper rear timing belt cover and install the timing belt on the camshaft sprocket.
24. Adjust timing belt tension.
25. Install the upper and lower front timing belt covers.
26. Install the engine fan and pulley.
27. Install the engine accessory drive belts.
28. Connect the negative battery cable.

1.8L ENGINE

1. Disconnect the negative battery cable. Remove the cam cover.
2. Remove the timing belt covers and timing belt. Remove the plug.
3. Install the fixing plate into the slot at the rear of the camshaft.
4. Remove the camshaft gear retaining bolt and using puller

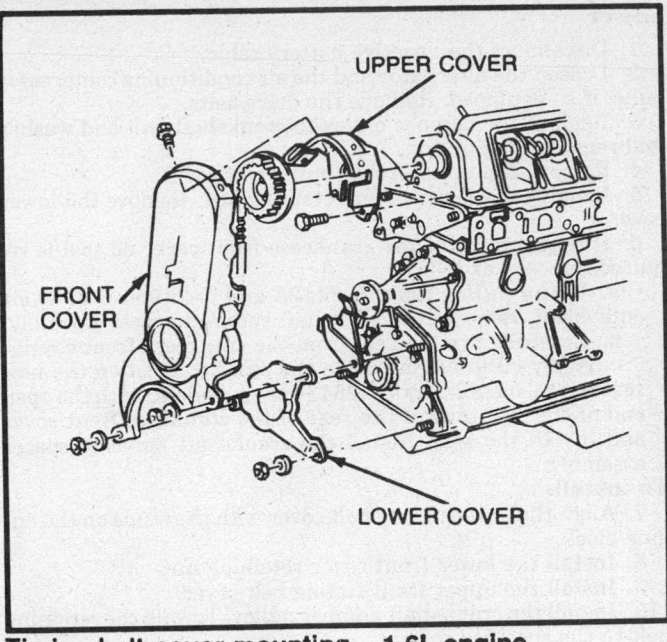

Timing belt cover mounting — 1.6L engine

J–22288 or equivalent, remove the cam gear.
5. Remove the rocker arms and shaft.
6. Remove the bolts attaching the front head plate and then remove the plate.
7. Remove the camshaft bearing cap retaining bolts and remove the bearing caps with the cap side bearings.
8. Lift out the camshaft oil seal and then remove the camshaft.

To install:
9. Coat the camshaft and cylinder head journals with clean engine oil.
10. Position the camshaft in the cylinder head with a new oil seal.
11. Apply a 3 mm bead of silicone sealer to the cylinder head face of the No. 1 camshaft bearing cap.
12. Install the remaining bearing caps. Install the rocker arm shaft assembly, leaving the adjusting screws loose.
13. Install the front head plate.
14. Install the timing belt.
15. Adjust the valve clearance to specifications and then install the cylinder head cover.

Timing Belt Covers/Oil Seal

Removal and Installation

1.6L ENGINE

Front

1. Disconnect the negative battery cable. Remove the radiator upper mounting panel on vehicles without air conditioning or fan shroud on models with A/C.
2. Remove engine accessory drive belts.
3. Remove the engine fan.
4. Remove the cover retaining screws and nuts and remove the cover.

To install:
5. Align the screw slots on the upper and lower parts of the cover.
6. Install the cover retaining screws and nuts.
7. Install the engine fan.
8. Install the engine accessory drive belts.
9. Connect the negative battery cable.

Lower

1. Disconnect the negative battery cable.
2. Loosen the alternator and the air conditioning compressor bolts, if so equipped. Remove the drive belts.
3. Remove the damper pulley-to-crankshaft bolt and washer and remove the pulley.
4. Remove the upper front timing belt cover.
5. Remove the lower cover retaining nut. Remove the lower cover.
6. If replacement of the crankcase front cover oil seal is required, proceed as follow:
   a. Using puller tools J–24420 and J–34984–6 or their equivalent, remove the crankshaft sprocket spacer assembly.
   b. Carefully pry the seal from the crankcase front cover.
   c. Apply clean engine oil to the seal lip. Position the new seal on seal installer tool J–26434 or equivalent, with the open end of the seal toward the rear of the crankcase front cover and install the seal. Install the crankshaft sprocket spacer assembly.

To install:

7. Align the lower timing belt cover with the studs on the engine block.
8. Install the lower front cover retaining nut.
9. Install the upper front timing belt cover.
10. Install the crankshaft damper pulley. Torque the retaining bolt to the specified torque.
11. Install the drive belts and tighten the alternator and compressor mounting bolts.
12. Connect the negative battery cable.

Upper

1. Crank the engine so that No. 1 cylinder is at TDC of the compression stroke.
2. Disconnect the negative battery cable.
3. Remove the upper and lower front cover, the timing belt and the camshaft timing sprocket.
4. Remove the 3 bolts retaining the camshaft sprocket cover to the camshaft carrier.
5. Inspect the condition of the cam seal. Replace the seal if necessary.
6. Position and align a new gasket over the end of the camshaft and against the camshaft carrier.
7. Install the 3 camshaft sprocket cover retaining screws.
8. Install the camshaft sprocket, timing belt and the upper and lower front covers.
9. Connect the negative battery cable.

1.8L ENGINE

Upper

1. Disconnect the negative battery cable. Remove the radiator upper mounting panel on vehicles without air conditioning or fan shroud on models with air conditioning.
2. Remove the bypass hose on the engine.
3. Remove the engine fan.
4. Remove the cover retaining screws and nuts and remove the cover.

To install:

5. Align the screw slots on the upper and lower parts of the cover.
6. Install the cover retaining screws and nuts.
7. Install the engine fan.
8. Install the engine bypass hose.
9. Connect the negative battery cable.

Lower

1. Disconnect the negative battery cable.
2. Loosen the alternator and the air conditioning compressor bolts, if equipped. Remove the drive belts.
3. Remove the damper pulley-to-crankshaft bolt and washer and remove the pulley.

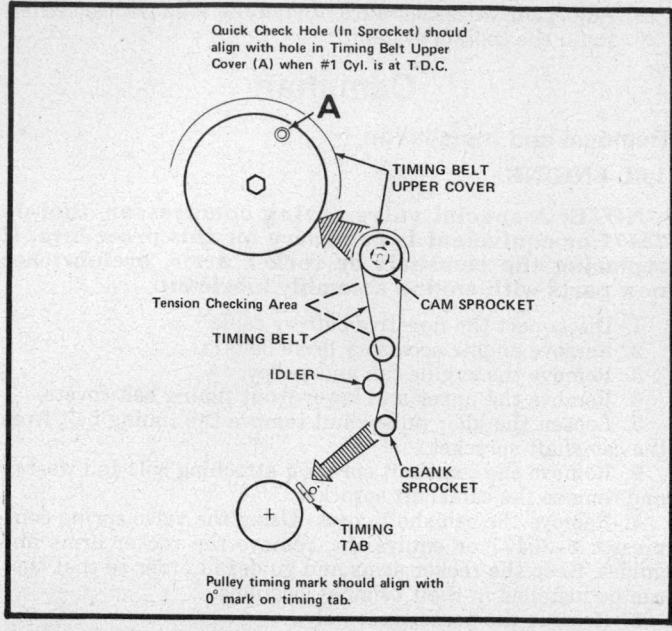

Quick Check Hole (In Sprocket) should align with hole in Timing Belt Upper Cover (A) when #1 Cyl. is at T.D.C.

Pulley timing mark should align with 0° mark on timing tab.

Timing belt installation—1.6L engine When camshaft is aligned at No. 1 cylinder TDC compression stroke, a $1/8$ in. drill bit should fit throught rear timing belt cover and into quick check hole in sprocket

4. Remove the upper front timing belt cover as outlined previously.
5. Remove the lower cover retaining bolts. Remove the lower cover.
6. If replacement of the crankcase front cover oil seal is required, proceed as follow:
   a. Using puller tools J–24420A or equivalent, remove the hub and crankshaft gear from the crankshaft.
   b. Carefully pry the seal from the front oil seal retainer.
   c. Apply clean engine oil to the lipped portion and face of the new seal. Install the new seal using tool J–33182 or equivalent. Install the crankshaft gear and hub to the crankshaft.

To install:

7. Align the cover with the studs on the engine block.
8. Install the lower front cover retaining bolts.
9. Install the upper front timing belt cover.
10. Install the crankshaft damper pulley. Torque the retaining bolt to the specified torque.
11. Install the drive belts and tighten the alternator and compressor mounting bolts.
12. Connect the negative battery cable.

Timing Belt and Sprockets

Removal and Installation

1.6L ENGINE

1. Rotate the engine to bring No. 1 cylinder to TDC. The timing mark should be at the **0** degree mark on the timing scale. With No. 1 cylinder at TDC, a ⅛ in. drill bit may be inserted through a hole in the timing belt upper rear cover into a hole in the camshaft drive sprocket. These holes are provided to facilitate and verify camshaft timing. Aligning these holes now will make installation of the new belt much easier.
2. Disconnect the negative battery cable.
3. Remove the alternator and air conditioning compressor drive belts.
4. Remove the engine fan and pulley.

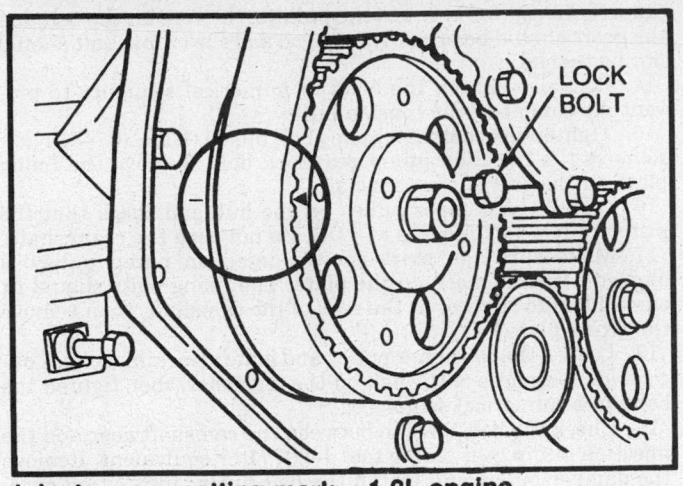

Injector gear setting mark —1.8L engine

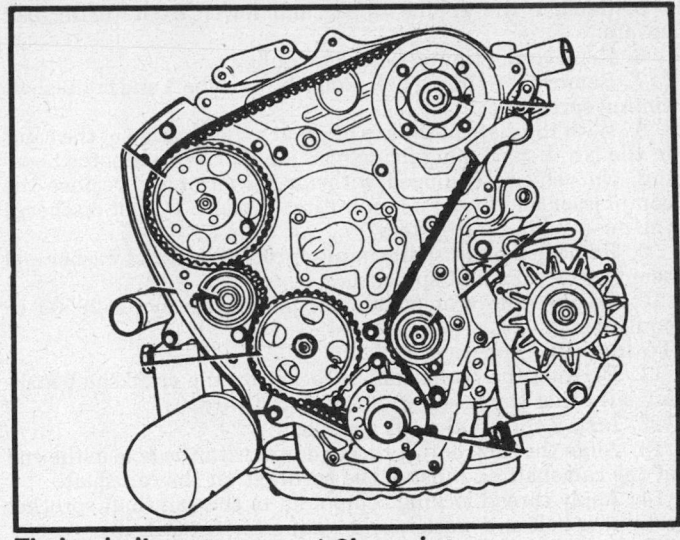

Timing belt sequence —1.8L engine

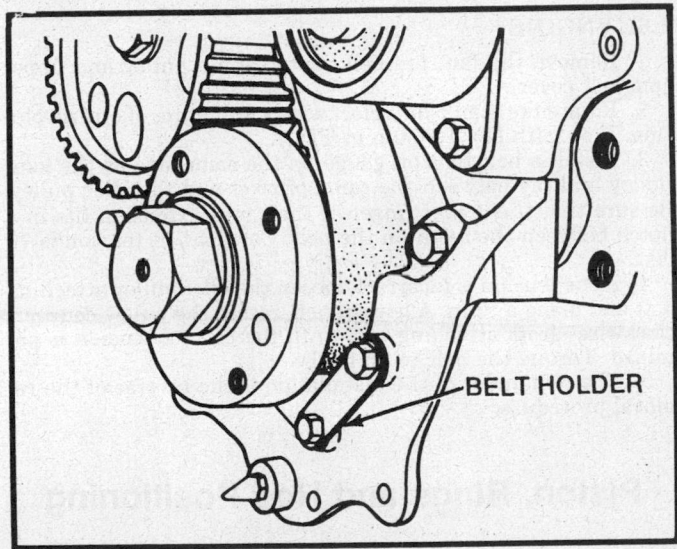

Timing belt holder —1.8L engine

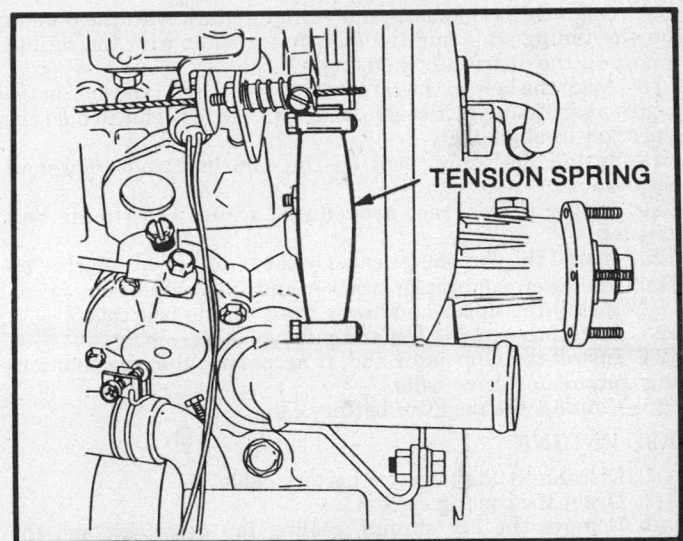

Tension spring —1.8L engine

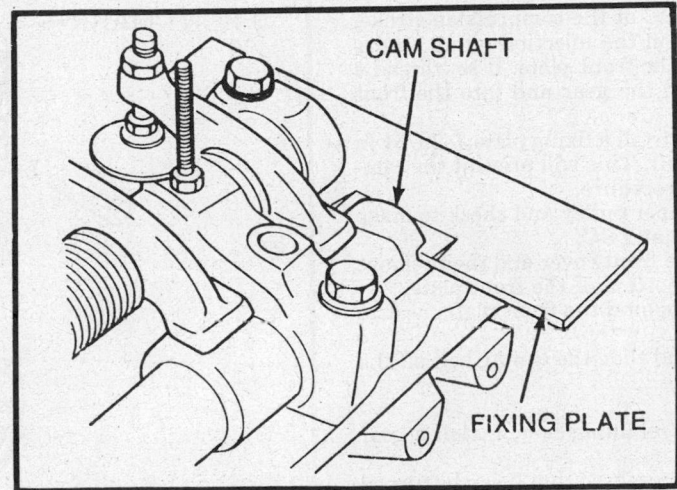

Camshaft fixing plate —1.8L engine

5. Remove the engine upper and lower front timing belt covers.

6. Remove the timing belt idler pulley.

7. Remove the timing belt from the camshaft and crankshaft timing sprockets.

8. With the distributor cap off, mark the location of the rotor in the No. 1 spark plug firing position on the distributor housing. On vehicles equipped with air conditioning, remove the compressor and lower its mounting bracket. Do not discharge the air conditioning system.

9. Remove the camshaft timing sprocket bolt and washer and remove the camshaft sprocket.

10. Remove the crankshaft sprocket using tool J–28509 or equivalent.

To install:

11. Position the crankshaft sprocket on the crankshaft making sure that the locating tabs face outward.

12. Install the crankshaft sprocket.

13. Align the camshaft sprocket dowel with the hole in the end of the camshaft and install the sprocket on the camshaft.

14. Apply thread locking compound to the camshaft sprocket retaining bolt and washer and torque to 65–85 ft. lbs.

15. Position the timing belt over the crankshaft sprocket.

16. Install the crankshaft pulley.

17. Align the crankshaft pulley timing mark with the **0** mark on the timing scale and the distributor rotor with the scribed mark on the distributor housing.

18. Align the hole in the camshaft sprocket with the hole in the upper rear timing belt cover. Insert a ⅛ in. drill bit to hold the sprocket in alignment.

19. Install the timing belt on the camshaft and crankshaft sprockets.

20. Using the correct procedure, adjust the timing belt tension.

21. Install the distributor cap. On air conditioned vehicles, install the lower compressor bracket and the compressor.

22. Install the upper and lower front timing belt covers.

23. Install the engine fan and pulley.

24. Install the alternator and, if necessary, the air conditioning compressor drive belts.

25. Connect the negative battery cable.

1.8L ENGINE

1. Disconnect the negative battery cable.

2. Drain the cooling system.

3. Remove the fan shroud, cooling fan drive belt and the pulley.

4. Disconnect the bypass hose and then remove the upper half of the front cover.

5. With the No. 1 piston at TDC of the compression stroke, make sure that the notch mark on the injection pump gear is aligned with the index mark on the front plate. If so, thread a lock bolt (8mm × 1.25) through the gear and into the front plate.

6. Remove the cam cover and install a fixing plate J–29761 in the slot at the rear of the camshaft. This will prevent the camshaft from rotating during the procedure.

7. Remove the crankshaft damper pulley and check to make sure that the No. 1 piston is still at TDC.

8. Remove the lower half of the front cover and then remove the timing belt holder from the bottom of the front plate.

9. Remove the tension spring behind the front plate, next to the injection pump.

10. Loosen the tension pulley and slide the timing belt off the pulleys.

To install:

11. Remove the camshaft gear retaining bolt, install a gear puller and remove the gear.

12. Reinstall the camshaft gear loosely so that it can be turned smoothly by hand.

13. Slide the timing belt over the gears. The belt should be properly tensioned between the pulleys, the cogs on the belt and the gears should be properly engaged and the crankshaft should not be turned.

14. Partially tighten the bolts in numerical sequence to prevent movement of the tension pulley.

15. Tighten the camshaft pulley bolt 50–60 ft. lbs. (67–81 Nm). Remove the injection pump gear lock bolt. Remove the fixing plate on the end of the camshaft.

16. Install the damper pulley on the hub and check that the piston in No. 1 cylinder is at TDC. Do not turn the crankshaft.

17. Make sure the mark on the injection pump pulley is aligned with the mark on the plate. The fixing plate should fit smoothly into the slot at the rear of the camshaft, then remove the fixing plate.

18. Loosen the tensioner pulley and plate attaching bolts. Concentrate looseness of the belt on the tensioner, then tighten the bolts in a numerical sequence.

19. Check the belt tension between the camshaft gear and the injection pump gear, using tool J–29771 or equivalent. Remove the damper pulley and install the belt holder in position away from the timing bolt.

20. Complete installation by reversing the removal procedure.

Adjustment

1.6L ENGINE

1. Remove the fan, fan belt, water pump pulley and upper cam belt cover.

2. Rotate the crankshaft clockwise a minimum of one revolution. Stop with No. 1 piston at TDC.

3. Install a belt tension gauge on the same side as the idler pulley midway between the cam sprocket and the idler pulley. Be sure that the center finger of the gauge extension fits in a notch between the teeth on the belt. Correct belt tension is 70 lbs..

4. If the tension is incorrect, loosen the idler pulley attaching bolt and using a ¼ in. Allen wrench, rotate the pulley counterclockwise on its attaching bolt until the correct tension is obtained. Torque the bolt to 15 ft. lbs.

5. The remainder of the installation is the reverse of the removal procedure.

Piston, Rings and Rod Positioning

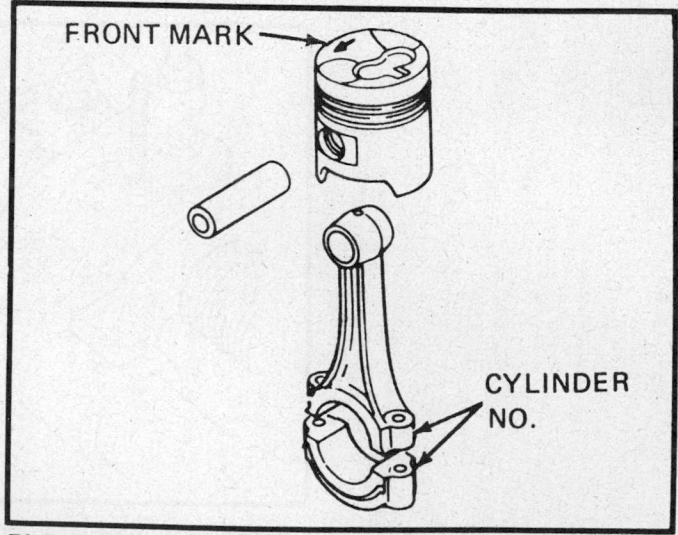

Piston and connecting rod position—1.8L engine

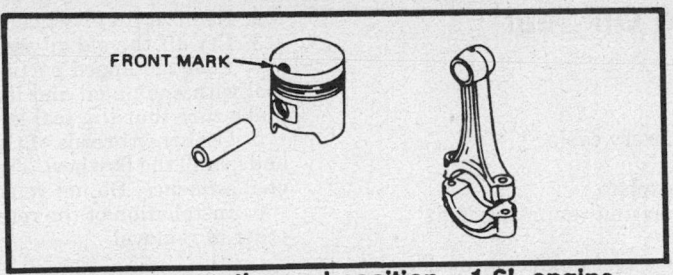

Piston and connecting rod position — 1.6L engine

ENGINE LUBRICATION SYSTEM

Oil Pan

Removal and Installation

1.6L ENGINE

1. Disconnect the negative battery cable.
2. Drain the cooling system.
3. Remove the upper radiator support and fan shroud.
4. Disconnect the heater hoses at the heater core.
5. Remove the heater core housing.
6. Remove the engine mount retaining nuts and clips.
7. Raise and safely support the vehicle.
8. Drain the engine oil.
9. Disconnect the power steering line, if equipped.
10. Disconnect the rack and pinion unit from the crossmember and steering shaft and pull it out of the way.
11. Remove the flywheel shield.
12. Remove the heater pipe at the oil pan.
13. Remove the oil pan retaining bolts.
14. Raise the engine.
15. Remove the oil pan, oil pipe and suction screen.
16. Installation is the reverse of the removal procedure. Fill the engine with oil and check for leaks. Start the engine and check for leaks.

1.8L ENGINE

1. Disconnect the negative battery cable. Remove the engine from the vehicle.
2. Support the engine on a stand.
3. Remove the bolts attaching the oil pan to the crankcase and remove the pan.
4. Clean the mating surfaces of the oil pan and the block. Install a new gasket.
5. Install the oil pan retaining bolts and tighten them to 5 ft. lbs.
6. Reinstall the engine.

Oil Pump

Removal and Installation

1.6L ENGINE

1. Disconnect the negative battery cable. Remove the ignition coil attaching bolts and lay the coil aside.
2. Raise and safely support the vehicle. Remove the fuel pump, pushrod and gasket. Note the direction the pushrod comes out for reference during installation.
3. Lower the vehicle and remove the distributor. On vehicles equipped with air conditioning, remove the compressor mounting bolts and lay it aside. Do not disconnect any refrigerant lines.
4. Raise and safely support the vehicle. Remove the oil pan.
5. Remove the oil pump pipe and screen assembly.
6. Remove the pipe and screen assembly from the oil pump.
7. Remove the pick-up tube seal from the oil pump.

8. Remove the oil pump attaching bolts and remove the oil pump.

To install:

9. Position the oil pump in place and torque the oil pump mounting bolts to 15 ft. lbs.

NOTE: Make certain that the pilot on the oil pump engages the case.

10. Install the pick-up tube seal in the oil pump.
11. Install the pick-up pipe and screen assembly in the oil pump. Install the pick-up pipe and screen clamp. Torque the clamp bolt 6–8 ft. lbs. Torque the pick-up tube and screen mounting bolt 19–25 ft. lbs.
12. Install the oil pan.
13. Install the fuel pump and pushrod in the same direction as removal.
14. Lower the vehicle and install the distributor and the ignition coil.

1.8L ENGINE

1. Disconnect the negative battery cable. Remove the timing belt cover(s) and timing belt.
2. Remove the 4 allen bolts attaching the oil pump to the front plate. Remove the pump with the pulley still attached.
3. Coat the pump vane with clean engine oil and then install it with the taper side toward the cylinder body.
4. Install a new O-ring, coated with engine oil, into the pump housing.
5. Position the rotor in the vane and then install the pump body together with the pulley. Tighten the allen bolts to 15 ft. lbs.
6. Complete installation by reversing the removal procedure.

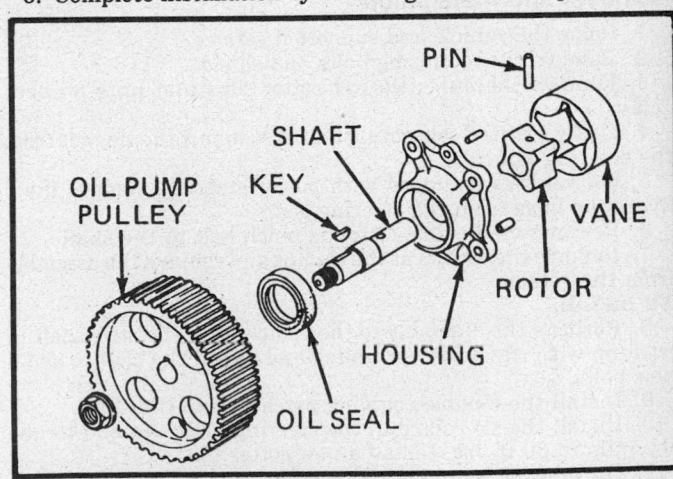

Oil pump assembly — 1.8L engine

Rear Main Oil Seal

Removal and Installation

1.6L ENGINE

1. Disconnect the negative battery cable.
2. Remove the transmission.
3. Remove the flywheel or flexplate.
4. Remove the rack and pinion unit mounting bolts.
5. Remove the left side strut.
6. Remove the flexible coupling and pull the gear down.
7. Drain the engine oil.
8. Remove the oil pan, suction pipe and screen.
9. Remove the rear main cap.
10. Remove the seal.

To install:

11. Before replacing the seal, clean all bearing cap and case surfaces.
12. Inspect the crankshaft seal surface for any wear or nicks.
13. Install the new seal against the rear main bearing bulkhead. Apply RTV sealer or equivalent to the verticle grooves of the bearing cap. Wipe off any excess sealer.
14. Torque the bearing bolts to 10–12 ft. lbs. Tap the end of the crankshaft rearward then forward. Retorque the bearing cap bolts to 40–52 ft. lbs.
15. Reverse the removal procedure for the remainder of the installation.

1.8L ENGINE

1. Disconnect the negative battery cable. Remove the transmission. If equipped with a manual transmission, remove the clutch.

2. Remove the flywheel.
3. Pry off the old oil seal.
4. Coat the lipped portion and the fitting face of the new oil seal with engine oil and install it into the crankshaft bearing. Make sure that the seal is properly seated.
5. Coat the threads of the new mounting bolts with Loctite® and install the flywheel. Tighten the bolts to 40 ft. lbs. in a diagonal sequence. Do not reuse the old bolts, they must be new.
6. Installation of the remaining components is in the reverse order of removal.

Connecting Rod and Main Bearing

Engine bearings are of the precision insert type. They are available for service in standard and various undersizes. Upper and lower bearing inserts may be different. Be careful to align holes. Do not obstruct any oil passages. Bearing inserts must not be shimmed. Do not touch the bearing surface of the insert with bare fingers. Skin oil and acids will etch the bearing surface.

Replacement

NOTE: Bearing failure, other than normal wear, must be investigated carefully. Inspect the crankshaft, connecting rods and the bearing bores. Avoid damage to the crankshaft journals during removal and installation.

—————— **CAUTION** ——————
Use care when handling the pistons. Worn piston rings are sharp and may cause injury.

FRONT SUSPENSION AND STEERING

For front suspension component removal and installation procedures, refer to Unit Repair Section.

For steering wheel removal and installation, refer to electrical control section.

Steering Rack and Pinion

Removal and Installation

1. Raise the vehicle and support it safely.
2. Remove the mounting bolts and shield.
3. Remove the outer tie rod cotter pins and nuts on both sides.
4. Using a tie rod separating tool, disconnect the tie rods from the steering knuckles.
5. On vehicles equipped with power steering, remove the 2 hydraulic lines from the steering gear.
6. Remove the flexible coupling pinch bolt to the shaft.
7. Remove the 4 bolts at the clamps and remove the assembly from the vehicle.

To install:

8. Position the assembly to the vehicle with the stub shaft in position with the flexible coupling and install the clamps and 4 new bolts.
9. Install the flexible coupling pinch bolt to the shaft.
10. Install the tie rods into the steering knuckles and torque the nuts to 30 ft. lbs. Install a new cotter pin.
11. On vehicles equipped with power steering, install the 2 hydraulic hoses and bleed the system.
12. Install the bolts and shield. Lower the vehicle.

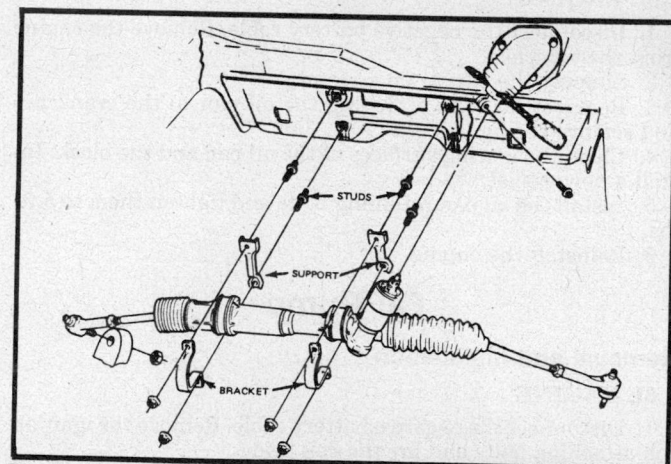

Rack and pinion attaching location—typical

Power Steering Pump

Removal and Installation

1. Disconnect the negative battery cable. Remove the upper adjusting bolt.
2. Remove the lower brace bolt to pump bracket.
3. Remove the left hand crossmember brace to body.

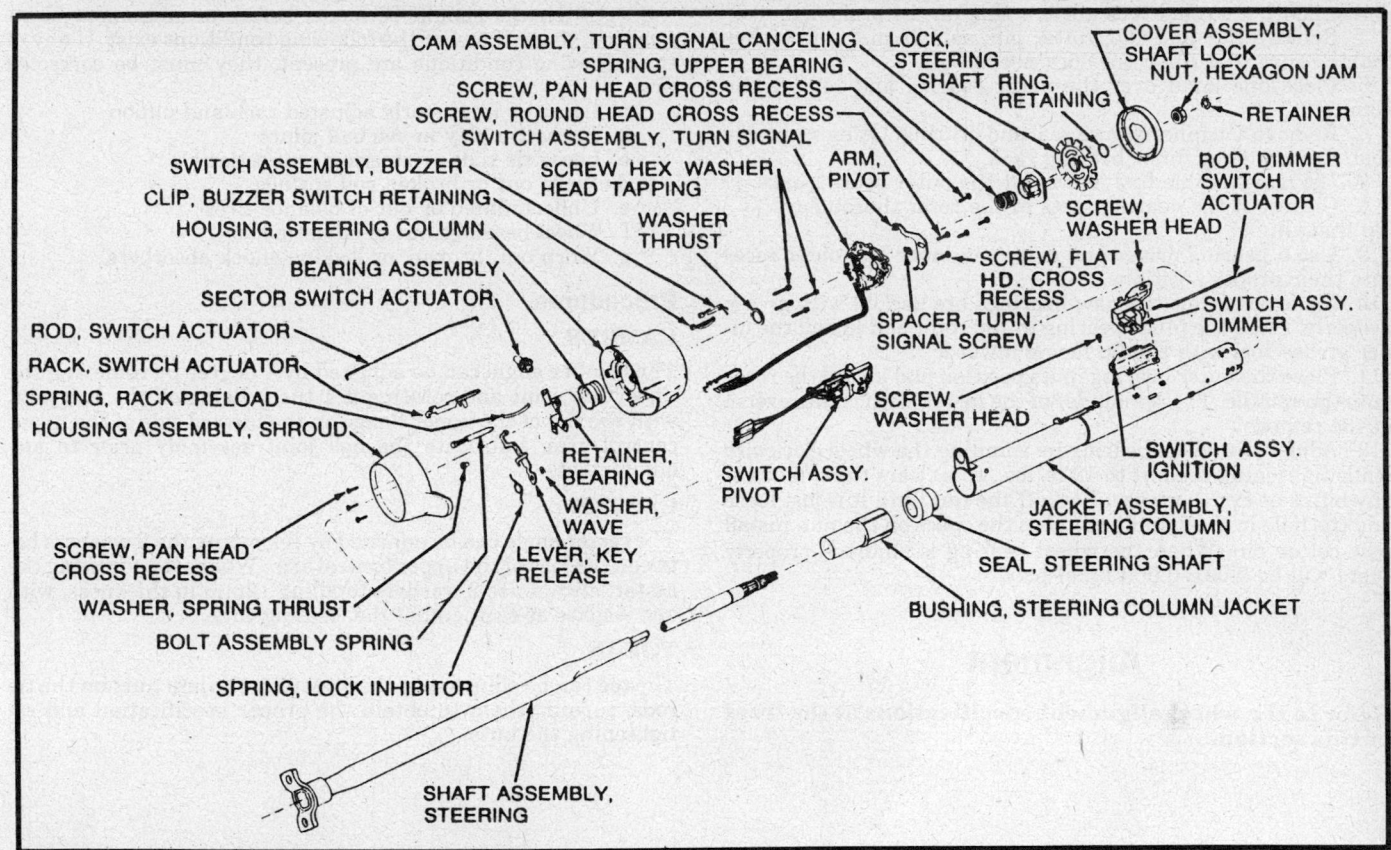

Steering column and related components

4. Remove the pressure line and the reservoir line at the pump.

5. Remove the rear pump adjusting bracket.

6. Remove the front pivot bolt at the pump and remove the bolt.

7. Remove the front pump bracket at the bolt to engine. Remove the bracket and pump.

8. Installation is the reverse of the removal procedure. In addition, adjust the belt tension, fill the reservoir and bleed the system.

Bleeding System

When the power steering system has been serviced, air must be bled from the system by using the following procedure:

1. Turn wheels all the way to the left, add power steering fluid to the **COLD** mark on the level indicator.

2. Start engine and run at fast idle momentarily, shut engine off and recheck the fluid level. If necessary add fluid to the **COLD** mark.

3. Start engine and bleed system by turning wheels from side to side without hitting stops. Keep the fluid level at the Cold mark. Fluid with air in it has a light tan or red appearance, this air must be eliminated before normal steering action can be achieved.

4. Return the wheels to the center position and continue running the engine for 2 or 3 minutes. Road test to check the operation of the steering.

5. Recheck the fluid level it should now be stabilized at the **HOT** level on the indicator.

Steering Column

Removal and Installation

1. Disconnect the negative battery cable.

2. Remove the steering wheel. Move the front seat rearward as far as possible.

3. Remove the floor pan bracket screws. Remove bolts securing steering column to rack and pinion assembly.

4. Remove the 2 column bracket to instrument panel nuts and lower the column far enough to disconnect the wiring harnesses.

5. Disconnect the directional signal and ignition switch wiring harnesses. Carefully pull the column rearward and remove the assembly from the vehicle.

NOTE: Do not hammer on the end of the steering shaft. The plastic injection break-away pins will shear, causing the shaft to collapse.

6. Installation is the reverse order of the removal. Special attention must be given to the installation of the bolts and brackets during the assembly.

Front Wheel Bearings

Removal and Installation

1. Raise and safely support the vehicle.

2. Remove the wheel and tire assembly.

3. Remove the brake caliper leaving the brake line attached

and support it so that it is not hanging on the brake line.

4. Remove the dust cap, cotter pin, spindle nut and washer making sure that the rotor does not fall off.

5. Place one hand over the outer bearing and remove the rotor.

6. Remove the inner grease seal and bearing. Using a suitable tool, drive out the inner bearing race.

7. Using a suitable tool, drive out the outer bearing race.

8. Clean out the bearing seats in the rotor thoroughly.

To install:

9. Use a bearing driver and drive the inner and outer races into their proper positions.

10. Make sure that the new bearings are packed with grease properly. Place the inner bearing in the rotor and install the inner grease seal with the lip facing inward.

11. Place the outer bearing in its position and install the rotor onto the spindle. The remainder of the installation is the reverse of the removal.

12. Adjust the wheel bearing by spinning the wheel clockwise while tightening the nut to 12 ft. lbs., this clears the threads of any burrs or excess grease. Backoff the nut until it is just loose and the hole in the spindle matches the space on the nut, install new cotter pin. When the wheel bearing is adjusted properly there will be 0.001–0.005 in. of play.

Alignment

Refer to the wheel alignment specifications at the front of this section.

Several checks should be made, before an alignment is attempted, to see if any of the following conditions exist. If any of the following conditions are present, they must be corrected first.

    a. Loose or improperly adjusted rack and pinion
    b. Excessive play in the ball joints
    c. Loose tie rods or steering connections
    d. Worn out or broken coil springs
    e. Underinflated or out of balance tires
    f. Wheel bearings out of adjustment
    g. Worn out, broken, or leaking shock absorbers

Procedures

CAMBER

The camber angle can be adjusted by 1 degree by removing the upper ball joint and rotating it 1 turn. Reinstall the ball joint with the flat of the upper flange on the inward side of the upper control arm. Lubricate the ball joint assembly prior to any adjustment.

CASTER

The caster angle can be adjusted by relocating the 2 washers between the legs of the upper control arm. Whenever adjusting the caster, always use 2 washers totalling 12mm in thickness, with one washer at each end of the locating tube.

TOE-IN

The toe can be adjusted by the loosening the jam nuts on the tie rods, turning them to obtain the proper specification and re-tightening the nuts.

BRAKE

Refer to the unit repair section for brake service information and drum/rotor specifications.

Master Cylinder

Removal and Installation

WITHOUT POWER BRAKE

1. Disconnect the negative battery cable. Disconnect the master cylinder pushrod from the brake pedal.

2. Remove the pushrod boot.

3. Remove the air cleaner.

4. Thoroughly clean all dirt from the master cylinder and the brake lines. Disconnect the brake lines from the master cylinder and plug them to prevent the entry of dirt.

5. Remove the master cylinder attaching nuts and remove the master cylinder.

To install:

6. Install the master cylinder with its spacer. Tighten the securing nuts.

7. Connect the brake lines to their ports.

8. Place the pushrod boot over the end of the pushrod. Secure the pushrod to the brake pedal with the pin and clip.

9. Fill the master cylinder and bleed the entire hydraulic system. After bleeding, fill the master cylinder to within ¼ in. from the top of the reservoir. Check for leaks.

10. Install the air cleaner.

11. Check brake operation before moving the car.

WITH POWER BRAKE

1. Disconnect the negative battery cable.

2. Remove the air cleaner assembly.

3. Thoroughly clean all dirt from the master cylinder and the brake lines. Disconnect the brake lines from the master cylinder and plug them to prevent the entry of dirt.

4. Remove the master cylinder attaching nuts and brace rod. Remove the master cylinder.

To install:

5. Place the master cylinder into position on the power brake booster. Install the brace rod and attaching nuts. Tighten the attaching nuts to 150 inch lbs. (17 Nm)

6. Connect the brake lines to their ports.

7. Fill the master cylinder and bleed the entire hydraulic system. After bleeding, fill the master cylinder to within ¼ in. from the top of the reservoir. Check for leaks.

8. Install the air cleaner assembly.

Bleeding the System

1. Clean the bleeder screw at each wheel.

2. Attach a small rubber hose to the bleed screw and place the end in a clear container of fresh brake fluid.

3. Fill the master cylinder with fresh brake fluid. The master cylinder reservoir level should be checked and filled often during the bleeding procedure.

4. Have an assistant slowly pump the brake pedal and hold the pressure.

5. Open the bleeder screw about ¼ turn. The pedal should fall to the floor as air and fluid are pushed out. Close the bleeder screw while the assistant holds the pedal to the floor, then slowly release the pedal and wait 15 seconds. Repeat the process until no more air bubbles are forced from the system when the brake pedal is applied. It may be necessary to repeat this 10 or more times to get all of the air from the system.

6. Repeat this procedure on the remaining wheel cylinders and calipers. Make sure that the master cylinder does not run out of brake fluid.

NOTE: Remember to wait 15 seconds between each bleeding and do not pump the pedal rapidly. Rapid pumping of the brake pedal pushes the master cylinder secondary piston down the bore in a manner that makes it difficult to bleed the system.

7. Check the brake pedal for sponginess and the brake warning light for an indication of unbalanced pressure. Repeat the entire bleeding procedure to correct either of these two conditions. Check the fluid level when finished.

Power Brake Booster

Removal and Installation

1. Disconnect the negative battery cable. Remove the air cleaner.
2. Disconnect the vacuum hose from the check valve.
3. Remove the master cylinder brace.
4. Remove the master cylinder-to-power cylinder nut and pull forward on the master cylinder until it clears the power cylinder mounting studs. Move the master cylinder aside and support it, being careful of the brake lines.
5. Remove the nuts securing the power cylinder to the firewall.
6. Remove the pushrod-to-pedal retainer and slip the pushrod off the pedal pin. Remove the power cylinder.
7. Installation is the reverse of removal.

Parking Brake

Adjustment

1. Raise the vehicle and support it safely.
2. Apply the parking brake 3 notches from the fully released position.
3. Tighten the parking brake cable equalizer adjusting nut under the car until a light drag is felt when the rear wheels are rotated forward.
4. Fully release the parking brake and rotate the rear wheels. There should be no drag.
5. Lower the vehicle.

CLUTCH AND TRANSMISSION

Refer to "Chilton's Transmission Service Manual" for addition coverage.

Clutch Cable

Adjustment

Adjustment is made at the firewall end of the outer clutch cable. Pedal free-play should be ½ in. at the pedal.
1. Pull the adjusting ring clip from the cable at the firewall.
2. To increase free-play, move the cable into the firewall, 1 notch at a time and replace the clip.
3. To decrease free-play, pull the cable out, 1 notch at a time and replace the clip.
4. If, after the adjustment, the pedal won't return tight against the bumper, the ball stud will have to be adjusted.

Clutch

Removal and Installation

1. Disconnect the negative battery cable. Raise the vehicle and support it safely.
2. Remove the transmission.
3. Remove the throwout bearing from the clutch fork by sliding the fork off the ball stud against spring tension. If the ball stud is to be replaced, remove the locknut and stud from the bellhousing.
4. If the balance marks on the pressure plate and the flywheel are not easily seen, remark them with paint or a centerpunch.
5. Alternately loosen the pressure plate to flywheel attaching bolts 1 turn at a time until spring tension is released.
6. Support the pressure plate and cover assembly, then remove the bolts and the clutch assembly.
7. Check the pressure plate, clutch plate and flywheel for wear. If the flywheel is scored, worn or discolored from overheating, it should be either refaced or replaced. Replace the clutch disc as necessary.
To install:
8. Align the balance marks on the clutch assembly and the flywheel. Place the clutch disc on the pressure plate with the long end of the splined hub facing forward and the damper

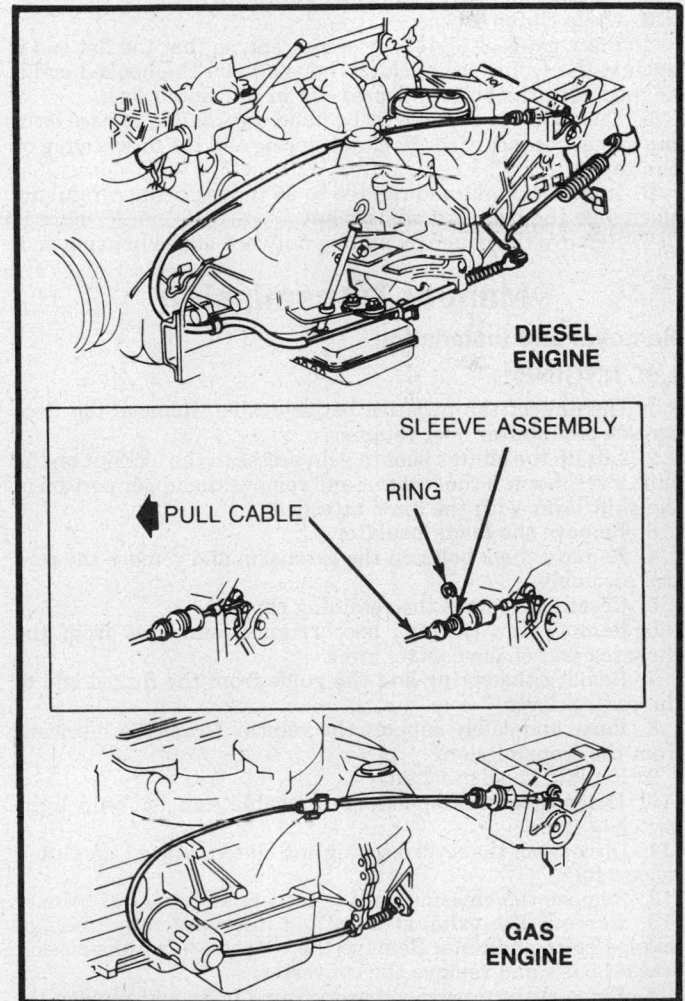

Clutch cable adjustment

springs inside the pressure plate. Insert a dummy shaft through the cover and clutch disc.

9. Position the assembly against the flywheel and insert the dummy shaft into the pilot bearing in the crankshaft.

10. Align the balance marks and install the pressure plate to flywheel bolts finger tight. Tighten all bolts evenly and gradually until tight, to avoid possible clutch distortion. Torque the bolts to 18 ft. lbs. and remove the dummy shaft.

11. Pack the groove on the inside of the throwout bearing with graphite grease. Also coat the fork groove and ball stud depression with the lubricant.

12. Install the throwout bearing and release fork assembly in the bellhousing with the fork spring hooked under the ball stud and the fork spring fingers inside the bearing groove.

13. Position the transmission and clutch housing and install the clutch housing attaching bolts and lockwashers. Torque the bolts to 25 ft. lbs.

14. Complete the transmission installation. Check the position of the engine in the front mounts and realign as necessary. A special gauge J–23644, or equivalent, is necessary to adjust ball stud position, if it has been removed.

15. Adjust clutch pedal free-play as required.

16. Lower the vehicle and check operation of the clutch and transmission.

Clutch Ball Stud Initial Adjustment

1. Install throw-out bearing assembly, clutch fork and ball stud to transmission.
2. Mount and secure transmission to engine.
3. Cycle clutch 1 time.
4. Place gauge J–28449, or equivalent, so that the flat end is against the front face of clutch housing and the hooked end is aligned with the bottom depression in the clutch fork.
5. Turn ball stud clockwise by hand until clutch release bearing makes contact with the clutch spring and the fork is snug on the gauge.
6. Install lock nut and tighten to 25 ft. lbs., being careful not to change the ball stud adjustment.
7. Remove the gauge by pulling outward at the housing end.

Manual Transmission

Removal and Installation

1.6L ENGINE

1. Disconnect the negative battery cable. Remove the floor console and shifter boot retainer.
2. Lift up the shifter boot to gain access to the locknut on the shift lever. Loosen the locknut and remove the upper portion of the shift lever with the knob attached.
3. Remove the foam insulator.
4. Remove the 3 bolts on the extension and remove the control assembly.
5. Carefully remove the retaining clip.
6. Remove the locknut, boot retainer and seat from the threaded end of the control lever.
7. Remove the spring and the guide from the forked end of the control lever.
8. Raise and safely support the vehicle. Drain the lubricant from the transmission.
9. Remove the driveshaft.
10. Disconnect the speedometer cable and back-up light switch.
11. Disconnect the return spring and clutch cable at the clutch release fork.
12. Remove the crossmember-to-transmission mount bolts.
13. Remove the exhaust manifold nuts and converter-to-tailpipe bolts and nuts. Remove the converter-to-transmission bracket bolts and remove the converter.
14. Remove the crossmember-to-frame bolts and remove the crossmember.

15. Remove the dust cover.
16. Remove the clutch housing-to-engine retaining bolts, slide the transmission and clutch housing to the rear and remove the transmission.

To install:

17. Place the transmission in gear, position the transmission and clutch housing and slide forward. Turn the output shaft to align the input shaft splines with the clutch hub.
18. Install the clutch housing retaining bolts and lockwashers. Torque the bolts to 25 ft. lbs.
19. Install the dust cover.
20. Position the crossmember to the frame and loosely install the retaining bolts. Install the crossmember-to-transmission mounting bolts. Torque the center nuts to 33 ft. lbs.; the end nuts to 21 ft. lbs. Torque the crossmember-to-frame bolts to 40 ft. lbs.
21. Install the exhaust pipe to the manifold and the converter bracket on the transmission.
22. Connect the clutch cable. Adjust clutch pedal free-play.
23. Connect the speedometer cable and back-up light switch.
24. Install the driveshaft.
25. Fill the transmission to the correct level with SAE 80W or SAE 80W–90 GL-5 gear lubricant. Lower the vehicle.
26. Install the shift lever and check operation of the transmission.

1.8L ENGINE

1. Disconnect the negative battery cable.
2. Remove the retaining screws and then remove the shift lever console.
3. Remove the mounting screws and remove the shift lever assembly.
4. Remove the upper starter mounting bolts.
5. Raise and safely support the front of the vehicle and drain the lubricant from the transmission.
6. Remove the driveshaft.
7. Disconnect the speedometer and the back-up light switch wires.
8. Disconnect the return spring and clutch cable at the clutch release fork.
9. Remove the starter lower bolt and support the starter.
10. Disconnect the exhaust pipe from the manifold.
11. Remove the flywheel inspection cover.
12. Remove the rear transmission support mounting bolt. Support the transmission underneath the case and then remove the rear support from the frame.
13. Lower the transmission approximately 4 inches.
14. Remove the transmission housing-to-engine block bolts. Pull the transmission straight back and away from the engine.
15. Installation of the remaining components is in the reverse order of removal.
16. Be sure to lubricate the drive gear shaft with a light coat of grease before installing the transmission.
17. After installation, fill the transmission to the level of the filler hole with 5W–30SF engine oil.

Automatic Transmission

NOTE: By September 1, 1991, Hydra-matic will have changed the name designation of the THM 180C automatic transmission. The new name designation for this transmission will be Hydra-matic 3L30. Transmissions built between 1989 and 1990 will serve as transitional years in which a dual system, made up of the old designation and the new designation will be in effect.

Removal and Installation

1. Disconnect the negative battery cable. Remove the T.V./detent cable at the bracket and carburetor or injection pump.

2. Remove the air cleaner and dipstick.

3. On vehicles with air conditioning, remove the heater core cover screws from the heater assembly. Disconnect the wire connector and with hoses attached, place the heater core cover out of the way.

4. Raise and safely support the vehicle. Remove the driveshaft.

5. Disconnect the speedometer cable, electrical lead to case connector and oil cooler pipes.

6. Disconnect the shift control linkage.

7. Support the transmission with suitable transmission jack and remove the rear transmission support bolts.

8. Remove the nuts holding the converter bracket to the support.

9. Disconnect the exhaust pipe at the rear of the catalytic converter.

10. Disconnect the exhaust pipe at manifold and remove the exhaust pipe, catalytic converter and converter bracket as an assembly.

11. Remove the torque converter dust cover, if equipped.

12. Remove converter to flexplate bolts.

13. Lower transmission until jack is just supporting it and remove the transmission to engine mounting bolts.

14. Raise the transmission to its normal position, then place a 2 in. block of wood between the rack-and-pinion housing and the engine oil pan.

15. Support the engine properly and slide the transmission rearward from the engine and lower it away from the vehicle.

NOTE: The use of a converter holding tool is necessary when lowering the transmission. If a converter holding tool is not available, keep the rear of the transmission lower than the front so the converter will not fall out.

16. Installation is the reverse of removal procedure.

17. When installing the flex plate to converter bolts, make certain that the weld nuts on the converter are flush with the flex plate and the converter rotates freely by hand in this position.

18. Hand start the 3 flex plate to converter bolts and tighten them finger tight, then torque to specifications. This will insure proper converter alignment. Install a new oil seal on the oil filler tube before installing the tube. Make all necessary linkage adjustments.

DRIVESHAFT

Driveshaft

Removal and Installation

1. Raise the vehicle and support it safely. Scribe reference marks on the driveshaft and the companion flange.

2. Disconnect the rear universal joint by removing the trunnion bearing straps.

3. Move the driveshaft to the rear under the axle to remove the slip yoke from the transmission. Watch for leakage from the transmission output shaft housing.

4. Install the driveshaft in the reverse order of removal. Tighten the trunnion strap bolts to 16 ft. lbs.

Universal Joints

Refer to unit repair section for overhaul procedures.

REAR AXLE AND REAR SUSPENSION

Refer to the unit repair section for axle overhaul procedures and rear suspension services.

Rear Axle Assembly

Removal and Installation

1. Disconnect the negative battery cable. Raise vehicle and support it safely.

2. Remove the rear wheels and tires.

3. Disconnect the parking brake equalizer spring.

4. Remove the equalizer bracket attaching nut and separate the parking brake cable(s).

5. Clean dirt from the brake line and separate the brake hose running from the frame to the axle. Plug both ends of the brake line to prevent contamination.

6. Disconnect the stabilizer bar, if equipped.

7. Safely support the rear axle with an adjustable lifting device.

8. Disconnect both rear shock obsorbers from the lower brackets.

9. Disconnect the rear axle extension bracket.

10. Lower the axle and remove the springs.

11. Remove the control arm front attaching bolts.

12. Lower the rear axle and remove from the vehicle.

13. Installation is the reverse of the removal procedure.

14. After the rear axle has been completely installed. Bleed the brake system and adjust the parking brake.

Axle Shaft/Wheel Bearing/Seal

Removal and Installation

1. Raise the vehicle and support it safely. Remove the wheel and the brake drum.

2. Clean the area around the differential carrier cover.

3. Remove the differential carrier cover to drain the rear axle lubricant.

4. Use a metric Allen wrench to remove the differential pinion shaft lockscrew and remove the differential pinion shaft. It may be necessary to shorten the Allen wrench to do this.

5. Push the flanged end of the axle shaft toward the center of the vehicle and remove the C-lock from the inner end of the shaft.

6. Remove the axle shaft from the housing making sure not to damage the oil seal.

7. If replacing the seal only, remove the oil seal by using the inner end of the axle shaft. Insert the end of the shaft behind the steel case of the oil seal and carefully pry the seal out of the bore.

8. To remove the bearings, insert a bearing and seal remover into the bore so that the tool head grasps behind the bearing. Slide the washer against the seal or bearing and turn the nut against the washer. Attach a slide hammer and remove the bearing.

9. Lubricate a new bearing with hypoid lubricant and install it into the housing with a bearing installer tool. Make sure that

the tool contacts the end of the axle tube to ensure that the bearing is at the correct depth.

10. Lubricate the cavity between the seal lips with a high temperature wheel bearing grease. Place a new oil seal on the seal installation tool and position the seal in the axle housing bore. Tap the seal into the bore flush with the end of the housing.

11. Slide the axle shaft into place making sure that the splines on the end of the shaft do not damage the oil seal and that they engage the splines of the differential side gear. Install the C-lock on the inner end of the axle shaft and push the shaft outward so that the shaft lock seats in the counterbore of the differential side gear.

12. Position the differential pinion shaft through the case and pinions, aligning the hole in the shaft with the lockscrew hole. Install the lockscrew.

13. Clean the gasket mounting surfaces on the differential carrier and the carrier cover. Install the carrier cover using a new gasket and tighten the cover bolts in a crosswise pattern to 22 ft. lbs.

14. Fill the rear axle with the correct lubricant to the bottom of the filler hole.

15. Install the brake drum and the wheel and tire assembly.

16. Lower the vehicle.

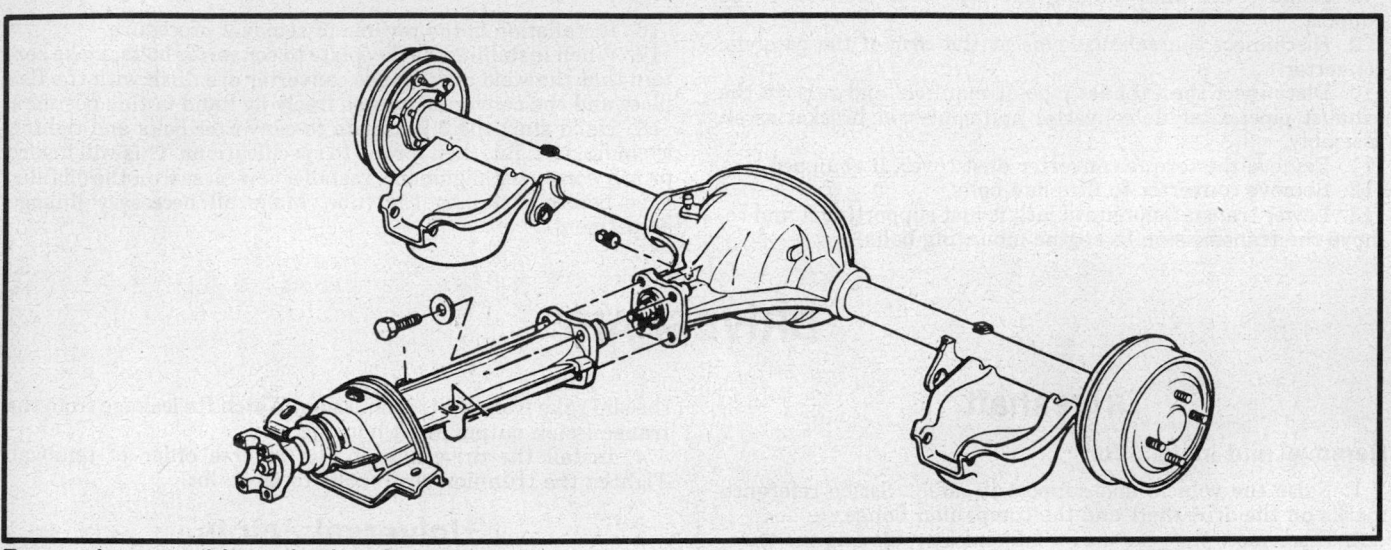

Rear axle assembly and related components

19–1

YEAR IDENTIFICATION

1986–90

VEHICLE IDENTIFICATION

It is important for servicing and ordering parts to be certain of the vehicle and engine identification. The VIN (vehicle identification number) is a 17 digit number visible through the windshield on the driver's side of the dash and contains the vehicle and engine identification codes. The tenth digit indicates model year, and the eighth digit indicates engine code. It can be interpreted as follows:

Engine Code

Code	Cu. In.	Liters	Cyl.	Fuel Sys.	Eng. Mfg.
Y	307	5.0	8	Carburetor	Oldsmobile

Model Year

Code	Year
G	1986
H	1987
J	1988
K	1989
L	1990

ENGINE IDENTIFICATION

Year	Model	Engine Displacement cu. in. (liter)	Engine Series Identification (VIN)	No. of Cylinders	Engine Type
1986	Fleetwood Brougham	8-307 (5.0)	Y	8	OHV
1987	Brougham	8-307 (5.0)	Y	8	OHV
1988	Brougham	8-307 (5.0)	Y	8	OHV
1989-90	Brougham	8-307 (5.0)	Y	8	OHV

GENERAL ENGINE SPECIFICATIONS

Year	VIN	No. Cylinder Displacement cu. in. (liter)	Fuel System Type	Net Horsepower @ rpm	Net Torque @ rpm (ft.lbs.)	Bore × Stroke (in.)	Compression Ratio	Oil Pressure @ rpm
1986	Y	8-307 (5.0)	4 bbl	140 @ 3200	255 @ 2000	3.800 × 3.390	8.0:1	30①
1987	Y	8-307 (5.0)	4 bbl	140 @ 3200	255 @ 2000	3.800 × 3.390	8.0:1	30①
1988	Y	8-307 (5.0)	4 bbl	140 @ 3200	255 @ 2000	3.800 × 3.390	8.0:1	30-45①
1989-90	Y	8-307 (5.0)	4 bbl	140 @ 3200	255 @ 2000	3.800 × 4.000	8.0:1	30-45①

① @ 1500 rpm

GASOLINE ENGINE TUNE-UP SPECIFICATIONS
Refer to Section 34 for all spark plug recommendations

Year	VIN	No. Cylinder Displacement cu. in. (liter)	Spark Plugs Gap (in.)	Ignition Timing (deg.) MT	Ignition Timing (deg.) AT	Compression Pressure (psi)	Fuel Pump (psi)	Idle Speed (rpm) MT	Idle Speed (rpm) AT	Valve Clearance In.	Valve Clearance Ex.
1986	Y	8-307 (5.0)	.060	—	20B	NA	5.5-6.5	—	475	Hyd.	Hyd.
1987	Y	8-307 (5.0)	.060	—	20B	NA	5.5-6.5	—	475	Hyd.	Hyd.
1988	Y	8-307 (5.0)	.060	—	20B	NA	6.0-7.5	—	450	Hyd.	Hyd.
1989	Y	8-307 (5.0)	.060	—	20B	NA	6.0-7.5	—	450	Hyd.	Hyd.
1990		SEE UNDERHOOD SPECIFICATIONS STICKER									

FIRING ORDERS

NOTE: To avoid confusion, always replace spark plug wires one at a time.

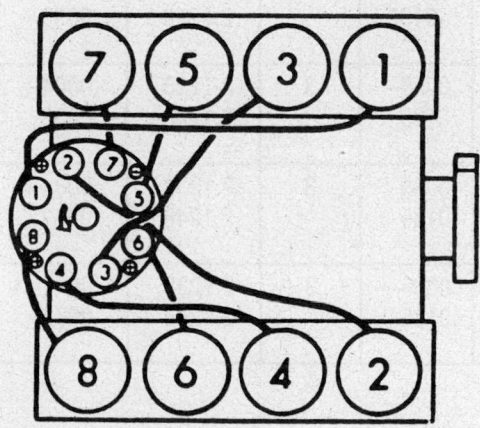

GM (Oldsmobile) 307 V8
Engine firing order: 1-8-4-3-6-5-7-2
Distributor rotation: counterclockwise

CAPACITIES

Year	Model	VIN	No. Cylinder Displacement cu. in. (liter)	Engine Crankcase with Filter	Engine Crankcase without Filter	Transmission (pts.) 4-Spd	Transmission (pts.) 5-Spd	Transmission (pts.) Auto.	Drive Axle (pts.)	Fuel Tank (gal.)	Cooling System (qts.)
1986	Brougham	Y	8-307 (5.0)	5.0	4.0	—	—	10.6	3.50	24.5	15.3
1987	Brougham	Y	8-307 (5.0)	5.0	4.0	—	—	10.6	3.50	20.7	15.3
1988	Brougham	Y	8-307 (5.0)	5.0	4.0	—	—	10.6	4.25	20.7	15.2①
1989-90	Brougham	Y	8-307 (5.0)	5.0	4.0	—	—	10.6	3.50②	20.7	15.2①

① Heavy duty—15.6
② Optional 3.23 ratio—4.25

CAMSHAFT SPECIFICATIONS
All measurements given in inches.

Year	VIN	No. Cylinder Displacement cu. in. (liter)	Journal Diameter 1	Journal Diameter 2	Journal Diameter 3	Journal Diameter 4	Journal Diameter 5	Lobe Lift In.	Lobe Lift Ex.	Bearing Clearance	Camshaft End Play
1986	Y	8-307 (5.0)	2.0352–2.0365	2.0152–2.0166	1.9952–1.9965	1.9752–1.9765	1.9552–1.9565	.247	.251	.0020–.0058	.006–.022
1987	Y	8-307 (5.0)	2.0352–2.0365	2.0152–2.0166	1.9952–1.9965	1.9752–1.9765	1.9552–1.9565	.247	.251	.0020–.0058	.006–.022
1988	Y	8-307 (5.0)	2.0352–2.0365	2.0152–2.0166	1.9952–1.9965	1.9752–1.9765	1.9552–1.9565	.247	.251	.0020–.0058	.006–.022
1989-90	Y	8-307 (5.0)	2.0352–2.0365	2.0152–2.0166	1.9952–1.9965	1.9752–1.9765	1.9552–1.9565	.247	.251	.0020–.0058	.006–.022

CRANKSHAFT AND CONNECTING ROD SPECIFICATIONS
All measurements are given in inches.

Year	VIN	No. Cylinder Displacement cu. in. (liter)	Crankshaft Main Brg. Journal Dia.	Crankshaft Main Brg. Oil Clearance	Crankshaft Shaft Endplay	Crankshaft Thrust on No.	Connecting Rod Journal Diameter	Connecting Rod Oil Clearance	Connecting Rod Side Clearance
1986	Y	8-307 (5.0)	2.4985–2.4995 ②	.0005–.0021 ①	.0035–.0135	3	2.1238 2.1248	.0004–.0033	.006–.020
1987	Y	8-307 (5.0)	2.4985–2.4995 ②	.0005–.0021 ①	.0035–.0135	3	2.1238 2.1248	.0004–.0033	.006–.020
1988	Y	8-307 (5.0)	2.4985–2.4995 ②	.0005–.0021 ①	.0035–.0135	3	2.1238 2.1248	.0004–.0033	.006–.020
1989-90	Y	8-307 (5.0)	2.4985–2.4995 ②	.0005–.0021 ①	.0035–.0135	3	2.1238 2.1248	.0004–.0033	.006–.020

① No. 5—.0015–.0031
② No. 1—2.4988–2.4998

VALVE SPECIFICATIONS

Year	VIN	No. Cylinder Displacement cu. in. (liter)	Seat Angle (deg.)	Face Angle (deg.)	Spring Test Pressure (lbs.)	Spring Installed Height (in.)	Stem-to-Guide Clearance (in.)		Stem Diameter (in.)	
							Intake	Exhaust	Intake	Exhaust
1986	Y	8-307 (5.0)	45①	44①	180–194 @ 1.27	1⁴³⁄₆₄	.0010–.0027	.0015–.0032	.3425–.3432	.3420–.3427
1987	Y	8-307 (5.0)	45①	44①	180–194 @ 1.27	1⁴³⁄₆₄	.0010–.0027	.0015–.0032	.3425–.3432	.3420–.3427
1988	Y	8-307 (5.0)	45①	44①	180–194 @ 1.27	1⁴³⁄₆₄	.0010–.0027	.0015–.0032	.3425–.3432	.3420–.3427
1989-90	Y	8-307 (5.0)	45①	44①	180–194 @ 1.27	1⁴³⁄₆₄	.0010–.0027	.0015–.0032	.3425–.3432	.3420–.3427

① Exhaust Valve—31° Seat, 30° Face

PISTON AND RING SPECIFICATIONS
All measurments are given in inches.

Year	VIN	No. Cylinder Displacement cu. in. (liter)	Piston Clearance	Ring Gap			Ring Side Clearance		
				Top Compression	Bottom Compression	Oil Control	Top Compression	Bottom Compression	Oil Control
1986	Y	8-307 (5.0)	.00075–.00175 ②	.009–.019	.009–.019	.015–.055	.0018–.0038	.0018–.0038	.001–.005
1987	Y	8-307 (5.0)	.00075–.00175 ②	.009–.019	.009–.019	.015–.055	.0018–.0038	.0018–.0038	.001–.005
1988	Y	8-307 (5.0)	.00075–.00175 ②	.009–.019	.009–.019	.015–.055	.0018–.0038	.0018–.0038	.001–.005
1989-90	Y	8-307 (5.0)	.00075–.00175 ②	.009–.019	.009–.019	.015–.055	.0018–.0038	.0018–.0038	.001–.005

② Clearance to bore (selective)

TORQUE SPECIFICATIONS
All readings in ft. lbs.

Year	VIN	No. Cylinder Displacement cu. in. (liter)	Cylinder Head Bolts	Main Bearing Bolts	Rod Bearing Bolts	Crankshaft Pulley Bolts	Flywheel Bolts	Manifold		Spark Plugs
								Intake	Exhaust	
1986	Y	8-307 (5.0)	125①	80 ④	42	200-310	60	40 ①	25	25
1987	Y	8-307 (5.0)	130①	80 ④	48	200-310	60	40 ①	25	25
1988	Y	8-307 (5.0)	130①	80 ④	48	200-310	60	40 ①	25	25
1989-90	Y	8-307 (5.0)	130①	80 ④	48	200-310	60	40 ①	25	25

① Dip bolt in oil before installation

④ Rear main bearing torque 120 ft. lbs.

WHEEL ALIGNMENT

Year	Model	Caster Range (deg.)	Caster Preferred Setting (deg.)	Camber Range (deg.)	Camber Preferred Setting (deg.)	Toe-in (in.)	Steering Axis Inclination (deg.)
1986	All	2P—4P	3P	$5/16$N—$1 5/16$P	$1/2$P	$1/8$	$10^{14}/_{32}$
1987	All	2P—4P	3P	$3/16$P—$13/16$P	$5/16$P	$3/64$	$10^{19}/_{32}$
1988	All	2P—4P	3P	$3/16$P—$13/16$P	$5/16$P	$3/64$	$10^{19}/_{32}$
1989-90	All	2P—4P	3P	$3/16$P—$13/16$P	$5/16$P	$3/64$	$10^{19}/_{32}$

ELECTRICAL

NOTE: Disconnecting the negative battery cable on some vehicles may interfere with the functions of the on board computer systems and may require the computer to undergo a relearning process, once the negative battery cable is reconnected.

For testing and overhaul procedures on starters, alternators and voltage regulators, refer to the Unit Repair Section.

Charging System

ALTERNATOR

Removal and Installation

1. Disconnect the negative battery cable.
2. Disconnect the electrical leads from the alternator.
3. Remove the screw from the alternator adjusting bracket.
4. Remove the screw from the rear of the alternator. If equipped with shims, save them for reinstallation.
5. Loosen the alternator pivot bolt and remove the drive belt.
6. Loosen the screws securing the front bracket to the engine.
7. Remove the alternator along with the spacer and lower through bolt.
8. Installation is the reverse of the removal procedure.

VOLTAGE REGULATOR

Removal and Installation

1. Disconnect the negative battery cable.
2. Remove alternator assembly.
3. Make scribe marks on end frames to facilitate reassembly.
4. Remove the retaining bolts and separate drive end frame assembly from rectifier end frame assembly.
5. Remove 3 attaching nuts and 3 regulator attaching screws.
6. Separate stator, diode trio and regulator from end frame.
7. Installation is the reverse of the removal procedure.

BELT TENSION

Gauge Method

Using belt tension gauge J–23600 or equivalent, adjust the alternator belt if the tension is below 300N, as indicated on the gauge. If the belt is used, the correct belt tension is 600N, as indicated on the gauge. If the belt is new, the correct tension is 900N, as indicated on the gauge.

Starting System

STARTER

Removal and Installation

1. Disconnect the negative battery cable.
2. Raise and support the vehicle safely.

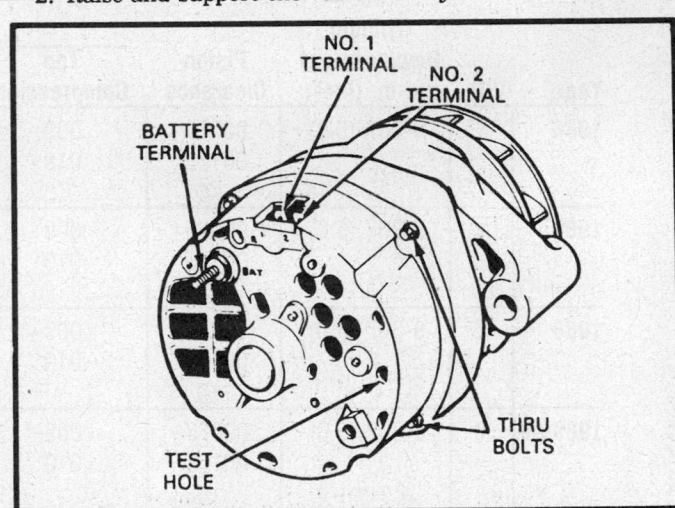

Alternator end frame view—typical

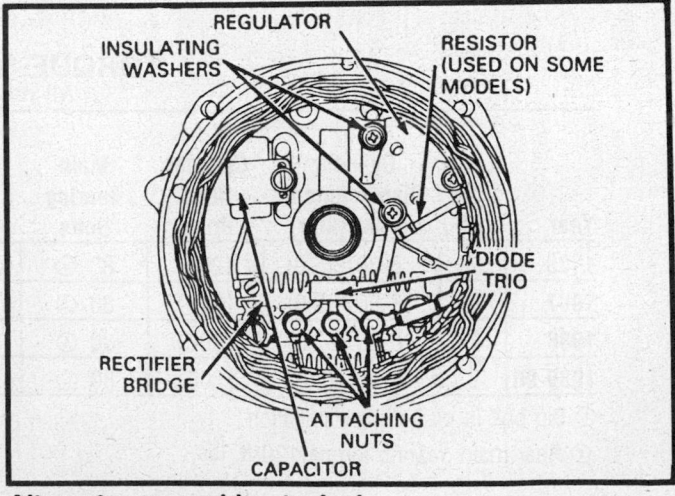

Alternator assembly—typical

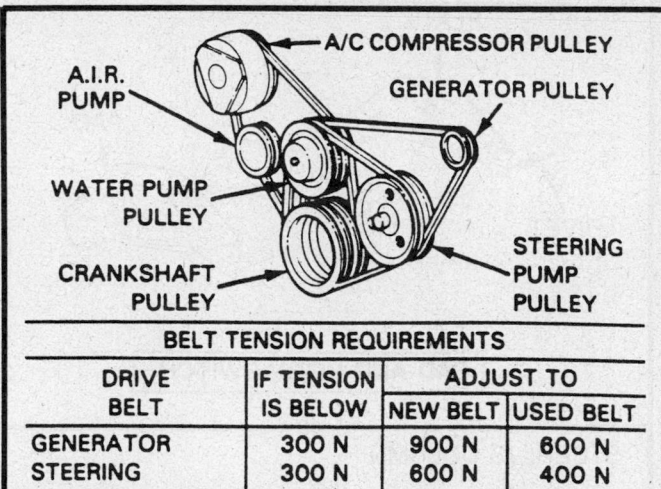

BELT TENSION REQUIREMENTS

DRIVE BELT	IF TENSION IS BELOW	ADJUST TO	
		NEW BELT	USED BELT
GENERATOR	300 N	900 N	600 N
STEERING	300 N	600 N	400 N
A/C COMPRESSOR	400 N	750 N	600 N

Belt tension

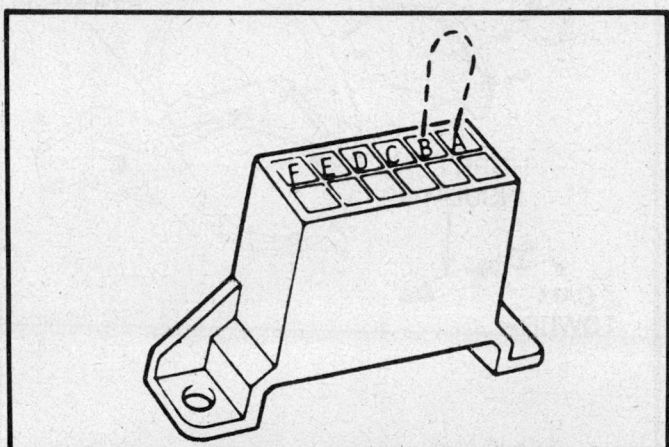

Grounding out the assembly line diagnostic lead connector

3. Remove the starter braces, shields, flywheel housing cover and other items that may interfere with the starter removal.
4. Remove the starter motor retaining bolts and allow the starter to be lowered.
5. Remove the solenoid wires and the battery cable while supporting the starter. Be sure to note the position of the wires for reinstallation. Remove the starter from the vehicle.
6. Installation is the reverse of the removal procedure.

Ignition System

DISTRIBUTOR

Removal and Installation

NOTE: Malfunction trouble codes must be cleared after the removal or adjustment of the distributor.

TIMING NOT DISTURBED

1. Disconnect the negative battery cable. Disconnect the electrical wires from the distributor cap. Disconnect the coil locking tab connectors.
2. Remove the distributor cap retaining screws. Remove the distributor cap and position it to the side.
3. Disconnect the terminal ECM harness from the distributor.

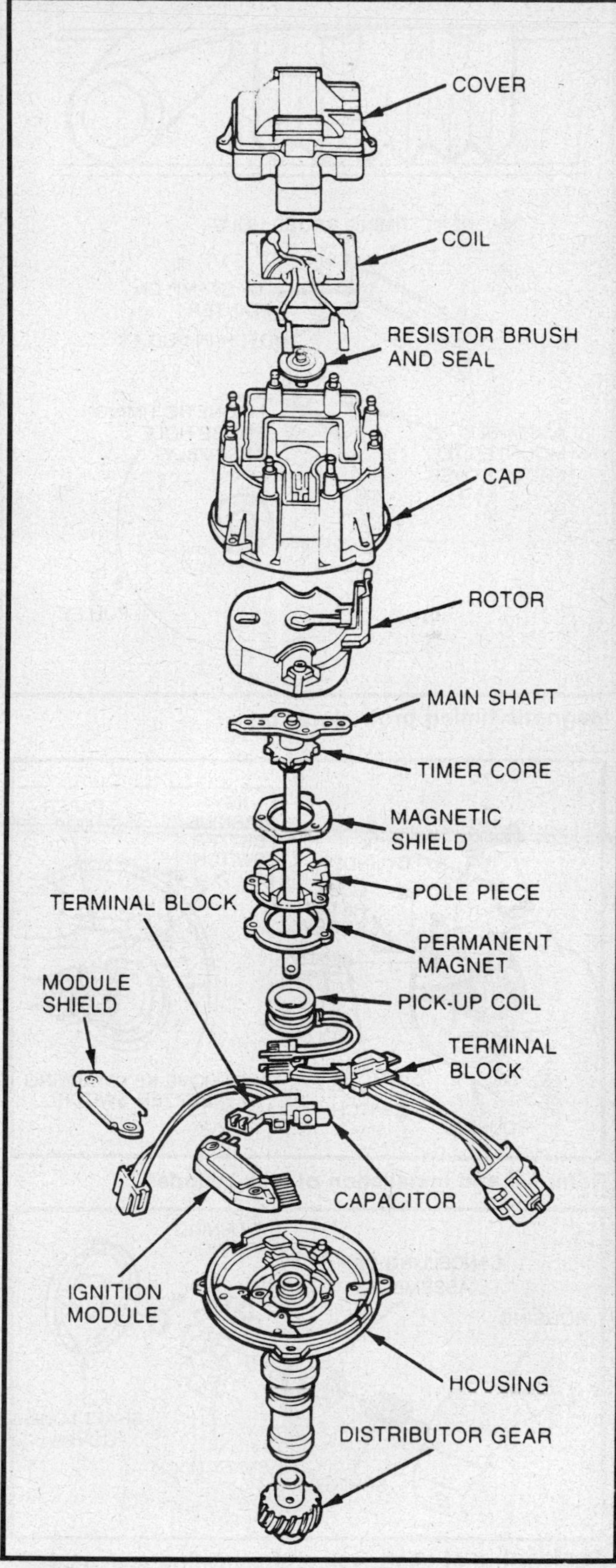

HEI (EST) distributor—exploded view

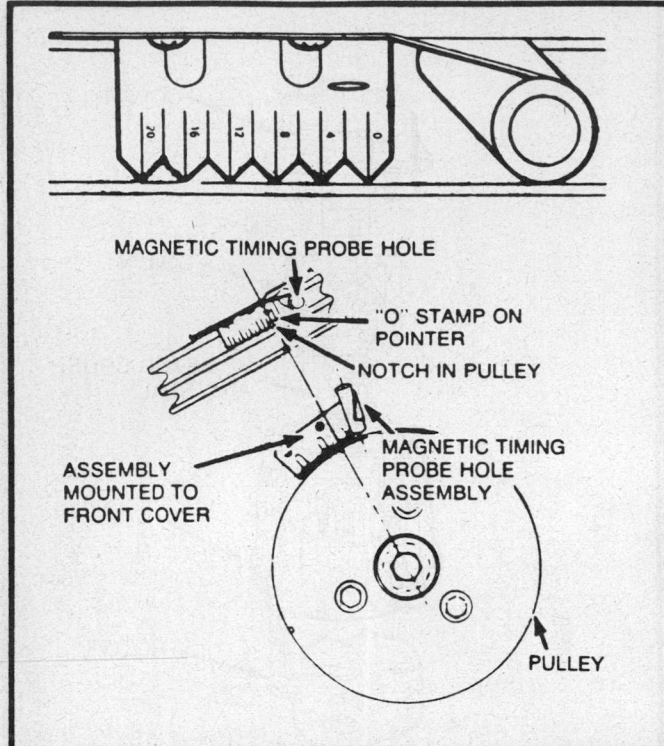

Magnetic timing probe location

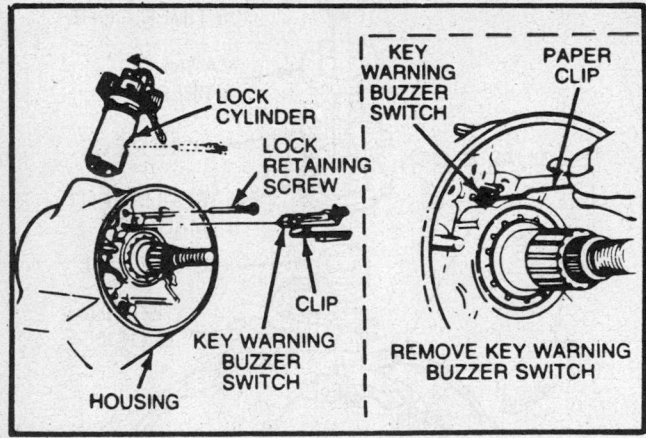

Removal and installation of lock cylinder

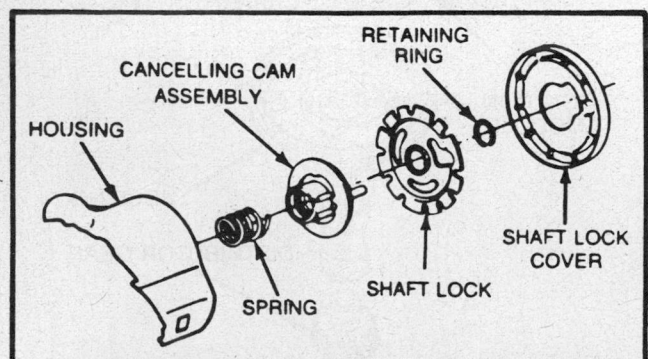

Positioning of shaft lock and canceling cam assembly, standard Column

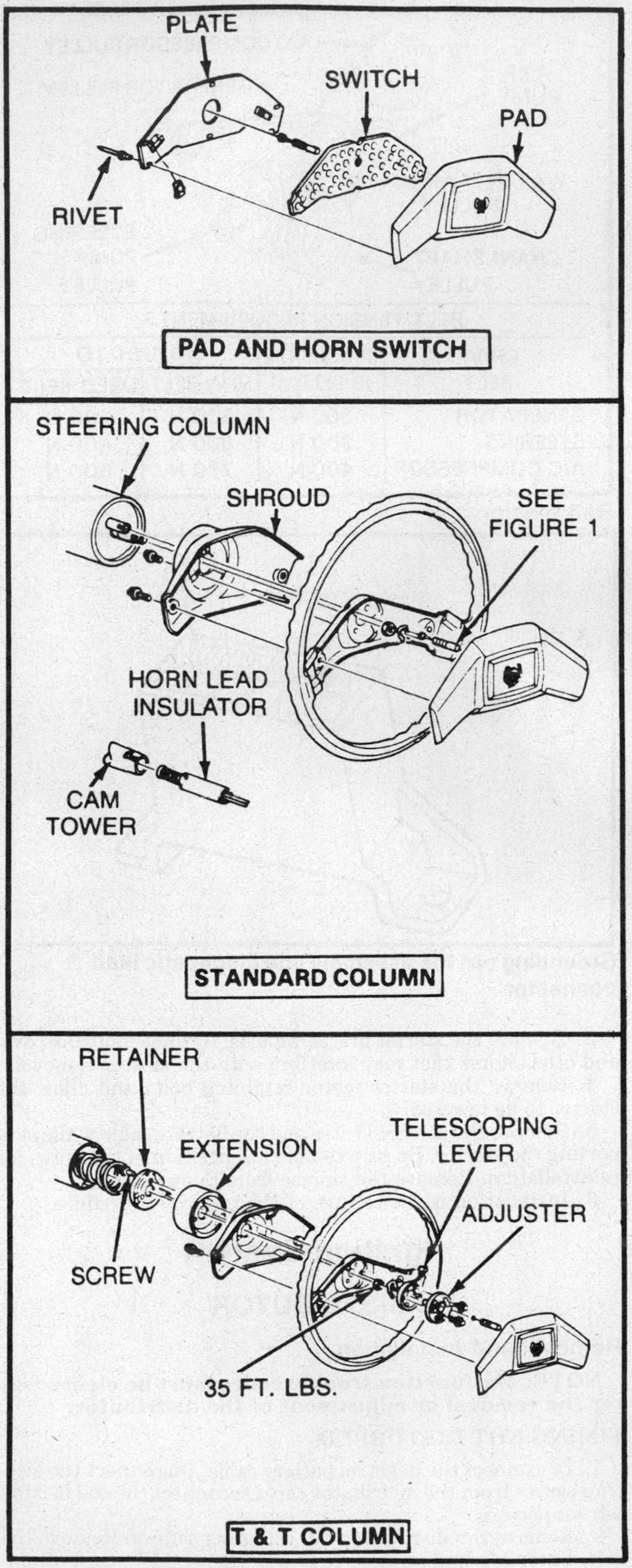

PAD AND HORN SWITCH

STANDARD COLUMN

T & T COLUMN

Steering wheel and related components

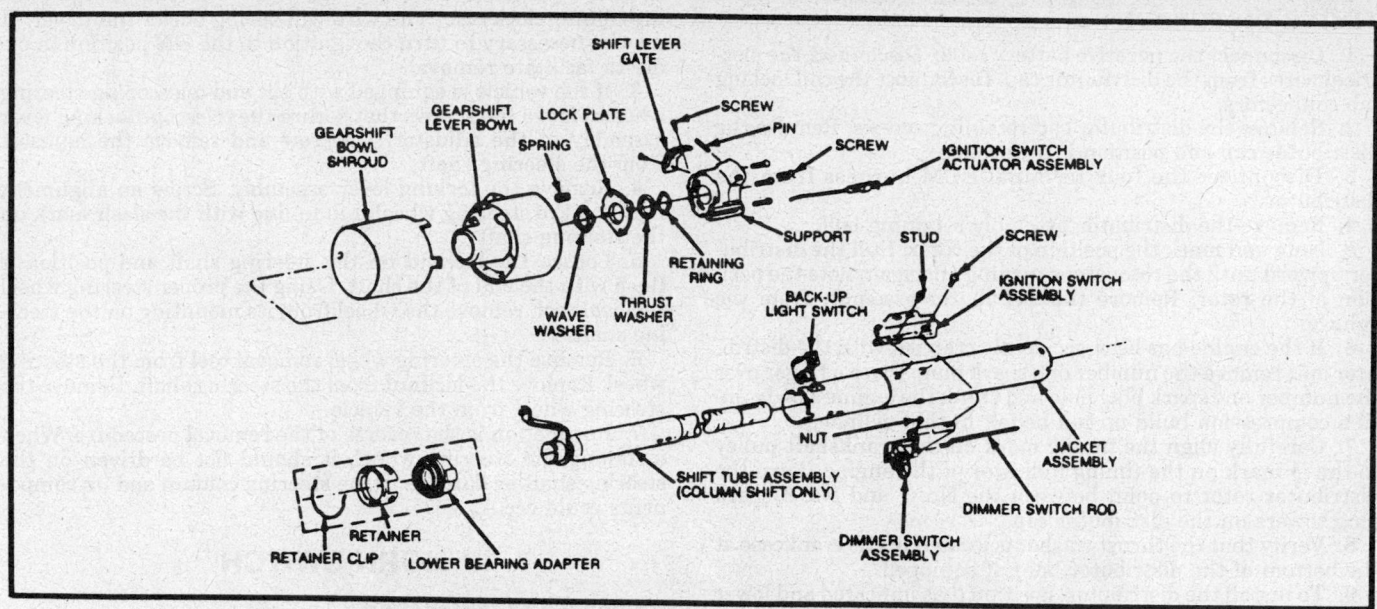

Exploded view of tilt and telescoping column bowl assembly and location of switches

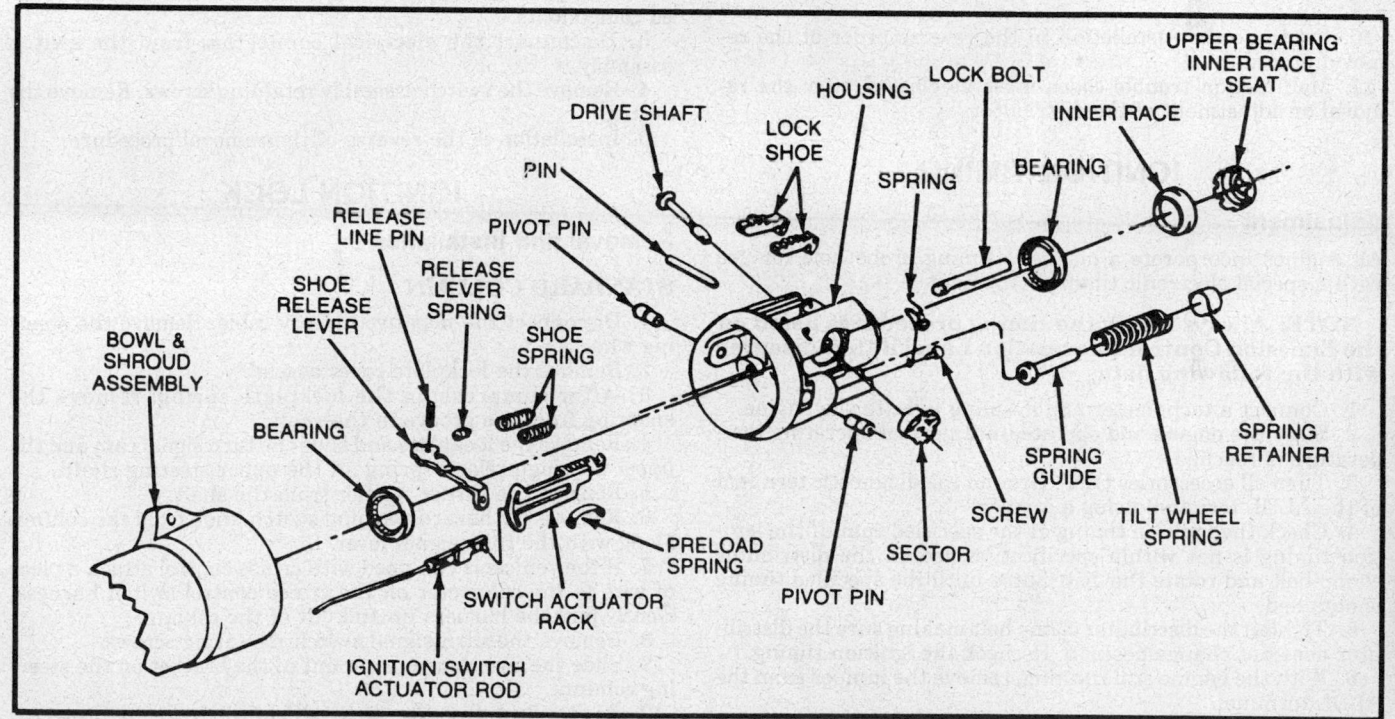

Exploded view of tilt and telescoping column housing assembly

4. Remove the distributor assembly retaining bolt.

5. Note and mark the position of the rotor. Pull the distributor upward until the rotor stops turning and again note the position of the rotor. Remove the distributor assembly from the vehicle.

6. Remove the thrust washer between the distributor drive gear and the crankcase, if equipped. This washer may stick to the bottom of the distributor as it is removed. Before distributor installation, verify that the thrust washer is located in the crankcase at the bottom of the distributor bore.

7. To install the distributor, position the rotor in the last position as marked and lower the assembly into the distributor bore of the engine. When the distributor rotor stops turning and the unit is seated, the rotor should be pointing to the first mark made.

8. Continue the installation in the reverse order of the removal procedure.

9. Malfunction trouble codes must be cleared after the removal or adjustment of the distributor.

TIMING DISTURBED

1. Disconnect the negative battery cable. Disconnect the electrical wires from the distributor cap. Disconnect the coil locking tab connectors.
2. Remove the distributor cap retaining screws. Remove the distributor cap and position it to the side.
3. Disconnect the four terminal ECM harness from the distributor.
4. Remove the distributor assembly retaining bolt.
5. Note and mark the position of the rotor. Pull the distributor upward until the rotor stops turning and again note the position of the rotor. Remove the distributor assembly from the vehicle.
6. If the engine has been accidently cranked with the distributor out, remove the number one spark plug. Place a finger over the number one spark plug hole and crank the engine slowly until a compression build up can be felt in that cylinder.
7. Carefully align the timing mark on the crankshaft pulley to the O mark on the timing indicator of the engine. Turn the distributor rotor to point between the No. 1 and No. 8 spark plug towers on the distributor cap.
8. Verify that the thrust washer is located in the crankcase at the bottom of the distributor bore, if equipped.
9. To install the distributor, position it as indicated and lower the assembly into the distributor bore of the engine. When the distributor rotor stops turning and the unit is seated, the rotor should be pointing to No. 1 cylinder segment on the distributor cap.
10. Continue the installation in the reverse order of the removal procedure.
11. Malfunction trouble codes must be cleared after the removal or adjustment of the distributor.

IGNITION TIMING

Adjustment

All engines incorporate a magnetic timing probe hole for use with a special electronic timing equipment.

NOTE: Always follow the timing procedures listed on the Emission Control Information Label if they disagree with the following data.

1. Connect a tachometer and a timing light to the engine.
2. Start the engine and operate until normal operating temperature is reached.
3. Turn all accessories OFF. Ground the diagnostic terminal of the ALDL terminal using a jumper.
4. Check the ignition timing at the specified rpm. If the ignition timing is not within specification, loosen the distributor clamp bolt and rotate the distributor until the specified timing is obtained.
5. Tighten the distributor clamp bolt making sure the distributor does not change position. Recheck the ignition timing.
6. With the engine still running, remove the jumper from the ALDL terminal.
7. Adjust the carburetor idle speed, as required.
8. Turn the engine OFF. Remove the tachometer and timing light.

Electrical Controls

STEERING WHEEL

Removal and Installation

1. Disconnect the negative battery cable.
2. Remove the horn pad retaining screws from back of spokes and remove the horn pad assembly. Remove the horn contact wire from the plastic tower by pushing in on the wire and turning counterclockwise. The wire will spring out of the tower. It may be necessary to turn the ignition to the ON position in order to facilitate removal.
3. If the vehicle is equipped with tilt and telescoping steering wheel remove the screws that secure the telescope locking lever assembly to the adjuster. Unscrew and remove the adjuster from the steering shaft.
4. Remove the locking lever assembly. Scribe an alignment mark on the steering wheel hub in line with the slash mark on the steering shaft.
5. Loosen the locknut on the steering shaft and position it flush with the end of the shaft. Using the proper steering wheel removal tool, remove the wheel from its mounting on the steering shaft.
6. Remove the steering wheel removal tool from the steering wheel. Remove the locknut from the steering shaft. Remove the steering wheel from the vehicle.
7. Installation is the reverse of the removal procedure. When installing the steering wheel, it should not be driven on the steering shaft as damage to the steering column and its components could occur.

HORN SWITCH

Removal and Installation

1. Disconnect the negative battery cable.
2. Remove the horn pad, contact assembly and all other related components.
3. Disconnect the electrical connectors from the switch assembly.
4. Remove the switch assembly retaining screws. Remove the switch.
5. Installation is the reverse of the removal procedure.

IGNITION LOCK

Removal and Installation

STANDARD COLUMN

1. Disconnect the negative battery cable. Remove the steering wheel.
2. Remove the lockplate cover assembly.
3. After compressing the lockplate spring, remove the snapring from the groove in the shaft.
4. Remove the lockplate and slide the turn signal cam and the upper bearing preload spring off the upper steering shaft.
5. Remove the thrust washer from the shaft.
6. Remove the hazard warning switch knob from the column along with the turn signal lever.
7. If the vehicle is equipped with cruise control attach a piece of wire to the connector on the cruise control switch harness. Gently pull the harness up and out of the column.
8. Remove the turn signal switch mounting screws.
9. Slide the switch connector out of the bracket on the steering column.
10. As required, free the turn signal switch wiring protector from its mounting after disconnecting the turn signal switch electrical connectors, then pull the turn signal switch straight up and out of the steering column along with the switch harness and the connector from the steering column.
11. Turn the ignition switch to the ON or RUN position. Insert a small drift pin into the slot next to the switch mounting screw boss. Push the lock cylinder tab and remove the lock cylinder.
12. Installation is the reverse of the removal procedure.

TILT AND TELESCOPING COLUMN

1. Disconnect the negative battery cable. Remove the steering wheel.

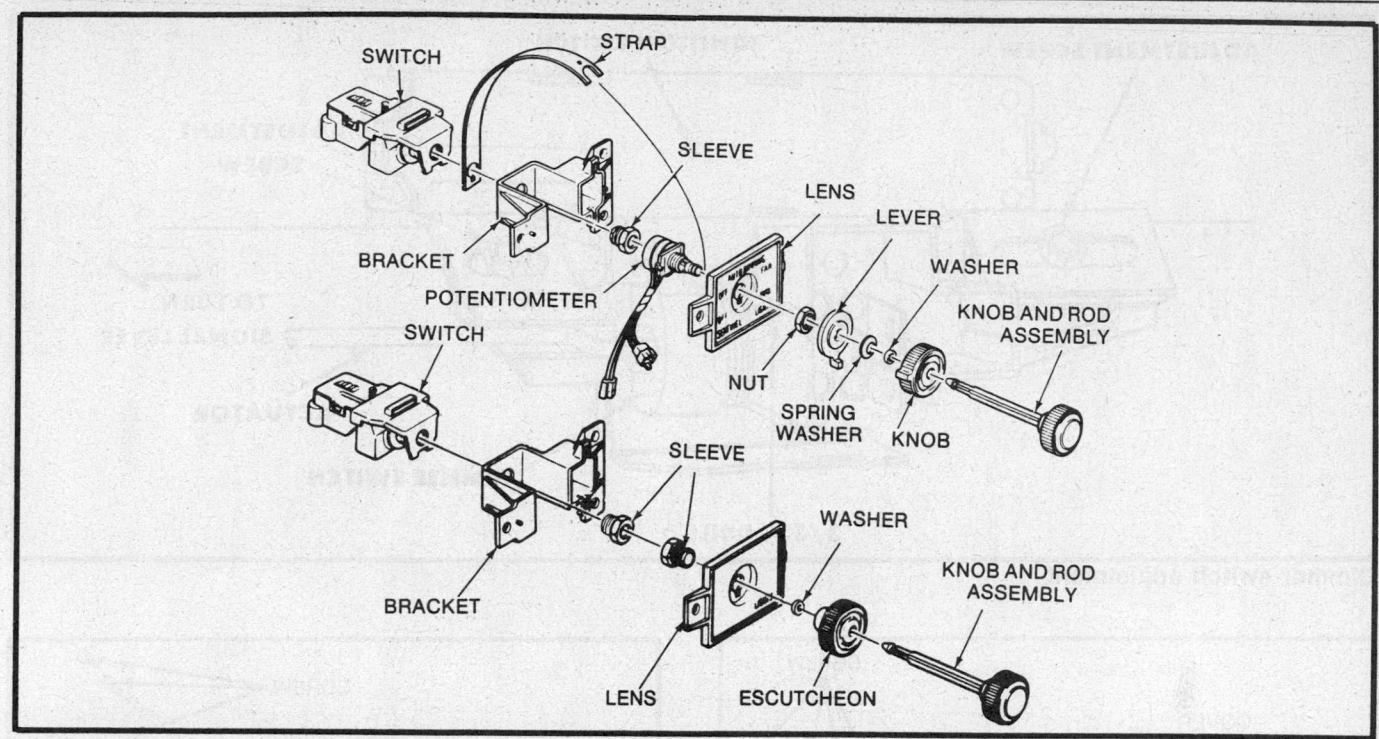

Headlight switches—exploded view

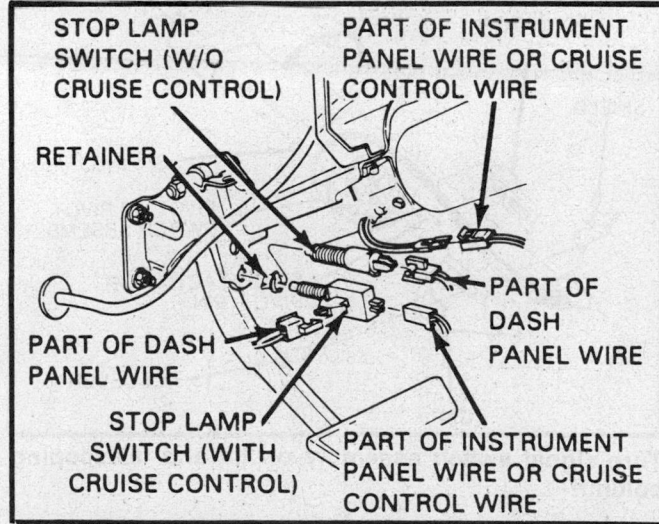

Location of stoplight switch, with or without cruise control

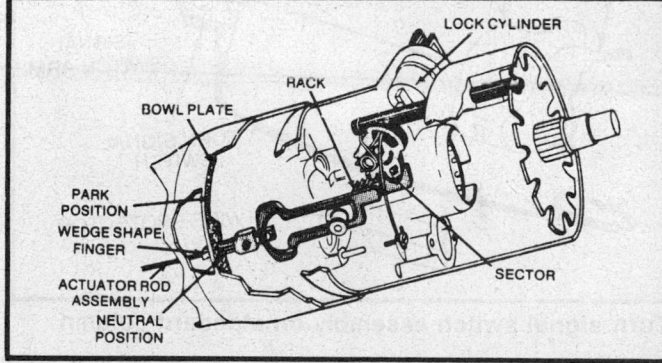

Mechanical start mechanism in steering column

2. Remove the rubber sleeve bumper from the steering shaft.

3. Using an appropriate tool, remove the plastic retainer.

4. Using a spring compressor, compress the upper steering shaft spring and remove the C-ring. Release the steering shaft lockplate, the horn contact carrier, and the upper steering shaft preload spring.

5. Remove the 4 screws which hold the upper mounting bracket and then remove the bracket.

6. Slide the harness connector out of the bracket on the steering column. Tape the upper part of the harness and connector.

7. Disconnect the hazard button and position the shift bowl in **P**. Remove the turn signal lever from the column.

8. If the vehicle is equipped with cruise control, remove the harness protector from the harness. Attach a piece of wire to the switch harness connector. Before removing the turn signal lever, loop a piece of wire and insert it into the turn signal lever opening. Use the wire to pull the cruise control harness out through the opening. Pull the rest of the harness up through and out of the column. Remove the guide wire from the connector and secure the wire to the column. Remove the turn signal lever.

9. Pull the turn signal switch up until the end connector is within the shift bowl. Remove the hazard flasher lever. Allow the switch to hang.

10. Place the ignition key in the **RUN** position.

11. Depress the center of the lock cylinder retaining tab with a suitable tool and then remove the lock cylinder.

12. Installation is the reverse of the removal procedure.

IGNITION SWITCH

Removal and Installation

1. Disconnect the negative battery terminal.

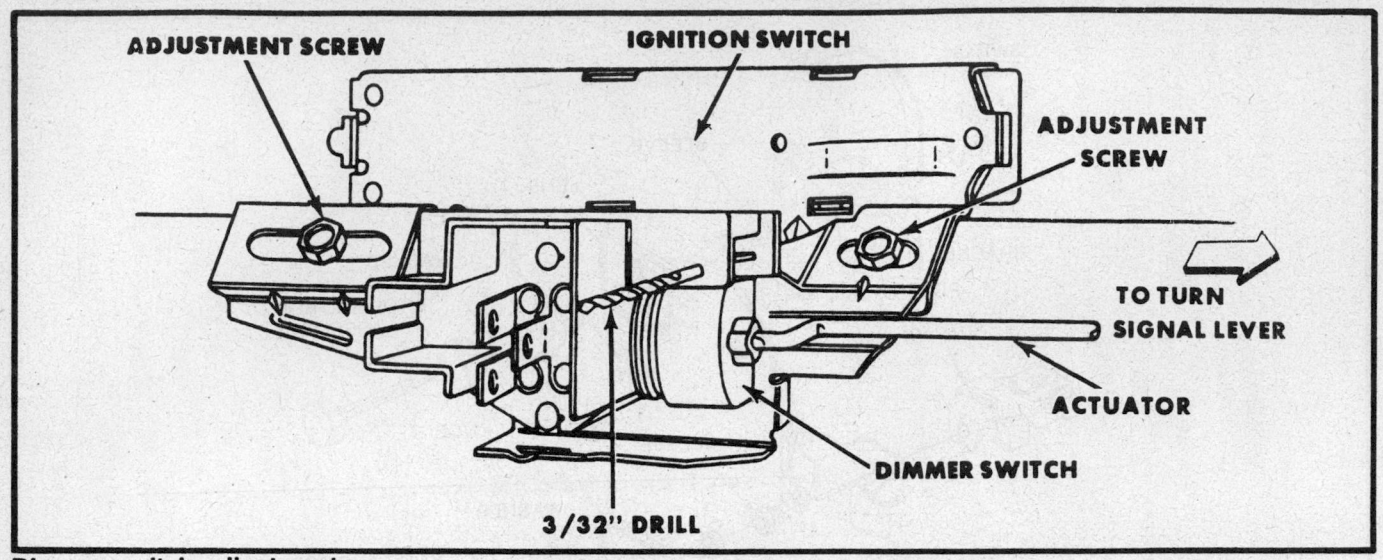

Dimmer switch adjustment

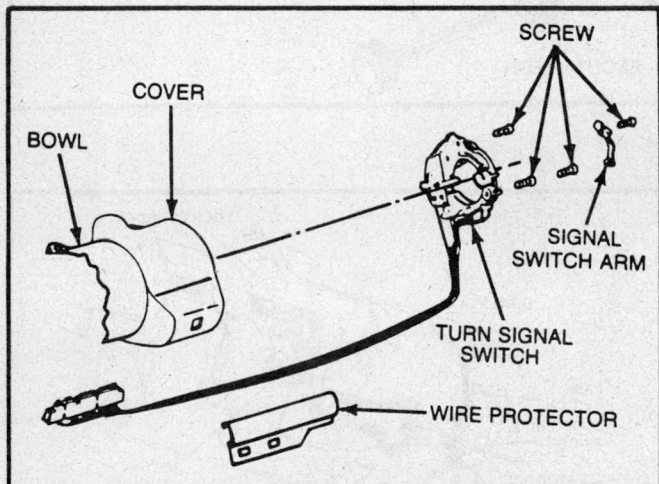

Turn signal switch assembly on standard column

2. Position lock cylinder in **LOCK** position.

3. Remove steering column lower cover.

4. Loosen the nuts on the upper steering column, allowing column to drop and support on the seat.

5. Disconnect the ignition switch connector at switch.

6. Remove the screws securing the dimmer switch and ignition switch to the steering column. Position the dimmer switch out of the way and remove the screw securing the ignition switch to the steering column. Remove the ignition switch from the vehicle.

To install:

7. Assemble the ignition switch on the actuator rod and adjust it to the **LOCK** position as follows.

8. If the vehicle is equipped with a standard column, hold the switch actuating rod stationary with one hand while moving the switch toward the bottom of the column until it reaches the end of its travel (**ACC** position). Back off 2 detents to the right (**OFF/UNLOCK** position), then with the key also in the **OFF/UNLOCK** position, tighten the switch mounting screws to 35 inch lbs.

9. If the vehicle is equipped with a tilt wheel, hold the switch actuating rod stationary with one hand while moving the switch toward the upper end of column until it reaches the end of its

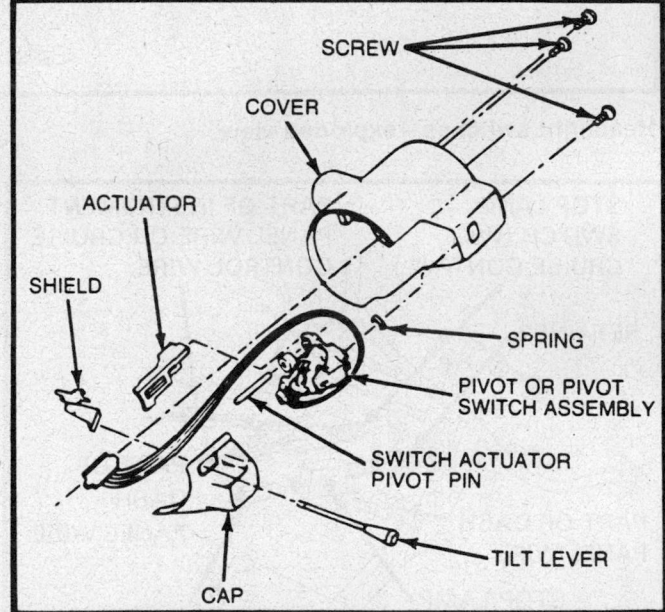

Turn signal switch assembly on tilt and telescoping column

travel (**ACC** position). Back off one detent and with the key in **LOCK** position, tighten the switch mounting screws to 35 inch lbs.

10. Continue the installation in the reverse order of the removal procedure. Test the starting system to start in **P** and **N** only.

NEUTRAL SAFETY SWITCH

These vehicles incorporate a mechanical neutral start system. This system relies on a mechanical block, rather than the starter safety switch to prevent starting the engine in other than **P** or **N** positions.

The mechanical block is achieved by a cast in finger added to the switch actuator rack, which interferes with the bowl plate in all shift positions except **N** or **P**. This interference prevents rotation of the lock cylinder into the **START** position.

In either **P** or **N**, this finger passes through the bowl plate slots allowing the lock cylinder full rotational travel into the **START** position.

STOPLIGHT SWITCH

Removal and Installation

NOTE: The cruise control release switch and the stoplight switch are adjusted or replaced in the same manner.

1. Disconnect the negative battery cable. Disconnect the wire harness connector from the switch.
2. Remove the switch from the clip and then remove the clip from the bracket.

To install:

3. Place the clip in its bore on the bracket.
4. With the brake pedal depressed, insert the switch into the clip and depress the switch body. Clicks can be heard as the threaded portion of the switch is pushed through the clip towards the brake pedal.
5. Pull the brake pedal fully rearward against the pedal stop until the clicking sounds cannot be heard. The switch can be moved in the clip to correct the adjustment.
6. Release the brake pedal and repeat Step 5 to assure that no clicking sounds remain. The switch is now correctly adjusted.
7. Install the harness connector and verify the stoplights operate correctly.

HEADLIGHT SWITCH

Removal and Installation

1. Disconnect the negative battery cable.
2. Remove the instrument panel insert.
3. Remove the screws securing the switch to the instrument panel.
4. On vehicles equipped with cruise control and twilight sentinel, remove the screws securing the cruise control switch to the instrument panel.
5. Slide the cruise control switch forward to remove the light switch. If equipped, disconnect the 2 piece connector from the headlight switch. Disconnect the guidematic and twilight sentinel electrical connectors from under the instrument panel.
6. Remove the headlight switch retaining screws. Remove the switch assembly from the vehicle.
7. Installation is the reverse of the removal procedure.

DIMMER SWITCH

Removal and Installation

1. Disconnect negative battery cable.
2. Remove left sound insulator.
3. Remove 2 nuts securing steering column to upper mounting bracket.
4. Lower steering column and remove 2 screws securing ignition switch and dimmer switch.
5. Disconnect electrical connections and remove switch.
6. Installation is the reverse of the removal procedure. Check the dimmer switch adjustment.

Adjustment

1. Insert a $3/32$ drill through the locating hole.
2. Loosen both screws attaching the dimmer switch mounting bracket.
3. Slide the dimmer switch firmly against the actuator arm and tighten both adjusting screws.

TURN SIGNAL SWITCH

Removal and Installation

STANDARD COLUMN

1. Disconnect the negative battery cable.
2. Remove the steering wheel.
3. Insert a suitable tool into the lockplate and remove the lockplate cover assembly.
4. Install a spring compressor onto the steering shaft. Tighten the tool to compress the lockplate and the spring. Remove the snapring from the groove in the shaft.
5. Remove the lockplate, the turn signal cam, and the upper bearing preload spring and the thrust washer off the upper steering shaft.
6. Remove the steering column lower cover.
7. Remove the turn signal lever from the column.
8. On vehicles equipped with cruise control, disconnect the cruise control wire from the harness near the bottom of the column. Remove the harness protector from the cruise control wire. Remove the turn signal lever. Do not remove the wire from the column.
9. Remove the vertical bolts at the steering column upper support. Remove the shim packs. Keep the shims in order for reinstallation.
10. Remove the screws securing the column upper mounting bracket to the column. Remove the bracket.
11. Disconnect the turn signal wiring and remove the wires from the plastic protector.
12. Remove the turn signal switch mounting screws.
13. Slide the switch connector out of the bracket on the steering column.
14. If the switch is known to be bad, cut the wires and discard the switch. Tape the connector of the new switch to the old wires, and pull the new harness down through the steering column while removing the old wires.
15. If the original switch is to be reused, wrap tape around the wire and connector and pull the harness up through the column. It may be helpful to attach a length of wire to the harness connector before pulling it up through the column to facilitate installation.
16. After freeing the switch wiring protector from its mounting, pull the turn signal switch straight up and remove the switch, switch harness and the connector from the column.
17. Installation is the reverse of the removal procedure.

TILT AND TELESCOPIC COLUMN

1. Disconnect the battery and remove the steering wheel.
2. Remove the rubber sleeve bumper from the steering shaft.
3. Remove the plastic retainer and disengage the tabs on the retainer from the C-ring.
4. Compress the upper steering shaft preload spring with a spring compressor and remove the C-ring. When installing the spring compressor, pull the upper shaft up about one inch and turn the ignition to the lock position to hold the shaft in place.
5. Remove the spring compressor and remove the upper steering shaft lock plate, horn contact carrier and the preload spring.
6. Remove the steering column lower cover. Unscrew and remove the turn signal lever.
7. If equipped with cruise control, disconnect the cruise control wire from the harness near the bottom of the steering column. Slide the protector off the cruise control wire. Remove the lever attaching screw and carefully pull the lever out enough to allow the removal of the turn signal switch.
8. Remove the nuts and shim packs from the upper column support. Keep the shims together as a unit for reinstallation.
9. Remove the bracket from the steering column by removing the two attaching screws from each side.
10. Disconnect the turn signal wiring harness and remove the wires from the plastic protector.

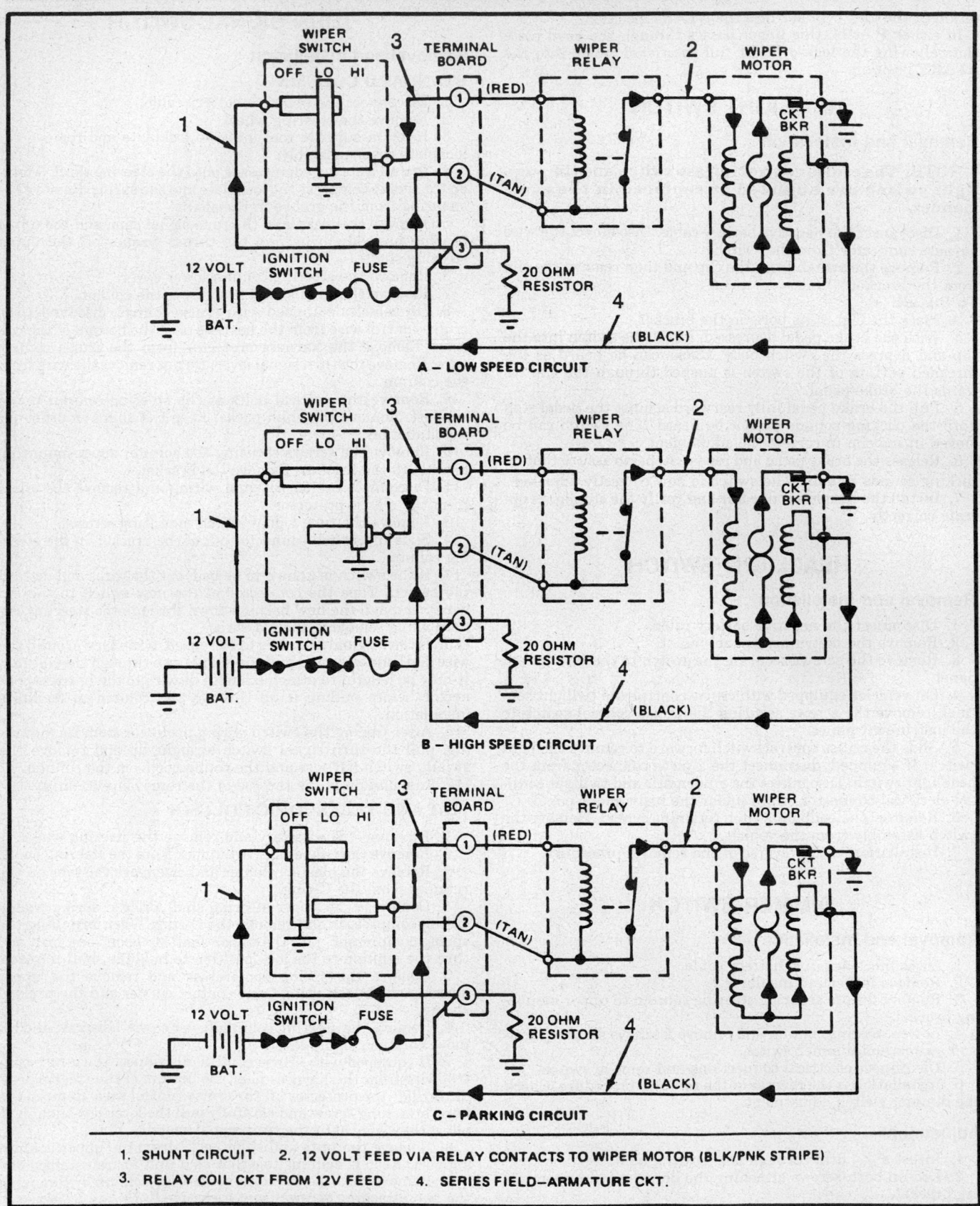

1. SHUNT CIRCUIT   2. 12 VOLT FEED VIA RELAY CONTACTS TO WIPER MOTOR (BLK/PNK STRIPE)
3. RELAY COIL CKT FROM 12V FEED   4. SERIES FIELD—ARMATURE CKT.

Delay wiper low/high speed and parking electrical schematic

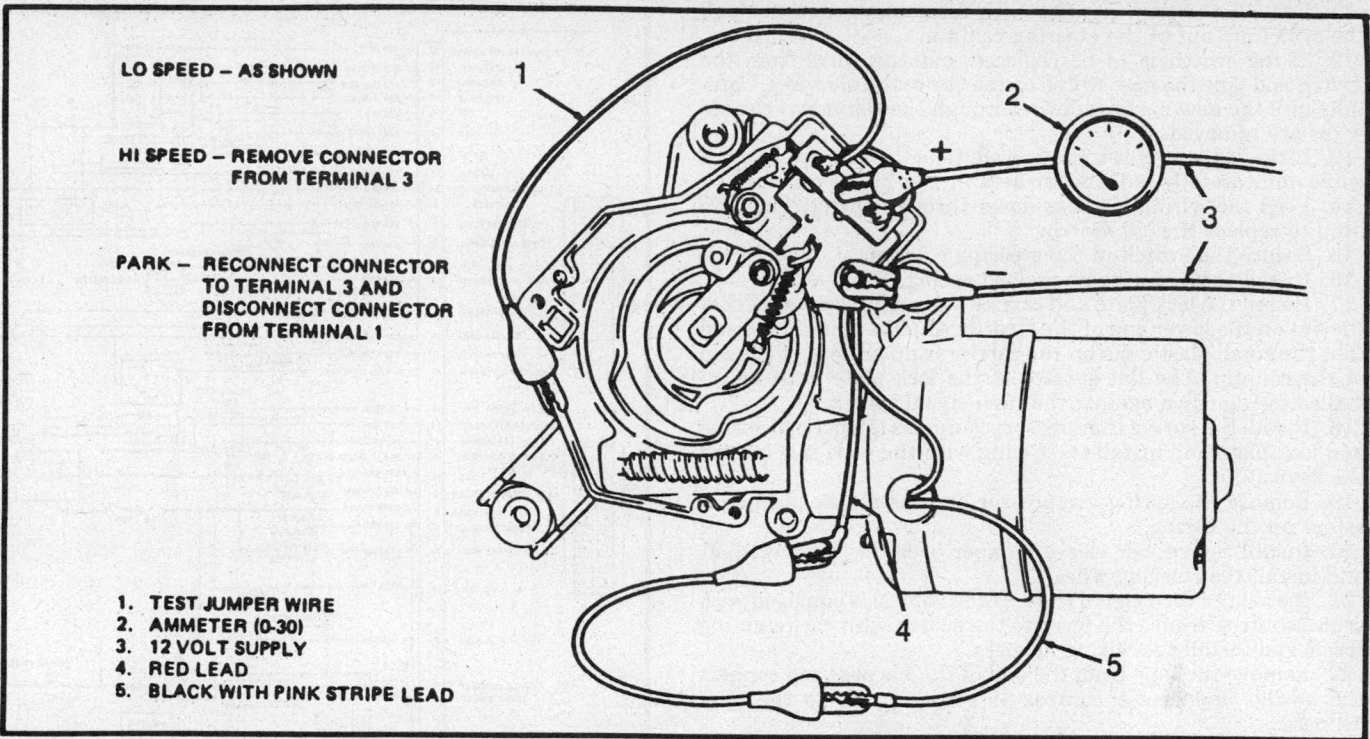

LO SPEED — AS SHOWN

HI SPEED — REMOVE CONNECTOR FROM TERMINAL 3

PARK — RECONNECT CONNECTOR TO TERMINAL 3 AND DISCONNECT CONNECTOR FROM TERMINAL 1

1. TEST JUMPER WIRE
2. AMMETER (0-30)
3. 12 VOLT SUPPLY
4. RED LEAD
5. BLACK WITH PINK STRIPE LEAD

Delay wiper motor bench test

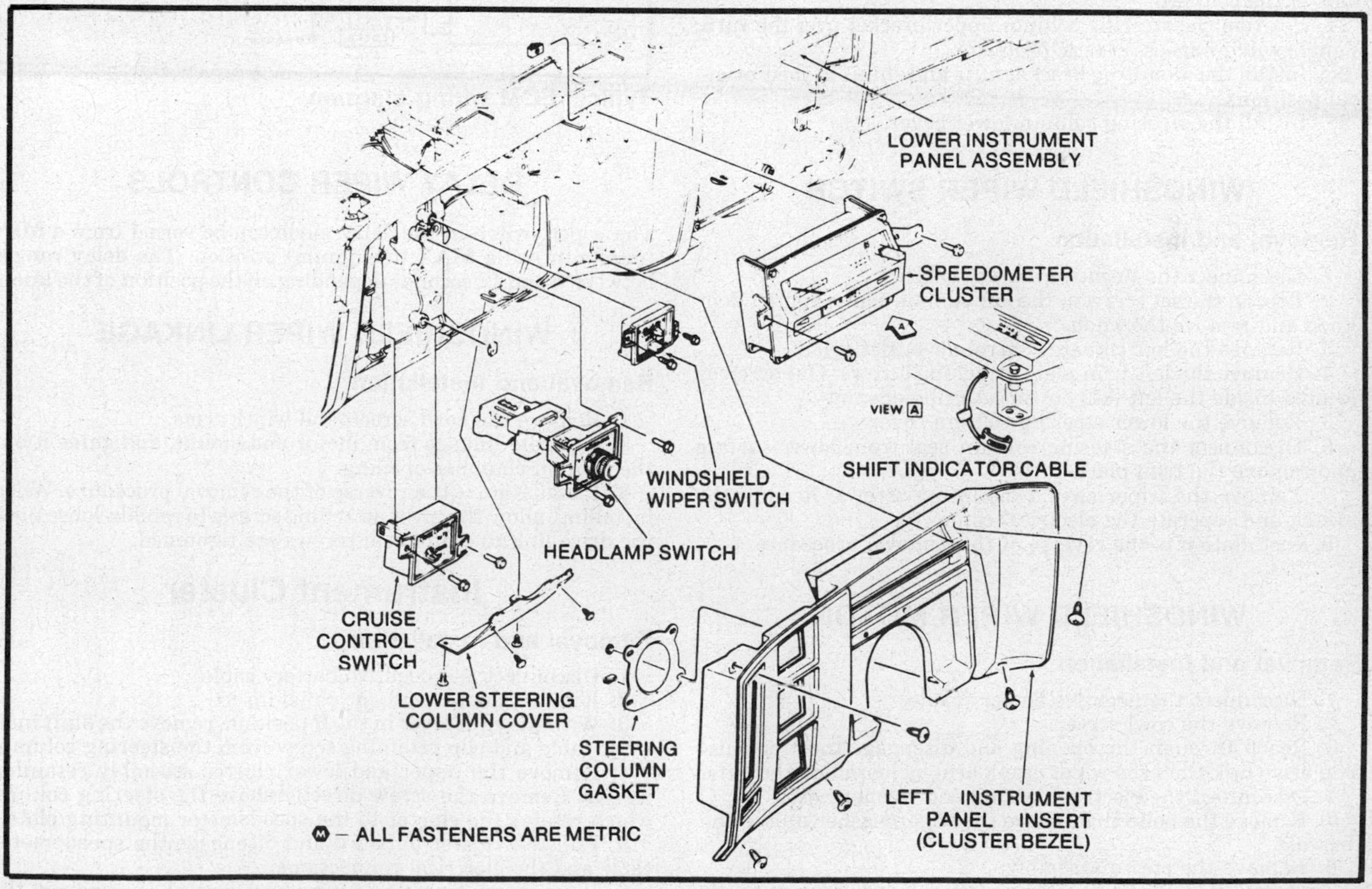

LOWER INSTRUMENT PANEL ASSEMBLY

SPEEDOMETER CLUSTER

VIEW A

SHIFT INDICATOR CABLE

WINDSHIELD WIPER SWITCH

HEADLAMP SWITCH

CRUISE CONTROL SWITCH

LOWER STEERING COLUMN COVER

STEERING COLUMN GASKET

LEFT INSTRUMENT PANEL INSERT (CLUSTER BEZEL)

Ⓜ — ALL FASTENERS ARE METRIC

Instrument cluster and related components

11. Remove the turn signal switch retaining screws and pull the switch up out of the steering column.

12. If the switch is to be replaced, cut the wires from the switch and tape the new switch connector to the old wires. Carefully pull the new harness down through the column as the old wires are removed.

13. If the old switch is to be reused, tape the connector to the wires and carefully pull the harness up out of the column.

14. Feed the wiring harness down through the steering column to replace the old switch.

15. Secure the switch in the steering column.

16. Install the upper shaft preload spring.

17. Install the lock plate and carrier assembly. Make sure that the flat on the lower end of the steering shaft is pointing up and that the small plastic tab on the carrier is up or nearest the top of the column. The flat surface of the lock plate must be installed facing down against the turn signal switch.

18. Install the spring compressor, compress the preload spring and lock plate and install the C-ring with the wide side toward the keyway.

19. Remove the spring compressor and install the plastic retainer on the C-ring.

20. Install the rubber sleeve bumper over the steering shaft and install the steering wheel.

21. Install the turn signal lever. If the vehicle is equipped with cruise control, secure the lever to the switch with the retaining screw and install the wiring harness.

22. Remove the tape from the end of the harness and connect the switch and cruise control, if so equipped, to the wire harness.

23. Cover both harnesses with the plastic protector and position it to the column. The turn signal connector slides on the tabs of the column.

24. Position the steering column upper bracket over the turn signal switch harness plastic protector.

25. Install the mounting bracket nuts and shims in their original positions.

26. Install the steering column lower cover.

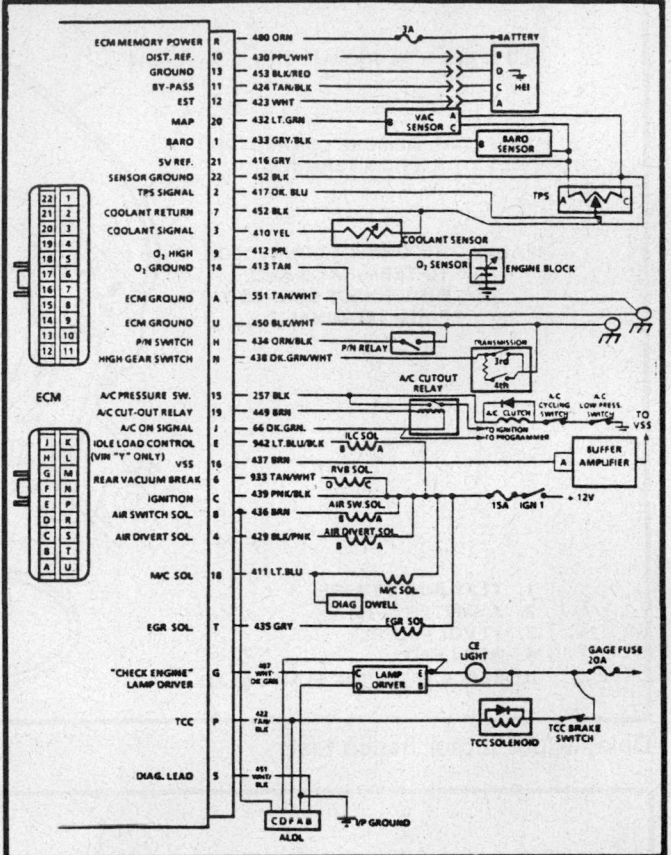

Typical ECM wiring diagram

WINDSHIELD WIPER SWITCH

Removal and Installation

1. Disconnect the negative battery cable.
2. Loosen the set screw in the left climate control outlet door knob and remove the knob.
3. Remove the left climate control air outlet grille.
4. Remove the left trim plate attaching screws. One screw is located inside the left A/C air outlet grille opening.
5. Remove the lower steering column cover.
6. Disconnect the steering column seal from lower surface and remove the trim plate.
7. Remove the wiper switch mounting screws. Remove the switch and seperate the electrical connector.
8. Installation is the reverse of the removal procedure.

WINDSHIELD WIPER MOTOR

Removal and Installation

1. Disconnect the negative battery cable.
2. Remove the cowl screen.
3. Reach through the opening and disengage the transmission drive link from the wiper crank arm by loosening the nuts.
4. Disconnect the electrical wiring and washer hoses.
5. Remove the bolts that secure the wiper/washer unit to the firewall.
6. Remove the entire assembly.
7. Installation is the reverse of the removal procedure. Be sure that the wiper crank arm is in the park position.

DELAY WIPER CONTROLS

The wiper switch in the delay mode can be varied from a **MIN** (minimum) to a **MAX** (maximum) position. The delay ranges between 0 and 12 seconds depending on the position of the knob.

WINDSHIELD WIPER LINKAGE

Removal and Installation

1. Remove the cowl screen and wiper arms.
2. Separate linkage from motor and mount, and guide it out the plenum chamber opening.
3. Installation is the reverse of the removal procedure. When installing, allow the pivot attaching screws to remain loose until the drive link to crank arm screws are tightened.

Instrument Cluster

Removal and Installation

1. Disconnect the negative battery cable.
2. Remove the instrument panel insert.
3. With the shift lever in the **P** position, remove the shift indicator cable and clip retaining screw from the steering column.
4. Remove the upper and lower cluster assembly retaining screws. Remove the screw directly above the steering column which retains the cluster to the speedometer mounting plate.
5. Pull the cluster outward and disengage the speedometer cable and the electrical connections.
6. If equipped, disconnect the speed control sensor from the cluster assembly. Disconnect other connectors as required.

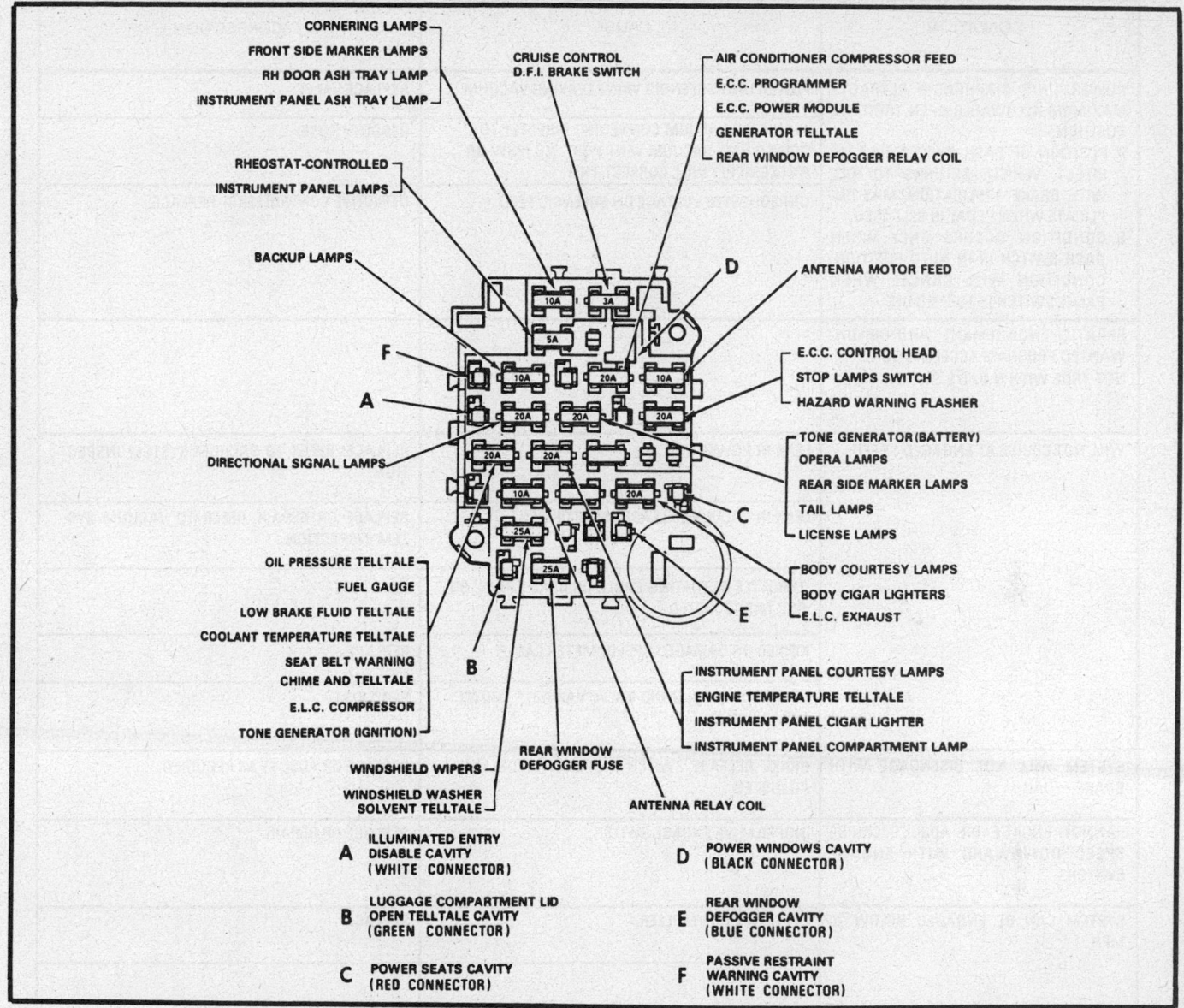

CORNERING LAMPS
FRONT SIDE MARKER LAMPS
RH DOOR ASH TRAY LAMP
INSTRUMENT PANEL ASH TRAY LAMP

CRUISE CONTROL
D.F.I. BRAKE SWITCH

AIR CONDITIONER COMPRESSOR FEED
E.C.C. PROGRAMMER
E.C.C. POWER MODULE
GENERATOR TELLTALE
REAR WINDOW DEFOGGER RELAY COIL

RHEOSTAT-CONTROLLED
INSTRUMENT PANEL LAMPS

BACKUP LAMPS

D

ANTENNA MOTOR FEED

E.C.C. CONTROL HEAD
STOP LAMPS SWITCH
HAZARD WARNING FLASHER

TONE GENERATOR (BATTERY)
OPERA LAMPS
REAR SIDE MARKER LAMPS
TAIL LAMPS
LICENSE LAMPS

DIRECTIONAL SIGNAL LAMPS

C

BODY COURTESY LAMPS
BODY CIGAR LIGHTERS
E.L.C. EXHAUST

E

OIL PRESSURE TELLTALE
FUEL GAUGE
LOW BRAKE FLUID TELLTALE
COOLANT TEMPERATURE TELLTALE
SEAT BELT WARNING
CHIME AND TELLTALE
E.L.C. COMPRESSOR
TONE GENERATOR (IGNITION)

B

INSTRUMENT PANEL COURTESY LAMPS
ENGINE TEMPERATURE TELLTALE
INSTRUMENT PANEL CIGAR LIGHTER
INSTRUMENT PANEL COMPARTMENT LAMP

WINDSHIELD WIPERS
WINDSHIELD WASHER
SOLVENT TELLTALE

REAR WINDOW
DEFOGGER FUSE

ANTENNA RELAY COIL

A   ILLUMINATED ENTRY
    DISABLE CAVITY
    (WHITE CONNECTOR)

D   POWER WINDOWS CAVITY
    (BLACK CONNECTOR)

B   LUGGAGE COMPARTMENT LID
    OPEN TELLTALE CAVITY
    (GREEN CONNECTOR)

E   REAR WINDOW
    DEFOGGER CAVITY
    (BLUE CONNECTOR)

C   POWER SEATS CAVITY
    (RED CONNECTOR)

F   PASSIVE RESTRAINT
    WARNING CAVITY
    (WHITE CONNECTOR)

Typical fuse panel with circuits indicated

7. Place the shift lever in the **L** position and if equipped with tilt wheel, place the wheel in its lowest position. Remove the cluster assembly from the dash.

8. Installation is the reverse of the removal procedure. Set the shift, indicator cable in the **N** position and adjust the cable accordingly.

SPEEDOMETER

Removal and Installation

1. Disconnect the negative battery cable.
2. Remove speedometer cluster as described above.
3. Remove 4 screws holding speedometer cluster lens to cluster housing.
4. Remove lens and faceplate.
5. Remove selector quadrant assembly from cluster housing by pulling straight out.
6. Remove 2 rubber mounted screws securing speedometer head and dial and remove from cluster housing.

7. Remove 2 screws securing dial to speedometer head and remove dial. Use care not to damage pointer.

8. Installation is the reverse of the removal procedure.

9. Check for proper operation of speedometer head and needle.

SPEEDOMETER CABLE

Removal and Installation

1. Disconnect the negative battery cable.
2. Remove the instrument panel insert.
3. With the shift lever in the **P** position, remove the shift indicator cable and clip retaining screw from the steering column.
4. Remove the upper and lower cluster assembly retaining screws. Remove the screw directly above the steering column which retains the cluster to the speedometer mounting plate.
5. Pull the cluster outward and disengage the speedometer cable and the electrical connections.

CONDITION	CAUSE	CORRECTION
POWER UNIT DIAPHRAGM RETRACTS MAXIMUM ALLOWABLE OPEN THROTTLE POSITION. A. POSITION OF DASH SWITCH HAS NO EFFECT. VEHICLE RETURNS TO IDLE WITH BRAKE APPLICATION, MAY DUPLICATE WHEN PEDAL IS RELEASED. B. CONDITION OCCURS ONLY WHEN DASH SWITCH IS IN AUTO POSITION. CONDITION WILL CANCEL WHEN PANEL SWITCH IS TURNED OFF.	POWER UNIT SOLENOID VALVE LEAKING VACUUM.	REPLACE VALVE.
	MANIFOLD VACUUM CONNECTED DIRECTLY TO POWER UNIT VACUUM VENT PORT. NO IPSW OR BRAKE APPLY WILL CORRECT THIS.	REROUTE HOSE.
	UNREQUESTED VOLTAGE ON SOLENOID FEED.	DEFECTIVE CONTROLLER — REPLACE.
ERRATIC ENGAGEMENT AND/OR UNWANTED PROGRAM ACCELERATION. NOT TRUE WITH N.O. T/S SWITCH		
WILL NOT CRUISE AT ENGAGED SPEED.	LEAK IN POWER UNIT.	REPLACE. REFER TO VACUUM SYSTEM INSPECTION.
	LEAK IN VACUUM RELEASE VALVE OR HOSE.	REPLACE OR REPAIR. REFER TO VACUUM SYSTEM INSPECTION.
	THROTTLE ACTUATING CABLE OR BEAD CHAIN, OR ROD MISADJUSTED.	READJUST
	KINKED OR DAMAGED SPEEDOMETER CABLE.	REPLACE.
	POWER UNIT SOLENOID VALVE VARIABLE ORIFICE MISADJUSTED.	READJUST.
SYSTEM WILL NOT DISENGAGE WITH BRAKE PEDAL.	BRAKE RELEASE SWITCH INOPERATIVE OR MISADJUSTED.	REPLACE OR ADJUST AS REQUIRED.
CANNOT ENGAGE OR ADJUST CRUISE SPEED DOWNWARD WITH ENGAGE SWITCH.	INOPERATIVE ENGAGE SWITCH.	REPLACE OR REPAIR.
SYSTEM CAN BE ENGAGED BELOW 20 MPH.	DEFECTIVE CONTROLLER.	REPLACE.
HISSING NOISE WHEN BRAKE PEDAL DISENGAGES SYSTEM.	VACUUM RELEASE VALVE OR, RELEASE SWITCH MISADJUSTED.	READJUST VALVE OR REPLACE.
AMBER "ON" LIGHT WILL NOT TURN ON EVEN THOUGH SYSTEM CRUISES SATISFACTORILY.	INOPERATIVE BULB.	REPLACE.
	OPEN PRINTED CIRCUIT ON DASH SWITCH.	REPLACE.
	WIRE HARNESS	REPAIR
"GREEN" OR "AUTO" LIGHT WILL NOT TURN ON EVEN THOUGH SYSTEM CRUISES SATISFACTORILY.	INOPERATIVE BULB.	REPLACE.
	OPEN PRINTED CIRCUIT ON DASH SWITCH OR OPEN IN CRUISE HARNESS.	REPLACE, OR REPAIR.
	DEFECTIVE CONTROLLER.	REPLACE.
	WIRE HARNESS	REPAIR

Cruise control trouble diagnosis chart

6. If equipped, disconnect the speed control sensor from the cluster assembly. Disconnect other connectors as required.

7. Place the shift lever in the **L** position and if equipped with tilt wheel, place the wheel in its lowest position. Remove the cluster assembly from the dash.

8. If only the cable is to be replaced, pull it from the cable housing.

9. If the cable housing is to be replaced, disconnect the cable housing from the mounting plate on the dash panel as required. Disconnect the cable housing from the transmission case. Remove the cable housing and the speedometer cable from the vehicle.

10. Installation is the reverse of the removal procedure.

Electrical Circuit Protectors

FUSIBLE LINKS

Fusible links are used to prevent major wire harness damage in the event of a short circuit or an overload condition in the wiring circuits which are normally not fused, due to carrying high amperage loads or because of their locations within the wiring harness. Each fusible link is of a fixed value for a specific electrical load and should a link fail, the cause of the failure must be determined and repaired prior to installing a new fusible link of the same value.

CIRCUIT BREAKERS

Various circuit breakers are located under the instrument panel. In order to gain access to these components, it may be necessary to first remove the under dash padding.

FUSE PANEL

The fuse panel is located on the left side of the vehicle. It is under the instrument panel assembly. In order to gain access to the fuse panel, it may be necessary to first remove the under dash padding.

COMPUTER (ECM)

The electronic control module is located on the right side of the vehicle. It is positioned in front of the right hand kick panel. In order to gain access to the assembly, the trim panel must first be removed.

COMPUTER (BCM)

The body computer module is located under the right side of the dash above the relay center. In order to gain access to the assembly, the trim panel must first be removed.

VARIOUS RELAYS

All vehicles use a combination of the following electrical relays in order to function properly.

DEFOGGER RELAY—is located on the relay panel under the instrument panel to the left of the fuse block.
DOOR LOCK RELAY—is attached to the lower right shroud panel behind the kick panel.
POWER ANTENNA RELAY—is located on the relay panel under the instrument panel to the left of the fuse block.
FUEL PUMP RELAY (Gas)—is located on the relay panel under the instrument panel to the left of the fuse block.
HORN RELAY—is located on the relay panel under the instrument panel to the left of the fuse block.

STARTER INTERRUPT RELAY—is located on a bracket under the left side of the dash panel, to the left of the steering column.
POWER SEAT RELAY—is located under the seat.
STOP/TURN LIGHT RELAYs—is located at the left rear quarter panel.
GUIDEMATIC POWER RELAY—is located under the dash panel, near the fuse block.
THEFT DETERRENT RELAY—is located behind a bracket under the left side of the instrument panel.
AIR CONDITION COMPRESSOR CONTROL RELAY (GAS)—is located on the right side of the firewall in the engine compartment.
ELECTRONIC LEVEL CONTROL RELAY—is located to the left of the level control compressor.
MEMORY DISABLE RELAY—is located behind the right side of the dash near the connector.
LOW BRAKE VACUUM RELAY—is located behind the right side of the dash near the connector.
ILLUMINATED ENTRY TIMER—is located behind the right side of the dash near the connector.
HORN RELAY—is located under the left side of the dash panel, to the left of the steering column.
HEADLIGHT WASHER RELAY—is located on the fluid reservoir on the front of the right front shock tower.
HIGH MOUNT STOP LIGHT RELAYS—are located on the left rear wheelwell inside the trunk.

TURN SIGNAL FLASHER

The turn signal flasher is located behind the instrument panel bracket to the right of the steering column. In order to gain access to the turn signal flasher, it may be necessary to first remove the under dash padding.

HAZARD FLASHER

The hazard flasher is located in the fuse block. It is positioned on the lower right hand corner of the fuse block assembly. In order to gain access to the turn signal flasher, it may be necessary to first remove the under dash padding.

ELECTRICAL SPEED SENSOR

Access to the speed sensor and harness assembly is gained by partially removing the speedometer cluster and disconnecting the electrical connector at the speed sensor amplifier pigtail connector. At this point, removal of the speed sensor can be accomplished.

Speed Controls

Refer to "Chilton 's Chassis Electronics Service Manual" for additional coverage.

Adjustment

1. Start the engine and operate to normal operating temperature.

2. Verify that the carburetor is on the slow idle screw.

3. Turn the engine **OFF** and remove the retainer from the servo rod.

4. Remove and plug the vacuum hose from the Idle Load Compensator (ILC) motor. Using a hand operated vacuum pump, apply 20 in. Hg. to fully retract motor.

5. Position the retainer in the servo rod to provide the minimum slack.

6. Remove the vacuum pump and reconnect the vacuum hose to the idle load compensator motor. Check cruise control operation.

COOLING AND HEATING SYSTEMS

Water Pump

Removal and Installation

1. Disconnect the negative battery cable.
2. Drain the radiator. Disconnect the lower radiator hose at the water pump. Remove the drive belts. Remove the radiator fan and water pump pulley.
3. Remove the front air condition compressor bracket. Remove the front alternator bracket. Remove the power steering pump adjusting bracket. Remove the air pump mounting bracket.
4. Remove the water pump retaining bolts. Remove the water pump from the engine.
5. Installation is the reverse of the removal procedure. Use a new gasket and apply a RTV sealant on the gasket. Install the drive belts and tighten them to the proper tension. Refill the cooling system with the correct mixture of antifreeze and water. Start the engine and check for leaks.

Blower Motor

Removal and Installation

1. Disconnect the negative battery cable.
2. Remove the rubber cooling hose from the nipple and blower motor.
3. Disconnect the electrical connections from the motor assembly.
4. Remove the screws that secure the heater motor to the heater case. Remove the heater motor from the vehicle.
5. Installation is the reverse of the removal procedure.

Heater Core

Refer to "Chilton's Auto Heating and Air Conditioning Manual" for additional coverage.

Removal and Installation

1. Disconnect the negative battery cable. Disconnect and tag all electrical wiring from the heater core housing, as required.
2. Remove the right windshield washer nozzle.
3. Remove the right air inlet screen from the plenum. Partially remove the rubber molding above the plenum (1 screw on the right hand side). Drain the radiator.
4. Remove the remaining screws and remove the primary inlet screen. Remove the blower motor.
5. Remove the 2 screws holding the compressor cycling switch to the module and carefully reposition the switch off of the module cover.
6. Remove the screws retaining the case module cover. Remove the cover. Remove and plug the heater hoses from the heater core nipples.
7. Remove the screw and the retainer holding the heater core to the frame at the top of the assembly.
8. With the temperature door in the max/hot position, reach through the temperature housing and push the lower forward corner of the heater core away from the housing.
9. Rotate the core parallel to the housing. This will cause the core to snap out of the lower clamp. The core can now be removed in a vertical direction due to the configuration of the component.
10. Installation is the reverse order of the removal procedure. Be sure to install a new module cover seal as required.

TEMPERATURE CONTROL/BLOWER SWITCH

Removal and Installation

1. Disconnect the negative battery cable.
2. Remove the radio knobs and retaining nuts.
3. Remove the center instrument panel trim assembly insert. Remove the 2 center air condition outlet grill screws, these screws are located inside the air condition outlet grills.
4. Remove the control assembly retaining screws. Pull the control assembly outward and disconnect the electrical connections. Remove the control assembly from the vehicle.
5. Installation is the reverse of the removal procedure.

FUEL SYSTEM

Fuel Pump

NOTE: Any time the fuel system is being worked on, disconnect the negative battery cable, except for those tests where battery voltage is required and always keep a dry chemical (Class B) fire extinguisher near the work area.

Removal and Installation

1. Disconnect the negative battery cable. Remove the air condition compressor drive belt.
2. If equipped with an air pump, loosen the air pump pulley bolts and remove the air pump hoses and electrical leads to the air pump. Remove the air pump pulley and the air pump from the engine.
3. Remove the compressor front bracket. Remove the fuel inlet hose from the fuel pump. Disconnect the vapor return hose, if so equipped.
4. Remove the fuel outlet pipe. Remove the nuts securing the fuel pump to the engine. Remove the fuel pump from the engine.
5. Installation is the reverse order of the removal procedure.

Carburetor

IDLE SPEED

Adjustment

1. Place the transmission in the **P** position, set the parking brake and block the drive wheels. Connect a suitable tachometer to the engine. Remove the air cleaner assembly and plug the vacuum hose to the Thermal Vacuum Valve (TVV).
2. Disconnect and plug the vacuum hose to the EGR valve and the vacuum hose to the canister purge port.
3. Disconnect and plug the vacuum hose to the idle load compensator (ILC). Back out the idle stop screw on the carburetor three turns.
4. Turn the air condition control switch to the **OFF** position. With the engine running and at normal operating temperature, place the transmission in the **D** position. Fully extend the idle load compensator plunger (no vacuum applied).
5. Using tool J–29607, Bt–8022 or equivalent, adjust the ILC plunger to obtain a 725 ± 50 rpm . The jam nut on the plunger

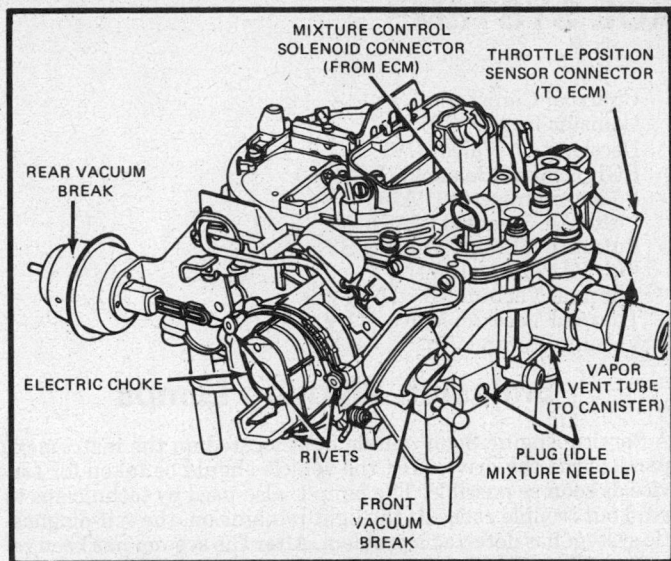

Carburetor and related components

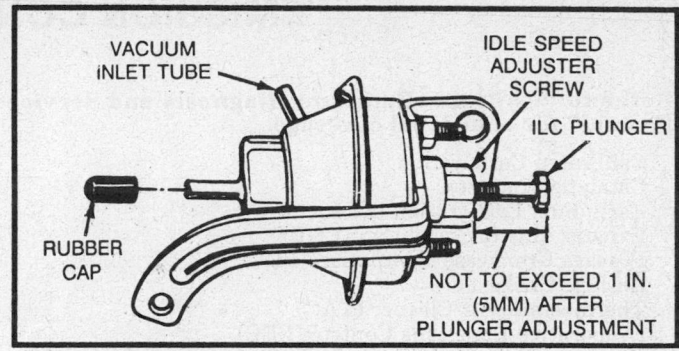

Idle load compensator

must be held with a suitable wrench to prevent damage to the guide tabs.

6. Measure the distance from the jam nut to the tip of the plunger. The dimension must not exceed one in. If the dimension does exceed one in. check for a low idle condition. Remove the plug from the ILC vacuum hose and plug the hose back into the ILC. Adjust the idle speed to specification in the **D** position.

7. If the idle speed is correct, then the adjustment is over. If the idle speed does not meet specifications, perform the following:

8. Stop the engine and remove the idle load compensator. It will not be necessary to remove the idle load compensator if a hex wrench is modified to clear the obstructions.

9. Remove the rubber cap from the center outlet tube. Using a $^3/_{32}$ in. hex key wrench, insert it through the open center tube to engage the idle speed adjusting screw inside the tube.

10. If the idle speed was low, turn the adjusting screw counter-clockwise one turn for every 75–100 rpm low. If the idle was too high, turn the adjusting screw clockwise one turn for every 75–100 rpm high. Reinstall the plug on the center of the outlet tube.

11. Reinstall the idle load compensator on the carburetor and attach the the throttle return spring and other related parts removed. Recheck the idle speed in the **D** position and closed loop mode. If the idle speed is still not within specification, repeat the procedure.

12. Disconnect the power feed (fuse) to the ECM with the ignition **OFF**, for 10 seconds. This will allow the ECM to reset the throttle position sensor value.

13. Disconnect and plug the vacuum source to the ILC. Apply a vacuum source using a hand held vacuum pump or equivalent to the ILC vacuum inlet tube to fully retract the plunger.

14. Adjust the idle stop screw on the carburetor float bowl to obtain a 450 rpm in the **D** position. Place the transmission in **P** and stop the engine.

15. Remove the plug from the vacuum hose and install the hose on the ILC vacuum inlet tube. Remove all the plugs from

the disconnected vacuum lines and reconnect the vacuum lines to their proper ports.

16. Install the air cleaner and gasket, remove the blocks from the drive wheels and road test the vehicle.

IDLE MIXTURE

Adjustment

NOTE: **All carburetors have mixture needles concealed under staked in plugs. Mixture adjustments should be performed only during carburetor overhaul or extreme circumstances.**

1. Start the engine and operate to normal operating temperature.

2. Remove the air cleaner assembly and plug the vacuum hose to the Thermal Vacuum Valve (TVV). Disconnect the vacuum hose to the canister purge valve and plug it.

3. Set the parking brake and block the drive wheels. Place the transmission in the **D** position. Connect a suitable tachometer to the engine and set on the 6 cylinder dwell scale.

4. Adjust both mixture needles equally in $^1/_8$ turn increments, until dwell reading varies within 25–35 degree range (30 degree preferred). Allow time for the dwell reading to stablize after each adjustment.

5. After adjustment is completed, seal the idle mixture needle opening in the throttle body with silicone sealant, RTV or equivalent.

6. Adjust the idle speed.

7. Turn the ignition **OFF**. Remove the tachometer. Reconnect all vacuum hoses and air cleaner assembly.

Removal and Installation

1. Disconnect the negative battery cable. Remove the air cleaner assembly and disconnect the accelerator linkage.

2. Disconnect the transmission detent cable, if so equipped. Disconnect the cruise control linkage, if so equipped.

3. Remove and tag all vacuum and electrical lines to the carburetor. Disconnect the choke heat pipe.

4. Remove the fuel line at the carburetor inlet. Remove the carburetor mounting bolts. Remove the carburetor from the manifold.

5. Installation is the reverse order of the removal procedure. Be sure to install a new carburetor base gasket.

EMISSION CONTROL SYSTEMS

Refer to "Chilton's Emission Diagnosis and Service Manual" for additional coverage.

- Calibrated Carburetion
- Catalytic Converter
- Early Fuel Evaporation (EFE)
- Exhaust Gas Recirculation (EGR)
- Positive Crankcase Ventilation (PCV)
- Electric Choke
- Thermostatic Air Cleaner (TAC)
- Evaporative Emissions Control (EEC)
- Computer Command Control (CCC)
- Electronic Spark Timing (EST)
- Oxygen Sensor
- Manifold Absolute Pressure Sensor (MAP)
- Air Management System
- Air Injection Reactor (AIR)
- Air Control Valve (ACV)
- Air Management Valve (AMV)
- Air Solenoid Valve (ASV)
- Air Temperature Sensor (ATS)
- Back Pressure EGR (BPEGR)
- Charcoal Canister
- Canister Purge (CP)
- Deceleration Valve (DV)
- EGR Control Solenoid (EGRCS)
- Pulse Air Injector (PAIR)
- Pulse Air Solenoid (PAS)
- Pulse Air Shutoff Valve (PSV)
- Pulse Air Valve (PV)
- Thermal Vacuum Switch (TVS)
- Thermal Vacuum Valve (TVV)
- Vacuum Pump (VP)

Emission Warning Lamps

A Service Engine Soon telltale light located on the instrument panel alerts the driver that the vehicle should be taken for service as soon as possible. The lamp is also used by technicians to read out trouble codes. If the light remains on, the self-diagnostic system has detected a problem. After the system has been repaired, all trouble codes must be cleared from the ECM memory.

To clear the trouble codes, remove the 3 amp ECM fuse for 10 seconds with the ignition switch turned **OFF**.

ENGINE

NOTE: Disconnecting the negative battery cable on some vehicles may interfere with the functions of the on board computer systems and may require the computer to undergo a relearning process, once the negative battery cable is reconnected.

Engine Assembly

Removal and Installation

1. Disconnect the negative battery cable.
2. Remove the hood, after scribing hood hinge outline for proper alignment.
3. Remove the air cleaner and heat shroud. Disconnect and plug the transmission oil cooler lines.
4. Drain the cooling system. Disconnect the heater hoses from the engine. Unfasten the fender struts from the radiator shroud. Remove the radiator hose bracket, radiator shroud and fan. Remove the radiator hoses. Remove the radiator.
5. If equipped, disconnect the throttle and cruise control linkage at the carburetor.
6. Disconnect the brake vacuum hose from the vacuum pipe. Remove the cruise control power unit, if equipped.
7. Disconnect the power steering pump bracket and position the pump out of the way with the hoses still connected.
8. Remove the air condition compressor bracket bolts and position the compressor out of the way with the hoses still connected. Do not discharge the system.
9. Disconnect all electrical wires and vacuum lines that will interfere with the removal of the engine.
10. Disconnect the automatic level control line, if equipped. Remove the alternator. Remove the air pump, if equipped.
11. Raise and support the vehicle safely. Remove the engine to transmission bolts. Remove each engine mount through bolt.
12. Remove the starter. Disconnect the exhaust pipes from the exhaust manifolds.
13. Remove the 4 bolts attaching the flywheel inspection cover to the transmission. Remove the cover. Remove the bolts attaching the flywheel to the converter.

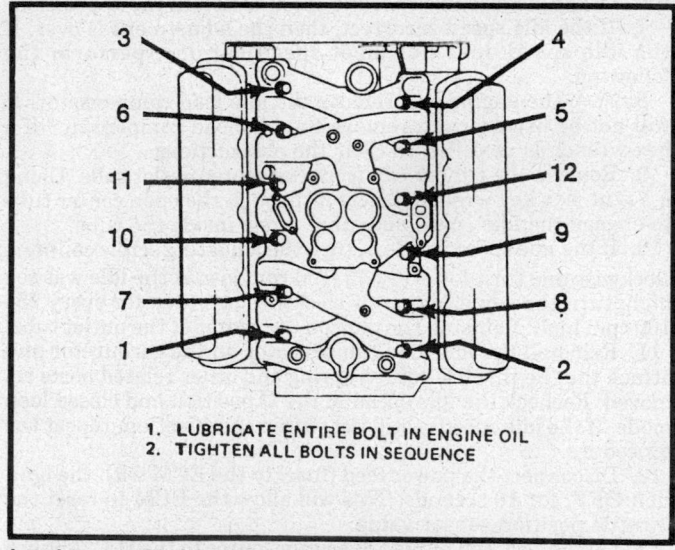

1. LUBRICATE ENTIRE BOLT IN ENGINE OIL
2. TIGHTEN ALL BOLTS IN SEQUENCE

Intake manifold torque sequence

16. Disconnect and plug the fuel line and the vapor return line at the fuel pump, as required.
17. Lower the vehicle. Install a lifting bracket to the engine. Support the transmission properly. Raise the engine slightly and pull it forward to disengage it from the transmission. Remove the engine from the vehicle.
18. Installation is the reverse of the removal procedure.

Engine Mounts

Removal and Installation

1. Disconnect the negative battery cable. Raise and support the vehicle safely.

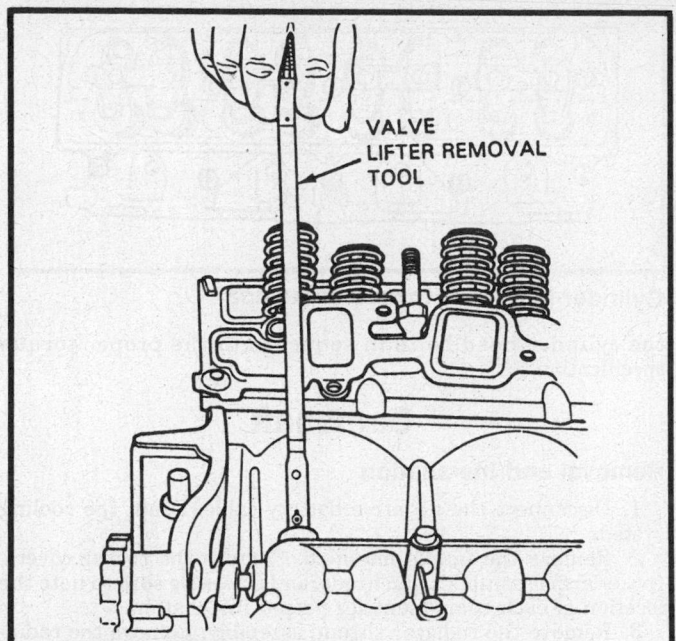

Valve lifter removal

2. Remove the engine through bolt. Properly raise the engine enough to remove the engine mount.

3. Installation is the reverse of the removal procedure.

Intake Manifold

Removal and Installation

1. Disconnect the negative battery cable. Drain the coolant.

2. Remove the air cleaner assembly. Remove the upper radia-tor hose, thermostat, bypass hose, and heater hose at the rear of the manifold. Remove and tag all vacuum lines from the intake manifold. Remove the fuel line.

3. Remove the throttle cable and the TV cable.

4. Remove the drive belts, alternator rear brace, air condition compressor rear brace and all necessary electrical leads.

5. Remove the computer command control solenoid assembly and the idle load compensator with bracket assembly. Remove the EGR valve.

6. Remove the intake manifold retaining bolts and remove the intake manifold from the vehicle.

7. Installation is the reverse order of the removal procedure. Be sure to apply a suitable RTV sealant to the head side of the manifold gasket and to the corners of the front and rear mani-fold seals. Tighten the intake manifold attaching bolts in se-quence to the proper specification.

8. Readjust the accessory drive belts, refill the cooling system and reconnect the negative battery cable.

Exhaust Manifold

Removal and Installation
LEFT SIDE

1. Disconnect the negative battery cable. Remove the air cleaner assembly.

2. Raise and support the vehicle safely. Flatten the exhaust manifold bolt lock tabs.

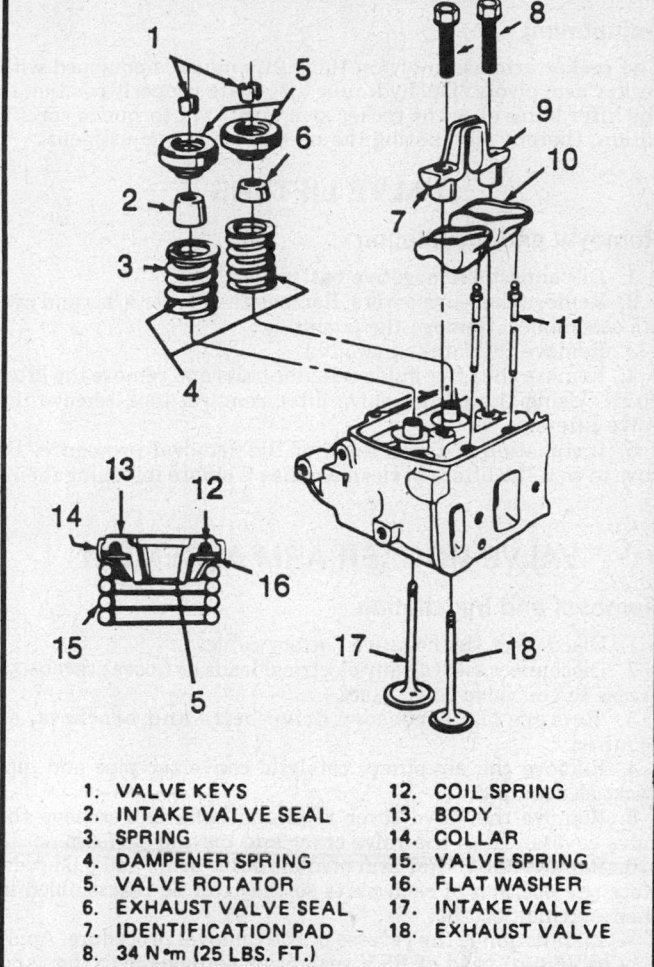

1. VALVE KEYS	12. COIL SPRING
2. INTAKE VALVE SEAL	13. BODY
3. SPRING	14. COLLAR
4. DAMPENER SPRING	15. VALVE SPRING
5. VALVE ROTATOR	16. FLAT WASHER
6. EXHAUST VALVE SEAL	17. INTAKE VALVE
7. IDENTIFICATION PAD	18. EXHAUST VALVE
8. 34 N•m (25 LBS. FT.)	
9. ROCKER ARM PIVOT	
10. ROCKER ARMS	
11. PUSH RODS	

Rocker arm assembly

3. Remove the exhaust pipe from the exhaust manifold. Low-er the vehicle.

4. Remove the hot air shroud. Loosen the alternator bracket bolts and lower the alternator bracket.

5. Remove the exhaust manifold retaining bolts and remove the exhaust manifold from the engine.

6. Installation is the reverse order of the removal procedure. Be sure to install new gaskets as required.

RIGHT SIDE

1. Disconnect the negative battery cable. Remove the air cleaner assembly.

2. Remove the oxygen sensor lead wire. Raise and support the vehicle safely.

3. Remove the crossover pipe. Remove the exhaust pipe from the exhaust manifold.

4. Remove the front wheel to gain access to the exhaust mani-fold bolts, if necessary. Flatten the exhaust manifold bolt lock tabs.

5. Remove the exhaust manifold retaining bolts and remove the exhaust manifold from the engine.

6. Installation is the reverse order of the removal procedure. Be sure to install new gaskets.

Valve System

Adjustment

The rocker arm assembly on the 5.0L engine is equipped with rocker arm pivots. The hydraulic lifters are properly position in the lifter bores once the rocker arm pivots are torque to specification, thereby eliminating the need for valve adjustment.

VALVE LIFTERS

Removal and Installation

1. Disconnect the negative battery cable.
2. Remove the valve covers. Remove the rocker arms and pivots assemblies. Remove the pushrods.
3. Remove the intake manifold.
4. Remove the lifter guide retainer bolts and remove the lifter guide. Using the proper valve lifter removal tool, remove the valve lifters.
5. Installation is the reverse of the removal procedure. Be sure to coat the lifters in clean engine oil before installing them.

VALVE ROCKER ARM ASSEMBLY

Removal and Installation

1. Disconnect the negative battery cable.
2. Disconnect and tag any electrical leads or hoses preventing access to the valve cover bolts.
3. Remove the accessory drive belts and brackets, as required.
4. Remove the air pump, catalytic converter pipe and dipstick, as required.
5. Remove the valve cover retaining bolts and remove the valve covers. Clean the valve cover and mating surfaces.
6. Remove the rocker arm pivots, rocker arms and pushrods. Note the position of each parts so they can be reassembled in their original location.
7. Installation is the reverse of the removal procedure. Apply a ¼ in. (6mm) bead of RTV sealant or equivalent to the valve cover.

NOTE: On some engines, the pushrods have a flag at the upper end so that the pushrod can only be installed one way. This is necessary as the ball hardness is not the same on both ends. Damage may result if the pushrods are installed incorrectly.

Cylinder Head

Removal and Installation

1. Disconnect the negative battery cable.
2. Drain the engine coolant. Disconnect the radiator hoses from the intake manifold.
3. Remove the intake manifold. Remove the exhaust manifold.
4. Remove the alternator lower mounting bolt. Remove the power steering pump and bracket to gain access.
5. Remove the rocker arm covers, rocker assemblies and pushrods. Note the position of each parts so they can be reassemble in their original location.

NOTE: If the rear cylinder head bolts or pushrods (No. 7 and 8 cylinders) can not be removed without interference, remove them together with the cylinder head.

6. Remove the cylinder head bolts. Remove the cylinder head and discard the old gasket.
7. Installation is the reverse of the removal procedure. Before installing the cylinder head bolts, dip them in engine oil. Torque

Cylinder head bolt torque sequence

the cylinder head bolts in sequence to the proper torque specification.

Camshaft

Removal and Installation

1. Disconnect the negative battery cable. Drain the cooling system.
2. Remove the intake manifold. Remove the rocker covers, rocker arm assemblies, pushrods, and lifters Be sure to note the location of each component for proper installation.
3. Remove the radiator shroud assembly. Remove the radiator. Remove the front grille if necessary. Remove the cooling fan and water pump pulley.
4. Remove the power steering pump. Remove the alternator. If equipped, remove the air pump. Remove the crankshaft pulley and torsional damper.
5. Discharge the air condition system. Remove the compressor mount bolts, brackets, and compressor assembly. Remove the condenser assembly and seal all openings.
6. Remove the water pump. Remove the fuel pump. Remove the front engine cover. Remove the camshaft thrust button and spring. Rotate the crankshaft and align the timing marks.
7. Remove the camshaft retaining bolt, gear and chain. Remove the camshaft retaining plate and camshaft flange adapter and carefully remove the camshaft. The camshaft sprocket is a tight fit. If the sprocket does not come off easily, a light blow on the lower edge of the sprocket with a soft face mallet should dislodge the sprocket.
8. Installation is the reverse order of the removal procedure. Lubricate the camshaft journals with a suitable engine oil supplement, before installing the camshaft.

Timing Case Cover/Oil Seal

Removal and Installation

1. Disconnect the negative battery cable. Drain the cooling the system.
2. Remove the drive belts. Remove the fan assembly and fan pulley. Use hub balancer puller J–8614 or equivalent to remove the hub balancer.
3. Remove the rear air conditioning compressor braces and lower the compressor mount bolts. Remove the compressor bracket and nuts at the water pump. Slide the mounting bracket forward and remove the compressor mount bolt. Disconnect the wires at the compressor and lay the unit aside. Disconnect the air injection hose at the right exhaust manifold.
4. Remove the compressor mount bracket. Remove the upper air injection pump bracket with the power steering reservoir. Remove the lower air injection pump bracket.
5. Disconnect the heater and radiator hoses at the water pump. Remove the water pump. Remove the front cover retaining bolts, timing indicator and front cover.

NOTE: It may be necessary to grind a flat surface on the dowel pins to aid in the removal of the front cover.

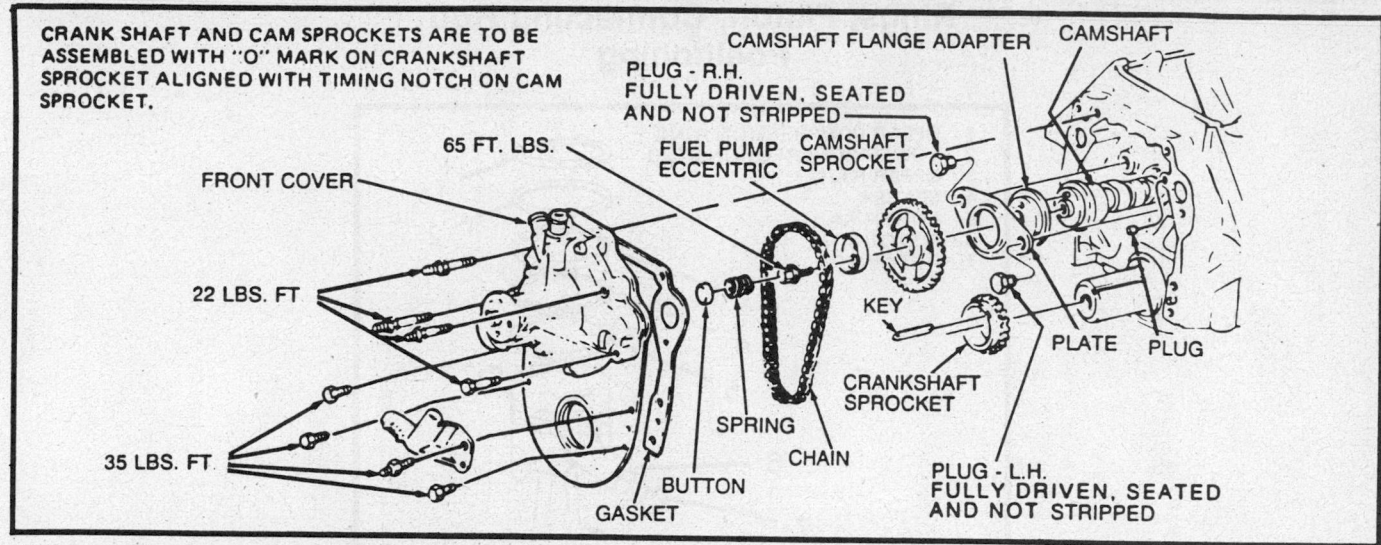

CRANK SHAFT AND CAM SPROCKETS ARE TO BE ASSEMBLED WITH "O" MARK ON CRANKSHAFT SPROCKET ALIGNED WITH TIMING NOTCH ON CAM SPROCKET.

CAMSHAFT FLANGE ADAPTER | CAMSHAFT

PLUG - R.H. FULLY DRIVEN, SEATED AND NOT STRIPPED

FUEL PUMP ECCENTRIC | CAMSHAFT SPROCKET

65 FT. LBS.

FRONT COVER

22 LBS. FT

KEY

35 LBS. FT.

PLATE | PLUG

CRANKSHAFT SPROCKET

SPRING

CHAIN

BUTTON

GASKET

PLUG - L.H. FULLY DRIVEN, SEATED AND NOT STRIPPED

Timing chain cover and related components

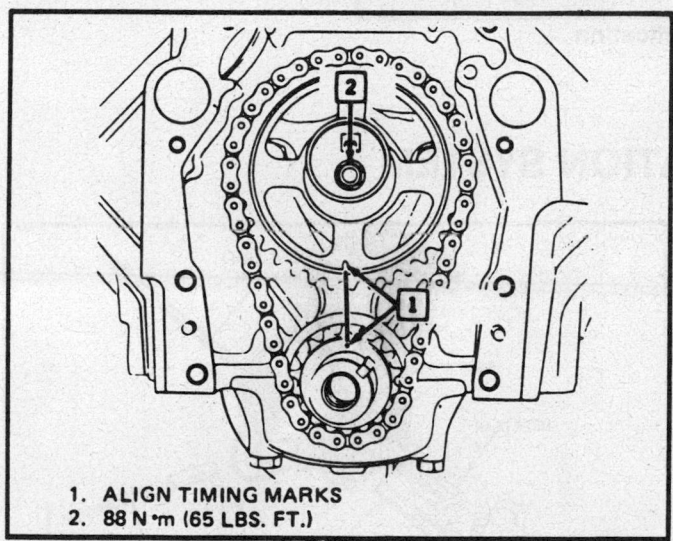

1. ALIGN TIMING MARKS
2. 88 N·m (65 LBS. FT.)

Timing mark alignment

6. Clean the front cover and engine mating surfaces. Remove the front cover oil seal using an appropriate oil seal removal tool.

To install:

7. Coat the outside diameter of the new seal with an approved sealer and install the seal using an approcate seal installer tool.

8. After installing the oil pan seal to the front cover, trim ⅛ in. (3.2mm) from each end of the seal.

9. Apply an approved sealer around coolant holes of the new front cover gasket and install the front cover. Install the timing indicator.

10. Apply a suitable sealer to crankshaft key and inside the crankshaft balancer hub. Apply a suitable seal lubricant to the seal contact area of the balancer hub.

11. Install the crankshaft balancer on the crankshaft. Check the clearance between the front of the engine and balancer hub while installing the hub. The proper balancer to engine clearance is 0.0007–0.001 in.

12. Torque the crankshaft hub bolt to 200–210 ft. lbs. and torque the crankshaft pulley bolts to 28 ft. lbs.

13. Complete installation by reversing the removal procedure.

Timing Chain/Gears

Removal and Installation

1. Disconnect the negative battery cable. Remove the engine front cover.

2. Remove the fuel pump.

3. Remove the crankshaft oil slinger, camshaft thrust button and spring.

4. Remove the camshaft sprocket retaining bolt, fuel pump eccentric and camshaft sprocket and chain assembly.

5. Remove the crankshaft key before attempting to pull off the sprocket. Using an appropriate puller tool, remove the crankshaft sprocket.

To install:

6. Insert the camshaft sprocket and crankshaft sprocket into the timing chain, with the timing marks aligned. Lube the thrust surface with Molykote or equivalent.

7. Grasp both sprockets and the timing chain together and put them into their prospective places. Rotate the camshaft sprocket and engage it on the camshaft.

8. Install the fuel pump eccentric, flat side toward the engine. Install the camshaft sprocket bolt finger tight. Rotate the crankshaft until the keyways are aligned. Install the crankshaft sprocket key, tap it in with a brass hammer until the key bottoms.

9. When the timing marks are in alignment, the No. 6 cylinder should be at TDC. When both timing marks are on the top, the No. 1 cylinder is at TDC of the compression stroke.

10. Slowly and evenly draw the camshaft sprocket onto the camshaft, using the mounting bolt and torque the bolt to 65 ft. lbs.

11. Lubricate the timing chain and finish the installation by reversing the order of the removal procedure.

12. When installing the front cover, apply a suitable RTV sealant around the coolant holes of the new front cover. Be sure to trim the ends of the oil pan seal and install the seal onto the timing chain cover.

Rings, Piston, Connecting Rod Positioning

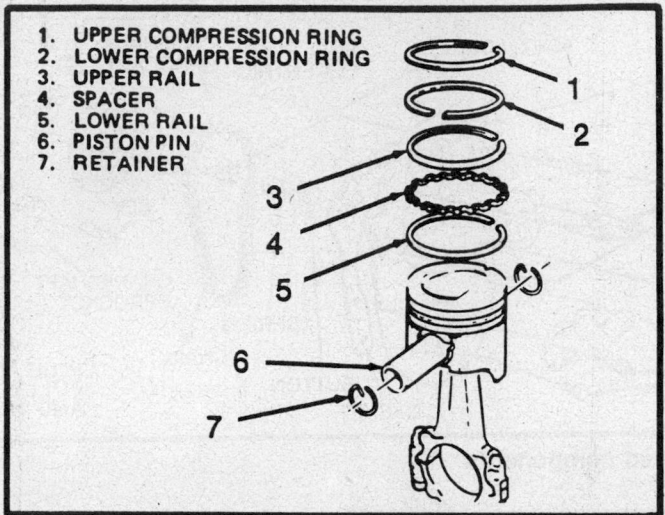

1. UPPER COMPRESSION RING
2. LOWER COMPRESSION RING
3. UPPER RAIL
4. SPACER
5. LOWER RAIL
6. PISTON PIN
7. RETAINER

Piston positioning and identification

ENGINE LUBRICATION SYSTEM

Oil Pan

Removal and Installation

1. Disconnect the negative battery cable. Remove the engine oil dipstick.
2. Remove the fan shroud attaching screws. Raise and support the vehicle safely.
3. Drain the engine oil. Remove the flywheel cover. Remove the exhaust crossover pipe.
4. Remove the starter. Using a jack, with a block of wood on top, place it under the crankshaft hub to support the engine. Remove the engine mounts at the cylinder block.
5. Carefully raise the front of the engine. Remove the oil pan retaining bolts and remove the oil pan from the engine.
6. Clean all the gasket material from the pan and the block mating surfaces. Use a new gasket kit and sealer. Make sure the seals are firmly positioned on the flange surfaces with each seal properly located in the cut out notches of the pan gasket.
7. Installation is the reverse of the removal procedure.

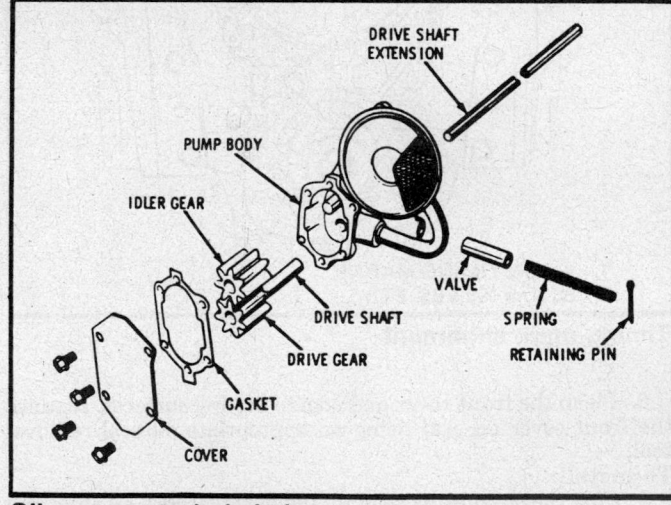

DRIVE SHAFT EXTENSION
PUMP BODY
IDLER GEAR
DRIVE SHAFT
DRIVE GEAR
VALVE
SPRING
RETAINING PIN
GASKET
COVER

Oil pump—exploded view

Oil Pump

Removal and Installation

1. Disconnect the negative battery cable. Drain the engine oil. Remove the oil pan.
2. Remove the oil pump retaining bolts. Remove the oil assembly with the pump driveshaft from the engine.
3. Before install the oil pump to the engine, fill the cavities with petroleum jelly and reassemble the pump.
4. Installation is the reverse of the removal procedure. Be sure that the oil pump driveshaft extension is fully engaged. The end of the oil pump driveshaft extension nearest the washers must be inserted into the driveshaft.

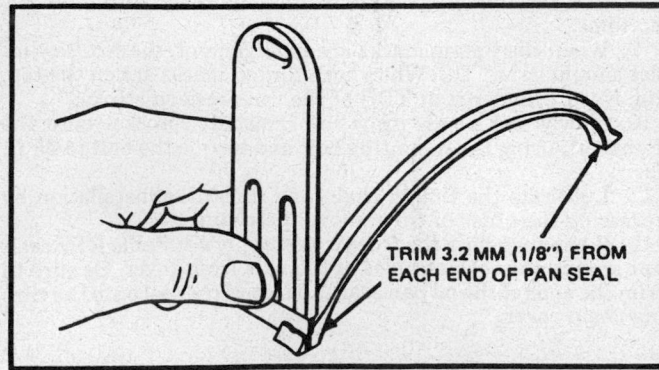

TRIM 3.2 MM (1/8") FROM EACH END OF PAN SEAL

Trimming the oil pan seal

5. After completing installation, remove the oil pressure sending unit and install an oil pressure guage. Start the engine and check the oil pressure.

Rear Main Oil Seal

Removal and Installation

1. Disconnect the negative battery cable. Remove the oil pan. Remove the rear main bearing cap.
2. Using packing tool BT-6433 or J-25282-2 or equivalent, drive both side of the old seal gently into the groove until it is packed tight.
3. Measure the amount of the seal that was driven up on one side and add $\frac{1}{16}$ in. Cut this length from the old seal that was removed from the main bearing cap.

4. Measure the amount of the seal that was driven up on the other side. Add a $\frac{1}{16}$ in. Cut another length from the old seal. Use the main bearing cap as a holding fixture when cutting the seal.
5. Work these 2 pieces of the seal into the cylinder block (one piece on each side) with the proper tools. Using the packing tool, pack these short pieces up into the block using tool BT-6436 or equivalent.
6. Place a piece of shim stock between the seal and the crankshaft to protect the bearing surface before trimming the seal.
7. Form a new rope seal in the rear main bearing cap. Place a drop of a suitable sealer on each end of the seal and cap. Install the main bearing cap. Do not use the attaching bolts to pull down the bearing cap. Tap gently into place with a suitable tool.
8. Continue the installation in the reverse order of the removal procedure.

FRONT SUSPENSION AND STEERING

For front suspension removal and installation services, refer to Unit Repair Section.

Steering Gear

Removal and Installation

1. Disconnect the negative battery cable. Position a drain pan under the steering gear. Disconnect the pressure and return lines from the steering gear assembly. Plug the opening to prevent the entrance of dirt.
2. If equipped, disconnect the stone shield from the return pipe.
3. Remove the pinch bolt from the flex coupling and disconnect the coupling from the gear.

NOTE: Failure to disconnect the flexible coupling from the steering gear stub shaft can result in damage to the steering gear and or the intermediate shaft. This damage can cause the loss of steering control which could result in a vehicle crash and bodily injuries.

4. Raise the vehicle and support it safely.
5. Remove the pitman arm nut and washer. Remove the pitman arm from the sector shaft with a pitman arm puller tool.
6. Remove the retaining bolts and washers holding the steering gear to the side rail. Lower the gear assembly from the vehicle.
7. The installation is the reverse of the removal procedure. Tighten the pitman arm nut to 185 ft. lbs., the mounting bolts to 70 ft. lbs. and the flex coupling pinch bolt to 30 ft. lbs.

Power Steering Pump

Removal and Installation

1. Disconnect the negative battery cable. Disconnect and relocate the air cleaner inlet tube and the upper radiator hose to gain access to the pump.
2. Loosen the alternator mounting bolts except for the long bolt. Rotate the unit upward to gain access by pivoting the long bolt.
3. Remove and plug the pressure and return hoses from the pump. Remove the front pump bracket mounting bolts and spacer. Remove the rear pump mounting nut.
4. Remove the pump and bracket from the engine as an assembly.
5. Installation is the reverse order of the removal procedure. Be sure to bleed the air from the system.

Bleeding System

1. Raise and support the front of the vehicle safely.
2. With the wheels turned all the way to the left add power steering fluid to the **COLD** mark on the dipstick.
3. Start the engine. Check the fluid level. Add fluid as necessary to bring the level to the **COLD** mark on the dipstick.
4. Bleed the system by turning the steering wheel from side to side without hitting the stops.
5. Be sure to maintain the fluid level at the **HOT/COLD** mark on the dipstick. Fluid with air in it will have a light tan appearance. This air must be expelled from the system before normal steering action can be obtained.
6. Return the wheels to the center position. Allow the engine to run for about two minutes and then shut it off.
7. Road test the vehicle and make sure that the steering performs properly and there is no noise from the power steering pump. Correct problems as required.
8. Recheck the power steering level. Be sure that the fluid level is at the **HOT** mark on the dipstick after the system has stabilized at its normal operating temperature.

Steering Column

Removal and Installation

1. Disconnect the negative battery cable.
2. Center the steering wheel and remove the upper coupling pinch bolt and nut.
3. Disconnect the transmission shift linkage at the lower shift lever.
4. Remove the steering column lower cover from the instrument panel, exposing the upper support nuts or bolts.
5. Disconnect the turn signal wiring connector. If equipped with cruise control, disconnect the harness.
6. Remove the screw securing the shift cable to the shift bowl.
7. Loosen bolts at the steering column upper support. Do not completely remove the upper support nuts or bolts as the steering column could bend under its own weight.
8. Move the rubber carpet seal up the steering column as far as possible and position the carpet to gain access to the toe plate.
9. Remove the screws retaining the toe plate to the floor pan.
10. Remove the bolts at the upper column bracket, disconnect the remaining electrical connectors and vacuum connectors while supporting the column.
11. Carefully pull the steering column up and out of the vehicle. If the shaft hangs up in the upper coupling, secure the upper

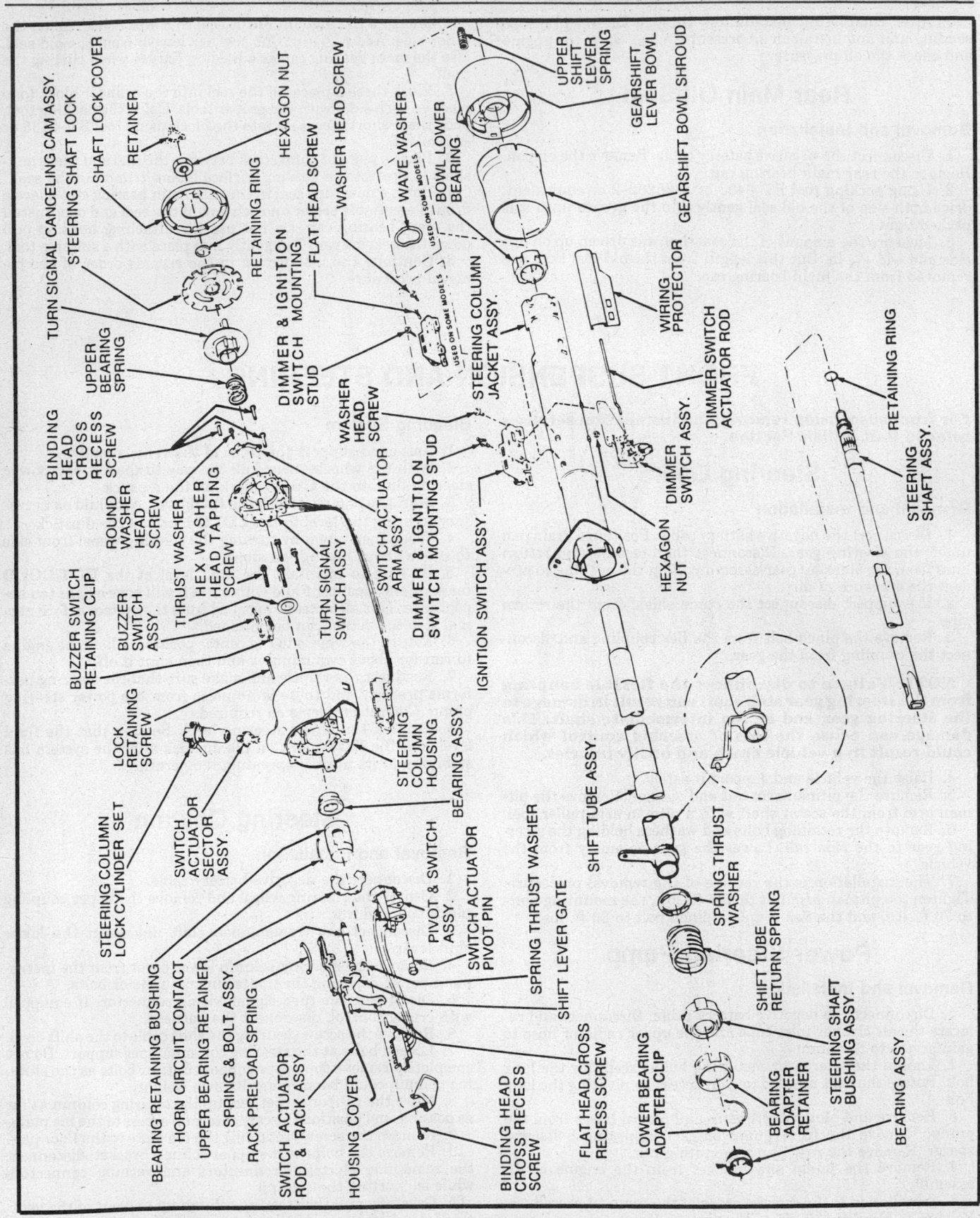

Exploded view of standard column assembly

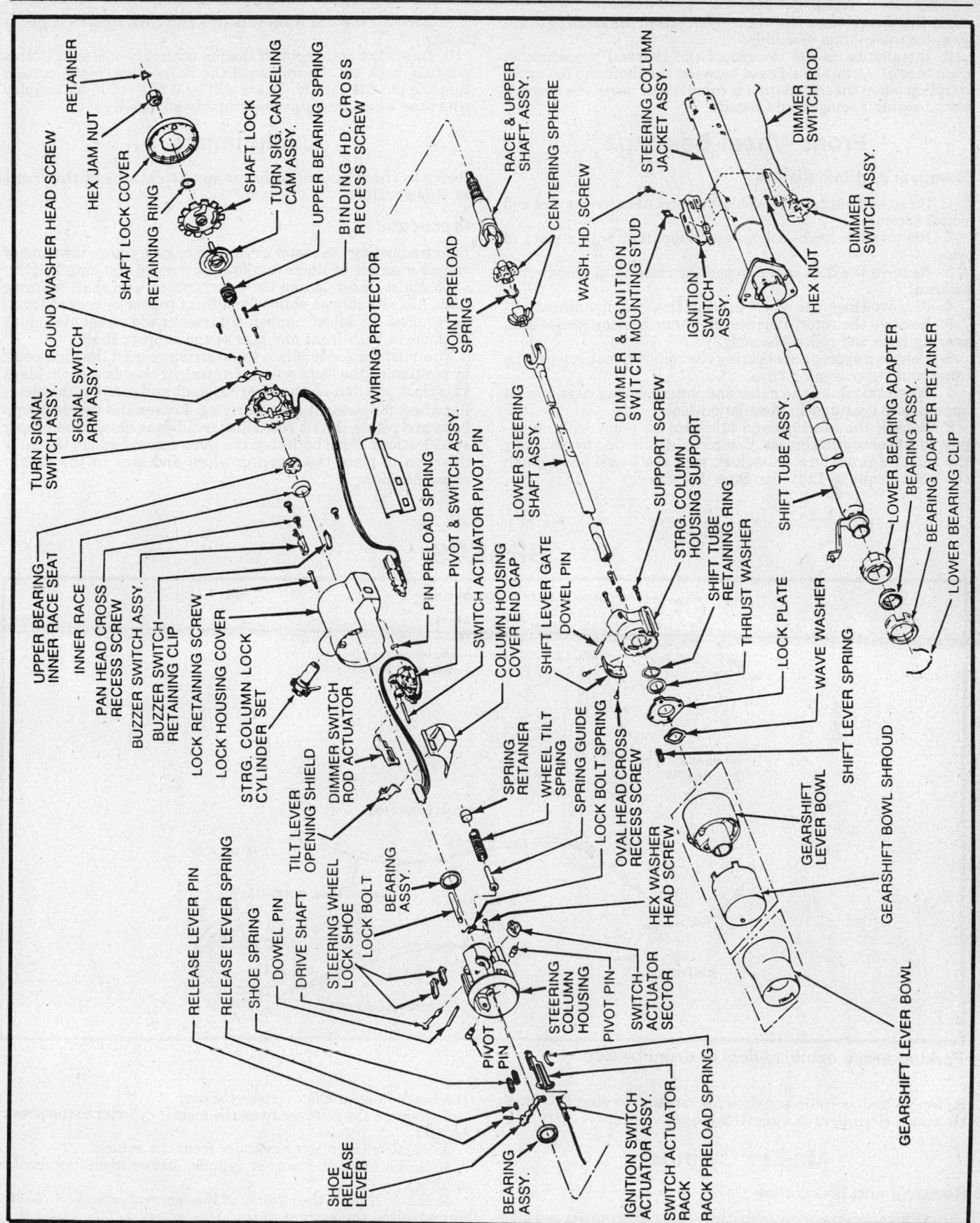

Exploded view of tilt and telescoping column assembly

mounting bracket and free the coupling from the steering shaft. Remove the column assembly.

12. Installation is the reverse of the removal procedure. A clearance of 5/16 in. should exist between the shaft and the upper coupling when the installation is complete or lower steering column bearing damage could result.

Front Wheel Bearings

Removal and Installation

1. Raise and support the vehicle safely. Remove the tire and wheel assembly.
2. Remove the brake caliper and support it with a piece of wire.
3. Remove the dust cap. Remove the cotter pin. Remove the locknut.
4. Remove the outer wheel bearing from its mounting.
5. Remove the rotor. Remove the inner bearing grease seal, bearing cone and roller assembly.
6. Using an appropriate bearing cup removal tool, remove the inner and outer bearing cups.
7. When installing the outer and inner bearing cups, use an appropriate bearing cup installation tool.
8. Repack the bearings and lubricate all parts with an approved wheel bearing grease. Complete installation by reversing the removal procedure. To adjust, spin the wheel and tighten the locknut nut to 12 ft. lbs. Stop the wheel.

9. Back off the nut until it is free and then tighten it finger tight.
10. Insert the cotter pin. If the pin cannot be installed in this position, back off the nut until the holes align. Make certain that the pin fits tightly. There will be 0.001–0.005 in. endplay when the wheel bearings are properly adjusted.

Alignment

Refer to the wheel alignment specifications at the front of this section.

Procedure

Before adjusting the caster or camber angles, jounce the front of vehicle a couple of times to allow for normal standing height.

To adjust caster, loosen the upper control arm shaft to frame nuts. Add or subtract shims from front to rear or rear to front, as required. To adjust camber, subtract or add an equal amount of shims at both front and rear of the support shaft.

To adjust the toe-in, place the steering gear on the high point by positioning the front wheels i a straight ahead position. Mark 12 o'clock position on the steering shaft and position the steering wheel for straight ahead driving. Loosen the tie rod clamp bolts and rotate the tie rod adjuster tubes to obtain the proper specifications. Turn both rods the same amount and in the same direction to place the steering wheel and gear in the stright ahead position.

BRAKES

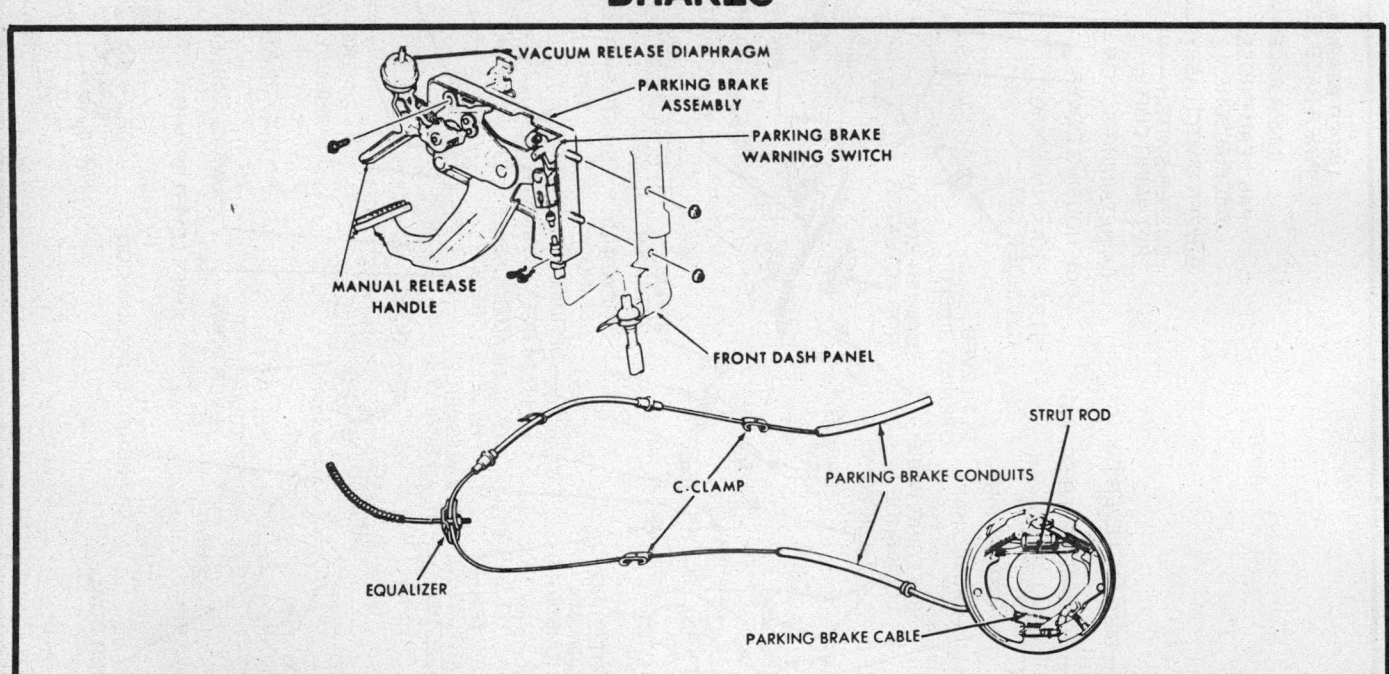

Parking brake cable, typical of drum brakes

Refer to unit repair section for brake service information and drum/rotor specifications.

Master Cylinder

Removal and Installation

1. Disconnect the negative battery cable. Disconnect and plug the brake lines at the master cylinder.
2. Remove the nuts securing the master cylinder to the power booster.
3. Remove the master cylinder from the vehicle.
4. Bench bleed the master cylinder before installing on the vehicle.
5. Installation is the reverse of the removal procedure. As required, bleed the system.

Bleeding System

1. Fill the master cylinder to within ¼ in. of the reservoir rim.
2. Raise and support the vehicle safely.
3. Bleed the system in the following sequence:—right rear, left rear, right front and left front.
4. Bleed 1 wheel at a time.
5. Install a transparent tube on the bleeder screw of the caliper or wheel cylinder to be bled and place the opposite end of the hose in a container partially fill with brake fluid.
6. Open the bleeder screw ¾ turn. Depress the brake pedal to the floor, then tighten the bleeder screw. Slowly release the brake pedal.
7. Repeat the bleeding operation until clear brake fluid flows without air bubbles.

NOTE: Check the master cylinder fluid level frequently during the bleeding procedure and refill if necessary.

8. After bleeding operation is completed, discard the fluid in the container. Fill the master cylinder to ¼ in. from the reservoir rim and check the brake operation.

Power Brake Vacuum Booster

Removal and Installation

1. Disconnect the negative battery cable. Remove the master cylinder retaining nuts and position the assembly out of the way.
2. Disconnect vacuum line from vacuum check valve on unit.
3. Remove steering column lower cover.
4. Remove cotter pin, washer and spring spacer that secures power unit pushrod to brake pedal arm.
5. Remove the nuts that secure the power unit to the firewall. Remove the power unit.
6. Installation is the reverse of the removal procedure. As required, bleed the system.

Parking Brake

Adjustment

1. Be sure that the rear brakes are properly adjusted before adjusting the parking brake. Check the parking brake linkage for the free movement of all the cables. Lubricate, if necessary.
2. Depress the parking brake pedal 3 ratchet clicks.
3. Raise and support the vehicle safely.
4. Holding the cable stud to keep it from turning, tighten the equalizer nut until the right rear wheel can just be turned rearward with two hands but cannot be turned forward.
5. When the parking brake is released there should be no brake shoe drag.

TRANSMISSION

Refer to the Transmission Manual for additional coverage.

Removal and Installation

1. Disconnect the negative battery cable. Position the selector lever in N.
2. Remove the air cleaner assembly. Disconnect the TV and detent cable at carburetor.
3. Remove the transmission dipstick and the dipstick tube retaining bolt.
4. Raise and support the vehicle safely.
5. Mark the driveshaft so it can be reinstalled in its original position. Remove the driveshaft.
6. Disconnect the shift linkage, speedometer cable and all electrical connections at the transmission.

7. Remove the flexplate cover and mark the flexplate and converter so they can be reinstalled in their original location. Remove the flexplate to converter bolts.
8. Position a transmission jack under the transmission and remove the transmission mount.
9. Remove the crossmember attaching bolts and remove the crossmember. If necessary, remove the floor pan reinforcement.
10. Remove the transmission to engine bolts. Support the engine with a suitable tool.
11. Lower the transmission slightly. Disconnect the transmission lines and TV cable. Plug all openings.
12. Install a torque converter holding tool and remove the transmission assembly.
13. Installation is the reverse of the transmission removal procedure.

DRIVESHAFT

Removal and Installation

1. Disconnect the negative battery cable. Position the selector lever in neutral. Raise and support the vehicle safely.
2. Mark the driveshaft so it can be reinstalled in its original position. Remove the rear driveshaft flange capscrews.

NOTE: Never let the full weight of the driveshaft be supported only by the front universal joint.

3. Push shaft forward to clear pinion flange, then pull the driveshaft rearward to disengage the slip yoke from the transmission. Plug the transmission to prevent oil leakage or the entry of dirt.
4. Installation is the reverse of the removal procedure.

Universal Joints

Refer to the unit repair section for overhaul procedures.

REAR AXLE AND REAR SUSPENSION

Refer to the unit repair section for axle overhaul procedures and rear suspension services.

Rear Axle Assembly

Removal and Installation

1. Raise and support the vehicle safely. Remove the rear wheels and drums. Properly support the rear axle.
2. Disconnect shock absorbers from axle. Matchmark the driveshaft and disconnect it from the rear axle pinion flange.
3. Remove the brake line junction block bolt at axle housing. Disconnect the brake lines at the junction block.
4. Disconnect the upper control arms from axle housing. Lower the rear axle assembly slightly and remove the springs.
5. Continue lowering the rear axle assembly and remove it from the vehicle.
6. Installation is the reverse of the removal procedure.

Axle Shaft, Wheel Bearing and Seal

Removal and Installation

1. Raise and support the vehicle safely. Remove the wheel and brake drum.
2. Clean any dirt from the differential cover and loosen the cover attaching bolts. Allow the lubricant to drain out into a drain container.
3. Remove the pinion cross shaft lockscrew and remove the cross shaft.
4. Push in on the flanged end of the axle shaft and remove the C-lock from the splined end of the axle shaft.
5. Remove the axle shaft from the housing, being cautious not to damage the oil seal.
6. Use a suitable tool to pry the oil seal out of the bore. Use an axle shaft bearing puller or a slide hammer to remove the axle bearing from the bearing bore.
7. Lubricate the new bearing with gear lubricant. Use bearing installer J-23690 or equivalent and install the bearing so that the tool bottoms out against the shoulder in the housing. Lubricate the lips of the seal with gear lubricant. Position the new seal on seal installer J-23771 or equivalent, and position the seal into the housing bore. Tap the seal into place so that it is flush with the axle tube.
8. Slide the axle shaft into the housing until the splines on the end of the shaft engage the splines of the differential side gear. Handle the shaft gently when trying to engage to splines.
9. Install the axle shaft C-lock on the splined end of the axle shaft in the differential. Push the shaft outward so that the shaft lock seats in the counterbore of the differential side gear.
10. Install the pinion cross shaft through the differential case and pinion gears. Align the lock screw hole and install the lock screw, tightening it to 25 ft. lbs.

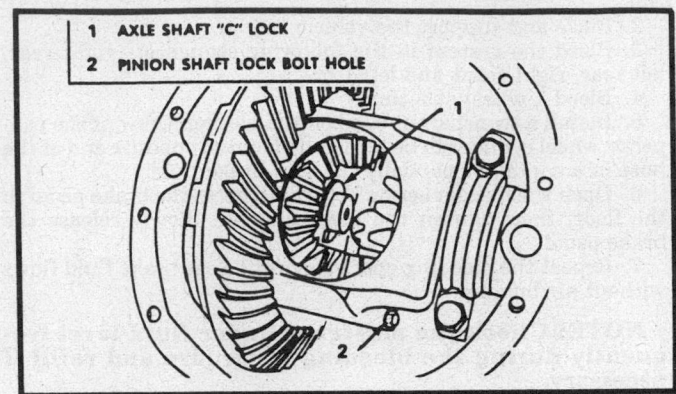

| 1 | AXLE SHAFT "C" LOCK |
| 2 | PINION SHAFT LOCK BOLT HOLE |

Location of axle "C" lock in the differential housing

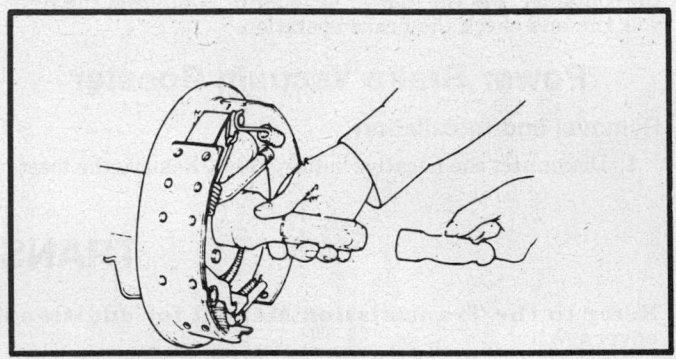

Installing axle seal

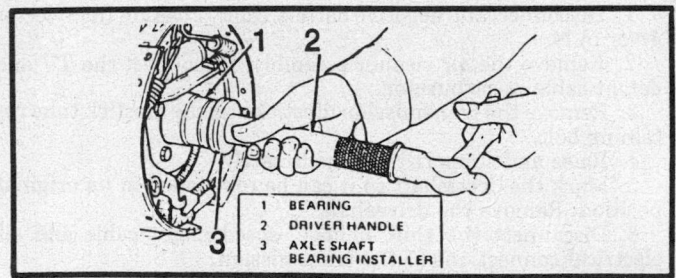

1	BEARING
2	DRIVER HANDLE
3	AXLE SHAFT BEARING INSTALLER

Axle bearing installer

11. Clean the differential housing and cover mating surfaces and install the cover with a new gasket.
12. Fill the differential with lubricant, install the brake drum and wheel and lower the vehicle.

20 GM "B" and "G" Body 20

ESTATE WAGON ● CAPRICE ● CUSTOM CRUISER ● SAFARI ● PARISIENNE—RWD
REGAL RWD ● MONTE CARLO ● CUTLASS ● 442 ● GRAND PRIX ● BONNEVILLE

YEAR IDENTIFICATION

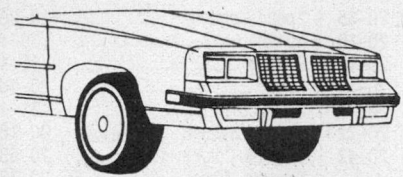

1986 Cutlass Supreme

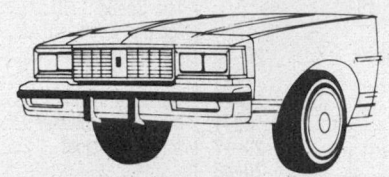

**1986–88 Cutlass Supreme Brougham
1986–90 Custom Cruiser**

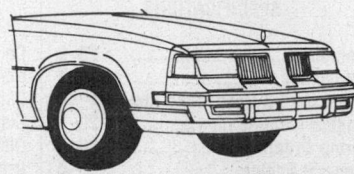

**1986–87 Cutlass Salon
1987–88 Cutlass Supreme**

1986 Bonneville

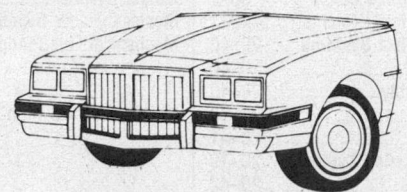

1986–87 Grand Prix

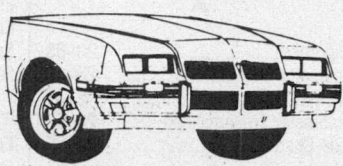

1987 Grand Prix 2 + 2

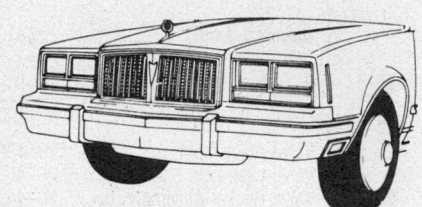

**1986 Parisienne
1987–90 Safari**

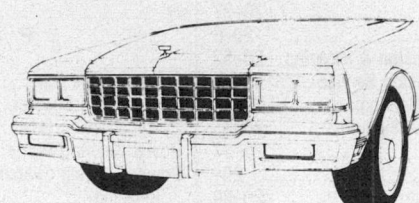

1986 Caprice

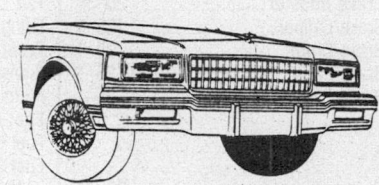

1987–90 Caprice

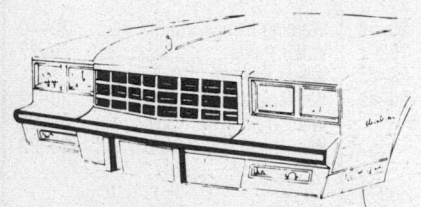

1986 Monte Carlo

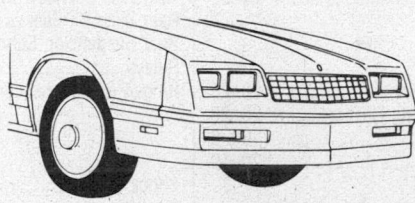

1987–88 Monte Carlo SS

1987–88 Monte Carlo

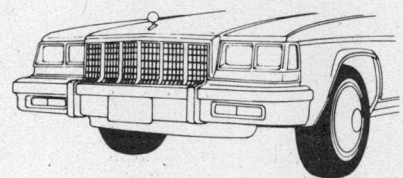

1986–90 Electra Estate Wagon

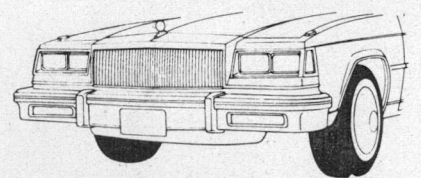

1986–90 LeSabre Estate Wagon

1986-87 Regal

VEHICLE IDENTIFICATION

It is important for servicing and ordering parts to be certain of the vehicle and engine identification. The VIN (vehicle identification number) is a 17 digit number visible through the windshield on the driver's side of the dash and contains the vehicle and engine identification codes. The tenth digit indicates model year and the eighth digit indicates engine code. It can be interpreted as follows:

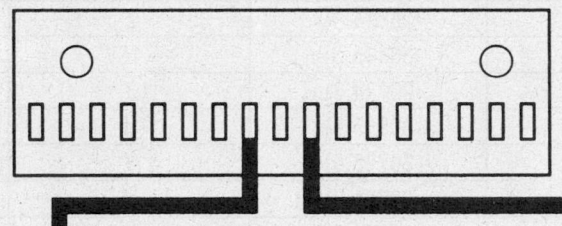

Engine Code						Model Year	
Code	Cu. In.	Liters	Cyl.	Fuel Sys.	Eng. Mfg.	Code	Year
A	231	3.8	V6	2 bbl	Buick	G	1986
7(86–87)	231	3.8	V6	SFI/Turbo	Buick	H	1987
Z	262	4.3	V6	EFI	Chevy	J	1988
E	305	5.0	V8	EFI	Chevy	K	1989
G	305	5.0	V8	4 bbl	Chevy	L	1990
H	305	5.0	V8	4 bbl	Chevrolet		
9	307	5.0	V8	4 bbl	Oldsmobile		
Y	307	5.0	V8	4 bbl	Oldsmobile		
6	350	5.7	V8	4 bbl	Chevy		
7(89–90)	350	5.7	V8	EFI	Chevy		

ENGINE IDENTIFICATION

Year	Model	Engine Displacement cu. in. (liter)	Engine Series Identification (VIN)	No. of Cylinders	Engine Type
1986	Estate Wagon	307 (5.0)	Y	8	OHV
	Regal	231 (3.8)	A	6	OHV
	Regal	231 (3.8)	7	6	OHV
	Regal	305 (5.0)	H	8	OHV
	Caprice	262 (4.3)	Z	6	OHV
	Caprice	305 (5.0)	H	8	OHV
	Caprice	307 (5.0)	Y	8	OHV
	Monte Carlo	231 (3.8)	A	6	OHV
	Monte Carlo	262 (4.3)	Z	6	OHV
	Monte Carlo	305 (5.0)	H	8	OHV
	Monte Carlo	307 (5.0)	Y	8	OHV
	Cutlass	231 (3.8)	A	6	OHV
	Cutlass	305 (5.0)	H	8	OHV
	Cutlass	307 (5.0)	Y	8	OHV
	Cutlass	307 (5.0)	9	8	OHV
	Custom Cruiser	307 (5.0)	Y	8	OHV
	Bonneville	262 (4.3)	Z	6	OHV
	Bonneville	305 (5.0)	H	8	OHV
	Bonneville	307 (5.0)	Y	8	OHV
	Grand Prix	231 (3.8)	A	8	OHV

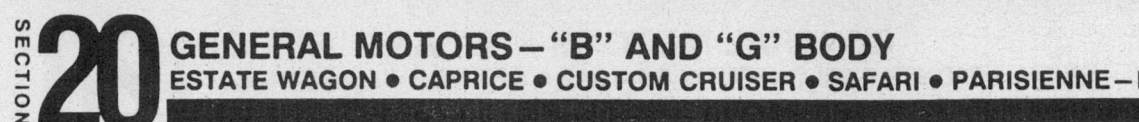
ENGINE IDENTIFICATION

Year	Model	Engine Displacement cu. in. (liter)	Engine Series Identification (VIN)	No. of Cylinders	Engine Type
1986	Grand Prix	262 (4.3)	Z	6	OHV
	Grand Prix	305 (5.0)	H	8	OHV
	Parisienne	262 (4.3)	Z	6	OHV
	Parisienne	305 (5.0)	H	8	OHV
	Parisienne	307 (5.0)	Y	8	OHV
	Safari	307 (5.0)	Y	8	OHV
1987	Estate Wagon	307 (5.0)	Y	8	OHV
	Regal	231 (3.8)	A	6	OHV
	Regal	231 (3.8)	7	6	OHV
	Caprice	262 (4.3)	Z	6	OHV
	Caprice	305 (5.0)	H	8	OHV
	Caprice	307 (5.0)	Y	8	OHV
	Monte Carlo	262 (4.3)	Z	6	OHV
	Monte Carlo	305 (5.0)	G	8	OHV
	Monte Carlo	305 (5.0)	H	8	OHV
	Cutlass	231 (3.8)	A	6	OHV
	Cutlass	305 (5.0)	H	8	OHV
	Cutlass	307 (5.0)	Y	8	OHV
	Cutlass	307 (5.0)	9	8	OHV
	Custom Cruiser	307 (5.0)	Y	8	OHV
	Grand Prix	231 (3.8)	A	6	OHV
	Grand Prix	262 (4.3)	Z	6	OHV
	Grand Prix	305 (5.0)	H	8	OHV
	Safari	307 (5.0)	Y	8	OHV
1988	Estate Wagon	307 (5.0)	Y	8	OHV
	Caprice	262 (4.3)	Z	6	OHV
	Caprice	305 (5.0)	H	8	OHV
	Caprice	307 (5.0)	Y	8	OHV
	Monte Carlo	262 (4.3)	Z	6	OHV
	Monte Carlo	305 (5.0)	H	8	OHV
	Monte Carlo	307 (5.0)	Y	8	OHV
	Cutlass	307 (5.0)	Y	8	OHV
	Custom Cruiser	307 (5.0)	Y	8	OHV
	Safari	307 (5.0)	Y	8	OHV
1989-90	Estate Wagon	307 (5.0)	Y	8	OHV
	Caprice	305 (5.0)	E	8	OHV
	Caprice	307 (5.0)	Y	8	OHV
	Caprice	350 (5.7)	7	8	OHV
	Custom Cruiser	307 (5.0)	Y	8	OHV
	Safari	307 (5.0)	Y	8	OHV

GENERAL ENGINE SPECIFICATIONS

Year	VIN	No. Cylinder Displacement cu. in. (liter)	Fuel System Type	Net Horsepower @ rpm	Net Torque @ rpm (ft. lbs.)	Bore × Stroke (in.)	Compression Ratio	Oil Pressure @ rpm
1986	A	6-231 (3.8)	2 bbl	110 @ 3800	190 @ 1600	3.800 × 3.400	8.0:1	37 @ 2400
	7	6-231 (3.8)	SFI/Turbo	235 @ 4400	330 @ 2800	3.800 × 3.400	8.0:1	37 @ 2400
	Z	6-262 (4.3)	EFI	140 @ 3800	225 @ 2200	4.000 × 3.480	9.3:1	45 @ 2000
	H	8-305 (5.0)	4 bbl	165 @ 4200	245 @ 2400	3.736 × 3.480	9.5:1	45 @ 2000
	G	8-305 (5.0)	4 bbl	105 @ 3200	240 @ 2400	3.736 × 3.480	9.5:1	45 @ 2000
	9	8-307 (5.0)	4 bbl	148 @ 3800	250 @ 2400	3.800 × 3.385	8.0:1	30 @ 1500
	Y	8-307 (5.0)	4 bbl	148 @ 3800	250 @ 2400	3.800 × 3.385	8.0:1	40 @ 2000
	6	8-350 (5.7)	4 bbl	205 @ 4200	290 @ 4200	4.000 × 3.480	8.2:1	45 @ 2000
1987	A	6-231 (3.8)	2 bbl	110 @ 3800	190 @ 1600	3.800 × 3.400	8.0:1	37 @ 2400
	7	6-231 (3.8)	SFI/Turbo	235 @ 4400	330 @ 2800	3.800 × 3.400	8.0:1	37 @ 2400
	Z	6-262 (4.3)	EFI	140 @ 3800	225 @ 2200	4.000 × 3.480	9.3:1	45 @ 2000
	H	8-305 (5.0)	4 bbl	165 @ 4200	245 @ 2400	3.736 × 3.480	9.5:1	45 @ 2000
	G	8-305 (5.0)	4 bbl	105 @ 3200	240 @ 2400	3.736 × 3.480	9.5:1	45 @ 2000
	9	8-307 (5.0)	4 bbl	148 @ 3800	250 @ 2400	3.800 × 3.385	8.0:1	30 @ 1500
	Y	8-307 (5.0)	4 bbl	148 @ 3800	250 @ 2400	3.800 × 3.385	8.0:1	40 @ 2000
	6	8-350 (5.7)	4 bbl	205 @ 4200	290 @ 4200	4.000 × 3.480	8.2:1	45 @ 2000
1988	Z	6-262 (4.3)	EFI	140 @ 4200	225 @ 2000	4.000 × 3.480	9.3:1	45 @ 2000
	H	8-305 (5.0)	4 bbl	165 @ 4200	245 @ 2400	3.736 × 3.480	8.6:1	45 @ 2000
	Y	8-307 (5.0)	4 bbl	148 @ 3800	250 @ 2400	3.800 × 3.385	8.0:1	40 @ 2000
1989–90	E	8-305 (5.0)	EFI	170 @ 4400	255 @ 2400	3.740 × 3.480	9.3:1	18 @ 2000
	Y	8-307 (5.0)	4 bbl	148 @ 3800	250 @ 2400	3.800 × 3.385	8.0:1	40 @ 2000
	7	8-350 (5.7)	EFI	NA	NA	3.740 × 3.480	9.3:1	18 @ 2000

GASOLINE ENGINE TUNE-UP SPECIFICATIONS

Year	VIN	No. Cylinder Displacement cu. in. (liter)	Spark Plugs Type	Spark Plugs Gap (in.)	Ignition Timing (deg.) MT	Ignition Timing (deg.) AT	Compression Pressure (psi)	Fuel Pump (psi)	Idle Speed (rpm) MT	Idle Speed (rpm) AT	Valve Clearance In.	Valve Clearance Ex.
1986	A	6-231 (3.8)	0.060	—	15	②	5.5–6.5	—	700	Hyd.	Hyd.	
	7	6-231 (3.8)	0.045	—	15	②	26–51	—	700	Hyd.	Hyd.	
	Z	6-262 (4.3)	0.035	—	0	②	—	—	400	Hyd.	Hyd.	
	H	8-305 (5.0)	0.045	—	0	②	7.5–9.0	—	500	Hyd.	Hyd.	
	G	8-305 (5.0)	0.045	—	6	②	7.5–9.0	—	500	Hyd.	Hyd.	
	9	8-307 (5.0)	0.060	—	20B	②	5.5–6.5	—	600	Hyd.	Hyd.	
	Y	8-307 (5.0)	0.060	—	20	②	6.0–7.5	—	425	Hyd.	Hyd.	
	6	8-350 (5.7)	0.035	—	6	②	—	—	650	Hyd.	Hyd.	
1987	A	6-231 (3.8)	0.060	—	15	②	5.5–6.5	—	700	Hyd.	Hyd.	
	7	6-231 (3.8)	0.035	—	①	②	26–51	—	700	Hyd.	Hyd.	
	Z	6-262 (4.3)	0.035	—	0	②	—	—	400	Hyd.	Hyd.	
	H	8-305 (5.0)	0.035	—	0	②	7.5–9.0	—	500	Hyd.	Hyd.	
	G	8-305 (5.0)	0.035	—	6	②	7.5–9.0	—	500	Hyd.	Hyd.	
	9	8-307 (5.0)	0.060	—	20B	②	5.5–6.5	—	600	Hyd.	Hyd.	

GASOLINE ENGINE TUNE-UP SPECIFICATIONS

Year	VIN	No. Cylinder Displacement cu. in. (liter)	Spark Plugs		Ignition Timing (deg.)		Compression Pressure (psi)	Fuel Pump (psi)	Idle Speed (rpm)		Valve Clearance	
			Type	Gap (in.)	MT	AT			MT	AT	In.	Ex.
1987	Y	8-307 (5.0)	0.060	—		20	②	6.0–7.5	—	450	Hyd.	Hyd.
	6	8-350 (5.7)	0.060	—		6	②	—	—	500	Hyd.	Hyd.
1988	Z	6-262 (4.3)	0.035	—		①	②	9.0–13.0	—	400	Hyd.	Hyd.
	H	8-305 (5.0)	0.035	—		①	②	7.5–9.0	—	500 ①	Hyd.	Hyd.
	Y	8-307 (5.0)	0.060	—		①	②	6.0–7.5	—	450	Hyd.	Hyd.
1989	E	8-305 (5.0)	0.035	—		①	②	11	—	①	Hyd.	Hyd.
	Y	8-307 (5.0)	0.060	—		①	②	6.0–7.5	—	①	Hyd.	Hyd.
	7	8-350 (5.7)	0.035	—		①	②	11	—	①	Hyd.	Hyd.
1990		See Underhood Specifications Sticker										

① See the Emission Control Label

② The lowest cylinder compression reading should not be less than 70% of the highest reading, and no cylinder should be less than 100 PSI

FIRING ORDERS

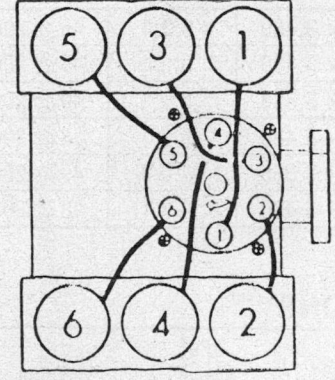

GM (Buick) 231 V6
Engine firing order: 1–6–5–4–3–2
Distributor rotation: clockwise

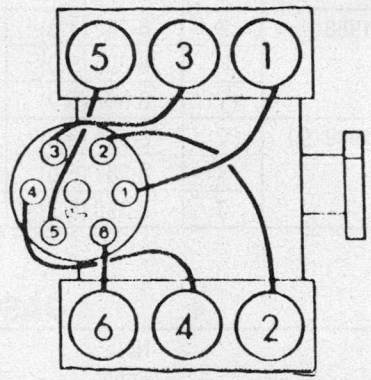

Chevrolet 262 V6 (4.3L)
Engine Firing Order: 1–6–5–4–3–2
Distributor Rotation: clockwise

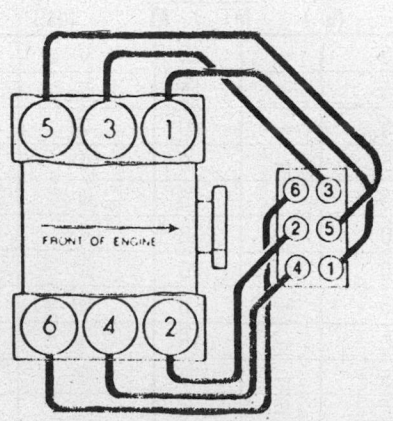

FRONT OF ENGINE

Buick 3.8L V6 turbo engine with C³I ignition
Firing order: 1–6–5–4–3–2

FIRING ORDERS

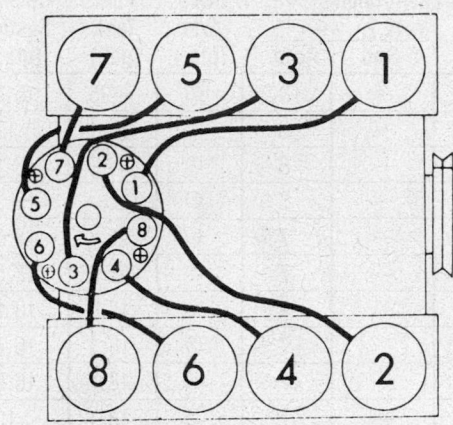

GM (Chevrolet) V8
Engine firing order: 1-8-4-3-6-5-7-2
Distributor rotation: clockwise

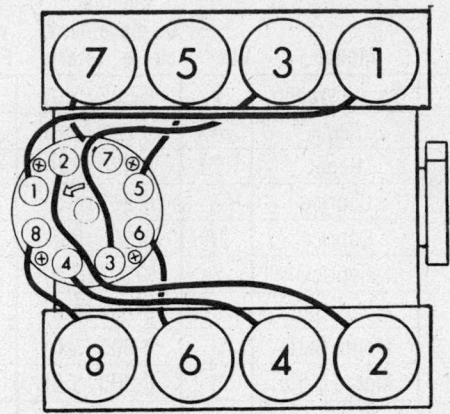

GM (Oldsmobile) 307 V8 (5.0L)
Engine Firing Order: 1-8-4-3-6-5-7-2
Distributor Rotation: counterclockwise

CAPACITIES

Year	Model	VIN	No. Cylinder Displacement cu. in. (liter)	Engine Crankcase with Filter	Engine Crankcase without Filter	Transmission (pts.) 4-Spd	Transmission (pts.) 5-Spd	Transmission (pts.) Auto.	Drive Axle (pts.)	Fuel Tank (gal.)	Cooling System (qts.)
1986	Estate Wagon	Y	8-307 (5.0)	5	4	—	—	8 ①	②	25	16.2
	Regal	A	6-231 (3.8)	5	4	—	—	8 ①	②	18.1	13
	Regal	7	6-231 (3.8)	6	5	—	—	8 ①	②	19	13.1
	Regal	H	8-305 (5.0)	5	4	—	—	8 ①	②	17.5	16.1
	Caprice	Z	6-262 (4.3)	5	4	—	—	6 ①	3.5	18	15
	Caprice	H	8-305 (5.0)	5	4	—	—	6 ①	3.5	18	15
	Caprice	Y	8-307 (5.0)	5	4	—	—	6 ①	3.5	18	15
	Monte Carlo	A	6-231 (3.8)	5	4	—	—	6 ①	3.5	18	15
	Monte Carlo	Z	6-262 (4.3)	5	4	—	—	6 ①	3.5	18	15
	Monte Carlo	H	8-305 (5.0)	5	4	—	—	6 ①	3.5	18	15
	Monte Carlo	Y	8-307 (5.0)	5	4	—	—	6 ①	3.5	18	15
	Cutlass	A	6-231 (3.8)	5	4	—	—	6 ①	3.5	18	13.3
	Cutlass	H	8-305 (5.0)	5	4	—	—	6 ①	3.5	18	16.1
	Cutlass	Y	8-307 (5.0)	5	4	—	—	6 ①	3.5	17.5	15.5
	Cutlass	9	8-307 (5.0)	5	4	—	—	6 ①	3.5	18	15.5
	Delta 88	Y	8-307 (5.0)	5	4	—	—	7 ①	②	25	15.5
	Bonneville	Z	6-262 (4.3)	5	4	—	—	7 ①	②	18	15
	Bonneville	H	8-305 (5.0)	5	4	—	—	6 ①	②	18.1	16.1
	Bonneville	Y	8-307 (5.0)	5	4	—	—	7 ①	⑦	19	15.5
	Grand Prix	A	6-231 (3.8)	5	4	—	—	7 ①	②	18	13.3
	Grand Prix	Z	6-262 (4.3)	5	4	—	—	7 ①	②	18	15
	Grand Prix	H	8-305 (5.0)	5	4	—	—	7 ①	②	18	16.1
	Parisienne	Z	6-262 (4.3)	5	4	—	—	7 ①	②	25	13.3
	Parisienne	H	8-305 (5.0)	5	4	—	—	7 ①	②	25	15.5
	Parisienne	Y	8-307 (5.0)	5	4	—	—	7 ①	②	25	18

GENERAL MOTORS — "B" AND "G" BODY
ESTATE WAGON • CAPRICE • CUSTOM CRUISER • SAFARI • PARISIENNE — RWD

CAPACITIES

Year	Model	VIN	No. Cylinder Displacement cu. in. (liter)	Engine Crankcase with Filter	without Filter	Transmission (pts.) 4-Spd	5-Spd	Auto.	Drive Axle (pts.)	Fuel Tank (gal.)	Cooling System (qts.)
1987	Estate Wagon	Y	8-307 (5.0)	5	4	—	—	8 [1]	[2]	25	16.2
	Regal	A	6-231 (3.8)	5	4	—	—	8 [1]	[2]	18.1	13
	Regal	7	6-231 (3.8)	6	5	—	—	8 [1]	[2]	19	13.1
	Caprice	Z	6-262 (4.3)	5	4	—	—	7 [4]	[2]	25	12.5
	Caprice	H	8-305 (3.0)	5	4	—	—	7 [4]	[2]	25	17.5
	Caprice	Y	8-307 (5.0)	5	4	—	—	7 [4]	[2]	25	17.5
	Monte Carlo	Z	6-262 (4.3)	5	4	—	—	7 [4]	[2]	17.6	13.1
	Monte Carlo	G	8-305 (5.0)	5	4	—	—	7 [4]	[2]	18.1	16.7
	Monte Carlo	H	8-305 (5.0)	5	4	—	—	7 [4]	[2]	18.1	16.5
	Cutlass	A	6-231 (3.8)	5	4	—	—	7	[2]	18.1	13
	Cutlass	H	8-305 (5.0)	5	4	—	—	7	[2]	18.1	16
	Cutlass	Y	8-307 (5.0)	5	4	—	—	7	[2]	18.1	15.5
	Cutlass	9	8-307 (5.0)	5	4	—	—	7	[2]	18.1	15.5
	Delta 88	Y	8-307 (5.0)	5	4	—	—	7	[2]	18.1	15.5
	Grand Prix	A	6-231 (3.8)	5	4	—	—	[5]	17.5	13.1	—
	Grand Prix	Z	6-262 (4.3)	5	4	—	—	[5]	17.5	13.1	—
	Grand Prix	H	8-305 (5.0)	5	4	—	—	[5]	17.5	16	—
	Safari	Y	8-307 (5.0)	5	4	—	—	[5]	22	15	—
1988	Estate Wagon	Y	8-307 (5.0)	5	4	—	—	10.1	4.25	22	15
	Caprice	Z	6-262 (4.3)	5	4	—	—	7 [4]	[2]	25	12.5
	Caprice	H	8-305 (5.0)	5	4	—	—	7 [4]	[2]	25	16.8
	Caprice	Y	8-307 (5.0)	5	4	—	—	7 [4]	[2]	25 [3]	17.1
	Monte Carlo	Z	6-262 (4.3)	5	4	—	—	7 [4]	[2]	17.6	13.1
	Monte Carlo	H	8-305 (5.0)	5	4	—	—	7 [4]	[2]	18.1	16.5
	Monte Carlo	Y	8-307 (5.0)	5	4	—	—	7 [4]	[2]	18.1	16.7
	Cutlass	Y	8-307 (5.0)	5	4	—	—	7	[2]	18.1	15.5
	Delta 88	Y	8-307 (5.0)	5	4	—	—	7	[2]	22	15.5
	Safari	Y	8-307 (5.0)	5	4	—	—	10.1	4.25	22	15
1989-90	Estate Wagon	Y	8-307 (5.0)	5	4	—	—	7 [4]	[2]	22	17.1
	Caprice	E	8-305 (5.0)	5	4	—	—	7 [4]	[2]	25	16.7
	Caprice	Y	8-307 (5.0)	5	4	—	—	7 [4]	[2]	22	17.1
	Caprice	7	8-350 (5.0)	5	4	—	—	7 [4]	[2]	25	14.9
	Delta 88	Y	8-307 (5.0)	5	4	—	—	7 [4]	[2]	22	17.1
	Safari	Y	8-307 (5.0)	5	4	—	—	7 [4]	[2]	22	17.1

[1] Additional transmission fluid may be required to bring level to full mark if overhauled or torque converter drained
[2] 7 ½ in. ring gear — 3.5 pts.
8 ½ in. ring gear — 4.25 pts.
8 ¾ in. ring gear — 5.4 pts.
[3] Wagon — 22 gals.
[4] 700R4 — 10 pts.
[5] 200R4 — 10.1 pts.
200C — 8.5 pts.

CAMSHAFT SPECIFICATIONS

Year	VIN	No. Cylinder Displacement cu. in. (liter)	Journal Diameter 1	2	3	4	5	Lobe Lift In.	Ex.	Bearing Clearance	Camshaft End Play
1986	A	6-231 (3.8)	1.785–1.786	1.785–1.786	1.785–1.786	1.785–1.786	1.785–1.786	NA	NA	0.001–0.003	NA
	7	6-231 (3.8)	1.785–1.786	1.785–1.786	1.785–1.786	1.785–1.786	1.785–1.786	NA	NA	0.001–0.003	NA
	Z	6-262 (4.3)	1.868–1.869	1.868–1.869	1.868–1.869	1.868–1.869	1.868–1.869	0.234	0.257	NA	0.004–0.012
	H	8-305 (5.0)	1.868–1.869	1.868–1.869	1.868–1.869	1.868–1.869	1.868–1.869	0.234	0.257	NA	0.004–0.012
	G	8-305 (5.0)	1.868–1.869	1.868–1.869	1.868–1.869	1.868–1.869	1.868–1.869	0.269	0.276	NA	0.004–0.012
	Y	8-307 (5.0)	2.036	2.0360	1.9959	1.9759	1.9559	0.247	0.251	0.0038–	0.006–0.022
	9	8-307 (5.0)	2.036	2.0360	1.9959	1.9759	1.9559	0.272	0.274	0.0038	0.006–0.022
	6	8-350 (5.7)	1.868–1.869	1.8682–1.8692	1.8682–1.8692	1.8682–1.8692	1.8682–1.8692	0.257	0.269	NA	0.004–0.012
1987	A	6-231 (3.8)	1.785–1.786	1.7850–1.7860	1.7850–1.7860	1.7850–1.7860	1.7850–1.7860	NA	NA	0.0010–0.0030	NA
	7	6-231 (3.8)	1.785–1.786	1.7850–1.7860	1.7850–1.7860	1.7850–1.7860	1.7850–1.7860	NA	NA	0.0010–0.0030	NA
	Z	6-262 (4.3)	1.868–1.869	1.8682–1.8692	1.8682–1.8692	1.8682–1.8692	1.8682–1.8692	0.234	0.257	NA	0.004–0.012
	H	8-305 (5.0)	1.868–1.869	1.8682–1.8692	1.8682–1.8692	1.8682–1.8692	1.8682–1.8692	0.234	0.257	NA	0.004–0.012
	G	8-305 (5.0)	1.868–1.869	1.8682–1.8692	1.8682–1.8692	1.8682–1.8692	1.8682–1.8692	0.269	0.276	NA	0.004–0.012
	Y	8-307 (5.0)	2.036	2.0360	1.9959	1.9759	1.959	0.247	0.251	0.0038–	0.006–0.022
	9	8-307 (5.0)	2.036	2.0360	1.9959	1.9759	1.9559	0.272	0.274	0.0038–	0.006–0.022
	6	8-350 (5.7)	1.868–1.869	1.8682–1.8692	1.8682–1.8692	1.8682–1.8692	1.8682–1.8692	0.257	0.269	NA	0.004–0.012
1988	Z	6-262 (4.3)	1.868–1.869	1.8682–1.8692	1.8682–1.8692	1.8682–1.8692	1.8682–1.8692	0.234	0.257	NA	0.004–0.012
	H	8-305 (5.0)	1.868–1.869	1.8682–1.8692	1.8682–1.8692	1.8682–1.8692	1.8682–1.8692	0.234	0.257	NA	0.004–0.012
	Y	8-307 (5.0)	2.036	2.0360	1.9959	1.9759	1.9559	0.247	0.251	0.0038–	0.006–0.022
1989-90 Ⓔ	E	8-305 (5.0)	1.868–1.869	1.8682–1.8692	1.8682–1.8692	1.8682–1.8692	1.8682–1.8692	NA	NA	NA	0.004–0.012
	Y	8-307 (5.7)	2.036	2.0360	1.9959	1.9759	1.9559	0.247	0.251	0.0038	0.006–0.022
	7	8-350 (5.7)	1.868–1.869	1.8682–1.8692	1.8682–1.8692	1.8682–1.8692	1.8682–1.8692	0.257	0.269	NA	0.004–0.012

GENERAL MOTORS—"B" AND "G" BODY
ESTATE WAGON • CAPRICE • CUSTOM CRUISER • SAFARI • PARISIENNE—RWD

CRANKSHAFT AND CONNECTING ROD SPECIFICATIONS
All measurements are given in inches.

| Year | VIN | No. Cylinder Displacement cu. in. (liter) | Crankshaft | | | | Connecting Rod | | |
			Main Brg. Journal Dia.	Main Brg. Oil Clearance	Shaft End-play	Thrust on No.	Journal Diameter	Oil Clearance	Side Clearance
1986	A	6-231 (3.8)	2.4995	0.0003–0.0018	0.003–0.011	2	2.2487–2.2495	0.0005–0.0026	0.003–0.015
	7	6-231 (3.8)	2.4995	0.0003–0.0018	0.003–0.011	2	2.2487–2.2495	0.0005–0.0026	0.003–0.015
	Z	6-262 (4.3)	2.4489–2.4493 ①	0.0008–0.0020 ③	0.002–0.006	4	2.2487–2.2498	0.0013–0.0035	0.006–0.014
	H	8-305 (5.0)	2.4484–2.4493 ①	0.0008–0.0020 ③	0.002–0.006	5	2.0986–2.0998	0.0013–0.0035	0.006–0.014
	G	8-305 (5.0)	2.4484–2.4493 ①	0.0008–0.0020 ③	0.002–0.006	5	2.0986–2.0998	0.0013–0.0035	0.006–0.014
	9	8-307 (5.0)	2.4990–2.4995 ①	0.0005–0.0021 ③	0.003–0.013	3	2.1238–2.2500	0.0004–0.0026	0.006 0.015
	Y	8-307 (5.0)	2.4985–2.4995 ⑤	0.0005–0.0021 ③	0.003–0.013	3	2.12438–2.1248	0.0004–0.0033	0.006–0.020
	6	8-350 (5.7)	2.4484–2.4493 ①	0.0008–0.0020 ②	0.002–0.006	5	2.0986–2.0998	0.0013–0.0035	0.006–0.014
1987	A	6-231 (3.8)	2.4995	0.0003–0.0018	0.003–0.011	2	2.2487–2.2495	0.0005–0.0026	0.003–0.015
	7	6-231 (3.8)	2.4995	0.0003–0.0018	0.003–0.011	2	2.2487–2.2495	0.0005–0.0026	0.003–0.015
	Z	6-262 (4.3)	2.4484–2.4493 ①	0.0008–0.0020 ③	0.002–0.006	4	2.2487–2.2498	0.0013–0.0035	0.006–0.014
	H	8-305 (5.0)	2.4484–2.4493 ①	0.0008–0.0020 ③	0.002–0.006	5	2.0986–2.0998	0.0013–0.0035	0.006–0.014
	G	8-305 (5.0)	2.4484–2.4493 ①	0.0008–0.0020 ③	0.002–0.006	5	2.0986–2.0998	0.0013–0.0035	0.006–0.014
	9	8-307 (5.0)	2.4990–2.4995 ①	0.0005–0.0021 ③	0.003–0.013	3	2.1238–2.1248	0.0004–0.0033	0.006 0.020
	Y	8-305 (5.0)	2.4985–2.4995 ⑤	0.0005–0.0221 ③	0.003–0.013	3	2.1238–2.1248	0.0004–0.0033	0.006–0.020
	6	8-350 (5.7)	2.4484–2.4493 ①	0.0008–0.0020 ②	0.002–0.006	5	2.0986–2.0998	0.0013–0.0035	0.006–0.014
1988	Z	6-262 (4.3)	2.4484–2.4493 ①	0.0008–0.0020 ③	0.002–0.006	4	2.2487–2.2498	0.0013–0.0035	0.006–0.014
	H	8-305 (5.0)	2.4484–2.4493 ①	0.0008–0.0020 ③	0.002–0.006	5	2.0986–2.0998	0.0013–0.0035	0.006–0.014

CRANKSHAFT AND CONNECTING ROD SPECIFICATIONS

All measurements are given in inches.

Year	VIN	No. Cylinder Displacement cu. in. (liter)	Crankshaft				Connecting Rod		
			Main Brg. Journal Dia.	Main Brg. Oil Clearance	Shaft End-play	Thrust on No.	Journal Diameter	Oil Clearance	Side Clearance
1988	Y	8-307 (5.0)	2.4985–2.4995 ①	0.0005–0.0021 ③	0.003–0.013	3	2.1238–2.1248	0.0004–0.0033	0.006–0.020
1989–90	E	8-305 (5.0)	2.4481–2.4490 ④	0.0011–0.0020 ⑤	0.001–0.007	5	NA	0.0013–0.0035	0.006–0.014
	Y	8-307 (5.0)	2.4985–2.4995 ①	0.0005–0.0021 ③	0.003–0.013	3	2.1238–2.1248	0.0004–0.0033	0.006–0.020
	7	8-350 (5.7)	2.4481–2.4990 ④	0.0011–0.0020 ⑤	0.001–0.007	5	NA	0.0013–0.0035	0.006–0.014

① Intermediate—2.4481–2.4490
Rear—2.4479–2.4488
② Intermediate—.0011–.0023
Rear—.0017–.0032
③ Intermediate—0.0011–0.0034
Rear—0.0015–0.0031

④ Front: 2.4488–2.4493
rear: 2.4481–2.4488
⑤ Rear: 0.0020–0.0032

VALVE SPECIFICATIONS

Year	VIN	No. Cylinder Displacement cu. in. (liter)	Seat Angle (deg.)	Face Angle (deg.)	Spring Test Pressure (lbs.)	Spring Installed Height (in.)	Stem-to-Guide Clearance (in.)		Stem Diameter (in.)	
							Intake	Exhaust	Intake	Exhaust
1986	A	6-231 (3.8)	45	45	182	1.73	0.0015–0.0035	0.0015–0.0032	0.3401 0.3412	0.3405 0.3412
	7	6-231 (3.8)	45	45	185	1.73	0.0015–0.0035	0.0015–0.0032	0.3401–0.3412	0.3405–0.3412
	Z	6-262 (4.3)	46	45	200	1.70	0.0010–0.0027	0.0010–0.0027	0.3414	0.3414
	H	8-305 (5.0)	46	45	200	1.70	0.0010–0.0027	0.0010–0.0027	0.3414	0.3414
	G	8-305 (5.0)	46	45	200	1.70	0.0010–0.0027	0.0010–0.0027	0.3414	0.3414
	Y	8-307 (5.0)	46	45	194	1.72	0.0010–0.0027	0.0015–0.0032	0.3425–0.3432	0.3420–0.3427
	9	8-307 (5.0)	46	45	194	1.72	0.0010–0.0027	0.0015–0.0032	0.3425–0.3432	0.3420–0.3427
	6	8-350 (5.7)	46	45	200	1.70	0.0010–0.0027	0.0015–0.0032	0.3414	0.3414
1987	A	6-231 (3.8)	46	45	182	1.73	0.0015–0.0035	0.0015–0.0032	0.3412–0.3401	0.3412–0.3401
	7	6-231 (3.8)	45	45	185	1.73	0.0015–0.0035	0.0015–0.0032	0.3401–0.3412	0.3405–0.3412
	Z	6-262 (4.3)	46	45	200	1.70	0.0010–0.0027	0.0010–0.0027	0.3414	0.3414
	H	8-305 (5.0)	46	45	200	1.70	0.0010–0.0027	0.0010–0.0027	0.3414	0.3414
	G	8-305 (5.0)	46	45	200	1.70	0.0010–0.0027	0.0010–0.0027	0.3414	0.3414

VALVE SPECIFICATIONS

Year	VIN	No. Cylinder Displacement cu. in. (liter)	Seat Angle (deg.)	Face Angle (deg.)	Spring Test Pressure (lbs.)	Spring Installed Height (in.)	Stem-to-Guide Clearance (in.) Intake	Stem-to-Guide Clearance (in.) Exhaust	Stem Diameter (in.) Intake	Stem Diameter (in.) Exhaust
	Y	8-307 (5.0)	46	45	194	1.72	0.0010–0.0027	0.0015–0.0032	0.3425–0.3432	0.3420–0.3427
	9	8-307 (5.0)	46	45	194	1.72	0.0010–0.0027	0.0015–0.0032	0.3425–0.3432	0.3420–0.3427
	6	8-350 (5.7)	46	45	200	1.70	0.0010–0.0027	0.0010–0.0027	0.3414	0.3414
1988	Z	6-262 (4.3)	46	45	200	1.70	0.0010–0.0027	0.0010–0.0027	0.3414	0.3414
	H	8-305 (5.0)	46	45	200	1.70	0.0010–0.0027	0.0010–0.0027	0.3414	0.3414
	Y	8-307 (5.0)	45	44	194	1.70	0.0010–0.0027	0.0015–0.0032	0.3425–0.3432	0.3420–0.3427
1989–90	E	8-305 (5.0)	46	45	200	1.72	0.0011–0.0027	0.0011–0.0027	NA	NA
	Y	8-307 (5.0)	46	45	194	1.72	0.0010–0.0027	0.0015–0.0032	0.3425–0.3432	0.3420–0.3427
	7	8-350 (5.7)	46	45	200	1.72	0.0011–0.0027	0.0011–0.0027	NA	NA

PISTON AND RING SPECIFICATIONS

Year	VIN	No. Cylinder Displacement cu. in. (liter)	Piston Clearance	Ring Gap Top Compression	Ring Gap Bottom Compression	Ring Gap Oil Control	Ring Side Clearance Top Compression	Ring Side Clearance Bottom Compression	Ring Side Clearance Oil Control
1986	A	6-231 (3.8)	0.0008–0.0020	0.010–0.020	0.010–0.020	0.015–0.055	0.0030–0.0050	0.0030–0.0050	0.0035 Max
	7	6-231 (3.8)	0.0008–0.0020	0.010–0.020	0.010–0.020	0.015–0.055	0.0030–0.0050	0.0030–0.0050	0.0035 Max
	Z	6-262 (4.3)	0.0012–0.0032	0.010–0.020	0.010–0.020	0.015–0.055	0.0012–0.0032	0.0012–0.0032	0.0020–0.0070
	H	8-305 (5.0)	0.0012–0.0032	0.010–0.020	0.010–0.025	0.015–0.055	0.0012–0.0032	0.0012–0.0032	0.0020–0.0070
	G	8-305 (5.0)	0.0012–0.0032	0.010–0.020	0.010–0.025	0.015–0.055	0.0012–0.0032	0.0012–0.0032	0.0020–0.0070
	9	8-307 (5.0)	0.00075–0.00175	0.009–0.019	0.009–0.019	0.015–0.055	0.0018–0.0038	0.0018–0.0038	0.0010–0.0050
	Y	8-307 (5.0)	0.0008–0.0018	0.009–0.019	0.009–0.019	0.015–0.055	0.0018–0.0038	0.0018–0.0038	0.0010–0.0050
	6	8-350 (5.7)	0.0012–0.0032	0.010–0.020	0.010–0.020	0.015–0.055	0.0012–0.0032	0.0012–0.0032	0.0020–0.0070
1987	A	6-231 (3.8)	0.0008–0.0020	0.010–0.020	0.010–0.020	0.015–0.055	0.0030–0.0050	0.0030–0.0050	0.0035 Max
	7	6-231 (3.8)	0.0008–0.0020	0.010–0.020	0.010–0.020	0.015–0.055	0.0030–0.0050	0.0030–0.0050	0.0035 Max
	Z	6-262 (4.3)	0.0012–0.0032	0.010–0.020	0.010–0.020	0.015–0.055	0.0012–0.0032	0.0012–0.0032	0.0020–0.0070
	H	8-305 (5.0)	0.0012–0.0032	0.010–0.020	0.010–0.025	0.015–0.055	0.0012–0.0032	0.0012–0.0032	0.0020–0.0070

PISTON AND RING SPECIFICATIONS

Year	VIN	No. Cylinder Displacement cu. in. (liter)	Piston Clearance	Ring Gap			Ring Side Clearance		
				Top Compression	Bottom Compression	Oil Control	Top Compression	Bottom Compression	Oil Control
1987	G	8-305 (5.0)	0.0012–0.0032	0.010–0.020	0.010–0.025	0.015–0.055	0.0012–0.0032	0.0012–0.0032	0.0020–0.0070
	9	8-307 (5.0)	0.00075–0.00175	0.009–0.019	0.009–0.019	0.015–0.055	0.0018–0.0038	0.0018–0.0038	0.0010–0.0050
	Y	8-307 (5.0)	0.0008–0.0018	0.009–0.019	0.009–0.019	0.015–0.055	0.0018–0.0038	0.0018–0.0038	0.0010–0.0050
	6	8-350 (5.7)	0.0012–0.0032	0.010–0.020	0.010–0.020	0.015–0.055	0.0012–0.0032	0.0012–0.0032	0.0020–0.0070
1988	Z	6-262 (4.3)	0.0027	0.010–0.020	0.010–0.025	0.015–0.055	0.0012–0.0032	0.0012–0.0032	0.0020–0.0070
	H	8-305 (5.0)	0.0027	0.010–0.020	0.010–0.025	0.015–0.055	0.0012–0.0032	0.0012–0.0032	0.0020–0.0070
	Y	8-307 (5.0)	0.0008–0.0018	0.009–0.019	0.009–0.019	0.015–0.055	0.0018–0.0038	0.0018–0.0038	0.0010–0.0050
1989–90	E	8-305 (5.0)	0.007–0.017	0.010–0.020	0.010–0.025	0.015–0.055	0.0012–0.0032	0.0012–0.0032	0.0020–0.0070
	Y	8-307 (5.0)	0.0008–0.0018	0.009–0.019	0.009–0.019	0.015–0.055	0.0018–0.0038	0.0018–0.0038	0.0010–0.0050
	7	8-350 (5.7)	0.007–0.017	0.010–0.020	0.010–0.025	0.015–0.055	0.0012–0.0032	0.0012–0.0032	0.0020–0.0070

TORQUE SPECIFICATIONS

All readings in ft. lbs.

Year	VIN	No. Cylinder Displacement cu. in. (liter)	Cylinder Head Bolts	Main Bearing Bolts	Rod Bearing Bolts	Crankshaft Pulley Bolts	Flywheel Bolts	Manifold		Spark Plugs
								Intake	Exhaust	
1986	A	6-231 (3.8)	④	100	40	200	60	45	20	20
	7	6-231 (3.8)	④	100	40	200	60	45	20	10
	Z	6-262 (4.3)	60–75	70–85	42–47	70	70	25–45	20	22
	H	8-305 (5.0)	60–75	70–85	42–47	70	70	25–45	20	22
	G	8-305 (5.0)	60–75	70–85	42–47	70	70	25–45	20	22
	9	8-307 (5.0)	125 ⑤	①	42	200–310	60	40	25	25
	Y	8-307 (5.0)	125 ⑤	80	42	300	60	40	25	25
	6	8-350 (5.7)	60–75	70–85	42–47	70	70	25–45	20	22
1987	A	6-231 (3.8)	④	100	40	219	60	45	37	20
	7	6-231 (3.8)	④	100	40	219	60	45	37	20
	Z	6-262 (4.3)	60–75	70–85	42–47	70	70	25–45	20	22
	H	8-305 (5.0)	60–75	70–85	42–47	70	70	25–45	20	22
	G	8-305 (5.0)	60–75	70–85	42–47	70	70	25–45	20	22
	9	8-307 (5.0)	130	80 ①	48	200–310	60	40	25	25
	Y	8-307 (5.0)	125 ⑤	80	42	300	60	40	25	25
	6	8-350 (5.7)	60–75	70–85	42–47	70	70	25–45	20	22
1988	Z	6-262 (4.3)	60–75	70–85	42–47	—	50–70	25–45	20	22
	H	8-305 (5.0)	60–75	70–85	42–47	—	70	25–45	14–26	22
	Y	8-307 (5.0)	130 ⑤	80 ①	18 ⑦	200–310	60	40 ⑤	25	25

TORQUE SPECIFICATIONS

All readings in ft. lbs.

Year	VIN	No. Cylinder Displacement cu. in. (liter)	Cylinder Head Bolts	Main Bearing Bolts	Rod Bearing Bolts	Crankshaft Pulley Bolts	Flywheel Bolts	Manifold Intake	Manifold Exhaust	Spark Plugs
1989–90	E	8-305 (5.0)	68	77	44	70	74	35	26	22
	Y	8-307 (5.0)	40 ⑥	80 ①	18 ⑦	200–310	60	40 ⑤	25	25
	7	8-350 (5.7)	68	77	44	70	74	35	26	22

① 80 on Nos. 1–4; 120 on No. 5
② Not used
③ Not used

④ Torque cylinder head bolts to 25 ft. lbs. in tightening sequence. Continue the torquing sequence, tightening each bolt ¼ turn (90 degrees) until 60 ft. lbs. is read on any one cylinder head bolt. Do not continue sequence at this point.

⑤ Dip in clean engine oil before tightening
⑥ Rotate position 1, 7 & 9—120°
Rotate position 8 & 10—95°
⑦ Torque in 2 steps:
1st step—18 ft.lbs.
2nd step—additional 70 degrees turn further

BRAKE SPECIFICATIONS

All measurements in inches unless noted

Year	Model	Lug Nut Torque (ft. lbs.)	Master Cylinder Bore	Brake Disc Minimum Thickness	Brake Disc Maximum Runout	Standard Brake Drum Diameter	Minimum Lining Thickness Front	Minimum Lining Thickness Rear
1986	Estate Wagon	④①	1.125①	0.965	0.004	11.00	0.125	0.125
	Regal	100	0.931	0.965	0.004	9.50	0.125	0.125
	Monte Carlo, Caprice	80②	NA	0.965	0.980	9.50	0.030	0.030
	Cutlass	100	0.931	0.980	0.004	9.50	0.030	0.030③
	Custom Cruiser	100	1.125	0.980	0.004	11.00	0.030	0.030③
	Parisienne	80	1.125	0.980	0.004	9.50	0.030	—
	Parisienne⑤	80	1.181	0.980	0.004	9.50	0.030	—
	Parisienne	80	1.125	0.980	0.004	9.50	0.030	—
	Bonneville, Grand Prix	100	0.931	0.980	0.004	9.50	0.030	—
	Bonneville, Grand Prix⑤	100	1.062	0.980	0.004	9.50	0.030	—
1987	Estate Wagon	④①	1.125	0.965	0.004	11.00	0.125	0.125
	Regal	100	0.931	0.965	0.004	9.50	0.125	0.125
	Monte Carlo, Caprice	80②	NA	0.965	0.980	9.50	0.030	0.030
	Cutlass	100	0.931	0.980	0.004	9.50	0.030	0.030③
	Custom Cruiser	100	1.125	0.980	0.004	11.00	0.030	0.030③
	Safari	100	1.125	0.980	0.004	9.50	0.030	
	Grand Prix	100	0.931	0.980	0.004	9.50	0.030	
1988	Estate Wagon	④①	1.125	0.965	0.004	11.00	0.125	0.125
	Monte Carlo, Caprice	80②	1.125④	0.965	0.004	11.00	0.030	0.030
	Cutlass	100	0.931	0.980	0.004	9.50	0.030	0.030③

BRAKE SPECIFICATIONS

All measurements in inches unless noted

Year	Model	Lug Nut Torque (ft. lbs.)	Master Cylinder Bore	Brake Disc Minimum Thickness	Brake Disc Maximum Runout	Standard Brake Drum Diameter	Minimum Lining Thickness Front	Minimum Lining Thickness Rear
1988	Custom Cruiser	100	1.125	0.980	0.004	11.00	0.030	0.030③
	Safari	100	1.125	0.980	0.004	9.50	0.030	
1989–90	Estate Wagon	④①	1.125	0.980	0.004	11.00	0.030	0.030③
	Caprice	80	1.125	0.980	0.004	11.00⑦	0.030	0.030③
	Custom Cruiser	100	1.125	0.980	0.004	11.00	0.030	0.030③
	Safari	100	1.125	0.980	0.004	11.00	0.030	0.030③

① Wheel lug type: $1/2 \times 20$—100 ft. lbs.
$7/16 \times 20$ Steel—80 ft. lbs.
$7/16 \times 20$ Aluminum—90 ft. lbs.
② 88 with $7/16$ in. stud; 100 with 11 in. brake drums
③ If Bonded use .062
④ Hydroboost—$1^3/16$ in.
⑤ With hydroboost
⑥ Not used
⑦ Sedan—9.50

WHEEL ALIGNMENT

Year	Model	Caster Range (deg.)	Caster Preferred Setting (deg.)	Camber Range (deg.)	Camber Preferred Setting (deg.)	Toe-in (in.)	Steering Axis Inclination (deg.)
1986	Estate Wagon	2P–4P	3P	$0–1^5/8$P	$^{13}/_{16}$P	$1/8$	NA
	Regal	2P–4P	3P	$5/16$N–$1^5/16$P	$1/2$P	$1/8$	8
	Monte Carlo	2–4P	3P	$3/10$N–$1^3/10$P	$1/2$P	$1/16$–$1/4$	$7^7/8$
	Caprice	2–4P	3P	$0–1^3/5$P	$1/2$P	$1/16$–$1/4$	$7^7/8$
	Cutlass	2P–3P	2P	$0–1^5/8$P	$3/4$P	$0–1/4$	—
	Custom Cruiser	2P–3P	2P	$0–1^3/5$P	$4/5$P	$0–1/4$P	—
	Grand Prix	2P–4P	3P	$5/16$N–$1^5/16$P	$1/2$P	$1/8$	8
	Bonneville	2P–4P	3P	$5/16$N–$1^5/16$P	$1/2$P	$1/8$	8
	Parisienne	2P–4P	3P	$0–1^5/8$P	$1/2$P	$1/8$	$9^3/4$
1987	Estate Wagon	2P–4P	3P	$0–1^5/8$P	$^{13}/_{16}$P	$1/8$	NA
	Regal	2P–4P	3P	$5/16$N–$1^5/16$P	$1/2$P	$1/8$	8
	Monte Carlo	2–4P	3P	$3/10$N–$1^3/10$P	$1/2$P	$1/16$–$1/4$	$7^7/8$
	Caprice	2–4P	3P	$0–1^3/5$P	$1/2$P	$1/16$–$1/4$	$7^7/8$
	Cutlass	2P–3P	2P	$0–1^5/8$P	$3/4$P	$0–1/4$	—
	Custom Cruiser	2P–3P	2P	$0–1^3/5$P	$4/5$P	$0–1/4$P	—
	Grand Prix	$2^{13}/_{16}$P–$3^{13}/_{16}$P	$2^{13}/_{16}$P	$5/16$N–$1^5/16$P	$1/2$P	$3/64$	8
	Safari	$2^3/16$P–$3^{13}/_{16}$P	$2^{13}/_{16}$P	$0–1^5/8$P	$^{13}/_{16}$P	$1/16$	$7^9/16$
1988	Monte Carlo	2–4P	3P	$3/10$N–$1^3/10$P	$1/2$P	$1/16$–$1/4$	$7^7/8$
	Caprice	2–4P	3P	$0–1^3/5$P	$1/2$P	$1/16$–$1/4$	$7^7/8$
	Estate Wagon	2P–4P	3P	$0–1^5/8$P	$^{13}/_{16}$P	$1/8$	NA
	Cutlass	2P–3P	2P	$0–1^5/8$P	$3/4$P	$0–1/4$	—
	Custom Cruiser	2P–3P	2P	$0–1^3/5$P	$4/5$P	$0–1/4$P	—
	Safari	$2^3/16$P–$3^{13}/_{16}$P	$2^{13}/_{16}$P	$0–1^5/8$P	$^{13}/_{16}$P	$1/16$	$7^9/16$

WHEEL ALIGNMENT

Year	Model	Caster Range (deg.)	Caster Preferred Setting (deg.)	Camber Range (deg.)	Camber Preferred Setting (deg.)	Toe-in (in.)	Steering Axis Inclination (deg.)
1989–90	Estate Wagon	2P–4P	3P	0–1$\frac{5}{8}$P	$\frac{13}{16}$P	$\frac{1}{8}$	NA
	Caprice	2–4P	3P	0–1$\frac{3}{5}$P	$\frac{1}{2}$P	$\frac{1}{16}$–$\frac{1}{4}$	7$\frac{7}{8}$
	Custom Cruiser	2P–3P	2P	0–1$\frac{3}{5}$P	$\frac{4}{5}$P	0–$\frac{1}{4}$P	—
	Safari	2$\frac{3}{16}$P–3$\frac{13}{16}$P	2$\frac{13}{16}$P	0–1$\frac{5}{8}$P	$\frac{13}{16}$P	$\frac{1}{16}$	7$\frac{9}{16}$

NA—Not Available
N—Negative
P—Positive

ELECTRICAL

NOTE: Disconnecting the negative battery cable on some vehicles may interfere with the functions of the on board computer systems and may require the computer to undergo a relearning process, once the negative battery cable is reconnected.

For Testing and Overhaul Procedures on starters, alternators and voltage regulators, Refer to the Unit Repair Section.

Charging System

ALTERNATOR

Removal and Installation

1. Disconnect the negative battery cable.
2. Remove the terminal plug and the battery lead from the back of the alternator assembly.
3. On engines without a serpentine belt, loosen the alternator adjusting bolts and remove the alternator belt. On engines with a serpentine belt, loosen the belt tensioner and remove the belt.
4. Remove the alternator mounting and adjusting bolts. Remove the alternator assembly from the vehicle.
5. Installation is the reverse of the removal procedure. Once the alternator belt is installed, check the belt for proper tension.

VOLTAGE REGULATOR

The voltage regulator is incorporated within the alternator assembly. There is no adjustment procedure. Should the regulator require service, the alternator must be disassembled.

BELT TENSION

Adjustment

GAUGE METHOD

1. Disconnect the negative battery cable.
2. Loosen the alternator pivot bolt and the adjustment bolt.
3. Using belt tension tool J–23600–B, BT 33–95–ACBN or equivalent, move the alternator until the correct tension is reached and tighten the bolts.

4. On engines equipped with a belt tension adjustment bolt, tighten the bolt to the proper tension on the gauge.
5. Tighten all bolts and connect the negative battery cable.

NOTE: Serpentine drive belts, installed on some engines, are adjusted automatically by a belt tensioner mounted on the engine.

Starting System

STARTER

Removal and Installation

1. Disconnect the negative battery cable.
2. Raise and support the vehicle safely.
3. Remove upper support attaching bolts and the brace and wire guide tube bolt, if equipped.
4. Remove the flywheel housing cover, as required.
5. If necessary, remove the exhaust crossover pipe.
6. If necessary, disconnect the transmission oil cooler lines.
7. Remove the starter mounting bolts and lower the starter.
8. Disconnect the wiring and remove starter.
9. If equipped with dual exhaust, it may be necessary to remove the left exhaust pipe.
10. Install by reversing the removal procedure.
11. If shims were removed, they must be installed in their original location to assure proper drive pinion to flywheel engagement.

Ignition System

Two types of ignition systems are used. Most engines use the High Energy Ignition (HEI) system. The Computer Controlled Coil Ignition (C^3I) is used with the 3.8L V6 turbocharged engine equipped with the SFI injection system. With the C^3I system, no distributor is used. The system utilizes a coil pack and ignition module, along with crankshaft and camshaft sensors.

NOTE: When troubleshooting a no start/no spark condition on vehicles equipped with C^3I system, make sure the ignition module is properly grounded to it's mounting bracket.

Belt Tension Chart

ENGINE	TENSION	GENERATOR		POWER STEERING	AIR CONDITIONING	A.I.R. PUMP	
		COGGED	PLAIN			.380" BELT	.312" BELT
V-6	NEW BELT		550 N Max. 125 Lbs. Max.	600 N Max. 135 Lbs. Max.	600 N Max. 135 Lbs. Max.		350 N Max. 80 Lbs. Max.
	USED BELT		300 N Min. 70 Lbs. Min.	350 N Min. 80 Lbs. Min.	350 N Min. 80 Lbs. Min.		200 N Min. 45 Lbs. Min.
5.0L (VIN Y & 9)	NEW BELT	650 N Max. 145 Lbs. Max.	700 N Max. 160 Lbs. Max.	750 N Max. 170 Lbs. Max.	750 N Max. 170 Lbs. Max.	650 N Max. 145 Lbs. Max.	350 N Max. 80 Lbs. Max.
	USED BELT	400 N Min. 90 Lbs. Min.	500 N Min. 110 Lbs. Min.	500 N Min. 110 Lbs. Min.	500 N Min. 110 Lbs. Min.	400 N Min. 90 Lbs. Min.	250 N Min. 55 Lbs. Min.
5.0L (VIN H)	NEW BELT	650 N Max. 145 Lbs. Max.			750 N Max. 170 Lbs. Max.	650 N Max. 145 Lbs. Max.	
	USED BELT	300 N Min. 70 Lbs. Min.			400 N Min. 90 Lbs. Min.	300 N Min. 70 Lbs. Min.	

*For belts driving more than one adjustable accessory, use highest tension specified.

DISTRIBUTOR

Removal and Installation

ENGINE TIMING NOT DISTURBED

1. Disconnect the negative battery cable.
2. Disconnect and tag the ignition wire (pink), tachometer wire if equipped and 3 terminal connector from distributor cap.

NOTE: Use care when releasing the connector locking tabs on the distributor cap.

3. Remove distributor cap with the spark plug wires attached and position it out of the way.
4. Disconnect the 4 terminal connector from the distributor.
5. Remove the distributor hold down bolt and clamp. Mark the position of the rotor in relation to the engine. Pull the distributor from the engine until the rotor just stops turning counterclockwise. Again mark the position of rotor.

NOTE: To insure correct ignition timing if the engine has not been disturbed, the distributor must be installed with the rotor in the same position as when removed.

6. Installation is the reverse of the removal procedure.
7. Align the rotor to the last mark made and install the distributor in the engine. The rotor should turn and end up at the first mark made. Check the timing when finished.

ENGINE TIMING DISTURBED

1. Remove the No. 1 spark plug. Place a finger over the spark plug hole and rotate the engine in the normal direction of rotation slowly, until compression is felt.
2. Align the timing mark on the pulley to the 0 on the engine timing indicator by rotating the engine in the same direction slowly.
3. Position the rotor between No. 1 and No. 8 spark plug towers on V8 engines and between No. 1 and No. 6 spark plug towers on V6 engines.
4. Install the distributor, distributor cap, spark plug, wiring and connectors.
5. Check the engine timing and adjust as required.

IGNITION TIMING

NOTE: On vehicles equipped with the C³I ignition system, the timing is adjusted automatically by the ECM. Manual adjustment of the C³I ignition timing is not possible.

Adjustment

V6 ENGINE

1. Run the engine until normal operating temperature is reached. Be sure that the air cleaner is installed and the air conditioner is off.
2. Connect a timing light with the pickup lead on the No. 1 plug wire.
3. Disconnect the 4 wire electrical connector at the distributor. The check engine light will come on.
4. If the timing requires adjustment, loosen the distributor

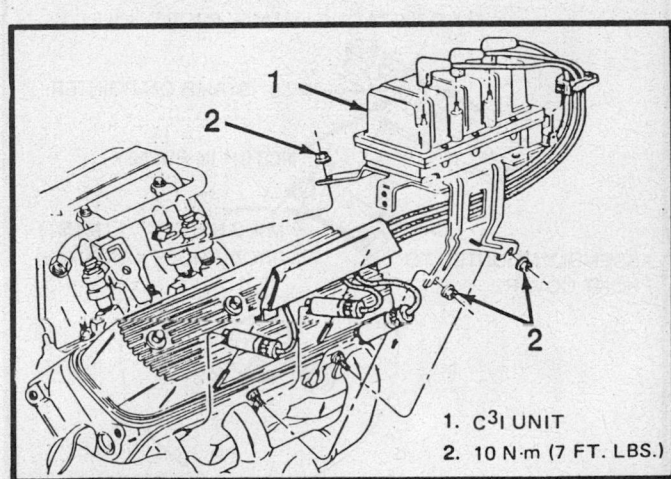

1. C³I UNIT
2. 10 N·m (7 FT. LBS.)

C³I ignition system coil mounting — 3.8L V6 turbo engine

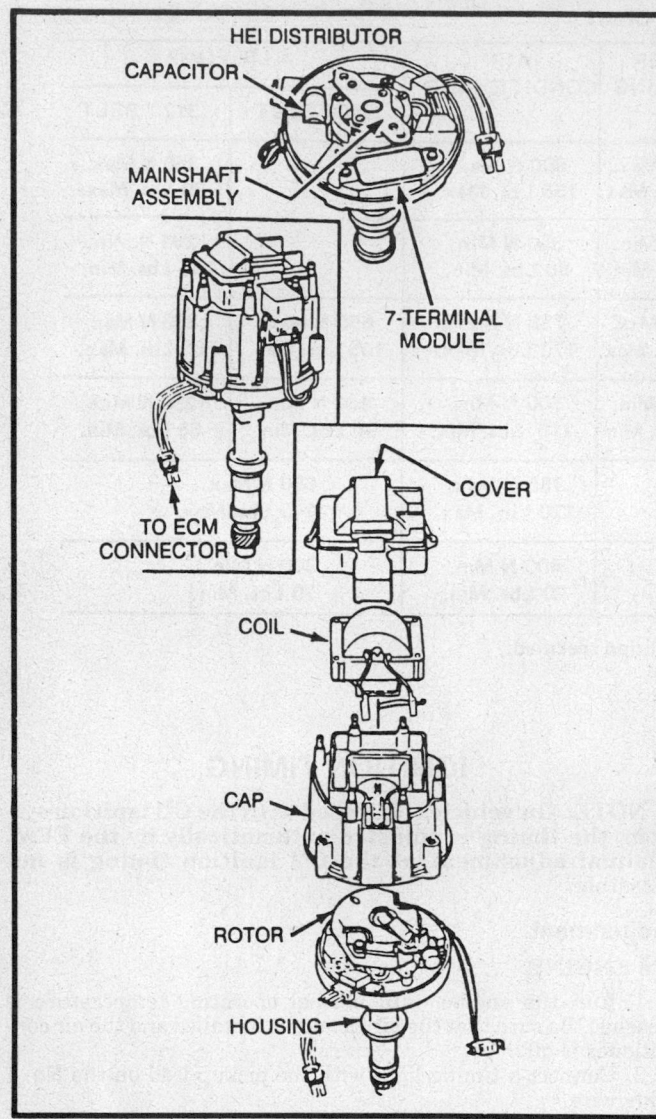

Exploded view of typical HEI distributor

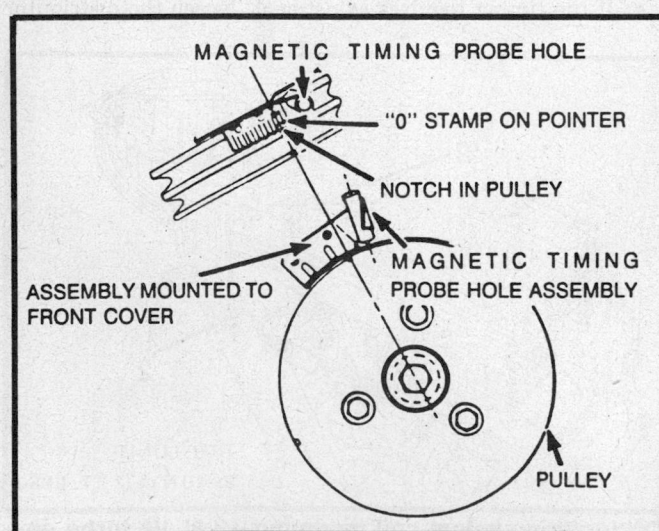

Timing marks and timing probe hole

and set the timing to the specifications as noted on the Vehicle Emission Information Label.

5. After the timing has been set, remove the ECM fuse from the fuse block for 15 seconds to cancel any stored trouble codes.

NOTE: Some engines will incorporate a magnetic timing probe hole for the use with electronic timing equipment. Be sure to consult the equipment manufactures instructions for the use of this equipment.

V8 ENGINE

1. Run the engine until operating temperature has been reached. Be sure that the choke is fully open and the air conditioner is off.

2. With the engine running, ground the diagnostic terminal of the twelve terminal ALCL connector.

3. Connect the timing light with the pickup lead on the No. 1 plug wire.

4. If the timing requires adjustment, loosen the distributor and set the timing to the specifications noted on the Vehicle Emission Information Label.

5. Once the timing has been set and with the engine still running, unground the diagnostic terminal.

6. Clear any stored trouble codes by removing the ECM fuse for 15 seconds.

Electrical Controls

STEERING WHEEL

Removal and Installation

NOTE: Do not pound on the steering wheel or the steering shaft. The collapsible column could be damaged enough to require replacement.

EXCEPT TILT AND TELESCOPE COLUMNS

1. Disconnect the battery ground cable.

2. On the stock wheel, remove the screws attaching the horn pad assembly to the wheel. Disconnect the horn contact from the pad assembly.

3. On the deluxe wheel, remove the pad attaching screws, lift up the pad, and disconnect the horn wire by pushing on the insulator and turning counterclockwise.

4. On the sport steering wheel, pull up on the emblem to remove it. Remove the contact assembly attaching screws and the contact assembly.

5. On all columns, remove the steering wheel nut retainer.

6. Remove the retaining nut and the steering wheel, using a puller.

7. Installation is the reverse of removal. Align the marks on the wheel hub and the steering shaft. Torque the attaching bolt to 30 ft. lbs.

TILT AND TELESCOPE COLUMNS

1. Disconnect the negative battery cable.

2. Remove the pad attaching screws, lift off the pad assembly and disconnect the horn wire.

3. Push the locking lever counterclockwise to full release.

4. Mark the plate assembly where the attaching screws attach the plate assembly to the locking lever and remove the screws.

5. Unscrew and remove the plate assembly. Remove the steering wheel nut.

6. Using a puller, remove the steering wheel.

7. Install a $\frac{5}{16}$ in. × 18 set screw into the upper shaft at the full extended position and lock.

8. Install the steering wheel, observing the aligning mark on the hub and the slash mark on the end of the shaft. Make certain that the unattached end of the horn upper contact assembly is seated flush against the top of the horn contact carrier button.

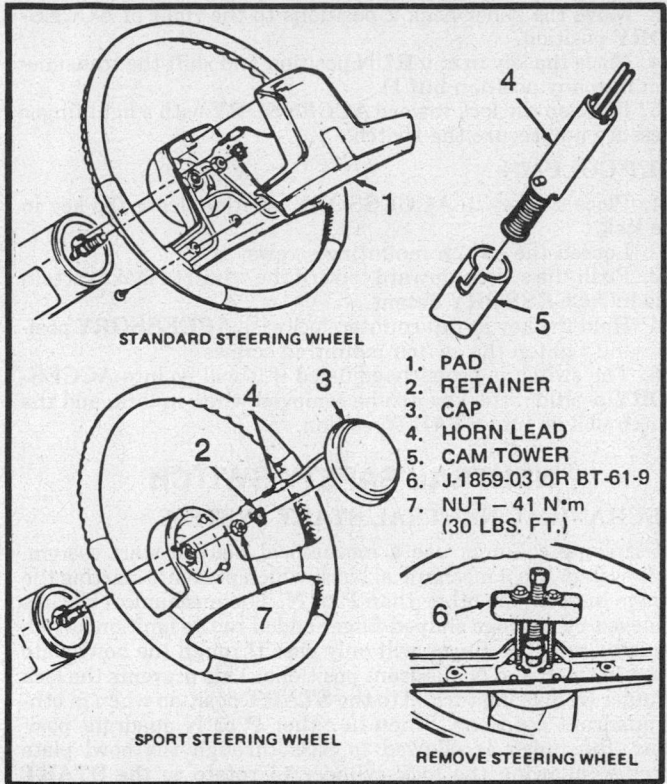

1. PAD
2. RETAINER
3. CAP
4. HORN LEAD
5. CAM TOWER
6. J-1859-03 OR BT-61-9
7. NUT — 41 N•m (30 LBS. FT.)

STANDARD STEERING WHEEL

SPORT STEERING WHEEL

REMOVE STEERING WHEEL

Steering wheel and horn contact assembly with standard steering column

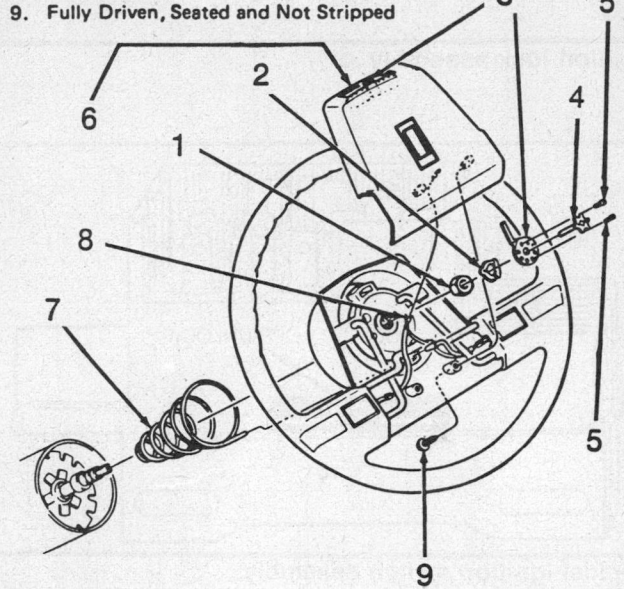

1. Steering Wheel Nut 41 N•m (30 Lbs. Ft.)
2. Steering Wheel Nut Retainer
3. Telescoping Adjuster Lever
4. Steering Shaft Lock Knob Bolt
5. Steering Shaft Lock Knob Bolt Positioning Screw (2)
6. Steering Wheel Pad
7. Horn Contact Spring
8. Horn Lead
9. Fully Driven, Seated and Not Stripped

Steering wheel and horn contact assembly with tilt and telescoping wheel

9. Install the nut on the upper steering shaft and torque to 30 ft. lbs.
10. Remove the set screw installed in Step 7.
11. Install the plate assembly finger tight.
12. Position the locking lever in the vertical position and move it counterclockwise until the holes in the plate align with the holes in the lever. Install the attaching screws.
13. Align the pad assembly with the holes in the steering wheel and install the retaining screws.
14. Connect the battery.
15. Make certain that the locking lever securely locks the wheel travel and that the wheel travel is free in the unlocked position.

HORN SWITCH

Removal and Installation

1. Disconnect the negative battery cable.
2. Remove the steering wheel.
3. Remove the contact assembly.
4. If the vehicle is equipped with tilt and telescopic steering column, remove the lock lever and plate.
5. Installation is the reverse of the removal procedure.

IGNITION LOCK

Removal and Installation

1. Disconnect the negative battery cable.
2. Position the ignition lock cylinder in the **RUN** position.
3. Remove the steering wheel. Remove the lock plate, turn signal switch and the buzzer switch.
4. Remove the lock cylinder retaining screw. Remove the lock cylinder.
5. To install, rotate the lock cylinder clockwise to align the cylinder key with the keyway in the lock housing.
6. Push the lock all the way in. Install the screw.
7. Continue the installation in the reverse order of the removal procedure.

IGNITION SWITCH

Removal and Installation

1. Disconnect the negative battery cable.
2. Loosen the toe pan screws on the steering column.
3. Remove the column to instrument panel trim plates and attaching nuts.
4. Lower the steering column. Disconnect the switch wire connectors.

NOTE: The steering column must be supported at all times to prevent damage.

5. Remove the switch attaching screws and remove the switch.
6. To replace, move the key lock to the **LOCK** position.
7. Move the actuator rod hole in the switch to the **LOCK** position.
8. Install the switch with the rod in the hole.
9. Position and reassemble the steering column in reverse of the disassembly procedure.

Adjustment

STANDARD COLUMN

1. Place the switch in the **OFF** position.
2. Position the switch on the column, then move the slider to the extreme left (toward the wheel).

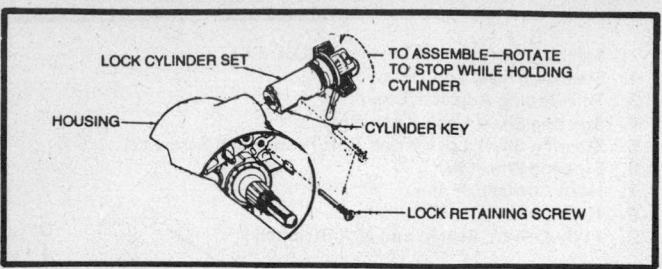

Ignition lock assembly

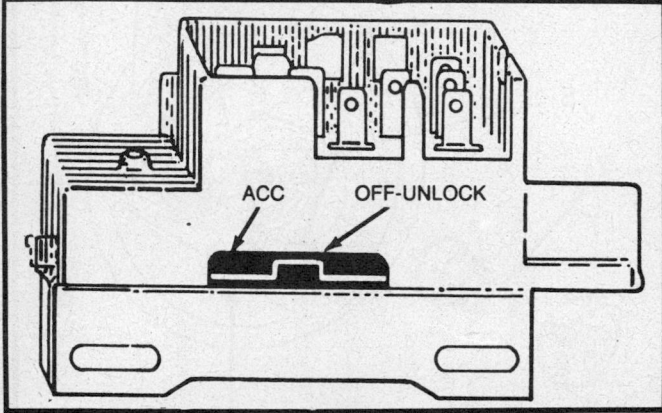

Typical ignition switch assembly

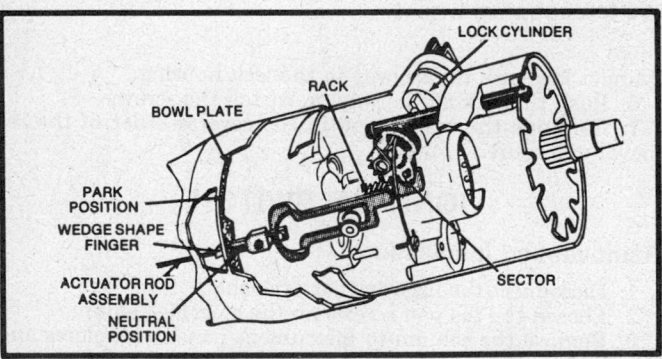

Mechanical neutral start system

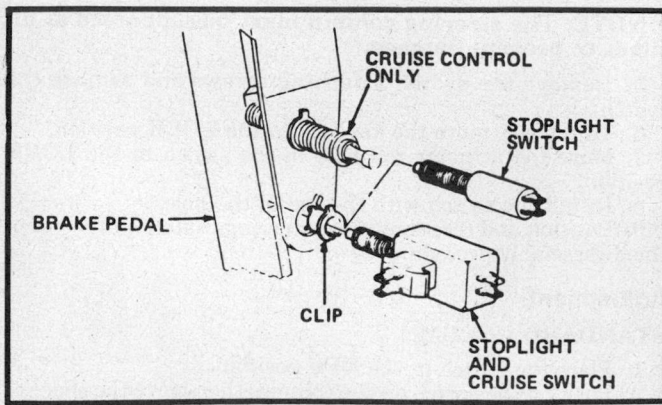

Stop light switch — typical

3. Move the slider back 2 positions to the right of **ACCESSORY** position.

4. Place the key in any **RUN** position and shift the transmission into any position but **P**.

5. Position the lock toward **ACCESSORY** with a light finger pressure and secure the switch.

TILT COLUMN

1. Place the key in **ACCESSORY** position; leave the key in the lock.

2. Loosen the switch mounting screws.

3. Push the switch upward toward the wheel to make certain it is in **ACCESSORY** detent.

4. Hold the key in full counterclockwise **ACCESSORY** position and tighten the switch mounting screws.

5. The switch is properly adjusted if it will go into **ACCESSORY** position, the key can be removed when in lock, and the switch will go into **START** position.

NEUTRAL SAFETY SWITCH

MECHANICAL NEUTRAL START SYSTEM

All steering columns use a mechanical neutral start system. This system has a mechanical block which prevents starting the engine in positions other than **P** or **N**. The mechanical block is achieved by a wedge shaped finger added to the ignition switch actuator rod. The finger will only pass through the bowl plate when in the **P** and **N** quadrant positions. This prevents the lock cylinder from being turned to the **START** position when in other quadrant positions. When in either **P** or **N** quadrant positions, the finger is allowed to pass through the bowl plate notches, allowing the lock cylinder to rotate to the **START** position.

STOPLIGHT SWITCH

Removal and Installation

1. Disconnect the negative battery cable.
2. Disconnect the electrical connection from the switch.

NOTE: If the vehicle is equipped with cruise control, there will be 2 switches mounted on the brake pedal support. The stoplight switch does not incorporate a vacuum hose.

3. Remove the switch from the tubular clip on the brake pedal mounting bracket.

4. To install and adjust, insert the switch into the clip until the switch body seats on the clip.

5. Pull the brake pedal rearwards against internal pedal stop. The switch will be moved in tubular clip, when no clicks are heard while pulling the pedal and the brake lamps do not stay on, proper adjustment has been reached.

HEADLAMP SWITCH

Removal and Installation

ROCKER SWITCH

1. Disconnect the negative battery cable.
2. Remove the left hand trim cover.
3. Remove the left side switch trim cover.
4. Remove the screws. Center screw shares the top of the switch and the bottom of the interior light rheostat.
5. Pull the switch and rheostat straight outwards, disconnect the wiring and remove the switch.
6. Installation is the reverse of the removal procedure.

KNOB SWITCH

1. Disconnect the negative battery cable.
2. Pull the headlamp switch to the **ON** position.

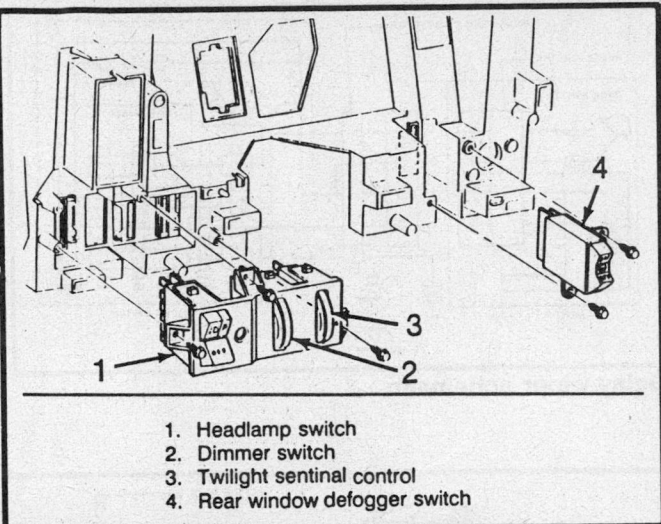

1. Headlamp switch
2. Dimmer switch
3. Twilight sentinal control
4. Rear window defogger switch

Headlamp switch mounting—rocker type

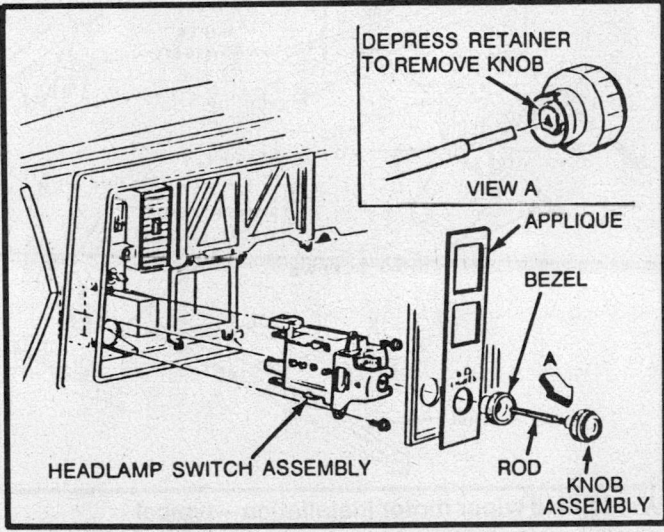

DEPRESS RETAINER TO REMOVE KNOB

VIEW A

APPLIQUE

BEZEL

A

HEADLAMP SWITCH ASSEMBLY   ROD   KNOB ASSEMBLY

Headlamp switch mounting—knob type

3. Depending upon the switch mechanism, pull the trim knob from the switch by either reaching under the dash and depressing the switch shaft release button while pulling the knob and shaft from the light switch or by using a suitable tool and pushing the tang under the trim knob while pulling the knob from the shaft.

4. Remove the ferrule nut retaining the switch to the dash panel. Disconnect the electrical connector and remove the switch.

5. Installation is the reverse of the removal procedure.

DIMMER SWITCH

Removal and Installation

1. Disconnect the negative battery cable.
2. The dimmer switch is attached to the lower steering column jacket. Disconnect all electrical connections from the switch.
3. Remove the nut and screw that attach the switch to the steering column jacket and remove switch.
4. Install the dimmer switch and depress it slightly to insert a

3/32 in. drill. Force switch up to remove lash, then tighten screw and nut to 4.0 ft. lbs.

TURN SIGNAL SWITCH

Removal and Installation

1. Disconnect the negative battery cable.
2. Disconnect turn signal switch wire connector at lower end of steering column.
3. Remove the steering wheel and shaft lock cover.
4. Remove retaining ring and shaft lock using tool J-23653 or equivalent.
5. Remove cancelling cam and spring assembly.
6. Remove screws attaching the switch to the housing. Pull switch out. If equipped with cruise control, the wiring harness will have to be pulled up through the steering column.
7. Installation is the reverse of the removal procedure.

COMBINATION SWITCH

The combination switch operates the turn signals, dimmer, cruise control if equipped and windshield washer/wipers switch.

Removal and Installation

1. Disconnect the negative battery cable. Remove the steering wheel. Remove the turn signal switch.
2. It may be necessary to loosen the column mounting nuts and remove the bracket-to-mast jacket screws. If so, separate the bracket from the mast jacket to allow the connector clip on the ignition switch to be pulled out of the column assembly.
3. Disconnect the washer/wiper switch lower connector.
4. Remove the screws attaching the column housing to the mast jacket. Be sure to note the position of the dimmer switch actuator rod for reassembly in the same position. Remove the column housing and switch as an assembly.

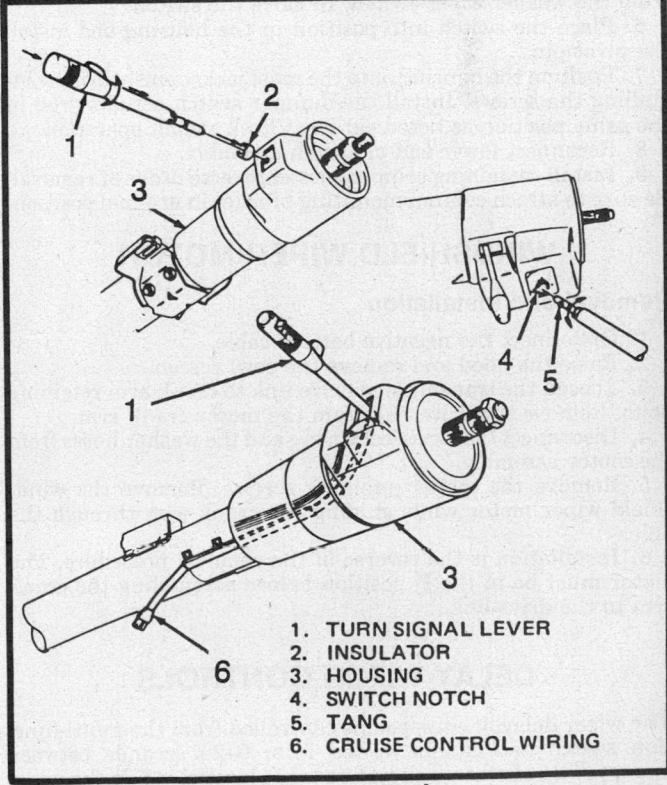

1. TURN SIGNAL LEVER
2. INSULATOR
3. HOUSING
4. SWITCH NOTCH
5. TANG
6. CRUISE CONTROL WIRING

Combination switch lever removal

NOTE: The tilt and travel columns have a removable plastic cover on the column housing. This provides access to the wiper switch without removing the entire column housing.

5. Turn the switch upside down and use a drift to remove the pivot pin from the washer/wiper switch. Remove the switch.

6. Place the switch into position in the housing and install the pivot pin.

7. Position the housing onto the mast jacket and attach by installing the screws. Install the dimmer switch actuator rod. Check switch operation.

8. Reconnect the lower end of switch assembly.

9. Install the remaining components in reverse order of removal. Be sure to attach column mounting bracket in original position.

WINDSHIELD WIPER SWITCH

Removal and Installation

1. Disconnect the negative battery cable. Remove the steering wheel.

2. It may be necessary to loosen the column mounting nuts and remove the bracket to mast jacket screws, then separate the bracket from the mast jacket to allow the connector clip on the ignition switch to be pulled out of the column assembly.

3. Disconnect the washer/wiper switch lower connector.

4. Remove the screws attaching the column housing to the mast jacket. Be sure to note the position of the dimmer switch actuator rod for reassembly in the same position. Remove the column housing and switch as an assembly.

NOTE: The tilt and travel columns have a removable plastic cover on the column housing. This provides access to the wiper switch without removing the entire column housing.

5. Turn upside down and use a drift to remove the pivot pin from the washer/wiper switch. Remove the switch.

6. Place the switch into position in the housing and install the pivot pin.

7. Position the housing onto the mast jacket and attach by installing the screws. Install the dimmer switch actuator rod in the same position as noted earlier. Check switch operation.

8. Reconnect lower end of switch assembly.

9. Install remaining components in reverse order of removal. Be sure to attach column mounting bracket in original position.

WINDSHIELD WIPER MOTOR

Removal and Installation

1. Disconnect the negative battery cable.

2. Raise the hood and remove the cowl screen.

3. Loosen the transmission drive link to crank arm retaining bolts. Remove the drive link from the motor crank arm.

4. Disconnect the electrical wiring and the washer hoses from the motor assembly.

5. Remove the motor retaining screws. Remove the windshield wiper motor while guiding the crank arm through the hole.

6. Installation is the reverse of the removal procedure. The motor must be in the **P** position before assembling the crank arm to the drive link.

DELAY WIPER CONTROLS

The wiper delay, if equipped, is controlled from the multi-function switch and can be varied from 0–25 seconds between sweeps. The electronic circuit board is located inside the wiper motor cover. The circuit board must be replaced as an assembly.

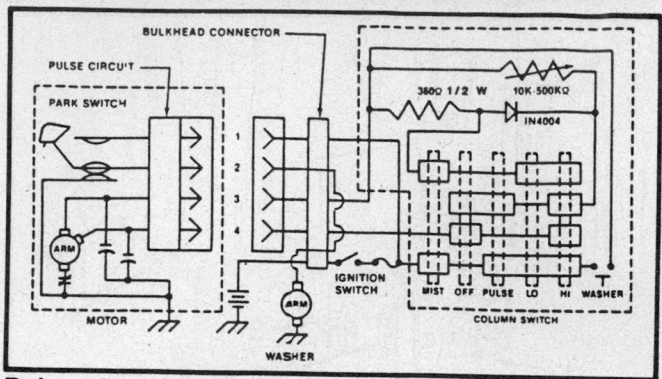

Delay wiper schematic

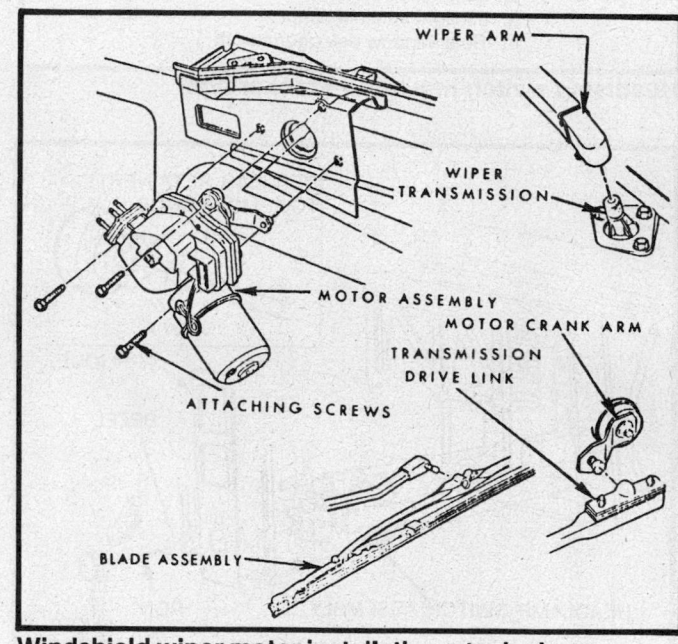

Windshield wiper motor installation—typical

WIPER WIPER LINKAGE

Removal and Installation

1. Disconnect the negative battery cable.

2. Raise the hood and remove the cowl vent screen. Remove both wiper arms and blade assemblies.

3. Loosen, but do not remove, the retaining nuts securing the transmission drive link to the motor crank arm.

4. Disconnect the transmission drive link from the motor crank arm. Remove the transmission to body retaining screws.

5. Remove the transmission and linkage assembly by guiding it through the plenum chamber opening or to the left side under the dash panel extension.

6. Installation is the reverse of the removal procedure. Be sure to seal all broken seams and cut welds with body caulk.

7. Check wiper operation, pattern and Park position.

Instrument Cluster

Refer to "Chilton's Electronic Instrumentation Service Manual" for additional coverage.

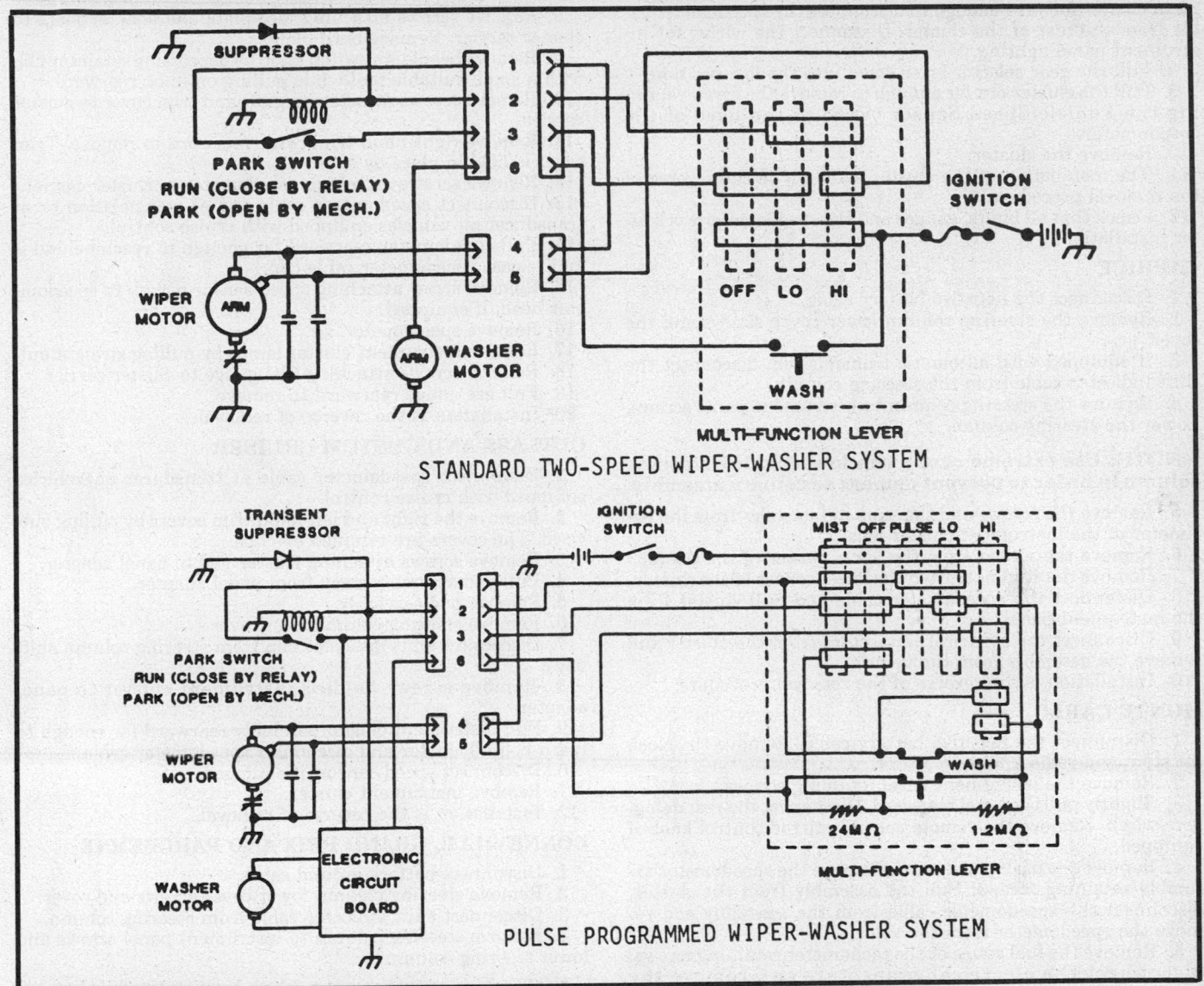

STANDARD TWO-SPEED WIPER-WASHER SYSTEM

PULSE PROGRAMMED WIPER-WASHER SYSTEM

Electrical schematic of standard and pulse wiper circuits

Removal and Installation
ESTATE WAGON

1. Disconnect the negative battery cable. Remove the defroster grille.
2. Remove the 10 screws retaining the instrument panel top cover to the instrument panel.
3. If the vehicle is equipped with a twilight sentinel, pop up the photocell retainer, turn the photocell counterclockwise in the retainer and pull it down and out.
4. Slide the instrument panel top cover out far enough to disconnect the aspirator hose, electrical connector to the in-vehicle sensor and the electrical connector to the electro-luminescent inverter.
5. Remove the instrument panel top cover from the instrument panel. On vehicles equipped with Quartz Electronic Speedometer clusters, remove the steering column trim cover, so that the shift indicator can be removed.
6. Remove the 5 screws from the instrument cluster to the instrument panel carrier.
7. Disconnect the speedometer cable and pull the cluster

housing assembly straight out, this will also separate the electrical connectors to the cluster.

NOTE: If equipped with Tilt Steering Wheel, it may be helpful to tilt the wheel all the way down and pull the gear select lever to low, when removing the cluster.

8. Installation is the reverse of the removal procedure.

REGAL

1. Disconnect the negative battery cable. Remove the left side trim cover.
2. Remove the retaining screws holding the cluster carrier to the instrument panel.
3. If a 2 piece speedometer cable is used, disconnect the speedometer cable at the split in the engine compartment.
4. Remove the steering column trim cover.
5. Disconnect the shift indicator clip.
6. Lower the steering column. If the vehicle is equipped with a tilt wheel it will be necessary to lower the wheel as far as possible and unscrew the tilt lever.
7. Remove the cluster mounting screws and pull the instru-

ment cluster forward enough to disconnect the speedometer cable from the rear of the cluster. Disconnect the wiring for instrument panel lighting.

8. Pull the gear selector lever down into the low position.

9. Pull the cluster out far enough to remove the screw retaining the Vehicle Speed Sensor (VSS) to the head of the speedometer.

10. Remove the cluster.

11. The installation of the cluster assembly is the reverse of the removal procedure.

12. Check that all lights, gauges and the speedometer work after installation.

CAPRICE

1. Disconnect the negative battery cable.

2. Remove the steering column lower cover screws and the cover.

3. If equipped with automatic transmission, disconnect the shift indicator cable from the steering column.

4. Remove the steering column to instrument panel screws. Lower the steering column.

NOTE: Use extreme care when lowering the steering column in order to prevent damage to column assembly.

5. Remove the screws and the snap in fasteners from the perimeter of the instrument cluster lens.

6. Remove the screws from the lower corner of the cluster.

7. Remove the stud nuts from the lower corner of the cluster.

8. Disconnect the speedometer cable and pull cluster from the instrument panel.

9. Disconnect the electrical connectors from the cluster and remove the assembly from the vehicle.

10. Installation is the reverse of the removal procedure.

MONTE CARLO

1. Disconnect the negative battery cable. Remove the clock set stem and radio knobs.

2. Remove the instrument bezel retaining screws.

3. Slightly pull the bezel rearward. Disconnect the rear defogger switch. Remove the remote control mirror control knob if equipped.

4. Remove the dash panel bezel. Remove the speedometer assembly retaining screws. Pull the assembly from the cluster, disconnect the speedometer cable from the assembly and remove the speedometer from the vehicle.

5. Remove the fuel gauge or the tachometer retaining screws, disconnect the electrical connectors and remove the components.

6. Remove the clock or voltmeter retaining screws, disconnect the electrical connectors and remove the components. Mark the electrical connectors.

7. Disconnect the transmission shift indicator cable from the steering column.

8. Disconnect all wiring connectors and remove the cluster case. Ensure that all electrical connectors are indentified to ensure proper reinstallation.

9. Installation is the reverse of the removal procedure.

88 AND 98

1. Disconnect the negative battery cable. Slide steering column collar up steering column.

2. Pull steering column trim cover rearward to remove. It is snapped into place.

3. Remove screws attaching gauge cluster to left hand trim cover.

4. Pull gauge cluster rearward far enough to reach behind it and disconnect gauge wiring connectors and both lamp sockets.

5. Remove gauge cluster.

6. Remove trip odometer knob, if equipped.

7. Remove screws attaching speedometer lens to cluster carrier. Remove speedometer lens.

8. Remove screws attaching face plate and adapter plate to cluster carrier. Remove both plates.

9. Remove headlamp switch knob by depressing retaining clip with a small suitable tool while pulling on knob rearward.

10. Remove screws attaching right hand trim cover to cluster carrier.

11. Remove right hand trim cover rearward to remove. Trim cover is held in place by clips.

12. Remove screws attaching speedometer to cluster carrier.

13. Disconnect speedometer cable end at transmission or at transducer on vehicles equipped with cruise control.

14. Pull speedometer rearward far enough to reach behind it and release speedometer cable clip.

15. Remove screw attaching speed sensor pickup to speedometer head, if equipped.

16. Remove speedometer.

17. Remove instrument cluster lamps by pulling straight out.

18. Remove screws attaching fuel gauge to cluster carrier.

19. Pull gas gauge rearward to remove.

20. Installation is the reverse of removal.

CUTLASS AND CUSTOM CRUISER

1. Disconnect speedometer cable at transducer on vehicles equipped with cruise control.

2. Remove the right and left hand trim covers by pulling outward. The covers are retained by clips.

3. Remove screws attaching cluster pad to panel adapter.

4. Pull pad assembly away from panel adapter.

5. Remove pad assembly.

6. Remove steering column trim cover.

7. Disconnect shift indicator clip from steering column shift bowl.

8. Remove screws holding instrument cluster to panel adapter.

9. Pull instrument cluster assembly rearward far enough to reach behind cluster and disconnect speedometer cable.

10. Disconnect speed sensor, if equipped.

11. Remove instrument cluster.

12. Installation is the reverse of removal.

BONNEVILLE, GRAND PRIX AND PARISIENNE

1. Disconnect battery ground cable.

2. Remove steering column lower cover screws and cover.

3. Disconnect shift indicator cable from steering column.

4. Remove steering column to instrument panel screws and lower steering column.

NOTE: Use extreme care when lower steering to prevent damage to column assembly.

5. Remove the screws and the snap-in fasteners from perimeter of instrument cluster lens.

6. Remove screws from upper surface of grey sheet metal trim plate.

7. Remove stud nuts from lower corner of cluster.

8. Disconnect speedometer cable and pull cluster from instrument panel.

9. Disconnect electrical connectors from cluster and remove from vehicle.

10. Reverse procedure to install.

SPEEDOMETER

Removal and Installation

1. Disconnect the negative battery cable.

2. Remove the instrument cluster as outlined in this section.

3. Remove the speedometer retaining screws. Pull the assembly forward in order to disconnect the speedometer cable. To gain slack, it may be necessary to disconnect the cable at the cruise control transducer or the transmission.

4. Remove the speedometer assembly from the vehicle.

5. Installation is the same as the removal procedure.

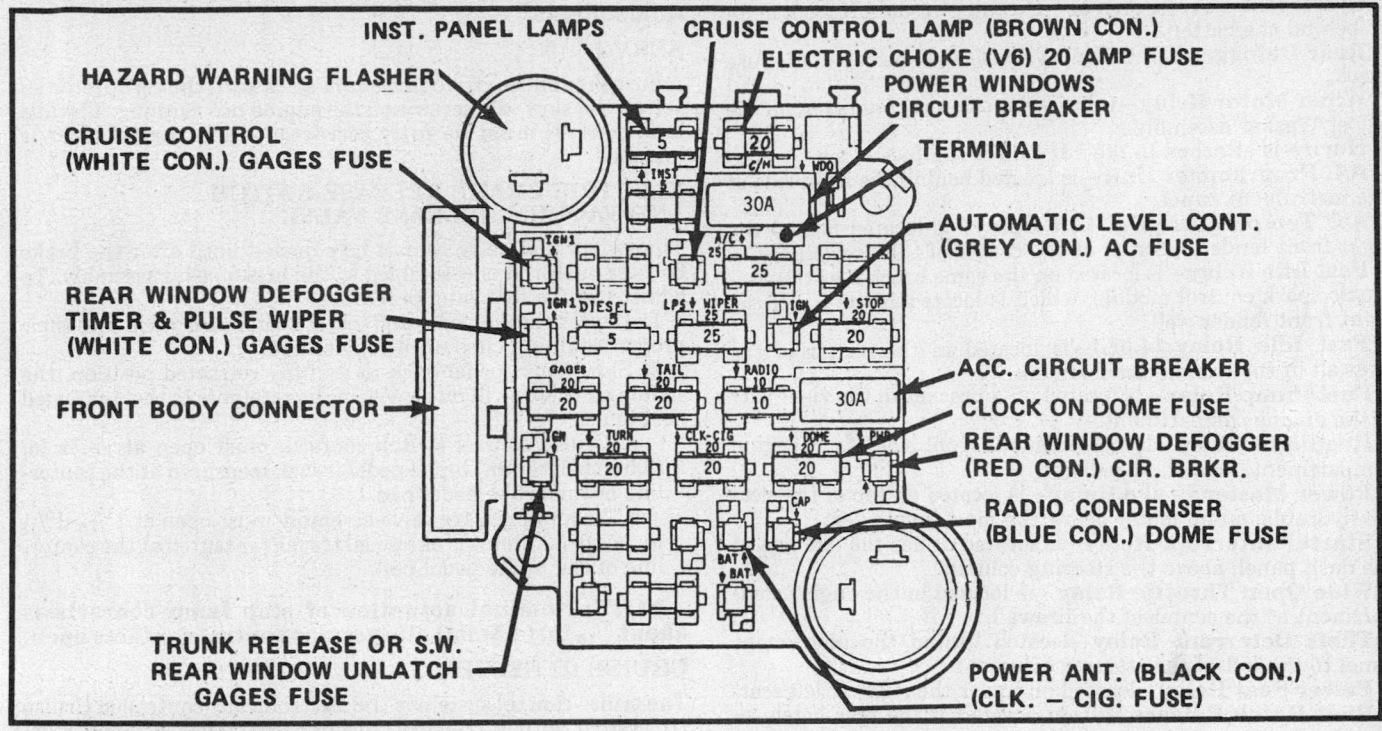

Typical fuse panel layout

ELECTRONIC SPEED SENSOR

1. Disconnect the negative battery cable.
2. Remove the steering column trim plate.
3. Disconnect the lower center air duct from the trim plate.
4. Remove the LH trim plate if equipped.
5. Remove the LH sound insulator.
6. Disconnect the speed sensor from the cluster carrier. Remove the tape securing the speed sensor to the wiring harness.
7. Disconnect the speed sensor connector at the rear of the speedometer.
8. Disconnect the speed sensor connector from the wiring harness.
9. Remove the speed sensor.
10. For installation, reverse the removal procedure.

SPEEDOMETER CABLE

Removal and Installation

1. Disconnect the negative battery cable.
2. Remove instrument cluster.
3. Remove any retainers and clips from cable casing.
4. Remove the casing from the cowl panel.
5. Raise vehicle and support safely.
6. Remove the casing from the transmission.
7. Remove the cable from the casing, clean and lubricate it.
8. Installation is the reverse of the removal procedure.

Electrical Circuit Protectors

FUSIBLE LINKS

Fusible links are used to prevent major wire harness damage in the event of a short circuit or an overload condition in the wiring circuits which are normally not fused, due to carrying high amperage loads or because of their locations within the wiring harness. Each fusible link is of a fixed value for a specific electrical load and should a link fail, the cause of the failure must be determined and repaired prior to installing a new fusible link of the same value.

CIRCUIT BREAKERS

Various circuit breakers are located under the instrument panel. In order to gain access to these components it may be necessary to first remove the under-dash padding.

FUSE PANEL

The fuse panel is located on the left side of the vehicle. It is under the instrument panel assembly. In order to gain access to the fuse panel, it may be necessary to first remove the under-dash padding.

COMPUTER (ECM)

The electronic control module is located in the passenger compartment. It is positioned in front of the right hand kick panel. In order to gain access to the assembly, first remove the trim panel.

VARIOUS RELAYS

A/C Blower—is located in the RH front of the dash, behind the accumulator.

A/C Compressor Control—is located on the RH front of the dash, near the blower motor.

Antenna—is located behind the RH side of the instrument panel compartment.

Choke Heater—is located on the LH front of the dash, beside the brake booster.

Power Door Locks—is located on the lower RH shroud, lower access hole.

Early Fuel Evaporation (EFE)—is located in the RH side of the engine compartment, top of the wheelhouse.

Electronic Level Control—is located on the LH front fender behind the battery.

Rear Defogger Timer Relay—is located on top of the fuse block.

Wiper Motor Relay—is located inside the connector, on the Wiper/Washer assembly.

Horn—is attached to the LH side of the fuse block.

A/C Programmer Unit—is located behind the right side of the instrument panel.

A/C Temperature Cut-Out Relay—is located behind the right front fender apron or at the center of the firewall.

Fast Idle Relay—is located on the same bracket as the electronic spark control module, which is located at the top of the right front fender well.

Fast Idle Relay (4.3L)—is located in the center of the firewall in the engine compartment.

Fuel Pump Relay—is located on a bracket in the right side of the engine compartment.

Headlight Relay—is located at the front side of the engine compartment, near the headlight.

Power Master Brake Relay—is located on top of the electro-hydraulic pump motor below the master cylinder.

Starter Interrupt Relay—is located under the left side of the dash panel, above the steering column.

Wide Open Throttle Relay—is located in the engine compartment at the center of the firewall.

Theft Deterrent Relay—located behind the instrument panel to the left of the steering column.

Power Seat Relay—located on under the right or left seat.

Rear Hatch Release Relay—located at the rear hatch release latch.

TURN SIGNAL FLASHER

The turn signal flasher is located inside the convenience center. In order to gain access to the turn signal flasher it may be necessary to first remove the under dash padding.

HAZARD FLASHER

The hazard flasher is located in the fuse block. It is positioned on the lower right hand corner of the fuse block assembly.

SPEED CONTROLS

Refer to "Chilton's Chassis Electronic Manual" for additional coverage..

Adjustments
SERVO

Adjust the rod length to minimum slack with the carburetor lever on the slow idle screw and the engine not running. The idle load control must be fully retracted when the retainer is installed.

ELECTRIC BRAKE RELEASE SWITCH AND VACUUM RELEASE VALVE

The switch and valve cannot be adjusted until after the brake booster push rod is assembled to the brake pedal assembly. To adjust use the following procedure.

1. Depress brake pedal and insert switch and valve into their proper retaining clips until fully seated.
2. Slowly pull pedal back to its fully retracted position, the switch and valve will move within the retainers to their adjusted position.

   a. Cruise control switch contacts must open at $\frac{1}{8}$–$\frac{1}{2}$ in. (3.5mm–12.5mm) brake pedal travel, measured at the centerline of the brake pedal pad.

   b. Vacuum release valve assembly must open at $1\frac{1}{16}$–$1\frac{5}{16}$ in. (27.0–33.0mm) brake pedal travel, measured at the centerline of the brake pedal pad.

NOTE: Nominal actuation of stop lamp contacts is about $\frac{3}{16}$ in. (4.5mm) after cruise control contacts open.

CRUISE III SYSTEM

The cruise control system is the electronically controlled Cruise III system with a memory. Vacuum controlled valving is retained to operate the throttle servo unit, since Cruise III can effectively operate at the lower manifold vacuum levels on the more fuel efficient engines.

Cruise III operates in any of the following modes:
1. Steady-state cruise—**COAST**.
2. Accelerate—**TAP UP**.
3. Decelerate—**TAP DOWN**.

The driver can disengage the cruise control system by braking the vehicle and resume a pre-set speed merely by moving the 3 position slide switch on the multi-function lever to the **RESUME** position. Steep grades, up or down however, may cause variations between the selected and actual vehicle speeds.

In addition to the multi-function switch on the steering column, the Cruise III Speed Control System includes:
1. An electronic control module (controller)
2. A two-valve (vent and vacuum) servo unit containing 2 solenoids

TEST		NORMAL REACTION
1	Apply 12 volts dc to servo pins A and E. Then ground servo pin C. NOTE: Pin A to pin C closes the normally-open vent valve; whereas, pin E to pin C opens the normally-closed vacuum valve.	Servo should full stroke. If not, check vacuum hoses to the vacuum supply.
2	Remove the 12 volts dc source voltage from SERVO pin E.	The servo should hold a full stroke. If not, go to step 3. If servo holds, go to step 4.
3	Disconnect vacuum brake release at servo and plug vacuum release port on the servo. Momentarily apply 12 volts dc to pin E to allow servo to full stroke.	If the servo holds its position, adjust the brake vacuum release valve or replace the valve.
4	Turn ignition "ON".	Vacuum release valve should engage.
5	Turn ignition "OFF" and disconnect vacuum valve harness connector at valve. Then turn ignition "ON".	If the brake switch is properly adjusted, battery voltage should be present across the two connector terminals on the switch. No battery voltage indicates an open circuit.

Cruise III system vacuum servo tests

CRUISE III SYSTEM ELECTRICAL TESTS
Connect: Volt-Ohmmeter; At: Cruise Control Module (Disconnected); Conditions: Ignition Switch—RUN

Test	Action	Using a Digital Meter		
		Meter Range	Connector Terminals	Correct Response
1	Cruise switch OFF	200 VDC	B & J	Battery voltage
		200 VDC	A & J	0 volts
		200 VDC	M & J	0 volts
2	Cruise switch ON	200 VDC	A & J	Battery voltage
		200 VDC	G & J	Battery voltage
		200 ohms	C & J	30 to 55 ohms
		200 ohms	K & J	30 to 55 ohms
		200 ohms	F & H	15 to 25 ohms
		200 VDC	M & J	0 volts
		200 VDC	L & J	0 volts
3	Cruise switch ON, Set switch pressed	200 VDC	L & J	Battery voltage
		200 ohms	K & J	30 to 55 ohms
4	Cruise switch in R/A	200 VDC	A & J	Battery voltage
		200 VDC	M & J	Battery voltage
		200 ohms	C & J	30 to 55 ohms
5	Cruise switch ON, Drive wheel turned by hand	200 VDC	A & D	Pulses between approx. battery voltage and less than 7 volts
6	Run engine for one minute, then turn it off. With ignition switch in RUN and holding Cruise switch in R/A, press and release Set switch	Connect fused jumper from C to M and from K to L before operating switches		Vacuum holds the servo at wide open throttle position
		200 ohms	F & J	Over range
		200 ohms	F & H	15 to 25 ohms

3. An electrical switch and a vacuum release valve
4. A vacuum supply
5. A speed sensing system
6. Electrical and vacuum harness

The servo unit maintains a desired vehicle speed by trapping vacuum in the servo unit at the proper servo-throttle position. The controller: (1) monitors vehicle speed and servo position and (2) operates the vacuum and vent valves in the servo to maintain desired speed. The controller has a low speed control limit which prevents system engagement below a 25 mph minimum speed. An electrical release switch disengages the cruise system; on vehicles equipped with automatic transmission the switch is mounted on the brake pedal bracket.

A vacuum release valve, also mounted on the brake pedal bracket, vents vacuum trapped in the servo to the atmosphere when the brake pedal is depressed and allows the throttle to return quickly to the idle position.

NOTE: Special testing tools are available to test the electronic circuits.

COOLING AND HEATING SYSTEMS

Water Pump

Removal and Installation

1. Disconnect the negative battery cable.
2. Drain the cooling system.
3. Unfasten the heater, bypass, and lower radiator hoses from the pump.
4. Loosen the drive belts and remove the fan assembly and the spacer bolts. On vehicles with A/C, remove the fan and clutch assembly.

NOTE: Keep the fan in an upright position during removal to prevent the silicone fluid from leaking out of the fan clutch.

5. Remove the alternator, A/C compressor and power steering brackets, if so equipped.

6. Unfasten the bolts which secure the water pump and remove it.
7. Clean all gasket mating surfaces and use a new gasket.
8. Installation is the reverse of the removal procedure.

Electric Cooling Fan

SYSTEM OPERATION

On the 3.8L turbocharged engine, 2 electric cooling fans are used. The fans are energized through a low speed, high speed and delay relay. Power to the fan motors comes from the fusible link to terminal 1 on all relays. The relays are energized when the current flows to ground, through the activation of the A/C coolant switches and/or ECM.

The low speed relay is energized by the ECM or A/C pressure

switch. The ECM energizes the relay through terminal D2 when the coolant temperature reaches 208°F and the vehicle speed is less than 45 mph. The relay can also be energized by the A/C pressure switch when the refrigerant pressure reaches 150 psi.

The high speed relay is energized by the A/C high pressure switch and coolant temperature override switch. If the A/C pressure reaches 27 psi or the coolant temperature reaches 226°F, the relay will be energized.

The delay relay is energized by the temperature switch. When the coolant temperature reaches 226°F or above and the ignition switch is turned OFF, the delay relay is energized for 10 minutes, or until the coolant temperature is below 226°F.

Removal and Installation

----------- CAUTION -----------
Always keep hands and tools away from the fan motors, even when the engine is not running. The fan motors will run at any time the coolant temperature is at 226°F and may cause injury. Always disconnect the negative battery cable before servicing the fan motors.

1. Disconnect the negative battery cable.
2. Disconnect the fan motor wiring.
3. Remove the fan and mounting bracket from the radiator supports.
4. Remove the motor from the mounting bracket and transfer the fan from the old motor to the new motor.
5. Installation is the reverse of the removal procedure.

Testing

NOTE: When testing the cooling fan system, refer to the schematic for test numbers.

1. Grounding of the diagnostic test terminal should cause the ECM to ground CKT 535 and the cooling fan should run in low speed.
2. Grounding the temperature switch harness will check CKT 335 and the high speed relay.
3. Check CKT 533 between the high speed relay terminal 4 and the fan motor. If the fan does not run, CKT 533 is open or the motor is faulty.
4. When the ignition switch is off, with the temperature switch grounded, the delay relay is activated. This will cause the fan to turn on for up to 10 minutes after the engine is off, depending on the coolant temperature.
5. Connect a set of A/C gauges to the system and start the engine. The low speed fan should operate when the high side pressure reaches 260 psi and the high speed fan should operate when the pressure reaches 300 psi.

Blower Motor

Removal and Installation

1. Disconnect the battery ground.
2. Disconnect the blower wiring.
3. Unbolt and remove the motor.
4. Installation is the reverse of removal. Replace any damaged sealer.

Heater Core

Refer to "Chilton's Heating and Air Conditioning Manual" for additional coverage.

Removal and Installation

1. Disconnect the battery ground. Drain the radiator.
2. Disconnect the blower wiring.
3. Remove the thermostatic switch and diagnostic connector.
4. Remove the right end of the hood seal and the air inlet screen screws.

5. Remove the case to firewall screws at the top, upper case to lower case screws at the flange and 2 more at the plenum.
6. Lift the upper case straight up and off.
7. Remove the pipe bracket screws from the case.
8. Disconnect the hoses and position them to prevent spillage.
9. Disconnect and lift out the heater core.
10. Installation is the reverse of removal.
11. Replace any damaged sealer.

TEMPERATURE CONTROL/BLOWER SWITCH

NOTE: If the vehicle is equipped with touch climate control air conditioning, extreme care should be used when disconnecting the electrical connections from the unit to avoid possible damage to the circuit board.

Removal and Installation

The removal and installation of the dash mounted temperature control unit is general in all vehicles. The outlined steps may not be in the correct order for specific model. Rearrange and delete the steps to suit the vehicle being repaired.

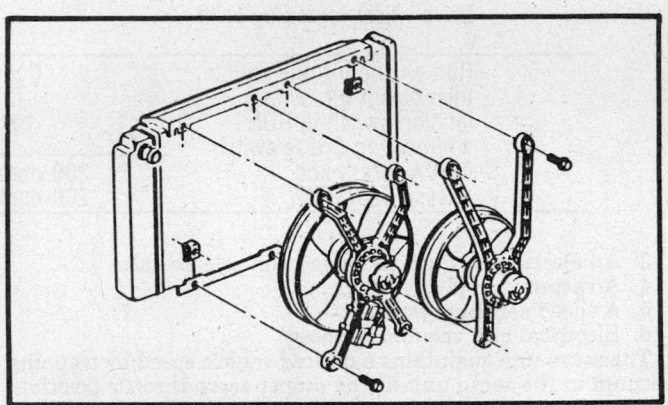

Electric cooling fan mounting

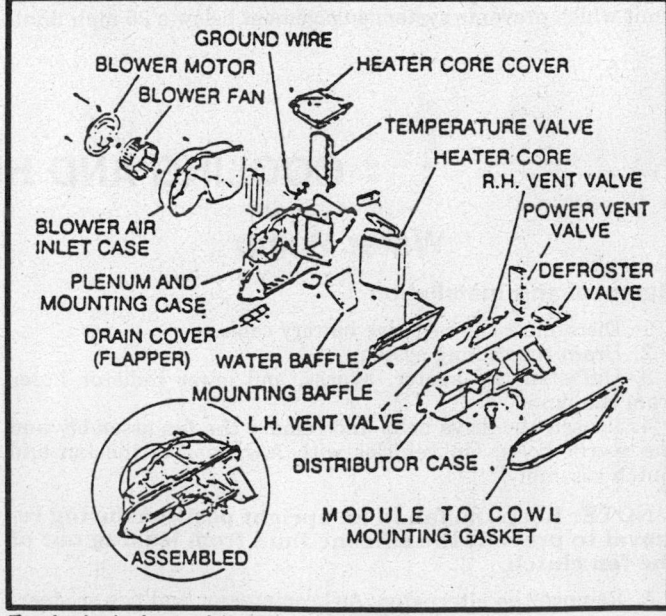

GROUND WIRE
BLOWER MOTOR
BLOWER FAN
HEATER CORE COVER
TEMPERATURE VALVE
HEATER CORE
R.H. VENT VALVE
POWER VENT VALVE
DEFROSTER VALVE
BLOWER AIR INLET CASE
PLENUM AND MOUNTING CASE
DRAIN COVER (FLAPPER)
WATER BAFFLE
MOUNTING BAFFLE
L.H. VENT VALVE
DISTRIBUTOR CASE
MODULE TO COWL MOUNTING GASKET
ASSEMBLED

Exploded view of heater assembly

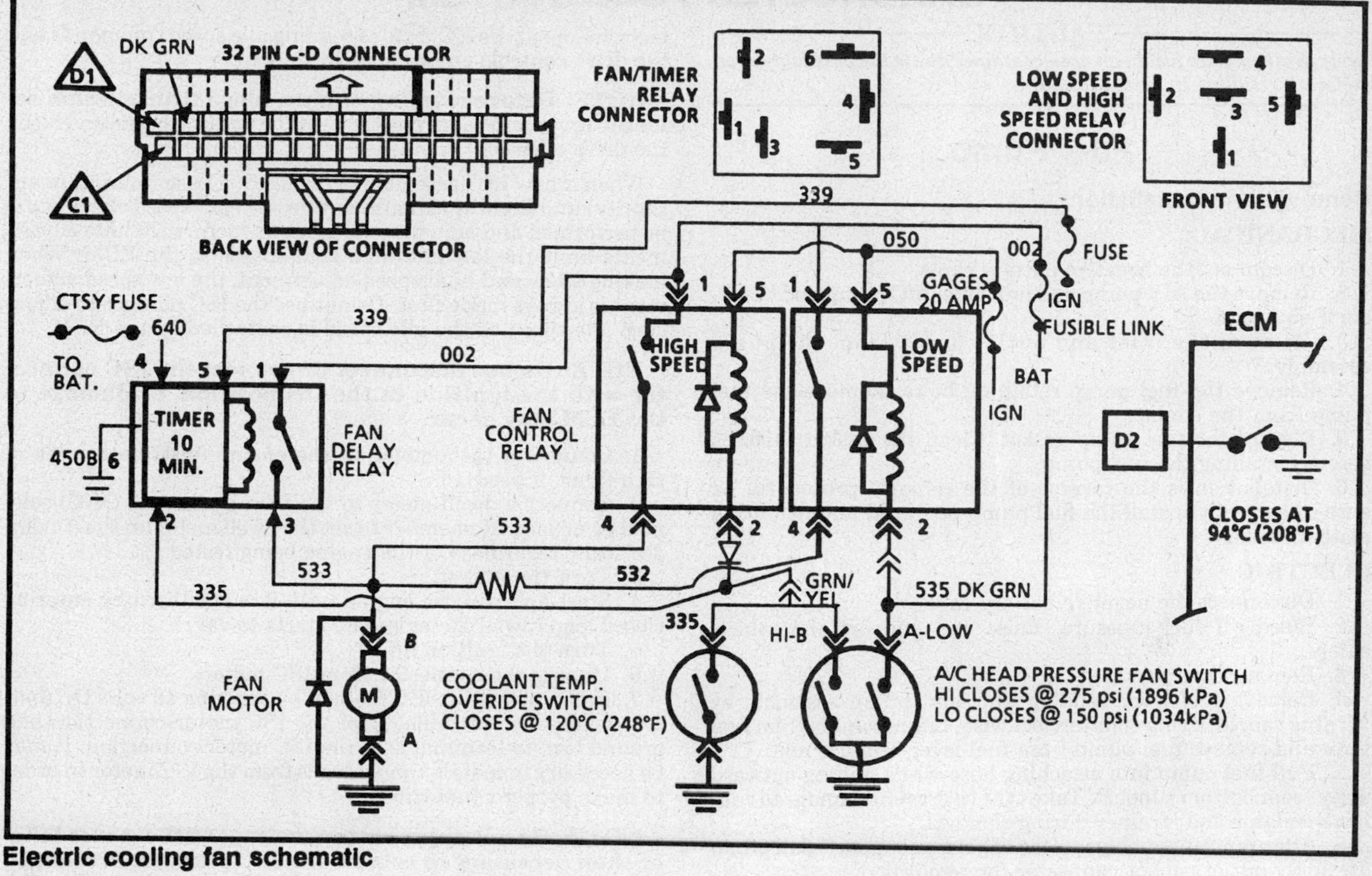

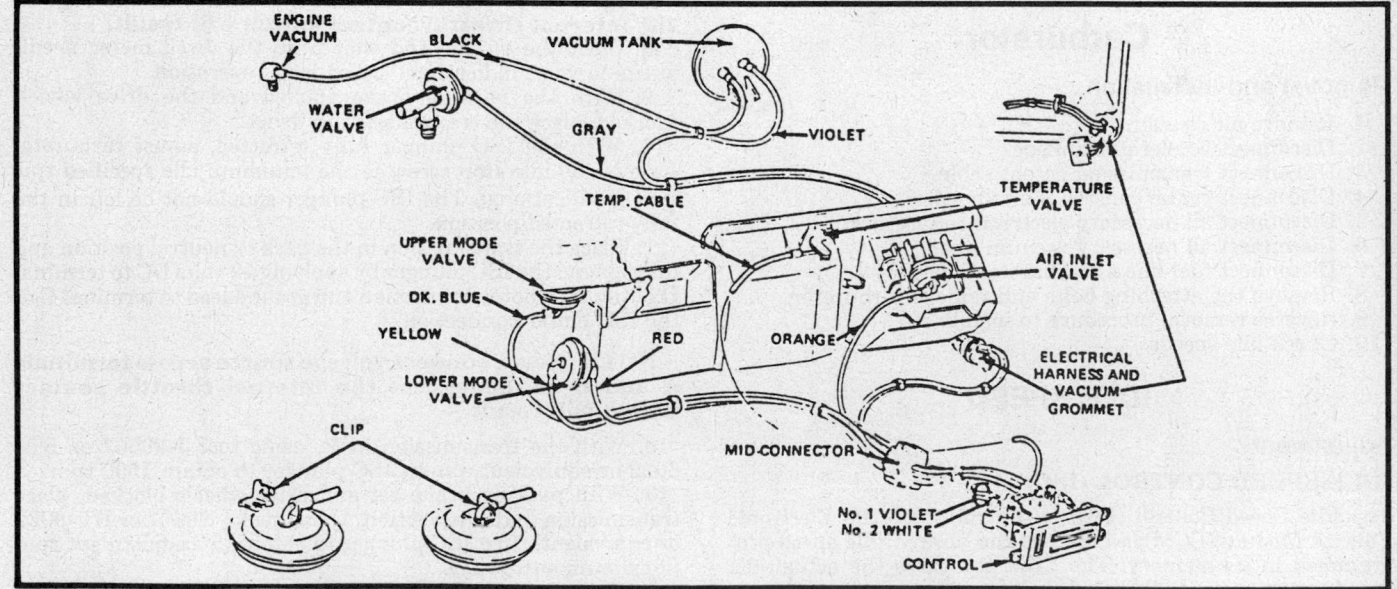

Electric cooling fan schematic

Heater and A/C vacuum control hoses

1. Disconnect the negative battery cable.
2. Remove the necessary instrument panel trim.
3. Remove the radio and/or knobs, radio speaker, ash tray, cigar lighter and the floor console trim plate (if equipped).
4. After exposing the control retaining screws, remove them and pull the control away from the dash. Disconnect the bowden

cable, electrical and vacuum connections. To ensure proper installation, identify each electrical and vacuum as they are removed.
5. Remove the control unit.
6. The installation of the control is the reverse of the removal procedure.

CARBRUETED FUEL SYSTEM

CAUTION

Never drain or store fuel in an open container due to the possibility of an explosion resulting in personal injury.

Fuel Pump

Removal and Installation

MECHANICAL

1. Disconnect the negative battery cable.
2. Remove the AIR pump and brackets, A/C pump and brackets if equipped.
3. Remove the inlet and outlet hoses from the pump assembly.
4. Remove the fuel pump retaining bolts. Remove the fuel pump from the engine.
5. Discard the fuel pump gasket. Clean the gasket surfaces before installing the fuel pump.
6. Installation is the reverse of the removal procedure. Be sure to correctly install the fuel pump push rod and mounting plate, if used.

ELECTRIC

1. Disconnect the negative battery cable.
2. Bleed off fuel pressure. Raise and support the vehicle safely.
3. Remove the fuel tank.
4. Remove fuel lever sending unit and pump assembly by turning cam lock ring counterclockwise. Lift assembly from fuel tank and remove fuel pump from fuel lever sending unit.
5. Pull fuel pump into attaching hose while pulling outward away from bottom support. Take care to prevent damage to rubber insulator and strainer during removal.
6. After pump assembly is clear of bottom support, pull pump assembly out of rubber connector for removal.
7. To install the fuel pump, reverse the removal procedure.

Carburetor

Removal and Installation

1. Remove air cleaner.
2. Disconnect accelerator linkage.
3. Disconnect transmission detent cable.
4. Disconnect cruise control, if equipped.
5. Disconnect all necessary electrical connectors.
6. Disconnect all necessary vacuum lines.
7. Disconnect fuel line at carburetor inlet.
8. Remove the attaching bolts and remove carburetor.
9. Reverse removal procedure to install.
10. Check idle speeds.

IDLE SPEED

Adjustment

IDLE SPEED CONTROL (ISC)

The Idle Speed Control (ISC) is controlled by the Electronic Control Module (ECM), which has the desired idle speed programmed in its memory. The ECM compares the actual idle speed to the desired idle speed and the plunger is moved in or out. This automatically adjusts the throttle to hold an idle rpm independent of the engine loads.

An integral part of the ISC is the throttle contact switch. The position of the switch determines whether or not the ISC should control idle speed. When the throttle lever is resting against the ISC plunger, the switch contacts are closed, at which time the ECM moves the ISC to the programmed idle speed. When the throttle lever is not contacting the ISC plunger, the switch contacts are open; the ECM stops sending idle speed commands and the drive controls engine speed.

NOTE: Before starting engine, place transmission selector lever in P or N position, set the parking brake and block the drive wheels.

When a new ISC assembly is installed, a base (minimum authority) and high (maximum authority) rpm speed check must be performed and adjustments made as required. These adjustments limit the low and high rpm speeds to the ECM. When making a low and high speed adjustment, the low speed adjustment is always made first. Do not use the ISC plunger to adjust curb idle speed as the idle speed is controlled by the ECM.

NOTE: Do not disconnect or connect the ISC connector with the ignition in the ON position, or damage to the ECM may occur.

1. Connect a tachometer to the engine (distributor side of tach filter, if used).
2. Connect a dwell meter to the mixture control (M/C) solenoid dwell lead. Remember to set the dwell meter on the 6 cylinder scale, regardless of the engine being tested.
3. Turn the A/C off.
4. Start and run the engine until it is stabilized by entering closed loop (dwell meter needle starts to vary).
5. Turn the ignition off.
6. Unplug the connector from ISC motor.
7. Fully retract the ISC plunger by applying 12 volts DC (battery voltage) to terminal **C** of the ISC motor connection and ground lead to terminal **D** of the ISC motor connection. It may be necessary to install jumper leads from the ISC motor in order to make proper connections.

NOTE: Do not apply battery voltage to the motor longer than necessary to retract the ISC plunger. Prolonged contact will damage the motor. Also, never connect a voltage source across terminals A and B or damage to the internal throttle contact switch will result.

8. Start the engine and wait until the dwell meter needle starts to vary, indicating "closed loop" operation.
9. With the parking brake applied and the drive wheels blocked, place the transmission in drive.
10. With the ISC plunger fully retracted, adjust carburetor base (slow) idle stop screw to the minimum idle specified rpm (see specifications). The ISC plunger should not be left in the fully retracted position.
11. Place the transmission in the park or neutral position and fully extend the ISC plunger by applying 12 volts DC to terminal **D** of the ISC motor connection and ground lead to terminal **C** of the ISC motor connection.

NOTE: Never connect voltage source across terminals A and B as damage to the internal throttle contact switch will result.

12. With the transmission in **P**, using tool J–29607 or BT–8022 or equivalent, preset ISC plunger to obtain 1500 rpm.
13. With parking brake set and drive wheels blocked, place transmission in drive position. Using tool J–29607 or BT–8022 or equivalent, turn ISC plunger to obtain ISC adjustment rpm (maximum authority).
14. Recheck ISC adjustment rpm with voltage applied to motor. Motor will ratchet at full extension with power applied.
15. Fully retract ISC plunger. Place transmission in **P** or **N** position and turn ignition in **OFF** position. Disconnect 12 volt power source, ground lead, tachometer and dwell meter. With ignition in **OFF** position, reconnect 4 terminal harness connector to ISC motor. To prevent internal damage to ISC, apply finger pressure to ISC plunger while retracting.
16. Remove block from drive wheels.

ISC CONTROL PLUNGER ADJUSTMENT CHART

Plunger Identification	Plunger Length Dimension "A"	Dimension "B" Must Not Exceed
None	9/16 inch	7/32 inch
None	41/64 inch	5/16 inch
X	47/64 inch	25/64 inch
A	49/64 inch	27/64 inch
Y	51/64 inch	15/32 inch
S	27/32 inch	1/2 inch
Z	7/8 inch	35/64 inch
G	29/32 inch	37/64 inch
E	1 inch	43/64 inch
L	13/32 inch	3/4 inch
J	13/16 inch	27/32 inch
N	1 17/64 inch	59/64 inch
T	1 11/32 inch	1 inch

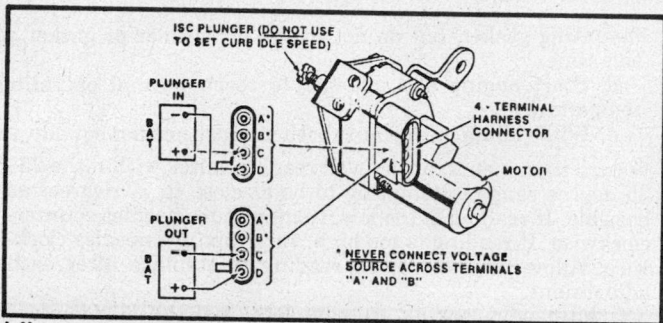

Idle speed control check ISC

IDLE AIR BLEED VALVE

1. Position the parking brake and block the drive wheels. Disconnect and plug the hoses as directed on the vehicle emission control label.

2. Check and adjust ignition timing. Connect a dwell meter to the carburetor mixture solenoid and a tachometer to the engine's distributor electrical system.

3. Start engine and with transmission in **P**, run engine at idle until fully warm and a varying dwell is noted on the dwell meter (engine now in closed loop operation). It is essential that the engine is operated for a sufficient length of time to ensure that the engine coolant sensor and the oxygen sensor in the exhaust, are at full operational temperature.

4. Check engine idle speed and compare to specifications on the underhood Emission Label. If necessary, adjust curb idle speed. On models with Idle Speed Control (ISC) or Idle Load Compensator (ILC), idle speeds are controlled by signals from the computer.

5. With engine idling in **D**, observe dwell reading on the 6 cylinder scale. If varying within the 10–50 degree range, adjustment is correct. If not, perform the following.

6. Remove the idle air bleed valve cover. If the cover is staked in place, pry it off using a suitable tool.

7. If the cover is riveted, cover the internal bowl vents to the bleed valve with masking tape.

8. Cover carburetor air intakes with masking tape to prevent metal chips from entering carburetor and engine.

9. Carefully align a No. 35 (0.110 in.) drill bit on a steel rivet head holding the idle air bleed valve cover in place. Drill only enough to remove rivet head. Drill the remaining rivet head located on the other side of the tower. Use a drift and small hammer to drive the remainder of the rivets out of the idle air bleed

valve tower in the air horn casting. Use care in drilling to prevent damage to the air horn casting.

10. Lift out cover over the idle air bleed valve and remove the rivet pieces from inside the idle air bleed valve tower.

11. Using shop air, carefully blow out any remaining chips from inside the tower. Discard cover after removal. A missing cover indicates that the idle air bleed valve setting has been changed from its original factory setting.

12. With cover removed, look for presence (or absence) of a letter identification on top of idle air bleed valve.

13. If an identifying letter appears on top of the valve proceed to the procedure outlined under Type 2. If an identifying letter does not appear on the top of the valve proceed to the procedure outlined under Type 1.

Type 1

1. Presetting the idle air bleed valve to a gauge dimension if the idle air bleed valve was serviced prior to on-vehicle adjustment.

   a. Install idle air bleed valve gauging tool J-33815-2, BT-8253-B, or equivalent, in throttle side D–shaped vent hole in the air horn casting. The upper end of the tool should be positioned over the open cavity next to the idle air bleed valve.

   b. While holding the gauging tool down lightly, so that the solenoid plunger is against the solenoid stop, adjust the idle air bleed valve so that the gauging tool will pivot over and just contact the top of the valve. The valve is now preset for on-vehicle adjustment.

   c. Remove the gauging tool.

2. Adjusting the idle air bleed valve on the vehicle to obtain correct dwell reading.

   a. Start engine and allow it to reach normal operating temperature.

   b. While idling in drive, use a suitable tool to slowly turn valve counterclockwise or clockwise, until the dwell reading varies within the 25–35 degree range, attempting to be as close to 30 degrees as possible. Perform this Step carefully. The air bleed valve is very sensitive and should be turned in 1/8 turn increments only.

   c. If, after performing Steps a and b above, the dwell reading does not vary and is not within the 25–35 degree range, it will be necessary to remove the plugs and to adjust the idle mixture needles.

3. Idle mixture needle plug removal, only if necessary.

   a. Remove the carburetor from the engine, following normal service procedures, to gain access to the plugs covering the idle mixture needles.

   b. Invert carburetor and drain fuel into a suitable container.

c. Place carburetor on a suitable holding fixture, with manifold side up. Use care to avoid damaging linkage, tubes, and parts protruding from air horn.

d. Make 2 parallel cuts in the throttle body, on each side of the locator points beneath the idle mixture needle plug (manifold side), with a hacksaw.

e. The cuts should reach down to the steel plug, but should not extend more than ⅛ in. beyond the locator points. The distance between the saw cuts depends on the size of the punch to be used.

f. Place a flat punch near the ends of the saw marks in the throttle body. Hold the punch at a 45 degrees angle and drive it into the throttle body until the casting breaks away, exposing the steel plug.

g. The hardened plug will break, rather than remaining intact. It is not necessary to remove the plug as a whole, but remove the loose pieces.

h. Repeat this procedure with the other mixture needle.

4. Setting the idle mixture needles (if necessary) where correct dwell reading could not be obtained with the idle air bleed valve adjustment.

a. Using tool J–29030, BT–7610B or equivalent, turn both idle mixture needles clockwise until they are lightly seated, then turn each mixture needle counterclockwise the number of turns specified.

b. Reinstall carburetor on engine using a new flange mounting gasket, but do not install air cleaner and gasket at this time.

5. Readjusting idle air bleed valve to finalize correct dwell reading. The following is necessary if idle mixture needles required setting in Step 4, above.

a. Start engine and run until fully warm, and repeat Step 2, above.

b. If unable to set dwell to 25–35 degrees, and the dwell is below 25 degrees, turn both mixture needles counterclockwise an additional turn. If dwell is above 35 degrees, turn both mixture needles clockwise an additional turn. Readjust idle air bleed valve to obtain dwell limits.

c. After adjustments are complete, seal the idle mixture needle openings in the throttle body, using silicone sealant, RTV rubber, or equivalent. The sealer is required to discourage unnecessary adjustment of the setting, and to prevent fuel vapor loss in that area.

d. On vehicles without a carburetor-mounted idle speed control or idle load compensator, adjust curb idle speed if necessary.

e. Check and only if necessary adjust, fast idle speed as described on emission control information label.

Type 2

1. Setting the idle air bleed valve to a gauge dimension;

a. Install air bleed valve, gauging tool J–33815–2, BT–8253–B, or equivalent, in throttle side **D** shaped vent hole in the air horn casting. The upper end of the tool should be positioned over the open cavity next to the idle air bleed valve.

b. While holding the gauging tool down lightly, so that the solenoid plunger is against the solenoid stop, adjust the idle air bleed valve so that the gauging tool will pivot over and just contact the top of the valve.

c. The valve is now set properly. No further adjustment of the valve is necessary.

d. Remove gauging tool.

2. Adjusting the idle mixture needles on the vehicle to obtain correct dwell readings.

a. Remove idle mixture needle plugs, following instructions in the information given for type one.

b. Using tool J–29030–B, BT–7610–B, or equivalent, turn each idle mixture needle clockwise until lightly seated, then turn each mixture needle counterclockwise 3 turns.

c. Reinstall carburetor on engine, using a new flange

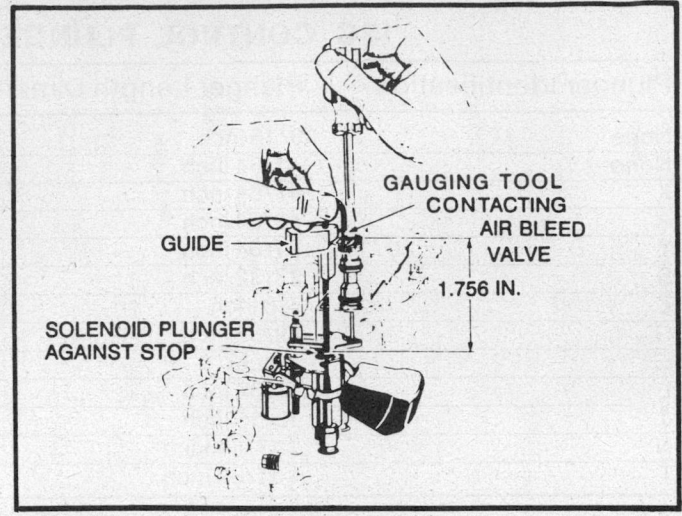

Adjusting air bleed valve assembly

mounting gasket, but do not install air cleaner or gasket at this time.

d. Start engine and allow it to reach normal operating temperature.

e. While idling in **D**, adjust both mixture needles equally, in ⅛ turn increments, until dwell reading varies within the 25–35 degree range, attempting to be as close to 30 degrees as possible. If reading is too low, turn mixture needles counterclockwise. If reading is too high, turn mixture needles clockwise. Allow time for dwell reading to stabilize after each adjustment.

f. After adjustments are complete, seal the idle mixture needle openings in the throttle body, using silicone sealant, RTV rubber, or equivalent. The sealer is required to discourage unnecessary readjustment of the setting, and to prevent fuel vapor loss in that area.

g. On vehicles without a carburetor-mounted idle speed control or idle load compensator, adjust curb idle speed if necessary.

h. Check, and if necessary, adjust fast idle speed, as described on the emission control information label.

IDLE LOAD COMPENSATOR (ILC)

1. Prepare vehicle for adjustments—see Vehicle Emission Information Label.

2. Connect tachometer (distributor side of tach filter, if used).

3. Remove air cleaner and plug vacuum hose to Thermal Vacuum Valve (TVV).

4. Disconnect and plug vacuum hose to EGR.

5. Disconnect and plug vacuum hose to canister purge port.

6. Disconnect and plug vacuum hose to ILC.

7. Back out idle stop screw on carburetor 3 turns.

8. Turn A/C to **OFF** position.

NOTE: Before starting engine, place transmission in P, set parking brake and block drive wheels.

9. With engine running (engine warm, choke off), transmission in drive and ILC plunger fully extended (no vacuum applied), using tool J–29607, BT–8022, or equivalent, adjust plunger to obtain 750 rpm on E2MC carburetor models, 725 rpm on E4MC carburetor models. Jam nut on plunger must be held with wrench to prevent damage to guide tabs when tightening.

10. Remove plug from vacuum hose, reconnect hose to ILC and observe idle speed. Idle speed should be 500 rpm in drive.

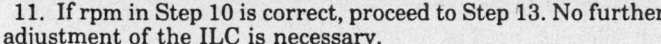

11. If rpm in Step 10 is correct, proceed to Step 13. No further adjustment of the ILC is necessary.

12. If rpm in Step 10 is not correct:

a. Stop engine and remove the ILC. Plug vacuum hose to ILC.

b. With the ILC removed, remove the rubber cap from the center outlet tube and then remove the metal plug if used from this same tube.

c. Install ILC on carburetor and re-attach throttle return spring and any other related parts removed during disassembly. Remove plug from vacuum hose and reconnect hose to ILC.

d. Using a spare rubber cap with hole punched to accept a 0.090 in. ($^3/_{32}$ in.) hex key wrench, install cap on center outlet tube (to seal against vacuum loss) and insert wrench through cap to engage adjusting screw inside tube. Start engine and turn adjusting screw with wrench to obtain 550 rpm in drive. Turning the adjusting screw will change the idle speed approximately 75–100 rpm for each complete turn. Turning the screw counterclockwise will increase the engine speed.

e. Remove wrench and cap (with hole) from center outlet tube and install new rubber cap.

f. Engine running, transmission in drive, observe idle speed. If a final adjustment is required, it will be necessary to repeat Steps 12a through 12e.

13. After adjustment of the ILC plunger, measure distance from the jam nut to tip of the plunger, dimension must not exceed 1.000 in. (25mm).

14. Disconnect and plug vacuum hose to ILC. Apply vacuum source, such as hand vacuum pump J–23768, BT–7517 or equivalent, to ILC vacuum inlet tube to fully retract the plunger.

15. Adjust the idle stop on the carburetor float bowl to obtain 500 rpm in drive.

16. Place transmission in **P** and stop engine.

17. Remove plug from vacuum hose and install hose on ILC vacuum inlet tube.

18. Remove plugs and reconnect all vacuum hoses.

19. Install air cleaner and gasket.

20. Remove block from drive wheels.

THROTTLE POSITION SENSOR (TPS)

NOTE: The plug covering the TPS adjustment screw is used to provide a tamper resistant design and retain the factory setting during vehicle operation. Do not remove the plug unless diagnosis indicates that the TPS sensor is not adjusted correctly or it is necessary to replace the air horn assembly, float bowl, TPS sensor to TPS adjustment screw. This is a critical adjustment that must be performed accurately and carefully to ensure proper vehicle performance and control of exhaust emissions.

1. If necessary to adjust the TPS sensor:

a. Using a $^5/_{64}$ in. (2mm) drill, drill hole in aluminum plug covering TPS adjustment screw, drilling only enough to start self-tapping screw.

b. Use care in drilling to prevent damage to adjustment screw head.

c. Start a No. 8, ½ in. long self-tapping screw in drilled hole in plug, turning screw in only enough to ensure good thread engagement in hole.

d. Using a suitable tool placed between the screw head and air horn casting, pry against screw head to remove plug. Discard plug.

e. Using tool J–28696, BT–7967A or equivalent, remove screw.

f. Connect digital voltmeter (such as J–29125) or equivalent from TPS connector center terminal (B) to bottom terminal (C). (Jumpers for access can be made using terminals 12014836 and 12014837).

g. With ignition on, engine stopped, reinstall TPS adjustment screw and with tool J–28696, BT7967A, or equivalent turn screw to obtain specified voltage at specified throttle position with A/C off.

h. After adjustment, install new plug (supplied in service kits) in air horn, driving plug in place until flush with raised pump lever boss on casting.

2. Remove ECM fuse from fuse block to clear any stored trouble codes.

NOTE: After TPS screw is adjusted, a new plug should be installed. If a new plug is not available, a locking type of sealer should be placed on the screw threads to prevent movement of the screw after installation.

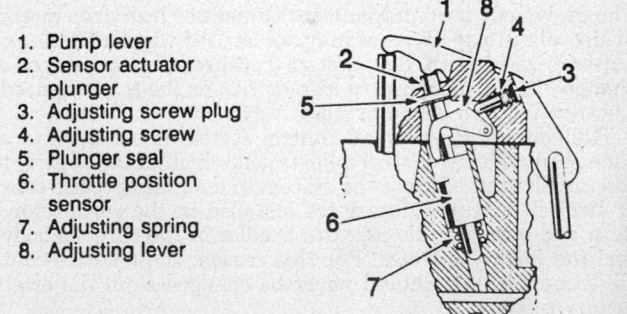

1. Pump lever
2. Sensor actuator plunger
3. Adjusting screw plug
4. Adjusting screw
5. Plunger seal
6. Throttle position sensor
7. Adjusting spring
8. Adjusting lever

Cross section of throttle position sensor assembly (TPS)

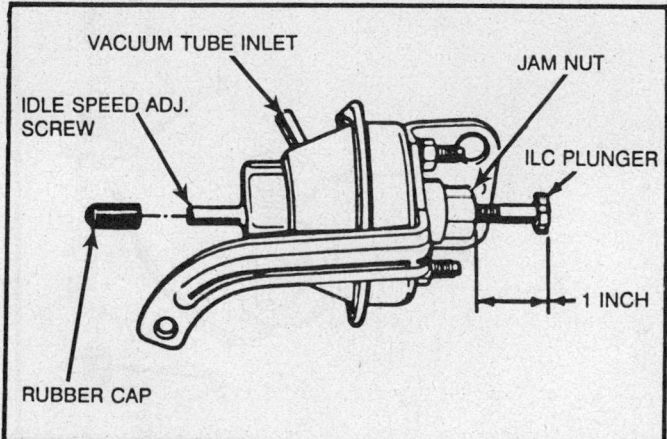

Idle load compensator—307 CID V8

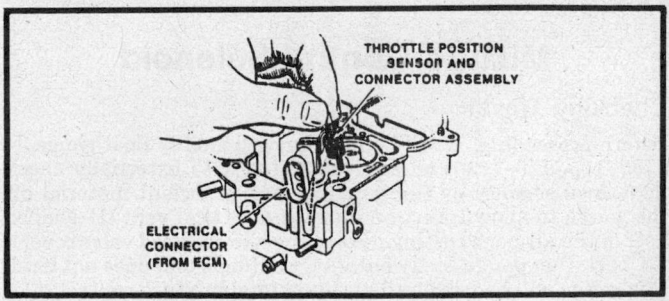

Throttle position sensor connectors

IDLE MIXTURE

Adjustment

1. Run the engine until it reaches normal operating temperature.
2. Check the ignition timing and set to specifications.
3. Remove the factory installed plugs from the mixture screws.

NOTE: Carburetor must be removed from engine to gain access to the idle mixture needle plugs.

4. Using tool J-29030-B, BT-7610-B, or equivalent, turn both mixture needles clockwise until lightly seated.
5. Turn each mixture needle counterclockwise 3 turns.
6. Remove air cleaner. Disconnect vacuum hose to canister purge valve and plug it.
7. Run engine until it reaches normal operating temperature.
8. Block rear wheels and put gear selector in **D**.
9. Adjust both mixture needles equally, in ⅛ turn increments, until dwell reading varies within the 25–35 degree range, as close to 30 degrees as possible.
10. If reading is too high, turn needles clockwise. If reading is too low, turn needles counterclockwise. Install new plugs over mixture needle adjustment holes.
11. Reconnect all lines and make all necessary adjustments.

Computer Command Control System (CCC)

MIXTURE CONTROL

The Computer Command Control System provides precise control of carburetor air/fuel mixtures during all ranges of engine operation. Because of this system control, the below listed mixture control adjustment procedures are to be used if required. The previously used propane enrichment or lean drop methods of idle mixture adjustment may not be used when adjusting carburetors used with this system because system control will change air/fuel mixtures to lean or rich as the mixture needles are adjusted rich or lean respectively.

The computer command control system is sensitive to any change in mixture control adjustment which, if improperly set, can impair the ability of the system to maintain precise control of air/fuel mixtures. Plugs are installed in the carburetor air horn and over the idle mixture needles in the throttle body to seal the factory settings. For this reason, the mixture control adjustment points should never be changed from the original factory setting.

However, if in diagnosis the system indicates the carburetor to be the cause of a driver performance complaint or emissions failure or critical parts such as air horn, float bowl, or throttle body are replaced, then the plugs may be removed and mixture control adjustments made, carefully following factory recommended procedures. After adjustment, replacement plugs (supplied in applicable service kits) must be installed.

Mixture Control Solenoid

Checking Travel

Before proceeding, it will be necessary to modify float gauge J-9789-130, BT-7720, or equivalent (used to externally check float level setting) by filing or grinding sufficient material off the gauge to allow insertion down the vertical vent (D-shaped hole in the air horn casting next to the idle air bleed valve cover).

Check that gauge freely enters D vent hole and does not bind. The gauge will be used to determine total mixture control solenoid travel.

With engine off, air cleaner removed, measure mixture control solenoid travel as follows:

a. Insert modified float gauge down D–shaped vent hole. Press down on gauge and release, observing that gauge moves freely and does not bind. With gauge released (solenoid up position), reading at eye level record mark on gauge (in in.) that lines up with top of air horn casting (upper edge).

b. Then, lightly press down on gauge until bottomed (solenoid down position). Record in in. mark on gauge that lines up with top of air horn casting.

c. Subtract gauge up dimension (item a) from gauge down position (item b) and record difference (in inches). The difference in dimensions is total solenoid travel.

d. If total solenoid travel (difference in item "c") is not within $\frac{2}{32}$–$\frac{6}{32}$ in., make mixture control solenoid adjustments as noted below. If difference is within the above specifications, proceed to idle air bleed valve adjustment.

Adjustment

1. Remove air horn, mixture control solenoid plunger, air horn gasket and plastic filler block, using normal service procedures.
2. Remove throttle side metering rod. Install mixture control solenoid gauging tool J-33815-1 and BT-8253-A, or equivalent over throttle side metering jet rod guide and temporarily reinstall the solenoid plunger into the solenoid body.
3. Holding the solenoid plunger in the down position, use tool J-28696-10 and BT-7928, or equivalent, to turn lean mixture (solenoid) screw counterclockwise until the plunger breaks contact with the gauging tool. Turn slowly clockwise until the plunger just contacts the gauging tool. The adjustment is correct when the solenoid plunger is contacting both the solenoid stop and the gauging tool.

NOTE: If the total difference in adjustment required less than ¾ turn of the lean mixture (solenoid) screw,

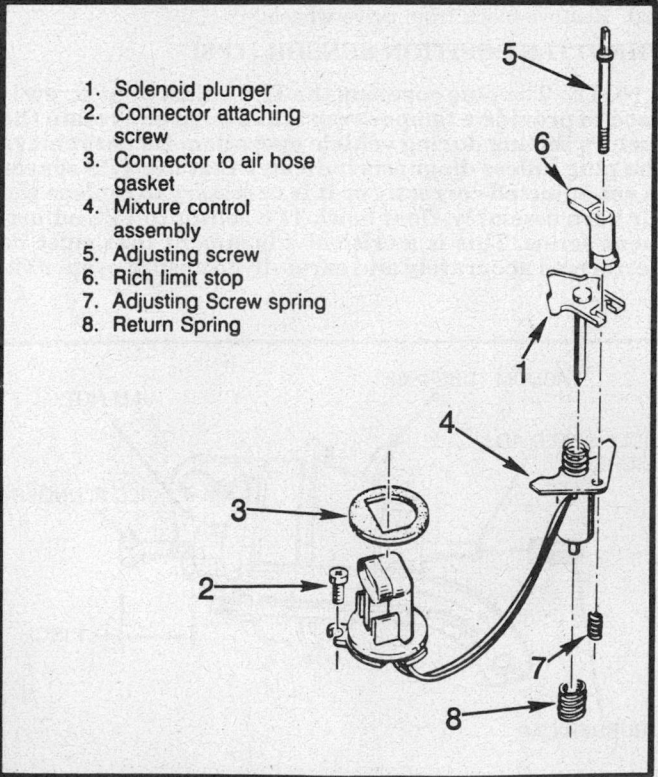

1. Solenoid plunger
2. Connector attaching screw
3. Connector to air hose gasket
4. Mixture control assembly
5. Adjusting screw
6. Rich limit stop
7. Adjusting Screw spring
8. Return Spring

Mixture control solenoid assembly

the original setting was within the manufacturer's specifications.

4. Remove solenoid plunger and gauging tool, and reinstall metering rod and plastic filler block.

5. Invert air horn and remove rich mixture stop screw and (if used) the rich authority adjusting spring from bottom side of air horn, using tool J-28696-4 and BT-7967A or equivalent.

6. Remove lean mixture screw plug and the rich mixture stop screw plug from air horn, using a suitable sized punch.

7. Reinstall rich mixture stop screw and (if used) the rich authority adjusting spring in air horn and bottom lightly, then back screw out ¼ turn.

8. Reinstall air horn gasket, mixture control solenoid plunger and air horn to carburetor.

9. Insert external float gauge in vent hole and, with tool J-28696-10 and BT-7928, or equivalent, adjust rich mixture stop screw to obtain ⅛ in. total plunger travel.

10. With solenoid plunger travel correctly set, install the plugs (supplied in service kits) in the air horn.

11. To install the lean mixture plug, position it hollow end down into the access hole of the lean mixture screw (solenoid), and use a suitably sized punch to drive plug into the air horn until the top of the plug is even with the lower plug.

12. To install the rich mixture stop screw, position it hollow end down, over the rich mixture stop screw access hole, and drive plug into place so that the top of the plug is ⅛ in. below the surface of the air horn casting.

FUEL INJECTION SYSTEM

Refer to "Chilton's Professional Electronic Engine Control Manual" for additional coverage.

Description

Turbocharged 3.8L V6 engines are equipped with Sequential Fuel Injection (SFI). Each fuel injector is opened independently of the others, 1 time for every 2 revolutions of the crankshaft and, prior to the opening of the intake valve for the cylinder to be fired. The Electronic Control Module (ECM) is in complete control of the system during all phases of engine operation.

On the 4.3L V6, 5.0L and 5.7L V8 engines, the EFI system centrally locates a single Model 220 throttle body injection (TBI) unit on the intake manifold where air and fuel are distributed through a single bore in the unit. The air used for combustion is controlled by a single throttle valve which is connected to the accelerator pedal linkage through a throttle shaft and lever assembly. A special plate is located underneath the throttle valve to aid in uniform mixture distribution. Fuel for combustion is supplied by a single fuel injector mounted on the TBI unit. The metering tip of the fuel injector is positioned directly above the throttle valve. The injector metering tip is "pulsed" or "timed" open or closed by an electronic output signal received from the ECM. The ECM receives inputs from the the various engine sensors concerning engine operating conditions (coolant temperature, exhaust gas oxygen content, etc.). The ECM uses this information to calculate the engines fuel requirements by controlling the injector pulse openings to provide an ideal fuel/air mixture ratio.

IDLE SPEED

Adjustment
3.8L ENGINE

NOTE: This adjustment should be performed only when the injection parts have been replaced. Engine must be at normal operating temperature before making an adjustment.

1. With a suitable tool, piece the idle stop screw plug and apply leverage to remove it.

2. Ground diagnostic lead and turn ignition to ON position, with out starting engine, for at least 30 seconds.

3. With the ignition still ON, disconnect Idle Air Control (IAC) electrical connector.

4. Remove the ground from diagnostic lead and start engine.

5. Adjust the idle speed to 500±50 rpm in drive position.

6. Turn the ignition OFF and reconnect connector at IAC motor.

7. Adjust the Throttle Position Sensor (TPS) to 0.36–0.44 volts.

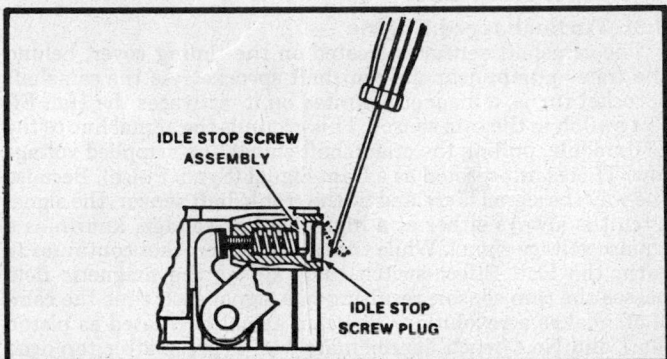

IDLE STOP SCREW ASSEMBLY

IDLE STOP SCREW PLUG

Removal of idle stop screw plug—fuel injection

8. Recheck the setting, start the engine and check for proper idle operation.

EXCEPT 3.8L ENGINE

1. Plug any vacuum ports as required.

2. Remove the idle speed stop screw cover (if installed).

3. Connect a tachometer to the engine.

4. Leaving the IAC valve connected, ground the ALDL diagnostic terminal.

5. Turn the ignition switch to the ON position but do not start the engine. Allow the ignition switch to remain in the ON position (engine off) for a period of 45 seconds. This allows the IAC valve pintle to extend and seat in the valve body.

6. With the ignition switch ON (engine stopped) and the diagnostic terminal grounded, disconnect the IAC valve electrical connector.

7. Remove the diagnostic terminal ground and start the engine. Place the transmission in P and allow the engine rpm to stabilize.

8. The tachometer should read between 400–450 rpm. Adjust the idle stop screw as required until the idle speed is within the specified range.

9. Turn the ignition switch OFF and reconnect the IAC valve connector.

10. Apply a bead of RTV sealant to cover the idle stop screw hole. Unplug and reconnect the vacuum hoses.

FUEL PRESSURE RELIEF

Procedure
3.8L ENGINE

1. Disconnect the fuel tank harness connector.

2. Crank the engine. The engine will start and run until the

fuel supply remaining in the fuel pipes is consumed.

3. Engage the starter for 3 seconds to assure the relief of any remaining pressure.

4. With the ignition **OFF**, connect the fuel tank harness connector.

5. Disconnect the negative battery cable.

EXCEPT 3.8L ENGINE

1. Disconnect the negative battery cable.
2. Loosen the fuel filler cap to relieve tank vapor pressure.

NOTE: The internal constant bleed feature of the TBI models relieves fuel pump system pressure when the engine is turned OFF. Therefore, no further relief procedure is required.

3. Disconnect the negative battery cable.

TIMING SENSORS

CAMSHAFT SENSOR

3.8L Turbocharged Engine

The camshaft sensor is located on the timing cover, behind the water pump, near the camshaft sprocket. As the camshaft sprocket turns, a magnet mounted on it, activates the Hall Effect switch in the cam sensor. This grounds the signal line to the C^3I module, pulling the crankshaft signal line's applied voltage low. This is interpreted as a Cam Signal (Sync. Pulse). Because the way the signal is created by the crankshaft sensor, the signal circuit is always either at a high or a low voltage, known as a square voltage signal. While the camshaft sprocket continues to turn, the Hall Effect switch turns off as the magnetic field passes the cam sensor, resulting in a signal each time the camshaft makes a revolution. The cam signal is created as piston No.1 and No.4 reach approximately 25 degrees after top dead center (ATDC). It is used by the C^3I module to begin the ignition coil firing sequence, starting with the No.3/6 ignition coil because the No.6 piston is now at the correct position in its compression stroke for the spark plug to be fired.

CRANKSHAFT SENSOR

3.8L Turbocharged Engine

A magnetic crankshaft sensor (Hall Effect switch) is used and is mounted in a pedestal on the front of the engine near the harmonic balancer. The sensor is a Hall Effect switch which depends on a metal interrupter ring, mounted on the balancer, to activate it. Windows in the interrupter activates the Hall Effect switch, as they provide a path for the magnetic field between the switch's transducer and magnet.

When the Hall Effect switch is activated, it grounds the signal line to the C^3I module, pulling the crankshaft signal line's applied voltage low, which is interpreted as a crankshaft signal. Because of the way the signal by the crank sensor is created, the signal circuit is always either at a high or low voltage (square wave signal) and 3 signal pulses are created during each crankshaft revolution. This signal is used by the C^3I module to create a reference signal, which is also a "square wave" signal, similar to the crank signal. The reference signal is used to calculate engine rpm and crankshaft position by the ECM. A misadjusted sensor or bent interrupter ring could cause rubbing of the sensor, resulting in potential driveability problems, such as rough idle, poor engine performance, or a no-start condition.

NOTE: Failure to have the correct clearance between the sensor and the interrupter ring could damage the sensor.

The crankshaft sensor is not adjustable for ignition timing but positioning of the interrupter ring is very important. A clearance of 0.025 in. is required on either side of the interrupter ring.

The C^3I ignition system consists of the ECM, ignition module, ignition coils and Hall Effect camshaft and crankshaft sensors.

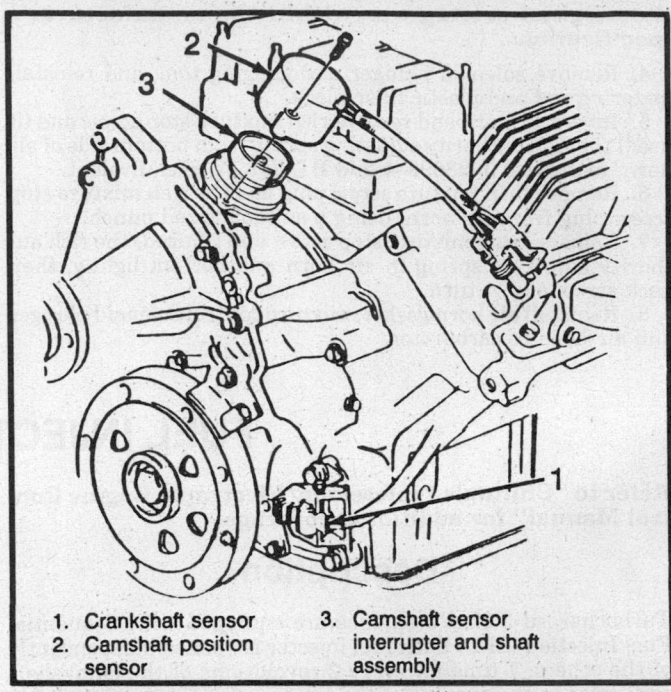

1. Crankshaft sensor
2. Camshaft position sensor
3. Camshaft sensor interrupter and shaft assembly

Camshaft and crankshaft sensor mounting—3.8L V6 turbo

The crankshaft sensor is mounted at the harmonic balancer and the camshaft sensor is mounted at the camshaft gear.

The spark distribution is accomplished by a signal from the crankshaft sensor which is used by the ignition module to determine the proper time to trigger the next ignition coil.

The camshaft sensor provides the C^3I module with a signal pulse as pistons No. 1 and 4 are approximately 25 degrees past TDC. The signal in fact, represents the camshaft's actual location, due to the sensors location. The camshaft sensor is also used to properly time the fuel injection system.

Removal and Installation

CAMSHAFT SENSOR

NOTE: If only the camshaft sensor is being replaced, it is not necessary to remove the entire drive assembly. The sensor can be replaced separately.

1. Disconnect the negative battery cable.
2. Disconnect the 14 way ignition module connector.
3. Disconnect the spark plug wire at the coil assemblies.
4. Remove the ignition module bracket assembly.
5. Disconnect the sensor wiring.
6. Remove the mounting screws and remove the sensor from the engine.
7. Install the sensor in the engine and install the mounting screws.
8. Connect the sensor wiring and install the ignition module mounting bracket.
9. Connect the spark plug wires, ignition module connector and negative battery cable.

NOTE: If the camshaft sensor drive was not removed, there is no reason to have to adjust the sensor's timing. If the sensor drive was removed, follow the adjustment procedure after installing the sensor and drive. The adjustment will not affect the spark timing.

CRANKSHAFT SENSOR

1. Disconnect the crankshaft sensor connector.
2. Slowly rotate the engine until any window (slot) in the

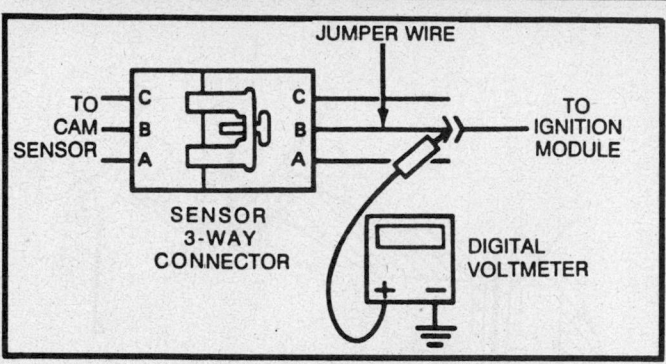

Camshaft sensor adjustment—3.8L V6 turbo

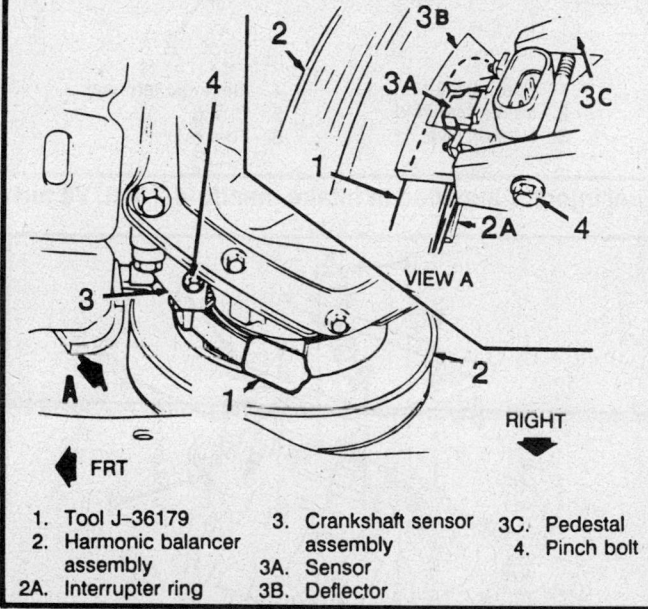

1. Tool J–36179
2. Harmonic balancer assembly
2A. Interrupter ring
3. Crankshaft sensor assembly
3A. Sensor
3B. Deflector
3C. Pedestal
4. Pinch bolt

Crankshaft sensor adjustment—3.8L V6 turbo

reluctor wheel on the balancer is aligned with the sensor.

3. Loosen the pinch bolt on the sensor pedestal until the sensor can freely slide in the pedestal.

4. Remove the pedestal to engine mounting bolts.

5. Carefully remove the pedestal and sensor as an assembly from the engine. The sensor will move in the pedestal and care must be used when removing.

6. Before installing the new sensor, loosen the sensor in the pedestal until it can be moved freely.

7. Verify that the reluctor is still in alignment and install the pedestal and sensor on the engine.

8. Tighten the pedestal mounting bolts to 22 ft. lbs.

9. Adjust the sensor when finished.

Adjustment

CAMSHAFT SENSOR

1. Remove the No. 1 spark plug and rotate the engine until the No. 1 cylinder is at TDC on the compression stroke.

2. Mark the harmonic balancer and rotate the engine an additional 25 degrees past TDC.

3. Remove the spark plug wires from the ignition coil.

4. Using tool J–28742–A or equivalent, remove terminal B of the camshaft sensor plug, on the ignition module side of the plug.

5. Insert a jumper wire into terminal B of the plug and connect a voltmeter between the wire and ground.

6. Place the ignition switch in the **ON** position with the engine **OFF**.

7. Rotate the sensor counterclockwise until the sensor switch just closes. This is indicated by a voltage going from a high of 5–12 volts, to a low of 0–2 volts. The low voltage indicates the switch is closed.

8. With voltage in the low range, tighten the mounting bolts and recheck the voltage.

9. Remove the jumper wire and voltmeter. Reconnect the sensor and run the engine.

CRANKSHAFT SENSOR

1. With the sensor installed on the engine, insert adjustment tool J–36179 or equivalent into the gap between the sensor and the reluctor wheel on the balancer.

2. Make sure that the interrupter is sandwiched between the blades of the adjustment tool and that both blades are properly inserted into the sensor slot.

3. Tighten the sensor pinch bolt to 30 inch lbs. while maintaining light pressure on the sensor and interrupter ring.

4. Check this clearance again at every 120 degree interval.

NOTE: If the sensor touches the interrupter ring at any point, the ring is bent and must be replaced.

FUEL INJECTOR

Removal and Installation

3.8L ENGINE

─────────────── **CAUTION** ───────────────

Before servicing the high pressure fuel system, the pressure in the system must be relieved. Failure to relieve the pressure, may cause a sudden spray of fuel when the system is opened that could cause fire and/or injury.

───

NOTE: Care must be taken when removing injectors to prevent damage to the electrical connector pins on the injector and the nozzle. The injectors are serviced as a complete assembly only. Injectors are an electrical component and should not be immersed in any type of cleaner.

1. Connect fuel gauge J–34730–1 or equivalent to the fuel pressure valve. Wrap a shop rag around fitting while connecting gauge to avoid fuel spill.

2. Install bleed hose into an approved container and open valve to bleed the excess system pressure.

3. With the ignition **OFF**, remove the electrical connections.

4. Remove the fuel rail.

NOTE: Precautions must be taken to prevent dirt and other contaminants from entering the fuel passages. It is recommended that fittings be capped and holes plugged, during servicing. The fuel rail assembly should be cleaned with AC-Delco® X–30A or equivalent engine spray cleaner before disassembly.

5. Remove the fuel injector retaining clips, if used.

6. Remove the injectors.

7. When installing the injectors, always use new O-rings and coat them with clean engine oil.

8. The remainder of the installation is the reverse of the removal procedure.

9. When finished, start and run the engine while checking for leaks.

EXCEPT 3.8L ENGINE

NOTE: Exercise care when removing the fuel injectors to prevent damage to the electrical connector ter-

minals, the injector filter and the fuel nozzle. Also, since the injectors are electrical components, they should not be immersed in any type of liquid solvent of cleaner as damage may occur.

1. Disconnect the electrical connectors from the fuel injectors by squeezing the plastic tabs and pulling straight up.
2. Remove the fuel meter cover assembly in the same manner as the electrical connectors.
3. With fuel meter cover gasket in place to prevent damage to casting, carefully lift out each injector and set aside.
4. Remove the lower (small) O-rings from the injector nozzles. Discard the O-rings and replace with new.
5. Remove the fuel meter cover gasket and discard.
6. Remove the upper (large) O-rings and steel backup washers from top of each fuel injector cavity. Discard the O-rings and replace with new.
7. Inspect the fuel injector filter for evidence of dirt and contamination. If present, check for presence of dirt in fuel lines and fuel tank.

NOTE: If replacements are required, ensure that the injector is replaced with an identical part. The model 220 TBI is capable of accepting other types of injectors, but other injectors are calibrated for different flow rates.

8. Lubricate new lower (small) O-ring with automatic transmission fluid and push on nozzle end of injector until it seats against injector fuel filter.
9. Install the steel injector backup washer in counterbore of fuel meter body.
10. Lubricate new upper (large) O-ring with automatic transmission fluid and install directly over the backup washer. Ensure that the O-ring is seated properly and is flush with top of fuel meter body surface.

NOTE: Backup washers and O-rings must be installed before the injectors, or improper seating of large O-ring could cause fuel to leak.

11. Align the raised lug on each injector base with notch in fuel meter body cavity and install the injector. Push down with moderate pressure on injector until it is fully seated in fuel meter body. The electrical terminals of injector should be parallel with throttle shaft.
12. Install the fuel meter cover gasket.
13. Install the fuel meter cover.
14. Coat the threads of the fuel meter attaching screw with a suitable thread locking compound. Install and tighten the screws.
15. Reconnect the electrical connectors to their respective fuel injectors.

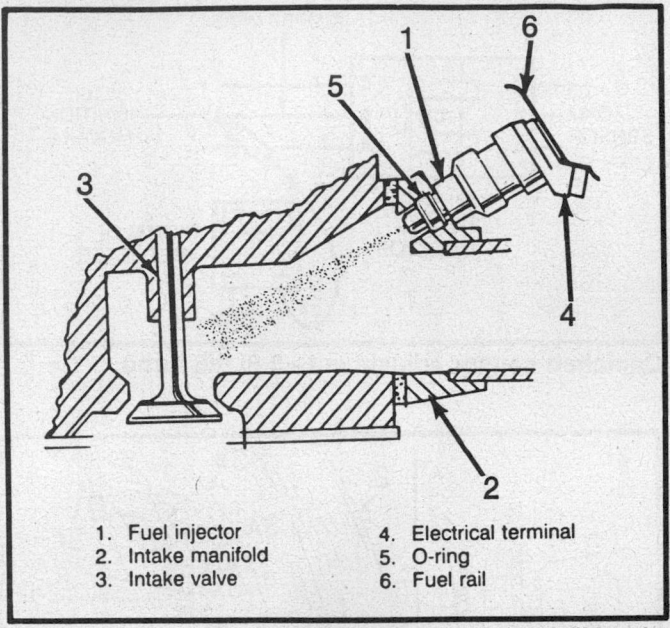

1. Fuel injector
2. Intake manifold
3. Intake valve
4. Electrical terminal
5. O-ring
6. Fuel rail

Fuel injector installed in intake manifold—3.8L V6 turbo

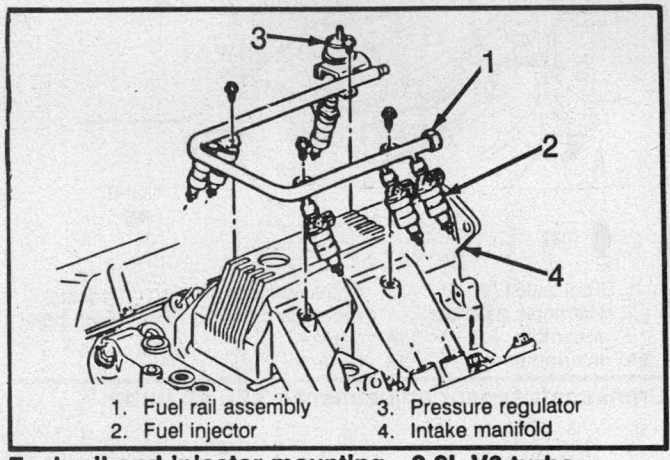

1. Fuel rail assembly
2. Fuel injector
3. Pressure regulator
4. Intake manifold

Fuel rail and injector mounting—3.8L V6 turbo

16. Turn the ignition switch to the **ON** position (engine not running) and check for fuel leaks.

TURBOCHARGER SYSTEM

Refer to "Chilton's Electronic Engine Controls Manual" for additional coverage

Description

The turbocharger is basically an air compressor or air pump. It consists of a turbine or hot wheel, a shaft, a compressor or cold wheel, a turbine housing, a compressor housing and a center housing. The center housing contains bearings, a turbine seal assembly and a compressor seal assembly.

Turbochargers are installed on an engine to put more and denser air into the engine's combustion chambers. Because of the increased volume and weight of compressed air, more fuel can be scheduled to produce more horsepower from an engine. The turbocharged version of an engine, when operated above sea level, will also maintain a higher level of power output than the non-turbocharged version.

4. Disconnect the compressor outlet pipe from the compressor.

5. Disconnect the oil breather and turbocharger heat shields.

6. Remove the exhaust pipe from the turbine outlet.

7. Remove the oil breather vent from the valve cover. Disconnect and plug the oil pressure feed line at the turbocharger assembly.

8. Remove the turbocharger mounting bracket nuts. Disconnect the turbine inlet pipe from the exhaust manifold.

9. Disconnect the oil return line from turbocharger.

10. Remove the vacuum line from the turbocharger wastegate actuator.

11. Disconnect the intercooler outlet to throttle body pipe.

12. Remove the turbocharger assembly from the manifold adapter.

13. Installation is the reverse of the removal procedure.

NOTE: Before installing the turbocharger assembly, be sure that it is first charged with oil. Failure to do this may cause damage to the assembly.

TURBOCHARGER WASTEGATE UNIT

Removal and Installation

1. Disconnect the negative battery cable.
2. Remove vacuum hose from actuator.
3. Remove retaining clip at actuator rod to wastegate lever.
4. Remove bolts attaching the mounting bracket to compressor housing.
5. Remove wastegate actuator.
6. Installation is the reverse of the removal procedure.

TURBOCHARGER UNIT

Removal and Installation

1. Disconnect the negative battery cable.
2. Relieve the fuel system pressure.
3. Remove the air inlet hose from the compressor section of the turbocharger.

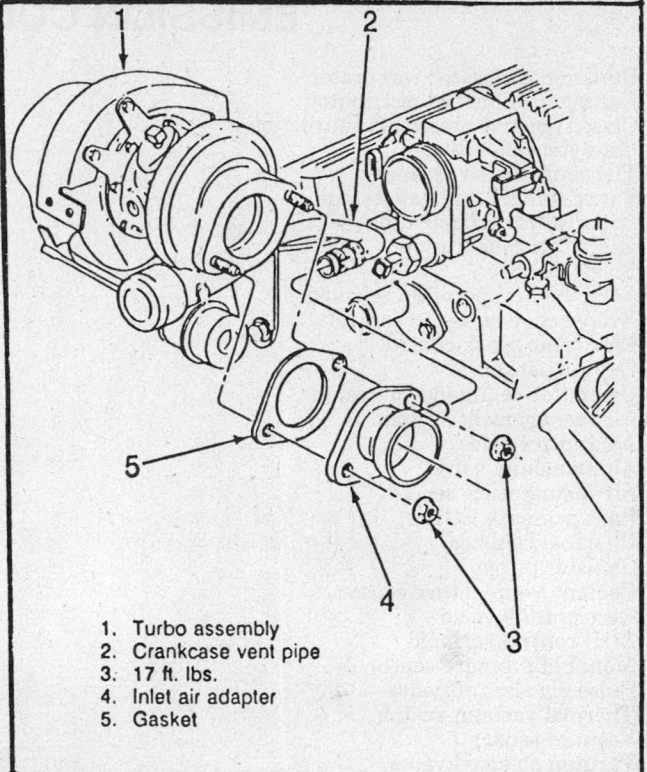

1. Turbo assembly
2. Crankcase vent pipe
3. 17 ft. lbs.
4. Inlet air adapter
5. Gasket

Air inlet adapter to turbocharger mounting—3.8L V6 engine

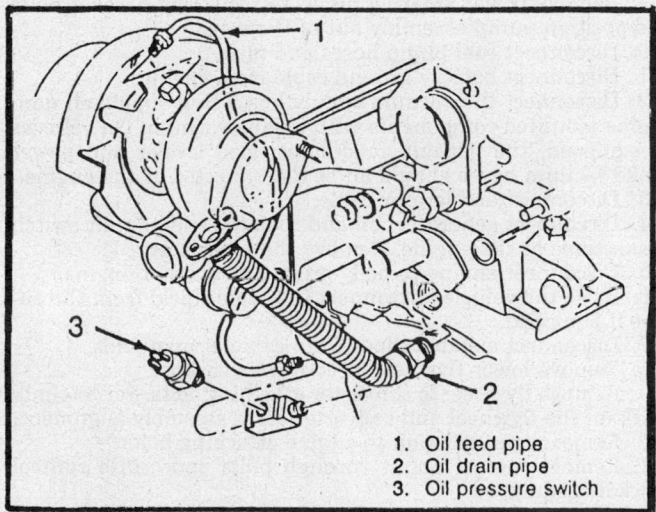

1. Oil feed pipe
2. Oil drain pipe
3. Oil pressure switch

Turbocharger oil supply line and feed pipe—3.8L V6 engine

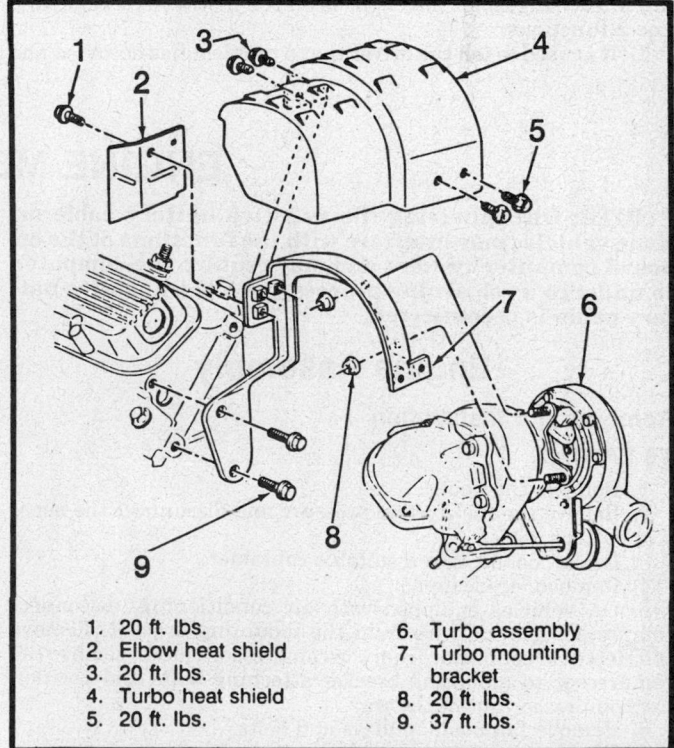

1. 20 ft. lbs.
2. Elbow heat shield
3. 20 ft. lbs.
4. Turbo heat shield
5. 20 ft. lbs.
6. Turbo assembly
7. Turbo mounting bracket
8. 20 ft. lbs.
9. 37 ft. lbs.

Turbocharger mounting—1986–87 3.8L V6 engine

EMISSION CONTROL SYSTEMS

Emission calibrated carburetor
Emission calibrated distributor
Closed positive crankcase ventilation
Catalytic converter
Thermostatic air cleaner
Vapor control canister storage
Exhaust gas recirculation
Early fuel evaporation
Electric choke
Early fuel evaporation solenoid
Evaporative emission control
Electronic spark control
Oxygen sensor
Computer command control
Air management system
Air control valve
Air switching valve
Air temperature sensor
Back pressure EGR
Charcoal canister
Canister purge
Coolant temperature sensor
Deceleration valve
EGR control solenoid
Manifold pressure sensor
Pulse air shut off valve
Thermal vacuum switch
Vacuum sensor
Vacuum solenoid valve

Resetting Emission Warning Lamps

Procedure

Although this light may indicate either wording depending on the vehicle, it has the same function in either case. The terms are interchangeable. This light is on the instrument panel and has 2 functions:

1. It is used to tell the driver that a problem has occurred and the vehicle should be taken for service as soon as reasonably possible.

2. It is also used by technicians to read out "Trouble Codes" when diagnosing system problems.

As a bulb and system check, the "Check Engine/Service Engine Soon" light will come on with the key on and the engine not running. When the engine is started, the "Check Engine/Service Engine Soon" light will turn off.

If the "Check Engine/Service Engine Soon" light remains on, the self-diagnostic system has detected a problem. If the problem goes away, the light will go out in most cases after 10 seconds, but a Trouble Code will remain in the ECM memory.

Clearing Trouble Codes

When the ECM finds a problem, the "Check Engine/Service Engine Soon" light will come on and a trouble code will be recorded in the ECM memory. If the problem is intermittent, the "Check Engine/Service Engine Soon" light will go out after 10 seconds, when the fault goes away. However, the trouble code will stay in the ECM memory until the battery voltage to the ECM is removed. Removing battery voltage for 10 seconds will clear all stored trouble codes. Do this by disconnecting the ECM harness from the positive battery pigtail for 10 seconds with the ignition OFF, or by disconnecting the ECM fuse, designated ECM or ECM/Bat., from the fuse holder.

NOTE: To prevent ECM damage, the key must be OFF when disconnecting or reconnecting power to ECM (for example battery cable, ECM pigtail, ECM fuse, jumper cables, etc.).

ECM Learning Ability

The ECM has a "learning" ability. If the battery is disconnected to clear diagnostic codes, or for repair, the "learning" process has to begin all over again. A change may be noted in the vehicle's performance to "teach" the vehicle, make sure the vehicle is at operating temperature and drive at part throttle, with moderate acceleration and idle conditions, until normal performance returns.

ENGINE MECHANICAL

NOTE: Disconnecting the negative battery cable on some vehicles may interfere with the functions of the on board computer systems and may require the computer to undergo a relearning process, once the negative battery cable is reconnected.

Engine Assembly

Removal and Installation

V6 ENGINE

1. Remove the hood.
2. Relieve the fuel system pressure and disconnect the negative battery cable.
3. Drain coolant into a suitable container.
4. Remove air cleaner.
5. On vehicles equipped with air conditioning, disconnect compressor ground wire from the mounting bracket. Remove the electrical connector from the compressor clutch, remove the compressor to mounting bracket attaching bolts and position the compressor out of the way.
6. Remove fan blade, pulleys and belts.
7. Disconnect radiator and heater hoses from engine.
8. Remove fan shroud assembly.
9. Remove power steering pump to mounting bracket bolts and position pump assembly out of the way.
10. Disconnect fuel pump hoses and plug.
11. Disconnect battery ground cable from engine.
12. Disconnect the vacuum supply hoses that supply all non-engine mounted components with engine vacuum. On vehicles so equipped, the vacuum modulator, load leveler and power brake vacuum hoses should all be disconnected at the engine.
13. Disconnect accelerator cable.
14. Disconnect generator, oil and coolant sending unit switch connections at the engine. Remove the alternator.
15. Disconnect engine to body ground strap(s) at engine.
16. Raise the vehicle, disconnect the cable shield from the engine if equipped.
17. Disconnect exhaust pipes from exhaust manifolds.
18. Remove lower flywheel or converter cover.
19. Remove flywheel to converter attaching bolts. Scribe chalk mark on the flywheel and converter for reassembly alignment.
20. Remove transmission to engine attaching bolts.
21. Remove motor mount through bolts and cruise control bracket if equipped.
22. Lower the vehicle and support the automatic transmission.
23. Attach a lifting device to the engine and raise the engine

enough so mounting through bolts can be removed. Make certain wiring harness, vacuum hoses and other parts are free and clear before lifting engine out of the vehicle.

24. Raise engine far enough to clear engine mounts, raise transmission support accordingly and alternately until engine can be disengaged from the transmission and removed.

25. Installation is the reverse of the removal procedure.

V8 ENGINE

1. Drain cooling system.
2. Remove air cleaner and hot air pipe.
3. Remove hood from hinges, mark hood for reassembly.
4. Disconnect the negative battery cable. Relieve the fuel system pressure.
5. Disconnect radiator hoses, automatic transmission cooler lines, heater hoses, vacuum hoses, power steering hose bracket from engine, air conditioning compressor with brackets and hoses attached, fuel hose from fuel line, wiring and throttle cable.

6. Remove upper radiator support and radiator.
7. Raise and support the vehicle.
8. Disconnect exhaust pipes at manifold.
9. Remove torque converter cover and the bolts holding converter to flywheel.
10. Remove engine mount bolts or nuts.
11. Remove the transmission to engine retaining bolts on the right side. Remove the starter.
12. Lower the vehicle. Secure lift chain to engine.
13. Place board on top of jack and slightly raise transmission.

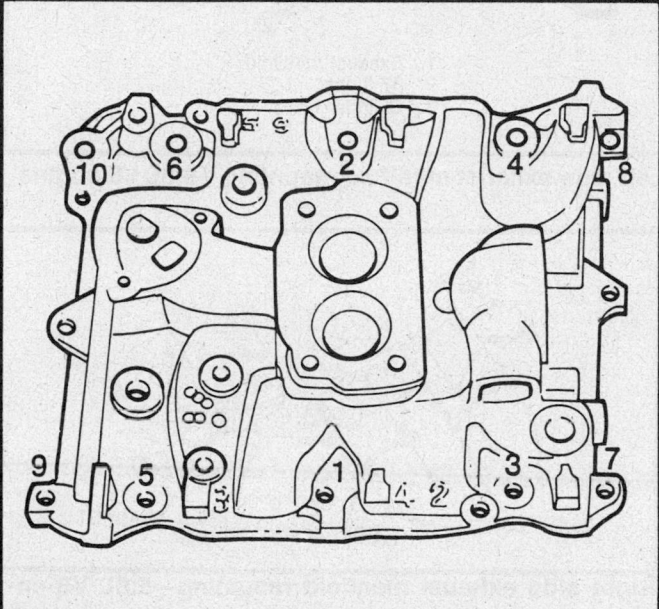

Intake manifold torque sequence—231 CID V6

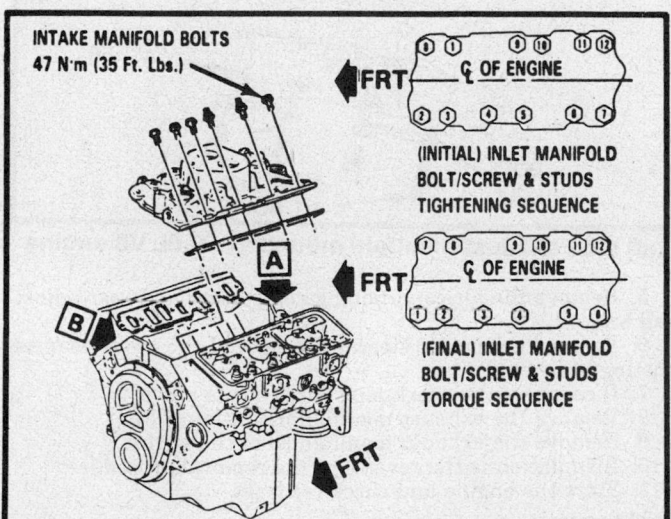

Intake manifold bolt torque sequence 262 cu. In. V6 gas engine

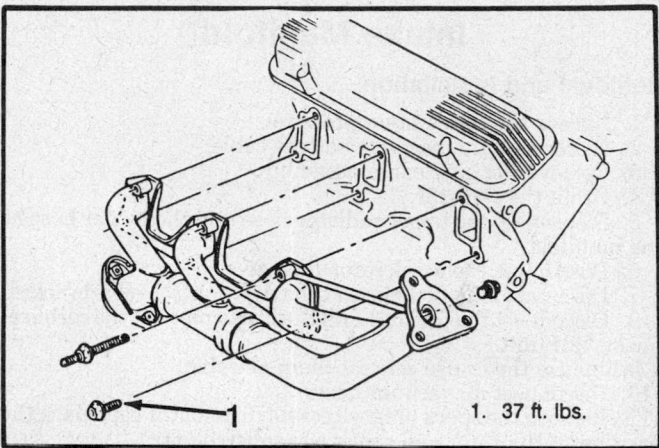

Right side exhaust manifold mounting—3.8L V6 engine—turbo shown-non turbo similar

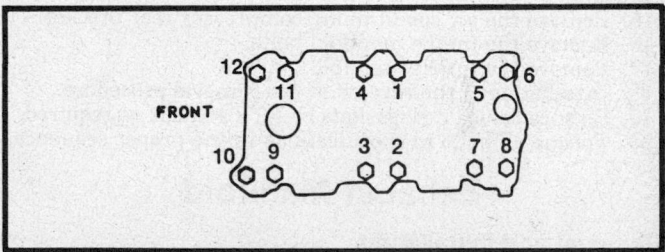

Intake manifold torque sequence—305 CID V8 and 350 CID V8

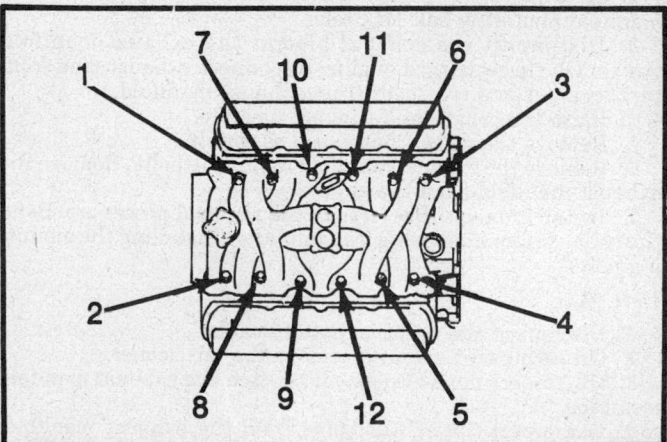

Intake manifold torque sequence—307 CID V8

Remove 3 left transmission to engine bolts. Remove engine.
14. Installation is the reverse of the removal procedure.

Engine Mounts

Removal and Installation

1. Disconnect the negative battery cable.
2. Raise and support the vehicle safely.
3. Properly support the weight of the engine at the forward edge of the oil pan.
4. Remove the mount to engine block bolts.
5. Raise the engine slightly and remove the mount to mount bracket bolt and nut. Remove the engine mount.
6. Installation is the reverse of the removal procedure.

Intake Manifold

Removal and Installation

1. Relieve the fuel system pressure.
2. Disconnect the negative battery cable.
3. Remove the air cleaner assembly.
4. Drain the radiator.
5. Disconnect the upper radiator hose and the heater hose at the manifold.
6. Disconnect the accelerator linkage.
7. Disconnect the fuel pipes at the AIR control valve bracket.
8. Disconnect the fuel line and the brake pipes at the carburetor or TBI unit.
9. Remove the cruise control chain or cable.
10. Disconnect all vacuum hoses.
11. Remove the spark plug wires and distributor cap. Mark the position of the rotor and remove the distributor.
12. Remove the carburetor or throttle body assembly.
13. Remove the EGR valve assembly.
14. On V6 engines, remove the coil.
15. Remove the air conditioning compressor rear bracket.
16. Remove the intake manifold bolts.
17. Remove the intake manifold.
18. Installation is the reverse of the removal procedure.
19. Be sure to use new gaskets or RTV sealant as required.
20. Torque all bolts to specifications in the proper sequence.

Exhaust Manifold

Removal and Installation

V6 ENGINE

Right Side
1. Disconnect the negative battery cable.
2. Disconnect the oxygen sensor and flatten the exhaust manifold mounting bolt lock tabs.
3. Disconnect the exhaust pipe at the exhaust manifold flange. On turbocharged engine, disconnect exhaust pipe from turbocharger and crossover from exhaust manifold.
4. Raise the vehicle and support it safely.
5. Remove the right front wheel assembly.
6. Remove the exhaust manifold mounting bolts. Remove the exhaust manifold from the engine.
7. Installation is the reverse of the removal procedure. Bend the exhaust manifold bolt's lock tabs after installing the mounting bolts.

Left Side
1. Disconnect the negative battery cable.
2. On carbureted engines, remove the air cleaner.
3. Disconnect the EFE pipe and flatten the exhaust manifold lock tabs.
4. Disconnect the exhaust pipe from the exhaust manifold. On turbocharged engines, disconnect the exhaust manifold from the crossover pipe.

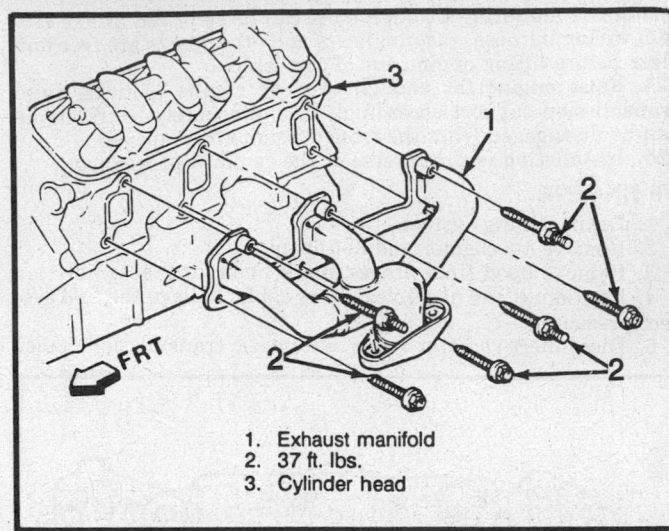

1. Exhaust manifold
2. 37 ft. lbs.
3. Cylinder head

Left side exhaust manifold mounting—3.8L V6 engine

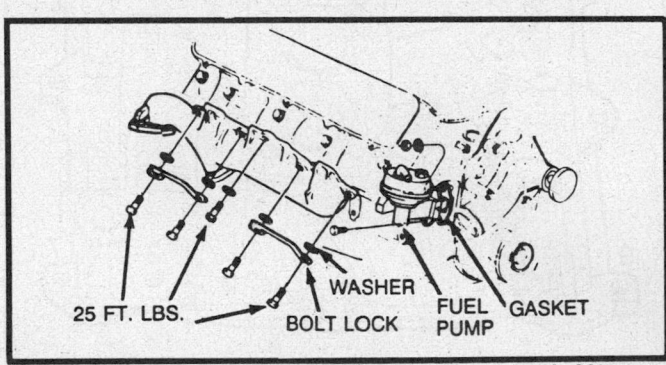

25 FT. LBS.   WASHER
BOLT LOCK   FUEL PUMP   GASKET

Right side exhaust manifold mounting—5.0L V8 engine

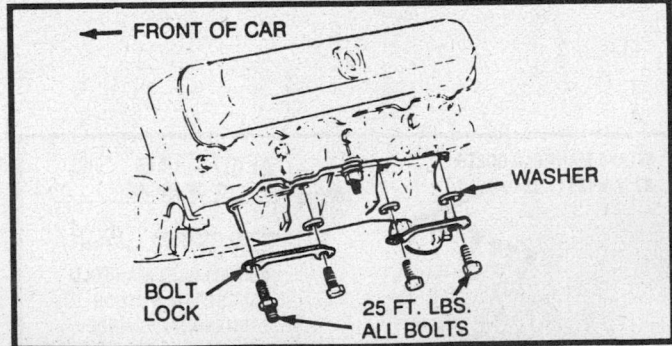

FRONT OF CAR

WASHER

BOLT LOCK   25 FT. LBS. ALL BOLTS

Left side exhaust manifold mounting—5.0L V8 engine

5. Remove the air conditioning compressor and rear adjusting bracket.
6. Remove the power steering pump and the lower rear adjusting bracket.
7. Disconnect the spark plug wires at the plugs.
8. Remove the exhaust manifold mounting bolts.
9. Remove the exhaust manifold from the engine.
10. Installation is the reverse of the removal procedure.
11. Start the engine and check for leaks.

V8 ENGINE

Right Side
1. Disconnect the negative battery cable.

2. Raise the vehicle and support it safely. Remove the right front wheel, the exhaust and crossover pipe(s).

3. Flatten the lock tabs on the manifold bolts and remove. If so equipped, disconnect the oxygen sensor lead.

4. Remove the lower engine mounting bolt and raise the engine slightly, if necessary for clearance.

5. Remove the manifold from below.

6. To install, use new gaskets and reverse the removal procedure. Torque the manifold bolts to specification, bend bolt lock tabs back into position.

Left Side

1. Remove the air cleaner.

2. Remove the hot air shroud and the hot air tube.

3. Remove the lower alternator bracket, A/C drive belt and the air pump pulley.

4. Remove all air pump hoses and the AIR switching valve.

5. Raise the vehicle and remove the crossover pipe.

6. Lower the vehicle and, flatten the lock tabs on the manifold bolts and remove.

7. To install, use a new gasket and reverse the removal procedures. Torque the exhaust manifold mounting bolts to specifications, bend bolt lock tabs back into position.

Valve Systems

VALVE ADJUSTMENT

Hydraulic valve lifters are used in all engines produced by General Motors Corporation. Certain engines have adjustable rocker arms, while others have no adjustment provisions, but rely upon a specific torque value. The following procedure applies to Chevrolet produced V6 and V8 engines.

1. Remove the valve covers.

2. By rotating the crankshaft and by positioning each valve on its base circle of the camshaft, remove the lash from each rocker arm and pushrod.

3. To adjust the valves, crank the engine until the mark on the vibration damper lines up with the center or **0** mark on the timing tab fastened to the crankcase front cover. The engine will be either in the No. 1 firing position or its opposite cylinder (No. 6 on V8 and No. 4 on V6 engines) firing position.

NOTE: The firing cylinder may be determined by placing a finger on the No. 1 cylinder valve rocker arms as the mark on the damper comes near the 0 mark on the crankcase front cover. If the valve rocker arms moves as the mark comes up to the timing tab, the engine is in the opposite cylinder (No. 6 on V8 and No. 4 on V6 engines) firing position and should be turned over a complete revolution to reach the No. 1 cylinder firing position.

4. With the engine in the No. 1 firing position, adjust the following valves:
   a. V8 engine—Exhaust—1, 3, 4, 8
   b. V8 engine—Intake—1, 2, 5, 7
   c. V6 engine—Exhaust—1, 5, 6
   d. V6 engine—Intake—1, 2, 3

5. Back out adjusting nut until lash is felt at the push rod, then turn in adjusting nut until all lash is removed. This can be determined by rotating push rod while turning adjusting nut. When play has been removed, turn adjusting nut in a full additional turn, which centers the lifter plunger.

6. Crank the engine 1 revolution until the pointer **0** mark and the vibration damper mark are again in alignment. This is the No. 1 firing position.

7. With the engine in this position, adjust the following valves:
   a. V8 engine—Exhaust—2, 5, 6, 7
   b. V8 engine—Intake—3, 4, 6, 8
   c. V6 engine—Exhaust—2, 3, 4
   d. V6 engine—Intake—4, 5, 6

8. Install the rocker arm covers.

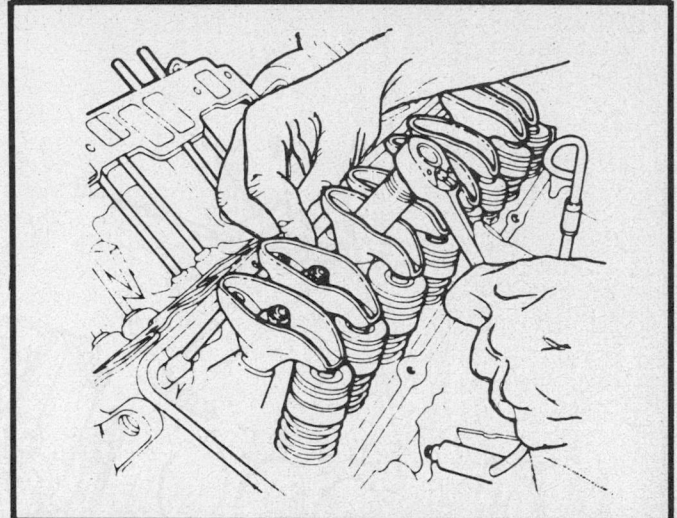

Typical valve adjustment

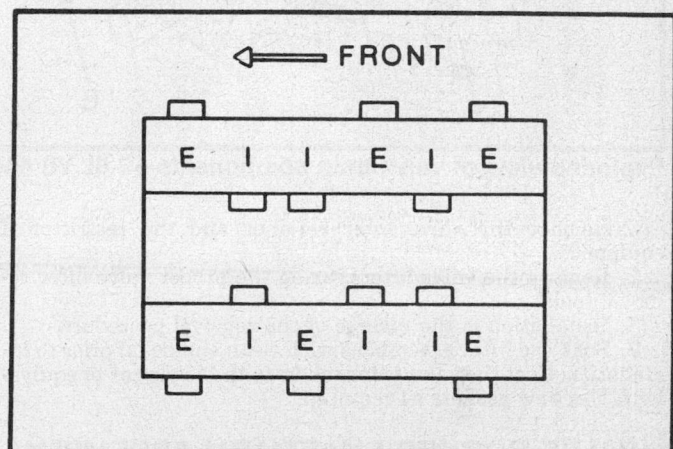

Intake and exhaust valve arrangements—V6

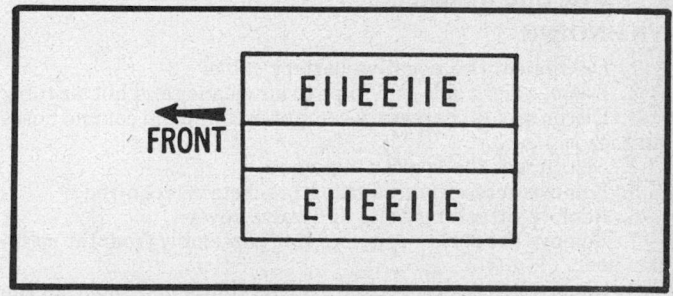

Intake and exhaust valve arrangements—V8

9. Start the engine and adjust the idle speed, as required.

VALVE LIFTERS

Removal and Installation

1. Disconnect the negative battery cable.

2. Drain the coolant.

3. Remove rocker arm covers.

4. Remove the intake manifold assembly.

5. Remove the rocker arm assembly or the rocker and pivot. Remove the pushrods. Be sure to keep them in order as they must be installed in the same bores as they were removed.

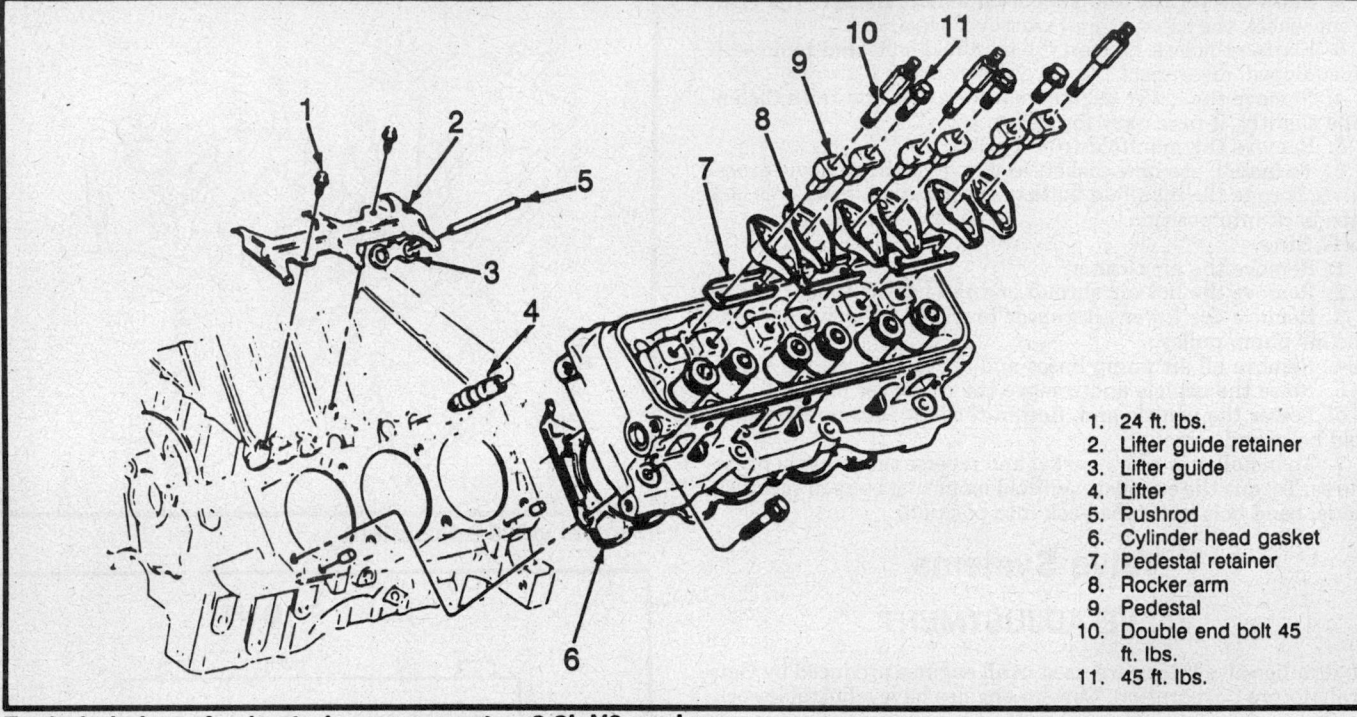

1. 24 ft. lbs.
2. Lifter guide retainer
3. Lifter guide
4. Lifter
5. Pushrod
6. Cylinder head gasket
7. Pedestal retainer
8. Rocker arm
9. Pedestal
10. Double end bolt 45 ft. lbs.
11. 45 ft. lbs.

Exploded view of valve train components—3.8L V6 engine

6. Remove the valve lifter retainer and the restrictor if equipped.
7. Remove the valve lifters, using the proper valve lifter removal tool.
8. Installation is the reverse of the removal procedure.
9. Soak the lifter assemblies with clean engine oil prior to installation. Coat the valve lifter rollers with Molykote® or equivalent. Use new gaskets as required.

VALVE ROCKER SHAFT/ARM ASSEMBLY

Removal and Installation

V6 ENGINE

1. Disconnect the negative battery cable.
2. Remove right side PCV pipe to air cleaner and hot air tube.
3. Disconnect all necessary computer command control hoses and leads.
4. Disconnect the spark plug wires.
5. Remove accessory mounting brackets as required.
6. Remove attaching bolts and valve cover.
7. Remove the rocker arm and shaft assembly from the cylinder head.
8. Remove the nylon rocker arm retainers and separate the rocker arms from the rocker shaft.
9. Installation is the reverse of the removal procedure. Be sure to use new valve cover gaskets, where required.
10. When installing the rocker arms onto the rocker shaft, be sure to position them in the correct sequence.

V8 ENGINE

1. Disconnect the negative battery cable.
2. Disconnect the spark plug wires.
3. Disconnect or remove all necessary hoses and electrical wiring to gain access to the valve cover.
4. Remove the generator drive belt and rear bracket.
5. Loosen exhaust manifold upper shroud only.
6. Remove the EGR valve.
7. Remove the oil level indicator.

8. Remove the AIR pump pulley and drive belt.
9. Remove the A/C compressor rear bracket.
10. Remove valve cover screws and install tool BT-8315 or J-34144 midway between the ends of the valve cover on the upper side. Tighten the screw to apply a load on the cover.
11. Using a rubber mallet, strike on the side of the valve cover, above where the tool is installed.

NOTE: Use a cloth to absorb the blow of the mallet. If a cloth is not used, the valve cover will be damaged.

12. Remove the valve cover.
13. Remove the rocker arm retaining bolts, rocker arm pivot and rocker arms.
14. Installation is the reverse of the removal procedure. Be sure to use new valve cover gaskets, as required.

CHECKING VALVE TIMING

There is no recommended procedure for valve timing adjustment. It is advisable to verify camshaft lobe lift and camshaft/crankshaft relationship through crankshaft pulley location and valve operation.

Procedure

NOTE: The following procedure applies to Chevrolet produced V6 and V8 engines only. For Buick and Oldsmobile produced engines, the camshaft lobe lift can be checked with the camshaft removed from the engine.

1. Remove the distributor cap. Remove the right valve cover. Remove the No. 4 intake and exhaust rocker arm assembly.
2. Remove the wire from the BAT terminal of the distributor cap.
3. Turn ignition switch on. Crank engine until rotor is in line with No. 4 spark plug wire position. No. 4 piston will be approximately at the top of cylinder.
4. Measure from pivot boss on head surface to top of No. 4 intake push-rod. Record measurement.
5. Slowly turn engine 1½ revolutions until rotor approaches

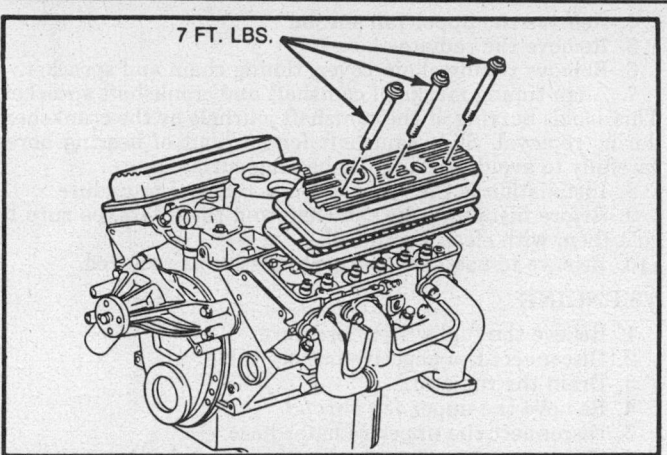

Rocker arm cover Installation—V6

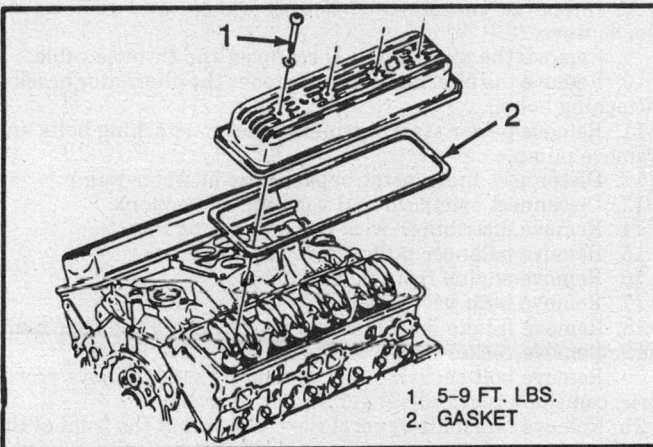

1. 5–9 FT. LBS.
2. GASKET

Rocker arm cover Installation—V8

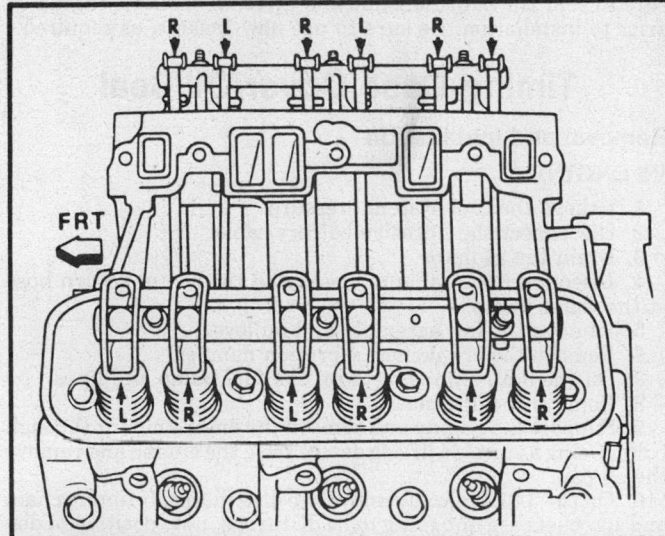

Positioning of rocker arms on 3.8L V6

No. 1 spark plug wire position. Continue to turn engine until timing mark on crank puller is aligned with 0 on indicator. This is top dead center of No. 1 piston.

6. Again measure from pivot boss surface to top of No. 4 cylinder intake push rod.

7. Measurement should increase over the first measurement.

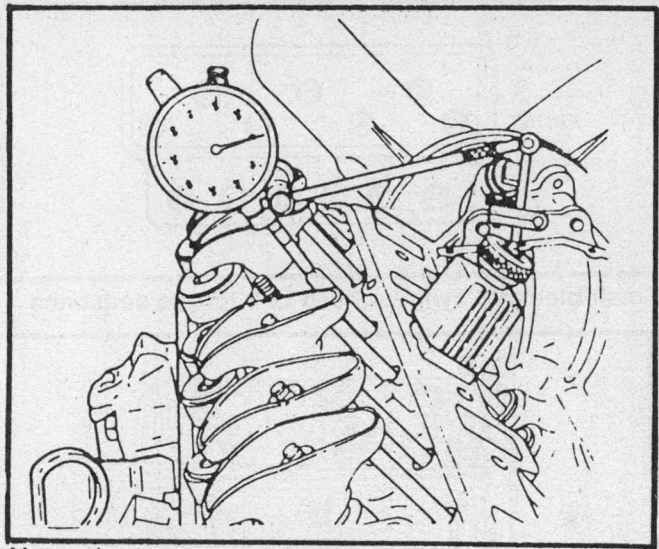

Measuring camshaft lobe lift

8. If measurement increase is not within $1/32$ in. of first measurement, camshaft is advanced or retarded.

Cylinder Heads

Removal and Installation

V6 ENGINE

1. Disconnect negative battery cable.
2. Remove intake manifold.
3. Loosen and remove belt(s).
4. When removing left cylinder head;
   a. Remove oil dipstick.
   b. Remove air and vacuum pumps with mounting bracket if present and move out of the way with hoses attached.
5. When removing right cylinder head:
   a. Remove alternator.
   b. Disconnect power steering gear pump and brackets attaching to cylinder head.
6. Disconnect wires from spark plugs, and remove the spark plug wire clips from the rocker arm cover studs.
7. Remove exhaust manifold bolts from the head being removed.
8. With air hose and cloths, clean dirt off cylinder head and adjacent area to avoid getting dirt into engine.
9. Remove rocker arm cover and rocker arm and shaft assembly from cylinder head. Lift out pushrods.
10. Loosen all cylinder head bolts, remove bolts and lift off the cylinder head.
11. Installation is the reverse of the removal procedure. Torque the cylinder head bolts to 80 ft. lbs., torque the exhaust manifold bolts to 25 ft. lbs. and torque the intake manifold bolts to 45 ft. lbs.

V8 ENGINE

1. Disconnect the negative battery cable. Drain the radiator.
2. Remove the intake manifold. Remove the exhaust manifold.
3. Remove the valve cover. Remove the ground strap from the left cylinder head.
4. Remove rocker arm bolts, pivots, rocker arms and push rods. Scribe pivots and keep rocker arms separated so they can be installed in their original locations.
5. Remove cylinder head bolts and remove cylinder head.
6. Installation is the reverse of the removal procedure. Torque the cylinder head bolts to 100 ft. lbs. and then to a final torque of 130 ft. lbs.

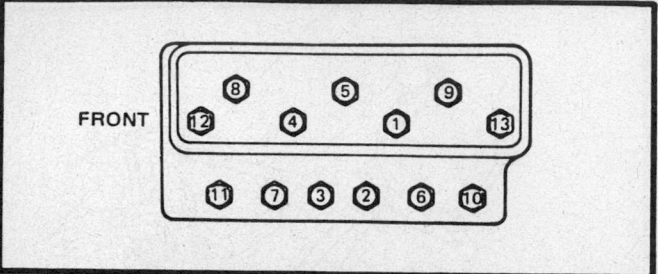

Small block V6 cylinder head bolt torque sequence

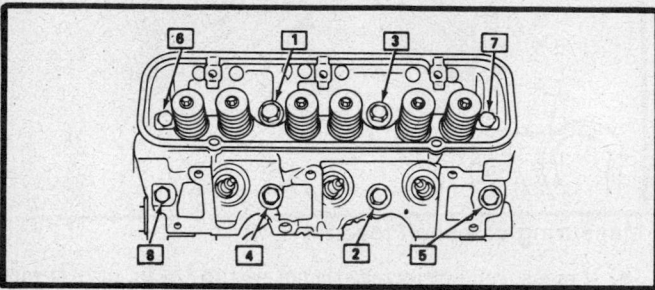

Cylinder head bolt torque sequence—3.8L V6 engine

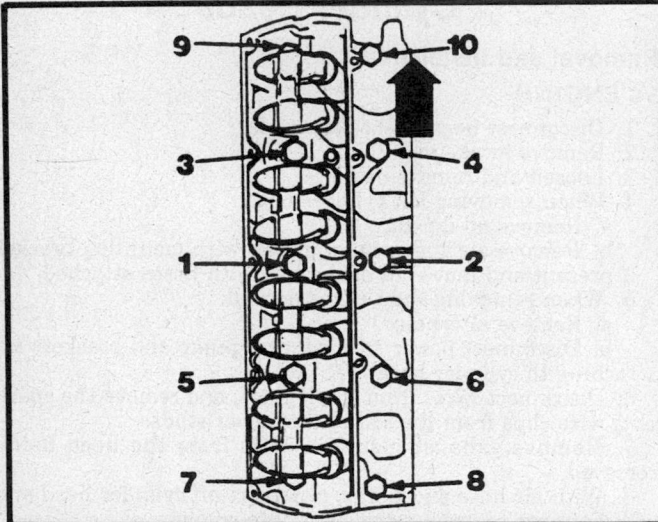

Cylinder head bolt torque sequence—307 CID V8

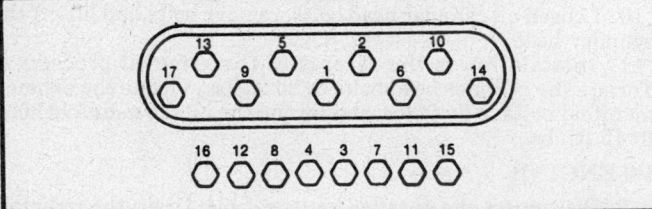

Small block V8 cylinder head torque sequence

Camshaft

Removal and Installation
V6 ENGINE

1. Disconnect the negative battery cable.
2. Drain the radiator.
3. Remove the intake manifold. Remove the rocker covers. Remove the rocker arm assemblies, push rods and valve lifters.

4. Remove the upper fan shroud.
5. Remove the radiator hoses.
6. Remove timing chain cover, timing chain and sprocket.
7. Align timing marks of camshaft and crankshaft sprocket. This avoids burring of the camshaft journals by the crankshaft during removal. Slide camshaft forward out of bearing bores carefully to avoid marring the bearing surfaces.
8. Installation is the reverse of the removal procedure.
9. Before installing the camshaft and the lifters, be sure to coat them with clean engine oil.
10. Be sure to use new gaskets and seals as required.

V8 ENGINE

1. Relieve the fuel system pressure.
2. Disconnect the negative battery cable.
3. Drain the radiator.
4. Remove the upper fan shroud.
5. Disconnect the upper radiator hose.
6. Disconnect the oil cooler lines and remove the radiator.
7. Disconnect the fuel line at the fuel pump.
8. Discharge the air conditioning system and remove the condensor.
9. Remove the air cleaner. Disconnect the throttle cable.
10. Remove the alternator belt. Remove the alternator bracket attaching bolts.
11. Remove power steering pump bracket attaching bolts and remove pump.
12. Disconnect thermostat bypass hose at water pump.
13. Disconnect electrical and vacuum connections.
14. Remove distributor with cap and wiring intact.
15. Remove balancer pulley. Remove balancer.
16. Remove engine front cover.
17. Remove both valve covers.
18. Remove intake manifold and gasket, front and rear seal.
19. Remove rocker arms, push rods and valve lifters.
20. Remove bolt securing fuel pump eccentric, remove eccentric, camshaft gear, oil slinger and timing chain.
21. Remove camshaft by carefully sliding it out the front of the engine.
22. Installation is the reverse of the removal procedure. Be sure to coat the camshaft and the lifters with clean engine oil prior to installation. Be sure to use new gaskets, as required.

Timing Case Cover/Oil Seal

Removal and Installation
V6 ENGINE

1. Relieve the fuel system pressure.
2. Disconnect the negative battery cable.
3. Drain the radiator.
4. Disconnect the radiator hoses and the heater return hose at the water pump.
5. Remove the fan assembly and pulleys.
6. Remove the crankshaft vibration damper.
7. On the 3.8L engine, remove the fuel pump and lines.
8. Remove the alternator.
9. Support the engine and remove the engine mount through bolts. Using a suitable lifting device raise the engine and remove the oil pan.
10. On the 3.8L engine, remove the distributor. If timing chain and sprockets are not going to be disturbed, note position of distributor rotor for reinstallation in same position.
11. Loosen and slide front clamp on thermostat bypass hose rearward.
12. Remove bolts attaching timing chain cover to cylinder block.
13. Remove the oil pan to timing chain cover bolts.
14. Remove timing chain cover assembly and gasket.
15. Thoroughly clean the cover, taking care to avoid damage to the gasket surface.

16. Installation is the reverse of the removal procedure.

17. On the 3.8L engine, remove oil pump cover and pack the space around the oil pump gears completely full of petroleum jelly. There must be no air space left inside the pump. Reinstall cover using new gasket.

18. To replace the front oil seal, use a punch and drive out the old seal and shedder. Drive the seal out from the front toward the rear of the timing chain cover.

19. On the 4.3L engine, support the rear of the cover at the seal area and drive in the new seal with the open end toward the inside of the cover using tool J–35468.

20. On the 3.8L engine, coil new packing around opening so ends of packing are at top. Drive in shedder using suitable punch. Stake the shedder in place in at least 3 places. Size the packing by rotating a hammer handle or similar tool around the packing until the balancer hub can be inserted through the opening.

V8 ENGINE

1. Relieve the fuel system pressure.
2. Disconnect the negative battery cable.
3. Drain the cooling system.
4. Disconnect the radiator hoses and the bypass hose.
5. On the 5.0L Oldsmobile produced engine, remove the radiator upper support. Remove the radiator.
6. Remove all belts, fan and fan pulley, crankshaft pulley and harmonic balancer.
7. On the 5.0L and 5.7L Chevrolet produced engines, remove the oil pan.
8. On the 5.0L Oldsmobile produced engine, remove the AIR pump pulley, the A/C compressor front bracket and move the A/C compressor aside. Remove the power steering pump with the hoses attached.
9. Remove cover to block attaching bolts and remove cover, timing indicator and water pump assembly.
10. Remove front cover and both dowel pins. It may be necessary to grind a flat on the pins to get a rough surface for gripping.
11. Installation is the reverse of the removal procedure.
12. To install the cover, grind a chamfer on an end of each dowel pin.
13. Cut excess material from front end of oil pan gasket on each side of engine block.
14. Clean block, oil pan and front cover mating surfaces with solvent.
15. Trim about ⅛ in. from each end of new front pan seal, using a sharp tool.
16. Install new front cover gasket on engine block and new front seal on front cover. Apply sealer to gasket around coolant holes and place on block. Apply RTV sealer or equivalent to both mating surfaces.
17. Place the cover on the front of the block and press downward to compress the seal.
18. Install the bolts finger tight to hold the cover in place. Install the the dowel pins, chamfered end first.
19. Continue the installation in the reverse order of the removal procedure.
20. To replace the front oil seal, use a punch and drive out the old seal. Drive the seal out from the front toward the rear of the timing chain cover. Support the rear of the cover at the seal area and drive in the new seal with the open end toward the inside of the cover using the proper seal installer tool.

Timing Chain and Gears

Removal and Installation
V6 ENGINE

1. Disconnect the negative battery cable.
2. Drain the cooling system. Remove the engine front cover.
3. With timing chain cover removed, temporarily install bal-

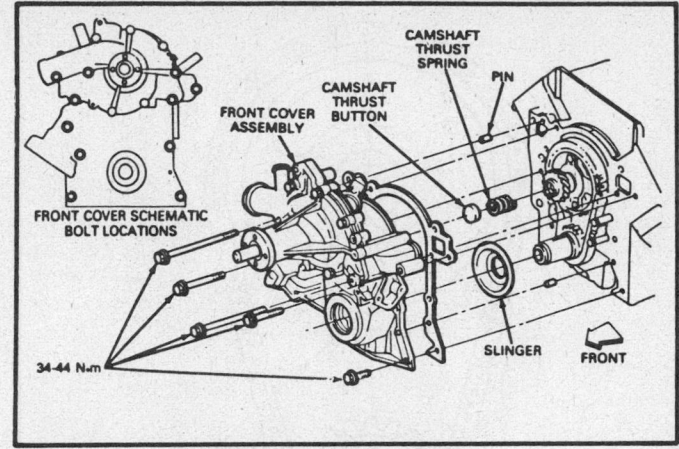

Timing chain cover—231 V6 engines

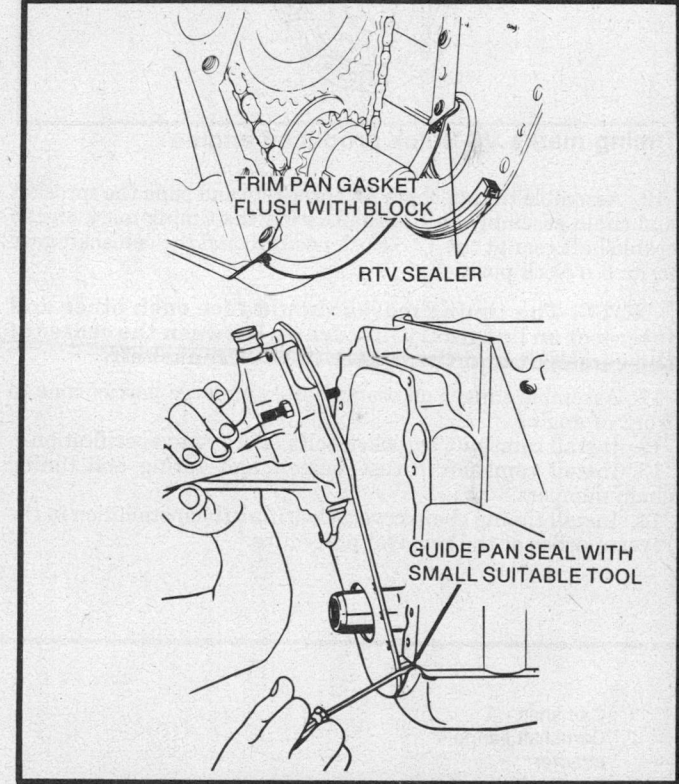

Timing cover installation—V8 engine

ancer bolt and washer in end of crankshaft. Turn crankshaft so that the timing marks on the sprockets are as close together as possible. Remove balancer bolt and washer.

4. Remove front crankshaft oil slinger. Remove the camshaft sprocket bolts.

5. Use 2 large suitable tools to alternately pry the camshaft sprocket from the camshaft while prying the crankshaft sprocket forward until the camshaft sprocket is free, remove the camshaft sprocket, chain and finish working crankshaft sprocket off crankshaft.

6. Thoroughly clean the timing chain, sprockets, distributor drive gear, fuel pump eccentric and crankshaft oil slinger.

7. If the crankshaft has not been turned in the engine, go to Step 10. If the crankshaft has been turned, start with Step 9.

8. Turn crankshaft so that No. 1 piston is at top dead center.

9. Turn camshaft so that with sprocket temporarily installed, timing mark is straight down. Remove sprocket.

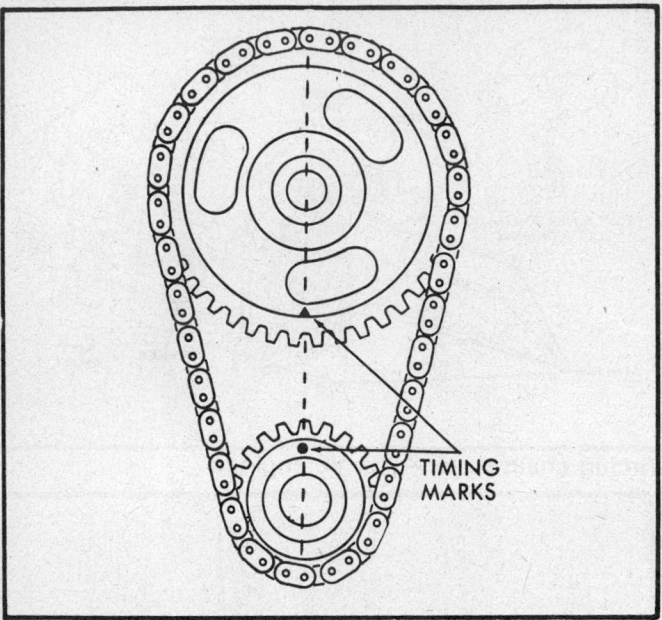

Timing marks V6 Buick produced engine

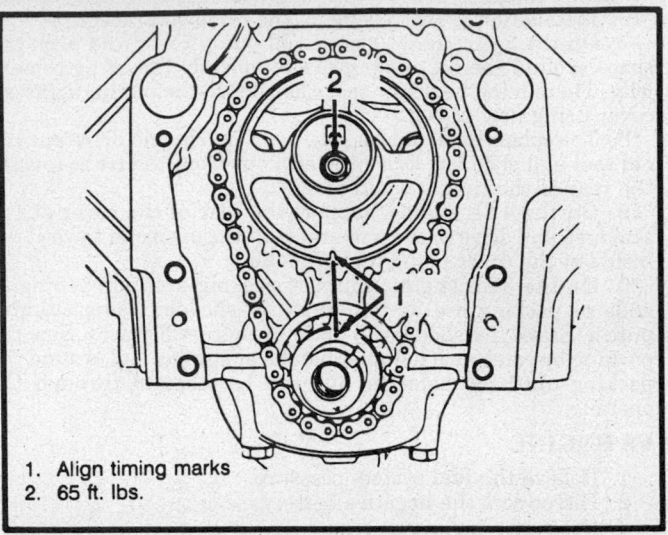

1. Align timing marks
2. 65 ft. lbs.

Timing gear alignment marks—5.0L V8 engine

10. Assemble timing chain on sprockets and slide the sprocket and chain assembly on the shafts with the timing mark on the crankshaft gear at the 12 o'clock position and the camshaft gear in its 6 o'clock position.

NOTE: The timing marks should face each other and intersect an imaginary line drawn between the center of the camshaft and the center of the crankshaft.

11. Assemble slinger on crankshaft with large part of cone to front of engine.
12. Install camshaft sprocket bolts. Torque to specification.
13. Install camshaft thrust button and spring and timing chain dampers.
14. Install timing chain cover. Continue the installation in the reverse order of the removal procedure.

V8 ENGINE

1. Disconnect the negative battery cable.
2. Remove the engine front cover.
3. Rotate the crankshaft and align the timing marks.
4. Remove the camshaft gear bolts. Remove the camshaft gear.

NOTE: Be sure the locating dowel is in place on the camshaft for the camshaft gear.

5. Remove the timing chain.
6. Remove the crankshaft gear sprocket.
7. Installation is the reverse of the removal procedure.
8. Align the timing marks and assemble the gears and chain in the following manner.
7. Assemble timing chain on sprockets and slide the sprocket and chain assembly on the shafts with the timing mark as close together as possible.

NOTE: The timing marks should face each other and intersect an imaginary line drawn between the center of the camshaft and the center of the crankshaft.

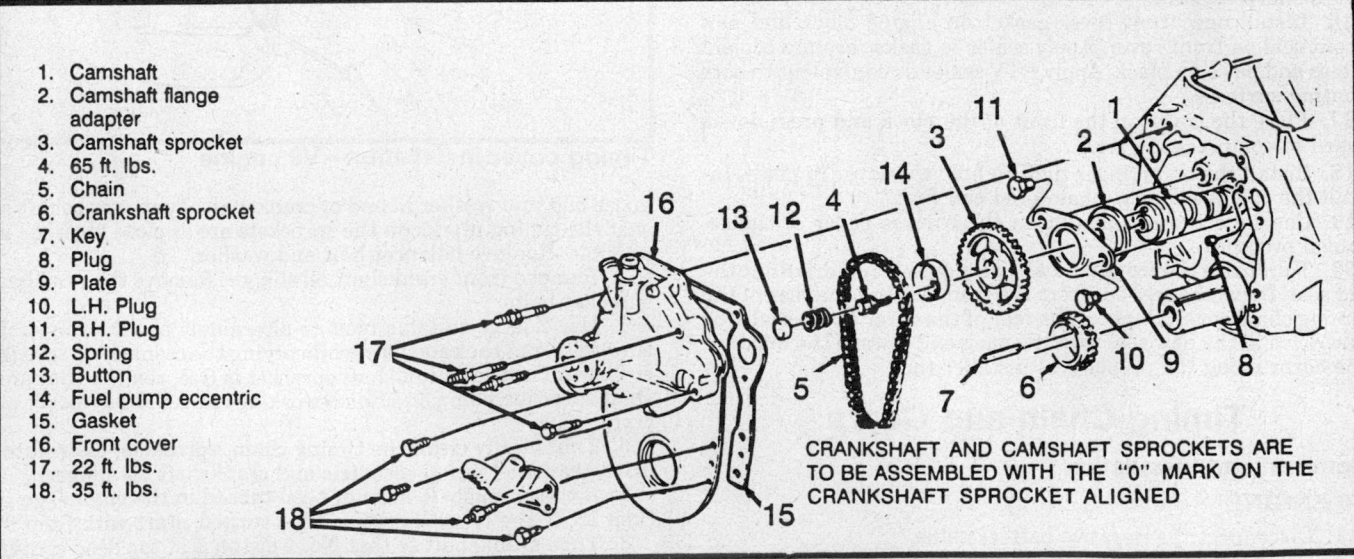

1. Camshaft
2. Camshaft flange adapter
3. Camshaft sprocket
4. 65 ft. lbs.
5. Chain
6. Crankshaft sprocket
7. Key
8. Plug
9. Plate
10. L.H. Plug
11. R.H. Plug
12. Spring
13. Button
14. Fuel pump eccentric
15. Gasket
16. Front cover
17. 22 ft. lbs.
18. 35 ft. lbs.

CRANKSHAFT AND CAMSHAFT SPROCKETS ARE TO BE ASSEMBLED WITH THE "0" MARK ON THE CRANKSHAFT SPROCKET ALIGNED

Timing chain and gears installation and alignment marks—5.0L V8 engine

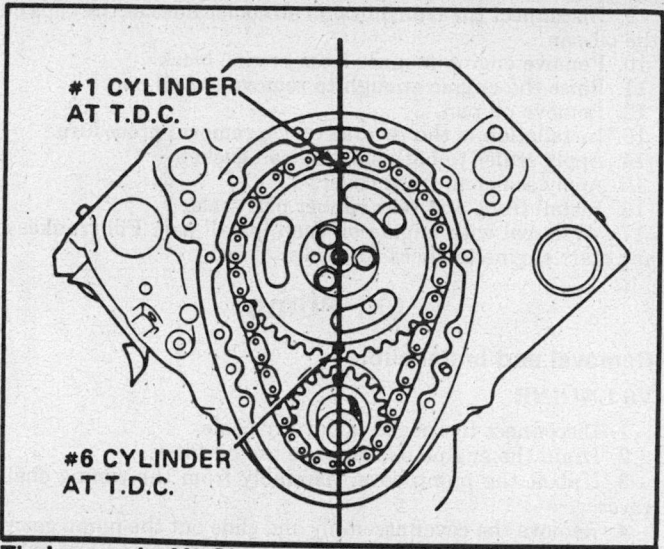

Timing marks V6 Chevy produced engine and all V8's except 307

Rings/Piston/Connecting Rod Positioning

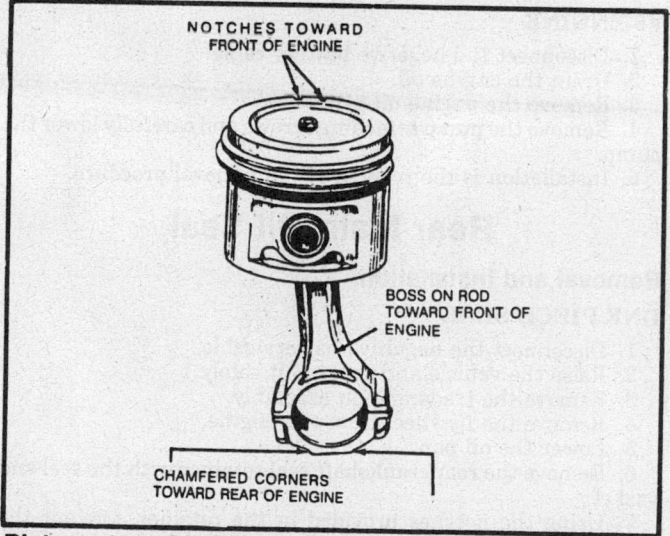

Piston assembly V6 engine

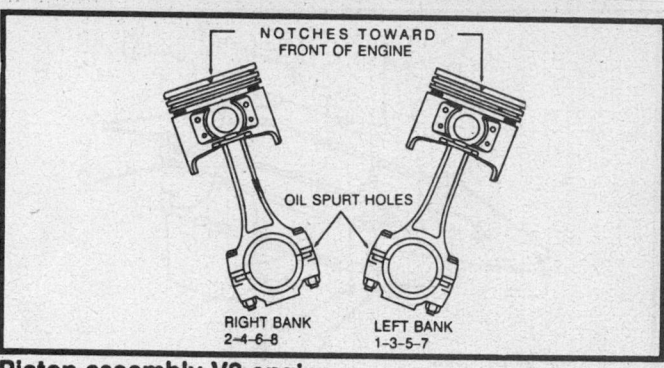

Piston assembly V8 engine

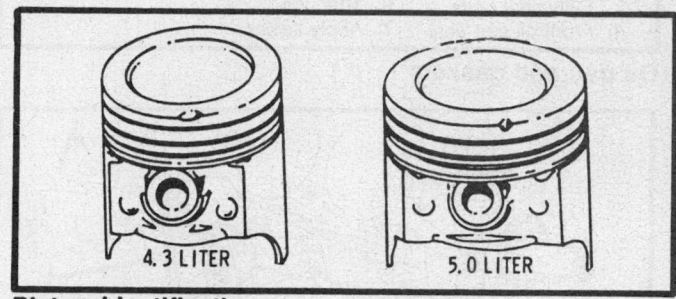

Piston identification

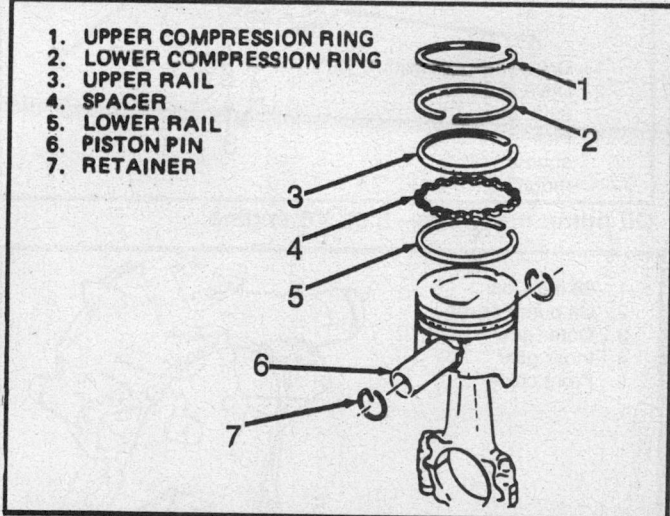

Piston assembly – 307 CID V8

ENGINE LUBRICATION SYSTEM

Oil Pan

Removal and Installation

V6 ENGINE

1. Disconnect the negative battery cable.
2. Raise the vehicle and support it safely.
3. Drain the engine oil.
4. Remove the flywheel cover and the engine crossover pipe.
5. Remove the oil cooler lines at the clips on the oil pan.
6. Disconnect the engine mounts from the frame brackets. Using a suitable lifting device, raise the engine.

7. Remove the oil pan bolts. Remove the oil pan from the engine assembly. It may be necessary to turn the crankshaft to move the forward crankshaft throw and counterbalance weight out of the way.
8. Raise the engine far enough to remove the oil pan.
9. Installation is the reverse of removal.

V8 ENGINE

1. Disconnect the negative battery cable.
2. Remove the oil level indicator.
3. Remove upper radiator support and fan shroud attaching screws.
4. Raise the vehicle and support it safely.

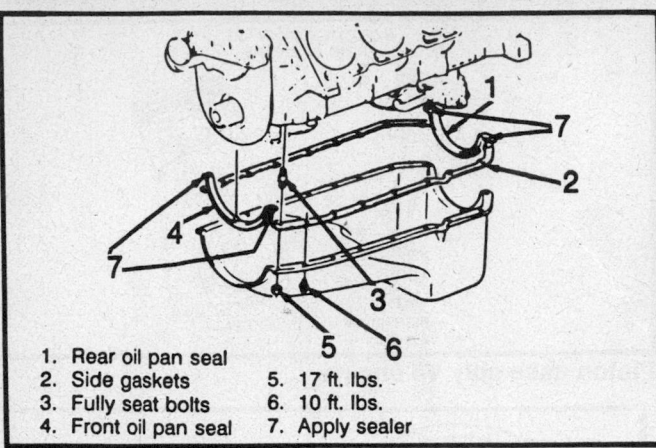

1. Rear oil pan seal
2. Side gaskets
3. Fully seat bolts
4. Front oil pan seal
5. 17 ft. lbs.
6. 10 ft. lbs.
7. Apply sealer

Oil pan and gaskets

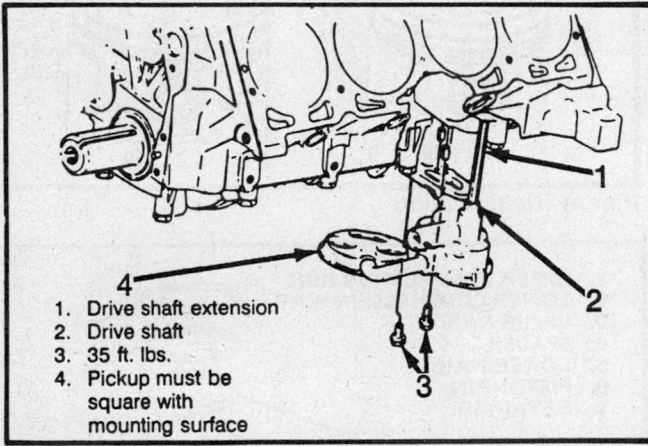

1. Drive shaft extension
2. Drive shaft
3. 35 ft. lbs.
4. Pickup must be square with mounting surface

Oil pump mounting—5.0L V8 engine

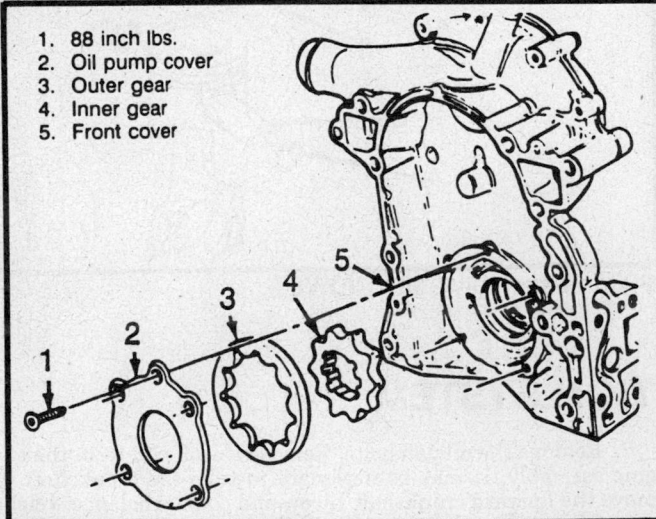

1. 88 inch lbs.
2. Oil pump cover
3. Outer gear
4. Inner gear
5. Front cover

Exploded view of oil pump and housing—3.8L V6 engine

5. Remove the flywheel cover and drain the engine oil.
6. Disconnect exhaust and crossover pipes.
7. On the 5.0L and 5.7L Chevrolet produced engines, disconnect the AIR pipes at the exhaust manifold and at the converter pipe.
8. Remove starter assembly.

9. Disconnect the transmission oil cooler lines at the clips on the oil pan.
10. Remove engine mounts from engine block.
11. Raise the engine enough to remove the oil pan.
12. Remove oil pan.
13. Installation is the reverse of the removal procedure.
14. Apply sealer to both sides of pan gasket.
15. Apply sealer to front cover.
16. Install front and rear rubber pan seals.
17. Wipe seal with engine oil then install pan. Fill crankcase and start engine to check for leaks.

Oil Pump

Removal and Installation

V6 ENGINE

1. Disconnect the negative battery cable.
2. Drain the engine oil. Remove the oil filter.
3. Unbolt the pump cover assembly from the timing chain cover.
4. Remove the cover assembly and slide out the pump gears.
5. Remove the oil pressure relief valve cap, spring, and valve. Do not remove the oil filter bypass valve and spring.
6. Check that the relief valve spring isn't worn on its side or collapsed. Check that the relief valve spring is no more than an easy slip fit in its bore in the cover. If there is any perceptible side play, replace the valve. If there is still side play, replace the cover.
7. Installation is the reverse of the removal procedure.

V8 ENGINE

1. Disconnect the negative battery cable.
2. Drain the engine oil.
3. Remove the engine oil pan.
4. Remove the pump attaching screws and carefully lower the pump.
5. Installation is the reverse of the removal procdure.

Rear Main Oil Seal

Removal and Installation

ONE PIECE SEAL

1. Disconnect the negaitive battery cable.
2. Raise the vehicle and support it safely.
3. Remove the transmission assembly.
4. Remove the flywheel from the engine.
5. Lower the oil pan.
6. Remove the rear crankshaft seal retainer with the seal and gasket.
7. Using the notches provided in the retainer, pry out the seal.
8. Installation is the reverse of the removal procedure.
9. Coat the new seal entirely with engine oil. Using tool J-35621, install the seal to the rear of crankshaft then install the retainer with the tool attached. Tighten the wingnut of the tool until it bottoms. Remove the tool from the retainer.

TWO PIECE SEAL

1. Disconnect the negative battery cable.
2. Raise the vehicle and support it safley.
3. Drain the engine oil and remove oil pan.
4. Remove the rear main bearing cap.
5. Pry the lower seal out of the bearing cap with a suitable tool, being careful not to gouge the cap surface.

NOTE: The following is a repair procedure for the upper oil seal with the engine in the vehicle. If upper seal replacement is necessary, crankshaft removal is required with the engine removed from the vehicle.

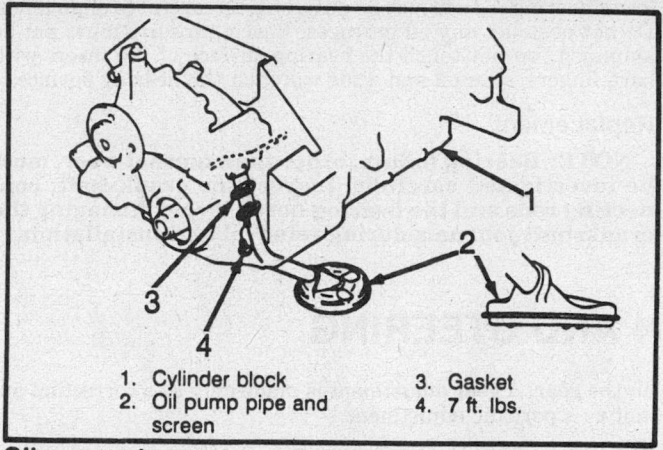

1. Cylinder block   3. Gasket
2. Oil pump pipe and   4. 7 ft. lbs.
     screen

Oil pump pipe and screen mounting—3.8L V6 engine

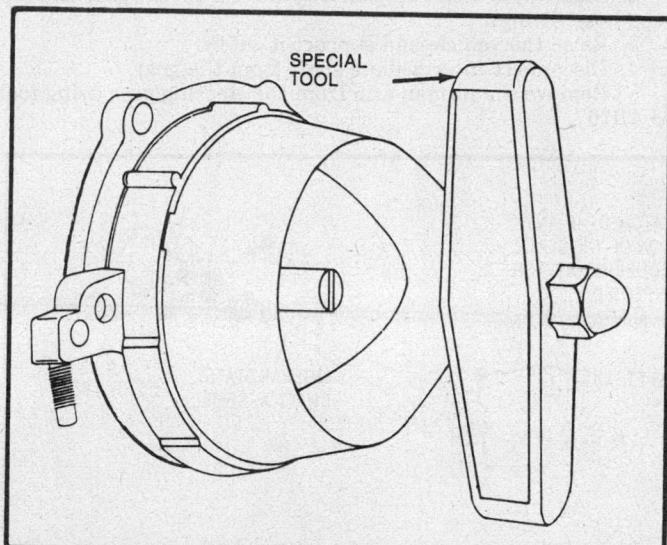

One piece rear main oil seal removal tool

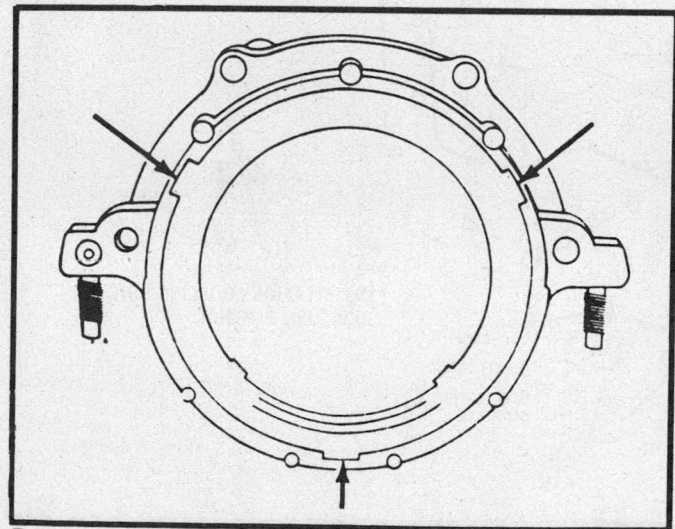

Removing the seal from the seal retainer

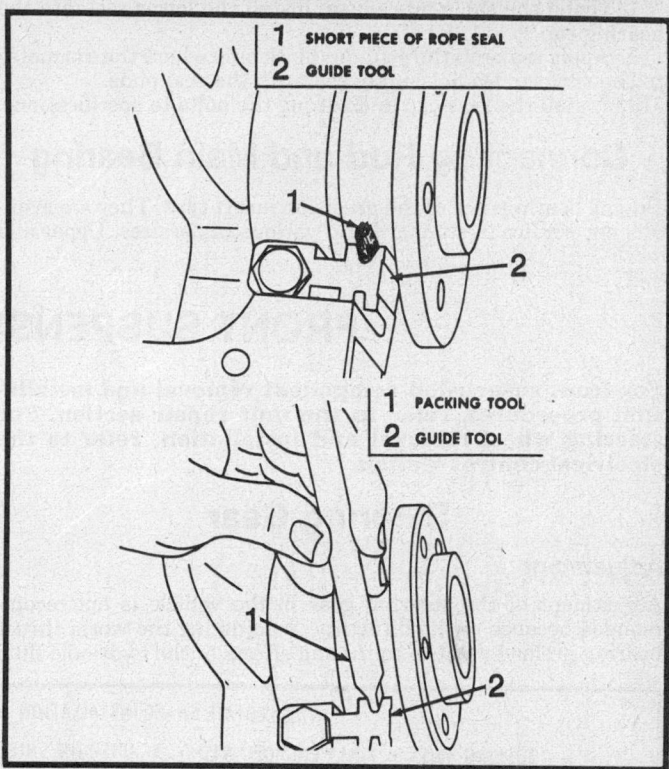

1. SHORT PIECE OF ROPE SEAL
2. GUIDE TOOL

1. PACKING TOOL
2. GUIDE TOOL

Rear main oil seal installation—V6 engine

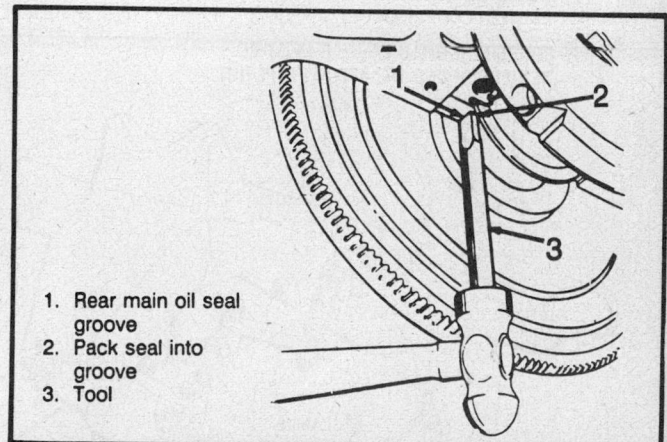

1. Rear main oil seal groove
2. Pack seal into groove
3. Tool

Installing rear main bearing upper seal—5.0L V8 engine

6. Remove the upper seal by lightly tapping on an end with a brass pin punch until the other end can be grasped and pulled out with pliers.

7. Apply light engine oil on the seal lips and bead, but keep the seal ends clean.

8. Insert the tip of the installation tool between the crankshaft and the seal of the cylinder block. Place the seal between the tip of the tool and the crankshaft, so that the bead contacts the tip of the tool.

9. Be sure that the seal lip is facing the front of the engine, and work the seal around the crankshaft using the installation tool to protect the seal from the corner of the cylinder block.

NOTE: Do not remove the tool until the opposite end of the seal is flush with the cylinder block surface.

10. Remove the installation tool, being careful not to pull the seal out at the same time.

11. Using the same procedure, install the lower seal into the bearing cap.

12. Apply sealer to the cylinder block only where the cap mates to the surface. Do not applly sealer to the seal ends.

13. Install the rear cap and torque the bolts to specifications.

Connecting Rod and Main Bearing

Engine bearings are of the precision insert type. They are available for service in standard and various undersizes. Upper and lower bearing inserts may be different. Be careful to align holes. Do not obstruct any oil passages. Bearing inserts must not be shimmed. Do not touch the bearing surface of the insert with bare fingers, skin oil and acids will etch the bearing surface.

Replacement

NOTE: Bearing failure, other than normal wear, must be investigated carefully. Inspect the crankshaft, connecting rods and the bearing bores. Avoid damaging the crankshaft journals during removal and installation.

FRONT SUSPENSION AND STEERING

For front suspension component removal and installation procedures, refer to the unit repair section. For steering wheel removal and installation, refer to the electrical control section.

Steering Gear

Adjustment

Adjustment of the steering gear in the vehicle is not recommended because of the difficulty in adjusting the worm thrust bearing preload and the confusing effects of the hydraulic fluid in the gear. A gear adjustment is made only as a correction and not as a periodic adjustment.

Removal and Installation

1. Disconnect the negative battery cable.
2. Disconnect the power steering hoses from the gear and cap the hose fittings.
3. Raise the vehicle and support it safely.
4. Disconnect intermediate shaft from the gear.
5. Remove the pitman arm from the steering gear using tool J–29107.

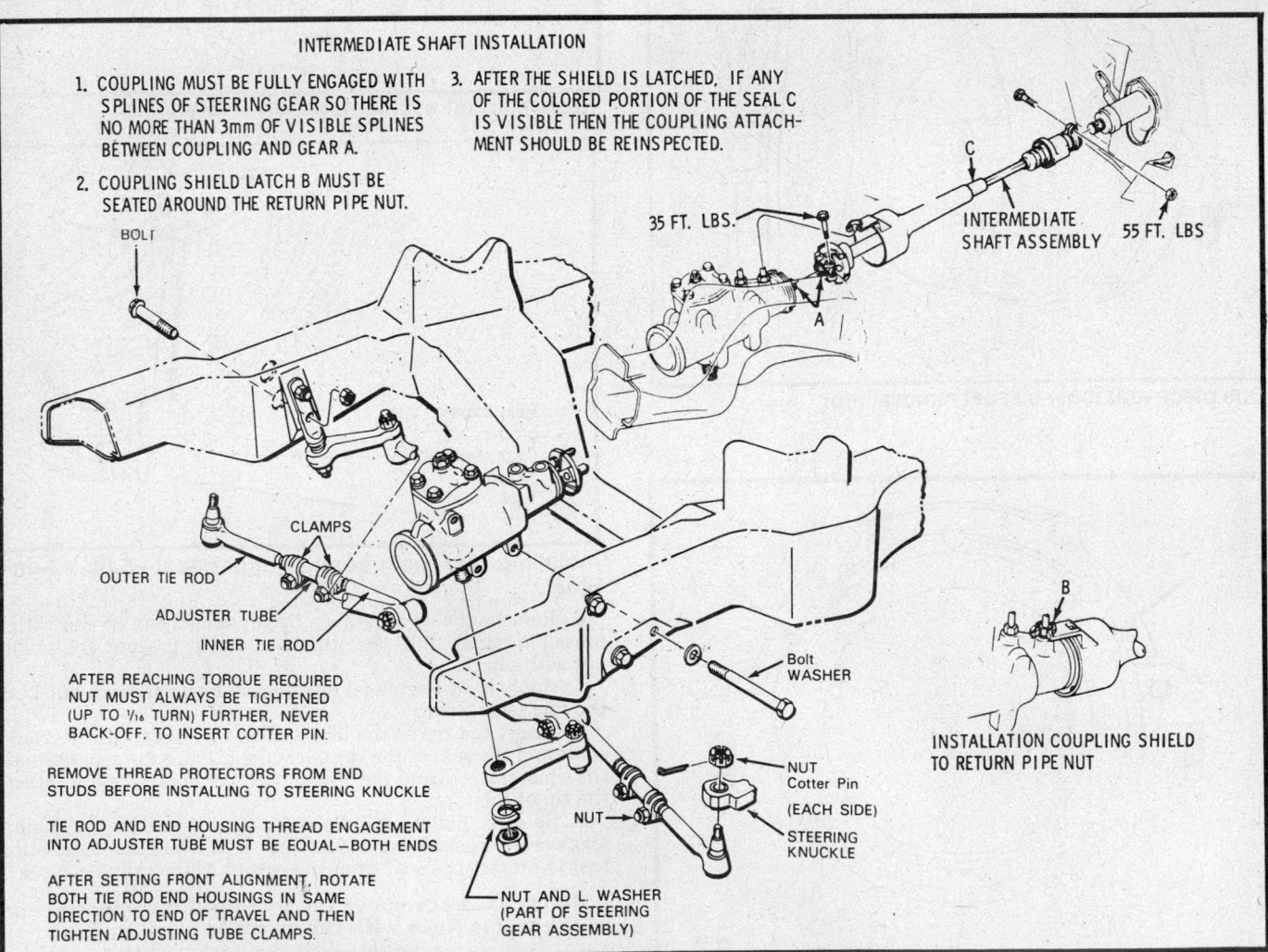

INTERMEDIATE SHAFT INSTALLATION

1. COUPLING MUST BE FULLY ENGAGED WITH SPLINES OF STEERING GEAR SO THERE IS NO MORE THAN 3mm OF VISIBLE SPLINES BETWEEN COUPLING AND GEAR A.

2. COUPLING SHIELD LATCH B MUST BE SEATED AROUND THE RETURN PIPE NUT.

3. AFTER THE SHIELD IS LATCHED, IF ANY OF THE COLORED PORTION OF THE SEAL C IS VISIBLE THEN THE COUPLING ATTACHMENT SHOULD BE REINSPECTED.

BOLT

35 FT. LBS.

C

INTERMEDIATE SHAFT ASSEMBLY

55 FT. LBS

A

B

INSTALLATION COUPLING SHIELD TO RETURN PIPE NUT

CLAMPS

OUTER TIE ROD

ADJUSTER TUBE

INNER TIE ROD

AFTER REACHING TORQUE REQUIRED NUT MUST ALWAYS BE TIGHTENED (UP TO 1/16 TURN) FURTHER, NEVER BACK-OFF, TO INSERT COTTER PIN.

REMOVE THREAD PROTECTORS FROM END STUDS BEFORE INSTALLING TO STEERING KNUCKLE

TIE ROD AND END HOUSING THREAD ENGAGEMENT INTO ADJUSTER TUBE MUST BE EQUAL—BOTH ENDS

AFTER SETTING FRONT ALIGNMENT, ROTATE BOTH TIE ROD END HOUSINGS IN SAME DIRECTION TO END OF TRAVEL AND THEN TIGHTEN ADJUSTING TUBE CLAMPS.

Bolt WASHER

NUT

NUT AND L. WASHER (PART OF STEERING GEAR ASSEMBLY)

NUT Cotter Pin (EACH SIDE)

STEERING KNUCKLE

Typical steering linkage and steering gear mounting

6. Remove the bolts that hold gear to frame and lower gear assembly down.

7. Installation is the reverse of the removal procedure.

8. Before positioning the gear, note that the flat on the gear lower shaft must index with the flat in the intermediate shaft.

9. Make certain there is a minimum of 0.040 in. (1.02mm) clearance between intermediate shaft coupling and steering gear upper seal. Tighten mounting bolts to 80 ft. lbs. (110 Nm).

Power Steering Pump

Removal and Installation

1. Disconnect the negative battery cable.
2. Loosen and remove power steering pump belt.
3. Remove bolts and nut from adjuster bracket.
4. Disconnect both lines at the pump and cap the lines.
5. Remove the pump assembly. Remove the pulley and bracket from the pump.
6. Installation is the reverse of the removal procedure. Connect power steering lines and tighten fittings to 20 ft. lbs. (27 Nm).
7. Fill with fluid and adjust belt to proper tension.

Bleeding System

When the power steering system has been serviced, air must be bled from the system by using the following procedure:
1. Turn wheels all the way to the left, add power steering fluid to the cold mark on the level indicator.
2. Start engine and run at fast idle momentarily, shut engine off and recheck the fluid level. If necessary add fluid to the cold mark.
3. Start engine and bleed system by turning wheels from side to side without hitting stops. Keep the fluid level at the cold mark. Fluid with air in it has a light tan or red appearance, this air must be eliminated before normal steering action can be achieved.
4. Return the wheels to the center position and continue running the engine for a few minutes. Roadtest to check the operation of the steering.
5. Recheck the fluid level it should now be stabilized at the Hot level on the indicator.

Steering Column

Removal and Installation

NOTE: Handle the steering column very carefully. Rapping on the end of it or leaning on it could shear off the inserts which allow the column to collapse in a crash.
1. Disconnect negative battery cable.
2. Disconnect flexible coupling.
3. Remove cover and toe-pan attaching screws.
4. If necessary, remove instrument panel lower trim.
5. Disconnect shift linkages, wiring, etc.
6. Remove lower column mounts, then upper column mounts, and pull column up and out of the vehicle.
7. When installing, check that flexible coupling alignment is correct.
NOTE: When installing, use only the specified hardware. Overlength bolts could prevent the column from properly collapsing in a crash.

Front Wheel Bearings

Removal and Installation

1. Raise the vehicle and support it safely.
2. Remove the tire and wheel assembly.
3. Using a C-clamp compress the caliper piston back into its bore. Rotate the disc until all the drag has been removed.

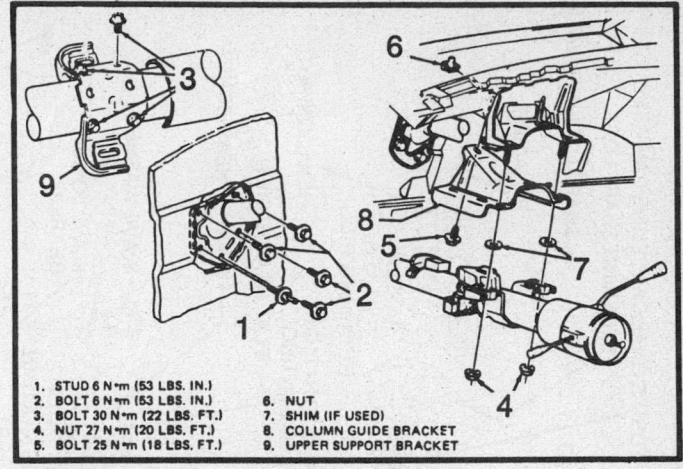

1. STUD 6 N·m (53 LBS. IN.)
2. BOLT 6 N·m (53 LBS. IN.)
3. BOLT 30 N·m (22 LBS. FT.)
4. NUT 27 N·m (20 LBS. FT.)
5. BOLT 25 N·m (18 LBS. FT.)
6. NUT
7. SHIM (IF USED)
8. COLUMN GUIDE BRACKET
9. UPPER SUPPORT BRACKET

Steering column mounting—typical

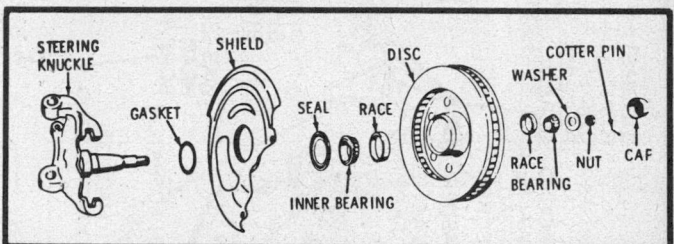

Hub and wheel bearings

4. Remove the caliper to adapter attaching bolts. Lift caliper assembly from disc and support so that brake hose is not damaged.
5. Remove the dust cap from the hub using tool BT-6507.
6. Remove cotter pin, nut, and washer from spindle. carefully pull hub from spindle and remove outer bearing.
7. Pry seal from hub, then remove inner bearing assembly.
8. Installation is the reverse of the removal procedure.
9. Tighten the spindle nut to 12 ft. lbs. (16 Nm) while turning the wheel forward by hand to fully seat the bearings.
10. Back off the nut to the just loose position. Hand tighten the spindle nut. Loosen nut until either hole in the spindle lines with a slot in the nut. (Not more than ½ flat).

Alignment

Procedures

CASTER AND CAMBER

1. Raise the vehicle and support it safely.
2. Loosen the upper control arm shaft to frame nuts.
3. Add or subtract shims as required per alignment correction charts.
4. Tighten the upper control arm shaft to frame nuts.
NOTE: A normal shim pack will leave at least 2 threads of the bolt exposed beyond the nut. If these requirements cannot be met in order to reach specifications, check for damaged suspension and steering components and replace parts as necessary.

TOE

1. Raise the vehicle and support it safely.
2. Loosen the clamp bolts at each end of the steering tie rod adjusting sleeves.
3. With steering wheel set in the straight ahead position, turn tie rod adjusting sleeves to obtain the proper toe-in adjustment.
4. When adjustment is completed, check to see that the number of threads showing on each end of the sleeve are equal.

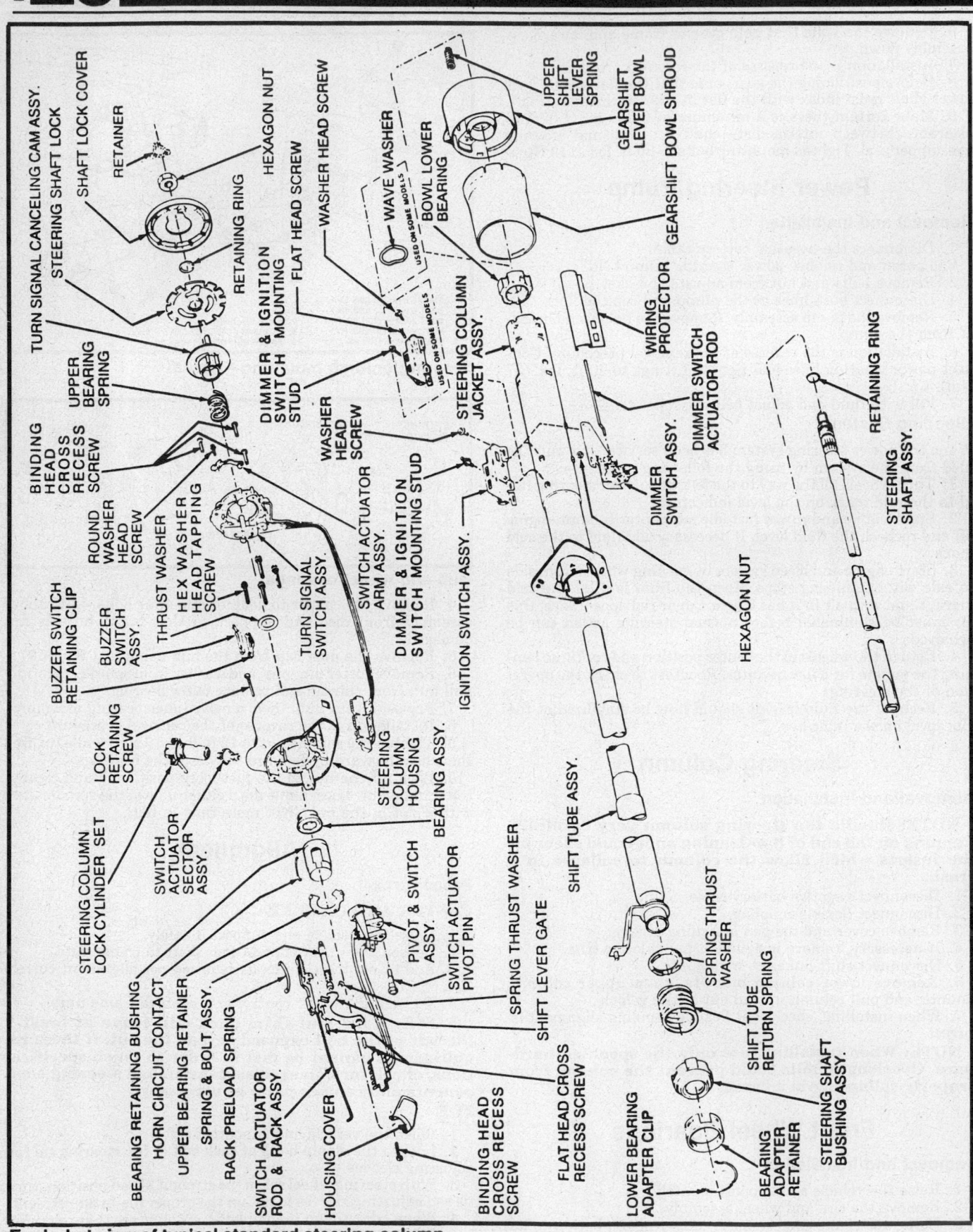

Exploded view of typical standard steering column

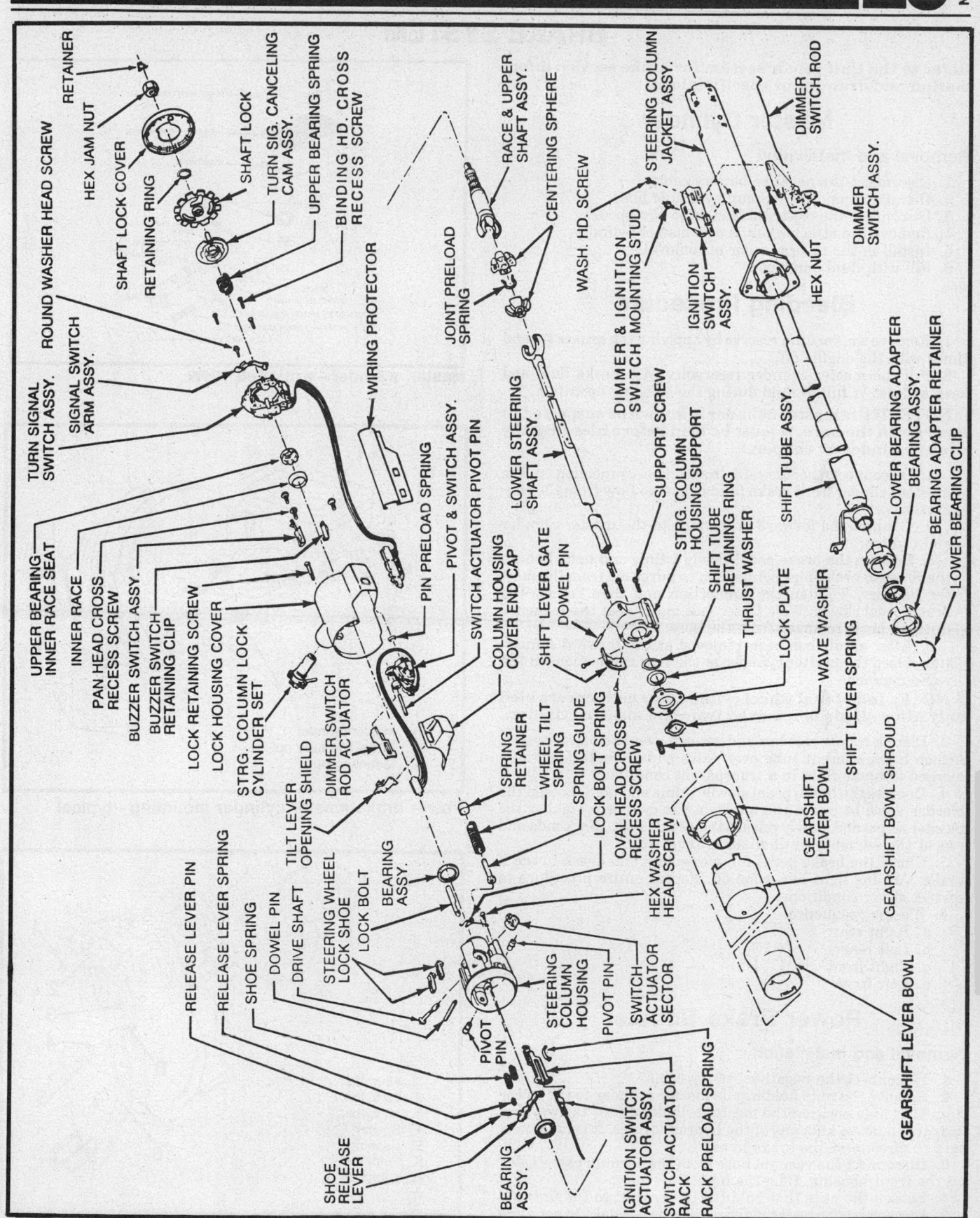

Exploded view of typical tilt wheel steering column

BRAKE SYSTEM

Refer to the Unit repair section for brake service information and drum/rotor specifications.

Master Cylinder

Removal and Installation

1. Disconnect the negative battery cable.
2. Disconnect and cap or plug hydraulic lines.
3. Disconnect the electrical lead, if so equipped.
4. Remove the attaching nuts and master cylinder.
5. Install in the reverse order of removal.
6. Fill with fluid and bleed.

Bleeding Procedure

1. Remove the vacuum reserve by applying the brakes several times with the engine off.
2. Fill the master cylinder reservoirs with brake fluid and keep at least ½ full of fluid during the bleeding operation.

NOTE: If the master cylinder is known or suspected to have air in the bore, it must be bled before bleeding any wheel cylinder or caliper.

    a. Disconnect the forward brake pipe connection at the master cylinder until brake fluid begins to flow from the connector port.

    b. Connect the forward brake pipe to the master cylinder and tighten.

    c. Depress the brake pedal slowly 1 time and hold. Loosen the forward brake pipe connection to purge air from the master cylinder. Tighten the connection and then release the brake pedal slowly. Wait 15 seconds and repeat the sequence until all air is removed from the bore.

    d. After all air has been removed at the forward connection, bleed the master cylinder at the rear connections in the same manner.

NOTE: Individual wheel cylinders or calipers are bled only after all air is removed from the master cylinder.

3. Place a proper size box end wrench over the bleeder valve. Attach a transparent tube over valve and allow to hang submerged in brake fluid in a transparent container.

4. Depress the brake pedal slowly 1 time and hold. Loosen the bleeder valve to purge the air from the cylinder. Tighten the bleeder screw and slowly release the pedal. Wait 15 seconds and repeat the sequence until all air is removed.

5. Check the brake pedal for sponginess and check to see if brake warning light has come on. Repeat entire procedure to correct either condition.

6. Bleeding sequence:
    a. Right rear
    b. Left rear
    c. Right front
    d. Left front

Power Brake Booster

Removal and Installation

1. Disconnect the negative battery cable.
2. Remove the nuts holding the master cylinder to the power unit. Carefully position the master cylinder out of the way, being careful not to kink any of the hydraulic lines. It is not necessary to disconnect the brake lines.
3. Disconnect the vacuum hose from the vacuum check valve on the front housing. Plug the hose.
4. Loosen the nuts that hold the power unit to the firewall.
5. Disconnect the pushrod from the brake pedal. Do not force the pushrod to the side when disconnecting.

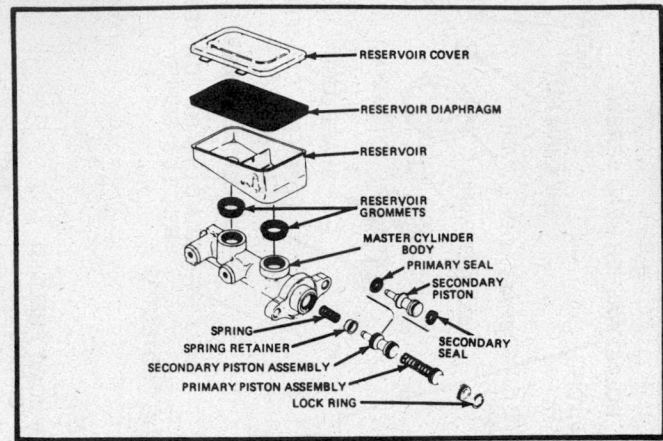

Master cylinder—exploded view

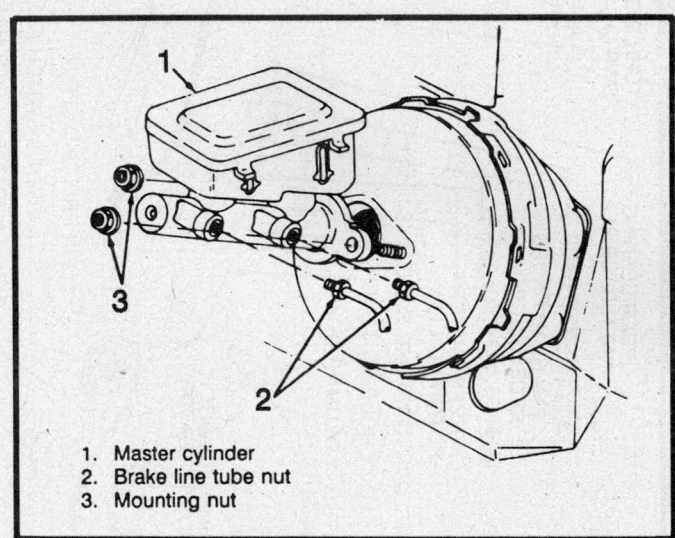

1. Master cylinder
2. Brake line tube nut
3. Mounting nut

Power brake master cylinder mounting—typical

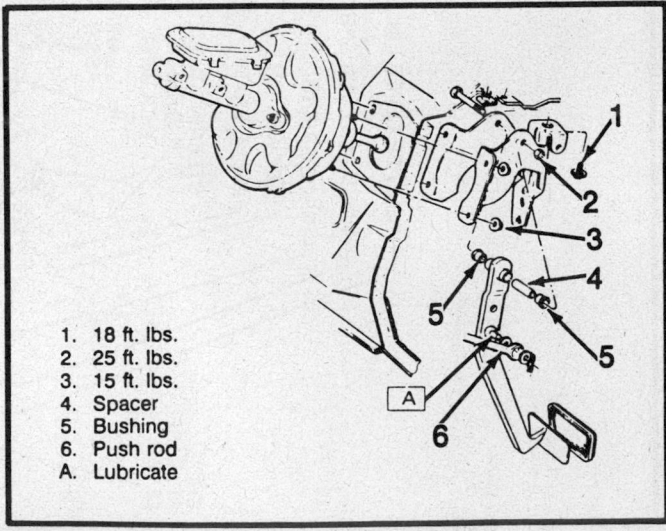

1. 18 ft. lbs.
2. 25 ft. lbs.
3. 15 ft. lbs.
4. Spacer
5. Bushing
6. Push rod
A. Lubricate

Power brake booster mounting—typical

6. Remove the mounting nuts and lift the power unit off the studs.

7. Installation is the reverse of removal. Torque the master cylinder to power brake unit mounting studs to 24 ft. lbs.

Parking Brake

Adjustment

Adjustment of the parking brake is necessary whenever the rear brake cables have been disconnected or the parking brake pedal can be depressed more than 8 ratchet clicks under heavy foot pressure. The rear of the vehicle should first be raised.

1. Make sure that the service brakes are properly adjusted.
2. Depress the parking brake pedal 2 ratchet clicks on all models.
3. Loosen the jam nut on the equalizer adjusting nut. Tighten the adjusting nut until the left rear wheel can just be turned rearward by hand, but not forward.
4. Release the ratchet 1 click; the rear wheel should rotate rearward freely and forward with a slight drag.
5. Release the ratchet fully; the rear wheel should turn freely in either direction.

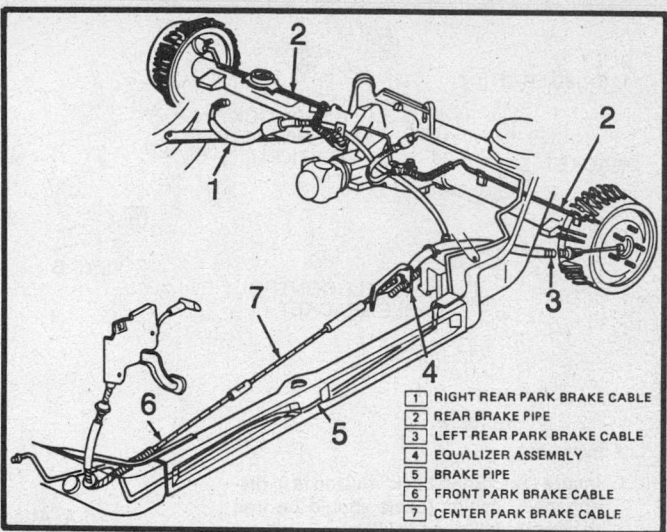

1	RIGHT REAR PARK BRAKE CABLE
2	REAR BRAKE PIPE
3	LEFT REAR PARK BRAKE CABLE
4	EQUALIZER ASSEMBLY
5	BRAKE PIPE
6	FRONT PARK BRAKE CABLE
7	CENTER PARK BRAKE CABLE

Parking brake cables

TRANSMISSION

Automatic Transmission

Removal and Installation

1. Disconnect the battery.
2. Disconnect the T.V. cable at the throttle lever.
3. Remove the transmission dipstick. Remove the bolt retaining the filler tube to the transmission.
4. Raise the vehicle and support it safely.
5. Remove the driveshaft. The floor pan reinforcement if used, may need to be removed if it interferes with the removal of the driveshaft.
6. Disconnect the speedometer cable and the shift linkage at the transmission.
7. Disconnect all electrical leads at the transmission and any clips that retain the leads to the transmission.
8. Remove the flywheel cover.
9. Mark flywheel and converter for installation reference.
10. Remove the torque converter to flywheel bolts.
11. Remove the catalytic converter support bracket.

12. Remove the transmission mount to support bolt and the transmission support to frame bolts and insulators.
13. Support and raise the transmission slightly.
14. Slide the transmission support rearward.
15. Lower the transmission to gain access to the oil cooler lines. Disconnect the lines and cap all openings.
16. Support the engine with a suitable jack. and remove the transmission to engine bolts.
17. Slide the transmission rearward and install tool J–21366 to the converter to hold it in place.
18. Remove the transmission assembly from the vehicle.
19. Installation is the reverse of the removal procedure.
20. Adjust the shift linkage, T.V. cable and check the fluid level.

SHIFT ROD

Adjustment

1. With shift rod clamp screw loosened, set transmission outer lever in **N** position.

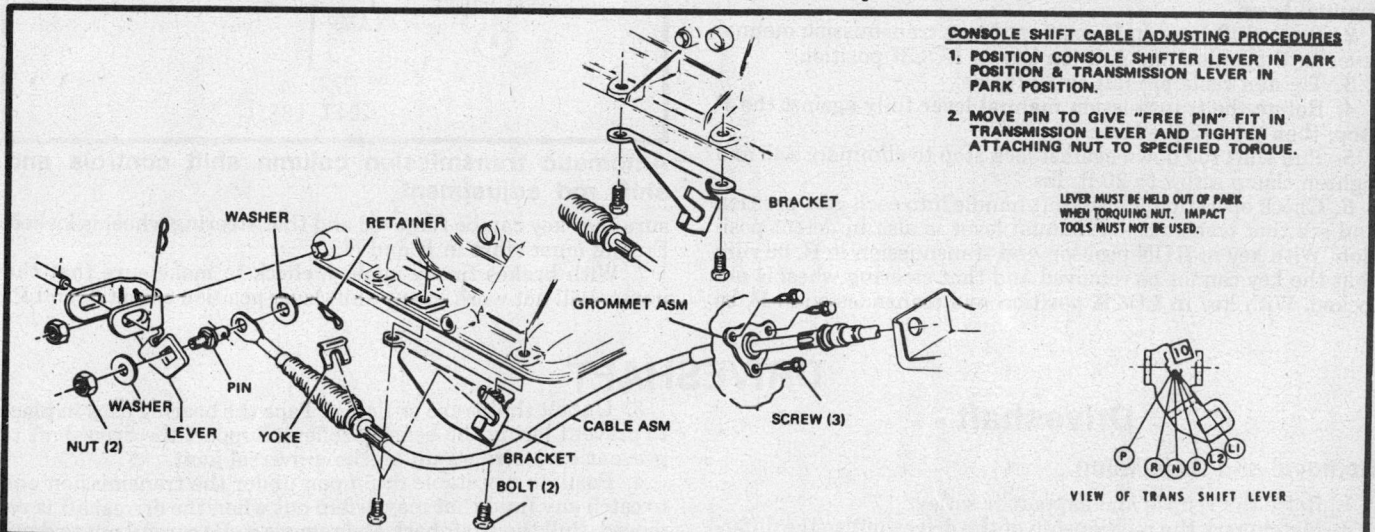

WASHER • RETAINER • BRACKET

NUT (2) • WASHER • PIN • LEVER • YOKE • BRACKET • BOLT (2) • CABLE ASM • GROMMET ASM • SCREW (3)

CONSOLE SHIFT CABLE ADJUSTING PROCEDURES

1. POSITION CONSOLE SHIFTER LEVER IN PARK POSITION & TRANSMISSION LEVER IN PARK POSITION.

2. MOVE PIN TO GIVE "FREE PIN" FIT IN TRANSMISSION LEVER AND TIGHTEN ATTACHING NUT TO SPECIFIED TORQUE.

LEVER MUST BE HELD OUT OF PARK WHEN TORQUING NUT. IMPACT TOOLS MUST NOT BE USED.

VIEW OF TRANS SHIFT LEVER

Linkage adjustment console shift

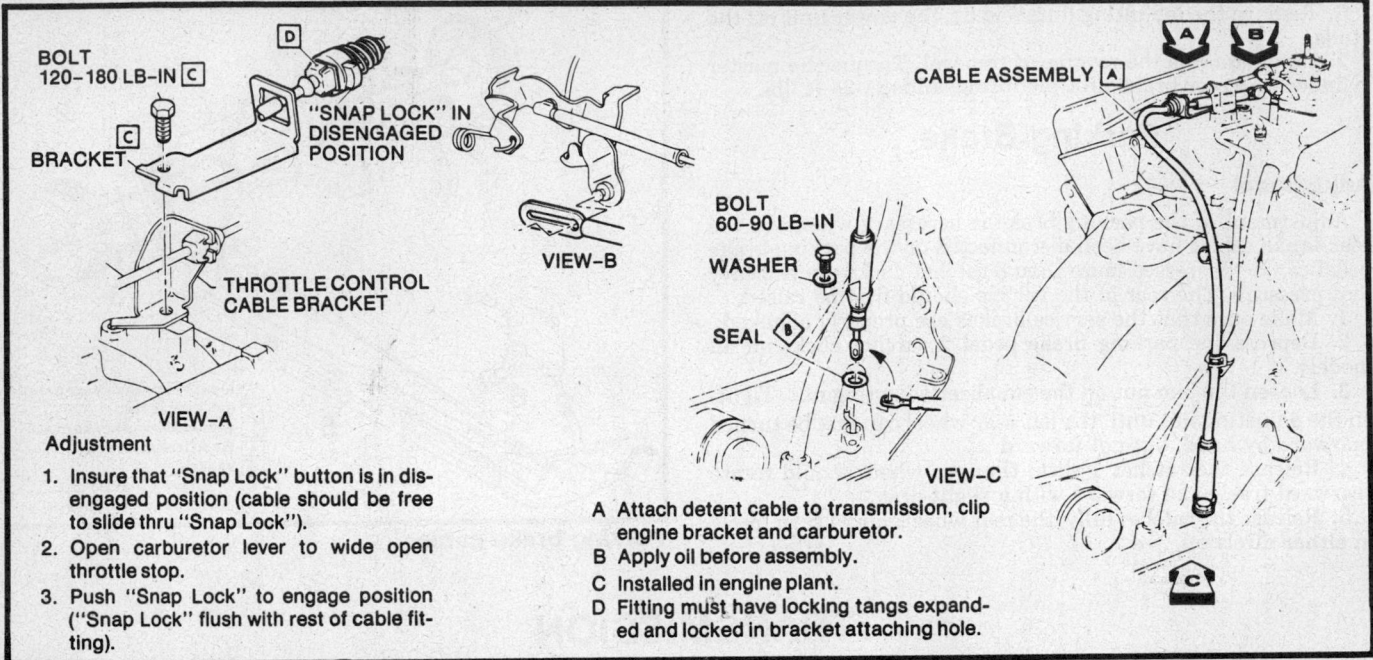

BOLT 120-180 LB-IN [C]

BRACKET [C]

"SNAP LOCK" IN DISENGAGED POSITION

THROTTLE CONTROL CABLE BRACKET

VIEW-A

VIEW-B

CABLE ASSEMBLY [A]

BOLT 60-90 LB-IN

WASHER

SEAL

VIEW-C

Adjustment

1. Insure that "Snap Lock" button is in disengaged position (cable should be free to slide thru "Snap Lock").
2. Open carburetor lever to wide open throttle stop.
3. Push "Snap Lock" to engage position ("Snap Lock" flush with rest of cable fitting).

A Attach detent cable to transmission, clip engine bracket and carburetor.
B Apply oil before assembly.
C Installed in engine plant.
D Fitting must have locking tangs expanded and locked in bracket attaching hole.

Detent cable adjustment in all car models

2. Hold upper shift lever against **N** position stop in upper steering column. Do not raise lever.
3. Tighten screw in clamp on lower end of shift rod to specified torque.
4. Check operation. With key in **RUN** position and transmission in **R**, be sure that the key cannot be removed and that the steering wheel is not locked. With key in **LOCK** position and shift lever in **P**, be sure that the key can be removed, that the steering wheel is locked and that the transmission remains in **P** when the steering column is locked.
5. With brakes firmly applied, check to make sure that the starter will not work in any shift lever position except **N** and **P**.

SHIFT CABLE

Adjustment

1. Loosen shift rod clamp screw, loosen pin in transmission manual lever.
2. Place shift lever in **P** position. Place transmission manual lever in **P** position and ignition key in **LOCK** position.
3. Tighten cable pin nut to 20 ft. lbs.
4. Rotate the transmission manual lever fully against the **P** stop, then release the lever.
5. Pull shift rod down against lock stop to eliminate lash and tighten clamp screw to 20 ft. lbs.
6. Check operation. Move shift handle into each gear position and see that transmission manual lever is also in detent position. With key in **RUN** position and transmission in **R**, be sure that the key cannot be removed and that steering wheel is not locked. With key in **LOCK** position and transmission in **P**, be

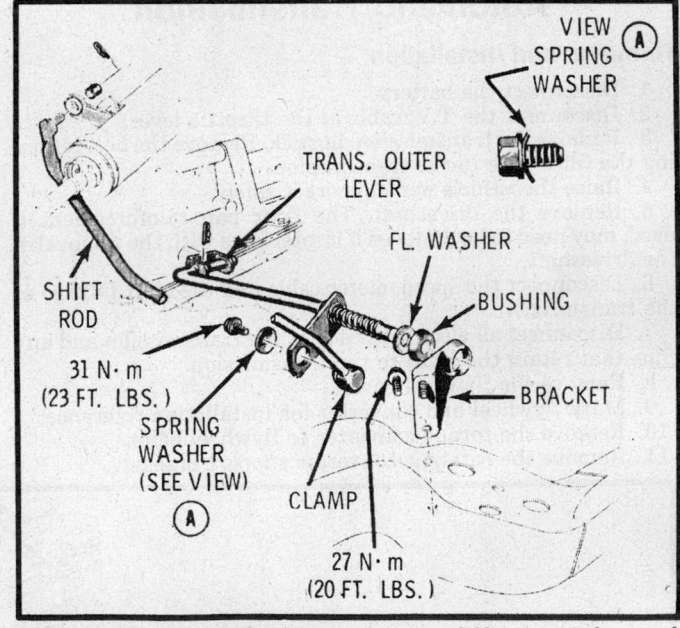

VIEW (A) SPRING WASHER

TRANS. OUTER LEVER

FL. WASHER

BUSHING

SHIFT ROD

31 N·m (23 FT. LBS.)

SPRING WASHER (SEE VIEW) (A)

BRACKET

CLAMP

27 N·m (20 FT. LBS.)

Automatic transmission column shift controls and shift rod adjustment

sure that key can be removed and that steering wheel is locked. Engine must start in **P** and **N**.
7. With brakes firmly applied, check to make sure that the starter will not work in any shift lever position except **N** and **P**.

DRIVESHAFT

Driveshaft

Removal and Installation

1. Raise the vehicle and support it safley.
2. Matchmark the relationship of the driveshaft to the differential flange.

3. Unbolt the straps or flange. Tape the bearing caps in place to prevent losing the bearing rollers. Support the driveshaft to prevent excessive strain on the universal joint.
4. Position a suitable drain pan under the transmission end to catch any fluid that may drfain out when the driveshaft is removed. Pull the shaft back and remove it. Be careful not to damage the splines at the transmission end.

5. If the transmission splined slip yoke does not have a vent hole at the center, it should be lubricated for installation with engine oil. If it does have a vent hole, it should be lubricated with grease. Slide the slip yoke into place.

6. Align the matchmarks and tighten the bolts. Tighten the U-bolts to 16 ft. lbs.

Universal Joints

Refer to the Unit Repair Section for overhaul procedures.

REAR AXLE AND REAR SUSPENSION

Refer to the Unit Repair Section for axle overhaul procedures and rear suspension services.

Rear Axle Assembly

Removal and Installation

1. Raise the vehicle and support it safely. Be sure that the rear axle assembly is supported safely.
2. Disconnect shock absorbers from axle.
3. Mark driveshaft and pinion flange, disconnect driveshaft and support it out of the way.
4. Remove brake line junction block bolt at axle housing, disconnect brake lines at junction block. On some vehicles, disconnect brake line at wheel cylinder.
5. Disconnect upper control arms from axle housing.
6. Lower rear axle assembly on hoist and remove springs.
7. Remove rear wheels and drums.
8. Disconnect brake lines from axle housing clips.
9. Disconnect lower control arms from axle housing.
10. Remove rear axle housing.
11. Installation is the reverse of the removal procedure.
12. Be sure to bleed the brake system, as required.

Axle Shaft

Removal and Installation

1. Raise vehicle and support it safely. Remove the tire and wheel assembly. Remove the brake drum.
2. Drain the fluid. Remove the rear carrier cover. Discard the gasket.
3. Remove the rear axle pinion shaft lock screw and the rear axle pinion shaft.
4. Push flanged end of axle shaft toward center of the vehicle and remove C-lock from button end of shaft.
5. Remove axle shaft from housing, being careful not to damage oil seal.
6. Installation is the reverse of the removal procedure. Be sure to fill the rear assembly with the proper grade and type gear oil.

Oil Seal/Bearing

Removal and Installation

1. Remove the axle shaft.
2. Remove seal from housing with a pry bar behind steel case of seal, being careful not to damage housing.
3. Insert tool J–23689 or equivalent into bore and position it behind bearing so that tangs on tool engage bearing outer race. Remove bearing, using slide hammer.
4. Lubricate the new bearing with gear lubricant and install bearing so that tool bottoms against shoulder in housing, using tool J–23690 or equivalent.
5. Lubricate seal lips with gear lubricant. Position seal on tool J–21128 or equivalent and position seal into housing bore. Tap seal into place so that it is flush with axle tube.

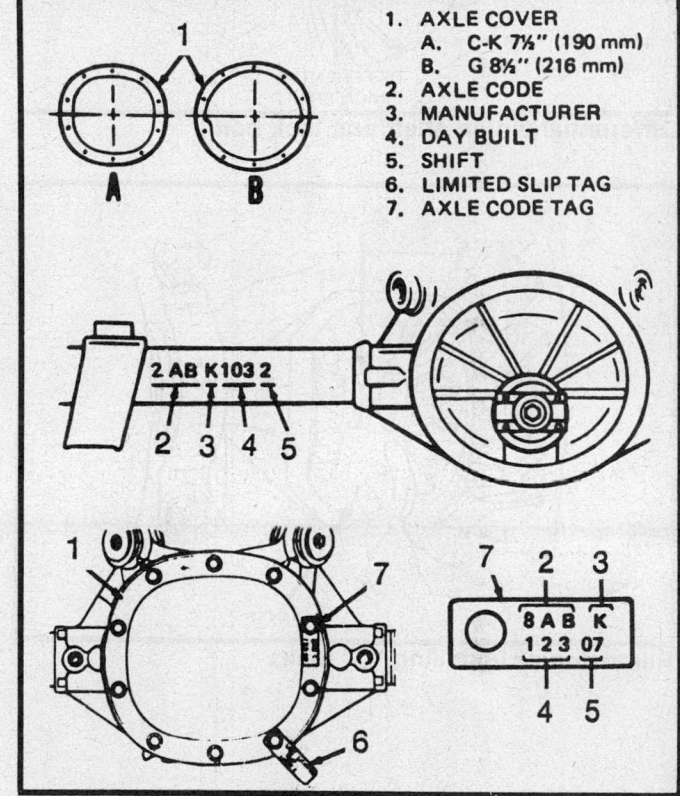

1. AXLE COVER
   A. C-K 7½" (190 mm)
   B. G 8½" (216 mm)
2. AXLE CODE
3. MANUFACTURER
4. DAY BUILT
5. SHIFT
6. LIMITED SLIP TAG
7. AXLE CODE TAG

Rear Axle Identification

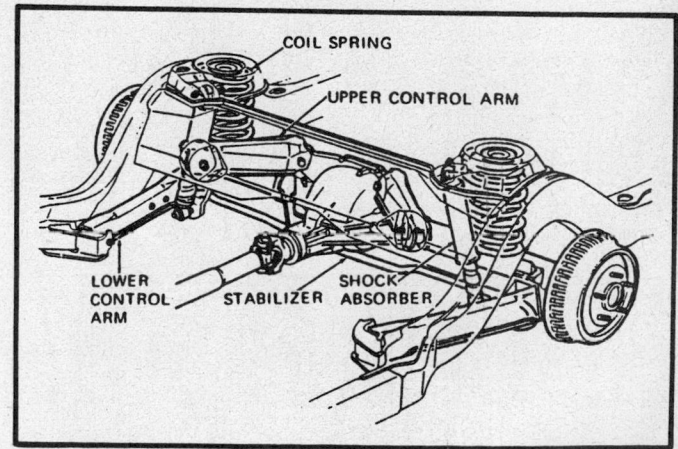

Rear axle mounting and rear suspension components

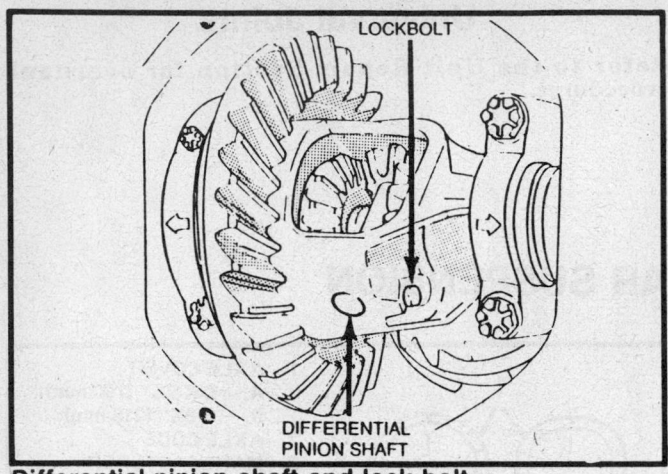

Differential pinion shaft and lock bolt

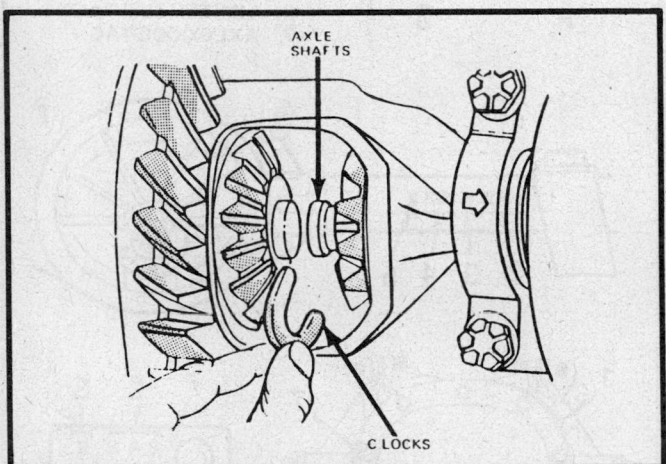

Removing or installing "C" locks

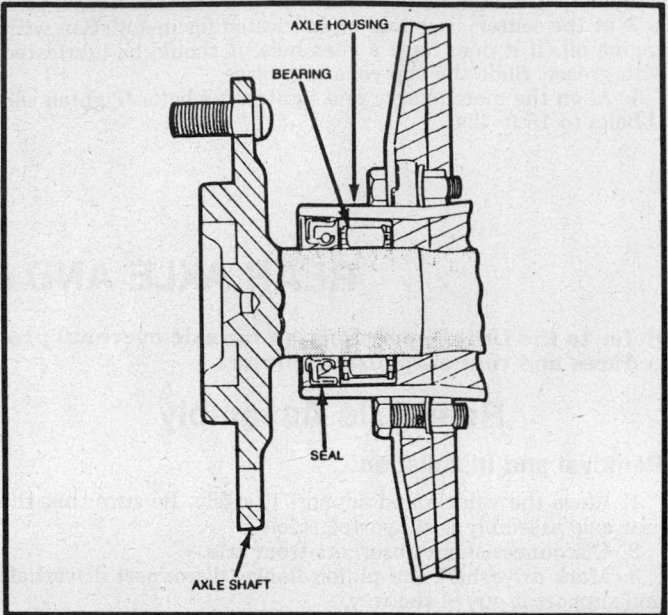

Rear axle shaft bearing and seal—cut away view

YEAR IDENTIFICATION

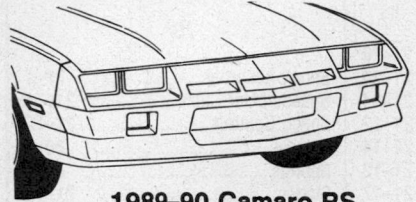

1989–90 Camaro RS

1986–88 Camaro Z28

1986–90 Camaro IROC

1987-89 Firebird Formula

1986 Firebird

1986–90 Firebird Trans AM/GTA

VEHICLE IDENTIFICATION

It is important for servicing and ordering parts to be certain of the vehicle and engine identification. The VIN (vehicle identification number) is a 17 digit number visible through the windshield on the driver's side of the dash and contains the vehicle and engine identification codes. The tenth digit indicates model year and the eighth digit indicates engine code. It can be interpreted as follows:

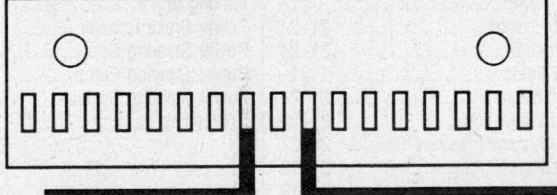

		Engine Code					Model Year	
Code	Cu. In.	Liters	Cyl.	Fuel Sys.	Eng. Mfg.		Code	Year
F	151	2.5	4	Carb.	Pontiac		G	1986
2	151	2.5	4	TBI	Pontiac		H	1987
1	173	2.8	6	Carb.	Chevrolet		J	1988
S	173	2.8	6	MFI	Chevrolet		K	1989
H	305	5.0	8	Carb.	Chevrolet		L	1990
G	305	5.0	8	Carb.	Chevrolet			
F	305	5.0	8	TPI	Chevrolet			
E	305	5.0	8	EFI	Chevrolet			
8	350	5.7	8	TPI	Chevrolet			

ENGINE IDENTIFICATION

Year	Model	Engine Displacement cu. in. (liter)	Engine Series Identification (VIN)	No. of Cylinders	Engine Type
1986	Camaro	151 (2.5)	2	4	OHV
	Firebird	151 (2.5)	2	4	OHV
	Camaro	173 (2.8)	5	6	OHV
	Firebird	173 (2.8)	5	6	OHV
	Camaro	305 (5.0)	G	8	OHV
	Firebird	305 (5.0)	G	8	OHV
	Camaro	305 (5.0)	H	8	OHV
	Firebird	305 (5.0)	H	8	OHV
	Camaro	305 (5.0)	F	8	OHV
	Firebird	305 (5.0)	F	8	OHV
	Camaro	350 (5.7)	8	8	OHV
	Firebird	350 (5.7)	8	8	OHV
1987	Camaro	173 (2.8)	5	6	OHV
	Firebird	173 (2.8)	5	6	OHV
	Camaro	305 (5.0)	H	8	OHV
	Firebird	305 (5.0)	H	8	OHV
	Camaro	305 (5.0)	F	8	OHV
	Firebird	305 (5.0)	F	8	OHV
	Camaro	350 (5.7)	8	8	OHV
	Firebird	350 (5.7)	8	8	OHV
1988	Camaro	173 (2.8)	S	6	OHV
	Firebird	173 (2.8)	S	6	OHV
	Camaro	305 (5.0)	F	8	OHV
	Firebird	305 (5.0)	F	8	OHV
	Camaro	305 (5.0)	E	8	OHV
	Firebird	305 (5.0)	E	8	OHV
	Camaro	350 (5.7)	8	8	OHV
	Firebird	350 (5.7)	8	8	OHV
1989-90	Camaro	173 (2.8)	S	6	OHV
	Firebird	173 (2.8)	S	6	OHV
	Camaro	305 (5.0)	F	8	OHV
	Firebird	305 (5.0)	F	8	OHV
	Camaro	305 (5.0)	F	8	OHV
	Firebird	305 (5.0)	F	8	OHV
	Camaro	350 (5.7)	8	8	OHV
	Firebird	350 (5.7)	8	8	OHV
	Camaro	191 (3.1)	—	6	OHV
	Firebird	191 (3.1)	—	6	OHV

OHV Over Head Valve

GENERAL ENGINE SPECIFICATIONS

Year	VIN	No. Cylinder Displacement cu. in. (liter)	Fuel System Type	Net Horsepower @ rpm	Net Torque @ rpm (ft.lbs.)	Bore × Stroke (in.)	Compression Ratio	Oil Pressure @ 2000 rpm
1986	2	4-151 (2.5)	EFI	92 @ 4000	134 @ 2800	4.000 × 3.000	9.0:1	40
	S	6-173 (2.8)	MFI	135 @ 5100	165 @ 3600	3.500 × 3.000	8.9:1	55
	G	8-305 (5.0)	Carb.	165 @ 4400	250 @ 2000	3.740 × 3.480	9.5:1	55
	H	8-305 (5.0)	Carb.	150 @ 4000	240 @ 2400	3.736 × 3.480	8.6:1	55
	F	8-305 (5.0)	TPI	190 @ 4800	240 @ 3200	3.740 × 3.480	9.5:1	55
	8	8-350 (5.7)	TPI	230 @ 4000	300 @ 3200	3.736 × 3.480	9.5:1	55
1987	S	6-173 (2.8)	MFI	135 @ 5100	165 @ 3600	3.500 × 3.000	8.9:1	55
	H	8-305 (5.0)	Carb.	150 @ 4000	240 @ 2400	3.736 × 3.480	8.6:1	55
	F	8-305 (5.0)	TPI	190 @ 4800	240 @ 3200	3.740 × 3.480	9.3:1	55
	8	8-350 (5.7)	TPI	230 @ 4000	300 @ 3200	4.000 × 3.480	9.5:1	55
1988	S	6-173 (2.8)	MFI	135 @ 5100	165 @ 3600	3.500 × 3.000	8.9:1	55
	F	8-305 (5.0)	TPI	190 @ 4800	240 @ 3200	3.736 × 3.480	9.3:1	55
	E	8-305 (5.0)	TBI	150 @ 4000	240 @ 3200	3.736 × 3.480	9.3:1	55
	8	8-350 (5.7)	TPI	230 @ 4000	300 @ 3200	4.000 × 3.480	9.5:1	55
1989-90	S	6-173 (2.8)	MFI	135 @ 5100	165 @ 3600	3.500 × 3.000	8.9:1	55
	F	8-305 (5.0)	TPI	190 @ 4800	240 @ 3200	3.736 × 3.480	9.3:1	55
	E	8-305 (5.0)	TBI	150 @ 4000	240 @ 3200	3.736 × 3.480	9.3:1	55
	8	8-350 (5.7)	TPI	230 @ 4000	300 @ 3200	4.000 × 3.480	9.5:1	55

GASOLINE ENGINE TUNE-UP SPECIFICATIONS
Refer to Section 34 for all spark plug recommendations

Year	VIN	No. Cylinder Displacement cu. in. (liter)	Spark Plugs Gap (in.)	Ignition Timing (deg.) MT	Ignition Timing (deg.) AT	Compression Pressure (psi)	Fuel Pump (psi)	Idle Speed (rpm) MT	Idle Speed (rpm) AT	Valve Clearance In.	Valve Clearance Ex.
1986	2	4-151 (2.5)	.060	8	8	NA	9.0-13.0	775	500	Hyd.	Hyd.
	S	6-173 (2.8)	.045	10	10	NA	40-47	600	500	Hyd.	Hyd.
	G	8-305 (5.0)	.045	6	6	NA	9.0-13.0	750	550	Hyd.	Hyd.
	H	8-305 (5.0)	.045	6	6	NA	9.0-13.0	750	550	Hyd.	Hyd.
	F	8-305 (5.0)	.045	—	6	NA	40-47	—	500	Hyd.	Hyd.
	8	8-350 (5.7)	.045	6	6	NA	34-39	450	400	Hyd.	Hyd.
1987	S	6-173 (2.8)	.045	10	10	NA	40-47	600	500	Hyd.	Hyd.
	H	8-305 (5.0)	.035	6	6	NA	9.0-13.0	500	500	Hyd.	Hyd.
	F	8-305 (5.0)	.035	6	6	NA	40-47	500	500	Hyd.	Hyd.
	8	8-350 (5.7)	.035	6	6	NA	40-47	450	400	Hyd.	Hyd.
1988	S	6-173 (2.8)	.045	10	10	NA	40-47	450	400	Hyd.	Hyd.
	F	8-305 (5.0)	.035	6	6	NA	40-47	500	500	Hyd.	Hyd.
	E	8-305 (5.0)	.035	①	①	NA	9.0-13.0	450	400	Hyd.	Hyd.
	8	8-350 (5.7)	.035	6	6	NA	40-47	450	400	Hyd.	Hyd.

GASOLINE ENGINE TUNE-UP SPECIFICATIONS
Refer to Section 34 for all spark plug recommendations

Year	VIN	No. Cylinder Displacement cu. in. (liter)	Spark Plugs Gap (in.)	Ignition Timing (deg.) MT	AT	Compression Pressure (psi)	Fuel Pump (psi)	Idle Speed (rpm) MT	AT	Valve Clearance In.	Ex.
1989	S	6-173 (2.8)	.045	10	10	NA	40-47	450	400	Hyd.	Hyd.
	F	8-305 (5.0)	.035	6	6	NA	40-47	500	500	Hyd.	Hyd.
	E	8-305 (5.0)	.035	①	①	NA	9.0-13.0	450	400	Hyd.	Hyd.
	8	8-350 (5.7)	.035	6	6	NA	40-47	450	400	Hyd.	Hyd.
1990		SEE UNDERHOOD SPECIFICATIONS									

① See Emission Decal

FIRING ORDERS

NOTE: To avoid confusion, replace spark plug wires 1 at a time.

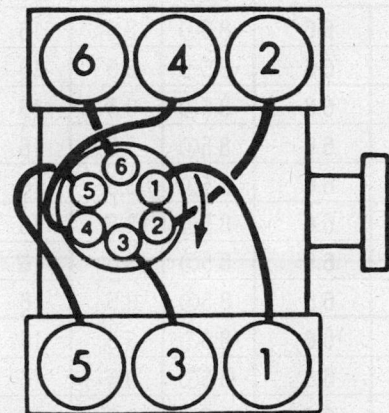

Chevrolet-built 173 V6 engine
Engine firing order: 1–2–3–4–5–6
Distributor rotation: clockwise

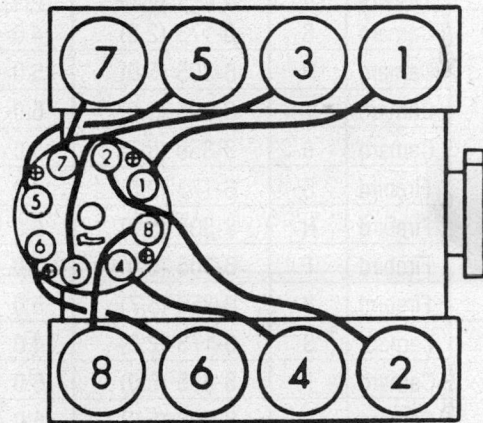

V8 engine
Engine firing order: 1-8-4-3-6-5-7-2
Distributor rotation: clockwise

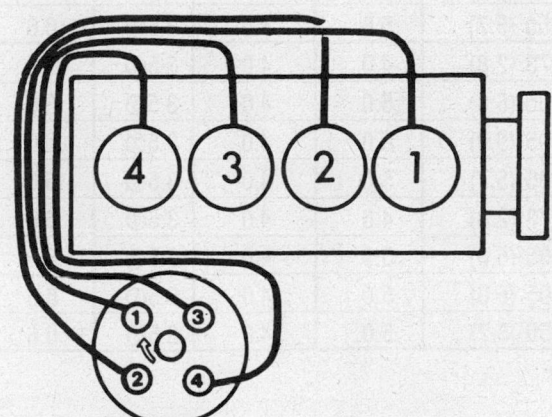

Pontiac-built 151–4 cylinder engine
Engine firing order: 1–3–4–2
Distributor rotation: clockwise

CAPACITIES

Year	Model	VIN	No. Cylinder Displacement cu. in. (liter)	Engine Crankcase with Filter	Engine Crankcase without Filter	Transmission (pts.) 4-Spd	Transmission (pts.) 5-Spd	Transmission (pts.) Auto.	Drive Axle (pts.)	Fuel Tank (gal.)	Cooling System (qts.)
1986	Camaro	2	4-151 (2.5)	3.5	3.0	3.5③	6.6	8.5①	3.5	16	9
	Camaro	S	6-173 (2.8)	4.0	4.0	3.5③	6.6	8.5①	3.5	16	15
	Camaro	G	8-305 (5.0)	5.0	4.0	3.5③	6.6	8.5①	3.5	16	17
	Camaro	H	8-305 (5.0)	5.0	4.0	3.5③	6.6	8.5①	3.5	16	17
	Camaro	F	8-305 (5.0)	5.0	4.0	3.5③	6.6	8.5①	3.5	16	17
	Camaro	8	8-350 (5.7)	5.0	4.0	3.5③	6.6	8.5①	3.5	16	17
	Firebird	2	4-151 (2.5)	3.5	3.0	3.5③	6.6	8.5①	3.5	16	9
	Firebird	S	6-173 (2.8)	4.0	4.0	3.5③	6.6	8.5①	3.5	16	15
	Firebird	G	8-305 (5.0)	5.0	4.0	3.5③	6.6	8.5①	3.5	16	17
	Firebird	H	8-305 (5.0)	5.0	4.0	3.5③	6.6	8.5①	3.5	16	17
	Firebird	F	8-305 (5.0)	5.0	4.0	3.5③	6.6	8.5①	3.5	16	17
	Firebird	8	8-350 (5.7)	5.0	4.0	3.5③	6.6	8.5①	3.5	16	17
1987	Camaro	S	6-173 (2.8)	4.0	4.0	3.5③	6.6	8.5①	3.5	16	13
	Camaro	H	8-305 (5.0)	5.0	4.0	3.5③	6.6	8.5①	3.5	16	17
	Camaro	F	8-305 (5.0)	5.0	4.0	3.5③	6.6	8.5①	3.5	16	17
	Camaro	8	8-350 (5.7)	5.0	4.0	3.5③	6.6	8.5①	3.5	16	17
	Firebird	S	6-173 (2.8)	4.0	4.0	3.5③	6.6	8.5①	3.5	16	13
	Firebird	H	8-305 (5.0)	5.0	4.0	3.5③	6.6	8.5①	3.5	16	17
	Firebird	F	8-305 (5.0)	5.0	4.0	3.5③	6.6	8.5①	3.5	16	17
	Firebird	8	8-350 (5.7)	5.0	4.0	3.5③	6.6	8.5①	3.5	16	17
1988	Camaro	S	6-173 (2.8)	4.0	4.0	3.5③	6.6	8.5①	3.5	16	13
	Camaro	F	8-305 (5.0)	5.0	4.0	3.5③	6.6	8.5①	3.5	16	17
	Camaro	E	8-305 (5.0)	5.0	4.0	3.5③	6.6	8.5①	3.5	16	15.5
	Camaro	8	8-305 (5.7)	5.0	4.0	3.5③	6.6	8.5①	3.5	16	17
	Firebird	S	6-173 (2.8)	4.0	4.0	3.5③	6.6	8.5①	3.5	16	13
	Firebird	F	8-305 (5.0)	5.0	4.0	3.5③	6.6	8.5①	3.5	16	17
	Firebird	E	8-305 (5.0)	5.0	4.0	3.5③	6.6	8.5①	3.5	16	15.5
	Firebird	8	8-350 (5.7)	5.0	4.0	3.5③	6.6	8.5①	3.5	16	17
1989-90	Camaro	S	6-173 (2.8)	4.0	4.0	3.5③	6.6	8.5①	3.5	16	13
	Camaro	F	8-305 (5.0)	5.0	4.0	3.5③	6.6	8.5①	3.5	16	17
	Camaro	E	8-305 (5.0)	5.0	4.0	3.5③	6.6	8.5①	3.5	16	15.5
	Camaro	8	8-305 (5.7)	5.0	4.0	3.5③	6.6	8.5①	3.5	16	17
	Firebird	S	6-173 (2.8)	4.0	4.0	3.5③	6.6	8.5①	3.5	16	13
	Firebird	F	8-305 (5.0)	5.0	4.0	3.5③	6.6	8.5①	3.5	16	17
	Firebird	E	8-305 (5.0)	5.0	4.0	3.5③	6.6	8.5①	3.5	16	15.5
	Firebird	8	8-350 (5.7)	5.0	4.0	3.5③	6.6	8.5①	3.5	16	17

① 10.0 if equipped with overdrive
② Not used
③ 6.6 if equipped with overdrive

CAMSHAFT SPECIFICATIONS
All measurements given in inches.

Year	VIN	No. Cylinder Displacement cu. in. (liter)	Journal Diameter					Lobe Lift		Bearing Clearance	Camshaft End Play
			1	2	3	4	5	In.	Ex.		
1986	2	4-151 (2.5)	1.8690	1.8690	1.8960	1.8960	1.8960	.3980	.3980	NA	.0015–.0050
	S	6-173 (2.8)	1.8976–1.8996	1.8976–1.8996	1.8976–1.8996	1.8976–1.8996	1.8976–1.8996	.2350	.2660	NA	NA
	G	8-305 (5.0)	1.8682–1.8692	1.8682–1.8692	1.8682–1.8692	1.8682–1.8692	1.8682–1.8692	.2340 ①②	.2570 ①②	NA	.004–.012
	H	8-305 (5.0)	1.8682–1.8692	1.8682–1.8692	1.8682–1.8692	1.8682–1.8692	1.8682–1.8692	.2340 ①②	.2570 ①②	NA	.004–.012
	F	8-305 (5.0)	1.8682–1.8692	1.8682–1.8692	1.8682–1.8692	1.8682–1.8692	1.8682–1.8692	.2340 ①②	.2570 ①②	NA	.004–.012
	8	8-350 (5.7)	1.8682–1.8692	1.8682–1.8692	1.8682–1.8692	1.8682–1.8962	1.8682–1.8962	.2730	.2828	NA	.004–.012
1987	S	6-173 (2.8)	1.8976–1.8996	1.8976–1.8996	1.8976–1.8996	1.8976–1.8996	1.8976–1.8996	.2350	.2660	NA	NA
	H	8-305 (5.0)	1.8682–1.8692	1.8682–1.8692	1.8682–1.8692	1.8682–1.8692	1.8682–1.8692	.2340 ①②	.2570 ①②	NA	.004–.012
	F	8-305 (5.0)	1.8682–1.8692	1.8682–1.8692	1.8682–1.8692	1.8682–1.8692	1.8682–1.8692	.2340 ①②	.2570 ①②	NA	.004–.012
	8	8-350 (5.7)	1.8682–1.8692	1.8682–1.8692	1.8682–1.8692	1.8682–1.8962	1.8682–1.8962	.2730	.2828	NA	.004–.012
1988	S	6-173 (2.8)	1.8976–1.8996	1.8976–1.8996	1.8976–1.8996	1.8976–1.8996	1.8976–1.8996	.2350	.2660	NA	NA
	F	8-305 (5.0)	1.8682–1.8692	1.8682–1.8692	1.8682–1.8692	1.8682–1.8692	1.8682–1.8692	.2690	.2760	NA	.004–.012
	E	8-305 (5.0)	1.8682–1.8692	1.8682–1.8692	1.8682–1.8692	1.8682–1.8692	1.8682–1.8692	.2340	.2570	NA	.004–.012
	8	8-350 (5.7)	1.8682–1.8692	1.8682–1.8692	1.8682–1.8692	1.8682–1.8692	1.8682–1.8692	.2730	.2820	NA	.004–.012
1989-90	S	6-173 (2.8)	1.8976–1.8996	1.8976–1.8996	1.8976–1.8996	1.8976–1.8996	1.8976–1.8996	.2350	.2660	NA	NA
	F	8-305 (5.0)	1.8682–1.8692	1.8682–1.8692	1.8682–1.8692	1.8682–1.8692	1.8682–1.8692	.2690	.2760	NA	.004–.012
	E	8-305 (5.0)	1.8682–1.8692	1.8682–1.8692	1.8682–1.8692	1.8682–1.8692	1.8682–1.8692	.2340	.2570	NA	.004–.012
	8	8-350 (5.7)	1.8682–1.8692	1.8682–1.8692	1.8682–1.8692	1.8682–1.8692	1.8682–1.8692	.2730	.2820	NA	.004–.012

① TBI — .2570-Intake; .2690-Exhaust
② 4 bbl HO — .2690-Intake; .2760-Exhaust

CRANKSHAFT AND CONNECTING ROD SPECIFICATIONS
All measurements are given in inches.

Year	VIN	No. Cylinder Displacement cu. in. (liter)	Crankshaft				Connecting Rod		
			Main Brg. Journal Dia.	Main Brg. Oil Clearance	Shaft End-play	Thrust on No.	Journal Diameter	Oil Clearance	Side Clearance
1986	2	4-151 (2.5)	2.300	.0005–.0022	.0035–.0085	5	2.000	.0005–.0026	.0060–.0020
	S	6-173 (2.8)	2.493–2.494	.0017–.0029	.0019–.0066	3	1.998–1.999	.0014–.0035	.0060–.0170
	G	8-305 (5.0)	①	②	.0020–.0060	5	2.098–2.099	.0018–.0039	.0080–.0140
	H	8-305 (5.0)	①	②	.0020–.0060	5	2.098–2.099	.0018–.0039	.0080–.0140
	F	8-305 (5.0)	①	②	.0020–.0060	5	2.098–2.099	.0018–.0039	.0080–.0140
	8	8-350 (5.7)	①	②	.0020–.0060	5	2.098–2.099	.0018–.0039	.0080–.0140
1987	S	6-173 (2.8)	2.493–2.494	.0017–.0029	.0019–.0066	3	1.998–1.999	.0014–.0035	.0060–.0170
	H	8-305 (5.0)	①	②	.0020–.0060	5	2.098–2.099	.0018–.0039	.0080–.0140
	F	8-305 (5.0)	①	②	.0020–.0060	5	2.098–2.099	.0018–.0039	.0080–.0140
	8	8-350 (5.7)	①	②	.0020–.0060	5	2.098–2.099	.0013–.0035	.0060–.0140
1988	S	6-173 (2.8)	2.493–2.494	.0017–.0029	.0019–.0066	3	1.998–1.999	.0014–.0035	.0060–.0170
	F	8-305 (5.0)	①	②	.0020–.0060	5	2.098–2.099	.0018–.0039	.0080–.0140
	E	8-305 (5.0)	①	②	.0020–.0060	5	2.098–2.099	.0018–.0039	.0080–.0140
	8	8-350 (5.7)	①	②	.0020–.0060	5	2.098–2.099	.0013–.0035	.0060–.0140
1989-90	S	6-173 (2.8)	2.493–2.494	.0017–.0029	.0019–.0066	3	1.998–1.999	.0014–.0035	.0060–.0170
	F	8-305 (5.0)	①	②	.0020–.0060	5	2.098–2.099	.0018–.0039	.0080–.0140
	E	8-305 (5.0)	①	②	.0020–.0060	5	2.098–2.099	.0018–.0039	.0080–.0140
	8	8-350 (5.7)	①	②	.0020–.0060	5	2.098–2.099	.0013–.0035	.0060–.0140

① No. 1 — 2.4484–2.4493
  Nos. 2, 3, 4 — 2.4481–2.4490
  No. 5 — 2.4479–2.4488
② No. 1 — .000–.0020
  Nos. 2, 3, 4 — .0011–.0023
  No. 5 — .0-017–.0032

VALVE SPECIFICATIONS

Year	VIN	No. Cylinder Displacement cu. in. (liter)	Seat Angle (deg.)	Face Angle (deg.)	Spring Test Pressure (lbs.)	Spring Installed Height (in.)	Stem-to-Guide Clearance (in.)		Stem Diameter (in.)	
							Intake	Exhaust	Intake	Exhaust
1986	2	4-151 (2.5)	46	45	122-180 @ 1.25	1.69	.0010–.0027	.0010–.0027	.3418–.3425	.3418–.3425
	S	6-173 (2.8)	46	45	194 @ 1.18	1.57	.0010–.0027	.3410–.0027	.0010–.3420	.3410–.3420
	G	8-305 (5.0)	46	45	194-206 @ 1.25	1.72	.0010–.0027	.0010–.0027	.3410–.3420	.3410–.3420
	H	8-305 (5.0)	46	45	194-206 @ 1.25	1.72	.0010–.0027	.0010–.0027	.3410–.3420	.3410–.3420
	F	8-305 (5.0)	46	45	194-206 @ 1.25	1.72	.0010–.0027	.0010–.0027	.3410–.3420	.3410–.3420
	8	8-350 (5.7)	46	45	194-206 @ 1.25	1.72	.0010–.0027	.0010–.0027	.3410–.3420	.3410–.3420
1987	S	6-173 (2.8)	46	45	194 @ 1.18	1.57	.0010–.0027	.3410–.0027	.0010–.3420	.3410–.3420
	H	8-305 (5.0)	46	45	194-206 @ 1.25	1.72	.0010–.0027	.0010–.0027	.3410–.3420	.3410–.3420
	F	8-305 (5.0)	46	45	194-206 @ 1.25	1.72	.0010–.0027	.0010–.0027	.3410–.3420	.3410–.3420
	8	8-350 (5.7)	46	45	194-206 @ 1.25	1.72	.0010–.0027	.0010–.0027	.3410–.3420	.3410–.3420
1988	S	6-173 (2.8)	46	45	194 @ 1.18	1.57	.0010–.0027	.3410–.0027	.0010–.3420	.3410–.3420
	E	8-305 (5.0)	46	45	194-206 @ 1.25	①	.0010–.0027	.0010–.0027	.3410–.3420	.3410–.3420
	F	8-305 (5.0)	46	45	194-206 @ 1.25	①	.0010–.0027	.0010–.0027	.3410–.3420	.3410–.3420
	8	8-350 (5.7)	46	45	194-206 @ 1.25	①	.0010–.0027	.0010–.0027	.3410–.3420	.3410–.3420
1989-90	S	6-173 (2.8)	46	45	194 @ 1.18	1.57	.0010–.0027	.3410–.0027	.0010–.3420	.3410–.3420
	E	8-305 (5.0)	46	45	194-206 @ 1.25	①	.0010–.0027	.0010–.0027	.3410–.3420	.3410–.3420
	F	8-305 (5.0)	46	45	194-206 @ 1.25	①	.0010–.0027	.0010–.0027	.3410–.3420	.3410–.3420
	8	8-350 (5.7)	46	45	194-206 @ 1.25	①	.0010–.0027	.0010–.0027	.3410–.3420	.3410–.3420

① Intake—1.72
 Exhaust—1.59

PISTON AND RING SPECIFICATIONS
All measurments are given in inches.

Year	VIN	No. Cylinder Displacement cu. in. (liter)	Piston Clearance	Ring Gap			Ring Side Clearance		
				Top Compression	Bottom Compression	Oil Control	Top Compression	Bottom Compression	Oil Control
1986	2	4-151 (2.5)	①	.0100–.0200	.0100–.0270	.0150–.0550	.0015–.0030	.0015–.0030	.0010–.0050
	S	6-173 (2.8)	.017–.043	.0098–.0196	.0098–.0196	.0020–.0550	.0011–.0027	.0015–.0037	.0078 Max.
	G	8-305 (5.0)	.0027	.0100–.0200	.0100–.0250	.0150–.0550	.0012–.0032	.0012–.0032	.0020–.0076
	H	8-305 (5.0)	.0027	.0100–.0200	.0100–.0250	.0150–.0550	.0012–.0032	.0012–.0032	.0020–.0076
	F	8-305 (5.0)	.0027	.0100–.0200	.0100–.0250	.0150–.0550	.0012–.0032	.0012–.0032	.0020–.0076
	8	8-350 (5.7)	.0045	.0100–.0200	.0100–.0250	.0150–.0550	.0012–.0032	.0012–.0032	.0020–.0076
1987	S	6-173 (2.8)	.017–.043	.0098–.0196	.0098–.0196	.0020–.0550	.0011–.0027	.0015–.0037	.0078 Max.
	H	8-305 (5.0)	.0027	.0100–.0200	.0100–.0250	.0150–.0550	.0012–.0032	.0012–.0032	.0020–.0070
	F	8-305 (5.0)	.0027	.0100–.0200	.0100–.0250	.0150–.0550	.0012–.0032	.0012–.0032	.0020–.0070
	8	8-350 (5.7)	.0045	.0100–.0200	.0100–.0250	.0150–.0550	.0012–.0032	.0012–.0032	.0020–.0070
1988	S	6-173 (2.8)	.017–.043	.0098–.0196	.0098–.0196	.0020–.0550	.0011–.0027	.0015–.0037	.0078 Max.
	F	8-305 (5.0)	NA	.0027 .0200	.0100–.0250	.0150–.0550	.0012–.0032	.0012–.0032	.0020–.0070
	E	8-305 (5.0)	.0027	.0100–.0200	.0100–.0250	.0150–.0550	.0012–.0032	.0012–.0032	.0020–.0070
	8	8-350 (5.7)	.0027	.0100–.0200	.0100–.0250	.0150–.0550	.0012–.0032	.0012–.0032	.0020–.0070
1989-90	S	6-173 (2.8)	.017–.043	.0250–.0430	.0508–.0500	.0510–1.400	.0300–.0070	.0040–.0950	.0510–1.400
	F	8-305 (5.0)	NA	.0027 .0200	.0100–.0250	.0150–.0550	.0012–.0032	.0012–.0032	.0020–.0070
	E	8-305 (5.0)	.0027	.0100–.0200	.0100–.0250	.0150–.0550	.0012–.0032	.0012–.0032	.0020–.0070
	8	8-350 (5.7)	.0027	.0100–.0200	.0100–.0250	.0150–.0550	.0012–.0032	.0012–.0032	.0020–.0070

① .036–.056 measured 1.8 in. down from piston top

TORQUE SPECIFICATIONS
All readings in ft. lbs.

Year	VIN	No. Cylinder Displacement cu. in. (liter)	Cylinder Head Bolts	Main Bearing Bolts	Rod Bearing Bolts	Crankshaft Pulley Bolts	Flywheel Bolts	Manifold Intake	Manifold Exhaust	Spark Plugs
1986	2	4-151 (2.5)	92	70	32	200	44	15	44	15-20
	S	6-173 (2.8)	③	83	34-45	75	50	13-25	19-31	7-15
	G	8-305 (5.0)	65-90	①	42-47	60	75	25-45	②	15-20
	H	8-305 (5.0)	65-90	①	42-47	60	75	25-45	②	15-20
	F	8-305 (5.0)	65-90	①	42-47	60	75	25-45	②	15-20
	8	8-350 (5.7)	65-90	①	42-47	60	75	25-45	②	15-20
1987	S	6-173 (2.8)	③	63-83	34-45	75	50	13-25	25	7-15
	H	8-305 (5.0)	60-70	63-85	42-47	60	75	25-45	②	15-20
	F	8-305 (5.0)	60-75	63-85	42-47	60	75	25-45	②	15-20
	8	8-350 (5.7)	60-75	63-85	42-47	60	75	25-45	②	15-20
1988	S	6-173 (2.8)	③	63-83	34-45	75	50	13-25	19-31	7-15
	F	8-305 (5.0)	60-75	63-85	42-47	60	75	25-45	②	15-20
	E	8-305 (5.0)	60-75	63-85	42-47	60	75	25-45	②	15-20
	8	8-350 (5.7)	60-75	63-85	42-47	60	75	25-45	②	15-20
1989-90	S	6-173 (2.8)	③	63-83	34-45	75	50	13-25	19-31	7-15
	F	8-305 (5.0)	60-75	63-85	42-47	60	75	25-45	②	15-20
	E	8-305 (5.0)	60-75	63-85	42-47	60	75	25-45	②	15-20
	8	8-350 (5.7)	60-75	63-85	42-47	60	75	25-45	②	15-20

① Inner—70-85
   Outer—60-75
② Outer bolts—14-26
   Inner bolts—20-32
③ Torque in 2 steps:
   1st step—Tighten to 40 ft. lbs.
   2nd step—Rotate wrench an additional 90 degrees.

WHEEL ALIGNMENT

Year	Model	Caster Range (deg.)	Caster Preferred Setting (deg.)	Camber Range (deg.)	Camber Preferred Setting (deg.)	Toe-in (in.)	Steering Axis Inclination (deg.)
1986	Camaro	2½P-3½P	3P	½P-1½P	1P	$5/32$P	NA
	Z28	3P-3½P	4P	½P-1½P	1P	$5/32$P	NA
	Firebird	3-3½	4	½-1½	1P	$1/16$	NA
1987	Camaro, Firebird	4½P-5½P	5P	½P-1½P	1P	$3/64$P	NA
1988	Camaro, Firebird	4½P-5½P	5P	½N-1½P	0	$3/64$P	NA
1989-90	Camaro, Firebird	$4^3/16$P-$5^3/16$P	$4^{11}/16$P	$3/16$N-$13/16$P	$5/16$P	0	NA

NA Not available
P Positive
N Negative

ELECTRICAL

For testing and overhaul procedures on starters, alternators and voltage regulators, refer to unit repair section.

Charging System

ALTERNATOR

Removal and Installation

1. Disconnect the negative battery cable.
2. Tag and disconnect the alternator wiring.
3. Remove the alternator brace bolt. As required, loosen the power steering pump brace and mount nuts. Remove the drive belts. If equipped with serpentine belt only loosen the belt tensioner and remove the serpentine belt.
4. Support the alternator and remove the mount bolts. Remove the unit from the vehicle.
5. Installation is the reverse of the previous steps. Tighten belt enough to allow approximately ½ in. of play on the longest run between pulleys.

VOLTAGE REGULATOR

All vehicles are equipped with an internal voltage regulator. Removal and installation requires complete alternator disassembly.

BELT TENSION

Adjustment

EXCEPT SERPENTINE BELT

Using belt tension gauge J–23600 or equivalent adjust, the alternator belt if the tension is below 300N, as indicated on the gauge. If the belt is used, the correct belt tension is 350N, on the gauge. If the belt is new, the correct tension is 575N.

SERPENTINE BELT

The correct belt tension is indicated on the indicator mark of the belt tensioner. If the indicator mark is not within specification, replace the belt or the tensioner.

NOTE: Routine inspection of the belt may reveal small cracks in the belt ribs. Small cracks will not impair belt performance and is not a basis for replacement. If sections of the belt are missing, the belt should be replaced.

Starting System

STARTER

Removal and Installation

1. Disconnect the negative battery cable.
2. As required, raise the vehicle and support it safely.
3. Disconnect all wiring from the starter.
4. Remove the frame support. This support runs from the corner of the frame to the front crossmember.
5. Remove the starter motor retaining bolts and any shims. If equipped, remove the solenoid heat shield.
6. Remove the starter from the vehicle.
7. Installation is the reverse of the removal procedure.
8. If shims were used, they must be replaced in their original locations.

Ignition System

DISTRIBUTOR

Removal and Installation

TIMING NOT DISTURBED

1. Disconnect the negative battery cable. Remove all the necessary components in order to gain access to the distributor assembly.
2. Remove all electrical connections from the unit. Release the coil connectors from the distributor cap.

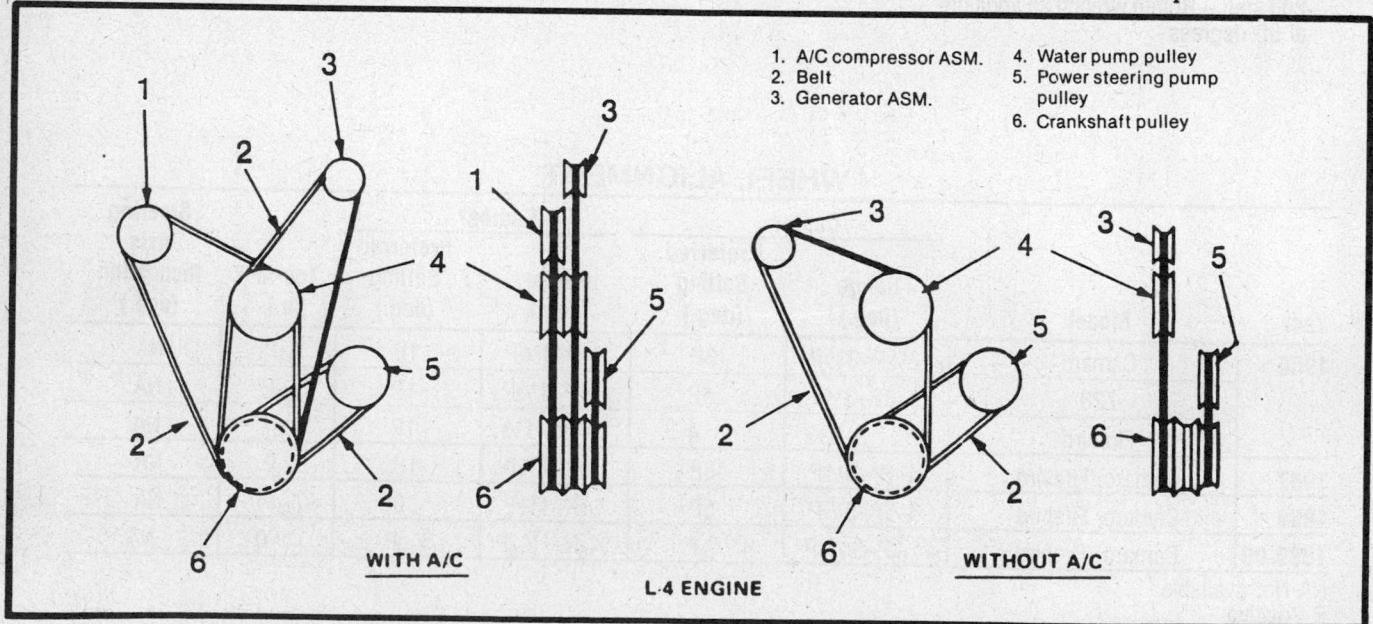

1. A/C compressor ASM.
2. Belt
3. Generator ASM.
4. Water pump pulley
5. Power steering pump pulley
6. Crankshaft pulley

WITH A/C   WITHOUT A/C

L-4 ENGINE

Proper belt installation for the 2.5L 4 cyl. engine

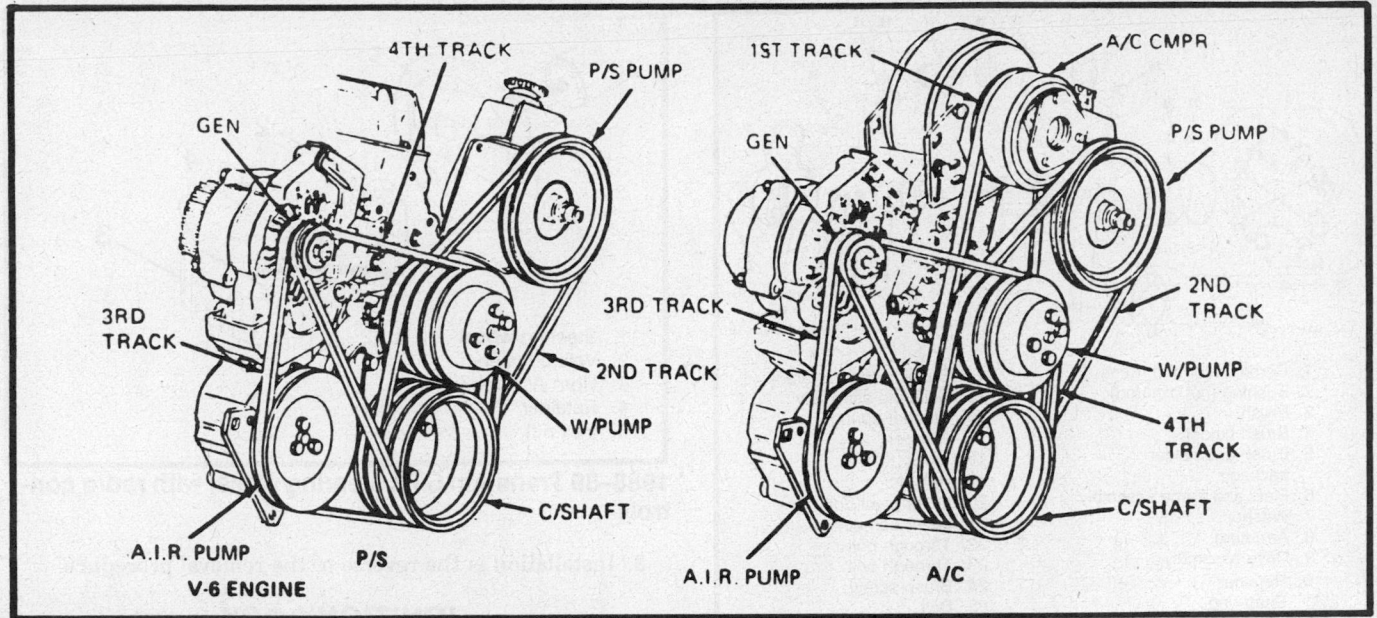

Proper belt installation for the 2.8L and 5.0L engine

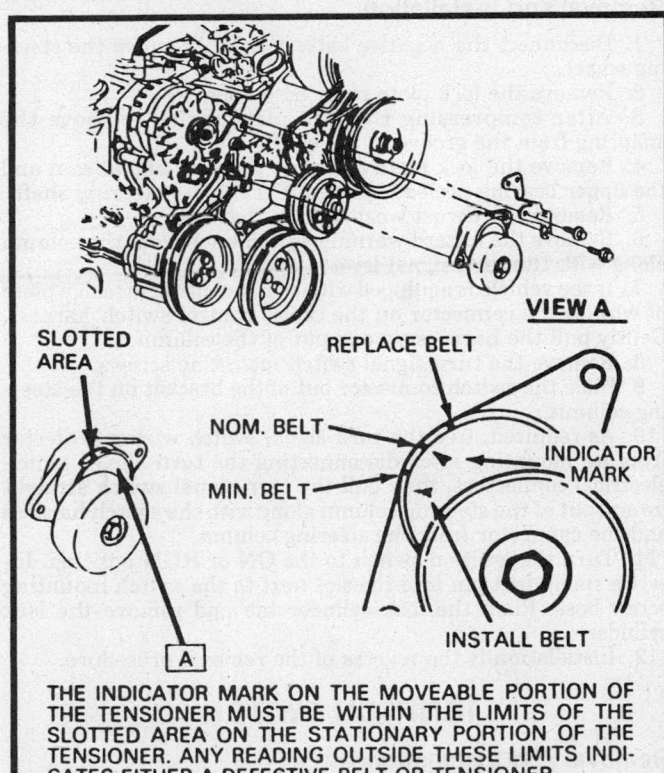

THE INDICATOR MARK ON THE MOVEABLE PORTION OF THE TENSIONER MUST BE WITHIN THE LIMITS OF THE SLOTTED AREA ON THE STATIONARY PORTION OF THE TENSIONER. ANY READING OUTSIDE THESE LIMITS INDICATES EITHER A DEFECTIVE BELT OR TENSIONER.

Serpentine drive belt tensioner and related components

3. Remove the distributor cap retaining screws and remove the cap. Disconnect the 4 terminal harness from the distributor. Mark the position of the distributor housing to the block.

4. Remove the distributor hold down bolt. Note the position of the rotor and then pull the distributor assembly from the engine.

5. To insure correct ignition timing, the distributor must be installed with the rotor in the same position as it was removed.

6. Installation is the reverse of the removal procedure. Check the engine timing and adjust as needed.

TIMING DISTURBED

1. Remove the No. 1 cylinder spark plug.

2. Place a finger over the spark plug hole while rotating the engine slowly by hand, until compression is felt.

3. Align the timing mark on the crankshaft pulley with the 0° mark on the timing scale attached to the front of the engine. This places the engine at TDC of the compression stroke for No. 1 cylinder.

4. Rotate the distributor shaft until the rotor points to the No. 1 spark plug tower on the distributor cap.

5. Install the distributor in the engine.

6. Install the hold down clamp and bolt. Start and run the engine.

7. Check and/or adjust the ignition timing.

IGNITION TIMING

Adjustment

NOTE: On all 1986–88 vehicles, it will be necessary to put the EST in the bypass mode by disconnecting the single wire timing connector. This wire is tan with a black tracer and breaks out of the wiring harness near the rear of the right hand valve cover. Do not disconnect the 4 prong EST connector from the distributor assembly. On 1989–90 vehicles, with the engine running, ground the diagnostic terminal (A and B) of the ALDL connector.

1. Refer to the Vehicle Emission Information label which is located on the radiator support panel, for the proper timing information.

2. Run engine to normal operating temperture. Disconnect the EST bypass mode connector or ground the diagnostic terminal of the ALDL connector.

3. If the engine timing requires adjustment, loosen the distributor hold down bolt and rotate the distributor slowly in either direction, to advance or retard the engine timing.

4. Tighten the hold down bolt and recheck the engine timing.

5. With the engine still running, unground the diagnostic terminal or reconnect the EST bypass mode connector.

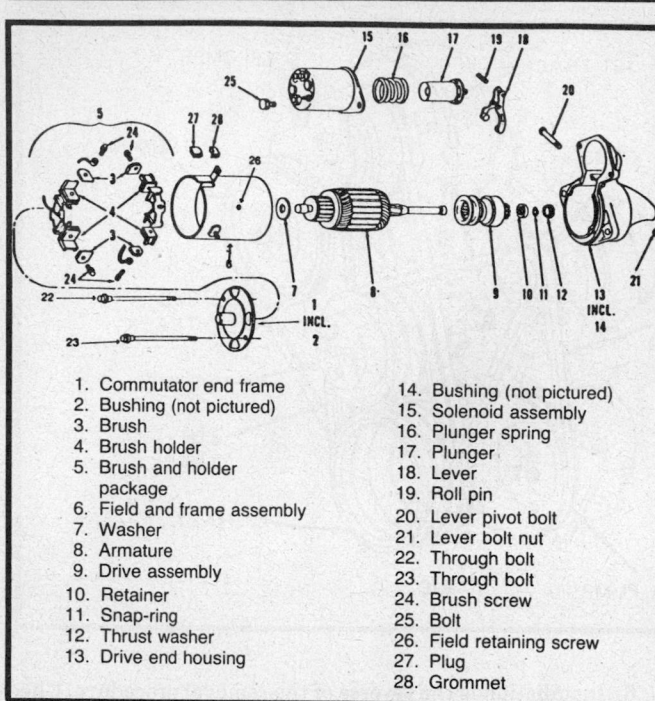

1. Commutator end frame
2. Bushing (not pictured)
3. Brush
4. Brush holder
5. Brush and holder package
6. Field and frame assembly
7. Washer
8. Armature
9. Drive assembly
10. Retainer
11. Snap-ring
12. Thrust washer
13. Drive end housing
14. Bushing (not pictured)
15. Solenoid assembly
16. Plunger spring
17. Plunger
18. Lever
19. Roll pin
20. Lever pivot bolt
21. Lever bolt nut
22. Through bolt
23. Through bolt
24. Brush screw
25. Bolt
26. Field retaining screw
27. Plug
28. Grommet

Exploded view of a typical starter

Electrical Controls

STEERING WHEEL

Removal and Installation

NOTE: If vehicle is equipped with an air bag restraint system care should be exercise when removing the steering wheel.

1. Disconnect the negative battery cable.
2. Remove the horn trim pad. Remove the horn contact wire from the plastic tower by pushing in on the wire and turning counterclockwise. The wire will spring out of the tower.
3. If vehicle is equipped with radio steering wheel controls gently lift each side of the horn pad to seperate the velcro attaching pads then disconnect the electrical connections.
4. Scribe an alignment mark on the steering wheel hub in line with the slash mark on the steering shaft.
5. Remove the steering wheel locknut retainer.
6. Loosen the locknut on the steering shaft and position it flush with the end of the shaft. Using the proper steering wheel removal tool, remove the wheel from its mounting on the steering shaft.
7. Remove the removal tool from the steering wheel. Remove the locknut from the steering shaft. Remove the steering wheel from the vehicle.
8. Installation is the reverse of the removal procedure. When installing the steering wheel, it should not be driven on the steering shaft as damage to the steering column and its components could occur.

HORN SWITCH

Removal and Installation

1. Disconnect the negative battery cable.
2. Remove the horn pad. Remove the contact assembly and all other related components. Disconnect the electrical connectors from the assembly.

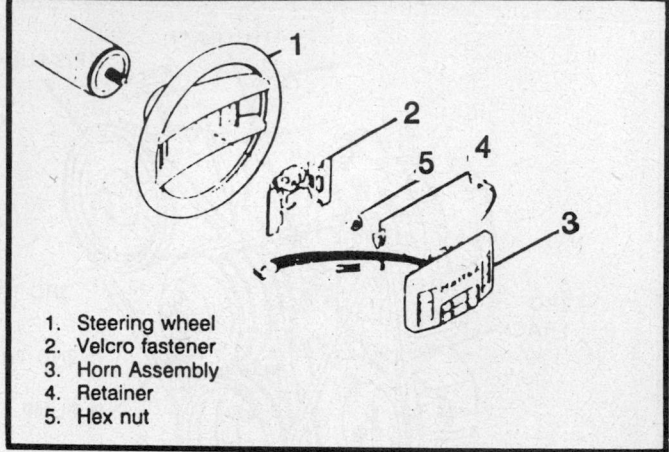

1. Steering wheel
2. Velcro fastener
3. Horn Assembly
4. Retainer
5. Hex nut

1988–89 Trans Am GTA steering wheel with radio controls

3. Installation is the reverse of the removal procedure.

IGNITION LOCK

Removal and Installation

1. Disconnect the negative battery cable. Remove the steering wheel.
2. Remove the lock plate cover assembly.
3. After compressing the lock plate spring, remove the snapring from the groove in the shaft.
4. Remove the lock plate and slide the turn signal cam and the upper bearing preload spring off the upper steering shaft.
5. Remove the thrust washer from the shaft.
6. Remove the hazard warning switch knob from the column along with the turn signal lever.
7. If the vehicle is equipped with cruise control, attach a piece of wire to the connector on the cruise control switch harness. Gently pull the harness up and out of the column.
8. Remove the turn signal switch mounting screws.
9. Slide the switch connector out of the bracket on the steering column.
10. As required, free the turn signal switch wiring protector from its mounting after disconnecting the turn signal switch electrical connectors, then pull the turn signal switch straight up and out of the steering column along with the switch harness and the connector from the steering column.
11. Turn the ignition switch to the **ON** or **RUN** position. Insert a small drift pin into the slot next to the switch mounting screw boss. Push the lock cylinder tab and remove the lock cylinder.
12. Installation is the reverse of the removal procedure.

IGNITION SWITCH

Removal and Installation

1. Disconnect the negative battery terminal.
2. Loosen the toe pan screws on the steering column.
3. Remove the column to instrument panel trim plates and attaching nuts.
4. Lower the steering column. Be sure that the steering column is supported at all times in order to prevent damage to the column. Disconnect the switch wire connectors.
5. Remove the switch attaching screws and remove the switch.
6. To replace, move the key lock to the **LOCK** position.
7. Move the actuator rod hole in the switch to the **LOCK** position.

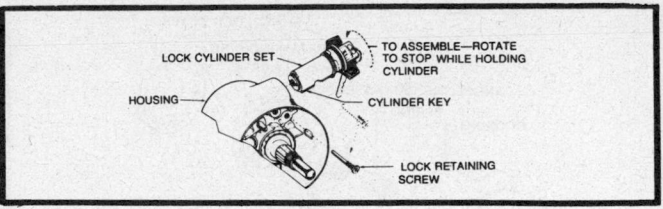

Removing the lock cylinder

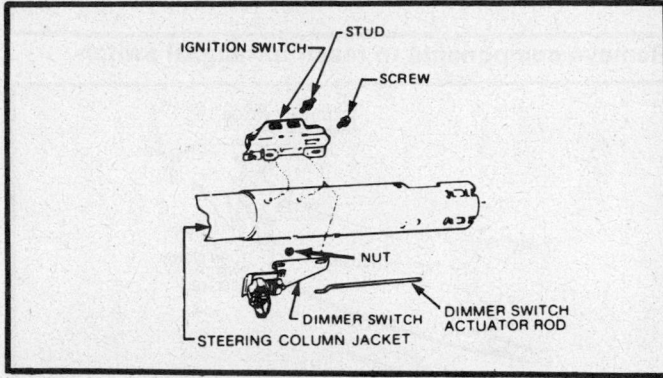

Removing ignition and dimmer switch

8. Install the switch with the rod in the hole.
9. Position and reassemble the steering column in reverse of the disassembly procedure.

NEUTRAL SAFETY SWITCH

These vehicles incorporate a mechanical neutral start system. This system relies on a mechanical block, rather than the starter safety switch to prevent starting the engine in other than **P** or **N**.

The mechanical block is achieved by a cast in finger added to the switch actuator rack, which interferes with the bowl plate in all shift positions except **N** or **P**. This interference prevents rotation of the lock cylinder into the **START** position.

In either **P** or **N**, this finger passes through the bowl plates lots allowing the lock cylinder full rotational travel into the **START** position.

CLUTCH START SWITCH

Removal and Installation

1. Disconnect the negative battery cable. Remove the hush pad from under the dash panel.
2. Remove the bolt and switch from the clutch bracket and rotate the switch slightly so that the actuating shaft retainer can be pulled from the hole of the clutch pedal.
3. Place a new switch in position so that the actuating shaft retainer is in line with the hole in the clutch pedal and reinstall the bolt.
4. Connect the electrical connector to the switch and depress the clutch pedal fully to the floor to adjust the switch.

Adjustment

The clutch operated starting switch is self adjusting. If there is a readjustment necessary, depress the detent on the adjuster block and slide the block to the full forward position on the switch rod. Depress clutch pedal fully to the floor to adjust the clutch switch.

STOPLIGHT SWITCH

Removal and Installation

NOTE: The cruise control release switch and the stoplight switch are adjusted or replaced in the same manner.

1. Disconnect the negative battery cable. Remove the under dash padding. Disconnect the wire harness connector from the switch.
2. Remove the switch from the clip and then remove the clip from the bracket.
3. To install, place the clip in its bore on the bracket.
4. With the brake pedal depressed, insert the switch into the clip and depress the switch body. Clicks can be heard as the threaded portion of the switch is pushed through the clip towards the brake pedal.
5. Pull the brake pedal fully rearward against the pedal stop until the clicking sounds cannot be heard. The switch can be moved in the clip to correct the adjustment.
6. Release the brake pedal and check the adjustment. Pull up on the brake pedal again to assure that no clicking sounds remain. The switch is now correctly adjusted.
7. Install the harness connector and verify the stoplights operate correctly.

HEADLAMP SWITCH

Removal and Installation

CAMARO EXCEPT BERLINETTA AND IROC-Z

1. Disconnect the negative battery cable. Remove the left and right lower trim plates.
2. Remove the instrument panel trim plate and the 2 switch assembly retaining screws.

NOTE: On some models, the headlamp switch knob can be removed by depressing the release button on the headlamp switch from underneath the instrument panel.

3. Depress the side tangs and remove the switch from the instrument panel.
4. Installation is the reverse order of the removal procedure.

BERLINETTA AND IROC-Z

NOTE: The headlight switch, is located in the left pod assembly. In order to replace the switch assembly, the pod assembly must be removed as a unit.

1. Disconnect the negative battery cable.
2. Remove the instrument panel trim plate screws. Remove the instrument panel trim plate.
3. Remove the lower steering column trim cover.
4. Remove the left control head attaching screw at the bottom front. Release the holding tab.
5. Disconnect the electrical connector located below the instrument panel.
6. Remove the pod assembly. Slide the control off the track to remove.
7. Installation is the reverse of the removal procedure.

FIREBIRD

1. Disconnect the negative battery cable. Remove the right and left lower trim plates. Remove the instrument panel lower cover, as required.
2. Remove the instrument panel cluster trim plate.
3. Remove the 2 switch mounting screws.
4. Depress the side tangs of the switch and pull the switch out of the instrument panel.

5. The individual switches of the headlamp switch assembly are now serviceable.

6. Installation is the reverse of the removal procedure.

CONCEALED HEADLAMPS

Manual Operation

1. Turn on the headlights and open the hood.

2. Rotate the manual control knob in the direction of the arrow on the headlamp door motor assembly. Turn the knob until it will not go any further or until resistance is stiff.

TURN SIGNAL SWITCH

Removal and Installation

NOTE: The dimmer switch is incorporated within the turn signal switch assembly and is removed together with the turn signal switch.

1. Disconnect the negative battery cable.

2. Remove the steering wheel.

3. Insert a suitable tool into the lock plate and remove the lock plate cover assembly.

4. Install a spring compressor onto the steering shaft. Tighten the tool to compress the lockplate and the spring. Remove the snapring from the groove in the shaft.

5. Remove the lock plate and slide the turn signal cam and the upper bearing preload spring and the thrust washer off the upper steering shaft.

6. Remove the steering column lower cover.

7. Remove the turn signal lever from the column.

8. On vehicles equipped with cruise control, disconnect the cruise control wire from the harness near the bottom of the column. Remove the harness protector from the cruise control wire. Remove the turn signal lever. Do not remove the wire from the column.

9. Remove the vertical bolts at the steering column upper support. Remove the shim packs. Keep the shims in order for reinstallation.

10. Remove the screws securing the column upper mounting bracket to the column. Remove the bracket.

11. Disconnect the turn signal wiring and remove the wires from the plastic protector.

12. Remove the turn signal switch mounting screws.

13. Slide the switch connector out of the bracket on the steering column.

14. If the switch is known to be bad, cut the wires and discard the switch. Tape the connector of the new switch to the old wires and pull the new harness down through the steering column while removing the old wires.

15. If the original switch is to be reused, wrap tape around the wire and connector and pull the harness up through the column. It may be helpful to attach a length of mechanic's wire to the harness connector before pulling it up through the column to facilitate installation.

16. After freeing the switch wiring protector from its mounting, pull the turn signal switch straight up and remove the switch, switch harness and the connector from the column.

17. Installation is the reverse of the removal procedure.

WINDSHIELD WIPER SWITCH

Removal and Installation

NOTE: On later models an multifunction turn signal lever incorporates the washer/wiper switch.

COLUMN MOUNTED

1. Disconnect the negative battery cable. Remove the steering wheel. Remove the turn signal switch.

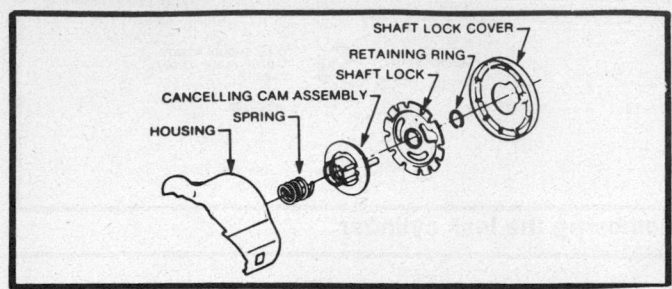

Remove components to reach turnsignal switch

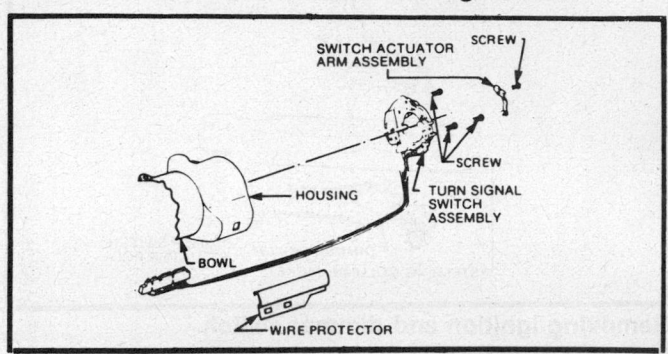

Turn signal switch assembly and related components

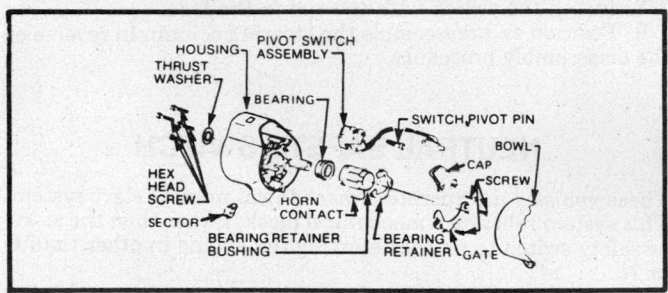

Removing the column mounted wiper switch

2. It may be necessary to loosen the 2 column mounting nuts and remove the 4 bracket to mast jacket screws, then separate the bracket from the mast jacket to allow the connector clip on the ignition switch to be pulled out of the column assembly.

3. Disconnect the washer/wiper switch lower connector.

4. Remove the screws attaching the column housing to the mast jacket. Be sure to note the position of the dimmer switch actuator rod for reassembly in the same position. Remove the column housing and switch as an assembly.

5. Turn the assembly upside down and use a drift to remove the pivot pin from the washer/wiper switch. Remove the switch.

6. Place the switch into position in the housing, then install the pivot pin.

7. Position the housing onto the mast jacket and attach by installing the screws. Install the dimmer switch actuator rod in the same position as noted earlier. Check switch operation.

8. Reconnect lower end of switch assembly.

9. Install remaining components in reverse order of removal. Be sure to attach column mounting bracket in original position.

DASH MOUNTED

1. Disconnect the negative battery cable.

2. Remove the trim panel. Remove the switch retaining screws.

3. Pull the switch forward and disconnect the electrical connection. Remove the switch from the vehicle.

4. Installation is the reverse of the removal procedure.

WINDSHIELD WIPER MOTOR

Removal and Installation

1. Disconnect the negative battery cable.
2. Remove the cowl screen.
3. Loosen the transmission drive link to crank arm retaining bolts. Remove the drive link from the motor crank arm.
4. Disconnect the electrical wiring and the washer hoses from the motor assembly.
5. Remove the motor retaining screws. Remove the windshield wiper motor while guiding the crank arm through the hole.
6. Installation is the reverse of the removal procedure. The motor must be in the park position before assembling the crank arm to the drive link.

WINDSHIELD WIPER LINKAGE

Removal and Installation

1. Disconnect the negative battery cable. Remove the cowl vent screen.
2. Remove the right and left wiper arm and blade.
3. Loosen but do not remove, the attaching nuts securing the transmission drive links to the motor crank arm.
4. Disconnect the transmission drive link from the motor crank arm.
5. Remove the wiper transmission to body attaching screws.
6. Remove the wiper transmission and linkage by guiding it through the plenum chamber opening or to the left side under the dash panel extension.
7. Installation is the reverse of the removal procedure.

Instrument Cluster

Refer to "Chilton's Electronic Instrumentation Service Manual" for additional coverage.

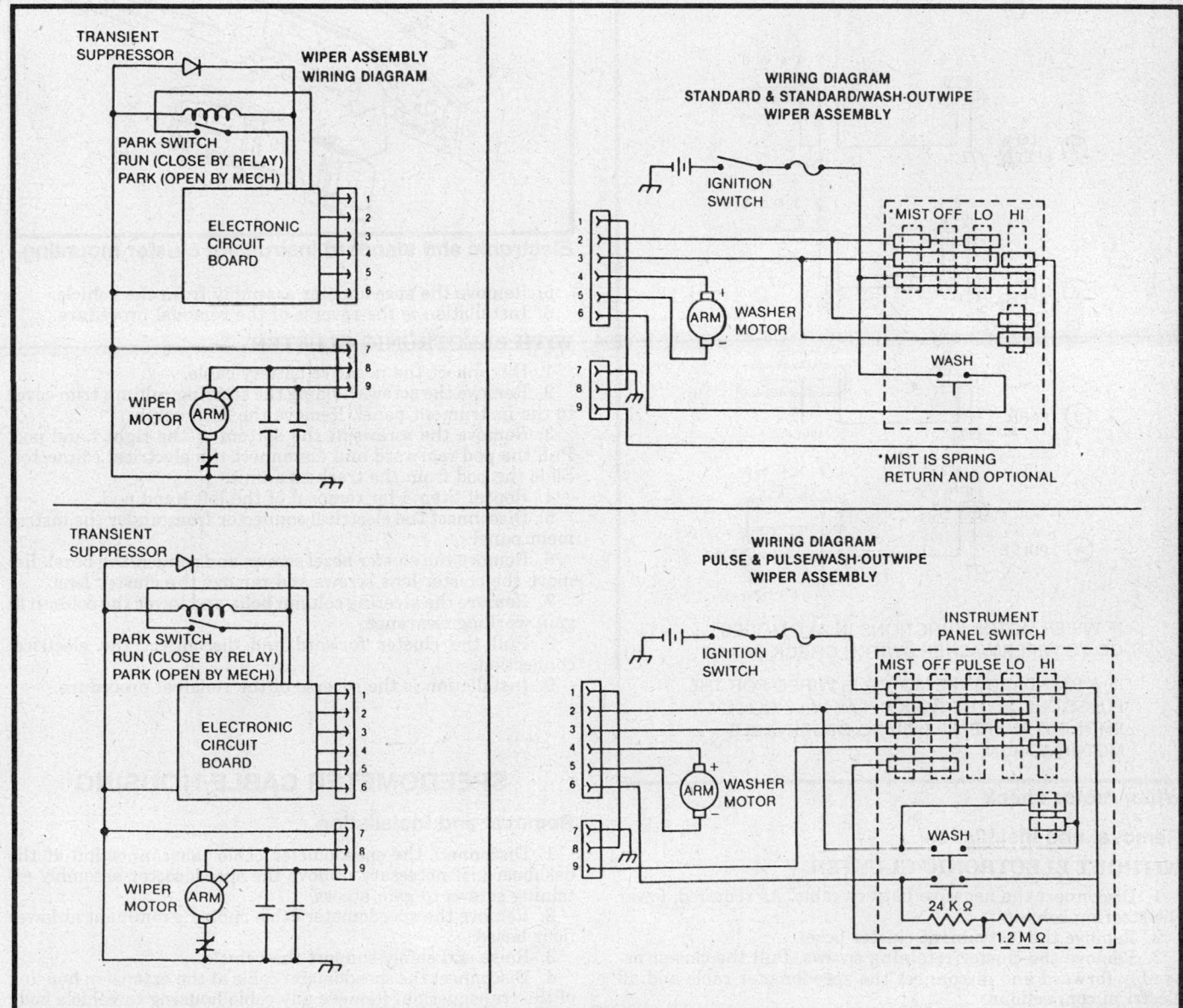

Wiper/washer wiring diagrams

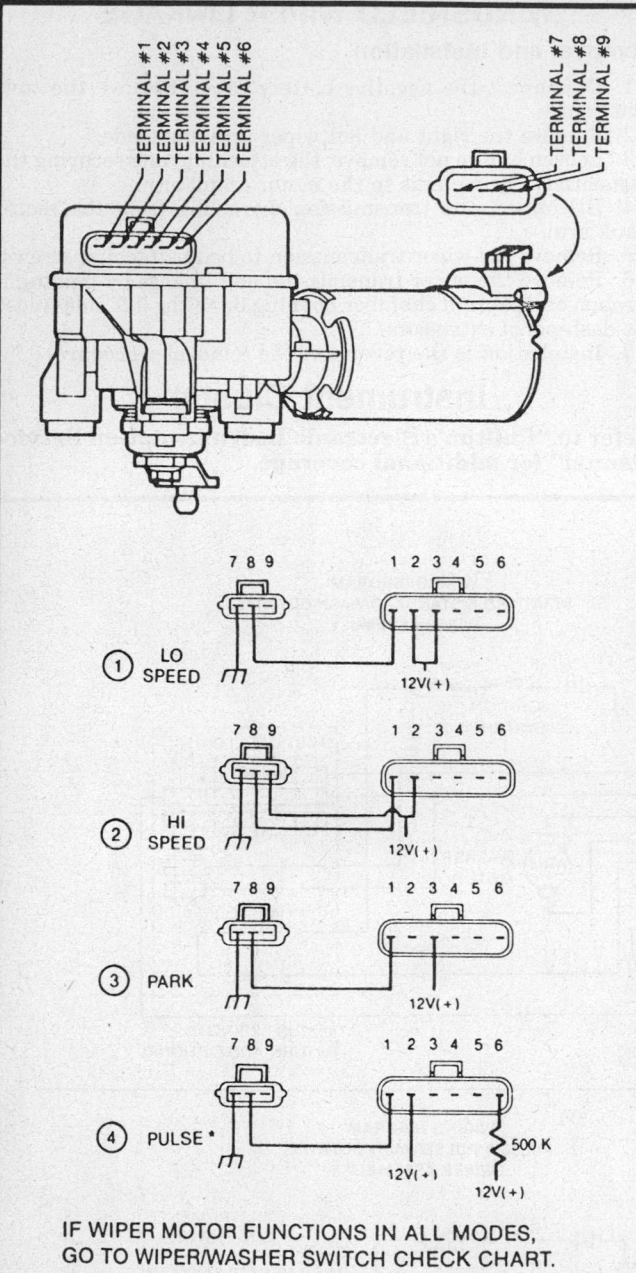

IF WIPER MOTOR FUNCTIONS IN ALL MODES,
GO TO WIPER/WASHER SWITCH CHECK CHART.

*IF A STANDARD TYPE MOTOR IS WIRED FOR THE
PULSE CHECK, THE PARK RELAY WILL CLICK
SHUT BUT THERE WILL BE NO OBSERVABLE
MOTOR ACTION.

Wiper motor check

Removal and Installation
WITHOUT ELECTRONIC CLUSTER

1. Disconnect the negative battery cable. As required, lower the steering column.
2. Remove the instrument cluster bezel.
3. Remove the cluster retaining screws. Pull the cluster assembly forward and disconnect the speedometer cable and all electrical connections.
4. As required, remove the trip odometer, reset knob and the cluster lens.

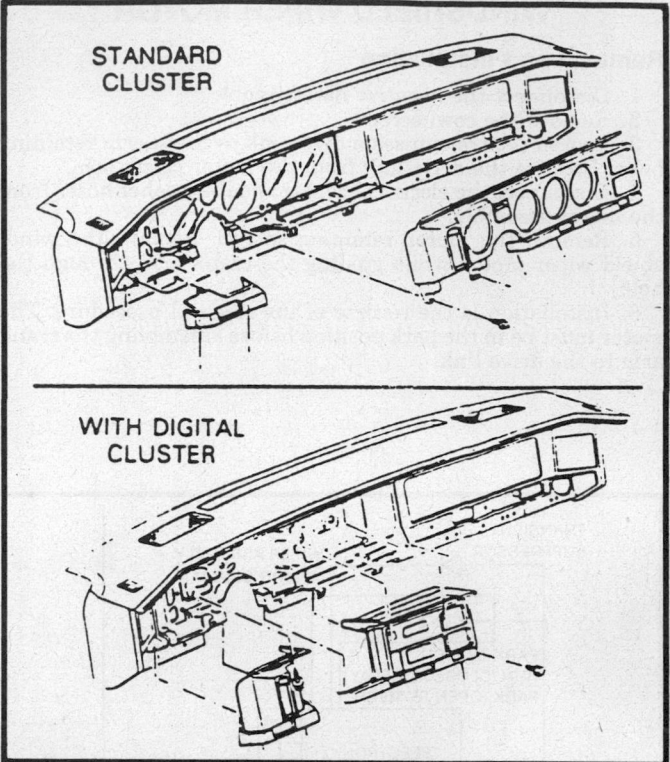

Electronic and standard instrument cluster mounting

5. Remove the speedometer assembly from the vehicle.
6. Installation is the reverse of the removal procedure.

WITH ELECTRONIC CLUSTER

1. Disconnect the negative battery cable.
2. Remove the screws holding the steering column trim cover to the instrument panel. Remove the trim cover.
3. Remove the screws at the bottom of the right hand pod. Pull the pod rearward and disconnect the electrical connector. Slide the pod from the track as a unit.
4. Repeat Step 3 for removal of the left hand pod.
5. Disconnect the electrical connector from under the instrument panel.
6. Remove the cluster bezel screws and remove the bezel. Remove the cluster lens screws and remove the cluster lens.
7. Remove the steering column bolts and lower the column to gain working clearance.
8. Pull the cluster forward and disconnect the electrical connection.
9. Installation is the reverse of the removal procedure.

SPEEDOMETER CABLE/HOUSING

Removal and Installation

1. Disconnect the speedometer cable tab connection at the dashboard. If necessary remove the speedometer assembly retaining screws to gain access.
2. Remove the speedometer cable rubber grommet at lower floor board.
3. Raise and safely support the vehicle.
4. Disconnect the speedometer cable at the extension housing of the transmission. Remove any cable housing to vehicle body retaining brackets.
5. Installation is the reverse of the removal procedure.

SWITCH MODE / TERMINAL #	MIST	OFF	PULSE	LO	HI †	WASH
PULSE 1	C	C	C	C	C	C
2	B(+)	—	B(+)	B(+)	—	*B(+)
3	B(+)	B(+)	—	B(+)	—	*B(+)
4	—	—	—	—	—	—
5	—	—	—	—	—	—
6	10-12V	10-12V	10-12V	10-12V	10-12V	B(+)
7	GROUND	GROUND	GROUND	GROUND	GROUND	GROUND
8	C	C	C	C	C	C
9	—	—	—	—	B(+)	—
STANDARD 1		C		C	C	C
2		—		B(+)	—	*B(+)
3		B(+)		B(+)	—	*B(+)
4		—		—	—	—
5		—		—	—	—
6		—		—	—	B(+)
7		GROUND		GROUND	GROUND	GROUND
8		C		C	C	C
9		—		—	B(+)	—

C = CONTINUITY   † TERMINALS #2 & #3 CONNECTED TOGETHER.   *EXCEPT ON HI.

Wiper/washer switch check

Electrical Circuit Protectors

FUSIBLE LINKS

Fusible links are used to prevent major wire harness damage in the event of a short circuit or an overload condition in the wiring circuits which are normally not fused, due to carrying high amperage loads or because of their locations within the wiring harness. Each fusible link is of a fixed value for a specific electrical load and should a link fail, the cause of the failure must be determined and repaired prior to installing a new fusible link of the same value.

CIRCUIT BREAKERS

Various circuit breakers are located under the instrument panel. In order to gain access to these components, it may be necessary to first remove the under dash padding.

FUSE PANEL

The fuse panel is located on the left side of the vehicle, under the instrument panel assembly. In order to gain access to the fuse panel it may be necessary to first remove the under dash padding.

COMPUTER (ECM)

The electronic control module is located on the right side of the vehicle, under the instrument panel. In order to gain access to the electronic control module, it may be necessary to remove the under dash padding.

VARIOUS RELAYS

All vehicles use a combination of the following electrical relays in order to function properly.

Throttle Kicker Relay (V8)—located on the left side of the engine cowl or the right front inner fender panel.

A/C Blower Speed High Speed Relay—located near the blower module on the A/C module.

A/C Blower Relay Assembly (Berlinetta)—located under the dash in the module on the A/C plenum housing.

Burn Off Relay—located behind the ECM.

Beam Change Relay (Berlinetta)—located inside the light module.

Choke Heater Relay—located in the convenience center.

Courtesy Light Relay (Berlinetta)—located in the light module.

Power Door Lock Relay—located behind the left kick panel in the lower opening.

Right turn Signal Relay (Berlinetta)—located inside the light module.

Left turn Signal Relay (Berlinetta)—located inside the light module.

A/C Compressor Relay—located on the left side engine cowl near the brake booster.

Power Antenna Relay—located behind the right side of the instrument panel lower cover.

Horn Relay—located in the convenience center.

Early Fuel Evaporation Relay—located on the upper right side of the engine cowl.

Hood Louver Relay (Z28)—located on the left side of the engine cowl.

Fuel Pump Relay—located on the left side of the engine cowl.

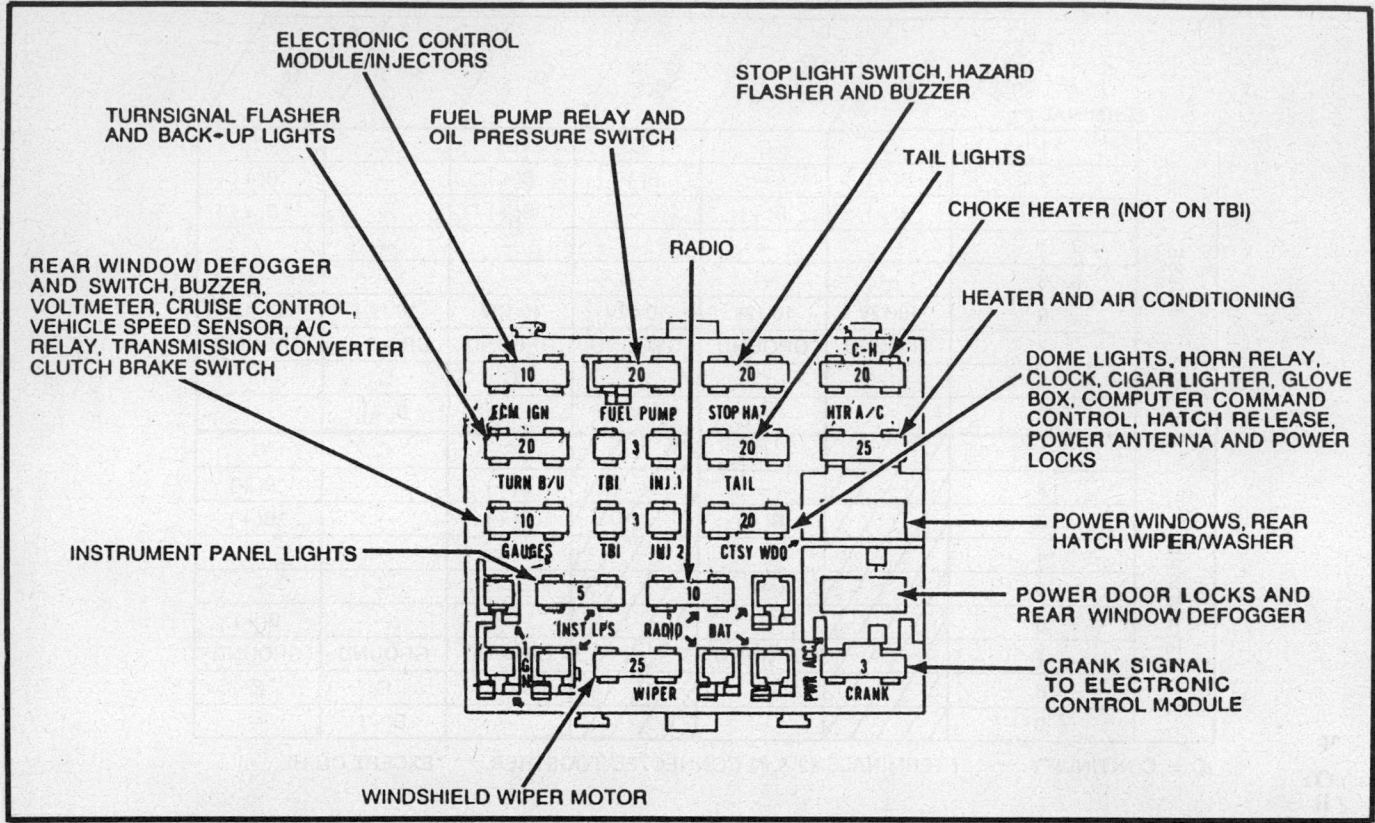

Typical fuse panel

Hatch Release Relay—located under the front part of the console.

Wide Open Throttle Relay—located in the left rear corner of the engine compartment.

Cooling Fan Relay (V6)—located on the left side of the firewall.

Cooling Fan Relay (V8)—located on the right side of the radiator or the left side of the firewall.

Flasher Select Relay (Berlinetta)—located inside the light module.

Fuel Pump Relay—located on the upper right side of the firewall.

Headlight Relay (Berlinetta)—located inside the light module.

Fast Idle Relay (V6)—located behind the right headlight on the side of the radiator.

Fast Idle Relay (V8)—located on the upper right side of the engine cowl.

Fog Light Relay—located on the left rear inner fender panel.

Isolation Relay—located behind the right headlight.

Low Blower Relay—located on the right side of the firewall, near the blower motor.

Rear Hatch Release Relay—located under the console.

Park/Turn Relay (Berlinetta)—located inside the light module.

Mass Air Flow Relay—located on the right side of the radiator support bracket.

Rear Defogger Timer/Relay—located below the right side of the dash, near the ECM.

CONVENIENCE CENTER

The convenience center is located on the underside of the in-strument panel. It is a swing down unit which provides access to buzzers, relays and flasher units. In order to gain access to the convenience center, it may be necessary to remove instrument panel sound absorber. On the later models, the flasher units are located on the right hand side of the steering column brace.

TURN SIGNAL FLASHER

The turn signal flasher is located inside the convenience center. In order to gain access to the turn signal flasher, it may be necessary to first remove the under dash padding.

HAZARD FLASHER

The hazard flasher is located inside the convenience center. In order to gain access to the hazard signal flasher, it may be necessary to first remove the under dash padding.

Speed Controls

Refer to "Chilton's Chassis Electronics Service Manual" for additional coverage.

Adjustment

1. With the cable assembly installed in the servo bracket, install the cable assembly end onto the stud of the lever assembly. Secure the component with the retainer.

2. Pull the servo assembly end of the cable toward the servo assembly without moving the lever assembly.

3. If one of the 6 holes in the servo assembly tab lines up with the cable assembly pin, connect the pin to the tab with the retainer.

4. If the tab hole does not line up with the pin, move the cable assembly away from the servo assembly until the next closest hole lines up. Secure the component with the retainer.

5. Do not stretch the cable assembly so as to make a particular tab hole connect to the pin, as this will prevent the engine from returning to idle.

COOLING AND HEATING SYSTEMS

Water Pump

Removal and Installation

1. Disconnect the negative battery cable. Drain the cooling system.
2. If equipped, remove the fan shroud and the upper radiator support.
3. Remove the drive belts or serpentine belt.
4. Remove the fan and the pulley from the water pump.

NOTE: Viscous drive fans should not be stored horizontally. The silicone fluid can leak out of the fan assemble if it is not kept upright.

5. As required, remove the upper and lower brackets, the air brace, the bracket and the lower power steering pump bracket.
6. Disconnect the heater and lower radiator hoses, from the water pump. On vehicles equipped with a bypass hose, remove it.
7. Remove the water pump retaining bolts. Remove the water pump.

NOTE: On the 2.5L engine, remove the pump by pulling it straight out of the block.

8. Installation is the reverse of the removal procedure. Use new gaskets or RTV sealant as required. Fill cooling system and run engine to normal operating temperature. Check pump area for leaks.

Electric Cooling Fan

——————— CAUTION ———————

Keep hands, tools and clothing away from cooling fan. Electric cooling fans can come on wheter or not the engine is running. The fan may start automatically in response to a heat sensor with the ignition in the ON position.

SYSTEM OPERATION

The electric cooling fan is activated by the coolant fan switch. This switch reads engine coolant temperature and activates the cooling fan. This occurs when the coolant temperature exceeds 222°F. The cooling fan may also be activated when the A/C control head pressure is greater than 233 psi. and the vehicle speed is less than 40mph.

Removal and Installation

1. Disconnect the negative battery cable.
2. Remove the fan harness connector from the fan motor and frame.
3. Remove the fan frame to radiator support mounting bolts and remove the fan assembly.
4. Install the cooling fan frame to the radiator support bolts. Reconnect the wiring harness and check fan operation.

NOTE: A/C equipped vehicles have 2 fan assemblies. This will require Steps 2 and 3 to be preformed for each assembly.

COOLANT TEMPERATURE SWITCH

The coolant temperature switch is located on the lower right side of the engine on 5.0 and 5.7L engines and on the top left side of the intake manifold on 2.5L and 2.8L engine.

COOLANT FAN RELAY

The coolant fan relay on 2.5L (VIN 2), 2.8L (VIN S) and 5.0L (VIN E) is located on the front of the dash under the engine compartment on the relay bracket (middle relay 2.8L and 5.0L) next to the fuel pump relay. On 5.0L (VIN F) and 5.7L (VIN 8) the coolant fan relay is located rear of the radiator support bracket in the engine compartment.

Blower Motor

Removal and Installation

1. Disconnect the negative battery cable. If necessary remove the fender brace to gain access to the blower motor.
2. Disconnect the electrical wiring from the blower motor.
3. Remove the blower motor cooling tube.
4. Remove the blower motor retaining screws.
5. Remove the blower motor and fan as an assembly from the case.
6. Installation is the reverse of the removal procedure.

Heater Core

Refer to "Chilton's Auto Heating and Air Conditioning Manual" for additional coverage.

Removal and Installation

1986

1. Disconnect the negative battery cable.
2. Drain the cooling system.
3. Disconnect the coolant hoses from the heater core.
4. Remove the right side lower hush panel.
5. Remove the right side lower instrument panel trim panel.
6. On fuel injected V8 engines, remove the electronic spark control (ESC) module from under the right side of the instrument panel.
7. Remove the right side lower instrument panel carrier to cowl screw.
8. Remove the 4 heater case cover screws.

NOTE: The upper left heater case cover screw may be reached with a long socket extension placed through the instrument panel openings which were exposed by the removal of the lower instrument panel trim panel. Carefully lift the lower right corner of the instrument panel to align the socket extension.

9. Remove the heater case cover.
10. Remove the heater core support plate and the baffle screws.
11. Remove the heater core, support plate and baffle from the heater case.
12. Installation is the reverse of the removal procedure.

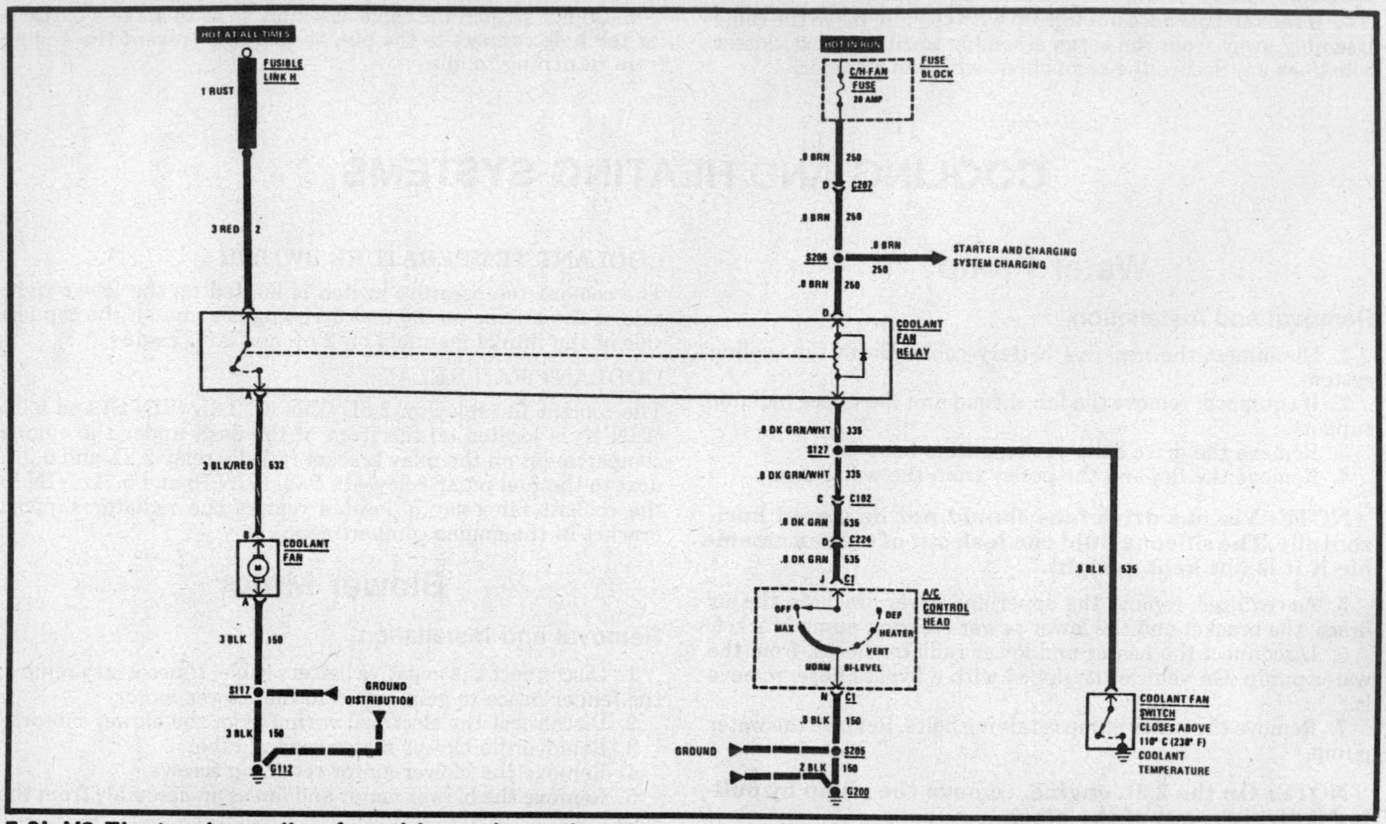

5.0L V8 Electronic cooling fan wiring schematic

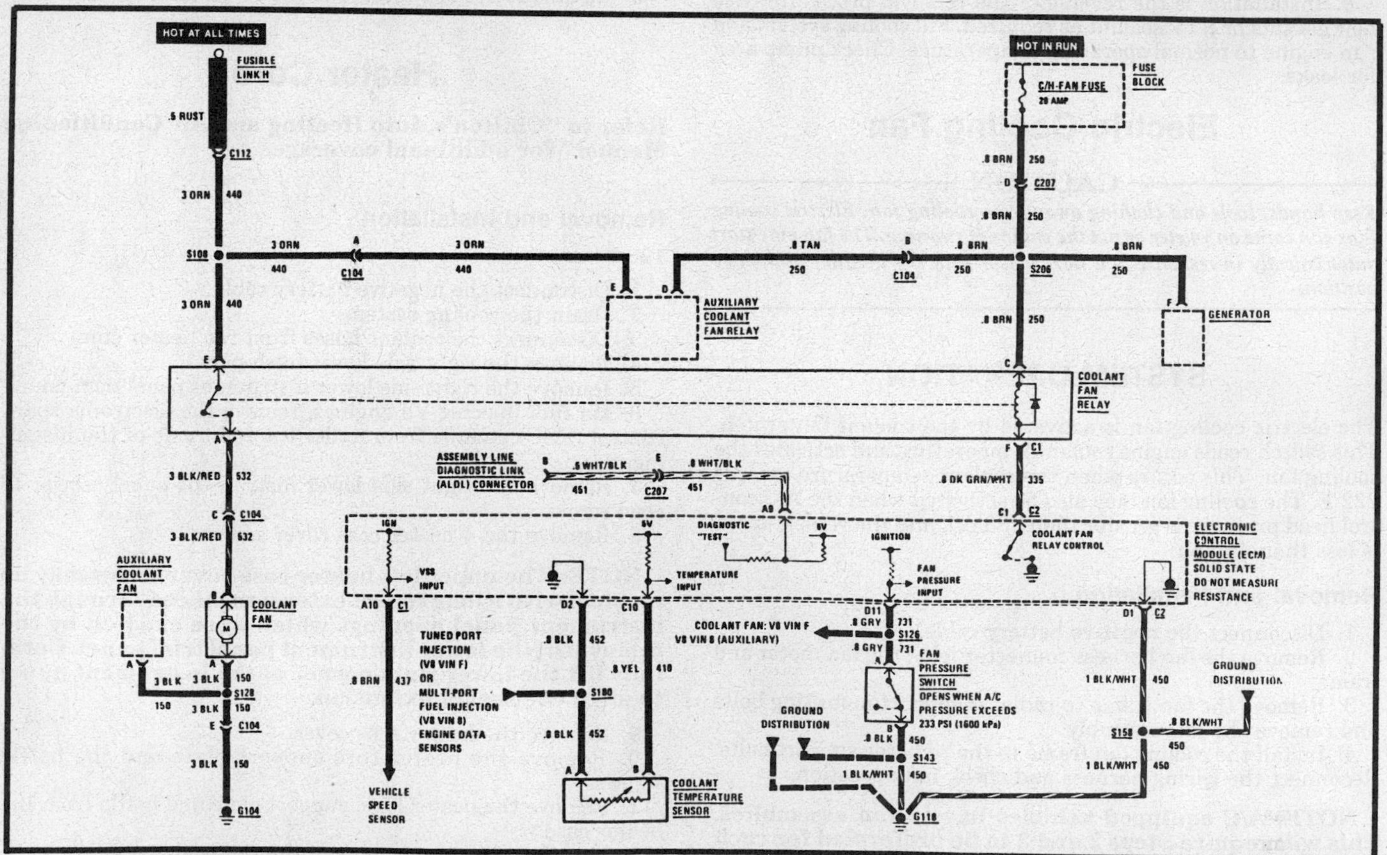

5.7L V8 Electronic cooling fan wiring schematic

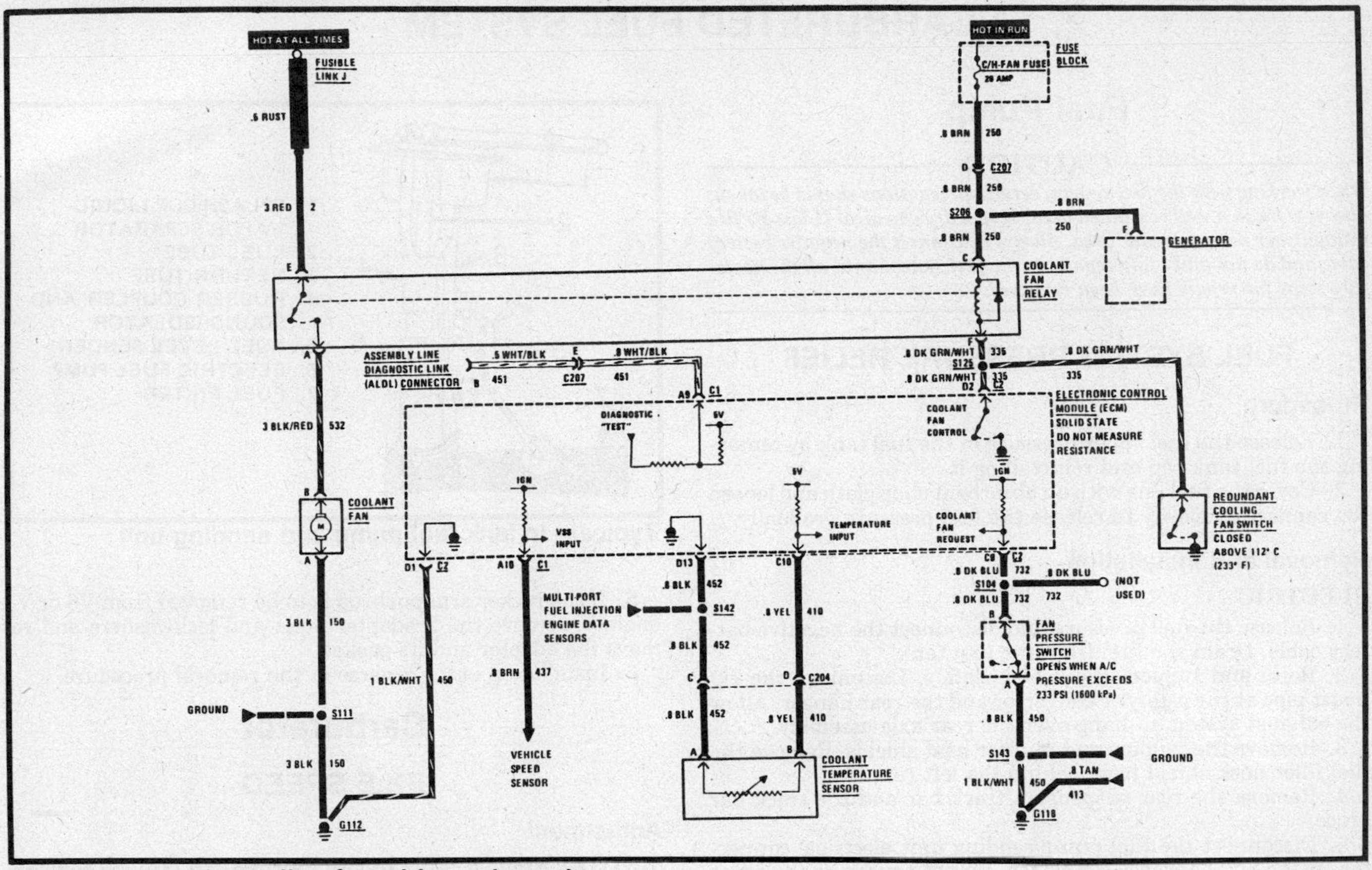

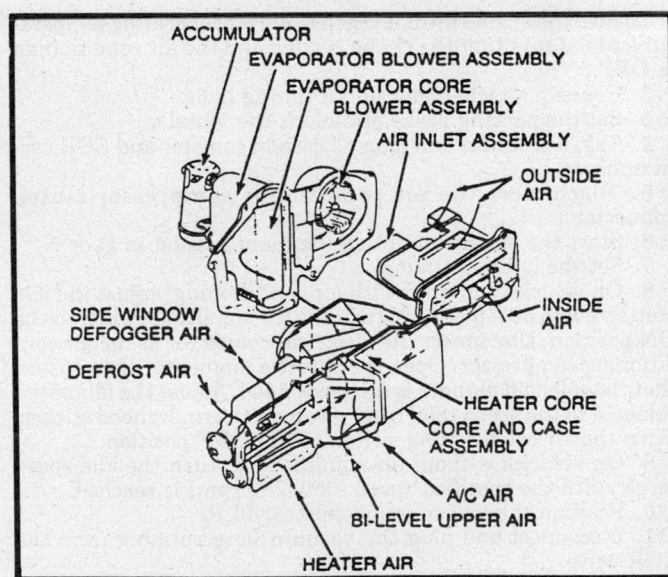

2.8L V6 Electronic cooling fan wiring schematic

Air condition components and duct work

1987–90

1. Disconnect the nagative battery cable. Drain the cooling system. Disconnect the heater hoses.

2. Remove the right and left lower hush panel. Remove the upper dash pad.

3. Remove both front speaker retaining nuts. Remove the side window defrost duct retaining nuts, front carrier braces and carrier shelf. Remove both side window defrost ducts.

4. Remove the 2 screws securing the right speaker and bracket. Disconnect the electronic control module and position it to the side.

5. Remove the radio trim plate. Remove the upper console trim. Remove the console glove box assembly. Remove the emergency brake handle grip.

6. Remove the screws that secure the console body and position the assembly out of the way.

7. Remove the trim plate from under the steering column. Remove the steering column retaining nuts and lower the column.

8. Remove the nuts and screws that retain the instrument panel carrier.

9. Move the instrument panel carrier back to gain access to the heater core and the heater core upper bolt.

10. Remove the screws that secure the heater core housing cover. Remove the screws that secure the heater core and shroud. Remove the heater core from the shroud assembly.

11. Installation is the reverse of the removal procedure.

TEMPERATURE CONTROL AND BLOWER SWITCH

Removal and Installation

1. Disconnect the negative battery cable.
2. Remove the air conditioning/radio console trim plate.
3. Remove the air conditioning control retaining screws.
4. Pull the assembly forward, disconnect the electrical and vacuum connections. Remove the temperature control cable.
5. Remove the control assembly from the vehicle.
6. Installation is the reverse of the removal procedure.

CARBURETED FUEL SYSTEM

Fuel Pump

CAUTION

When working with the fuel system, certain precautions should be taken; always work in a well ventilated area, keep a dry chemical (Class B) fire extinguisher near the work area. Always disconnect the negative battery cable and do not make any repairs to the fuel system until all the necessary steps for repair have been reviewed.

FUEL SYSTEM PRESSURE RELIEF

Procedure

1. Release the fuel vapor pressure in the fuel tank by removing the fuel tank cap and reinstalling it.
2. Cover the fuel line with an absorbent shop cloth and loosen the connection slowly to release the fuel pressure gradually.

Removal and Installation

ELECTRIC

1. Release the fuel pressure and disconnect the negative battery cable. Drain the fuel from the fuel tank.
2. Raise and support the vehicle safely. Disconnect the exhaust pipe at the catalytic convertor and the rear hanger. Allow the exhaust system to hang over the rear axle assembly.
3. Remove the tailpipe and muffler heat shields. Remove the fuel filler neck shield from behind the left rear tire.
4. Remove the rear suspension track bar and the track bar brace.
5. Disconnect the fuel pump/sending unit electrical connector, at the body harness connector. Do not pry up on the cover connector, as the pump/sending unit wiring harness is an integral part of the sending unit.
6. Disconnect the fuel pipes. Remove the fuel pipe retaining bracket on the left side and the brakeline clip from the retaining bracket.
7. Position a jack under the rear axle assembly in order to support the rear axle.
8. Disconnect the lower ends of the shock absorbers, lower the axle assembly enough to release the tension on the coil springs. Remove the coil springs.
9. Lower the rear axle assembly as far as possible without causing damage to the brake lines and cables.
10. Remove the fuel tank strap bolts. Remove the tank by rotating the front of the tank downward and sliding it to the right side.
11. Remove the fuel pump/sending unit from the tank, by loosening the cam nut. When removing the cam nut, use brass tool or equivalent to tap the nut loose.
12. Remove the O-ring from beneath the unit. Replace the O-ring if defective.
13. Separate the fuel pump from the sending unit and install the new pump in the same manner.

MECHANICAL

1. Disconnect the negative battery cable. Remove all the necessary components in order to gain access to the fuel pump assembly.
2. Disconnect and plug the fuel intake and outlet lines at the fuel pump.
3. On V6 and V8 engines, remove the upper bolt from the right front mounting boss. Insert a longer bolt (⅜–16 × 2 in.) in this hole to hold the fuel pump pushrod.
4. Remove the 2 pump mounting bolts and lockwashers. Remove the fuel pump from the vehicle.

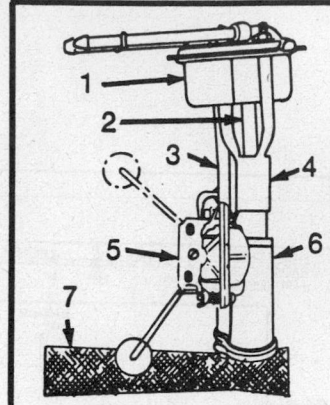

1. SPLASH CUP LIQUID VAPOR SEPARATOR
2. FUEL TUBE
3. RETURN TUBE
4. RUBBER COUPLER AND SOUND ISOLATOR
5. FUEL LEVEL SENDER
6. ELECTRIC FUEL PUMP
7. FUEL FILTER

Typical—in tank fuel pump and sending unit

5. If the rocker arm pushrod is to be removed from V6 or V8 engines, remove the 2 adapter bolts and lockwashers and remove the adapter and its gasket.
6. Installation is the reverse of the removal procedure.

Carburetor

IDLE SPEED

Adjustment

NOTE: Always refer to the underhood sticker for correct engine and tune-up specifications.

1. Run the engine until it reaches normal operating temperature. Make sure that the choke is open and the air conditioning is **OFF**.
2. Connect a tachometer and a timing light.
3. Set the parking brake and block the wheels.
4. Tag, disconnect and plug all carbon canister and EGR vacuum hoses.
5. Disconnect the air conditioner compressor clutch connector.
6. Start the engine and place the transmission in **D** or **N**.
7. Set the ignition timing.
8. On vehicles equipped with air conditioning, adjust the idle stop screw to 500–600 rpm, turn the air condition switch to the **ON** position. Disconnect the electrical connector at the air conditioning compressor. Open the throttle momentarily to ensure that the solenoid plunger is fully extended. Adjust the idle speed solenoid to the speed (800 rpm) given on the underhood sticker. Turn the air conditioning switch to the **OFF** position.
9. On vehicles without air conditioning, turn the idle speed screw until the specified speed (650–750 rpm) is reached.
10. Position the transmission selector in **P**.
11. Disconnect and plug the vacuum hose running from the EGR valve.
12. Adjust the fast idle screw on the second step of the fast idle cam until you obtain the specified rpm (1800 rpm).
13. Stop the engine and reconnect the EGR vacuum hose, the vapor canister hose and the air conditioner compressor clutch connector.

IDLE MIXTURE

The computer controlled carburetor systems are designed to provide precise control of carburetor air/fuel mixtures during all ranges of engine operation. Because of this system control, new mixture control adjustment procedures are required. Previously used propane enrichment or lean drop methods of idle mixture adjustment may not be used when adjusting carburetors with a computer system because system control will change air/fuel mixtures to lean or rich as the mixture screws are adjusted rich or lean, respectively.

The system is sensitive to any change in mixture control adjustment which, if improperly set, can impair the ability of the system to maintain precise control of carburetor air/fuel mixtures. Plugs are installed in the carburetor air horn and over the idle mixture needles in the throttle body to seal the factory settings. For this reason, the mixture control adjustment points should never be changed from the original factory setting. However, if in diagnosis, the "preliminary system performance check" indicates the carburetor to be the cause a driver performance complaint or emissions failure, or critical parts such as air horn, float bowl, throttle body, needle and seat, may be removed and the mixture control adjustments made.

External Gauge Check

Before proceeding, a check of mixture control solenoid adjustments can be made on the vehicle. It will be necessary to modify float gauge tool J-9789-130 (used to externally check float level setting on Dualjet and Quadrajet carburetors) by filing or grinding sufficient material off the gauge to allow insertion down the vertical vent **D** shaped hole in the air horn casting (next to the idle air bleed valve plug).

Check that gauge freely enters **D** vent hole and does not bind. The gauge will be used to determine total mixture control solenoid travel.

With engine off, air cleaner and gasket removed, measure mixture control solenoid travel as follows.

1. Insert modified float gauge tool J-9789-130 down **D** shaped vent hole. Press down on gauge and release, observing that gauge moves freely and does not bind. With the gauge released (solenoid up position), record mark on gauge (in inches) that lines up with top of air horn casting.

2. Lightly press down on gauge until bottom (solenoid down positon). Record in in. the mark on gauge that lines up with top of air horn casting.

3. Subtract gauge up dimension (Step 1) from gauge down dimension (Step 2) and record difference in inches. The difference in dimensions is total solenoid travel.

4. If total solenoid travel (Step 3) is greater or less than $^3/_{32}$ ± $^1/_{32}$ in., make mixture control solenoid adjustments as noted below.

Mixture Control Solenoid Adjustment

If external gauge check shows the total solenoid travel is incorrect, proceed as follows.

1. Remove air horn.

2. Using special tool No. J-28696 or equivalent, on upper end of mixture control solenoid screw (in float bowl), turn screw clockwise until it bottom lightly in bowl, counting number of turns until screw is bottomed. If number of turns counted is greater than 2½ turns, or less than 1½ turns, solenoid travel was incorrect. In this case, reset mixture control solenoid screw (Step 3). If solenoid screw setting is correct (1½–2½ turns), it will be necessary to reset solenoid stop screw to air horn (Step 4). Return solenoid screw back to its previous position.

NOTE: Do not bottom solenoid screw by forcing. To do so may result in breakage of the screw head. Do not use pliers, which would damage or break the screw.

3. From bottomed position, turn solenoid screw counterclockwise until the screw is backed out of the bowl exactly 2 turns.

4. Invert air horn and using a suitable wrench, remove the solenoid stop screw and spring (if used), from air horn. With

stop screw removed, drive out small plug located between **D** shaped vent holes to gain access to the solenoid stop screw (when installed). Reinstall solenoid stop screw and spring (if used), in air horn until screw is bottomed lightly.

5. Reinstall air horn and new gasket on float bowl.

6. Install external gauge in vent hole and with a suitable tool inserted in small hole in air horn, turn mixture control solenoid stop screw clockwise until total solenoid travel is within specified limits.

Idle Air Bleed Valve Adjustment

1. Set parking brake and block drive wheels. Disconnect and plug hoses as directed on the Vehicle Emission Information Label. Check and adjust ignition timing. Connect a dwell meter and tachometer to engine and mixture solenoid.

2. Start engine and run at idle until fully warm and a varying dwell is noted on the dwell meter. It is absolutely essential that the engine is operated for a sufficient length of time to ensure the engine coolant sensor and the oxygen sensor in the exhaust, are at full operational temperature.

3. Adjust curb idle speed, if necessary. With engine idling, observe dwell reading on the 6 cylinder scale. If within, or varying between 25–35 degree range, no further adjustment is necessary. If dwell does not vary and/or falls outside of the 10–50 degree range, perform the following.

   a. With engine off, cover primary and secondary carburetor air intake with a shop cloth to prevent metal chips from entering carburetor and engine, also place masking tape over side air top vents on bleed valve tower.

   b. Carefully align a No. 35 drill (0.110 in.) on the steel rivet head holding the idle air bleed valve cover in place and drill only enough to remove rivet head. Use a drift and small hammer to drive the remainder of the rivets out of the idle air bleed value tower in the air horn casting. Use care in drilling to prevent damage to the air horn casting.

   c. Remove idle air bleed valve cover and remove remainder of rivets from inside tower in air horn casting. Discard cover after removal. Carefully blow out any chips or dirt which may be in air bleed valve cavity. A missing cover indicates the idle air bleed valve setting has been changed from its original factory setting.

   d. While idling in **D** or **N**, slowly turn valve up or down until dwell reading varies within the 25–35 degree range, attempting to be as close to 30 degree as possible. Perform this step carefully. The idle air bleed valve is very sensitive and should be turned only in ⅛ turn increments.

   e. If after performing Step d, the dwell reading does not vary and is not within the 25–35 degree range, it will be necessary to remove the carburetor to gain access to the plugs covering the idle mixture needles and readjust the idle mixture.

Idle Mixture Adjustment

If total solenoid travel and the idle air bleed valve dwell are correct, proceed with idle mixture adjustment.

1. Remove carburetor from the engine.

2. Invert carburetor and drain fuel in container.

3. Place inverted carburetor on suitable holding fixture.

4. Remove idle mixture needle plug as follows. Using a punch between the 2 locator points in throttle body beneath idle mixture needle plus (manifold side), break out throttle body to gain access to the idle mixture needle plugs. Drive out hardened steel plugs covering mixture needles. Hardened plugs will shatter rather than remaining intact. It is not necessary to remove the plug completely; instead, remove loose pieces to allow use of the idle mixture adjusting tool J-29030 or equivalent. Use same procedure for both plugs over idle mixture needles.

5. Using Tool J-29030 or equivalent, turn each idle mixture needle inward until lightly seated. Back out each mixture needle 4½ turns.

6. Reinstall the carburetor. Do not install the air cleaner and

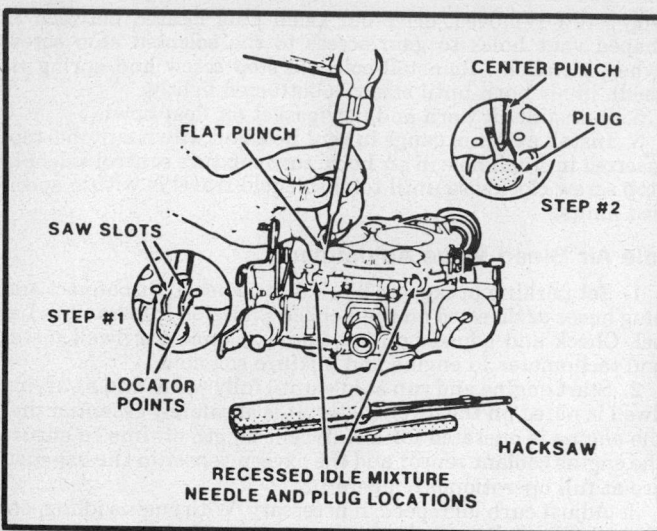

Removing idle mixture screw plugs—caburetor

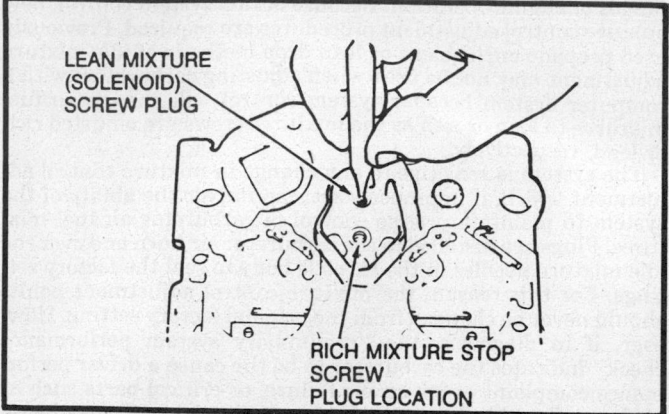

Idle mixture screw locations—carburetor

gasket. Start engine, run until fully warm and repeat idle air bleed valve adjustment until dwell reading is varying and within specified limits. If unable to achieve varying dwell and specified limits, turn each mixture needle out an additional ½ turn. Reset idle air bleed valve to obtain dwell limit specifications.

7. If necessary, reset curb idle speed to specification.

8. Check and, if necessary, adjust fast idle speed. Disconnect dwell meter and tachometer. Unplug and reconnect vacuum hoses.

Carburetor

Removal and Installation

1. Disconnect the negative battery cable. Remove the air cleaner assembly.

2. Disconnect the accelerator linkage and the detent cable.

3. Separate the necessary electrical connectors and remove vacuum lines.

4. Remove the fuel line at the carburetor inlet.

5. Remove the 4 attaching bolts. Remove the carburetor from the vehicle.

6. Installation is the reverse of removal. Be sure to use a new gasket. Tighten hold down bolts in an "X" pattern.

FUEL INJECTION SYSTEM

Refer to "Chilton's Electronic Engine Control Manual" for additional coverage.

Description

THROTTLE BODY INJECTION (TBI)

With throttle body injection TBI, an injection unit is placed on the intake manifold where the carburetor is normally mounted. The TBI unit is computer controlled and supplies the correct amount of fuel during all engine operating conditions. In the TBI system, a single fuel injector mounted at the top of the throttle body, sprays fuel through the throttle valve and into the intake manifold. The activating signal for the injector originates with the electronic control module ECM, which monitors engine temperature, throttle position, vehicle speed and several other engine related conditions. A fuel pressure regulator inside the throttle body maintains fuel pressure at 9–13 psi and routes unused fuel back to the fuel tank through a fuel return line.

MULTI-PORT FUEL INJECTION (MPFI)

This system uses Bosch or Multex fuel injectors, one at each intake port. The injectors are mounted on a fuel rail and are activated by a signal from the electronic control module ECM. The injector is a solenoid operated valve which remains open depending on the width of the electronic pulses (length of the signal) from the ECM; the longer the open time, the more fuel is injected. In this manner, the air/fuel mixture can be precisely controlled for maximum performance with minimum emissions. A pressure regulator maintains about 28–36 psi in the fuel line to the injectors and the excess fuel is fed back to the tank.

IDLE SPEED

Adjustment

The idle speed and mixture are electronically controlled by the Electronic Control Module (ECM). All adjustments are preset at the factory. The only time the idle speed should need adjustment is when the throttle body assembly has been replaced. The throttle stop screw, used in regulating the minimum idle speed, is adjusted at the factory and is not necessary to perform. This adjustment should be performed only when the throttle body has been replaced

TBI SYSTEM

1. Block the drive wheels and apply the parking brake. Remove the air cleaner assembly and or air duct. Remove and plug any vacuum hoses on the tube manifold assembly, if so equipped. Disconnect the throttle cable.

NOTE: If present, pierce the idle stop screw plug with an awl and apply leverage to remove it.

2. Ground the diagnostic test terminal in the ALCL connector. Turn the ignition **ON** and leave the engine **OFF**. Wait at least 30 seconds, this will allow the IAC pintle to seat in the throttle body.

3. With the ignition still in the **ON** position and the engine **OFF**, with the ALCL test terminal still grounded, disconnect the IAC valve electrical connector.

4. Connect a tachometer to the engine (a Scan tool can also be used) to monitor the engine speed.

5. Remove the ground from the ALCL connector test terminal.

6. Place the transmission in the **P** or **N** position. Start and run the engine until it reaches normal operating temperature. It may be necesary to depress the accelerator pedal in order to start the engine. Allow the engine idle speed to stabilize.

NOTE: The engine should be at normal operating temperature with the accessories and cooling fan off.

7. The idle speed should be set at 600 ± 50 rpm, if not within specification adjust as necesary.

8. Install the throttle cable, be sure that the minimum idle speed is not affected by the throttle cable. If so correct this condition.

9. Turn the ignition **OFF** and reconnect the IAC valve electrical connector. Unplug and reconnect and disconnected vacuum lines. Install the air cleaner assembly.

MPFI SYSTEM

1. Apply the parking brake and block the drive wheels. Remove the plug from the idle stop screw by piercing it first with a suitable tool, then applying leverage to the tool to lift the plug out.

2. Leave the Idle Air Control (IAC) valve connected and ground the diagnostic terminal (ALCL).

3. Turn the ignition switch to the **ON** position, do not start the engine. Wait for at least 30 seconds (this allows the IAC valve pintle to extend and seat in the throttle body).

4. With the ignition switch still in the **ON** position, disconnect IAC electrical connector.

5. Remove the ground from the diagnostic terminal. Disconnect the distributor set-timing connector (5.0L and 5.7L engines). Start the engine and allow the engine to reach normal operating temperature.

6. Apply the parking brake and block the drive wheels.

7. With the engine in the drive position adjust the idle stop screw to obtain the correct specifications (500rpm).

8. Turn the ignition **OFF** and reconnect the connector at the IAC motor.

9. Adjust the TPS if necessary. Start the engine and inspect for proper idle operation.

FUEL SYSTEM PRESSURE RELIEF

Procedure

1. Release the fuel vapor pressure in the fuel tank by removing the fuel tank cap and reinstalling it.

2. With the engine running, remove the connector of the fuel pump and wait until the engine stops.

3. Once the engine is stopped, crank it a few times with the starter for about 5 seconds with the pump disconnected.

4. If the fuel pressure can't be released in the above manner because the engine failed to run, disconnect the negative battery cable, cover the union bolt of the fuel line with an absorbent shop cloth and loosen the union bolt slowly to release the fuel pressure gradually.

FUEL INJECTORS

Removal and Installation

TBI

1. Release the fuel pressure and remove the air cleaner. Disconnect the negative battery cable.

2. Disconnect injector electrical connector by squeezing 2 tabs together and pulling straight up.

NOTE: Use care in removing to prevent damage to the electrical connector pins on top of the injector, injector fuel filter and nozzle. The fuel injector is only serviced

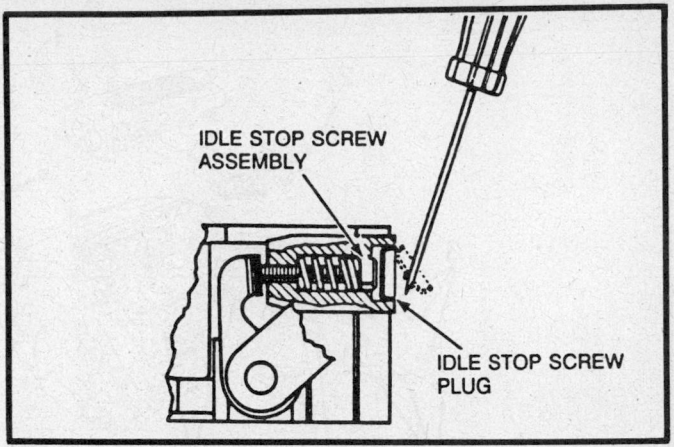

Removing idle stop screw plug—fuel injected models

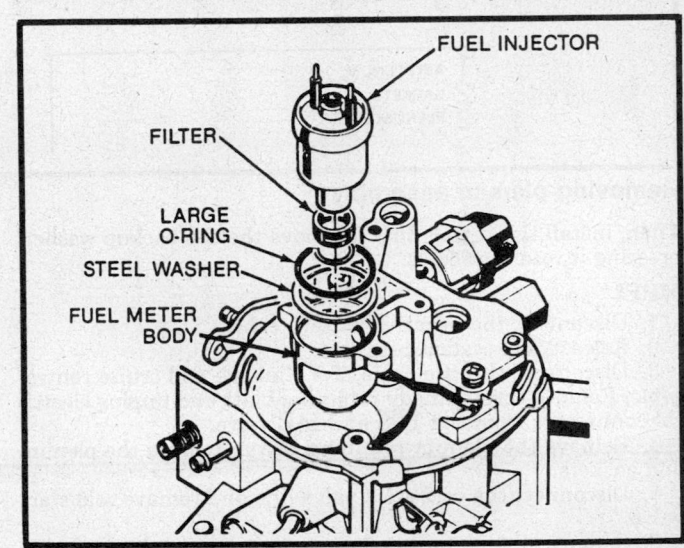

TBI injector assembly

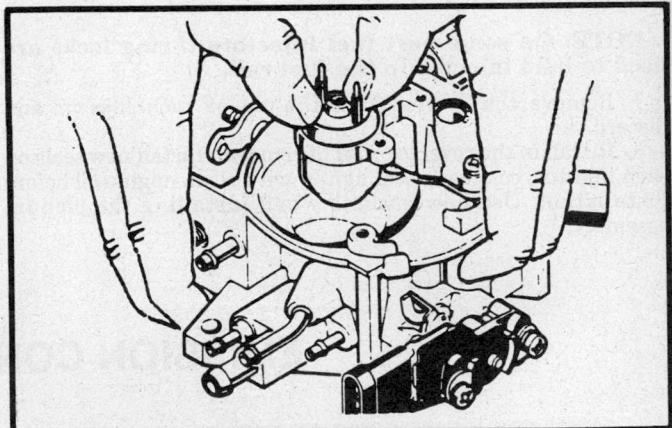

Install injector by firmly pushing in on housing

as a complete assembly. Do not immerse it in any type of cleaner.

3. Remove the fuel meter cover.

4. Using a small awl, gently pry up on the injector and carefully remove it.

5. Installation is the reverse of the removal procedure. Install the steel backup washer in the recess of the fuel meter body.

21–27

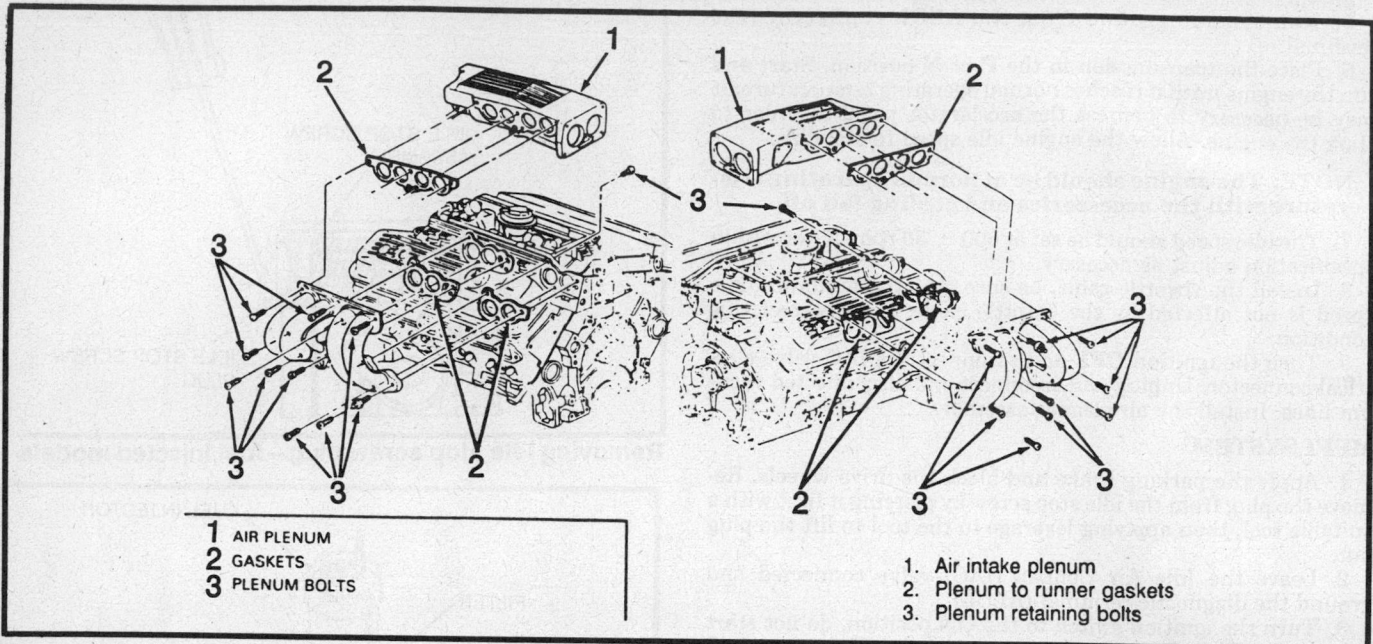

1 AIR PLENUM
2 GASKETS
3 PLENUM BOLTS

1. Air intake plenum
2. Plenum to runner gaskets
3. Plenum retaining bolts

Removing plenum assembly

Then, install the O-ring directly above the the backup washer, pressing it into the recess.

MPFI

1. Disconnect the negative battery cable.
2. Release fuel system pressure.
3. Disconnect throttle cable, T.V. linkage and cruise control cable. Remove throttle body retaining bolts and unplug electrical connectors from the TPS and IAC valve.
4. Remove the plenum retaining bolts. Remove the plenum and gaskets.
5. Disconnect the cold start valve line and remove cold start valve.
6. Remove all fuel lines and disconnect injector harness connectors. Loosen fuel rail retaining bolts. Remove the fuel rail and the injectors.

NOTE: On some port fuel injectors U-ring locks are used to hold injector to the fuel rail.

7. Remove the O-ring from the tip of each injector and discard.
8. Install in the reverse order of removal. Install new seals on each injector, coat each seal lightly with clean engine oil before installation. Use new gaskets when installing the plenum assembly.

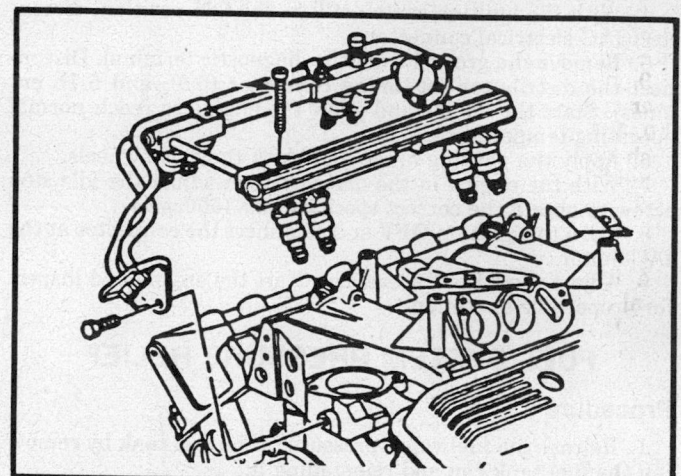

Fuel rail and injector assembly

EMISSION CONTROL SYSTEMS

ALL ENGINES

Refer to "Chilton's Emission Diagnosis and Service Manual" for additional coverage.

Air Injector System (AIR)
Assembly Line Communication Link (ALCL)
Barometric Absolute Pressure Sensor (BARO)
Computer Command Control (CCC)
Controlled Canister Purge (CCP)
Closed Loop Carburetor Control (CLCC)

Coolant Temperature Sensor (CTS)
Catalytic Converter
Electric Air Control (EAC)
Electric Air Switching (EAS)
Electronic Control Module (ECM)
Exhaust Gas Recirculation (EGR)
Evaporative Emissions Control System (EECS)
Electronic Module Retard (EMR)
Electronic Spark Control (ESC)
Idle Air Bleed Valve (IABV)

Idle Speed Control Motor (ISC)
Manifold Vacuum Sensor
Manifold Pressure Sensor (MAP)
Mixture Control Solenoid (M/C)
Oxygen Sensor, Exhaust

Pulse Air Injection Reactor System (PAIR)
Positive Crankcase Ventilation (PCV)
Programmable Read Only Memory (PROM)
Thermostatic Air Cleaner (THERMAC)
Throttle Position Sensor (TPS)

ENGINE MECHANICAL

Engine Assembly

Removal and Installation

2.5L ENGINE

1. Disconnect the negative battery cable.
2. Mark the location of the hood on the hood hinges and remove the hood.
3. Drain the cooling system.
4. Remove the A/C compressor and any necessary brackets to gain working clearance.
5. Remove the radiator hoses from the engine. Remove the fan assembly. Remove the radiator shroud and radiator.
6. If equipped, remove the power steering pump.
7. Tag and disconnect the electrical connector at the bulkhead connector.
8. Relieve the fuel line pressure. Disconnect and plug the fuel lines.
9. Remove the brake hoses and the ground strap from the rear of the cylinder head.
10. Working from inside the vehicle, remove the right hand hush panel and the ECM harness at the main ECM connector. Remove the right hand splash shield from the right fender and feed the ECM harness out from inside the vehicle.
11. Disconnect the heater hoses from the heater core. Remove the canister hose and the throttle cable.
12. Raise the vehicle and support safely. Disconnect the electrical connections from the transmission.
13. Remove the flywheel dustcover. If the vehicle is an automatic, remove the torque converter to flywheel holding bolts.
14. Remove the bolts holding the bellhousing to the engine. Remove the bellhousing to engine exhaust pipe support.
15. Remove the exhaust pipe at the manifold. Remove the catalytic converter assembly.
16. Remove the starter assembly.
17. Remove the clutch fork return spring if vehicle is equipped with a manual transmission.
18. Remove the motor mount bolts.
19. Lower the vehicle and install a suitable engine lifting device.
20. Position a floor jack under the transmission to support the transmission.
21. Lift the engine from the vehicle and place in a suitable engine holding fixture.
22. Installation is the reverse of the removal procedure.

2.8L, 5.0L AND 5.7L ENGINES

1. Disconnect the negative battery cable.
2. Mark the hood location on the hood supports and remove the hood from the vehicle.
3. Drain the cooling system. Remove the lower radiator hose and the upper fan shroud. Remove the fan assembly.
4. Remove the upper radiator hose and the coolant recovery hose. Remove the radiator.
5. Remove the transmission cooler lines. Remove the heater hoses.
6. Disconnect the carburetor linkage. If the vehicle is equipped with cruise control, disconnect the detent cable.

7. If equipped with fuel injection, properly relieve the fuel line pressure. Disconnect and plug the fuel lines.
8. Remove the vacuum brake booster line.
9. As required, remove the distributor cap and lay aside with the wiring to gain working clearance.
10. Disconnect all necessary wires and hoses.
11. Remove the power steering pump and lay aside.
12. Raise the vehicle and support it safely.
13. Remove the exhaust pipes from the manifold. Remove the dust cover from the vehicle. Remove the converter bolts.
14. Disconnect the starter wires and remove the starter assembly.
15. Remove the bellhousing bolts. Remove the motor mount through bolts.
16. On carbureted engines, disconnect the fuel lines at the fuel pump.
17. Lower the vehicle and support the transmission using a suitable fixture.
18. Remove the air injection reaction system, if equipped.
19. Attach a suitable engine lifting device and remove the engine from the vehicle.
20. Installation is the reverse of the removal procedure.

Engine Mounts

Removal and Installation

2.5L ENGINE

1. Disconnect the negative battery cable. Raise and support the vehicle safely.
2. Remove the engine to mount attachment bolt on the left and right side.
3. Using a suitable lifting device, raise the engine until the engine mount is clear. Remove the mount bolts and the mount.
4. Installation is the reverse order of the removal procedure. Torque the mount bolt to 34 ft. lbs. and torque the engine mount attaching bolt to 48 ft. lbs.

2.8L ENGINE

1. Disconnect the negative battery cable. Remove the top half of the radiator shroud. Raise and support the vehicle safely.
2. Remove the engine mount through bolt. Using a suitable engine lift, raise the front of the engine and remove the mount to engine bolts and remove the mount.

NOTE: Raise the engine only enough for sufficient clearance. Check for interference between the rear of the engine and the cowl panel which could cause distributor damage.

3. Installation is the reverse order of the removal procedure.

5.0L AND 5.7L ENGINES

1. Disconnect the negative battery cable.
2. Raise the vehicle and support safely.
3. Remove the engine mount retaining bolt from below the the frame mounting bracket.
4. Using a suitable engine lift, raise the front of the engine and remove the mount to engine bolts and remove the mount.

NOTE: Raise the engine only enough for sufficient clearance. Check for interference between the rear of the engine and the cowl panel which could cause distributor damage.

5. Installation is the reverse of the removal procedure.

Intake Manifold

Removal and Installation

2.5L ENGINE

1. Disconnect the negative battery cable. Relieve fuel pressure as necessary.
2. Remove the air cleaner, PCV valve and hose.
3. Drain the cooling system. Tag and disconnect the vacuum hoses.
4. Disconnect the fuel line from throttle body.
5. Remove the throttle linkage and wiring.
6. Disconnect the transmission downshift linkage.
7. Disconnect the cruise control linkage, as required.
8. Remove the heater hoses to gain working clearance.
9. Disconnect the alternator bracket and lay aside.
10. Disconnect the ignition coil assembly.
11. Remove the intake manifold retaining bolts and remove the intake manifold.
12. Installation is the reverse of the removal procedure. Fill the cooling system and check for leaks. Tighten in correct order, outside bolts to 25–28 ft. lbs. and inside bolts to 37 ft. lbs.

2.8L ENGINE

1. Disconnect the negative battery cable. Remove the air cleaner assembly. Drain the coolant system.
2. Relieve fuel pressure as necessary.
3. Remove the following subassemblies: plenum, fuel rail and runner.
4. Remove the spark plug wires from the spark plugs and disconnect the wires at the coil.
5. Remove the distributor cap along with the spark plug wires, mark the position of the distributor, remove the distributor hold down bolt and lift the distributor out of the vehicle.
6. If equipped, remove the air management hose and bracket.
7. Disconnect the emission canister hoses. Remove the pipe bracket on the front left valve cover and remove the left valve cover.
8. Remove the right valve cover and the upper radiator hose. Disconnect the coolant switches.
9. Remove the manifold bolts along with the intake manifold. Discard the old gaskets and any loose RTV sealant from the front and rear ridges of the cylinder case.
10. Installation is the reverse order of the removal procedure. Be sure to apply a $^3/_{16}$ in. bead of RTV sealant on the front and rear ridge of the cylinder case. Torque all retaining bolts in proper order and to the correct specifications.
11. Install the new gaskets on the cylinder heads. Hold the gaskets in place by extending the RTV bead up onto the gasket ends. Certain GM intake gaskets will have to be cut to be install behind the pushrods. Cut these gaskets as required and only where necessary.

5.0L AND 5.7L ENGINES

1. Disconnect the negative battery cable. Remove the air cleaner assembly.
2. Relieve fuel pressure as necessary. Drain the radiator. Disconnect the upper radiator hose and the heater hoses at the manifold.
3. If equipped, disconnect the carburetor linkage and fuel line at the carburetor. Remove the carburetor as required.
4. On vehicles equipped with fuel injection, remove the following sub-assemblies: plenum, fuel rail and runner.
5. Remove and tag the spark plug wires and remove all necessary wires and hoses.

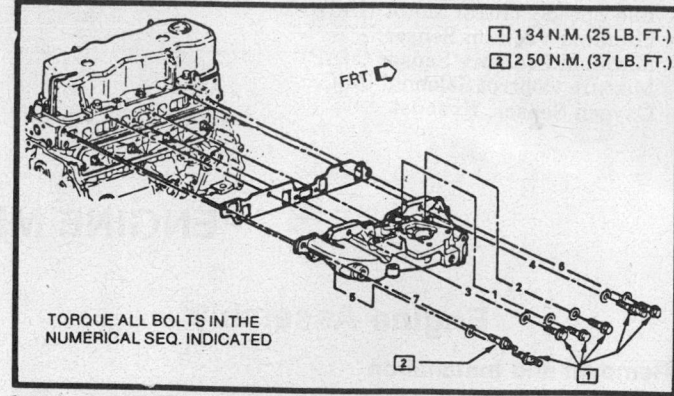

TORQUE ALL BOLTS IN THE NUMERICAL SEQ. INDICATED

① 34 N.M. (25 LB. FT.)
② 50 N.M. (37 LB. FT.)

FRT

Intake manifold bolt tightening sequence—4 cylinder

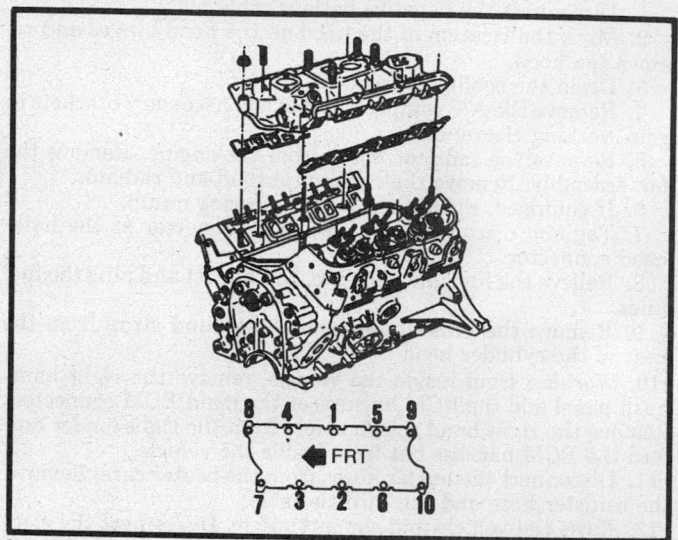

FRT

8 4 1 5 9
7 3 2 6 10

Intake manifold bolt tightening sequence V6 engine

6. Remove the distributor cap. Mark the position of the rotor and remove the distributor.
7. If the vehicle is equipped with A/C and/or cruise control, remove the A/C compressor with brackets and the cruise control servo assembly with bracket.
8. Loosen the alternator belt and remove the upper mounting bracket. Remove the EGR solenoids and brackets. Remove the vacuum brake line.
9. Remove the intake manifold attaching bolts. Remove the intake manifold.
10. Installation is the reverse of the removal procedure. Apply a $^3/_{16}$ in. bead of RTV sealant on the front and rear ridge of the cylinder case. Extend the bead about ½ in. up each cylinder head in order to seal and retain the manifold side gaskets. On carbureted engines, use sealer at water passages.
11. Torque all retaining bolts in proper order and to the correct specifications.

Exhaust Manifold

Removal and Installation

2.5L ENGINE

1. Disconnect the negative battery cable. Raise and safely support the vehicle.
2. Remove the air cleaner and EFI preheat tube. Remove the oxygen sensor electrical connection.
3. Disconnect the exhaust pipe from the exhaust manifold.

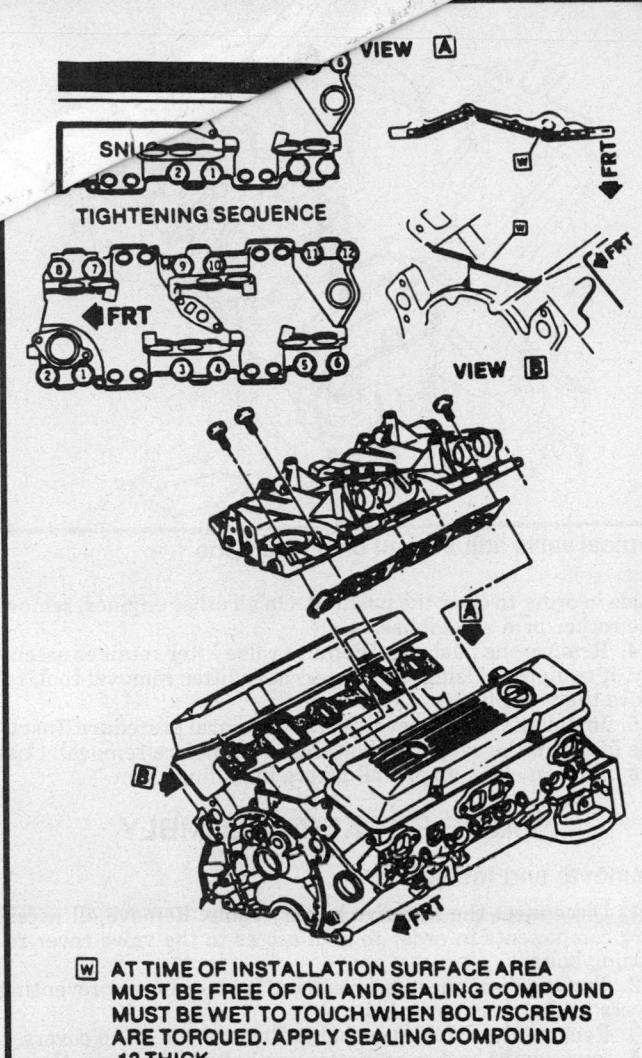

W AT TIME OF INSTALLATION SURFACE AREA MUST BE FREE OF OIL AND SEALING COMPOUND MUST BE WET TO TOUCH WHEN BOLT/SCREWS ARE TORQUED. APPLY SEALING COMPOUND .12 THICK.

Intake manifold torque sequence V8 engine with fuel injection

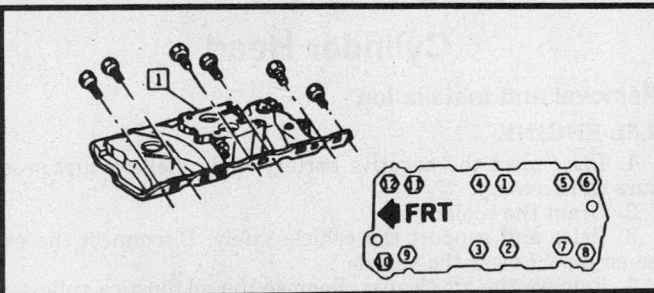

Intake manifold torque sequence V8 engine with carburetor

4. Remove the oil dipstick tube to gain working clearance.
5. Remove the exhaust manifold bolts. Remove the exhaust manifold.
6. Installation is the reverse of the removal procedure. Tighten outside bolts (No. 1, 2, 6, 7) to 32 ft. lbs., inside bolts (No. 3, 4, 5) to 37 ft. lbs.
7. Start the engine and check for exhaust leaks.

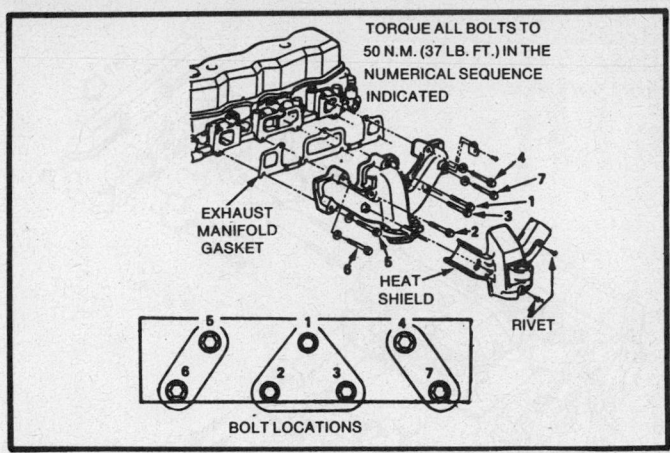

Exhaust manifold bolt tightening sequence 4 cylinder engine

2.8L ENGINE

1. Disconnect the negative battery cable. Raise and support the vehicle safely.
2. Disconnect the exhaust pipe from the exhaust manifold. Lower the vehicle.
3. Remove the following components on the right side:
   a. Disconnect the air management valve bracket.
   b. Disconnect the AIR hoses and AIR converter pipe.
   c. Disconnect the AIR pipe at the cylinder heads and at the manifold. Disconnect the spark plug wires.
4. Remove the following components on the left side:
   a. Remove the A/C compressor and the power steering pump.
   b. Remove the rear A/C adjusting brace and the lower power steering adjusting brace. Disconnect the spark plug wires.
5. Remove the exhaust manifold bolts and remove the exhaust manifold.
6. Installation is the reverse order of the removal procedure. Tighten all manifold bolts to 18–30 ft. lbs.

5.0L AND 5.7L ENGINES

1. Disconnect the negative battery cable and raise and support the vehicle safely.
2. Disconnect the exhaust pipe from the exhaust manifold and lower the vehicle.
3. On the right side, remove the air cleaner, spark plugs and disconnect the vacuum hoses at the early fuel evaporator canister.
4. On the left side, remove the power steering pump and loosen the A/C bracket at the front of the head. Remove the rear A/C bracket and the A/C compressor. Remove the lower power steering adjusting bracket.
5. Remove the vacuum hose at the AIR valve.
6. On the right side, remove the alternator belt and lower alternator bracket, also remove the AIR valve. Disconnect the converter AIR pipe at the back of the manifold.
7. Remove the exhaust manifold bolts and on the left side, remove the wire loom holder at the valve cover. Remove the exhaust manifold.
8. Installation is the reverse order of the removal procedure. Torque the 4 outside bolts to 14–26 ft. lbs., inside bolts to 20–32 ft. lbs.

Valve System

Adjustment

Hydraulic valve lifters are used in all engines produced by Gen-

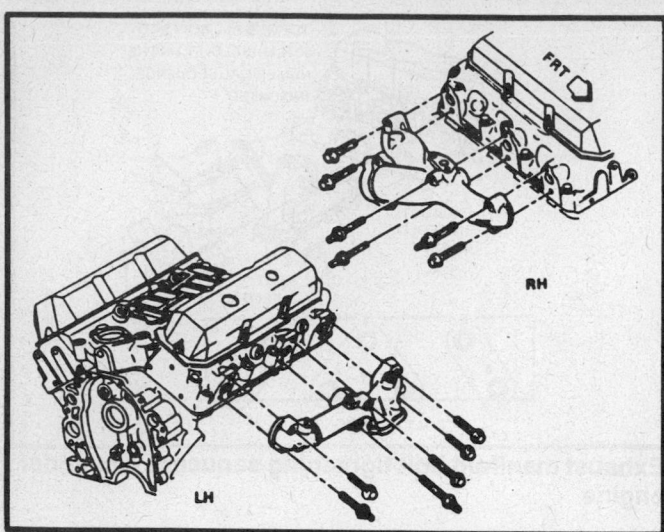

2.8L V6 exhaust manifold mounting

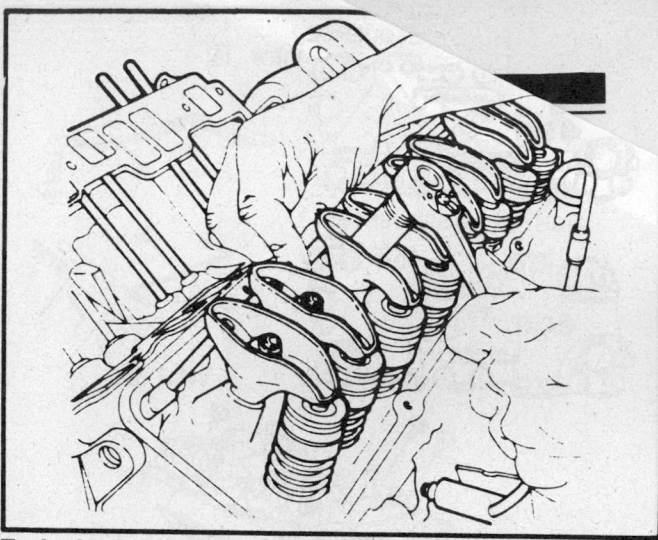

Typical valve adjustment on a V8 engine

eral Motors Corporation. Valve adjustments are not possible on the 2.5L engine.

2.8L, 5.0L AND 5.7L ENGINES

1. Disconnect the negative battey cable. Remove the valve covers.
2. Tighten the rocker arm nuts until all lash is eliminated if necessary.
3. Adjust the valves when the lifter is on the base circle of the camshaft lobe by cranking the engine until the mark on the vibration damper lines up with the center or **0** mark on the timing tab fastened to the crankcase front cover and the engine is in the No.1 firing position.

NOTE: **This may be determined by placing a finger on the No. 1 valve as the mark on the damper comes near the 0 mark on the crankcase front cover. If the valves move as the mark comes up to the timing tab, the engine is in the No. 6 (No. 4—V6) firing position and should be turned over one more time to reach to No. 1 firing position.**

4. With the engine in the No. 1 firing position, adjust the following valves. V6 engine: intake—1, 5, 6 exhaust—1, 2, 3. V8 engine: exhaust—1, 3, 4, 8 intake—1, 2, 5, 7.
5. Back out adjusting nut until lash is felt at the push rod, then turn in adjusting nut until all lash is removed. This can be determined by rotating push rod while turning adjusting nut. When play has been removed, turn adjusting nut in one full additional turn.
6. Crank the engine one revolution until the pointer, **0** mark and the vibration damper mark are again in alignment. This is the No. 6 (No. 4–V6) firing position.
7. With the engine in this position, adjust the following valves. V6 engine: intake—2, 3, 4 exhaust—4, 5, 6. V8 engine: exhaust—2, 5, 6, 7 intake—3, 4, 6, 8.
8. Install the rocker arm covers.
9. Start the engine and adjust the idle speed as required.

VALVE LIFTERS

Removal and Installation

1. Disconnect the negative battery cable.
2. Remove the intake manifold assembly. Remove the valve covers.
3. On 2.5L engine, loosen the rocker arms and move them

aside in order to clear the pushrod. On all other engines, remove the rocker arm assemblies.
4. Remove the pushrods. Remove valve lifter retainer assembly, if equipped. Using the proper valve lifter removal tool, remove the valve lifters.
5. Installation is the reverse of the removal procedure. Install the lifters in the same position they were before removal. Coat the lifters in clean engine oil before installing them.

VALVE ROCKER ASSEMBLY

Removal and Installation

1. Disconnect the negative battery cable. Remove all necessary components in order to gain access to the valve cover retaining bolts.
2. Tag and disconnect any electrical leads or hoses preventing access to the valve cover bolts.
3. Remove the valve cover bolts. Remove the valve covers.
4. Remove the rocker arm retaining bolts and remove the assembly from the engine.
5. Installation is the reverse of the removal procedure. Install the rocker arms in the same position they were in before removal. Adjust valve lash as necessary.

Cylinder Head

Removal and Installation

2.5L ENGINE

1. Disconnect the negative battery cable. Relieve fuel pressure as necessary.
2. Drain the coolant.
3. Raise and support the vehicle safely. Disconnect the exhaust pipe. Lower the vehicle.
4. Remove the air cleaner. Remove the oil dipstick tube.
5. Tag and disconnect all electrical connections and fuel lines. Remove any vacuum hoses and the throttle linkage.
6. Remove the EGR base plate and the heater hose from the intake manifold.
7. Remove the ignition coil and any other wiring connections from the intake manifold and cylinder head. Tag all wiring for identification.
8. Remove the A/C compressor, alternator brackets and position them in order to gain working clearance. Remove the alternator and bracket.
9. Remove the power steering upper bracket, if so equipped.

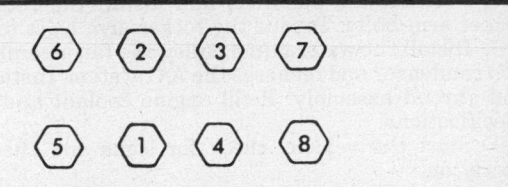

Cylinder head bolt tightening sequence—V6 engine

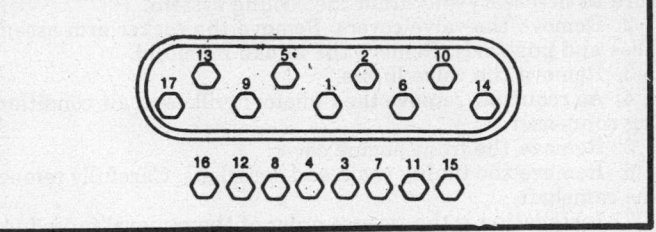

Cylinder head bolt tightening sequence—Chevrolet V8 engine

NOTE: Do not use any sealer on composite head gaskets.

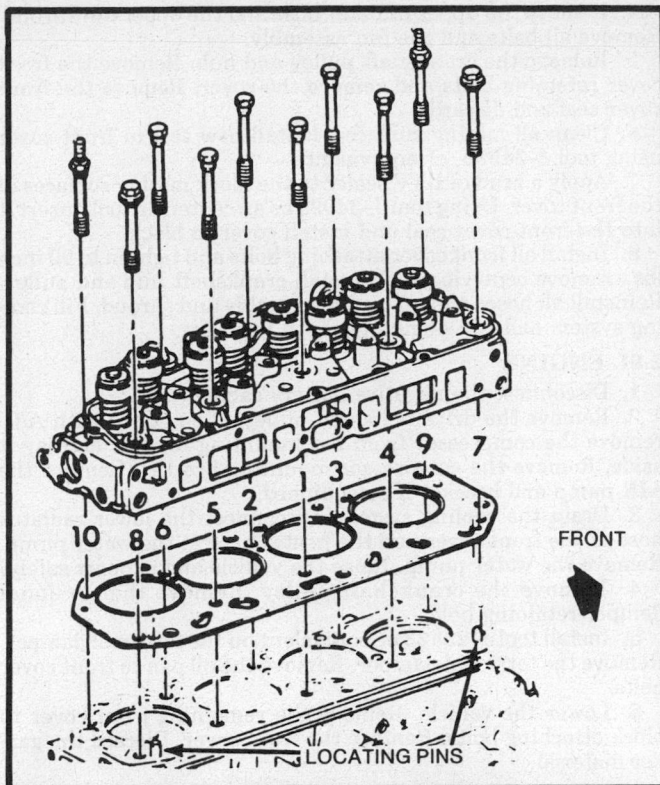

Cylinder head bolt tightening sequence — 4 cylinder

10. Remove the radiator hoses and valve cover.

11. Remove the rocker arms and pushrods (keep all parts in order). Remove the cylinder head bolts.

12. Remove the cylinder head and discard the gasket.

13. Installation is the reverse of the removal procedure. Use new gasket material prior to installing the cylinder head. Apply a suitable thread sealer to the stud bolts at both ends of the head. Torque the cylinder head bolts gradually and in sequence until a final torque of 92 ft. lbs. has been reached.

2.8L, 5.0L AND 5.7L ENGINES

1. Disconnect the negative battery cable. Relieve fuel pressure as necessary.

2. Drain the engine coolant from the radiator. Disconnect the radiator hoses from the intake manifold.

3. Remove the intake manifold. Remove the exhaust manifold.

4. Remove the alternator lower mounting bolt and lay aside to gain working clearance.

5. If the vehicle is equipped with power steering, remove the pump and bracket to gain access.

6. Remove the rocker arm covers and the rocker assemblies. Remove the pushrods (keep all parts in order).

7. Remove all vacuum hoses from the engine assembly. Tag and disconnect spark plug wires.

8. Remove the cylinder head bolts. Remove the cylinder head and discard the gasket.

9. Installation is the reverse of the removal procedure. Install the head gasket over the dowel pins, with the note **"This Side Up"** showing. On engines using a steel gasket, coat both sides with a suitable sealer. Spread the sealer evenly. Too much sealer may hold the gasket away from the head or block thus causing a bad seal. Carefully guide the cylinder head over the dowel pins and onto the cylinder block. Apply a suitable thread sealer to the head bolts and tighten the head bolts finger tight. Torque all cylinder retaining bolts gradually in proper order and to the correct specifications.

Camshaft

Removal and Installation

2.5L ENGINE

1. Disconnect the negative battery cable. Relieve fuel pressure as necessary.

2. Drain the engine oil and coolant from the engine. Remove the radiator. If equipped with A/C, discharge the system and remove the condenser.

3. Remove the water pump pulley and the fan assembly.

4. Remove the valve cover and discard the gasket. Loosen and remove the valve rocker bolts as required.

5. Remove the oil pump drive shaft and gear assembly. On some vehicles, it may be necessary to remove the spark plugs.

6. Mark the location of the distributor and remove it.

7. Remove the pushrod cover, pushrods, guides and valve lifters (keep in order).

8. Remove the crankshaft pulley and hub assembly. Remove the timing gear cover. Remove the timing gears.

9. Remove the 2 camshaft thrust plate screws, by working through the holes in the camshaft gear. Remove the camshaft assembly by pulling it out through the front of the engine block.

10. To install, coat the camshaft journals with a high quality engine oil supplement.

11. Install the camshaft assembly into the engine block, being careful not to damage the bearings or the cam.

12. Turn the crankshaft and camshaft so that the valve timing marks on the gear teeth will line up. The engine is now up on the No. 4 cylinder firing position.

13. Install the thrust plate the engine block retaining screws and torque the screws to 88 ft. lbs. Install the timing gear cover.

14. Line up and slide the crankshaft hub onto the shaft. Install the center bolt and torque it to 162 ft. lbs.

15. Install the valve lifters, pushrods, pushrod cover, oil pump shaft and gear assembly. Install the distributor.

16. Turn the crankshaft 360 degrees to the firing position of the No. 1 cylinder (No. 1 exhaust and intake valve lifters both are on the base circle of the camshaft and timing mark on the harmonic balancer indexed with the top dead center mark on the timing pad). Install the distributor in the original position and align the shaft with the rotor towards the No. 1 plug contact.

17. Position the pushrods and install the rocker arms and rocker arm bolts. Torque the rocker arm bolts to 20 ft. lbs.

18. Install the water pump pulley and fan assembly. Install the A/C condenser and recharge the A/C system. Install the radiator and shroud assembly. Refill engine coolant and engine oil to specifications.

19. Start the vehicle, check for leaks and check for proper operation.

2.8L ENGINE

1. Disconnect the negative battery cable. Relieve fuel pressure as necessary and drain the cooling system.

2. Remove the valve covers. Remove the rocker arm assemblies and pushrods. Remove the intake manifold.

3. Remove the valve lifters.

4. As required, remove the radiator, grille and air conditioning condenser.

5. Remove the front engine cover.

6. Remove the timing chain and sprockets. Carefully remove the camshaft.

7. Installation is the reverse order of the removal procedure. Be sure to coat the lifters and the camshaft with clean engine oil before installation.

5.0L AND 5.7L ENGINES

1. Disconnect the negative battery cable. Relieve fuel pressure as necessary and drain the cooling system.

2. Remove the intake manifold. Remove the rocker covers, rocker arm assemblies, pushrods and lifters (keep all parts in order).

3. Remove all necessary wires and hoses. Disconnect the upper and lower transmission cooler lines.

4. Remove the radiator shroud assembly and radiator. Remove the front grille, if necessary. Remove the cooling fan.

5. Remove the power steering pump, if so equipped. Remove the drive belts, crankshaft pulley and torsional damper.

6. Remove the A/C compressor mount bolts, brackets, accumulator and compressor and position it out of the way. Remove the air injection pump with brackets and set it aside.

7. Remove the water pump assembly, remove the front engine cover. Remove the fuel pump pushrod if equipped with mechanical pump. Rotate the crankshaft and align the timing marks.

8. Remove the camshaft bolts, gear and chain. Install 2 ⁵⁄₁₆ in. × 4 in. bolts or equivalent in the camshaft bolt holes and carefully remove the camshaft.

NOTE: The camshaft sprocket is a tight fit. If the sprocket does not come off easily, a light blow on the lower edge of the sprocket with a soft face mallet should dislodge the sprocket.

9. Installation is the reverse order of the removal procedure. Lubricate the camshaft journals with a suitable engine oil supplement, before installing the camshaft. Once the camshaft has been installed, install the chain on the camshaft sprocket. Hold the sprocket vertically with the chain hanging down and align the marks on the camshaft and crankshaft sprockets.

10. Align the dowel in the camshaft sprocket with the dowel hole in the camshaft sprocket, then install the sprocket on the camshaft. Draw the camshaft sprocket onto the camshaft, using the mounting bolts.

Timing Case Cover/Oil Seal

Removal and Installation
2.5L ENGINE

1. Disconnect the negative battery terminal.

2. Raise and safely support vehicle. Drain the cooling system.

3. Remove the lower radiator hose and lower fan shroud. Lower vehicle.

4. Remove the upper radiator hose and the upper fan shroud. Remove all belts and the fan assembly.

5. Remove the crankshaft pulley and hub. Remove the front cover retaining bolts and remove the cover. Remove the front cover seal and discard.

6. Clean all mating surfaces. Install new seal to front cover using tool J–34995, or equivalent.

7. Apply a bead of RTV sealer to the block mating surfaces of the front cover. Using tool J–34995 as an centering tool, insert it into the front cover seal and install cover to block.

8. Install all front cover attaching bolts and tighten to 90 inch lbs., remove centering tool. Install crankshaft hub and pulley. Reinstall all hoses and belts, fan assembly and shroud. Fill cooling system and run engine to check for leaks.

2.8L ENGINE

1. Disconnect the negative battery cable.

2. Remove the drive belts and pulley. If equipped with A/C, remove the compressor from the mounting bracket and lay it aside. Remove the compressor mounting bracket. Remove the AIR pump and bracket if so equipped.

3. Drain the cooling system. Disconnect the lower radiator hose at the front cover and the heater hose at the water pump. Remove the water pump. Raise the vehicle and support safely.

4. Remove the crankshaft pulley. Remove the torsional damper retaining bolt.

5. Install tool J–23523 or equivalent on the torsional damper. Remove the torsional damper. Remove the oil pan to front cover bolts.

6. Lower the vehicle. Remove the remaining front cover to block attaching bolts. Remove the front cover. Discard the gasket material.

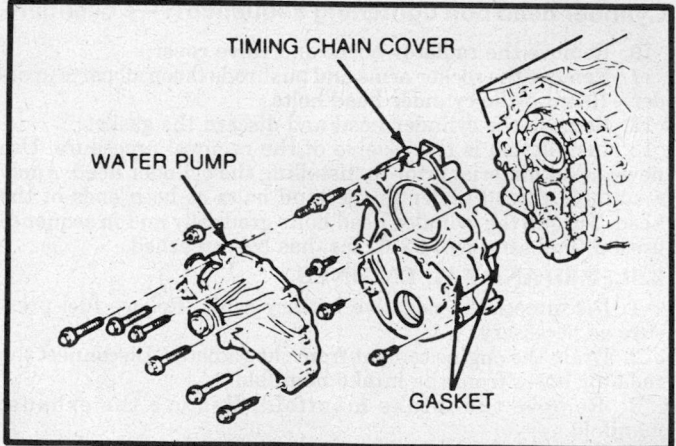

Front cover assembly V6 engine

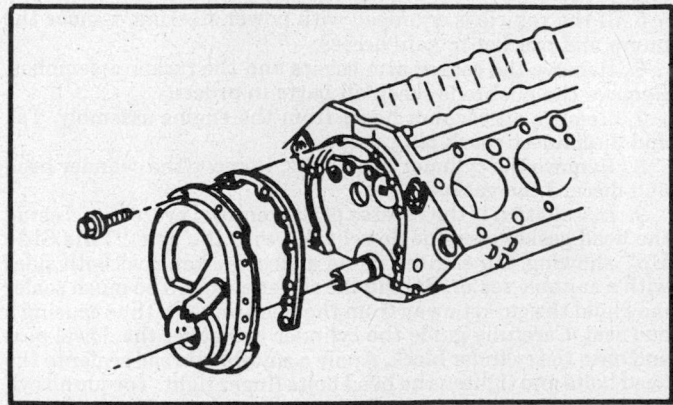

Front cover assembly V8 engine

7. Remove the front oil seal from the front cover using a suitable tool.

8. Installation is the reverse of the removal procedure. Be sure to apply a continuous bead of a suitable sealant to the front cover sealing surface. Apply a continuous bead of a suitable sealer to the oil pan surface of the front cover. Install the new oil seal so that the open end of the seal is facing the inside of the cover. Torque the front cover retaining bolts to 6–8 ft. lbs.

5.0L AND 5.7L ENGINES

1. Disconnect the negative battery cable. Drain the cooling the system.

2. Remove the drive belts and accessory belts. Remove the fan assembly and fan pulley. Using torsional damper puller J–23523 or equivalent, remove the torsional damper.

3. On engines equipped with TBI, remove the air injection pump pulley and air management valve adapter. Remove the air injection pump. Relieve fuel pressure as necessary. Disconnect the fuel inlet and outlet lines at the TBI unit.

4. On vehicles equipped with A/C, remove the rear A/C compressor braces and lower the A/C mount bolts. Remove the compressor bracket and nuts at the water pump. Slide the mounting bracket forward and remove the compressor mount bolt. Disconnect the wires at the compressor and lay the unit aside. Disconnect the air injection hose at the right exhaust manifold.

5. Remove the compressor mount bracket. Remove the upper air injection pump bracket with the power steering reservoir. Remove the lower air injection pump bracket.

6. Disconnect the heater and radiator hoses to the water pump. Remove the water pump. Remove the front cover retaining bolts, cover and old gasket.

7. To install clean the gasket surfaces. Apply a suitable sealer to the new gasket. Apply a suitable RTV sealant to the joint formed where the oil pan meets the cylinder block, be sure to trim the excess material the sticks out from the junction. Place the gasket on the cover and install the cover to oil pan seal. The rest of the installation procedure is the reverse order of the removal procedure. Torque the front cover retaining bolts to 6–8 ft. lbs.

Timing Gears

Removal and Installation

2.5L ENGINE

1. Disconnect the negative battery cable.

2. Remove the camshaft.

3. With the camshaft removed, use a press plate and Adapter J–971 or equivalent on the press to remove the timing gear from the camshaft. Be sure to place the camshaft through the opening in the tools on the table of the press and press the camshaft out of the timing gear. Position the thrust plate so that the Woodruff key in the camshaft does no damage during removal.

4. If the crankshaft gear needs to be replaced, use a suitable gear puller to remove it from the crankshaft.

5. To install, support the camshaft at the back of the front journal in a arbor press using the press plate adaptors. Install the spacer ring and thrust plate over the end of the camshaft.

6. Install the Woodruff key in the shaft keyway. Install the timing gear on the camshaft until it bottoms against the gear ring spacer ring. Measure the end clearance of the thrust plate. The clearance should be 0.0015–0.0050 in.

7. If the clearance is less than specified, replace the spacer ring. If the clearance is more than specified, replace the thrust plate.

8. Coat the camshaft journals with a high quality engine oil supplement.

9. Install the camshaft assembly into the engine block, being careful not to damage the bearings or the cam.

10. Turn the crankshaft and camshaft so that the valve timing

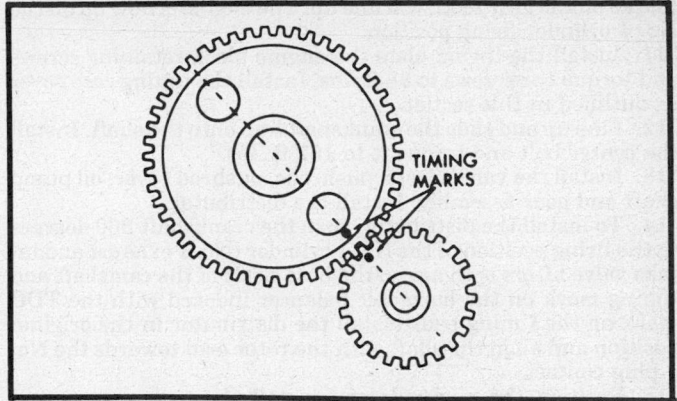

Timing mark location- 4 cylinder engine

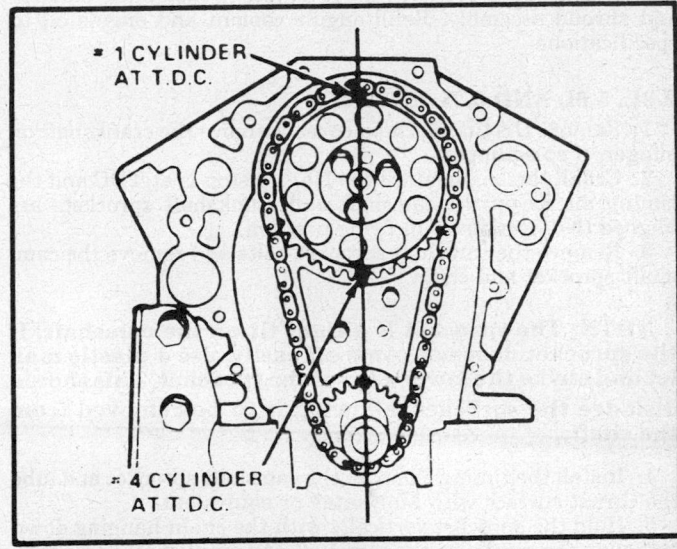

Aligning the timing gears on the V6 engine

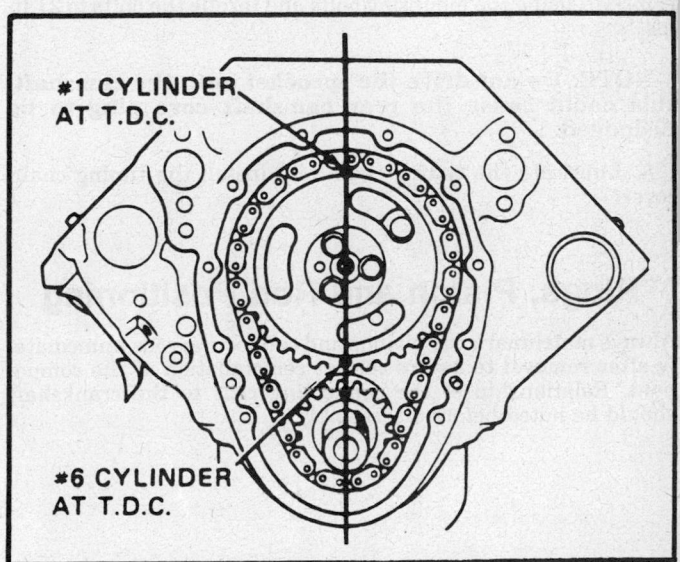

Aligning the timing gears on the V8 engine

marks on the gear teeth will line up. The engine is now up on the No. 4 cylinder firing position.

11. Install the thrust plate the engine block retaining screws and torque the screws to 88 ft. lbs. Install the timing case cover as outlined in this section.

12. Line up and slide the crankshaft hub onto the shaft. Install the center bolt and torque it to 162 ft. lbs.

13. Install the valve lifters, pushrods, pushrod cover, oil pump shaft and gear assembly. Install the distributor.

14. To install the distributor, turn the crankshaft 360 degrees to the firing position of the No. 1 cylinder (No. 1 exhaust and intake valve lifters both are on the base circle of the camshaft and timing mark on the harmonic balancer indexed with the TDC mark on the timing pad) Install the distributor in the original position and align the shaft with the rotor arm towards the No. 1 plug contact.

15. Position the pushrods and install the rocker arms and rocker arm bolts. Torque the rocker arm bolts to 20 ft. lbs.

16. Install the water pump pulley and fan assembly. Install the A/C condenser and recharge the A/C system. Install the radiator and shroud assembly. Refill engine coolant and engine oil to specifications.

2.8L, 5.0L AND 5.7L ENGINES

1. Remove the timing chain cover. Remove the crankshaft oil slinger, if so equipped.

2. Crank the engine until the No. 1 piston is at TDC and the timing marks on the camshaft and crankshaft sprockets are aligned (No. 4 cylinder in firing position).

3. Remove the camshaft sprocket bolts and remove the camshaft sprocket and chain.

NOTE: The sprocket is a tight fit on the camshaft. If the sprocket does not come off easily, use a plastic mallet and strike the lower edge of the sprocket. This should dislodge the sprocket, allowing it to be removed from the shaft.

4. Install the timing chain on the camshaft sprocket and lube the thrust surface with Molykote® or equivalent.

5. Hold the sprocket vertically with the chain hanging down and align the marks on the camshaft and crankshaft sprockets.

6. Align the dowel in the camshaft with the dowel hole in the camshaft sprocket and install the sprocket on the camshaft.

7. Slowly and evenly draw the camshaft sprocket onto the camshaft using the mounting bolts and torque the bolts to 21 ft. lbs.

NOTE: Do not drive the sprocket onto the camshaft, this could cause the rear camshaft core plug to be dislodged.

8. Lubricate the timing chain and install the timing chain cover.

Rings, Piston and Rod Positioning

Always matchmark the pistons and connecting rods immediately after removal to assure correct reinstallation of the component. Relationship of the connecting rods to the crankshaft should be noted before disassembly.

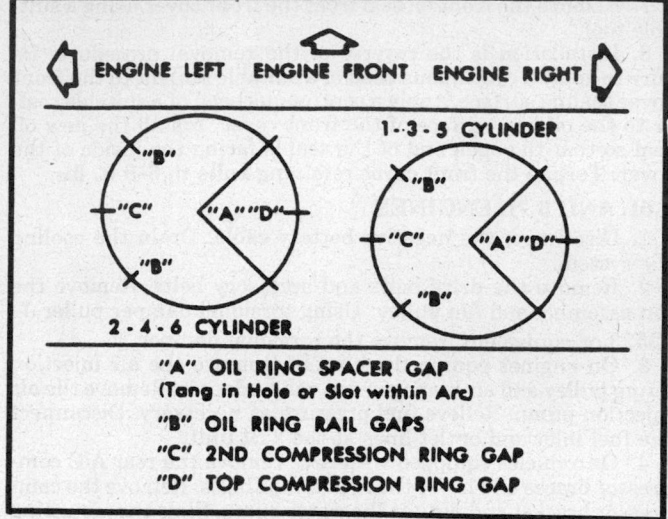

V6 engine ring gap locations

Piston and rod positioning for the V8 engine notches facing forward

Piston and rod positioning for the V6 engine

ENGINE LUBRICATION SYSTEM

Oil Pan

Removal and Installation

2.5L ENGINE

1. Disconnect the negative battery cable.
2. Raise the vehicle and support it safely.
3. Drain the engine oil.
4. Disconnect the exhaust pipe at the manifold.
5. Loosen the exhaust pipe at the manifold.
6. Remove the starter assembly, if necessary.
7. Remove the flywheel dust cover, if necessary.
8. Remove the front engine mount through bolts.
9. Carefully raise the engine enough to provide sufficient clearance to lower the oil pan.
10. Remove the oil pan retaining bolts and remove the oil pan.
11. Clean all old RTV from the mating surfaces.
12. Install the rear gasket into the rear main bearing cap and apply a small amount of RTV where the gasket engages into the engine block.
13. Install the front gasket.
14. Install the side gaskets, using grease as retainer. Apply a small amount of RTV where the side gaskets meet the front gasket.
15. Install the oil pan. Torque oil pan retaining bolts to about 6–8 ft. lbs.

NOTE: Install the oil pan to timing cover bolts last, as these holes will not align until the other pan bolts are snug.

16. The remainder of the installation procedure is performed in the reverse of removal.

2.8L, 5.0L AND 5.7L ENGINES

1. Disconnect the negative battery cable. Remove the air cleaner assembly. Remove the distributor cap and lay it aside.
2. Remove the upper half of the fan shroud assembly.
3. Raise the vehicle and support it safely. Drain the engine oil.
4. Remove the air injection pipe at the catalytic convertor. Remove the catalytic converter hanger bolts.
5. Remove the torque converter dust shield. On some vehicles equipped with manual transmissions, it may be necesary to remove the oil filter in order to remove the dust shield.
6. Remove the exhaust pipe at the manifolds.
7. Remove the starter bolts, loosen the starter brace, then lay the starter aside. On V8 engines, remove the front starter brace.
8. Remove the front engine mount through bolts.
9. Raise the engine enough to provide sufficient clearance for oil pan removal.
10. Remove the oil pan bolts. If the front of the crankshaft prohibits removal of the pan, turn the crankshaft to position it horizontally.
11. Remove the oil pan from the vehicle.
12. Remove all old RTV from the oil pan and engine block.
13. Run a ⅛ in. bead of RTV around the oil pan sealing surface. Remember to keep the RTV on the inside of the bolt holes.
14. Installation is the reverse of the removal procedure. Torque all retaining bolts to the correct specifications.

Oil Pump

Removal and Installation

1. Raise the vehicle and support safely.
2. Drain the oil.

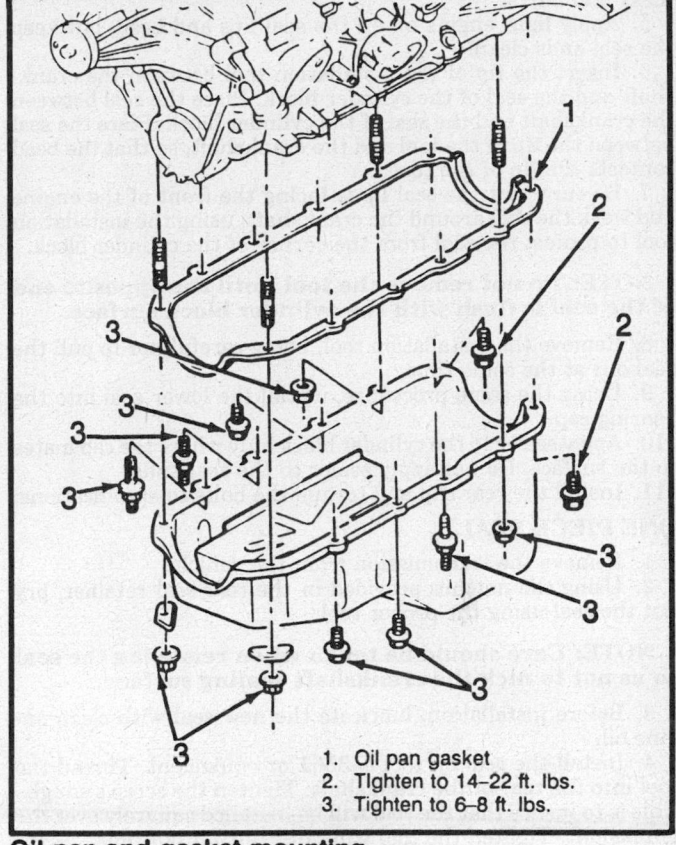

1. Oil pan gasket
2. Tighten to 14–22 ft. lbs.
3. Tighten to 6–8 ft. lbs.

Oil pan and gasket mounting

3. Remove the oil pan. Discard the old gasket material.
4. Remove the oil pump bolts and the bolt or nuts from the main bearing cap. Remove the oil pump. On 2.8L, 5.0L and 5.7L engines, remove the pump with the extension shaft.
5. Installation is the reverse of the removal procedure. Use a new gasket or equivalent prior to installing. All parts should be coated with clean engine oil before installation.

Inspection

1. Inspect pump body and cover for cracks, scoring, casting imperfectons and damaged threads.
2. Check idler gear shaft for play in pump body. If loose replace the oil pump.
3. Check pressure regulator valve for sticking and pressure regulator spring for loss of tension.
4. Inspect pick-up screen and pipe assembly for broken wire mesh or looseness. The pick-up screen and pipe are serviced as an assembly.

Rear Main Oil Seal

Removal and Installation

EXCEPT ONE PIECE SEAL

1. Remove the oil pan. Remove the oil pump where required. Remove the rear main bearing cap.
2. Pry the lower seal out of the bearing cap with a suitable tool, being careful not to gouge the cap surface.
3. Remove the upper seal by lightly tapping on one end with a

brass pin punch until the other end can be grasped and pulled out with pliers.

4. Clean the bearing cap, cylinder block and crankshaft mating surfaces with solvent. Inspect all these surfaces for gouges, nicks and burrs.

5. Apply light engine oil on the seal lips and bead, but keep the seal ends clean.

6. Insert the tip of the installation tool between the crankshaft and the seal of the cylinder block. Place the seal between the crankshaft and the seal of the cylinder block. Place the seal between the tip of the tool and the crankshaft, so that the bead contacts the tip of the tool.

7. Be sure that the seal lip is facing the front of the engine and work the seal around the crankshaft, using the installation tool to protect the seal from the corner of the cylinder block.

NOTE: Do not remove the tool until the opposite end of the seal is flush with the cylinder block surface.

8. Remove the installation tool, being careful not to pull the seal out at the same time.

9. Using the same procedure, install the lower seal into the bearing cap.

10. Apply sealer to the cylinder block only where the cap mates to the surface. Do not apply sealer to the seal ends.

11. Install the rear cap and torque the bolts to specifications.

ONE PIECE SEAL

1. Remove the transmission from the vehicle.

2. Using the notches provided in the rear seal retainer, pry out the seal using the proper tool.

NOTE: Care should be taken when removing the seal so as not to nick the crankshaft sealing surface.

3. Before installation, lubricate the new seal with clean engine oil.

4. Install the seal on tool J–3561 or equivalent. Thread the tool into the rear of the crankshaft. Tighten the screws snugly. This is to insure that the seal will be installed squarely over the crankshaft. Tighten the tool wing nut until it bottoms.

5. Remove the tool from the crankshaft.

6. Install the transmission.

ONE PIECE SEAL RETAINER AND GASKET

Removal and Installation

1. Remove the transmission from the vehicle. Drain the engine oil.

2. Remove the oil pan bolts. Lower the oil pan.

3. Remove the retainer and seal assembly.

4. Remove the gasket.

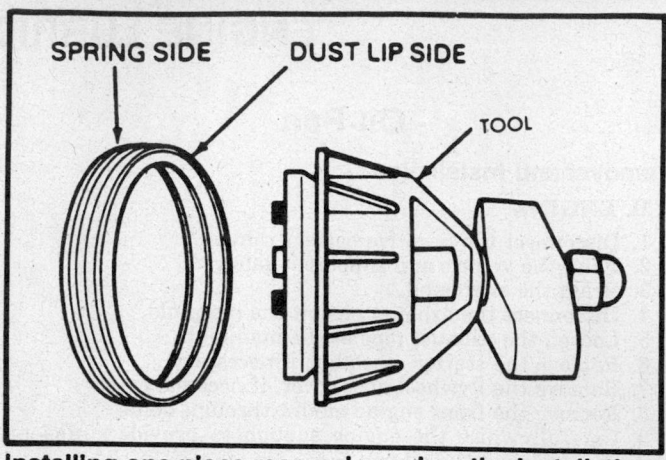

Installing one piece rear main seal on the installation tool

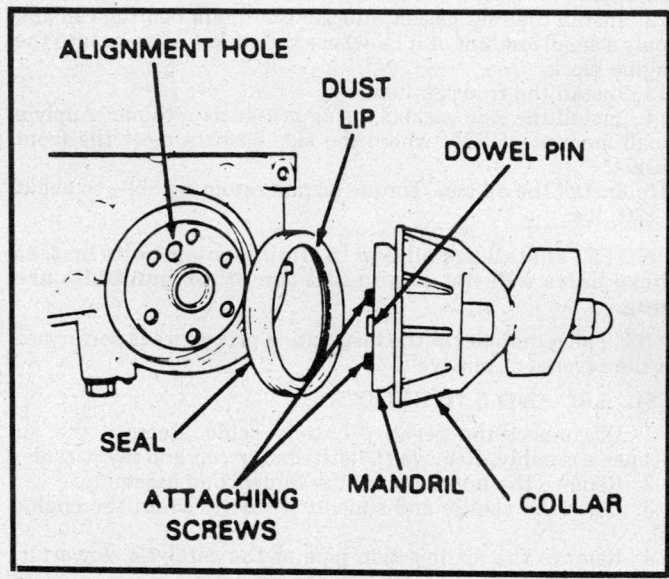

Installing one piece rear main seal

NOTE: Whenever the retainer is removed, a new retainer gasket and rear main seal must be installed.

5. Installation is the reverse of the removal procedure. After the oil pan has been installed, the new rear main oil seal can be installed.

FRONT SUSPENSION AND STEERING

For front suspension component removal and installation procedures, refer to unit repair section.

For steering wheel removal and installation, refer to electrical control section.

Steering Gear

Removal and Installation

1. Disconnect the negative battery cable. Remove coupling shield, if equipped.

2. Remove the retaining nuts, lock washers and bolts at the steering coupling to steering shaft flange.

3. Disconnect and plug the pressure and return lines from the steering gear box. Plug the hoses and gearbox openings. Raise and safely support the vehicle.

4. Remove the pitman arm nut and washer. Matchmark the arm to the shaft.

5. With a puller, remove the pitman arm from the shaft.

6. Remove the bolts retaining the steering gear box to the side frame rail and remove the gear box from the vehicle.

7. Installation is the reverse of the removal procedure.

8. Fill and bleed the hydraulic system. Note the coupling shield must be installed to prevent foreign material from jamming in the steering coupler.

Power Steering Pump

Removal and Installation

1. Disconnect the negative battery cable. Remove the hoses at the pump and tape the openings shut to prevent contamination. Position the disconnected lines in a raised position to prevent leakage.
2. Remove any components in order to gain access to the power steering pump retaining bolts. Remove the pump belt.
3. Loosen the retaining bolts and any braces. Remove the pump.
4. Installation is the reverse of removal.

System Bleeding

1. With the wheels turned all the way to the left, add power steering fluid to the **COLD** mark on the fluid level indicator.
2. Start the engine and run at fast idle momentarily, shut engine off and recheck fluid level. If necessary, add fluid to to bring level to the **COLD** mark.
3. Start the engine and bleed the system by turning the wheels from side to side without hitting the stops.

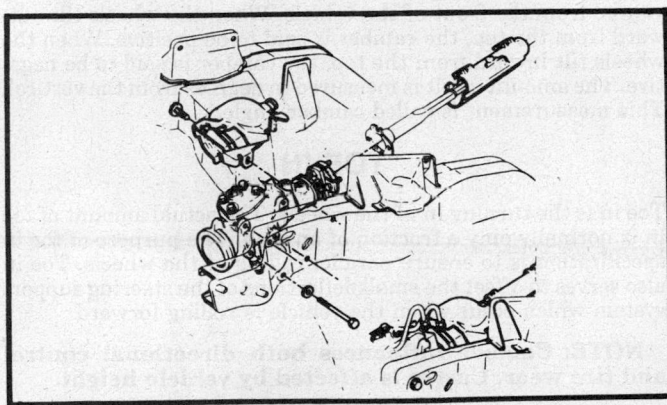

Typical steering gear mounting

4. Return the wheels to the center position and keep the engine running for a few minutes.
5. Road test the vehicle and recheck the fluid level making sure it is at the **HOT** mark.

Steering Column

Removal and Installation

NOTE: Handle the steering column very carefully. Rapping on the end of it or leaning on it could shear off the inserts which allow the column to collapse in a collision. If equipped with an air bag restraint system care should be exercise when removing the steering column.

1. Disconnect the negative battery cable. Remove the nut and bolt from the upper intermediate shaft coupling. Separate the coupling from the lower end of steering column.
2. Disconnect the shift linkage from the lower shift lever, as required.
3. Disconnect all electrical connectors from the column assembly.
4. Remove the screws securing the toe pan cover to the floor.

NOTE: Some vehicles equipped with tilt steering column may experience a squeaking noise when turning the steering wheel in a tilted position. This can be cause by insufficient grease in the tilting mechanism.

5. Remove the nuts securing the bracket to the instrument panel. Disconnect the shift position indicator pointer (where applicable), then withdraw column.
6. Installation is the reverse of the removal procedure. Use only the specified hardware. Overlength bolts could prevent the column from properly collapsing in a collision.

Front Wheel Bearings

Removal and Installation

1. Raise the vehicle and support safely.
2. Remove the dust cap from the hub. Remove the cotter pin and discard it. Remove the locknut.
3. Remove the outer wheel bearing from its mounting.
4. Remove the rotor. Remove the inner wheel bearing from its mounting.

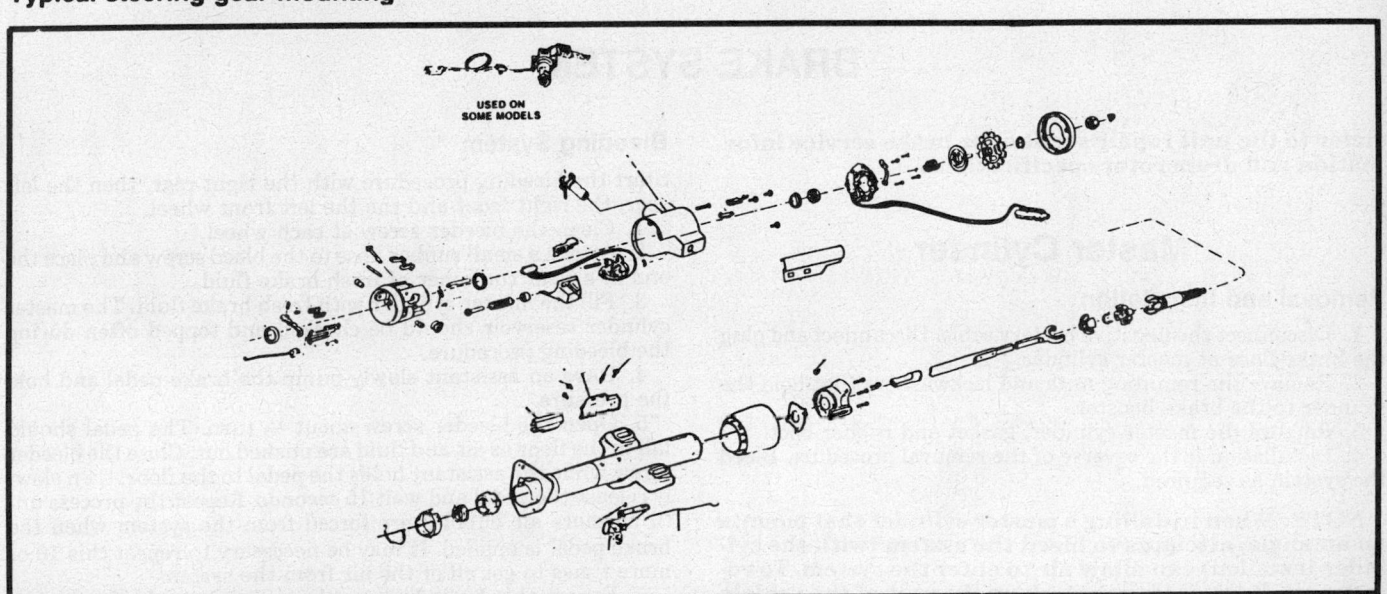

USED ON SOME MODELS

Exploded view of typical tilt steering column

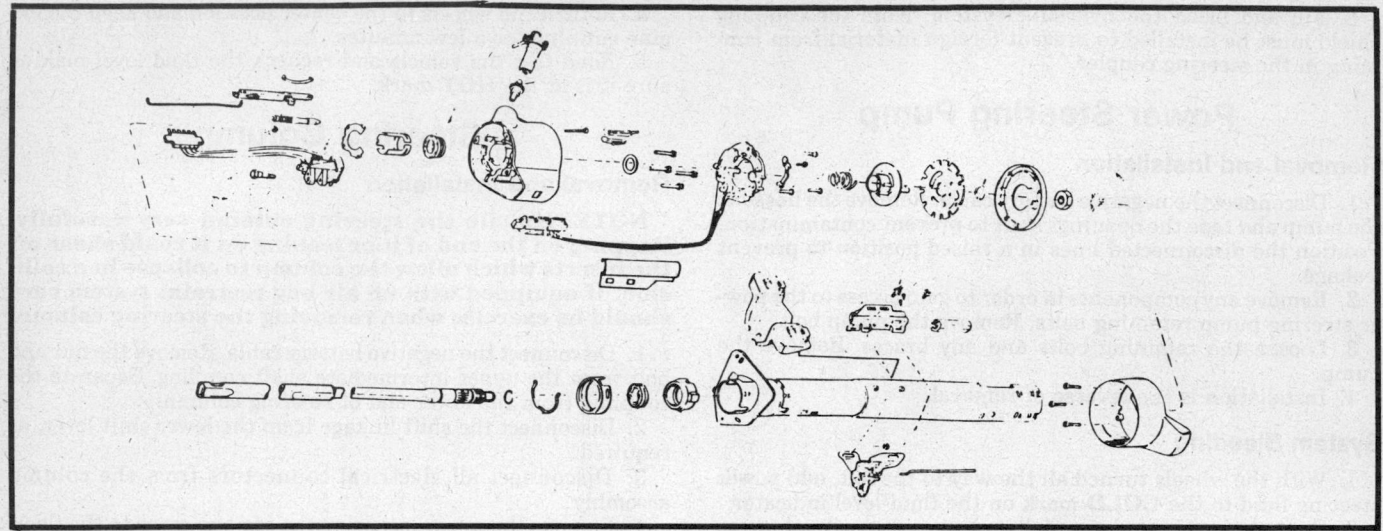

Exploded view of standard steering column

5. Installation is the reverse of the removal procedure. To adjust, tighten the spindle nut to 12 ft. lbs. while turning the wheel. Back off the nut ¼–½ turn.

6. Retighten the nut by hand until it is finger tight.

7. Loosen the nut no more than ⅙ of a turn until the nearest hole in the spindle lines up with the slot in the spindle nut and insert a new cotter pin.

8. Feel the looseness in the hub assembly. There should be 0.001–0.005 in. endplay.

Front Wheel Alignment

CASTER

Caster is the tilting of the steering axis either forward or backward from the vertical, when viewed from the side of the vehicle. A backward tilt is said to be positive and a forward tilt is said to be negative.

CAMBER

Camber is the tilting of the wheels from the vertical when viewed from the front of the vehicle. When the wheels tilt outward from the top, the camber is said to be positive. When the wheels tilt inward from the top, the camber is said to be negative. The amount of tilt is measured in degrees from the vertical. This measurement is called camber angle.

TOE IN

Toe in is the turning in of the wheels. The actual amount of toe in is normally only a fraction of an inch. The purpose of toe in specification is to ensure parallel rolling of the wheels. Toe in also serves to offset the small deflections of the steering support system which occur when the vehicle is rolling forward.

NOTE: Camber influences both directional control and tire wear. Caster is affected by vehicle height.

BRAKE SYSTEM

Refer to the unit repair section for brake service information and drum/rotor specifications.

Master Cylinder

Removal and Installation

1. Disconnect the negative battery cable. Disconnect and plug the brake lines at master cylinder.

2. Remove the retaining nuts and lockwashers that hold the cylinder to the brake booster.

3. Remove the master cylinder, gasket and rubber boot.

4. Installation is the reverse of the removal procedure. Bleed the system as required.

NOTE: When installing a master cylinder that mounts on an angle, attempts to bleed the system (with the cylinder installed) can allow air to enter the system. To remove air, it is necesary to jack up the rear of the vehicle until the master cylinder bore is level.

Bleeding System

Start the bleeding procedure with the right rear, then the left rear, the right front and the the left front wheel.

1. Clean the bleeder screw at each wheel.

2. Attach a small rubber hose to the bleed screw and place the end in a clear container of fresh brake fluid.

3. Fill the master cylinder with fresh brake fluid. The master cylinder reservoir should be checked and topped often during the bleeding procedure.

4. Have an assistant slowly pump the brake pedal and hold the pressure.

5. Open the bleeder screw about ¼ turn. The pedal should fall to the floor as air and fluid are pushed out. Close the bleeder screw while the assistant holds the pedal to the floor, then slowly release the pedal and wait 15 seconds. Repeat the process until no more air bubbles are forced from the system when the brake pedal is applied. It may be necessary to repeat this 10 or more times to get all of the air from the system.

6. Repeat this procedure on the remaining wheel cylinders and calipers.

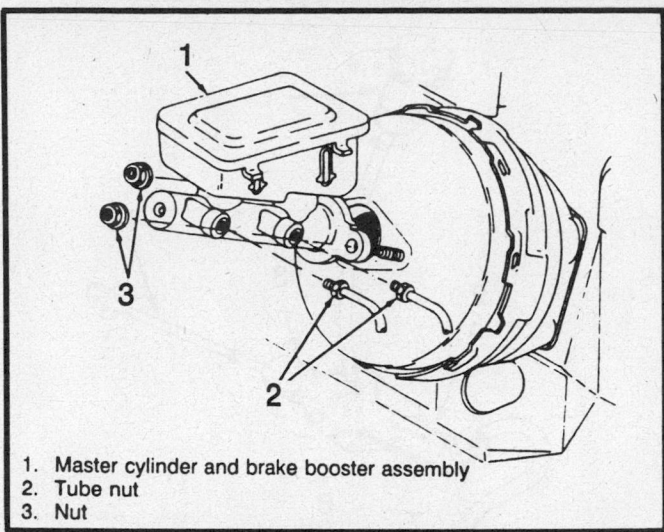

1. Master cylinder and brake booster assembly
2. Tube nut
3. Nut

Master cylinder and booster mounting

NOTE: Remember to wait 15 seconds between each bleeding and do not pump the pedal rapidly. Rapid pumping of the brake pedal pushes the master cylinder secondary piston down the bore in a manner that makes it difficult to bleed the system.

Power Brake Vacuum Booster

Removal and Installation

1. Disconnect the negative battery cable. Remove the master cylinder retaining nuts and position the assembly out of the way.
2. Disconnect vacuum line from vacuum check valve on unit.
3. Remove steering column lower cover, as required.
4. Remove cotter pin, washer and spring spacer that secures power unit pushrod to brake pedal arm.

5. Remove the nuts that secure the power unit to the firewall. Remove the power brake unit.
6. Installation is the reverse of the removal procedure.

Parking Brake

Adjustment
EXCEPT REAR DISC BRAKES

1. Depress the parking brake pedal exactly 2 ratchet clicks.
2. Raise the rear of the vehicle and support it safely.
3. Tighten the brake cable adjusting nut until the left rear wheel can be turned rearward with both hands, but locks when forward rotation is attempted.
4. Release the parking brake pedal; both rear wheels must turn freely in either direction without brake drag. Be sure that the parking brake cables are not adjusted too tightly causing the brakes to drag.
5. Lower the vehicle.

REAR DISC BRAKES

1. Check for free movement of the parking brake cables and lubricate the underbody rub points of the cables. Also lubricate the equalizer hooks.
2. Release the parking brake pedal completely.
3. Raise the rear of the vehicle and support it safely.
4. Hold the brake cable stud from turning, then tighten the adjusting nut until all cable slack is taken up.

NOTE: Check that the parking brake levers on the rear calipers are against the stops on the caliper housing. If the levers are not contacting the stops, loosen the cable adjusting nut until the levers just contact the stops.

5. Operate the parking brake cable several times. Parking brake pedal travel should be 14 clicks with approximately 150 ± 20 lbs. of forced applied to the pedal.
6. Readjust if necessary.
7. Make sure that the levers contact the caliper stops after adjustment.
8. Lower the vehicle.

CLUTCH AND TRANSMISSION

Refer to "Chilton's Transmission Service Manual" for additional coverage.

Clutch

Removal and Installation

1. Raise and safely support the vehicle. Support engine and remove the transmission.
2. Disconnect the clutch fork push rod and spring.
3. Remove the flywheel housing.
4. Slide the clutch fork from the ball stud and remove the fork from the dust boot. The ball stud is threaded into the clutch housing and may be replaced, if necessary. As required, remove the clutch fork from the slave cylinder.
5. Install an alignment tool to support the clutch assembly during removal. Mark the flywheel and clutch cover for reinstallation.
6. Loosen the clutch to flywheel attaching bolts evenly, one turn at a time, until spring pressure is released. Remove the bolts and clutch assembly.

7. Installation is the reverse of removal. Be sure to install the driven disc with the damper springs facing the transmission. Torque the pressure plate to flywheel bolts 30 ft. lbs. on V8 engines and 15 ft. lbs. on V6 engine.

Clutch Master Cylinder

Removal and Installation

1. Disconnect the negative battery cable. Remove the steering column trim cover and hush panel.
2. Remove the master cylinder pushrod from the clutch pedal.
3. Remove the clutch master cylinder to cowl nuts.
4. Remove the brake booster to cowl nuts. Remove the clutch fluid reservoir from the bracket.
5. Pull the brake master cylinder forward for access to the clutch master cylinder. Disconnect the hydraulic line. Remove the clutch master cylinder from the cowl.
6. Installation is the reverse of removal. Bleed the system.

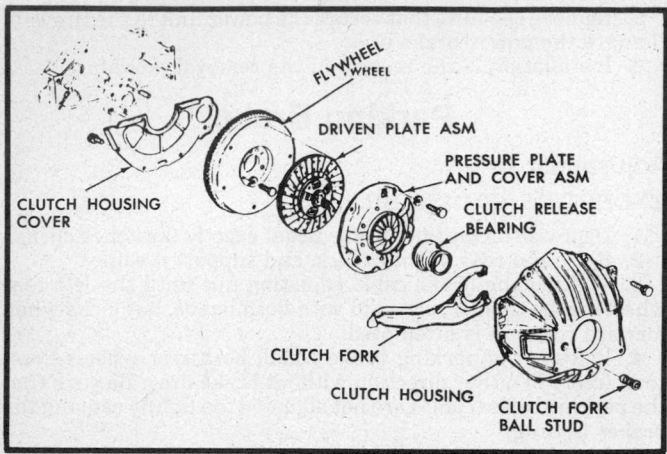

Exploded view of clutch assembly

Clutch Slave Cylinder

Removal and Installation

NOTE: **Do not depress the clutch pedal when slave cylinder is disconnected.**

1. Raise and support the vehicle safely. Remove the slave cylinder heat shield.
2. Disconnect the pressure line.
3. Disconnect the slave cylinder from the clutch fork. Remove the slave cylinder retaining bolts and remove the slave cylinder from the bell housing.
4. Installation is the reverse order of the removal procedure. Bleed the system.

System Bleeding

1. Clean all dirt and grease from the cap to make sure that no foreign subtances enter the system.
2. Remove the cap and diaphragm and fill the reservoir to the top with the approved DOT 3 brake fluid. Fully loosen the bleed screw which is in the slave cylinder body next to the inlet connection.
3. At this point, bubbles of air will appear at the bleed screw outlet. When the slave cylinder is full and a steady stream of fluid comes out of the slave cylinder bleeder, tighten the bleed screw.
4. Assemble the diaphragm and cap to the reservoir, fluid in the reservoir should be level with the step. Exert a light load of about 20 lbs. to the slave cylinder piston by pushing the release lever towards the cylinder and loosen the bleed screw. Maintain a constant light load, fluid and any air that is left will be expelled through the bleed port. Tighten the bleed screw when a steady flow of fluid and no air is being expelled.
5. Fill the reservoir fluid level back to normal capacity.
6. Exert a light load to the release lever, but do not open the bleeder screw as the piston in the slave cylinder will move slowly down the bore. Repeat this operation 2–3 times. The fluid movement will force any air left in the system into the reservoir. The hydraulic system should now be fully bled.
7. Check the the operation of the clutch hydraulic system and repeat this procedure if necesary. Check the push rod travel at the slave cylinder to insure the minimum travel is 0.57 in. for V8 engines and 0.43 for V6 engine.

Manual Transmission

Removal and Installation

1. Disconnect the negative battery cable at the battery.

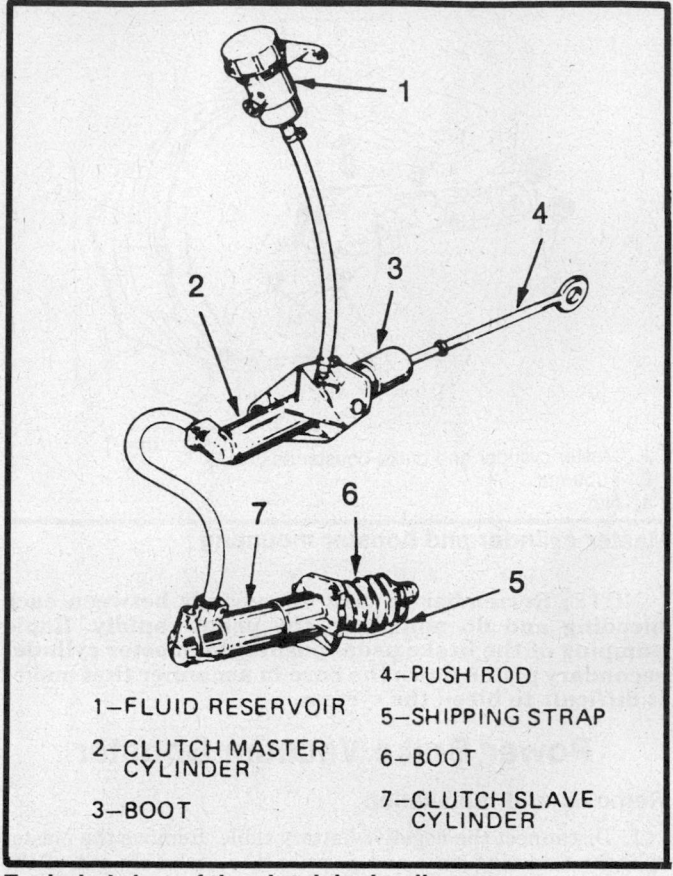

1—FLUID RESERVOIR	4—PUSH ROD
2—CLUTCH MASTER CYLINDER	5—SHIPPING STRAP
3—BOOT	6—BOOT
	7—CLUTCH SLAVE CYLINDER

Exploded view of the clutch hydraulic system

2. Remove the shift lever boot attaching screws and slide the boot up the shift lever.
3. Remove the shift lever from the transmission.
4. Raise the vehicle and support it safely.
5. Drain the lubricant from the transmission.
6. Remove the torque arm from the vehicle.
7. Mark the driveshaft and the rear axle pinion flange to indicate their relationship. Remove the driveshaft from the vehicle.
8. Disconnect the speedometer cable and the electrical connectors from the transmission.
9. Remove the catalytic converter hanger.
10. Remove the exhaust pipe brace.
11. Remove the transmission shifter support attaching bolts from the transmission.
12. Disconnect the shift linkage at the shifter.
13. Raise the transmission slightly with a jack, then remove the crossmember attaching bolts.
14. Remove the transmission mount attaching bolts and remove the mount and crossmember from the vehicle.
15. Remove the transmission attaching bolts and carefully move the transmission rearward and downward out of the vehicle.
16. Installation is the reverse of the removal procedure. Torque the transmission to the flywheel housing bolts to 55 ft. lbs.

Automatic Transmission

NOTE: **By September 1, 1991, Hydra-matic will have changed the name designation of the THM 700-R4 automatic transmission. The new name designation for this transmission will be Hydra-matic 4L60. Transmissions** built between 1989 and 1990 will serve as transitional years in which a dual system, made up of the old designation and the new designation will be in effect.

Removal and Installation

1. Disconnect the negative battery cable.
2. Remove the air cleaner assembly.
3. Disconnect the throttle valve (T.V.) control cable at the throttle lever.
4. Remove the transmission oil dipstick. Unbolt and remove the dipstick tube.
5. Raise the vehicle and support it safely.
6. Mark the relationship between the driveshaft and the rear pinion flange so that the driveshaft may be reinstalled in its original position.
7. Remove the driveshaft from the vehicle.
8. Disconnect the catalytic converter support bracket at the transmission.
9. Disconnect the speedometer cable, electrical connectors and the shift control cable from the transmission.
10. Remove the torque arm to transmission bolts.

NOTE: The rear spring force will cause the torque arm to move toward the floor pan. When disconnecting the arm from the transmission, carefully place a piece of wood between the floor pan and the torque arm. This will prevent possible personal injury and/or floor pan damage.

11. Remove the flywheel cover, then mark the relationship between the torque converter and the flywheel.
12. Remove the torque converter to flywheel attaching bolts.
13. Support the transmission with a jack, then remove the transmission mount bolt.
14. Unbolt and remove the transmission crossmember.
15. Lower the transmission slightly. Disconnect the T.V. cable and oil cooler lines from the transmission.
16. Support the engine. Remove the transmission to engine mounting bolts.
17. Remove the transmission from the vehicle. Keep the rear of the transmission lower than the front to avoid the possibility of the torque converter disengaging from the transmission.
18. Installation is the reverse of the removal procedure. Torque the converter to flywheel bolts to 46 ft. lbs. and the transmission to engine bolts to 35 ft. lbs.

Adjustment

1. Raise and safely support the vehicle.
2. Loosen the shift control cable attachment at the shift lever.
3. Rotate the shift lever clockwise to **P** detent and then back to the **N**.
4. Tighten the cable attaching nut to 11 ft. lbs. The lever must be held out of **P** when tightening nut.
5. Check cable adjustment by rotating control lever through the detents.

DRIVESHAFT

Removal and Installation

1. Raise and support the vehicle safely. Matchmark the pinion flange and driveshaft for assembly.
2. Unbolt the flange or remove the U-bolts or straps. If straps or U-bolts are used, tape the bearing cups in place.
3. Drop the driveshaft down at the rear, then pull it back-wards out from the transmission extension housing. The transmission housing should be plugged to prevent leakage.
4. Installation is the reverse of the removal procedure.

Universal Joints

Refer to the unit repair section for overhaul procedures.

REAR AXLE AND SUSPENSION

Refer to the unit repair section for axle overhaul procedures and for rear suspension services.

Rear Axle Assembly

Removal and Installation

1. Raise the vehicle and support it safely. Be sure that the rear axle assembly is supported safely.
2. Disconnect shock absorbers from axle. Remove the tire and wheel assemblies.
3. Mark driveshaft and pinion flange, then disconnect driveshaft and support out of the way.
4. Remove brake line junction block bolt at axle housing. If necessary, disconnect the brake lines at the junction block.
5. Disconnect the upper control arms from the axle housing.
6. Lower the rear axle assembly. Remove the springs.
7. Continue lowering the rear axle assembly and remove it from the vehicle.
8. Installation is the reverse of the removal procedure.

Axle Shaft, Bearing/Oil Seal

Removal and Installation
EXCEPT BORG WARNER REAR ASSEMBLY

The Borg Warner axle assembly can be quickly identified, by checking the axle number (found on the left or right axle tube). The Borg Warner axle numbers are 4EW, 4EU and 4ET.

1. Raise the vehicle and support it safely. Remove the rear wheels and drums.
2. Remove the carrier cover and drain.
3. Remove the rear axle pinion shaft lock screw. Remove the rear axle pinion shaft.
4. Remove the C-lock clip from the bottom end of the pinion shaft.
5. Remove the axle shaft from the axle housing.
6. Using a suitable tool, remove the oil seal from the axle housing. Be careful not to damage the housing.
7. Install tool J–22813–01 or equivalent, into the bore of the

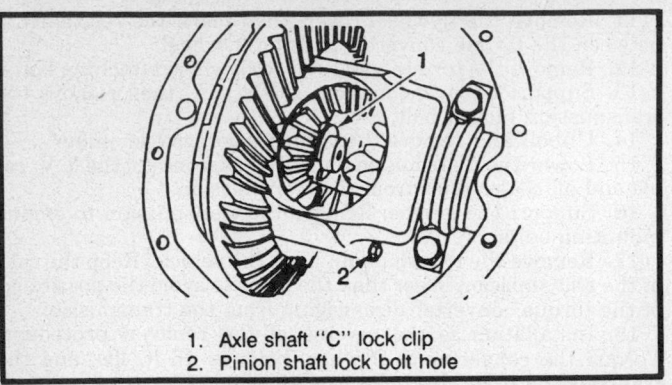

1. Axle shaft "C" lock clip
2. Pinion shaft lock bolt hole

To remove axle shaft assembly—first remove C-lock clip

axle housing, making sure that it engages the bearing outer race. Remove the bearing, using slide hammer.

8. Installation is the reverse of the removal procedure. Lubricate the new bearing with gear lube before installing.

BORG WARNER REAR ASSEMBLY

1. Raise the vehicle and support it safely.

2. Remove the rear wheels and drums. Remove the brake components as required.

3. Remove the 4 nuts holding the brake anchor plate and outer bearing retainer.

4. Remove the axle shaft and wheel bearing assembly using axle shaft removal tool J–21597 and slide hammer J–2619 or equivalent.

5. To remove the inner bearing retainer and the bearing from the axle shaft, split the retainer with a chisel and remove it from the shaft. Using tool J–22912–01, press the bearing off the shaft.

6. Installation is the reverse of the removal procedure

HEEL CONTACT
DECREASE BACKLASH—
MOVES AREA OF
PINION CONTACT
TOWARD TOE

DESIRED PATTERN—
IN CENTER OF
RING GEAR TOOTH

HIGH FACE CONTACT
INCREASE PINION
SHIM THICKNESS—
MOVES LARGER DIAMETER
OF PINION IN TOWARD
CENTER OF RING GEAR

LOW FACE CONTACT
DECREASE PINION
SHIM THICKNESS—
MOVES SMALLER DIAMETER
OF PINION OUT TOWARD
RING GEAR CENTER LINE

TOE CONTACT
INCREASE BACKLASH—
MOVES AREA OF
PINION CONTACT
TOWARD HEEL

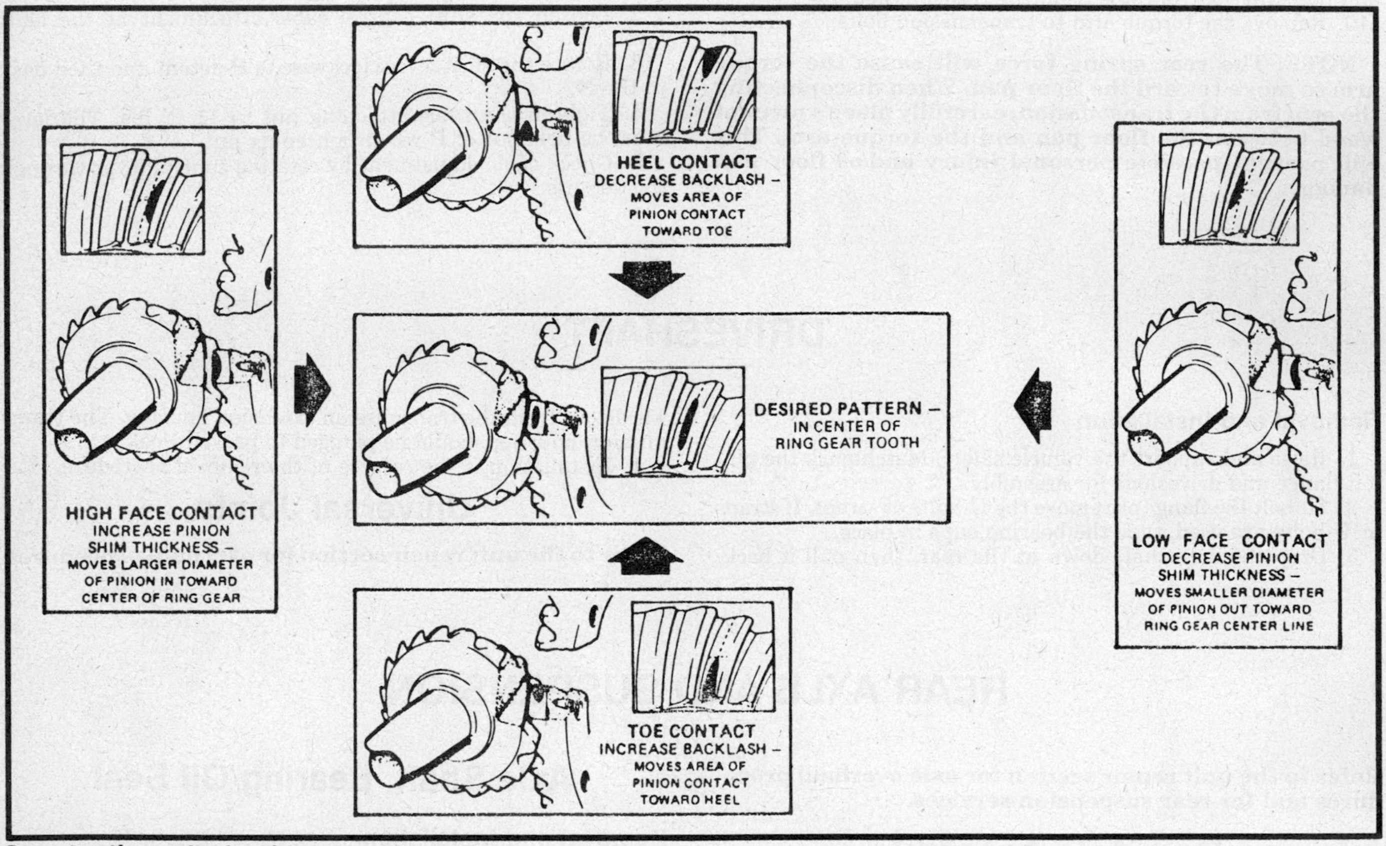

Gear tooth contact patern

YEAR IDENTIFICATION

1986–88 Fiero

1986–88 Fiero GT

VEHICLE IDENTIFICATION

It is important for servicing and ordering parts to be certain of the vehicle and engine identification. The VIN (vehicle identification number) is a 17 digit number visible through the windshield on the driver's side of the dash and contains the vehicle and engine identification codes. The tenth digit indicates model year, and the eighth digit indicates engine code. It can be interpreted as follows:

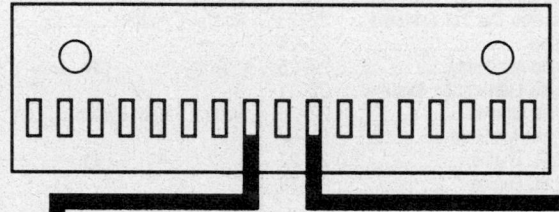

Engine Code						Model Year	
Code	Cu. In.	Liters	Cyl.	Fuel Sys.	Eng. Mfg.	Code	Year
R	151	2.5	4	TBI	Pontiac	G	1986
9	173	2.8	6	MFI	Chevrolet	H	1987
						J	1988

ENGINE IDENTIFICATION

Year	Model	Engine Displacement cu. in. (liter)	Engine Series Identification (VIN)	No. of Cylinders	Engine Type
1986	Fiero	151 (2.5)	R	4	OHV
	Fiero	173 (2.8)	9	4	OHV
1987	Fiero	151 (2.5)	R	4	OHV
	Fiero	173 (2.8)	9	4	OHV
1988	Fiero	151 (2.5)	R	4	OHV
	Fiero	173 (2.8)	9	4	OHV

GENERAL ENGINE SPECIFICATIONS

Year	VIN	No. Cylinder Displacement cu. in. (liter)	Fuel System Type	Net Horsepower @ rpm	Net Torque @ rpm (ft.lbs.)	Bore × Stroke (in.)	Compression Ratio	Oil Pressure @ rpm
1986	R	4-151 (2.5)	TBI	92 @ 4400	134 @ 2800	4.000 × 3.000	9.0:1	36–41 @ 2000
	9	6-173 (2.8)	MFI	140 @ 5200	170 @ 3600	3.500 × 3.000	8.5:1	30–45 @ 2000
1987	R	4-151 (2.5)	TBI	92 @ 4400	134 @ 2800	4.000 × 3.000	8.3:1	36–41 @ 2000
	9	6-173 (2.8)	MFI	140 @ 5200	170 @ 3600	3.500 × 3.000	8.5:1	30–45 @ 2000
1988	R	4-151 (2.5)	TBI	98 @ 4500	134 @ 2800	4.000 × 3.000	8.3:1	36-41 @ 2000
	9	6-173 (2.8)	MFI	135 @ 4500	170 @ 3600	3.500 × 3.000	8.5:1	30-45 @ 2000

TBI—Throttle Body Fuel Injection
MFI—Multiport Fuel Injection

GASOLINE ENGINE TUNE-UP SPECIFICATIONS
See chart at end of manual for spark plug recommendations

Year	VIN	No. Cylinder Displacement cu. in. (liter)	Spark Plugs Gap (in.)	Ignition Timing (deg.) MT	Ignition Timing (deg.) AT	Compression Pressure (psi)	Fuel Pump (psi)	Idle Speed (rpm) MT	Idle Speed (rpm) AT	Valve Clearance In.	Valve Clearance Ex.
1986	R	4-151 (2.5)	.060	①	①	NA	9-13	①	①	Hyd.	Hyd.
	9	6-173 (2.8)	.045	①	①	NA	41-47	①	①	Hyd.	Hyd.
1987	R	4-151 (2.5)	.060	①	①	NA	9-13	①	①	Hyd.	Hyd.
	9	6-173 (2.8)	.045	①	①	NA	41-47	①	①	Hyd.	Hyd.
1988	R	4-151 (2.5)	.060	①	①	NA	9-13	①	①	Hyd.	Hyd.
	9	6-173 (2.8)	.045	①	①	NA	41-47	①	①	Hyd.	Hyd.

NOTE: The underhood specifications sticker often reflects tune-up specification changes made in production. Sticker figures must be used if they disagree with those in this chart
NA—Not available
① See underhood sticker

FIRING ORDERS

NOTE: To avoided confusion always replace spark plug wires 1 at a time.

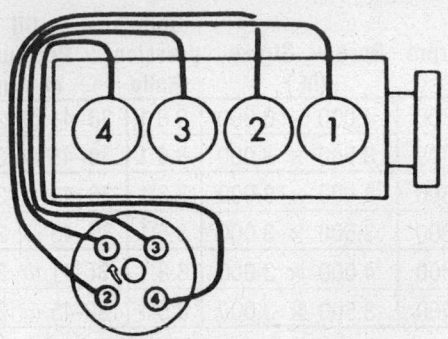

2.5L engine
Engine firing order: 1-3-4-2
Distributor rotation: clockwise

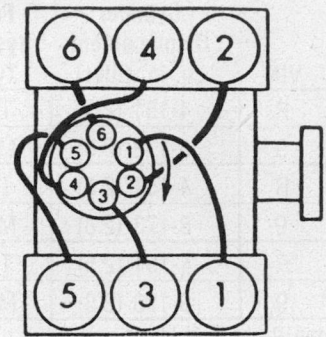

2.8L engine
Engine firing order: 1-2-3-4-5-6
Distributor rotation: clockwise

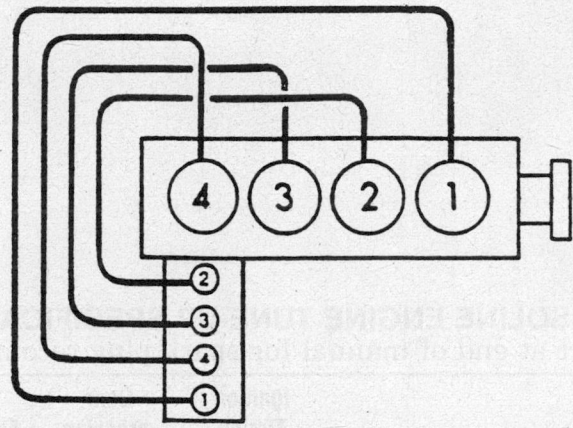

2.5L engine
Engine firing order: 1-3-4-2
Distributorless ignition

CAPACITIES

Year	Model	VIN	No. Cylinder Displacement cu. in. (liter)	Engine Crankcase with Filter	Engine Crankcase without Filter	Transmission (pts.) 4-Spd	Transmission (pts.) 5-Spd	Transmission (pts.) Auto.	Drive Axle (pts.)	Fuel Tank (gal.)	Cooling System (qts.)
1986	Fiero	R	4-151 (2.5)	3	3	—	5.9	8.0	—	10.3	13.8
	Fiero	9	6-173 (2.8)	4	4	—	5.3	8.0	—	10.3	13.8
1987	Fiero	R	4-151 (2.5)	3	3	—	4.1	8.0	—	11.9	13.8
	Fiero	9	6-173 (2.8)	4	4	—	5.3	8.0	—	11.9	13.8
1988	Fiero	R	4-151 (2.5)	4	4	—	4.1②	8.0①	—	11.9	13.8
	Fiero	9	6-173 (2.8)	4	4	—	5.3②	8.0①	—	11.9	13.8

① Overhaul – 10.0
② Isuzu – 5.3

CAMSHAFT SPECIFICATIONS
All measurements given in inches.

Year	VIN	No. Cylinder Displacement cu. in. (liter)	Journal Diameter 1	2	3	4	5	Lobe Lift In.	Ex.	Bearing Clearance	Camshaft End Play
1986	R	4-151 (2.5)	1.869	1.869	1.869	1.869	—	0.232	0.232	.0007–.0027	.0015–.0050
	9	6-173 (2.8)	1.869	1.869	1.869	1.869	—	0.231	0.231	.0010–.0040	—
1987	R	4-151 (2.5)	1.869	1.869	1.869	1.869	—	0.232	0.232	.0007–.0027	.0015–.0050
	9	6-173 (2.8)	1.869	1.869	1.869	1.869	—	0.231	0.231	.0010–.0040	—
1988	R	4-151 (2.5)	1.869	1.869	1.869	1.869	—	0.232	0.232	.0007–.0027	.0015–.0050
	9	6-173 (2.8)	1.869	1.869	1.869	1.869	—	0.231	0.263	.0010–.0040	—

CRANKSHAFT AND CONNECTING ROD SPECIFICATIONS
All measurements are given in inches.

Year	VIN	No. Cylinder Displacement cu. in. (liter)	Crankshaft Main Brg. Journal Dia.	Main Brg. Oil Clearance	Shaft End-play	Thrust on No.	Connecting Rod Journal Diameter	Oil Clearance	Side Clearance
1986	R	4-151 (2.5)	2.2995–2.3005	.0003–.0022	.0035–.0085	5	1.9995–2.0005	.0005–.0026	.006–.022
	9	6-173 (2.8)	2.585–2.586	.0016–.0031	.002–.0067	3	1.9984–1.9994	.0014–.0037	.006–.017
1987	R	4-151 (2.5)	2.2995–2.3005	.0005–.0022	.0035–.0085	5	1.9995–2.0005	.0005–.0026	.006–.022
	9	6-173 (2.8)	2.6473–2.6482	.0016–.0031	.0023–.0082	3	1.9984–1.9994	.0014–.0037	.006–.017
1988	R	4-151 (2.5)	2.3000–2.3005	.0005–.0022	.0035–.0085	5	2.0000–2.0005	.0005–.0026	.006–.022
	9	6-173 (2.8)	2.6473–2.6482	.0016–.0031	.0023–.0082	3	1.9984–1.9994	.0014–.0037	.006–.017

VALVE SPECIFICATIONS

Year	VIN	No. Cylinder Displacement cu. in. (liter)	Seat Angle (deg.)	Face Angle (deg.)	Spring Test Pressure (lbs.)	Spring Installed Height (in.)	Stem-to-Guide Clearance (in.) Intake	Exhaust	Stem Diameter (in.) Intake	Exhaust
1986	R	4-151 (2.5)	46	45	176	1.69	.0010–.0027	.0010–.0027	.3418–.3425	.3418–.3425
	9	6-173 (2.8)	46	45	195	1.57	.0010–.0027	.0010–.0027	.3410–.3425	.3418–.3426
1987	R	4-151 (2.5)	45	45	176	1.69	.0010–.0027	.0010–.0027	.3418–.3425	.3418–.3425
	9	6-173 (2.8)	46	45	195	1.57	.0010–.0027	.0010–.0027	.3410–.3425	.3410–.3426
1988	R	4-151 (2.5)	46	45	178	1.44	.0010–.0027	0.010–.0027	.3130–.3140	.3120–.3130
	9	6-173 (2.8)	46	45	195	1.57	.0010–.0027	.0010–.0027	.3410–.3425	.3410–.3426

PISTON AND RING SPECIFICATIONS
All measurments are given in inches.

Year	VIN	No. Cylinder Displacement cu. in. (liter)	Piston Clearance	Ring Gap Top Compression	Bottom Compression	Oil Control	Ring Side Clearance Top Compression	Bottom Compression	Oil Control
1986	R	4-151 (2.5)	.0014–.0022 ①	.010–.020	.010–.020	.020–.060	.002–.003	.001–.003	.015–.055
	9	6-173 (2.8)	.0007–.0017	.0098–.0197	.0098–.0197	.020–.055	.0012–.0028	.0016–.0037	.008 Max
1987	R	4-151 (2.5)	.0014–.0022 ①	.010–.020	.010–.020	.020–.060	.002–.003	.001–.003	.015–.055
	9	6-173 (2.8)	.0007–.0017	.0098–.0197	.0098–.0197	.020–.055	.0012–.0028	.0016–.0037	.008 Max

PISTON AND RING SPECIFICATIONS
All measurments are given in inches.

Year	VIN	No. Cylinder Displacement cu. in. (liter)	Piston Clearance	Ring Gap			Ring Side Clearance		
				Top Compression	Bottom Compression	Oil Control	Top Compression	Bottom Compression	Oil Control
1988	R	4-151 (2.5)	.0014–.0022 ①	.010–.020	.010–.020	.020–.060	.002–.003	.002–.003	.015–.055
	9	6-173 (2.8)	.0007–.0017	.0098–.0197	.0098–.0197	.020–.055	.0012–.0028	.0016–.0037	.008 Max

① Measured 1.8 in. down from piston top

TORQUE SPECIFICATIONS
All readings in ft. lbs.

Year	VIN	No. Cylinder Displacement cu. in. (liter)	Cylinder Head Bolts	Main Bearing Bolts	Rod Bearing Bolts	Crankshaft Pulley Bolts	Flywheel Bolts	Manifold Intake	Manifold Exhaust	Spark Plugs
1986	R	4-151 (2.5)	①	70	32	162	44	25	44	7-15
	9	6-173 (2.8)	65-90	63-74	34-40	66-84	45-55	20-25	22-28	7-15
1987	R	4-151 (2.5)	①	70	32	162	44	25	44	7-15
	9	6-173 (2.8)	65-90	63-74	34-40	66-84	45-55	20-25	22-28	7-15
1988	R	4-151 (2.5)	①	70	32	162	44	25	44	7-15
	9	6-173 (2.8)	65-90	63-74	34-40	66-84	45-55	22-28	44	7-15

① Stage 1—18
Stage 2—35 except bolts 9–18
Stage 3—Torque all bolts 90 degrees

WHEEL ALIGNMENT

Year	Model	Caster Range (deg.)	Caster Preferred Setting (deg.)	Camber Range (deg.)	Camber Preferred Setting (deg.)	Toe-in (in.)	Steering Axis Inclination (deg.)
1986	Fiero	3N-7P	5P	5/16N-1 5/16P	1/2P	1/16 ± 1/32	NA
1987	Fiero	3N-7P	5P	5/16N-1 5/16P	1/2P	1/16 ± 1/32	NA
1988	Fiero	3N-7P	5P	5/16N-1 5/16P	1/2P	1/16 ± 1/32	NA

N Negative
P Positive

ELECTRICAL

NOTE: Disconnecting the negative battery cable on some vehicles may interfere with the functions of the on board computer systems and may require the computer to undergo a relearning process, once the negative battery cable is reconnected.

For testing and overhaul procedures on starters, alternators and voltage regulators, refer to the Unit Repair Section.

Charging System

ALTERNATOR

Removal and Installation

2.5L ENGINE

1. Disconnect the negative battery cable.
2. Remove the air cleaner, as required.
3. Disconnect the upper strut mount, as required.
4. Disconnect the alternator adjusting bolts and upper adjusting bracket. remove the drive belt.
5. Disconnect the wiring from the back of the alternator.
6. Lower the alternator mounting bracket and remove the alternator from the vehicle.
7. Installation is the reverse of the removal procedure. Adjust the drive belt, as required.

2.8L ENGINE

1. Disconnect the negative battery cable.
2. Loosen the top alternator bracket retaining bolts.
3. Raise and support the vehicle safely. Remove the right rear tire and wheel assembly.
4. Remove the splash guards. Remove the toe link rod outer end and swing it up and to the left.
5. Remove the lower alternator bracket. Remove the alternator adjusting bolt.
6. Remove the drive belt. Disconnect the upper alternator bracket bolt.
7. Disconnect the electrical connections from the alternator.
8. Rotate the alternator bracket lower end toward the engine. Remove the alternator from the vehicle. Remove the alternator shield.
9. Installation is the reverse of the removal procedure. Adjust the drive belt, as required.

VOLTAGE REGULATOR

An alternator with an integral voltage regulator is standard equipment. There are no adjustments possible with this unit. The alternator must be disassembled in order to service the regulator.

BELT TENSION

2.5L ENGINE

On 1986 vehicles the drive belt tension is 145 lbs. for a new belt and 70 lbs. for a used belt.

A single (serpentine) belt is used to drive all engine mounted components on 1986–88 vehicles. Drive belt tension is maintained by a spring loaded tensioner. The drive belt tensioner can control belt tension over a wide range of belt lengths; however, there are limits to the tensioner's ability to compensate. Using the tensioner outside its operating range can result in poor tension control and/or damage to the tensioner.

2.8L ENGINE

The drive belt tension is 145 lbs. for a new belt and 70 lbs. for a used belt.

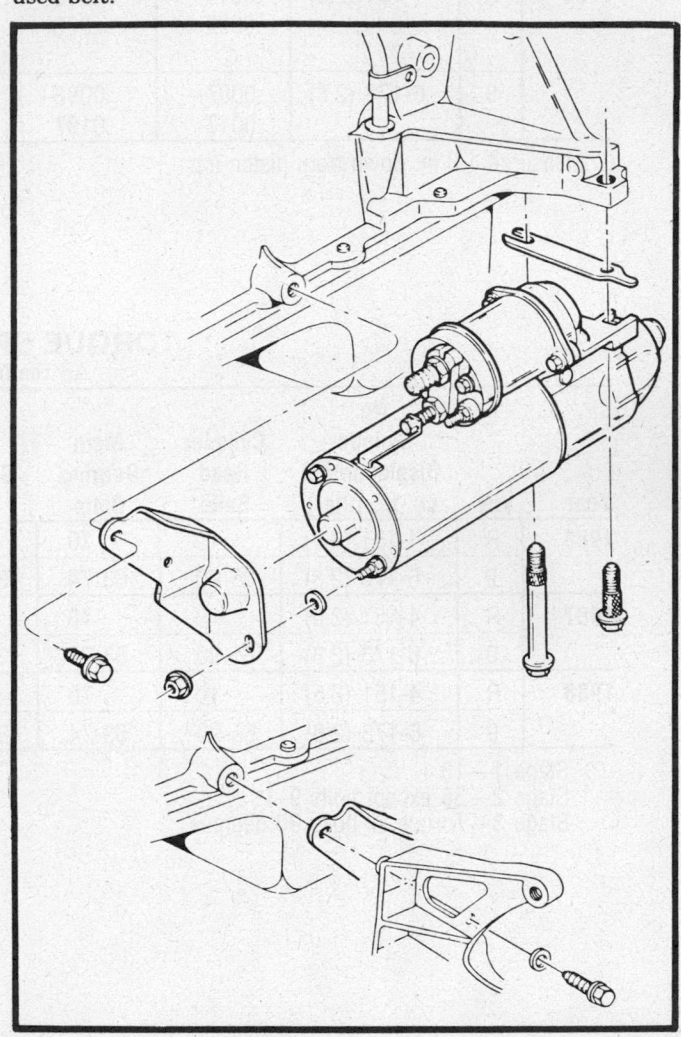

Starter motor mounting

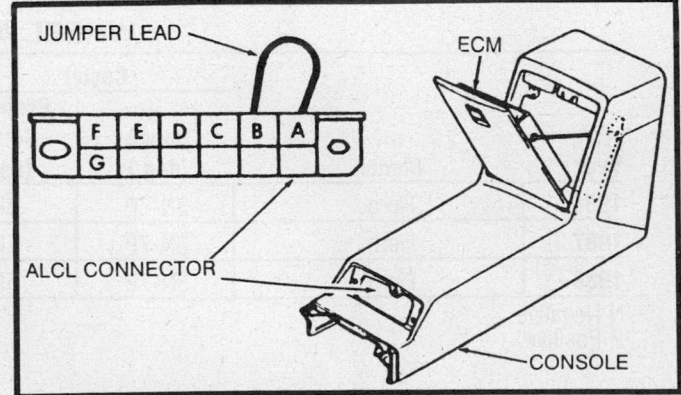

ALCL connector location

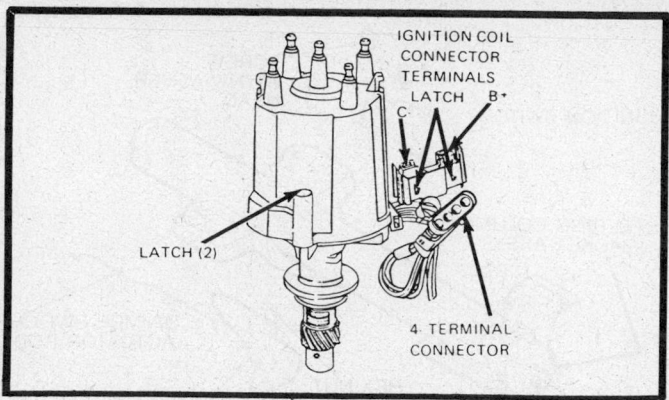

Typical distributor used with a separately mounted coil

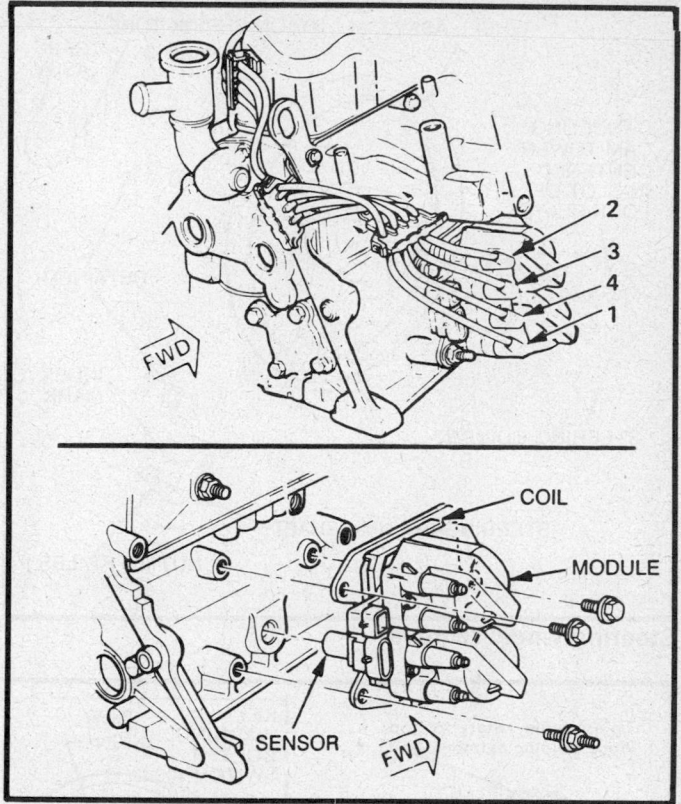

Distributorless ignition assembly—2.5L engine

Starting System

STARTER

Removal and Installation

1. Disconnect the negative battery cable.
2. Raise and support the vehicle safely.
3. Disconnect all wires at solenoid terminals. Note color coding of wires for reinstallation.
4. Remove the starter support bracket mount bolts, as required. Loosen the front bracket bolt or nut and rotate the bracket clear.
5. Remove the starter retaining bolts. Remove the starter. Note the location of any shims so that they may be replaced in the same positions upon installation.
6. Installation is the reverse of the removal procedure.

Ignition System

DISTRIBUTOR

Removal and Installation
TIMING NOT DISTURBED

1. Position the engine at TDC on the compression stroke. Disconnect the negative battery cable.
2. If required, remove the air cleaner assembly. Tag and disconnect all electrical wires.
3. Remove the spark plug wires. Remove the distributor cap.
4. Matchmark the distributor assembly in relation to where the rotor is pointing, to aid in reassembly.
5. Remove the distributor retaining bolt. Carefully remove the distributor from the engine.
6. Installation is the reverse of the removal procedure. Check and adjust the engine timing as required.

TIMING DISTURBED

If the engine was cranked while the distributor was removed, place the engine on TDC of the compression stroke to obtain proper ignition timing.
1. Remove the No. 1 spark plug.
2. Place a thumb or finger over the spark plug hole. Crank the engine slowly until compression is felt.
3. Align the timing mark on the crankshaft pulley with the 0 degree mark on the timing scale attached to the front of the engine. This places the engine at TDC of the compression stroke.
4. Turn the distributor shaft until the rotor points between the No. 1 and No. 3 spark plug towers on the cap for the 2.5L engine. If equipped with the 2.8L engine, turn the distributor

shaft until the rotor points between the No. 1 and No. 6 spark plug towers on the cap.
5. Continue the installation in the reverse order of the removal.

IGNITION TIMING
EXCEPT DISTRIBUTORLESS IGNITION

NOTE: *If these timing procedures differ from the information found on the vehicle identification label, use the data on the vehicle information label.*

1. Connect a timing light according to the manufacturer's instructions.
2. Follow the instructions on the underhood engine decal.
3. The **ALCL** terminal must be grounded before the ignition timing can be properly checked. The **ALCL** terminal is located in the front lower section of the console. Connect terminals **A** and **B** with a jumper wire. The engine is now in the bypass mode, thus enabling the engine timing to be checked. Do not disconnect the 4 wire connector at the distributor.
4. Start the engine and run it at idle speed.
5. Aim the timing light at the degree scale just over the harmonic balancer.
6. Adjust the timing by loosening the securing clamp and rotating the distributor until the desired ignition advance is achieved, then tighten the clamp.
7. Loosen the distributor clamp outer bolt, then slide the clamp back slightly. Do not remove the retaining bolt.
8. Adjust the timing, then replace and tighten the clamp. To advance the timing, rotate the distributor opposite the normal direction of rotor rotation. Retard the timing by rotating the distributor in the normal direction of rotor rotation.

DISTRIBUTORLESS IGNITION

Distributorless ignition systems use a Waste Spark method of

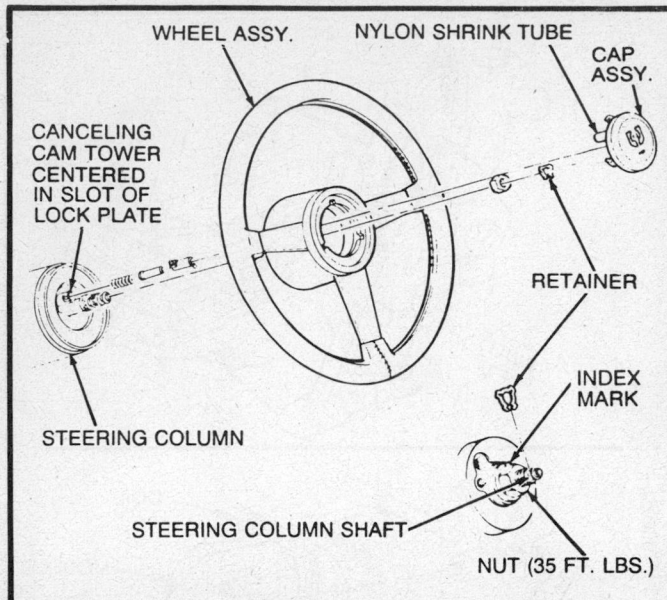

Steering wheel removal

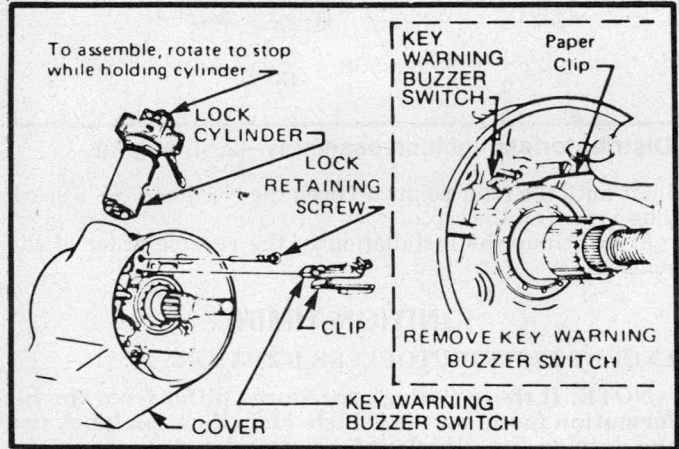

Ignition lock cylinder removal

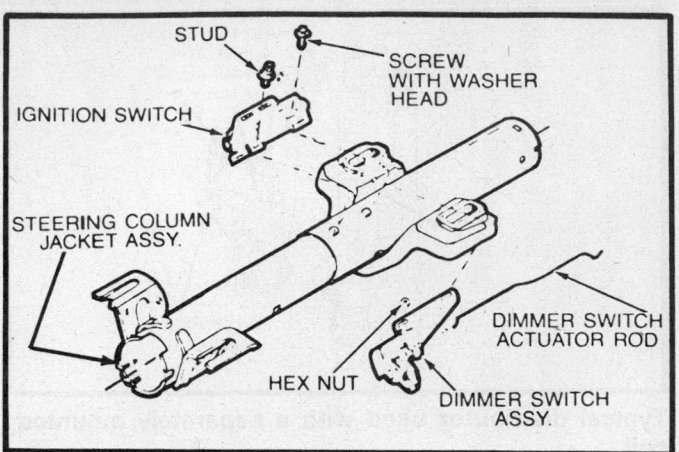

Ignition switch removal

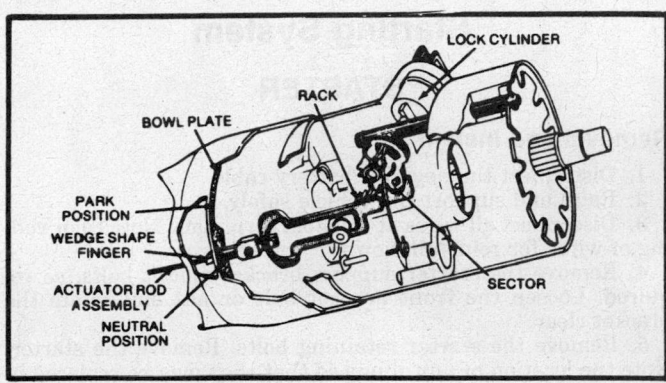

Mechanical neutral start system

spark distribution making the timing non adjustable. Each cylinder is paired with its opposing cylinder in the firing order, so that 1 cylinder on compression fires at the same time with its opposing cylinder on exhaust. The process reverses when the cylinders reverse roles. 1 coil per cylinder is needed, since 1 coil fires 2 cylinders. An ignition module is located under the coil pack and is connected to the Electronic Control Module (ECM), by a 6 pin connector. The ignition module controls the primary circuit to the coils, by turning them on and off. It also controls spark timing below 400 rpm and if the ECM bypass circuit becomes open or grounded.

The magnetic pickup sensor inserts through the engine block, just above the pan rail, in proximity to the crankshaft reluctor ring. Notches in the crankshaft reluctor ring trigger the magnetic pickup sensor to provide timing information to the ECM. The magnetic pickup sensor provides a cam signal to identify correct firing sequence and crank signal to trigger each coil at the proper time.

This system uses EST and control wires from the ECM, as with distributor systems. The ECM controls timing using crankshaft position, engine rpm, engine temperature and manifold absolute pressure, (MAP), sensing.

Electrical Controls

STEERING WHEEL

Removal and Installation

1. Disconnect the negative battery cable. Remove the center cap, retainer clip and nut.
2. Remove the steering wheel retaining nut. Remove the wheel using a steering wheel puller.
3. When installing, align the index mark on the steering wheel with the index mark on the steering shaft. Torque the retaining nut to 35 ft. lbs.
4. The canceling cam tower must be centered in the slot of the lock plate cover before assembling the wheel.

IGNITION LOCK

Removal and Installation

1. Disconnect the negative battery cable. Remove the steering wheel.
2. Turn the lock to the **RUN** position.
3. Remove the lock plate, turn signal switch or combination switch and the key warning buzzer switch. The warning buzzer switch can be fished out using a suitable tool.
4. Remove the lock cylinder retaining screw and lock cylinder. If the screw is dropped on removal, it could fall into the column, requiring complete disassembly to retrieve the screw.
5. Position the lock assembly in the column. Rotate the cylinder clockwise to align the cylinder key with the keyway in the housing.
6. Push the lock all the way in.

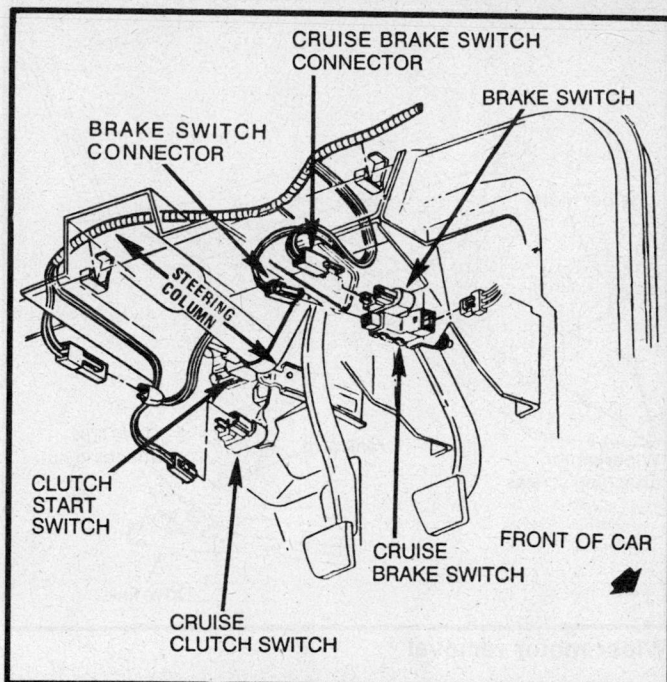

Clutch and brake switch location

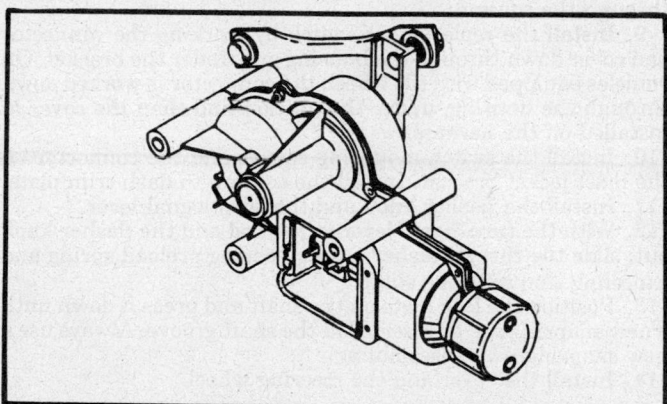

Headlight door motor

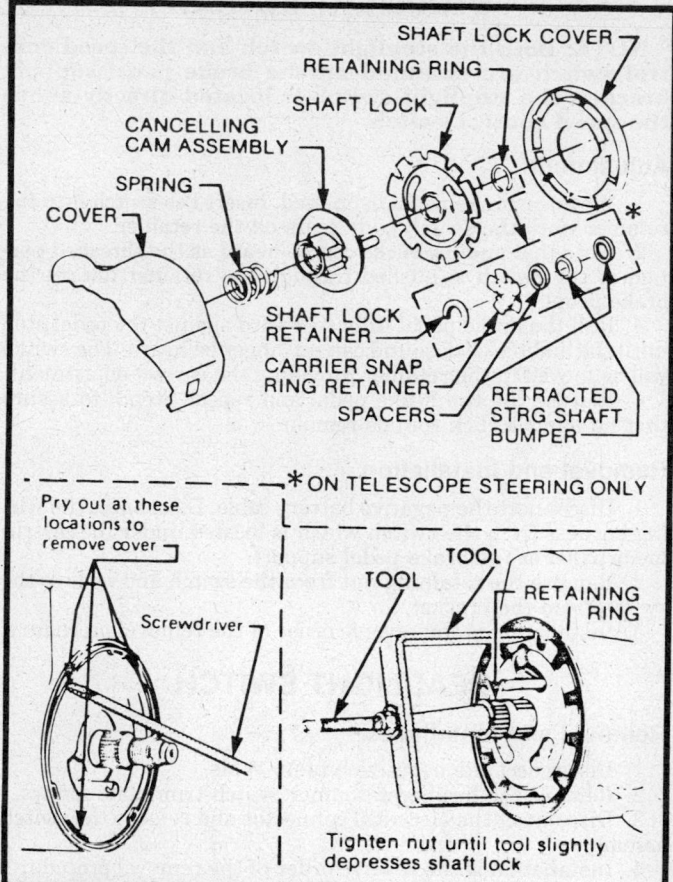

Turn signal switch removal

the specified screws, since overlength screws could impair the collapsibility of the column.

6. Reinstall the steering column.

NEUTRAL SAFETY SWITCH

This vehicle is equipped with a mechanical neutral start system. This system relies on a mechanical block, rather than the starter safety switch to prevent starting the engine in any gear except **P** or **N**. This unit is mounted on top of the steering column and has a manual actuated cable leading from the shifter to the column. When the shifter is in the **P** or **N** position the cable positions a locking pin against a cam in relationship to the ignition switch, thus preventing the ignition from moving to the start position.

CLUTCH START SWITCH

Removal and Installation

1. Disconnect the negative battery cable. Disconnect the electrical connector at the clutch switch, which is located at the top of the clutch pedal.

2. Remove the bolt attaching the switch to the clutch bracket.

3. Rotate the clutch switch slightly to disconnect the shaft from the clutch pedal hole.

4. Installation is the reverse order of the removal procedure.

7. Install the screw. Tighten to 15 inch lbs.

8. The rest of installation is the reverse of the removal procedure.

9. Turn the lock to the **RUN** position and install the key warning buzzer switch, which is simply pushed down into place.

IGNITION SWITCH

Removal and Installation

1. Disconnect the negative battery cable. Lower the steering column and support it properly.

2. Put the switch in the **OFF/UNLOCK** position. With the cylinder removed, the rod is in an **OFF/UNLOCK** position when it is in the next to the uppermost detent.

3. Remove the 2 switch screws and remove the switch assembly.

4. Before installing, place the new switch in **OFF/UNLOCK** position and make sure the lock cylinder and actuating rod are in **OFF/UNLOCK** position (second detent from the top).

5. Install the activating rod into the switch and assemble the switch on the column. Tighten the mounting screws. Use only

STOPLIGHT SWITCH

NOTE: Both the stoplight switch and the speed control switch are mounted on the brake pedal support bracket, the stoplight switch is located directly above the speed control switch.

Adjustment

1. With the brake pedal depressed, insert the switch into the retainer until the switch body seats on the retainer.
2. Note that audible clicks can be heard as the threaded portion of the switch is pushed through the retainer toward the brake pedal.
3. Pull the brake pedal fully rearward against the pedal stop until the audible click sound can no longer be heard. The switch will be moved in the retainer providing the correct adjustment.
4. Release the the brake pedal and repeat Step 3 to assure that no audible click sounds remain.

Removal and Installation

1. Disconnect the negative battery cable. Disconnect the wiring harness from the switch which is located under the instrument panel at the brake pedal support.
2. Remove the retaining nut from the switch and remove the switch from the bracket.
3. Installation is the reverse order of the removal procedure.

HEADLIGHT SWITCH

Removal and Installation

1. Disconnect the negative battery cable.
2. Remove the headlight/dimmer switch trim plate screws.
3. Disconnect the electrical connector and remove the switch assembly.
4. Installation is the reverse order of the removal procedure.

CONCEALED HEADLAMPS

Manual Operation

In the event of system failure, the headlights may be raised or lowered manually.
1. Locate the headlight door motors in each headlight assembly under the front compartment.
2. Rotate the knob on each headlight door motor in the direction of the arrow until each headlight door fully open.

COMBINATION SWITCH

Removal and Installation

1. Disconnect the negative battery cable. Remove the steering wheel.
2. Remove the trim cover from the steering column.
3. Position a U-shaped lockplate compressing tool on the end of the steering shaft and compress the lock plate by turning the shaft nut clockwise. Pry the wire snapring out of the shaft groove.
4. Remove the tool and lift the lockplate off the shaft.
5. Slip the canceling cam, upper bearing preload spring and thrust washer off the shaft.
6. Remove the turn signal lever. Remove the hazard flasher button retaining screw and remove the button, spring and knob.
7. Pull the switch connector out of the mast jacket and tape the upper part to facilitate switch removal. Attach a long piece of wire to the turn signal switch, feed this wire through the column first and then use this wire to pull the switch connector into position. On vehicles equipped with tilt wheel, place the turn signal and shifter housing in low position and remove the harness cover.

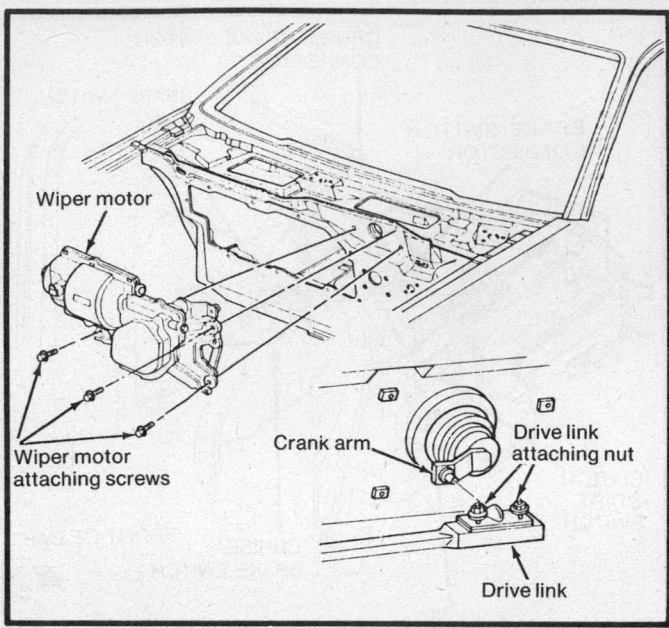

Wiper motor removal

8. Remove the 3 switch mounting screws. Remove the switch by pulling it straight up while guiding the wiring harness cover through the column.
9. Install the replacement switch by working the connector and cover down through the housing and under the bracket. On vehicles equipped with tilt wheel, the connector is worked down through the housing, under the bracket and then the cover in installed on the harness.
10. Install the switch mounting screws and the connector on the mast jacket bracket. Install the column to dash trim plate.
11. Install the flasher knob and the turn signal lever.
12. With the turn signal lever in neutral and the flasher knob out, slide the thrust washer, upper bearing preload spring and canceling cam onto the shaft.
13. Position the lock plate on the shaft and press it down until a new snapring can be inserted in the shaft groove. Always use a new snapring when assembling.
14. Install the cover and the steering wheel.

WINDSHIELD WIPER MOTOR

Removal and Installation

1. Disconnect the negative battery cable. Remove the wiper arms and the shroud top vent grille, as necessary.
2. Loosen, but do not remove the transmission drive link to motor crank arm retaining nuts.
3. Detach the drive link from the motor crank arm.
4. Disconnect the electrical leads.
5. Remove the attaching screws and remove the wiper motor.
6. Installation is the reverse of removal. Be sure the wiper motor is in the park position before installing the wiper arms and the shroud top screen.

DELAY WIPER CONTROLS

Operation
PULSE POSITION

With the wiper/washer switch in **PULSE** voltage is applied to the solid state pulse/speed/wash control through the gray (No. 91) wire. This voltage signals the solid state pulse/speed/wash control to momentarily ground the coil of the park/run relay.

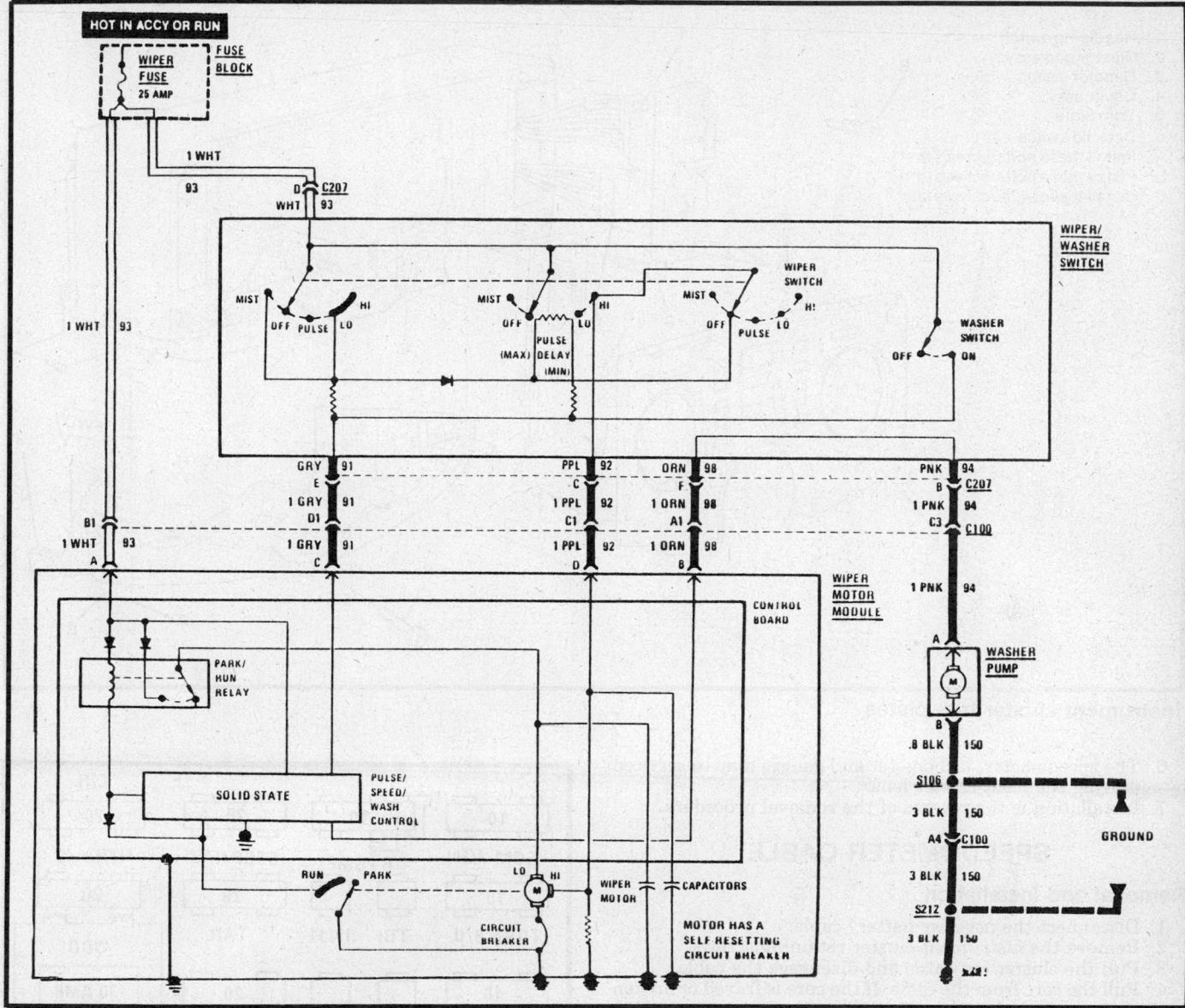

Delay wiper system electrical schematic

With the park/run relay energized, voltage is applied through the contacts of the relay to the wiper motor.

After the wipers have started, the park/run switch supplies battery voltage until the wipers return to park position. The wipers remain parked until the solid state pulse/speed/wash control again grounds the park/run relay coil.

The length of the delay time between strokes is controlled by the variable pulse delay resistor. From the low position, the delay cycles are 18, 10, 6, 3 and 1.25 seconds.

MIST POSITION

When the control is moved to the mist position and released, the wipers make 1 sweep at low speed and return to the park position. The circuit operation is the same as that of the low speed.

WINDSHIELD WIPER LINKAGE

Removal and Installation

1. Disconnect the negative battery cable. Remove the wiper arms.

2. Remove the shroud top vent screen.
3. Remove the drive link from the crank arm.
4. Remove the transmission to cowl panel attaching bolts.
5. Remove wiper transmission.
6. Installation is the reverse of the removal procedure.

Instrument Cluster

Refer to "Chilton's Electronic Instrumentation Service Manual" for additional coverage.

Removal and Installation

1. Disconnect the negative battery cable.
2. Remove the rear cluster cover.
3. Remove the front trim plate.
4. Remove the steering column cover.
5. Remove the cluster attaching screws. Disconnect the wiring harness and remove the cluster assembly.

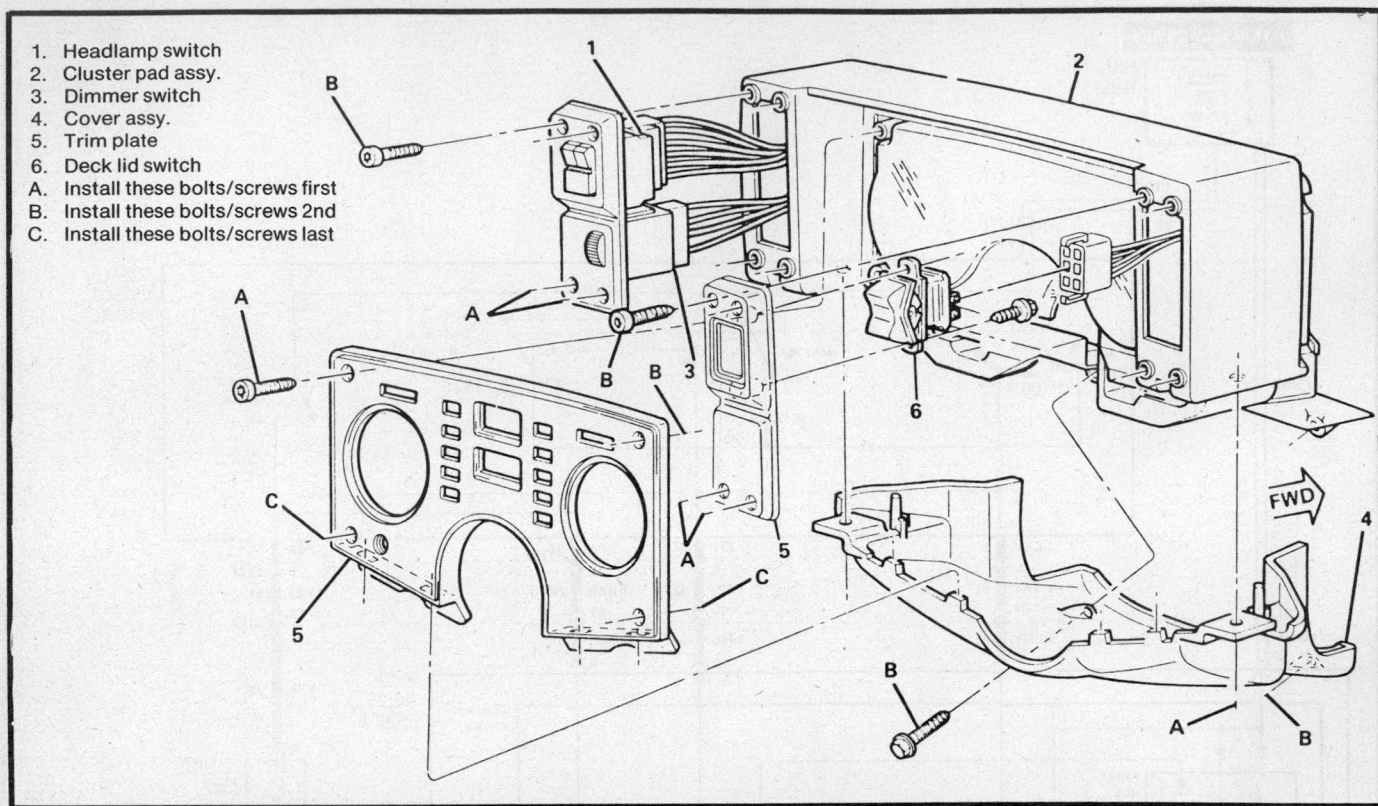

1. Headlamp switch
2. Cluster pad assy.
3. Dimmer switch
4. Cover assy.
5. Trim plate
6. Deck lid switch
A. Install these bolts/screws first
B. Install these bolts/screws 2nd
C. Install these bolts/screws last

Instrument cluster trim plates

6. The speedometer, tachometer and gauges may be serviced by removing the front cluster lens.
7. Installation is the reverse of the removal procedure.

SPEEDOMETER CABLE

Removal and Installation

1. Disconnect the negative battery cable.
2. Remove the instrument cluster retaining screws.
3. Pull the cluster outwards and disengage the cable.
4. Pull the core from the cable. If the core is frayed or broken on the transaxle end, raise and support the vehicle safely. Disconnect the cable from the transaxle. Make sure that the entire cable has been removed.
5. Installation is the reverse order of the removal procedure.

Electrical Circuit Protectors

FUSIBLE LINK

Added protection is provided in all battery feed circuits and other selected circuits by a fusible link. This link is a short piece of copper wire approximately 4 in. long inserted in series with the circuit and acts as a fuse. The link is 2 or more gauges smaller in size than the circuit wire it is protecting and will burn out without damage to the circuit in case of current overload.

Location

1. Fuse block—Behind the left side of instrument panel.
2. Fusible link B—right front of engine compartment at battery junction block.
3. Fusible link C—In front lights harness, right of master cylinder.

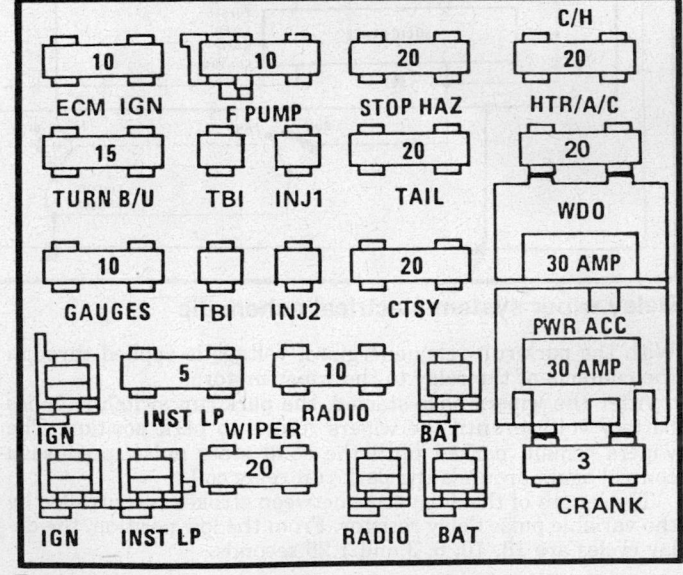

Front face of fuse block

4. Fusible link D—In front lights harness, right of master cylinder.

FUSE PANEL

The fuse panel is a swing down unit located in the underside of the instrument panel, left of the steering column. The fuse panel uses miniaturized fuses, designed for increased circuit protec-

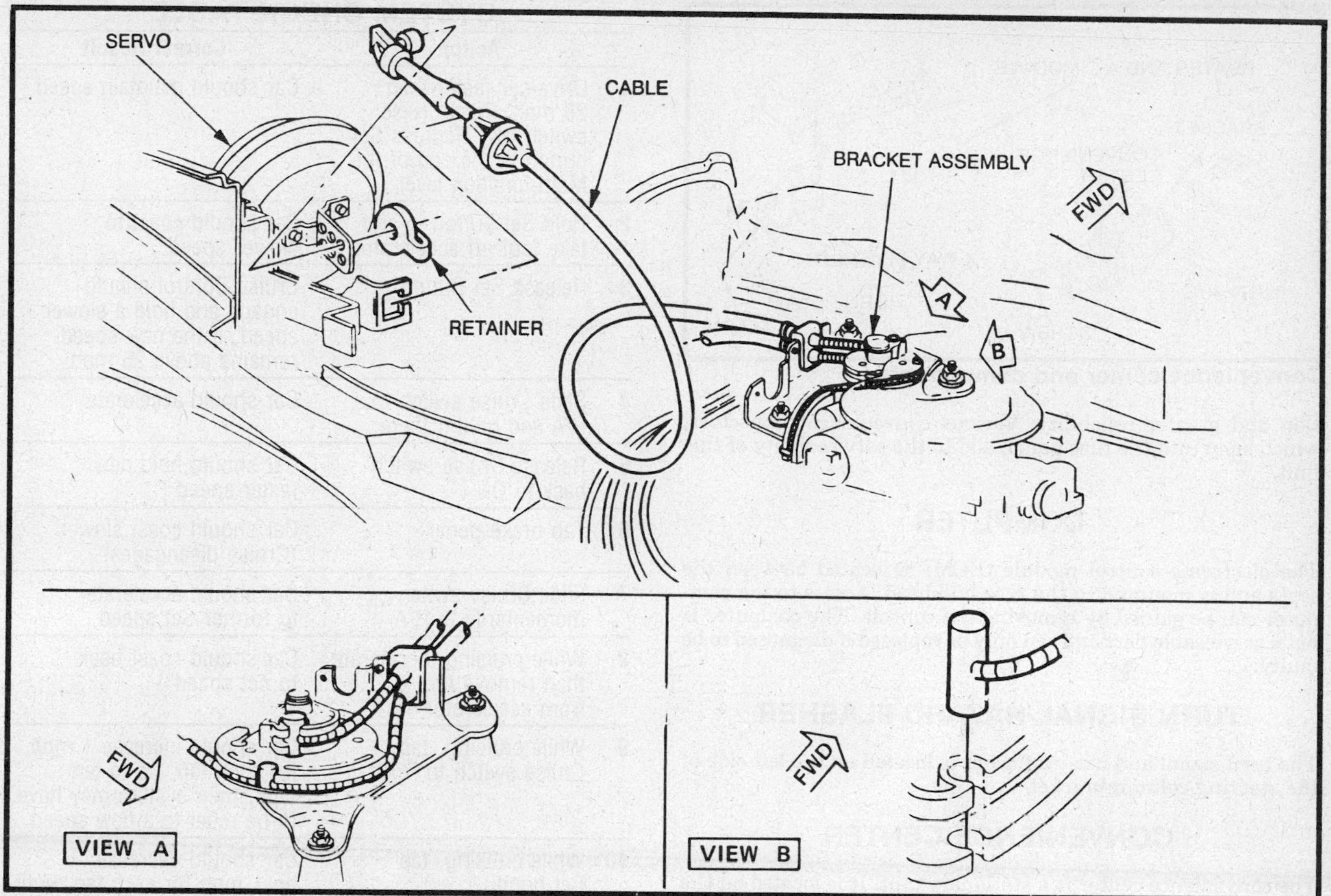

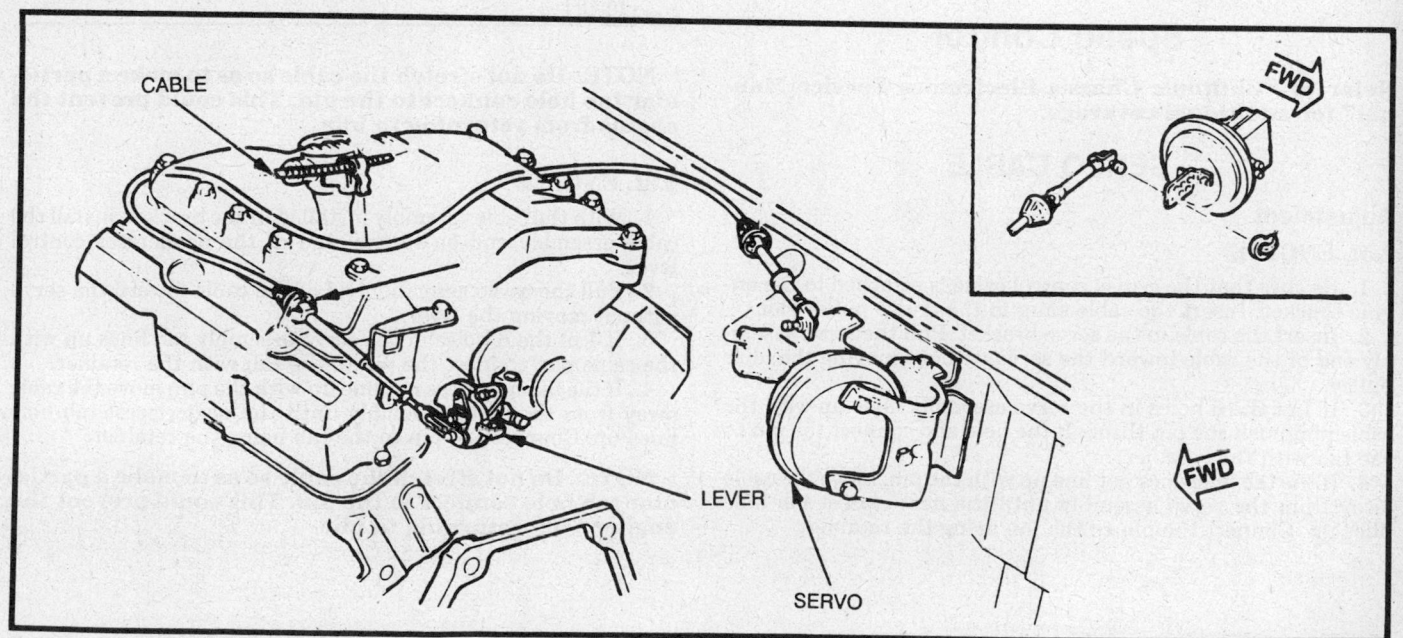

Cruise control cable adjustment—2.5L engine

Cruise control cable adjustment—2.8L engine

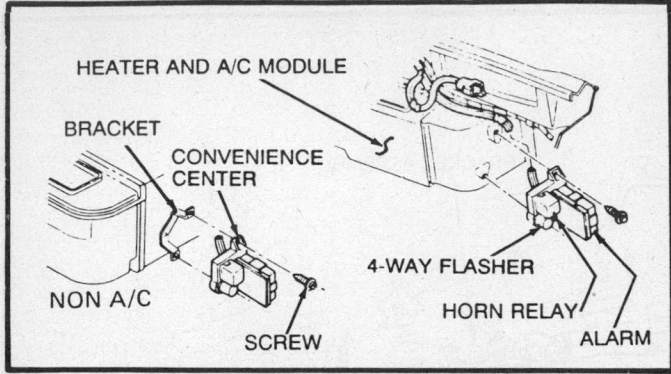

Convenience center and components

tion and greater reliability. Various convenience connectors, which snap into the fuse panel, add to the serviceability of this unit.

COMPUTER

The electronic control module (ECM) is located between the seats and is mounted to the rear bulkhead. Access to the computer can be gained by removing the console. The computer is not a serviceable part and can only be replaced if diagnosed to be faulty.

TURN SIGNAL/HAZARD FLASHER

The turn signal and hazard flasher is located on the left side of the steering column bracket

CONVENIENCE CENTER

The convenience center is a stationary unit. It is located on the right side of the heater or air conditioning module in the vehicle under the instrument panel. This location provides easy access to the audio alarm, hazard warnings, the horn relay and the seatbelt key and headlamp warning alarm. All units are serviced by plug-in replacements.

Speed Control

Refer to "Chilton's Chassis Electronics Service Manual" for additional coverage.

SERVO CABLE

Adjustment
2.5L ENGINE

1. Be sure that the cruise control cable is attached to the engine bracket. Insert the cable snug in the cruise pulley slot.
2. Insert the cable in the servo bracket. Pull the servo assembly end of the cable toward the servo without moving the idler pulley.
3. If 1 of the 6 holes in the servo assembly lines up with the cable pin, push the pin through the hole and connect the pin to the tab with the retainer.
4. If the tab hole does not line up with the pin, move the cable away from the servo assembly until the next closest tab hole lines up. Connect the pin to the tab using the retainer.

SYSTEM CHECK TABLE

	Action	Correct Result
1	Drive car faster than 25 mph. Turn Cruise switch ON. Depress Set button at the end of the Multi-function lever	Car should maintain speed
2	Hold Set button in and take foot off accelerator	Car should coast to slower speed
3	Release Set Button	Cruise Control should engage and hold a slower speed, if the new speed remains above 25 mph
4	Slide Cruise switch to R/A and hold it there	Car should accelerate
5	Release Cruise switch back to ON	Car should hold new faster speed
6	Tap brake pedal	Car should coast slower (Cruise disengages)
7	Slide Cruise switch momentarily to R/A	Car should accelerate to former Set speed
8	While cruising, accelerate, then remove foot from accelerator	Car should coast back to set speed
9	While cruising, tap Cruise switch to R/A	Car should increase 1 mph for each tap, up to ten taps, then system may have to be reset to a new speed
10	While cruising, tap Set button	Car should decrease by 1 mph for each tap, until 25 mph is reached when Cruise Control will not operate
11	Slide Cruise switch to OFF	Cruise Control turns off

NOTE: Do not stretch the cable so as to make a particular tab hole connect to the pin. This could prevent the engine from returning to idle.

2.8L ENGINE

1. With the cable assembly installed in the bracket, install the cable assembly end on to the stud of the accelerator control lever.
2. Pull the servo assembly end of the cable toward the servo without moving the lever.
3. If 1 of the 6 holes in the servo assembly tab lines up with the cable pin, connect the pin to the tab with the retainer.
4. If the tab hole does not line up with the pin, move the cable away from the servo assembly until the next closest tab hole lines up. Connect the pin to the tab using the retainer.

NOTE: Do not stretch the cable so as to make a particular tab hole connect to the pin. This could prevent the engine from returning to idle.

COOLING AND HEATING SYSTEMS

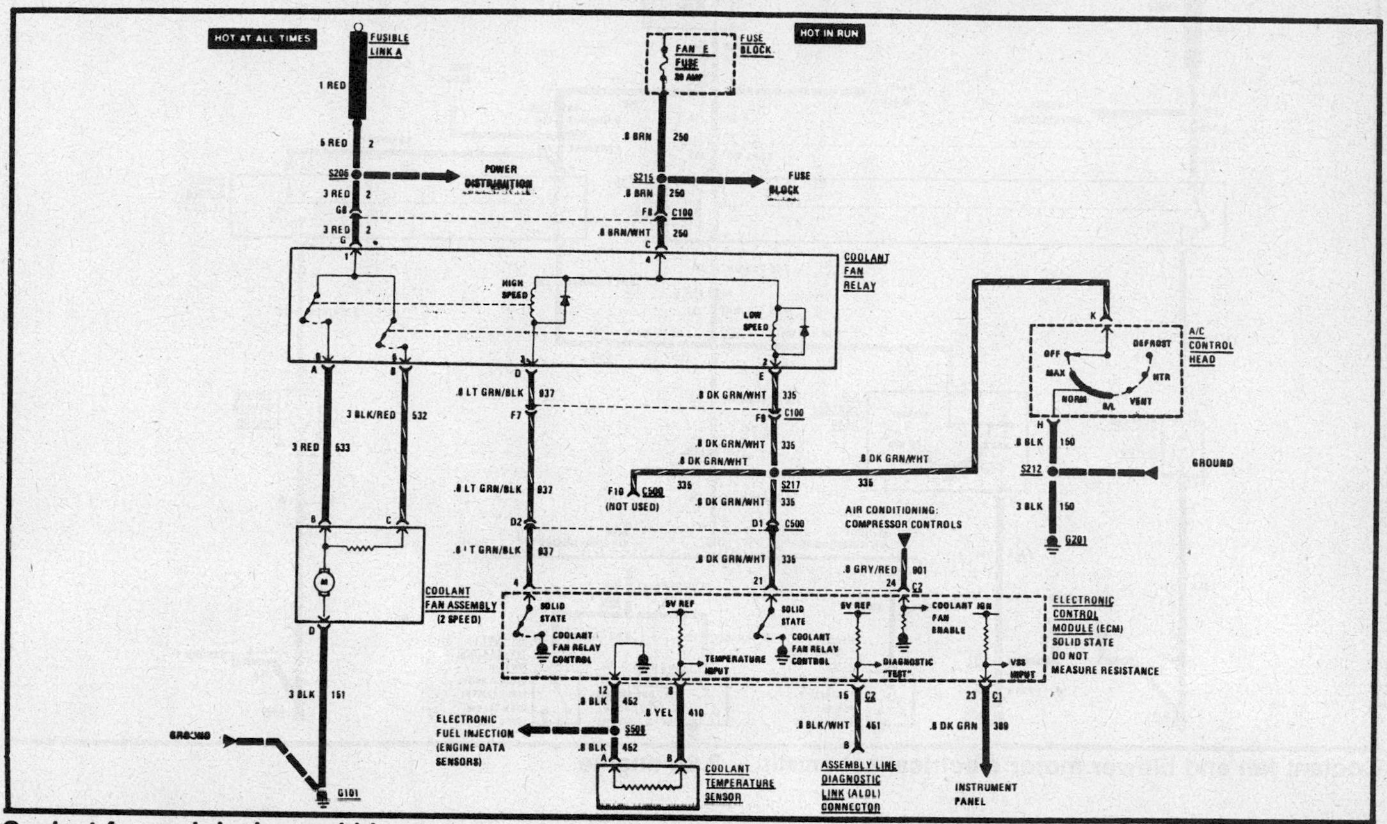

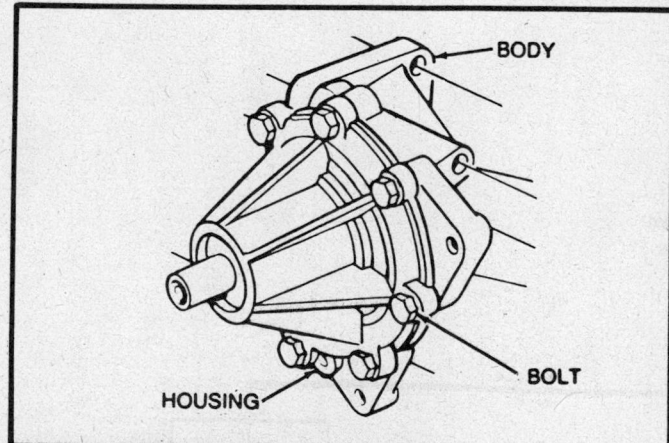

Coolant fan and dual speed blower motor electrical schematic—2.5L engine

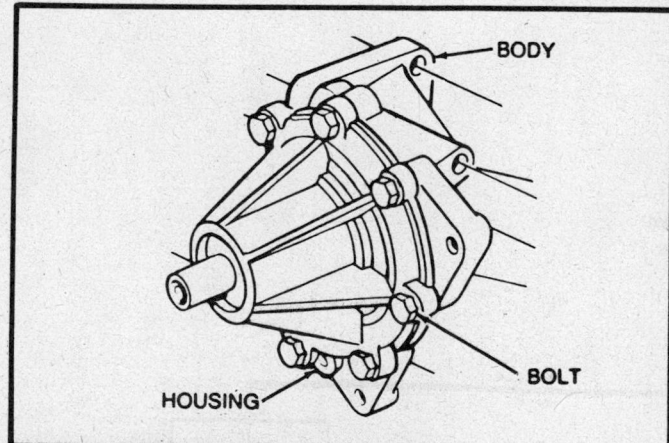

Water pump assembly—2.5L engine

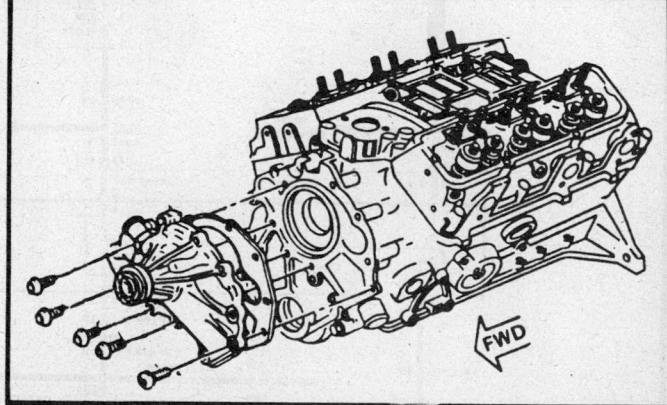

Water pump assembly—2.8L engine

Water Pump

Removal and Installation

2.5L ENGINE

1. Disconnect battery negative cable. Drain the engine coolant.

2. Remove accessory drive belts. Remove all components in order to gain access to the water pump retaining bolts.

3. Remove the water pump attaching bolts and remove the pump.

4. If installing a new water pump, transfer the pulley from the old unit. With sealing surfaces cleaned, place a ⅛ in. bead of RTV gasket sealant or an equivalent, on the water pump sealing surface. While sealer is still wet, install pump and torque bolts to 6 ft. lbs. Be sure to coat the bolts with RTV sealant in order to prevent coolant leakage.

5. Install accessory drive belts.

6. Connect battery negative cable.

2.8L ENGINE

1. Disconnect the negative battery cable. Drain the engine coolant.

2. Remove the fan shroud and the drive belts. Remove all the

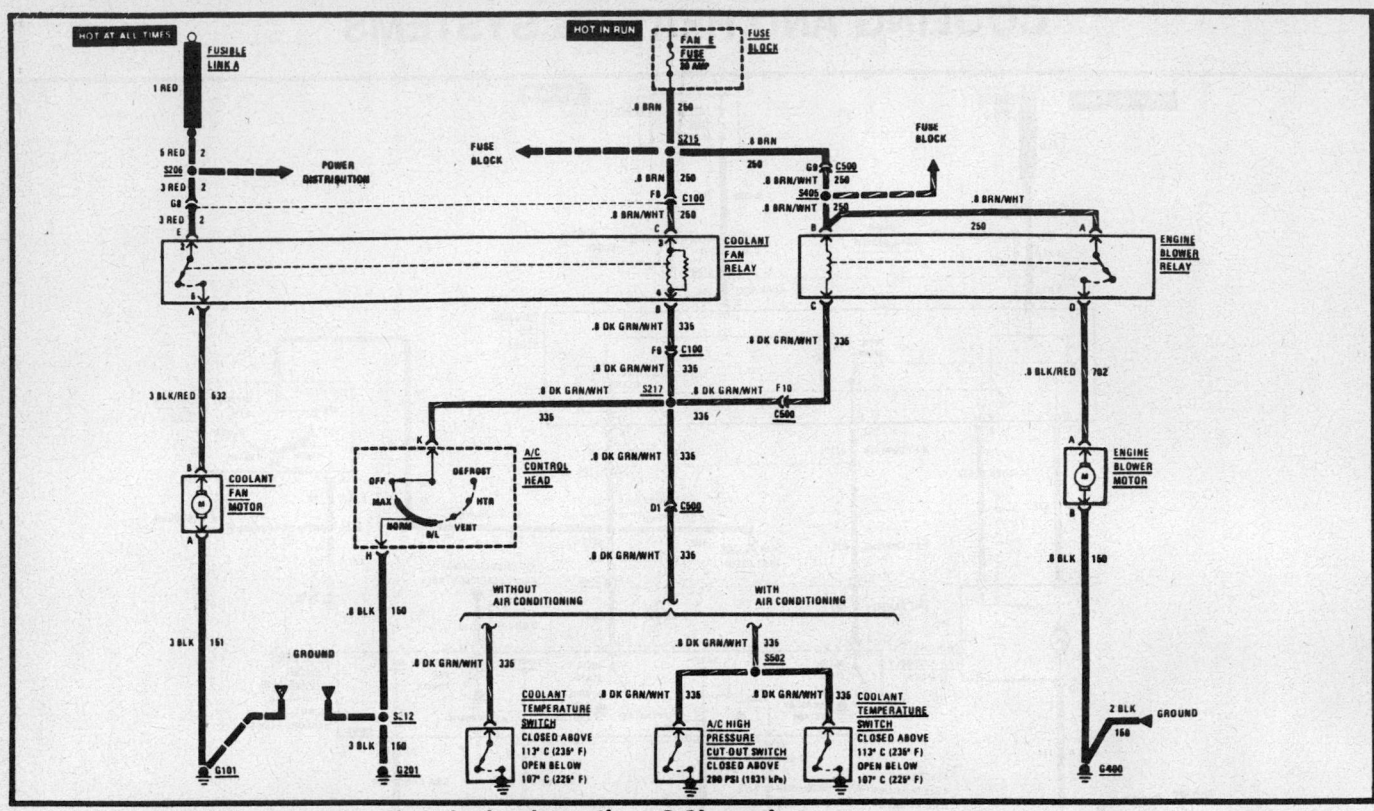

Coolant fan and blower motor electrical schematic— 2.8L engine

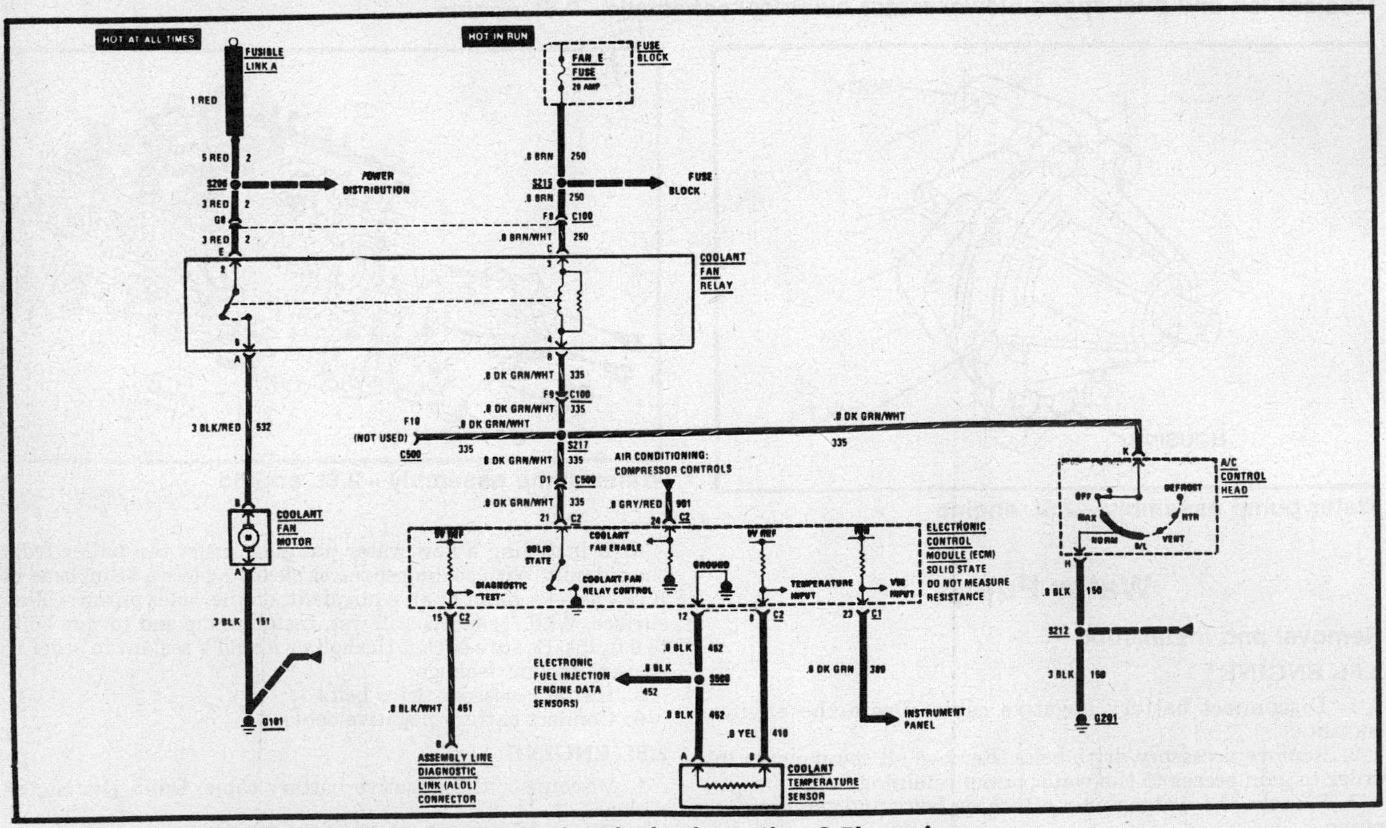

Coolant fan and single speed blower motor electrical schematic—2.5L engine

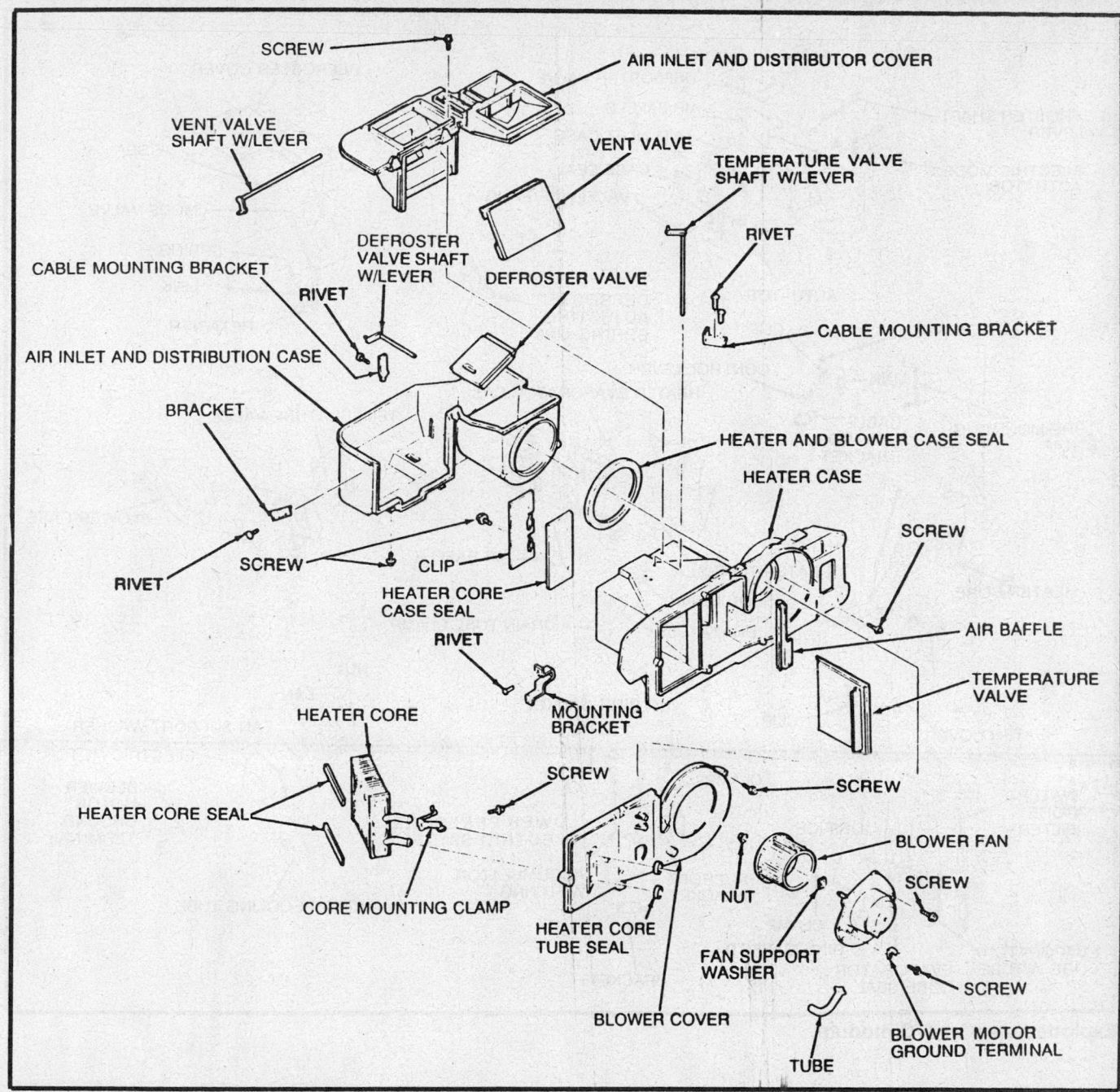

SCREW — AIR INLET AND DISTRIBUTOR COVER

VENT VALVE SHAFT W/LEVER

VENT VALVE

TEMPERATURE VALVE SHAFT W/LEVER

RIVET

CABLE MOUNTING BRACKET

CABLE MOUNTING BRACKET

DEFROSTER VALVE SHAFT W/LEVER

DEFROSTER VALVE

RIVET

AIR INLET AND DISTRIBUTION CASE

HEATER AND BLOWER CASE SEAL

HEATER CASE

BRACKET

SCREW

RIVET

SCREW — CLIP

HEATER CORE CASE SEAL

AIR BAFFLE

TEMPERATURE VALVE

RIVET

MOUNTING BRACKET

HEATER CORE

SCREW

SCREW

HEATER CORE SEAL

BLOWER FAN

SCREW

NUT

CORE MOUNTING CLAMP

HEATER CORE TUBE SEAL

FAN SUPPORT WASHER

SCREW

BLOWER COVER

TUBE

BLOWER MOTOR GROUND TERMINAL

Exploded view of heater module

necessary components in order to gain access to the water pump retaining bolts.

3. Remove the radiator hoses and the heater hose running to the water pump.

4. Remove the bolts attaching the water pump to the engine block and remove the water pump and gasket.

5. Installation is the reverse order of the removal procedure, be sure to apply a thin bead of RTV sealant or an equivalent, to the water pump mounting surface and the water pump bolts. Torque the bolts to 6–9 ft. lbs. Do not over torque the water pump bolts, because the pump is aluminum and will crack very easily.

Electric Cooling Fan

SYSTEM OPERATION

The fan motor is activated by a coolant temperature fan switch. If the vehicle is equipped with A/C, a second switch can activate the circuit, depending upon A/C compressor head pressure to the condenser. The coolant temperature fan switch regulates voltage to the coolant fan relay, which operates the fan whenever the coolant temperature exceeds 230°F (110°C).

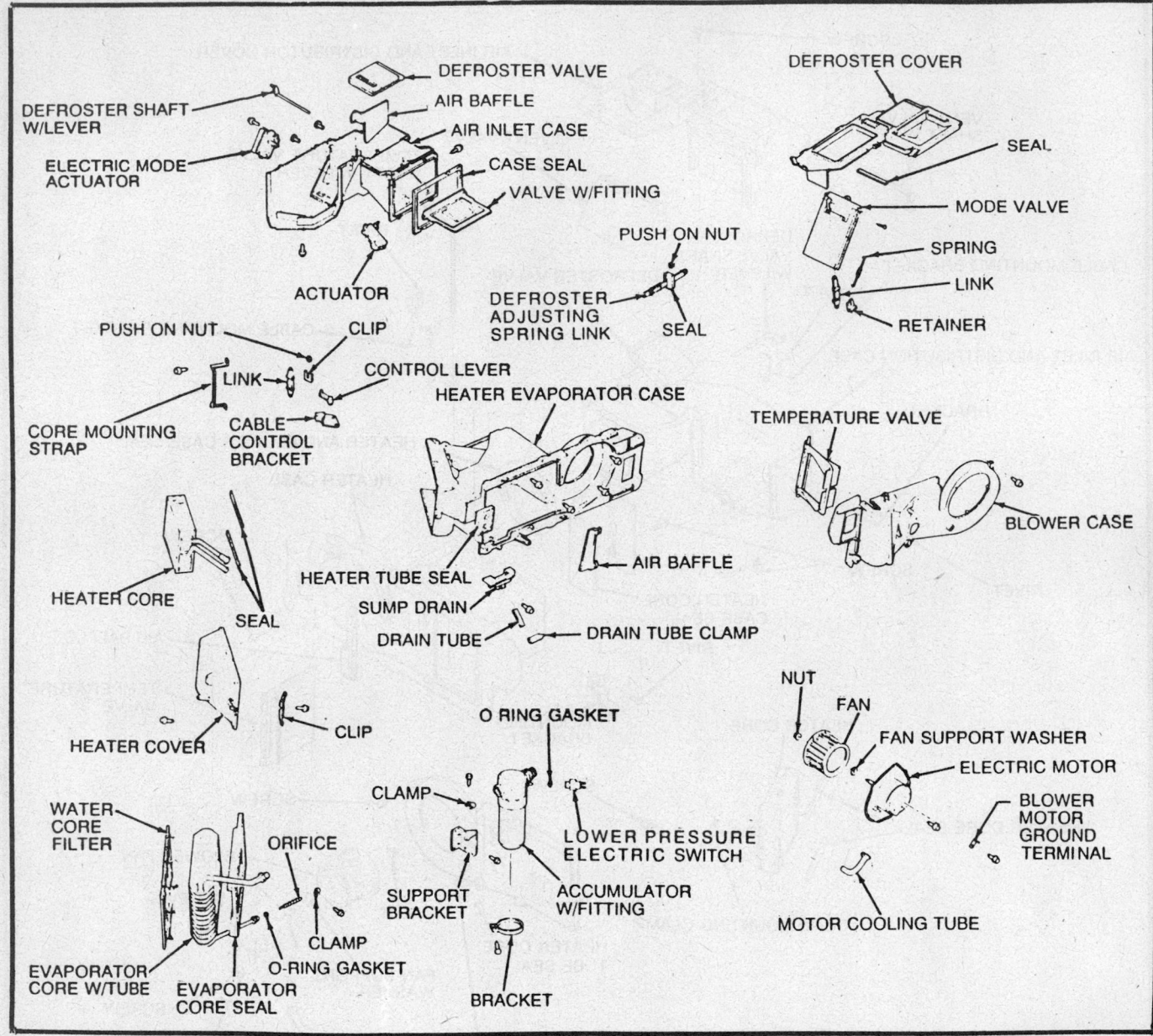

Exploded view of A/C module

Removal and Installation

1. Disconnect the negative battery cable.
2. Disconnect the harness from the fan motor and the fan frame.
3. Remove the fan frame to radiator support attaching bolts.
4. Remove the fan and frame assembly.
5. Installation is the reverse order of the removal procedure.

Testing

1. With the engine cold and idling, move the A/C Function selector to the **NORM** position. The coolant fan and engine blower will turn on.
2. With the engine coolant below operating temperature, move the A/C function selector to the **OFF** position. The coolant fan and engine blower will turn off.
3. With the engine warm, run the engine at a fast idle for sev-

eral minutes. The coolant fan and the engine blower will turn on before the coolant temperature indicator on the instrument panel comes on.

Thermostat

Removal and Installation

1. Disconnect the negative battery cable. As required, drain the coolant. Remove the thermostat cap.
2. Grasp the thermostat handle and gently pull up.
3. Before installing, clean the thermostat housing and O-ring. Apply a suitable lubricant to the O-ring for easier installation.
4. Push the thermostat down into the housing until it is properly seated and install the cap.

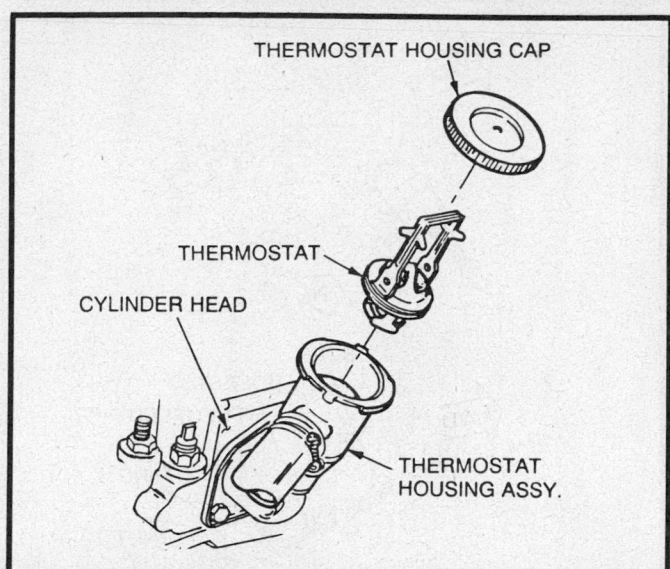

Thermostat and housing

Heater Blower Motor

Removal and Installation

1. Disconnect the negative battery cable.
2. Remove the cooling tube.
3. Disconnect all electrical connections.
4. Remove the heater motor retaining screws. Remove the heater motor from its mounting.
5. Installation is the reverse order of the removal procedure.

Heater Core

Refer to "Chilton's Auto Heating and Air Conditioning Manual" for additional coverage.

Removal and Installation

WITH AIR CONDICTIONING

1. Disconnect the negative battery cable. Drain the cooling system. Disconnect and plug the heater hoses at the heater.
2. Remove the speaker grille and the speaker.
3. Remove the heater core cover retainers and the heater core.
4. Installation is the reverse order of the removal procedure.
5. Refill the cooling system as required.

WITHOUT AIR CONDICTIONING

1. Disconnect the negative battery cable.
2. Disconnect the following wire connections, heater relay, heater blower resistor, heater blower switch, heater ground connection and forward courtesy lamp socket.
3. Remove the windshield washer fluid container.
4. Drain the radiator. Disconnect the heater core inlet and outlet hoses.
5. Remove the heater core grommets.
6. Remove the heater case cover.
7. Remove the heater core retainer and remove the heater core.
8. Installation is the reverse order of the removal procedure.
9. Refill the cooling system as required.

Temperature Control Assembly and Blower Switch

Removal and Installation

1. Disconnect the negative battery cable.
2. Remove the front pad and trim plate assembly.
3. Remove the 3 controller retaining screws.
4. Disconnect the electrical connection at the switch and remove the blower switch from the controller.
5. Installation is the reverse order of the removal procedure.

FUEL INJECTION SYSTEM

Refer to "Chilton's Electronic Engine Control Manual" for additional coverage.

Description

TBI SYTEM

This system, is used on the 2.5L engine and has a single fuel injector mounted above a throttle body assembly. The entire assembly is mounted to the intake manifold. This type of system is referred to as Throttle Body Injection (TBI).

MPI SYSTEM

This system, is used on the 2.8L engine and has a fuel injector in the intake manifold near the intake valve for each cylinder. It is commonly referred to as Port Fuel Injection (PFI).

IDLE SPEED

Idle speed is controlled by the ECM and therefore not adjustable.

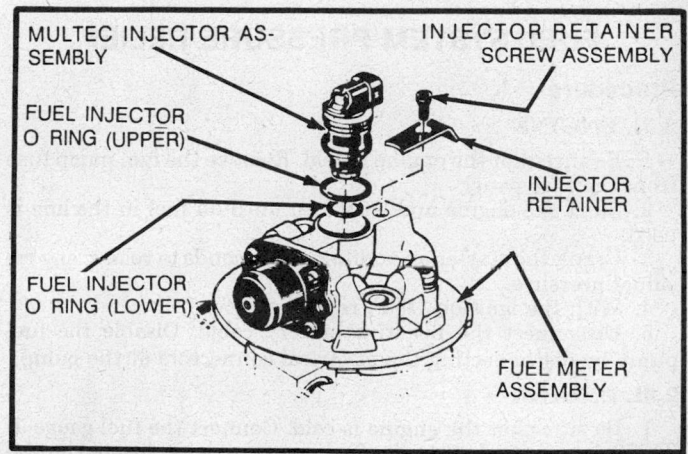

Throttle body injection system—2.5L engine

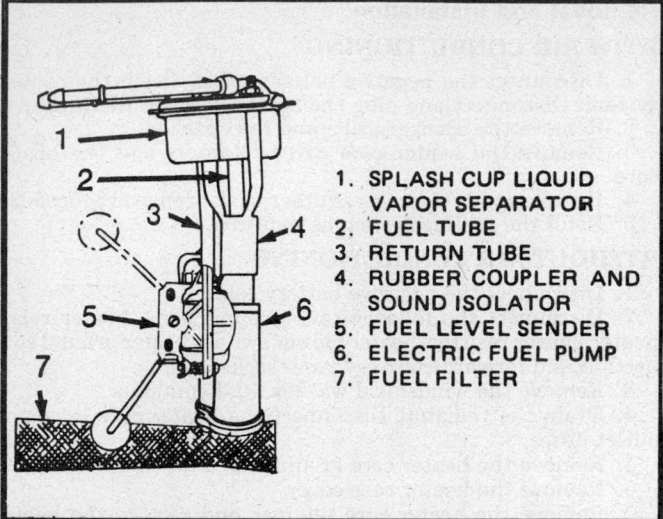

1. SPLASH CUP LIQUID VAPOR SEPARATOR
2. FUEL TUBE
3. RETURN TUBE
4. RUBBER COUPLER AND SOUND ISOLATOR
5. FUEL LEVEL SENDER
6. ELECTRIC FUEL PUMP
7. FUEL FILTER

Typical electric fuel pump and sending unit

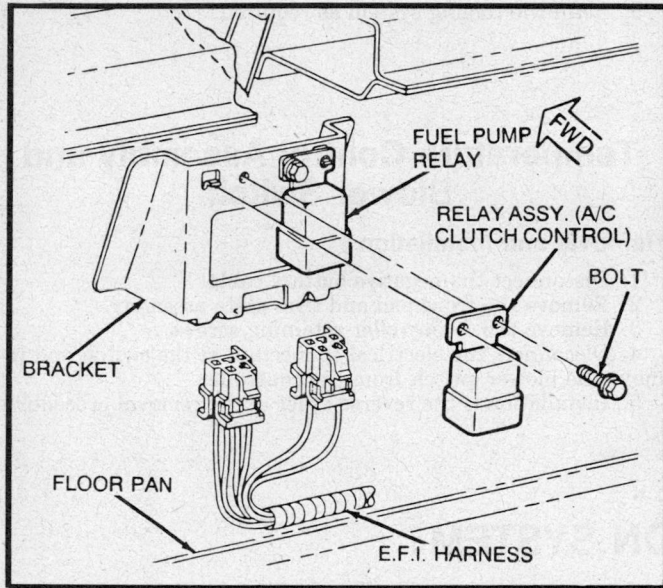

Fuel pump relay location

FUEL SYSTEM PRESSURE RELIEF

Procedure

2.5L ENGINE

1. Be sure that the engine is cold. Remove the fuel pump fuse from the fuse panel.
2. Start the engine and let it run until all fuel in the line is used.
3. Crank the starter an additional 3 seconds to relieve any residual pressure.
4. With the ignition **OFF**, replace the fuse.
5. Disconnect the negative battery cable. Disable the fuel pump by disconnecting the electrical connectors at the pump.

2.8L ENGINE

1. Be sure that the engine is cold. Connect the fuel gauge J-34730-1 or equivalent to the fuel pressure valve, located on the fuel rail.

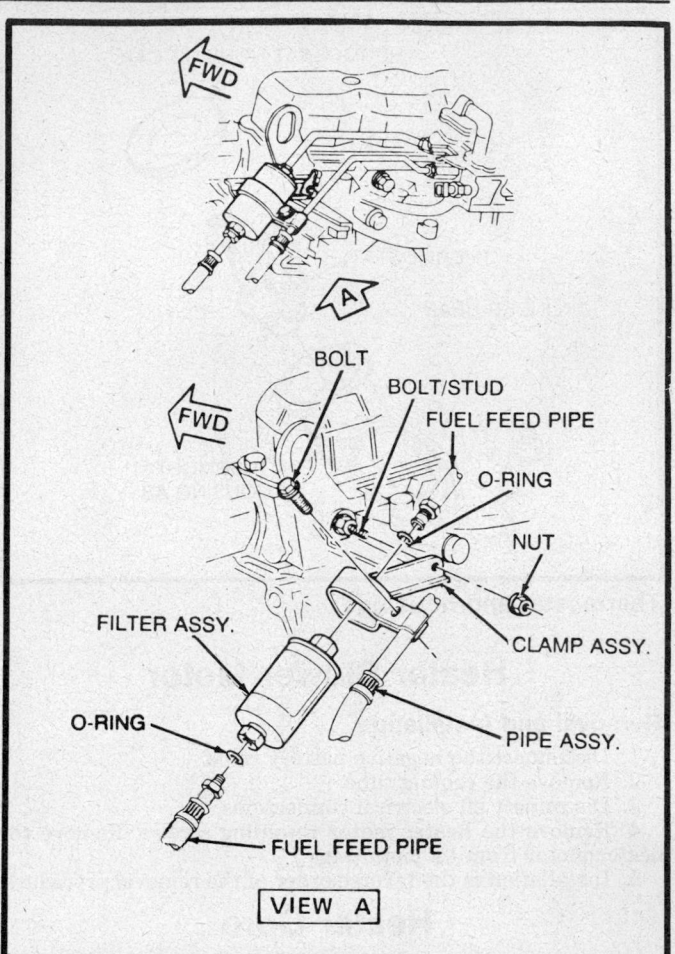

Fuel filter and related components

2. Wrap a shop towel around the fitting while connecting the gauge to avoid any spillage.
3. Install the bleed hose into a suitable container and open the valve to bleed off the fuel pressure.
4. Disconnect the negative battery cable. Disable the fuel pump by disconnecting the electrical connectors at the pump.

Electric Fuel Pump

Removal and Installation

1. Relieve the fuel system pressure. Disconnect the negative battery cable.
2. Drain the fuel tank. Raise and support the vehicle safely.
3. Disconnect the wiring from the tank.
4. Remove the ground wire retaining screw from under the body.
5. Disconnect all hoses from the tank.
6. Properly support the tank and remove the retaining strap nuts.
7. Remove the fuel tank from the vehicle.
8. Remove the fuel gauge/pump retaining ring using spanner wrench tool J-24187 or equivalent.
9. Remove the gauge unit and the pump.
10. Installation is the reverse of removal. Always replace the O-ring under the gauge/pump retaining ring.

TIMING SENSORS

DIS REFERENCE—CKT 430

The crankshaft sensor generates a signal to the ignition module

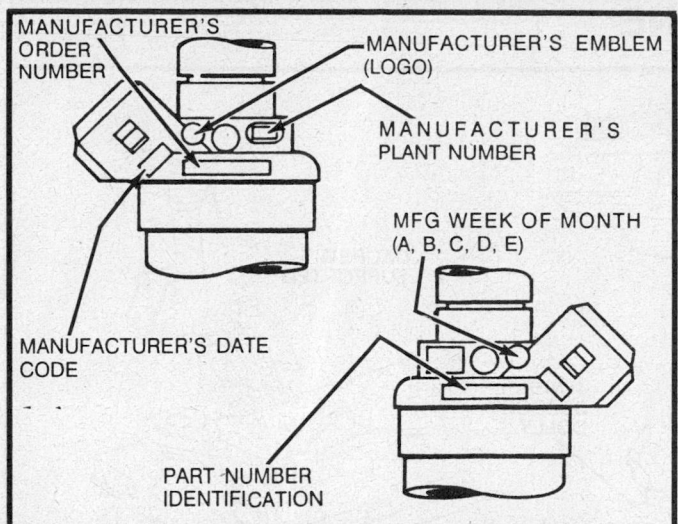

Part information—multi port fuel injection system

which results in a reference pulse being sent to the ECM. The ECM uses this signal to calculate crankshaft position, engine speed and injector pulse width.

REFERENCE GROUND—CKT 453

This wire is grounded through the module and insures that the ground circuit has no voltage drop between the ignition module and the ECM, which could affect performance.

BYPASS—CKT 424

At about 400 rpm, the ECM applies 5 volts to this circuit to switch spark timing control from the DIS module to the ECM. An open or grounded bypass circuit will set a Code 42 and result in the engine operating in a back-up ignition timing mode (module timing) at a calculated timing value. This may cause poor performance and reduced fuel economy.

FUEL INJECTOR

Removal and Installation

2.5L ENGINE

NOTE: Use care in removing the injector in order to prevent damage to the electrical connector on top of the injector and nozzle. Also, because the fuel injector is an electrical component, it should not be immersed in any type of liquid solvent or cleaner, as damage may occur. The fuel injector is serviced only as a complete assembly.

1. Relieve the fuel system pressure. Disconnect the negative battery cable. Remove the air cleaner assembly.
2. Disconnect the electrical connector to the fuel injector. Remove the injector retainer screw and the retainer.
3. Using a fulcrum, place a flat blade tool under the ridge opposite the connector end and carefully pry the injector out.
4. Remove the upper and lower O-rings from the injector and in fuel injector cavity and discard.
5. Inspect the fuel injector filter for evidence of dirt and contamination. If present, check for presence of dirt in the fuel lines and the fuel tank.

NOTE: Be sure to replace the injector with an identical part. Other injectors will fit, but are calibrated for different flow rates.

To Install:

6. Lubricate the new upper and lower O-rings with automatic transmission fluid and place them on injector. (Make sure the upper O-ring is in the groove and the lower 1 is flush up against filter.)
7. Install the injector assembly, pushing it straight into fuel injector cavity.
8. Install the injector retainer and attaching screw, using an appropriate thread locking compound.
9. Reconnect the electrical connector to the fuel injector. Torque the injector retainer attaching screw to 27 inch lbs.
10. Be sure the electrical connector end on the injector is facing in the general direction of the cut-out in the fuel meter body to accommodate the wire grommet.

2.8L ENGINE

NOTE: Use care in removing the injectors to prevent damage to the electrical connector pins on the injector and the nozzle. The fuel injector is serviced as a complete assembly. Since it is an electrical component, it should not be immersed in any type of cleaner. Support the fuel rail to avoid damaging other components while removing the injector. Also, to prevent dirt from entering the engine, the area around the injectors should be clean before servicing.

1. Relieve the fuel system pressure. Disconnect the negative battery cable. As required, remove the air cleaner assembly. Remove the plenum and fuel rail assembly.
2. Rotate the injector retainer clip to the release position.
3. Remove the fuel injector.
4. Remove the injector O-ring seals from both ends of injector and discard.

NOTE: When ordering new fuel injectors, be sure to check part number information.

To Install:

5. Lubricate the new injector O-ring seals with engine oil and install on the injector.
6. Secure the retainer clip onto the injector.
7. Install the injectors to the fuel rail and pressure regulator assembly.
8. Rotate the injector retainer clip to locking position.
9. Install the plenum and fuel rail assembly.

EMISSION CONTROL SYSTEMS

Refer to "Chilton's Emission Diagnosis and Service Manual" for additional coverage.

EMISSION EQUIPMENT USED

Electronic Control Module
Throttle Body Injection
Evaporative Emission Control System (EEEC)
Electronic Spark Timing Control System (EST)

Exhaust Gas Recirculation System (EGR)
Transaxle Converter Clutch (TCC)
Positive Crankcase Ventilation (PCV)
Thermostatic Air Cleaner (TAC)

ENGINE

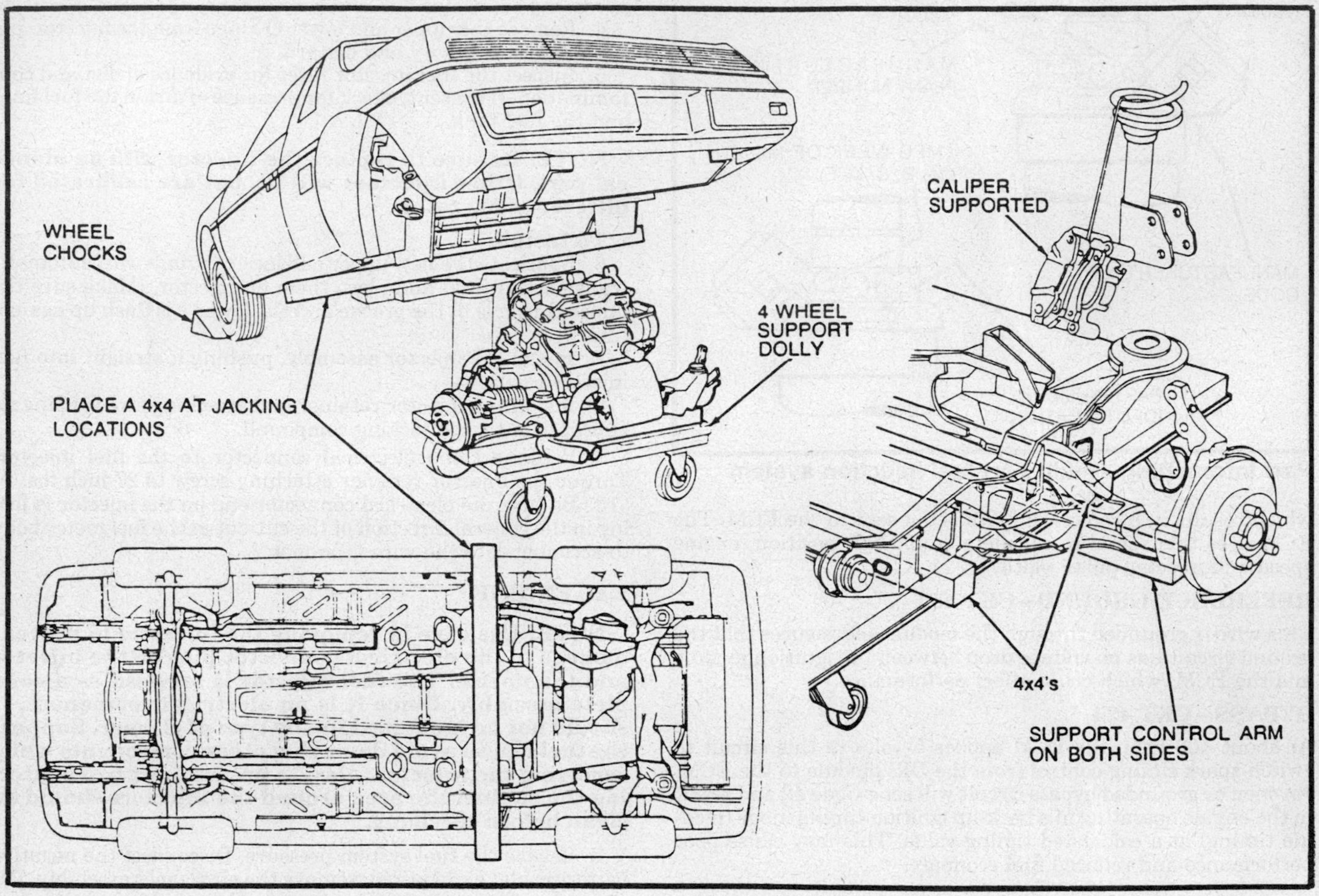

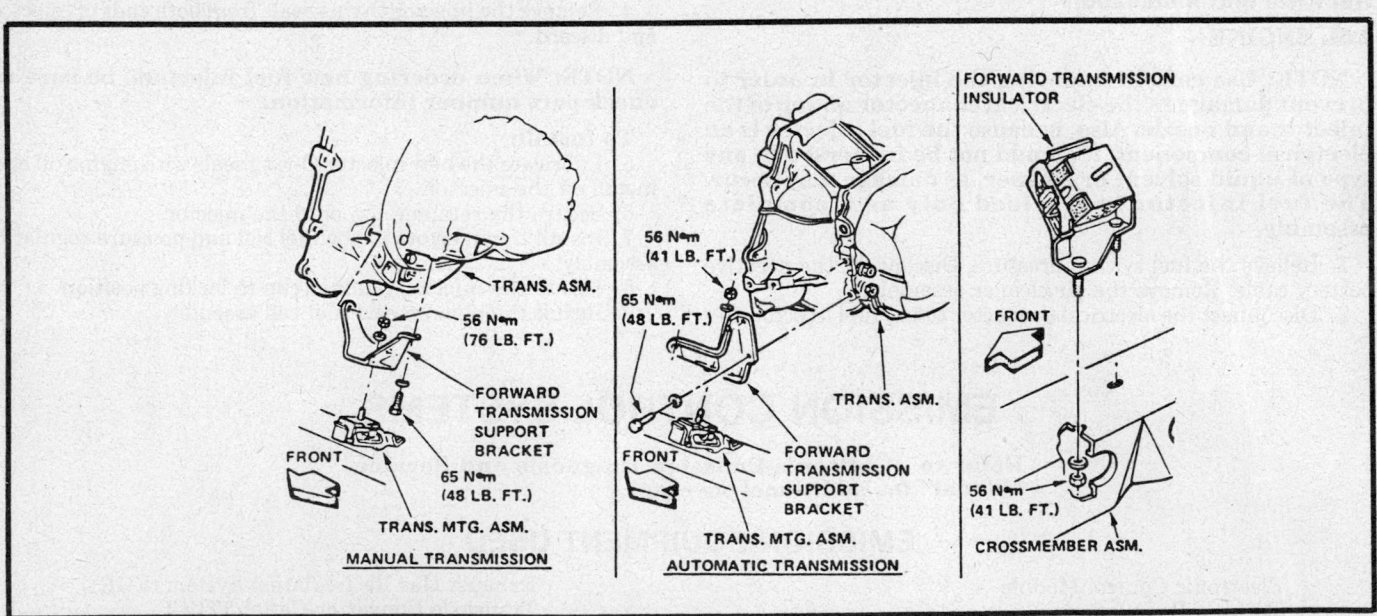

Engine removal and cradle support points

WHEEL CHOCKS

PLACE A 4x4 AT JACKING LOCATIONS

CALIPER SUPPORTED

4 WHEEL SUPPORT DOLLY

4x4's

SUPPORT CONTROL ARM ON BOTH SIDES

TRANS. ASM.

56 N•m (76 LB. FT.)

FORWARD TRANSMISSION SUPPORT BRACKET

65 N•m (48 LB. FT.)

FRONT

TRANS. MTG. ASM.

MANUAL TRANSMISSION

56 N•m (41 LB. FT.)

65 N•m (48 LB. FT.)

TRANS. ASM.

FORWARD TRANSMISSION SUPPORT BRACKET

FRONT

TRANS. MTG. ASM.

AUTOMATIC TRANSMISSION

FORWARD TRANSMISSION INSULATOR

FRONT

56 N•m (41 LB. FT.)

CROSSMEMBER ASM.

Forward transaxle mount and mounting brackets

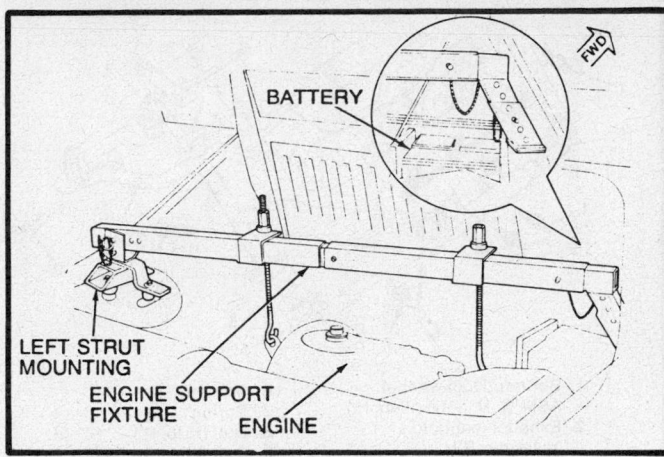

Engine holding fixture mounting

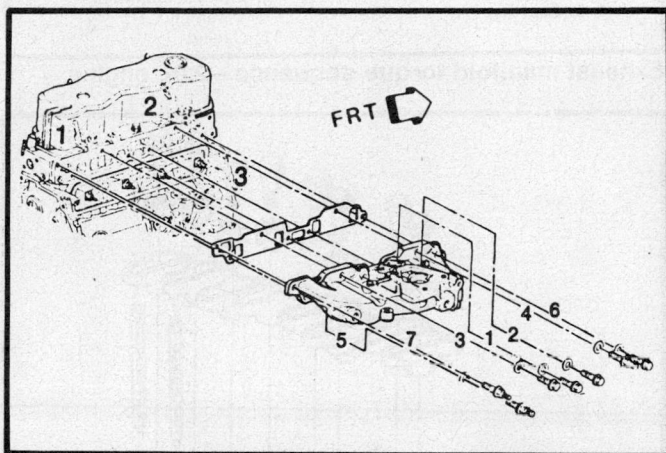

Intake manifold torque sequence—2.5L engine

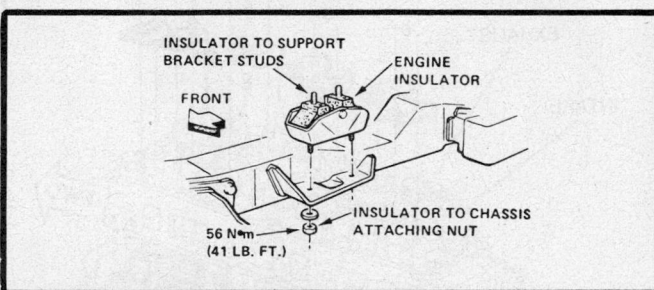

Engine mount to crossmember

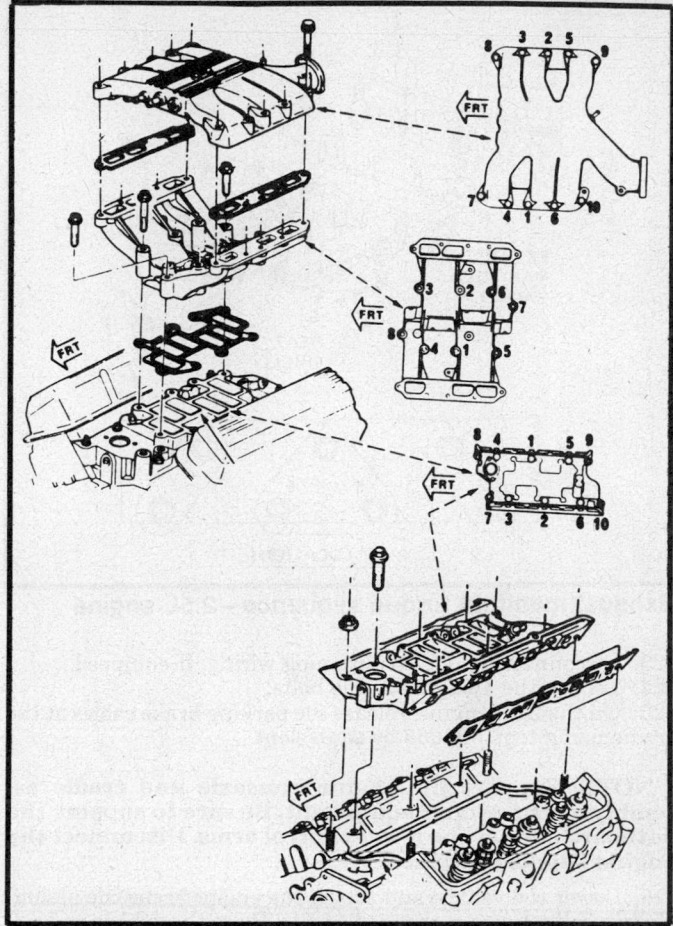

Intake manifold torque sequence—2.8L engine

NOTE: **Disconnecting the negative battery cable on some vehicles may interfere with the functions of the on board computer systems and may require the computer to undergo a relearning process, once the negative battery cable is reconnected.**

Engine Assembly

Removal and Installation

NOTE: **The engine assembly is removed from underneath the vehicle.**

1. Disconnect the negative battery cable.
2. Drain the engine coolant.
3. Remove the rear compartment lid and also the side panels. Do not remove the torsion rod retaining bolts.

4. Remove the air cleaner assembly.
5. Disconnect the throttle and shift cables.
6. Disconnect the heater hose at the intake manifold.
7. Disconnect the vacuum hoses from all non-engine components.
8. Properly relieve the fuel system pressure. Disconnect the fuel lines and filter.
9. Disconnect the fuel pump relay and the oxygen sensor.
10. On vehicles equipped with automatic transaxle, disconnect the transaxle cooler lines.
11. Disconnect the slave cylinder from the manual transaxle equipped vehicles.
12. Disconnect the engine to chassis ground strap.
13. If equipped with airconditioning, properly discharge the system. Disconnect and plug the refrigerant lines at the compressor and seal the end.
14. Remove the rear console.
15. Remove the ECM harness through the bulkhead panel.
16. Install an engine support fixture.
17. Remove the engine strut bracket and mark the bolt and bracket for reassembly.
18. Raise and support the vehicle safely.
19. Remove the rear wheels.
20. On vehicles equipped with an automatic transaxle, remove the torque converter bolts.
21. Remove the parking brake cable and calipers. Do not disconnect the brake hoses. Support the caliper out of the way.
22. Remove the strut bolts and mark the struts for realignment.

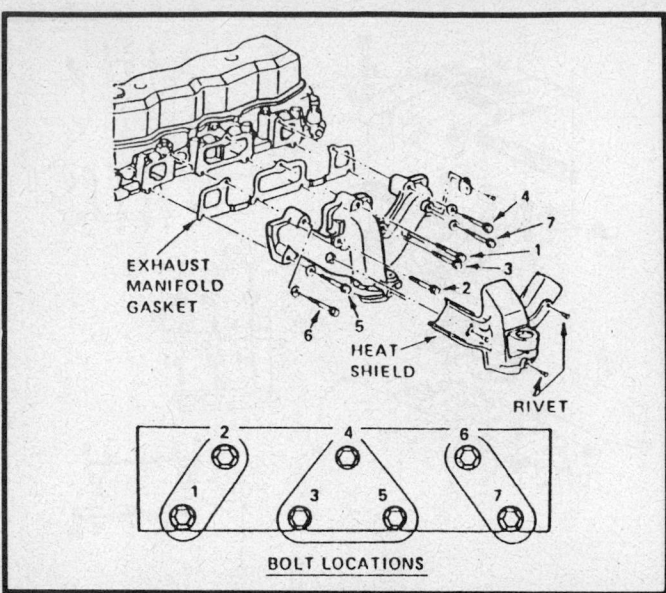

Exhaust manifold torque sequence – 2.5L engine

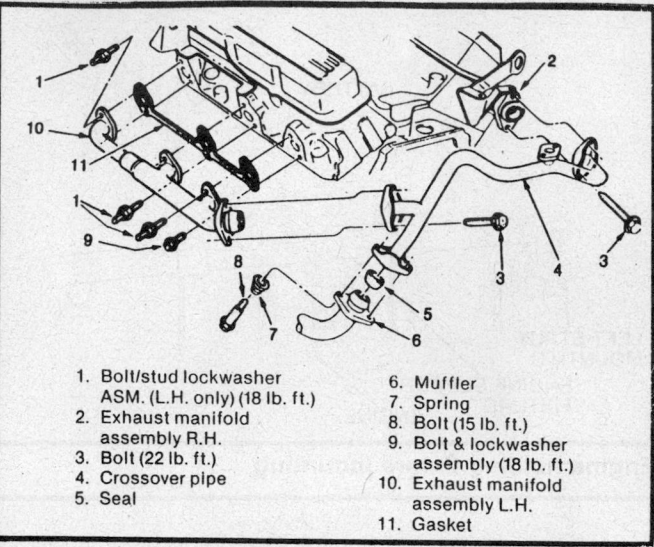

1. Bolt/stud lockwasher ASM. (L.H. only) (18 lb. ft.)
2. Exhaust manifold assembly R.H.
3. Bolt (22 lb. ft.)
4. Crossover pipe
5. Seal
6. Muffler
7. Spring
8. Bolt (15 lb. ft.)
9. Bolt & lockwasher assembly (18 lb. ft.)
10. Exhaust manifold assembly L.H.
11. Gasket

Exhaust manifold torque sequence – 2.8L engine

23. Disconnect the air conditioning wiring, if equipped.
24. Loosen the 4 engine cradle bolts.
25. On the 2.5L engine, release the parking brake cables at the cradle using tool J-34065 or equivalent.

NOTE: Support the engine/transaxle and cradle assembly on the proper equipment. Be sure to support the outboard ends of the lower control arms. Disconnect the engine support fixture.

26. Lower the vehicle and attach the engine/transaxle assembly to a dolly. Remove the cradle bolts. Raise the vehicle and roll the dolly from under the vehicle.
27. Separate the engine and transaxle.
28. Installation is the reverse of removal.

Engine Mounts

Removal and Installation

1. Disconnect the negative battery cable. Support engine using and engine support tool.
2. Remove the bolt for the forward torque reaction rod.
3. Raise the vehicle and support it safely.
4. Remove the engine mount to chassis nuts.
5. Remove the upper engine mount to support bracket nuts.
6. Remove the mount.
7. Installation is the reverse order of the removal procedure.
8. Torque engine mount to specification.
9. Torque engine mount to support bracket to specification.

Intake Manifold

Removal and Installation

2.5L ENGINE

1. Relieve the fuel pump pressure. Disconnect the negative battery cable. Remove the air cleaner assembly.
2. Remove the PCV valve and hose.
3. Drain the cooling system.
4. Disconnect the fuel lines.
5. Disconnect the vacuum hoses.
6. Disconnect the wiring and the throttle linkage from the throttle body assembly.
7. Disconnect the cruise control and linkage, if equipped.

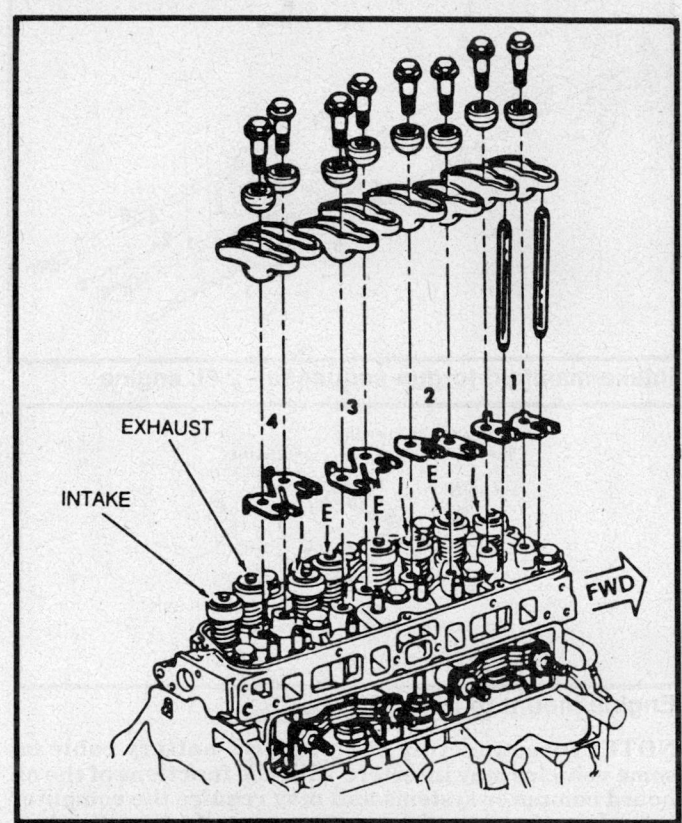

Valve arrangement – 2.5L engine

8. Disconnect the throttle linkage and bell crank and place to the side.
9. Disconnect the heater hose.
10. Remove the generator upper bracket.
11. Remove the ignition coil.
12. Remove the retaining bolts and remove the manifold.
13. Installation is the reverse of removal. Be sure to use new gaskets, as required. Torque all bolts in the proper sequence.

2.8L ENGINE

1. Position the engine at TDC on the compression stroke.

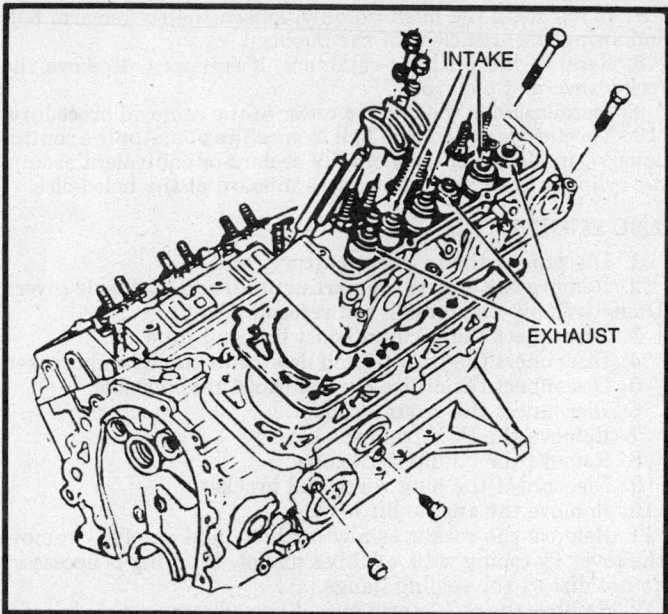

Valve arrangement—2.8L engine

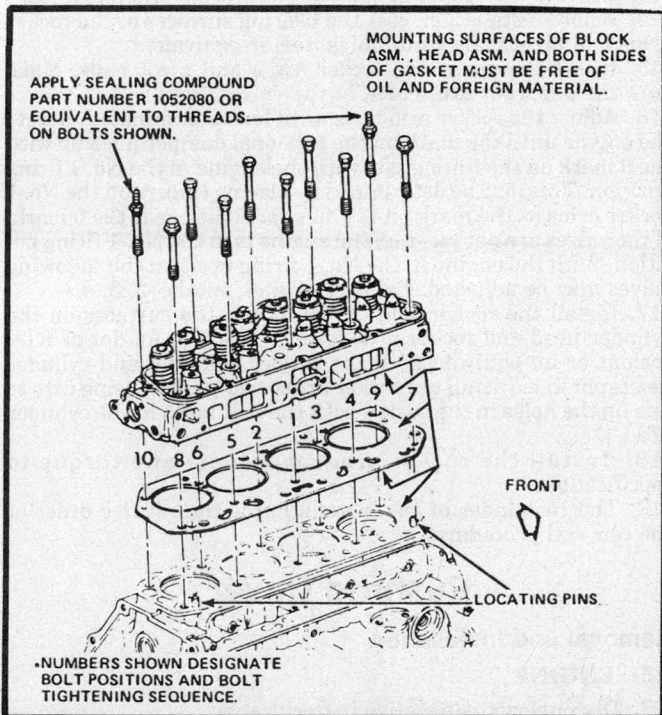

APPLY SEALING COMPOUND PART NUMBER 1052080 OR EQUIVALENT TO THREADS ON BOLTS SHOWN.

MOUNTING SURFACES OF BLOCK ASM., HEAD ASM. AND BOTH SIDES OF GASKET MUST BE FREE OF OIL AND FOREIGN MATERIAL.

FRONT

LOCATING PINS

•NUMBERS SHOWN DESIGNATE BOLT POSITIONS AND BOLT TIGHTENING SEQUENCE.

Cylinder head torque sequence—2.5L engine

Properly relieve the fuel system pressure.

2. Disconnect the negative battery cable. Remove the valve covers.

3. Drain the engine coolant.

4. Disconnect the throttle body to elbow intake hose.

5. Remove the distributor. Disconnect the vacuum booster pipe and bracket.

6. Disconnect the shift and throttle linkage.

7. Remove the throttle body to upper plenum.

8. Disconnect the heater and radiator hoses.

9. Disconnect all wiring harness and vacuum hoses while noting their locations for reassembly.

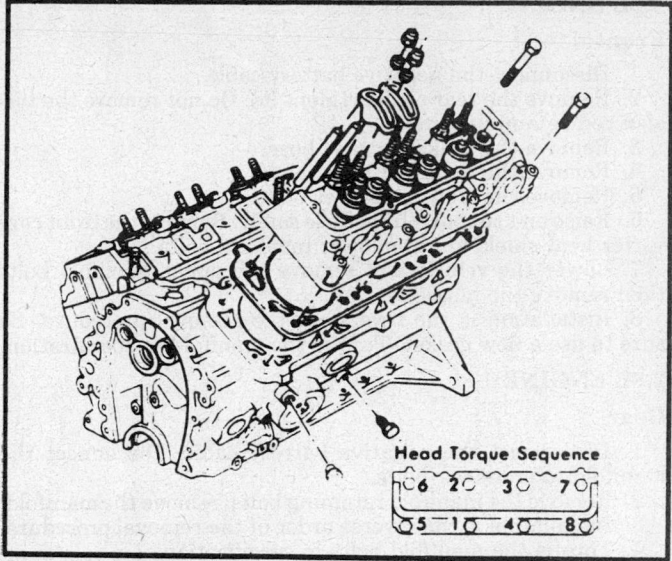

Cylinder head torque sequence—2.8L engine

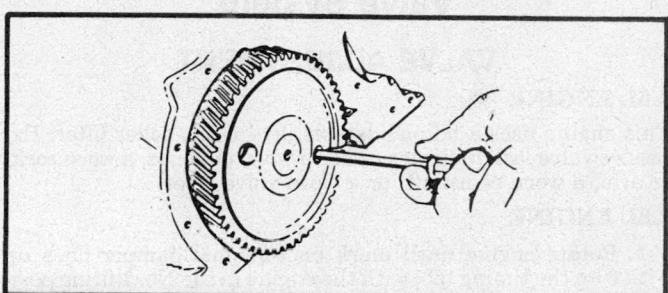

Removing the camshaft thrust screws—2.5L engine

10. Disconnect the EGR pipe.

11. Remove the upper manifold plenum and gaskets.

12. Remove the intermediate intake manifold and gasket.

13. Remove the lower intake manifold and gaskets.

14. Clean all gasket surfaces on the intake manifolds and cylinder head.

15. Install the lower intake manifold and gasket and torque to specification in the proper sequence.

16. Install the intermediate intake manifold and gaskets and torque in sequence to specification.

17. Install the upper manifold plenum and gaskets and torque in sequence.

18. The remainder of the installation is the reverse of the removal. Check engine timing, coolant level and for leaks.

Exhaust Manifold

Removal and Installation

2.5L ENGINE

1. Disconnect the negative battery cable. Remove the air cleaner and the EFI bracket tube.

2. Raise and support the vehicle safely.

3. Remove the exhaust pipe and lower the vehicle. As required, remove the battery side cover.

4. Remove the exhaust manifold retaining bolts. Remove the exhaust manifold and gasket from the engine.

5. Installation is the reverse of removal. Clean the sealing surfaces and use a new gasket. Torque the retaining bolts in sequence.

2.8L ENGINE

Front

1. Disconnect the negative battery cable.
2. Remove the rear compartment lid. Do not remove the torsion rod retaining bolts.
3. Remove the brake vacuum hose.
4. Remove the manifold heat shield.
5. Remove the front crossover bolts.
6. Raise and support the vehicle safely. Remove the front converter heat shield and the lower manifold bolts.
7. Lower the vehicle and remove the upper manifold bolts then remove the manifold.
8. Installation is the reverse of the removal procedure. Be sure to use a new gasket. Torque the manifold to specification.

2.8L ENGINE

Rear

1. Disconnect the negative battery cable. Disconnect the manifold to crossover bolts.
2. Remove the manifold retaining bolts. remove the manifold.
3. Installation is the reverse order of the removal procedure.
4. Torque the manifold bolts to specification.

Valve System

VALVE ADJUSTMENT

2.5L ENGINE

This engine uses a non-adjustable, hydraulic, roller lifter. Excessive valve lash indicates either a worn pushrod, a worn rocker arm, a worn camshaft, or a worn valve lifter.

2.8L ENGINE

1. Rotate engine until mark on torsional damper lines up with **0** on the timing tab, with the engine in the No. 1 firing position. This can be determined by placing fingers on the No. 1 rocker arms as the mark on the damper comes near the **0** mark. If the valves are not moving, the engine is in the No. 1 firing position.
2. With the engine in the No. 1 firing position the following valves may be adjusted: Exhaust–1, 2, 3; Intake–1, 5, 6.
3. Back out the adjusting nut until lash is felt at the pushrod.
4. Turn in adjusting nut until all lash is removed.
5. When all lash has been removed, turn in adjusting nut 1½ additional turns.
6. Crank the engine 1 turn until the timing tab **0** mark and torsional damper mark are again in alignment. This is the No. 4 firing position.
7. With the engine in the No. 4 firing position the following valves may be adjusted: exhaust–4, 5, 6; intake–2, 3, 4.
8. Install rocker arm covers.
9. Start engine, check timing and idle speed, check for oil leaks.

Rocker Arm and Pushrod

Removal and Installation

2.5L ENGINE

1. Disconnect the negative battery cable. Remove the air cleaner.
2. Remove the PCV valve and hose.
3. Disconnect the wires from the spark plugs and clips.
4. Remove the valve cover retaining bolts.
5. Remove the valve cover by tapping lightly with a rubber hammer. Prying on the cover could cause damage to the sealing surfaces.
6. Remove the rocker arm bolt.

7. If replacing the pushrod only, loosen the rocker arm bolt and swing the arm clear of the pushrod.
8. Remove the pushrod retainers, if equipped. Remove the rocker arm and pushrod.
9. Installation is the reverse order of the removal procedure.
10. Torque the rocker arm bolt to specification. Apply a continuous $\frac{3}{16}$ in. diameter bead of RTV sealant or equivalent around the cylinder head sealant surfaces inboard at the bolt holes.

2.8L ENGINE

1. Disconnect the negative battery cable.
2. Remove the engine compartment lid and both side covers. Do not remove the torsion rod retaining bolts.
3. Disconnect the vacuum boost line and tube.
4. Disconnect the throttle and downshift cables and bracket.
5. Disconnect the cruise control cable, if applicable.
6. Disconnect the ground cable.
7. Remove the PCV from the cover.
8. Remove the oil dip stick tube.
9. Disconnect the plug wires and bracket.
10. Remove the engine lift hook.
11. Remove the rocker arm cover bolts and carefully remove the cover by taping with a rubber mallet. If prying is necessary do not distort the sealing flange.
12. Remove the rocker arm nuts. Keep all components in order so that they may be reinstalled in the same location.
13. Remove the rocker arm pivot balls, arms and pushrods.
14. Before installation, coat the bearing surfaces of the rocker arms and pivot balls with Molykote® or equivalent.
15. Insert the pushrods, rocker arms and pivot balls. Make sure the pushrods are seated in the valve lifters.
16. Adjust the rocker arm nuts until lash is eliminated. Rotate the engine until the mark on the torsional damper lines up with the **0** mark on the timing tab, with the engine in the No. 1 firing position. This may be determined by placing fingers on the No. 1 rocker arms as the mark on the damper comes near the 0 mark. If the valves are not moving, the engine is in the No. 1 firing position. With the engine in the No. 1 firing position the following valves may be adjusted, Exhaust–4, 5, 6; Intake–2, 3, 4.
17. Install the rocker arm covers. Clean the surfaces on the cylinder head and rocker arm cover. Place a ⅛ in. dot of RTV sealant or an equivalent, at the intake manifold and cylinder head split line. Install the rocker arm cover gasket, using care to line up the holes in the gasket with the bolt holes in the cylinder head.
18. Install the rocker arm cover bolts and torque to specification.
19. The remainder of the installation is the reverse order of the removal procedure

Pushrod Cover

Removal and Installation

2.5L ENGINE

1. Disconnect the negative battery cable.
2. Remove the intake manifold assembly.
3. Remove the pushrod cover retaining bolts. Remove the pushrod cover.
4. Installation is the reverse of the removal procedure. Be sure to use new gaskets or RTV sealant, as required.

Cylinder Head

Removal and Installation

2.5L ENGINE

1. Relieve the fuel system pressure. Disconnect the negative battery cable. Drain the cooling system.
2. Raise the vehicle and support it safely.

3. Remove the exhaust pipe.

4. Lower the vehicle.

5. Remove the oil level indicator tube.

6. Remove the air cleaner assembly.

7. Disconnect the EFI electrical connections and vacuum hoses.

8. Remove the EGR base plate.

9. Remove the heater hose from the intake manifold.

10. Remove the ignition coil lower mounting bolt and wiring connections.

11. Remove all wiring connections from the intake manifold and cylinder head.

12. Remove the engine strut bolt from the upper support. Remove the power steering pump and position it to the side, as required.

13. Remove the alternator belt. Remove the air conditioning compressor and position to the side, as required.

14. Remove the throttle cables from the intake manifold. Remove the intake manifold.

15. Remove the valve cover, rocker arms and pushrods.

16. Remove the cylinder head bolts and remove the cylinder head.

17. Before installing, clean the gasket surfaces of the head and block.

18. Make sure the retaining bolt threads and the cylinder block threads are clean since dirt could affect bolt torque.

19. Install a new gasket over the dowel pins in the cylinder block. Install the cylinder head into place over the dowel pins.

20. Tighten the cylinder head bolts to specification gradually and in the proper sequence.

21. The remainder of the installation is the reverse order of the removal procedure.

2.8L ENGINE

1. Relieve the fuel system pressure. Disconnect the negative battery cable. Drain the radiator.

2. Remove the intake manifold. Remove the exhaust manifolds, as necessary.

3. If removing the left cylinder head, disconnect the alternator bracket and the oil level indicator tube. If removing the right cylinder head, disconnect the cruise control servo bracket.

4. Remove the valve covers. Remove the pushrods.

5. Remove the cylinder head retaining bolts. Remove the cylinder head from the engine.

6. Before installing, clean the gasket surfaces on the head, cylinder head and intake manifold.

7. Place the gasket in position over the dowel pins with the note **THIS SIDE UP** showing.

8. Place the cylinder head into position. Coat the cylinder head bolts threads with a sealer and install the bolts. Tighten the bolts to specification and in the proper sequence.

9. Install the pushrods and loosely retain with the rocker arms. Make sure the lower ends of the pushrods are in the lifter seals then adjust the valves.

10. The remainder of the installation is the reverse of the removal.

Camshaft

Removal and Installation

2.5L ENGINE

1. Disconnect the negative battery cable. Remove the engine from the vehicle and position it in a suitable holding fixture.

2. Remove the valve cover. Remove the pushrods.

3. Remove the distributor and fuel pump.

4. Remove the pushrod cover, and valve lifters.

5. Remove the alternator, lower alternator bracket and front engine mount bracket assembly.

6. Remove the oil pump driveshaft and gear assembly. Remove the front pulley hub and timing gear cover.

7. Remove the 2 camshaft thrust plate screws by working through holes in the camshaft gear.

8. Remove the camshaft and gear assembly by pulling it out through the front of the block. Support the camshaft carefully when removing so as not to damage camshaft bearings.

9. As required, remove the gear from the camshaft.

10. Installation is the reverse of the removal procedure. The end clearance of the thrust plate should be 0.0015–0.0050 in. If less than 0.0015 in., the spacer ring should be replaced. If more than 0.0050 in., the thrust plate should be replaced.

11. Thoroughly coat the camshaft journals with a high quality engine oil supplement.

12. Install the camshaft assembly in the engine block, be careful not to damage the cam bearings or the camshaft.

13. Turn crankshaft and camshaft so that the valve timing marks on the gear teeth will line up. The engine is now in the No. 4 cylinder firing position. Install camshaft thrust plate to block screws and tighten to 75 inch lbs.

14. Install timing gear cover and gasket. Line up keyway in hub with key on crankshaft and slide hub onto shaft. Install center bolt and torque to 160 ft. lbs. (212 Nm).

15. Install the lifters, pushrods, pushrod cover, oil pump shaft and gear assembly and fuel pump. Install the distributor.

16. Install front mount assembly lower alternator bracket and alternator.

17. Install the engine in the vehicle.

2.8L ENGINE

1. Disconnect the negative battery cable. Remove the engine from the vehicle and position it in a suitable holding fixture.

2. Remove the intake manifold. Remove the valve covers. Remove rocker arm assemblies, pushrods and lifters.

3. Remove the crankcase front cover.

4. Remove the timing chain and sprocket.

5. Remove the engine rear cover.

6. Carefully remove the camshaft to avoid damage to the cam bearings.

7. Before installation, lubricate the camshaft journals with engine oil. If a new camshaft is to be installed, coat the lobes with clean engine oil.

8. The remainder of the installation is the reverse of removal.

Timing Cover and Oil Seal

Removal and Installation

2.5L ENGINE

1. Disconnect the negative battery cable. Remove the engine compartment lid and side panels. Remove the trim at the sail panel below the battery side panel.

2. Remove the drive belt. Raise and support the vehicle safely.

3. Remove the right rear tire and wheel assembly. Remove the inner splash shield.

4. Remove the starter assembly. Remove the flywheel cover.

5. Remove the pulley and hub. Lower the vehicle.

6. Properly support the engine using the required equipment. Remove the engine torque strut.

7. Raise and support the vehicle safely. Remove the engine mounts.

8. Remove the timing gear cover bolts. Remove the timing gear cover.

9. Installation is the reverse of the removal procedure. Be sure to use new gaskets or RTV sealant, as required.

2.8L ENGINE

1. Disconnect the negative battery cable.

2. Remove the air conditioning compressor and bracket, without disconnecting the refrigerant lines and position out of the way.

3. Remove the water pump.

Timing gear alignment—2.5L engine

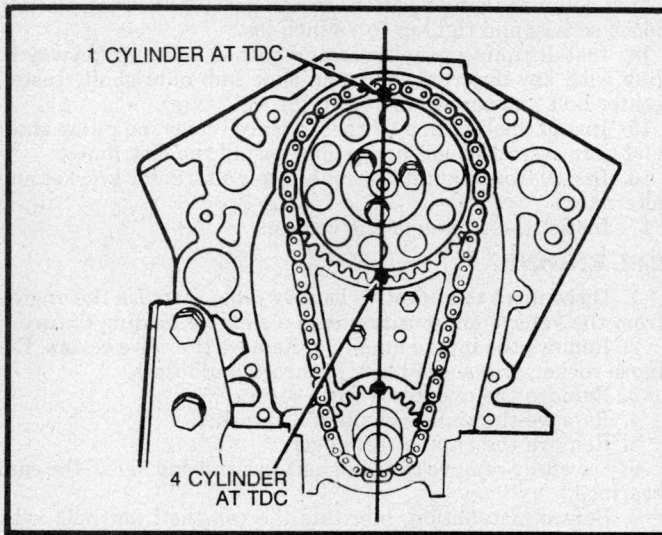

Timing chain and gear alignment—2.8L engine

4. Raise the vehicle and support it safely. Remove the torsional damper.

5. If replacing the seal, pry the old seal out using a suitable tool. When installing a new seal, lubricate the seal with clean engine oil. Insert the seal in the front cover with the lip facing the engine. Using the proper tool, drive the seal into place.

6. Remove the oil pan to cover bolts.

7. Lower the vehicle and remove the front cover.

8. Before installing, clean the sealing surfaces on the front cover and cylinder block. Install a new gasket and apply a ⅛ in. bead of RTV sealer to the oil pan sealing surface of the front cover.

9. Place the front cover on the engine and install the stud bolt and bolts.

10. The remainder of the installation is the reverse order of the removal procedure.

Timing Chain and Sprockets

Removal and Installation

2.5L ENGINE

Camshaft Sprocket

1. Disconnect the negative battery cable. Remove the engine from the vehicle.

2. Position the engine assembly in a suitable holding fixture.

3. Position the engine at TDC on the compression stroke. Remove the front cover. Remove the camshaft.

4. Using the proper equipment, press the camshaft sprocket from the camshaft.

5. Installation is the reverse of the removal procedure.

6. The end clearance of the thrust plate should be 0.0015–0.0050 in. If less than 0.0015 in., the spacer ring should be replaced. If more than 0.0050 in., the thrust plate should be replaced.

Crankshaft Sprocket

1. Disconnect the negative battery cable. Position the engine at TDC on the compression stroke.

2. Remove the engine front cover.

3. Remove the crankshaft gear from its mounting.

4. Installation is the reverse of the removal procedure.

2.8L ENGINE

1. Disconnect the negative battery cable. Remove the crankcase front cover.

2. Align the No. 1 piston at TDC, with the marks on the camshaft and crankshaft sprockets aligned.

3. Remove the camshaft sprocket and chain. It may be necessary to use a plastic mallet on the lower edge of the sprocket to dislodge it.

4. Remove the camshaft sprocket using the proper tool. Remove the crankshaft sprocket, using the proper tool.

5. Install the sprockets.

6. Apply Molykote® or equivalent to the sprocket thrust surface.

7. Hold the sprocket with the chain hanging down and align the marks on the camshaft and crankshaft sprockets.

8. Align the dowel in the camshaft with the dowel hole in the camshaft sprocket.

9. Draw the camshaft sprocket onto the camshaft, using the mounting bolts and torque 15–25 ft. lbs.

10. Lubricate the timing chain with engine oil.

11. Install the crankcase front cover.

Piston and Connecting Rod Position

To properly install the piston and connecting rod assembly. Align the piston and connecting rod assembly with the piston mark (notch) toward the front of the engine.

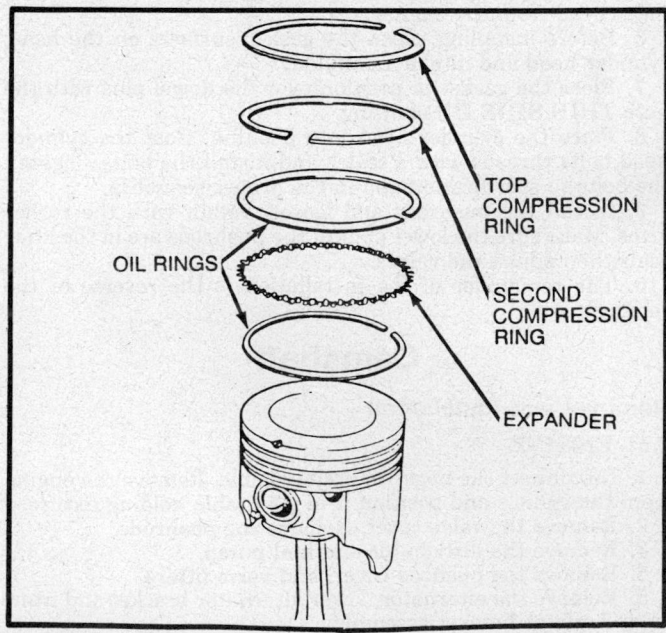

Typical piston and rod assembly

ENGINE LUBRICATION

Force Balancer Assembly

Removal and Installation

2.5L ENGINE

1. Disconnect the negative battery cable. Raise and support the vehicle safely.
2. Drain the engine oil. Remove the oil pan.
3. Remove the balancer assembly.
4. Installation is the reverse of the removal procedure. Torque the short bolts to 9 ft. lbs. plus a 75 degree turn. Torque the long bolts 9 ft. lbs. plus a 90 degree turn.
5. Rotate the engine to TDC on the No. 1 and No. 4 cylinders. Measure from the block to the first cut of the double notch on the reluctor ring.
6. The measurement should be $1^{11}/_{16}$ in. Mount the balancer with the counterweights parallel and pointing away from the crankshaft. Be sure not to move the crankshaft.
7. Be sure to use new gaskets or RTV sealant, as required.

Oil Pan

Removal and Installation

2.5L ENGINE

1. Disconnect the negative battery cable. Remove the engine compartment lid and side panels.
2. On 1988 vehicles, remove the sail panel below the battery side panel trim. Remove the battery side shield.
3. Raise and support the vehicle safely. Drain the engine oil. On 1988 vehicles, remove the oil filter. On 1988 vehicles, remove the serpentine drive belt.
4. Remove the engine mount to cradle nuts. Remove the fly wheel cover. Remove the starter.
5. As required, remove the right rear tire and wheel assembly. Remove the splash shield. Loosen the alternator bracket. As required, remove the alternator.
6. On 1988 vehicles, remove the heat shield at the air conditioning compressor. Remove the air conditioning compressor mounting bolts. Position the compressor to the side.
7. Lower the vehicle. Remove the engine strut. Properly support the engine using tool J28467, or equivalent.
8. Raise and support the vehicle safely. Remove the engine front support bracket and mount.

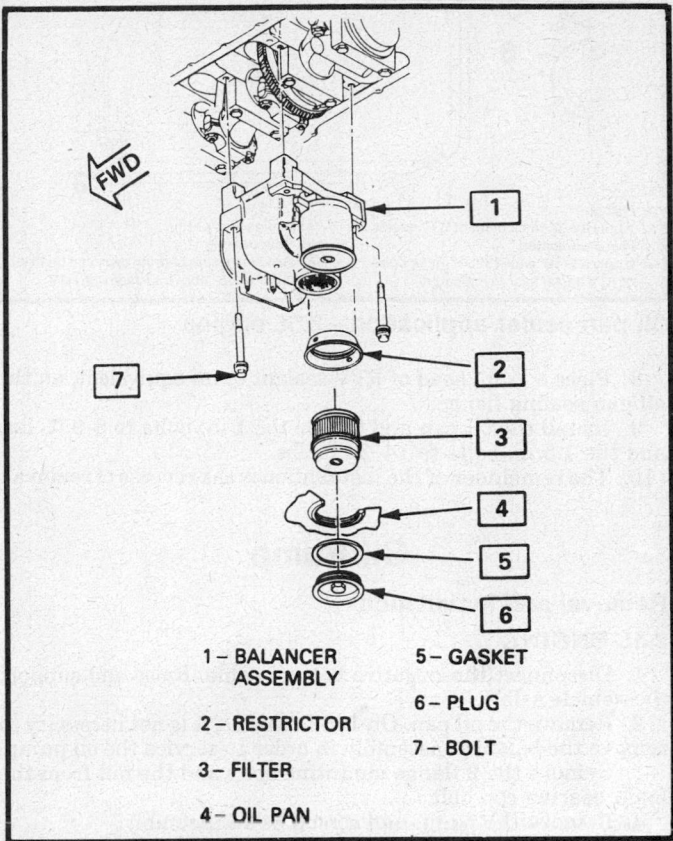

Balancer assembly—2.5L engine

1 – BALANCER ASSEMBLY
2 – RESTRICTOR
3 – FILTER
4 – OIL PAN
5 – GASKET
6 – PLUG
7 – BOLT

Correct counterweight installation

9. Remove the oil pan retaining bolts. Remove the oil pan from the vehicle.
10. Installation is the reverse of the removal procedure. Be sure to use new gaskets or RTV sealant, as required.

2.8L ENGINE

1. Disconnect the negative battery cable.
2. Raise the vehicle and support it safely.
3. Drain the oil.
4. Remove the flywheel shield or clutch housing cover.
5. Remove the starter.
6. Remove the oil pan retaining bolts. Remove the oil pan from the engine.
7. Before installation, clean all mating surfaces.

Crankshaft position movement

1-11/16" (42.9mm)

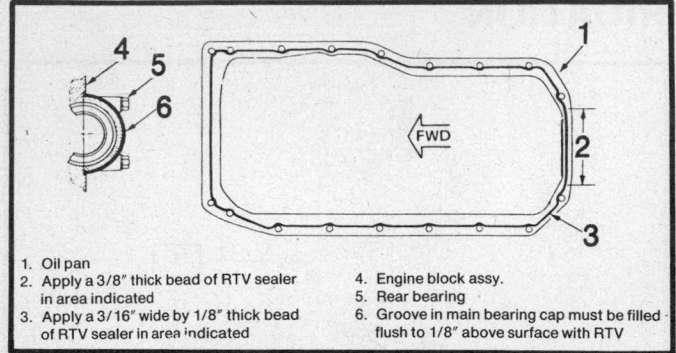

1. Oil pan
2. Apply a 3/8" thick bead of RTV sealer in area indicated
3. Apply a 3/16" wide by 1/8" thick bead of RTV sealer in area indicated
4. Engine block assy.
5. Rear bearing
6. Groove in main bearing cap must be filled flush to 1/8" above surface with RTV

Oil pan sealer application—2.5L engine

8. Place a ⅛ in. bead of RTV sealant or an equivalent, on the oil pan sealing flange.
9. Install the oil pan and torque the 1 in. bolts to 6–9 ft. lbs. and the 1.5 in. bolts to 14–22 ft. lbs.
10. The remainder of the installation is the reverse of removal.

Oil Pump

Removal and Installation

2.5L ENGINE

1. Disconnect the negative battery cable. Raise and support the vehicle safely.
2. Remove the oil pan. On 1988 vehicles, it is not necessary to remove the balancer assembly in order to service the oil pump.
3. Remove the 2 flange mounting bolts and the nut from the main bearing cap bolt.
4. Remove the pump and screen as an assembly.
5. Installation is the reverse of removal. Align the pump shaft with the drift shaft tang. Torque the pump retaining bolts to 20 ft. lbs.

2.8L ENGINE

1. Disconnect the negative battery cable. Raise and support the vehicle safely. Remove the oil pan.
2. Remove the oil pump retaining bolts. Remove the oil pump and driveshaft extension.
3. To install, engage the driveshaft extension in the cover end of the distributor drive gear.
4. Install the pump to rear bearing cap bolt and torque 26 to 35 ft. lbs.
5. Install the oil pan and refill with oil.

Rear Main Oil Seal

ONE PIECE SEAL

Removal and Installation

1. Disconnect the negative battery cable. Raise and support the vehicle safely.
2. Remove the transaxle assembly. Remove the flywheel.
3. If equipped with a manual transaxle, remove the pressure plate and clutch.
4. Pry out of the rear main seal.
5. Before installing, clean the block and crankshaft to seal mating surfaces.
6. Lubricate the outside of the seal for ease of installation and press into the block with fingers.
7. Install the flywheel and torque the bolts to 44 ft. lbs.
8. Install the transaxle assembly.

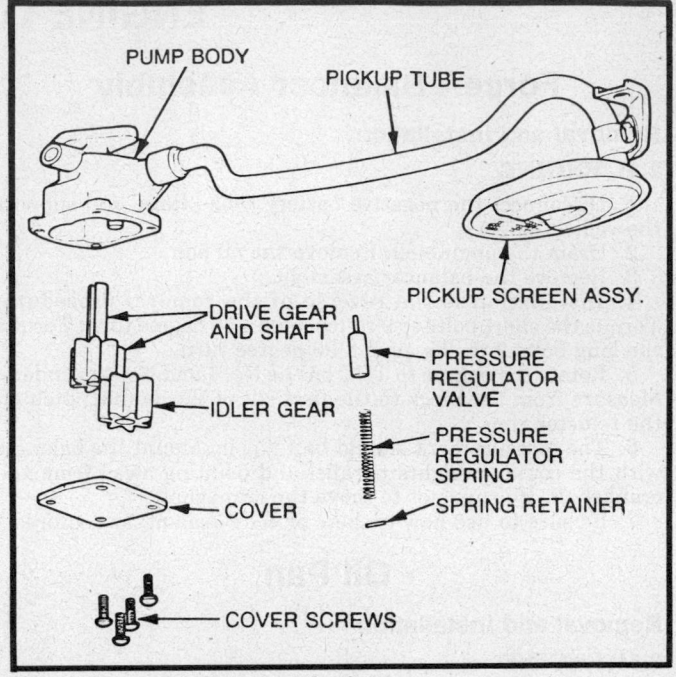

Oil pump assembly—typical

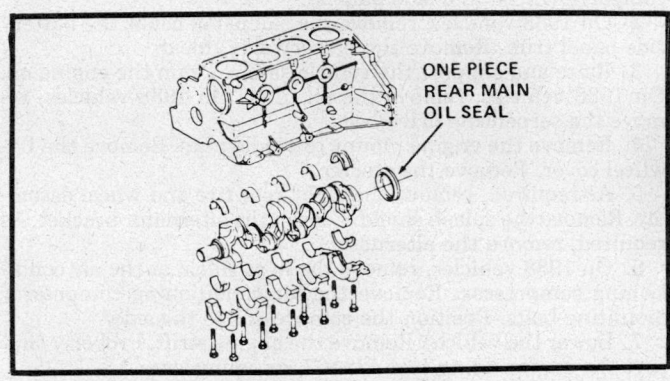

Lower block assembly—2.5L engine

THIN SEAL

Removal and Installation

1. Remove the engine and mount on a suitable stand.
2. Remove the oil pan and oil pump assembly.
3. Remove the front cover, then the lock chain tensioner with a pin.
4. Rotate the crankshaft until the timing marks on the cam and crank sprockets align.
5. Remove the camshaft bolt, cam sprocket and timing chain.
6. Rotate the crankshaft to the horizontal position.
7. Remove the rod bearing nuts, caps and bolts.
8. Remove the crankshaft and the old oil seal.
9. Apply a light coat of GM 1052726 or equivalent to the outside of the seal.
10. Install the new seal and tool in the rear area of the crankshaft.
11. Install the crankshaft and tool in the engine.
12. Position the seal tool so that the arrow points towards the cylinder block and remove the tool.
13. Put a light coat of oil on the crankshaft journals.

14. Seal the rear main bearing split line surface with GM 1052726 or equivalent.
15. The remainder of the installation is the reverse of removal. Torque to specifications.

Connecting Rod and Main Bearing

Replacement

1. Remove the engine from the vehicle. Position the assembly in a suitable holding fixture.
2. Remove the cylinder head assembly, as required. Remove the flywheel.

3. Remove the timing belt covers. Remove the timing belt. Remove the oil pan. Remove the oil screen assembly.
4. Matchmark and remove the main bearing caps. Remove the upper half of the main bearing shells.
5. Matchmark and remove the connecting rod caps. Remove the upper half of the connecting rod bearing shells.
6. Carefully push the pistons up into the cylinder head or remove them.
7. Remove the lower half of the connecting rod bearing shells.
8. Carefully lift the crankshaft from its mounting. Remove the lower half of the main bearing shells.
9. Installation is the reverse of the removal procedure.

FRONT SUSPENSION AND STEERING

For front suspension component removal and installation procedures, refer to the unit repair section. For steering wheel removal and installation procedures, refer to electrical controls section.

Steering Rack and Pinion

Removal and Installation

1. Disconnect the negative battery cable. Raise the vehicle and support it safely.
2. Disconnect both front crossmember braces.
3. Disconnect the flexible coupling pinch bolt to the shaft.
4. Remove the outer tie rod cotter pins and nuts on the left and right sides.
5. Disconnect the tie rods from the steering knuckle.
6. Remove the 4 bolts retaining the steering assembly to the crossmember and remove the steering assembly.
7. Installation is the reverse of removal. Tighten the flexible coupling bolt to 46 ft. lbs., the 4 new steering assembly bolts to 21 ft. lbs., the 4 crossmember brace bolts to 20 ft. lbs. and the tie rod nut at each knuckle to 29 ft. lbs., turn nut to align the cotter pin.

Steering Column

Removal and Installation

1. Disconnect the battery negative cable.
2. Remove the left instrument panel sound absorber. Remove the left instrument panel trim pad and steering column trim collar.
3. Remove the bolt at the flex joint. Remove 2 nuts from the lower support and 2 bolts from the upper support.
4. Remove the shift indicator cable. Disconnect all electrical connectors. Remove the shift cable at the actuator and housing holder.
5. Remove the steering column.
6. Installation is the reverse of removal procedure.
7. Center the steering shaft within the steering column jacket bushing and tighten lower attaching bolt. This can be done by moving the steering column jacket assembly up and down or side to side until the steering shaft is centered.

Front Wheel Bearings

Adjustment

TAPERED WHEEL BEARINGS

1. Raise the vehicle and support it safely.
2. Remove the wheel and tire assembly.
3. Remove the dust cap from the hub.
4. Remove cotter pin from spindle and spindle nut.

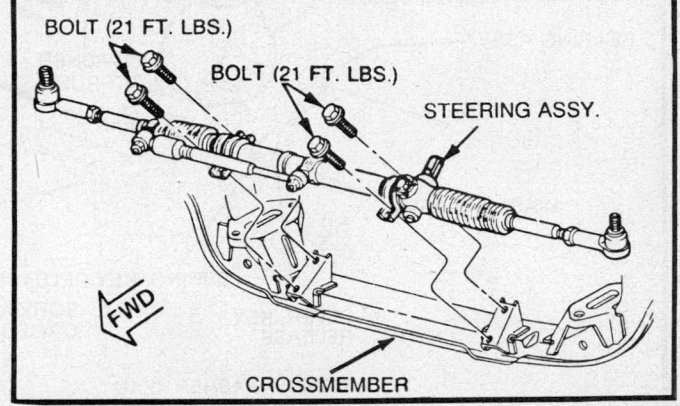

Rack and pinion assembly

5. Tighten the spindle nut to 12 ft. lbs. while turning the wheel assembly forward by hand to fully seat the bearings. This will remove any grease or burrs which could cause excessive wheel bearing play later.
6. Back off the nut to the just loose position.
7. Hand tighten the spindle nut. Loosen the spindle nut until either hole in the spindle lines up with a slot in the nut. (Not more than ½ flat).
8. Install a new cotter pin. Bend the ends of the cotter pin against nut, cut off extra length to ensure ends will not interfere with the dust cap.
9. Measure the looseness in the hub assembly. There will be from 0.001–0.005 in. endplay when properly adjusted.
10. Install the dust cap on the hub.
11. Replace the wheel cover or hub cap.
12. Lower the vehicle to the floor.

SEALED WHEEL BEARINGS

1. Raise and support the vehicle safely. Remove the tire and wheel assemblies.
2. Remove the disc brake linings and position the calipers out of the way. Complete removal of the caliper, may be required.
3. Reinstall the disc, use 2 wheel nuts to secure the disc to the bearing.
4. Mount a dial indicator gauge, tool J8001 to the disc and hub assembly.
5. Grasp the disc and use a push pull movement to check the specification.
6. If specification exceeds 0.005 in. (0.1270mm), replace the hub and bearing assembly.

Front Wheel Alignment

Camber Adjustment

Camber is the tilting of the wheels from the vertical when

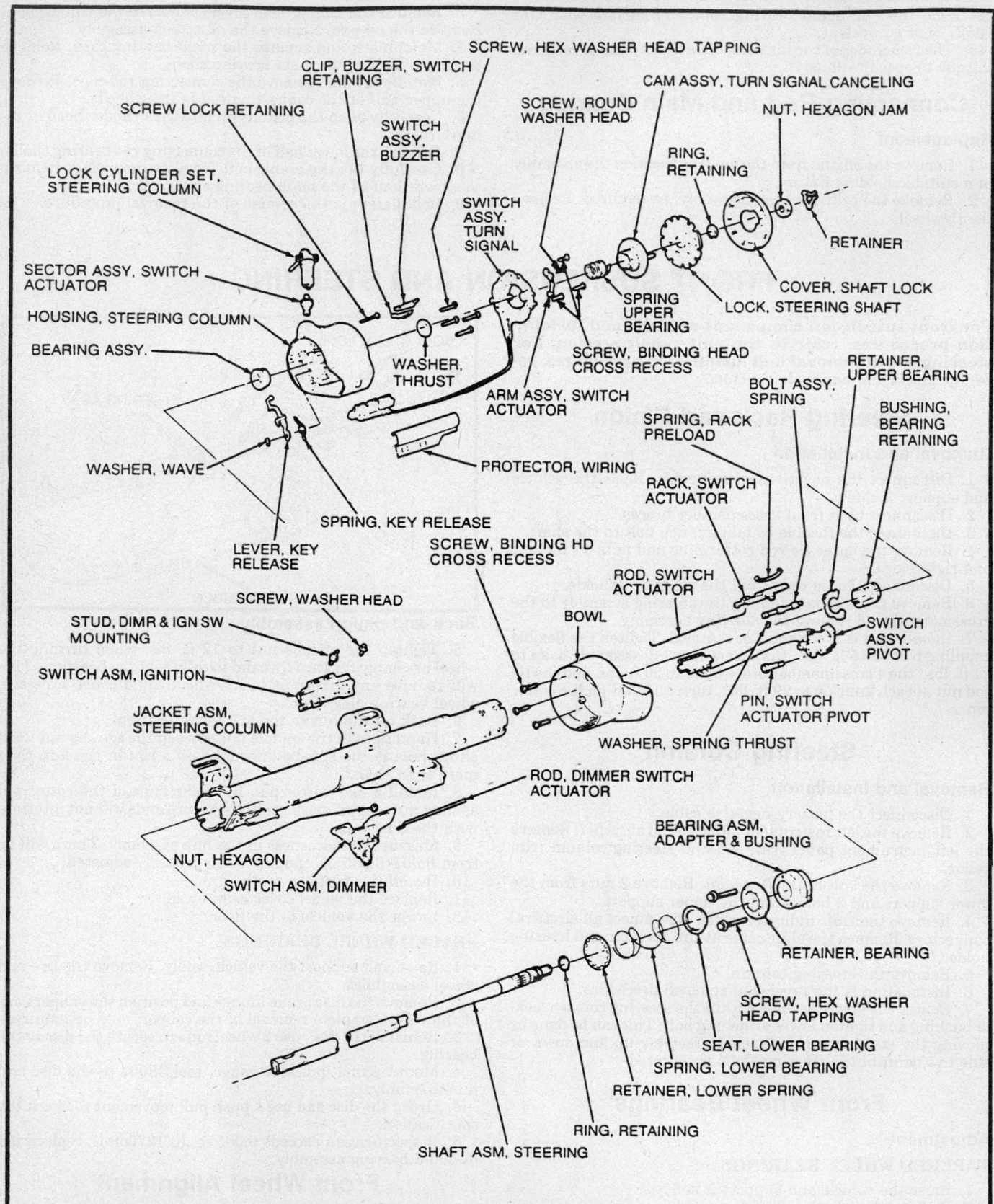

Exploded view of standard steering column

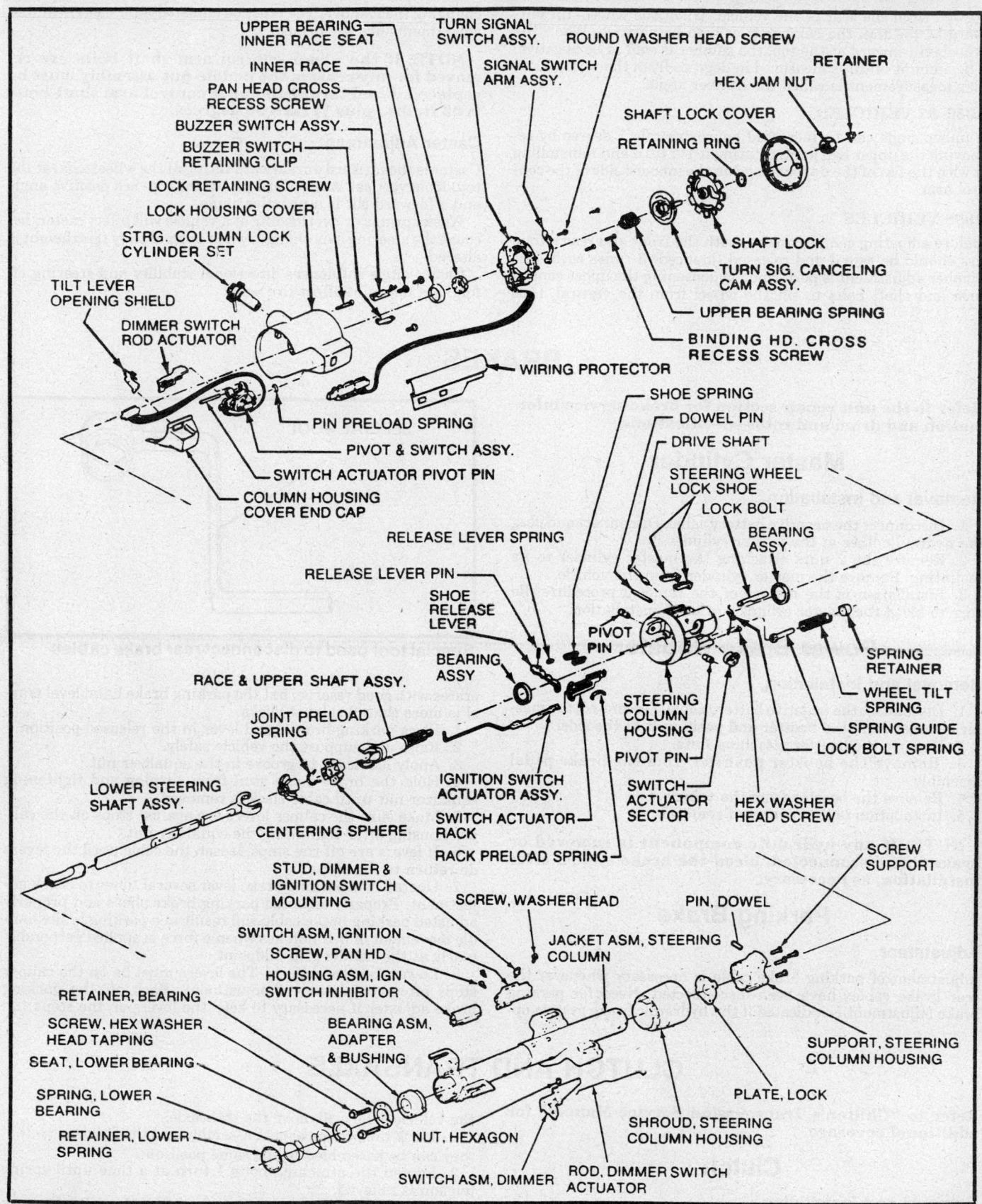

UPPER BEARING INNER RACE SEAT
INNER RACE
PAN HEAD CROSS RECESS SCREW
BUZZER SWITCH ASSY.
BUZZER SWITCH RETAINING CLIP
LOCK RETAINING SCREW
LOCK HOUSING COVER
STRG. COLUMN LOCK CYLINDER SET
TILT LEVER OPENING SHIELD
DIMMER SWITCH ROD ACTUATOR
TURN SIGNAL SWITCH ASSY.
SIGNAL SWITCH ARM ASSY.
ROUND WASHER HEAD SCREW
RETAINER
HEX JAM NUT
SHAFT LOCK COVER
RETAINING RING
SHAFT LOCK
TURN SIG. CANCELING CAM ASSY.
UPPER BEARING SPRING
BINDING HD. CROSS RECESS SCREW
WIRING PROTECTOR
PIN PRELOAD SPRING
PIVOT & SWITCH ASSY.
SWITCH ACTUATOR PIVOT PIN
COLUMN HOUSING COVER END CAP
SHOE SPRING
DOWEL PIN
DRIVE SHAFT
STEERING WHEEL LOCK SHOE
LOCK BOLT
BEARING ASSY.
RELEASE LEVER SPRING
RELEASE LEVER PIN
SHOE RELEASE LEVER
BEARING ASSY
RACE & UPPER SHAFT ASSY.
JOINT PRELOAD SPRING
PIVOT PIN
STEERING COLUMN HOUSING
PIVOT PIN
SWITCH ACTUATOR SECTOR
HEX WASHER HEAD SCREW
SPRING RETAINER
WHEEL TILT SPRING
SPRING GUIDE
LOCK BOLT SPRING
LOWER STEERING SHAFT ASSY.
CENTERING SPHERE
IGNITION SWITCH ACTUATOR ASSY.
SWITCH ACTUATOR RACK
RACK PRELOAD SPRING
STUD, DIMMER & IGNITION SWITCH MOUNTING
SCREW, WASHER HEAD
JACKET ASM, STEERING COLUMN
SCREW SUPPORT
PIN, DOWEL
SWITCH ASM, IGNITION
SCREW, PAN HD
HOUSING ASM, IGN SWITCH INHIBITOR
RETAINER, BEARING
SCREW, HEX WASHER HEAD TAPPING
SEAT, LOWER BEARING
SPRING, LOWER BEARING
RETAINER, LOWER SPRING
BEARING ASM, ADAPTER & BUSHING
NUT, HEXAGON
SWITCH ASM, DIMMER
ROD, DIMMER SWITCH ACTUATOR
SHROUD, STEERING COLUMN HOUSING
PLATE, LOCK
SUPPORT, STEERING COLUMN HOUSING

Exploded view of tilt steering column

viewed from the rear of the vehicle. When the wheels tilt outward at the top, the camber is said to be positive. When the wheels tilt inward at the top, the camber is said to be negative. The amount of tilt is measured in degrees from the vertical and this measurement is called the camber angle.

1986–87 VEHICLES

Camber angle can be increased approximately 1 degree by removing the upper ball joint, rotating it 1½ turn and reinstalling it with the flat of the upper flange on the inboard side of the control arm.

1988 VEHICLES

Before adjusting camber angles, both the front and rear bumpers should be raised and released (jounced) 3 times each. The camber adjustment is performed by loosening the upper control arm and shaft bolts to tilt the wheel from the vertical, thus

changing the camber. Toe must be adjusted after caster/camber adjustments are performed.

NOTE: If the upper control arm shaft bolts are removed for any reason, the paddle nut assembly must be replaced. Final torque to upper control arm shaft bolts is 52 ft. lbs., plus ¼ turn 90 degrees.

Caster Adjustment

Caster is the forward or rearward tilting of the wheel axis (at the top) from vertical. A rearward tilt (at the top) is a positive angle and a forward tilt is a negative angle.

Weak springs or overloading of a vehicle will affect caster, because the steering axis changes when normal body trim height is altered.

Caster angle influences directional stability and steering effort, but does not affect tire wear.

BRAKES

Refer to the unit repair section for brake service information and drum and rotor specifications.

Master Cylinder

Removal and Installation

1. Disconnect the negative battery cable. Disconnect and plug the hydraulic lines at the master cylinder.
2. Remove the 2 nuts attaching the master cylinder to its mounting. Remove the master cylinder from the vehicle.
3. Installation is the reverse of the removal procedure. Be sure to bleed the master cylinder, prior to installation.

Power Brake Booster

Removal and Installation

1. Disconnect the negative battery cable. Disconnect the master cylinder from the booster and position it to the side.
2. Remove the booster attaching nuts.
3. Remove the booster pushrod from the brake pedal assembly.
4. Remove the booster from the vehicle.
5. Installation is the reverse of removal.

NOTE: If any hydraulic component is removed or brake line disconnected, bleed the brake system after installation, as necessary.

Parking Brake

Adjustment

Adjustment of parking brake cable is necessary whenever the rear brake cables have been disconnected. Need for parking brake adjustment is indicated if the hydraulic brake system op-

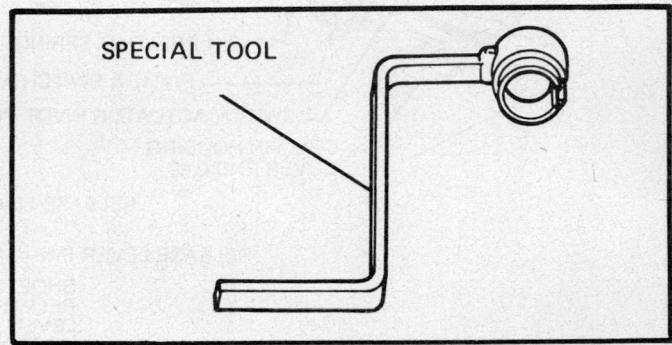

SPECIAL TOOL

Special tool used to disconnect rear brake cables

erates with good reserve, but the parking brake hand level travel is more than 9 ratchet clicks.

1. Place parking brake hand lever in the released position.
2. Raise and support the vehicle safely.
3. Apply lubricant to groove in the equalizer nut.
4. Hold the brake cable stud from turning and tightening equalizer nut until cable slack is removed.
5. Make sure the caliper levers are against stops on the caliper housing after tightening the equalizer nut.
6. If levers are off the stops, loosen the cable until the levers do return to the stops.
7. Operate the parking brake lever several times to check adjustment. Properly adjusted parking brake shoes and properly adjusted parking brake cable will result in a parking brake handle movement of 5–8 notches when a force is applied perpendicularly at the handle grip midpoint.
8. Lower the rear wheels. The levers must be on the caliper stops after completion of adjustment. Back off the parking brake adjuster if necessary to keep the levers on the stops.

CLUTCH AND TRANSAXLE

Refer to "Chilton's Transmission Service Manual" for additional coverage.

Clutch

Removal and Installation

1. Disconnect the negative battery cable. Raise and support

the vehicle safely. Remove the transaxle.
2. Mark the pressure plate assembly and the flywheel so that they can be assembled in the same position..
3. Loosen the attaching bolts 1 turn at a time until spring tension is relieved.
4. Support the pressure plate and remove the bolts. Remove the pressure plate and clutch disc. Do not disassemble the pres-

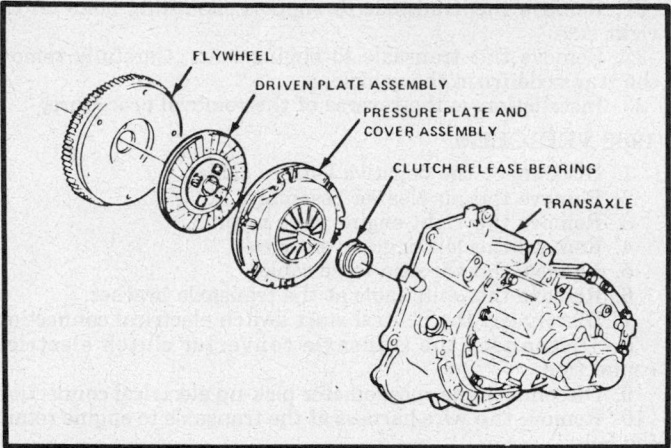

Exploded view of clutch assembly

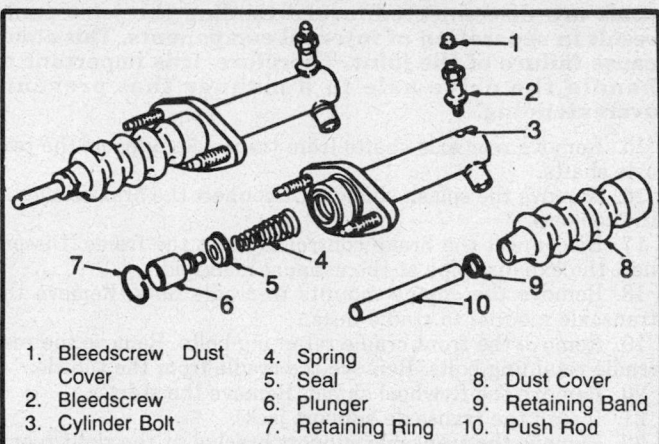

1. Bleedscrew Dust Cover
2. Bleedscrew
3. Cylinder Bolt
4. Spring
5. Seal
6. Plunger
7. Retaining Ring
8. Dust Cover
9. Retaining Band
10. Push Rod

Clutch slave cylinder—exploded view

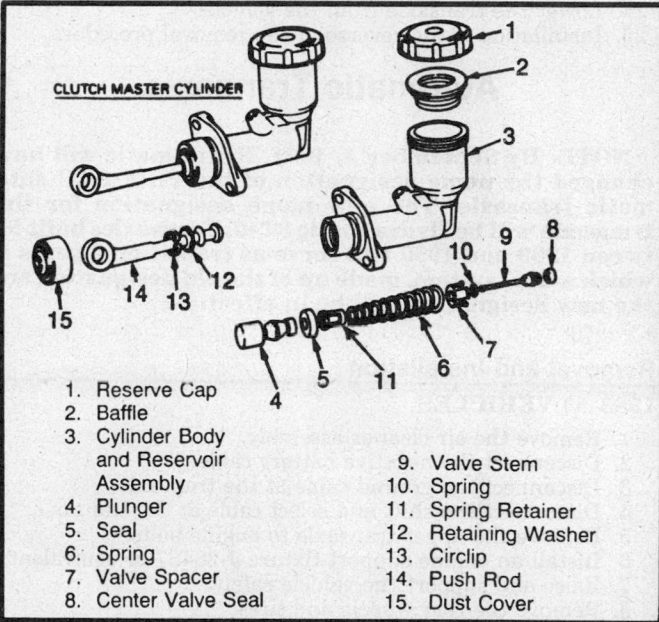

1. Reserve Cap
2. Baffle
3. Cylinder Body and Reservoir Assembly
4. Plunger
5. Seal
6. Spring
7. Valve Spacer
8. Center Valve Seal
9. Valve Stem
10. Spring
11. Spring Retainer
12. Retaining Washer
13. Circlip
14. Push Rod
15. Dust Cover

Clutch master cylinder—exploded view

sure plate assembly, replace it if defective.

5. Inspect the flywheel, clutch disc, pressure plate, throwout bearing and the clutch fork and pivot shaft assembly for wear. Replace the parts as required. If the flywheel shows any signs of overheating, or if it is badly grooved or scored, it should be replaced.

6. Clean the pressure plate and flywheel mating surfaces thoroughly. Position the clutch disc and pressure plate into the installed position and support with a dummy shaft or clutch aligning tool. The clutch plate is assembled with the damper springs offset toward the transaxle. One side of the factory supplied clutch disc is stamped **FLYWHEEL SIDE**.

7. Install the pressure plate to flywheel bolts. Tighten them gradually in a crisscross pattern.

8. Lubricate the outside groove and the inside recess of the release bearing with high temperature grease. Wipe off any excess. Install the release bearing.

9. Install the transaxle.

Manual Transaxle

Removal and Installation

1986–87 VEHICLES

1. Remove the air cleaner assembly.
2. Disconnect the negative battery cable.
3. Disconnect the ground cable at the transaxle.
4. Disconnect the shift and select cable at the transaxle.
5. Remove the upper transaxle to engine bolts.
6. Install an engine support fixture J–28467 or equivalent.
7. Raise and support the vehicle safely.
8. Remove the rear wheels and tires.
9. Remove the axle shafts.
10. Remove the heat shield from the catalytic converter.
11. Disconnect the exhaust pipe at the exhaust manifold.
12. Remove the engine mount to cradle nuts.
13. Support the cradle with an adjustable stand.
14. Remove the rear cradle to body bolts.
15. Remove the forward cradle to body through bolts.
16. Lower the cradle and move out of the way.
17. Remove the starter and inspection cover shields and remove the starter.
18. Position a transaxle jack under the transaxle.
19. Remove the transaxle to engine bolts. Carefully remove the transaxle from the vehicle.
20. Installation is the reverse of the removal procedure.

1988 VEHICLES

1. Disconnect the negative battery cable.
2. Remove the air cleaner assembly.

3. Remove the right engine vent cover.
4. Remove the left engine vent cover.
5. Remove the throttle valve cable.
6. Remove the shift cable at the transaxle bracket.
7. Disconnect the neutral start switch electrical connection.
8. Disconnect the transaxle converter clutch electrical connection.
9. Disconnect the speedometer pick-up electrical connection.
10. Remove the wire harness at the transaxle to engine retaining bolts.
11. Remove the transaxle to engine retaining bolts. Remove the shift cable bracket to remove the neutral start switch harness.
12. Install the engine fixture tool J–28467–A or equivalent. Raise the vehicle and support it safely. Remove the rear wheels.
13. Install rear axle boot protectors. Remove the fixed adjusting link/lateral control arm through bolts.
14. Disconnect the trailing arms at knuckles.

NOTE: On vehicles equipped with Tri-Pot joints, care must be exercised not to allow the Tri-Pot joints to become overextended. When either end or both ends of the

shaft are disconnected, overextending the joint could result in separation of internal components. This could cause failure of the joint. Therefore, it is important to handle the drive axle in a manner that prevents overextending.

15. Remove rear axle shafts from transaxle. Support the rear axle shafts.
16. Remove the splash shields. Disconnect the brake cables at the calipers.
17. Disconnect the brake control cable at the frame. Disconnect the exhaust pipe at the exhaust manifold.
18. Remove the engine mounts to cradle nuts. Remove the transaxle mounts to cradle nuts.
19. Remove the front cradle retaining bolts. Remove the rear cradle retaining bolts. Remove the cradle from the vehicle.
20. Remove the flywheel shield. Remove the starter.
21. Install the transaxle support jack.
22. Remove the transaxle support bracket at the right rear.
23. Remove the remaining transaxle to engine retaining bolts including the ground wire.
24. Lower the transaxle from the vehicle.
25. Installation is the reverse of the removal procedure.

Automatic Transaxle

NOTE: By September 1, 1991, Hydra-matic will have changed the name designation of the THM 125C automatic transaxle. The new name designation for this transaxle will be Hydra-matic 3T40. Transaxles built between 1989 and 1990 will serve as transitional years in which a dual system, made up of the old designation and the new designation will be in effect.

Removal and Installation
1986–87 VEHICLES

1. Remove the air cleaner assembly.
2. Disconnect the negative battery cable.
3. Disconnect the ground cable at the transaxle.
4. Disconnect the shift and select cable at the transaxle.
5. Remove the upper transaxle to engine bolts.
6. Install an engine support fixture J-28467 or equivalent.
7. Raise and support the vehicle safely.
8. Remove the rear wheels and tires.
9. Remove the axle shafts.
10. Remove the heat shield from the catalytic converter.
11. Disconnect the exhaust pipe at the exhaust manifold.
12. Remove the engine mount to cradle nuts.
13. Support the cradle with an adjustable stand.
14. Remove the rear cradle to body bolts.
15. Remove the forward cradle to body through bolts.
16. Lower the cradle and move out of the way.
17. Remove the starter and inspection cover shields and remove the starter.
18. Remove the flywheel to converter bolts.
19. Disconnect and plug the cooler lines.
20. Position a transaxle jack under the transaxle.

21. Remove the transaxle to support mounting bolts on the right side.
22. Remove the transaxle to engine bolts. Carefully remove the transaxle from the vehicle.
23. Installation is the reverse of the removal procedure.

1988 VEHICLES

1. Disconnect the negative battery cable.
2. Remove the air cleaner assembly.
3. Remove the right engine vent cover.
4. Remove the left engine vent cover.
5. Remove the throttle valve cable.
6. Remove the shift cable at the transaxle bracket.
7. Disconnect the neutral start switch electrical connection.
8. Disconnect the transaxle converter clutch electrical connection.
9. Disconnect the speedometer pick-up electrical connection.
10. Remove the wire harness at the transaxle to engine retaining bolts.
11. Remove the transaxle cooler line support bracket.
12. Remove the transaxle to engine retaining bolts.
13. Remove the shift cable bracket to remove the neutral start switch harness.
14. Install the engine fixture tool J-28467-A or equivalent.
15. Raise the vehicle and support it safely.
16. Remove the rear wheels.
17. Install rear axle boot protectors.
18. Remove the fixed adjusting link/lateral control arm through bolts.
19. Disconnect the trailing arms at knuckles.

NOTE: On vehicles equipped with Tri-Pot joints, care must be exercised not to allow the Tri-Pot joints to become overextended. When either end or both ends of the shaft are disconnected, overextending the joint could result in separation of internal components. This could cause failure of the joint. Therefore, it is important to handle the drive axle in a manner that prevents overextending.

20. Remove rear axle shafts from transaxle.
21. Support the rear axle shafts.
22. Remove the splash shields.
23. Disconnect the brake cables at the calipers.
24. Disconnect the brake control cable at the frame.
25. Disconnect the exhaust pipe at the exhaust manifold.
26. Remove the engine mounts to cradle nuts.
27. Remove the transaxle mounts to cradle nuts.
28. Remove the front cradle retaining bolts.
29. Remove the rear cradle retaining bolts.
30. Remove the cradle from the vehicle.
31. Remove the flywheel shield. Remove the starter.
32. Remove the flexplate bolts.
33. Disconnect and plug the cooler lines.
34. Install the transaxle support jack.
35. Remove the transaxle support bracket at the right rear.
36. Remove the remaining transaxle to engine retaining bolts including the ground wire.
37. Lower the transaxle from the vehicle.
38. Installation is the reverse of the removal procedure.

HALFSHAFTS

Drive Axle

Removal and Installation
1986–87 VEHICLES

1. Remove the hub nut and discard.

2. Raise the vehicle and remove the wheel and tire.
3. Install a drive boot seal protector on the outer seal.
4. Disconnect the toe link rod at the knuckle assembly.
5. Disconnect the parking brake cables at the cradle.
6. Disconnect the brake line bracket at the underbody in the inner wheel housing opening.

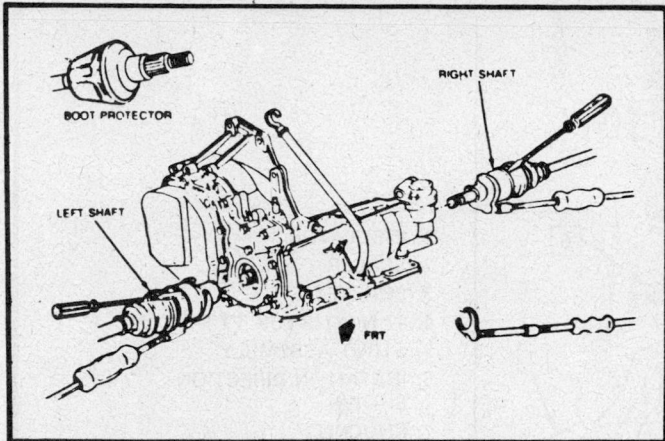

Pressing the Drive Axle from the Hub

7. Using tool J-28733 or equivalent, remove the axle shaft from the hub and bearing assembly.
8. Support the axle shaft.
9. Remove the clamp bolt from the lower control arm ball stud.
10. Separate the knuckle from the lower control arm.
11. Pull the strut, knuckle and caliper assembly away from the body and secure in this position.
12. Using tool J-33008 and J-2619-01 or equivalents, disengage the snaprings which are retaining the drive axle at the transaxle and remove the drive axle. If the drive axle is being replaced, replace the knuckle seal.
13. When installing the drive to the transaxle, seat the axle positioning a suitable tool inside the groove provided on the inner retainer. The remainder of the installation is the reverse of removal. Torque the hub nut to 225 ft. lbs.

1988 VEHICLES

NOTE: Vehicles equipped with a silicone (gray) boot on the drive axle joints, use boot protector J-33162 on these boots. All other boots are made of thermoplastic material (black) and do not require use of the boot protector.

1. Position the selector lever in the **N** detent.
2. Raise and support the vehicle safely.
3. Remove the tire and wheel assembly.
4. Install a drift punch through rotor and remove hub nut and washer (discard nut).
5. Remove the caliper and rotor.
6. Disconnect the trailing arm at the knuckle.
7. Remove the fixed adjusting link, lateral control arm through bolt.
8. Scribe a matchmark on the strut and knuckle assembly.
9. Remove the strut mounting bolts.
10. Press the hub from the halfshaft.

NOTE: On vehicles equipped with Tri-Pot joints, care must be exercised not to allow Tri-Pot joints to become overextended. When either end or both ends of the shaft are disconnected, overextending the joint could result in separation of internal compounds. This could cause failure of the joint. Therefore, it is important to handle the drive axle in a manner that prevents overextending.

11. Install special tools J-28468 or J-33008 with J-29794 and J-2619-01 or equivalent slide and remove haftshaft from the transaxle.
12. Installation is the reverse of removal. Install the hub and washer and replace with a new nut. Torque the nut to 183–208 ft. lbs.

REAR SUSPENSION

Refer to the unit repair section for axle overhaul procedures and rear suspension services.

Rear Wheel Bearing and Oil Seal

Removal and Installation

1. Remove the hub cap and loosen the hub nut.
2. Raise and support the vehicle safely and remove the tire and wheel assembly.
3. Install the drive axle boot protectors. Remove and discard the hub nut.
4. Remove the caliper and rotor and remove the hub and bearing attaching bolts. If the bearing assembly is being reused, mark the attaching bolts and corresponding holes for installation.
5. Install tool J-28733 or equivalent and remove the hub and bearing assembly.
6. If installing a new bearing, be sure to replace the knuckle seal. Clean and inspect the bearing mating surfaces and knuckle bore for dirt, nicks and burrs.
7. If installing a knuckle seal, use tool J-28671 or equivalent and apply grease to the seal and knuckle bore.
8. Place the hub and bearing on the axle shaft and install all other components at this time.

9. Apply a torque of 74 ft. lbs. to the new hub nut, until the hub and bearing assembly is seated properly.
10. Install the rotor and caliper and apply a final torque of 200 ft. lbs. to the hub nut.
11. Install the tire and wheel assembly and lower the vehicle.

Rear Wheel Alignment

The rear alignment refers to the angular relationship between the rear wheels, the rear suspension attaching parts and the ground. Camber and toe are the only adjustments required. Specifications can be found in the front of the section.

Adjustment

CAMBER

The camber can be adjusted by loosening both the strut to knuckle bolts enough to allow movement between the strut and knuckle and grasping the top of the tire and moving it inboard or outboard until the correct camber is obtained.

TOE ADJUSTMENT

Toe-in is adjusted by loosening the jam nuts on the toe link rods, then rotating the toe link rods to adjust to specifications.

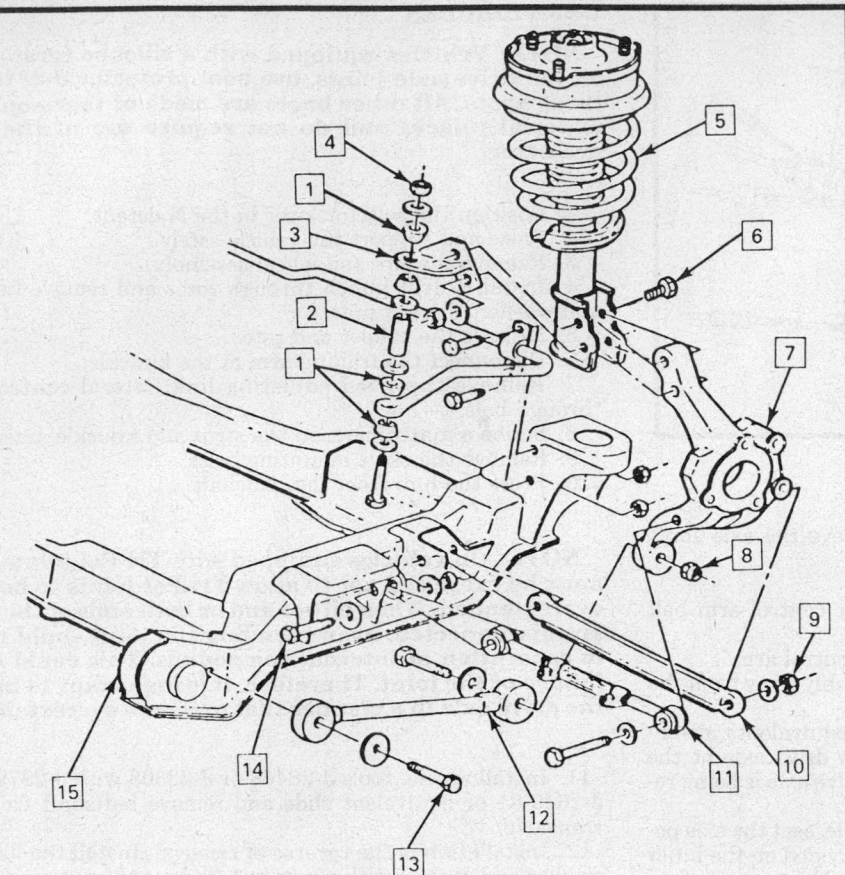

1. INSULATOR
2. SPACER
3. BRACKET
4. 17 N·m (13 LBS. FT.)
5. STRUT ASSEMBLY
6. INSTALL IN DIRECTION SHOWN
7. KNUCKLE
8. 60 N·m (44 LBS. FT.) + 90°
9. 50 N·m (37 LBS. FT.) + 90°
10. LATERAL CONTROL ARM
11. FIXED ADJUSTING LINK
12. TRAILING ARM
13. 51 N·m (37 LBS. FT.)
14. 55 N·m (41 LBS. FT.)
15. FRAME

SCRIBE

| STRUT MOUNT |
| JOUNCE BUMPER |
| STRUT SHIELD |
| SPRING SEAT |
| SPRING INSULATOR |
| DRIVE AXLE REMOVAL |

DO NOT SCRIBE

| REAR RIDE SPRING |
| STRUT DAMPER |
| KNUCKLE |

CHECK/ADJUST BOTH CAMBER AND TOE-IN.

SCRIBING PROCEDURE

1. USING A SHARP TOOL, SCRIBE THE KNUCKLE ALONG THE LOWER OUTBOARD STRUT RADIUS, AS IN VIEW A.
2. SCRIBE THE STRUT FLANGE ON THE INBOARD SIDE, ALONG THE CURVE OF THE KNUCKLE, AS IN VIEW B.
3. MAKE A CHISEL MARK ACROSS THE STRUT/KNUCKLE INTERFACE, AS IN VIEW C.
4. ON REASSEMBLY, CAREFULLY MATCH THE MARKS TO THE COMPONENTS.

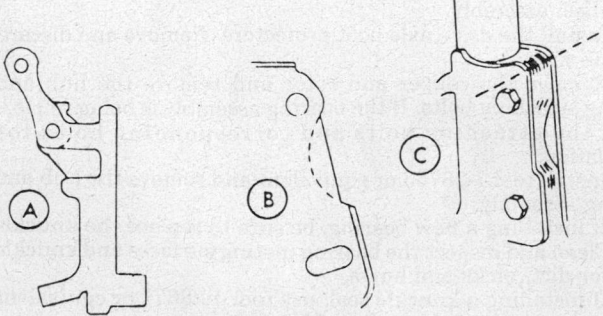

Rear suspension and related components

YEAR IDENTIFICATION

1986–90 Corvette

VEHICLE IDENTIFICATION

It is important for servicing and ordering parts to be certain of the vehicle and engine identification. The VIN (vehicle identification number) is a 17 digit number visible through the windshield on the driver's side of the dash and contains the vehicle and engine identification codes. The tenth digit indicates model year, and the eighth digit indicates engine code. It can be interpreted as follows:

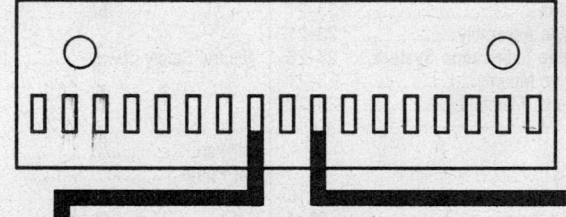

	Engine Code						Model Year	
Code	Cu. In.	Liters	Cyl.	Fuel Sys.	Eng. Mfg.		Code	Year
8	350	5.7	8	PFI	Chevy		G	1986
							H	1987
							J	1988
							K	1989
							L	1990

ENGINE IDENTIFICATION

Year	Model	Engine Displacement cu. in. (liter)	Engine Series Identification (VIN)	No. of Cylinders	Engine Type
1986	Corvette	350 (5.7)	8	8	OHV
1987	Corvette	350 (5.7)	8	8	OHV
1988	Corvette	350 (5.7)	8	8	OHV
1989-90	Corvette	350 (5.7)	8	8	OHV

GENERAL ENGINE SPECIFICATIONS

Year	VIN	No. Cylinder Displacement cu. in. (liter)	Fuel System Type	Net Horsepower @ rpm	Net Torque @ rpm (ft.lbs.)	Bore × Stroke (in.)	Compression Ratio	Oil Pressure @ rpm
1986	8	8-350 (5.7)	PFI	230 @ 4000	330 @ 3200	4.000 × 3.480	9.0:1	50-65 @ 2000
1987	8	8-350 (5.7)	PFI	230 @ 4000	330 @ 3200	4.000 × 3.480	9.5:1	50-65 @ 2000
1988	8	8-350 (5.7)	PFI	245 @ 4300	340 @ 3200	4.000 × 3.480	9.5:1	50-65 @ 2000
1989-90	8	8-350 (5.7)	PFI	240 @ 4300	335 @ 3200	4.000 × 3.480	9.5:1	50-65 @ 2000

TBI Throttle Body Injection
PFI—Port Fuel Injection

GASOLINE ENGINE TUNE-UP SPECIFICATIONS
Refer to Section 34 for all spark plug recommendations

Year	VIN	No. Cylinder Displacement cu. in. (liter)	Spark Plugs Gap (in.)	Ignition Timing (deg.) MT	AT	Compression Pressure (psi)	Fuel Pump (psi)	Idle Speed (rpm) MT	AT	Valve Clearance In.	Ex.
1986	8	8-350 (5.7)	0.035	6B	6B①	②	9-13	450	400①	Hyd.	Hyd.
1987	8	8-350 (5.7)	0.035	6B @	6B @ 450 400①	②	9-13	450	400①	Hyd.	Hyd.
1988	8	8-350 (5.7)	0.035	④	④	②	3-10	450③	450③	Hyd.	Hyd.
1989	8	8-350 (5.7)	0.035	④	④	②	3-10	450③	450③	Hyd.	Hyd.
1990		SEE UNDERHOOD SPECIFICATIONS STICKER									

① In Drive
② When checking cylinder compression pressures, the throttle should be open, all spark plugs should be removed and the battery should be near or at full charge. The lowest reading cylinder should not be less than 70% of the highest cylinder. No individual cylinder reading should be less than 100 lbs.
③ Minimum idle speed specification shown. Idle speed is usually a non-adjustable specification controlled by the ECM
④ Refer to Vehicle Emission Control Information label for ignition timing specifications. If no specifications are shown, no adjustment is required

FIRING ORDERS

NOTE: To avoid confusion, replace the spark plug wires one at a time.

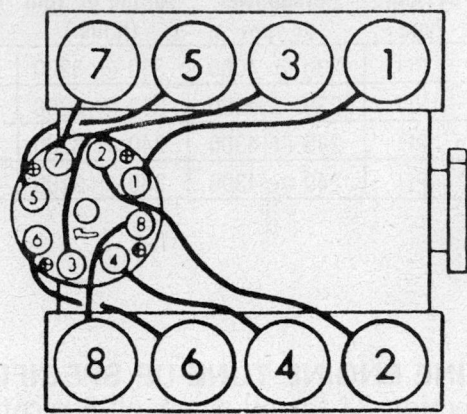

GM (Chevrolet) 350 V8 (5.7L)
Engine Firing Order: 1–8–4–3–6–5–7–2
Distributor Rotation: clockwise

CAPACITIES

Year	Model	VIN	No. Cylinder Displacement cu. in. (liter)	Engine Crankcase with Filter	Engine Crankcase without Filter	Transmission (pts.) 4-Spd	Transmission (pts.) 5-Spd	Transmission (pts.) Auto.	Drive Axle (pts.)	Fuel Tank (gal.)	Cooling System (qts.)
1986	Corvette	8	8-350 (5.7)	5	4	3.5①	—	10	3.75	20	14
1987	Corvette	8	8-350 (5.7)	5	4	3.5①	—	10	3.75	20	14
1988	Corvette	8	8-350 (5.7)	5	4	3.5①	—	10	3.75	20	14
1989-90	Corvette	8	8-350 (5.7)	5	4	—	②	10	3.75	20	14

① 4 speed overdrive uses Dexron®II in the overdrive section and 80WGL5 in the transmission section
② ZF 6 speed transmission—4.4 pts.

CAMSHAFT SPECIFICATIONS
All measurements given in inches.

Year	VIN	No. Cylinder Displacement cu. in. (liter)	Journal Diameter 1	2	3	4	5	Lobe Lift In.	Lobe Lift Ex.	Bearing Clearance	Camshaft End Play
1986	8	8-350 (5.7)	1.8682–1.8692	1.8682–1.8692	1.8682–1.8692	1.8682–1.8692	1.8682–1.8692	0.2733①	0.2820①	—	0.004–0.012
1987	8	8-350 (5.7)	1.8682–1.8692	1.8682–1.8692	1.8682–1.8692	1.8682–1.8692	1.8682–1.8692	0.2733①	0.2820①	—	0.004–0.012
1988	8	8-350 (5.7)	1.8682–1.8692	1.8682–1.8692	1.8682–1.8692	1.8682–1.8692	1.8682–1.8692	0.2733①	0.2820①	—	0.004–0.012
1989-90	8	8-350 (5.7)	1.8682–1.8692	1.8682–1.8692	1.8682–1.8692	1.8682–1.8692	1.8682–1.8692	0.2733①	0.2820①	—	0.004–0.012

① ± 0.002

CRANKSHAFT AND CONNECTING ROD SPECIFICATIONS
All measurements are given in inches.

Year	VIN	No. Cylinder Displacement cu. in. (liter)	Crankshaft				Connecting Rod		
			Main Brg. Journal Dia.	Main Brg. Oil Clearance	Shaft End-play	Thrust on No.	Journal Diameter	Oil Clearance	Side Clearance
1986	8	8-350 (5.7)	2.4484–2.4493 ①	0.0008–0.0020 ②	0.002–0.006	5	2.0988–2.0998	0.0013–0.0035	0.006–0.014
1987	8	8-350 (5.7)	2.4484–2.4493 ①	0.0008–0.0020 ②	0.002–0.006	5	2.0988–2.0998	0.0013–0.0035	0.006–0.014
1988	8	8-350 (5.7)	2.4484–2.4493 ①	0.0008–0.0020 ②	0.002–0.006	5	2.0988–2.0998	0.0013–0.0035	0.006–0.014
1989-90	8	8-350 (5.7)	2.4484–2.4493 ①	0.0008–0.0020 ②	0.002–0.006	5	2.0988–2.0998	0.0013–0.0035	0.006–0.014

① Specification applies to the No. 1 bearing.
Nos. 2, 3, 4—2.4481-2.4490
No. 5—2.4479-2.4488

② Specification applies to the No. 1 bearing.
Nos. 2, 3, 4—.0011-.0023

No. 5—.0017-.0032
Specifications shown apply to new components

VALVE SPECIFICATIONS

Year	VIN	No. Cylinder Displacement cu. in. (liter)	Seat Angle (deg.)	Face Angle (deg.)	Spring Test Pressure (lbs.)	Spring Installed Height (in.)	Stem-to-Guide Clearance (in.)		Stem Diameter (in.)	
							Intake	Exhaust	Intake	Exhaust
1986	8	8-350 (5.7)	46	45	194-206 @ 1.25①	1²³⁄₃₂②	0.0010–0.0027	0.0010–0.0027	0.3410–0.3417	0.3410–0.3417
1987	8	8-350 (5.7)	46	45	194-206 @ 1.25①	1²³⁄₃₂②	0.0010–0.0027	0.0010–0.0027	0.3410–0.3417	0.3410–0.3417
1988	8	8-350 (5.7)	46	45	194-206 @ 1.25①	1²³⁄₃₂②	0.0010–0.0027	0.0010–0.0027	0.3410–0.3417	0.3410–0.3417
1989-90	8	8-350 (5.7)	46	45	194-206 @ 1.25①	1²³⁄₃₂②	0.0010–0.0027	0.0010–0.0027	0.3410–0.3417	0.3410–0.3417

① Exhaust valve—1.16
② Exhaust—1¹⁹⁄₃₂

PISTON AND RING SPECIFICATIONS
All measurments are given in inches.

Year	VIN	No. Cylinder Displacement cu. in. (liter)	Piston Clearance	Ring Gap			Ring Side Clearance		
				Top Compression	Bottom Compression	Oil Control	Top Compression	Bottom Compression	Oil Control
1986	8	8-350 (5.7)	0.0025–0.0035	0.010–0.020	0.010–0.025	0.015–0.055	0.0012–0.0032	0.0012–0.0032	0.002–0.007
1987	8	8-350 (5.7)	0.0007–0.0017 ①	0.010–0.020	0.013–0.025	0.015–0.055	0.0012–0.0029	0.0012–0.0029	0.002–0.008

PISTON AND RING SPECIFICATIONS
All measurments are given in inches.

Year	VIN	No. Cylinder Displacement cu. in. (liter)	Piston Clearance	Ring Gap			Ring Side Clearance		
				Top Compression	Bottom Compression	Oil Control	Top Compression	Bottom Compression	Oil Control
1988	8	8-350 (5.7)	0.0007–0.0017 ①	0.010–0.020	0.013–0.025	0.015–0.055	0.0012–0.0029	0.0012–0.0029	0.002–0.008
1989-90	8	8-350 (5.7)	0.0007–0.0017 ②	0.010–0.020	0.013–0.017	0.010–0.030	0.0012–0.0029	0.0012–0.0029	0.0012–0.0029

① 0.0025 maximum
② 0.0027 maximum

TORQUE SPECIFICATIONS
All readings in ft. lbs.

Year	VIN	No. Cylinder Displacement cu. in. (liter)	Cylinder Head Bolts	Main Bearing Bolts	Rod Bearing Bolts	Crankshaft Pulley Bolts	Flywheel Bolts	Manifold		Spark Plugs
								Intake	Exhaust	
1986	8	8-350 (5.7)	65①	80	45	60	60	30	20	22
1987	8	8-350 (5.7)	65①	80	45	60	60	30	20	22
1988	8	8-350 (5.7)	65	80	45	59-81	60	35	20	22
1989-90	8	8-350 (5.7)	67	80	45	70	60	35	19	22

① Long and medium; short—60 ft.lbs.

WHEEL ALIGNMENT

Year	Model		Caster		Camber		Toe-in (in.)	Steering Axis Inclination (deg.)
			Range (deg.)	Preferred Setting (deg.)	Range (deg.)	Preferred Setting (deg.)		
1986	Corvette	Front	5½-6½	6	⁵/₁₆-1⁵/₁₆	¹³/₁₆	⁵/₃₂	8¾
		Rear	—	—	¹/₃₂N-²⁹/₃₂P	¹³/₃₂	⁵/₃₂	—
1987	Corvette	Front	4¹¹/₁₆-6⁵/₁₆	5½	⁵/₁₆-1⁵/₁₆	¹³/₁₆	³/₃₂	8¾
		Rear	—	—	¹/₁₆N-²⁹/₃₂P	¹³/₃₂	³/₃₂	—
1988	Corvette	Front	4¹¹/₁₆-6⁵/₁₆	5½	⁵/₁₆-1⁵/₁₆	¹³/₁₆	³/₃₂	8¾
		Rear	—	—	¹/₁₆N-²⁹/₃₂P	¹³/₃₂	³/₃₂	—
1989-90	Corvette	Front	5⁵/₁₆-6⁵/₁₆	5¹³/₁₆	0–1	½	³/₆₄	—
		Rear	—	—	⁵/₁₆N-¹¹/₁₆P	³/₁₆	³/₆₄	—

N—Negative
P—Positive

ELECTRICAL

NOTE: Disconnecting the negative battery cable on some vehicles may interfere with the functions of the on board computer systems and may require the computer to undergo a relearning process, once the negative battery cable is reconnected.

For testing and overhaul procedures on starters, alternators and voltage regulators, refer to Unit Repair Section.

Charging System

ALTERNATOR

Removal and Installation

1. Disconnect the negative battery cable.
2. Remove all necessary components in order to gain access to the alternator assembly.
3. Disconnect the 2 terminal plugs and the battery leads from the back of the alternator assembly. Identify each wire with its respective connection to ensure proper reinstallation.
4. Loosen the adjusting bolts.
5. Remove the serpentine drive belt.
6. Remove the alternator retaining bolts.
7. Remove the alternator assembly from the vehicle.
8. Installation is the reverse of the removal procedure. Check for the proper belt tension.

VOLTAGE REGULATOR

The CS type alternator uses a built-in regulator with fault detection. There are no adjustments possible with this unit. To replace the voltage regulator, the alternator must be removed and disassembled.

BELT TENSION

A single serpentine belt is used to drive all accessories. Belt tension is maintained by a spring loaded tensioner which has the ability to maintain belt tension over a broad range of belt lengths. There is an indicator to make sure the tensioner is adjusted to within its operating range.

To check the belt tension, install belt tension gauge J–23600 between the alternator and the air pump. The correct belt tension should be 120–140 lbs. (534–623N).

Starting System

STARTER

Removal and Installation

1. Disconnect the negative battery cable.
2. Raise and support the vehicle safely.
3. Remove the flywheel cover.
4. Disconnect the wiring from the starter solenoid. Replace each connector nut as the terminals are removed as the thread sizes differ between connectors. Tag the wiring positions to avoid improper connections during installation.
5. Loosen the 2 starter mounting bolts, support the starter and remove the bolts. Lower the starter from the vehicle.
6. Installation is the reverse of the removal procedure.
7. Check the flywheel to pinion clearance. The clearance should be 0.020 in. (0.5mm).
8. Torque the 2 starter mounting bolts to 35 ft. lbs. (47 Nm).

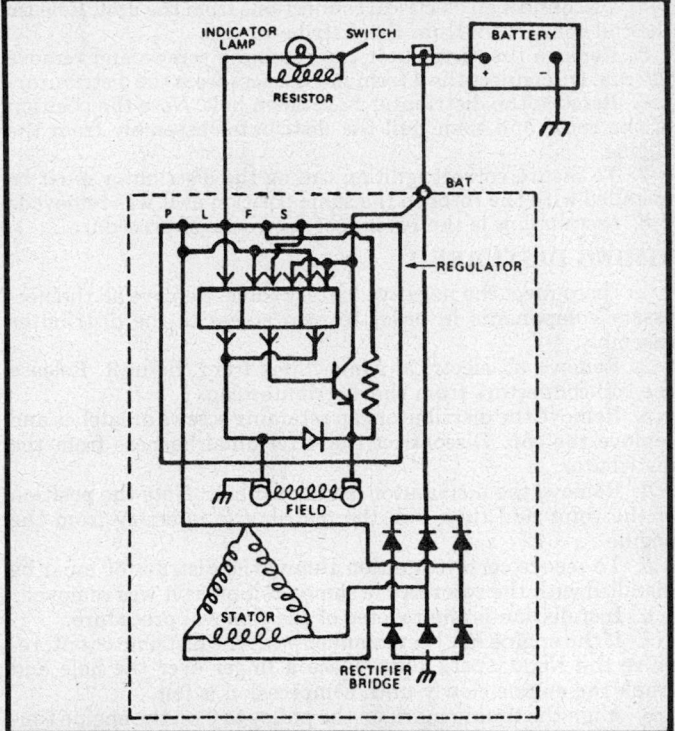

CS charging system wiring schematic

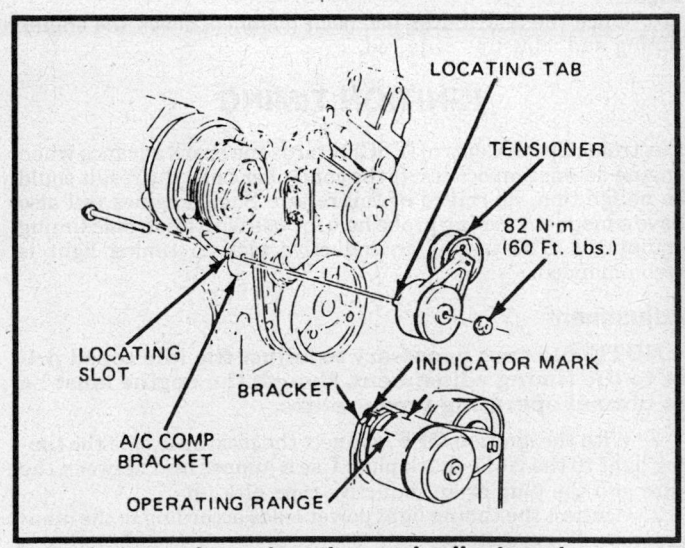

Drive belt tensioner location and adjustment

Ignition System

DISTRIBUTOR

Removal and Installation
TIMING NOT DISTURBED

1. Disconnect the negative battery cable.

2. Remove the air cleaner cover and distributor shield.

3. Disconnect the ignition switch battery feed wire and tachometer wire from the distributor cap, if equipped.

4. Disconnect all electrical connections from the unit. Release the coil connectors from the distributor cap.

5. Remove the distributor cap retaining screws and remove the cap. Disconnect the 4 terminal harness from the distributor.

6. Remove the distributor hold down bolt. Note the position of the rotor and then pull the distributor assembly from the engine.

7. To insure correct ignition timing the distributor must be installed with the rotor in the same position as it was removed.

8. Installation is the reverse of the removal procedure.

TIMING DISTURBED

1. Disconnect the negative battery cable. Remove all the necessary components in order to gain access to the distributor assembly.

2. Remove all electrical connections from the unit. Release the coil connectors from the distributor cap.

3. Remove the distributor cap retaining screws or latches and remove the cap. Disconnect the 4 terminal harness from the distributor.

4. Remove the distributor hold down bolt. Note the position of the rotor and then pull the distributor assembly from the engine.

5. To insure correct ignition timing the distributor must be installed with the rotor in the same position as it was removed.

6. Installation is the reverse of the removal procedure.

7. If the engine has been cranked with the distributor out, remove the No. 1 spark plug. Place a finger over the hole and crank the engine slowly until compression is felt.

8. Align the timing mark on the pulley to **0** on the engine timing indicator. Position the rotor between the No. 1 and No. 8 spark plug towers.

9. The distributor can now be correctly installed in the engine.

10. Once the distributor has been installed, check the engine timing and adjust as required.

IGNITION TIMING

Electronic Spark Control (ESC) retards the spark advance when engine detonation occurs. If the controller fails, the result could be no ignition, no retard or full retard. Some engines will also have a magnetic timing probe hole for use with electronic timing equipment. The use of an inductive pick-up timing light is recommended.

Adjustment

NOTE: It is not necessary to adjust the idle speed prior to the timing adjustment, though the engine must be at normal operating temperature.

1. With the ignition **OFF**, connect the pick-up lead of the timing light to the No. 1 spark plug. Use a jumper lead between the wire and the plug or an inductive type pick-up.

2. Connect the timing light power leads according to the manufacturers instructions.

3. Disconnect the ECM harness connector at the distributor.

4. Start the engine and run it at idle speed. Aim the timing light at the timing mark. The line on the balancer or pulley will align with the timing mark.

5. If required, adjust the timing by loosening the securing clamp hold-down bolt and rotating the distributor until the desired ignition advance is achieved, then tighten the bolt.

6. To advance the timing, rotate the distributor opposite to the normal direction of rotor rotation. Retard the timing by rotating the distributor in the normal direction of rotor rotation.

7. Tighten the hold down bolt to 25 ft. lbs. (34 Nm).

8. Turn the ignition **OFF** and remove the timing light. Re-

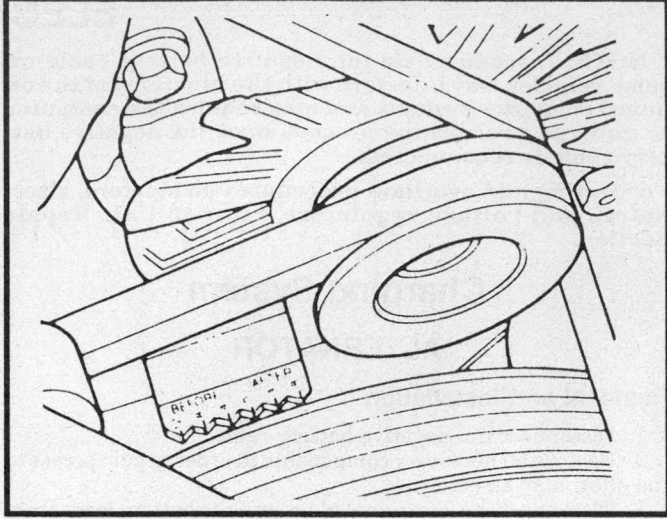

Timing mark—typical

connect the No. 1 spark plug wire and connect the ECM harness connector.

Electrical Controls

STEERING WHEEL

Removal and Installation

1. Disconnect the negative battery cable.

2. Squeeze the horn cap (top and bottom), disengage the locking fingers and remove the cap.

3. Remove the retaining screws and remove the upper horn contact assembly. Disconnect the horn lead wire connector.

4. If used, remove the shim then remove the screw securing the center star screw. Remove the star screw and telescope adjusting lever assembly.

5. Remove the snapring and nut from the shaft. Remove the steering wheel assembly with a wheel puller.

6. Installation is the reverse of the removal procedure.

HORN SWITCH

Removal and Installation

1. Disconnect the negative battery cable.

2. Squeeze the horn cap (top and bottom), disengage the locking fingers and remove the cap.

3. Remove the retaining screws and remove the upper horn contact assembly.

4. Disconnect the horn lead wire connector.

5. Installation is the reverse of the removal procedure.

IGNITION LOCK

Removal and Installation

1. Disconnect the negative battery cable.

2. Remove the steering wheel.

3. Remove the rubber sleeve bumper from the steering shaft.

4. Using an appropriate tool, remove the plastic retainer.

5. Using a spring compressor, compress the upper steering shaft spring and remove the C-ring. Release the steering shaft lockplate, the horn contact carrier and the upper steering shaft preload spring.

6. Remove the 4 screws which hold the upper mounting bracket and then remove the bracket.

7. Slide the harness connector out of the bracket on the steer-

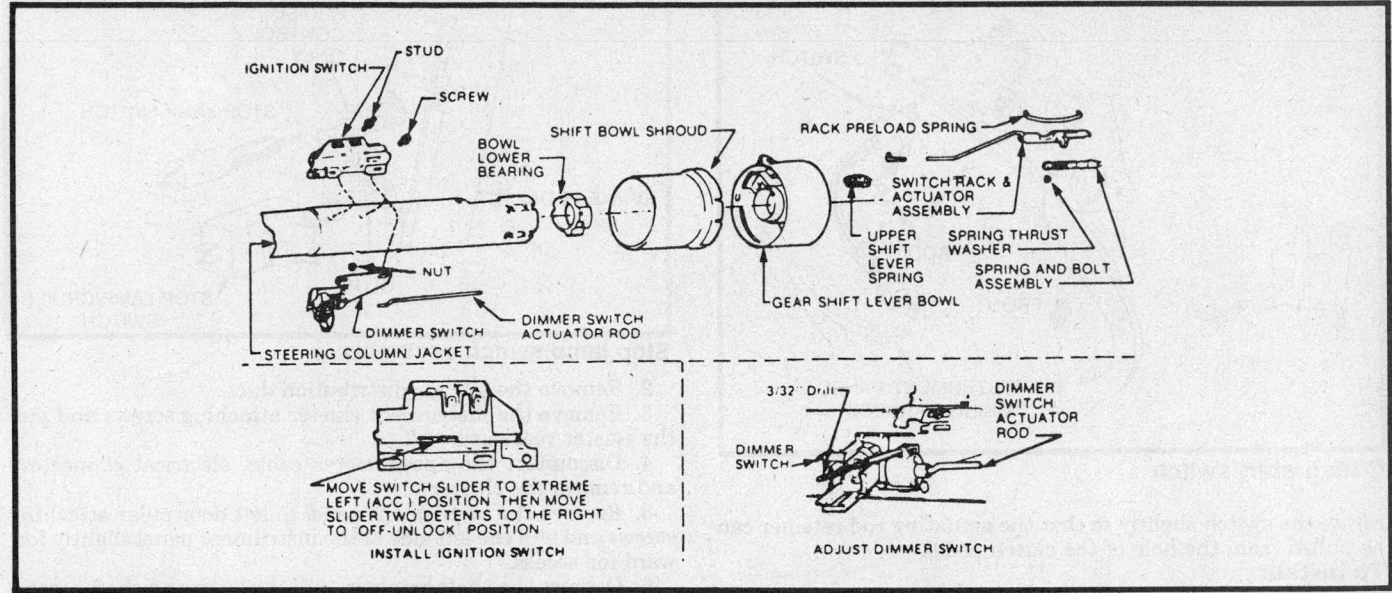

Ignition and dimmer switches installation

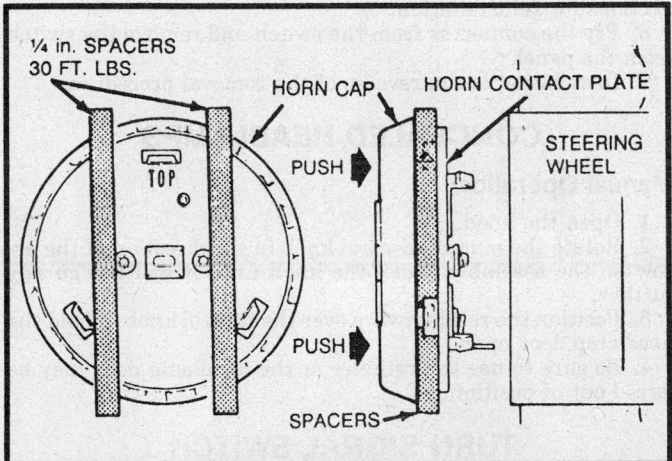

Horn cap and contact plate assembly (typical)

ing column. Tape the upper part of the harness and connector.

8. Disconnect the hazard button and position the shift bowl in park.

9. Remove the turn signal lever from the column.

10. If the vehicle is equipped with cruise control, remove the harness protector from the harness. Attach a piece of wire to the switch harness connector. Before removing the turn signal lever, loop a piece of wire and insert it into the turn signal lever opening. Use the wire to pull the cruise control harness out through the opening. Pull the rest of the harness up through and out of the column.

11. Remove the guide wire from the connector and secure the wire to the column.

12. Remove the turn signal lever.

13. Pull the turn signal switch up until the end connector is within the shift bowl.

14. Remove the hazard flasher lever. Allow the switch to hang.

15. Place the ignition key in the run position.

16. Depress the center of the lock cylinder retaining tab with a suitable tool and then remove the lock cylinder.

17. On some vehicles it will be necessary to cut and splice an electrical wire which is a part of the lock cylinder.

18. Installation is the reverse of the removal procedure.

IGNITION SWITCH

Removal and Installation

1. Disconnect the negative battery terminal.
2. Loosen the retaining screws on the steering column.
3. Remove the column to instrument panel trim plates and attaching nuts.
4. Lower the steering column.

NOTE: Be sure that the steering column is supported at all times in order to prevent damage to the column.

5. Disconnect the switch wire connectors.
6. Remove the switch attaching screws and remove the switch.

To install:

7. Move the key lock to the **LOCK** position.
8. Move the actuator rod hole in the switch to the **LOCK** position.
9. Install the switch with the rod in the hole.
10. Position and reassemble the steering column in reverse of the disassembly procedure.

NEUTRAL SAFETY SWITCH

These vehicles incorporate a mechanical neutral start system. This system relies on a mechanical block, rather than the starter safety switch to prevent starting the engine in other than **P** or **N**.

The mechanical block is achieved by a metal finger that has been added to the switch actuator rack, which interferes with the bowl plate in all shift positions except **N** or **P**. This interference prevents rotation of the lock cylinder into the **START** position.

In either **P** or **N**, this finger passes through the bowl plates slots allowing the lock cylinder full rotational travel into the **START** position.

CLUTCH START SWITCH

Removal and Installation

1. Disconnect the negative battery cable.
2. Remove the hush pad from under the dash panel.
3. Remove the bolt and switch from the clutch bracket and

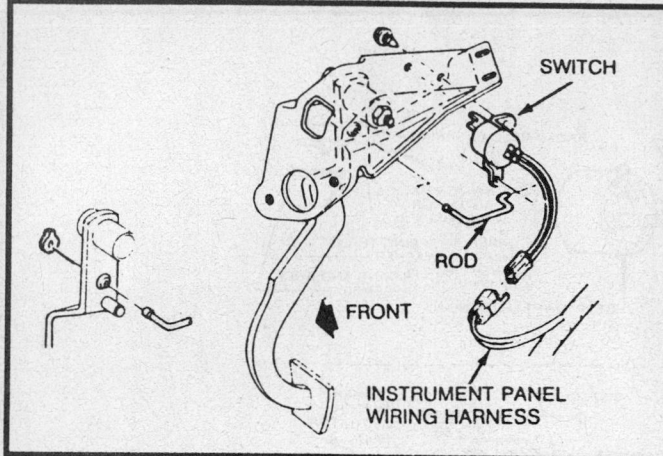

Clutch start switch

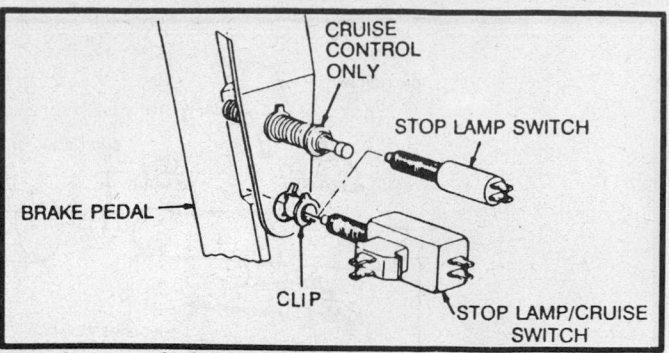

Stop lamp switch assembly

rotate the switch slightly so that the actuating rod retainer can be pulled from the hole of the clutch pedal.

To install:

4. Place a new switch in position so that the actuating rod retainer is in line with the hole in the clutch pedal and reinstall the bolt.

5. Connect the electrical connector to the switch and depress the clutch pedal fully to the floor to adjust the switch.

NOTE: The clutch operated starting switch is self adjusting after initial installation. If there is a readjustment necessary, depress the detent on the adjuster block and slide the block to the full forward position on the actuating rod. Depress clutch pedal fully to the floor to adjust the clutch switch.

STOPLIGHT SWITCH

Adjustment

NOTE: Do not use excessive force while adjusting the stop lamp switch as damage to the power booster may occur.

Pull the brake pedal fully rearward against the pedal stop until the clicking sounds cannot be heard. The switch can be moved in the clip to correct the adjustment.

Electrical contact should be made when the brake pedal is depressed $3/8$–$5/8$ in. from the fully released position. Release the brake pedal and make sure that no clicking sounds remain. When no clicks can be heard with the brake pedal pulled up, the stop lamp switch is correctly adjusted.

Removal and Installation

1. Disconnect the negative battery cable.
2. Disconnect the wire harness connector from the switch.
3. Remove the switch from the clip and then remove the clip from the bracket.

To Install:

4. Install the clip in its bore on the bracket.
5. With the brake pedal depressed, insert the switch into the clip and depress the switch body.
6. Adjust the switch.
7. Install the harness connector and verify the stoplights operate correctly.

HEADLAMP SWITCH

Removal and Installation

1. Disconnect the negative battery terminal.

2. Remove the left air distribution duct.
3. Remove the instrument cluster attaching screws and pull the cluster rearward.
4. Disconnect the speedometer cable, electrical connectors and remove the cluster.
5. Remove the instrument panel to left door pillar attaching screws and pull the left side of the instrument panel slightly forward for access.
6. Depress the shaft retainer, pull the knob and shaft assembly out and remove the switch bezel.
7. Disconnect all connections from the switch. Mark the connections for reinstallation.
8. Pry the connector from the switch and remove the switch from the panel.
9. Installation is the reverse of the removal procedure.

CONCEALED HEADLAMPS

Manual Operation

1. Open the hood.
2. Rotate the manual control knob in the direction of the arrow on the assembly. Turn the knob until it will not go any further.
3. Position the retainer wire over the control knob to hold the headlamp door open.
4. Be sure to use the retainer or the headlamp door may be jarred out of position.

TURN SIGNAL SWITCH

Removal and Installation

1. Disconnect the negative battery cable.
2. Remove the steering wheel.
3. Remove the steering column/dash trim cover.
4. Remove the C-ring plastic retainer.
5. Install the special lockplate compressing tool (J–23653 and J–23063) over the steering shaft. Position a $5/16$ in. nut under each tool leg and reinstall the star screw to prevent the shaft from moving.
6. Compress the lock plate by turning the shaft nut clockwise until the C-ring can be removed.
7. Remove the tool and lift out the lockplate, horn contact carrier and the upper bearing preload spring.
8. Pull the switch connector out of the mast jacket and tape the upper part to facilitate switch removal.
9. Remove the turn signal lever. Push the flasher in and unscrew it.
10. Position the turn signal and shifter housing in **LOW** position. Remove the switch by pulling it straight up while guiding the wiring harness out of the housing.

To install:

11. Install the replacement switch by working the harness connector down through the housing and under the mounting bracket.

WIPER & WASHER MOTOR DIAGNOSTIC CHART

PROBABLE CAUSE \\ SYMPTOM	Wiper system inoperative—all modes	Wiper won't shut off	Blades cycle in and out of park position	Wiper has Hi speed only—won't delay	Wiper inop in "Delay" mode, functions OK in other modes	Wiper won't delay between delay wipes	Wiper has Lo speed only	Wiper intermittent operation	Washer does not operate properly in demand or program modes
Defective cover/board	XX*				X	X			X
Motor defective	X			X			X	XX*	
Park switch defective			X	X					
Gear train damaged								X	

*Denotes most probable cause.

12. Install the harness cover and clip the connector to the mast jacket.

13. Install the switch mounting screws, signal lever and the flasher knob.

14. With the turn signal lever in neutral and the flasher knob out, install the upper bearing preload spring, horn contact carrier and lock plate onto the shaft.

15. Position the tool as in Step 4 and compress the plate far enough to allow the C-ring to be installed.

16. Remove the tool. Install the plastic C-ring retainer.

17. Install the column/dash trim cover. Install the steering wheel.

WINDSHIELD WIPER SWITCH

Removal and Installation

1. Disconnect the negative battery cable.
2. Remove the drivers door panel, as required.
3. Disconnect the electrical connections from the switch.
4. Remove the switch retaining screws. Remove the switch from the panel.
5. Installation is the reverse of the removal procedure.

WINDSHIELD WIPER MOTOR

Removal and Installation

1. Disconnect the negative battery cable.
2. Remove wiper arms.
3. Remove air inlet leaf screen.
4. Turn ignition ON and activate motor with wiper switch. Allow motor crank arm to rotate to point to a position between 4 and 5 o'clock as viewed from passenger compartment. Stop crank arm in this position by turning OFF ignition switch.
5. Disconnect battery ground cable.
6. Disconnect upper motor electrical connectors.
7. Remove motor mounting bolts.
8. With crank arm in position described in Step 4 above, motor may now be removed from vehicle. Lower electrical connector may be disconnected as motor is partially removed.
9. Installation is the reverse of the removal procedure.

DELAY WIPER CONTROLS

Operation

The electronic printed circuit board controls all the timing and washer commands. Moving the switch to the LO or HI speed position completes the respective brush circuit to 12V at the switch and the wiper motor runs at that speed.

Moving the switch to the DELAY position operates the motor intermittently. The delay time can be varied by moving the switch back and forth in the DELAY mode.

An instantaneous wipe can be obtained by moving the switch to the MIST position and a continuous wipe will be performed if the switch is held.

WINDSHIELD WIPER LINKAGE

Removal and Installation

1. Raise the hood. Turn the windshield wipers ON.
2. With the wipers ON, turn the ignition switch OFF when the wipers are at the mid-wipe position.
3. Lift the wiper arm from the windshield and pull the retaining latch.
4. Lift the wiper from the transmission shaft.
5. Disconnect the wiper hose at the wiper transmission end of the wet arm.
6. Remove the screen over the left cowl.
7. Remove the nuts holding the wiper motor crank arm in the wiper transmission link sockets.
8. Remove the wiper transmission to body attaching screws.
9. Remove the wiper transmission and linkage by guiding it through the plenum chamber opening or to the left side under the dash panel extension.
10. Installation is the reverse of the removal procedure.

Instrument Cluster

Refer to "Chilton's Electronic Instrumentation Service Manual" for additional coverage.

Removal and Installation

1. Disconnect battery ground cable.
2. Remove light switch knob (spring loaded) and light switch nut.
3. Remove steering column trim cover.
4. Remove the steering column attaching bolts and lower steering column for access.
5. Remove cluster bezel front and left side attaching screws.
6. Remove cluster bezel from instrument panel.
7. Remove the cluster to instrument panel attaching screws.

COVER
786
CASTING
3 2 1
END CAP
45
1 LO SPEED
7 8 6
4 5
3 2 1
12V
2 HI SPEED
7 8 6
4 5
3 2 1
12V
3 PARK
7 8 6
4 5
3 2 1
12V
4 PULSE
7 8 6
4 5
3 2 1
500K
12V
12V

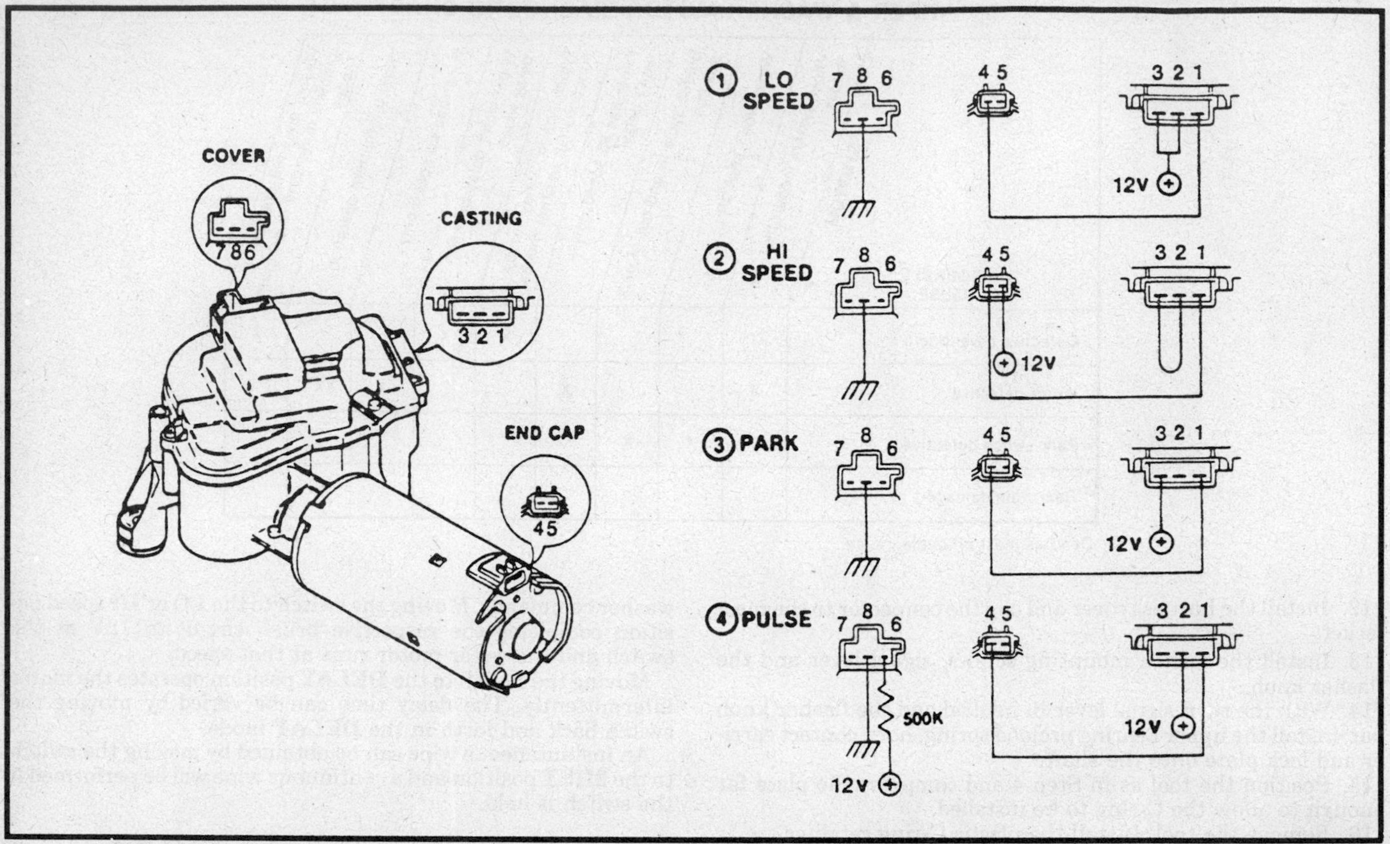

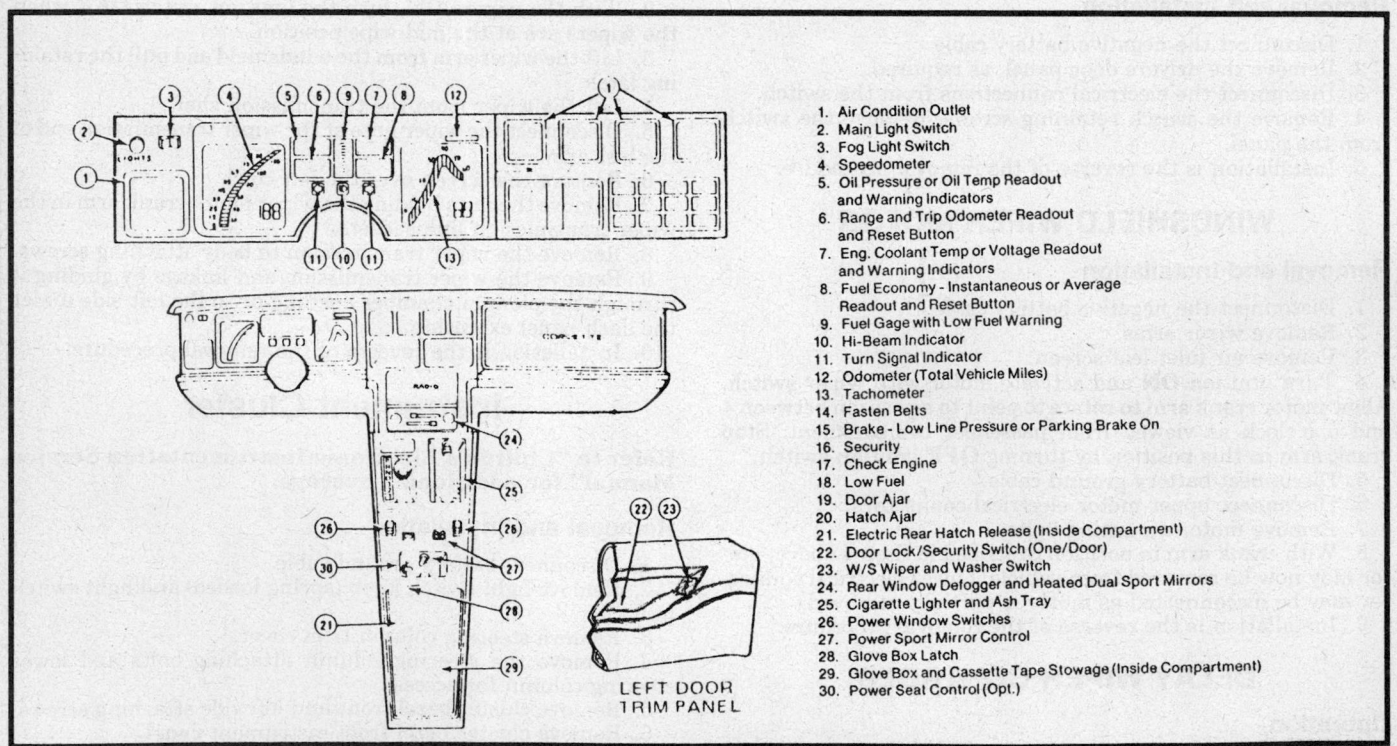

Delay wiper motor test

LEFT DOOR TRIM PANEL
1. Air Condition Outlet
2. Main Light Switch
3. Fog Light Switch
4. Speedometer
5. Oil Pressure or Oil Temp Readout and Warning Indicators
6. Range and Trip Odometer Readout and Reset Button
7. Eng. Coolant Temp or Voltage Readout and Warning Indicators
8. Fuel Economy - Instantaneous or Average Readout and Reset Button
9. Fuel Gage with Low Fuel Warning
10. Hi-Beam Indicator
11. Turn Signal Indicator
12. Odometer (Total Vehicle Miles)
13. Tachometer
14. Fasten Belts
15. Brake - Low Line Pressure or Parking Brake On
16. Security
17. Check Engine
18. Low Fuel
19. Door Ajar
20. Hatch Ajar
21. Electric Rear Hatch Release (Inside Compartment)
22. Door Lock/Security Switch (One/Door)
23. W/S Wiper and Washer Switch
24. Rear Window Defogger and Heated Dual Sport Mirrors
25. Cigarette Lighter and Ash Tray
26. Power Window Switches
27. Power Sport Mirror Control
28. Glove Box Latch
29. Glove Box and Cassette Tape Stowage (Inside Compartment)
30. Power Seat Control (Opt.)

Instrument cluster assembly

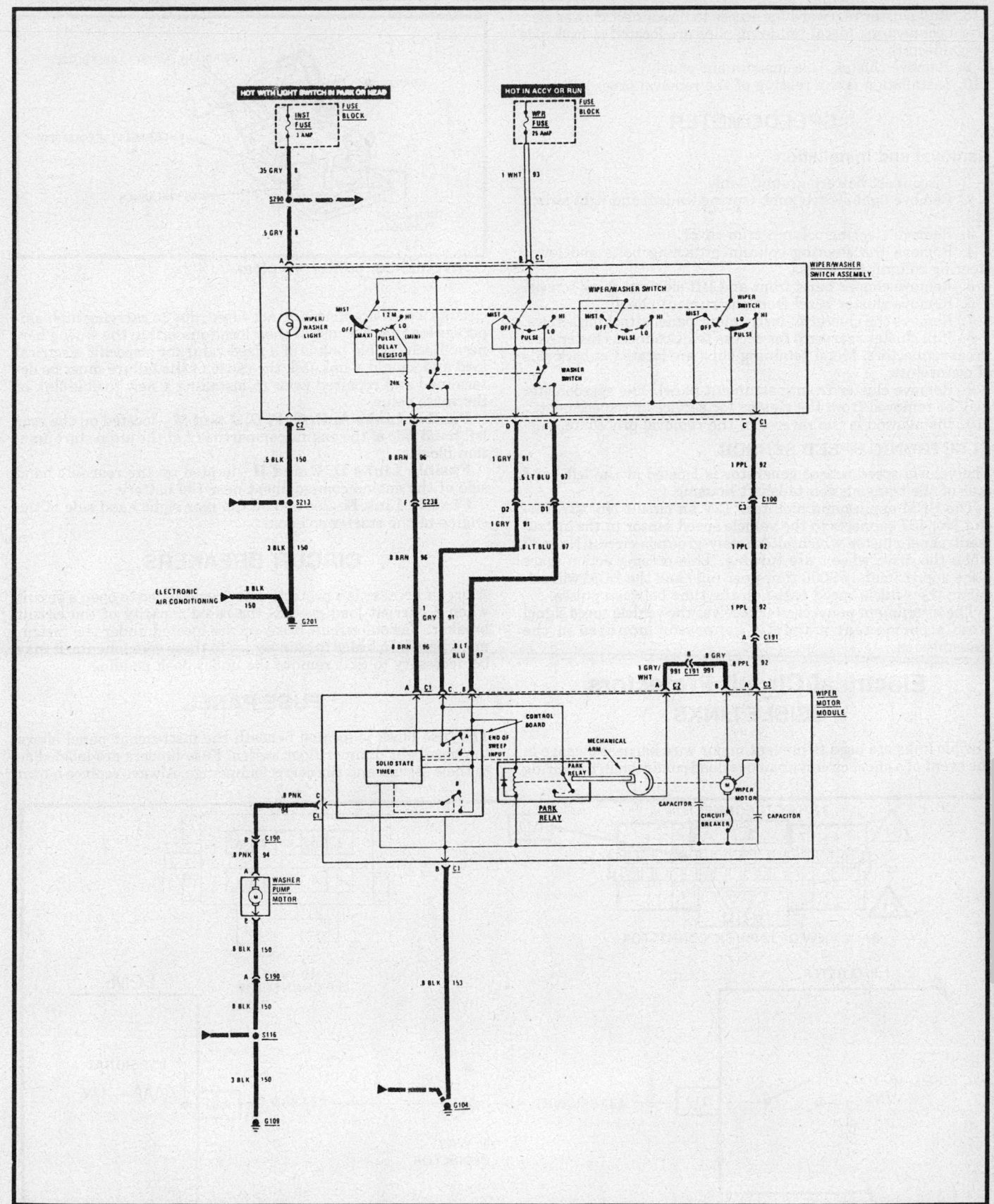

Wiper/washer circuit schematic

8. Pull cluster rearward for access to disconnect cluster electrical connectors. Metal retaining clips are located at back side of connectors.

9. Remove cluster from instrument panel.

10. Installation is the reverse of the removal procedure.

SPEEDOMETER

Removal and Installation

1. Disconnect battery ground cable.

2. Remove light switch knob (spring loaded) and light switch nut.

3. Remove steering column trim cover.

4. Remove the steering column attaching bolts and lower steering column for access.

5. Remove cluster bezel front and left side attaching screws.

6. Remove cluster bezel from instrument panel.

7. Remove the cluster to instrument panel attaching screws.

8. Pull cluster rearward for access to disconnect cluster electrical connectors. Metal retaining clips are located at back side of connectors.

9. Remove cluster from instrument panel. The speedometer may be removed from the cluster for service or replacement.

10. Installation is the reverse of the removal procedure.

ELECTRONIC SPEED SENSOR

The vehicle speed sensor generator is located at the left hand rear of the transmission tailshaft housing.

The ECM applies and monitors 12V on circuit No. 437. Circuit No. 437 connects to the vehicle speed sensor in the instrument panel cluster which alternately grounds circuit No. 437 when the drive wheels are turning. This pulsing action takes place approximately 2000 times per mile and the ECM will calculate the vehicle speed based on the time between pulses.

The instrument panel cluster receives the vehicle speed signal from a permanent magnetic generator mounted in the transmission.

Electrical Circuit Protectors
FUSIBLE LINKS

Fusible links are used to prevent major wire harness damage in the event of a short circuit or an overload condition in the wiring

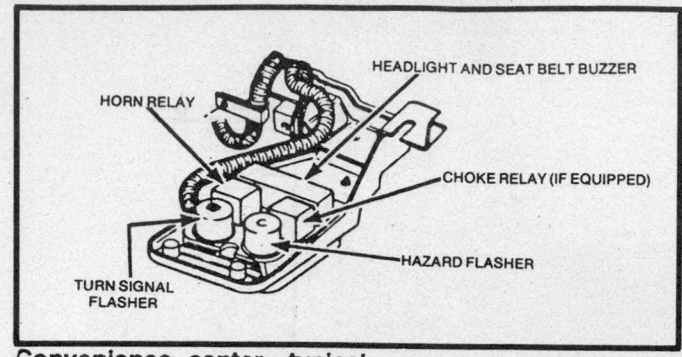

Convenience center—typical

circuits which are normally not fused, due to carrying high amperage loads or because of their locations within the wiring harness. Each fusible link is of a fixed value for a specific electrical load and should a link fail, the cause of the failure must be determined and repaired prior to installing a new fusible link of the same value.

Fusible Links A, B, C, F, G, J and M—located on the rear left hand side of the engine compartment at the jump start junction block.

Fusible Links D, E and H—located on the rear left hand side of the engine compartment near the battery.

Fusible Link K—located on the rear right hand side of the engine at the starter solenoid.

CIRCUIT BREAKERS

A circuit breaker is a protective device designed to open a circuit when a current load exceeds the rated capacity of the circuit breaker. Various circuit breakers are located under the instrument panel. In order to gain access to these components, it may be necessary to first remove the under dash padding.

FUSE PANEL

The fuse block is located beneath the instrument panel above the headlight dimmer floor switch. Fuse holders are labeled as to their service and the correct amperage. Always replace blown

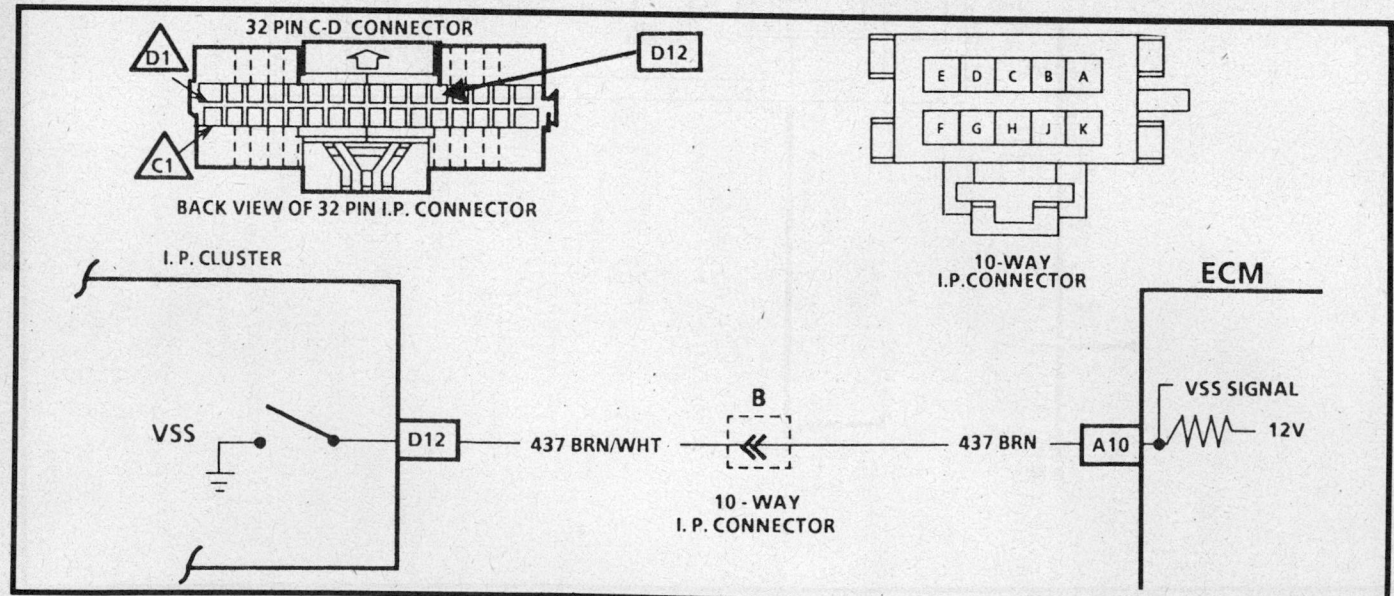

fuses with new ones of the correct amperage. Otherwise electrical overloads and possible wiring damage will result.

The fuse block on some models is a swing down unit located in the underside of the instrument panel adjacent to the steering column. Access to the fuse block on some models is gained through the glove box opening. The convenience center on some models is a swing down unit located on the underside of the instrument panel. The swing down feature provides center location and easy access to buzzers, relays and flasher units. All units are serviced by replacement components. Location of convenience center on specific models may vary.

COMPUTER

The Electronic Control Module (ECM) is located up under the dash. In order to gain access to the assembly, remove the trim panel. The ECM contains the electronic circuitry that functions to monitor and control the air/fuel and emissions systems.

VARIOUS RELAYS

All vehicles use a combination of the following electrical relays in order to maintain a properly functioning electrical system.

Amplifier Relay — located behind the center of the dash panel.

Anti-Theft Relay — located in the convenience center.

Auxiliary Engine Cooling Fan Relay — located in the left rear corner of the engine compartment.

Engine Cooling Fan Relay — located under the brake booster assembly.

Fuel Pump Relay — located on the left side of the firewall in the engine comaprtment.

Headlight Actuator Relays — located on the support in the front of the left front wheel well.

High Speed Blower Relay — located on the A/C-Heater blower assembly.

Horn Relay — located in the convenience center.

Overdrive Relay — located on the rear of the right front fender apron.

Power Antenna Relay — located on the rear of the center console.

Power Door Lock Relay — located in the convience center.

Rear Hatch Release Relay — located at the rear hatch release latch.

TURN SIGNAL FLASHER

The turn signal flasher is located inside the convenience center. In order to gain access to the turn signal flasher it may be necessary to first remove the under dash padding.

HAZARD FLASHER

The hazard flasher is located inside the convenience center. In order to gain access to the turn signal flasher it may be necessary to first remove the under dash padding.

Speed Controls

Refer to "Chilton's Chassis Electronic Service Manual" for additional coverage.

COMPONENTS

Electronic cruise control is a speed control system which maintains a desired vehicle speed under normal driving conditions.

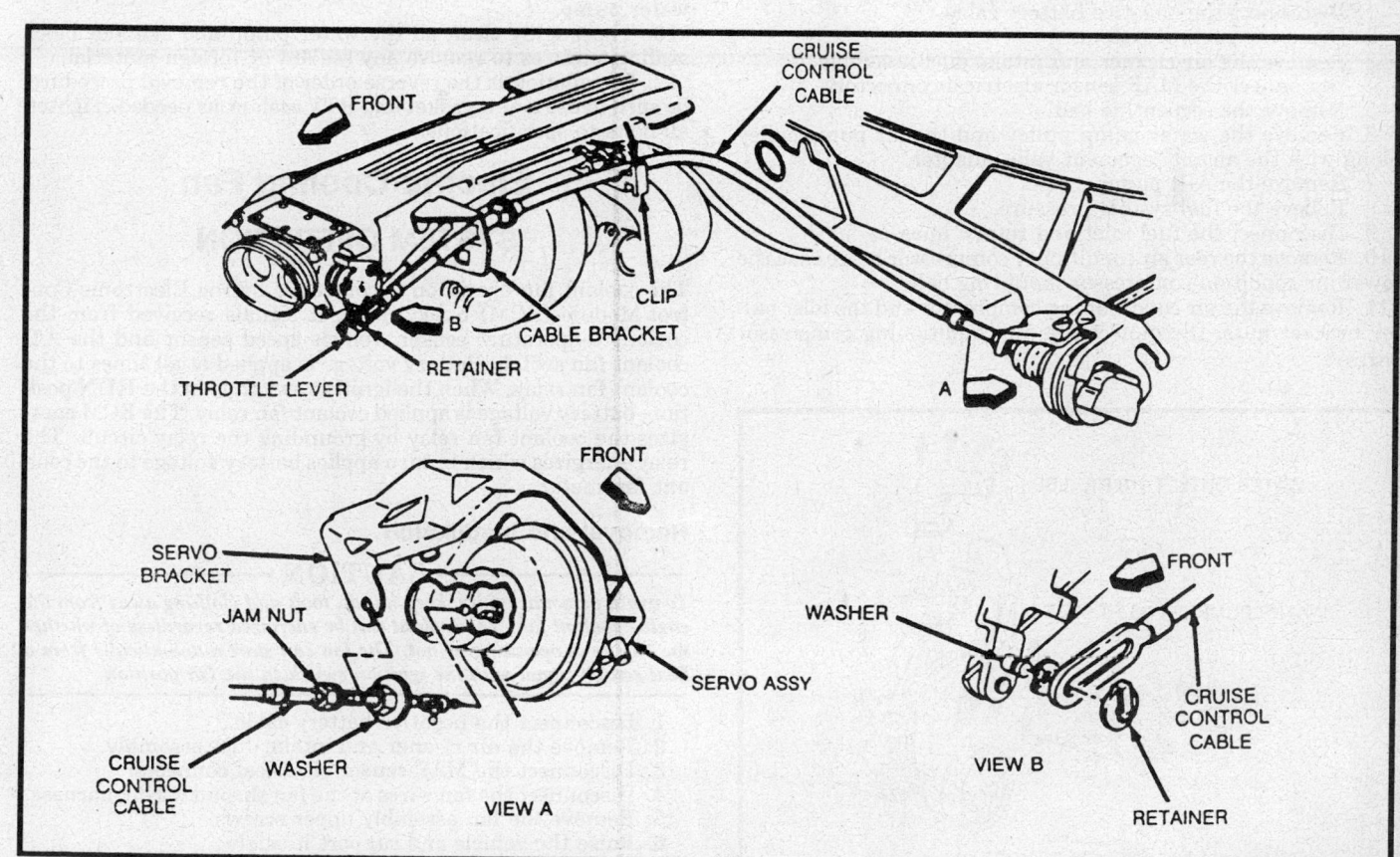

Cruise control cable routing and adjustment

The main parts of the cruise control system are:

Mode control switches
Controller (module)
Servo unit
Servo cable
Speed sensor
Vacuum supply
Electrical and vacuum release switches
Electrical harness

Adjustments

RELEASE VALVE AND SWITCH

1. With the brake pedal depressed, insert the valve into the tubular retainer until the valve seats on the retainer.

NOTE: Audible clicks can be heard as the threaded portion of the valve is pushed through the retainer toward the brake pedal.

2. Pull the brake pedal fully rearward against the pedal stop until the audible click sounds can no longer be heard. The valve will be moved in the tubular retainer providing adjustment.

3. Release the brake pedal, then repeat Step 2 to assure that no audible click sounds remain.

SERVO LINKAGE

1. With the cable installed to the cable bracket and throttle lever, install the cable to the clip and servo bracket using the first ball on the servo chain.

2. Connect the servo chain to the cable assembly connector leaving a space of 4 ball links.

3. With the ignition **OFF**, close the throttle completely.

4. Adjust the cable jam nuts until the cable sleeve at the throttle lever is tight but not holding the throttle open.

5. Tighten the jam nuts.

6. Pull the servo boot over the washer on the cable.

COOLING AND HEATING SYSTEMS

Water Pump

Removal and Installation

NOTE: If the compressor lines do not have enough slack to move the compressor out of the way without disconnecting the refrigerant lines, the air conditioning system must be evacuated, use the required tools and proper procedures, before the refrigerant lines can be disconnected.

1. Disconnect the negative battery cable.
2. Drain the cooling system.
3. Remove the air cleaner and intake duct assembly.
4. Disconnect the MAF sensor electrical connector.
5. Remove the serpentine belt.
6. Remove the water pump pulley and the air pump pulley along with the air management valve adapter.
7. Remove the AIR pump.
8. Relieve the fuel system pressure.
9. Disconnect the fuel inlet and return lines.
10. Remove the rear air conditioner compressor braces and the lower air condition compressor mounting bolt.
11. Remove the air conditioning compressor and the idler pulley bracket nuts. Disconnect the air conditioning compressor wires.

12. Slide the mounting bracket forward and remove the rear air conditioning compressor bolt along with the compressor.

13. Remove the right and left AIR hoses at the check valve and remove the AIR pipe at the intake and power steering reservoir bracket including the top alternator bolt.

14. Remove the lower AIR bracket on the water pump and the lower radiator and heater hose at the water pump.

15. Remove the water pump retaining bolts. Remove the water pump and gasket from the vehicle. If a new water pump is being installed, transfer the existing heater hose fitting onto the new water pump.

16. Thoroughly clean all the water pump and cylinder block sealing surfaces to remove any sealant or foreign material.

17. Installation is the reverse order of the removal procedure, be sure to use a new gasket and RTV sealant as needed. Tighten all bolts to specifications.

Electric Cooling Fan

SYSTEM OPERATION

The coolant fan operation is controlled by the Electronic Control Module (ECM) based on input signals received from the coolant tenperature sensor, vehicle speed sensor and the A/C coolant fan switch. Battery voltage is applied at all times to the coolant fan relay. When the ignition switch is in the **RUN** position, battery voltage is applied coolant fan relay. The ECM energizes the coolant fan relay by grounding the relay circuit. The relay energizes which in turn applies battery voltage to the coolant fan motor.

Removal and Installation

--- CAUTION ---

To avoid personal injury, keep hands, tools and clothing away from the engine coolant fan. The coolant can be energized regardless of whether the engine is operating or not. The fan can start automatically from a heat sensor signal with the ignition switch in the On position.

1. Disconnect the negative battery cable.
2. Remove tha air cleaner and intake duct assembly.
3. Disconnect the MAF sensor electrical connector.
4. Disconnect the fan wires at the fan shroud wiring harness.
5. Remove the fan assembly upper screws.
6. Raise the vehicle and support it safely.
7. Remove the fan assembly lower screws.
8. Lower the vehicle.

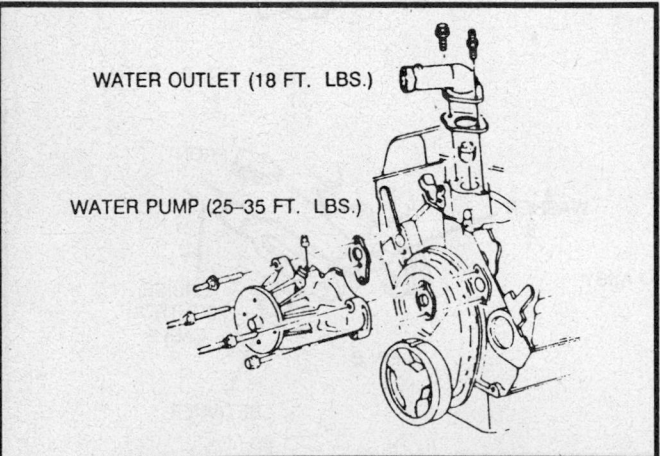

WATER OUTLET (18 FT. LBS.)

WATER PUMP (25–35 FT. LBS.)

Water pump assembly

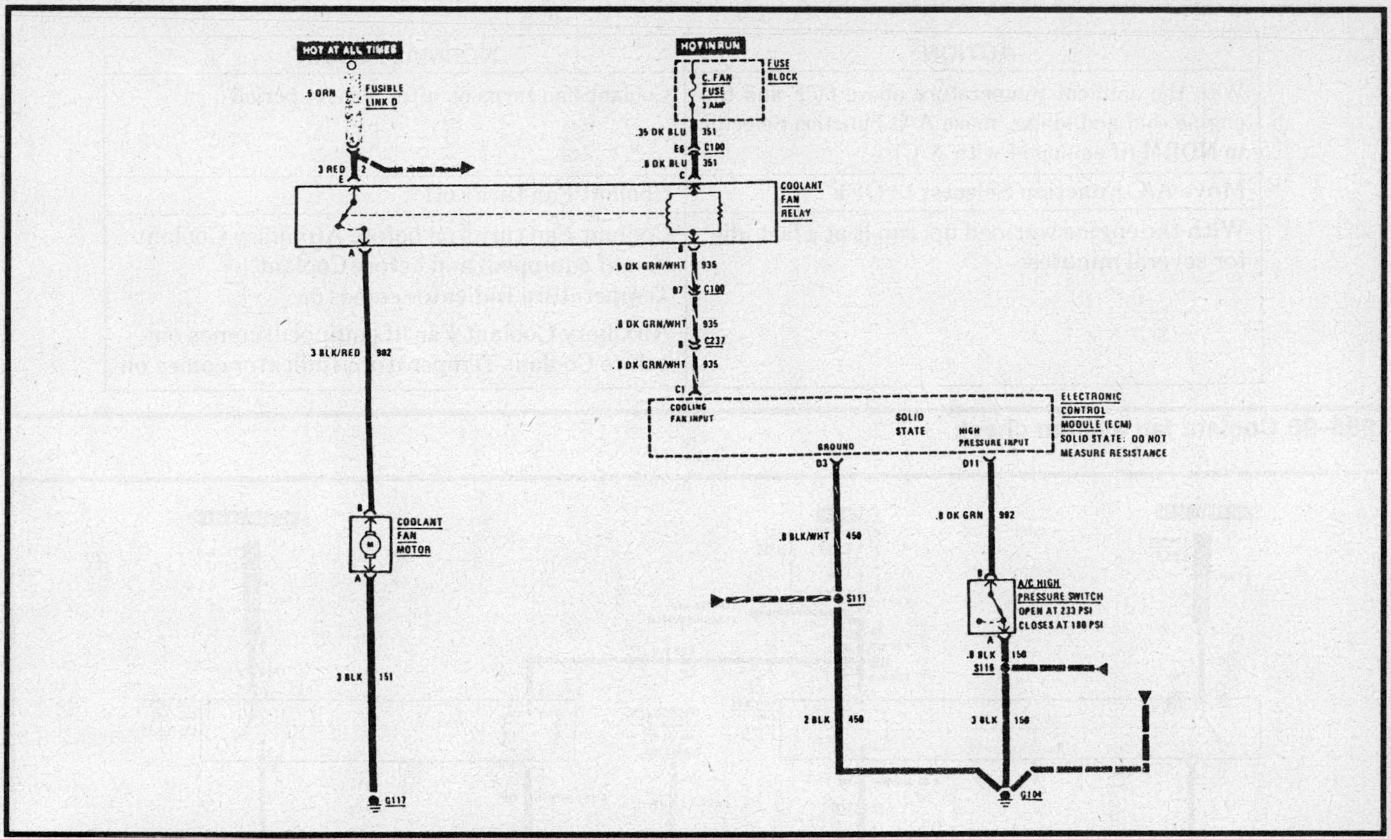

Coolant fan eletrical schematic—1986 Corvette

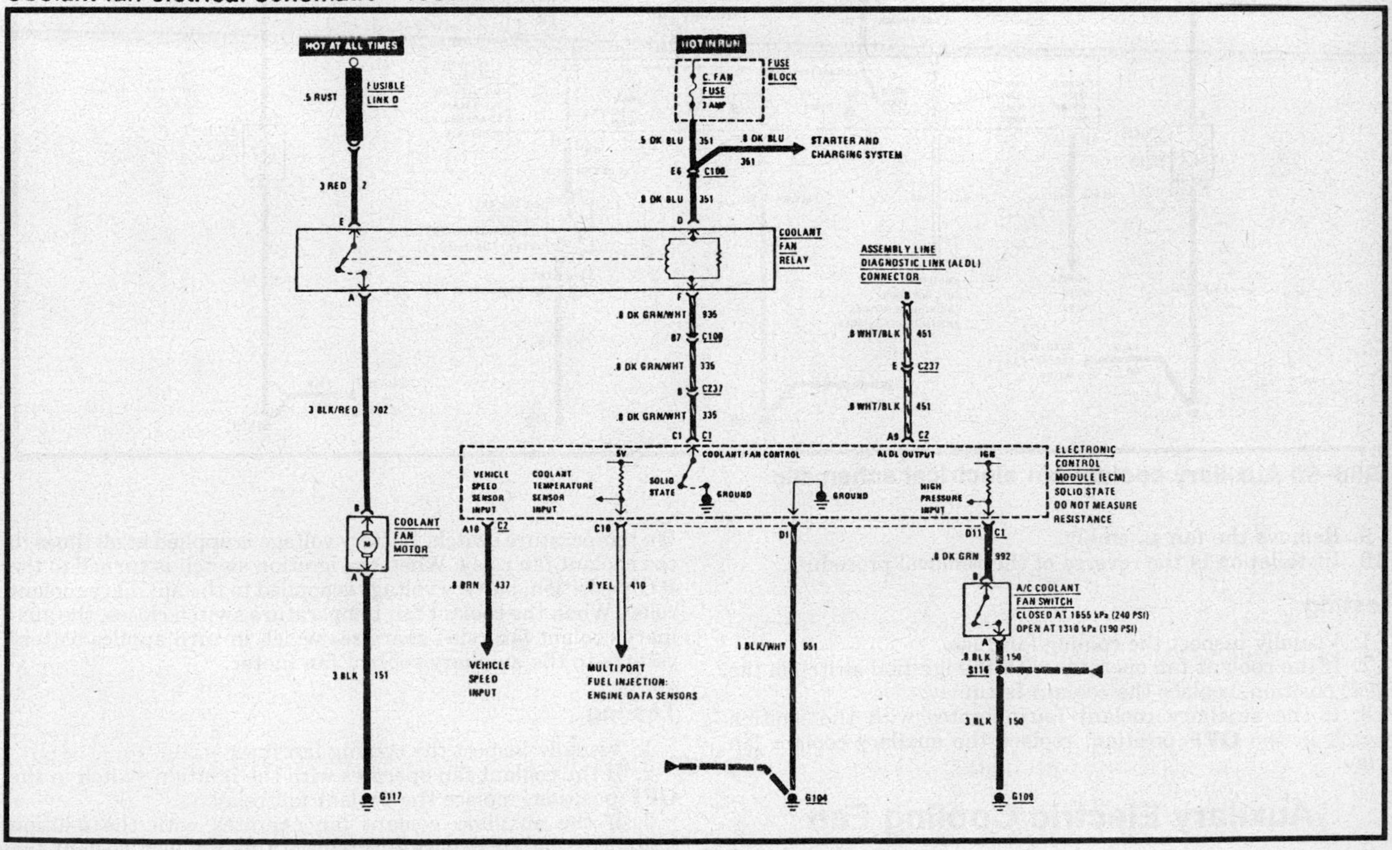

1988-90 Coolant fan system schematic

ACTION	NORMAL RESULT
With the ambient temperature above 60°F and the engine cold and idling, move A/C Function Selector to NORM (if equipped with A/C)	Coolant Fan turns on after a short period
Move A/C Function Selector to OFF	Coolant Fan turns off
With the engine warmed up, run it at a fast idle for several minutes	Coolant Fan turns on before Auxiliary Coolant Fan (if equipped) and before Coolant Temperature Indicator comes on. Auxiliary Coolant Fan (if equipped) comes on before Coolant Temperature Indicator comes on

1988–90 Coolant fan system check

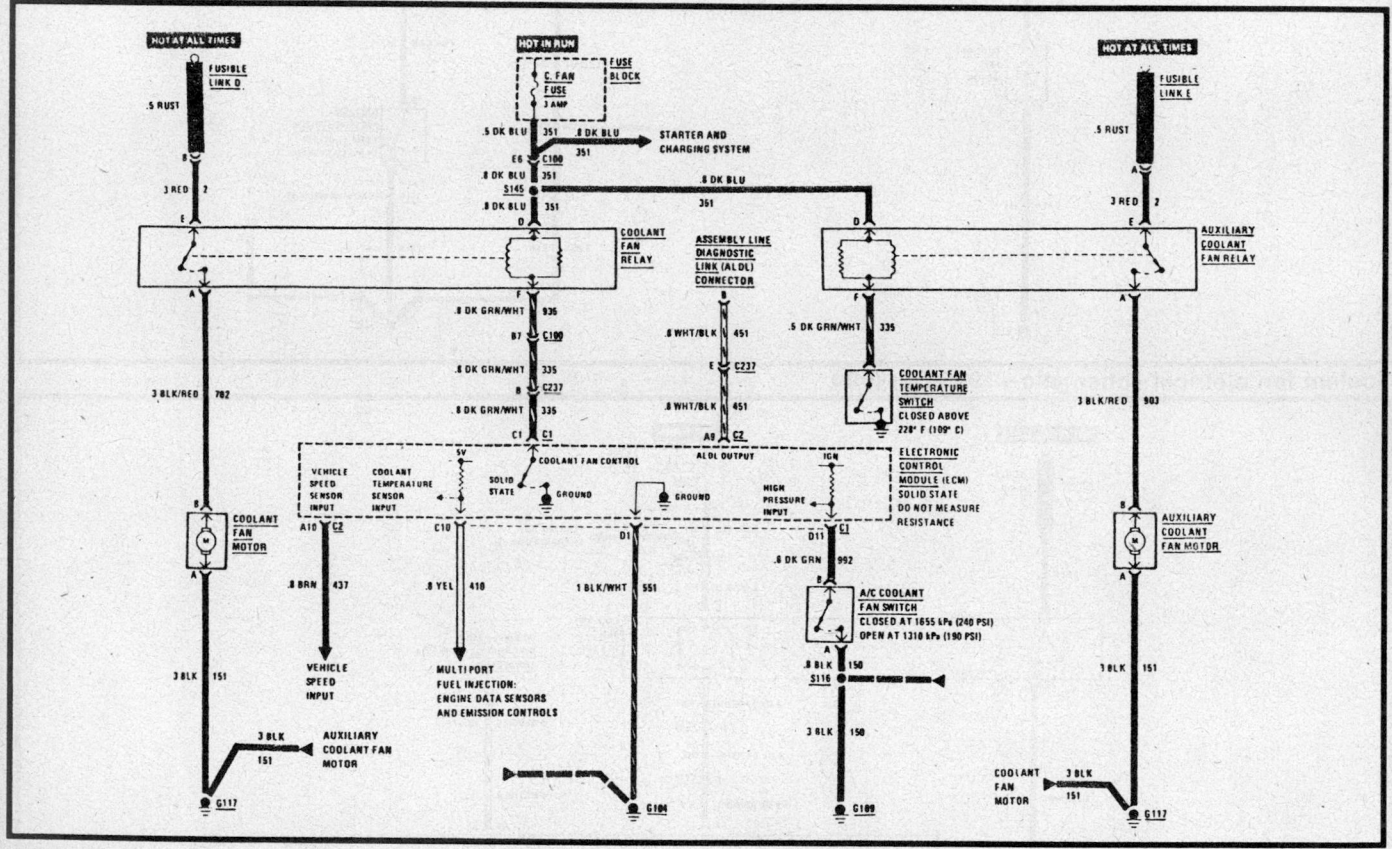

1988–90 Auxiliary coolant fan electrical schematic

9. Remove the fan assembly.
10. Installation is the reverse of the removal procedure.

Testing

1. Visually inspect the cooling fan fuse.
2. If the coolant fan operates with the ignition switch in the **OFF** position, replace the coolant fan relay.
3. If the auxiliary coolant fan operates with the ignition switch in the **OFF** position, replace the auxiliary coolant fan relay.

Auxilary Electric Cooling Fan

The auxiliary cooling fan operation is controlled by the coolant fan temperature switch. Battery voltage is applied at all times to the coolant fan relay. When the ignition switch is turned to the **RUN** position, battery voltage is applied to the auxiliary coolant relay. When the coolant fan temperature switch closes, the auxiliary coolant fan relay energizes which in turn applies battery voltage to the auxiliary coolant fan motor.

Testing

1. Visually inspect the cooling fan fuse.
2. If the coolant fan operates with the ignition switch in the **OFF** position, replace the coolant fan relay.
3. If the auxiliary coolant fan operates with the ignition switch in the **OFF** position, replace the auxiliary coolant fan relay.

Removal and Installation

1. Disconnect the negative battery cable.
2. Remove tha air cleaner and intake duct assembly.
3. Disconnect the MAF sensor electrical connector.
4. Disconnect the fan wires at the fan shroud wiring harness.
5. Remove the fan assembly upper screws.
6. Raise the vehicle and support it safely.
7. Remove the fan assembly lower screws.
8. Lower the vehicle.
9. Remove the fan assembly.
10. Installation is the reverse of the removal procedure.

Blower Motor

Removal and Installation

1. Disconnect the negative battery cable.
2. Remove the front wheel hose rear panel. Move the wheel hose seal aside.
3. Remove the heat motor cooling tube.
4. Remove the heater motor relay.
5. Remove the motor retaining screws and remove the motor assembly from the vehicle.
6. Installation is the reverse of the removal procedure.

HEATER CORE

Refer to "Chilton's Auto Heating and Air Conditioning Manual" for additional coverage.

Removal and Installation

1. Disconnect the negative battery cable.
2. Drain the cooling system.
3. Remove the instrument cluster bezel including the tilt wheel lever and instrument panel pad.

4. Remove the A/C distributor duct and disconnect the flex hose.
5. Remove the right side hush panel.
6. Remove the side window defroster flex hose.
7. Remove the side window defroster to heater cover screws and disconnect the extension.
8. Remove the temperature control cable and bracket assembly at heater cover including disconnecting heater door control shaft.
9. Remove the Electric Control Module (ECM) and disconnect the electrical connectors. Be sure that the ignition switch is off when disconnecting ECM.
10. Remove the tubular support brace from the door pillar to aluminum, instrument panel reinforcement brace.
11. Remove heater core cover attaching screws.
12. Remove heater pipe and heater water control bracket attaching screws.
13. Remove heater hose at heater core pipes.
14. Remove the heater core.
15. Installation is the reverse of the removal procedure.

TEMPERATURE CONTROL BLOWER SWITCH

Removal and Installation

1. Disconnect the negative battery cable.
2. Remove the cluster bezel.
3. Remove the tilt wheel lever.
4. Remove the center bezel above the console assembly.
5. Remove the screws attaching the control assembly to its carrier.
6. Rotate the control assembly to gain access to the electrical connectors, temperature control cable and vacuum hoses.
7. Installation is the reverse of the removal procedure.

FUEL INJECTION SYSTEM

Refer to "Chilton's Professional Electronic Engine Control Manual" for additional coverage.

Description

The Corvette uses the tuned port injection (TPI) system. The introduction of this new TPI system has improved the torque and power of the Corvette's 350 V8 engine.

The induction system for the TPI is made up of large forward mounted air cleaners, a new mass airflow sensor, a cast aluminum throttle body assembly with dual throttle blades, a large extended cast aluminum plenum, individial aluminum tuned runners and a protruding dual fuel rail assembly with computer controlled injectors.

The base plate is cast aluminum and incorporates the crossover portion of the tuned runners. The base plate also serves as a mounting base for the fuel injectors. The individual aluminum runners are designed to provide the best tuning or frequency of air pulses within the runners and for the optimum throttle response throughout the driving range, thus the name Tuned Port Injection. The runners are selected by length and size to take advantage of the air pulses set up by the opening and closing of the intake valves.

The high pressure pulses result in denser air at each intake valve and timing the pressure pulses to occur during the valve open period forces more air into the combustion chamber, which results in a more efficient cylinder charging and improved volumetric efficiency.

IDLE SPEED

Adjustment

NOTE: The idle stop screw used to adjust the minimum engine idle speed is adjusted at the factory. The idle speed should only be adjusted if it is absolutely necessary. Prior to adjusing the idle speed, ensure that the ignition timing is correct and that the throttle body is clean around the throttle plates.

1. Using the proper tool, pierce the idle stop plug and remove it.
2. Leave the idle air control motor connected and ground the diagnostic lead. Turn the ignition to the **ON** position, but do not start the engine.
3. Wait 30 seconds and with the ignition switch still in the **ON** position disconnect the idle air control connector.
4. Remove the ground from the diagnostic lead and start the engine.
5. Allow the engine to go into the closed loop mode and adjust the idle screw to 450 rpm in **N**.
6. Turn the ignition **OFF** and reconnect the idle speed control connector.
7. Adjust the throttle position sensor as follows:
   a. With the ignition switch in the **ON** position, connect a scan tool or 3 jumper wires to the TPS.
   b. Adjust the TPS to obtain a reading from 0.46–0.62 volts.
8. Start the engine and check for proper idle operation.

FUEL SYSTEM PRESSURE RELIEF

Procedure

NOTE: This procedure must be performed to relieve the fuel system pressure before any work is done to the fuel system which requires that a fuel line be disconnected.

1. Disconnect the negative battery cable.
2. Loosen the fuel filler cap to relieve the tank pressure.
3. Connect fuel gauge J34730-1 or equivalent to the fuel pressure tap.
4. Wrap a shop towel around the fitting while connecting the gauge to catch any fuel spray.
5. Install a bleed hose into a suitable container, then open the valve to bleed the fuel system pressure.

Fuel Pump

The electric fuel pump is located inside the fuel tank attached to the fuel tank sending unit. The fuel pump takes its suction directly from the tank through a plastic micron filter. The pump is both cooled and lubricated by the incoming fuel.

Fuel from the pump is delivered to the fuel rails, fuel injectors and then to the pressure regulator. The pump may be serviced separately and access to the fuel pump is gained through the filler door in the body.

Removal and Iinstallation

1. Disconnect the negative battery cable.
2. Relieve the fuel system pressure.
3. Remove the fuel tank filler door and drain tube.
4. Disconnect the feed, return and vapor hoses from the sending unit.
5. Remove the license plate to gain access for removal of the 2 bolts securing the fascia to impact bar.
6. Raise the vehicle and support it safely.
7. Remove the spare tire and carrier from the frame.
8. Disconnect the intermediate exhaust pipe at the converter. Remove the intermediate pipe and mufflers as an assembly from the vehicle.
9. Remove both rear inner fender braces at the frame.
10. Remove both rear inner fender panels.
11. Remove the antenna ground strap and clip.
12. Disconnect the fuel vapor pipe from the left hand fuel tank strap.
13. Disconnect the fuel tank cables from the rear stabilizer shaft brackets.
14. Remove the screws securing the bottom edge of the fascia to the energy absorber pad.
15. Remove all rear lamps.
16. Disconnect each side of the fascia from the horizontal body retainer.

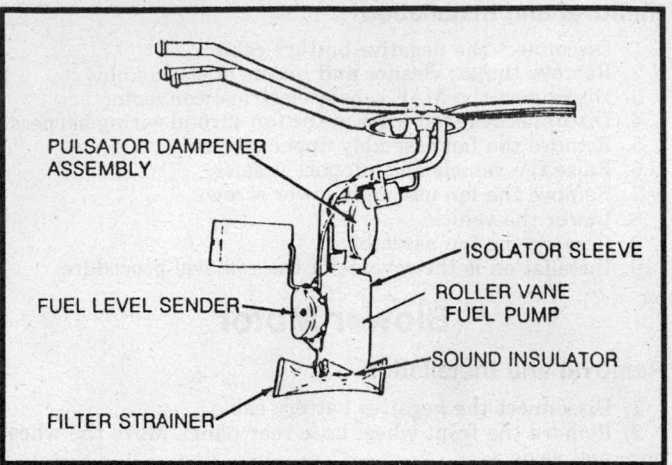

Electric in-tank fuel pump

17. Disconnect the right and left vertical retainers securing the fascia to the body.
18. Remove the 6 frame bolts and loosen the 2 front frame bolts.
19. Remove the front frame bolts. Pull the tank and frame assembly to the rear pushing the cover outward and letting the rear of the frame assembly down to clear the cover.
20. Remove the vapor hose from the vapor connector and remove the tank and frame assembly.
21. Remove the fuel sending unit and pump assembly by turning the cam lock ring counterclockwise. Lift the assembly from the fuel tank.
22. Disconnect the fuel pump from the fuel level sending unit.
23. Installation is the reverse of the removal procedure. Always use a new gasket when the sending unit has been removed from the tank.

FUEL INJECTOR

Removal and Installation

1. Relieve the fuel system pressure.
2. Disconnect the negative battery cable.
3. Remove the plenum, cold start valve line, runners and cold start valve.
4. Disconnect the fuel lines and the fuel line connectors.
5. Loosen the fuel injector rail retaining bolts and raise the rail (with fuel injectors) upward and away from the manifold.
6. Rotate the injector retaining clips to the unlocked position to release the injector. Withdraw the injector from the fuel rail opening.
7. Remove the O-ring seals from both ends of the injector. Discard and replace the seals.
8. Installation is the reverse of the removal procedure.

EMISSION CONTROL SYSTEM

Refer to "Chilton's Emission Diagnosis and Service Manual" for additional coverage.

Electronic control module
Fuel control system
Evaporative emission control system
Ignition system/EST
Electonic spark control system
Air injection reaction system
Exhaust gas recirculation system
Torque converter clutch system
1–4 Upshift system
Electric cooling fan
Positive crankcase ventilation system

Resetting Emission Warning Lamps

SERVICE ENGINE SOON LIGHT

This light is on the instrument panel and has the following functions:

It informs the driver that a problem has occurred and that the vehicle should be serviced as soon as possible.

It displays trouble codes stored by the ECM.

It indicates Open Loop or Closed Loop operation.

The light will come **ON** with the key **ON** and the engine not running. When the engine is started, the light will turn **OFF**. If the light remains **ON**, the self-diagnostic system has detected a problem. If the problem goes away, the light will go out in most cases after 10 seconds, but a trouble code will remain stored in the ECM.

To clear the codes from the memory of the ECM, either to determine if the malfunction will occur again or because repair has been completed, the ECM power feed must be disconnected for at least 30 seconds.

Depending on how the vehicle is equipped, the ECM power feed can be disconnected at the positive battery terminal "pigtail". The inline fuseholder that originates at the positive connection at the battery, or the ECM fuse in the fuse block.

If the negative battery terminal is disconnected, other onboard memory data, such as pre-set radio tuning will also be lost.

ENGINE

NOTE: Disconnecting the negative battery cable on some vehicles may interfere with the functions of the on board computer systems and may require the computer to undergo a relearning process, once the negative battery cable is reconnected.

Engine Assembly

Removal and Installation

NOTE: Fuel injection lines and components may be under considerable pressure even when the engine is secured. To avoid injury to personnel, be sure to relieve the fuel pressure before disconnecting any fuel lines. Replace all worn fuel line connection O-rings as required.

1. Mark the relationship between each hood hinge and the hood. Remove the hood.
2. Disconnect the negative battery cable.
3. Drain the coolant.
4. Disconnect the throttle, T.V. and cruise control cables at the engine.
5. Disconnect the spark plug wires from the plugs. Remove the wires and distributor cap as an assembly.
6. Remove the distributor.
7. Remove the cowl screen. Remove the nut from the wiper motor arm.
8. Disconnect the wiper motor wires, remove the wiper motor cover and remove the wiper motor.
9. Remove the air intake duct with the MAF sensor.
10. Disconnect the brake booster vacuum hose.
11. Disconnect the canister hose at the PCV pipe.
12. Disconnect all necessary wiring and vascuum hoses at the engine.
13. Disconnect the injection harness at the intake manifold.
14. Disconnect the heater hoses at the pipe.
15. Disconnect the upper radiator hose at the thermostat housing.
16. Remove the serpentine belt.
17. Remove the AIR control valve at the A/C compressor.
18. Relieve the fuel system pressure.
19. Disconnect the fuel lines at the rail.
20. Disconnect the catalytic converter AIR pipe.
21. Remove the A/C brace at the exhaust manifold.
22. Remove the accumulator at the fan shroud and brace.
23. Disconnect the fuel lines at the block.
24. Disconnect the lower radiator hose and the heater hose from the water pump.
25. Remove the alternator.
26. Remove the AIR pump with the bracket.
27. Remove the power steering pump from the engine and wire it aside.
28. Remove the water pump pulley and the crankshaft pulley.
29. Raise the vehicle and support it safely.
30. Disconnect the wires at the oxygen, Electronic Spark Control (ESC) system harness and temperature sensors.
31. Remove the temperature sensor wire retainer at the block.
32. Disconnect the ground wires at the engine.
33. Disconnect the transmission oil cooler lines at the transmission.
34. Remove the starter.
35. Disconnect the front crossover pipe at the exhaust manifolds.
36. Drain the engine oil and remove the oil filter.
37. Remove the oil cooler adapter and lines at the block.
38. Remove the flywheel cover.
39. Disconnect the exhaust system at the converter hanger.
40. Disconnect the clutch system, if equipped with a manual transmission.
41. Remove the engine mount through bolts and nuts.
42. Remove the transmission to engine bolts, if equipped with an automatic transmission.
43. Lower the vehicle.
44. Support the transmission with a transmission jack.
45. Install a suitable lifting device and remove the engine from the vehicle.
46. Installation is the reverse of the removal procedure.

Engine Mounts

Removal and Installation
RIGHT

1. Disconnect the negative battery cable.
2. Raise and support the vehicle safely.
3. Remove engine mount through bolt.
4. Disconnect catalytic converter AIR pipe at exhaust manifold.
5. Disconnect catalytic converter AIR pipe at exhaust pipe.
6. Disconnect AIR pipe at converter.
7. Raise engine enough to allow for sufficient clearance.
8. Remove motor mount bolts.
9. Remove engine mount.
10. Replace mount to engine and lower engine into place.
11. Install and tighten the retaining bolts.
12. Installation is the reverse of the removal procedure.

LEFT

1. Disconnect the negative battery cable.
2. Raise and support the vehicle safely.
3. Remove engine mount through bolt.
4. Raise the engine enough to allow for sufficient clearance.
5. Remove engine mount to block bolts.
6. Remove 1 exhaust manifold shroud screw.

7. Remove engine mount.

8. Replace mount to engine and lower engine into place.

9. Install and tighten the retaining bolts.

10. Install the remaining components in the reverse of the removal procedure.

Intake Manifold

Removal and Installation

1. Disconnect the negative battery cable.

2. Relieve the fuel system pressure.

3. Drain the cooling system.

4. Remove the fuel injection subassembly: mass air flow sensor, plenum, runners and the fuel rail assembly.

5. Disconnect and mark all necessary vacuum and electrical connections.

6. Remove the distributor cap, mark the position of the rotor and the distributor. Remove the distributor.

7. Disconnect the upper radiator hose at the thermostat outlet opening.

8. Remove the air pump brace.

9. Disconnect the EGR pipe at the inlet opening.

10. Disconnect the heater control vacuum line at the intake.

11. Remove the thermostat outlet.

12. Remove the intake manifold retaining bolts.

13. Lift the intake manifold upward and away from the intake surface.

14. Remove the gaskets from the cylinder head surfaces.

To install

15. Thoroughly clean the cylinder block, intake manifold and cylinder head surfaces with the proper cleaning compound to remove any traces of gasket material and RTV sealant. Any material left on these surfaces will cause installation interference and improper sealing.

16. Install the cylinder head gaskets so that the blocked openings are positioned toward the rear of the engine. Locate the gasket tabs and bend the tabs so that they are flush with the rear surface of the cylinder head. After the tabs are bent into place, apply a $^3/_{16}$ bead of RTV onto the front and rear cylinder case ridges.

17. Apply Loctite to the threads of the intake manifold retaining bolts.

18. Install the intake manifold in the reverse order of the removal procedure. Torque the intake manifold retaining bolts in sequence to 35 ft. lbs. (47 Nm).

Exhaust Manifold

Removal and Installation

RIGHT SIDE

1. Disconnect the negative battery cable.

2. Remove the plenum extension.

3. Disconnect the EGR sensor wire.

4. Remove the EGR pipe bolts at the intake manifold.

5. Remove the rear A/C compressor brace and allow it to hang from the compressor.

6. Disconnect the dipstick tube at the manifold and remove the dipstick/tube as an assembly.

7. Remove the AIR check valve at the manifold.

8. Disconnect the AIR hose at the catalytic air pipe opening.

9. Disconnect the temperature sending unit wire.

10. Disconnect the spark plug wires from the plugs, cylinder head and the valve covers.

11. Remove the spark plugs.

12. Raise and properly support the vehicle.

13. Remove the catalyic coverter AIR pipe at the manifold.

14. Disconnect the exhaust crossover pipe at the manifold.

15. Remove the bolts from the catalytic front support hanger.

16. Remove the catalytic converter AIR pipe.

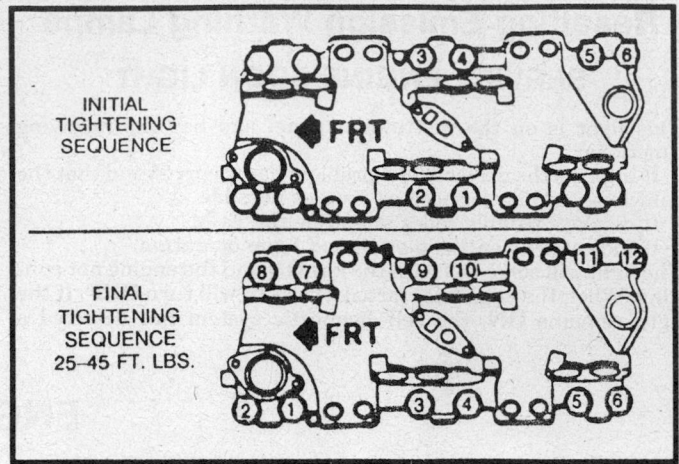

Intake manifold bolt torque sequence

17. Lower the vehicle.

18. Support the exhaust manifold and remove the retaining bolts.

19. Remove the exhaust manifold and EGR assembly from the vehicle. If the manifold is being replaced, remove the EGR pipe clamp and EGR pipe.

20. Replace all gaskets as required and ensure that all gasket contact surfaces are cleaned prior to reinstallation. Installation is the reverse of the removal procedure. Torque the manifold retaining bolts to 15–24 ft. lbs..

LEFT SIDE

1. Disconnect the negative battery cable.

2. Remove the air cleaner.

3. Disconnect the PCV hose from the intake and rocker arm cover.

4. Disconnect the AIR at the exhaust check valve.

5. Disconnect the rear alternator brace and allow to hang from the alternator.

6. Raise and properly support the vehicle.

7. Disconnect the exhaust pipe at the manifold.

8. Lower the vehicle.

9. Support the manifold and remove the retaining bolts.

10. Remove the exhaust manifold from the vehicle.

11. Replace all gaskets as required and ensure that all gasket contact surfaces are cleaned prior to reinstallation. Installation is the reverse of the removal procedure. Torque the manifold retaining bolts to 15–24 ft. lbs..

Valve System

Adjustment

NOTE: This engine utilizes hydraulic lifters that normally require very little maintenance or adjustment. These components are simple in design and are best maintained through regular, scheduled engine oil changes. If the engine is running well and no audible clicking sounds are heard from the valve train, do not attempt to remove or disassemble the valve lifters.

1. Disconnect the negative battery cable.

2. Remove the valve covers.

3. Tighten the rocker arm nuts until all lash is eliminated.

4. Adjust the valves when the lifter is on the base circle of the camshaft lobe by cranking the engine until the mark on the vibration damper lines up with the center or **0** mark on the timing tab fastened to the crankcase front cover and the engine is in the No. 1 firing position.

NOTE: This may be determined by placing your fingers on the No. 1 valve as the mark on the damper comes near the 0 mark on the crankcase front cover. If the valves move as the mark comes up to the timing tab, the engine is in the No. 6 firing position and should be turned over one more time to reach to No. 1 firing position.

5. With the engine in the No. 1 firing position, adjust the following valves:
   a. Exhaust—1, 3, 4, 8
   b. Intake—1, 2, 5, 7

6. Back out adjusting nut until lash is felt at the push rod then turn in adjusting nut until all lash is removed. This can be determined by rotating push rod while turning adjusting nut. When play has been removed, turn adjusting nut in one full additional turn.

7. Crank the engine one revolution until the pointer **0** mark and the vibration damper mark are again in alignment. This is the No. 6 firing position.

8. With the engine in this position, adjust the following valves:
   a. Exhaust—2, 5, 6, 7
   b. Intake—3, 4, 6, 8

9. Install the rocker arm covers.

10. Start the engine and adjust the idle speed as required.

VALVE LIFTERS

Removal and Installation

1. Disconnect the negative battery cable.
2. Drain the cooling system.
3. Remove the intake manifold assembly.
4. Remove the rocker arm covers.
5. Remove the rocker arms and pushrods. Be sure to keep them in order as they must be installed in the same bores as they were removed.
6. As required, remove the valve lifter guide retaining bolts. Remove the valve lifter guide, if equipped with roller lifters.
7. Remove the valve lifters using the proper valve lifter removal tool.
8. Place the lifters in a rack so that they may be installed in their original locations.
9. Coat the base of the lifters with Molycoat® or equivalent prior to installation.
10. Installation is the reverse of the removal procedure.

VALVE ROCKER ARM ASSEMBLY

Removal and Installation

1. Disconnect the negative battery cable. Remove the air cleaner.
2. Remove the right rocker arm cover as follows:
   a. Remove the right exhaust manifold on 1986–87 vehicles only. Remove the EGR pipe assembly.
   b. Remove the fresh air pipe.

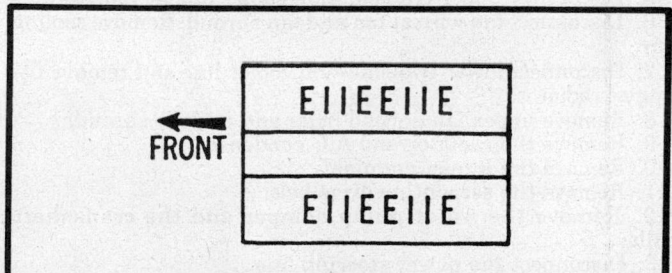

Intake and exhaust valve arrangements

c. Loosen the spark plug wire retainer on the right cylinder head and remove the remaining wire retainers.
   d. Remove the injector harness retaining nuts and position the harness off to the side.
   e. Disconnect the heater control valve harness vacuum hose.
   f. Remove the rocker arm retaining bolts. Remove the rocker arm cover and gasket. Replace the gasket as required.

3. Remove the left rocker arm cover as follows:
   a. Disconnect the PCV valve and hose.
   b. Disconnect the injector harness and position to the side.
   c. Disconnect the canister hose at the purge pipe.
   d. Disconnect the power brake booster vacuum line. Disconnect the brake booster pipe at the plenum.
   e. Loosen the AIR pump pulley bolts and disconnect the serpentine belt from the AIR pump.
   f. Remove the AIR pump pulley and loosen the AIR pump lower mounting bolt.
   g. Remove the rocker cover retaining bolts and remove the cover and cover gasket.

4. Remove the rocker arm nuts, rocker arm balls and the rocker arms. Indentify the rocker arm nuts, rocker arm balls, rocker arms and push rods so that they may be installed in their original locations. If new rocker arms and/or rocker arm balls are being installed, place a coat of Molycoat® or equivalent onto the bearing surfaces prior to installation.

5. Install the push rods making certain that they seat in the lifter sockets.

6. Install the rocker arms, rocker arm balls and rocker arm nuts in their original positions.

7. Tighten the rocker arm nuts until all lash is eliminated.

8. Adjust the valves and the A/C belt tension.

9. Reinstall the rocker arm covers.

10. Start the engine and inspect for leaks. Check and adjust the curb idle speed.

Cylinder Head

Removal and Installation

RIGHT SIDE

1. Disconnect the negative battery cable.
2. Drain the cooling system.
3. Remove the intake manifold.
4. Disconnect the rear A/C brace at the exhaust manifold.
5. Disconnect and remove the dipstick tube assembly.
6. Remove the check valve from the AIR manifold.
7. Disconnect the AIR hose at the catalytic converter AIR pipe.

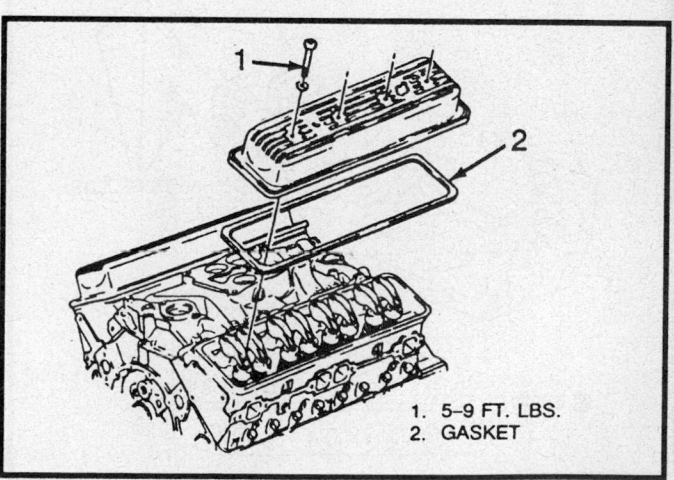

1. 5–9 FT. LBS.
2. GASKET

Valve cover installation

8. Disconnect the temperature sending unit wire.
9. Disconnect the plug wires from the spark plugs and cylinder head/rocker arm attachment points.
10. Remove the spark plugs.
11. Raise and properly support the vehicle.
12. Disconnect the converter AIR pipe clamp at the manifold.
13. Disconnect the exhaust pipe at both manifolds.
14. Remove the front converter hanger bolts.
15. Remove the converter AIR pipe.
16. Lower the vehicle.
17. Remove the exhaust manifold bolts.
18. Remove the exhaust manifold with the EGR pipe.
19. Remove the spark plug wire retainers.
20. Remove the rocker arm cover.
21. Disconnect the serpentine belt at the A/C compressor.
22. Disconnect the A/C wire connectors.
23. Loosen the rear A/C mounting bolts.
24. Loosen and remove the A/C bracket nuts from the water pump studs.
25. Loosen the front A/C mounting bolt and slide the A/C unit with bracket forward.
26. Remove the pushrods.
27. Loosen and remove the head bolts.
28. Remove the right cylinder head from the cylinder head from the engine block surface.
29. Remove and discard the cylinder head gasket. Thoroughly clean all gasket mating surfaces.

To install:

NOTE: The cylinder head and engine block surfaces must be completely free of existing gasket material and free of nicks and grooves. Throughly clean and inspect the cylinder head bolt threads for damage and wear. The use of dirty or damaged bolts may produce false and inaccurate torque readings. Replace all damaged bolts as required.

30. Use a new cylinder head gasket installed with the bead facing up. Installation of the cylinder head is the reverse of the removal procedure.

NOTE: If the steel type gaskets were removed, coat both sides of the new steel gasket (lightly but thoroughly) with a suitable sealing compound. If composite type gaskets were removed, the new gaskets must be installed dry.

31. Coat the threads of the cylinder head bolts with a suitable sealing compound. Install the bolts finger tight.

32. Torque the bolts to the proper specification and in the proper sequence.

LEFT SIDE

1. Disconnect the negative battery cable.
2. Drain the cooling system.
3. Remove the intake manifold.
4. Disconnect the AIR hose at the check valve.
5. Remove the alternator brace.
6. Disconnect the fan temperature sensor wire.
7. Raise and safely support the vehicle.
8. Disconnect the exhaust pipe at the manifold.
9. Lower the vehicle.
10. Remove the exhaust manifold bolts.
11. Support and remove the left hand exhaust manifold.
12. Disconnect the serpentine belt at the AIR pump.
13. Remove the rocker arm cover.
14. Remove the spark plugs.
15. Disconnect the power steering, alternator mounting bracket at the cylinder head.
16. Remove the pushrods.
17. Loosen and remove the head bolts. Remove the left cylinder head from the engine block surface.
18. Remove the cylinder head gasket and discard. Thoroughly clean all gasket mating surfaces.

To install:

NOTE: The cylinder head and engine block surfaces must be completely free of existing gasket material and free of nicks and grooves. Throughly clean and inspect the cylinder head bolt threads for damage and wear. The use of dirty or damaged bolts may produce false and inaccurate torque readings. Replace all damaged bolts as required.

19. Use a new cylinder head gasket installed with the bead facing up. Installation of the cylinder head is the reverse of the removal procedure.

NOTE: If steel type gaskets were removed, coat both sides of the new steel gasket (thinly and evenly) with a suitable sealing compound. It is important to apply the proper amount of sealant because too much can cause the gasket to move away from the cylinder head and block surfaces. If composite type gaskets were removed, the new gaskets must be installed dry.

20. Coat the threads of the cylinder head bolts with a suitable sealing compound. Install the bolts finger tight.

Camshaft

Removal and Installation

1. Disconnect the negative battery cable.
2. Relieve the fuel system pressure.
3. Drain the cooling system.
4. Disconnect air conditioning accumulator from shroud and lay aside.
5. Disconnect upper transmission cooler line at radiator.
6. Disconnect fan wire at fan and fan shroud. Remove cooling fan.
7. Disconnect lower transmission cooler line and remove fitting at radiator.
8. Remove upper fan shroud bolts and remove shroud.
9. Remove the radiator and A/C condenser.
10. Remove the intake manifold.
11. Remove the serpentine drive belt.
12. Remove the water pump damper and the crankshaft pulley.
13. Disconnect the power steering line.
14. Remove the vibration damper.
15. Raise the vehicle and support it safely.

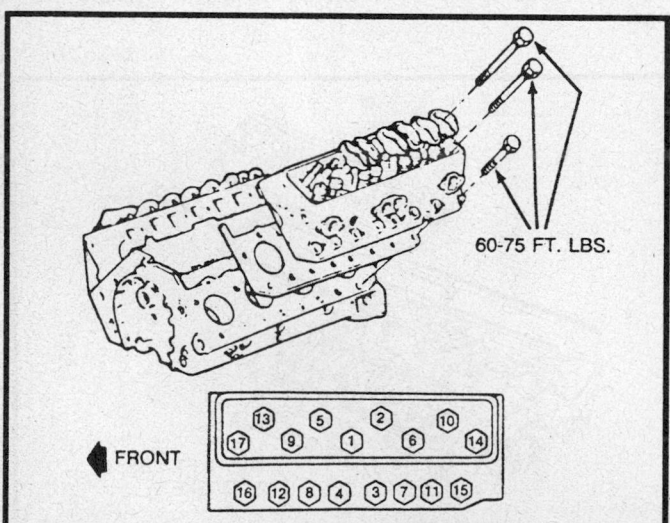

60-75 FT. LBS.

FRONT

13 5 2 6 10
17 9 1 4 14
16 12 8 4 3 7 11 15

Cylinder head bolt torque sequence

16. Drain the engine oil and remove the oil pan.
17. Lower the vehicle.
18. Remove the AIR pump.
19. Disconnect the fuel inlet and return lines.
20. Remove the air conditioning compressor brackets and position the compressor to the side.
21. Remove the water pump.
22. Remove front cover bolts. Remove front cover.
23. Rotate crankshaft and align timing marks.
24. Remove cam gear bolts remove chain and gear.
25. Remove camshaft, using care not to damage the camshaft bearings.
26. Installation is the reverse of the removal procedure.

Timing Case Cover

Removal and Installation

1. Disconnect the negative battery cable.
2. Disconnect the drive belt and remove the crankshaft pulley.
3. Install tool J–23523 onto the vibration dampener assembly. Remove the vibration damper from the face of the crankcase front cover.

NOTE: The use of pullers (such as the universal claw type) that pull on the outside of the hub may damage the torsional dampener. The outside ring of the dampener is bonded to the hub with rubber. The use of the wrong type puller may disturb this bond.

4. Raise the vehicle and support it safely.
5. Drain the engine oil and remove the oil pan.
6. Lower the vehicle. Remove the AIR management valve adapter.
7. Remove the AIR pump pulley and air pump retaining bolts. Remove the air pump.
8. Relieve the fuel system pressure and disconnect the fuel inlet and return pipes.
9. Disconnect the air conditioner compressor mounting bracket nuts at the water pump. Slide the mounting bracket forward and remove the compressor mounting bolt. Disconnect the electrical wires and position the unit to the side.
10. Drain the radiator and disconnect the radiator and heater hoses at the water pump. Remove the water pump.
11. Remove the front cover retaining screws. Remove the front cover and discard the gasket.
12. Thoroughly clean the gasket mating surfaces on the cylinder block and front cover. Inspect the front cover for damage and distortion. Replace the front cover if necessary. Replace the oil seal.
13. With a suitable cutting tool, remove any excess gasket material that may be protruding at the oil pan to engine block surface.

To install

14. Coat the new cover gasket with a suitable sealing compound and apply the gasket onto the front cover sealing surface.
15. Position the front cover and gasket onto the cylinder block surface and hold in place. Install the cover retaining screws and make them finger tight.
16. Tighten the retaining screws evenly in an alternate pattern. While tightening the retaining screws, readjust the position of the front cover as required to ensure that the cylinder block locating dowels are evenly aligned with the holes in the cover. Do not force the cover over the locating dowels.
17. When the front cover is properly in place, torque the retaining screws to 90 inch lbs. (9 Nm).
18. Prior to installing the oil pan, apply an even coating of sealant GM part number 1052080 or equivalent onto the front corners where the front cover and the rear main seal mate with the crankcase. Reinstall the oil pan and pan gasket.
19. Install the remaining components in reverse of the removal procedure.

Oil Seal

Replacement
FRONT COVER REMOVED

1. Pry the oil seal from the front cover with the appropriate tool.

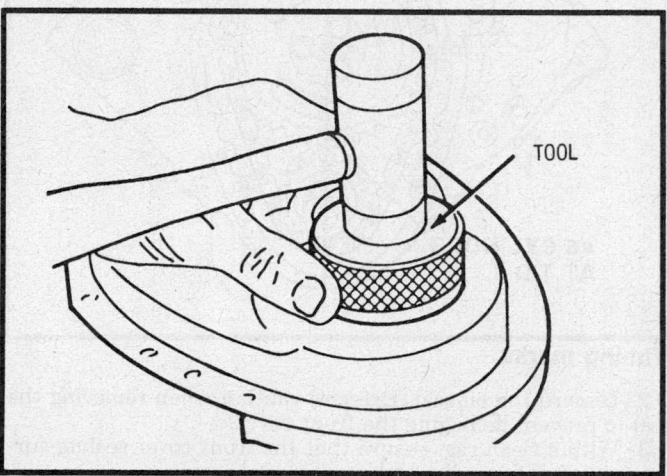

Installing front cover oil seal

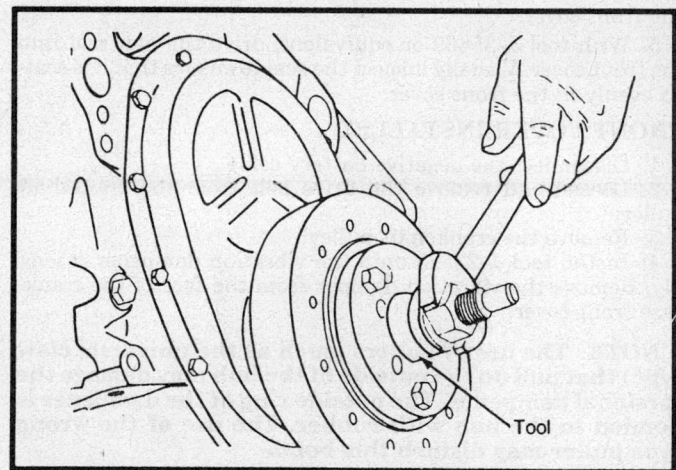

Installing the torsional damper

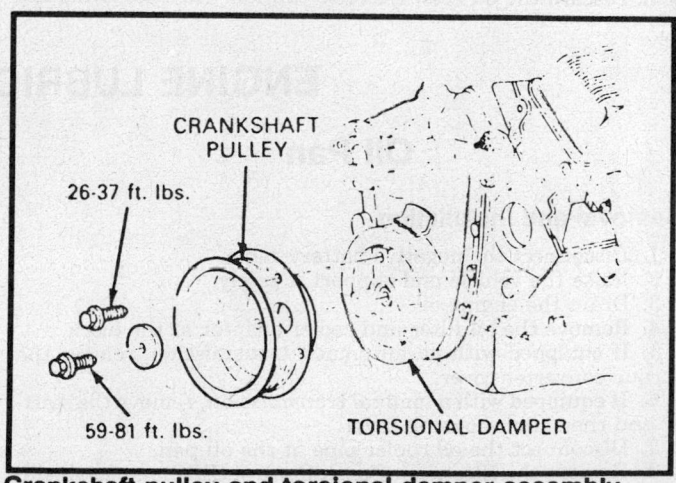

Crankshaft pulley and torsional damper assembly

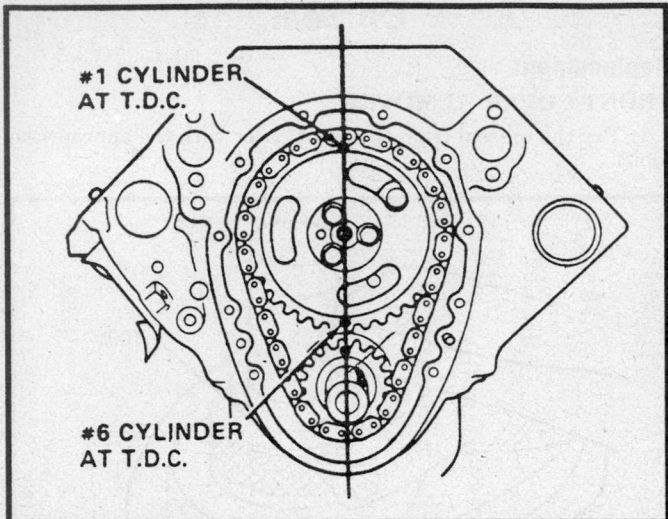

Timing marks

2. Discard the oil seal. Exercise caution when removing the seal to prevent damaging the front cover.

3. With a clean rag, ensure that the front cover sealing surfaces are free from dirt and grease.

4. Support the rear of the front cover and position the new seal so that the open end of the seal is toward the the inside of the front cover.

5. With tool J–35468 or equivalent, drive the new seal into the front cover. Visually inspect the seal to ensure that it is seated evenly in the front cover.

FRONT COVER INSTALLED

1. Disconnect the negative battery cable.

2. Loosen and remove the drive belt from the crankshaft pulley.

3. Remove the crankshaft pulley.

4. Install tool J–23523 onto the vibration dampener assembly. Remove the vibration damper from the face of the crankcase front cover.

NOTE: The use of pullers (such as the universal claw type) that pull on the outside of the hub may damage the torsional dampener. The outside ring of the dampener is bonded to the hub with rubber. The use of the wrong type puller may disturb this bond.

5. Pry the oil seal from the front cover with the appropriate tool. Discard the oil seal. Exercise caution when removing the

seal to prevent damaging the front cover and crankshaft surfaces.

6. With a clean rag, ensure that the front cover sealing surfaces are free from dirt and grease.

7. With tool J–35468 or equivalent, drive the new seal into the front cover. Visually inspect the seal to ensure that it is seated evenly in the front cover.

8. With the removal tool, reinstall the vibration dampener.

9. Reinstall the crankshaft pulley and reconnect the drive belt. Adjust the drive belt tension.

Timing Gears and Chain

Removal and Installation

1. Disconnect the negative battery cable.

2. Remove the engine front cover.

3. Rotate the crankshaft and align the timing marks.

4. Remove the camshaft gear bolts. Remove the camshaft gear.

5. Remove the timing chain.

6. With a suitable puller, carefully remove the crankshaft gear sprocket. Remove the key from the end of the crankshaft keyway. Inspect the keyway surface for excessive wear or rounding. Replace if necessary.

7. Visually inspect the crankshaft and camshaft gear teeth for chipped, missing and cracked teeth. Replace all damaged parts, as the use of a damaged gear will result in timing chain failure.

8. Installation is the reverse of the removal procedure.

Rings/Piston/Connecting Rod Positioning

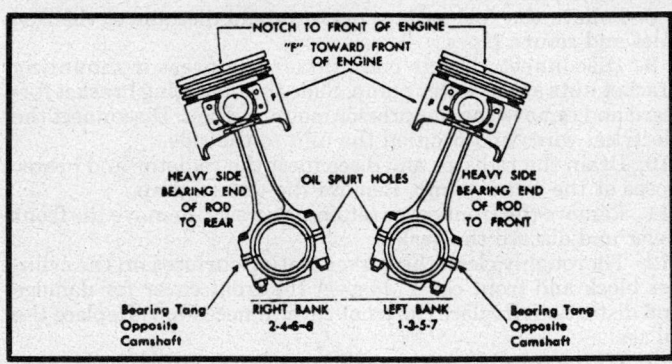

Piston assembly

ENGINE LUBRICATION SYSTEM

Oil Pan

Removal and Installation

1. Disconnect the negative battery cable.

2. Raise the vehicle and support it safely.

3. Drain the engine oil.

4. Remove the oil filter and cooler adapter at the block.

5. If equipped with an automatic transmission, remove the torque converter cover.

6. If equipped with a manual transmission, remove the starter and the clutch housing cover.

7. Disconnect the oil cooler pipe at the oil pan.

8. Remove the Electronic Spark Control (ESC) sensor shield.

9. Remove the front crossmember braces.

10. Remove the oil pan bolts and the pan.

11. Installation is the reverse of the removal procedure. Tighten the bolts to 16 ft. lbs. (22 Nm).

Oil Pump

Removal and Installation

1. Disconnect the negative battery cable.

2. Raise the vehicle and support it safely.

3. Drain the engine oil and remove the oil pan.

4. Support the oil pump by hand and remove the main bearing cap bolt.

5. Carefully remove the pump with the extension shaft.

To install:

6. Support the oil pump with extension shaft and assemble to

the rear main bearing cap.

7. Ensure that the slot on the top of the extension shaft is aligned with the drive tang on the lower end of the distributor drive shaft.

8. Torque the main bearing cap bolt to 80 ft. lbs. (108 Nm).

Rear Main Oil Seal

Removal and Installation

1. Disconnect the negative battery cable.
2. Raise the vehicle and support it safely.
3. Remove the transmission.
4. Drain the engine oil and remove the oil pan.
5. Remove the studs from the retainer.
6. Remove the retainer and seal assembly.
7. Using the notches provided in the retainer, pry out the seal.
8. Remove the gasket.

NOTE: Whenever the retainer is removed, a new retainer gasket and rear main seal must be installed.

To install:

9. Clean the mating surfaces of the case and the retainer assembly.
10. Install a new gasket on the studs in the engine case.

NOTE: It is not necessary to use any type of sealant to retain the gasket in place.

11. Install the retainer-to-case bolts. Torque the bolts to 90–120 inch lbs. (10–13 Nm).
12. Install a new gasket on the oil pan. Apply sealant onto the 2 front corners where the cover meets the case and where the rear seal retainer meets the case.
13. Install the oil pan and gasket.
14. Lubricate the inside and outside diameters of the oil seal with engine oil.
15. Install the seal on tool J–35621.
16. Thread the screws into the rear of the crankshaft. Tighten the screws snugly to insure that the seal will be installed squarely over the crankshaft.
17. Tighten the wing nut on the tool until it bottoms.
18. Remove the tool from the crankshaft.

Connecting Rod and Main Bearing

Replacement

1. Remove the engine from the vehicle and position it in a suitable holding fixture.
2. Remove the oil pan.
3. Remove the oil pump.
4. Remove the cylinder head.
5. For the cylinder being serviced, turn the crankshaft until the piston is at the bottom of the stroke. Place a cloth on the top of the piston.
6. Remove any ridge or deposits from the upper end of the cylinder bore.
7. Turn the crankshaft until the piston is at the top of the stroke and remove the cloth and cuttings.
8. Remove the connecting rod cap and install tool J–5239 on the studs.
9. Push the connecting rod and piston assembly out of the top of the cylinder block.
10. Remove the bearings from the connecting rods and rod caps.
11. Use the following procedure for measuring the maximum diameter of the crankpin to determine the new bearing size required:

    a. Place a piece of gauging plastic, the length of the bearing, parallel to the crankshaft on the crankpin or bearing surface.

NOTE: Plastic gauge should be positioned in the middle of the bearing shell. The bearing are eccentric and false readings could occur if placed elsewhere.

    b. Install the bearings in the connecting rod and cap.
    c. Install the bearing cap and tighten the nuts to 45 ft. lbs. (60 Nm).

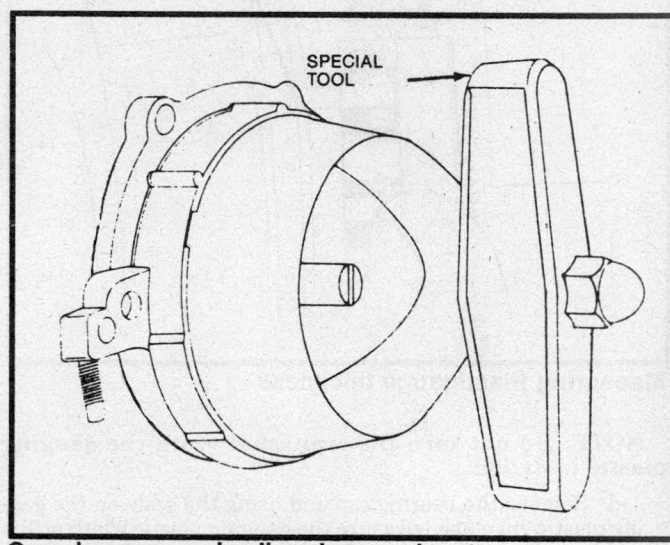

One piece rear main oil seal removal tool

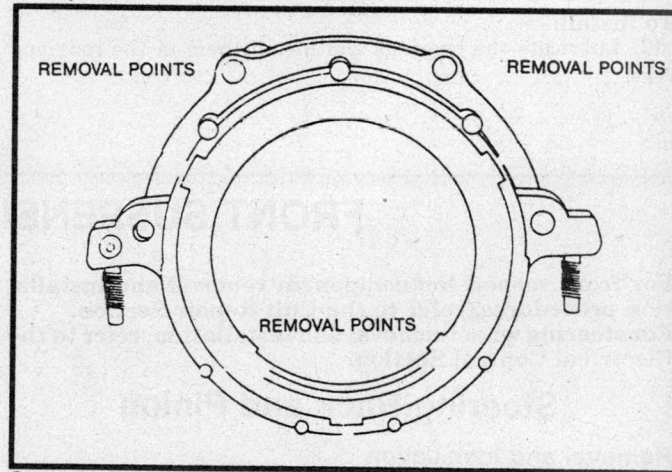

One piece rear main oil seal removal procedure

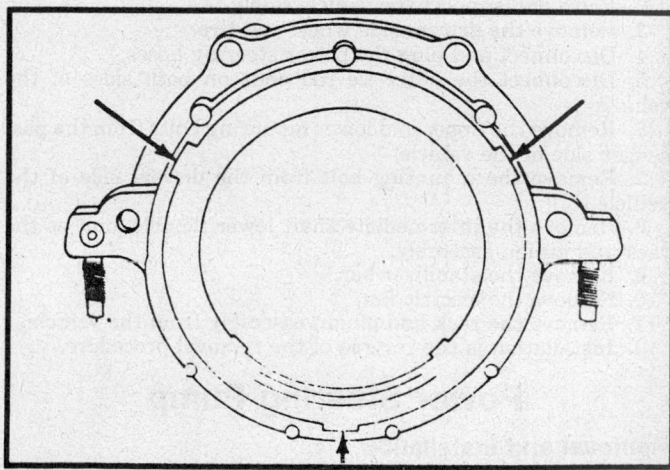

Removing the seal from the seal retainer

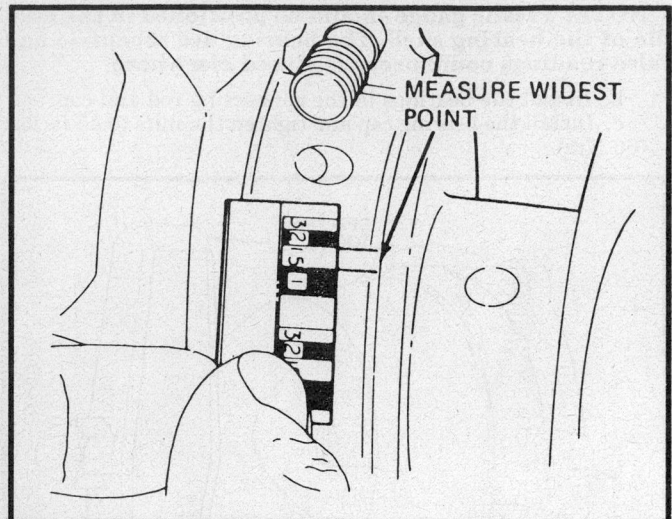

Measuring Plastigauge thickness

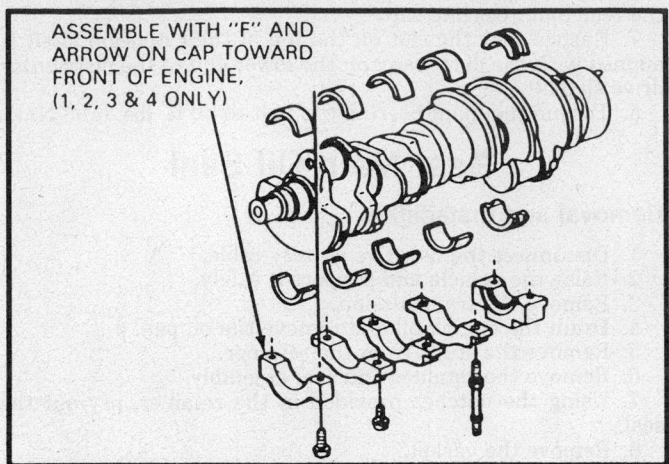

Crankshaft and bearing assembly

NOTE: Do not turn the crankshaft with the gauging plastic installed.

d. Remove the bearing cap and using the scale on the gaging plastic envelope, measure the gauging plastic width at the widest point.

To install:

12. Lubricate the bearings and install them in the rods and caps.

13. Lightly coat the pistons, rings and cylinder walls with light engine oil.

14. With the bearing caps removed, install tool J–5239 on the connecting rod bolts.

15. Install each connecting rod and piston assembly in its respective bore. Install them with the connecting rod bearing tang slots on the side opposite the camshaft.

16. Compress the piston rings using the proper tool while guiding the connecting rod into place on the crankshaft journal.

17. Install the bearing caps and tighten the nuts to 45 ft. lbs. (60 Nm).

FRONT SUSPENSION AND STEERING

For front suspension component removal and installation procedures, refer to the Unit Repair Section.
For steering wheel removal and installation, refer to the Electrical Control Section.

Steering Rack and Pinion

Removal and Installation

1. Disconnect the negative battery cable.
2. Raise and support the vehicle safely.
3. Remove the drivers side wheel and tire.
4. Disconnect and plug the power steering hoses.
5. Disconnect the outer tie rod ends on both sides of the vehicle.
6. Remove the upper and lower mounting bolts from the passenger side of the vehicle.
7. Remove the mounting bolt from the drivers side of the vehicle.
8. Remove the intermediate shaft lower flexible joint at the rack and pinion assembly.
9. Remove the stabilizer bar.
10. Remove the electric fan.
11. Remove the rack and pinion assembly from the vehicle.
12. Installation is the reverse of the removal procedure.

Power Steering Pump

Removal and Installation

1. Disconnect the negative battery cable.

2. Remove the serpentine drive belt.
3. Disconnect and plug the fluid lines.
4. Remove the pump pulley.
5. Remove the pump retaining bolts. Remove the pump from the vehicle.

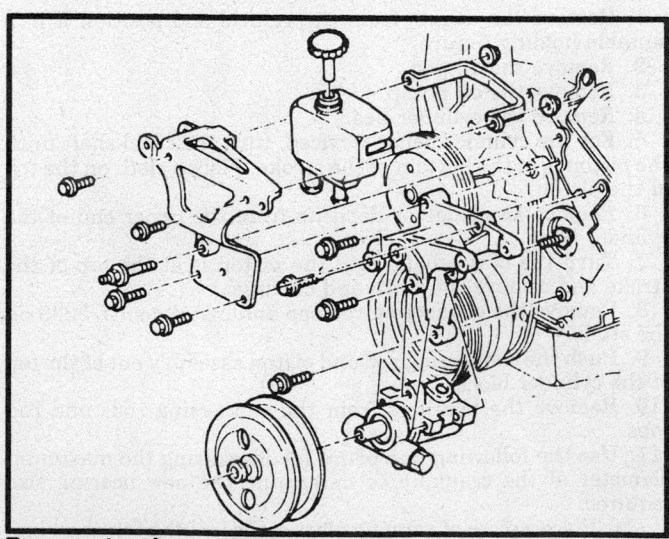

Power steering pump assembly

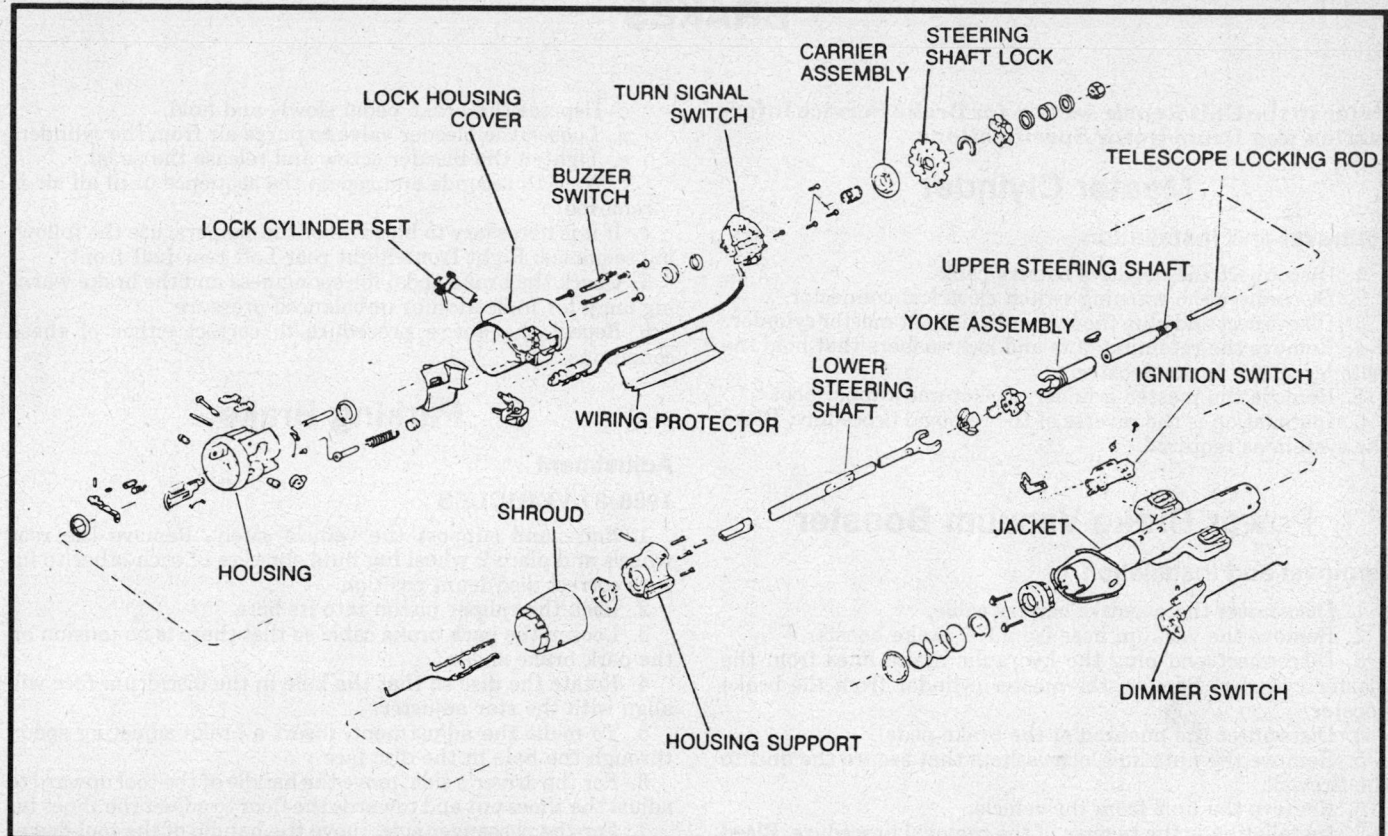

Steering column and related components—column shift

6. Installation is the reverse of the removal procedure. Bleed the system, as required.

Steering Column

Removal and Installation

NOTE: Handle the steering column very carefully. Hammering the end of it or leaning on it could shear off the plastic type inserts which allow the column to collapse in a collision.

1. Disconnect the negative battery cable.
2. Remove the steering wheel.
3. Remove the nut and bolt from the upper intermediate shaft coupling.
4. Separate the coupling from the lower end of steering column.
5. Remove the left hand instrument panel sound insulator and lower trim pad.
6. Disconnect all electrical connectors from the column assembly.
7. Remove the screws securing the toe pan cover to the floor.
8. Remove the nuts securing the bracket to the instrument panel.
9. Withdraw the steering column.
10. Installation is the reverse of the removal procedure. Use only the specified hardware. Overlength bolts could prevent the column from properly collapsing in a crash.

Front Wheel Bearings

Removal and Installation

1. Raise and support the vehicle safely.

2. Remove the tire and wheel assembly.
3. Remove the caliper assembly and position it out of the way.
4. Remove the rotor and bearing assembly.
5. Installation is the reverse of the removal procedure. The bearings do not require adjustment.

Alignment

Procedure

CASTER

Caster is the tilting of the steering axis either forward or backward from the vertical, when viewed from the side of the vehicle. A backward tilt is said to be positive and a forward tilt is said to be negative. Weak springs or overloading of a vehicle effect caster due to the effect these conditions have on the normal body trim height. Changes to the trim height result in changes to the inclination of the steering axis. Caster angle influences directional stability and steeering effort, but does not effect tire wear.

CAMBER

Camber is the tilting of the wheels from the vertical when viewed from the front of the vehicle. When the wheels tilt outward from the top, the camber is said to be positive. When the wheels tilt inward from the top the camber is said to be negative. The amount of tilt is measured in degrees from the vertical. This measurement is called camber angle.

TOE-IN

Toe in is the turning in of the wheels. The actual amount of toe in is normally only a fraction of an inch. The purpose of toe in specification is to ensure parallel rolling of the wheels. Toe in also serves to offset the small deflections of the steering support system which occur when the vehicle is rolling forward.

BRAKES

Refer to the Unit Repair section for Brake Service Information and Drum/Rotor Specifications.

Master Clyinder

Removal and Installation

1. Disconnect the negative battery cable.
2. Disconnect the warning switch electrical connector.
3. Disconnect and plug the hydraulic lines at master cylinder.
4. Remove the retaining nuts and lockwashers that hold the cylinder to the brake booster.
5. Remove the master cylinder, gasket and rubber boot.
6. Installation is the reverse of the removal procedure. Bleed the system as required.

Power Brake Vacuum Booster

Removal and Installation

1. Disconnect the negative battery cable.
2. Remove the vacuum hose from the brake booster.
3. Disconnect and plug the hydraulic brake lines from the master cylinder. Remove the master cylinder from the brake booster.
4. Disconnect the pushrod at the brake pedal.
5. Remove the nuts and lockwashers that secure the unit to the firewall.
6. Remove the unit from the vehicle.
7. Installation is the reverse of the removal procedure. Bleed the system.

Bleeding Procedure

1. Fill the master cylinder reservoirs with brake fluid and keep them at least ½ full of fluid during the bleeding operation.
2. Bleed the master cylinder before any caliper is bled using the following procedure:
   a. Disconnect the forward brake line from the master cylinder.
   b. When brake fluid begins to flow from the forward brake line port, connect the brake line to the master cylinder and tighten.
   c. Depress the brake pedal slowly and hold. Loosen the forward brake line connection to purge air from the bore. Tighten the connection and then release the brake pedal slowly.
   d. Wait 15 seconds and repeat the sequence until all air is removed from the bore.
   e. When clear fluid flows from the forward connection, repeat the procedure for the rear connection.
3. After bleeding the master cylinder, bleed individual calipers using the following procedure:
   a. Position the proper size box wrench over the caliper bleeder valve.
   b. Attach a clear tube over the valve. Submerge the other end of the tube in a clear container partially filled with brake fluid.

   c. Depress the brake pedal slowly and hold.
   d. Loosen the bleeder valve to purge air from the cylinder.
   e. Tighten the bleeder screw and release the pedal.
   f. Wait 15 seconds and repeat the sequence until all air is removed.
4. If it is necessary to bleed all of the calipers, use the following sequence: Right front-Right rear-Left rear-Left front.
5. Check the brake pedal for sponginess and the brake warning lamp for indication of unbalanced pressure.
6. Repeat the entire procedure to correct either of these conditions.

Parking Brake

Adjustment
1986–87 VEHICLES

1. Raise and support the vehicle safely. Remove the rear wheels and place 2 wheel lug nuts opposite of each other to insure correct disc/drum position.
2. Back the caliper piston into its bore.
3. Loosen the park brake cable so that there is no tension on the park brake shoes.
4. Rotate the disc so that the hole in the disc/drum face will align with the star adjuster.
5. To make the adjustment, insert a brake adjusting spoon through the hole in the disc face.
6. For the driver's side, move the handle of the tool upward to adjust the shoes out and towards the floor to adjust the shoes in.
7. For the passenger side, move the handle of the tool downward to adjust the shoes out and towards the ceiling to adjust them in.
8. Adjust 1 side at a time until there is no rotation of the disc/drum, then back the star adjuster off 5–7 notches. Then go to the opposite side and do the same procedure.
9. Apply the park brake lever 2 notches.
10. Adjust the cable at the equalizer so that the wheel has a drag.
11. Release the park brake lever and check the wheel for free rotation.
12. Correct adjustment will result in no drag on the wheel.

1988–90 VEHICLES

The parking brake lever/cable adjustment is automatic. The only adjustment required is a free-travel adjustment and should only be made if the caliper housing has been disassembled.

The adjustment process requires a second person to apply a light brake pedal load. Lever free-travel is set by the position of the adjusting screw. Turning the adjustment screw clockwise increases the free-travel; turning the adjustment screw counterclockwise decreases the free-travel. Measure the free-travel between the lever and the caliper housing. Free-travel must be 0.024–0.028 in. (0.6–0.7mm).

NOTE: Cycling the lever 3 times should result in parking brake lever movement of 7–9 notches when a 50 lb. (220 N) force is applied.

CLUTCH AND TRANSMISSION

Refer to "Chilton's Transmission Service Manual" for additional coverage.

Clutch Linkage

HYDRAULIC

Bleeding

1. Fill the master cylinder reservoir with the proper grade and type brake fluid.
2. Raise the vehicle and support it safely.
3. Remove the clutch slave cylinder.
4. Hold the slave cylinder at a 45 degree angle with the bleeder valve at the highest point.
5. Fully depress the clutch pedal and open the bleeder valve. Close the bleeder valve and release the clutch pedal.
6. Repeat Step 5 until all air is expelled from the system.
7. Check the fluid reservoir and replenish as required.

Clutch

Removal and Installation

1. Remove the transmission from the vehicle.
2. Disconnect the clutch fork pushrod and spring.
3. Remove the slave cylinder attaching bolts.
4. Remove the flywheel housing.
5. Slide the clutch fork from the ball stud and remove the fork from the dust boot. The ball stud is threaded into the clutch housing and is easily replaced, if necessary.
6. Install a clutch pilot tool.

NOTE: Look for the assembly markings X on the flywheel and the clutch cover (pressure plate assembly). If there are none, scribe marks to identify the position of the clutch cover relative to the flywheel.

7. Loosen the clutch cover bolts evenly until the spring pressure is relieved, then remove the bolts and clutch assembly.
8. Clean the pressure plate and the flywheel face.

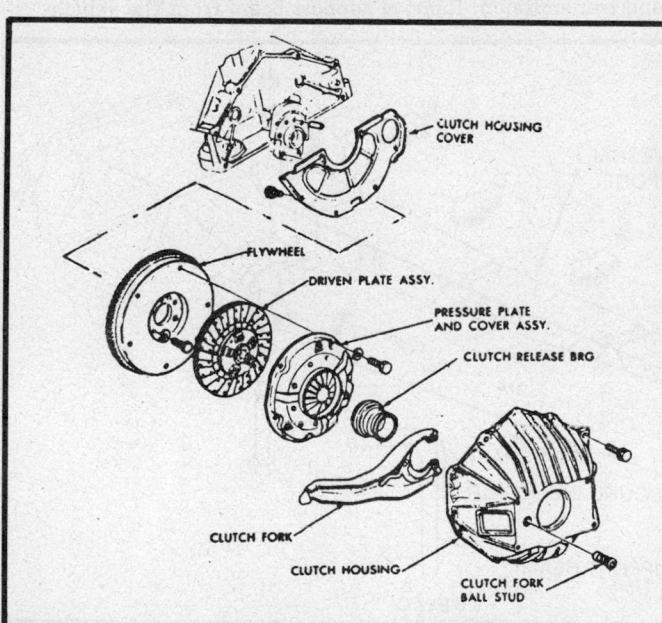

Exploded view of the clutch assembly

CLUTCH HOUSING COVER
FLYWHEEL
DRIVEN PLATE ASSY.
PRESSURE PLATE AND COVER ASSY.
CLUTCH RELEASE BRG
CLUTCH FORK
CLUTCH HOUSING
CLUTCH FORK BALL STUD

To install:

9. Position the disc and pressure plate assembly on the flywheel and install a pilot tool.
10. Install the pressure plate assembly bolts. Make sure the mark on the cover is aligned with the mark on the flywheel. Tighten the bolts alternately and evenly to 30 ft. lbs. (41 Nm).
11. Remove the pilot tool.
12. Remove the release fork and lubricate the ball socket and the fork fingers at the throwout bearing with graphite or Molycoat® grease. Reinstall the release fork.
13. Lubricate the inside recess and the fork groove of the throwout bearing with a light coat of graphite or Molycoat® grease.
14. Install the clutch release fork and dust boot in the clutch housing and the throwout bearing on the fork, then install the flywheel housing. Tighten flywheel housing bolts to 30 ft. lbs. (41 Nm). Reinstall the slave cylinder.
15. Connect the fork pushrod and spring.
16. Adjust the shift linkage.
17. Adjust the clutch pedal free play. Bleed the hydraulic clutch system.

Clutch Master Cylinder

Removal and Installation

1. Disconnect the negative battery cable.
2. Remove the hush panel from underneath of the dash.
3. Disconnect the pushrod from the clutch pedal.
4. Disconnect the hydraulic line at the master cylinder.
5. Remove the clutch master cylinder retaining bolts. Remove the clutch master cylinder from the vehicle.
5. Installation is the reverse of the removal procedure. Bleed the system, as required.

Clutch Slave Cylinder

Removal and Installation

1. Disconnect the negative battery cable.
2. Raise and support the vehicle safely.
3. Disconnect the hydraulic line at the slave cylinder.
4. Remove the slave cylinder mounting bolts from the clutch housing.
5. Remove the pushrod and the slave cylinder from the vehicle.
6. Installation is the reverse of the removal procedure. Bleed the system, as required.

Manual Transmission

Removal and Installation

1. Disconnect the negative battery cable.
2. Remove the distributor cap.
3. Raise the vehicle and support it safely.
4. Remove the upper and lower underbody braces on vehicles equipped with a convertible top.
5. Remove the complete exhaust system as an assembly.
6. Remove the exhaust hanger at the transmission.
7. Support the transmission using the proper equipment.
8. Remove the bolts attaching the driveline support beam at the axle and the transmission. Remove the driveline support beam from the vehicle.
9. Mark the relationship of the driveshaft to the axle companion flange. Remove the trunnion bearing straps and disengage the rear universal joint from the axle. Slide the driveshaft slip yoke out of the overdrive unit and remove the shaft from the vehicle.

10. Disconnect the transmission cooler lines at the overdrive unit, if equipped.

11. Disconnect the shift linkage at the side cover.

12. Disconnect the electrical connectors at the side cover. Disconnect the back up light switch, 1st gear switch, overdrive unit and speedometer sensor switch.

13. Lower the transmission and support the engine.

14. Remove the bolts attaching the transmission to the bellhousing. Slide the transmission to the rear to disengage the input shaft from the clutch. Remove the transmission from the vehicle.

To install:

15. Clean and repack the clutch release bearing.

16. Install the transmission and attaching bolts.

17. Connect the oil cooler line pipes to the overdrive unit, if equipped. Torque the connector fittings to 8–12 ft. lbs. (11–16 Nm).

18. Install and align the driveline support beam.

19. Install the driveshaft shaft.

20. Connect and adjust the throttle shift linkage.

21. Connect the backup light switch, overdrive unit, if equipped speedometer sensor and 1st gear electrical connectors.

22. Refill transmission to proper level. The 4 or 6 Speed section uses SAE-80 W or SAE-80 W-90 GL-5 gear lube. The overdrive unit, if equipped uses Dextron II® automatic transmission fluid.

23. Install the exhaust system components. Reinstall upper and lower underbody braces, if removed.

Automatic Transmission

Removal and Installation

1. Disconnect the negative battery cable.
2. Raise and support the vehicle safely.
3. Disconnect the T.V. cable at the transmission.
4. Disconnect the oil cooler lines at the transmission.
5. Remove the complete exhaust system.
6. Remove the transmission inspection cover.

7. Remove the torque convertor to flywheel bolts. The relationship between the flywheel and convertor must be marked so that proper balance is maintained after installation.

8. Matchmark the driveshaft and the rear yoke (for reinstallation purposes). With a drain pan positioned under the front yoke, unbolt and remove the drive shaft.

9. Mark and disconnect vacuum lines, wiring and the speedometer cable from the transmission as required.

10. Place a transmission jack up against the transmission oil pan, then secure the transmission to the jack.

11. Remove the transmission mounting pad bolt(s), then carefully raise the transmission just enough to take the weight of the transmission off of the supporting crossmember. Remove the transmission mounting pad.

NOTE: Exercise extreme care to avoid damage to underhood components while raising or lowering the transmission.

12. Remove the transmission dipstick, then unbolt and remove the filler tube.

13. Disconnect the floor shift cable. Disconnect the oil cooler lines from the transmission.

14. Support the engine using a jack placed beneath the engine oil pan. Be sure to put a block of wood between the jack and the oil pan, to prevent damage to the pan.

15. With the proper gauge wire, fasten the torque convertor to the transmission case.

16. Remove the transmission to engine mounting bolts, then carefully move the transmission rearward, downward and out from beneath the vehicle.

NOTE: If interference is encountered with the cable(s), cooler lines, etc., remove the component(s) before finally lowering the transmission.

17. Installation is the reverse of the removal procedure. Adjust the shift control cable and T.V. cable. Refill the transmission to the proper level with Dexron II® automatic transmission fluid.

DRIVESHAFT

Removal and Installation

1. Raise the vehicle and support it safely.

2. Remove the complete exhaust system.

3. Remove the bolts attaching the support beam at the axle and transmission. Remove support beam from the vehicle.

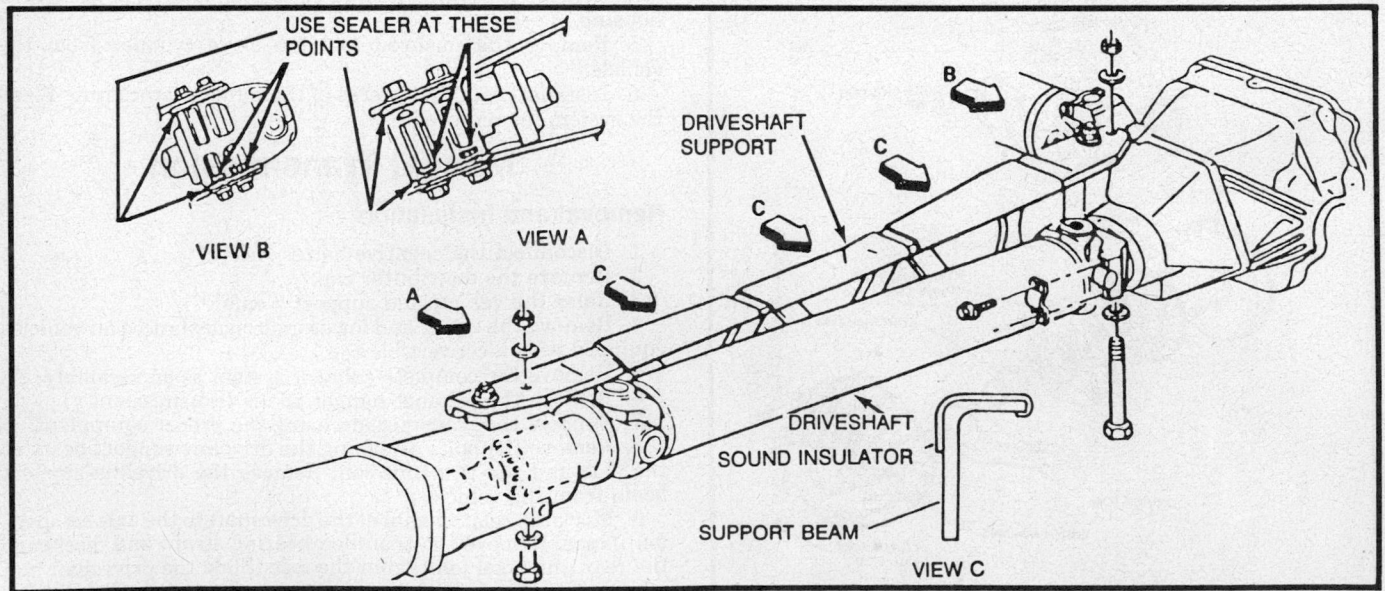

USE SEALER AT THESE POINTS

VIEW B   VIEW A

DRIVESHAFT SUPPORT

DRIVESHAFT SOUND INSULATOR

SUPPORT BEAM

VIEW C

Driveshaft alignment check

4. Mark relationship of shaft to companion flange and disconnect the rear universal joint by removing trunnion bearing straps. Tape bearing cups to trunnion to prevent dropping and loss of bearing rollers.

5. Slide slip yoke from the transmission and remove shaft. Watch for oil leakage from transmission output shaft housing.

6. Installation is the reverse of the removal procedure.

Universal Joints

For universal joint overhaul and service procedures, refer to the Unit Repair Section.

REAR AXLE AND SUSPENSION

Refer to the Unit Repair Section for Axle Overhaul Procedures and Rear Suspension Services.

Rear Axle Assembly

Removal and Installation

1. Remove air cleaner.
2. Disconnect distributor cap from distributor.
3. Raise and support the vehicle safely.
4. Remove spare tire cover by removing support hooks.
5. Remove spare tire.
6. Remove the complete exhaust system as an assembly.
7. Disconnect leaf spring at the knuckles and remove attaching bolts at the cover. Remove leaf spring from vehicle.
8. Scribe mark on cam bolts and mounting bracket so they can be realigned in the same position. Remove cam bolts and then mounting bracket from carrier.
9. Disconnect both tie rod ends from the knuckles.
10. Remove the axle shaft union straps from the side gear yokes. Push the wheel assemblies outboard to disengage the trunnions from the side gear yokes.
11. Remove drive shaft trunnion straps at pinion flange. Push drive shaft forward into transmission and tie shaft to the support beam.
12. Properly support the transmission.
13. Remove differential cover/beam attaching bolts at frame brackets.
14. Remove support beam attaching bolts at the front of the differential carrier. Remove differential carrier assembly from the vehicle.
15. Installation is the reverse of removal.

Axle Shaft, Bearing and Oil Seal

Removal and Installation

1. Raise the vehicle and support it safely.
2. Disconnect the leaf spring from the knuckle.
3. Disconnect the tie rod end from the knuckle.
4. Scribe a mark on the cam bolt and the knuckle for realignment.
5. Remove the cam bolt.
6. Separate the spindle support rod from the mounting bracket at the carrier.
7. Remove the axle shaft trunnion straps at the spindle and side gear yoke.
8. Push out on the wheel and tire assembly.
9. Remove the axle shaft.
10. Installation is the reverse of the removal procedure.
11. Tighten the trunnion strap retaining bolts to 26 ft. lbs. (35 Nm). Tighten the cam bolt to 187 ft. lbs. (253 Nm).

REAR WHEEL BEARING

Removal and Installation

1. Raise the vehicle and support it safely.

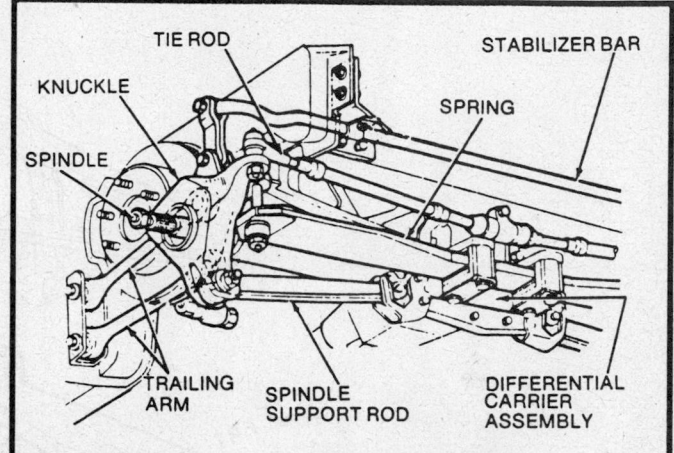

Rear suspension and related components

2. Remove the tire and wheel assembly. Remove the center cap.
3. Remove the cotter pin, spindle nut and washer.
4. Remove the brake caliper and support. Remove the rotor.
5. Disconnect the tie rod end from the knuckle. Disconnect the transverse spring from the knuckle.
6. Scribe a mark on the dam bolt and mounting bracket.
7. Remove the cam bolt and separate the spindle support rod from the mounting bracket.
8. Remove the trunnion straps at the side gear yoke shaft. Separate and remove the axle shaft.

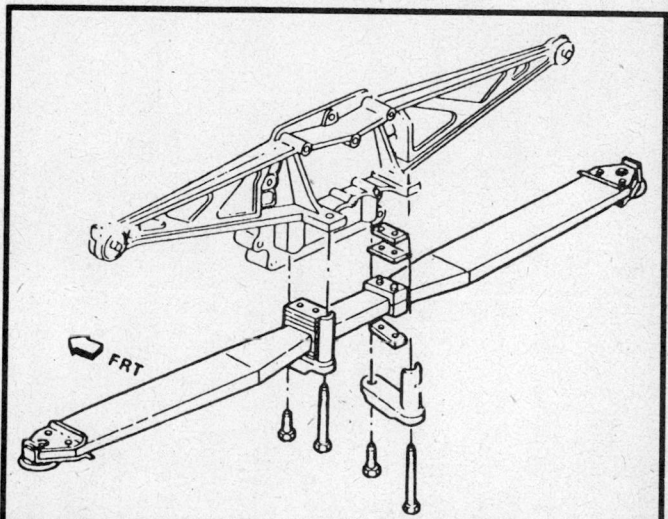

Rear suspension

9. Remove the hub and bearing mounting bolts using a number 45 Torx® head socket, or equivalent.

10. Remove the hub and bearing from the vehicle. Be sure to support the parking brake backing plate.

11. Installation is the reverse of removal.

Adjustment

The rear wheel bearing should have endplay of 0.001–0.008 in. When necessary, adjust using the following procedure.

1. Raise and support the vehicle safely.

2. Remove the tire and wheel assembly.

3. Remove the axle driveshaft.

4. Mark the camber cam in relation to the bracket. Loosen and turn the camber bolt until the strut rod forces the torque control arm outward.

5. Mount a dial indicator on the torque control surface and rest the pointer on the flange end.

6. Grasp the rotor and move it, in and out. If the bearing movement is within specification, no adjustment is necessary. If adjustment is necessary and the bearing is not within specification, add or subtract shims accordingly.

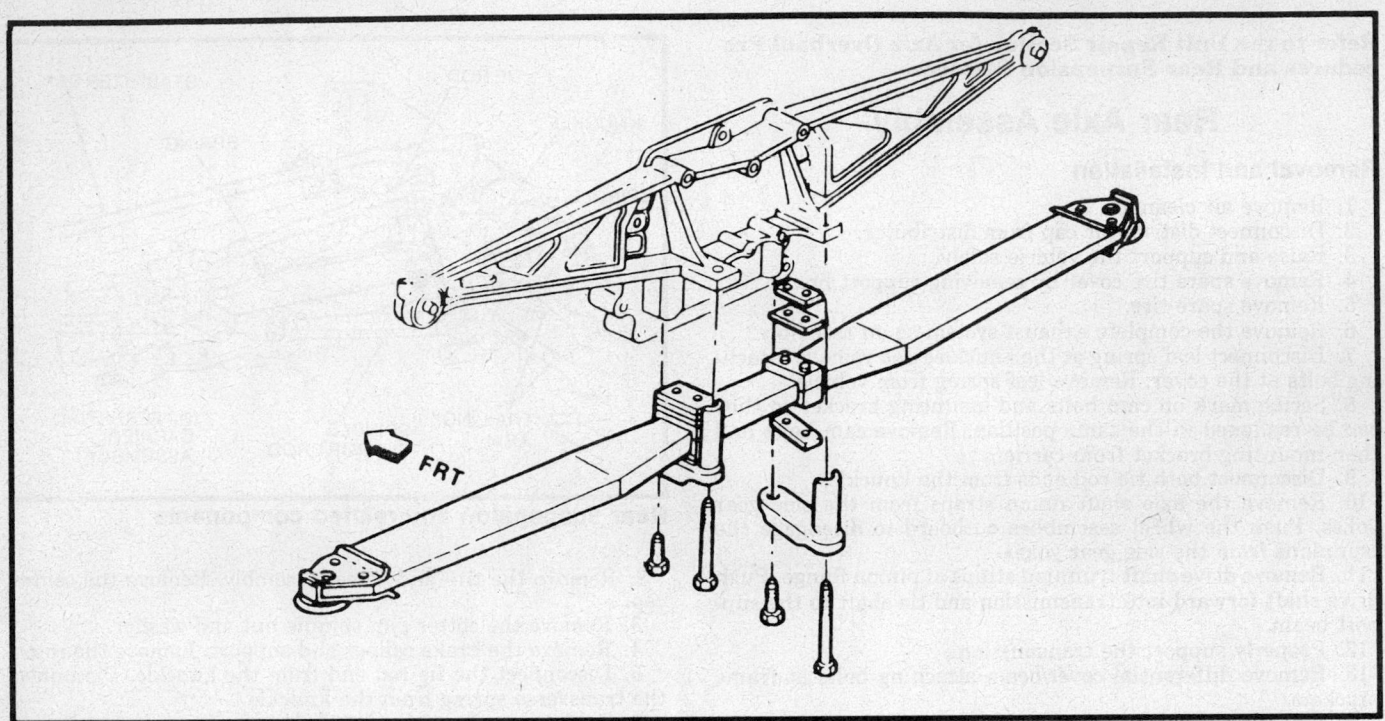

Rear transverse spring assembly

ELECTRICAL DIAGNOSIS

To satisfy the growing trend toward organized engine diagnosis and tune-up, the following gauge and meter hook-ups, as well as diagnosis procedures are covered. The most sophisticated tune-up and diagnostic facilities are no more than a complex of the basic gauges and meters in common, everyday use. Therefore, to understand gauge and meter hook-ups, their applications and procedures, is to be equipped with the know how to perform the most exacting diagnosis.

KNOW YOUR INSTRUMENTS

OHMMETER

An ohmmeter is used to measure electrical resistance in a unit or circuit. The ohmmeter has a self contained power supply. In use, it is connected across (or in parallel with) the terminals of the unit being tested.

AMMETER

An ammeter is used to measure the amount of electricity flowing through a unit, or circuit. Ammeters are always connected in series with the unit or circuit being tested.

VOLTMETER

A voltmeter is used to measure voltage pushing the current through a unit, or circuit. The meter is connected across the terminals of the unit being tested.

ALTERNATORS AND REGULATORS

Diagnosis

The first step in diagnosing troubles of the charging system, is to identify the source of failure. Does the fault lie in the alternator or the regulator? The next move depends upon preference or necessity, either repair or replace the offending unit.

If the system is equipped with an external voltage regulator, it is easy to separate an alternator, electrically, from the regulator. Alternator output is controlled by the amount of current supplied to the field circuit of the system.

An alternator is capable of producing substantial current at idle speed. Higher maximum output is also a possibility. This presents a potential danger when testing. As a precaution, a field rheostat should be used in the field circuit when making the following isolation test. The field rheostat permits positive control of the amount of current allowed to pass through the field circuit during the isolation test. Unregulated alternator capacity could ruin the unit.

Most manufacturers of precision gauges offer special test connectors, in sets, that will adapt to the leads and connections of any charging system.

ALTERNATOR TEST PLANS

The following is a procedure pattern for testing the various alternators and their control systems.

There are certain precautionary measures that apply to alternator tests in general. These items are listed in detail to avoid repetition when testing each make of alternator and to encourage a habit of good test procedure.

1. Check alternator drive belt for condition and tension.
2. Disconnect the battery cables. Check physical, chemical and electrical condition of battery.
3. Be absolutely sure of polarity before connecting any battery in the circuit. Reversed polarity will ruin the diodes.
4. Never use a battery charger to start the engine.
5. Disconnect both battery cables when making a battery recharge hook-up.

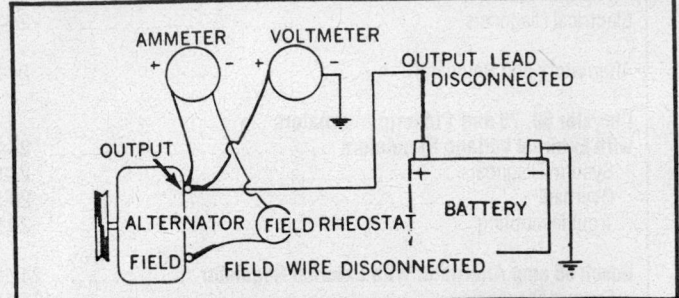

Checking field circuit current draw-As a precaution, a field rheostat should be used to control the amount of current allowed to pass through the circuit during isolation test

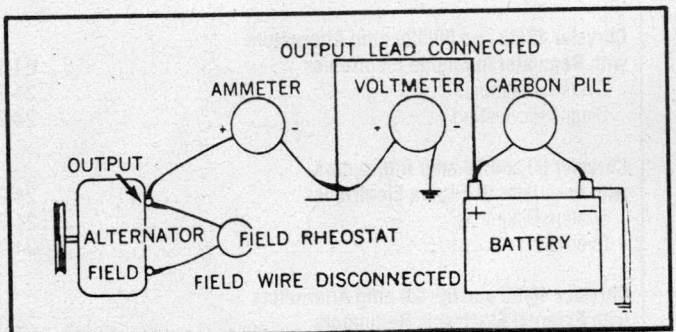

Checking current output of the charging system—if an overcharge of 10-15 amps is indicated, check for a faulty regulator

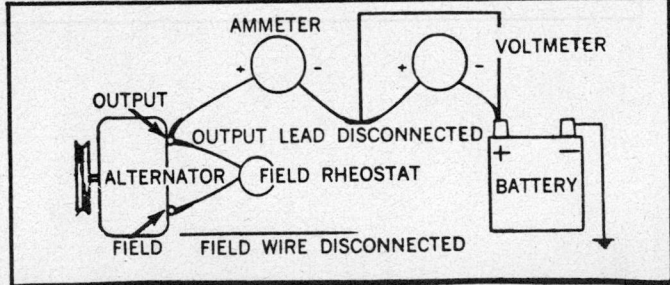

Checking charging system resistance to determine the amount of "voltage drop" between the alternator output terminal wire and the battery

6. Be sure of polarity hook-up when using a booster battery for starting.
7. Never ground the alternator output or battery terminal.
8. Never ground the field circuit between alternator and regulator.
9. Never run any alternator on an open circuit with the field energized.
10. Never try to polarize an alternator, unless directed by the manufacturer.
11. Do not attempt to motor an alternator.
12. When making engine idle speed adjustments, always consider potential load factors that influence engine rpm. To compensate for electrical load, switch **ON** the lights, radio, heater, air conditioner, etc.

Diagnosis

LOW OR NO CHARGING

1. Blown fuse
2. Broken or loose fan belt
3. Voltage regulator not working
4. Brushes sticking
5. Slip ring dirty
6. Open circuit
7. Bad wiring connections
8. Bad diode rectifier
9. High resistance in charging circuit
10. Grounded stator
11. May be open rectifiers (check all 3 phases)
12. If rectifiers are found or open, check capacitor

NOISY UNIT

1. Damaged rotor bearings
2. Poor alignment of unit
3. Broken or loose belt
4. Open diode rectifiers.

CHRYSLER 60 AMP, 78 AMP AND 114 AMP WITH EXTERNAL REGULATOR

The 60 and 78 amp alternators are equipped with 6 built-in silicon rectifiers, while the 114 amp alternator is equipped with 12 built-in silicon rectifiers.

System Diagnosis

ON VEHICLE SERVICE

System Operation

NOTE: If the current indicator is to give an accurate reading, the battery cables must be of the same gauge and length as the original equipment.

1. With the engine running and all electrical systems **OFF**, place a current indicator over the positive battery cable.

2. If a charge of about 5 amps is recorded, the charging system is working. If a draw of about 5 amps is recorded the system is not working. The needle moves toward the battery when a charge condition is indicated and away from the battery when a draw condition is indicated. If a draw is indicated, proceed to the next testing procedure. If an overcharge of 10–15 amps is indicated, check for a faulty regulator.

Ignition Switch to Regulator Circuit Check

1. Disconnect the regulator wires at the regulator.
2. Turn the key **ON** but do not start the engine.

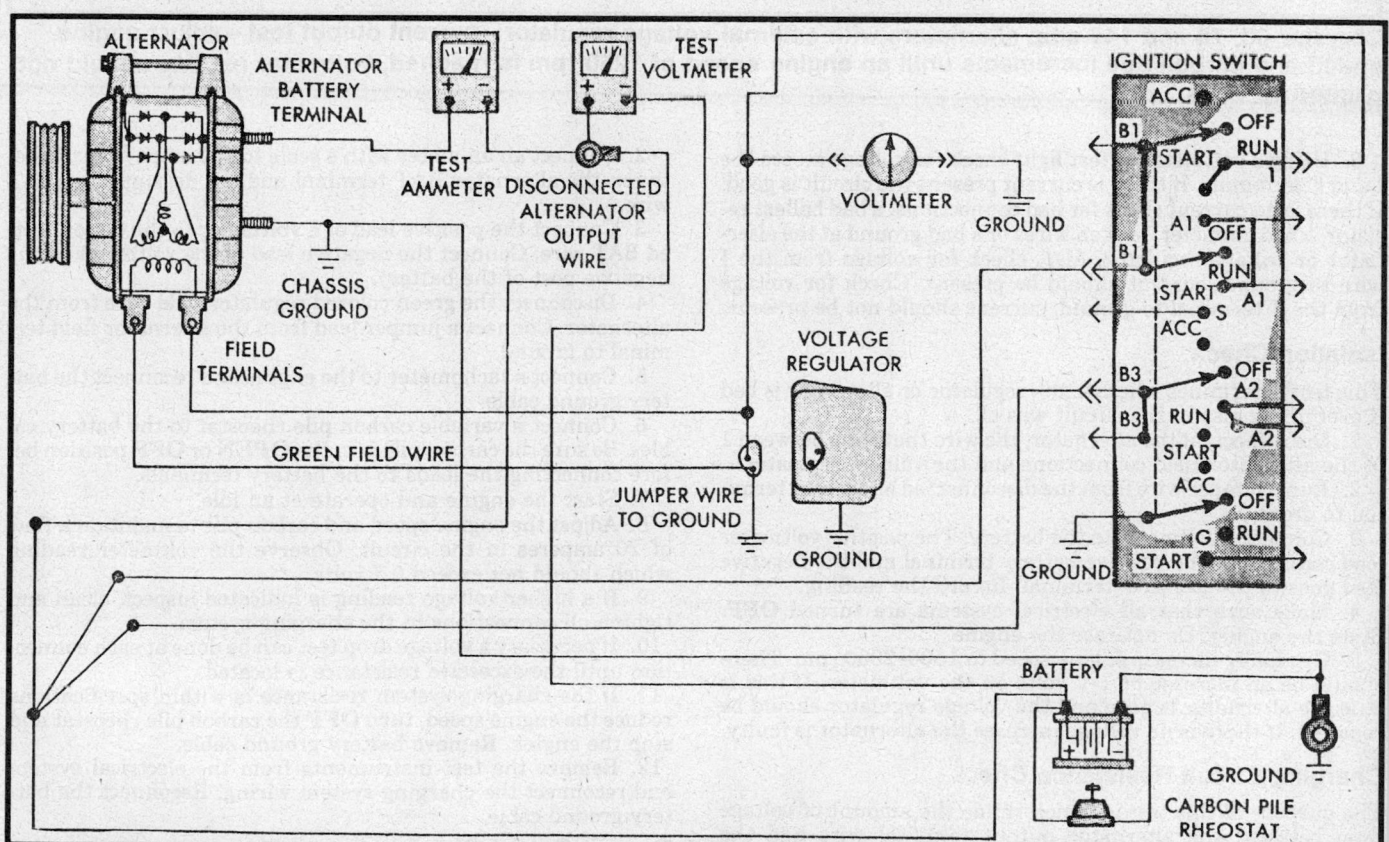

Chrysler 60, 78 and 114 amp alternators with external voltage regulator—charging system resistance test—adjust engine speed and carbon pile to maintain 20 amps, voltmeter reading should not exceed 0.5 volts

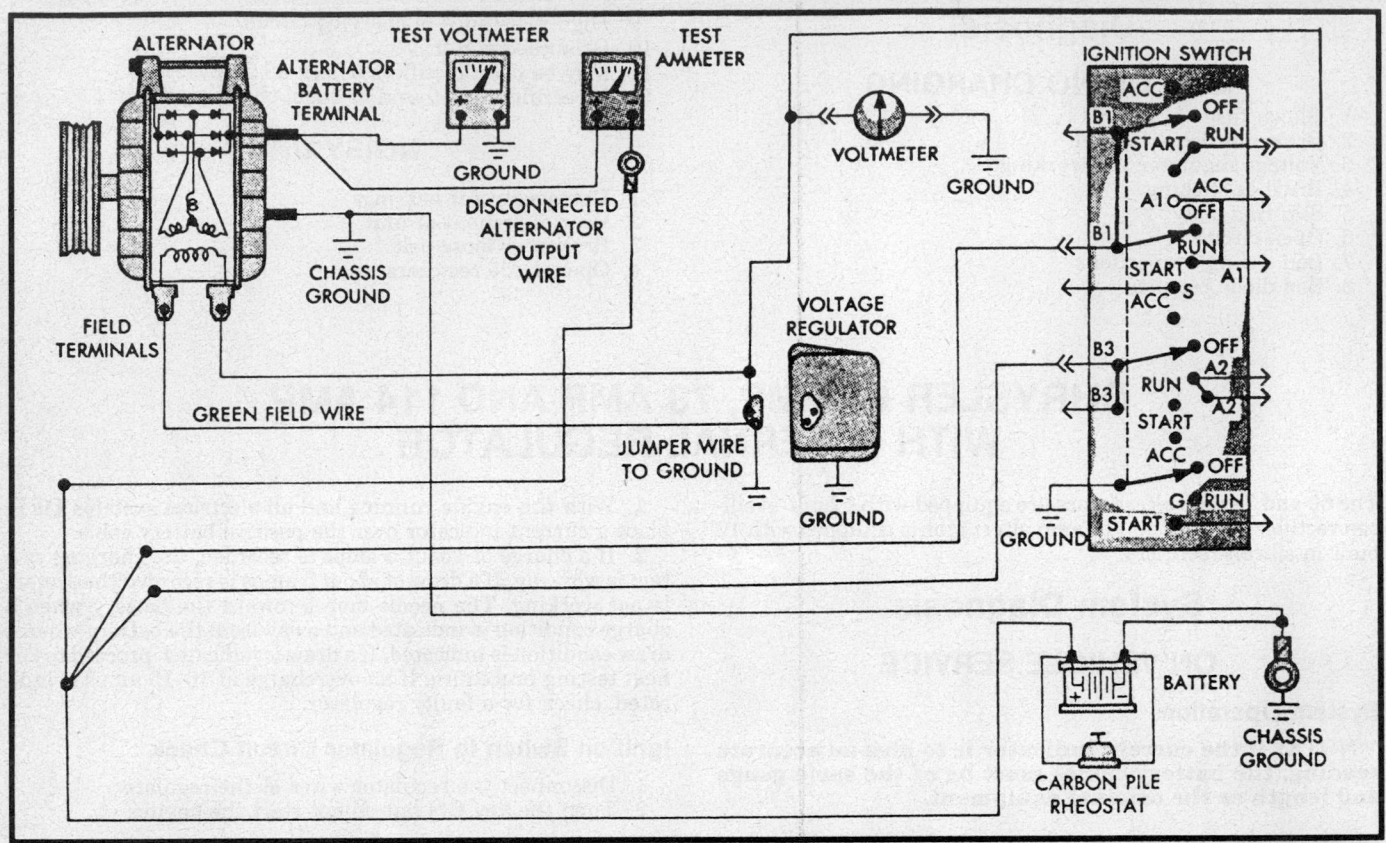

Chrysler 60, 78 and 144 amp alternators with external voltage regulator—current output test—adjust engine speed and carbon pile increments until an engine speed of 1250 rpm is reached, voltmeter reading should not exceed 15 volts

3. Using a voltmeter or test light check for voltage across the I and F terminals. If there is current present the circuit is good. If there is no current check for bad connections, a bad ballast resistor, a bad ammeter, broken wires or a bad ground at the alternator or voltage regulator. Also, check for voltage from the I wire to ground, current should be present. Check for voltage from the F terminal to ground, current should not be present.

Isolation Check

This test determines whether the regulator or alternator is bad if everything else in the circuit was ok.

1. Disconnect, at the alternator, the wire that runs between 1 of the alternator field connections and the voltage regulator.
2. Run a jumper wire from the disconnected alternator terminal to ground.
3. Connect a voltmeter to the battery. The positive voltmeter lead connects to the positive battery terminal and the negative lead goes to the negative terminal. Record the reading.
4. Make sure that all electrical systems are turned **OFF**. Start the engine. Do not race the engine.
5. Gradually increase engine speed to 1500–2000 rpm. There should be an increase of 1–2 volts on the voltmeter. If this is true the alternator is good and the voltage regulator should be repaired. If there is no voltage increase the alternator is faulty.

Charging Circuit Resistance Check

The purpose of this test is to determine the amount of voltage drop between the alternator output terminal wire and the battery.

1. Disconnect the battery ground cable and the BAT lead at the alternator output terminal.

2. Connect an ammeter with a scale to 100 amps in series between the alternator BAT terminal and the disconnected BAT wire.
3. Connect the positive lead of a voltmeter to the disconnected BAT wire. Connect the negative lead of the voltmeter to the negative post of the battery.
4. Disconnect the green colored regulator field wire from the alternator. Connect a jumper lead from the alternator field terminal to ground.
5. Connect a tachometer to the engine and reconnect the battery ground cable.
6. Connect a variable carbon pile rheostat to the battery cables. Be sure the carbon pile is in the **OPEN** or **OFF** position before connecting the leads to the battery terminals.
7. Start the engine and operate at an idle.
8. Adjust the engine speed and carbon pile to maintain a flow of 20 amperes in the circuit. Observe the voltmeter reading which should not exceed 0.7 volts.
9. If a higher voltage reading is indicated inspect, clean and tighten all connections in the charging system.
10. If necessary a voltage drop test can be done at each connection until the excessive resistance is located.
11. If the charging system resistance is within specifications reduce the engine speed, turn **OFF** the carbon pile rheostat and stop the engine. Remove battery ground cable.
12. Remove the test instruments from the electrical system and reconnect the charging system wiring. Reconnect the battery ground cable.

Current Output Check

This test determines if the alternator is capable of delivering its rated current output.

1. Disconnect the battery ground cable and the BAT lead wire at the alternator output terminal.

2. Connect an ammeter in series between the alternator output terminal and the disconnected BAT lead wire. The ammeter must have a scale of 100 amps.

3. Connect the positive lead of a voltmeter to the output terminal of the alternator and the negative lead to a good ground.

4. Disconnect the green colored wire at the voltage regulator and connect a jumper wire from the alternator field terminal to ground.

5. Connect a tachometer to the engine and reconnect the battery ground wire.

6. Connect a variable carbon pile rheostat between the positive and negative battery cables. Be sure the rheostat control is in the **OPEN** or **OFF** position before connecting the leads to the battery cables.

7. Start the engine and operate at idle. Adjust the carbon pile rheostat control and the engine speed in increments until the voltmeter reading is 15 volts (13 volts for the 114 amp alternators) and the engine speed is 1250 rpm (900 rpm for the 114 amp alternators). Do not allow the voltage to rise above 16 volts.

8. The ammeter readings must be within the following specifications.

NOTE: If measured at the battery, current output will be approximately 5 amperes lower than specified.

9. If the readings are less than specified, the alternator should be removed and checked during a bench test.

10. After the current output test is completed, reduce the engine speed, turn the carbon pile rheostat **OFF** and then stop the engine.

11. Disconnect the battery ground cable, remove the ammeter, voltmeter and carbon pile. Remove the jumper wire from the field terminal and reconnect the green colored wire to the alternator field terminal.

12. Reconnect the battery cable, if no further testing is to be done to the charging circuit.

Rotor Field Coil Draw Check

1. If on the vehicles remove the drive belt and wiring connections from the alternator.

2. Connect a jumper wire from the negative terminal of the battery to 1 of the field terminals of the alternator.

3. Connect the test ammeter positive lead to the other field terminal of the alternator and the negative ammeter lead to the positive battery terminal.

4. Connect a jumper wire between the alternator end shield and the battery negative terminal.

5. Slowly rotate the alternator pulley by hand and observe the ammeter reading.

6. The field coil draw should be 4.5–6.5 amperes at 12 volts. (4.75–6.0 amperes at 12 volts 114 amp alternators).

7. A low rotor coil draw is an indication of high resistance in the field coil circuit (brushes, slip-rings or rotor coil). A higher rotor coil draw indicates possible shorted rotor coil or grounded rotor. No reading indicates an open rotor or defective brushes.

8. Remove the test equipment and jumper leads.

Electronic Voltage Regulator Check

1. Make sure battery terminals are clean and battery is charged.

2. Connect the positive lead of a test voltmeter to ignition terminal No. 1 of the ballast resistor.

3. Connect the negative voltmeter lead to a good body ground.

4. Start engine and allow it to idle at 1250 rpm, all lights and accessories turned **OFF**. Voltage should be as indicated.

5. If the voltage is below specification check the following. Voltage regulator ground check, voltage drop between regulator cover and ground. Harness wiring, disconnect regulator plug

Current Rating	Identification	Current Output
60 amp	Blue, natural or yellow	47 amps min.
78 amp	Brown tag	58 amps min.
114 amp	Yellow	97 amps min.

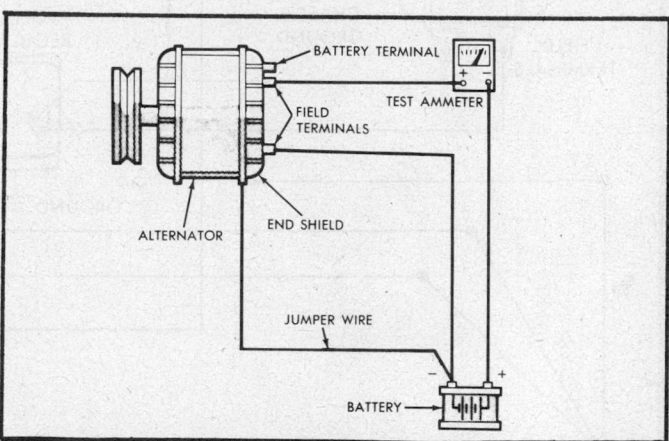

Chrysler alternator w/external regulator-rotor field coil current draw test. Connect ammeter as shown, rotate alternator pulley slowly by hand and observe the field coil draw reading

(ignition switch **OFF**), then turn **ON** ignition switch and check for battery voltage at the terminals having the red and green leads. Wiring harness must be disconnected from the regulator when checking individual leads. If no voltage is present in either lead the problem is in the wiring or alternator field.

6. If Step 5 tests showed no malfunctions, install a new regulator and repeat Step 4.

7. If voltage is above specifications (Step 4), or fluctuates, check the following. Ground between regulator and body, between body and engine. Ignition switch circuit between switch and regulator.

8. If voltage is still more than ½ volt above specifications install a new regulator and repeat Step 4.

OVERHAUL

Alternator disassembly, repair and assembly procedures are basically the same for all Chrysler alternators. Certain variations in design, or production modifications, could require slightly different procedures that should be obvious upon inspection of the unit being serviced.

Disassembly

To prevent damage to the brush assemblies (114 amp), they should be removed before proceeding with the disassembly of the alternator. The brushes are mounted in a plastic holder that positions the brushes vertically against the slip-rings.

1. Remove the retaining screw, flat washer, nylon washer and field terminal and carefully lift the plastic holder containing the spring and brush assembly from the end housing.

2. The ground brush (60 amp) is positioned horizontally against the slip-ring and is retained in the holder that is integral with the end housing. Remove the retaining screw and lift the clip, spring and brush assembly from the end housing. The stator is laminated so don't burr the stator or end housings.

3. Remove the through bolts and pry between the stator and

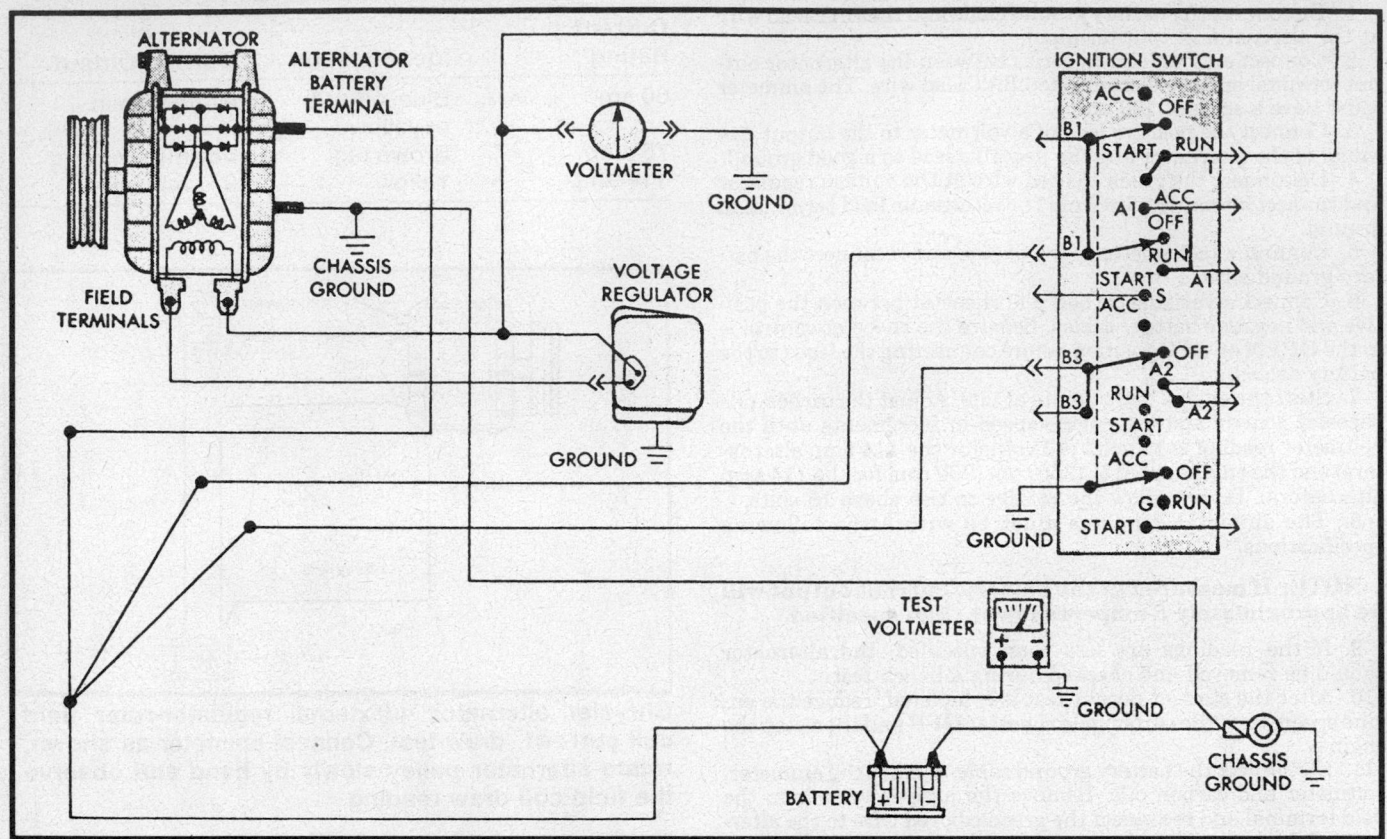

Chrysler 60, 78 and 114 amp alternators with external voltage regulator—voltage regulator test—idle engine at 1250 rpm with all lights and accessories off, voltmeter readings should equal shown in table

drive end housing with a suitable tool. Carefully separate the drive end housing, pulley and rotor assembly from the stator and rectifier housing assembly.

4. The pulley is an interference fit on the rotor shaft. Remove with a puller and special adapters.

5. Remove the nuts and washers and, while supporting the end frame, tap the rotor shaft with a plastic hammer and separate the rotor and end housing.

6. The drive end ball bearing is an interference fit with the rotor shaft. Remove the bearing with puller and adapters.

NOTE: Further dismantling of the rotor is not advisable, as the remainder of the rotor assembly is not serviced separately.

7. Remove the DC output terminal nuts and washers and remove terminal screw and inside capacitor (on units so equipped).

8. Remove the insulator.

NOTE: Positive rectifiers are pressed into the heat sink and negative rectifiers in the end housing. When removing the rectifiers it is necessary to support the end housing and the heat sink in order to prevent damage to the castings. Another caution is in order relative to the diode rectifiers. Don't subject them to unnecessary jolting. Heavy vibration or shock may ruin them. Cut rectifier wire at point of crimp. Support rectifier housing. The factory tool is cut away and slotted to fit over the wires and around the bosses in the housing. Be sure that the bore of the tool completely surrounds the rectifier, then press the rectifier out of the housing. The roller bearing in the rectifier end frame is a press fit. To protect the end housing, it is necessary to support the housing with a tool when pressing out the bearing.

Inspection

RECTIFIERS OPEN IN ALL 3 PHASES

Testing with Ohmmeter

Disassemble the alternator and separate the wires at the Y-connection of the stator.

There are 6 diode rectifiers mounted in the back of the alternator (60 amp). Three of them are marked with a plus (+) and 3 are marked with a minus (−). These marks indicate diode case polarity. The 114 amp alternator has 12 silicon diodes; 6 positive and 6 negative.

To test, set ohmmeter to its lowest range. If case is marked positive (+), place positive meter probe to case and negative probe to the diode lead. Meter should read between 4–10 ohms. Now, reverse leads of ohmmeter, connecting negative meter probe to positive case and positive meter probe to wire of rectifier. Set meter on a high range. Meter needle should move very little, if any (infinite reading). Do this to all positive diode rectifiers.

The diode rectifiers with minus (−) marks on their cases are checked the same way as above. Only now the negative ohmmeter probe is connected to the case for a reading of 4–10 ohms. Reverse leads as above for the other part to test. If a reading of 4–10 ohms is obtained in 1 direction and no reading (infinity) is read on the ohmmeter in the other direction, diode rectifiers are good. If either infinity or a low resistance is obtained in both directions on a rectifier it must be replaced. If meter reads more than 10 ohms when ohmmeter positive probe is connected to positive on diode and negative probe to negative diode, replace diode rectifier.

NOTE: With this test it is necessary to determine the

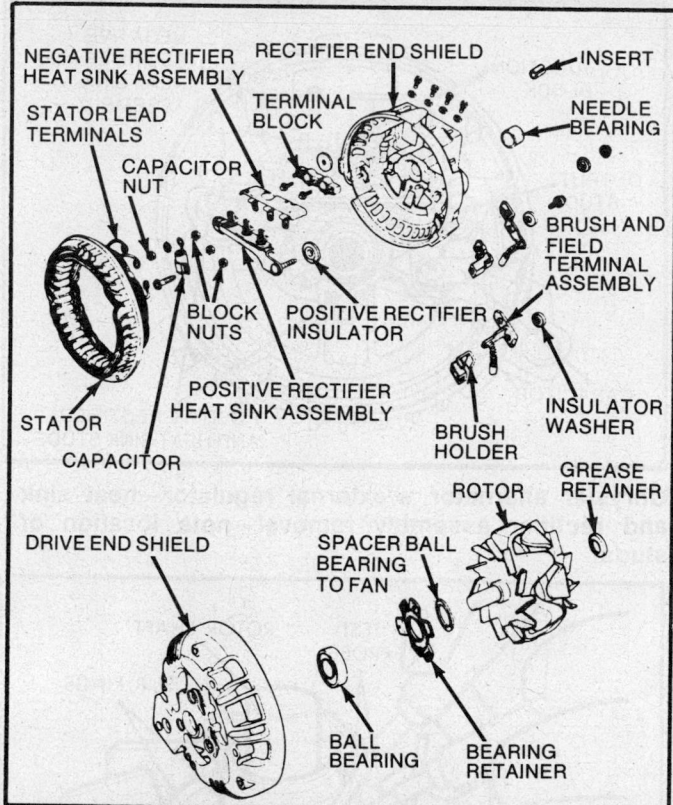

Typical Chrysler alternator—showing assembly sequence of components

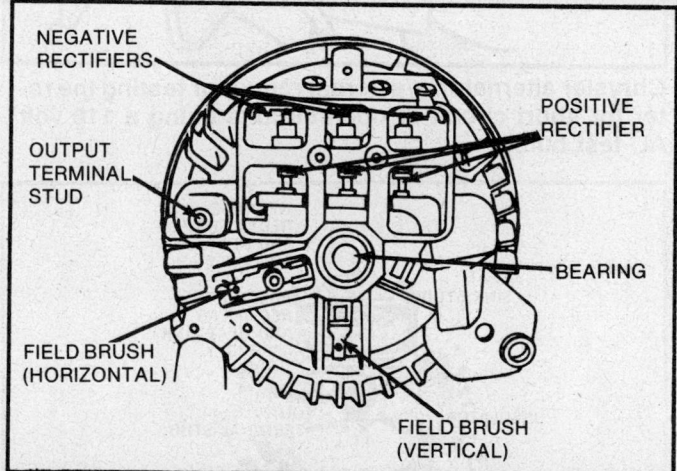

Chrysler alternator rear housing showing locations of rectifiers and field bushings

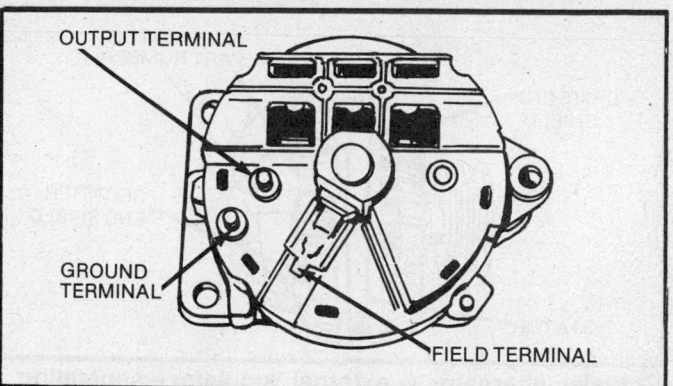

View of the rear housing terminal loaction—Chrysler alternator 114 amp

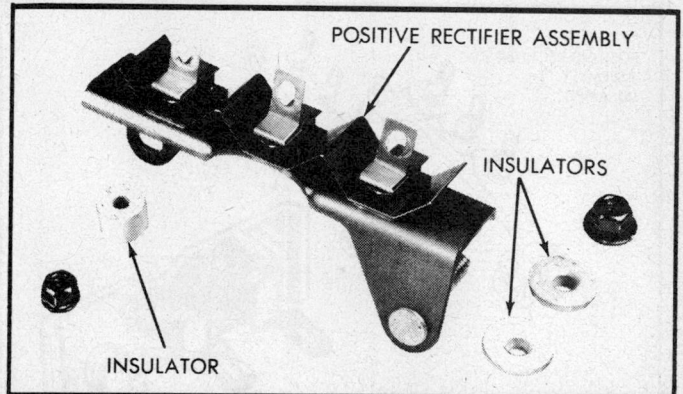

Positive rectifier assembly—114 amp alternator—note position of insulators. Positive rectifier is pressed into the heat sink

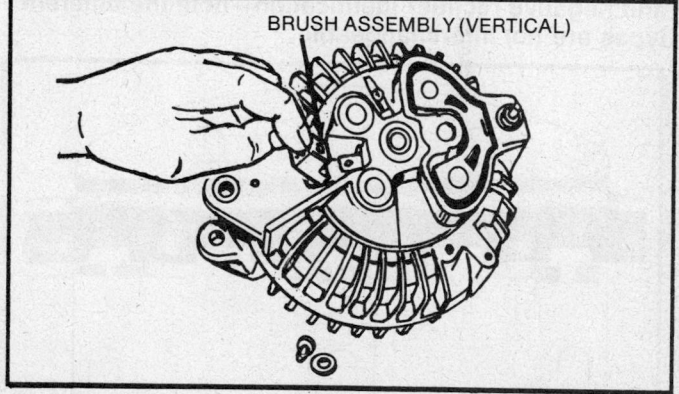

Chrysler alternator w/external regulator removing alternator field brush (vertical)

polarity of the ohmmeter probes. This can be done by connecting the ohmmeter to a DC voltmeter. The voltmeter will read up scale when the positive probe of the ohmmeter is connected to the positive side of the voltmeter and the negative probe of the ohmmeter is connected to the negative side of the voltmeter.

Alternate Method with Test Lamp

Be sure that the lead from the center of the diode rectifiers is disconnected. To test rectifiers with positive cases, touch the positive probe of tester to case and the negative probe to lead wire of rectifier. Bulb should light if rectifier is good. If bulb does not light, replace rectifier. Now reverse tester probe connections to rectifier. Bulb should not light. If bulb does light, replace rectifier. For testing minus (−) marked cases follow the above procedure except that now bulb should light with negative probe of tester touching rectifier case and positive probe touching lead wire. Rectifier is good if the bulb lights when tester probes are connected one way and does not light when tester connections are reversed. Rectifier must be replaced if the bulb does not light either way. Also, replace rectifier if bulb lights both ways.

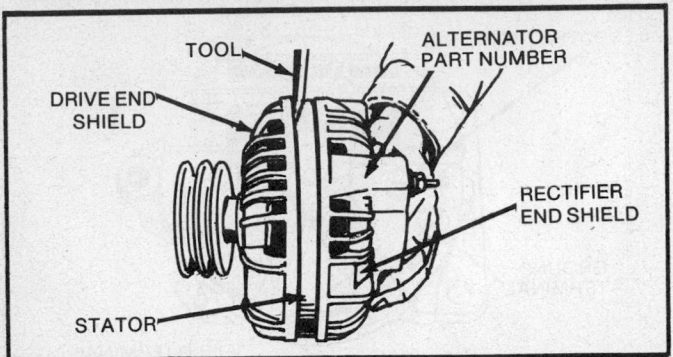

Chrysler alternator w/external regulator—separating alternator drive end shield from stator, using a pry tool

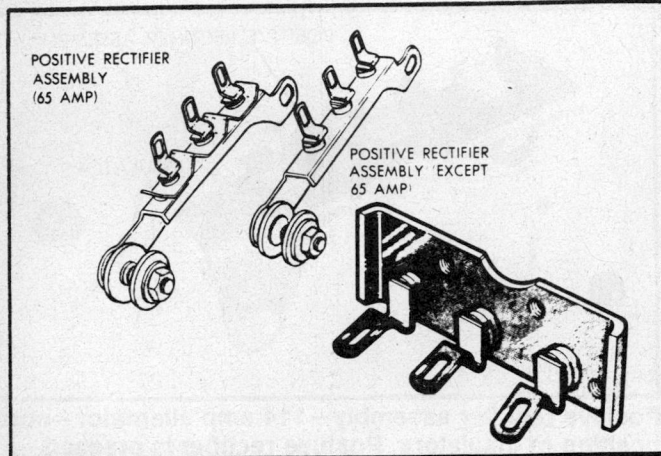

Chrysler altermator w/external regulator—positive and negative rectifier idetification—note the different types are not interchangeable

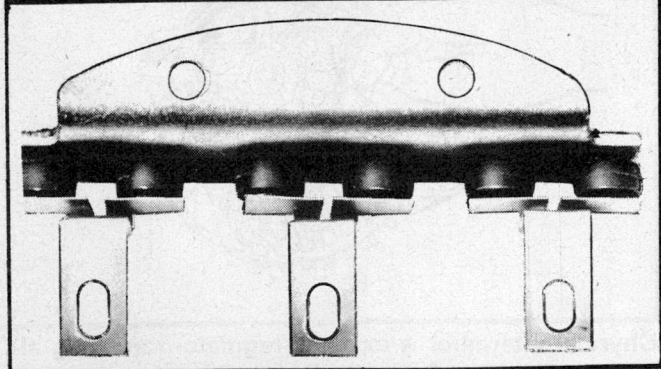

Negative rectifier assembly—114 amp alternator. Negative rectifier is pressed into the end housing

NOTE: The usual cause of an open diode or rectifier is a defective capacitor or a battery that has been installed in reverse polarity. If the battery is installed properly and the diodes are open, test the capacitor.

FIELD COIL DRAW TEST

1. Connect a jumper between one FLD terminal and the positive terminal of a fully charged 12 volt battery.
2. Connect the positive lead of a test ammeter to the other

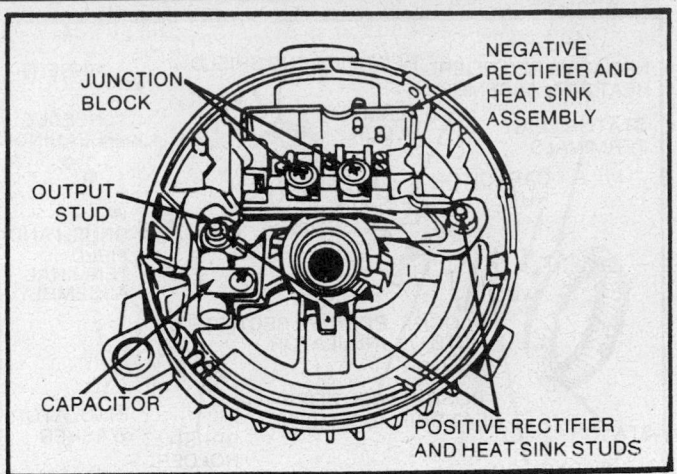

Chrysler alternator w/external regulator—heat sink and rectifier assembly removal—note location of studs

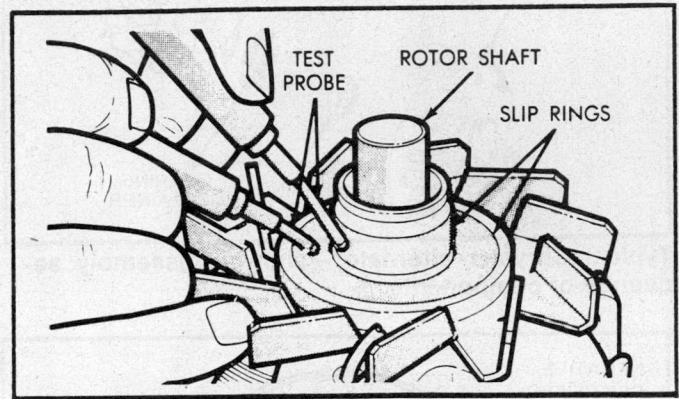

Chrysler alternator w/external regulator testing the rotor for short circuit or open circuits using a 110 volt AC test bulb

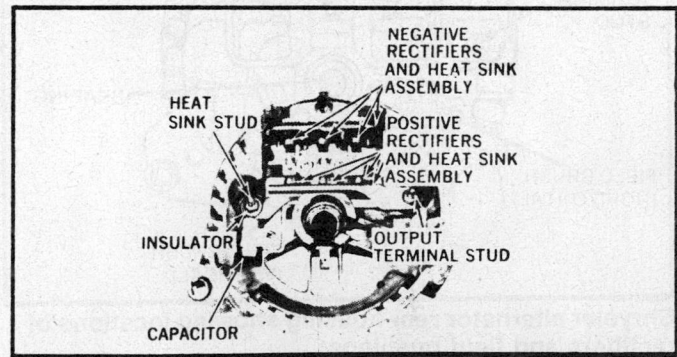

Chrysler alternator w/external regulator—location of negative and positive rectifiers check part number of rectifier to be sure correct rectifier is being used

field (Fld) terminal and the negative test lead to the negative battery terminal.

3. Slowly rotate the rotor by hand and observe the ammeter. The proper field coil draw is 2.3–2.7 amps at 12 volts.

NOTE: Field coil draw for the 114 ampere alternators should be 4.75–6.0 amperes at 12 volts.

TROUBLESHOOTING
CHRYSLER ISOLATED FIELD ALTERNATOR
(WITH EXTERNAL ELECTRONIC REGULATOR)

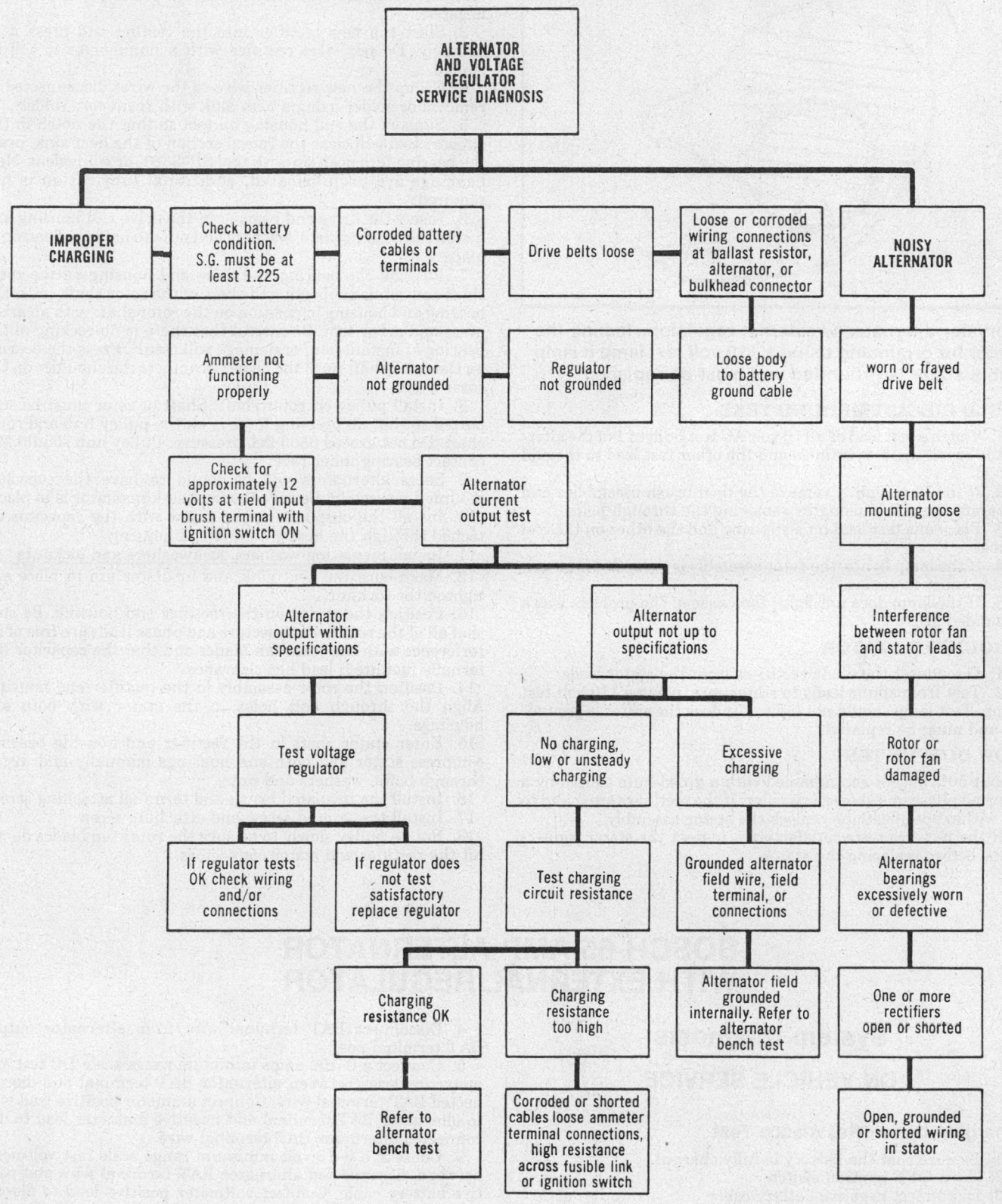

ALTERNATOR AND VOLTAGE REGULATOR SERVICE DIAGNOSIS

IMPROPER CHARGING — Check battery condition. S.G. must be at least 1.225 — Corroded battery cables or terminals — Drive belts loose — Loose or corroded wiring connections at ballast resistor, alternator, or bulkhead connector — NOISY ALTERNATOR

Ammeter not functioning properly — Alternator not grounded — Regulator not grounded — Loose body to battery ground cable — worn or frayed drive belt

Check for approximately 12 volts at field input brush terminal with ignition switch ON — Alternator current output test — Alternator mounting loose

Alternator output within specifications — Alternator output not up to specifications — Interference between rotor fan and stator leads

Test voltage regulator — No charging, low or unsteady charging — Excessive charging — Rotor or rotor fan damaged

If regulator tests OK check wiring and/or connections — If regulator does not test satisfactory replace regulator — Test charging circuit resistance — Grounded alternator field wire, field terminal, or connections — Alternator bearings excessively worn or defective

Charging resistance OK — Charging resistance too high — Alternator field grounded internally. Refer to alternator bench test — One or more rectifiers open or shorted

Refer to alternator bench test — Corroded or shorted cables loose ammeter terminal connections, high resistance across fusible link or ignition switch — Open, grounded or shorted wiring in stator

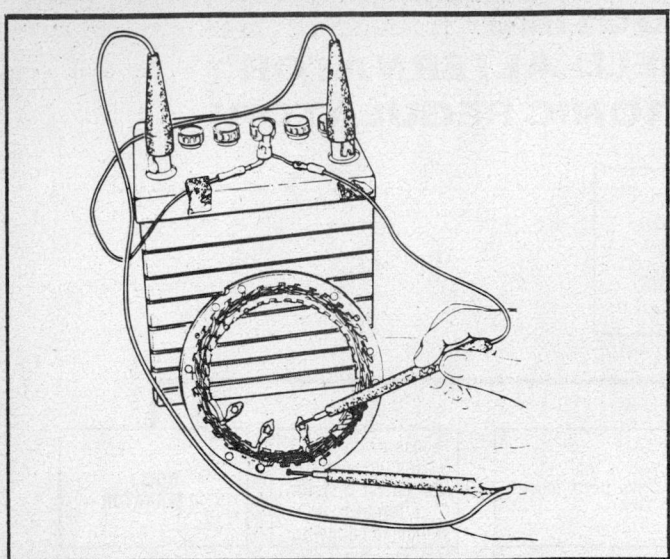

Chrysler alternator w/external regulator—testing the stator for grounding using a 110 volt test lamp if lamp lights stator is grounded and must be replaced

FIELD CIRCUIT GROUND TEST

1. Touch a test lead of a 110 volt AC test bulb to 1 of the alternator brush (field) terminals and the other test lead to the end shield.
2. If the lamp lights, remove the field brush assemblies and separate the end housing by removing the through bolts.
3. Place one test lead on a slip-ring and the other on the end shield.
4. If the lamp lights, the rotor assembly is grounded internally and must be replaced.
5. If the lamp does not light, the cause of the problem was a grounded brush.

GROUNDED STATOR

1. Disconnect the diode rectifiers from the stator leads.
2. Test from stator leads to stator core, using a 110 volt test lamp. Test lamp should not light. If it does, the stator is grounded and must be replaced.

LOW OUTPUT TEST

About 50% output accompanied with a growl-hum caused by a shorted phase or a shorted rectifier. If the rectifiers are found to be within specifications replace the stator assembly.

If the rectifier tests satisfactorily, inspect the stator connections before replacing the stator.

Assembly

1. Support the heat sink or rectifier end housing on circular plate.
2. Check rectifier identification to be sure the correct rectifier is being used. The part numbers are stamped on the case of the rectifier. They are also marked red for positive and black for negative.
3. Start the new rectifier into the casting and press it in squarely. Do not start rectifier with a hammer or it will be ruined.
4. Crimp the new rectifier wire to the wires disconnected at removal or solder using a heat sink with rosin core solder.
5. Support the end housing on tool so that the notch in the support tool will clear the raised section of the heat sink, press the bearing into position with tool SP-3381, or equivalent. New bearings are prelubricated, additional lubrication is not required.
6. Insert the drive end bearing in the drive end housing and install the bearing plate, washers and nuts to hold the bearing in place.
7. Position the bearing and drive end housing on the rotor shaft and, while supporting the base of the rotor shaft, press the bearing and housing in position on the rotor shaft with an arbor press and arbor tool. Be careful that there is no cocking of the bearing at installation; or damage will result. Press the bearing on the rotor shaft until the bearing contacts the shoulder on the rotor shaft.
8. Install pulley on rotor shaft. Shaft of rotor must be supported so that all pressing force is on the pulley hub and rotor shaft. Do not exceed 6800 lbs. pressure. Pulley hub should just contact bearing inner race.
9. Some alternators will be found to have the capacitor mounted internally. Be sure the heat sink insulator is in place.
10. Install the output terminal screw with the capacitor attached through the heat sink and end housing.
11. Install insulating washers, lockwashers and locknuts.
12. Make sure the heat sink and insulator are in place and tighten the locknut.
13. Position the stator on the rectifier end housing. Be sure that all of the rectifier connectors and phase leads are free of interference with the rotor fan blades and that the capacitor (internally mounted) lead has clearance.
14. Position the rotor assembly in the rectifier end housing. Align the through bolt holes in the stator with both end housings.
15. Enter stator shaft in the rectifier end housing bearing, compress stator and both end housings manually and install through bolts, washers and nuts.
16. Install the insulated brush and terminal attaching screw.
17. Install the ground screw and attaching screw.
18. Rotate pulley slowly to be sure the rotor fan blades do not hit the rectifier and stator connectors.

BOSCH 65 AMP ALTERNATOR WITH EXTERNAL REGULATOR

System Diagnosis

ON VEHICLE SERVICE

Charging Circuit Resistance Test

1. Be sure that the battery is fully charged.
2. Turn **OFF** ignition switch.
3. Disconnect negative battery cable.

4. Disconnect BAT terminal wire from alternator output BAT terminal post.
5. Connect a 0–100 amps minimum range scale DC test ammeter in series between alternator BAT terminal and disconnected BAT terminal wire. Connect ammeter positive lead wire to alternator BAT terminal and negative ammeter lead to disconnected alternator BAT terminal wire.
6. Connect a 0–18 volt minimum range scale test voltmeter between disconnected alternator BAT terminal wire and positive battery cable. Connect voltmeter positive lead to discon-

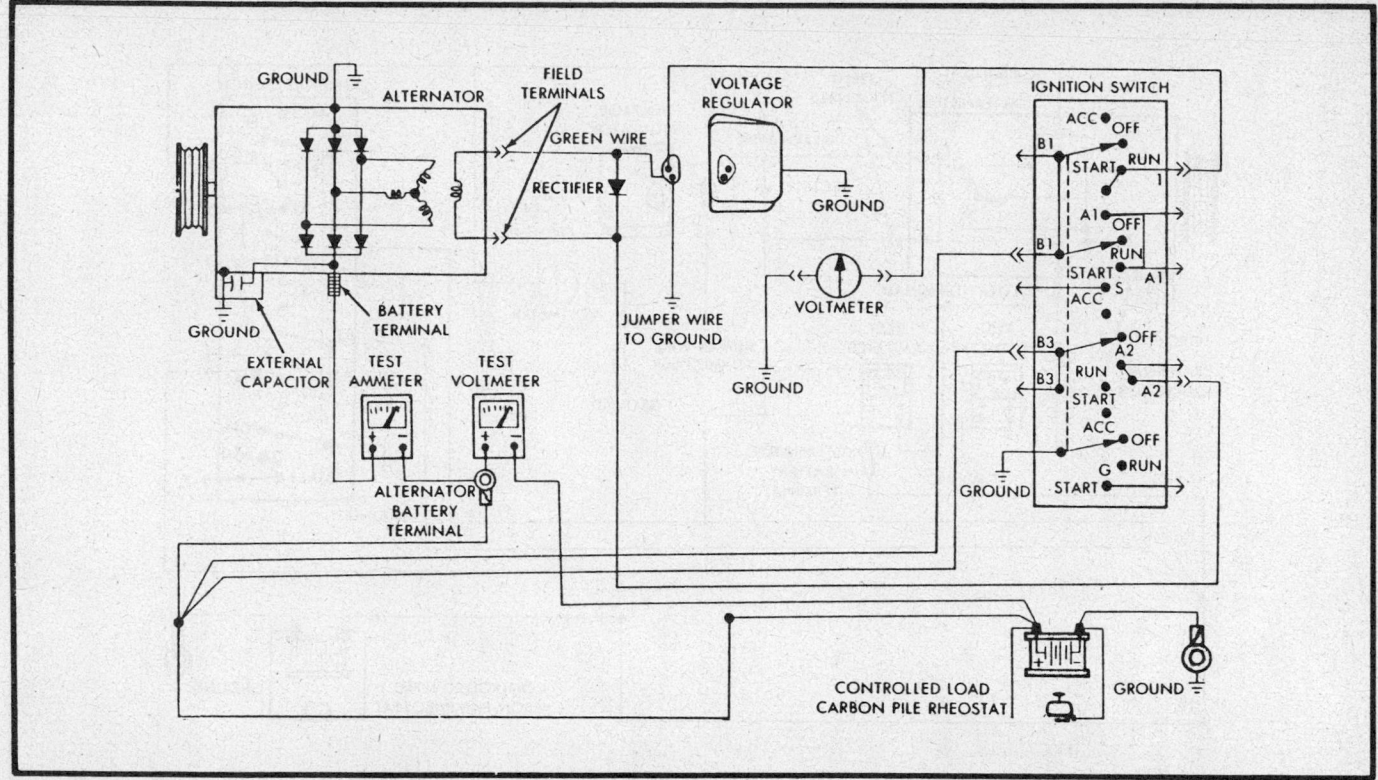

Bosch alternator with external regulator—charging circuit resistance test—adjust engine speed and carbon test—adjust engine speed and carbon pile to maintain 20 amps., voltmeter should not exceed 0.5 volts

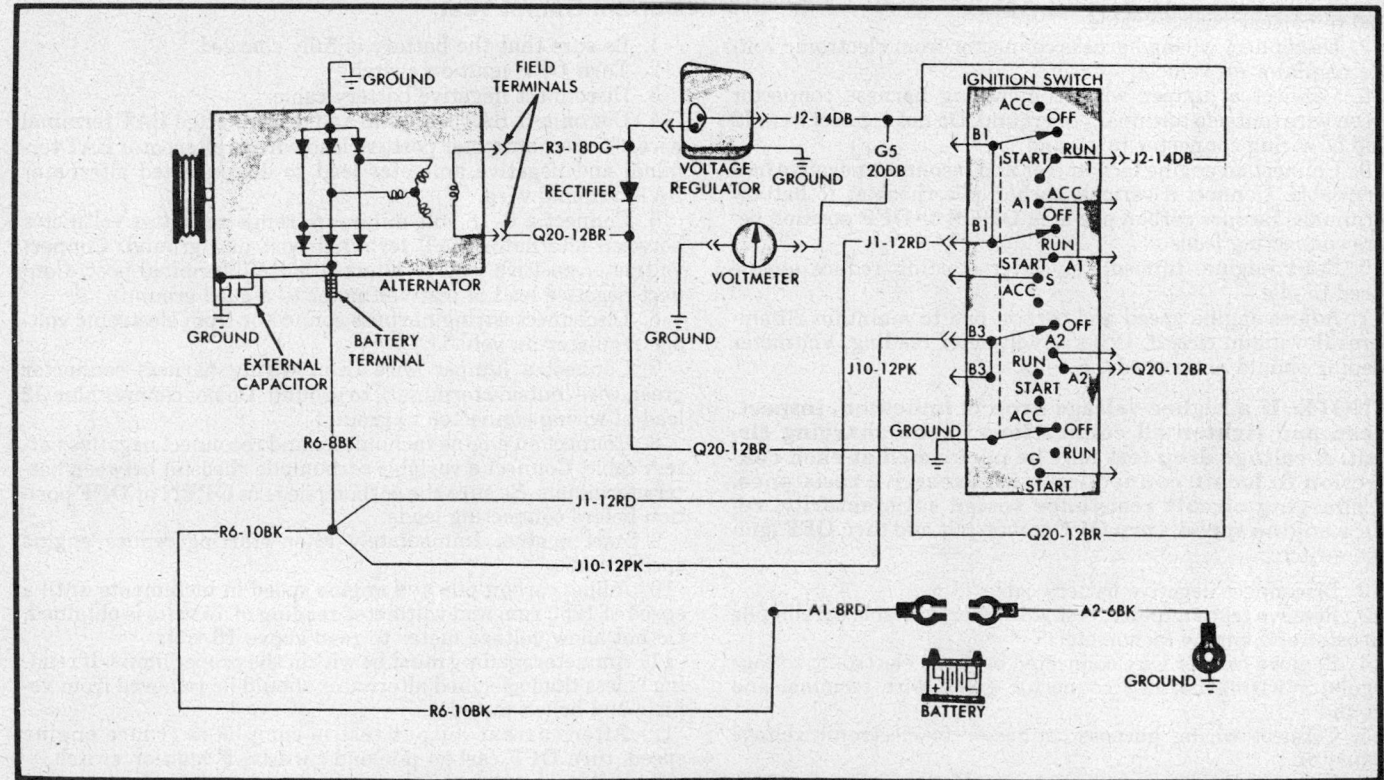

Bosch alternator with external regulator—charging system schematic showing ignition switch wiring details

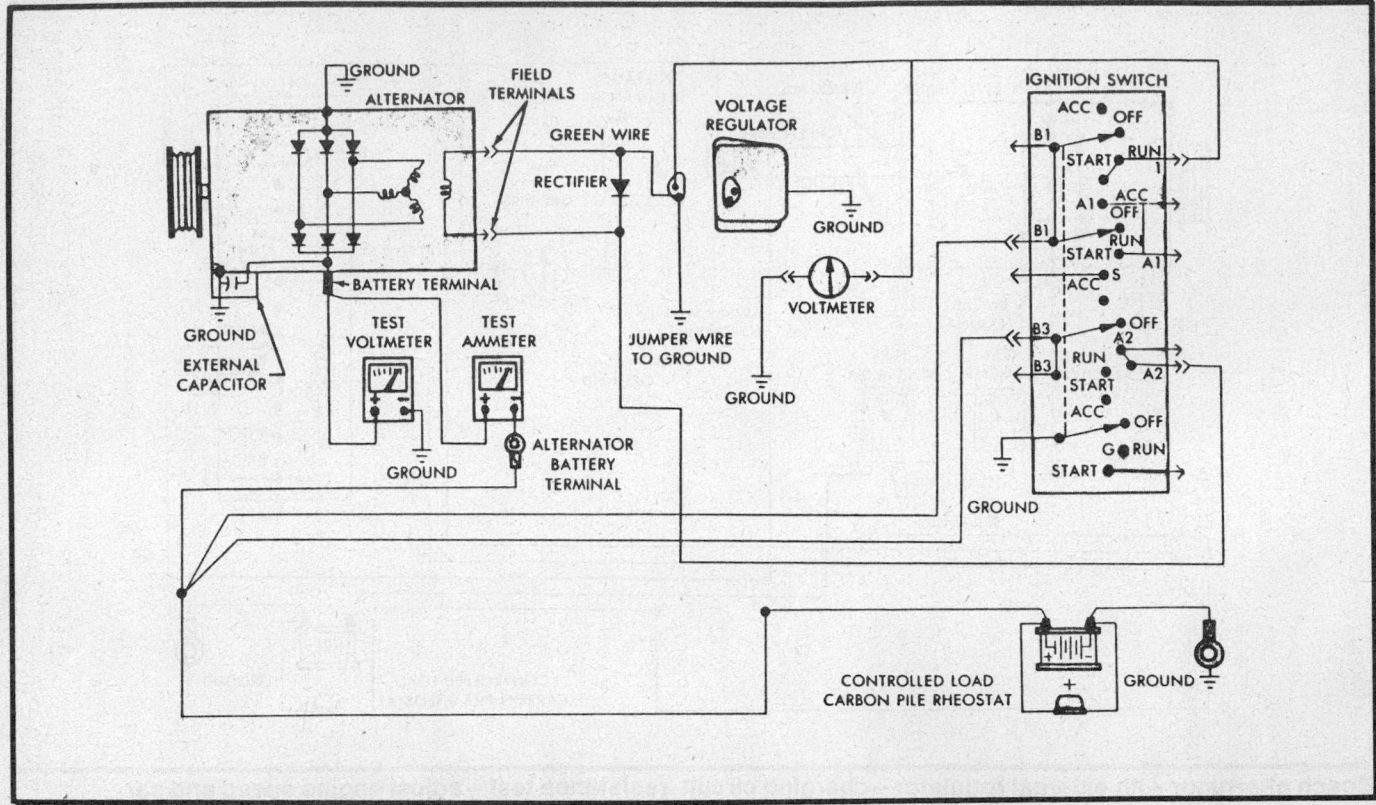

Bosch alternator with external regulator—current output test—if ammeter reading is less than specified, alternator should be removed and bench tested

nected alternator BAT terminal wire and negative voltmeter lead to battery positive cable.

7. Disconnect wiring harness connector from electronic voltage regulator on vehicle.

8. Connect a jumper wire from wiring harness connector green wire (outside terminal), to ground. Do not connect blue J2 lead of wiring connector to ground.

9. Connect an engine tachometer and reconnect negative battery cable. Connect a variable carbon pile rheostat to battery terminals. Be sure carbon pile is in **OPEN** or **OFF** position before connecting leads.

10. Start engine. Immediately after starting reduce engine speed to idle.

11. Adjust engine speed and carbon pile to maintain 20 amperes flowing in circuit. Observe voltmeter reading. Voltmeter reading should not exceed 0.5 volts.

NOTE: If a higher voltage drop is indicated, inspect, clean and tighten all connections in the charging circuit. A voltage drop test may be performed at each connection to locate connection with excessive resistance. If charging circuit resistance tested satisfactorily, reduce engine speed, turn OFF carbon pile and turn OFF ignition switch.

12. Disconnect negative battery cable.

13. Remove test ammeter, test voltmeter, variable carbon pile rheostat and engine tachometer.

14. Remove jumper wire connected between electronic voltage regulator wiring harness connector green wire terminal and ground.

15. Connect wiring harness connector to electronic voltage regulator.

16. Connect BAT terminal wire to alternator output BAT terminal.

17. Connect negative battery cable.

Current Output Test

1. Be sure that the battery is fully charged.
2. Turn **OFF** ignition switch.
3. Disconnect negative battery cable.
4. Disconnect BAT terminal and disconnected BAT terminal wire. Connect ammeter positive lead wire to alternator BAT terminal and negative ammeter lead to disconnected alternator BAT terminal wire.
5. Connect a 0–18 volt minimum range scale test voltmeter between alternator BAT terminal post and ground. Connect voltmeter positive lead to alternator BAT terminal post. Connect negative lead of test voltmeter to a good ground.
6. Disconnect wiring harness connector from electronic voltage regulator on vehicle.
7. Connect a jumper wire from wiring harness connector green wire (outside terminal), to ground. Do not connect blue J2 lead of wiring connector to ground.
8. Connect an engine tachometer and reconnect negative battery cable. Connect a variable carbon pile rheostat between battery terminals. Be sure the carbon pile is in **OPEN** or **OFF** position before connecting leads.
9 Start engine. Immediately after starting reduce engine speed to idle.
10. Adjust carbon pile and engine speed in increments until a speed of 1250 rpm and voltmeter reading of 15 volts is obtained. Do not allow voltage meter to read above 16 volts.
11. Ammeter reading must be within the proper limits. If reading is less than specified alternator should be removed from vehicle and bench tested.
12. After current output test is completed reduce engine speed, turn **OFF** carbon pile and turn **OFF** ignition switch.
13. Disconnect negative battery cable.
14. Remove test ammeter, test voltmeter, tachometer and variable carbon pile rheostat.

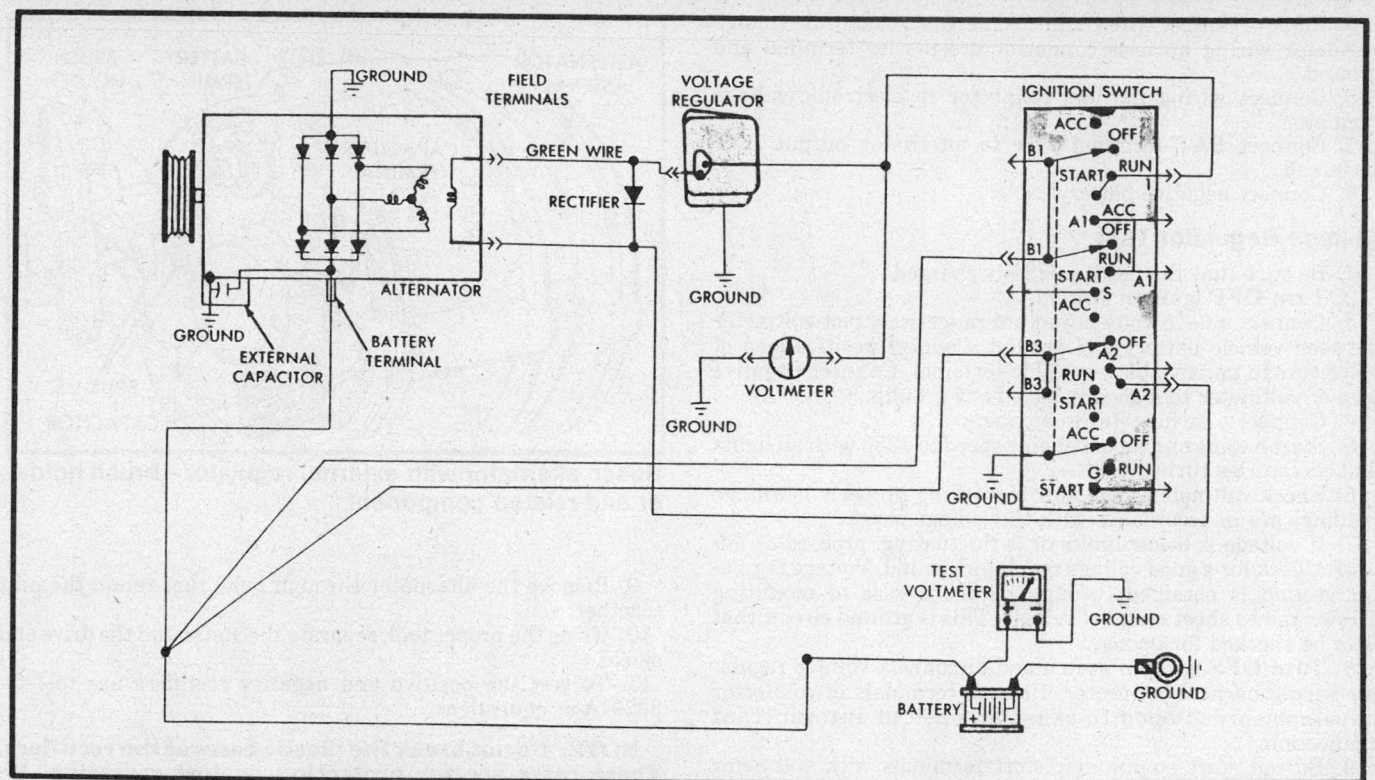

Bosch alternator with external regulator—voltage regulator test. Check voltmeter, regulator is working properly if voltage readings are in accordance with the voltage chart

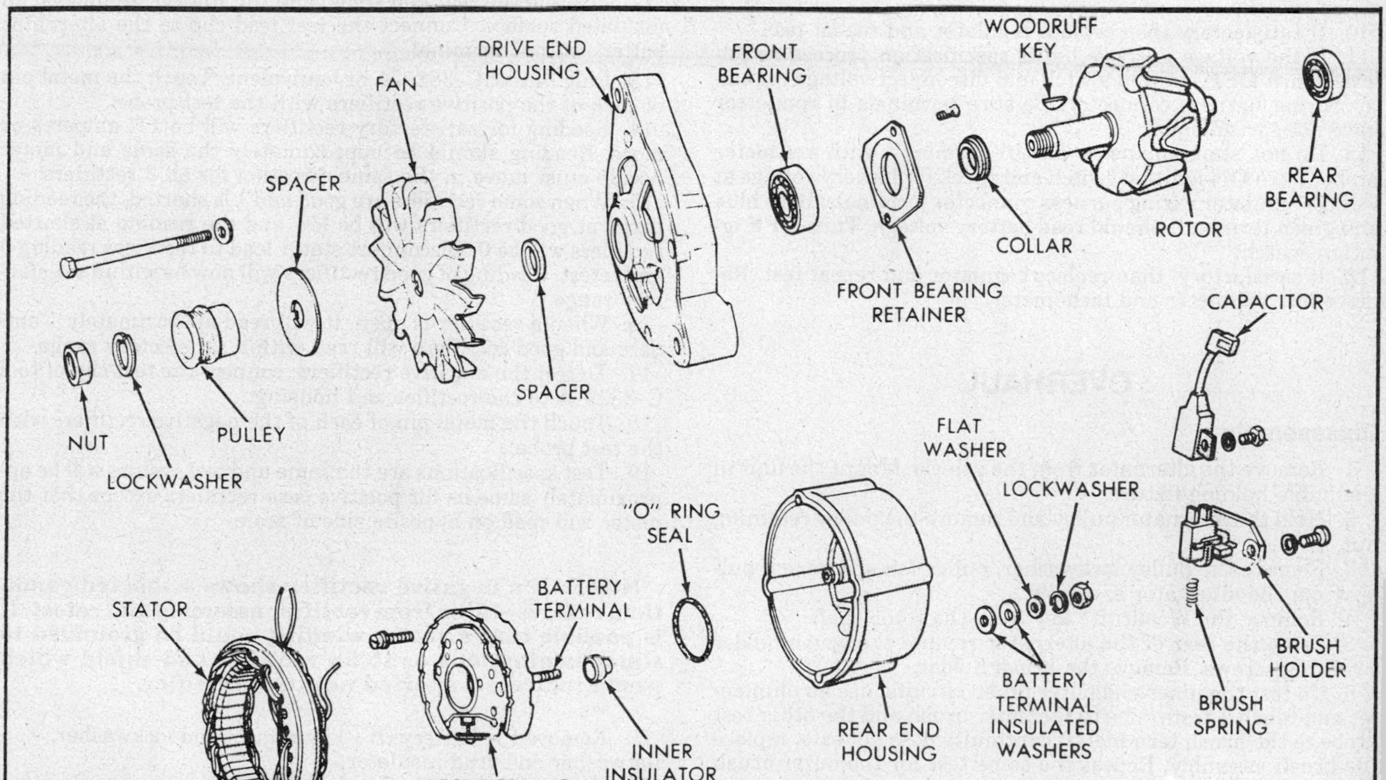

Bosch alternator with external regulator—exploded view showing assembly sequence

15. Remove jumper wire connected between electronic voltage regulator wiring harness connector green wire terminal and ground.

16. Connect wiring harness connector to electronic voltage regulator.

17. Connect BAT terminal wire to alternator output BAT terminal.

18. Connect negative battery cable.

Voltage Regulator Test

1. Be sure that the battery is fully charged.
2. Turn **OFF** ignition switch.
3. Connect a 0–18 volts minimum range scale test voltmeter between vehicle battery and ground. Connect positive lead of voltmeter to positive battery cable terminal. Connect negative lead of voltmeter to a good vehicle body ground.
4. Connect a tachometer to engine.
5. Start engine and adjust engine speed to 1250 with all lights and accessories turned **OFF**.
6. Check voltmeter, regulator is working properly if voltage readings are in accordance with the voltage chart.
7. If voltage is below limits or is fluctuating, proceed as follows. Check for a good voltage regulator ground. Voltage regulator ground is obtained through regulator case to mounting screws and to sheet metal of vehicle. This is ground circuit that is to be checked for opens.
8. Turn **OFF** ignition switch and disconnect voltage regulator wiring harness connector. Be sure terminals of connector have not spread open to cause an open or intermittant connection.
9. Do not start engine or distort terminals with voltmeter probe: turn **ON** ignition switch and check for battery voltage at voltage regulator wiring harness connector terminals. Both blue and green terminals should read battery voltage. Turn **OFF** ignition switch.
10. If satisfactory then replace regulator and repeat test.
11. If the voltage is above limits specification proceed as follows. Turn **OFF** ignition switch and disconnect voltage regulator wiring harness connector. Be sure terminals in connector have not spread open.
12. Do not start engine or distort terminals with voltmeter probe. Turn **ON** ignition switch and check for battery voltage at voltage regulator wiring harness connector terminals. Both blue and green terminals should read battery voltage. Turn **OFF** ignition switch.
13. If satisfactory, then replace regulator and repeat test. Remove test voltmeter and tachometer.

OVERHAUL

Disassembly

1. Remove the alternator from the vehicle. Mount the unit in a suitable holding fixture.
2. Hold the alternator pulley and remove the pulley retaining nut.
3. Remove the pulley lockwasher, pulley fan spacer and pulley from the alternator assembly.
4. Remove the Woodruff® key from the rotor shaft.
5. From the rear of the alternator remove the brush holder retaining screws. Remove the brush holder.
6. To test the inner and outer brush circuits, use an ohmmeter and touch 1 test probe to the inner brush and the other test probe to the brush terminal. If continuity does not exist replace the brush assembly. Repeat the same test for the outer brush circuit.
7. Disconnect the capacitor electrical connection and remove the capacitor retaining screw. Remove the capacitor from its mounting on the alternator.
8. Remove the ground stud nut and stud washer.

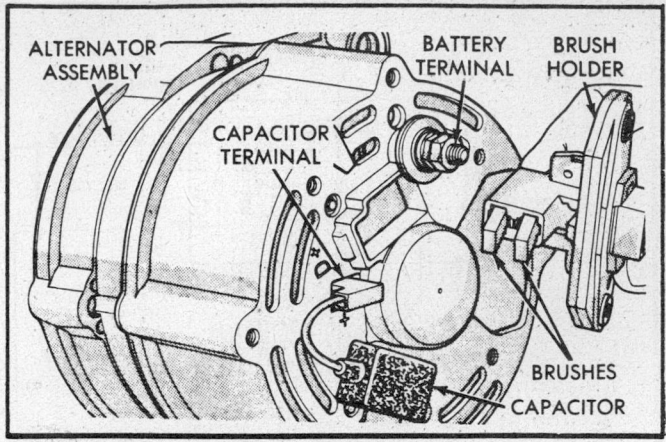

Bosch alternator with external regulator—brush holder and related component

9. Remove the alternator through bolts that retain the unit together.
10. Using the proper tool, separate the stator and the drive end shield.
11. To test the positive and negative rectifiers use tool C–3929–A or equivalent.

NOTE: Do not break the plastic cases of the rectifiers. These cases are for protection against corrosion. Be sure to always touch the test probe to the metal pin of the nearest rectifier.

12. Position the rear end shield and the stator assembly on an insulated surface. Connect the test lead clip to the alternator battery output terminal.
13. Plug in tool C–3829–A or equivalent. Touch the metal pin of each of the positive rectifiers with the test probe.
14. Reading for satisfactory rectifiers will be 1¾ amperes or more. Reading should be approximately the same and meter needle must move in the same direction for all 3 rectifiers.
15. When some rectifiers are good and 1 is shorted, the reading taken at good rectifiers will be low and the reading at shorted rectifiers will be 0. Disconnect stator lead to rectifiers reading 0 and retest. Reading of good rectifiers will now be within satisfactory range.
16. When a rectifier is open, it will read approximately 1 ampere and good rectifiers will read within satisfactory range.
17. To test the negative rectifiers, connect the test clip of tool C–3829–A to the rectifier end housing.
18. Touch the metal pin of each of the negative rectifiers with the test probe.
19. Test specifications are the same and test results will be approximately same as for positive case rectifiers except that the meter will read on opposite side of scale.

NOTE: If a negative rectifier shows a shorted condition, remove stator from rectifier assembly and retest. It is possible that a stator winding could be grounded to stator laminations or to an rectifier end shield which would indicate a shorted negative rectifier.

20. Remove the battery (B+) stud nut, stud lockwasher, flatwasher and stud insulator.
21. Remove the rectifier assembly retaining screws. Remove the stator assembly along with the rectifier unit. Unsolder the stator to rectifier leads.
22. Check for continuity between stator coil leads. Press test probe firmly to each of 3 phase (stator) lead terminals separate-

ly. If there is no continuity, stator coil is defective. Replace stator assembly.

23. To test stator for ground, check for continuity between stator coil leads and stator coil frame. If there is continuity stator is grounded. Replace stator assembly.

24. Remove the rear bearing oil and dust seal. Check the rotor bearing surface for wear and scoring. Replace as required.

25. Remove the inner battery (B+) stud insulator.

26. Press the rotor out of the drive end shield and remove the spacer.

27. Check outside circumference of slip-ring for dirtiness and roughness. Clean or polish with fine sandpaper, if required. A badly roughened slip-ring or a worn down slip-ring should be replaced.

28. Check for continuity between field coil and slip-rings. If there is no continuity, field coil is defective. Replace rotor assembly.

29. Check for continuity between slip-rings and shaft (or core). If there is continuity, it means that coil or slip-ring is grounded. Replace rotor assembly.

30. Using a puller remove the rotor bearing.

31. Remove the front bearing from the drive end shield by removing the front bearing retaining screws.

32. Press out the drive end shield bearing. Remove the front drive bearing from the front drive end shield.

Assembly

1. Be sure to check all parts for wear and replace the defective components as required.

2. Install the rear rotor bearing oil and dust seal.

3. Install the inner alternator battery terminal insulator.

4. Solder the stator leads to the rectifier assembly; be sure to use needle nose pliers as a heat sink.

5. Position the stator and rectifier assembly. Install the rectifier mounting screws, both terminal insulators, the insulator washer, the insulator lockwasher and the insulator nut.

6. Position and press the front bearing into the drive end shield. Install the bearing retainer.

7. Position the drive end shield and spacer over the rotor. Press the drive end shield onto the rotor.

8. Install the rectifier end shield over the drive end shield. Install the through bolts and tighten.

9. Install the capacitor and terminal plug onto the alternator assembly.

10. Push the brushes into the brush holder and install the brush holder onto the alternator assembly.

11. Install the Woodruff key into the shaft and the fan over the shaft.

12. Install the drive pulley-to-fan spacer, the pulley, the lockwasher and the nut over the shaft. Secure the pulley and tighten the nut.

BOSCH 35/75, 40/90, 90 RS AND 40/100 AMP ALTERNATORS

The alternators are alike, except, the 35/75 has 6 built-in silicon rectifiers, the 40/90 has 12 (1986–87) or 8 (1988–90) built-in silicon rectifiers and the 40/100 (1986) has 14 built-in silicon rectifiers.

The voltage regulator is built into the power and logic modules for 1986–88 or the Single Module Engine Controller (SMEC) for 1989–90.

System Diagnosis
ON VEHICLE SERVICE

Charging Circuit Resistance Test

1. Be sure that the battery is fully charged.

2. Disconnect negative battery cable.

3. Disconnect BAT lead at alternator output terminal.

4. Connect a 0–150 ampere scale DC ammeter in series between alternator output BAT terminal and disconnected BAT terminal wire. Connect positive lead to alternator output BAT terminal and negative lead to disconnected alternator BAT lead.

5. Connect positive lead of a test voltmeter (range 0–18 volts minimum) to alternator BAT terminal. Connect negative lead of test voltmeter to battery positive post.

6. Remove air hose between power module (1986–88) or single module engine controller (1989–90) and air cleaner.

7. Connect an end of a jumper wire to ground and with other end, probe the green R3 lead wire of black 8-way connector (1986–88) or back of the alternator (1989–90). Do not connect blue J2 lead of 8-way wiring connector (1986–88) or back of the atlernator (1989–90) to ground.

NOTE: On the 1986–88 vehicles, both R3 and J2 leads are green on alternator side of 8-way wiring connector. At dash end of 8-way connector, R3 is green and J2 is blue.

8. Connect an engine tachometer and reconnect negative battery cable.

9. Connect a variable carbon pile rheostat to the battery terminals. Be sure carbon pile is in **OPEN** or **OFF** position before connecting leads.

10. Start engine. Immediately after starting, reduce engine speed to idle.

11. Adjust engine speed and carbon pile to maintain 20 amperes flowing in circuit. Observe voltmeter reading. Voltmeter reading should not exceed 0.5 volts.

NOTE: If a higher voltage drop is indicated, inspect, clean and tighten all connections in charging circuit. A voltage drop test may be performed at each connection to locate connection with excessive resistance. If charging circuit resistance tested satisfactorily, reduce engine speed, turn OFF carbon pile and turn OFF ignition switch.

12. Disconnect negative battery cable.

13. Remove test ammeter, voltmeter, carbon pile and tachometer.

14. Remove jumper wire between 8-way black connector (1986–88) or the back of the alternator (1989–90) and ground.

15. Connect BAT lead to alternator output BAT terminal post.

16. Reconnect negative battery cable.

17. Reconnect hose between power module (1986–88) or single module engine controller (1989–90) and air cleaner.

Current Output Test

1. Be sure that the battery is fully charged.

2. Disconnect negative battery cable.

3. Disconnect the BAT lead wire at the alternator output terminal.

4. Connect a 0–150 ampere scale DC ammeter in series between alternator output BAT terminal and negative lead to disconnected BAT terminal.

5. Connect positive lead of a test voltmeter (range 0–18 volts minimum) to alternator output BAT terminal.

6. Connect negative lead of test voltmeter to a good ground.

7. Connect an engine tachometer and reconnect negative battery cable.

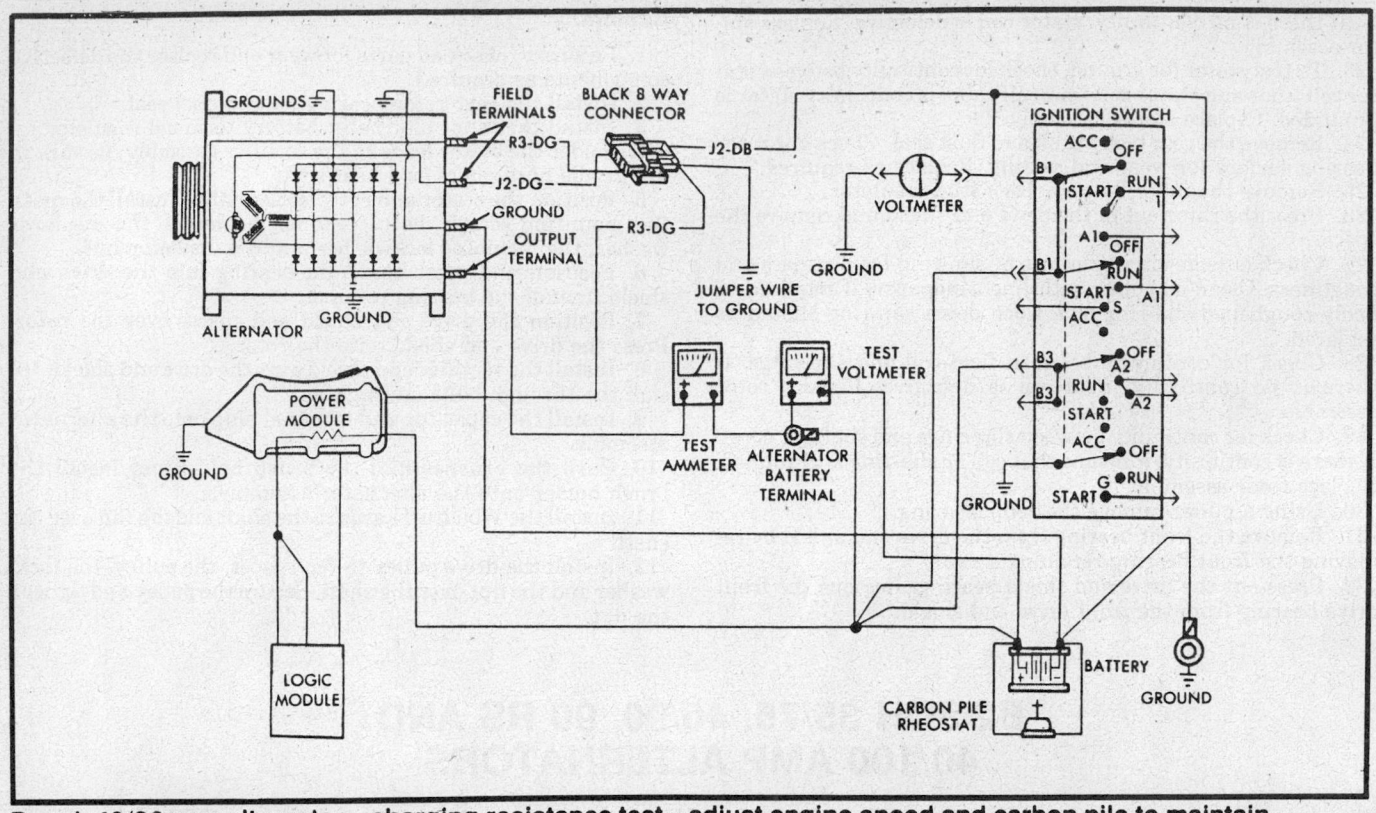

Bosch 40/90 amp alternator—charging resistance test—adjust engine speed and carbon pile to maintain 20 amps flowing in circuit. Voltmeter reading should not exceed 0.5 volts

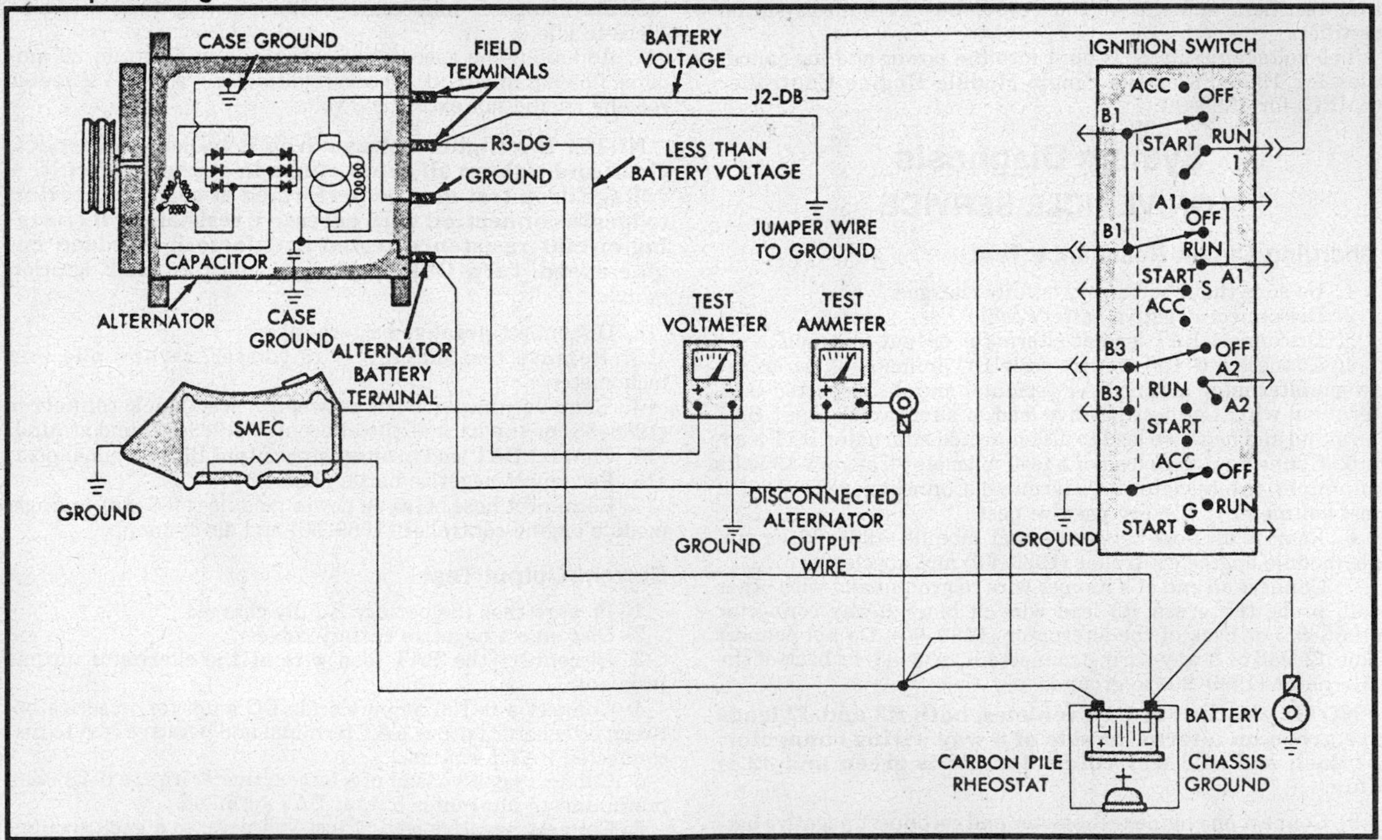

Bosch 90 RS amp alternator—charging system resistance test—adjust engine speed and carbon pile to maintain 20 amps, voltmeter reading should not exceed 0.5 volts

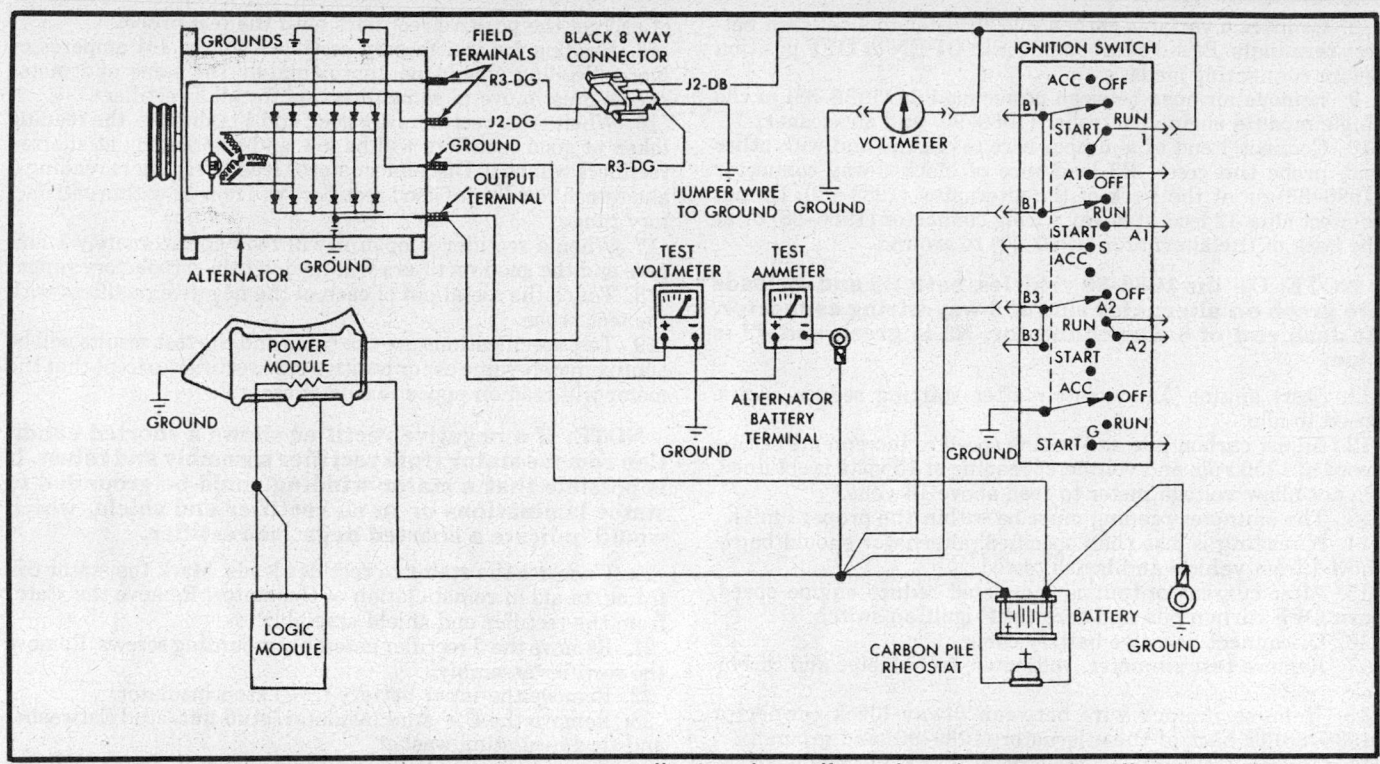

Bosch 40/90 amp. alternator—current output test—adjust carbon pile and engine speed until a speed of 1250 rpm and voltmeter reading of 15 volts is obtained. The ammeter reading must be within proper limits

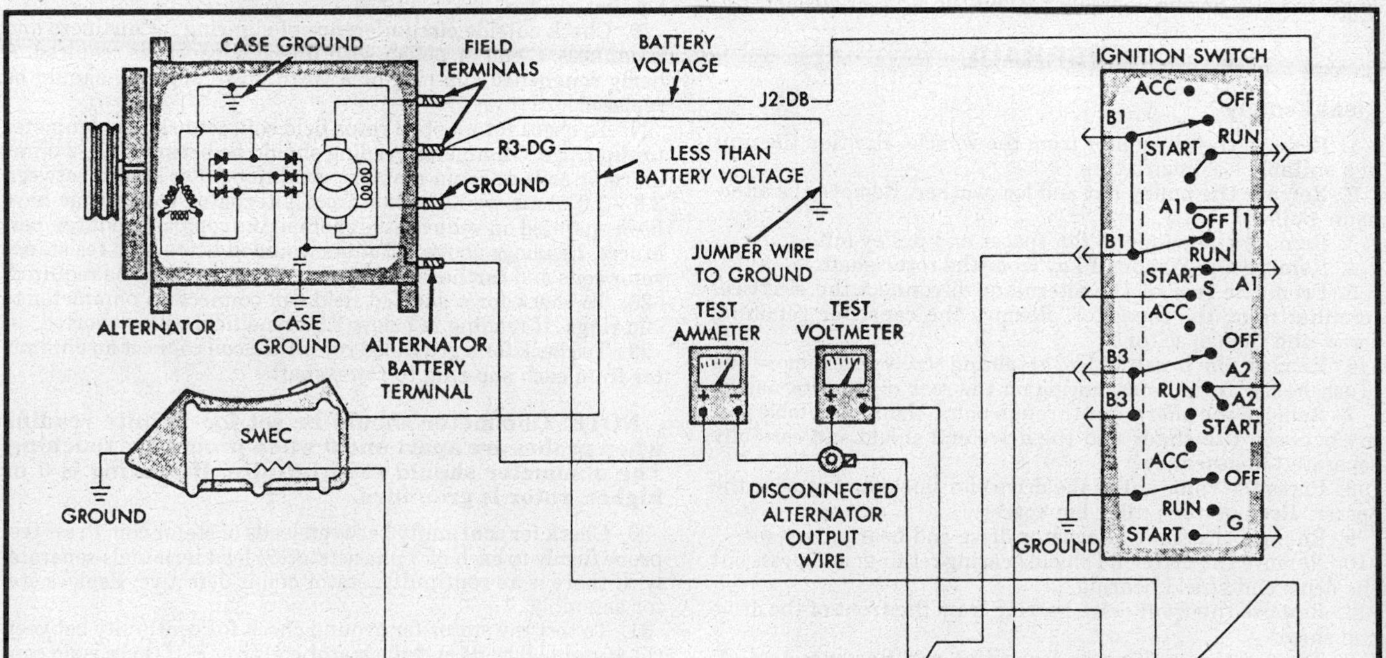

Bosch 90 RS amp alternator—current output test—adjust engine speed and carbon pile increments until an engine speed of 1250 rpm is reached, voltmeter reading should not exceed 15 volts

8. Connect a variable carbon pile rheostat tool between battery terminals. Be sure carbon pile is in **OPEN** or **OFF** position before connecting leads.

9. Remove air hose between power module (1986–88) or the single module engine controller (1989–90) and air cleaner.

10. Connect 1 end of a jumper wire to ground and with other end, probe the green R3 lead wire of black 8-way connector (1986–88) or at the back of the alternator (1989–90). Do not connect blue J2 lead of 8-way wiring connector (1986–88) or at the back of the alternator (1989–90) to ground.

NOTE: On the 1986–88 vehicles, both R3 and J2 leads are green on alternator side of 8-way wiring connector. At dash end of 8-way connector, R3 is green and J2 is blue.

11. Start engine. Immediately after starting reduce engine speed to idle.

12. Adjust carbon pile and engine speed in increments until a speed of 1250 rpm and voltmeter reading of 15 volts is obtained. Do not allow voltage meter to read above 16 volts.

13. The ammeter reading must be within the proper limits.

14. If reading is less than specified, alternator should be removed from vehicle and bench tested.

15. After current output is completed reduce engine speed, turn **OFF** carbon pile and turn **OFF** ignition switch.

16. Disconnect negative battery cable.

17. Remove test ammeter, voltmeter, tachometer and carbon pile.

18. Remove jumper wire between 8-way black connector (1986–88) or back of the atlernator (1989–90) and ground.

19. Connect BAT lead to alternator output BAT terminal post.

20. Reconnect negative battery cable.

21. Reconnect hose between power module (1986–88) or the single module engine controller (1989–90) and air cleaner.

OVERHAUL

Disassembly

1. Remove the alternator from the vehicle. Position the unit in a suitable holding fixture.

2. Remove the pulley nut and lockwasher. Remove the alternator pulley.

3. Remove the pulley to fan spacer and pulley fan.

4. Remove the Woodruff key from the rotor shaft.

5. From the rear of the alternator disconnect the electrical terminal from the capacitor. Remove the capacitor retaining screw and the capacitor.

6. Remove the brush holder retaining screw and remove the brush holder from its mounting on the rear of the alternator.

7. Remove the alternator through bolts. Using a suitable tool pry between the stator and the drive end shield and carefully separate the assembly.

8. Press the rotor out of the drive end shield and remove the spacer. Remove the pulley fan spacer.

9. Remove the front alternator drive end bearing screws.

10. Remove the drive end shield bearing retainer and press out the drive end shield bearing.

11. Remove the front drive bearing from the front of the drive end shield.

12. To test the positive and negative rectifiers use tool C–3929-A or equivalent.

NOTE: Do not break the plastic cases of the rectifiers. These cases are for protection against corrosion. Be sure to always touch the test probe to the metal pin of the nearest rectifier.

13. Position the rear end shield and the stator assembly on an insulated surface. Connect the test lead clip to the alternator battery output terminal.

14. Plug in tool C–3829-A or equivalent. Touch the metal pin of each of the positive rectifiers with the test probe.

15. Reading for satisfactory rectifiers will be 1¾ amperes or more. Reading should be approximately the same and meter needle must move in same direction for all 3 rectifiers.

16. When some rectifiers are good and 1 is shorted, the reading taken at good rectifiers will be low and the reading at shorted rectifiers will be 0. Disconnect stator lead to rectifiers reading 0 and retest. Reading of good rectifiers will now be within satisfactory range.

17. When a rectifier is open it will read approximately 1 ampere and the good rectifiers will read within satisfactory range.

18. Touch the metal pin of each of the negative rectifiers with the test probe.

19. Test specifications are the same and the test results will be approximately same as for positive case rectifiers except that the meter will read on opposite side of scale.

NOTE: If a negative rectifier shows a shorted condition remove stator from rectifier assembly and retest. It is possible that a stator winding could be grounded to stator laminations or to an rectifier end shield, which would indicate a shorted negative rectifier.

20. Unsolder the stator to rectifier leads. Mark the stator coil frame, to aid in reinstallation of the stator. Remove the stator from the rectifier end shield assembly.

21. Remove the 3 rectifier assembly mounting screws. Remove the rectifier assembly.

22. Remove the inner battery (B+) stud insulator.

23. Remove the D+ stud insulator, stud nut, stud flatwasher and stud insulating washer.

24. Remove the rear bearing oil and dust seal. Check the rotor bearing surface for scoring.

25. Using puller C–4068 or equivalent, remove the rear rotor bearing.

26. Check outside circumference of slip-ring for dirtiness and roughness. Clean or polish with fine sandpaper, as required. A badly roughened slip-ring or a worn down slip-ring should be replaced.

27. To check for an open rotor field coil, connect an ohmmeter to slip-rings. Ohmmeter reading should be between 1.5–2 ohms on rotor coils at room ambient conditions. Resistance between 2.5–3.0 ohms would result from alternator rotors that have been operated on vehicle at higher engine compartment temperatures. Readings above 3.5 ohms would indicate high resistance rotor coils and further testing or replacement may be required.

28. To check for a shorted field coil connect an ohmmeter to slip-rings. If reading is below 1.5 ohms field coil is shorted.

29. To check for a grounded rotor field coil connect an ohmmeter from each slip-ring to rotor shaft.

NOTE: Ohmmeter should be set for infinite reading when probes are apart and 0 when probes are touching. The ohmmeter should read infinite. If reading is 0 or higher, rotor is grounded.

30. Check for continuity between leads of stator coil. Press test probe firmly to each of 3 phase (stator) lead terminals separately. If there is no continuity, stator coil is defective. Replace stator assembly.

31. To test the stator for ground check for continuity between the stator coil leads and the stator coil frame. If there is no continuity the stator is grounded and must be replaced.

32. To test the inner and outer brush circuit, use an ohmmeter and touch 1 test probe to the inner brush and the other test probe to the brush terminal. If continuity does not exist replace the brush assembly. Repeat the same procedure for the outer brush.

Assembly

1. Be sure to check all parts for wear and replace the defective components as required.

2. Install the rear rotor bearing oil and dust seal.

3. Install the inner alternator battery B + terminal insulator.

4. Position the rectifier assembly. Install the rectifier mounting screws, the insulator, the insulator washer, the insulator lockwasher and the insulator nut.

5. Position the stator assembly into the rectifier end shield. Align the scribe marks on the stator and the rectifier end shield.

6. Solder the stator leads to the rectifier assembly; be sure to use needle nose pliers as a heat sink.

7. Position and press the front bearing into the drive end shield. Install the bearing retainer and the pulley fan spacer onto the drive end shield.

8. Position the drive end shield and spacer over the rotor. Us-

ing a socket wrench, press the drive end shield onto the rotor.

9. Install the rectifier end shield and stator assembly into the drive end shield and rotor assembly. Install the through bolts and tighten.

10. Push the brushes into the brush holder and install the brush holder onto the alternator assembly.

11. Install the capacitor and terminal plug onto the alternator assembly.

12. Install the Woodruff key into the shaft and the fan over the shaft.

13. Install the drive pulley-to-fan spacer, the pulley, the lockwasher and the nut over the shaft. Secure the pulley and tighten the nut.

CHRYSLER 40/90 AND 50/120 AMP ALTERNATOR WITH VOLTAGE REGULATOR IN ENGINE ELECTRONICS

The charging system consists of a battery, alternator, voltmeter and connecting wires. The 40/90 has 6 built-in silicon rectifiers, while the 50/120 has 12 built-in silicon rectifiers. The voltage regulator is built into the power and logic modules. The rectifiers convert AC current into DC current. Current at the alternator battery terminal is DC. The alternator's main components are rotor, stator, capacitor, rectifiers, end shields, brushes, bearings, poly-vee drive pulley and fan.

The electronic voltage regulator is contained within engine electronics power module and logic module. It is a device that regulates vehicle electrical system voltage by limiting output voltage that is generated by the alternator. This is accomplished

by controlling amount of current that is allowed to pass through alternator field winding. The alternator field is turned **ON** by a driver in power module which is controlled by a predriver in the logic module. The logic module looks at battery temperature to determine control voltage. The field is then driven at a duty cycle proportional to the difference between battery voltage and desired control voltage. One important feature of the electronic regulator is the ability of its control circuit to vary regulated system voltage up or down as temperature changes. This provides varying charging conditions for battery throughout seasons of the year.

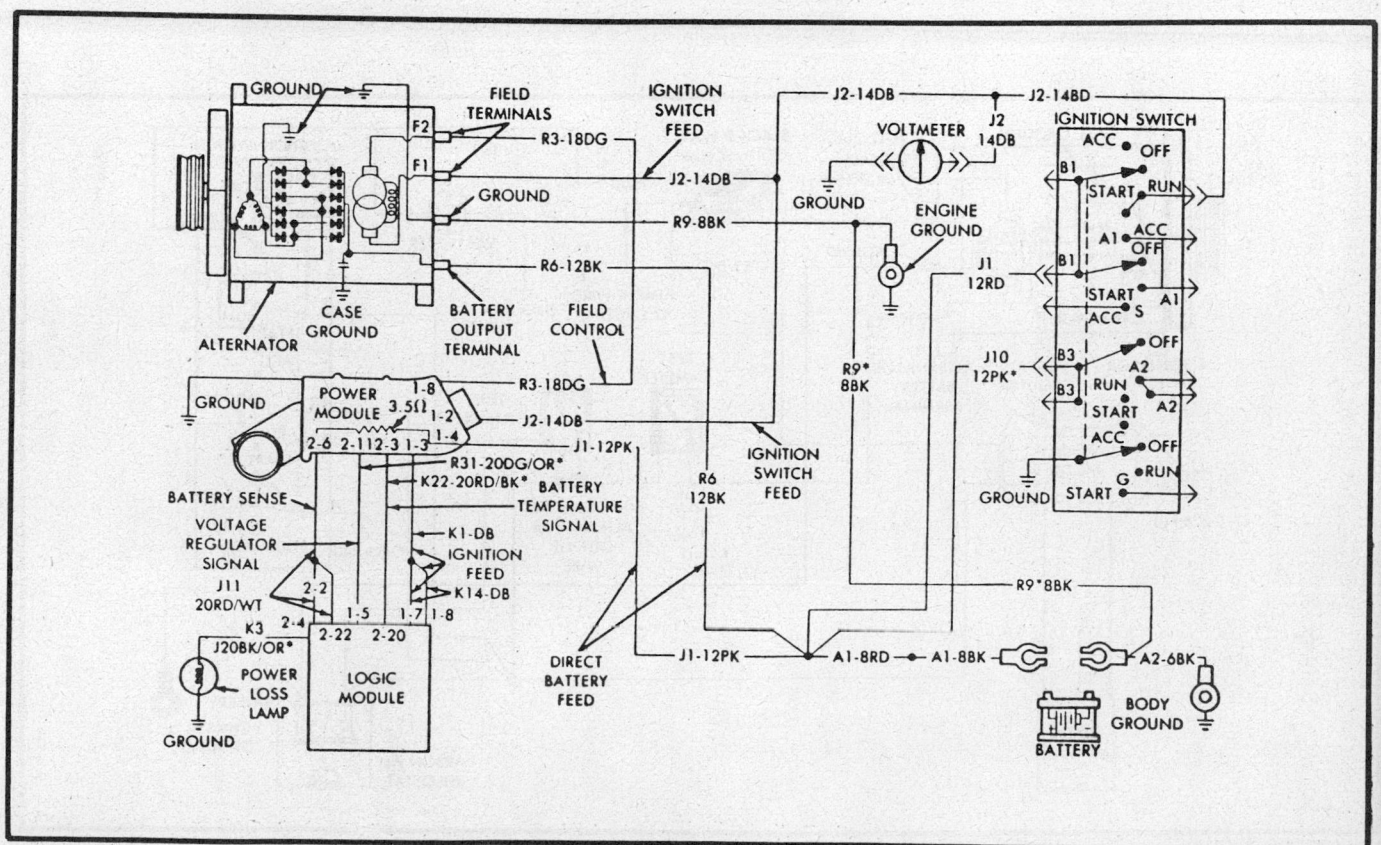

1987–88 Chrysler 50/120 amp alternator electrical schematic

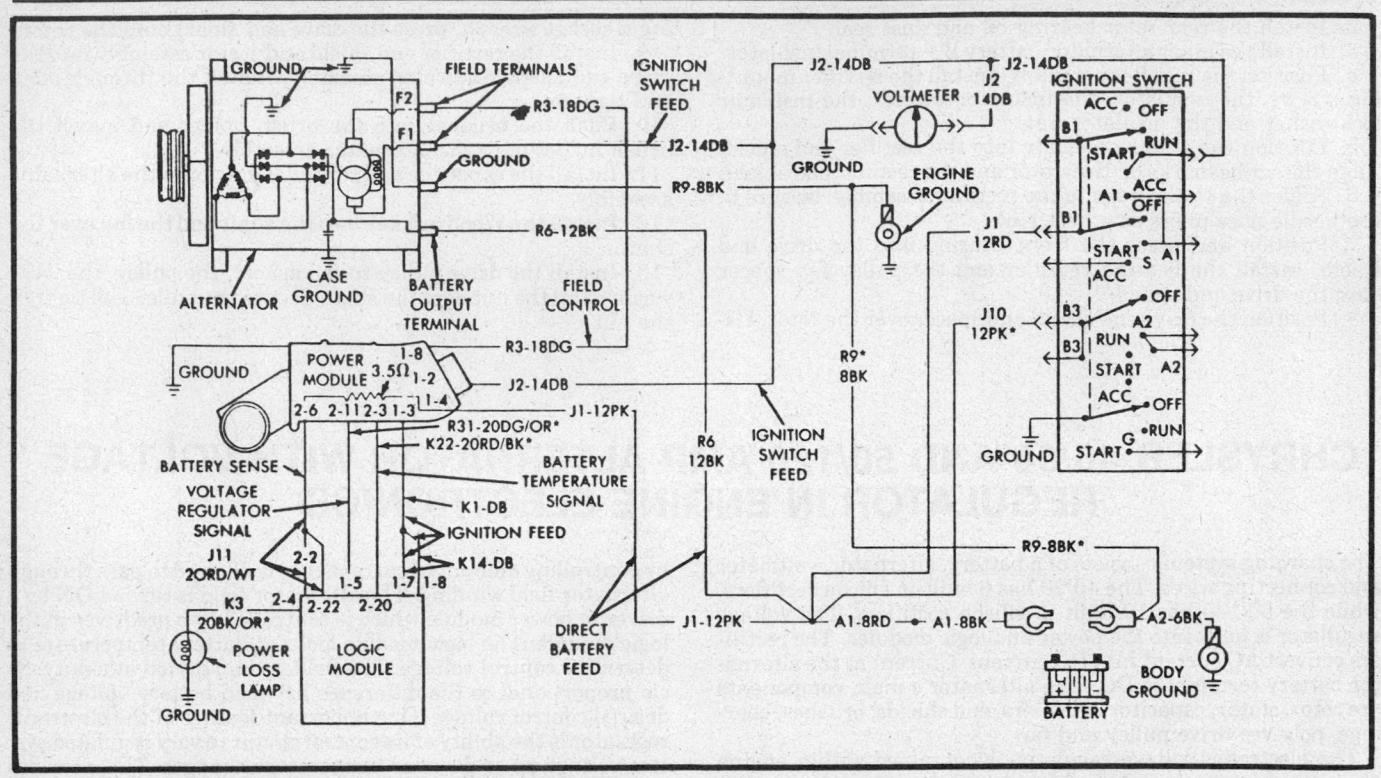

Chrysler 40/90 amp alternator electrical schematic

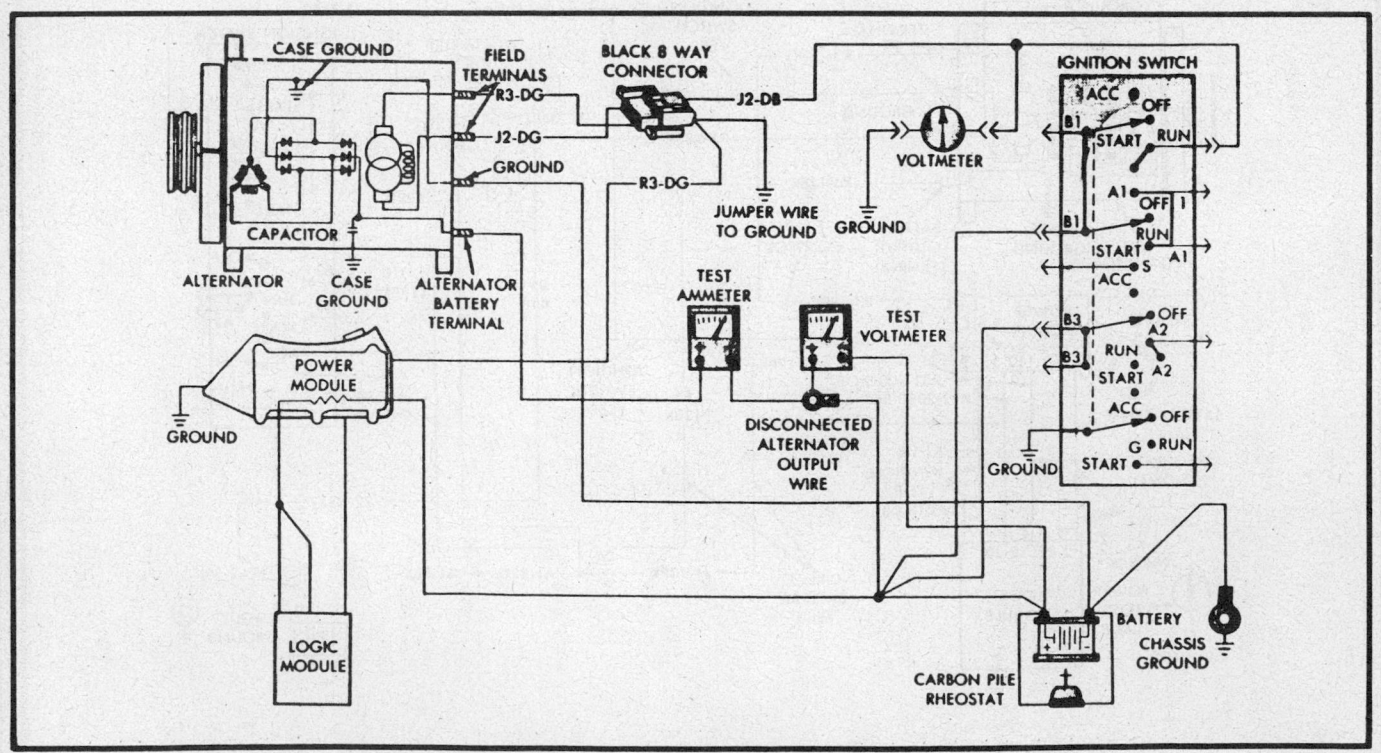

1986 Chrysler 40/90 amp alternator with engine electronics—output wire resistance test

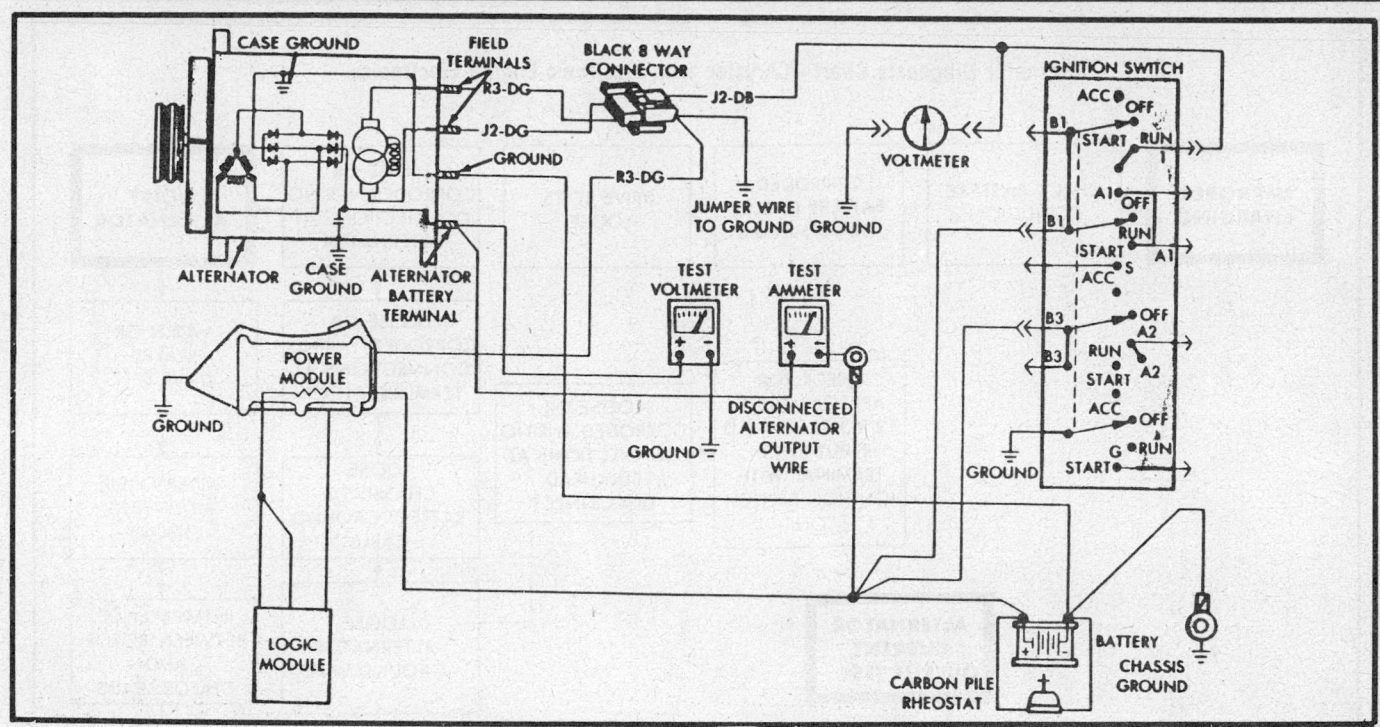

1986 Chrysler 40/90 amp alternator with engine electronics—current output test

System Diagnosis

ON VEHICLE SERVICE

Alternator Output Wire Resistance Test

Alternator output wire resistance test will show amount of voltage drop across alternator output wire between alternator BAT terminal and positive battery post.

1. Before starting test, make sure vehicle has a fully charged battery.
2. Turn **OFF** ignition switch.
3. Disconnect negative battery cable.
4. Disconnect alternator output wire from alternator output battery terminal.
5. Connect a 0–150 ampere scale DC ammeter in series between alternator BAT terminal and disconnected alternator output wire. Connect positive lead to alternator BAT terminal and negative lead to disconnected alternator output wire.
6. Connect positive lead of a test voltmeter (Range 0–18 volts minimum) to disconnected alternator output wire. Connect negative lead of test voltmeter to positive battery cable at positive post.
7. Remove air hose between power and module and air cleaner.
8. Connect an end of a jumper wire to ground and with other end probe green R3 lead wire on dash side of black 8-way connector.

NOTE: Do not connect the blue J2 lead of the 8-way connector to ground. Both R3 and J2 leads are green on the alternator side of the 8-way connector. At the dash end of the connector, R3 is green and J2 is blue.

9. Connect an engine tachometer and reconnect negative battery cable.
10. Connect a variable carbon pile rheostat between battery terminals. Be sure carbon pile is in **OPEN** or **OFF** position before connecting leads.

11. Start engine. Immediately after staring, reduce engine speed to idle. Adjust engine speed and carbon pile to maintain 20 amperes flowing in circuit. Observe voltmeter reading. Voltmeter reading should not exceed 0.5 volts.
12. If a higher voltage drop is indicated, inspect, clean and tighten all connections between alternator BAT terminal and positive battery post.
13. A voltage drop test may be performed at each connection to locate connection with excessive resistance. If resistance tested satisfactorily, reduce engine speed, turn **OFF** carbon pile and turn **OFF** ignition switch.
14. Disconnect negative battery cable. Remove test ammeter, voltmeter, carbon pile and tachometer. Remove jumper wire between 8-way black connector and ground.
15. Connect alternator output wire to alternator BAT terminal post. Tighten 45–75 inch lbs. Reconnect negative battery cable. Reconnect hose between power module and air cleaner.

Current Output Test

Current output test determines whether or not alternator is capable of delivering its rated current output.

1. Before starting any tests, make sure vehicle has a fully charged battery.
2. Disconnect negative battery cable.
3. Disconnect alternator output wire at the alternator battery terminal.
4. Connect a 0–150 ampere scale DC ammeter in series between alternator BAT terminal and disconnected alternator output wire. Connect positive lead to alternator BAT terminal and negative lead to disconnected alternator output wire.
5. Connect positive lead of a test voltmeter (range 0–18 volts minimum) to alternator BAT terminal.
6. Connect negative lead of test voltmeter to a good ground.
7. Connect an engine tachometer and reconnect negative battery cable.
8. Connect a variable carbon pile rheostate between battery terminals. Be sure carbon pile is in **OPEN** or **OFF** position before connecting leads.
9. Remove air hose between power module and air cleaner.

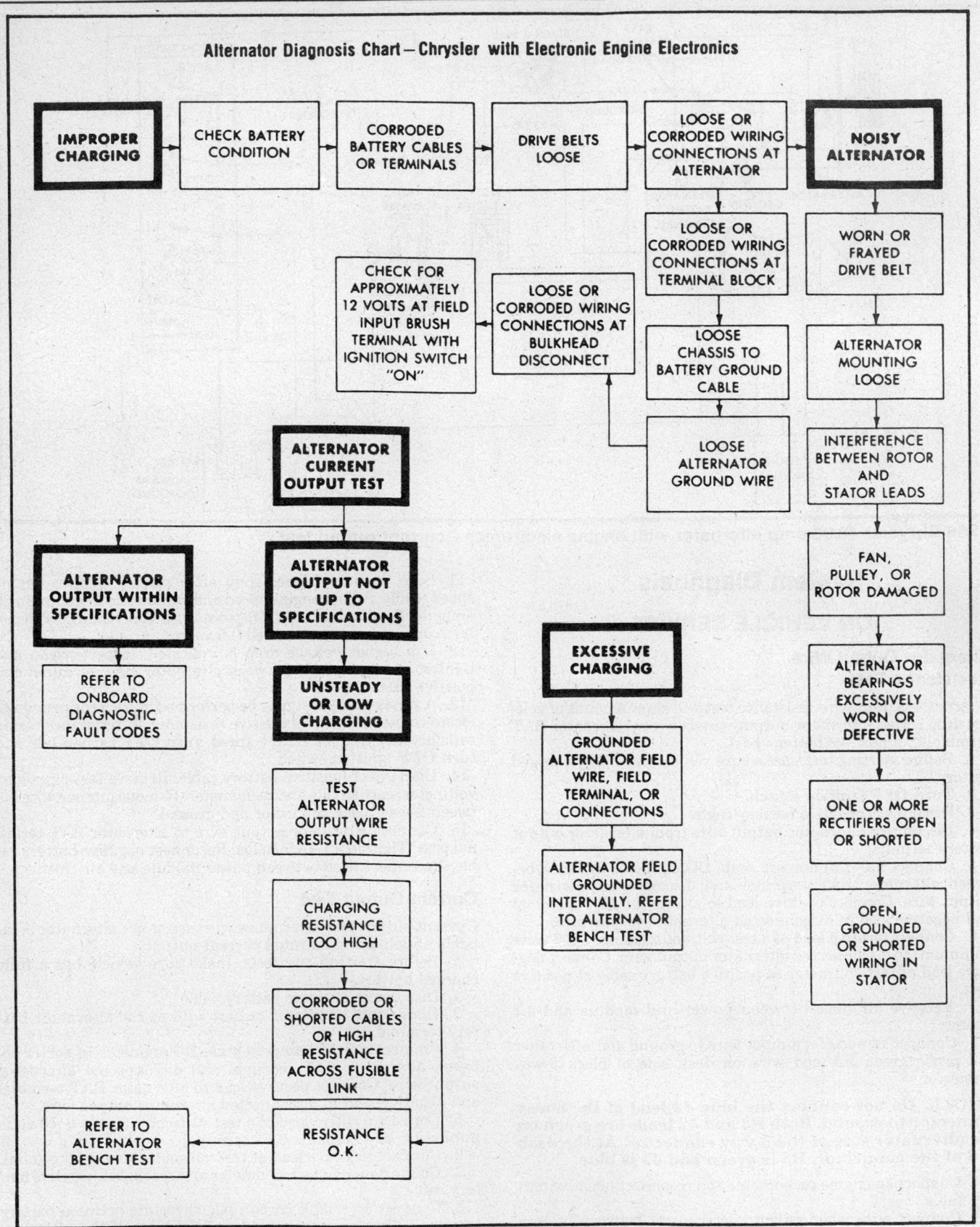

Alternator Diagnosis Chart—Chrysler with Electronic Engine Electronics

Alternator fault code chart 1987-90

10. Connect 1 end of a jumper wire to ground and with other end probe green R3 lead wire on dash side of Black 8-way connector.

NOTE: Do not connect the blue J2 lead of the 8-way connector to ground. Both R3 and J2 leads are green on the alternator side of the 8-way connector. At the dash end of the connector, R3 is green and J2 is blue.

11. Start engine. Adjust carbon pile and engine speed in increments until a speed of 1250 rpm and voltmeter reading of 15 volts is obtained. Do not allow the voltage meter to read above 16 volts.

12. The ammeter reading must be within the proper limits.

13. If reading is less than specified and alternator output wire resistance is not excessive alternator should be removed from vehicle and bench tested.

14. After current output test is completed, reduce engine speed, turn **OFF** carbon pile and ignition switch. Disconnect negative battery cable.

15. Remove test ammeter, voltmeter, tachometer and carbon pile. Remove jumper wire between 8-way black connector and ground. Disconnect alternator output wire to alternator BAT terminal post.

16. Reconnect negative battery cable. Reconnect air hose between power module and air cleaner.

Voltage Regulator Test

On board diagnostic fault codes play a major role in case of a charging system failure.

Fault codes are 2 digit numbers that identify which circuit is bad. In most cases, they do not identify which component in a circuit is bad. Therefore, a fault code is only a result, not necessarily a reason for the problem. It is important that the test procedure be followed in order to understand the fault codes of the on-board diagnostic system.

DIAGNOSTIC READOUT BOX OPERATION

The diagnostic readout box is used to put the on-board diagnostic system in 3 different modes of testing as called for in the driveability test procedure, only one of which is used in charging system diagnosis.

DIAGNOSTIC MODE

1. Connect diagnostic readout box C–4805 to the mating connector located in the wiring harness by right front shock tower.

2. Place read/hold switch on readout box in **READ** position.

3. Turn ignition switch **ON/OFF, ON/OFF,** on within 5 seconds.

4. Record all codes, displaying of codes may be stopped by moving read/hold button to **HOLD** position. Returning to **READ** position will continue displaying of codes.

5. If for some reason diagnostic readout box is not available, logic module can show fault codes by means of flashing power loss lamp on instrument cluster.

HOW TO USE POWER LOSS OR POWER LIMIT LAMP FOR CODES

To activate this function, turn ignition key **ON/OFF/ON/OFF/ON** within 5 seconds. The power loss lamp will turn **ON** for 2 seconds as a bulb check. Immediately following this it will display a fault code by flashing on and off. There is a short pause between flashes and a longer pause between digits. All codes displayed are 2 digit numbers with a 4 second pause between codes. An example of a code is as follows.

1. Lamp on for 2 seconds then turns off.
2. Lamp flashes 4 times, pauses and flashes once.
3. Lamp pauses for 4 seconds, flashes 4 times, pauses and flashes 7 times.
4. The 2 codes are 41 and 47. Any number of codes can be displayed as long as they are in memory. The lamp will flash until all of them are displayed.

CHARGING SYSTEM FAULT CODES

Perform test procedure categories using the following guide lines.

1. Each category is made up of many tests. Always start at the first test of a category. Starting at any other test will only give incorrect results.

2. Each test may have many steps. Only perform steps indicated under action required. It is not necessary to perform all steps in a test.

3. At the end of each test (not step) reconnect all wires and turn the engine **OFF** and reinstall any components that were removed for testing.

4. The vehicle being tested must have a fully charged battery.

Diagnostic Testing with Readout Box

TEST 1

Checking Battery Sensing Circuit Code 16

This test will check for direct battery feed to logic module. Circuit is also memory feed to logic module. Code 16 with lower battery voltage will turn **ON** power loss lamp.

1. Turn the ignition switch **OFF**.

2. Disconnect the (black on EFI, blue on turbo models) connector from the logic module.

3. Connect a voltmeter to cavity No. 22 of logic module connector and ground.

4. Voltmeter should read within 1 volt of battery voltage. Voltage okay, replace logic module. Before replacing logic module, make sure the terminal in cavity No. 22 is not crushed so that it cannot touch logic module pin.

5. Zero volts, repair wire of cavity No. 22 for an open circuit to the wiring harness splice.

TEST 2

Checking Charging System
Fault Codes 41 and 46

STEP A

1. Disconnect the power module 10-way connector.

2. Connect a voltmeter between cavity No. 8 of 10-way connector and ground.

3. Turn ignition switch to **RUN** position.

4. Voltmeter should read within 1 volt of battery voltage. Not within 0–1 volts, repair alternator field circuit for short to ground. Voltage okay, perform Step B.

STEP B

1. Turn the ignition switch **OFF**.

2. Reconnect the power module 10-way connector.

3. Disconnect the power module 12-way connector.

4. Connect a voltmeter between F2 terminal on alternator and ground.

5. Turn the ignition switch to the **RUN** position.

6. Voltage should read within 1 volt of battery voltage. Not within 0–1 volt, replace power module. Voltage okay, perform Step C.

STEP C

1. Turn the ignition switch **OFF**.

2. With power module 12-way connector disconnected.

3. Disconnect the logic module (white on EFI, red on Turbo models) connector.

4. Connect an ohmmeter between cavity No. 11 of power module 12-way connector and ground.

5. Ohmeter should not show continuity. No continuity, replace logic module. Continuity repair wire of cavity No. 11 for short circuit to ground.

TEST 3

Checking Codes 41 and 47

STEP A

1. Conenct a voltmeter between battery positive and ground.
2. Connect an end of jumper wire to a good engine ground.
3. Start the engine and note reading of voltmeter.
4. Very quickly touch other end of jumper wire to F2 terminal on alternator and watch voltmeter.
5. Voltmeter should show an increase in voltage. Voltage increases, this indicates alternator is operating correctly. Move on to Step B, for field circuit check. Voltage does not increase, this indicates alternator is not operating. If this is the case, perform Step E which checks for voltage to alternator field.

STEP B

1. Connect a voltmeter between cavity No. 2 of logic module (black on EFI, blue on turbo models) connector and ground.
2. Connect an end of a jumper wire to cavity No. 5 of the logic module white connector.
3. Very quickly touch other end of jumper wire to logic module mounting stud and watch voltmeter.
4. Voltmeter should show an increase in voltage. If voltage increases, this indicates all components of system, except logic module, are operating correctly.
5. Before replacing the logic module, be sure that the terminal in cavity No. 5 is not crushed so that it cannot touch the logic module pin. If terminal in cavity 5 is not damaged, replace logic module. If no increase is indicated, move on to Step C.

STEP C

1. Turn the engine OFF.
2. Disconnect logic module (white on EFI, red on turbo models) connector.
3. Connect a voltmeter between cavity No. 5 of logic module connector and ground.
4. Turn the ignition switch to RUN position. Voltmeter should read within 1 volt of battery voltage. 0 volts, disconnect power module 12-way and connect an ohmmeter between cavity 5 of logic module (white on EFI, red on turbo models) connector and cavity 11 of power module. If open, repair wire or connector. If meter shows continuity replace power module. If voltage shown is within 1 volt of battery voltage, go on to Step D.

STEP D

1. Turn ignition switch OFF.
2. Disconnect 10-way connector from power module.
3. Connect a voltmeter between cavity No. 8 of 10-way connector and ground.
4. Turn ignition switch to RUN position. Voltmeter should read within 1 volt of battery voltage. If voltage shown is within 1 volt of battery voltage, replace power module.
5. 0 volts, turn ignition switch OFF and place an ohmmeter between cavity 8 of power module 10-way connector and F2 terminal of alternator. If open, repair wire or connector. If meter shows continuity, proceed to Step E.

STEP E

1. Turn ignition switch to OFF position.
2. Connect a voltmeter between F1 terminal of alternator and ground.
3. Turn ignition switch to RUN position.
4. Voltmeter should read within 1 volt of battery voltage. If voltage shown is within 1 volt of battery voltage, alternator is not functioning properly and must be removed form vehicle and repaired.
5. If no voltage is shown, this indicates an open circuit and the wire from the F1 terminal to ignition switch must be repaired.

TEST 4

Checking Code 44

STEP A

1. Turn the ignition switch OFF.
2. Disconnect the logic module (black connector on EFI, blue connector on turbo models).
3. Connect an ohmmeter between cavity No. 20 of logic module (black on EFI, blue on turbo models) connector and ground.
4. Ohmmeter should show resistance, amount of resistance should be 8–29K ohms. Correct resistance, replace logic module. If 0 resistance, perform Step B. Open circuit, perform Step C.

STEP B

1. Ohmmter connected between cavity No. 20 of logic module (black on EFI, blue on turbo models) connector and ground.
2. Disconnect power module 12-way connector.
3. Ohmmeter should show an open circuit. Open circuit, replace power module. If 0 resistance, repair wire of cavity No. 20 and cavity No. 3 of power module 12-way connector.

STEP C

1. Disconnect power module 12-way connector.
2. Connect an ohmmeter between pin 3 of power module 12-way and ground.
3. Ohmmeter should show resistance, amount of resistance should be between 8–29K ohms.
4. Correct resistance, repair wire in cavity No. 20 of logic module (black on EFI, blue on turbo models) and cavity No. 3 of power module 12-way connector. Open circuit, replace power module.

OVERHAUL

Disassembly

1. Remove the dust cover mounting nut. Remove the dust cover.
2. Remove the brush holder assembly mounting screws. Remove the brush holder assembly.
3. Remove the stator to rectifier mounting screws. Remove the stator-to-rectifier assembly mounting screws. Remove the rectifier insulator. Remove the capacitor mounting screw. Remove the rectifier assembly.
4. Remove the through bolts. Carefully pry between the stator and the drive end shield, using a suitable tool and separate the end shields. The stator is laminated, do not burr the stator or the end shield.
5. Position the drive end of the alternator over the bosses of the holding fixture. Do not position the rotor plastic termination plate over the fixture boss or damage to the assembly will result.
6. Bolt the drive end of the assembly to shield fixture. Loosen the pulley mounting nut. Remove the pulley mounting nut. Remove the pulley washer.
7. Remove the poly-vee pulley. Remove the fan. Remove the front bearing spacer. Press the rotor assembly out of the drive end shield.
8. Remove the inner bearing spacer. Position the alternator bearing puller tool under the rear rotor bearing. Tighten the right puller bolt a ½ turn. Tighten the left puller bolt a ½ turn. Continue tightening the tool a ½ turn on each bolt until the rear rotor bearing is free. Remove the rear rotor bearing assembly from the rotor.
9. Position the rotor assembly in the holding fixture. Position the rear rotor bearing onto the rotor shaft.
10. Drive the rear rotor bearing onto the rotor until it bottoms. The rear rotor position is critical and must be installed using special tools C–4885 and C–4894.
11. Remove the front bearing retaining screws. Press the front bearing out of the drive end shield.
12. Carefully remove the stator from the rectifier end shield.

Inspection
ROTOR ASSEMBLY TEST

Check the outside circumference of slip-ring for dirtiness and roughness. Clean or polish with fine sandpaper, if required. A badly roughened slip-ring or a worn down slip-ring should be replaced.

Slip-rings are not serviced as a separate item. They are serviced with the rotor assembly.

ROTOR FIELD COILS FOR OPENS AND SHORTS TEST

To check for an open rotor field coil connect an ohmmeter between slip-rings. Ohmmeter readings should be between 1.5-2 ohms on rotor field coils at room ambient conditions. Resistance between 2.5-3.0 ohms would result from alternator rotor field coils that have been operated on vehicle at higher engine compartment temperatures. Readings about 3.5 ohms would indicate high resistance rotor field coils and further testing or replacement may be required.

To check for a shorted rotor field coil, connect an ohmmeter between both slip-rings. If the reading is below 1.5 ohms, the rotor field coil is shorted.

ROTOR FIELD COIL FOR GROUND TEST

To check for a grounded rotor field coil, connect an ohmmeter from each slip-ring to rotor shaft. Ohmmeter should be set for infinite reading when probes are apart and 0 when probes are shorted. The ohmmeter should read infinite. If the reading is 0 or low in value, rotor is grounded.

STATOR ASSEMBLY TEST

Stator Coil for Ground Test

1. Remove varnish from a spot on the stator frame.
2. Press an ohmmeter test probe firmly onto cleaned spot on frame. Be sure varnish has been removed from stator so that spot is bare.
3. Press the other ohmmeter test probe firmly to each of the 3 phase (stator) lead terminals 1 at a time. If ohmmeter reads 0 or low in value stator lead is grounded.
4. Replace stator if stator tested grounded.

Stator for Open or Short Circuit Test

The stator windings are Delta wound. Therefore, they cannot be tested for opens or shorts with an ohmmeter. They can only be tested for these items with test equipment not common to automotive service test equipment. If stator is not grounded and all other electrical circuits and components of alternator test okay, it can be suspected that stator could possibly be open or shorted and must be replaced.

Rectifier Assemblies Test

When testing rectifiers with an ohmmeter, disconnect the 3 phase stator lead terminals from rectifier assembly. Pry stator lead terminals away from rectifier assembly.

Positive Rectifier Test

With an ohmmeter check for continuity between each positive (+) rectifier strap and positive (+) heat sink. Reverse test probes and retest. There should be continuity in one direction only. If there is continuity in both directions, rectifier is short circuited. If there is no continuity in either direction, rectifier is open. If rectifier is shorted or open, replace rectifier assembly.

Negative Rectifier Test

With an ohmmeter, check for continuity between each negative (−) rectifier strap and negative (−) sink. Reverse test probes and retest. There should be continuity in one direction only. If there is continuity in both directions, rectifier is short circuited. If there is no continuity in either direction, rectifier is open. If

rectifier is shorted or open, replace rectifier assembly. When installing a new rectifier assembly, apply 3 dabs (0.1 grams each) of heat sink compound to bottom of negative rectifier prior to mounting rectifier assembly to rectifier end shield.

Brushes and Brush Springs Continuity Test

When testing brushes and brush springs make sure that brushes move smoothly in brush holder. Sticking brushes require replacement of brush holder assembly.

Inner Brush Circuit Test

With an ohmmeter, touch a test probe to inner brush and another probe to field terminal. If there is no continuity, replace the brush assembly.

Outer Brush Circuit Test

With an ohmmeter, touch a test probe to outer brush and other probe to field terminal. If there is no continuity, replace brush assembly.

Cleaning Alternator Parts

Do not immerse stator field coil assembly, rotor assembly or rectifier assembly in cleaning solvent, as solvent will damage these parts.

Assembly

1. Be sure to repair or replace defective components as required.
2. To the front of the rotor, install the inner bearing spacer and press the drive end shield onto the rotor.

NOTE: The front drive end shield bearing must be replaced anytime the rotor or drive end shield is removed, for the front bearing is a press fit and may be damaged upon removal.

3. Position the drive end shield into a holding fixture so the fixture bosses do not contact the rotor plastic termination plate and tighten the holding bolt.
4. At the front of the drive end shield, install the pulley spacer (flat side up), the fan, the pulley, the washer and the pulley nut. Torque the pulley nut to 80-105 ft. lbs. (108-125 Nm).
5. Remove the drive end shield and rotor assembly from the holding fixture.
6. To assemble the rear end housing for the 40/90, perform the following procedures:
    a. Apply joint compound to the rectifier end shield surface, under the rectifier mounting position.
    b. Position the rectifier assembly to the rectifier drive end housing.
    c. Install the rectifier insulator, the insulator mounting screws and torque the screws to 36-46 inch lbs. (4-6 Nm).
    d. Install the capacitor terminal over the rectifier assembly battery terminal stud and torque the mounting screw to 36-48 inch lbs. (4-6 Nm).
    e. Install the alternator battery terminal nut and torque to 30-50 inch lbs. (3-6 Nm).
    f. Install the stator-to-rectifier screws and torque to 12-18 inch lbs. (1-2 Nm).
    g. Slide the brushes into their cavity, Install the brush holder assembly and torque the screws to 12-18 inch lbs. (1-2 Nm).
    h. Install the dust cover and torque the nut to 12-18 inch lbs. (1-2 Nm).
7. To assemble the rear end housing for the 50/120, perform the following procedures:
    a. Apply joint compound to the rectifier end shield surface, under the rectifier mounting position.
    b. Position the rectifier assemblies No. 1 and No. 2 to the rectifier drive end housing.

c. Install the rectifier insulators, the insulator mounting screws and torque to 36–46 inch lbs. (4–6 Nm).

d. Install the capacitor terminal over the rectifier assembly No. 2 battery terminal stud and torque the mounting screw to 36–48 inch lbs. (4–6 Nm).

e. Install the alternator battery terminal nut and torque to 30–50 inch lbs. (3–6 Nm).

f. Position a jumper strap between the rectifier assemblies No. 1 and No. 2.; torque the nut to 36–48 inch lbs. (4–6 Nm) and the screw to 15–35 inch lbs. (2–4 Nm).

g. Position the 3 buss bars to the rectifier assemblies and torque the screws to 12–18 inch lbs. (1–2 Nm).

h. Slide the brushes into their cavity, Install the brush holder assembly and torque the screws to 12–18 inch lbs. (1–2 Nm).

i. Install the dust cover and torque the nut to 12–18 inch lbs. (1–2 Nm).

8. Assemble the rear end housing to the drive end shield and rotor assemlby. Install the through bolts and torque to 48–72 inch lbs. (5–8 Nm).

9. Install the rear bearing oil seal.

CHRYSLER 60 AND 78 AMP ALTERNATOR WITH VOLTAGE REGULATOR IN ENGINE ELECTRONICS

Charging system consists of a battery alternator voltage regulator voltmeter and connecting wires. Alternator has 6 built in silicon rectifiers, that convert AC current into DC current. Current at alternator battery terminal is DC. Alternator main components are rotor, stator, capacitor, rectifiers, end shields, brushes, bearings, poly-vee drive pulley and fan.

The electronic voltage regulator is contained within engine electronics power and logic modules. It is a device that regulates vehicle electrical system voltage by limiting output voltage that is generated by the alternator. This is accomplished by controlling amount of current that is allowed to pass through alternator field winding. The alternator field is turned on by a driver in power module which is controlled by a predriver in the logic module. The logic module looks at battery temperature to determine control voltage. The field is then driven at a duty cycle proportional to the difference between battery voltage and desired

control voltage. One important feature of the electronic regulator is the ability of its control circuit to vary regulated system voltage up or down as temperature changes. This provides varying charging conditions for battery throughout seasons of the year.

System Diagnosis

ON VEHICLE SERVICE

Output Wire Resistance Test

Alternator output wire resistance test will show amount of voltage drop across alternator output wire between alternator BAT terminal and positive battery post.

1. Before starting test, make sure vehicle has a fully charged battery.

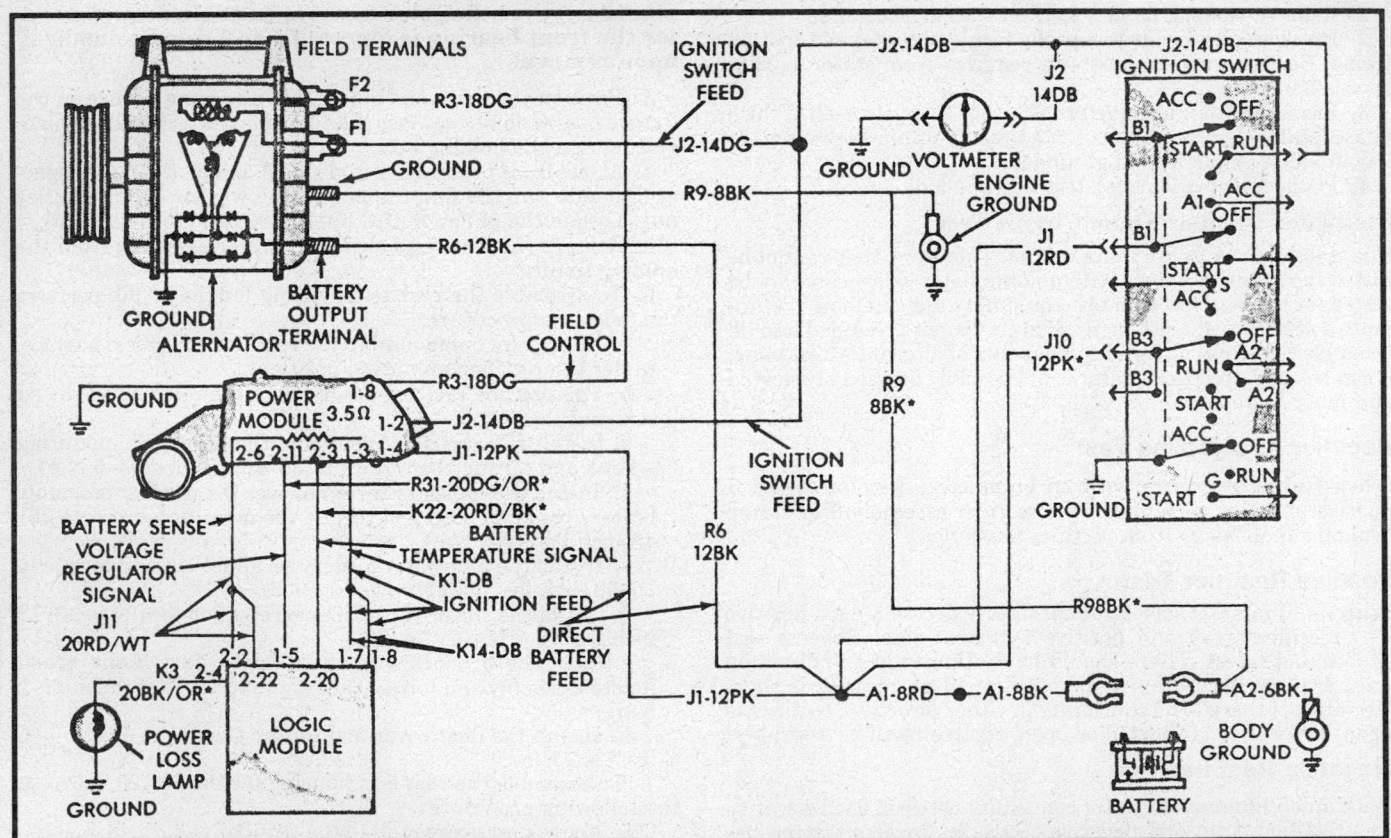

View of the Chrysler 60 and 78 amp alternator electrical system with voltage regulator in power and logic modules

2. Turn **OFF** ignition switch.

3. Disconnect negative battery cable.

4. Disconnect alternator output wire from alternator output battery terminal.

5. Connect a 0–150 ampere scale DC ammeter in series between alternator BAT terminal and disconnected alternator output wire. Connect positive lead to alternator BAT terminal and negative lead to disconnected alternator output wire.

6. Connect positive lead of a test voltmeter (range 0–18 volts minimum) to disconnected alternator output wire. Connect negative lead of test voltmeter to positive battery cable at positive post.

7. Remove air hose between power and module and air cleaner.

8. Connect an end of a jumper wire to ground and with other end probe green R3 lead wire on dash side of black 8-way connector.

NOTE: Do not connect the blue J2 lead of the 8-way connector to ground. Both R3 and J2 leads are green on the alternator side of the 8-way connector. At the dash end of the connector, R3 is green and J2 is blue.

9. Connect an engine tachometer and reconnect negative battery cable.

10. Connect a variable carbon pile rheostat between battery terminals. Be sure carbon pile is in **OPEN** or **OFF** position before connecting leads.

11. Start engine. Immediately after starting, reduce engine speed to idle. Adjust engine speed and carbon pile to maintain 20 amperes flowing in circuit. Observe voltmeter reading. Voltmeter reading should not exceed 0.5 volts.

12. If a higher voltage drop is indicated, inspect, clean and tighten all connections between alternator BAT terminal and positive battery post.

13. A voltage drop test may be performed at each connection to locate connection with excessive resistance. If resistance tested satisfactorily, reduce engine speed, turn **OFF** carbon pile and turn **OFF** ignition switch.

14. Disconnect negative battery cable. Remove test ammeter, voltmeter, carbon pile and tachometer. Remove jumper wire between 8-way black connector and ground.

15. Connect alternator output wire to alternator BAT terminal post. Tighten 45–75 inch lbs. Reconnect negative battery cable. Reconnect hose between power module and air cleaner.

Current Output Test

Current output test determines whether or not alternator is capable of delivering its rated current output.

1. Before starting any tests, make sure vehicle has a fully charged battery.

2. Disconnect negative battery cable.

3. Disconnect alternator output wire at the alternator battery terminal.

4. Connect a 0–150 ampere scale DC ammeter in series between alternator BAT terminal and disconnected alternator output wire. Connect positive lead to alternator BAT terminal and negative lead to disconnected alternator output wire.

5. Connect positive lead of a test voltmeter (range 0–18 volts minimum) to alternator BAT terminal.

6. Connect negative lead of test voltmeter to a good ground.

7. Connect an engine tachometer and reconnect negative battery cable.

8. Connect a variable carbon pile rheostate between battery terminals. Be sure carbon pile is in **OPEN** or **OFF** position before connecting leads.

9. Remove air hose between power module and air cleaner.

10. Connect an end of a jumper wire to ground and with other end probe green R3 lead wire on dash side of black 8-way connector.

NOTE: Do not connect the blue J2 lead of the 8-way

connector to ground. Both R3 and J2 leads are green on the alternator side of the 8-way connector. At the dash end of the connector, R3 is green and J2 is blue.

11. Start engine. Adjust carbon pile and engine speed in increments until a speed of 1250 rpm and voltmeter reading of 15 volts is obtained. Do not allow the voltage meter to read above 16 volts.

12. The ammeter reading must be within the proper limits.

13. If reading is less than specified and alternator output wire resistance is not excessive alternator should be removed from vehicle and bench tested.

14. After current output test is completed, reduce engine speed, turn **OFF** carbon pile and ignition switch. Disconnect negative battery cable.

15. Remove test ammeter, voltmeter, tachometer and carbon pile. Remove jumper wire between 8-way black connector and ground. Disconnect alternator output wire to alternator BAT terminal post.

16. Reconnect negative battery cable. Reconnect air hose between power module and air cleaner.

Voltage Regulator Test

On-board diagnostic fault codes play a major role in case of a charging system failure.

Fault codes are 2 digit numbers that identify which circuit is bad. In most cases, they do not identify which component in a circuit is bad. Therefore, a fault code is only a result, not necessarily a reason for the problem. It is important that the test procedure be followed in order to understand what the fault codes of the on board diagnostic system are trying to tell.

DIAGNOSTIC READOUT BOX OPERATION

The diagnostic readout box is used to put the on board diagnostic system in 3 different modes of testing as called for in the driveability test procedure, only one of which is used in charging system diagnosis.

DIAGNOSTIC MODE

1. Connect diagnostic readout box C–4805 to the mating connector located in the wiring harness by right front shock tower.

2. Place read/hold switch on readout box in **READ** position.

3. Turn ignition switch **ON/OFF, ON/OFF, ON** within 5 seconds.

4. Record all codes, displaying of codes may be stopped by moving read/hold button to **HOLD** position. Returning to **READ** position will continue displaying of codes.

5. If for some reason diagnostic readout box is not available, logic module can show fault codes by means of flashing power loss lamp on instrument cluster.

HOW TO USE POWER LOSS OR POWER LIMIT LAMP FOR CODES

To activate this function, turn ignition key **ON/OFF/ON/OFF/ON** within 5 seconds. The power loss lamp will then come **ON** for 2 seconds as a bulb check. Immediately following this it will display a fault code by flashing **ON** and **OFF**. There is a short pause between flashes and a longer pause between digits. All codes displayed are 2 digit numbers with a 4 second pause between codes. An example of a code is as follows.

1. Lamp **ON** for 2 seconds then turns **OFF**.

2. Lamp flashes 4 times, pauses and flashes once.

3. Lamp pauses for 4 seconds, flashes 4 times, pauses and flashes 7 times.

4. The 2 codes are 41 and 47. Any number of codes can be displayed as long as they are in memory. The lamp will flash until all of them are displayed.

CHARGING SYSTEM FAULT CODES

Perform test procedure categories using the following guide lines.

1. Each category is made up of many tests. Always start at

the first test of a category. Starting at any other test will only give incorrect results.

2. Each test may have many steps. Only perform steps indicated under action required. It is not necessary to perform all steps in a test.

3. At the end of each test (not step) reconnect all wires and turn the engine **OFF** and reinstall any components that were removed for testing.

4. The vehicle being tested must have a fully charged battery.

TEST 1

CHECKING BATTERY SENSING CIRCUIT CODE 16

This test will check for direct battery feed to logic module. Circuit is also memory feed to logic module. Code 16 with lower battery voltage will turn **ON** Power Loss lamp.

1. Turn the ignition switch **OFF**.

2. Disconnect the (black on EFI, blue on turbo models) connector from the logic module.

3. Connect a voltmeter to cavity No. 22 of logic module connector and ground.

4. Voltmeter should read within 1 volt of battery voltage. Voltage okay, replace logic module. Before replacing logic module, make sure the terminal in cavity No. 22 is not crushed so that it cannot touch logic module pin.

5. Zero volts, repair wire of cavity No. 22 for an open circuit to the wiring harness splice.

TEST 2

Checking Charging System
Fault Codes 41 and 46
STEP A

1. Disconnect the power module 10-way connector.

2. Connect a voltmeter between cavity No. 8 of 10-way connector and ground.

3. Turn ignition switch to **RUN** position.

4. Voltmeter should read within 1 volt of battery voltage. Not within 0–1 volts, repair alternator field circuit for short to ground. Voltage okay, perform Step B.

STEP B

1. Turn the ignition switch **OFF**.

2. Reconnect the power module 10-way connector.

3. Disconnect the power module 12-way connector.

4. Connect a voltmeter between F2 terminal on alternator and ground.

5. Turn the ignition switch to the **RUN** position.

6. Voltage should read within 1 volt of battery voltage. Not within 0–1 volt, replace power module. Voltage okay, perform Step C.

STEP C

1. Turn the ignition switch **OFF**.

2. With power module 12-way connector disconnected.

3. Disconnect the logic module (white on EFI, red on Turbo models) connector.

4. Connect an ohmmeter between cavity No. 11 of power module 12-way connector and ground.

5. Ommeter should not show continuity. No continuity, replace logic module. Continuity repair wire of cavity No. 11 for short circuit to ground.

TEST 3

Checking Codes 41 and 47
STEP A

1. Connectct a voltmeter between battery positive and ground.

2. Connect an end of jumper wire to a good engine ground.

3. Start the engine and note reading of voltmeter.

4. Very quickly touch other end of jumper wire to F2 terminal on alternator and watch voltmeter.

5. Voltmeter should show an increase in voltage. Voltage increases, this indicates alternator is operating correctly. Move on to Step B, for field circuit check. Voltage does not increase, this indicates alternator is not operating, if this is the case perform Step E which checks for voltage to alternator field.

STEP B

1. Connect a voltmeter between cavity No. 2 of logic module (black on EFI, blue on turbo models) connector and ground.

2. Connect an end of a jumper wire to cavity No. 5 of the logic module white connector.

3. Very quickly touch other end of jumper wire to logic module mounting stud and watch voltmeter.

4. Voltmeter should show an increase in voltage. If voltage increases, this indicates all components of system, except logic module, are operating correctly.

5. Before replacing the logic module be sure that the terminal in cavity No. 5 is not crushed so that it cannot touch the logic module pin. If terminal in cavity No. 5 is not damaged, replace logic module. If no increase is indicated, move on to Step C.

STEP C

1. Turn the engine **OFF**.

2. Disconnect logic module (white on EFI, red on turbo models) connector.

3. Connect a voltmeter between cavity No. 5 of logic module connector and ground.

4. Turn the ignition switch to **RUN** position. Voltmeter should read within 1 volt of battery voltage. 0 volts, disconnect power module 12-way and connect an ohmmeter between cavity No. 5 of logic module (white on EFI, red on turbo models) connector and cavity No. 11 of power module. If open, repair wire or connector. If meter shows continuity replace power module. If voltage shown is within 1 volt of battery voltage, go on to Step D.

STEP D

1. Turn ignition switch **OFF**.

2. Disconnect 10-way connector from power module.

3. Connect a voltmeter between cavity No. 8 of 10-way connect and ground.

4. Turn ignition switch to **RUN** position. Voltmeter should read within 1 volt of battery voltage. If voltage shown is within 1 volt of battery voltage, replace power module.

5. Zero volts, turn ignition switch **OFF** and place an ohmmeter between cavity No. 8 of power module 10-way connector and F2 terminal of alternator. If open, repair wire or connector. If meter shows continuity, proceed to Step E.

STEP E

1. Turn ignition switch to **OFF** position.

2. Connect a voltmeter between F1 terminal of alternator and ground.

3. Turn ignition switch to **RUN** position.

4. Voltmeter should read within 1 volt of battery voltage. If voltage shown is within 1 volt of battery voltage, alternator is not functioning properly and must be removed form vehicle and repaired.

5. If no voltage is shown, this indicates an open circuit and the wire from the F1 terminal to ignition switch must be repaired.

TEST 4

Checking Code 44
STEP A

1. Turn the ignition switch **OFF**.

2. Disconnect the logic module (black connector on EFI, blue connector on turbo engines).

3. Connect an ohmmeter between cavity No. 20 of logic module (black on EFI, blue on turbo models) connector and ground.

4. Ohmmeter should show resistance, amount of resistance should be between 8–29K ohms. Correct resistance, replace logic module. Zero resistance, perform Step B. Open circuit, perform Step C.

STEP B

1. Ohmmter connected between cavity No. 20 of logic module (black on EFI, blue on turbo engines) connector and ground.

2. Disconnect power module 12-way connector.

3. Ohmmeter should show an open circuit. Open circuit, replace power module. Zero resistance, repair wire of cavity No. 20 and cavity No. 3 of power module 12-way connector.

STEP C

1. Disconnect power module 12-way connector.

2. Connect an ohmmeter between pin 3 of power module 12-way and ground.

3. Ohmmeter should show resistance, amount of resistance should be between 8–29K ohms.

4. Correct resistance, repair wire in cavity No. 20 of logic module (black on EFI, blue on turbo) and cavity No. 3 of power module 12-way connector. Open circuit, replace power module.

OVERHAUL

Disassembly

1. Remove the retaining screw, flat washer, nylon washer and field terminal and carefully lift the plastic holder containing the spring and brush assembly from the end housing.

2. The ground brush (60 amp) is positioned horizontally against the slip-ring and is retained in the holder that is integral with the end housing. Remove the retaining screw and lift the clip, spring and brush assembly from the end housing. The stator is laminated so don't burr the stator or end housings.

3. Remove the through bolts and pry between the stator and drive end housing with a suitable tool. Carefully separate the drive end housing, pulley and rotor assembly from the stator and rectifier housing assembly.

4. The pulley is an interference fit on the rotor shaft. Remove with a puller and special adapters.

5. Remove the nuts and washers and, while supporting the end frame, tap the rotor shaft with a plastic hammer and separate the rotor and end housing.

6. The drive end ball bearing is an interference fit with the rotor shaft. Remove the bearing with puller and adapters.

NOTE: Further dismantling of the rotor is not advisable, as the remainder of the rotor assembly is not serviced separately.

7. Remove the DC output terminal nuts and washers and remove terminal screw and inside capacitor (on units so equipped).

8. Remove the insulator.

NOTE: Positive rectifiers are pressed into the heat sink and negative rectifiers in the end housing. When removing the rectifiers it is necessary to support the end housing and the heat sink in order to prevent damage to the castings. Another caution is in order relative to the diode rectifiers. Don't subject them to unnecessary jolt-ing. Heavy vibration or shock may ruin them. Cut rectifier wire at point of crimp. Support rectifier housing. The factory tool is cut away and slotted to fit over the wires and around the bosses in the housing. Be sure that the bore of the tool completely surrounds the rectifier, then press the rectifier out of the housing. The roller bearing in the rectifier end frame is a press fit. To protect the end housing, it is necessary to support the housing with a tool when pressing out the bearing.

Assembly

1. Support the heat sink or rectifier end housing on circular plate.

2. Check rectifier identification to be sure the correct rectifier is being used. The part numbers are stamped on the case of the rectifier. They are also marked red for positive and black for negative.

3. Start the new rectifier into the casting and press it in squarely. Do not start rectifier with a hammer or it will be ruined.

4. Crimp the new rectifier wire to the wires disconnected at removal or solder using a heat sink with rosin core solder.

5. Support the end housing on tool so that the notch in the support tool will clear the raised section of the heat sink, press the bearing into position with tool SP–3381, or equivalent. New bearings are prelubricated, additional lubrication is not required.

6. Insert the drive end bearing in the drive end housing and install the bearing plate, washers and nuts to hold the bearing in place.

7. Position the bearing and drive end housing on the rotor shaft and, while supporting the base of the rotor shaft, press the bearing and housing in position on the rotor shaft with an arbor press and arbor tool. Be careful that there is no cocking of the bearing at installation; or damage will result. Press the bearing on the rotor shaft until the bearing contacts the shoulder on the rotor shaft.

8. Install pulley on rotor shaft. Shaft of rotor must be supported so that all pressing force is on the pulley hub and rotor shaft. Do not exceed 6800 lbs. pressure. Pulley hub should just contact bearing inner race.

9. Some alternators will be found to have the capacitor mounted internally. Be sure the heat sink insulator is in place.

10. Install the output terminal screw with the capacitor attached through the heat sink and end housing.

11. Install insulating washers, lockwashers and locknuts.

12. Make sure the heat sink and insulator are in place and tighten the locknut.

13. Position the stator on the rectifier end housing. Be sure that all of the rectifier connectors and phase leads are free of interference with the rotor fan blades and that the capacitor (internally mounted) lead has clearance.

14. Position the rotor assembly in the rectifier end housing. Align the through bolt holes in the stator with both end housings.

15. Enter stator shaft in the rectifier end housing bearing, compress stator and both end housings manually and install through bolts, washers and nuts.

16. Install the insulated brush and terminal attaching screw.

17. Install the ground screw and attaching screw.

18. Rotate pulley slowly to be sure the rotor fan blades do not hit the rectifier and stator connectors.

CHRYSLER 40/90 AND 50/120 AMP ALTERNATOR WITH EXTERNAL ELECTRONIC REGULATOR

The 40/90 alternator is used as standard equippment. When the vehicle is equipped with for lamps or a police/taxi package, the 50/120 alternator is used.

System Diagnosis

ON VEHICLE SERVICE

Charging Circuit Resistance Test

1. Be sure that the battery is fully charged.
2. Turn **OFF** ignition switch.
3. Disconnect negative battery cable.
4. Disconnect BAT terminal wire from alternator output BAT terminal post.
5. Connect a 0–100 amps minimum range scale DC test ammeter in series between alternator BAT terminal and disconnected BAT terminal wire. Connect ammeter positive lead wire to alternator BAT terminal and negative ammeter lead to disconnected alternator BAT terminal wire.
6. Connect a 0–18 volt minimum range scale test voltmeter between disconnected alternator BAT terminal wire and positive battery cable. Connect voltmeter positive lead to disconnected alternator BAT terminal wire and negative voltmeter lead to battery positive cable.
7. Disconnect wiring harness connector from electronic voltage regulator on vehicle.
8. Connect a jumper wire from wiring harness connector green wire (outside terminal), to ground. Do not connect blue J2 lead of wiring connector to ground.

9. Connect an engine tachometer and reconnect negative battery cable. Connect a variable carbon pile rheostat to battery terminals. Be sure carbon pile is in **OPEN** or **OFF** position before connecting leads.
10. Start engine. Immediately after starting reduce engine speed to idle.
11. Adjust engine speed and carbon pile to maintain 20 amperes flowing in circuit. Observe voltmeter reading. Voltmeter reading should not exceed 0.5 volts.

NOTE: If a higher voltage drop is indicated, inspect, clean and tighten all connections in the charging circuit. A voltage drop test may be performed at each connection to locate connection with excessive resistance. If charging circuit resistance tested satisfactorily, reduce engine speed, turn OFF carbon pile and turn **OFF** ignition switch.

12. Disconnect negative battery cable.
13. Remove test ammeter, test voltmeter, variable carbon pile rheostat and engine tachometer.
14. Remove jumper wire connected between electronic voltage regulator wiring harness connector green wire terminal and ground.
15. Connect wiring harness connector to electronic voltage regulator.
16. Connect BAT terminal wire to alternator output BAT terminal.
17. Connect negative battery cable.

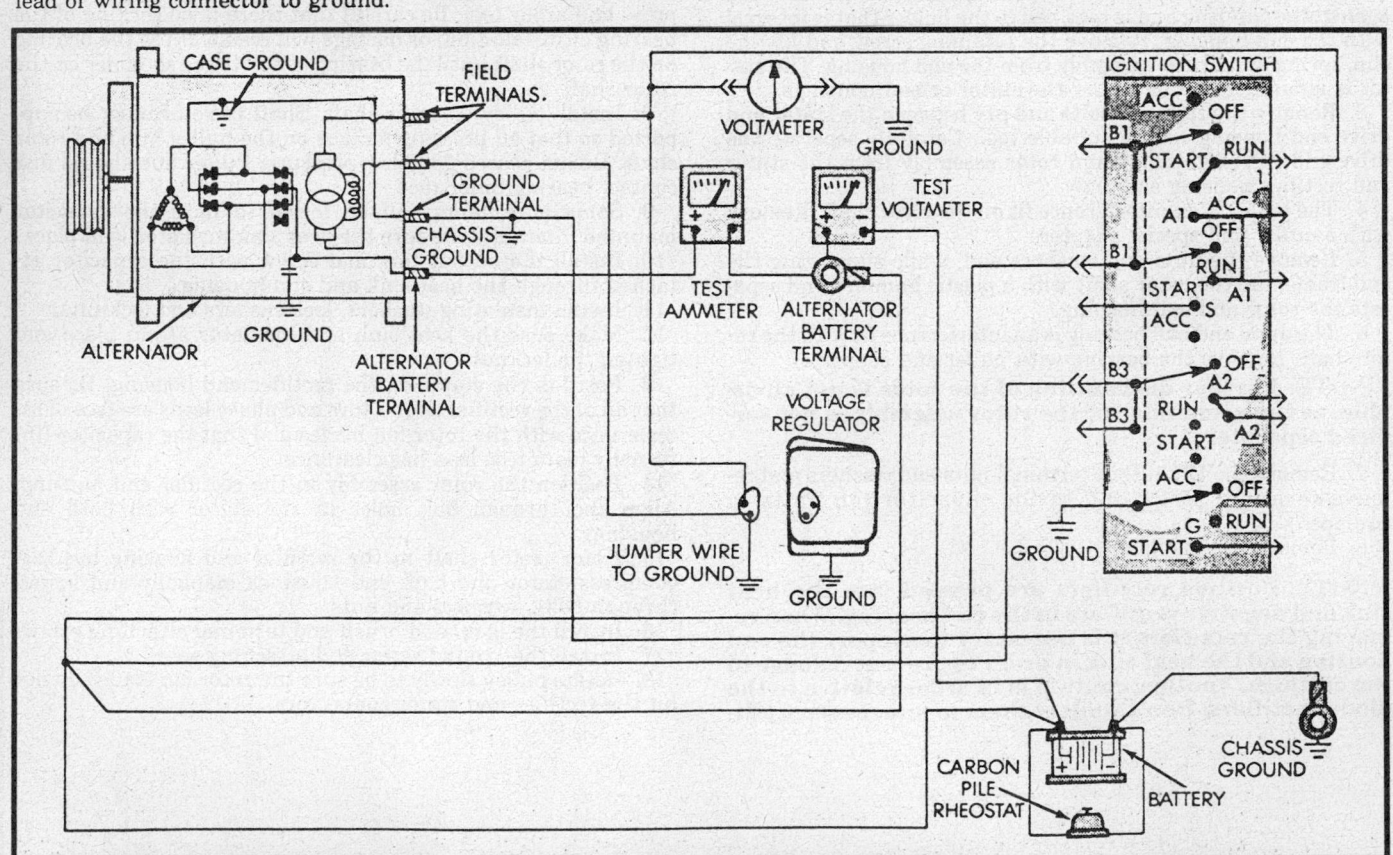

Chrysler 90 and 120 amp alternators with external voltage regulator—charging system resistance test—adjust engine speed and carbon pile to maintain 20 amps, voltmeter reading should not exceed 0.5 volts

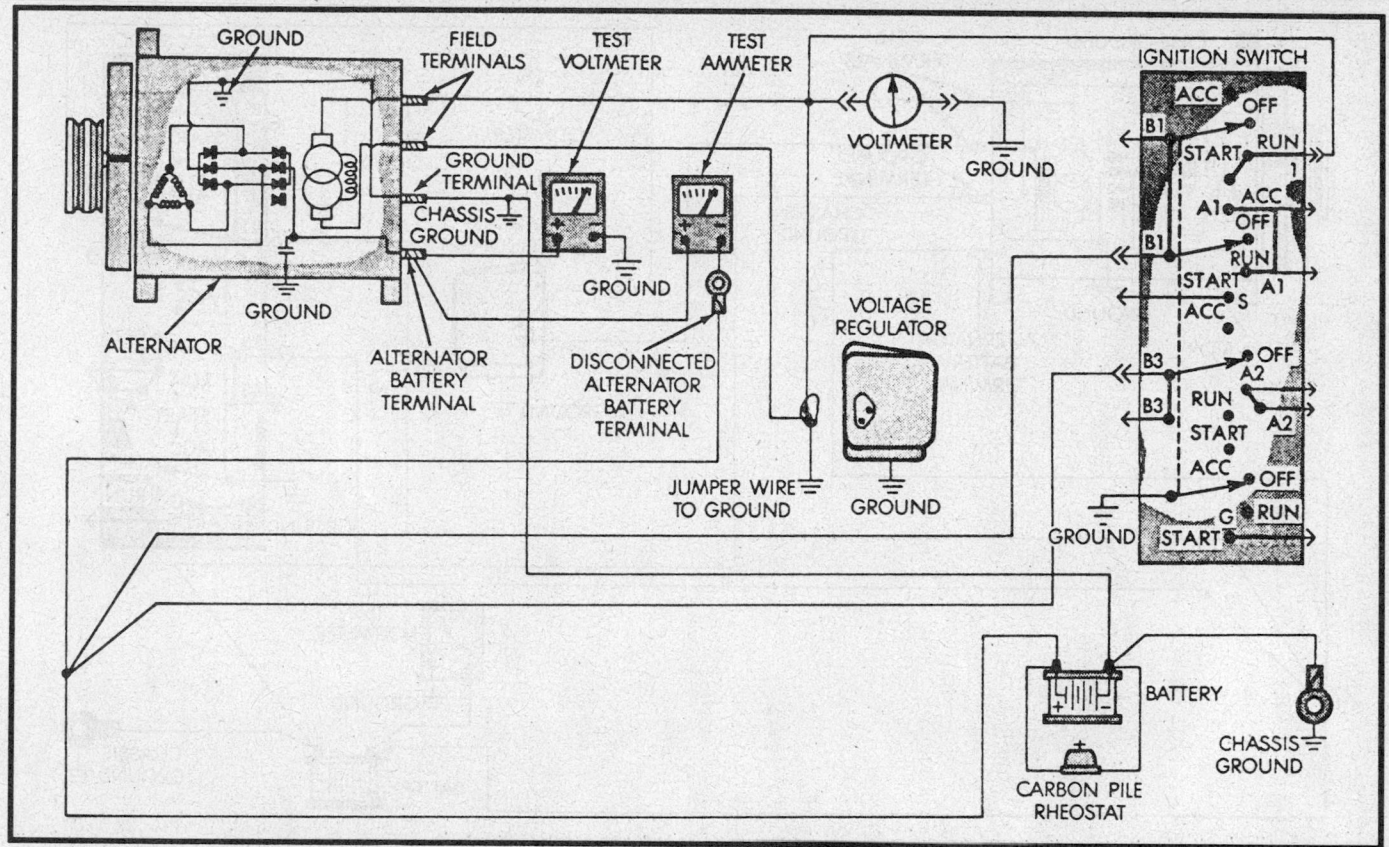

Chrysler 90 and 120 amp alternators with external voltage regulator—current output test—adjust engine speed and carbon pile increments until an engine speed of 1250 rpm is reached, voltmeter reading should not exceed 15 volts

Current Output Test

1. Be sure that the battery is fully charged.
2. Turn **OFF** ignition switch.
3. Disconnect negative battery cable.
4. Disconnect the output wire from the alternator BAT terminal. Connect a 0-100 ammeter positive lead wire to alternator BAT terminal and negative ammeter lead to disconnected alternator BAT terminal wire.
5. Connect a 0–18 volt minimum range scale test voltmeter between alternator BAT terminal post and ground. Connect voltmeter positive lead to alternator BAT terminal post. Connect negative lead of test voltmeter to a good ground.
6. Disconnect wiring harness connector from electronic voltage regulator on vehicle.
7. Connect a jumper wire from wiring harness connector green wire (outside terminal) to ground. Do not connect blue J2 lead of wiring connector to ground.
8. Connect an engine tachometer and reconnect negative battery cable. Connect a variable carbon pile rheostat between battery terminals. Be sure the carbon pile is in **OPEN** or **OFF** position before connecting leads.
9. Start the engine. Immediately after starting reduce engine speed to idle.
10. Adjust carbon pile and engine speed in increments until a speed of 1250 rpm and voltmeter reading of 15 volts is obtained. Do not allow voltage meter to read above 16 volts.
11. Ammeter reading must be within the proper limits. If reading is less than specified alternator should be removed from vehicle and bench tested.
12. After current output test is completed reduce engine speed, turn **OFF** carbon pile and turn **OFF** ignition switch.

13. Disconnect negative battery cable.
14. Remove test ammeter, test voltmeter, tachometer and variable carbon pile rheostat.
15. Remove jumper wire connected between electronic voltage regulator wiring harness connector green wire terminal and ground.
16. Connect wiring harness connector to electronic voltage regulator.
17. Connect BAT terminal wire to alternator output BAT terminal.
18. Connect negative battery cable.

Voltage Regulator Test

1. Be sure that the battery is fully charged.
2. Turn **OFF** ignition switch.
3. Connect a 0–18 volts minimum range scale test voltmeter between vehicle battery and ground. Connect positive lead of voltmeter to positive battery cable terminal. Connect negative lead of voltmeter to a good vehicle body ground.
4. Connect a tachometer to engine.
5. Start engine and adjust engine speed to 1250 rpm with all lights and accessories turned **OFF**.
6. Check voltmeter, regulator is working properly if voltage readings are in accordance with the voltage chart.
7. If voltage is below limits or is fluctuating, proceed as follows. Check for a good voltage regulator ground. Voltage regulator ground is obtained through regulator case to mounting screws and to sheet metal of vehicle. This is ground circuit that is to be checked for opens.
8. Turn **OFF** ignition switch and disconnect voltage regulator wiring harness connector. Be sure terminals of connector have not spread open to cause an open or intermittant connection.

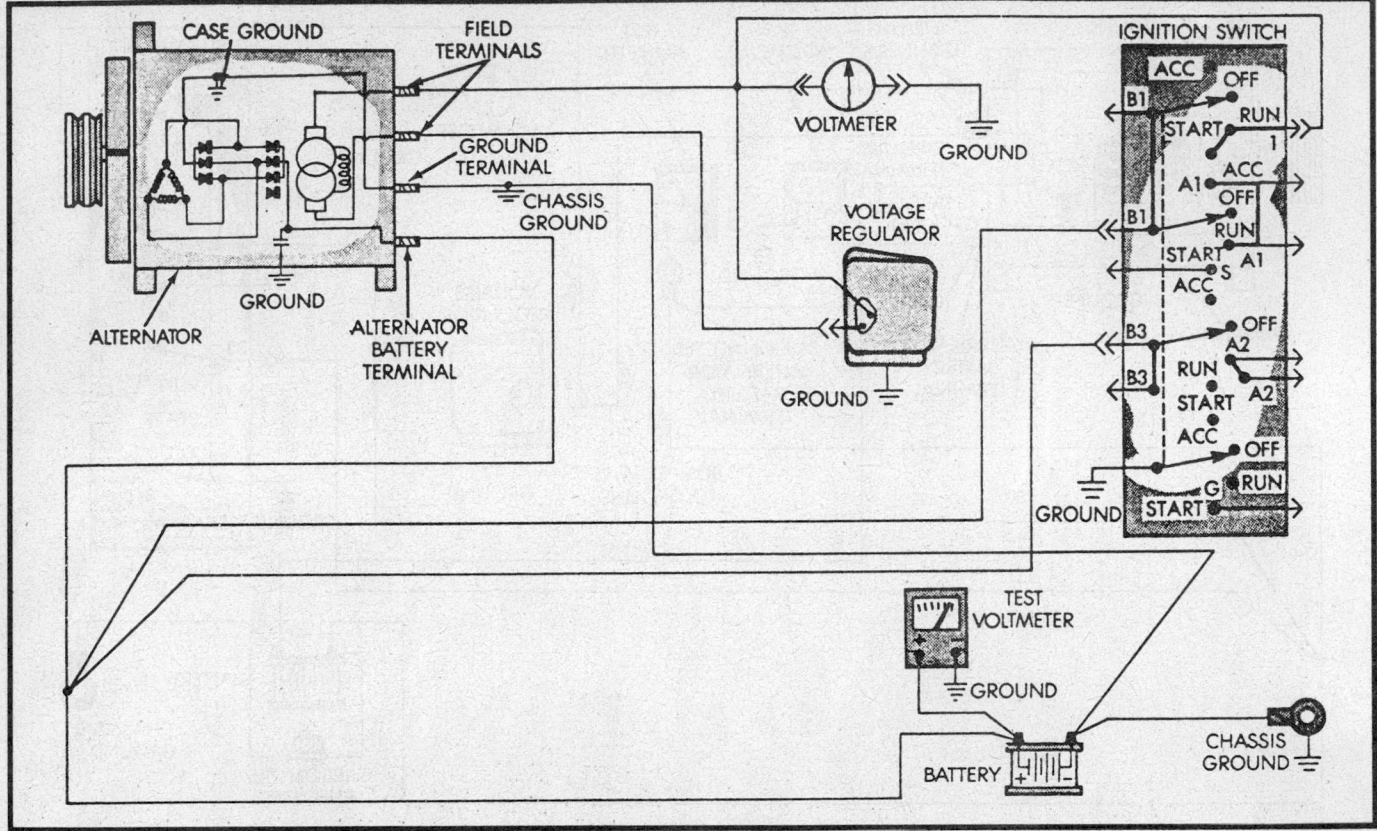

Chrysler 90 and 120 amp alternators with external voltage regulator—voltage regulator test—idle engine at 1250 rpm with all lights and accessories off, voltmeter readings should equal shown in table

9. Do not start engine or distort terminals with voltmeter probe: turn **ON** ignition switch and check for battery voltage at voltage regulator wiring harness connector terminals. Both blue and green terminals should read battery voltage. Turn **OFF** ignition switch.

10. If satisfactory, replace the regulator and repeat the test.

11. If the voltage is above limits specification proceed as follows. Turn **OFF** ignition switch and disconnect voltage regulator wiring harness connector. Be sure terminals in connector have not spread open.

12. Do not start engine or distort terminals with voltmeter probe. Turn **ON** ignition switch and check for battery voltage at voltage regulator wiring harness connector terminals. Both blue and green terminals should read battery voltage. Turn **OFF** ignition switch.

13. If satisfactory, then replace regulator and repeat test. Remove test voltmeter and tachometer.

OVERHAUL

Disassembly

1. Remove the rectifier dust cover nut and separate the cover from the alternator.

2. Remove the brush holder bolts and separate it from the alternator.

3. Remove the stator lead, the rectifier and capacitor bolts. Separate the rectifier and insulator from the alternator.

4. If disassembling a 50/120 alternator rectifier, perform the following procedures:

    a. Remove the connecting strap from between the rectifiers.

    b. Remove the buss bar and insulator screws.

    c. Separate the insulators from the rectifier.

5. From the shield end, remove the through bolts.

6. From the drive end shield, separate the stator and rectifier end shield.

7. Separate the stator from the rectifier end shield.

8. Remove the drive pulley nut, the washer, the pulley and the fan.

9. Press the rotor shaft from the drive end shield.

NOTE: If the bearing is defective, replace the drive end shield as an assembly.

10. If necessary to remove the rectifier end bearing from the rotor assembly, use a bearing puller to press the bearing from the rotor shaft.

Inspection

BRUSH HOLDER TESTS

1. Make sure the brushes move smoothly and return fully to the stops when released; if not, replace the brush holder assembly.

2. Using an ohmmeter, test inner brush-to-field terminals continuity; a field terminal should be open and the other closed. If not, replace the brush holder.

3. Using an ohmmeter, test outer brush-to-field terminals continuity; 1 field terminal should be open and the other closed. If not, replace the brush holder.

ROTOR TESTS

1. Check the field slip rings for excessive wear or roughness; fine emery cloth may be used to repair minor damage. If the rings are excessively damaged, replace the rotor.

2. Using an ohmmeter, test for continuity between the slip rings; the circuit should be closed. If not, replace the rotor.

3. Using an ohmmeter, test for continuity between the slip

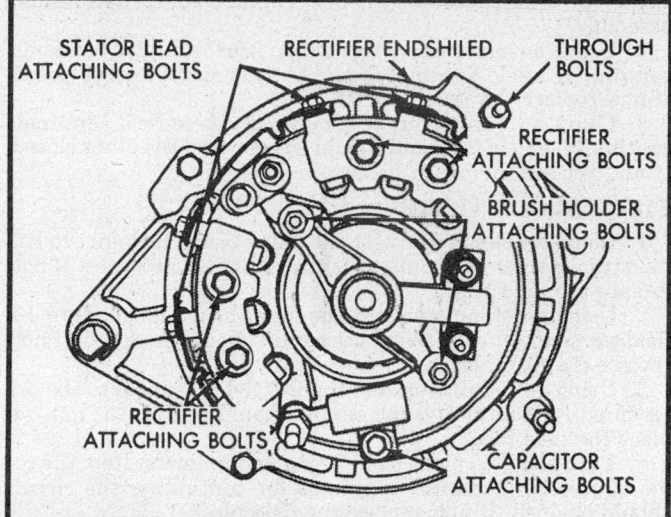

View of the rectifier end shield assembly bolts—Chrysler 90 and 120 amp alternator

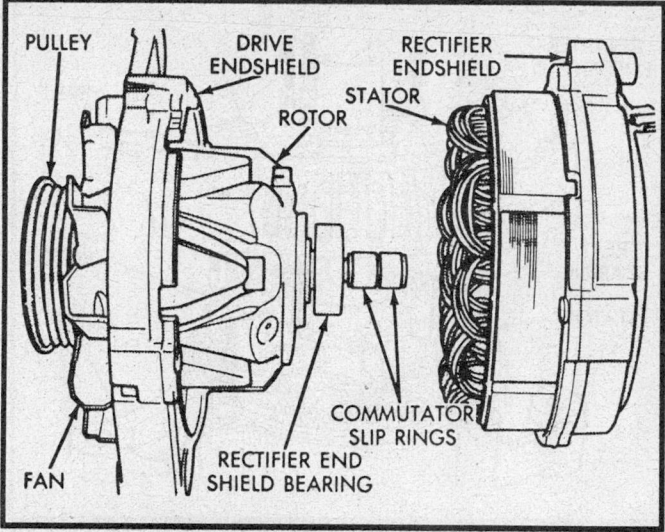

View of the stator and drive end shield assemblies—Chrysler 90 and 120 amp alternator

rings and the rotor shaft or core; the circuit should be open. If not, replace the rotor.

STATOR TESTS

1. Check the stator for signs damage—weak or broken leads, distorted frame or burned windings; if necessary, replace the stator.

NOTE: **Using a scraping device, clean a portion of the stator frame to assure good electrical contact.**

2. Using an ohmmeter, test for continuity between the stator leads and frame; the circuit should be open. If not, replace the stator.
3. Using an ohmmeter, test for continuity between the stator leads; the circuit should be closed. If not, replace the stator.

RECTIFIER TESTS

1. Separate the positive diode leads from the negative diode leads.
2. Using an ohmmeter, test for continuity between the positive heat sink to each of the positive diode leads. Reverse the test probes and repeat the test; the diodes should show continuity in 1 direction. If not, replace the rectifier assembly.

3. Using an ohmmeter, test for continuity between the negative heat sink to each of the negative diode leads. Reverse the test probes and repeat the test; the diodes should show continuity in 1 direction. If not, replace the rectifier assembly.

Assembly

1. If the rectifier end bearing was removed, support the rotor assembly in a holding fixture and drive the bearing onto the rotor shaft with a bearing driver.
2. Press the drive end shield onto the rotor shaft and install the fan, the pulley, the washer and the drive pulley nut.
3. Assemble the stator to the rectifier end shield and the stator to the drive end shield. Install the through bolts.
4. If assembling a 50/120 alternator rectifier, perform the following procedures:
   a. Install the insulators on the rectifier.
   b. Install the insulator screws and the buss bar.
   c. Attach the connecting strap between the rectifiers.
5. Assemble the rectifier and insulator to the alternator. Install the capacitor, the rectifier and the stator lead bolts.
6. Install the brush holder and tighten the bolts.
7. Install the rectifier dust cover and nut.

NIPPONDENSO 75, 90 AND 120 AMP ALTERNATORS

The alternators appear to be the same, except, the 75 amp alternator is equipped with 3 sets of diodes and the 90 amp and 120 amp alternators are equipped with 4 sets.

OVERHAUL

Disassembly

1. Remove the B+ insulator nut and insulator. Remove the rear cover nuts and cover.
2. Remove the brush holder screws and the brush holder.
3. Remove the field block screws and the block.
4. Remove the rectifier and stator terminal screws and the rectifier.
5. Remove the stator terminal rubber insulators and the end shield through stud nuts.
6. With the drive pulley facing downward, tap rectifier end shield upward and separate the 2 end shields.
7. Remove the drive pulley nut and the drive pulley.

NOTE: **Do not handle the slip rings of the rotor with the bare hands for oil or grease may restrict contact.**

8. Pull the rotor assembly from the drive end shield.
9. Using a wheel puller, press the rectifier end shield bearing from the rotor shaft.

NOTE: **When removing the bearing, be careful not to damage the slip rings.**

10. From the drive end shield, remove the bearing retainer screws and the retainer.
11. Using a socket and a light hammer, place the drive end shield on a work surface and tap the bearing from the shield.

Inspection

BRUSH HOLDER TESTS

1. Make sure the brushes move smoothly and return fully to

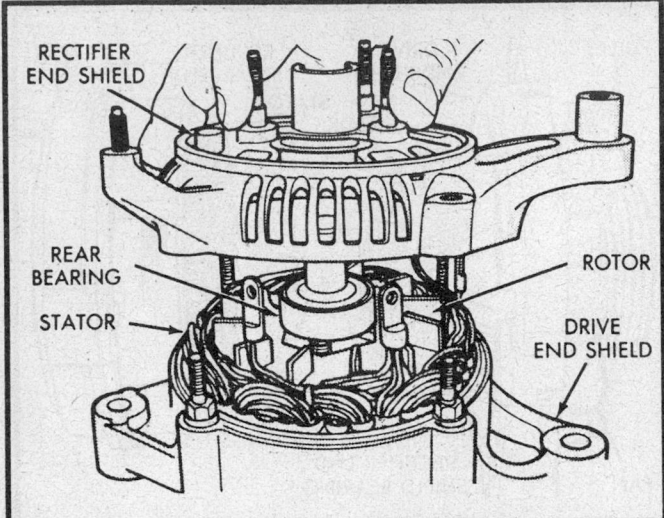

Separating the end shields—Nippondenso 75, 90 and 120 amp alternators

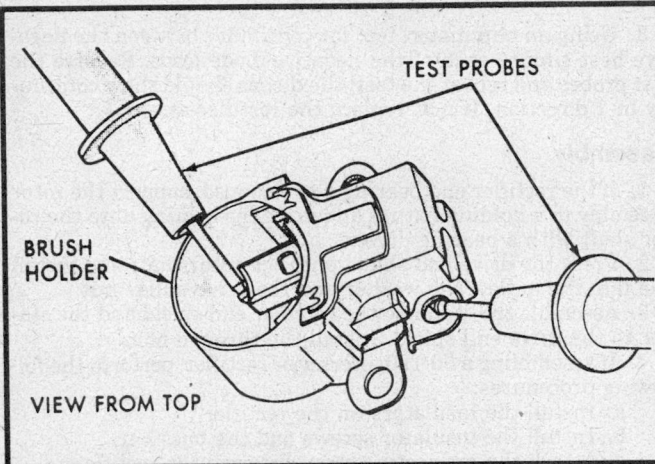

Testing the inner brush continuity—Nippondenso 75, 90 and 120 amp alternators

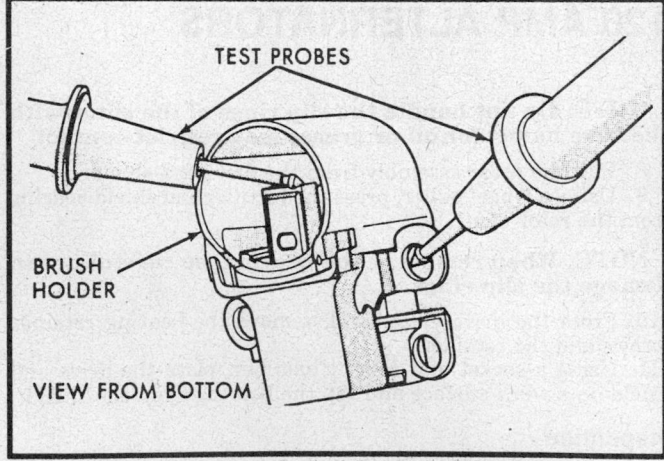

Testing the outer brush continuity—Nippondenso 75, 90 and 120 amp alternators

the stops when released; if not, replace the brush holder assembly.

2. Using an ohmmeter, test inner brush-to-field terminals continuity; 1 field terminal should be open and the other closed. If not, replace the brush holder.

3. Using an ohmmeter, test outer brush-to-field terminals continuity; a field terminal should be open and the other closed. If not, replace the brush holder.

FIELD BLOCK TESTS

1. Using an ohmmeter, test the outer brush terminal to R-3 field terminal for continuity; the circuit should be closed. If not, replace the field block.

2. Using an ohmmeter, test the inner brush terminal to J-2 field terminal for continuity; the circuit should be closed. If not, replace the field block.

3. Using an ohmmeter, test the R-3 field terminal to the J-2 terminal for continuity; the circuit should be open. If not, replace the field block.

4. Turn the field block over. Using an ohmmeter, test the radio supression capacitor terminals for continuity; the circuit should be open. If not, replace the field block.

ROTOR TESTS

1. Check the field slip rings for excessive wear or roughness; fine emery cloth may be used to repair minor damage. If the rings are excessively damaged, replace the rotor.

2. Using an ohmmeter, test for continuity between the slip rings; the circuit should be closed. If not, replace the rotor.

3. Using an ohmmeter, test for continuity between the slip rings and the rotor shaft or core; the circuit should be open. If not, replace the rotor.

STATOR TESTS

1. Check the stator for signs damage—weak or broken leads, distorted frame or burned windings; if necessary, replace the stator.

NOTE: Using a scraping device, clean a portion of the stator frame to assure good electrical contact.

2. Using an ohmmeter, test for continuity between the stator leads and frame; the circuit should be open. If not, replace the stator.

3. Using an ohmmeter, test for continuity between the stator leads; the circuit should be closed. If not, replace the stator.

RECTIFIER TESTS

1. Inspect the rectifier assembly for poor solder joints, cracks, loose terminals or signs of overheating.

2. At each diode location, scrape a small area of the coating to assure good electrical contact while testing.

NOTE: Using an analog ohmmeter or a Digital Volt Ohmmeter (DVOM), perform the following tests.

3. Position the negative test probe on the stator terminal and the positive test probe on a negative diode; the resistance should be 7–11 ohms or 0.4–0.6 volts. Position the positive test probe on a positive diode; there should be no continuity. Perform this procedure on each terminal to diode set. If failure is detected, replace the rectifier.

4. Position the positive test probe on the stator terminal and the negative test probe on a positive diode; the resistance should be 7–11 ohms or 0.4–0.6 volts. Position the negative test probe on a negative diode; there should be no continuity. Perform this procedure on each terminal to diode set. If failure is detected, replace the rectifier.

Assembly

1. Using a socket, slightly smaller than the bearing, tap the bearing into the drive end shield.

2. Install the bearing retainer in the drive end shield.

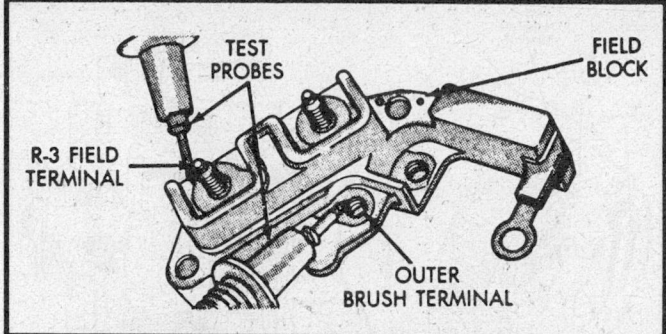

Testing the field block R-3 terminal—Nippondenso 75, 90 and 120 amp alternators

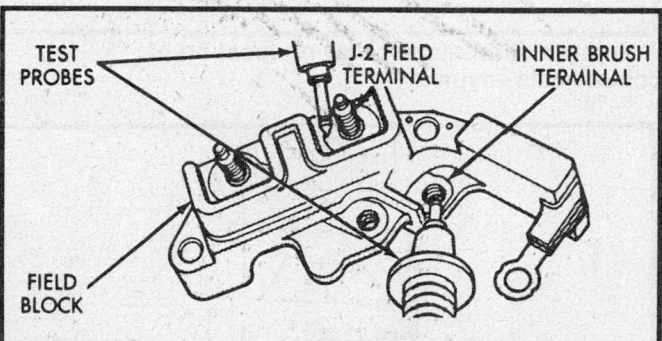

Testing the field block J-2 terminal—Nippondenso 75, 90 and 120 amp alternators

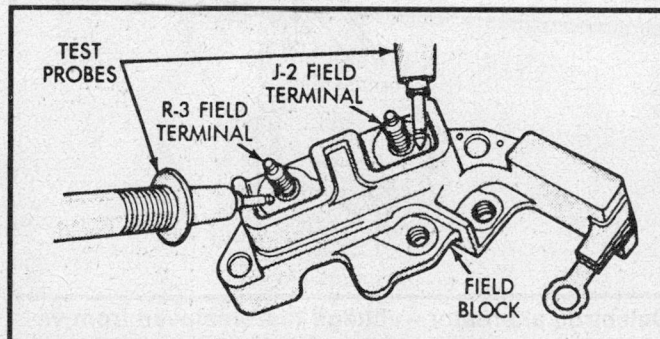

Testing the field block R-3 to J-2 terminals—Nippondenso 75, 90 and 120 amp alternators

3. Using a shop press, press the rectifier end shield bearing onto the rotor shaft.

NOTE: When installing the bearing, be careful not to damage the slip rings.

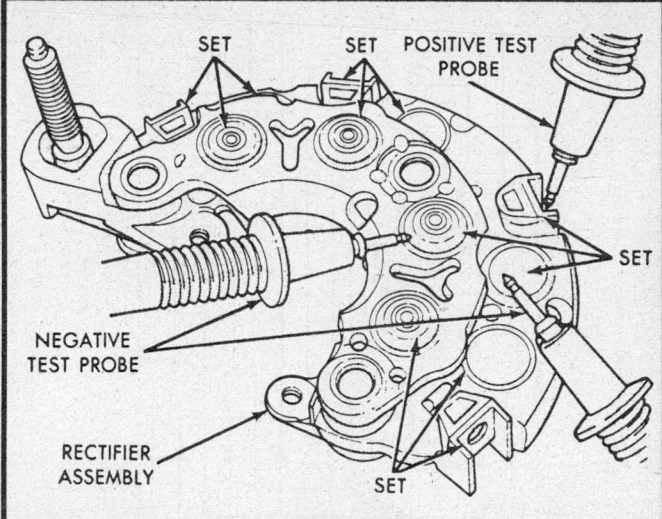

Testing the diodes—Nippondenso 75, 90 and 120 amp alternators

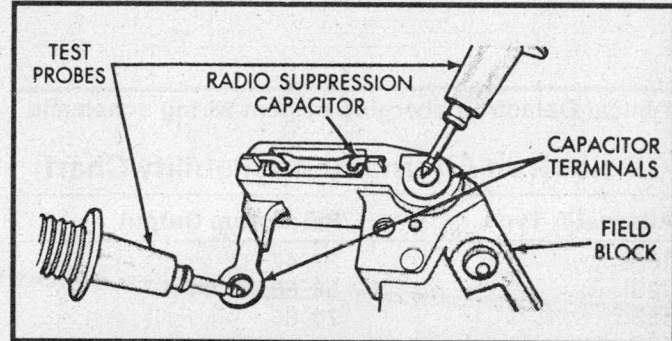

Testing the field block radio capacitor—Nippondenso 75, 90 and 120 amp alternators

4. Install the rotor assembly into the drive end shield.
5. Install the drive pulley and nut.
6. Using solvent, clean the slip rings on the rotor shaft.
7. Align the rectifier end shield and assemble it to the drive end shield.
8. Install the through stud nuts and the stator terminal insulators.
9. Position the rectifier and install the screws.
10. Position the field block and install the screws.
11. Retract the brushes into the brush holder, slide the assembly over the commutator rings and install the screws.
12. Install the rear cover and nuts.
13. Align the B+ insulator guide boss into the rear cover hole and install the nut.

GM SI ALTERNATORS

Delcotron alternators are available with different idle outputs and rated amp outputs.

All alternators incorporate a solid state voltage regulator which is mounted inside the alternator. The construction and operation of each alternator is basically the same. The Delcotron alternator consists of a forward and rear end frame assembly, a rotor, a stator, brushes, slip-rings and diodes. The rotor is supported in the drive end frame by ball bearings and in the slip-ring end frame by roller bearings. The bearings do not require periodic lubrication.

There are 2 brushes which carry current through the slip-rings to the field coil. The field coil is mounted on the rotor. The stator windings are assembled on the inside of a laminated core that is part of the alternator frame. The rectifier bridge which is connected to the stator windings contains 6 diodes, 3 of which are negative and 3 of which are positive. The positive and nega-

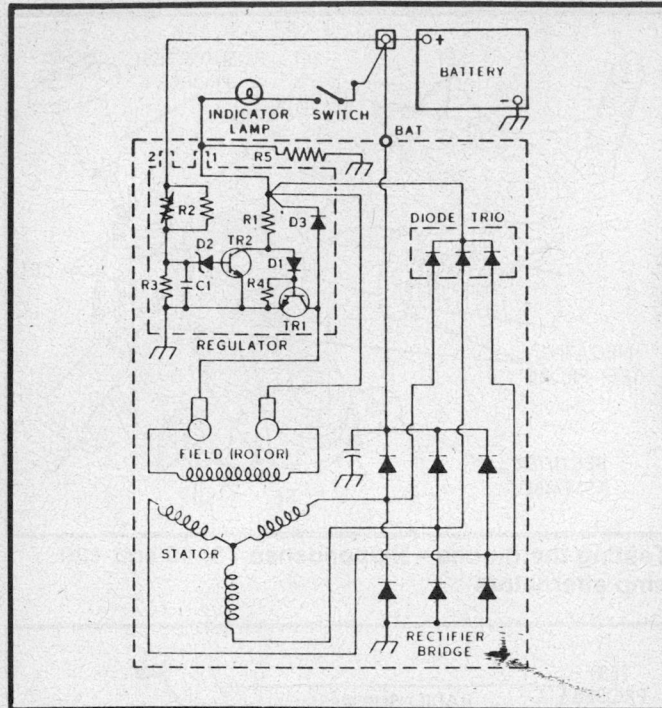

Typical Delcotron charging system wiring schematic

Delcotron Alternator Availability Chart

Alternator Type	Rated Amp Output
10SI	37, 42, 63
12SI	56, 66, 78, 94
15SI	70, 85
17SI	—
27SI	65, 80, 100

tive diodes are moulded into the assembly. The rectifier bridge changes stator AC voltage into DC voltage which appears at the output BAT terminal.

The blocking action of the diodes prevents the battery from discharging, back through the alternator. The need for a cutout relay is eliminated because of this blocking action. The alternator field current is supplied through a diode trio, which is connected to the stator windings. A capacitor is mounted in the end frame to protect the rectifier bridge and the 6 diodes from high voltage and radio interference. Periodic alternator adjustment or maintenance is not required. The voltage regulator is preset and needs no adjustment.

System Diagnosis

ON VEHICLE SERVICE

Indicator Lamp Operation Test

1. Check the indicator lamp for normal operation. If the indicator lamp operates properly, refer to the undercharged battery test. If the indicator lamp does not operate properly, proceed accordingly.

2. Switch **OFF**, lamp **ON**. Unplug the connector from the generator No. 1 and No. 2 terminals. If the lamp stays **ON**, there is a short between these 2 leads. If the lamp goes out, replace the rectifier bridge.

3. Switch **ON**, lamp **OFF**, engine stopped. This condition can

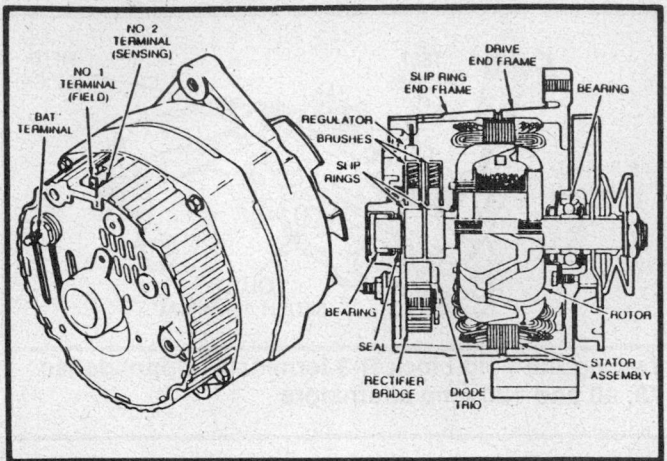

Delcotron alternator — showing location of components — typical

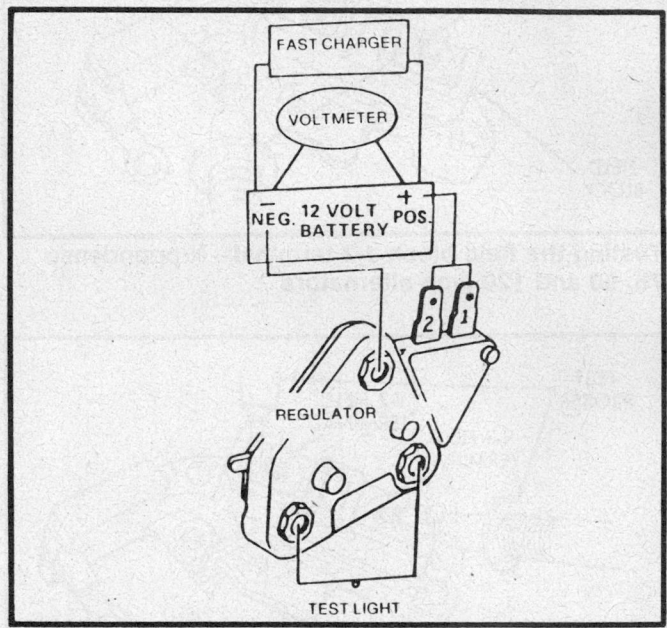

Delcotron alternator — voltage test (removed from vehicle) follow outlined test procedures

be caused by the defects listed above or by an open in the circuit. To determine where an open exists proceed as follows. Check for a blown fuse, or fusible link, a burned out bulb, defective bulb socket, or an open in No. 1 lead circuit between generator and ignition switch. If no defects have been found, proceed to undercharged battery test.

4. Switch **ON**, lamp **ON**, engine running. Check for a blown fuse, (where used), between indicator lamp and switch and also

Undercharged Battery Test

1. Be sure that the undercharged battery condition has not been caused by accessories that have been left **ON** for an extended period of time.

2. Check the alternator belt for proper belt tension. Inspect the battery for physical defects replace as required.

3. Inspect the wiring for defects. Check all connections for proper contact and cleanliness, including the slip connectors at the generator and baulkhead connections.

4. With ignition switch **ON** and all wiring harness leads connected, connect a voltmeter from the generator BAT terminal to

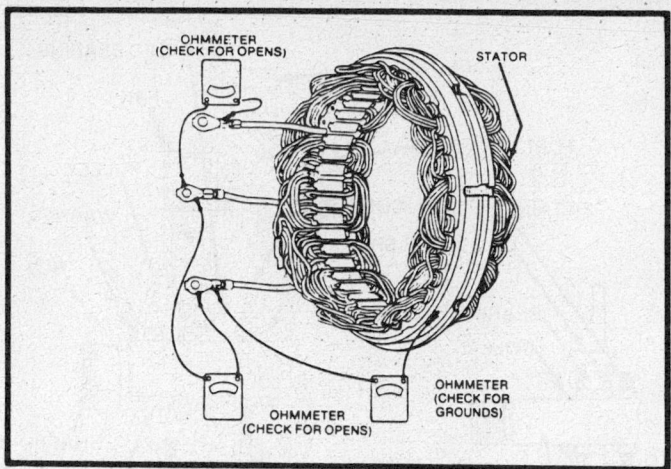

Testing Delcotron alternator stator — use an ohmmeter to check for opens or grounds

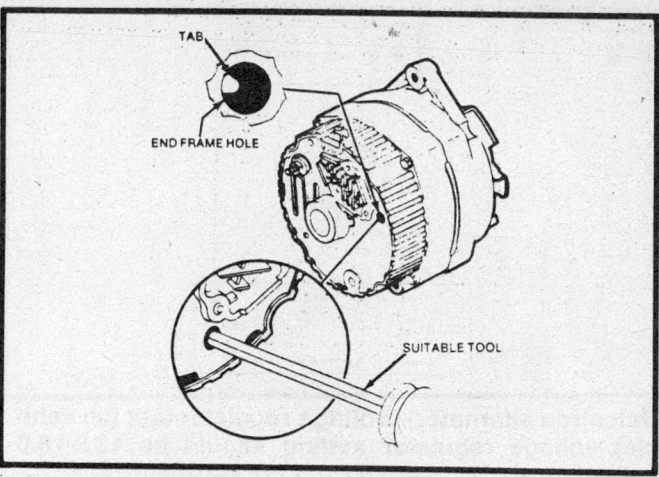

Delcotron alternator — if test hole is accessible, ground the field winding by inserting a suitable tool into the test hole (max of 1 in.)

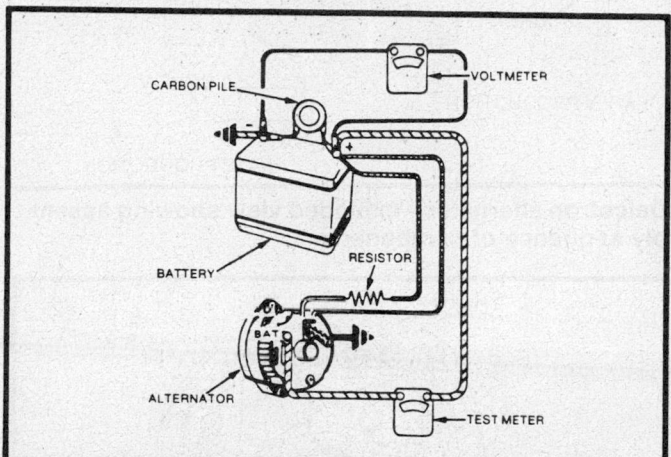

Bench test hook-up for testing the delcotron alternator

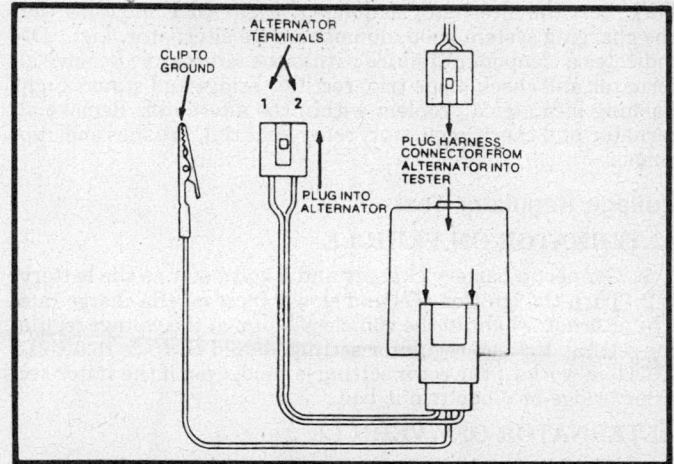

Delcotron alternator diagnostic tester (J-26290) use tester according to maufacturers instructions

ground, from the generator No. 1 terminal to ground and from the generator No. 2 terminal to ground. A zero reading indicates an open circuit between voltmeter connection and battery.

5. Delcotron alternators have a built in feature, which prevents overcharge and accessory damage by preventing the alternator from turning on if there is an open circuit in the wiring harness connected to the No. 2 alternator terminal.

6. If Steps 1–5 check out okay, check the alternator as follows. Disconnect negative battery cable. Connect an ammeter or alternator tester in the circuit at the BAT terminal of the alternator. Reconnect negative battery cable.

7. Turn **ON** radio, windshield wipers, lights high beam and blower motor on high speed. Connect a carbon pile across the battery (or use alternator tester). Operate engine about 2000 rpm and adjust carbon pile as required, to obtain maximum current output. If ampere output is within 10 amperes of rated output as stamped on generator frame, alternator is not defective. Recheck Steps 1–5.

8. If ampere output is not within 10 percent of rated output, determine if test hole is accessible. Ground the field winding by inserting a suitable tool into the test hole. Tab is within ¾ in. of casting surface. Do not force suitable tool deeper than 1 in. into end frame to avoid damaging alternator.

9. Operate engine at moderate speed as required and adjust carbon pile as required to obtain maximum current output.

10. If output is within 10 amperes of rated output, check field winding, diode trio and rectifier bridge. Test regulator with an approved regulator tester.

11. If output is not within 10 amperes of rated output, check the field winding, diode trio, rectifier bridge and stator. If test hole is not accessible, disassemble alternator and repair as required.

Overcharged Battery Test

1. Check the condition of the battery before any testing is done.

2. If an obvious overcharging condition exists, remove the alternator from the vehicle and check the field windings for grounds or shorts. If defective, replace the rotor. Test the regulator.

Alternator Diagnostic Tester (J-26290)

This special diagnostic tester is designed to determine if the alternator should be removed from the vehicle.

1. Install tester J-26290 according to manufacturers instructions.

2. With the engine **OFF** and all lights and accessories **OFF**, test the alternator as follows. Light flashes, go to Step 3. Light **ON**, indicates fault in tester which should be replaced. Light **OFF**, pull plug from generator. One flashing light, indicates that the alternator should be removed and the rectifier bridge replaced. Light **OFF**, indicates faulty tester or no voltage to tester. Check for 12 volts at No. 2 terminal of harness connec-

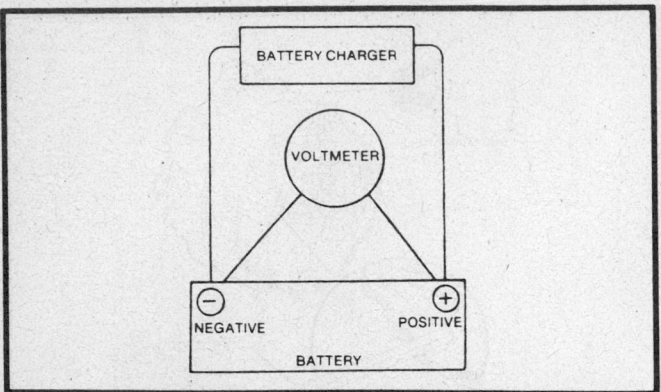

Delcotron alternator – voltage regulator test (on vehicle) voltage regulator setting should be 13.5-16.0 volts

tor. Repair wiring or terminals if 12 volts is not available. Replace tester if 12 volts is available.

3. With the engine at fast idle and all accessories and lights **OFF**, test the alternator as follows. Light **OFF** indicates that the charging system good, do not remove alternator. Light **ON** indicates a component failure within the alternator. Remove alternator and check diode trio, rectifier bridge and stator. Light flashing indicates a problem within the alternator. Remove alternator and check regulator, rotor field coil, brushes and sliprings.

Voltage Regulator Test

ALTERNATOR ON VEHICLE

1. Connect a battery charger and a voltmeter to the battery.
2. Turn the ignition **ON** and slowly increase the charge rate. The alternator light in the vehicle will dim at the voltage regulator setting. Voltage regulator setting should be 13.5–16.0 volts. This test works if the rotor setting is good, even if the stator rectifier bridge or diode trio is bad.

ALTERNATOR OFF VEHICLE

1. Remove the alternator from the vehicle.
2. Disassemble the alternator and remove the voltage regualtor.
3. Connect a voltmeter and a fast charger to a 12 volt battery. Connect a test light to the regulator and observe the battery polarity.
4. The test light should light.
5. Turn **ON** the fast charger and slowly increase the charge rate. Observe the voltmeter, the light should go out at the voltage regualtor setting. The voltage regulator setting specification

OVERHAUL

Alternator Bench Test

1. Remove the alternator from the vehicle. Position the unit in a suitable test stand.
2. Connect the alternator in series, but leave the carbon pile disconnected.

NOTE: Ground polarity of the battery must be the same as the alternator. Be sure to use a fully charged battery and a 10 ohm resistor rated at 6 watts or more between the alternator No. 1 terminal and the battery.

3. Increase the alternator speed slowly and observe the voltage.
4. If the voltage is uncontrolled with speed and increases above 15.5 volts on a 12 volt system, or 31 volts on a 24 volt system, test regulator with an approved regulator tester and check

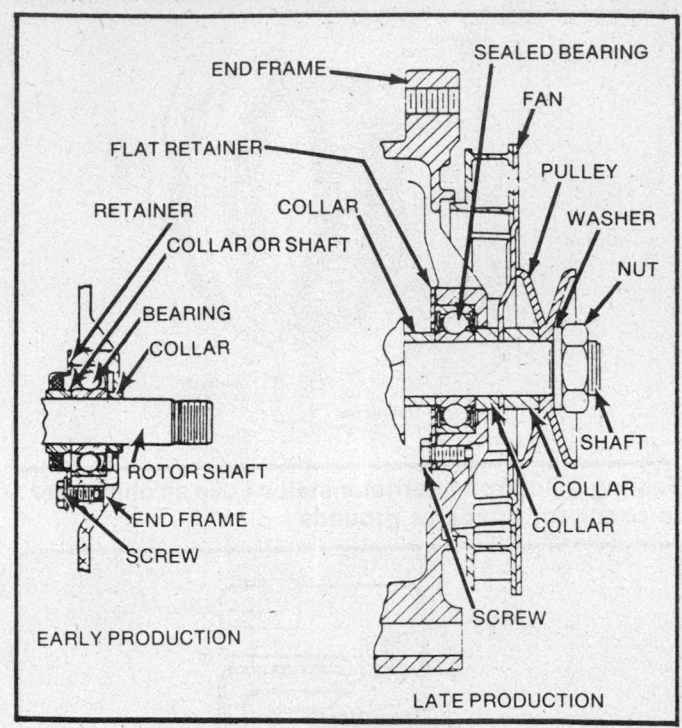

Delcotron alternator – exploded view showing assembly sequence of components

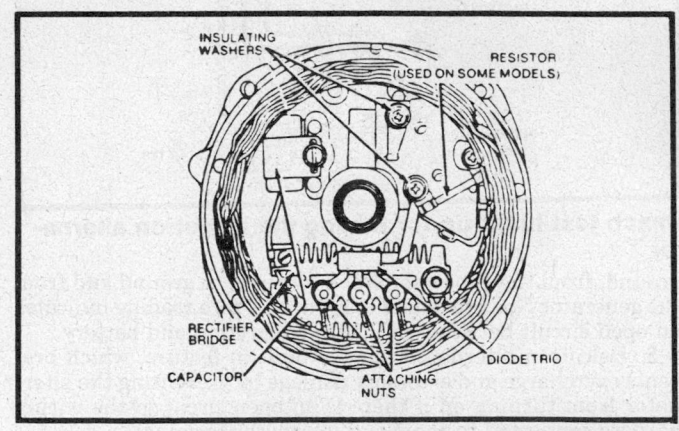

Delcotron alternator end frame – showing location of related components

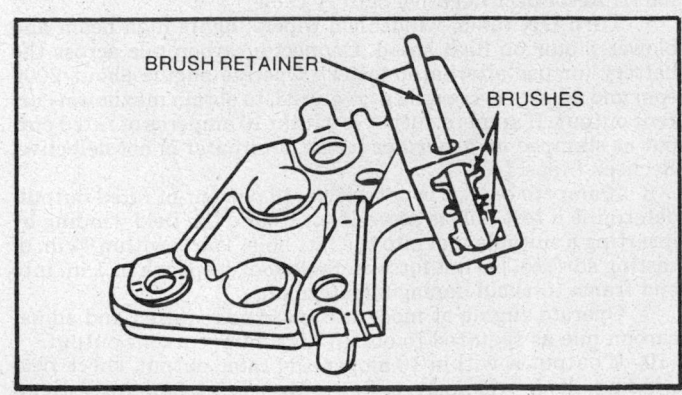

Delcotron alternator brush installation

field winding. If voltage is below 15.5 volts on a 12 volt system, or 31 volts on a 24 volt system, connect the carbon pile.

5. Operate the alternator at moderate speed as required and adjust the carbon pile as required to obtain maximum current output.

6. If output is within 10 amperes of rated output as stamped on alternator frame, alternator is good. If output is not within 10 amperes of rated output, keep battery loaded with carbon pile and ground alternator field.

7. Operate alternator at moderate speed and adjust carbon pile as required to obtain maximum output. If output is within 10 amperes of rated output, test regulator with an approved regulator tester and check field winding.

8. If output is not within 10 amperes of rated output, check the field winding, diode trio, rectifier bridge and stator.

Disassembly

1. Remove the alternator from the vehicle. Position the assembly in a suitable holding fixture.

2. Make scribe marks on the alternator case end frames to aid in reassembly.

3. Remove the through bolts that retain the assembly together. Separate the drive end frame assembly from the rectifier end frame assembly.

4. Remove the rectifier attaching nuts and the regulator attaching screws from the end frame assembly.

5. Separate the stator, diode trio and voltage regulator from the end frame assembly.

6. On the 10SI alternator, check the stator for opens using an ohmmeter. If high readings are obtained, replace the stator.

7. Check the stator for grounds using an ohmmeter. If readings are low, replace the stator.

8. Using an ohmmeter check the rotor for grounds. The ohmmeter reading should be very high. If not, replace the rotor.

9. Using an ohmmeter, check the rotor for opens. If the ohmmeter reading is not 2.4–3.5 ohms replace the rotor.

10. To check the diode trio connect the ohmmeter to the diode trio and then reverse the lead connections. The ohmmeter should read high and low if not replace the diode trio. Repeat the same test between the single connector and each of the other connectors.

11. Check rectifier bridge with ohmmeter connected from grounded heat sink to flat metal on terminal. Reverse leads. If both readings are the same replace rectifier bridge.

12. Repeat test between grounded heat sink and other 2 flat metal clips.

13. Repeat test between insulated heat sink and 3 flat metal clips.

14. Clean or replace the alternator brushes as required. Position the brushes in the brush holder and retain them in place using the brush retainer wire or equivalent.

15. To remove the rotor and drive end bearing, remove the shaft nut, washer and pulley, fan and collar. Push the rotor from the housing.

16. Remove the retainer plate from inside the drive end frame. Push the bearing out. Clean or replace parts as required.

Assembly

1. Press against the outer bearing race to push the bearing in. On early production alternators it will be necessary to fill the bearing cavity with lubricant. Late production alternators use a sealed bearing and lubricant is not required for assembly.

2. Press rotor into end frame. Assemble collar, fan, pulley, washer and nut. Torque shaft nut 40–60 ft. lbs.

3. Push slip-ring end bearing out from outside toward inside of end frame.

4. On 10SI and 15SI, place flat plate over new bearing and press from outside toward inside until bearing is flush with end frame.

5. On 15SI alternators use the thin wall tube in the space be-

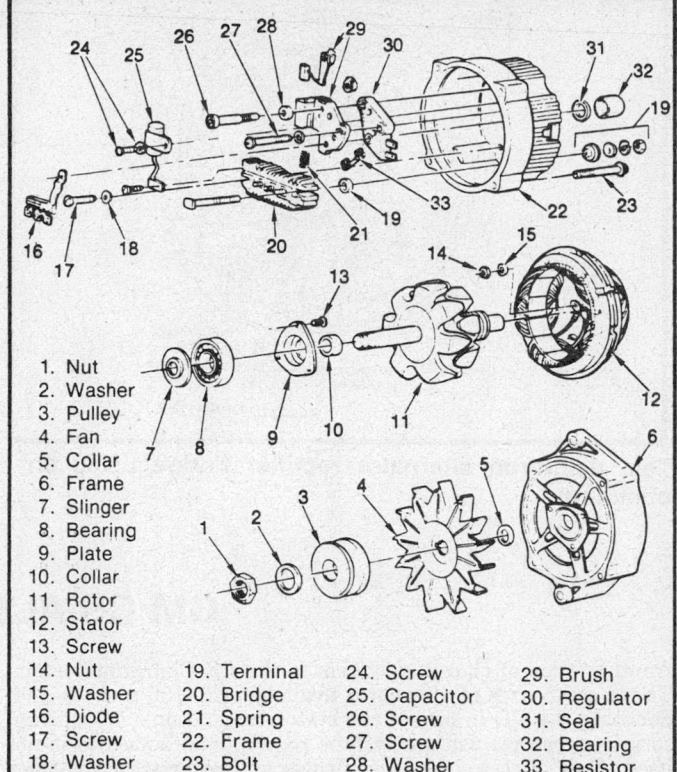

1. Nut
2. Washer
3. Pulley
4. Fan
5. Collar
6. Frame
7. Slinger
8. Bearing
9. Plate
10. Collar
11. Rotor
12. Stator
13. Screw
14. Nut
15. Washer
16. Diode
17. Screw
18. Washer
19. Terminal
20. Bridge
21. Spring
22. Frame
23. Bolt
24. Screw
25. Capacitor
26. Screw
27. Screw
28. Washer
29. Brush
30. Regulator
31. Seal
32. Bearing
33. Resistor

Delcotron alternator drive end bearing and related components

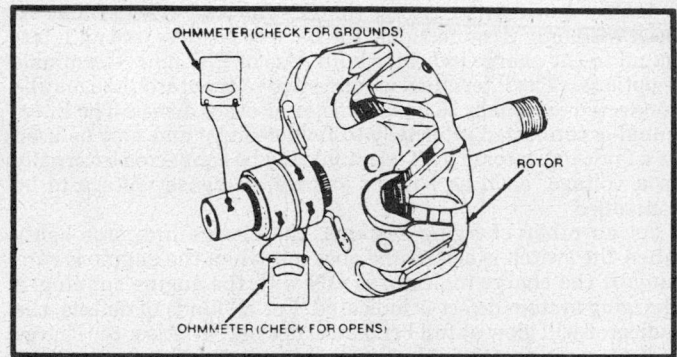

Delcotron alternator—rotor test use an ohmmeter to check for opens or grounds

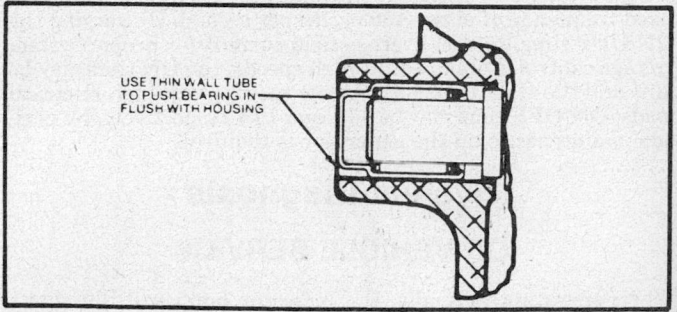

Delcotron 155 alternator rectifier end bearing installation

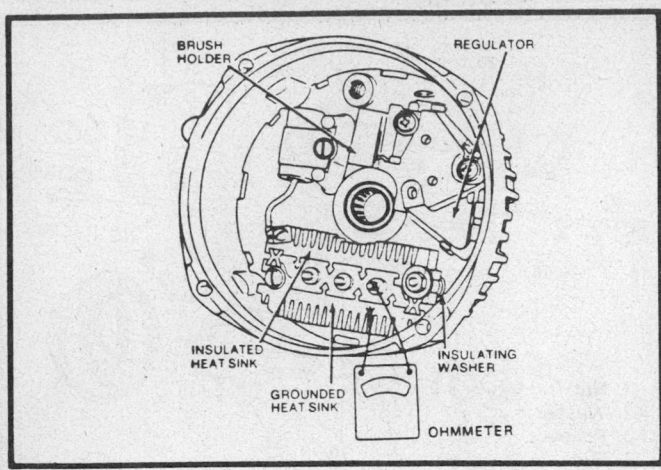

Test delcotron alternator rectifier bridge using an ohmmeter

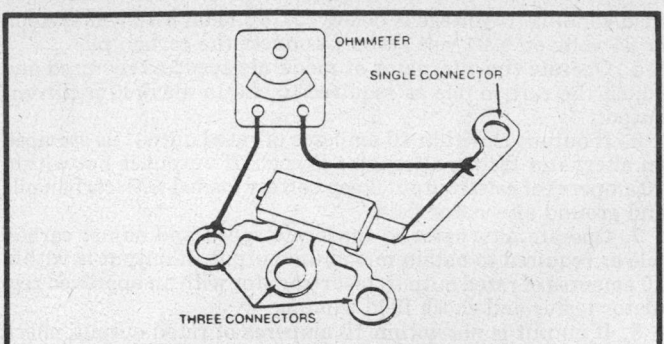

Testing delcotron alternator diode trio using an ohmmeter

tween the grease cup and the housing to push the bearing in flush with the housing.

6. Assemble brush holder, regulator, resistor, diode trio, rectifier bridge and stator to slip-ring end frame.

7. Assemble end frames together with through bolts. Remove brush retainer wire.

GM CS ALTERNATORS

Another type of charging system is the CS Charging System. There are 2 sizes of alternator available, CS-130 and CS-144, denoting the OD in mm of the stator laminations. CS alternators (generators) use a new type regulator a diode trio is not used. A delta stator, rectifier bridge and rotor with slip-rings and brushes are electrically similar to earlier alternators (generators). A regular pulley and fan is used and, on the CS-130, an internal fan cools the slip-ring end frame, rectifier bridge and regulator.

Unlike 3 wire alternators, the CS-130 and CS-144 may be used with only 2 connections, the battery positive and an L terminal to the charge indicator bulb. Use of P, F and S terminals is optional. The P terminal is connected to the stator and may be connected externally to a tachometer or other device. The F terminal is connected internally to field positive and may be used as a fault indicator. The S terminal may be connected externally to a voltage, such as battery voltage, to sense voltage to be controlled.

As on other charging systems, the charge indicator lights when the switch is closed and goes out when the engine is running. If the charge indicator is **ON** with the engine running, a charging system defect is indicated. For all kinds of defects, the indicator will glow at full brilliance, not half lit. Also, the charge indicator will be **ON** with the engine running if system voltage is too high or too low. The regulator voltage setting varies with temperature and limits system voltage by controlling rotor field current.

This regulator switches rotor field current **ON** and **OFF** at a fixed frequency of about 400 cycles per second. By varying the **ON/OFF** time, correct average field current for proper system voltage control is obtained. At high speeds, the **ON** time may be 10% and the **OFF** time 90%. At low speeds, with high electrical loads, **ON/OFF** time may be 90% and 10% respectively. No periodic maintenance on the generator is required.

System Diagnosis

ON VEHICLE SERVICE

When operating normally, the indicator lamp will illuminate when the ignition switch is turned **ON** and go out when the engine starts. If the lamp operates abnormally, or if an undercharged or overcharged battery condition occurs, the following

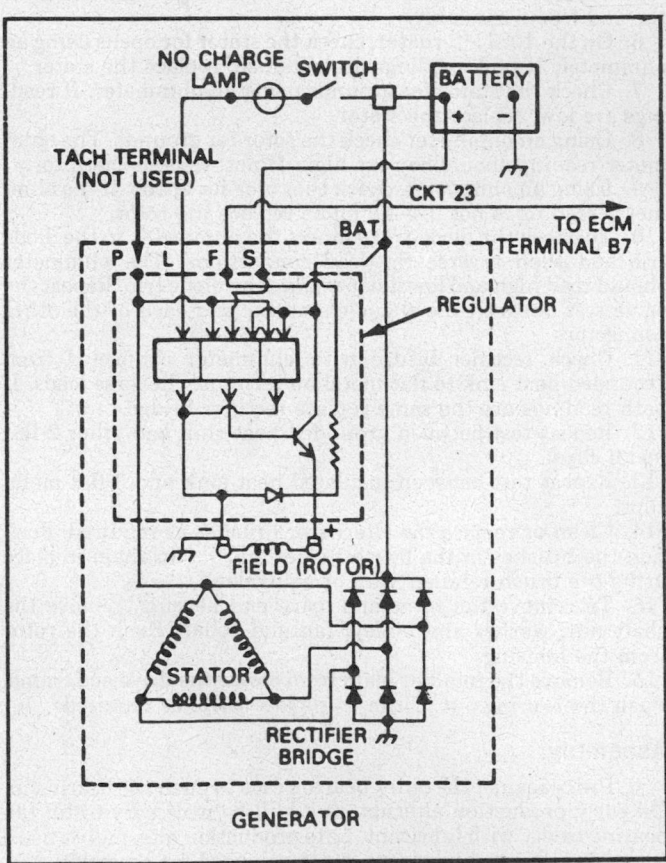

Delcotron—CS series charging system

procedure may be used to diagnose the charging system.

To diagnose the CS-130 and CS-144 charging systems, use the following procedure.

1. Visually check the belt and wiring.

2. For vehicles without charge indicator lamp, go to Step 5.

3. With switch **ON**, engine stopped, lamp should illuminate. If not, detach harness at generator and ground L terminal. If

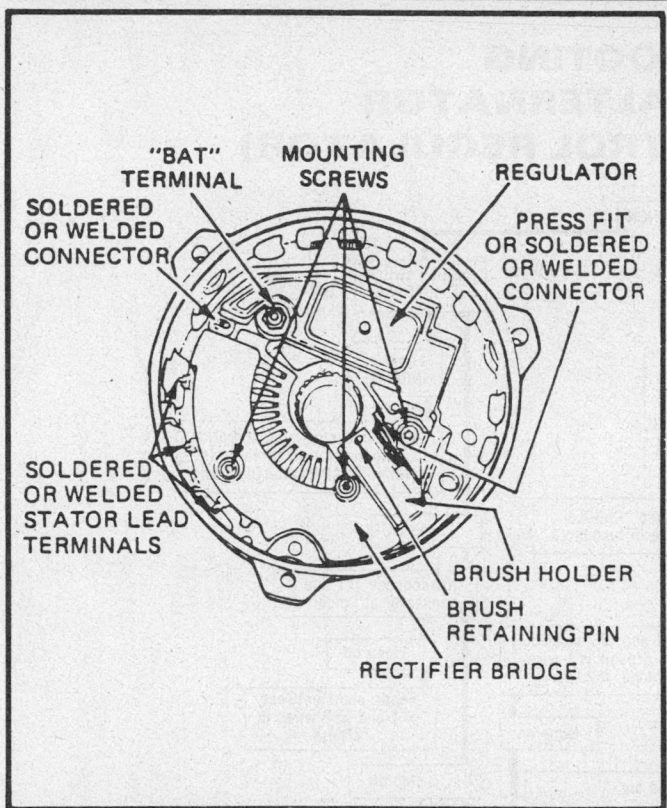

CS130 alternator component location

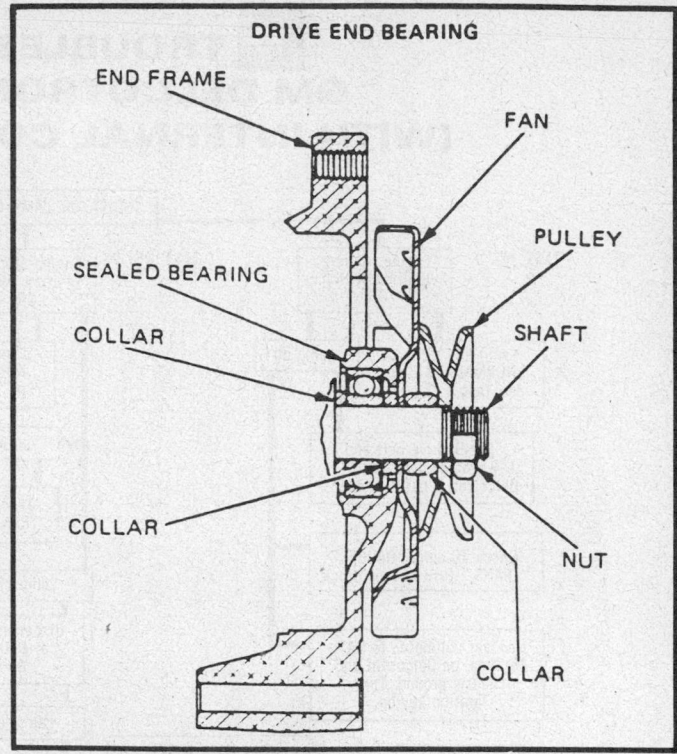

Delcotron CS130 alternator drive end bearing assembly

the lamp lights, repair or replace the generator. If the lamp does not light locate open circuit between grounding lead and ignition switch. Lamp may be open.

4. With switch **ON**, engine running at moderate speed, lamp should illuminate. If not, detach wiring harness at generator. If the lamp goes off, replace or repair generator. If the lamp stays on, check for grounded L terminal wire in harness.

5. Battery undercharged or overcharged. Detach wiring harness connector from generator. With switch **ON**, engine not running, connect voltmeter from ground to L terminal. Zero reading indicates open circuit between terminal and battery. Correct as required. Reconnect harness connector to generator, run engine at moderate speed. Measure voltage across battery. If above 16 V, replace or repair generator.

6. Turn **ON** accessories, load battery with carbon pile to obtain maximum amperage. Maintain voltage at 13 V or above. If within 15 amperes of rated output, generator is fine. If not within 15 amperes of rated output, repair or replace the generator.

OVERHAUL

Alternator Bench Test

1. Make the proper connections but leave the carbon pile disconnected. The ground polarity of generator and battery must be the same. The battery must be fully charged. Use a 30–500 ohm resistor between battery and L terminal.

2. Slowly increase generator speed and observe voltage.

3. If the voltage is uncontrolled and increases above 16.0 volts, the rotor field is shorted, the regulator is defective or both. A shorted rotor field coil can cause the regulator to become defective. The battery must be fully charged when making this test.

4. If voltage is below 16.0 volts, increase speed and adjust carbon pile to obtain maximum amperage output. Maintain voltage above 13.0 volts.

5. If output is within 15 amperes of rated output, generator is good.

6. If output is not within 15 amperes of rated output, generator is faulty and requires repair or replacement.

Disassembly and Assembly

The alternator is serviced as an assembly only.

CS-144

1. Remove the alternator from the vehicle. Scribe marks on the end frames to facilitate assembly.

2. Remove the through bolts and separate the end frames.

3. Check the rotor for grounds using an ohmmeter. The reading should be infinite, if not, replace the rotor.

4. Check the rotor for shorts and opens. Replace the rotor as required.

5. Remove the attaching nuts and the stator from the end frame.

6. Check the stator for grounds using an ohmmeter. If the reading is low replace the stator.

7. Unsolder the connections, remove the retaining screws and connector from the end frame. Separate the regulator and the brush holder from the end frame.

8. Check the rectifier bridge using an ohmmeter. Replace as required. Check the heat sink, using an ohmmeter. Replace as required. Clean the brushes. Replace them as required.

9. To remove the rotor and drive end bearing, Hold the rotor using a hex wrench in the shaft end while removing the nut. Push the rotor from the housing. Remove the plate and push the bearing out.

10. Assembly is the reverse of the disassembly procedure. Repair or replace defective components as required.

CS-130

1. Remove the alternator from the vehicle. Scribe marks on the end frames to facilitate assembly. Remove the through bolts and separate the end frames.

TROUBLESHOOTING
GM DELCOTRON ALTERNATOR
(WITH INTERNAL CONTROL REGULATOR)

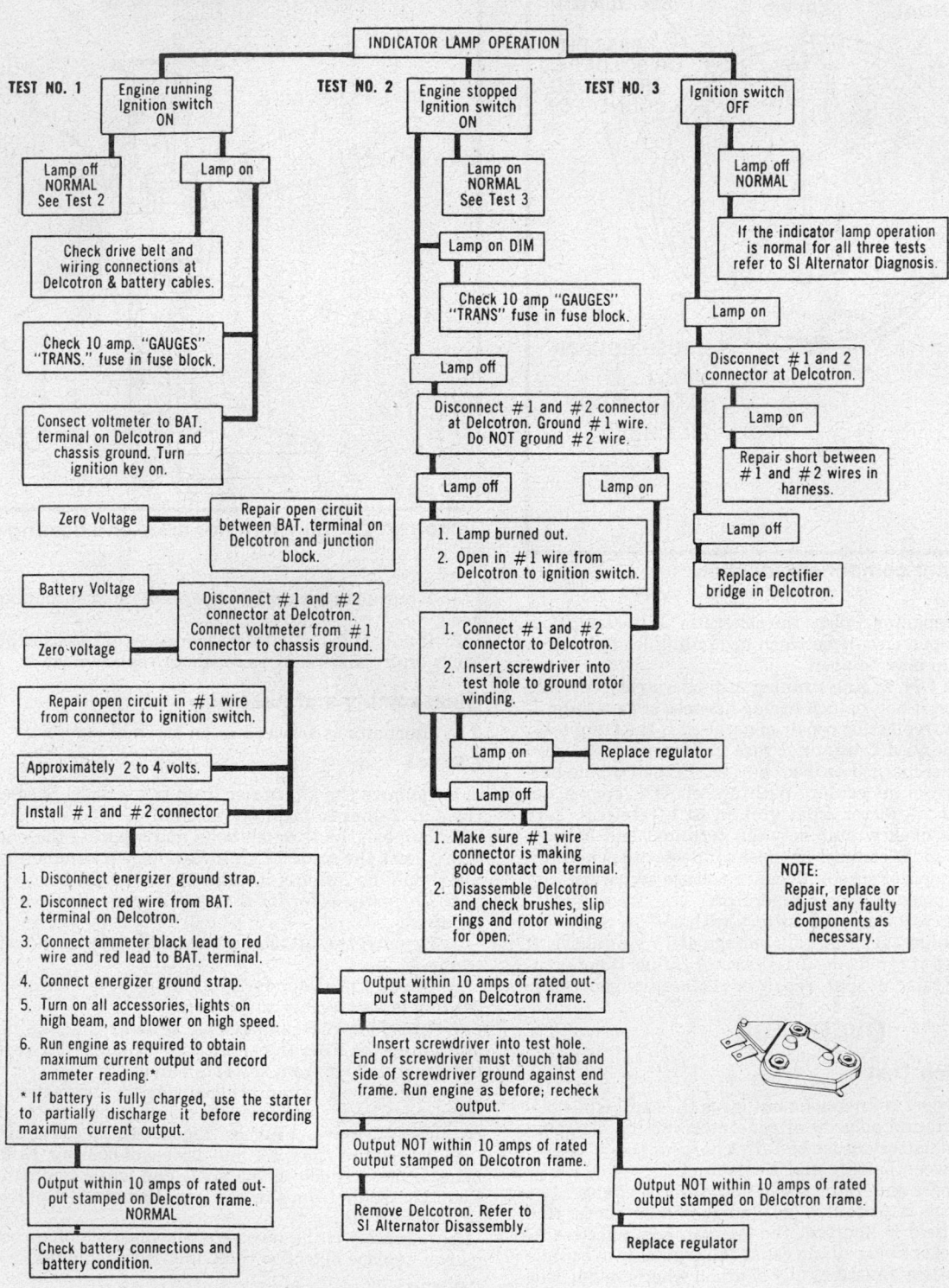

INDICATOR LAMP OPERATION

TEST NO. 1 Engine running Ignition switch ON

TEST NO. 2 Engine stopped Ignition switch ON

TEST NO. 3 Ignition switch OFF

Lamp off NORMAL See Test 2

Lamp on

Lamp on NORMAL See Test 3

Lamp off NORMAL

Check drive belt and wiring connections at Delcotron & battery cables.

Lamp on DIM

If the indicator lamp operation is normal for all three tests refer to SI Alternator Diagnosis.

Check 10 amp. "GAUGES" "TRANS." fuse in fuse block.

Check 10 amp "GAUGES" "TRANS" fuse in fuse block.

Lamp on

Consect voltmeter to BAT. terminal on Delcotron and chassis ground. Turn ignition key on.

Lamp off

Disconnect #1 and 2 connector at Delcotron.

Disconnect #1 and #2 connector at Delcotron. Ground #1 wire. Do NOT ground #2 wire.

Lamp on

Zero Voltage

Repair open circuit between BAT. terminal on Delcotron and junction block.

Lamp off

Lamp on

Repair short between #1 and #2 wires in harness.

Battery Voltage

Disconnect #1 and #2 connector at Delcotron. Connect voltmeter from #1 connector to chassis ground.

1. Lamp burned out.
2. Open in #1 wire from Delcotron to ignition switch.

Lamp off

Zero voltage

Replace rectifier bridge in Delcotron.

Repair open circuit in #1 wire from connector to ignition switch.

1. Connect #1 and #2 connector to Delcotron.
2. Insert screwdriver into test hole to ground rotor winding.

Approximately 2 to 4 volts.

Install #1 and #2 connector

Lamp on

Replace regulator

Lamp off

1. Disconnect energizer ground strap.
2. Disconnect red wire from BAT. terminal on Delcotron.
3. Connect ammeter black lead to red wire and red lead to BAT. terminal.
4. Connect energizer ground strap.
5. Turn on all accessories, lights on high beam, and blower on high speed.
6. Run engine as required to obtain maximum current output and record ammeter reading.*

* If battery is fully charged, use the starter to partially discharge it before recording maximum current output.

1. Make sure #1 wire connector is making good contact on terminal.
2. Disassemble Delcotron and check brushes, slip rings and rotor winding for open.

NOTE:
Repair, replace or adjust any faulty components as necessary.

Output within 10 amps of rated output stamped on Delcotron frame.

Insert screwdriver into test hole. End of screwdriver must touch tab and side of screwdriver ground against end frame. Run engine as before; recheck output.

Output within 10 amps of rated output stamped on Delcotron frame. NORMAL

Output NOT within 10 amps of rated output stamped on Delcotron frame.

Output NOT within 10 amps of rated output stamped on Delcotron frame.

Check battery connections and battery condition.

Remove Delcotron. Refer to SI Alternator Disassembly.

Replace regulator

2. Remove the cover rivets or pins. Remove the cover on the slip-ring end frame.

3. Unsolder the stator leads at the 3 terminals on the rectifier bridge. Avoid excessive heat, as damage to the assembly will occur. Remove the stator.

4. Drive out the 3 baffle pins. Remove the baffle from inside of the slip-ring end frame.

5. Check the rotor for grounds using an ohmmeter. The reading should be infinite, if not, replace the rotor. Check the rotor for shorts and opens, the ohmmeter should read 1.7–2.3 ohms. Replace the rotor as required.

6. Check the stator for grounds using an ohmmeter. If the reading is low replace the stator.

7. Remove the brush holder screw. Disconnect the terminal and remove the brush holder assembly. Check and replace the brushes, as required.

8. Unsolder and pry open the terminal between the regulator and the rectifier bridge. Remove the terminal and the retaining screws. Remove the regulator and the rectifier bridge from the end frame.

9. To check the rectifier bridge, connect the proper (analog reading) ohmmeter, using the low scale, to a terminal and the heat sink, record the reading. Reverse the test leads and record the reading. If both readings are the same replace the rectifier bridge. Check the other diodes in the same manner.

10. To remove the rotor and drive end bearing, Hold the rotor using a hex wrench in the shaft end while removing the nut. Push the rotor from the housing. Remove the plate and push the bearing out.

11. Assembly is the reverse of the disassembly procedure. Repair or replace defective components as required.

GM ALTERNATOR WITH REAR VACUUM PUMP

The Delcotron alternator with rear vacuum pump, manufactured by Mitsubishi, is basically the same as the other Delcotron alternators, with the exception of a rear vacuum pumpo which is mounted on the back of the alternator assembly. The vacuum pump is driven by the alternator shaft and is used to provide vacuum to various control systems throughtout the vehicle.

Disassembly and Assembly

1. Remove the alternator from the vehicle. Position the unit in a suitable holding fixture.

2. Remove the vacuum pump retaining bolts. Remove the vacuum pump from the rear of the alternator while holding the center plate.

3. Remove the brush cover retaining bolts and brushes. Wrap the pump drive shaft spline with tape in order to protect the rear seal from damage.

4. Inspect the vacuum pump for wear and damage, replace defective components as required. Measure the length of the vanes, replace if not within specification (0.511–0.531 in.) Measure the inside diameter of the housing and replace if not within specification (2.440–2.441 in.).

5. Examine the check valve for damage. Apply light pressure to the valve and make sure the valve operates properly. Replace as required.

6. Check the inner face of the rear cover on the vacuum pump for oil leakage. Check the inner face of the oil seal for wear and damage. Replace the oil seal in the rear end housing of the vacuum pump as required.

7. Remove the alternator through bolts which hold the unit together. Matchmark the assembly to aid in reassembly. Separate the front end housing from the stator and rear end housing.

8. Remove the pulley nut, fan and front end housing from the rotor.

9. Remove the front bearing retainer screws. Remove the front bearing retainer and the bearing from the front end housing.

10. Remove the bolt and nuts retaining the stator, diodes and brush holder to the rear end housing. Note the position of the insulating washers for reassembly.

11. Separate the rear end housing from the stator and diode assembly.

12. Remove the diodes from the stator by melting the solder from the terminals. Be sure to protect the diodes while melting the solder.

13. Remove the solder from the voltage regulator holder plate terminal. Remove the voltage regulator.

14. Check the slip-ring surfaces of the rotor for wear and damage, repair or replace as required.

15. Measure the outside diameter of the rotor slip-rings. If ring diameter is not 1.18–1.24 in., replace the rotor.

16. Connect the ohmmeter test leads to each slip-ring. Resistance should be 4.2 ohms at 68°F. If continuity does not exist the coil is open and the rotor must be replaced.

17. Connect the ohmmeter to either slip-ring and the rotor core. If continuity exists the coil is grounded and the rotor must be replaced.

18. Check the front and rear rotor bearings for wear and damage. Replace defective parts as required.

19. Check for continuity across the stator coils. If continuity does not exist in any 1 stator coil replace the stator assembly.

20. Check for continuity across any of the stator coils and the stator core. If continuity exists, 1 of the stator coils is grounded and the stator must be replaced.

21. Coil resistance should be 0.05 ohms at 68°F and should be measured from the coil lead to terminal N.

22. Inspect the alternator brush assembly for wear and damage. Replace defective components as required.

23. Check for continuity of positive diodes between each stator coil terminal and the battery terminal of rectifier assembly. Reverse the ohmmeter leads and recheck for continuity.

24. If continuity exists in both polarity directions or does not exist in both directions diode is defective and must be replaced.

25. Check for continuity of negative diodes between each stator lead and E terminal or rectifier assembly. Reverse ohmmeter leads and recheck for continuity. Continuity should exist in 1 direction only.

26. Assemble a test circuit using the following components: One 10 ohm 3 watt resistor (R_1) one 0–300 ohm 3 watt variable resistor (R_2), two 12 volt batteries (BAT_1 and BAT_2) and one 0–30 volt DC voltmeter.

27. Adjust variable resistor (R_2) until voltage at V_4 reads the same as voltage at V_3 (this should be all the way to 1 end of travel or 0 ohms).

28. Connect the test circuit to the integrated circuit regulator terminals. Measure voltage at V_1 and V_2. Voltage should measure 10–13 volts at V_1 and 0–2 volts at V_2.

29. Disconnect terminal S from circuit and measure voltage at V_3. Voltage at V_3 should be 20–26 volts. Reconnect terminal S.

30. Measure voltage at V_4 while increasing resistance at R_2 from 0 ohms. V_4 voltmeter reading should increase from 2 volts to 10–13 volts. Stop increasing R_2 when voltage reaches 10–13 volts.

31. If increase at V_4 is interrupted at any point up to 10–13 volts, while increasing resistance at R_2, regulator is defective.

32. Measure voltage at V_4 with R_2 at same setting as previous step that produced 10–13 volt reading at V_2. If V_4 not within 14–14.6 volts, regulator is defective.

33. Disconnect wire at terminal S. Connect it to terminal B.

Repeat Step 30. If V_2 does not vary or V_4 is not within 14.5–16.6 volts, regulator is defective.

34. To assemble the alternator reverse the disassembly procedure. Be sure to check all parts for wear and damage. Replace defective components as required.

35. Insert the brushes into the brush holder and insert a wire to retain them in place. Install the rotor and remove the retaining wire.

GM ALTERNATOR
METRO, PRIZM, SPRINT, SPECTRUM AND NOVA

The basic charging system is the IC integral regulator charging system. The alternator features a solid state regulator that is located inside the alternator assembly. All regulator components are enclosed in a solid mold and this unit along with the brush holder assembly is attached to the slip-ring end frame.

The alternator rotor bearings contain enough grease to eliminate the need for periodic lubrication. Two brushes carry current through the 2 slip-rings to the field coil that is mounted on the rotor.

The stator windings are assembled on the inside of a laminated core that forms part of the alternator frame. A rectifier bridge is connected to the stator windings and contains 6 diodes and electrically changes the stator AC voltages to DC voltages which appear at the alternator output terminal. The neutral diodes convert the voltage fluctuation at the neutral point to direct current in order to increase the alternator output.

System Diagnosis
ON VEHICLE SERVICE

Charging Circuit Test
WITHOUT LOAD

1. Properly connect an ammeter and a voltmeter to the alternator assembly.

2. Disconnect the wire from terminal B of the alternator. Connect it to the negative terminal of the ammeter. Connect the test lead from the positive terminal of the ammeter to terminal B of the alternator.

3. Connect the positive lead of the voltmeter to terminal B of the alternator. Connect the negative lead of the voltmeter to ground.

4. Check the charging circuit, as follows. Run the engine from idle to 2000 rpm. Check the reading on the test equipment. Amperage should be less than 10A and voltage should be 13.5–15.1 volts.

5. If the voltage reading is greater than specification, replace the IC regulator.

6. If the voltage reading is less than specification check the IC regulator as follows. With terminal F grounded, start the engine and check the voltage reading at terminal B.

7. If the voltage reading is greater than specification, replace the IC regulator.

8. If the voltage reading is less than specification, check the alternator assmbly.

WITH LOAD

1. With the engine running at 2000 rpm turn the headlights **ON** along with the high beams and position the heater switch in the **HI** position.

2. Check the reading on the ammeter, it should be 30A or more. If not within specification, repair the alternator assembly.

NOTE: If the battery is not fully charged, the reading will be less than 30A.

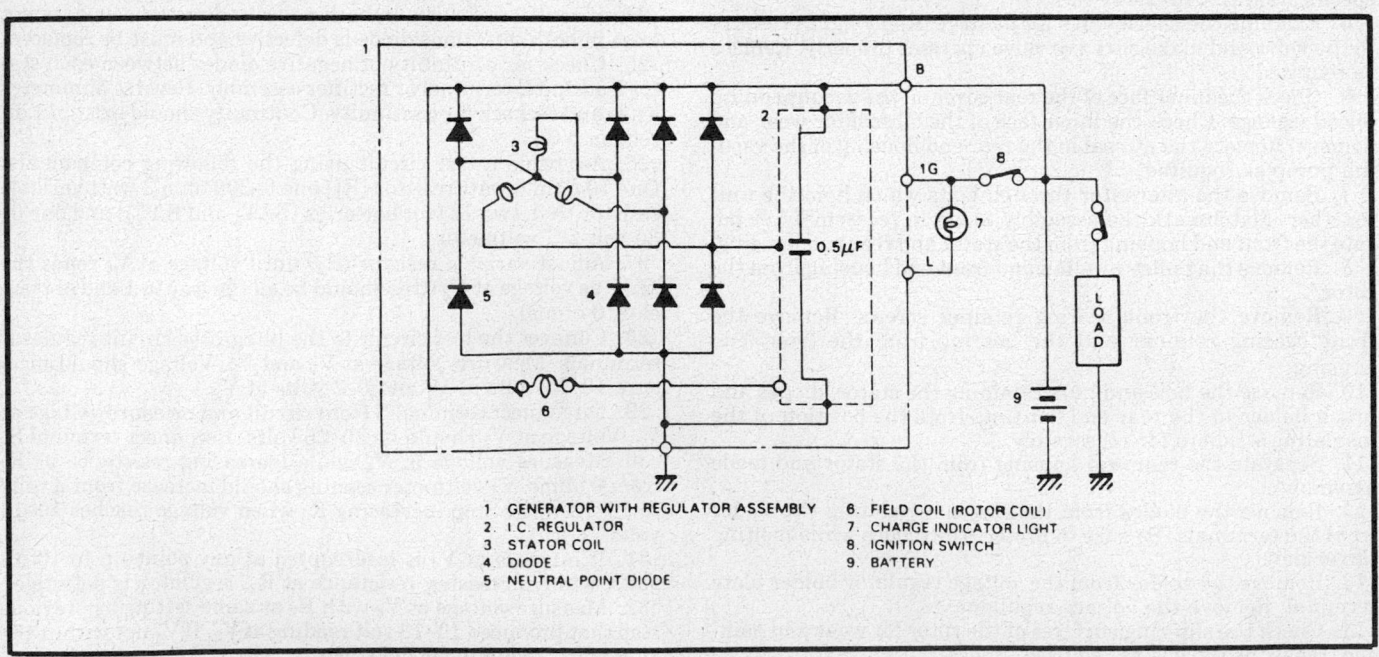

1. GENERATOR WITH REGULATOR ASSEMBLY 6. FIELD COIL (ROTOR COIL)
2. I.C. REGULATOR   7. CHARGE INDICATOR LIGHT
3. STATOR COIL   8. IGNITION SWITCH
4. DIODE   9. BATTERY
5. NEUTRAL POINT DIODE

Schematic of the 1985–88 Sprint alternator

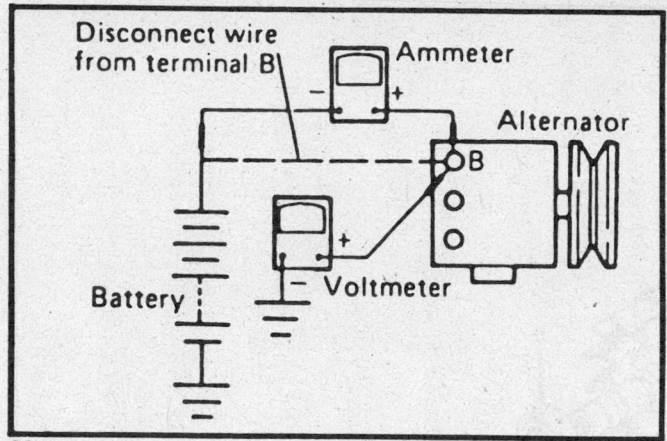

Metro, Prizm, Sprint, Spectrum and Nova test connections

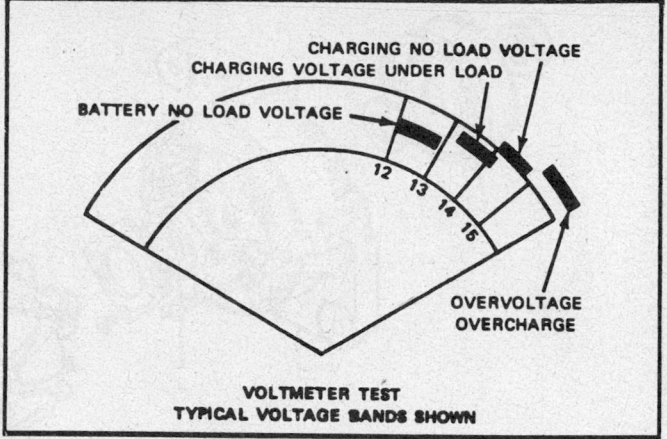

Voltmeter test patterns—typical

OVERHAUL

Disassembly and Assembly

1. Remove the alternator from the vehicle. Position the assembly in a suitable holding fixture.

2. Remove the nut and the terminal insulator. Remove the nuts and the end cover.

3. Remove the screws, brush holder and IC regulator. Remove the screws securing the rectifier holder and rubber insulators.

4. Using tool J–35452 and a breaker bar loosen and remove the alternator pulley.

5. Using an ohmmeter inspect the rotor assembly for an open circuit. Check for continunity between the slip-rings. If continunity does not exist, replace the rotor.

6. Using an ohmmeter inspect the rotor assembly for ground. Check for non- continunity between the slip-ring and the rotor. If continunity exists, replace the rotor.

7. Check that the slip-rings are not rough or scored. If the slip-rings are rough or scored replace the rotor.

8. Using a measuring caliper, measure the slip-ring diameter. If not within specification, replace the rotor assembly.

9. Using an ohmmeter inspect the stator assembly for an open circuit. Check all leads for continuity. If continuity does not exist, replace the drive end.

10. Using an ohmmeter inspect the stator assembly to insure that it is not grounded. Check that there is no continuity between the coil leads and the drive end frame. If continuity exists, replace the drive end frame.

11. Replace the brush assembly if less than 0.177 in. Check the front bearing and if necessary, replace it.

12. Install the stator and stud bolts and torque to 6 ft. lbs. (8 Nm).

13. Install the drive end bearing, the bearing retainer and screws.

14. Install the rear end bearing, the bearing cover and the wave washer.

15. Install the rotor into the drive end frame and mate the drive end frame-to-rear end frame. Torque the bolts and nuts to 22 ft. lbs. (30 Nm).

16. Install the rectifier screws. Install the alternator B terminal insulator and nut; torque the nut to 3.7 ft. lbs. (5 Nm).

17. Install the voltage regulator and the brush holder assembly.

18. Install the rear end cover.

19. Using a hexagonal socket to hold the shaft, install the pulley and nut; torque the nut to 83 ft. lbs. (113 Nm).

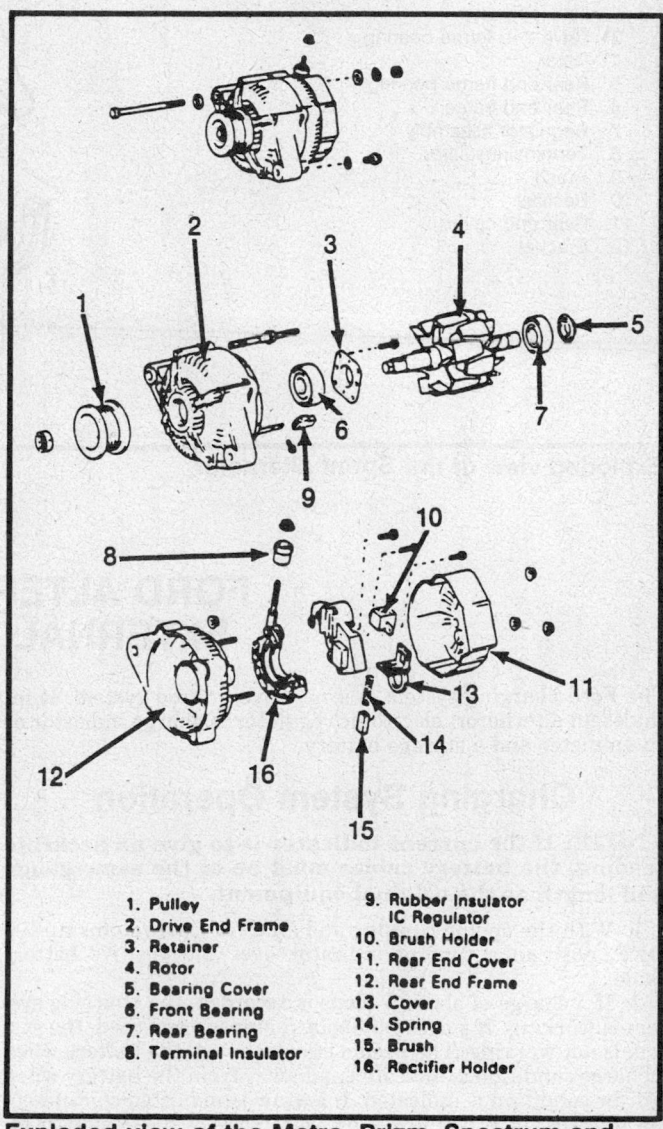

1. Pulley	9. Rubber Insulator IC Regulator
2. Drive End Frame	10. Brush Holder
3. Retainer	11. Rear End Cover
4. Rotor	12. Rear End Frame
5. Bearing Cover	13. Cover
6. Front Bearing	14. Spring
7. Rear Bearing	15. Brush
8. Terminal Insulator	16. Rectifier Holder

Exploded view of the Metro, Prizm, Spectrum and Nova alternator assembly

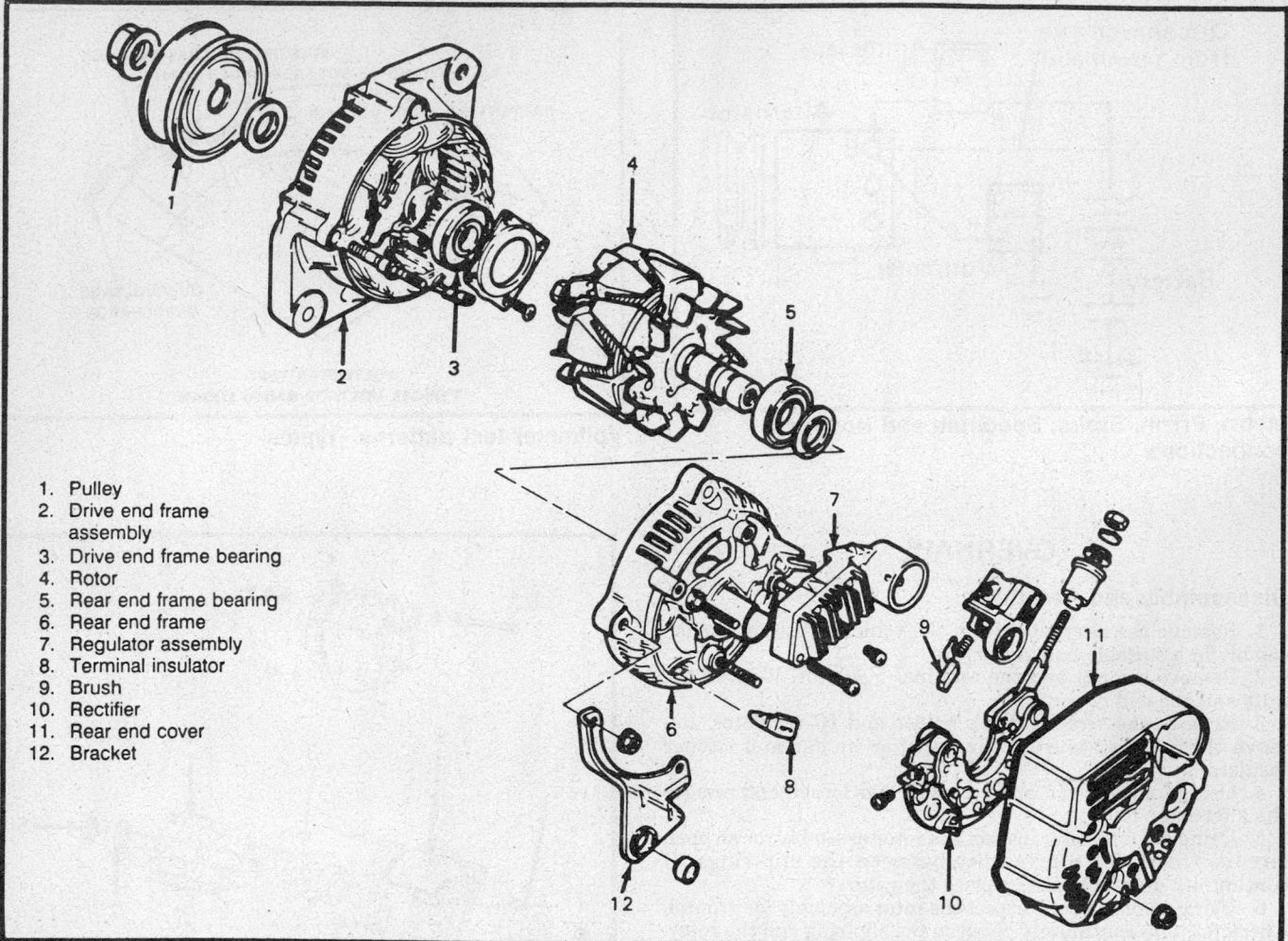

1. Pulley
2. Drive end frame assembly
3. Drive end frame bearing
4. Rotor
5. Rear end frame bearing
6. Rear end frame
7. Regulator assembly
8. Terminal insulator
9. Brush
10. Rectifier
11. Rear end cover
12. Bracket

Exploded view of the Sprint alternator

FORD ALTERNATOR WITH EXTERNAL REGULATOR

The Ford charging system is a negative ground system. It includes an alternator, electronic regulator, a charge indicator or an ammeter and a storage battery.

Charging System Operation

NOTE: If the current indicator is to give an accurate reading, the battery cables must be of the same gauge and length as the original equipment.

1. With the engine running and all electrical systems turned **OFF**, position a current indicator over the positive battery cable.

2. If a charge of about 5 amps is recorded, the charging system is working. If a draw of about 5 amps is recorded, the system is not working. The needle moves toward the battery when a charge condition is indicated and away from the battery when a draw condition is indicated. If a draw is indicated continue to the next testing procedure. If an overcharge of 10–15 amps is indicated check for a faulty regulator or a bad ground at the regulator or the alternator.

Ignition Switch to Regulator Circuit Test

1. Disconnect the regulator wiring harness from the regulator.

2. Turn **ON** the key. Using a test light or voltmeter check for voltage between the I wire and ground. Check for voltage between the A wire and ground. If voltage is present at this part of the system the circuit is OK. If there is no voltage at the I wire check for a burned out charge indicator bulb, a burned-out resistor, or a break or short in the wiring. If there is no voltage present at the A wire check for a bad connection at the starter relay or a break or short in the wire.

Isolation Test

This test determines whether the regulator or the alternator is faulty after the rest of the circuit is found to be in good working order.

1. Disconnect the regulator wiring harness from the regulator.

2. Connect a jumper wire from the A wire to the F wire in the wiring harness plug.

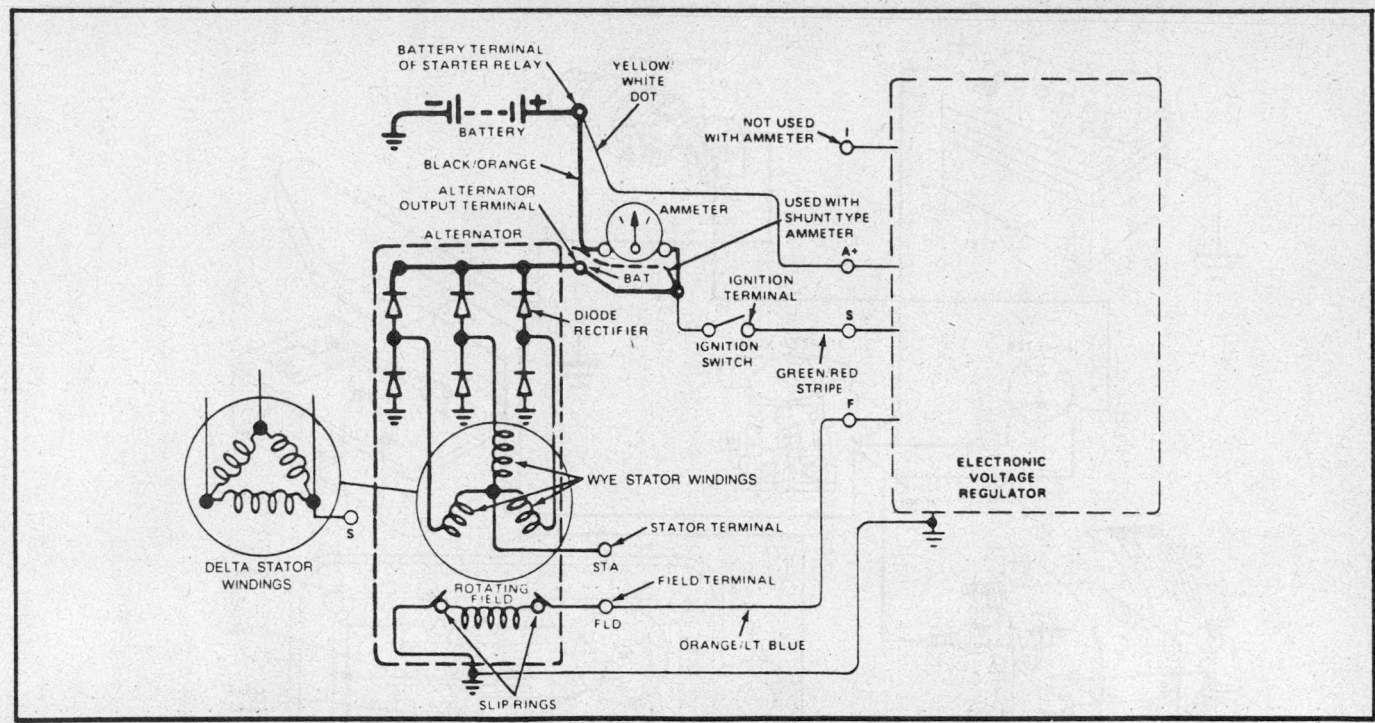

Ford alternator w/external regulator—rear terminal alternator charging system schematic with ammeter—typical side terminal alternator. Wye stator windings on 40, 60, and 65 amp alternators. Delta stator windings on 70, 90, and 100 amp alternators

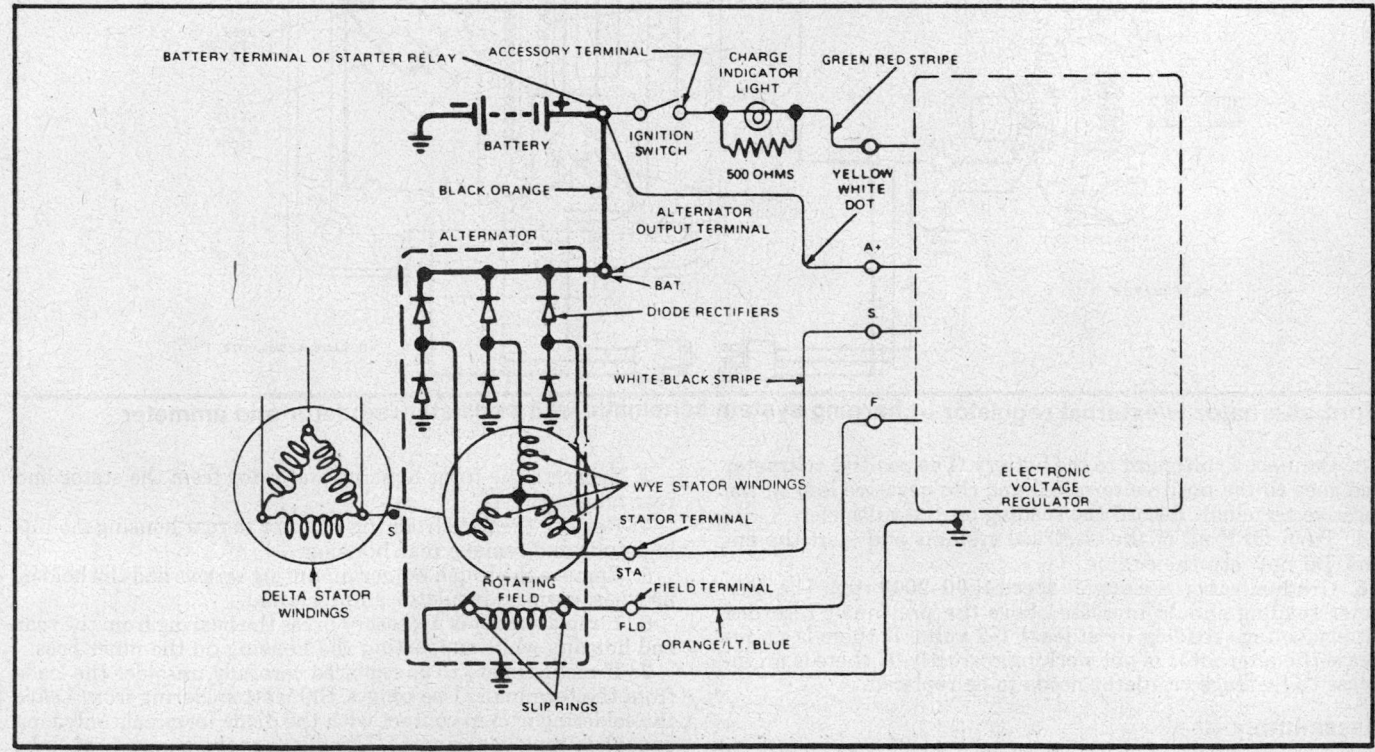

Ford alternator w/external regulator—rear terminal alternator charging system schematic with indicator light—typical of side terminal alternator. Wye stator windings on 40, 60 and 65 amp alternators

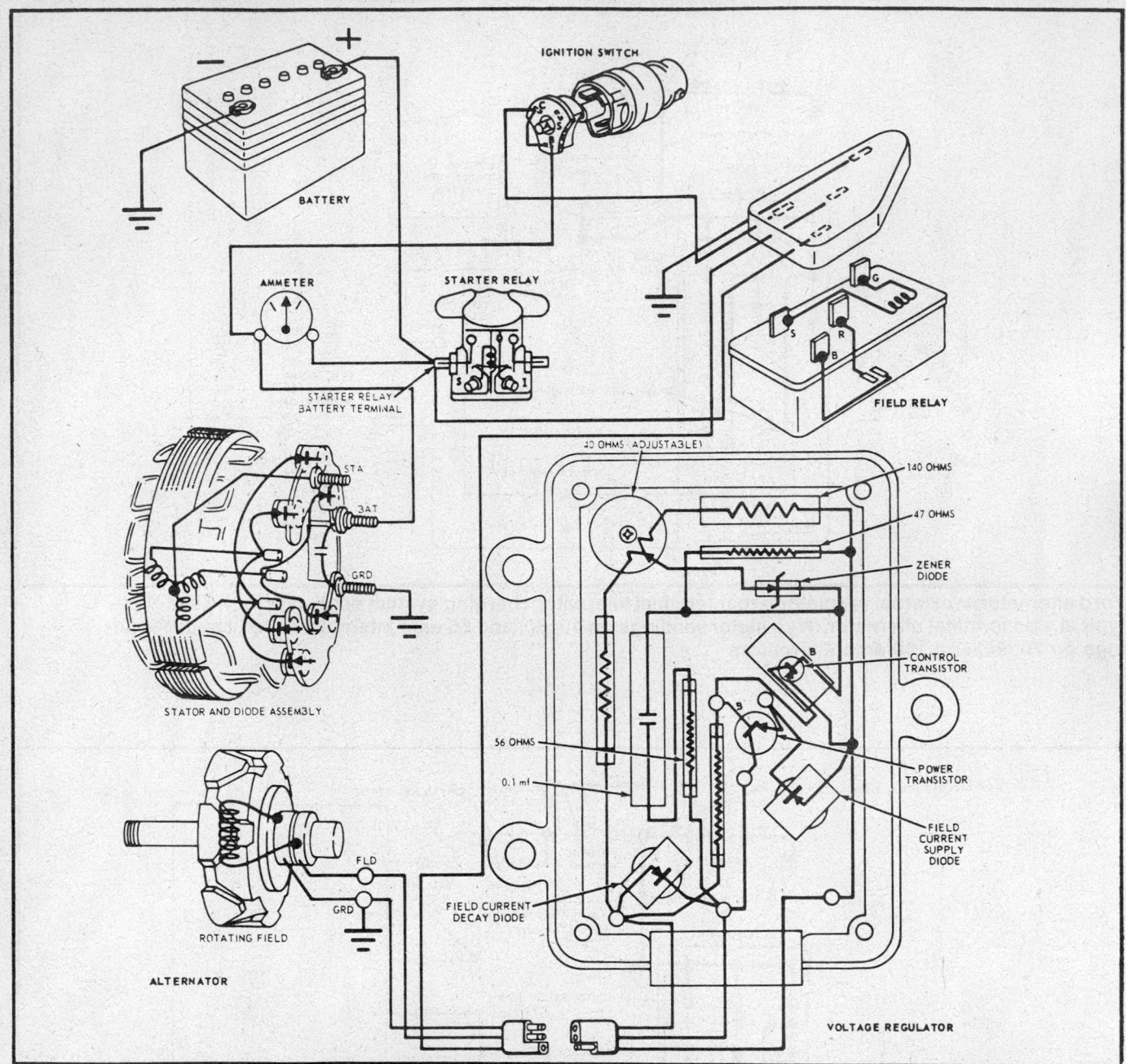

Ford alternator w/external regulator—charging system schematic with transistor regulator and ammeter

3. Connect a voltmeter to the battery. The positive voltmeter lead goes to the positive terminal and the negative lead to the negative terminal. Record the reading on the voltmeter.

4. Turn **OFF** all of the electrical systems and start the engine. Do not race the engine.

5. Gradually increase engine speed 1500–2000 rpm. The voltmeter reading should increase above the previously recorded battery voltage reading by at least 1–2 volts. If there is no increase the alternator is not working correctly. If there is an increase the voltage regulator needs to be replaced.

Disassembly
EXCEPT 65, 70, 90 AND 100 AMP ALTERNATORS
1. Matchmark both end housings for assembly.
2. Remove the housing through bolts.

3. Separate the front housing and rotor from the stator and rear housing.

4. Remove the nuts from the rectifier to rear housing mounting studs and remove rear housing.

5. Remove the brush holder mounting screws and the holder, brushes, springs, insulator and terminal.

6. If replacement is necessary press the bearing from the rear end housing while supporting the housing on the inner boss.

7. If rectifiers are to be replaced carefully unsolder the leads from the terminals. Use only a 100 watt soldering iron. Leave the soldering iron in contact with the diode terminals only long enough to remove the wires. Use pliers as temporary heat sinks in order to protect the diodes.

8. There are various types of rectifier assembly circuit boards installed in production. One type has the circuit board spaced

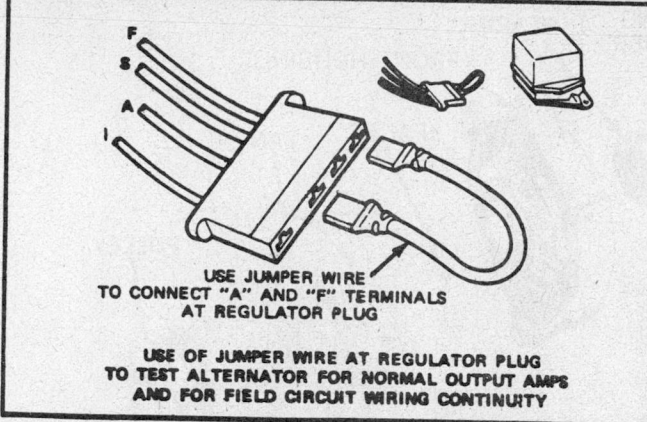

Ford alternator w/external regulator—use a jumper wire at regulator plug to test alternator for normal output amps and for field circuit wiring continuity

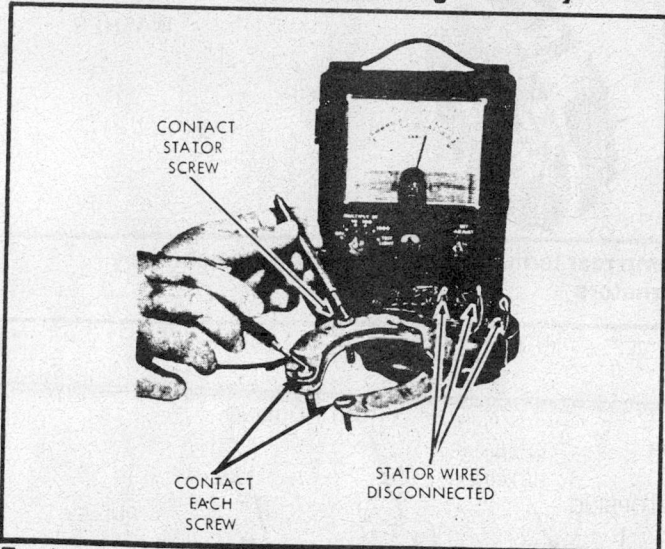

Ford alternator w/external regulator—testing diodes—typical of flat type rectifiers

away from the diode plates and the diodes are exposed. Another type consists of a single circuit board with integral diodes; and still another has integral diodes with an additional booster diode plate containing 2 diodes.

9. This last type is used only on the 8 diode (61 amp) alternator. To disassemble use the following procedures. Exposed diodes remove the screws from the rectifier by rotating bolt heads ¼ turn clockwise to unlock and unscrewing. Integral diodes, press out the stator terminal screw, making sure not to twist it while doing this. Do not remove grounded screw. Booster diodes, press out the stator terminal screw about ¼ in., remove the nut from the end of the screw and lift screw from circuit board. Be sure not to twist it as it comes out.

10. Remove the drive pulley and fan. On alternator pulleys with threaded holes in the outer end of the pulley use a standard puller for removal.

11. Remove the front bearing retainer screws and the front housing. If the bearing is to be replaced press it from the housing.

65, 70, 90 AND 100 AMP ALTERNATORS

NOTE: When disassembling the side terminal alternator, the brush holder would be removed after the rectifier is removed. During the assembly, the brush holder would be installed in the reverse order.

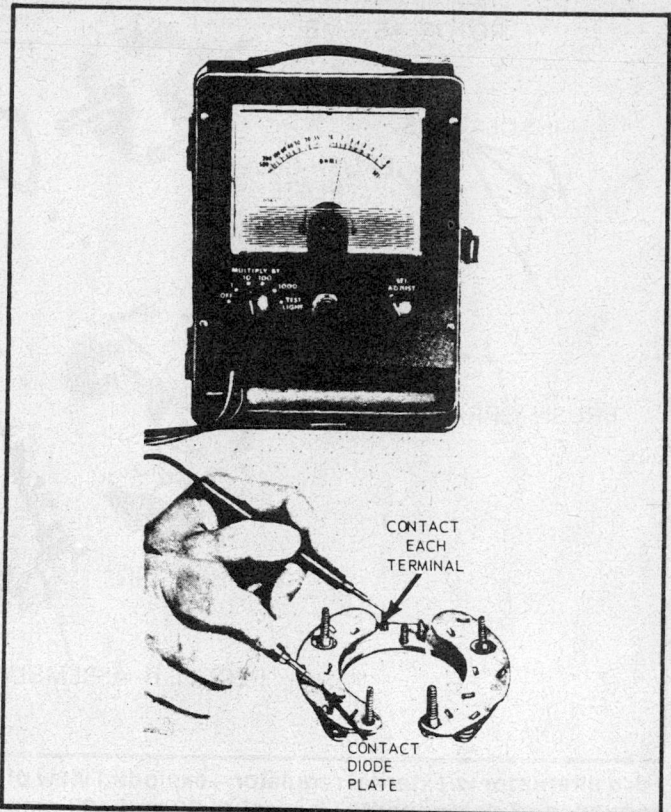

Ford alternator w/external regulator—testing diodes—typical of bridge type rectifiers

1. Remove the brush holder and cover assembly from the rear housing.

2. Mark both end housings and the stator.

3. Remove the housing through bolts.

4. Separate the front housing and rotor from the stator and rear housing.

5. Remove the drive pulley nut, lockwasher, flat washer, pulley, fan, fan spacer and rotor from the front housing.

6. Remove the front bearing retainer screws and the retainer. If the bearing is damaged or has lost its lubricant, support the housing close to the bearing boss and press out the bearing.

7. Remove all the nut and washer assemblies and insulators from the rear housing and remove the rear housing from the stator and rectifier assembly.

8. If necessary press the rear bearing from the housing while supporting the housing on the inner boss.

9. Unsolder the 3 stator leads from the rectifier assembly and separate the stator from the assembly. Use a 200 watt soldering iron. Perform a diode test and an open and grounded stator coil test.

Cleaning and Inspection

1. The rotor, stator, diode rectifier assemblies and bearings are not to be cleaned with solvent. These parts are to be wiped off with a clean cloth. Cleaning solvent may cause damage to the electrical parts or contaminate the bearing internal lubricant. Wash all other parts in solvent and dry them.

2. Rotate the front bearing on the driveshaft. Check for any scraping noise, looseness or roughness that indicates that the bearing is excessively worn. As the bearing is being rotated look for excessive lubricant leakage. If any of these conditions exist replace the bearing. Check rear bearing and rotor shaft.

3. Place the rear end housing on the slip-ring end of the shaft and rotate the bearing on the shaft. Make a similar check for noise, looseness or roughness. Inspect the rollers and cage for

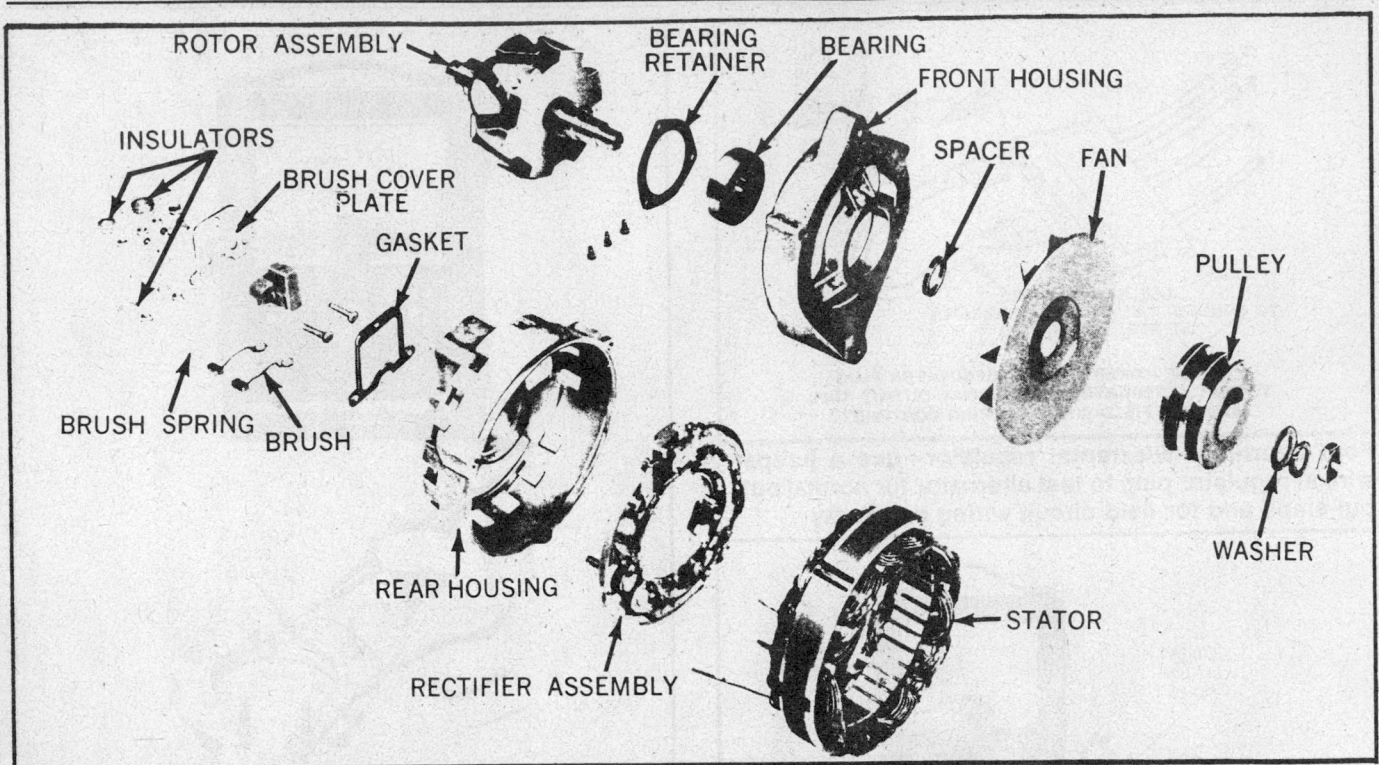

Ford alternator w/external regulator—exploded view of 70 amp rear terminal alternator showing assembly sequence of components—typical of 90 and 100 amp alternators

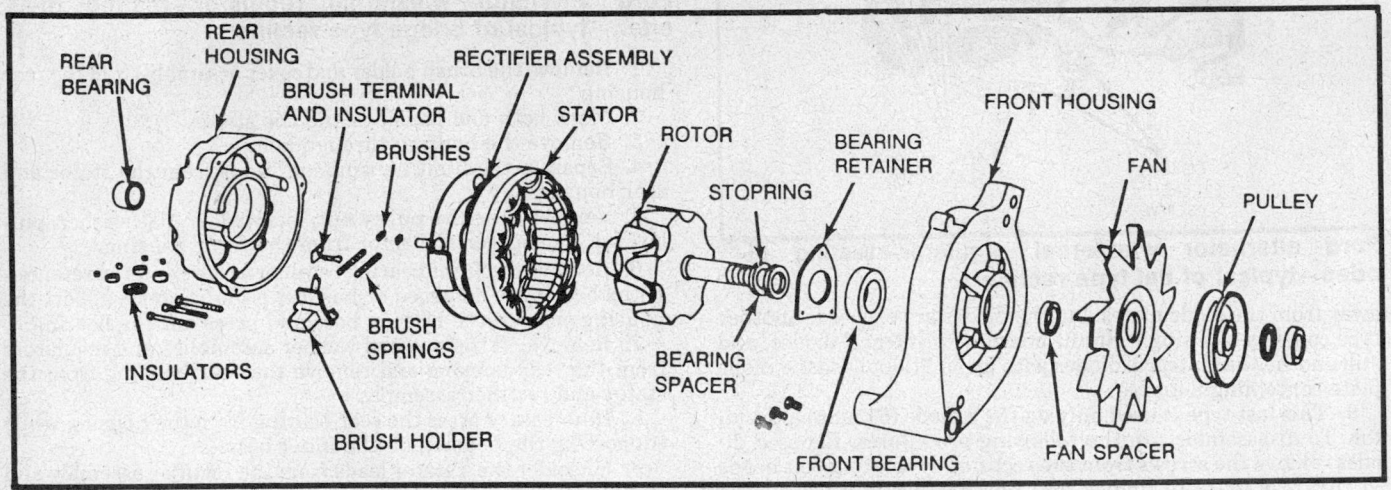

Exploded view of the rear terminal alternator with an external voltage regulator

damage. Replace the bearing if these conditions exist or if the lubricant is missing or contaminated.

4. Check both the front and rear housings for cracks.

5. Check all wire leads on both the stator and rotor assemblies for loose soldered connections and for burned insulation. Solder all poor connections. Replace parts that show burned insulation.

6. Check the slip-rings for damaged insulation and runout. If the slip-rings are more than 0.005 in. out of round, take a light cut (minimum diameter limit 1.220 in.) from the face of the rings to true them. If the slip-rings are badly damaged the entire rotor will have to be replaced as an assembly.

7. Replace any parts that are burned or cracked. Replace brushes that are worn to less than $5/16$ in. in length. Replace the brush spring if it has less than 7–12 oz. tension.

Field Current Draw Test

1. Remove the alternator from the vehicle. Connect a test ammeter between the alternator frame and the positive post of a 12 volt test battery.

2. Connect a jumper wire between the negative test battery post and the alternator field terminal.

3. Observe the ammeter. Little or no current flow indicates high brush resistance, open field windings, or high winding resistance. Current in excess of specifications (approximately 2.9 amps for most models) indicates shorted or grounded field windings, or brush leads touching.

NOTE:The alternator, may produce current output at low engine speeds, but ceases to produce current at higher speeds. This can be caused by centrifugal force

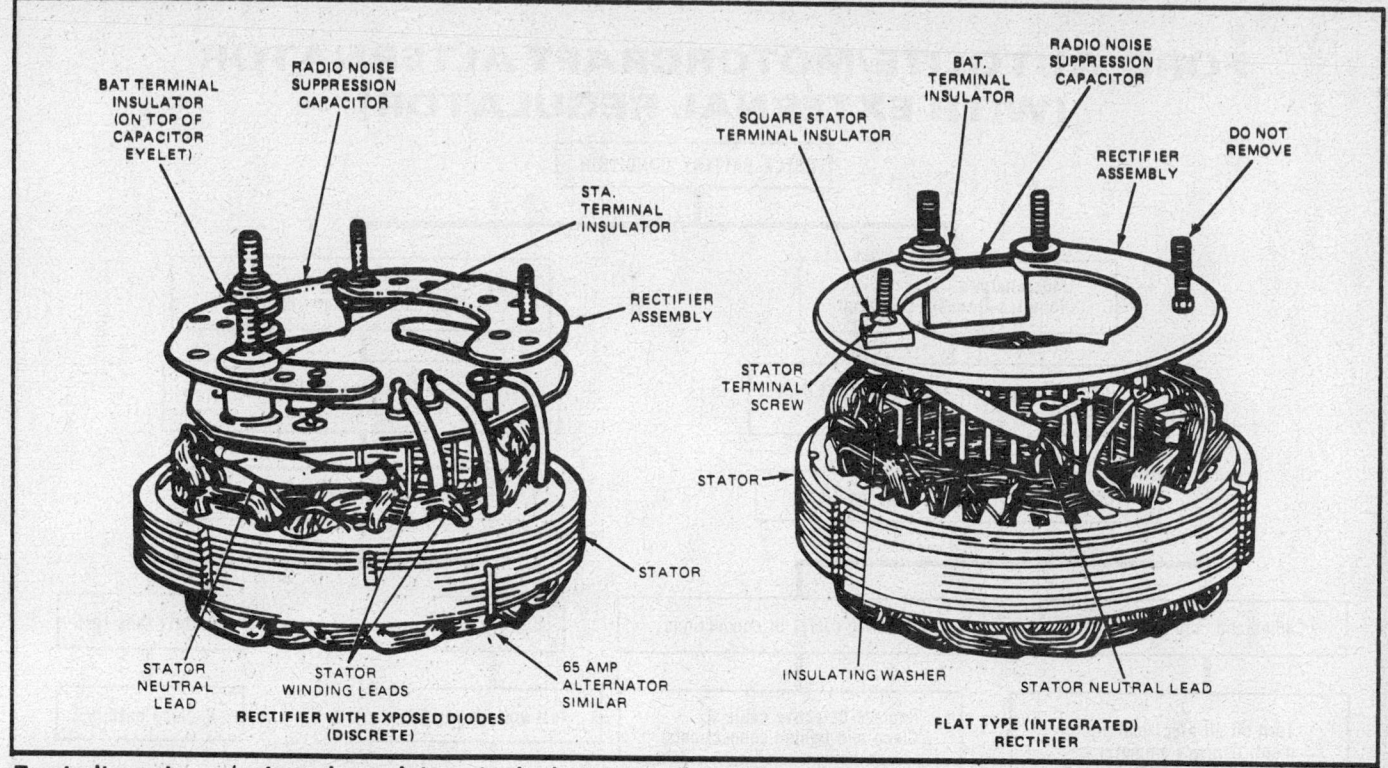

Ford alternator w/external regulator—typical stator and rectifier assemblies and related terminals

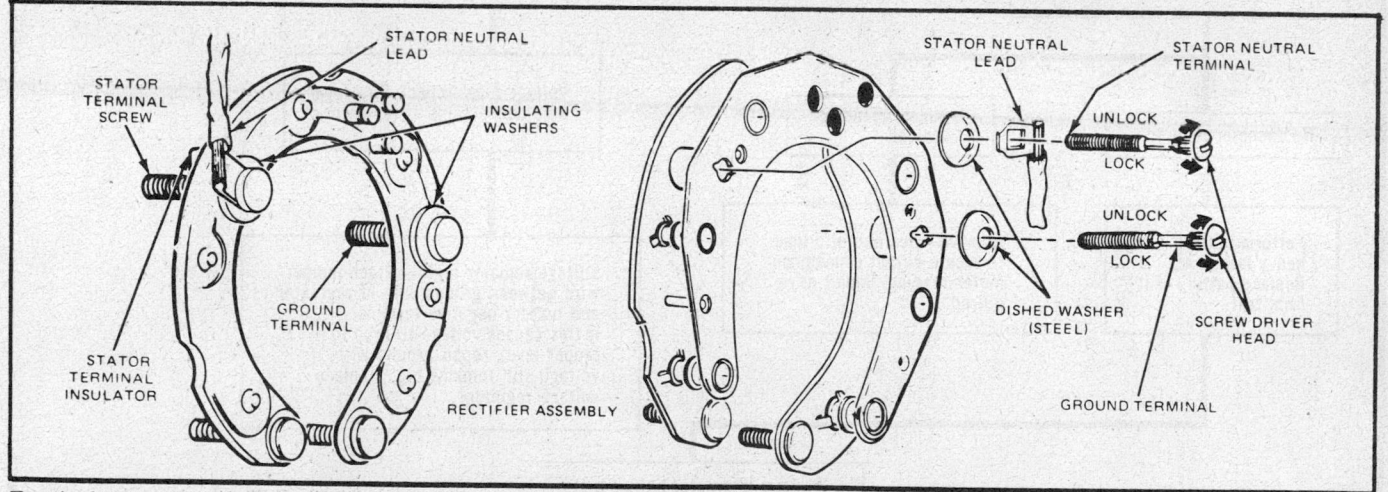

Ford alternator w/external regulator—rectifier assemblies and related components

expanding the rotor windings to the point where they short to ground. Place in a test stand and check field current draw while spinning alternator.

Diode Tests

Disassemble the alternator. Disconnect diode assembly from stator and make tests. To test one set of diodes contact 1 ohmmeter probe to the diode plate and contact each of the 3 stator lead terminals with the other probe. Reverse the probes and repeat the test. All 6 tests (eight for 61 amp 8-diode models) should show a reading of about 60 ohms in one direction and infinite ohms in the other. If 2 high readings or 2 low readings are obtained after reversing probes, the diode is faulty and must be replaced.

Stator Tests

Disassemble the stator from the alternator assembly and rectifiers. Connect test ohmmeter probes between each pair of stator leads. If the ohmmeter does not indicate equally between each pair of leads the stator coil is open and must be replaced.

Connect test ohmmeter probes between one of the stator leads and the stator core. The ohmmeter should not show any reading. If it does show continuity the stator winding is grounded and must be replaced.

Assembly

EXCEPT 65, 70, 90 AND 100 AMP ALTERNATORS

1. Press the front bearing into the front housing boss by put-

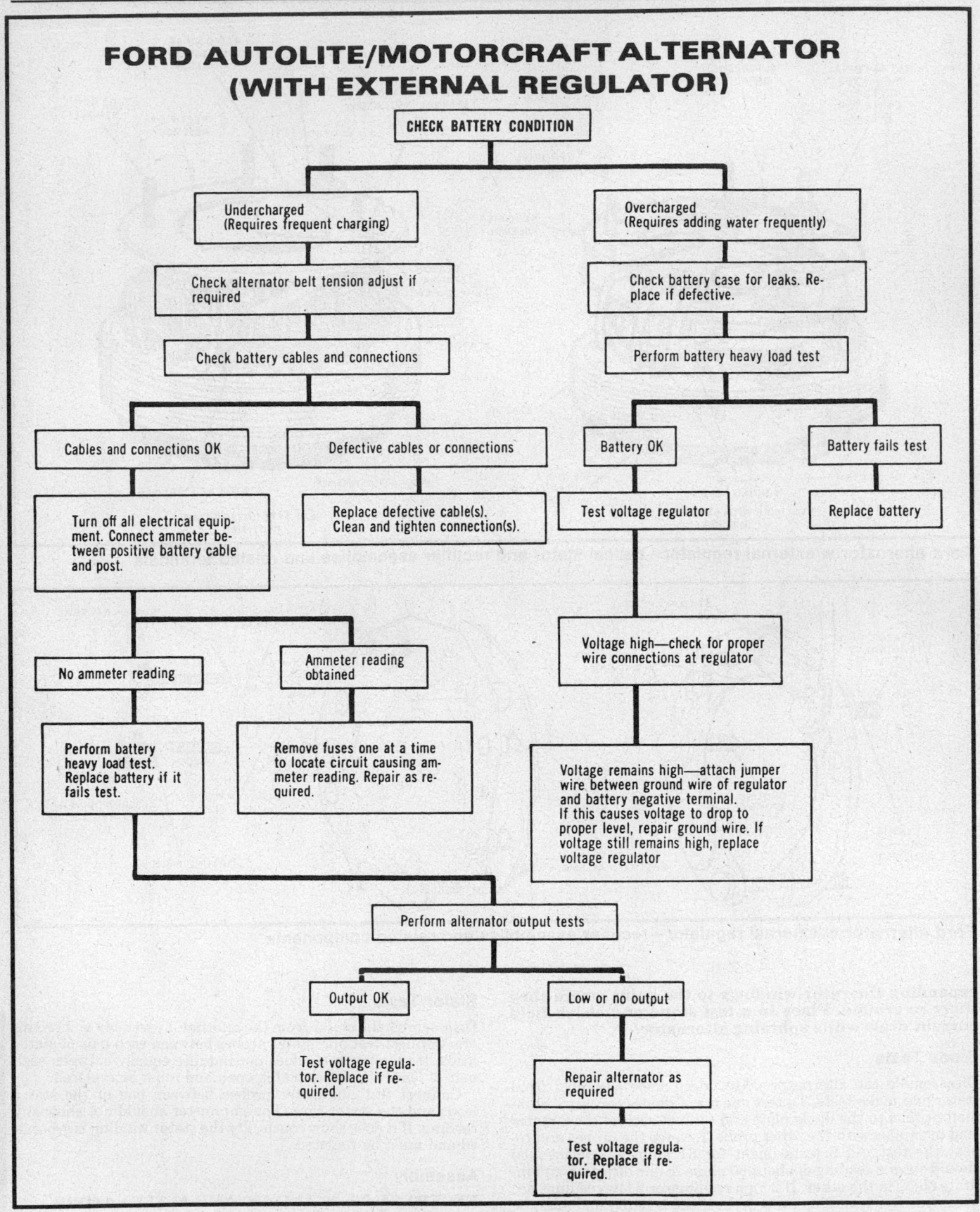

FORD AUTOLITE/MOTORCRAFT ALTERNATOR (WITH EXTERNAL REGULATOR)

CHECK BATTERY CONDITION

- Undercharged (Requires frequent charging)
  - Check alternator belt tension adjust if required
  - Check battery cables and connections
    - Cables and connections OK
      - Turn off all electrical equipment. Connect ammeter between positive battery cable and post.
        - No ammeter reading
          - Perform battery heavy load test. Replace battery if it fails test.
        - Ammeter reading obtained
          - Remove fuses one at a time to locate circuit causing ammeter reading. Repair as required.
    - Defective cables or connections
      - Replace defective cable(s). Clean and tighten connection(s).

- Overcharged (Requires adding water frequently)
  - Check battery case for leaks. Replace if defective.
  - Perform battery heavy load test
    - Battery OK
      - Test voltage regulator
        - Voltage high—check for proper wire connections at regulator
          - Voltage remains high—attach jumper wire between ground wire of regulator and battery negative terminal. If this causes voltage to drop to proper level, repair ground wire. If voltage still remains high, replace voltage regulator
    - Battery fails test
      - Replace battery

Perform alternator output tests
- Output OK
  - Test voltage regulator. Replace if required.
- Low or no output
  - Repair alternator as required
    - Test voltage regulator. Replace if required.

ting pressure on outer race only. Install bearing retainer.

2. If the stop ring on the driveshaft was damaged install a new stop ring. Push the new ring onto the shaft and into the groove.

3. Position the front bearing spacer on the driveshaft against the stop ring.

4. Place the front housing over the shaft with the bearing positioned in the front housing cavity.

5. Install fan spacer, fan, pulley, lockwasher and retaining nut and tighten nut 60–100 ft. lbs. while holding the driveshaft with an Allen key.

6. If rear bearing was removed, press a new one into rear housing.

7. Assemble brushes, springs, terminal and insulator in the brush holder, retract the brushes and insert a short length of ⅛ in. rod or stiff wire through the hole in the holder to hold the brushes in the retracted position.

8. Position the brush holder assembly in the rear housing and install mounting screws. Position brush leads to prevent shorting.

9. Wrap the 3 stator winding leads around the circuit board terminals and solder them using only rosin core solder and a solder iron. Position the stator neutral lead eyelet on the stator terminal screw and install the screw in the rectifier assembly.

10. Exposed diodes, insert the special screws through the wire lug, dished washers and circuit board. Turn ¼ turn counterclockwise to lock in place. Integral diodes, insert the screws straight through the holes.

NOTE: The dished washers are to be used on the molded circuit boards only. Using these washers on a fiber board will result in a serious short circuit, as only a flat insulating washer between the stator terminal and the board is used on fiber circuit boards.

11. Booster diodes, position the stator wire terminal on the stator terminal screw, then position screw on rectifier. Position square insulator over the screw and into the square hole in the rectifier, rotate terminal screw until it locks, then press it in fingertight. Position the stator wire, then press the terminal screw into the rectifier and insulator with a vise.

12. Place the radio noise suppression condenser on the rectifier terminals. With molded circuit board and install the STA and BAT terminal insulators. With fiber circuit board place the square stator terminal insulator in the square hole in the rectifier assembly, then position BAT terminal insulator.

13. Position the stator and rectifier assembly in the rear housing, making sure that all terminal insulators are seated properly in the recesses. Position STA, BAT and FLD insulators on terminal bolts and install the nuts.

14. Clean the rear bearing surface of the rotor shaft with a rag and then position rear housing and stator assembly over rotor. Align matchmarks made during disassembly and install the through bolts. Remove brush retracting wire and place a dab of silicone sealer over the hole.

65, 70, 90 AND 100 AMP ALTERNATORS

1. If the front bearing is being replaced press the new bearing into the bearing boss by putting pressure on the outer race only. Install the bearing retainer and tighten the retainer screws until the tips of the retainer touch the housing.

2. Position the rectifier assembly to the stator, wrap the 3 stator leads around the diode plate terminals and solder them using a 200 watt soldering iron.

3. If the rear housing bearing was removed press in a new bearing from the inside of the housing by putting pressure on the other race only.

4. Install at the BAT/GRD insulator and position the stator and rectifier assembly in the rear housing.

5. Install the STA (purple) and BAT (red) terminal insulators on the terminal bolts and install the nut and washer assemblies. Make certain that the shoulders on all insulators, both inside and outside of the housing, are seated properly before tightening the nuts.

6. Position the front housing over the rotor and install the an spacer, fan, pulley, flat and lockwasher and nut on the rotor shaft.

7. Wipe the rear bearing surface of the rotor shaft with a clean rag.

8. Position the rotor with the front housing into the stator and rear housing assembly and align the matchmarks made during disassembly. Seat the machined portion of the stator core into the step in both housings and install the through bolts.

9. If the field brushes have worn to less than ⅜ in., replace both brushes. Hold the brushes in position by inserting a stiff wire into the brush holder.

10. Position the brush holder assembly into the rear housing and install the mounting screws. Remove the brush retracting wire and put a dab of silicone cement over the hole.

Brush Replacement

1. Remove the brush holder and cover assembly from the rear housing.

2. Remove the terminal bolts from the brush holder and cover assembly. Remove the brush assemblies.

3. Position the new brush terminals on the terminal bolts and assemble the terminals, bolts, brush holder washers and nuts. The insulating washer mounts under the FLD terminal nut. The entire brush and cover assembly also is available for service.

4. Depress the brush springs in the brush holder cavities and insert the brushes on top of the springs. Hold the brushes in position by inserting a stiff wire in the brush holder as shown. Position the brush leads as shown.

5. Install the brush holder and cover assembly into the rear housing. Remove the brush retracting wire and put a dab of silicone cement over the hole.

FORD ALTERNATOR WITH
INTERNAL REGULATOR

The Ford alternator with Internal Regulator is manufactured by Motorcraft, which is a division of the Ford Motor Company. The Field current is supplied from the alternator regulator which is mounted on the rear of the alternator, to the rotating field of the alternator through 2 brushes and 2 slip-rings.

The alternator produces power in the form of alternating current. The alternating current is rectified to direct current by 6 diodes. The alternator regulator automatically adjusts the alternator field current to maintain the alternator output voltage within prescribed limits to correctly charge the battery. The alternator is self current limiting.

The regulator voltage control circuit is turned on when the ignition switch is **ON** and voltage is applied to the regulator I terminal through a resistor in the I circuit. When the ignition switch is **OFF** the control circuit is turned off and no field current flows to the alternator.

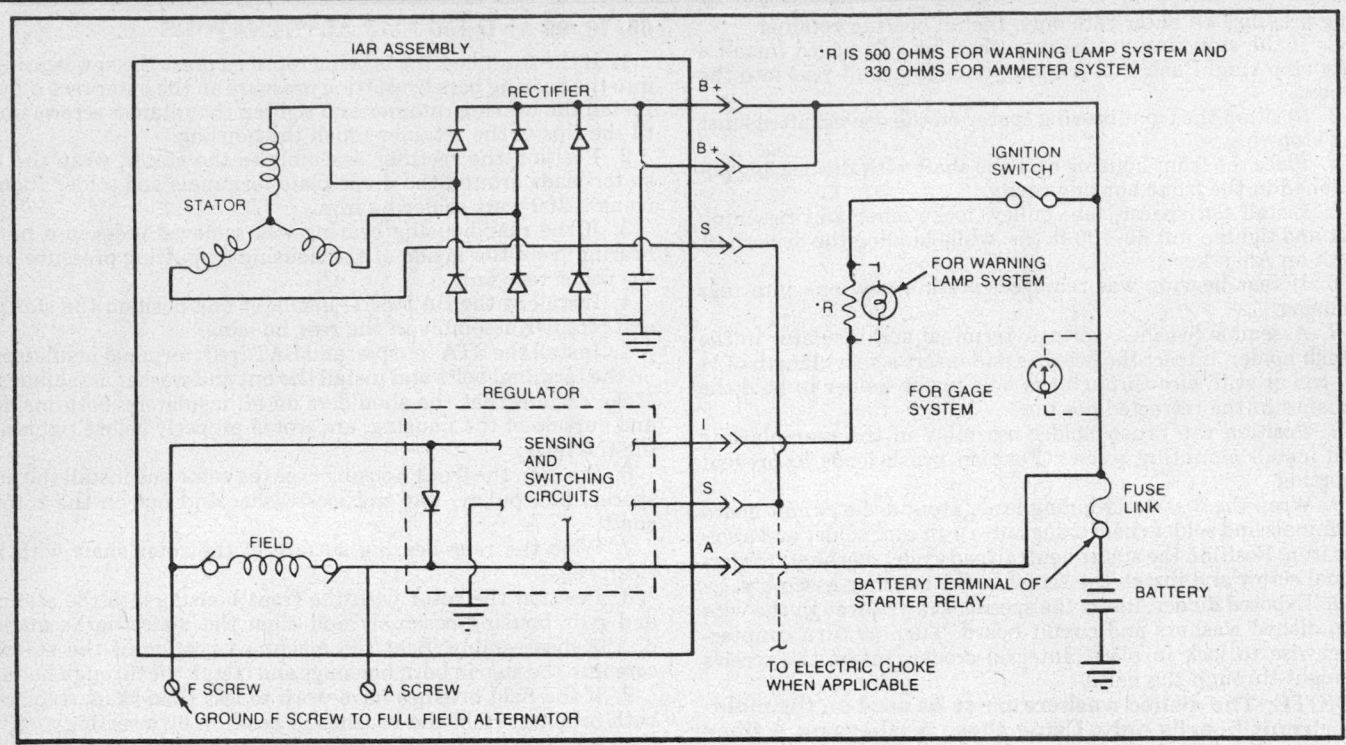

Ford alternator w/internal regulator—charging system wiring

On warning lamp equipped vehicles, the warning lamp is connected across the terminals of a 500 ohm resistor at the instrument cluster. Current passes through the warning lamp when the ignition switch is in the **RUN** position and there is no voltage at terminal S. When voltage at S rises to a preset value the regulator switching circuits stop the flow of current into terminal I and the lamp turns off.

System voltage is sensed and alternator field current is drawn through terminal A. The regulator switching circuits will turn the warning lamp on, indicating a system fault, if terminal A voltage is excessively high or low, or if the terminal S voltage signal is abnormal. A fusible link is included in the charging system wiring on all models. The fusible link is used to prevent damage to the wiring harness and alternator if the wiring harness should become grounded, or if a booster battery is connected to the charging system with the wrong polarity.

Diagnostic Testing

NOTE: The following diagnostic tests are made with the alternator installed in the vehicle. Be sure that the battery is fully charged before any testing is done.

Battery Voltage Test

1. Connect a voltmeter to the positive and negative battery terminals.
2. Record the battery voltage. If battery voltage is not within specification, correct as required.

Load Test

1. Be sure that the battery is fully charged before performing this test.
2. Connect the tachometer to the engine.
3. Start the engine. Turn the heater/air condition switch to the **HIGH** blower position. Turn **ON** the headlights with the high beams. Increase engine speed to 2000 rpm.
4. Voltmeter should indicate a minimum of a 0.5 volt increase over battery voltage.

5. If the system is working the above readings will be obtained. Be sure not to ground the A terminal of the voltage regulator.

No Load Test

1. Be sure that the battery is fully charged before performing this test.
2. Connect a tachometer to the engine. Start the engine and increase the engine speed to 1500 rpm with no electrical load.
3. The voltmeter reading should be taken when the voltmeter needle stops moving. The voltmeter reading should be 1–2 volts above the voltage of the battery.
4. If the voltage increased properly proceed with another test.

High Voltage Test

1. Be sure that the battery is fully charged before performing this test.
2. Turn the ignition switch to the **ON** position. Connect the voltmeter negative lead to the rear of the alternator housing.
3. Connect voltmeter positive lead to alternator output terminal and record voltage. Connect voltmeter positive lead to the A terminal of regulator. Compare voltage difference recorded at alternator output terminal.
4. If voltage difference is greater than 0.5 volt, repair or replace wiring circuit to A terminal.
5. If high voltage condition still exists check ground connections at regulator to alternator, alternator to engine, firewall to engine and engine to battery.
6. If high voltage condition still exists connect voltmeter negative lead to rear of alternator housing. With ignition to **OFF** position connect voltmeter positive lead to A terminal of regulator and record reading. Connect voltmeter positive lead to F terminal of regulator.
7. Check if different voltage is present at A and F terminals. Different voltage readings indicate a defective regulator, grounded brush leads or grounded rotor coil.
8. If same voltage is present at both terminals and circuits tested in previous steps are good replace the regulator.

Low Voltage Test

1. Be sure that the battery is fully charged before performing this test.
2. Disconnect the wiring plug from the voltage regulator and install the ohmmeter between terminals A and F.
3. The ohmmeter reading should indicate more than 2.2 ohms. If the reading is less than 2.2 ohms, replace the voltage regulator and check the alternator for a shorted rotor or open field circuit. Repeat the load test. Do not replace the voltage regulator before a shorted rotor coil or field circuit has been determined not to be the problem. If not, damage to the new regulator could occur.
4. If the field circuit is okay, more than 2.2 ohms, reconnect the voltage regulator wiring plug and connect the voltmeter negative lead to the rear of the alternator. Connect the positive lead of the voltmeter to terminal A of the voltage regulator. Battery voltage should be present, if so go on. If not, repair wiring in circuit A.
5. With the ignition switch in the **OFF** position connect the positive lead of the voltmeter to the F terminal of the voltage regulator.
6. If battery voltage is present, go on. If not, replace the voltage regulator. Repeat the load test.
7. Turn the ignition switch to the **ON** position. The voltmeter should indicate 1.5 volts or less. If the reading is more than 1.5 volts, perform the regulator I circuit test. Repair the voltage regulator as required. Repeat the load test.
8. If the voltmeter reading is 1.5 volts or less, disconnect the alternator wiring plug and connect a twelve gauge jumper wire between the alternator plug terminal and the wiring harness connector.
9. Connect the positive lead of the voltmeter to 1 of the B terminals. Repeat the load test.
10. If the reading is 0.5 volt above battery voltage, repair the wiring harness from the alternator to the starter relay.
11. If the voltmeter reading is less than 0.5 volt above battery voltage, connect a jumper wire from the rear of the alternator housing to terminal F of the voltage regulator.
12. Repeat the load test. If the voltmeter reading is more than 0.5 volt, replace the voltage regulator. If the reading is less than 0.5 volt, repair the alternator.

Voltage Regulator Circuit I Test

1. Disconnect the voltage regulator wiring plug harness.
2. Connect the voltmeter negative lead to the battery ground. Connect the voltmeter positive lead to the harness side of terminal I.
3. With the ignition switch in the **OFF** position, voltage should not be present. If voltage is present repair the circuit as necessary.
4. With the ignition switch in the **ON** position, battery voltage should be present. If voltage is not present, check the wiring for an open or grounded circuit. Repair as required.
5. If the voltage readings are within specification, check the resistance of the I circuit resistor. If the vehicle is equipped with an indicator light the resistance is 500 ohms. If the vehicle is equipped with a gauge, the resistance is 300 ohms. If the specification obtained is not within plus or minus 50 ohms, replace the resistor. Repeat the load test.
6. Disconnect the voltage regulator wiring plug and remove the indicator light bulb, if equipped, before performing this test.

Field Circuit Drain Test

1. Connect the negative lead of the voltmeter to the rear of the alternator housing. Turn the ignition switch to the **OFF** position. Connect the positive lead of the voltmeter to the F terminal of the voltage regulator.
2. Battery voltage should be present. If no voltage is present, proceed.
3. If voltage is less than battery voltage, check I circuit. Dis-

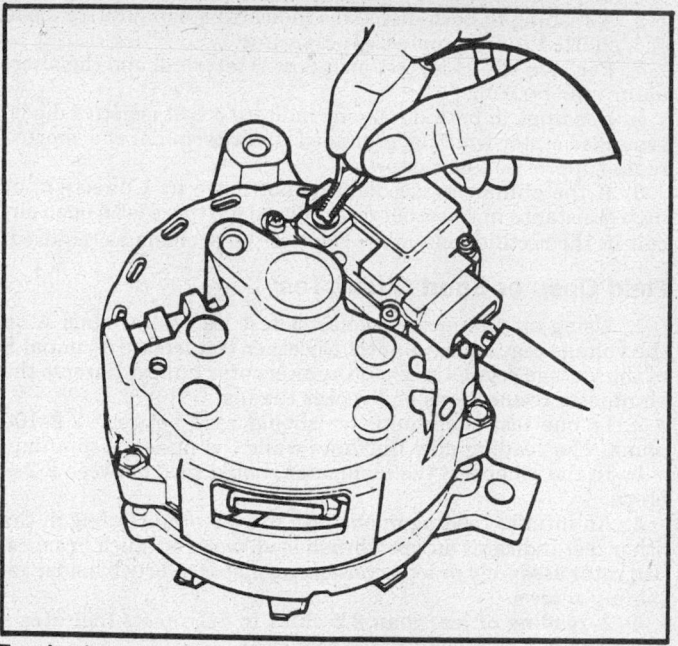

Ford alternator w/internal regulator

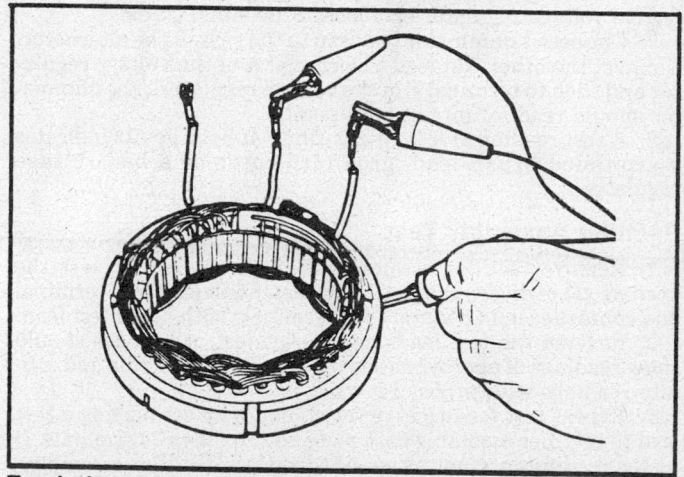

Ford alternator w/internal regulator—stator coil open test, using an ohmmeter. If meter doesnot respond an open is present and the stator should be replaced

connect regulator wiring harness. Connect voltmeter positive lead to S terminal of wiring plug. If voltage is present, proceed to Step 4. If no voltage is present replace regulator.
4. Disconnect wiring plug from alternator. Check S terminal for voltage. If no voltage is present, replace alternator rectifier assembly. If voltage is still present, replace or repair wiring between alternator and regulator plugs.

ALTERNATOR BENCH TESTS

NOTE: In performing the following tests, digital meters cannot be used.

Stator Ground Test

1. Using an ohmmeter connect 1 test lead to the B terminal and the other test lead to the S terminal.
2. Reverse the test leads and repeat the test. The ohmmeter should read about 6.5 ohms in 1 direction and infinity when the test probes are reversed.

3. A reading in both directions indicates a bad positive diode or a shorted radio suppression capacitor.

4. Perform the same test using the S terminal and the alternator rear housing.

5. Readings in both directions indicate a bad negative diode, grounded stator winding, grounded stator terminal or a shorted radio suppression capacitor.

6. If the ohmmeter needle does not move in 1 direction, or high resistance in the other direction exists, there is an open circuit in the rectifier assembly. Correct the problem as required.

Field Open or Short Circuit Test

1. Using an ohmmeter connect 1 test lead to terminal A on the voltage regulator. Connect the other test lead to terminal F of the voltage regulator. Spin the alternator pulley. Reverse the ohmmeter connections and repeat the test.

2. In one test the ohmmeter should read between 2.2–100 ohms. The reading may fluctuate while the pulley is spinning.

3. In the other test the ohmmeter should read between 2.2–9 ohms.

4. An infinite reading in one test and a 9 ohm reading in the other test indicates an open brush lead, worn or stuck brushes, bad rotor assembly or loose voltage regulator to brush holder retaining screws.

5. A reading of less than 2.2 ohms in both tests indicates a shorted rotor or a bad voltage regulator.

6. A reading greater than 9 ohms in both tests indicates a defective voltage regulator or a loose F terminal screw.

7. Connect 1 ohmmeter test lead to the rear of the alternator. Connect the other test lead to terminal A of the voltage regulator and then to terminal F of the voltage regulator. The ohmmeter should read infinity at both points.

8. A test reading of less than infinity at both points indicates a grounded brush lead, grounded rotor or a bad voltage regulator.

Rectifier Assembly Test

1. Remove rectifier assembly from alternator. To test the positive set of diodes contact 1 ohmmeter test lead to B terminal and contact each of 3 stator lead terminals with other test lead.

2. Reverse the test leads and repeat test. All diodes should show readings of approximately 6.5 ohms in 1 direction and infinite readings with probes reversed.

3. Repeat test for negative set of diodes by connecting a test lead to rectifier assembly base plate and to other 3 terminals. If meter readings are not as specified replace rectifier assembly.

Radio Suppression Capacitor Test

NOTE: This is an open or shorted circuit test only and does not measure capacitance value.

1. Contact the ohmmeter test leads to the B terminal and the rectifier base plate assembly. Reverse the test leads while observing the indicator needle.

2. If the needle jumps momentarily and then returns to previous position, capacitor is okay. If needle does not jump replace rectifier assembly. Radio suppression capacitor must be replaced as a complete rectifier assembly.

Stator Coil Ground Test

1. Remove the stator from the alternator.

2. Using an ohmmeter connect a test lead to a stator lead and the other test lead to the stator laminated core. The reading should be infinity.

3. If the meter needle moves then the stator winding is shorted to the core. Replace the stator. Repeat this test for each stator lead.

NOTE: Do not touch the metal test leads or the stator leads, an incorrect test reading will result.

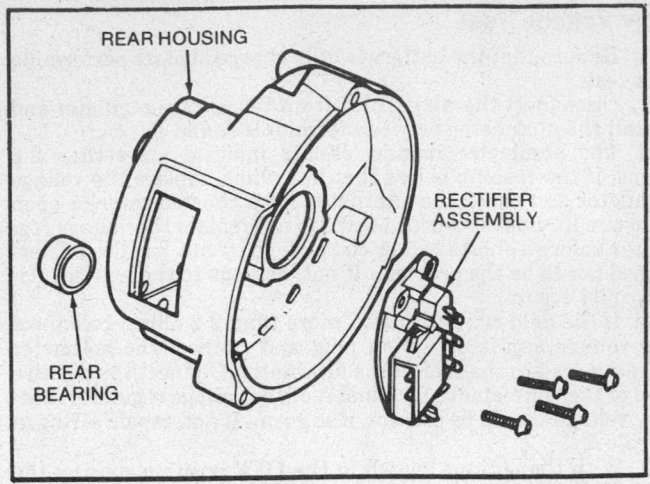

Ford alternator w/internal regulator rear housing and related components

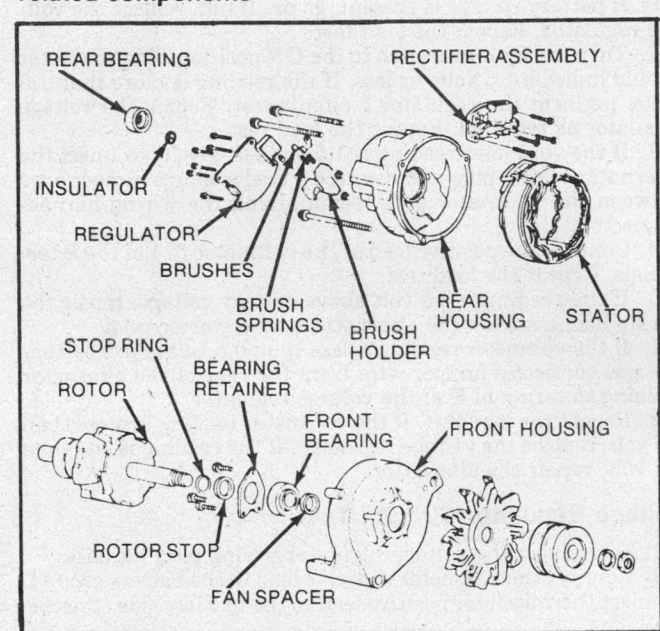

Ford alternator w/internal regulator—exploded view showing assembly sequence of components

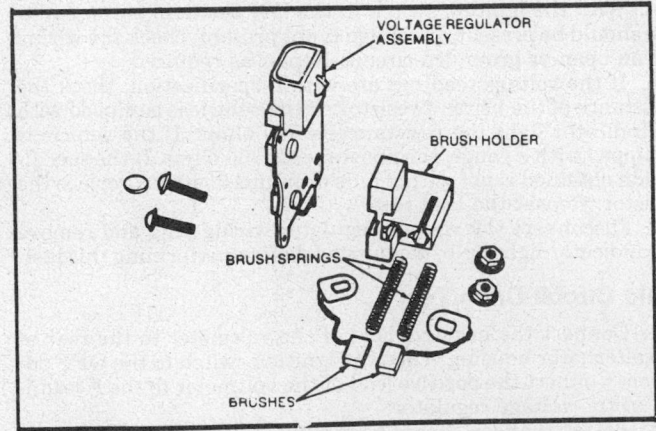

Ford alternator w/internal regulator—voltage regulator and brush holder

Stator Coil Open Test

1. Disconnect the stator from the rectifier assembly.
2. Using an ohmmeter, connect a test lead to a stator lead and the other test lead to another stator lead.
3. If the meter does not respond, an open circuit is present and the stator should be replaced. Repeat the test with the other wire combinations. A single open phase cannot be detected on alternators using a delta connected stator.

Rotor Open Or Short Circuit Test

1. Remove the rotor assembly from the alternator.
2. Using an ohmmeter contact each test lead to a rotor slip-ring. The ohmmeter should read 2.0–3.9 ohms.
3. If the readings are higher than specification it would indicate a damaged slip-ring solder connection or a broken wire.
4. If the readings are lower than specification it would indicate a shorted wire or slip-ring.
5. Replace the rotor if it is damaged. Connect an test lead of the ohmmeter to a rotor slip-ring and the other test lead to the rotor shaft.
6. The ohmmeter reading should be infinity. If this is not the case, the rotor is shorted to the shaft. Replace the rotor if the unit is shorted.

Disassembly and Assembly

1. Remove the alternator from the vehicle. Position the unit in a suitable holding fixture.
2. Remove the voltage regulator and the brush holder from the rear of the alternator assembly.
3. Remove the brush holder-to-voltage regulator screws and separate the components.
4. Matchmark the alternator end housings and stator frame to aid in installation.
5. Remove the alternator through bolts. Separate the front housing and the rotor assembly from the stator and the rear housing.
6. Unsolder the 3 stator leads from the rectifier assembly. Be careful that the rectifiers are not in contact with the solder iron, overheating them will cause damage.
7. Remove the rectifier assembly from the rear of the alternator housing. Press the rear alternator housing bearing from the rear housing.
8. From the front housing of the alternator remove the drive pulley nut from the rotor shaft.
9. Remove the lockwasher, drive pulley, fan and fan spacer from the rotor shaft.
10. Remove the rotor from the front housing. Remove the front bearing spacer from the rotor shaft. Do not remove the rotor stop ring unless it must be replaced.
11. Remove the front housing bearing retainer and bearing.
12. Assembly of the alternator is the reverse of the disassembly procedure. Be sure to clean and check all parts for wear and defects. Repair or replace defective components as required.

FORD SIDE TERMINAL ALTERNATOR

The warning lamp control circuit passes current to the warning lamp when the ignition switch is in the **RUN** position and there is no alternator voltage at terminal S. When the voltage at terminal S rises to a preset value, current is cut off to the warning lamp. This circuit is not included in the regulator for vehicles equipped with an ammeter rather than a warning lamp.

A 500 ohm, ¼ watt resistor is connected across the terminals of the lamp at the instrument cluster in vehicles equipped with an indicator warning lamp. The regulator switching circuit receives voltage from the ignition switch through the warning lamp at terminal I on vehicles equipped with an indicator warning lamp or through terminal S on vehicles equipped with an ammeter. With an input voltage present, the switching circuit turns on the voltage control circuit which, in turn, adjusts field current to control alternator output voltage.

Fuse links are included in the charging system wiring on all models. This fuse link is used to prevent damage to the wiring harness and alternator if the wiring harness should become grounded or if a booster battery is connected to the charging system with the wrong polarity.

Diagnostic Testing

Rectifier Short Grounded and Stator Grounded Test

NOTE: These tests are performed with an ohmmeter. Digital meters cannot be used to perform rectifier tests

1. Connect an ohmmeter probe to alternator BAT terminal (red insulator) and other probe to STA terminal (rear blade terminal). Then reverse ohmmeter probes and repeat test. Normally, there will be no needle movement in one direction, indicating rectifier diodes are being checked in reverse current direction and are not shorted. A low reading with probes reversed indicates that rectifier positive diodes are being checked in forward current direction. Using referenced tester, low reading should be about 6 ohms, but may vary if another type of test is used. A reading in both directions indicates a damaged positive diode, a grounded positive diode plate, or a grounded BAT terminal.

2. Perform same test using STA and GND (ground) terminals of alternator. A reading in both directions indicates either a damaged negative diode, a grounded positive diode plate or a grounded BAT terminal.

3. If there is no needle movement with probes in 1 direction and no needle movement or high resistance (significantly over 6 ohms) in opposite direction, a bad connection exists in stator circuit inside alternator.

Field Open or Short Circuit Test

1. Using an ohmmeter, contact the alternator field terminal with 1 probe and ground terminal with other probe. Then, spin alternator pulley. Ohmmeter reading should be between 2.4–100 ohms and should fluctuate while pulley is turning.

2. An infinite reading (no meter movement) indicates a grounded brush lead, worn or stuck brushes or a worn or damaged rotor assembly.

3. An ohmmeter reading less than 2.4 ohms indicates a grounded brush assembly, a grounded field terminal or a worn or damaged rotor.

Diode Test

1. Remove the rectifier assembly from the alternator stator. To test a set of diodes, contact one probe to a terminal screw and contact each of 3 stator lead terminals with other probe. Reverse probes and repeat test. All diodes should show a low reading of about 6 ohms in one direction and an infinite reading (no needle movement) with probes reversed. Low reading may vary with type of ohmmeter used.

2. Repeat preceding tests for other set of diodes by contacting the other terminal screw and 3 stator lead terminals.

3. If meter readings are not as specified, replace rectifier assembly.

Stator Coil Grounded Test

1. Connect ohmmeter probes to a stator lead and to stator

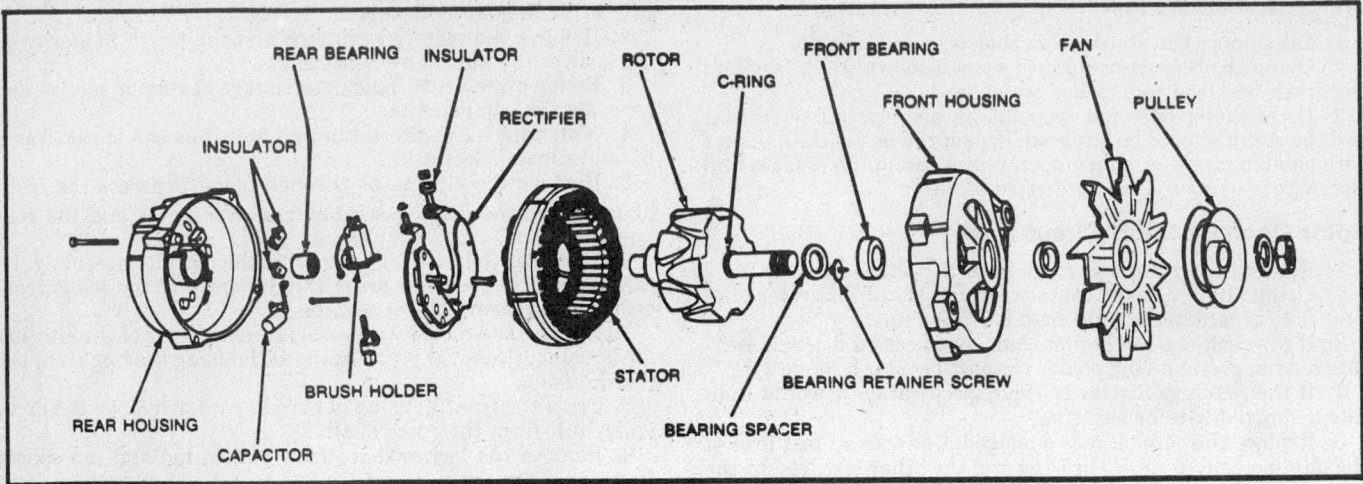

Ford side terminal alternator—exploded view

laminated core. Ensure that probe makes a good electrical connection with stator core. The meter should show an infinite reading (no meter movement).

2. If meter does not indicate an infinite reading (needle moves), stator winding is shorted to core and must be replaced.

3. Repeat this test for each stator lead. Do not touch the metal probes or stator leads with the hands. Such contact will result in an incorrect reading.

Stator Coil Open Test

NOTE: A single open phase will not be diagnosed by this test on a 100 amp alternator that has a delta connected stator.

1. Connect ohmmeter probe to a stator phase lead and touch other probe to another stator lead. Check meter reading.

2. Repeat this test with the other 2 stator lead combinations. If no meter movement occurs (infinite resistance) on a lead paired with either of the other phase leads, that phase is open and the stator should be replaced.

Rotor Open or Short Circuit Test

1. Contact each ohmmeter probe to a rotor slip-ring. The meter reading should be 2.3–2.5 ohms.

2. A higher reading indicates a damaged slip-ring solder connection or a broken wire.

3. A lower reading indicates a shorted wire or slip-ring. Replace rotor if it is damaged and cannot be serviced.

4. Contact an ohmmeter probe to a slip-ring and the other probe to rotor shaft. Meter reading should be infinite (no deflection).

5. A reading other than infinite indicates rotor is shorted to shaft. Inspect slip-ring soldered terminals to assure they are not bent and not touching rotor shaft, or that excess solder is not grounding rotor coil connections to shaft. Replace the rotor if it is shorted and cannot be serviced.

Disassembly and Assembly

1. Mark both end housings and stator with a scribe mark for assembly.

2. Remove housing through bolts and separate front housing and rotor from rear housing and stator. Slots are provided in front housing to aid in disassembly. Do not separate rear housing from stator at this time.

3. Remove drive pulley nut, lockwasher, pulley, fan and fan spacer from rotor shaft.

4. Pull rotor and shaft from front housing and remove spacer from rotor shaft.

5. Remove the screws retaining bearing to front housing. If bearing is damaged or has lost lubricant, remove bearing from housing. To remove bearing, support housing close to bearing boss and press bearing from housing.

6. Unsolder and disengage 3 stator leads from rectifier. Work quickly to prevent overheating rectifier.

7. Lift stator from rear housing.

8. Unsolder and disengage brush holder lead from rectifier. Work quickly to prevent overheating rectifier.

9. Remove screw attaching capacitor lead to rectifier.

10. Remove the screws attaching rectifier to rear housing.

11. Remove the terminal nuts and insulator from outside housing. Remove rectifier from housing.

12. Remove the screws attaching brush holder to housing. Remove brushes and holder.

13. Remove any sealing compound from rear housing and brush holder.

14. Remove the screw attaching capacitor to rear housing and remove capacitor.

15. If bearing replacement is necessary, support rear housing close to bearing boss and press bearing out of housing.

16. Wipe rotor, stator and bearings with a clean cloth. Do not clean these parts with solvent.

17. Rotate front bearing on drive end of rotor shaft. Check for any scraping noise, looseness or roughness. Look for excessive lubricant leakage. If any of these conditions exist, replace bearing.

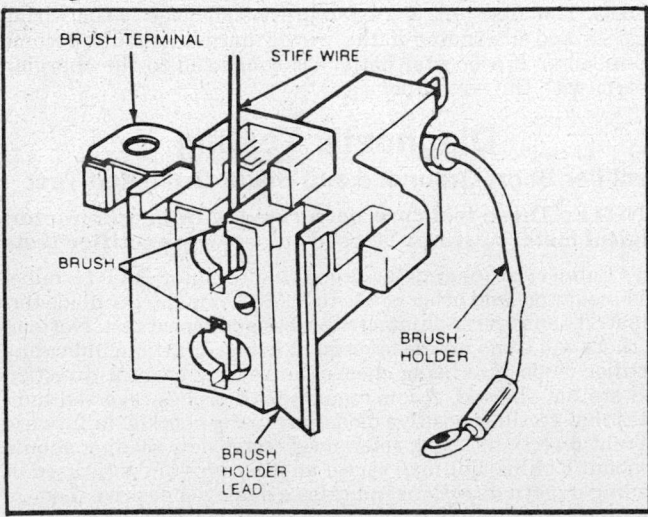

Ford side terminal alternator brush holder assembly

18. Inspect rotor shaft rear bearing surface for roughness or sever chatter marks. Replace rotor assembly if shaft is not smooth.

19. Place rear bearing on slip-ring end of rotor shaft and rotate bearing. Make the same check for noise, looseness, or roughness as was made for front bearing. Inspect rollers and cage for damage. Replace bearing if these conditions exist, or if lubricant is lost or contaminated.

20. Check pulley and fan for excessive looseness on rotor shaft. Replace any pulley that is loose or bent out of shape.

21. Check both front and rear housing for cracks, particularly in webbed areas and at mounting ear. Replace damaged or cracked housing.

22. Check all wire leads on both stator and rotor assemblies for loose or broken soldered connections and for burned insulation. Resolder poor connections. Replace parts that show signs of burned insulation.

23. Check slip-rings for nicks and surface roughness. Nicks and scratches may be removed by turning down slip-rings. Do not go beyond minimum diameter of 1.220 in. If rings are badly damaged, replace rotor assembly.

24. Replace brushes if they are worn shorter than ¼ in..

25. If front housing bearing is being replaced, press new bearing in housing. Apply pressure on bearing outer race only. Install bearing retaining screws and tighten to 25–40 inch lbs.

26. Place inner spacer on rotor shaft and insert rotor shaft into front housing and bearing.

27. Install fan spacer, fan, pulley, lockwasher and nut on rotor shaft. Use the proper tool to tighten pulley nut.

28. If rear bearing is being replaced, press a new bearing in from inside housing until rear bearing face is flush with boss outer surface.

29. Position brush terminal on brush holder. Install springs and brushes in brush holder and insert a piece of stiff wire to hold brushes in place.

30. Brushes and springs are serviced as part of brush holder assembly. Position brush holder in rear housing and install attaching screws. Brush retaining wire must stick out enough to be grabbed and pulled from housing assembly.

31. Waterproof glue sealer may have to be pushed out of pin hole in housing. Push brush holder toward brush holder attaching screws. Reseal crack between brush holder and brush cavity in rear housing with Caulking Cord or equivalent body sealer. Do not use silicone base sealer for this application.

32. Position capacitor to rear housing and install attaching screw. Place 2 rectifier insulators on bosses inside housing.

33. Place insulator on BAT (large) terminal of rectifier and position rectifier in rear housing. Place outside insulator on BAT terminal and install nuts on BAT and Grd terminals fingertight. Install, but do not tighten, the rectifier attaching screws.

34. Tighten the BAT terminal nuts to 35–50 inch lbs. and GRD terminal nuts to 25–35 inch lbs. on outside of rear housing. Then, tighten rectifier attaching screws to 40–50 inch lbs.

35. Position capacitor lead to rectifier and install attaching screw.

36. Press brush holder lead on rectifier pin and solder securely. Work quickly to prevent overheating of rectifier.

37. Position stator in rear housing and align scribe marks. Press 3 stator leads on rectifier pins and solder securely using resin core electrical solder. Work quickly to prevent overheating rectifier.

38. Position rotor and front housing into stator and rear housing. Align scribe marks and install through bolts. Tighten 2 opposing bolts and the remaining bolts.

39. Spin fan and pulley to be sure nothing is binding within alternator.

40. Remove brush retracting wire and place a daub of waterproof cement over hole to seal it. Do not use silicone sealer on hole.

INTERNAL FAN ALTERNATOR
WITH INTERNAL REGULATOR

1989–90 Festiva, Probe and Tracer

Disassembly

1. Remove the alternator housing screws.

2. Using a 200W soldering iron, heat the rear bearing area of the rear housing; the heat will expand the rear housing to allow the rear bearing to be removed from the housing.

3. Using a small pry bar, separate the rear housing and stator assembly from the front housing; be careful not to lose the stopper spring which fits around the circumference of the rear bearing.

4. Place the rotor in a soft-jawed vise with the jaws around the outside of the rotor. Remove the pulley retaining nut, the pulley, both front seals and the spacer.

5. Separate the rotor from the front housing.

6. If necessary to remove the front bearing, perform the following procedures:

a. Remove the front bearing retainer plate-to-housing screws and the plate.

b. Using a shop press and the socket, press the bearing from the front housing.

7. To disassemble the rear housing, perform the following procedures:

a. Remove the nut and insulator from the B terminal.

b. Remove the rectifier-to-housing screw and the brush holder/regulator assembly-to-housing screws.

c. Using a small pry bar, separate the stator from the rear housing.

d. Remove the stator assembly, with the rectifier and brush holder/regulator assembly attached.

e. From the brush holder, remove both plastic shields.

f. Using a soldering iron, unsolder the stator-to-rectifier leads; work quickly to avoid overheating the diodes.

On Vehicle Testing

NOTE: Before performing the following test, be sure to firmly apply the parking brake, place the transaxle in P or N and turn OFF all electrical loads. Make sure the battery posts and cables are clean and tight. The battery must be fully charged and the alternator connectors cleaned.

AMPERAGE OUTPUT

1. Using a starting/charging system analyzer, connect the red lead to the positive battery terminal, the black lead to the negative battery terminal and the current probe on the analyzer's red lead with the arrow pointing toward the battery of the on the black lead with the arrow pointing away from the battery.

2. Start and operate the engine at 2500–3000 rpm.

3. Record the maximum alternator amperage output.

4. If the output is within 10 percent of it's rated output, the alternator is working properly.

5. If the output is less than 5 amps, perform the voltage output test.

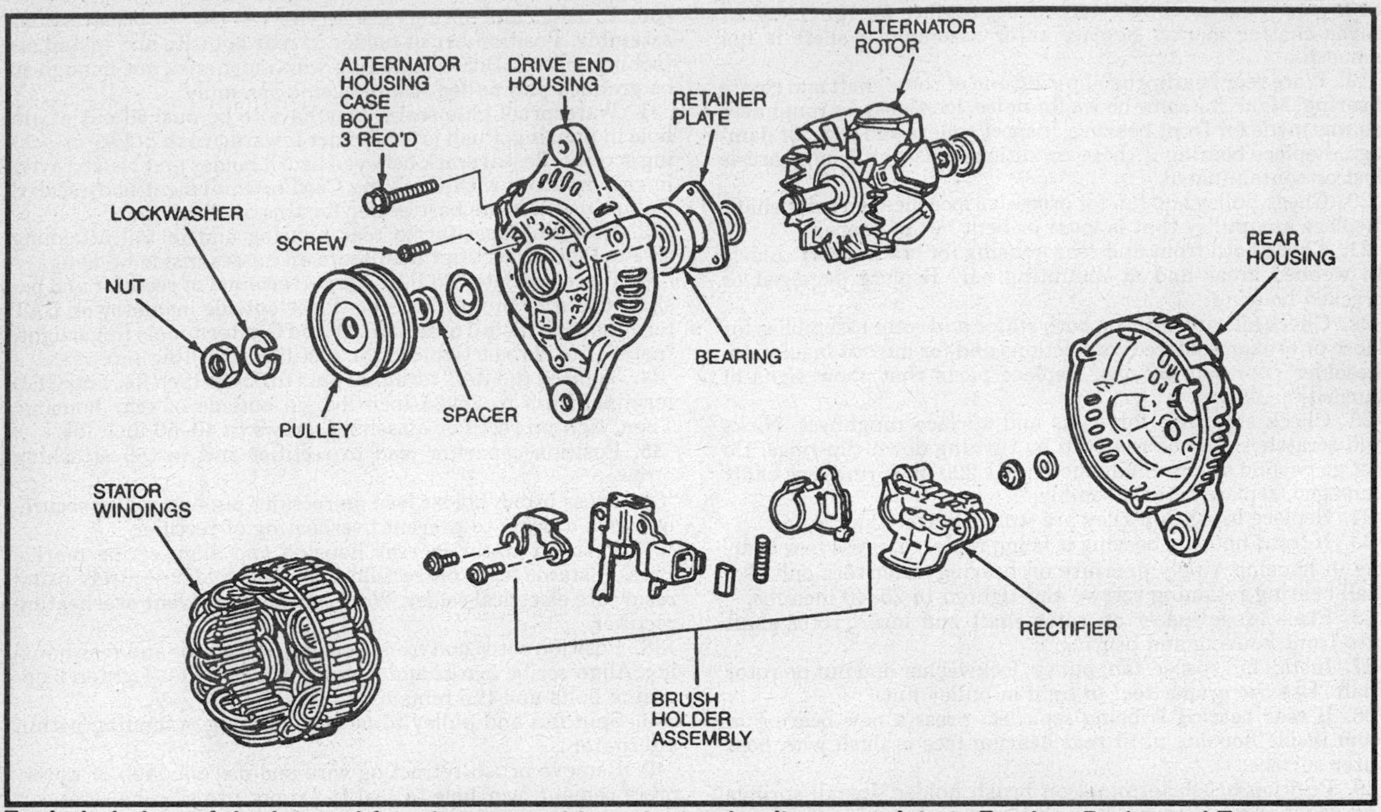

Exploded view of the internal fan alternator with an internal voltage regulator—Festiva, Probe and Tracer

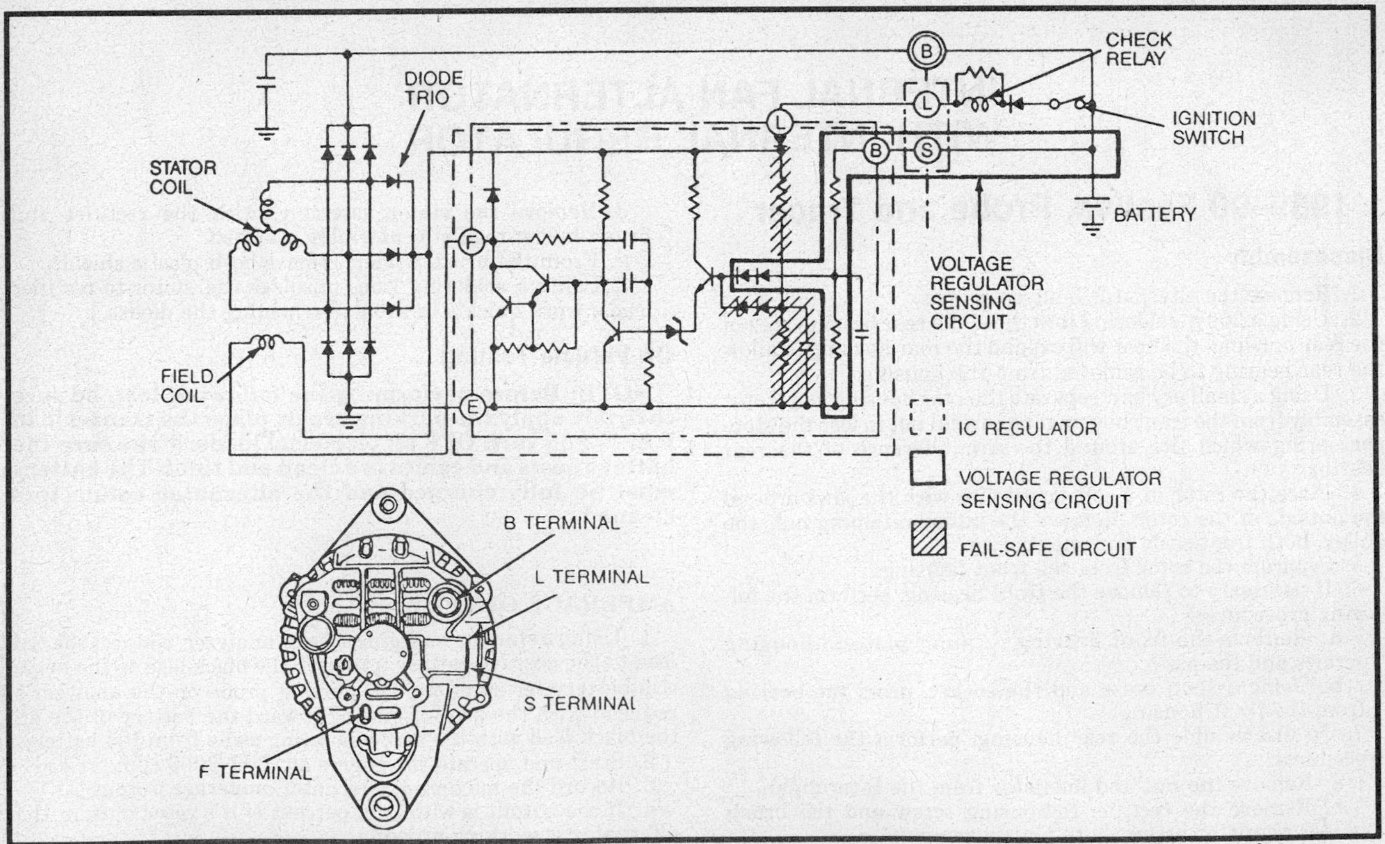

Electrical schematic and terminal locations of the internal fan alternator with an internal voltage regulator—1989–90 Festiva, Probe and Tracer

VOLTAGE OUTPUT

1. Using a starting/harging system analyzer, connect the red lead to the positive battery terminal, the black lead to the negative battery terminal and the current probe on the analyzer's red lead with the arrow pointing toward the battery of the on the black lead with the arrow pointing away from the battery.

2. Start and operate the engine at approximately 2500 rpm.

3. Using a voltmeter, touch the (+) positive lead to the alternator's L-terminal (leave the 2-wire connector attached) and the (−) negative lead to the alternator's case.

4. If the reading is less than 14.4 volts at 68°F (20°C), perform the regulator power source test. If the reading is 14.4–15.0 volts at 68°F (20°C), the alternator is operating properly. If the reading is 14.4–15.0 volts at 68°F (20°C) and the amperage is less than 5 amps, inspect the stator and/or rectifier.

REGULATOR POWER SOURCE

1. Turn the ignition switch to the **ON** position but do not start the engine.

2. At the rear of the alternator, disconnect the 2-wire electrical connector from the L and S-terminals.

3. Using a voltmeter, touch the (+) positive lead to the alternator's S-terminal and the (−) negative lead to the alternator's case.

4. If the reading is less than 14.4 volts at 68°F (20°C), the problem is in the circuit between the battery and the S-terminal. If the reading is 14.4–15.0 volts at 68°F (20°C), perform the rotor field coil test.

ROTOR FIELD COIL

1. Disconnect the negative battery cable.

2. At the rear of the alternator, disconnect the electrical connector from the B-terminal; be sure the wire end does not touch the alternators output terminal.

3. At the rear of the alternator, disconnect the 2-wire electrical connector from the L and S-terminals.

4. Using a digital volt/ohmmeter, position it on the Multiply By setting **1** and calibrate it.

5. Connect the digital volt/ohmmeter to the alternator's S and F-terminals.

NOTE: The F-terminal is internal and accessed through the hole at the rear of the alternator. Be sure the test lead does not touch the alternator housing while performing this test.

6. If the reading is 3–6 ohms, the field coil is good; perform the voltage regulator test. If the reading is less than 3 ohms or greater than 6 ohms, inspect the rotor field coil, slip rings or brushes.

7. Reconnect the electrical connectors to the alternator and the battery.

VOLTAGE REGULATOR

1. Turn the ignition switch to the **ON** position but do not start the engine.

2. Using a voltmeter, touch the (+) positive lead to the alternator's L terminal (leave the 2-wire connector attached) and the (−) negative lead to the alternator's case.

3. If the reading is 1–3 volts, inspect the stator and/or rectifier. If the reading is greater than 3 volts, inspect and/or replace the voltage regulator.

Bench Testing

ROTOR

1. Using an ohmmeter, measure the resistance of the slip rings, the reading should be 2.0–2.6 ohms; if not, replace the rotor.

2. Using an ohmmeter, check for continuity between the slip ring(s) and the rotor core; if continuity exists, replace the rotor.

3. If the slip rings appear dark, use fine emery paper to clean them. If the slip rings are grooved, refinish them on a lathe.

STATOR

1. Inspect the stator laminations for signs of overheating; a burnt spot usually indicates a shorted winding and the stator should be replaced.

2. Using an ohmmeter, check for continuity between the stator winding leads; no continuity indicates an open winding and the stator should be replaced.

3. Using an ohmmeter, check for continuity between the stator winding leads and the core; if continuity exists, a ground is indicated and the stator should be replaced.

BRUSHES

1. The brushes are equipped with a wear limit line of 0.315 in.; if they are worn close to this measurement, replace the brushes.

2. When installing new brushes, be sure to solder the brushes into the brush holder (at the pigtails) so the brush wear limit protrudes 0.079–0.118 in. (2–3mm) from the brush holder.

3. Using a spring pressure gauge, measure the brush spring pressure by pushing the brushes into the brush holder; the spring pressure should be 10.9–15.2 oz. (3.0–4.2 N) whit the brush protruding 0.079 in. from the brush holder.

BEARINGS

Inspect the bearings for abnormal noise, looseness or insufficient lubrication; if necessary, replace them.

RECTIFIER

1. Using an ohmmeter, check for continuity between each positive diode and the heat sink; while reversing the test probes, continuity should exist in one direction only. Should the diodes exhibit continuity in both directions or no continuity in either direction, replace the rectifier.

2. Using an ohmmeter, check for continuity between each negative diode and the heat sink; while reversing the test probes, continuity should exist in one direction only. Should the diodes exhibit continuity in both directions or no continuity in either direction, replace the rectifier.

3. Using an ohmmeter, check for continuity between the diode trio (the 3 smaller diodes located between the 3 main diode leads; while reversing the test probes, continuity should exist in one direction only. Should the diode trio exhibit continuity in both directions or no continuity in either direction, replace the trio.

Assembly

1. To assemble the rear housing, perform the following procedures:

   a. Using a soldering iron and rosin core solder, solder the stator leads to the rectifier assembly; work quickly to avoid overheating the diodes.

   b. Install both plastic shields to the brush holder/regulator assembly.

   c. Install the stator assembly, with the rectifier and brush holder attached, to the rear housing. Position the stator into the housing so one of the shallow lamination ridges aligns with the case bolt holes.

   d. Install the rectifier and brush holder screws.

   e. Install the "B" terminal insualtor and nut. Torque the nut to 1.0–4.6 ft. lbs. (4.2 Nm).

2. Using a straight, stiff wire, depress the brushes and insert the wire through the rear housing, to hold the brushes for assembly purposes.

3. If the front bearing was removed, use a shop press and a socket to press the bearing into the front housing. Install the bearing retainer plate.

4. Position the rotor in a soft-jawed vise, with the clamp around the outside of the rotor. Install the spacer the inner shield, the front housing, the outer shield, the pulley, the lock-

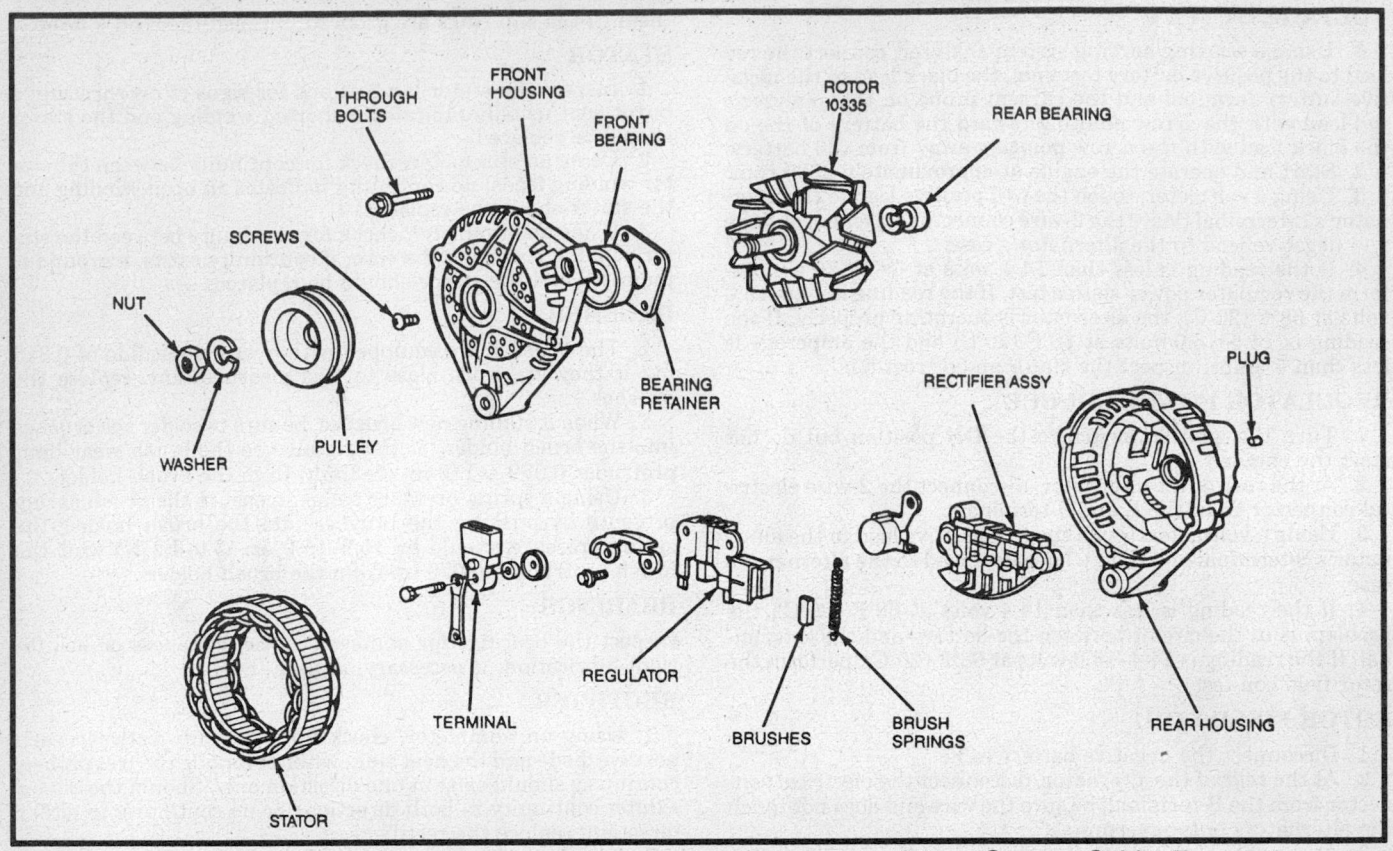

Exploded view of the internal fan alternator with an internal voltage regulator—Cougar, Sable, Taurus and Thunderbird

washer and the nut. Torque the nut to 36–65 ft. lbs. (49–88 Nm).

5. Using a 200W soldering iron, heat the bearing area of the rear housing; be sure to heat the housing to 122–144°F (50–60°C). Install the front housing assembly to the rear housing assembly by indexing the larger mounting brackets.

6. Install the case bolts and tighten gradually to draw the halves together uniformly.

7. Remove the wire used to retain the brushes.

8. Rotate the alternator to be sure there is no drag and the rotor spins freely; if resistance or drag is present, disassemble the alternator and determine the cause.

1989–90 Cougar, Sable, Taurus and Thunderbird

Disassembly

1. Remove the alternator housing screws.

2. Using a 200W soldering iron, heat the rear bearing area of the rear housing; the heat will expand the rear housing to allow the rear bearing to be removed from the housing.

3. Using a small pry bar, separate the rear housing and stator assembly from the front housing; be careful not to lose the stopper spring which fits around the circumference of the rear bearing.

4. Place the rotor in a soft-jawed vise with the jaws around the outside of the rotor. Remove the pulley retaining nut and the pulley.

5. Separate the rotor from the front housing.

6. If necessary to remove the front bearing, perform the following procedures:

   a. Remove the front bearing retainer plate-to-housing screws and the plate.

b. Using a shop press and the socket, press the bearing from the front housing.

7. To disassemble the rear housing, perform the following procedures:

   a. Remove the nut and insulator from the B terminal.

   b. Remove the rectifier-to-housing screws and the brush holder/regulator assembly-to-housing screw.

   c. Using a small pry bar, separate the stator from the rear housing.

   d. Remove the stator assembly, with the rectifier and brush holder/regulator assembly attached.

   e. From the brush holder, remove both plastic shields.

   f. Using a soldering iron, unsolder the stator-to-rectifier leads; work quickly to avoid overheating the diodes.

Testing
ROTOR

1. Using an ohmmeter, measure the resistance of the slip rings, the reading should be 2.0–3.9 ohms; if not, replace the rotor.

2. Using an ohmmeter, check for continuity between the slip ring(s) and the rotor core; if continuity exists, replace the rotor.

3. If the slip rings appear dark, use fine emery paper to clean them. If the slip rings are grooved, refinish them on a lathe.

STATOR

1. Inspect the stator laminations for signs of overheating; a burnt spot usually indicates a shorted winding and the stator should be replaced.

2. Using an ohmmeter, check for continuity between the stator winding leads; no continuity indicates an open winding and the stator should be replaced.

3. Using an ohmmeter, check for continuity between the sta-

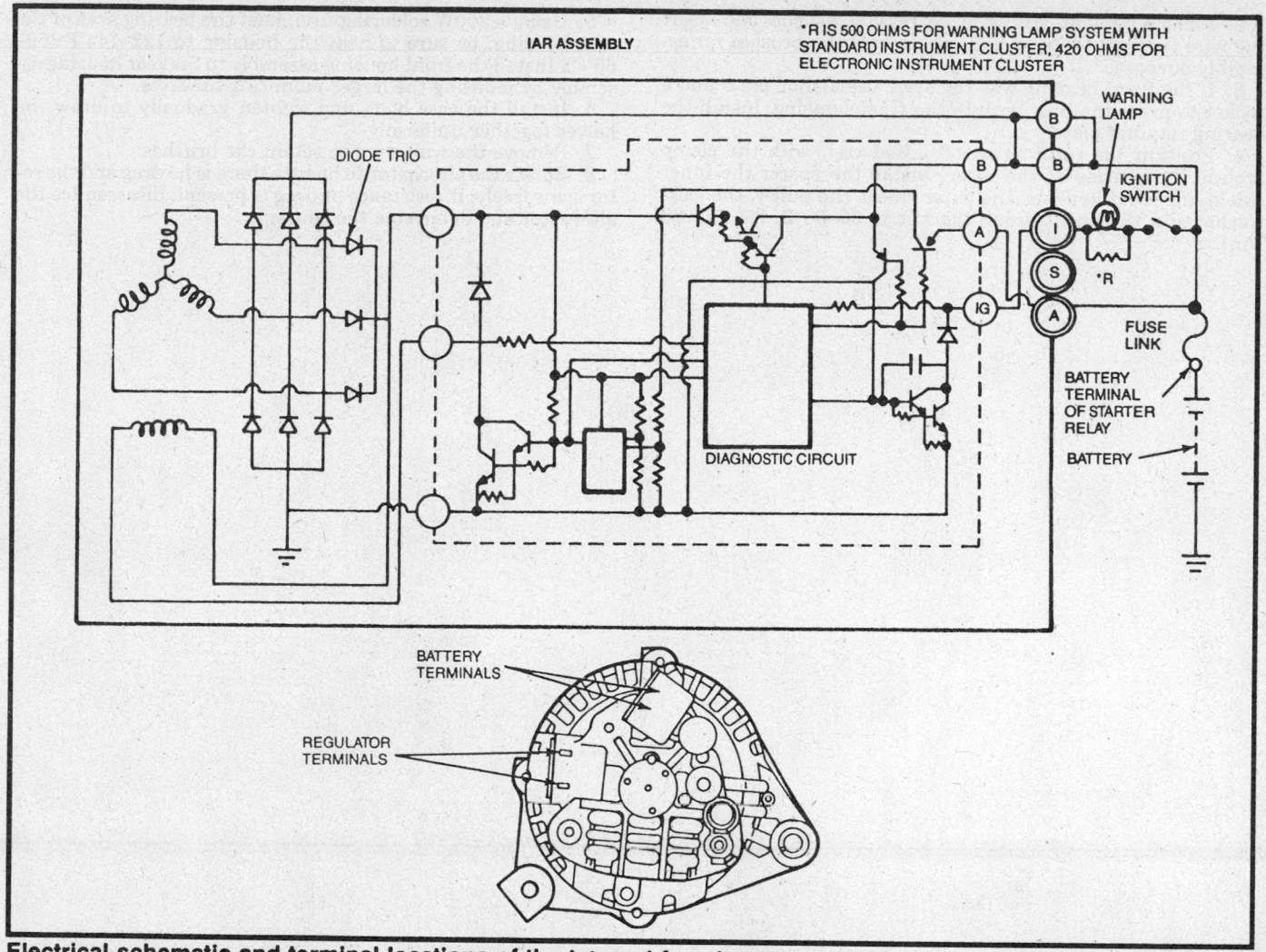

IAR ASSEMBLY

*R IS 500 OHMS FOR WARNING LAMP SYSTEM WITH STANDARD INSTRUMENT CLUSTER, 420 OHMS FOR ELECTRONIC INSTRUMENT CLUSTER

Electrical schematic and terminal locations of the internal fan alternator with an internal voltage regulator—1989–90 Cougar, Sable, Taurus and Thunderbird

tor winding leads and the core; if continuity exists, a ground is indicated and the stator should be replaced.

BRUSHES

1. The brushes are equipped with a wear limit line of 0.30 in.; if they are worn close to this measurement, replace the brushes.

2. When installing new brushes, be sure to solder the brushes into the brush holder (at the pigtails) so the brush wear limit protrudes 0.08–0.12 in. (2–3mm) from the brush holder.

3. Using a spring pressure gauge, measure the brush spring pressure by pushing the brushes into the brush holder; the spring pressure should be 10.9–15.9 oz. (3.0–4.2 N) whit the brush protruding 0.079 in. from the brush holder.

BEARINGS

Inspect the bearings for abnormal noise, looseness or insufficient lubrication; if necessary, replace them.

RECTIFIER

1. Using an ohmmeter, check for continuity between each positive diode and the heat sink; while reversing the test probes, continuity should exist in one direction only. Should the diodes exhibit continuity in both directions or no continuity in either direction, replace the rectifier.

2. Using an ohmmeter, check for continuity between each negative diode and the heat sink; while reversing the test probes, continuity should exist in one direction only. Should the diodes exhibit continuity in both directions or no continuity in either direction, replace the rectifier.

3. Using an ohmmeter, check for continuity between the diode trio (the 3 smaller diodes located between the 3 main diode leads; while reversing the test probes, continuity should exist in one direction only. Should the diode trio exhibit continuity in both directions or no continuity in either direction, replace the trio.

Assembly

1. To assemble the rear housing, perform the following procedures:

   a. Using a soldering iron and rosin core solder, solder the stator leads to the rectifier assembly; work quickly to avoid overheating the diodes.

   b. Install both plastic shields to the brush holder/regulator assembly.

   c. Install the stator assembly, with the rectifier and brush holder attached, to the rear housing. Position the stator into the housing so one of the shallow lamination ridges aligns with the case bolt holes.

   d. Install the rectifier and brush holder screws.

   e. Install the B terminal insulator and nut. Torque the nut to 1.0–4.6 ft. lbs. (4.2 Nm).

2. Using a straight, stiff wire, depress the brushes and insert the wire through the rear housing, to hold the brushes for assembly purposes.

3. If the front bearing was removed, use a shop press and a socket to press the bearing into the front housing. Install the bearing retainer plate.

4. Position the rotor in a soft-jawed vise, with the clamp around the outside of the rotor. Install the spacer the inner shield, the front housing, the outer shield, the pulley, the lockwasher and the nut. Torque the nut to 36–65 ft. lbs. (49–88 Nm).

5. Using a 200W soldering iron, heat the bearing area of the rear housing; be sure to heat the housing to 122–144°F (50–60°C). Install the front housing assembly to the rear housing assembly by indexing the larger mounting brackets.

6. Install the case bolts and tighten gradually to draw the halves together uniformly.

7. Remove the wire used to retain the brushes.

8. Rotate the alternator to be sure there is no drag and the rotor spins freely; if resistance or drag is present, disassemble the alternator and determine the cause.

HYDRAULIC BRAKE SERVICE

GENERAL DESCRIPTION

All vehicles are equipped with 2 separate brake systems, so that if either system should fail, the other will provide enough braking power to safely stop the vehicle. The standard approach has been to use a tandem master cylinder and separate hydraulic circuits for the front and rear brakes, or a diagonally split system separating opposite front and rear wheels. A tandem master cylinder uses a pair of piston-and-seal assemblies in-line within a single bore.

The dual system includes a warning lamp on the instrument panel and, to activate it, a pressure differential valve which is connected to both sides of the system. The valve is sensitive to any loss of hydraulic pressure which results from a braking failure on either side of the system and alerts the driver by switching on the lamp, which is connected to the ignition switch. With the switch in **START** position, the lamp is lit, furnishing a bulb check, but in **RUN** position, it will light only if a brake failure occurs.

All vehicles are provided with pressure regulating units. Pressure-regulating units refine the braking balance, by changing the ratio of front-to-rear pressure, regulating it for moderate or severe stops as required to lessen skidding and diving. The pressure metering valve inhibits pressure to front disc brakes during easy, rolling stops. The proportioning or proportioner valve(s) proportion outlet pressure to the rear brakes after a predetermined master cylinder pressure has been reached. This is used when more apply force is needed in the front to obtain normal braking. Either or both types of valves are found in various systems.

NOTE: Unless the proportioning valve is integral with the master cylinder, overhaul parts may not be available. Check for overhaul kit availability. When replacing the valve components, make sure the new part is an exact duplicate of the original part.

The dual master cylinder is equipped with a pair of pistons. This type of master cylinder has the secondary piston in front of the primary piston. The primary piston is actuated directly by mechanical linkage from the brake pedal. The secondary piston is actuated by fluid trapped between the front and rear pistons. If a leak develops in front of the secondary piston, it moves forward until it bottoms against the front of the master cylinder. The fluid trapped between the pistons will operate the front side of the split system. If the other side of the system develops a leak, the primary piston will move forward until direct contact with the secondary piston takes place and it will force the secondary piston to actuate the other side of the split system. In either case the brake pedal drops closer to the floor and less braking power is available.

Master Cylinder Systems

The master cylinder unit is a highly calibrated unit specifically designed for the vehicle it is on. Although the cylinders may look alike there are many differences in calibration. If replacement is necessary, make sure the replacement unit is specified for the vehicle.

Many GM vehicles are equipped with Quick Take-Up or Composite master cylinders which provide a large volume of fluid to the brakes at low pressure when the brake pedal is initially applied. This large volume of fluid is needed because of the new self retracting piston seals at the front disc brake calipers which pull the pistons into the calipers after the brakes are released, thereby preventing the brake pads from causing a drag on the rotors. Overhaul procedures on the Quick Take-Up master cylinders are basically the same as those on conventional master cylinder. Other GM vehicles are using a Compact master cylinder designed for use with diagonally split systems. It incorporates the functions of a standard dual master cylinder and in addition it has a fluid sensor switch and integral proportioners.

The master cylinder used on some GM front wheel drive vehicles has a fluid level operated brake warning light switch incorporated in the master cylinder body. The piston is accessible by removing the large plug at the front of the master cylinder body.

Brake system schematic

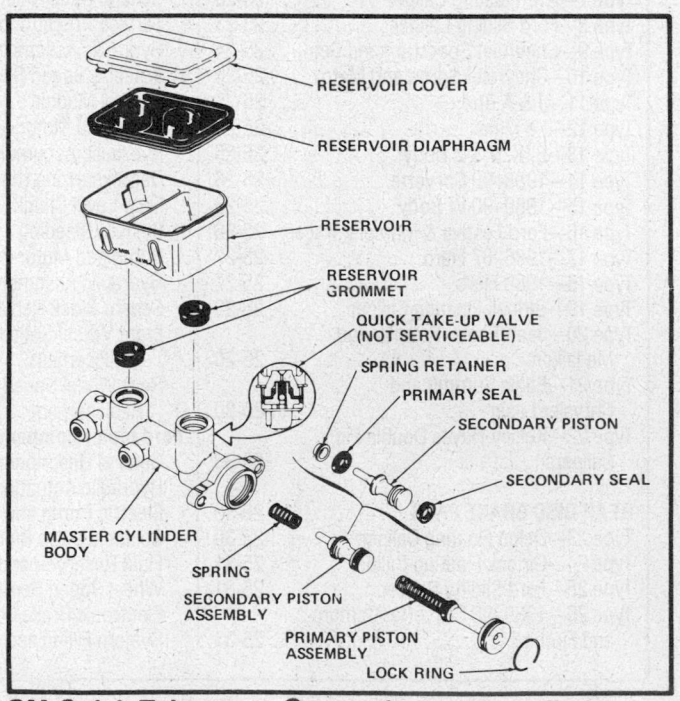

GM Quick Take-up or Composite master cylinder

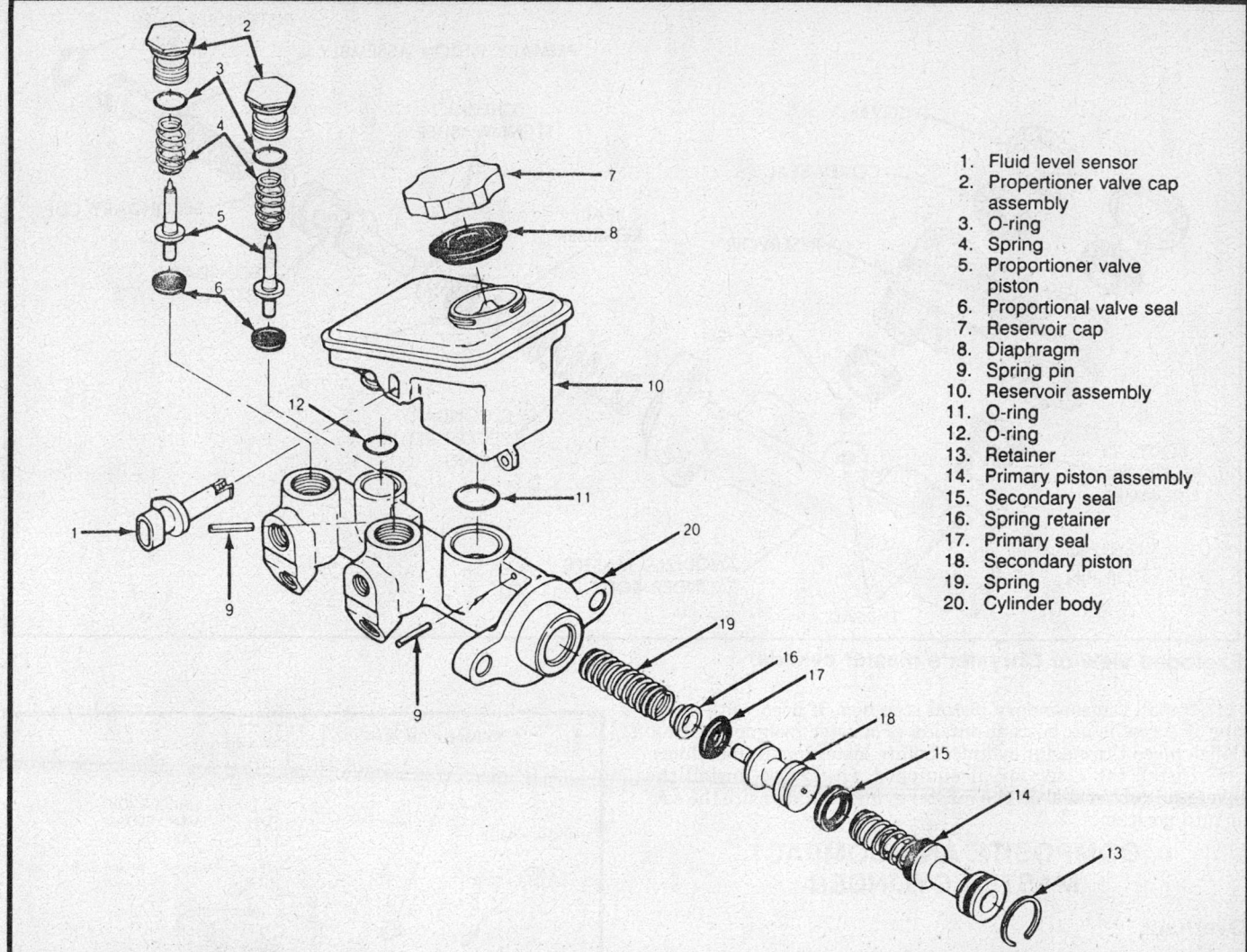

1. Fluid level sensor
2. Proportioner valve cap assembly
3. O-ring
4. Spring
5. Proportioner valve piston
6. Proportional valve seal
7. Reservoir cap
8. Diaphragm
9. Spring pin
10. Reservoir assembly
11. O-ring
12. O-ring
13. Retainer
14. Primary piston assembly
15. Secondary seal
16. Spring retainer
17. Primary seal
18. Secondary piston
19. Spring
20. Cylinder body

GM Compact master cylinder

Only remove the plug when overhauling the cylinder, as brake fluid will escape. Other manufacturers use a floating device in the master cylinder in specially equipped vehicles to inform the driver of a low fluid situation.

QUICK TAKE-UP AND CONVENTIONAL DUAL MASTER CYLINDER

Overhaul

NOTE: If the Quick Take-Up valve is defective on GM units, the entire master cylinder assembly must be replaced. The plastic reservoir may be reused if it is not damaged.

1. On Chysler vehicles, remove the plastic reservoir from the master cylinder. Remove the secondary piston stop bolt or pin from the bottom or inside the reservoir, if equipped.

2. Depress the primary piston and remove the snapring from the retaining groove at the rear of the master cylinder bore.

3. Remove the pushrod and primary piston assembly from the master cylinder bore. Do not remove the screw that secures the primary return spring retainer, return spring, primary cup and protector on the primary piston. This assembly is factory pre-adjusted and should not be disassembled.

4. Remove the secondary piston assembly, but do not remove the outlet tube seats from the master cylinder body.

5. Inspect all parts for chipping, excessive wear or damage. When using a master cylinder repair kit, install all the parts supplied.

6. Be sure that all recesses, openings and internal passages are open and clean.

7. Inspect the master cylinder bore for signs of pitting, scoring or rust. If necessary to hone the master cylinder bore to repair damage, do not exceed the 0.003 in. allowable hone specification.

8. To assemble, dip all parts except the master cylinder body in clean brake fluid.

9. Carefully insert the complete secondary piston and return spring assembly in the master cylinder bore.

10. Install the primary piston assembly in the master cylinder bore.

11. Depress the primary piston and install the snap ring in the cylinder bore groove.

12. Install the pushrod, boot and retainer on the pushrod, if so equipped. Install the pushrod assembly into the primary piston. Make sure the retainer is properly seated and holding the pushrod securely.

13. Position the inner end of the pushrod boot, if equipped, in the master cylinder body retaining groove.

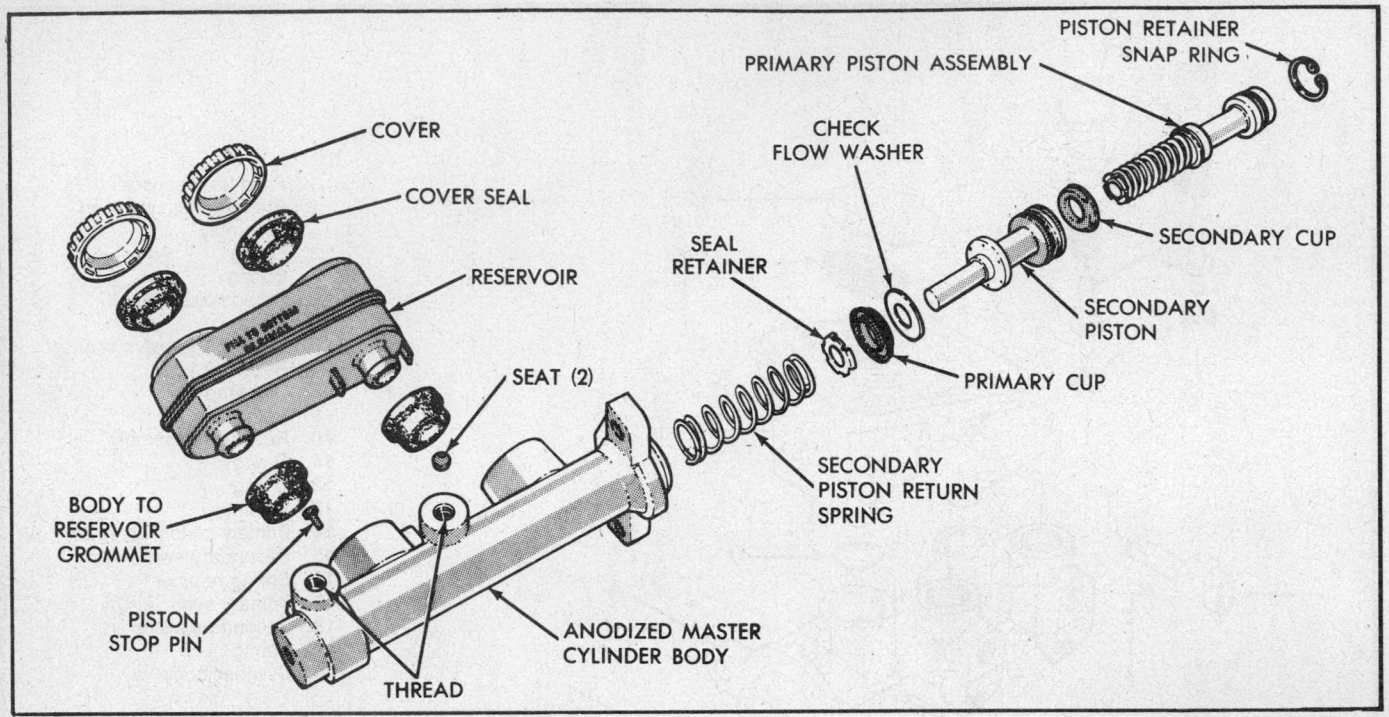

Exploded view of Chrysler's master cylinder

14. Install the secondary piston stop bolt, if used, with an O-ring if screw is on bottom outside of master cylinder casting. Bench bleed the master cylinder before installing in the vehicle.

15. Install the reservoir, if equipped. Otherwise, install the cover and rubber seal on the master cylinder and secure the cover into position.

COMPOSITE AND COMPACT MASTER CYLINDER

Overhaul

1. Do not remove the plastic reservoir(s) unless there is damage to the reservoir or seals.

2. Remove the fluid sensor switch.

3. Remove the proportioner valve cap assembly, O-ring, spring, piston and seal.

4. Push the primary piston in and remove the snapring.

5. Apply low pressure compressed air to the upper outlet port at the blind end of the bore with all other ports plugged in order to remove the primary piston assembly, secondary piston, spring and spring retainer.

6. Inspect all parts for chipping, excessive wear or damage. When using a master cylinder repair kit, install all the parts supplied.

7. Be sure that all recesses, openings and internal passages are open and clean. Check all rubber parts that can be reused for rips, swelling and other damage.

8. Inspect the master cylinder bore for signs of pitting, scoring or rust. If necessary to hone the master cylinder bore to repair damage, do not exceed the 0.003 in. allowable hone specification.

—— CAUTION ——

Do not hone aluminum master cylinders. There is a special coating on the aluminum which will be removed if honed. This will damage the master cylinder and could cause personal injury if the vehicle is driven.

9. When assembling, dip all parts except the master cylinder body in clean brake fluid.

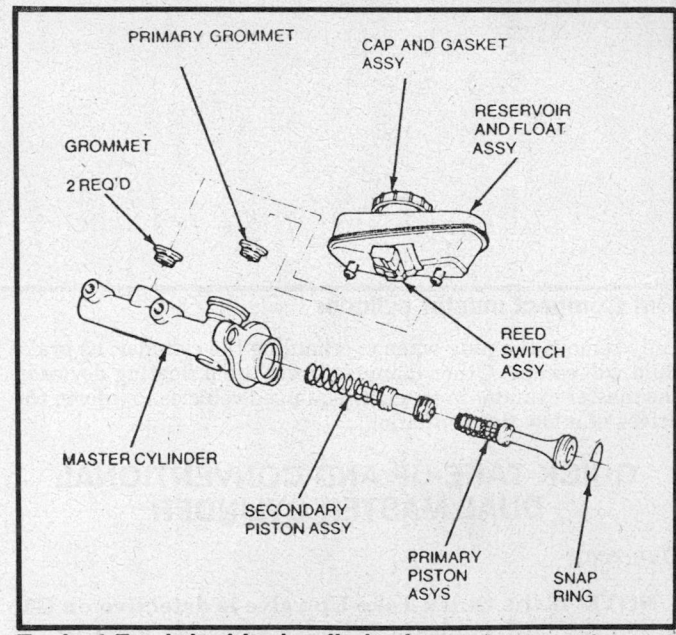

Typical Ford dual hydraulic brake system master cylinder

10. Assemble the secondary piston assembly with new seals.

11. Install the secondary piston assembly and spring into the master cylinder.

12. Install the primary piston assembly into the master cylinder.

13. Install the snapring.

14. Install the proportioner valve assemblies with new O-rings.

15. Install the fluid level switch.

16. Install the reservoir, if removed, with new seals and install the cap(s).

17. On GM vehicles with a fluid level switch, remove the plug and remove the switch assembly. If any corrosion is present in the bore, the master cylinder must be replaced. Otherwise, remove the O-rings and retainers from the piston. Install new O-rings and retainers and install the piston in its bore. Install the Allen head plug with a new O-ring.

Disc Brake Calipers

DESCRIPTION

Caliper disc brakes can be divided into 3 types: the 2-piston, floating caliper type; single-piston, floating-caliper type; and the single-piston sliding-caliper type. With the floating-caliper type, the inboard shoe is pushed hydraulically into contact with the disc, while the reaction force generated is used to pull the outboard shoe into frictional contact, made possible by letting the caliper move slightly along the axle centerline. 2 pistons are used to accomodate more severe braking conditions with heavier or faster vehicles and give more positive stopping power.

In the sliding caliper (single piston) type, the caliper assembly slides along the machined surfaces of the anchor plate. A steel key located between the machined surfaces of the caliper and the machined surfaces of the anchor plate is held in place with either a retaining screw or 2 cotter pins. The caliper is held in place against the anchor plate with 1 or 2 support springs.

Some new developments in brake equipment materials include the use of aluminum calipers for the purpose of saving weight. A variety of anti-rattle springs and clips are used by the manufacturers to prevent the pads from making any noise while the vehicle is in motion. Also, virtually all quality brake pads are now comprised of a semi-metallic material for improved stopping ability. A problem frequently encountered with these brake pads is an annoying brake squeal caused by the high metallic content of the pad. Some pad kits include anti-squeal plates. Aftermarket sprays and spreads are also available to quiet noisy brakes.

Another fairly recent development in brakes is the wide use of rear discs brakes. In the past, rear discs were mostly used mostly on fairly exotic vehicles and sports cars. Presently, they can be purchased as an option on a majority of domestic vehicles. An advantage of having rear disc brakes is that they require no adjustment; all disc brake systems are self-adjusting. Since most drivers do not adjust their rear drum brakes, the shoes get out of adjustment quickly and become less efficient. This can become potentially dangerous in time and causes the front pads to wear out faster than they should under normal circumstances.

A disadvantage, however, of rear disc brakes is that the parking brake mechanism has to be built into the caliper, except in some applications. This makes the construction of the caliper more complex than the conventional front caliper and, in turn, makes overhaul procedures more involved and replacement parts more expensive. The attraction of more efficient braking has overcome these disadvantages and made rear disc brakes popular.

DISC BRAKE CALIPERS

————— **CAUTION** —————

When servicing brake parts, do not create dust by grinding or sanding the brake pads, or by cleaning brake parts with a dry brush or compressed air. Many brake parts contain asbestos fibers which can become airborne if dust is created during servicing. Breathing this dust can cause serious bodily harm. A dampened cloth can be used to remove brake dust. Equipment is also commercially available for safe brake servicing.

Removal and Installation

Before servicing the calipers, try to loosen both bleeder screws using light pressure. Spray the bleeder screw liberally with rust penetrant if it does not come out easily. If the bleeder screw breaks, it is usually very difficult to remove the siezed piece neatly and rethread the bore, in which case the caliper must be replaced.

Before the calipers are removed from the vehicle, clamp the brake hoses with the proper tools so the brake fluid will not run out of the hoses. Remove the caliper mounting hardware and slide the caliper from the brake pads, prying with a suitable pry bar if necessary. Remove parking brake cable retaining clips and disconnect the cable from its pivot, if removing rear disc brake calipers. Mark the caliper so it is reinstalled on the same side of the vehicle.

Use new copper washers, if equipped, when installing new or overhauled calipers on the vehicle. Lubricate sliding components with suitable high temperature lubricant to prevent the brakes from hanging up while in operation. Make sure all anti-rattle clips are installed correctly. Torque all mounting bolts to specification and bleed the system completely to finish the operation.

FRONT CALIPERS

Overhaul

NOTE: Some late G and J body Chrysler vehicles and 1986–87 Corvettes are equipped with rear disc brakes, but do not have the parking brake mechanism integrated into the rear calipers. Instead, they have small parking brake shoes under the rear rotors. Follow the procedures for front caliper overhaul for these units.

1. Remove the bleeder screw. Drain the brake fluid from the caliper and clean the outside of the caliper.

NOTE: When cleaning brake components, use only brake fluid or denatured Isopropyl alcohol. Never use a mineral-based solvent, such as gasoline or paint thinner, since it will swell and quickly deteriorate rubber parts. All alcohol must be completely removed from system; any alcohol mixed with brake fluid will lower its boiling point.

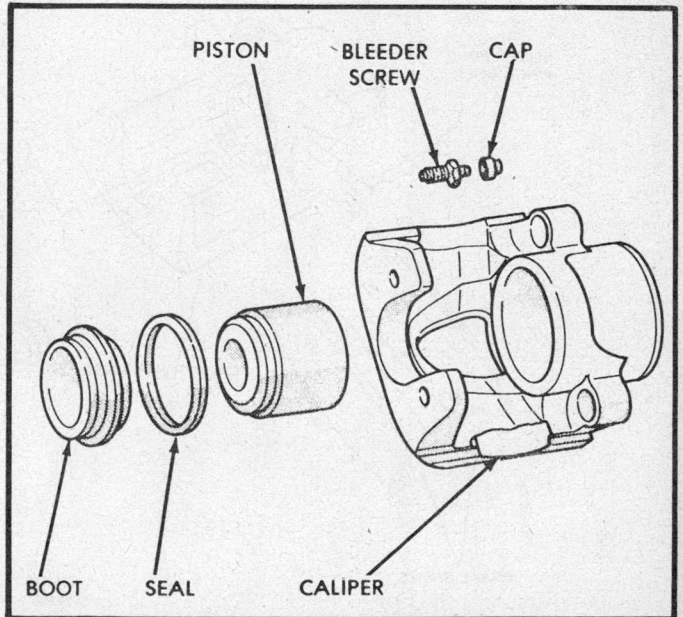

Typical single piston caliper components

2. Remove the piston dust boot(s) from the caliper with the retaining spring, if equipped.

3. Position a shop rag opposite the top of the piston. Apply low pressure compressed air to the fluid inlet and carefully blow the piston out of its bore.

4. If pistons on dual-piston caliper do not come out at the same time, install the extracted piston back into its bore just enough to seal and hold in place with a spacer. Repeat the procedure and or extract the remaining piston.

5. Remove the seal from inside the bore.

6. Blow out all caliper passages with low pressure compressed air.

7. Slight corrosion or rust can be removed with commutator paper or crocus cloth. Metallic pistons that are pitted, scored, or worn, must be replaced; replacement plastic piston are normally included in the overhaul kit. A corroded or deeply scored caliper should also be replaced.

NOTE: If a fine stone honing of a caliper bore is necessary it should be done with skill and caution. Some vehicles can develop 800 psi. hydraulic pressure on severe application so the honing must never exceed 0.003 in. Also the dust seal groove must be free of rust or nicks so that a perfect mating surface is possible on piston and casting.

8. When assembling, use all parts in the overhaul kit, lubricating everything liberally with brake fluid or special brake assembly lube. Install the piston seal and the dust boot to the caliper, using the proper tools.

9. Position the piston on top of the dust boot.

10. Using the proper technique, use low pressure compressed air to blow the dust boot around the piston. If compressed air is not available, compress the lip on the dust boot into the groove in the caliper. Be sure the boot is fully seated in the groove, as poor sealing will allow contaminants to ruin the bore.

11. Push the piston in the bore fully, until it bottoms. If this cannot be done by hand, then the piston is probably cocked in the bore. If necessary, use an old brake pad and hammer and lighty tap the piston into place. If working with a dual piston caliper, keep the first piston in place with a spacer so it will not become dislodged when installing the other piston.

12. Apply rust penetrant to the bleeder screw threads and install to the caliper. Tighten until it is snug against its seat.

REAR CALIPERS

Overhaul

FORD MOTOR CO. EXCEPT MARK VII, PROBE AND TRACER

1. Remove the bleeder screw. Drain the brake fluid from the caliper and clean the outside of the caliper. Mount the caliper in a vise.

2. Using a brake piston turning tool T75P-2588-B or equivalent turn the piston counterclockwise to remove the piston from the bore.

3. Remove the snapring retaining the pushrod from the caliper.

─────────── **CAUTION** ───────────

The snapring and spring cover are under spring load. Be careful when removing the snapring.

──────────────────────────────────

4. Remove the spring cover, spring, washer, key plate and pull out the pushrod strut pin from the piston bore.

5. Remove the parking brake lever return spring, unscrew

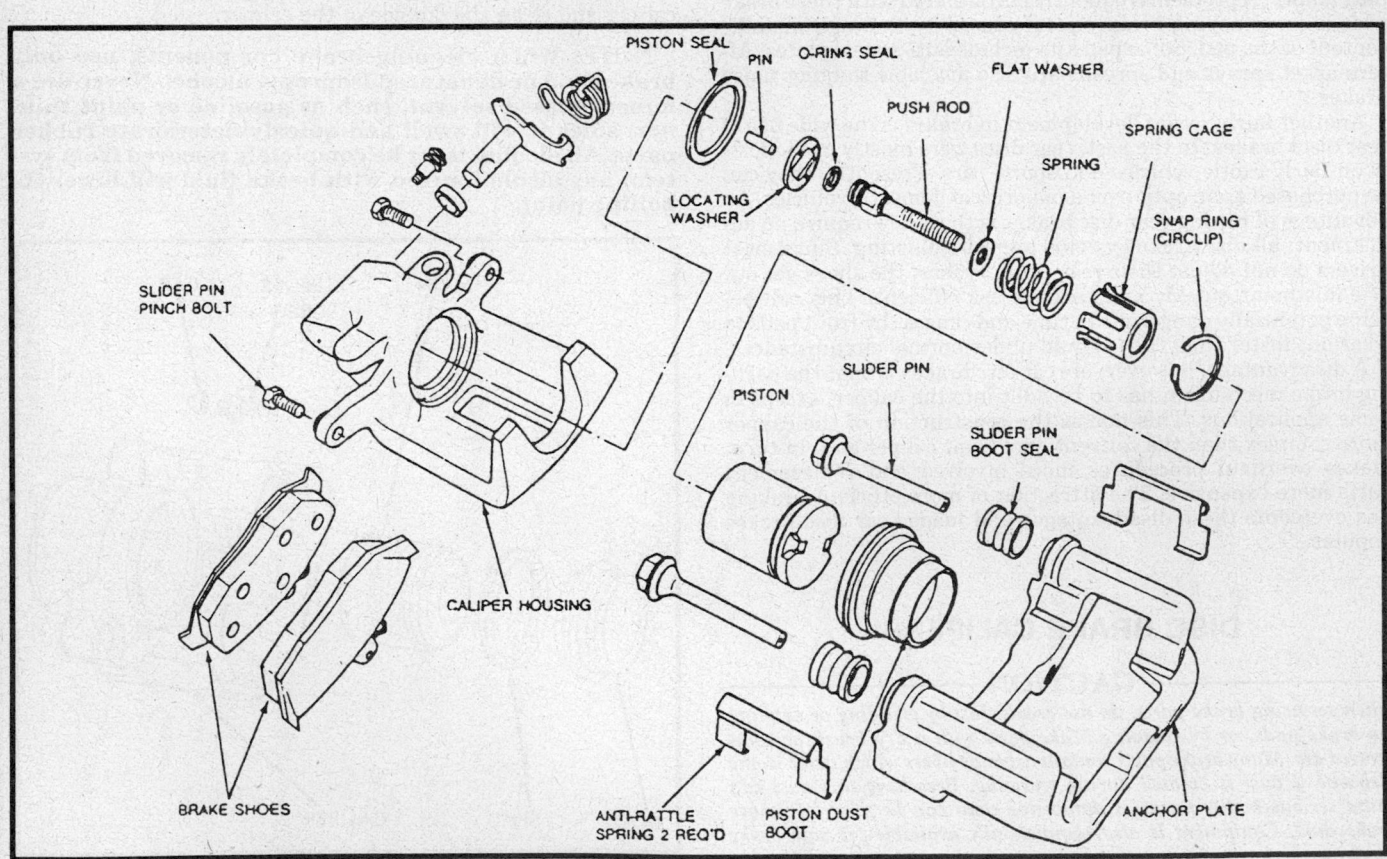

Ford rear caliper, except Mark VII, Probe and Tracer

the parking brake lever stop bolt and pull the parking brake lever out of the caliper housing.

6. Clean all metal parts with isopropyl alcohol. Use clean dry compressed air to clean the grooves and passages. Inspect the caliper bore for damage or excessive wear. If the piston is pitted, scratched, or scored replace the piston.

7. To assemble, lightly grease the parking brake lever bore and the lever shaft seal with silicone dielectric compound or equivalent. Press the parking brake lever shaft seal into the caliper bore.

8. Grease the parking brake shaft recess and slightly grease the parking brake lever shaft. Install the shaft into the caliper housing.

9. Install the lever stop bolt into the caliper housing and torque the bolt to 60-84 in. lbs.

10. Attach the parking brake lever return spring to the stop bolt and install the free end into the parking brake lever slot.

11. Install a new O-ring seal in the groove of the pushrod. Grease the pushrod end with silicone dielectric compound or equivalent.

12. Position the strut pin into the caliper housing and in the recess of the parking brake lever shaft. Install the pushrod into the bore. Make sure the pin is positioned correctly between the shaft recess. Install the flat washer, pushrod, spring and spring cover in order.

13. Apply rust penetrant to the bleeder screw threads and install to the caliper. Tighten until it is snug against its seat.

MARK VII

1. Remove the bleeder screw. Drain the brake fluid from the caliper and clean the outside of the caliper. Remove the parking brake cable bracket and caliper end retainer.

2. Lift out the operating shaft, thrust bearing and balls.

3. Remove the thrust screw anti-rotation pin. Remove the thrust screw by rotating it counterclockwise with a ¼-inch Allen wrench.

4. Remove the piston adjuster assembly by installing piston

remover tool T75B-2588-A or equivalent through the back of the caliper and pushing the piston out.

5. Remove and discard the piston seal, boot, thrust screw C-ring, end retainer lip seal and pin insulators.

6. Clean all metal parts with isopropyl alcohol. Use clean dry compressed air to clean the grooves and passages. Inspect the caliper bore for damage or excessive wear. If the piston is pitted, scratched, or scored replace the piston. Inspect all other parts for excessive wear.

NOTE: Do not attempt to service the adjuster at any time. When service is necessary, replace the piston and adjuster assembly.

7. Apply a coat of clean brake fluid to the new caliper piston seal and install it in the bore.

8. Install a new dust boot.

9. Coat the piston/adjuster assembly with brake fluid and install it in the bore. Spread the dust boot over the piston and seat the boot in the piston groove.

10. Clamp the caliper in a vise. Fill the assembly with brake fluid to the bottom edge of the thrust screw bore.

11. Install a new thrust screw O-ring in the groove in the thrust screw.

12. Install the thrust screw by turning it into the piston/adjuster assembly with a ¼-inch Allen wrench until the top surface of the thrust screw is flush with the bottom of the threaded bore.

13. Index the thrust screw, so that the notches of the thrust screw and caliper housing are aligned. Install the anti-rotation pin.

NOTE: Do not confuse the right and left side thrust screw and operating shaft. The pocket surface of the operating shaft and thrust screw are stamped with the proper letter (R or L) indicated the side from which it came.

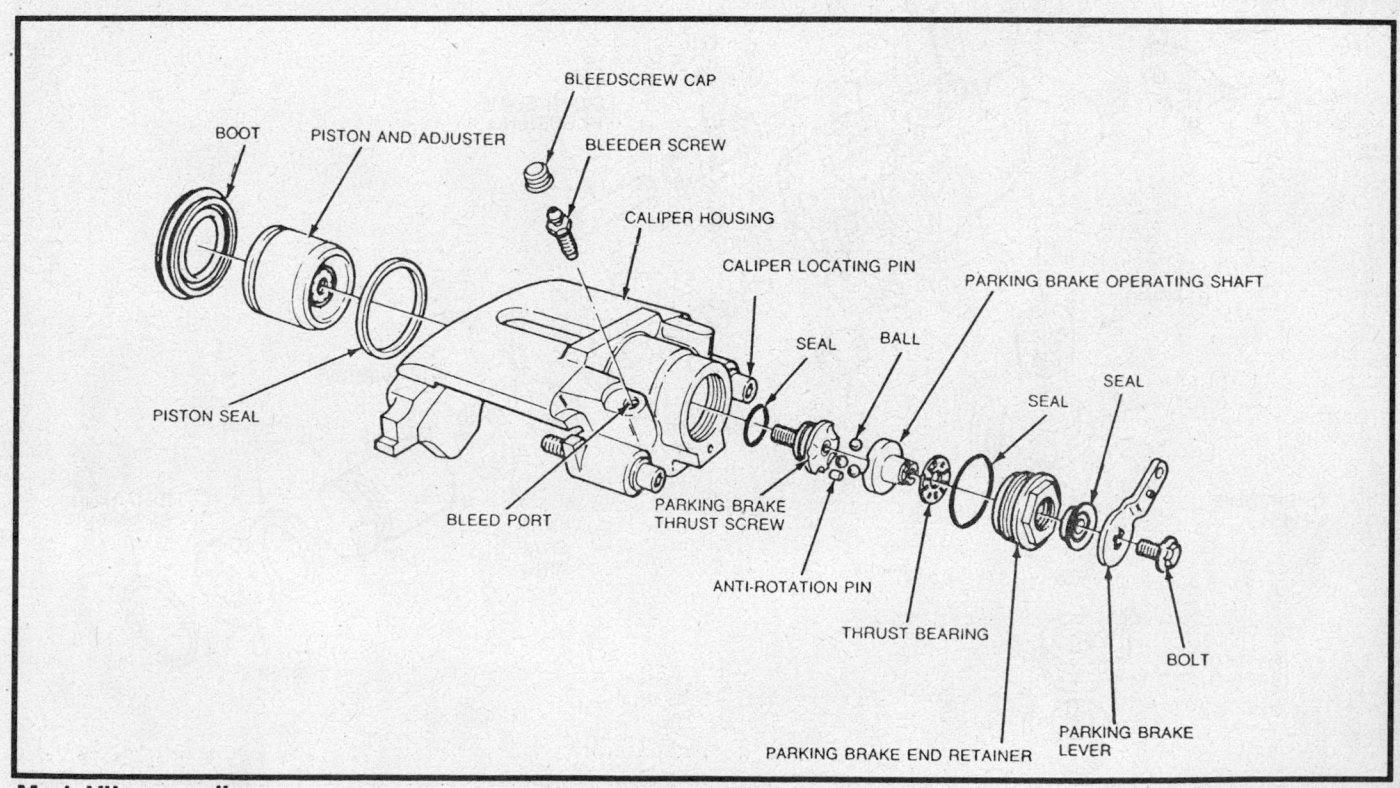

Mark VII rear caliper

14. Place a ball in each of the 3 pockets and apply a liberal amount of silicone dielectric compound or equivalent on all components in the parking brake mechanism.

15. Install the shaft on the balls.

16. Coat the thrust bearing with silicone dielectric compound or equivalent and install on the operating shaft.

17. Install a new lip seal and O-ring on the end retainer.

18. Coat the O-ring seal and lip seal with silicone grease and install the end retainer in the caliper. Hold the operating shaft firmly seated against the internal mechanism while installing the end retainer to prevent mislocation of the balls. Tighten the end retainer to 75–96 ft. lbs. (101–130 Nm).

19. Clamp the caliper in a vise and bottom the piston with modified brake piston turning tool T75P-2588-B or eqivalent. Apply rust penetrant to the bleeder screw threads and install to the caliper. Tighten until it is snug against its seat.

20. Install new pin insulators in the caliper housing. Check to see that both insulator flanges straddle the housing holes.

21. When the caliper is installed on the vehicle, pull the caliper out until the inner pad is firmly seated against the rotor. Measure the clearance between the outer pad and the caliper. The clearance must be $\frac{1}{32}$–$\frac{3}{32}$. If is is not within specification, remove the caliper and adjust the

PROBE AND TRACER

1. Remove the bleeder screw. Drain the brake fluid from the caliper and clean the outside of the caliper. Remove the caliper guide bushing and dust boots.

2. Pry the retaining spring off of the dust boot.

3. Rotate the piston counterclockwise with piston turning tool T75P-2588-B and remove the piston from the adjuster spindle.

4. Remove and discard the piston seal and dust seal.

5. Remove the stopper snapring.

6. Remove the adjustring spindle, stopper and connecting link. Separate the adjuster spindle and the stopper.

7. Remove and discard the O-ring from the adjuster spindle.

8. Remove the parking brake return spring

9. Remove the operating lever nut and lockwasher.

10. Matchmark the operating lever and the shaft. Remove the lever from the shaft.

11. Remove the seal, shaft and needle bearing assembly from the caliper housing.

12. Clean all metal parts with isopropyl alcohol. Use clean dry compressed air to clean the grooves and passages. Inspect the caliper bore for damage or excessive wear. If the piston is pitted, scratched, or scored replace the piston. Inspect all other parts for excessive wear.

13. To assemble, lubricate the needle bearing with the orange grease in the overhaul kit.

14. Align the opening in the bearing with the bore in the caliper housing. Install the needle bearings.

15. Install the operating shaft into the caliper housing.

16. Install the operating lever, aligning the marks made previously.

17. Install the lock washer nut.

18. Install the connecting link into the operating shaft.

19. Install the O-ring onto the adjuster spindle. Position the stopper on the adjuster spindle so the pins will align with the caliper housing.

20. Install the adjuster spindle and the stopper.

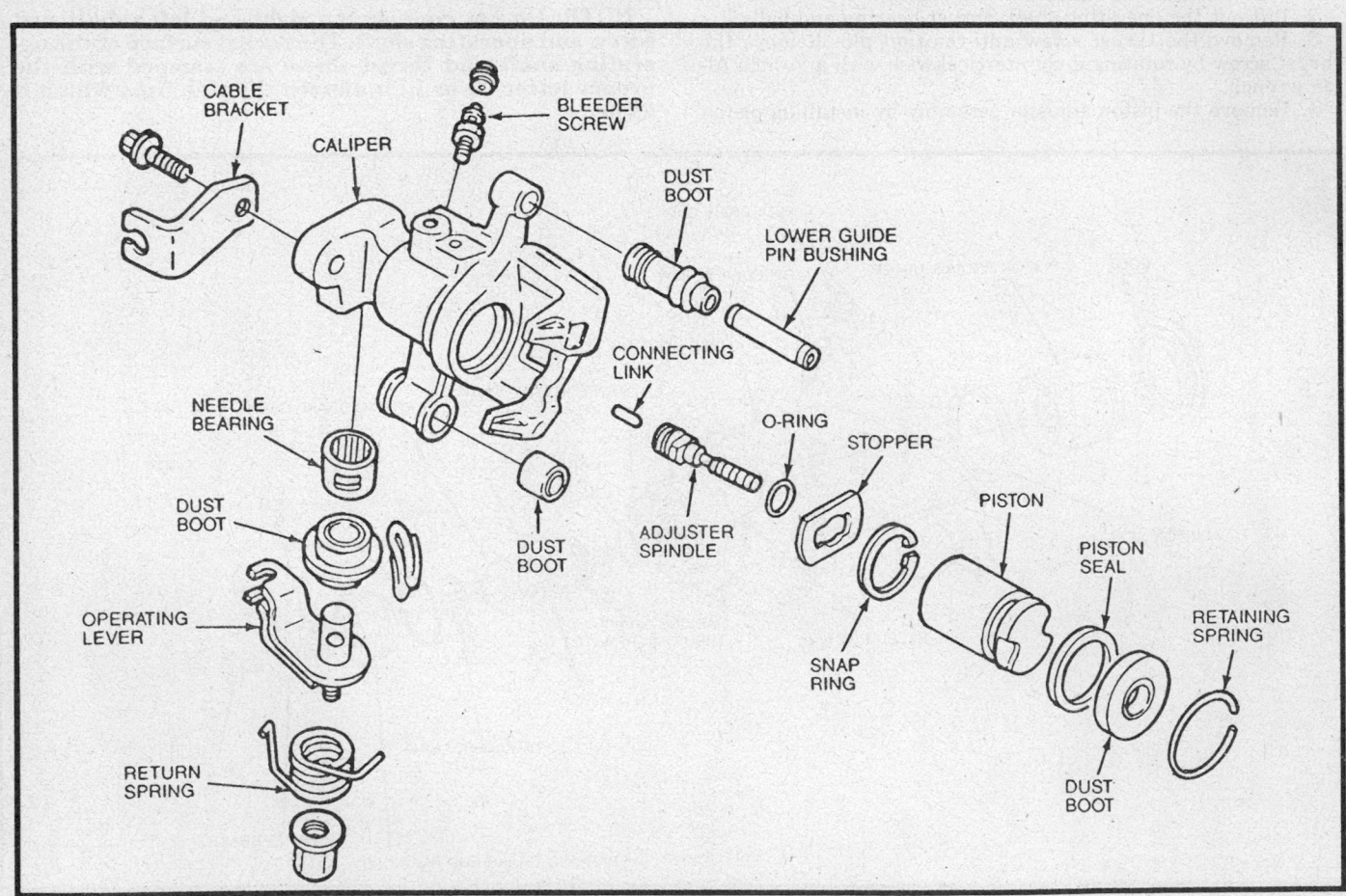

Probe rear caliper

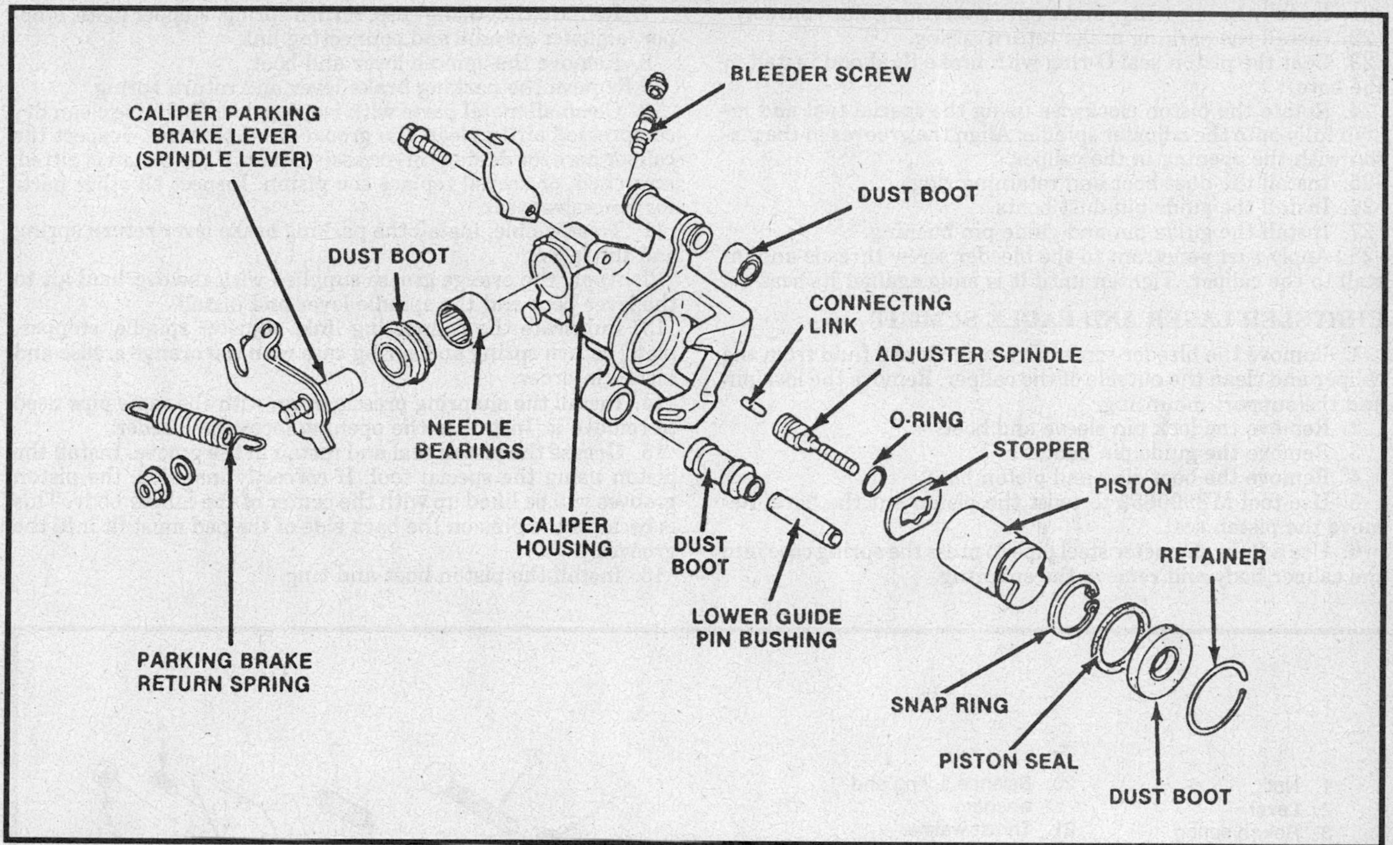

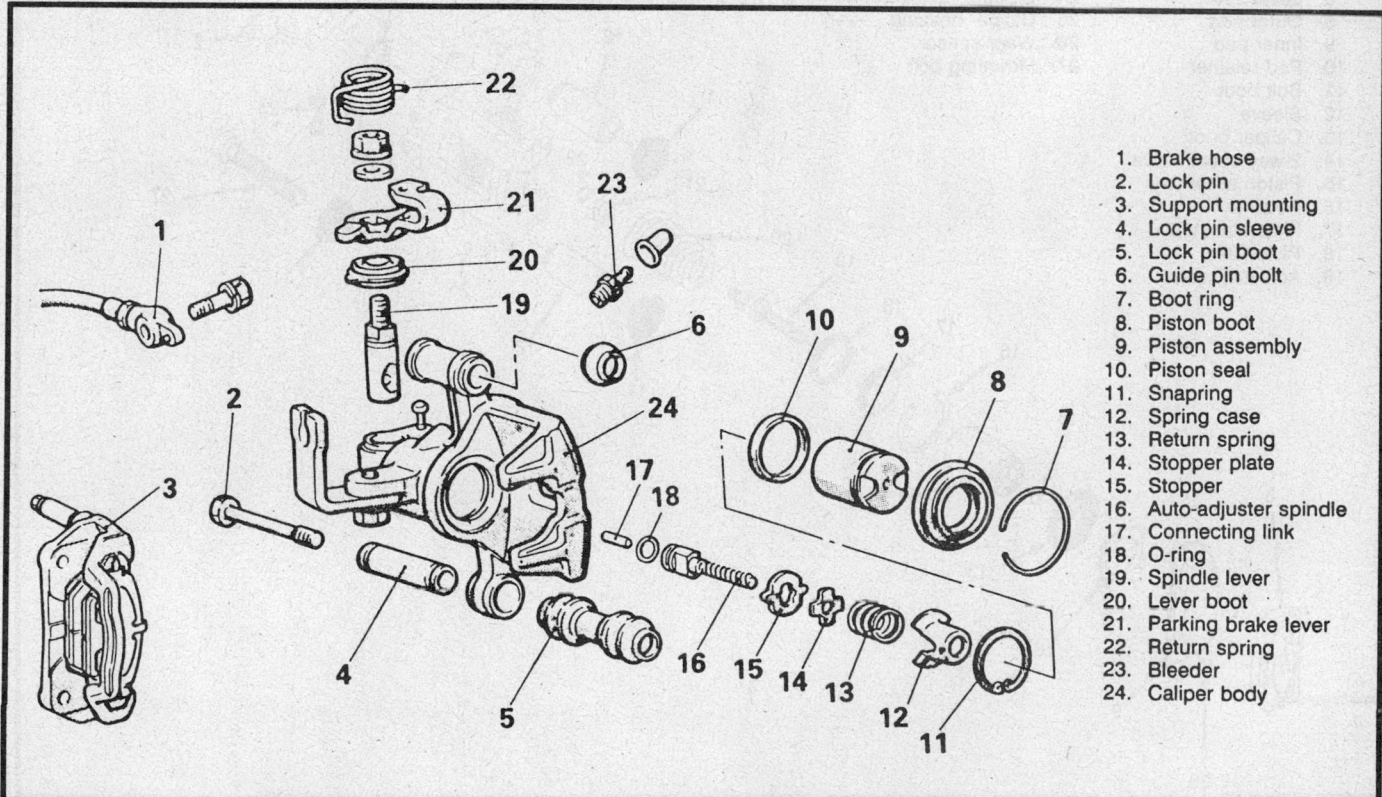

Tracer rear caliper

1. Brake hose
2. Lock pin
3. Support mounting
4. Lock pin sleeve
5. Lock pin boot
6. Guide pin bolt
7. Boot ring
8. Piston boot
9. Piston assembly
10. Piston seal
11. Snapring
12. Spring case
13. Return spring
14. Stopper plate
15. Stopper
16. Auto-adjuster spindle
17. Connecting link
18. O-ring
19. Spindle lever
20. Lever boot
21. Parking brake lever
22. Return spring
23. Bleeder
24. Caliper body

Chrysler Laser and Eagle Summit rear caliper

21. Install the snapring. Make sure everything moves freely.

22. Install the parking brake return spring.

23. Coat the piston seal O-ring with brake fluid and install in the bore.

24. Rotate the piston clockwise using the special tool and install fully onto the adjuster spindle. Align the grooves in the piston with the opening in the caliper.

25. Install the dust boot and retaining ring.

26. Install the guide pin dust boots.

27. Install the guide pin and guide pin bushing.

28. Apply rust penetrant to the bleeder screw threads and install to the caliper. Tighten until it is snug against its seat.

CHRYSLER LASER AND EAGLE SUMMIT

1. Remove the bleeder screw. Drain the brake fluid from the caliper and clean the outside of the caliper. Remove the lock pin and the support mounting.

2. Remove the lock pin sleeve and boot.

3. Remove the guide pin boot.

4. Remove the boot ring and piston boot.

5. Use tool MB990652 to twist the piston out the bore. Remove the piston seal.

6. Use a ¾-in. diameter steel pipe to press the spring case into the caliper body and remove the snapring.

7. Remove the spring case, return spring, stopper plate, stopper, adjuster spindle and connecting link.

8. Remove the spindle lever and boot.

9. Remove the parking brake lever and return spring.

10. Clean all metal parts with isopropyl alcohol. Use clean dry compressed air to clean the grooves and passages. Inspect the caliper bore for damage or excessive wear. If the piston is pitted, scratched, or scored replace the piston. Inspect all other parts for excessive wear.

11. To assemble, install the parking brake lever return spring and the lever.

12. Apply the orange grease supplied with the overhaul kit to the lever boot and the spindle lever and install.

13. Lubricate the connecting link, adjuster spindle, stopper, plate, return spring and spring case with the orange grease and install in order.

14. Install the snapring pressig down with the same pipe used to remove it. Install so the opening faces the bleeder.

15. Grease the piston seal and install in the groove. Install the piston using the special tool. If correctly installed, the piston grooves will be lined up with the center of the caliper body. This is because the pins on the back side of the pad must fit into the grooves.

16. Install the piston boot and ring.

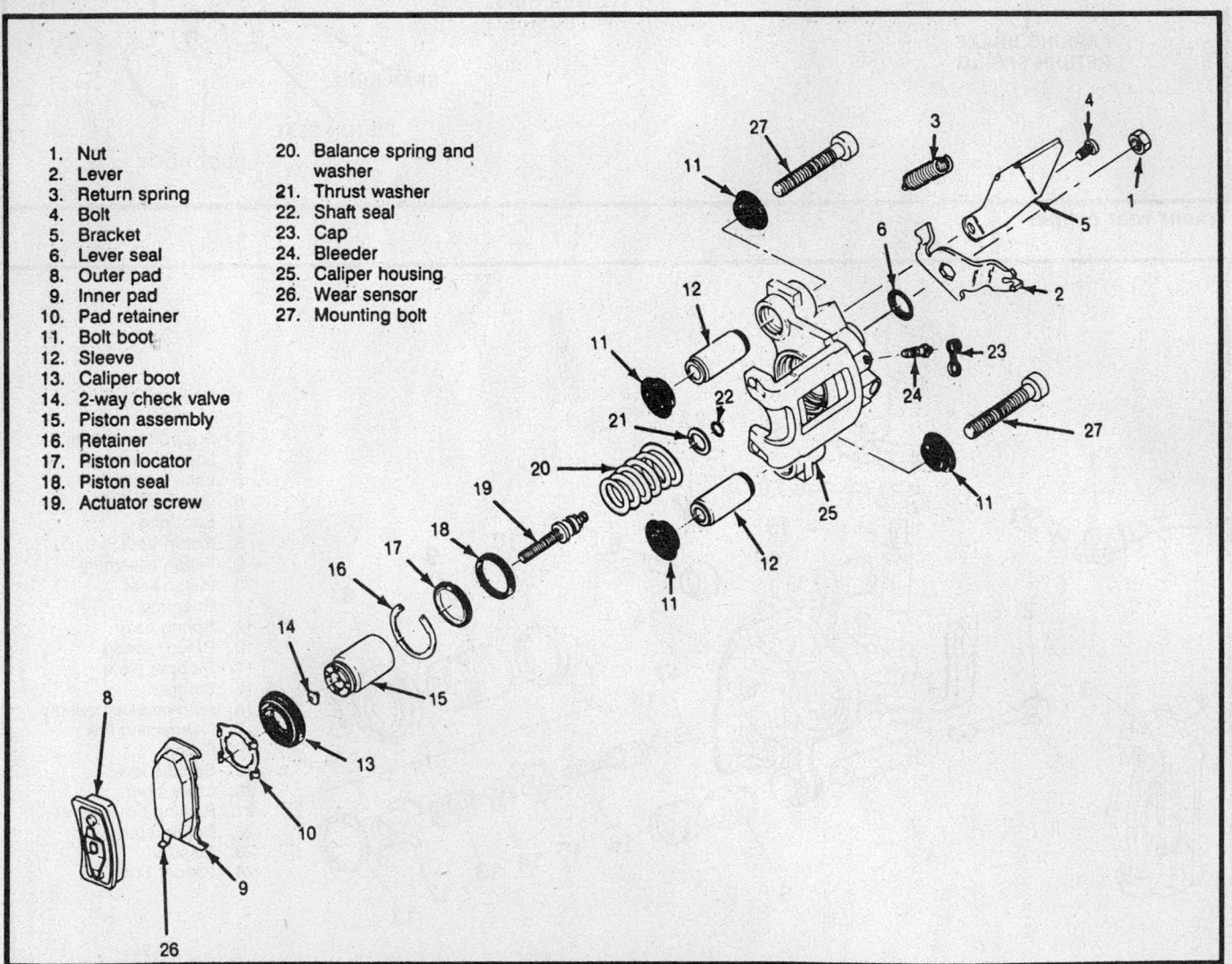

1. Nut
2. Lever
3. Return spring
4. Bolt
5. Bracket
6. Lever seal
8. Outer pad
9. Inner pad
10. Pad retainer
11. Bolt boot
12. Sleeve
13. Caliper boot
14. 2-way check valve
15. Piston assembly
16. Retainer
17. Piston locator
18. Piston seal
19. Actuator screw
20. Balance spring and washer
21. Thrust washer
22. Shaft seal
23. Cap
24. Bleeder
25. Caliper housing
26. Wear sensor
27. Mounting bolt

GM front wheel drive except 1989–90 Pontiac 6000 and 1988 Fiero rear caliper

17. Grease the guide pin boot, lock pin boot, lock pin sleeve and lock pin and install on the caliper.

18. Apply rust penetrant to the bleeder screw threads and install to the caliper. Tighten until it is snug against its seat.

GENERAL MOTORS EXCEPT 1988 FIERO, 1988–90 CORVETTE, 1989 CAMARO AND FIREBIRD AND 1989–90 PONTIAC 6000

NOTE: Some differences may exist between rear calipers in the various model lines, but all except those noted are basically the same. Careful and organized workmanship will fill in the gaps that any discrepancies may present.

1. Remove the bleeder screw. Drain the brake fluid from the caliper and clean the outside of the caliper. Remove the shoe retainer from the end of the piston.

2. Remove the nut, parking brake lever and seal.

3. Support the caliper in a vise. Using a wrench, rotate the actuator screw to remove the piston from the bore.

4. Remove the balance spring. Remove the actuator screw by pressing on the threaded end. Remove the shaft seal and thrust washer.

5. Remove the piston boot with a suitable prying tool.

6. Remove the snapring and piston locator, if equipped.

7. Remove the piston seal.

8. Inspect the caliper bore and seal groove for scoring or nicks. Inspect the piston for scores or deterioration in the chrome finish. If these conditions can not be polished out with soft crocus cloth, replace as necessary.

9. Clean all parts in denatured alcohol and dry with compressed air.

10. To assemble, install the parking brake bracket, if removed. Lubricate the new seals and caliper housing with new brake fluid. Install the piston seal.

11. Install new piston locator on the piston using tool No. J36627 or equivalent, if necessary.

12. Install the thrust washer on the actuator screw with the copper side of the washer towards the piston.

13. Install the shaft seal on the actuator screw. Install the actuator screw into the piston assembly.

14. Install the balance spring and retainer into the piston recess.

15. Install the piston boot onto the piston with the inside lip of the boot in the piston groove and fold the boot toward the end of the piston that contacts the inboard brake pad.

16. Push the piston until it bottoms in the bore with the special tool, or equivalent.

17. Install the lever seal over the back end of the actuator screw. Make sure the sealing bead on the lever seal is against the housing.

18. Install the lever on the actuator screw. Rotate the lever away from stop slightly and hold while installing the nut. Then rotate the lever back to contact stop.

19. Install the boot in the caliper counterbore and seat using tool No. J-28678 or equivalent.

20. Install the sleeve and bolt boots, making sure everything is well lubricated upon installation.

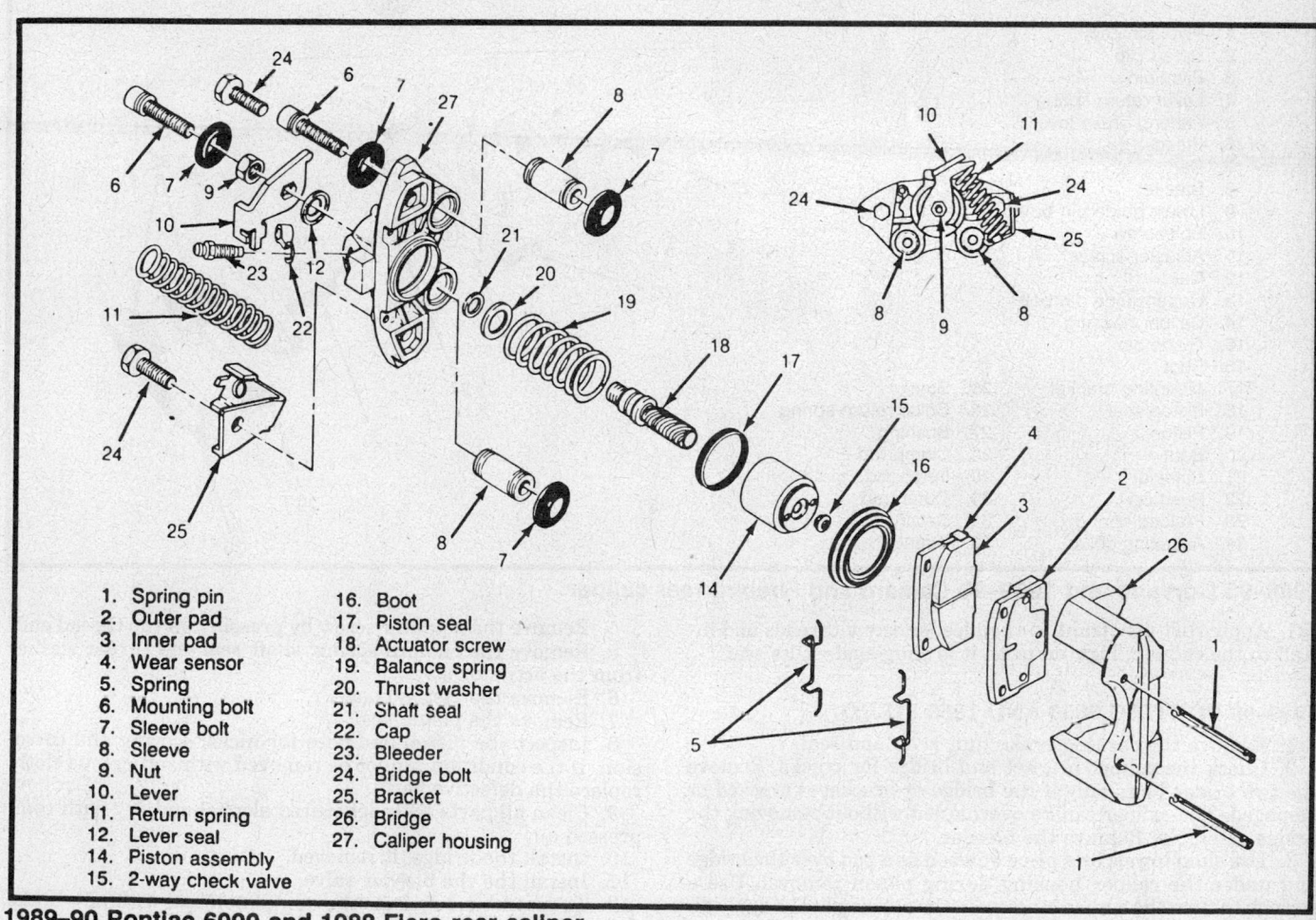

1. Spring pin
2. Outer pad
3. Inner pad
4. Wear sensor
5. Spring
6. Mounting bolt
7. Sleeve bolt
8. Sleeve
9. Nut
10. Lever
11. Return spring
12. Lever seal
14. Piston assembly
15. 2-way check valve
16. Boot
17. Piston seal
18. Actuator screw
19. Balance spring
20. Thrust washer
21. Shaft seal
22. Cap
23. Bleeder
24. Bridge bolt
25. Bracket
26. Bridge
27. Caliper housing

1989–90 Pontiac 6000 and 1988 Fiero rear caliper

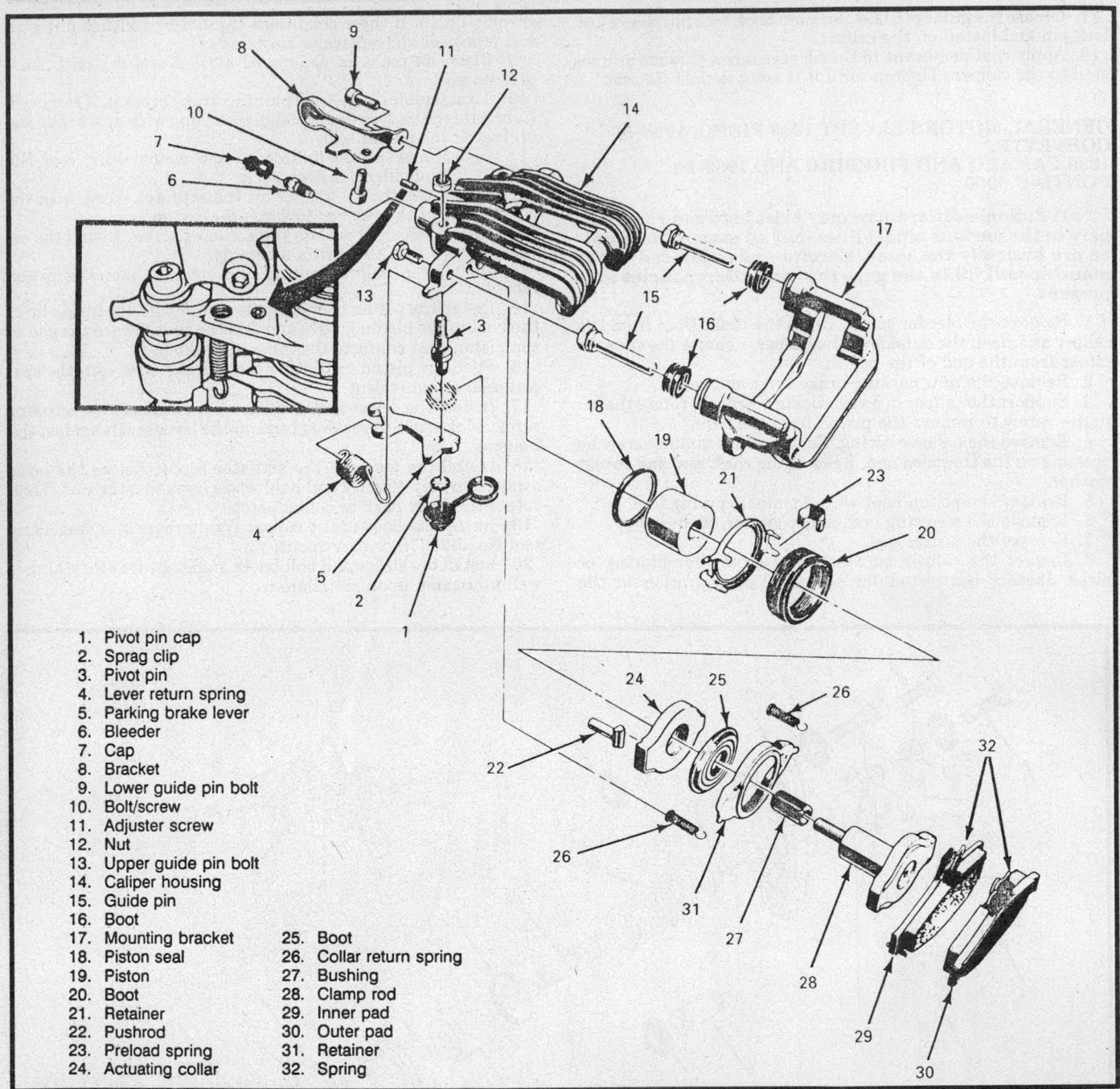

1. Pivot pin cap
2. Sprag clip
3. Pivot pin
4. Lever return spring
5. Parking brake lever
6. Bleeder
7. Cap
8. Bracket
9. Lower guide pin bolt
10. Bolt/screw
11. Adjuster screw
12. Nut
13. Upper guide pin bolt
14. Caliper housing
15. Guide pin
16. Boot
17. Mounting bracket
18. Piston seal
19. Piston
20. Boot
21. Retainer
22. Pushrod
23. Preload spring
24. Actuating collar
25. Boot
26. Collar return spring
27. Bushing
28. Clamp rod
29. Inner pad
30. Outer pad
31. Retainer
32. Spring

1988–90 Corvette and 1989–90 Camaro and Firebird rear caliper

21. Apply rust penetrant to the bleeder screw threads and install to the caliper. Tighten until it is snug against its seat.

1989–90 PONTIAC 6000 AND 1988 FIERO

1. Remove the parking brake nut, lever and seal.
2. Check the caliper bracket and bridge for cracks. Remove the two bridge bolts only if the bridge or bracket is cracked or damaged. The caliper can be overhauled without removing the bridge assembly. Remove the bleeder.
3. Use shop towels or a piece of wood as a pad over the bridge and under the caliper housing during piston removal. Use a wrench to turn the actuator screw in the parking brake apply direction to work the piston assembly out of the caliper housing.

4. Remove the actuator screw by pressing on the thread end.
5. Remove the balance spring, shaft seal and thrust washer from the actuator screw.
6. Remove the piston boot.
7. Remove the piston seal.
8. Inspect the piston and bore for nicks, scoring and corrosion. If the condition cannot be removed with soft crocus cloth, replace the defective part.
9. Clean all parts with denatured alcohol and dry with compressed air.
10. Install the bridge, it removed.
11. Install the the bleeder valve.
12. To assemble, lubricate the new piston seal with new brake fluid and install into the seal groove.

13. Install the thrust washer onto the actuator screw with the copper side of washer towards the piston.

14. Lubricate the shaft seal and piston boot. Install the boot onto the piston.

15. Lubricate the actuator screw and install with the shaft seal and thrust washer into the caliper housing.

16. Install the balance spring into the housing bore with the end of the spring in the recess at the bottom of the bore.

17. Lubricate the piston and boot. Install the assembly by pushing the piston toward the bottom of the bore using a piston installer tool J-36623 or equivalent. Turn the actuator screw as necessary to move the piston to the bottom of the bore.

18. Lubricate the parking lever seal and install so that the rubber sealing bead on the seal is against the lever and the copper side is against the housing.

19. Hold the lever back against the stop on the housing while tightening the nut. Install the lever.

20. Set the piston boot to the housing by pressing down with a boot tool J-36622 and J-36623 or equivalent.

1988–90 CORVETTE AND 1989–90 CAMARO AND FIREBIRD

1. Remove the collar return springs from the actuating collar.

2. Pull the actuating collar with assembled parts out of the caliper housing by pulling on both ends of the collar.

3. Remove the clamp rod and bushing from the collar.

4. Bend back the retainer tabs and separate the retainers. Remove the boots and pushrod from the collar.

5. Remove the preload spring from the retainer.

6. Remove the piston by carefully applying low pressure compressed air to the fluid inlet.

7. Remove the piston seal.

8. Remove the bleeder screw.

9. Remove the pivot pin cap, sprag clip and lever from the pivot pin.

10. Remove the pivot pin and nut, if worn.

11. Remove the adjuster screw from the caliper housing.

12. Remove the guide pins and boots from the mounting bracket.

13. Inspect the piston and bore for nicks, scoring and corrosion. If the condition cannot be removed with soft crocus cloth, replace the defective part.

14. Clean all parts with denatured alcohol and dry with compressed air.

15. To assemble, lubricate the new seal with brake fluid and install seal in the caliper bore.

16. Install the piston until it bottoms in the bore.

17. Lightly coat the actuating collar with the lubricant provided in the kit. Install the pushrod, new boots and clamp the new boot retainers to the actuating collar. Bend the tabs on the retainer to hold the assembly together.

18. Install the preload spring into the boot retainers.

19. Lightly coat the clamp rod with the lubricant and slide it throught the actuating collar and boot assembly. The boot must be against the reation plate on the clamp rod.

20. Install the new bushing to the clamp rod.

21. Lubricate the grooved bead of the inner boot and the groove in the housing with the lubricant. Also, coat the actuating collar, especially around the center hole.

22. Push the clamp rod to the bottom of the mating hole of the piston.

23. Pull on the actuatring collar and seat the inner boot in the groove on the housing. Make sure the pushrod enteres the hole in the caliper housing.

24. Apply rust penetrant to the bleeder screw threads and install to the caliper. Tighten until it is snug against its seat.

25. Install anew pivot pin and nut to housing, if removed.

26. Install the pivot pin cap, lever and new sprag clip in order. The sprag clip teeth must face away from the lever. Snap the pivot pin seal cap over the pivot pin.

27. Install the collar return springs to the boot retainer.

28. Install the adjustment screw into the caliper until the actuating collar is about even with the piston bore face of the housing.

29. Install and lubricate new guide pin boots and guide pns.

Rear Wheel Cylinders

WHEEL CYLINDER

Overhaul

1. Raise the vehicle and support safely. Remove the wheel and drum from the side to be serviced.

NOTE: It is a good idea to overhaul or replace both wheel cylinders at the same time for smooth, even braking.

2. Remove the brake shoes and clean the backing plate and wheel cylinder. Depending on the design of the backing plate, overhauling may be able to be done on the vehicle. If the backing plate is recessed to the point that it is impossible to get a hone into the cylinder, the cylinder must be removed.

3. To remove the cylinder, disconnect the brake line from the rear of the cylinder, remove the mounting bolts or retainers and remove the cylinder. Use rust penetrant and/or heat where necessary to break the lines free from the wheel cylinders. Do not twist the brake lines when removing.

4. Remove the rubber boots from the ends of the cylinder. Remove the pistons, piston cups or expanders and spring from the inside of the cylinder. Remove the bleeder screw and make sure it is not clogged.

5. Discard all of the parts that the rebuilding kit will replace.

6. Examine the inside of the cylinder. If it is severely rusted, pitted or scratched, install a new or rebuilt cylinder.

7. If the condition of the cylinder indicates that it can be rebuilt, hone the bore. Light honing will provide a new surface on the inside of the cylinder which promotes better cup sealing.

8. Wash out the cylinder with brake fluid after honing. Reassemble the cylinder using the new parts provided in the kit. When assembling the cylinder, dip all parts in brake fluid.

9. Install the cylinder. Reinstall the shoes and drum. Bleed the brake system and road test the vehicle.

Hydraulic Control Valves

PRESSURE DIFFERENTIAL VALVE

The pressure differential valve activates a dash panel warning light if pressure loss in the brake system occurs. If pressure loss occurs in half of the split system the other system's normal pressure causes the piston in the switch to compress a spring until it touches an electrical contact. This turns the warning lamp on the dash panel to light, thus warning the driver of possible brake failure.

On some vehicles the spring balance piston automatically recenters as the brake pedal is released, warning the driver only upon brake application. On others, the light remains on until manually cancelled. Valves may be located separately or as part of a combination valve. On GM front wheel drive vehicles, the valve and switch are usually incorporated into the master cylinder.

Resetting Valves

On some vehicles, the valve piston(s) remain off-center after failure until necessary repairs are made. The valve will automatically reset itself after repairs are made, when pressure is equal on both sides of the system.

If the light does not go out, bleed the brake system that is opposite the failed system. If front brakes failed, bleed the rear brakes; this should force the light control piston toward center. If this fails, remove the terminal switch. If brake fluid is present in the electrical area, the seals are gone, replace the complete valve assembly.

METERING VALVE

The metering valve's function is to improve braking balance between the front and rear brakes, especially during light brake application. The metering valve prevents application of the front disc brakes until the rear brakes overcome the return spring pressure. Thus, when the front disc pads contact the rotor, the rear brakes will contact the braking surface at the same time.

Inspect the metering valve each time the brakes are serviced. A slight amount of moisture inside the boot does not indicate a defective valve, however, fluid leakage indicates a damaged or worn valve. If fluid leakage is present, the valve must be replaced.

PROPORTIONING VALVE

The proportioning or proportioner valve, is used to transmit full input pressure to the rear brakes up to a certain point, called the split point. Beyond that point it reduces the amount of pressure increase to the rear brakes according to a certain ratio. On light pedal applications, equal brake pressure is transmitted to the front and rear brakes. During heavier brake applications, the pressure transmitted to the rear will be lower than that to the front to prevent premature rear wheel lockup and skid.

Whenever the brakes are serviced, the valve should be inspected for leakage. Premature rear brake application during light braking may indicate a defective proportioning valve. Repair is by replacement of the valve, unless overhaul kits are available. On most GM master cylinders, the proportioning valves are integral with the master cylinder. Since these vehicles have a diagonally split brake system, 2 valves are required.

COMBINATION VALVE

The combination valve may perform 2 or 3 functions. They are: metering, proportioning and brake failure warning. Variations of the two-way combination valve are: proportioning and brake failure warning or metering and brake failure warning. A three-way combination valve directs the brake fluid to the appropriate wheel, performs necessary valving and contains a brake failure warning. The combination valve is usually mounted under the hood close to the master cylinder, where the brake lines can easily be connected and routed to the front or rear wheels. The combination valve is non-serviceable and must be replaced if malfunctioning.

BRAKE BLEEDING

The hydraulic brake system must be free of air to operate properly. Air can enter the system when hydraulic parts are defective, disconnected for servicing or replacement, or when the fluid level in the master cylinder reservoirs is too low. Air in the system will give the brake pedal a spongy feeling upon application.

The quickest and easiest way to bleed the system is the pressure method, but special equipment is needed to externally pressurize the hydraulic system. The more commonly used method of brake bleeding is done manually.

Bleeding may be required at only 1 or 2 wheels or at the master cylinder, depending upon what point the system was opened. If after bleeding the component that was rebuilt or replaced and the pedal still has a spongy feeling upon application, it will be necessary to bleed the entire system.

Procedure

NOTE: If using a pressure bleeder, follow the instructions furnished with the unit and choose the correct adaptor for the application. Do not substitute an adapter that "almost fits" as it will not work and could be dangerous.

MASTER CYLINDER

If the master cylinder is off the vehicle it can be bench bled.

1. Connect 2 short pieces of brake line to the outlet fittings, bend them until the free end is below the fluid level in the master cylinder reservoirs.

2. Fill the reservoirs with fresh brake fluid. Pump the piston slowly until no more air bubbles appear in the reservoirs.

3. Disconnect the 2 short lines, refill the master cylinder and securely install the cylinder cap(s).

4. If the master cylinder is on the vehicle, it can still be bled, using a flare nut wrench.

5. Open the brake lines slightly with the flare nut wrench while pressure is applied to the brake pedal by a helper inside the vehicle.

6. Be sure to tighten the line before the brake pedal is released.

7. Repeat the process with every line until no air bubbles out.

CALIPERS AND WHEEL CYLINDERS

1. Fill the master cylinder with fresh brake fluid. Check the level often during the procedure.

2. Start with the wheel farthest from the master cylinder. Pop the cap off of the bleeder screw, if equipped and place where it will not be lost. Clean the bleed screw.

CAUTION

When bleeding the brakes, keep face away from the brake area. Spewing fluid may cause facial and/or visual damage. Do not allow brake fluid to spill on the car's finish, it will remove the paint.

3. If the system is empty, the most effecient way to get fluid down to the wheel is to loosen the bleeder about ½-¾ turn, place a finger firmly over the bleeder and have a helper pump the brakes slowly until fluid comes out the bleeder. Once fluid is at the bleeder, close it before the pedal is released inside the vehicle.

NOTE: If the pedal is pumped rapidly, the fluid will churn and create small air bubbles, which are almost impossible to remove from the system. These air bubbles will eventually congregate and a spongy pedal will result.

4. Once fluid has been pumped to the caliper or wheel cylinder, open the bleed screw again, have the helper press the brake pedal to the floor, lock the bleeder and have the helper slowly release the pedal. Wait 15 seconds and repeat the procedure (including the 15 second wait) until no more air comes out of the bleeder upon application of the brake pedal. Remember to close the bleeder before the pedal is released inside the vehicle each time the bleeder is opened. If not, air will be induced into the system.

5. If a helper is not available, connect a small hose to the bleeder, place the end in a container of brake fluid and proceed to pump the pedal from inside the vehicle until no more air comes out the bleeder. The hose will prevent air from entering the system.

6. Repeat the procedure on remaining wheel cylinders and calipers still working from the wheel farthest away from the master cylinder.

7. On diagonally split systems, start with the right rear fol-

lowed by the left front. Then the left rear followed by the right front.

8. Hydraulic brake systems must be totally flushed if the fluid becomes contaminated with water, dirt or other corrosive chemicals. To flush, simply bleed the entire system until all fluid has been replaced with the correct type of new fluid.

9. Install the bleeder cap(s), if equipped, on the bleeder to keep dirt out. Always road test the vehicle after brake work of any kind is done.

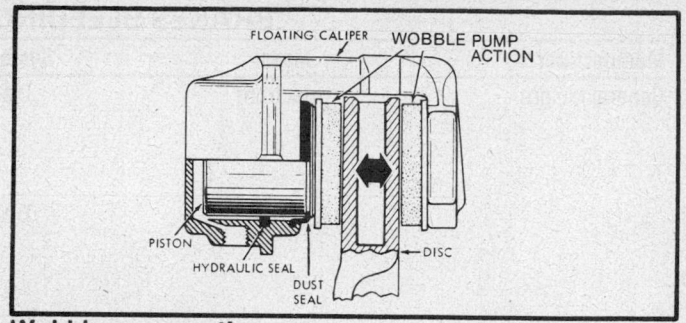

Wobble pump action

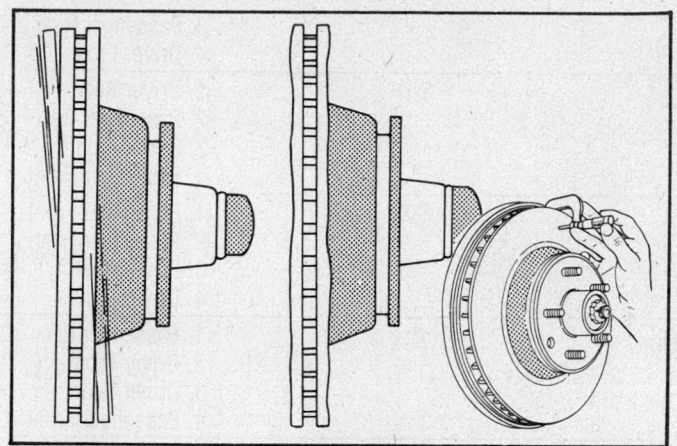

Excessive runout or parallelism

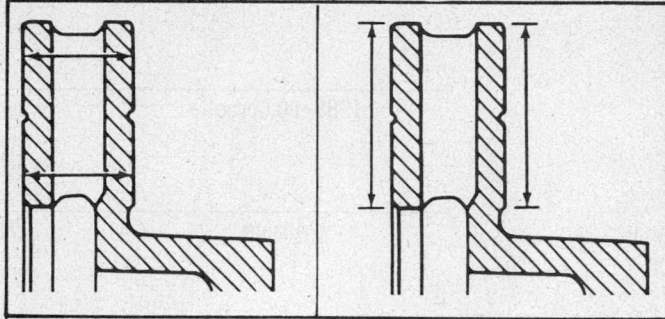

Taper variation not to exceed .003 in.

These surfaces to be flat and within .002 in.

BRAKES BLEEDING SEQUENCE CHART

Manufacturer	Model	System Split	Special Procedures	Bleeding Sequence
AMC-Eagle	Eagle	Front-to-Rear	①	1. Passenger Rear 2. Driver Rear 3. Passenger Front 4. Driver Front
	Medallion, Premier, Summit	Diagonal	⑥	1. Passenger Rear 3. Driver Front 2. Driver Rear 4. Passenger Front
Chrysler Corp.	All except ABS	Front-to-Rear and Diagonal	①	1. Passenger Rear 2. Driver Rear 3. Passenger Front 4. Driver Front
	With ABS II	—	⑦	1. Driver Rear 2. Passenger Rear 3. Driver Front 4. Driver Rear
Ford Motor	Rear Drive except ABS	Front-to-Rear	①	1. Passenger Rear 2. Driver Rear 3. Passenger Front 4. Driver Front
	Front Drive	Diagonal	—	1. Passenger Rear 2. Driver Front 3. Driver Rear 4. Passenger Front
	With ABS	—	⑦	1. Passenger Front 2. Driver Front 3. Passenger Rear 4. Driver Rear

BRAKES BLEEDING SEQUENCE CHART

Manufacturer	Model	System Split	Special Procedures	Bleeding Sequence
General Motors	Spectrum	Diagonal	—	1. Driver Front 2. Passenger Rear 3. Passenger Front 4. Driver Rear
	Sprint	Diagonal	—	1. Driver Rear 2. Passenger Front 3. Passenger Rear 4. Driver Front
	1986–87 Corvette		④⑦	1. Driver Rear 2. Passenger Rear 3. Driver Front 4. Passenger Front
	1988–90 Corvette		④⑦	1. Passenger Front 2. Passenger Rear 3. Driver Rear 4. Driver Front
	Allante	Diagonal	⑦	1. Passenger Rear 2. Driver Front 3. Driver Rear 4. Passenger Front
	Rear Drive and E & K Body except above and ABS ⑤	Front-to-Rear	①	1. Passenger Rear 2. Driver Rear 3. Passenger Front 4. Driver Front
	Front Drive except E & K Body ⑤	Diagonal	②③	1. Passenger Rear 2. Driver Front 3. Driver Rear 4. Passenger Front
	With Teves—ABS		⑦	1. Passenger Front 2. Driver Front 3. Driver Rear 4. Passenger Rear

① It may be necessary to push on or pull out a button or rod on the metering valve to bleed front disc brakes, particularly when pressure bleeding

② Use **SLOW** strokes when manually bleeding the quick take-up system

③ Always bleed the master cylinder first in the quick take-up system. Bleed the left front caliper fitting first and then the right front fitting.

④ Raise the front of the vehicle slightly when bleeding the rear brakes

⑤ E body—Riviera, Eldorado and Toronado K body—Seville

⑥ Rear wheel must not hang down on models equipped with compensator-limiter valve

⑦ Use procedure shown in "Anti-Lock Brakes"

DISC BRAKE SPECIFICATIONS

Car Manufacturer, Year & Model	Text Reference Type	Caliper Style	Brake manufacturer	Anchor Bolt (ft. lbs.)	Brige, Pin or Key Bolts (ft. lbs.)	Wheels Lugs (ft. lbs.)	Normal Std.	Minimum Thickness Machine To	Discard At	Rotor Parallel Variation	Max. Run-out
					AMC/Eagle						
1988–90 Premier	20	Floating	—	70	18.5	63	0.866	—	0.807	—	.003
1988–89 Medallion	20	Floating	—	48	18	67	0.775	—	0.697	—	.002
1986–87 AMC Eagle	1	Sliding	Bendix	100	30	75	.880	.815	0.810	.0005	.003
1989–90 Summit with rear disc	21	Floating	—	58–72	16–23	65–80	0.510	—	0.449	—	.006
				58–72	16–23	65–80	0.940	—	0.882	—	.006
Rear	33	Floating	—	36–43	16–23	65–80	0.390	—	0.331	—	.006

DISC BRAKE SPECIFICATIONS

Car Manufacturer, Year & Model	Text Reference Type	Caliper Style	Brake manufacturer	Anchor Bolt (ft. lbs.)	Brige, Pin or Key Bolts (ft. lbs.)	Wheels Lugs (ft. lbs.)	Normal Std.	Minimum Thickness Machine To	Discard At	Rotor Parallel Variation	Max. Run-out
CHRYSLER—FRONT WHEEL DRIVE											
1986–90 Aries, Reliant and 1986–87 Daytona, Laser, 600 and Caravelle	7	Floating	ATE	70–100	18–22	80	.935	912	.882	.0005	.004
1988–90 D, C, V and TC											
with Std.	22	Floating	K/H	130–190	18–26	95	.935	.912	.882	.0005	.005
with H/D	22	Floating	K/H	130–190	25–35	95	.935	.912	.882	.0005	.005
Rear	31 or 32	Floating	K/H	130–190	18–26	95	.345	.312	.291	.0005	.003
1986–90 Shadow, Sundance, Lancer, LeBaron	6	Floating	K/H	70–100	25–40	80	.500	.461	.431	.0005	.004
1986–90 M and Z	6	Floating	K/H	130–190	18–26	95	.935	.912	.882	.0005	.005
1989–90 Laser	21	Floating	—	58–72	16–23	65–80	0.510	—	0.449	—	.006
with rear disc				58–72	16–23	65–80	0.940	—	0.882	—	.006
Rear	33	Floating	—	36–43	16–23	65–80	0.390	—	0.331	—	.006
CHRYSLER CORP.—REAR WHEEL DRIVE											
1986–89 All	3	Sliding	Chrysler	95–125	15–20	85	1.010	.955	.940	.0005	.004
FORD MOTOR CO.—FRONT WHEEL DRIVE											
1988–90 Festiva	16	Sliding	Ford	—	29–36	65–87	—	.463	.433	.0006	.003
1988–90 Tracer											
Front	16	Sliding	Ford	—	20–36	65–87	.710	.660	.630	.001	.004
Rear	29	Sliding	Ford	—	29–36	65–87	.390	.380	.350	.001	.004
1988–90 Lincoln Continental											
Front	5	Sliding	Ford	—	18–25	80–105	1.02	—	.974	.0004	.002
Rear	30	Sliding	Ford	—	23–36	80–105	1.02	—	.974	.0005	.002
1988–90 Taurus, Sable	5	Sliding	Ford	—	24–34	80–105	1.024	—	.974	.0005	.002
1988–90 Taurus SHO											
Rear	30	Sliding	Ford	80–100	23–26	80–105	1.020	—	0.974	.0005	.002
1988–90 Escort, Tempo, Topaz	5	Sliding	Ford	—	18–25	80–105	.945	.896	.882	.0004	.002
1986–87 Taurus, Sable	5	Sliding	Ford	—	18–25	80–105	.945	.896	.882	.0005	.003
1985–87 Escort, Lynx, LN7, EXP, Tempo, Topaz	5	Sliding	Ford	—	18–25	80–105	.945	.896	.882	.0004	.002
FORD MOTOR CO.—REAR WHEEL DRIVE											
1988–90 Mark VII											
Front	8	Floating	Ford	—	45–65	80–105	1.030	—	.972	.0005	.003
Rear	25	Sliding	K/H	80–110	29–37	80–105	.945	—	.895	.0005	.004
1988–90 Cougar, Mustang exc. 5.0L Thunderbird exc. Turbo	8	Floating	Ford	—	45–65	80–105	.870	—	.810	.0005	.003
1987–90 Mustang 5.0L, Thunderbird Turbo											
Front	8	Floating	Ford	—	45–65	80–105	1.030	—	.972	.0005	.003
Rear	30	Sliding	Ford	—	23–26	80–105	1.02	—	.974	.0005	.002
1986–87 Lincoln Continental, Mark VII											
Front	8	Floating	Ford	—	40–60	80–105	1.030	—	.972	.0005	.003
Rear	25	Sliding	K/H	85–115	15–20	80–105	.945	—	.895	.0004	.004

DISC BRAKE SPECIFICATIONS

Car Manufacturer, Year & Model	Text Reference Type	Caliper Style	Brake manu-facturer	Anchor Bolt (ft. lbs.)	Brige, Pin or Key Bolts (ft. lbs.)	Wheels Lugs (ft. lbs.)	Normal Std.	Minimum Thickness Machine To	Discard At	Rotor Parallel Varia-tion	Max. Run-out
FORD MOTOR CO.—REAR WHEEL DRIVE											
1986–90 Lincoln Town Car, Crown Victoria, Grand Marquis	8	Floating	Ford	—	40–60	80–105	1.030	—	.972	.0005	.003
1986–87 All Models except noted	8	Floating	Ford	—	30–40	80–105	.870	—	.810	.0005	.003
GENERAL MOTORS—BUICK											
1988–90 Regal											
Front	15	Floating	Delco	79	—	100	1.040	1.019	.972	.0005	.003
Rear	27	Floating	Delco	79	—	100	.492	.476	.429	.0005	.003
1986–90 Riviera											
Front	13	Floating	Delco	83	63	100	1.943	.971	.956	.0005	.004
Rear	23	Floating	Delco	83	63	100	.494	.444	.429	.0005	.003
1986–90 Electra Limited, Park Avenue FWD	2	Floating	Delco	—	35	70	1.043	.972	.957	.0005	.004
1986–90 Electra, Estate Wagon RWD	2	Floating	Delco	—	35	80①	1.037	.980	.965	.0005	.004
1986–90 Century											
With H.D.	2	Floating	Delco	—	28	100	1.043	.972	.957	.0005	.004
w/o H.D.	2	Floating	Delco	—	28	100	.885	.830	.815	.0005	.004
1986–90 Skyhawk	11	Floating	Delco	—	28	100	.885	.830	.815	.0005	.004
1986–87 Regal	2	Floating	Delco	—	35	70–80	1.043	.980	.965	.0005	.004
1986–90 Skylark	15	Floating	Delco	—	21–35	102	.885	.830	.815	.0005	.004
GENERAL MOTORS—CADILLAC											
1987–90 Allante											
Front	13	Floating	Delco	83	63	100	1.035	.971	.956	.0005	.004
Rear	23	Floating	Delco	83	63	100	.494	.444	.429	.0005	.003
1986–90 Eldorado, Seville											
Front	13	Floating	Delco	83	63	100	1.035	.971	.956	.0005	.004
Rear	23	Floating	Delco	83	63	100	.494	.444	.429	.0005	.003
1986–88 Cimarron	11	Floating	Delco	—	28	100	.885	.830	.815	.0005	.004
1986–90 Brougham, Fleetwood, DeVille RWD	2	Floating	Delco	—	30	100	1.037④	.980	.965	.0005	.004
1986–90 CC, Limousine	2	Floating	Delco	—	30	100	1.250	1.230	1.215	.0005	.004
GENERAL MOTORS—CHEVROLET AND GEO											
1986–90 Nova, Prizm	9	Floating	Delco	65	18	76	.531	.507	.472	.0005	.006
1986–88 Camaro											
Front	2	Floating	Delco	—	21–35	80	1.030	.980	.965	.0005	.004
Rear	26	Floating	Delco	—	30–45	80	1.030	.980	.965	.0005	.004
1988–89 Corvette and 1989–90 Camaro											
Front w/o H.D.	14	Floating	—	137	⑤	100	.795	.744	.724	.0005	.006
Front with H.D.	14	Floating	—	137	⑤	100	1.110	1.059	1.039	.0005	.006
Rear	26	Floating	—	70	⑤	100	.795	.744	7.24	.0005	.006
1986–90 B Body	2	Floating	Delco	—	35	80②	1.030	.980	.965	.0005	.004
1986–90 Malibu, Monte Carlo	2	Floating	Delco	—	35	80③	1.030	.980	.965	.0005	.004

DISC BRAKE SPECIFICATIONS

Car Manufacturer, Year & Model	Text Reference Type	Caliper Style	Brake manufacturer	Anchor Bolt (ft. lbs.)	Brige, Pin or Key Bolts (ft. lbs.)	Wheels Lugs (ft. lbs.)	Normal Std.	Minimum Thickness Machine To	Discard At	Rotor Parallel Variation	Max. Runout
GENERAL MOTORS—CHEVROLET AND GEO											
1986–87 Corvette											
Front	18	Floating	Girlock	70	24	100	.780	.739	.724	.0005	.006
Rear	24	Floating	Girlock	44	24	100	.780	.739	.724	.0005	.006
1986–90 Celebrity, Cavalier	11	Floating	Delco	—	28	100		Vented		.0005	.004
1986–90 Spectrum	9	Floating	—	40	36	65	.433	.393	.378	.0005	.006
1986–90 Sprint, Metro	10	Floating	—	—	26	50	.394	.330	.315	.0005	.003
1990 Lumina	15	Floating	—	—	26	50	.394	.330	.315	.0005	.003
1986–87 Chevette	4	Floating	Delco	—	21–25	70	—	.390	.374	.0005	.005
1987–89 Corsica, Beretta	11	Floating	Delco	—	38	100	.880	.830	.815	.0005	.005
GENERAL MOTORS—OLDSMOBILE											
1986–90 Toronado											
Front	13	Floating	Delco	83	63	100	1.035	.971	.956	.0005	.004
Rear	23	Floating	Delco	83	63	100	.494	.444	.429	.0005	.003
1988–90 Cutlass Supreme											
Front	15	Floating	Delco	79	—	100	1.040	1.019	.972	.0005	.003
Rear	27	Floating	Delco	79	—	100	.492	.476	.429	.0005	.003
1988–90 Delta 88	2	Floating	Delco	—	38	100	1.043	.972	.957	.0005	.004
1986–90 98 Regency Brougham FWD	2	Floating	Delco	—	35	70	1.0443	.972	.957	.0005	.004
1986–90 Full Size	2	Floating	Delco	—	35	80①	1.040	.960	.965	.0005	.005
1986–90 Ciera, Firenza	2	Floating	Delco	—	28	100	1.043	.972	.957	.0005	.004
GENERAL MOTORS—PONTIAC											
1986–90 B Body	2	Floating	Delco	—	35	80②	1.030	.980	.965	.0005	.004
1988 Fiero & 1989–90 6000											
Front	17	Floating	—	74	74	100	.756	.702	.681	.0005	.003
Rear	28	Floating	—	74	74	100	.756	.702	.681	.0005	.003
1988–89 Grand Prix											
Front	15	Floating	—	79	—	100	1.040	1.019	.972	.0005	.003
Rear	27	Floating	—	79	—	100	.492	.476	.429	.0005	.003
1987–88 6000											
Front w/rear drum	2	Floating	Delco	—	38	100	—	.830	.815	.0005	.004
Front w/rear disc	2	Floating	Delco	—	38	100	1.043	.972	.957	.0005	.004
Rear	23	Floating	Delco	—	38	100	—	.444	.429	.0005	.004
1988–90 Grand Am	2	Floating	Delco	—	35	100	1.030	.980	.965	.0005	.004
1987–90 Bonneville	2	Floating	Delco	—	38	80	1.043	.972	.957	.0005	.004
1986–87 Grand Prix	2	Floating	Delco	—	35	80	1.030	.980	.965	.0005	.004
1988–90 Lemans	12	Floating	—	—	—	65	.500	.460	.420	.0004	.004
1986–88 Firebird											
Front	2	Floating	Delco	—	21–35	80	1.030	.980	.965	.0005	.004
Rear	26	Floating	Delco	—	30–45	80	1.030	.980	.965	.0005	.004
1989–90 Firebird											
Front w/o H.D.	14	Floating	—	137	⑤	100	.795	.744	.724	.0005	.006
Front with H.D.	14	Floating	—	137	⑤	100	1.110	1.059	1.039	.0005	.006
Rear	26	Floating	—	70	⑤	100	.795	.744	7.24	.0005	.006

DISC BRAKE SPECIFICATIONS

Car Manufacturer, Year & Model	Text Reference Type	Caliper Style	Brake manufacturer	Anchor Bolt (ft. lbs.)	Brige, Pin or Key Bolts (ft. lbs.)	Wheels Lugs (ft. lbs.)	Normal Std.	Minimum Thickness Machine To	Discard At	Rotor Parallel Variation	Max. Runout
GENERAL MOTORS—PONTIAC											
1989–90 T1000	4	Floating	Delco	—	21–25	70	.440	.390	.374	.0005	.005
1986–87 Fiero											
Front	17	Floating	Delco	—	35	81	—	.444	.390	.0005	.004
Rear	23	Floating	Delco	—	35	81	—	.444	.390	.0005	.004

① 100 with ½ in studs
② 100 on s/w
③ 90 with aluminum wheels
④ 80 with aluminum wheels

Disc Brakes

ROTORS

Resurfacing

Manufacturers differ widely on permissible runout, but too much can sometimes be felt as a pulsation at the brake pedal. A wobble pump effect is created when a rotor is not perfectly smooth and the pad hits the high spots forcing fluid back into the master cylinder. This alternating pressure causes a pulsating feeling which can be felt at the pedal when the brakes are applied. This excessive runout also causes the brakes to be out of adjustment because disc brakes are self-adjusting; they are designed so that the pads drag on the rotor at all times and therefore automatically compensate for wear.

To check the actual runout of the rotor, first tighten the wheel spindle nut to a snug bearing adjustment, endplay removed. Fasten a dial indicator on the suspension at a convenient place so that the indicator stylus contacts the rotor face approximately 1 in. from its outer edge. Set the dial at zero. Check the total indicator reading while turning the rotor 1 full revolution. If the rotor is warped beyond the runout specification, it is unlikely that it can be successfully remachined.

Lateral Runout—A wobbly movement of the rotor from side to side as it rotates. Excessive lateral runout causes the rotor faces to knock back the disc pads and can result in chatter, excessive pedal travel, pumping or fighting pedal and vibration during the breaking action.

Parallelism (lack of)—Refers to the amount of variation in the thickness of the rotor. Excessive variation can cause pedal vibration or fight, front end vibrations and possible grab during the braking action; a condition comparable to an out-of-round brake drum. Check parallelism with a micrometer. Measure the thickness at 8 or more equally spaced points, equally distant from the outer edge of the rotor, preferably at mid-points of the braking surface. Parallelism then is the amount of variation between maximum and minimum measurements.

Surface or Micro-inch finish, flatness, smoothness—Different from parallelism, these terms refer to the degree of perfection of the flat surface on each side of the rotor; that is, the minute hills, valleys and swirls inherent in machining the surface. In a visual inspection, the remachined surface should have a fine ground polish with, at most, only a faint trace of non-directional swirls.

Removal and Installation

1. Raise the vehicle, support safely and remove the wheel assemblies.

2. Remove the caliper mounting bolts. Slide the caliper away from the disc and suspend it using a wire loop. In some vehicles, it is advisable to install a cardboard spacer between the pads to prevent the piston from coming out of its cylinder.

3. On rear wheel drive vehicles, remove the cotter pin, castellated nut lock, if equipped, wheel bearing nut and washer from the spindle and remove the outer wheel bearing from the hub. Remove the hub and disc assembly from the spindle. Installation of hub and disc is the reverse order of removal.

4. On front wheel drive vehicles, remove any adaptors or brackets preventing the remval of the rotor. Some vehicles require the removal of the axle locknut for the rotor to be removed from the vehicle using a puller. Then the rotor may be unbolted from the hub.

DISC BRAKE PADS

Inspection

Disc pads should be replaced in axle sets (both wheels) when the lining on any pad is worn to $\frac{1}{16}$ in. at any point. If lining is allowed to wear past $\frac{1}{16}$ in. minimum thickness, severe damage to disc may result. Individual state safety inspection specifications take precedence over these general recommendations.

Note that disc pads in floating caliper type brakes may wear at an angle and measurement should be made at the narrow end of the taper. Tapered linings should be replaced if the taper exceeds $\frac{1}{8}$ in. from end to end (the difference between the thickest and thinnest points).

To prevent costly paint damage, remove some brake fluid from the reservoir and install the reservoir cover before replacing the disc pads. When replacing the pads, the piston is depressed and fluid is forced back through the lines to squirt out of the fluid reservoir.

When the caliper is unbolted from the hub, do not let it dangle by the brake hose. It can be rested on a suspension member or wired to the frame. All disc brake systems are self-adjusting and have no provision for manual adjustment.

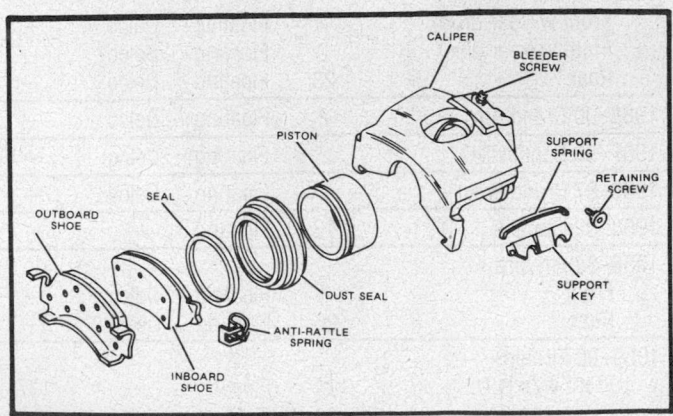

Type 1—Bendix sliding caliper

DISC PAD SERVICE

NOTE: All of the following procedures are under the assumption that the vehicle has been raised and safely supported and that the wheels have been removed. It is recommended that 2 lug nuts be installed over the rotor to keep it in place while working on the brakes. When the work is done, lower the vehicle and always pump up the brakes before moving the vehicle. If they will not pump up, bleed the hydraulic system. Road test the vehicle completely after any brake work has been completed.

Type 1

KELSEY–HAYES OR BENDIX SLIDING CALIPER DISC BRAKES

Removal and Installation

1. Remove half of the brake fluid from the master cylinder.
2. Remove the retaining screw holding the caliper support key.
3. Drive the caliper retaining key and support spring out of the anchor plate.
4. Lift the caliper off of the rotor and support so there is no stress on the hose.
5. Use a large C-clamp to force the piston back into its bore, being careful not to scratch the piston or bore and being careful not to cut or tear the dust boot.
6. Remove the inboard disc pad and anti-rattle spring from the caliper support adapter.
7. Remove the outboard disc pad from the caliper. Check the condition of the rotor. If rotor measurements exceed manufacturer's specifications or has deep scratches, machine the rotor.
8. Clean and lubricate all sliding surfaces on the adapter and caliper.
9. Install the inboard brake pad and anti-rattle spring in the caliper support adapter.
10. Position the outboard brake pad in the caliper. Bend ears if necessary to provide slight interference fit in caliper.
11. Position the caliper over the rotor.
12. Install the caliper support spring and support key into the slot and drive them into the opening between the lower end of the caliper and the lower anchor plate abutment.
13. Install and tighten the key retaining screw.
14. Fill the master cylinder with brake fluid.

Type 2

DELCO FLOATING CALIPER DISC BRAKES

Removal and Installation

1. Remove half of the brake fluid from the master cylinder.
2. Position a large C-clamp over the caliper with the screw end against the outboard brake pad. Tighten the clamp until the caliper is pushed out enough to bottom the piston.
3. Remove the C-clamp. Remove the 2 caliper guide pin mounts and lift the caliper off of the rotor.
4. Support the caliper so there is no strain on the brake hose.
5. Press the inboard pad outward, then lift from the caliper.
6. Remove and discard the 4 O-ring bushings and steel sleeves if new ones are to be installed. Check the condition of the rotor. If rotor measurements exceed manufacturer's specifications or has deep scratches, machine the rotor.
7. Lubricate and install the 4 O-ring bushings. Install the sleeves pressing them through the O-rings until the sleeve end on the pad side is flush with caliper ear. Position the inboard

pad so the pad contacts the piston and the 2 support spring ends. The inboard and outboard pads are similar, but not interchangeable.
8. Press down on the ears at the top of the inboard pad until the pad lies flat and the spring ends are just inside the lower edge of the pad.
9. Position the outboard pad with the ears toward the positioning pin holes and the tab on the inner edge of the pad resting in the notch in the edge of the caliper. Bend the ears to provide a slight interference fit in the caliper.
10. Press the outboard pad tightly into position and use a pair of pliers to clinch the ears of the outboard pad over the outboard caliper half.
11. Position the caliper over the rotor.
12. Install the caliper mounting bolts and tighten to specification.
13. Fill the master cylinder with brake fluid.

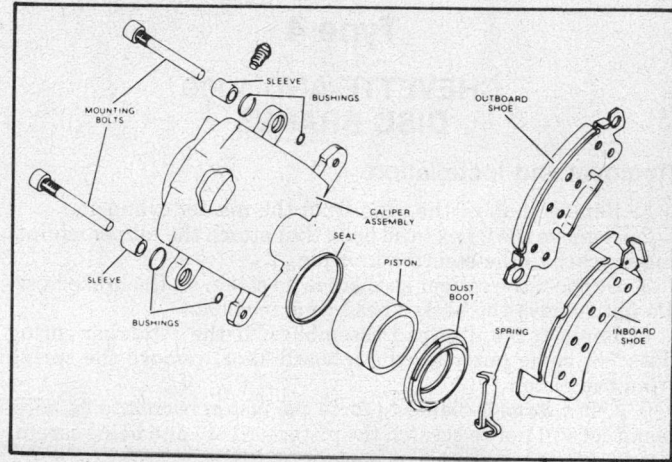

Type 2—Delco floating caliper

Type 3

KELSEY–HAYES/CHRYSLER SLIDING CALIPER DISC BRAKES

Removal and Installation

1. Remove half of the brake fluid from the master cylinder.
2. Remove the caliper retaining clips and anti-rattle springs.
3. Lift the caliper off of the rotor.
4. Support the caliper so there is no strain on the brake hose.
5. Use a large C-clamp to force the piston back into its bore,

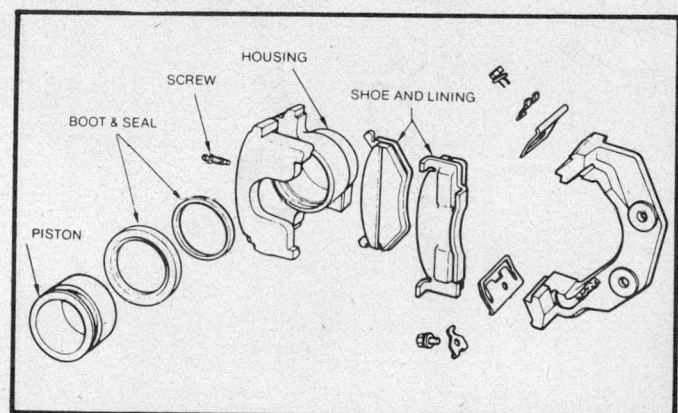

Type 3—Kelsey Hayes sliding caliper

being careful not to scratch the piston or bore and being careful not to cut or tear the dust boot.

6. Pry the outboard pad from caliper.

7. Remove the inboard pad from the adapter.

8. Check the condition of the rotor. If rotor measurements exceed manufacturer's specifications or has deep scratches, machine the rotor.

9. Adjust the ears of the outboard pad to provide a tight fit in the caliper recess and install in the caliper.

10. Install inboard pad in the adapter.

11. Position the caliper on the rotor with the caliper engaging the adapter properly.

12. Install the anti-rattle springs and caliper retaining clips and torque retaining screws to 180 inch lbs.

13. Fill the master cylinder with brake fluid.

Type 4

CHEVETTE AND 1000 DISC BRAKES

Removal and Installation

1. Remove half of the fluid from the master cylinder.

2. Remove the 2 hex head bolts that attach the caliper mounting bracket to the steering knuckle.

3. Support the caliper so there is no strain on the brake hose. Do not remove the socket head retainer bolt.

4. Remove the disc pad assemblies. If the retaining spring does not come out with the inboard shoe, remove the spring from the piston.

5. Use a large C-clamp to force the piston back into its bore, being careful not to scratch the piston or bore and being careful not to cut or tear the dust boot.

6. If rotor measurements exceed manufacturer's specifications or has deep scratches, machine the rotor.

7. Before installing the inboard shoe, make sure that the shoe retaining spring is properly installed. Push the tab on the single-leg end of the spring down into the shoe hole, then snap the other 2 legs over the edge of the shoe notch.

8. Position the caliper over the rotor, lining up the bracket mounting holes. Install the mounting bolts.

9. Clinch the outboard shoe to the caliper.

10. Add brake fluid to the master cylinder.

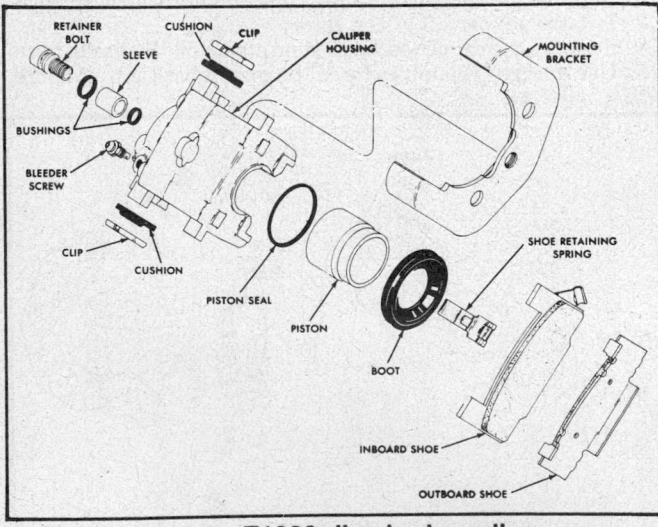

Type 4 — Chevette, T1000 disc brake caliper

Type 5

FORD MOTOR CO. FRONT WHEEL DRIVE DISC BRAKES

Removal and Installation

1. Remove half of the fluid from the master cylinder.

2. Remove the brake caliper anti-rattle spring by applying upward pressure to center portion of spring until the spring tabs are free of the caliper holes.

3. Back out the caliper locating pins. Do not remove pins completely unless new bushings are to be installed. Reinstalling pins after complete removal can be difficult.

4. Lift caliper assembly from integral knuckle and anchor plate and rotor and use a C-clamp to bottom the piston. Suspend the caliper from inside the fender housing.

5. Remove the disc pads and inspect both rotor braking surfaces. If rotor measurements exceed manufacturer's specifications or has deep scratches, machine the rotor. Minor scoring or build-up of lining material does not require machining or replacement of the rotor.

6. Use care not to damage caliper or stretch the brake hose.

7. Install the inner disc pad assembly in the piston. Do not bend shoe clips during installation in the piston or distortion and rattle can occur.

8. Install the outer disc pad assembly making sure clips are properly seated. Replace caliper anti-rattle spring.

9. Install the locating pin and torque to specification.

10. Refill master cylinder to at least ¼ in. from the top in both reservoirs.

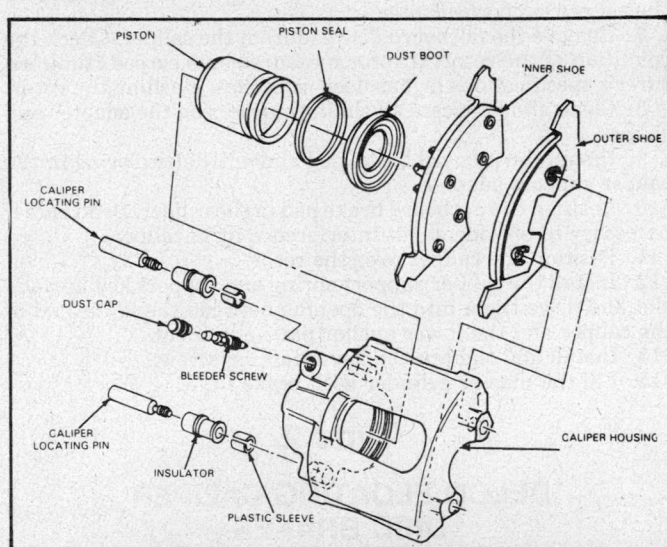

Type 5 — Ford front wheel drive caliper

Type 6

KELSEY-HAYES SINGLE PIN CALIPER DISC BRAKES

Pad Removal

1. Remove half of the brake fluid from each master cylinder reservoir.

2. Remove the caliper guide pin. Do not remove any of the anti-rattle springs.

3. Lift the caliper from the rotor and support to prevent strain on the brake hose.

4. Use a C-clamp to bottom the piston.

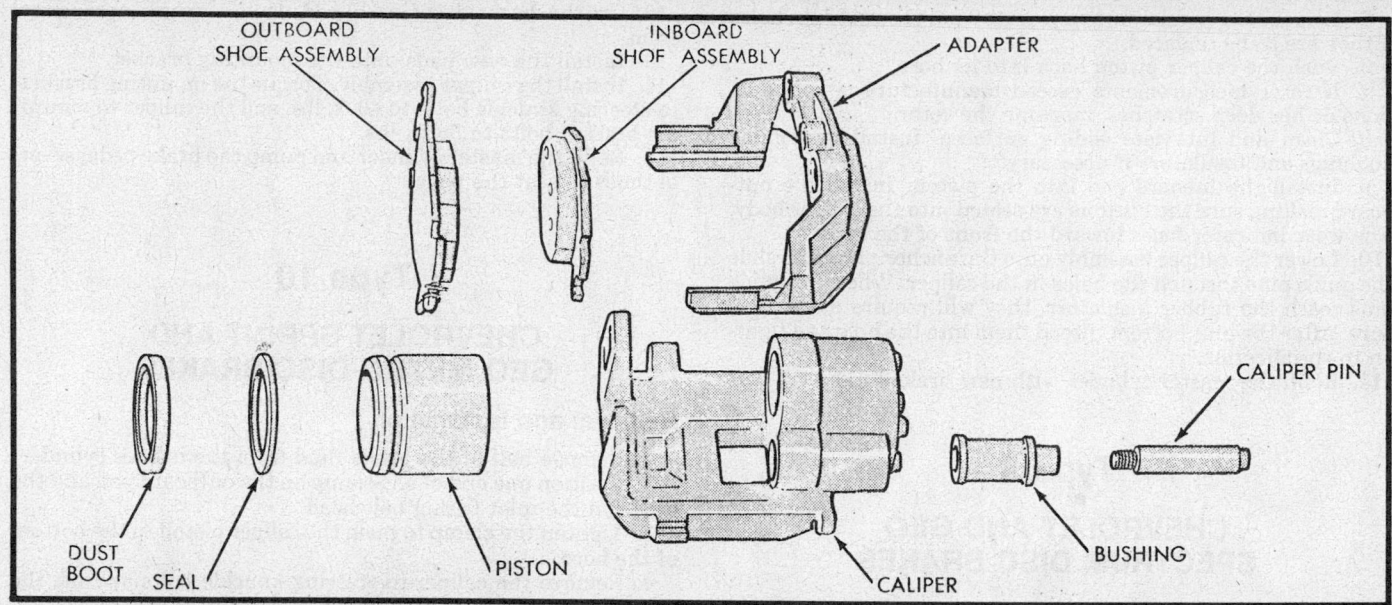

Type 6—Kelsey-Hayes single piston caliper

5. Remove the brake pads from the caliper adaptor. Remove and discard the bushings if they are to be replaced.
6. If rotor measurements exceed manufacturer's specifications or has deep scratches, machine the rotor.
7. Clean and lubricate the caliper guide pin and sliding surfaces. Install new guide bushings if necessary.
8. Position the new brake pads in the caliper adaptor. Some new pads kits have anti-rattle clips installed on the pads. If not, transfer the clips from the old pads to the new.
9. Carefully lower the caliper over the adaptor.
10. Align and install the guide pin.
11. Fill the master cylinder with new fluid.

Type 7

ATE FLOATING CALIPER DISC BRAKES

Removal and Installation

1. Remove the anti-rattle clip and the guide pin.
2. Remove the caliper from the rotor by slowly sliding it up and away. Support the caliper so there is no strain on the brake hose.
3. Remove the outer pad from the caliper. Remove the inner pad from the adaptor.
4. Push the caliper piston back into its bore.
5. If rotor measurements exceed manufacturer's specifications or has deep scratches, machine the rotor.

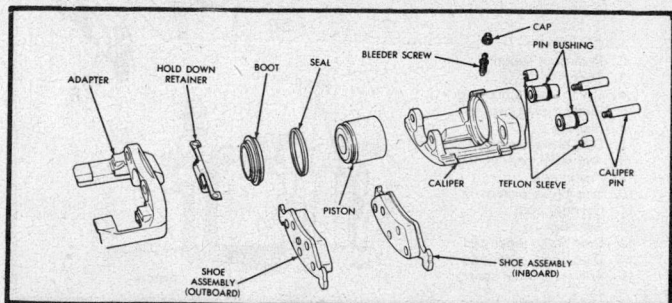

Type 7—ATE floating disc brake caliper

7. Clean and lubricate the sliding surfaces. Install the inner pad and onto the adaptor.
8. Install the outer pad on the piston.
9. Position the caliper over the rotor. Align and install the guide pins and anti-rattle clip.
10. Fill the master cylinder with brake fluid.

Type 8

FORD SLIDING CALIPER DISC BRAKES

Removal and Installation

1. Remove half of the brake fluid from the master cylinder reservoirs.
2. Remove the caliper guide pins.
3. Lift the caliper assembly from the rotor. Support the caliper so there is no strain on the brake hose.
4. Remove the outboard pad from the caliper. Remove the inboard pad from the piston.

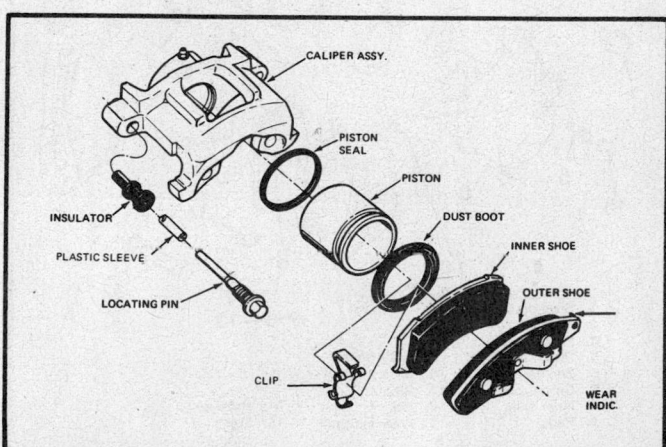

Type 8—Ford floating disc brake caliper

5. Remove the insulators and inserts from the guide pin holes if they are to be replaced.

6. Push the caliper piston back into its bore.

7. If rotor measurements exceed manufacturer's specifications or has deep scratches, machine the rotor.

8. Clean and lubricate sliding surfaces. Install new guide bushings and insulators if necessary.

9. Install the inboard pad into the piston. Install the outboard making sure the buttons are seated into the caliper body. The wear indicator faces toward the front of the car.

10. Lower the caliper assembly onto the anchor plate and slide the guide pins through the holes in the caliper. When the guide pins reach the rubber insulators, they will require more pressure. After the pins bottom thread them into the hole and tighten to specification.

11. Refill the master cylinder with new brake fluid.

Type 9

CHEVROLET AND GEO SPECTRUM DISC BRAKES

Removal and Installation

1. Remove half of the brake fluid from the master cylinder.

2. Position a C-clamp over the caliper, with an end on the outboard pad and the other on the inlet fitting bolt head.

3. Tighten the clamp to push the caliper piston to the bottom of the bore.

4. Remove the caliper-to-mounting bracket bolts and lift the caliper from the steering knuckle.

5. Using a wire, support the caliper from the vehicle.

6. Remove the inner and outer pads, pad wear indicators, anti-squeal shims and retainers from the caliper.

9. Clean the pad mounting frame on the caliper. If rotor measurements exceed manufacturer's specifications or has deep scratches, machine the rotor.

10. Install grease inside of the slide pin bushing and the new inner and outer pads in position on the caliper.

11. Install new pad wear indicator plates to each pad.

NOTE: When installing the pad wear indicator plates, be sure the arrow on the pad wear indicator is facing the rotating direction of the rotor.

12. On the backside of each pad, install a new anti-squeal shim.

13. Install the new pads onto the mounting bracket.

14. Install the caliper assembly. Torque the mounting bracket-to-steering knuckle bolts to 40 ft. lbs. and the caliper to mounting bracket bolts to 36 ft. lbs.

15. Refill the master cylinder and pump the brake pedal several times to seat the pads.

Type 10

CHEVROLET SPRINT AND GEO METRO DISC BRAKES

Removal and Installation

1. Remove half of the brake fluid from the master cylinder.

2. Position one end of a C-clamp on the outboard pad and the other on the inlet fitting bolt head.

3. Tighten the clamp to push the caliper piston to the bottom of the bore.

4. Remove the caliper-to-steering knuckle bolts and lift the caliper from the steering knuckle.

5. Using a wire, support the caliper from the vehicle.

6. From the caliper, remove the inner/outer pads and the anti-squeal shims.

7. Clean the pad mounting frame on the caliper. Inspect the caliper for signs of fluid leakage, the rotor thickness and runout. Remove and service the caliper if necessary.

8. Install new inner and outer pads into position on the caliper.

9. On the backside of each pad, install a new anti-squeal shim.

10. Install the new outer pad onto the mounting bracket.

11. Install the new inner pad onto the caliper.

12. Install the caliper assembly onto the mounting bracket and the springs onto the caliper. Torque the caliper-to-mounting bracket bolts to 17–26 ft. lbs.

13. Refill the master cylinder and pump the brake pedal several times to seat the pads. Bleed the brakes if necessary.

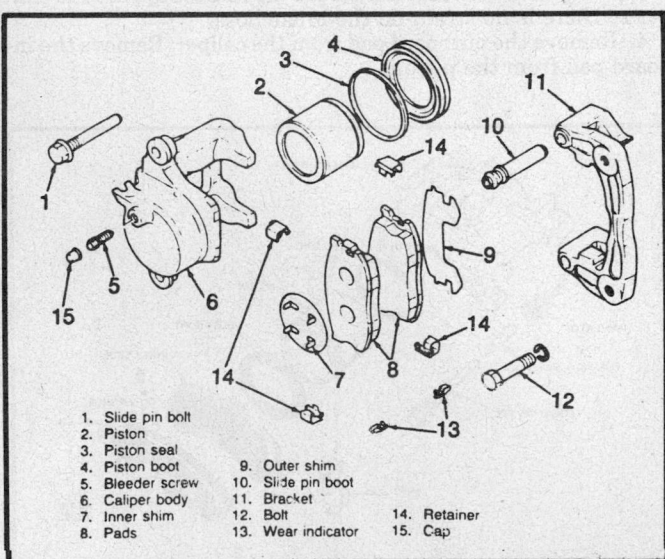

1. Slide pin bolt
2. Piston
3. Piston seal
4. Piston boot
5. Bleeder screw
6. Caliper body
7. Inner shim
8. Pads
9. Outer shim
10. Slide pin boot
11. Bracket
12. Bolt
13. Wear indicator
14. Retainer
15. Cap

Type 9 – Spectrum disc brake caliper

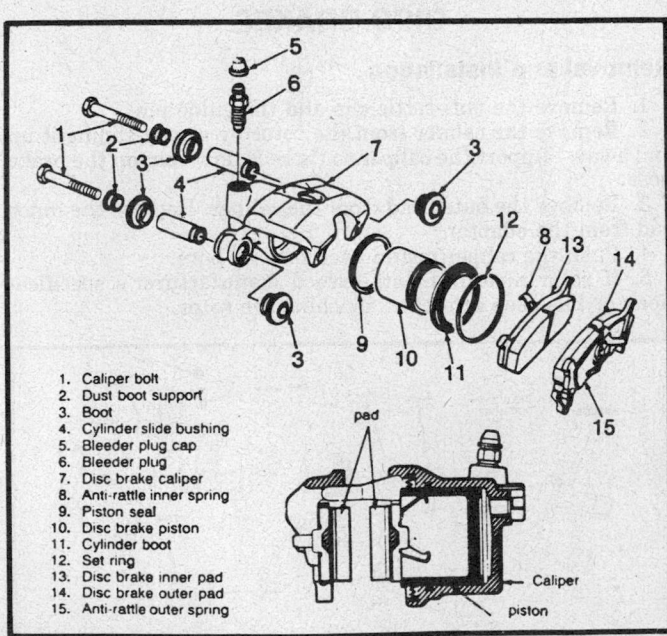

1. Caliper bolt
2. Dust boot support
3. Boot
4. Cylinder slide bushing
5. Bleeder plug cap
6. Bleeder plug
7. Disc brake caliper
8. Anti-rattle inner spring
9. Piston seal
10. Disc brake piston
11. Cylinder boot
12. Set ring
13. Disc brake inner pad
14. Disc brake outer pad
15. Anti-rattle outer spring

pad

Caliper

piston

Type 10 – Sprint disc brake caliper

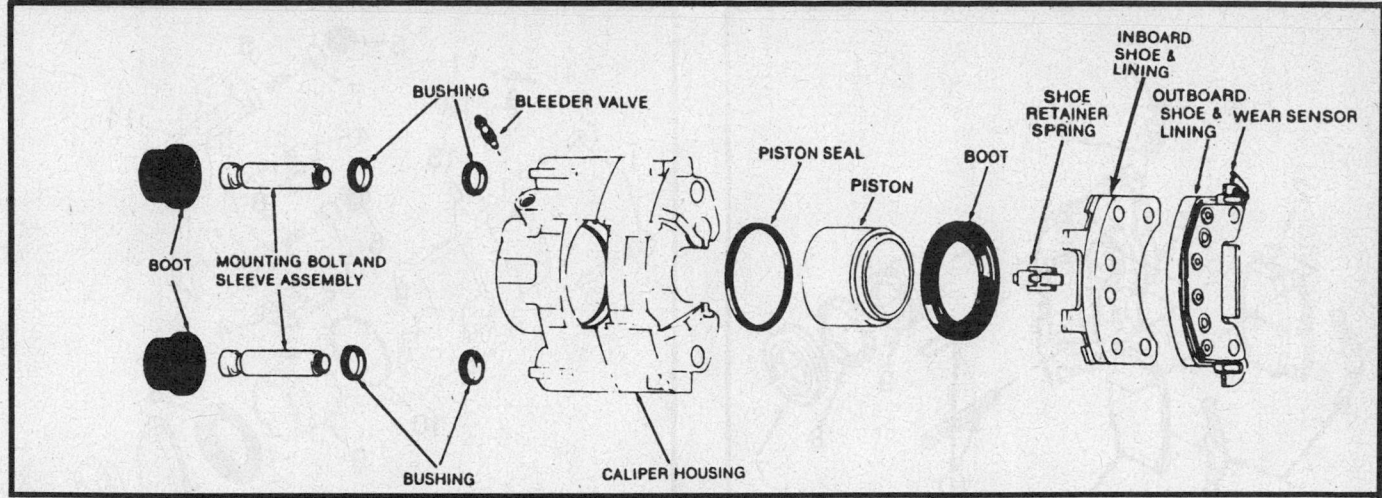

Type 11—GM J and A-body disc brake caliper

Type 11

GM J AND A-BODY DISC BRAKES

Pad Removal

1. Remove half of the brake fluid from the master cylinder.
2. Remove mounting bolt boots and bolt and sleeve assemblies.
3. Remove caliper from the rotor and mounting bracket.
4. Remove the inboard and outboard pads.
5. Remove the bushings from the grooves inside the mounting bolt holes.
6. If rotor measurements exceed manufacturer's specifications or has deep scratches, machine the rotor.
7. Clean and lubricate all sliding surfaces.
8. Fill both cavities in the caliper housing with silicone grease and install new bushings.
9. Unless already mounted, install the retainer spring on the inner pad. Install the pad to the piston.
10. Install the outer pad with the wear sensor on the leading edge of the pad.
11. Position the caliper over the rotor in the mounting bracket. Install the mounting boot and sleeve assemblies.
12. Clinch outer shoe tightly in place.
13. Refill the master cylinder.

Type 12

PONTIAC LEMANS FRONT DISC BRAKES

Removal and Installation

1. Remove ⅔ of brake fluid from the master cylinder.
2. Using a brass drift and hammer and working from the inner side of the caliper, drive out the pad and lining retaining pins.

NOTE: The expanding springs in the caliper are held under tension from the retaining pins. Exercise caution when removing the pins.

3. Position a C-clamp over the caliper, connecting the outboard pad and the inlet fitting bolt head.

4. Tighten the clamp to push the caliper piston to the bottom of the bore.
5. Remove the brake pads.
6. Install new inner and outer pads and wear sensor in position on the caliper. Check that the pads and linings can be moved slightly backwards and forwards in the caliper.
7. Install the expanding springs.
8. Working from the outer side of the caliper, install the retaining pins so that the openings align.
9. Check the brake fluid level and add if necessary.

Type 13

GM E, K, V AND Z-BODY DISC BRAKES

Removal and Installation

1. Remove ⅔ of the brake fluid from the master cylinder.
2. Remove the caliper retaining bolts. Remove the caliper from the mounting bracket and suspend it out of the way with a metal hook or wire.
3. Remove the metal insulators from the top and bottom of the caliper mounting bracket.
4. Position a C-clamp over the caliper, contacting the outboard pad and the other on the inlet fitting bolt head.
5. Tighten the clamp to push the caliper piston to the bottom of the bore.
6. Remove the brake pads. Remove the bushings from the mounting bolt holes in the caliper mounting bracket.
7. If rotor measurements exceed manufacturer's specifications or has deep scratches, machine the rotor.
8. Lubricate and install new bushings in the mounting bolt holes in the caliper mounting bracket.
9. Install the inboard disc pad by snapping the shoe retaining spring into position. The shoe must lay flat against the piston.
10. Install the outboard disc pad by snapping the shoe springs into the holes in the caliper housing.
11. Install the wear sensors.

NOTE: Wear sensors should be at the trailing edge of the brake shoe during forward wheel rotation. The back of the brake shoe must lay flat against the caliper.

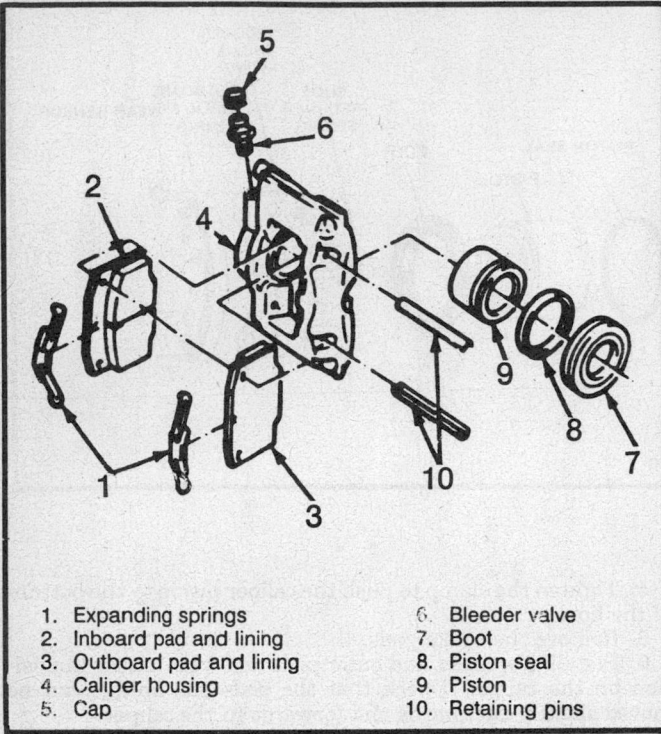

1. Expanding springs
2. Inboard pad and lining
3. Outboard pad and lining
4. Caliper housing
5. Cap
6. Bleeder valve
7. Boot
8. Piston seal
9. Piston
10. Retaining pins

Type 12—LeMans disc brake caliper

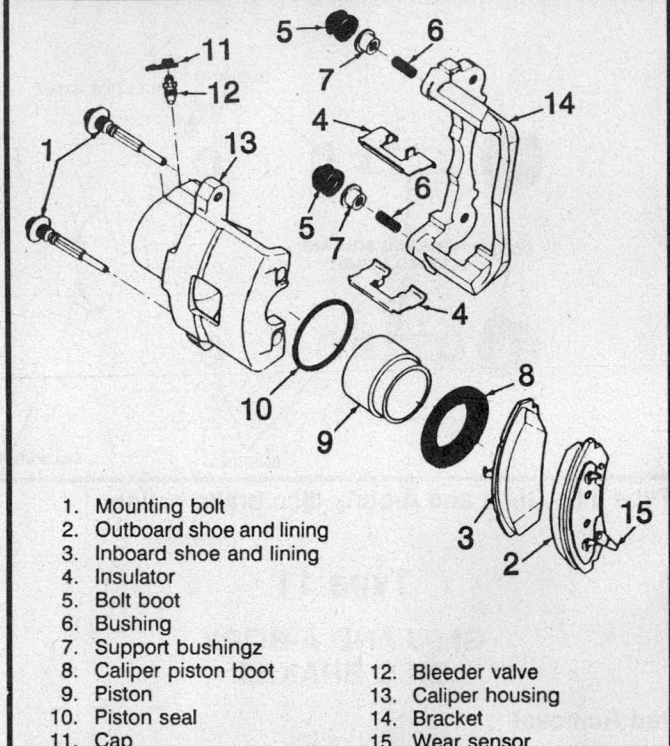

1. Mounting bolt
2. Outboard shoe and lining
3. Inboard shoe and lining
4. Insulator
5. Bolt boot
6. Bushing
7. Support bushingz
8. Caliper piston boot
9. Piston
10. Piston seal
11. Cap
12. Bleeder valve
13. Caliper housing
14. Bracket
15. Wear sensor

Type 13—GM E, K, V and Z-body disc brake caliper

12. Install the caliper onto the mounting bracket.
13. Install and tighten the mounting bolt and sleeve assemblies.
14. Refill the master cylinder.

Type 14

1988–90 CORVETTE DISC BRAKES

Removal and Installation

1. Remove ⅔ of brake fluid from the master cylinder.
2. Remove the circlip from inside of the retaining pin.
3. Remove caliper retaining pins.
4. Place caliper on upper control arm to avoid damaging the brake hose.
5. Bottom the caliper pistons using C-clamp or pliers.

NOTE: The C-clamp or pliers must be placed at the center of the brake pad to press both pistons evenly.

6. Remove the brake pads.
7. If rotor measurements exceed manufacturer's specifications or has deep scratches, machine the rotor.
8. Install new inner and outer outer pads. the outboard pad with insulator is installed in the caliper housing. The inboard shoe and lining with wear sensor is pressed into the caliper pistons.
9. Install the caliper over the rotor.
10. Install 1 new retainer pin and circlip.

NOTE: There are 2 types of replacement retainer pins. The circlip grooves are cut in different positions for standard and heavy duty calipers.

11. Press the caliper housing down to compress bias springs and install second retainer pin and circlip.
12. Check the brake fluid level and add if necessary.

Type 15

1988–90 GM W BODY DISC BRAKES

Removal and Installation

1. Remove ⅔ of brake fluid from the master cylinder.
2. Remove the 2 caliper mounting bolts from the mounting bracket.
3. Support the caliper so there is no stress on the hose.
4. Remove the brake pads.
5. If rotor measurements exceed manufacturer's specifications or has deep scratches, machine the rotor.
6. Clean and lubricate all sliding surfaces. Install new inner and outer pads on the mounting bracket.
7. Install new wear sensors. Be sure the arrow on the pad wear indicator is pointing in the rotating direction of the disc.
8. Press the caliper piston back into the bore.
9. Install the caliper onto the rotor.
10. Tighten caliper guide bolts to proper torque.
11. Check the brake fluid level and add if necessary.

Type 16

FORD FESTIVA AND MERCURY TRACER DISC BRAKES

Removal and Installation

1. Remove ⅔ of brake fluid from the master cylinder. Caliper removal is not required to replace the pads.

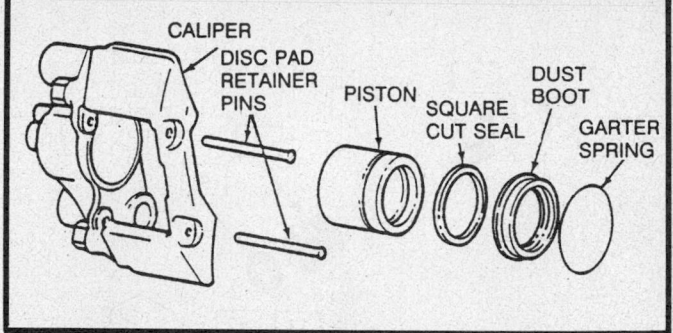

Type 16—Ford Festiva and Tracer front caliper

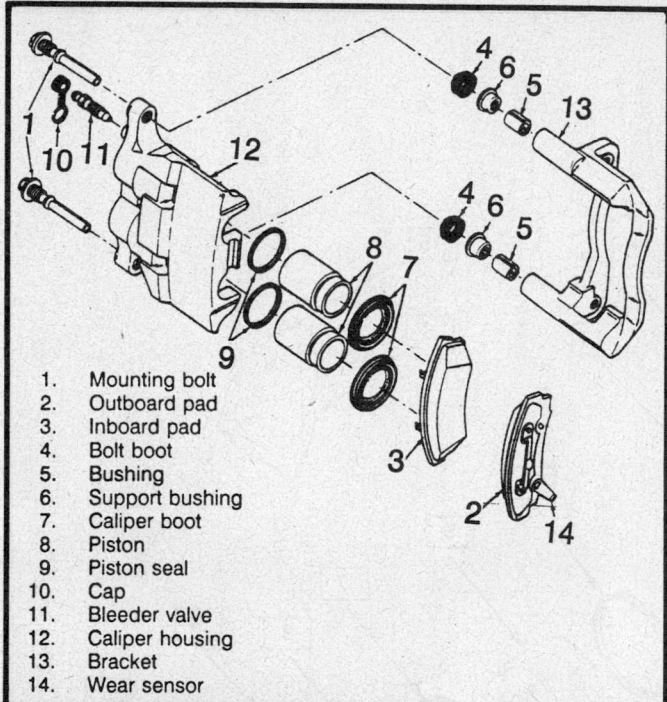

1. Mounting bolt
2. Outboard pad
3. Inboard pad
4. Bolt boot
5. Bushing
6. Support bushing
7. Caliper boot
8. Piston
9. Piston seal
10. Cap
11. Bleeder valve
12. Caliper housing
13. Bracket
14. Wear sensor

Type 15—GM W-Body front caliper

2. Remove the pad retainer spring that locks the disc pad retainer pins.

3. Tap out the disc pad retainer pins.

4. Pry the caliper outboard and remove the outboard pad and shim. Mark the shims so they can be installed in their original position.

5. Push the caliper inboard and remove the inboard pad and shim.

6. Remove the anchor plate clips and label them top and bottom.

7. If rotor measurements exceed manufacturer's specifications or has deep scratches, machine the rotor.

8. Install anchor plate clips in original locations.

9. Push caliper inboard and Install new inner pad and shim.

10. Pry caliper outboard and Install the outer pad and shim.

11. Lightly lubricate and install pad retaining pins.

12. Install pin retaining springs.

13. Check the brake fluid level and add if necessary.

Type 17

1986–87 FIERO
DISC BRAKES

Removal and Installation

1. Remove half of the brake fluid from the master cylinder reservoir.

2. Remove the 2 boots and mounting bolts.

3. Position adjustable pliers over the inboard surface of the caliper housing and caliper support bracket and compress the piston back into the caliper bore.

4. Remove the caliper from the rotor and suspend with a wire hook from the suspension.

5. Remove the pads assemblies from the caliper. To remove the outboard pad use a suitable tool to disengage the buttons on the shoe from the holes in the caliper.

6. Remove the sleeves from the mounting bolt holes.

7. Remove the bushings from the grooves in the mounting bolt holes.

8. If rotor measurements exceed manufacturer's specifications or has deep scratches, machine the rotor.

9. Use new bushings and sleeves and lubricate with a silicone lubricant.

10. Install the inboard pad.

11. Install the outboard pad with the wear sensor at the leading edge of the shoe during forward wheel rotation.

12. Liberally fill both cavities in the caliper housing between the bushings with silcone grease.

13. Install the sleeves and boots in the caliper.

14. Install the caliper over the rotor in the mounting bracket.

15. Install the mounting bolts and torque to 21–35 ft.lb. (28–41 Nm).

Type 18

1988 FIERO
DISC BRAKES

Removal and Installation

1. Remove ⅔ of brake fluid from the master cylinder.

2. Remove the caliper mounting pins using tools J-36620 and J-6125-1b or equivalent. Insert J-36620 slide hammer though pin and install tool J-6125-1b on the end. Thrust weight away from caliper to pull pins out.

--- CAUTION ---

Be prepared to catch springs when removing spring pins. Springs may fly out causing injury.

3. Remove spings from pad flanges.

4. Remove brake pads.

5. If rotor measurements exceed manufacturer's specifications or has deep scratches, machine the rotor.

6. Press the caliper piston back into the bore.

7. Install new wear sensors.

NOTE: Wear sensor should be at trailing edge of pad during forward wheel rotation.

8. Install new inner and outer pads.

9. Install the caliper onto the rotor.

10. Align 1 spring pin with pads and caliper. Tap in pin with soft brass drift until end of pin just emerges from inboard face of caliper.

11. Install springs one at a time. Hook end of spring under pin with center of spring over shoe flange.

12. Press down on other end of spring and install second pin through caliber and pad far enough to hold spring. Install second spring following the same procedure and finish tapping the pin through caliber.

13. Check the brake fluid level and add if necessary.

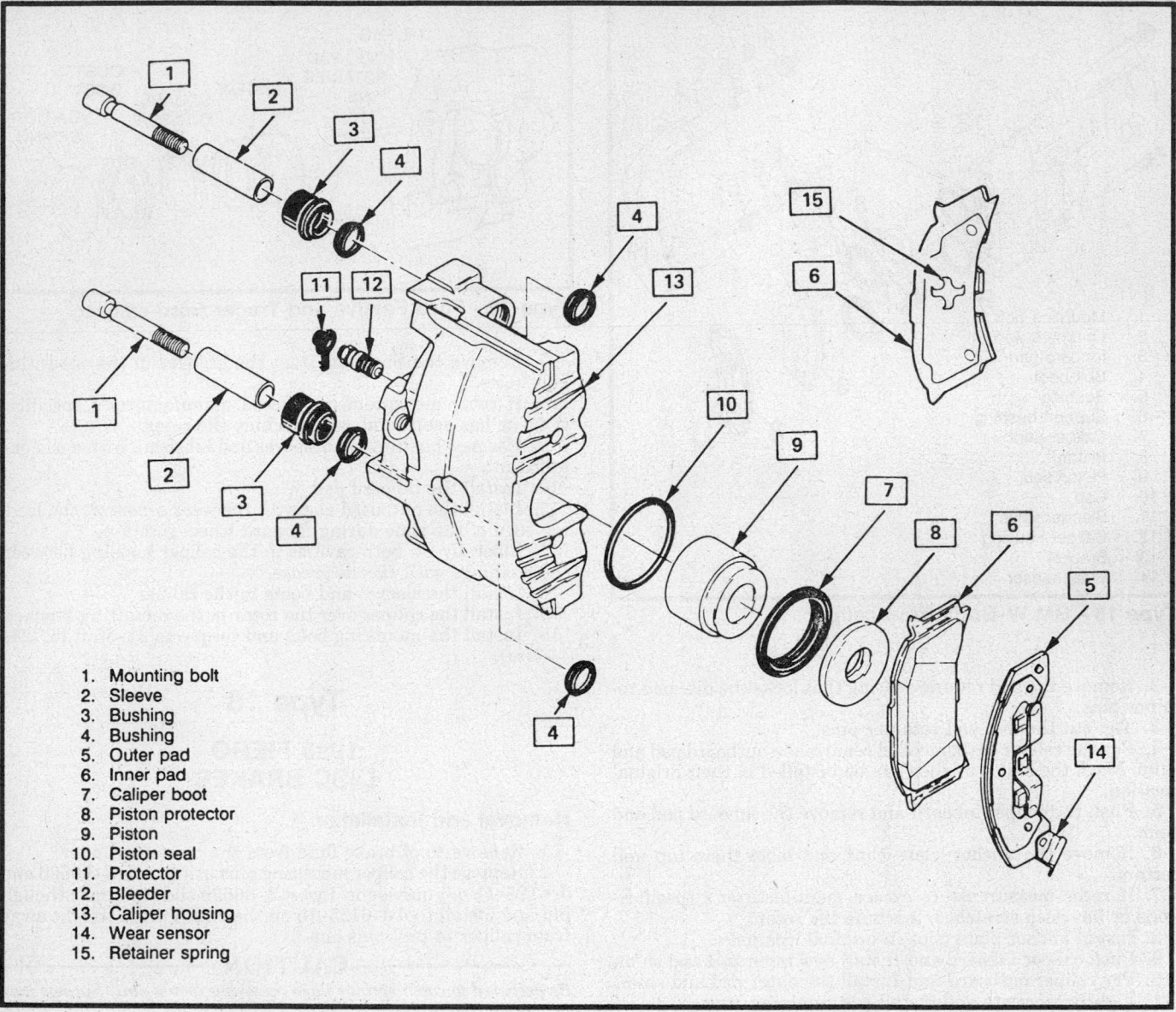

1. Mounting bolt
2. Sleeve
3. Bushing
4. Bushing
5. Outer pad
6. Inner pad
7. Caliper boot
8. Piston protector
9. Piston
10. Piston seal
11. Protector
12. Bleeder
13. Caliper housing
14. Wear sensor
15. Retainer spring

Type 17 — 1986–87 Fiero disc brakes

Type 19

GIRLOCK FLOATING CALIPER DISC BRAKES

Removal and Installation

1. Remove ⅔ of the brake fluid from the master cylinder.

2. If working on the rear, loosen the tension on the parking brake cable by backing off the equalizer. After cable tension has been released, remove the cable end from the apply lever at the caliper. Hold the apply lever in position and remove the retaining nut. Remove the lever, lever seal and anti-friction washer.

NOTE: If the parking brake levers are not disconnected from the caliper during pad removal and installation, damage to the piston assembly will occur when it is moved back in the caliper bore.

3. Position a C-clamp over the caliper and tighten until the piston bottoms in the caliper bore. Take care not to allow the C-clamp to contact the actuator screw on the caliper. Reinstall anti-friction washer, seal and lever.

4. Remove the caliper mounting bolts using a ⅜ in. allen head socket or wrench.

5. Remove the caliper by lifting up and off the rotor. Do not permit the caliper to be suspended by the brake hose.

6. Remove the pads from the caliper. A suitable tool is required to pry the outboard pad from the caliper since it is retained by a spring button.

7. Remove the pin bushings and sleeves from the caliper ears.

8. If rotor measurements exceed manufacturer's specifications or has deep scratches, machine the rotor.

9. Lubricate and install new sleeves and bushings. Insure that the sleeve is flush with the pad side of the caliper ear.

10. Install the inboard pad. Make sure that the D-shaped retainer on the pad engages the D-shaped slot in the caliper piston. Turn piston if necessary for correct alignment.

11. Be sure that the wear indicator is mounted on the leading edge of the pad for forward rotation of the wheel.

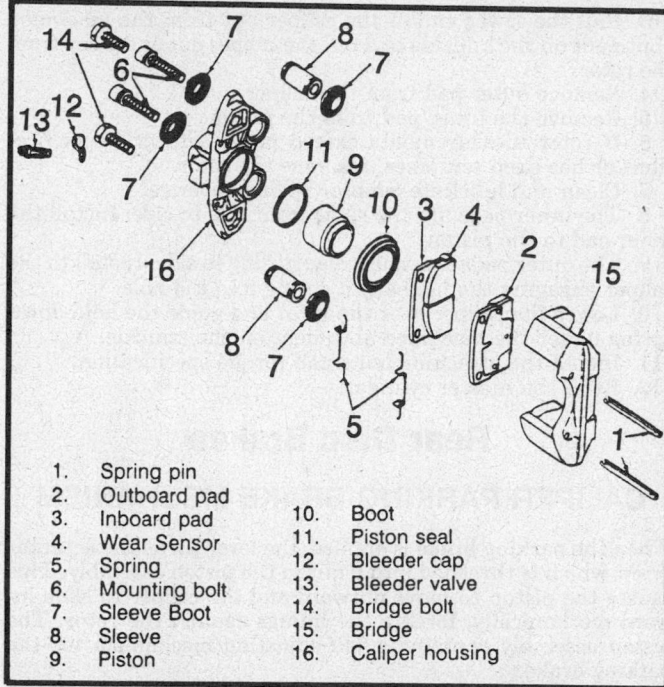

1. Spring pin
2. Outboard pad
3. Inboard pad
4. Wear Sensor
5. Spring
6. Mounting bolt
7. Sleeve Boot
8. Sleeve
9. Piston

10. Boot
11. Piston seal
12. Bleeder cap
13. Bleeder valve
14. Bridge bolt
15. Bridge
16. Caliper housing

Type 18—1988–90 Fiero front disc brake caliper

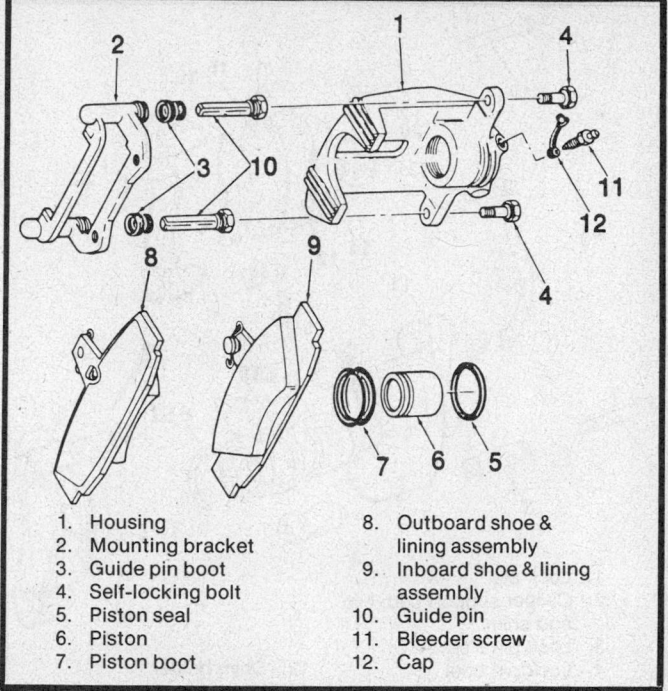

1. Housing
2. Mounting bracket
3. Guide pin boot
4. Self-locking bolt
5. Piston seal
6. Piston
7. Piston boot

8. Outboard shoe & lining assembly
9. Inboard shoe & lining assembly
10. Guide pin
11. Bleeder screw
12. Cap

Type 19—Girlock front and rear disc brake caliper

12. Slide the edge of the metal shoe under the ends of the dampening spring and snap the pad into position flat against the caliper piston.

13. Mount the outboard pad in position. Be sure it snaps into the caliper recess.

14. Install the caliper over the disc rotor in the reverse order of removal. Apply the brakes several times to seat the linings, after filling the master cylinder.

Type 20

JEEP/EAGLE PREMIER AND MEDALLION FRONT DISC BRAKES

Removal and Installation

1. Remove ⅔ of brake fluid from the master cylinder.
2. Force the piston back into the bore to allow clearance between pads and rotor.
3. On Medallion, remove just the lower caliper bolt using T40 Torx® head tool. On Premier, remove both caliper bolts.
4. On the Medallion rotate caliper up on the upper bolt to clear the rotor, on Premier, lift the caliper off of rotor and carefully suspend with wire.
5. Remove brake pads.

NOTE: Rotors must not be resurfaced; if rotor does not meet specifications it must be replaced.

6. To install, press the piston back into bore using piston installer or equivalent tool.
7. Install new inner and outer pads and anit-rattle clips.

NOTE: The anti-rattle clips must be located at the bottom of each disc brake pad.

8. Install caliper over rotor and pads.
9. Lubricate and install caliper bolts and tighten to proper torque.
10. Check the brake fluid level and add if necessary.

NOTE: If bleeding is necessary on the Medallion, do not let the rear wheels hang down due to the compensator-limiter valve.

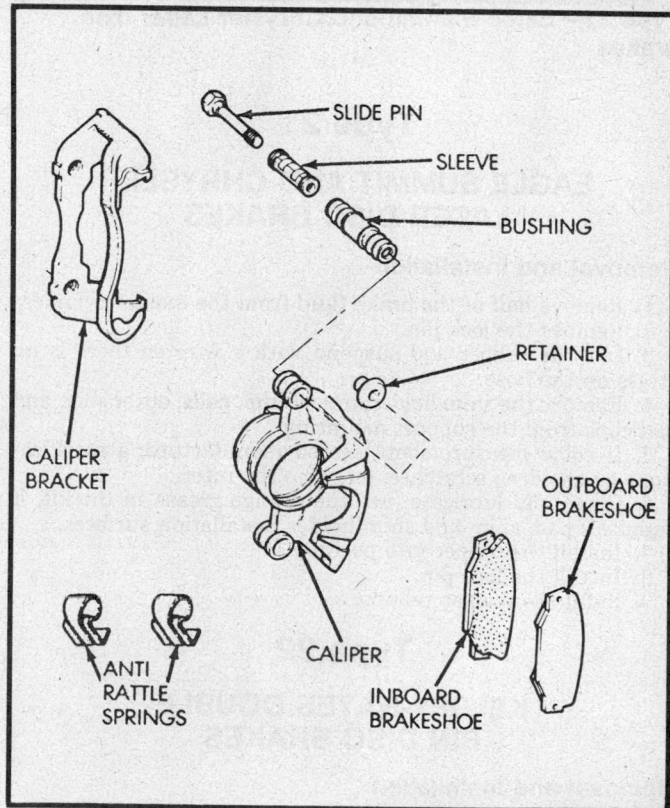

SLIDE PIN
SLEEVE
BUSHING
RETAINER
CALIPER BRACKET
OUTBOARD BRAKESHOE
ANTI RATTLE SPRINGS
CALIPER
INBOARD BRAKESHOE

Type 20—Eagle Premier and Medallion disc brakes

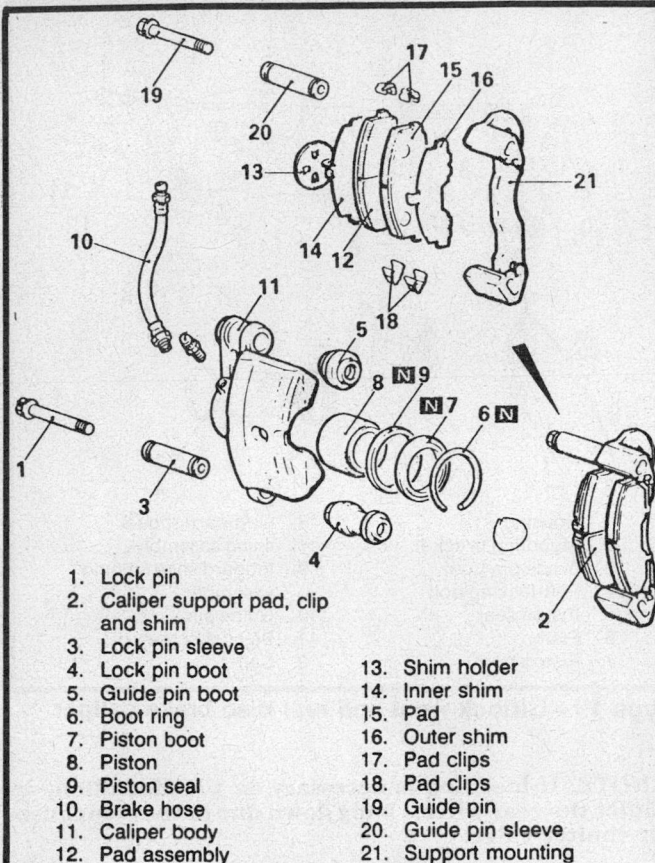

1. Lock pin
2. Caliper support pad, clip and shim
3. Lock pin sleeve
4. Lock pin boot
5. Guide pin boot
6. Boot ring
7. Piston boot
8. Piston
9. Piston seal
10. Brake hose
11. Caliper body
12. Pad assembly
13. Shim holder
14. Inner shim
15. Pad
16. Outer shim
17. Pad clips
18. Pad clips
19. Guide pin
20. Guide pin sleeve
21. Support mounting

Type 21—Eagle Summit and Chrysler Laser disc brakes

Type 21

EAGLE SUMMIT AND CHRYSLER LASER DISC BRAKES

Removal and Installation

1. Remove half of the brake fluid from the master cylinder.
2. Remove the lock pin.
3. Lift the caliper and suspend with a wire so there is no stress on the hose.
4. Remove the shim holder, inner shim, pads, outer shim and pad clips from the support mounting.
5. If rotor measurements exceed manufacturer's specifications or has deep scratches, machine the rotor.
6. Clean and lubricate (use the orange grease in the kit, if supplied) pad, shim and shim holder installation surfaces.
7. Install the caliper into position.
8. Install the lock pin.
9. Refill the master cylinder.

Type 22

KELSEY-HAYES DOUBLE PIN DISC BRAKES

Removal and Installation

1. Remove half of the fluid from the master cylinder.
2. Remove the caliper to knuckle attaching bolts.

3. Pull the lower end of the caliper out from the machined abutment on the knuckle and roll the caliper out and away from the rotor.
4. Remove outer pad from the caliper.
5. Remove the inner pad from the piston.
6. If rotor measurements exceed manufacturer's specifications or has deep scratches, machine the rotor.
7. Clean and lubricate adaptor sliding surfaces.
8. The inner pads are the same from side to side. Install the inner pad to the piston.
9. The outer pads are marked according to side. Install to the caliper engaging the hold-down spring into the hole.
10. Lower the caliper over the rotor and guide the hold-down spring under the machined abutment on the knuckle.
11. Install the attaching bolts and torque specification.
12. Refill the master cylinder.

Rear Disc Brakes

CALIPER PARKING BRAKE MECHANISM

When the parking brake is applied, the lever turns the actuator screw which is threaded into a nut in the piston assembly. This causes the piston to move outward and the caliper to slide inward mechanically, forcing the linings against the rotor. The piston assembly contains a self-adjusting mechanism for the parking brake.

REAR DISC PAD SERVICE

NOTE: All of the following procedures are under the assumption that the vehicle has been raised, safely supported and that the wheels have been removed. It is recommended that 2 lug nuts be installed over the rotor to keep it in place while working on the brakes. When the work is done, lower the vehicle and always pump up the brakes before moving the vehicle. If they will not pump up, bleed the hydraulic system. Road test the vehicle completely after any brake work has been completed.

Type 23

DELCO FLOATING CALIPER DISC BRAKES

NOTE: The removal and installation procedures for the Cadillac Allante and 1986–87 Pontiac Fiero rear disc brake assembly are exactly the same as the Delco floating rear brake assembly. The following procedures apply to both, even though their calipers and mounting brackets are different in appearance.

Removal and Installation

1. Remove ⅔ of the brake fluid from the master cylinder.
2. Loosen the tension on the parking brake cable by backing off the equalizer.
3. After cable tension has been released, remove the cable end from the apply lever at the caliper.
4. Hold the apply lever in position and remove the retaining nut.
5. Remove the lever, lever seal and anti-friction washer.

NOTE: If the parking brake levers are not disconnected from the caliper during pad removal and installation, damage to the piston assembly will occur when it is moved back in the caliper bore.

6. Position a C-clamp over the caliper and tighten until the piston bottoms in the caliper bore. Take care not to allow the C-

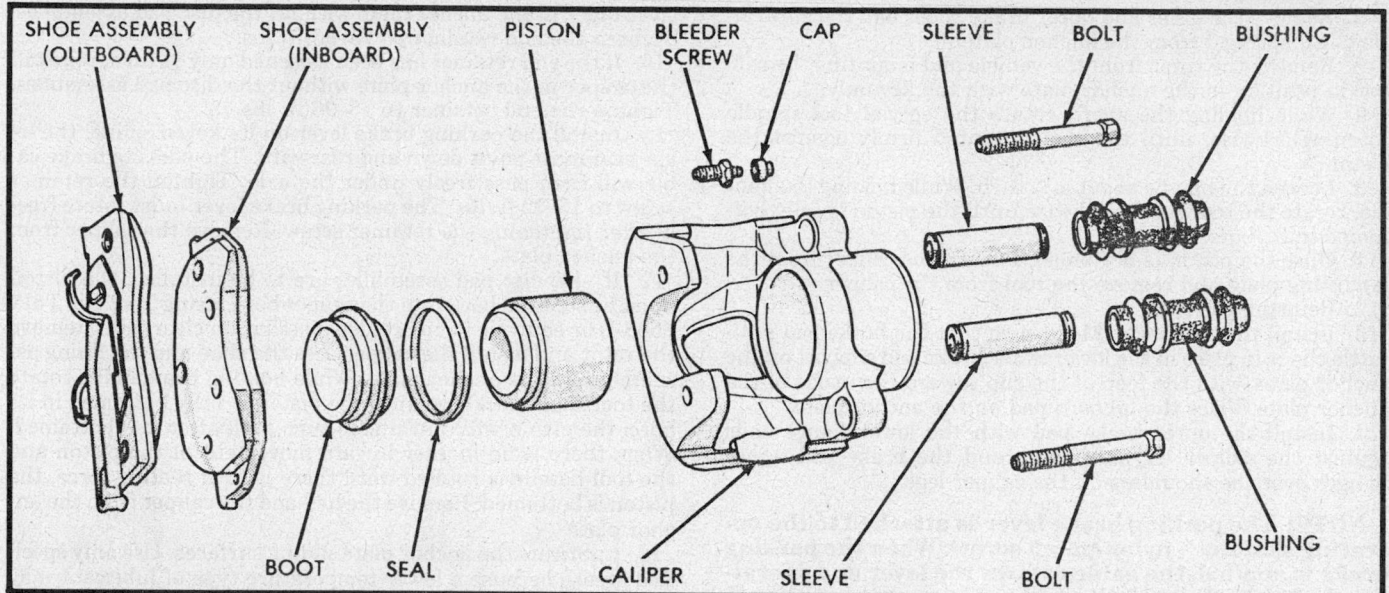

SHOE ASSEMBLY (OUTBOARD) — SHOE ASSEMBLY (INBOARD) — PISTON — BLEEDER SCREW — CAP — SLEEVE — BOLT — BUSHING

BOOT — SEAL — CALIPER — SLEEVE — BOLT — BUSHING

Type 22—Kelsey-Hayes double pin caliper

clamp to contact the actuator screw on the caliper. Reinstall anti-friction washer, seal and lever.

7. Remove the caliper mounting bolts using a ⅜ in. Allen head socket or wrench.

8. Remove the caliper by lifting up and off the rotor. Suspend it so no stress is placed on the hose.

9. Remove the pads from the caliper. A suitable tool is required to pry the outboard pad from the caliper since it is retained by a spring button.

10. Remove the pin bushings and sleeves from the caliper ears.

11. Lubricate and install new sleeves and bushings. Insure that the sleeve is flush with the pad side of the caliper ear.

12. Install the inboard pad. Make sure that the D-shaped retainer on the pad engages the D-shaped slot in the caliper piston. Turn the piston if necessary for correct alignment.

13. Be sure that the wear indicator is mounted on the leading edge of the pad for forward rotation of the wheel.

14. Slide the edge of the metal shoe under the ends of the dampening spring and snap the pad into position flat against the caliper piston.

15. Mount the outboard pad in position. Be sure it snaps into the caliper recess.

16. Install the caliper over the disc rotor.

8. Rotate the caliper back into position over the disc brake rotor.

9. Install a new self-locking bolt.

10. Install wheel assemblies and lower vehicle.

11. Fill the master cylinder and pump the brake pedal several times to seat the pads. Bleed the brakes if necessary.

Parking Brake Adjustment

1. Raise the rear of the vehicle and support it safely, remove the rear wheels and place a couple of lug nuts opposite of each other to ensure proper disc/drum position.

2. Loosen the parking brake cable to release any tension on the parking brake shoes. Rotate the disc so that the hole in the disc/drum face will be aligned with the star adjuster.

3. Using a brake spoon or equivalent, adjust the parking brake by inserting the tool into the hole in the disc face on the drivers side and move the handle of the tool toward the top of the fender skirt to adjust the shoes out and toward the ground to adjust the shoes in. Reverse this procedure on the passenger side.

4. Adjust the shoes until the disc/drum cannot rotate and back the star adjuster off 5–7 notches on both sides.

5. Reinstall the rear wheels, lower the vehicle and road test.

Type 24

GIRLOCK FLOATING CALIPER DISC BRAKES

Removal and Installation

1. Remove ⅔ of the brake fluid from the master cylinder.

2. Position a C-clamp over the caliper, contacting the outboard pad and the inlet fitting bolt head.

3. Tighten the clamp to push the caliper piston until it bottoms in the bore.

4. Remove and discard the upper caliper self-locking bolt. Rotate the caliper on the lower bolt to expose the brake pads.

5. Remove the inner and outer pads from the caliper.

6. Clean the pad mounting frame on the caliper.

7. Install the new inner and outer pad in position on the caliper.

Type 25

FORD SLIDING CALIPER DISC BRAKES

Removal and Installation

EXCEPT MARK VII CONTINENTAL AND MUSTANG SVO

1. Remove the screw retaining the brake hose bracket to the shock absorber bracket.

2. Remove the retaining clip from the parking brake cable at the caliper.

3. Remove the cable end from the parking brake.

4. Hold the slider pin hex heads with an open end wrench. Remove the upper pinch bolt.

5. Loosen, but do not remove the lower pinch bolt.

6. Rotate the caliper away from the rotor.

7. Remove the inner and outer brake shoes and the anti-rattle clips (springs) from the anchor plate.

8. Remove the rotor from the vehicle and mounting the caliper in position in the anchor plate with the key only.

9. While holding the shaft, rotate the special tool spindle counterclockwise, until the tool is seated firmly against the piston.

10. Loosen the handle about a ¼ turn. While holding the handle, rotate the tool shaft clockwise until the piston is fully bottomed in its bore.

11. Once the piston is bottomed, remove the caliper from the mounting plate and remove the tool from the caliper.

12. Reinstall the rotor.

13. Install the new pads. Make sure that the brake pad anti-rattle clip is in place in the lower inner brake pad support on the anchor plate, with the loop of the clip toward the inside of the anchor plate. Place the inboard pad on the anchor plate.

14. Install the outer brake pad with the lower flange ends against the caliper leg abutments and the brake pad upper flanges over the shoulders on the caliper legs.

NOTE: The parking brake lever is attached to the operating shaft by a nylon-patch screw. When the parking brake is applied, the cable rotates the lever and operating shaft. The 3 steel balls, located in pockets on the opposing heads of the operating shaft and thrust screw, roll between ramps formed in these ball pockets. The balls force the thrust screw away from the operating shaft, driving the piston and pad against the rotor, creating the parking brake force.

MARK VII CONTINENTAL AND MUSTANG SVO

1. Disconnect the parking brake cable from the lever and bracket. Use care to avoid kinking or cutting the cable or return spring.

2. Remove the caliper locating pins.

3. Lift the caliper assembly away from the anchor plate by pushing the caliper upward toward the anchor plate, then rotate the lower end out of the anchor plate.

4. If insufficient clearance between the caliper, the shoe and the lining assemblies prevents removal of the caliper, it is necessary to loosen the caliper end retaining ½ turn, maximum, to allow the piston to be forced back into its bore. To loosen the end retainer, remove the parking brake lever, then mark or scribe the end retainer and caliper housing to be sure that the end retainer is not loosened more than ½ turn. Force the piston back in its bore and remove the caliper.

NOTE: If the retainer must be loosened more than ½ turn, the seal between the thrust screw and the housing may be broken and the brake fluid may leak into the parking brake mechanism chamber. In this case, the end retainer must be removed, then the internal parts cleaned and lubricated.

5. Remove the outer disc pad assembly from the anchor plate.

6. Remove the 2 rotor retainer nuts and the rotor from the axle shaft.

7. Remove the inner brake shoe and the lining assembly from the anchor plate. Remove anti-rattle clip from the anchor plate.

8. Clean the caliper, the anchor plate and the rotor assemblies, then inspect for signs of brake fluid leakage, excessive ear or damage. The caliper must be inspected for leakage both in the piston boot area and at the operating shaft seal area. Lightly sand or wire brush any rust or corrosion from the caliper and anchor plate sliding surfaces as well as the outer and inner brake shoe abutment surfaces. Inspect the brake shoes for wear. If either lining is worn to within ⅛ in. of the shoe surface, both the shoe and the lining assemblies must be replaced using the disc pad removal procedures.

9. If the end retainer has been loosened only ½ turn, reinstall the caliper in the anchor plate without the disc pad assemblies. Tighten the end retainer to 75–96 ft. lbs.

10. If the end retainer has been loosened only ½ turn, reinstall the caliper in the anchor plate without the disc pad assemblies. Tighten the end retainer to 75–96 ft. lbs.

11. Install the parking brake lever on its keyed spline; the lever arm must point down and rearward. The parking brake cable will then pass freely under the axle. Tighten the retainer screw to 16–22 ft. lbs. The parking brake lever must rotate freely after tightening the retainer screw. Remove the caliper from the anchor plate.

12. If new disc pad assemblies are to be installed, the piston must be screwed back into the caliper bore, using Tool No. T5P-2588-B or equivalent, to provide installation clearance. Remove the rotor and install the caliper, less the shoe and the lining assemblies, in the anchor plate. While holding the handle, rotate the tool shaft clockwise until the piston is fully bottomed in its bore; the piston will continue to turn even after it is bottomed. When there is no further inward movement of the piston and the tool handle is rotated until there is firm seating force, the piston is bottomed. Remove the tool and the caliper from the anchor plate.

13. Lubricate the anchor plate sliding surfaces. Use only specified grease because a lower temperature type of lubricant may melt and contaminate the brake pads. Use care to prevent any lubricant from getting on the braking surface. Install the antirattle clip on the lower rail of the anchor plate.

14. Install the inner brake shoe and the lining assembly on the anchor plate with the lining toward the rotor. Be sure shoes are installed in their original positions as marked for identification before removal. Install the rotor and the 2 retainer nuts.

15. Install the correct hand outer disc pad assembly on the anchor plate with the lining toward the rotor and wear indicator toward the upper portion of the brake.

16. Position the upper tab of the caliper housing on the anchor plate upper abutment surface.

17. Rotate the caliper housing until it is completely over the rotor. Use care so that the piston dust boot is not damaged.

18. To adjust the piston position, pull the caliper outboard until the inner disc pad is firmly seated against the rotor, then measure the clearance between the outer shoe and caliper; the clearance must be ¹⁄₃₂–³⁄₃₂ in. If not, remove the caliper and readjust the piston to obtain required gap. Follow the procedure given in Step 14, then rotate the shaft counterclockwise to narrow the gap and clockwise to widen the gap (¼ turn of the piston moves it approximately ¹⁄₁₆ in.).

NOTE: A clearance greater than ³⁄₃₂ in. may allow the adjuster to be pulled out of the piston when the service brake is applied. This will cause the parking brake mechanism to fail to adjust. It is then necessary to replace the piston/adjuster assembly.

19. Lubricate the locating pins and the inside of insulator with silicone grease. Add 1 drop of Locite® or equivalent, to locating pin threads.

20. Install the locating pins through the caliper insulators and into the anchor plate; the pins must be hand inserted and hand started. Torque to 29–37 ft. lbs.

21. Connect the parking brake cable to the bracket and the lever on the caliper.

22. Fill the master cylinder reservoir.

23. To adjust the caliper, have the engine running and pump the service brake lightly (approximately 14 lbs. pedal effort) about 40 times. Allow at least 1 second between pedal applications. As an alternative, with the engine **OFF**, pump the service brake lightly (approximately 87 lbs. pedal effort) about 30 times. Now check the parking brake for excessive travel or very light effort. In either case, repeat the pumping the service brake or (if necessary) check the parking brake cable for proper tension. The caliper levers must return to the **OFF** position when the parking brake is released.

Type 26

1988–90 CORVETTE, 1989–90 CAMARO AND FIREBIRD DISC BRAKES

Removal and Installation

1. Remove ⅔ of brake fluid from the master cylinder.
2. Bottom the caliper pistons using a C-clamp. The end of the C-clamp must be placed on the inlet fitting bolt and the other end against the center of the outboard brake pad.

NOTE: It is not necessary to remove the parking brake caliper lever return spring.

3. Remove the upper caliper guide bolt.
4. Rotate the caliper housing on the lower caliper bolt.
5. Remove the brake pads.
6. Clean and lubricate the sliding surfaces.
7. Install the new inner pad with wear sensor in the piston. The wear sensor must be in the trailing position with forward wheel rotation.
8. Install the new outer pad in the caliper housing. The springs on the outer pad must not stick through the inspection hole in the caliper housing.
9. Rotate the caliper over the rotor.
10. Install a new caliper guide bolt.
11. Tighten caliper guide bolts to proper torque.
12. Check the brake fluid level and add if necessary.

Type 27

GM W BODY REAR DISC BRAKES

Removal and Installation

1. Remove ⅔ of brake fluid from the master cylinder.
2. Relieve the tension on the parking brake cable at equalizer.
3. Remove the cable and return spring from the lever.
4. Remove the locknut, lever and seal.
5. Remove the parking cable bracket to allow access to upper mounting bolt.
6. Remove the mounting bolts, using GM torque wrench adapter J–36581 or equivalent.
7. Remove the caliper from the rotor.
8. Disconnect the brake hose support bracket and suspend with wire.
9. Using an appropriate tool disengage the buttons on the pad from the holes in the caliper and remove the outer pad.
10. From the open side of the caliper, press in on the edge of the inner pad and tilt outward to release the pad from the retainer. Remove the pad.
11. Remove the 2-way valve from piston end.
12. Press piston back into bore using 12 in. pliers.

NOTE: Do not allow the pliers to contact actuator screw. Protect piston so as not to damage surface.

13. Lubricate the new 2-way check valve and install into piston end.
14. Install the pads onto caliper. the piston must be properly aligned with 1 of the D-shaped notches is nearest the bridge of the caliper. Turn the piston with spanner wrench J–7624 or equivalent, if necessary.
15. Install the caliper onto the rotor.
16. Tighten the caliper guide bolts to proper torque.
17. Install parking cable bracket.
18. Lubricate and install seal with bead against caliper housing.
19. Install lever, nut and return spring. Hold the lever against

stop on caliper while tightening nut to prevent accidental application of the parking brake.
20. Connect the parking brake cables. Parking brake levers should be against the lever stops on the caliper housing. Tighten cable at adjuster until either right or left lever begins to move off the stop; then loosen adjustment until lever is barely touching the stop.
21. Check the brake fluid level and add if necessary.

Type 28

1988 FIERO AND 1989–90 PONTIAC 6000 DISC BRAKES

Removal and Installation

1. Remove ⅔ of brake fluid from the master cylinder.
2. Remove the 2 caliper mounting pins using tools J–36620 and J–6125–1b or equivalent.
3. Insert J–36620 slide hammer though pin and install tool J–6125–1b on the end. Thrust weight away from caliper to pull pins out.

─────────── **CAUTION** ───────────

Be prepared to catch springs when removing spring pins. Springs may fly out causing injury.

───────────────────────────────

4. Remove springs from pad flanges.
5. Remove brake pads.
6. Bottom the piston in the bore using tool J–36621 or equivalent to turn piston. Turn the right caliper piston clockwise and the left caliper piston counterclockwise to move piston back.
7. Install new wear sensors. Wear sensor should be at trailing edge of pad during forward wheel rotation.
8. Install new inner and outer pads.
9. Install the caliper onto the rotor.
10. Align 1 spring pin with pads and caliper. Tap in pin with soft brass drift until end of pin just emerges from inboard face of caliper.
11. Install springs one at a time. Hook the end of the spring under the pin with center of spring over shoe flange.
12. Press down on the other end of spring and install second pin through the caliper and pad far enough to hold the spring. Install second spring following the same procedure and finish tapping pin through caliper.
13. Check the brake fluid level and add if necessary.

Type 29

MERCURY TRACER DISC BRAKES

Removal and Installation

1. Remove ⅔ of brake fluid from the master cylinder.
2. Remove parking brake return spring.
3. Loosen the parking brake cable housing adjusting nut and remove the cable housing from the bracket on thr rear lower control arm.
4. Loosen the bolt connecting the parking brake cable bracket to the rear caliper.
5. Remove the parking brake cable from the rear caliper.
6. Loosen the lower caliper bolt and pivot the caliper upward.
7. Remove the pad retaining springs.
8. Remove the brake pads and shims.
9. Remove the anchor plate clips and label them top and bottom.
10. Install anchor plate clips in original locations.
11. Install shims onto the back of the pads and install brake pads.

12. Pivot the caliper over rotor and pads. Rotate disc brake piston if necessary.
13. Install lower caliper bolt and torque to specification.
14. Install parking brake cable in the caliper parking brake lever.
15. Position the parking brake bracket against the rear caliper and install the attaching bolt.
16. Check the brake fluid level and add if necessary.

Type 30

LINCOLN CONTINENTAL (FWD), COUGAR TURBO COUPE, THUNDERBIRD, 5.0L MUSTANG AND TAURUS SHO REAR DISC BRAKES

Removal and Installation

1. Remove ⅔ of brake fluid from the master cylinder.
2. Remove the brake hose bracket from the shock absorber bracket.
3. Remove the retaining clip from parking brake cable at caliper and remove the cable from brake lever.
4. Hold the slider pin with open end wrench and remove the upper pinch bolt.
5. Hold the slider pin with open end wrench and loosen, but do not remove the lower pinch bolt.
6. Rotate caliper away from rotor.
7. Remove the brake pads and anti-rattle clips from anchor plate.
8. Using tool T87P-2588-A or equivalent, rotate piston clockwise until it is fully seated.

NOTE: Ensure that 1 of the 2 slots in piston face is positioned so it will engage nib on brake pad.

9. Install the anti-rattle clips and pads on anchor plate.
10. Pivot the caliper over rotor and pads. Rotate disc brake piston if necessary.
11. Apply threadlock or equivalent to pinch bolts.
12. Install the pinch bolts and torque.
13. Install the parking brake cable in the caliper parking brake lever.
14. Check the brake fluid level and add if necessary.

Type 31

CHRYSLER DYNASTY, NEW YORKER AND LANDAU DISC BRAKES

Removal and Installation

1. Remove ⅔ of brake fluid from the master cylinder.
2. Using a brass drift and hammer and working from the inner side of the caliper, drive out the pad retaining pin.
3. Remove the 2 caliper mounting bolts.
4. Lift the caliper off of rotor and carefully suspend with wire to prevent damage to ABS sensor wire, brake hose and parking cable.
5. Remove the brake pads.
6. Bottom the caliper piston in the bore.
7. Install new inner and outer pads.
8. Install the anti-rattle clips over the pads.
9. Rest caliper on adapter plate and insert the anti-rattle clip through the opening in the caliper. The lower portion must be placed in position first and then released. The clip should fall into the correct position on the brake pads.
10. Install the retainer pin through the pads and caliper.
11. Push down on upper portion of caliper, align and install upper mounting bolt.

12. Push down on lower portion of caliper, align and install lower mounting bolt.
13. Torque mounting bolts.
14. Check the brake fluid level and add if necessary.

Type 32

CHRYSLER DAYTONA AND TC REAR DISC BRAKES

Removal and Installation

1. Remove ⅔ of brake fluid from the master cylinder.
2. Remove access plug and insert a 4mm allen wrench through hole.
3. Turn the retraction shaft counterclockwise a few turns ro increase clearance between pads and rotor.
4. Remove the anti-rattle spring from outboard pad taking care not to damage it.
5. Back the caliper guide pins out just enought to free caliper from adapter.
6. Lift the caliper off of rotor and carefully suspend with wire.
7. Remove the brake pads.
8. Insert allen wrench through access hole and turn clockwise, if necessary to retract piston further to increase clearance for new pads.
9. Install new inner and outer pads.

NOTE: The outboard pads are marked for right and left hand sides and must be properly installed.

10. Lower the caliper over rotor and pads.
11. Install the guide pins and tighten to proper torque.
12. Insert allen wrench through the access hole and turn clockwise until snug, (no clearance between pads and rotors) and back off ⅓ turn to obtain proper clearance.
13. Check the brake fluid level and add if necessary.

Type 35

EAGLE SUMMIT AND CHRYSLER LASER REAR DISC BRAKE

Removal and Installation

1. Loosen the parking brake cable from inside the vehicle.
2. Disconnect the parking brake cable from the caliper.
3. Remove the lock pin.
4. Remove the caliper and hold with a wire.
5. Remove the outer shim, pads and pad clips.
6. Use the special tool to thread the piston back into the bore. The stopper groove of the piston must correctly fit into the projection on the rear surface of the pad.
7. Clean and lubricate all sliding surfaces.
8. Install the pad clips, pads and outer shim.
9. Install the caliper and install the lock pin.
10. Connect the parking brake cable and adjust. Check the parking brake lever stroke after 5 or 6 brake applications.
11. Refill the master cylinder if necessary.

Drum Brakes

DRUM CONDITION AND RESURFACING

The condition of the brake drum surface is just as important as the surface of the brake lining. All drum surfaces should be clean, smooth, free from hard spots, heat checks, score marks and foreign matter imbedded in the drum surface. They should not be out of round, bell-mouthed or barrel shaped. It is recommended that all drums be first checked with a drum micrometer to see if they are within over-size limits. If the drum is within safe limits, even though the surface appears smooth, it should be turned not only to assure a true drum surface but also to remove any possible contamination in the surface from previous brake linings, road dusts, etc. Too much metal removed from a drum is unsafe and may result in brake fade due to the thin drum being unable to absorb the heat generated, vibration from drum distortion and generally unsafe conditions.

Brake drum run-out should not exceed 0.005 inch. Drums machined to more than 0.060 in. oversize are unsafe and should be replaced with new drums, except for some heavy ribbed drums which have an 0.080 in. limit. It is always good practice to replace the drums on both wheels at the same time. If the drums are true, smooth up any slight scores by polishing with fine emery cloth. If deep scores or grooves are present which cannot be removed by this method, then the drum must be machined.

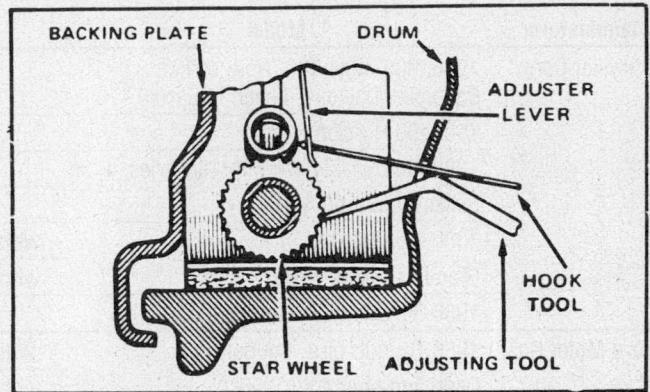

Release of adjusting lever with adjusting slot in brake drum

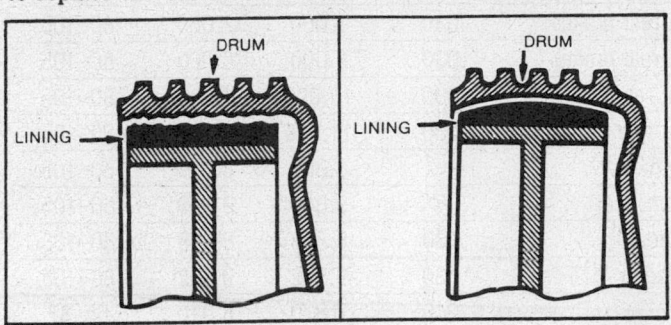

Scored drum surface   **Concave drum**

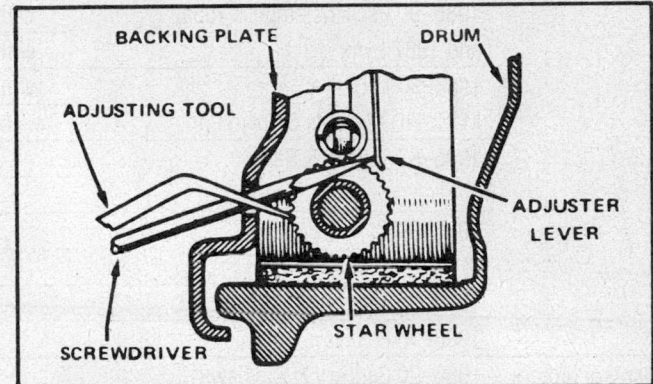

Release of adjusting lever with adjusting slot in backing plate

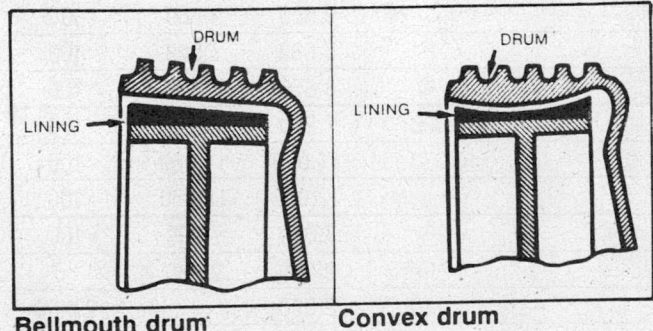

Bellmouth drum   **Convex drum**

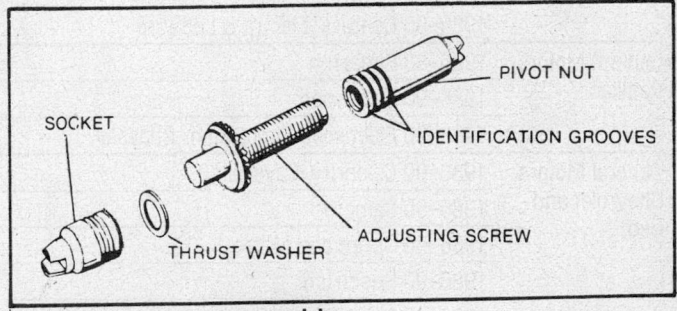

Adjusting screw assembly

DRUM BRAKE SPECIFICATIONS

Manufacturer	Model	Brake Shoe Minimum Lining Thickness	Brake Drum Diameter Standard Size	Brake Drum Diameter Machine To	Wheel Lugs or Nuts Torque (ft. lbs.)
AMC-Eagle	1986–87 Eagle	.030	10.000	10.060	75
	1988–90 Premier	.132	8.858	8.917	63
	1988–89 Medallion	.098	9.000	9.030	67

DRUM BRAKE SPECIFICATIONS

Manufacturer	Model		Brake Shoe Minimum Lining Thickness	Brake Drum Diameter		Wheel Lugs or Nuts Torque (ft. lbs.)
				Standard Size	Machine To	
Chrysler Corp.	1986–90 Dodge 600, New Yorker, Caravelle, Daytona, Laser, LeBaron		.030	8.861	8.920	95
	1986–90 Horizon & Omni		.030	7.870	7.900	95
	1988–90 Dynasty, New Yorker, Aries,	Std.	.030	7.870	7.90	95
	Reliant, LeBaron & TC	H.D.	.030	8.861	8.920	95
	1986–89 Diplomat,	with 10 in. rear brakes	.030	10.000	10.060	85
	Gran Fury, New Yorker	with 11 in. rear brakes	.030	11.000	11.060	85
	1986–90 Shadow & Sundance		①	7.835	7.935	95
Ford Motor Co.	1986 Thunderbird, Cougar,	with 9 in. rear brakes	.030	9.000	9.060	80–105
	Capri and Mustang	with 10 in. rear brakes	.030	10.000	10.060	80–105
	1987 Cougar, Mustang and Thunderbird		.030	9.000	9.060	70–115
	1986–90 Escort, Tempo & Topaz	with 7 in. rear brakes	.030	7.000	7.060	80–105
	and 1987 Lynx	with 8 in. rear brakes	.030	8.000	8.060	80–105
	1986–90 LTD	with 10 in. rear brakes	.030	10.000	10.060	80–105
	Mark VII, Marquis & Town Car	with 11 in. rear brakes	.030	11.000	11.060	80–105
	1986–87 Taurus & Sable	Sedan, rear	①	8.850	8.909	80–105
		Wagon, rear	①	9.840	9.899	80–105
	1988–90 Taurus & Sable	Sedan	.030	8.858	8.918	80–105
		Wagon	.030	9.842	9.902	80–105
	1988–90 Tracer		.040	7.870	8.910	65–87
	1988–90 Festiva		.040	6.690	6.750	65–87
General Motors Buick	1986–90 Century & Skyhawk		①	7.880	7.899	100
	1986–90 LeSabre & Regal		①	9.500	9.560	80③
	1986–90 Skylark & Regal (FWD)		①	7.880	7.899	103
	1986–90 Century, Electra & LeSabre		①	8.858	8.880	100
General Motors Cadillac	1986–88 Cimarron		.030	7.880	7.899	100
	1986–90 Fleetwood		.030	11.000	11.060	100
	1986–90 Fleetwood Limo, Com. Chassis			12.000	12.060	100
General Motors Chevrolet and Geo	1986–90 Celebrity, Cavalier		①	7.880	7.899	100
	1986–90 Camaro		①	9.500	9.560	80
	1986–90 Sprint and Metro		.110	7.090	—	29–50
	1986–90 Spectrum		.039	7.090	—	65
	1986–88 Nova, 89–90 Prizm		.039	7.913	—	76
	1986–90 Impala & Caprice	with 9½ in. rear brakes	①	9.500	9.560	80
		with 11 in. rear brakes	①	11.000	11.060	100
	1986–87 Chevette		①	7.874	7.899	70
	1987–90 Beretta & Corsica		①	7.870	7.895	100
Oldsmobile	1986–90 Calais & Firenza		①	7.880	7.899	100
	1986–90 Cutlass Supreme & 88		①	9.500	9.560	100⑤
	1986–90 Toronado		①	9.500	9.560	100
	1986–90 Custom Cruiser,	with 9.5 in. rear brakes	①	9.500	9.560	100
	88 (w/403) & 98	with 11 in. rear brake	①	11.000	11.060	100

DRUM BRAKE SPECIFICATIONS

Manufacturer	Model	Brake Shoe Minimum Lining Thickness	Brake Drum Diameter		Wheel Lugs or Nuts Torque (ft. lbs.)
			Standard Size	Machine To	
Oldsmobile	1986–90 Cutlass Ciera	①	8.858	8.880	100
	1988–90 Delta 88	①	8.860	8.880	100
Pontiac	1986–90 6000, J2000	①	7.880	7.899	100
	1986–90 Firebird	①	9.500	9.560	80④
	1986–87 T1000	①	7.874	7.899	70
	1988–90 LeMans	①	7.870	7.900	65
	1988–90 Grand Am	①	7.880	7.899	100
	1987–90 Bonneville	①	8.860	8.880	100

① .030 in. over rivet head, if bonded lining use .062 in.
③ With Aluminum wheels
LeSabre—90 ft. lbs.
Regal—100 ft. lbs.
④ Aluminum wheels
Corvette—80
Camaro—105
Others—90

DUO-SERVO BRAKES

In the Duo-Servo design, the force which the wheel cylinder applies to the shoes is multiplied by the primary lining friction to provide a large force applied to the secondary shoe. Thus the 2 braking forces are applied to each drum every time the brakes are activated. Adjustment is automatic during reverse brake applications.

NON-SERVO BRAKES

With a non-servo, leading-trailing shoe design, the leading shoe does the majority of the work because only it is used to stop forward motion. The trailing shoe works in the same fashion during rearward motion. It is common for the front shoe in a non-servo system to wear out faster than the rear shoe.

STAR AND SCREW ADJUSTER

Star and screw type self-adjusters are used on most late-model domestic vehicles. This braking system requires manual adjustment only when the shoes have been replaced or when the star and screw adjuster has been disturbed. The drum brakes on most vehicles can be initially adjusted by removing the brake drum, measuring its internal diameter with a drum micrometer and adjusting the shoes to slightly less than that measurement.

The main difference, other than size, among units used on different models is the mechanism that is used to activate the self-adjusting system.

Adjustment

1. Remove the access slot plug from the backing plate. Upon Completion of the adjustment, cover the hole with a plug to prevent entrance of dirt and water.
2. While spinning the wheel, use a brake adjusting spoon to pry downward on the end of the tool (starwheel teeth moving up) to tighten the brakes, or upward on the end of the tool (starwheel teeth moving down) to loosen the brakes. Normally, the adjusting lever will prevent the starwheel from being turned in the loosening direction.

NOTE: It may be necessary to use a small rod or fabricated tool to hold the adjusting lever away from the star wheel.

3. When the brakes start to drag fairly heavily, stop turning the starwheel. If necessary, tap on the back of the backing plate or pull on the parking brake cables to unbind the shoes. Repeat the procedure. Bring both wheel to the same drag feeling to prevent brake pull from side to side.
4. Adjust the parking brake cables.
5. When all the brakes are adjusted, check brake pedal travel and then make several stops, while backing the vehicle up, to equalize all the wheels.

Rear Brake Shoes

Disassemble and assemble one side at a time to prevent improper assembly. All of the following procedures are under the assumption that the vehicle has been raised and safely supported and the drums have been removed. Always complete the brake adjustment with the wheels installed and road test the vehicle after the work is completed.

——— CAUTION ———

Dust and dirt on brake parts generated during normal use of the vehicle can contain asbestos fibers. Breathing these fibers can cause serious bodily harm, such as cancer or asbestosis. Take the proper precautions. Do not create dust by sanding the linings and do not use compressed air to clean the assembly before working on it. Either use a vacuum specifically designed for the purpose or spray the assembly down with water to prevent the creation of asbestos dust. Also, wearing a particle mask while working with rear brakes is recommended.

REAR WHEEL DRIVE VEHICLES

Removal and Installation

EXCEPT 1989–90 COUGAR AND THUNDERBIRD

1. Remove the primary and secondary shoe return springs from the anchor pin, but leave them installed in the shoes.
2. Lift on the adjuster lever and remove the adjuster cable. On GM vehicles remove the actuating lever link and pawl return spring.
3. Remove the hold down pin return springs and cups. Remove the parking brake strut and spring. On GM vehicles, remove the actuating lever and pawl.
4. Remove the shoes (held together by the lower spring) while separating the parking brake actuating lever from the shoe with a twisting motion.
5. Lift the wheel cylinder dust boots and inspect for fluid leakage.
6. Thoroughly clean the backing plate.
7. Remove, clean and dry all parts still on the old shoes. Lubricate the starwheel shaft threads and transfer all the parts to the new shoes in their proper locations.
8. To prepare the backing plate, lubricate the bosses, anchor pin and parking brake actuating lever pivot surface lightly with the proper lubricant.
9. Spread the shoes apart, engage the parking brake actuating lever and position them on the backing plate so the wheel cylinder pins engage properly and the anchor pin holds the shoes up.
10. Install the parking brake strut and the hold down pin assemblies. On GM vehicles, install the actuating lever with the hold down pin assembly.
11. Install the anchor plate. Lubricate the sliding surface of the adjuster cable plate and install the adjuster cable.
12. Install the shoe return spring opposite the cable, then the remaining spring. On GM vehicles, install the actuating lever link, the shoe return springs and assemble the pawl and return spring.
13. Adjust the starwheel.
14. Remove any grease from the linings and install the drum.
15. Complete the brake adjustment with the wheels installed and adjust the parking brake cable.

1989–90 COUGAR AND THUNDERBIRD

1. Install a wheel cylinder clamp over the ends of the wheel cylinder.
2. Disconnect the parking brake cable from the parking brake lever.
3. Remove the shoe hold down retainers, springs and pins.
4. Spread the shoes over the piston shoe guide slots. Lift the shoes, springs and adjuster off as an assembly.
5. Remove the adjuster spring.
6. To separate the shoes, remove the retracting springs.
7. Remove the parking brake lever retaining clip and spring washer. Remove the lever from the pin.
8. Lift the wheel cylinder dust boots and inspect the cylinder for leakage.
9. Thoroughly clean the backing plate.
10. Apply a light coat of the proper lubricant to the bosses on the backing plate.
11. Clean, dry and lubricate the adjuster assembly. Lubricate the threads of the starwheel shaft and assemble the adjuster with the stainless steel thrustwasher. Turn the socket all the way down on the screw, then back off ½ turn.
12. Install the parking brake lever to the trailing shoe with the spring washer and new retaining clip. Crimp the clip to securely retain the lever.
13. Position the trailing shoe on the backing plate and attach the parking brake cable.
14. Position the leading shoe on the backing plate and attach the lower retracting spring to the shoes.

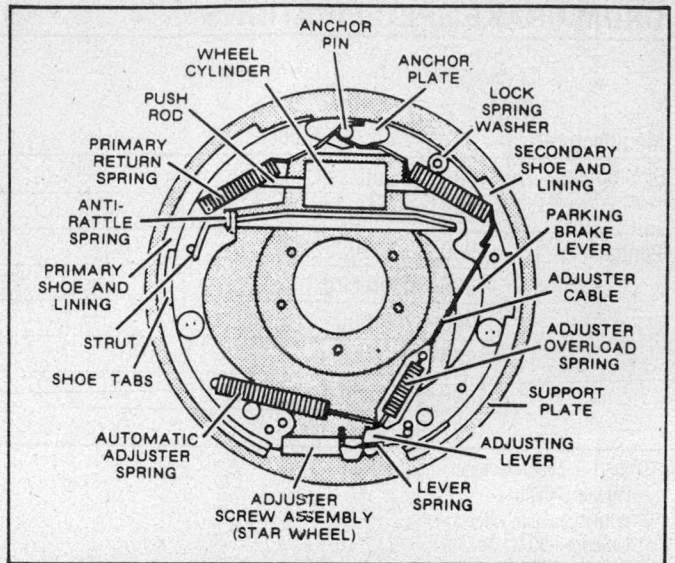

Chrysler rear wheel drive drum brakes

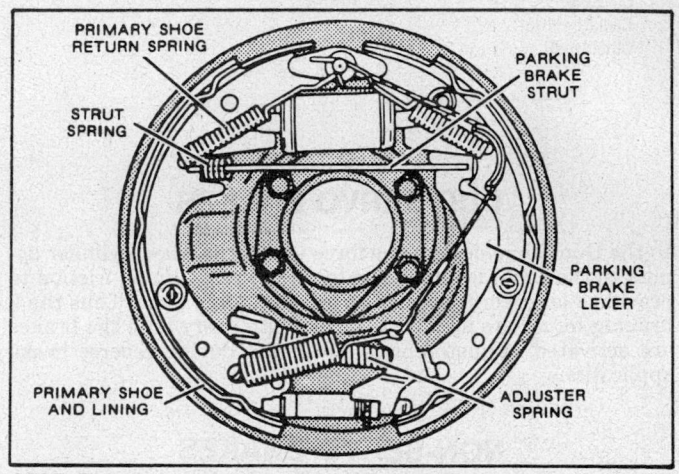

AMC Eagle and Ford rear wheel drive except 1989–90 Thunderbird and Cougar drum brakes

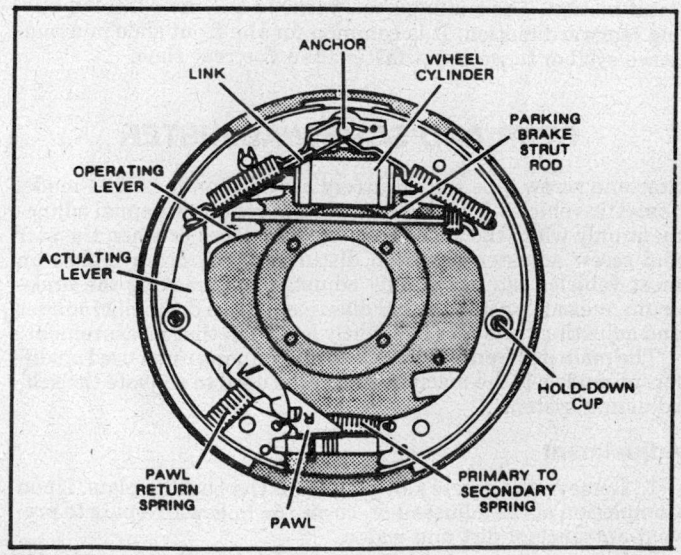

GM type rear drum brake assembly

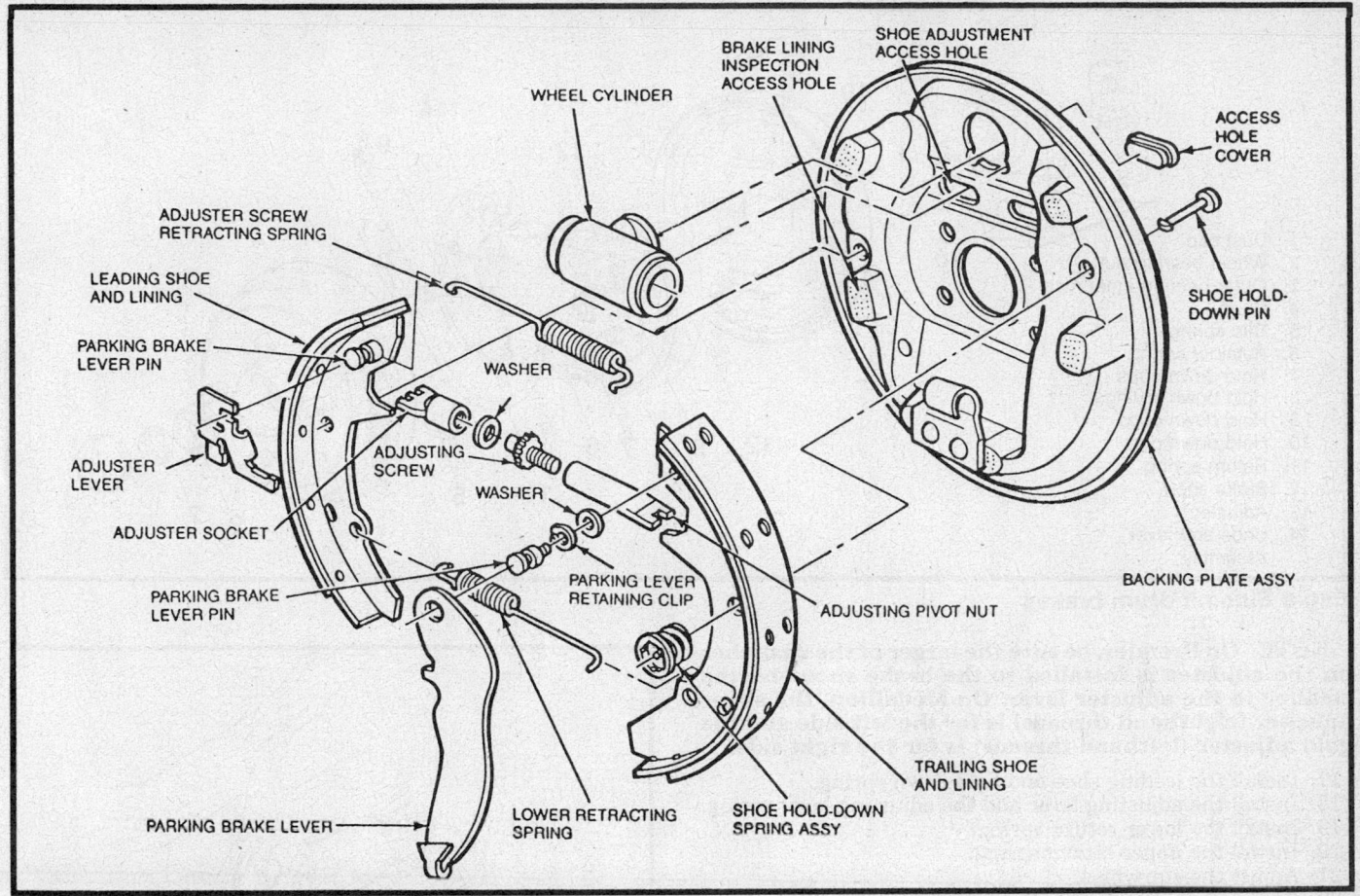

1989–90 Thunderbird and Cougar drum brakes

15. Install the adjuster assmbly to the slots in the shoes. The socket end must fit into the slot in the leading shoe (wider slot). The slot in the adjuster nut must fit into the slots in the trailing shoe and parking brake lever.

16. Install the adjuster lever on the pin on the leading shoe and to the slot in the adjuster socket.

17. Install the upper retracting spring in the slot on the training shoe and slot in adjuster lever. The adjuster lever should contact the star and adjuster assembly.

18. Install the shoe anchor pins, springs and retainers. Remove the cylinder clamp.

19. Adjust the starwheel.

20. Remove any grease from the linings and install the drum.

21. Complete the brake adjustment with the wheels installed and adjust the parking brake cable.

EAGLE PREMIER AND MEDALLION

Removal and Installation

NOTE: The brake components are different for right and left sides, so it is important not to interchange them.

1. Remove the upper return spring.
2. Remove the lower return spring.
3. Remove the adjuster lever spring and adjuster lever.
4. Remove the parking brake cable from lever.
5. To remove the shoe hold down springs, compress them slightly and slide them off of the hold-down pins or push in and twist them from the mount pin.

6. Remove the adjuster screw assembly by spreading the shoes apart.

7. Remove the brake shoes.

8. Remove the parking brake lever from the rear brake shoe if not included with new shoes.

9. Lift the wheel cylinder dust boots and inspect the cylinder for leakage.

10. Thoroughly clean the backing plate.

11. Lubricate the shoe contact areas on the brake backing plate and the web end of the brake shoe which contacts the anchor plate. Use a brake component lubricant or a high temperature brake grease made for the purpose. Lightly lubricate the self-adjuster threads.

12. If the hub was removed, clean, check and repack the rear wheel bearings. Make sure to properly torque the axle nut when reinstalling the hub, if removed.

13. Install the old parking brake lever on trailing shoe if not included with the new brake shoes.

NOTE: If the brakes exhibit a howling noise upon application, procure 6 silencer pads from the dealer and install under the pads at the contact points of the backing plate.

14. Install the trailing shoe and hold down spring.

15. Install the parking brake cable onto the the parking brake lever.

16. Install adjuster screw.

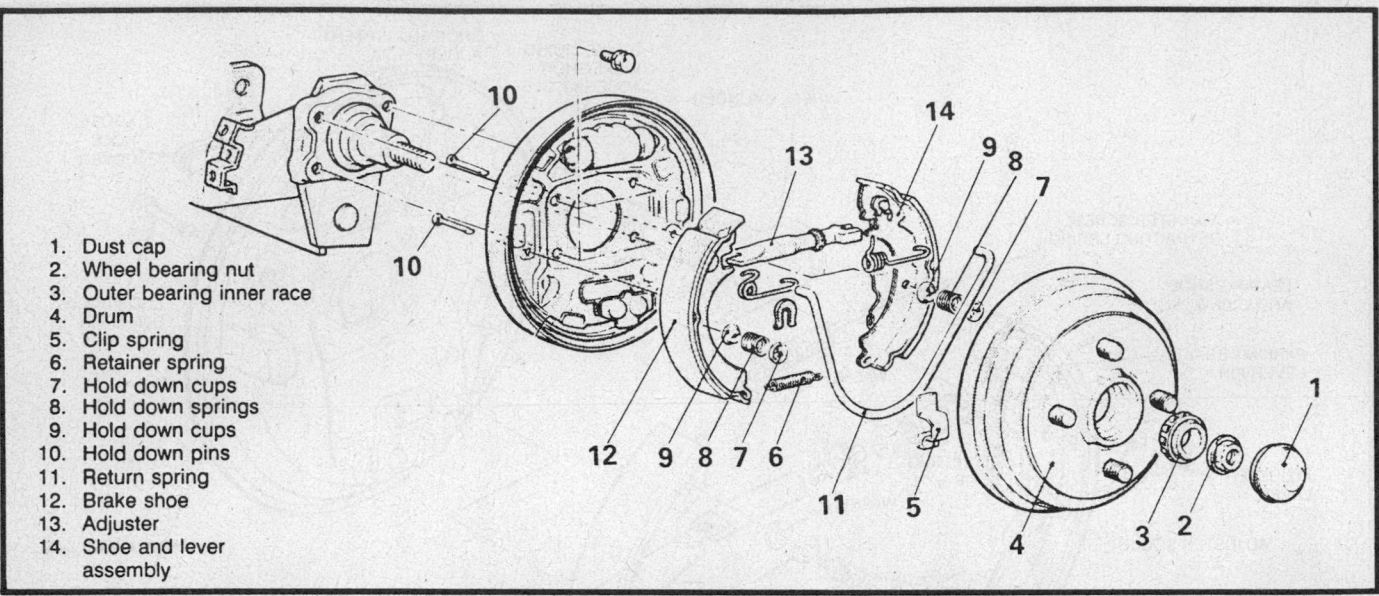

1. Dust cap
2. Wheel bearing nut
3. Outer bearing inner race
4. Drum
5. Clip spring
6. Retainer spring
7. Hold down cups
8. Hold down springs
9. Hold down cups
10. Hold down pins
11. Return spring
12. Brake shoe
13. Adjuster
14. Shoe and lever
assembly

Eagle Summit drum brakes

NOTE: On Premier, be sure the larger of the 2 notches on the adjuster is installed to the brake shoe and the smaller to the adjuster lever. On Medallion, the silver adjuster (righthand threads) is for the left side and the gold adjuster (lefthand threads) is for the right side.

17. Install the leading shoe and hold down spring.
18. Install the adjusting lever and the adjusting lever spring.
19. Install the lower return spring.
20. Install the upper return spring.
21. Adjust the starwheel.
22. Remove any grease from the linings and install the drum.
23. Complete the brake adjustment with the wheels installed and adjust the parking brake cable.

EAGLE SUMMIT

Removal and Installation

1. Remove the clip spring.
2. Remove the retainer spring.
3. Remove the U-shaped shoe-to-shoe spring.
4. Remove the hold down springs and cups.
5. Disconnect the parking brake cable and remove the shoes with the adjuster assembly still intact.
6. Lift the wheel cylinder dust boots and inspect the cylinder for leakage.
7. Completely clean the backing plate.
8. Remove, clean and dry all parts still installed on the old shoes and not on the new shoes.
9. Lubricate the threads of the adjuster shaft. Transfer the parts to the new shoes in their proper locations.
10. Lubricate the raised bosses on the backing plate with the proper lubricant.
11. Install the shoes and connect the parking brake cable.
12. Install the U-shaped spring.
13. Install the hold down spring assemblies.
14. Install the U-shaped spring
15. Install the retainer spring.
16. Install the clip spring.
17. Adjust the starwheel until the distance from the outer surface of one shoe to the other is almost the same as the inner diameter of the drum. There is no external adjustment on this application.
18. Remove any grease from the surface of the linings.

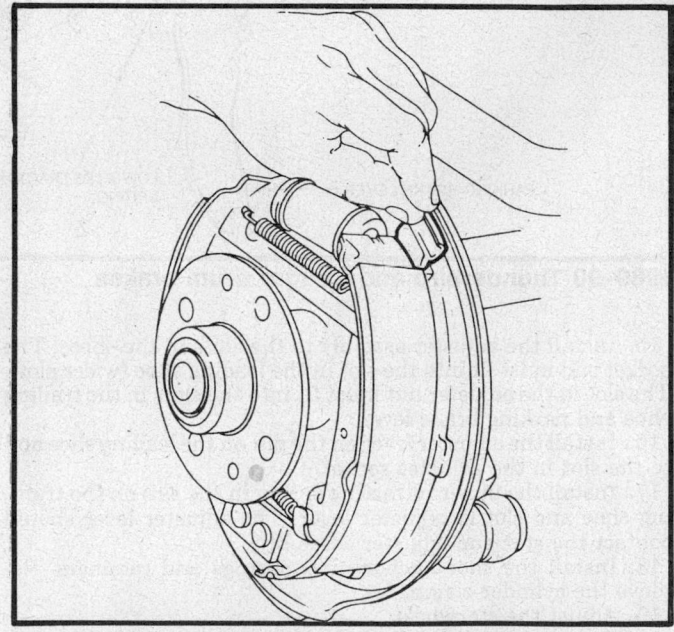

Installing Premier and Medallion silencer pads

19. After installing the drum, torque the bearing nut to 108–145 ft. lbs. (150–200Nm).

FORD FRONT WHEEL DRIVE EXCEPT PROBE, TRACER AND FESTIVA

The star and screw adjuster is used on models with 8 in. diameter brake drums while the strut and pin adjuster is used on 7 in. diameter drums.

Removal and Installation

7 INCH (180mm) BRAKES

1. Remove the hold down springs and pins.
2. Lift the assembly up and away from the anchor block and shoe guide.

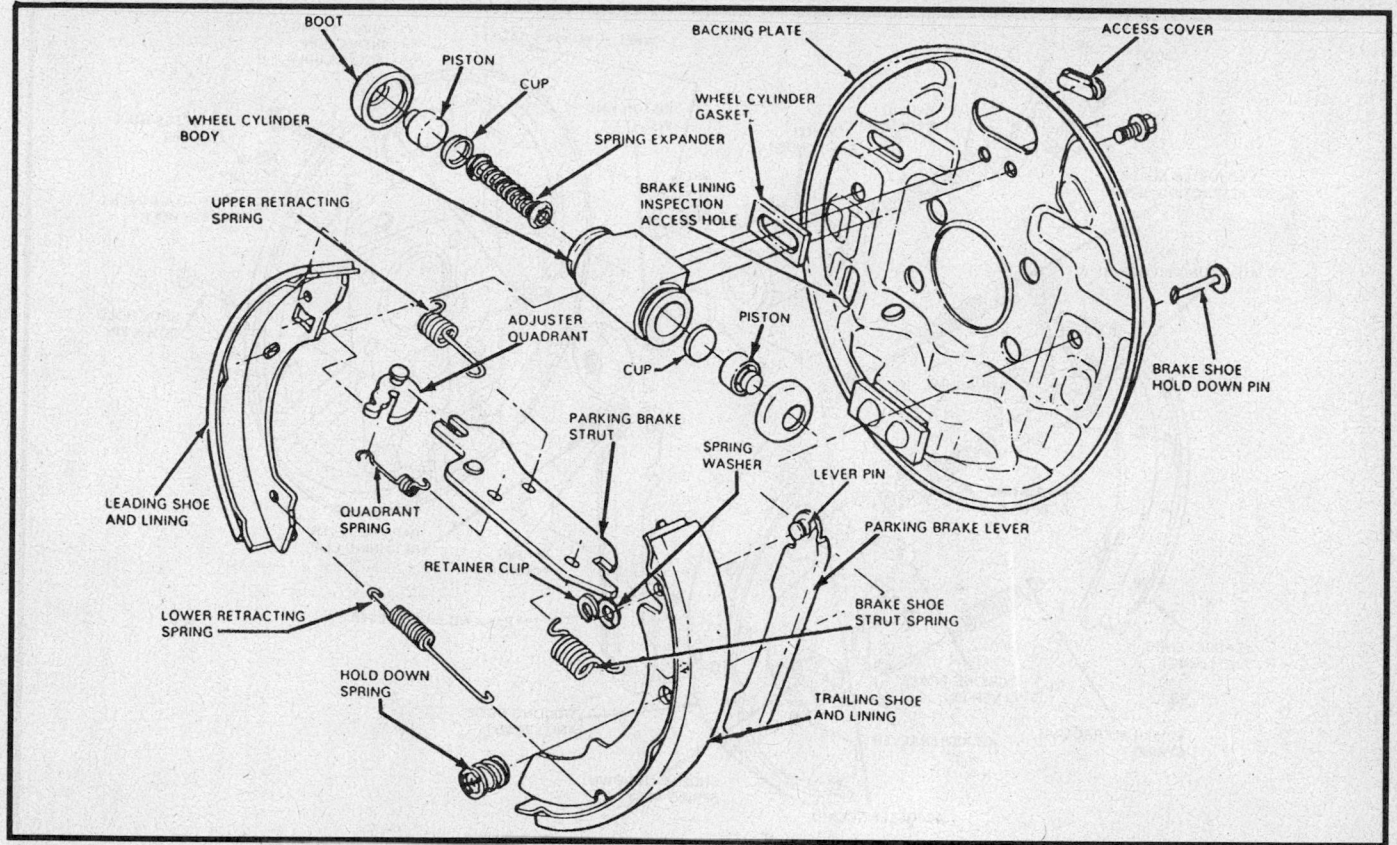

Ford front wheel drive 7 in. drum brakes

3. Remove the parking brake cable end from the parking brake lever.

4. Remove the lower retracting spring.

5. While holding the assembly, remove the leading shoe-to-adjuster strut retracting spring.

6. Remove the trailing shoe-to-parking brake strut retracting spring.

7. Disassembly the adjuster, if necessary. Pull the quadrant away from the knurled pin in the strut and rotate the quadrant in either direction until the teeth are no longer meshed. Remove the spring and slide the quadrant out of the slot.

8. Remove the parking brake lever from the trailing shoe by remove the horseshoe clip and spring washer and lifting the lever off the shoe.

9. Lift the wheel cylinder dust boots and inspect the cylinder for leakage.

10. Thoroughly clean the backing plate.

11. Apply a light coating of the proper lubricant to the bosses on thebacking plate.

12. Lightly lubricate the strut at the contact surface between the strut and the adjuster quadrant.

13. Install the adjuster quadrant pin into the slot in the strut and install the adjuster spring. Pivot the quadrant until it meshed with the knurled pin in the third and forth notch on the quadrant.

14. Assembly the parking brake lever to the trailing shoe. Install the spring washer and a new horseshoe clip.

15. Install the trailing shoe-to-parking brake strut retracting spring by attaching the spring to slots in each part and pivoting the strut into position to place tension on the spring. The installed spring should be flat against the shoe web and parallel to the strut.

16. Install the lower retracting spring.

17. Install the leading shoe-to-adjuster strut retracting spring.

18. Expand the assembly so it fits over the anchor plate and wheel cylinder inserts.

19. Attach the parking brake cable to the lever.

20. Install the hold down pins and springs.

21. Remove any grease from the linings and install the drum.

22. Complete the brake adjustment with the wheels installed and adjust the parking brake cable.

8-INCH (203MM) BRAKES

1. Remove the hold down springs and pins.

2. Lift the assembly up and away from the backing plate.

3. Remove the parking brake cable end from the parking brake lever.

4. Remove the retracting springs. This will separate the shoes and disengage the adjuster machanism.

5. Remove the horseshoe clip and spring washer and slide the lever off of the parking brake lever pin on the trailing shoe.

6. Lift the wheel cylinder dust boots and inspect the cylinder for leakage.

7. Thoroughly clean the backing plate.
Apply a light coating of the proper lubricant to the bosses on the backing plate.

8. Lightly lubricate the adjuster shaft threads and the socket at the end of the adjuster screw. Install the stainless steel washer and install the socket. Turn the adjusting screw to the end and back off ½ turn.

9. Assemble the parking brake lever to the trailing shoe with a new horseshoe clip.

10. Attach the parking brake cable to the lever.

11. Attach the lower retracting spring to the shoes and install on the backing plate.

12. Install the adjuster assembly between the leading shoe slot, the trailing shoe slot and the parking lever.

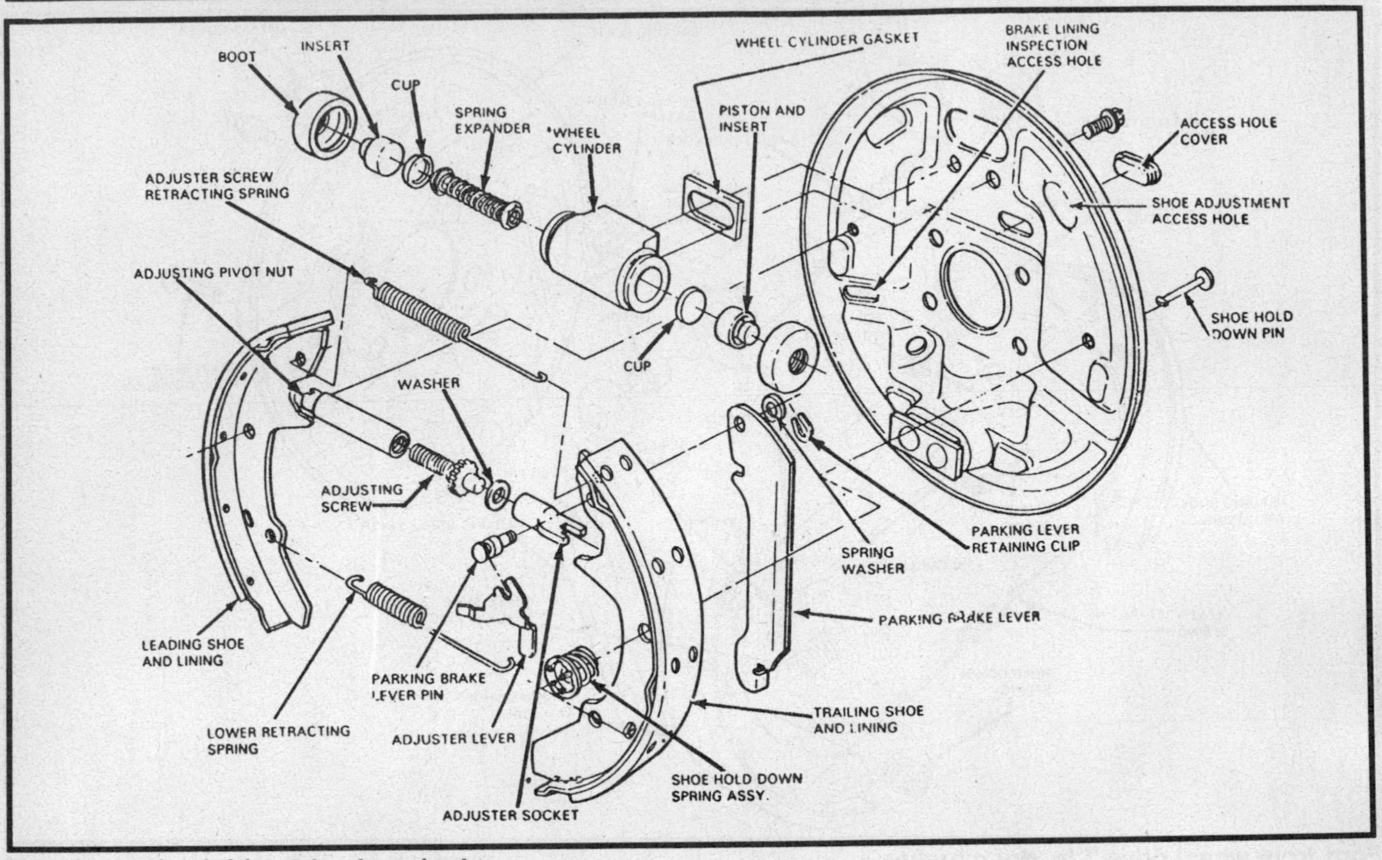

Ford front wheel drive 8 in. drum brakes

NOTE: The adjuster socket blade is marked according to side. The R or L adjuster blade must be installed with the letter R or L in the upright position and on the correct side to ensure that the deeper of the 2 slots in the adjuster sockets fits into the parking brake lever.

13. Assemble the adjuster lever in the groove located in the parking brake lever pin and into the slot of the adjuster socket that fits into the trailing shoe web.
14. Install the upper retracting spring.
15. Remove any grease from the linings and install the drum.
16. Complete the brake adjustment with the wheels installed and adjust the parking brake cable.

PROBE, FESTIVA AND TRACER

Removal and Installation

1. Remove hold down springs.
2. Pull the front shoe away from the backing plate and disconnect from springs.
3. Remove the return springs from the rear shoe.
4. Disconnect the anti–rattle spring from the parking brake strut and the rear shoe.
5. Unless broken, leave the parking brake strut, adjuster mechanism and adjuster spring in place. If damaged, service the assembly as required.
6. Lift the wheel cylinder dust boots and inspect the cylinder for leakage.
7. Thoroughly clean the backing plate.
8. Position the new rear shoe in the parking brake strut and install the hold down spring.
9. Hook the return springs in position on the rear shoe.
10. Connect the return springs onto the front shoe.

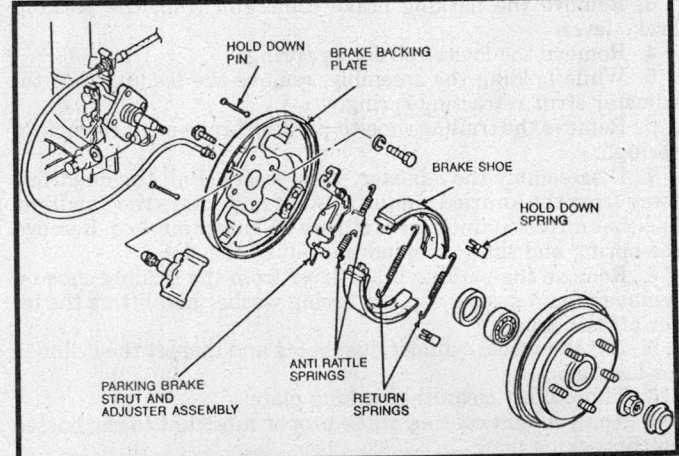

Probe, Festiva and Tracer drum brakes

11. Push the rear shoe down against the backing plate and install the hold down spring.
12. Insert an appropriate tool between the knurled quadrant and the parking brake strut and twist until the quadrant just touches the backing plate.
13. Install the drum and tighten the bearing nut to a slight bearing preload. With a torque wrench on the lug nut at the twelve o'clock position, measure the amount of force needed to rotate the drum. The proper specification are a drum drag of 1.3–4.3 inch lbs. not including seal drag.
14. Mount wheel assembly and torque lug nuts.
15. Press the brake pedal down firmly several times to adjust and center the brakes.

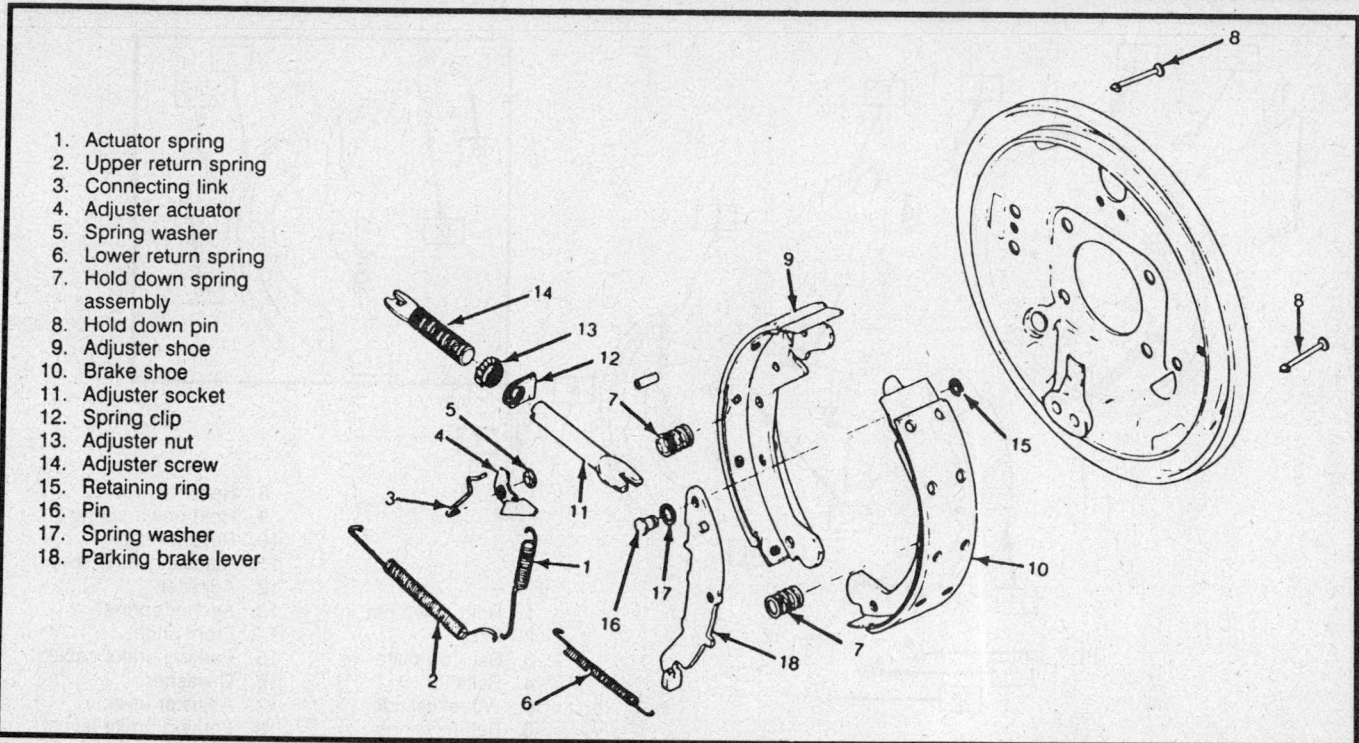

1. Actuator spring
2. Upper return spring
3. Connecting link
4. Adjuster actuator
5. Spring washer
6. Lower return spring
7. Hold down spring assembly
8. Hold down pin
9. Adjuster shoe
10. Brake shoe
11. Adjuster socket
12. Spring clip
13. Adjuster nut
14. Adjuster screw
15. Retaining ring
16. Pin
17. Spring washer
18. Parking brake lever

GM front wheel drive non-servo drum brakes

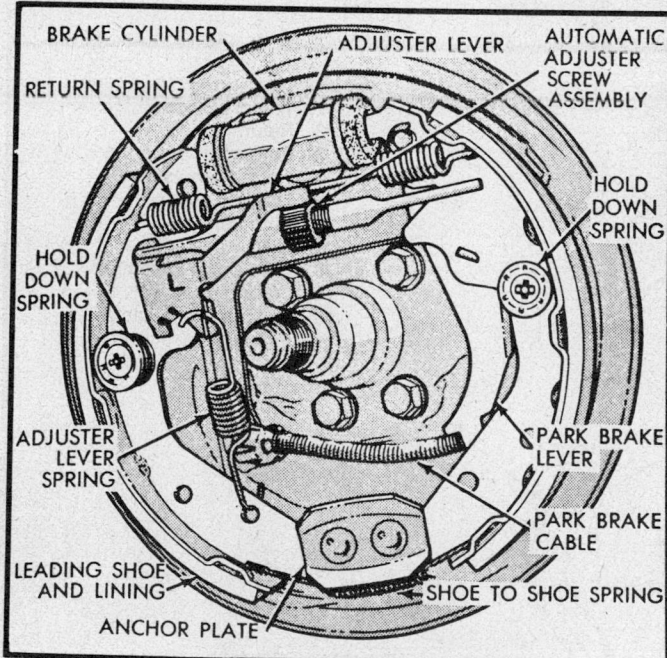

Chrysler front wheel drive drum brakes

CHRYSLER CORP. FRONT WHEEL DRIVE BRAKES

Removal and Installation

1. Remove the automatic adjuster spring and lever.
2. Rotate the adjuster screw enough so that each shoe mives out far enough to be free from the wheel cylinder boots.

3. Disconnect the parking brake cable from the parking brake lever.
4. Remove the hold down springs and lower spring.
5. Remove the adjuster assembly and shoes, still held together by the upper return spring.
6. Lift the wheel cylinder dust boots and inspect the cylinder for leakage.
7. Completely clean the backing plate.
8. Remove, clean and dry the parts still on the old shoes. Lubricate the threads on the starwheel shaft. Transfer the parts to the new shoes.
9. Lubricate the raised bosses on the backing plate and the side of the anchor plate where the bottom of the shoes contact it.
10. Expand the automatic adjuster so the ends of the shoes will clear the wheel cylinder boots.
11. Install the assembly on the backing plate and install the hold down springs.
12. Install the self adjuster lever and spring.
13. Connect the parking brake cable. Make sure the spring-end washer is properly seated in the bottom of the lever.
14. Adjust the starwheel.
15. Remove any grease from the linings.
16. Complete the brake adjustment with the wheels installed and adjust the parking brake cable.

GENERAL MOTORS FRONT WHEEL DRIVE DUO-SERVO BRAKES

Many GM front wheel drive vehicles are equipped with a smaller version of GM's rear wheel drive duo-servo drum brakes. An easy way to tell duo-servo brakes from non-servo brakes on these vehicles is by the location of the adjuster. If the adjuster is at the bottom, the brakes are the duo-servo design. Removal and installaton procedures for them is the same as for rear wheel drive.

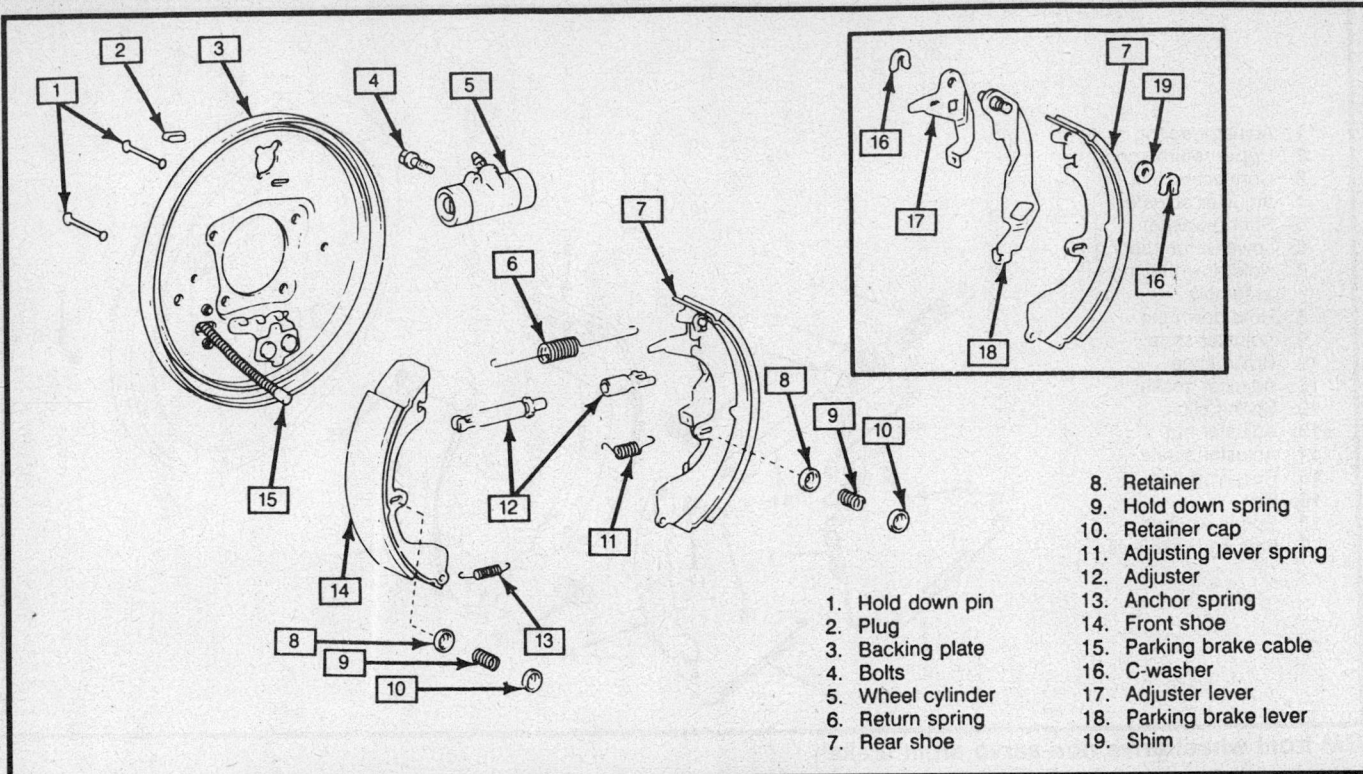

1. Hold down pin
2. Plug
3. Backing plate
4. Bolts
5. Wheel cylinder
6. Return spring
7. Rear shoe

8. Retainer
9. Hold down spring
10. Retainer cap
11. Adjusting lever spring
12. Adjuster
13. Anchor spring
14. Front shoe
15. Parking brake cable
16. C-washer
17. Adjuster lever
18. Parking brake lever
19. Shim

Chevrolet Nova and Geo Prizm drum brakes

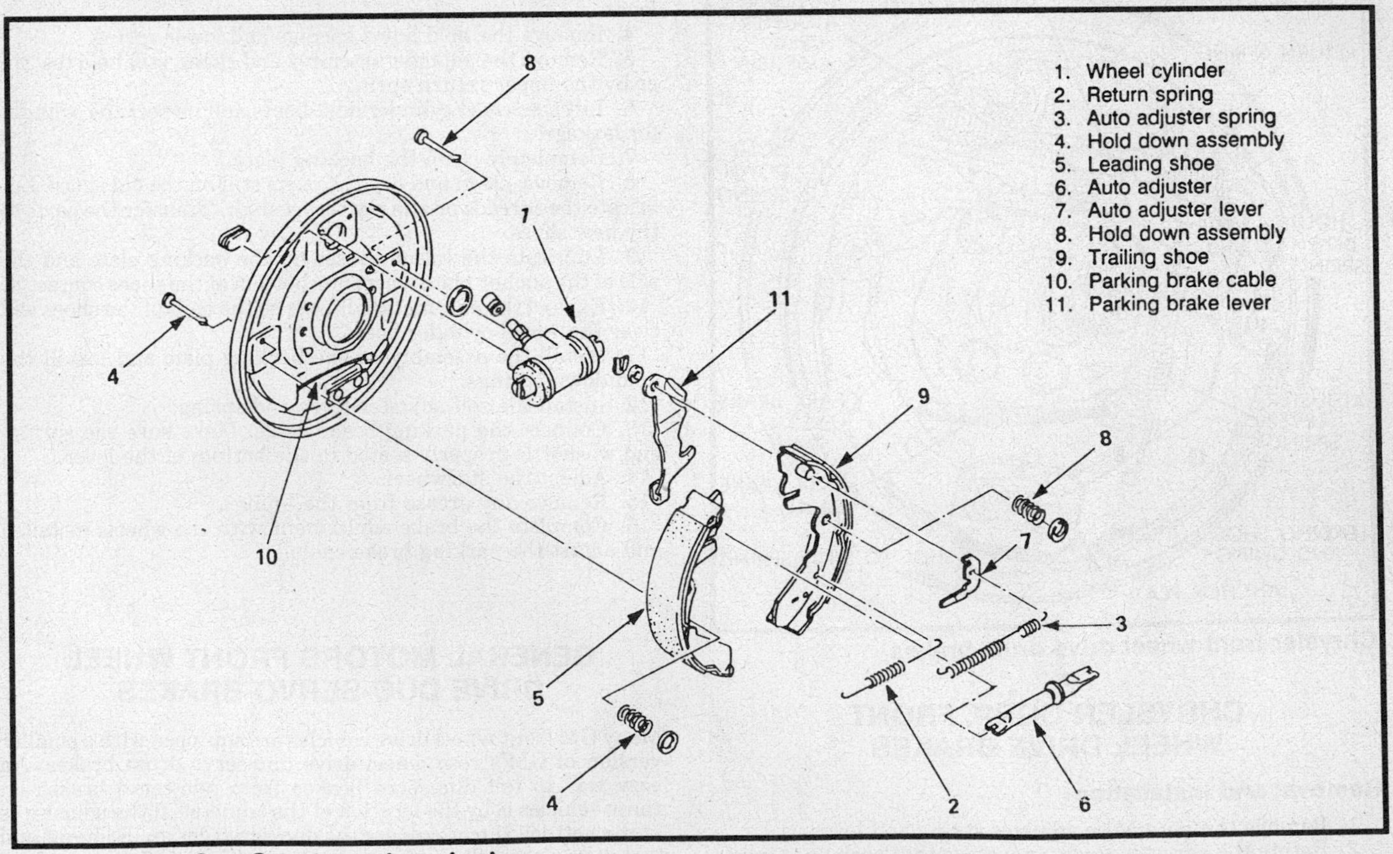

1. Wheel cylinder
2. Return spring
3. Auto adjuster spring
4. Hold down assembly
5. Leading shoe
6. Auto adjuster
7. Auto adjuster lever
8. Hold down assembly
9. Trailing shoe
10. Parking brake cable
11. Parking brake lever

Chevrolet and Geo Spectrum drum brakes

GENERAL MOTORS FRONT WHEEL DRIVE NON-SERVO BRAKES

Removal and Installation

1. Remove the adjuster lever spring.
2. Remove the return springs.
3. Remove the spring connecting link, adjuster actuator and spring washer, if equipped.
4. Remove the hold down spring assemblies.
5. Disconnect the parking brake cable and remove the shoes with the adjuster still intact.
6. Lift the wheel cylinder dust boots and inspect the cylinder for leakage.
7. Completely clean the backing plate.
8. Remove, clean and dry the parts still on the old shoes. Lubricate the threads on the starwheel shaft. Transfer the parts to the new shoes.
9. Lubricate the raised bosses on the backing plate and the side of the anchor plate where the bottom of the shoes contact it.
10. Install the shoes and connect the parking brake cable.
11. Install the hold down spring assemblies.
12. Install the adjuster connecting link, actuator and spring washer, if equipped.
13. Install the return springs and adjuster lever spring.
14. Adjust the starwheel.
15. Remove any grease from the linings.
16. Complete the brake adjustment with the wheels installed and adjust the parking brake cable.

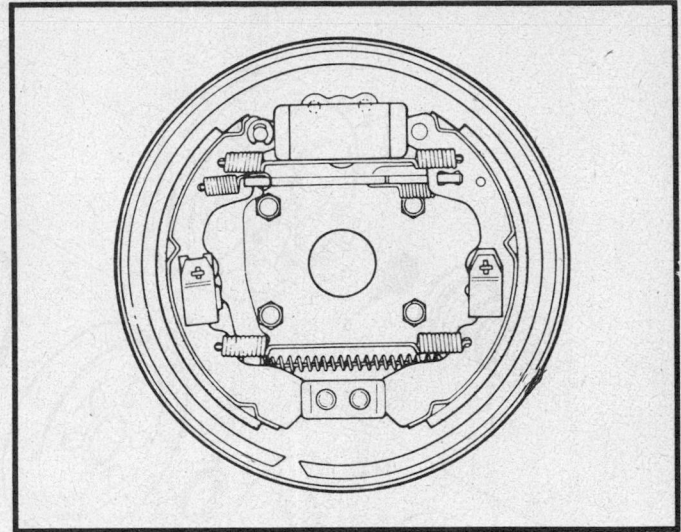

Chevrolet Sprint and Geo Metro drum brakes

POWER BRAKE SYSTEMS

VACUUM OPERATED BOOSTER

Description

Power brakes operate just as standard brake systems except in the actuation of the master cylinder pistons. A vacuum diaphragm is located behind the master cylinder and assists the driver in applying the brakes, reducing both the effort and travel put into moving the brake pedal.

The vacuum diaphragm housing is connected to the intake manifold by a vacuum hose. A check valve/filter is placed between the manifold and the unit so that during periods of low manifold vacuum brake assist vacuum will not be lost.

Depressing the brake pedal closes off the vacuum source and allows atmospheric pressure to enter a side of the diaphragm. This causes the master cylinder pistons to move and apply the brakes. When the brake pedal is released, vacuum is applied to both sides of the diaphragm and return springs. This return the diaphragm and master cylinder pistons to the released position. If the vacuum fails, the brake pedal rod will butt against the end of the master cylinder actuating rod and direct mechanical application will occur as the pedal is depressed.

Troubleshooting

If diagnosis indicates an internal malfunction in the power brake unit, service the unit as an assembly only. Do not attempt to disassemble, repair or adjust any power brake unit. If a unit must be replaced, use all parts supplied with the new unit.

HARD PEDAL

1. Faulty vacuum check valve
2. Vacuum hose kinked, collapsed, plugged, leaky, or improperly connected
3. Internal leak in unit
4. Damaged vacuum cylinder

5. Damaged valve plunger
6. Broken or faulty springs
7. Broken plunger stem

GRABBING BRAKES

1. Damaged vacuum cylinder
2. Faulty vacuum check valve
3. Vacuum hose leaky or improperly connected
4. Broken plunger stem
5. Misadjusted pushrod

ROUGH ENGINE IDLE

1. Damaged vacuum cylinder
2. Leaky vacuum hose
3. Misadjusted pushrod

Removal and Installation

1. Remove the brake lines from the master cylinder.
2. Remove the master cylinder.
3. Inspect and remove all hoses from the vacuum unit.
4. From inside the vehicle, disconnect the pushrod from the brake pedal and unbolt the unit from the firewall.
5. Remove the unit from the vehicle.
6. Install the new unit with all parts included in the package.
7. Install all vacuum hoses to the unit. Use replacement hoses if any damage is detected.
8. Install the master cylinder and connect the lines.
9. Fill the master cylinder and bleed the brakes.

Adjustment

Pushrod length can be adjusted, if necessary, on Ford units. A pushrod that is too long will prevent the master cylinder piston from releasing hydraulic pressure, eventually causing the brakes to drag. A properly adjusted pushrod that remains as-

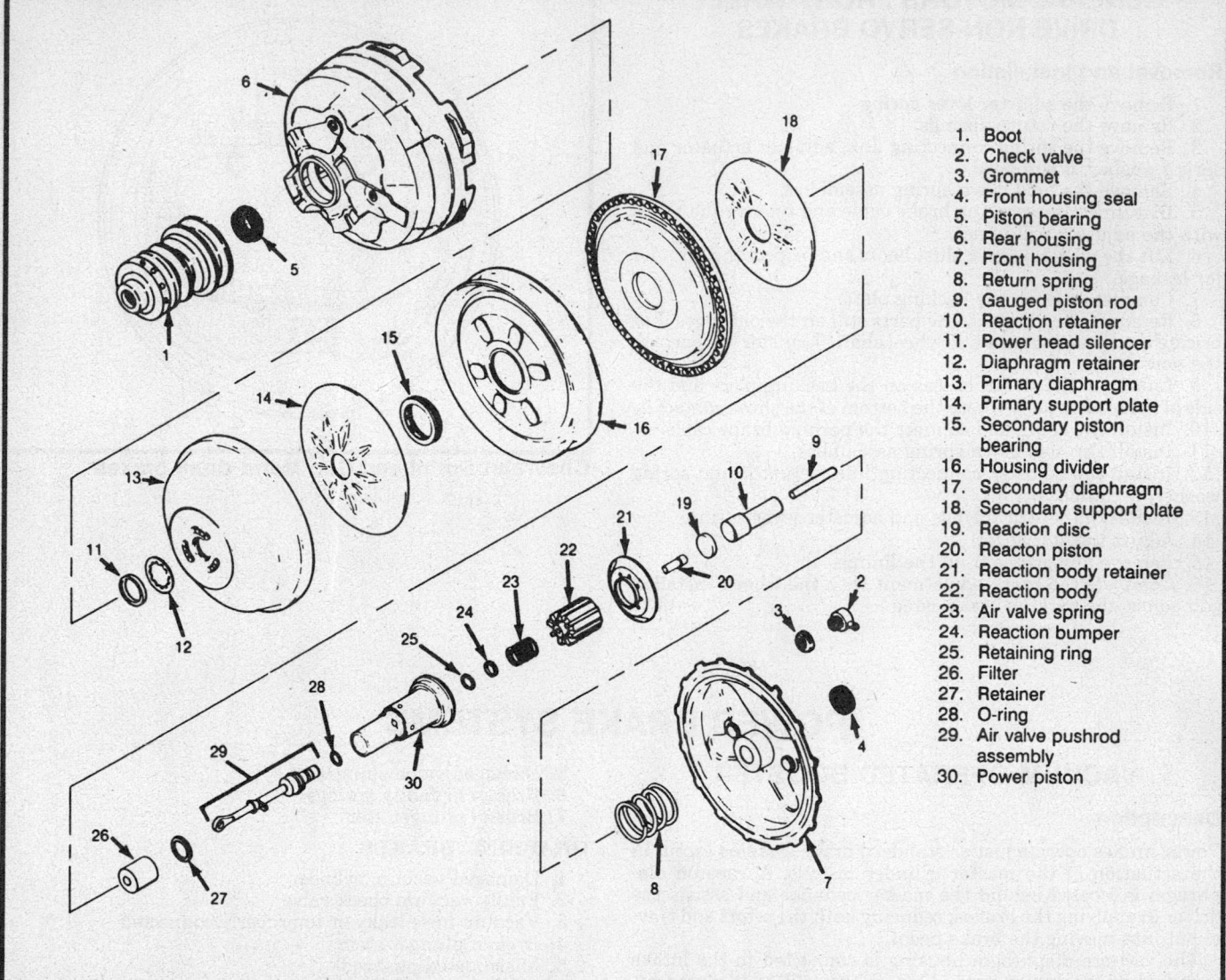

1. Boot
2. Check valve
3. Grommet
4. Front housing seal
5. Piston bearing
6. Rear housing
7. Front housing
8. Return spring
9. Gauged piston rod
10. Reaction retainer
11. Power head silencer
12. Diaphragm retainer
13. Primary diaphragm
14. Primary support plate
15. Secondary piston bearing
16. Housing divider
17. Secondary diaphragm
18. Secondary support plate
19. Reaction disc
20. Reacton piston
21. Reaction body retainer
22. Reaction body
23. Air valve spring
24. Reaction bumper
25. Retaining ring
26. Filter
27. Retainer
28. O-ring
29. Air valve pushrod assembly
30. Power piston

Exploded view of GM tandem diaphram power brake booster

sembled to the booster with which it was matched in production should never need adjustment.

If an incorrectly adjusted pushrod is suspected, remove the master cylinder with the brake lines still attached to gain access to the pushrod adjusting nut. When adjusting the nut, grip the rod only by the knurled area. After adjusting, reinstall the master cylinder and remove the reservoir covers. With the engine running, observe the fluid surface in the reservoirs upon rapid brake pedal applications. Some fluid movement in the forward reservoir. If no movement occurs, the pushrod is too long. A pushrod that is too short will increase pedal travel and may cause a groaning noise from the booster. Readjust the pushrod as necessary.

GENERAL MOTORS TANDEM DIAPHRAGM POWER BRAKE BOOSTER

Description

This booster is a tandem vacuum suspended unit. It is used on virtually all late model GM vehicles equipped with power (not ABS) brakes. In its normal operating mode, with the service

brakes in the released position, the booster operates with vacuum on both sides of its diaphragms. When the brakes are applied, air at atmospheric pressure is admitted to one side of each diaphragm to provide power assist. When the brake pedal is releases, the atmospheric air is shut off from one side of each diaphragm. The air is then drawn from the booster through the vacuum check valve to the vacuum source.

Overhaul of this unit requires the use of many special tools and could be dangerous if the technician is not familiar with the unit. Replacement of the faulty unit is recommended. Overhaul is only possible when the proper parts and special tools have been procured.

Overhaul

1. Remove the power booster from the vehicle, remove the push rod boot, silencer, front housing seal, grommet and vacuum check valve.
2. Scribe a line on the front and rear housing for alignment purposes when reassembling the unit.
3. Install the front housing into a suitable holding fixture. On Cadillac, press down on the holding tool and turn counterclockwise to unlock the housing.

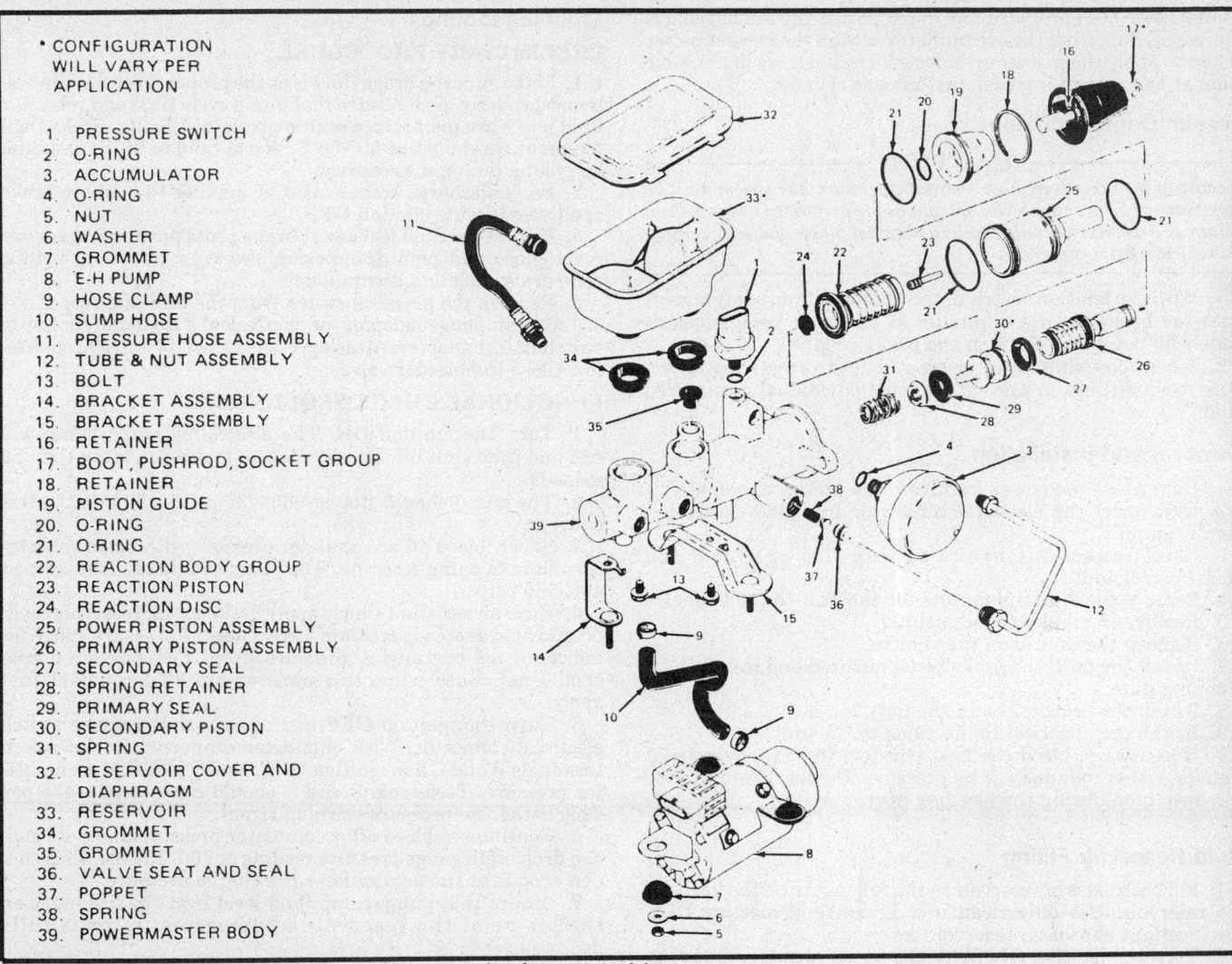

• CONFIGURATION
WILL VARY PER
APPLICATION

1. PRESSURE SWITCH
2. O-RING
3. ACCUMULATOR
4. O-RING
5. NUT
6. WASHER
7. GROMMET
8. E-H PUMP
9. HOSE CLAMP
10. SUMP HOSE
11. PRESSURE HOSE ASSEMBLY
12. TUBE & NUT ASSEMBLY
13. BOLT
14. BRACKET ASSEMBLY
15. BRACKET ASSEMBLY
16. RETAINER
17. BOOT, PUSHROD, SOCKET GROUP
18. RETAINER
19. PISTON GUIDE
20. O-RING
21. O-RING
22. REACTION BODY GROUP
23. REACTION PISTON
24. REACTION DISC
25. POWER PISTON ASSEMBLY
26. PRIMARY PISTON ASSEMBLY
27. SECONDARY SEAL
28. SPRING RETAINER
29. PRIMARY SEAL
30. SECONDARY PISTON
31. SPRING
32. RESERVOIR COVER AND
    DIAPHRAGM
33. RESERVOIR
34. GROMMET
35. GROMMET
36. VALVE SEAT AND SEAL
37. POPPET
38. SPRING
39. POWERMASTER BODY

Exploded view of the powermaster power brake assembly

4. On all other vehicles, place the special spanner wrench (J-9504) or equivalent over the rear housing studs, press down and turn counterclockwise to unlock the housing.

5. Remove the power piston group, power piston return spring and power piston bearing.

6. Remove the piston rod, reaction retainer and power head silencer.

7. Hold the assembly at the outside edge of the divider and diaphragms. Holding the pushrod down against a hard surface, apply a light impact to dislodge the diaphragm retainer.

8. Remove the primary diaphragm, primary support plate, secondary support plate and diaphragm and power piston assembly.

NOTE: Before reassembling the unit, be sure to clean all plastic, metal and rubber parts in denatured alcohol. Air dry all parts and do not reinstall any rubber parts with cuts, nicks or distortion. Use all of the parts included in the overhaul kit. Before installing any of the rubber, plastic or metal friction parts, lubricate them with silicone lube.

9. Assembly is the reverse order of the disassembly procedure.

10. After the housing has been installed, align the scribe marks and press down with the holding fixture handle on Cadil-lac, or the spanner wrench on the other vehicles, clockwise to lock the housing together. Stake the housing tabs into sockets at 2 new locations, 180 degrees apart.

11. Gauge the booster before installing to make sure the pushrod is the correct length. Position the appropriate push rod height gauge over the piston rod. Apply 25 inches vacuum to the booster. If the piston rod does not fall between the GO-NO GO limits, obtain a service adjustable piston rod to obtain the correct length.

12. Install the assembly on the vehicle, bleed the brake system and road test the vehicle.

POWERMASTER POWER BRAKE UNIT

Description

The Powermaster unit, used in some 1986 full size vehicles, is a complete, integral power brake apply system, consisting of an electro-hydraulic pump, fluid accumulator, pressure switch, fluid reservoir and a hydraulic booster, with an integral dual master cylinder. The nitrogen charged accumulator stores fluid at 510–675 psi for the hydraulic booster operation. The electro-hydraulic operates between pressure limits with the ignition switch on. When the pressure switch senses accumulator pressure is below 510 psi, the 12 volt pump operates to increase the accumulator fluid pressure to 675 psi. When the brake pedal is depressed, fluid from the accumulator acts on the booster power piston to apply the master cylinder which functions in the same manner as the conventional dual master cylinder.

System Depressurizing

CAUTION

Because of the excessively high hydraulic pressure, the system must be depressurized before any service operations are performed on the system. Failure to depressurize could result in personal injury and/or damage to the vehicle's painted surfaces.

1. With the ignition switch in the **OFF** position, apply and release the brake pedal a minimum of 10 times, using approximately 50 pounds of force on the brake pedal.
2. When loosening hoses or pipe fittings, wrap shop towels close to the fittings to prevent spraying of residual pressurized fluid.

Removal and Installation

1. Disconnect the power lead from the pressure switch.
2. Disconnect the electrical connector from the electro-hydraulic pump.
3. Disconnect the brake tubing fittings from the Powermaster unit.
4. Remove the 2 retaining nuts for the unit to dash panel.
5. Remove the brake pedal pushrod.
6. Remove the unit from the vehicle.
7. Install the unit, the brake pedal pushrod and install the 2 retaining nuts.
8. Install the brake pipes to the unit.
9. Install the electrical connections to the unit.
10. If necessary, bleed the brake system in the conventional manner, either manually or by pressure. Do not leave the ignition switch on during the bleeding operation.

Fluid Reservoir Filling

1. Fill both sides of reservoir to the full marks on the inside of the reservoir. Use only clean new brake fluid meeting DOT specifications shown on reservoir cover.
2. Turn the ignition **ON**. With the pump running, the brake fluid level in the booster side of the reservoir should decrease as brake fluid is moved to the accumulator.
3. If the booster side of the reservoir begins to run dry, add brake fluid to just cover the reservoir pump port until the pump stops.

NOTE: The pump must be shut OFF within 20 seconds. Turn the ignition OFF after 20 seconds have elapsed. Check for leaks or flow back into reservoir from booster return port.

4. Properly install the reservoir cover assembly to reservoir.
5. Turn the ignition **OFF** and apply and release brake pedal 10 times. Remove the reservoir cover and adjust booster fluid level to full mark.
6. Turn the ignition **ON**. The pump will run and refill accumulator. Make sure that pump does not run longer than 20 seconds and that fluid level remains above pump sump port in reservoir.
7. Properly install the reservoir cover. With the ignition **ON**, apply and release the brake pedal to cycle pump on and off 10–15 cycles and remove air from booster section. Do not allow the pump to run more than 20 seconds for each cycle.
8. Recheck high and low reservoir fluid levels. Check power master diagnosis if fluid levels do not stabilize or if the pump runs for more than 20 seconds. The pump should not cycle without brake applications.

Troubleshooting

PRELIMINARY PROCEDURE

1. Make sure the brake fluid is at the proper level and the system is properly bled. Assure that pump cycle time and reservoir fluid levels are maintained within prescribed limits. Brake fluid temperature should be 60°–80°F. Warm fluid to 60°F minimum by cycling pump, if necessary.
2. Fully discharge accumulator by making 10 medium brake applications with ignition **OFF**.
3. Inspect for fluid leakage at brake pedal push rod, reservoir cover, hose and pipe connections, reservoir attaching points, pressure switch and accumulator.
4. Remove the pressure switch from the unit and install J–35126 test gauge adapter or equivalent. Reinstall pressure switch in test adapter. Attach pressure switch electrical connector. Close the bleeder valve.

FUNCTIONAL CHECK SEQUENCE

1. Turn the ignition **ON**. The electro-hydraulic pump will run and then shut off. Do not allow pump to run more than 20 seconds.
2. The pump should stop at 635–735 psi reading on the test gauge.
3. Slowly bleed off accumulator pressure with bleed valve return fluid to pump reservoir. The pump should turn on again at 490–530 psi.
4. Have an assistant slowly apply brake pedal, reservoir cover off and hold at steady medium force. Observe pressure gauge for indication of continuous pressure drop. Pressure drop rate should not cause pump to recycle within 30 seconds of first apply.
5. Turn the ignition **OFF** and remove the pressure switch electrical connector. With ohmmeter connected to the switch terminals B and C and ignition **OFF**, slowly bleed off accumulator pressure. Terminals B and C should close at 355–435 psi. This is the low pressure warning signal.
6. Continue to bleed off accumulator pressure and note sudden drop off in gauge pressure reading at 200–330 psi. This sudden drop is at the accumulator pre-charge pressure.
7. Assure that pump sump fluid level is at the full mark on the inside of the reservoir when accumulator is fully depressurized.
8. Turn ignition **ON** and cycle the pump several times to remove air by opening and closing bleed valve. Pump on time should now be less than 10 seconds each cycle.
9. During pump on/off cycles, note sump reservoir fluid level. It normally will be just covering the sump hose port when pump is off and ½ full when pump comes on.
10. Depressurize the accumulator and remove J–35126 or equivalent test gauge adapter. Reinstall the pressure switch, electrical connector and the reservoir cover.
11. With the unit functioning normally, apply the brake pedal and note pedal travel. Pedal should not creep at steady pressure. The brake warning light should not indicate any pressure differential between pressure circuits.
12. Observe running motor and pump sound from driver's seat.

BRAKE LIGHT ON

Apply and release the parking brake. Reapply if light remains on. This indicates a partial failure in brake hydraulic pressure circuit. Evaluate for excessive brake pedal travel. Evaluate for hard brake pedal force to stop. Evaluate for excessive stopping distances and early wheel lock-up tendency. Repair as necessary.

LOW PRESSURE IN POWERMASTER ACCUMULATOR

First check for low fluid in the reservoir. If the level is correct, check for a possible electrical failure. Check the ignition circuit,

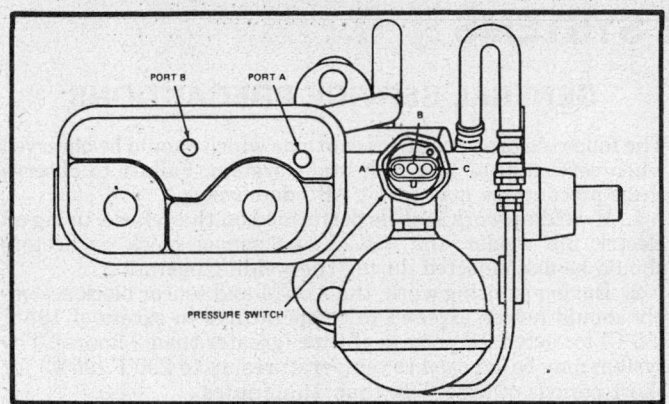

Powermaster vacuum ports and electrical terminals

30 amp fuse, pressure switch A/C terminals motor relay, connectors and wiring. Check for a faulty warning light pressure switch. Check warning switch actuation pressure at Terminals B and C.

PUMP MOTOR WILL NOT RUN

This indicates a possible electrical failure. Check the ignitioncircuit, 30 amp fuse, pressure switch terminals A/C closed, connector terminals, motor/relay and wiring.

PUMP MOTOR RUNS BUT DOES NOT SHUT OFF IN 20 SECONDS

Turn ignition off after 20 seconds. Check reservoir fluid level. Check reservoir port A for backflow and replace power piston, if necessary. Check pump pressure. If pressure is low, check pressure line for obstruction and replace pump and motor, if necessary. If pressure is high, replace switch if higher than normal. Replace pump if lower than normal cut-off.

PUMP CYCLES WITHOUT BRAKE APPLICATION

Check for accumulator precharge pressure. Replace accumulator if low. Recheck self cycle.

PUMP CYCLES WHILE APPLYING STEADY BRAKE PRESSURE

Check for accumulator precharge pressure. Replace accumulator if low, then recheck self cycle. Check for fluid backflow at reservoir port and replace the power piston, if necessary.

PUMP AND MOTOR NOISY

Check for grounded tube and motor. Check for reservoir fluid level. Replace motor mount grommets or the unit itself, if necessary.

PUMP CYCLE TIME AT PRESSURE SWITCH LIMIT EXCEEDS 10 SECONDS

Check for air in system. Recycle 5 to 10 pump cycles to remove air. Check for normal pressure switch points. Check for obstructed pump inlet and outlet fluid circuits. Check for a faulty pump.

Overhaul

1. Depressurize the system and remove the unit from the vehicle.
2. Remove the reservoir cover with the diaphragm and empty the brake fluid from the reservoir.

3. Remove the pressure switch, accumulator, electro-hydraulic pump, pressure hose assembly, sump hose, clamps, tube and nut assembly and all brackets.
4. Remove the retainer from the groove in the unit body.
5. Remove the boot, retainer, pushrod, power piston group, remove the power piston group by pulling on the pushrod.
6. Disassemble the retainer and boot, pushrod, socket assembly and the piston guide from the power piston assembly.
7. Remove the O-ring from the piston guide and the O-rings from the power piston assembly and piston guide.
8. Remove the reaction body assembly from the power piston assembly and the reaction piston and disc from the reaction body assembly.

NOTE: Neither the reaction body assembly or the power piston assembly can be disassembled any further. If there is any major problem with either of these assemblies, they must be replaced as a complete assembly.

9. Disassemble the primary piston from the secondary piston assembly, by blowing a small amount of compressed air into an outlet port at the blind end of the body. The other outlet port must be plugged.
10. Remove the secondary seal, spring retainer and primary seal from the secondary piston. Remove the spring from the body core.
11. Place the unit body in a vise; be sure not to clamp across the body.
12. Using the proper tools, remove the reservoir and the reservoir grommets.
13. Remove the valve seat and seal.
14. Remove the poppet and spring and discard them. Before re-assembling the unit, be sure to clean all parts in denatured alcohol, except for the pressure switch and the electro-hydraulic pump.
15. Use the clean fresh brake fluid to lubricate all parts before assembling the unit. Be sure to lubricate the new O-rings also. With the body still in the vise, install the new spring, poppet, valve seat and seal.
16. Bottom out the valve seat and seal by threading the nut of the tube and nut assembly in the body port.
17. Remove the body from the vise and install the grommets and the reservoir.
18. Install the spring into the body, along with the secondary seal, primary seal and spring retainer on the secondary piston.
19. Install the secondary piston assembly into the body.
20. Install the primary piston assembly into the body.
21. Assemble the reaction piston and disc into the reaction body assembly.
22. Install the 2 O-rings on the power piston assembly and install the reaction body assembly into the power piston assembly.
23. Install the power piston assembly into the body.
24. Install the O-ring on the piston guide and the O-ring in the piston guide.
25. Install the piston guide over the power piston in the body.
26. While depressing the piston guide, install the retainer and the power piston.
27. Install the boot, pushrod, socket assembly, socket into the end of the power piston assembly and secure it with the retainer.
28. Install the brackets, sump hose, clamps, tube and nut assembly, electro-hydraulic pump and pressure hose assembly, accumulator and pressure switch.
29. Install the reservoir cover and diaphragm on the reservoir and bench bleed the unit.
30. Install the powermaster unit on the vehicle and bleed the system. Properly fill the powermaster unit with brake fluid.

ABS BRAKING SYSTEMS

Chrysler Corp. and Cadillac Allante

BOSCH III ANTI-LOCK BRAKE SYSTEM

Description

The purpose of the anti-lock brake system (ABS) is to prevent wheel lockup under heavy braking conditions on virtually any type of road surface. ABS is beneficial because a vehicle which is stopped without locking the wheels will normally stop in a shorter distance than a vehicle with locked wheels, while retaining directional stability and some steering capability. This allows the driver to retain greater control of the vehicle during heavy braking or under slippery conditions.

Under normal braking conditions, the ABS functions much the same as a standard brake system with a diagonally split master cylinder. The primary difference is that the power assist is provided by the hydraulic power assist instead of the conventional vacuum assist. The system also provides a means for preventing excessive pedal travel in the event of a brake system hydraulic leak.

If a wheel locking tendency is noticed during a brake application, the system will enter ANTI-LOCK mode. During anti-lock braking, hydraulic pressure in the 4 wheel circuits is modulated to prevent any wheel from locking. Each wheel is designed with a separate electrical valve and hydraulic line to provide modulation, although for vehicle stability, both rear wheel valves receive the same electrical signal. The system can build, hold or reduce pressure at each wheel, depending on the signals generated by the wheel speed sensors (WSS) at each wheel and received at the Anti-lock Brake Control Module (ABCM).

System Components

HYDRAULIC ASSEMBLY

The hydraulic assembly provides the function of an integral master cylinder and hydraulic booster assembly and contains the wheel circuit valves used for brake pressure modulation.

WHEEL SPEED SENSORS

A wheel speed sensor is located at each wheel to transmit wheel speed information to the control module.

ANTI-LOCK BRAKE CONTROL MODULE (ABCM)

The ABCM is a small control computer which receives wheel speed information, controls anti-lock operation and monitors system performance.

PUMP/MOTOR ASSEMBLY

The pump/motor assembly is an electrically driven pump that takes low pressure brake fluid from the hydraulic assembly reservoir and pressurizes it for storage in an accumulator for power assist and anti-lock braking.

HYDRAULIC ACCUMULATOR

A hydraulic accumulator is used to store brake fluid at high pressure (approximately 2100-2600 psi) so that a supply of pressurized fluid is available for anti-lock operation and for power assisted normal braking.

GENERAL SERVICE PRECAUTIONS

The following are general precautions which should be observed when servicing the anti-lock brake system. Failure to observe these precautions may result ABS damage.

1. If welding work is to be performed on the vehicle, using an electric arc welder, the ABCM and sensor block connectors should be disconnected during the welding operation.

2. During painting work, the ABCM and sensor block assembly should not be exposed to temperatures in excess of 185°F (85°C) for extended periods of time (greater than 2 hours). The system may be exposed to temperatures up to 200°F (95°C) for short periods of time (less than 15 minutes).

3. The ABCM and sensor block connectors should never be connected or disconnected with the ignition ON.

4. Many components of the ABS are not serviceable and must be replaced as an assembly. Do not disassemble any component which is not designed to be serviced.

DEPRESSURIZING HYDRAULIC ACCUMULATOR

The pump/motor assembly will keep the hydraulic accumulator charged to a pressure between approximately 2100-2600 psi (14,480-17,930 kPa) anytime that the ignition is in the ON position. The pump/motor assembly cannot run if the ignition is OFF or if either battery cable is disconnected. Disconnecting the sensor block connector from the hydraulic unit will also prevent the pump from operating.

Unless otherwise specified, the hydraulic accumulator should be depressurized before disassembling any portion of the hydraulic system. The following procedure should be used to depressurize the hydraulic accumulator.

1. With the ignition OFF, sensor block connector disconnected from the hydraulic assembly, or negative battery cable disconnected, pump the brake pedal a minimum of 25 times, using approximately 50 lbs. (222 N) pedal force. A noticeable change in pedal feel will occur when the accumulator is discharged.

2. When a definite increase in pedal effort is felt, stroke the pedal a few additional times. This should remove all hydraulic pressure from the system.

CHECKING BRAKE FLUID LEVEL

NOTE: Do not use any fluid which contains a petroleum base. Do not use a container which has been used for petroleum based fluids of a container which is wet with water. Petroleum based fluids will cause swelling and distortion of rubber parts in the hydraulic brake system and water will mix with brake fluid, lowering the fluid boiling point. Keep all fluid containers capped to prevent contamination.

The hydraulic assembly is equipped with a plastic fluid reservoir with a filter/strainer in the filler neck.

ABS requires that the hydraulic accumulator be depressurized when checking the fluid level. To check the brake fluid level, the following procedure should be used:

1. Depressurize the hydraulic accumulator.
2. Thoroughly clean the reservoir cap and surrounding area.
3. Inspect the fluid level; see instructions on the side of the reservoir.
4. Fill the reservoir to the top of the white screen in the filter/strainer as required. Use brake fluid conforming to DOT 3.
5. Replace the reservoir cap.

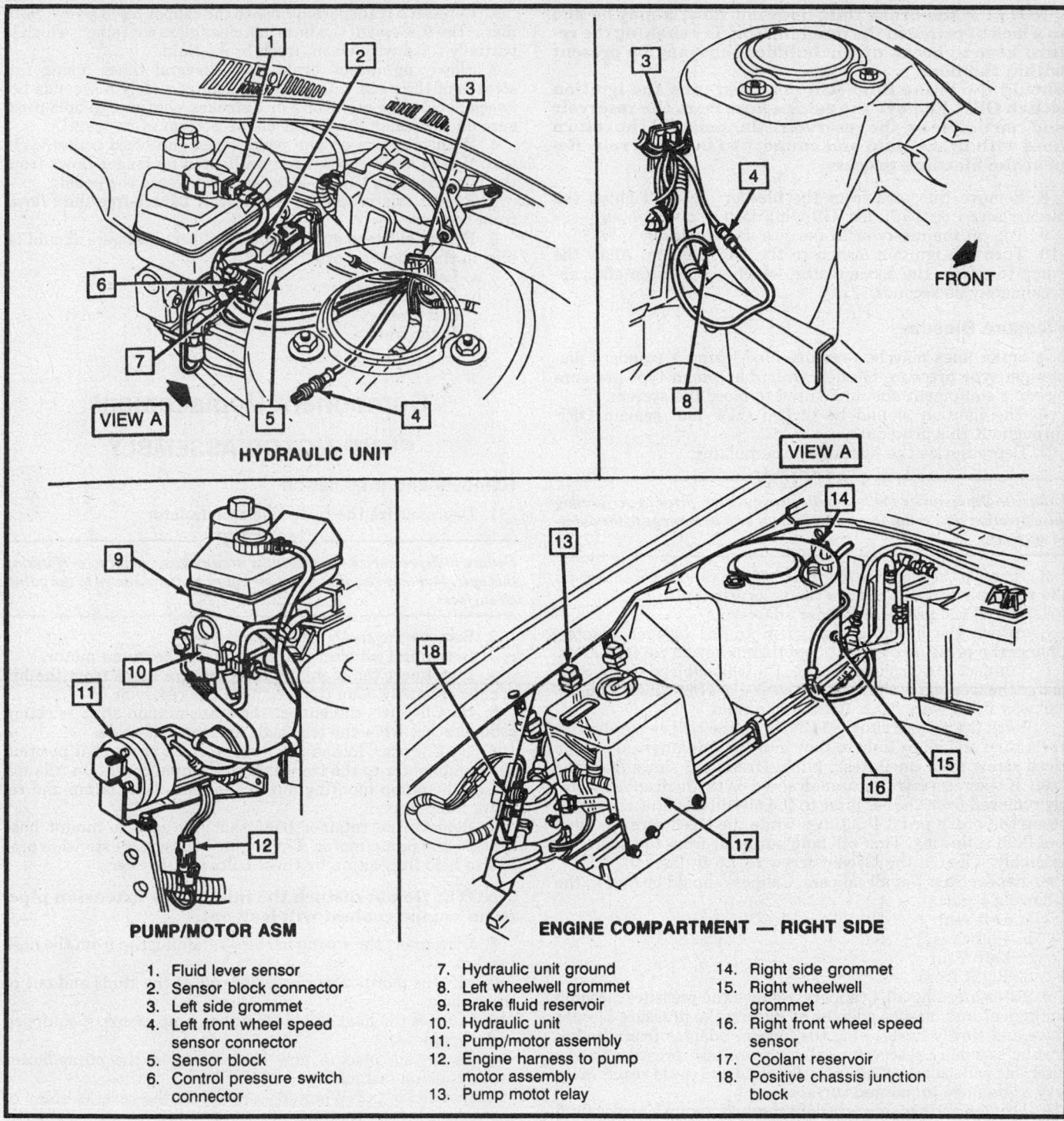

HYDRAULIC UNIT

VIEW A

FRONT

VIEW A

PUMP/MOTOR ASM

ENGINE COMPARTMENT — RIGHT SIDE

1. Fluid lever sensor
2. Sensor block connector
3. Left side grommet
4. Left front wheel speed sensor connector
5. Sensor block
6. Control pressure switch connector

7. Hydraulic unit ground
8. Left wheelwell grommet
9. Brake fluid reservoir
10. Hydraulic unit
11. Pump/motor assembly
12. Engine harness to pump motor assembly
13. Pump motot relay

14. Right side grommet
15. Right wheelwell grommet
16. Right front wheel speed sensor
17. Coolant reservoir
18. Positive chassis junction block

Underhood components — Cadillac Allante

FILLING AND BLEEDING

Booster Bleeding

1. The hydraulic accumulator must be depressurized.
2. Connect all pump/motor and hydraulic assembly electrical connections if previously disconnected. Be sure that all brake lines and hose connections are tight.
3. Fill the reservoir to the full level.
4. Connect a transparent hose to the bleeder screw location on the right side of the hydraulic assembly. Place the other end of the hose into a clear container to receive brake fluid.
5. Open the bleeder screw ½–¾ of a turn.
6. Turn the ignition switch to the **ON** position. The pump/motor should run, discharging fluid into the container. After a good volume of fluid has been forced through the hose, an air-free flow in the plastic hose and container will indicate a good bleed.
7. Turn the ignition switch **OFF**.

NOTE: If the brake fluid does not flow, it may be due to a lack of prime to the pump/motor. Try shaking the return hose to break up air bubbles that may be present within the hose.

Should the brake fluid still not flow, turn the ignition switch OFF. Remove the return hose from the reservoir and cap nipple on the reservoir. Manually fill the return hose with brake fluid and connect to the reservoir. Repeat the bleeding process.

8. Remove the hose from the bleeder screw. Tighten the bleeder screw to 7.5 ft. lbs. (10 Nm). Do not overtighten.

9. Top off the reservoir to the correct fluid level.

10. Turn the ignition switch to the **ON** position. Allow the pump to charge the accumulator, which should stop after approximately 30 seconds.

Pressure Bleeding

The brake lines may be pressure bled, using a standard diaphragm type pressure bleeder. Only diaphragm type pressure bleeding equipment should be used to bleed the system.

1. The ignition should be turned **OFF** and remain **OFF** throughout this procedure.

2. Depressurize the hydraulic accumulator.

CAUTION

Failure to depressurize the hydraulic accumulator, prior to performing this operation may result in personal injury and/or damage to the painted surfaces.

---

3. Remove the electrical connector from fluid level sensor on the reservoir cap and remove the reservoir cap.

4. Install the pressure bleeder adapter.

5. Attach the bleeding equipment to the bleeder adapter. Charge the pressure bleeder to approximately 20 psi (138 kPa).

6. Connect a transparent hose to the caliper bleed screw. Submerge the free end of the hose in a clear glass container, which is partially filled with clean, fresh brake fluid.

7. With the pressure turned **ON**, open the caliper bleed screw ½–¾ turn and allow fluid to flow into the container. Leave the bleed screw open until clear, bubble-free fluid slows from the hose. If the reservoir has been drained or the hydraulic assembly removed from the car prior to the bleeding operation, slowly pump the brake pedal 1–2 times while the bleed screw is open and fluid is flowing. This will help purge air from the hydraulic assembly. Tighten the bleeder screw to 7.5 ft. lbs. (10 N).

8. Repeat Step 7 at all calipers. Calipers should be bled in the following order:
   a. Left rear
   b. Right rear
   c. Left front
   d. Right front

9. After bleeding all 4 calipers, remove the pressure bleeding equipment and bleeder adapter by closing the pressure bleeder valve and slowly unscrewing the bleeder adapter from the hydraulic assembly reservoir. Failure to release pressure in the reservoir will cause spillage of brake fluid and could result in injury or damage to painted surfaces.

10. Using a syringe or equivalent method, remove excess fluid from the reservoir to bring the fluid level to full level.

11. Install the reservoir cap and connect the fluid level sensor connector. Turn the ignition **ON** and allow the pump to charge the accumulator.

Manual Bleeding

1. Depressurize the hydraulic accumulator.

CAUTION

Failure to depressurize the hydraulic accumulator, prior to performing this operation may result in personal injury and/or damage to the painted surfaces.

---

2. Connect a transparent hose to the caliper bleed screw. Submerge the free end of the hose in a clear glass container, which is partially filled with clean, fresh brake fluid.

3. Slowly pump the brake pedal several times, using full strokes of the pedal and allowing approximately 5 seconds between pedal strokes. After 2 or 3 strokes, continue to hold pressure on the pedal, keeping it at the bottom of its travel.

4. With pressure on the pedal, open the bleed screw ½–¾ turn. Leave bleed screw open until fluid no longer flows from the hose. Tighten the bleed screw and release the pedal.

5. Repeat this procedure until clear, bubble-free fluid flows from the hose.

6. Repeat all steps at each of the calipers. Calipers should be bled in the following order:
   a. Left rear
   b. Right rear
   c. Left front
   d. Right front

Component Replacement

PUMP/MOTOR ASSEMBLY

Removal and Installation

1. Depressurize the hydraulic accumulator.

CAUTION

Failure to depressurize the hydraulic accumulator, prior to performing this operation may result in personal injury and/or damage to the painted surfaces.

---

2. Remove the fresh air intake ducts.

3. Disconnect all electrical connectors the pump motor.

4. Disconnect the high and low pressure hoses from the hydraulic assembly. Cap the spigot on the reservoir.

5. On Chrysler, disconnect the transmission shift selection cable bracket from the transaxle and move it aside.

6. On Chrysler, loosen the nuts on the 2 studs that position the pump/motor to the transaxle differential cover. On Allante, loosen the pump monting nut at the rear of the pump and remove the pump.

7. Remove the retainer bolts that are used to mount hose bracket and pump/motor. The engine inlet water extension pipe is also held in position by these bolts on Chrysler.

NOTE: Do not disturb the inlet water extension pipe, or an engine coolant will leak out.

8. Disconnect the wiring harness retaining clip from the hose bracket.

9. Lift the pump/motor assembly off of the studs and out of the vehicle.

10. Remove the heat shield from the pump/motor, if equipped and discard.

11. To install, place a new heat shield to the pump/motor bracket, using fasteners provided.

12. Install the pump/motor assembly in the reverse order of the removal.

13. Readjust the gearshift linkage, if it was disturbed..

HYDRAULIC ASSEMBLY

Removal and Installation

1. Depressurize the hydraulic accumulator.

CAUTION

Failure to depressurize the hydraulic accumulator, prior to performing this operation may result in personal injury and/or damage to the painted surfaces.

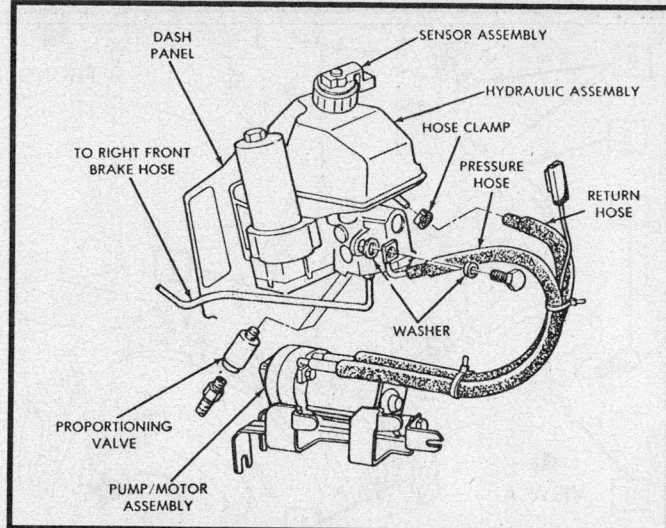

Brake tube and hose routing

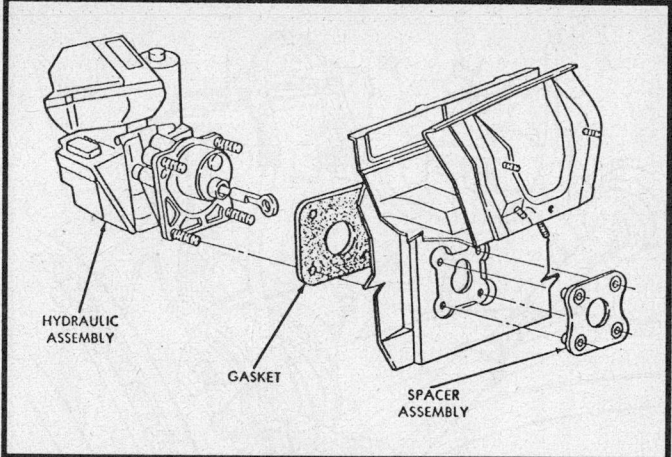

Hydraulic assembly mounting

2. Remove the fresh air intake ducts. Reposition the cross-car brace on Allante.

3. Disconnect all electrical connectors from the hydraulic unit and pump/motor.

4. Remove as much of the fluid as possible from the reservoir on the hydraulic assembly.

5. Remove the pressure hose fitting (banjo bolt) from the hydraulic assembly. Use care not to drop the two washers used to seal the pressure hose fitting to the hydraulic assembly inlet.

6. Disconnect the return hose from the reservoir nipple. Cap the spigot on the reservoir.

7. Disconnect all brake tubes from the hydraulic assembly.

8. Remove the driver's side sound insulation panel.

9. Disconnect the pushrod from the brake pedal.

10. Remove the 4 hydraulic assembly mounting nuts. They are underdash on Chrysler and underhood on Allante.

11. Remove the hydraulic assembly.

12. To install, position the hydraulic assembly on the vehicle.

13. Install and torque the mounting nuts to 21 ft. lbs. (28 Nm).

14. Using lubriplate or equivalent, coat the bearing surface of the pedal pin.

15. Connect the pushrod to the pedal and install a new retainer clip.

16. Install the brake tubes. If the proportioning valves were removed from the hydraulic assembly, reinstall valves and tighten to 20 ft. lbs. (27 Nm).

NOTE: Be sure that the brake tubes are installed to the proper proportioning valve. The longer tube goes on the inboard proportioning valve.

17. Install the return hose to the nipple on the reservoir.

18. Install the pressure hose to the hydraulic assembly, be sure that the 2 washers are in there proper position. Tighten the bango bolt to 13 ft. lbs. (18 Nm).

19. Fill the reservoir to the top of the screen.

20. Connect all electrical connectors to the hydraulic assembly.

21. Bleed the entire brake system.

22. Install the crosscar brace, if disturbed. Install the fresh air intake duct.

SENSOR BLOCK

Removal and Installation

1. Depressurize the hydraulic accumulator.

CAUTION

Failure to depressurize the hydraulic accumulator, prior to performing this operation may result in personal injury and/or damage to the painted surfaces.

---

2. Disconnect all electrical connectors from the reservoir on the hydraulic assembly.

3. Working from under the dash, disconnect the pushrod from the brake pedal.

4. Remove the driver's side sound insulator panel.

5. Remove the 4 hydraulic assembly mounting nuts.

6. Working from under the hood, pull the hydraulic assembly away from the dash panel and rotate the assembly enough to gain access to the sensor block cover.

NOTE: The brake lines should not be removed or deformed during this procedure.

7. Remove the sensor block cover retaining bolt and remove the sensor block cover. Care should be used not to damage the cover gasket during removal.

8. Disengage the locking tabs and disconnect the valve block connector (12 pin) from the sensor block.

9. Disengage the reed block connector (marked PUSH) by carefully pulling outward on the orange connector body. The connector is partially retained by a plastic clip and will only move outward approximately ½ in. (13mm).

10. Remove the 3 block retaining bolts.

11. Carefully disengage the sensor block pressure port from the hydraulic assembly and remove the sensor block from the vehicle. The sensor block pressure port is sealed with an O-ring and extra care should be taken to prevent damage to the seal.

12. Inspect the sensor block pressure port O-ring for damage. Replace the O-ring if cut or damaged. Check the sensor block wiring for any mispositioning or damage. Correct any damage or replace the sensor block if damage cannot be corrected.

13. To install, pull the reed block connector (2 pin) outward to the disengage position prior to installing the sensor block on the hydraulic unit.

14. Throughly lubricate the sensor block pressure port O-ring with fresh, clean brake fluid. Carefully insert the pressure port into the hydraulic assembly's orifice, taking care not to cut or damage the O-ring. Position the sensor block for installation of the mounting bolts.

15. Install the sensor block mounting bolts. Tighten to 11 ft. lbs. (15 Nm).

16. Engage the reed block connector by pressing on the orange connector body marked PUSH.

17. Connect the valve block connector (12 pin) to the sensor block.

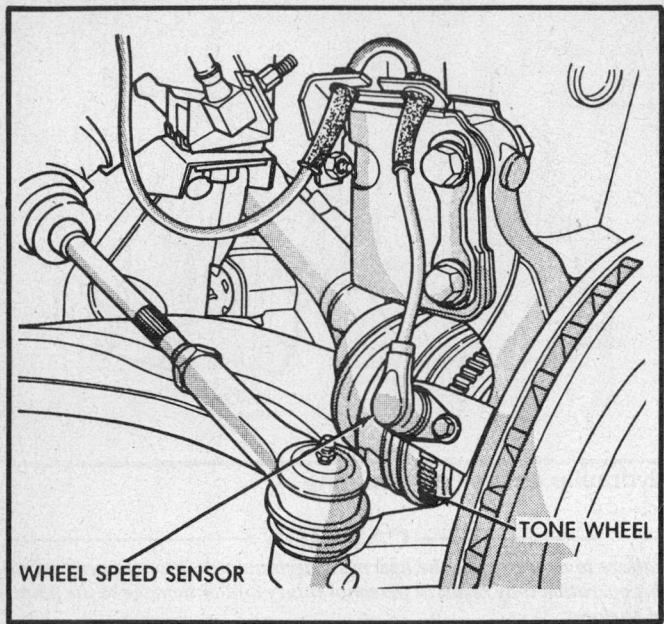

Chrysler front wheel speed sensor

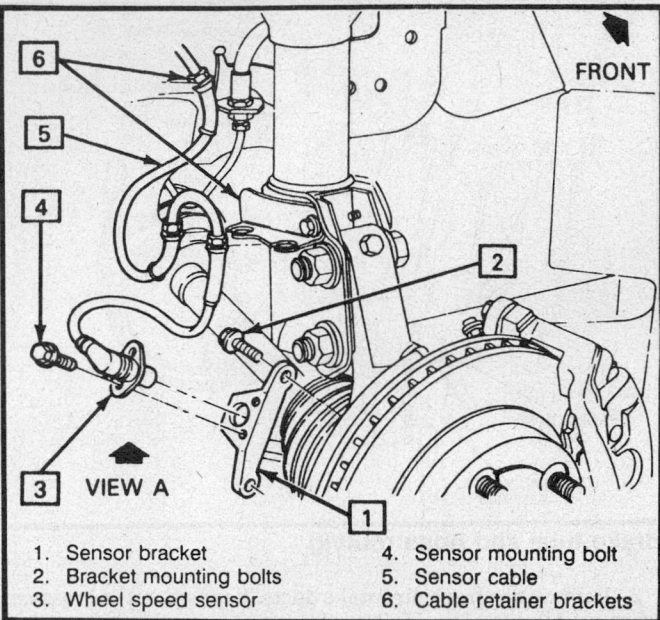

1. Sensor bracket
2. Bracket mounting bolts
3. Wheel speed sensor
4. Sensor mounting bolt
5. Sensor cable
6. Cable retainer brackets

Allante front wheel speed sensor

18. Install the sensor block cover, gasket and mounting bolt.
19. Connect the sensor block and control pressure switch connectors.
20. Install the hydraulic assembly by reversing the removal procedure.

FRONT WHEEL SPEED SENSOR

Removal and Installation

1. Raise the vehicle and remove the wheel and tire assembly.
2. Remove the screw from the sensor cable retainer clip.
3. Carefully pull the sensor assembly grommet from the fender shield.
4. Unplug the connector from the harness.
5. Remove the retainer clip from the bracket on the strut damper.
6. Remove the 3 sensor assembly grommets from the retainer brackets.
7. Remove the sensor head screw.
8. Carefully remove the sensor head from the steering knuckle.

NOTE: Do not use pliers on the sensor head.

9. To install, coat the sensor with high temperature multi-purpose anti-corrosion compound at all areas that it contacts the bracket before installing into the steering knuckle. Install the screw and tighten to 60 inch lbs. (7 Nm).
10. Connect the sensor connector to the harness and install the sensor connector lock.
11. Push the sensor assembly grommet into the hole in the fender shield. Install the clip and screw.
12. Install the sensor grommets in the brackets on the fender shield and strut damper. Install the retainer clip on the retainer at the strut damper.

NOTE: Proper installation of the wheel speed sensor cables is critical to continued system operation. Be sure that the cables are installed in retainers. Failure to install the cables in the retainers may result in contact with moving parts and/or over-extension of the cables, resulting in an open circuit.

REAR WHEEL SPEED SENSOR

Removal and Installation

1. Raise the vehicle and remove the wheel and tire assembly.
2. Remove the sensor assembly grommet from underbody and pull the harness through the hole in underbody.
3. Unplug the connector from the harness.
4. Remove the sensor spool grommet clip retaining screw from the body hose bracket.
5. Remove the sensor assembly clip.
6. Remove the outboard sensor assembly retainer nut.
7. Remove the sensor head screw.
8. Carefully remove the sensor head from the adapter assembly.

NOTE: Do not use pliers on the sensor head.

9. Installation is the reverse of the removal procedure. Be sure to coat the sensor with high temperature multi-purpose anti-corrosion compound before installing into the adapter assembly. Tighten the screw to 60 inch lbs. (7 Nm).

Ford Motor Co.

4 WHEEL ANTI-LOCK BRAKE SYSTEM

Description

The Anti-lock brake system works on all 4 wheels. A combination of wheel speed sensors and a microprocessor can determine when a wheel is about to lock-up and adjust the brake pressure to maintain the best braking. This system helps the driver maintain the control of the vehicle under heavy braking conditions.

The 1988–90 Continental ABS system controls each front brake separately, but the rear brakes as a pair whenever wheel lockup begins. The brake pedal force required to engage the ABS function may vary with the road surface conditions. A dry surface requires a higher force, while a slippery surface requires much less force.

During ABS operation, the driver will sense a slight pulsation in the brake pedal, accompanied by a rise in the pedal height and

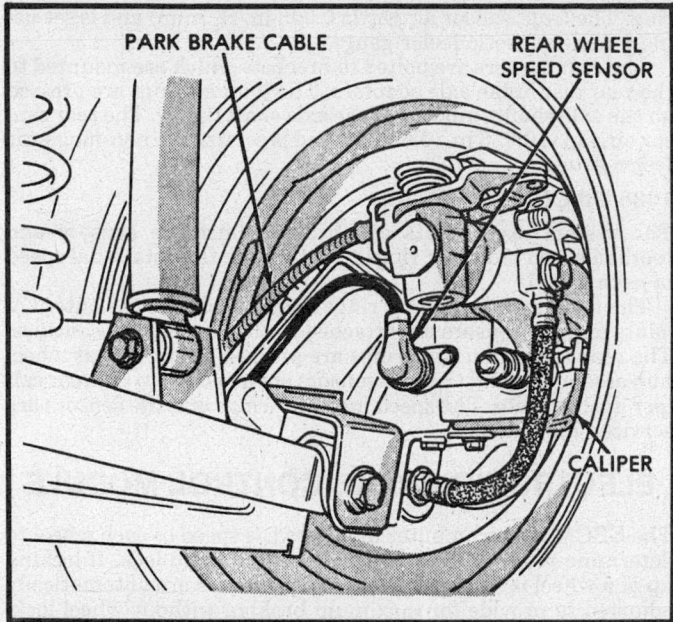

Chrysler rear wheel sensor

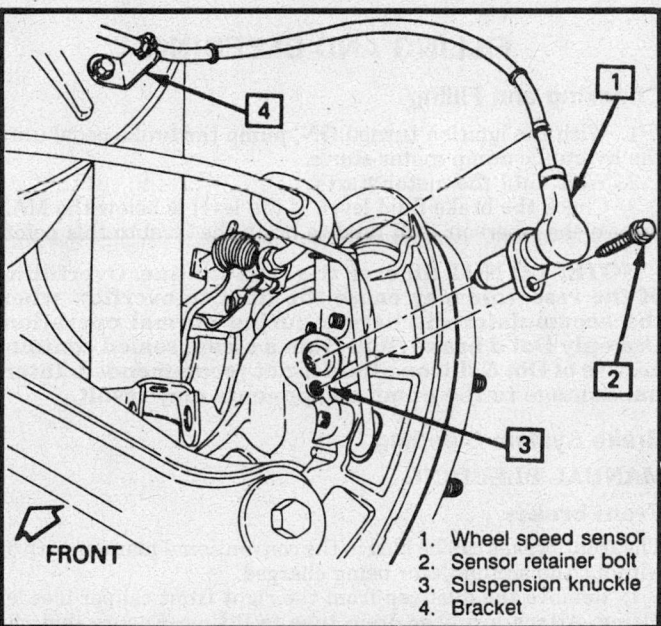

1. Wheel speed sensor
2. Sensor retainer bolt
3. Suspension knuckle
4. Bracket

FRONT

Allante rear wheel sensor

a clicking sound. The pedal effort and pedal feel during normal braking are similar to that of a conventional power brake system.

CAUTION

Some procedures in this section require that hydraulic lines, hoses and fitting be disconnected for inspection or testing purposes. Before disconnecting any hydraulic lines, hoses or fittings, be sure that the accumulator is fully depressurized as described in this section. Failure to depressurize the hydraulic accumulator may result in personal injury.

The hydraulic pump maintains a pressure between 2030–2610 psi in the accumulator and is connected by a high pressure hose to the booster chamber and a control valve. When the brakes are applied, a scissor-lever mechanism activates the control valve and a pressure, proportional to the pedal travel, enters the booster chamber. This pressure is transmitted through the normally open solenoid valve through the proportioning valve to the rear brakes. The same pressure moves the booster piston against the master cylinder piston, shutting off the central valves in the master cylinder. This applies pressure to the front wheels through the 2 front normally open solenoid valves.

The electronic brake control module monitors the electromechanical components of the system. A malfunction in the anti-lock brake system will cause the module to shut off or inhibit the anti-lock system. However, normal power assisted braking remains operational. Malfunctions are indicated by one of the 2 warning lights inside the vehicle.

The 4 wheel anti-lock brake system is self monitoring. When the ignition switch is turned to the **RUN** position, the electronic brake control module will perform a eliminary self check on the anti-lock electrical system indicated by a 3–4 second illumination of the CHECK ANTILOCK BRAKES light in the over head console. During operation of the vehicle, including both normal and anti-lock braking, the electronic brake control module continually monitors all electrical anti-lock functions as well as many hydraulic performance characteristics.

System Components

HYDRAULIC ACTUATION UNIT

The master cylinder and brake booster are connected in the conventional front-to-back position with the booster mounted behind the master cylinder. The booster control valve is located in a parallel bore above the master cylinder centerline and is operated by a lever connected to the brake pedal push rod.

ELECTRIC PUMP AND ACCUMULATOR

The electric pump is a high pressure pump designed to run at frequent intervals for short periods to charge the hydraulic accumulator that supplies the service brake system.

The accumulator is a gas-filled pressure chamber that is part of the pump and motor assembly. The electric motor, pump and accumulator assembly is shock mounted to the master cylinder/booster assembly.

SOLENOID VALVE BLOCK ASSEMBLY

The valve block contains 3 pairs of solenoid valves, one pair for each front wheel and the third pair for both rear wheels. The paired solenoid valves are inlet/outlet valves with the inlet valve normally open and the outlet valve normally closed. The valve body is bolted to the hydraulic actuation unit assembly.

FLUID RESERVOIR AND WARNING SWITCHES

1986–90 MARK VII, 1986–87 CONTINENTAL AND 1988–89 THUNDERBIRD TURBO COUPE

The reservoir assembly is a translucent plastic container which is mounted on top of the hydraulic actuation unit. Integral fluid level switches are part of the reservoir cap assembly with one electrical connector pointing forward for the wire harness connections. Two low pressure hoses lead from the reservoir, one is attached to the hydraulic pump assembly and the other to the master cylinder housing.

The reservoir is mounted to the hydraulic unit with a screw and bracket and a push-in tube outlet that seats in a grommet located in the brake booster housing.

1988–90 CONTINENTAL

The reservoir assembly and fluid level indicator assembly is a translucent plastic container which is mounted on top of the hy-

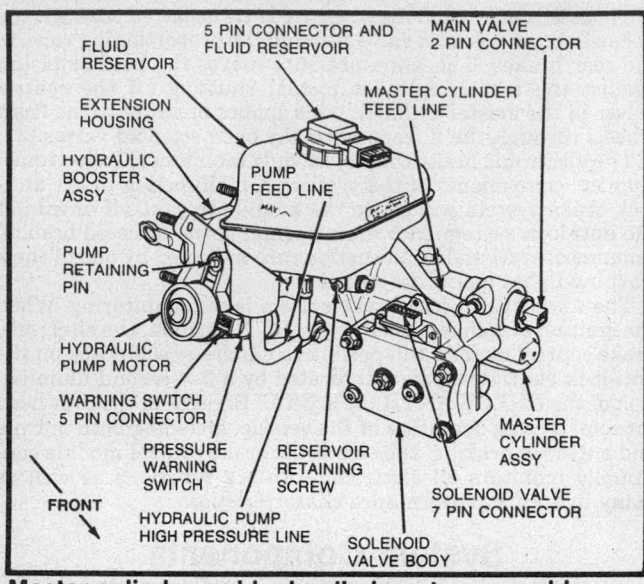

Master cylinder and hydraulic booster assembly

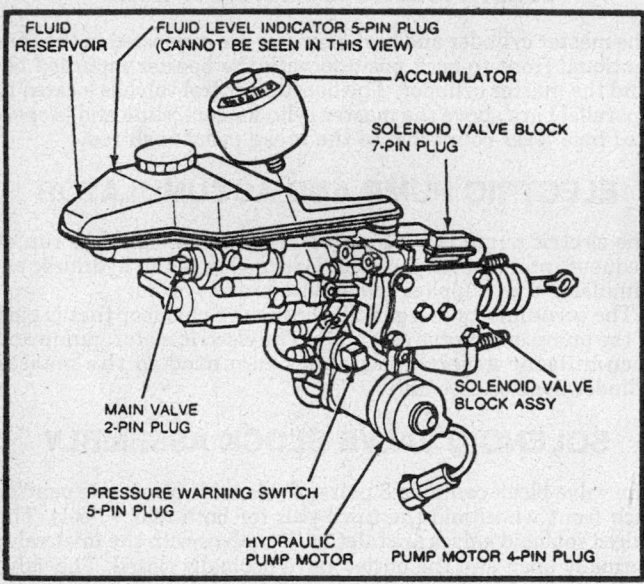

Actuator assembly — Continental

draulic actuation unit. The reservoir is connected to the pump inlet port by a low pressure hose and to the master cylinder by a sealed feed port. The level indicator provides a warning signal to the driver (BRAKE light on the instrument panel) should the brake fluid level fall below minimum. Further loss of fluid will cause the amber CHECK ANTI-LOCK BRAKE light to come on and the vehicle anti-lock function will stop functioning.

WHEEL SPEED SENSORS

1986–90 MARK VII, 1986–87 CONTINENTAL AND 1988–90 THUNDERBIRD TURBO COUPE

There are 4 electronic sensor assemblies, each with a 104 tooth ring in the anti-lock brake system. Each sensor is connected to the electronic brake control module through a wiring harness. The front sensors are bolted to brackets which are mounted to the front spindles. The front toothed sensor rings are pressed onto the inside of the front rotors. Each sensor has an adjustable air gap between the sensor head and the toothed sensor ring. The front sensor air gap is 0.043 in. (1.1mm) and is set using a non-magnetic feeler gauge.

The rear sensors are bolted to brackets which are mounted to the rear disc brake axle adapters. The toothed rings are pressed on the axle shafts, inboard of the axle shaft flange. The rear sensor air gap is 0.026 in. (0.65mm) and is set using a non-magnetic feeler gauge.

1988–90 CONTINENTAL

The system uses 4 sets of variable reluctance sensors and toothed speed indicator rings to determine the rotational speed of each wheel.

The front speed indicator rings are pressed onto the outer CV joints and the sensors are attached to the suspension knuckles. The rear speed indicator rings are pressed onto the rear wheel hub assemblies and the rear sensors are attached to the rear caliper anchor plate. The speed indicator rings and the sensors are serviced individually.

ELECTRONIC BRAKE CONTROL MODULE

The EBCM microcomputer monitors the speed of each wheel to determine if any of the wheels are beginning to lock. If locking up of a wheel is detected, the brake pressures are automatically adjusted to provide for maximum braking without wheel lock. The EBCM monitors system operation during normal driving as well as during anti-lock braking.

FILLING AND BLEEDING

Checking and Filling

1. With the ignition turned **ON**, pump the brake pedal until the hydraulic pump motor starts.
2. Wait until the motor starts.
3. Check the brake fluid level. If the level is below the MAX line on the reservoir, add fluid to bring the level to this point.

NOTE: DO NOT fill over the MAX fill line. Overfilling of the reservoir may cause the fluid to overflow when the accumulator discharges during normal operation. Use only Dot 3 brake fluid from a clean, sealed container. Use of Dot 5 silicone fluid is not recommended. Internal damage to the pump components may result.

Brake System Bleeding
MANUAL BLEEDING
Front brakes

The front brakes can be bled in the conventional manner with or without the accumulator being charged.
1. Remove the dust cap from the right front caliper bleeder fitting. Attach a rubber drain tube to fitting. Ensure that the end of the tube fits snugly around the fitting.
2. Submerge the free end of the tube in a container partially filled with clean brake fluid.
3. Loosen the bleeder fitting approximately ¾ turn. Have an assistant push the brake pedal down slowly through full travel and hold at that position.
4. Close the bleeder fitting, then return the pedal to the full release position.
5. Wait 5 seconds, then repeat the operation until all the air bubbles cease to appear at the submerged end of the bleeder tube.
6. Repeat the operation at the left front caliper.

Rear Brakes

Bleed the rear brakes with a fully charged accumulator.
1. Remove the dust cap from the right rear caliper bleeder fitting. Attach a rubber drain tube to fitting. Ensure that the end of the tube fits snugly around the fitting.

2. Turn the ignition switch to the **RUN** position. This will turn on the electric pump to charge the accumulator as required.

3. Hold the brake pedal in the applied position. Open the right rear caliper bleeder fitting for 10 seconds at a time until all the air bubbles cease to appear from the stream of brake fluid.

─────────── CAUTION ───────────

Care must be used when opening the bleeder screws due to the high pressures available from a fully charged accumulator, or personal injury may result.

──────────────────────────────

4. Repeat the procedure at the left rear caliper.

5. Pump the brake pedal several times to complete the bleeding procedure and to fully charge the accumulator.

6. Adjust the fluid level in the reservoir to the MAX mark with a fully charged accumulator.

NOTE: If the pump motor is allowed to run continuously for approximately 20 minutes, a thermal safety switch inside the motor may shut the motor off to prevent the motor from overheating. If this happens, a cool down period of 2–10 minutes may be required before normal operation can resume.

BLEEDING WITH A PRESSURE BLEEDER

1. Clean all the dirt from the reservoir filler cap area. Attach the pressure bleeder to reservoir cap opening.

2. Maintain 35 psi (240 kPa) pressure on the system.

3. Bleed the brakes in the following order:
   a. Right front
   b. Left front
   c. Right rear
   d. Left rear

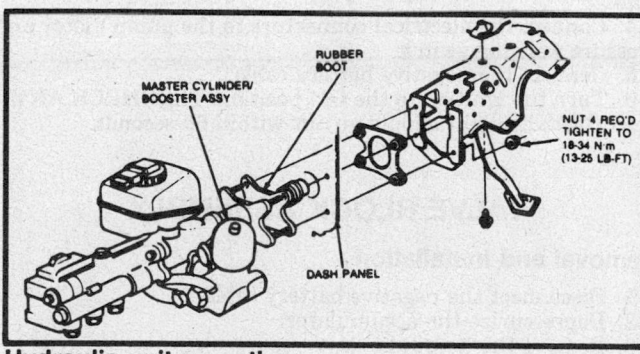

Hydraulic unit mounting

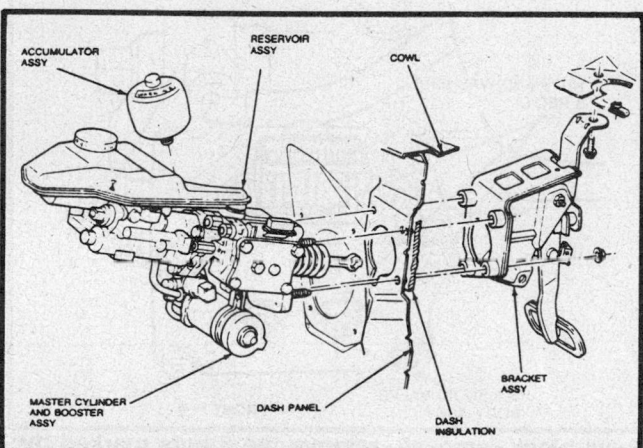

Actuator assembly servicing— Continental

4. Remove the dust cap from the caliper bleeder fitting. Attach a rubber drain tube to fitting. Ensure that the end of the tube fits snugly around the fitting. With the ignition switch **OFF** and the brake pedal in the fully released position, open the caliper bleeder fitting for 10 seconds at a time until all the air bubbles cease to appear from the stream of brake fluid.

5. Repeat the procedure at each wheel in order.

6. Place the ignition switch in the **RUN** position and pump the brake pedal several times to complete the bleeding procedure and to fully charged accumulator.

7. Remove the excess fluid in the reservoir to adjust the level to the MAX mark with a fully charged accumulator.

Component Replacement

─────────── CAUTION ───────────

Some procedures in this section require that hydraulic lines, hoses and fitting be disconnected for inspection or testing purposes. Before disconnecting any hydraulic lines, hoses or fittings, be sure that the accumulator is fully depressurized as described in this section. Failure to depressurize the hydraulic accumulator may result in personal injury.

──────────────────────────────

Depressurizing Hydraulic Accumulator

1. Disconnect the negative battery cable.

2. Apply and release the brake pedal a minimum of 20 times using approximately 50 lbs. (224 N) force on the pedal.

3. A noticeable change in pedal feel will occur when the accumulator is completely discharged.

HYDRAULIC UNIT

Removal and Installation

1986–90 MARK VII, 1986–87 CONTINENTAL AND 1988–90 THUNDERBIRD TURBO COUPE

1. Disconnect the negative battery cable.

2. Depressurize the accumulator.

3. Label and disconnect all electrical connections to the unit.

4. Disconnect the brake lines connected to the solenoid valve body. Plug the threaded tube openings in the valve body to prevent the loss of brake fluid.

5. From the inside of the vehicle, disconnect the pushrod from the brake pedal.

6. Inside the engine compartment, remove the booster from the dash panel.

7. To install, place the hydraulic unit with the rubber boot to the engine side of the dash panel with the 4 mounting studs and the pushrod inserted in the proper holes.

8. Inside the passenger compartment, loosely start the 4 retaining locknuts on the hydraulic unit studs.

9. Connect the pushrod to the brake pedal pin as follows:

10. Connect the brake lines to the valve body one at a time starting with the rear brake line (line to the right front wheel), while removing the plugs.

11. Install all the electrical connections to the unit.

12. Connect the negative battery cable.

13. Bleed the brake system.

1988–90 CONTINENTAL

1. Disconnect the negative battery cable.

2. Remove the air cleaner housing and the duct assembly.

3. Disconnect the electrical connectors from the fluid level indicator, main valve, solenoid valve block, pressure warning switch, hydraulic pump motor and the ground connector from master cylinder portion of the actuation assembly.

4. Disconnect the 3 brake tube fittings. Immediately plug each threaded port to prevent fluid loss and contamination.

NOTE: Do not allow any brake fluid to come into contact with any of the electrical connectors.

5. Remove the trim panel under steering column. Disconnect actuation assembly pushrod from brake pedal by removing hairpin connector next to the stop light switch. Slide the switch, push rod and plastic bushings off the pedal pin.

6. Remove the 4 retaining nuts that hold the actuation assembly to the brake pedal support to the bracket.

7. Remove the actuation assembly from the engine compartment.

8. To install, place the actuation assembly with the rubber boot and foam gasket to the engine side of the dash panel with 4 mounting studs and pushrod inserted in proper holes.

9. From the passenger compartment, loosely start the 4 retaining nuts attaching the actuation assembly to the pedal support bracket.

10. Connect the pushrod to the brake pedal pin by sliding the flanged plastic bushing, pushrod and washer onto the brake pedal pin.

11. Position the stop light switch so that the slot on the switch bracket straddles the pushrod on the brake pedal pin, with the hole on the opposite leg of the switch bracket just clearing pin. Slide the switch onto pedal pin until bottoming. Install the outer nylon bushing and secure assembly with hairpin retainer.

12. Tighten 4 locknuts securing hydraulic unit to the pedal support to 13–25 ft. lbs. (18–34 Nm).

13. From the engine compartment, connect the solenoid valve block brake tubes 1 at a time, while removing the plugs. Tighten the brake tube locknuts to 13–25 ft. lbs. (18–34 Nm).

14. Connect the electrical connectors to the fluid level indicator, main valve, solenoid valve block, pressure switch and electric pump. Secure the ground wire to the master cylinder of the actuation assembly. Ensure that all the connections are clean and all seals are in place.

15. Install the air cleaner and duct assembly.

16. Connect the negative battery cable and bleed the brake system.

HYDRAULIC ACCUMULATOR

Removal and Installation

1. Disconnect the negative battery cable.
2. Depressurize the accumulator.
3. Using an 8mm hex wrench unscrew the hydraulic accumulator from the hydraulic unit.
4. Remove the O-ring from the accumulator.
5. To install, lubricate a new O-ring with clean brake fluid and install it on the accumulator.
6. Install the accumulator and tighten to 30–34 ft. lbs. (40–46 Nm)
7. Connect the negative battery cable.
8. Turn the ignition to the ON position. The BRAKE, ANTILOCK and/or CHECK ANTILOCK BRAKE light(s) should go out within 60 seconds.
9. Check for leakage around the accumulator.
10. Top off the fluid reservoir to the MAX mark with a fully charged accumulator.

PUMP AND MOTOR ASSEMBLY

Removal and Installation

1986–90 MARK VII, 1986–87 CONTINENTAL AND 1988–90 THUNDERBIRD TURBO COUPE

1. Disconnect the negative battery cable.
2. Depressurize the accumulator.
3. On all except 1988–90 Continental, disconnect the electrical connector from the pressure switch and the electric motor. Remove the fluid from the reservoir.
4. Remove the hydraulic accumulator and O-ring.
5. Remove the suction line between the reservoir and the pump at the reservoir by twisting the hose and pulling.

6. On all except 1988–90 Continental, disconnect the high pressure hose fitting connected to the pump. Remove the pressure hose assembly and O-rings. On 1988–90 Continental, disconnect the low pressure line between the fluid reservoir and the pump suction port. With the vehicle safely on a hoist, disconnect the electrical connector for the pump motor and the pressure warning switch.

7. Using a 6mm hex wrench remove the pump and motor retaining bolt. Check and save the thick spacer between the extension housing and the shock mount, if equipped.

8. Move the pump and motor assembly inboard (toward the engine) to remove the assembly from the retaining pin, located on the inboard side of the extension housing.

9. To install, position the pump and motor assembly onto the retaining pin and swing the pump outboard into position. Install the Allen head bolt and thick spacer and tighten to 5–7 ft. lbs. (7–10 Nm).

NOTE: A gap of 0.06–0.13 in. (1.5–3.5mm) must be between the washer on the Allen head bolt and isolator bushing retainer cap. A vibration may be heard from the pump during normal operation if direct contact occurs.

10. Install the sealing bolt on the pressure hose to the booster housing under the reservoir. Inspect and replace the O-rings, if necessary. Be sure that the O-rings are on each side of the banjo fitting. Tighten the bolt to 12–15 ft. lbs. (16–22 Nm).

11. On 1988–90 Continental, Install the low pressure line between the reservoir and the pump inlet. On all other vehicles, connect the suction hose to the fluid reservoir being careful to minimize fluid loss when removing the vacuum nipple and installing the hose.

12. Lubricate a new O-ring with clean brake fluid and install it on the accumulator.

13. Install the accumulator and tighten to 30–34 ft. lbs. (40–46 Nm).

14. Connect the electrical connectors to the pump motor and pressure warning switch.

15. Connect the negative battery cable.

16. Turn the ignition to the ON position. The CHECK ANTI-LOK BRAKES light should go out within 60 seconds.

VALVE BLOCK ASSEMBLY

Removal and Installation

1. Disconnect the negative battery cable.
2. Depressurize the accumulator.
3. Remove the hydraulic unit.

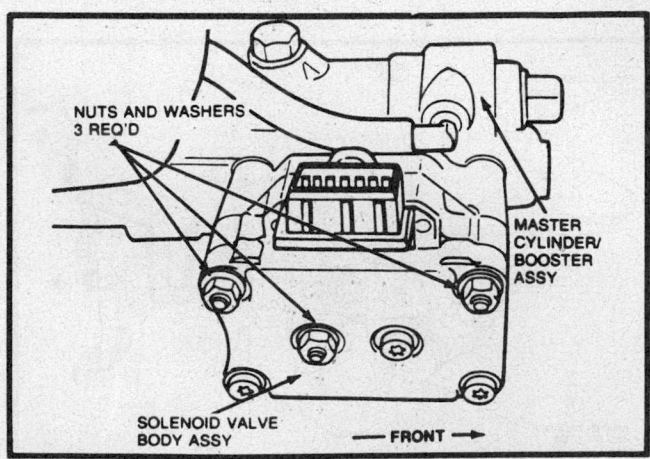

Valve block removal—remove the 3 nuts marked by the arrows

4. Using a 13mm hex socket, remove the 3 nuts and washers which are holding the valve block to the master cylinder.

5. Remove the valve block assembly and O-rings by sliding the valve block off of the studs.

6. To install, fit 4 new square-cut O-rings lubricated with brake fluid, in the 4 ports of the valve block mounting face.

7. Install the valve block and O-rings onto the master cylinder body.

8. Install the 3 nuts and new washers, tighten to 15–21 ft. lbs. (21–29 Nm).

9. Install the hydraulic unit.

10. Install the negative battery cable.

11. Refill and bleed the brake system.

12. Check for leaks at the valve block mating surfaces and tube seats.

FRONT WHEEL SENSORS

Removal and Installation

1986–90 MARK VII, 1986–87 CONTINENTAL AND 1988–90 THUNDERBIRD TURBO COUPE

1. From the inside of the engine compartment, disconnect the electrical connector from the sensor.

2. Raise the vehicle and support safely. Disengage the wire grommet at the shock tower and pull the sensor cable connector through the hole. Be careful not to damage the connector.

3. Remove the sensor wire from the bracket on the shock strut and the side rail.

4. Loosen the 5mm set screw holding the sensor to the sensor bracket post. Remove the sensor through the hole in the disc brake splash shield.

5. To remove the sensor bracket or the sensor bracket post, in case of damage, the caliper and the hub and rotor assembly must be removed. After removing the hub and rotor assembly, remove the 2 brake splash shield attaching bolts which attach the sensor bracket.

NOTE: If the toothed sensor ring is damaged, replace the ring.

6. To install, position the sensor bracket to the sensor bracket post, if it was removed. Tighten the post retaining bolt to 40–60 inch lbs. (4.5–6.8 Nm) and the splash shield attaching bolts to 10–15 ft. lbs. (13–20 Nm). Install the hub and rotor assembly and the caliper.

7. If a sensor is to be re-used or adjusted, the pole face must be clean of all foreign material. Carefully scrape the pole face with a dull knife, or similar tool to ensure that the sensor slides freely on the post. Glue a new front paper spacer on the pole face (front paper spacer is marked with an F and is 0.043 in. (1.1mm) thick). Also the steel sleeve around the post bolt must be rotated to provide a new surface for the set screw to indent and lock onto.

8. Install the sensor through the brake shield onto the sensor

bracket post. Be sure the paper spacer on the sensor is intact and does not come off during installation.

9. Push the sensor bracket toward the sensor ring until the new paper spacer contacts the ring. Hold the sensor against the sensor ring and tighten the 5mm set screw to 21–26 inch lbs. (2.4–3.0 Nm).

10. Insert the sensor cable into the bracket on the shock strut, rail bracket; then through the inner fender apron to the engine compartment and seat the grommet.

11. Lower the vehicle and from inside the engine compartment, connect the sensor electrical connection.

12. Check the function of the sensor by driving the vehicle and observing the CHECK ANTI LOCK BRAKES light in the overhead console.

1988–89 CONTINENTAL

1. From the engine compartment, disconnect the sensor connector.

2. For the right front sensor, remove the 2 plastic push studs to loosen the front section of the splash shield in the wheel well. For the left front sensor, remove the 2 plastic push studs to loosen the rear section of the splash shield.

3. Thread the sensor wire through the holes in the fender apron. For the right front sensor, remove the 2 retaining clips behind the splash shield.

4. Raise the vehicle and support safely. Remove the wheel and tire assembly.

5. Disengage the sensor wire grommets at the height sensor bracket and from the retainer clip at the shock tower.

6. Loosen the sensor retainer screw and remove the sensor assembly from the front knuckle.

7. To install, align the sensor with its mounting holes an the front knuckle. Tighten the retainer screw to 40–60 inch lbs. (4.6–6.8 Nm).

8. Install the grommets at the height sensor bracket and the retainer clip at the shock tower.

9. Thread the wire through the holes in the fender apron. Install the retainer clip (for the right front sensor only). Secure the splash shield with the plastic push studs.

10. Connect the sensor connector to the wiring harness from the engine compartment.

REAR WHEEL SENSORS

Removal and Installation

1986–90 MARK VII, 1986–87 CONTINENTAL AND 1988–90 THUNDERBIRD TURBO COUPE

1. From inside the luggage compartment, disconnect the wheel sensor electrical connector, located behind the forward luggage compartment trim panel.

2. Lift the luggage compartment carpet and push the sensor wire grommet through the hole in the luggage compartment floor.

3. Raise the vehicle and support safely. Remove the wheel and tire assembly.

4. Carefully remove the wheel sensor wiring from the axle shaft housing. The wiring harness has 3 different types of retainers. The inboard retainer is a clip located on top of the differential housing. The second retainer is a C-clip located in the center of the axle shaft housing. Pull rearward on the clip to disengage the clip from the axle housing.

NOTE: Do not bend the clip open beyond the amount necessary to remove the clip from the axle housing.
The third clip is at the connection between the rear wheel brake tube and the flexible hose. Remove the hold-down bolt and open the clip to remove the harness.

5. Remove the rear wheel caliper and rotor assemblies.

6. Remove the wheel speed sensor 10mm hex head retaining

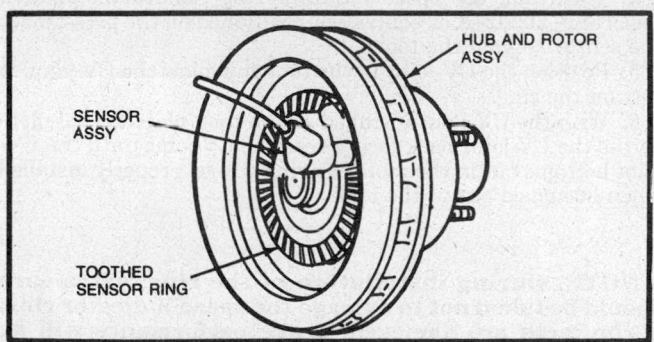

Front wheel speed sensor

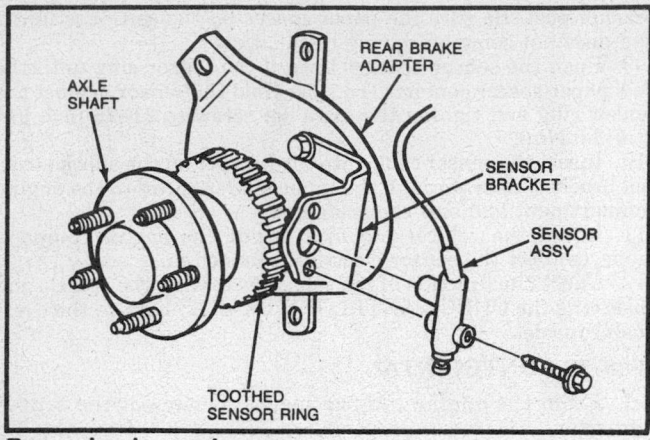

Rear wheel speed sensor

bolt. Slip the grommet out of the rear brake splash shield and pull the sensor wire outward through the hole.

7. Inspect the sensor bracket for possible damage. If damaged, remove the 6mm self tapping screws (2) attaching the bracket to the axle adapter and remove the bracket.

NOTE: If the toothed sensor ring is damaged, replace the ring.

8. To install, position the sensor bracket with the sensor bracket post, if removed. Tighten the screws to 11–15 ft. lbs. (15–20 Nm).

9. Loosen the 5mm set screw on the sensor and ensure that the sensor slides freely on the sensor bracket post.

10. If a sensor is to be re-used or adjusted, the pole face must be clean of all foreign material. Carefully scrape the pole face with a dull knife, or similar tool to ensure that the sensor slides freely on the post. Glue a new rear paper spacer on the pole face (rear paper spacer is marked with an R and is 0.026 in. (0.65mm) thick).

If desired, a feeler gauge may be used instead of a paper spacer (if used, remove the paper spacer prior to adjusting). Also the steel sleeve around the post bolt must be rotated to provide a new surface for the set screw to indent and lock onto.

11. Insert the sensor into the large hole in the sensor bracket and install the 10mm hex head retaining bolt into the sensor bracket post. Tighten the bolt to 40–60 inch lbs. (4.5–6.8 Nm).

12. Push the sensor toward the toothed ring until the new paper sensor makes contact with the sensor ring. Hold the sensor against the toothed ring and tighten the 5mm set screw to 21–26 inch lbs. (2.4–3.0 Nm).

13. Install the caliper and rotor.

14. Push the wire and connector through the splash shield hole and engage the grommet into the shield eyelet. Install the sensor wire in the retainers along the axle housing.

15. Push the connector through the hole in the luggage compartment and seat the grommet in the luggage compartment floorpan.

16. From inside the luggage compartment, connect the cable electrical connector. Install the carpet as necessary.

17. Check the function of the sensor by driving the vehicle and observing the CHECK ANTI LOCK BRAKES light in the overhead console.

1988-90 CONTINENTAL

1. From the luggage compartment, disconnect the sensor connector.

2. Push the rubber grommet through the sheet metal floor pan.

3. From the luggage compartment, turn the air suspension switch OFF. Raise the vehicle and support safely. Remove the

retainer clips for the sensor wire and remove the wire from its routing position.

4. Loosen the sensor retainer screw at the caliper anchor plate and remove the sensor.

5. To install, with the suspension arm in its lowered position, thread the sensor wire connector through the opening above the arm. Install the front suspension arm.

6. Align the sensor with its mounting holes on the caliper anchor plate. Tighten the sensor retainer screw to 40–60 inch lbs. (4.6–6.8 Nm).

7. Position the sensor wire in its normal routing position and install the retaining clips.

8. Thread the sensor connector through the hole in the floorpan. Push the center portion of the rubber grommet on the sensor wire until it is properly seated.

9. Connect the electrical connector in the luggage compartment and turn ON the air suspension switch.

FRONT INDICATOR RING

Removal and Installation

1986-90 MARK VII, 1986-87 CONTINENTAL AND 1988-90 THUNDERBIRD TURBO COUPE

1. Raise the vehicle and support safely.

2. Remove the wheel and tire assembly.

3. Remove the caliper and rotor assemblies.

4. Position the rotor assembly on an arbor press with the wheel studs facing up.

NOTE: Press each stud individually and carefully only until they contact the surface of the sensor ring.

5. Position the special anti-lock ring gear remover tool T85P-20202-A, or equivalent, on top of the studs and press the 5 studs and sensor ring out of the rotor assembly together.

6. To install, place the wheel studs into the rotor, one stud at a time.

7. Position the sensor ring on the rotor. Press the sensor ring onto the rotor using the special anti-lock ring gear remover tool T85P-20202-B, or equivalent, until the sensor ring is seated.

8. Install the rotor and caliper assemblies.

9. Install the wheel and tire assembly. Lower the vehicle.

1988-90 CONTINENTAL

1. Remove the outboard CV-joint.

2. Position the speed sensor ring removal/installation tool T88P-20202-A or equivalent on a press. Position the CV-joint on the tool.

3. Use a press arm to apply pressure to the CV-joint and remove the speed indicator ring.

4. To install, use speed indicator ring removal/installation tool T88P-20202-A or equivalent positioned on the press, place the sensor ring on the tool.

5. Position the CV-joint in the tool and allow the CV-joint to rest on the ring.

6. With the CV-joint installed in the tool, place a steel plate across the CV-joint back face. Press the CV-joint until the CV-joint bottoms out in the tool. The ring will be properly installed when bottomed out in the tool.

NOTE: During installation of the ring, extra care should be taken not to damage the speed indicator ring. If the teeth are damaged, brake performance will be affected.

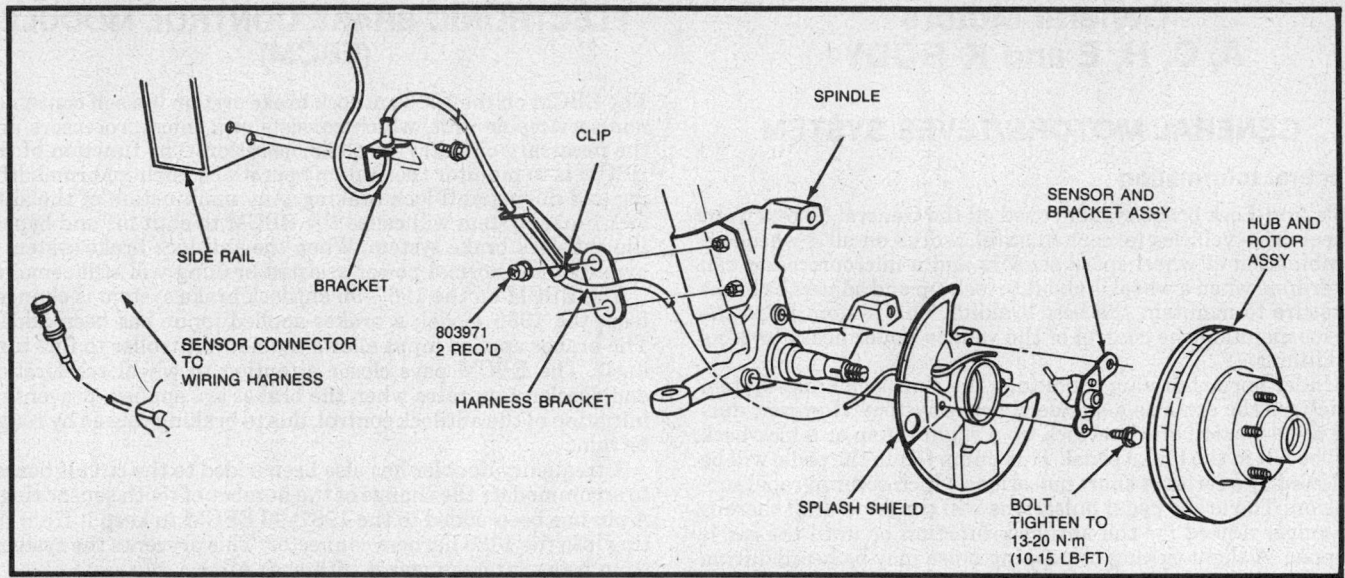

Front wheel sensor mounting

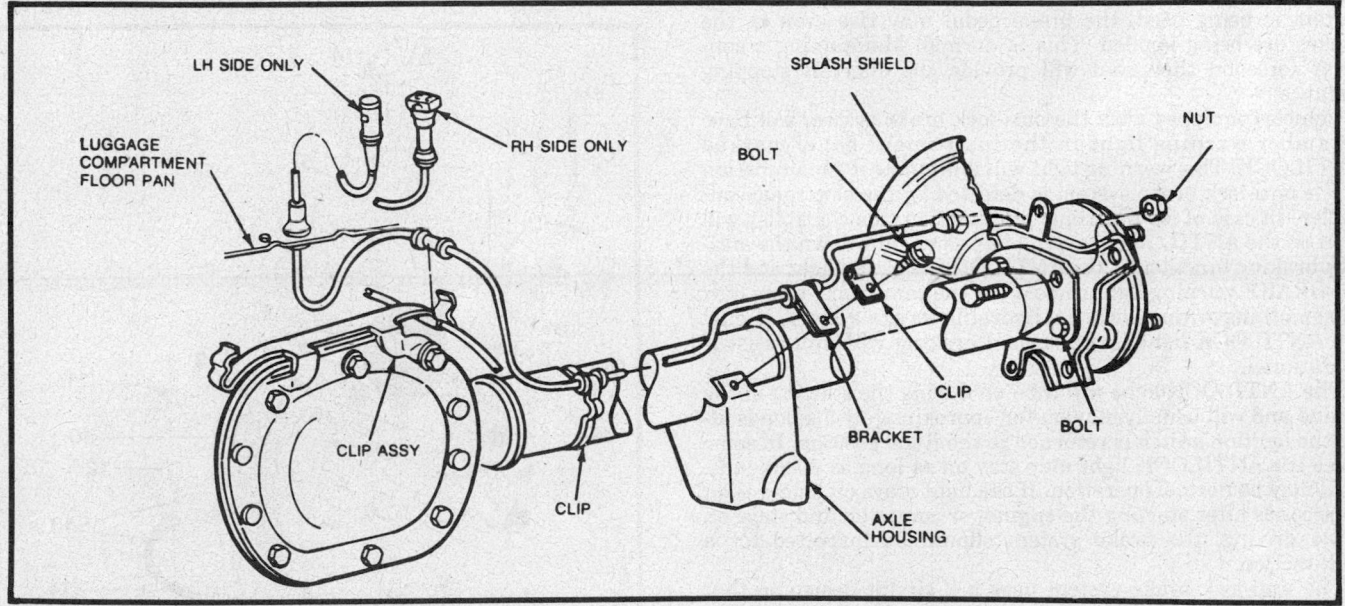

Rear wheel sensor mounting

REAR SPEED INDICATOR RINGS

1986–90 MARK VII, 1986–87 CONTINENTAL AND 1988–90 THUNDERBIRD TURBO COUPE

1. Remove the rear axle shaft.
2. Install the special pinion bearing cone remover tool T71P–4621–A, or equivalent, between the axle shaft flange and the sensor ring.

NOTE: Install the tool with the recessed portion of the inner surface toward the axle flange.

3. Position the axle in an arbor press and press the axle out of the sensor ring.
4. To install, position the sensor ring with the recessed side facing inboard, on the axle and install the special pinion bearing cone remover tool T71P–4621–A, or equivalent, on the axle shaft.
5. With a piece of bar stock on the top of the axle flange, press the sensor ring onto the axle shaft.

NOTE: Press the sensor ring onto the axle shaft until a gap of 1.8 in. (47mm) between the face of the sensor ring and the face of the flange is obtained.

6. Install the axle shaft and related parts.

1988–90 Continental

1. Raise the vehicle and support safely. Remove the wheel and tire assembly.
2. Remove the caliper, rotor and rear hub assemblies.
3. Remove the spring retainer for the sensor ring.
4. Position hub assembly in an arbor press and press hub out of the speed sensor ring.
4. To install, position the speed sensor ring over the hub.
5. Position installation tool T88P–20202–A or equivalent over the speed sensor ring. Gradually press the sensor ring onto the hub until tool is bottomed out over the rim of the hub.
6. Install the spring retainer ring.
7. Install the rear hub, rotor, caliper and wheel/tire assemblies.

General Motors
A, C, H, E and K-BODY

GENERAL MOTORS/TEVES SYSTEM

General Information

This Anti-Lock brake system, used on the General Motors front wheel drive vehicles (except Allante), works on all 4 wheels. A combination of wheel speed sensors and a microprocessor can determine when a wheel is about to lock-up and adjust the brake pressure to maintain the best braking. This system helps the driver maintain the control of the vehicle under heavy braking conditions.

Under normal driving conditions the Anti-lock brake system functions the same as a standard brake system. However, during the detection of wheel lock-up a slight bump or a kick-back will be felt in the brake pedal. This bump felt in the pedal will be followed by a series of short pulsations which occur in rapid succession. The brake pedal pulsations will continue until there is no longer a need for the anti-lock function or until the car is stopped. A slight ticking or popping noise may be heard during brake applications with anti-lock. This noise is normal and indicates that the anti-lock system is being used. When the anti-lock system is being used, the brake pedal may rise even as the brakes are being applied. This is normal. Maintaining a constant force on the pedal will provide the shortest stopping distance.

Vehicles equipped with the anti-lock brake system will have an amber warning light in the instrument panel marked ANTILOCK. This warning light will illuminate if a malfunction in the anti-lock brake system is detected by the electronic controller. In case of an electronic malfunction, the controller will turn on the ANTILOCK warning light and shut-down the anti-lock braking function. If the ANTILOCK warning light and the red BRAKE warning light come on at the same time, there may be something wrong with the hydraulic brake system. If only the ANTILOCK light is on, normal braking with full assist is operational.

The ANTILOCK light will turn on during the starting of the engine and will usually stay on for approximately 3 seconds after the ignition switch is returned to the RUN position. In some cases the ANTILOCK light may stay on as long as 30 seconds. This may be normal operation. If the light stays on longer than 30 seconds after starting the engine, or comes on and stays on while driving, the brake system should be inspected for a malfunction.

The anti-lock brake system uses a 2 circuit design so that some braking capacity is still available if hydraulic pressure is lost in 1 circuit. A BRAKE warning light is located at the left hand side of the instrument cluster and is designed to alert the driver of conditions that could result in reduced braking ability.

The BRAKE warning light should turn on briefly during engine starting and should remain on whenever the parking brake is not fully released. If the BRAKE warning light stays on longer than 30 seconds after starting the engine, or comes on and stays on while driving, there may be a malfunction in the brake hydraulic system.

System Components

The Anti-lock brake system consists of a pump motor assembly, fluid accumulator, pressure switch, fluid reservoir with an integral filter, hydraulic booster/master cylinder, 4 wheel speed sensors, Electronic Brake Control Module (EBCM) and a valve block assembly. A wiring harness with specific fuses and relays connects the major system components to the EBCM which controls the Anti-lock brake system.

ELECTRONIC BRAKE CONTROL MODULE (EBCM)

The EBCM on the 1986 antilock brake system is a self contained non-serviceable unit, which consists of 2 microprocessors and the necessary circuitry for their operation. The function of the EBCM is to monitor the system operations during normal driving and during anti-lock braking. Any malfunction of the anti-lock brake system will cause the EBCM to shut off and bypass the anti-lock brake system. When the anti-lock brake system is bypassed the normal power assisted braking will still remain.

The EBCM on the 1987–90 antilock brake system is changed from the 1986 model; a brakes-applied input has been added. The brakes applied input allows the new controller to fine tune itself. The EBCM pays closer attention to wheel acceleration and deceleration rates when the brakes are applied, preventing initiation of the antilock control, due to braking caused by rough terrain.

A frequency doubler has also been added to the circuit boards to accommodate the change of the number of tooth sensor rings. A pin has been added to the 1987–90 EBCM to keep it from fitting into the 1986 harness connector. This prevents the systems from being interchangable with each other.

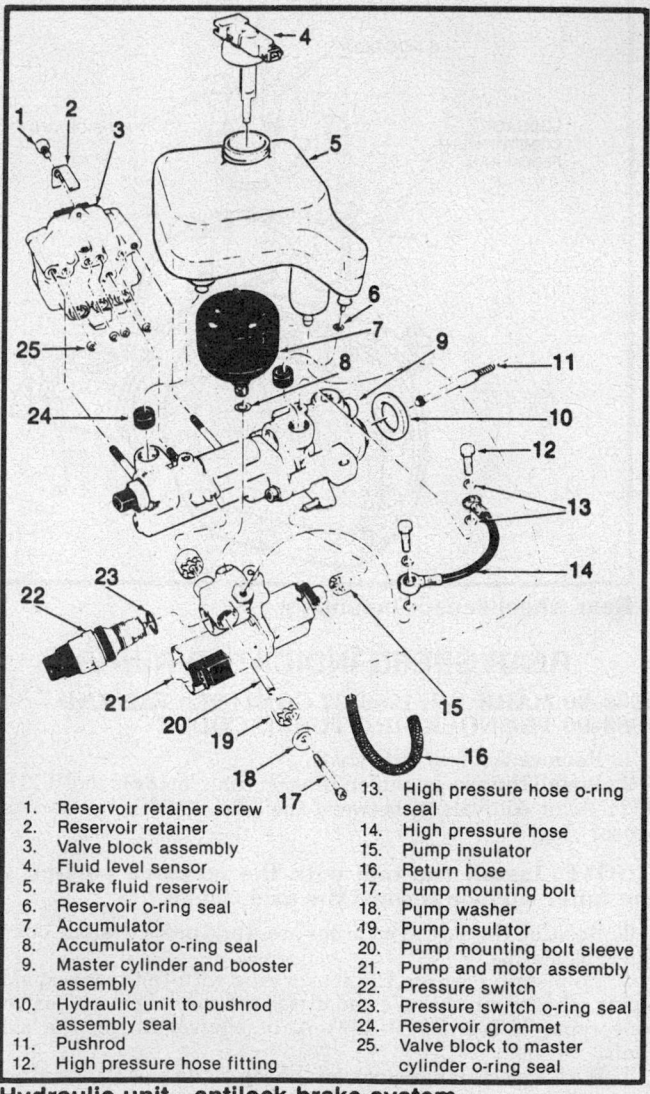

1. Reservoir retainer screw	13. High pressure hose o-ring seal
2. Reservoir retainer	14. High pressure hose
3. Valve block assembly	15. Pump insulator
4. Fluid level sensor	16. Return hose
5. Brake fluid reservoir	17. Pump mounting bolt
6. Reservoir o-ring seal	18. Pump washer
7. Accumulator	19. Pump insulator
8. Accumulator o-ring seal	20. Pump mounting bolt sleeve
9. Master cylinder and booster assembly	21. Pump and motor assembly
10. Hydraulic unit to pushrod assembly seal	22. Pressure switch
11. Pushrod	23. Pressure switch o-ring seal
12. High pressure hose fitting	24. Reservoir grommet
	25. Valve block to master cylinder o-ring seal

Hydraulic unit—antilock brake system

WHEEL SPEED SENSORS

A wheel speed sensor is located at each wheel and transmits wheel speed information to the EBCM by means of a small AC voltage that is dependent on the wheel speed.

The 1986 sensors are 4 variable reluctance electronic sensor assemblies, each with a 104 tooth ring in the anti-lock system. The 1987–90 front wheel sensors are different from the earlier model. The 1987–90 model has a 47 tooth sensor ring and a different bearing assembly. The location of the sensor tooth on the bearing assembly has also changed. Externally the 1986 and the 1987–90 front wheel sensors look identical, but, they are not interchangable. The 1987–90 rear wheel sensors are different in appearance from their front wheel sensors and are different in appearance from the 1986 front and rear wheel sensors. A new rear knuckle was designed to accommodate the new bearing design.

LOW FLUID AND LOW PRESSURE SENSORS

The low brake fluid and low brake pressure inputs consist of a continuous loop circuit which runs through the fluid level sensor and pressure switch on the hydraulic unit. If a low fluid condition is detected, the fluid sensor will open the circuit. Likewise if low pressure is detected at the accumulator, the pressure switch will open the circuit. Any time an open circuit is detected on the low fluid/pressure input circuit, the anti-lock function is inhibited.

SOLENOID VALVES (VALVE BLOCK)

Each hydraulic brake circuit, left front, right front and rear, is equipped with 2 non-serviceable solenoid valves for fluid intake and output. These valve are actuated by a 12 volt signal from the EBCM when the anti-lock mode is activated and act singly or in combination to provide pressure increase, holding pressure, or decrease depending on the wheel speed sensor signal.

During normal braking (not in the anti-lock mode), no voltage is sent to these valves. The inlet valve is normally open and the outlet valve is normally closed.

MAIN VALVE SOLENOID

The main valve solenoid is located in the hydraulic unit and is activated by the EBCM main valve solenoid circuit only when anti-lock braking is required. During anti-lock braking, The EBCM provides 12 volts to the main valve solenoid output.

HYDRAULIC UNIT

The main components of the hydraulic unit are the hydraulic booster/master cylinder, valve block assembly, pump motor assembly, pressure switch, accumulator and the fluid level sensor.

When the brake pedal is depressed, the booster/master cylinder operates the front brakes in the normal manner and also provides modulated accumulator pressure to the rear brakes.

The valve block assembly is a series of solenoid controlled valves which can cycle very quickly to increase and reduce hydraulic pressure to each wheel. The pump and the motor assembly supplies high pressure brake fluid to the accumulator. This high pressure fluid is used for the power assist and also to apply the rear brakes.

The pressure switch monitors the pressure that is maintained in the accumulator. When the pressure drops below the pressure limit, the pressure switch activates the pump motor relay which turns on the pump. Once the pressure reaches the upper pressure limit the pressure switch deactivates the relay and shuts down the pump. In the event of a pressure leak or a pump failure, the pressure switch will signal the EBCM to shut-down

the Anti-lock function. The pressure switch will also light the BRAKE lamp located in the instrument panel.

The accumulator is a pressure storage device which can hold brake fluid under very high pressures. The accumulator has an internal diaphragm with nitrogen trapped on 1 side. As the pump fills the accumulator, the diaphragm moves and compresses the trapped nitrogen.

The fluid level sensor is located in the fluid reservoir cap. It has 2 functions. It can signal the EBCM that there is a low fluid condition. The EBCM with then shut-down the Anti-lock function. The fluid level sensor will also light the red BRAKE lamp located in the instrument panel.

FILLING AND BLEEDING

CAUTION

Some procedures in this section require that hydraulic lines, hoses and fitting be disconnected for inspection or testing purposes. Before disconnecting any hydraulic lines, hoses or fittings, be sure that the accumulator is fully depressurized. Failure to depressurize the hydraulic accumulator may result in personal injury.

DEPRESSURIZING THE ACCUMULATOR

1. Disconnect the negative battery cable.
2. Apply and release the brake pedal a minimum of 25 times with a force of approximately 50 lbs. (222 N).
3. A noticable change in pedal feel will occur when the accumulator is fully depressurized.

Checking and Filling Brake Fluid

NOTE: Do not use any brake fluid which may contain a petroleum base. Do not use a container which has been used for petroleum based fluids or a container which is wet with water. Petroleum based fluids will cause swelling and distortion of rubber parts in the hydraulic brake system and water will mix with brake fluid, lowering the fluid boiling point. Keep all fluid containers capped to prevent contamination.

The plastic fluid reservoir, on the ABS hydraulic unit, has a label marking the proper FULL level. The hydraulic accumulator must be depressurized when checking the brake fluid level. Use the following procedure to check the brake fluid level.
1. Depressurize the hydraulic accumulator.
2. Inspect the fluid level.
3. Thoroughly clean the reservoir cap and surrounding area prior to cap removal to avoid contamination of the reservoir.
4. Fill the reservoir to the FULL mark using DOT–3 brake fluid. Use of DOT–5 silicone fluid is not allowed, as internal damage to the pump components may result.

Brake Bleeding

Only the front brakes should be pressure bled. The rear brakes will bleed without the use of pressure equipment. Only diaphragm type pressure bleeding equipment should be used to prevent air, moisture and other contaminants from entering the system.

NOTE: The front brakes may be manually bled by conventional bleeding methods. The rear brakes should be bled according to the procedures given below.

FRONT BRAKES

1. Disconnect the wiring sensor from the fluid level sensor and remove the sensor.
2. Install the special tool J–35798 in place of the sensor.
3. Attach the brake bleeder to the adapter tool J–35798 and charge to 20 psi (138 kPa).

4. Attach a bleeder hose to 1 front bleeder valve and submerge the other end in a container of clean brake fluid.

5. Open the bleeder valve.

6. Allow the fluid to flow from the bleeder until no air bubbles are seen in the brake fluid.

7. Close the bleeder valve.

8. Repeat Steps 4–7 on the other front bleeder valve.

9. Check the fluid level and adjust as necessary.

10. Remove the brake bleeding equipment and adapters, install and connect the fluid level sensor.

REAR BRAKES

1. Turn the ignition on and allow the system to charge. (Listen for the pump motor, it will stop when the system is charged.)

2. Attach a bleeder hose to 1 of the rear bleeder valves and submerge the other end in a container of clean brake fluid.

3. Open the bleeder valve.

4. With the ignition on, slightly depress the brake pedal for at least 10 seconds.

5. Allow the fluid to flow from the bleeder until no air bubbles are seen in the brake fluid. Repeat the Step above if necessary.

6. Close the bleeder valve.

7. Repeat Steps 2–6 on the other rear bleeder valve.

8. Fill the fluid reservoir to the maximum level mark.

Component Replacement

HYDRAULIC UNIT

Removal and Installation

1. Disconnect the negative battery cable.

2. Depressurize the accumulator.

3. Label and disconnect all electrical connections to the unit.

4. Remove the pump bolt and move the energy unit to the side to gain access to the brake lines.

5. Disconnect the 3 lines connected to the valve block. Use a second wrench to prevent the line from twisting.

6. Disconnect the line attaching the hydraulic unit to the combination valve.

7. From the inside of the vehicle, disconnect the pushrod from the brake pedal.

8. Push the dust boot forward, past the hex on the pushrod.

9. Separate the pushrod halves by unthreading the 2 pieces.

10. Remove the 2 unit-to-pushrod bracket bolts and remove the hydraulic unit.

NOTE: The front half of the pushrod will remain locked into the hydraulic unit.

11. To install, position the hydraulic unit to the support bracket.

12. Install the support bracket bolts and torque them to 37 ft. lbs. (50 Nm).

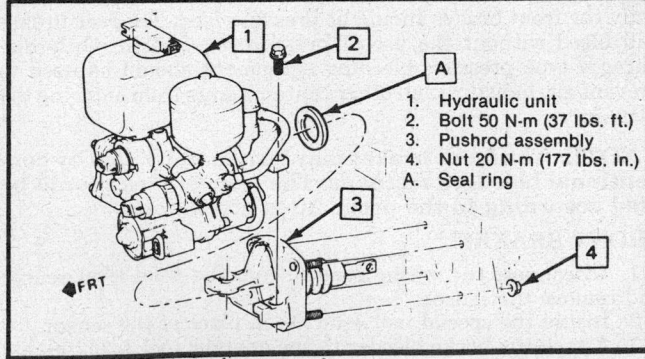

1. Hydraulic unit
2. Bolt 50 N-m (37 lbs. ft.)
3. Pushrod assembly
4. Nut 20 N-m (177 lbs. in.)
A. Seal ring

Hydraulic unit replacement

13. Thread the 2 halves of the pushrod together and tighten.

14. Reposition the dust boot.

15. Connect the line from the combination valve to the hydraulic unit.

16. Connect the 3 lines to the valve block, reposition the energy unit as necessary.

17. Install all the electrical connections to the unit.

18. Connect the negative battery cable.

19. Bleed the brake system.

PUMP AND MOTOR ASSEMBLY

Removal and Installation

1. Disconnect the negative battery cable.

2. Depressurize the accumulator.

3. Disconnect the electrical connector from the pressure switch and the electric motor. Remove the fluid from the reservoir.

4. Remove the hydraulic accumulator and O-ring.

5. Disconnect the high pressure hose fitting connected to the pump.

6. Remove the pressure hose assembly and O-rings.

7. Disconnect the wire clip then, pull the return hose fitting out of the pump body.

8. Remove the bolt attaching the pump and motor assembly to the main body.

9. Remove the pump and motor assembly by sliding it off of the locating pin.

NOTE: Replace the insulators, if damaged or deteriorated.

10. To install, position the pump and motor assembly to the main body.

11. Install the bolt attaching the pump and motor assembly to the main body.

12. Connect the pressure hose assembly.

13. Connect the return hose and fitting into the pump body. Install the wire clip.

14. Install the bolt, O-rings and fitting of the high pressure hose to the pump body.

15. Connect the electrical connector to the pump motor.

16. Connect the negative battery cable.

VALVE BLOCK ASSEMBLY

Removal and Installation

1. Disconnect the negative battery cable.

2. Depressurize the accumulator.

3. Remove the hydraulic unit.

4. Remove the 3 nuts and washers show in the illustration.

5. Remove the valve block assembly and O-rings by sliding the valve block off of the studs.

6. To install, lubricate the O-rings with brake fluid.

7. Install the valve block and O-rings onto the master cylinder body.

8. Install the 3 nuts and washers removed in Step 4.

9. Install the hydraulic unit.

10. Install the negative battery cable.

11. Refill and bleed the system.

PRESSURE WARNING SWITCH

Removal and Installation

1. Disconnect the negative battery cable.

2. Depressurize the accumulator.

3. Disconnect the electrical connector from the pressure/warning switch.

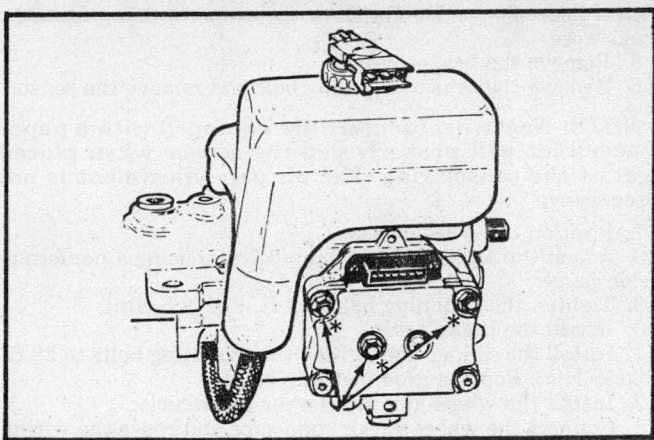

Valve block removal—remove the 3 nuts marked by the arrows

4. Remove the pressure/warning switch using special tool J–35804.
5. Remove the O-ring from the switch.
6. To install, lubricate the O-ring with clean brake fluid.
7. Install the O-ring on the pressure/warning switch.
8. Install the switch and tighten to 17 ft. lbs. (23 Nm). using special tool J–35804.
9. Connect the electrical connector to the pressure/warning switch.
10. Connect the negative battery cable.
11. Turn the ignition to the **ON** position. The BRAKE light should go out within 60 seconds.
12. Check for leakage around the switch.

HYDRAULIC ACCUMULATOR

Removal and Installation

1. Disconnect the negative battery cable.
2. Depressurize the accumulator.
3. Unscrew the hydraulic accumulator from the hydraulic unit.
4. Remove the O-ring from the accumulator.
5. To install, lubricate a new O-ring with clean brake fluid and install it on the accumulator.
6. Install the accumulator and tighten to 17 ft. lbs. (23 Nm).
7. Connect the negative battery cable.
8. Turn the ignition to the **ON** position. The BRAKE light should go out within 60 seconds.
9. Check for leakage around the accumulator.

BRAKE FLUID RESERVOIR AND SEAL

Removal and Installation

1. Disconnect the negative battery cable.
2. Depressurize the accumulator.
3. Remove the return hose and drain the brake fluid into a container and discard the fluid.
4. Disconnect the 2 wire connectors from the fluid level sensor assembly.
5. Remove the reservoir to block mounting bolt.
6. Remove the reservoir by carefully prying between the reservoir and the master cylinder.
7. To install, lubricate the seals with clean brake fluid.
8. Install the seals and O-ring into the master cylinder body.
9. Push the reservoir into the master cylinder until it is fully seated.

10. Install the reservoir to valve block mounting bracket bolt.
11. Connect the 2 wire connectors to the reservoir cap.
12. Connect the sump hose to the reservoir.
13. Refill the reservoir with clean brake fluid.
14. Connect the negative battery cable.

FRONT WHEEL SPEED SENSOR

Removal and Installation

A, C AND H-BODY

1. Raise and safely support the vehicle.
2. Disconnect the wheel sensor connector from the wiring harness.
3. Remove the sensor retaining screw.
4. Remove the wheel sensor.

NOTE: New wheel sensors are equipped with a paper spacer that will properly gap the sensor when placed against the sensor ring. The air gap adjustment is not necessary.

5. To install, position the sensor and install the retaining bolt.
6. Tighten the sensor retaining bolt to 7 ft. lbs. (9.5 Nm).

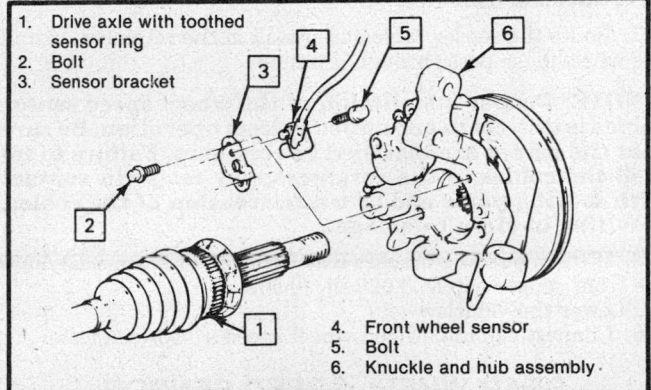

1. Drive axle with toothed sensor ring
2. Bolt
3. Sensor bracket
4. Front wheel sensor
5. Bolt
6. Knuckle and hub assembly

Front wheel speed sensor mounting—A & C Body

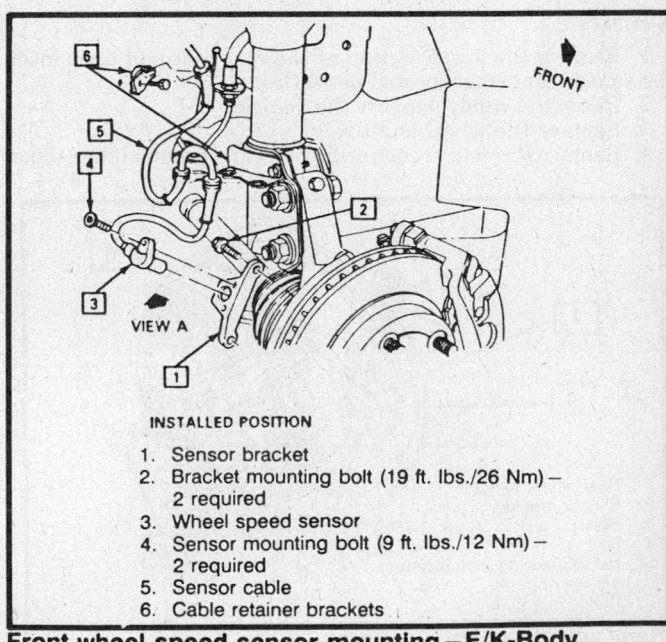

INSTALLED POSITION

1. Sensor bracket
2. Bracket mounting bolt (19 ft. lbs./26 Nm)— 2 required
3. Wheel speed sensor
4. Sensor mounting bolt (9 ft. lbs./12 Nm)— 2 required
5. Sensor cable
6. Cable retainer brackets

Front wheel speed sensor mounting—E/K-Body

7. Adjust the air gap to 0.028 in. (0.7mm) using a nonferous feeler gauge, if necessary.

8. Tighten the sensor lock bolt to 22 inch lbs. (2.5 Nm).

9. Connect the wheel sensor connector and route the wiring to avoid contact with the suspension components.

E AND K-BODY

1. Disconnect the sensor connector from the underhood area near the strut tower.

2. Raise the vehicle and safely support.

3. Disengage the sensor cable grommet from the wheel house pass-through hose and remove the sensor cable from the retaining brackets.

4. Remove the sensor with or without the mounting bracket, as required.

5. To install, if the mounting bracket was removed from the knuckle, install the mounting bracket and bolts. Install the bracket bolts finger tight. Do not tighten at this time.

6. If the sensor was removed from the mounting bracket, thoroughly coat the sensor with anti-corrosion compound or equivalent in all areas where the sensor contacts the mounting bracket. Install the sensor in the mounting bracket and tighten to 9 ft. lbs. (12 Nm).

NOTE: Failure to coat the sensor with anti-corrosion compound prior to installation in the bracket will result in reduced sensor life.

7. Route the sensor cable and install in the retainers. Install the wheelhouse pass-through grommet.

NOTE: Proper installation of the wheel speed sensor cables is critical to continued system operation. Be sure that the cables are installed in retainers. Failure to install the cables in the retainers may result in contact with moving parts and/or over-extension of the cables, resulting in circuit damage.

8. If the mounting bracket was loosened or removed, adjust the front sensor gap to 0.020 in. (0.50mm).

9. Lower the vehicle.

10. Connect the underhood wheel speed sensor connector.

REAR WHEEL SPEED SENSOR

Removal and Installation

A-BODY

1. Remove the lower section of the rear seat and disconnect the sensor connector located beneath it.

2. Raise and safely support the vehicle.

3. Remove the wheel and tire.

4. Remove the caliper mounting bolts and suspend the caliper

with a piece of wire. Do not allow the caliper to hang from the brake hose.

5. Remove the brake rotor.

6. Remove the sensor retaining bolt and remove the sensor.

NOTE: New wheel sensors are equipped with a paper spacer that will properly gap the sensor when placed against the sensor ring. The air gap adjustment is not necessary.

7. Position the wheel sensor.

8. Adjust the air gap to 0.028 in. (0.7mm) using a nonferous feeler gauge.

9. Tighten the retaining bolt to 7 ft. lbs. (9.5 Nm).

10. Install the brake rotor.

11. Install the caliper and tighten the mounting bolts to 28 ft. lbs. (38 Nm). Pop the grommet into place.

12. Install the wheel and tire. Lower the vehicle.

13. Connect the wheel sensor connector and route the wiring to avoid contact with the suspension components.

14. Install the rear seat.

C AND H-BODY

1. Disconnect the sensor connector located in the trunk area.

2. Raise and safely support the vehicle.

3. Remove the wheel and tire.

4. Drill out the 2 grommet retaining rivets.

5. Remove the brake drum, shoes and hardware.

6. Remove the sensor retaining screw and remove the sensor.

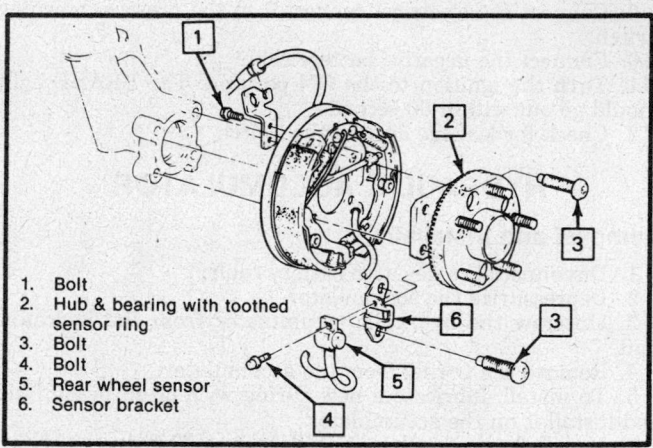

1. Bolt
2. Hub & bearing with toothed sensor ring
3. Bolt
4. Bolt
5. Rear wheel sensor
6. Sensor bracket

Rear wheel sensor—C-Body

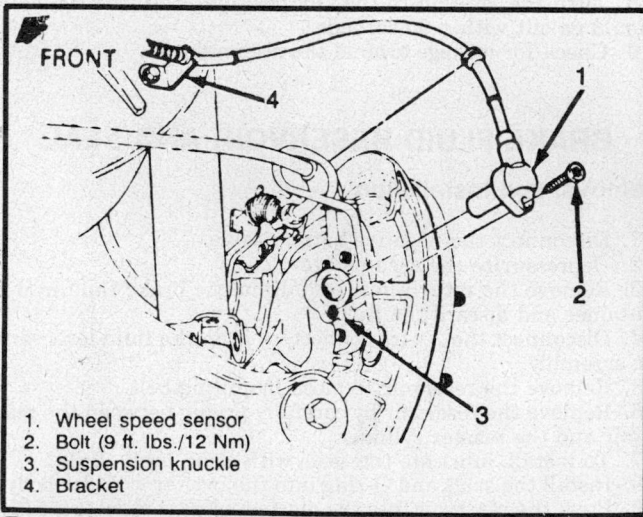

1. Wheel speed sensor
2. Bolt (9 ft. lbs./12 Nm)
3. Suspension knuckle
4. Bracket

Rear wheel speed sensor mounting—E/K-Body

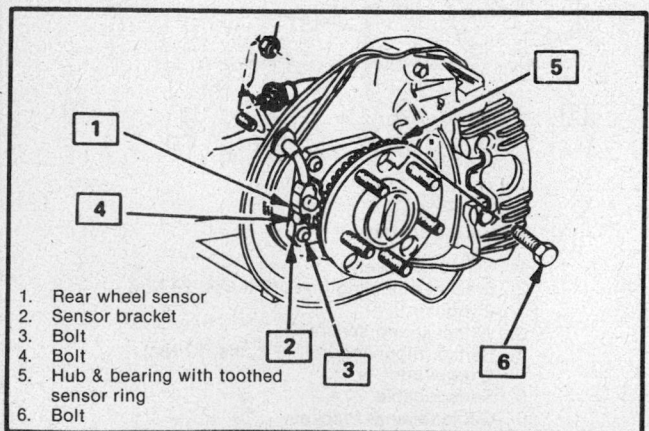

1. Rear wheel sensor
2. Sensor bracket
3. Bolt
4. Bolt
5. Hub & bearing with toothed sensor ring
6. Bolt

Rear wheel sensor—A-Body

NOTE: New wheel sensors are equipped with a paper spacer that will properly gap the sensor when placed against the sensor ring. The air gap adjustment is not necessary.

7. Position the wheel sensor.
8. Adjust the air gap to 0.028 in. (0.7mm) using a nonferous feeler gauge.
9. Tighten the retaining bolt to 7 ft. lbs. (9.5 Nm).
10. Install the brake shoes, hardware and drum.
11. Pop rivet the grommet into place.
12. Install the wheel and tire. Lower the car.
13. Connect the wheel sensor connector and route the wiring to avoid contact with the suspension components.

E AND K-BODY

1. Raise the vehicle and support safely.
2. Disconnect the sensor connector and remove the sensor cable from the retainer brackets.
3. Remove the sensor mounting bolt and remove the sensor from the vehicle.
4. To install, position the sensor in the knuckle and install the mounting bolt. Tighten mounting bolt to 9 ft. lbs. (12 Nm).
5. Install the wheel speed sensor cable in the retainers.

NOTE: Proper installation of the wheel speed sensor cables is critical to continued system operation. Be sure that the cables are installed in retainers. Failure to install the cables in the retainers may result in contact with moving parts and/or over-extension of the cables, resulting in circuit damage.

6. Connect the wheel speed sensor connector.

General Motors W-BODY

DELCO MORAINE SYSTEM

Description

The W-Body is optionally equipped with the Delco Moraine Anti-lock Brake System (DM ABS–III) which operates on all 4 wheels. The system is designed to reduce the tendency of a wheel (or wheels) to lose traction (lock) while braking. ABS occurs only when a combination of wheel speed sensors and a microprocessor determines a wheel (or wheels) is about to lose traction during braking. The DM ABS–III then adjusts the brake pressure to both front wheels independently and/or both rear wheels to reduce the tendency of the wheel (or wheels) to lock-up. This system helps the driver maintain steerability during braking over a wide range of road surfaces and driving conditions. Thus, the driver can minimize stopping distance and bring the vehicle to a controlled stop. The DM ABS–III can not increase the brake pressure above the master cylinder pressure and can never apply the brakes by itself.

When the ABS system operates, the DM ABS–III automatically pumps the brakes for the driver to adjust brake line pressure (or pressures) for optimum stopping distance and vehicle control. While the system is cycling, the brake pedal pulsates as brake line pressures change and clicking sounds can be heard from the solenoids controlling the cycling.

The ignition switch, when turned to the RUN position, initializes the system and a functional DM ABS–III will turn on the solenoids 3 times. The clicking sound caused by solenoid operation can be heard and is normal. In addition, when the brakes are applied moderately and held while turning the ignition switch ON, the brake pedal pulsates, which is caused by the initial cycling of the solenoids. These pulsations are similar to those felt during ABS braking. These pulsations are normal and indicate that the ABS system is functioning properly.

To minimize stopping distance during ABS operation, the operator should steadily and firmly apply the brake pedal and al-low the system to pump the brakes; the operator should not pump the brakes. During ABS operation, intermittent screeching noise from the tires may be heard. This noise is normal and results from slippage of the tire on the road surface. The amount of tire noise will vary with the road and tire conditions. A tire(s) may appear to lock momentarily during ABS stopping. This results from rapid changes in wheel speed (rotation) and is also normal.

However, a wheel that completely locks and stays locked for more than one second is not normal. A vehicle with this problem should be serviced as soon as possible. The DM ABS–III cannot operate properly if the base power brake system is defective. Dragging brakes, defective wheel bearings, etc. will not allow proper ABS operation.

SYSTEM COMPONENTS

The main components of the system are the Powermaster III hydraulic booster/master cylinder (The Powermaster III includes an electric pump assembly, fluid accumulator, pressure switch, front and rear solenoid, fluid reservoir and fluid level sensor) 4 wheel speed sensors, 4 wheel speed rings (only the 2 front wheel speed sensor rings are visible), remote proportioner valve assembly, anti-lock brake controller and interconnect wiring.

FILLING AND BLEEDING

If the hydraulic unit has been replaced, or if air has entered (or is suspected in) the brake lines, the entire brake system (hydraulic unit, lines and calipers) must be bled at each wheel brake.

If only a hydraulic part of the hydraulic unit has been replaced (bleeder valve, tube and nut assembly, accumulator, reservoir, solenoid, or pressure switch) and no air has entered the brake lines, it may only be necessary to bleed the hydraulic unit by performing an ABS solenoid bleed and checkout test using a bi-directional scan tool or by bleeding the booster section of the hydraulic unit at its bleeder valves. (Neither performing an ABS solenoid bleed and checkout test nor bleeding the hydraulic unit at its bleeder valves will remove air from the brake lines.)

CAUTION

Failure to fully depressurize the ABS system before performing service operations could result in brake fluid under high pressure being sprayed on the technician and the vehicle. This can result in serious personal injury and vehicle damage.

DEPRESSURIZING THE SYSTEM

1. To depressurize the ABS system, turn the ignition switch OFF or disconnect the battery. Then firmly apply and release the brake pedal a minimum of 40 times.
2. The pedal should become noticeably hard, which will occur when the accumulator is completely discharged.
3. Do not turn the ignition switch ON after depressurizing the system unless all service operations have been performed.

Checking Fluid Level

1. Park the vehicle on a level surface.
2. Depressurized the ABS system.
3. Clean the reservoir cover and remove the cover and diaphragm assembly from the hydraulic unit.
4. Note the fluid level in the hydraulic reservoir chambers.
5. If any reservoir chamber is underfilled, look for signs of leakage. Make repairs as necessary. Fill the reservoir chambers with clean, DOT 3 brake fluid until the levels reach the full marks. Install the reservoir cover and diaphragm assembly.
6. If a reservoir chamber is overfilled, correct the fluid level,

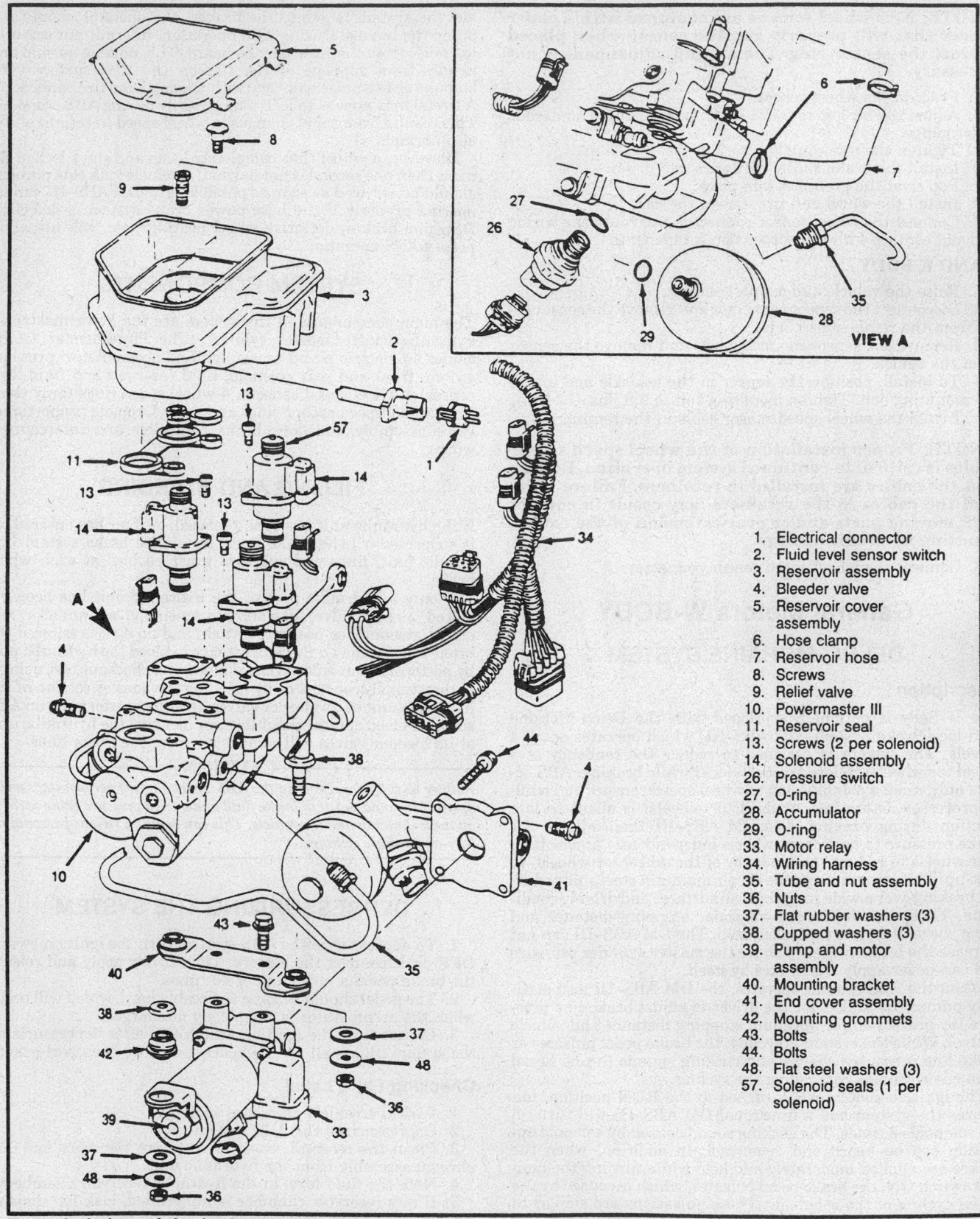

Exploded view of the hydraulic assembly

1. Electrical connector
2. Fluid level sensor switch
3. Reservoir assembly
4. Bleeder valve
5. Reservoir cover assembly
6. Hose clamp
7. Reservoir hose
8. Screws
9. Relief valve
10. Powermaster III
11. Reservoir seal
13. Screws (2 per solenoid)
14. Solenoid assembly
26. Pressure switch
27. O-ring
28. Accumulator
29. O-ring
33. Motor relay
34. Wiring harness
35. Tube and nut assembly
36. Nuts
37. Flat rubber washers (3)
38. Cupped washers (3)
39. Pump and motor assembly
40. Mounting bracket
41. End cover assembly
42. Mounting grommets
43. Bolts
44. Bolts
48. Flat steel washers (3)
57. Solenoid seals (1 per solenoid)

VIEW A

install the cover and diaphragm assembly, turn the ignition switch **ON** and allow the system to pressurize.

7. Again, depressurize the hydraulic unit and check the fluid level.

8. If a reservoir chamber is again overfilled, check the hydraulic system.

Pressure Bleeding

NOTE: The pressure bleeding equipment must be the diaphragm type. It must have a rubber diaphragm between the air supply and the brake fluid to prevent air, moisture and other contaminants from entering the hydraulic system.
Use only DOT 3 brake fluid from a sealed container. Do not use any suspect or contaminated (wet, dirty, etc.) fluid. Do not use DOT 5 silicone fluid.

1. Depressurize the hydraulic unit before pressure bleeding.

NOTE: Make sure the vehicle ignition switch is OFF, unless otherwise noted. This will prevent the hydraulic unit pump from starting during the bleeding procedure.

2. Clean the reservoir cover and diaphragm assembly. Then remove the assembly.

3. Check the fluid level in both the reservoir sections and fill to the correct level using clean brake fluid, if necessary.

4. Install the bleeder adapter J–37115 and secure with attachment cable. Make sure attachment cable does not interfere with access to the bleeder valves on the hydraulic unit.

5. Attach adapter J–37115 to pressure bleed equipment and charge to 5–10 psi (35–70 kPa) for approximately 30 seconds, then slowly increase the pressure to 30–35 psi (205–240 kPa).

6. Bleed the adapter (J–37115).

   a. Connect a clear plastic bleeder line to the adapter bleeder screw and submerge the opposite end in a clean container of partially filled brake fluid.

   b. Slowly open the bleeder valve and allow the fluid to flow until no air is seen in the fluid.

   c. Close the valve when the fluid begins to flow without any air bubbles.

7. Raise the vehicle and support safely.

8. Bleed the wheel brakes in sequence: Right rear, left rear, right front and left front.

   a. Attach the bleeder hose to the bleeder valve and submerge the opposite end in a clean container of partially filled brake fluid.

   b. Slowly open the bleeder valve and allow the fluid to flow until no air is seen in the fluid.

   c. Allow the brake fluid to flow for at least 20–30 seconds at each wheel when checking for entrapped air.

   d. To assist in freeing entrapped air, tap LIGHTLY on the caliper castings with a rubber mallet.

   e. Close the valve when the fluid begins to flow without any air bubbles.

9. Lower the vehicle.

10. Bleed the booster section of the hydraulic unit.

   a. Attach the bleeder hose to the bleeder valve on the inboard side of the hydraulic unit and submerge the opposite end in a clean container of partially filled brake fluid.

   b. Slowly open the bleeder valve and allow the fluid to flow until no air is seen in the fluid.

   c. Allow the brake fluid to flow for at least 20–30 seconds at each wheel when checking for entrapped air.

   d. Close the valve when the fluid begins to flow without any air bubbles.

   e. Repeat the procedure on the outboard side of the bleeder valve.

11. Remove the bleeder adapter J–37115 from the hydraulic unit.

12. Check the fluid level in both the reservoir sections. Using clean brake fluid, fill the reservoirs to the proper level, if necessary.

13. Replace the reservoir cover and snap all 4 cover tabs in place on the reservoir.

14. Bleed the hydraulic unit solenoids. This Step will insure that the brake pedal applies firmly and smoothly.

NOTE: This Step can also be performed using a bidirectional scan tool.

   a. Apply moderate to heavy force on the brake pedal.

   b. With the pedal applied, turn the ignition switch **ON** for 5 seconds, then turn **OFF**. Do this 10 times in succession to cycle the solenoids, but do not start the engine.

15. Depressurize the hydraulic unit and wait 2 minutes for the air to clear from within the reservoir.

16. Bleed the hydraulic unit of air accumulated from the solenoids.

   a. Attach the bleeder hose to the bleeder valve on the inboard side of the hydraulic unit and submerge the opposite end in a clean container of partially filled brake fluid.

   b. With the ignition switch **ON**, apply light force to the brake pedal.

   c. With the pedal applied, slowly open the bleeder valve and allow the fluid to flow until no air is seen in the fluid.

   d. Close the valve when the fluid begins to flow without any air bubbles.

   e. Repeat the procedure on the outboard side of the hydraulic unit.

17. Turn the ignition switch **OFF**, depressurize the hydraulic unit.

18. Remove the reservoir cover and diaphragm assembly.

19. Check the fluid level in both reservoir sections. Using clean brake fluid, fill the reservoirs to their proper level, if necessary.

20. Install the reservoir cover and snap all 4 tabs in place on the reservoir.

21. Turn the ignition switch **ON** and allow the pump motor to run. (Shut the ignition switch **OFF** if the pump motor runs for more than 60 seconds and check the hydraulic system.)

Manual Bleeding

1. Depressurize the hydraulic unit before pressure bleeding.

NOTE: Make sure the vehicle ignition switch is OFF, unless otherwise noted. This will prevent the hydraulic unit pump from starting during the bleeding procedure.

2. Clean the reservoir cover and diaphragm assembly. Then remove the assembly.

3. Check the fluid level in both the reservoir sections and fill to the correct level using clean brake fluid, if necessary.

4. Raise the vehicle and support safely.

5. Bleed the right front wheel brake.

   a. Attach a bleeder hose to the bleeder valve and submerge the opposite end in a clean container partially filled with brake fluid.

   b. Open the bleeder valve.

   c. Slowly depress the brake pedal.

   d. To assist in freeing entrapped air, tap lightly on the caliper castings with a rubber mallet.

   e. Close the valve and release the brake pedal.

   f. Check the fluid level and add new brake fluid, if necessary.

6. Repeat Step 5 until the brake pedal feels firm at half travel and no air bubbles are observed in the bleeder hose.

7. Repeat Steps 5 and 6 on the left front wheel brake.

8. Turn the ignition switch **ON** and allow the pump motor to run. (Shut ignition switch **OFF** if the pump runs for more than 60 seconds and check the hydraulic system.)

9. Bleed the right rear wheel brake.

   a. Attach a bleeder hose to the bleeder valve and submerge

the opposite end in a clean container partially filled with brake fluid.

b. Open the bleeder valve.

c. With the ignition switch **ON**, slowly depress the brake pedal part way, until the brake fluid begins to flow from the bleeder hose. Hold for 15 seconds.

NOTE: Do not fully depress the brake pedal.

d. To assist in freeing entrapped air, tap lightly on the caliper castings with a rubber mallet.

e. Close the valve and release the brake pedal.

f. Repeat these Steps until no air bubbles are observed in the bleeder hose.

g. Check the fluid level and add new brake fluid, if necessary. (Turn the ignition **OFF** and depressurize the hydraulic unit before checking the fluid level.)

10. Repeat Steps 8 and 9 on the left rear wheel brake.

11. Lower the vehicle.

12. Bleed the booster section of the hydraulic unit.

a. Repeat procedure described in Steps 8 and 9 on the inboard bleeder valve of the hydraulic unit.

b. Repeat the procedure on the outboard side of the bleeder valve.

c. Check the fluid level and add new brake fluid, if necessary. (Turn the ignition **OFF** and depressurize the hydraulic unit before checking the fluid level.)

13. Bleed the hydraulic unit solenoids. This Step will insure that the brake pedal applies firmly and smoothly.

NOTE: This Step can also be performed using a bidirectional scan tool.

a. Apply moderate to heavy force on the brake pedal.

b. With the pedal applied, turn the ignition switch **ON** for 5 seconds, then turn **OFF**. Do this 10 times in succession to cycle the solenoids, but do not start the engine.

14. Depressurize the hydraulic unit and wait 2 minutes for the air to clear from within the reservoir.

15. Bleed the hydraulic unit of air accumulated from the solenoids.

a. Attach the bleeder hose to the bleeder valve on the inboard side of the hydraulic unit and submerge the opposite end in a clean container of partially filled brake fluid.

b. With the ignition switch **ON**, apply light force to the brake pedal.

c. With the pedal applied, slowly open the bleeder valve and allow the fluid to flow until no air is seen in the fluid.

d. Close the valve when the fluid begins to flow without any air bubbles.

e. Repeat the procedure on the outboard side of the hydraulic unit.

16. Turn the ignition switch **OFF**, depressurize the hydraulic unit.

17. Remove the reservoir cover and diaphragm assembly.

18. Check the fluid level in both reservoir sections. Using clean brake fluid, fill the reservoirs to their proper level, if necessary.

19. Install the reservoir cover and snap all 4 tabs in place on the reservoir.

20. Turn the ignition switch **ON** and allow the pump motor to run. (Shut the ignition switch **OFF** if the pump motor runs for more than 60 seconds and check the hydraulic system.

Component Replacement

HYDRAULIC UNIT (POWERMASTER III UNIT)

Removal and Installation

NOTE: Do not lift or pull the hydraulic unit using the hydraulic unit wiring harness.

1. Depressurize the hydraulic unit. Disconnect the 3 electrical connectors from the hydraulic unit.

2. Disconnect the 3 brake pipes from the hydraulic unit. Plug the open lines to prevent fluid loss and contamination.

3. Remove the hair pin clip (inside the vehicle) and pushrod from the brake pedal.

4. Remove the 2 attaching nuts from the cowl bracket studs.

5. Remove the hydraulic unit.

NOTE: To avoid damage to the protruding hydraulic unit parts, install unit on J–37116 (or equivalent) holding fixture.

6. To install, lightly lubricate the entire outer surface of the pushrod with silicone grease. Position the hydraulic unit in the vehicle. Guide the pushrod through the grommet. Position the mounting bracket on the cowl bracket studs. Loosely install the attaching nuts. Install the pushrod on the brake pedal mounting pin and install the hair pin clip.

7. Install the 2 attaching nuts. Torque the nuts to 15–25 ft. lbs. (20–34 Nm).

8. Install the 3 brake pipes to the hydraulic unit and torque to 10–15 ft. lbs. (14–20 Nm).

9. Connect the 3 electrical connectors to the hydraulic unit. Make sure all connector position assurance locking pins are installed, if equipped.

10. Adjust the stop light switch.

11. Bleed the hydraulic system.

ACCUMULATOR

Removal and Installation

NOTE: The accumulator is a nitrogen-charged pressure vessel which holds brake fluid under high pressure. It can not be repaired and must be serviced as an assembly.

1. Depressurize the hydraulic unit.

2. Remove the accumulator by turning the hex nut on the end of the accumulator with a 17mm socket. Remove from the vehicle by sliding out from underneath the hydraulic unit, towards the left front wheel well.

3. Remove the O-ring from the accumulator.

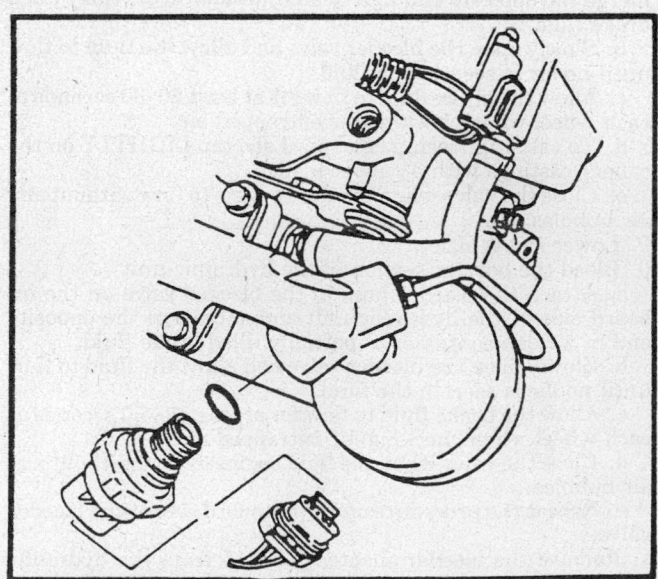

Replacing the pressure switch

4. To install, lightly lubricate and install a new O-ring on the accumulator.

5. Install the accumulator and torque to 23–36 ft. lbs. (31–35 Nm).

6. Bleed the system.

PRESSURE SWITCH

Removal and Installation

1. Depressurize the hydraulic unit.

2. Disconnect the 3 pin electrical connector from the pressure switch.

3. Loosen, but do not completely, remove the attaching nuts from the cowl bracket studs. Pull the hydraulic unit forward.

4. Raise the vehicle and support safely. Using tool J–37117, swivel joint and extensions, remove the switch through the bottom of the engine compartment.

5. Remove the O-ring from the pressure switch.

6. To install, lightly lubricate and install a new O-ring on the pressure switch.

7. Install the pressure switch and torque to 15–20 ft. lbs. (20–27 Nm).

8. Lower the vehicle.

9. Connect the 3 pin electrical connector to the pressure switch. Make sure the connector position assurance locking pin is installed.

10. Tighten the 2 attaching nuts on the cowl bracket studs and torque to 15–25 ft. lbs. (20–34 Nm).

11. Adjust the stop light switch.

12. Bleed the system.

SOLENOID ASSEMBLIES

Removal and Installation

NOTE: Wipe the reservoir cover assembly and surrounding area clean before removing. A clean work area is essential to completing this procedure without damaging the hydraulic unit.

1. Depressurize the hydraulic unit.

2. Remove the reservoir cover assembly and reservoir assembly.

3. Disconnect the 3 pin electrical connector from the solenoid assembly.

4. Remove the screws attaching the solenoid assembly.

5. Remove the solenoid assembly. Make sure both lower solenoid O-rings (2 per solenoid) are removed from the hydraulic unit.

6. To install, place the solenoid assembly into position. Make sure the lower solenoid O-rings are in place and in good condition before installing a solenoid assembly.

7. Install the screws attaching the solenoid assembly and torque to 33–45 inch lbs. (4–5 Nm).

8. Connect the electrical connector to the solenoid assembly. Make sure all connector position assurance locking pins are installed.

9. Install the reservoir cover and reservoir assembly.

10. Adjust the stop light switch.

11. Bleed brake system.

FRONT WHEEL SPEED SENSORS

Removal and Installation

1. Raise the vehicle and support safely.

2. Disconnect the sensor connector from the wiring harness.

3. Remove the 2 front wheel speed sensor bolts. Remove 1 connector bracket bolt.

4. Remove the front wheel speed sensor.

5. To install, position the front wheel speed sensor into place.

6. Install the sensor retaining bolts. Torque the 15mm bolts to 52–65 ft. lbs. (70–90 Nm). Torque the 10mm connector bracket bolt to 6–9 ft. lbs. (8–12 Nm).

7. Connect the sensor connector to the wiring harness. Install the connector position assurance locking pin.

8. If necessary, route the wire to avoid unwanted contact with the suspension components.

9. Lower the vehicle.

REAR WHEEL SPEED SENSORS

Removal and Installation

The rear wheel speed sensors are integral with the hub and bearing assemblies. Should a speed sensor require replacement, the entire hub and bearing assembly must be replaced.

WHEEL SPEED SENSOR RINGS

Removal and Installation

The front wheel speed sensor rings are integral with the outer CV-joint housing. Should a front wheel speed sensor ring require replacement, the entire CV-joint must be replaced.

The rear wheel speed sensors rings are integral with the hub and bearing assemblies. Should a ring require replacement, the entire hub and bearing assembly must be replaced.

Chevrolet Corvette

GENERAL MOTORS/BOSCH SYSTEM

Description

The purpose of the Corvette anti-lock brake system is to maintain vehicle steerability, directional stability and optimum deceleration under severe braking conditions on most road surfaces. The anti-lock brake system performs this function by monitoring the rotational speed of each wheel and controlling the brake line pressure to each wheel during a braking maneuver to prevent the wheel from locking up.

When the ignition is switched to the on position, the amber ANTILOCK warning light in the instrument panel lights. When the engine is started it goes out similar to the battery charge warning light. If the anti-lock brake system warning light does not go out or illuminates permanently while driving, it indicates a problem with the anti-lock brake system.

Upon starting the vehicle, the control module performs a functional check of the electrical circuitry (Self-Test). The test cycle itself checks the components of the monitoring circuit as well as the logic section. For this reason the control module is fed with given test sample signals to check if the correct output signals are available.

Since the anti-lock brake system may not be used everyday, there is an additional test which actually runs the modulator valve. This check is done to insure that the system is functioning correctly. Each time the ignition is first turned on and the vehicle reaches 4 mph, the test begins. This can be heard and, if the driver's foot is on the brake pedal, it can be felt.

The electronic control module monitors its own supply voltage. If the supply voltage drops below a specified value, the anti-lock brake system will be shut off and the amber ANTILOCK warning light comes on. When the supply voltage returns to or exceeds the specified minimum value, the light will go off. If a problem occurs with the anti-lock brake system, the ANTILOCK light will come on and the system will be shut off. The system will remain off until the car is restarted at which time the functional (self-test) check is repeated.

NOTE: During a problem with the anti-lock brake system, the conventional system remains fully operational providing it is not faulty.

System Components

MODULATOR VALVE

The modulator valve consists of 3 rapidly switching solenoid valves, 2 accumulator chambers, (one for each brake circuit) and the return pump. One solenoid valve is assigned to each of the front wheel brakes. The third solenoid valve is assigned to the rear brakes. This design is known as a three-channel system. The modulator valve receives its instructions from the control module.

Independent of the pressure in the tandem master cylinder, the modulator valve can maintain or reduce the brake hydraulic pressure to the brake calipers during regulation. The modulator valve cannot increase the pressure above that transmitted to the master cylinder, nor can it apply the brakes by itself.

Two replaceable relays are mounted on the top of the modulator valve. One controls the return pump and the other controls the power supply to the solenoid valves. The modulator valve is mounted in the rear storage compartment located behind the driver's seat.

NOTE: The modulator valve cannot be repaired. Only the relays may be replaced. If a problem occurs in the modulator valve, it must be replaced as an assembly.

ELECTRONIC BRAKE CONTROL MODULE

The EBCM is constructed of 2 circuit boards. Components such as resistors, diodes, transistors and large integrated circuits are mounted on the boards. These intergrated circuits contain thousands of transistors, resistors and diodes mounted on a single silicon (IC) chip. The circuit boards are housed in the control module and are surrounded by a light alloy case.

Wheel acceleration, deceleration and slip values are calculated from the electronic signals generated by the wheel speed sensors, which are proportional to the speed of the tire/wheel. The control module calculates these values and produces control commands for the electro-mechanically controlled hydraulic modulator valves.

The control module is located in the rear storage compartment behind the driver's seat.

NOTE: The control module cannot be repaired. If a problem occurs in the control module, it must be replaced as an assembly.

LATERAL ACCELERATION SWITCH

The lateral acceleration switch is basically 2 mercury switches connected in series. It is used to detect if the vehicle is traveling faster than a given cornering speed. When this speed is exceeded, 1 of the 2 mercury switches opens up and sends a signal to the control module.

The lateral acceleration switch is located underneath the A/C control head on the floorpan.

NOTE: The lateral acceleration switch cannot be repaired and can only be tested using the ABS TESTER. If a problem occurs in the switch it must be replaced.

WHEEL SPEED SENSORS

The rotational speed of the wheels is detected by the inductive wheel speed sensors, one at each wheel and the resulting electric signal is passed on to the control module. In a system of this type with 4 wheel speed sensors, the rotational speed of each wheel is measure individually.

On the 3-channel system, the front wheels are controlled individually and the rear wheels together. The control of the rear wheels works on the Select Low principle. Select Low means that the tire with the lower tire to road co-efficient, (i.e., the greater tendency to lock) determines the level of control.

The wheel speed sensors are mounted in the knuckles. The toothed rings are pressed into the front hub and bearing assemblies and the rear halfshaft spindles.

NOTE: The Wheel Speed Sensors cannot be repaired or adjusted. If a problem occurs in the sensor it must be replaced.

CIRCUIT PROTECTION

A fuse located in the main fuse block, labeled BRAKE, provides protection for the main power feed circuit of the ABS electrical

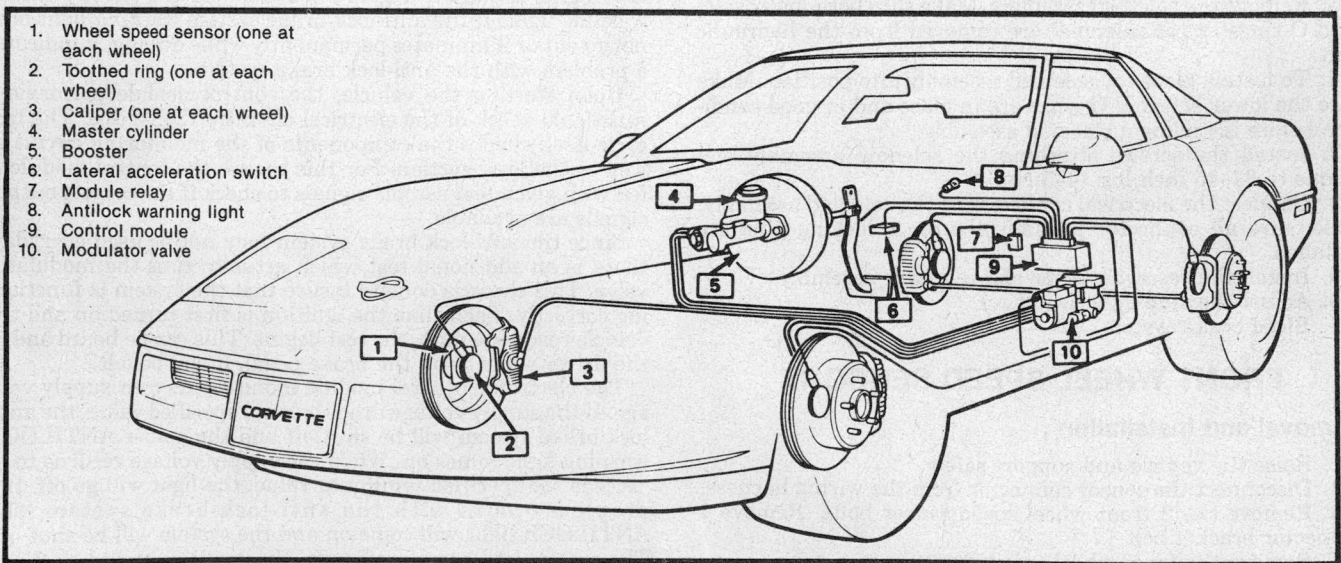

1. Wheel speed sensor (one at each wheel)
2. Toothed ring (one at each wheel)
3. Caliper (one at each wheel)
4. Master cylinder
5. Booster
6. Lateral acceleration switch
7. Module relay
8. Antilock warning light
9. Control module
10. Modulator valve

Corvette antilock brake system

system. The GAUGE fuse is also tied into the main power feed to the anti-lock brake system.

FILLING AND BLEEDING

NOTE: It may be necessary to bleed the hydraulic system at all 4 wheels if air has been introduced through a low fluid level or by disconnecting brake pipes at the master cylinder. If a brake pipe is disconnected at any wheel, then only the wheel needs bleeding. If pipes are disconnected at any fitting location between the master cylinder and wheel, then all the wheels served by the disconnected pipe must be bled.

When bleeding the rear brake system, the front of the car should be raised higher than the rear. This will position the bleeder valve near the 12 O'CLOCK position and will prevent air from being trapped in the caliper.

Manual Bleeding

NOTE: Deplete the vacuum reserve by applying the brakes several times.

1. Fill the master cylinder with brake fluid and keep at least ½ full of fluid during the bleeding operation. Bleed the brakes in the following sequence:
   Left rear
   Right rear
   Left front
   Right front
2. With the proper size box end wrench over the bleeder valve, attach the bleeder tube to the valve. Allow the tube to hang submerged in the brake fluid in a clean glass container.
3. Open the bleeder valve and fully depress the brake pedal.
4. Close the bleeder valve and release the brake pedal.
5. Repeat Steps 3 and 4 until all the air is evacuated. Check the refill master cylinder reservoir as required to prevent air from being drawn through the master cylinder.
6. Repeat the bleeding procedure at all wheels if the entire system is to be bled.
7. Check the brake pedal feel for sponginess and repeat the entire bleeding procedure, if necessary.

Pressure Bleeding

NOTE: Pressure bleeding equipment must be of the diaphragm type. It must have a rubber diaphragm between the air supply and the brake fluid to prevent air, moisture, oil and other contaminants from entering the hydraulic system

1. Install the correct bleeding adapter to the master cylinder, Tool J–35690 or equivalent.
2. Make sure the pressure tank is at least ⅓ full of Supreme No. 11 brake fluid or its equivalent. The bleeder ball must be re-bled each time fluid is added.
3. Charge the bleeder ball to between 20–25 psi (140–175 kPa).
4. When ready to begin bleeding, connect the hose to the master cylinder bleeder adapter and open the tank valve.
5. Bleed the brakes in the following sequence:
   Left rear
   Right rear
   Left front
   Right front

NOTE: Stroke the brake pedal while pressure bleeding.

6. With the proper size wrench over the bleeder valve, attach the bleeder tube. The discharge end must hang submerged in a clean container partially filled with brake fluid.

7. Open the bleeder valve at least ¾ turn and allow flow to continue until no air is seen in the fluid.
8. Close the bleed valve; be sure it seals.
9. Repeat Steps 6–8 for the remaining bleeder valves.
10. Check the pedal feel for sponginess and repeat the entire procedure, if necessary.
11. Dispose of all removed brake fluid.
12. Disconnect the bleeder equipment from the brake bleeder adapter.
13. Remove the bleeder adapter. Wipe all areas dry if fluid was spilled during adapter removal.
14. Fill the master cylinder reservoir to the proper level and install the master cylinder diaphragm and cover.

Component Replacement

MODULATOR VALVE

Removal and Installation

1. Disconnect the negative battery cable.
2. Remove the storage tray and insulation.
3. Disconnect and remove the entire ABS wiring harness from the storage compartment.
4. Disconnect the modulator valve ground from the body harness.
5. Label, then disconnect the 5 brake lines from the modulator valve.
6. Loosen the 3 nuts holding the modulator valve to the bracket.

NOTE: When removing the modulator valve from the storage compartment, protect the interior from possible damage caused by the spillage of brake fluid.

7. Remove the modulator valve from the storage compartment.
8. Wipe any brake fluid from the bottom of the storage compartment.
9. To install, transfer the ground wire and the insulators to the new modulator valve.
10. Install the modulator valve to the bracket and tighten the nuts to 7 ft. lbs. (9.5 Nm).
11. Remove the shipping caps from the modulator valve and connect the brake lines to their correct positions. Tighten the brake lines to 13 ft. lbs. (17.6 Nm).
12. Connect the modulator valve ground wire.
13. Install the ABS wiring harness.

NOTE: When installing the wiring harness, be certain that all the connectors are securely connected.

14. Connect the negative battery cable.
15. Bleed the brake system.
16. Install the insulation and the storage tray.

ELECTRONIC CONTROL MODULE

Removal and Installation

1. Disconnect the negative battery cable.
2. Remove the storage tray and insulation.
3. Disconnect the electronic control module connector by depressing the spring clip located under the neck of the connector.
4. Remove the module relay from the electronic control module.
5. Remove the 2 electronic control module mounting bolts.
6. Remove the control module.
7. To install, reverse the removal procedure.

NOTE: The electronic control module must be installed correctly to insure the wiring harness connector comes in from the correct side. The electronic control module connector must be securely connected.

LATERAL ACCELERATION SWITCH

Removal and Installation

1. Disconnect the negative battery cable.
2. Remove the screws retaining the instrument cluster trim plate.
3. Remove the screw retaining the instrument panel accessory trim plate and then remove the trim plate.
4. Remove the screws retaining the console trim plate.
5. Rotate the trim plate and disconnect the lighter.
6. Remove the A/C control head.
7. Remove the lateral acceleration switch mounting bolts.
8. Disconnect the wiring harness and remove the switch.
9. To install, reverse the removal procedure.

WHEEL SPEED SENSORS

Removal and Installation

1. Raise the vehicle and support safely.
2. Remove the wheel and tire assembly.
3. Unclip the sensor connector from the bracket and disconnect it.
4. Remove the sensor wire grommets from the brackets, take note of the sensor wire routing for installation.
5. Remove the sensor hold down bolt(s) from the knuckle and remove the sensor.
6. To install, coat the new wheel speed sensor with anti-corrosion compound prior to installation.
7. Install the sensor into the knuckle.

NOTE: Do not hammer the sensor into the knuckle.

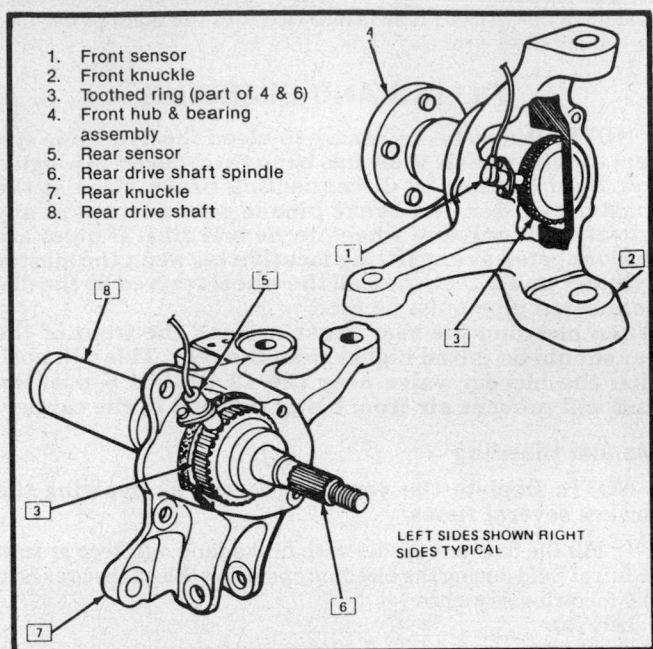

1. Front sensor
2. Front knuckle
3. Toothed ring (part of 4 & 6)
4. Front hub & bearing assembly
5. Rear sensor
6. Rear drive shaft spindle
7. Rear knuckle
8. Rear drive shaft

LEFT SIDES SHOWN RIGHT SIDES TYPICAL

Wheel speed sensor mounting

8. Install the sensor hold down bolt(s) and tighten to 27 inch lbs. (3 Nm).
9. Install the sensor wire grommets to the brackets and route the sensor wire as noted during Step 4.
10. Connect the sensor connector and clip into the bracket.
11. Install the wheel and tire assembly.
12. Lower the vehicle.

CARBURETOR APPLICATION CHART AND INDEX

The carburetor manufacturer, model and identification numbers which are listed in the specifications chart, appear either on a tag on the carburetor or stamped on the carburetor body.

Car Manufacturer	Year	Carburetor Manufacturer	Carburetor Model	Page Numbers	
				Adjustments	Specifications
American Motors	1986	Carter	YF, YFA	26-2	26-4
	1986	Rochester	2SE, E2SE	26-3	26-3
Chrysler Corp.	1986–89	Holley	2280, 6280	26-13	26-15
	1986–88	Holley	5220	26-15	26-18
	1986–88	Holley	6520	26-15	26-18
	1986–88	Rochester	Quadrajet	26-19	26-31
Ford Motor Co.	1986	Carter	YF, YFA, YFA-FB	26-2	26-4
	1986	Motorcraft	740	26-4	26-7
	1986–89	Motorcraft	7200VV	26-6	26-9
	1986–87	Holley	1949	26-9	26-13
	1986–89	Aisan (Festiva)	NA	26-40	26-40
General Motors	1986	Holley	6510C	26-17	26-19
	1986–87	Holley	5210C	26-14	26-16
	1986–89	Rochester	Angle Degree to Decimal Conversion		26-20
	1986	Rochester	2SE, E2SE	26-20	26-23
	1986–87	Rochester	M2ME, E2ME, E2MC	26-22	26-27
	1986–89	Rochester	Quadrajet	26-19	26-31
	1986–89	Nippon Kikaki (Spectrum)	NA	26-33	26-33
	1986–88	Hitachi (Sprint)	MR08	26-36	26-36
	1986–88	Aisan (Nova)	NA	26-38	26-38

NOTE: New model carburetor part numbers and specifications are not released by the manufacturers until well after the press date for this manual. These will be included in the next edition. New model carburetor part numbers are obtained from the most current factory sources, however, carburetors which are new or redesigned by the manufacturer during the production year and designated with new part numbers may not appear.
NA Not available

CARTER CARBURETORS

Model YF and YFA

The YF and YFA carburetors are single barrel downdraft carburetors with a diaphragm type accelerator pump and diaphragm operated metering rods.

FLOAT LEVEL

Adjustment

1. Invert the air horn assembly and check the clearance from the top of the float to the surface of the air horn with a T-scale. The air horn should be held at eye level when gauging and the float arm should be resting on the needle pin.
2. Do not exert pressure on the needle valve when measuring or adjusting the float. Bend the float arm as necessary to adjust the float level.

NOTE: Do not bend the tab at the end of the float arm as it prevents the float from striking the bottom of the fuel bowl when empty and keeps the needle in place.

METERING ROD

Adjustment

1. Remove the air horn. Back out the idle speed adjusting screw until the throttle plate is seated fully in its bore.
2. Press down on the upper end of the diaphragm shaft until the diaphragm bottoms in the vacuum chamber.
3. The metering rod should contact the bottom of the metering rod well. The lifter link at the outer end nearest the springs and at the supporting link should be bottomed.
4. On carburetors not equipped with an adjusting screw, adjust by bending the lip of the metering rod is attached.
5. On models with an adjusting screw, turn the screw until

the metering rod just bottoms in the body casting. For final adjustment, turn the screw an additional turn clockwise.

FAST IDLE CAM

Adjustment

1. Put the fast idle screw on the second highest step of the fast idle cam against the shoulder of the high step.
2. Adjust by bending the choke plate connecting rod to obtain the specified clearance between the lower edge of the choke plate and the air horn wall.

CHOKE UNLOADER

Adjustment

1. Hold the throttle valve wide open and hold the choke valve in the closed position.

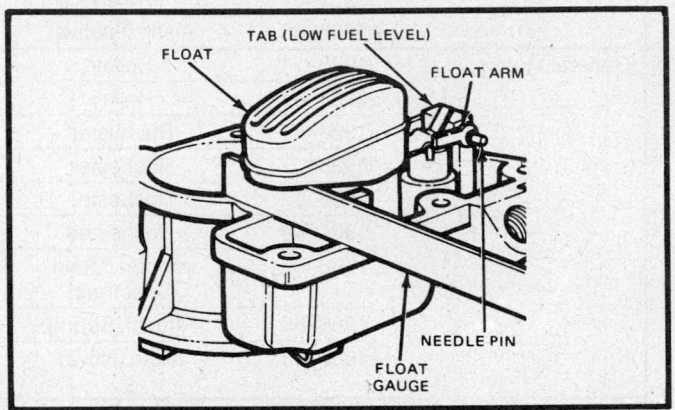

YFA float level adjustment

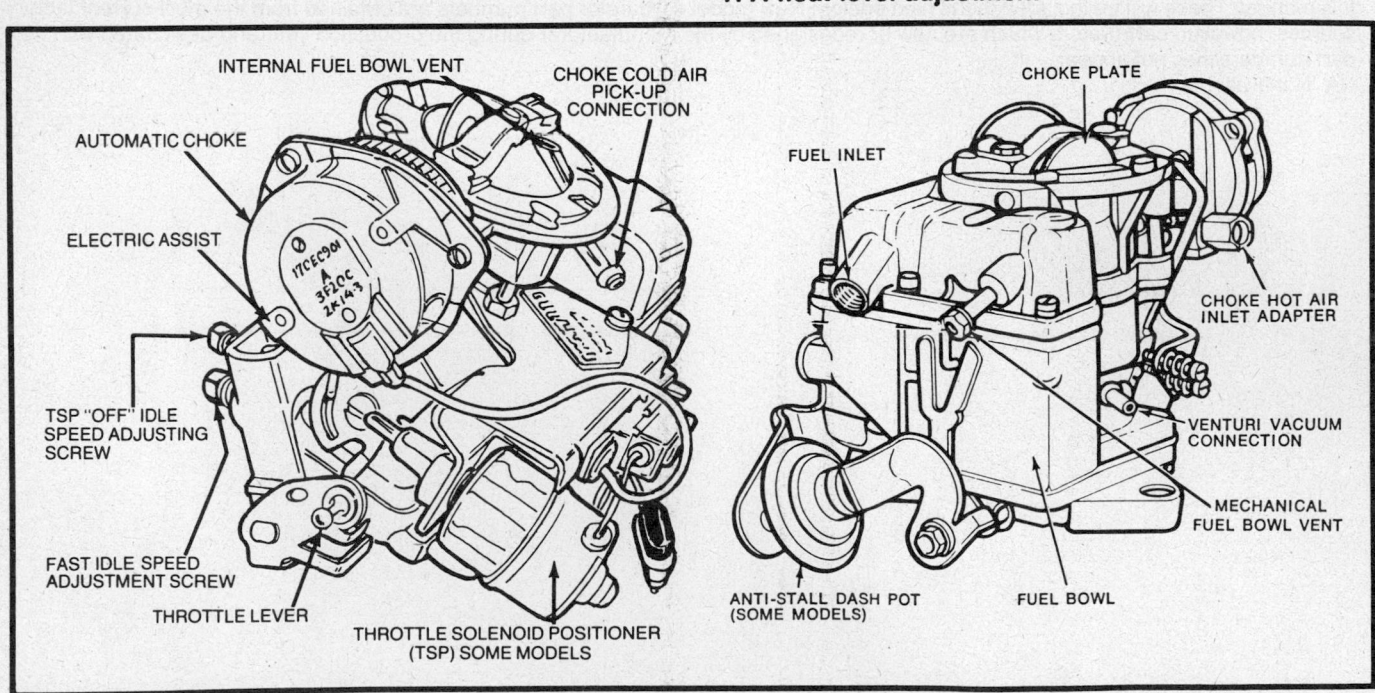

Carter YFA carburetor—typical

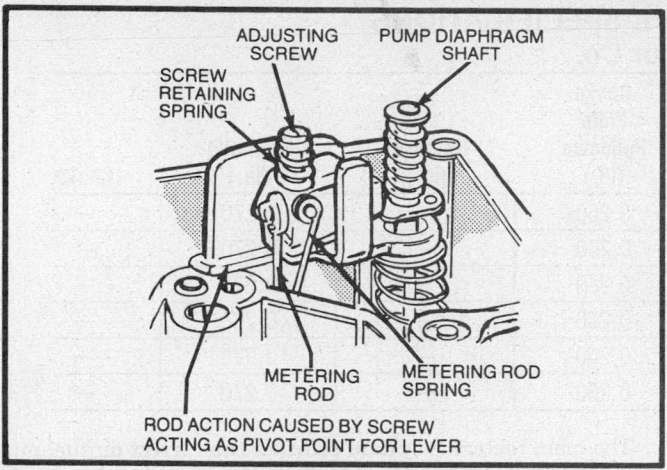

YFA metering rod adjustment

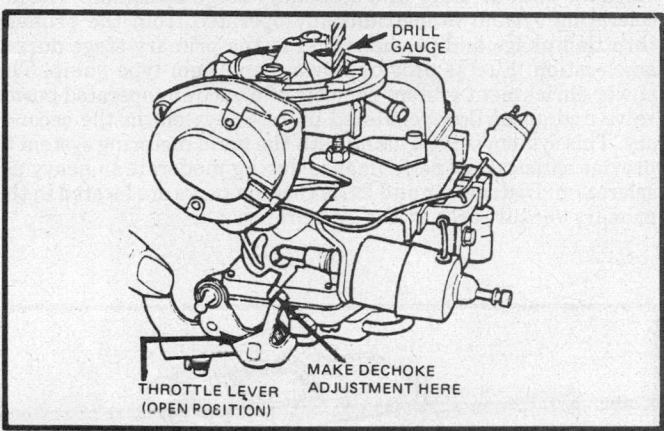

YFA choke unloader adjustment

2. Bend the unloader tang on the throttle lever to obtain the specified clearance between the lower edge of/the choke valve and the air horn wall.

AUTOMATIC CHOKE

Adjustment

1. Loosen the choke cover retaining screws.
2. Turn the choke cover so that the index mark on the cover lines up with the specified mark on the choke housing.

CHOKE PLATE

Adjustment

DIAPHRAGM TYPE CHOKE

1. Activate the pulldown motor by applying an external vacuum source.
2. Close the choke plate as far as possible without forcing it.
3. Using a drill of the specified size, measure the clearance between the lower edge of the choke plate and the air horn wall.
4. If adjustment is necessary bend the choke diaphragm link as required.

CHOKER PLATE CLEARANCE (DECHOKE)

Adjustment

1. Remove the air cleaner assembly.
2. Hold the throttle plate fully open and close the choke plate

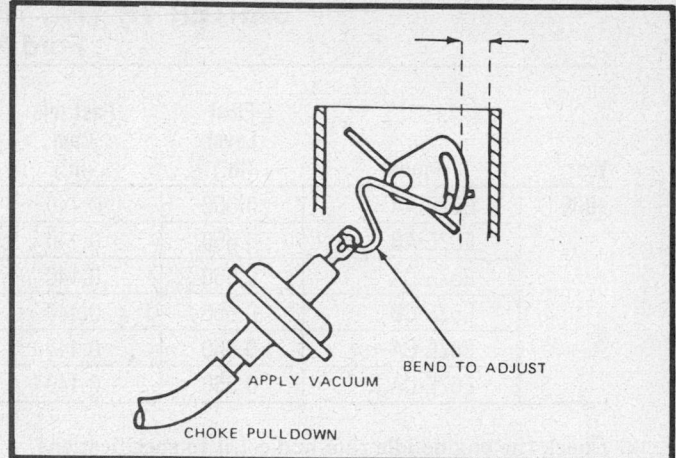

Choke plate pulldown—diaphragm type choke—FYA

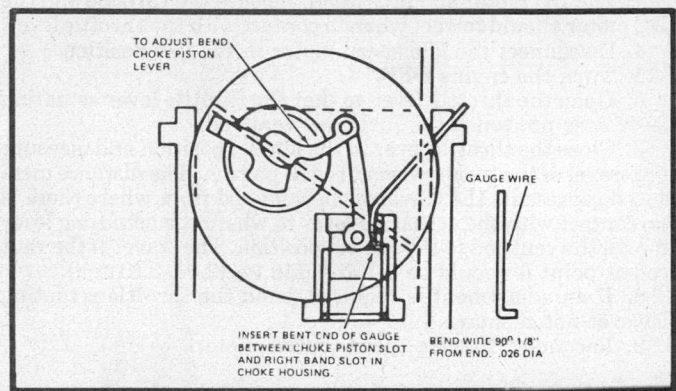

Choke plate pulldown—piston type choke—YFA

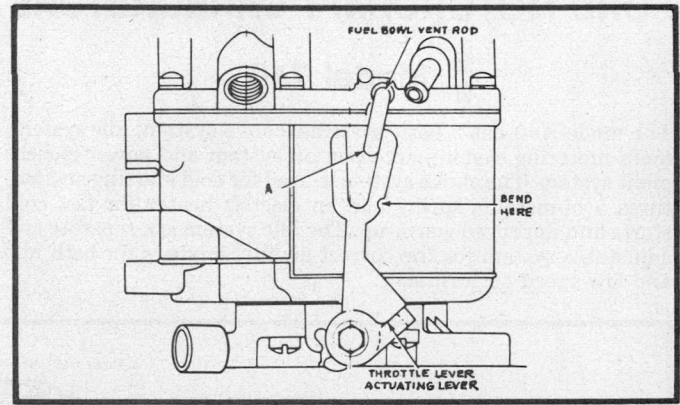

Mechanical fuel bowl vent adjustment—YFA

as far as possible without forcing it. Use a drill of the proper diameter to check the clearance between the choke plate and air horn.
3. If the clearance is not within specification, adjust the clearance by bending the arm on the choke lever of the throttle lever. Bending the arm downward will decrease the clearance and bending it upward will increase the clearance. Always recheck the clearance after making any adjustment.

MECHANICAL FUEL BOWL VENT

Adjustment

1. Start the engine and wait until it has reached normal operating temperature before proceeding.

CARTER YF, YFA, YFA-FB SPECIFICATIONS
Ford Motor Co.

Year	Model	Float Level (in.)	Fast Idle Cam (in.)	Choke Plate Pulldown (in.)	Unloader (in.)	Dechoke (in.)	Choke
1986	E5ZE-AA	0.650	0.140	0.260	—	0.270	—
	E5ZE-AB	0.650	0.140	0.260	—	0.270	—
	E5ZE-CA	0.650	0.140	0.260	—	0.270	—
	E5ZE-CB	0.650	0.140	0.260	—	0.270	—
	E6ZE-EA	0.650	0.140	0.260	—	0.270	—
	E6ZE-DA	0.650	0.140	0.260	—	0.270	—

2. Check the engine idle rpm and set it to specifications.

3. Check the DC motor operation by opening the throttle off idle. The DC motor should extend. Release the throttle and the DC motor should retract when in contact with the throttle lever.

4. Disconnect the idle speed motor in the idle position.

5. Turn the engine OFF.

6. Open the throttle lever so that the throttle lever actuating lever does not touch the fuel bowl vent rod.

7. Close the throttle lever to the idle set position and measure the travel of the fuel bowl vent rod at point A. The distance measured represents the travel of the vent rod from where there is no contact with the actuating lever to where the actuating lever moves the vent rod to the idle set position. The travel of the vent rod at point A should be 0.100–0.150 in. (2.54–3.81mm).

8. If an adjustment is required, bend the throttle actuating lever at notch shown.

9. Reconnect the idle speed control motor.

FORD MOTORCRAFT CARBURETORS

Model 740

The model 740 has 5 basic systems: choke system, idle system, main metering system, acceleration system and power enrichment system. The choke system is used for cold starting and features a bi-metallic spring and an electric heater for fast cold starts and improved warm-up. The idle system is a separate and adjustable system for the correct air/fuel mixture for both idle and low speed performance.

The main metering system provides the correct air/fuel mixture for normal cruising speeds. A main metering system is provided for both primary and secondary stage operation. The accelerating system is mechanically operated from the primary throttle linkage and provides fuel to the primary stage during acceleration. Fuel is provided by a diaphragm-type pump. The power enrichment system consists of a vacuum operated power valve and an airflow-regulated pullover system in the secondary. This system is used along with the main metering system to provide satisfactory performance during moderate to heavy acceleration. Distributor and EGR vacuum ports are located in the primary venturi area of the carburetor.

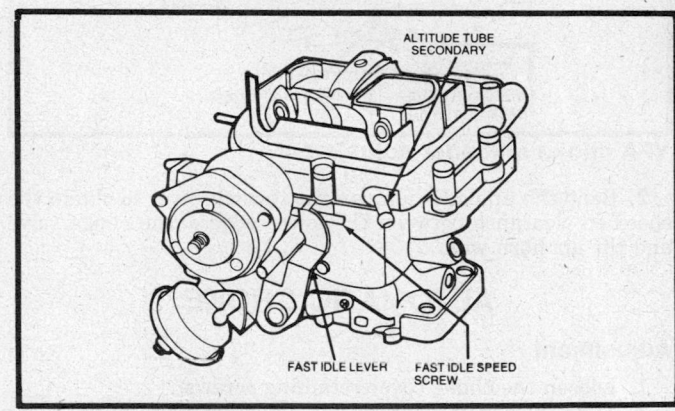

Model 740 carburetor — 3/4 front view

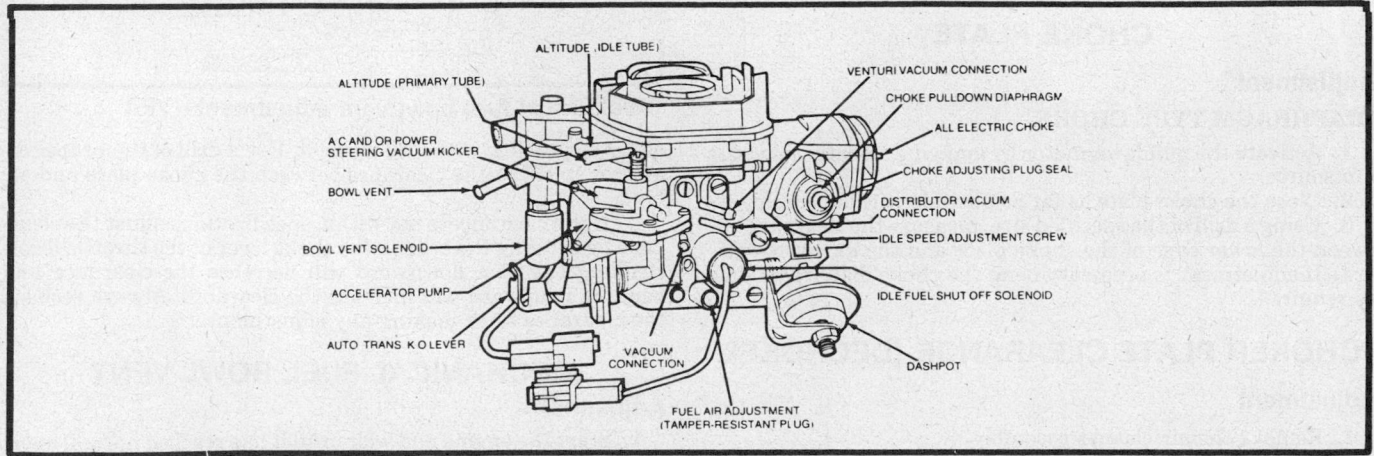

Model 740 carburetor — full rear

FAST IDLE CAM

Adjustment

1. Set the fast idle screw on the kickdown step of the cam against the shoulder of the top step.
2. Manually close the primary choke plate and measure the distance between the downstream side of the choke plate and the air horn wall.
3. Adjust the right fork of the choke bimetal shaft, which engages the fast idle cam, by bending the fork up and down to obtain the specified clearance.

FAST IDLE

Adjustment

1. Place the transmission in **N** or **P**.
2. Bring the engine to normal operating temperature.
3. Disconnect and plug the vacuum hose at the EGR and purge valves.
4. Identify the vacuum source to the air bypass section of the air supply control valve. If a vacuum hose is connected to the carburetor, disconnect the hose and plug the hose at the air supply control valve.
5. Place the fast idle adjustment on the second step of the fast idle cam. Run the engine until the cooling fan comes on.
6. While the cooling fan is on, check the fast idle rpm. If an adjustment is necessary, loosen the locknut and adjust to the idle to the specification on the underhood decal.
7. Remove all plugs and reconnect the hoses to their original position.

DASHPOT

Adjustment

With the throttle set at the curb idle position, fully depress the dashpot stem and measure the distance between the stem and the throttle lever. Adjust by loosening the locknut and turning the dashpot.

CHOKE PLATE PULLDOWN

Adjustment

NOTE: The following procedure requires the removal of the carburetor and also the choke cap which is retained by rivets.

1. Remove the carburetor air cleaner.
2. Remove the choke cap as follows:
   a. Check the rivets to determine if mandrel is well below the rivet head. If mandrel is within the rivet head thickness, drive it down or out with a $1/16$ in. diameter tip punch.
   b. With a $1/8$ in. diameter drill, drill into the rivet head until the rivet head comes loose from the rivet body. Use light pressure on the drill bit or the rivet will just spin in the hole.
   c. After drilling off the rivet head, drive the remaining rivet out of the hole with a $1/8$ in. diameter punch.
3. Connect an external vacuum source to the vacuum tube on the choke pulldown cover.
4. Set the fast idle adjusting screw on the high step of the fast idle cam by temporarily opening the throttle lever and rotating the choke bimetal shaft lever counterclockwise until the choke plates are in the fully closed position.
5. While applying the external vacuum, lightly force the choke thermostat actuating lever counterclockwise.
6. Using the drill diameter specified in the carburetor specifications table at the end of this section, measure the clearance between the down-stream side of the choke plate and the air horn wall.

7. If an adjustment is necessary, turn the vacuum diaphragm adjusting screw in or out as required.

NOTE: The choke pulldown adjustment screw is sealed with a limiting plug.

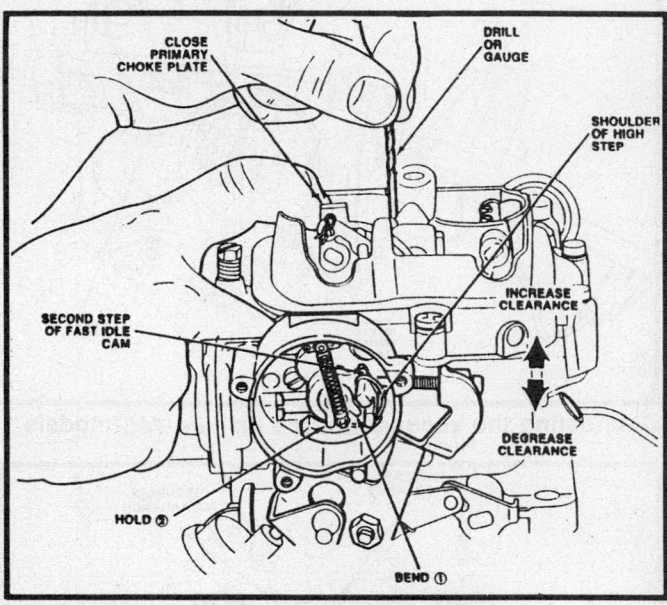

Fast idle cam adjustment—model 740

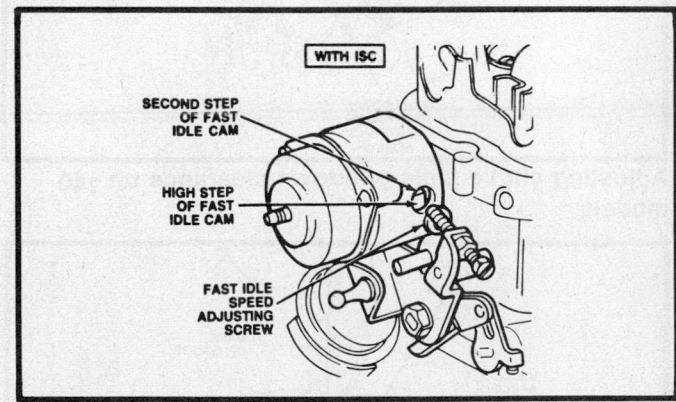

Fast idle speed adjusting screw and fast idle cam—model 740

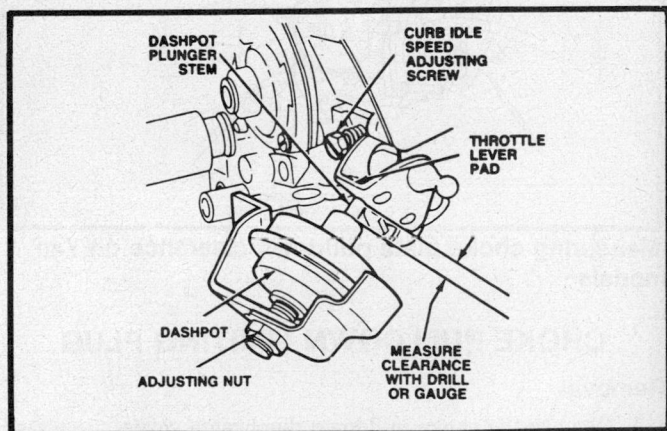

Dashpot assembly—model 740

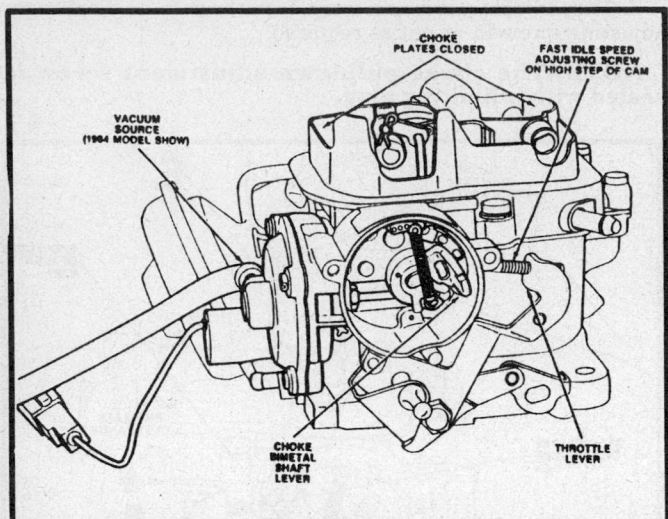

Connecting the vacuum source on late 740 models

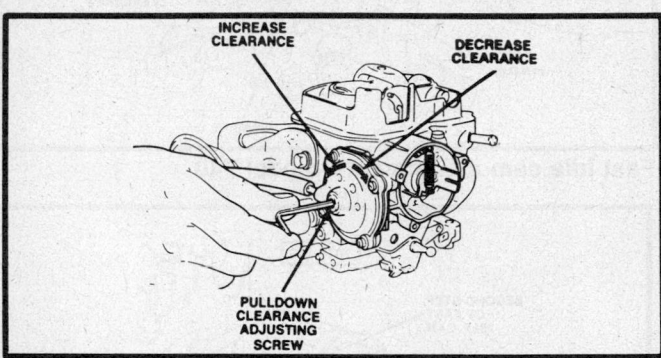

Adjusting choke plate pulldown clearance on 740 models

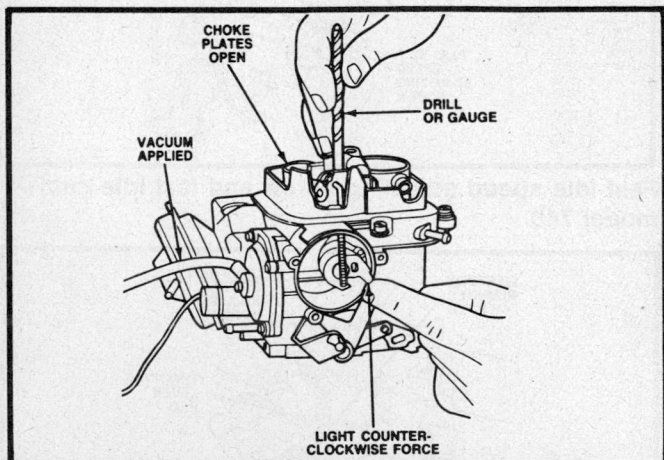

Measuring choke plate pulldown clearance on 740 models

CHOKE PULLDOWN LIMITING PLUG

Removal

1. Remove the choke pulldown diaphragm cover.
2. Using pliers, grasp the back of the adjustment screw and turn it out of the cover.

3. Drive the plugs out of the cover, using a punch and a hammer.

— CAUTION —

Always wear eye protection when driving out plugs.

DRY FLOAT LEVEL

Adjustment

1. Place the air horn assembly upside down and at a 45 degree angle with the air horn gasket in place. The float tang should rest lightly on the inlet needle.
2. Measure the clearance with a suitable gauge at the extreme end or toe of the float.
3. Remove the float and adjust to specification by bending the float level adjusting tang up or down.

NOTE: Care must be taken not to scratch or damage the float tang while adjusting.

FLOAT DROP

Adjustment

1. Suspend the air horn assembly in the normal position with the air horn gasket in position.
2. The distance from the air horn gasket to the bottom of the float should be 1.690 ± 0.310 in. (43 ± 8mm).
3. Remove the float and adjust to specification by bending the float drop tang.

WIDE OPEN THROTTLE (WOT) AIR CONDITIONING CUT-OUT SWITCH

Adjustment

A visual inspection is required to ensure adequate pin and actuating arm overlap with the carburetor linkage in the WOT position.

Adjustments to the switch position are made by bending it's support bracket outboard. A 0.120 in. (3mm) minimum overlap is desired. Precaution is required to ensure adequate clearance between the tip of the carburetor fast idle lever and switch housing.

Model 7200 VV

Since the design of the 7200 VV (variable venturi) carburetor differs considerably from the other carburetors in the Ford line-up, an explanation in the theory and operation is presented here.

In exterior appearance, the variable venturi carburetor is sim-

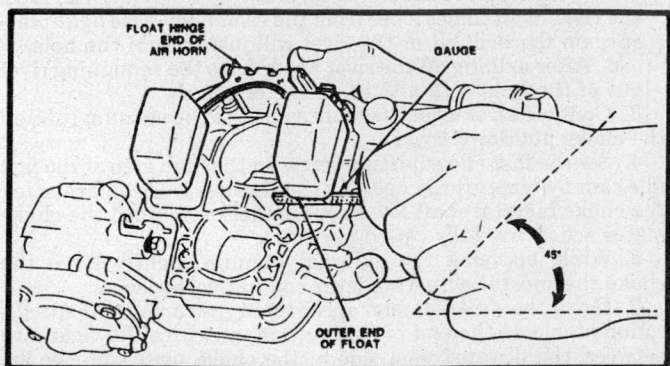

Measuring float clearance—Model 740

MOTORCRAFT MODEL 740 SPECIFICATIONS
Escort, Lynx, Exp, Lynx

Year	Carburetor Identification	Dry Float Level (in.)	Choke Plate Pulldown (in.)	Fast Idle Cam Linkage (in.)	Fast Idle (rpm)	Dechoke (in.)	Choke Setting	Dashpot (in.)
1986	E5GE-AAA	0.300	0.300	0.110	①	0.140	NA	0.060
	E5GE-ADA	0.300	0.300	0.100	①	0.140	NA	0.020
	E5GE-ACA	0.300	0.300	0.100	①	0.140	NA	0.020
	E5GE-AEC	0.300	0.280	0.080	①	0.140	NA	0.080
	E5GE-AFC	0.300	0.280	0.080	①	0.140	NA	0.060

NA—Not available
① See underhood decal.

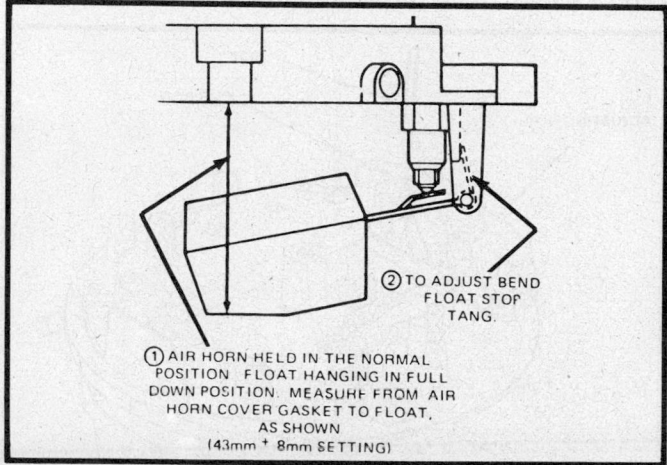

Float drop adjustment—Model 740

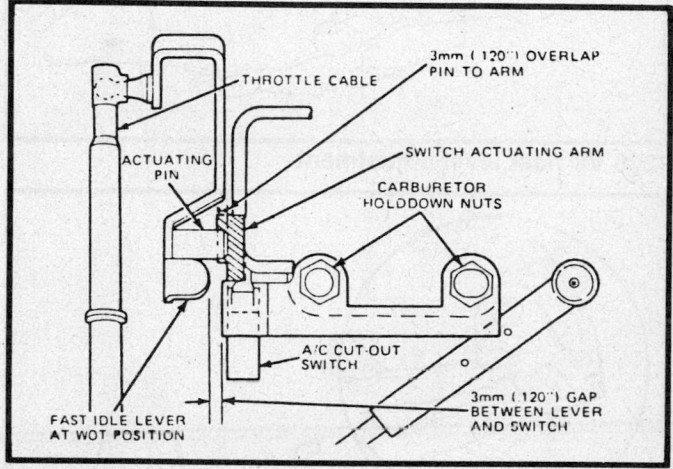

(WOT) A/C cut-off switch adjustment—Model 740

ilar to conventional carburetors and like a conventional carburetor, it uses a normal float and fuel bowl system. However, the similarity ends there. In place of a normal choke plate and fixed area venturis, the 7200 VV carburetor has a pair of small oblong castings in the top of the upper carburetor body where the choke plate would normally be located. These castings slide back and forth across the top of the carburetor in response to air/fuel demands. Their movement is controlled by a spring-loaded diaphragm valve regulated by a vacuum signal taken below the venturis in the throttle bores. As the throttle is opened, the strength of the vacuum signal increases, opening the venturis and allowing more air to enter the carburetor.

Fuel is admitted into the venturi area by means of tapered metering rods that fit into the main jets. These rods are attached to the venturis and the venturis open or close in response to air demand. The fuel needed to maintain the proper mixture increases or decreases as the metering rods slide in the jets. In comparison to a conventional carburetor with fixed venturis and a variable air supply, this system provides much more precise control of the fuel/air supply during all modes of operation. Because of the variable venturi principle, there are fewer fuel metering systems and fuel passages. The only auxiliary fuel metering systems required are an idle trim, accelerator pump (similar to a conventional carburetor), starting enrichment and cold running enrichment.

NOTE: Adjustment, assembly and disassembly of this carburetor require special tools for some of the operations. Do not attempt any operations on this carburetor without first obtaining special tools needed for that particular operation. Special tools needed for the following adjusments are identified in the procedure.

FLOAT LEVEL

Adjustment

1. Remove and invert the upper part of the carburetor, with the gasket in place.
2. Measure the vertical distance between the carburetor body, outside the gasket and the bottom of the float.
3. To adjust, bend the float operating lever that contacts the needle valve. Make sure that the float remains parallel to the gasket surface.

FLOAT DROP

Adjustment

1. Remove and hold the upper part of the carburetor upright.
2. Measure the vertical distance between the carburetor body, outside the gasket and the bottom of the float.
3. Adjust by bending the stop tab on the float lever that contacts the hinge pin.

FAST IDLE SPEED

Adjustment

1. With the engine warmed up and idling, place the fast idle lever on the step of the fast idle cam specified on the engine compartment sticker or in the specifications chart. Disconnect and plug the EGR vacuum line.
2. Make sure the high speed cam positioner lever is disengaged.

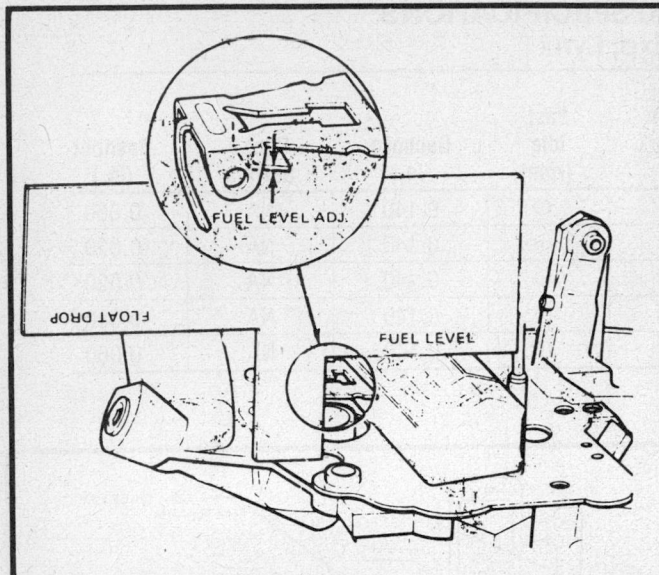

7200 VV float level adjustment

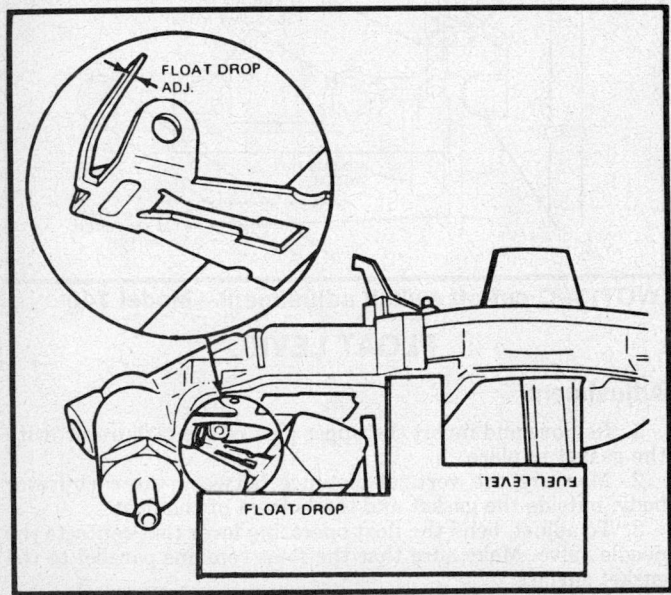

7200 VV float drop adjustment

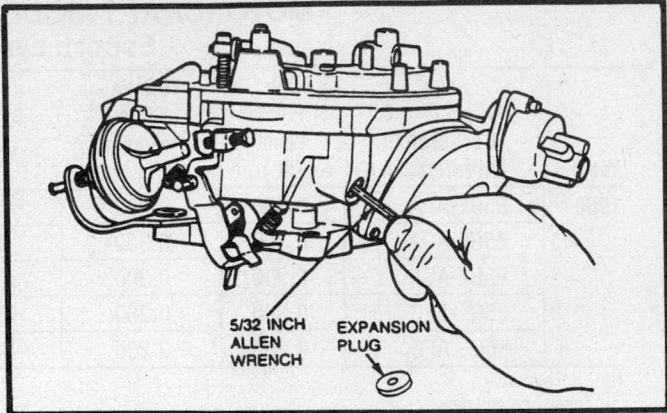

7200 VV wide open throttle limiter adjustment

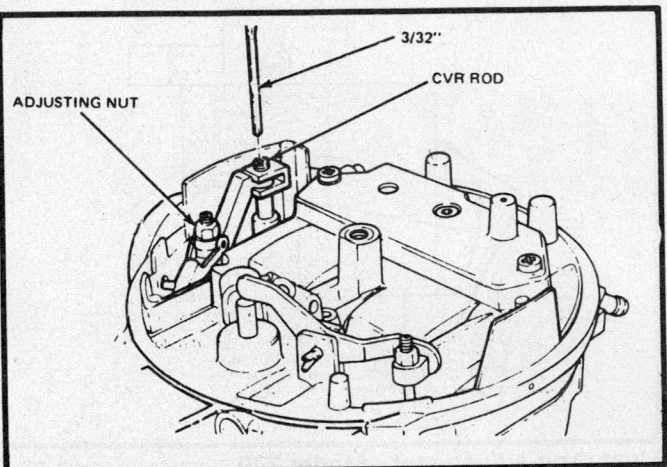

7200 VV vacuum control regulator adjustment

4. Turn the stator cap tool clockwise until the lever contacts the fast idle cam adjusting screw.

5. Turn the fast idle cam adjusting screw until the index mark on the cap lines up with the specified mark on the casting.

6. Remove the stator cap tool. Install the choke coil cap and set to the specified housing mark.

COLD ENRICHMENT METERING ROD

Adjustment

A dial indicator and a stator cap tool T77L–9848–A or equivalent, are required for this adjustment.

1. Remove the choke coil cap.

2. Attach a weight to the choke coil mechanism to seat the cold enrichment rod.

3. Install and zero a dial indicator with the tip on top of the enrichment rod. Raise and release the weight to verify zero on the dial indicator.

4. With the stator cap at the index position, the dial indicator should read the specified dimension on the specification tag. If needed, turn the adjusting nut to correct.

5. Install the choke cap at the correct setting.

VENTURI VALVE LIMITER

Adjustment

1. Remove the carburetor. Take off the venturi valve cover and the 2 rollers.

2. Use a center punch to loosen the expansion plug at the rear

3. Turn the fast idle speed screw to adjust to the specified speed.

FAST IDLE CAM

Adjustment

Use of a stator cap special tool T77L–9848–A or equivalent, is required for this procedure. It fits over the choke thermostatic lever when the choke cap is removed.

1. Remove the choke coil cap. The top rivets will have to be drilled out; the bottom rivet will have to be driven out from the rear. New rivets must be used upon installation.

2. Place the fast idle lever in the corner of the specified step of the fast idle cam (the highest step is first) with the high speed cam positioner retracted.

3. If the adjustment is being made with the carburetor removed, hold the throttle lightly closed with a rubber band.

MOTORCRAFT MODEL 7200 VV SPECIFICATIONS

Year	Model	Float Level (in.)	Float Drop (in.)	Fast Idle Cam Setting/Step	Cold Enrichment Metering Rod (in.)	Control Vacuum (in. H₂O)	Venturi Valve Limiter (in.)	Choke Cap Setting (notches)
1986	E2AE-AJA	1.010–1.070	1.430–1.490	0.360/2nd step	③	②	①	Index
	E2AE-APA	1.010–1.070	1.430–1.490	0.360/2nd step	③	②	①	Index
1987	E2AE-AJA	1.010–1.070	1.430–1.490	0.360/2nd step	④	②	①	Index
	E2AE-APA	1.010–1.070	1.430–1.490	0.360/2nd step	④	②	①	Index
1988	E7AE-AA	1.010–1.070	1.430–1.490	0.360/2nd step	④	②	①	Index
	E8AE-AA	1.010–1.070	1.430–1.490	0.360/2nd step	④	②	①	Index
1989	ALL	1.010–1.070	1.430–1.490	0.360/2nd step	④	②	①	Index

① Maximum opening: .99/1.01
 Wide open on throttle: .39/.41
② See text

③ 0°F—0.490 @ starting position
 75°F—0.460 @ starting position
④ Maximum opening: .99/1.01
 Wide open on throttle: .74/.76

of the carburetor main body on the throttle side and remove the expansion plug.

3. Use an Allen wrench to remove the venturi valve wide open stop screw.

4. Hold the throttle wide open.

5. Apply a light closing pressure on the venturi valve and check the gap between the valve and the air horn wall. To adjust, move the venturi valve to the wide open position and insert an Allen wrench into the stop screw hole. Turn clockwise to increase the gap. Remove the wrench and check the gap again.

6. Replace the wide open stop screw and turn it clockwise until it contacts the valve.

7. Push the venturi valve wide open and check the gap. Turn the stop screw to bring the gap to specifications.

8. Reassemble the carburetor with a new expansion plug.

CONTROL VACUUM REGULATOR (CVR)

Adjustment

The cold enrichment metering rod adjustment must be checked and set before making this adjustment.

1. After adjusting the cold enrichment metering rod, leave the dial indicator in place but remove the stator cap. Do not re-zero the dial indicator.

2. Press down on the CVR rod until it bottoms on its seat. Measure this amount of travel with the dial indicator.

3. If the adjustment is incorrect, hold the ⅜ in. CVR adjusting nut with a box wrench to prevent it from turning. Use a ³⁄₃₂ in. Allen wrench to turn the CVR rod; turning counter-clockwise will increase the travel and vice versa.

HOLLEY CARBURETORS

Model 1949

The Holley model 1949 is a single venturi booster style carburetors. The carburetor is used on the 2.3L High Swirl Combustion (HSC) engine, in the 1986–87 Tempo and Topaz. The model 1949 is used in Canada. The model 1949 carburetor uses 13 basic systems.

DRY FLOAT LEVEL

Adjustment

1. Remove the carburetor air horn.

2. With the air horn assembly removed, place a finger over float hinge pin retainer and invert the main body. Catch the accelerator pump check ball and weight.

3. Using a straight edge, check the position of the floats. The correct dry float setting is that both pontoons at the extreme outboard edge by flush with the surface of the main body casting (without gasket). If adjustment is required, bend the float tabs to raise or lower the float level.

4. Once adjustment is correct, turn main body right side up and check the float alignment. The float should move freely throughout its range without contacting the fuel bowl walls. If the float pontoons are misaligned, straighten them by bending the float arms. Recheck the float level adjustment.

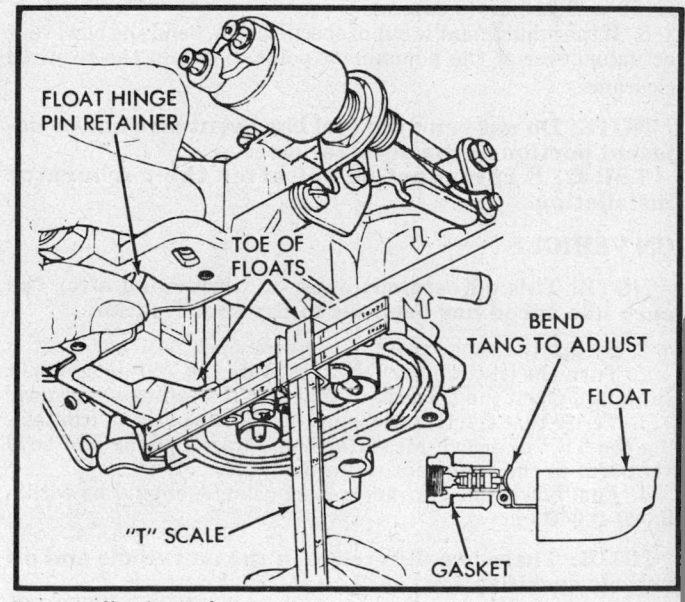

Float adjustment

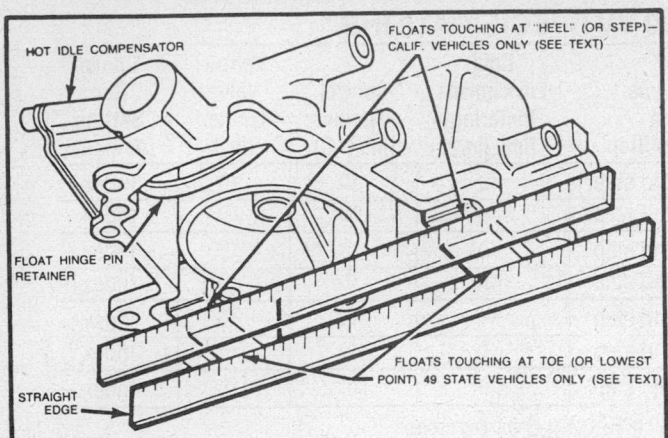

Float adjustment

5. During assembly, insert the check ball first and then the weight.

AUXILIARY MAIN JET/PULLOVER VALVE

Adjustment

The length of the auxiliary main jet/pullover valve adjustment screw which protrudes through the back side (side opposite the adjustment screw head) of the throttle pick-up lever must be 0.345 ±0.010 in. (8.76mm). To adjust, turn screw in or out as required.

MECHANICAL FUEL BOWL VENT (LEVER CLEARANCE)

Adjustment

OFF VEHICLE

1. Secure the choke plate in the wide-open position.
2. Set the throttle at the TSP **OFF** position.
3. Turn the TSP **OFF** idle adjustment screw counterclockwise until the throttle plate is closed in the throttle bore.
4. Fuel bowl vent clearance: Dimension A should be within 0.120 ± 0.010 in. (3.05mm).
5. If the adjustment is out of specification, bend the bowl vent actuator lever at the adjustment point to obtain the required clearance.

NOTE: Do not bend the fuel bowl vent arm and/or adjacent portion of the actuator lever.

TSP OFF rpm must be set after the carburetor installation.

ON VEHICLE

NOTE: This adjustment must be performed after the curb idle speed has been set to the specification.

1. Secure the choke plate in the wide open position.
2. Turn the ignition key **ON** to activate the TSP (engine not running). Open the throttle so that the TSP plunger extends.
3. Verify that the throttle is in the idle set position (contacting the TSP plunger). Measure the clearance of the fuel bowl vent arm to the bowl vent actuating lever.
4. Fuel bowl vent clearance: Dimension A should be within 0.020–0.040 in.

NOTE: There is a difference in the on vehicle and off vehicle specification.

5. If the dimension is out of specification, bend the bowl vent

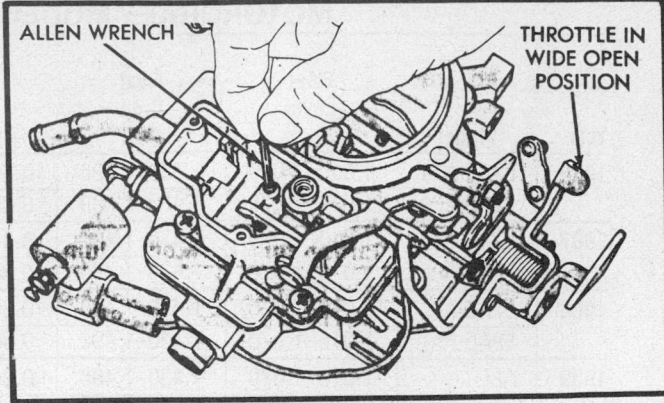

Mechanical power valve adjustment

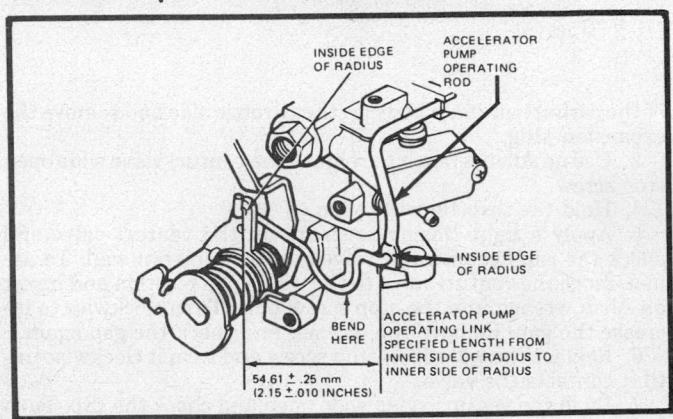

Auxiliary main jet/Pullover valve (timing adjustment)—Models 1949 and 6149

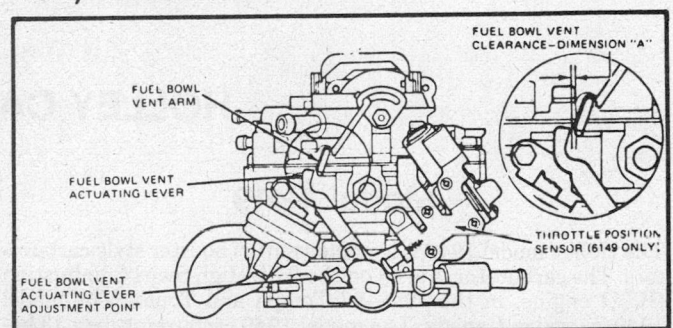

Mechanical fuel pump vent adjustment—Model 1949

actuator lever at the adjustment point to obtain the required clearance.

NOTE: Do not bend the fuel bowl vent arm and/or adjacent portion of the actuating lever.

ACCELERATOR PUMP STROKE

Adjustment

1. Check the length of the accelerator pump operating link from its inside edge at the accelerator pump operating rod to its inside edge at the throttle lever hole. The dimension should be 2.150 ±0.010 in. (54.61 ±.25 mm).
2. Adjust to the proper length by bending the loop in the operating link.

CHOKE PLATE PULLDOWN

Adjustment

This adjustment is preset at the factory and protected by a tamper resistant plug.

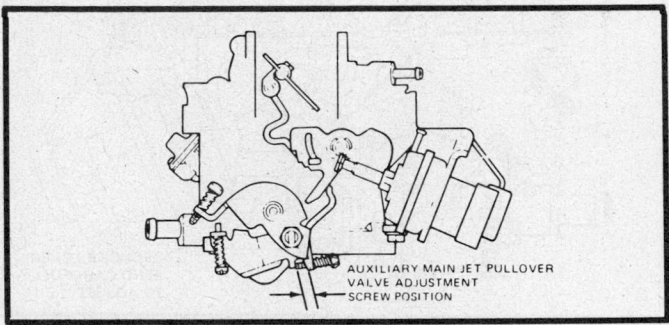

Accelerator pump stroke adjustment—Model 1949

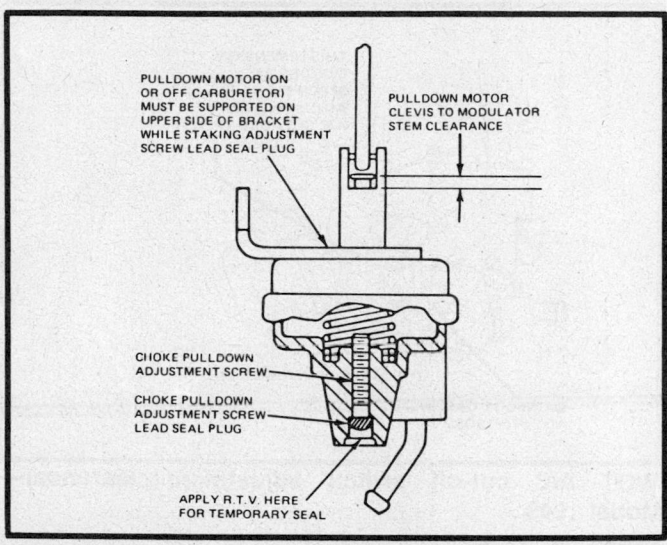

Choke pulldown adjustment—Model 1949

FAST IDLE CAM INDEX

Adjustment

1. With the engine cool, position the fast idle screw on the high step of the fast idle cam.
2. Activate the pulldown motor by applying an external vacuum source of 15–20 in. Hg.
3. Apply light pressure to the upper edge of the choke plate in the closing direction to remove clearance between the pulldown motor clevis and the modulator stem.
4. Open the throttle slightly and allow the fast idle cam to drop.
5. Close the throttle and measure the clearance between the top edge of the fast idle rpm adjusting screw and the shoulder of the fast idle cam highest step (Dimension A is the fast idle cam index shown in the illustration).
6. Remove the light closing pressure from the upper edge of the choke plate.
7. Open the throttle to the wide open position and return slowly.
8. The fast idle adjustment screw must contact the lower end of the fast idle cam kickdown step by at least half of its diameter on carburetors with 4 step cams, or must contact the third step by at least half of its diameter without contacting the second or fourth steps on carburetors with 5 step cams.
9. If Steps 5 and 8 are okay, the fast idle cam index is within specification. If adjustment is necessary, bend the fast idle cam link at the loop to obtain 0.020–0.030 in. at Dimension A.

DECHOKE

Adjustment

1. With the engine off and cool, hold the throttle in the wide open position.
2. Use a drill of the specified size and measure the clearance between the upper edge of the choke plate and the air horn wall.
3. With slight pressure against the choke shaft, a slight drag should be felt when the gauge is withdrawn.
4. To adjust, bend the tang on the throttle lever as required.

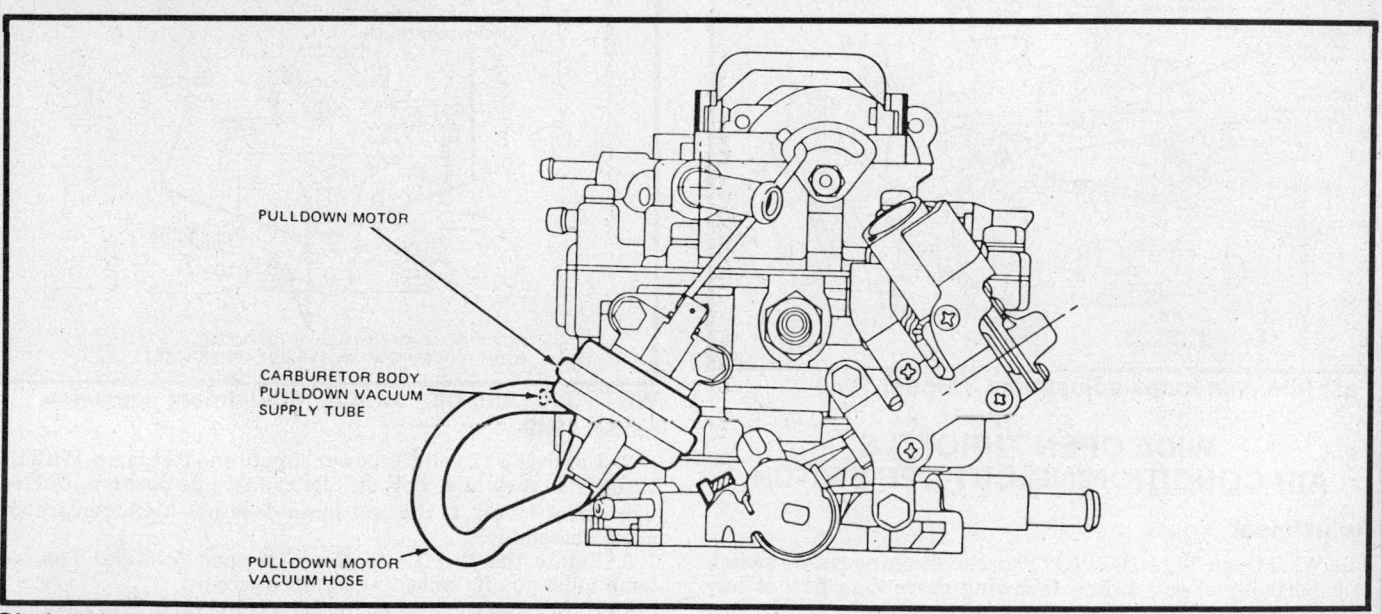

Choke plate pulldown motor—Model 1949

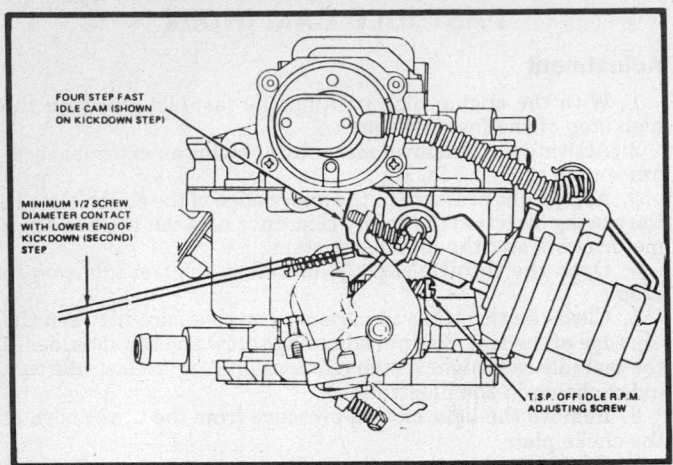

Fast idle cam index (4 step idle cams)—Model 1949

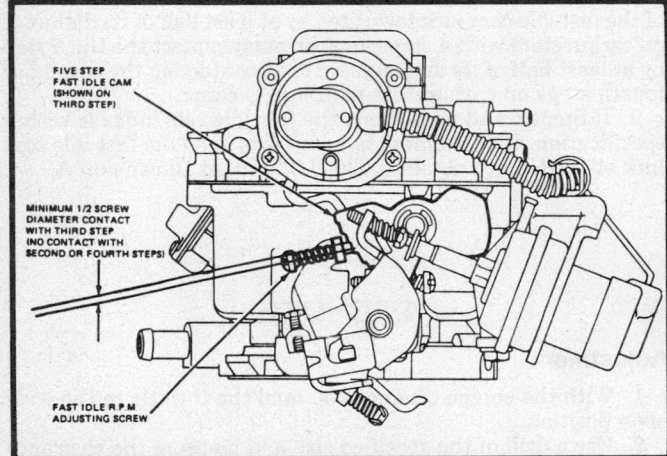

Fast idle cam index (5 step idle cams)—Model 1949

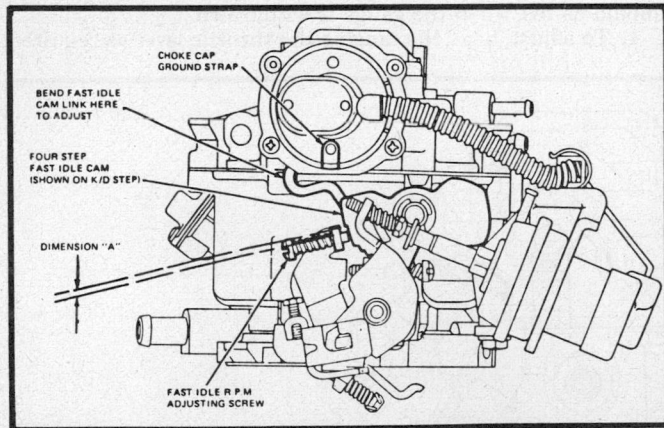

Fast idle cam index adjustment—Model 1949

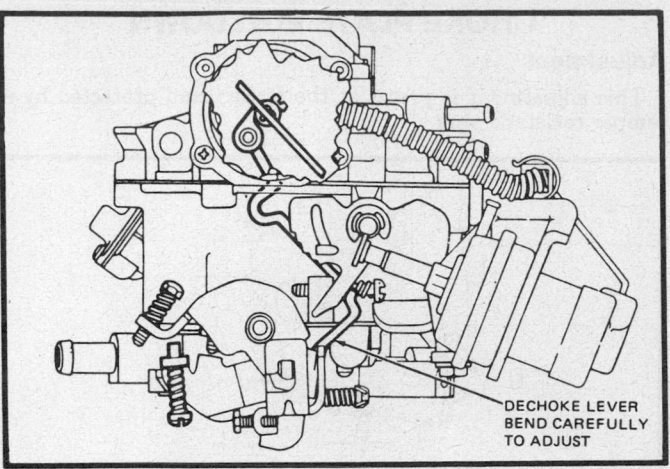

Dechoke adjustment—Model 1949

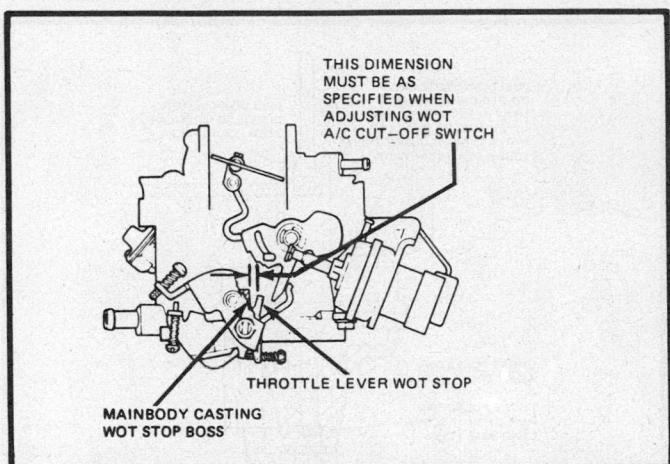

WOT A/C cut-off switch adjustment (clearance)—Model 1949

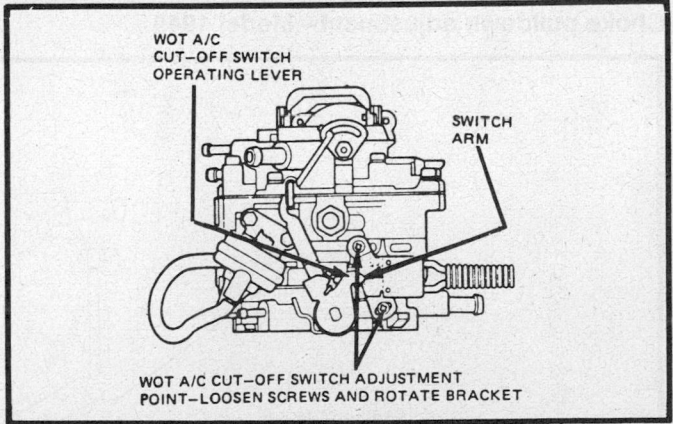

WOT A/C cut-off switch adjustment screws—Model 1949

WIDE OPEN THROTTLE
AIR CONDITIONING CUT-OFF SWITCH

Adjustment

The Wide Open Throttle (WOT) air conditioning cut-off switch is a normally closed switch (allowing current to flow at any throttle position other than wide-open throttle).

1. Disconnect the wiring harness at the switch connector.

2. Connect a 12 volt DC power supply and test lamp. With the throttle at curb idle, TSP off idle or fast idle position, the test light must be on. If the test lamp does not light, replace the switch assembly.

3. Rotate the throttle to the wide-open position. The test lamp must go off, indicating an open circuit.

4. If the lamp remains on, insert a 0.165 in. drill or gauge between the throttle lever WOT stop and the WOT stop boss on

HOLLEY MODEL 1949
Ford Motor Co.

Year	Carb. Iden.	Dry Float Level (in.)	Pump Hole No. Setting	Choke Plate Pulldown (in.)	Fast Idle Cam Linkage (in.)	Dechoke (in.)	Choke Setting
1986	E43E-ADA	①	2	0.080–0.120	0.020–0.030	0.180–0.220	2 Rich
	E43E-AEA	①	2	0.080–0.120	0.020–0.030	0.180–0.220	2 Rich
	E73E-AV ②	①	2	0.090–0.120	0.020–0.030	0.180–0.220	1 Rich
	E73E-BB ②	①	2	0.090–0.120	0.020–0.030	0.180–0.220	1 Rich
1987	E43E-ADA	①	2	0.080–0.120	0.020–0.030	0.180–0.220	2 Rich
	E43E-AEA	①	2	0.080–0.120	0.020–0.030	0.180–0.220	2 Rich
	E73E-AV ②	①	2	0.090–0.120	0.020–0.030	0.180–0.220	1 Rich
	E73E-BB ②	①	2	0.090–0.120	0.020–0.030	0.180–0.220	1 Rich

① Both float pontoons at outboard edge flush with surface of main body casting (without gasket)

the carburetor main body casting. Hold the throttle open as far as possible against the gauge. Loosen the switch mounting screws sufficiently to allow the switch to pivot. Rotate the switch assembly so the test lamp just goes out with the throttle held in the above referenced position. If the lamp does not go **OFF** within the allowable adjustment rotation, replace the switch. If the lamp goes out, tighten the switch bracket-to-carburetor screws to 45 inch lbs. (5 Nm) and remove drill or gauge and repeat Step 3.

Model 2280 and 6280
FLOAT LEVEL

Adjustment

1. Remove the carburetor air horn.
2. Invert the carburetor body taking care to catch the pump intake check ball so that only the weight of the floats is forcing the needle against the seat. Hold a finger against the hinge pin retainer to fully seat the float in the float pin cradle.
3. Lay a straight edge across the float bowl. The toe of each float should be as per specifications from the straight-edge. If necessary, bend the float tang to adjust.

ACCELERATOR PUMP STROKE

Measurement

MODEL 2280

1. Remove the bowl vent cover plate and vent valve lever spring. Take care to avoid loosening the vent valve retainer.
2. Make sure that the accelerator pump connector rod is in the inner hole of the pump operating lever and the throttle is at curb idle.
3. Place a straight edge on the bowl vent cover surface of the air horn, over the accelerator pump lever.
4. The lever surface should be flush with the air horn. If not, adjust it by bending the pump connector rod at the 90 degree bend.

NOTE: If this adjustment is changed, both the bowl vent and the mechanical power valve adjustments must be reset.

MODEL 6280

1. Remove the bowl vent cover plate and gasket.
2. With all pump links and levers installed, adjust the accelerator pump cap nut for zero clearance between the pump lever and the cap nut. Check that the wide open throttle can be reached without binding.

3. Install the gasket and the bowl vent cover plate.

CHOKE UNLOADER
Adjustment

1. Hold the throttle valves in the wide open position.
2. Lightly press a finger against the control lever to move the choke valve toward the closed position.
3. Insert the specified gauge between the top of the choke valve and the air horn wall.
4. Adjust, if necessary, by bending the tang on the accelerator pump lever.

CHOKE VACUUM KICK
Adjustment

1. Open the throttle, close the choke, then close the throttle to trap the fast idle cam at the closed choke position.
2. Disconnect the vacuum hose from the carburetor and connect it to an auxiliary vacuum source with a length of hose. Apply at least 15 in. Hg.
3. Completely compress the choke lever spring in the diaphragm stem without distorting the linkage.
4. Insert the specified gauge between the top of the choke valve and the air horn wall.
5. Adjust by bending the diaphragm link. Check for free movement. Replace the vacuum hose.

FAST IDLE CAM POSITION
Adjustment

1. Position the adjusting screw on the second highest step of the fast idle cam.

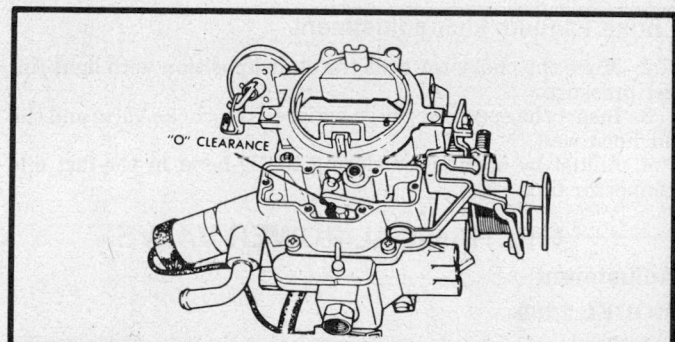

Accelerator pump stroke adjustment—model 6280

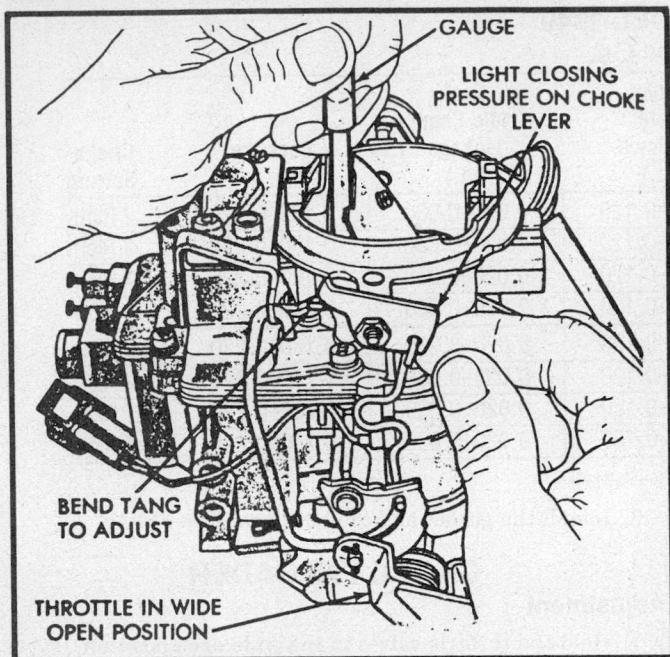

Choke unloader adjustment

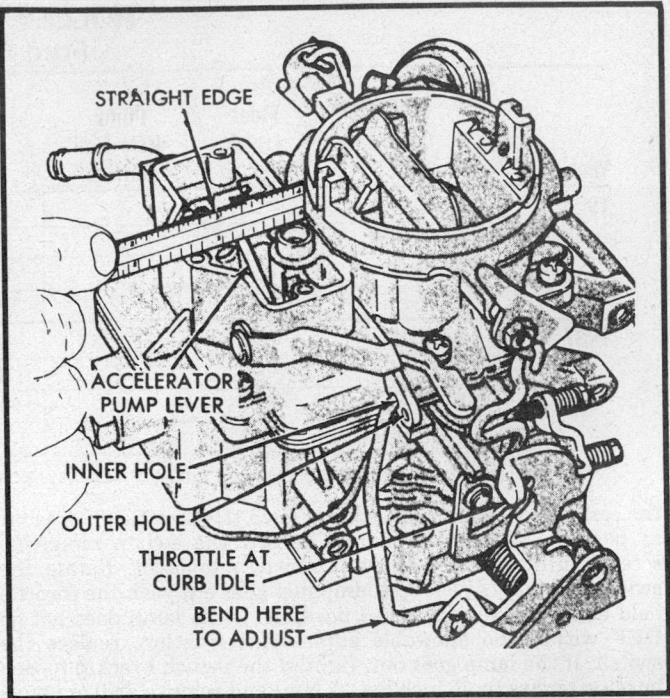

Fast idle adjustment—measure the clearance between the lower edge of the choke plate and the air horn wall

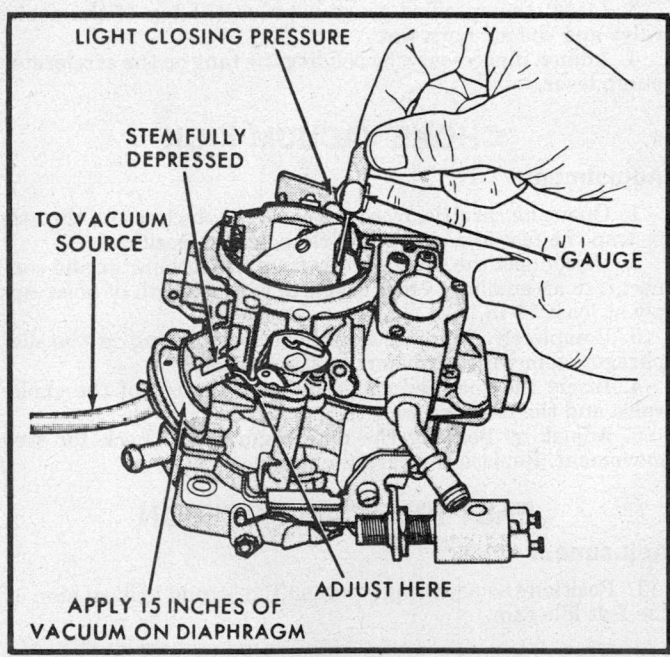

Choke vacuum kick adjustment

2. Move the choke towards the closed position with light finger pressure.

3. Insert the specified gauge between the choke valve and the air horn wall.

4. Adjust by opening or closing the U-bend in the fast idle connector link.

MECHANICAL POWER VALVE

Adjustment

MODEL 2280

1. Remove the bowl vent cover plate, vent valve lever, spring and retainer. Remove the lever pivot pin.

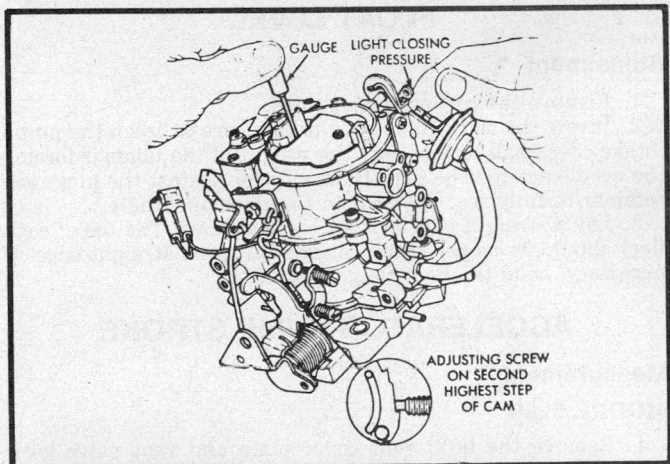

Fast idle cam position adjustment

2. Hold the throttle in the wide open position.

3. Using a 5/64 in. Allen wrench, press the mechanical power valve adjustment screw down and release it to determine if clearance exists. Turn the screw clockwise until clear is zero.

4. Adjust by turning the screw a turn counterclockwise.

5. Install all parts.

Model 5210-C

The Holley 5210–C is a progressive 2 barrel carburetor with an automatic choke system which is activated by a water heated thermostatic coil. An electrically heated choke is used on most later models. It also has an exhaust gas recirculation system with the valve located in the intake manifold. It is used on 1986–87 Chevettes (Canada).

HOLLEY MODEL 2280/6280
Chrysler Corporation

Year	Carb. Part No.	Float Level (in.)	Accelerator Pump Adjustment (in.)	Fast Idle (rpm)	Choke Unloader Clearance (in.)	Vacuum Kick (in.)	Fast Idle Cam Position (in.)	Choke
1986	R-40276A	9/32	0.180	①	0.280	0.130	0.060	Fixed
	R-40245A	9/32	0.050	①	0.200	0.140	0.052	Fixed
1987	R-40276A	9/32	0.180	①	0.280	0.130	0.060	Fixed
	R-40245A	9/32	0.050	①	0.200	0.140	0.052	Fixed
1988	R-40276A	9/32	0.180	①	0.280	0.130	0.060	Fixed
	R-40354A	9/32	0.050	①	0.200	0.140	0.052	Fixed
1989	R-40354A	9/32	0.180	①	0.280	0.130	0.060	Fixed

① Refer to underhood sticker

FLOAT LEVEL

Adjustment

1. With the carburetor air horn inverted and the float tang resting lightly on the inlet needle, insert the specified gauge between the air horn and the float.
2. Bend the float tang if an adjustment is needed.

FAST IDLE CAM

Adjustment

1. Place the fast idle screw on the second step of the fast idle cam and against the shoulder of the high step.
2. Place the specified drill or gauge on the down side of the choke plate.
3. To adjust, bend the choke lever tang.

CHOKE PLATE PULLDOWN (VACUUM BREAK)

Adjustment

1. Attach a hand vacuum pump to the vacuum break diaphragm; apply vacuum and seat the diaphragm.
2. Push the fast idle cam lever down to close the choke plate.
3. Take any slack out of the linkage in the open choke position.
4. Insert the specified gauge between the lower edge of the choke plate and the air horn wall.
5. If the clearance is incorrect, turn the vacuum break adjusting screw, located in the break housing, to adjust.

CHOKE UNLOADER

Adjustment

1. Position the throttle lever at the wide open position.
2. Insert a gauge of the size specified in the chart between the lower edge of the choke valve and the air horn wall.
3. Bend the unloader tang for adjustment.

FAST IDLE SPEED

Adjustment

1. The engine must be at normal operating temperature with the air cleaner off.
2. With the engine running, position the fast idle screw on the high step of the cam. Plug the EGR Port on the carburetor.
3. Adjust the speed by turning the fast idle screw.

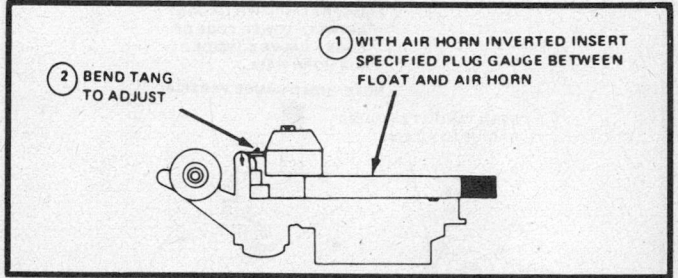

5210-C Float level adjustment

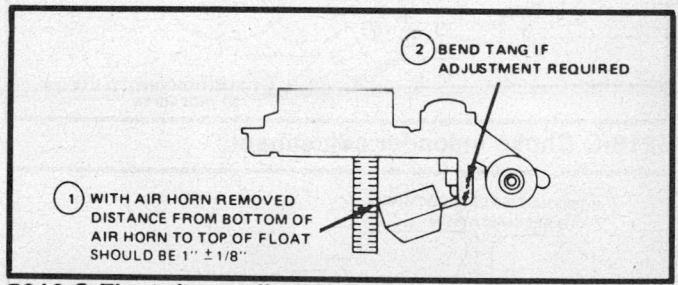

5210-C Float drop adjustment

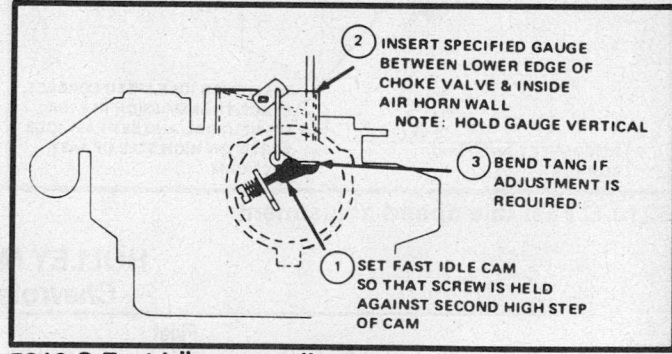

5210-C Fast idle cam adjustment

Model 5220 and 6520

Both carburetors are staged dual venturi carburetors. The model 6520 has the electronic feedback system while the model 5220 is of the conventional design. On the 6520, always check the

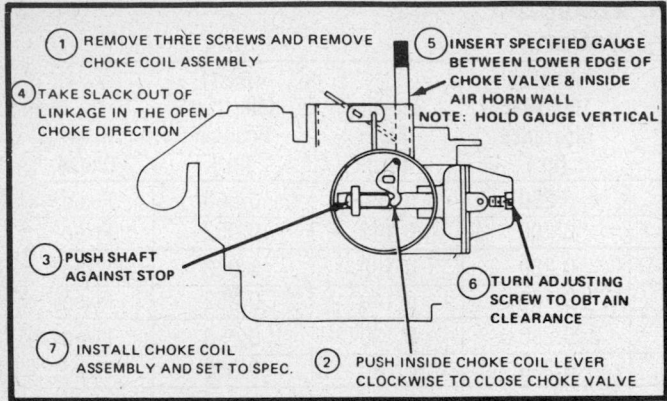

5210-C Vacuum break (choke plate pulldown) adjustment

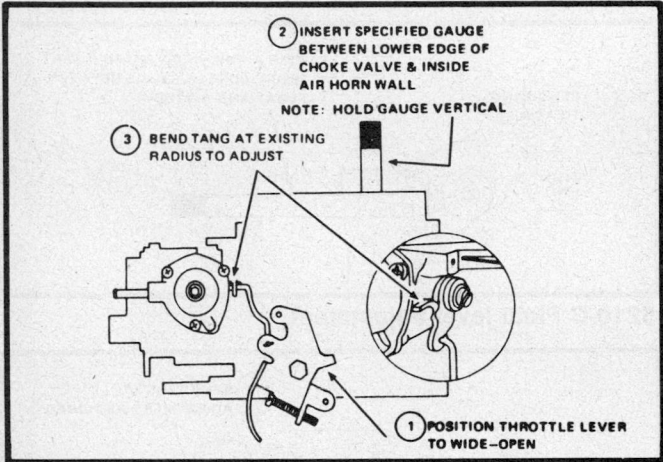

5210-C Choke unloader adjustment

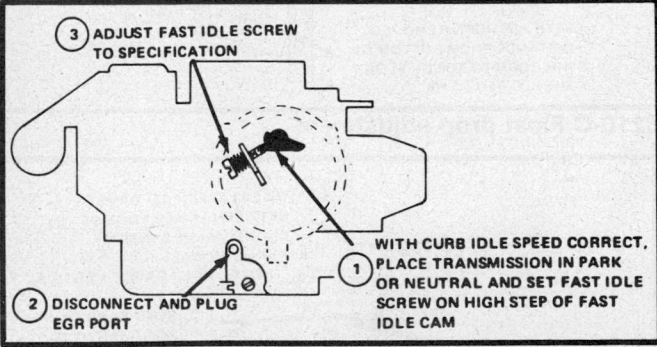

5210-C Fast idle speed adjustment

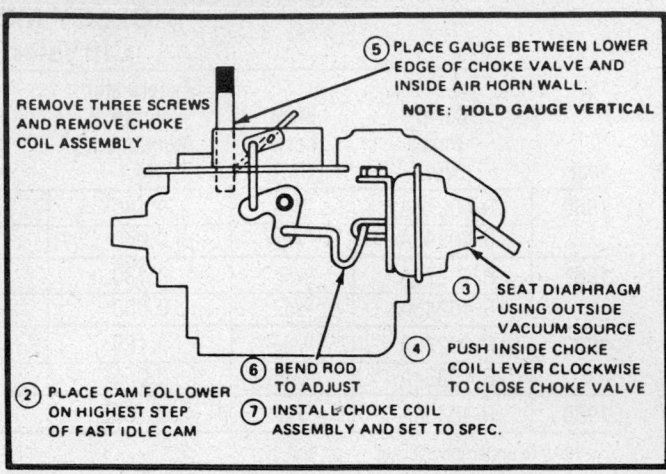

5210-C Secondary vacuum break adjustment

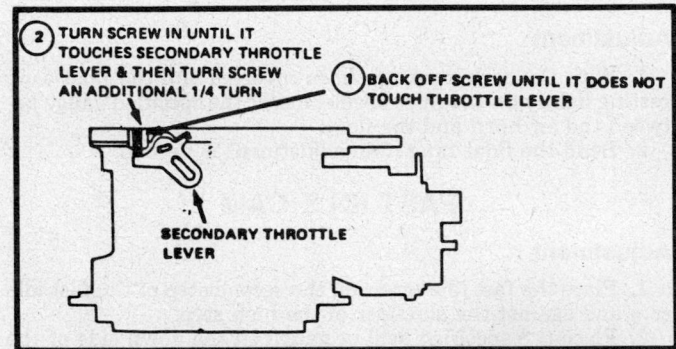

5210-C Secondary throttle stop screw adjustment

condition of hoses and related wiring before making any carburetor adjustments.

FLOAT SETTING AND FLOAT DROP

Adjustment

1. Remove and invert the air horn.
2. Insert a 0.480 in. gauge between the air horn and float.
3. If necessary, bend the tang on the float arm to adjust.
4. Turn the air horn right side up and allow the float to hang freely. Measure the float drop from the bottom of the air horn to the bottom of the float. It should be exactly 1⅛ in. Correct by bending the float tang.

HOLLEY MODEL 5210-C
Chevrolet Chevette

Year	Carb. Part No. ① ②	Float Level (Dry) (in.)	Fast Idle Cam (in.)	Secondary Vacuum Break (in.)	Fast Idle Setting (rpm)	Choke Unloader (in.)	Choke Setting
1986 (Canada)	14076393	0.50	0.100	④	③	0.325	Fixed
	14076394	0.50	0.090	④	③	0.275	Fixed
1987 (Canada)	14076393	0.50	0.100	④	③	0.325	Fixed
	14076394	0.50	0.090	④	③	0.275	Fixed

① Located on tag attached to the carburetor, or on the casting or choke plate
② GM identification numbers are used in place of the Holley numbers
③ See underhood sticker
④ Hot: 0.250 Cold: 0.100

VACUUM KICK

Adjustment

1. Open the throttle, close the choke, then close the throttle to trap the fast idle system at the closed choke position.

2. Disconnect the vacuum hose to the carburetor and connect it to an auxiliary vacuum source.

3. Apply at least 15 in. Hg vacuum to the unit.

4. Apply sufficient force to close the choke valve without distorting the linkage.

5. Insert a gauge between the top of the choke plate and the air horn wall.

6. Adjust by rotating the Allen screw in the center diaphragm housing.

7. Replace the vacuum hose.

FAST IDLE SPEED

Adjustment

1. Remove the air cleaner, disconnect and plug the EGR line, but do not disconnect the spark control computer vacuum line. Turn the air conditioning off.

2. Disconnect the radiator fan electrical connector and use a jumper wire to complete the circuit at the fan. Do not short to ground, as this will damage the system.

3. With the parking brake set and the transmission in **N**, (engine still off), open the throttle and place the fast idle screw on the slowest step of the cam.

4. Start the engine and check the idle speed. If it continues to rise slowly, the idle stop switch is not grounded properly.

5. Adjust the fast idle with the screw, moving the screw off the cam each time to adjust. Allow the screw to fall back against the cam and the speed to stabilize between each adjustment.

Model 6510-C

The 6510-C is used on the Chevrolet Chevette and Pontiac 1000. This is a staged, 2 barrel unit which incorporates a feedback air/fuel metering system.

VACUUM BREAK

Adjustment

Refer to the illustration for the adjustment procedures.

FAST IDLE CAM

Adjustment

1. Set the fast idle cam so that the screw is on the second highest step of the fast idle cam.

2. Insert the specified gauge between the lower edge of the choke valve and the air horn wall.

3. Bend the tang on the arm to adjust.

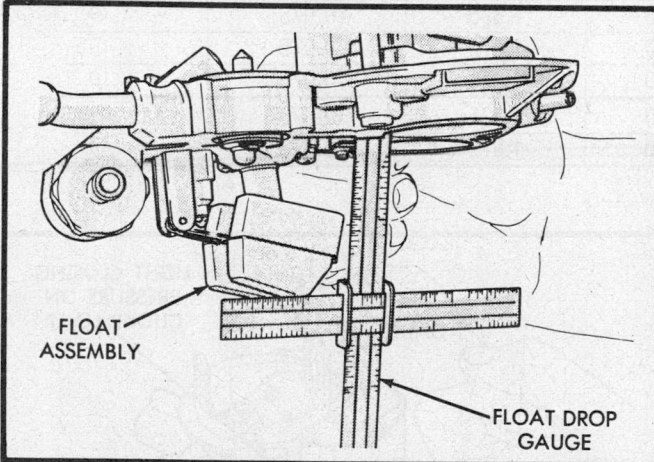

Float drop measurement

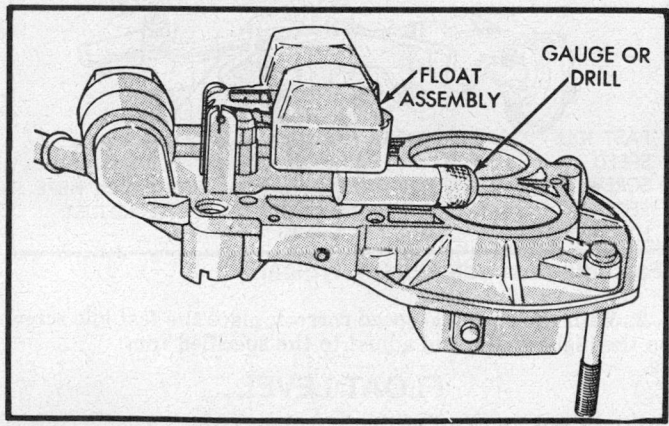

Float setting adjustment

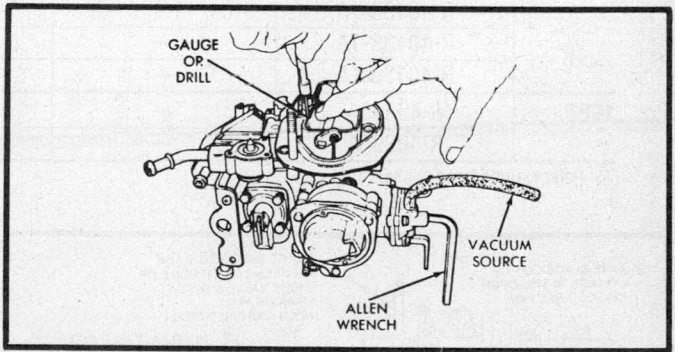

Vacuum kick adjustment

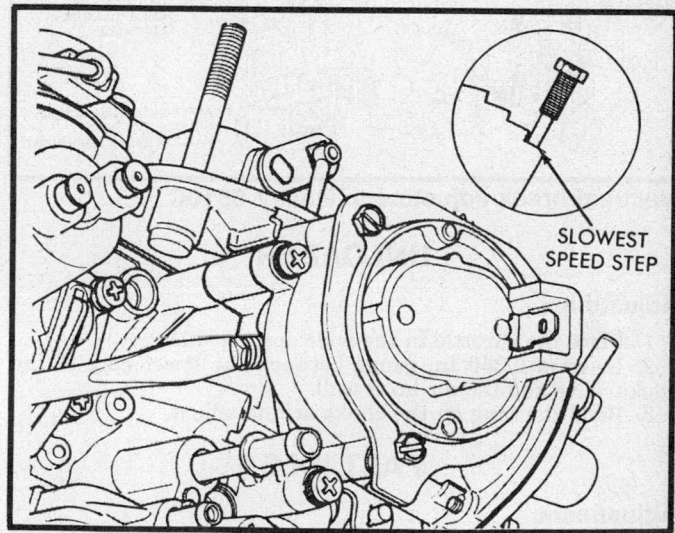

Fast idle speed adjustment

HOLLEY MODEL 5220
Chrysler Corporation

Year	Carb. Part No.	Accelerator Pump Hole No.	Dry Float Level (in.)	Vacuum Kick (in.)	Fast Idle RPM (w/fan)	Throttle Stop Speed RPM	Choke
1986	R-40060-2A	—	0.480	0.055	①	—	Fixed
	R-40116-A	—	0.480	0.095	①	—	Fixed
	R-40117-A	—	0.480	0.095	①	—	Fixed
1987	R-40060-2	—	0.480	0.055	①	—	Fixed
	R-40233	—	0.480	0.095	①	—	Fixed
	R-40234	—	0.480	0.095	①	—	Fixed
	R-40240	—	0.480	0.095	①	—	Fixed

① See underhood sticker

HOLLEY MODEL 6520
Chrysler Corporation

Year	Carb. Part No.	Accelerator Pump Hole No.	Dry Float Level (in.)	Float Drop (in.)	Vacuum Kick (in.)	Fast Idle RPM
1986	R-40058-1A	—	0.480	1.875	0.070	①
	R-40134-A	—	0.480	1.875	0.075	①
	R-40135-1A	—	0.480	1.875	0.075	①
	R-40138-1A	—	0.480	1.875	0.075	①
	R-40139-1A	—	0.480	1.875	0.075	①
1987	R-40295A	—	0.480	1.875	0.075	①
	R-40296A	—	0.480	1.875	0.075	①

① Refer to underhood sticker

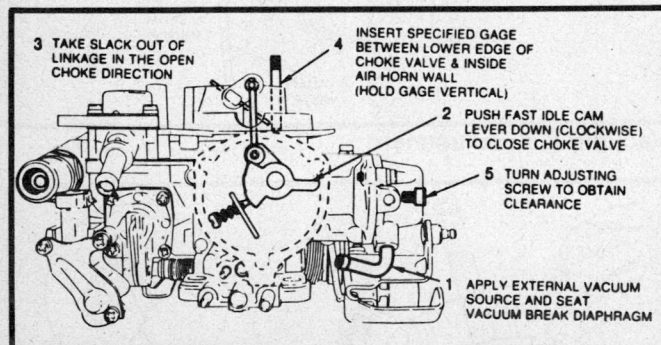

Vacuum break adjustment, Holley 6510C

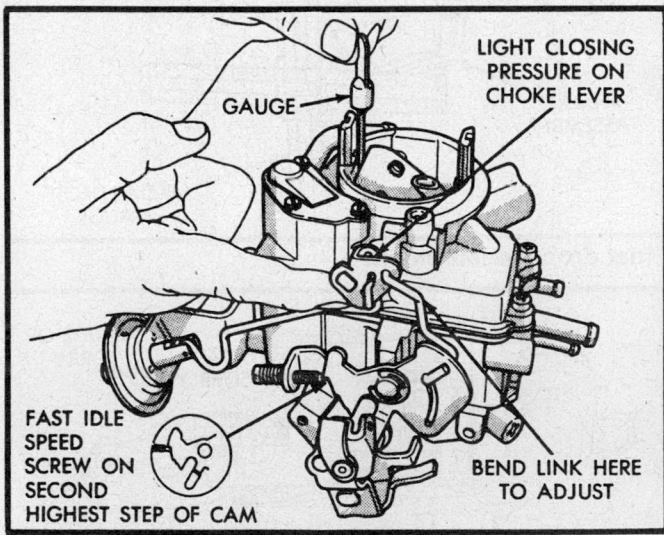

Fast idle cam adjustment, typical

UNLOADER

Adjustment

1. Place the throttle in the wide open position.
2. Insert a 0.350 in. gauge between the lower edge of the choke valve and the air horn wall.
3. Bend the tang on the choke arm to adjust.

FAST IDLE

Adjustment

1. Disconnect and plug the EGR line.

2. With the curb idle speed correct, place the fast idle screw on the highest step and adjust to the specified rpm.

FLOAT LEVEL

Adjustment

1. Remove and invert the air horn.

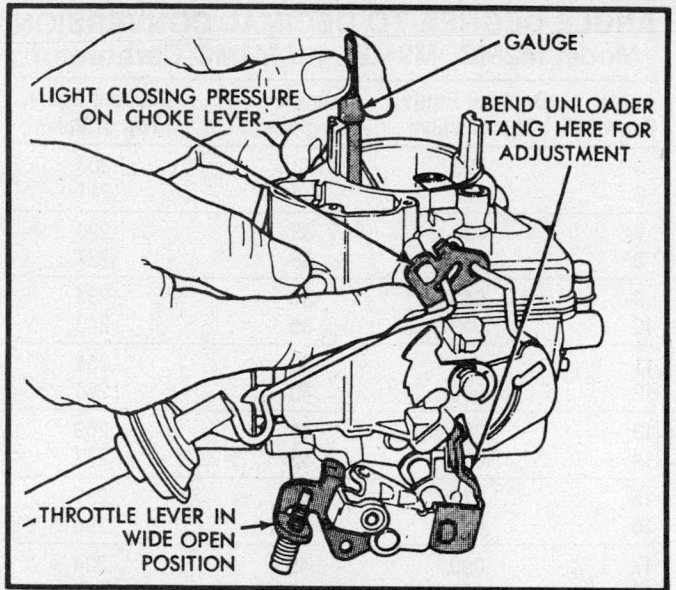

Choke unloader adjustment, typical

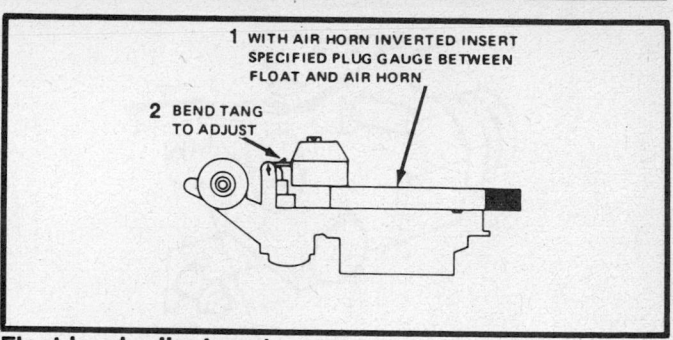

Float level adjustment

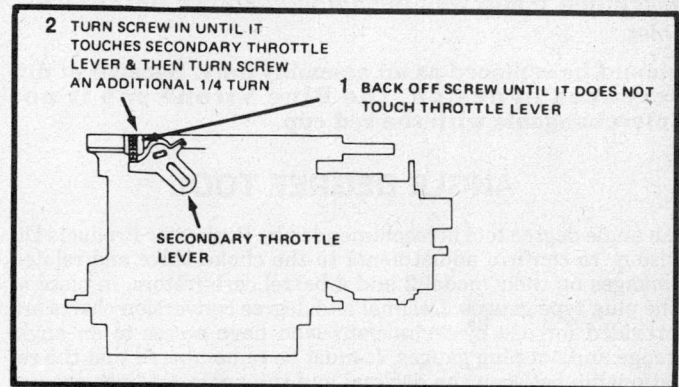

Secondary throttle stop screw adjustment

2. Place the specified gauge between the air horn and the float.

3. If necessary, bend the float arm tang to adjust.

SECONDARY THROTTLE STOP SCREW

Adjustment

1. Back off the screw until it does not touch the lever.

2. Turn the screw in until it touches the lever, then turn it an additional ¼ turn.

HOLLEY MODEL 6510-C
General Motors Corporation

Year	Part Number	Vacuum Break Adjustment (in.)	Fast Idle Cam Adjustment (in.)	Unloader Adjustment (in.)	Fast Idle Adjustment (rpm)	Float Level Adjustment (in.)	Choke Setting
1986	14068690	0.270	0.080	0.350	①	0.500	Fixed
	14068691	0.270	0.080	0.350	①	0.500	Fixed
	14068692	0.300	0.080	0.350	①	0.500	Fixed
	14076363	0.300	0.080	0.350	①	0.500	Fixed

① See underhood decal

ROCHESTER CARBURETORS

General Information

Model Identification

Rochester carburetors used by General Motors are identified by their model number. The first number indicates the number of barrels, while the last letters indicates the type of choke used. These are V for the manifold mounted choke coil, C for the choke coil mounted on the carburetor and E for electric choke, also mounted on the carburetor. Model numbers ending in A indicate an altitude-compensating carburetor.

NOTE: Due to the presence of ethyl alcohol in some gasolines, the black rubber pump cup swells causing driveability complaints. In order to correct this problem, all Varajet, Dualjet and Quadrajet carburetors with a MW designation (machined pump well) stamped on the carburetor next to the fuel inlet should use a Red Viton® pump cup when rebuilding the carburetor. The Red Viton® cup is not to be used on carburetors with tapered pump wells (no MW stamped on the fuel inlet). All Monojet, Dualjet and Quadrajet carburetors with a tapered pump well should use a Blue Viton® pump and

Machined pump well designation shown next to fuel inlet

should be replaced as an assembly only. Because of differences in design, the Blue Viton® cup is not interchangable with the red cup.

ANGLE DEGREE TOOL

An angle degree tool is recommended by Rochester Products Division, to confirm adjustments to the choke valve and related linkages on their model 2 and 4 barrel carburetors, in place of the plug type gauges. Decimal and degree conversion charts are provided for use by technicians who have access to an angle gauge and not plug gauges. It must be remembered that the relationship between the decimal and the angle readings are not exact, due to manufacturers tolerances.

To use the angle gauge, rotate the degree scale until zero (0) is opposite the pointer. With the choke valve completely closed, place the gauge magnet squarely on top of the choke valve and rotate the bubble until it is centered. Make the necessary adjustments to have the choke valve at the specified degree angle opening as read from the degree angle tool.

The carburetor may be off the engine for adjustments. Be sure the carburetor is held firmly during the use of the angle gauge.

Models 2SE and E2SE

The Rochester 2SE and E2SE Varajet II carburetors are 2 barrel, 2 stage downdraft units. Most carburetor components are aluminum. In that installation the E2SE is equipped with an electrically operated mixture control solenoid, controlled by the electronic control module.

FLOAT LEVEL

Adjustment

1. Remove the air horn from the throttle body.
2. Hold the retainer in place and to push the float down into light contact with the needle.
3. Measure the distance from the toe of the float (furthest from the hinge) to the top of the carburetor with the gasket removed.
4. To adjust, remove the float and gently bend the arm to specification. After adjustment, check the float alignment in the chamber.

NOTE: Some carburetors have a float stabilizer spring. If used, remove the spring with float. Use care when removing.

ACCELERATOR PUMP

Adjustment

No accelerator pump adjustment is required.

ANGLE DEGREE TO DECIMAL CONVERSION
Model M2MC, M2ME and M4MC Carburetor

Angle Degrees	Decimal Equiv. Top of Valve	Angle Degrees	Decimal Equiv. Top of Valve
5	.023	33	.203
6	.028	34	.211
7	.033	35	.220
8	.038	36	.227
9	.043	37	.234
10	.049	38	.243
11	.054	39	.251
12	.060	40	.260
13	.066	41	.269
14	.071	42	.277
15	.077	43	.287
16	.083	44	.295
17	.090	45	.304
18	.096	46	.314
19	.103	47	.322
20	.110	48	.332
21	.117	49	.341
22	.123	50	.350
23	.129	51	.360
24	.136	52	.370
25	.142	53	.379
26	.149	54	.388
27	.157	55	.400
28	.164	56	.408
29	.171	57	.418
30	.179	58	.428
31	.187	59	.439
32	.195	60	.449

FAST IDLE

Adjustment

1. Set the ignition timing and curb idle speed and disconnect and plug hoses as directed on the emission control decal.
2. Place the fast idle screw on the second step of the cam.
3. Start the engine and adjust the engine speed to specification with the fast idle screw.

NOTE: On carburetors using a clip to retain the pump rod in the pump lever, no pump adjustment is required. On models using the clipless pump rod, the pump rod adjustment should not be changed from the original factory setting unless gauging shows it to be out of specification. The pump lever is made from heavy duty, hardened steel making bending difficult. Do not remove the pump lever for bending unless absolutely necessary.

CHOKE COIL LEVER

Adjustment

1. Remove the retaining screws and remove the choke cover and coil. On carburetors with a riveted choke cover, drill out the rivets and remove the cover and choke coil.

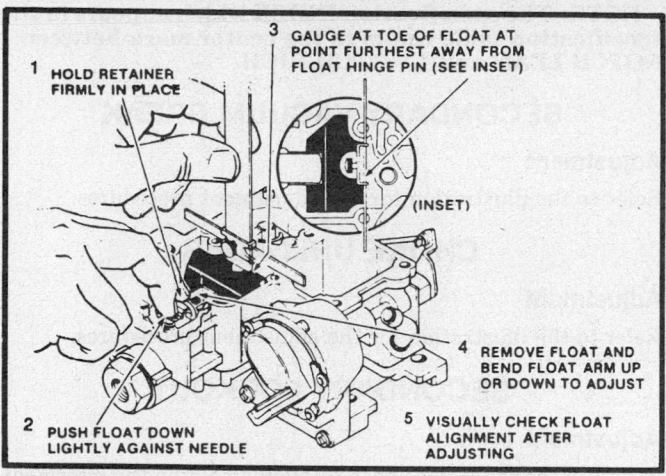

2SE, E2SE float adjustment

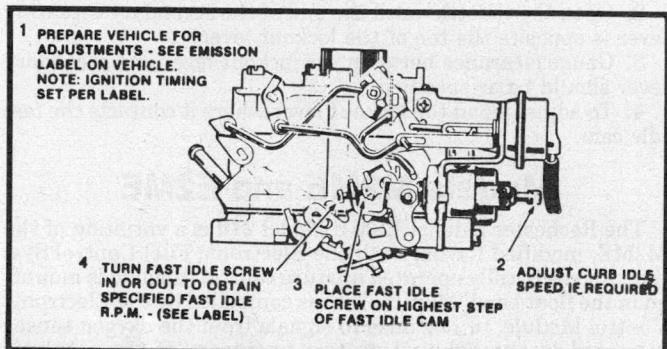

2SE, E2SE fast idle adjustment

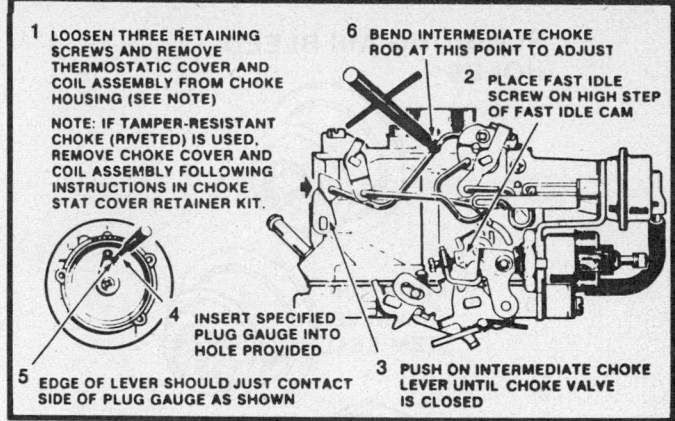

2SE, E2SE choke coil lever adjustment

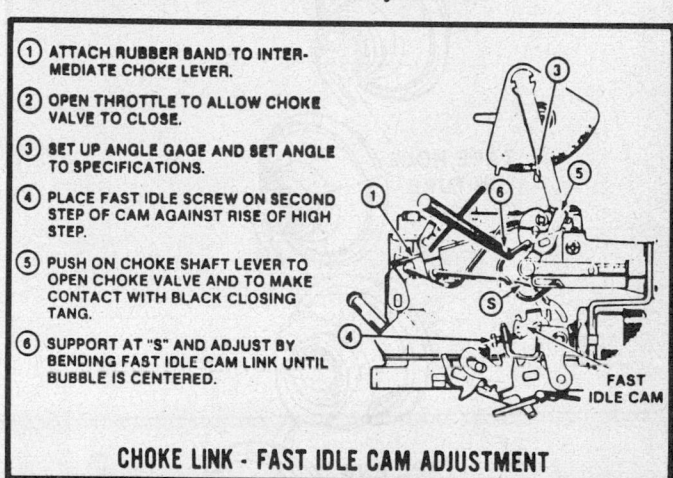

CHOKE LINK — FAST IDLE CAM ADJUSTMENT

Choke link—Fast idle cam adjustment

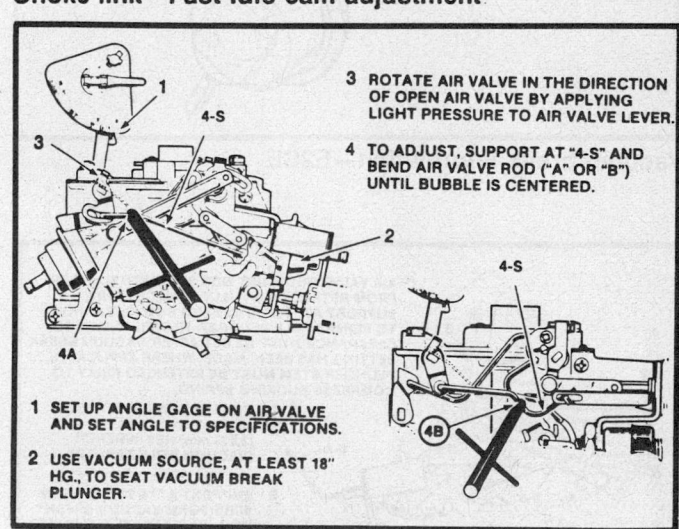

E2SE air valve rod adjustment

NOTE: A choke stat cover retainer kit is required for reassembly.

2. Place the fast idle screw on the high step of the cam.

3. Close the choke by pushing in on the intermediate choke lever. On FWD, the intermediate choke lever is behind the choke vacuum diaphragm.

4. Insert a drill or gauge of the specified size into the hole in the choke housing. The choke lever in the housing should be up against the side of the gauge.

5. If the lever does not just touch the gauge, bend the intermediate choke rod to adjust.

FAST IDLE CAM (CHOKE ROD)

Adjustment

Refer to the illustration for the adjustment procedures.

AIR VALVE ROD

Adjustment

Refer to the illustration for the adjustment procedures.

PRIMARY SIDE VACUUM BREAK

Adjustment

Refer to the illustration for the adjustment procedures.

ELECTRIC CHOKE SETTING

This procedure is only for those carburetors with choke covers retained by screws. Riveted choke covers are preset and nonadjustable.

1. Loosen the retaining screws.

2. Place the fast idle screw on the high step of the cam.

3. Rotate the choke cover to align the cover mark with the specified housing mark.

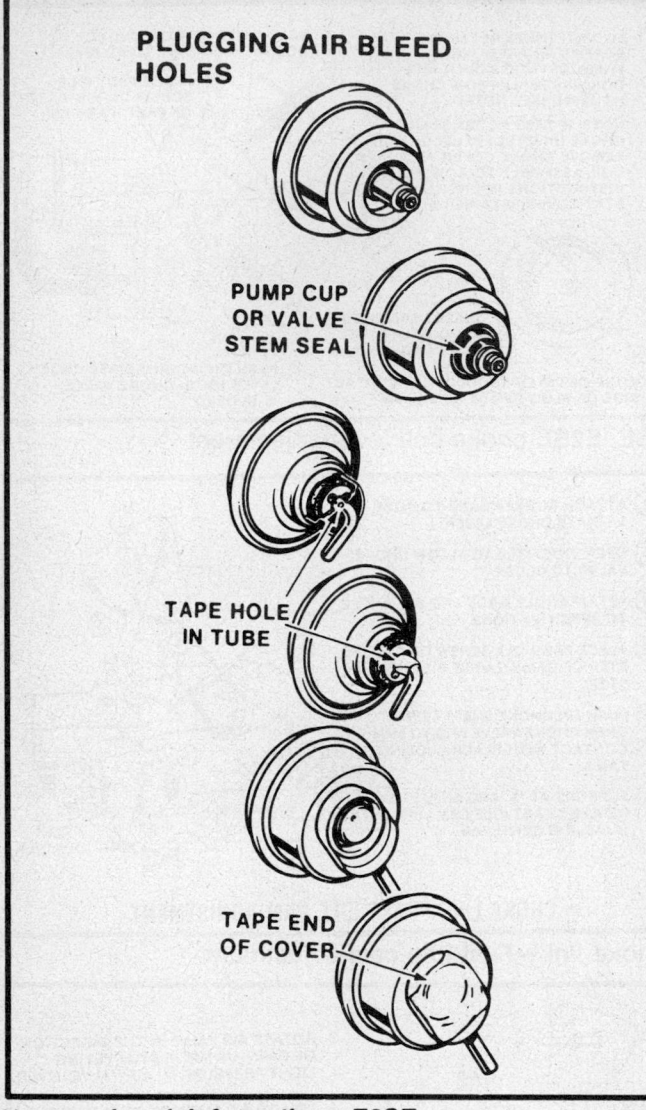

PLUGGING AIR BLEED HOLES

PUMP CUP OR VALVE STEM SEAL

TAPE HOLE IN TUBE

TAPE END OF COVER

Vacuum break information—E2SE

NOTE: The specification INDEX which appears in the specification table refers to the center mark between 1 NOTCH LEAN and 1 NOTCH RICH.

SECONDARY VACUUM BREAK

Adjustment

Refer to the illustration for the adjustment procedures.

CHOKE UNLOADER

Adjustment

Refer to the illustration for the adjustment procedures.

SECONDARY LOCKOUT

Adjustment

1. Pull the choke wide open by pushing out on the intermediate choke lever.
2. Open the throttle until the end of the secondary actuating lever is opposite the toe of the lockout lever.
3. Gauge clearance between the lockout lever and secondary lever should be as specified.
4. To adjust, bend the lockout lever where it contacts the fast idle cam.

Models M2ME and E2ME

The Rochester Dualjet E2ME Model 210 is a variation of the M2ME, modified for use with the Electronic Fuel Control System. An electrically operated mixture control solenoid is mounted in the float bowl. Mixture is thus controlled by the Electronic Control Module, in response to signals from the oxygen sensor mounted in the exhaust system upstream of the catalytic converter.

FLOAT LEVEL

Adjustment

The E2ME procedure is the same except for the method that the float arm is adjusted. For the E2ME only, if the float level is too high, hold the retainer firmly in place and push down on the center of the float to adjust.

1. If float level is low on the E2ME, lift out the metering rods.
2. Remove the solenoid connector screws.
3. Turn the lean mixture solenoid screw in clockwise, counting the exact number of turns until the screw is lightly bottomed in the bowl.

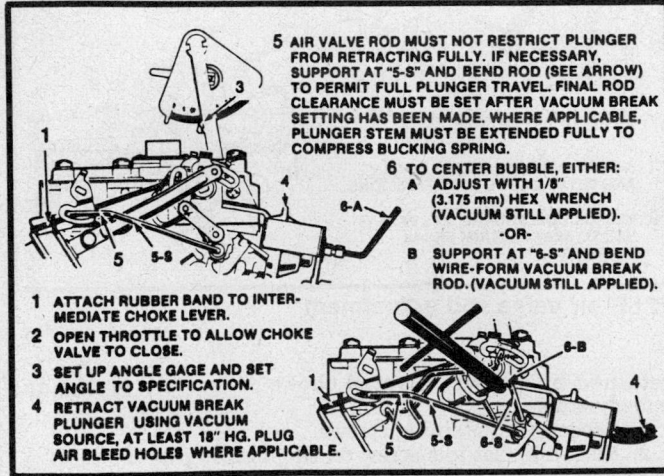

5 AIR VALVE ROD MUST NOT RESTRICT PLUNGER FROM RETRACTING FULLY. IF NECESSARY, SUPPORT AT "5-S" AND BEND ROD (SEE ARROW) TO PERMIT FULL PLUNGER TRAVEL. FINAL ROD CLEARANCE MUST BE SET AFTER VACUUM BREAK SETTING HAS BEEN MADE. WHERE APPLICABLE, PLUNGER STEM MUST BE EXTENDED FULLY TO COMPRESS BUCKING SPRING.

6 TO CENTER BUBBLE, EITHER:
A ADJUST WITH 1/8" (3.175 mm) HEX WRENCH (VACUUM STILL APPLIED).
-OR-
B SUPPORT AT "6-S" AND BEND WIRE-FORM VACUUM BREAK ROD. (VACUUM STILL APPLIED).

1 ATTACH RUBBER BAND TO INTERMEDIATE CHOKE LEVER.
2 OPEN THROTTLE TO ALLOW CHOKE VALVE TO CLOSE.
3 SET UP ANGLE GAGE AND SET ANGLE TO SPECIFICATION.
4 RETRACT VACUUM BREAK PLUNGER USING VACUUM SOURCE, AT LEAST 18" HG. PLUG AIR BLEED HOLES WHERE APPLICABLE.

E2SE primary vacuum break adjustment

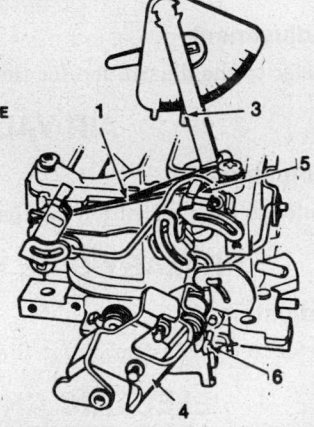

1 ATTACH RUBBER BAND TO INTERMEDIATE CHOKE LEVER.
2 OPEN THROTTLE TO ALLOW CHOKE VALVE TO CLOSE.
3 SET UP ANGLE GAGE AND SET ANGLE TO SPECIFICATIONS.
4 HOLD THROTTLE LEVER IN WIDE OPEN POSITION.
5 PUSH ON CHOKE SHAFT LEVER TO OPEN CHOKE VALVE AND TO MAKE CONTACT WITH BLACK CLOSING TANG.
6 ADJUST BY BENDING TANG UNTIL BUBBLE IS CENTERED.

E2SE choke unloader adjustment

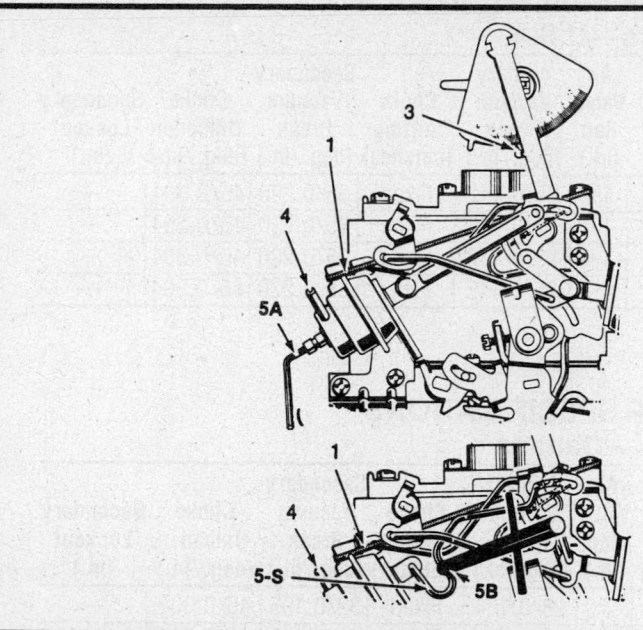

1. ATTACH RUBBER BAND TO INTER-MEDIATE CHOKE LEVER.
2. OPEN THROTTLE TO ALLOW CHOKE VALVE TO CLOSE.
3. SET UP ANGLE GAGE AND SET ANGLE TO SPECIFICATION.
4. RETRACT VACUUM BREAK PLUNGER USING VACUUM SOURCE, AT LEAST 18" HG. PLUG AIR BLEED HOLES WHERE APPLICABLE.

   WHERE APPLICABLE, PLUNGER STEM MUST BE EXTENDED FULLY TO COM-PRESS PLUNGER BUCKING SPRING.
5. TO CENTER BUBBLE, EITHER:

   A. ADJUST WITH 1/8" (3.175 mm) HEX WRENCH (VACUUM STILL APPLIED)
      -OR

   B. SUPPORT AT "5-S", BEND WIRE-FORM VACUUM BREAK ROD (VACUUM STILL APPLIED)

E2SE secondary vacuum break adjustment

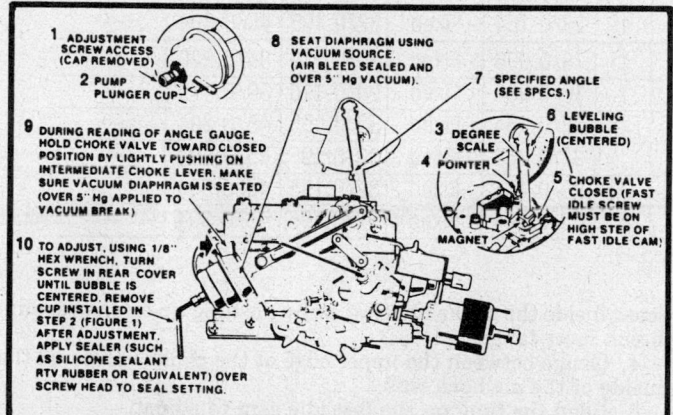

E2SE secondary vacuum break adjustment GM A and X series

4. Turn the screw out counterclockwise and remove it.
5. Lift out the solenoid and connector.
6. Remove the float and bend the arm up to adjust.
7. Install the parts, installing the mixture solenoid screw in until it is lightly bottomed, then turning it out the exact number of turns counted earlier.

FAST IDLE SPEED

Adjustment

1. Place the fast idle lever on the high step of the fast idle cam.
2. Turn the fast idle screw out until the throttle valves are closed.
3. Turn the screw in to contact the lever, then turn it in the number of turns listed in the specifications. Check this preliminary setting against the sticker figure.

2SE, E2SE CARBURETOR SPECIFICATIONS
American Motors

Year	Carburetor Identification	Float Level (in.)	Pump Rod (in.)	Fast Idle (rpm)	Choke Coil Lever (in.)	Fast Idle Cam (deg./in.)	Air Valve Rod (in.)	Primary Vacuum Break (deg./in.)	Choke Setting (notches)	Choke Unloader (deg./in.)	Secondary Lockout (in.)
1986	17085006	4/32	0.128	②	0.085	22/0.123	1①	21/0.117	Fixed	40/0.260	0.025
	17085380	5/32	0.128	②	0.085	22/0.123	1①	26/0.149	Fixed	40/0.260	0.025
	17085381	5/32	0.128	②	0.085	22/0.123	1①	26/0.149	Fixed	40/0.260	0.025
	17085382	5/32	0.128	②	0.085	22/0.123	1①	26/0.149	Fixed	40/0.260	0.025
	17085383	5/32	0.128	②	0.085	22/0.123	1①	26/0.149	Fixed	40/0.260	0.025
	17085385	5/32	0.128	②	0.085	22/0.123	1①	26/0.149	Fixed	40/0.260	0.025
	17085388	4/32	0.128	②	0.085	22/0.123	1①	21/0.117	Fixed	30/0.179	0.025
	17086081	4/32	0.128	②	0.085	22/0.123	1①	25/0.142	Fixed	30/0.179	0.025

① Degrees
② See underhood decal

2SE, E2SE CARBURETOR SPECIFICATIONS
General Motors—U.S.A.

Year	Carburetor Identification	Float Level (in.)	Pump Rod (in.)	Fast Idle (rpm)	Choke Coil Lever (in.)	Fast Idle Cam (deg./in.)	Air Valve Rod (in.)	Primary Vacuum Break (deg./in.)	Choke Setting (notches)	Secondary Vacuum Break (deg./in.)	Choke Unloader (deg./in.)	Secondary Lockout (in.)
1986	17084534	5/32	Fixed	①	0.085	28/0.164	1 ②	25/0.142	Fixed	35/0.220	45/0.304	—
	17084535	5/32	Fixed	①	0.085	28/0.164	1 ②	25/0.142	Fixed	35/0.220	45/0.304	—
	17084540	5/32	Fixed	①	0.085	28/0.164	1 ②	25/0.142	Fixed	35/0.220	45/0.304	—
	17084542	5/32	Fixed	①	0.085	28/0.164	1 ②	25/0.142	Fixed	35/0.220	45/0.304	—

① See underhood decal
② Measurement in degrees

2SE, E2SE CARBURETOR SPECIFICATIONS
General Motors—Canada

Year	Carburetor Identification	Float Level (in.)	Pump Rod (in.)	Fast Idle (rpm)	Choke Coil Lever (in.)	Fast Idle Cam (deg./in.)	Air Valve Rod (in.)	Primary Vacuum Break (deg./in.)	Choke Setting (notches)	Secondary Vacuum Break (deg./in.)	Choke Unloader (deg./in.)	Secondary Lockout (in.)
1986	17086484	12/32	Fixed	①	0.085	—	1	28/0.164	Fixed	32/0.195	45/0.304	—
	17086485	12/32	Fixed	①	0.085	—	1	28/0.164	Fixed	32/0.195	45/0.304	—
	17086486	4/32	Fixed	①	0.085	—	1	28/0.164	Fixed	32/0.195	45/0.304	—
	17086487	4/32	Fixed	①	0.085	—	1	28/0.164	Fixed	32/0.195	45/0.304	—
1987	17084312	5/16	Fixed	①	0.085	—	1	18/0.096	Fixed	20/0.110	35/0.220	—
	17084314	5/16	Fixed	①	0.085	—	1	16/0.083	Fixed	20/0.110	30/0.179	—
	17085482	3/8	Fixed	①	0.085	—	1	28/0.164	Fixed	32/0.195	45/0.304	—
	17085483	3/8	Fixed	①	0.085	—	1	28/0.164	Fixed	32/0.195	45/0.304	—
	17085484	3/8	Fixed	①	0.085	—	1	28/0.164	Fixed	32/0.195	45/0.304	—
	17085485	3/8	Fixed	①	0.085	—	1	28/0.164	Fixed	32/0.195	45/0.304	—

① See underhood decal

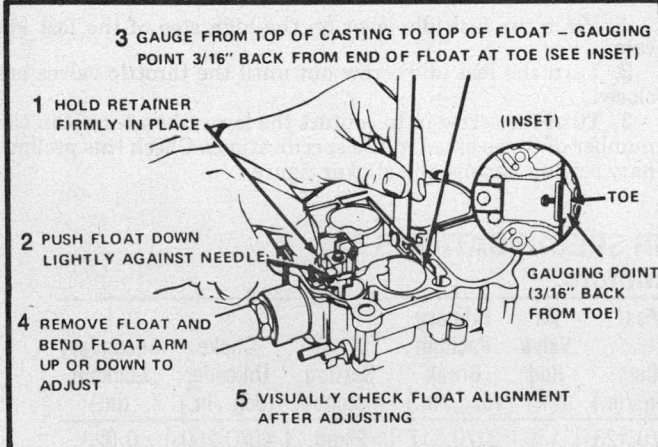

3 GAUGE FROM TOP OF CASTING TO TOP OF FLOAT – GAUGING POINT 3/16" BACK FROM END OF FLOAT AT TOE (SEE INSET)

1 HOLD RETAINER FIRMLY IN PLACE

(INSET)

TOE

2 PUSH FLOAT DOWN LIGHTLY AGAINST NEEDLE

GAUGING POINT (3/16" BACK FROM TOE)

4 REMOVE FLOAT AND BEND FLOAT ARM UP OR DOWN TO ADJUST

5 VISUALLY CHECK FLOAT ALIGNMENT AFTER ADJUSTING

M2ME, E2ME float level adjustment

FAST IDLE CAM (CHOKE ROD)

Adjustment

1. Adjust the fast idle speed.
2. Place the cam follower lever on the second step of the fast idle cam, holding it firmly against the rise of the high step.
3. Close the choke valve by pushing upward on the choke coil lever inside the choke housing, or by pushing up on the vacuum break lever tang.
4. Gauge between the upper edge of the choke valve and the inside of the air horn wall.
5. Bend the tang on the fast idle cam to adjust.

ACCELERATOR PUMP

Adjustment

This adjustment is not required on E2ME carburetors used in conjunction with the computer controlled systems.

1. With the fast idle cam follower off the steps of the fast idle cam, back out the idle speed screw until the throttle valves are completely closed.
2. Place the pump rod in the proper hole of the lever.
3. Measure from the top of the choke valve wall, next to the vent stack, to the top of the pump stem.
4. Bend the pump lever to adjust.

CHOKE COIL LEVER

Adjustment

1. Remove the choke cover and thermostatic coil from the choke housing. On carburetors with a fixed choke cover, drill out the rivets and remove the cover. A stat cover kit will be required for assembly.
2. Push up on the coil tang (counterclockwise) until the choke valve is closed. The top of the choke rod should be at the bottom

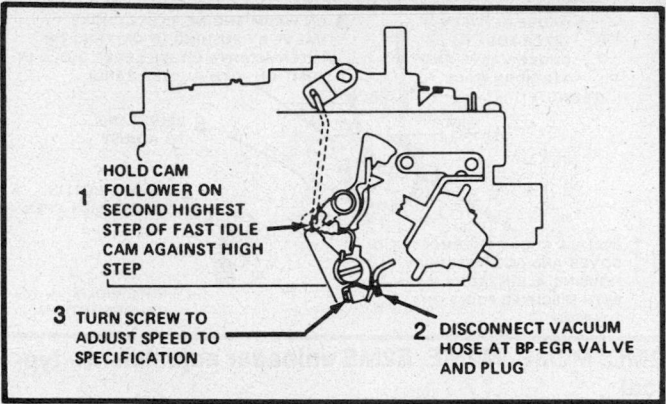

M2ME, E2ME fast idle speed adjustment—typical

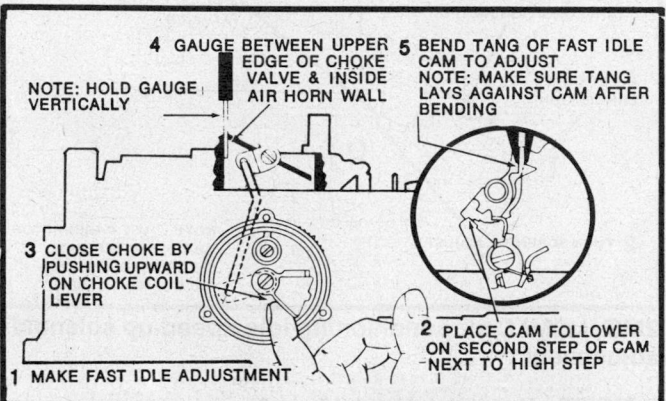

M2ME, E2ME fast idle cam adjustment—typical

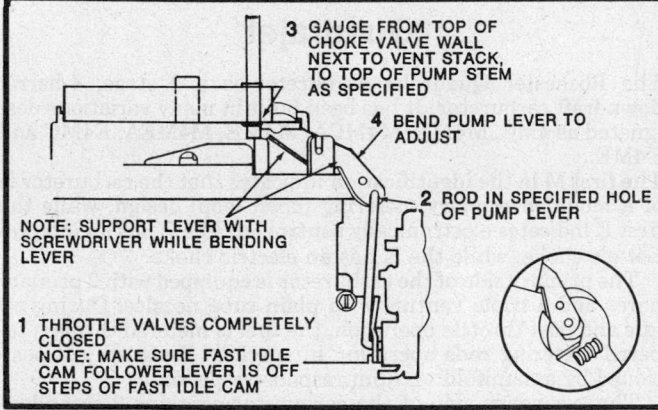

Pump adjustment

of the slot in the choke valve lever. Place the fast idle cam follower on the high step of the cam.

3. Insert a 0.120 in. plug gauge in the hole in the choke housing.

4. The lower edge of the choke coil lever should just contact the side of the plug gauge.

5. Bend the choke rod to adjust.

FRONT/REAR VACUUM BRAKE

Adjustment

A choke valve measuring gauge J–26701 or equivalent is used to measure angle (degrees instead of inches).

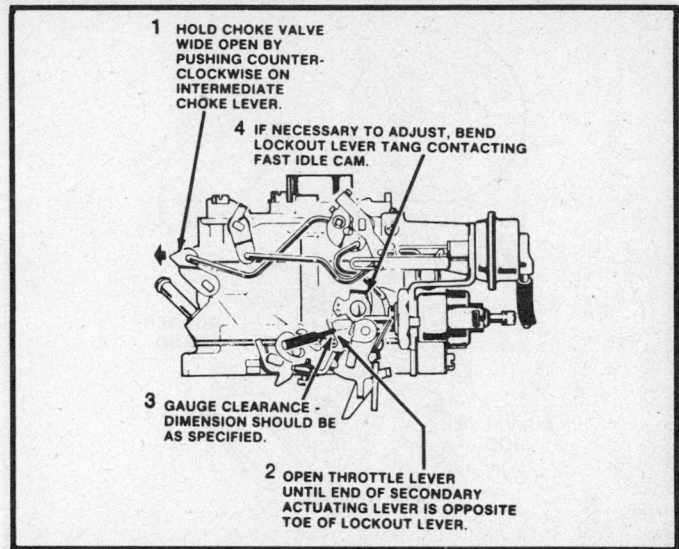

2SE and E2SE secondary lockout adjustment—typical

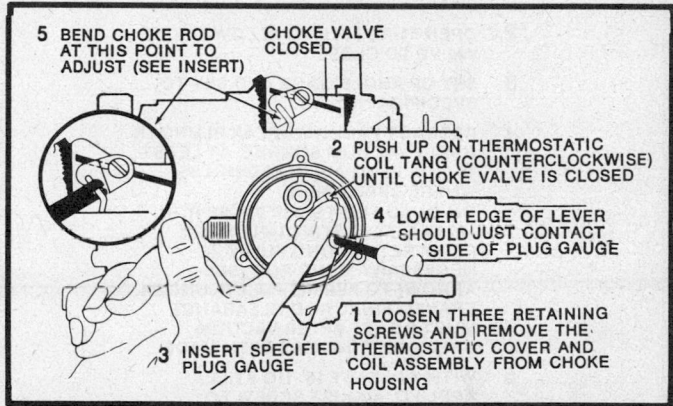

M2ME, E2ME choke coil lever adjustment—typical

CHOKE UNLOADER

Adjustment

1. With the choke valve completely closed, hold the throttle valves wide open.

2. Measure between the upper edge of the choke valve and air horn wall.

3. Bend the tang on the fast idle lever to obtain the proper measurement.

AIR CONDITIONING IDLE SPEED-UP SOLENOID

Adjustment

1. With the engine at normal operating temperature and the air conditioning turned on but the compressor clutch lead disconnected, the solenoid should be electrically energized (plunger stem extended). Open the throttle slightly to allow the solenoid plunger to fully extend.

2. Adjust the plunger screw to obtain the specified idle speed.

3. Turn off the air conditioner. The solenoid plunger should move away from the tang on the throttle lever.

4. Adjust the curb idle speed with the idle speed screw, if necessary.

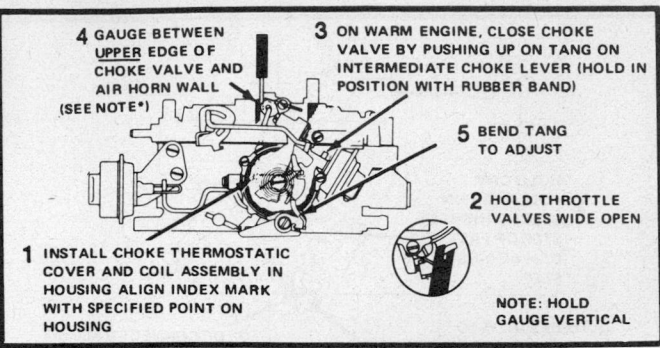

4 GAUGE BETWEEN UPPER EDGE OF CHOKE VALVE AND AIR HORN WALL (SEE NOTE*)

3 ON WARM ENGINE, CLOSE CHOKE VALVE BY PUSHING UP ON TANG ON INTERMEDIATE CHOKE LEVER (HOLD IN POSITION WITH RUBBER BAND)

5 BEND TANG TO ADJUST

2 HOLD THROTTLE VALVES WIDE OPEN

1 INSTALL CHOKE THERMOSTATIC COVER AND COIL ASSEMBLY IN HOUSING ALIGN INDEX MARK WITH SPECIFIED POINT ON HOUSING

NOTE: HOLD GAUGE VERTICAL

2MC, M2MC, M2ME, E2ME unloader adjustment—typical

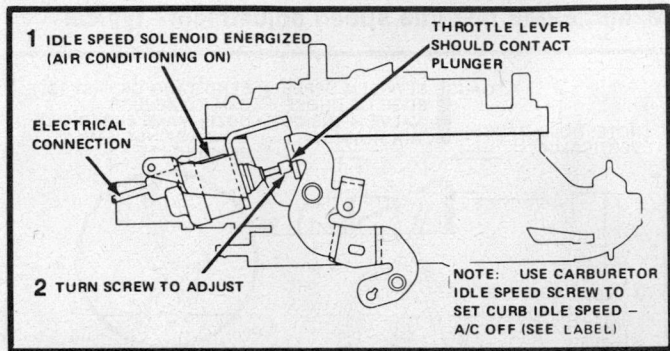

1 IDLE SPEED SOLENOID ENERGIZED (AIR CONDITIONING ON)

THROTTLE LEVER SHOULD CONTACT PLUNGER

ELECTRICAL CONNECTION

2 TURN SCREW TO ADJUST

NOTE: USE CARBURETOR IDLE SPEED SCREW TO SET CURB IDLE SPEED — A/C OFF (SEE LABEL)

2MC, M2MLC air conditioning idle speed-up solenoid adjustment

NOTE: Do not adjust if carburetor is computer controlled.

Quadrajet

The Rochester Quadrajet carburetor is a 2 stage, 4-barrel downdraft carburetor. It has been built in many variations designated as 4MC, M4MC, M4MCA, M4ME, M4MEA, E4MC and E4ME.

The first M in the identification indicates that the carburetor is of a modified primary metering (open loop) design, while the first E indicates electronically controlled. The C has an integral hot air choke, while the E has an electric choke.

The primary side of the carburetor is equipped with 2 primary bores and a triple venturi with plain tube nozzles. During off idle and part throttle operation, the fuel is metered through tapered metering rods operating in specially designed jets positioned by a manifold vacuum responsive piston.

The secondary side of the carburetor contains 2 secondary bores. An air valve is used on the secondary side for metering control and supplements the primary bore. The secondary air valve operates tapered metering rods which regulate the fuel in constant proportion to the air being supplied.

FAST IDLE SPEED

Adjustment

1. Position the fast idle lever on the high step of the fast idle cam.

2. Be sure that the choke is wide open and the engine warm. Plug the EGR vacuum hose. Disconnect the vacuum hose to the front vacuum break unit, if there are 2.

3. Make a preliminary adjustment by turning the fast idle screw out until the throttle valves are closed, then turning it in the specified number of turns after it contacts the lever.

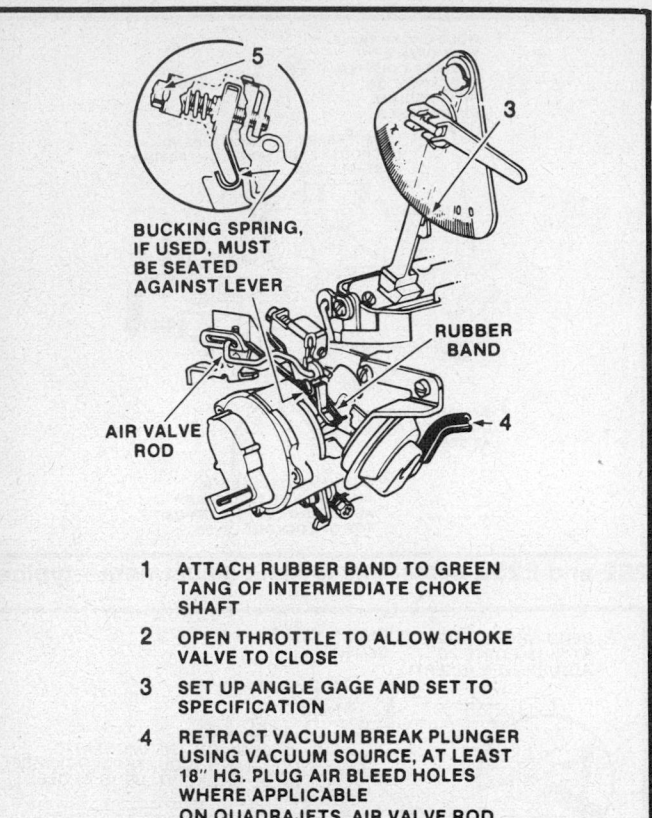

5

BUCKING SPRING, IF USED, MUST BE SEATED AGAINST LEVER

3

RUBBER BAND

AIR VALVE ROD

4

1 ATTACH RUBBER BAND TO GREEN TANG OF INTERMEDIATE CHOKE SHAFT

2 OPEN THROTTLE TO ALLOW CHOKE VALVE TO CLOSE

3 SET UP ANGLE GAGE AND SET TO SPECIFICATION

4 RETRACT VACUUM BREAK PLUNGER USING VACUUM SOURCE, AT LEAST 18" HG. PLUG AIR BLEED HOLES WHERE APPLICABLE ON QUADRAJETS, AIR VALVE ROD MUST NOT RESTRICT PLUNGER FROM RETRACTING FULLY. IF NECESSARY, BEND ROD (SEE ARROW) TO PERMIT FULL PLUNGER TRAVEL. FINAL ROD CLEARANCE MUST BE SET AFTER VACUUM BREAK SETTING HAS BEEN MADE.

5 WITH AT LEAST 18" HG STILL APPLIED, ADJUST SCREW TO CENTER BUBBLE

E2ME front vacuum break adjustment

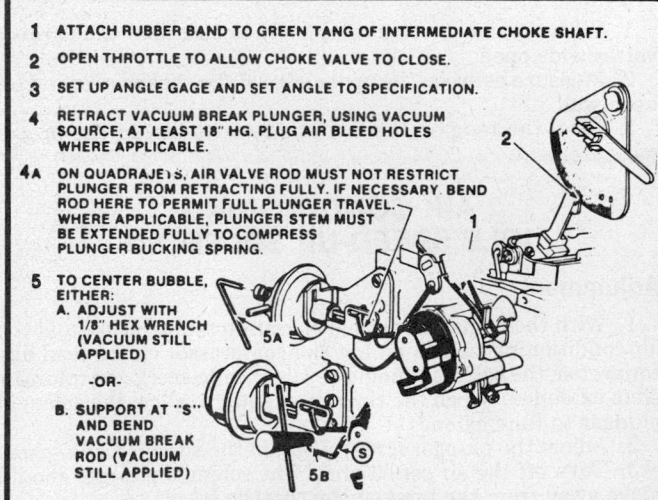

1 ATTACH RUBBER BAND TO GREEN TANG OF INTERMEDIATE CHOKE SHAFT.

2 OPEN THROTTLE TO ALLOW CHOKE VALVE TO CLOSE.

3 SET UP ANGLE GAGE AND SET ANGLE TO SPECIFICATION.

4 RETRACT VACUUM BREAK PLUNGER, USING VACUUM SOURCE, AT LEAST 18" HG. PLUG AIR BLEED HOLES WHERE APPLICABLE.

4A ON QUADRAJETS, AIR VALVE ROD MUST NOT RESTRICT PLUNGER FROM RETRACTING FULLY. IF NECESSARY, BEND ROD HERE TO PERMIT FULL PLUNGER TRAVEL. WHERE APPLICABLE, PLUNGER STEM MUST BE EXTENDED FULLY TO COMPRESS PLUNGER BUCKING SPRING.

2

1

5 TO CENTER BUBBLE, EITHER:
A. ADJUST WITH 1/8" HEX WRENCH (VACUUM STILL APPLIED)
-OR-
B. SUPPORT AT "S" AND BEND VACUUM BREAK ROD (VACUUM STILL APPLIED)

5A

S

5B

E2ME rear vacuum break adjustment

M2ME, E2ME CARBURETOR SPECIFICATIONS
General Motors—U.S.A.

Year	Carburetor Identification	Float Level (in.)	Choke Rod (in.)	Choke Unloader (deg./in.)	Vacuum Break Lean or Front (deg./in.)	Vacuum Break Rich or Rear (deg./in.)	Pump Rod (in.)	Choke Coil Lever (in.)	Automatic Choke (notches)
1986	17086190	10/32	0.096	35/0.195	28/0.164	24/0.136	①	0.120	Fixed
1987	17086190	10/32	0.096	35/0.195	28/0.164	24/0.136	①	0.120	Fixed

① Not Adjustable

M2ME, E2ME CARBURETOR SPECIFICATIONS
General Motors—Canada

Year	Carburetor Identification	Float Level (in.)	Choke Rod (in.)	Choke Unloader (in.)	Vacuum Break Lean or Front (deg./in.)	Vacuum Break Rich or Rear (deg./in.)	Pump Rod (in.)	Choke Coil Lever (in.)	Automatic Choke (notches)
1986	17086170	9/32	0.139	0.243	17/0.090	19/0.103	9/32 ①	0.120	Fixed
1987	17087170	9/32	0.139	0.243	17/0.090	19/0.103	9/32 ①	0.120	Fixed

① Inner hole

4. Use the fast idle screw to adjust the fast idle to the speed and under the conditions, specified on the engine compartment sticker or in the specifications chart.

FAST IDLE CAM CHOKE ROD

Adjustment

1. Adjust the fast idle and place the cam follower on the highest step of the fast idle cam against the shoulder of the high step.
2. Close the choke valve by exerting counter-clockwise pressure on the external choke lever. Remove the coil assembly from the choke housing and push upon the choke coil lever. On models with a fixed (riveted) choke cover, push up on the vacuum brake lever tang and hold in position with a rubber band.
3. Insert a gauge of the proper size between the upper edge of the choke valve and the inside air horn wall.
4. To adjust the valve, bend the tang on the fast idle cam. Be sure that the tang rests against the cam after bending.

PRIMARY (FRONT) VACUUM BREAK

Adjustment

A choke valve measuring gauge J–26701 or equivalent is used to measure angle (degrees instead of inches).

SECONDARY (REAR) VACUUM BRAKE

Adjustment

A choke valve measuring gauge J–26701 or equivalent is used to measure the angle (degrees instead of inches).

CHOKE LINK

Adjustment

Refer to the illustration for E4MC fast idle cam adjustment.

CHOKE UNLOADER

Adjustment

1. Push up on the vacuum break lever to close the choke valve and fully open the throttle valves.

2. Measure the distance from the upper edge of the choke valve to the air horn wall.
3. To adjust, bend the tang on the fast idle lever.

CHOKE COIL LEVER

Adjustment
MC AND ME CARBURETORS

1. Remove the choke cover and thermostatic coil from the

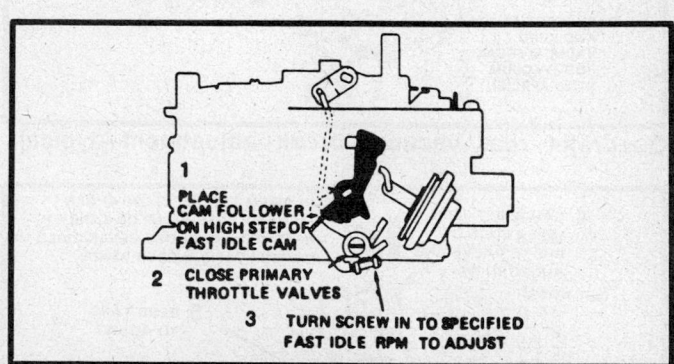

Quadrajet fast idle adjustment

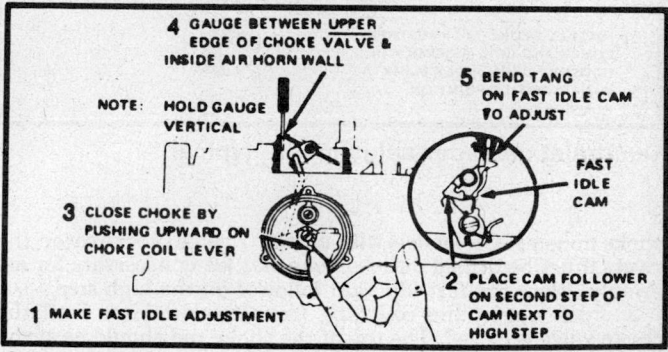

Quadrajet choke rod (fast idle cam) adjustment—typical

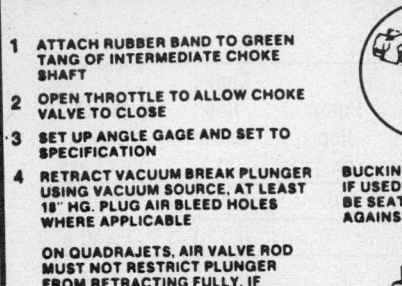
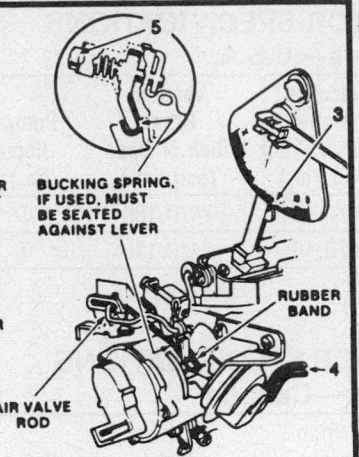

1 ATTACH RUBBER BAND TO GREEN TANG OF INTERMEDIATE CHOKE SHAFT

2 OPEN THROTTLE TO ALLOW CHOKE VALVE TO CLOSE

3 SET UP ANGLE GAGE AND SET TO SPECIFICATION

4 RETRACT VACUUM BREAK PLUNGER USING VACUUM SOURCE, AT LEAST 18" HG. PLUG AIR BLEED HOLES WHERE APPLICABLE

ON QUADRAJETS, AIR VALVE ROD MUST NOT RESTRICT PLUNGER FROM RETRACTING FULLY. IF NECESSARY, BEND ROD (SEE ARROW) TO PERMIT FULL PLUNGER TRAVEL. FINAL ROD CLEARANCE MUST BE SET AFTER VACUUM BREAK SETTING HAS BEEN MADE.

5 WITH AT LEAST 18" HG STILL APPLIED, ADJUST SCREW TO CENTER BUBBLE

BUCKING SPRING, IF USED, MUST BE SEATED AGAINST LEVER

RUBBER BAND

AIR VALVE ROD

Quadrajet front vacuum break adjustment

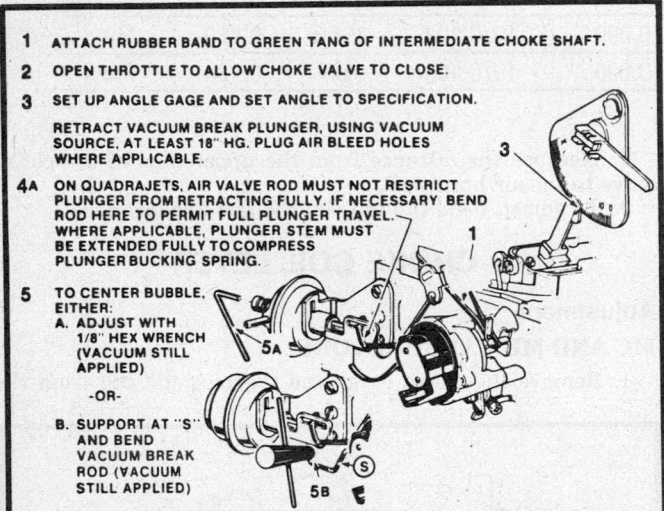

1 ATTACH RUBBER BAND TO GREEN TANG OF INTERMEDIATE CHOKE SHAFT.

2 OPEN THROTTLE TO ALLOW CHOKE VALVE TO CLOSE.

3 SET UP ANGLE GAGE AND SET ANGLE TO SPECIFICATION.

RETRACT VACUUM BREAK PLUNGER, USING VACUUM SOURCE, AT LEAST 18" HG. PLUG AIR BLEED HOLES WHERE APPLICABLE.

4A ON QUADRAJETS, AIR VALVE ROD MUST NOT RESTRICT PLUNGER FROM RETRACTING FULLY. IF NECESSARY BEND ROD HERE TO PERMIT FULL PLUNGER TRAVEL. WHERE APPLICABLE, PLUNGER STEM MUST BE EXTENDED FULLY TO COMPRESS PLUNGER BUCKING SPRING.

5 TO CENTER BUBBLE, EITHER:
A. ADJUST WITH 1/8" HEX WRENCH (VACUUM STILL APPLIED)
-OR-
B. SUPPORT AT "S" AND BEND VACUUM BREAK ROD (VACUUM STILL APPLIED)

Quadrajet rear vacuum break adjustment—typical

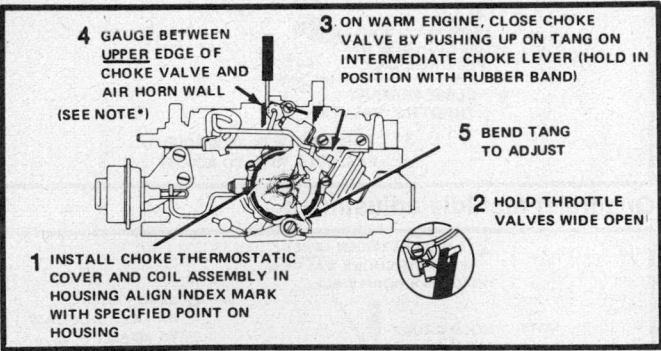

4 GAUGE BETWEEN UPPER EDGE OF CHOKE VALVE AND AIR HORN WALL (SEE NOTE*)

3 ON WARM ENGINE, CLOSE CHOKE VALVE BY PUSHING UP ON TANG ON INTERMEDIATE CHOKE LEVER (HOLD IN POSITION WITH RUBBER BAND)

5 BEND TANG TO ADJUST

2 HOLD THROTTLE VALVES WIDE OPEN

1 INSTALL CHOKE THERMOSTATIC COVER AND COIL ASSEMBLY IN HOUSING ALIGN INDEX MARK WITH SPECIFIED POINT ON HOUSING

Quadrajet unloader adjustment—typical

choke housing. On models with a fixed (riveted) choke cover, the rivets must be drilled out. A choke stat kit is necessary for assembly. Place the fast idle cam follower on the high step.

2. Push up on the coil tang (counter-clockwise) until the choke valve is closed. The top of the choke rod should be at the bottom of the slot in the choke valve lever.

3. Insert a 0.120 in. drill bit in the hole in the choke housing.

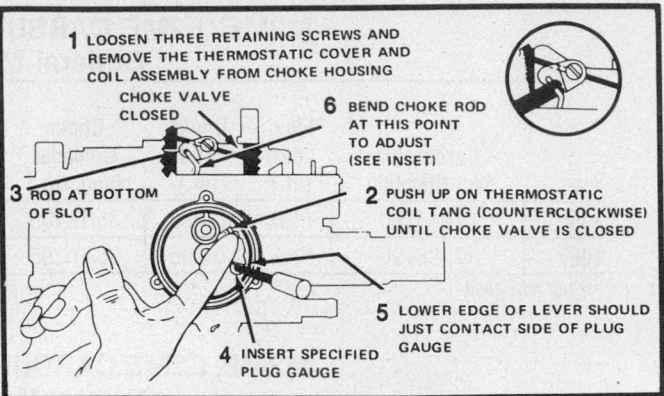

1 LOOSEN THREE RETAINING SCREWS AND REMOVE THE THERMOSTATIC COVER AND COIL ASSEMBLY FROM CHOKE HOUSING

CHOKE VALVE CLOSED

6 BEND CHOKE ROD AT THIS POINT TO ADJUST (SEE INSET)

3 ROD AT BOTTOM OF SLOT

2 PUSH UP ON THERMOSTATIC COIL TANG (COUNTERCLOCKWISE) UNTIL CHOKE VALVE IS CLOSED

4 INSERT SPECIFIED PLUG GAUGE

5 LOWER EDGE OF LEVER SHOULD JUST CONTACT SIDE OF PLUG GAUGE

Quadrajet choke coil lever adjustment—typical

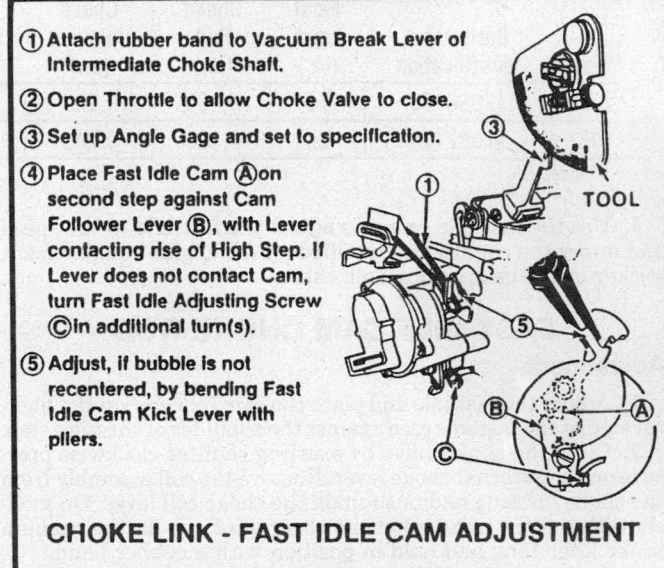

① Attach rubber band to Vacuum Break Lever of Intermediate Choke Shaft.

② Open Throttle to allow Choke Valve to close.

③ Set up Angle Gage and set to specification.

④ Place Fast Idle Cam Ⓐ on second step against Cam Follower Lever Ⓑ, with Lever contacting rise of High Step. If Lever does not contact Cam, turn Fast Idle Adjusting Screw Ⓒ in additional turn(s).

⑤ Adjust, if bubble is not recentered, by bending Fast Idle Cam Kick Lever with pliers.

TOOL

CHOKE LINK - FAST IDLE CAM ADJUSTMENT

Feedback Quadrajet—Fast idle cam adjustment

4. The lower edge of the choke coil lever should just contact the side of the plug gauge.

5. Bend the choke rod at the top angle to adjust.

SECONDARY CLOSING

Adjustment

This adjustment assures proper closing of the secondary throttle plates.

1. Set the slow idle as per instructions in the appropriate car section. Make sure that the fast idle cam follower is not resting on the fast idle cam and the choke valve is wide open.

2. There should be 0.020 in. clearance between the secondary throttle actuating rod and the front of the slot on the secondary throttle lever with the closing tang on the throttle lever resting against the actuating lever.

3. Bend the secondary closing tang on the primary throttle actuating rod or lever to adjust.

SECONDARY OPENING

Adjustment

1. Open the primary throttle valves until the actuating link contacts the upper tang on the secondary lever.

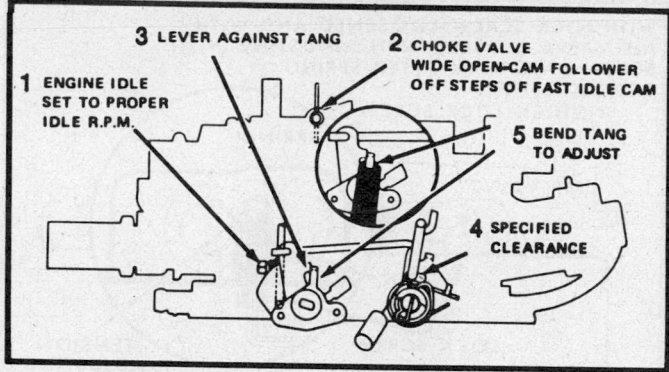

Quadrajet Secondary Closing Adjustment

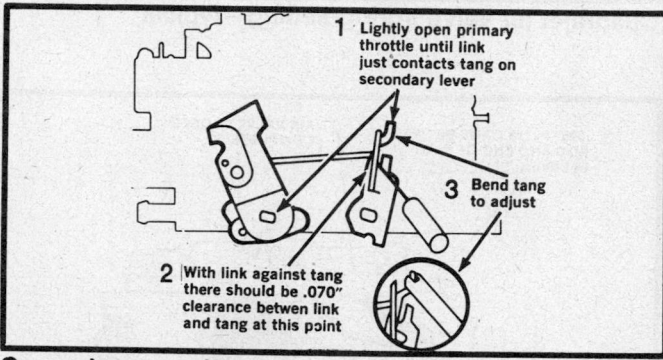

Secondary opening adjustment—three point linkage

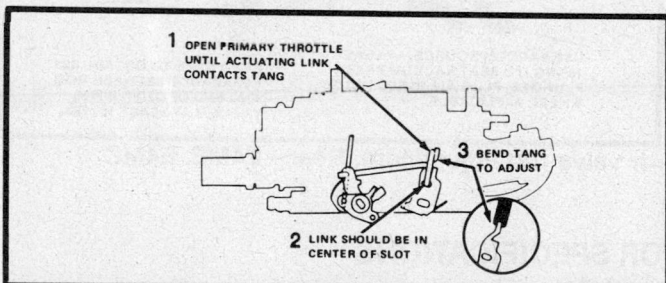

Quadrajet secondary opening adjustment, two point linkage

2. With the 2 point linkage, the bottom of the link should be in the center of the secondary lever slot.

3. With the 3 point linkage, there should be 0.070 in. clearance between the link and the middle tang.

4. Bend the upper tang on the secondary lever to adjust as necessary.

FLOAT LEVEL

Adjustment

With the air horn assembly removed, measure the distance from the air horn gasket surface (gasket removed) to the top of the float at the toe (³⁄₁₆ in. back from the toe).

NOTE: Make sure the retaining pin is firmly held in place and that the tang of the float is lightly held against the needle and seat assembly.

On carburetors without the computer controlled systems, remove the float and bend the float arm to adjust. For (E4MC and E4ME) the computer controlled systems carburetors, use the following steps:

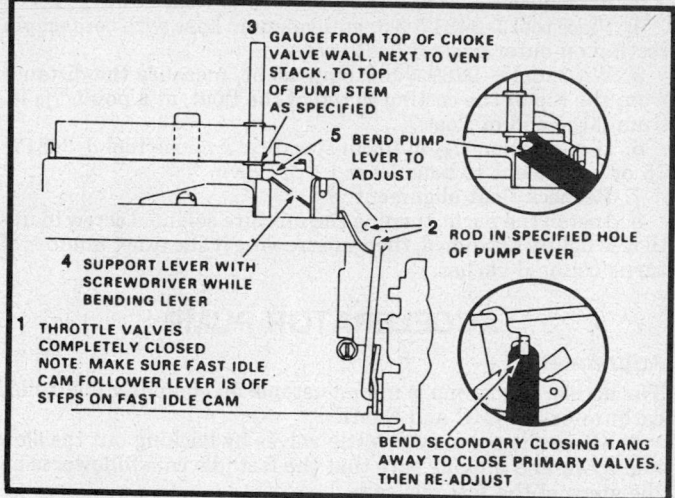

Quadrajet accelerator pump rod adjustment

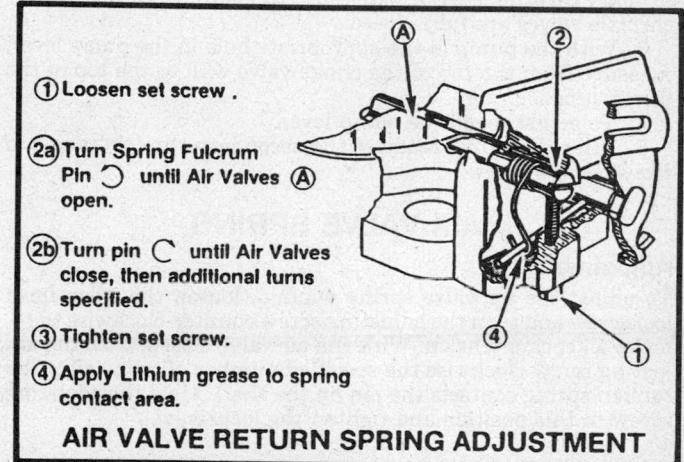

AIR VALVE RETURN SPRING ADJUSTMENT

Typical E4MC air valve return spring adjustment

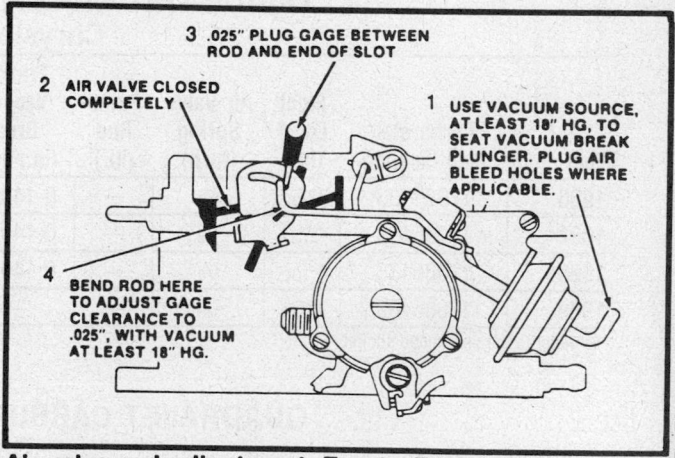

Air valve rod adjustment, Front—E4ME, E4MC

1. Remove air horn and gasket.
2. Remove solenoid plunger, metering rods and float bowl insert.

NOTE: If necessary to remove solenoid lean mixture adjusting screw count and record the number of turns it takes to lightly bottom the screw and return to the exact position when reassembling.

3. Attach tool J–34817 or equivalent to float bowl.

4. Place tool J–34817–3 or equivalent in base with contact pin resting on outer edge of float lever.

5. With tool J–9789–90 or equivalent, measure the distance from the top of the casting to top of the float, at a point 3/16 in. from large end of float.

6. If more than 2/32 in. from specification, use tool J–34817–15 or equivalent to bend lever up or down.

7. Recheck float alignment.

8. Install the parts, turning the mixture solenoid screw in until it is lightly bottomed, then unscrewing it the exact number of turns counted earlier.

ACCELERATOR PUMP

Adjustment

The accelerator pump is not adjustable on computer controlled carburetors (E4MC and E4ME).

1. Close the primary throttle valves by backing out the slow idle screw and making sure that the fast idle cam follower is off the steps of the fast idle cam.

2. Bend the secondary throttle closing tang away from the primary throttle lever, if necessary, to insure that the primary throttle valves are fully closed.

3. With the pump in the appropriate hole in the pump lever, measure from the top of the choke valve wall to the top of the pump stem.

4. To adjust, bend the pump lever.

5. After adjusting, readjust the secondary throttle tang and the slow idle screw.

AIR VALVE SPRING

Adjustment

To adjust the air valve spring windup, loosen the Allen head lockscrew and turn the adjusting screw counter-clockwise to remove all spring tension. With the air valve closed, turn the adjusting screw clockwise the specified number of turns after the torsion spring contacts the pin on the shaft. Hold the adjusting screw in this position and tighten the lockscrew.

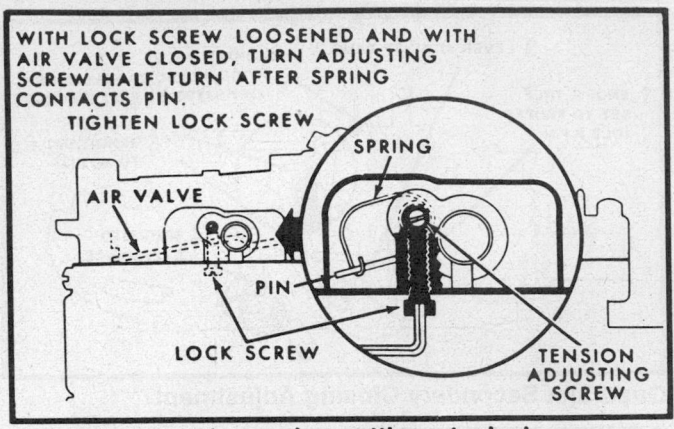

WITH LOCK SCREW LOOSENED AND WITH AIR VALVE CLOSED, TURN ADJUSTING SCREW HALF TURN AFTER SPRING CONTACTS PIN.
TIGHTEN LOCK SCREW

SPRING
AIR VALVE
PIN
LOCK SCREW
TENSION ADJUSTING SCREW

Quadrajet air valve spring setting—typical

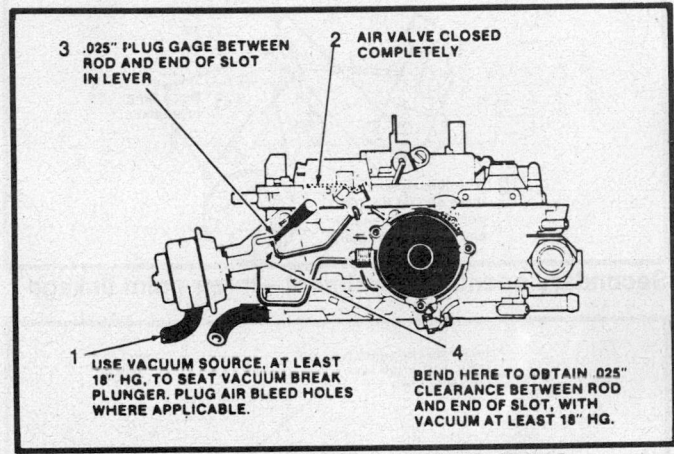

3 .025" PLUG GAGE BETWEEN ROD AND END OF SLOT IN LEVER
2 AIR VALVE CLOSED COMPLETELY
1 USE VACUUM SOURCE, AT LEAST 18" HG, TO SEAT VACUUM BREAK PLUNGER. PLUG AIR BLEED HOLES WHERE APPLICABLE.
4 BEND HERE TO OBTAIN .025" CLEARANCE BETWEEN ROD AND END OF SLOT, WITH VACUUM AT LEAST 18" HG.

Air valve rod adjustment, Rear—E4ME, E4MC

QUADRAJET CARBURETOR SPECIFICATIONS
Chrysler Products

Year	Carburetor Identification	Float Level (in.)	Air Valve Spring (turn)	Pump Rod (in.)	Primary Vacuum Break (in./deg.)	Secondary Vacuum Break (in./deg.)	Secondary Opening (in.)	Choke Rod (in./deg.)	Choke Unloader (in./deg.)	Fast Idle Speed (rpm)
1986	17085433	14/32	7/8	—	0.140/25	—	—	0.120/20	0.179/30	①
1987	17085433	14/32	7/8	—	0.140/25	—	—	0.120/20	0.179/30	①
1988	17085433	14/32	7/8	—	0.140/25	—	—	0.120/20	0.179/30	①
1989	17085433	14/32	7/8	—	—	—	—	0.120/20	0.180/30	①

① Refer to the underhood sticker

QUADRAJET CARBURETOR SPECIFICATIONS
Cadillac

Year	Carburetor Identification	Float Level (in.)	Air Valve Spring (turn)	Pump Rod (in.)	Primary Vacuum Break (deg.)	Secondary Vacuum Break (deg.)	Secondary Opening (in.)	Choke Rod (in./deg.)	Choke Unloader (in./deg.)	Fast Idle Speed (rpm)
1986	17086008	11/32	1/2	Fixed	25°	43°	①	14°	35°	②
	17086009	14/32	1/2	Fixed	25°	43°	①	14°	35°	②

QUADRAJET CARBURETOR SPECIFICATIONS
Cadillac

Year	Carburetor Identification	Float Level (in.)	Air Valve Spring (turn)	Pump Rod (in.)	Primary Vacuum Break (deg.)	Secondary Vacuum Break (deg.)	Secondary Opening (in.)	Choke Rod (in./deg.)	Choke Unloader (in./deg.)	Fast Idle Speed (rpm)
1987	17086008	11/32	1/2	Fixed	25°	43°	①	14°	35°	②
	17086009	14/32	1/2	Fixed	25°	43°	①	14°	35°	②
1988	17086008	11/32	1/2	Fixed	25°	43°	①	14°	35°	②
	17086009	14/32	1/2	Fixed	25°	43°	①	14°	35°	②
	17088115	11/32	1/2	Fixed	25°	43°	①	14°	35°	②
1989	17086008	11/32	1/2	Fixed	25°	43°	①	14°	35°	②
	17086009	14/32	1/2	Fixed	25°	43°	①	14°	35°	②
	17086115	11/32	1/2	Fixed	25°	43°	①	14°	35°	②

① No measurement necessary on two point linkage
② See underhood decal

QUADRAJET CARBURETOR SPECIFICATIONS
Buick

Year	Carburetor Identification	Float Level (in.)	Air Valve Spring (turn)	Pump Rod (in.)	Primary Vacuum Break (deg.)	Secondary Vacuum Break (deg.)	Secondary Opening (in.)	Choke Rod (deg.)	Choke Unloader (deg.)	Fast Idle Speed (rpm)
1986	17086008	11/32	1/2	Fixed	25°	43°	①	14°	35°	②
1987	17086008	11/32	1/2	Fixed	25°	43°	①	14°	35°	②
1988	17086008	11/32	1/2	Fixed	25°	43°	①	14°	35°	②
	17088115	11/32	1/2	Fixed	25°	43°	①	14°	35°	②
1989	17088115	11/32	1/2	Fixed	25°	43°	①	14°	35°	②

① No measurement necessary on two point linkage
② See underhood decal

QUADRAJET CARBURETOR SPECIFICATIONS
Chevrolet

Year	Carburetor Identification	Float Level (in.)	Air Valve Spring (turn)	Pump Rod (in.)	Primary Vacuum (deg./in.)	Secondary Vacuum (deg./in.)	Secondary Opening (in.)	Choke Rod (deg./in.)	Choke Unloader (deg./in.)	Fast Idle Speed (rpm)
1986	17086003	11/32	7/8	Fixed	0.157/27	—	①	20°	0.243/38°	②
	17086004	11/32	7/8	Fixed	0.157/27	—	①	20°	0.243/38°	②
	17086005	11/32	7/8	Fixed	0.157/27	—	①	38°	0.243/38°	②
	17086006	11/32	7/8	Fixed	0.157/27	—	①	20°	0.243/38°	②
1987	17086008	11/32	7/8	Fixed	0.157/27	—	①	14°	0.243/35°	②
	17087129	11/32	7/8	Fixed	0.157/27	—	①	20°	0.243/38°	②
	17087130	11/32	7/8	Fixed	0.157/27	—	①	20°	0.243/38°	②
	17087132	11/32	7/8	Fixed	0.157/27	—	①	20°	0.243/38°	②
1988	17087306	11/32	7/8	Fixed	27°	—	①	20°	32°	②
	17087129	11/32	7/8	Fixed	27°	—	①	20°	32°	②
	17087132	11/32	7/8	Fixed	27°	—	①	20°	32°	②
1989	17088115	11/32	1/2	Fixed	25°	43°	①	14°	35°	②

① No measurement necessary on two point linkage
② See underhood decal.

QUADRAJET CARBURETOR SPECIFICATIONS
Oldsmobile

Year	Carburetor Identification	Float Level (in.)	Air Valve Spring (turn)	Pump Rod (in.)	Primary Vacuum Break (in./deg.)	Secondary Vacuum Break (in./deg.)	Secondary Opening (in.)	Choke Rod (in./deg.)	Choke Unloader (in./deg.)	Fast Idle Speed (rpm)
1986	17086008	11/32	1/2	Fixed	0.142/25	0.287/43	①	0.171/14°	0.220/35°	②
	17086009	14/32	1/2	Fixed	0.142/25	0.287/43	①	0.171/14°	0.220/35°	②
1987	17086008	11/32	1/2	Fixed	0.142/25	0.287/43	①	0.171/14°	0.220/35°	②
	17086009	14/32	1/2	Fixed	0.142/25	0.287/43	①	0.171/14°	0.220/35°	②
1988	17086008	11/32	1/2	Fixed	25°	43°	①	14°	35°	②
	17088115	11/32	1/2	Fixed	25°	43°	①	14°	35°	②
1989	17088115	11/32	1/2	Fixed	25°	43°	①	14°	35°	②

① No measurement necessary on two point linkage
② See underhood decal.

QUADRAJET CARBURETOR SPECIFICATIONS
Pontiac

Year	Carburetor Identification	Float Level (in.)	Air Valve Spring (turn)	Pump Rod (in.)	Primary Vacuum Break (in./deg.)	Secondary Vacuum Break (in./deg.)	Secondary Opening (in.)	Choke Rod (in./deg.)	Choke Unloader (in./deg.)	Fast Idle Speed (rpm)
1986	17086003	11/32	7/8	Fixed	0.157/27	—	①	0.110	0.243/38	②
	17086004	11/32	7/8	Fixed	0.157/27	—	①	0.110	0.243/38	②
	17086005	11/32	7/8	Fixed	0.157/27	—	①	0.243	0.243/38	②
	17086006	11/32	7/8	Fixed	0.157/27	—	①	0.110	0.243/38	②
	17086007	11/32	1/2	Fixed	0.142/25	0.287/43	①	0.071	0.220/35	②
	17086008	11/32	1/2	Fixed	0.142/25	0.287/43	①	0.071	0.220/35	②
	17086040	11/32	7/8	Fixed	0.157/27	—	①	0.110	0.243/38	②
1987	17087130	11/32	7/8	Fixed	0.157/27	—	①	0.110	0.243/38	②
	17087131	11/32	7/8	Fixed	0.157/27	—	①	0.110	0.243/38	②
	17087133	11/32	7/8	Fixed	0.157/27	—	①	0.110	0.243/38	②
	17086008	11/32	1/2	Fixed	0.142/25	0.287/43	①	0.071	0.220/35	②
1988	17086008	11/32	1/2	Fixed	25°	43°	—	14°	35°	②
	17088115	11/32	1/2	Fixed	25°	43°	—	14°	35°	②
1989	17088115	11/32	1/2	Fixed	25°	43°	①	14°	35°	②

① No measurement necessary on two point linkage; see text
② See underhood decal

QUADRAJET CARBURETOR SPECIFICATIONS
All Canadian Models

Year	Carburetor Identification	Float Level (in.)	Air Valve Spring (turn)	Pump Rod (in.)	Primary Vacuum Break (deg./in.)	Secondary Vacuum Break (deg.)	Secondary Opening (deg./in.)	Choke Rod (deg./in.)	Choke Unloader (deg./in.)	Fast Idle Speed (rpm)
1986	17086246	13/32	7/8	9/32 ①	20/0.110	—	②	0.096	30/0.179	③
	17086247	13/32	7/8	9/32 ①	20/0.110	—	②	0.096	30/0.179	③
	17086248	13/32	7/8	9/32 ①	20/0.110	—	②	0.096	30/0.179	③
	17086249	13/32	7/8	9/32 ①	20/0.110	—	②	0.096	30/0.179	③
	17086580	3/8	7/8	9/32 ①	21/0.117	—	②	0.077	30/0.179	③
	17086581	3/8	7/8	9/32 ①	21/0.117	—	②	0.077	30/0.179	③
	17086582	3/8	7/8	9/32 ①	21/0.117	—	②	0.077	30/0.179	③
	17086583	3/8	7/8	9/32 ①	21/0.117	—	②	0.077	30/0.179	③

QUADRAJET CARBURETOR SPECIFICATIONS
All Canadian Models

Year	Carburetor Identification	Float Level (in.)	Air Valve Spring (turn)	Pump Rod (in.)	Primary Vacuum Break (deg./in.)	Secondary Vacuum Break (deg./in.)	Secondary Opening (deg./in.)	Choke Rod (deg./in.)	Choke Unloader (deg./in.)	Fast Idle Speed (rpm)
1986	17086584	3/8	7/8	9/32 ①	21/0.117	—	②	0.077	30/0.179	③
	17086586	3/8	7/8	9/32 ①	21/0.117	—	②	0.077	30/0.179	③
	17086588	3/8	7/8	9/32 ①	21/0.117	—	②	0.077	30/0.179	③
	17086590	3/8	7/8	9/32 ①	21/0.117	—	②	0.077	30/0.179	③
	17086596	1/2	7/8	9/32 ①	21/0.117	—	②	0.077	30/0.179	③
	17086598	1/2	7/8	9/32 ①	21/0.117	—	②	0.077	30/0.179	③
1987	17087117	1/2	7/8	9/32	23/0.129	—	②	0.077	26/0.149	③
	17087118	1/2	7/8	9/32	23/0.129	—	②	0.077	26/0.149	③
	17087119	1/2	7/8	9/32	23/0.129	—	②	0.077	26/0.149	③
	17087120	1/2	7/8	9/32	23/0.129	—	②	0.077	26/0.149	③
	17087123	1/2	7/8	9/32	23/0.129	—	②	0.077	26/0.149	③
	17087124	1/2	7/8	9/32	23/0.129	—	②	0.077	26/0.149	③
	17087125	1/2	7/8	9/32	25/0.142	—	②	0.077	26/0.149	③
	17087126	1/2	7/8	9/32	25/0.142	—	②	0.077	26/0.149	③
	17087207	13/32	1/2	9/32	21/0.117	—	②	0.077	28/0.164	③
	17087211	13/32	1/2	9/32	21/0.117	—	②	0.077	28/0.164	③
1988	17086008	11/32	1/2	Fixed	25/0.142	43°	②	14°	35°	③
	17088115	11/32	1/2	Fixed	25/0.142	43°	②	14°	35°	③
	17087211	11/32	1/2	9/32	21/0.117	—	②	14°	28/0.164	③
1989	17086008	11/32	1/2	Fixed	25/0.142	43°	②	14°	35°	③
	17088115	11/32	1/2	Fixed	25/0.142	43°	②	14°	35°	③
	17087211	11/32	1/2	9/32	21/0.117	—	②	14°	28/0.164	③

① Inner hole
② No measurement necessary on two point linkage
③ See underhood decal

NIPPON KIKAKI CARBURETORS

Spectrum 2 Barrel

PRIMARY THROTTLE VALVE OPENING (FULL OPENING)

Adjustment

1. Inspect the angle of the primary throttle valve when the throttle valve has been fully opened. The valve angle should be 90 degrees from the horizontal plane.
2. If adjustment is needed, bend the throttle adjusting arm.

SECONDARY THROTTLE VALVE OPENING

Adjustment

1. Open the throttle lever, fully open the secondary throttle valve and inspect the angle. The valve angle should be 87 degrees from the horizontal plane.

2. If necessary, bend the secondary shaft lever to adjust.

CHOKE VALVE (THIRD STAGE)

Adjustment

Check the choke valve in the third stage of the fast idle cam.

NOTE: If removing the choke cover, note the relationship between the punched mark and the scribed line on the choke pinion plate. During reassembly the line and punch mark must be aligned to this position.

1. Set the choke valve to full open.
2. Slowly open the throttle lever while lightly pushing the choke valve in the closing direction with a finger and set the choke valve to the third stage of the fast idle cam.
3. The choke valve clearance should be 0.093 in.
4. If adjustment is needed, remove the rivet of the automatic choke and adjust by bending the choke lever in the housing. Reinstall the choke lever by riveting.

PRIMARY THROTTLE VALVE OPENING (SECOND STAGE)

Adjustment

Check the clearance of the primary throttle valve in the second stage of the fast idle cam.

1. Set the choke valve to full open.
2. Open the throttle valve slowly while pushing the choke valve lightly in the closing direction with a finger and set the choke valve to the second stage of the fast idle cam.
3. The primary throttle valve clearance should be: automatic transaxle – 0.692 in., manual transaxle – 0.543 in.
4. Adjustment is made with the fast idle screw.

CHOKE UNLOADER

Adjustment

1. Check the clearance of the choke valve when the primary throttle valve has been fully opened. The clearance should be 0.071 in.
2. If adjustment is necessary, remove the rivet of the automatic choke and adjust it by bending the choke lever in the housing. Reinstall the choke lever by riveting.

CHOKE BREAKER

Adjustment

1. Apply a vacuum of about 15.75 in.(400mm) Hg to the choke breaker diaphragm unit.
2. Lightly push the choke valve to the closing side. The clearance should be 0.057 in.
3. Adjust by bending the choke lever.

THROTTLE POSITION SENSOR (TPS)

Adjustment

NOTE: After the connection of the ohmmeter is made to the TPS, this test should be performed in as short of time as possible.

1. Check that the TPS bracket screws are tight.
2. Check that there is no play in the TPS arm and primary throttle valve arm.
3. Connect an ohmmeter to the green and black leads of the TPS.
4. Open the throttle lever about one-third (no continuity in this case) and then gradually close the lever and check that there is continuity when the primary slot valve reaches the the prescribed clearance of 0.015 (automatic transaxle), 0.011 (manual transaxle).
5. Adjust by loosening the TPS screws. After adjustment check the clearance as in Step 4.

SECONDARY TOUCH ANGLE

Adjustment

1. Measure the primary throttle valve opening at the same time the secondary throttle valve starts to open.
2. The clearance should be 0.023 in. Adjust by bending the throttle adjusting arm.

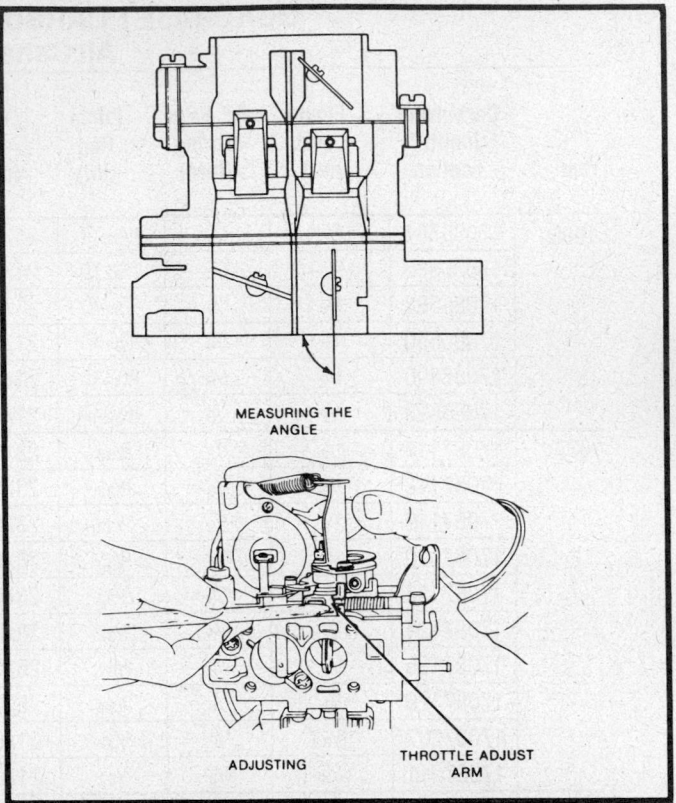

Primary throttle valve angle (full-open) – Spectrum

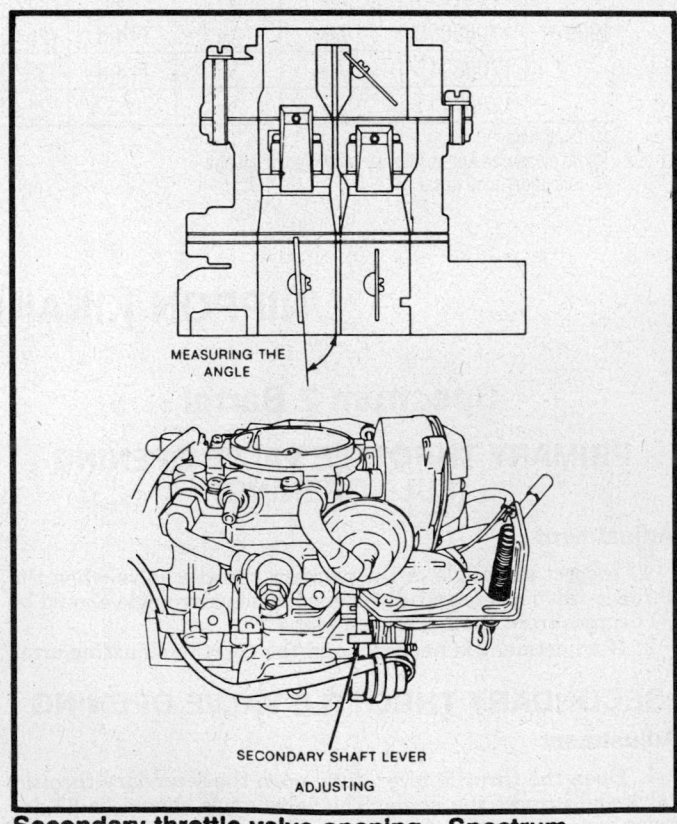

Secondary throttle valve opening – Spectrum

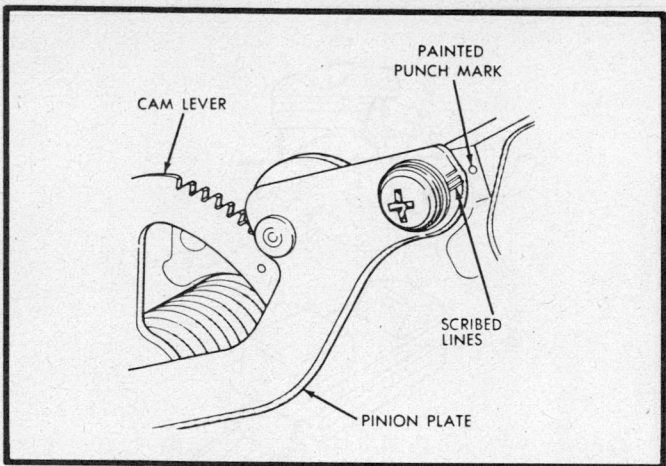

Pinion plate alignment

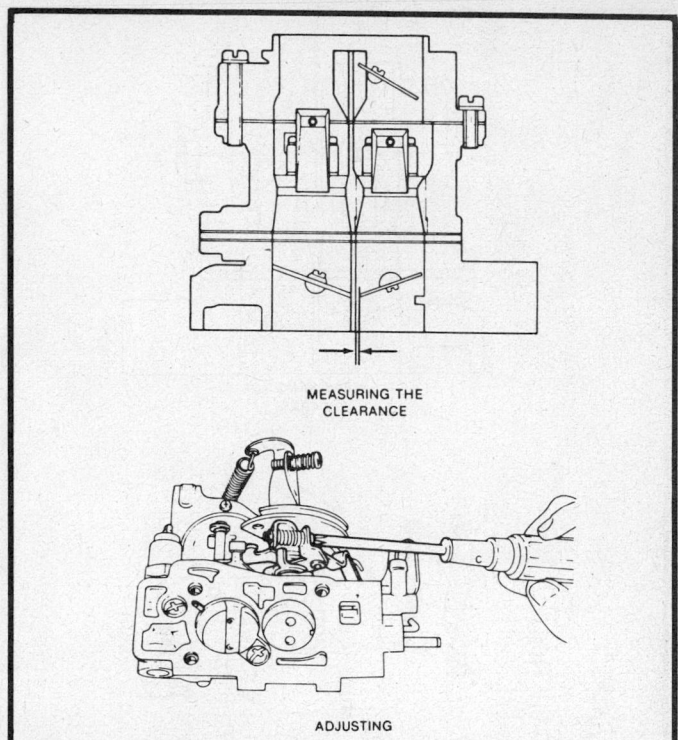

MEASURING THE CLEARANCE

ADJUSTING

Primary throttle valve opening (second stage) — Spectrum

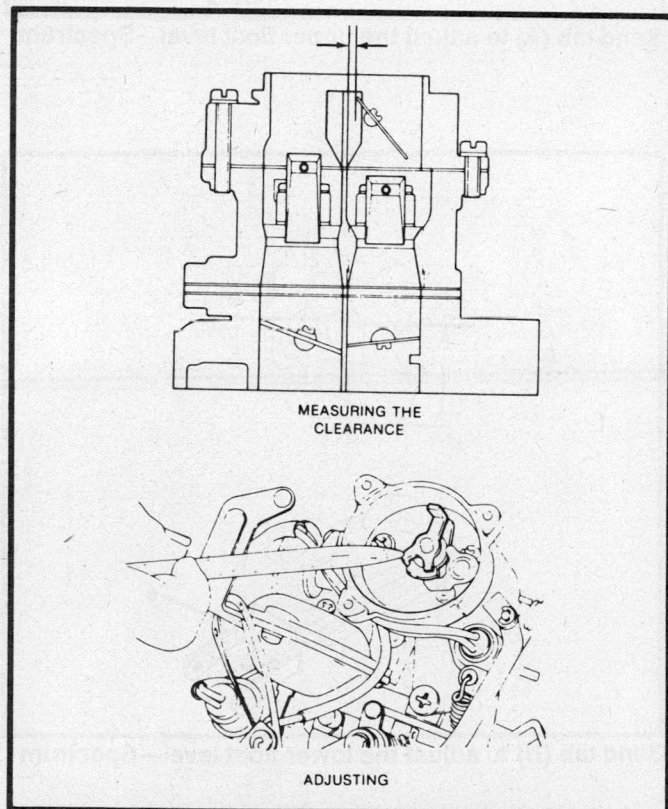

MEASURING THE CLEARANCE

ADJUSTING

Choke valve adjustment (third stage) — Spectrum

FLOAT LEVEL

Adjustment

1. Measure the clearance between the float top and gasket when the float is in the raised position. The clearance should be 0.059 in.
2. Bend float tab (A) to adjust.

NOTE: Care should be taken not to damage the needle valve when adjusting the float level.

3. Measure the clearance between the float bottom and gasket at the lowered position of the float. the clearance should be 1.7 in. Adjust by bending float tap.

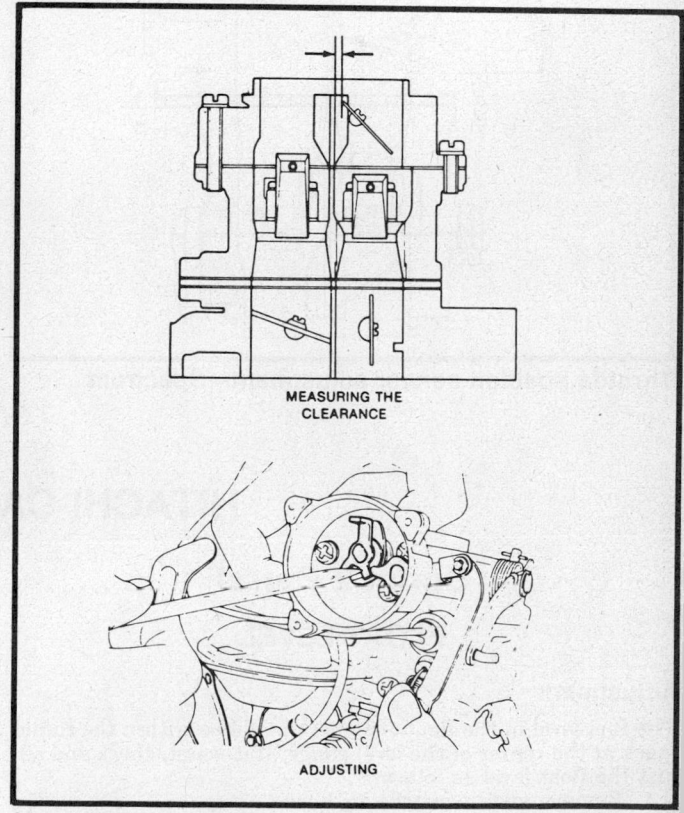

MEASURING THE CLEARANCE

ADJUSTING

Unloader adjustment — Spectrum

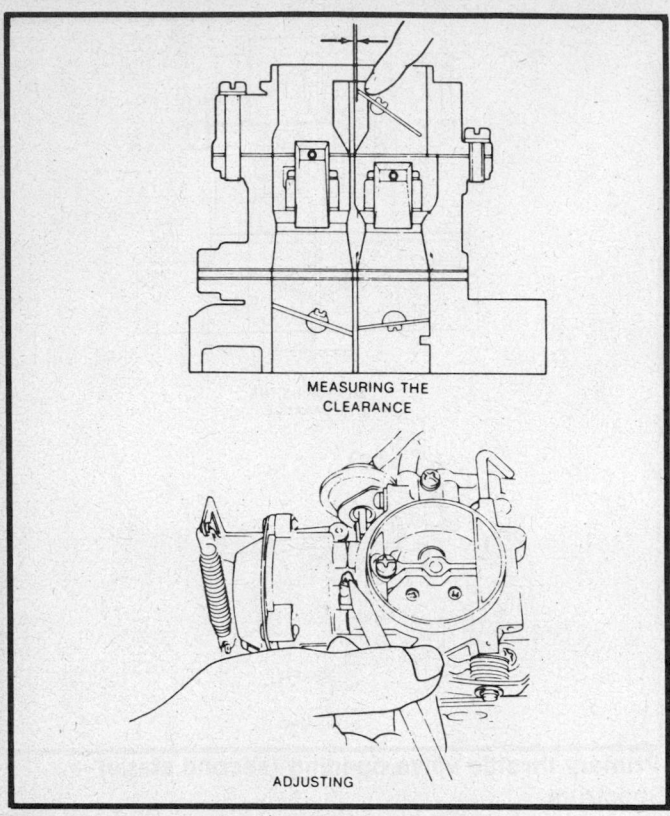

Choke breaker adjustment — Spectrum

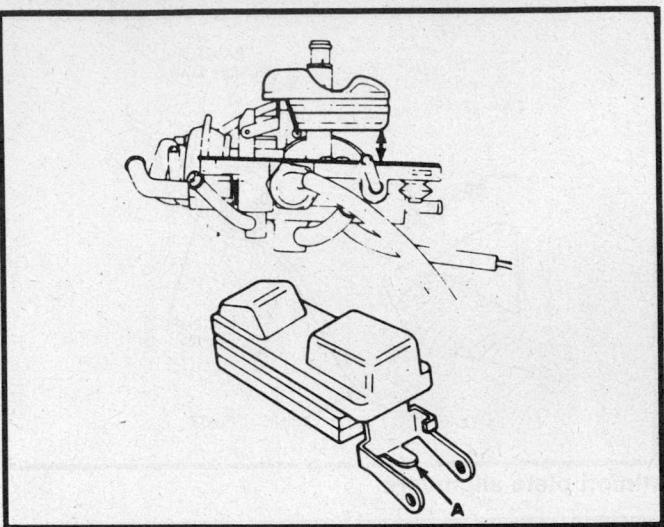

Bend tab (A) to adjust the upper float level — Spectrum

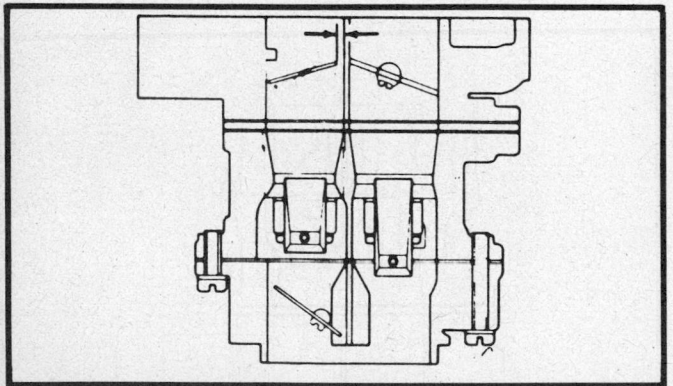

Throttle position sensor adjustment — Spectrum

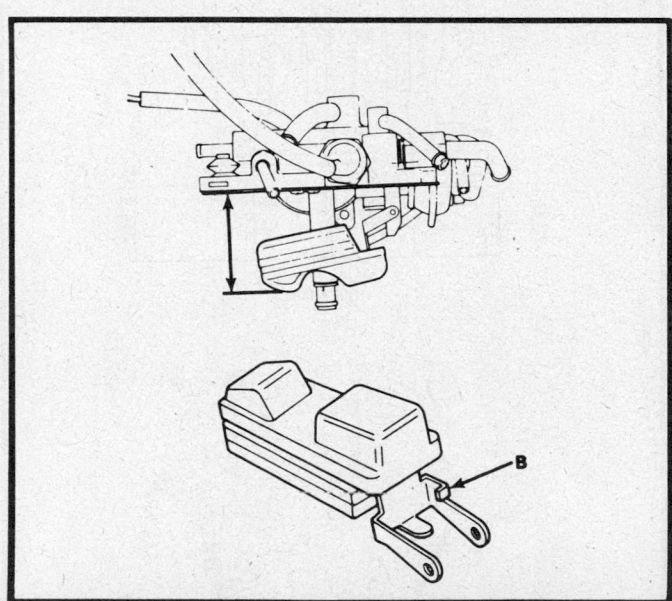

Bend tab (B) to adjust the lower float level — Spectrum

HITACHI CARBURETORS

Sprint 2 Barrel

FLOAT LEVEL

Adjustment

The fuel level in the float chamber should be within the round mark at the center of the level gauge. If it is not, check and adjust the float level as follows:
1. Remove and invert the air horn.
2. Measure the distance between the float and the gasketed surface of the choke chamber. The measured distance is the float level and it should be 0.210–0.240 in. The measurement should be made without the gasket on the air horn.
3. Adjustment is made by bending the tongue up and down.

IDLE-UP

Adjustment

The idle-up actuator operates even when the cooling fan is running. Therefore the idle-up adjustment must be performed when the cooling fan is not running.

MANUAL TRANSAXLE

1. Warm up the engine to normal operating temperature.
2. After warming up, run the engine at idle speed.
3. Check to make sure that the idle-up adjusting screw moves down (indicating that the idle-up is at work) when the lights are turned **ON**.
4. With the lights turned **ON**, check the engine rpm (idle-up speed). Be sure that the heater fan, rear defogger (if equipped), engine cooling fan and air conditioner (if equipped) are all turned **OFF**. The idle-up speed should be 750–850 rpm. Adjust by turning the adjusting screw.
5. After making the idle-up adjustment, make sure the idle-up adjusting screw moves as in Step 3 when only the heater fan is operated and then only the rear defogger or engine cooling fan is operated (lights should be off).

AUTOMATIC TRANSAXLE

1. Warm up the engine to normal operating temperature.
2. After warming up, run the engine at idle speed.
3. Apply the parking brake and block the drive wheels.
4. Turn all accessories **OFF**.
5. With the brake pedal depressed, shift the selector lever to **D**. Check to make sure that the idle-up adjusting screw moves down (indicating that the idle-up is at work).
6. Check the idle-up speed (do not depress the accelerator pedal). The Idle-up speed should be between 700–800 rpm. Adjustment is made by turning the adjusting screw.

CHOKE

Adjustment

Perform the following check and adjustments with the air cleaner top removed and the engine cold.

CHOKE VALVE

1. Check the choke valve for smooth movement by pushing it with a finger.

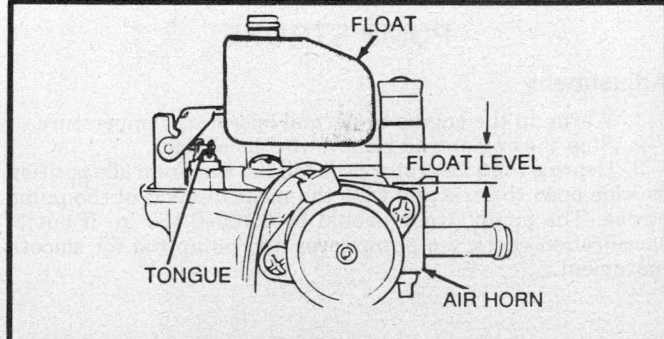

Float level adjustment – Sprint

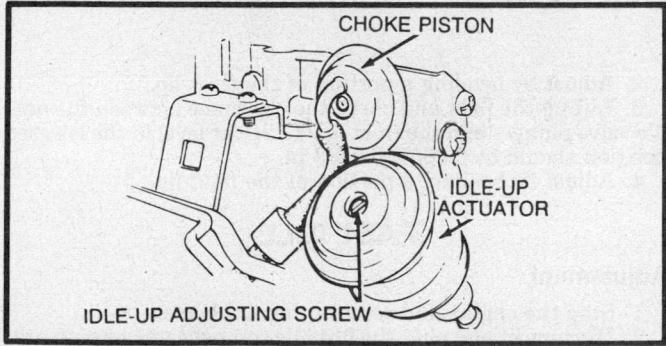

Idle-up adjusting screw – Sprint

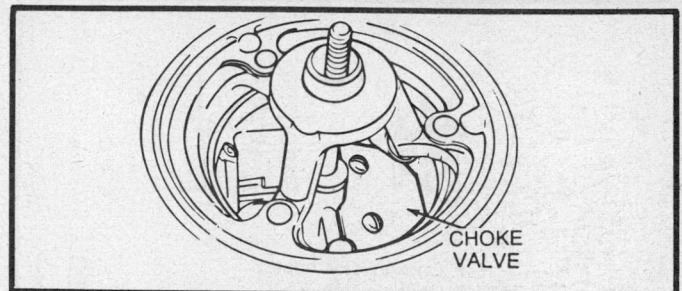

Choke valve – Sprint

Ambient temperature	Clearance
25°C (77°F)	0.1—0.5 mm 0.004—0.019 in
35°C (95°F)	0.7—1.7 mm 0.03—0.06 in

Choke valve to bore clearance – Sprint

2. Make sure that the choke valve is closed almost completely when ambient temperature is below 77°F and the engine is cold.
3. Check that the choke valve to carburetor bore clearance is within specifications when the ambient temperature is above 77°F and the engine is cool.
4. If clearance is found to be excessively large or small in the above check, remove the air cleaner case and check the strangler spring, choke piston and each link in the choke system for smooth operation. Lubricate the choke valve shaft and each link with a spray lubricant if necessary. Do not remove the riveted choke lever guide.
5. If after lubrication the clearance is still out of specification, remove the carburetor from the intake manifold and remove the idle-up actuator from the carburetor. Turn the fast idle cam counterclockwise and insert an available pin into the holes on the cam and bracket to lock the cam. In this state, bend the choke lever up or down with pliers. Bending up causes the choke valve to close and vice versa.

CHOKE PISTON

1. Disconnect the choke piston hose at the throttle chamber.
2. While lightly pushing down on the choke valve to the closing position with a finger, apply vacuum to the choke piston hose and check to make sure that the choke valve to the carburetor bore clearance is 0.090–0.100 in.
3. With vacuum applied as in Step 2, move the choke piston rod with a small tool and check to see that the choke valve to carburetor bore clearance is within 0.160–0.180 in.

CHECKING FAST IDLE CAM

Adjustment

NOTE: Ambient temperature must be between 72–82°F before performing this check.

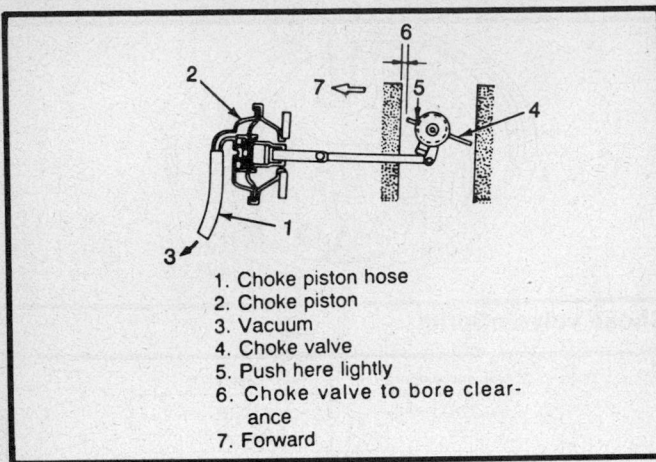

1. Choke piston hose
2. Choke piston
3. Vacuum
4. Choke valve
5. Push here lightly
6. Choke valve to bore clearance
7. Forward

Checking choke piston — Sprint

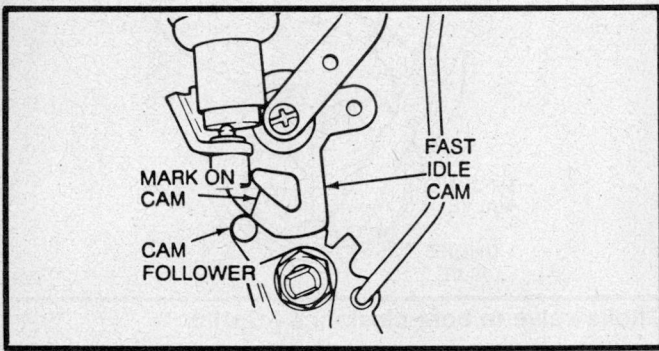

Mark on cam and cam follower

1. Drain the cooling system when the engine is cold and remove the carburetor from the intake manifold.
2. Leave the carburetor in a place where the ambient temperature is between 72–82°F for an hour.
3. After an hour, make sure that the mark on the cam and the center of the cam follower are in alignment.

CHOKE UNLOADER

Adjustment

NOTE: Perform this check and adjustment when the engine is cool.

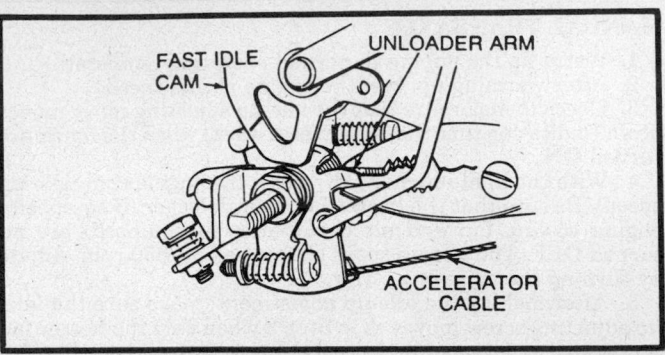

Unloader level arm — Sprint

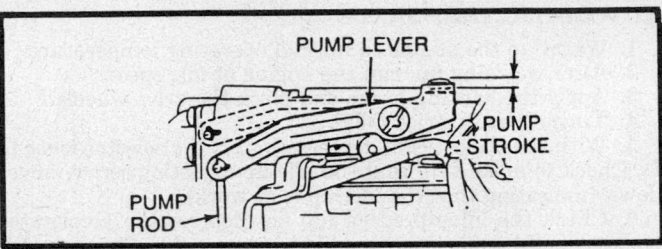

Pump stroke — Sprint

1. Remove the air cleaner cover.
2. Make sure that the choke valve is closed.
3. Fully open the throttle valve and check the choke valve to carburetor bore clearance is within 0.100–0.120 in.
4. If the clearance is out of specification adjust by bending the unloader arm.

PUMP STROKE

Adjustment

1. Warm up the engine to normal operating temperature.
2. Stop the engine and remove the air cleaner.
3. Depress the accelerator pedal all the way from idle position to wide open throttle and take the measurement of the pump stroke. The pump stroke should be 0.160–0.180 in. If out of specification check the pump lever and pump rod for smooth movement.

AISAN CARBURETORS

Nova 2 Barrel
FLOAT LEVEL

Adjustment

1. Allow the float the hang down by its own weight. Check the clearance between the float tip and air horn. The float level should be 0.075 in.

NOTE: This measurement should be made without a gasket on the air horn.

2. Adjust by bending a portion of the float lip.
3. Lift up the float and check the clearance between the needle valve plunger and the float lip. The float level in the lowered position should be 0.0657–0.0783 in.
4. Adjust by bending a portion of the float lip.

FAST IDLE

Adjustment

1. Stop the engine and remove the air cleaner.
2. Disconnect and plug the hot idle compensator hose to prevent rough idle.

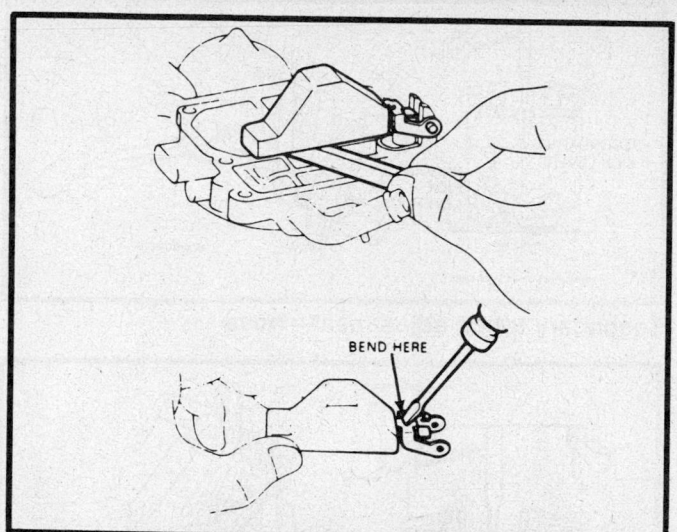

Checking the float level in the upper position—Nova

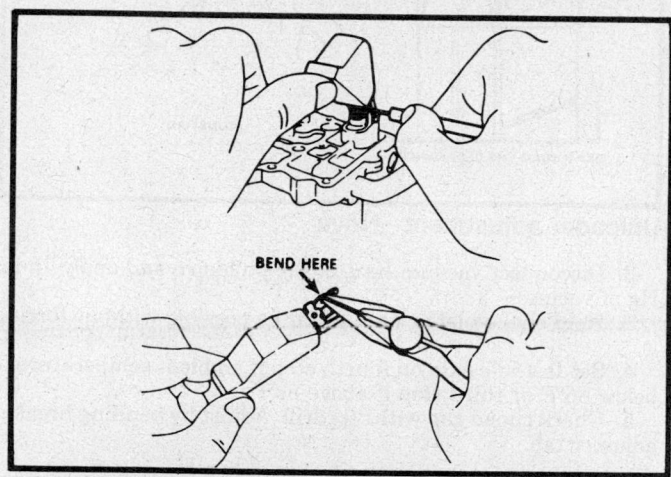

Checking the float level in the lower position—Nova

3. Shut off the choke opener and EGR systems by disconnecting the hose from the thermo vacuum switching valve M and plugging the M port.

4. Hold the throttle slightly open, push the choke valve closed and hold it closed while releasing the throttle valve.

5. Start the engine without depressing the accelerator pedal.

6. Set the fast idle speed by turning the fast idle screw.

7. Fast idle speed should be: 3000 rpm.

THROTTLE VALVE OPENING

Adjustment

1. Check the full opening angle of the primary throttle valve, with a T scale. The standard angle should be 90 degrees from the horizontal plane.

2. Adjust by bending the 1st throttle lever stopper.

3. Check the full opening clearance between the secondary throttle valve and the body. The standard clearance should be 0.500 in.

4. Adjust by bending the secondary throttle lever stopper.

KICK-UP

Adjustment

1. With the primary throttle valve fully opened, check the

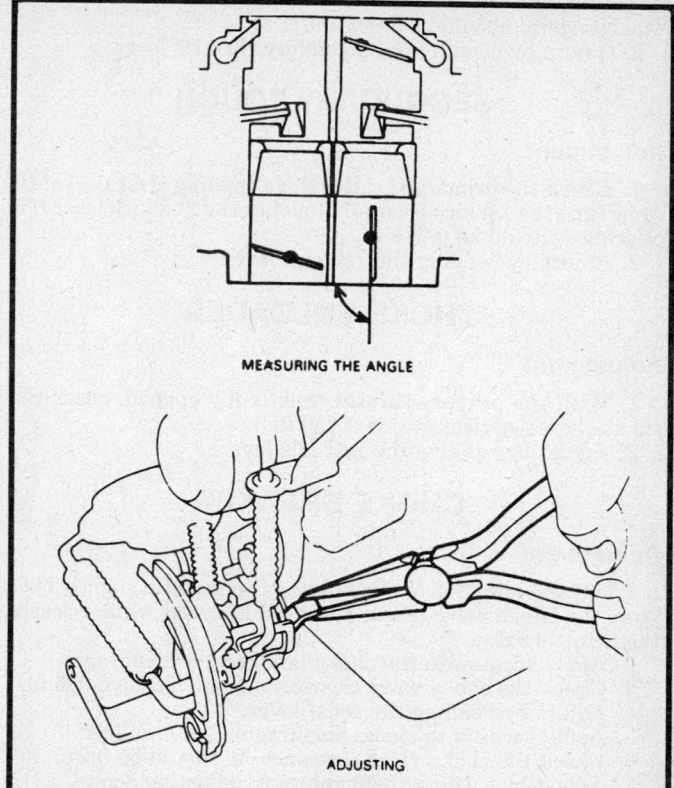

Primary throttle valve adjustment—Nova

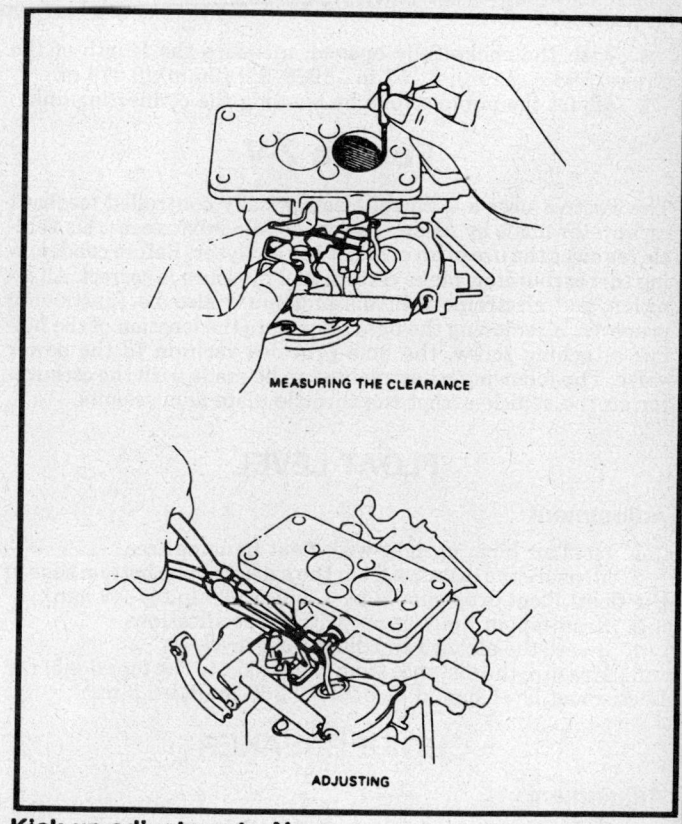

Kick-up adjustment—Nova

clearance between the secondary throttle valve and the body. The clearance should be 0.006 in.
2. Adjust by bending the secondary throttle lever.

SECONDARY TOUCH

Adjustment

1. Check the primary throttle valve opening clearance at the same time the 1st kick lever just touches the 2nd kick lever. The clearance should be 0.230 in.
2. Adjust by bending the 1st kick lever.

CHOKE UNLOADER

Adjustment

1. With the primary throttle valve fully opened, check that the choke valve clearance is 0.120 in.
2. Adjust by bending the fast idle lever.

CHOKE BREAKER

Adjustment

1. Set the idle cam. While holding the throttle slightly open, push the choke valve closed and hold it closed while releasing the throttle valve.
2. Apply vacuum to the choke breaker 1st diaphragm.
3. Check the choke valve clearance. It should be 0.095 in.
4. Adjust by bending the relief lever.
5. Apply vacuum to choke diaphragms 1st and 2nd.
6. Check the choke valve clearance. It should be 0.245 in.
7. Adjust by turning the diaphragm adjusting screw.

ACCELERATOR PUMP STROKE

Adjustment

1. With the choke fully opened, measure the length of the stroke. 1985: (4mm); 0.157 in., 1986–89: (2mm); 0.079 in.
2. Adjust the pump stroke by bending the connecting link.

Festiva 2-V

The Festiva uses a 2 barrel electronically controlled feedback carburetor made by Aisan. To set the idle mixture on this vehicle requires the use of an exhaust gas analyzer. Before condemning this carburetor, make certain fuel pressure is correct. All ignition and electronic controls and must also be functioning properly. If removing the base plate note the location of the hollow attaching screw, the hole provides vacuum to the power valve. The following adjustments can be made with the carburetor on the vehicle except the throttle plate adjustments.

FLOAT LEVEL

Adjustment

1. Hold air horn upright with float hanging free.
2. Measure the distance from the gasket to the bottom edge of the float. Float drop should be 1.850–1.929 in.(47–49 mm).
3. Bend tap on hinge if not within specifications.
4. Invert the airhorn to adjust float level.
5. Measure the distance from the gasket to the top edge of the float. Float level should be 0.327–0.366 in.(8.3–9.3 mm).

CHOKE BREAKER

Adjustment

1. Set choke plate to fully closed position.

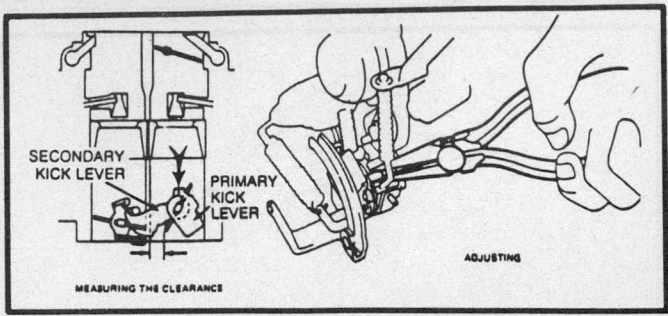

Secondary touch adjustment – Nova

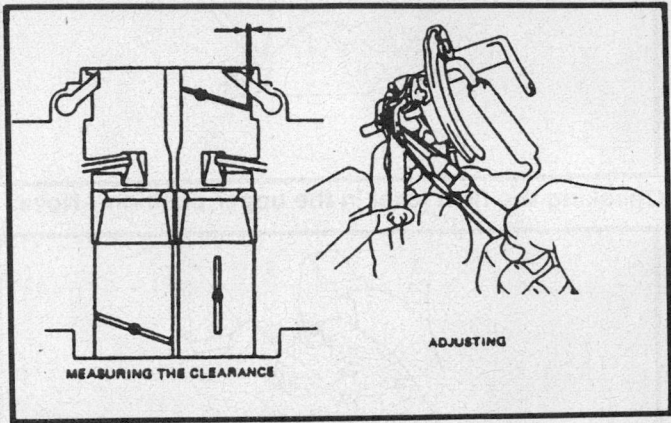

Unloader adjustment – Nova

2. Disconnect vacuum hose at the pulldown and apply 16 in. Hg of vacuum.
3. Hold choke plate closed as far as possible without forcing it.
4. Set fast idle cam on fourth step if ambient temperature is below 86°F or third step if above 86°F.
5. Check choke gap with $^5/_{16}$ drill. Adjust by bending breaker adjuster tab.

CHOKE UNLOADER

Adjustment

1. Hold the choke plate closed as far as possible without forcing it.
2. Distance between choke plate and air horn should be 0.059–0.076 in.(drill size $^1/_{16}$) while holding throttle wide open.
3. Adjust clearance by bending rod.

CHOKE PLATE CLEARANCE

Adjustment

1. Set fast idle on third step of cam.
2. Distance between choke plate and air horn should be 0.024–0.037 in.(drill size $^1/_{32}$).
3. Adjust clearance by bending the tap.

SECONDARY THROTTLE PLATE

Adjustment

1. With carburetor assembly removed from engine, slowly open throttle while watching the secondary plate.
2. When the secondary plate just starts to open the clearance to the throttle wall should be .0372 in. (³⁄₈ drill size).
3. Adjust clearance by bending tap at secondary shaft.

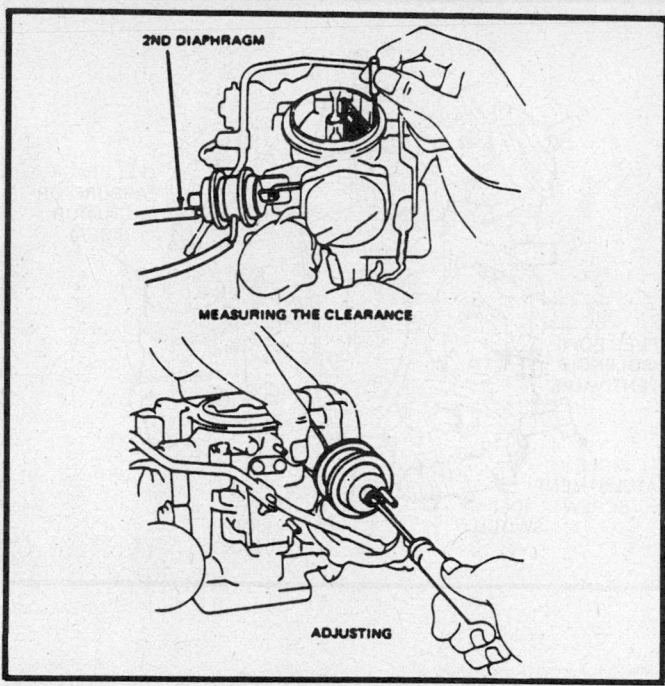

Choke breaker 1st and 2nd diaphragm adjustment— Nova

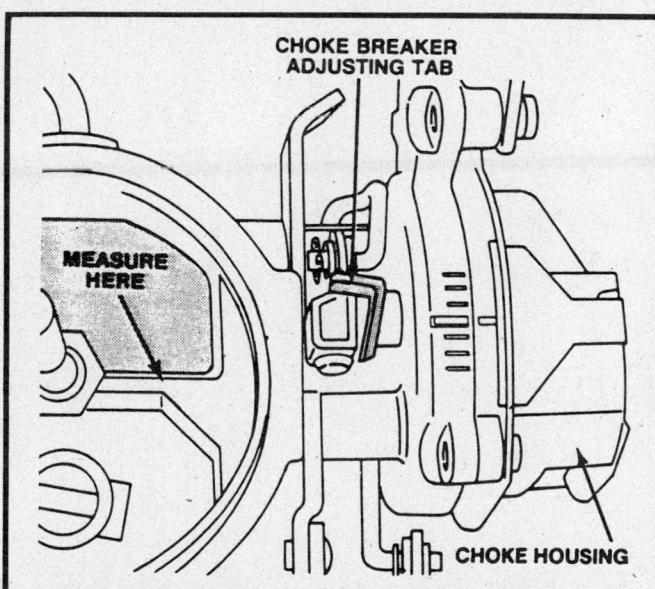

Festiva choke breaker diaphragm adjustment

THROTTLE OPENING

Adjustment

1. With carburetor assembly removed from engine, position idle cam against the third step.
2. The distance between the throttle and venturi wall should be 0.009–0.014 in.(0.25–0.36mm).
3. Adjust to specifications using the fast idle cam screw.

IDLE MIXTURE

Adjustment

NOTE: To perform the idle mixture adjustment an

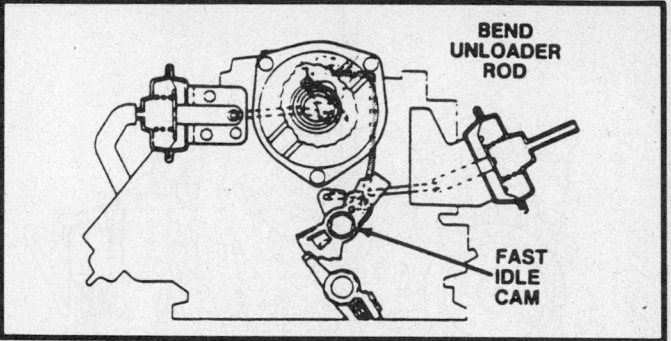

Festiva choke unloader adjustment

emission analyzer must be used to identify CO concentration.

1. Run engine to reach normal temperature.
2. Insert probe into the secondary air hose and plug hose to prevent leaking past the probe lead.
3. Adjust mixture screw until analyzer shows CO concentration of 1.5–2.5%.

CURB IDLE

Adjustment

1. Run engine to reach normal temperature, place transaxle in **N** and set parking brake.
2. Adjust idle to 700–760 rpm using idle adjusting screw.

FAST IDLE BREAKER

Adjustment

1. Run engine to reach normal temperature.
2. Set fast idle cam on 2nd step.
3. Turn fast idle cam breaker adjusting screw to obtain an engine speed of 1650–2150 rpm.

FAST IDLE ADJUSTMENT

Adjustment

1. Disconnect and plug vacuum hose at the fast idle cam servo.
2. Set fast idle cam on 2nd step.
3. Adjust engine speed to 1650–2150 rpm using fast idle screw.

ELECTRICAL LOAD IDLE-UP

Adjustment

1. Run engine to reach normal temperature.
2. Disconnect brown electrical connector at electrical vacuum solenoid.
3. Increase engine speed to 2000 rpm and let return to idle.
4. Adjust servo nut to obtain at idle of 750–850 rpm.

AIR CONDITIONING IDLE-UP

Adjustment

1. Run engine to reach normal temperature.
2. Disconnect orange electrical connector at air conditioning vacuum solenoid.
3. Increase engine speed to 2000 rpm and let return to idle.
4. Adjust A/C idle-up screw to obtain 1200–1300 rpm.

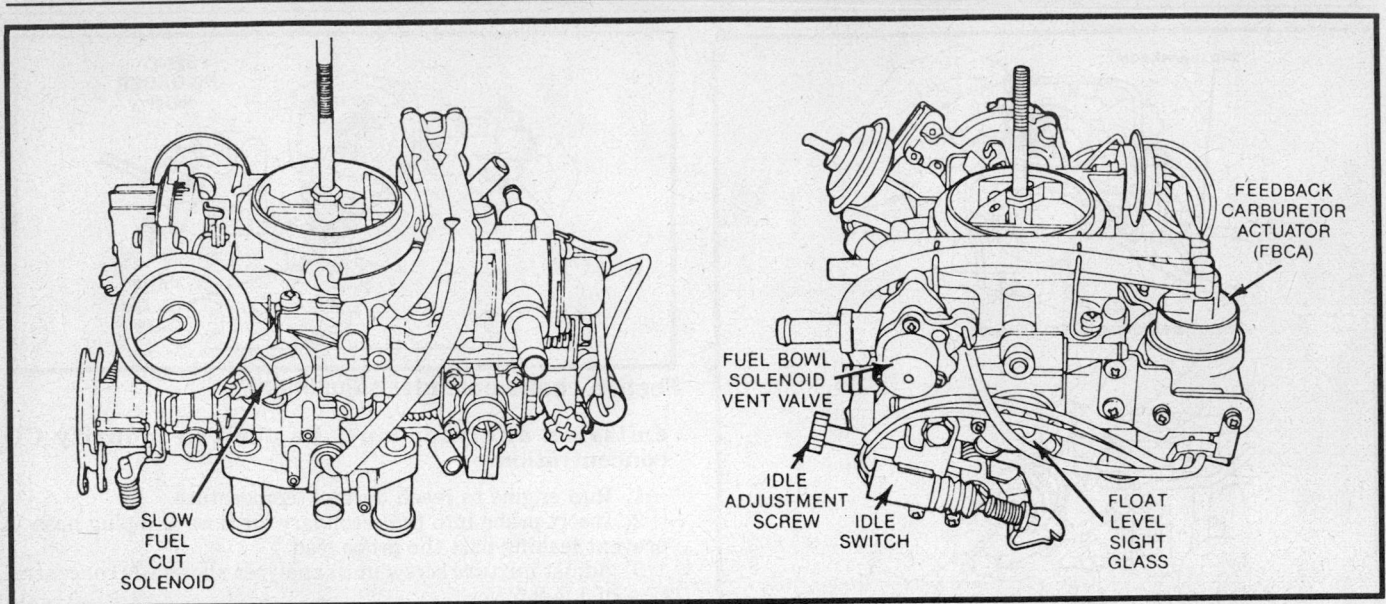

Carburetor assembly—Festiva

SLOW
FUEL
CUT
SOLENOID

FUEL BOWL
SOLENOID
VENT VALVE

IDLE
ADJUSTMENT
SCREW

IDLE
SWITCH

FLOAT
LEVEL
SIGHT
GLASS

FEEDBACK
CARBURETOR
ACTUATOR
(FBCA)

REAR AXLES

General Information

The drive pinion, which is turned by the driveshaft, turns the ring gear. The ring gear, which is bolted to the differential carrier, rotates the carrier. The differential pinion forces the carrier pinion gears against the side gears. When both wheels have equal traction, the pinion gears do not rotate on the pinion shaft because the input force of the pinion gear is divided equally between both side gears. Consequently, the pinion gears revolve with the pinion shaft, although they do not revolve on the pinion shaft. The side gears, which are splined to the axle shafts and meshed with the pinion gears in turn rotate the axle shafts.

Limited slip differentials provide driving force to the wheel with the best traction before the other wheel begins to spin. This is accomplished by the use of clutch plates or cones. The clutch plates or cones are located between the side gears and the inner wall of the differential case. When they are squeezed together, through spring tension and outward force from the side gears, multiple reactions occur. Resistance on the side gears cause more torque to be exerted on the clutch packs or clutch cones. Rapid single wheel spin cannot occur, because the side gear is forced to turn at the same speed as the case. Most important, with the side gear and the differential case turning at the same speed, the other wheel is forced to rotate in the same direction and at the same speed as the differential case. This applies driving force to the wheel with the better traction.

All drive axles have a certain axle ratio. This ratio, usually represented by a whole number and a decimal fraction, is a comparison between the number of teeth on the ring gear and the number of teeth on the pinion gear. For example, a 4.11 axle ratio would mean that, in theory, there would be 4.11 teeth on the ring gear and 1 tooth on the pinion gear. Actually, with a 4.11 axle ratio, there are 37 teeth on the ring gear and 9 teeth on the pinion gear. By dividing the number of teeth on the pinion gear into the number of teeth on the ring gear, the numerical axle ratio of 4.11 is obtained. This provides a good method of determining exactly what axle ratio is in the vehicle.

Noise Diagnosis

Any gear driven unit will produce a certain amount of noise, therefore, a specific diagnosis for each individual unit is the best practice. Acceptable or normal noise can be classified as a slight noise heard only at certain speeds or unusual conditions. This noise tends to reach a peak at 40–60 mph, depending on the road condition, vehicle load, gear ratio and tire size. Frequently, other noises are mistakenly diagnosed as rear axle noises. Vehicle noises from tires, transmissions, driveshafts, U-joints or front and rear wheel bearings will often be mistaken as rear axle noises. Raise the tire pressure to eliminate tire noise, (although this will not silence mud or snow treads) and listen for the noise at various speeds and road conditions. Listen for noise during drive and coast conditions. These checks will aid in determining if the noise is coming from the rear axle or elsewhere.

Eliminate the possibility of external noise by making a thorough road test to determine whether the noise originates in the rear axle or whether it originates from the tires, engine, transmission, driveshaft, wheel bearings or road surface.

FRONT WHEEL BEARING NOISE

Front wheel bearing noises are sometimes confused with rear axle noises. This noise will not change when comparing drive and coast conditions. Hold the vehicle speed steady and lightly apply the foot brake. This will often cause the front wheel bearing noise to lessen as some of the weight is taken off the bearing. Front wheel bearings are easily checked by raising the vehicle, grabbing the tire and shaking it from side-to-side to determine if the wheel bearings are excessively loose.

REAR AXLE NOISE

If a logical test of the vehicle shows that the noise is not caused by external items, it can be assumed that the noise originates from the rear axle. The rear axle should be tested on a smooth level road to avoid road noise. Do not test the rear axle by raising the rear wheels and running the vehicle.

True rear axle noises generally fall into 2 classes; gear noises and bearing noises. These noises can be caused by one or a combination of, the following: a faulty driveshaft, faulty wheel bearings, worn differential or pinion shaft bearings, U-joint failure or misalignment, worn differential side and pinion gears or ring and pinion gears that are mismatched, improperly adjusted, or scored.

REAR WHEEL BEARING NOISE

A rough rear wheel bearing causes a vibration or growl that will continue while the vehicle is coasting in D‹cf1 or N. A brinelled rear wheel bearing will cause a knock or click approximately every 2 revolutions of the rear wheel. This is because the bearing rollers do not travel at the same speed as the rear wheel and axle. Raise the rear wheels and spin the wheel by hand slowly while listening for signs of a rough or brinelled wheel bearing.

DIFFERENTIAL SIDE AND PINION GEAR NOISE

Differential side and pinion gears seldom cause noise since their movement is relatively slight on straight ahead driving. Noise produced by these gears will be most noticeable on turns.

PINION BEARING NOISE

Pinion bearing failures can be distinguished by the speed of the gear rotation, which is higher than side bearings or axle bearings. A rough or brinelled pinion bearing causes a continuous low pitch whirring or scraping noise beginning at low speeds.

SIDE BEARING NOISE

Side bearings produce a constant rough noise that is slower than the pinion bearing noise. Side bearing noise may also fluctuate in the above rear wheel bearing test.

GEAR NOISE

There are 2 basic types of gear noises. The first type is produced by bent or broken gear teeth which have been forcibly damaged. The noise from this type of damage can be heard over the entire speed range. Scored or damaged hypoid gear teeth generally result from insufficient or improper lubricant, improper break in, incorrect gear backlash, improper ring and pinion gear alignment or loss of torque on the drive pinion nut. Unless corrected, the scoring will lead to eventual erosion or fracture of the gear teeth. Hypoid gear tooth fracture can also be caused by extended overloading (fatigue fracture), of the gear set or by shock overloading, (sudden failure). Differential side gears rarely give trouble but, common causes of differential failure are shock loading, extended overloading and differential pinion seizure at the cross shaft, resulting from excessive wheel spin and consequent lubricant breakdown.

The second type of gear noise pertains to the mesh pattern between the ring and pinion gear. This type of abnormal gear noise

TAPERED WHEEL BEARING DIAGNOSIS

GOOD BEARING

BENT CAGE

CAGE DAMAGE DUE TO IMPROPER HANDLING OR TOOL USAGE.

REPLACE BEARING.

BENT CAGE

CAGE DAMAGE DUE TO IMPROPER HANDLING OR TOOL USAGE.

REPLACE BEARING

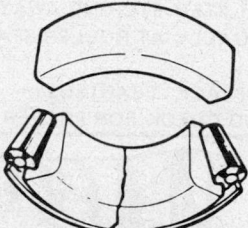

CRACKED INNER RACE

RACE CRACKED DUE TO IMPROPER FIT, COCKING, OR POOR BEARING SEATS.

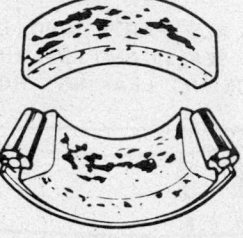

SMEARS

SMEARING OF METAL DUE TO SLIPPAGE. SLIPPAGE CAN BE CAUSED BY POOR FITS, LUBRICATION, OVERHEATING, OVERLOADS OR HANDLING DAMAGE.

REPLACE BEARINGS, CLEAN RELATED PARTS AND CHECK FOR PROPER FIT AND LUBRICATION.

REPLACE SHAFT IF DAMAGED.

FRETTAGE

CORROSION SET UP BY SMALL RELATIVE MOVEMENT OF PARTS WITH NO LUBRICATION.

REPLACE BEARING. CLEAN RELATED PARTS. CHECK SEALS AND CHECK FOR PROPER LUBRICATION.

HEAT DISCOLORATION

HEAT DISCOLORATION CAN RANGE FROM FAINT YELLOW TO DARK BLUE RESULTING FROM OVERLOAD OR INCORRECT LUBRICANT.

EXCESSIVE HEAT CAN CAUSE SOFTENING OF RACES OR ROLLERS.

REPLACE BEARINGS IF OVER HEATING DAMAGE IS INDICATED. CHECK SEALS AND OTHER PARTS.

STAIN DISCOLORATION

DISCOLORATION CAN RANGE FROM LIGHT BROWN TO BLACK CAUSED BY INCORRECT LUBRICANT OR MOISTURE.

RE-USE BEARINGS IF STAINS CAN BE REMOVED BY LIGHT POLISHING OR IF NO EVIDENCE OF OVERHEATING IS OBSERVED.

CHECK SEALS AND RELATED PARTS FOR DAMAGE.

TAPERED WHEEL BEARING DIAGNOSIS

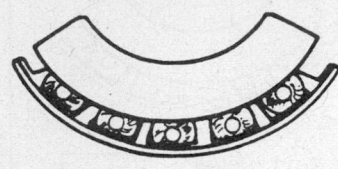

GALLING

METAL SMEARS ON ROLLER ENDS DUE TO OVERHEAT, LUBRICANT FAILURE OR OVERLOAD.

REPLACE BEARING — CHECK SEALS AND CHECK FOR PROPER LUBRICATION.

ABRASIVE STEP WEAR

PATTERN ON ROLLER ENDS CAUSED BY FINE ABRASIVES.

CLEAN ALL PARTS AND HOUSINGS, CHECK SEALS AND BEARINGS AND REPLACE IF LEAKING, ROUGH OR NOISY.

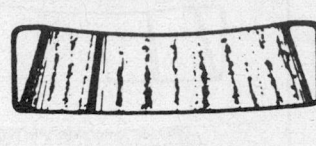

ETCHING

BEARING SURFACES APPEAR GRAY OR GRAYISH BLACK IN COLOR WITH RELATED ETCHING AWAY OF MATERIAL USUALLY AT ROLLER SPACING.

REPLACE BEARINGS — CHECK SEALS AND CHECK FOR PROPER LUBRICATION.

MISALIGNMENT

OUTER RACE MISALIGNMENT DUE TO FOREIGN OBJECT.

CLEAN RELATED PARTS AND REPLACE BEARING. MAKE SURE RACES ARE PROPERLY SEATED.

INDENTATIONS

SURFACE DEPRESSIONS ON RACE AND ROLLERS CAUSED BY HARD PARTICLES OF FOREIGN MATERIAL.

CLEAN ALL PARTS AND HOUSINGS, CHECK SEALS AND REPLACE BEARINGS IF ROUGH OR NOISY.

FATIGUE SPALLING

FLAKING OF SURFACE METAL RESULTING FROM FATIGUE.

REPLACE BEARING — CLEAN ALL RELATED PARTS.

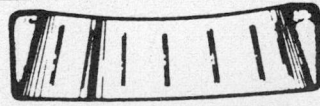

BRINELLING

SURFACE INDENTATIONS IN RACEWAY CAUSED BY ROLLERS EITHER UNDER IMPACT LOADING OR VIBRATION WHILE THE BEARING IS NOT ROTATING.

REPLACE BEARING IF ROUGH OR NOISY.

CAGE WEAR

WEAR AROUND OUTSIDE DIAMETER OF CAGE AND ROLLER POCKETS CAUSED BY ABRASIVE MATERIAL AND INEFFICIENT LUBRICATION. CHECK SEALS AND REPLACE BEARINGS.

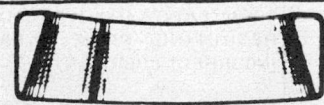

ABRASIVE ROLLER WEAR

PATTERN ON RACES AND ROLLERS CAUSED BY FINE ABRASIVES.

CLEAN ALL PARTS AND HOUSINGS, CHECK SEALS AND BEARINGS AND REPLACE IF LEAKING, ROUGH OR NOISY.

ROLLER WHEEL BEARING DIAGNOSIS

WEAR (MINOR)

LIGHT PATTERN ON RACES AND ROLLERS CAUSED BY FINE ABRASIVES.

CLEAN ALL PARTS AND HOUSINGS. CHECK SEALS AND REPLACE BEARINGS IF ROUGH OR NOISY.

REPLACE SHAFT IF DAMAGED

WEAR (MAJOR)

HEAVY PATTERN ON RACES AND ROLLERS CAUSED BY FINE ABRASIVES.

CLEAN ALL PARTS AND HOUSINGS. CHECK SEALS AND REPLACE BEARINGS IF ROUGH OR NOISY.

REPLACE SHAFT IF DAMAGED

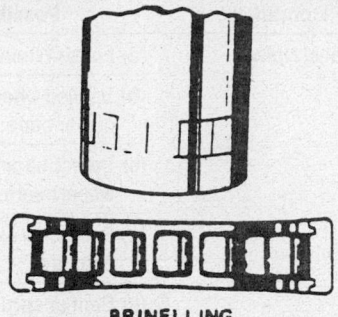

BRINELLING

SURFACE INDENTATIONS IN RACEWAY CAUSED BY ROLL EITHER UNDER IMPACT LOADING OR VIBRATION WHILE THE BEARING IS NOT ROTATING.

REPLACE BEARING IF ROUGH OR NOISY.

REPLACE SHAFT IF DAMAGED

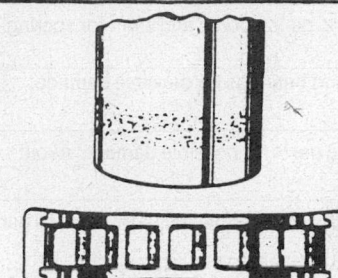

INDENTATIONS

SURFACE DEPRESSIONS ON RACE AND ROLLERS CAUSED BY HARD PARTICLES OF FOREIGN MATERIAL.

CLEAN ALL PARTS AND HOUSINGS. CHECK SEALS AND REPLACE BEARINGS IF ROUGH OR NOISY.

REPLACE SHAFT IF DAMAGED

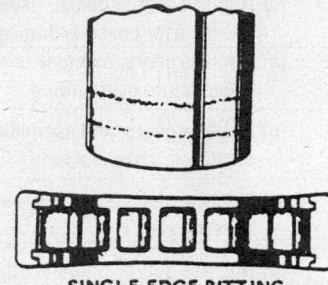

SINGLE EDGE PITTING

FLAKING OF SURFACE METAL RESULTING FROM FATIGUE. USUALLY AT ONE EDGE OF RACE AND ROLLERS.

REPLACE BEARING — CLEAN ALL RELATED PARTS.

REPLACE SHAFT IF DAMAGED

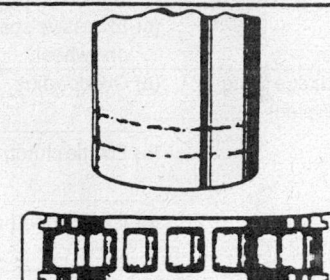

DOUBLE EDGE PITTING

FLAKING OF SURFACE METAL RESULTING FROM FATIGUE. USUALLY AT BOTH EDGES OF RACE AND ROLLERS.

REPLACE BEARING — CLEAN ALL RELATED PARTS.

REPLACE SHAFT IF DAMAGED

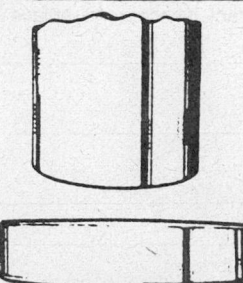

MISALIGNMENT

REPLACE BEARING AND MAKE SURE RACES ARE PROPERLY SEATED.

REPLACE SHAFT IF BEARING OPERATING SURFACE DAMAGED.

FRETTAGE

CORROSION SET UP BY SMALL RELATIVE MOVEMENT OF PARTS WITH NO LUBRICATION.

REPLACE BEARING. CLEAN RELATED PARTS. CHECK SEALS AND CHECK FOR PROPER FIT AND LUBRICATION.

REPLACE SHAFT IF DAMAGED.

SMEARS

SMEARING OF METAL DUE TO SLIPPAGE. SLIPPAGE CAN BE CAUSED BY POOR FITS. LUBRICATION. OVERHEATING, OVERLOADS OR HANDLING DAMAGE.

REPLACE BEARINGS. CLEAN RELATED PARTS AND CHECK FOR PROPER FITS AND LUBRICATION.

GENERAL DRIVE AXLE DIAGNOSTIC GUIDE

Condition	Possible Cause	Correction
Rear Wheel Noise	(a) Loose Wheel.	(a) Tighten loose wheel nuts.
	(b) Spalled wheel bearing cup or cone.	(b) Check rear wheel bearings. If spalled or worn, replace.
	(c) Defective or brinelled wheel bearing.	(c) Defective or brinelled bearings must be replaced. Check rear axle shaft endplay.
	(d) Excessive axle shaft endplay.	(d) Readjust axle shaft endplay.
	(e) Bent or sprung axle shaft flange.	(e) Replace bent or sprung axle shaft.
Scoring of Differential Gears and Pinions	(a) Insufficient lubrication.	(a) Replace scored gears. Scoring marks on the pressure face of gear teeth or in the bore are caused by instantaneous fusing of the mating surfaces. Scored gears should be replaced. Fill rear axle to required capacity with proper lubricant.
	(b) Improper grade of lubricant.	(b) Replace scored gears. Inspect all gears and bearings for possible damage. Clean and refill axle to required capacity with proper lubricant.
	(c) Excessive spinning of one wheel.	(c) Replace scored gears. Inspect all gears, pinion bores and shaft for scoring, or bearings for possible damage.
Tooth Breakage (Ring Gear and Pinion)	(a) Overloading.	(a) Replace gears. Examine other gears and bearings for possible damage. Avoid future overloading.
	(b) Erratic clutch operation.	(b) Replace gears, and examine remaining parts for possible damage. Avoid erratic clutch operation.
	(c) Ice-spotted pavements.	(c) Replace gears. Examine remaining parts for possible damage. Replace parts as required.
	(d) Improper adjustment.	(d) Replace gears. Examine other parts for possible damage. Be sure ring gear and pinion backlash is correct.
Rear Axle Noise	(a) Insufficient lubricant.	(a) Refill rear axle with correct amount of the proper lubricant. Also check for leaks and correct as necessary.
	(b) Improper ring gear and pinion adjustment.	(b) Check ring gear and pinion tooth contact.
	(c) Unmatched ring gear and pinion.	(c) Remove unmatched ring gear and pinion. Replace with a new matched gear and pinion set.
	(d) Worn teeth on ring gear or pinion.	(d) Check teeth on ring gear and pinion for contact. If necessary, replace with new matched set.
	(e) End-play in drive pinion bearings.	(e) Adjust drive pinion bearing preload.
	(f) Side play in differential bearings.	(f) Adjust differential bearing preload.
	(g) Incorrect drive gear lash.	(g) Correct drive gear lash.
	(h) Limited-Slip differential—moan and chatter.	(h) Drain and flush lubricant. Refill with proper lubricant.
Loss of Lubricant	(a) Lubricant level too high.	(a) Drain excess lubricant.
	(b) Worn axle shaft oil seals.	(b) Replace worn oil seals with new ones. Prepare new seals before replacement.
	(c) Cracked rear axle housing.	(c) Repair or replace housing as required.
	(d) Worn drive pinion oil seal.	(d) Replace worn drive pinion oil seal with a new one.
	(e) Scored and worn companion flange.	(e) Replace worn or scored companion flange and oil seal.

GENERAL DRIVE AXLE DIAGNOSTIC GUIDE

CONDITION	POSSIBLE CAUSE	CORRECTION
Loss of Lubricant	(f) Clogged vent.	(f) Remove obstructions.
	(g) Loose carrier housing bolts or housing cover screws.	(g) Tighten bolts or cover screws to specifications and fill to correct level with proper lubricant.
Overheating of Unit	(a) Lubricant level too low.	(a) Refill rear axle.
	(b) Incorrect grade of lubricant.	(b) Drain, flush and refill rear axle with correct amount of the proper lubricant.
	(c) Bearings adjusted too tightly.	(c) Readjust bearings.
	(d) Excessive wear in gears.	(d) Check gears for excessive wear or scoring. Replace as necessary.
	(e) Insufficient ring gear-to-pinion clearance.	(e) Readjust ring gear and pinion backlash and check gears for possible scoring.

REPAIR PROCEDURES INDEX

Manufacturer	Ring Gear Size (in.)	R&R Rear Hub	Pressed-on Bearing from Axle	R&R Axle and Bearing	Install Outer Oil V	Install Inner Oil V	Axle Shaft Endplay Adjust.	Install Pinion Seal	Replace Yoke Bearing and Side Gear Seal	Set Pinion Depth	Ring Gear Backlash Adjust.	Pinion Bearing Preload
AMC	$7^9/_{16}$	1	8	2	3	4	5	6	None	13	14	15
Chrysler Corp.	$7^1/_4$	②	8	7	12	4	9	6	None	13	14	15
	$8^1/_4$	②	8	7	12	4	9	6	None	13	14	15
Ford Motor Corp.	$7^1/_2$	②	8	7	12	4	9	6	None	13	14	15
	$8^1/_2, 8^3/_4$	②	8	7	12	4	9	6	None	13	14	15
General Motors	$7^1/_2$	②	8	7	12	4	9	6 ①	None	13	14	15
	$8^1/_2$	②	8	7	12	4	9	6	None	13	14	15

① See Procedure No. 11 for Chevette
② Hub is not separate, but part of the axle shaft assembly

can be recognized by a cycling pitch or whine audible in either drive, float or coast conditions. These gear noises can usually be recognized as they tend to peak out in a narrow speed range and remain constant in pitch.

Bearing Diagnosis

Bearing diagnosis can be very helpful in determining the cause of rear axle failure.

When disassembling a rear axle, the general condition of all bearings should be noted and classified where possible. Proper recognition of the cause of bearing failure will help in correcting the problem and avoiding a repetition of the failure.

Some of the most common causes of bearing failure are:
1. Abuse during assembly or disassembly
2. Improper assembly
3. Improper or inadequate lubrication
4. Contact with dirt or water
5. Wear caused by dirt or metal chips
6. Corrosion or rust
7. Seizing due to overloading
8. Overheating
9. Frettage of the bearing seats
10. Brinelling from impact or shock loading
11. Manufacturing defects
12. Pitting due to fatigue

Avoid damage to bearings from improper handling. Treat a

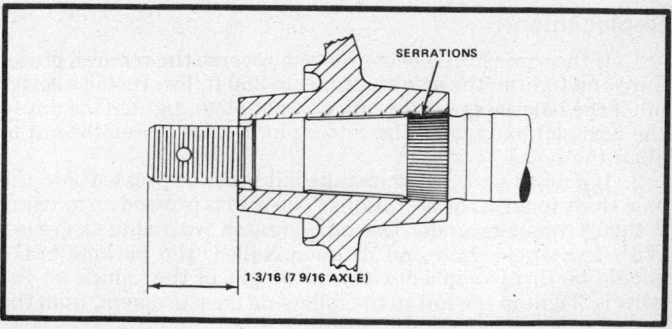

Hub installation measurement

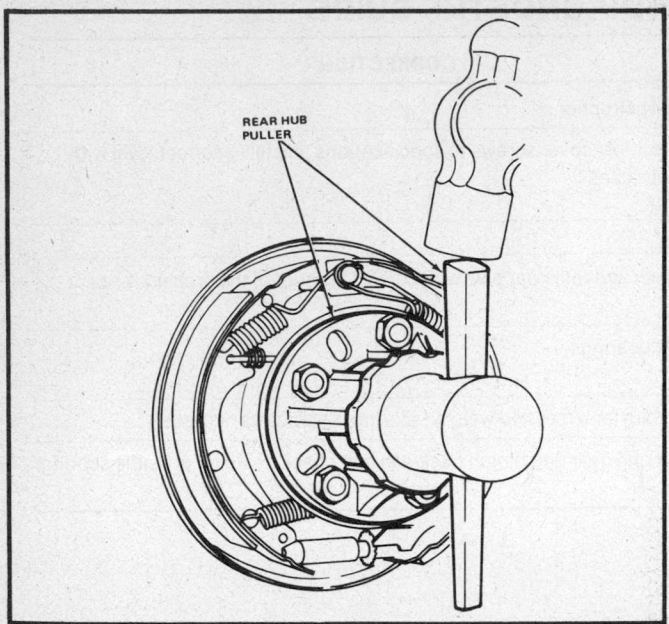

Removing axle

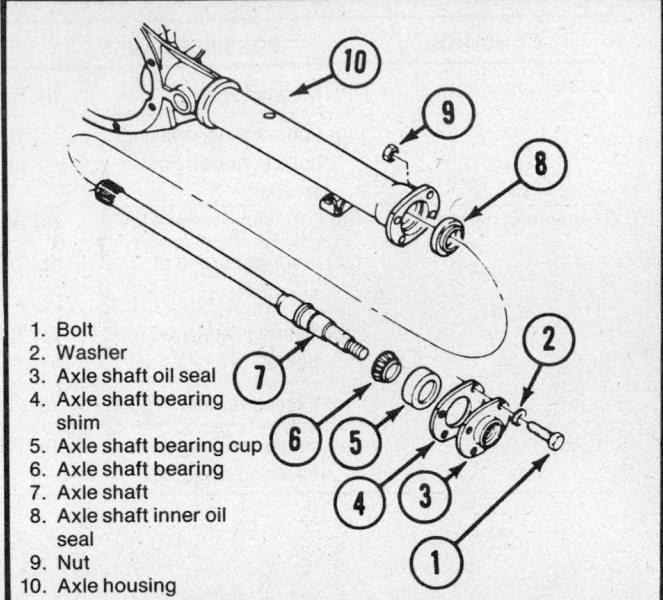

1. Bolt
2. Washer
3. Axle shaft oil seal
4. Axle shaft bearing shim
5. Axle shaft bearing cup
6. Axle shaft bearing
7. Axle shaft
8. Axle shaft inner oil seal
9. Nut
10. Axle housing

Exploded view of AMC axle, bearing assembly, inner and outer oil seal assembly

used bearing with the same care as a new bearing. Always work in a clean area with clean tools. Remove all outside dirt from the housing before exposing a bearing and clean all bearing seats before installing a bearing.

NOTE: Never spin a bearing with compressed air, as this will lead to almost certain bearing seizure and/or failure.

Service Procedures

PROCEDURE NO. 1

Removal and Installation Rear Hub

AMC EAGLE

1. With the weight of the vehicle on the wheels, remove the axle shaft nut and loosen each lug nut ¼ turn.
2. Raise and support the vehicle safely.
3. Remove the lug nuts, wheel and brake drum.
4. Attach a hub puller and remove the hub.

NOTE: Do not use the type of puller that screws into the end of the axle and provides a surfaces for striking. The heavy blows necessary with this type of puller may damage the rear wheel bearings and differential thrust block. A screw type or wedge type puller must be used.

Replacement

1. If the same hub is being reused, reverse the removal procedure and tighten the axle shaft nut to 250 ft. lbs. Install a cotter pin if the holes align. If the holes do not align, tighten the nut to the next slot and install the cotter pin. Do not loosen the nut to align the holes.
2. If a new hub is being installed, it must be pressed onto the axle shaft to form the serrations. The hub is pressed on by using 2 thrust washers under the nut, greased with chassis grease. With the wheel, hub and drum installed, the parking brake should be firmly applied with the weight of the vehicle on the wheels. Tighten the nut to the following measurement, from the end of axle to the end of the hub.

$7\frac{9}{16}$ in. axle = $1\frac{3}{16}$ in.

3. Remove the axle shaft nut and 1 thrust washer. Reinstall the nut and tighten it to 250 ft. lbs. Install a cotter key if the holes align. If the holes do not align, tighten the nut to the next slot and install the cotter key; do not loosen it to align the holes.

PROCEDURE NO. 2

Removing Tapered Axle and Bearing

AMC EAGLE

1. Raise and support the vehicle safely. Remove the wheel, brake drum and hub.
2. Disconnect and plug the brake line from the wheel cylinder.
3. Remove the housing flange bolts and nuts, the brake backing plate, oil, seal and retainer. Remove the shims if the left side shaft is being removed.

NOTE: Axle shaft endplay shims are installed on the left side of the axle only.

4. Using a screw type puller or slide hammer, press or pull the axle shaft and bearing from the housing.

NOTE: If equipped with a self locking differential, do not rotate the other axle while one axle is removed. The side gear splines may misalign if the differential is rotated, preventing insertion of the replacement axle.

5. Continue the installation in the reverse order of the removal procedure. On $7\frac{9}{16}$ in. axles, the outer oil seal and retainer is installed between the housing flange and the brake backing plate. Bleed the brakes system.

PROCEDURE NO. 3

Replacing Outer Axle Oil Seal

AMC EAGLE

1. Raise and support the vehicle safely. Remove the wheel, brake drum and hub.
2. Disconnect and plug the brake line from the wheel cylinder.

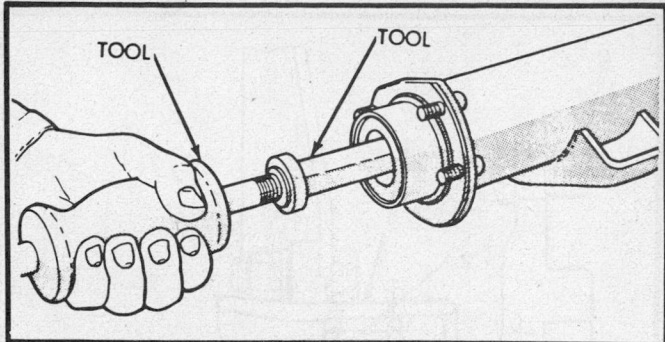

Removing inner seal from axle tube, typical

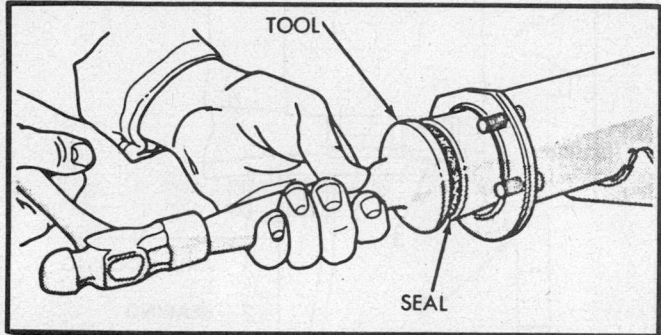

Installing the axle shaft seal, typical

3. Remove the housing flange bolts/nuts, the brake backing plate, oil seal and retainer. If the left side is being removed, make note of any shims next to the backing plate.

4. Installation is the reverse order of the removal procedure. Use a new seal and replace the shims in the original position. On $7^9/_{16}$ in. axles, the outer seal and retainer is installed between the housing flange and the brake backing plate. Bleed the brake system.

PROCEDURE NO. 4

Replacing Inner Axle Oil Seal

ALL VEHICLES

NOTE: Some vehicles do not use an inner seal.

1. Raise and support the vehicle safely.
2. Remove the rear wheel assemblies and rear axle.
3. Use a slide hammer puller tool that will hook onto the seal and pull it out of the axle housing. The end of the axle may be used to pry the seal out but be careful not to gouge or damage the housing. In the some designs, it may be necessary to remove the bearing also because the puller will not grab the seal alone. Clean the inside of the housing and remove any old sealer.

To install:

4. Coat the seal lips with rear axle lubricant and the outer metal shell with nonhardening sealer.
5. Use a driver that fits the seal and with the seal lip pointing inwards, drive the seal into the axle housing to the same depth as the old seal.
6. Complete the installation in the reverse order of the removal procedure.
7. Check the level of the rear axle lubricant.

PROCEDURE NO. 5

Adjusting Axle Shaft Endplay

AMC EAGLE

1. Raise and support the vehicle safely. Remove the brake drum and hub.

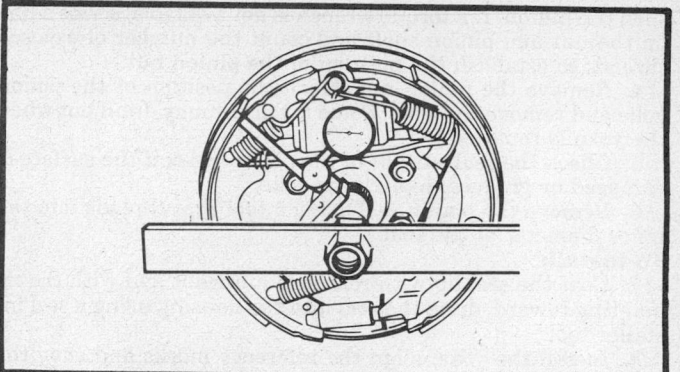

Checking axle shaft endplay

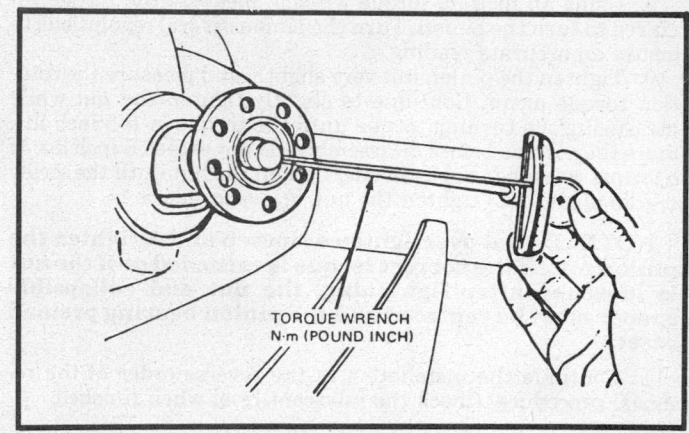

Checking pinion preload

2. Using a lead hammer, strike the end of each axle shaft to seat the bearing cups against the support plates.
3. Attach a large 18 in. bar with a hole in the middle, to the end of the axle. The bar will be used as a handle to move the axle in and out while checking the endplay.
4. Attach a dial indicator to the axle housing backing plate so it will read the in and out movement of the axle.
5. Alternately, pull and push on the bar so the axle moves in and out to the limit of its endplay. Correct endplay is 0.006 in. Allowable endplay is 0.004–0.008 in.
6. If the endplay needs to be adjusted, place shims on the left side of the axle only. Adding shims will increase endplay. Removing shims will decrease endplay.
7. The outer oil seal housing acts as a bearing retainer. To be effective, shims must be installed inboard from the oil seal. Any other parts that install inboard from the bearing retainer will affect the endplay of the axle. On axles that the shims are inboard from the brake backing plate, the backing plate must be removed to take out or install the shims.
8. Install the hub and drum by the correct procedure under axle shaft removal.

PROCEDURE NO. 6

Pinion Oil Seal Replacement

ALL VEHICLES

1. Raise and support the vehicle safely. Remove the wheels and brake drums.
2. Matchmark the driveshaft and rear yoke for correct reassembly. Disconnect the driveshaft from the yoke.
3. Rotate the pinion several revolutions. Use an inch lb. torque wrench to measure the amount of torque required to

turn the pinion. If a torque wrench is not available, scribe a line on the nut and pinion shaft and count the number of exposed threads to establish the position of the pinion nut.

4. Remove the pinion nut. Mark the position of the pinion yoke and remove the yoke. Some lubricant may drain out when the yoke is removed.

5. Check the seal surface of the pinion yoke; if the surface is damaged or grooved, replace the yoke.

6. Remove the pinion seal using a tool that threads into the inner diameter of the seal.

To install:

7. Coat the seal lip with rear axle lubricant and with the lip pointing inward, drive the seal into the housing using a seal installer tool.

8. Install the yoke, align the reference marks and snug the nut; do not tighten the nut. As required, use a new retaining nut.

9. Using an inch lb. torque wrench, measure the torque required to turn the pinion. Turn the pinion several revolutions to insure an accurate reading.

10. Tighten the pinion nut very slightly and measure the rotation torque again. Continue to slightly tighten the nut while measuring the turning torque until the torque is 1–5 inch lbs. more than it was before disassembly; do not exceed 5 inch lbs. If a torque wrench is not available, tighten the nut until the scribe marks align, then tighten the nut $1/16$–$1/8$ in. more.

NOTE: Do not overtighten or loosen and retighten the pinion nut. If the correct torque is exceeded or if the nut is loosened after tightening, the nut and collapsible spacer must be replaced and the pinion bearing preload reset.

11. Continue the installation in the reverse order of the removal procedure. Check the lubricant level when finished.

PROCEDURE NO. 7

Replacing Flanged Axle and Bearing

NOTE: There are 2 types of axle shaft designs used: the C-lock and the retainer plate types. The C-lock type axle is retained in the housing by a C-lock at the inner end of the axle. To remove the axle, the differential housing cover must be removed. The retainer plate type of axle is retained in the housing by a retainer plate held by the same bolts that hold the brake backing plate. On the retainer plate type, the removal of the axle shaft is done at the wheel end of the axle housing.

To determine which type of axle is used, remove a rear wheel and brake drum. Inspect the area behind the axle flange. If the axle is a retainer type, the retainer can be seen. On the C-lock type, the housing will stick out more and there is no retainer plate.

RETAINER PLATE TYPE

1. Raise and support the vehicle safely. Remove the wheel and brake drum.

2. Using a socket and extension through the hole in the axle flange, remove the retainer plate-to-backing plate nuts.

3. Using a slide hammer puller, pull the axle shaft and bearing from the axle housing. Once the bearing is free, support the axle while removing it. Dragging the axle may damage the inner seal.

4. Clean the retainer plate mounting area before replacing the axle. Make sure the backing plate is seated flat against it and that no dirt is caught between the flanges.

5. Continue the installation in the reverse order of the removal procedure.

NOTE: The retainer plate gasket is usually not available. If the gasket is not available, replace the plate without a gasket or use the old gasket.

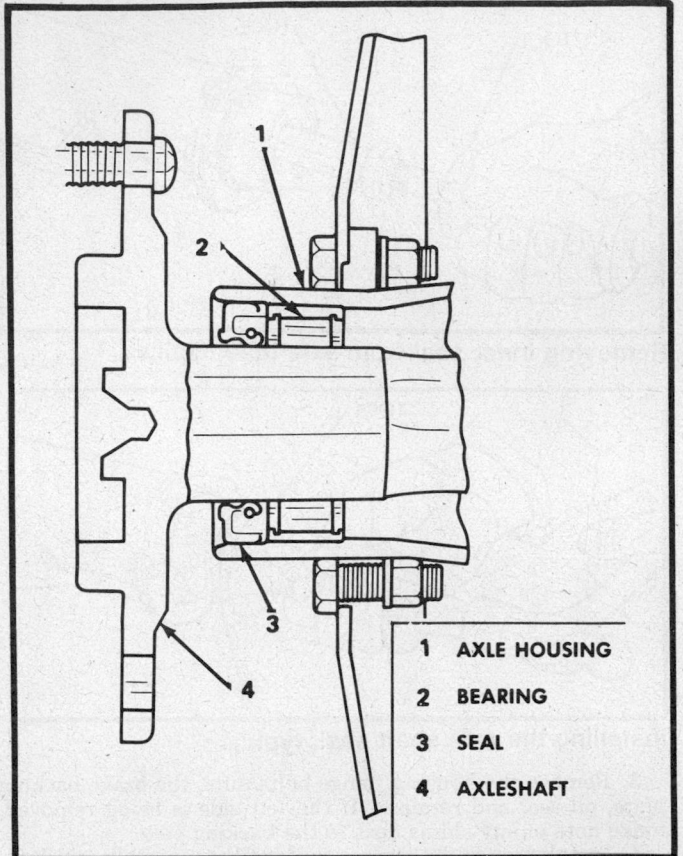

1	AXLE HOUSING
2	BEARING
3	SEAL
4	AXLESHAFT

Cross section of bearing and seal used with C-type axles, typical

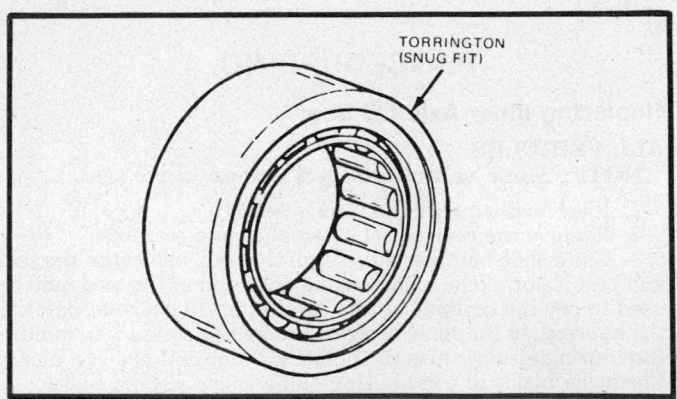

TORRINGTON (SNUG FIT)

Typical axle tube bearing assembly

C-LOCK TYPE

1. Raise and support the vehicle safely. Remove the wheel and brake drum.

2. Remove the differential cover and drain the lubricant.

3. Remove the pinion shaft lock bolt and pinion shaft.

4. Push the axle shaft inward to permit removal of the C-lock and pull the axle out of the housing.

5. The axle shaft bearing is press fit into the housing. Using a slide hammer puller tool, remove the axle shaft bearing; the seal will be removed with it.

6. To install the new bearing, pack it in axle grease and drive it into the housing to the same depth as the old one. A new seal should be driven into the end of the housing; be sure to lubricate the seal lips.

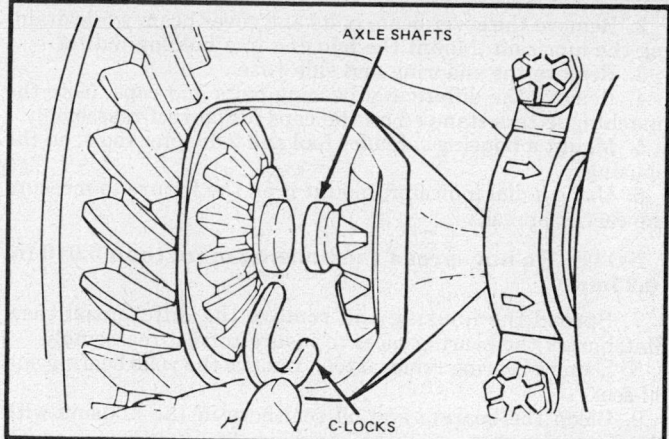

Removal or installation of C locks

7. Continue the installation in the reverse order of the removal procedure. Be sure to avoid any gasket leaks at the differential cover. Refill the differential with the correct lubricant.

PROCEDURE NO. 8

Removing Pressed On Bearing From Axle

NOTE: A hydraulic or mechanical press is necessary. The press should be one that is recommended for axle bearing work.

1. Raise and support the vehicle safely. Remove the axle and bearing assembly from the vehicle.
2. The retainer ring that is pressed against the bearing, must be V grooved with a chisel and a heavy hammer to relieve the pressure so that it can be slipped off the shaft, on vehicles with tapered axle.

NOTE: Do not attempt to split the ring because the chisel might damage the shaft. Several deep V grooves will usually loosen the ring enough that it can be removed by hand.

3. Use a press setup, using press blocks that fit the bearing and a cage or bearing cap that will contain the bearing pieces in case it factures.

─────────── **CAUTION** ───────────
Always wear eye protection when pressing the bearings.
───────────────────────────────────

4. Press the bearing off the axle.
5. Remove the seal from the retainer plate, not applicable on some vehicles. Install a new seal, with the lip facing inward. Slip the retainer plate and seal over the axle, with the seal lip facing inward. On some models, the retainer plate does not contain a seal.
6. Press a new bearing on the axle following the same precautions as when removing the old bearing. Press a new retaining ring up against the bearing.
7. Continue the installation in the reverse order of the removal procedure.

PROCEDURE NO. 9

Adjusting Axle EndPlay

There is no endplay adjustment on these axles. If the endplay is excessive, the bearing is worn and must be replaced.

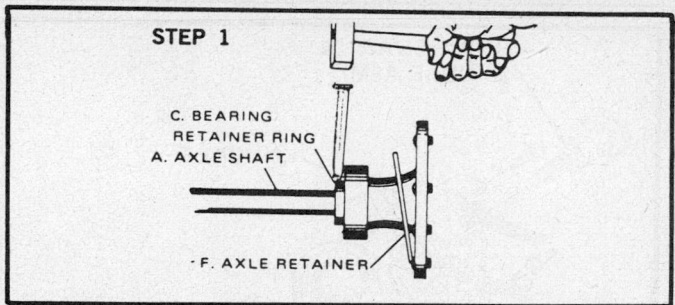

1. Mount axle shaft (A) in vise. Remove the bearing retainer ring

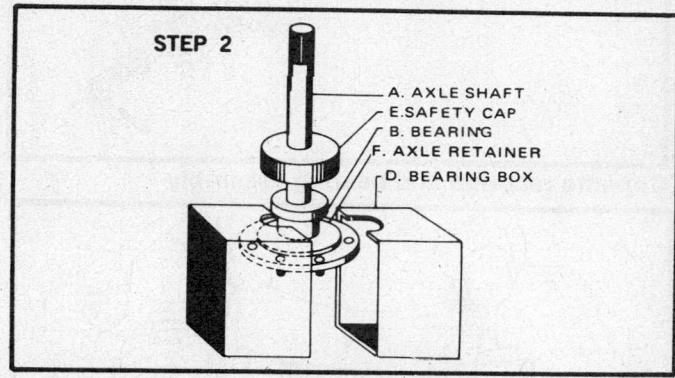

2. At the press table, insert the axle flange and retainer (F) within the removal box (D). Both sections of the box should rest against the axle under the bearing (B). Place safety cap (E) over the shaft on top of the bearing. Press against shaft end to remove bearing. If it does not easily break loose, tap shaft with a ballpean hammer.

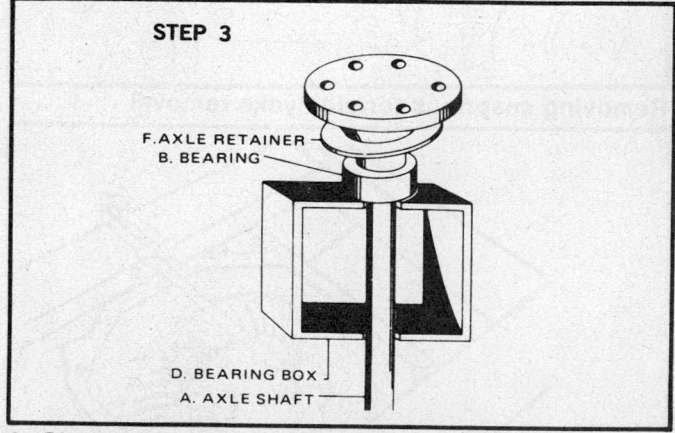

3. Clean shaft and retainer (F) and replace retainer against axle flange. Slip new bearing (B) over the shaft. Be sure a sealed bearing faces the proper directions. Locate axle shaft (A) in the removal box (D) and press the bearng to its seat on the shaft. Also press a new retaining ring (C) against the bearng ends. To remove the axles, the differential housing cover must be removed. The other type of axle is retained in the housing by a retainer plate held by the same bolts that hold the brake backing plate. On the retainer plate type, all the work of removing the axle shafts is done at the wheel ends of the axle housing

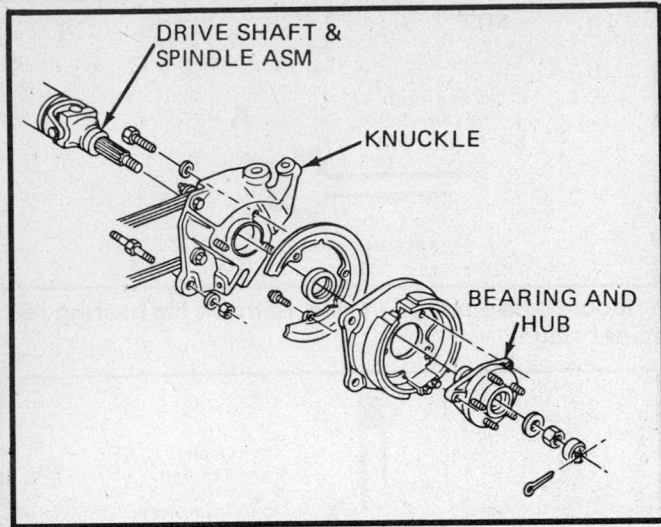

Corvette rear hub and bearing assembly

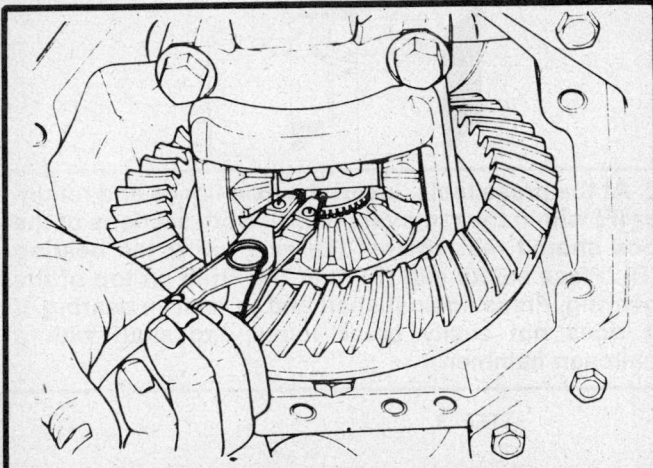

Removing snaprings for side yoke removal

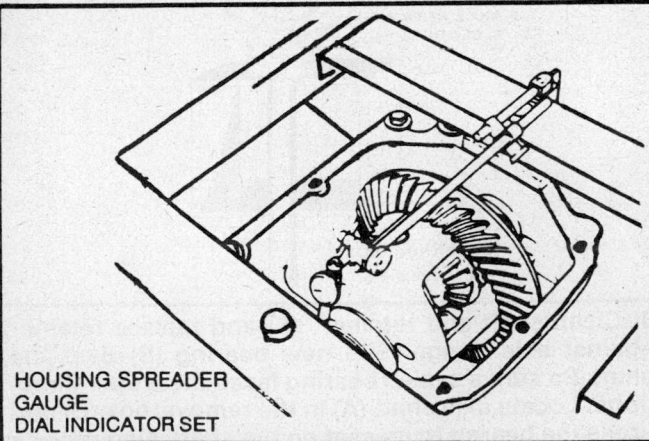

HOUSING SPREADER
GAUGE
DIAL INDICATOR SET

Checking carrier spread with dial indicator

PROCEDURE NO. 10

Replacing Yoke Bearing and Seal
CORVETTE

1. Raise and support the vehicle safely. Remove the differential housing from the vehicle.

2. Remove the cover beam bolts and cover beam while draining the lubricant. Mount the housing in a holding fixture.
3. Remove the snapring and side yoke.
4. Remove the differential bearing bolts and caps. Note the matching letters stamped on the caps for correct reassembly.
5. Mount a housing spreader tool and 2 adapter tools, on the housing.
6. Using a dial indicator, mount it on the fixture to measure the carrier spread.

NOTE: Do not spread the housing more than 0.010 in. (0.25mm).

7. Spread the housing and remove the differential case. Matchmark the bearing races to insure correct reassembly.
8. Using a bearing removal tool, remove the yoke bearing and oil seal.
9. Clean the bearing and oil seal bore in the housing with cleaning solvent.
10. Using a bearing installation tool, drive the new bearing into the housing.
11. Apply a light coat of gear lubricant to the new seal and using a seal driver tool, install the new seal into the housing.
12. Reinstall the differential in the housing making sure the bearing races are replaced on the same side they were on before removal. Remove the housing spreader. For the $7\frac{7}{8}$ in. axle, torque the differential bolts to 42–48 ft. lbs. For the $8\frac{1}{2}$ in. axle, torque the bolts to 58–68 ft. lbs. Install the yoke and snapring in the housing.
13. Continue the installation in the reverse order of the removal procedure. Fill the housing with the correct lubricant.

NOTE: To control yoke shaft endplay, snaprings come in 7 sizes and colors for the $7\frac{7}{8}$ in. axle and 8 sizes and colors for the $8\frac{1}{2}$ in. axle.

$7\frac{7}{8}$ IN. AXLE

1. Plain—0.050 in.
2. Blue—0.055 in.
3. Yellow—0.060 in.
4. Green—0.065 in.
5. Orange—0.070 in.
6. Red—0.075 in.
7. Purple—0.080 in.
8. Endplay—0.0005–0.0085 in.

$8\frac{1}{2}$ IN. AXLE

1. Red—0.075 in.
2. Purple—0.080 in.
3. Pink—0.085 in.
4. Plain—0.090 in.
5. Blue—0.095 in.
6. Yellow—0.100 in.
7. Green—0.105 in.
8. Orange—0.110 in.
9. Endplay—0.0005–0.0085 in.

PROCEDURE NO. 11

Installing Pinion Oil Seal
CHEVETTE AND PONTIAC 1000

1. Raise and support the vehicle safely. Disconnect the driveshaft from the rear U-joint and remove the shaft by pulling the slip joint from the transmission.
2. Position a safety stand or other firm support under the front of the rear axle housing. Place another support under the extension housing to hold it in place before it is disconnected.
3. Disconnect the center support bracket from the underbody.
4. Disconnect the extension housing flange from the axle carrier housing.

5. Remove the extension housing carefully. If necessary, use pry bar to pry the extension housing away from the carrier housing.

6. Using a slide hammer puller or pry bar, remove the seal from the front of the carrier housing.

NOTE: Be careful not damage the splines on the drive coupling.

7. With the seal lip pointing inwards, drive a new seal into the housing to the same depth as the old one. Continue the installation in the reverse order of the removal procedure. Check the lubricant level when finished.

PROCEDURE NO. 12

Installing Outer Oil Seal In Retainer Flange

NOTE: Some vehicles do not use a seal in the retainer flange.

1. Raise and support the vehicle safely.
2. Remove the rear wheel assemblies. Remove the axle.
3. Press the bearing from the axle.
4. Remove the axle retainer and install a new seal in the retainer.
5. Install the retainer and bearing on the axle.
6. Continue the installation in the reverse order of the removal procedure. Check and/or refill the lubricant level.

PROCEDURE NO. 13

Setting Pinion Depth

NOTE: If the original pinion gear and bearings are to be reinstalled, the original shims can be reused to provide the correct shim thickness providing the ring and pinion gear teeth wear pattern is acceptable.

The methods of adjusting the pinion to obtain the proper depths will vary by axle types and manufacturer's recommendations. Pinion depth settings and gear tooth contact may be determined by the use of pinion setting gauges or by the use of marking dye on the gear teeth while observing the meshing pattern of the teeth.

When using the gauge method, backlash is established after the pinion has been properly set. With the marking dye method, backlash is established first, then the proper pinion tooth contact is established.

Terms Used

Certain dimensions must be determined when using the pinion setting gauge:

1. **NOMINAL ASSEMBLY DIMENSION** – Standard pinion depth. This dimension, (varying with axle model), is the distance between the center line of the drive gear, (or differential carrier bore) and the end of the drive pinion. This dimension may be marked on the pinion.

2. **INDIVIDUAL VARIATION DISTANCE** – Pinion depth variance. This dimension is a plus or minus variation of the nominal assembly dimension on each individual pinion which may be caused by manufacturing variations.

3. **CORRECTED NOMINAL DIMENSION** – Desired pinion depth. This dimension is the nominal assembly dimension plus or minus the individual variation distance.

4. **CORRECTED MICROMETER DISTANCE IS THE CORRECTED NOMINAL DIMENSION** – Less the thickness of the gauge set step plate 0.400 in. mounted on end of pinion.

5. **INITIAL MICROMETER READING** – Is the dimension taken by the micrometer to the gauge step plate.

6. **SHIM PACK CORRECTION** – Is determined by the difference between the corrected micrometer distance and the

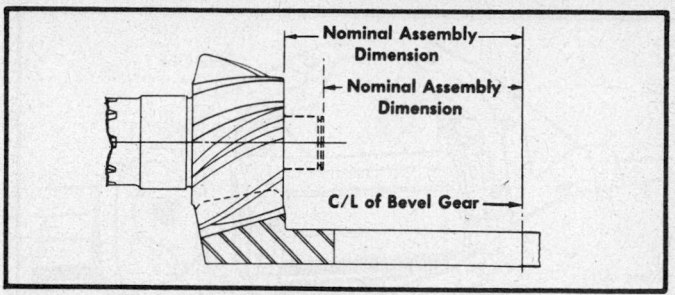

Nominal assembly dimension

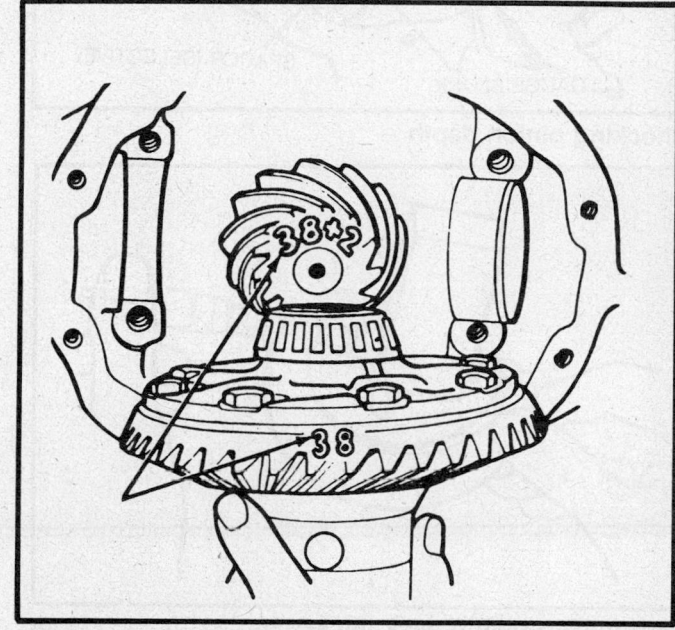

Markings etched on pinion and ring gear

intial micrometer reading. This represents the amount of shim pack to be added or removed as later explained.

7. **MEASURED PINION DEPTH** – This measurement is the distance between the axle center line and the top of the pinion gear. If a step plate or other type of gauge tool is used, this measurement is included in the total.

Markings On Ring and Pinion Gears

Ring and pinion gears are tested at the time of manufacture to detect machining variances and to obtain desirable tooth contact and quietness. When the correct setting is achieved, the gears are considered a matched set and a set of numbers, along with other identifying marks, are etched on the gear set.

A plus or minus sign are used, followed by a digit to represent the factory setting where to tooth contact and quietness were the best. This is called the pinion depth variance or the individual variation distance.

For example, if the pinion gear is marked +5, this means the distance from the pinion gear rear face to the axle shaft center line is 0.005 in. more than the standard setting. If the pinion gear is marked −5, the distance is 0.005 in. less than the standard setting. To move the pinion to the standard setting, compensating for the variation, shims must be either added or subtracted from the total shim pack. This shim pack is located under the rear pinion bearing cup, between the pinion cage and the differential carrier or under the rear pinion bearing, depending upon the differential being serviced.

If the addition or removal of shims is necessary for the pinion depth adjustment, draw a diagram as shown and determine

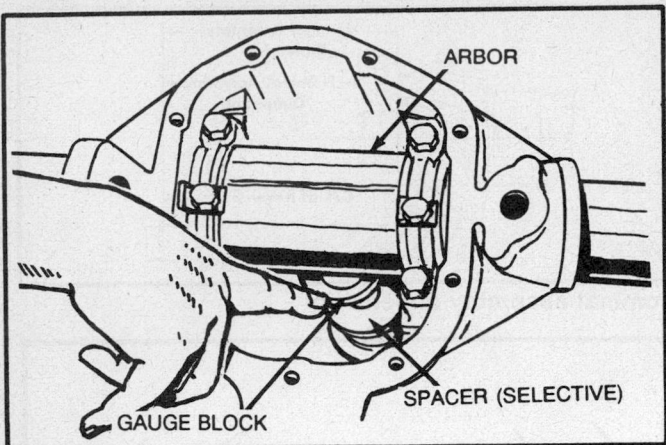

Checking pinion depth

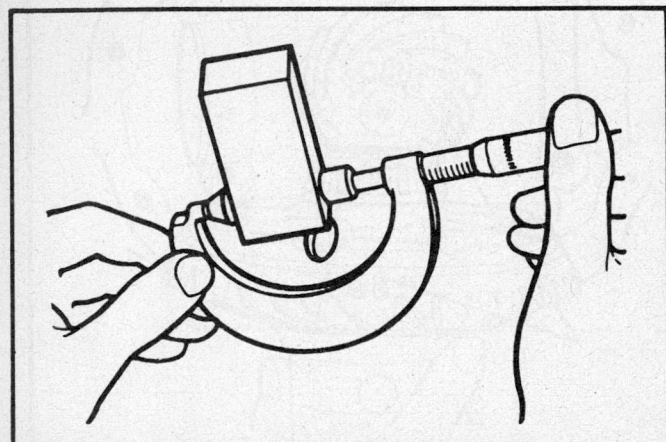

Determining pinion pack thickness

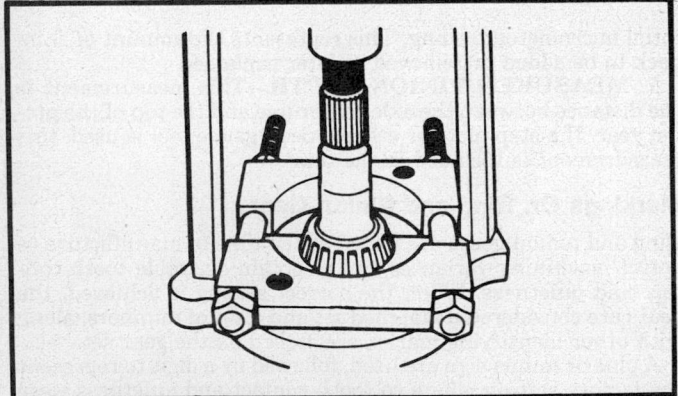

Rear pinion bearing removal-typical

which way the pinion must be moved to obtain the desired pinion depth.

NOTE: When a pinion has a plus or minus reading, the reading is etched on the head of the pinion gear along with other pertinent information. The plus or minus reading can be expressed in either metric or standard measurement. The metric measurement will have a letter M after the measurement digit.

Pinion Gauge Method

The pinion gauge method uses a direct reading micrometer

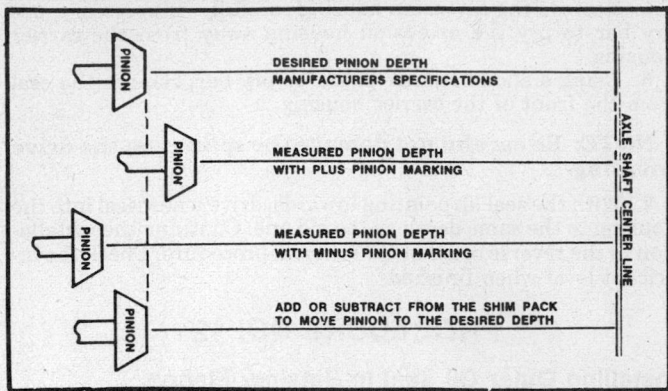

Movement of pinion to obtain desired pinion depth

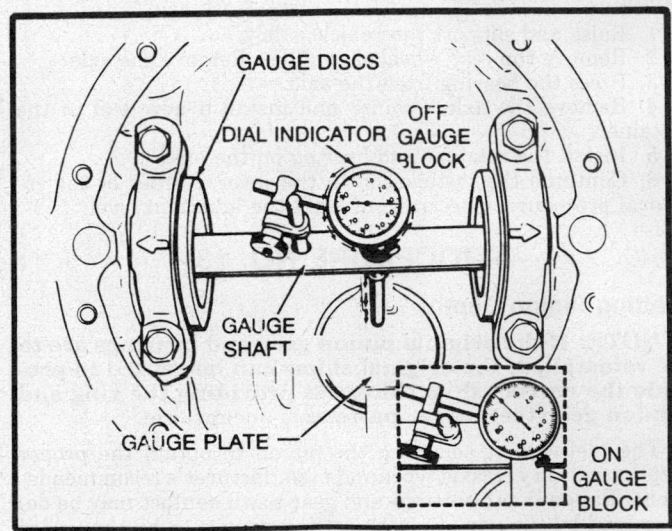

Use of typical pinion depth gauge assembly

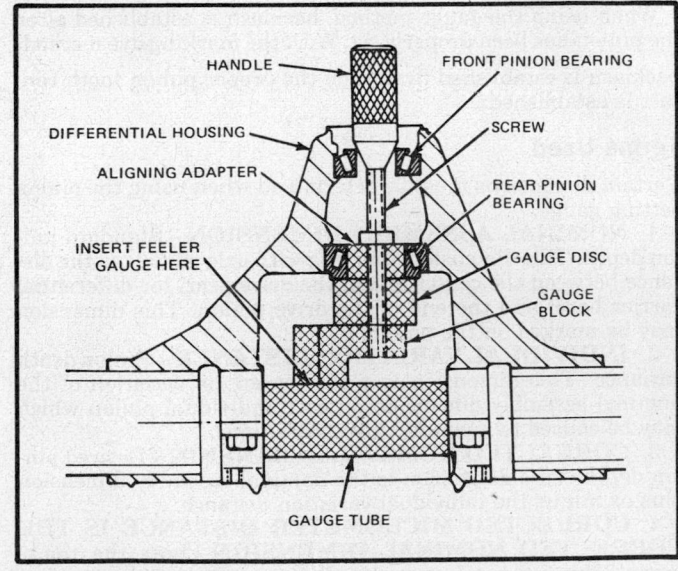

Use of typical pinion depth gauge assembly

mounted on or through an arbor bar set in adaptor discs and located in the side carrier bearing cup locations on the differential housing and held in place by the bearing cup caps. The arbor bar coincides and represents the center line of the axle shafts. A reading is taken by a mounted micrometer from the arbor bar to the head of the pinion. This reading is used to determine the need to add or subtract shims from the shim pack total in order to adjust the pinion to the proper nominal assembly dimension or standard pinion depth.

Another method, that uses the arbor bar and discs, is the use of a gauge block with a spring loaded plunger and thumb screw to lock the plunger upon expansion. A micrometer is used to measure the gauge block after the plunger has been allowed to expand between the arbor bar and the pinion head. As in the mounted micrometer procedure, the shim pack thickness is determined by the reading obtained.

A third method is the use of a gauge block tool, installed in the differential housing in place of the pinion gear and a large arbor bar placed in the axle housing differential bearing seats and tightened securely. A measurement is taken between the arbor bar and the pinion tool by either a dial indicator, feeler gauge blades or the use of individual shims from the shim pack. This measurement represents the shim pack needed for a 0 marked pinion. If the pinion is marked either plus or minus, the shim pack is adjusted accordingly.

Setting New Pinion Without Gauge

Whenever a pinion gauge is not available, measure the thickness of the pinion shim pack at the rear pinion bearing cup or between the pinion rear bearing and pinion gear head. Change the sign of the marking, (individual variation distance), on the new pinion, (plus-to-minus or minus-to-plus), then add or subtract the variation on the old pinion (sign unchanged). This will determine the amount that the original shim pack must be changed when installing the new pinion.

Differential units that have shims located between the pinion cage and differential carrier, change the sign of the marking, (individual variation distance), on the pinion, (plus to minus or minus to plus). Add the variation of the new pinion, (sign unchanged), which will determine how much the original shim pack must be altered when installing a new pinion.

When the approximate thickness of shim pack has been determined, a final check of the tooth contact must be made by using the marking dye method.

NOTE: Never put a differential unit in service until the tooth contact pattern is satisfactory.

Marking Dye Method

The marking dye method takes extra time, due to the numerous times the ring and pinion components may have to be assembled and disassembled in search of the correct shim pack thickness to give the proper tooth contact pattern between the teeth of the ring and pinion gears. Usually, the only time this method is

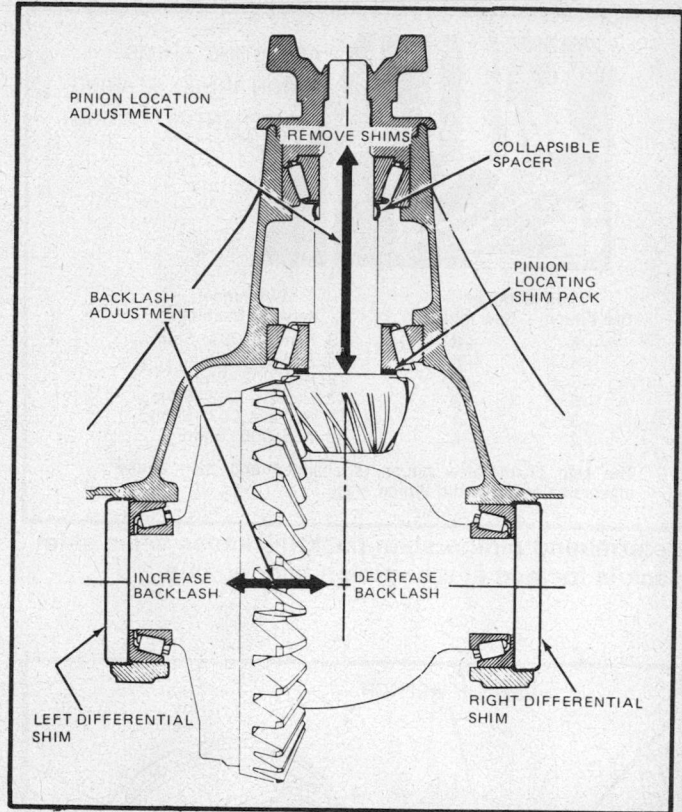

Typical pinion and ring gear tooth contact used with integral carrier axles

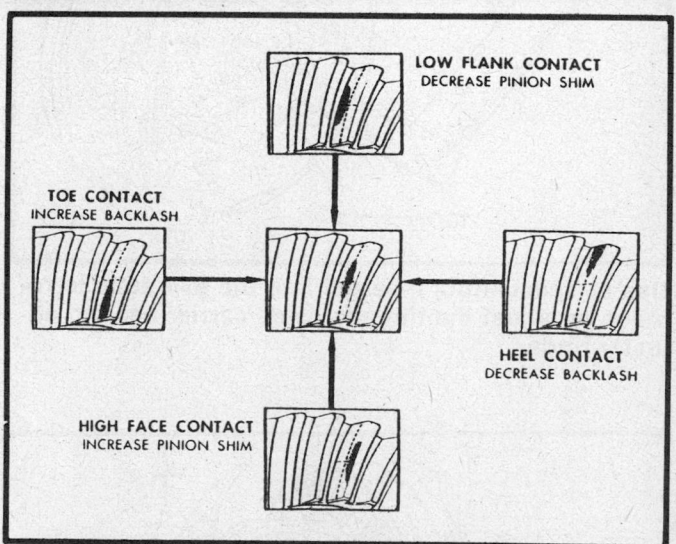

Typical gear tooth pattern check

used, is when special tools or rebuilding specifications are not available for a specific unit.

PROCEDURE NO. 14

Ring Gear Backlash Adjustment

Operating clearance is needed between the ring gear and the pinion gear. This clearance is known as backlash and is measured in either the standard inch or metric measurements. Two

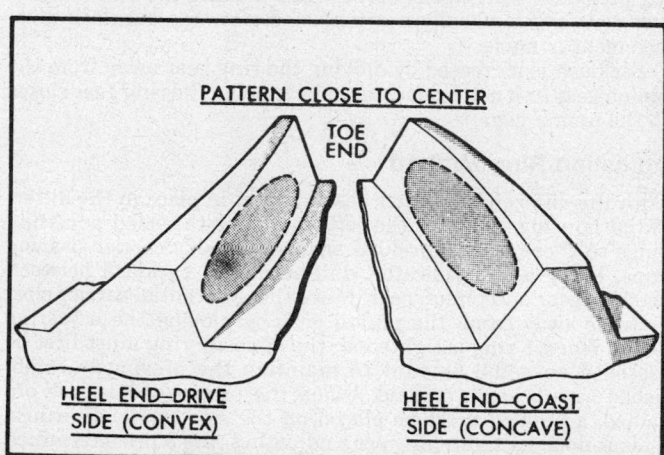

Desired tooth contact

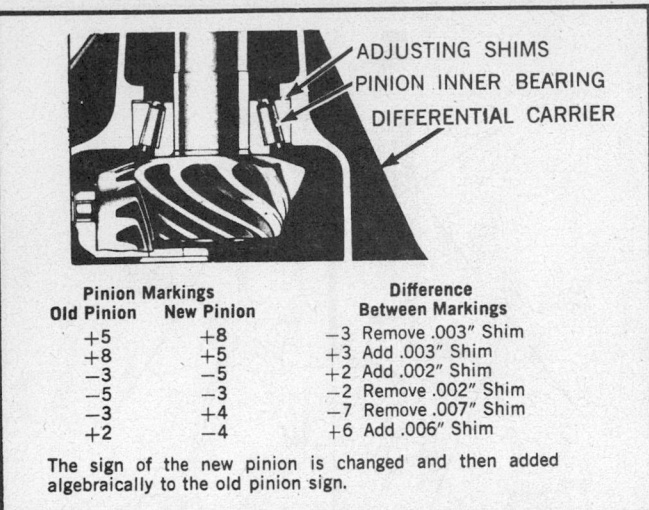

Pinion Markings		Difference
Old Pinion	New Pinion	Between Markings
+5	+8	−3 Remove .003″ Shim
+8	+5	+3 Add .003″ Shim
−3	−5	+2 Add .002″ Shim
−5	−3	−2 Remove .002″ Shim
−3	+4	−7 Remove .007″ Shim
+2	−4	+6 Add .006″ Shim

The sign of the new pinion is changed and then added algebraically to the old pinion sign.

Determining pinion shim pack thickness when shim pack is located at rear pinion bearing cup

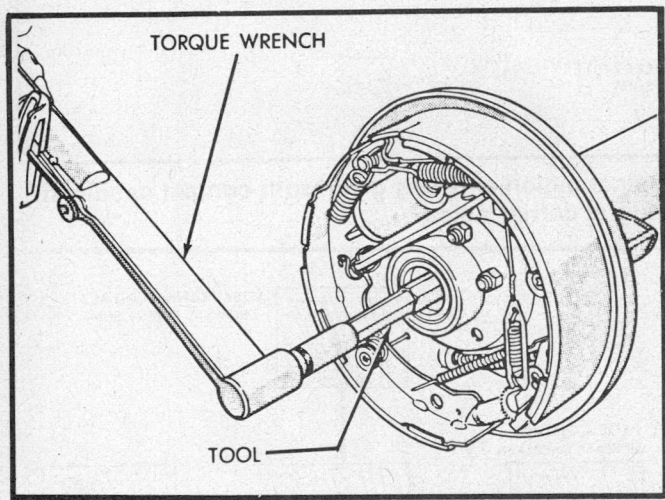

Use of special tool inserted into the axle tube to remove or adjust the threaded side carrier bearing adjuster rings

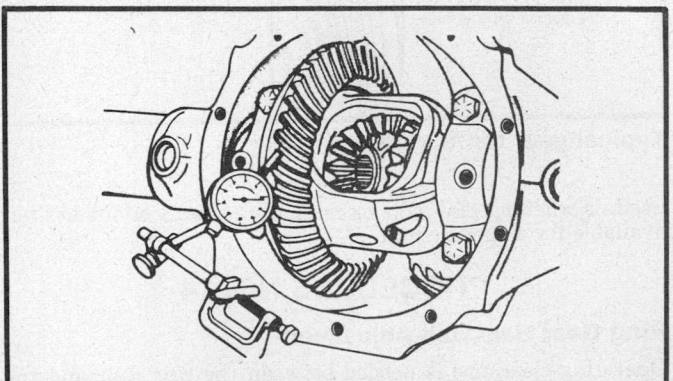

Checking backlash with dial indicator

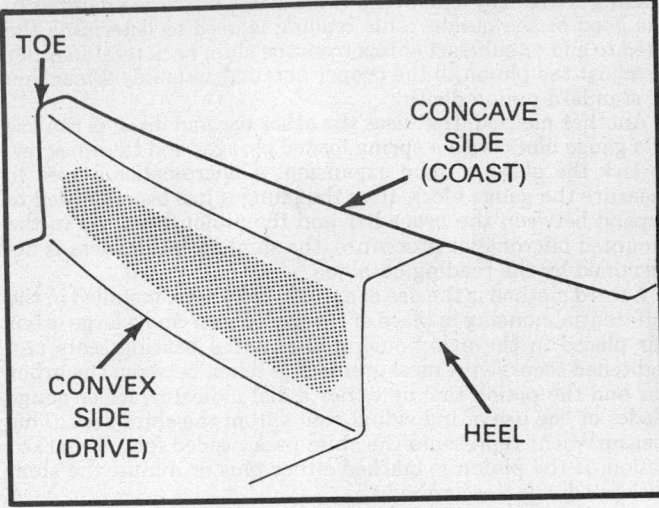

Desired ring gear tooth contact under light load

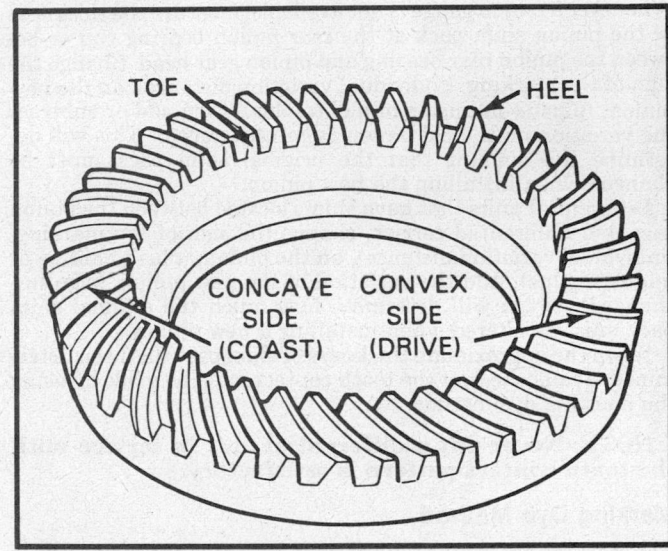

Ring gear tooth nomenclature

adjustment procedures are used to control the backlash tolerance, either adjusting rings or shim packs. The differential bearing preload must be considered when making the backlash adjustment and is usually accomplished after the backlash measurement is made.

Backlash is increased by moving the ring gear away from the pinion gear or it can be decreased by moving the ring gear closer to the pinion gear.

Adjusting Ring Method

With the differential carrier assembly set in place in the differential housing, position the left and right threaded adjusting rings so there is zero preload against the side carrier bearing cups. Using a dial indicator, determine the backlash between the ring gear and pinion gear. Move the differential carrier closer to or away from, the pinion gear by moving the adjusting rings. When 1 ring is tightened, the opposite ring must first be loosened an equal amount to maintain the previously established zero bearing preload. When the proper backlash is obtained, a preload must be placed on the side carrier bearings. This is done by tightening each adjusting ring a predetermined distance or to a specific torque, usually 1 opening of the ring locking lug from the zero bearing preload.

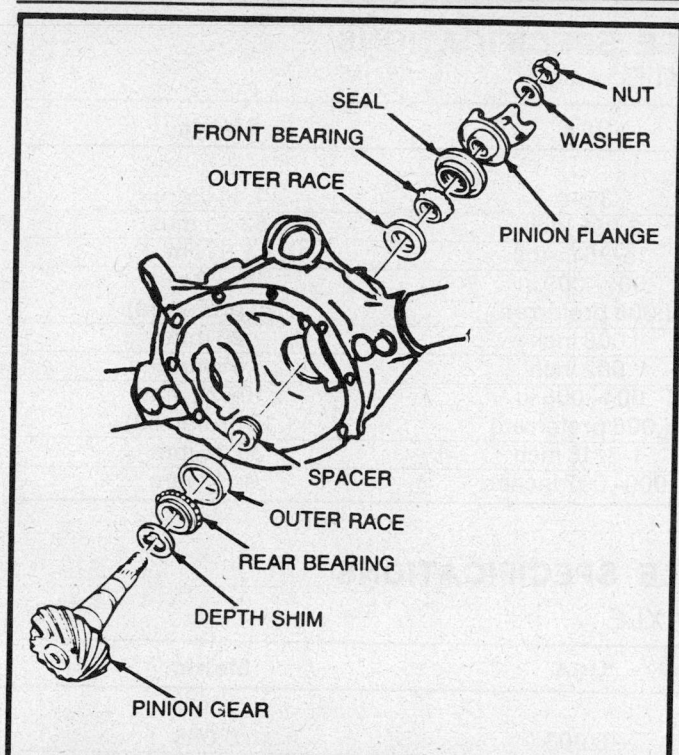

Typical standard rear axle using shims for pinion adjustment

Shim Pack Method

Shims are used to control the backlash in numerous differential assemblies. Special tools are available to find zero bearing preload before the backlash is obtained. If the original shim pack is available, the measurements can be used to arrive at a starting point to determine zero bearing preload. As a rule of thumb, 0.004 in. is used to preload the differential side bearings after the backlash has been adjusted and, therefore, subtract 0.002 in. from each side of the shim pack and the zero preload should be obtained or only small changes in the shim packs would be needed to obtain the zero bearing preload. Measure the gear backlash and adjust the left and right shim packs to move the ring gear closer to or away from the pinion gear until the correct backlash is obtained.

The amount of change in the shim thickness needed to correct the backlash must be subtracted from 1 side and added to the other. This keeps the total shim thickness (left side + right side = total) the same. When the proper backlash is obtained, add the specified bearing preload measurement to each side shim pack. Recheck the backlash and the tooth contact pattern.

PROCEDURE NO. 15

Pinion Bearing Preload

As with other bearing applications, the pinion bearings must be preloaded after the pinion depth has been corrected. Shims and/or crushable sleeves are used to provide the necessary preload adjustments.

The preload is usually determined by the rotating torque reading of the pinion, less the pinion oil seal, using a torque wrench. When using shims, the pinion nut, yoke and front pinion bearing must be removed when adjusting the shim pack thickness. When the crushable sleeve is used, the pinion nut is tightened, less pinion oil seal, until the correct turning torque is obtained.

NOTE: Should the turning torque be loose because the spacer is crushed too far, a new spacer must be used and the procedure repeated. Never back the nut off to obtain the correct torque reading.

LIMITED SLIP DIFFERENTIALS

General Information

LUBRICATION

The use of proper lubricant is critical in limited slip type drive axles. Force is applied when cornering to the clutch pack or clutch cones and the use of the wrong lubricant can cause the clutch surfaces to grab and chatter while turning. Always follow the manufacturer's recommendations regarding drive axle lubrication. When chatter is encountered, the 1st step should be to drain the lubricant and refill it using the proper lubricant.

Testing

The clutch operation on all limited slip type axles can be tested as follows:

CHRYSLER CORPORATION SURE GRIP

1. Raise and support the vehicle safely. Turn the engine **OFF** and place the automatic transmission in **L**.
2. Grip the tire and attempt to rotate the wheel by hand.
3. If it is extremely difficult, if not impossible, to rotate either wheel the Sure Grip differential can be assumed to be performing satisfactorily.
4. If it is relatively easy to continuously turn either rear wheel, the unit should be removed and replaced.

NOTE: The Sure Grip differential is serviced as a unit only. Under no circumstances should the unit be disassembled and reinstalled.

FORD MOTOR COMPANY TRACTION LOK

A Traction Lok differential can be checked for proper operation without removing the differential from the axle housing.

1. Raise a rear wheel and support it under the axle housing. Remove the wheel cover.
2. Install a Traction Lok torque tool on the axle shaft flange studs.
3. Using a 200 ft. lb. torque wrench, rotate the axle shaft. Be sure that the transmission is in **N** with 1 rear wheel on the floor and the other raised off the floor.
4. The break away torque required to start rotation should be at least 30–40 ft. lbs. The initial break away torque may be higher than the continuous turning torque but normal.
5. The axle shaft should turn with even pressure throughout the check without slipping or binding. If the torque reading is less than specified, check the differential for proper assembly.

——————————— **CAUTION** ———————————

A vehicle equipped with a Traction Lok Differential will always have both wheels driving. If the engine is being used to drive the rear axle while servicing the vehicle, be sure to have both rear wheels OFF the ground. Failure to do this will cause the vehicle to surge OFF the support and could cause injury.

AMERICAN MOTORS AXLE SPECIFICATIONS
REAR AXLE

Operation	USA	Metric
7-9/16 in. Ring Gear		
Lubricant Capacity	3 pts.	1.41 liters
Pinion Depth Standard Setting	2.095 inch	53.21 mm
Pinion Bearing Preload	15-25 in-lbs	2.3 N·m
Ring and Pinion Backlash	.005-.009 in. (.008 preferred)	.13-.23 mm (.20 preferred)
Differential Bearing Preload	.008 inch	.20 mm
Differential Case Face Runout	.002 inch	.05 mm
Axle Shaft End Play	.004-.008 in. (.006 preferred)	.10-.20 mm (.15 preferred)
Axle Hub Installation Dimension	1-3/16 inch	30.16 mm
Differential Side Gear to Case Clearance	.000-.007 inches	.0-.17 mm

AMERICAN MOTORS AXLE SPECIFICATIONS
FRONT AXLE

Operation	USA	Metric
7-9/16 in. Ring Gear		
Axle Shaft End Play	0.003	0.088
Differential Bearing Preload	0.15 in	0.38 mm
Differential Side Gear-to Case Clearance	.000-.006 inn	0.000-0.15 mm
Ring Gear Backlash	0.005-0.010	0.12-0.25 mm
Pinion Bearing Break-Away Preload		
Original Bearings	15-25 in-lbs	2-3 N·m
New Bearings	20-40 in-lbs	2-5 N·m
Pinion Depth		
Standard Setting	2.250	57.1 mm
Lubricant Capacity	2.5 pts.*	1.2 liters
Lubricant Type	SAE 85W-90**	SAE 85W-90**

* add 5 ounces (148 ml) to front axle shift housing
** use SAE 80W-140 lubricant during prolonged trailer towing

AMERICAN MOTORS AXLE TORQUE SPECIFICATIONS
(Service Set-To Torques should be used when assembling components. Service In-Use Recheck Torques should be used for checking a pre-tightened item.)

Rear Axle Differential Torque Specifications

	USA (ft-lbs)		Metric (N·m)	
	Service Set-To Torque	In-Use Recheck Torque	Service Set-To Torque	In-Use Recheck Torque
Brake Tubing-to-Rear Wheel Brake Cylinder	97 in-lb	90-105 in-lb	11	10-12
Differential Bearing Cap Bolt	57	52-67	77	71-91
Drive Gear-to-Case Bolt	52	42-65	71	57-88
Rear Brake Support Plate Screw Nut	32	25-40	43	34-54
Rear Wheel Hub-to-Axle Shaft Nut	250 min.	250 min.	339 min.	339 min.
Axle Cover Screw	15	10-18	20	14-27
Clamp Strap Bolt	14	10-18	19	14-24

Front Axle Differential Torque Specifications

	USA (ft-lbs)		Metric (N·m)	
Axle Housing Cover Bolts	20	15-25	27	20-34

AMERICAN MOTORS AXLE TORQUE SPECIFICATIONS

(Service Set-To Torques should be used when assembling components. Service In-Use Recheck Torques should be used for checking a pre-tightened item.)

	Set-To (ft-lbs)	Recheck (ft-lbs)	Set-To (N·m)	Recheck (N·m)
Axle Housing to left Engine Mounting Bracket	33	27-38	45	36-51
Axle Tube to right Engine Mounting Bracket Bolt and Nut	33	27-38	45	36-51
Differential Bearing Cap Bolts	40	35-50	54	47-68
Front Axle Support-to-Engine and Axle Housing Bolts	33	27-38	45	36-51
Pinion Nut	210	200-220	271	285-298
Propeller Shaft Flange Bolt Four-Cylinder Engine	15	12-18	20	16-24
Ring Gear-to-Case Bolts	55	45-65	75	61-88
Universal Joint Clamp Strap Bolts	17	15-20	23	20-27

All Torque values given in foot-pounds and newton-meters with dry fits unless otherwise specified.

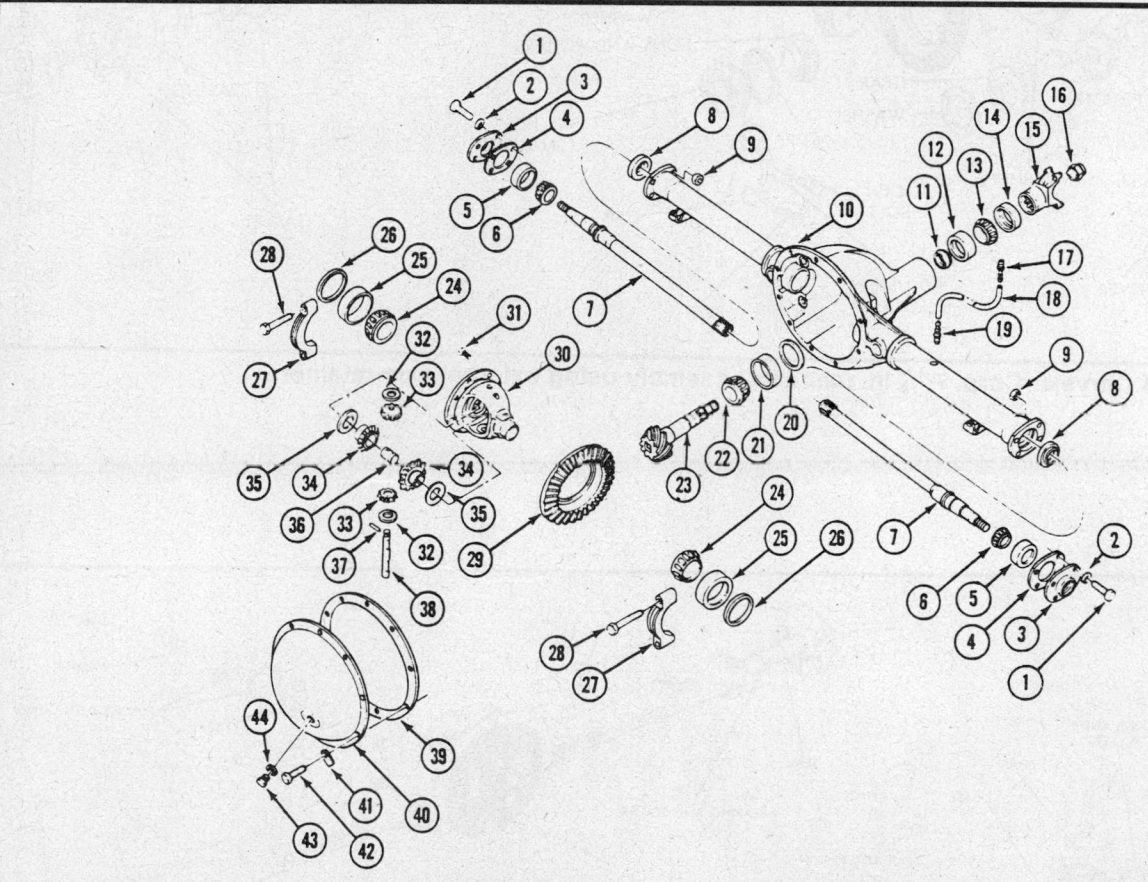

1. Bolt
2. Washer
3. Axle shaft oil seal and retainer assembly
4. Axle shaft bearing shim
5. Axle shaft bearing cup
6. Axle shaft bearing
7. Axle shaft
8. Axle shaft inner oil seal
9. Nut
10. Axle housing
11. Collapsible spacer
12. Pinion bearing cup-front
13. Pinion bearing-front
14. Pinion oil seal
15. Universal joint yoke
16. Pinion nut
17. Breather
18. Breather hose
19. Breather
20. Pinion depth adjusting shim
21. Pinion rear bearing cup
22. Pinion bearing-rear
23. Pinion gear
24. Differential bearing
25. Differential bearing cup
26. Differential bearing shim
27. Differential bearing cap
28. Differential bearing cap bolt
29. Ring gear
30. Differential case
31. Ring gear bolt
32. Differential pinion washer
33. Differential pinion
34. Differential side gear
35. Differential side gear thrust washer
36. Differential pinion shaft thrust block
37. Differential pinion shaft pin
38. Differential pinion shaft
39. Axle housing cover gasket
40. Axle housing cover
41. Axle identification tag
42. Bolt
43. Axle housing cover fill plug
44. Washer

Exploded view of AMC 7⁹/₁₆ in. rear axle with standard differential

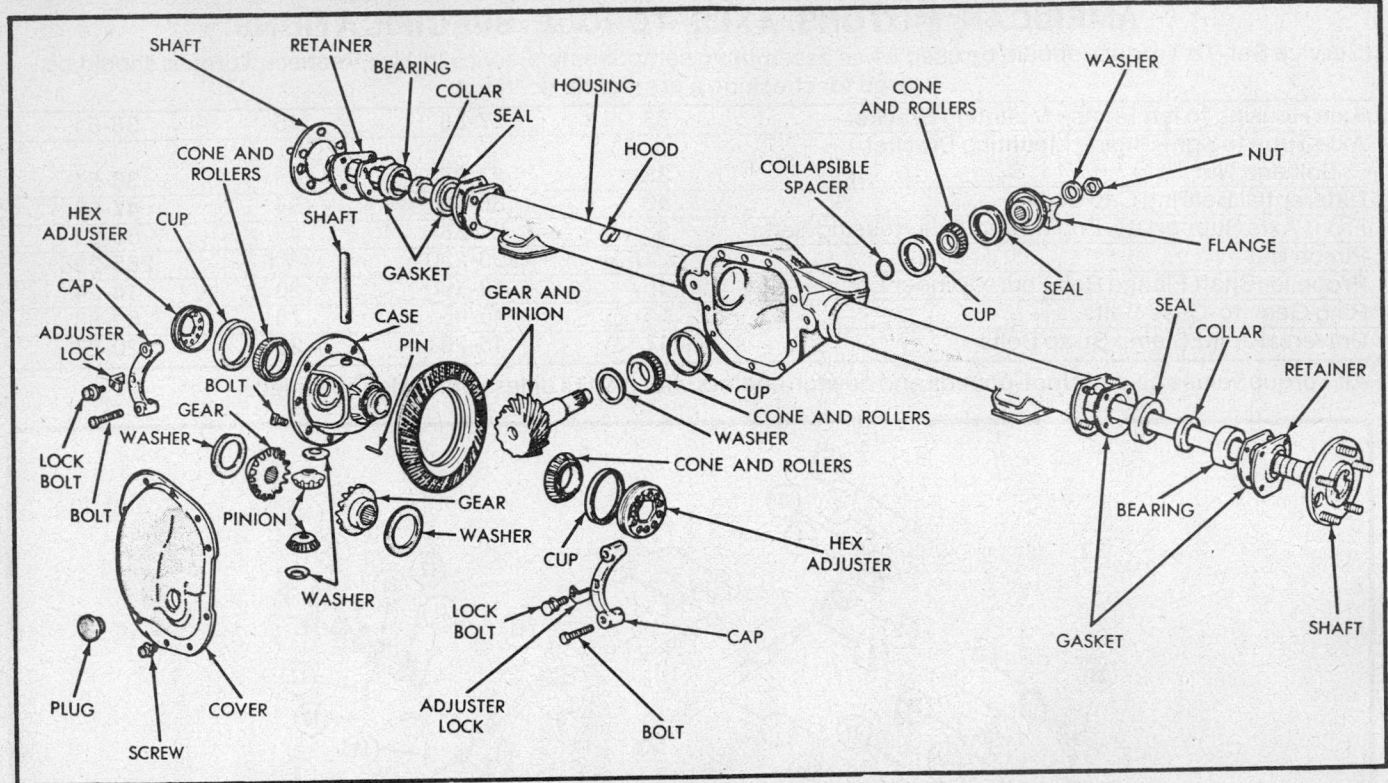

Exploded view of Chrysler Corp. 7 $\frac{1}{4}$ in. rear axle assembly using external axle retainers

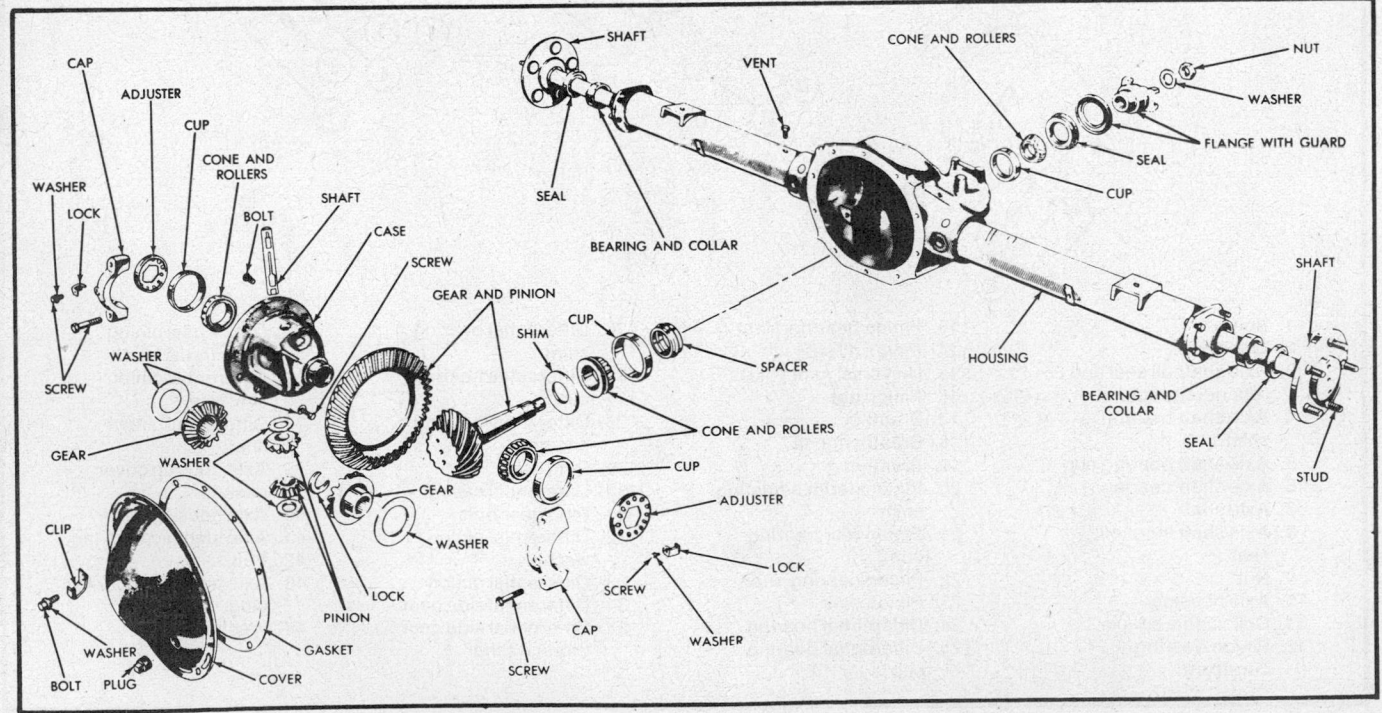

Chrysler 8 $\frac{1}{4}$ in. ring gear rear axle assembly

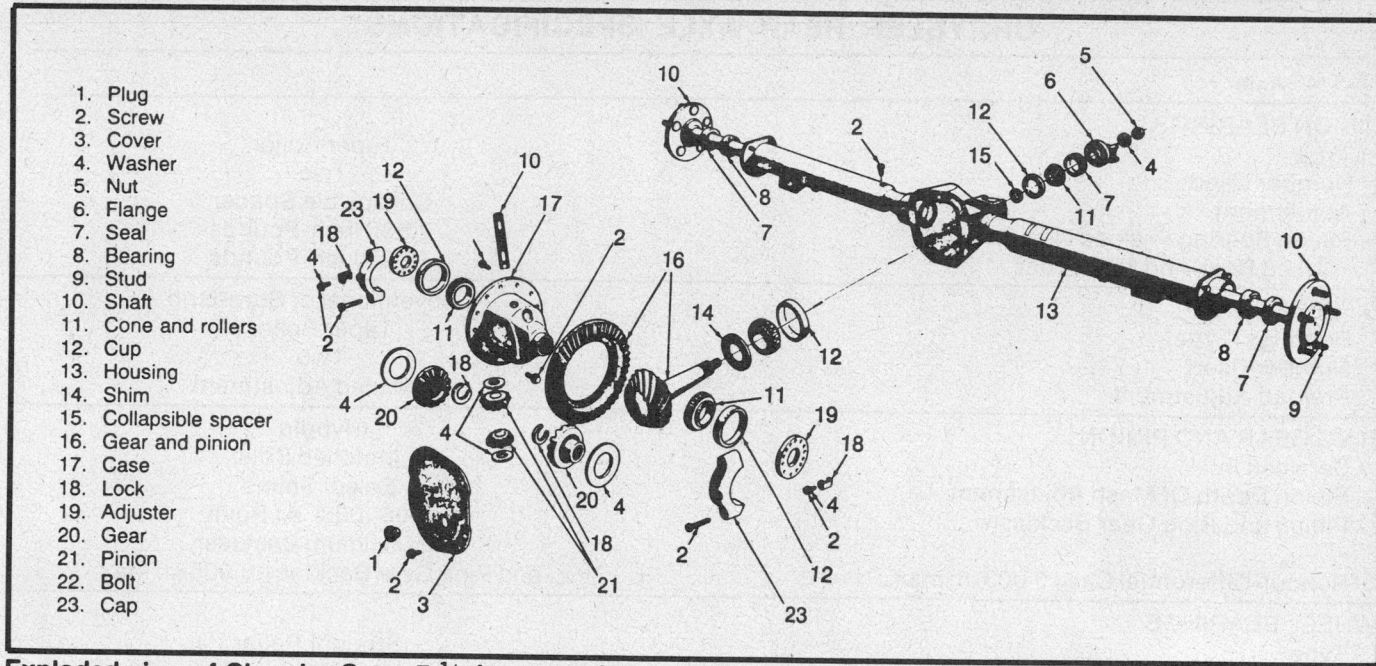

1. Plug
2. Screw
3. Cover
4. Washer
5. Nut
6. Flange
7. Seal
8. Bearing
9. Stud
10. Shaft
11. Cone and rollers
12. Cup
13. Housing
14. Shim
15. Collapsible spacer
16. Gear and pinion
17. Case
18. Lock
19. Adjuster
20. Gear
21. Pinion
22. Bolt
23. Cap

Exploded view of Chrysler Corp. 7 ¼ in. rear axle assembly using C locks to retain axles

CHRYSLER REAR AXLE SPECIFICATIONS

7-1/4″ Axle

TYPE	Semi-Floating Hypoid
Ring Gear Diameter	7.250″
Number of Teeth	
Drive Gear	43
Pinion	19
Ratio to 1	2.26
DIFFERENTIAL BEARINGS	
Adjustment by	Threaded Adjustment
PINION AND DRIVE GEAR BACK LASH	.004-.006″ at point of minimum back lash
PINION BEARING PRELOAD ADJUSTMENT BY	Collapsible Spacer
PINION BEARING DRAG TORQUE	15-25 inch-pounds
PINION DEPTH OF MESH ADJUSTMENT BY	Selected Shims
	.020-.038 inch in .001 inch graduations
RUNOUT-CASE AND DRIVE GEAR	.005 inch Maximum
WHEEL BEARING TYPE	Single Row Sealed Ball
LUBRICATION	
Capacity	2.5 Pints (2 Imperial) 1.18 litres
Type	Multi-Purpose Gear Lubricant

CHRYSLER REAR AXLE SPECIFICATIONS

8-1/4″ Axle

TYPE	Semi-Floating Hypoid
Ring Gear Diameter	8.250″
Number of Teeth	
Drive Gear	47
Pinion	21
Ratio to 1	2.24

CHRYSLER REAR AXLE SPECIFICATIONS

8-1/4" Axle

PINION BEARINGS	
Type	Taper Roller
Number Used	Two
Adjustment	Collapsible Spacer
Pinion Bearing Preload New Bearings	20-35 Inch-Pounds
Used Rear And New Front	10-25 Inch-Pounds
DIFFERENTIAL	Conventional or Sure-Grip
Bearings (Type)	Taper Roller
Number Used	Two
Preload Adjustment	Threaded Adjustment
RING GEAR AND PINION	Hypoid
Serviced In	Matched Sets
Pinion Depth Of Mesh Adjustment	Select Shims
Pinion and Ring Gear Backlash	.006-.008" At Point
	Of Minimum Backlash
Runout-Differential Case 0.003 in. max.,	and Ring Gear Backface 0.005 in. Max.
WHEEL BEARINGS	
Type	Straight Roller
Adjustment	None
End Play	Built-In
Lubrication	Rear Axle Lubricant
LUBRICATION	
Capacity	4.4 PTS. (3-1/2 Imperial) 2.08 litres
Type	Multi-Purpose Gear Lubricant. In Sure-Grip Differentials 4 ounces (.1183 litres) of MOPAR Hypoid Gear Oil Additive Friction Modifier, Part No. 4057100 or equivalent must be included with every refill.

CHRYSLER REAR AXLE
TORQUE SPECIFICATIONS

Components	Ft. lbs.	Inch lbs.	Nm
7-1/4 inch Axle			
Differential Bearing Cap Bolts	45		61
Ring Gear to Differential Case Bolts (Left Hand Thread)	70		95
Drive Pinion Flange Nut	210 (Min.)		285
Carrier Cover Bolts		250	28
Axle Shaft Retainer Nuts	35		47
Propeller Shaft Bolts (Rear)		170-200	19-23
Spring Clip (U Bolt) Nuts	45 (Max.)		61
Wheel Stud Nuts	85		115
Shock Absorber Stud Nuts (Lower)	50		68
8-1/4 inch Axle			
Differential Bearing Cap Bolts	100		136
Ring Gear to Differential Case Bolts	70		95
Drive Pinion Flange Nut	210 (Min.)		285
Carrier Cover Bolts		250	28
Brake Support Plate Retainer Nuts	35		47
Propeller Shaft Bolts (Rear)		170-200	19-23
Spring Clip (U Bolt) Nuts	45		61
Wheel Stud Nuts	85		115
Shock Absorber Stud Nuts	50		68

FORD REAR AXLE SPECIFICATIONS
Integral Carrier—7-1/2 Inch Ring Gear

CLEARANCE, TOLERANCE AND ADJUSTMENTS

Description	mm	Inches	Description	mm	Inches
Maximum Runout of Backface of Ring Gear	.010	.004	Backlash Between Ring Gear and Pinion Teeth	.203-.4	.008-.015
Differential Side Gear Thrust Washer Thickness	.762-.812	.030-.032	Maximum Backlash Variation Between Teeth	.10	.004
Differential Pinion Gear Thrust Washer Thickness	.762-.812	.030-.032	Maximum Radial Runout of Companion Flange in Assembly	.25 TIR	.010 TIR
Differential Carrier Spread	.041	.016	Available Pinion Gear Shims in Steps of: .0254mm (0.001 inch) 191mm (7.5 inch)		
Nominal Pinion Locating Shim	.762	.030		.533-.94	.021-.037

LUBRICANT CAPACITIES AND CHECKING PROCEDURES (INTEGRAL CARRIER)—CONVENTIONAL

Vehicle	Engine	Axle	U.S. Measure Capacity (Pints) ①	Imperial Capacity (Pints) ①
Mustang/Capri, Fairmont/Zephyr	2.3L	171.45mm (6-3/4 inch) Ring Gear	2.50 ②	2.08

① All conventional axles use ESP-M2C154-A (E0AZ-19580-A, B, C) lubricant or equivalent.

② Approximate refill capacity—actual lubricant capacities are determined by filling to the bottom of the filler plug hole.

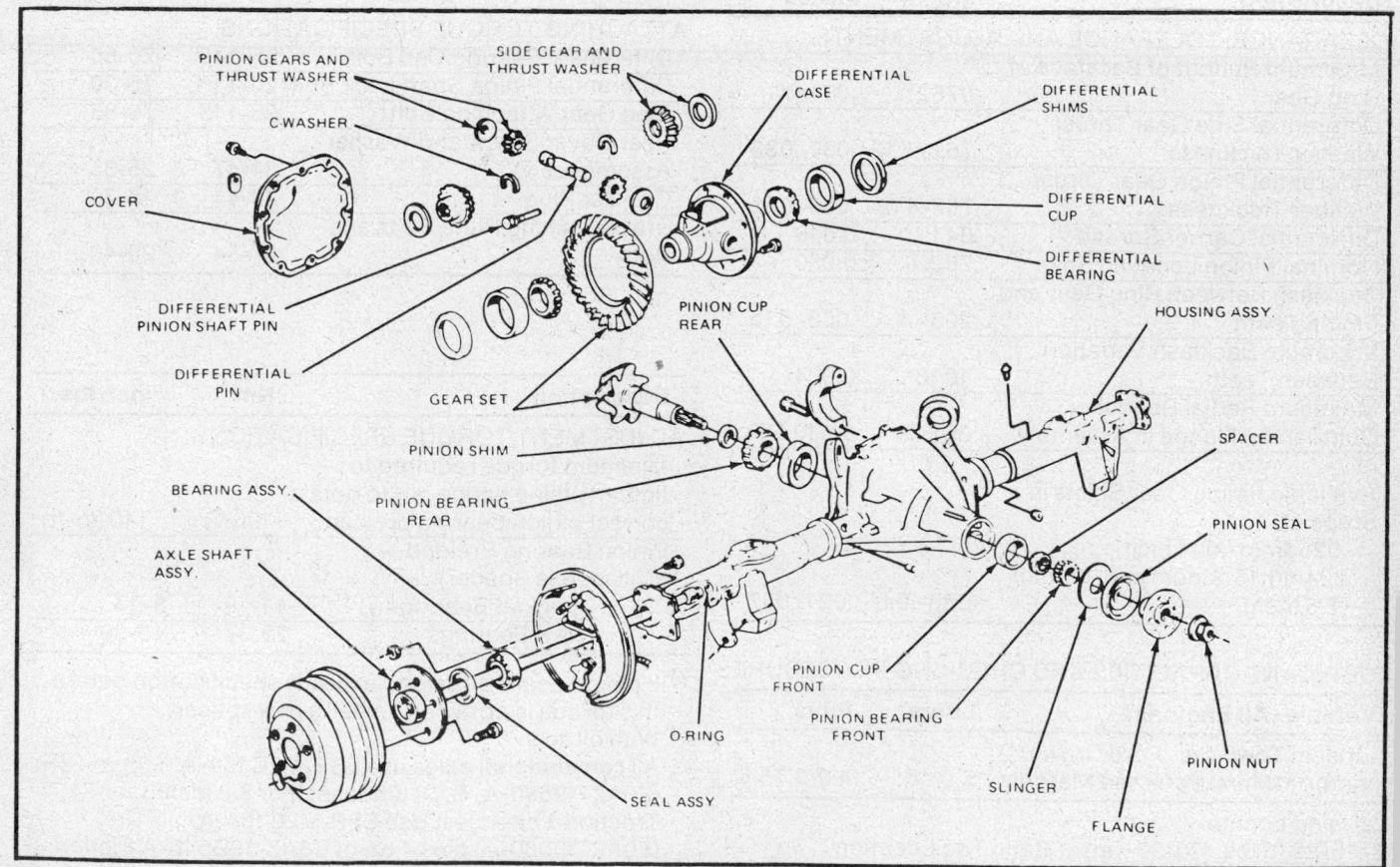

Exploded view of Ford Motor Co. 8.5 and 8.8 in. rear axle assembly

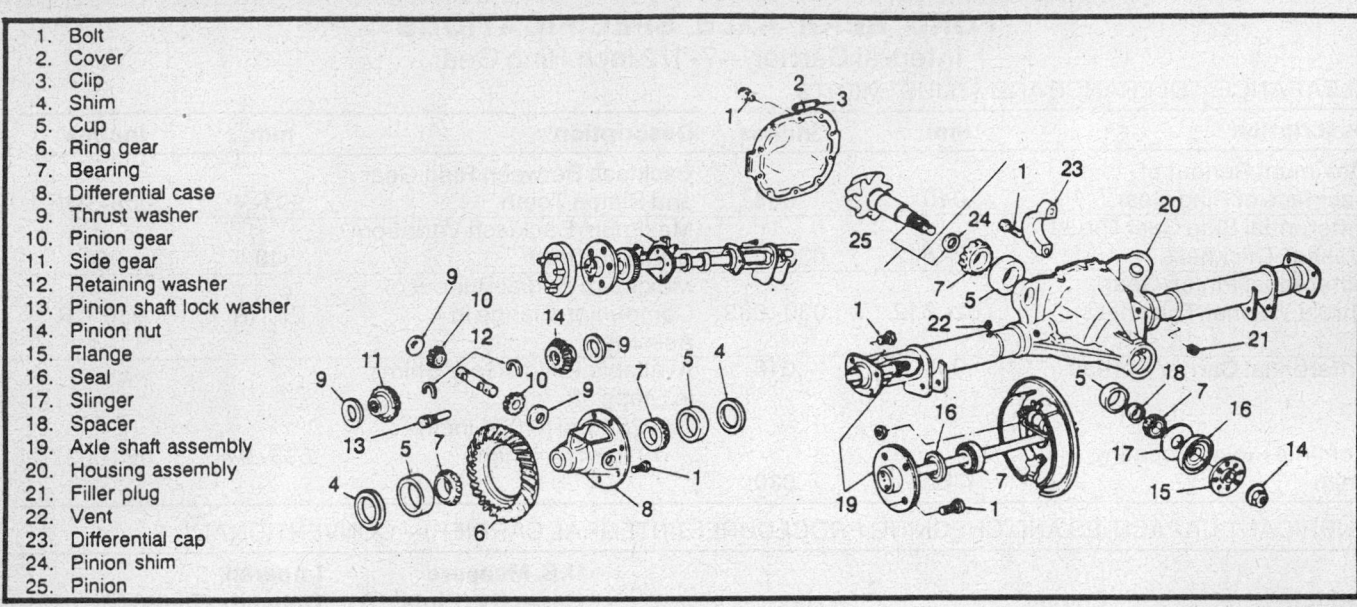

1. Bolt
2. Cover
3. Clip
4. Shim
5. Cup
6. Ring gear
7. Bearing
8. Differential case
9. Thrust washer
10. Pinion gear
11. Side gear
12. Retaining washer
13. Pinion shaft lock washer
14. Pinion nut
15. Flange
16. Seal
17. Slinger
18. Spacer
19. Axle shaft assembly
20. Housing assembly
21. Filler plug
22. Vent
23. Differential cap
24. Pinion shim
25. Pinion

Exploded view of Ford Motor Co. 7 ¹/₂ in. rear axle assembly

FORD REAR AXLE SPECIFICATIONS
INTEGRAL CARRIER—8.5 AND 8.8 IN. RING GEAR

Description	mm	Inches
CLEARANCE, TOLERANCE AND ADJUSTMENTS		
Maximum Runout of Backface of Ring Gear	.0762	.004
Differential Side Gear Thrust Washer Thickness	.762-.812	.030-.032
Differential Pinion Gear Thrust Washer Thickness	.762-812	.030-.032
Differential Carrier Spread	.041	0.016
Nominal Pinion Locating Shim	.762	0.030
Backlash Between Ring Gear and Pinion Teeth	.203-.4	.008-.015
Maximum Backlash Variation Between Teeth	.1016	0.004
Maximum Radial Runout of Companion Flange in Assembly	.25 TIR	0.010 TIR
Available Pinion Gear Shims in Steps of: .0254mm (.001 inch) 224mm (8.8 inch) and 191mm (7.5 inch)	.533-.94	.021-.037

LUBRICANT CAPACITIES AND CHECKING PROCEDURES

Vehicle (All Engines)	Liters	Pints
Lincoln Town Car, Ford Crown Victoria/Mercury Grand Marquis	1.9	4.0/3.75 ⑤

① Using Loctite
② 15-25 ft. lbs. (20-33 Nm) at Ratio Tag Location (Two O'clock Position).

Description	Nm	ft. lbs.
ATTACHING TORQUE SPECIFICATIONS		
Differential Bearing Cap Bolt	95-115	70-85
Differential Pinion Shaft Lock Bolt	20-41	15-30
Ring Gear Attaching Bolt ①	95-115	70-85
Rear Cover Screw and Washer Assemblies ②	34-47	25-35
Oil Filler Plug	20-41	15-30
Brake Backing Plate Bolts and Nuts	27-54	20-40

Description	Nm	inch lbs.
ADJUSTMENT TORQUE SPECIFICATIONS		
Minimum torque required to tighten pinion flange nut to obtain correct pinion bearing preload.	190 ③	140 (lb-ft)
Pinion Bearing Preload— (Collapsible Spacer)		
Original Bearings ④	11-19	8-14
New Bearings	23-37	16-29

③ If pinion bearing preload exceeds specification before this torque is obtained, install a new spacer.
④ With oil seal.
⑤ All conventional axles use ESP-M2C154-A (E0AZ-19580-A, B, C) lubricant. For 8.8 inch Traction-Lok Axles: Use ESP-M2C154-A (E0AZ-19580-A) plus 4 oz. of C8AZ-19B546-A friction modifier (or equivalent).

ATTACHING TORQUE SPECIFICATIONS

Description	Nm	ft. lbs.
Differential Bearing Cap Bolt	95-115	70-85
Differential Pinion Shaft Lock Bolt	20-41	15-30
Ring Gear Attaching Bolts ①	95-115	70-85
Rear Cover Screw and Washer Assemblies	34-47	25-35
Oil Filler Plug	20-41	15-30
Brake Backing Plate Bolts and Nuts	27-54	20-40

① Using Loctite

LUBRICANT CAPACITIES AND CHECKING PROCEDURES

Vehicles	Liters	Pints
All — All Engines	①1.5	3.5

① All conventional axles use ESP-M2C154-A (E0AZ-19580-A, B, C) lubricant or equivalent.

ADJUSTMENT TORQUE SPECIFICATIONS

Description	Nm	inch lbs.
Minimum torque required to tighten pinion flange nut to obtain correct pinion bearing preload.	① 230	170 (lb-ft)
Pinion Beaing Preload— (Collapsible Spacer)②		
Original Bearings	.9-1.6	8-14
New Bearings	1.8-3.2	16-29

① If pinion bearing preload exceeds specification before this torque is obtained, install a new spacer.
② With oil seal.

1. Race
2. Roller assembly
3. Shim
4. Carrier and cap assembly
5. Race (pinion front)
6. Roller assembly (pinion front)
7. Seal assembly
8. Flange assembly
9. Washer
10. Nut
11. Flange
12. Spacer
13. Race (pinion rear)
14. Roller assembly (pinion rear)
15. Shim
16. Drive pinion gear
17. Case
18. Screw
19. Side gear thrust washer
20. Side gear
21. Differential pinion
22. Pinion thrust washer
23. Shaft

Exploded view of General Motors Corp. standard rear axle assembly

BUICK REAR AXLE SPECIFICATIONS

Rear Axle Type	Semi-Floating Hypoid
Drive and Torque (All)	Through 4 Arms
Rear Axle Oil Capacity -	
7-1/2 in. Ring Gear Axle	1.66 Liters, 3.5 Pints
8-1/2 in. Ring Gear Axle	2.0 Liters, 4.25 Pints
8-3/4 in. Ring Gear Axle	2.0 Liters, 4.25 Pints
Ring and Pinion Gear Set Type	Hypoid
Differential Lubricant (All Axles)	GM 1052271 or Equivalent

LIMITS FOR FITTING AND ADJUSTMENTS

Pinion Bearing Pre-Load (Measured at Pinion Flange Nut) New Bearings	2.26 - 2.82 N·m (20-25 Lb. In.) Rotating Torque With New Seal
Reused Bearings - All	1.69 N·m (10-15 Lb. In.) Rotating Torque With New Seal

BUICK REAR AXLE SPECIFICATIONS

Total Assembly Preload (Measured at Pinion Flange Nut)	
New Bearings	3.95 - 4.52 N·m (35-40 Lb. In.) Rotating Torque W/New Seal-Ring Gear
Reused Bearings	2.26 - 2.82 N·m (20-25 Lb. In.) Rotating Torque W/New Seal-Ring Gear
Ring Gear Position	.006"-.008" Backlash

BUICK REAR AXLE TORQUE SPECIFICATIONS

		Nm(ft. lbs.)
Bolt Rear universal joint to pinion flange strap or u-bolt—All		20(15)
Bolt Rear axle housing cover to carrier		41(30)
Nut Brake assembly to rear axle housing		48(35)
Bolt Ring gear to differential tail case		120(90)
Bolt Bearing cap to carrier		81(60)
Nut Rear wheel to axle shaft		108(80)
Nut Upper and lower control arm		108(80)

Use a reliable torque wrench to tighten the parts listed to insure proper tightening without staining or distorting parts. These specifications are for clean and lightly lubricated threads only. Dirt of dirty threads produce increased friction which prevents accurate measurement of tightness

CADILLAC REAR AXLE SPECIFICATIONS

8-1/2 INCH MEASUREMENTS

Ring Gear Position Backlash	.13-.23mm	.005-.009 in.
Lash must not vary over .05mm (.002 in) around ring gear		
Pinion Depth	.50 to 1.27mm	.020-.050 in.

8-7/8 INCH MEASUREMENTS

Pinion Flange Radial Runout	Zero to .076 mm (.000" to .003")
Side Bearing Pre-load	Slip Fit Plus .203 mm (.008")
Pinion Bearing Pre-load (Rotating Torque)	
New Bearings	2.7 to 3.6 N·m (24-32 in. lbs.)
Used Bearings	1.0 to 1.4 N·m (8-12 in. lbs.)
Ring Gear to Pinion Backlash	
New Gears	.127 to .228 mm (.005" to .009")
Used Gears (More than 3,000 mi.)	Original "Pre-checked" reading
Lubricant Capacity	2 Liters (4-1/4 Pints)

CADILLAC REAR AXLE TORQUE SPECIFICATIONS

8-1/2 INCH TORQUE SPECIFICATIONS

Bearing Cap Bolts	75 N·m	55 ft. lbs.
Carrier Cover Bolts	27 N·m	20 ft. lbs.
Pinion Shaft Lock Screw	27 N·m	20 ft. lbs.
Strap Bolts	21 N·m	16 ft. lbs.
Pinion Bearing Pre-Load		
New Bearings	2.26-2.82 N·m	20-25 in. lbs.
Used Bearings	1.13-1.69 N·m	10-15 in. lbs.
Total Assembly Pre-Load		
(measured at pinion flange nut)		
*New Bearings	3.95-4.52 N·m	35-40 in. lbs.
*Reused Bearings	2.26-2.82 N·m	20-25 in. lbs.

CADILLAC REAR AXLE TORQUE SPECIFICATIONS

8-1/2 INCH TORQUE SPECIFICATIONS

Pinion Depth Measurement Gage Plate Assembly Nut	1.6-2.2 N·m	15-25 in. lbs.

*Rotating Torque With New Seal - Ring Gear

8-7/8 INCH TORQUE SPECIFICATIONS

Bearing Cap Bolts	90 N·m	65 ft. lbs.
Ring Gear-to-Gear Case Bolts	120 N·m	90 ft. lbs.
Housing Rear Cover Screws	27 N·m	20 ft. lbs.
Wheel Mounting Nuts	125 N·m	90 ft. lbs.
Pinion Cross Shaft Lock Screw	27 N·m	20 ft. lbs.
Pinion Flange to Driveshaft Screws	90 N·m	65 ft. lbs.
Differential Filler Plug	27 N·m	20 ft. lbs.
Lower Shock Absorber Bolts	90 N·m	65 ft. lbs.

CHEVROLET REAR AXLE SPECIFICATIONS

Ring Gear to Pinion Backlash		.005″-.008″
Pinion Bearing Preload — Inch/Pounds of Rotating	New	15-30
Torque	Used	10-10

CHEVROLET REAR AXLE TORQUE SPECIFICATIONS

B-G-F CARLINE

BOLT TORQUES—FOOT/POUNDS	7-1/2″	8-1/2″	8-3/4″	LUBRICANT CAPACITIES
				Complete Drain and Refill
Carrier Cover	15-25	15-25	20-30	
Filler Plug	15-25	15-25	20-30	7-1/2″ Ring Gear .... 3.5 pints
Pinion Lock Screw	15-25	15-25	15-25	8-1/2″ Ring Gear .... 4.25 pints
Bearing Caps	46-65	45-65	60-75	8-3/4″ Ring Gear .... 5.4 pints
Ring Gear Bolts	80-95	70-90	70-90	

T CARLINE

Rear Cover-to-Axle Housing	30 N·m	22 Ft. Lbs.
Bearing Caps	75 N·m	55 Ft. Lbs.
Ring Gear-to-Case	65 N·m	48 Ft. Lbs.
Pinion Bearing Rotational Torque		10-20 in. lbs. (NDH) 5-15 in. lbs.
New Bearings	1.2-22 N·m (NDH) .6-1.6 N·m (Timken)	(Timken)
Used Bearings	0.56-1.13 N·m	5-10 in. lbs.
Lubricant Capacity	0.8 litres	(28 oz.)
Axle Shaft End-Play	0.5 mm	(.020 in.)

OLDSMOBILE REAR AXLE SPECIFICATIONS

Capacity	
7-1/2″ Ring Gear	1-3/4L (3-1/2 Pts.) approx.
8-1/2″ Ring Gear	2L (4-1/4 Pts.) approx.
8-3/4″ Ring Gear	2L (4-1/4 Pts.) approx.

OLDSMOBILE REAR AXLE SPECIFICATIONS

Replenish (Conventional)	Lubricant No. SAE 80W GL-5, SAE 80W-90 GL-5, 1052271, or equivalent
Replenish (Limited Slip)	Special Lubricant No. 1052271, 1052272 or equivalent
	On 8-1/2" and 8-3/4" Axle Add 4 Ounces Lubricant Additive 1052358

Adjustments	
Backlash	.13-.23mm (.005"-.009")
Drive Pinion Bearing Pre-Load	
New Bearings	2.7 to 3.6 N·m (24 to 32 in. lbs.)
Old Bearings	1.0 to 1.4 N·m (8 to 12 in. lbs.)

OLDSMOBILE REAR AXLE TORQUE SPECIFICATIONS

Application	N·m	Ft. Lbs.
Cover to Carrier	30	20
Ring Gear Bolts	120	90
Side Bearing Cap Bolts	75	55
Pinion Gear Shaft Retaining Bolt	27	20

PONTIAC REAR AXLE SPECIFICATIONS

Rear Axle Type	Semi-Floating Hypoid
Drive and Torque (All)	Through 4 Arms
Rear Axle Oil Capacity -	
7-1/2" Ring Gear	3.50 Pints
8-1/2" Ring Gear	4.25 Pints
8-3/4" Ring Gear	5.40 Pints
Ring and Pinion Gear Set Type	Hypoid
Differential Lubricant (All Axles)	GM 1052271 or Equivalent

LIMITS FOR FITTING AND ADJUSTMENTS

Pinion Bearing Pre-Load (Measured at Pinion Flange Nut)	
New Bearings	15-30 inch lbs. Rotating Torque With New Seal
Reused Bearings - All	10-10 inch lbs. Rotating Torque With New Seal
Total Assembly Preload (Measured at Pinion Flange Nut)	
New Bearings	3.95 - 4.52 N·m (35-40 Lb. In.) Rotating Torque W/New Seal-Ring Gear
Reused Bearings	2.26 - 2.82 N·m (20-25 Lb. In.) Rotating Torque W/New Seal-Ring Gear
Ring Gear Backlash	.005 in.-.008 in. Backlash

PONTIAC REAR AXLE TORQUE SPECIFICATIONS

		Nm(ft. lbs.)
Bolt	Rear universal joint to pinion flange strap or u-bolt – All	20(15)
Bolt	Rear axle housing cover to carrier	41(30)
Nut	Brake assembly to rear axle housing	48(35)
Bolt	Ring gear to differential tail case	120(90)
Bolt	Bearing cap to carrier	81(60)
Nut	Rear wheel to axle shaft	108(80)
Nut	Upper and lower control arm	108(80)

Use a reliable torque wrench to tighten the parts listed to insure proper tightening without staining or distorting parts. These specifications are for clean and lightly lubricated threads only. Dirt of dirty threads produce increased friction which prevents accurate measurement of tightness

CHEVROLET REAR AXLE TORQUE SPECIFICATIONS
1986 and Later B-G Carlines
Bolt Torques (ft. lbs.)

Ring Gear (in.)	Carrier Cover	Filler Plug	Case Lock Screw		Bearing Caps	Ring Gear Bolts	Lubricant* Capacities (pints)
			Std. Slip	Ltd. Slip			
7½	15-25	15-25	15-25	23-30	45-65	80-95	3.5
7⅝	15-25	15-25	15-25	23-30	45-65	80-95	3.5
8½	15-25	15-25	15-25	23-30	45-65	70-90	4.25

Ring Gear to Pinion Backlash....................005"-.008"
Pinion Bearing Preload (inch lbs. of
   rotating torque   New 15-30
                           Used 10-10

*Complete drain and refill

GENERAL MOTORS POSITRACTION EXCEPT CADILLAC

1. Place the transmission in **N**.
2. Raise and support the vehicle safely, with 1 rear wheel off the floor and block the other wheels, (front and rear), to prevent the vehicle from moving.
3. Using a torque wrench and extension on the lug nut, note the turning torque required to continuously rotate the rear wheel. The breakaway torque figure will be a great deal higher and should not be considered.

NOTE: Make sure that the wheel studs and lug nuts are in good condition before attempting this operation.

4. The minimum torque to continuously rotate the rear wheel should be at least 35 ft. lbs.; if not, the rear axle is in need of service.

CADILLAC CONTROLLED DIFFERENTIAL

This unit should not be serviced. If a malfunction exists that cannot be cured by changing the fluid, remove the unit and install a new one.

GENERAL DIAGNOSIS

Improper operation of a limited slip type rear axle is generally indicated by clutch slippage or grabbing, which will sometimes produce a whirring or chatter sound. Occasionally, this condition is induced by improper lubrication. Check the unit for the wrong type of lubricant or lubricant which has broken down or become contaminated. Replace the lubricant with the type specified by the manufacturer.

During normal operation, such as straight ahead driving, both rear wheels are rotating at equal speeds. The driving force is distributed equally between both wheels. When cornering, the inside wheel delivers extra driving force, causing slippage in both clutch packs. Therefore, if the wheel rotation of both rear wheels is not equal, the unit will constantly be functioning as if the vehicle were cornering. This will cause constant slippage and lead to eventual failure of the unit. It is important that there be no excessive differences in wheel and tire size, wear pattern or tire pressures between both rear wheels. A vehicle driving to 1 side or the other during acceleration is an indication of 1 or more of the above conditions. Before attempting an overhaul or replacement operation, check both rear wheels for identical tire sizes, tire pressure, tire tread depth and wear pattern.

CHRYSLER SURE GRIP DIFFERENTIAL

GENERAL INFORMATION

NOTE: Anytime rear axle servicing is necessary or an axle is being rotated through use of the engine or other means, elevate both rear wheels.

The Sure Grip differential is being offered as a special equipment option in 7¼ in. and 8¼ in. rear axles.

The Sure Grip differential design is basic and simple. It consists of a 2 piece case construction and is completely interchangeable with the conventional differential.

A conventional differential allows the driving wheels to rotate at different speeds while dividing the driving torque equally between them. This function is ordinarily desirable and satisfactory. However, the total driving torque can be no more than double the torque at the lower traction wheel. When traction conditions are not the same for both driving wheels, a portion of the available traction cannot be used.

The Sure Grip differential allows the driving wheel with the better traction to develop more driving torque than the wheel with less traction. This makes the total driving torque significantly greater than with a conventional differential.

Sure Grip is not a locking differential. Under normal driving conditions the controlled internal friction is easily overcome

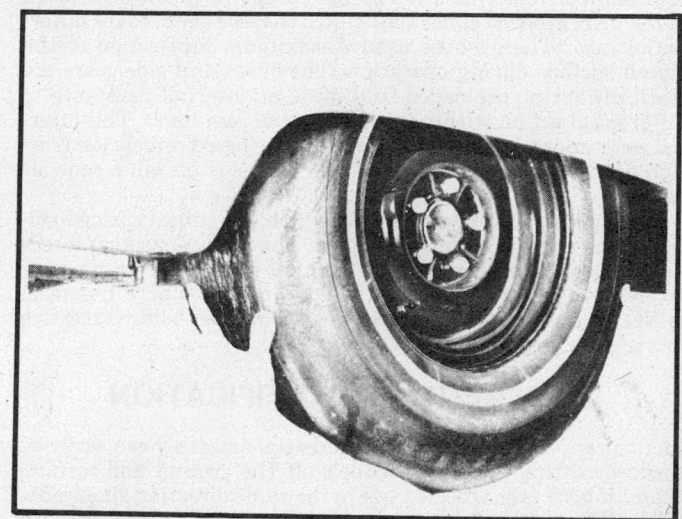

Testing sure grip differential effectiveness

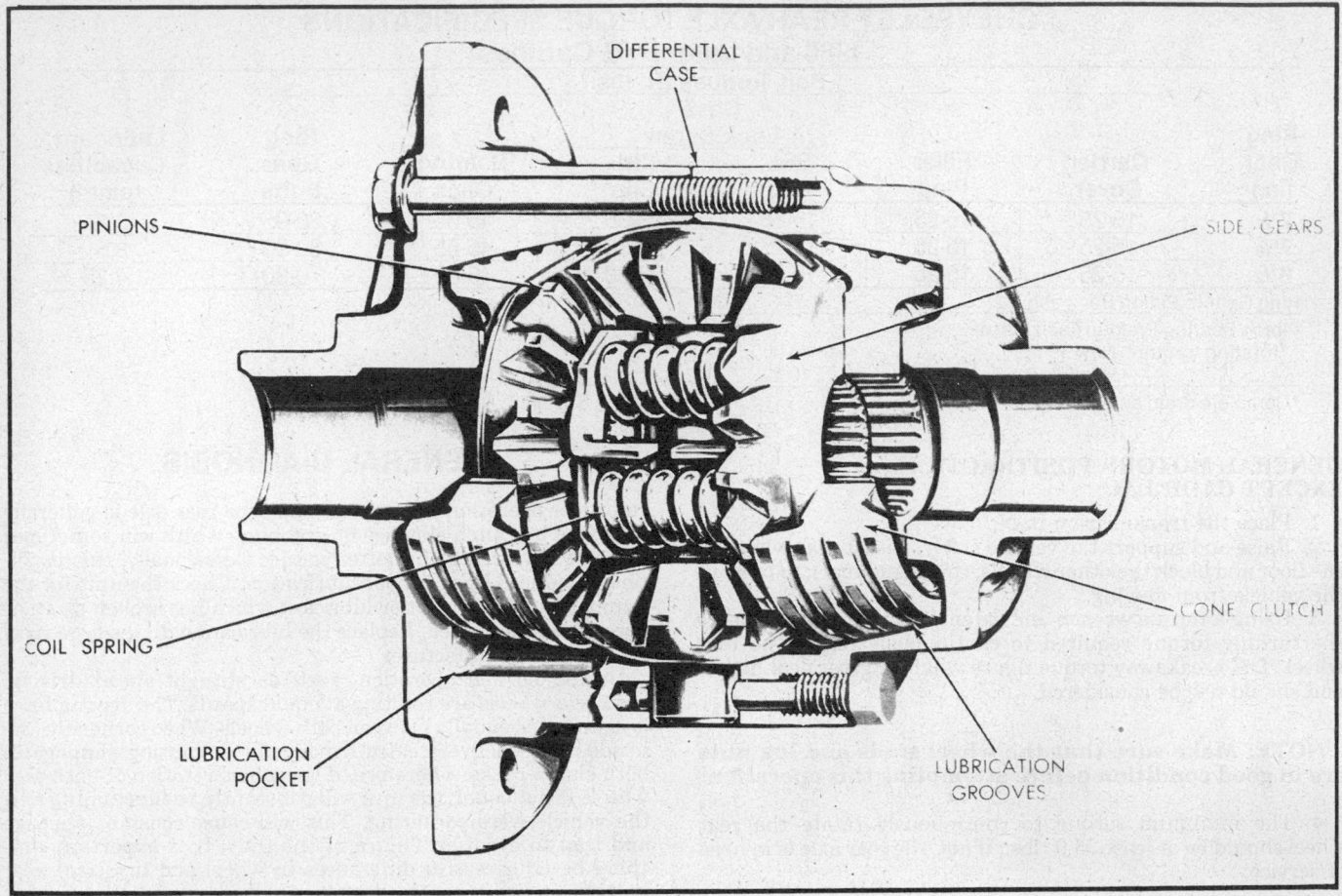

Sure Grip differential (schematic)

during cornering and turning; this allows the driving wheels to turn at different speeds. Extreme differences in traction conditions at the driving wheels may permit a wheel to spin.

The Sure Grip differential has been engineered to perform its specialized functions with a minimal effect on normal vehicle operations.

The cone clutch Sure Grip differentials are similar to corresponding conventional differentials except for the incorporation of the helix grooved cones that clutch the side gears to the differential case. The grooves assure maximum lubrication of the clutch surface during operation. The cones and side gears are statically spring preloaded to provide an internal resistance to differential action within the differential case itself. This internal resistance provides pulling power during extremely low traction conditions such as when a rear wheel is on mud, snow or ice.

During torque application to the axle, the initial spring loading of the cones is supplemented by the gear separating forces between the side gears and differential pinions which progressively increases the friction in the differential. This differential is NOT a positive locking type and will release before excessive driving force can be applied to 1 wheel.

DIFFERENTIAL IDENTIFICATION

Identification of a Sure Grip differential assembly can easily be made by lifting both rear wheels off the ground and turning them. If both rear wheels turn in the same direction simultaneously, the vehicle is equipped with a Sure Grip differential. Another means of identification is by removing the filler plug and using a flashlight to look through the filler plug hole to identify the type of differential case.

DIFFERENTIAL NOISE

Noise complaints related to rear axles equipped with cone clutch Sure Grip should always be checked to determine the source of the noise. If a vehicle ride check produces the noise in turns but not while going straight, the probable cause is an incorrect or dissipated rear axle lubricant. The following draining and flushing procedure has been established for the Sure Grip differential before it is removed from the vehicle and replaced.

CAUTION

When servicing vehicles equipped with Sure Grip differentials do not use the engine to rotate axle components unless BOTH rear wheels are OFF the ground and the vehicle is safely supported. Sure Grip equipped axles can exert a significant driving force and cause the vehicle to move if 1 wheel is in contact with floor.

1. With the lubricant of the rear axle assembly at operating temperature, raise and support the vehicle safely, so the rear wheels are free to turn.
2. Remove the rear cover. Drain and discard the lubricant. Rotate the differential so the hole in the case is facing downward. Wipe out all of the accessible areas in the carrier.

NOTE: Draining and discarding the old lubricant will rid the axle of any solid particles or liquid contaminants that may be contributing to the noise condition.

3. Scrape all gasket material from the housing cover and thoroughly clean the surface with mineral spirits or equivalent and dry it completely. Apply a $\frac{1}{16}$–$\frac{3}{32}$ in. bead of silicone rubber sealant.

Allow the sealant to cure while cleaning the carrier gasket flange with mineral spirits or equivalent. Dry the surface completely. Install the cover on axle and torque the cover screws to 250 inch lbs. (28 Nm). Beneath 1 of the cover screws, install the axle ratio identification tag.

If for any reason the cover is not installed within 20 minutes after applying the sealant, the old sealant should be removed and a new bead installed.

4. Remove the safety stands if used. Raise or lower the hoist until the vehicle is in a level position.

5. Remove the filler plug. Install 4 ounces (0.12L), of gear oil additive friction modifier in the axle. Refill the axle to the proper level with with gear lubricant.

6. Install the filler plug. Lower the vehicle.

TESTING

The Sure Grip differential can be checked to determine if its performance is satisfactory without removing the differential and carrier assembly from the vehicle.

1. Raise and support the vehicle safely. Turn the engine **OFF** and place the transmission in **P** automatic transmission or **1st** for manual transmission.

2. Apply a turning force by gripping the tire tread area and turning the wheel.

3. If it is extremely difficult, if not impossible, to manually turn either wheel, consider the Sure Grip differential to be performing satisfactorily. If it is relatively easy to continuously turn either wheel, the differential is not performing properly and should be removed and replaced. The Sure Grip differential and internal parts are serviced as a complete assembly only. Under no circumstances should the differential be removed, disassembled, assembled and/or reinstalled.

Removal

NOTE: During the removal and installation of the axle shafts, do not rotate an axle shaft unless both axles are in position. Rotation of 1 axle shaft without the other in place may result in a misalignment of the 2 spline segments with which the axle shaft spline engages and will make realignment procedures difficult when the shaft is installed.

1. Raise and support the vehicle safely.

2. Remove the rear wheels and brake drums. Loosen the rear housing cover and drain the fluid. Remove the rear cover. Flush the axle housing with solvent.

3. Using a pry bar, pry between the differential case flange and the housing to determine if side play is present; there should be no side play. Side play can be eliminated by tightening the threaded adjuster nuts.

4. Using a dial indicator, mount the plunger at a right angle to the ring gear. Turn the ring gear several revolutions to determine runout; mark the ring gear and differential at the maximum runout point. The runout should not exceed 0.005 in.

5. Rotate the differential to provide access to the pinion lock screw. Remove the pinion lock screw and the pinion shaft.

6. Push the axle shafts toward the center of the differential. Remove the C-locks from the shafts and the axle shafts from the axle housing.

7. Mark the housing/differential bearing caps for installation purposes. From the bearing caps, remove the adjuster locks. Loosen the bearing caps; do not remove them. Through each axle tube, insert a hex adjuster tool and loosen the hex adjusters.

8. Remove the bearing caps and differential assembly; keep the caps and cups in order. Place the differential assembly in a

soft jawed vise. Remove and discard the ring gear bolts; the bolts have a left hand thread. Using a mallet, tap the ring gear from the differential case.

9. If replacing the differential side bearings, perform the following procedures:

a. Use a bearing removal tool and an adapter tool for the 7¼ in. axle, use a bearing removal tool and a plug tool for the 8¼ in. axle and remove the differential side bearings.

b. Lubricate the new parts.

c. Using an arbor press and a bearing installation tool for the 7¼ in. axle or 8¼ in. axle, install the differential bearing cones; do not exert pressure against the bearing cage, for damage will result.

Cleaning and Inspection

1. Clean the Sure Grip differential assembly in a fast evaporating mineral spirits or a dry cleaning solvent. With exception of bearings, dry the assembly with compressed air.

2. Inspect the differential bearing cones, cups and rollers for pitting, spalling or other visible damage. If replacement is necessary, remove the bearing cones from the differential case and renew at this time.

3. Visually inspect the differential case for cracks or other visible damage which might render it unfit for further service.

Assembly

1. On axles requiring the ring gear to be installed on the differential case, relieve the sharp edge of the chamfer on the inside diameter of the ring gear with an Arkansas stone or equivalent. This is very important, otherwise during the installation of ring gear on differential case, the sharp edge will remove metal from the pilot diameter of case, which can get imbedded between the differential case flange and gear. This will cause the ring gear not to seat properly.

2. Heat the ring gear with a heat lamp or by immersing the gear in a hot fluid (water or oil). The temperature should not exceed 300°F (149.0°C); Do not use and torch to heat the ring gear. Use pilot studs equally spaced in 3 positions to align the gear to the case.

3. Using new ring gear screws, (left hand threads), insert the screws through the case flange and into the ring gear.

4. Position the unit between brass jaws of a vise and alternately tighten each screw to 70 ft. lbs. (95 Nm).

5. Set the drive pinion depth, drive gear backlash adjustment and bearing preload adjustment.

Installation

1. Position the differential assembly into the case and install the bearing caps and bolts. Torque the bearing cap-to-housing bolts to 45 ft. lbs. (7¼ in.) or 100 ft. lbs. (8¼ in.).

2. Using a pry bar, pry between the differential case flange and the housing to determine if side play is present; there

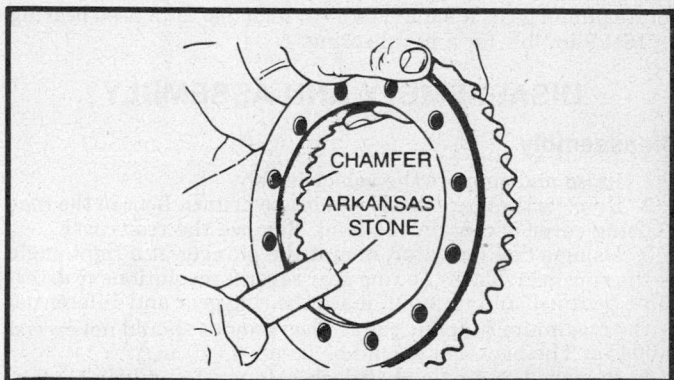

Using Arkansas stone on ring gear chamfer

should be no side play. Side play can be eliminated by tightening the threaded adjuster nuts.

3. Continue the installation in the reverse order of the removal procedure. Use a new gasket, sealant and reverse the removal procedures. Torque the housing cover bolts to 250 inch lbs. Refill the differential with clean fluid.

LUBRICATION

Multi purpose gear lubricant, should be used in all rear axles with conventional differentials. A hypoid type lubricant in all others.

In Sure Grip differentials 4 oz., (0.1183L), of hypoid gear oil additive friction modifier, must be included when refilling the differential.

Fluid Level Check

For normal passenger vehicle service, periodic fluid level checks

are not required. However, at each engine oil change, the exterior surfaces of the axle assembly should be inspected for any evidence of gear oil leakage. A fluid level check will confirm any suspected leakage. When this check is made, the vehicle must be in a level position, supported by the suspension, on an axle, heel type hoist or ground. The fluid level for the 8¼ in. and 7¼ axles should be at the bottom of the filler hole.

NOTE: When the fluid level check is made with the vehicle on a frame contact type hoist with the axle hanging free, the fluid level should not be lower than the bottom of the filler plug opening. Confirmed leakage should be repaired as soon as possible. Should the rear axle become submerged in water, the lubricant must be changed immediately to avoid the possibility of early bearing or gear failure resulting from contamination of the lubricant due to water being drawn in through the vent hole.

FORD DIFFERENTIAL AXLE 7½ AND 8¾ IN. RING GEAR

DESCRIPTION AND OPERATION

The axle consists of a hypoid design with ring and pinion encased in a cast iron housing. The differential case consists of a 2 piece differential assembly. The axle shafts are retained by C-locks at the splined end of the shaft.

NOISE ACCEPTABILITY

A gear driven unit, especially a drive axle, will produce a certain amount of noise. Some noise is acceptable and may be audible at certain speeds or under various driving conditions. For example; on a newly paved blacktop road. This slight noise will in no way effect the operation of the rear axle and must be considered normal.

Adjustments

If new components have been install, the correct pinion shim thickness must be determined using a axle pinion gauge tool and the bearing cups must be seated in the bores so a 0.0015 in. feeler gauge cannot be inserted between the cup and the bore bottom.

Bench Check

Using an inch lb. torque wrench, check the torque required to rotate pinion gear; it should be 8–14 inch lbs. for a used bearing or 16–29 in. lbs. for a new bearing.

DISASSEMBLY AND ASSEMBLY

Disassembly

1. Raise and support the vehicle safely.
2. Remove the rear wheels and brake drums. Loosen the rear housing cover and drain the fluid. Remove the rear cover.
3. Using a dial indicator, mount the plunger at a right angle to the ring gear. Turn the ring gear several revolutions to determine backlash and runout; mark the ring gear and differential at the maximum runout point. The runout should not exceed 0.004 in. The backlash should be 0.008–0.015 in.
4. Remove the pinion shaft lock bolt and the pinion shaft.
5. Push the axle shafts toward the center of the differential.

Remove the C-locks from the shafts and the axle shafts from the axle housing.
6. Mark the differential bearing caps for installation purposes. Loosen the bearing cap bolts.
7. Using a pry bar, pry the differential case, the bearing cups and shims loose in the bearing caps.
8. Remove the bearing caps and differential assembly; keep the caps and cups in order. Place the differential assembly in a soft jawed vise.
9. Mark the ring gear and the differential housing for installation purposes. Remove and discard the ring gear bolts; the bolts have a left hand thread. Using a mallet, tap the ring gear loose from the differential case.
10. If replacing the differential side bearings, perform the following procedures:
    a. Using a bearing puller tool, remove the differential side bearings.
    b. Lubricate the new parts.
    c. Using an arbor press and the bearing installation tool, install the differential bearing.

Cleaning and Inspection

1. Wipe all parts clean with a shop towel. Do not use cleaners or solvents on this locking differential.
2. Inspect all mating parts for surface condition. Excessive scoring or wear should not be accepted. Very slight grooves or scratches are acceptable and the parts can be reused.
3. Any condition worse than the preceding inspection requires complete replacement of the unit.

Assembly

1. Position the differential assembly into the case and install the bearing the caps and bolts. Install new ring gear bolts. Torque the bearing cap-to-housing bolts to 70–85 ft. lbs.

NOTE: The new ring gear bolts should have a green coating about ½ in. on the threads; if not, apply Loctite® on the threads.

2. Continue the installation in the reverse order of the removal procedure. Use a new gasket and silicone sealant. Torque the housing cover bolts to 25–35 inch lbs. Refill the differential with clean fluid.

FORD TRACTION LOK LIMITED SLIP
DIFFERENTIAL AXLE 7½ AND 8¾ IN. RING GEAR

DESCRIPTION

The Traction Lok axle assembly, except for the differential case and its internal components, is identical to the conventional axle.

Traction Lok differentials use 2 sets of multiple disc clutches to control the differential action. The side gear mounting distance is controlled by 9 plates; 5 steel and 4 friction. Use 1 steel shim selected by size to control the side gear position.

The plates are stacked on the side gear hub and are housed in the differential case. Also located in the differential case, between the side gears, is a 1 piece preload spring, which applies an initial force to the clutch packs. Additional clutch capacity is delivered from the side gears thrust loads. The 4 friction plates are splined to the side gear hub which, in turn, is splined to the left and right axle shafts. The geared steel plates are dogged to the case making the clutch packs always engaged.

The pressure between the clutch plates opposes the differential action at all times. When the vehicle turns a corner, the clutch plates slip allowing normal differential action to take place. Under adverse weather conditions, where 1 or both wheels may be on a low traction surface, the friction between the clutch plates will transfer a portion of the usable torque to the wheel with the most traction. This makes the wheel with less traction have a tendency to operate with the opposite wheel in a combined driving effort.

NOTE: Never drive a vehicle with the new mini spare tire on the rear, if equipped with a Traction Lok rear axle. The 2 different size tires cause differentiation in the unit and will cause excessive damage to the clutches.

NOISE ACCEPTABILITY

Drive axles will produce a certain amount of noise. Some noise is acceptable and may be heard at certain speeds or under various driving conditions. For example; on a newly paved blacktop road. The slight noise is in no way detrimental to operation of the rear axle and must be considered normal.

NOTE: If equipped with a Traction Lok differential, a slight stick slip noise on tight turns after extended highway driving is considered acceptable and has no detrimental effect.

Operation Check

A Traction Lok differential can be checked for proper operation without removing the differential from the axle housing.

1. Raise a rear wheel and support it under the axle housing. Remove the wheel cover.

2. Install a differential torque tool, on the axle shaft flange studs.

3. Using a 200 ft. lb. torque wrench, rotate the axle shaft. Be sure that the transmission is in **N** with 1 rear wheel on the floor and the other raised off the floor.

4. The break away torque required to start rotation should be at least 30–40 ft. lbs. The initial break away torque may be higher than the continuous turning torque but normal.

5. The axle shaft should turn with even pressure throughout the check without slipping or binding. If the torque reading is less than specified, check the differential for proper assembly.

——— CAUTION ———

A vehicle equipped with a Traction Lok differential will always have both wheels driving. If the engine is being used to drive the rear axle while servicing the vehicle, be sure to have both rear wheels OFF the ground. Failure to do this will cause the vehicle to surge OFF the support and could cause injury.

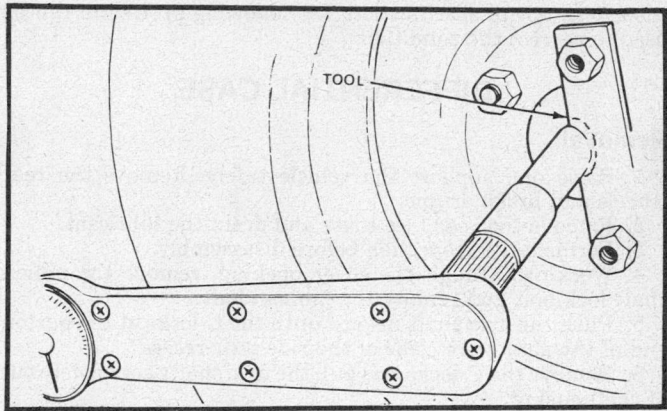

Traction-lok differential check

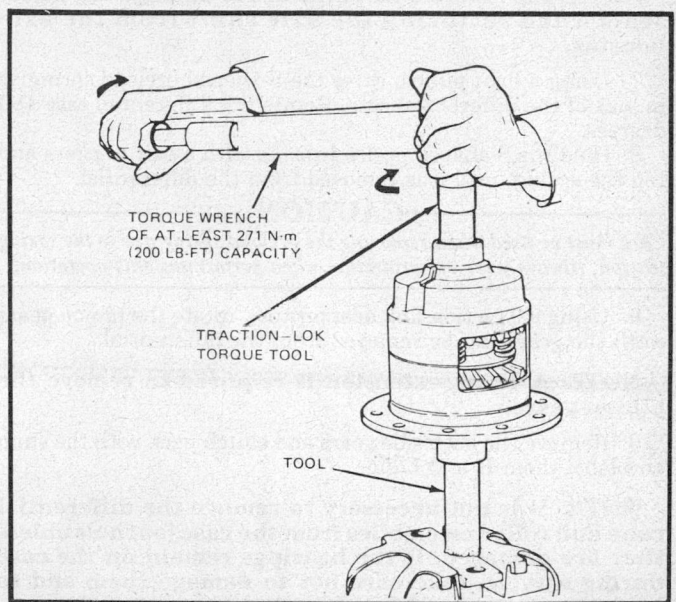

TORQUE WRENCH OF AT LEAST 271 N·m (200 LB-FT) CAPACITY

TRACTION–LOK TORQUE TOOL

TOOL

Bench torque check

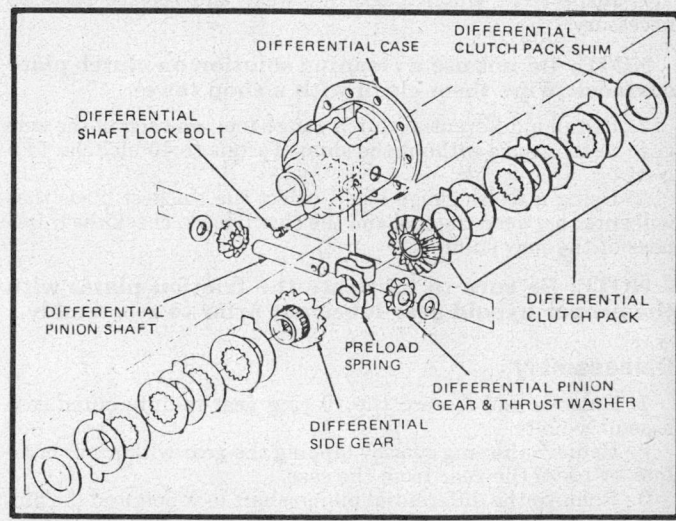

DIFFERENTIAL CASE

DIFFERENTIAL CLUTCH PACK SHIM

DIFFERENTIAL SHAFT LOCK BOLT

DIFFERENTIAL PINION SHAFT

PRELOAD SPRING

DIFFERENTIAL SIDE GEAR

DIFFERENTIAL PINION GEAR & THRUST WASHER

DIFFERENTIAL CLUTCH PACK

Differential assembly components

ADJUSTMENTS

On vehicle adjustment are possible on this unit without removing the differential case from the axle assembly. If the testing check was not to specification, the following procedure can be used to correct the condition:

DIFFERENTIAL CASE

Removal

1. Raise and support the vehicle safely. Remove the rear wheels and brake drums.
2. Remove the rear face cover and drain the lubricant.
3. Perform the inspection before disassembly.
4. Working through the cover opening, remove the pinion shaft lock bolt and remove the pinion shaft.
5. Push the axle shaft inward until the C-locks at the button end of the shafts are clear of the side gear recess.
6. Remove the C-locks and pull the axle shafts completely out of the housing.

NOTE: Care should be taken not to damage the wheel seals when removing the axle shaft from the axle housing.

7. Using a drift punch, drive the S-shaped preload spring ½ in. out of the differential case. Rotate the differential case 180 degrees.
8. Hold the S-shaped preload spring with a pair of pliers and tap the spring until it is removed from the differential.

───────────── CAUTION ─────────────

Care must be used when removing the preload spring due to the spring tension. Always wear eye protection when performing this operation.

9. Using a Traction Lok adapter tool, rotate the pinion gears until the gears can be removed from the differential.

NOTE: A 12 in. extension is required to remove the pinion gears.

10. Remove the both side gears and clutch pack with the shim and label them **R** and **L** side.

NOTE: It is not necessary to remove the differential cone and roller assemblies from the case journals unless they are damaged. If the bearings remain on the case during service, take care not to damage them and to keep them clean and free from foreign material.

11. Inspect the clutch packs for wear and replace parts as necessary.

NOTE: Do not use a cleaning solution on clutch plate surfaces. Wipe them clean with a shop towel.

12. Install a differential clutch gauge tool, on each of the side gear clutch packs without the shim. Torque to 40 inch lbs. (4.5 Nm).
13. Using a feeler gauge blade, select the thickest blade that will enter between the tool and the clutch pack, check the thickness of the new shim.

NOTE: Be sure to lubricate the friction plates with the proper hypoid gear lubricant prior to reassembly.

Disassembly

1. Remove and discard the 10 ring gear-to-differential case assembly bolts.
2. Remove the ring gear by tapping the gear with a soft hammer or press the gear from the case.
3. Remove the differential pinion shaft lock bolt and the pinion shaft.
4. Using a drift punch, drive out the S-shaped preload spring.

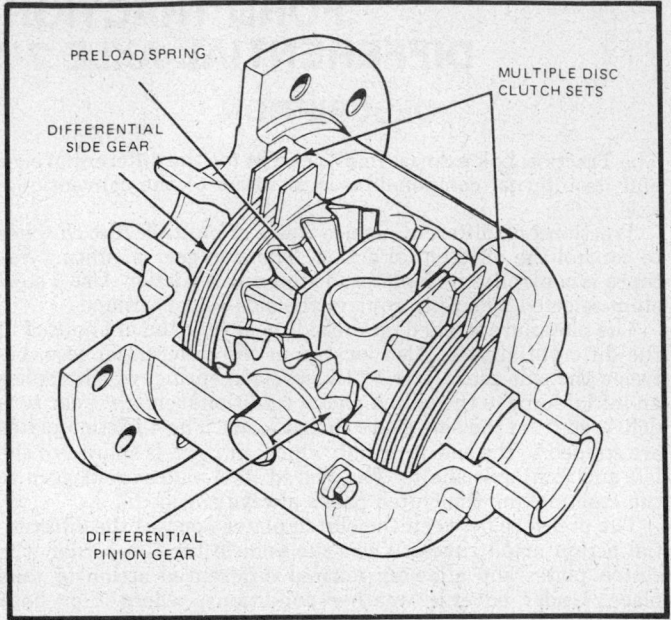

Differential assembly—exploded view

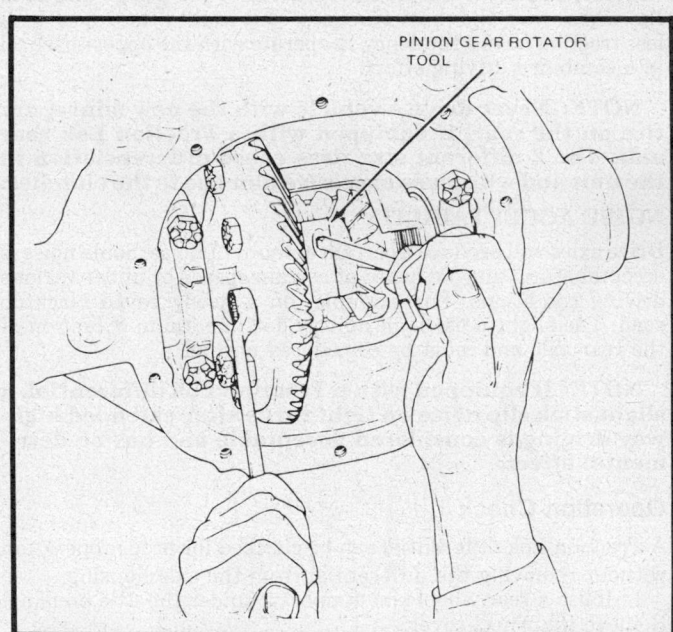

Differential pinion gears and thrust washers removal or installation

───────────── CAUTION ─────────────

Care must be used when removing the preload spring due to the spring tension. Always wear eye protection when performing this operation.

5. Using a gear rotator tool, rotate the pinion gears until the gears and thrust washers can be removed.
6. Remove the side gears, clutch plates and shims from the right and left cavities and label them **R** and **L**.
7. Clean and inspect all parts for wear or damage, replace as necessary.

Clutch Pack Preload

1. Assemble the clutch pack on the side gear, no shim is required at this point. All plates must be prelubricated with a com-

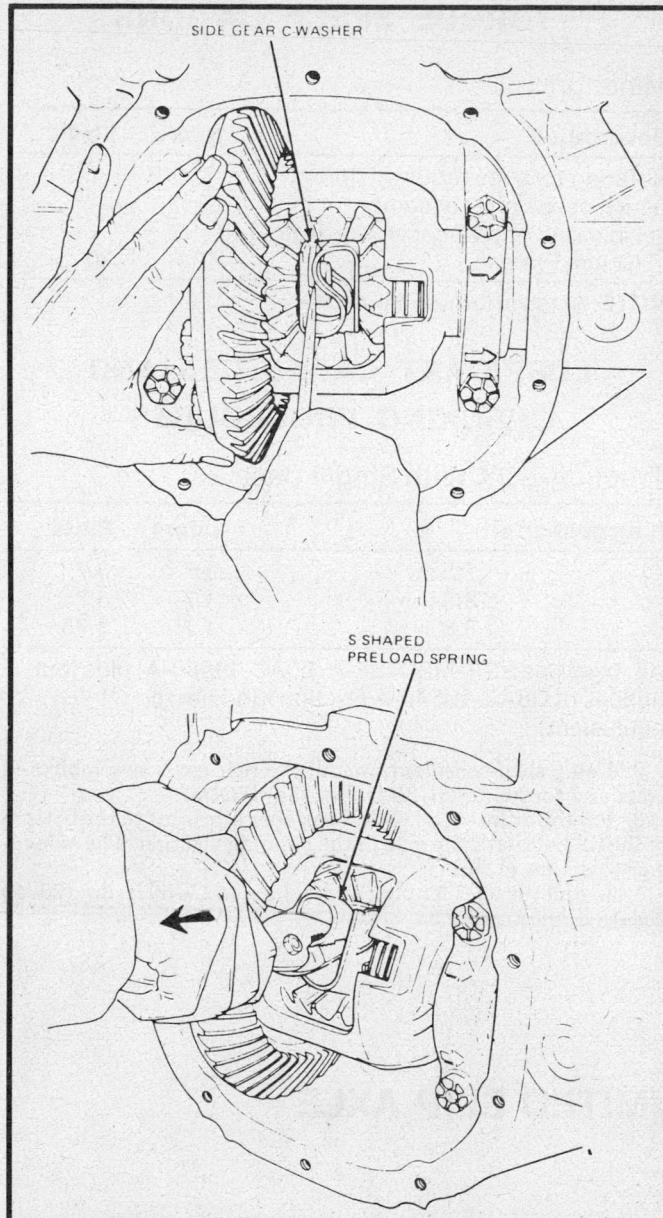

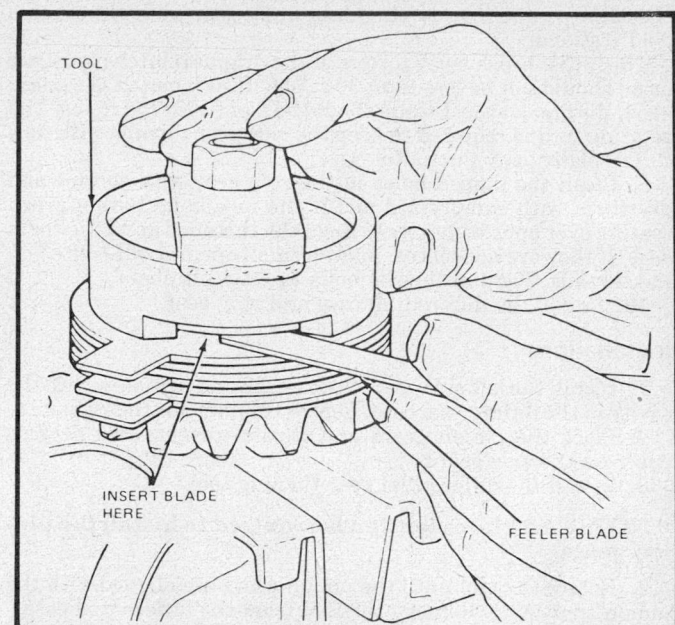

Checking clutch pack clearance

Side gear "C" lock and S-shaped pre-load spring re moval or installation

bination of a friction modifier and hypoid gear lubricant.

2. Assemble a differential clutch gauge tool on the side gear clutch pack.

3. Using a feeler gauge blade, select the thickest blade that will enter between the tool and the clutch pack.

4. Note the thickness; this will be the shim required for that clutch pack.

NOTE: Do not mix the clutches or shims.

5. Repeat Steps 1–4 for the opposite clutch pack.

Assembly

1. Lubricate all parts with a hypoid gear lubricant prior to assembly.

2. Mount the differential case in a soft jaw vise and place the clutch packs and side gears in their proper cavities in the differential case.

3. Place the pinion gears and thrust washers on the side gears.

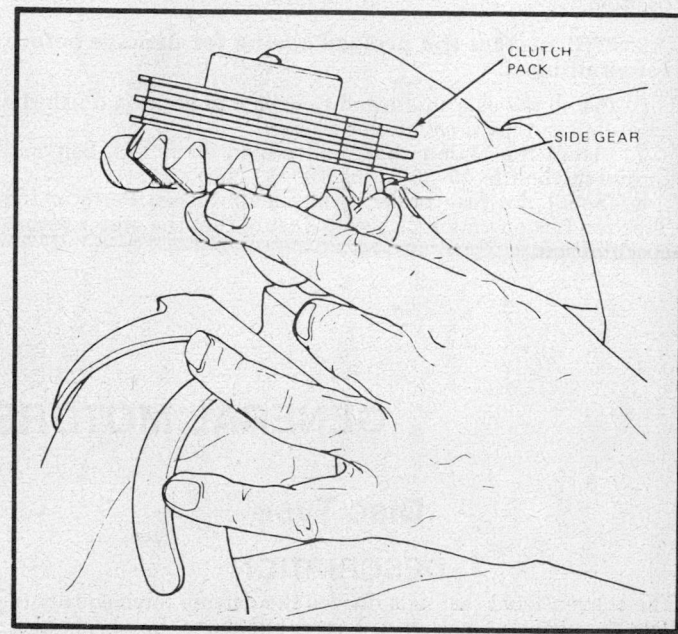

Installation of clutch pack on side gear

4. Install a differential gear rotator tool, in the differential case.

5. Rotate the pinion gears until the bores in the gears are aligned with the pinion shaft holes in the differential case. Remove the tool from the differential case.

6. With a soft faced hammer, install the S-shaped preload spring into the differential case.

NOTE: The S-shaped preload spring should be inspected before installing it. If there are any signs of wear it should be replaced.

7. Install the pinion shaft and lock bolt; do not tighten the lock bolt at this point.

8. Prior to installation of the locking differential into a vehicle, a bench torque check must be made. Using the locker tools,

check the torque required to rotate 1 side gear while the other is held stationary.

The initial break away torque, if the original clutch plates are used, should not be less than 30 ft. lbs. If new clutch plates are used, the break away torque should be from 150–250 ft. lbs. The rotating torque required to keep the side gear turning with new clutch plates may fluctuate.

9. Clean the tapped holes in the ring gear with solvent and dry them with compressed air. If the new bolts have a green coating over approximately ½ in. of the threaded area, use them as is. If they are not coated, apply a small amount of Loctite® on the threads. Tighten the the bolts to 70–85 ft. lbs.

10. Install the differential case and ring gear.

Installation

1. Install the left side gear, clutch pack and new shim into the cavity in the differential case. Repeat this step for the right side.

2. Place the pinion gears and thrust washers 180 degrees apart on the side gears.

3. Install the differential gear turning tool.

NOTE: A 12 in. extension is required to install the pinion gears.

4. Rotate the tool until the pinion gears are aligned with the pinion shaft hole. Remove the tool from the differential case.

5. Hold the S-shaped preload spring up to the differential case window and with a soft faced hammer, tap the spring into position.

NOTE: Inspect the preload spring for damage before reinstalling it.

6. Install the axle shafts and C-locks into position. Push the axle shaft outboard as far as possible.

7. Install the pinion shaft and pinion shaft lock bolt and torque the bolt to 15–30 ft. lbs. (20–40 Nm).

8. Install the rear brake drums and wheels. Perform the Traction Lok operational check to insure that the unit is within specification.

TORQUE SPECIFICATIONS

Minimum

Description	N·m	Lb-Ft
Rotating torques required during bench check after assembly or in vehicle with one wheel on the ground.		
Clutch Plates	41	30

NOTE: Rotating torque may fluctuate.

LUBRICANT CAPACITIES AND CHECKING PROCEDURES

Traction-LOK With Single Case

Ring gear size	Liters	Pints
7.5 in.	1.7	3.75
8.5 in.	1.7	3.75
8.8 in.	1.7	3.75

All Axles use ESP-M2C154-A (E0AZ-19580-A) plus four ounces of C8AZ-19546-A Friction Modifier (or equivalent).

9. Using slicone sealant, install the rear cover assembly and bolts and torque to 25–35 ft. lbs. (34–47 Nm).

10. Fill the differential with the proper lubricant to the bottom of the fill hole with the axle in the running position. The axle capacity is 4 pt. (1.9L).

11. Install the oil filler plug and tighten to 15–30 ft. lbs. (20–40 Nm).

GENERAL MOTORS LIMITED SLIP AXLE

Disc Type

DESCRIPTION

The conventional rear axle divides the driving force equally to both rear wheels. The driving force is applied to the wheel which has the least amount of traction; therefore, if a wheel is on snow or mud, the wheel will spin and driving force is lost.

The limited slip rear axle uses clutch plates to direct the driving force to the wheel with the best traction thus improving the ability of the vehicle to pull out of mud or snow.

——————— CAUTION ———————

On vehicles equipped with limited slip rear axles, do not run the engine with only one rear wheel OFF the ground and the transmission in gear. Also, on car type wheel balancers should not be used on the rear wheels unless both rear wheels are OFF the floor and the vehicle safely supported. Leaving 1 wheel on floor may cause vehicle to move forward and possibly cause damage or injury.

OPERATION

The limited slip rear axle transmits torque from the drive pinion gear to the ring gear and case in the same manner as a conventional rear axle. In addition, the limited slip rear axle incorporates the use of clutch plates which tend to lock the axle shafts to the case or in effect, to each other.

As driving torque is developed at the rear wheels, side gear separating loads are developed which load the rear axle clutch packs. This induced clutch torque capacity resists relative motion between the side gears and the rear axle case. Therefore, if 1 wheel is on slippery pavement, such as ice or snow, the other wheel must develop considerably more torque before the case assembly will differentiate and allow the wheel to spin.

The axle shaft torques developed are designed to overcome the clutch capacities and allow differentiation when turning corners.

LIMITED SLIP CONVERSION INFORMATION

The case assembly, less ring gear and side bearings, is available for converting a conventional rear axle to limited slip. The ring gear and side bearings of the conventional rear axle, if in good condition, can be used with the limited slip case assembly.

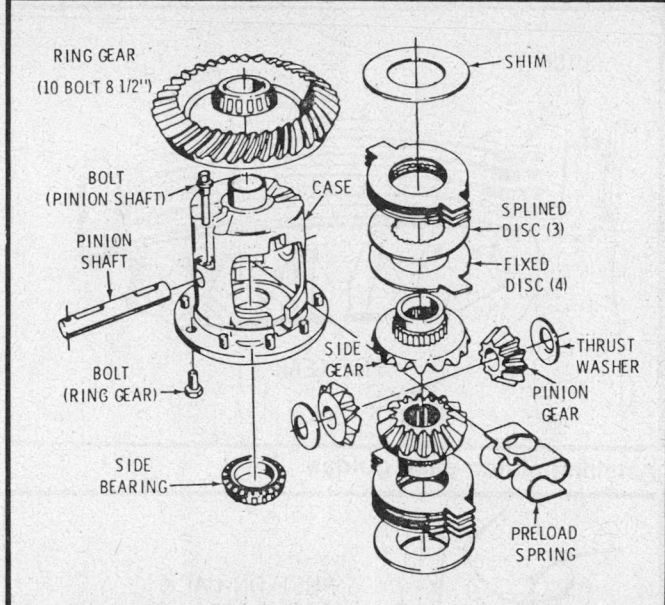

"G" type limited slip differential exploded veiw

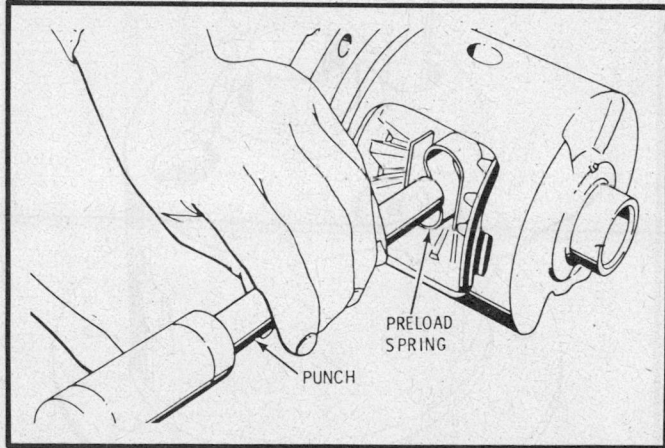

Removing pre-load spring

Four Disc Types

1. The General Motors type plates are on both differential side gears.
2. The Eaton type plates on 1 differential side gear are locked with preload springs.
3. The Corvette type (Dana) plates on 1 differential side gear are tensioned by 1 disked washer in clutch pack.
4. The Eaton type with governor plates are both differential side gears, using governor and latching bracket.

GENERAL MOTORS TYPE

Disassembly

1. If the side bearings are to be removed, they can be removed in the coventional manner.
2. If the rear axle case is going to be replaced, remove the ring gear from the case.
3. Remove the pinion shaft lock screw and the pinion shaft from the case.
4. Drive the preload spring from the case.
5. Rotate the side gears until the pinion gears are in the open

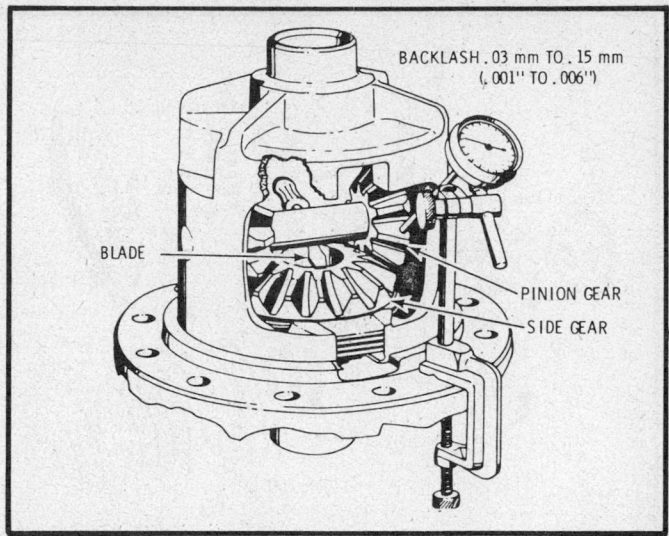

Removing clutch pack

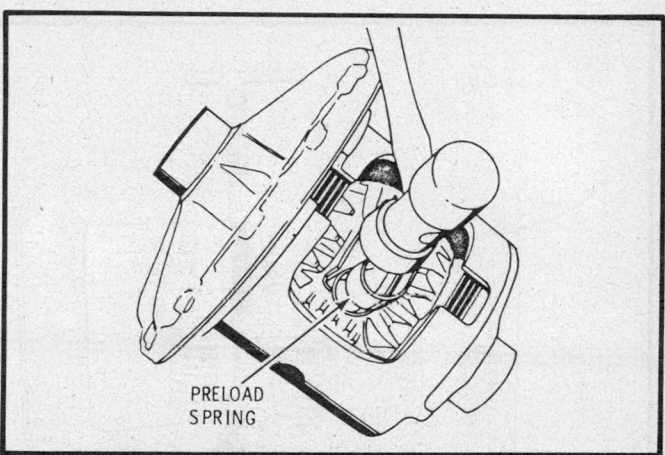

Installing pre-load spring

area of the case. Remove the pinion gears and thrust washers.
6. Remove a side gear, clutch pack and shims from the case, noting its location in the case for reassembly.
7. Remove the side gear clutch pack and shims from the opposite side.
8. Remove the shims and clutch plates from the side gears. Keep the clutch plates in their original location in the clutch pack.

Assembly

1. If the side bearings were removed, lubricate the bearings with hypoid gear lubricant and install them on the case hubs.
2. Apply lubricant, to the clutch plates.
3. Assemble the clutch pack as follows:
   a. Alternately position 7 clutch plates on the side gear, starting and ending with a clutch plate having external lugs.
   b. Place the spacer against the plate having the external lugs, positioning the shims last. Be careful to install the same spacer and shims or an equal amount on the clutch pack for a starting point.
   c. Repeat the previous steps for the other clutch pack.
4. Check the pinion to side gear clearance as follows:
   a. Install a side gear with the clutch pack and shims in the case.
   b. Position the 2 pinion gears and thrust washers on the side gear and install the pinion shaft.

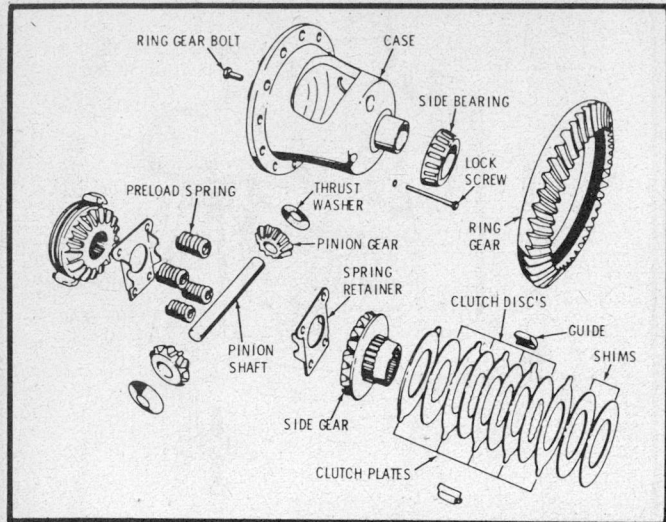

"P" type limited slip differential

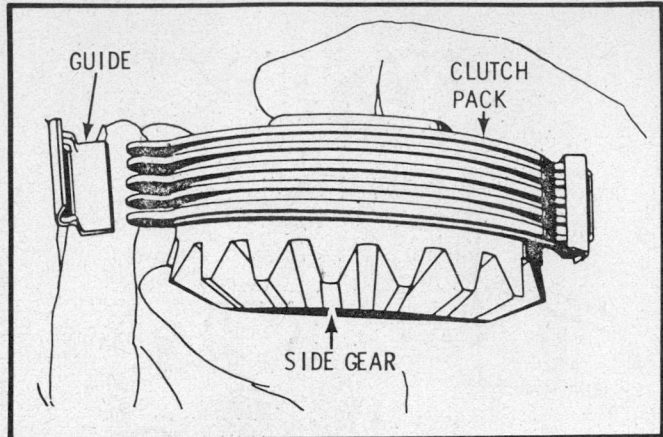

Installing clutch pack guides

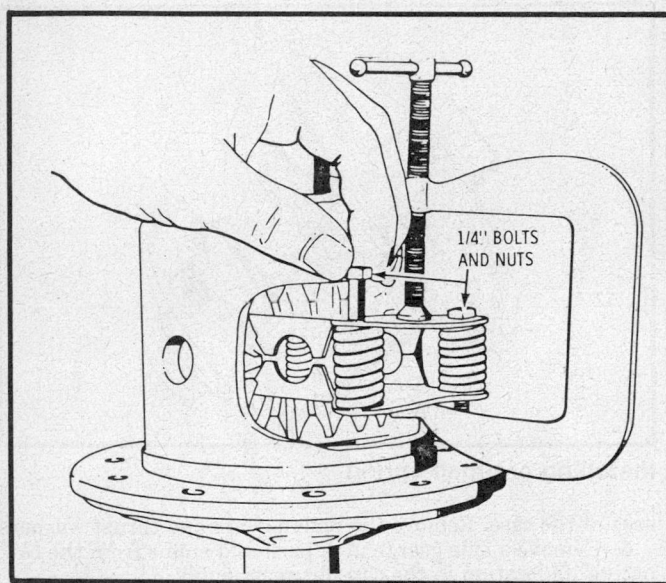

Removing pre-load springs and retainers

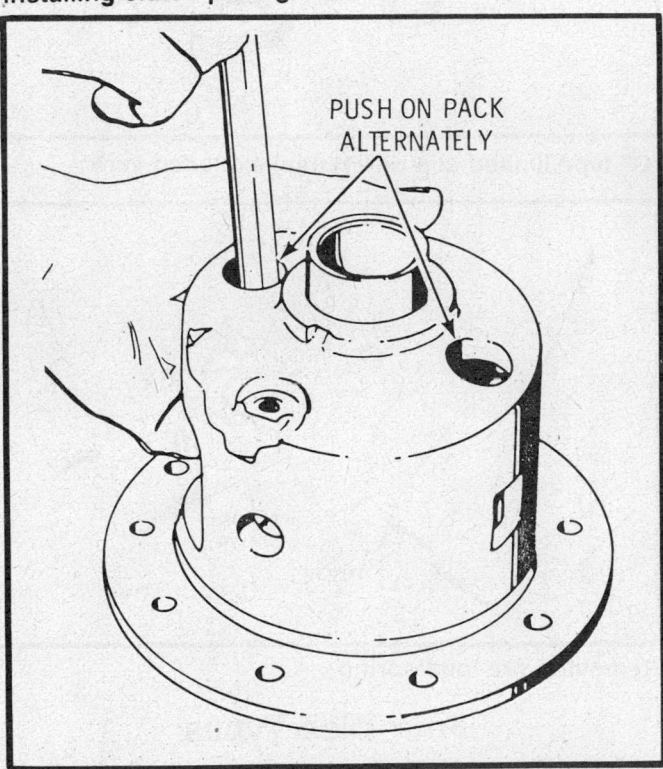

Checking side gear to pinion backlash

c. Compress the clutch pack by inserting a wedge between the side gear and pinion shaft.

d. Install a dial indicator with the contact button against the pinion gear.

e. Rotate the pinion gear. Clearance should be 0.001–0.006 in. (0.03–0.15mm).

f. If the clearance is more than 0.006 in. (0.15mm), add shims between the clutch pack and the case. If the clearance is less than 0.001 in. (0.03mm), remove the shims. A 0.002 in. (0.05mm) shim will change the clearance approximately 0.001 in. (0.03mm). Recheck the clearance after adding or subtracting shims.

g. Remove the side gear and repeat the procedure with the opposite clutch pack, on the opposite side of case.

5. Remove the pinion shaft, pinions and thrust washers.

6. Install the remaining side gear and clutch pack with the correct shims in the case.

7. Place the pinion gears on the gears and rotate them into the correct position.

8. Install the thrust washers behind the pinion gears and align them properly.

9. Insert the pinion shaft into the case through the thrust washer and part way into the pinion gear. This will keep the pinion gears aligned while driving the preload spring into place.

10. Position the preload spring next to the side gears and drive it into place.

11. Push the pinion shaft into position and align the lock screw hole in the shaft with the hole in the case. Install the pinion shaft lock screw and torque it to 20 ft. lbs. (27 Nm).

12. If the ring gear was removed, position the gear on the case flange and install new bolts. Torque the bolts evenly and alternately across the diameter in progressive stages to 90 ft. lbs. (120 Nm); do not hammer on the ring gear to seat it.

EATON TYPE

Disassembly

1. If necessary to remove the ring gear and side bearings, fol-

low the procedures established for the conventional rear axle unit.

2. Drive the preload spring retainer and springs through the observation hole in the case only far enough to secure a C-clamp. Install ¼ in. bolts through the retainers and secure them enough to remove the retainer and spring pack.

3. If necessary to disassemble the retainer and spring, position the retainer and spring pack in a vise and remove the ¼ in. bolts and C-clamp and loosen the vise slowly until the spring compression is relieved.

4. Remove the pinion thrust washer from behind the pinion gears.

5. Remove the pinion gears from the case. The pinion gears can be removed by rotating them in one direction. Rotate the rear axle case clockwise to remove the 1st gear; rotate case counterclockwise to remove the 2nd gear. To remove 2nd gear, it may be necessary to assist the pinion gear from its seat by prying on the gear through the observation hole in the case.

6. Remove the side gear, clutch pack, shims and guides from the case. Tap the assembly from the case, using a brass drift. Repeat the removal on the opposite gear.

7. Separate the clutch pack assembly from the side gear. Retain the clutch pack assembly with the original side gear.

Assembly

1. Lubricate the clutch plates and discs with a hypoid gear lubricant.

2. Alternately position the clutch plate and clutch disc on the side gear, beginning and ending with the clutch plate, until assembly to the clutch pack is complete.

3. Install the clutch pack guides on the clutch plate lugs. Make sure that the clutch disc lugs engage with the side gear teeth.

4. Select shims of equal thickness to those removed from the case. Use the old shims if necessary and reinstall them over the side gear hub.

5. Lubricate and assemble the opposite side gear as above.

6. Install 1 side gear, clutch pack assembly and shims in the rear axle case.

7. Position the pinion gears and thrust washers on the side gears, install the pinion shaft through the case and gears.

8. Install a dial indicator on the case so that the contact button rests against the pinion gear.

9. Compress the clutch pack using a suitable pry bar. Move the pinion gear to obtain the proper tooth clearance.

10. The tooth clearance should be 0.001–0.006 in. (0.03–0.15mm). If required, change the shims to obtain the proper tooth clearance.

11. Remove the side gear assembly and repeat the tooth clearance procedure for the gear on the opposite side of the case.

12. Remove the pinion shaft, gears and thrust washers.

13. Install the remaining side gear, clutch pack assembly and shims in the case.

14. Install the pinion gears and thrust washers. Installation of the pinion gears can be performed by reversing the pinion gear removal procedure.

15. Assemble the springs in the spring retainer and clamp the assembly in a vise. Install a C-clamp and bar stock on the spring retainer then install a ¼ in. bolt and nut in each front spring.

16. Position the spring pack between the side gears and remove the bar stock and C-clamp.

17. Drive the spring pack into the side gear enough to retain the front springs and remove the ¼ in. bolts from the springs. Drive the spring pack completely into position.

18. Check the alignment of the spring retainer with the side gears. Move the spring pack slightly, if necessary.

19. If the side bearings and ring gear were removed, install them onto the case using the procedure outlined for the conventional rear axle.

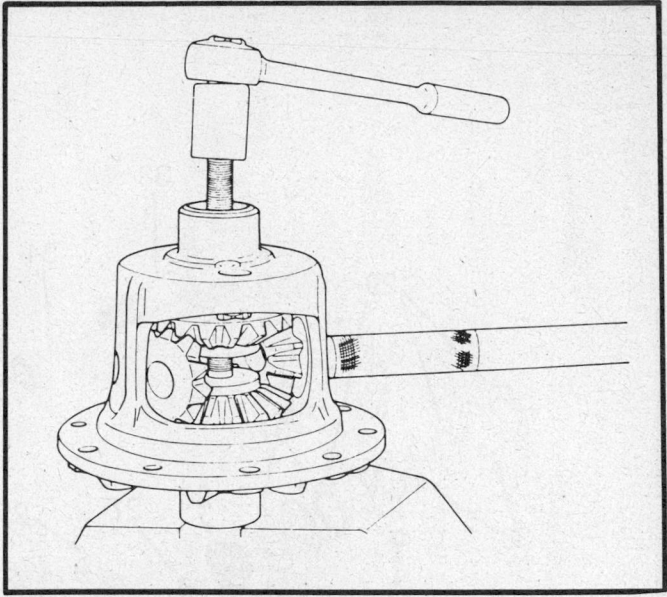

Removing or installing side and pinion gears with special tools, Corvette type

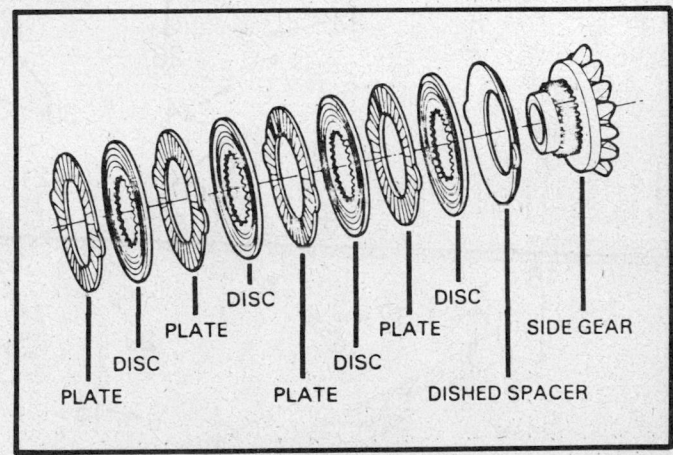

Arrangement of clutch pack in Corvette type rear axle

DANA AXLES 36 AND 44

Dana model 36 is a 7⅞ in. ring gear and Dana model 44 is a 8½ in. ring gear. Disassembly and assembly procedures are the same for both size differentials.

Disassembly

1. Reposition the differential case onto the axle shaft. Remove the 2 snaprings from the cross pin. Use a pin punch, push the retaining pin from the pinion pin; place a shop towel behind the case to prevent the pin from flying out of the case.

2. Using a hammer and a punch, drive the pinion pin from the differential case.

3. Using the adapter plate tool, assemble it into the bottom side gear.

4. Using the threaded adapter plate tool, install it into the top side gear. Thread the forcing screw into the threaded adapter until it becomes centered into the bottom adapter plate.

5. Torque the forcing screw until it becomes slightly tight; the dished spacers will collapse and will provide loose condition between the side gears and pinion gears.

6. Using a shim stock of 0.020 in. (0.51mm) thickness or an

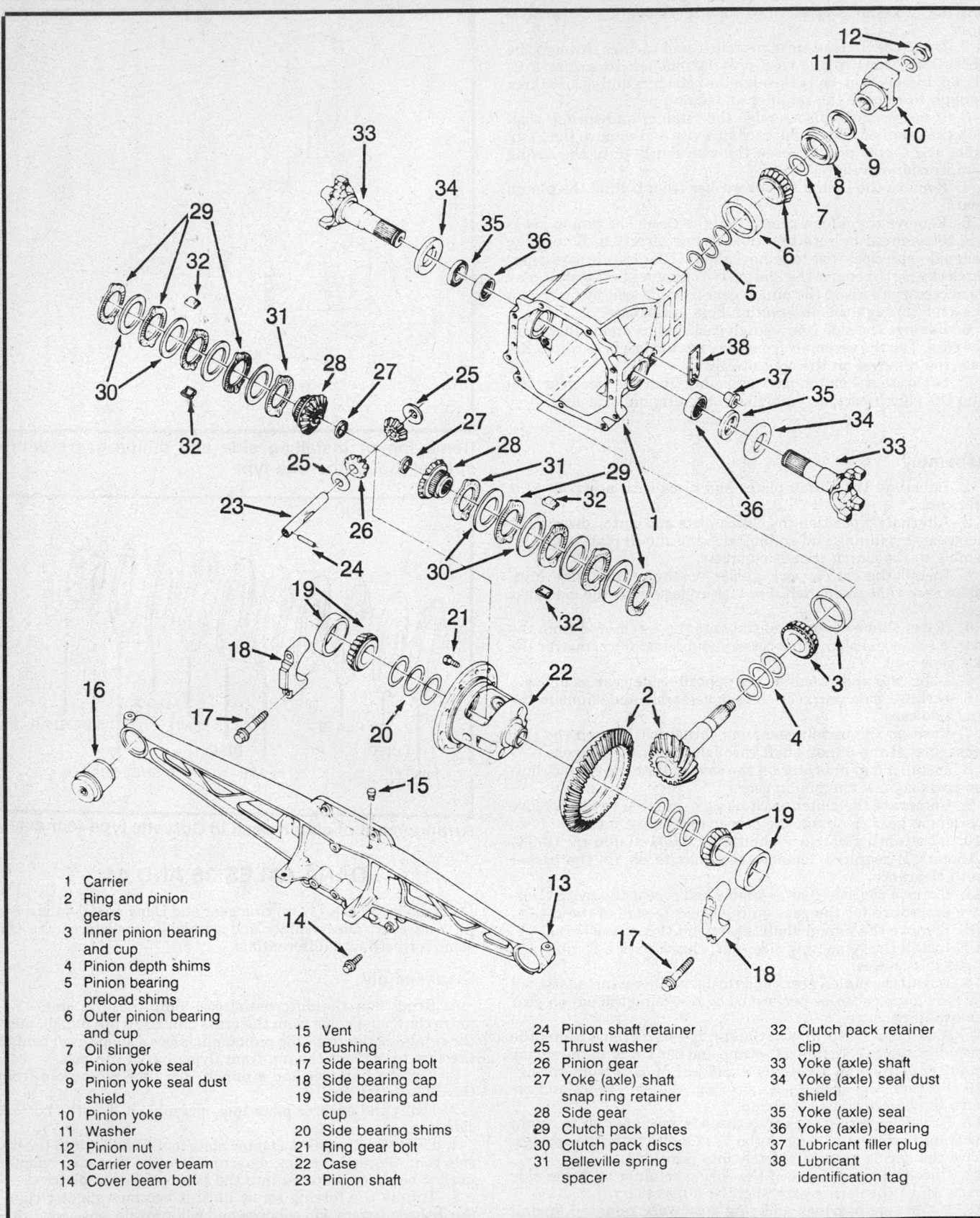

1 Carrier
2 Ring and pinion gears
3 Inner pinion bearing and cup
4 Pinion depth shims
5 Pinion bearing preload shims
6 Outer pinion bearing and cup
7 Oil slinger
8 Pinion yoke seal
9 Pinion yoke seal dust shield
10 Pinion yoke
11 Washer
12 Pinion nut
13 Carrier cover beam
14 Cover beam bolt

15 Vent
16 Bushing
17 Side bearing bolt
18 Side bearing cap
19 Side bearing and cup
20 Side bearing shims
21 Ring gear bolt
22 Case
23 Pinion shaft

24 Pinion shaft retainer
25 Thrust washer
26 Pinion gear
27 Yoke (axle) shaft snap ring retainer
28 Side gear
29 Clutch pack plates
30 Clutch pack discs
31 Belleville spring spacer

32 Clutch pack retainer clip
33 Yoke (axle) shaft
34 Yoke (axle) seal dust shield
35 Yoke (axle) seal
36 Yoke (axle) bearing
37 Lubricant filler plug
38 Lubricant identification tag

Exploded view of the corvette differential components

equivalent tool, push the spherical washers to remove them from both pinion gears.

7. Loosen the forcing screw to relieve the tension on the dished spacers; it may be necessary to adjust the forcing screw slightly to allow the case to rotate.

8. Using a turning adapter tool, insert the small end of the adapter into the cross pin hole of the case. Pull on the bar to rotate the case until the pinion gears can be removed and remove them.

9. While holding the top clutch pack in place, remove the tools.

10. Keeping the plates and discs in exactly the same position, remove the top side gear and clutch pack.

11. Remove the case from the axle shaft.

12. Turn the case with the flange or ring gear side upward and remove the adapter plate, side gear and clutch pack from the case.

13. Remove the clutch pack retaining clips and the separate of the plates and discs; keep the stack of plates and discs in exactly the same order as they were removed.

Assembly

1. Using the limited slip rear axle lubricant, prelubricate the clutch plates, discs and thrust face of the side gear.

2. Be sure to assemble the plates and discs in exactly the same position as they disassembled, regardless of whether they are new parts or original parts.

3. Install the retainer clips onto the plate ears. Make sure both clips are completely assembled and seated onto the plate ears. Assemble the clutch pack and side gear into the top side gear splines and the retainer clips completely seated into the case pockets.

NOTE: To prevent the clutch pack from falling out of the case, hold them in place by hand while repositioning the case on a bench.

4. Using the adapter plate tool, position it onto the side gear.

5. Assemble the other clutch pack and side gear. Make sure the clutch pack stays assembled to the side gear splines and the retainer clips are seated completely into the case pockets.

6. Using a special tool, install it into the clutch pack to hold it in position. Lightly torque the forcing screw into the bottom adapter; this will hold the clutch packs in position. With the tools assembled in the case, position the case into the axle shaft and align the side gear splines to the shaft splines.

7. Compress the clutch packs by torquing the forcing screw. With the clutch pack compressed, insert the pinion gears.

8. While holding the gears in place, insert the adapter tool, with the handle tool, into the cross pin hole in the case. Pull the handle and rotate the case allowing the gears to turn. Make sure the pinion gear holes are aligned with the case holes; if necessary, adjust the forcing screw tension to rotate the case.

9. Using the proper lubricant, prelubricate the spherical washers. Assemble the spherical washers into the case, using a small tool to push the washers into place. Remove the installation tools.

10. Position the pinion pin shaft into the case and drive it in with a hammer. Be sure the retaining pin holes are aligned and install the retaining pin.

Cleaning and Inspecting

1. Thoroughly clean the side bearings in a clean solvent (do not use a brush). Examine the bearings visually and by feel for signs of wear. Oil the bearings and, while rotating them, apply as much hand pressure as possible making sure that the bearings feel smooth.

Minute scratches and/or pits that appear on the rollers and races at low mileage are due to the initial preload. Bearings having these marks should not be rejected.

2. Carefully examine the ring and pinion gear teeth for nicks,

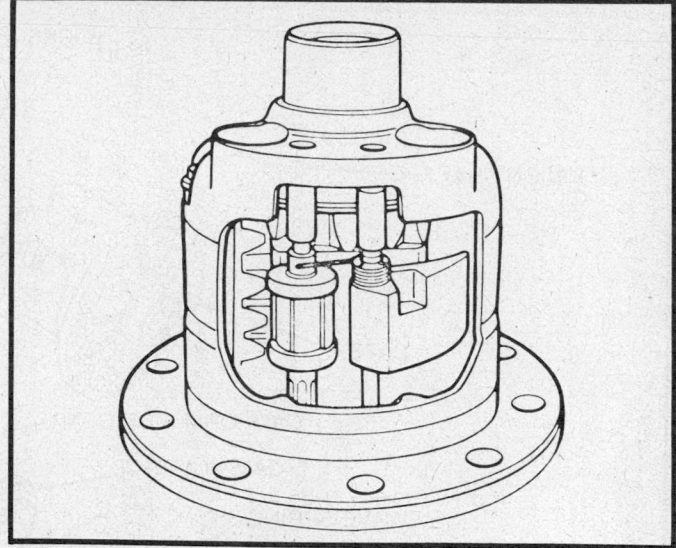

Positioning of governor and latching bracket

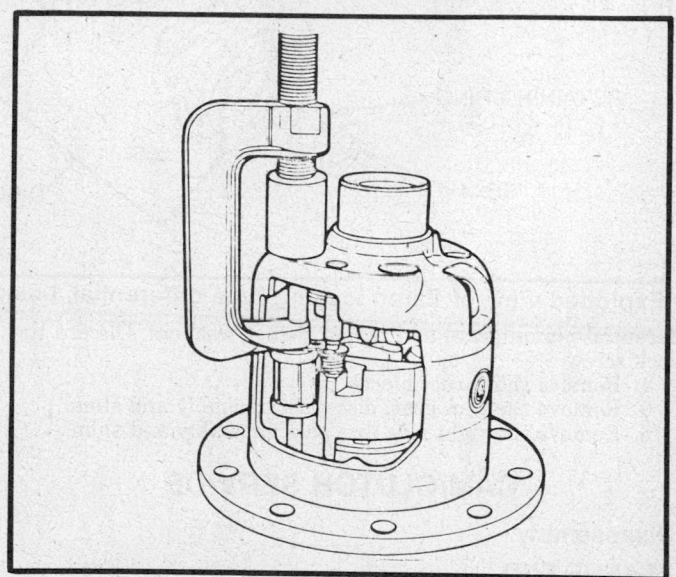

Removal of governor shaft

cracks, burrs or scoring. Any of these conditions will require replacement of the entire gear set.

3. Inspect the pinion shaft, pinion gears and side gears. Replace them if they are excessively scored, pitted or worn.

4. Check the press fit of the side bearing inner race on the rear axle case. The side bearings must have a tight press fit on the hub.

5. Inspect the clutch plates for scores, wear, cracks or a distorted condition. If any of these conditions exist, new clutch plates must be installed.

EATON TYPE WITH GOVERNOR

Disassembly

1. Note the position of the governor and latching bracket assembly. Remove the ring gear and side bearings following the procedures established for the standard differential.

2. Using a bushing puller tool, remove the governor assembly and latching bracket by pulling the retaining bushings. Hold the latching bracket spring out of the way while pulling the governor assembly to prevent damage.

3. Remove the lock screw and pinion shaft. Roll out the dif-

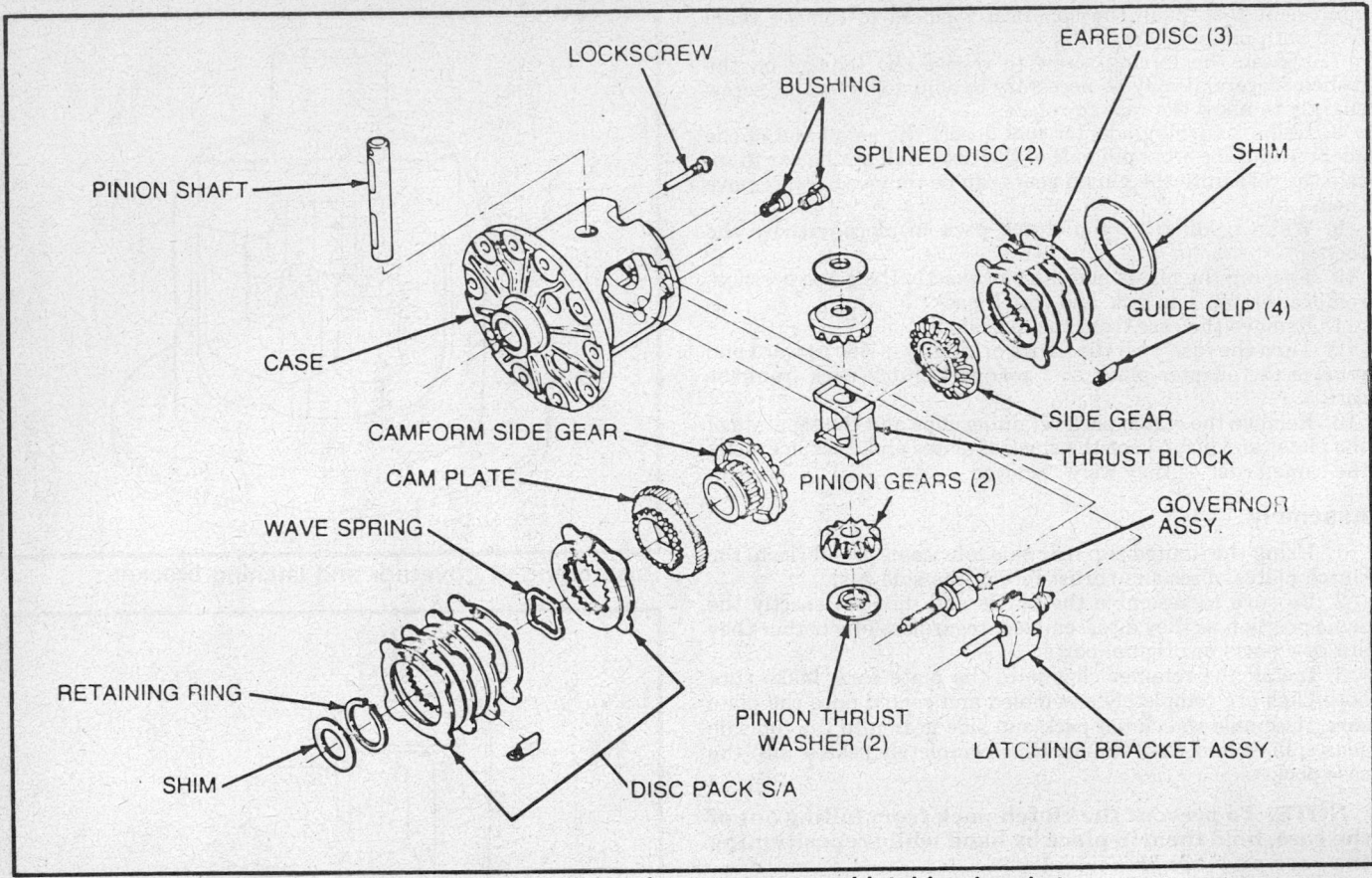

PINION SHAFT

LOCKSCREW

BUSHING

EARED DISC (3)

SPLINED DISC (2)

SHIM

CASE

GUIDE CLIP (4)

CAMFORM SIDE GEAR

SIDE GEAR

CAM PLATE

THRUST BLOCK

PINION GEARS (2)

WAVE SPRING

GOVERNOR ASSY.

RETAINING RING

PINION THRUST WASHER (2)

LATCHING BRACKET ASSY.

SHIM

DISC PACK S/A

Exploded view of Eaton locking type differential, using governor and latching bracket

ferential pinion gears and pinion thrust washers. Discard the lock screw.
4. Remove the thrust block.
5. Remove the cam gear, disc pack assembly and shim.
6. Remove the right side disc pack assembly and shim.

CAM/CLUTCH SERVICE

Disassembly

FLANGE END

If the cam plate or clutch discs must be replaced, the cam gear sub assembly must be serviced as follows:
1. Remove the retaining ring using external snapring pliers.
2. Keeping all components in the proper order, remove the discs and cam plate.

CLUTCH PACK

Remove the disc pack and shim from the side gear. Keeping the discs in order.

Assembly

FLANGE END

Replace the cam plate and wave spring or clutch discs as necessary and reassemble as follows:
1. Place the gear on a bench with the hub end up.
2. Assembly the cam plate with the cam form down to mate with the cam form on the gear.
3. Assemble onto cam plate: 2 eared discs, 1 splined disc and 1 wave spring alternately.
4. Assemble on to gear hub 2 splined discs and 3 eared discs alternately. Begin and end with an eared disc.
5. Install the retaining ring.

CLUTCH PACK

1. Replace the discs and/or clips, as required.
2. Reassemble the discs onto the gear hub (2 splined discs and 3 eared discs) alternately. Maintain the original sequence if new discs are not used. Reinstall the original shim or a new shim with the original thickness.

NOTE: If the gear hubs are scored, rough or have abnormal wear, check the condition of the bores in case. If damaged or oversized, the entire unit must be replaced.

PINION GEARS

Installation

If it is necessary to replace the pinion gears due to pitting of the teeth, scoring of the pinion shaft bearing surface or breakage, it will be necessary to disassemble the unit. Install new pinion gears and pinion thrust washers and reassemble the unit.

If the cam gear, side gear or pinion gears are broken or damaged, check for other damage and replace the parts as needed. If the case is damaged, the entire unit must be replaced.

CAM GEAR LEFT SIDE

Installation

If it is necessary to replace the cam gear due to pitting of the teeth, scoring of the hub or breakage, it will be necessary to disassemble the unit. When replacing the cam gear, it will be necessary to adjust (by selecting the correct shim) the cam gear to pinion gear backlash using the following procedure:
1. Using the original shim, install the new cam gear and disc

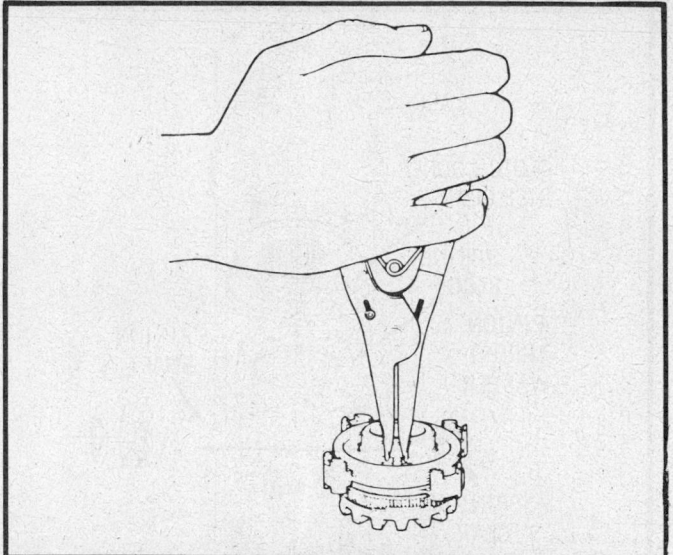

Removing or installing clutch plate retaining ring

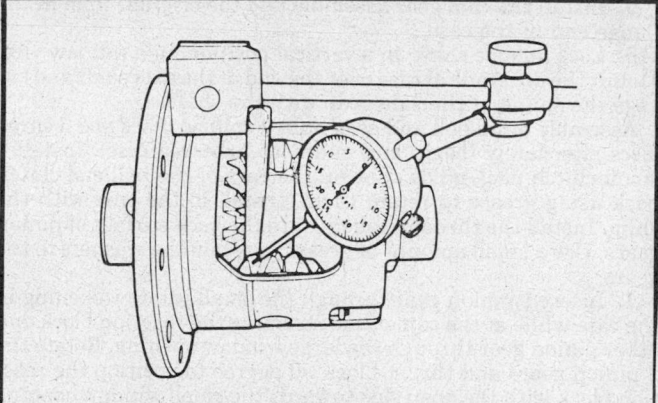

Measuring cam gear backlash

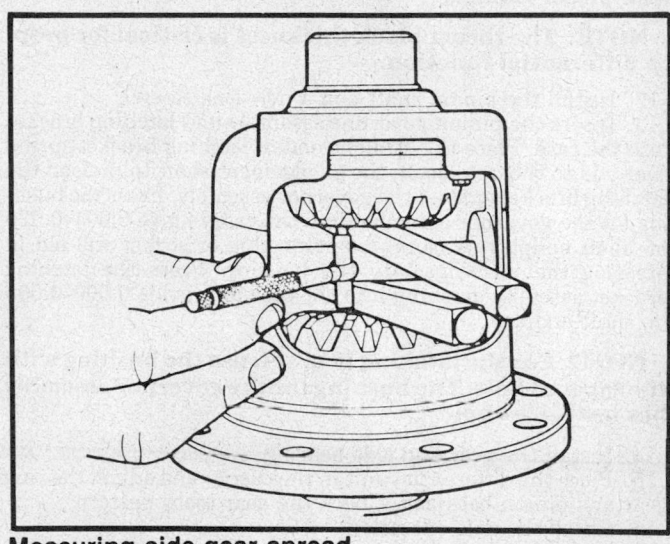

Measuring side gear spread

pack sub assembly into the flange end of the case. Place the pinion gears and pinion thrust washers into their respective locations in the case. Depress the cam gear into its bore and slide the pinion shaft through the case and both pinion gears.

If the installation of the pinion shaft is prevented by the pinion gears, it will be necessary to replace the original shim with 1 of less thickness.

2. Once the pinion shaft is installed with the lockscrew in place, index 1 tooth of the pinion gear nearest the pinion shaft lockscrew so it points downward and perpendicular to the case flange. Use a large tapered tool and firmly wedge it between the cam gear and pinion shaft.

3. Using a dial indictor mounted to the case flange, check the pinion to cam gear backlash by pulling the pinion gear firmly into its seat and rotating it back and forth while reading the gauge. Note the reading. Repeat the above procedure of indexing and checking the backlash of the pinion gear opposite the pinion shaft lockscrew while noting the reading. If the backlash is not between 0.010–0.018 in., change the shim size and repeat the backlash procedure until the correct backlash is obtained. The thinner the shim is, the greater the backlash reading will be.

When the cam gear and/or side gear is replaced, the thrust block replacement and clearance procedure must be followed during reassembly of the unit. Failure to do so may disturb the critical clearances and could result in differential complaints.

SIDE GEAR RIGHT SIDE

Installation

If it is necessary to replace the right side gear due to pitting of the teeth, scoring of the hub or breakage, it will be necessary to disassemble the unit. When replacing the side gear, it will be necessary to adjust the side-to-pinion gear backlash by selecting a correct shim and using a similar procedure as described in the cam gear replacement section. However, different from the cam gear, the backlash for the side gear should be adjusted to within 0.002–0.010 in., with the right side gear wedged against case.

THRUST BLOCK

Installation

If it is necessary to replace only the thrust block, replace it with a new block of identical thickness. If the thrust block is broken, check for other damage and replace parts as necessary. If the case is damaged, replace the entire unit.

If the cam gear and/or side gears are replaced, it will be necessary to check the side gear spread dimension and adjust the block clearance as follows:

1. Install the cam gear and disc pack with the cam gear shim into the flange end of the case.

2. Install the side gear and disc pack with the shim into the bell end of the case.

3. Install the pinion shaft with a new lockscrew into the case. Firmly wedge a large tapered tool between the pinion shaft and cam gear. Wedge another similar tool between the pinion shaft and side gear.

4. Using a 1–2 in. telescoping gauge, measure the distance between the cam gear face and side gear face. This is the side gear spread. Make sure telescoping gauge ends rest on the gear face, not on the gear teeth. Measure the telescoping gauge with a 1–2 in. micrometer and note the reading.

5. Measure the thickness of the original thrust block at the outer corner and note the reading.

6. If the thrust block thickness is not within a range of 0–0.006 in. less than the side gear spread, adjust the clearance with 1 of the following procedures:

   a. Reshim the right side clutch disc pack.

NOTE: Backlash of 0.002–0.010 in. must be maintained.

   b. Select a new thrust block of the correct size to obtain 0.000–0.006 in. clearance.

8. Install 4 clutch pack guide clips on the ears of the cam gear clutch pack using grease to retain them.

9. Install the cam gear assembly and the original shim in the flange end of the case.

10. Lock an axle shaft, in a vertical position, in a soft jaw vice. Mount the differential case over the end of the axle shaft and engage the spline of the side gear with the shaft.

Assemble on to bell and gear hub; 2 splined discs and 3 eared discs alternately (begin and end with an eared disc). Install 4 small clutch pack guide clips on the ears of the bell end clutch pack using grease to retain them. Install in the case with the shim. Install the thrust washers onto the back surface of pinion gears. Use a small amount of grease to retain the washers to the gears.

11. Insert 1 pinion gear through the small window opening in the case while at the same time inserting the reaction block and other pinion gear through the large window opening. Rotate the 2 pinion gears and thrust block 90 degree to position the reaction block with the open side towards the small window opening in the case. Be sure the 2 pinion gears and thrust washers are in their proper location.

NOTE: The thrust block thickness is critical for proper differential function.

12. Install the pinion shaft and a new lock screw.

13. Insert the pinion governor assembly and latching bracket into the case. Place the straight end of latching bracket spring over and to the outside of, the engagement shaft to preload the latching bracket against the governor assembly. Press the bushing for the governor assembly into the case to give 0.004–0.020 in. shaft endplay. A ³⁄₈ in. diameter plug or socket will aid in pressing the bushings into the housing. Press the latching bracket assembly bushing into the case to provide 0.000–0.003 in. shaft endplay.

NOTE: For the latching bracket, use the bushing with the tapered hole. The bushing for the governor assembly has a straight hole.

14. Install the gear and side bearing.

15. Place the differential unit in the carrier and adjust the ring gear and pinion backlash. Check the gear tooth pattern.

16. Check the axle operation.

NOTE: Use only the rear axle lubricant recommended. The usage of any other lubricant or additive may result in damage to the differential.

Cone Type Locking Differential Borg Warner

The limited slip rear axle can be identified by a tag attached to the lower right section of the axle cover. It is designed to direct the majority of the driving force to the wheel with greater traction. In doing so it reduces the possibility of the vehicle becoming stuck while driving under adverse conditions.

All rear axle parts of a vehicle equipped with the limited slip rear axle are interchangeable with those equipped with the conventional rear axle, except for the case assembly. It is similar in all respects to the conventional case assembly, with the addition of cone clutches splined to each side gear.

SERVICE PROCEDURES

Rear axle service procedures are the same for the limited slip as for the conventional rear axle, except for the servicing of the case assembly.

If the case, clutch cone/side gears, or pinion gears are damaged, it is necessary to replace case assembly.

——— CAUTION ———
Never raise a wheel and operate the engine with the transmission in gear. The driving force to the wheel on the floor will cause the vehicle to

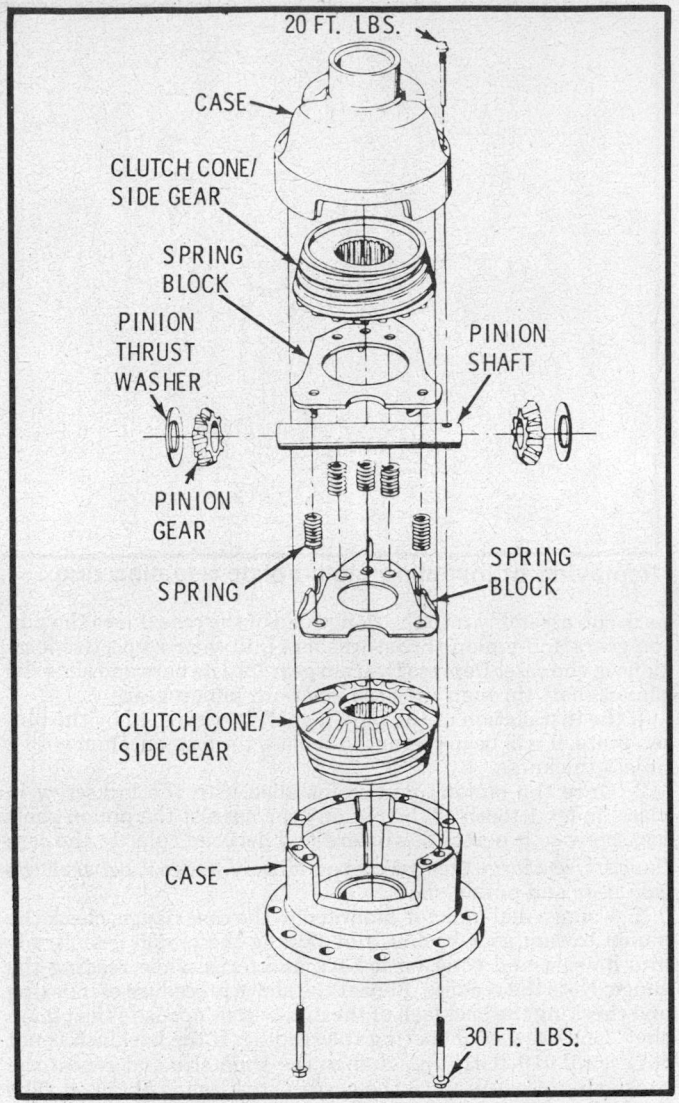

Limited slip differential (cone type) — exploded view

move. Do not use on car type wheel balancers on the rear wheels, unless both wheels are OFF the floor and the vehicle is properly supported. Leaving a wheel on floor may cause vehicle to move forward and possibly cause damage or injury.

REAR AXLE CASE

Disassembly

1. Before disassembling the rear axle case, inspect, visibly and by feel, the rear axle side bearings for damage to the rollers and outer races.

2. Place an outer race into its matched inner race and roller assembly and turn slowly, applying a strong load by hand.

3. If the bearing outer race turns smoothly and there is no visible damage found, the bearing can be reused.

4. Repeat the above operation with the outer race and matched bearing and check for smoothness.

NOTE: Both side bearings and their outer races are matched parts. If either bearing is to be replaced, its matching outer race must also be replaced.

5. Inspect the fit of the inner races on the case hubs by prying against shoulders at the puller recesses. The bearing inner races

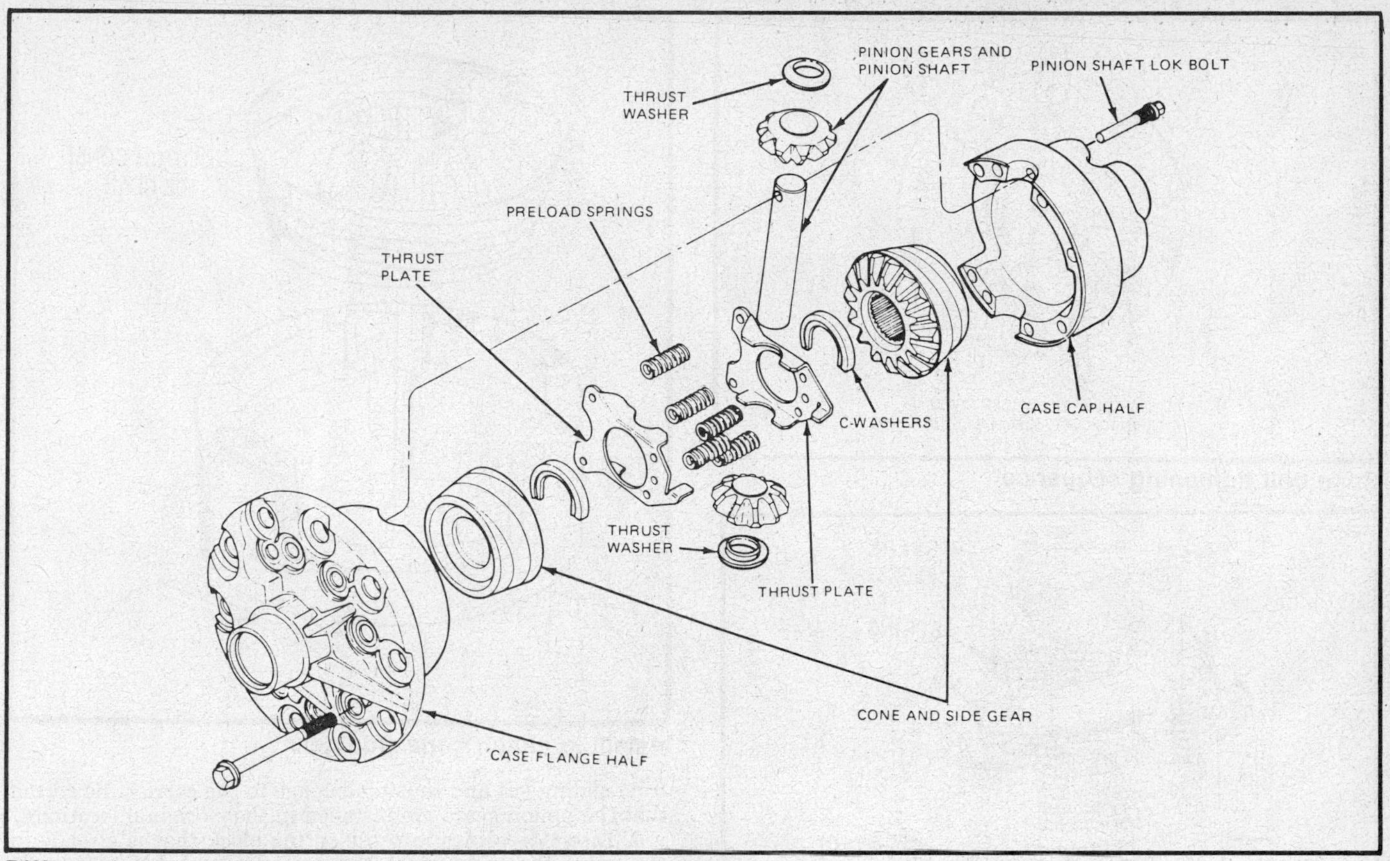

Differential assembly—sectional view

Labels: THRUST WASHER · PINION GEARS AND PINION SHAFT · PINION SHAFT LOK BOLT · PRELOAD SPRINGS · THRUST PLATE · C-WASHERS · CASE CAP HALF · THRUST WASHER · THRUST PLATE · CONE AND SIDE GEAR · CASE FLANGE HALF

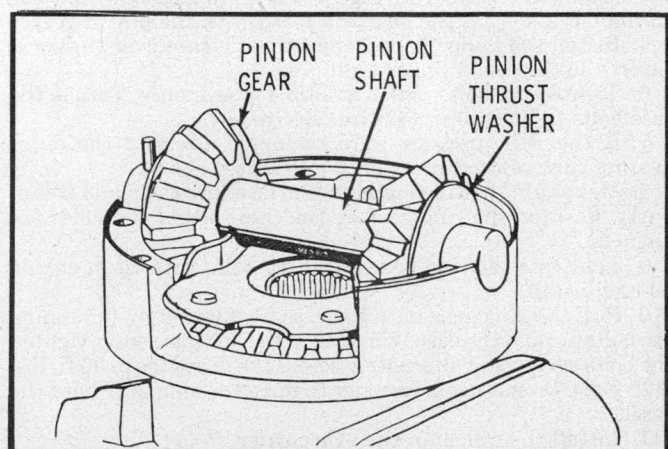

Installing parts in case half

Labels: PINION GEAR · PINION SHAFT · PINION THRUST WASHER

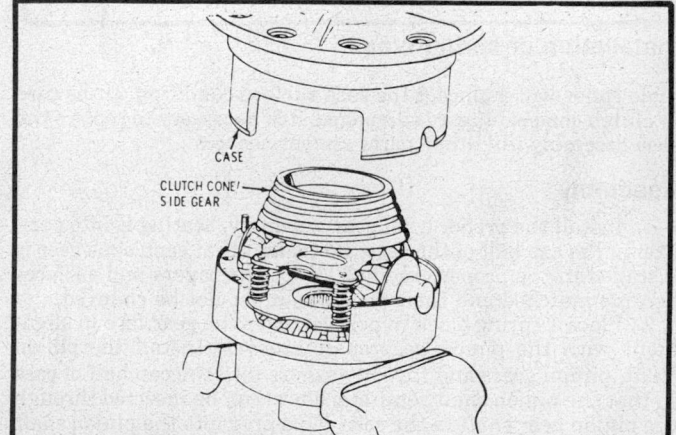

Case flange installation

Labels: CASE · CLUTCH CONE/SIDE GEAR

must be tight on the case hubs. If either bearing is loose on the case, the entire case must be replaced.

6. If the bearing inspection indicates that the bearings should be replaced, remove the side bearings using the proper tools.

7. If the ring gear is being removed, clamp the case in a vise so the jaws are 90 degree to the pinion shaft holes and remove the ring gear retaining bolts.

8. Partially install 2 bolts on opposite sides of the ring gear.

9. Remove the ring gear from case by alternately tapping on the bolts. Do not hammer directly on the ring gear or pry between the case and the ring gear.

10. Remove the case half attaching bolts.

11. Lift the cap half of case from the flange half. Remove the

clutch cone/side gears, spring blocks, preload springs, pinion gears and shaft.

Be certain that each clutch cone/side gear and pinion gear is marked so they can be installed in their original location.

Cleaning and Inspection

1. Make certain that all parts are absolutely clean and dry.

2. Inspect the pinion shaft, pinion and side gears, brake cone surfaces and corresponding cone seats in case. The cone seats in case should be smooth and free of any excessive scoring. Slight grooves or scratches, indicating passage of foreign material, are permissible and normal. The land surface on the heavy spirals of

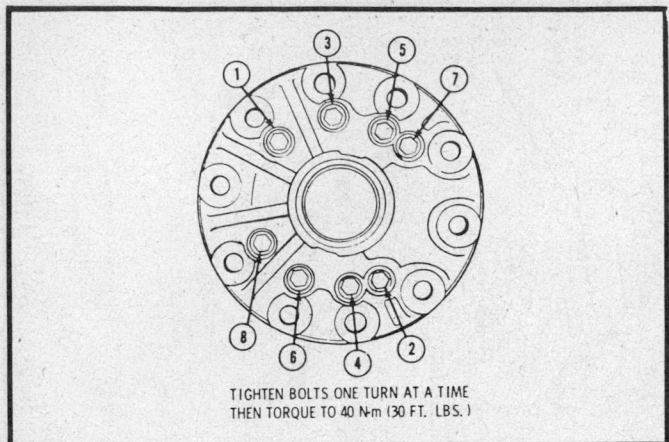

TIGHTEN BOLTS ONE TURN AT A TIME
THEN TORQUE TO 40 N·m (30 FT. LBS.)

Case bolt tightening sequence

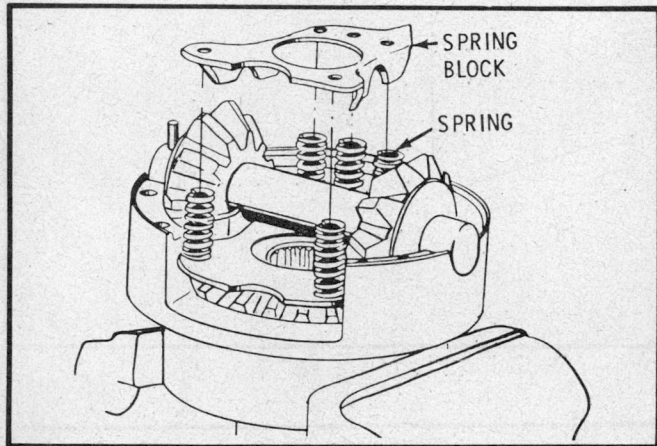

SPRING
BLOCK

SPRING

Installation of spring block

male cones will duplicate the case surface condition. If the case or clutch cone/side gear is damaged, it is necessary to replace the case assembly. All other parts are serviceable.

Assembly

1. Install the proper cone/gear assembly, seating it into position in the cap half of the case. Be certain that each cone/gear is installed in the proper case half, since the tapers and surfaces become matched and their positions must not be changed.
2. Place 1 spring block in position over the gear face in alignment with the pinion gear shaft grooves. Install the pinion shaft, pinion gears and thrust washers into the cap half of case so that the pinion shaft retaining dowel can be inserted through the pinion gear shaft in the case. This prevents the pinion shaft

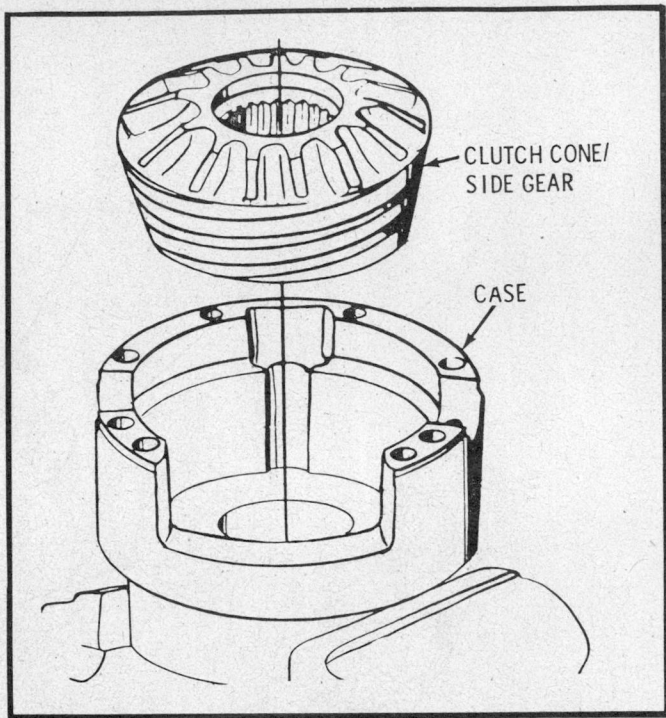

CLUTCH CONE/
SIDE GEAR

CASE

Installing clutch cone/side gear

from sliding out and causing damage to the carrier. Be certain that the pinion gears are installed in their original locations.

3. Insert 5 springs into the spring block that is already installed in the case. Place the second spring block over the springs.
4. Install the second cone/gear assembly face down on the spring block so that the gear will mesh with the pinion gears.
5. Install the flange half of the rear axle case over the cone. Insert the case bolts finger tight.
6. Tighten the bolts 1 turn at a time in sequence. Torque the case bolts to 30 ft. lbs., (40 Nm) alternately.
7. If the side bearings were removed, lubricate the outer bearing surfaces and press on the bearings.
8. Make sure that the matching surfaces are clean and free of burrs. Position the ring gear on the case so that the holes are aligned.
9. Lubricate the ring gear attaching bolts with clean engine oil and install.
10. Pull the ring gear onto the case by alternately tightening the bolts around the case. When all of the bolts are snug, tighten the bolts evenly and alternately across the diameter to 90 ft. lbs. (120 Nm). Do not use a hammer to force the ring gear onto the case.
11. Install the unit into the axle carrier.

UNIVERSAL JOINTS AND DRIVESHAFTS

GENERAL INFORMATION

Universal joints provide flexibility between the driveshaft and axle housing to accommodate changes in the angle between them. Changes in driveshaft length are accommodated by the sliding splined yoke between the driveshaft and transmission. The engine and transmission are mounted rigidly on the vehicle frame, while the driving wheels are free to move up and down in relation to the frame. The angles between the transmission,

driveshaft and axle are constantly changing as the vehicle responds to various road conditions.

Several types of universal joints are used to give flexibility and transmit power as smoothly as possible.

The most common type of universal joint is the cross and yoke type. Yokes are used on the ends of the driveshaft with the yoke arms opposite each other. Another yoke is used opposite the driveshaft. When placed together, both yokes engage a center member or cross, with 4 arms spaced 90 degrees apart. The U-

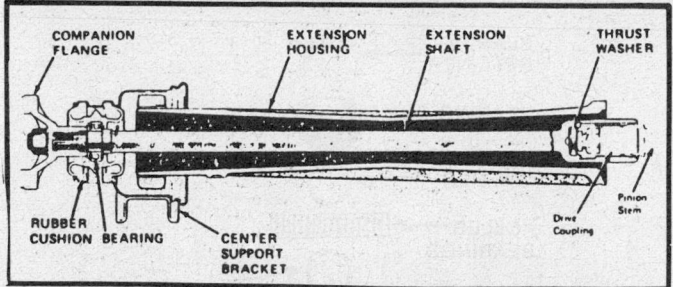

Chevette and 1000 model rear extention assembly

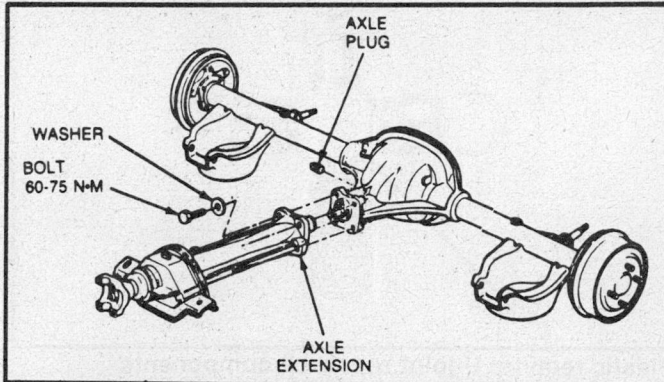

Mounting of rear axle extension on rear axle assembly — Chevette and 1000 models

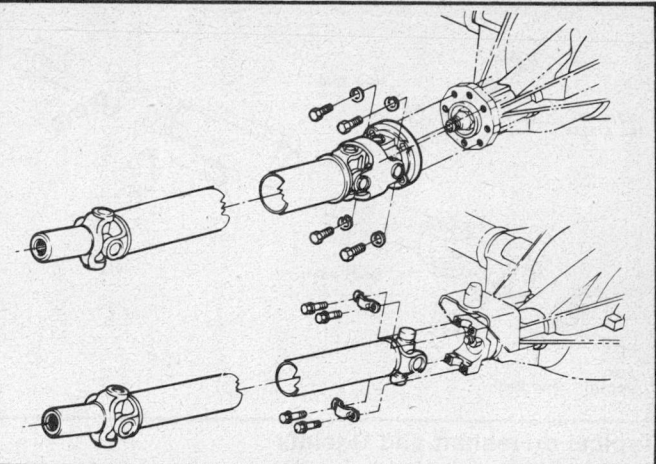

The driveshaft may be retained to the differential pinion by a flange (top or by U-bolts or straps (bottom)

joint cross is alternately referred to as a spider and the arms are called trunnions. A bearing cup (or cap) is used on each arm of the cross to allow movement as the driveshaft rotates. The bearings used are invariably needle bearings.

The second type of universal joint is the ball and trunnion universal joint. A T-shaped shaft is enclosed in the body of the joint and the trunnion ends are each equipped with a ball mounted in needle bearings. The trunnion ends move freely in grooves in the outer body of the joint creating a slip joint. This type of joint is always sealed and enclosed. On domestic vehicles, it is only used on front wheel drive axles, Toronado, Eldorado, etc. and because of the complexities of service will not be considered here.

A conventional universal joint causes the driveshaft to speed up and slow down through each revolution and causes a corresponding change in the velocity of the driven shaft. This change in speed causes natural vibrations to occur throughout the driveline making it necessary a third type of universal joint: the constant velocity joint. A rolling ball moves in and out of a curved groove, located between 2 yoke and cross universal joints, connected to each other by a coupling yoke. The result is a uniform motion as the driveshaft rotates, avoiding the fluctuations in driveshaft speed. This type of joint is found in vehicles with sharp driveline angles or where the extra measure of isolation is desirable.

Cross and Yoke U-Joint

There are 2 types of cross and yoke U-joints. One type is found on all American Motors, Chrysler and Ford vehicles. This type retains the cross within the yoke with C-shaped snaprings. General Motors cars generally use the second type of joint, which is held together by injection molded plastic (delrin) rings. The second type cannot be reassembled with the same parts once disassembled. However, repair kits are available.

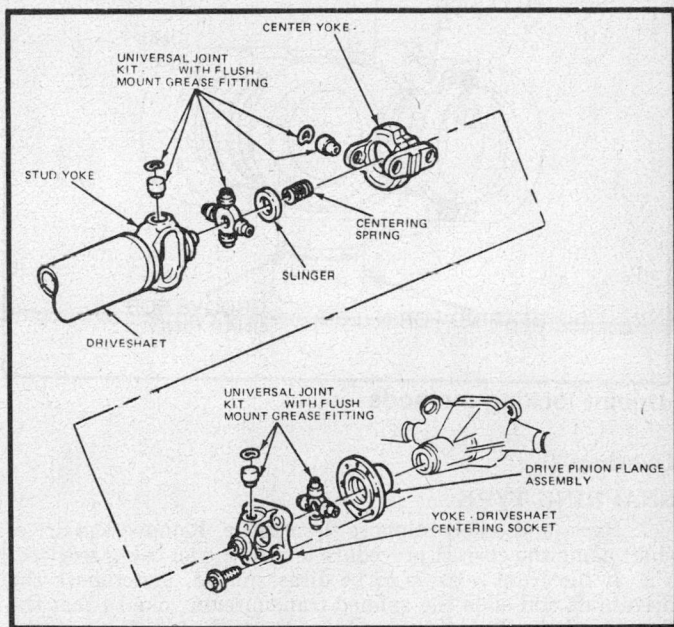

Typical driveshaft with constant velocity joints

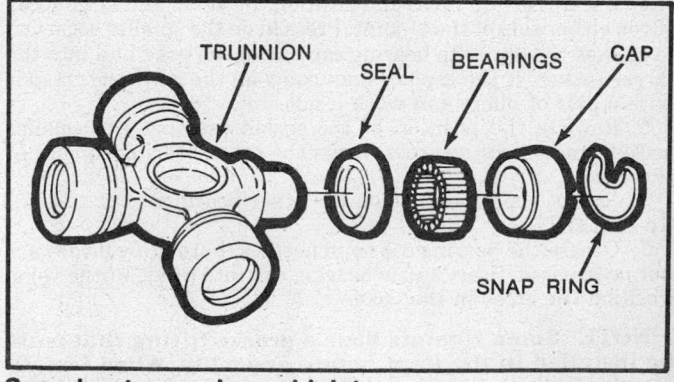

Snapring type universal joint

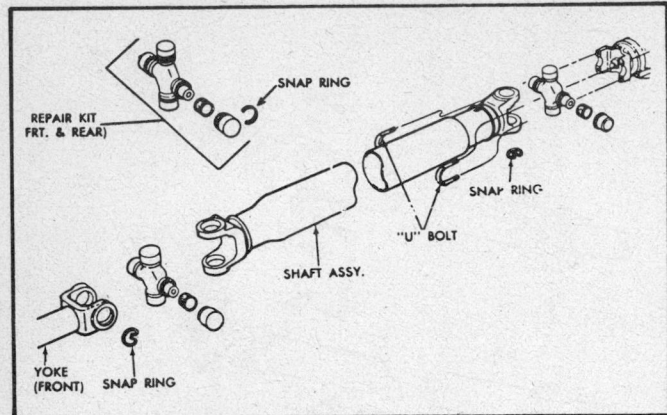

Typical driveshaft and U-joints

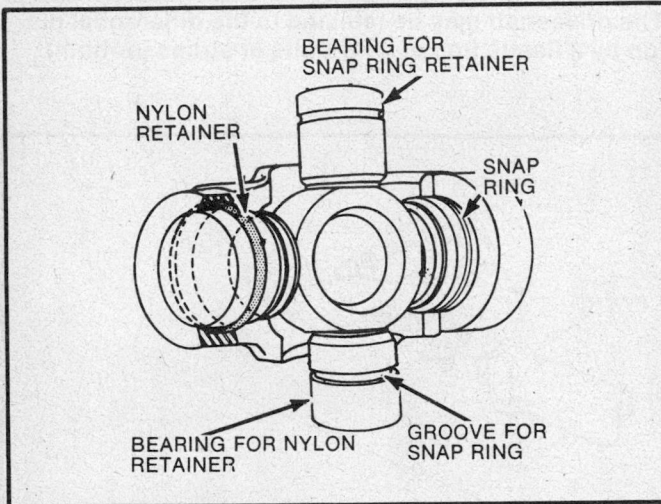

U-joint locking methods

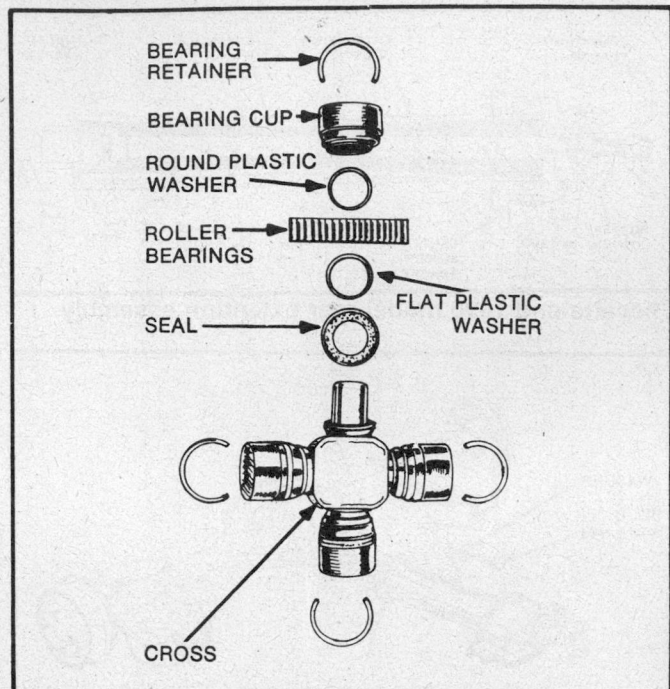

Plastic retainer U-joint repair kit components

Overhaul

SNAPRING TYPE

1. Raise and safely support the vehicle. Remove the driveshaft using the correct procedure for the model being serviced.

2. If the front yoke is to be disassembled, matchmark the driveshaft and slide the splined transmission yoke so that the driveline balance is preserved upon reassembly. Remove the snaprings that retain the bearing caps.

3. Select 2 sockets, use impact sockets preferably, with 1 small enough to pass through the yoke holes for the bearing caps and the other large enough to receive the bearing cap.

4. Use a vise or a press and position the small and large sockets on either side of the U-joint. Press in on the smaller socket so it presses the opposite bearing cap out of the yoke and into the larger socket. If the cap does not come all the way out, grasp it with a pair of pliers and work it out.

5. Reverse the position of the sockets so that the smaller socket presses on the cross. Press the other bearing cap out of the yoke.

6. Repeat the procedure on the other bearings.

To install:

7. Grease the bearing caps and needles thoroughly if they are not pregreased. Start a new bearing cap into a side of the yoke. Position the cross in the yoke.

NOTE: Some U-joints have a grease fitting that must be installed in the joint before assembly. When installing the fitting, make sure that once the driveshaft is in- stalled in the vehicle that the fitting is accessible to be greased at a later date.

8. Select 2 sockets small enough to pass through the yoke holes. Put the sockets against the cross and the cap and press the bearing cap ¼ in. below the surface of the yoke. If there is a sudden increase in the force needed to press the cap into place or if the cross starts to bind, the bearings are cocked. They must be removed and restarted in the yoke. Failure to do so will cause premature bearing failure.

9. Install a new snapring.

10. Start the new bearing into the opposite side. Place a socket on it and press in until the opposite bearing contacts the snapring.

11. Install a new snapring. It may be necessary to grind the facing surface of the snapring slightly to permit easier installation.

12. Install the other bearings in the same manner.

13. Check the joint for free movement. If binding exists, smack the yoke ears with a brass or plastic faced hammer to seat the bearing needles. If binding still exists, disassemble the joint and check to see if the needles are in place. Do not strike the bearings unless the shaft is supported firmly. Do not install the driveshaft until free movement exists at all joints.

PLASTIC RETAINER TYPE

Remove and install the bearing caps and trunnion cross. On an original universal joint, the bearing caps will be secured in the yokes with injected plastic. The plastic will shear when the bearing caps are pressed. Service snaprings are installed in the groove on the inside (of yoke) of the installed caps.

NOTE: The plastic which retains the bearing will be sheared when the bearing cup is pressed out. Be sure to remove all remains of the plastic retainer from the ears of the yoke. It is easier to remove the remains if a small pin or punch is 1st driven through the injection holes in the yoke. Failure to remove all of the plastic remains may prevent the bearing cups from being pressed into place and the bearing retainers from being properly seated.

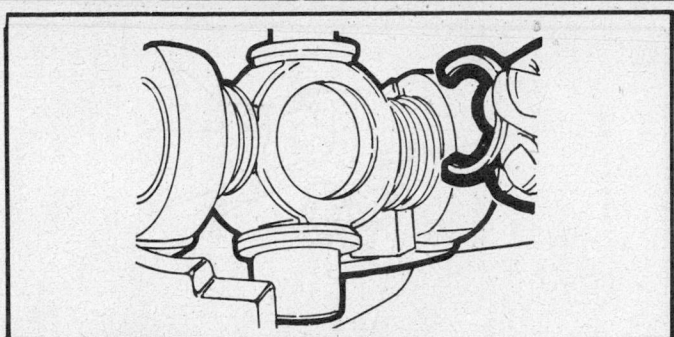

Service snap rings are installed

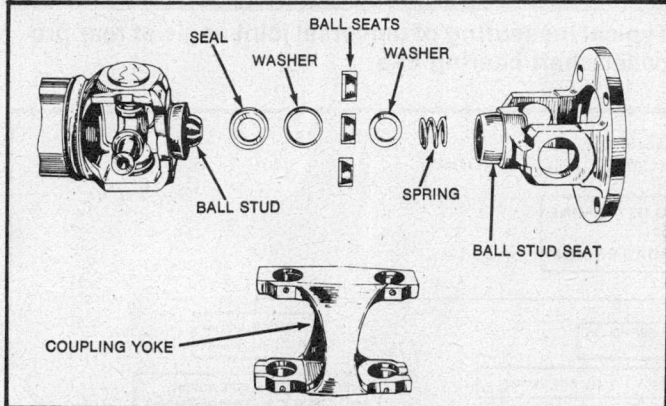

Constant velocity joint

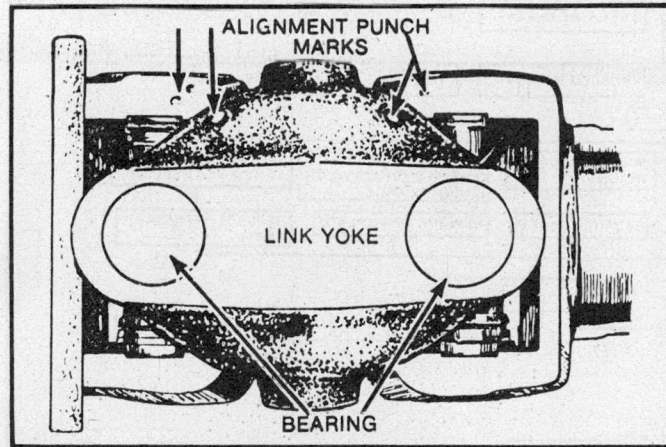

Match marks for double cardan joint

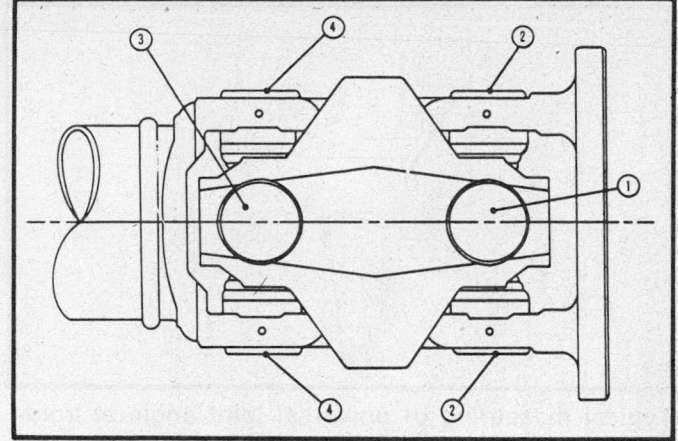

C.V. joint disassembly sequence

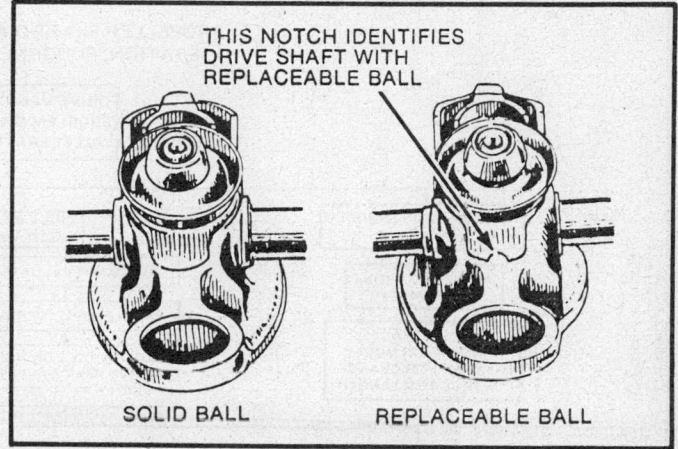

Solid and replaceable U-joint balls

CONSTANT VELOCITY JOINT

Ford and Chrysler products with constant velocity joints use snaprings to retain the bearing cups in the yokes. Most General Motors cars have plastic retainers. Be sure to obtain the correct rebuilding kit.

Overhaul

1. Use a punch to mark the coupling yoke and the adjoining yokes before disassembly to ensure proper reassembly and driveline balance.
2. Remove the bearings from the coupling yoke.
3. Support the driveshaft horizontally on a press stand or a the workbench if a vise is being used.

4. Remove the snaprings if they are used to retain the bearings cups. Place the rear ear of the coupling yoke over a socket large enough to receive the cup. Place a smaller socket or a cross press made for the purpose, over the opposite cup. Press the bearing cup out of the coupling yoke ear. If the cup is not completely removed, insert a spacer and complete the operation or grasp the cup with a pair of slip joint pliers and work it out. If the cups are retained by plastic, this will shear the retainers. Remove any bits of plastic.
5. Rotate the driveshaft and repeat the operation on the opposite cup.
6. Disengage the trunnions of the spider, still attached to the flanged yoke, from the coupling yoke and pull the flanged yoke and spider from the center ball on the ball support tube yoke.

NOTE: The joint between the shaft and coupling yoke can be serviced without disassembly of the joint between the coupling yoke and flanged yoke.

7. Pry the seal from the ball cavity and remove the washers, spring and 3 seats. Examine the ball stud seat and the ball stud for signs of scoring or wear. Worn parts can be replaced with a kit. Clean the ball seat cavity and fill it with grease. Install the spring, washer, ball seats and spacer washer over the ball.
8. To assemble, insert a bearing cup part way into an ear of the ball support tube yoke and turn this cup to the bottom.
9. Insert the spider cross into the tube yoke so the trunnion arm seats freely in the cup.
10. Install the opposite cup part way, making sure that both cups are straight.

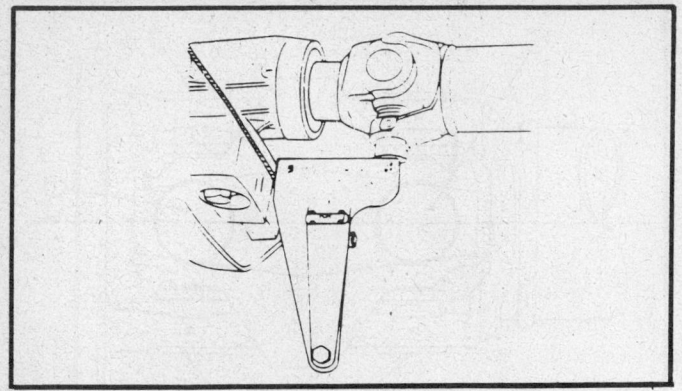

Typical measuring of universal joint angle at front propeller shaft bearing cap

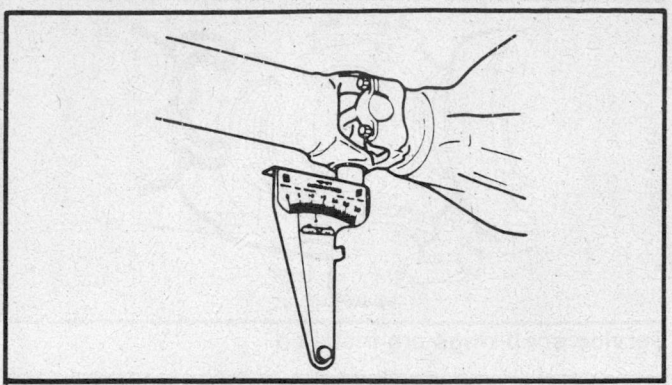

Typical measuring of universal joint angle at rear propeller shaft bearing cap

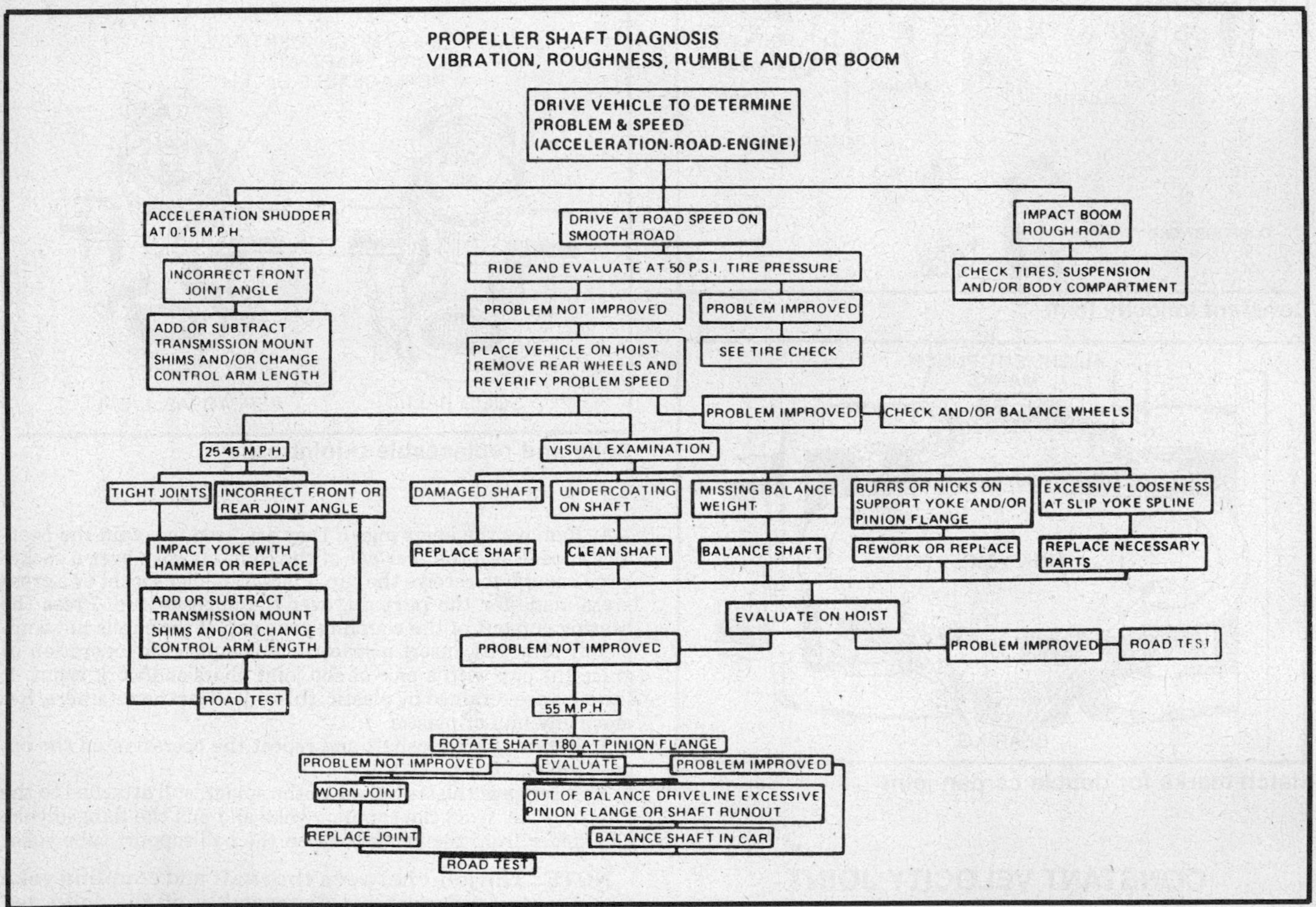

PROPELLER SHAFT DIAGNOSIS
VIBRATION, ROUGHNESS, RUMBLE AND/OR BOOM

DRIVE VEHICLE TO DETERMINE PROBLEM & SPEED (ACCELERATION-ROAD-ENGINE)

ACCELERATION SHUDDER AT 0-15 M.P.H.
INCORRECT FRONT JOINT ANGLE
ADD OR SUBTRACT TRANSMISSION MOUNT SHIMS AND/OR CHANGE CONTROL ARM LENGTH

DRIVE AT ROAD SPEED ON SMOOTH ROAD
RIDE AND EVALUATE AT 50 P.S.I. TIRE PRESSURE
PROBLEM NOT IMPROVED
PROBLEM IMPROVED
SEE TIRE CHECK
PLACE VEHICLE ON HOIST, REMOVE REAR WHEELS AND REVERIFY PROBLEM SPEED
PROBLEM IMPROVED — CHECK AND/OR BALANCE WHEELS

IMPACT BOOM ROUGH ROAD
CHECK TIRES, SUSPENSION AND/OR BODY COMPARTMENT

25-45 M.P.H.
TIGHT JOINTS | INCORRECT FRONT OR REAR JOINT ANGLE
IMPACT YOKE WITH HAMMER OR REPLACE
ADD OR SUBTRACT TRANSMISSION MOUNT SHIMS AND/OR CHANGE CONTROL ARM LENGTH
ROAD TEST

VISUAL EXAMINATION
DAMAGED SHAFT | UNDERCOATING ON SHAFT | MISSING BALANCE WEIGHT | BURRS OR NICKS ON SUPPORT YOKE AND/OR PINION FLANGE | EXCESSIVE LOOSENESS AT SLIP YOKE SPLINE
REPLACE SHAFT | CLEAN SHAFT | BALANCE SHAFT | REWORK OR REPLACE | REPLACE NECESSARY PARTS
EVALUATE ON HOIST
PROBLEM IMPROVED — ROAD TEST
PROBLEM NOT IMPROVED
55 M.P.H.
ROTATE SHAFT 180 AT PINION FLANGE
PROBLEM NOT IMPROVED | EVALUATE | PROBLEM IMPROVED
WORN JOINT | OUT OF BALANCE DRIVELINE EXCESSIVE PINION FLANGE OR SHAFT RUNOUT
REPLACE JOINT | BALANCE SHAFT IN CAR
ROAD TEST

Propeller shaft diagnosis

11. Press the cups into position, making sure both cups squarely engage the spider. Back them off if there is a sudden increase in resistance, indicating that a cup is cocked or a needle bearing is out of place.

12. As soon as a bearing retainer groove clears the yoke, stop and install the retainer on plastic retainer models. On models with snaprings, press the cups into place and install the snaprings over the cups.

13. If difficulty is encountered installing the plastic retainers or snaprings, smack the yoke sharply with a hammer to spring the ears slightly.

14. Install a bearing cup part way into the ear of the coupling yoke. Make sure that the alignment marks are matched, engage the coupling yoke over the spider and press in the cups. Install the retainers or snaprings.

15. Install the cups and spider into the flanged yoke as done with the previous yoke.

NOTE: The flange yoke should snap over center to the right or left and up or down by the pressure of the ball seat spring.

NOTE:
RUN OUT SHOULD NOT
EXCEED 1mm (.040 IN.)
105mm
(4.0 IN.)
105mm
(4.0 IN.)
105mm
(4.0 IN.)
FRT
105mm
(4.0 IN.)

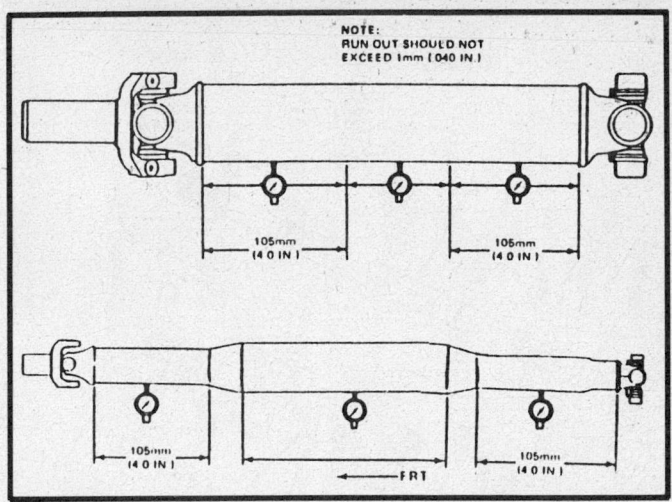

Allowable propeller shaft runout on two different type shafts

ROTATING CLAMP HEADS
AWAY FROM EACH OTHER
REAR U-JOINT
HOSE CLAMP HEADS
180° FROM CRAYON
MARK
CRAYON MARK

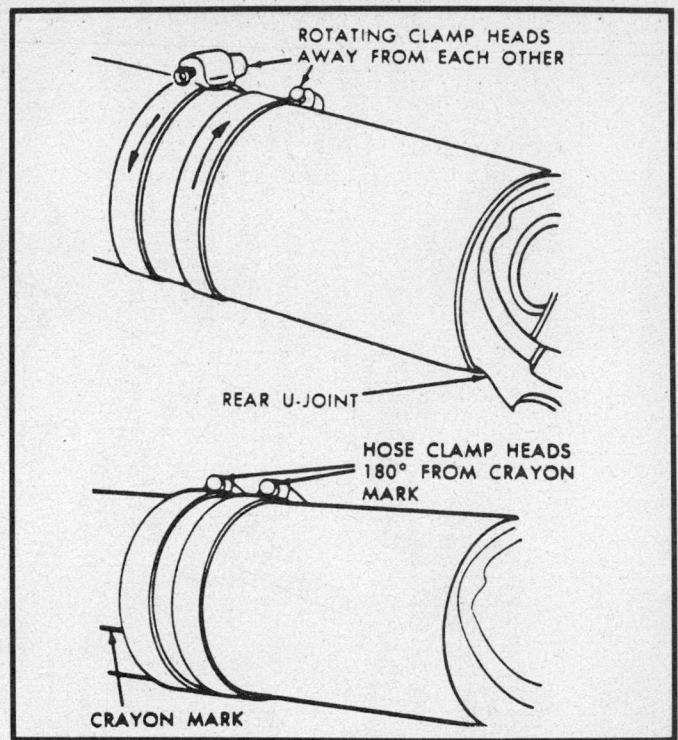

Rotation of hose clamps to balance a propeller shaft. A third clamp may be needed, but the shaft should be replaced if balancing cannot be accomplished

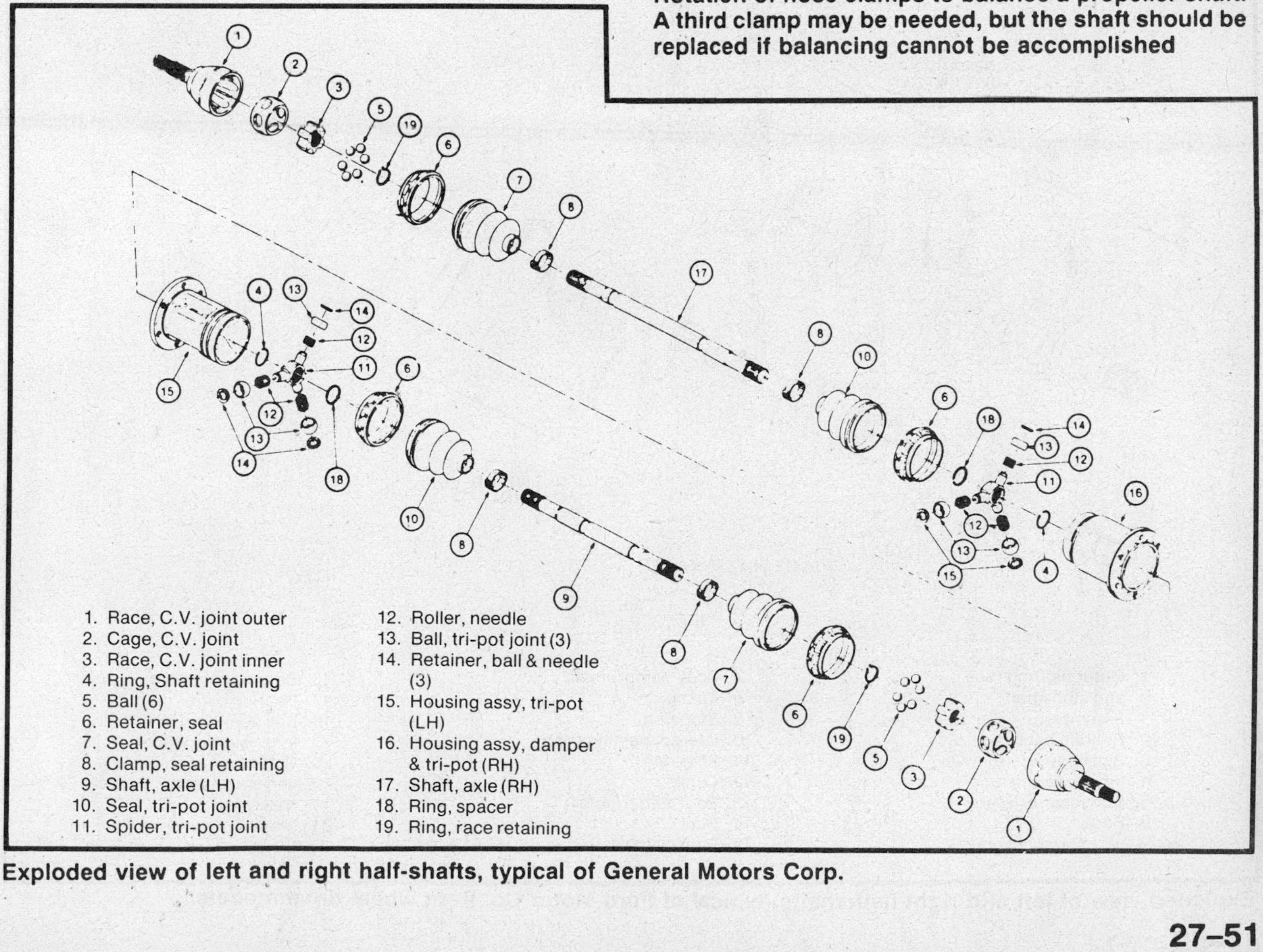

1. Race, C.V. joint outer
2. Cage, C.V. joint
3. Race, C.V. joint inner
4. Ring, Shaft retaining
5. Ball (6)
6. Retainer, seal
7. Seal, C.V. joint
8. Clamp, seal retaining
9. Shaft, axle (LH)
10. Seal, tri-pot joint
11. Spider, tri-pot joint
12. Roller, needle
13. Ball, tri-pot joint (3)
14. Retainer, ball & needle (3)
15. Housing assy, tri-pot (LH)
16. Housing assy, damper & tri-pot (RH)
17. Shaft, axle (RH)
18. Ring, spacer
19. Ring, race retaining

Exploded view of left and right half-shafts, typical of General Motors Corp.

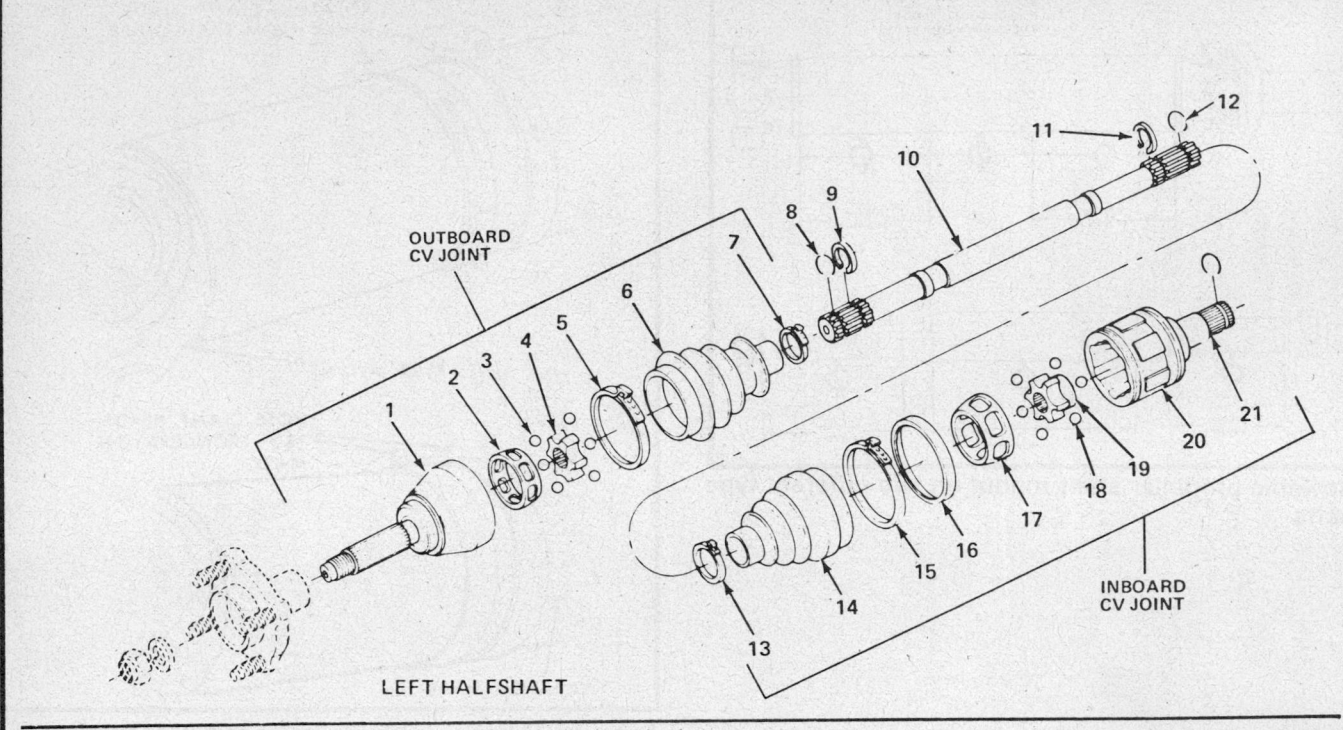

LEFT HALFSHAFT

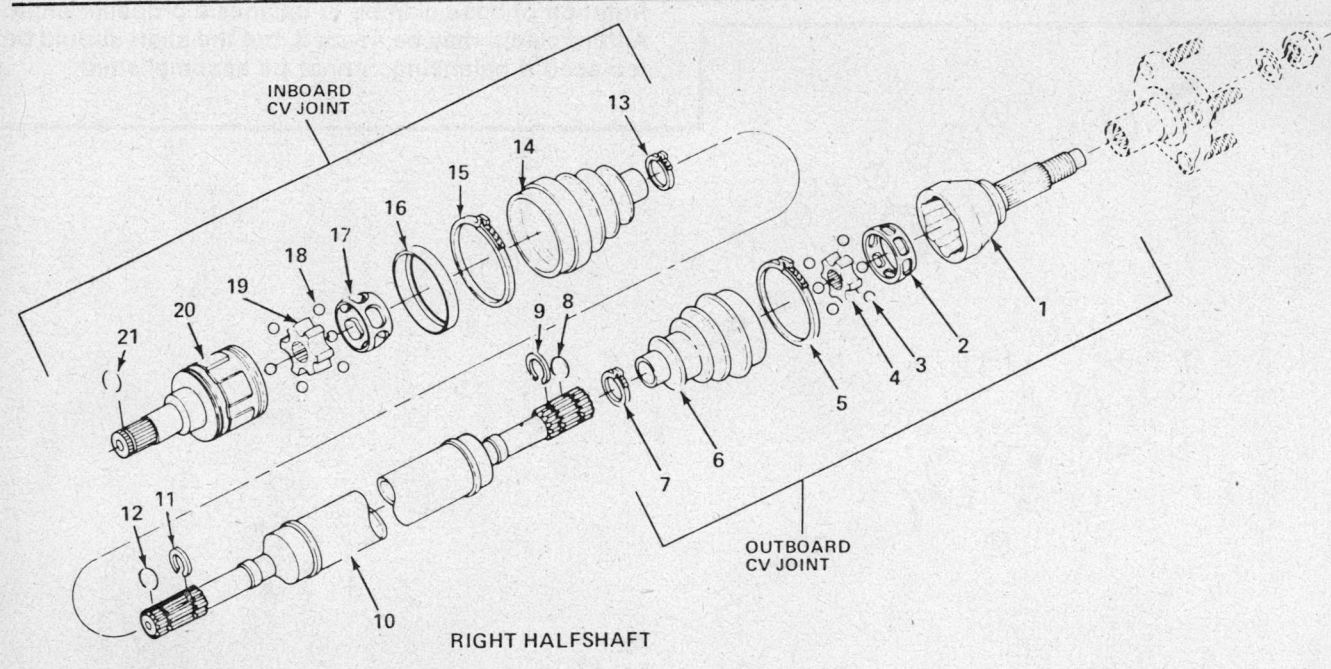

RIGHT HALFSHAFT

1. Outer bearing race
   and stub shaft
   assembly
2. Bearing cage
3. Ball bearings (6)
4. Inner bearing race
5. Boot clamp (large)
6. Boot

7. Boot clamp (small)
8. Circlip
9. Stop ring
10. Interconnecting shaft
11. Stop ring
12. Circlip
13. Boot clamp (small)
14. Boot
15. Boot clamp (large)

16. Bearing retainer
17. Bearing cage
18. Ball bearings (6)
19. Inner bearing race
20. Outer bearing race
    and stub shaft
    assembly
21. Circlip

Exploded view of left and right half-shafts, typical of Ford Motor Co. front wheel drive models

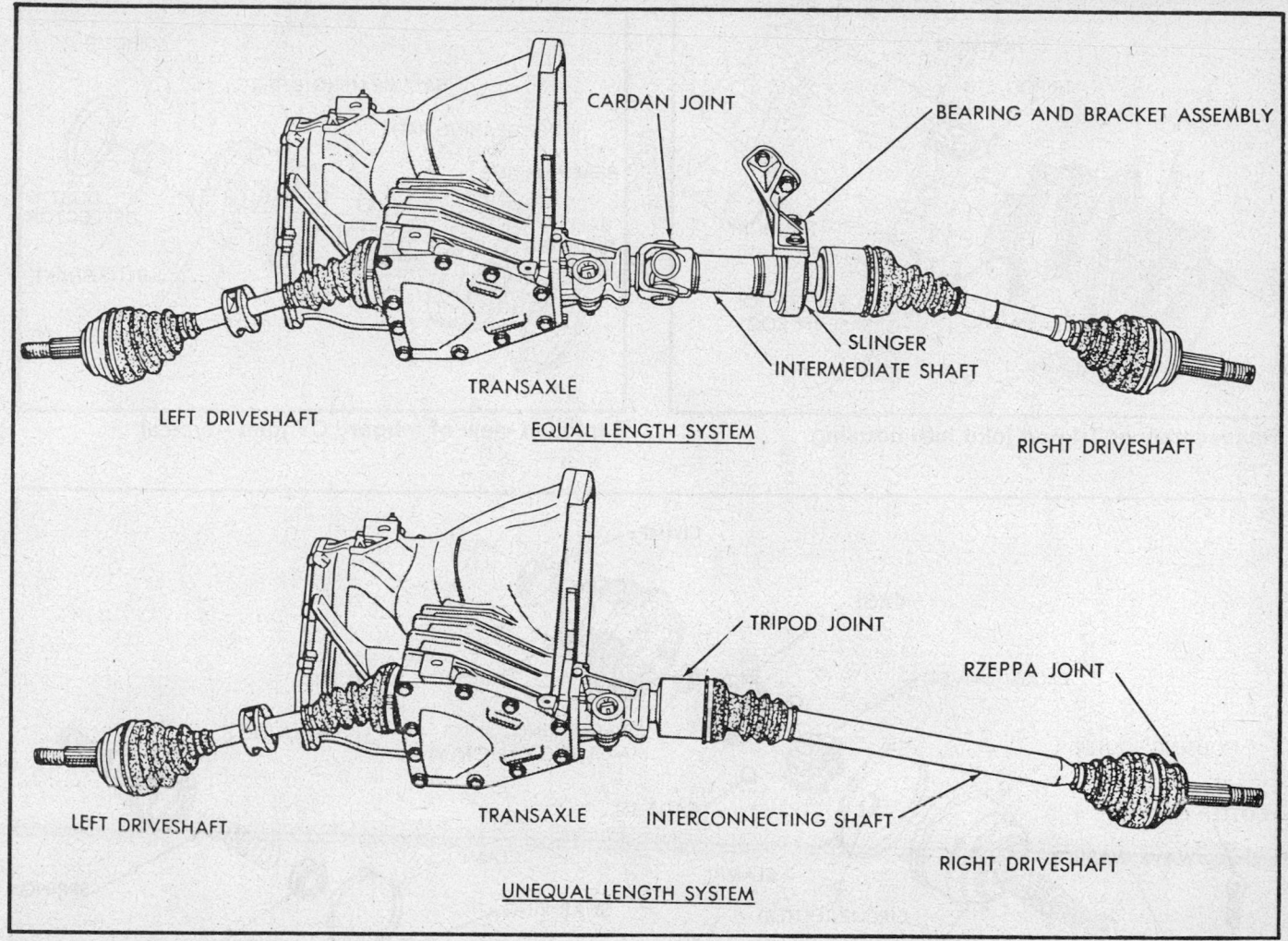

Typical front wheel drive system

Front Wheel Drive

GENERAL INFORMATION

Natural drive line vibrations are created by the fluctuations in the speed of the halfshaft as the drive line angle is changed during a single revolution of the shaft. The halfshafts and universal joints must transfer the driving power to the front wheels and at the same time, compensate for steering action on turns. Two special universal joints are used, one a constant velocity CV or double offset type and a second type known as the Tri-pot joint.

The constant velocity joint or CV joint, uses rolling balls that move in and out of curved grooves to obtain a uniformed motion. As the joint rotates in the driving or steering motion, the balls, which are in driving contact between the 2 halves of the joint coupling, remain in a plane which bisects the angle between the 2 shafts, cancelling out the fluctuations of speed in the driveshaft.

The Tripot type uses a 3 legged spider with needle bearings and balls incased in a 3 grooved housing. With the spider attached to the halfshaft, the joint assembly is free to roll back and forth in the housing grooves as the shaft length varies during normal drive line operation.

The front halfshafts are normally 2 different lengths from the transaxle to the drive wheels. This is due to the mounting location of the engine/transaxle in the vehicle. Mark the halfshafts

locations when removing or replacing them. When removing the halfshafts, handle them carefully so as not to damage the boots covering the universal joints or if equipped, with boots covering the transaxle halfshaft opening. Should the boots become torn or damaged, replace the boots before reinstalling the halfshafts. Premature failure of the universal joint would result due to the loss of lubricant and the entrance of contaminates if the boots are not replaced.

ATTACHMENT OF THE HALFSHAFT TO THE TRANSAXLE

NOTE: The halfshafts are attached to the transaxle in a various ways. If not familiar with the particular shaft attachment, do not pry or hammer until the correct procedure is known.

The shafts can be attached by one of the following methods:
1. Halfshaft flange to transaxle stub shaft flange, bolted together. Mark the flanges and remove the bolts.
2. Circlips inside the differential housing. Remove the differential cover, compress the circlips and push the axle shaft outward.
3. Spring loaded circlip mounted in a groove on the axle shaft and mating with a groove in the differential gear splines. It is usually pried or tapped from differential gear with care.

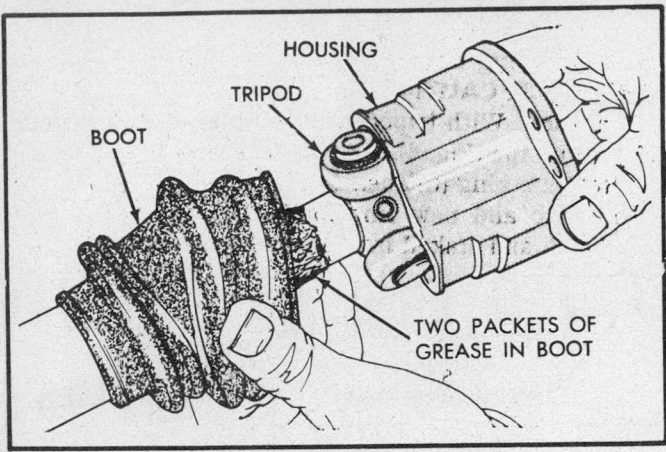

Reassembly of Tri-pod joint into housing

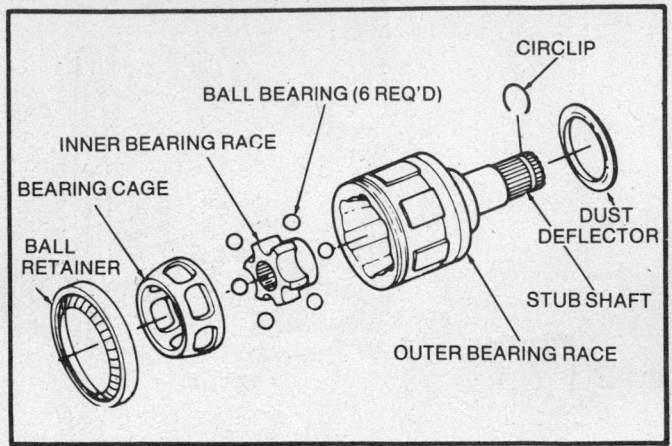

Exploded view of inboard CV joint – typical

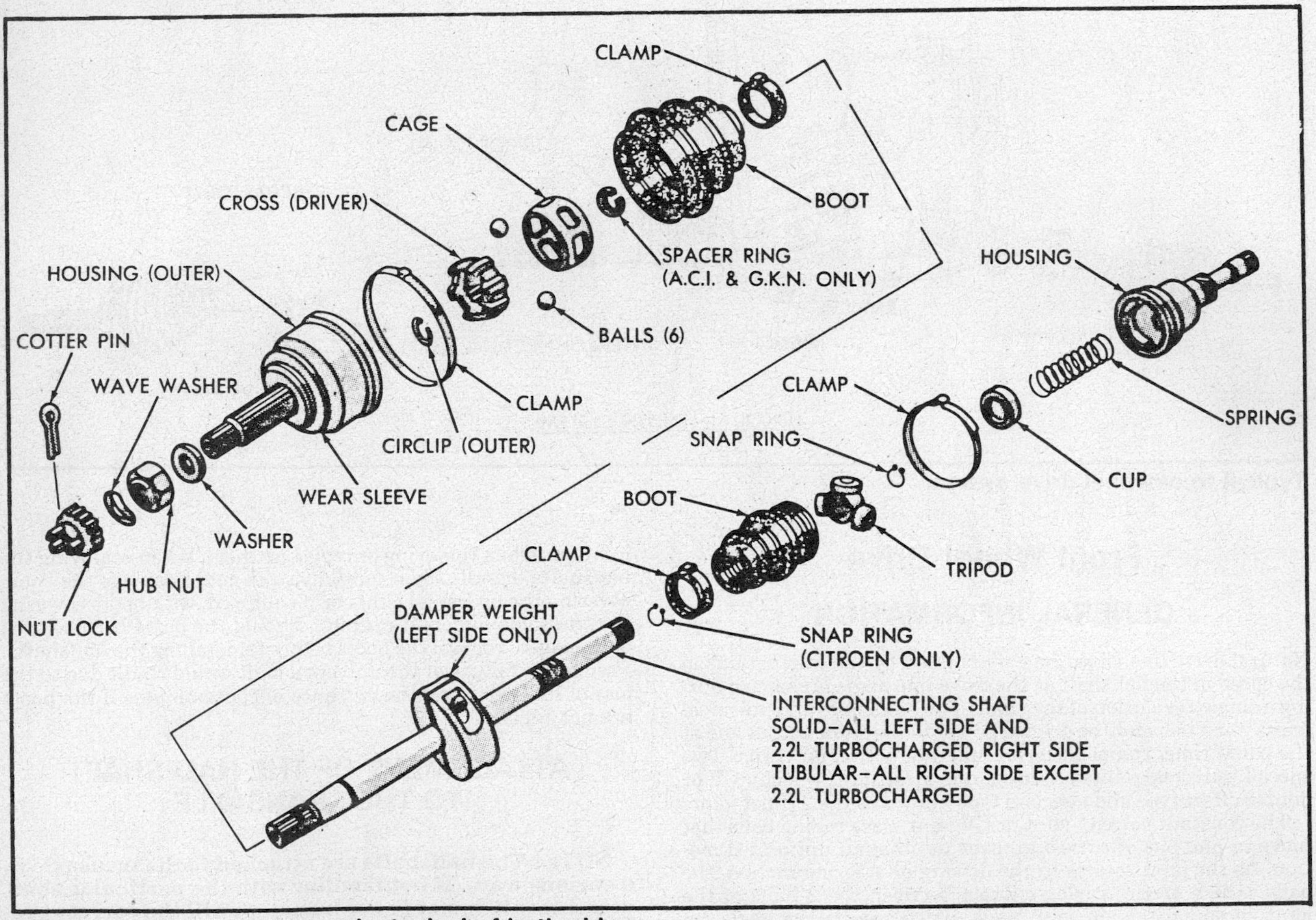

Exploded view of the drive axle, typical of both sides

4. Universal joint housing, the axle shaft flange or axle shaft stub end is pinned to either the differential stub shaft or the differential gear flange with a roll pin. Mark the 2 components and drive the pin from the units.

BOOT REPLACEMENT

One of the most common repairs to the front halfshafts are CV-joint boot and retaining ring replacements. Many repair shops are requested to perform this type of repairs for their customers. OEM and after market replacement boots are available, with special tools used to crimp and tighten the retaining rings. Most boot replacement procedures require the removal of the halfshafts and disassembly of the joint assembly. A boot kit is available that provides a split boot that can be installed without halfshaft removal. The boot is sealed with a special adhesive along its length and the procedure is finished with the installation of the boot retaining rings.

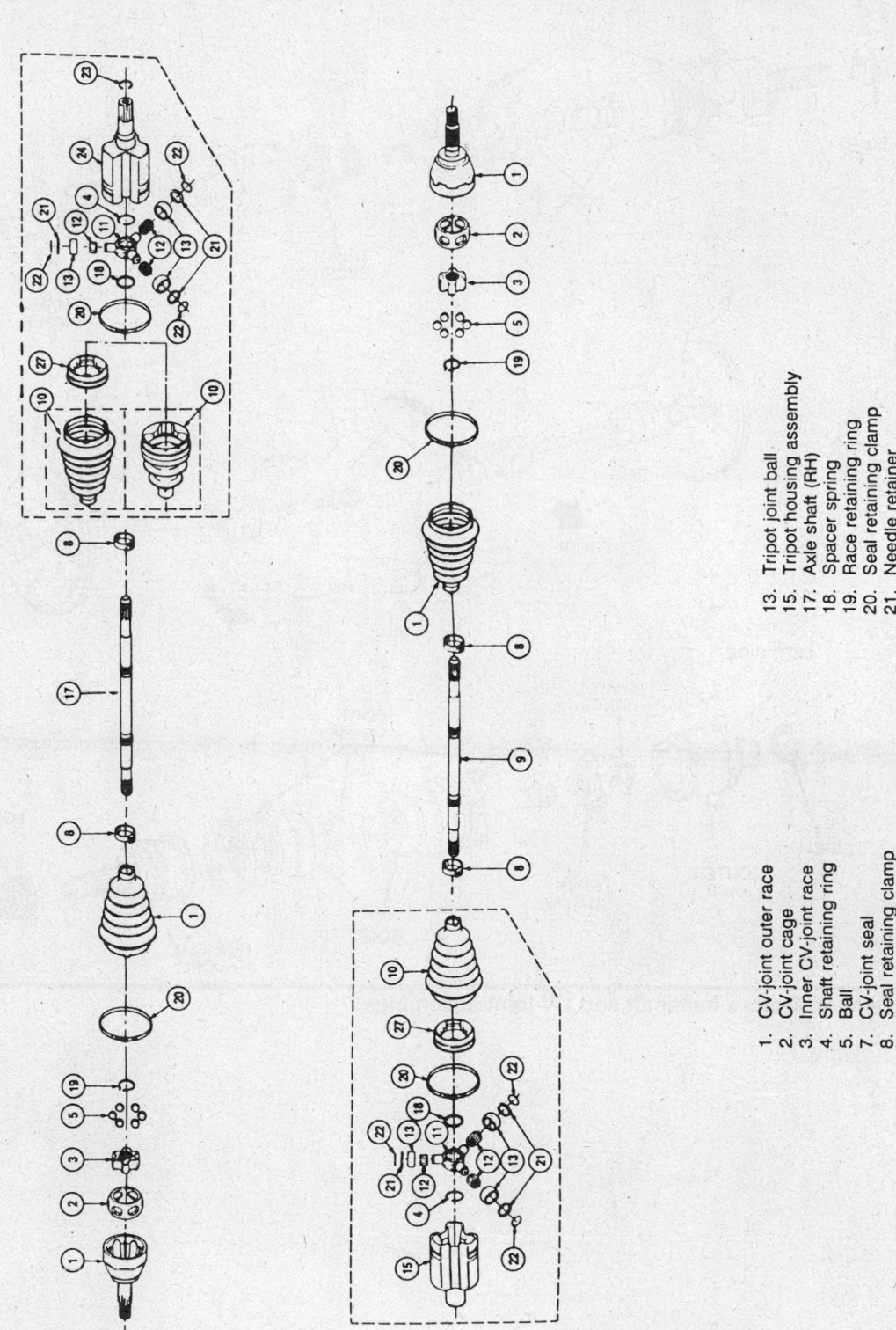

1. CV-joint outer race
2. CV-joint cage
3. Inner CV-joint race
4. Shaft retaining ring
5. Ball
7. CV-joint seal
8. Seal retaining clamp
9. Axle shaft (LH)
10. Tripot joint seal
11. Tripot joint spider
12. Needle roller
13. Tripot joint ball
15. Tripot housing assembly
17. Axle shaft (RH)
18. Spacer spring
19. Race retaining ring
20. Seal retaining clamp
21. Needle retainer
22. Needle retainer ring
23. Joint retaining ring
24. Tripot housing
27. Trilobal Tripot bushing

1989–90 Ford halfshaft and CV-joint assemblies

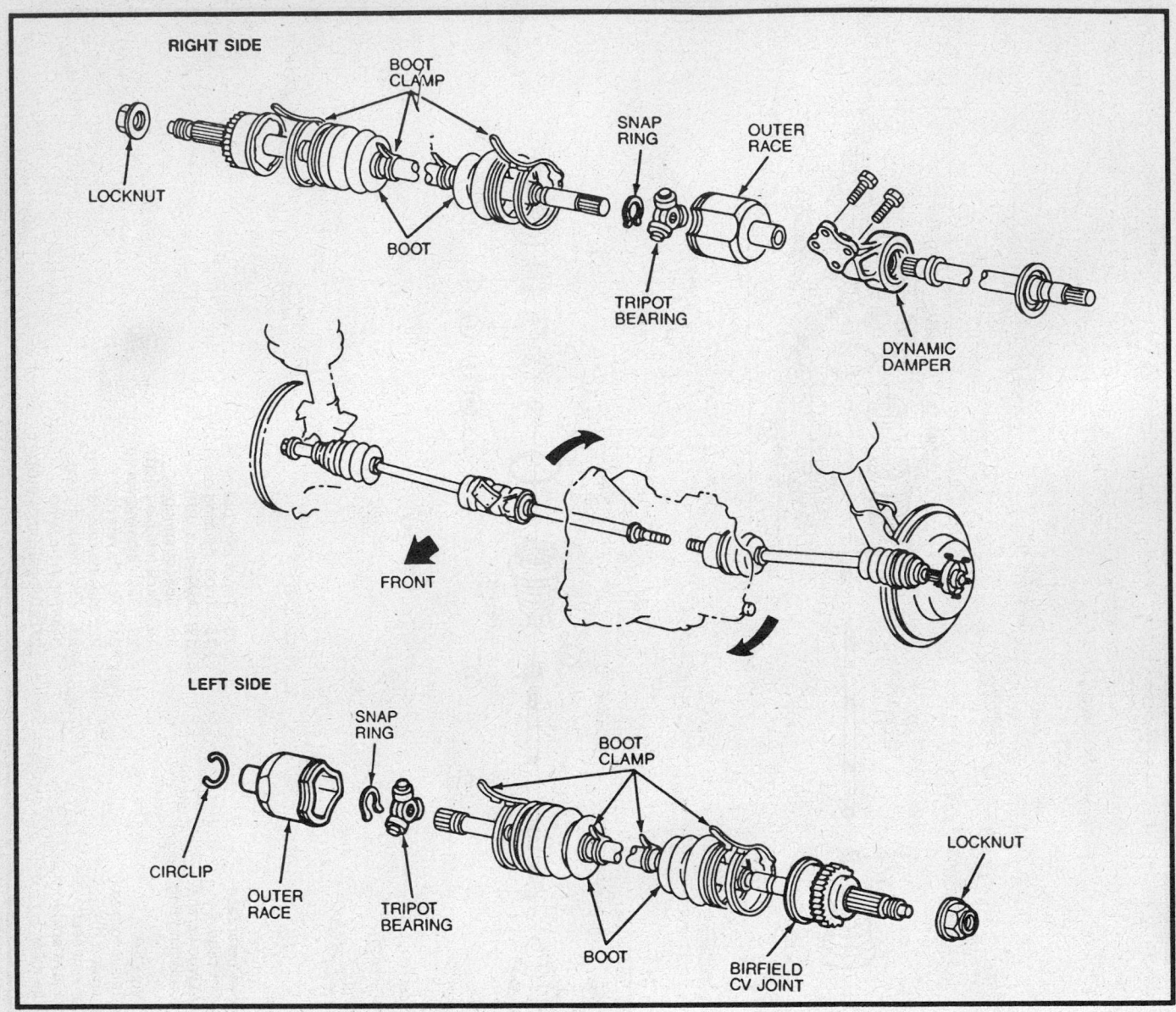

RIGHT SIDE

LOCKNUT

BOOT CLAMP

BOOT

SNAP RING

TRIPOT BEARING

OUTER RACE

DYNAMIC DAMPER

FRONT

LEFT SIDE

SNAP RING

CIRCLIP

OUTER RACE

TRIPOT BEARING

BOOT CLAMP

BOOT

LOCKNUT

BIRFIELD CV JOINT

1989–90 General Motors halfshaft and CV-joint assembles

AMERICAN MOTORS COMPUTERIZED EMISSION CONTROL SYSTEM

General Information

The Computerized Emission Control system (CEC) is used on both 4 and 6 cylinder engines to maintain the ideal air/fuel ratio to provide an optimum balance between emission and engine performance.

This is accomplished by the use of a microcomputer unit (MCU), several MCU input components and several MCU output components. The MCU monitors various engine operating conditions and based on these conditions, the MCU may, depending upon the mode of operation, generate output signals to provide the proper air/fuel mixture, proper ignition timing and engine speed.

Two modes of operation are used, the open loop and the closed loop. In open loop, the air/fuel ratio is predetermined by the MCU for a number of engine operating conditions, such as start up, cold engine operation or Wide Open Throttle (WOT) position. The closed loop system is used when the air/fuel ratio is varied, according to the oxygen content in the exhaust gas. When the engine is started, the MCU determines which mode of operation is initiated, either open or closed loop, by monitoring the input signals from the various input components, such as the air and coolant temperature information, engine rpm information and vacuum levels.

If the MCU determines that the engine control system should be operated in the open loop mode, the engine's operation is based on priority ratings for the various predetermined engine operating conditions. It will continue to operate the system in the open loop mode until such time as a closed loop mode of operation is indicated.

At this time, the MCU shifts the operation to the closed loop mode. Based on oxygen content of the exhaust gas and other inputs, it continues to operate the system in the closed loop mode, constantly varying the air/fuels ratio to obtain the optimum 14.7:1 ratio.

As the engine operating conditions are constantly monitored by the MCU, any change in conditions, such as the engine being placed in the wide open throttle position, is immediately detected by the MCU and the engine is appropriately placed into the open loop mode until the WOT position is relieved and the engine would then return the the closed loop mode.

INPUT DATA SENSORS

Oxygen sensor
Thermal electric switch
Coolant temperature switch
4 in. Hg. vacuum switch
10 in. Hg. vacuum switch
Wide open throttle switch
Closed throttle switch
Knock sensor
Distributor
Altitude jumper wire

OUTPUT COMPONENTS

Mixture control solenoid (4 cylinder)
Stepper motor (6 cylinder)
Idle relay
Idle solenoid
Upstream and downstream air switch solenoids
Positive crankcase ventilation valve shut-off solenoid
Sole-vac throttle positioner
Bowl vent solenoid

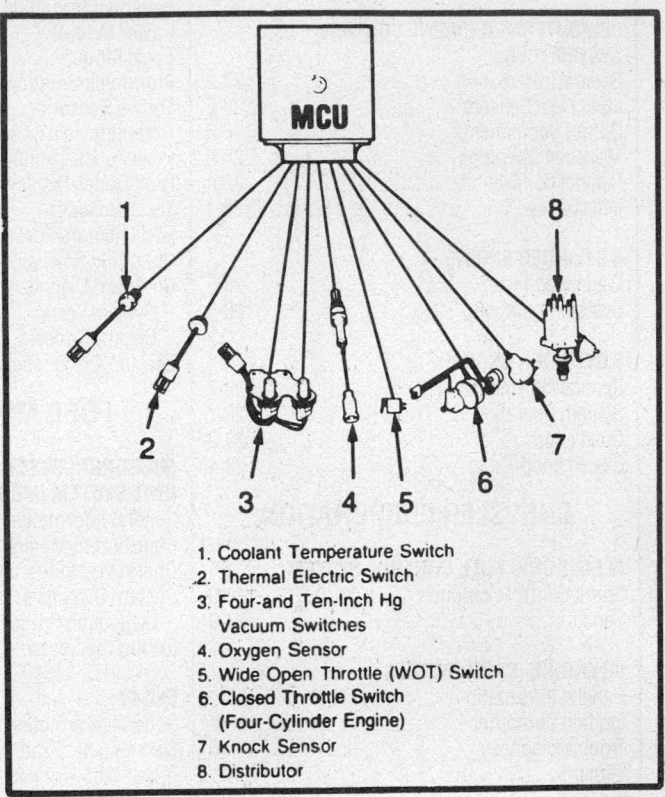

1. Coolant Temperature Switch
2. Thermal Electric Switch
3. Four-and Ten-Inch Hg Vacuum Switches
4. Oxygen Sensor
5. Wide Open Throttle (WOT) Switch
6. Closed Throttle Switch (Four-Cylinder Engine)
7. Knock Sensor
8. Distributor

MCU input components

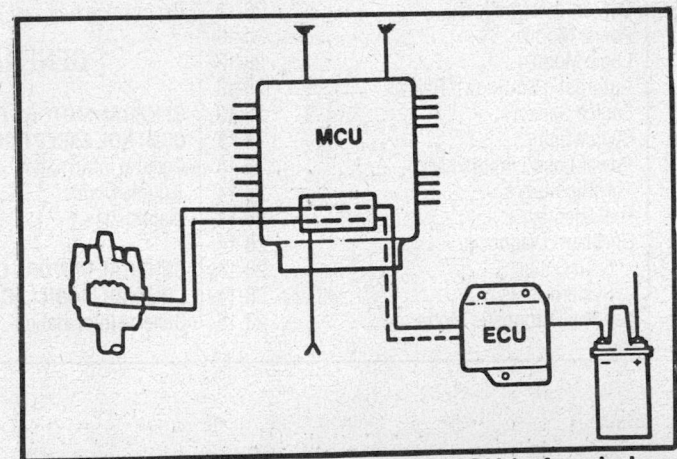

Electronic Ignition circuit through MCU before being routed to ECU

Intake manifold heater switch

MODES OF OPERATION

Each engine has 4 modes of operation for the fuel feedback system. They are as follows:
1. Key-on mode
2. Start-up mode
3. Warm-up mode
4. Cruise mode

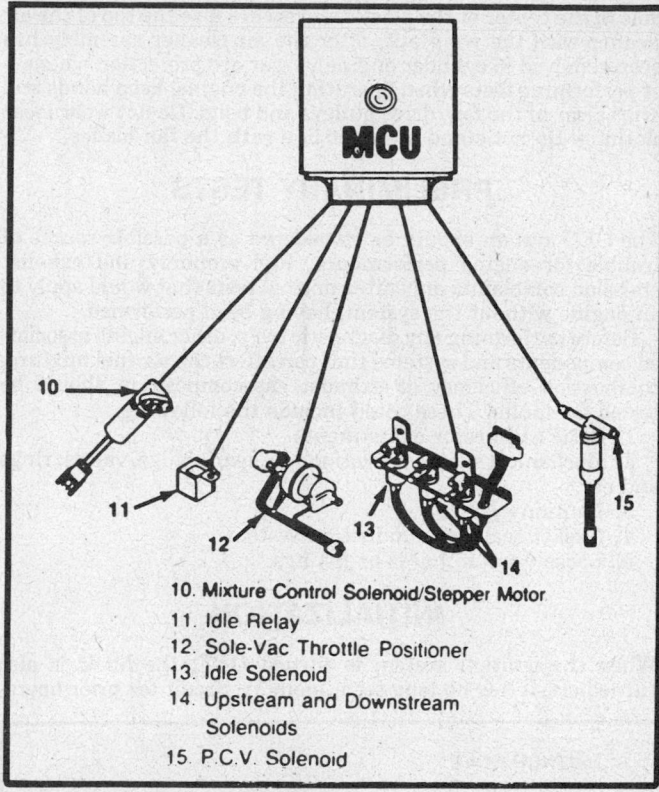

10. Mixture Control Solenoid/Stepper Motor
11. Idle Relay
12. Sole-Vac Throttle Positioner
13. Idle Solenoid
14. Upstream and Downstream Solenoids
15. P.C.V. Solenoid

MCU output components

KEY-ON MODE

In the key-on mode, the system operates as follows:
1. The ignition switch is in the **ON** position.
2. The MCU is energized.
3. The bowl vent solenoid is energized.
4. The Sole-Vac holding solenoid is energized.
5. The idle relay is activated by voltage applied, although there is no ground supplied.
6. The PCV valve shut-off solenoid is energized by the MCU via the anti-diesel relay (4 cylinder engines).

START-UP MODE

In the start-up mode, the system operates as follows:
1. The key is in the **START** position.
2. The starter motor solenoid is energized.
3. The choke relay is energized by alternator voltage output.
4. The intake manifold heater switch is closed to activate the heater, if the coolant is cold.
5. The starting signal is provided to the MCU.
6. The engine rpm voltage from the distributor is provided to the MCU.
7. The MCU controls the ignition timing.

WARM-UP MODE

In the warm-up mode, the system operates as follows:
1. The system is in the open loop mode operation.
2. The MCU receives varied inputs.
3. The 4 in. Hg. vacuum switch is open if the ported vacuum is less than 4 in. Hg.
4. The 10 in. Hg. vacuum switch is closed below 10 in. Hg. vacuum level and open above 10 in. Hg. vacuum level.
5. The coolant temperature switch closes at 135°F.
6. The wide open throttle (WOT) switch is open.
7. Thermal electric switch opens at 65°F.
8. The closed throttle switch is closed (4 cylinder engine).
9. Manifold heater switch opens at 160°F.

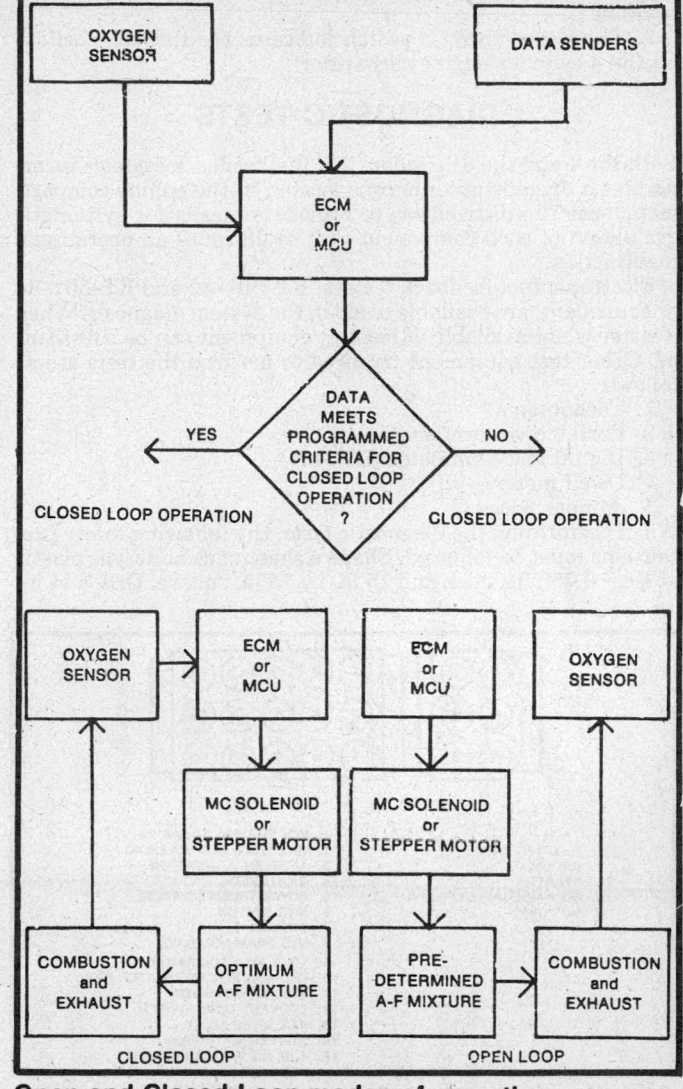

Open and Closed Loop modes of operation

10. The stepper motor or mixture control solenoid is controlled by the MCU to provide a pre-programmed amount of air for the air/fuel mixture.
11. Upstream and downstream solenoids are controlled by the MCU to distribute air to either the exhaust of the catalytic converter.
12. The Sole-vac vacuum actuator unit is activated if the headlamps or certain accessories (such as the air conditioning or rear window defogger) are in operation. It is also activated when the steering wheel is turned to the full-stop position on the 4 cylinder engine, if equipped with power steering.

CRUISE MODE

In the cruise mode, the system operates as follows:
1. The system is in the closed loop mode of operation.
2. The MCU is producing output information.
3. The components are controlled as in the warm-up mode.
4. The oxygen sensor input is being accepted by the MCU.
5. The MCU controls the stepper motor or mixture control solenoid, according to the inputs.
6. The MCU may receive input from the knock sensor to advance or retard the ignition timing.
7. Upstream and downstream solenoids route air to the exhaust pipe or catalytic converter.

8. The wide open throttle (WOT) switch indicates the throttle position.

9. The closed throttle switch indicates the throttle position on the 4 cylinder engine carburetor.

DIAGNOSTIC TESTS

Both the 4 and the 6 cylinder CEC fuel feedback systems incorporates a diagnostic connector, located in the engine compartment near the distributor, to provide a means for systematic evaluation of each component that could cause an operational malfunction.

Electronic fuel feedback testers, ET–501–82 and ET–501–84 or equivalent, are available to aid in the system diagnosis. When a tester is not available, other test equipment can be substituted. Other test equipment required to perform the tests are as follows:

1. Tachometer
2. Portable vacuum source
3. Digital volt-ohmmeter (DVOM)
4. Dwell meter
5. Jumper wires

When performing the diagnostic tests, the following safety precautions must be followed. Shape a sheet of clear acrylic plastic at least 0.250 in. thick and 15 in. by 15 in. square. Drill a ¼ in.

hole in the center of the plastic and secure it to the top of the air cleaner with the wing nut, after the air cleaner assembly has been removed (6 cylinder engine). Wear eye protection whenever performing tests when operating the engine, keep hands and arms clear of the fan, drive pulleys and belts. Do not wear loose clothing. Do not stand in direct line with the fan blades.

PRELIMINARY TESTS

The CEC system should be considered as a possible source of trouble for engine performance, fuel economy and exhaust emission complaints only after normal tests that would apply to an engine without the system, having been performed.

Before performing any diagnostic tests, other engine associated components and systems that can effect the air/fuel mixture, combustion efficiency or exhaust gas composition should be tested for faults. These could include the following:

1. Basic carburetor adjustments
2. Mechanical engine operation (i.e. spark plugs, valves, rings and etc.)
3. Ignition system
4. Gasket sealing on induction system
5. Loose vacuum hoses or fittings.

INITIALIZATION

When the ignition system is turned **OFF**, the MCU is also turned off. It has no long term memory circuit for prior opera-

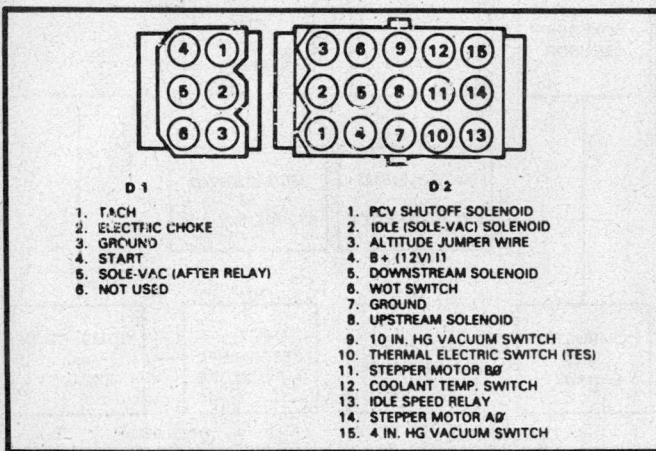

```
D1
1. TACH
2. ELECTRIC CHOKE
3. GROUND
4. START
5. SOLE-VAC (AFTER RELAY)
6. NOT USED

D2
1. PCV SHUTOFF SOLENOID
2. IDLE (SOLE-VAC) SOLENOID
3. ALTITUDE JUMPER WIRE
4. B+ (12V) I1
5. DOWNSTREAM SOLENOID
6. WOT SWITCH
7. GROUND
8. UPSTREAM SOLENOID
9. 10 IN. HG VACUUM SWITCH
10. THERMAL ELECTRIC SWITCH (TES)
11. STEPPER MOTOR BØ
12. COOLANT TEMP. SWITCH
13. IDLE SPEED RELAY
14. STEPPER MOTOR AØ
15. 4 IN. HG VACUUM SWITCH
```

CEC diagnostic connector usage – 6 cylinder engine

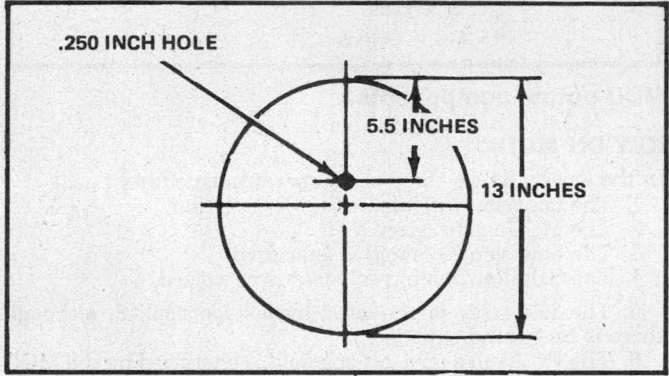

Fabricating plastic cover for the top of 6 cylinder engine

D2 Pin	Function	Definition	MCU Pin	D1 Pin	Function
1	PCV Shut-Off Sol.	High Current 2	J1-18	1	Tach
2	Shift Light*	Aux 1*	J1-15	2	Electric Choke
3	Altitude Jumper Wire	B4	J2-15	3	Body Gnd.
4	I_1 Power	Power	J2-11 & 12	4	Start
5	Downstream Sol.	Aux 3	J1-11	5	Idle Solenoid
6	WOT Switch	B3	J2-10	6	Not Used
7	Ground	Ground	J2-1 & 2		
8	Upstream Sol.	Aux 4	J1-13		**Definition**
9	10 in. Hg Vac. Sw.	B2	J2-8		Ign. Coil Neg. —
10	Thermal Elect. Sw.	B5	J2-14		After Oil Pres. Sw. —
11	Sole-Vac Solenoid	I_3 Power	—		Extra Gnd. Reference —
12	Coolant Temp. Sw.	B1	J2-6		Start Circuit J2-7
13	Idle Relay	Aux 2	J1-17		Idle Relay Voltage —
14	MC Sol.	High Current 1	J1-20		
15	4 in. Hg Vac. Sw.	B0	J2-4		

*NOTE: Aux 1 must be present at the diagnostic connector regardless of the presence of a shift light

CEC diagnostic connector usage – 4 cylinder engine

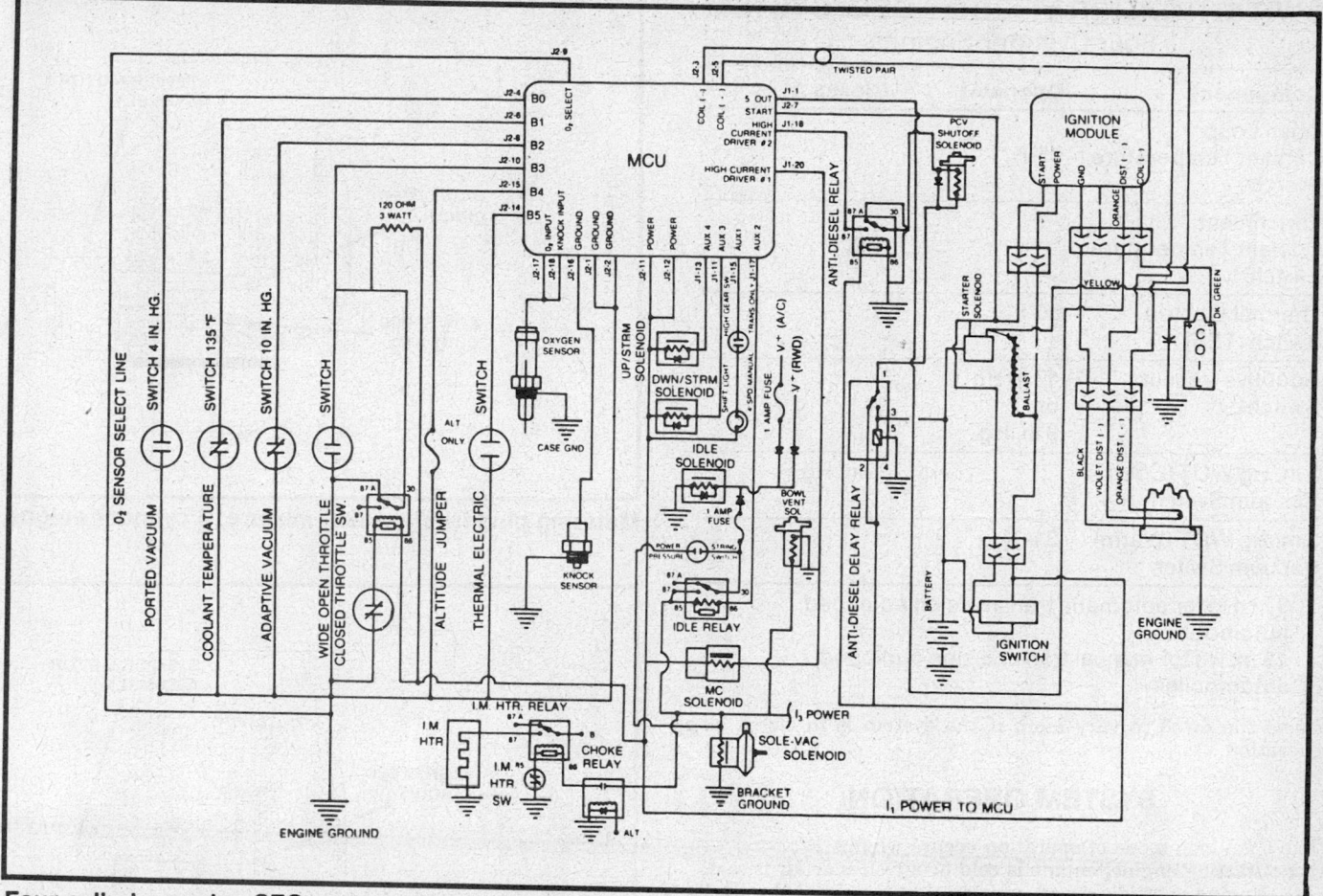

Four cylinder engine CEC system wiring schematic

tion or storing of fault codes. As a result, it has an initialization function that is activated when the ignition switch is turned **ON**.

The MCU initialization function for the 6 cylinder engine moves the metering pins to a predetermined starting position by first driving them all the way to the rich end stop and then driving them in the lean direction by a predetermined number of steps. No matter where they were before initialization, they will be at the correct position at the end of every initialization period. Because each open loop operation metering pin position is dependent on the initialization function, this function is the first test in the diagnostic procedure.

During open loop operation, the air supplied by the mixture control solenoid is pre-programmed.

NOTE: The use of a voltmeter with less than 10 megohms per volt input independence can destroy the oxygen sensor. A digital volt-ohm meter must be used.

CEC System — 4 Cylinder Engine

DIAGNOSTIC TESTS

The CEC System should be considered as a possible source of trouble for engine performance, fuel economy and exhaust emission complaints only after normal tests and inspections that would apply to an automobile without the system have been performed.

The steps in each test will provide a systematic evaluation of each component that could cause an operational malfunction.

Refer to the Switch Calibrations chart during tests. To determine if fault exists with the system, a system operational test is necessary. This test should be performed when the CEC System is suspected because no other reason can be determined for a specific complaint. A dwell meter, digital volt-ohmmeter, tachometer, vacuum gauge and jumper wires are required to diagnose system problems. Although most dwell meters should be acceptable, if one causes a change in engine operation when it is connected to the mixture control (MC) solenoid dwell pigtail wire test connector, it should not be used.

The dwell meter, set for the 6 cylinder engine scale and connected to a pigtail wire test connector leading from the mixture control (MC) solenoid, is used to determine the air/fuel mixture dwell. When the dwell meter is connected, do not allow the connector terminal to contact any engine component that is connected to engine ground. This includes hoses because they may be electrically conductive. With a normally operating engine, the dwell at both idle speed and partial throttle will be between 10–50 degrees and will be varying. Varying means the pointer continually moves back and forth across the scale. The amount it varies is not important, only the fact that it does vary.

The variance of the pointer indicates closed loop operation, indicating the mixture is being varied according to the input voltage to the MCU from the oxygen sensor. With wide open throttle (WOT) and/or cold engine operation, the air/fuel mixture ratio will be predetermined and the pointer will only vary slightly. This is open loop operation, indicating the oxygen sensor output has no effect on the air/fuel mixture.

If there is a question whether or not the system is in closed loop operation, enriching or leaning the air/fuel mixture will

SWITCH CALIBRATIONS—CEC SYSTEM
Four Cylinder Engines

Component	Opens At	Closes At
Open Loop Coolant Temperature Switch	95°F	
Enrichment Coolant Temperature Switch		135°F
Thermal Electric Switch (TES)	65°F	55°F
Adaptive Vacuum Switch ①	13 in Hg or 9 in. Hg	
5 in. Hg WOT (Cold) Vacuum Switch		5 in. Hg
3 in. Hg WOT (Warm) Vacuum Switch	3 in. Hg	

①9 in. Hg for automatic transmission equipped automobiles
13 in. Hg for manual transmission equipped automobiles

cause the dwell to vary more if the system is in closed loop operation.

SYSTEM OPERATION

The open loop mode of operation occurs when:
1. Starting engine, engine is cold or air cleaner air is cold.
2. Engine is at idle speed, accelerating to partial throttle or decelerating from partial throttle to idle speed.
3. Carburetor is either at or near wide open throttle (WOT), predetermined air/fuel mixture ratio for each condition. Because the air/fuel ratios are predetermined and no feedback relative to the results is accepted, this type of operation is referred to as open loop operation. All open loop operations are characterized by predetermined air/fuel mixture ratios.

OPERATIONAL PRIORITIES

Each operation (except closed loop) has a specific air/fuel ratio and because more than one of the engine operational selection conditions can be present at one time, the MCU is programmed with a priority ranking for the operations. It complies with the conditions that pertain to the operation having the highest priority. The priorities are as described below.

COLD WEATHER ENGINE START-UP AND OPERATION

If the air cleaner air temperature is below the calibrated value (55°F) of the thermal electric switch (TES), the air/fuel mixture is at a rich ratio. Lean air/fuel mixtures are not permitted for a preset period following a cold weather start-up.

AT OR NEAR WIDE OPEN THROTTLE (WOT) OPERATION WITH COLD ENGINE

This open loop operation occurs whenever the coolant temperature is below the calibrated switching value (95°F) of the open loop coolant temperature switch and the WOT vacuum switch (cold) has been closed because of the decrease in manifold vacuum (i.e., less than 5 in. Hg or 17 kPa). When this open loop condition occurs, the MC solenoid provides a rich air/fuel mixture for cold engine operation at wide open throttle.

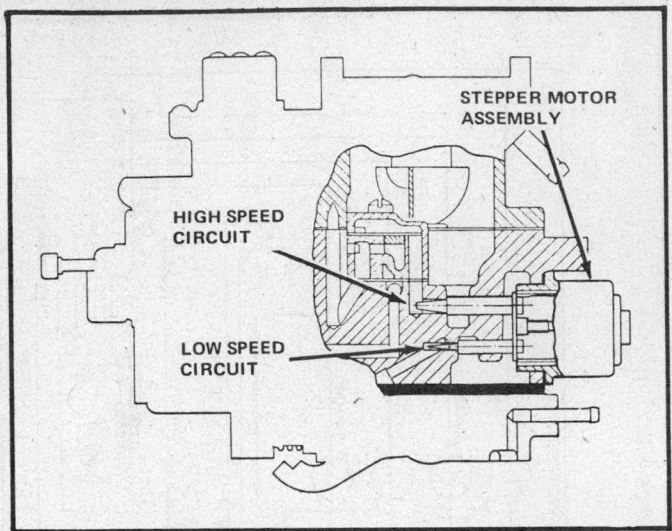

Metering pins IN allow rich mixture, 6 cylinder enigne

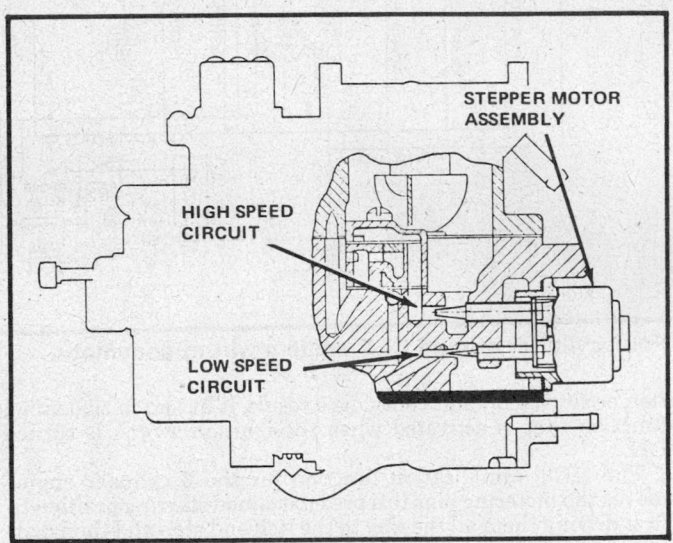

Metering pins OUT allow lean mixture, 6 cylinder engine

Temperature and switching vacuum levels are nominal values. The actual switching temperature or vacuum level will vary slightly from switch to switch.

AT OR NEAR WIDE OPEN THROTTLE (WOT) OPERATION WITH WARM ENGINE

This open loop operation occurs whenever the coolant temperature is above the calibrated switching temperature (135°F) of the enrichment coolant temperature switch and the WOT vacuum switch (warm) has been opened because of the decrease in manifold vacuum (i.e., less than 3 in. Hg or 10 kPa). When this open loop condition occurs, the MC solenoid provides a rich air/fuel mixture for warm engine operation at wide open throttle.

ADAPTIVE MODE OF OPERATION

This open loop operation occurs when the engine is either at idle speed, accelerating from idle speed or decelerating to idle speed. If the engine rpm (tach) voltage is less than the calibrated value and manifold vacuum is above the calibrated switching level for the adaptive vacuum switch (i.e., switch closed), an engine idle condition is assumed to exist. If the engine rpm (tach) voltage is

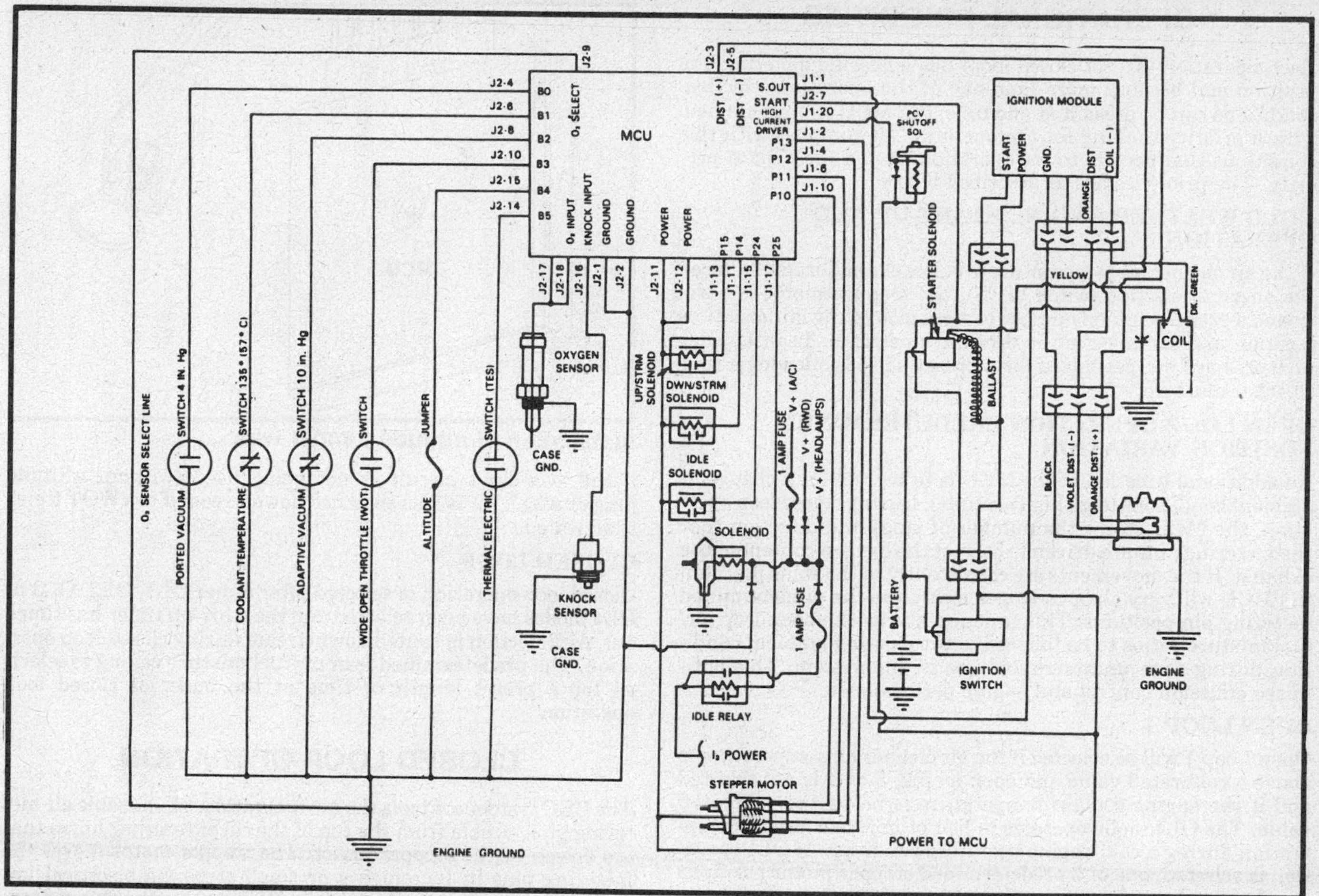

Six cylinder engine CEC system wiring schematic

greater than the calibrated value and manifold vacuum is below the calibrated switching level for the adaptive vacuum switch (i.e., switch open), an engine-acceleration-from-idle speed condition is assumed to exist.

If the engine rpm (tach) voltage is greater than the calibrated value and manifold vacuum is above the calibrated switching level of the adaptive vacuum switch (i.e., switch closed), an engine-deceleration-to-idle speed condition is assumed to exist. During the adaptive mode of operation, the MC solenoid provides a predetermined air/fuel mixture.

CLOSED LOOP

Closed loop operation occurs whenever none of the open loop engine operating conditions exist. The MCU causes the MC solenoid to vary the air/fuel mixture in reaction to the voltage input from the oxygen sensor, located in the exhaust manifold. The oxygen sensor voltage varies in reaction to changes in oxygen content present in the exhaust gas. Because the content of oxygen in the exhaust gas indicates the completeness of the combustion process, it is a reliable indicator of the air/fuel mixture that is entering the combustion chamber.

Because the oxygen sensor only reacts to oxygen, manifold air leak or malfunction between the carburetor and sensor may cause the sensor to provide an erroneous voltage output.

The engine operation characteristics never quite permit the MCU to compute a single air/fuel mixture ratio that constantly provides the optimum air/fuel mixture. Therefore, closed loop operation is characterized by constant variation of the air/fuel mixture because the MCU is forced constantly to make small corrections in an attempt to create an optimum air/fuel mixture ratio.

CEC System—6 Cylinder Engine

Since it is necessary to look inside the carburetor on the 6 cylinder engine, observe the following precautions:

1. Shape a sheet of clear acrylic plastic at least 0.250 in. thick and 15 × 15 in.
2. Secure the acrylic sheet with an air cleaner wing nut after the top of the air cleaner has been removed.
3. Wear eye protection whenever performing checks and tests.
4. When engine is operating, keep hands and arms clear of fan, drive pulleys and belts. Do not wear loose clothing. Do not stand in line with fan blades.
5. Do not stand in front of running vehicle.

SYSTEM OPERATION

The open loop mode of operation occurs when:
1. Starting engine, engine is cold or air cleaner air is cold.
2. Engine is at idle speed.
3. Carburetor is either at or near wide open throttle (WOT). When any of these conditions occur, the metering pins are driven to a predetermined (programmed) position for each condition. Because the positions are predetermined and no feedback relative to the results is accepted, this type of operation is referred to as open loop operation.
4. The 5 open loop operations are characterized by the metering pins being driven to a position where they are stopped and remain stationary.

OPERATIONAL PRIORITIES

Each operation (except closed loop) has a specific metering pin position and because more than one of the operation selection conditions can be present at one time, the MCU is programmed with a priority ranking for the operation. It complies with the conditions that pertain to the operation having the highest priority. The priorities are as described below.

COLD WEATHER ENGINE START-UP AND OPERATION

If the air cleaner air temperature is below the calibrated value of the thermal electric switch (TES), the stepper motor is positioned a predetermined number of steps rich of the initialization position and air injection is diverted upstream. Lean air/fuel mixtures are not permitted for a preset period following a cold weather start-up.

OPEN LOOP OPERATION PREDETERMINED POSITION VARIATION

An additional function of the MCU is to correct for a change in ambient conditions (e.g., high altitude). During closed loop operation, the MCU stores the number of steps and direction that the metering pins are driven to correct the oxygen content of the exhaust. If the movements are consistently to the same position, the MCU will vary all open loop operation to the predetermined metering pin positions. This function allows the open loop air/fuel mixture ratios to be tailored to the existing ambient condition during each uninterrupted use of the system. This optimizes emission control and engine performance.

OPEN LOOP 1

Open Loop 1 will be selected if the air cleaner air temperature is above a calibrated value and open loop 2, 3 or 4 is not selected and if the engine coolant temperature is below the calibrated value. The OL1 mode operates in lieu of normal closed loop operation during a cold engine operating condition. If OL1 operation is selected, one of 2 predetermined stepper motor positions are chosen, dependent if the altitude circuit (lean limit) jumper wire is installed. With each engine start-up, a start-up timer is activated. During this interval, if the engine operating condition would otherwise trigger normal closed loop operation, OL1 operation is selected.

OPEN LOOP 2, WIDE OPEN THROTTLE (WOT)

Open loop 2 is selected whenever the air cleaner air temperature is above the calibrated value of the thermal electric switch (TES) and the WOT switch has been engaged. When the Open Loop 2 mode is selected, the stepper motor is driven to a calibrated number of steps rich of initialization and the air control valve switches air downstream. However, if the lean limit circuit (with altitude jumper wire) is being used, the air is instead directed upstream. The WOT timer is activated whenever OL2 is selected and it remains active for a preset period of time. The WOT timer remains inoperative if the lean limit circuit is being used.

OPEN LOOP 3

Open Loop 3 is selected when the ignition advance vacuum level falls below a predetermined level. When the OL3 mode is selected, the engine rpm is also determined. If the rpm (tach) voltage is greater than the calibrated value, an engine deceleration condition is assumed to exist. If the rpm (tach) voltage is less than the calibrated value, an engine idle speed condition is assumed to exist.

OPEN LOOP 4

Open Loop 4 is selected whenever manifold vacuum falls below a predetermined level. During OL4 operation, the stepper motor is positioned at the initialization position. Air injection is switched upstream during OL4 operation. However, air is switched downstream if the extended OL4 timer is activated and

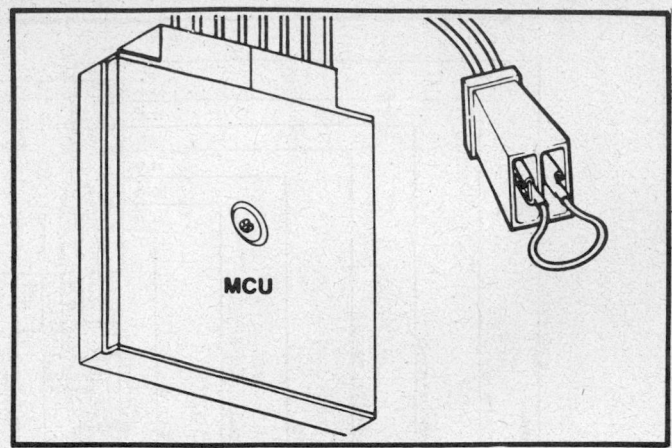

Installation of altitude jumper wire

if the lean limit circuit is not being used (without altitude jumper wire). Air is also switched downstream if the WOT timer is activated.

CLOSED LOOP

Closed loop operation is selected after either OL1, OL2, OL3 or OL4 modes have been selected and the start-up timer has timed out. Air injection is routed downstream during closed loop operation. The predetermined lean air/fuel mixture ceiling is selected for a preset length of time at the onset of closed loop operation.

CLOSED LOOP OPERATION

The CEC system controls the air/fuel ratio with movable air metering pins, visible from the top of the carburetor air horn, that are driven by the stepper motor. The stepper motor moves the metering pins in increments or small steps via electrical impulses generated by the MCU. The MCU causes the stepper motor to drive the metering pins to a richer or leaner position in reaction to the voltage input from the oxygen sensor located in the exhaust manifold.

The oxygen sensor voltage varies in reaction to changes in oxygen content present in the exhaust gas. Because of the content of oxygen in the exhaust gas indicates the completeness of the combustion process, it is a reliable indicator of the air/fuel mixture that is entering the combustion chamber. Because the oxygen sensor only reacts to oxygen, any air leak or malfunction between the carburetor and sensor may cause the sensor to provide an erroneous voltage output. This could be caused by a manifold air leak or malfunctioning secondary air check value.

The engine operation characteristics never quite permit the MCU to compute a single metering pin position that constantly provides the optimum air/fuel mixture. Therefore, closed loop operation is characterized by constant movement of the metering pins because the MCU is forced constantly to make small corrections in the air/fuel mixture in an attempt to create an optimum air/fuel mixture ratio.

ALTITUDE PERFORMANCE

EAGLE WITH 4.2L ENGINE AND AUTOMATIC TRANSMISSION

On the above listed vehicles, originally sold for operation at altitudes below 4,000 feet that are being operated above 4,000 feet, the ignition timing must be advanced 7 degrees and the idle speed reset. In addition, a jumper wire must be added to the MCU circuit to activate the altitude compensating circuit in the MCU. An emission control update label must be installed along side the original emission certification label, stating the modification done to the engine.

EAGLE WITH 4.2L ENGINE AND MANUAL TRANSMISSION

On the above listed vehicles, originally sold for operation at altitudes below 4,000 feet that are being operated above 4,000 feet, the ignition timing must be advanced 7 degrees, the engine idle speed reset and a jumper wire added to the MCU circuit. In addition, the idle/decel switch must be connected to the carburetor EGR port, instead of the spark port. An emission control update label must be installed along side the original emission certification label, stating the modifications done to the engine.

NOTE: Whenever these vehicles are returned to operation at altitudes below 4000 feet, the MCU jumper wire must be removed, the idle/decel switch reconnected to the carburetor spark port (6 cylinder engines), the ignition timing and idle speed reset to original specifications and the vehicle emission control update label must be removed. Do not remove the original emission certification information label

CHRYSLER ELECTRONIC FUEL CONTROL SYSTEM

1.6L and 2.2L Carbureted Engines

The electronic fuel control system consists of a spark control computer, various engine sensors and a specially calibrated carburetor. The function of the system is to provide a way for the engine to burn the correct air/fuel mixture, providing performance, economy and cleaner emissions.

SPARK CONTROL COMPUTER (SCC)

The spark control computer is the heart of the complete system. It gives the capability of igniting the fuel mixture according to different modes of engine operation by delivering an infinite amount of variable advance curves. The computer consists of 1 electronic printed circuit board which simultaneously receives signals from all the sensors and within milliseconds, analyzes them to determine how the engine is operating and then advances or retards the ignition timing. It then signals the ignition coil to produce the electrical impulses to fire the spark plugs.

SENSORS

There are as many as 5 sensors on the engine that supply the ignition computer with the necessary information needed to fire the spark plugs at the right time and when equipped with a feedback carburetor, to change the air/fuel ratio. The senors are as follows:

HALL EFFECT PICK-UP ASSEMBLY

The 4 cylinder hall effect pick-up is located in the distributor and supplies the basic timing signal to the computer, also, the computer can determine from this signal, engine speed (rpm), when each piston is coming up on its compression stroke, or when the engine is in the cranking mode.

COOLANT SENSOR

The coolant sensor is located on the thermostat housing and supplies a signal to the computer. The resistance of the sensor is inversely proportional to coolant temperature. This information is required to prevent changing of the air/fuel ratio until the engine reaches normal operating temperature on the feedback carbureted engines. It also controls the amount of spark advance with a cold engine.

VACUUM TRANSDUCER

The vacuum transducer is located on the spark control computer. Its signal informs the computer how much engine vacuum is present. Engine vacuum is one of the factors that will determine how the computer will advance/retard the ignition timing and with feedback carbureted vehicles, what change of air/fuel ratio is required.

CARBURETOR SWITCH

When equipped, this switch is located on the end of the idle stop. It tell the computer when the engine is at idle.

OXYGEN SENSOR

The oxygen senor is used on feedback carburetor equipped vehicles. It is located in the exhaust manifold and tell the computer how much oxygen is present in the exhaust gases. Since the amount of oxygen is proportional to rich and lean mixtures, the computer will adjust the air/fuel ratio to a level which will maintain operating efficiency of the 3-way catalyst system and engine.

SPARK CONTROL COMPUTER (SCC)

During cranking, an electrical signal from the distributor is fed to the computer. This signal will cause the computer to fire the spark plugs at a fixed amount of advance. Once the engine has started, the timing will then be controlled by the computer, based on the information received from the various sensors.

The amount of spark advance is determined by 3 factors, coolant temperature, engine speed and manifold vacuum. The computer determines the spark advance, based on these factors in the following manner:

1. Coolant temperature modifies the vacuum advance schedule. It has a different schedule for a hot or cold engine.
2. Advance from vacuum is programmed into the computer. On a cold engine, the vacuum advance depends only on the amount of manifold vacuum. In a hot engine, the vacuum advance depends on both manifold vacuum and engine speed.
3. Advance from speed is programmed into the computer and depends only on engine rpm.

NOTE: This electronic system has no internal memory to recognize, store, or to display defect codes in any manner. The system has a general diagnosis program that must be followed when malfunctions are noted.

5.2L Carbureted Engine

The electronic fuel control system is used on Federal and California emission related vehicles, while the basic system is used for Canadian vehicles and is named the spark control computer, SCC.

The system contains various sensors, a specially calibrated carburetor and dual pick-up distributor. The function of the system is to provide a way for the engine to burn a correct air/fuel mixture.

The 2 functional modes of the computer are START and RUN. The START mode will only function during engine cranking and starting. The RUN mode only function after the engine has started and during the engine operation. The 2 modes will never operate together at the same time.

In the event of a RUN mode failure, the START mode will take over the engine operation. The engine will keep running, but since the START mode timing remains fixed, performance will be below standard.

If for some reason a failure occurs within the computer, the system will go into what is known as the LIMP-IN mode. This

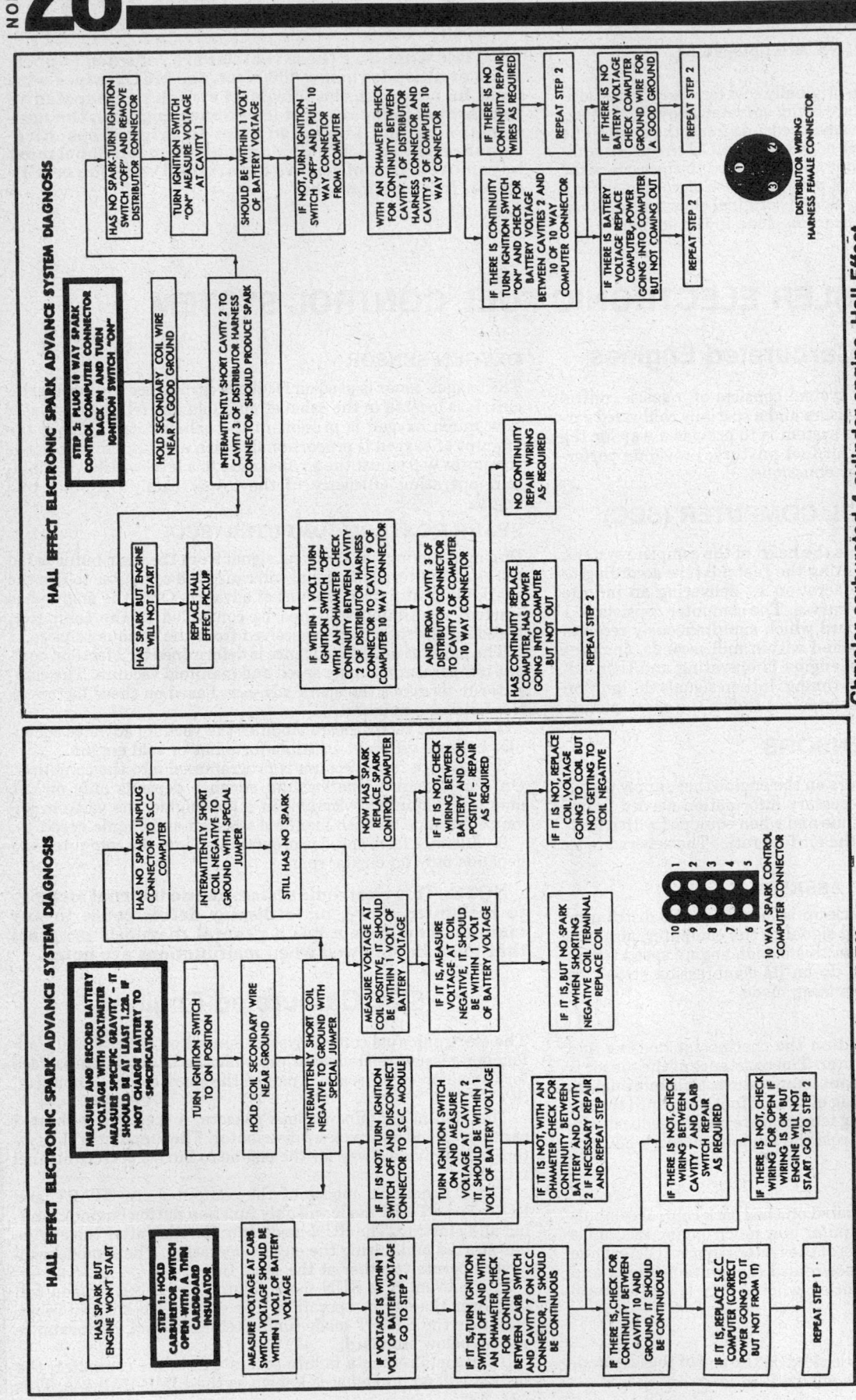

HALL EFFECT ELECTRONIC SPARK ADVANCE SYSTEM DIAGNOSIS

HAS NO SPARK-TURN IGNITION SWITCH "OFF" AND REMOVE DISTRIBUTOR CONNECTOR

TURN IGNITION SWITCH "ON" MEASURE VOLTAGE AT CAVITY 1

SHOULD BE WITHIN 1 VOLT OF BATTERY VOLTAGE

IF NOT, TURN IGNITION SWITCH "OFF" AND PULL 10 WAY CONNECTOR FROM COMPUTER

WITH AN OHMMETER CHECK FOR CONTINUITY BETWEEN CAVITY 1 OF DISTRIBUTOR HARNESS CONNECTOR AND CAVITY 3 OF COMPUTER 10 WAY CONNECTOR

IF THERE IS NO CONTINUITY REPAIR WIRES AS REQUIRED

REPEAT STEP 2

IF THERE IS NO BATTERY VOLTAGE CHECK COMPUTER GROUND WIRE FOR A GOOD GROUND

REPEAT STEP 2

IF THERE IS CONTINUITY TURN IGNITION SWITCH "ON" AND CHECK FOR BATTERY VOLTAGE BETWEEN CAVITIES 2 AND 10 OF 10 WAY COMPUTER CONNECTOR

IF THERE IS BATTERY VOLTAGE REPLACE COMPUTER, POWER GOING INTO COMPUTER BUT NOT COMING OUT

REPEAT STEP 2

STEP 2: PLUG 10 WAY SPARK CONTROL COMPUTER CONNECTOR BACK IN AND TURN IGNITION SWITCH "ON"

HOLD SECONDARY COIL WIRE NEAR A GOOD GROUND

INTERMITTENTLY SHORT CAVITY 2 TO CAVITY 3 OF DISTRIBUTOR HARNESS CONNECTOR, SHOULD PRODUCE SPARK

HAS SPARK BUT ENGINE WILL NOT START

REPLACE HALL EFFECT PICKUP

IF WITHIN 1 VOLT TURN IGNITION SWITCH "OFF" WITH AN OHMMETER CHECK CONTINUITY BETWEEN CAVITY 2 OF DISTRIBUTOR HARNESS CONNECTOR TO CAVITY 9 OF COMPUTER 10 WAY CONNECTOR

AND FROM CAVITY 3 OF DISTRIBUTOR CONNECTOR TO CAVITY 5 OF COMPUTER 10 WAY CONNECTOR

NO CONTINUITY REPAIR WIRING AS REQUIRED

HAS CONTINUITY REPLACE COMPUTER, HAS POWER GOING INTO COMPUTER BUT NOT OUT

REPEAT STEP 2

DISTRIBUTOR WIRING HARNESS FEMALE CONNECTOR

Chrysler carbureted 4 cylinder engine, Hall Effect spark advance system diagnosis, chart 2

HALL EFFECT ELECTRONIC SPARK ADVANCE SYSTEM DIAGNOSIS

HAS NO SPARK UNPLUG CONNECTOR TO S.C.C. COMPUTER

INTERMITTENTLY SHORT COIL NEGATIVE TO GROUND WITH SPECIAL JUMPER

STILL HAS NO SPARK

NOW HAS SPARK REPLACE SPARK CONTROL COMPUTER

IF IT IS NOT, CHECK WIRING BETWEEN BATTERY AND COIL POSITIVE – REPAIR AS REQUIRED

IF IT IS, BUT NO SPARK WHEN SHORTING NEGATIVE COIL TERMINAL REPLACE COIL

IF IT IS, NOT REPLACE COIL, VOLTAGE GOING TO COIL BUT NOT GETTING TO COIL NEGATIVE

MEASURE VOLTAGE AT COIL POSITIVE, IT SHOULD BE WITHIN 1 VOLT OF BATTERY VOLTAGE

IF IT IS, MEASURE VOLTAGE AT COIL NEGATIVE, IT SHOULD BE WITHIN 1 VOLT OF BATTERY VOLTAGE

MEASURE AND RECORD BATTERY VOLTAGE WITH VOLTMETER MEASURE SPECIFIC GRAVITY – IT SHOULD BE AT LEAST 1.220, IF NOT CHARGE BATTERY TO SPECIFICATION

TURN IGNITION SWITCH TO ON POSITION

HOLD COIL SECONDARY WIRE NEAR GROUND

INTERMITTENTLY SHORT COIL NEGATIVE TO GROUND WITH SPECIAL JUMPER

HAS SPARK BUT ENGINE WON'T START

STEP 1: HOLD CARBURETOR SWITCH OPEN WITH A THIN CARDBOARD INSULATOR

MEASURE VOLTAGE AT CARB SWITCH VOLTAGE SHOULD BE WITHIN 1 VOLT OF BATTERY VOLTAGE

IF VOLTAGE IS WITHIN 1 VOLT OF BATTERY VOLTAGE GO TO STEP 2

IF IT IS, TURN IGNITION SWITCH OFF AND DISCONNECT CONNECTOR TO S.C.C. MODULE

TURN IGNITION SWITCH ON AND MEASURE VOLTAGE AT CAVITY 2 IT SHOULD BE WITHIN 1 VOLT OF BATTERY VOLTAGE

IF IT IS NOT, WITH AN OHMMETER CHECK FOR CONTINUITY BETWEEN BATTERY AND CAVITY 2 IF NECESSARY REPAIR AND REPEAT STEP 1

IF IT IS, TURN IGNITION SWITCH OFF AND WITH AN OHMMETER CHECK BETWEEN CARB SWITCH AND CAVITY 7 ON S.C.C. CONNECTOR, IT SHOULD BE CONTINUOUS

IF IT IS NOT, CHECK FOR CONTINUITY BETWEEN CAVITY 7 AND CARB SWITCH SWITCH REPAIR AS REQUIRED

IF THERE IS, CHECK FOR CONTINUITY BETWEEN CAVITY 10 AND GROUND, IT SHOULD BE CONTINUOUS

IF THERE IS NOT, CHECK WIRING BETWEEN CAVITY 10 AND GROUND WILL REPAIR AS REQUIRED

IF THERE IS NOT, CHECK WIRING FOR OPEN IF ENGINE WILL NOT START GO TO STEP 2

IF IT IS, REPLACE S.C.C. COMPUTER (CORRECT POWER GOING TO IT BUT NOT FROM IT)

REPEAT STEP 1

10 WAY SPARK CONTROL COMPUTER CONNECTOR

Chrysler carbureted 4 cylinder engine, Hall Effect spark advance system diagnosis, chart 1

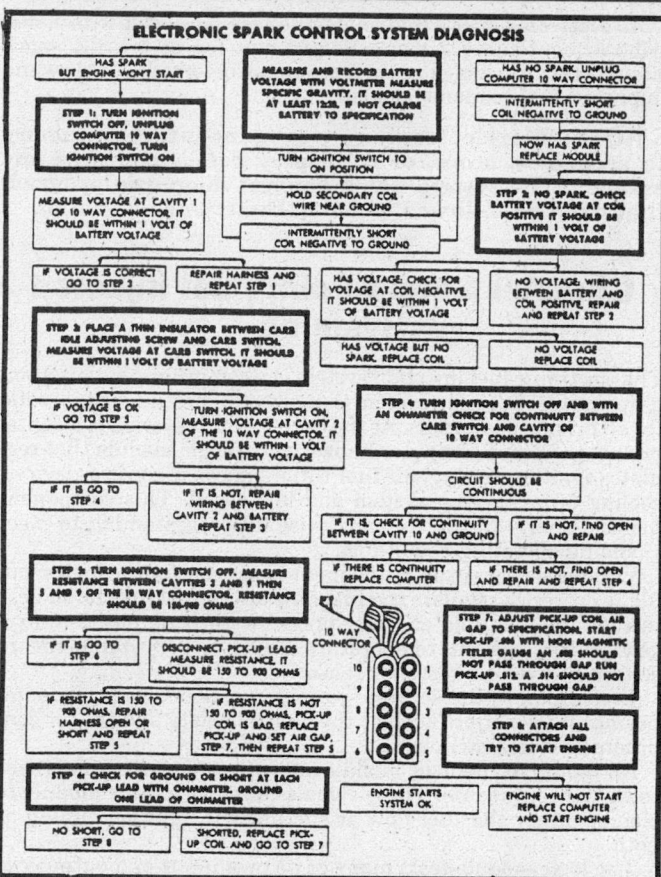

Chrysler carbureted V-8 engine electronic spark control system diagnosis

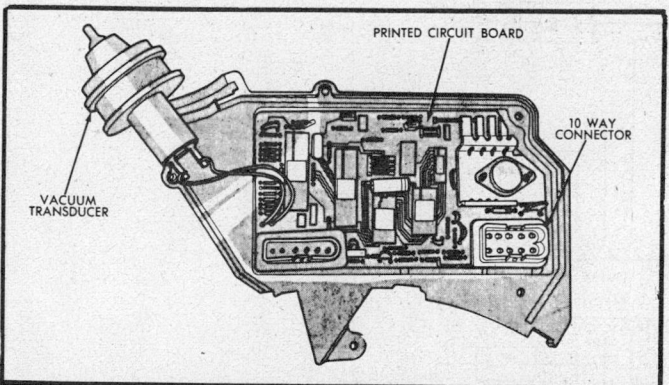

Electronic Spark Control computer

will enable the operator to continue to drive the vehicle until it can be repaired. However, while in this mode, very poor engine performance and poor fuel economy will result. Should a failure of the pick-ups within the distributor or the START mode of the computer, the engine will not start and run.

IGNITION COMPUTER (SCC)

The Spark Control Computer (SCC) is the heart of the entire system. It has the capability of igniting the fuel mixture according to different modes of engine operation, by delivering an infinite amount of variable advance curves.

The computer consists of 1 electronic printed circuit board, which simultaneously receives signals from all the sensors and within milliseconds, analyzes them to determine how the engine is operating and then advances or retards the ignition timing to determine the exact instant when the ignition is required and then signals the ignition coil to produce the electrical impulses which fire the spark plugs.

SENSORS

There are as many as 7 sensors on the engine that supply the ignition computer with the necessary information needed to fire the spark plugs at the correct time and when equipped with a feedback carburetor, to change the air/fuel ratio as required. The sensors are as follows.

MAGNETIC PICK-UP ASSEMBLY

The engines use 2 pick-up coils within the distributor. A start pick-up coil supplies a signal to the computer which will cause the spark plugs to be fired at a fixed amount of advance during the cranking mode only. The amount of advance is determined by the position of the start pick-up coil.

The run pick-up coil functions in the same manner, except that its signal is not recognized during the cranking mode.

COOLANT SENSOR

The coolant sensor is located in the intake manifold and supplies a signal to the computer when the engine has reached its predetermined temperature, to prevent changing the air/fuel ratio on a feedback carburetor equipped engine and the help control the amount of spark advance with a cold engine.

VACUUM TRANSDUCER

The vacuum transducer is located on the spark control computer and its signal informs the computer at what level the manifold vacuum is being developed. Engine vacuum is one of the factors that will determine how the computer will advance or retard the ignition timing and when equipped with a feedback carburetor, changing of the air/fuel ratio.

CARBURETOR SWITCH

The carburetor switch is located at the end of the idle stop and informs the computer when the engine is in the idle mode. When ever the curb switch contacts the throttle lever ground, there will be a cancellation of spark advance and an idle control of the air/fuel ratio of the carburetor. Not all carburetors are equipped with the carburetor switch.

DETONATION SUPPRESSOR SYSTEM

The detonation suppressor system helps to provide protection from spark knock. The system employs a detonation sensor, mounted in the No. 2 branch of the intake manifold. The sensor is tuned to the frequency that is characteristic of engine knocking.

When the knock frequencies are detected, the detonation sensor sends a low voltage signal to the electronic spark control computer, which then retards the timing a maximum of 20 degrees. The amount of decrease in timing is directly proportional to the strength and frequency of the detonation condition. When the condition is removed, the timing is advanced to the original value and the detonation suppression system will no longer influence the ignition timing.

OXYGEN SENSOR

The oxygen sensor is used in conjunction with the feedback carburetors. It is located in the exhaust manifold and signals the computer of the oxygen content in the exhaust gases. Since the amount of oxygen is proportional to rich and lean mixtures, the computer will adjust the air fuel ratio to a level which maintains the operating efficiency of a 3 way catalyst system and the engine

CHARGE TEMPERATURE SWITCH

The charge temperature switch is installed on the No. 8 intake

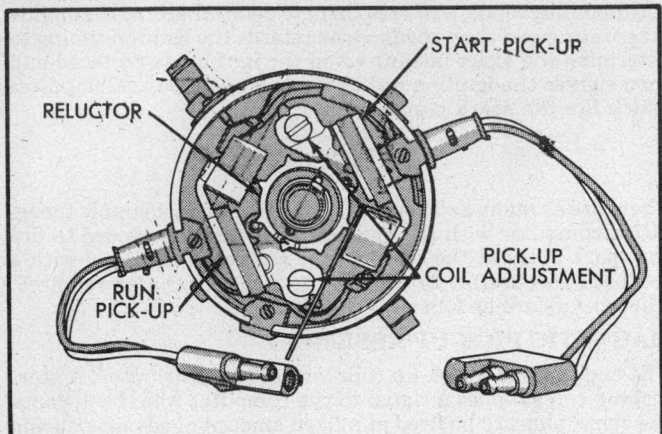

Dual pick-up distributor

manifold runner. When the intake air temperature is below approximately 60°F, the charge temperature switch will be closed, allowing no EGR timer function, no EGR valve operation and switches the air injection to the upstream mode and into the exhaust manifold.

The charge temperature switch will be open when the intake charge temperature is above approximately 60°F thus allowing the EGR timer to time out, the EGR valve to operate and will switch the air injection to the downstream mode and into the exhaust system.

MICROPROCESSOR ELECTRONIC SPARK CONTROL

The microprocessor is an electronic module located within the computer that processes the signals from the engine sensors for accurate engine spark timing, Its digital electronic circuitry offers more operating precision and programming flexibility than the voltage dependent analog system used previously.

All electronic spark control engines are equipped with a distributor containing 2 magnetic pick-ups for better idle spark timing stability, which in turn promotes better idle quality and improved fuel economy at idle.

NOTE: This electronic system has no internal memory to recognize, store, or to display defect codes in any manner. The system has a general diagnosis program that must be followed when malfunctions are noted.

Chrysler Single Point Fuel Injected Systems

The electronic fuel injection system is a computer regulated single point fuel injection system that provides precise air/fuel ratio for all driving conditions. At the center of this system is a digital pre-programmed computer known as the logic module that regulates ignition timing, air/fuel ratio, emission control devices, cooling fan, charging system and idle speed. This component has the ability to update and revise its programming to meet changing operating conditions.

Various sensors provide the input necessary for the logic module to correctly regulate the fuel flow at the fuel injector. These include the manifold absolute pressure, throttle position, oxygen sensor, coolant temperature, throttle body temperature sensor and vehicle distance sensor.

In addition to the sensors, various switches also provide important information, such as the neutral/safety and the air conditioning clutch switches.

All inputs to the logic module are converter into signals sent to the power module. These signals cause the power module to change either the fuel flow at the injector, ignition timing or both.

The logic module tests many of its own input and output circuits, If a fault is reading a numbered display code, which directly relates to a general fault.

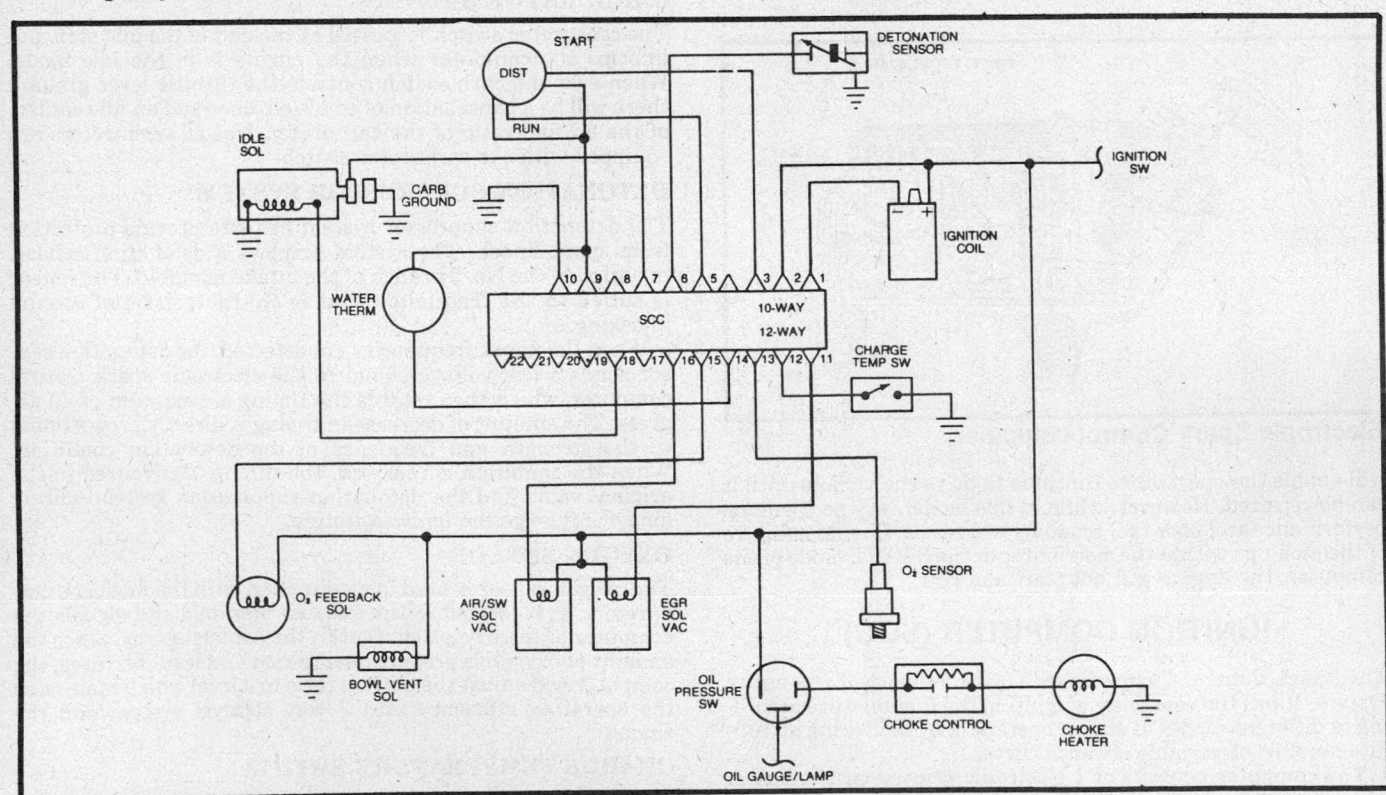

Typical schematic of electronic Spark Control computer

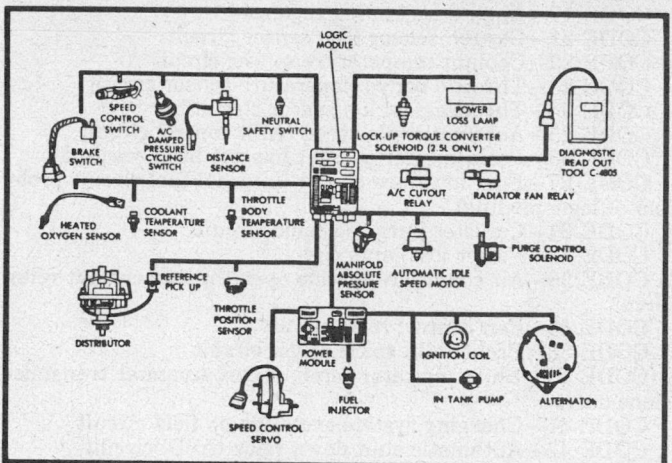

Chrysler electronic single point fuel injection system

POWER MODULE

The power module circuits powers the ignition coil, the alternator and the fuel injector. These units are high current devices and have been isolated to minimize any electrical noise reaching the logic module. The power module also energizes the automatic shutdown (ASD) relay, which activates the fuel pump, ignition coil, the power module and the injector.

The distributor pick-up signal is sent to the logic module only. Again, if no distributor signal is sent, the ASD relay is not activated and the power is shut off from the fuel and the ignition coil.

The Power module contains a voltage converter which reduces battery voltage to a regulated 8.0V output. This 8.0V output powers the distributor and the logic module.

LOGIC MODULE

The logic module is a digital computer containing a microprocessor. The logic module then computes the fuel injector pulse width, spark advance, ignition coil dwell, idle speed and purge and EGR control solenoid cycles.

The logic module receives its input signals from sensors and switches. It then computes the fuel injector pulse width spark advance, ignition coil dwell, idle speed, purge, cooling fan turn on and alternator charge rate.

The logic module tests many of its own input and output circuits. If a fault is found in a major system, this information is stored in the logic module. Information on this fault can be displayed for a technician by means of the instrument panel power loss lamp or by connecting a diagnostic read-out tester and reading a numbered display code, which directly relates to a general fault.

AUTOMATIC SHUTDOWN RELAY (ASD)

The ASD relay is incorporated within the power module, but is turned off and on by the logic module. The distributor signal is sent to the logic module and in the event of no distributor signal, the ASD relay is not activated and the power is shut off from the fuel components and ignition coil.

ENGINE SENSORS

MANIFOLD ABSOLUTE PRESSURE (MAP) SENSOR

The manifold absolute pressure (MAP) sensor is a device which monitors manifold vacuum. The sensor is mounted on the logic module. it is connected to a vacuum nipple on the throttle body and electrically to the logic module. The sensor transmits infor-

mation on manifold vacuum conditions and barometric pressure to the logic module. The MAP sensor data on engine load is used with data from other sensors to determine the correct air mixture.

OXYGEN SENSOR

The oxygen sensor is a device which produces an electrical voltage when exposed to the oxygen present in the exhaust gases. The sensor is mounted in the exhaust manifold and must be heated by the exhaust gases before producing the voltage. When there is a large amount of oxygen present (lean mixture), the sensor produces a low voltage. When there is a lesser amount present (rich mixture) it produces a higher voltage. By monitoring the oxygen content and converting it to electrical voltage, the sensor acts as a rich-lean switch. The voltage is transmitted to the logic module. The logic module signals the power module to change the fuel injector pulse width and the injector changes the mixture.

COOLANT TEMPERATURE SENSOR

The coolant temperature sensor is mounted in the thermostat housing. This sensor provides data on engine operating temperature to the logic module. This data along with data provided by the charge temperature switch allows the logic module to demand slightly richer air mixtures and higher idle speeds until normal operating temperatures are reached. The coolant temperature sensor is also used to control the cooling fan.

SWITCH INPUT

Various switches provide information to the logic module. These include the air conditioning clutch and brake light switches. If one or more of these switches is sensed as being in the ON position, the logic module signals the automatic idle speed motor to increase idle speed to a scheduled rpm.

With the air conditioning engaged and the throttle blade above a specific angle, the wide open throttle cut-out relay prevents the air conditioning clutch from engaging until the throttle blade is below this angle.

POWER LOSS/LIMITED LAMP

The power loss lamp comes on each time the ignition key is turned ON and stays on for 3 seconds as a bulb test. If the logic module receives an incorrect signal or no signal from either the coolant temperature sensor, manifold absolute pressure sensor, or the throttle position sensor, the power loss lamp on the instrument panel is illuminated. This is a warning that the logic module has gone into LIMP-IN mode in an attempt to keep the system operational and a signal for immediate service.

DISPLAY OF FAULT CODES BY POWER LOSS LAMP

The power loss lamp is also used to display fault codes. To enter the system, cycle the ignition switch ON, OFF, ON, OFF, ON within 5 seconds and any fault codes stored in the logic module will be displayed.

LIMP-IN MODE

The LIMP-IN mode is the attempt by the logic module to compensate for the failure of certain components by substituting information from other sources. If the logic module senses incorrect data or no data at all from the MAP sensor, throttle position sensor or coolant temperature sensor, the system is placed into LIMP-IN Mode and the power loss lamp on the instrument panel is activated.

THROTTLE POSITION SENSOR (TPS)

The Throttle Position Sensor (TPS) is an electric resistor which is activated by the movement of the throttle-shaft. It is mounted on the throttle body and senses the angle of the throttle blade

28-13

opening. The voltage that the sensor produces increases or decreases according to the throttle blade opening. This voltage is transmitted to the logic module where it is used along with data from other sensors to adjust the air ratio to varying conditions and during acceleration, deceleration, idle and wide open throttle operations.

AUTOMATIC IDLE SPEED (AIS) MOTOR

The Automatic Idle Speed motor (AIS) is operated by the logic module. Data from the throttle position sensor, speed sensor, coolant temperature sensor and various switch operations, (electric backlite, air conditioning safety/neutral, brake) are used by the logic module to adjust engine idle to an optimum during all idle conditions. The AIS adjusts the air portion of the air/fuel mixture through an air bypass on the back of the throttle body. Basic (no load) idle is determined by the minimum air flow through the throttle body.

The AIS opens or closes off the air bypass as an increase or decrease is needed due to engine loads or ambient conditions. The logic module senses an air/fuel change and increases or decreases fuel proportionally to change engine idle. Deceleration die out is also prevented by increasing engine idle when the throttle is closed quickly after a driving (speed) condition.

THROTTLE BODY

The throttle body replaces a conventional carburetor and is mounted on top of the intake manifold. The throttle body houses the fuel injector, pressure regulator, throttle position sensor, automatic idle speed motor and the throttle body temperature sensor.

The air flow through the throttle body is controlled by a cable operated throttle blade, located in the base of the body. The throttle body provides the chamber for metering atomized fuel to mix with the air entering the engine.

FUEL INJECTOR

The fuel injector is an electrical solenoid, driven by the power module, but controlled by the logic module. The logic module, based on sensor input, determines when and how long the power module should operate the injector. The injector operates at a pressure of 14.5 psi.

ON-BOARD DIAGNOSTICS

The logic module has been programmed to monitor several different circuits of the fuel injection system. This monitoring is called on-board diagnosis. If a problem is sensed with a monitored circuit, often enough to indicate an actual problem, its fault code is stored in the logic module for eventual display to the service technician. If the problem is repaired or ceases to exist, the logic module cancels the fault code after 20–40 ignition key **ON/OFF** cycles.

FAULT CODES

When a fault code appears (either by flashes of the light emitting diode or by watching the diagnostic readout, tool C–4805 or equivalent, it indicates that the logic module has recognized an abnormal signal in the system. Fault codes indicate the results of a failure but do not always identify the failed component.

CODE 88 – Start of test
CODE 11 – Engine not cranked since battery disconnected
CODE 12 – Memory standby power lost
CODE 13 – MAP Sensor pneumatic circuit*
CODE 14 – MAP sensor electrical system*
CODE 15 – Vehicle Speed Sensor circuit
CODE 16 – Lose of battery voltage sense*

CODE 17 – Engine is running too cool
CODE 21 – Oxygen sensor (O_2) sensor circuit
CODE 22 – Coolant temperature sensor circuit*
CODE 23 – Throttle body temperature sensor circuit
CODE 24 – Throttle position sensor circuit*
CODE 25 – Automatic idle speed (AIS) control circuit
CODE 26 – Peak injector current has not been reached
CODE 27 – Fuel interface circuit (internal fuel circuit problem of logic module)
CODE 31 – Canister purge solenoid circuit
CODE 32 – Power loss lamp circuit
CODE 33 – Air conditioning wide open throttle cut out relay circuit
CODE 35 – Fan control relay circuit
CODE 36 – Problem in spare driver circuit
CODE 37 – Shift indicator lamp circuit (manual transmissions only)
CODE 41 – Charging system excess or no field circuit
CODE 42 – Automatic shut down relay (ASD) circuit
CODE 43 – Spark interface (internal) circuits
CODE 44 – Indicate battery temperature is out of range
CODE 46 – Battery voltage too high*
CODE 47 – Battery voltage too low
CODE 51 – Closed loop fuel system problem: O_2 signal stuck at lean position
CODE 52 – The O_2 signal stuck at the rich position
CODE 53 – Logic module problem or failure
CODE 55 – means end of message
CODE 88 – means start of message: only appears on the diagnostic readout tool C–4805 or equivalent

NOTE: * indicates the power loss/limited lamp is on.

SYSTEMS TEST

Obtaining Fault Codes

1. Connect diagnostic readout box tool C–4805 or equivalent, to the diagnostic connector located in the engine compartment near the passenger side strut tower.

2. Start the engine if possible, cycle the transmission selector and the A/C switch if applicable. Shut off the engine.

3. Turn the ignition switch **ON, OFF, ON, OFF, ON.** Within 5 seconds record all the diagnostic codes shown on the diagnostic readout box tool, observe the power loss lamp on the instrument panel the lamp should light for 3 seconds, then go out (bulb check).

Switch Test

After all codes have been shown and has indicated Code 55 end of message, actuate the following component switches. The digital display must change its numbers when the switch is activated and released:

Brake pedal
Gear shift selector park, reverse, park
A/C switch (if applicable)

OBTAINING CIRCUIT ACTUATION TEST MODE (ATM TEST)

1. Put the system into the diagnostic test mode and wait for code 55 to appear on the display screen.

2. Press ATM button on the tool to activate the display. If a specific ATM test is desired, hold the ATM button down until the desired test code appears.

3. The computer will continue to turn the selected circuit on and off for as long as 5 minutes or until the ATM button is pressed again or the ignition switch is turned to the **OFF** position.

4. If the ATM button is not pressed again, the computer will continue to cycle the selected circuit for 5 minutes and then

shut the system off. Turning the ignition to the **OFF** position will also turn the test mode off.

ACTUATOR TEST DISPLAY CODES

01 — Spark activation — once every 2 seconds
02 — Injector activation — once every 2 seconds
03 — AIS activation — one step open, one step closed every 4 seconds
04 — Radiator fan relay — once every 2 seconds
05 — A/C WOT cutout relay — once every 2 seconds
06 — ASD relay activation — once every 2 seconds
07 — Purge solenoid activation — one toggle every 2 seconds

OBTAINING SENSOR READ TEST MODE DISPLAY CODES

With the diagnostic readout box, tool number C–4805 or its equivalent, sensor voltage, degrees F, vacuum, rpm and mileage reading can be determined with the vehicle's engine both **OFF** and **On**.

Since each available diagnostic readout box may differ in its interpretation and display of the sensor results, refer to the instructional procedure that accompanies each tester unit.

LEAVING DIAGNOSTIC MODE

By turning the ignition switch to the **OFF** position, the test mode system is turned off and exited.

With a diagnostic readout box attached to the system and the ATM control button not pressed, the computer will continue to cycle the selected circuits for 5 minutes and then automatically shut the system down.

Chrysler Multi-Point Fuel Injected Systems

The turbocharged multi-point electronic fuel injection system combines an electronic fuel and spark advance control system with a turbocharged intake system.

At the center of the system is a digital, pre-programmed computer, identified as the logic module. It regulates ignition timing, air ratio, emission control devices and idle speed. This electronic component has the ability to update and revise its programming to meet changing operating conditions.

Various sensors provide the input necessary for the logic module to correctly regulate the fuel flow at the fuel injectors. These include the manifold absolute pressure, throttle position, oxygen feedback, coolant temperature, charge temperature and vehicle speed sensors. In addition to the sensors, various switches also provide important information. The switches are the transmission neutral safety, the air conditioning clutch and the brake switch.

Inputs to the logic module are converted into signals sent to the power module. These signals cause the power module to change either the fuel flow at the injector, ignition timing or both.

The logic module tests many of its own inputs and output circuits. If a fault is found in a major circuit, this information is stored in the logic module. Information of this fault can be displayed to a technician by means of the instrument panel POWER LOSS lamp or by connecting a diagnostic readout and observing a numbered display code which directly relates to a general fault.

POWER MODULE

The power module circuits powers the ignition coil, the fuel injectors and the alternator field circuit. These units are high current devices and have been isolated to minimize any electrical noise reaching the logic module. The power module also ener-

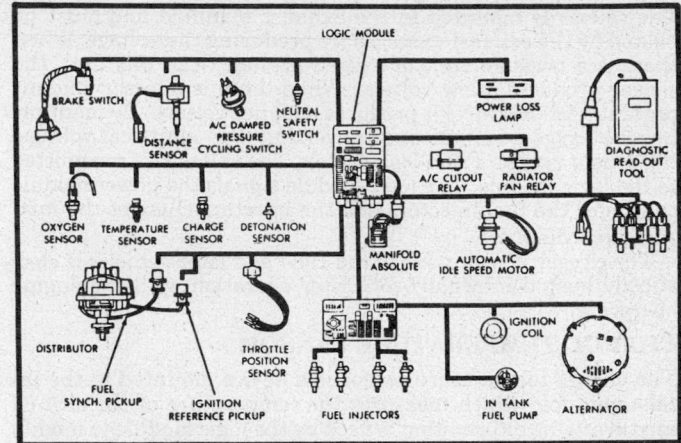

Chrysler electronic multi point fuel injection system

gizes the Automatic Shutdown (ASD) Relay, which activates the fuel pump, ignition coil, the power module and the injector.

NOTE: The ASD is turned OFF and ON by the logic module.

The distributor pick-up signal is sent to the logic module only. Again, if no distributor signal is sent, the ASD relay is not activated and the power is shut off from the fuel and the ignition coil.

The power module contains a voltage converter which reduces battery voltage to a regulated 8.0V output. This 8.0V output powers the distributor and the logic module.

LOGIC MODULE

The logic module receives its input signals from sensors and switches. It then computes the fuel injector pulse width spark advance, ignition coil dwell, idle speed, purge, cooling fan turn on and alternator charge rate.

The logic module tests many of its own input and output circuits If a fault is found in a major system, this information is stored in the logic module . Information on this fault can be displayed by a technician by means of the instrument panel power loss lamp or by connecting a diagnostic read-out tester and reading a numbered display code, which directly relates to a general fault.

AUTOMATIC SHUTDOWN RELAY (ASD)

The ASD relay is incorporated within the power module, but is turned off and on by the logic module. The distributor signal is sent to the logic module and in the event of no distributor signal, the ASD relay is not activated and the power is shut off from the fuel components and ignition coil.

SENSORS

MANIFOLD ABSOLUTE PRESSURE (MAP) SENSOR

The Manifold Absolute Pressure (MAP) sensor is a device which monitors manifold vacuum. The MAP sensor is mounted on the logic module. Both are connected to a vacuum nipple on the throttle body and electrically to the logic module. The sensor transmits information on manifold vacuum conditions and barometric pressure to the logic module. The MAP sensor data on engine load is used with data from other sensors to determine the correct air mixture.

OXYGEN SENSOR

The oxygen sensor is a device which produces an electrical voltage when exposed to the oxygen present in the exhaust gases.

The sensor is mounted in the exhaust manifold and must be heated by the exhaust gases before producing the voltage. When there is a large amount of oxygen present (lean mixture), the sensor produces a low voltage. When there is a lesser amount present (rich mixture) it produces a higher voltage. By monitoring the oxygen content and converting it to electrical voltage, the sensor acts as a rich-lean switch. The voltage is transmitted to the logic module. The logic module signals the power module to trigger the fuel injectors and the injectors changes the mixture accordingly.

The oxygen sensor used in the 1987 and later vehicles is electrically heated internally for faster operation with the engine operating.

CHARGE TEMPERATURE SENSOR

The charge temperature sensor is a device mounted in the intake manifold which measures the temperature of the air/fuel mixture. This information is used by the logic module to modify the fuel/air ratio and the boost level.

COOLANT TEMPERATURE SENSOR

The coolant temperature sensor is mounted in the thermostat housing. This sensor provides data on engine operating temperature to the logic module. This data along with data provided by the charge temperature switch allows the logic module to demand slightly richer air mixtures and higher idle speeds until normal operating temperatures are reached. The coolant temperature sensor is also used to control the cooling fan.

DETONATION SENSOR

The detonation sensor is a device that generates a signal when spark knock occurs in the combustion chamber/s. It is mounted at a position on the intake manifold where detonation on each cylinder can be detected. The sensor provides information used by the logic module to modify spark advance and boost schedules in order to eliminate detonation.

SWITCH INPUT

Various switches provide information to the logic module. These include the idle and brake light switches. If one or more of these switches is sensed as being in the on position, the logic module signals the automatic idle speed motor to increase idle speed to a scheduled rpm.

With the air conditioning on and the throttle blade above a specific angle, the wide open throttle cut-out relay prevents the air conditioning clutch from engaging until the throttle blade is below this angle.

THROTTLE POSITION SENSOR (TPS)

The Throttle Position Sensor (TPS) is an electric resistor which is activated by the movement of the throttle-shaft. It is mounted on the throttle body and senses the angle of the throttle blade opening. The voltage that the sensor produces increases or decreases according to the throttle blade opening. This voltage is transmitted to the logic module where it is used along with data from other sensors to adjust the air ratio to varying conditions and during acceleration, deceleration, idle and wide open throttle operations.

AUTOMATIC IDLE SPEED (AIS) MOTOR

The Automatic Idle Speed motor (AIS) is operated by the logic module. Data from the throttle position sensor, speed sensor, coolant temperature sensor and various switch operations, (electric backlite, air conditioning safety/neutral, brake) are used by the logic module to adjust engine idle to an optimum during all idle conditions. The AIS adjusts the air portion of the air/fuel mixture through an air bypass on the back of the throttle body. Basic (no load) idle is determined by the minimum air flow through the throttle body.

The AIS opens or closes off the air bypass as an increase or de-

crease is needed due to engine loads or ambient conditions. The logic module senses an air/fuel change and increases or decreases fuel proportionally to change engine idle. Deceleration die out is also prevented by increasing engine idle when the throttle is closed quickly after a driving (speed) condition.

POWER LOSS/LIMITED LAMP

The power loss lamp comes on each time the ignition key is turned on and stays on for 3 seconds as a bulb test. If the logic module receives an incorrect signal or no signal from either the coolant temperature sensor, charge temperature sensor, manifold absolute pressure sensor, the throttle position sensor, or the battery voltage sensor input, the power loss lamp on the instrument panel is illuminated. This is a warning that the logic module has gone into LIMP-IN mode in an attempt to keep the system operational and is a signal for immediate service.

DISPLAY OF FAULT CODES BY POWER LOSS LAMP

The power loss lamp is also used to display fault codes. To enter the system, cycle the ignition switch ON, OFF, ON, OFF, ON within 5 seconds and any fault codes stored in the logic module will be displayed.

LIMP-IN MODE

The LIMP-IN mode is the attempt by the logic module to compensate for the failure of certain components by substituting information from other sources. If the logic module senses incorrect data or no data at all from the MAP sensor, throttle position sensor or coolant temperature sensor, the system is placed into LIMP-IN Mode and the power loss lamp on the instrument panel is activated.

THROTTLE BODY

The throttle body replaces a conventional carburetor and is mounted on top of the intake manifold. The throttle body houses the fuel injector, pressure regulator, throttle positioner sensor, automatic idle speed motor and the throttle body temperature sensor.

The air flow through the throttle body is controlled by a cable operated throttle blade, located in the base of the body. The throttle body provides the chamber for metering atomized fuel to mix with the air entering the engine.

FUEL INJECTORS AND FUEL RAIL

The 4 fuel injectors are retained in the fuel rail by lock rings. The rail and injector assembly is then bolted into position with the injectors inserted in the recessed holes in the intake manifold.

The fuel injector is an electrical solenoid, driven by the power module, but controlled by the logic module. The logic module, based on sensor input, determines when and how long the power module should operate the injector. The system operates at a pressure of 55 psi.

OPERATING SOLENOIDS

Various solenoids are used to control the charcoal canister purge (L body—black dot), the EGR system (L body—white dot), a combination of purge/EGR (Turbo I and II), barometric read solenoid (one for L body — blue dot and one for Turbo I and II) and wastegate control solenoid (one for L body and one for other models). These solenoids are controlled by the logic module in their operation and timing.

ON-BOARD DIAGNOSTICS

The logic module has been programmed to monitor several different circuits of the fuel injection system. This monitoring is called On-Board Diagnosis. If a problem is sensed with a monitored circuit, often enough to indicate an actual problem, its fault code is stored in the logic module for eventual display to the service technician. If the problem is repaired or ceases to exist, the logic module cancels the fault code after 30 ignition key **ON/OFF** cycles.

FAULT CODES

When a fault code appears (either by flashes of the light emitting diode or by watching the diagnostic readout, tool C–4805 or equivalent, it indicates that the logic module has recognized an abnormal signal in the system. Fault codes indicate the results of a failure but do not always identify the failed component.

CODE 88 — Start of test
CODE 11 — Engine not cranked since battery disconnected
CODE 12 — Memory standby power lost
CODE 13 — MAP Sensor pneumatic circuit*
CODE 14 — MAP sensor electrical system*
CODE 15 — Vehicle Speed Sensor circuit
CODE 16 — Lose of battery voltage sense*
CODE 17 — Engine is running too cool
CODE 21 — Oxygen sensor (O_2) sensor circuit.
CODE 22 — Coolant temperature sensor circuit*
CODE 23 — Charge temperature sensor circuit
CODE 24 — Throttle position sensor circuit*
CODE 25 — Automatic idle speed (AIS) control circuit
CODE 26 — No. 1 injector circuit
CODE 27 — No. 2 injector circuit
CODE 31 — Canister purge solenoid circuit (1986) EGR/purge solenoid circuit (1987–90)
CODE 33 — A/C wide cut out relay circuit
CODE 34 — Problem in the EGR solenoid circuit (1986): Speed control malfunction (1987–90)
CODE 35 — Fan control relay circuit
CODE 36 — Wastegate solenoid circuit*
CODE 37 — Barometric read solenoid circuit
CODE 41 — Charging system excess or no field circuit
CODE 42 — Automatic shutdown relay driver (ASD) circuit
CODE 43 — Spark interface (internal) circuits
CODE 44 — Indicate battery temperature is out of range models
CODE 45 — Overboost shut-off circuit*
CODE 46 — Battery voltage too high*
CODE 47 — Battery voltage too low
CODE 51 — O_2 signal stuck at the lean position
CODE 52 — O_2 signal stuck at the rich position
CODE 53 — Logic module problem or failure
CODE 54 — Distributor sync pick-up circuit
CODE 55 — means "end of message"

NOTE: * indicates the power loss/limited lamp is on.

SYSTEMS TEST

Obtaining Fault Codes

1. Connect diagnostic readout box tool C–4805 or equivalent, to the diagnostic connector located in the engine compartment near the passenger side strut tower.
2. Start the engine if possible, cycle the transmission selector and the A/C switch, if applicable. Shut off the engine.
3. Turn the ignition switch **ON, OFF, ON, OFF, ON** within 5 seconds. Record all the diagnostic codes shown on the diagnostic readout box tool, observe the power loss lamp on the instrument panel the lamp should light for 3 seconds, then go out (bulb check).

Switch Test

After all codes have been shown and has indicated Code 55 (end of message), actuate the following component switches. The digital display must change its numbers when the switch is activated and released:
Brake pedal.
Gear shift selector P, R, P.
A/C switch (if applicable).

OBTAINING CIRCUIT ACTUATION TEST MODE (ATM TEST)

1. Put the system into the diagnostic test mode and wait for code 55 to appear on the display screen.
2. Press ATM button on the tool to activate the display. If a specific ATM test is desired, hold the ATM button down until the desired test code appears.
3. The computer will continue to turn the selected circuit on and off for as long as 5 minutes or until the ATM button is pressed again or the ignition switch is turned to the **OFF** position.
4. If the ATM button is not pressed again, the computer will continue to cycle the selected circuit for 5 minutes and then shut the system off. Turning the ignition to the **OFF** position will also turn the test mode off.

ACTUATOR TEST DISPLAY CODES

CODE 01 — Spark activation — once every 2 seconds
CODE 02 — Injector activation — once every 2 seconds
CODE 03 — AIS activation — one pulse open, 1 pulse closed every 4 seconds
CODE 04 — Radiator fan relay — 1 pulse every 2 seconds
CODE 05 — A/C WOT cutout relay — 1 pulse every 2 seconds
CODE 06 — ASD relay activation — 1 toggle every 2 seconds
CODE 07 — EGR/Purge solenoid activation — 1 toggle every 2 seconds
CODE 08 — Speed control switch ON, S/C vacuum and vent solenoid activation — every 2 seconds
CODE 09 — Wastegate solenoid activation — 1 toggle every 2 seconds
CODE 10 — Barometric read solenoid activation — 1 toggle every 2 seconds
CODE 11 — Alternator full field activation — 1 toggle every 2 seconds

OBTAINING SENSOR READ TEST MODE DISPLAY CODES

With the diagnostic readout box, tool number C–4805 or its equivalent, sensor voltage, degrees F., vacuum, rpm and mileage reading can be determined with the vehicle's engine both off and on.
Since each available diagnostic readout box may differ in its interpretation and display of the sensor results, refer to the instructional procedure that accompanies each tester unit.

LEAVING DIAGNOSTIC MODE

By turning the ignition switch to the **OFF** position, the test mode system is turned off and exited.
With a diagnostic readout box attached to the system and the ATM control button not pressed, the computer will continue to cycle the selected circuits for 5 minutes and then automatically shut the system down.

FORD MOTOR COMPANY MICROPROCESSOR CONTROL UNIT (MCU) SYSTEM

General Information

The MCU system's primary task is to maintain a balance between the engine's performance, the vehicle emissions and fuel economy. To accomplish this, the MCU system regulates the air/fuel mixture at the carburetor for the best engine performance, while controlling the vehicle's catalyst system with the addition of the thermactor air for maximum catalytic efficiency.

The MCU system uses sensors similar to those used on the EEC systems. The major difference between the 2 systems is that, unlike the EEC systems, the MCU systems do not control engine timing. However, some of the MCU applications do provide inputs to retard ignition timing during periods of spark knock.

Unlike the EEC systems, the MCU system receives, rather than sends a timing signal imput from the ignition module. The ground pulse signal from, the ignition module is the same signal applied to the ignition coil's primary circuit. The frequency of this signal is proportional to the engine speed and is used by the MCU module to control the damping of the air/fuel mixture output signal.

For the system to operate at peak engine and catalyst performance, the MCU system receives information from the various sends so that it can analyze the engine operation. After the analysis, the system will forward output signals to the regulation components to manage the vehicle's air/fuel ratio, thermactor system and the canister purge system.

MCU MODULE

The MCU module is the main controller of the MCU system. It operates similar to the electronic control unit used on the EEC systems. However, it does not perform as many functions as an ECA.

Since good emissions and fuel economy do not mix to provide good engine performance, the MCU module operates in 3 fuel control modes. This allows it to assist in the compatibility of good emissions, fuel economy and engine performance.

MCU MODULE OPERATING MODES

The MCU system has 3 operating modes. These modes are system initialization (start-up), open loop and closed loop.

SYSTEM INITIALIZATION (START-UP)

The MCU module will initialize when battery power is applied to the computer prior to engine cranking and again immediately with engine starting. During initialization, the duty cycle to the vacuum regulator solenoid is maintained at 50%. After starting, initialization lasts for only a fraction of a second. Then, the MCU system goes into the open or closed loop.

OPEN LOOP MODE

The system is in the open loop mode when either the cold temperature vacuum switch or idle tracking switch is activated. In the open loop mode, the MCU module will control the duty cycle with ON time signals to the vacuum regulator solenoid. These will provide a calibrated air mixture.

CLOSED LOOP MODE

With the proper signals from the idle tracking switch and the cold temperature switch, the MCU module changes to the closed loop mode for close range monitoring and control of the air ratio. The exhaust gas oxygen sensor monitors the exhaust gas to determine if the engine is running rich or lean.

This information is used by the MCU module to adjust the carburetor to the air ratio desired for the operating condition. Signals from the MCU module, which produce carburetor adjustments, are calibrated. This provides a damping effect to minimize over-correction and abrupt changes in the air/fuel ratio.

System Diagnosis

PRELIMINARY INSPECTION

A routine inspection should be the first procedure the technician should use to begin the diagnosis of the MCU system. Broken or frayed wires, loose connections, obvious shorts, disconnected or damaged vacuum hoses are among the areas that should be inspected and corrected before any tests are done.

SELF-TEST CAPABILITIES

The MCU has the capability to diagnose a malfunction within its own system. However, it is not designed to diagnose malfunctions outside the MCU system.

Through the use of trouble code indications, the system will indicate to the technician where to look for MCU problems through the use of a self-test computer program, built into the MCU module. Standard test equipment, such as an analog voltmeter, can be used to check the system, or a special tester can be used to simplify the testing procedure on the MCU self-test connector.

When the analog voltmeter or the special tester is connected to the test connector and the system is triggered, the self-test simulates a variety of engine operating conditions and evaluates all the responses received from the various MCU components, so that any abnormal operating condition can be detected.

SELF-TEST PROCEDURE

The MCU system incorporates a self-test connector, located near the MCU module in the engine compartment on one of the fender aprons, for isolating problems in the system.

A received response to the initiated self-test is reported, through the self-test connector to one of 2 testing devices, an analog voltmeter or a Self-Test Automatic Readout (STAR) tester, which in turn indicate service codes as a pulsing series of electrical outputs, displayed on the meters of the testers.

The service codes are displayed by the series of electrical pulses which indicate a 2 digit number. This 2 digit service code indicates to the technician the nature of the MCU system's problem.

CONNECTION OF ANALOG VOLTMETER

1. With the ignition key in the **OFF** position, connect a jumper wire between circuits 60 and 201 on the self-test connector.
2. Connect an analog voltmeter from the battery positive post to the self-test output on the self-test connector.
3. Set the voltmeter on the DC volt range to read from 0–15 volts.

NOTE: One quick initialization pulse may occur on the voltmeter immediately after turning the ignition key to the ON position. The output service code will occur in approximately 5 seconds.

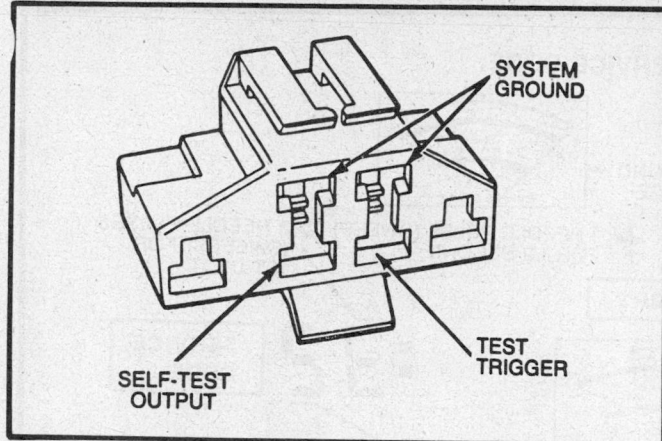

MCU Self-Test connector

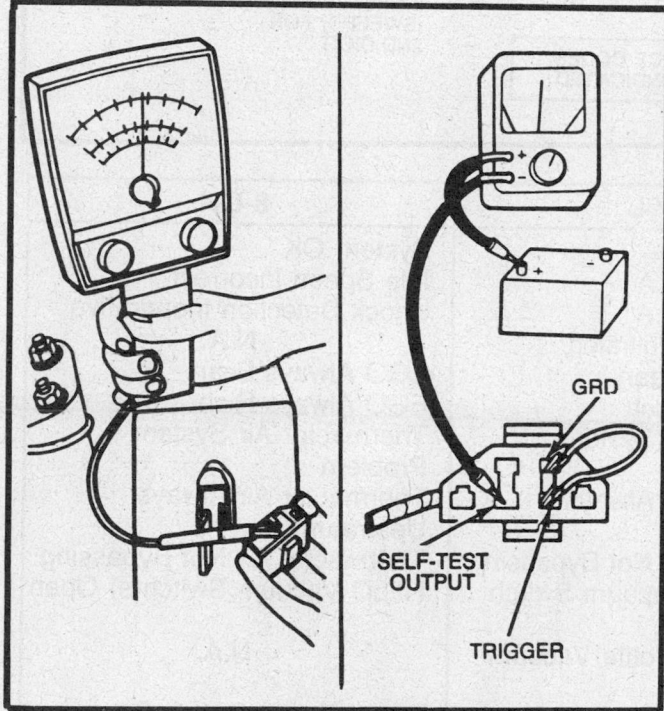

MCU Self-Test with analog voltmeter

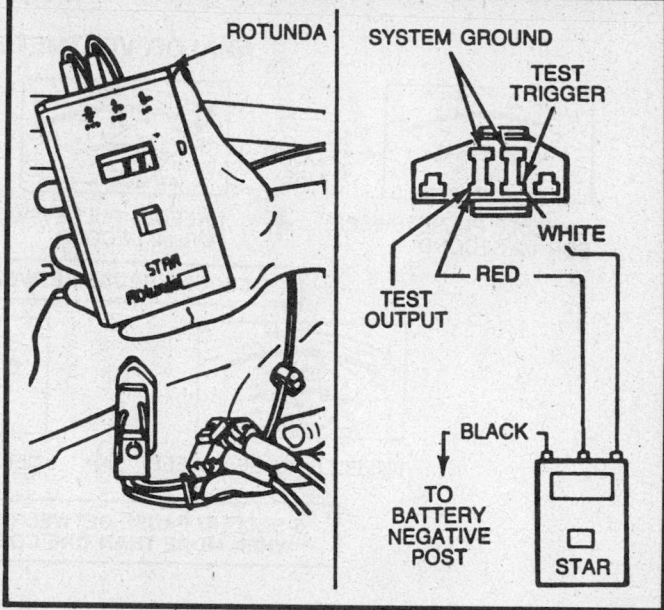

MCU Self-Test with STAR tester

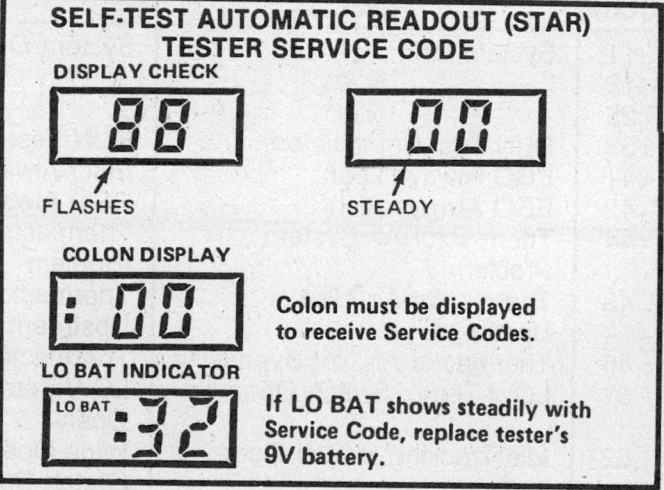

SELF-TEST AUTOMATIC READOUT (STAR)
TESTER SERVICE CODE

MCU Service Code display on STAR tester

CONNECTION OF STAR TESTER

NOTE: Operating instruction for the STAR tester are located on the back panel of the tester.

1. With the ignition key in the **OFF** position, connect the black negative lead to the battery's negative post.
2. Connect the red lead to the self-test output terminal on the self-test connector.
3. Connect the white lead to the self-test trigger on the self-test connector.

DIAGNOSTIC PROCEDURE

ANALOG VOLTMETER

With the analog voltmeter connected and the ignition switch turned to the **ON** position, without the engine operating, the MCU system is placed in its reporting service code mode.

When a service code is reported on the analog meter, it will represent itself as a pulsing or sweeping movement of the volt-meter scale's needle across the dial face of the meter. Therefore, a single digit number of 3 will be indicated by 3 pulses (sweeps) of the needle across the dial. Since the service codes are indicated by a 2 digit number, such as 32, the self-test's service code of 32 will be displayed as 3 pulses (sweeps) of the meter's needle with a one-half second pause between pulses (sweeps) and a 2 second pause between digits. When more than one service code is indicated, a 5 second pause between service codes will occur.

SELF-TEST AUTOMATIC READOUT (STAR) TESTER

After connecting the tester and turning on its power switch, the tester will run a display check with the numerals 88 beginning to flash in the display window. A steady 00 will then appear to signify that the tester is ready to start the self-test and receive the stored service codes.

In order to receive the service codes, press the pushbutton on the front of the tester. The button will latch down and a colon will appear in the display window in the front of the 00 numerals (:00). The colon MUST be displayed before the trouble codes can be received.

Follow the instruction accompanying the tester to complete the self-test procedure.

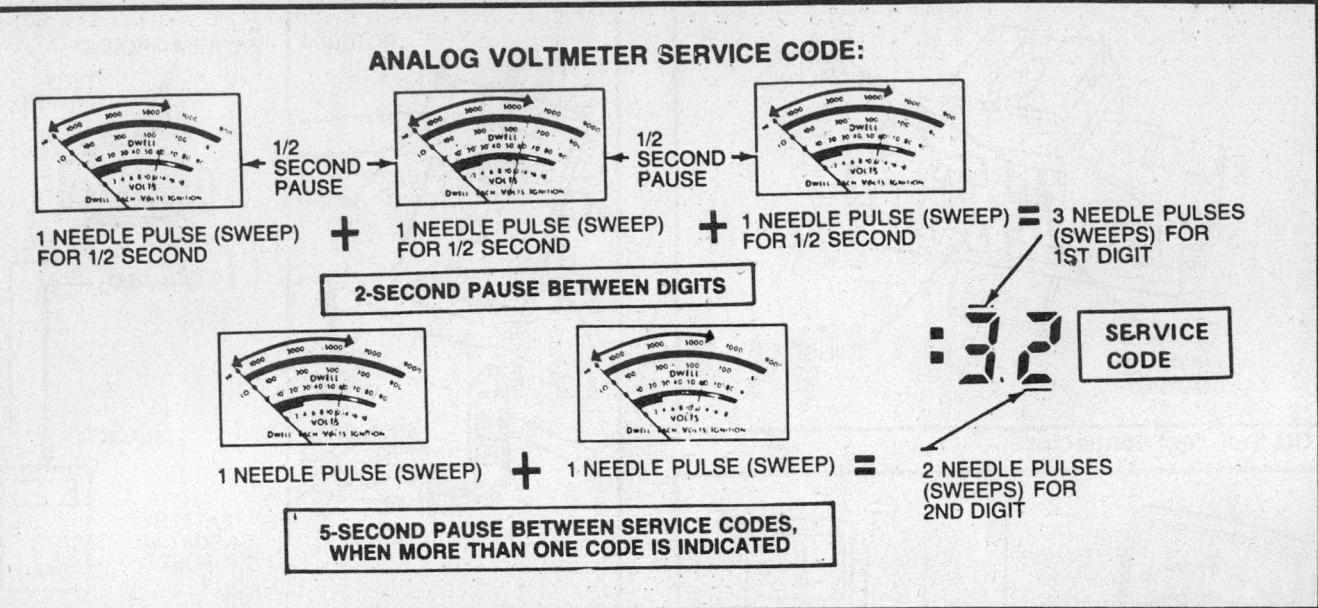

ANALOG VOLTMETER SERVICE CODE:

MCU Service Code display on analog voltmeter

Code	2.3L	4.9L	8-Cyl.
11	System OK	System OK	System OK
12	N.A.	N.A.	Idle Speed Incorrect
25	N.A.	N.A.	Knock Detection Inoperative
33	RUN Test Not Initiated	RUN Test Not Initiated	N.A.
41	EGO Always Lean	EGO Always Lean	EGO Always Lean
42	EGO Always Rich	EGO Always Rich	EGO Always Rich
44	Thermactor Air System Problem	Thermactor Air System Problem	Thermactor Air System Problem
45	Thermactor Air Always Upstream	Thermactor Air Always Upstream	Thermactor Air Always Upstream
46	Thermactor Air Not Bypassing	Thermactor Air Not Bypassing	Thermactor Air Not Bypassing
51	LOW-Temp. Switch Open	LOW-Temp. Vacuum Switch Open	HI/LO Vacuum Switch(s) Open
52	Idle Tracking Switch Open	Wide-Open-Throttle Vacuum Switch Open	N.A.
53	Wide-Open-Throttle Vacuum Switch Open	Crowd Vacuum Switch Open	DUAL-Temp. Switch Open
54	N.A.	N.A.	MID-Temp. Switch Open
55	N.A.	N.A.	MID-Vacuum (MIDVAC) Switch Open
56	N.A.	Closed-Throttle Vacuum Switch Open	N.A.
61	N.A.	N.A.	HI/LO Vacuum Switch(es) Closed
62	Idle Tracking Switch Closed	Wide-Open-Throttle Vacuum Switch Closed	Altitude Switch*
63	Wide-Open-Throttle Vacuum Switch Closed	Crowd Vacuum Switch Closed	N.A.
65	Altitude Switch*	N.A.	MID-Vacuum (MIDVAC) Switch Closed
66	N.A.	Closed-Throttle Vacuum Switch Closed	N.A.

MCU Service Code explanation

OTHER CIRCUIT AND SELF-TEST UNITS

Numerous other self-test units have been developed to aid the technician in obtaining the stored trouble codes. Should these units be used in determining malfunctions or to retrieve stored trouble codes from the system, the manufacturer's operating procedures must be followed to prevent damage to the MCU system and/or the test unit.

EXITING THE MCU SYSTEM

To exit the MCU system, turn the ignition key to the **OFF** position and disconnect the read-out meter from the self-test connnector.

FORD MOTOR COMPANY EEC-IV ELECTRONIC ENGINE CONTROL SYSTEM

General Information

The EEC-IV system is the fifth generation of electronic engine controls developed and produced by Ford Motor Company. In the past, the engine's air/fuel mixture, ignition and emission systems were controlled by independently functioning vacuum and/or mechanical devices. With the EEC-IV system, these processes are now controlled by the Electronic Control Assembly (ECA), a small electronic computer. This integrated control provides for optimal engine performance and driveability, maximum fuel efficiency and minimum noxious emissions under any operating condition.

In order to control these many different processes that are part of the engine control system, the EEC-IV system must have the ability to monitor each process individually. In addition, the EEC-IV system needs devices which allow it to control these processes. The EEC-IV system allows the ECA to read and evaluate the signals it receives from each of its system inputs.

NOTE: System inputs are sensors that transmit signals to the ECA. These signals indicate what is taking place at key locations in and around the engine.

The ECA uses these same input signals as the basis for commands sent to the system output.

NOTE: System outputs are actuating devices that perform a specific function whenever the ECA signals them to do so.

BASE ENGINE STRATEGY

The base engine strategy for the EEC-IV system controls the system in a wide range of conditions found during normal driving and is divided into the same 4 sub-modes as was controlled by the EEC-III system. They are as follows:
  Crank mode
  Closed throttle mode
  Part throttle mode
  Wide open throttle mode
EEC-IV also has the provisions for an underspeed mode. When the engine is operating and begins to stumble, the underspeed mode is entered to help the engine recover and is used to prevent the engine from stalling. A unique strategy is used in underspeed mode, in place of the normal engine run operation.

The ECA will determine the proper mode, based on information received from its sensors. It then controls the system by way of its actuators according to its internal calibration.

MODULAR STRATEGY

This strategy is used for uncommon operating conditions, as was used in the EEC-III system.

LIMITED OPERATIONAL STRATEGY

The limited operational strategy on the EEC-IV system is different than that used on the EEC-III system. When the ECA can

no longer operate under a normal strategy, the ECA will enter an alternate strategy. Also, if the central processing unit (CPU) should fail, the ECA will control the outputs on a fixed mode, such as: no EGR system, fixed base timing, no canister purge, etc.

ADAPTIVE STRATEGY

Adaptive strategy is a new feature added to the EEC-IV system. This feature continually adjusts the calibration strategy to correct for wear and aging of calibration components. This adaptive strategy then retains the adjustments in the KEEP ALIVE MEMORY so they will not be lost or cancelled when the engine is turned off.

LEARNING PERIOD

A short learning period will occur on new vehicles, when the battery has been disconnected during normal service and when an EEC-IV component is disconnected or replaced.

If, due to age or damage, an EEC-IV component is replaced, the memory may need to be cleared to eliminate the adjustments that were made to correct for the replaced component. It is possible for the engine operation to actually deteriorate because the new component will be controlled as if it were still the replaced aged or damaged component.

During the adjustment or learning period, usually under 5 miles of driving, some vehicles could exhibit abnormal drive symptoms, such as surge, hesitation, high idle speed, etc., which should clear up after the learning period.

FAILURE MODE EFFECTS MANAGEMENT

Improvements have been made on the EEC-IV system to provide better driveability when one or more sensors fail. The basic improvement within the ECA is that each sensor now has an input operating range. The ECA monitors whether the sensor is operating within it operating limits. When an out of limit condition occurs, the ECA will store a diagnostic code in its memory and will substitute an in-limit signal.

By substituting an in-limit signal, an alternate system strategy comes into operation, which allows the vehicle to continue running. Prior to this change, the engine may have stalled or may not have run at all. With the addition of the failure mode effects management, the vehicle can now be started and operated. It may not run well, but it will allow the operator to drive the vehicle to a service center.

KEEP ALIVE MEMORY

The EEC-IV system has a KEEP ALIVE MEMORY, which the other systems did not have. The ECA retains any intermittent trouble codes stored within the last 20 engine restarts. With this system, the memory is not erased when the key is turned off. Trouble codes retained in the ECA are used by the technicians to evaluate and diagnose the EEC-IV system.

NOTE: In the EEC-IV system, the reference voltage is

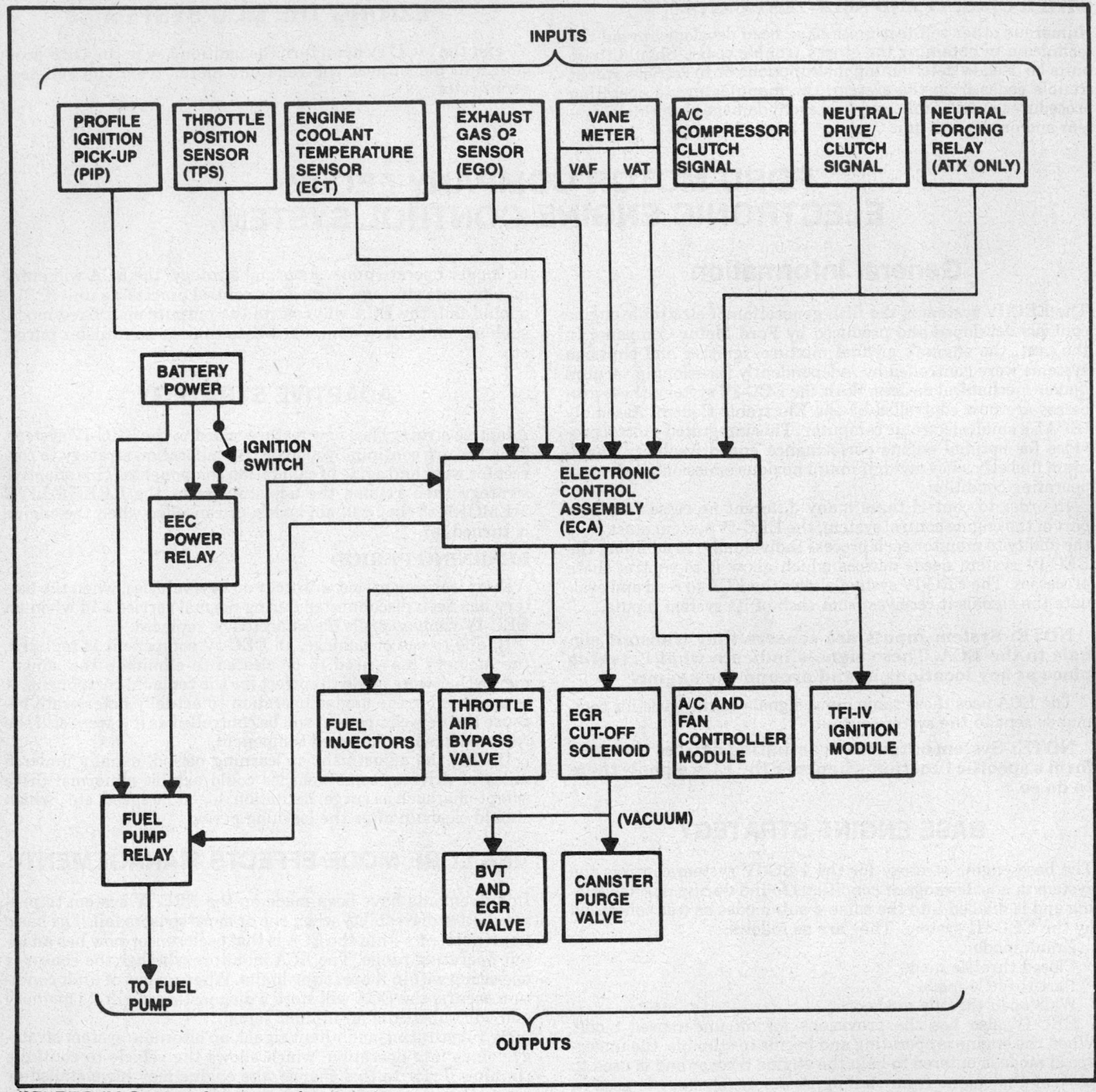

EFI-EEC IV System Inputs and outputs

5 volts, instead of the 9 volts used with the other EEC systems and a power relay is used to provide all necessary power required for the EEC-IV system.

EEC-IV SELF-TEST

The EEC-IV system has the capability of checking the electronic components in the system. This self-test, often referred to as a QUICK TEST, is an internal function performed by the Electronic Control Assembly (ECA), in which the ECA checks the operational status of every circuit and component in the EEC-IV system.

NOTE: The EEC-IV self-test only checks the system components, such as sensors, relays, switches and solenoids. It cannot provide information on driveability/engine performance problems, unless related to one of the system's components.

During the self-test, the ECA reads and evaluates signals received from the system input components. The input components are checked by the ECA during a KEY ON/ENGINE OFF and during the ENGINE RUNNING portion of the test.

This self-test also allows the technician to determine if the ECA is capable of controlling the ignition timing of the engine, since different engine operating modes require the timing be advanced or retarded. The ECA must do this automatically or the engine will not perform properly.

NOTE: EEC-IV system engines have an in-line base timing connector that must be disconnected to check the base ignition timing. The connector is part of the SPOUT circuit and when disconnected, interrupts the electronic timing signal and locks the system into a fixed timing base. The SPOUT connector is located within 6 inches of the distributor on all EEC-IV applications.

SELF-TEST PROCEDURE

The EEC-IV system self-test can be performed by either an analog voltmeter or by the Self-Test Automatic Readout (STAR) tester or its equivalent. Other types of automatic testers are marketed and are available to the technicians. With each of the automatic testers, it is imperative that the technician follows the manufacturer's instructions on hook-up and display procedures.

KEY ON/ENGINE OFF (KOEO)

In this segment of the test, the system inputs and outputs are checked for existing faults. These type of faults are referred to as HARD FAULTS in this test procedure because they represent a failure that is always present. Also, the system is checked for INTERMEDIATE FAULTS, which indicate that a problem did exist recently somewhere in the system. The fault is not now present, but it did occur some time recently. This usually indicates a loose wire, a bad connection, a broken wire that opens periodically, or some failure similar to these. Some times, recent work that may have been done to the vehicle is good place to start when trying to determine the root of an intermediate problem.

KEY ON/ENGINE RUNNING (KOER)

In this portion of the test, the system is checked under all operating conditions. The output devices are all activated to check for proper operation. Only HARD FAULTS are noted during this test.

INTERMITTENT FAULT CONFIRMATION CHECK

This test is also referred to as the WIGGLE TEST because connectors, wires and components are wiggled during the check. This test is performed if intermittent faults are indicated during the KEY ON/ENGINE OFF segment of the self-test.

ANALOG VOLTMETER CONNECTION

1. Set the analog voltmeter on a DC voltage range to read from 0 to 15 volts. Insert one end of a jumper wire into the No.4 pin on the self-test output connector. Clamp the negative lead from the analog voltmeter to the other end of the jumper wire.
2. Clamp the positive lead from the voltmeter to the positive terminal of the battery.
3. Insert the end of a second jumper wire into the No. 2 terminal of the self-test output connector. Insert the other end of the jumper wire into the self-test input wire connector.

NOTE: The final connection to the self-test input wire connector also activates the self-test sequence inside the ECA when the ignition switch is turned ON.

SERVICE CODES

After the EEC-IV system completes its self-test, it communicates with the service technician by way of the analog voltmeter needle and scale.

When a service code is reported on the analog meter, it will represent itself as a pulsing or sweeping movement of the voltmeter scale's needle across the dial face of the meter. Therefore,

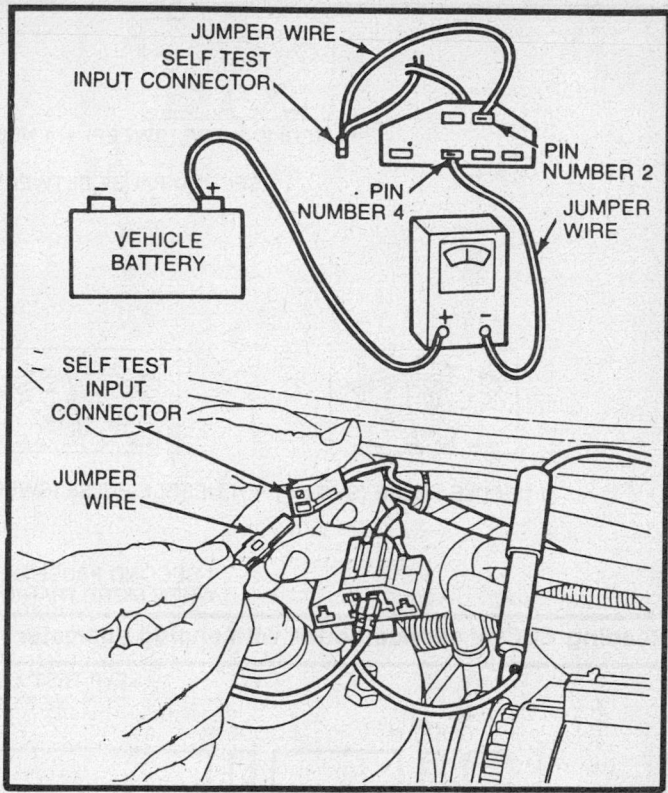

Connection of analog voltmeter to Self-Test input and output connectors

a single digit number of 3 will be indicated by 3 pulses (sweeps) of the needle across the dial. Since the service codes are indicated by a 2 digit number, such as 32, the self-test's service code of 32 will be displayed as 3 pulses (sweeps) of the meter's needle with a ½ second pause between pulses (sweeps) and a 2 second pause between digits. When more than one service code is indicated, a 4 second pause between service codes will occur.

Separator and dynamic response codes (numeral 10 in both cases), are represented by a single pulse or sweep of the needle. There are no pulses or sweeps generated for the digit 0. There will be a 6 second pause before each one of these.

The key to sorting out the service codes on the voltmeter is to keep the pulses and the pauses straight.

1. Each digit is separated by a 2 second pause.
2. Each code is separated by a 4 second pause.
3. Separator and dynamic response codes are separated from previous and subsequent codes by 6 second (or longer) pauses.

SERVICE CODE SEQUENCE

The self-test consists of 2 segments: key on/engine off and engine running. Each segment displays its own set of service codes.

KEY ON/ENGINE OFF SEQUENCE

FAST CODES

At the very beginning of the key on/engine off self-test sequence, the ECA generates standard service codes at a rate of approximately 100 times faster than a voltmeter can respond. These fast codes are read by special computer type machines in the assembly plants and maybe observed on the voltmeter by a slight deflection of the needle. They have no practical application in the service field.

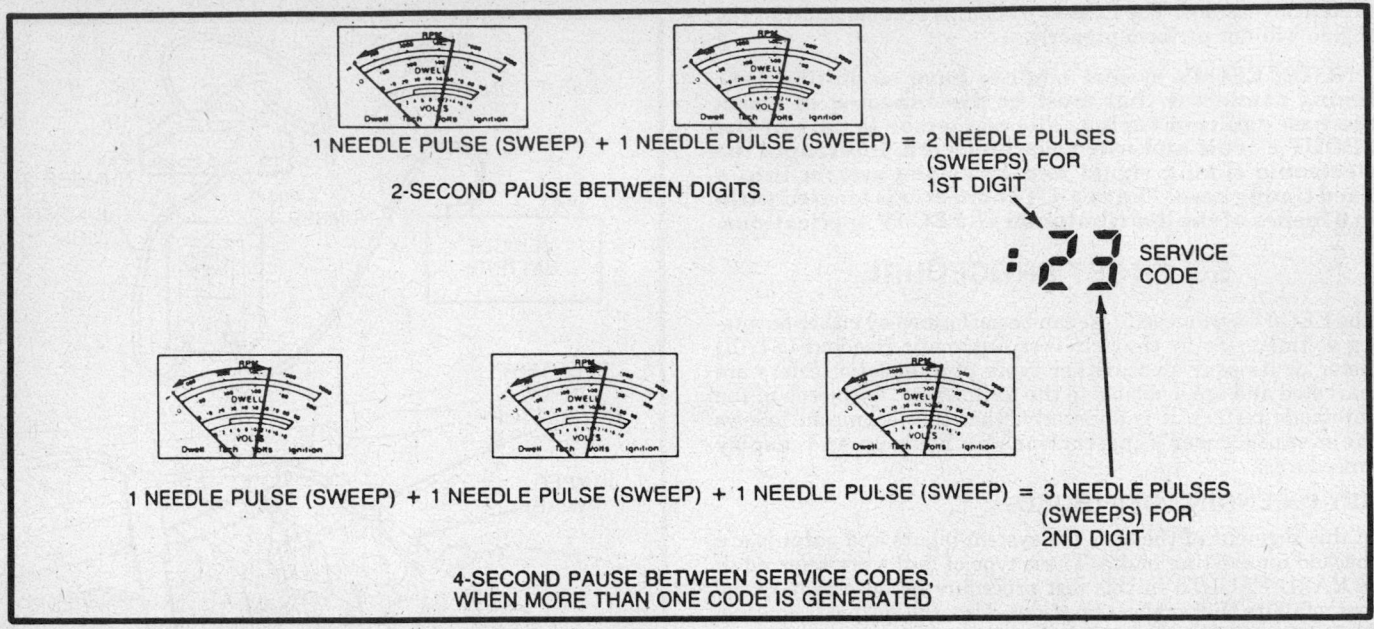

1 NEEDLE PULSE (SWEEP) + 1 NEEDLE PULSE (SWEEP) = 2 NEEDLE PULSES (SWEEPS) FOR 1ST DIGIT

2-SECOND PAUSE BETWEEN DIGITS

:23 SERVICE CODE

1 NEEDLE PULSE (SWEEP) + 1 NEEDLE PULSE (SWEEP) + 1 NEEDLE PULSE (SWEEP) = 3 NEEDLE PULSES (SWEEPS) FOR 2ND DIGIT

4-SECOND PAUSE BETWEEN SERVICE CODES, WHEN MORE THAN ONE CODE IS GENERATED

Reading EEC-IV service codes with analog voltmeter

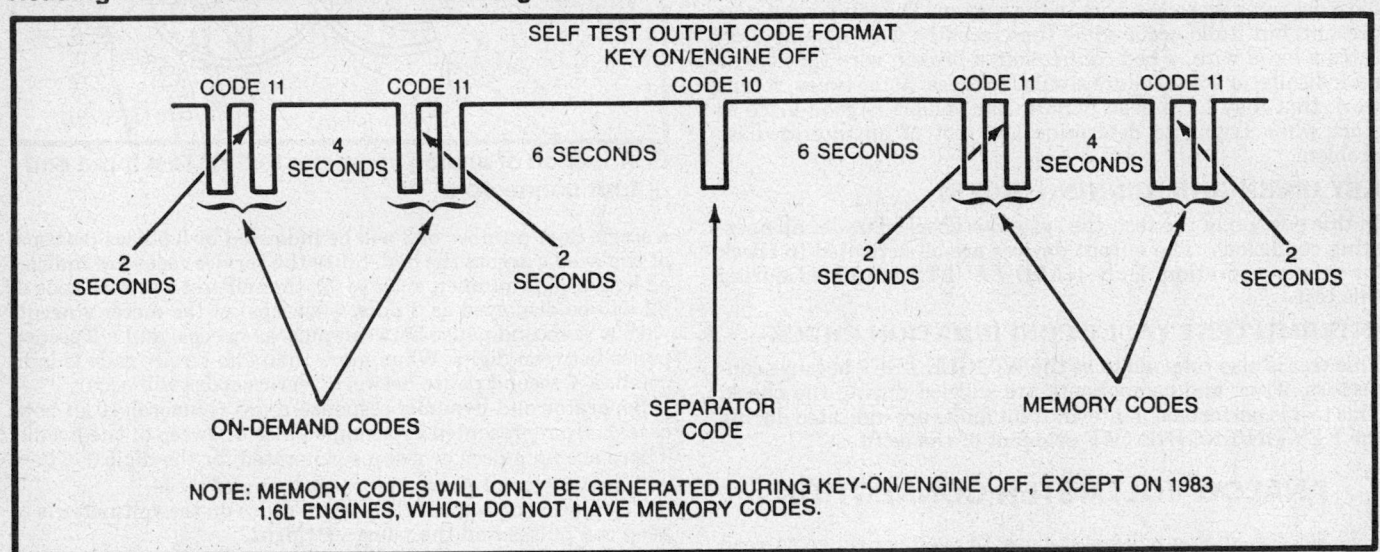

SELF TEST OUTPUT CODE FORMAT
KEY ON/ENGINE OFF

NOTE: MEMORY CODES WILL ONLY BE GENERATED DURING KEY-ON/ENGINE OFF, EXCEPT ON 1983 1.6L ENGINES, WHICH DO NOT HAVE MEMORY CODES.

EEC-IV KEY ON/ENGINE OFF self-test output code format

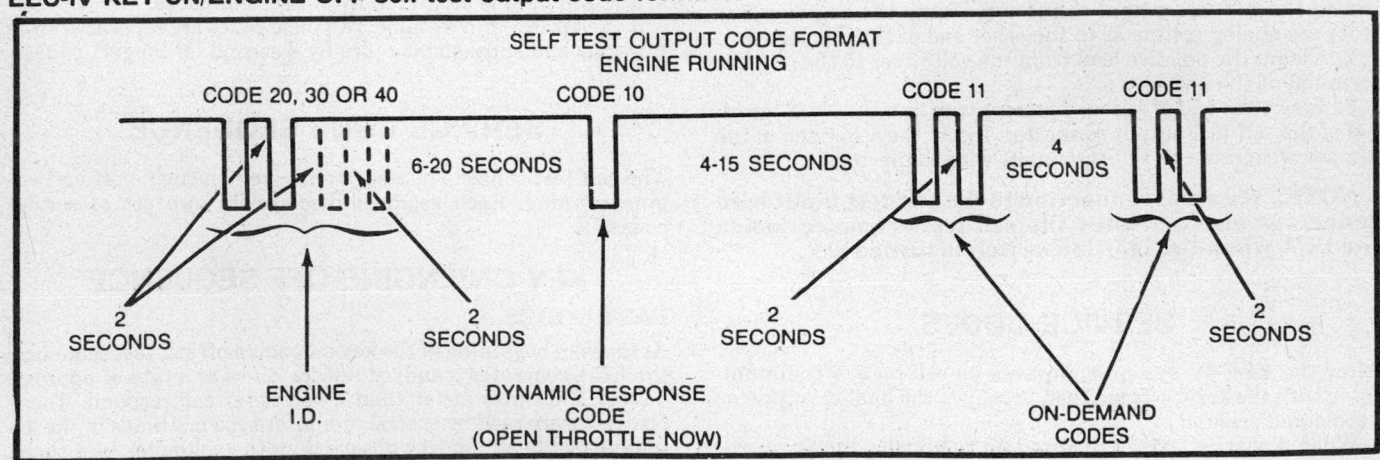

SELF TEST OUTPUT CODE FORMAT
ENGINE RUNNING

EEC-IV engine running self-test output code format

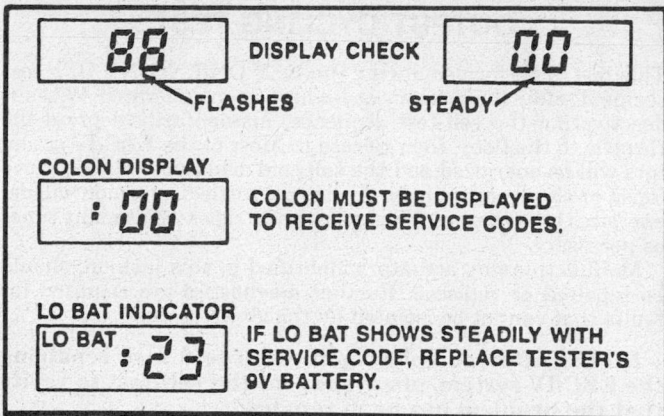

Self test output code format (Star Tester)

ON-DEMAND CODES

The on-demand codes indicate there is something wrong somewhere in the EEC-IV system at the time of the self-test. This type of malfunction is considered to be a HARD FAULT.

SEPARATOR CODES

The separator codes or pulses, cause the voltmeter needle to sweep once, indicating that on-demand codes have ceased and memory codes are about to begin.

MEMORY CODES

Memory codes indicate there was a recent problem, somewhere in the EEC-IV system, such as an open or short circuit, though it is not present at the time of the self-test. These codes are often referred to as intermediate faults.

ENGINE RUNNING SEGMENT

ENGINE IDENTIFICATION CODES

The engine identification codes have no practical application in the service field, but are part of the assembly process. When the self-test is initiated at the beginning of the engine running segment, the voltmeter needle will sweep 2, 3 or 4 times to denote a 4, 6 or 8 cylinder engine. The identification code multiplied by 2 equals the number of engine cylinders.

DYNAMIC RESPONSE CODE

The dynamic response code is indicated by the needle sweeping once, signals the operator to perform a brief wide open throttle. This allows the ECA to check for proper movement of the throttle position sensor and operation of the manifold absolute pressure sensor, The operator has 15 seconds to goose the engine after the dynamic response code appears. Otherwise a code 77 (operator did not do goose test) will appear.

ON-DEMAND CODES

The on-demand codes indicate there is something wrong in the EEC-IV system at this time. These faults or malfunctions are referred to as hard faults.

PERFORMING THE SELF-TEST

These 3 conditions must be met before performing the self-test procedures. They are as follows:
1. Preliminary check out of the engine, associated systems and vehicle systems and engine preparation must be performed.
2. Voltmeter must be connected and functioning properly.
3. The technician performing the self-test must know what to expect when the self-test is activated and what to do when the service codes begin being read out.

KEY ON/ENGINE OFF SEGMENT

1. Set the voltmeter to a range that covers 0–15 volts DC and connected as previously explained.
2. Connect a jumper wire from the No. 2 pin on the self-test connector to the self-test input connector.
3. Turn the ignition switch to the **ON** position.
4. Assuming the system inputs check out OK for hard and intermediate faults, service codes should be registering as follows:
   a. The needle will fluctuate from 0 to approximately 3 volts for fast codes.
   b. Next the needle will sweep twice, with a 2 second pause in between, representing a code 11 (system pass). The code 11 will be repeated once (in case it was missed the first time). There is a 4 second pause in between the codes.
   c. A 6 second pause is next, followed by a single sweep of the needle (representing the separator code). Another 6 second pause follows the separator pulse.
   d. Finally, the code 11 is repeated twice, again with a 4 second pause in between.

ENGINE RUNNING SEGMENT

1. Start the engine and run at approximately 1500 rpm for 2 minutes to warm the EGO sensor.
2. Turn the engine **OFF** and insert the jumper wire from the No. 2 pin on the self-test output connector to the self-test input wire connector.
3. Wait 10 seconds and then start the engine.
4. Assuming the system checks out OK for hard faults, the service codes should register as follows:
   a. The needle will sweep 2, 3 or 4 times without a pause, depending upon the number of cylinders in the engine.
   b. The needle will then sweep once after a 6 second to 20 second pause. This is the dynamic response code and the technician has 15 seconds to goose the throttle.
   c. A pause of 4–15 seconds will follow the goose test, after which the needle will fluctuate from 0–3 volts for the fast codes.
   d. Finally, the needle will sweep twice with a 2 second pause in between sweeps, representing another code 11. After 4 seconds, the code will be repeated.

INTERMITTENT FAULT CONFIRMATION CHECK (WIGGLE TEST)

The ECA is continually looking for shorts, open circuits and other problems within the EEC-IV system and when noted, stores them in the memory, when they occur. Memory codes obtained during the KEY ON/ENGINE OFF segment of the self test, recalls intermittent faults from the ECA memory. To make final diagnosis and repair as easy as possible, it is recommended that the technician do 2 things before proceeding to further diagnostics.
1. Repeat the self-test segment when any code other than SYSTEM PASS (code 11), is generated by the ECA.
2. Attempt to re-create intermittent faults while the test equipment is still connected to the system. This is called an intermittent fault confirmation check.
3. During the KEY ON/ENGINE OFF segment, perform this check with self-test sequence de-activated (ECA not in the self-test mode). A fault is indicated when the VOM deflection is 10.5 volts or greater.
4. During the KEY ON/ENGINE RUNNING mode, perform this check with self-test sequence activated (ECA in self-test mode). A fault will be indicated in the same way as it is with the KEY ON/ENGINE OFF mode.

Re-Creating Intermittent Faults

Intermittent faults can generally be re-created by the following methods:
1. Wiggling connectors and harnesses.
2. Manipulating moveable sensors and actuators.
3. Heating thermistor-type sensors with a heat gun.

Suspected components, such as the sensors, actuators and harnesses, are identified by matching service codes obtained during the KEY ON/ENGINE OFF segment of the self-test.

When an intermittent fault is re-created, the voltmeter needle will sweep back and forth across the scale or sweep to the right and stay there.

Malfunctioning components identified with this procedure can be repaired or replaced without further diagnostic testing. Further testing must be done for hard faults and for intermittent faults that can not be re-created by the above method.

OUTPUT CYCLING TEST

This test is performed during the KEY ON/ENGINE OFF test segment, after the memory codes have been generated. Without deactivating the self-test sequence, momentarily depress the throttle to the floor, then release it. Most of the EEC-IV actuators will be energized and the solenoid armatures should move (open or close) accordingly. Another throttle depression will de-energize the actuators. This cycle can be repeated as many times as necessary.

Malfunctiuoning actuators identified in this fashion, should be repaired or replaced. Further diagnostics are required for faults that cannot be isolated by the above method.

NOTE: After completing the self-test and repairing the EEC-IV system, always repeat the self-test to verify that the problem has been repaired.

CONTINUOUS CODES

SERVICE CODE	EXPLANATION OF SERVICE CODE	POSSIBLE CAUSES OF CONCERN		POSSIBLE SYMPTOMS
13 Cont.	Indicates that during recent operation, while in the normal operating mode an ISC command to extend the ISC motor shaft occurred without a corresponding TP sensor change.	Non-EEC:	— Throttle shaft binding. — Improper ISC adjustment.	— Improper idle speed. — Possible stalls.
		EEC:	— ISC motor problems. — TP sensor problems. — Wire harness problems. — ECA problems.	
14 Cont.	Indicates that erratic operation or intermittent loss of PIP information to the ECA has occurred during recent operation.	Non-EEC:	— Distributor pickup problems. — TFI module problems.	— Engine miss. — Surge. — Rough idle. — Stall.
		EEC:	— Wire harness problems. — ECA problems.	
15 Cont.	Indicates loss of Keep-Alive-Memory during recent operation.	EEC:	— Loss of Keep-Alive-Memory battery power. — ECA problems.	— No codes in memory.
18 Cont.	Indicates that during recent operation the ECA received a PIP signal input without receiving a corresponding tach signal input.	Non-EEC:	— Ignition coil problems. — TFI module problems. — Vehicle wire harness.	— No start. — Stalls. — Idles/runs rough.
		EEC:	— Wire harness problems. — ECA problems.	
21 Cont.	Indicates that during a single drive cycle the engine has reached normal operating temperature and then has cooled down.	Non-EEC:	— Thermostat failure. — Coolant loss.	— Reduced MPG. — Heater output loss.
		EEC:	— ECT sensor problems. — Wire harness problems. — ECA problems.	
22 Cont.	Indicates that a gross MAP/BP sensor signal error has occurred during recent operation.	Non-EEC:	Basic engine problems. ● Compression problems. ● Improper timing. ● Vacuum leaks.	— Detonation. — Poor performance. — Reduced MPG. — Surge. — Stumbles.
		EEC:	— MAP/BP sensor problems. — Wire harness problems. — ECA problems.	

Cont: Continuous Test.

CONTINUOUS CODES

continued

SERVICE CODE	EXPLANATION OF SERVICE CODE	POSSIBLE CAUSES OF CONCERN	POSSIBLE SYMPTOMS
31 Cont.	Indicates that the EVP sensor signal has been off scale at the high or low end during recent operation.	Non-EEC: — EGR valve sticks at wide open. EEC: — EGR over travel (normal condition on some applications, refer to diagnostics manual). — EVP sensor problems. — Wire harness problems. — ECA problems.	— Detonation. — Hard to start. — No start. — Stalls. — Dies at idle.
53 Cont.	Indicates that the TP sensor signal has been off scale at the high end during recent operation.	EEC: — Wire harness problems. • Open signal return. • Signal short circuit to Vref. — TP sensor problems. — ECA problems.	— No start (CFI/EFI). — Detonation. — Poor performance.
54 Cont.	Indicates that the ACT/VAT sensor signal has been off scale at the high end during recent operation.	— ACT/VAT sensor problems. — Wire harness open circuit. — ECA problems.	— Runs rough. — Black smoke. — Reduced MPG.
56 Cont.	Indicates that the VAF meter signal has been off scale at the high end during recent operation.	EEC: — VAF sensor problems. — Wire harness problems. — ECA problems.	— No start. — Stumbles. — Stalls. — Runs only at WOT.
61 Cont.	Indicates that the ECT sensor signal has been off scale at the low end during recent operation.	EEC: — ECT sensor problems. — Wire harness shorted to ground. — ECA problems.	— Runs rough. — Stalls. — Erratic idle.
63 Cont.	Indicates that the TP sensor signal has been off scale at the low end during recent operation.	EEC: — Wire harness problems. • Vref open. • Signal line open. • Signal shorted to sensor return. — TP sensor problems. — ECA problems.	— Poor performance. — Stumbles. — Detonation.
64 Cont.	Indicates that the ACT/VAT sensor signal has been off scale at the low end during recent operation.	— ACT/VAT sensor problems. — Wire harness shorted to ground. — ECA problems.	— Runs rough. — Stalls. — Erratic idle.
65 Cont.	Indicates that during recent operation a charging system over-voltage condition (greater than 17.5 v) has occurred.	Non-EEC: — Voltage regulator problems. — Alternator problems. EEC: — Wire harness problems. — ECA problems.	— Lamp burnout. — Electronic component burnout (e.g. TFI, ECA, Radio, etc.).
66 Cont.	Indicates that the VAF meter signal has been off scale at the low end during recent operation.	EEC: — Wire harness problems. • Vref circuit open. • Signal circuit open. • Signal circuit shorted to signal return. — VAF meter problems. — ECA problems.	— No start. — Lacks power. — Runs only at WOT.

Cont: Continuous Test.

ON-DEMAND SERVICE CODES

SERVICE CODE	EXPLANATION OF SERVICE CODE	POSSIBLE CAUSES OF CONCERN	POSSIBLE SYMPTOMS
12 KOER	Indicates the system is not capable of raising engine speed above curb idle.	Non-EEC: — Engine running rough/missing. — Throttle linkage binding. — Improper vehicle prep. (e.g., warm-up). EEC: — ISC motor/TKS system/ISC solenoid problems. — Wire harness problems. — ECA problems.	— Rough idle or stalls due to lack of rpm increase with added loads (e.g. Power Steering lock or A/C 'on').
13 KOER	Indicates that the engine did not return to a specified lower rpm prior to entering the "goose" test portion of Quick Test.	Non-EEC: — Improper curb idle set. — Throttle/TVS linkage binding. — Improper throttle stop set. EEC: — ISC motor/ISC solenoid problems. — Idle tracking switch problems. — Wire harness problems. — ECA problems.	— Idle speed concerns (may be accompanied by code 58).
15 KOEO	Indicates an ECA failure.	EEC: — ECA problems.	— Erratic operation or no start.
16 KOER	Indicates that the fuel system has been driven "lean" until the rpm drops, but the EGO sensor continues to indicate "rich."	EEC: — Contaminated EGO sensor. — Wire harness problems. — ECA problems.	— System may correct "lean" inducing stumbles or hesitation.
17 KOER	Indicates that with thermactor air upstream the fuel system has been driven "lean" until the rpm drops, but the EGO sensor continues to indicate "rich" (5.0L CFI only).	EEC: — Contaminated or disconnected EGO sensor. — Wire harness problems. — ECA problems.	— System may correct "rich" causing reduced MPG or black smoke.
21 KOEO	Indicates that the engine coolant temperature is out of range.	Non-EEC: — Engine not up to operating temperature or, in the case of a no-start, test performed in cool ambient conditions. — Engine over operating temperature. • Low coolant. • Stuck thermostat. • Cooling fan problems. EEC: — ECT sensor problems. — Wire harness problems. — ECA problems.	— Reduced MPG. — Rough idle. — Improper idle speed. — Detonation.
21 KOER	Indicates that the engine coolant is not at normal operating temperature.	Non-EEC: — Engine not warmed up. — Thermostat stuck open. — Low coolant level. — Coolant fan not operating. — Thermostat stuck closed. — Radiator blockage (internal or external). — Improper spark timing. — Fuel problems. EEC: — ECT sensor problems. — Wire harness problems. — ECA problems.	— Reduced MPG. — Rough idle. — Improper idle speed. — Detonation.

KOEO: Key On Engine Off.
KOER: Key On Engine Running.

ON-DEMAND SERVICE CODES

continued

SERVICE CODE	EXPLANATION OF SERVICE CODE		POSSIBLE CAUSES OF CONCERN	POSSIBLE SYMPTOMS
22 KOEO	Indicates that the MAP/BP sensor is out of range. The sensor(s) should read atmospheric pressure.	Non-EEC:	— Unusually high atmospheric pressure. — Vacuum trapped at MAP sensor.	— No-start. — Stalls. — Detonation. — Reduced MPG. — Loss of power.
		EEC:	— MAP/BP sensor problems. — Wire harness problems. — ECA problems.	
22 KOER	Indicates that the MAP/BP sensor is not at normal vacuum levels for Quick Test. The MAP sensor should indicate engine manifold vacuum. The BP sensor should indicate atmospheric pressure.	Non-EEC:	— Base engine problems (MAP). • Compression problems. • Improper timing. • Vacuum leaks. • Excess EGR. — Vacuum line connected to BP sensor (BP).	— Stalls. — Detonation. — Reduced MPG. — Loss of power.
		EEC:	— MAP/BP sensor problems. — Wire harness problems. — ECA problems.	
23 KOEO	Indicates that the TP sensor is not at the proper closed throttle position. Failure may occur either above or below the proper closed throttle position.	Non-EEC:	— Improper base adjustment of curb set, ISC motor, TSP, TKS, or cruise control linkage.	— No-start (EFI/CFI). — Hesitation. — Stalls. — Low/high idle. — Poor performance. — Reduced MPG.
		EEC:	— TKS/ISC motor problems. — Wire harness problems. — TP sensor problems. — ECA problems.	
23 KOER	Indicates that the TP sensor is not at the normal throttle position for Quick Test conditions.	Non-EEC:	— Improper base adjustment of curb set, ISC motor, TSP, TKS, or cruise control linkage.	— Hesitation. — Stalls. — Low/high idle. — Poor performance. — Reduced MPG.
		EEC:	— TKS/ISC motor problems. — TP sensor problems. — ECA problems.	
24 KOEO	Indicates that the Air Charge/Vane Air temperature is out of range.	Non-EEC:	— Vehicle testing performed in ambient temperature less than +50 deg. F. — Improper air cleaner duct/door operation.	— Poor idle. — Reduced MPG.
		EEC:	— ACT sensor problems. — Wire harness problems. — ECA problems.	
24 KOER	Indicates that the ACT/VAT sensor is not at normal engine operating temperature.	Non-EEC:	— Improper operation of the air cleaner duct door. — Cooling system problems. — Base timing problems.	— Poor idle. — Reduced MPG.
		EEC:	— ACT/VAT sensor problems. — Wire harness problems. — ECA problems.	
25 KOER	Indicates that knock was not sensed during the "goose" test.	Non-EEC:	— Base timing problems.	— Detonation. — Poor performance.
		EEC:	— Knock sensor problems. — Wire harness problems. — ECA problems.	
26 KOEO	Indicates that the VAF meter is not in its closed position.	Non-EEC:	— Obstruction in VAF meter.	— No-start. — Stalls. — Runs rough. — Hesitates.
		EEC:	— VAF Meter problems. — Wire harness problems. — ECA problems.	

KOEO: Key On Engine Off.
KOER: Key On Engine Running.

continued

SERVICE CODE	EXPLANATION OF SERVICE CODE		POSSIBLE CAUSES OF CONCERN	POSSIBLE SYMPTOMS
26 KOER	Indicates that the VAF meter is not at the normal position for Quick Test conditions.	Non-EEC:	— Unmetered air leaks. — Improper idle speeds. — Engine not at normal operating temperature.	— Stalls. — Runs rough. — Hesitates.
		EEC:	— VAF meter problems. — Wire harness problems. — ECA problems.	
31 KOEO/ KOER	Indicates that the EGR valve is not in its normal closed position.	Non-EEC:	— Sticking/damaged EGR valve. — Vacuum trapped at EGR valve.	— Stalls. — Runs rough. — Dies at idle. — Detonation.
		EEC:	— EGR solenoid problems. — EVP sensor problems. — Wire harness problems. — ECA problems.	
32 KOER	Indicates that the system is not able to open and maintain a specified EGR valve position.	Non-EEC:	— Stuck or damaged EGR valve. — Vacuum leaks.	— Detonation. — Poor performance.
		EEC:	— EGR solenoid problems. — EVP sensor problems. — Wire harness problems. — ECA problems.	
33 KOER	Indicates that the EGR valve has not returned to its normal closed position after the EGR test.	Non-EEC:	— Stuck or damaged EGR valve.	— Decel stall. — Runs rough.
		EEC:	— EGR solenoid problems. — EVP sensor problems.	
34 KOER	Indicates that, with engine rpm elevated and stabilized, a specified rpm drop did not occur when EGR was turned "on."	Non-EEC:	— Stuck or damaged EGR valve. — BVT/EGR problems. — Vacuum leaks. — Improper exhaust back-pressure	— Detonation.
		EEC:	— EGR solenoid problems. — Wire harness problems. — ECA problems.	
35 KOER	Indicates that the engine rpm is too low for the EGR test.	Non-EEC:	— Base engine problems.	— May run rough. — Lacks power.
		EEC:	— ISC problems.	
41* KOER	Indicates that the EGO sensor output voltage is always less than 0.5 volts ("lean") during the fuel test.	Non-EEC:	— Improper fuel delivery. — Carburetor/Throttle-Body injector problem. — Vacuum leaks. — Unmetered air. — Thermactor air is always upstream.	— Runs rough. — Stalls. — Hesitates. — Runs "lean". — May correct "rich" if sensor or harness related. • Spark plugs fouled. • Reduced MPG.
		EEC:	— EGO sensor problems. — Wire harness problems. — ECA problems.	

KOEO: Key On Engine Off.
KOER: Key On Engine Running.
*On 3.8L engines this condition refers to the left bank.

ON-DEMAND SERVICE CODES

continued

SERVICE CODE	EXPLANATION OF SERVICE CODE	POSSIBLE CAUSES OF CONCERN	POSSIBLE SYMPTOMS
42* KOER	Indicates that the EGO sensor output voltage is always greater than 0.5 volts ("rich") during the fuel test.	Non-EEC: — Improper fuel delivery. — Carburetor/Throttle-Body injector problems. — Obstructed air intake. — Ignition system problems. — Canister purge problems. EEC: — EGO sensor problems. — Wire harness problems. — ECA problems.	— Runs rough. — Runs "rich". — Reduced MPG. — Spark plugs fouled. — May correct "lean" if sensor or harness related. • Hesitations. • Stalls.
43* KOER	Indicates that the EGO sensor has cooled down and may not have given the proper responses during Quick Test.	Non-EEC: — Vehicle not properly prepared for test (Run at 2000 rpm for 2 minutes prior to test). — Engine below operating temperature.	— Usually no drive complaint.
44* KOER	Indicates that there is a thermactor problem.	Non-EEC: — Air pump problems. — Thermactor valve problems. EEC: — Thermactor solenoid problems. — Wire harness problems. — ECA problems.	— Usually no drive complaint.
45* KOER	Indicates that thermactor air is always upstream during Quick Test.	Non-EEC: — Air pump problems. — Thermactor valve problems. EEC: — Thermactor solenoid problems. — Wire harness problems. — ECA problems.	— Catalyst over temperature.
46* KOER	Indicates that the system is unable to bypass (vent to atmosphere) thermactor air.	Non-EEC: — Air pump problems. — Thermactor valve problems. EEC: — Thermactor solenoid problems. — Wire harness problems. — ECA problems.	— Catalyst over temperature.
47* KOER	Indicates that, even though thermactor air is upstream and fuel control is max. "lean", the EGO sensor indicates "rich".	Non-EEC: — Improper fuel delivery. — Carburetor/Throttle-Body injector problems. — Obstructed air intake. — Ignition system problems. EEC: — EGO sensor problems. — Wire harness problems. — ECA problems.	— Runs "rich". — Runs rough. — Reduced MPG. — Spark plugs fouled. — May correct "lean" if sensor or harness related. • Hesitations. • Stalls.

KOEO: Key On Engine Off.
KOER: Key On Engine Running.
*On 3.8L engine this condition refer to the left bank.

On-Demand service codes —

continued

SERVICE CODE	EXPLANATION OF SERVICE CODE	POSSIBLE CAUSES OF CONCERN	POSSIBLE SYMPTOMS
48 KOER	Indicates that the system does not have proper side-to-side fuel control. (3.8L only.)	Non-EEC: — Catalyst blockage. — Stuck injector. — Plugged injector. EEC: — Wire harness problems. • Injector connections reversed. • EGO connections reversed. • One injector disconnected. • One EGO disconnected. — EGO sensor problems. — ECA problems.	— Stumbles. — Stalls. — Reduce MPG. — Black smoke.
51 KOEO	Indicates that the ECT signal failed at the high end (approximately 5.0 volts). Failure mode indicates − 40 deg. F.	EEC: — ECT sensor problems. — Wire harness problems. — ECA problems.	— Hard to start Hot. — Black smoke. — Reduced MPG.
53 KOEO	Indicates that the TP signal has failed at the high end (approximately 5.0 volts). Failure mode indicates WOT.	EEC: — Wire harness problems. • Open signal return circuit. • TP signal shorted to VREF. — TP sensor problems. — ECA problems.	— No start (EFI/CFI). — Poor part throttle performance.
54 KOEO	Indicates that the ACT signal has failed at the high end (approximately 5.0 volts). Failure mode indicates − 40 deg. F.	EEC: — Wire harness problems. • Vref open. • ACT signal shorted to signal return. • ACT signal open. — ECA problems.	— Reduced MPG. — Black smoke.
56 KOEO	Indicates that the VAF signal has failed at the high end (approximately 5.0 volts). Failure mode indicates wide open throttle.	EEC: — Wire harness problems. — VAF sensor problems. — ECA problems.	— Black smoke.
58 KOER	Indicates that the ITS is not in contact with the throttle lever with the ISC motor extended.	Non-EEC: — Improper throttle plate stop adjustment. — Throttle linkage binding. — Cruise control misadjusted. — Improper ISC adjustment. EEC: — ITS problems. — Wire harness problems. — ECA problems.	— Improper idle speeds. — Stalls.
61 KOEO	Indicates that the ECT signal has failed at the low end (approximately 0.0 volts). Failure mode indicates + 240 deg. F.	EEC: — ECT sensor problems. — Wire harness problems. — ECA problems.	— Hard start/no start (cold).
63 KOEO	Indicates that the TP signal has failed at the low end (approximately 0.0 volts). Failure mode indicates closed throttle.	EEC: — Wire harness problems. • Vref open. • TP signal shorted to signal return. — TP sensor problems. — ECA problems.	— Runs rough. — Stumbles. — Stalls.

KOEO: Key On Engine Off.
KOER: Key On Engine Running.

ON-DEMAND SERVICE CODES

continued

SERVICE CODE	EXPLANATION OF SERVICE CODE	POSSIBLE CAUSES OF CONCERN	POSSIBLE SYMPTOMS
64 KOEO	Indicates that the ACT/VAT signal has failed at the low end (approximately 0.0 volts). Failure mode indicates +240 deg.	EEC: — ACT/VAT sensor problems. — Wire harness problems. — ECA problems.	— Runs rough. — Stumbles. — Stalls.
66 KOEO	Indicates that the VAF signal has failed at the low end (approximately 0.0 volts). Failure mode indicates closed throttle.	EEC: — Wire harness problems. — VAF sensor problems. — ECA problems.	— Stumbles. — Stalls.
67 KOEO	Indicates that the system is receiving an improper neutral/drive or A/C clutch status input.	Non-EEC: — Vehicle in gear or A/C "on." EEC: — Neutral/drive switch problems. — Wire harness problems. — ECA problems.	— Improper ISC.
68 KOEO	Indicates that the ITS is in contact with the throttle lever with the ISC motor retracted.	Non-EEC: — Improper ISC motor adjustment. EEC: — ITS problems. — Wire harness problems. — ECA problems.	— Improper idle speed control. — Stalls.
72 KOER	Indicates that the MAP sensor has not detected a sufficient manifold vacuum change during the "goose" test.	Non-EEC: — Vacuum leaks. — Base engine problems. EEC: — Map sensor problems. — ECA problems.	— Stumbles. — Hesitations. — Stalls.
73 KOER	Indicates that the system has not detected a sufficient TP change during the "goose" test.	EEC: — TP sensor stuck at WOT. — TP sensor not tracking throttle shaft. — ECA problems.	— Stumbles. — Hesitations.
76 KOER	Indicates that the system has not detected a sufficient VAF change during the "goose" test.	Non-EEC: — Unmetered air entering engine. EEC: — VAF meter sticking. — Wire harness problems. — ECA problems.	—
77 KOER	Indicates that the operator did not do the "goose" test.	Non-EEC: — Operator did not do a brief WOT. EEC: — ECA problems.	—
81 KOEO	Indicates a TAD circuit fault. (For 2.8L only, code indicates 8 TAB circuit fault.)	EEC: — Open/shorted TAD solenoid. — Wire harness problems. — ECA problems.	— Thermactor service code KOER.
82 KOEO	Indicates a TAB circuit fault. (For 2.8L only, code indicates 8 TAD circuit fault.)	EEC: — Open/shorted TAB solenoid. — Wire harness problems. — ECA problems.	— Thermactor service code KOER.
83 KOEO	Indicates an EGRC circuit fault.	EEC: — Open/shorted EGRC solenoid. — Wire harness problems. — ECA problems.	— No EGR control. — Detonation.
84 KOEO	Indicates an EGRV circuit fault.	EEC: — Open/shorted EGRV solenoid. — Wire harness problems. — ECA problems.	— Improper EGR control. — Stalls. — Runs rough.
85 KOEO	Indicates a CANP circuit fault.	EEC: — Open/shorted CANP valve. — Wire harness problems. — ECA problems.	— Customer complaints of gasoline odor.
86 KOEO	Indicates a WAC circuit fault.	EEC: — Open/shorted WAC controller. — Wire harness problems. — ECA problems.	— No A/C operation. — No WOT-A/C cutoff.

KOEO: Key On Engine Off.
KOER: Key On Engine Running.

continued

SERVICE CODE	EXPLANATION OF SERVICE CODE	POSSIBLE CAUSES OF CONCERN	POSSIBLE SYMPTOMS
87 KOEO	Indicates a fuel pump relay circuit fault or a TCP circuit fault (2.8L only).	EEC: — Inertia switch problems. — Open/short fuel pump relay. — Wire harness problems. — ECA problems. EEC: — TCP solenoid problems. — Wiring harness problems. — ECA problems.	— No start. — Pump runs with key in "off" position. — Poor cold start/driveaway.
88 KOEO	Indicates a TKS circuit fault (5.0L CFI only) or a VVC circuit fault (2.8L only).	EEC: — Open/shorted TKS solenoid. — Wiring harness problems. — ECA problems. EEC: — VVC relay problems. — Wiring harness problems. — ECA problems.	— High idle speeds. — Stalls (low idle speeds). — Poor cold start/driveaway. — Spark plug loading. — Reduced MPG. — Black smoke.
89 KOEO	Indicates an exhaust heat control circuit fault.	EEC: — Open/shorted EHC solenoid. — Wire harness problems. — ECA problems.	— Stumbles. — Hesitations cold.
91 KOER	Indicates that the right EGO sensor output voltage is always less than 0.5 volts ("lean") during the fuel test (3.8L only).	Non-EEC: — Improper fuel delivery. — Carburetor/Throttle-Body injector problems. — Vacuum leaks. — Unmetered air. — Thermactor air is always upstream. EEC: — EGO sensor problems. — Wire harness problems. — ECA problems.	— Runs rough. — Stalls. — Hesitates. — Runs "lean." — May correct "rich" if sensor or harness related. • Spark plugs fouled. • Reduced MPG.
92 KOER	Indicates that the right EGO sensor output voltage is always greater than 0.5 volts ("rich") during the fuel test (3.8L only).	Non-EEC: — Improper fuel delivery. — Carburetor/Throttle-Body injector problems. — Obstructed air intake. — Ignition system problems. EEC: — EGO sensor problems. — Wire harness problems. — ECA problems.	— Runs rough. — Runs "rich". — Reduced MPG. — Spark plugs fouled. — May correct "lean" if sensor or harness related. • Hesitations. • Stalls.
93 KOER	Indicates that the right EGO sensor has cooled down and may not have given the proper responses during Quick Test (3.8L only).	Non-EEC: — Vehicle not properly prepared for test (Run at 2000 rpm for 2 minutes prior to test). — Engine below operating temperature.	— Usually no drive complaint.
94 KOER	Indicates that there is a thermactor problem on the right bank (3.8L only).	Non-EEC: — Air pump problems. — Thermactor valve problems. EEC: — Thermactor solenoid problems. — Wire harness problems. — ECA problems.	— Usually no drive complaint.
95 KOER	Indicates that the right bank thermactor air is always upstream during Quick Test (3.8L only).	Non-EEC: — Air pump problems. — Thermactor valve problems. EEC: — Thermactor solenoid problems. — Wire harness problems. — ECA problems.	— Catalyst over temperature.
96 KOER	Indicates that the system is unable to bypass (vent to atmosphere) thermactor air on the right bank (3.8L only).	Non-EEC: — Air pump problems. — Thermactor valve problems. EEC: — Thermactor solenoid problems. — Wire harness problems. — ECA problems.	— Catalyst over temperature.
97 KOER	Indicates that, even though thermactor air is upstream and fuel control is max. "lean," the right EGO sensor indicates "rich" (3.8L only).	Non-EEC: — Improper fuel delivery. — Carburetor/Throttle-Body injector problems. — Obstructed air intake. — Ignition system problems. EEC: — EGO sensor problems. — Wire harness problems. — ECA problems.	— Runs "rich." — Runs rough. — Reduced MPG. — Spark plugs fouled. — May correct "lean" if sensor or harness related. • Hesitations. • Stalls.

KOEO: Key On Engine Off.
KOER: Key On Engine Running.

GENERAL MOTORS
COMPUTER COMMAND CONTROL (CCC) SYSTEM

General Information

Each General Motors engine has system controls to reduce exhaust emissions while maintaining good driveability and fuel economy.

The engines all have an Electronic Control Module (ECM) to control the fuel system. The ECM varies the air/fuel ratio depending on whether the fuel control is carbureted, Throttle Body Fuel Injected (TBI) or Port Fuel Injected (PFI).

In addition, the ECM controls the ignition timing system, as well as other systems, such as the Exhaust Gas Recirculation (EGR) system, the purge system and numerous others.

SERVICE ENGINE SOON LIGHT

The ECM is equipped with a self-diagnostic capability, which can detect system failures and aids the technician by identifying the fault via a trouble code system and a dash mounted indicator lamp, called the SERVICE ENGINE SOON light.

The lamp is mounted on the instrument panel and has 2 functions:

1. It is used to inform the operator that a problem has occurred and the vehicle should be taken in for service as soon as reasonably possible.

2. It is used by the technician to read out trouble codes in order to localize malfunction areas during the diagnosis and repair phases.

As a bulb and system check, the light will come on with the ignition key in the **ON** position and the engine not operating. When the engine is started, the light will turn off. If the light does not turn off, the self diagnostic system has detected a problem in the system. If the problem goes away, the light will go out, in most cases after 10 second, but a trouble code will be set in the ECM's memory.

INTERMITTENT OR HARD TROUBLE CODES

An intermittent code is one which does not reset itself and is not present when initiating the trouble codes. It is often be caused by a loose connection, which with vehicle movement can possibly cure its self, but intermittently, re-appear.

A hard code is an operational malfunction which remains in the ECM memory and will be presented when calling for the trouble code display.

BASIS OF TROUBLE CODE DETERMINATION

The Electronic Control Module (ECM) is actually a computer. It uses numerous sensors to look at many engine operating conditions. It has been programmed to know what certain sensor readings should be under most all operating conditions and if the sensor readings are not what the ECM thinks it should be, the ECM will turn on the SERVICE ENGINE SOON indicator light and will store a trouble code in its memory. When called up, the trouble code directs the technician to examine a particular circuit in order to locate and repair the trouble code setting defect.

ASSEMBLY LINE COMMUNICATION LINK (ALCL)

In order to access the ECM to provide the trouble codes stored in its memory, the Assembly Line Communication Link (ALCL, also known as the Assembly Line Diagnostic Link, ALDL) is used.

NOTE: **This connector is utilized at the assembly plant to insure the engine is operating properly before the vehicle is shipped.**

Terminal **B** of the diagnostic connnector is the diagnostic terminal and it can be connected to terminal **A**, or ground, to enter the diagnostic mode, or the field service mode on fuel injected vehicles.

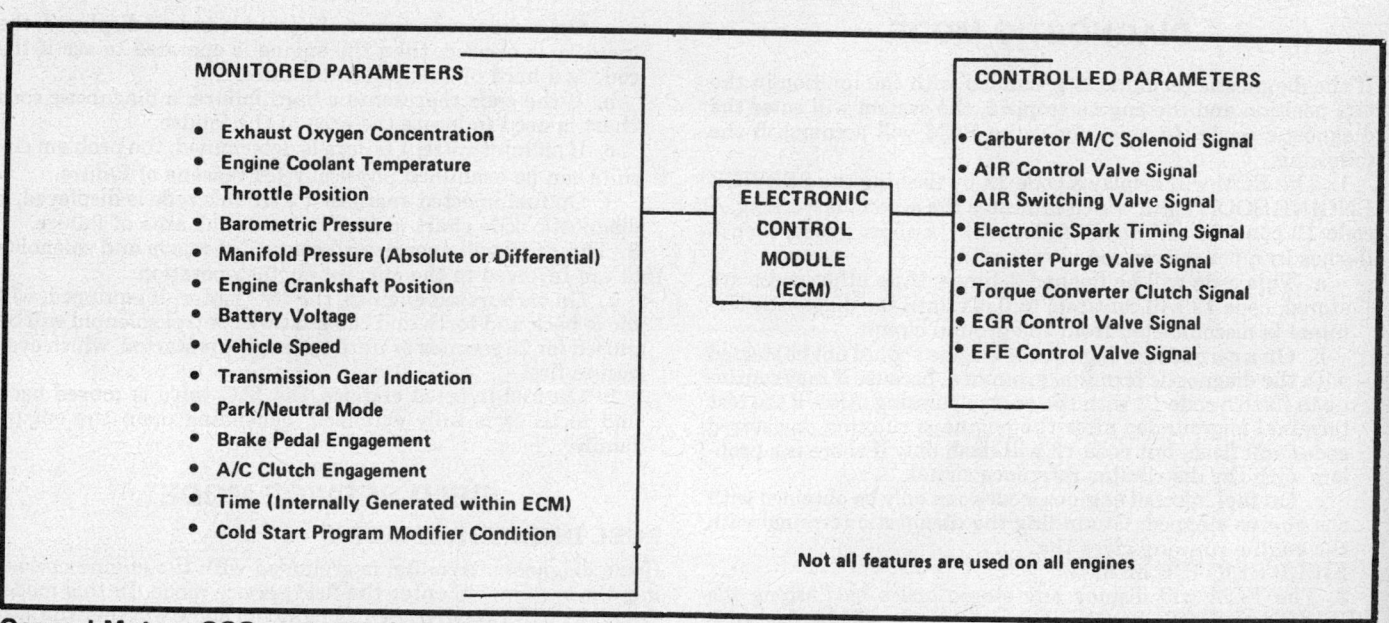

MONITORED PARAMETERS

- Exhaust Oxygen Concentration
- Engine Coolant Temperature
- Throttle Position
- Barometric Pressure
- Manifold Pressure (Absolute or Differential)
- Engine Crankshaft Position
- Battery Voltage
- Vehicle Speed
- Transmission Gear Indication
- Park/Neutral Mode
- Brake Pedal Engagement
- A/C Clutch Engagement
- Time (Internally Generated within ECM)
- Cold Start Program Modifier Condition

ELECTRONIC CONTROL MODULE (ECM)

CONTROLLED PARAMETERS

- Carburetor M/C Solenoid Signal
- AIR Control Valve Signal
- AIR Switching Valve Signal
- Electronic Spark Timing Signal
- Canister Purge Valve Signal
- Torque Converter Clutch Signal
- EGR Control Valve Signal
- EFE Control Valve Signal

Not all features are used on all engines

General Motors CCC system schematic

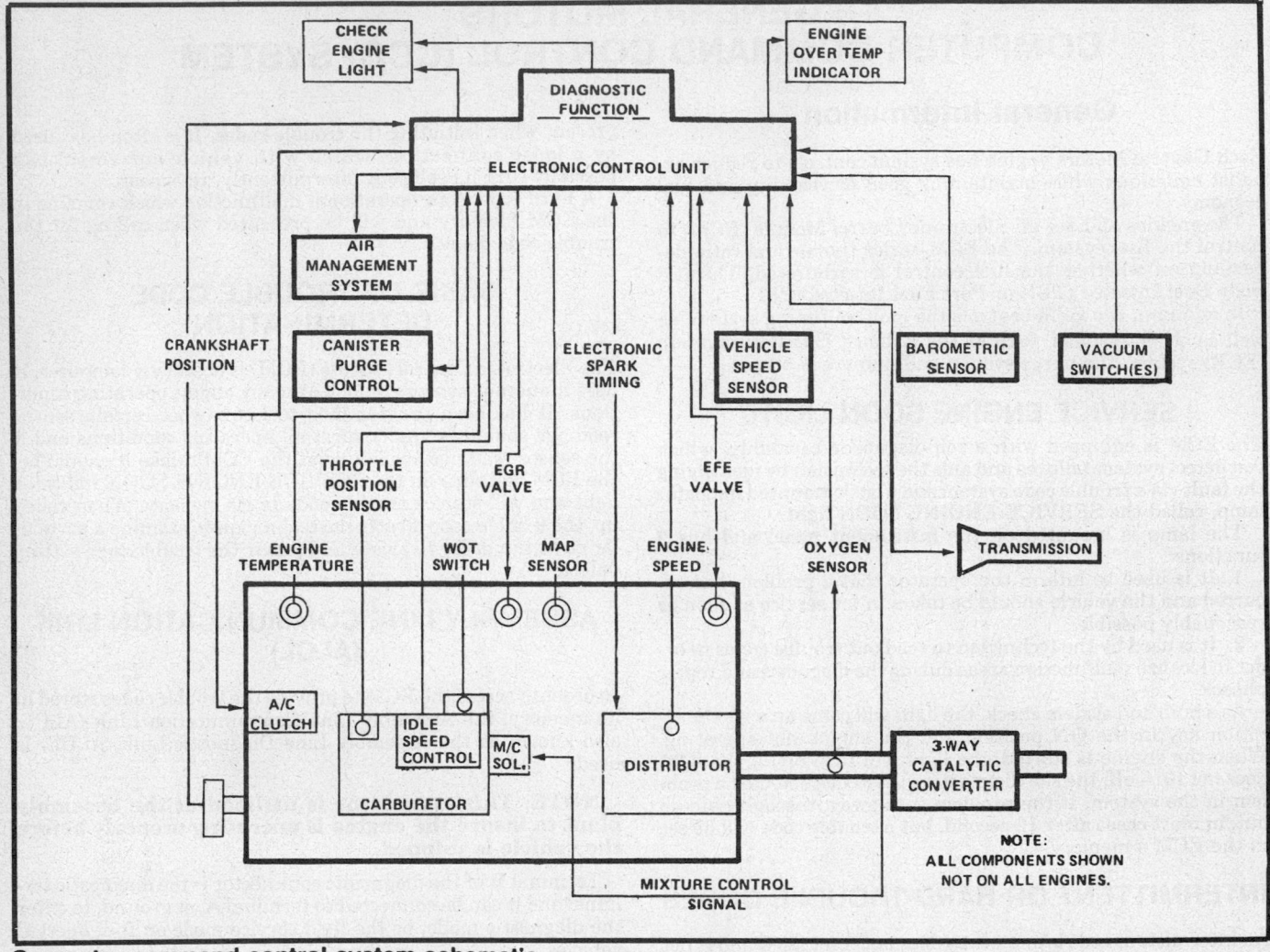

Computer command control system schematic

DIAGNOSTIC MODE

If the diagnostic terminal is grounded with the ignition in the **ON** position and the engine stopped, the system will enter the diagnostic mode. In this mode, the ECM will accomplish the following:

1. The ECM will display a code 12 by flashing the SERVICE ENGINE SOON light, which indicates the system is working. A code 12 consists of 1 flash, followed by a short pause, then 2 flashes in quick succession.

    a. This code will be flashed 3 times. If no other codes are stored, code 12 will continue to flash until the diagnostic terminal is disconnected from the ground circuit.

    b. On a carbureted engine, the engine should not be started with the diagnostic terminal grounded, because it may continue to flash a code 12 with the engine running. Also, if the test terminal is grounded after the engine is running any stored codes will flash, but code 12 will flash only if there is a problem with the distributor reference signal.

    c. On fuel injected engines, codes can only be obtained with the engine stopped. Grounding the diagnostic terminal with the engine running gives the FIELD SERVICE MODE.

2. The ECM will display any stored codes by flashing the SERVICE ENGINE SOON light. Each code will be flashed 3 times, then code 12 will be flashed again.

    a. On carbureted engines, if a trouble code is displayed, the memory is cleared, then the engine is operated to see if the code is a hard or intermittent failure.

    b. If the code represents a hard failure, a diagnostic code chart is used to locate the area of the failure.

    c. If an intermittent failure is determined, the problem circuits can be examined physically for reasons of failure.

    d. On fuel injected engines, if a trouble code is displayed, a diagnostic code chart is used to locate the area of failure.

3. The ECM will energize all controlled relays and solenoids that are involved in the current engine operation.

    a. On carbureted engines, the ISC motor, if equipped, will move back and forth and the mixture control solenoid will be pulsed for 25 seconds or until the engine is started, which ever occurs first.

    b. On fuel injected engines, the IAC valve is moved back and forth or is fully extended, depending upon the engine family.

FIELD SERVICE MODE

FUEL INJECTED ENGINES

If the diagnostic terminal is grounded with the engine operating, the system will enter the field service mode. In this mode, the SERVICE ENGINE SOON light will show whether the system is in open or closed loop.

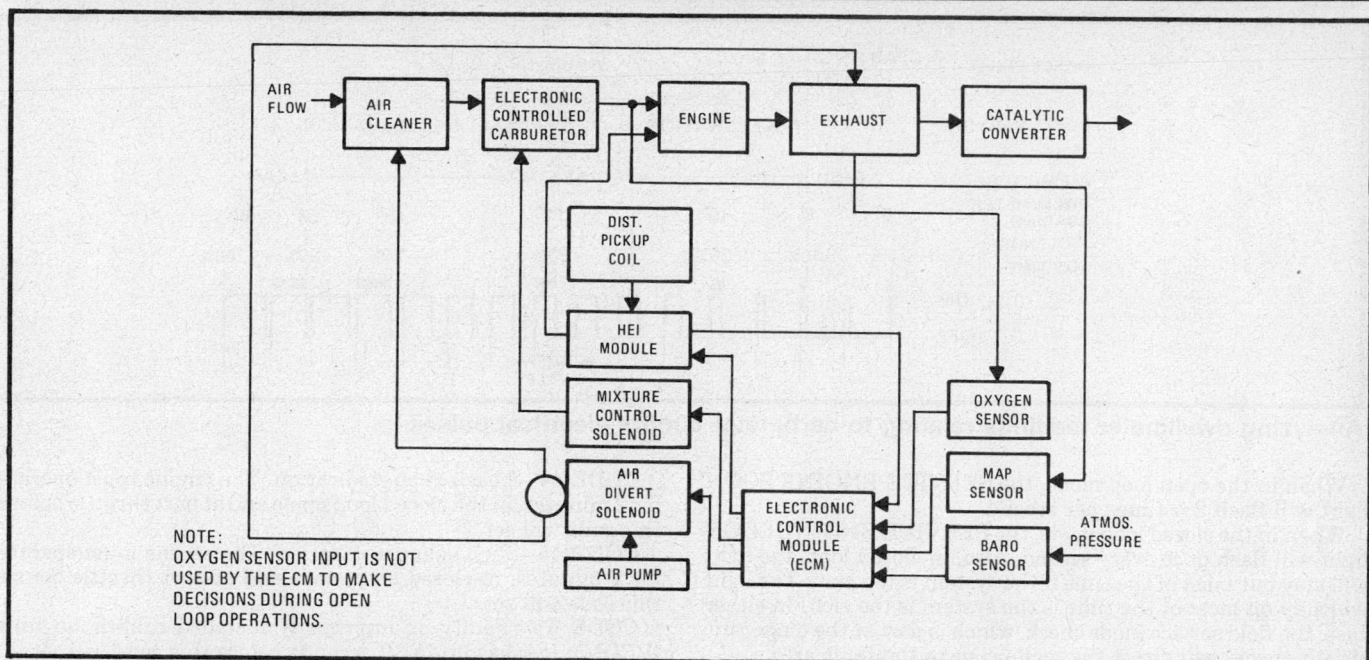

Non-turbocharged functional block diagram

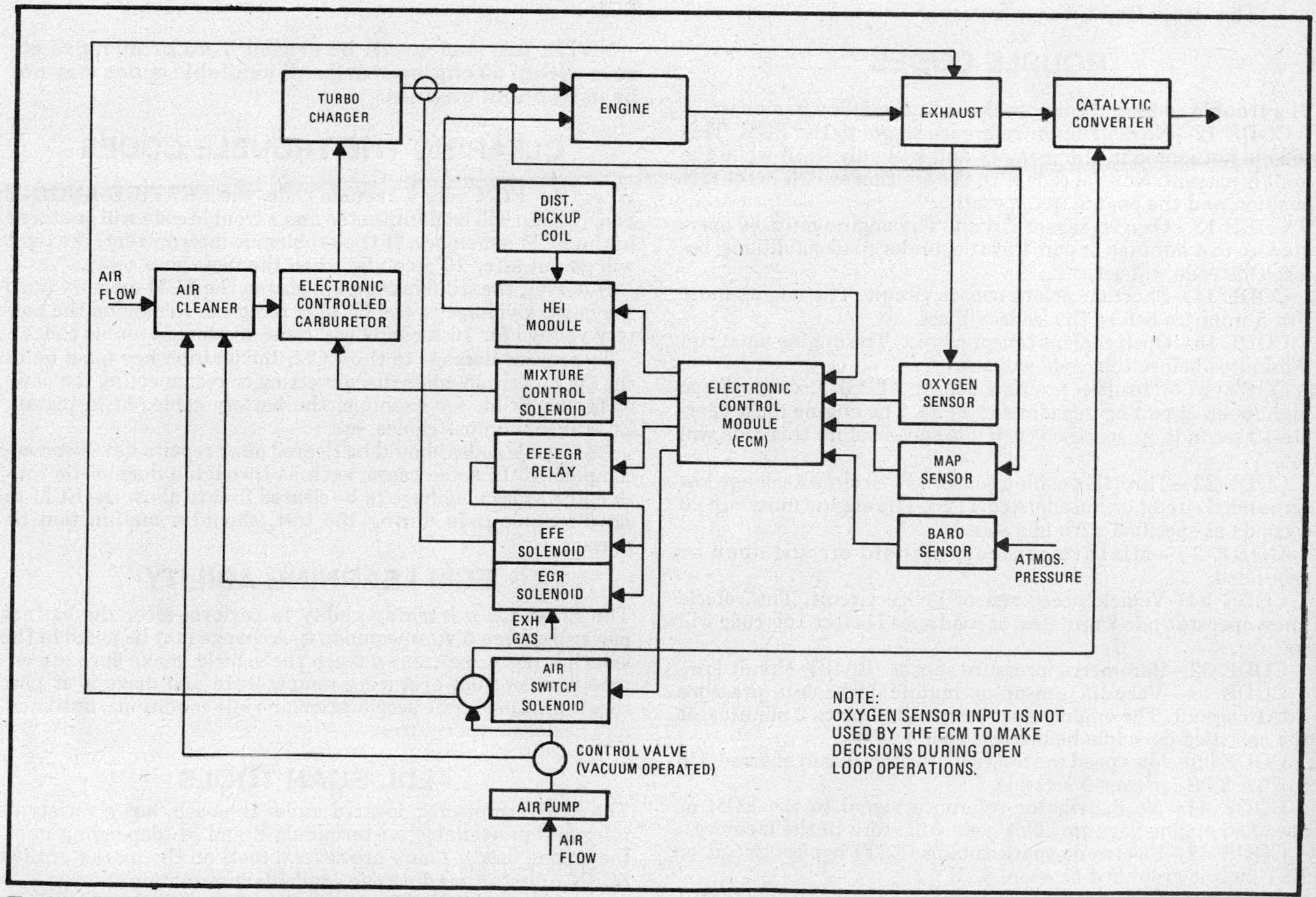

Turbocharged functional block diagram

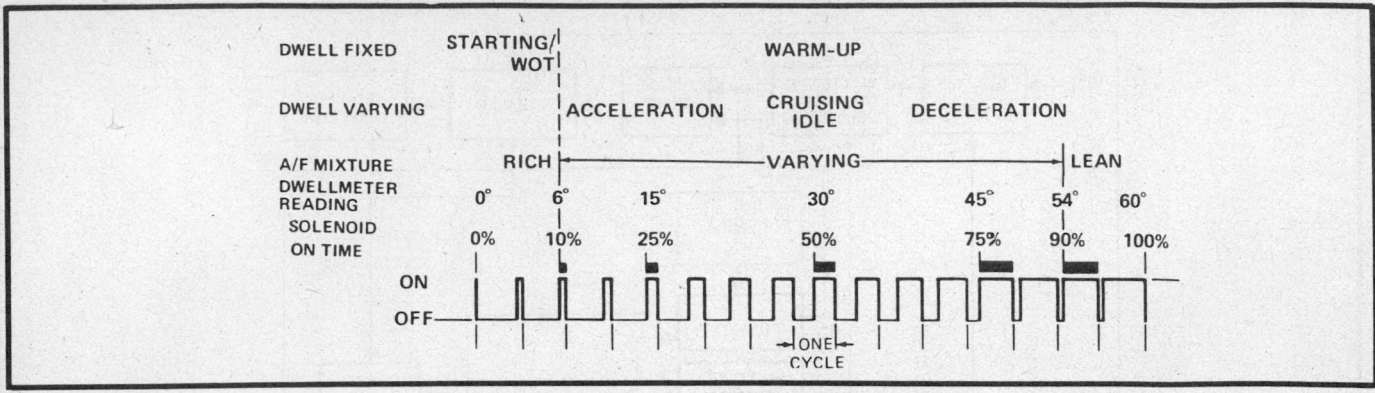

Analyzing dwellmeter readings relating to carburetor control electrical pulses

When in the open loop mode, the SERVICE ENGINE SOON light will flash 2½ times per second.

When in the closed loop mode, the SERVICE ENGINE SOON light will flash once every second. Also, in closed loop, the light will stay out most of the time if the system is too lean. The light will stay on most of the time is the system is too rich. In either case, the field service mode check, which is part of the diagnostic circuit check, will direct the technician to the fault area.

While in the field service mode, the ECM will be in the following mode:

1. The distributor will have a fixed spark advance.
2. New trouble codes cannot be stored in the ECM.
3. The closed loop timer is bypassed.

TROUBLE CODES

The trouble codes indicate problems in the following areas:

CODE 12 – No distributor reference signal to the ECM. This code is not stored in the memory and will only flash while the fault is present. Normal code with the ignition switch in the **ON** position and the engine not operating.

CODE 13 – Oxygen sensor circuit. The engine must be operated up to 4 minutes at part throttle, under road conditions, before this code will set.

CODE 14 – Shorted coolant sensor circuit. The engine must run 5 minutes before this code will set.

CODE 15 – Open coolant sensor circuit. The engine must run 5 minutes before this code will set.

CODE 21 – Throttle position sensor (TPS) circuit voltage high (open circuit or misadjusted TPS). The engine must operate 10 seconds, at specified curb idle speed before this code will set.

CODE 22 – Throttle position sensor (TPS) circuit voltage low (grounded circuit or misadjusted TPS). The engine must run 20 seconds at specified curb idle speed.

CODE 23 – Mixture control solenoid circuit open or grounded.

CODE 24 – Vehicle speed sensor (VSS) circuit. The vehicle must operate up to 2 minutes, at road speed before this code will set.

CODE 32 – Barometric pressure sensor (BARO) circuit low.

CODE 34 – Vacuum sensor or manifold absolute pressure (MAP) circuit. The engine must be operated up to 2 minutes, at the specified curb idle before this code will set.

CODE 35 – Idle speed control (ISC) switch circuit shorted. Up to 70% TPS for over 5 seconds.

CODE 41 – No distributor reference signal to the ECM at specified engine vacuum. This code will store in the memory.

CODE 42 – Electronic spark timing (EST) bypass circuit or EST circuit grounded or open.

CODE 43 – Electronic spark cntrol (ESC) retard signal for too long of a time, will cause retard in EST signal.

CODE 44 – Lean exhaust idication. The engine must operate for 2 minutes, in the closed loop mode and at part throttle before this code will set.

CODE 45 – Rich exhaust idication. The engine must operate for 2 minutes, in closed loop mode and at part throttle before this code will set.

CODE 51 – Faulty or improperly installed calibration unit (PROM). It takes up to 30 seconds before this code will set.

CODE 53 – Exhaust gas recirculation (EGR) valve vacuum sensor has noted improper EGR control vacuum.

CODE 54 – Mixture cntrol solenoid voltage high at the ECM as a result of a shorted M/C solenoid circuit and/or a faulty ECM.

NOTE: Any codes will be erased if no problem re-occurs within 50 engine starts. All available codes may not be used on all engines.

CLEARING THE TROUBLE CODES

When the ECM sets a trouble code, the SERVICE ENGINE SOON lamp will be illuminated and a trouble code will be stored in the ECM's memory. If the problem is intermittent, the light will go out after 10 seconds, when the fault goes away.

However, the trouble code will stay in the ECM memory until the battery voltage to the ECM is removed. Removing the battery voltage for 10 seconds will clear all stored trouble codes.

To prevent damage to the ECM, the ignition key must be in the **OFF** position when disconnecting or reconnecting the power to the ECM, for example, the battery cable, ECM pigtail, ECM fuse, Jumper cables, etc.

All trouble codes should be cleared after repairs have been accomplished. In some cases, such as through a diagnoistic routine, the codes may have to be cleared first to allow the ECM to set a trouble code during the test, should a malfunction be present.

ECM LEARNING ABILITY

The ECM has a learning ability to perform after the battery power has been disconnected to it. A change may be noted in the vehicle's performance. To teach the vehicle, make sure the engine is at normal operating temperature and drive it at part throttle, at moderate acceleration and idle conditions, until normal performance returns.

ALDL SCAN TOOLS

The ALDL connector, located under the dash, has a variety of information available on terminals E and M (depending upon the engine used). There are several tools on the market, called SCAN units for reading the available information.

It must be emphasized that each type scanner instrument must be used in accordance with the manufacturers instructions.

BUICK RIVERIA SEQUENTIAL FUEL INJECTION (SFI) SYSTEM

ELECTRONIC CONTROL MODULE

The Electronic Control Module (ECM) is the controlling unit of the electronic engine control system. Though it communicates with the other vehicle computers, it alone has the primary responsibility of maintaining proper emissions while delivering optimum driveability characteristics.

The ECM monitors inputs from the engine as well as other vehicle sensors. It then correlates this information with data stored in the PROM. After all the information is evaluated, the ECM calulates the necessary changes to compensate for all driving conditions.

The ECM is able to detect malfunctions in most of the systems it monitors. It will turn on the SERVICE ENGINE SOON indicator lamp, set a trouble code, or both if it detects a fault.

NOTE: Always repair all code malfunctions before any driveability or emission problem repairs are attempted. If more than one code is set, always repair the lowest numbered code first.

The ECM trouble codes are displayed on the Cathode Ray Tube (CRT) when in the diagnostic mode. Other service related information that can be displayed are as follows:
ECM data
ECM Discrete inputs
ECM output cycling
ECM trouble codes
All displays, except for the output mode cycling, can be viewed under the following conditions:
The ignition switch in the **ON** position
The engine not operating
The engine at idle
The vehicle being driven
The output mode cycling function is only operational with the ignition switch in the **ON** position and the engine not operating

ACCESSING THE BCM SELF-DIAGNOSTICS

In order to access and control the BCM self-diagnostic features, 2 additional electronic components are necessary, the CRTC and the CRT picture tube. As part of the CRT's SERVICE MODE page, a 22 character display area is used to display diagnostic information. When a malfunction is sensed by the computer system, one of the driver warning messages is displayed on the CRT under the DIAGNOSTIC category. When the service mode is entered, the various BCM, ECM, or IPC parameters, fault codes, inputs, outputs as well as override commands and clearing code capability are displayed when commanded through the CRT.

The CRT becomes the device to enter the diagnostics and access the service diagnostic routines. The CRTC is the device which controls the display on the CRT and interprets the switches touched on the CRT and passes this information along to the BCM. This communication process allows the BCM to transfer any of its available diagnostic information to the CRT for display during SERVICE MODE.

By touching the appropriate pads on the CRT, data messages can be sent to the BCM from the CRTC over the data line, requesting the specific diagnostic feature required.

CATHODE RAY TUBE

The systems consists of a Cathode Ray Tube (CRT) monitor, a Cathode Ray Tube Controller (CRTC) and a Body Computer Module (BCM). The information is sent to and from the BCM, the CRTC and the electronic A/C controller with the serial data link.

SERVICE ENGINE SOON INDICATOR

The SERVICE ENGINE SOON indicator lamp warns that an engine problem has occurred and the vehicle needs service. With the ignition switch in the **RUN** position, but the engine not operating, the lamp will turn on as a bulb test. When the engine is started, the lamp should turn off. If the Electronic Control Module (ECM) detects an engine problem. the amber SERVICE ENGINE SOON lamp is turned on. If the lamp turns off in approximately 10 seconds, the engine problem has disappeared, but the ECM stores a trouble code. The trouble code will stay in the ECM memory until the battery is disconnected from the ECM or until the memory is cleared, using the service mode.

CRT TESTER

A cathode ray tube tester (Kent Moore J-34914 or its equivalent) is available to help isolate faults that may occur during the CRT operation. Substituting the tool in place of the CRTC will verify the integrity of the picture tube and switching the circuitry that make up the CRT. By connecting the tester directly to the CRT, the CRT can be checked as a unit. Connecting the tester to the vehicle harness, after the CRT has been independently checked out, will determine if the fault is in the wiring or the CRTC. The tester will run automatic tests and then allow individual switch tests.

Should the service facility obtain this type of tester to be used with the CRT system, instructions on its use will be included with the tester. Follow the manufacturer's recommended operating procedures to obtain the tester's maximum potential.

COMPUTER SYSTEM SERVICE PRECAUTIONS

The computer system is designed to withstand normal current draws associated with vehicle operation. However, care must be taken to avoid overloading any of these circuits. In testing for open or short circuits, do not ground or apply voltage to any of the circuits unless instructed to do so by the diagnosis procedures. These circuits should only be tested by using a high impedance mulimeter (Kent Moore J-29125A or its equivalent), if the tester remains connected to one of the computers. Power should never be applied or removed to one of the computers with the key in the **ON** position. Before removing or connecting battery cables, fuses or connectors, always turn the ignition switch to the **OFF** position.

ALDL CONNECTOR

The Assembly Line Diagnostic Link (ALDL) is a diagnostic connector located in the passenger compartment. Along with the assembly plant usage for proper engine operation before leaving the plant, it may also be used to access the SERIAL DATA circuit, using a service diagnostic tool, specifically designed and calibrated for that purpose.

The ALDL cover contains a jumper, which is part of the redundant SERIAL DATA CKT 800 and if removed for any reason, must be replaced before returning the vehicle to service. The missing ALDL cover could create a loss of SERIAL DATA communication if CKT 800 was already open elsewhere. This would result in the message ELECTRICAL PROBLEM, accompanied by a SERIAL DATA loss code and potential driveability complaints.

TROUBLE CODES

In the process of controlling the various subsystems, the ECM

ECM DIAGNOSTIC CODES

CODE	DESCRIPTION	COMMENTS
E013	Open Oxygen Sensor Circuit *Canister Purge	A
E014	Coolant Sensor High Temp. Indicated	A – B
E015	Coolant Sensor Low Temp. Indicated	A – B
E016	System Voltage Out of Range *All Solenoids	A
E021	TPS Signal Voltage High *TCC	A
E022	TPS Signal Voltage Low *TCC	A
E024	Vehicle Speed Sensor Circuit Failure *TCC	A
E029	Fourth Gear Switch Circuit Open	A
E032	EGR Vacuum Control System Fault	A
E033	MAF Sensor Signal Frequency High	A
E034	MAF Sensor Signal Frequency Low	A
E037	MAT Sensor High Temperature Indicated	A
E038	MAT Sensor Low Temperature Indicated	A
E040	Power Steering Pressure Switch Circuit Open - *A/C Clutch and Cruise	A
E041	CAM Sensor Circuit Failure (C³I Module to ECM)	A
E042	C³I-EST or Bypass Circuit Failure	A – D
E043	ESC System Failure	A
E044	Lean Exhaust Indication	A – C
E045	Rich Exhaust Indication	A – C
E047	ECM–BCM Data *A/C Clutch and Cruise	A
E051	ECM PROM Error	A – D – E
E052	Calpak Error	A
E055	ECM Error	A

DIAGNOSTIC CODE COMMENTS

"A"	"Service Engine Soon" Message Displayed
"B"	Forces Cooling Fans "ON"
"C"	Forces Open Loop Operation
"D"	Causes System to Operate in Bypass Spark Mode (Module Timing)
"E"	Causes System to Operate in Back up Fuel Mode

* These functions are disengaged while specified malfunctions remains current.

ECM diagnostic codes—Riviera

and the BCM continually monitor operating conditions for possible malfunctions. By comparing systems conditions against standard operating limits, certain circuit and component malfunctions can be detected. A 3 digit numerical TROUBLE CODE is stored in the computer memory when a problem is detected by this self-diagnostic system. These TROUBLE CODES can later be displayed by the service technician as an aid in system repair.

The occurrence of certain system malfunctions require that the vehicle operator be alerted to the problem so as to avoid prolonged operation of the vehicle under degrading system operations. The computer controlled diagnostic messages and/or telltales will appear under these conditions which indicate that service or repairs are required.

If a particular malfunction would result in unacceptable system operation, the self-diagnostics will attempt to minimize the effect by taking a FAIL-SOFT action. FAIL-SOFT action refers to any specific attempt by the computer system to compensate for the detected problem. A typical FAIL-SOFT action would be the substitution of a fixed input value when a sensor is detected to have an open or shorted circuit.

HOW TO ENTER THE DIAGNOSTIC SERVICE MODE

To enter the diagnostic service mode, proceed as follows:
1. Turn the ignition switch to the ON position.
2. Touch the OFF and the WARM pads on the CRT's climate control page, simultaneously and hold until a double BEEP is heard or a page entitled SERVICE MODE appears on the CRT.

NOTE: Operating the vehicle in the SERVICE MODE for an extended time period without the engine operating or without a trickle battery charger attached to the battery, can cause the battery to become discharged and possibly relate false diagnostic information or cause an engine no-start. Avoid lengthy (over ½ hour) SERVICE MODE operation.

TROUBLE CODE DISPLAY

After the SERVICE MODE is entered, any trouble codes stored

STEERING KNUCKLE

Removal and Installation

1986-87

1. Raise and safely support the vehicle. Support the lower control arm; this will keep the coil spring compressed. Remove the wheel assembly.
2. Remove the brake caliper and position it aside.
3. Remove the hub and disc. Remove the splash shield. Remove both ball stud nuts.
4. Remove the tie rod end from the steering knuckle. Using tool J-26407 or equivalent, press the upper ball stud from the steering knuckle.
5. Reverse the tool and press the lower ball stud from the steering knuckle. Remove the ball stud nuts. Remove the steering knuckle. Remove the steering knuckle from the vehicle.
6. To install, reverse the removal procedures.
7. Disconnect the tie rod end from the steering knuckle.
8. Remove the cotter pins and loosen the stud nuts attaching the upper and lower ball joints to the steering knuckle.
9. Separate the upper ball joint from the steering knuckle.
10. Release the lower ball joint from the steering knuckle. Remove the steering knuckle.
11. To install, reverse the removal procedures. Torque the hub and bearing bolts to 220 ft. lbs.

9. Install the ball joint through the lower control arm and into the steering knuckle. Install nut to ball joint stud and torque to 55 ft. lbs. Install a new cotter pin.
10. Connect the stabilizer bar and torque the bolt to 16 ft. lbs. Connect the tie rod and torque to 29 ft. lbs. Install the shock absorber to the lower control arm and torque the bolt to 35 ft. lbs.
11. If the bolts were removed or loosened at the steering assembly replace with new bolts and torque to 21 ft. lbs.
12. With the suspension system in its normal standing height, torque the lower control arm-to-body bolt to 62 ft. lbs. and the lower control arm-to-crossmember nut to 52 ft. lbs. Check and set alignment as necessary.

1988

1. Raise the vehicle and properly support the lower control arm with a jack.
2. Remove the wheel assembly.
3. Remove the brake caliper and the rotor.
4. Support the brake caliper with a piece of wire. Do not allow the caliper to hang by the brake hose.
5. Remove splash shield retaining bolts.
6. Unbolt the hub and bearing assembly from the steering knuckle.
7. Disconnect the tie rod end from the steering knuckle.

REAR WHEEL ALIGNMENT

Rear Suspension

Adjustment

CAMBER

1. Position the vehicle on alignment equipment and follow the manufacturers instructions to obtain a camber reading.
2. Use appropriate sockets and extensions to reach around both sides of the tire and loosen both strut-to-knuckle bolts enough to allow movement between the strut and the knuckle. Remove the tools.
3. Grasp the top of the tire firmly and move it inboard or outboard until the correct camber is obtained.
4. Again reach around the tire, as in Step 2, and tighten both bolts to 140 ft. lbs.
5. If the accessibility to the bolts prevents applying complete torque, it will be necessary to apply only partial torque, just

---

REAR WHEEL BEARINGS

Removal and Installation

STEEL WHEEL

1. Raise and safely support the vehicle. Remove the wheel assembly.
2. Install drive axle boot protectors.
3. Remove hub nut and discard. Remove caliper and rotor.
4. Remove hub and bearing attaching bolts. If bearing assembly is being reused, mark attaching bolt and corresponding holes for installation.
5. Install tool J-28733 or equivalent, and remove hub and bearing assembly. If excessive corrosion is present make sure hub and bearing is loose in knuckle before using tool.

To install:

6. If installing new bearing, replace knuckle seal. The vehicle must be moved without hub nut installed to proper torque.
7. Clean and inspect bearing mating surfaces and knuckle bore for dirt, nicks and burrs.
8. If installing knuckle seal, use tool J-28671 or equivalent, apply grease to seal and knuckle bore. Push hub and bearing on axle shaft.
9. Continue the installation in the reverse order of the removal procedure. Apply partial hub torque, about 74 ft. lbs., to new hub nut until hub and bearing assembly is seated.
10. Lower the vehicle and apply final torque, 200 ft. lbs. to the hub nut.

ALUMINUM WHEEL

1. Set parking brake. Raise and safely support the vehicle.

Rear wheel camber adjustment

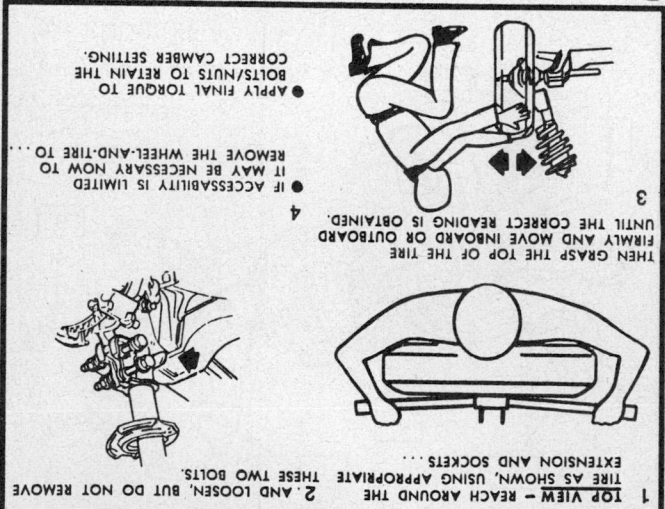

1 TOP VIEW — REACH AROUND THE TIRE AS SHOWN, USING APPROPRIATE EXTENSION AND SOCKETS . . .

2. AND LOOSEN, BUT DO NOT REMOVE THESE TWO BOLTS.

3 THEN GRASP THE TOP OF THE TIRE FIRMLY AND MOVE INBOARD OR OUTBOARD UNTIL THE CORRECT READING IS OBTAINED.

4 • IF ACCESSABILITY IS LIMITED IT MAY BE NECESSARY NOW TO REMOVE THE WHEEL-AND-TIRE TO . . .

• APPLY FINAL TORQUE TO BOLTS/NUTS TO RETAIN THE CORRECT CAMBER SETTING.

enough to hold the correct camber position, then to remove the wheel in order to apply final torque. After complete torquing, install the wheel.
6. Repeat on other side. Whenever adjusting caster, it is important to always use 2 washers totaling 12mm thickness, with a washer at each end of locating tube.

TOE

1. Position the vehicle on the alignment equipment and obtain an alignment reading.
2. If the reading is not within specification, loosen the adjuster tube clamps.
3. Rotate the adjuster tube as required to obtain the proper toe angle.
4. Tighten the adjuster clamps and torque the clamp bolts to 47 ft. lbs.

MacPherson strut design rear suspension

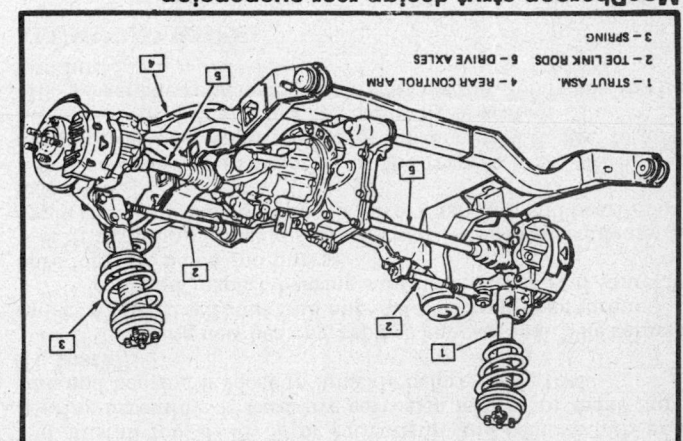

1 — STRUT ASM.
2 — TOE LINK RODS
3 — SPRING
4 — REAR CONTROL ARM
6 — DRIVE AXLES

Rear wheel bearing arrangement

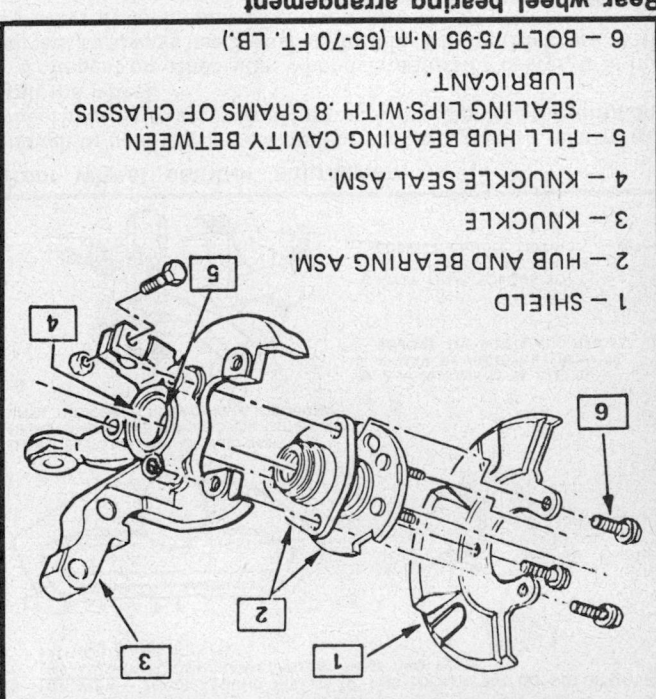

1 — SHIELD
2 — HUB AND BEARING ASM.
3 — KNUCKLE
4 — KNUCKLE SEAL ASM.
5 — FILL HUB BEARING CAVITY BETWEEN SEALING LIPS WITH .8 GRAMS OF CHASSIS LUBRICANT.
6 — BOLT 75-95 N·m (55-70 FT. LB.)

2. Remove wheel assembly. Remove hub nut. Install drive axle boot protectors.

3. Remove hub nut and discard. Remove caliper and rotor.

4. Remove hub and bearing attaching bolts. If bearing assembly is being reused, mark attaching bolt and corresponding holes for installation.

5. Install tool J-28733 or equivalent, and remove hub and bearing assembly. If excessive corrosion is present make sure hub and bearing is loose in knuckle before using tool.

To install:

6. If installing new bearing, replace knuckle seal. The vehicle must be moved without hub nut installed to proper torque.

7. Clean and inspect bearing mating surfaces and knuckle bore for dirt, nicks and burrs.

8. If installing knuckle seal, use tool J-28671 or equivalent, apply grease to seal and knuckle bore. Push hub and bearing on axle shaft.

9. Continue the installation in the reverse order of the removal procedure. Apply partial torque, about 74 ft. lbs., to new hub nut until hub and bearing assembly is seated.

STRUT ASSEMBLY

Removal and Installation

1. Remove the engine compartment lid from inside the vehicle.
2. Raise the vehicle and support at rear control arm.
3. Remove upper strut nuts and washers. Remove brake line clip.
4. Scribe mark strut and knuckle to assure proper assembly.
5. Remove strut mounting bolts. Remove the strut and the spacer plate.
6. To install, reverse the removal procedures.

Strut and knuckle scribe marks

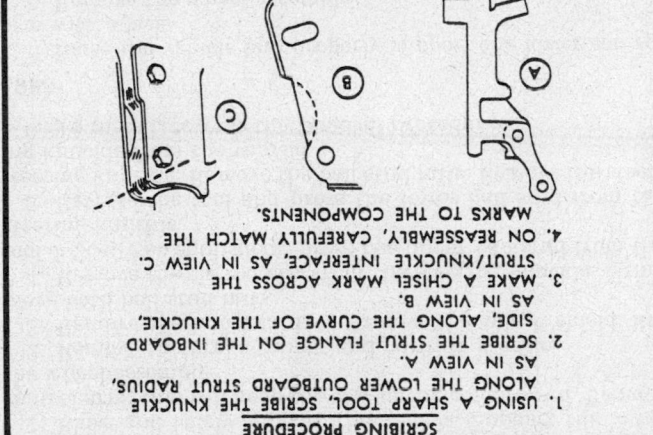

SCRIBING PROCEDURE
1. USING A SHARP TOOL, SCRIBE THE KNUCKLE ALONG THE LOWER OUTBOARD STRUT RADIUS, AS IN VIEW A.
2. SCRIBE THE STRUT FLANGE ON THE INBOARD SIDE, ALONG THE CURVE OF THE KNUCKLE, AS IN VIEW B.
3. MAKE A CHISEL MARK ACROSS THE STRUT/KNUCKLE INTERFACE, AS IN VIEW C.
4. ON REASSEMBLY, CAREFULLY MATCH THE MARKS TO THE COMPONENTS.

BALL JOINT

Removal and Installation

1. Raise and safely support the vehicle. Remove the wheel assembly.
2. Remove clamp bolt from lower control arm ball stud.
3. Disconnect the ball joint from the knuckle. It may be necessary to tap the stud with a mallet. Using a drill, remove the rivets.
4. Remove the ball from the lower control arm assembly.
5. To install, reverse the removal procedures.

LOWER CONTROL ARM

Removal and Installation

1. Raise and safely support the vehicle. Remove the wheel assembly.
2. Remove ball joint clamping bolt. Separate knuckle from assembly.
3. Remove lower control arm pivot bolts at frame. Remove control arm.
4. To install, reverse the removal procedures.

KNUCKLE ASSEMBLY

Removal and Installation

1986-87

1. Remove the rear wheel bearing assembly.

10. Lower the vehicle and apply final torque, 200 ft. lbs. to the hub nut.

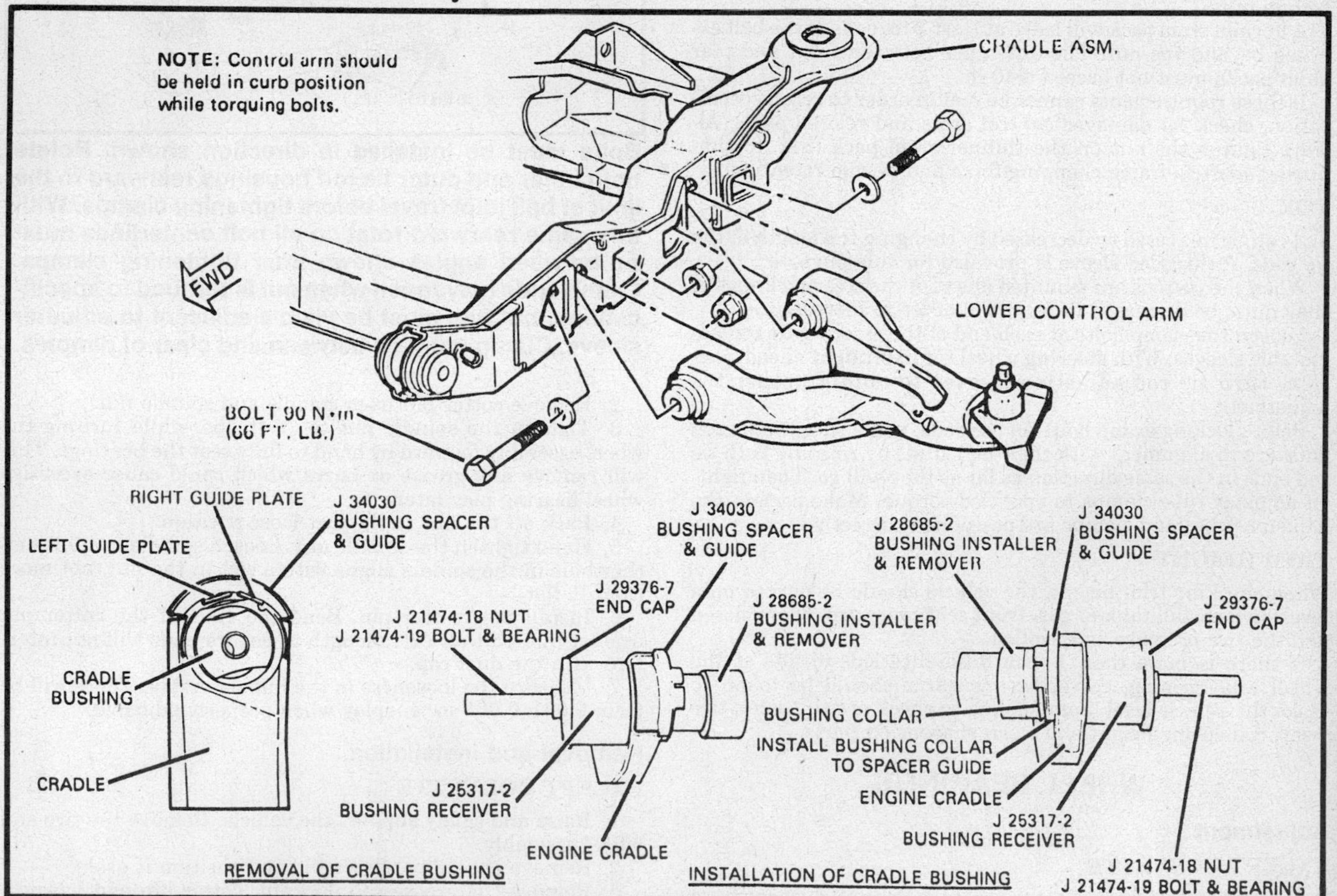

Remove/Install lower control arm

REMOVAL OF CRADLE BUSHING

- CRADLE
- CRADLE BUSHING
- LEFT GUIDE PLATE
- RIGHT GUIDE PLATE
- J 34030 BUSHING SPACER & GUIDE
- J 21474-18 NUT
- J 21474-19 BOLT & BEARING
- J 29376-7 END CAP
- J 25317-2 BUSHING RECEIVER
- ENGINE CRADLE

INSTALLATION OF CRADLE BUSHING

- J 21474-18 NUT
- J 21474-19 BOLT & BEARING
- J 25317-2 BUSHING RECEIVER
- ENGINE CRADLE
- J 29376-7 END CAP
- J 34030 BUSHING SPACER & GUIDE
- J 28686-2 BUSHING INSTALLER & REMOVER
- BUSHING COLLAR
- INSTALL BUSHING COLLAR TO SPACER GUIDE
- J 28686-2 BUSHING INSTALLER & REMOVER
- J 34030 BUSHING SPACER & GUIDE
- J 29376-7 END CAP

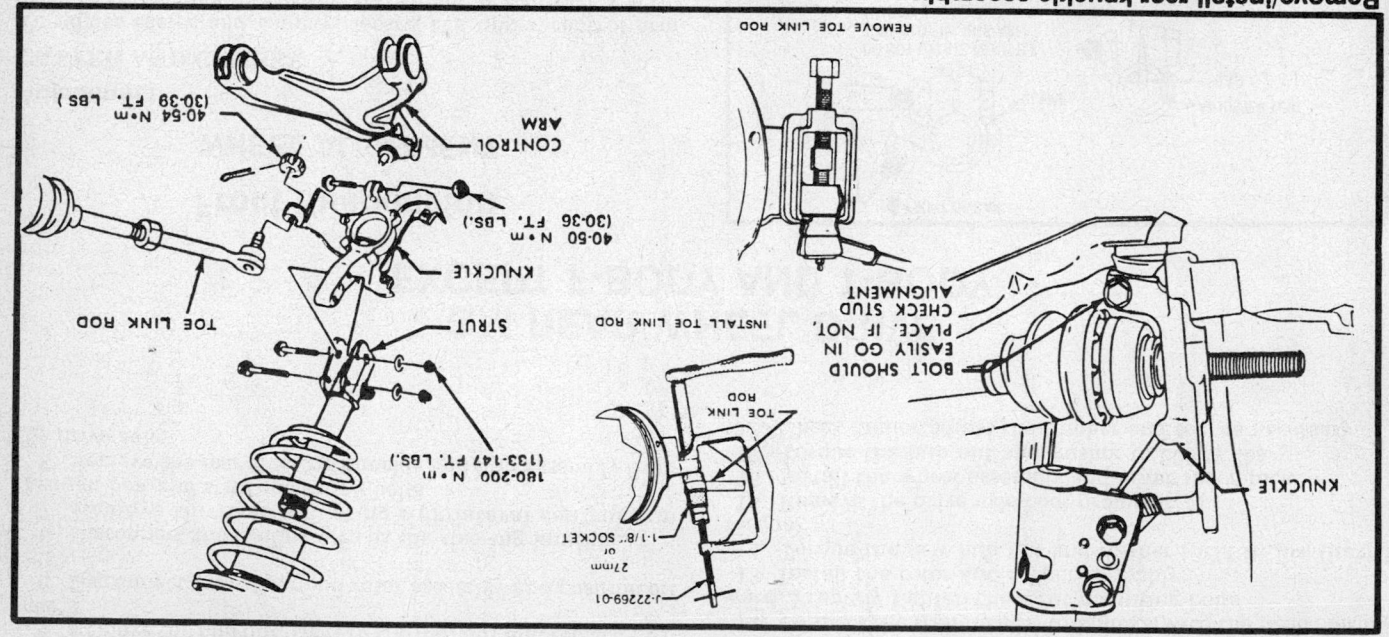

- LOWER CONTROL ARM
- CRADLE ASM.
- BOLT 90 N·m (66 FT. LBS.)
- FWD

NOTE: Control arm should be held in curb position while torquing bolts.

Remove/Install rear knuckle assembly

- CONTROL ARM
- 40-54 N·m (30-39 FT. LBS)
- TOE LINK ROD
- 40-50 N·m (30-36 FT. LBS.)
- KNUCKLE
- STRUT
- 180-200 N·m (133-147 FT. LBS.)
- 27mm or 1-1/8" SOCKET
- J-22269-01

- REMOVE TOE LINK ROD
- INSTALL TOE LINK ROD
- TOE LINK ROD
- BOLT SHOULD EASILY GO IN PLACE. IF NOT, CHECK STUD ALIGNMENT
- KNUCKLE

2. Remove the toe link rod at the knuckle. Remove clamp bolt and disconnect knuckle from the ball stud.
3. Remove the bolts holding the strut to the knuckle. Remove the rear knuckle. Whenever separating the ball joint from the knuckle, be careful not to cut or tear the ball joint seal, or damage to the ball joint could occur. If the seal is cut or torn, the ball joint must be replaced.
4. To install, reverse the removal procedures.

1. Raise and safely support the vehicle.
2. Install a drive axle boot protectors.
3. Remove the wheel assembly.
4. Remove the hub nut. Discard the hub nut and replace with new.
5. Disconnect the caliper and rotor assembly and position off aside.
6. Disconnect the trailing arm at the steering knuckle.
7. Remove the fixed adjusting link/lateral control arm through bolt and strut mounting bolts.
8. Remove the rear steering knuckle and hub assembly from the drive axle.

To install:
9. Install the hub and knuckle assembly to the drive axle.
10. Loosely install the strut mounting bolts with the bolt heads to the rear.
11. Install the fixed/lateral control arm through bolt.
12. Connect the trailing arm-to-knuckle with the head bolt inward. Properly tighten the strut mounting bolts.
13. Install the rotor and caliper assembly.
14. Torque the new hub nut and washer to 74 ft. lbs. (initial torque).
15. Remove the drive axle boot protector.
16. Install the wheel assembly and lower the vehicle.
17. Torque the hub nut and washer to 200 ft. lbs.
18. Check and/or adjust the camber and toe, as necessary.

GM REAR WHEEL DRIVE EXCEPT F-BODY AND T-BODY

Front Suspension

WHEEL ALIGNMENT

Adjustment

CASTER AND CAMBER

To adjust caster and camber, loosen the upper control arm shaft-to-frame nuts, add and/or subtract shims, as required, and re-torque nuts.

A normal shim pack will leave at least 2 threads of the bolt exposed beyond the nut. The difference between front and rear shim packs must not exceed .040 in.

If these requirements cannot be met in order to reach specification, check for damaged control arms and related parts. Always tighten the nut on the thinner shim pack first, for improved shaft-to-frame clamping force and torque retention.

TOE

Toe can be increased or decreased by changing the length of the tie rods. A threaded sleeve is provided for this purpose.

When the tie rods are mounted ahead of the steering knuckle, they must be decreased in length in order to increase toe.

Loosen the clamp bolts at each end of the steering tie rod adjustable sleeves. With steering wheel set in straight ahead position, turn tie rod adjusting sleeves to obtain proper toe adjustment.

Before locking clamp bolts on the rods, make sure the tie rod ends are in alignment with their ball studs by rotating both tie rod ends in the same direction as far as they will go. Then tighten adjuster tube clamps to specified torque. Make certain the adjuster tubes and clamps are positioned correctly.

TRIM HEIGHT

When checking trim height, the vehicle should be parked on a level surface, full tank of gas, front seat rearward, doors closed and the tire pressure as specified.

If there is more than 1 inch difference side-to-side at the wheel well opening, corrective measures should be taken to make the vehicle level. Some points to check are tire sizes, tire wear, coil spring height and worn suspension parts.

WHEEL BEARINGS

Adjustment

EXCEPT CORVETTE

1. Raise and safely support the vehicle. Remove dust cap from hub.

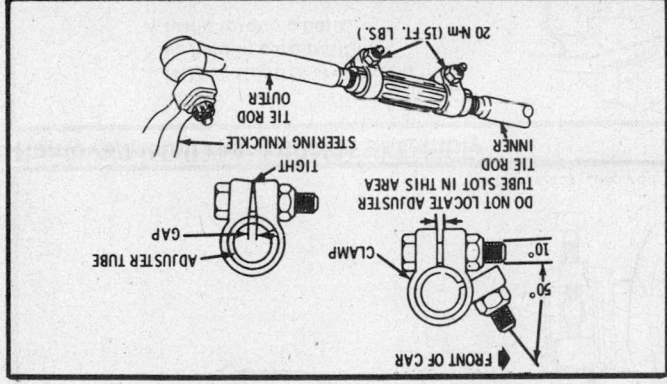

FRONT OF CAR — CLAMP — 10° — 50° — DO NOT LOCATE ADJUSTER TUBE SLOT IN THIS AREA — TIE ROD INNER — STEERING KNUCKLE — TIGHT — GAP — ADJUSTER TUBE — TIE ROD OUTER — 20 N·m (15 FT. LBS.)

Bolts must be installed in direction shown. Rotate both inner and outer tie rod housings rearward to the limit of ball joint travel before tightening clamps. With this same rearward rotation all bolt centerlines must be between angles shown after tightening clamps. Clamp ends may touch when nut is torqued to specifications, but gap must be visible adjacent to adjuster sleeve. Clamp must be between and clear of dimples.

2. Remove cotter pin from spindle and spindle nut.
3. Tighten the spindle nut to 12 ft. lbs. while turning the wheel assembly forward by hand to fully seat the bearings. This will remove any grease or burrs which could cause excessive wheel bearing play later.
4. Back off the nut to the just loose position.
5. Hand tighten the spindle nut. Loosen spindle nut until either hole in the spindle aligns with a slot in the nut, not more than ½ flat.
6. Install new cotter pin. Bend the ends of the cotter pin against it. Cut off extra length to ensure ends will not interfere with the dust cap.
7. Measure the looseness in the hub assembly. There will be from 0.001–0.005 in. endplay when properly adjusted.

EXCEPT CORVETTE

Removal and Installation

1. Raise and safely support the vehicle. Remove the tire and wheel assembly.
2. Remove the caliper assembly and position it aside.
3. Remove the grease cap, cotter pin, locknut, and locknut. Remove the outer wheel bearing assembly.

Caster and camber adjustment—except Corvette

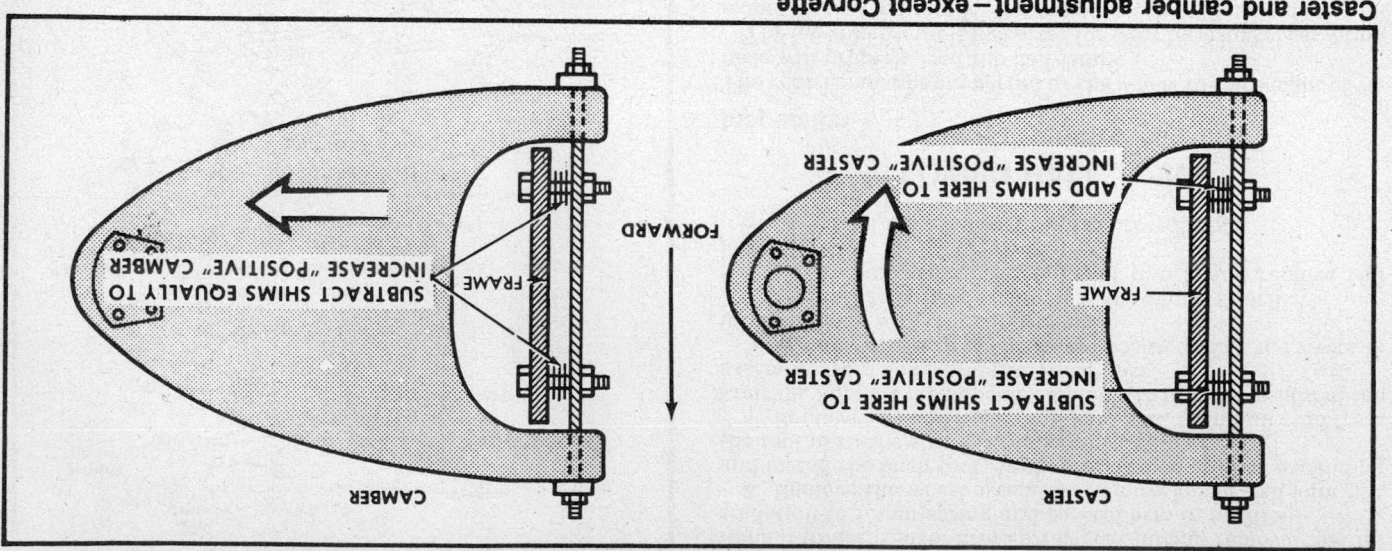

CASTER

SUBTRACT SHIMS HERE TO INCREASE "POSITIVE" CASTER

FRAME

ADD SHIMS HERE TO INCREASE "POSITIVE" CASTER

CAMBER

SUBTRACT SHIMS EQUALLY TO INCREASE "POSITIVE" CAMBER

FRAME

FORWARD

Front wheel alignment—Corvette

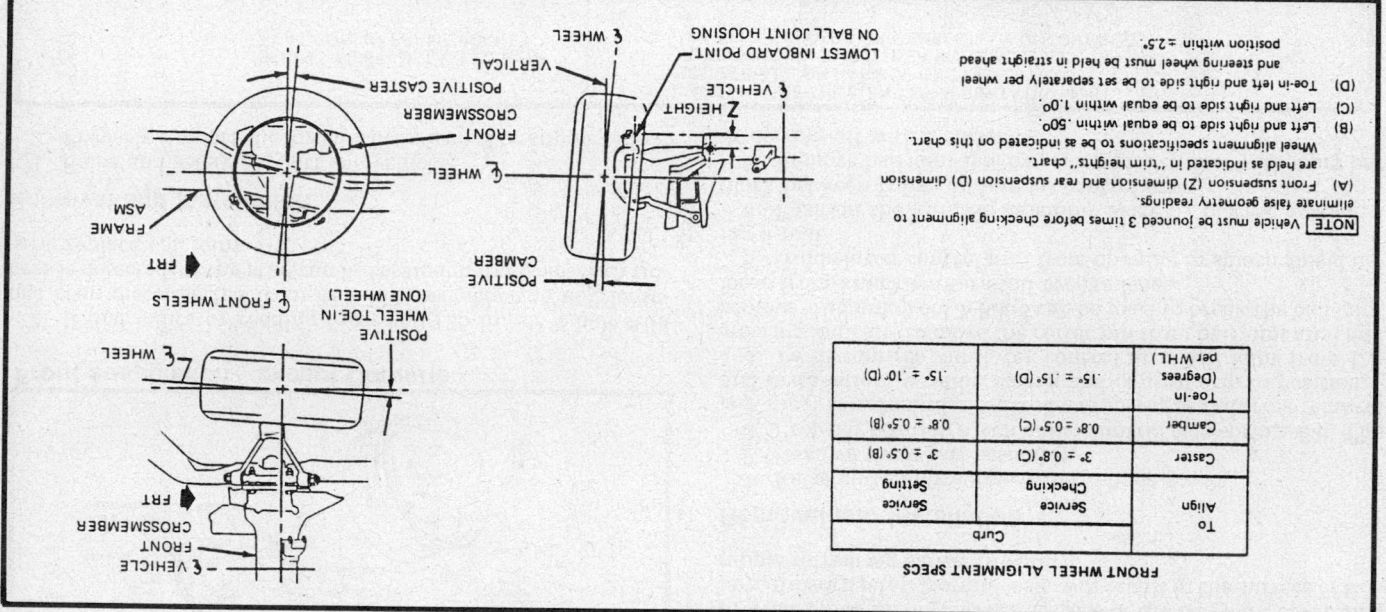

FRONT WHEEL ALIGNMENT SPECS

To Align	Service Checking	Service Setting
Caster	3° ± 0.8° (C)	3° ± 0.5° (B)
Camber	0.8° ± 0.5° (C)	0.8° ± 0.5° (B)
Toe-in (Degrees per WHL.)	.15° = .15° (D)	.15° = .10° (D)

Curb

NOTE Vehicle must be jounced 3 times before checking alignment to eliminate false geometry readings.

(A) Front suspension (Z) dimension and rear suspension (D) dimension are held as indicated in "trim heights" chart.
Wheel alignment specifications to be as indicated on this chart.
(B) Left and right side to be equal within .50°.
(C) Left and right side to be equal within 1.0°.
(D) Toe-in left and right side to be set separately per wheel and steering wheel must be held in straight ahead position within ±2.5°.

FRAME ASM

FRT

← FRONT CROSSMEMBER

₵ FRONT WHEELS

POSITIVE CASTER

VERTICAL

₵ WHEEL

POSITIVE WHEEL TOE-IN (ONE WHEEL)

POSITIVE CAMBER

₵ WHEEL

LOWEST INBOARD POINT ON BALL JOINT HOUSING

₵ VEHICLE

Z HEIGHT

₵ VEHICLE

FRT

FRONT CROSSMEMBER

₵ WHEEL

CORVETTE

1. Raise and safely support the vehicle.
2. Remove the wheel assembly.
3. Remove the caliper assembly and position it aside.
4. Remove the hub and bearing assembly.
5. To install, reverse the removal procedures.

4. Remove the rotor. Remove the inner wheel bearing assembly using the proper removal tools.
5. To install, reverse the removal procedures. Be sure to use a new grease seal and properly repack the bearings.

UPPER BALL JOINT

Inspection

1. Raise the vehicle and position jackstands under the left and right lower control arm as near as possible to each lower ball joint. The vehicle must be stable and should not rock on the jackstands. Upper control arm bumper must not contact frame.
2. Grasp front wheel and push in on bottom of tire while pulling out at the top. Read dial gauge, then reverse the push-pull procedure. Horizontal deflection on dial indicator should not exceed 0.125 in.

SHOCK ABSORBER

Removal and Installation

1. Remove the upper stem nut while holding the stem to keep it from turning.

2. Raise and safely support the vehicle.
3. Remove the shock absorber-to-lower control arm bolts.
4. Remove the shock absorber from the vehicle.
5. To install, reverse the removal procedures.

VIEW A

LOWER SUSPENSION ARM

AFTER ASSEMBLY, END OF SPRING COIL MUST COVER ALL OR PART OF ONE INSPECTION DRAIN HOLE. THE OTHER HOLE MUST BE PARTLY EXPOSED OR COMPLETELY UNCOVERED.

VIEW B

LOWER SUSPENSION ARM

WHEN COMPRESSING A PORTION OF THE SPRING, DO NOT COMPRESS TO GAP BETWEEN ACTIVE COILS OF LESS THAN 6mm (.22 INCHES)—C-CAR

IF ENTIRE SPRING IS COMPRESSED, THE OVERALL DIMENSION MUST NEVER BE LESS THAN 244mm (9.62 INCHES)—C-CAR

FRONT OF CAR

FRAME

SPRING TO BE INSTALLED WITH FLAT COIL IN FRAME POCKET.

LOWER SUSPENSION ARM

Removal and Installation

1. Raise and safely support the vehicle.
2. Properly support the lower control arm. The support must remain under spring seat during removal and installation to retain spring and control arm in position.
3. Remove the wheel assembly. Remove upper ball joint nut and install the push tool. Apply pressure on stud by expanding the tool until the stud breaks loose.
4. Remove tool and upper ball joint nut, then pull stud from knuckle. Support the knuckle assembly to prevent weight of the assembly from damaging the brake hose.
5. With control arm in the raised position, drill the rivets 1/4 in. deep using a 1/8 in. diameter drill.
6. Drill off rivet heads using a 1/2 in. diameter drill.
7. Punch out rivets using a small punch and remove ball joint.
8. To install, reverse the removal procedures.

LOWER BALL JOINT

Inspection

The vehicle must be supported by the wheel so the weight of vehicle will properly load the ball joints.

The lower ball joint is inspected for wear by visual observation alone. Wear is indicated by protrusion of the 1/2 in. diameter nipple into which the grease fitting is threaded. This round nipple projects 0.050 in. beyond the surface of the ball joint cover on a new, unworn joint. Normal wear will result in the surface of this nipple retreating slowly inward.

Removal and Installation

1. Raise and safely support the vehicle.
2. Remove the wheel assembly.
3. Properly position a jack under control arm spring seat. The jack must remain under control arm spring seat during removal and installation to retain spring and control arm in position.
4. To disconnect the lower control arm ball joint from the steering knuckle. Remove the cotter pin from ball joint stud and remove stud nut. Tool J-8806 can be used to break the ball joint loose from knuckle after stud breaks loose.
5. Guide lower control arm from opening in splash shield using a tool.
6. Position the knuckle assembly aside by placing a wooden block between frame and upper control arm.
7. Remove ball joint seal by prying off retainer with a pry bar or driving off with a chisel.

Front suspension—except Corvette

4. If dial indicator reading exceeds 0.125 in., or if ball stud has been disconnected from knuckle assembly and any looseness is detected, or the stud can be twisted in its socket with fingers, replace ball joint.

WHEEL ASM — CAP — WASHER — BEARING — HUB & ROTOR ASSEMBLY — BEARING — SEAL — LINK BOLT — SPLASH SHIELD — STEERING KNUCKLE GASKET — BRAKE CALIPER — FITTING — SPHERICAL JOINT — LOWER SUSPENSION ARM — SHOCK ABSORBER — COIL SPRING — BUSHING — STABILIZER BAR — BRACKET — BUSHING — SHAFT — NUT — SHIM — UPPER BUMPER — UPPER SUSPENSION ARM — BUSHING — RETAINER — SPHERICAL JOINT

COIL SPRING

EXCEPT CORVETTE

Removal and Installation

1. Raise and safely support the vehicle. Remove the wheel assembly.
2. If equipped, remove stabilizer link nut, grommets washers and bolt.
3. Remove the shock absorber from the vehicle.
4. Install coil spring tool. Make sure the tool is fully seated into lower control arm spring seat.
5. Rotate nut until spring is compressed enough so it is free in its seat.
6. Remove the lower control arm pivot bolts and disengage lower control arm from frame. Rotate the arm with spring rearward. Remove the spring from the vehicle.
7. To install, reverse the removal procedures.

CORVETTE

1. Raise and safely support the vehicle.
2. Remove both the wheel assemblies.
3. Remove both front spring protectors. Remove the spring mounting nuts.
4. Install a spring compressing tool.
5. Disconnect both lower ball joints using tool J-33436 or equivalent.
6. Compress the spring assembly.
7. Remove the lower shock/stabilizer bracket from the lower control arm, on one side of the vehicle.
8. Remove the lower shock and stabilizer-to-bracket retaining bolts. Remove the bracket from the lower control arm, on one side of the vehicle.
9. Release and remove the compressing tool from its mounting on the vehicle.
10. Pull both lower control arms down to their full travel. It may be necessary to use the help of another person to accomplish this.
11. Remove the spring assembly from the vehicle.
12. To install, reverse the removal procedures. After installation, check and/or adjust wheel alignment as required.

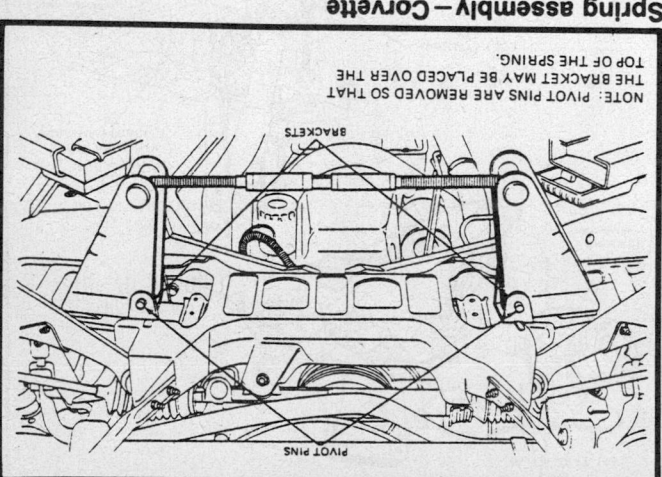

Upper control arm bushing installation — except Corvette

13.3 ± 0.5 mm (.5 ± .02 IN.)
BOTH ENDS

UPPER CONTROL ARM

EXCEPT CORVETTE

Removal and Installation

1. Raise and safely support the vehicle. Support the lower control arm; the control arm must be properly supported during this procedure.
2. Remove the tire wheel assembly. Remove the upper ball joint nut. Apply pressure on stud by expanding the tool until the stud breaks loose.
3. Remove the tool and upper ball joint nut, then pull stud free from knuckle. Support the knuckle assembly to prevent weight of the assembly from damaging the brake hose.
4. Remove the upper control arm attaching bolts to allow clearance to remove upper control arm assembly.
5. Remove upper control arm from the vehicle.
6. To install, reverse the removal procedures.

CORVETTE

1. Raise and safely support the vehicle. Remove the wheel assembly.
2. Remove spring protector.
3. Using a spring compressor, compress and loosen the spring.
4. Use tool J-33436 or equivalent, to disconnect the upper ball joint from the knuckle.
5. Remove the upper control arm.
6. To install, reverse the removal procedures. Torque upper control arm bolts to specification and the ball joint nut to specification. The cotter pin at the ball joint must be installed from rear to front. Do not back off the nut for the cotter pin.

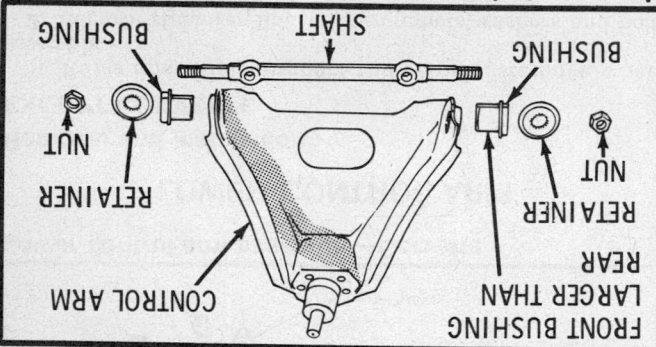

Upper control arm assembly — except Corvette

BUSHING
SHAFT
BUSHING
NUT
NUT
RETAINER
RETAINER
FRONT BUSHING LARGER THAN REAR
CONTROL ARM

Spring assembly — Corvette

BRACKETS
PIVOT PINS

NOTE: PIVOT PINS ARE REMOVED SO THAT THE BRACKET MAY BE PLACED OVER THE TOP OF THE SPRING.

8. Remove grease fittings and install special tool to remove lower ball joint from lower control arm.
9. To install, reverse the removal procedures.

STEERING KNUCKLE

Removal and Installation

EXCEPT CORVETTE

1. Raise and safely support the vehicle and the lower suspension arm.
2. Remove wheel assembly. Remove tie rod end from steering knuckle.
3. Remove brake caliper and rotor assembly. Position the caliper assembly aside.
4. Remove the splash shield. Remove upper and lower ball joint studs from the steering knuckle.

CORVETTE

1. Raise and safely support the vehicle. Remove the wheel assembly.
2. Remove spring protector.
3. Using tool J-33432 or equivalent, compress the spring.
4. Remove lower shock bracket.
5. Using tool J-33436 or equivalent, disconnect lower ball joint.
6. Remove lower control arm.
7. To install, reverse the removal procedures. Torque the ball joint nut to specification.

LOWER CONTROL ARM

Removal and Installation

EXCEPT CORVETTE

1. Raise and safely support the vehicle. Remove wheel assembly.
2. Remove stabilizer link nut, grommets washers and bolt. Remove the shock absorber.
3. Loosen the lower ball joint nut and use tool J-8806 or equivalent. Apply pressure on stud by expanding the tool until the stud breaks loose.
4. Install spring compressor in through front spring. Compress spring until all tension is off lower control arm.
5. Remove pivot bolts and ball joint. Remove the control arm assembly.
6. To install, reverse the removal procedures.

CORVETTE

1. Raise and safely support the vehicle.
2. Remove the brake caliper. Position the caliper assembly aside.
3. Properly support the control arm assembly. Remove the hub and bearing assembly.
4. Disconnect the brake sensor. Disconnect the upper and lower ball joints, using the proper tools.
5. Disconnect the steering ball joint. Remove the knuckle from the vehicle.
6. To install, reverse the removal procedures. Check front wheel alignment.

5. Remove the steering knuckle from the vehicle.

Stabilizer bar assembly—except Corvette

STABILIZER SHAFT — SPACER — GROMMET — RETAINER — NUT — BOLT — BUSHING — BRACKET

VIEW A

INSTALL BUSHING WITH SLIT TO FRONT OF CAR

Steering knuckle assembly—except Corvette

CAP — COTTER PIN — NUT — WASHER — RACE — BEARING — INNER BEARING — RACE — SEAL — DISC — GASKET — SHIELD — STEERING KNUCKLE

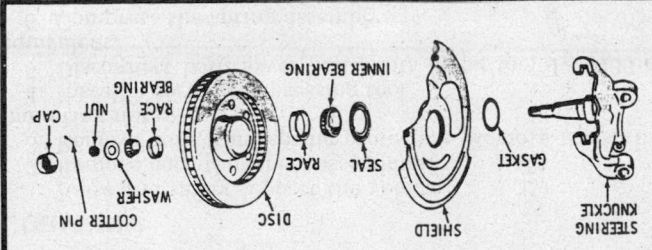

Upper control arm assembly—Corvette

KNUCKLE ASSEMBLY
85 N·m (63 FT. LBS.)
43 N·m (32 FT. LBS.)
UPPER CONTROL ARM
SHIMS
SPECIAL THICK WASHER IS LOCATED AT REAR INBOARD POSITION

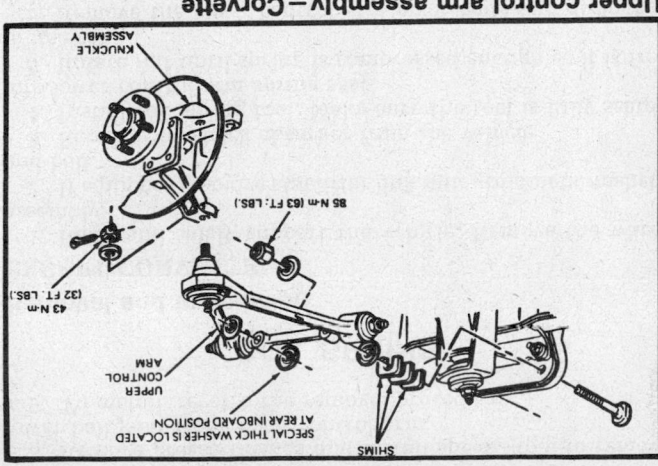

Lower control arm assembly—Corvette

40 N·m (30 FT. LBS.)
LOWER CONTROL ARM
30 N·m (22 FT. LBS.)
40 N·m (30 FT. LBS.)
SHOCK ABSORBER MOUNTING BRACKET
KNUCKLE ASSEMBLY
130 N·m (96 ft. lbs.)
130 N·m (96 ft. lbs.)
65 N·m (48 FT. LBS.)

6. To install, reverse the removal procedures.

STABILIZER SHAFT

Removal and Installation

1. Raise and safely support the vehicle.
2. On all but Corvette, disconnect each side of stabilizer linkage by removing nut from link bolt. Pull bolt from linkage and remove retainers, grommets and spacer.
3. On Corvette, remove the upper link mounting bolt, the lower mounting bracket and the bracket.
4. Remove bracket-to-frame or body bolts and remove stabilizer shaft, rubber bushings and brackets. Some models require a special tool to remove stabilizer shaft bolt.
5. To install, reverse the removal procedures. On Corvette, be sure the upper link mounting bolt and the lower bracket mounting bolt are installed in the same direction they were removed in.

Rear Suspension Except Corvette

SHOCK ABSORBER

Removal and Installation

1. Raise and safely support the vehicle and the rear axle.
2. Remove the top shock absorber retaining bolts. Remove the lower shock absorber retaining bolts.
3. Remove the shock absorber from the vehicle.
4. To install, reverse the removal procedures.

COIL SPRING

Removal and Installation

1. Raise and safely support the vehicle and the rear axle assembly.
2. Disconnect the brake line mount at axle housing. Do not open the brake line unless necessary.
3. Disconnect the upper control arms at the axle housing. Remove the shock lower mount.
4. Carefully lower the rear axle assembly enough to remove the springs. Do not allow the rear axle to remain in the lowered position.
5. To install, reverse the removal procedures.

UPPER CONTROL ARM

Removal and Installation

NOTE: If both control arms are to be replaced, remove and replace 1 control arm at a time to prevent the axle from rolling or slipping sideways. This might occur with both upper control arms removed, making replacement difficult.

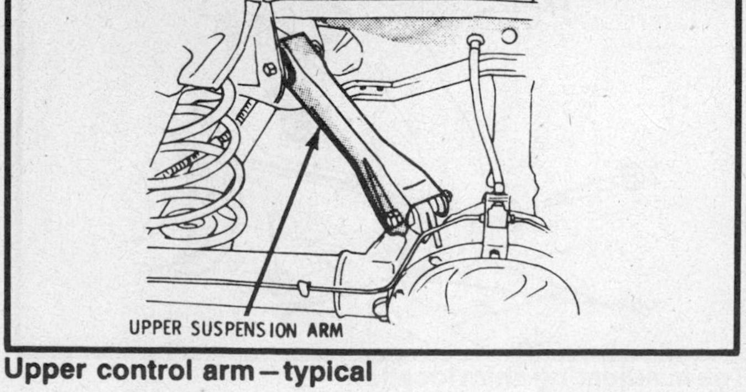
UPPER SUSPENSION ARM
Upper control arm—typical

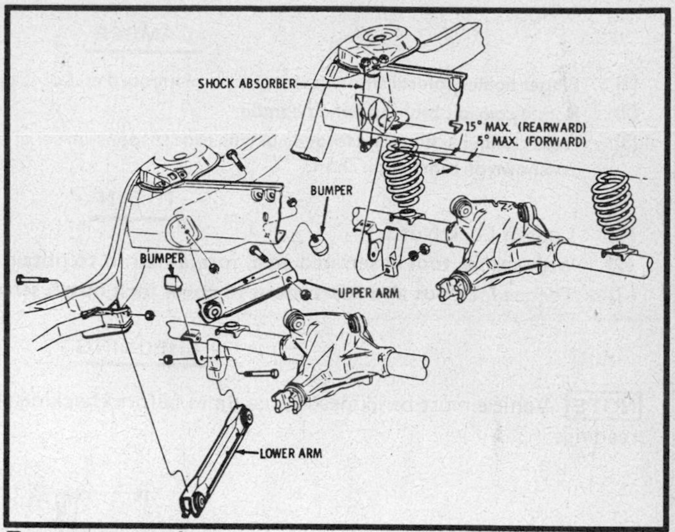
SHOCK ABSORBER
15° MAX. (REARWARD)
5° MAX. (FORWARD)
BUMPER
BUMPER
UPPER ARM
LOWER ARM
Rear suspension

1. Raise and safely support the vehicle and the rear axle assembly.
2. Remove the nut from the rear arm-to-rear axle housing bolt and while rocking rear axle, remove the bolt. On some vehicles disconnecting lower shock absorber stud will provide clearance. Use support under rear axle nose to aid in bolt removal.
3. Remove the upper control arm attaching bolts. Remove upper control arm from the vehicle.
4. To install, reverse the removal procedures.

LOWER CONTROL ARM

Removal and Installation

NOTE: If both control arms are to be replaced, remove and replace 1 control arm at a time to prevent the axle from rolling or slipping sideways. This might occur with both lower control arms removed, making replacement difficult.

1. Raise and safely support the vehicle and the rear axle assembly.
2. Remove the rear arm-to-axle housing bracket bolt.
3. Remove front arm-to-bracket bolts. Remove the lower control arm from the vehicle.
4. To install, reverse the removal procedures.

Rear Suspension Corvette

REAR WHEEL ALIGNMENT

To align the rear suspension, back the vehicle onto the machine normally used to align front suspension. Camber will now be read in the normal manner. However, with the vehicle backed in, toe-in will now read as toe-out, while toe-out will be read as toe-in. Check condition of strut rods. They should be straight. Rear wheel alignment could be affected if they are bent.

Adjustment

CAMBER

Wheel camber angle is obtained by adjusting the eccentric cam and bolt assembly located at the inboard mounting of the strut rod. Place rear wheels on alignment machine and determine camber angle. To adjust, loosen cam bolt nut and rotate cam and bolt assembly until specified camber is reached. Tighten nut securely and torque to specifications.

Rear wheel camber adjustment

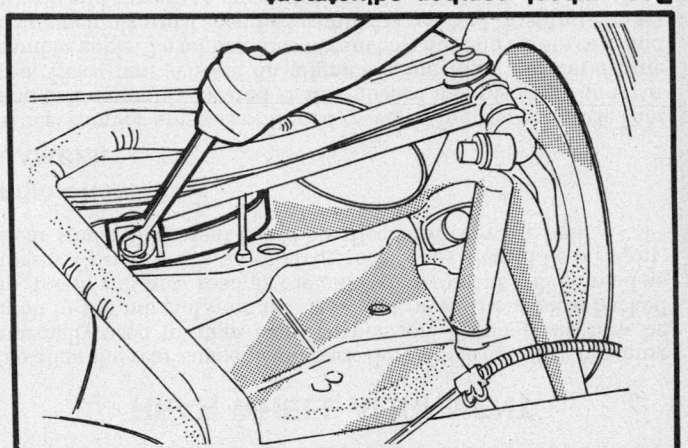

TOE

Wheel toe is adjusted by inserting shims of varying thickness inside the frame side member on both sides of the torque control arm pivot bushing. Shims are available in thickness of $1/64$ in., $1/32$ in., $1/8$ in. and $1/4$ in.

To adjust toe, loosen torque control arm pivot bolt. Remove cotter pin retaining shims and remove shims. Position torque control arm to obtain specified toe-in. Shim the gap toward vehicle centerline between torque arm bushing and frame side inner wall. Do not use thicker shim than necessary and do

Toe in adjusting shim location

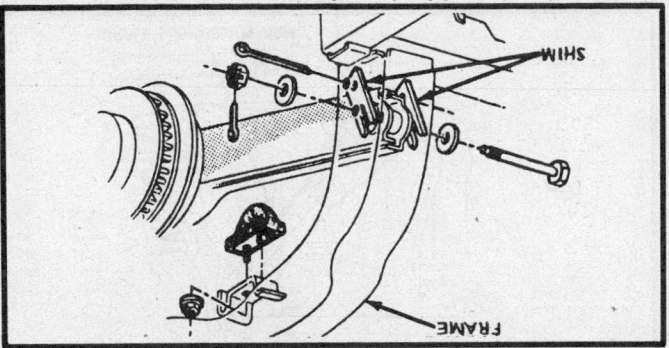

2. Disengage bolt tabs and disconnect outboard end of axle drive shaft from wheel spindle flange.

1. Raise and safely support the vehicle.

Adjustment

REAR WHEEL BEARING

mit cotter pin insertion, tighten nut to next flat.

fications and install cotter pin. If specified torque does not permit cotter pin (with loop outboard) through shims. Torque nut to specifications. After correct shim stack has been selected, install cotter pin (with loop outboard) through shims. Torque nut to specifications and install cotter pin. If specified torque does not permit member. After correct shim stack has been selected, install cotter pin (with loop outboard) through shims. Torque nut to specifications tween torque control arm bushing and inner wall of frame side member. After correct shim stack has been selected, install cotter pin (with loop outboard) through shims.

Shim outboard gap as necessary to obtain solid stackup between torque control arm bushing and inner wall of frame side member.

arm. To do so may cause toe setting to change.

not use undue force when shimming inner side of torque control arm.

Rear wheel alignment

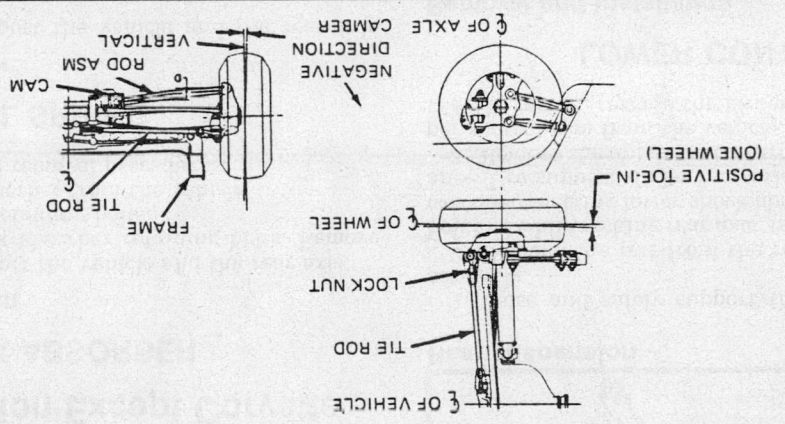

NOTE Vehicle must be jounced three times before checking alignment, to eliminate false geometry readings.

CHECKING

TOE IN

(1) Loosen Lock Nut

(2) With special tool in serrated area, rotate tie rod to obtain specified toe-in.

(3) Torque lock nut and adjust boot to cover lock nut & serrations.

CAMBER

(1) Finger tighten lateral strut attaching parts at inboard end of strut asm.

(2) Rotate cam to obtain specified camber.

(3) Hold camber setting and torque nut with rear suspension set at "D" height of 71.0. As shown on trim height chart.

REAR WHEEL ALIGNMENT SPECS

To Align	Service Setting
Camber	$0° \pm .5°$
Toe-in (Deg per WHL)	$0.15° \pm .06°$

3. Mark camber cam in relation to bracket. Loosen and turn camber bolt until strut rod forces torque control arm outward. Position loose end of axle drive shaft aside for access to spindle.

4. Remove wheel assembly. Mount dial indicator on torque control arm adjacent surface and rest pointer on flange or spindle end.

5. Grasp brake disc and move axially (in and out) while reading movement on dial indicator. If end movement is within the 0.001-0.008 in., bearings do not require adjustment.

Removal and Installation

1. Raise and safely support the vehicle. Remove center cap from wheel.
2. Remove cotter pin, spindle nut and washer. Remove the wheel assembly.
3. Remove caliper and support. Remove the rotor.
4. Disconnect tie rod end from the knuckle.
5. Disconnect transverse spring from the knuckle.
6. Scribe mark on cam bolt and mounting bracket so they can be realigned in the same position.
7. Remove cam bolt and separate spindle support rod from the mounting bracket.
8. Remove the trunnion straps at the side yoke shaft. Push out on the knuckle and separate axle shaft from the side gear yoke shaft. Remove the axle shaft from the vehicle.
9. Using tool J-34161 or equivalent, remove the hub and bearing mounting bolts.
10. Remove hub and bearing from the vehicle. Properly support the parking brake backing plate.
11. To install, reverse the removal procedures. Check suspension alignment and adjust as needed.

SHOCK ABSORBER

Removal and Installation

1. Raise and safely support the vehicle. If necessary, remove the rear wheels.
2. Remove the upper bolt and nut.
3. Remove the lower mounting nut and washers.
4. Pivot the top of the shock absorber from the frame bracket and pull the bottom off the strut shaft.
5. Slide the upper shock absorber eye into the frame bracket and install the bolt, lockwasher and nut.
6. Install the rubber grommets on the lower shock eye and place the shock over the strut shaft. Install the washers and nut.

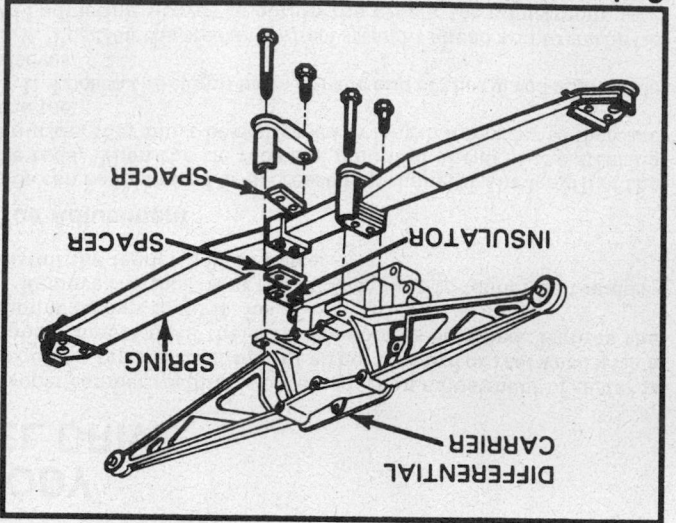

Spring attachment at cover beam

SPACER
SPACER
INSULATOR
SPRING
DIFFERENTIAL CARRIER

SPINDLE ASSEMBLY

Removal and Installation

1. Raise and safely support the vehicle. Remove the rear wheel assembly.
2. Disconnect the spring from the knuckle. Remove the cotterpin, spindle nut and washer.
3. Remove the trunnion straps at the spindle yoke. Push out on the knuckle and separate the axle shaft from the spindle.

Control arms

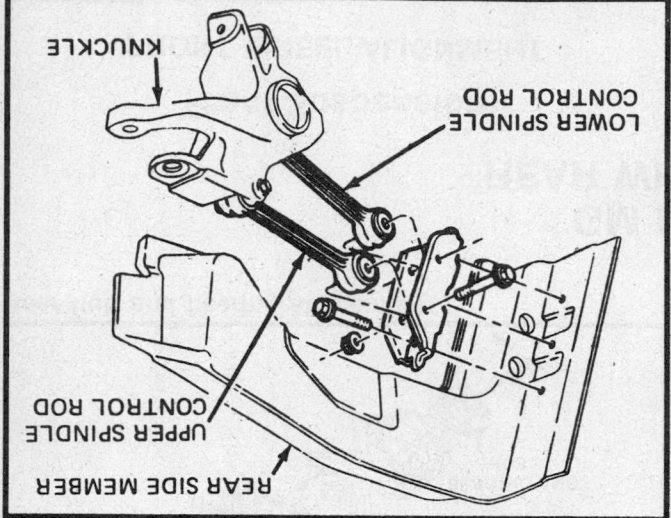

KNUCKLE
LOWER SPINDLE CONTROL ROD
UPPER SPINDLE CONTROL ROD
REAR SIDE MEMBER

5. To install, reverse the removal procedures.

CONTROL ARM

Removal and Installation

1. Raise and safely support the vehicle.
2. Disconnect the spring at the knuckle.
3. Remove the control arm nut and bolt at the knuckle.
4. Remove control arm nut and bolt at the body bracket. Remove the control arm.
5. To install, reverse the removal procedures.

SPRING

Removal and Installation

1. Raise and safely support the vehicle.
2. Remove both wheel assemblies.
3. Remove the spring-to-knuckle cotter pins, retaining nuts, rubber bushings and the link bolt.
4. Remove the spring retaining bolts, spacers and insulators. Remove the spring from the carrier beam.
5. To install, reverse the removal procedures.

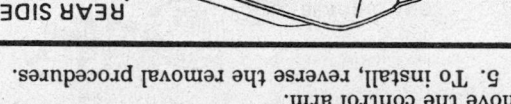

Corvette rear suspension

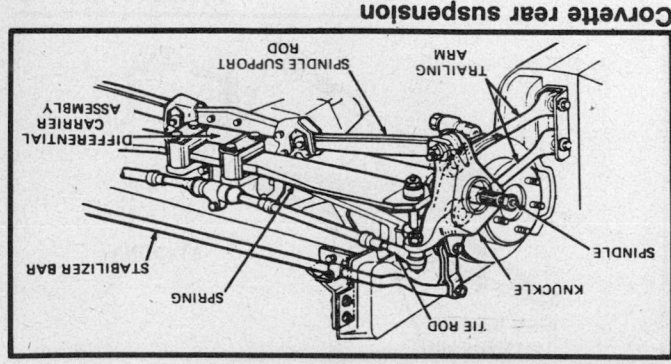

DIFFERENTIAL CARRIER ASSEMBLY
SPINDLE SUPPORT ROD
TRAILING ARM
STABILIZER BAR
SPRING
KNUCKLE
SPINDLE
TIE ROD

Front Suspension

FRONT WHEEL ALIGNMENT

Adjustment

CASTER AND CAMBER

Caster and camber can be adjusted by moving the position of the upper strut mount assembly. Moving the strut mount forward/rearward adjusts the caster while moving the strut mount inward and outward, adjusts the camber.

The position of the strut mount can be changed after loosening the retaining nuts. The weight of the vehicle will normally cause the strut assembly to move to the full inboard position. Install tool J-29724 or equivalent, between the strut mount and a fender bolt and tighten the tool's turnbuckle until the proper camber reading is obtained. If an adjustment of caster is required, tap the strut mount either forward or rearward with a rubber mallet until the caster reading is obtained. Tighten the mount screws to 20 ft. lbs. Remove the tool from the strut mount-to-fender bolt and re-install the fender bolt in place.

Toe Adjustment

Toe can be increased or decreased by changing the length of the tie rods. When the tie rods are mounted ahead of the steering knuckle, they must be decreased in length ion order to increase the toe.

1. Loosen the clamp bolts at each end of the tie rod adjustable sleeves.
2. Position the steering wheel straight ahead and turn the tie rod adjusting sleeves to obtain the proper toe adjustment.
3. After the proper toe adjustment is obtained, check to en-

GM F-BODY
REAR WHEEL DRIVE

KNUCKLE ASSEMBLY

Removal and Installation

1. Raise and safely support the vehicle. Remove the wheel assembly.
2. Remove the caliper. Remove the rotor.
3. Disconnect tie rod end from the knuckle. Disconnect transverse spring from the knuckle.
4. Remove the spindle from the hub and bearing assembly.
5. To install, reverse the removal procedures. It may be necessary to remove the parking brake plate prior to installation. Check and adjust the alignment as necessary.

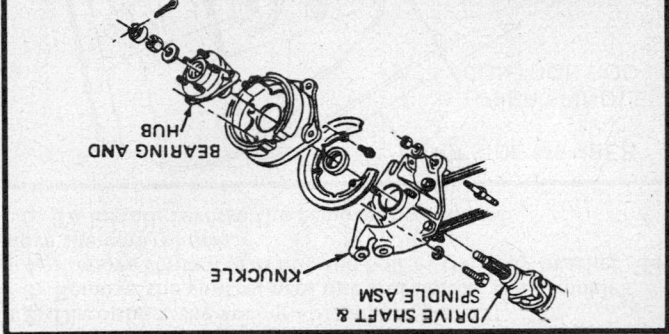

Rear hub and bearing attachment

BEARING AND HUB — KNUCKLE — DRIVE SHAFT & SPINDLE ASM

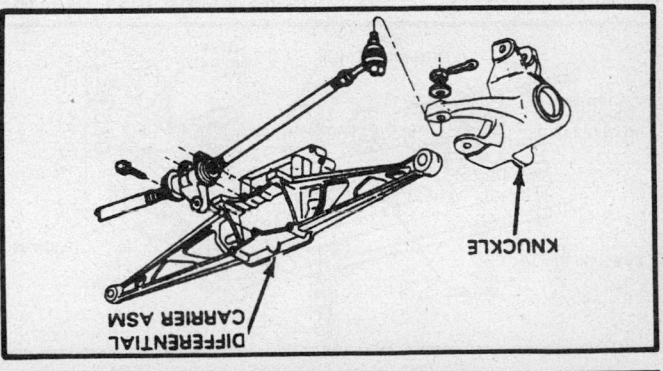

Tie rod assembly

KNUCKLE — DIFFERENTIAL CARRIER ASM

4. Disconnect stabilizer bar from the knuckle. Disconnect parking brake cable from the backing plate.
5. Disconnect shock absorber from the knuckle. Disconnect spindle support rod from the knuckle.
6. Disconnect upper and lower control arms from the knuckle. Lower the knuckle assembly and slide spindle out from the hub and bearing.
7. Using tool J-34161 or equivalent, remove the hub and bearing bolts. Remove hub and bearing with parking brake backing plate from the knuckle.
8. Remove the splash shield from the knuckle.
9. To install, reverse the removal procedures.

STABILIZER BAR

Removal and Installation

1. Raise and safely support the vehicle. Remove the spare tire and the tire carrier.
2. Disconnect the stabilizer bar from the knuckles.
3. Remove the stabilizer bar bushing retainers, bushings and stabilizer bar from the vehicle.
4. To install, reverse the removal procedures.

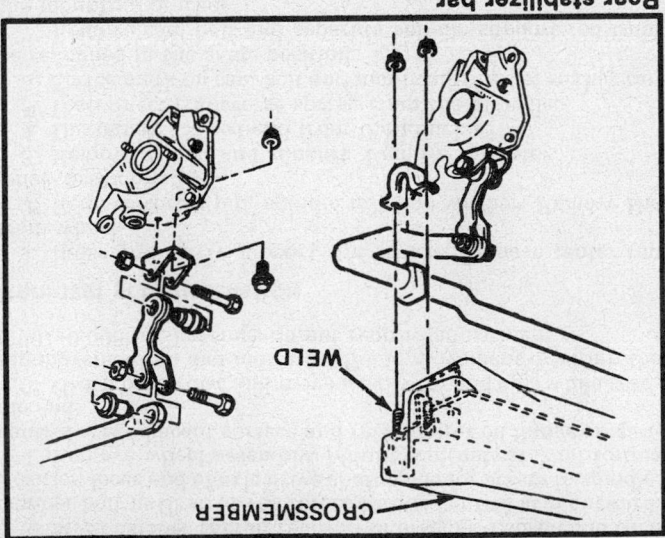

Rear stabilizer bar

WELD — CROSSMEMBER

Front end alignment procedure

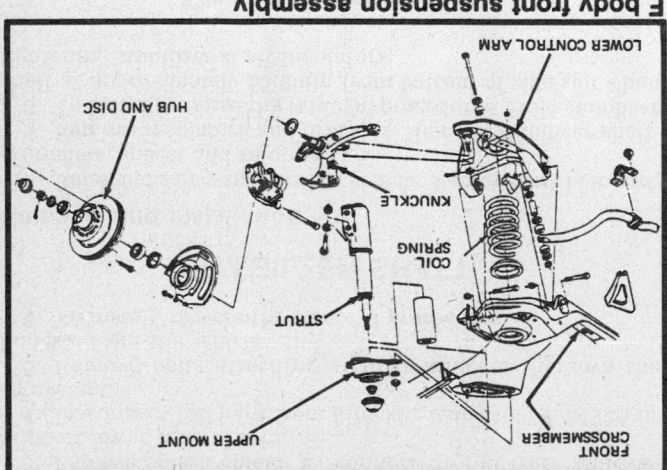

① REMOVE DUST CAP. USE ORIGINAL FENDER BOLT TO ATTACH TOOL. UPPER MOUNT ASSEMBLY. LOOSEN THESE THREE NUTS.

② MOVE INBOARD TO DECREASE CAMBER. MOVE OUTBOARD TO INCREASE CAMBER.

③ MOVE FORWARD TO DECREASE CASTER. MOVE REARWARD TO INCREASE CASTER.

WHEEL BEARINGS

Adjustment

1. Raise and safely support the vehicle. Remove dust cap from hub.
2. Remove cotter pin from spindle and spindle nut.
3. Tighten the spindle nut to 12 ft. lbs. while turning the wheel assembly forward by hand to fully seat the bearings. This will remove any grease or burrs which could cause excessive wheel bearing play later.
4. Back off the nut to the just loose position.
5. Hand tighten the spindle nut. Loosen spindle nut until either hole in the spindle aligns with a slot in the nut. Not more than ½ flat.
6. Install new cotter pin. Bend the ends of the cotter pin against nut, cut off extra length to ensure ends will not interfere with the dust cap.
7. Measure the looseness in the hub assembly. There will be from 0.001–0.005 in. endplay when properly adjusted.
8. Install dust cap on hub.

STRUT ASSEMBLY

Removal and Installation

1. Raise and safely support the vehicle. Remove wheel assembly.
2. Support lower control arm with jackstand. Remove brake hose bracket.
3. Remove strut-to-knuckle bolts. Remove cover from upper mount assembly.
4. Remove nut from upper end of strut. Remove strut and shield.
5. To install, reverse the removal procedures.

LOWER BALL JOINT

Removal and Installation

1. Raise and safely support the vehicle.
2. Remove the wheel assembly. A floor jack must remain under control arm spring during removal and installation to retain spring and control arm in position.
3. Remove cotter pin and loosen castellated nut. Use tool J-24292A or equivalent, to break ball joint loose from knuckle. Remove tool and separate joint from knuckle.
4. Guide lower control arm from opening in splash shield. Remove grease fittings. Press ball joint from lower control arm.
5. To install, reverse the removal procedures.

KNUCKLE ASSEMBLY

Removal and Installation

1. Siphon master cylinder to avoid leakage. Raise and safely support the vehicle.
2. Remove wheel assembly and the brake from the strut. Remove caliper support, the hub and disc.

sure the number of threads showing on each end of the sleeve are equal. Also, check to ensure the tie rod end housings are at right angles to the steering arm.
4. Properly tighten the clamp bolts.

COIL SPRING/LOWER CONTROL ARM ASSEMBLY

F body front suspension assembly

UPPER MOUNT. FRONT CROSSMEMBER. STRUT. COIL SPRING. KNUCKLE. HUB AND DISC. LOWER CONTROL ARM.

Removal and Installation

1. Raise and safely support the vehicle. Remove the wheel assembly.
2. Remove stabilizer link and bushings at lower control arm.
3. Remove pivot bolt nuts. Do not remove pivot bolts at this time.
4. Install the adaptor tool J-23028 or equivalent, to jack and place into position with tool J-23028 or equivalent, supporting bushings.
5. Install jackstand under outside frame rail on opposite side of vehicle.
6. Raise tool J-23028 or equivalent, enough to remove both pivot bolts. Lower tool J-23028 or equivalent, carefully.
7. Remove the spring and insulator, tape insulator-to-spring.
8. Remove ball joint from knuckle using tool J-24924 or equivalent.
9. To install, reverse the removal procedures. After assembly, end of spring coil must cover all or part of one inspection drain hole. The other hole must be partly exposed or completely uncovered.

Front Suspension

WHEEL ALIGNMENT

Adjustment

CAMBER

Camber angle can be increased approximately 1 degree. Remove the upper ball joint, rotate it ¾ turn and reinstall it with the flat of the upper flange on the inboard side of the control arm.

CASTER

Shims placed between the upper control arm and legs control caster. Always use 2 washers totalling 12mm thickness, placing a washer at each end of the locating tube.

TOE

Adjust by changing tie rod position Loosen the nuts at the steering knuckle end of the tie rod and the rubber cover at the lower end. Rotate tie rod to to change adjustment.

WHEEL BEARINGS

Adjustment

1. Raise and safely support the vehicle. Remove the dust cap from hub. Remove cotter pin from spindle and spindle nut.
2. Tighten the spindle nut to 12 ft. lbs. while turning the wheel assembly forward by hand to fully seat the bearings. This will remove any grease or burrs which could cause excessive wheel bearing play later.
3. Back off the nut to the just loose position.
4. Hand tighten the spindle nut. Loosen spindle nut until either hole in the spindle aligns with a slot in the nut, not more than ½ flat.
5. Install new cotter pin. Bend the ends of the cotter pin

GM T-BODY
REAR WHEEL DRIVE

3. Remove splash shield. Disconnect tie rod from knuckle. Support lower control arm.
4. Disconnect ball joint from knuckle, using tool J-2492A or equivalent.
5. Remove bolts attaching strut-to-knuckle. Remove the knuckle from the vehicle.
6. To install, reverse the removal procedures.

STABILIZER SHAFT

Removal and Installation

1. Raise and safely support the vehicle. Remove link bolt, nut, grommets, spacer and retainers.
2. Remove insulators and brackets. Remove stabilizer shaft.
3. To install, reverse the removal procedures. Hold stabilizer shaft at approximately 55.0mm from bottom of side rail when tightening stabilizer shaft insulators.

Rear Suspension

SHOCK ABSORBERS

Removal and Installation

1. Pull back all necessary carpeting and remove shock absorber upper mounting nut.
2. Raise and safely support the rear axle.
3. Loosen and remove shock absorber lower mounting nut from shock absorber and remove shock.
4. To install, reverse the removal procedures.

COIL SPRING

Removal and Installation

1. Raise and safely support the vehicle and the rear axle assembly.
2. Remove track bar mounting bolt at axle assembly and loosen track bar bolt at body brace.
3. Disconnect rear brake hose clip at underbody to allow additional axle drop.
4. Remove right and left shock absorber lower attaching nuts.
5. Remove the driveshaft, if equipped with a 4 cylinder engine.
6. Carefully lower rear axle and remove the springs. Do not suspend rear axle by brake hose. Damage to hose could result.
7. To install, reverse the removal procedures.

TRACK BAR

Removal and Installation

1. Raise and safely support the vehicle and the rear axle, at curb height position.
2. Remove track bar mounting bolt and nut at rear axle and at body bracket.
3. Remove the track bar from the vehicle.
4. To install, reverse the removal procedures.

LOWER CONTROL ARM

NOTE: If both control arms are being replaced, remove and replace 1 control arm at a time to prevent the axle from rolling or slipping sideways making replacement difficult.

Removal and Installation

1. Raise and safely support the vehicle and the rear axle at curb height position.
2. Remove lower control arm-to-axle housing bolt and control arm-to-underbody bolt.
3. Remove the control arm from the vehicle.
4. To install, reverse the removal procedures.

TORQUE ARM

Removal and Installation

1. Raise and safely support the vehicle and the rear axle assembly. Remove the springs.
2. Remove track bar mounting bolt at axle assembly and loosen track bar bolt at body brace.
3. Remove torque arm rear attaching bolts. Remove front torque arm outer bracket. Remove the torque arm from the vehicle.
4. To install, reverse the removal procedures.

against nut, cut off extra length to ensure ends will not interfere with the dust cap.

6. Measure the looseness in the hub assembly. There will be from 0.001-0.005 in. endplay when properly adjusted. Install dust cap on hub.

SHOCK ABSORBER

Removal and Installation

1. Hold the shock absorber upper stem and remove the nut, upper retainer and rubber grommet.
2. Raise and safely support the vehicle.
3. Remove the bolts from the lower end of the shock absorber.
4. Remove the shock absorber from the vehicle.
5. To install, reverse the removal procedures.

UPPER BALL JOINT

Inspection

1. Raise the vehicle and position jackstands under the left and right lower control arm as near as possible to each lower ball joint. The vehicle must be stable and should not rock on the jackstands. Upper control arm bumper must not contact frame.
2. Position dial indicator against the wheel rim.
3. Grasp front wheel and push in on bottom of tire while pull-ing out at the top. Read gauge, then reverse the push-pull procedure. Horizontal deflection on dial indicator should not exceed 0.125 in.
4. If dial indicator reading exceeds 0.125 in., or if ball stud has been disconnected from knuckle assembly and any looseness is detected, or the stud can be twisted in its socket with fingers, replace ball joint.

Removal and Installation

1. Raise and safely support the vehicle. Remove the wheel assembly. Properly support the lower control arm.
2. Remove the upper ball stud nut. Reinstall the nut finger tight.
3. Install the spreader tool and push stud loose from the knuckle. Remove tool and remove nut from ball stud.
4. Remove nuts and bolts attaching ball joint-to-upper control arm, then remove the ball joint.
5. To install, reverse the removal procedures.

LOWER BALL JOINT

Inspection

The vehicle must be supported by the wheel so the weight of vehicle will properly load the ball joints.

The lower ball joint is inspected for wear by visual observation alone. Wear is indicated by protrusion of the 1/2 in. diameter nipple into which the grease fitting is threaded. This round nipple projects 0.050 in. beyond the surface of the ball joint cover on a new, unworn joint. Normal wear will result in the surface of this nipple retracting slowly inward.

Removal and Installation

1. Raise and safely support the vehicle. Remove the wheel assembly. Properly support the lower control arm.
2. Remove lower ball stud nut, then reinstall nut finger tight.
3. Install spreader tool and push the ball joint stud until it is free of the steering knuckle. Remove tool and remove nut from ball stud.
4. Remove ball joint from lower control arm.
5. To install, reverse the removal procedures.

COIL SPRING

Removal and Installation

1. Raise and safely support the vehicle and the lower control arm.
2. Disconnect stabilizer from lower control arm. Disconnect tie rod from steering knuckle.
3. Remove the nut from the lower ball joint. Install spreader tool and push the ball joint stud loose in the steering knuckle. Position the knuckle and hub assembly aside.
4. Loosen lower control arm pivot bolts. Install chain through coil spring as a safety precaution. The coil spring is under load.
5. Slowly lower the jack. When the spring is extended as far as possible, use a prybar to carefully lift the spring over the lower control arm seat.
6. Remove the spring from the vehicle.
7. To install, reverse the removal procedures.

LOWER CONTROL ARM

Removal and Installation

1. Raise and safely support the vehicle and the lower control arm.
2. Disconnect stabilizer from lower control arm. Disconnect tie rod from steering knuckle.

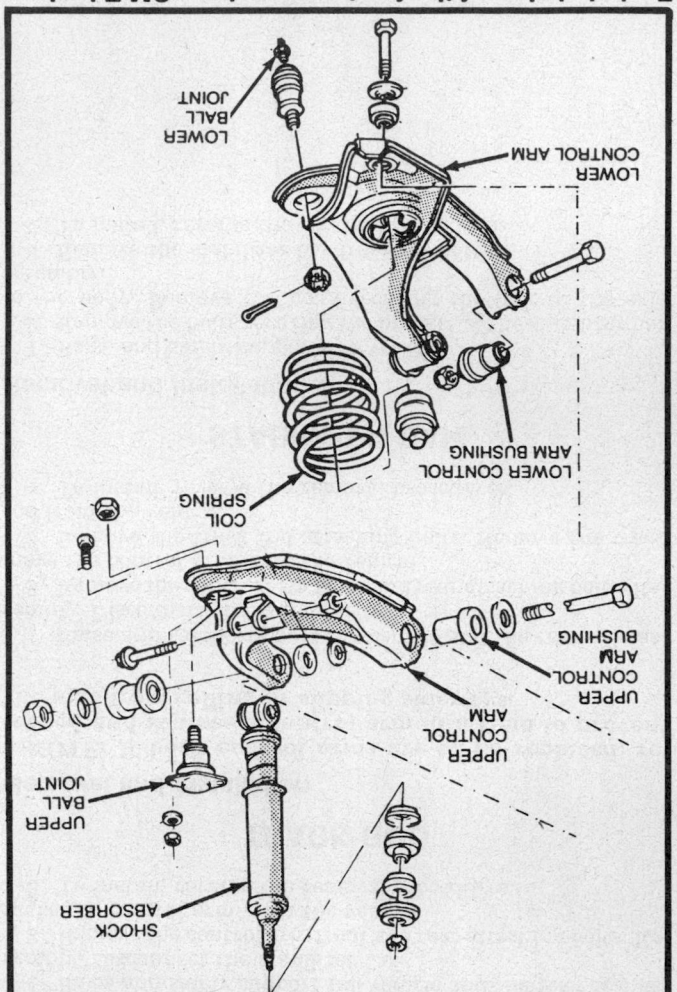

Exploded view of the front suspension—GM T-body

3. Remove the nut from the lower ball joint. Install spreader tool and push the ball joint stud loose in the steering knuckle. Position the knuckle and hub assembly aside.

4. Loosen lower control arm pivot bolts. Install chain through coil spring as a safety precaution. The coil spring is under load.

5. Slowly lower the jack. When the spring is extended as far as possible, use a prybar to carefully lift the spring over the lower control arm seat.

6. Remove the spring from the vehicle.

7. Remove the control arm pivot bolts. Remove the lower control arm from the vehicle.

8. To install, reverse the removal procedures.

UPPER CONTROL ARM

Removal and Installation

1. Raise and safely support the vehicle. Remove the wheel assembly and support the lower control arm.

2. Remove the upper ball joint from the steering knuckle.

3. Remove control arm pivot bolts. Remove the control arm from the vehicle.

4. To install, reverse the removal procedures. Be sure to use new ball joint retaining nuts.

STEERING KNUCKLE

Removal and Installation

1. Raise and safely support the vehicle and the lower control arm; this will keep the coil spring compressed.

2. Remove the wheel assembly. Remove the caliper and position it aside.

3. Remove the hub and rotor. Remove the splash shield. Remove the tie rod end from the steering knuckle.

4. Loosen both ball stud nuts. Using a spreader tool, push both the upper and lower ball studs from the steering knuckle.

5. Remove ball stud nuts and remove the steering knuckle from the vehicle.

6. To install, reverse the removal procedures.

STABILIZER BAR

Removal and Installation

1. Raise and safely support the vehicle.

2. Remove the stabilizer bar nut and bolt from lower control arm.

3. Remove stabilizer bar bracket. Remove the stabilizer bar from the vehicle.

4. To install, reverse the removal procedures.

Rear Suspension

SHOCK ABSORBER

Removal and Installation

1. Raise and safely support the vehicle and the rear axle assembly.

2. Remove upper attaching bolts, remove the lower attaching bolt and nut.

3. Remove shock absorber from the vehicle.

4. To install, reverse the removal procedures.

COIL SPRING

Removal and Installation

1. Raise and safely support the vehicle and the rear axle assembly.

2. Disconnect both shock absorbers from lower brackets. As required, disconnect the rear brake line from its mounting.

3. Disconnect the rear axle extension bracket. Be sure to safely support the assembly.

4. Lower the axle and remove springs and spring insulators. Do not leave the axle in the lowered position once the springs are removed.

5. To install, reverse the removal procedures.

LOWER CONTROL ARM

Removal and Installation

NOTE: If both control arms are to be replaced, removed and replace 1 control arm at a time to prevent the axle from rolling or slipping sideways.

1. Raise and safely support the vehicle and the rear axle assembly. Disconnect the stabilizer bar.

2. Remove the control arm front and rear attaching bolts. Remove the control arm from the vehicle.

3. To install, reverse the removal procedures.

TRACK ROD

Removal and Installation

NOTE: If both control arms are to be replaced, removed and replace 1 control arm at a time to prevent the axle from rolling or slipping sideways.

1. Raise and safely support the vehicle and the rear axle assembly. Disconnect the stabilizer bar.

2. Remove the control arm front and rear attaching bolts. Remove the control arm from the vehicle.

3. Remove the track rod attaching bolts. Remove the track rod from the vehicle.

4. To install, reverse the removal procedures.

STABILIZER BAR

Removal and Installation

1. Raise and safely support the vehicle.

2. Remove the bolts securing the bracket of the stabilizer bar to the body. Remove the bolts securing the link to the axle assembly.

3. Remove the stabilizer bar from the vehicle.

4. To install, reverse the removal procedures.

33 Steering 33

STEERING MANUAL STEERING ASSEMBLIES
33 SECTION

CHRYSLER MANUAL STEERING RACK AND PINION ASSEMBLY

Front Wheel Drive Vehicles

The manual steering rack and pinion gear cannot be adjusted or serviced. Should a malfunction occur, the complete rack and pinion assembly must be replaced.

FORD MANUAL STEERING RACK AND PINION ASSEMBLY

TIE ROD ENDS, BELLOWS AND TIE ROD BALL JOINT SOCKETS

Disassembly

1. Remove the steering gear from the vehicle. Position the steering assembly in a suitable holding fixture.
2. Loosen the jam nuts on the outer ends of the tie rods. Remove the tie rod ends and the jam nuts.
3. Remove the wires that retain the bellows to the gear housing. Drain the lubricant and remove the bellows.
4. Remove the set screw from the ball housing. Install ball housing torque adapter tool T78P-3504-AA or equivalent on the ball housing.
5. Locate the point of the locking screw in the large hole midway along the length of the housing. Tighten firmly. Use care not to place the point of the locking screw into the tapped set screw hole.
6. Attach a drive ratchet handle to the tool. Expose enough rack teeth to install an adjustable wrench over the flat formed by the tops of the rack teeth.
7. Loosen the ball housing tie rod assembly by holding the adjustable wrench and turning the ball housing tool.

NOTE: If the rack is not restrained by the adjustable wrench, damage to the pinion will occur.

8. Clean and inspect the condition of the threads on the rack and in the ball housing socket. Lubricate the inner seat with multi-purpose lubricant.

Assembly

1. Be sure that the ball housing is seated firmly into ball housing socket and on the tie rod ball. It is important that the back of the rack and the face of the rack are wiped clean of grease to avoid a hydraulic lock and improper assembly.
2. Thread the tie rod assembly onto the end of the rack assembly.
3. Install the ball housing torque adapter tool on the ball housing. Locate the point of the locking screw in the large hole midway along the length of the housing, and tighten it firmly. Use care not to place the point of the locking screw into the tapped set screw hole.
4. Hold the rack with an adjustable wrench on the flat of the rack, as near to the end of the rack as possible.
5. If the pinion has not been removed, use care not to load the pinion during tightening.
6. Hold the rack using an adjustable wrench and tighten the ball housing to 40–51 ft. lbs. by turning the ball housing torque adapter tool with a torque wrench.
7. Rotate the tie rod at least 10 times, do not force the tie rod against the limits of articulation travel, before measuring articulation effort.
8. To measure articulation effort, loop a piece of wire through the hole in the rod end stud. Insert the hook of a pull scale, through the wire loop. Effort to move the tie rod should be 1–5 lbs.
9. If articulation effort is not within specification, replace the tie rod assembly.
10. Install the set screw in the ball housing. Tighten the screw to 20–40 inch lbs.
11. Install the large bellows and new clamp on the right side only (opposite end from pinion). Use service, screw type clamps. Do not reuse original production wire retainers. Install small clamps to used bellows to retain bellows to tie rod.
12. Place gear in a vertical position with pinion end of gear up. Fill housing with 3.2 ounces of D8AZ-19578-A fluid grease or equivalent lubricant. Install left large bellows and new clamp, fastening bellows in the gear housing. Do not reuse original production wire retainers.
13. Install jam nuts and tie rod ends on tie rods.

INPUT SHAFT SEAL

Disassembly and Assembly

1. Remove the steering gear from the vehicle. Position the assembly in a suitable holding fixture.
2. Clean the input shaft and the input seal area. Do not scratch or damage the pinion shaft. Pry the pinion seal from its bore.
3. Check to be sure that the pinion cover is centered using tool T81P-3504-Y or an equivalent centering tool.
4. If the pinion cover is not centered, loosen the bolts, center the cover and tighten the bolts.
5. Lubricate the new pinion seal with lubricant and install the seal over the shaft.
6. Use a piece of tubing to engage the outer flange of the seal. Press the seal into its bore until the flange is flush with the shoulder of the bore. If the outer edge of the seal is not engaged when assembling, the seal will be damaged.

RACK SUPPORT YOKE, SPRING, GASKET, SHIMS AND COVER

Disassembly

1. Remove the steering gear from the vehicle. Position the rack and pinion assembly in a suitable holding fixture.
2. Remove the yoke cover. Remove the shims, gasket and yoke spring.

Assembly

1. Clean the cover and the flange areas. Assemble the yoke and the yoke spring.
2. Position a new gasket next to the housing flange. If new shims are used, adjust the support yoke to rack.
3. To adjust the support yoke to rack, install the yoke and the cover, omitting the gasket, shims and spring.

4. Tighten the bolts lightly until the cover just touches the yoke.

5. Measure the gap between the cover and the housing flange. With the gasket add selected shims to give a combined pack thickness of 0.005-0.006 in. greater than the measured gap.

6. Assemble the shim pack and the cover. Add sealant to the cover bolt threads.

PINION COVER, GASKET, PINION SHAFT, SPACER, SHIMS, UPPER BEARING, RACK, LOWER BEARING AND HOUSING

Disassembly

1. Remove the steering gear from the vehicle. Position the assembly in a suitable holding fixture. Clean the exterior of the gear.

2. Remove the bolts, yoke cover, gasket, shims, spring and yoke from the gear housing.

3. Remove the right ball housing and the tie rod assembly from the rack.

NOTE: Be sure that the rack is restrained with an adjustable wrench during removal or damage to the pinion will occur.

4. Move the rack to the right turn stop. The flat on the input shaft should be facing straight up.

NOTE: It is important that the flat be in the same position when assembling the gear. If not the steering gear will not be centered.

5. Remove the pinion cover bolts, pinion cover, gasket, pinion shaft, spacer, shims and upper bearing from the gear assembly.

6. Remove the pinion shaft from the cover. Discard the seal. Remove the rack from the housing.

7. Remove the lower bearing through the pinion shaft bore. Access to the pinion shaft lower bearing is easiest through the support yoke bore.

Assembly

1. Assembly of the rack and pinion steering gear is the reverse of the disassembly procedure.

2. Be sure to coat the entire length of the rack with the proper grade and type lubricant on assembly.

3. When installing the upper bearing, turn the pinion from lock to lock counting the number of turns. Turn the pinion back from 1 of the locks exactly 1/2 the total number of turns, with the steering gear on center.

4. The flat must be in the 3 o'clock position, as viewed from the drivers position. If not, repeat and recheck.

AMC MANUAL STEERING ASSEMBLY

WORM BEARING PRELOAD

NOTE: Do not turn steering wheel hard against stops as damage to ball nut assembly may result.

Adjustment

1. Disconnect the ball stud from the pitman arm, and retighten the pitman arm nut.

2. Loosen the pitman shaft adjusting screw locknut and back off adjusting screw a few turns.

3. Attach spring scale to the steering wheel and measure the pull needed to move the steering wheel when off the high point. The pull should be between 1/8-3/8 lbs.

4. To adjust the worm bearing, loosen the worm bearing adjuster locknut with a brass drift and turn the adjuster screw until the proper pull is obtained. When adjustment is correct, tighten the adjuster locknut, and recheck with the spring scale again.

SECTOR AND BALL NUT BACKLASH

Adjustment

1. After the worm bearing preload has been adjusted correctly, loosen the pitman shaft adjusting screw locknut and turn the pitman shaft adjusting screw clockwise until a pull of 3/4 to 1 1/8 lbs. is shown on the spring scale. When the adjustment is correct, tighten the pitman shaft adjusting screw locknut and recheck the adjustment.

NOTE: A torque wrench calibrated in inch lbs. may be substituted for the spring scale in adjusting steering gear.

2. Turn the steering wheel to the center of its turning limits (pitman arm disconnected). If the steering wheel is removed, the mark on the steering shaft should be at top center.

3. Connect the ball stud to the pitman arm, tightening the attaching nut to 115 ft. lbs.

STEERING GEAR

Disassembly and Assembly

1. After removing the steering gear from the vehicle, place the steering gear assembly in a bench vise.

NOTE: Worm seal may be replaced without disassembling gear. Be careful not to damage shaft or housing when removing seal.

2. Rotate the worm shaft until it is centered with the mark facing upward. Remove the cover attaching screws and the adjusting screw locknut. Remove the cover and gasket by turning adjusting screw clockwise through the cover.

3. Remove the adjusting screw with its shim from the slot in the end of the pitman shaft. Remove the pitman shaft from the housing being careful not to damage the seal in the housing.

4. Loosen the worm bearing adjuster locknut with a brass drift and remove the adjuster and bearing. Remove the bearing retainer.

5. Remove the worm and shaft assembly with the ball nut assembly and bearing. Remove the ball nut return guide clamp by removing screws. Remove the guides, turn ball nut over, and remove the steel balls by rotating the shaft from side to side. After all steel balls have been removed, take the ball nut off the worm shaft.

6. Clean all parts in solvent. Inspect all bearings, bearing cups, bushings, seals, worm groove, and gear teeth for signs of wear, scoring, pitting, etc.

7. Remove the pitman shaft seal. If there is leakage around the threads of the bearing adjuster, apply a non-hardening sealer.

8. Remove faulty bushings from the pitman shaft with puller and slide hammer. Install new bushings, seating the inner end of the bushing flush with the inside surface of the housing.

9. Remove the steering shaft seal. Tap new seal in place, using a section of tubing to seat the seal.

10. Remove the upper or lower bearing cup from the worm bearing adjuster or steering gear housing using puller and slide hammer. Install the new bearing cups.

11. Lubricate all seals, bushings, and bearings before installing into the steering gear assembly.

12. Position the ball nut on the worm shaft. Install the steel balls in the return guides and the ball nut, placing an equal number in each circuit of the ball nut. Install the return guide clamp and screws.

NOTE: Do not rotate the worm shaft while installing the steel balls since the balls may enter the crossover passage between the circuits, causing incorrect operation of the ball nut.

13. Place bearing on shaft above the worm gear, center ball nut on worm gear; then, slide the steering shaft, bearing, and ball nut into the housing. Do not damage the steering shaft seal in the housing.

14. Place the bearing in the worm adjuster, install the bearing retainer, and install the adjuster and locknut on the housing, tightening it just enough to hold the bearing in place.

15. Install the pitman shaft adjusting screw and selective shim in the pitman shaft. Be sure there is no more than 0.002 in. of endplay of the screw in the slot. If the end-play is more than 0.002 in., install a new selective shim to get the proper clearance. Shims are available in 4 thickness: 0.063 in., 0.065 in., 0.067 in. and 0.069 in.

16. Install the pitman shaft and adjusting screw with the sector and ball nut positioned as shown.

17. Install the cover and gasket on the adjusting screw, turning screw counterclockwise until it extends through the cover from 5/8-3/4 in. Install the cover attaching screws and torque to 35 ft. lbs.

18. Tighten the pitman shaft adjusting screw so that the teeth on the shaft and the ball nut engage but do not bind. Final adjustment must be made later.

19. Wrap the pitman shaft splines with tape to protect the seal and install the seal.

20. Fill steering gear with a good quality steering gear lubricant. Turn the steering gear from 1 extreme to the other to make sure it does not bind. Do not allow the ball nut to strike the ends of the ball races on the worm gear to avoid damaging the ball return guides.

21. Install the steering gear. Perform the final adjustments on the worm bearing preload and the sector and ball nut backlash adjustments.

GENERAL MOTORS MANUAL STEERING RACK AND PINION ASSEMBLY

Spectrum

Disassembly

1. Place the steering unit in a soft jawed vise.
2. Remove the tie rod end.
3. Remove the boot.
4. Using a chisel, bend back (straighten) the bent (staked) part of the locking washer between the inner tie rod and the rack. A new washer should be used when reassembled.
5. Remove the tie rod from the rack.
6. Loosen the adjusting plug nut and remove the spring and plunger.
7. Remove the pinion seal.
8. Remove the snapring.

NOTE: Rotate the pinion gear shaft until the pinion flat is parallel or aligned with the rack. Then carefully measure dimension A. Record this measurement. This relationship must be used for reassembly.

9. Using a plastic hammer, gently tap and withdraw the pinion assembly.
10. Be careful not to damage the housing and pull the rack.

Assembly

Before reassembly, lubricate with lithium grease: The sliding part of the rack against the steering housing (all around the rack plunger, rack bushing and rack, steering pinion, grease seal lip, needle bearing, steering rack and pinion teeth, pinion bearing, inside the small opening of the boots and the inner tie rod ball sockets.

1. With the housing in a vise, install the rack into the steering housing.

NOTE: Carefully set the rack to dimension A noted during disassembly. Install the pinion, aligning the flat parallel as shown, ± 5 degrees from parallel is acceptable.

2. Install the pinion retaining snapring.
3. Lubricate well with grease, and install the plunger, spring, adjusting plug and locknut. Tighten the adjusting plug to 4 ft. lbs.
4. With the adjusting plug torqued to 4 ft. lbs., back off the adjusting nut to 25 degrees.
5. Install the pinion shaft seal. Tighten the locknut snug.
6. Measure the pinion shaft preload (0.4-0.9 ft. lbs.). If preload is not within specifications, loosen the locknut and readjust the plug torque. When an acceptable preload is achieved, apply liquid thread lock to the locknut and torque the locknut to 49 ft. lbs.
7. Install the inner tie rod and new locking washer to the rack end. Torque to 65 ft. lbs. Protect the rack mounted in a vise. Stack the locking washer to the flat of the inner tie rod. Apply grease to the inner surface of the small opening in the boot.
8. Install the new boot over the inner tie rod.
9. Install the tie rod nut and attach the tie rod end.
10. Adjust the rod to length to 7.5 in. (L dimension)
11. Torque the tie rod locking nut to 40 ft. lbs.
12. Install the boot clamp and wire.

Sprint

STEERING RACK PLUNGER

Removal

1. Remove the rack damper screw cap.
2. Remove the damper screw.
3. Remove the rack plunger spring.
4. Remove the rack plunger.

Installation

1. Apply grease lightly to the sliding part of the plunger against the rack.
2. Install the parts in the reverse of removal.
3. After tightening the the rack damper screw to the tightest point, turn it back 0-90 degrees and check for rotation torque of the pinion. Also check if the rack as a hole moves smoothly. Pinion torque is 0.58-0.94 ft. lbs.
4. After adjustment, put the rack damper screw cap as deeply as possible.

STEERING PINION

Removal

1. Remove the rack plunger.
2. Remove the gear case packing.

3. Using a 43mm socket, remove the bearing plug.
4. Tap gently with a plastic hammer and separate the pinion assembly from the housing.

Installation

1. Apply grease to all around the pinion teeth, pinion needle bearing and gear case oil seal lip.
2. Install the pinion assembly.
3. Tighten the pinion bearing plug to 58-79.5 ft. lbs.
4. Install the gear case packing.
5. Install the rack plunger.

PINION BEARING

Removal

With the steering rack removed from the case, pull out the pinion bearing from the gear case with special tools J-34839 bearing remover and J-6125-1B sliding shaft.

Installation

1. Apply grease to the rollers of the pinion bearing.
2. Press-fit the pinion bearing into the gear case with special tool J-34840 Bearing Installer.
3. After press-fitting, make sure that the bearing rollers are installed properly.
4. Install the steering rack assembly.

RACK BUSHING

Removal

1. With the steering rack removed from the case.
2. Remove the snapring.
3. Pull out the bushing using special tool J-34869 bushing remover.

NOTE: Be careful not to pull out the bushing by holding the gear case in a vise or the housing (pipe) may come off the gear case. Use the special tool.

Installation

1. Apply grease lightly to the entire inner surface of the bushing.
2. Press-fit the bushing as far into the rack housing using special tool J-34868 bushing installer.
3. Install the snapring.
4. Install the rack assembly

Chevette And T-1000

Disassembly

1. Position assembly in vise, clamping housing near center. Use soft jaws to prevent damage to housing.
2. Loosen jam nuts. Remove outer tie rod.

NOTE: Hold housing while loosening nuts so as not to damage internal gear components.

3. Remove inner boot clamp by cutting. Remove the outer clamp by relieving tension in clamp. Remove boot by pulling. Repeat procedure for other end.
4. Position rack in soft jaw vise, and remove inner tie rod assemblies (both ends).

NOTE: To prevent internal gear damage when removing housing, turn housing counterclockwise until assembly separates from rack.

5. Remove adjuster plug locknut, adjuster plug, and spring.
6. Remove rack bearing from housing.

7. Clean surface at seal. Pierce seal at 1 of the 2 round spots on surface. Pry out seal.
8. Using snapring pliers, remove retaining ring from bore.
9. Position end of shaft in soft jaw vise. Tap housing to separate pinion assembly from housing.
10. With pinion separated, rack may slide from housing and be damaged. Remove rack from housing.
11. The rack and pinion assembly is now disassembled. Clean all components, except inner tie rod assemblies, with an approved solvent. Air dry and inspect. Replace any seals which are cut or badly worn. If the pinion seal is removed, it must be replaced.

NOTE: Check major wear areas for cracking, chipping, etc. Replace as required.

MOUNTING GROMMETS

Do not remove grommets unless replacement is required. Replace both grommets if either requires replacement. Cut through grommet and remove. Lube inside of seals lightly with chassis lube. Start with left seal first and force it past the right side (smaller inside diameter) boss. Start right hand grommet and seat. Remove housing from vise and slide grommet to left hand mounting. Assemble grommet to housing.

GUIDE BUSHINGS

No attempt to replace the guide bushing should be made unless it is damaged or broken. If this occurs, replace the housing.

RACK BUSHING

The rack bushing should only be replaced if evidence of heavy wear is observed.

Remove retaining ring. Using a suitable size socket and extension, drive the bushing out of the housing. If a puller is available, position fingers of puller behind bushing and remove bushing using slide hammer.

Using a suitable size socket, press new rack bushing into housing until it bottoms. Install retaining ring.

ROLLER BEARING ASSEMBLY

Check condition of pinion pilot. If scored or badly worn, replace pinion and roller bearing assembly.

Press or tap out bearing using drift and press or hammer. Using a suitable size socket, press or drive new bearing into housing until it bottoms.

BEARING AND PINION ASSEMBLY

Inspect roller bearing pilot, pinion teeth, and rotor bearing assembly. If pilot is scored, teeth are chipped, or is loose on pinion shaft, the bearing and pinion assembly should be replaced.

INNER TIE RODS

The inner tie rod assemblies cannot be serviced. If the pivot is loose, replace the tie rod assembly. If the joint rocking or turning torque exceeds 150 inch lbs. (17 Nm) replace the inner tie rod assembly.

Assembly

1. Install rack with teeth facing pinion into housing. The flat on the teeth should be parallel with pinion shaft. Measure and set 2.70 in. (68.5mm) from lip of housing to end of rack.

NOTE: Insert pinion with flat at 75° from vertical. Tap

on pinion shaft with soft hammer until pinion seats. Re-set 2.70 in. (68.5mm) dimension of rack position. Flat should now be vertical. If flat is at plus or minus 30° from vertical, restart procedure. The rack must be centered as described. If not, the steering wheel cannot travel fully, causing unequal turning radius.

2. Install retaining ring using tool J-4245 or equivalent. Beveled edge of retaining ring should be up.
3. Liberally coat top of pinion bearing with anhydrous calcium grease.
4. Install rack bearing. Coat bearing with lithium based grease, then seat pinion seal flush with housing. Seal can be seated by tapping on alternate sides with hammer.
5. Coat both ends of preload spring and threads of adjuster plug with lithium based grease.
6. Assemble adjuster plug and spring assembly into housing. Turn adjuster plug clockwise until it bottoms, then counterclockwise 45–60 degrees. Torque required to turn pinion should be between 8–10 inch lbs. (0.9–1.1 Nm). Turn plug in or out to adjust as required. Tighten locknut to 50 ft. lbs. (68 Nm).
7. Lube both ends of rack with lithium based grease. Fill rack teeth with lube. Move rack back and front several times by turning pinion shaft, adding grease to rack teeth each time.
8. Install inner tie rod assemblies to rack. Turn inner tie rod assemblies until they bottom out. Support rack in vise or with another wrench to avoid internal gear damage.
9. Use wood block or vise support and stake tie rod housing to rack flat. Stake both sides.
10. Position 1 of the large clamps on the housing. Place boot lip into position over undercut. Position clamp over boot at undercut and secure using side cutter type pliers or tool J-22610.
11. Slip end of boot into rod undercut. Do not assemble clamp over boot until toe adjustment is made. Straighten boots if twisted before assembling clamps.
12. Thread jam nuts (both sides) onto tie rods.
13. Thread on tie rod ends. Do not tighten jam nuts until toe adjustment is made. Then tighten to 50 ft. lbs. (67 Nm).
14. Slip on coupling assembly. Flat on inside diameter of coupling mates with flat on pinion shaft. Install pinch bolt, but do not tighten until vehicle installation, then tighten to 30 ft. lbs. (41 Nm).

Celebrity, 6000, Ciera And Century

OUTER TIE ROD

Removal
1. Loosen the jam nut and remove the tie rod from the steering knuckle. Count the number of turns needed to remove.
2. Remove the outer tie rod.

Installation
1. Install the outer tie rod by screwing it on the inner tie rod the same amount of turns as was needed to remove the outer tie rod.
2. Adjust the toe-in/out by turning the inner tie rod. Tighten the locknut to 50 ft. lbs.
3. Install the outer boot clamp and secure.

BOOT SEAL

Removal and Installation
To remove the boot seal from either side of the steering assembly, the outer tie rod must be removed. Remove the locknut and the boot clamps. Remove the boot by sliding it off the inner tie rod.

To install the boot, reverse the removal procedure. Secure the boot clamps.

INNER TIE ROD

Removal
1. The steering assembly must be out of the vehicle.
2. Position a wrench on the rack and hold it as the inner tie rod is unscrewed.

Installation
1. Screw the inner tie rod into the rack and with a wrench holding the rack to avoid teeth damage, tighten the inner tie rod to 70 ft. lbs.
2. Stake the housing on both sides.

NOTE: Be sure the tie rod rocks freely in the housing before staking.

3. When staking is completed, a 0.010 in. feeler gauge must not pass between the rack and the housing stakes. Check both sides.

RACK BEARING

Removal
Remove the adjuster plug locknut, the adjuster plug, spring and the rack bearing.

Installation
1. Lubricate the metal parts before installation, install then in the housing in the reverse order of their removal.
2. Turn the adjuster plug in until it bottoms and then back off approximately 40–60 degrees.
3. Check the torque on the pinion by turning it with a torque wrench. The correct pinion torque is 8–10 inch. lbs.
4. Tighten the locknut to 50 ft. lbs. while holding the adjuster plug.

PINION SEAL

Removal and Installation
Pierce the seal in 1 or 2 round spots and pry it from the housing. Lubricate the seal and seat the seal flush with the housing.

PINION SHAFT ASSEMBLY

Removal
1. Remove the seal and the retaining ring from the housing assembly.
2. Place the pinion shaft in a soft jawed vise and tap on the housing to separate the two.
3. With the pinion removed from the housing, the rack can slide from the housing and be damaged.

Installation
1. Lubricate and slide the rack into the housing.
2. Position the rack that 63.5mm protrudes from the pinion shaft end of the housing.
3. Position the pinion so that the center of the flat is facing the 4 o'clock position and install it into the housing.
4. When the pinion is seated properly, the center of the flat will be facing the 9 o'clock position.
5. Install the retainer ring and install the seal.

NOTE: The distance between the holes in the retaining ring should be 7.0mm apart.

RACK AND PINION BOOT, RACK GUIDE, BEARING GUIDE, MOUNTING GROMMET OR HOUSING END COVER

Removal

1. Separate right-hand mounting grommet and remove. Left-hand mounting grommet need not be removed unless replacement is required.
2. Cut both boot clamps and discard.
3. Using constant pressure, slide rack and pinion boot over boot retaining bushing and off housing.
4. The boot retaining bushing on housing tube end need not be removed unless damaged.
5. Remove housing end cover only if damaged.

Installation

1. Remove boot retaining bushing from pinion end of boot.
2. Slide new boot clamp on boot. Install bushing into boot.
3. Install new bearing guide on rack guide if necessary.
4. Install new boot retaining bushing on housing if necessary.
5. Install rack guide on rack.
6. Coat inner lip of boot retaining bushing lightly with grease for ease of assembly.
7. Install boot on housing.
8. Be sure center housing washers are in place on boot.
9. For ease of assembly, install inner tie rod bolts through cover washers and boot. Screw into rack lightly. This will keep rack, rack guide and boot in proper alignment.
10. Slide boot and boot retaining bushing until seated in bushing groove at pinion end of housing. Crimp new boot clamp.
11. Slide other end of boot onto boot retaining bushing in housing at tube end. Crimp new boot clamp.

FLANGE AND STEERING COUPLING ASSEMBLY

Removal

1. Loosen and remove the pinch bolt.
2. Remove the coupling.

NOTE: The dash seal can be removed or installed with the coupling off the steering assembly.

Installation

1. Install the flange and steering coupling assembly on the pinion shaft.
2. Install the pinch bolt and torque to 29 ft. lbs.

RACK BEARING

Removal

1. Remove the adjuster plug locknut.
2. Remove the adjuster plug, the spring, O-ring and rack bearing.

Installation

1. Install the parts in the reverse order of the removal procedure.
2. With the rack centered, tighten the adjuster plug to a torque of 6-11 ft. lbs. Back off adjuster plug to 50-70 degrees.
3. Assemble locknut and tighten while holding the adjuster plug stationary. Tighten to 50 ft. lbs.
4. Rotate the pinion with an inch pound torque wrench and socket. The turning torque should be 8-20 inch lbs. Adjust as required.

OUTER TIE ROD
Cavalier, 2000, Skyhawk And Firenza

Removal

With the steering assembly removed from the vehicle, loosen the outer rod pinch bolt and turn the tie rod from the adjuster stud, counting the number of turns until the tie rod separates from the adjuster stud.

Installation

1. Turn the tie rod onto the adjuster stud the same number of turns as was needed to remove.
2. Tighten the pinch bolt until the toe-out can be verified. Re-loosen and adjust as required.

INNER TIE ROD AND INNER PIVOT BUSHING

Removal

1. Bend back the lock plate tabs and loosen the inner tie rod bolt and remove.
2. Remove the inner tie rod by sliding it out between the bolt support plate and rack/pinion boot.

NOTE: If both inner tie rods are to be removed, re-install the inner tie rod bolt in the first tie rod retaining bolt hole to keep the rack and pinion boot and other parts aligned, while tie rods are out.

3. With the tie rod disconnected, the pivot bushings can be pressed out and new ones pressed in.

Installation

1. Be sure the center housing cover washers are fitted into the rack and pinion boot, before rod installation.
2. Remove the locating bolt from the rack and position 1 inner tie rod assembly in place over the rack. Place the bolt through the lock plate and install the bolt through the lock plate and the tie rod. Place the second inner tie rod in place and install the bolt through the lock plate and the tie rod.
3. Tighten the inner tie rod bolts to 65 ft. lbs. and bend the lock tabs against the flats of the inner tie rod bolts after torquing.

RACK BUSHING

Removal

1. Remove the pinion and rack assembly from the housing.
2. Remove the retaining ring from the housing and with a special long legged puller, remove the bushing from the housing.

Installation

1. Press a new bushing into the housing until it is firmly seated.
2. Install the retaining ring and complete the rack and pinion installation.

ROLLER BEARING

Removal and Installation

The pinion must be out of the housing. Drive the bearing from the housing and press the new bearing in place. Complete the pinion installation.

Fiero

Disassembly

1. Remove the steering gear from the vehicle. Position the assembly in a suitable holding fixture. Clean the exterior of the gear.
2. Loosen the jam nut. Remove the outer tie rods from the steering gear inner tie rods.
3. Remove the damper assembly retaining bolts and remove the damper assembly from the steering gear. Upon installation, torque the retaining nuts to 32 ft. lbs.
4. To remove the boot seal, remove the jam nut and cut the boot clamp. Remove the boot.
5. When removing the right boot the shock damper stud must be removed before the boot is removed. Upon installation torque the shock damper stud to 35 ft. lbs.
6. To remove the inner tie rod, position an adjustable wrench on the flat of the rack teeth. Using an open end wrench remove the inner tie rod. Upon installation torque the retaining bolt to 70 ft. lbs.
7. To remove the rack bearing, remove the adjuster plug locknut, adjuster plug and the spring from the steering gear housing.
8. Remove the pinion seal from its bore on the steering gear assembly.
9. To remove the pinion shaft, remove the pinion shaft retaining ring. Tap on the housing and separate the pinion from the housing. Once the pinion is removed from its bore the rack can slide from its mounting, be careful as damage to the rack can occur.
10. To remove the roller bearing, position the housing assembly in a suitable vise. Using an arbor press, press the bearing from its bore.
11. To remove the rack bushing, remove the bushing retaining nut. Slide the rack bushing from its mounting.
12. Remove the grommets from the housing as necessary. Replace as required.

Assembly

1. Assembly is the reverse of the disassembly procedure.
2. When installing the inner tie rod, support the housing in a suitable vise. Stake both sides of the housing to the adapter flats using a drift.
3. To check the staking procedure, use a 0.010 in. feeler gauge and be sure that it will not pass between the rack and housing stake.
4. Pinion preload is 18 ft. lbs.
5. When installing the pinion shaft bolt, start at the 4 o'clock position and finish at the 3 o'clock position.

Nova

Disassembly

1. Place the steering unit into a vise using wood or soft metal to line the vise jaws.
2. Mark the left and right tie rod ends for ease of reassembly. Remove the boots and discard. Upon reassembly, new boots should be installed.
3. Using a suitable tool, bend back (straighten) the bent part of the locking washer between the inner tie rod and the rack. Remove the inner tie rods from the rack marking the left and right rack ends.
4. Loosen the rack guide spring cap locknut, remove the spring and rack guide. Remove the pinion dust cover.
5. Remove the pinion bearing adjusting screw locknut. Remove the pinion bearing adjusting screw.

VISCOUS STEERING DAMPER ASSEMBLY

Removal

1. Using a three-fingered wheel puller on flange of viscous damper, remove damper.

NOTE: Three finger puller must be used or damage to damper will occur.

2. Replace dust seal if necessary.

Installation

1. Remove retaining shield from damper.
2. Be sure dust seal is installed on damper.
3. Line up flat on damper with adjuster plug.
4. Using a press, press on inner hub of damper with suitable pipe. Be sure tabs on damper line up with slots in housing. Press until seated on pinion shaft.
5. Using suitable pipe, press on outer housing of damper until fully seated in rack and pinion housing.
6. Reinstall retaining shield.

PINION SHAFT ASSEMBLY

Removal

1. Turn the pinion shaft until the rack guide is equal distance from both sides of the housing opening.
2. Mark the location of the stub shaft flat on the housing. Remove the retaining ring.
3. Remove the pinion by placing it in a soft jawed vise and tapping on the housing with a soft faced hammer.

Installation

1. Measure the rack guide so it is equal distance on both sides of the housing opening.
2. Install the pinion assembly so when the pinion is fully seated, the pinion shaft flat and the mark on the housing line up and the rack guide is centered in the housing opening.
3. Install the retaining ring.

RACK

Removal

1. With the pinion out of the steering housing, thread an inner tie rod bolt into the rack.
2. Slide the rack back and forth until the housing end and cover is forced from the end of the tube.
3. Unthread the bolt and slide the rack from the steering housing.

Installation

Slide rack into the housing and seat the end cover into the end of the housing tube.

PINION SHAFT ROLLER BEARING

Removal and Installation

The roller bearing is pressed out and the new bearing is pressed into the housing.

RACK BUSHING

Removal and Installation

With the rack out of the housing, remove the internal retaining ring from the tube. A long legged puller is used to remove the bushing from the tube. A press is used to install the new bushing. Press the bushing into position and install the retaining ring.

CHRYSLER FULL TIME CONSTANT CONTROL POWER STEERING GEAR

Rear Wheel Drive Vehicles

Disassembly and Assembly

1. Drain gear by turning worm shaft from limit to limit with oil connections held downward. Thoroughly clean outside.
2. Remove valve body attaching screws, body and the 3 O-rings.
3. Remove pivot lever and spring. Pry under spherical head with a suitable tool. Use care not to collapse slotted end of valve lever as this will destroy bearing tolerances of the spherical head.
4. Remove steering gear arm from sector shaft.
5. Remove snapring and seal backup washer.
6. Remove seal, using proper tool to prevent damage to relative parts.
7. Loosen gear shaft adjusting screw locknut and remove gear shaft cover nut.
8. Rotate wormshaft to position sector teeth at center of piston travel.
9. Loosen power train retaining nut.
10. Turn worm shaft either to full left or full right (depending on vehicle application) to compress power train parts. Then remove power train retaining nut.
11. Remove housing head tang washer.
12. While holding power train completely compressed, pry on piston teeth with a suitable tool, using shaft as a fulcrum, and remove complete power train.

NOTE: Maintain close contact between cylinder head, center race and spacer assembly and the housing head. This will eliminate the possibility of reactor rings becoming disengaged from their grooves in cylinder and housing head. It will prohibit center spacer from separating from center race and cocking in the housing. This could make it impossible to remove the power train without damaging involved parts.

13. Place power train in soft-jawed vise in vertical position. The worm bearing rollers will fall out. Use of arbor tool will hold roller when the housing is removed.
14. Raise housing head until wormshaft oil shaft just clears the top of wormshaft and position arbor tool on top of shaft and into seal. With arbor in position, pull up on housing head until arbor is positioned in bearing. Remove when the housing is removed.
15. Remove large O-ring from housing head groove.
16. Remove reaction seal from groove in face of head with air pressure directed into ferrule chamber.
17. Remove reactor spring, reactor ring, worm balancing ring and spacer.
18. While holding wormshaft from turning, turn nut with enough force to release staked portions from knurled section and remove nut.
19. Remove upper thrust race (thin) and upper thrust bearing.
20. Remove center bearing race.
21. Remove lower thrust bearing and lower thrust bearing race (thick).
22. Remove lower reaction ring and reaction spring.
23. Remove cylinder head assembly.
24. Remove O-rings from outer grooves in head.
25. Remove reaction O-ring from groove in face of cylinder head. Use air pressure in oil hole located between O-ring grooves.
26. Remove snapring, sleeve and rectangular oil seal from cylinder head counterbore.
27. Test wormshaft operation. Not more than 2 inch lbs. should be required to turn it through its entire travel, and with a 15 ft. lb. side load.

NOTE: The worm and piston is serviced as a complete assembly and should not be disassembled.

Assembly

1. Assembly is the reverse of the disassembly.

removal.

7. Remove the rack from the pinion side. Do not attempt to remove the rack from the tube side or twist the tube during removal.
6. Remove the pinion with their upper bearing being careful not to damage the pinion serrations.

2. Inspect all mating surfaces for excessive wear or signs of damage. Inspect the rack for runout. Runout should not exceed 0.012 in. (0.3 mm). Check bearings and seals. Replace as required.
3. Lubricate all sliding parts and sealing surfaces using lithium grease.

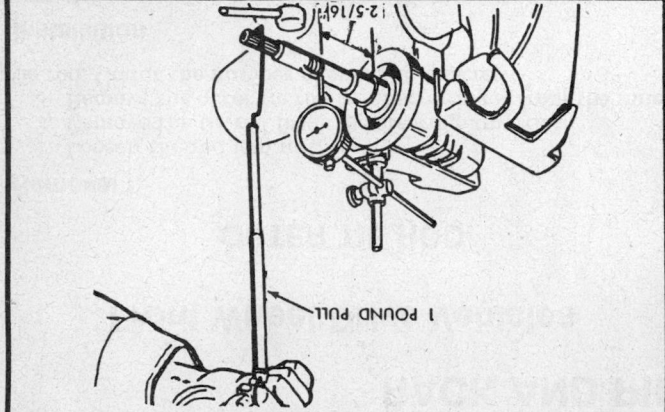

Checking the wormshaft side play

2-5/16"

1 POUND PULL

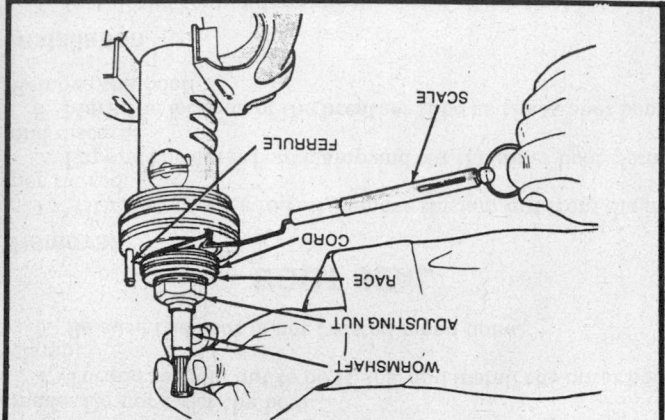

Checking the center bearing preload

SCALE
FERRULE
CORD
RACE
ADJUSTING NUT
WORMSHAFT

CHRYSLER POWER STEERING RACK AND PINION ASSEMBLY

Front Wheel Drive Vehicles

OUTER TIE ROD

Removal

1. Loosen the rod jam nut.
2. Remove the tie rod from the steering knuckle.
3. Remove the outer tie rod by unscrewing it from the inner tie rod. Count the number of turns to unscrew.

Installation

1. Screw the outer tie rod onto the inner tie rod the same number of turns necessary to remove.
2. Expand the outer boot clamp and leave loose on the tie rod.
3. Do not tighten the jam nut until the toe adjustment is made. Do not twist the boot.
4. Torque the jam nut to 50 ft. lbs. and install the outer boot clamp.
5. Be sure the boot is not twisted when done.

BOOT SEAL

Removal

1. With the outer tie rod off, remove the jam nut from the inner tie rod.
2. Expand the outer boot clamp and cut the inner boot clamp and discard.
3. Mark the location of the breather tube on the rubber boot. Remove the boot.

Installation

1. Install the boot and inner boot clamp. Align the boot mark and breather tube.
2. Install thee boot seal over the housing lip with the hole in the boot aligned with the breather tube.
3. Install the inner boot clamp. Lubricate the tie rod boot groove with a silicone type lubricant before installing the outer clamp.

INNER TIE ROD

Removal

1. With the steering unit out of the vehicle, remove the shock dampener ring from the inner tie rod housing and slide it back on the rack Saginaw gears.
2. On TRW gears, remove the roll pin from the inner tie rod to the rack.
3. Put a wrench on the tie rod pivot housing flats and turn the housing counterclockwise until the inner tie rod assembly separates from the rack.

Installation

1. Install the inner tie rod onto the rack and bottom the threads.
2. Torque the housing while holding the rack with a wrench. Torque to 70 ft. lbs. for the Saginaw gear, while torquing the inner tie rod to 60 ft. lbs. for the TRW gear. Install roll pin as required.
3. Support the rack and housing and stake the housing in a couple of places for the Saginaw gear.
4. Inspect the stake, a 0.010 in. feeler gauge must not pass between the rack and the housing stake on each side.
5. On the Saginaw gear, slide the shock dampener over the inner tie rod housing until it engaged.

Removing the valve body assembly

28. Shaft side play should not exceed 0.008 in. under light pull applied 2⁵⁄₁₆ in. from piston flange.
29. Assemble in reverse of above, noting proper adjustments and preload requirements following.
30. When cover nut is installed, tighten to 20 ft. lbs. torque.
31. Valve mounting screws should be tightened to 200 inch lbs.
32. With hoses connected, system bled, and engine idling

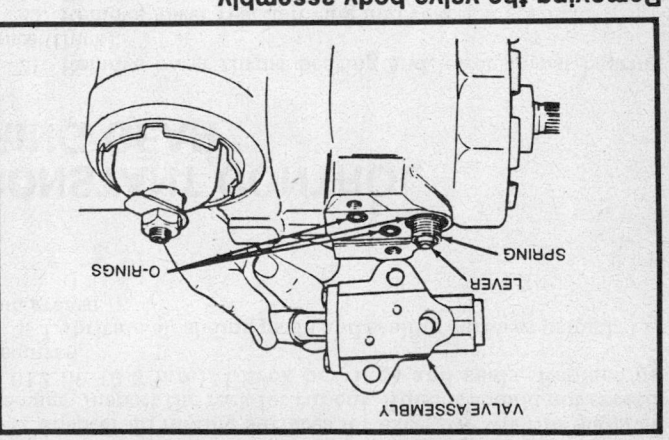

Staking the wormshaft bearing adjusting nut

roughly, center valve unit until it not self-steering. Tap on head of valve body attaching screws to move valve body up, and tap on end plug to move valve body down.

33. With steering gear on center, tighten gear shaft adjusting screw until lash just disappears.
34. Continue to tighten ³⁄₈-½ turn and tighten locknut to 50 ft. lbs.

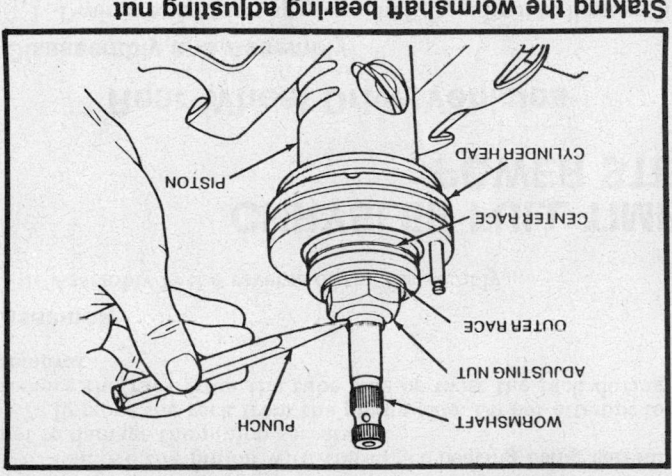

RACK BEARING

Removal

1. Loosen the locknut for the adjuster plug.
2. Remove the adjuster plug from the housing. Remove the spring and rack bearing.

Installation

1. Lubricate the metal parts and install the rack bearing, the spring, the adjuster plug and the locknut.
2. Turn the adjuster plug in until it bottoms and then back off 40–60 degrees.
3. Tighten the locknut while holding the adjuster plug in place. The torque must be 50 ft. lbs.

Exploded view of TRW power steering gear

1. Housing
2. Bushing, pinion
3. Seal
4. Bearing, pinion
5. Lock nut, pinion
6. Plug, pinion
7. Seal
8. Bearing yoke
9. Spring
10. Plug
11. Lock nut
12. Valve assembly
13. Bearing
14. Seal, shaft
15. Retaining ring
16. Tube assembly
17. Retaining wire
18. Rack assembly
19. Piston
20. Piston ring
21. O-ring
22. Retaining ring
23. O-ring, bushing
24. Bushing, rack
25. Seal
26. Lock ring
27. Valve rings
28. Inner tie rod
29. Inboard clamp
30. Boot
31. Outboard clamp
32. Lock nut
33. Tie rod, outer
34. Spring pin
35. Shock damper
36. Breather tube
37. Oil lines, cylinder
38. Bolt, gear mounting
39. Bracket, gear mounting
40. Bushing, gear mounting
41. Bracket, inner

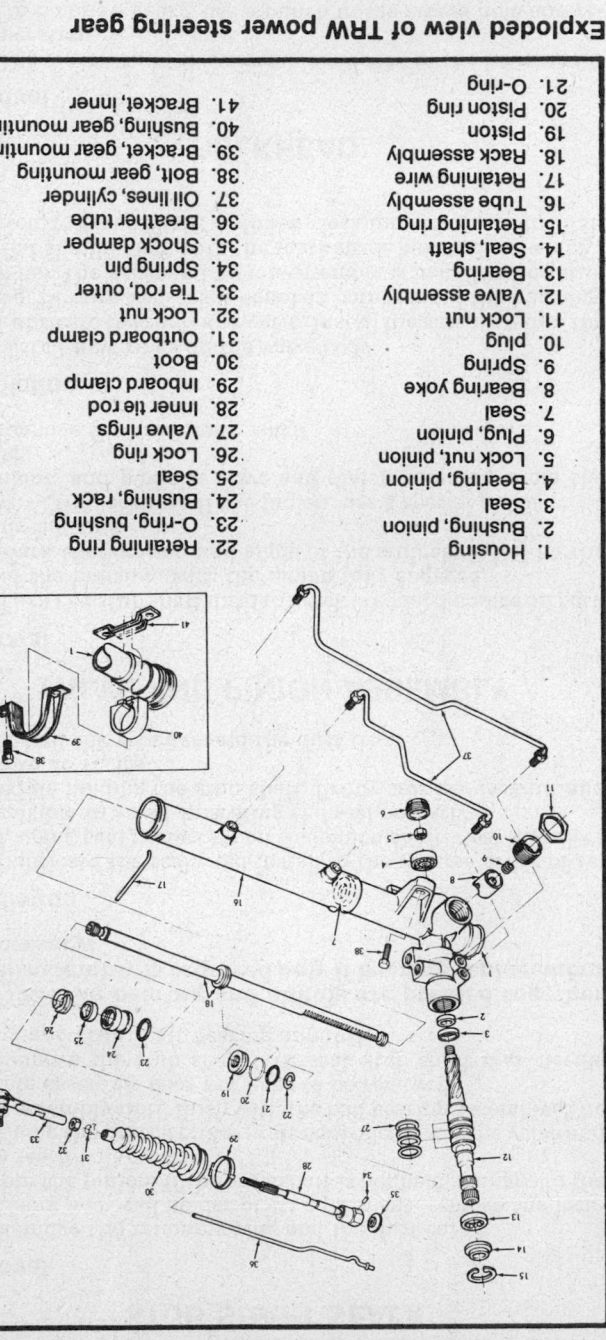

Exploded view of Saginaw power steering gear

1. Gear assembly
2. Housing assembly
3. Bushing, upper pinion
4. Seal, rack and pinion
5. Pinion, with valve assembly
6. Ring, valve body
7. Ring, spool, shaft retaining
8. Annulus, stub shaft
9. Bearing, needle bearing
10. Seal, stub shaft
11. Seal, stub shaft dust
12. Ring, seal retaining
13. Bearing, rack
14. Spring, adjuster
15. Plug, adjuster
16. Nut, adjuster plug lock
17. Ring, shock dampener
18. Rod assembly, inner
19. Clamp, boot
20. Boot, rack and pinion
21. Clamp, boot (tie rod end)
22. Nut, hex jam
23. Tie rod, outer, left
24. Fitting, lubrication
25. Seal, tie rod
26. Nut, outer tie rod
27. Pin, cotter
28. Bearing, ball
29. Ring, pinion bearing retaining
30. Nut, hex lock
31. Cover, dust
32. Tube, breather
33. Seal, cylinder oil line
34. Kit, cylinder oil line, left, w/"O" ring seal
35. Kit, cylinder oil line, right with/"O" ring seal
36. Seal, inner rack
37. Rack, assembly
38. Ring, piston
39. Bulkhead, cylinder inner
40. Seal, rack and pinion (bulkhead) inner
41. Bulkhead, cylinder outer
42. Seal, "O" ring
43. Ring, bulkhead retaining
44. Rod, assembly, inner tie, right
45. Tie rod, outer, right
46. Spring, wave washer
47. Bolt, rack and pinion, steering gear mounting, left
48. Bolt, rack and pinion, steering gear mounting, right
49. Bracket, rack and pinion steering, gear mounting, outer
50. Bushing, rack and pinion steering gear
51. Bracket, rack and pinion steering gear mounting, inner

STUB SHAFT SEALS

Removal

1. Remove the retaining ring and the dust cover.
2. Using a special holder or its equivalent, remove the locknut from the pinion. If the stub shaft is not held, damage to the pinion teeth will occur.
3. Using the special puller or its equivalent, pull the valve and pinion assembly until flush with the ball bearing assembly. The complete assembly does not have to be removed.
4. Remove the stub shaft dust seal, stub shaft seal, needle bearing and stub shaft bearing annulus.

NOTE: The bearing and annulus are pressed together and disassembly is required only if bearing replacement is necessary.

Installation

1. Lubricate the seals and install in the reverse order of removal, using seal protectors on the pinion shaft. Seal installers are available to assist in seating the seal properly.
2. While holding the stub shaft, firmly seat the locknut and torque to 26 ft. lbs.
3. Install the retainer and the dust cover.

VALVE AND PINION ASSEMBLY

Removal

1. Turn the stub shaft until the rack is equal distance on both sides of the housing, with the pinion fully engaged.
2. Mark the location and angle of the stub shaft flat on the steering housing.
3. With the locknut off the pinion, use a special puller or its equivalent, and pull the valve and pinion assembly from the steering housing.
4. Remove the valve body rings.

Installation

1. Install new rings on the valve body.
2. Lubricate the rings and valve. Install the assembly into the housing. Be sure the rack is equal on both sides of the housing.
3. When the valve and pinion assembly is installed, the stub shaft flat should align with the mark made before disassembly.
4. Hold the stub shaft, install the locknut and torque to 26 ft. lbs.

BULKHEAD

Removal

1. The pinion and valve assembly must be in the housing for this operation.
2. On Saginaw gears, use a punch in the access hole and remove the bulkhead retaining ring. Discard the ring.
3. On TRW gears, use a punch to rotate the retaining wire clockwise to expose the end. Pull the retaining wire to remove.
4. Loosen and remove both cylinder lines. Plug fittings at the cylinder.
5. Turn the stub shaft so that the rack moves to the right, forcing the bulkhead from the housing. Use a drain pan to catch the power steering fluid.
6. If the inner rack seal or piston rings are to be replaced, use special seal remover tools as required.
7. The piston and pinion can be removed.

Installation

1. Install the inner rack seal with special seal installer tools or equivalent.
2. Install the plastic retainer onto the inner rack seal.
3. Install the bulkhead outer seal into the bulkhead.
4. Install the bulkhead onto the rack.
5. On Saginaw gears, be sure the open end of the new bulkhead retaining ring is approximately 0.50 in. from the access hole.
6. On Saginaw gears, turn the rack to full right turn to fully seat the retaining ring.
7. The remaining models, install the retaining wire by rotating the bulkhead assembly counterclockwise.

PINION BALL BEARING, UPPER PINION BUSHING AND SEAL

Removal and Installation

1. The pinion and piston must be out of the housing.
2. The bearing is removed by the use of a drift and hammer. To install, a bearing installer is available.
3. To remove the seal and bushing, a drift and hammer is used. To install, the use of special installing tools are necessary.

POWER STEERING PUMP OVERHAUL

Disassembly

1. With the power steering pump removed from the vehicle, drain the reservoir and reinstall the filler cap to prevent contamination. Clean the exterior of the pump before starting the disassembly procedures.
2. Secure the pump in a suitable vise at the mounting bracket.
3. Using special puller tool C-4068A or equivalent remove the pulley from the pump. Be sure that the puller screw is perfectly aligned with the shaft end and to prevent cocking.

NOTE: The pump pulley is a press fit on the shaft and must be removed and replaced with the aid of puller tools. Do not hammer on the puller, pulley or shaft for this could cause internal damage to the pump components. To aid in pulley removal it is advisable to apply a light oil on the pulley shaft. If a hydraulic press is available, place the power steering pump into the press and press the pulley off of the pump shaft. If there is not a hydraulic press available, remove the pulley with the puller.

4. Remove the brackets from the pump and using a soft jaw vise or equivalent, clamp the pump (shaft end down) in the vise between the square boss and shaft housing.
5. Remove the mounting studs and pressure hose fitting. Tap the reservoir filler tube back and forth with a plastic mallet to loosen. Remove the reservoir off of the pump body and discard the O-rings from the reservoir along with the mounting studs and the pressure fitting.
6. Using a punch, tap the end cover retainer ring around until 1 end of the ring is near the hole in the pump body. Insert the punch far enough to disengage the ring from the groove in the pump bore and pry the ring out of the pump body.
7. Tap the end cover with a plastic mallet to dislodge it, the spring under the cover should push the cover up.
8. Remove the pump body from the vise, place the pump body upside down on a flat surface and tap the end of the driveshaft with a plastic mallet to loosen the pressure plate, rotor and thrust plate assembly from the pump body.
9. Lift the pump body off of rotor assembly. Flow control valve and spring should slide out of the bore.
10. Replace and discard cover and pressure plate O-rings, place pump body on a flat surface and pry the driveshaft oil seal out with a suitable tool.
11. Inspect the seal bore in housing for burrs, nicks or gouge marks that would allow oil to bypass outer seal surface.
12. Remove the 10 vanes from the slots in the rotor, after lift-

the seal bottoms on shoulder.

Assembly

1. With the pump body laying on a flat surface, drive a new driveshaft seal into the bore, using a 7/8 or 15/16 in. socket until the seal bottoms on shoulder.

NOTE: Inspect and wash all parts in clean solvent, blow out all passages with compressed air and dry the cleaned parts.

14. Slide the rotor and thrust plate off of the shaft and remove the shaft from the vise.

13. Remove the rotor lock ring, pry the ring off the driveshaft and be sure to avoid nicking the rotor end face. Discard the lock ring.

ing out the pressure plate and cam ring from the rotor. Clamp the driveshaft in a soft jaw vise or equivalent, with the rotor and thrust plate facing up.

Power steering pump disassembled

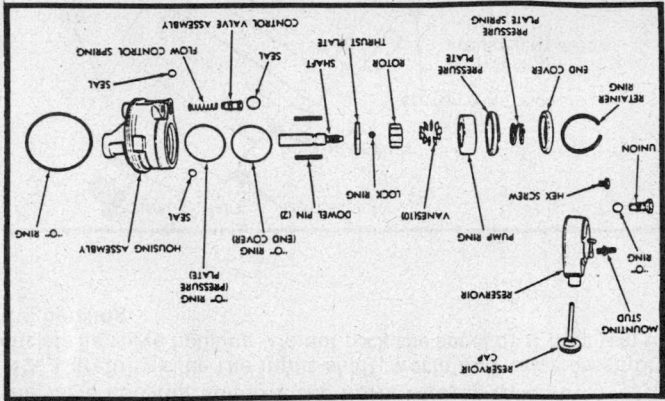

Removing the end cover retaining ring

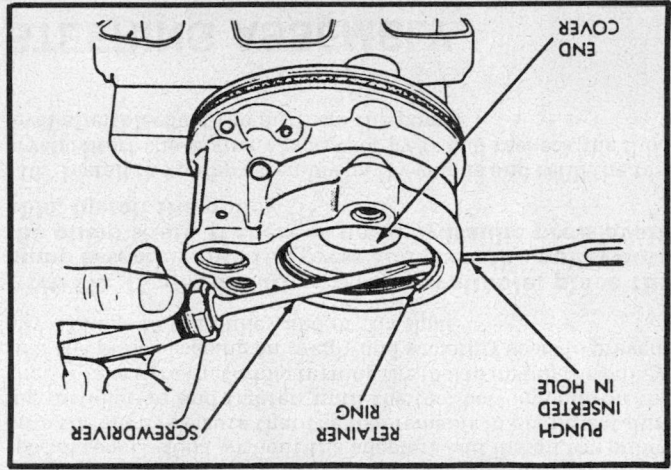

Thrust plate installation

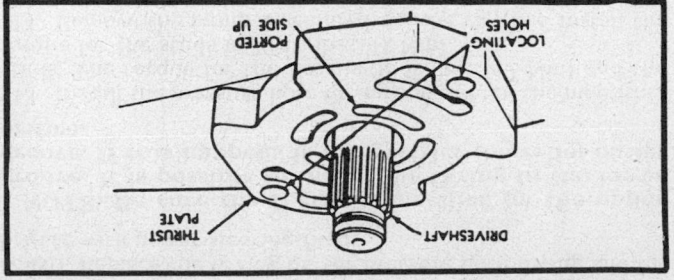

---

2. Lubricate the seal with power steering fluid and clamp the pump body shaft end down into a vise.

3. Install the end cover and pressure plate O-rings in the grooves in the pump cavity. (These rings are the same size.) Be sure to lubricate the O-rings in power steering fluid.

4. With the driveshaft clamped in a soft jaw vise or equivalent with the splined end up, install the thrust plate on the driveshaft with the counterbore of the rotor facing down. Using special tool C-4090 or equivalent. Slide rotor over splines with the counterbore of the rotor facing down.

5. Install the dowel pins in holes in the pump cavity. Insert

NOTE: Do not use excessive force when installing the seal, because the seal will become distorted.

The rotor and thrust plate installed

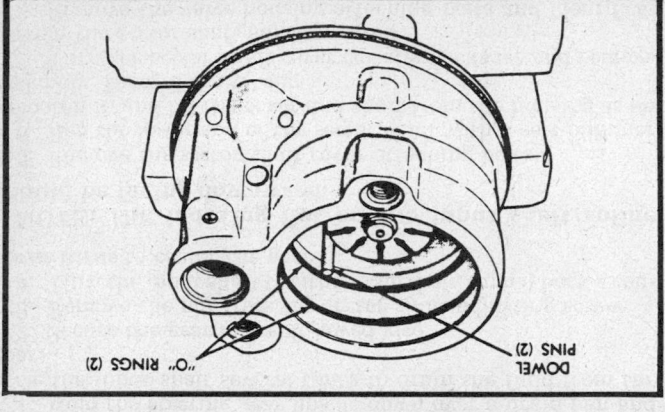

Rotor vanes installation

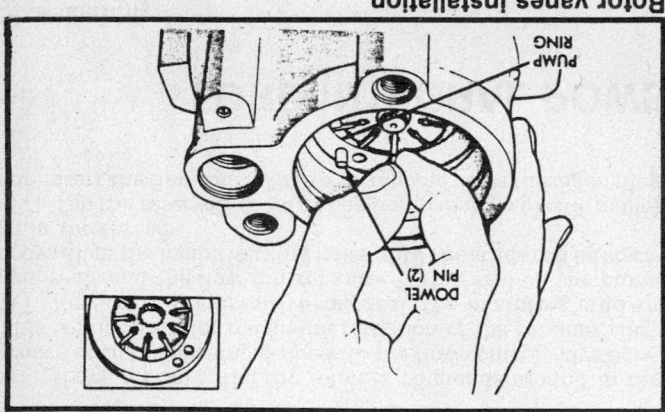

Drive shaft removal

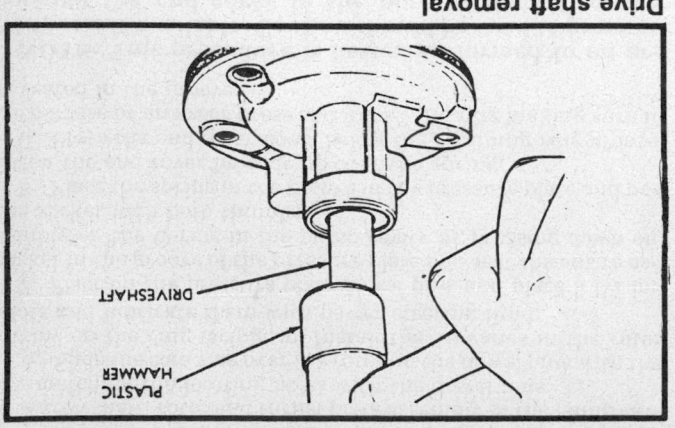

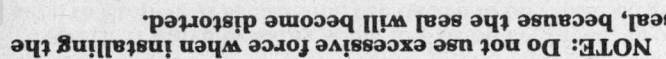

the driveshaft, rotor and thrust plate assembly in the pump cavity matching the locating holes with the dowel pins.

6. Slide the cam ring over the rotor on the dowel pins with the arrow on the ring facing up. Install the 10 vanes in the rotor slots and lubricate them with power steering fluid.

7. Position the pressure plate dowel pins and place a 1/4 in. socket in the groove of the pressure plate and seat the entire assembly in the pump cavity by pressing down on the O-ring with the socket with both thumbs.

8. Place the spring in the groove in the pressure plate and position the end cover lip edge up over the spring.

9. Press the end cover down below the retaining ring groove with a vise or an arbor press and install the ring making sure it is seated in the groove.

NOTE: This procedure is better performed in an arbor press if available. Caution should be used to prevent cocking the end cover in the bore or distorting the assembly.

10. Using a punch, tap the retainer ring ends around in the groove until the opening is opposite the flow control valve bore. This is important for maximum retention of the retainer ring.

11. Replace the reservoir O-ring seal, the mounting stud O-ring seals and the flow control valve O-ring seal on the pump body. Align the mounting stud holes until the studs can be started in the threads.

12. Tap the reservoir down on the pump using a plastic mallet and insert the flow control valve spring and valve (hexagon plug

down). Replace the O-ring on the pressure hose fitting and lubricate with power steering fluid.

NOTE: Be sure the O-ring is installed on the upper groove. It is possible to install the O-ring in the lower groove. If this happens it will restrict the relief outlet orifice.

13. Install the pressure hose fitting and tighten the mounting studs. The torque for the hose is 35 ft. lbs. (47 Nm) and the torque for the studs is 30 ft. lbs. (41 Nm).

14. Remove the pump assembly from the vise and install the mounting brackets. After the brackets are installed clamp the pump assembly into the vise at the mounting bracket.

15. Apply a thin coat of light oil to the pump shaft and using special tool C-4063 without the adapters and install the pulley onto the shaft. Be sure that the tool remains in alignment during installation and tighten until the tool bottoms out on the shaft. Make sure that while turning the tool to install the pulley, that the pulley is going on evenly and smoothly so as to prevent any damage to the pulley and or the shaft.

NOTE: If a hydraulic press is available, place the pump assembly into the press and press the pulley onto the pump shaft. If there is not a hydraulic press available, install the pulley.

16. Install the pump assembly on the engine and refill the reservoir. Start the engine, inspect for leaks and recheck the fluid level after bleeding the air from the pump.

FORD INTEGRAL POWER STEERING ASSEMBLY

Disassembly

1. Hold the steering gear upside down over a drain pan and cycle the input shaft several times to drain the fluid from the gear.

2. Secure the gear in a soft-jawed vise.

3. Remove the nut from the sector shaft adjusting screw.

4. Turn the input shaft to either stop then, turn it back a couple of turns to center the gear.

NOTE: The indexing flat on the input shaft spline should be facing downward.

5. Remove the sector shaft cover attaching bolts.

6. Rap the lower end of the sector shaft with a soft-hammer to loosen it, and lift the cover and shaft from the housing as an assembly. Discard the O-ring.

7. Turn the sector shaft cover counterclockwise and remove it from the sector shaft adjuster screw.

8. Remove the valve housing bolts and identification tag. Hold the piston to keep it from spinning off the shaft, and lift the valve housing off the steering gear housing. Remove the valve housing and control valve gasket. Discard the gasket.

NOTE: If valve housing seals are to be replaced, proceed to Step 12. If sector shaft seals are to be replaced go to steering gear housing section. Balls need only to be removed if valve sleeve rings are to be replaced.

9. With the piston held so that the ball guide faces up, remove the ball guide clamp screws and ball guide clamp. With a finger over the opening in the ball guide, turn the piston so that the ball guide faces down over a clean container. Let the guide tubes drop into the container.

10. Rotate the input shaft from stop to stop until all balls fall from the piston into the container. The valve assembly can then be removed from the piston. Inspect the piston bore to insure all balls have been removed.

11. Install the valve body assembly in the bench mounted

holding fixture, and loosen the Allen head race nut screw from the valve housing. Remove the worm bearing race nut.

12. Carefully slide the input shaft, worm and valve assembly out of the valve housing. Do not cock the spool or it may jam in the housing.

Ford integral power steering gear assembly — exterior view

SECTOR SHAFT
IDENTIFICATION TAG
LOCK NUT
SECTOR SHAFT ADJUSTMENT SCREW
SECTOR SHAFT COVER
CONTROL VALVE HOUSING
INLET PORT
OUTLET PORT
INPUT SHAFT

STEERING GEAR HOUSING

Disassembly and Assembly

1. Remove the snapring from the lower end of the housing.
2. Remove dust seal using puller tools attachment and slide hammer.
3. Remove pressure seal in the same manner. Discard the seal.
4. Lubricate the new pressure seal dust seal with clean Ford polyethylene grease.
5. Apply Ford polyethylene grease to the sector shaft seal bore.
6. Place the dust seal on sector shaft replacement tool so the raised lip of the seal is towards the tool. Place the pressure seal on the tool lip away from the tool. The flat back side of the pressure seal should be against the flat side of the dust seal.
7. Insert the seal driver tool into the sector shaft bore and drive the seal tool until the seals clear the snapring groove. Do not bottom seals against bearing. The seal will not function properly when bottomed against the bearing.
8. Install snapring in the groove in the housing.

Differences in worm and piston ratios – Ford integral power steering

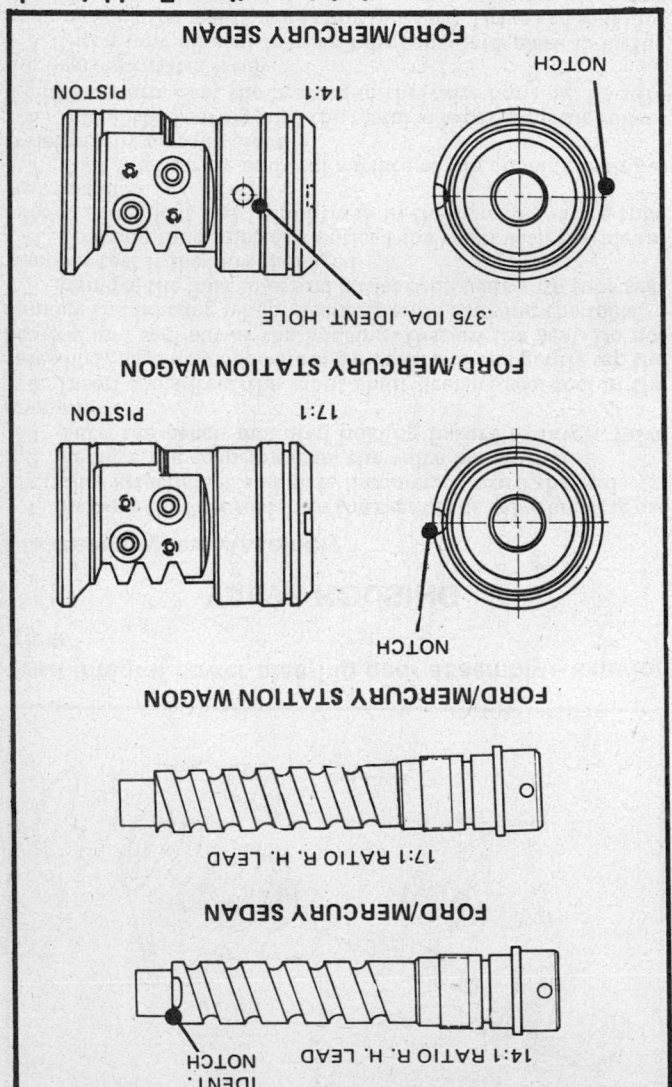

FORD/MERCURY SEDAN

14:1

PISTON

NOTCH

.375 DIA. IDENT. HOLE

FORD/MERCURY STATION WAGON

17:1

PISTON

NOTCH

FORD/MERCURY STATION WAGON

17:1 RATIO R. H. LEAD

FORD/MERCURY SEDAN

14:1 RATIO R. H. LEAD

IDENT. NOTCH

Assembling ball in piston and piston on worm shaft – Ford integral power steering

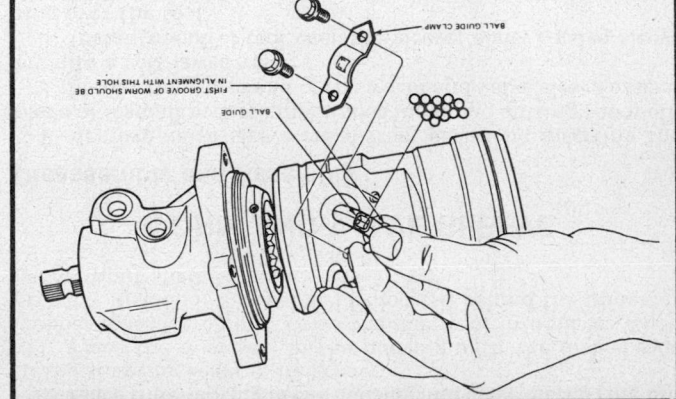

BALL GUIDE CLAMP

FIRST GROOVE OF WORM SHOULD BE IN ALIGNMENT WITH THIS HOLE

BALL GUIDE

Assembly

1. Mount the valve housing in the bench mounted holding fixture with the flanged end up.
2. Apply a light coat of gear lubricant to the teflon rings on the valve sleeve.
3. Carefully install the worm shaft and valve in the housing.
4. Install the worm bearing race nut in the housing and torque to specification.
5. Install the Allen head race nut screw through the valve housing and tighten to specification 15-25 inch lbs. (1.7-2.8 Nm).
6. Place the power cylinder piston on the bench with the ball guide holes facing up. Insert the worm shaft into the piston so that the first groove is in line with the hole nearest the center of the piston.
7. Place the ball guide in the piston. Turning the worm shaft counterclockwise as viewed from the input end of the shaft, place the same balls as removed in Step 9 in the ball guide. A minimum of 27 balls is required. If all the balls have not been inserted upon reaching the left stop, rotate the input shaft in 1 direction then the other while inserting the remaining balls. Do not rotate the input shaft or piston more than 3 turns from the left stop, or the balls will fall out of the circuit.
8. Secure the guides in the ball nut with the clamp. Tighten screws to specification.
9. Apply petroleum jelly or equivalent to the teflon seal on the piston.
10. Place a new control valve O-ring on the valve housing.
11. Slide the piston and valve into the gear housing being careful not to damage the piston ring.
12. Align the oil passage in the valve housing with the passage in the gear housing. Place a new O-ring onto the oil passage hole of the gear housing. Install identification tag onto the housing. Install but do not tighten, the attaching bolts. Identification tag is to be installed under upper right valve housing bolt.
13. Rotate the ball nut so that the teeth are in the same plane as the sector teeth. Tighten the valve housing attaching bolts to specification.
14. Position the sector shaft cover O-ring in the steering gear housing. Turn the input shaft to center the piston.
15. Apply petroleum jelly or equivalent to the sector shaft journal, and position the sector shaft and cover assembly in the gear housing. Install the sector shaft cover attaching bolts. Tighten the bolts to specification 55-70 ft. lbs. (75-94 Nm).
16. Attach an inch lb. torque wrench to the input shaft. Adjust mesh load to specification.

VALVE HOUSING

Disassembly and Assembly

1. Remove the dust seal from the rear of the valve housing using puller attachment and slide hammer. Discard the seal.
2. Remove the snapring from the valve housing.
3. Turn the bench mounted holding fixture to invert valve housing.
4. Insert tools from the input shaft bearing seal tool in the valve body assembly opposite the oil seal end and gently tap the bearing seal out of the housing. Discard the seal. Do not damage the housing when inserting and removing the tools.
5. Remove the fluid inlet and outlet tube seats with tube seat remover tool if they are damaged.
6. Coat the fluid inlet and outlet tube seats with petroleum jelly or equivalent and install them in the housing with a tube seat installer.
7. Coat the bearing and seal surface of the housing with petroleum jelly or equivalent.
8. Install the bearing with the metal side covering the rollers facing outward. Seat the bearing in the valve housing. Be sure the bearing rotates freely.
9. Dip a new oil seal in gear lubricant, and place it in the housing with the metal side facing inward. Drive the seal into the housing until the outer edge does not quite clear the snapring groove.
10. Place the snapring in the housing and drive in the ring until the snapring seats in its groove.
11. Place the dust seal in the housing with the dished side (rubber side) facing out. Drive the dust seal into place. When properly installed, the seal will be located behind the undercut in the input shaft.

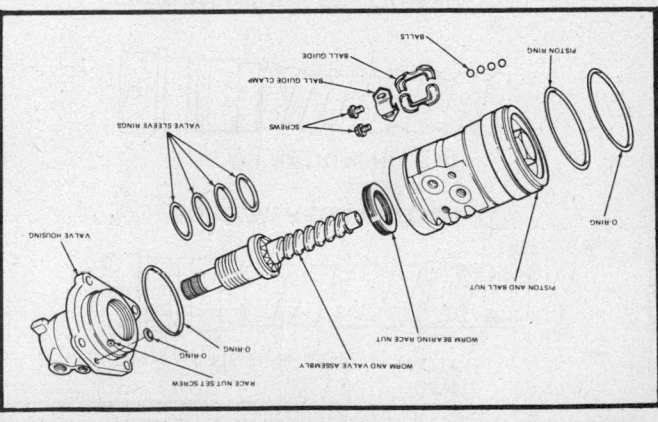

Ford integral power steering gear assembly — exterior view

TIE ROD BALL SOCKETS

Disassembly

1. Remove the rack and pinion steering gear from the vehicle. Position the gear in a suitable holding fixture. Clean the exterior of the gear.
2. Remove the tie rod outer ends and locknuts.
3. Remove the bellow clamps. Remove the bellows and the breather tube. Be careful not to damage the bellows. Discard the breather tube.
4. Using a left hand threaded easy out tool, remove the spiral pin that locks each tie rod socket to the rack.
5. Using tool T74P-3504-U or equivalent and a torque wrench, as well as an adjustable wrench, remove the ball socket.

NOTE: If the rack is not restrained by the adjustable wrench damage to the pinion will occur.

Assembly

1. Assembly is the reverse of the removal procedure.
2. Tighten the tie rod ball socket to 55–65 ft. lbs.

VALVE AND VALVE HOUSING

Disassembly and Assembly

1. Remove the steering gear from the vehicle. Position the assembly in a suitable holding fixture. Clean the exterior of the gear.
2. Remove the external pressure lines from the valve and the gear housing. Remove the 4 flare gaskets from the ports.
3. Loosen the yoke plug locknut and the yoke plug. This is done to relieve the preload on the rack. Remove the pinion bearing plug.
4. Install tool T47P-3504-R or an equivalent pinion shaft torque tool on the input shaft.

TRW RACK AND PINION POWER STEERING ASSEMBLY

WORM AND VALVE SLEEVE

Disassembly and Assembly

1. Remove valve sleeve rings from sleeve by inserting the blade of a small pocket knife under them and cutting them off.
2. Mount the worm end of the worm and valve sleeve assembly into a soft-jawed vise.
3. Install mandrel tool over the sleeve; slide 1 valve sleeve ring over the tool.
4. Slide the pusher tool over the mandrel; rapidly push down on the pusher tool, forcing the ring down the ramp and into the fourth groove of the valve sleeve. Repeat this step 3 more times, and each time add the spacers under the mandrel tool. By adding the spacer each time, the mandrel tool will line up with the next groove of the valve sleeve.
5. After installing the 4 valve sleeve rings, apply a light coat of gear lubricant to the sleeve and rings.
6. Install a spacer over the input shaft as a pilot for installing the sizing tube. Slowly install the sizing tube over the sleeve valve end of the worm shaft onto the valve sleeve rings. Make sure that the rings are not being bent over as the tube is slid over them.
7. Remove the sizing tube and check the condition of the rings. Make sure that the rings turn freely in the grooves.

NOTE: No further service or disassembly of the worm valve assembly is possible.

PISTON AND BALL NUT

Disassembly and Assembly

1. Remove the teflon piston ring and O-ring from the piston and ball nut. Discard both rings.
2. Dip a new O-ring in gear lubricant and install it on the piston and ball nut.
3. Install a new teflon piston ring on the piston and ball nut being careful not to stretch it any more than necessary.

5. Hold the input shaft, and remove the pinion bearing locknut and discard it.

6. Remove the bolts and washers retaining the valve housing to the gear housing.

7. Move the rack to the left stop (rack teeth exposed). With a file or chalk, mark the relative position of the indexing flat surface on the input shaft splines to the valve housing face.

NOTE: It is important when subsequent assembly of the input shaft is made that the flat be aligned in the same position.

8. The valve housing cannot be removed as a single component because of the pinion seal design. To service the valve housing, valve assembly, or the pinion seal, the complete valve housing and valve assembly must be removed as a unit.

9. Carefully work the valve housing and the valve assembly, as a unit, out and away from the gear assembly.

NOTE: The pinion bearing locknut must be removed before attempting to remove the valve housing.

10. Position the valve and housing assembly in a suitable vise. Grip the protruding pinion seal with a pair of interlocking pliers.

11. Rotate the seal in the clockwise direction, this will cause the seal to twist out of the valve housing. Do not hammer or pry on the pliers or the input shaft, as damage may occur.

12. Discard the pinion oil seal and any other damaged or worn components.

13. Using a slide hammer, remove the pinion bearing from the gear housing.

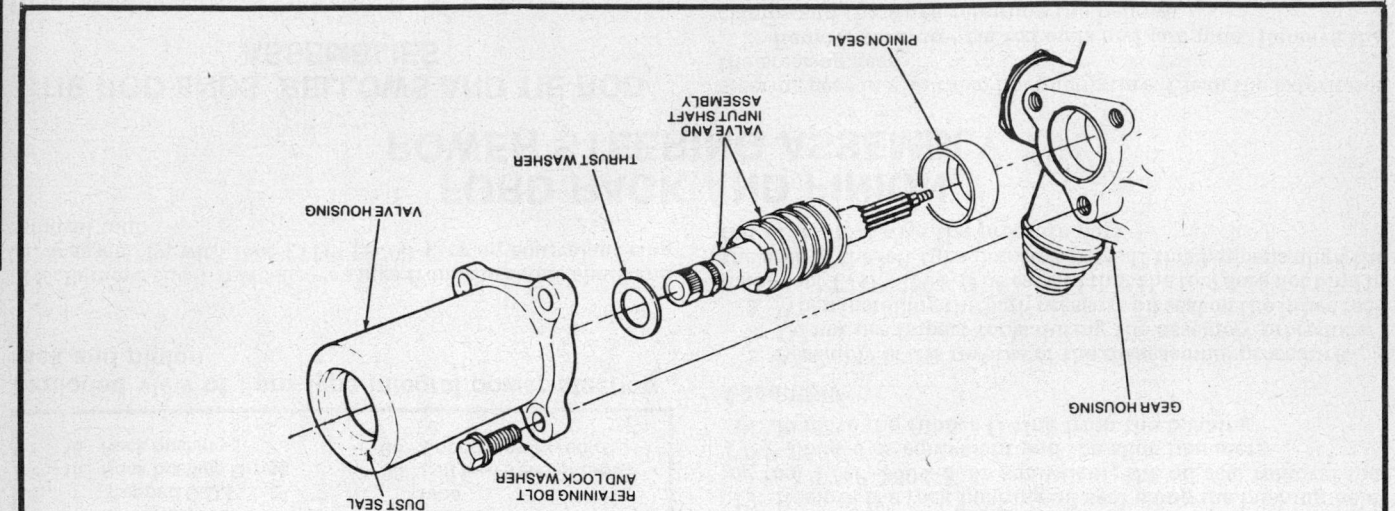

TRW power rack and pinion valve housing assembly

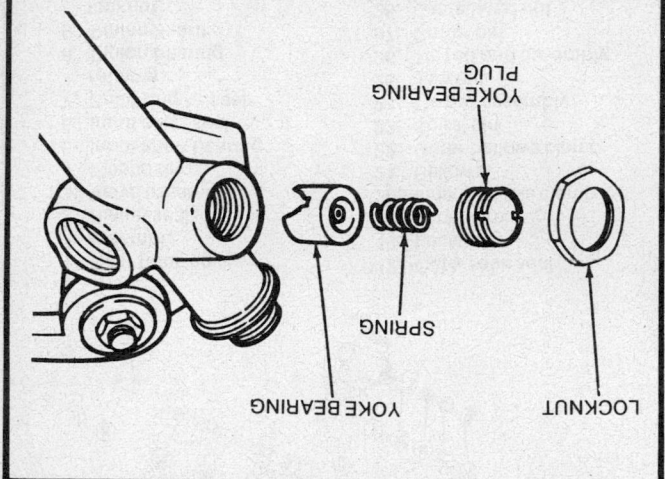

TRW rack and pinion yoke bearing and related components

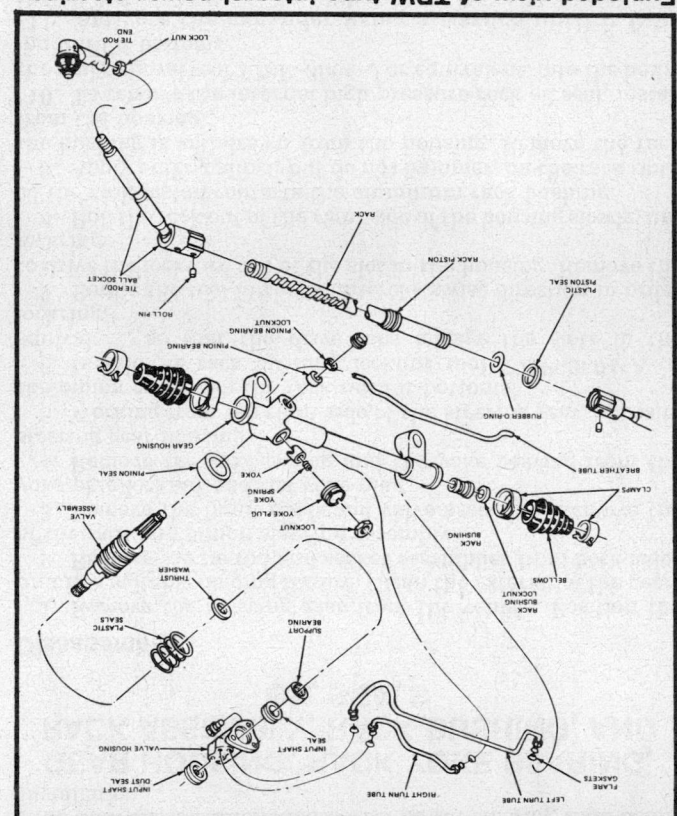
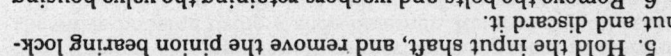

Exploded view of TRW type integral power steering rack and pinion

14. Remove the 4 valve sleeve rings from the input shaft and valve assembly, with tool T71P-19703-C or an equivalent ring removal tool.

FORD RACK AND PINION POWER STEERING ASSEMBLY

TIE ROD ENDS, BELLOWS AND TIE ROD ASSEMBLIES

Disassembly

1. Remove the steering gear from the vehicle. Position the steering gear in a suitable holding fixture. Clean the exterior of the steering gear.
2. Remove the outer tie rod ends and jam nuts. Remove the clamps and the wires retaining the bellows.
3. Remove the bellows. Remove the breather tube. Use care not to cause damage to the bellows.

Assembly

1. Assembly is the reverse of the disassembly procedure.
2. Do not use impact tools during the assembly procedure.
3. When installing the high pressure oil seal on the inner rack using tool T74P-3504-D be careful that the tool does not bind in the area of the left turn pressure port. If this happens align the flat of the tool with the pressure port.

Exploded view of Ford type integral power steering rack and pinion

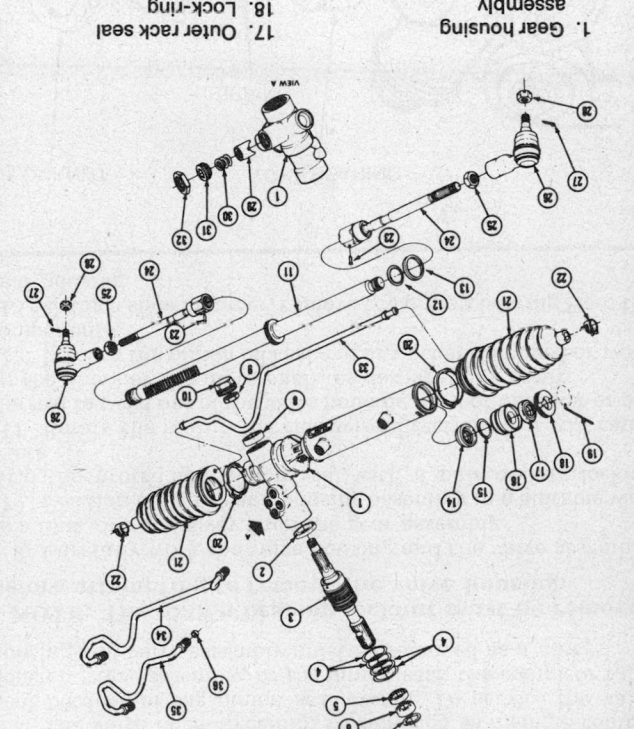

1. Gear housing assembly	19. Lock-wire
2. Pinion seal	20. Inner bellows clamp
3. Valve assembly	21. Bellows
4. Plastic rings	22. Outer bellows clamp
5. Input shaft bearing	23. Spiral pin
6. Input shaft seal	24. Tie rod assembly
7. Snap ring — seal retainer	25. Jam nut
8. Pinion bearing	26. Tie rod end assembly
9. Pinion bearing locknut	27. Cotter pin
10. Housing cap	28. Castellated nut
11. Rack assembly	29. Rack yoke
12. Back up O-ring (rubber)	30. Yoke spring
13. Piston seal (plastic)	31. Yoke plug
14. Inner rack seal (stepped O.D.)	32. Yoke plug lock nut
15. Rack bushing O-ring	33. Breather tube
16. Rack bushing	34. Right turn transfer tube
17. Outer rack seal	35. Left turn transfer tube
18. Lock-ring	36. Copper seal (4 req'd)

GEAR HOUSING, RACK YOKE BEARING, RACK ASSEMBLY, RACK BUSHING, AND OIL SEALS

Disassembly

1. Remove the steering gear from the vehicle. Position the unit in a suitable holding fixture. Clean the exterior of the gear.
2. Remove the tie rod and socket assemblies from both sides of the rack and pinion steering assembly.
3. Remove the input shaft and valve assembly. Remove the yoke plug locknut and the yoke plug.
4. Remove the yoke spring and the yoke bearing from the steering gear housing.
5. Working from the right side of the steering gear, opposite the pinion end, push the rack until it bottoms.
6. Install the rack bushing locknut tool T77P-3504-A or equivalent, so that the drive tabs engage the slots in the locknut.
7. Rotate the tool in the counterclockwise direction in order to drive the lockwire out of the slot in the housing. Remove the lockwire.
8. Pull the rack out of the right side of the housing slowly, until the rack piston contacts the aluminum rack bushing.
9. Apply pulling effort, but do not hammer, on the rack until the bushing is withdrawn from the housing. Remove the rack from the housing.
10. To remove the internal high pressure rack oil seal, install the seal removal tool T78P-3504-J or equivalent, into the housing.
11. Activate the expander using a wrench until it fully bottoms. Remove the tool and the oil seal from the housing using a slide hammer. Discard the oil seal.
12. Remove the plastic O-ring and the rubber O-ring from the rack piston assembly.
13. Remove the rack bushing oil seal using the bushing holding tool T74P-3504-E or equivalent, the oil seal removal tool T78P-3504-J or equivalent, and the slide hammer.
14. Remove the rubber O-ring from the bushing.
15. Remove the input shaft support bearing from its bore in the valve housing using a slide hammer. Remove the oil seal.
16. Pry the input shaft dust seal out of the valve housing. Be careful not to damage the surfaces of the valve housing.

Assembly

1. Assemble the steering gear in the reverse order of the disassembly procedure.
2. Be sure to fill the input shaft dust seal bore with lubricant, before installing the dust seal.
3. Coat all new components with power steering fluid before installation.

4. Using a left hand threaded easy out tool, remove the spiral pin that locks the tie rod assembly to the rack. Repeat the procedure to the other side of the rack assembly.

5. Push out the rack to expose several rack teeth. Hold the rack with an adjustable wrench positioned on the rack teeth against the rack shoulder. Remove both tie rod assemblies using the adjustable wrench and tool T81P-3504-G or equivalent.

Assembly

1. Assembly is the reverse of the disassembly procedure.

2. Be sure to repair or replace all defective components as required.

3. Torque the tie rod ball housing to 50-55 ft. lbs.

INPUT SHAFT AND VALVE ASSEMBLY WITH GEAR IN VEHICLE

Disassembly

1. Set the steering in the straight ahead position. Lock the steering wheel. Raise the vehicle and support it safely.

2. Remove the bellow clamps and slide the bellows outboard from the gear housing. Clean the fluid from the boots.

3. Remove the pinion cap. Position a drain pan under the pinion area and lower the vehicle to the ground.

4. Remove the column boot from the dash panel. Disconnect the intermediate shaft from the gear. It may be necessary to loosen the steering column in order to separate the intermediate shaft from the steering gear.

5. Turn the gear input shaft to the on center position so that the D flat is in the the 3 o'clock position and the wheels are in the straight ahead position.

6. Remove the snapring that retains the shaft seal to the gear housing.

7. Install the input shaft and valve body puller tool T81P-3504-T or equivalent to the input shaft. Turn the nut and remove the valve assembly.

8. Remove the valve assembly slowly in order to prevent oil spillage. Be sure to protect the carpet inside the vehicle, before removing the shaft.

9. Both the input shaft seal and the bearing will come out of the valve body.

10. To remove the lower pinion shaft oil seal, insert the protective sleeve tool T81P-3504-E and T78P-3504-E or equivalent into the steering gear housing. Tap the tool to bottom it. Activate the expander tool by holding the large nut and turning the small nut until it is fully expanded.

11. Pull the tool and the seal out using a pair of pliers. Oil will drain out of the valve bore.

Assembly

1. Assembly of the input shaft and valve is the reverse of the disassembly procedure.

2. Install the pinion oil seal in the valve bore, seating the seal against the shoulder.

NOTE: To protect seal outer diameter from sharp edge of step inside valve bore, use sizing tool T81P-3504-M3 or equivalent as a guide with its small diameter end in valve bore.

3. Insert valve sizing tube tool T81P-3504-M3 or equivalent into valve housing. Position D-flat on input shaft to right and vertical (3 o'clock position), and insert valve assembly in bore.

NOTE: D-flat surface must be in the 3 o'clock position in vehicle with gear on center (straight ahead position). Rotate input shaft slightly, if necessary, to mesh pinion with rack teeth. Push valve assembly in by hand until seated properly. Remove sizing tool.

4. With wheels off floor, using tool T81P-3504-R or equivalent to turn input shaft, check if pinion is centered by counting number of turns from center to each stop (approximately 1-1/2 turns). If number of turns is unequal, pull valve assembly out far enough to free pinion teeth. Rotate input shaft 60 degrees (one tooth) in direction which required less turns. Reinsert valve assembly and check if on center. Repeat procedure if not on center.

INPUT SHAFT AND VALVE ASSEMBLY— GEAR OUT OF VEHICLE

Disassembly

1. Remove the steering gear from the vehicle. Position the assembly in a suitable holding fixture. Clean the exterior of the gear.

2. The external pressure lines should not be removed if there is no evidence of leakage at the fittings. If the lines require removal, the copper seals must be replaced.

3. Loosen the yoke plug locknut. Remove the plug and lift out the spring and plug. Remove the steering gear housing cap.

4. Install input shaft removal tool T81P-3504-R or equivalent on the input shaft. Hold the input shaft and remove the pinion bearing locknut. Discard the locknut.

5. Do not allow the rack teeth to reach full travel when loosening or tightening the locknut.

6. Remove the snapring retaining the shaft seal to the gear housing.

7. Install the input shaft and valve body puller tool T81P-3504-T or equivalent to the input shaft.

8. Turn the nut and remove the valve assembly. Tap the tool in order to bottom it. Activate the expander by holding the large nut until it fully expands. Remove the tool and the seal using a slide hammer.

9. If necessary, remove the pinion bearing from the gear housing using the lower pinion bearing removal tool T81P-3505-S, T58L-101-A and T81P-3504-T or equivalent.

10. Remove the input shaft and valve assembly seal rings, by pushing the rings to the side with a small pointed tool. Be careful not to nick or scratch the valve sleeve. Do not replace the rings unless they are damaged.

Assembly

1. Assembly of the input shaft and valve is the reverse of the disassembly procedure.

2. Install the pinion oil seal in the valve bore, seating the seal against the shoulder.

NOTE: To protect seal outer diameter from sharp edge of step inside valve bore, use sizing tool T81P-3504-M3 or equivalent as a guide with its small diameter end in valve bore.

3. Insert valve sizing tube tool T81P-3504-M3 or equivalent into valve housing. Position D-flat on input shaft to right and vertical (3 o'clock position), and insert valve assembly in bore.

NOTE: D-flat surface must be in the 3 o'clock position in vehicle with gear on center (straight ahead position). Rotate input shaft slightly, if necessary, to mesh pinion with rack teeth. Push valve assembly in by hand until seated properly. Remove sizing tool.

4. With wheels off floor, using tool T81P-3504-R or equivalent to turn input shaft, check if pinion is centered by counting number of turns from center to each stop (approximately 1-1/2 turns). If number of turns is unequal, pull valve assembly out far enough to free pinion teeth. Rotate input shaft 60 degrees (one tooth) in direction which required less turns. Reinsert valve assembly and check if on center. Repeat procedure if not on center.

FORD MOTOR COMPANY
POWER STEERING PUMP

POWER STEERING PUMP RESERVOIR

Disassembly

1. With the pump removed from the vehicle, place the pump assembly in a soft jaw vise or equivalent and remove the outlet fitting, flow control valve and spring.
2. Remove the fiberglass reservoir, discard the O-ring seal on the pump housing. Do not use a hammer on the fiberglass reservoir.

Assembly

1. Install a new O-ring seal on the pump housing and apply petroleum jelly or equivalent to the reservoir O-ring seal and on the inside edge of the reservoir.
2. Place the reservoir over the pump body and align the outlet fitting hole in the reservoir with the hole in the valve cover.
3. Place new O-ring seals on the outlet fitting. Install the flow control spring, flow control valve and the outlet fitting into the reservoir and valve cover. Torque the fitting to 25–34 ft. lbs. (34–46 Nm).

NOTE: If the valve is cocked, it may become stuck in the valve cover. Do not force the valve forward, because in doing so the valve may shear off metal which in turn would allow metal chips to enter the valve bore.

POWER STEERING PUMP

Disassembly

NOTE: The pulley on the power steering pump must be removed before the pump can be removed from the vehicle.

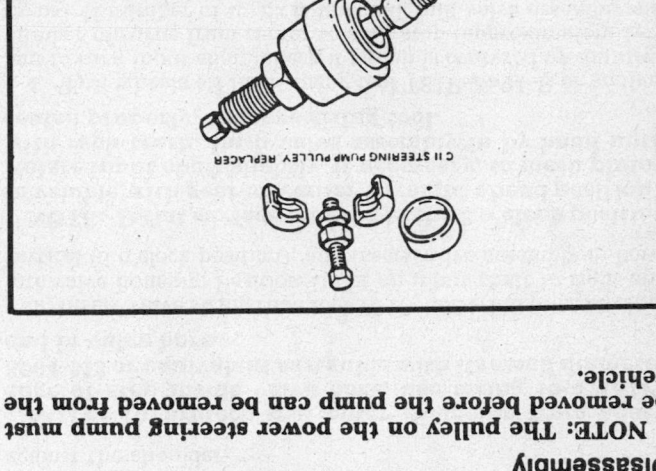

Power steering pump pulley removal and installation tools

5. If the valve sleeve rings were removed, installation is as follows:

a. Install sleeve tool T8IP-3503-M1 over valve assembly. Lubricate tool with automatic transmission and power steering fluid Type F, or equivalent.

b. Place a ring over the tool. Rapidly push down on pusher tool T8IP-3405-M2 or equivalent forcing the ring down into the fourth groove.

c. Lubricate inside of sizing tool T8IP-3504-M3 or equivalent with power steering fluid. Slowly work the sizing tool over the ring taking care not to deform the ring. This step should be performed after each ring is installed.

d. Install a spacer tool T8IP-3504-M4 or equivalent with the thin lip toward the input shaft splines over input shaft. This aligns the sleeve tool T8IP-3504-M1 or equivalent with the third groove. Repeat Steps a, b and c.

e. Install the second spacer on top of the first with lip in the same direction. Repeat Steps a, b and c.

f. Flip the second spacer so the thin lips are together. Repeat Steps a, b and c.

6. Remove the sizing tube and check the condition of the rings. Make sure that the rings turn freely in the grooves.

Removing the reservoir

Positioning the pump assembly in the C-clamp tool

33-20

1. Disconnect the fluid return hose at the reservoir and drain the fluid into a suitable drain pan.

2. Remove the pressure hose from the pump fitting (leave the fitting in the pump) and remove the drive belt from the pump pulley.

3. Install the special pump pulley remover tool T75L-3733-A or equivalent onto the pulley hub.

4. Hold the small hex head on the tool, and rotate the tool nut counterclockwise to remove the pulley. Do not apply in and out pressure on the pump shaft for this could cause damage to the internal thrust area.

5. Remove the pump from the vehicle (refer to the individual vehicle section for more information on pump removal) and remove the outlet fitting, flow control valve, and flow control spring from the pump and remove the pump reservoir.

6. Place a C-clamp tool T74P-3044-A1 or equivalent in a bench vise. Place the lower support plate tool T78P-3733-A2 or equivalent over the pump rotor shaft.

7. Install the upper compression plate tool T78P-3733-A1 or equivalent, into the upper portion of the C-clamp. Holding the upper compression tool, place the pump assembly into the C-clamp with the rotor shaft facing down.

8. Tighten the C-clamp until a slight bottoming of the valve is felt. Located in the side of the pump housing is a small hole, through this hole, insert a small drift or a suitable tool and push inward on the valve cover retaining ring.

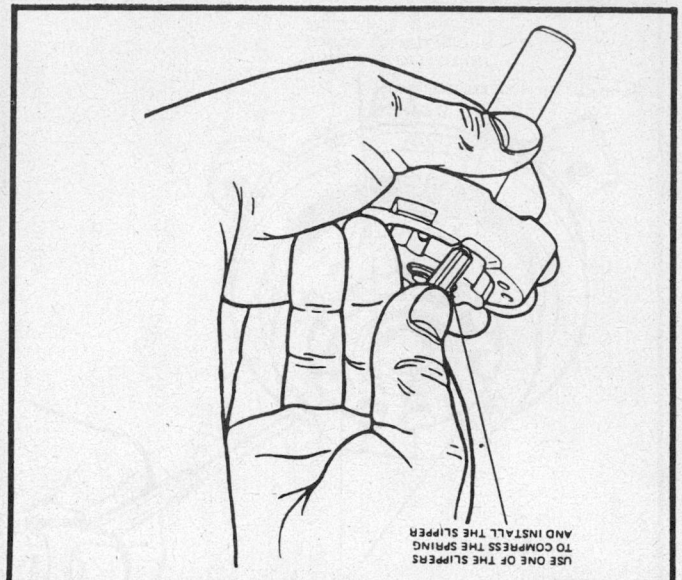

The slippers and springs assembly

INDEX THE ROTOR EITHER RIGHT OR LEFT TO THE NEXT CAVITY AND INSTALL ANOTHER SPRING AND SLIPPER UNTIL ALL (10) CAVITIES ARE FILLED

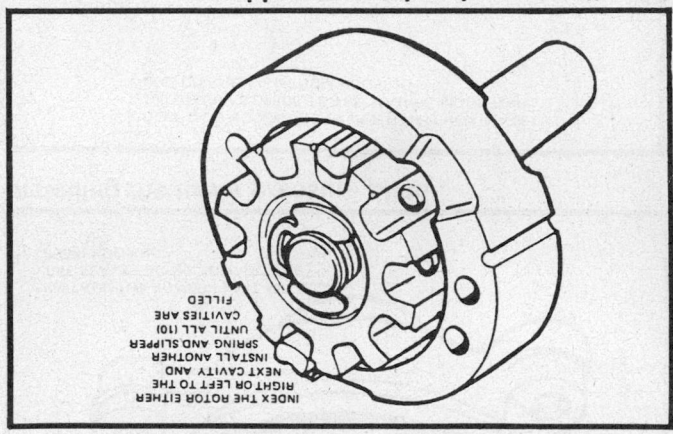

Installing the slipper

USE ONE OF THE SLIPPERS TO COMPRESS THE SPRING AND INSTALL THE SLIPPER

9. While applying inward pressure on the retaining ring, place a suitable tool under the edge of the retaining ring and remove the ring.

10. Loosen the C-clamp, remove the upper compression plate and remove the pump assembly. Remove the pump valve cover and discard the O-ring seal.

11. Apply downward pressure on the rotor shaft to remove the rotor shaft, upper plate, rotating group assembly and the dowel pins.

12. The lower plate and the belleville spring will remain in the pump housing. To remove them, place the pump housing on a flat surface, raise it slightly and slam the housing down until the lower plate and the belleville spring fall out. Discard the O-ring seals.

13. Remove the rotor shaft seal and the seal retainer ring at the same time by prying them out with a suitable tool.

NOTE: Inspect and wash all parts in clean solvent, blow out all passages with compressed air and air dry the cleaned parts.

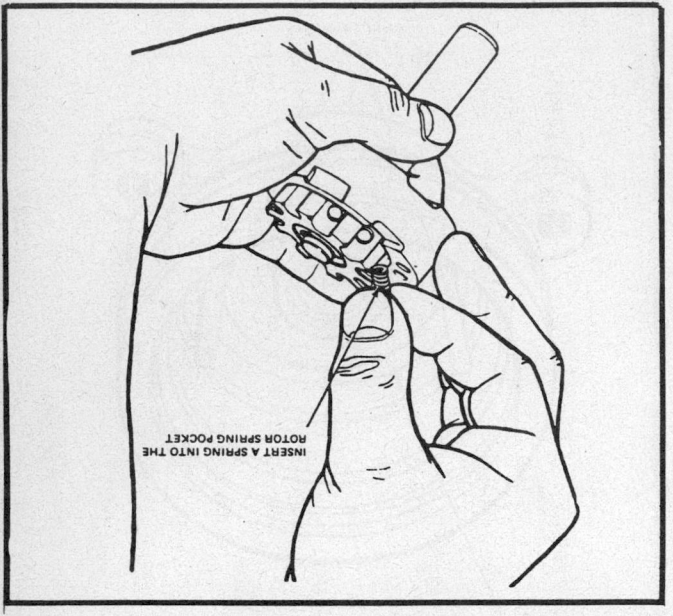

Disassembled pump components

HOUSING
DOWEL PIN
LOWER PLATE
UPPER PLATE
COVER

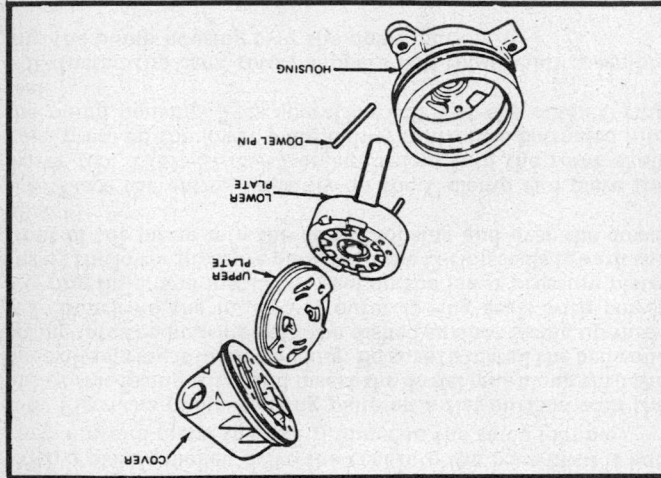

Rotor spring installation

INSERT A SPRING INTO THE ROTOR SPRING POCKET

Installing the belleville spring and dowel pins

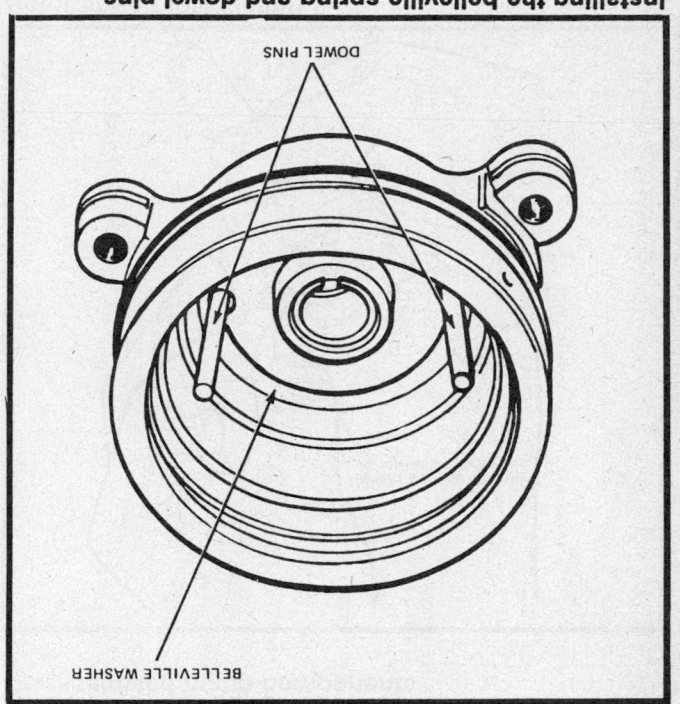

DOWEL PINS

BELLEVILLE WASHER

Assembly

NOTE: The first 4 steps are to be used only if the rotating group was disassembled for cleaning and inspection.

1. Place the rotor of the shaft splines with the triangle detent in the rotor counterbore facing upwards. Install the retaining ring in the groove at the end of the rotor shaft.

2. Place the insert cam over the rotor and be sure the recessed notch on the insert cam faces up. With the rotor extended upward, halfway out of the cam, insert a spring into a rotor spring pocket. Work the spring into the rotor cavity directly beneath the recessed flats on the cam.

3. Use 1 of the slippers to compress the spring and install the slipper with the groove facing the cam profile. Repeat Step two on the slipper cavity beneath the opposite inlet recess.

4. Holding the cam stationary, index the rotor either right or left a space, and install another spring and slipper until all 10 rotor cavities have been filled.

NOTE: Turn the rotor slow and carefully, so that the springs and slippers already installed do not fall out.

5. Using a suitable seal driver, install a new rotor shaft seal. With a plastic mallet, drive the seal into the bore until it bottoms out and install the seal retainer in the same manner.

6. Place the pump housing plate on a flat surface with the pulley side facing down and insert the dowel pins along with the belleville spring into the housing. Be sure to install the belleville spring into the housing with the dished surface facing upward.

7. Lubricate the inner and outer O-ring seals with power steering fluid, and install the seal on the lower pressure plate. Insert the lower pressure plate with the O-ring seals toward the front of the pump into the pump housing and over the dowel pins.

8. Place the entire assembly on the C-clamp and place the driver tool T78P-3733-A3 or equivalent into the rotor shaft hole, press on the lower plate lightly, until it is bottomed into the pump housing. This operation will seat the outer O-ring seal.

9. Install the cam, rotor, slippers and rotor shaft assembly into the pump housing over the dowel pins.

Installing the lower pressure plate

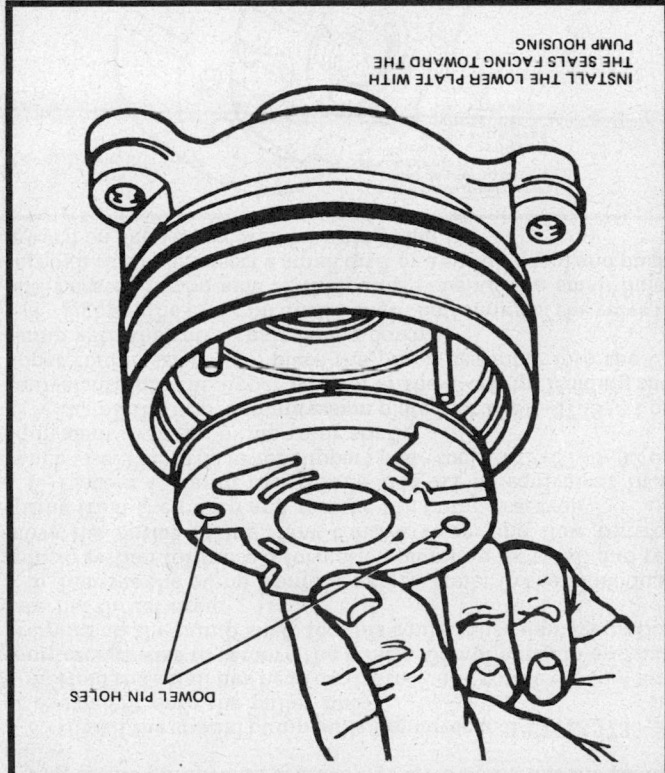

NOTE: When installing this assembly into the pump housing, the holes in the assembly must be used for the pump housing.

DOWEL PIN HOLES

PUMP HOUSING

INSTALL THE LOWER PLATE WITH THE SEALS FACING TOWARD THE PUMP HOUSING

Rotor, cam and slippers assembly installed

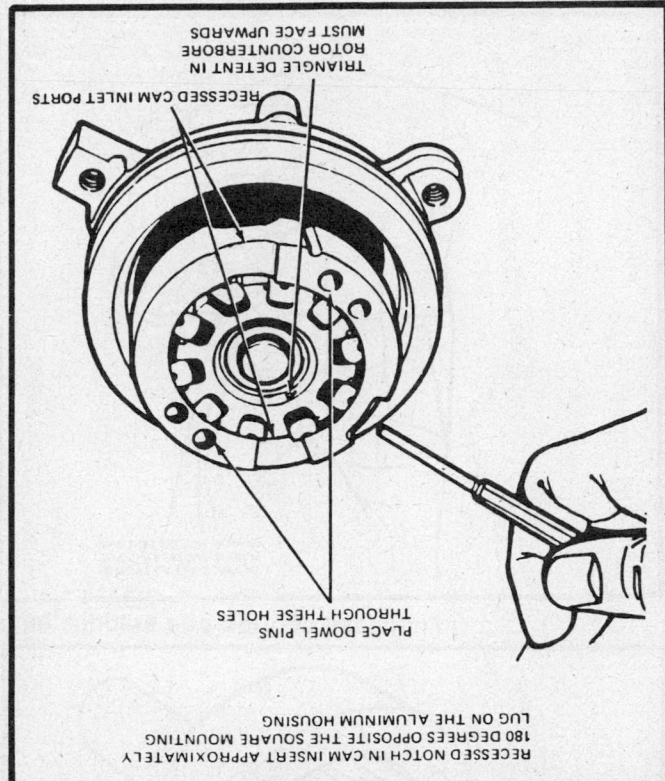

RECESSED CAM INLET PORTS

TRIANGLE DETENT IN ROTOR COUNTERBORE MUST FACE UPWARDS

PLACE DOWEL PINS THROUGH THESE HOLES

RECESSED NOTCH IN CAM INSERT APPROXIMATELY 180 DEGREES OPPOSITE THE SQUARE MOUNTING LUG ON THE ALUMINUM HOUSING

Install the pitman arm and draw the arm into position with the nut.

ADJUSTER PLUG AND ROTARY VALVE

Removal and Installation

1. Thoroughly clean exterior of gear assembly. Drain by holding valve ports down and rotating worm back and forth through entire travel.
2. Place gear in vise.
3. Loosen adjuster plug locknut with punch. Remove adjuster plug.
4. Remove rotary valve assembly by grasping stub shaft and pulling it out.
5. Installation is the reverse of the removal procedure.

ADJUSTER PLUG

Disassembly and Assembly

1. Remove upper thrust bearing retainer using the proper tool. Be careful not to damage bearing bore. Discard retainer.
   Remove spacer, upper bearing and races. Discard adjuster plug O-ring.
3. Remove stub shaft seal retaining ring and remove and discard dust seal.
4. Remove stub shaft seal by prying out with a suitable tool and discard.
5. Examine needle bearing and, if required, remove same by pressing from thrust bearing end.
6. Inspect thrust bearing spacer, bearing rollers and races.
7. Reassembly is the reverse of above.

ROTARY VALVE

Disassembly

Repairs are seldom needed. Do not disassemble unless absolutely necessary. If the O-ring seal on valve spool dampener needs replacement, perform this portion of operation only.

1. Remove cap-to-worm O-ring seal and discard.
2. Remove valve spool spring by prying on small coil with a

GENERAL MOTORS SAGINAW ROTARY TYPE POWER STEERING MODEL 605

dowel pins, and the recessed notch in the cam insert must face the reservoir and approximately 180 degrees opposite the square mounting lug on the aluminum housing.

10. Place the upper pressure plate over the dowel pins, with the recess directly over the recessed notch on the cam insert and approximately 180 degrees opposite the square mounting lug.
11. Place a new O-ring seal on the valve cover and lubricate the seal with power steering fluid. Be sure that the plastic baffle is placed securely in the valve cover. If the baffle is loose, apply a coat of petroleum jelly or equivalent on the baffle and install it in its location on the valve cover.
12. Insert the valve cover over the dowel pins and be sure the outlet fitting hole in the valve cover is directly in line with the square mounting lug of the aluminum housing.
13. Place the entire assembly in the C-clamp tool and compress the valve cover into the pump housing, until the retaining ring groove is exposed in the pump housing.
14. Install the valve cover retaining ring with the ends near the access hole in the pump housing. Remove the pump assembly from the C-clamp tool.
15. Place a new O-ring seal on the pump housing and lubricate the seal with power steering fluid.
16. Install the flow control spring and flow control valve into the valve cover and install the power steering pump reservoir.
17. Place a new O-ring seal on the outlet fitting and lubricate the seal with power steering fluid. Install the outlet fitting into the valve cover, and torque it to 25–34 ft. lbs. (34–46 Nm).
18. Install the pump assembly on the vehicle and place the pulley onto the pump shaft.
19. Install special pulley tool T65P-3A733-C or equivalent onto the pump pulley, the small diameter threads on the tool should be engaged in the pump shaft.
20. Hold the small hex head of the tool nut and rotate the tool clockwise to install the pulley on the shaft. The pulley face must be flush within 0.010 in. (0.25mm). Remove the tool.

NOTE: Do not apply in and out pressure on the pump shaft for this could cause damage to the internal thrust area.

21. Install all lines to the pump and refill the reservoir (with the specified power steering fluid). Start the engine, inspect for leaks and recheck the fluid level after bleeding the air from the pump.

Checking Steering Effort

Run the engine to attain normal operating temperatures. With the wheels on a dry floor, hook a pull scale to the spoke of the steering wheel at the outer edge. The effort required to turn the steering wheel should be 3½–5 lbs. If the pull is not within these limits, check the hydraulic pressure.

Pressure Test

To check the hydraulic pressure, disconnect the pressure hose from the gear. Now connect the pressure gauge between the pressure hose from the pump and the steering gear housing. Run the engine to attain normal operating temperatures, then turn the wheel to a full right and a full left turn to the wheel stops.

Hold the wheel in this position only long enough to obtain an accurate reading.

The pressure gauge reading should be within the limits specified. If the pressure reading is less than the minimum pressure needed for proper operation, close the valve at the gauge and see if the reading increases. If the pressure is still low, the pump is defective and needs repair. If the pressure reading is at or near the minimum reading, the pump is normal and needs only an adjustment of the power steering gear or power assist control valve.

Worm Bearing Preload and Sector Mesh Adjustments

Disconnect the pitman arm from the sector shaft, then back off on the sector shaft adjusting screw on the sector shaft cover. Center the steering on the high point, then attach a pull scale to the spoke of the steering wheel at the outer edge. The pull required to keep the wheel moving for a complete turn should be ½–⅔ lbs.

If the pull is not within these limits, loosen the thrust bearing locknut and tighten or back off on the valve sleeve adjuster locknut to bring the preload within limits. Tighten the thrust bearing the preload and recheck the preload.

Slowly rotate the steering wheel several times, then center the steering on the high point. Now, turn the sector shaft adjusting screw until a steering wheel pull of 1–1½ lbs. is required to move the worm through the center point. Tighten the sector shaft adjusting screw and recheck the sector mesh adjustment.

Correct installation of thrust bearing races

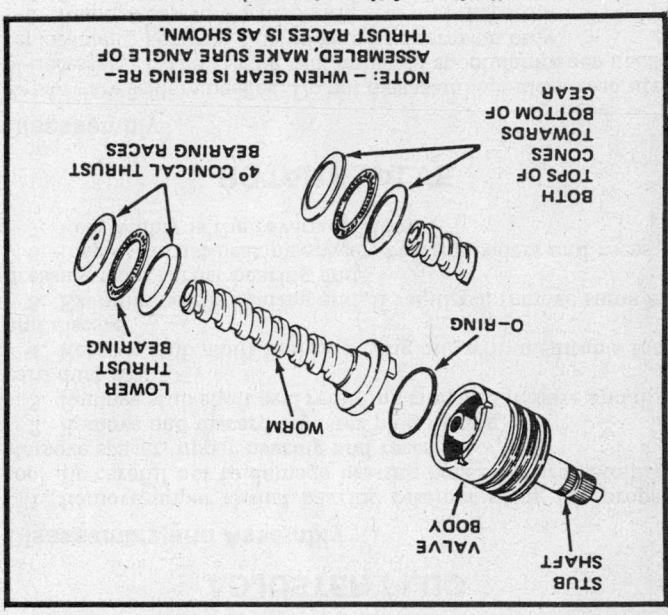

NOTE: — WHEN GEAR IS BEING RE-
ASSEMBLED, MAKE SURE ANGLE OF
THRUST RACES IS AS SHOWN.

BOTH
TOPS OF
CONES
TOWARDS
BOTTOM OF
GEAR

4° CONICAL THRUST
BEARING RACES

LOWER
THRUST
BEARING

WORM

O-RING

STUB SHAFT

VALVE
BODY

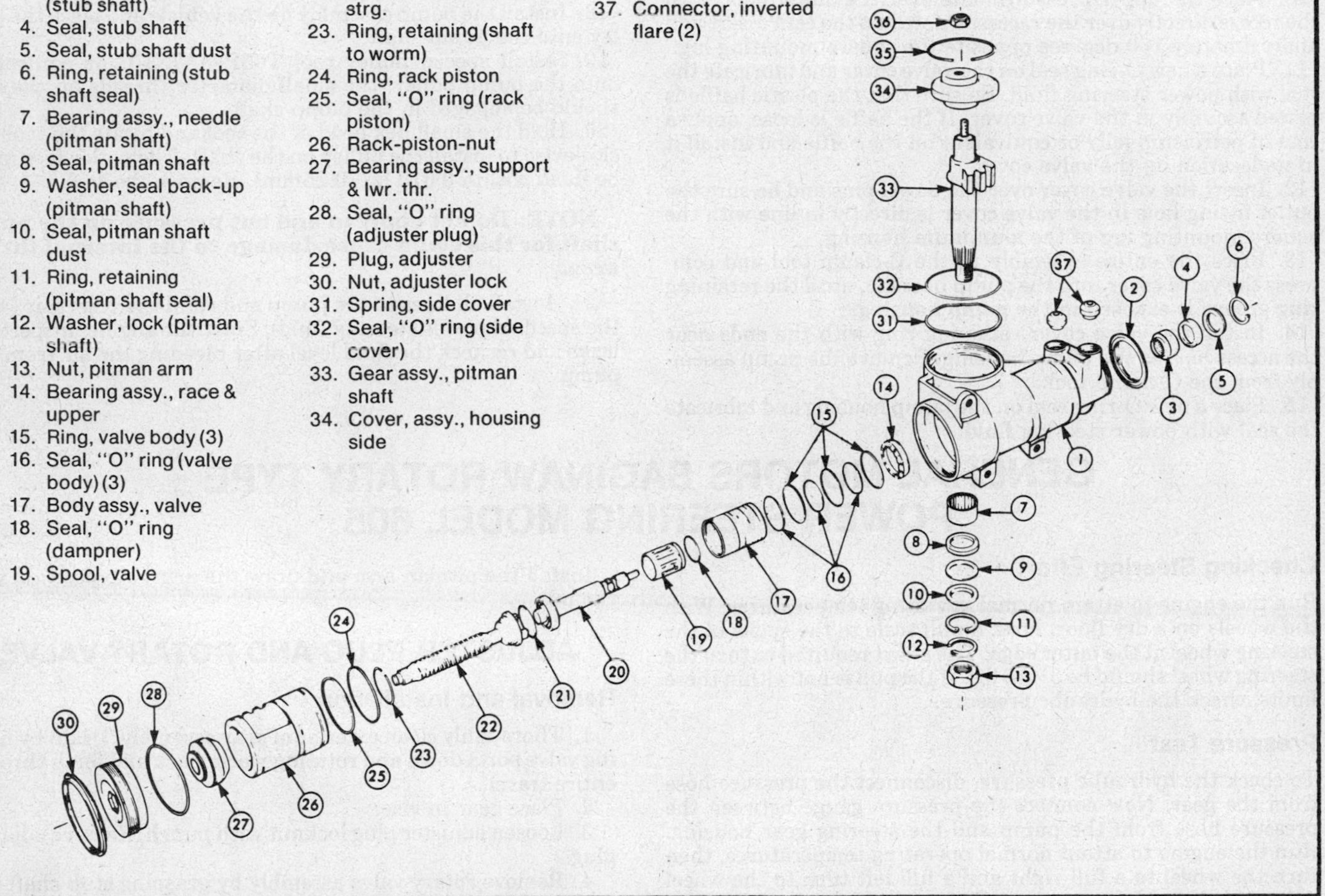

Exploded view of model 605 power steering gear

1. Housing, steering gear.
2. Retainer, strg. coupling shield
3. Bearing assy., needle (stub shaft)
4. Seal, stub shaft
5. Seal, stub shaft dust
6. Ring, retaining (stub shaft seal)
7. Bearing assy., needle (pitman shaft)
8. Seal, pitman shaft back-up
9. Washer, seal back-up (pitman shaft)
10. Seal, pitman shaft dust
11. Ring, retaining (pitman shaft seal)
12. Washer, lock (pitman shaft)
13. Nut, pitman arm
14. Bearing assy., race & upper
15. Ring, valve body (3)
16. Seal, "O" ring (valve body) (3)
17. Body assy., valve
18. Seal, "O" ring
19. Spool, valve (damper)
20. Shaft assy., stub
21. Seal, "O" ring (shaft to worm)
22. Worm assy., pin & to worm)
23. Ring, retaining (shaft to worm
24. Ring, rack piston
25. Seal, "O" ring (rack piston)
26. Rack-piston-nut
27. Bearing assy., support & lwr. thr.
28. Seal, "O" ring (adjuster plug)
29. Plug, adjuster
30. Nut, adjuster lock
31. Spring, side cover
32. Seal, "O" ring (side cover)
33. Gear assy., pitman shaft
34. Cover, assy., housing side
35. Ring, retaining (side cover)
36. Nut, preload adjuster
37. Connector, inverted flare (2)

Assembly

NOTE: All parts must be free of dirt, chips, etc., before assembly and must be protected after assembly.

1. Lubricate 3 new back-up O-ring seals with power steering fluid, or equivalent and reassemble in the ring grooves of valve body. Assemble 3 new valve body rings in the grooves over the O-ring seals by carefully slipping over the valve body.

NOTE: If the valve body rings seem loose or twisted in the grooves, the heat of the oil during operation will cause them to straighten.

2. Lubricate a new dampener O-ring with power steering fluid, or equivalent and install in valve spool groove.

3. Assemble stub shaft torsion bar and cap assembly in the valve body, aligning the groove in the valve cap with the pin in the valve body. Tap lightly with soft hammer until cap is against

3. Remove valve spool by holding the valve assembly in 1 hand with the stub shaft pointing down. Insert the end of pencil or wood rod through opening in valve body cap and push spool until it is out far enough to be removed. In this procedure, rotate to prevent jamming. If spool becomes jammed it may be necessary to remove stub shaft, torsion bar and cap assembly.

small pry bar, work the spring onto the bearing surface of the stub shaft. Slide spring off shaft. Be careful not to damage shaft surface.

GENERAL MOTORS/AMC SAGINAW ROTARY TYPE POWER STEERING MODEL 800/808

ADJUSTER PLUG AND ROTARY VALVE

Removal

1. Thoroughly clean exterior of gear assembly. Drain by holding valve ports down and rotating worm back and forth through entire travel.
2. Place gear in vise.
3. Loosen adjuster plug locknut with punch. Remove adjuster plug.
4. Remove rotary valve assembly by grasping stub shaft and pulling it out.
5. Installation is the reverse of the removal procedure.

Installation

1. Align narrow pin slot on valve body with valve body drive pin on the worm. Insert the valve assembly onto gear housing by pressing against valve body with finger tips. Do not press on stub shaft or torsion bar. The return hole in the gear housing should be fully visible when properly assembled.

NOTE: Do not press on stub shaft as this may cause shaft and cap to pull out of valve body, allowing the spool dampener O-ring seal to slip into valve body oil grooves.

2. With protector over end of stub shaft, install adjuster plug assembly snugly into gear housing then back plug off approximately one-eighth turn. Install plug locknut but do not tighten. Adjust preload.
3. After adjustment, tighten locknut.

ADJUSTER PLUG

Disassembly and Assembly

1. Remove upper thrust bearing retainer using the proper tool. Be careful not to damage bearing bore. Discard retainer. Remove spacer, upper bearing and races.
2. Remove and discard adjuster plug O-ring.
3. Remove stub shaft seal retaining ring and remove and discard dust seal.
4. Remove stub shaft seal.
5. Examine needle bearing and, if required, remove same by pressing from thrust bearing end.
6. Inspect thrust bearing spacer, bearing rollers and races.
7. Reassemble in reverse of above.

ROTARY VALVE

Disassembly

Repairs are seldom needed. Do not disassemble unless absolutely necessary. If the O-ring seal on valve spool dampener needs replacement, perform this portion of operation only.

1. Remove cap-to-worm O-ring seal and discard.
2. Remove valve spool spring by prying on small coil with small screw driver to work spring onto bearing surface of stub shaft. Slide spring off shaft. Be careful not to damage shaft surface.
3. Remove valve spool by holding the valve assembly in 1 hand with the stub shaft pointing down. Insert the end of pencil or wood rod through opening in valve body cap and push spool until it is out far enough to be removed. In this procedure, rotate to prevent jamming. If spool becomes jammed it may be necessary to remove stub shaft, torsion bar and cap assembly.

Assembly

NOTE: All parts must be free of dirt, chips, etc., before assembly and must be protected after assembly.

1. Lubricate 3 new back-up O-ring seals with power steering valve body shoulder. Valve body pin must be in the cap groove. Hold parts together during the remainder of assembly.
4. Lubricate spool. With notch in spool toward valve body, slide the spool over the stub shaft. Align the notch on the spool with the spool drive pin or stub shaft and carefully engage spool with the spool drive pin in valve body bore. Push spool evenly and with slight rotating motion until spool reaches drive pin. Rotate spool slowly, with some pressure, until notch engages drive pin. Be sure dampener O-ring seal is evenly distributed in the spool groove.

NOTE: Use extreme care because spool-to-valve body clearance is very small. Damage is easily caused.

5. With seal protector tool over stub shaft, slide valve spool spring over stub shaft, with small diameter of spring going over shaft last. Work spring onto shaft until small coil is located in studshaft groove.
6. Lubricate a new cap-to-O-ring seal and install in valve body.

RACK—PISTON NUT AND WORM ASSEMBLY

Removal and Installation

1. Completely drain the gear assembly and thoroughly clean the outside.
2. Remove pitman shaft assembly.
3. Rotate housing end plug retaining ring so that 1 end of ring is over hole in gear housing. Spring 1 end of ring so a suitable tool can be inserted to lift out ring.
4. Rotate stub shaft to a full left turn position to force end plug out of housing.
5. Remove and discard housing end plug O-ring seal.
6. Remove rack-piston nut end plug with $\frac{1}{2}$ in. square drive.
7. Insert tool in end of worm. Turn stub shaft so that rack-piston nut will go into tool and remove rack-piston nut from gear housing.
8. Remove adjuster plug and rotary valve assemblies.
9. Remove worm and lower thrust bearing and races.
10. Remove cap-to-O-ring seal and discard.
11. Installation is the reverse of the removal procedure.

Disassembly and Assembly

1. Remove and discard piston ring and back-up O-ring on rack-piston nut.
2. Remove ball guide clamp and return guide.
3. Place nut on clean cloth and remove ball retaining tool. Make sure all balls are removed.
4. Inspect all parts for wear, nicks, scoring or burrs. If worm or rack-piston nut need replacing, both must be replaced as a matched pair.
5. In assembling, reverse the above.

NOTE: When assembling, alternate black and white balls, and install guide and clamp. Packing with grease helps in holding during assembly. When new balls are used, various sizes are available and a selection must be made to secure proper torque when making the high point adjustment.

Exploded view of the valve body and shaft assembly

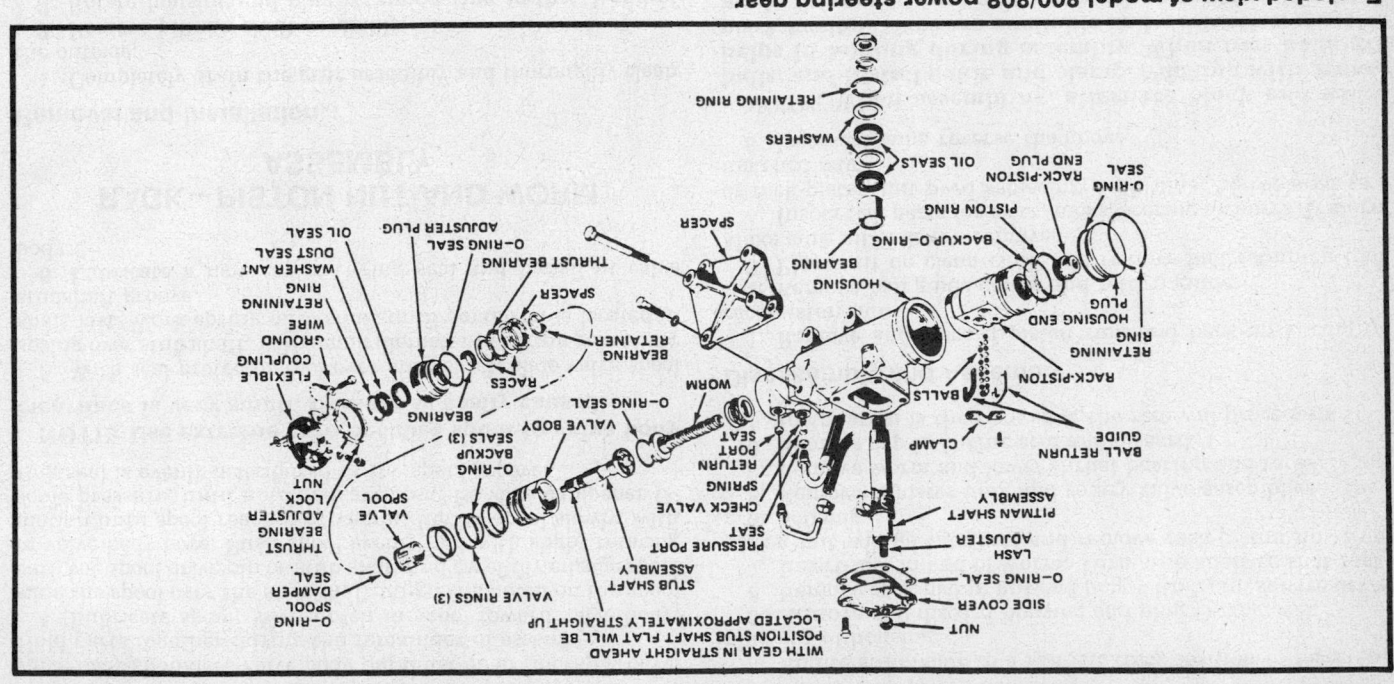

5. With seal protector tool over stub shaft, slide valve spool spring over stub shaft, with small diameter of spring going over shaft last. Work spring onto shaft until small coil is located in stubshaft groove.

NOTE: Use extreme care because spool-to-valve body clearance is very small. Damage is easily caused.

4. Lubricate spool. With notch in spool toward valve body, slide the spool over the stub shaft. Align the notch on the spool with the spool drive pin on stub shaft and carefully engage spool in valve body bore. Push spool evenly and with slight rotating motion until spool reaches drive pin. Rotate spool slowly, with some pressure, until notch engages pin. Be sure dampener O-ring seal is evenly distributed in the spool groove.

3. Assemble stub shaft torsion bar and cap assembly in the valve body, aligning the groove in the valve cap with the pin in the valve body. Tap lightly with soft hammer until cap is against valve body shoulder. Valve body pin must be in the cap groove. Hold parts together during the remainder of assembly.

2. Lubricate a new dampener O-ring with power steering fluid, or equivalent and install in valve spool groove.

NOTE: If the valve body rings seem loose or twisted in the grooves, the heat of the oil during operation will cause them to straighten.

fluid, or equivalent and reassemble in the ring grooves of valve body. Assemble 3 new valve body rings in the grooves over the O-ring seals by carefully slipping over the valve body.

Installation of ball nut or shaft

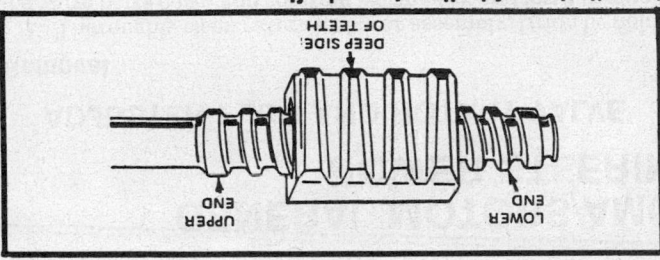

Exploded view of stub shaft and wormshaft assembly

NOTE: — WHEN GEAR IS BEING REASSEMBLED, MAKE SURE ANGLE OF THRUST RACES IS AS SHOWN.

Exploded view of model 800/808 power steering gear

WITH GEAR IN STRAIGHT AHEAD POSITION STUB SHAFT FLAT WILL BE LOCATED APPROXIMATELY STRAIGHT UP

Typical power steering rack and pinion assembly

1. Housing assy, R&P
2. Bushing, upper pinion
3. Seal, rack & pinion
4. Valve assy, pinion &
5. Ring, valve body (4)
6. Ring, retaining
7. Annulus, stub shaft bearing
8. Bearing assy, needle
9. Seal, stub shaft
10. Seal, stub shaft dust
11. Ring, retaining
12. Adapter, seal
13. Bearing, rack
14. Spring, adjuster
15. Plug, adjuster
16. Nut, adjuster plug lock
17. Ring, shock dampener
18. Rod assy, inner tie (LT)
19. Clamp, boot
20. Boot, rack & pinion
21. Nut, hex jam
22. Rod assy, outer tie (LT)
23. Fitting, lubrication
24. Seal, tie rod
25. Nut, hexagon slotted
26. Pin, cotter
27. Bearing assy, ball
28. Ring, retaining
29. Nut, hex lock
30. Cover, dust
31. Grommet, mounting (LT)
32. Ring, retaining
33. Grommet assembly, mounting (RT)
34. Tube, breather
35. Seal, O-ring
36. Seal, O-ring
37. Line assy, cylinder (LT)
38. Line assy, cylinder (RT)
39. Cap, dust
40. Seal, inner rack
41. Rack assy, piston & steering
42. Ring, piston
43. Bulkhead, cylinder inner
44. Seal, rack & pinion (bulkhead)
45. Seal, O-ring (bulkhead)
46. Bulkhead, cylinder outer
47. Ring, bulkhead retaining
48. Rod assy, inner tie (RT)
49. Rod assy, outer tie (RT)

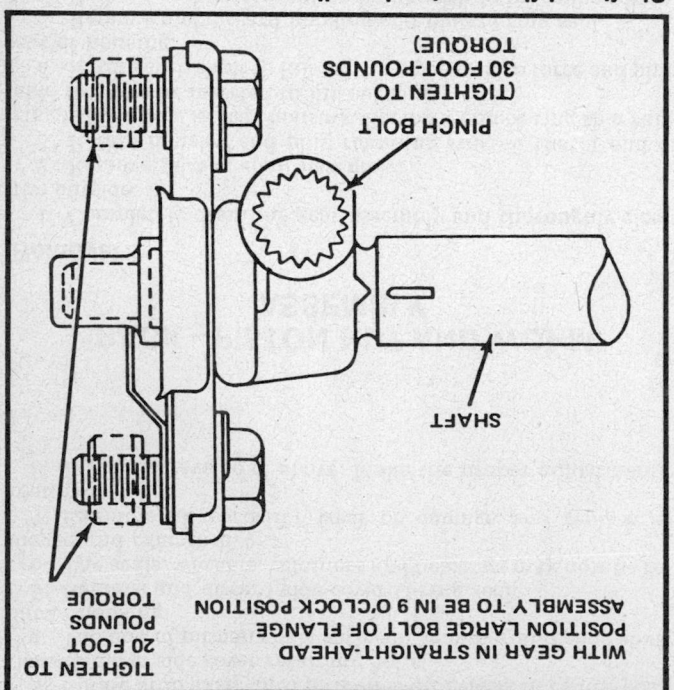

PITMAN SHAFT

Removal and Installation

1. Completely drain the gear assembly and thoroughly clean the outside.
2. Place gear in vise.

6. Lubricate a new cap-to-O-ring seal and install in valve body.

Position of pitman shaft and ball nut

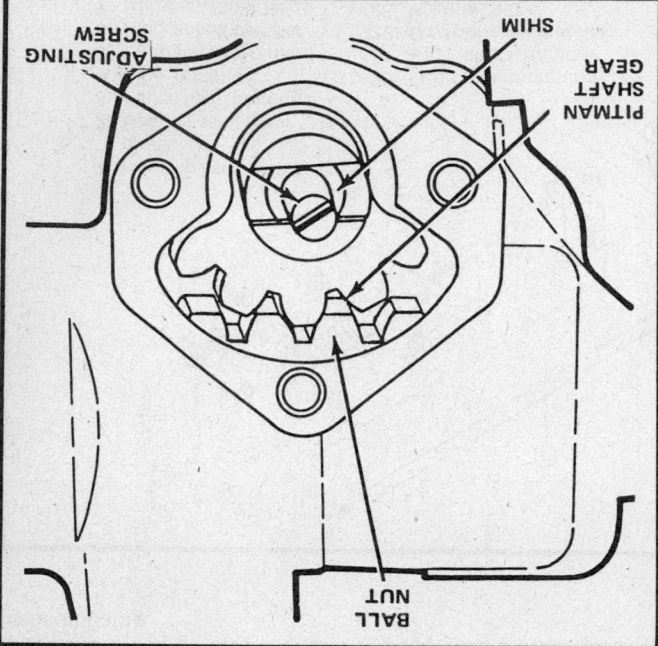

ADJUSTING SCREW

SHIM

PITMAN SHAFT GEAR

BALL NUT

Shaft and flange steering alignment

PINCH BOLT (TIGHTEN TO 30 FOOT-POUNDS TORQUE)

SHAFT

WITH GEAR IN STRAIGHT-AHEAD POSITION LARGE BOLT OF FLANGE ASSEMBLY TO BE IN 9 O'CLOCK POSITION

TIGHTEN TO 20 FOOT POUNDS TORQUE

Adjuster plug assembly sequence

RETAINER

SPACER

SMALL THRUST WASHER

UPPER THRUST BEARING

LARGE THRUST WASHER

O-RING

ADJUSTER PLUG

NEEDLE BEARING

OIL SEAL

DUST SEAL

RETAINING RING

1. Housing asm, rack & pinion
2. Bearing asm, roller pinion
3. Pinion asm, bearing &
4. Ring, retaining
5. Seal, steering pinion
6. Ring, shock damper
7. Rod asm, inner tie
8. Clamp, boot
9. Boot, rack & pinion
10. Nut, hex
11. Rod asm, outer tie
12. Fitting, lubrication
13. Seal, tie rod
14. Nut, hex
15. Pin, cotter
16. Bearing, rack
17. Spring, adjuster
18. Plug, adjuster
19. Nut, adjuster plug lock
20. Grommet, mounting
21. Stud, shock damper
22. Damper asm, steering
23. Washer, flat
24. Nut, hex
25. Bushing, rack
26. Ring, retaining
27. Rack, steering
28. Ring, shock damper
29. Adapter, steering damper
30. Rod asm, inner tie
31. Clamp, boot
32. Boot, rack & pinion
33. Support, boot
34. Rod asm, outer tie

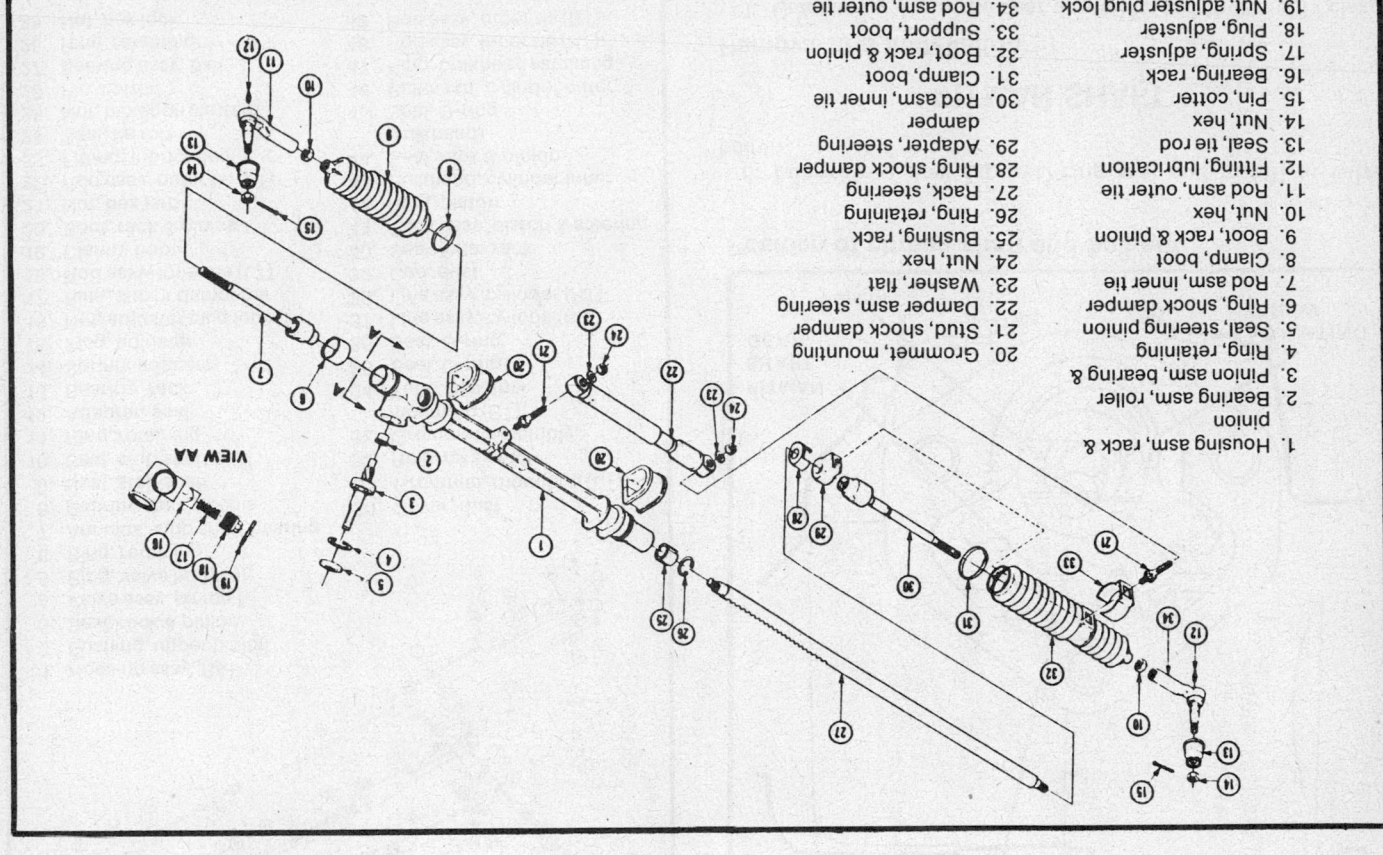

VIEW AA

RACK–PISTON NUT AND WORM ASSEMBLY

Removal

1. Completely drain the gear assembly and thoroughly clean the outside.
2. Remove pitman shaft assembly.
3. Rotate housing end plug retaining ring so that 1 end of ring is over hole in gear housing. Spring 1 end of ring so that a suitable tool can be inserted to lift out ring.
4. Rotate stub shaft to full left turn position to force end plug out of housing.
5. Remove and discard housing end plug O-ring seal.
6. Remove rack-piston nut end plug with 1/2 in. square drive. Insert tool in end of worm. Turn stub shaft so that rack-piston nut will go into tool and remove rack-piston nut from gear housing.

---

3. Rotate stub shaft until pitman shaft gear is in center position. Remove side cover retaining bolts.
4. Tap end of pitman shaft with soft hammer and slide shaft out of housing.
5. Remove and discard side cover O-ring seal.
6. The seals, washers, retainers and bearings may now be removed and examined.
7. Examine all parts for wear or damage and replace as required.
8. Install in reverse of above. Make the proper adjustment.

RACK–PISTON NUT AND WORM

Disassembly and Assembly

1. Remove and discard piston back-up ring and O-ring on rack-piston nut.
2. Remove ball guide clamp and return guide.
3. Place nut on clean cloth and remove ball retaining tool. Make sure all balls are removed.
4. Inspect all parts for wear, nicks, scoring or burrs. If worm or rack-piston nut need replacing, both must be replaced as a matched pair.
5. In assembling, reverse the above.

NOTE: When assembling, alternate black and white balls, and install guide clamp. Packing with grease helps in holding during assembly. When new balls are used, various sizes are available and a selection must be made to secure proper torque when making the high point adjustment.

---

8. Remove adjuster plug and rotary valve assemblies.
9. Remove worm and lower thrust bearing and races.
10. Remove cap-to-O-ring seal and discard.

Installation

1. Install in reverse of removal procedure.
2. In all cases use new O-ring seals.
3. Make adjustments are required.

NOTE: For information on overhauling the power steering pump on AMC vehicles, refer to the GM power steering pump overhaul section.

GENERAL MOTORS POWER STEERING RACK AND PINION ASSEMBLY

Outer Tie Rod Take Off Type

A difference exists between the power steering rack and pinion assemblies used on front wheel drive GM vehicles. The major difference is in the manner of attachment of the steering unit to the vehicle body. The early model is attached by wrap around type brackets and rubber grommets, while the later model is attached by bolts through eyelets and grommets, in the steering housing.

Minor variations exist between the units, both externally and internally, but the basic disassembly and assembly remains the same.

OUTER TIE ROD

Removal
1. Loosen the jam nut and remove the tie rod from the steering knuckle.
2. Remove the outer tie rod by turning it off the inner tie rod. Count the number of turns needed to unscrew the outer tie rod.

Installation
1. Screw the outer tie rod onto the inner tie rod the same number of turns as was needed to remove it.
2. Do not tighten the jam nut until the toe-in/out adjustment has been made. Torque to 50 ft. lbs.
3. Be sure the boot is not twisted when done.

BOOT SEAL AND BREATHER TUBE

Removal
1. Remove the outer tie rod and the jam nut from the inner tie rod shaft.
2. Cut the boot clamp and discard. Mark the breather tube location on the steering housing before removing the tube.

Installation
1. Install the breather tube in the same location before removal.
2. Install a new clamp on before installing the boot.
3. Push the boot elbow on the breather tube and engage the boot onto the housing.
4. Secure the boot clamp.
5. Install the boot tube and the outer tie rod. Adjust the toe-in/out as required and tighten the jam nut to 50 ft. lbs.

INNER TIE ROD

Removal
1. The steering assembly must be out of the vehicle.
2. Remove the shock damper ring from the inner tie rod housing and slide it back on the rack.
3. Position a wrench on the rack flat to prevent rack damage when removing the tie rod.
4. Position a wrench on the tie rod pivot housing flats.
5. Turn the inner tie rod housing counterclockwise until the tie rod assembly separates.

Installation
1. Screw the inner tie rod into the steering rack. Be sure the shock damper is positioned on the rack.
2. Torque the tie rod housing to the rack by holding the rack and tie rod with 2 wrenches. Tighten to 70 ft. lbs. torque. The tie rod must rock freely in the housing before staking.
3. Support the rack and housing and stake the tie rod housing flat. To inspect the stake, a 0.010 in. feeler gauge should not pass between the rack and the housing stakes on both sides.
4. Slide the shock dampener over the inner tie rod housing until it engages.

RACK BEARING

Removal
1. Loosen the adjuster plug locknut.
2. Remove the adjuster plug, spring and the rack bearing.

Installation
1. Lubricate the metal parts and install the rack bearing, spring, adjuster plug and the locknut.
2. Turn the adjuster plug in until it bottoms and then back off 50-70 degrees.
3. Check the turning torque of the pinion. The correct turning torque is 8-10 inch lbs.
4. Torque the locknut to 50 ft. lbs.

STUB SHAFT SEALS

Removal
1. Remove the retaining ring and the dust cover.
2. While holding the stub shaft, remove the locknut from the pinion. If the stub shaft is not held, damage to the pinion teeth will occur.
3. Using a press, press on the threaded end of the pinion until flush with the ball bearing assembly. Complete removal of the valve and pinion assembly is not necessary.

Installation
1. Install the shaft protector over the stub shaft and install the stub shaft bearing annulus, needle bearing, stub shaft seal, stub shaft dust seal and the retaining ring.
2. While holding the stub shaft securely, firmly seat the locknut and torque to 26 ft. lbs.

VALVE AND PINION ASSEMBLY

Removal
Turn the stub shaft until the rack has equal distance on both sides of the housing, with the pinion fully engaged. The valve and pinion locknut must be removed.

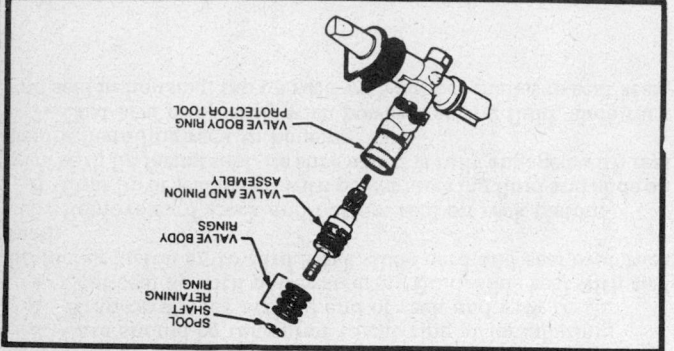

Installing valve and pinion assembly

BALL BEARING ASSEMBLY

Removal

1. With the piston and pinion assembly out of the housing, remove the bearing retaining ring.
2. Use a drift and gently tap on the bearing and remove it from the housing.

Installation

1. Using a suitable block, install the bearing in the housing and press it to its seat.
2. Install the retaining ring.

UPPER PINION BEARING AND SEAL

Removal

1. With the piston and pinion assembly out of the housing, remove the upper bushing and seal with a drift.

Installation

1. Install the new bushing to its seat.
2. Install the new seal, using an installer tool. Seat the seal in the housing with the lip of the seal facing up.

CYLINDER LINES

Removal and Installation

The lines are removed and replaced in a conventional manner, using tubing flare wrenches and using the normal precautions when working with fittings and piping. The fittings should be torqued to 15 ft. lbs.

Tie Rod Center Take Off Type

OUTER TIE ROD

Removal

1. With the steering assembly from the vehicle, loosen the outer rod pinch bolt and turn the tie rod from the adjuster stud, counting the number of turns until the tie rod separates from the adjuster stud.

Installation

1. Turn the tie rod onto the adjuster stud the same number of turns as was needed to remove.
2. Tighten the pinch bolt until the toe-out can be verified. Re-loosen and adjust as required.

INNER TIE ROD AND INNER PIVOT BUSHING

Removal

1. Bend back the lock plate tabs and loosen the inner tie rod bolt and remove.
2. Remove the inner tie rod by sliding it out between the bolt support plate and rack/pinion boot.

NOTE: If both inner tie rods are to be removed, reinstall the inner tie rod bolt in the first tie rod retaining bolt hole to keep the rack and pinion boot and other parts aligned, while the tie rods are out.

3. With the tie rod disconnected, the pivot bushings can be pressed out and new ones pressed in.

2. Mark the location of the stub shaft flat surface on the housing.
3. Using a press, press on the threaded end of the pinion until it is possible to remove the valve and pinion assembly.
4. Remove the valve body rings, if the replacement is required.

Installation

1. Install new valve body rings, if required.
2. Be sure that both ends of the rack are at equal distance from the housing.
3. Install the pinion and valve assembly, being careful not to damage the rings during the installation.
4. The valve and pinion assembly must be fully seated and the flat section of the pinion must line up with the previously marked location indicator on the housing.

BULKHEAD

Removal

1. Use punch in access hole to remove bulkhead retaining ring.
2. If only the bulkhead, bulkhead O-ring seal or rack seal (bulkhead) are to be replaced. Loosen (left) fitting and remove cylinder line.
3. Plug (left) cylinder line hole at cylinder using a finger or plastic cap with $7/16 \times 20$ internal threads over hole to prevent oil leaking from cylinder.
4. Using a $11/16$ in.–12 point socket turn stub shaft. Move rack to the right forcing the bulkhead out of the housing. Use drain pan to catch hydraulic oil from assy.
5. If inner rack seal or piston ring are to be replaced, use rack to remove bulkhead instead of compressed oil method.

Installation

1. Install the cylinder inner bulkhead, the O-ring seal, the cylinder outer bulkhead, the bulkhead retaining ring and the shock dampener. A seal protector should be used on the rack end.
2. Make sure that the open end of the retaining ring is approximately 0.50 in. from the access hole.
3. Fully seat the retaining ring.

RACK INNER SEAL AND PISTON RING

Removal

1. Remove the rack from the housing.
2. Remove the piston rings and discard.
3. Fit seal remover tool in place and using a long rod, tap the seal from its seat.

Installation

1. Install new piston ring on rack.
2. Care should be taken not to cut ring at installation.
3. Wrap card stock around end of rack and rack teeth.
4. Coat seal lip with power steering fluid, slide seal with seal lip facing piston on to card stock, slide card and seal over rack teeth.
5. Remove card stock and bottom seal on rack piston.
6. Coat lip of seal insert with power steering fluid and slide on rack with lip facing seal. Be sure insert is fully engaged with seal before installing rack in housing.
7. Coat seal completely with power steering fluid, slide rack and seal in housing, tap on rack with rubber mallet to seat seal.

NOTE: Seal must be fully seated in housing.

RACK BEARING

Removal
1. Remove the adjuster plug locknut.
2. Remove the adjuster plug from the housing.
3. Remove the spring, O-ring seal and the rack bearing.

Installation
1. Lubricate the metal parts before installation and install in the reverse order of the removal procedure.
2. With the rack centered, tighten the adjuster plug to a torque of 6–11 ft. lbs. Back off the adjuster plug 50 to 70 degrees. Check the pinion torque.
3. The pinion torque should be 8–16 inch lbs., turning.
4. Assemble the locknut and while holding the adjusting plug stationary, tighten the adjusting plug locknut to 50 ft. lbs.

STUB SHAFT SEALS AND UPPER BEARING

Removal
1. Remove retaining ring.
2. Remove dust cover.
3. While holding the stub shaft remove locknut from pinion.

NOTE: If stub shaft is not held, damage to the pinion teeth will occur.

4. Using a press, press on threaded end of pinion until flush with ball bearing assembly.
5. Complete removal of valve and pinion assembly is not necessary.

NOTE: Bearing and annulus are pressed together. Disassemble only if bearing replacement is required.

Installation
1. Install the seals and bearing in the reverse order of the removal.
2. While holding the stub shaft, firmly seat the lock at 26 ft. lbs.

VALVE AND PINION ASSEMBLY

Removal
1. Turn stub shaft until rack guide is equal distance from both sides of housing opening.
2. Mark location of stub shaft flat on housing.
3. Using a press, press on threaded end of pinion until it is possible to remove valve and pinion assembly.
4. Remove valve body rings if replacement is necessary.

Installation
1. Install new valve body rings if required.
2. Care should be taken not to cut rings at installation.
3. Measure rack guide so that it is equal from both sides of housing.
4. Install valve and pinion assembly so that when full seated stub shaft flat and mark on housing line up and the rack guide is centered in housing.

CYLINDER ASSEMBLY

Removal
1. The cylinder outer bulkhead and housing must be marked before removal to insure proper location in housing at assembly so cylinder lines will fit correctly.
2. Use a small punch in access hole to unseat retaining ring. Then use a suitable tool to bring out retaining ring enough to be

Installation
1. Be sure the center housing cover washers are fitted into the rack and pinion boot, before rod installation.
2. Remove the locating bolt from the rack and position 1 inner tie rod assembly in place over the rack. Place the bolt through the lock plate and the tie rod. Place the second inner tie rod in place and install the bolt through the bolt and the tie rod.
3. Tighten the inner tie rod bolts to 65 ft. lbs. and bend the lock tabs against the flats of the inner tie rod bolts after torquing.

FLANGE AND STEERING COUPLING ASSEMBLY

Removal
1. Loosen and remove the pinch bolt.
2. Remove the coupling.

Installation
1. Install the flange and steering coupling assembly on the stub shaft.
2. Install the pinch bolt and torque to 37 ft. lbs.

NOTE: With the flange and steering coupling assembly off the stub shaft, the dash seal can be replaced.

HYDRAULIC LINES

Removal and Installation
For ease of line removal and installation, remove the lines from the valve end first and install them on the cylinder end first. Torque to 13 ft. lbs.

RACK AND PINION BOOT, RACK GUIDE, BEARING GUIDE, MOUNTING GROMMET, OR HOUSING END COVER

Removal
1. Separate the right hand mounting grommet and remove. The left hand mounting grommet need not be removed unless replacement is required.
2. Cut both boot clamps and discard.
3. For ease of rack and pinion boot removal slide cylinder end of boot toward center of gear enough to expose boot groove in cylinder. Place a rubber band in groove. This fills the groove and allows easy removal of rack and pinion boot from gear. Rack bearing or rack guide can now be removed or replaced if necessary.
5. Remove housing end cover only if damaged.

Installation
1. Remove boot retaining bushing from rack and pinion boot.
2. Slide new boot clamp on rack and pinion boot. Install boot retaining bushing into rack and pinion boot.
3. Install new bearing guide on rack guide if necessary.
4. Install rack guide on rack.
5. Coat inner lip of boot retaining bushing lightly with grease for ease of assembly.
6. Install boot on housing.
7. Be sure center housing cover washers are in place on boot.
8. For ease of assembly, install inner tie rod bolts through cover washers, and rack and pinion boot. Screw into rack lightly. This will keep rack, and boot in proper alignment.
9. Slide boot and boot retaining bushing until seated in bushing groove in housing. Crimp new boot clamp.
10. Slide other end of boot into boot groove on cylinder end of housing. Crimp new boot clamp.

able to remove retaining ring with suitable pliers, discard retaining ring.

3. By threading an inner tie rod into bolt into rack, rack can be used in a slide hammer fashion to remove rack and cylinder assembly from housing.

Installation

1. Replace both O-ring seals before assembly.
2. Using crocus cloth remove burrs or sharp edges from retaining ring groove in housing. This must be done to insure that the new O-ring seals are not damaged at assembly.
3. Coat O-ring seals with hydraulic fluid and install rack and cylinder assembly in housing.
4. Line up marks on housing and cylinder outer bulkhead. Gently tap on cylinder outer bulkhead until it is seated far enough in housing to install retaining ring. It may be necessary to use a press to hold bulkhead far enough in housing to install retaining ring.
5. Open end of retaining ring should be approx. 0.50 in. (13mm) from access hole. Be sure retaining ring is fully seated in housing.

PISTON RING

Removal

1. Hold on to cylinder, using rack and piston rod guide assembly as a slide hammer. Piston rod guide assembly will disengage from cylinder assembly.

Installation

1. Install new piston ring coat lightly with hydraulic steering fluid.
2. Slide piston into cylinder assembly.
3. Lightly tap piston rod guide assembly until fully seated in cylinder assembly.

RACK, PISTON ROD AND PISTON ROD GUIDE ASSEMBLY

Removal

1. Put steering rack in soft-jawed vise.
2. Using a tool J-29811 or equivalent unscrew rod and piston assembly from rack.
3. Because of close tolerances, it may be necessary to use piston rod guide assembly as a slide hammer to separate rod and piston assembly from rack.
4. Do not remove piston rod guide assembly from rod and piston assembly unless piston rod seal or rod and piston assembly require replacement, because the piston rod seal will be damaged.

Installation

1. Install new piston rod seal in piston rod guide, if required.
2. Using crocus cloth remove any burrs or sharp edges from rod and piston assembly. Put seal protector J-29812 or equivalent on rod and piston assembly.
3. Coat piston rod seal with hydraulic fluid and slide piston rod guide assembly on piston and rod assembly.
4. Gently tap guide assembly into rack and piston rod until threads engage.
5. Tighten to specifications.
6. Stake rack against piston rod flats.

PINION BEARING ASSEMBLY

Removal

1. Remove bearing retaining ring.
2. Use drift or punch and gently tap on bearing until bearing is removed.

Installation

1. Install new pinion bearing assembly. Using a suitable socket, press on outer race. Be careful not to cock bearing in housing.
2. Install retaining ring. Note position of large lug to be sure beveled side of ring is properly located.

UPPER PINION BEARING AND PINION SHAFT SEAL

Removal

1. Remove upper pinion bushing and seal with a punch.
2. Remove and discard the bushing and seal.

Installation

1. Install the new bushing.
2. Install the new seal with an installer tool. Seat the seal with the seal lip facing up.

Nova

Disassembly

1. Place the rack and pinion unit in a soft jawed vise.
2. Mark the left and right tie rod ends for ease of reassembly. Remove the boots and discard. Upon reassembly, new boots should be installed.
3. Using a suitable tool, bend back (straighten) the bent portion of the locking washer between the inner tie rod and the rack. Remove the inner tie rods from the rack.
4. Disconnect the right and left pipe assemblies between the cylinder and valve housing.
5. Remove the adjusting plug locknut. Using tool J-35692 and J-35423 or equivalent, remove the cap, spring and rack guide.
6. Remove the dust cover and snapring. Remove the self locking nut from the lower end of the pinion gear.
7. Remove the pinion assembly along with the upper bearing and oil seal. Remove the cylinder end stopper retaining snapring. Remove the rack assembly and cylinder end stopper together.

NOTE: While removing the rack from the housing, exercise care so as to avoid damage to the piston bore inner housing face.

8. Using tool J-35434 or equivalent, remove the inner rack seal and spacer. Remove the piston and O-ring seals from the rack.
9. Remove the inner bushing from the valve housing using tool J-35420 or equivalent. Remove the inner valve housing seal.

Assembly

1. Using an arbor press, install inner bushing tools J-35695 and J-8092 or equivalent, and install the bushing to a depth of 2.736 in. (69.5 mm).
2. Lubricate the valve and inner bushing with power steering fluid. Install the control valve pinion and check that the valve rotates smoothly.
3. The remainder of assembly is the reverse of the disassembly.
4. Inspect all mating surfaces for excessive wear or signs of damage. Inspect the rack for runout and tooth wear. Runout should not exceed 0.012 in. (0.33 mm). Check bearings and seals. Replace as required.
5. Replace the housing if the inner piston cylinder walls are damaged.

6. Lubricate all sliding parts and sealing surfaces using lithium grease.

7. Inspect the inner tie rod and the tie rod end for looseness and replace if worn or defective.

Spectrum

Disassembly

1. Place the steering unit in a soft jawed vise.
2. Remove the tie rod end.
3. Remove the boot.
4. Using a chisel, bend back (straighten) the bent (staked) part of the locking washer between the inner tie rod and the rack. A new washer should be used when reassembled.
5. Remove the tie rod from the rack.
6. Disconnect the right and left pipe assemblies between the valve housing and cylinders.
7. Loosen the adjusting plug nut and remove the spring and plunger.

NOTE: Rotate the pinion gear shaft until the pinion flat is parallel or aligned with the rack. Then carefully measure dimension A. Record this measurement. This relationship must be used for reassembly.

8. Remove the valve/pinion housing assembly.
9. Remove the adjusting shims.
10. Remove the retaining ring from the right side.
11. Carefully withdraw the rack assembly (right side) and seal holder together.
12. Remove the inner rack seal and shock dampener.
13. Remove the piston and O-ring seals from the rack.
14. Using a plastic hammer, drive the valve assembly from the housing.
15. Using tool J-33997, drive the bearing and seal from the valve housing.
16. Remove the snapring from the spool end of the valve assembly, then slide the spool, seals and spacer.

NOTE: Do not remove the teflon seals. The valve is serviced as an assembly.

Assembly

1. Install the spacer, then using tool J-33997-7, slide the oil seal onto the shaft (flat side of the seal toward the spacer).
2. Slide the valve spool onto the pinion shaft. If the spool will not slide onto the pinion shaft, do not force it. Using tool J-33997-5 to size, (compress) the seal ring, then install the seal.
3. Install the snapring on the shaft at the spool.
4. Use a press to install the upper bearing and seal into the valve housing, with the help of tool J-33997-4 (flat side of seal toward the bearing).
5. Before installing the pinion/valve assembly into the valve housing, use tool J-33997-8 to compress the seal rings on the spool housing.
6. Place tool J-33997-10 on the upper pinion shaft. Install the pinion/valve assembly into the valve housing.
7. Using tool J-33997-6 to size, (compress) the seal ring, then install the seal onto the valve piston.
8. Apply grease to the rack gear surfaces. Install the seal into the seal holder, flat end of the seal in first, then install the seal holder using seal protector tool J-33997-9.
9. Install the shock damping ring using tools J-35527 and J-7079-2.
10. Install the inner rack seal, gear side of rack. Shim stock should be used to protect the seal from the rack gear surface. Flat end of the seal away from the rack piston.
11. Install the rack assembly and push the seal holder into the housing. Install the retaining ring.
12. Move the rack assembly into the housing as far as possible and measure the distance between the end of the holder (A) and the tip of the rack shaft (B). The seals are positioned correctly when this dimension (L) is 10mm or more.

NOTE: When replacing the valve housing, or any internal valve components, it is necessary to check and adjust the clearance between the valve assembly and the housing.

13. Center the rack. Measure between the end of the seal holder and the end of the rack (2.5 in.).
14. Apply grease to the pinion gear teeth and the pinion ball bearings.
15. Using a valve assembly repair kit, install all 7 adjusting shims.
16. Install the pinion/valve assembly to the housing and carefully snug up the 2 bolts, 1/4 turn each until snug.
17. Using a feeler gauge, measure the clearance between the valve and the gear housings.

NOTE: The purpose of Step 11 is to reduce the clearance as close to zero as possible by removing shims. This minimizes endplay for pinion gear assembly.

18. As noted, calculate and remove the necessary shims. Install the pinion/valve assembly following the procedure in Step 19. Check the clearance again, as in Step 11. The final clearance should be 0.002 in. or less.
20. When final clearance is reached, use RTV No. 1052366 or equivalent, to seal the mating surfaces of the valve and steering housing. Torque to 18 ft. lbs.
21. Lubricate well with grease, and install the plunger, spring, adjusting plug and locknut. Tighten the adjusting plug to 3.6 ft. lbs.
22. Loosen the plug and once again tighten the plug to 3.6 ft. lbs.
23. With the adjusting plug torqued to 3.6 ft. lbs., back off the plug 30-35 degrees. Tighten the locknut snug.
24. Measure the pinion shaft preload. (0.4-1.2 ft. lbs.). If preload is not within specifications, loosen the locknut and readjust the plug torque. When an acceptable preload is achieved, apply liquid thread lock to the locknut and torque the locknut to 49 ft. lbs.
25. Install the right and left cylinder pipes.
26. Install the inner tie rod and new locking washer to the rack end. Torque to 65 ft. lbs. Protect the rod mounted in a vise. Stack the locking washer to the flat of the inner tie rod. Apply grease to the inner surface of the small opening in the boot.
27. Install the new boot over the inner tie rod.
28. Install the tie rod nut and attach the the tie rod end.
29. Adjust the rod length to 7.5 in. (''L'' dimension shown)
30. Torque the tie rod locking nut to 40 ft. lbs.
31. Install the boot clamp and wire.

GENERAL MOTORS POWER STEERING PUMP OVERHAUL

Disassembly

1. With the power steering pump removed from the vehicle, drain the reservoir and reinstall the filler cap to prevent contamination. Clean the exterior of the pump before starting the disassembly procedures.
2. Secure the pump in a suitable vise at the mounting bracket.
3. Install special puller J-25034 or BT-7515 or equivalent and be sure the pilot bolt bottoms out in the pump shaft by turning the nut at the top of the pilot bolt.
4. Install the puller jaws and retainer sleeve that go with the special puller tool and remove the pulley by holding the pilot bolt and turning it out counterclockwise.

NOTE: The pump pulley is a press fit on the shaft and must be removed and replaced with the aid of puller tools. Do not hammer on the pulley, pulley or shaft for this could cause internal damage to the pump components.

5. Remove the brackets from the pump and using a soft jaw vise or equivalent, clamp the pump (shaft end down) in the vise between the square boss and shaft housing.

6. Remove the mounting studs and pressure hose fitting. Tap the reservoir filler tube back and forth with a rubber mallet to loosen. Remove the reservoir off of the pump body and discard the O-rings from the reservoir along with the mounting studs and the pressure fitting.

7. Using a punch, tap the end cover retainer ring around until 1 end of the ring is near the hole in the pump body. Insert the punch far enough to disengage the ring from the groove in the pump bore and pry the ring out of the pump body.

8. Tap the end cover with a plastic mallet to dislodge it, the spring under the cover should push the cover up.

9. Remove the pump body from the vise, place the pump upside down on a flat surface and tap the end of the driveshaft with a rubber mallet to loosen the pressure plate, rotor and thrust plate assembly from the pump body.

10. Lift the pump body off of rotor assembly. Flow control valve and spring should slide out of the bore.

11. Replace and discard end cover and pressure plate O-rings, place pump body on a flat surface and pry the driveshaft oil seal nut with a suitable tool.

12. Inspect the seal bore in housing for burrs, nicks or gouge marks that would allow oil to bypass outer seal surface.

13. Remove the 10 vanes from the slots in the rotor, after lifting out the pressure plate and cam ring from the rotor. Clamp the driveshaft in a soft jaw vise or equivalent, with the rotor and thrust plate facing up.

14. Remove the rotor lock ring, pry the ring off the driveshaft and be sure to avoid nicking the rotor end face. Discard the lock ring.

15. Slide the rotor and thrust plate off of the shaft and remove the shaft from the vise.

NOTE: Inspect and wash all parts in clean solvent, blow out all passages with compressed air and air dry the cleaned parts.

Assembly

1. With the pump body laying on a flat surface, drive a new driveshaft seal into the bore, using a suitable tool until the seal bottoms on shoulder.

NOTE: Do not use excessive force when installing the seal, because the seal will become distorted.

2. Lubricate the seal with power steering fluid and clamp the pump body shaft end down into a vise.

3. Install the end cover and pressure plate O-rings in the grooves in the pump cavity. (These rings are the same size.) Be sure to lubricate the O-rings in power steering fluid.

4. With the driveshaft clamped in a soft jaw vise or equivalent with the splined end up, install the thrust plate on the driveshaft (ported side up). Slide rotor over splines with the counterbore of the rotor facing down. Install the rotor lock ring making sure the ring is seated in the groove.

5. Install the dowel pins in holes in the pump cavity. Insert the driveshaft, rotor and thrust plate assembly in the pump cavity matching the locating holes with the dowel pins.

6. Slide the cam ring over the rotor on the dowel pins with the arrow on the ring facing up. Install the 10 vanes in the rotor slots and lubricate them with power steering fluid.

7. Position the pressure plate dowel pins and place a 1¼ in. socket in the groove of the pressure plate and seat the entire assembly on the O-ring in the pump cavity by pressing down on the socket with both thumbs.

8. Place the spring in the groove in the pressure plate and position the end cover lip edge up over the spring.

9. Press the end cover down below the retaining ring groove with a vise or an arbor press and install the ring making sure it is seated in the groove.

NOTE: This procedure is better performed in an arbor press. Caution should be used to prevent cocking the end cover in the bore or distorting the assembly.

10. Using a punch, tap the retainer ring ends around in the groove until the opening is opposite the flow control valve bore. This is important for maximum retention of the retainer ring.

11. Replace the reservoir O-ring seals and the flow control valve O-ring seal on the pump body. Align the mounting stud holes until the studs can be started in the threads.

12. Tap the reservoir down on the pump using a rubber mallet and insert the flow control valve spring and valve (hexagon plug down). Replace the O-ring on the pressure hose fitting and lubricate with power steering fluid.

NOTE: Be sure the O-ring is installed on the upper groove. It is possible to install the O-ring in the lower groove. If this happens it will restrict the relief outlet orifice.

13. Install the pressure hose fitting and tighten the mounting studs. The torque for the hose is 37 ft. lbs. (50 Nm) and the torque for the studs is 26 ft. lbs. (35 Nm).

14. Remove the pump assembly from the vise and install the mounting brackets. After the brackets are installed clamp the pump assembly into the vise at the mounting bracket.

15. Place the pulley on the end of the pump shaft and install special tool J-25034 or BT-7515 or equivalent. Be sure the pilot bolt bottoms in the shaft by turning the nut at the top of the pilot bolt.

16. Install the pulley by holding the pilot bolt and turning the nut clockwise.

17. Install the pump assembly on the engine, refill the reservoir and start engine, inspect for leaks and recheck the fluid level after bleeding the air from the pump.

Spark Plugs

AMERICAN MOTORS

MAKE/ENGINE	YEAR(S)	AC DELCO	AUTOLITE	BOSCH	CHAMPION	MOTOR-CRAFT	NGK	ND
L4-96 (1.5L) VIN X	1989	R42XLS	63		RN9YC4	AGR22C		W20EXR-U11
L4-98 (1.6L) VIN Y	1989							
L4-98 (1.6L) VIN Z	1989		64		RN9YC4			
L4-132 (2.2L) VIN F	1989	R42LTS	103	HR7DC	RS9YC	AGRF22C		T20EPR-U
L4-132 (2.2L) VIN F	1988	R42LTS	103	HR7DC	RS12YC	AGR22	TR5	T20EPR-U
L4-150 (2.5L) VIN H	1989	FR3LM	985	FR9HC	RC12YC	AGRP54		QJ16HR-U
L4-150 (2.5L) VIN Z	1988	FR3LM	103	FR9HC	RC12YC	AGRP54		QJ16HR-U
V6-182 (3.0L) VIN J	1988	R42LTS	103	HR7DC	RS9YC	AGRP54	BCPR6ES-11	T20EPR-U
V6-182 (3.0L) VIN U	1989	R42LTS	103	HR7DC	RS9YC	AGRF22C		T20EPR-U
L6-258 (4.2L) VIN C	1986	FR4LE	985	FR9HC	RFN14LY	AGRP54		QJ16HR-V
L6-258 (4.2L) VIN C	1987-88	FR4LE	985	FR9HC	RFN14LY	AGRP54		QJ16HR-U

BUICK (General Motors)

MAKE/ENGINE	YEAR(S)	AC DELCO	AUTOLITE	BOSCH	CHAMPION	MOTOR-CRAFT	NGK	ND
L4 111 (1.8L) VIN J Turbo	1986	R42XLS	63	WR9DC	WRFDC	AGR22C	BPR6ES	W22EPR-U
L4 111 (1.8L) VIN O	1986	R44XLS	65	WR8DC	RN12YC	AGR42C	BPR5ES	W16EXR-U
L4 121 (2.0L) VIN 1	1989	R44LTSM	985	HR9D	RS13YC	AGRP54		T16EPR-U
L4 122 (2.0L) VIN P	1986	R42TS	24	HR8BC	RV12YC	ARF22C	BPR6FS	T20PR-U
L4 122 (2.0L) VIN K	1987	R44XLS6		WR9DCY	RN12YC		BPR5ES	
L4 122 (2.0L) VIN K	1988	R44XLS6	646		RN12YC	AGR52C-6	BPR5ES	W16EXR-U11
L4 122 (2.0L) VIN M Turbo	1987	R42XLS6		WR9DCY	RN9YC4		BPR6ES-11	
L4 122 (2.0L) VIN I High Output	1987	FR3LM	985	WR7DC	RC12YC	AGRP54		
L4 122 (2.0L) VIN I High Output	1988	FR3LM	985	FR9HC	RC12YC	AGRP54	GR5	QJ16HR-U
L4 138 (2.3L) VIN D	1989	FR3LS	3924	FR8DCX	RC12YC	AGSP32C		Q16PR-U11
L4 140 (2.3L) VIN D	1988	FR3LS	3924	FR9HC	RC12YC	AGSP32C	BCPR5ES-11	Q16PR-U11
L4 151 (2.5L) VIN R, U	1986	R43TS6	664	HR9BCY	RV12YC	ARF32C-6	BPR6FS-15	T20PR-U15
L4 151 (2.5L) VIN R, U	1987	R43TS6	664	HR9BCY	RV12YC	ARF32C-6		T16PR-U15
L4 151 (2.5L) VIN R, U	1988	R43TS6	664	HR9BCY	RV12YC	ASF32C-6	UR55	T20PR-U15
L4 151 (2.5L) VIN R, U	1989	R43TS6	664		RV12YC	ARF32C-6		T20PR-U15

BUICK (General Motors)

MAKE/ENGINE	YEAR(S)	AC DELCO	AUTOLITE	BOSCH	CHAMPION	MOTOR-CRAFT	NGK	ND
V6 173 (2.8L) VIN W	1987	R43LTSE		HR9LCX	RS13LYC			
V6 173 (2.8L) VIN W	1988	R43LTSE	5164	HR9LCX	RS13LYC		TR4-2	T20EPR-U
V6 173 (2.8L) VIN W	1989	R43LTSE	5164	HR5DC	RS13LYC	AGSF33C		T20EPR-U
V6 173 (2.8L) VIN X	1986	R43TS	24	HR8BC	RV12YC	ASF32C	BPR6FS	T20PR-U11
V6 181 (3.0L) VIN L High Output	1986	R44LTS	105	HR9DC	RS12YC	AGR32C	BPR5EFS	T16EPR-U
V6 181 (3.0L) VIN L High Output	1987	R44LTS	105	HR9DC	RS12YC	AGRF42	BPR5EFS	T16EPR-U
V6 181 (3.0L) VIN L High Output	1988	R44LTS	105	HR9DCX	RS12YC	AGRF42	TR5	T16EPR-U
V6 189 (3.1L) VIN T	1989	R43LTSE	5164	HR5DC	RS13LYC	AGSF33C		T20EPR-U
V6 204 (3.3L) VIN N	1989	R44TS6	605	HR9DCX	RS12YC6	AGRF42-6		T16EPR-U15
V6 231 (3.8L) VIN A	1986-87	R45TSX	666	HR9BCY	RV15YC6	ARF52-6	BPR4FS-15	T16PR-U15
V6 231 (3.8L) VIN C	1988	R44LTS6	605	HR9DCY	RS12YC6	AGRF42	TR5	T16EPR-U15
V6 231 (3.8L) VIN C	1989	R44LTS6	605	HR9DCX	RS12YC6	AGRF42-6		T16EPR-U15
V6 231 (3.8L) VIN 7 SFI	1986-87	R44TS	25	HR8BC	RS12YC	ARF42	BPR5FS	T16PR-U
V6 231 (3.8L) VIN 3, BMFI	1986-87	R44LTS	105	HR9DCX	RS12YC	AGRF42	BPR5FS	T16EPR-U
V6 231 (3.8L) VIN 3, BMFI	1988	R44LTS	105	HR9DCX	RS12YC	AGRF42	TR5	T16EPR-U
V8 305 (5.0L) VIN H	1987	R45TS		HR10BC			BPR4FS	T16PR-U
V8 307 (5.0L) VIN Y	1986-87	FR3LS6	3924	FR8DCX	RC12YC5	AGSP32C	BCPR5ES-11	016PR-U15
V8 307 (5.0L) VIN Y	1988	FR3LS6	5184	FR8DCY	RC12YC5	AGSP32C	BCPR5ES-11	016PR-U15
V8 307 (5.0L) VIN Y	1989	FR3LS6	5184		RC12YC5	AGSP32C		016PR-U15

CADILLAC (General Motors)

MAKE/ENGINE	YEAR(S)	AC DELCO	AUTOLITE	BOSCH	CHAMPION	MOTOR-CRAFT	NGK	ND
L4 121 (2.0L) VIN P	1986	R42TS	24	HR8BC	RV12YC	ARF22C	BPR6FS	T20PR-U
L4 121 (2.0L) VIN I High Output	1987	FR3LM	985	FR9HC	RC12YC	AGRP54		
V6 173 (2.8L) VIN W	1986	R42TS	24	HR8BC	RV12YC	ARF22C	BPR6FS	T20PR-U
V6 173 (2.8L) VIN W	1987	R43LTSE		HR9LCX	RS13LYC			
V6 173 (2.8L) VIN W	1988	R43LTSE	5164	HR9LCX	RS13LYC		TR4-2	T20EPR-U
V8 250 (4.1L) VIN 7, 8	1986-87	R44LTS6	605	HR9DCY	RS12YC6	AGRF42-6	BPR5EFS	T16EPR-U15
V8 250 (4.1L) VIN 7	1988	R44LTS6	605	HR9DCY	RS12YC6	AGRF42-6	TR5	T16EPR-U15
V8 273 (4.5L) VIN 5	1988	R44LTS6	605	HR9DCY	RS12YC6	AGRF42-6	TR5	T16EPR-U15
V8 273 (4.5L) VIN 5, 8	1989	R44LTS6	605	HR9DCX	RS12YC6	AGRF42-6		T16EPR-U15
V8 307 (5.0L) VIN Y, 9	1986-87	FR3LS6	3924	FR8DCX	RC12YC5	AGSP32C	BCPR5ES-11	016PR-U15
V8 307 (5.0L) VIN Y	1988	FR3LS6	5184	FR8DCX	RC12YC5	AGSP32C	BCPR5ES-11	016PR-U15
V8 307 (5.0L) VIN Y, 9	1989	FR3LS6	5184		RC12YC5	AGSP32C		016PR-U15

CHEVROLET (General Motors)

MAKE/ENGINE	YEAR(S)	AC DELCO	AUTOLITE	BOSCH	CHAMPION	MOTOR-CRAFT	NGK	ND
L3 61 (1.0L) VIN 2	1987	R42XLS	63	WR7DC	RN9YC	AGR22C	BPR6ES-11	W20EXR-U11
L3 61 (1.0L) VIN 2	1988	R42XLS	63	WR7DC	RN9YC	AGR22C	GR5	W20EXR-U11
L3 61 (1.0L) VIN 2	1989	R42XLS	63		RN9YC4	AGR22C		W20EXR-U11
L3 61 (1.0L) VIN 5	1986	R43XLS	64	WR9DC	RN11YC	AGR32C	BPR6ES	W20EXR-U11
L3 61 (1.0L) VIN 5	1987	R43XLS	64	WR9DCX	RN11YC4	AGR32C	BPR6ES-11	W20EXR-U11
L3 61 (1.0L) VIN 5	1988	R43XLS	64	WR9DCX	RN11YC4	AGR32C	GR5	W20EXR-U11
L3 61 (1.0L) VIN 6	1989	R42XLS	63		RN11YC4	AGR22C		W16EXR-U11
L3 61 (1.0L) VIN F	1986	R43TS	64	WR8DCX	RV12YC	AGR32C	BPR6ES-11	W20EXR-U11
L4 92 (1.5L) VIN F, 9	1987	R42XLS		WR8DCX	RV12YC			
L4 92 (1.5L) VIN 7, 9	1988	R42XLS	63	WR8DCX	RN11YC4	AGR22C	GR5	W20EXR-U11
L4 92 (1.5L) VIN 7, 9	1989	R42XLS	63		RN11YC4	AGR22C		W20EXR-U11
L4 97 (1.6L) VIN 4	1986-88	R43XLS	64	WR9DCX	RN11YC4	AGS32C	GR5	W16EXR-U11
L4 97 (1.6L) VIN 5	1988	R43XLS	3924	WR9DCX	RC9YC	AGSP32C	GR5	PO16R
L4 97 (1.6L) VIN 5	1989	R43XLS	3924		RC9YCN4	AGS32C		K16R-U
L4 121 (2.0L) VIN P	1986	R42TS	23	HR8BC	RV12YC	ARF22C	BPR6FS	T20PR-U
L4 121 (2.0L) VIN 1 High Output	1987	FR3LM	985	FR9HC	RC12LYC	AGRP54		
L4 121 (2.0L) VIN 1 High Output	1988	FR3LM	985	FR9HC	RC13LYC	AGRP54		QJ16HR-U
L4 121 (2.0L) VIN 1 High Output	1989	R44LTSM	985		RS13LYC	AGRP54		T16EPR-U
L4 151 (2.5L) VIN R, 2	1986	R43TSX	664	HR9BCY	RV12YC6	ARF32C-6	BPR6FS-15	T20PR-U15
L4 151 (2.5L) VIN R	1987	R43TS6	664	HR9BCY	RV12YC6	ARF32C-6	BPR6FS-15	T20PR-U15
L4 151 (2.5L) VIN R	1988	R43TS6	664	HR9BCY	RV12YC6	ASF32C-6	UR55	T20PR-U15
L4 151 (2.5L) VIN R	1989	R43TS6	664		RV12YC6	ASF32C-6		T20PR-U15
V6 173 (2.8L) VIN S	1986-87	R42TS	23	HR8BC	RV12YC	ARF22-C	BPR6FS	T20PR-U11
V6 173 (2.8L) VIN S	1988	R42TS	23	HR8BC	RV12YC	ARF22-C	UR5	T20PR-U11
V6 173 (2.8L) VIN S	1989	R43TSK	24		RV12YC	ASF32-C		T20PR-U11
V6 173 (2.8L) VIN W	1986	R42TS	23	HR8BC	RV12YC	ARF22C	BPR6FS	T20PR-U11
V6 173 (2.8L) VIN W	1987	R43LTSE		HR9LCX	RS13LYC			
V6 173 (2.8L) VIN W	1988	R43LTSE	5164	HR9LCX	RS13LYC		TR4-2	T20EPR-U
V6 173 (2.8L) VIN W	1989	R43LTSE	5164		RS13LYC	AGSF33C		T20EPR-U
V6 173 (2.8L) VIN X	1986	R43TS	24	HR8BC	RV12YC	ASF32C	BPR6FS	T20PR-U11
V6 231 (3.8L) VIN A	1987	R45TSX		HR10BCY				
V6 262 (4.3L) VIN Z	1987-88	R45TS	26	HR10BC	RV15YC	ASF52	UR4	T16PR-U
V6 262 (4.3L) VIN Z	1989	R45TS	26		RV15YC	ASF52C		T16PR-U
V8 305 (5.0L) VIN E, F	1988	R45TS	26	HR10BC	RV12YC	ASF52	UR4	T16PR-U
V8 305 (5.0L) VIN E, F	1989	R45TS	26		RV15YC	ASF52C		T16PR-U
V8 305 (5.0L) VIN F	1986	R43TS	24	HR8BC	RV12YC	ASF32C	BPR6FS	T20PR-U
V8 305 (5.0L) VIN F	1987	R43TS	24	HR10BC	RV12YC	ARF32	BPR6FS	T20PR-U
V8 305 (5.0L) VIN G	1986	R43TS	24	HR8BC	RV12YC	ASF32C	BPR6FS	T20PR-U
V8 305 (5.0L) VIN H	1986	R43TS	24	HR10BCX	RV15YC	ASF32C	BPR6FS	T16PR-U11
V8 305 (5.0L) VIN G, H	1987	R45TS	26	HR10BC	RV15YC	ARF52	BPR4FS	T16PR-U

CHEVROLET (General Motors)

MAKE/ENGINE	YEAR(S)	AC DELCO	AUTOLITE	BOSCH	CHAMPION	MOTOR-CRAFT	NGK	ND
V8 305 (5.0L) VIN G, H	1988	R45TS	26	HR10BC	RV15YC	ASF52	UR4	T16PR-U
V8 307 (5.0L) VIN Y	1986-87	FR3LS6	5184	FR8DCX	RC12YC5	AGSP32C	BCPR5ES-11	016PR-U15
V8 307 (5.0L) VIN Y	1988	FR3LS6	5184	FR8DCX	RC12YC5	AGSP32C	BCPR5ES-11	016PR-U15
V8 307 (5.0L) VIN Y	1989	FR3LS6	5184		RC12YC5	AGSP32C		016PR-U15
V8 350 (5.7L) VIN 6	1986-88	R45TS	26	HR10BC	RV15YC	ASF52	BCPR5ES-11	T16PR-U
V8 350 (5.7L) VIN 7	1989	R45TS	26			ASF52C		
V8 350 (5.7L) VIN 8 Alum. Heads	1986-87	FR3LS	3926	FR8DCX	RC12YC	AGSP52	BCPR5ES-11	016PR-U11
V8 350 (5.7L) VIN 8 Alum. Heads	1988	FR5LS	3926	FR10DCX	RC12YC	AGSP52	BCPR5ES-11	016PR-U11
V8 350 (5.7L) VIN 8 Alum. Heads	1989	FR5LS	3926		RC12YC	AGSP52		016PR-U11
V8 350 (5.7L) VIN 8 Cast Heads	1986-88	R45TS	26	HR10BC	RV15YC	ASF52	UR5	T16PR-U
V8 350 (5.7L) VIN 8 Cast Heads	1989	R45TS	26		RV15YC	ASF52C		T16PR-U
V8 350 (5.7L) VIN J	1989	FR2LS	26			ASF52C		

CHRYSLER

MAKE/ENGINE	YEAR(S)	AC DELCO	AUTOLITE	BOSCH	CHAMPION	MOTOR-CRAFT	NGK	ND
L4 135 (2.2L) VIN A, D	1989	R44XLS	65		RN12YC	AGR42C		W16EXR-U
L4 135 (2.2L) VIN D, E	1986-87	R44XLS	65	WR9DC	RN12YC	AGR42C	BPR5ES	W16EXR-U
L4 135 (2.2L) VIN D, E	1988	R44XLS	65	WR9DC	RN12YC	AGR42C	GR4	W16EXR-U
L4 153 (2.5L) VIN J, K	1989	R44XLS	65		RN12YC	AGR42C		W16EXR-U
L4 153 (2.5L) VIN K	1986-87	R44XLS	65	WR9DC	RN12YC	AGR42C	BPR5ES	W16EXR-U
L4 153 (2.5L) VIN K	1988	R44XLS	65	WR9DC	RN12YC	AGR42C	GR4	W16EXR-U
L4 156 (2.6L) VIN N	1989	R42XLS	62		RN7YC	AGR12		W22EPR-U11
V6 181 (3.0L) VIN 3	1988	FR3JM	65	WR9DCX	RN11YC4	AGR42C	GR4	W16EXR-U
V6 181 (3.0L) VIN 3	1989	R43XLS	64		RN11YC4	AGS32C		W16EXR-U11
V8 318 (5.2L) VIN P,R,S,4	1986-87	R44XLS	65	WR9DC	RN12YC	AGR42C	BPR5ES	W16EXR-U
V8 318 (5.2L) VIN P,S,4	1988	R44XLS	65	WR9DC	RN12YC	AGR42C	GR4	W16EXR-U
V8 318 (5.2L) VIN P	1989	R44XLS	65		RN12YC	AGR42C		W16EXR-U

DODGE

MAKE/ENGINE	YEAR(S)	AC DELCO	AUTOLITE	BOSCH	CHAMPION	MOTOR-CRAFT	NGK	ND
L4 90 (1.5L) VIN K	1988	R42XLS	63	WR8DCX	RN9YC	AGR32C	GR4	W20EXR-U11
L4 98 (1.6L) VIN A	1986	R44XLS	65	WR7DC	RN12YC	AGR42C	BPR5ES	W16EXR-U

DODGE

MAKE/ENGINE	YEAR(S)	AC DELCO	AUTOLITE	BOSCH	CHAMPION	MOTOR-CRAFT	NGK	ND
L4 98 (1.6L) VIN F	1988	R42XLS	63	WR7DC	RN7YC	AGR12	GR4	W22EPR-U11
L4 122 (2.0L) VIN D	1988	R42XLS	63	WR8DCX	RN9YC	AGR22C	GR4	W20EXR-U11
L4 135 (2.2L) VIN A,C,D,E,8	1986-87	R44XLS	65	WR9DC	RN12YC	AGR42C	BPR5ES	W16EXR-U
L4 135 (2.2L) A,C,D,E	1988	R44XLS	65	WR9DC	RN12YC	AGR42C	GR4	W16EXR-U
L4 135 (2.2L) A, D	1989	R44XLS	65		RN12YC	AGR42C		W16EXR-U
L4 153 (2.5L) VIN J, K	1989	R44XLS	65		RN12YC	AGR42C		W16EXR-U
L4 153 (2.5L) VIN K	1986	R44XLS	65	WR9DC	RN12YC	AGR22C	BPR5ES	W16EXR-U
L4 153 (2.5L) VIN K	1987	R44XLS	65	WR9DC	RN12YC	AGR42C	BPR5ES	W16EXR-U
L4 153 (2.5L) VIN K	1988	R44XLS	65	WR9DC	RN12YC	AGR42C	GR4	W16EXR-U
V6 181 (3.0L) VIN 3	1988	R43XLS	65	WR8DCX	RN11YC4	AGR42C	GR4	W16EXR-U
V6 181 (3.0L) VIN 3	1989	R43XLS	64		RN12YC	AGS32C		W16EXR-U11
V8 318 (5.2L) VIN P,S,4	1986-87	R44XLS	65	WR9DC	RN12YC	AGR42C	BPR5ES	W16EXR-U
V8 318 (5.2L) VIN P,S,4	1988	R44XLS	65	WR9DC	RN12YC	AGR42C	GR4	W16EXR-U
V8 318 (5.2L) VIN P, S	1989	R44XLS	65		RN12YC	AGS42C		W16EXR-U

FORD

MAKE/ENGINE	YEAR(S)	AC DELCO	AUTOLITE	BOSCH	CHAMPION	MOTOR-CRAFT	NGK	ND
L4 79 (1.3L) VIN K	1987	R42XLS	64	WR8DCX	RN11YC4	AGS32C	GR4	W16EXR-U11
L4 79 (1.3L) VIN K	1988	R42XLS	64	WR8DCX	RN11YC4	AGS32C	GR4	W16EXR-U11
L4 79 (1.3L) VIN K, M	1989	R42XLS	64		RN11YC4	AGS32C		W16EXR-U11
L4 116 (1.9L) VIN 9	1986	R43NTSE	2544		RE10LC	AWSF34C		T20NR-U11
L4 116 (1.9L) VIN 9	1987-88	R43LTSE	5144	HR10HCO	RS10LC	AGSF34C	TR5-1	T20EPR-U
L4 116 (1.9L) VIN 9	1989		5144		RS10LC	AGSF34C		T20EPR-U
L4 116 (1.9L) VIN J	1986	R43NTSE	2543	HR9LCO	RE10LC	AWSF24C		T20NR-U11
L4 116 (1.9L) VIN J	1987-88		5143	HR9CO	RS10LC	AGSF24C	TR5-1	T20EPR-U
L4 116 (1.9L) VIN J	1989		5143		RS10LC	AGSF24C		T20EPR-U
L4 135 (2.2L) VIN C, L	1989		5224		RC9YC	AGSP33C		QJ20CR11
L4 140 (2.3L) VIN A	1986	R44NTSE	2545	HR10LCO	RE10LC			T16NR-U11
L4 140 (2.3L) VIN A	1987	R44NTSE	2545	HR10HCO	RS10LC	AWSF44C	SR5	T16NR-U11
L4 140 (2.3L) VIN A	1988	R44NTSE	2545	HR10HCO	RS10LC	AWSF44C	SR5	T16NR-U11
L4 140 (2.3L) VIN A	1989	R42LTS	2545		RS10LC	AWSF44C		T16NR-U11
L4 140 (2.3L) VIN R	1985	R44LTS			RS12YC		BPR5EFS	
L4 140 (2.3L) VIN R	1986	R44NTSE	2545			AWSF52C	BPR5EFS	T16EPR-U
L4 140 (2.3L) VIN R	1987	R44LTS				AWSF52C	BPR5EFS	T16EPR-U
L4 140 (2.3L) VIN R	1989	R44NTSE	765		RS12YC	AWSF42C		T16EPR-U15
L4 140 (2.3L) VIN S	1986-87	R42LTS	764/104	HR8DCX	RS12YC	AWSF32C	BPR6EFS	T20EPR-U
L4 140 (2.3L) VIN S	1988	R42LTS	765/865	HR9DCX	RS12YC	AWSF32C	TR5	T16EPR-U

FORD

MAKE/ENGINE	YEAR(S)	AC DELCO	AUTOLITE	BOSCH	CHAMPION	MOTOR-CRAFT	NGK	ND
L4 140 (2.3L) VIN S	1989	R44NTSE	765			AWSF42C		T16EPR-U15
L4 140 (2.3L) VIN T,W Turbo	1986-87	R42LTS	764/104	HR8DCX	RS12YC	AWSF32C	BPR6EFS	T20EPR-U
L4 140 (2.3L) VIN T,W Turbo	1988	R42LTS	764/104	HR8DCX	RS12YC	AWSF32C	TR5	T20EPR-U
L4 140 (2.3L) VIN X	1986-87	R44LTS	766/106	HR9DCX	RS14YC	AWSF52C	BPR5EFS	T16EPR-U
L4 140 (2.3L) VIN X	1988	R44LTS	765/865	HR9DCX	RS14YC	AWSF42C	TR5	T16EPR-U
L4 140 (2.3L) VIN X	1989	R44NTSE	765			AWSF42C		T16EPR-U15
L4 153 (2.5L) VIN D	1986-87	R42LTS	764/104	HR9DCX	RS12YC	AWSF32C	BPR6EFS	T20EPR-U
L4 153 (2.5L) VIN D	1988	R42LTS	764/104	HR8DCX	RS12YC	AWSF32C	BPR6EFS	T20EPR-U
L4 153 (2.5L) VIN D	1989	R42LTS	764		RS12YC	AWSF32C		T20EPR-U
V6 183 (3.0L) VIN 2	1989	R42LTS	3924			AGSP32PP		PQ20R
V6 183 (3.0L) VIN U	1986	R42LTS	764/104	HR8DCX	RS12YC	AWSF32C	TR5	T20EPR-U
V6 183 (3.0L) VIN U	1987	R42LTS	764/104	HR8DCX	RS9YC	AWSF32C	BPR6EFS	T16EPR-U
V6 183 (3.0L) VIN U	1988	R42LTS	764/104	HR8DCX	RS9YC	AWSF32P	BPR6EFS	T20EPR-U
V6 183 (3.0L) VIN U	1989	R42LTS	764		RS9YC	AWSF32P		T20EPR-U
V6 232 (3.8L) VIN C, 3	1986	R45NTSE	2546	HR10LCO	RE10LC	AWSF54C		T16NR-U11
V6 232 (3.8L) VIN C, 3	1987	R45NTSE	2546	HR10HCO	RS10LC	AWSF54C		T16NR-U11
V6 232 (3.8L) VIN C, R	1989	R45NTSE	2544		RS12YC	AWSF34PP		T20NR-U11
V6 232 (3.8L) VIN 4	1988	R45NTSE	2545	HR10HCO	RS10LC	AWSF44C	TR5	T16NR-U11
V6 232 (3.8L) VIN 4	1989	R43NTSE	2545		RS10LC	AWSF44C		T16NR-U11
V8 302 (5.0L) VIN F,M	1986	R44NTSE	2545	HR10HCO	RE10LC	AWSF44C		T16NR-U11
V8 302 (5.0L) VIN F exc H.O.	1987-88	R44NTSE	2545	HR10HCO	RS10LC	AWSF44C	SR5	T16NR-U11
V8 302 (5.0L) VIN E,M, H.O.	1987	R43TS	725/25	HR10BCY	RV15YC4	ASF42C	BPR5FS-15	T16PR-U15
V8 302 (5.0L) VIN E, H.O.	1988	R43TS	725/25	HR10BCY	RV15YC6	ASF42C	UR45	T16PR-U15
V8 302 (5.0L) VIN E	1989	R44NTSE	2545		RV15YC6	ASF42C		T16PR-U15
V8 302 (5.0L) VIN F	1989	R43TS	2545		RS10LC	AWSF44C		T16NR-U11
V8 351 (5.8L) VIN G H.O.	1986	R44TS	725/25	HR9BC	RV12YC	ASF42	BPR5FS-11	T16PR-U11
V8 351 (5.8L) VIN G H.O.	1987	R43TS	725/25	HR9BC	RV12YC	ASF42	BPR5FS-11	T16PR-U11
V8 351 (5.8L) VIN G H.O.	1988	R43TS	725/25	HR9BC	RV12YC	ASF42	UR4	T16PR-U11
V8 351 (5.8L) VIN G	1989	R44LTS	725/25		RV12YC	ASF42		T16PR-U11

LINCOLN

MAKE/ENGINE	YEAR(S)	AC DELCO	AUTOLITE	BOSCH	CHAMPION	MOTOR-CRAFT	NGK	ND
V6 232 (3.8L) VIN 4	1988	FR3LS	2545	HR10HCO	RS10LC	AWSF44C	SR5	T16NR-U11
V6 232 (3.8L) VIN 4	1989	R44NTSE	2545		RS10LC	AWSF44C		T16NR-U11
V8 302 (5.0L) VIN F.M	1986	R44NTSE	2545	HR10HCO	RE10LC	AWSF44C		T16NR-U11
V8 302 (5.0L) VIN F exc H.O.	1987-88	R44NTSE	2545	HR10HCO	RS10LC	AWSF44C	SR5	T16NR-U15
V8 302 (5.0L) VIN F	1989	R43TS	2545		RS10LC	AWSF44C		T16NR-U11

LINCOLN

MAKE/ENGINE	YEAR(S)	AC DELCO	AUTOLITE	BOSCH	CHAMPION	MOTOR-CRAFT	NGK	ND
V8 302 (5.0L) VIN E,M,H.O.	1987	R44TSE	725/25	HR10BCY	RS10LC	AWSF44C	UR45	T16NR-U11
V8 302 (5.0L) VIN E, H.O.	1988	R44TSE	725/25	HR10BCY	RV15YC6	ASF42C	UR45	T16PR-U15
V8 302 (5.0L) VIN E, H.O.	1989	R44TSE	725/25		RV15YC6	ASF42C		T16PR-U15

MERCURY

MAKE/ENGINE	YEAR(S)	AC DELCO	AUTOLITE	BOSCH	CHAMPION	MOTOR-CRAFT	NGK	ND
V8 302 (5.0L) VIN F	1989	R44NTSE	2545		RS10LC	AWSF44C		T16NR-U11
V8 302 (5.0L) VIN F	1987-88	R44NTSE	2545	HR10HCO	RS10LC	AWSF44C	SR5	T16NR-U11
V8 302 (5.0L) VIN F,M	1986	R44NTSE	2545	HR10HCO	RE10LC	AWSF44C		T16NR-U11
V6 232 (3.8L) VIN 4	1989	R44NTSE	2545		RS10LC	AWSF44C		T16NR-U11
V6 232 (3.8L) VIN 4	1988	R45NTSE	2545	HR10HCO	RS10LC	AWSF44C	SR5	T16NR-U11
V6 232 (3.8L) VIN C, R	1989	R43NTSE	2544		RS10LC	AWSF34PP		T20NR-U11
V6 232 (3.8L) VIN C,3	1987	R45NTSE	2546	HR10HCO	RS10LC	AWSF54C	SR5	T16NR-U11
V6 232 (3.8L) VIN C,3	1986	R45NTSE	2546	HR10HCO	RE10LC	AWSF54C		T16NR-U11
V6 183 (3.0L) VIN U	1989	R42LTS	764		RS9YC	AWSF32P		T20EPR-U
V6 183 (3.0L) VIN U	1988	R42LTS	764/104	HR8DCX	RS9YC	AWSF32P	TR5	T20EPR-U
V6 183 (3.0L) VIN U	1987	R42LTS	764/104	HR8DCX	RS10LC	AWSF32C	BPR6EFS	T16EPR-U
V6 183 (3.0L) VIN U	1986	R42LTS	764/104	HR8DCX	RS12YC	AWSF32C	BPR6EFS	T20EPR-U
L4 153 (2.5L) VIN D	1988-89	R42LTS						
L4 153 (2.5L) VIN D	1986-87	R42LTS	764/104	HR9DCX	RS12YC	AWSF32C	BPR6EFS	T20EPR-U
L4 140 (2.3L) VIN X	1989	R44LTS	765-		RS12YC	AWSF42C		T16EPR-U15
L4 140 (2.3L) VIN X	1988	R44LTS	765/865	HR9DCX	RS14YC	AWSF42C	TR5	T16EPR-U
L4 140 (2.3L) VIN X	1986-87	R44LTS	766/106	HR9DCX	RS14YC	AWSF52C	BPR5EFS	T16EPR-U
L4 140 (2.3L) VIN T,W Turbo	1986-87	R42LTS	764/104	HR8DCX	RS12YC	AWSF32C	BPR6EFS	T20EPR-U
L4 140 (2.3L) VIN S	1989	R44LTS	765		RS12YC	AWSF42C		T16EPR-U15
L4 140 (2.3L) VIN S	1988	R44LTS	765/865	HR9DCX	RS12YC	AWSF42C	TR5	T16EPR-U
L4 140 (2.3L) VIN S	1986-87	R42LTS	764/104	HR8DCX	RS12YC	AWSF32C	BPR6EFS	T20EPR-U
L4 140 (2.3L) VIN R	1986-87	R44NTSE	2545		RS12YC	AWSF52C	BPR5EFS	T16EPR-U
L4 140 (2.3L) VIN A	1986	R44NTSE	2545	HR10LCO	RE10LC			T16NR-U11
L4 140 (2.3L) VIN 6 LPG	1986	R42LTS	764/104	HR9DC	RS12YC	AWSF42		T16EPR-U
L4 116 (1.9L) VIN J	1987		5143	HR9HCO	RS10LC	AGSF24C	SR5	T20EPR-U
L4 116 (1.9L) VIN 9	1987	R43LTSE	5144	HR10HCO	RS10LC	AGSF34C	SR5	T20EPR-U
L4 116 (1.9L) VIN J EFI	1986	R43NTSE	2543	HR9HCO	RE10LC	AWSF24C		T20NR-U11
L4 116 (1.9L) VIN 9 exc EFI	1986	R43NTSE	2543	HR9HCO	RE10LC	AWSF34C		T20NR-U11
L4 98 (1.6L) VIN 5	1989	R42XLS	64		RN11YCA	AGS32C		W16EXR-U11
L4 98 (1.6L) VIN 5, 7	1987-88	R42XLS	64	WR8BCX	RN11YC4	AGS32C	GR4	W16EXR-U11

MERCURY

MAKE/ENGINE	YEAR(S)	AC DELCO	AUTOLITE	BOSCH	CHAMPION	MOTOR-CRAFT	NGK	ND
V8 351 (5.8L) VIN G H.O.	1986	r44TS	725/25		RV12YC	ASF42	BPR5FS-11	T16PR-U11
V8 351 (5.8L) VIN G H.O.	1987	R43TS	725/25		RV12YC	ASF42	BPR5FS-11	T16PR-U11
V8 351 (5.8L) VIN G H.O.	1988	R43TS	725/25		RV12YC	ASF42	UR4	T16PR-U11
V8 351 (5.8L) VIN G	1989	R43TS	725		RV12YC	ASF42C		T16PR-U11

OLDSMOBILE

MAKE/ENGINE	YEAR(S)	AC DELCO	AUTOLITE	BOSCH	CHAMPION	MOTOR-CRAFT	NGK	ND
L4 112 (1.8L) VIN O	1986	R44XLS	65	WR8DC	RN12YC	AGR42C	BPR5ES	W16EXR-U
L4 112 (1.8L) VIN J Turbo	1986	R42XLS	63					
L4 121 (2.0L) VIN P	1986	R42TS	23	HR8BC	RV12YC	ARF22C	BPR6F5	T20PR-U
L4 121 (2.0L) VIN K	1987	R44XL56	646	WR9DCY	RN12YC6	AGR52C-6	BPR5ES-15	W16EXR-U11
L4 121 (2.0L) VIN K	1988	R44XL56	646	WR9DCY	RN12YC6	AGR52C-6	GR4	W16EXR-U11
L4 121 (2.0L) VIN 1 H.O.	1987-88	FR3LM	985	FR9HC	RS13YC	AGRP54	TR4-2	QJ16HR-U
L4 138 (2.3L) VIN A, D	1989	FR3LS	3924		RC12YC	A6SP32C		016PR-U11
L4 138 (2.3L) VIN D	1988	FR3LS	605	HR9DCX	RC12YC	A6SP32C	BPR5ES-11	016PR-11
L4 151 (2.5L) VIN R, U	1986-87	R43TS6	664	HR9BCY	RV12YC6	ARF32C-6	BPR5ES-15	T20PR-U15
L4 151 (2.5L) VIN R, U	1988	R43TS6	664	HR9BCY	RV12YC6	ASF32C-6	UR55	T20PR-U15
L4 151 (2.5L) VIN R, U	1989	R43TS6	664		RV12YC6	ASF32C-6		T20PR-U15
V6 173 (2.8L) VIN W H.O.	1986	R42TS	23	HR8BC	RV12YC	ARF22C	BPR6F5	T20PR-U11
V6 173 (2.8L) VIN X	1986	R43TS	24	HR8BC	RV12YC	ASF32C	BPR6F5	T20PR-U11
V6 173 (2.8L) VIN W	1987-88	R43LTSE	5164	HR9LCX	RS13YC	ARF22C	TR4-2	T20EPR-U
V6 173 (2.8L) VIN W	1989	R43LTSE	5164		RS13YC	AGSP533C		T20EPR-U
V6 181 (3.0L) VIN L	1986-87	R44LTS	105	HR9DCX	RS12YC	AGRF42	BPR5EF5	T16EPR-U
V6 181 (3.0L) VIN L	1988	R44LTS	105/104	HR9DCX	RS12YC	AGRF42	TR5	T16EPR-U
V6 189 (3.1L) VIN T	1989	R43LTSE	5164		RS13YC	AGSP533C		T20EPR-U
V6 204 (3.3L) VIN N	1989	R44LTS6	605		RS12YC6	AGRF42-6		T16PR-U15
V6 231 (3.8L) VIN A	1986-87	R45TSX	666	HR9BCY	RV15YC6	ARF52-6	BPR4F5-15	T16PR-U15
V6 231 (3.8L) VIN B	1986	R44LTS	105	HR9DCX	RS12YC	AGRF42	BPR5EF5	T16EPR-U
V6 231 (3.8L) VIN C	1988	R44LTS6	605	HR9DCX	RS12YC6	AGRF42-6	TR5	T16EPR-U11
V6 231 (3.8L) VIN C	1989	R44LTS6	605		RS12YC6	AGRF42-6		T16EPR-U15
V6 231 (3.8L) VIN 3	1986-87	R44LTS	105	HR9DCX	RS12YC	AGRF42	BPR5EF5	T16EPR-U
V6 231 (3.8L) VIN 3	1988	R44LTS	105/104	HR9DCX	RS12YC	AGRF42	TR5	T16EPR-U
V8 305 (5.0L) VIN H	1987	R45TS	26	HR10BC			BPR4F5	T16PR-U
V8 307 (5.0L) VIN Y	1986-87	FR3LSX	3924	FR8DCX	RC12YC5	A6SP32C	BCPR5ES-11	016PR-U15
V8 307 (5.0L) VIN Y	1988	FR3L56	5184	FR8DCY	RC12YC5	A6SP32C	BCPR5ES-11	016PR-U15
V8 307 (5.0L) VIN Y	1989	FR3L56	5184	FR8DCY	RC12YC5	A6SP32C		016PR-U15
V8 307 (5.0L) VIN 9 H.O.	1986-87	FR3LSX	3924	FR8DCX	RJ18YC6	A6SP32C	BCPR5ES-11	016PR-U15

PONTIAC

MAKE/ENGINE	YEAR(S)	AC DELCO	AUTOLITE	BOSCH	CHAMPION	MOTOR-CRAFT	NGK	ND
L4 98 (1.6L) VIN C	1986-87	R42TS	23	HR8BC	RV12YC	ARF22C	BPR5ES	T20PR-U
L4 98 (1.6L) VIN 6	1988	R44XLS6	646	WR9DCY	RN12YC6	AGR52C-6	GR4	W16EXR-U11
L4 98 (1.6L) VIN 6	1989	R44XLS6	646		RN12YC6	AGR52C-6		W16EXR-U11
L4 112 (1.8L) VIN O EFI	1986	R44XLS	65	WR8DC	RN12YC	AGR42C	BPR5ES	W16EXR-U
L4 112 (1.8L) VIN J Turbo	1986	R42XLS	63	WR7DC	RN9YC	AGR22C	BPR6ES	W22EPR-U
L4 121 (2.0L) VIN P	1986	R42TS	23	HR8BC	RV12YC	ARF22C	BPR6FS	T20PR-U
L4 121 (2.0L) VIN K	1987	R44XLS6	646	WR9DCY	RN12YC6	AGR52C-6	BPR5ES-15	W16EXR-U11
L4 121 (2.0L) VIN K	1988	R44XLS6	646	WR9DCY	RN12YC6	AGR52C-6	GR4	W16EXR-U11
L4 121 (2.0L) VIN K	1989	R44XLS	65		RN12YC6	AGR42C		W16EXR-U
L4 121 (2.0L) VIN M Turbo	1987	R42XLS6	63	WR7DC	RN9YC4	AGR22C	BPR6ES-11	W22EPR-U
L4 121 (2.0L) VIN M Turbo	1988	R42XLS	63	WR7DC	RN9YC	AGR22C	GR5	W22EPR-U
L4 121 (2.0L) VIN M Turbo	1989	R42XLS	63		RN9YC	AGR22C		W22EPR-U
L4 138 (2.3L) VIN A, D	1989	FR3LS	3924		RC12YC	AGSP32C		Q16PR-U11
L4 138 (2.3L) VIN D	1988	FR3LS	3924		RC12YC	AGSP32C	BCPR5ES-11	Q16PR-U11
L4 151 (2.5L) VIN R,U,Z	1986-87	R43TS6	664	HR9BCY	RV12YC6	ARF32C-6	BPRFS-15	T20PR-U15

PLYMOUTH

MAKE/ENGINE	YEAR(S)	AC DELCO	AUTOLITE	BOSCH	CHAMPION	MOTOR-CRAFT	NGK	ND
L4 90 (1.5L) VIN K	1988	R42XLS	63	WR8DCX	RN9YC	AGR22C	GR4	W20EXR-U11
L4 90 (1.5L) VIN K	1989	R42XLS	63		RN9YC	AGR22C		W20EXR-U11
L4 98 (1.6L) VIN A	1986	R44XLS	65	WR7DC	RN12YC	AGR42C	BPR5ES	W16EXR-U
L4 98 (1.6L) VIN F	1988	R42XLS	63	WR7DC	RN7YC	AGR12	GR4	W22EPR-U11
L4 98 (1.6L) VIN F	1989	R42XLS	63		RN9YC	AGR22C		W20EXR-U11
L4 105 (1.8L)	1989	R42XLS	63		RN9YC	AGR22C		W20EXR-U11
L4 122 (2.0L) VIN D	1988	R42XLS	63	WR8DCX	RN9YC	AGR22C	GR4	W20EXR-U11
L4 122 (2.0L) VIN D,R,U,V	1989	R42XLS	63		RN9YC	AGR22C		W20EXR-U11
L4 135 (2.2L) B,C,D,E,8	1986-87	R44XLS	65	WR9DC	RN12YC	AGR42C	BPR5ES	W16EXR-U
L4 135 (2.2L) A,C,D,E	1988	R44XLS	65	WR9DC	RN12YC	AGR42C	GR4	W16EXR-U
L4 135 (2.2L) D	1989	R44XLS	65		RN12YC	AGR42C		W16EXR-U
L4 153 (2.5L) VIN K	1986	R44XLS	65	WR9DC	RN12YC	AGR22C	BPR5ES	W16EXR-U
L4 153 (2.5L) VIN K	1987	R44XLS	65	WR9DC	RN12YC	AGR42C	BPR5ES	W16EXR-U
L4 153 (2.5L) VIN K	1988	R44XLS	65	WR9DC	RN12YC	AGR42C	GR4	W16EXR-U
L4 153 (2.5L) VIN K, J	1989	R44XLS	65		RN12YC	AGR42C		W16EXR-U
V6 181 (3.0L) VIN 3	1988	R44XLS	65	WR9DCX	RN11YC4	AGR42C	GR4	W16EXR-U
V6 181 (3.0L) VIN 3	1989	R43XLS	64		RN11YC4	AGS32C		W16EXR-U11
V8 318 (5.2L) VIN P,R,S,4	1986-87	R44XLS	65	WR9DC	RN12YC	AGR42C	BPR5ES	W16EXR-U
V8 318 (5.2L) VIN P,R,S,4	1988	R44XLS	65	WR9DC	RN12YC	AGR42C	GR4	W16EXR-U
V8 318 (5.2L) VIN P, S	1989	R44XLS	65		RN12YC	AGR42C		W16EXR-U

PONTIAC

MAKE/ENGINE	YEAR(S)	AC DELCO	AUTOLITE	BOSCH	CHAMPION	MOTOR-CRAFT	NGK	ND
L4 151 (2.5L) VIN R, U	1988	R43TS6	664	HR9BCY	RV12YC6	ASF32C-6	UR55	T20PR-U15
L4 151 (2.5L) VIN R, U	1989	R43TS6	664		RV12YC6	ARF32C-6		T20PR-U15
V6 173 (2.8L) VIN 9	1986	R42TS	23	HR8BC	RV9YC	ASF32C		T20PR-U
V6 173 (2.8L) VIN 9	1987-88	R42TS	23	HR8BC	RV9YC	ARF22C	UR5	T20PR-U11
V6 173 (2.8L) VIN S	1986	R42TS	23	HR8BC	RV12YC	ARF22C		T20PR-U
V6 173 (2.8L) VIN S	1987	R42TS	23	HR8BC	RV12YC	ARF22C	BPR6FS	T20PR-U11
V6 173 (2.8L) VIN S	1988	R42TS	23	HR8BC	RV12YC	ARF22C	UR5	T20PR-U11
V6 173 (2.8L) VIN S	1989	R43TS-K	23		RV12YC	ASF32C		T20PR-U11
V6 173 (2.8L) VIN W	1987	R43LT5E	23	HR8BC	RS13LVC		TR4-2	T20EPR-U
V6 173 (2.8L) VIN W	1988	R43LT5E	5164	HR9LCX	RS13LVC		TR4-2	T20EPR-U
V6 173 (2.8L) VIN W	1989	R43LT5E	5164		RS13LVC	AGSF33C		T20EPR-U
V6 173 (2.8L) VIN X	1986	R43TS	24	HR8BC	RV12YC	ASF32C		T20PR-U
V6 181 (3.0L) VIN L	1986-87	R44LTS	105	HR9DCX	RS12YC	AGRF42	BPR5EFS	T16EPR-U
V6 189 (3.1L) VIN T	1988	R43LT5E	26	HR9LCX	RS13LVC		TR4-2	T20EPR-U
V6 189 (3.1L) VIN T	1989	R43LT5E	5164		RS13LVC	AGSF33C		T20EPR-U
V6 189 (3.1L) VIN V	1989	R42LTS	103		RS9YC	AGRF22		T20EPR-U
V6 231 (3.8L) VIN A	1986-87	R45TSX	666	HR9BCY	RV15YC6	ARF52-6	BPR4FS-15	T16EPR-U15
V6 231 (3.8L) VIN B,3	1986		24					
V6 231 (3.8L) VIN C	1988	R44LTS6	605	HR9DCY	RS12YC6	AGRF42-6	TR5	T16PR-U15
V6 231 (3.8L) VIN C	1989	R44LTS6	605		RS12YC6	AGRF42-6		T16PR-U15
V6 231 (3.8L) VIN 3	1987	R44LTS	105	HR9DCX	RV15YC6	AGRF52-6	BPR5EFS	T16EPR-U
V6 231 (3.8L) VIN 3	1988	R44LTS	105/104	HR9DCX	RS12YC	AGRF42	TR5	T16EPR-U
V6 231 (3.8L) VIN 7	1989		103		RS9YC	AGRF22		T20EPR-U
V6 262 (4.3L) VIN Z	1986	R43TS	24	HR8BC	RV15YC	ASF32C		T20PR-U
V6 262 (4.3L) VIN Z	1987	R45TS	26	HR10BC	RV15YC	ARF52	BPR4FS	T16PR-U
V8 305 (5.0L) VIN E	1988	R45TS	26	HR10BC	RV12YC	ASF52	UR5	T16PR-U
V8 305 (5.0L) VIN E	1989	R45TS	26		RV15YC	ASF52C		T16PR-U
V8 305 (5.0L) VIN F	1986	R43TS	24	HR8BC	RV12YC	ASF32C	BPR6FS	T20PR-U
V8 305 (5.0L) VIN F	1987	R43TS	24	HR10BC	RV12YC	ARF32	BPR6FS	T20-PR-U
V8 305 (5.0L) VIN F	1988	R45TS	26	HR10BC	RV12YC	ASF52	UR5	T16PR-U
V8 305 (5.0L) VIN F	1989	R45TS	26		RV15YC	ASF52C		T16PR-U
V8 305 (5.0L) VIN G	1986	R43TS	24	HR8BC	RV12YC	ASF32C	BPR6FS	T20PR-U
V8 305 (5.0L) VIN H	1986	R43TS	24	HR10BCX	RV15YC	ASF32C	BPR6FS	T16PR-U11
V8 305 (5.0L) VIN H	1987	R45TS	26	HR10BC	RV15YC	ARF52	BPR4FS	T16PR-U
V8 307 (5.0L) VIN Y	1986-87	FR3LS6	3924	FR8DCX	RC12YC5	AGSF32C	BCPR5ES-11	Q16PR-U15
V8 307 (5.0L) VIN Y	1988	FR3LS6	5184	FR8DCY	RC12YC5	AGSF32C	BCPR5ES-11	Q16PR-U15
V8 307 (5.0L) VIN Y	1989		5184			AGSF32C		Q16PR-U15
V8 350 (5.7L) VIN 8 exc. Alum. Heads 1986-87		R43TS	24		RV15YC	ARF32	BPR6FS	T20PR-U
V8 350 (5.7L) VIN 8 w/Alum. Heads 1986-87		FR3LS	3924		RC12YC		BCPR5ES-11	Q16PR-U11
V8 350 (5.7L) VIN 8	1988	R45TS	26	HR10BC	RV15YC	ASF52	UR4	T16PR-U
V8 350 (5.7L) VIN 8	1989	R45TS	26		RV15YC	ASF52C		T16PR-U

SECTION 35 — MECHANIC'S DATA

STANDARD TORQUE SPECIFICATIONS AND CAPSCREW MARKINGS

Newton-Meter has been designated as the world standard for measuring torque and will gradually replace the foot-pound and kilogram-meter torque measuring standard. Torquing tools are still being manufactured with foot-pounds and kilogram-meter scales, along with the new Newton-Meter standard. To assist the repairman, foot-pounds, kilogram-meter and Newton-Meter are listed in the following charts, and should be followed as applicable.

U.S. BOLTS

Capscrew Head Markings — Manufacturer's marks may vary. Three-line markings on heads below indicate SAE Grade 5.

SAE Grade Number	1 or 2			5			6 or 7			8		
Usage	Used Frequently			Used Frequently			Used at Times			Used at Times		
Quality of Material	Indeterminate			Minimum Commercial			Medium Commercial			Best Commercial		
Capacity Body Size (inches)-(thread)	Ft-Lb	kgm	Nm	Ft-Lb	kgm	Nm	Ft-Lb	kgm	Nm	Ft-Lb	kgm	Nm
1/4-20	5	0.6915	6.7791	10	1.3830	13.5582				12	1.6596	16.2698
1/4-28	6	0.8298	8.1349	8	1.1064	10.8465	10	1.3830	13.5582	14	1.9362	18.9815
5/16-18	11	1.5213	14.9140	17	2.3511	23.0489	19	2.6277	25.7605	24	3.3192	32.5396
5/16-24	13	1.7979	17.6256	19	2.6277	25.7605				27	3.7341	36.6071
3/8-16	18	2.4894	24.4047	31	4.2873	42.0304	34	4.7022	46.0978	44	6.0852	59.6560
3/8-24	20	2.7660	27.1164	35	4.8405	47.4536				49	6.7767	66.4351
7/16-14	28	3.8132	37.9629	49	6.7767	66.4351	55	7.6065	74.5700	70	9.6810	94.9073
7/16-20	30	4.1490	40.6745	55	7.6065	74.5700				78	10.7874	105.7538
1/2-13	39	5.3937	52.8769	75	10.3725	101.6863	85	11.7555	115.2445	105	14.5215	142.3609
1/2-20	41	5.6703	55.5885	85	11.7555	115.2445				120	16.5860	162.6960
9/16-12	51	7.0533	69.1467	110	15.2130	149.1380	120	16.5960	162.6960	155	21.4365	210.1490
9/16-18	55	7.6065	74.5700	120	16.5960	162.6960				170	23.5110	230.4860
5/8-11	83	11.4789	112.5329	150	20.7450	203.3700	167	23.0961	226.4186	210	29.0430	284.7180
5/8-18	95	13.1385	128.8027	170	23.5110	230.4860				240	33.1920	325.3920
3/4-10	105	14.5215	142.3609	270	37.3410	366.0060	280	38.7240	379.6240	375	51.8625	508.4250
3/4-16	115	15.9045	155.9170	295	40.7985	399.9610				420	58.0860	568.4360
7/8-9	160	22.1280	216.9280	395	54.6285	535.5410	440	60.8520	596.5520	605	83.6715	820.2590
7/8-14	175	24.2025	237.2650	435	60.1605	589.7730				675	93.3525	915.1650
1-8	236	32.5005	318.6130	590	81.5970	799.9220				910	125.6530	1233.7780
1-14	250	34.5750	338.9500	660	91.2780	849.8280				990	136.9170	1342.2420

METRIC BOLTS

Description	Torque ft-lbs. (Nm)	
Thread for general purposes (size x pitch (mm))	Head Mark 4	Head Mark 7
6 x 1.0	2.2 to 2.9 (3.0 to 3.9)	3.6 to 5.8 (4.9 to 7.8)
8 x 1.25	5.8 to 8.7 (7.9 to 12)	9.4 to 14 (13 to 19)
10 x 1.25	12 to 17 (16 to 23)	20 to 29 (27 to 39)
12 x 1.25	21 to 32 (29 to 43)	35 to 53 (47 to 72)
14 x 1.5	35 to 52 (48 to 70)	57 to 85 (77 to 110)
16 x 1.5	51 to 77 (67 to 100)	90 to 120 (130 to 160)
18 x 1.5	74 to 110 (100 to 150)	130 to 170 (180 to 230)
20 x 1.5	110 to 140 (150 to 190)	190 to 240 (260 to 320)
22 x 1.5	150 to 190 (200 to 260)	250 to 320 (340 to 430)
24 x 1.5	190 to 240 (260 to 320)	310 to 410 (420 to 550)

CAUTION: Bolts threaded into aluminum require much less torque.

ENGLISH TO METRIC CONVERSION: TORQUE

Torque is now expressed as either foot-pounds (ft./lbs.) or inch-pounds (in./lbs.). The metric measurement unit for torque is the Newton-meter (Nm). This unit—the Nm—will be used for all SI metric torque references, both the present ft./lbs. and in./lbs.

ft lbs	N-m	ft lbs	N-m	ft lbs	N-m	ft lbs	N-m
0.1	0.1	33	44.7	74	100.3	115	155.9
0.2	0.3	34	46.1	75	101.7	116	157.3
0.3	0.4	35	47.4	76	103.0	117	158.6
0.4	0.5	36	48.8	77	104.4	118	160.0
0.5	0.7	37	50.7	78	105.8	119	161.3
0.6	0.8	38	51.5	79	107.1	120	162.7
0.7	1.0	39	52.9	80	108.5	121	164.0
0.8	1.1	40	54.2	81	109.8	122	165.4
0.9	1.2	41	55.6	82	111.2	123	166.8
1	1.3	42	56.9	83	112.5	124	168.1
2	2.7	43	58.3	84	113.9	125	169.5
3	4.1	44	59.7	85	115.2	126	170.8
4	5.4	45	61.0	86	116.6	127	172.2
5	6.8	46	62.4	87	118.0	128	173.5
6	8.1	47	63.7	88	119.3	129	174.9
7	9.5	48	65.1	89	120.7	130	176.2
8	10.8	49	66.4	90	122.0	131	177.6
9	12.2	50	67.8	91	123.4	132	179.0
10	13.6	51	69.2	92	124.7	133	180.3
11	14.9	52	70.5	93	126.1	134	181.7
12	16.3	53	71.9	94	127.4	135	183.0
13	17.6	54	73.2	95	128.8	136	184.4
14	18.9	55	74.6	96	130.2	137	185.7
15	20.3	56	75.9	97	131.5	138	187.1
16	21.7	57	77.3	98	132.9	139	188.5
17	23.0	58	78.6	99	134.2	140	189.8
18	24.4	59	80.0	100	135.6	141	191.2
19	25.8	60	81.4	101	136.9	142	192.5
20	27.1	61	82.7	102	138.3	143	193.9
21	28.5	62	84.1	103	139.6	144	195.2
22	29.8	63	85.4	104	141.0	145	196.6
23	31.2	64	86.8	105	142.4	146	198.0
24	32.5	65	88.1	106	143.7	147	199.3
25	33.9	66	89.5	107	145.1	148	200.7
26	35.2	67	90.8	108	146.4	149	202.0
27	36.6	68	92.2	109	147.8	150	203.4
28	38.0	69	93.6	110	149.1	151	204.7
29	39.3	70	94.9	111	150.5	152	206.1
30	40.7	71	96.3	112	151.8	153	207.4
31	42.0	72	97.6	113	153.2	154	208.8
32	43.4	73	99.0	114	154.6	155	210.2

ENGLISH TO METRIC CONVERSION: PRESSURE

The basic unit of pressure measurement used today is expressed as pounds per square inch (psi). The metric unit for psi will be the kilopascal (kPa). This will apply to either fluid pressure or air pressure, and will be frequently seen in tire pressure readings, oil pressure specifications, fuel pump pressure, etc.

To convert pounds per square inch (psi) to kilopascals (kPa): multiply the number of psi by 6.89.

Psi	kPa	Psi	kPa	Psi	kPa	Psi	kPa
0.1	0.7	37	255.1	82	565.4	127	875.6
0.2	1.4	38	262.0	83	572.3	128	882.5
0.3	2.1	39	268.9	84	579.2	129	889.4
0.4	2.8	40	275.8	85	586.0	130	896.3
0.5	3.4	41	282.7	86	592.9	131	903.2
0.6	4.1	42	289.6	87	599.8	132	910.1
0.7	4.8	43	296.5	88	606.7	133	917.0
0.8	5.5	44	303.4	89	613.6	134	923.9
0.9	6.2	45	310.3	90	620.5	135	930.8
1	6.9	46	317.2	91	627.4	136	937.7
2	13.8	47	324.0	92	634.3	137	944.6
3	20.7	48	331.0	93	641.2	138	951.5
4	27.6	49	337.8	94	648.1	139	958.4
5	34.5	50	344.7	95	655.0	140	965.2
6	41.4	51	351.6	96	661.9	141	972.2
7	48.3	52	358.5	97	668.8	142	979.0
8	55.2	53	365.4	98	675.7	143	985.9
9	62.1	54	372.3	99	682.6	144	992.8
10	69.0	55	379.2	100	689.5	145	999.7
11	75.8	56	386.1	101	696.4	146	1006.6
12	82.7	57	393.0	102	703.3	147	1013.5
13	89.6	58	399.9	103	710.2	148	1020.4
14	96.5	59	406.8	104	717.0	149	1027.3
15	103.4	60	413.7	105	723.9	150	1034.2
16	110.3	61	420.6	106	730.8	151	1041.1
17	117.2	62	427.5	107	737.7	152	1048.0
18	124.1	63	434.4	108	744.6	153	1054.9
19	131.0	64	441.3	109	751.5	154	1061.8
20	137.9	65	448.2	110	758.4	155	1068.7
21	144.8	66	455.0	111	765.3	156	1075.6
22	151.7	67	461.9	112	772.2	157	1082.5
23	158.6	68	468.8	113	779.1	158	1089.4
24	165.5	69	475.7	114	786.0	159	1096.3
25	172.4	70	482.6	115	792.9	160	1103.2
26	179.3	71	489.5	116	799.8	161	1110.0
27	186.2	72	496.4	117	806.7	162	1116.9
28	193.0	73	503.3	118	813.6	163	1123.8
29	200.0	74	510.2	119	820.5	164	1130.7
30	206.8	75	517.1	120	827.4	165	1137.6
31	213.7	76	524.0	121	834.3	166	1144.5
32	220.6	77	530.9	122	841.2	167	1151.4
33	227.5	78	537.8	123	848.0	168	1158.3
34	234.4	79	544.7	124	854.9	169	1165.2
35	241.3	80	551.6	125	861.8	170	1172.1
36	248.2	81	558.5	126	868.7	171	1179.0

ENGLISH TO METRIC CONVERSION: PRESSURE

The basic unit of pressure measurement used today is expressed as pounds per square inch (psi). The metric unit for psi will be the kilopascal (kPa). This will apply to either fluid pressure or air pressure, and will be frequently seen in tire pressure readings, oil pressure specifications, fuel pump pressure, etc.

To convert pounds per square inch (psi) to kilopascals (kPa): multiply the number of psi by 6.89

Psi	kPa	Psi	kPa	Psi	kPa	Psi	kPa
172	1185.9	216	1489.3	260	1792.6	304	2096.0
173	1192.8	217	1496.2	261	1799.5	305	2102.9
174	1199.7	218	1503.1	262	1806.4	306	2109.8
175	1206.6	219	1510.0	263	1813.3	307	2116.7
176	1213.5	220	1516.8	264	1820.2	308	2123.6
177	1220.4	221	1523.7	265	1827.1	309	2130.5
178	1227.3	222	1530.6	266	1834.0	310	2137.4
179	1234.2	223	1537.5	267	1840.9	311	2144.3
180	1241.0	224	1544.4	268	1847.8	312	2151.2
181	1247.9	225	1551.3	269	1854.7	313	2158.1
182	1254.8	226	1558.2	270	1861.6	314	2164.9
183	1261.7	227	1565.1	271	1868.5	315	2171.8
184	1268.6	228	1572.0	272	1875.4	316	2178.7
185	1275.5	229	1578.9	273	1882.3	317	2185.6
186	1282.4	230	1585.8	274	1889.2	318	2192.5
187	1289.3	231	1592.7	275	1896.1	319	2199.4
188	1296.2	232	1599.6	276	1903.0	320	2206.3
189	1303.1	233	1606.5	277	1909.8	321	2213.2
190	1310.0	234	1613.4	278	1916.7	322	2220.1
191	1316.9	235	1620.3	279	1923.6	323	2227.0
192	1323.8	236	1627.2	280	1930.5	324	2233.9
193	1330.7	237	1634.1	281	1937.4	325	2240.8
194	1337.6	238	1641.0	282	1944.3	326	2247.7
195	1344.5	239	1647.8	283	1951.2	327	2254.6
196	1351.4	240	1654.7	284	1958.1	328	2261.5
197	1358.3	241	1661.6	285	1965.0	329	2268.4
198	1365.2	242	1668.5	286	1971.9	330	2275.3
199	1372.0	243	1675.4	287	1978.8	331	2282.2
200	1378.9	244	1682.3	288	1985.7	332	2289.1
201	1385.8	245	1689.2	289	1992.6	333	2295.9
202	1392.7	246	1696.1	290	1999.5	334	2302.8
203	1399.6	247	1703.0	291	2006.4	335	2309.7
204	1406.5	248	1709.9	292	2013.3	336	2316.6
205	1413.4	249	1716.8	293	2020.2	337	2323.5
206	1420.3	250	1723.7	294	2027.1	338	2330.4
207	1427.2	251	1730.6	295	2034.0	339	2337.3
208	1434.1	252	1737.5	296	2040.8	340	2344.2
209	1441.0	253	1744.4	297	2047.7	341	2351.1
210	1447.9	254	1751.3	298	2054.6	342	2358.0
211	1454.8	255	1758.2	299	2061.5	343	2364.9
212	1461.7	256	1765.1	300	2068.4	344	2371.8
213	1468.7	257	1772.0	301	2075.3	345	2378.7
214	1475.5	258	1778.8	302	2082.2	346	2385.6
215	1482.4	259	1785.7	303	2089.1	347	2392.5

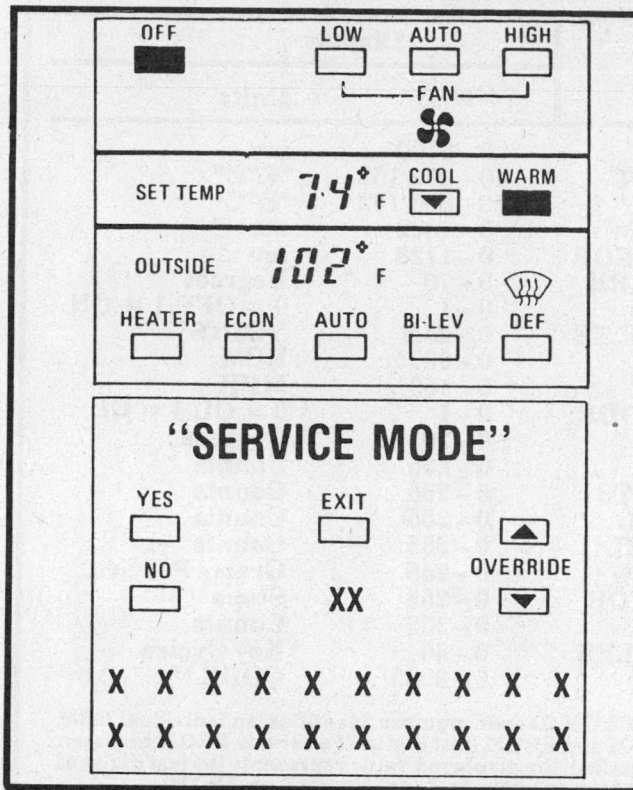

Service mode entrance—Riviera

in the computer memory will be displayed. ECM codes will be displayed first. If no ECM codes are stored, the CRT will display a NO ECM CODES message for approximately 2 seconds. All ECM codes will be prefixed with an E (Example—EO13, EO23 and etc.)

The lowest numbered ECM code will be displayed first, followed by progressively higher numbered codes present. Codes will be displayed consecutively for 2 second intervals until the highest code present has been displayed. When all ECM codes have been displayed, BCM codes will be displayed. Following the highest ECM code present or the NO ECM CODES message, the lowest numbered BCM code will be displayed for approximately 2 seconds. BCM codes displayed will also be accompanied by CURRENT or HISTORY. HISTORY indicates the failure was not present the last time the code was tested and CURRENT indicates the fault still exists. Since the ECM is not capable of making this determination, these messages do not appear when the ECM codes are being displayed. All BCM codes will be prefixed with the letter B (Example—B110 and etc.). Progressively higher numbered BCM codes, if present, will be displayed for approximately 2 second intervals until the highest code present has been displayed. If no BCM trouble codes are stored, NO BCM CODES message will be displayed. At any time during the display of the ECM or BCM codes, if the NO pad is touched, the display will bypass the codes. At any time during the display of trouble codes, if the EXIT pad is touched, the CRT will exit the SERVICE MODE and go back to normal vehicle operation.

CLIMATE CONTROL OPERATION

Upon entering the SERVICE MODE, the climate control will operate in whatever setting was being commanded just prior to depressing the OFF and WARM pads. Even though the display may change just as the pads are touched, the prior operating setting is remembered and will resume after the SERVICE MODE is entered.

During the SERVICE MODE, the climate control can be operated the same as normally by touching the climate control border pad and calling up climate control page. To get back to SERVICE MODE page, simply touch the border pad marked DIAGNOSTICS. This will take the system back to the exact same spot in the SERVICE MODE as what it was before the climate control border pad was touched. The climate control and the diagnostic border pads are the only 2 border pads that will operate while in the SERVICE MODE.

HOW TO OPERATE THE SERVICE MODE

After trouble codes have been displayed, the SERVICE MODE can be used to perform several tests on different systems one at a time. Upon completion of code display, a specific system may be selected for testing or a segment check can be performed.

Selecting The System

Following the display of trouble codes, the first available system will be displayed (i.e. ECM?). While selecting a system to test, any of the following actions may be taken to control the display.

1. Touching the EXIT pad will stop the system selection process and return the display to the beginning of the trouble code sequence.

2. Touching the NO pad will display the next available system selection. This allows the display to be stepped through all systems choices. This list of systems can be repeated following the display of the last system.

3. Touching the YES pad will select the displayed system for testing. At this point, the first available test type will appear with the selected name above it.

Selecting The Test Type

Having selected a system, the first available test type will be displayed (i.e. ECM data?). While selecting a specific test type, any of the following actions may be taken to control the display.

1. Touching the EXIT pad will stop the test type selection process and return the display to the next available system selection.

2. Touching the NO pad will display the next available test type for the selected system. This allows the display to be stepped through all available test type choices. The list of test types can be repeated following the display of the last test type.

3. Touching the YES pad will select the displayed test type. At this point, the display will either indicate the at the selected test type is in progress or the first of several specific tests will appear. If NO DEVICES is displayed, no tests are available.

Selecting The Test

Selection of the DATA, INPUTS?, OUTPUTS? or OVERRIDE? test types will result in the first available test being displayed, If a SELECT ERR message ever appears, this test is not allowed with the engine operating. Turn the engine **OFF** and try again. The 4 characters of the display will contain a test code to identify the selection. The first 2 characters are letters which identify the system and the test type (i.e. ED01 for throttle position). While selecting a specific test, any of the following actions may be taken to control the display.

1. Touching the EXIT pad will stop the test selection process and return the display to the next available test type for the selected system.

2. Touching the NO pad will display the next smaller test number for the selected test type. If this pad is touched with the lowest test number displayed, the highest test number will then appear.

3. Touching the YES pad will display the next larger test number for the selected test type. If this pad is touched with the highest test number displayed, the lowest test number will then appear.

Data Number	Description	Message	Display Range	Units
ED01	Throttle Position	TPS	0 – 5100	mv
ED04	Coolant Temperature	COOLANT	−40 – 306/152	°F/°C*
ED05	Air Temperature	MAT	−40 – 306/152	°F/°C*
ED06	Injector Pulse Width	MS INJ PW	0 – 1002	ms
ED07	Oxygen Sensor Voltage	OXY SENSOR	0 – 1128	mv
ED08	Spark Avance	DEG SPARK	0 – 70	Degrees
ED09	Transaxle Convertor Clutch	TCC SOL	0 – 1	0 = OFF 1 = ON
ED10	Battery Voltage	BATT VOLTS	0 – 25.5	VOLTS
ED11	Engine RPM	RPM	0 – 6375	RPM
ED12	Vehicle Speed	MPH	0 – 159	MPH
ED15	Closed or Open Loop	OPER MODE	0 – 1	0 = OL 1 = CL
ED16	ESC (Knock Retard)	ESC	0 – 20	Degrees
ED17	OLDPA3 (Knock Signal)	OLD PA3	0 – 255	Counts
ED18	Cross Counts 0^2	CROSS CTS	0 – 255	Counts
ED19	Fuel Integrator	INT FUEL	0 – 255	Counts
ED20	Block Learn Memory (Fuel)	BLM FUEL	0 – 255	Counts
ED21	Air Flow	AIR FLOW	0 – 255	Grams Per Sec.
ED22	Idle Air Control	IAC MOTOR	0 – 255	Steps
ED23	LV8 (Engine Load)	LV8	0 – 255	Counts
ED98	Ignition Cycle Counter	IGN CYCLES	0 – 50	Key Cycles
ED99	ECM PROM ID	PROM ID	0 – 9999	CODE **

*°F or °C selectable with the E/M button on the Left Switch Assy.

**PROM ID code number identifies an individual OEM ECM and PROM (last digits).If a service PROM has been installed, the displayed value represents the last digits of the service package # (not stamped on PROM).

ECM diagnostic data—Riviera

ECM OUTPUT CYCLING

Output Number	Description	Message	Status
EO00	No Outputs	None	
EO01	Canister Purge Solenoid	Purge	HI/LO
EO02	TCC Solenoid	TCC	HI/LO
EO04	EGR Solenoid	EGR	HI/LO
EO07	IAC Motor Set	IAC	Pintle Fully Extended*
EO08	A/C Clutch	A/C Clutch	HI/LO
EO09	Coolant Fan Relay	Fan	Hi/LO

*Minimum air adjustment can be made when pintle is fully extended.

ECM output cycling—Riviera

ECM DISCRETE INPUTS

Input Number	Description	Message	Status	Ign. "ON" * Display
EI60	EVRV EGR Vac. Switch	EVRV	HI/LO	HI
EI74	Park/Neutral Switch	P/N	HI/LO	LO
EI78	Power Steering Press.Switch	PS	HI/LO	HI
EI82	Fourth Gear Switch	4TH	HI/LO	LO

* In park, engine not running.
In the Input mode, four switches can be monitored relative to their "HI" and "LO" status.

ECM discreet inputs—Riviera

Selecting CODE RESET?

Selection of CODE RESET? test type will result in the message CODES CLEAR being displayed with the selected system name above it after the YES pad has been touched. This message will appear for 3 seconds to indicate all stored trouble codes have been erased from that system's memory. After 3 seconds, the display will automatically return to the next available test type for the selected system

IPC Segment Check

Whenever the key is **ON** and the vehicle is in the **PARK** position, pressing the TEST button on the instrument panel cluster, will cause the IPC to sequentially illuminate and blank all segments and telltales in the cluster. This is helpful in determining if any bulbs or segments or the cluster's vacuum fluorescent display are out or always on. To provide more time to study the various segments, whenever in the SERVICE MODE and not in the middle of running a test, such as when the CRT displays ECM?, if the TEST button on the ICP is depressed, the segment check will run 10 times slower than when not in the SERVICE MODE.

Exiting SERVICE MODE

To exit the service mode, repeatedly touch the EXIT pad until the SERVICE MODE page disappears or turn the ignition switch to the **OFF** position. Trouble codes are not erased when this is done.

INPUT DISPLAYS

When troubleshooting a malfunction, the ECM, BCM or IPC input display can be used to determine if the switched inputs can be used to determine if the switched inputs can be properly interpreted. When one of the various input tests is selected, the state of that device is displayed as HI or LO. In general, the HI and LO refer to the input terminal voltage for that circuit. The display also indicates if the input changed state so that the technician could activate or deactivate any listed device and return to the display to see if it changed state. If a change of state occurred, an X will appear next to the HI/LO indicator, otherwise, an O will remain displayed. The X will only appear once per selected input, although the HI/LO indication will continue to change as the input changes. Some tests are momentary and the X can be used as an indication of a change.

COMPUTER COMMAND CONTROL – CADILLAC RWD VEHICLES

General Information

ELECTRONIC CONTROL MODULE SERVICE PRECAUTIONS

The ECM is designed to withstand normal current draws associated with the vehicle operation. However, care must be exercised to avoid overloading any of these circuits. In testing for opens or shorts, do not ground or apply voltage to any of the ECM circuits, unless instructed to do so by a diagnostic procedure. These circuits should only be tested using a high impedance Mulimeter, should they remain connected to the ECM.

Power should never be applied to the ECM with the ignition in the **ON** position. Before removing or connecting battery cables, ECM fuses or ECM connectors, always turn the ignition to the **OFF** position.

ECM LEARNING ABILITY

The ECM has a learning ability that allows the fuel control calibration to be tailored to account for minor differences in the fuel control system and the engine mechanical system. This allows the ECM to better adapt the vehicle to changing environmental conditions. If the battery is disconnected or if an ECM is replaced, the ECM in the vehicle will have to begin the learning process all over again . A change in vehicle driveability may be noted after a battery disconnect or ECM replacement. To teach the ECM, operate the vehicle at normal operating temperature, at part throttle and at idle until driveability and performance returns

TROUBLE CODES

NOTE: Cadillac rear wheel drive vehicles have carbureted engines and are equipped with the CCC Engine Control system.

The dash mounted SERVICE NOW and SERVICE SOON indicator lamps are used to inform the technician of detected system malfunctions or system abnormalities. These malfunctions

may be related to the various operating sensors or to the ECM itself. The light that comes on will automatically go out if the fault clears, such as an intermediate malfunction. However, the ECM stores the trouble code associated with the detected failure until the diagnostic system is CLEARED or until 50 OFF-ON ignition switch cycles have occurred without any fault reappearing.

Proper operation of SERVICE NOW or the SERVICE SOON indicator lamps are as follows:

1. Both lamps are normally off.

2. A bulb check is performed with both bulbs on, when the ignition switch is in the CRANK position only. When the engine starts, both lamps go out.

3. Depending upon the trouble code set, either the SERVICE SOON or the SERVICE NOW lamps will come on and stay on when a constant malfunction is detected.

4. If the malfunction is intermittent, the lamp that came on previously, will go out when the malfunction is no longer detected. The lamp will come on each time the malfunction is again detected and will either be on bright or flickering.

5. When a SERVICE SOON malfunction is detected at the same time a SERVICE NOW malfunction is detected, only the SERVICE NOW lamp will be on.

6. Both lamps will stay on when the system is displaying the diagnostic routines.

The dash mounted digital display panel, normally used for the ECC system, can be temporarily directed to display trouble codes stored in the ECM.

INTERMITTENT CODES VERSUS HARD FAILURES CODES

For codes 12 through 51, the SERVICE indicator lamp will go out automatically if the malfunction clears. However, the ECM stores the trouble code associated with the detected failure until the diagnostic system is cleared or until 50 ignition cycles have occurred without any fault reappearing. This condition is known as an intermediate failure.

Therefore, the ECM may have 2 types of trouble codes stored in its memory. These 2 codes types are:

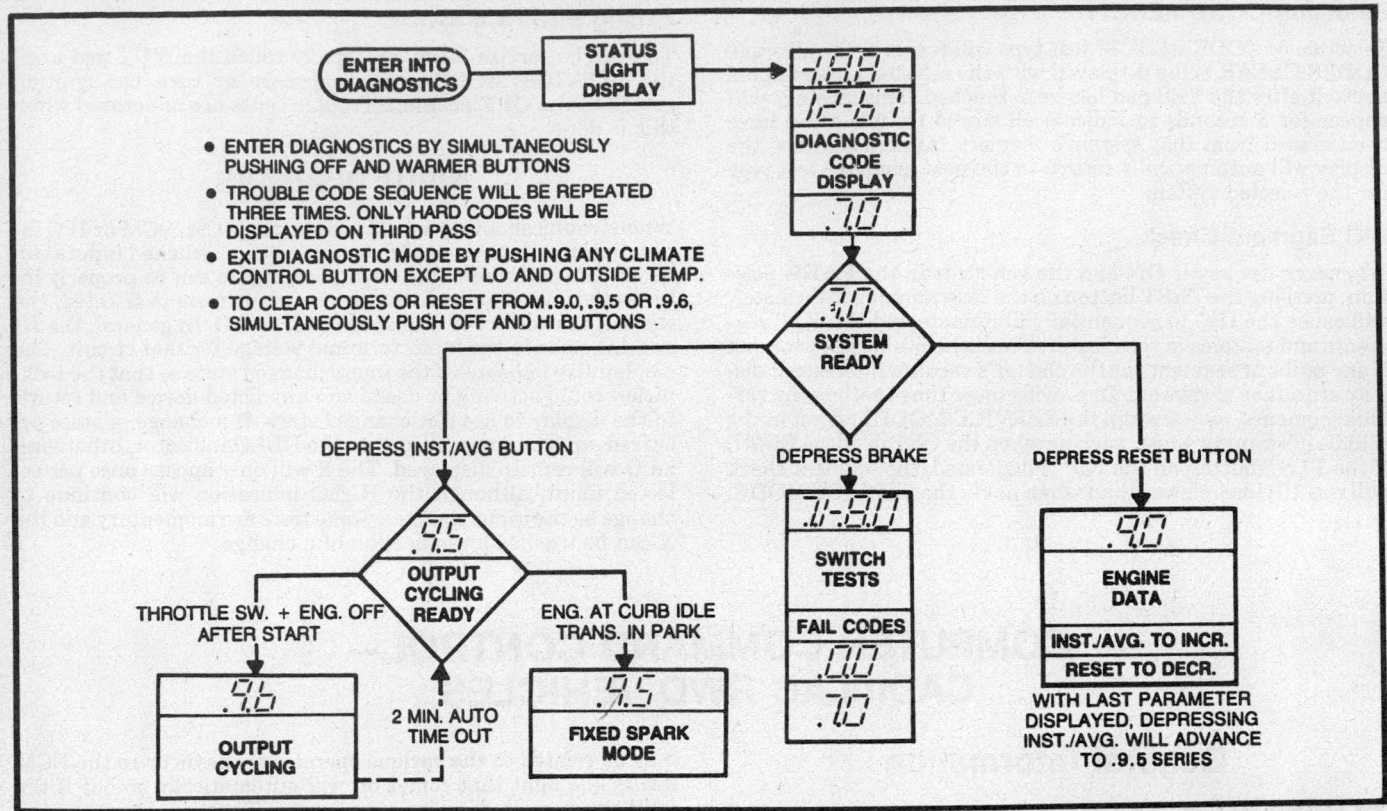

Diagnostic data Cadillac — RWD

1. A code for malfunction which is a hard failure. A hard failure turns on the appropriate SERVICE indicator lamp and keeps it on as long as the malfunction is present.

2. A code for intermediate malfunction which has occurred within the last 50 ignition cycles. An intermediate failure turns off the SERVICE lamp when the malfunction clears up.

For codes 52 through 67, the SERVICE indicator lamp will never come on. These codes indicate that a specific condition occurred of which the technician should be aware. Since these codes can be operator induced, a judgement must be made whether or not the code requires investigation. These codes will also be stored until the diagnostic system is cleared or until 50 ignition cycles have occurred without any faults reappearing.

INTERMITTENT PROBLEM DIAGNOSIS

It should be noted that diagnostic charts cannot be used to diagnose intermittent failures. The testing required at various points of the chart depends upon the fault to be present in order to locate its source in order to correct it.

If the fault is intermittent, an unnecessary ECM replacement could be indicated and the problem could remain.

Exceptions to this rule includes trouble codes 13, 20, 30, 33, 39, 44 and 45. The nature of these codes or the design of their charts allow them to be treated as hard failures.

Since many of the intermittent problems are caused at electrical connections, diagnosis of intermittent problems should start with a visual and physical inspection of the connectors involved in the circuit. Disconnect the connectors, examine and reconnect before replacing any component of the system.

Some causes of connector problems are:
1. Improperly formed terminals or connector bodies.
2. Damaged terminals or connector bodies.
3. Corrosion, body sealer, or other foreign matter on the terminal mating surfaces which could insulate the terminals.

4. Incomplete mating of the connector halves.
5. Connectors not fully seated in the connector body.
6. Terminals not tightly crimped to the wire.

If an affected circuit is one that may be checked by the status light on the ECC, the switch tests, the output cycling tests, or the engine data displays, make the check on the appropriate circuit. Some of the trouble codes include a Note On Intermittents describing a suggested procedure for isolating the location of intermittent malfunctions.

HOW TO ENTER THE DIAGNOSTIC MODE

To enter diagnostics, proceed as follows.
1. Turn ignition **ON**.
2. Depress OFF and WARMER buttons on the ECC panel simultaneously and hold until .. appears. –1.8.8 will then be displayed, which indicates the beginning of the diagnostic readout.
3. If –1.8.8 does not display or is partially displayed, a malfunction is indicated and a misdiagnose of codes could occur due to segments of the display inoperative. The display head would then have to be replaced.

NOTE: Some vehicles may not display one or both of the decimal points. This is a normal condition and the control head should not be replaced because of it.

4. Trouble codes will be displayed on the digital ECC panel beginning with the lowest numbered code. Note that the Fuel Data panel goes blank when the system is in the diagnostic mode.
5. The lowest numbered code will be displayed for approximately 2 seconds. Progressively higher numbered codes, if present, will be displayed consecutively for 2 seconds until all stored code have been displayed.
6. The code –1.8.8 will be displayed again.
7. A second pass will be repeated of the first pass.

8. On the third pass, only HARD trouble codes will be displayed. These are the codes which indicate a malfunction and keep the indicator lamp on.

NOTE: Codes which were displayed on the first and second pass, but not the third, are intermittent codes.

9. The –1.8.8 will be displayed again. When the trouble codes are displayed again, code .7.0 will then be displayed. Code .7.0 indicates that the ECM is ready for the next diagnostic feature to be selected.

10. If a code 51 (PROM error) is present, it will be displayed continuously until the diagnostic mode is exited. During the display of code 51, none of the other diagnostic features will be possible.

11. If a code 16 (alternator voltage out of range) is present, this must be diagnosed first, since this malfunction can affect the setting of other codes.

12. If no trouble codes are present, –1.8.8 will be displayed for 2 seconds and then the ECM will display the code .7.0, which indicates the ECM is ready for the next diagnostic feature to be selected.

DISPLAY OF CODE .7.0

Code .7.0 is a decision point for the technician. When code .7.0 is displayed, the technician should select the diagnostic feature that he wants to display. The following choices are available:
1. Switch tests
2. Engine data display
3. Output cycling tests
4. Fixed spark mode
5. Exit diagnostics or clear codes and then exit.

Switch Test Procedure

Code .7.0 must be displayed on the ECC control head before the switch tests can begin. To start the switch tests sequence, depress and release the brake pedal. The switch tests begin as the display switches from code .7.0 to code .7.1. If the display codes do not advance, the ECM is not processing the brake signal.

As each code is displayed, the associated switch must be cycled within 10 seconds or the code will be recorded in the ECM's memory as a failure.

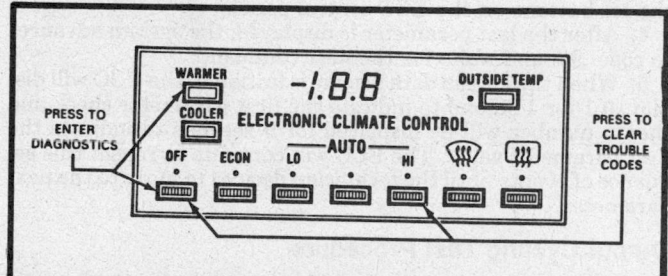

Electronic Climate Control head (ECC) Cadillac—RWD

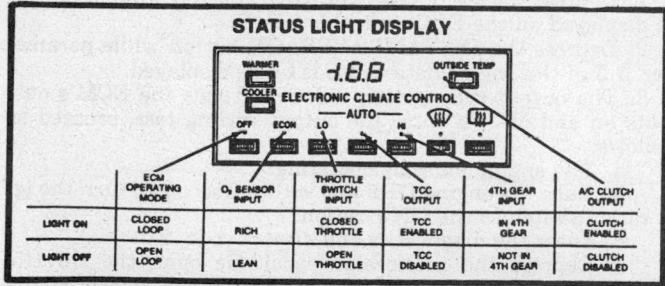

ECC control head status light display Cadillac—RWD

CODE	CIRCUIT AFFECTED
■■ 12	NO DISTRIBUTOR (TACH) SIGNAL
□ 13	O$_2$ SENSOR NOT READY
□ 14	SHORTED COOLANT SENSOR CIRCUIT
□ 15	OPEN COOLANT SENSOR CIRCUIT
■■ 16	GENERATOR VOLTAGE OUT OF RANGE
□ 18	OPEN CRANK SIGNAL CIRCUIT
□ 19	SHORTED FUEL PUMP CIRCUIT
■■ 20	OPEN FUEL PUMP CIRCUIT
□ 21	SHORTED THROTTLE POSITION SENSOR CIRCUIT
□ 22	OPEN THROTTLE POSITION SENSOR CIRCUIT
□ 23	EST/BYPASS CIRCUIT PROBLEM
□ 24	SPEED SENSOR CIRCUIT PROBLEM
□ 26	SHORTED THROTTLE SWITCH CIRCUIT
□ 27	OPEN THROTTLE SWITCH CIRCUIT
□ 28	OPEN FOURTH GEAR CIRCUIT
□ 29	SHORTED FOURTH GEAR CIRCUIT
□ 30	ISC CIRCUIT PROBLEM
■■ 31	SHORTED MAP SENSOR CIRCUIT
■■ 32	OPEN MAP SENSOR CIRCUIT
■■ 33	MAP/BARO SENSOR CORRELATION
■■ 34	MAP SIGNAL TOO HIGH
□ 35	SHORTED BARO SENSOR CIRCUIT
□ 36	OPEN BARO SENSOR CIRCUIT
□ 37	SHORTED MAT SENSOR CIRCUIT
□ 38	OPEN MAT SENSOR CIRCUIT
□ 39	TCC ENGAGEMENT PROBLEM
■■ 44	LEAN EXHAUST SIGNAL
■■ 45	RICH EXHAUST SIGNAL
■■ 51	PROM ERROR INDICATOR
▼ 52	ECM MEMORY RESET INDICATOR
▼ 53	DISTRIBUTOR SIGNAL INTERRUPT
▼ 60	TRANSMISSION NOT IN DRIVE
▼ 63	CAR AND SET SPEED TOLERANCE EXCEEDED
▼ 64	CAR ACCELERATION EXCEEDS MAX. LIMIT
▼ 65	COOLANT TEMPERATURE EXCEEDS MAX. LIMIT
▼ 66	ENGINE RPM EXCEEDS MAXIMUM LIMIT
▼ 67	SHORTED SET OR RESUME CIRCUIT
.7.0	SYSTEM READY FOR FURTHER TESTS
.7.1	CRUISE CONTROL BRAKE CIRCUIT TEST
.7.2	THROTTLE SWITCH CIRCUIT TEST
.7.3	DRIVE (ADL) CIRCUIT TEST
.7.4	REVERSE CIRCUIT TEST
.7.5	CRUISE ON/OFF CIRCUIT TEST
.7.6	"SET/COAST" CIRCUIT TEST
.7.7	"RESUME/ACCELERATION" CIRCUIT TEST
.7.8	"INSTANT/AVERAGE" CIRCUIT TEST
.7.9	"RESET" CIRCUIT TEST
.8.0	A/C CLUTCH CIRCUIT TEST
-1.8.8	DISPLAY CHECK
.9.0	SYSTEM READY TO DISPLAY ENGINE DATA
.9.5	SYSTEM READY FOR OUTPUT CYCLING OR IN FIXED SPARK MODE
.9.6	OUTPUT CYCLING
.0.0	ALL DIANOSTICS COMPLETE
■■	TURNS ON "SERVICE NOW" LIGHT
□	TURNS ON "SERVICE SOON" LIGHT
▼	DOES NOT TURN ON ANY TELLTALE LIGHT

NOTE: CRUISE IS DISENGAGED WITH ANY "SERVICE NOW" LIGHT OR WITH CODES 60-67.

Diagnostic codes Cadillac—RWD

After the ECM recognizes a test as passing or after the 10 second time-out elapses without the proper cycling being recognized, the display will automatically advance to the next switch test code.

1. With code .7.0 displayed to start the test sequence, depress and release the brake pedal.

2. With code .7.1 displayed, depress the throttle from the idle position to an open throttle position and slowly release the throttle.

3. With code .7.3 displayed, shift the transmission lever into D and then the N position.

4. On vehicles without cruise control, codes .7.5, .7.6. and .7.7 will be displayed, but cannot be performed during the switch tests.

5. On vehicles with cruise control, code .7.5 will be displayed. With the cruise instrument panel switch in the ON position, depress and release the SET/COAST button.

6. With code .7.6 displayed and with the cruise instrument panel switch in the ON position, depress and release the RESUME/ACCELERATION switch.

7. With code .7.8 displayed, depress and release the INSTANT/AVERAGE button on the fuel data panel.

8. With code .7.9 displayed, depress and release the RESET button on the fuel data panel.

9. With code .8.0 displayed, depress and release the OUTSIDE TEMPERATURE button twice. This operation works in conjunction with the air conditioning compressor clutch.

10. When all the tests are completed, the ECM will then go back to display the switch codes that did not test properly, from the lowest number to the highest. The switch codes will not disappear until the affected switch circuit has been repaired and retested.

11. After the switch tests are completed and all circuits pass, the ECC panel will display .0.0 and then return to code .7.0.

NOTE: 0.0 indicates that all switch circuits are operating properly.

Engine Data Display Procedure

The code .7.0 must be displayed on the ECC control head before the engine data can be displayed. To begin the display procedure, proceed as follows:

1. Depress and release the RESET button on the fuel data panel. The engine data series begins as the display switches from code .7.0 to code .9.0.

2. To advance the display, depress the INSTANT/AVERAGE button on the fuel data panel.

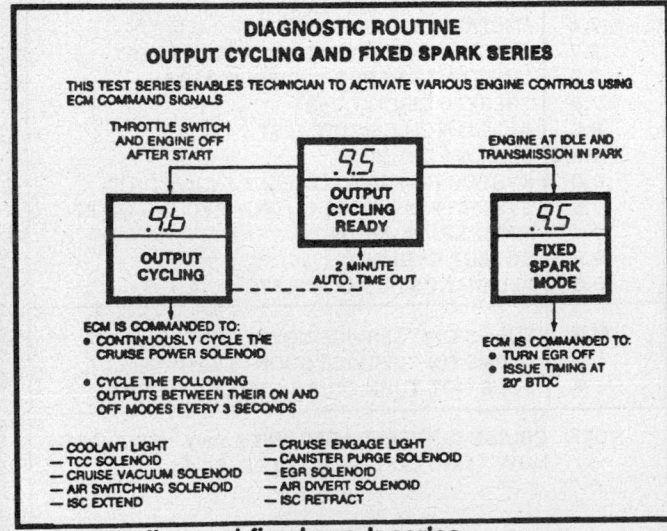

Output cycling and fixed spark series

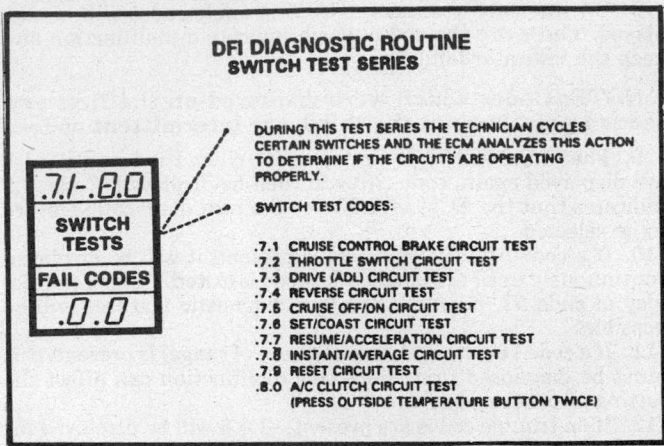

Switch test series Cadillac—RWD

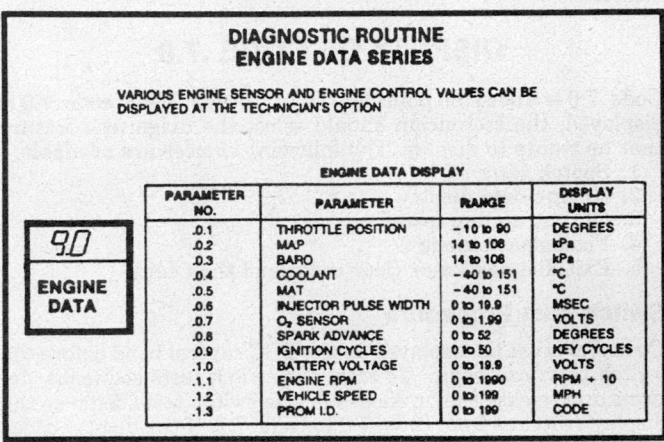

Engine data display RWD models

3. It is possible to leave the engine data series at any time and return to code .7.0 by simultaneously depressing the OFF and the HI buttons on the ECC control panel.

4. After the last parameter is displayed, the system advances to code .9.5 and waits for the next command.

5. When the engine data display is initiated, the ECC will display .0.1 for 1 second to indicate the first parameter check and then a number will be displayed for 9 seconds to indicate the first parameter value. The ECC will continue to repeat this sequence of events until the technician decides to move to the next parameter.

Output Cycling Test Procedure

This series of tests can be initiated after .9.5 is displayed on the ECC panel. The display of .9.5 can be reached by either of the following methods:

1. Depress the INSTANT/AVERAGE button while code .7.0 is displayed on the ECC control head.

2. Depress the INSTANT/AVERAGE button while parameter .1.3 of the engine data series is being displayed.

3. The output cycling test, code .9.6, turns the ECM's outputs on and off. To enter the output cycling test, proceed as follows:

a. The engine must be operating.

b. Turn the engine OFF and within 2 seconds, turn the ignition switch to the ON position.

c. Enter the diagnostics and display code .9.5.

d. Depress the accelerator pedal the open the throttle switch and release it to close it. Code .9.6 will appear on the display.

e. Turn the cruise control instrument panel switch to the **ON** position so that the cruise control outputs will cycle.

f. The output cycling test will end automatically after 2 minutes of cycling and display will switch from code .9.6 to code .9.5.

4. The outputs will cycle ON and OFF every 3 seconds until the 2 minute automatic shut-off occurs. The only exception to this 3 second cycle is the cruise control power valve, which cycles continuously. If additional output cycling is desired, recycle the throttle switch.

Fixed Spark Mode Procedure

To verify proper adjustment of the spark timing, the ECM will command a fixed 20 degrees of spark advance and disable the EGR valve operation when ever the following conditions are met:

1. The engine must be operating and to normal operating temperature.
2. Code .9.5 must be displayed on the ECC control head.
3. Engine speed must be under 900 rpm.
4. The transmission must be in the **P** position.

Code 9.5

The display of code .9.5 can be reached by either of the following methods:

1. Depress the INSTANT/AVERAGE button while the .7.0 is displayed on the ECC control head.
2. Depress the INSTANT/AVERAGE BUTTON while the parameter .1.3. of the engine data series is being displayed.

As long as these conditions are met, codes 23 and 25 are not set and the HEI system is operating correctly, a timing light can be used to verify that the engine timing is adjusted correctly. If the engine timing is not at 20° ± 2° BTDC under the above conditions, the base timing of 10° BTDC should be adjusted.

STATUS DISPLAY

While in the diagnostic mode, the mode indicators on the CCP are used to indicate the status of certain operating systems. These different modes of operation are indicated by the status light either being turned OFF or ON.

DIGITAL FUEL INJECTION (DFI) SYSTEM—
FWD DE VILLE AND FLEETWOOD

General Information

Several electronic components are used to provide the technician with valuable diagnostic information as part of an electronic network designed to control various engine and body subsystems.

At the center of the self-diagnostic system is the Body Computer Module (BCM), located behind the glove compartment opening. An internal microprocessor is used to control various vehicle function, based on monitored sensor and switch inputs.

When equipped with the digital fuel injection system, an electronic Control Module (ECM) is used to provide a microprocessor control for the various engine and emission related functions. The ECM is located on the right side of the instrument panel and is the major factor in providing self-diagnostic capabilities for those subsection which it controls.

When both the BCM and ECM are used, a communication process has been incorporated which allows the 2 modules to share information and thereby provide for additional control capability. In a method similar to a telegraph key operator, each module's internal circuitry rapidly switches a circuit between 0 and 5 volts. This process is used to convert information into a series of pulses which represent coded data messages understood by the other components.

One of the data messages transferred from the BCM is a request for specific ECM diagnostic action. This action may affect the ECM controlled output or require the ECM to transfer some information back to the BCM. This communication gives the BCM control over the ECM's self-diagnostic capabilities in addition to its own.

In order to access and control the self-diagnostic features, available to the BCM, 2 additional electronic components are utilized by the service technician. Located to the right of the steering column is the Climate Control Panel (CCP) and located to the left of the steering column is either the Fuel Data Center (FDC), used with DFI equipped vehicles.

These devices provide displays and keyboard switches used with several BCM controlled subsystems. This display and keyboard information is transferred over the single wire data circuits which carry coded data back and forth between the BCM and the display panels. This communication process allows the BCM to transfer any of its available diagnostic information to

BCM/ECM DATA TRANSFER

CIRCUIT 459-ECM TO BCM DATA

- REQUESTED DIAGNOSTIC DATA
- FUEL ECONOMY DATA
- VEHICLE SPEED
- COOLANT TEMPERATURE
- ENGINE RUN STATUS
- WIDE OPEN THROTTLE STATUS

BODY COMPUTER MODULE

ELECTRONIC CONTROL MODULE

CIRCUIT 491-BCM TO ECM DATA

- DIAGNOSTIC ACTION REQUEST
- OUTSIDE AIR TEMPERATURE
- A/C HIGH SIDE TEMPERATURE
- A/C CLUTCH STATUS
- REAR DEFOG STATUS
- HIGH BLOWER STATUS
- HIGH COOLING FANS STATUS

BCM/ECM data transfer method—DeVille and Fleetwood

the instrument panel for display during service. By depressing the appropriate buttons on the CCP, data messages can be sent to the BCM, requesting the specific diagnostic features required.

ECM/BCM SERVICE PRECAUTIONS

The ECM/BCMs are designed to withstand normal current draws associated with the vehicle operation. However, care must be exercised to avoid overloading any of these circuits. In testing for opens or shorts, do not ground or apply voltage to any of the ECM/BCM circuits, unless instructed to do so by a diagnostic procedure. These circuits should only be tested using a high impedance Mulimeter, should they remain connected to the ECM/BCM.

Power should never be applied to the ECM with the ignition in the **ON** position. Before removing or connecting battery cables, ECM/BCM fuses or ECM/BCM connectors, always turn the ignition to the **OFF** position.

Self-Diagnostic System

INTERMITTENT CODES VERSUS HARD FAILURES

For codes 12 through 51, the SERVICE SOON or SERVICE NOW will go out automatically if the malfunction clears. However, the ECM stores the trouble code associated with the detected failure until the diagnostic system is cleared or until 50 ignition cycles have occurred without any fault reappearing. This condition is known as an intermediate failure.

Therefore, the ECM may have 2 types of trouble codes stored in its memory. These 2 codes types are:

1. A code for malfunction which is a hard failure. A hard failure turns on the appropriate SERVICE indicator lamp and keeps it on as long as the malfunction is present.

2. A code for intermediate malfunction which has occurred within the last 50 ignition cycles. An intermediate failure is one that was previously present, but was not detected the last time the ECM tested the circuit. The SERVICE indicator lamp turns out after the ECM tests the circuit without the defect being detected.

The first pass of the diagnostic codes, preceded by ..E, will contain all history codes, both hard and intermittent. The second pass contains only the hard codes that are present and will be preceded by .E.E.

For codes 52 through 67, the SERVICE indicator lamp will never come on. These codes indicate that a specific condition occurred of which the technician should be aware. Since these codes can be operator induced, a judgement must be made whether or not the code requires investigation. These codes will also be stored until the diagnostic system is cleared or until 50 ignition cycles have occurred without any faults reappearing.

INTERMITTENT PROBLEM DIAGNOSIS

It should be noted that diagnostic charts cannot be used to diagnose intermittent failures. The testing required at various points of the chart depends upon the fault to be present in order to locate its source in order to correct it.

If the fault is intermittent, an unnecessary ECM replacement could be indicated and the problem could remain.

Since many of the intermittent problems are caused at electrical connections, diagnosis of intermittent problems should start with a visual and physical inspection of the connectors involved in the circuit. Disconnect the connectors, examine and reconnect before replacing any component of the system.

Some causes of connector problems are:

1. Improperly formed terminals or connector bodies
2. Damaged terminals or connector bodies
3. Corrosion, body sealer, or other foreign matter on the terminal mating surfaces which could insulate the terminals
4. Incomplete mating of the connector halves
5. Connectors not fully seated in the connector body
6. Terminals not tightly crimped to the wire

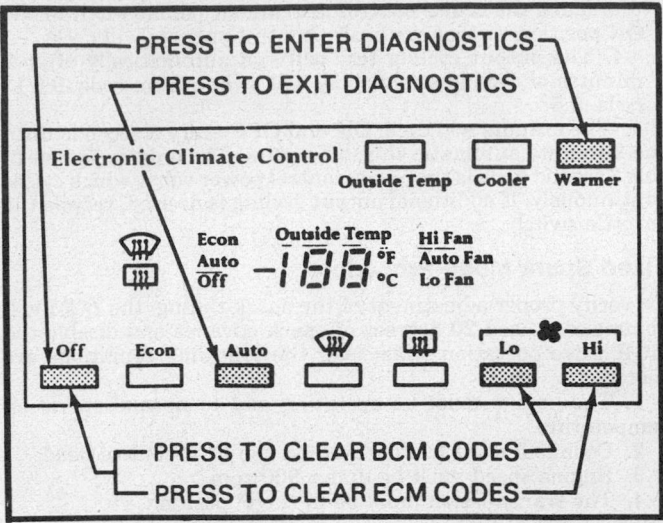

Entering the diagnostic system on ECC—DeVille and Fleetwood

BCM DIAGNOSTIC CODES	
CODE	CIRCUIT AFFECTED
▼ F10	OUTSIDE TEMP SENSOR CKT
▼ F11	A/C HIGH SIDE TEMP SENSOR CKT
▼ F12	A/C LOW SIDE TEMP SENSOR CKT
▼ F13	IN-CAR TEMP SENSOR CKT
▼ F30	CCP TO BCM DATA CKT
▼ F31	FDC TO BCM DATA CKT
▼ F32	ECM-BCM DATA CKT'S
▼ F40	AIR MIX DOOR PROBLEM
▼ F41	COOLING FANS PROBLEM
☑ F46	LOW REFRIGERANT WARNING
☑ F47	LOW REFRIGERANT CONDITION
☑ F48	LOW REFRIGERANT PRESSURE
▼ F49	HIGH TEMP CLUTCH DISENGAGE
▼ F51	BCM PROM ERROR

☑ TURNS ON "SERVICE AIR COND" LIGHT

▼ DOES NOT TURN ON ANY LIGHT

COMMENTS:

F11 TURNS ON COOLING FANS WHEN A/C CLUTCH IS ENGAGED

F12 DISENGAGES A/C CLUTCH

F32 TURNS ON COOLING FANS

F30 TURNS ON FT. DEFOG AT 75° F

F41 TURNS ON "COOLANT TEMP/FANS" LIGHT WHEN FANS SHOULD BE ON

F47 & F48 SWITCHES FROM "AUTO" TO "ECON"

BCM diagnostic codes—DeVille and Fleetwood

If an affected circuit is one that may be checked by the status light on the ECC, the switch tests, the output cycling tests, or the engine data displays, make the check on the appropriate circuit. Some of the trouble codes include a Note On Intermittents describing a suggested procedure for isolating the location of intermittent malfunctions.

TROUBLE CODES

In the process of controlling its various subsystems, the ECM and BCM continually monitor the operating conditions for possible system malfunctions. By comparing system conditions against standard operating limits, certain circuit and component malfunctions can be detected. A 2 digit numerical TROUBLE CODE is stored in the computer's memory when a problem is detected by this self-diagnostic system. These trouble codes can later be displayed by the service technician as an aid in system repair.

If a particular malfunction would result in unacceptable system operation, the self-diagnostics will attempt to minimize the effect by taking FAIL-SAFE action. FAIL-SAFE action refers to any specific attempt by the computer system to compensate for the detected problem. A typical FAIL-SAFE action would be the substitution of a fixed input value when a sensor/circuit is detected to be open or shorted.

HOW TO ENTER THE DIAGNOSTIC MODE

To enter the diagnostic mode, proceed as follows:
1. Turn the ignition switch to the **ON** position.
2. Depress the OFF and the WARMER buttons on the CCP, simultaneously and hold them in until all display segments illuminate, which indicated the beginning of the diagnostic readout.

NOTE: If any of the segments are inoperative, the diagnosis should not be attempted, as this could lead to misdiagnosis. The display in question would have to be replaced before the diagnosis procedure is initiated.

TROUBLE CODE DISPLAY

After the display segment check is completed, any trouble codes stored in the computer memory will be displayed on the Data Center panel as follows:
1. Display of the trouble codes will begin with an 1.8.8 on the data center panel for approximately 1 second. ..E will then be displayed which indicates the beginning of the ECM stored trouble codes.
2. This first pass of ECM codes includes all detected malfunctions whether they are currently present or not. If no ECM trouble codes are stored, the ..E display will be bypassed.
3. Following the display of ..E, the lowest numbered ECM trouble code will be displayed for approximately 2 seconds. All ECM trouble codes will be prefixed with the letter E. (i.e. E12, E13, etc.).
4. Progressively higher numbered trouble codes will be displayed, until the highest code present has been displayed.
5. .E.E' will then be displayed, which indicates the beginning of the second pass of the ECM trouble codes.
6. On the second pass, only HARD trouble codes will be displayed. These are the codes which indicate a currently present malfunction.
7. Codes which are displayed during the first pass, but not on the second, are classified as intermittent trouble codes. If all the ECM codes are considered intermittent, the .E.E display will be bypassed.
8. When all the ECM trouble codes have been displayed, the BCM codes will then displayed in a similar fashion. The only exceptions during the BCM code display are as follows:
   a. ..F precedes the first display pass.

ECM DIAGNOSTIC CODES

CODE	MALFUNCTION
■■ E12	NO DISTRIBUTOR SIGNAL
□ E13	OXYGEN SENSOR NOT READY (CANISTER PURGE)
□ E14	SHORTED COOLANT SENSOR CIRCUIT
□ E15	OPEN COOLANT SENSOR CIRCUIT
■■ E16	GENERATOR VOLTAGE OUT OF RANGE (ALL SOLENOIDS)
□ E18	OPEN CRANK SIGNAL CIRCUIT
□ E19	SHORTED FUEL PUMP CIRCUIT
■■ E20	OPEN FUEL PUMP CIRCUIT
□ E21	SHORTED THROTTLE POSITION SENSOR CIRCUIT
□ E22	OPEN THROTTLE POSITION SENSOR CIRCUIT
□ E23	EST/BYPASS CIRCUIT PROBLEM (AIR)
□ E24	SPEED SENSOR CIRCUIT PROBLEM (VCC)
□ E26	SHORTED THROTTLE SWITCH CIRCUIT
□ E27	OPEN THROTTLE SWITCH CIRCUIT
□ E28	OPEN THIRD OR FOURTH GEAR CIRCUIT
□ E30	ISC CIRCUIT PROBLEM
■■ E31	SHORTED MAP SENSOR CIRCUIT (AIR)
■■ E32	OPEN MAP SENSOR CIRCUIT (AIR)
■■ E34	MAP SENSOR SIGNAL TOO HIGH (AIR)
□ E37	SHORTED MAT SENSOR CIRCUIT
□ E38	OPEN MAT SENSOR CIRCUIT
□ E39	VCC ENGAGEMENT PROBLEM
□ E40	OPEN POWER STEERING PRESSURE CIRCUIT
■■ E44	LEAN EXHAUST SIGNAL (AIR & CL & CANISTER PURGE)
■■ E45	RICH EXHAUST SIGNAL (AIR & CL & CANISTER PURGE)
□ E47	BCM - ECM DATA PROBLEM
■■ E51	ECM PROM ERROR
▼ E52	ECM MEMORY RESET INDICATOR
▼ E53	DISTRIBUTOR SIGNAL INTERRUPT
▼ E59	VCC TEMPERATURE SENSOR CIRCUIT
▼ E60	TRANSMISSION NOT IN DRIVE
▼ E63	CAR SPEED AND SET SPEED DIFFERENCE TOO HIGH
▼ E64	CAR ACCELERATION TOO HIGH
▼ E65	COOLANT TEMPERATURE TOO HIGH
▼ E66	ENGINE RPM TOO HIGH
▼ E67	CRUISE SWITCH SHORTED DURING ENABLE

ECM AND CRUISE CONTROL COMMENTS:

■■	TURNS ON "SERVICE NOW" LIGHT
□	TURNS ON "SERVICE SOON" LIGHT
▼	DOES NOT TURN ON ANY TELLTALE LIGHT
( )	FUNCTIONS WITHIN BRACKETS ARE DISENGAGED WHILE SPECIFIED MALFUNCTION REMAINS CURRENT (HARD)

E16 & E24 DISABLE VCC FOR ENTIRE IGNITION CYCLE

E24 & E67 DISABLE CRUISE FOR ENTIRE IGNITION CYCLE

CRUISE IS DISENGAGED WITH CODE(S) E16, E51 OR E60 - E67

ECM diagnostic codes—DeVille and Fleetwood

ECM DIAGNOSTIC CODES

CODE	DESCRIPTION	COMMENTS
E12	No Distributor Signal	Ⓐ
E13	Oxygen Sensor Not Ready [AIR, CL & Canister Purge]	Ⓑ
E14	Shorted Coolant Sensor Circuit [AIR]	ⒷⒼ
E15	Open Coolant Sensor Circuit [AIR]	ⒷⒼ
E16	Generator Voltage Out Of Range [All Solenoids]	ⒶⒻ
E18	Open Crank Signal Circuit	Ⓑ
E19	Shorted Fuel Pump Circuit	Ⓑ
E20	Open Fuel Pump Circuit	Ⓐ
E21	Shorted Throttle Position Sensor Circuit	Ⓑ
E22	Open Throttle Position Sensor Circuit	Ⓑ
E23	EST/Bypass Circuit Problem [AIR]	ⒷⒺ
E24	Speed Sensor Circuit Problem [VCC & Cruise]	ⒷⒹⒻ
E26	Shorted Throttle Switch Circuit	Ⓑ
E27	Open Throttle Switch Circuit	Ⓑ
E28	Open Third Or Fourth Gear Circuit	Ⓑ
E30	ISC Circuit Problem	Ⓑ
E31	Shorted MAP Sensor Circuit [AIR]	Ⓐ
E32	Open MAP Sensor Circuit [AIR]	Ⓐ
E34	MAP Sensor Signal Too High [AIR]	Ⓐ
E37	Shorted MAT Sensor Circuit [AIR]	Ⓑ
E38	Open MAT Sensor Circuit [AIR]	Ⓑ
E39	VCC Engagement Problem	Ⓑ
E40	Open Power Steering Pressure Switch Circuit	Ⓑ
E44	Lean Exhaust Signal [AIR, CL & Canister Purge]	Ⓐ
E45	Rich Exhaust Signal [AIR, CL & Canister Purge]	Ⓐ
E47	BCM — ECM Data Problem	Ⓑ
E48	EGR System Fault [EGR]	Ⓑ
E51	ECM PROM Error	Ⓐ
E52	ECM Memory Reset Indicator	Ⓒ
E53	Distributor Signal Interrupt	Ⓒ
E55	TPS Misadjusted	Ⓒ
E59	VCC Temperature Sensor Circuit Problem	Ⓒ
E60	Cruise - Transmission Not In Drive [Cruise]	Ⓒ
E63	Cruise - Car Speed And Set Speed Difference Too High [Cruise]	Ⓒ
E64	Cruise - Car Acceleration Too High [Cruise]	Ⓒ
E65	Cruise - Coolant Temperature Too High [Cruise]	Ⓒ
E66	Cruise - Engine RPM Too High [Cruise]	Ⓒ
E67	Cruise - Cruise Switch Shorted During Enable [Cruise]	ⒸⒹ

DIAGNOSTIC CODE COMMENTS

A	Turns On "SERVICE NOW" Light.
B	Turns On "SERVICE SOON" Light.
C	Does Not Turn On Any Telltale Light.
D	Disables Cruise For Entire Ignition Cycle.
E	Causes System To Operate On Bypass Spark.
F	Disengages VCC For Entire Ignition Cycle.
G	Forces Cooling Fans On Full Speed.
H	Turns On Cooling Fans Whenever A/C Clutch Is Engaged.
I	Displays "c" for Clock Problem Or "d" for Data Problem.
J	Turns On Front Defog At 75°F.
K	Turns On "COOLANT TEMP/FAN" Light Whenever Cooling Fans Should Be Operating.
L	Turns On "SERVICE AIR COND" Light For A Period Of Time.
M	Turns On "SERVICE AIR COND" Light For A Period Of Time, & Switches ECC Mode To ECON.
N	Displays "-151" On CCP And Turns On Front Defog.
[ ]	Functions Within Bracket Are Disengaged While Specified Malfunction Remains Current.

ECM diagnostic codes—DeVille and Fleetwood

b. The BCM codes are prefixed by an F.

c. .F.F precedes the second display pass.

9. After all the ECM and BCM trouble codes have been displayed or if no codes are present, code .7.0 will be displayed. This code indicates that the system is ready for the next diagnostic feature to be selected.

NOTE: If a code E51 is detected, it will be displayed continuously until the diagnostic mode is exited. During this display of code E51, none of the other diagnostic features will be possible.

CLEARING TROUBLE CODES

Trouble codes stored in the ECM's memory may be cleared (erased) by entering the diagnostic mode and then depressing the OFF and HI buttons on the CCP simultaneously. Hold the buttons in until E.0.0 appears on the display. Trouble codes stored in the BCM's memory may be cleared by depressing the OFF and LO buttons simultaneously until F.0.0 appears. After E.0.0 or F.0.0 is displayed, .7.0. will appear. With the .7.0 displayed, turn the ignition OFF for at least 10 seconds before re-entering the diagnostic mode.

EXITING THE DIAGNOSTIC MODE

To get out of the diagnostic mode, depress the AUTO button or turn the ignition switch OFF for 10 seconds. Trouble codes are not erased when this is done. The temperature setting will reappear in the display panel.

NOTE: The climate control system will operate in whatever mode was commanded prior to depressing the necessary buttons to enter the diagnostic system. The prior operating mode will be remembered and will resume after the diagnostic mode is entered.

STATUS DISPLAY

While in the diagnostic mode, the mode indicators on the CCP are used to indicate the status of certain operating systems. These different modes of operation are indicated by the status light either being turned OFF or ON.

EEC PROGRAM OVERRIDE

During the BCM display of data, a manual override of the system can be accomplished by the technician, for different levels of heating and cooling effort. Since this is not in the realm of this diagnostic coverage, no procedural explanation is given.

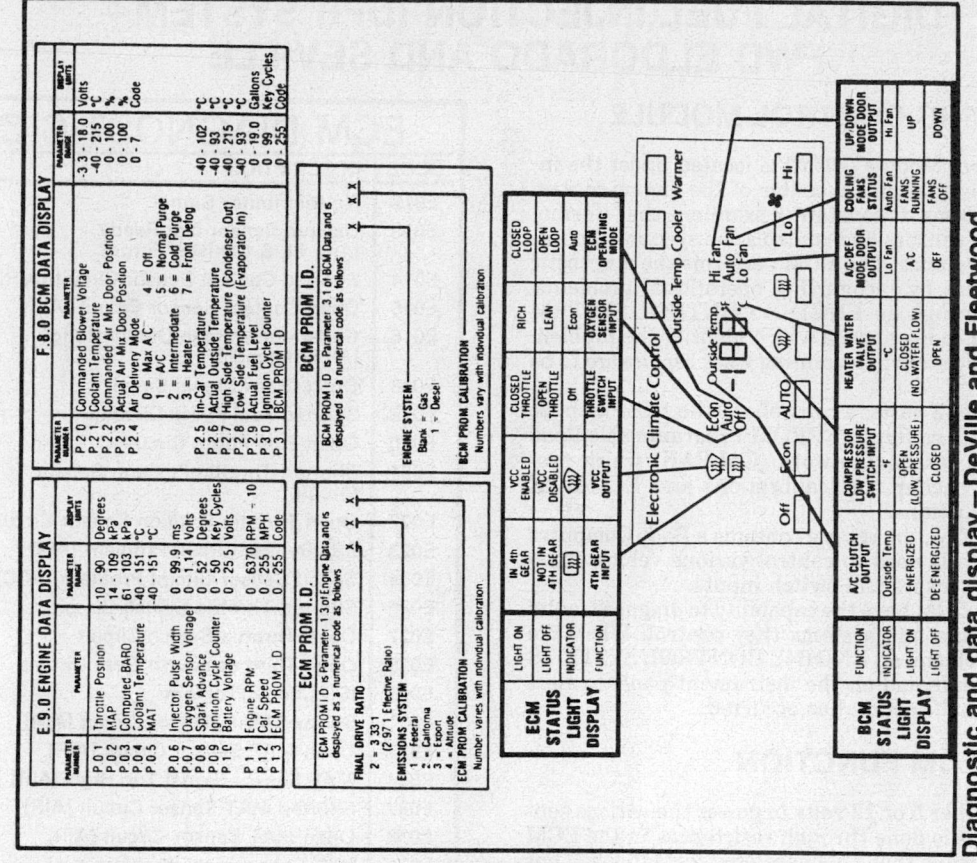

Diagnostic and data display—DeVille and Fleetwood

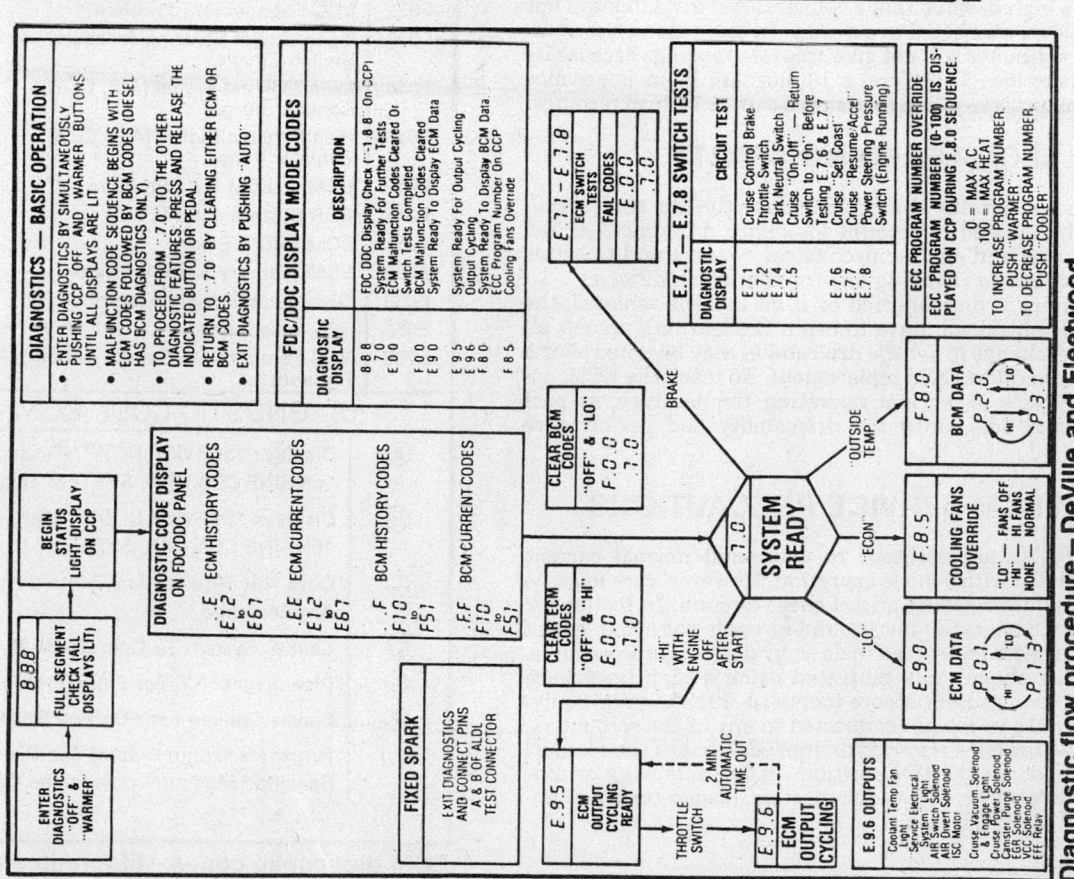

Diagnostic flow procedure—DeVille and Fleetwood

DIGITAL FUEL INJECTION (DFI) SYSTEM — FWD ELDORADO AND SEVILLE

ELECTRONIC CONTROL MODULE

The Electronic Control Module (ECM) is located under the instrument panel and is the control center of the engine control and fuel injection systems. It constantly examines the information from the various sensors and controls the systems that affect the vehicle performance. The ECM performs the diagnostic function of the system by recognizing operational problems, alert the operator through an ENGINE CONTROL SYSTEM lamp and will store a code or codes which identify the problem areas to aid the technician in determining what repairs are to be made.

The ECM consists of 3 parts; a controller, (the ECM without the PROM), A separate calibrator (PROM-Programmable Read Only Memory) and a resistor network (CALPAK) which provides the calibrated backup fuel calibrations and ECM/BCM communication instructions.

In addition to the ECM, the vehicle contains a Body Computer Module (BCM), which is used to control various vehicle functions, based on data sensors and switch inputs.

Both the ECM and BCM have the capability to diagnose faults with the various inputs and systems they control. When the ECM recognizes a problem, an ENGINE CONTROL SYSTEMS indicator lamp is illuminated on the instrument panel to alert the operator that a malfunction has occurred.

ECM FUNCTION

The ECM supplies either 5 or 12 volts to power the various sensors or switched. This is done through resistances in the ECM which are so high in value that a conventional test lamp will not illuminate when connected to a circuit. In some cases, a conventional shop voltmeter will not give accurate readings because its resistance is to low. Therefore, a 10 megohm input impedance digital voltmeter is required to assure accurate voltage readings.

ECM LEARNING ABILITY

The ECM has a learning ability that allows the fuel control calibration to be tailored to account for minor differences in fuel control systems and engine mechanical systems and to better adapt the vehicle to changing environmental conditions.

If the battery is disconnected or if an ECM is replaced, the ECM in the vehicle will have to begin the learning process all over again. A change in vehicle driveability may be noted after a battery disconnect or ECM replacement. To teach the ECM, operate the vehicle at normal operating temperature, at part throttle and at idle, until the driveability and performance returns.

ECM/BCM SERVICE PRECAUTIONS

The ECM/BCMs are designed to withstand normal current draws associated with vehicle operation. However, care must be taken to avoid overloading any of these circuits. In testing for open or short circuits, do not ground or apply voltage to any of the circuits, unless instructed to do so by diagnostic procedures. These circuits should only be tested using a high impedance multimeter, such as Kent Moore tool no. J-29125A or its equivalent, if they are to remain connected to any of the computers. Power should never be removed or applied to one of the computers with the key in the ON position. Before removing or connecting battery cables, fuses or connectors, always turn the ignition to the LOCK position.

ECM DIAGNOSTIC CODES

CODE	DESCRIPTION	COMMENTS
E012	No Distributor Signal	Ⓐ
E013	Oxygen Sensor Not Ready [AIR, CL & Canister Purge]	Ⓑ
E014	Shorted Coolant Sensor Circuit [AIR]	Ⓑ Ⓕ
E015	Open Coolant Sensor Circuit [AIR]	Ⓑ Ⓕ
E016	Generator Voltage Out Of Range [All Solenoids]	Ⓐ Ⓔ
E018	Open Crank Signal Circuit	Ⓑ
E019	Shorted Fuel Pump Circuit	Ⓑ
E020	Open Fuel Pump Circuit	Ⓐ
E021	Shorted Throttle Position Sensor Circuit	Ⓑ
E022	Open Throttle Position Sensor Circuit	Ⓑ
E023	EST/Bypass Circuit Problem [AIR]	Ⓑ Ⓓ
E024	Speed Sensor Circuit Problem [VCC]	Ⓑ Ⓔ
E026	Shorted Throttle Switch Circuit	Ⓑ
E027	Open Throttle Switch Circuit	Ⓑ
E028	Open Third or Fourth Gear Circuit	Ⓑ
E030	ISC Circuit Problem	Ⓑ
E031	Shorted MAP Sensor Circuit [AIR]	Ⓐ
E032	Open MAP Sensor Circuit [AIR]	Ⓐ
E034	MAP Sensor Signal Too High [AIR]	Ⓐ
E037	Shorted MAT Sensor Circuit [AIR]	Ⓑ
E038	Open MAT Sensor Circuit [AIR]	Ⓑ
E039	VCC Engagement Problem	Ⓑ
E040	Open Power Steering Pressure Switch Circuit	Ⓑ
E044	Lean Exhaust Signal [AIR, CL & Canister Purge]	Ⓐ
E045	Rich Exhaust Signal [AIR, CL & Canister Purge]	Ⓐ
E047	BCM — ECM Data Problem	Ⓑ
E048	EGR System Fault [EGR]	Ⓑ
E051	ECM PROM Error	Ⓐ Ⓕ
E052	ECM Memory Reset Indicator	Ⓒ
E053	Distributor Signal Interrupt	Ⓒ
E055	TPS Misadjusted	Ⓒ
E059	VCC Temperature Sensor Circuit Problem	Ⓒ

DIAGNOSTIC CODE COMMENTS

Ⓐ	Displays "SERVICE NOW" Message And Turns On "ENGINE CONTROL SYSTEM" Light.
Ⓑ	Displays "SERVICE SOON" Message And Turns On "ENGINE CONTROL SYSTEM" Light.
Ⓒ	Does Not Turn On Any Telltale Light Or Display Any Message.
Ⓓ	Causes System To Operate On Bypass Spark.
Ⓔ	Disengages VCC For Entire Ignition Cycle.
Ⓕ	Forces Cooling Fans On Full Speed.
[ ]	Functions Within Bracket Are Disengaged While Specified Malfunction Remains Current.

ECM diagnostic codes—Eldorado and Seville

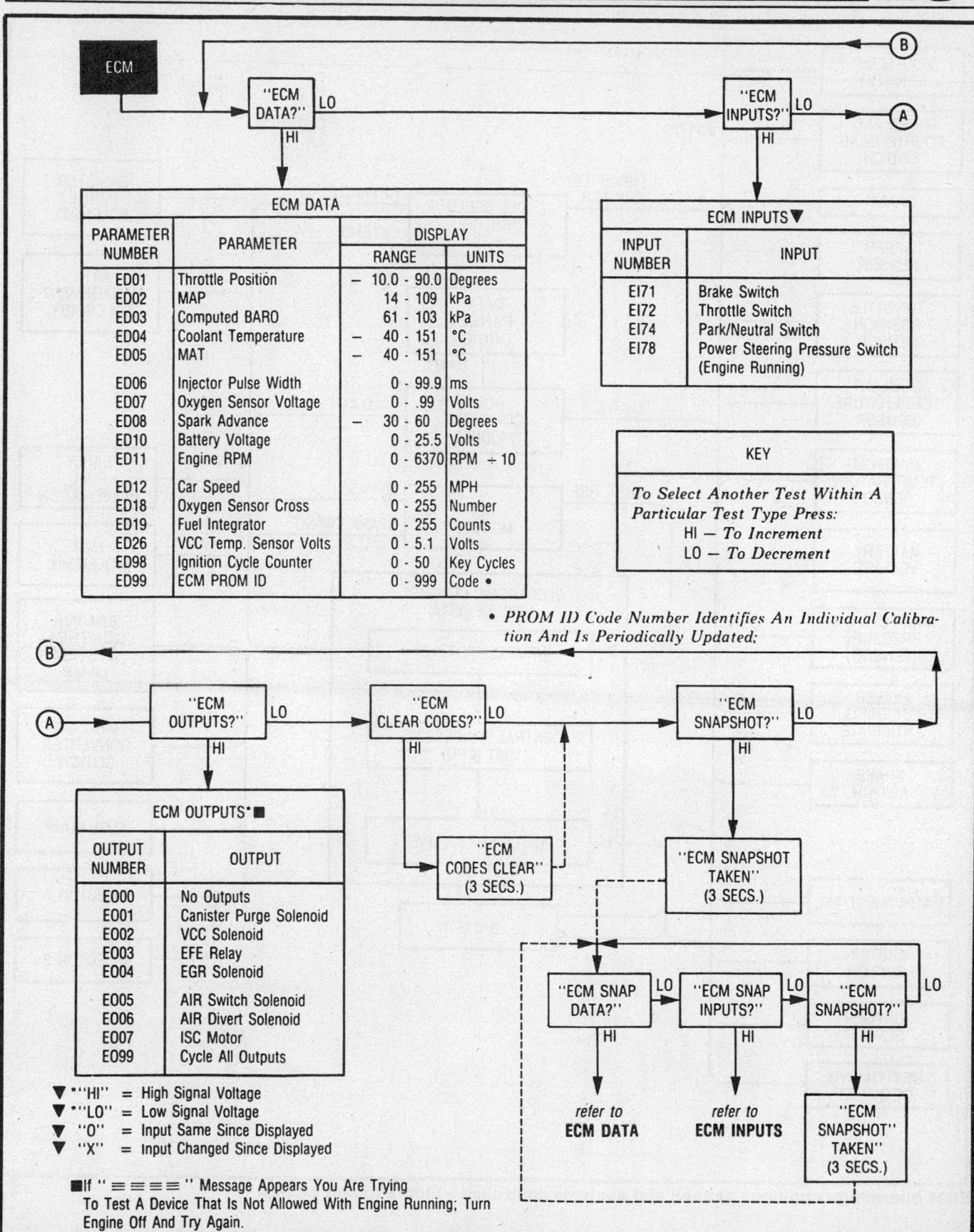

ECM DATA

PARAMETER NUMBER	PARAMETER	DISPLAY	
		RANGE	UNITS
ED01	Throttle Position	− 10.0 - 90.0	Degrees
ED02	MAP	14 - 109	kPa
ED03	Computed BARO	61 - 103	kPa
ED04	Coolant Temperature	− 40 - 151	°C
ED05	MAT	− 40 - 151	°C
ED06	Injector Pulse Width	0 - 99.9	ms
ED07	Oxygen Sensor Voltage	0 - .99	Volts
ED08	Spark Advance	− 30 - 60	Degrees
ED10	Battery Voltage	0 - 25.5	Volts
ED11	Engine RPM	0 - 6370	RPM ÷ 10
ED12	Car Speed	0 - 255	MPH
ED18	Oxygen Sensor Cross	0 - 255	Number
ED19	Fuel Integrator	0 - 255	Counts
ED26	VCC Temp. Sensor Volts	0 - 5.1	Volts
ED98	Ignition Cycle Counter	0 - 50	Key Cycles
ED99	ECM PROM ID	0 - 999	Code •

ECM INPUTS ▼

INPUT NUMBER	INPUT
EI71	Brake Switch
EI72	Throttle Switch
EI74	Park/Neutral Switch
EI78	Power Steering Pressure Switch (Engine Running)

KEY

To Select Another Test Within A Particular Test Type Press:
HI — To Increment
LO — To Decrement

• *PROM ID Code Number Identifies An Individual Calibration And Is Periodically Updated;*

ECM OUTPUTS* ■

OUTPUT NUMBER	OUTPUT
EO000	No Outputs
EO001	Canister Purge Solenoid
EO002	VCC Solenoid
EO003	EFE Relay
EO004	EGR Solenoid
EO005	AIR Switch Solenoid
EO006	AIR Divert Solenoid
EO007	ISC Motor
EO099	Cycle All Outputs

▼ *"HI" = High Signal Voltage
▼ *"LO" = Low Signal Voltage
▼ "O" = Input Same Since Displayed
▼ "X" = Input Changed Since Displayed

■ If "≡ ≡ ≡ ≡" Message Appears You Are Trying To Test A Device That Is Not Allowed With Engine Running; Turn Engine Off And Try Again.

Data, Input and output tests, ECM diagnostics – Eldorado and Seville

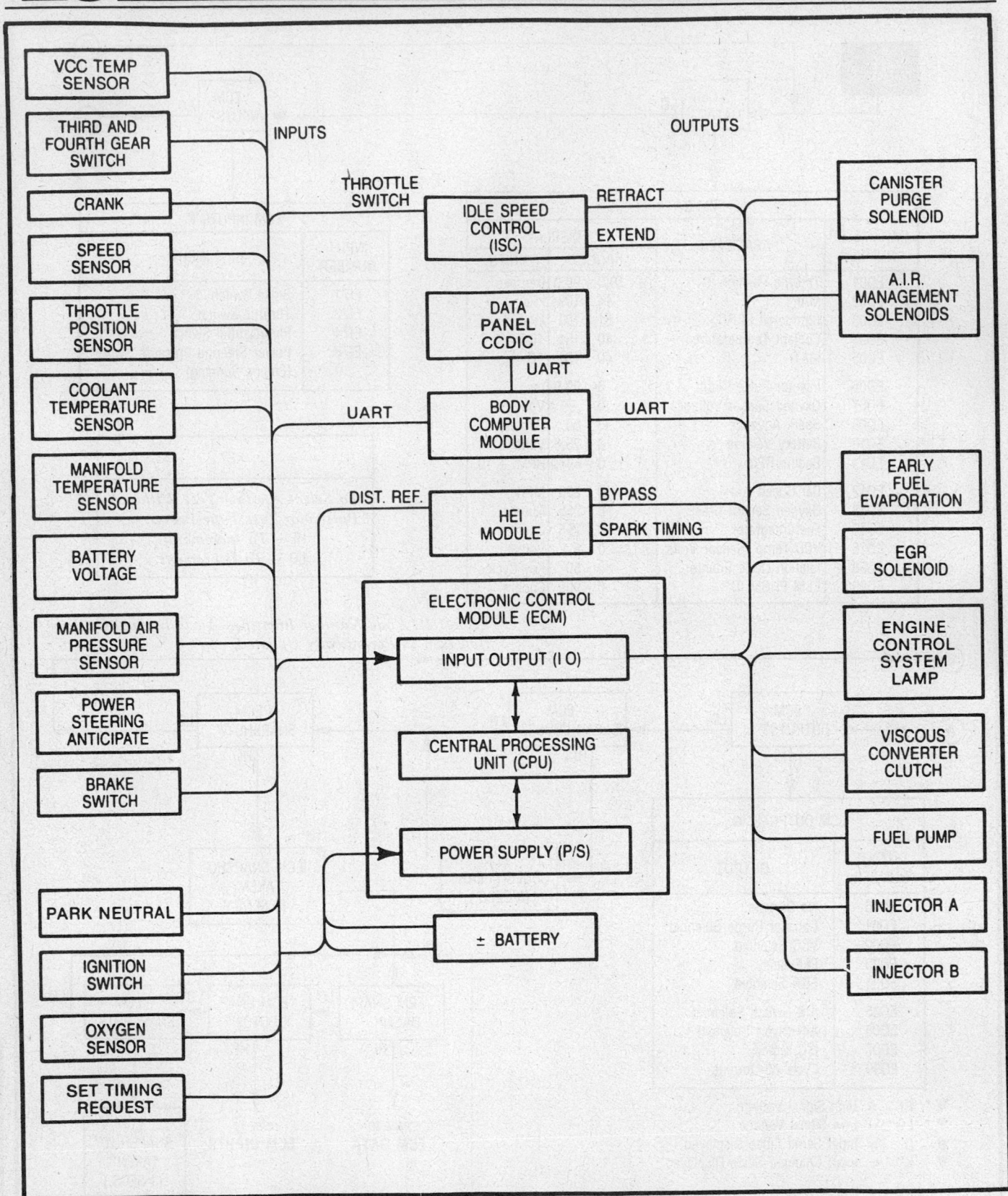

INPUTS

OUTPUTS

VCC TEMP SENSOR

THIRD AND FOURTH GEAR SWITCH

CRANK

SPEED SENSOR

THROTTLE POSITION SENSOR

COOLANT TEMPERATURE SENSOR

MANIFOLD TEMPERATURE SENSOR

BATTERY VOLTAGE

MANIFOLD AIR PRESSURE SENSOR

POWER STEERING ANTICIPATE

BRAKE SWITCH

PARK NEUTRAL

IGNITION SWITCH

OXYGEN SENSOR

SET TIMING REQUEST

THROTTLE SWITCH

IDLE SPEED CONTROL (ISC)

RETRACT

EXTEND

DATA PANEL CCDIC

UART

UART

BODY COMPUTER MODULE

UART

DIST. REF.

HEI MODULE

BYPASS

SPARK TIMING

ELECTRONIC CONTROL MODULE (ECM)

INPUT OUTPUT (I O)

CENTRAL PROCESSING UNIT (CPU)

POWER SUPPLY (P/S)

± BATTERY

CANISTER PURGE SOLENOID

A.I.R. MANAGEMENT SOLENOIDS

EARLY FUEL EVAPORATION

EGR SOLENOID

ENGINE CONTROL SYSTEM LAMP

VISCOUS CONVERTER CLUTCH

FUEL PUMP

INJECTOR A

INJECTOR B

ECM operating conditions sensed and systems controlled—Eldorado and Seville

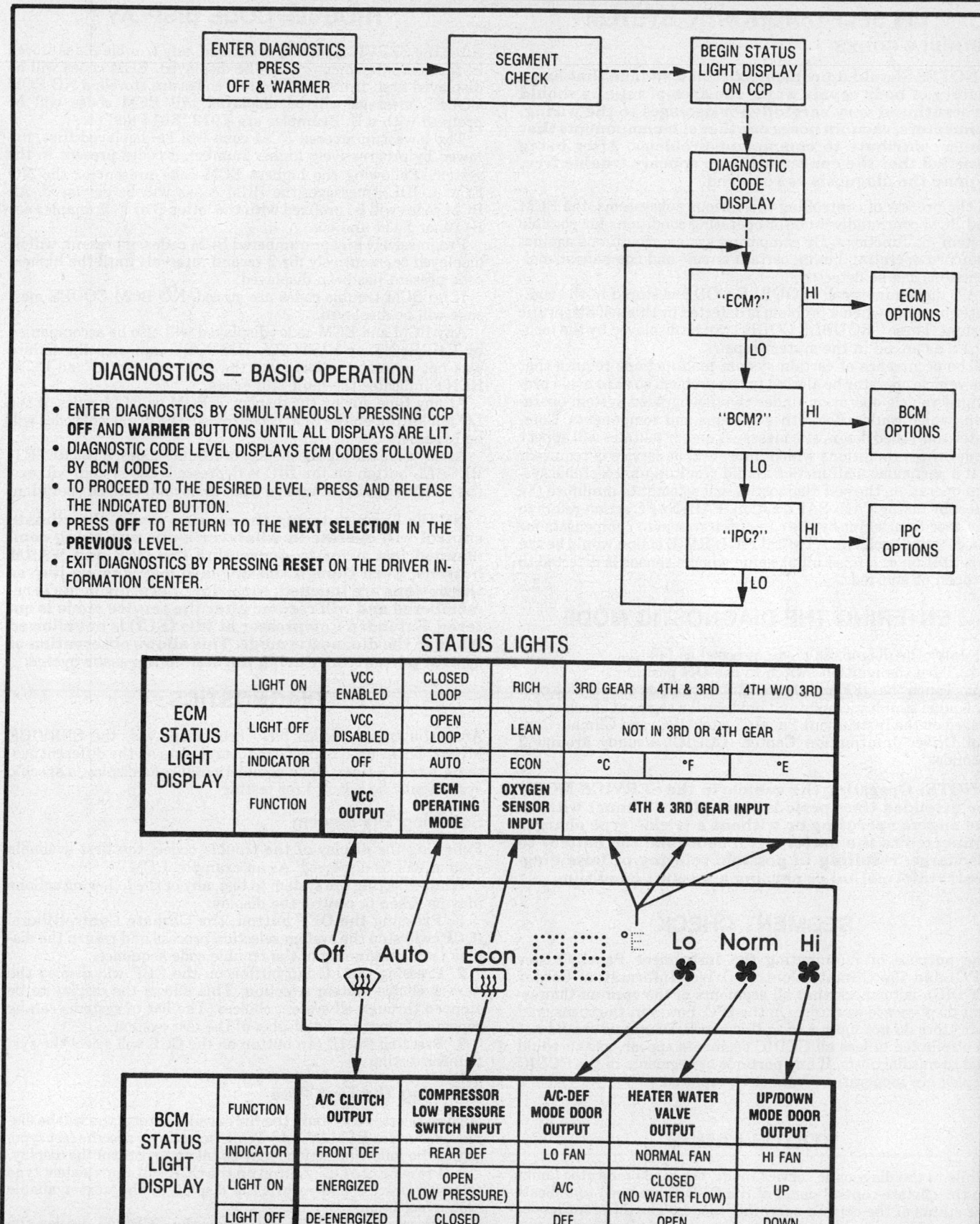

DIAGNOSTIC CODE DISPLAY flow:
ENTER DIAGNOSTICS PRESS OFF & WARMER → SEGMENT CHECK → BEGIN STATUS LIGHT DISPLAY ON CCP → DIAGNOSTIC CODE DISPLAY → "ECM?" (HI → ECM OPTIONS / LO) → "BCM?" (HI → BCM OPTIONS / LO) → "IPC?" (HI → IPC OPTIONS / LO)

DIAGNOSTICS — BASIC OPERATION

- ENTER DIAGNOSTICS BY SIMULTANEOUSLY PRESSING CCP **OFF** AND **WARMER** BUTTONS UNTIL ALL DISPLAYS ARE LIT.
- DIAGNOSTOC CODE LEVEL DISPLAYS ECM CODES FOLLOWED BY BCM CODES.
- TO PROCEED TO THE DESIRED LEVEL, PRESS AND RELEASE THE INDICATED BUTTON.
- PRESS **OFF** TO RETURN TO THE **NEXT SELECTION** IN THE **PREVIOUS** LEVEL.
- EXIT DIAGNOSTICS BY PRESSING **RESET** ON THE DRIVER IN-FORMATION CENTER.

STATUS LIGHTS

ECM STATUS LIGHT DISPLAY	LIGHT ON	VCC ENABLED	CLOSED LOOP	RICH	3RD GEAR	4TH & 3RD	4TH W/O 3RD
	LIGHT OFF	VCC DISABLED	OPEN LOOP	LEAN	NOT IN 3RD OR 4TH GEAR		
	INDICATOR	OFF	AUTO	ECON	°C	°F	°E
	FUNCTION	VCC OUTPUT	ECM OPERATING MODE	OXYGEN SENSOR INPUT	4TH & 3RD GEAR INPUT		

Off Auto Econ °E Lo Norm Hi

BCM STATUS LIGHT DISPLAY	FUNCTION	A/C CLUTCH OUTPUT	COMPRESSOR LOW PRESSURE SWITCH INPUT	A/C-DEF MODE DOOR OUTPUT	HEATER WATER VALVE OUTPUT	UP/DOWN MODE DOOR OUTPUT
	INDICATOR	FRONT DEF	REAR DEF	LO FAN	NORMAL FAN	HI FAN
	LIGHT ON	ENERGIZED	OPEN (LOW PRESSURE)	A/C	CLOSED (NO WATER FLOW)	UP
	LIGHT OFF	DE-ENERGIZED	CLOSED	DEF	OPEN	DOWN

ECM diagnostoc based operatio and status lights — Eldorado and Seville

DFI SELF-DIAGNOSTIC SYSTEM

TROUBLE CODES

NOTE: Should a problem exist in a vehicle that has a history of body repair work, the area of repairs should be scrutinzed very carefully for damages to the wiring, connectors, vacuum hoses or other sub-components that could contribute to component problems. After being satisfied that the concerned area appears trouble free, expand the diagnosis as required.

In the process of controlling the various subsystems, the ECM and BCM continually monitor operating conditions for possible system malfunctions. By comparing system conditions against standard operating limits, certain circuit and component malfunctions can be detected.

A 3 digit numerical TROUBLE CODE is stored in the computer memory when a problem is detected by this self diagnostic system. These TROUBLE CODES can be displayed by the technician as an aid in the system repairs.

The occurrence of certain system malfunctions require that the vehicle operator be alerted to the problem so as to avoid prolonged vehicle operation under the downgraded system operation, which could affect other systems and components. Computer controlled diagnostic messages and/or telltales will appear under these conditions which indicate that service is required.

If a particular malfunction would result in unacceptable system operation, the self diagnostics will attempt to minimize the effect by taking FAIL-SAFE action. FAIL-SAFE action refers to any specific attempt by the computer system to compensate for the detected problem. A typical FAIL-SAFE action would be the substitution of a fixed input value when a sensor is detected to be open or shorted.

ENTERING THE DIAGNOSTIC MODE

To enter the diagnostic mode, proceed as follows:
1. Turn the ignition switch to the **ON** position.
2. Touch the OFF and the WARM buttons on the climate control panel simultaneously and hold until a segment check is displayed on the Instrument Panel Cluster (IPC) and Climate Control Driver Information Center (CCDIC), usually around 3 seconds.

NOTE: Operating the vehicle in the SERVICE MODE for extended time periods (exceeding ½ hour) without the engine operating or without a trickle type charger connected to the battery, can cause the the battery to discharge, resulting in possible relaying of false diagnostic information or causing a no-start condition.

SEGMENT CHECK

The purpose of illuminating the Instrument Panel Cluster (IPC) and the Climate Control Driver Information Center (CCDIC), is to check that all segments of the vacuum fluorescent displays are working. On the IPC, however, the turnsignal indicators do not light during this check. Diagnosis should not be attempted unless all CCDIC segments appear, as this could lead to misdiagnosis, If any portions or segments of the CCDIC display are inoperative, it must be replaced.

STATUS LAMPS

While in the diagnostic service mode, the mode indicator lamps on the climate control panel of the CCDIC are used to indicate the status of the certain operating modes. The different modes of operation are indicated by the status lamp being turned on or off.

TROUBLE CODE DISPLAY

After the SERVICE MODE is entered, any trouble codes stored in the computer memory will be displayed. ECM codes will be displayed first. If no ECM trouble codes are stored, a NO ECM CODES message will be displayed. All ECM codes will be prefixed with a E. Examples are E013, E014 and etc.

The lowest numbered ECM code will be displayed first, followed by progressively higher numbered codes present in the system. Following the highest ECM code present or the NO ECM CODES message, the BCM codes will be displayed. All BCM codes will be prefixed with the letter B or F. Examples are B110, or F111 and etc.

Progressively higher numbered BCM codes, if present, will be displayed consecutively for 2 second intervals until the highest code present has been displayed.

If no BCM trouble codes are stored, NO BCM CODES message will be displayed.

Any BCM and ECM codes displayed will also be accompanied by CURRENT or HISTORY. HISTORY indicates the failure was not present the last time the code was tested and CURRENT indicates the fault still exists.

At any time during the display of ECM or BCM codes, if the LO fan button on the ECC is depressed, the display of codes will be bypassed.

At any time during the display of trouble codes, if the RESET/RECALL button on the DIC is depressed, the system will exit the SERVICE MODE and go back to normal vehicle operation.

NOTE: Upon entering the service mode, the climate control will operate in whatever mode was being commanded just prior to depressing the OFF and WARM buttons. Even though the displays may change just as the buttons are touched, the prior operating mode is remembered and will resume after the service mode is entered. Extended Compressor at Idle (ECI) is not allowed while in the diagnostic mode. This allows observation of system parameters during normal compressor cycles.

DIAGNOSTICS

After the trouble codes have been displayed, the SERVICE MODE can be used to perform several tests on the different systems, one at a time. Upon completion of code display, a specific system may be selected for testing.

Selecting The System

Following the display of the trouble codes, the first available system will be displayed. As an example, ECM.

While selecting the system to test, any of the following actions may be taken to control the display.
1. Pressing the OFF button, the Climate Control Panel (CCP) will stop the system selection process and return the display to the beginning of the trouble code sequence.
2. Pressing the LO fan button on the CCP will display the next available system selection. This allows the display to be stepped through all system choices. The list of systems can be repeated following the display of the last system.
3. Pressing the HI fan button on the CCP will select the system for testing.

Selecting The Test Type

Having selected a system, the first available test type will be displayed, such as ECM DATA?. While selecting a specific test type, any of the following actions may be taken to control the display.
1. Pressing the OFF button on the CCP will stop the test type selection process and return the display to the next available system selection.
2. Pressing the LO fan button on the CCP will display the next available test type for the selected system. This allows the

display to be stepped through all available test type choices. The list of test types can be repeated following the display of the last test type.

3. Pressing the HI fan button on the CCP will select the displayed test type.

4. At this point, the first of several specific tests will appear.

Selecting The Test

Selection of the DATA, INPUTS?, OUTPUTS? or OVERRIDE test types will result in the first available test being displayed.

If dashes ever appears, this test is not allowed with the engine running. Turn the engine **OFF** and try again. The 4 characters of the display will contain a test code to identify the selection. The first 2 characters are letters which identify the system and test type, such as ED for ECM DATA and the last 2 characters are letters which identify the test, such as ED01 for Throttle Position. While selecting a specific test, any of the following actions may be taken to control the display.

1. Pressing the OFF button on the CCP will stop the test selection process and return the display to the next available test type for the selected system.

2. Pressing the LO fan button on the CCP will display the next smaller test number for the selected test type. If this button is pressed with the lowest test number displayed, the highest test number will then appear.

3. Pressing the HI fan button on the CCP will display the next larger test number for the selected test type. If this pad is touched with the highest test number displayed, the lowest test number will then appear.

Override Test

Upon selecting an OVERRIDE test function, current operation will be represented as a percentage of its full range and this value will be displayed on the ECC panel. This display will alternate between – – and the normal program value. This alternating display is a reminder that the function is not currently being overridden.

Pressing the WARM or COOL buttons on the ECC panel begins the override at which time the display will no longer alternate to – –. Pressing the WARM button increases the value while the COOL button decreases the value. Normal program control can be resumed in one of 3 ways.

1. Selection of another override test will cancel the current override.

2. Selection of another system (ECM, BCM or IPC) will cancel the current overide.

3. Overriding the value beyond either extreme (0 or 99) will display – – momentarily and then jump to the opposite extreme. If the button is released while – – is displayed, normal program control will resume and the display will again alternate.

The override test type is unique in that any other test type within the selected system may be active at the same time. After selecting an override test, pressing the OFF button will allow selection of another test type, DATA, INPUTS or OUTPUTS. The ECC panel will continue to display the selected override.By selecting another test type and test, while at the same time pressing the WARM or COOL button, it is possible to monitor the effects of the override on different vehicle parameters.

Selecting CLEAR CODES?

Selection of the CLEAR CODES? test type will result in the message CODES CLEAR being displayed along with the selected system name. This message will appear for 3 seconds to indicate that all stored trouble codes have been erased from that system's memory. After 3 seconds, the display will automatically return to the next available test type for the selected system

Selecting SNAPSHOT?

Selection of SNAPSHOT? test type will result in the message SNAPSHOT TAKEN being displayed with the selected system name proceeding it. This message will appear for 3 seconds to indicate that all system data and inputs have been stored in memory. After 3 seconds, the display will automatically proceed to the first available snapshot test type, for example SNAP DATA. While selecting a snapshot test type, any of the following actions can be taken to control the display;

1. Pressing the OFF button on the CCP will stop the test type selection process and return the display to the next available system selection.

2. Pressing the LO button on the CCP will display the next available snapshot test type.

3. This allows the display to be stepped through all available choices. This list of snapshot test types can be repeated following the display of the last choice.

4. Pressing the HI button with SNAP DATA? or SNAP INPUT? displayed, will select that test type. At this point, the display is controlled as it would be for non-snapshot data and inputs displays. However, all values and status information represents memorized vehicle conditions.

5. Pressing the HI button on the CCP with SNAPSHOT? displayed will again display the SNAPSHOT TAKEN message to indicate that new information has been stored in the memory. Access to this information is obtained the same as previously outlined.

How To Exit SERVICE MODE

To exit the service mode, press the RESET/RECALL button on the DIC or turn the ignition switch to the **OFF** position. Trouble codes are not erased when this is done.

OLDSMOBILE TORONADO SEQUENTIAL FUEL INJECTION (SFI) SYSTEM

ELECTRONIC CONTROL MODULE

The Electronic Control Module (ECM) is the controlling unit of the electronic engine control system. Though it communicates with the other vehicle computers, it alone has the primary responsibility of maintaining proper emissions while delivering optimum driveability characteristics.

The ECM monitors inputs from the engine as well as other vehicle sensors. It then correlates this information with data stored in the PROM. After all the information is evaluated, the ECM calculates the necessary changes to compensate for all driving conditions.

The ECM is able to detect malfunctions in most of the systems it monitors. It will turn on the SERVICE ENGINE SOON indicator lamp, set a trouble code, or both if it detects a fault.

NOTE: Always repair all code malfunctions before any driveability or emission problem repairs are attempted. If more than one code is set, always repair the lowest numbered code first.

The ECM trouble codes are displayed on the Instrument Panel Cluster (IPC) when in the diagnostic mode. Other service related information that can be displayed are as follows:
ECM data
ECM Discrete inputs
ECM output cycling

ECM trouble codes

All displays, except for the output mode cycling, can be viewed under the following conditions:

The ignition switch in the **ON** position

The engine NOT operating

The engine at idle

The vehicle being driven

The output mode cycling function is only operational with the ignition **ON** and the engine not operating.

ECM DATA

While in this mode, the display will show 21 data messages and the data value of each. This information assists in tracing down emission and driveability problems, since the displays can be viewed while the vehicle is being driven.

BODY COMPUTER MODULE (BCM)

The Body Computer Module (BCM) is located behind the glove box. The BCM has an internal microprocessor, which is the center for communication with all other components in the system. All sensors and switches are monitored by the BCM or 1 of the 5 other major components that complete the computer system. The 5 components are as follows:

1. Electronic Control Module (ECM)
2. Instrument Panel Cluster (IPC)
3. Electronic Climate Control Panel (ECC)
4. Programmer/Heating/Ventilation/AC
5. Chime/Voice module

Between the BCM and the other 5 major components of the computer system, a communication process has been incorporated which allows the devices to share information and thereby provide additional control capabilities.

In order to access and control the self diagnostic features, 2 additional electronic components are necessary, the Instrument Panel Cluster (IPC) and the Electronic Climate Control panel (ECC). As part of the IPC, a 20 character display area called the Information Center is used. During normal engine operation, this area displays Toronado or is a tachometer, displaying the engine rpm. When a malfunction is sensed by the ECM/BCM, one of the driver warning messages is displayed in this area. When the diagnostic mode is entered, the various BCM or ECM diagnostic codes are displayed. In addition to the codes of the ECM/BCM data parameters, discrete inputs and outputs, as well as output override messages are also displayed when commanded for, through the ECC.

The Electronic Comfort Control Panel (ECC) provides the controls for the heating and air conditioning systems. It also becomes the controller to enter the diagnostics and access the BCM self-diagnostics. This communication process allows the BCM to transfer any of its available diagnostic information to the top of the instrument panel for display during service. By pressing the appropriate buttons on the ECC, data messages can be sent to the BCM over the serial data line requesting the specific diagnostic features desired. When in the override mode of the BCM diagnostics, the amount of override is displayed at the ECC where the outside and set temperatures are normally displayed.

SYSTEM DIAGNOSIS

A systematic approach is needed to begin the vehicle's self diagnostic capabilities along with an understanding of the basic operation and procedures, necessary to determine external or internal malfunctions of the computer operated circuits and systems. A systematic beginning is to determine if the SERVICE ENGINE SOON telltale lamp is illuminated when the ignition key is in the **ON** position and the engine not operating. If the lamp is off, a problem could be in the power supply circuits of the systems.

If the lamp is illuminated, can the SERVICE MODE be accessed? If the Electronic Climate Control panel is not operating, the self diagnostics cannot be used.

Is there a trouble code displayed? If a trouble code is identified, using the self diagnostics mode, a malfunction or problem has been detected by the system.

COMPUTER SYSTEM SERVICE PRECAUTIONS

The computer control system is designed to withstand normal current draws associated with vehicle operation. However, care must be taken to avoid overloading any of these circuits. In testing for open or short circuits, do not ground or apply voltage to any of the circuits, unless instructed to do so by diagnostic procedures. These circuits should only be tested using a high impedance Multimeter, such as Kent Moore tool no. J–29125A or its equivalent, if they are to remain connected to any of the computers. Power should never be remove or applied to one of the computers with the key in the **ON** position. Before removing or connecting battery cables, fuses or connectors, always turn the ignition to the **LOCK** position.

SELF DIAGNOSTIC SYSTEM

Trouble Codes

In the process of controlling the various subsystems, the ECM and BCM continually monitor operating conditions for possible system malfunctions. By comparing system conditions against standard operating limits, certain circuit and component malfunctions can be detected. A 3 digit numerical TROUBLE CODE is stored in the computer memory when a problem is detected by this self diagnostic system. These TROUBLE CODES can be displayed by the technician as an aid in the system repairs.

The occurrence of certain system malfunctions require that the vehicle operator be alerted to the problem so as to avoid prolonged vehicle operation under the downgraded system operation, which could affect other systems and components. Computer controlled diagnostic messages and/or telltales will appear under these conditions which indicate that service is required.

If a particular malfunction would result in unacceptable system operation, the self diagnostics will attempt to minimize the effect by taking FAIL-SAFE action. FAIL-SAFE action refers to any specific attempt by the computer system to compensate for the detected problem. A typical FAIL-SAFE action would be the substitution of a fixed input value when a sensor is detected to be open or shorted.

ENTERING THE DIAGNOSTIC MODE

To enter the diagnostic mode, proceed as follows:
1. Turn the ignition switch to the **ON** position.
2. Touch the OFF and the WARM buttons on the Electronic Climate Control (ECC) panel simultaneously and hold until a segment check is displayed on the Instrument Panel Cluster (IPC) and Electronic Climate Control (ECC), usually around 3 seconds.

—————————— CAUTION ——————————

Operating the vehicle in the SERVICE MODE for extended time periods (exceeding ½ hour) without the engine operating or without a trickle type charger connected to the battery, can cause the the battery to discharge, resulting in possible relaying of false diagnostic information or causing a no-start condition.

TROUBLE CODE DISPLAY

After the SERVICE MODE is entered, any trouble codes stored in the computer memory will be displayed. ECM codes will be

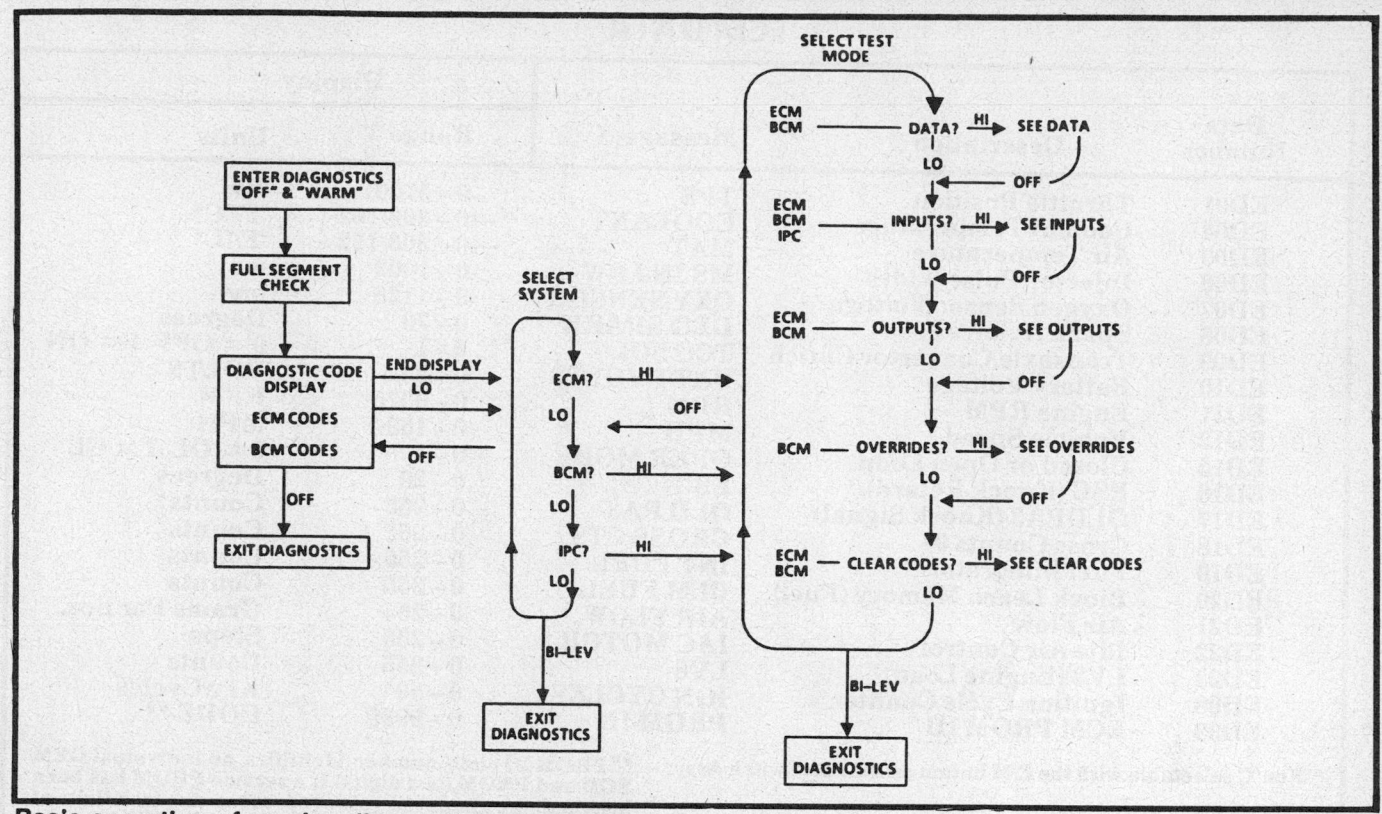

Basic operation of service diagnsotics—Toronado

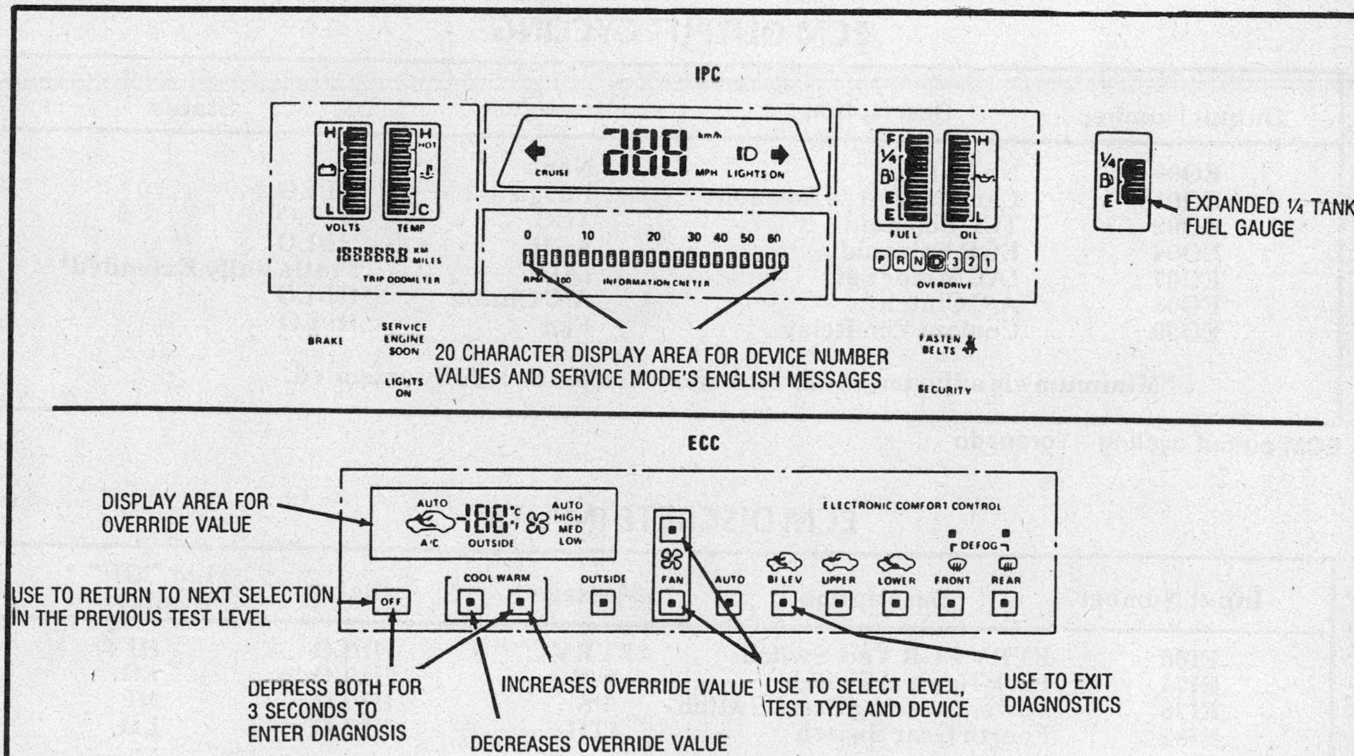

IPC

20 CHARACTER DISPLAY AREA FOR DEVICE NUMBER
VALUES AND SERVICE MODE'S ENGLISH MESSAGES

EXPANDED ¼ TANK FUEL GAUGE

ECC

ELECTRONIC COMFORT CONTROL

DISPLAY AREA FOR OVERRIDE VALUE

USE TO RETURN TO NEXT SELECTION IN THE PREVIOUS TEST LEVEL

DEPRESS BOTH FOR 3 SECONDS TO ENTER DIAGNOSIS

INCREASES OVERRIDE VALUE

DECREASES OVERRIDE VALUE

USE TO SELECT LEVEL, TEST TYPE AND DEVICE

USE TO EXIT DIAGNOSTICS

Diagnostic displays—Toronado

ECM DATA

Data Number	Description	Message	Display Range	Units
ED01	Throttle Position	TPS	0 – 5100	mv
ED04	Coolant Temperature	COOLANT	–40 – 306/152	°F/°C*
ED05	Air Temperature	MAT	–40 – 306/152	°F/°C*
ED06	Injector Pulse Width	MS INJ PW	0 – 1002	ms
ED07	Oxygen Sensor Voltage	OXY SENSOR	0 – 1128	mv
ED08	Spark Avance	DEG SPARK	0 – 70	Degrees
ED09	Transaxle Convertor Clutch	TCC SOL	0 – 1	0 = OFF 1 = ON
ED10	Battery Voltage	BATT VOLTS	0 – 25.5	VOLTS
ED11	Engine RPM	RPM	0 – 6375	RPM
ED12	Vehicle Speed	MPH	0 – 159	MPH
ED15	Closed or Open Loop	OPER MODE	0 – 1	0 = OL 1 = CL
ED16	ESC (Knock Retard)	ESC	0 – 20	Degrees
ED17	OLDPA3 (Knock Signal)	OLD PA3	0 – 255	Counts
ED18	Cross Counts 0^2	CROSS CTS	0 – 255	Counts
ED19	Fuel Integrator	INT FUEL	0 – 255	Counts
ED20	Block Learn Memory (Fuel)	BLM FUEL	0 – 255	Counts
ED21	Air Flow	AIR FLOW	0 – 255	Grams Per Sec.
ED22	Idle Air Control	IAC MOTOR	0 – 255	Steps
ED23	LV8 (Engine Load)	LV8	0 – 255	Counts
ED98	Ignition Cycle Counter	IGN CYCLES	0 – 50	Key Cycles
ED99	ECM PROM ID	PROM ID	0 – 9999	CODE **

*°F or °C selectable with the E/M button on the Left Switch Assy.

**PROM ID code number identifies an individual OEM ECM and PROM (last digits). If a service PROM has been installed, the displayed value represents the last digits of the service package # (not stamped on PROM).

ECM diagnostic data — Toronado

ECM OUTPUT CYCLING

Output Number	Description	Message	Status
EO00	No Outputs	None	
EO01	Canister Purge Solenoid	Purge	HI/LO
EO02	TCC Solenoid	TCC	HI/LO
EO04	EGR Solenoid	EGR	HI/LO
EO07	IAC Motor Set	IAC	Pintle Fully Extended*
EO08	A/C Clutch	A/C Clutch	HI/LO
EO09	Coolant Fan Relay	Fan	Hi/LO

*Minimum air adjustment can be made when pintle is fully extended.

ECM output cycling — Toronado

ECM DISCRETE INPUTS

Input Number	Description	Message	Status	Ign. "ON" * Display
EI60	EVRV EGR Vac. Switch	EVRV	HI/LO	HI
EI74	Park/Neutral Switch	P/N	HI/LO	LO
EI78	Power Steering Press. Switch	PS	HI/LO	HI
EI82	Fourth Gear Switch	4TH	HI/LO	LO

* In park, engine not running.

ECM discreet inputs — Toronado

displayed first. If no ECM trouble codes are stored, the IPC will display a NO ECM CODES message for approximately 2 seconds. All ECM codes will be prefixed with an E. Examples are E013, E014 and etc. The lowest numbered ECM code will be displayed first, followed by progressively higher numbered codes present in the system.

The codes will be displayed consecutively for 2 second intervals until the highest code present has been displayed. When all ECM codes have been displayed, the BCM codes will be displayed. The lowest numbered BCM code will be displayed for appropriately 2 seconds. BCM codes accompanied by CURRENT indicates the fault still exits. Since the ECM is not capable of making this determination, this message does not appear when the ECM codes are being displayed. All BCM codes will be prefixed with a letter B. Examples are B110, B111 and etc.

Progressively higher numbered BCM codes, if present, will be displayed consecutively for 2 second intervals until the highest code present has been displayed. If no BCM trouble codes are stored, NO BCM CODES message will be displayed. At any time during the display of ECM or BCM codes, if the LO fan button on the ECC is depressed, the display of codes will be bypassed. At any time during the display of trouble codes, if the BI-LEV button is depressed, the BCM will exit the SERVICE MODE and go back to normal vehicle operation.

NOTE: Upon entering the service mode, the climate control will operate in whatever mode was being commanded just prior to depressing the OFF and WARM buttons. Even though the displays may change just as the buttons are touched, the prior operating mode is remembered and will resume after the service mode is entered.

OPERATION OF THE SERVICE DIAGNOSTICS

After the trouble codes have been displayed, the SERVICE MODE can be used to perform several tests on the different systems, one at a time. Upon completion of code display, a specific system may be selected for testing.

Selecting The System

Following the display of the trouble codes, the first available system will be displayed. As an example, ECM.

While selecting the system to test, any of the following actions may be taken to control the display.

1. Pressing the OFF button will stop the system selection process and return the display to the beginning of the trouble code sequence.

2. Pressing the LO fan button will display the next available system selection. This allows the display to be stepped through all system choices. The list of systems can be repeated following the display of the last system.

3. Pressing the HI fan button will select the displaced system for testing. At this point, the first available test type will appear with the selected system name above it.

4. Pressing the BI-LEV button will exit diagnostics and return to normal IPC and ECC operation.

Selecting The Test Type

Having selected a system, the first available test type will be displayed, such as ECM DATA?. While selecting a specific test type, any of the following actions may be taken to control the display.

1. Pressing the OFF button will stop the test type selection process and return the display to the next available system selection.

2. Pressing the LO fan button will display the next available test type for the selected system. This allows the display to be stepped through all available test type choices. The list of test types can be repeated following the display of the last test type.

3. Pressing the HI fan button will select the displayed test type. At this point, the display will either indicate that the se-

lected test type is in progress or the first of several specific tests will appear.

4. Pressing the BI-LEVEL button will exit the diagnostics.

Selecting The Test

Selection of the DATA, INPUTS?, or OUTPUTS? test types will result in the first available test being displayed. If a EEEE message ever appears, this test is not allowed with the engine running. Turn the engine **OFF** and try again. The last 4 characters of the display will contain a test code to identify the selection. The first 2 characters are letters which identify the system and test type, such as ED for ECM DATA. and the last 2 characters are letters which identify the test, such as ED01 for Throttle Position. While selecting a specific test, any of the following actions may be taken to control the display.

1. Pressing the OFF button will stop the test selection process and return the display to the next available test type for the selected system.

2. Pressing the LO fan button will display the next smaller test number for the selected test type. If this button is touched with the lowest test number displayed, the highest test number will then appear.

3. Pressing the HI fan button will display the next larger test number for the selected test type. If this pad is touched with the highest test number displayed, the lowest test number will then appear.

4. Upon selecting an OVERRIDE test function, current operation will be represented as a percentage of its full range and this value will be displayed on the ECC panel. This display will alternate between — and the normal program value. This alternating display is a reminder that the function is not currently being overridden.

5. Pressing the WARM or COOL buttons on the ECC panel begins the override at which time the display will no longer alternate to —. Pressing the WARM button increases the value while the COOL button decreases the value. Normal program control can be resumed in one of 3 ways:

   a. Selection of another override test will cancel the current override.

   b. Selection of another system (ECM, BCM or IPC) will cancel the current override.

   c. Overriding the value beyond either extreme (0 or 99) will display – – momentarily and then jump to the opposite extreme. If the button is released while – – is displayed, normal program control will resume and the display will again alternate.

6. The override test type is unique in that any other test type within the selected system may be active at the same time. After selecting an override test, pressing the OFF button will allow selection of another test type, DATA, INPUTS or OUTPUTS. The ECC panel will continue to display the selected override. By selecting another test type and test, while at the same time pressing the WARM or COOL button, it is possible to monitor the effects of the override on different vehicle parameters.

Selecting CLEAR CODES

Selecting reset codes will result in the message CLEAR ECM CODES? or CLEAR BCM CODES? depending which system was being tested. At this point, the following action may be taken:

1. Pressing the OFF button will stop the test selection process and return the display to the next available test type for the selected system.

2. Pressing the LO fan button will display the next test type available.

3. Pressing the HI fan button will select CLEAR CODES. A message ECM CODES CLEARED or BCM CODES CLEARED will appear to indicate those codes have been cleared from memory.

4. Pressing BI-LEV will exit diagnostics.

IPC Segment Check

Whenever the key is **ON**, pressing the SYSTEM MONITOR button on the left switch assembly will cause the IPC and the ECC to sequentially illuminate and darken all segments and telltales in the clusters. This is helpful in determining if any bulbs or segments or the clusters vacuum fluorescent display are out or always on. To provide more time to study the various segments, whenever service diagnostics are entered, a total illumination of all segments and bulbs on the IPC and ECC will also occur.

Exiting SERVICE MODE

To exit the service mode, press the BI-LEV button. Trouble codes are not erased when this is done. Any mode button will exit diagnostics, however, BI-LEV was chosen for procedural consistency.

Battery Electrical Drain

If the vehicle is equipped with both the Body Control Module (BCM) and the Electronic Control Module (ECM) and exhibits a low or dead battery after being parked overnight, or the battery goes down over a period of 2 or 3 days, the electrical system should be checked for excessive electrical drain.

The following test procedures are outlined to provide a complete check of the basic electronic controlling components that are capable of retaining electrical current until needed by the start-up of the vehicle.

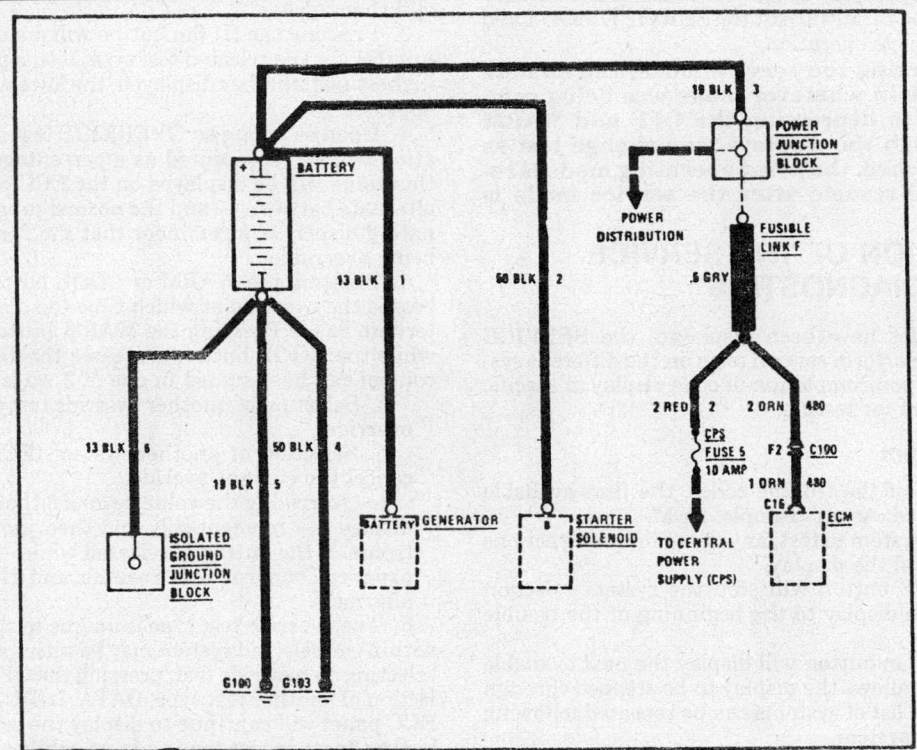

BATTERY ELECTRICAL DRAIN CHECK

Battery current should be less than 50 milliamps with no circuits active. This test determines the value of battery current with all systems off.

(1) A current drain over 50 milliamps indicates a fault.

(2) A current drain under 50 milliamps is OK.

(3) A current drain drop under 10 milliamps indicates the problem is not BCM related.

(4) A current drain drop over 10 milliamps indicates the problem is BCM related.

(5) A current drain drop under 10 milliamps indicates the problem is not ECM related. Remove other fuses one at a time to determine which component is causing the excessive amperage drain.

(6) A current drain drop over 10 milliamps indicates the problem is ECM related.

Battery electrical drain check

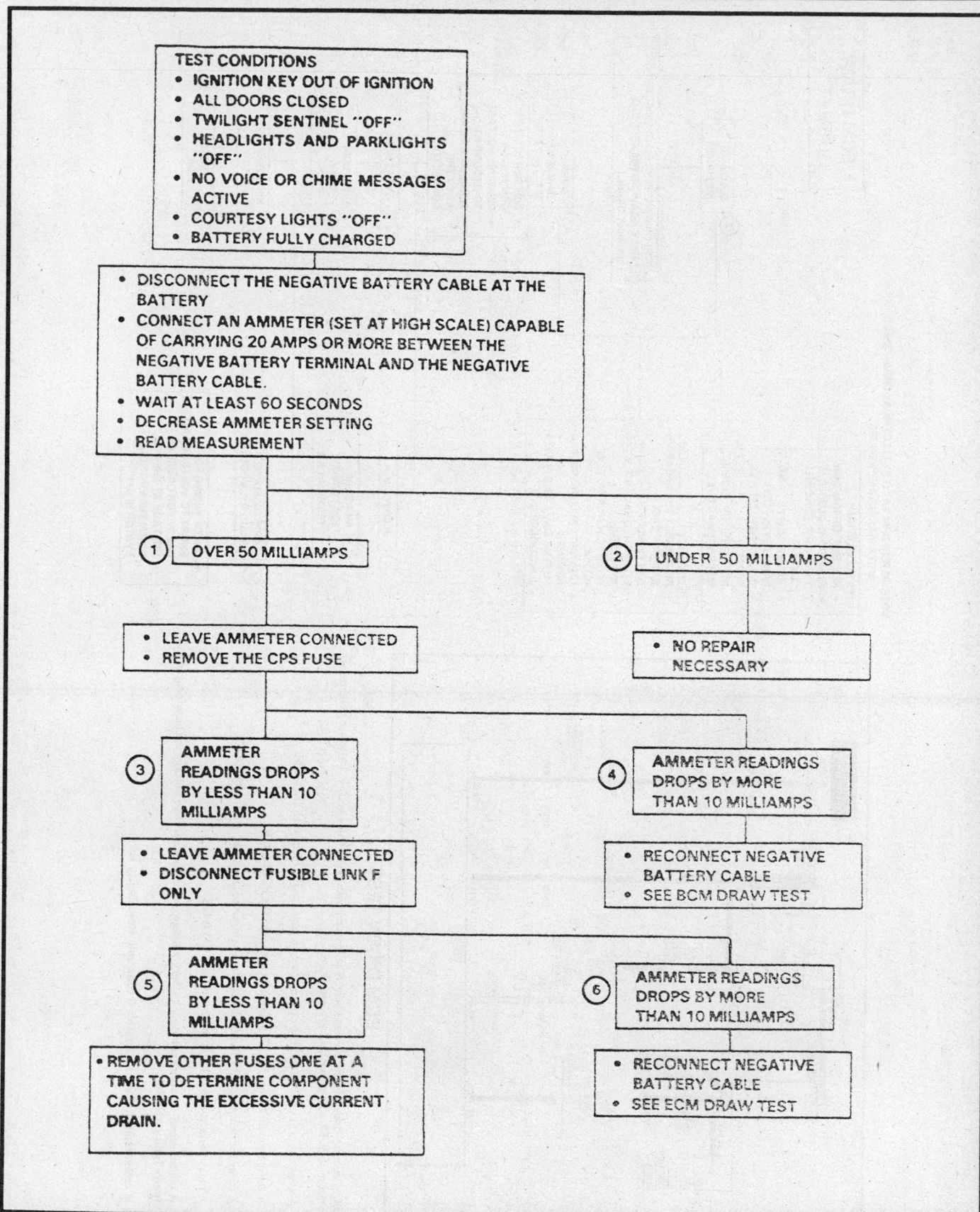

TEST CONDITIONS
- IGNITION KEY OUT OF IGNITION
- ALL DOORS CLOSED
- TWILIGHT SENTINEL "OFF"
- HEADLIGHTS AND PARKLIGHTS "OFF"
- NO VOICE OR CHIME MESSAGES ACTIVE
- COURTESY LIGHTS "OFF"
- BATTERY FULLY CHARGED

- DISCONNECT THE NEGATIVE BATTERY CABLE AT THE BATTERY
- CONNECT AN AMMETER (SET AT HIGH SCALE) CAPABLE OF CARRYING 20 AMPS OR MORE BETWEEN THE NEGATIVE BATTERY TERMINAL AND THE NEGATIVE BATTERY CABLE.
- WAIT AT LEAST 60 SECONDS
- DECREASE AMMETER SETTING
- READ MEASUREMENT

(1) OVER 50 MILLIAMPS

(2) UNDER 50 MILLIAMPS

- LEAVE AMMETER CONNECTED
- REMOVE THE CPS FUSE

- NO REPAIR NECESSARY

(3) AMMETER READINGS DROPS BY LESS THAN 10 MILLIAMPS

(4) AMMETER READINGS DROPS BY MORE THAN 10 MILLIAMPS

- LEAVE AMMETER CONNECTED
- DISCONNECT FUSIBLE LINK F ONLY

- RECONNECT NEGATIVE BATTERY CABLE
- SEE BCM DRAW TEST

(5) AMMETER READINGS DROPS BY LESS THAN 10 MILLIAMPS

(6) AMMETER READINGS DROPS BY MORE THAN 10 MILLIAMPS

- REMOVE OTHER FUSES ONE AT A TIME TO DETERMINE COMPONENT CAUSING THE EXCESSIVE CURRENT DRAIN.

- RECONNECT NEGATIVE BATTERY CABLE
- SEE ECM DRAW TEST

Battery electrical drain check

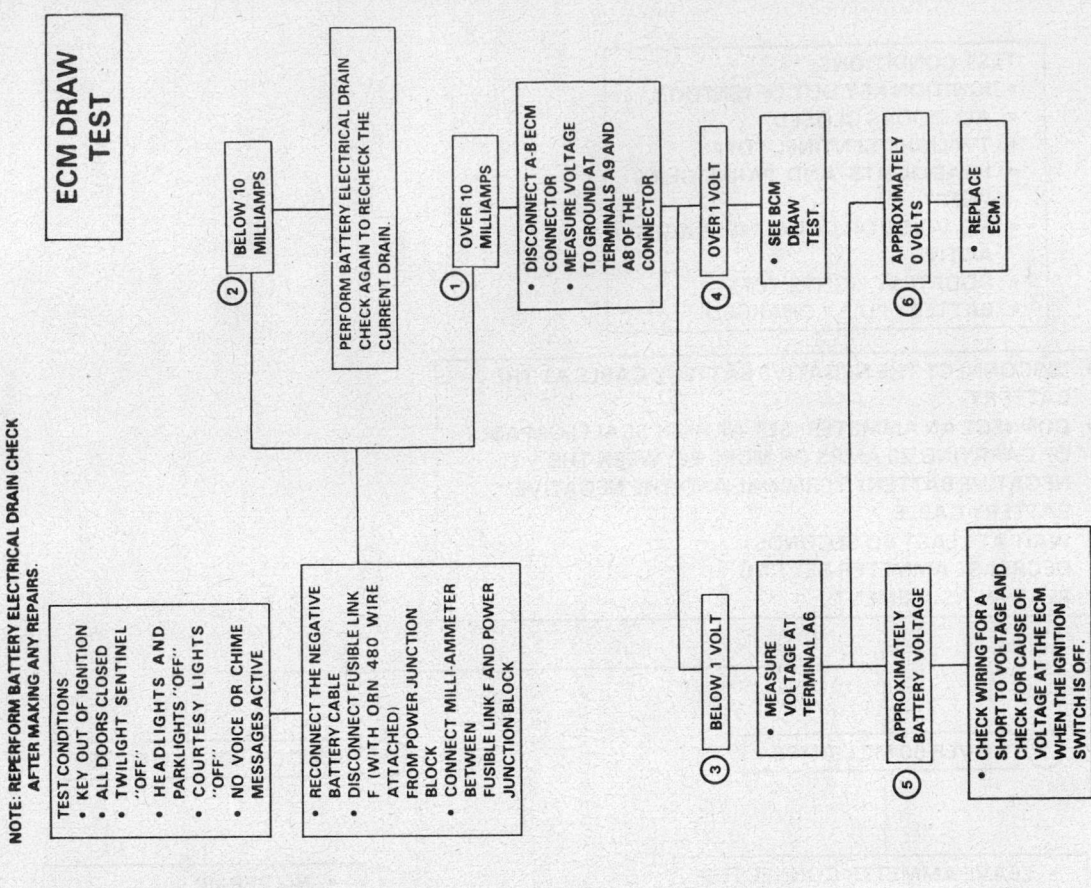

ECM DRAW TEST

NOTE: REPERFORM BATTERY ELECTRICAL DRAIN CHECK AFTER MAKING ANY REPAIRS.

TEST CONDITIONS:
- KEY OUT OF IGNITION
- ALL DOORS CLOSED
- TWILIGHT SENTINEL "OFF"
- HEADLIGHTS AND PARKLIGHTS "OFF"
- COURTESY LIGHTS "OFF"
- NO VOICE OR CHIME MESSAGES ACTIVE

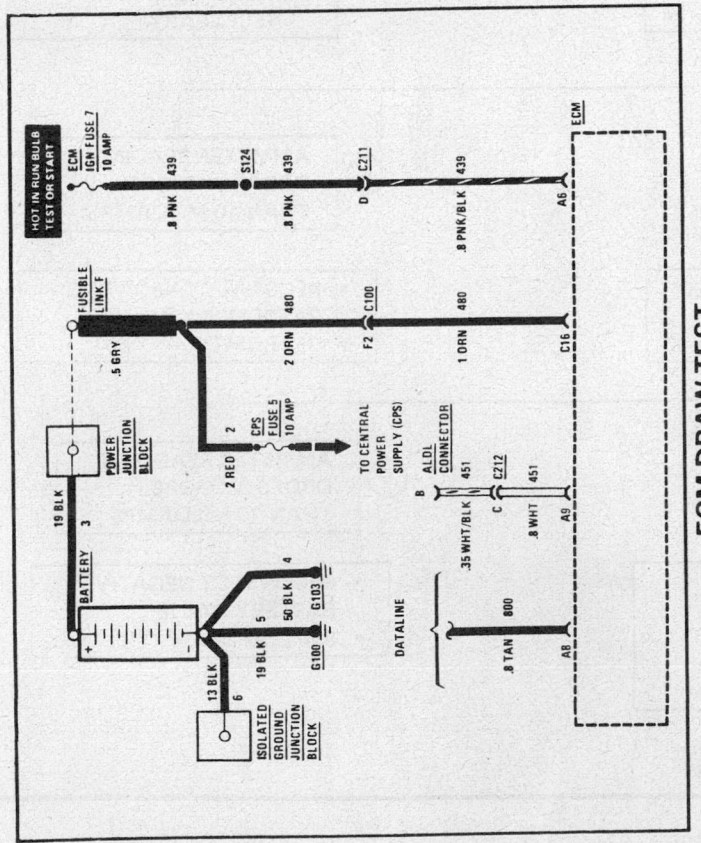

ECM DRAW TEST

ECM current draw should be less than 10 milliamps with no circuits active. This test determines the value of ECM current with all system off.

(1) A measurement above 10 milliamps indicates a possible problem with the ECM.

(2) A measurement below 10 milliamps indicates that the ECM is OK.

(3) A measurement below 1 volt indicates a faulty input to the ECM or a faulty ECM.

(4) A measurement above 1 volt indicates the ECM is OK.

(5) A measurement of approximately battery voltage indicates a short to voltage in the wiring or a faulty Ignition Switch.

(6) A measurement of approximately 0 volts indicates a faulty ECM.

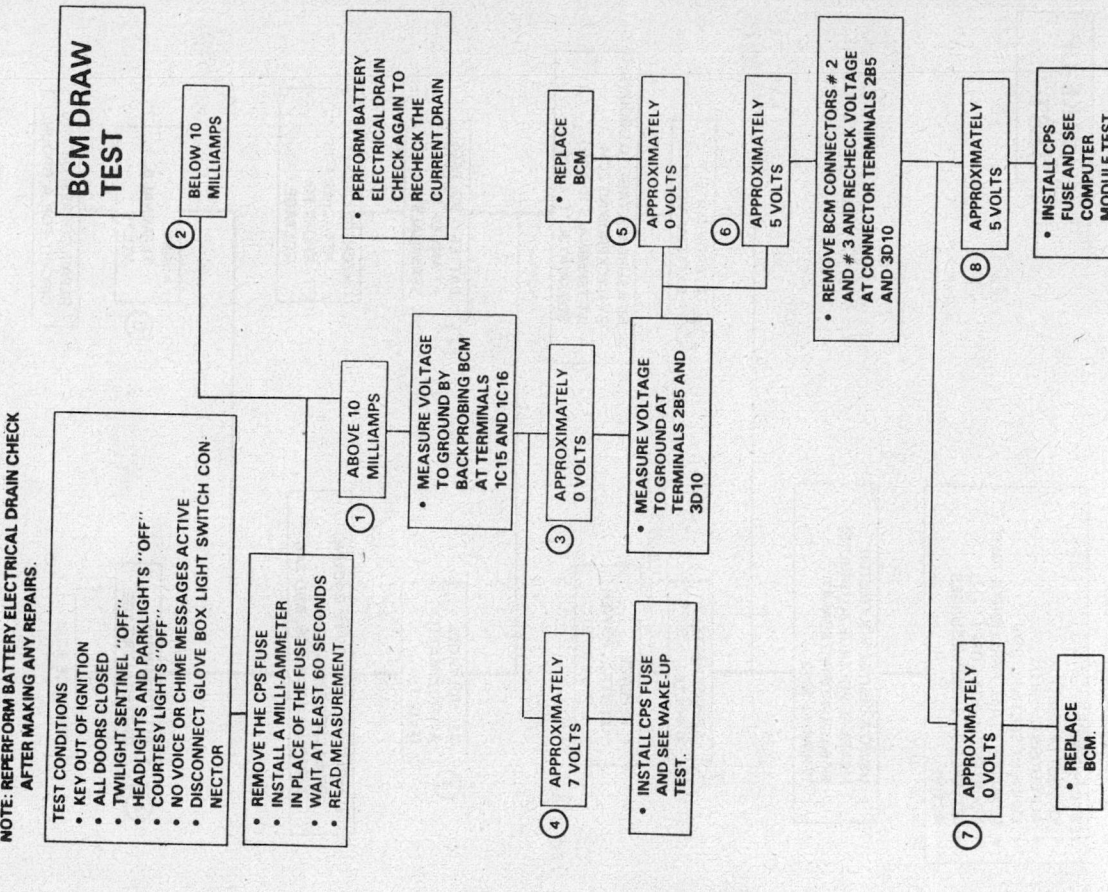

BCM DRAW TEST

Current draw through the CPS Fuse to the Central Power Supply (CPS) should be less than 10 milliamps with no circuits active. This test determines the value of current to the Central Power Supply (CPS) with all system off. The BCM may be the cause of this current.

(1) A measurement above 10 milliamps indicates a problem with the BCM or one of the other computer modules.

(2) A measurement below 10 milliamps indicates a problem with a non micro-processer system.

(3) A measurement of approximately 0 volts may indicate a faulty BCM.

(4) A measurement of approximately 7 volts may indicate a fault in the Wake-Up System.

(5) A measurement of approximately 0 volts indicates a faulty BCM.

(6) A measurement of approximately 5 volts indicates that the BCM or one of the other computer modules is faulty.

(7) A measurement of approximately 0 volts indicates a faulty BCM.

(8) A measurement of approximately 5 volts indicates the problem is in one of the other computer modules.

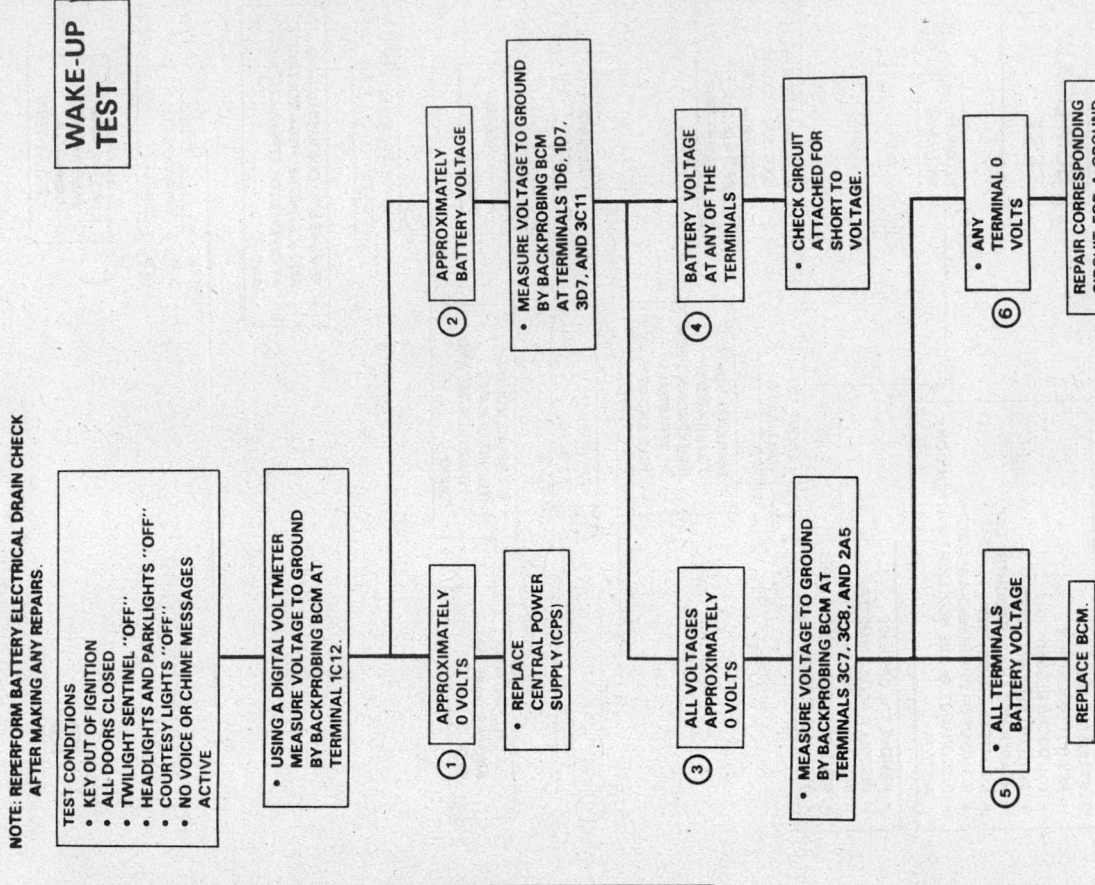

WAKE-UP TEST

The Wake-Up Test determines why the BCM is awake with all systems off. The test checks the Central Power Supply (CPS), the BCM and the BCM Wake-Up Inputs.

(1) A measurement of approximately 0 volts indicates a faulty Central Power Supply (CPS).

(2) A measurement of approximately battery voltage indicates a faulty BCM input or a faulty BCM.

(3) A measurement of approximately 0 volts at all terminals indicates a faulty Wake-Up Input or a faulty BCM.

(4) A measurement of approximately battery voltage indicates a faulty BCM input.

(5) A measurement of battery voltage at all terminals indicates the fault is in the BCM.

(6) A measurement of 0 volts at any terminals indicates a faulty Wake-Up Input.

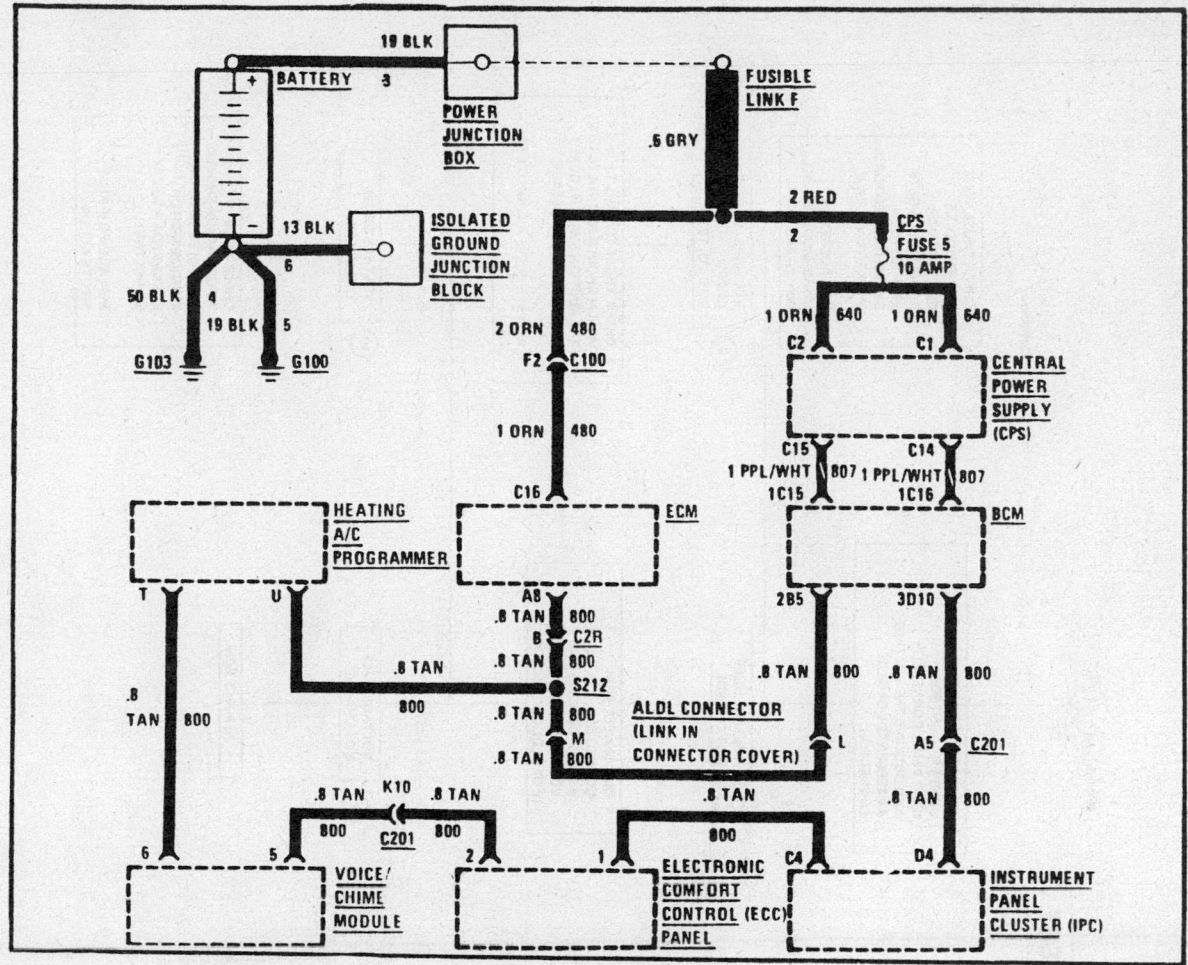

COMPUTER MODULE TEST

The Computer Module Test determines why the Data Line is high with all systems off.

(1) If the voltage does not change, the ECM is OK.

(2) If the voltage drops to 0 volts, an ECM input which should be 0 volts with the Ignition Switch locked may be shorted to voltage.

(3) If the voltage does not change, the Heating-A/C Programmer is OK.

(4) If the voltage drops to 0 volts, a Heating-A/C Programmer input, which should be 0 volts with the Ignition Switch locked, may be shorted to voltage.

(5) If the voltage does not change, the Voice/Chime module is OK.

(6) If the voltage drops to 0 volts a Voice/Chime module input, which should be 0 volts with the Ignition Switch locked may be shorted to voltage.

(7) If the voltage does not change, the ECC is OK.

(8) If the voltage drops to 0 volts, an ECC input which should be 0 volts with the Ignition Switch locked, may be shorted to voltage.

(9) If the voltage does not change, the BCM is faulty.

(10) If the voltage drops to 0 volts, an IPC input, which should be 0 volts with the Ignition Switch locked, may be shorted to voltage.

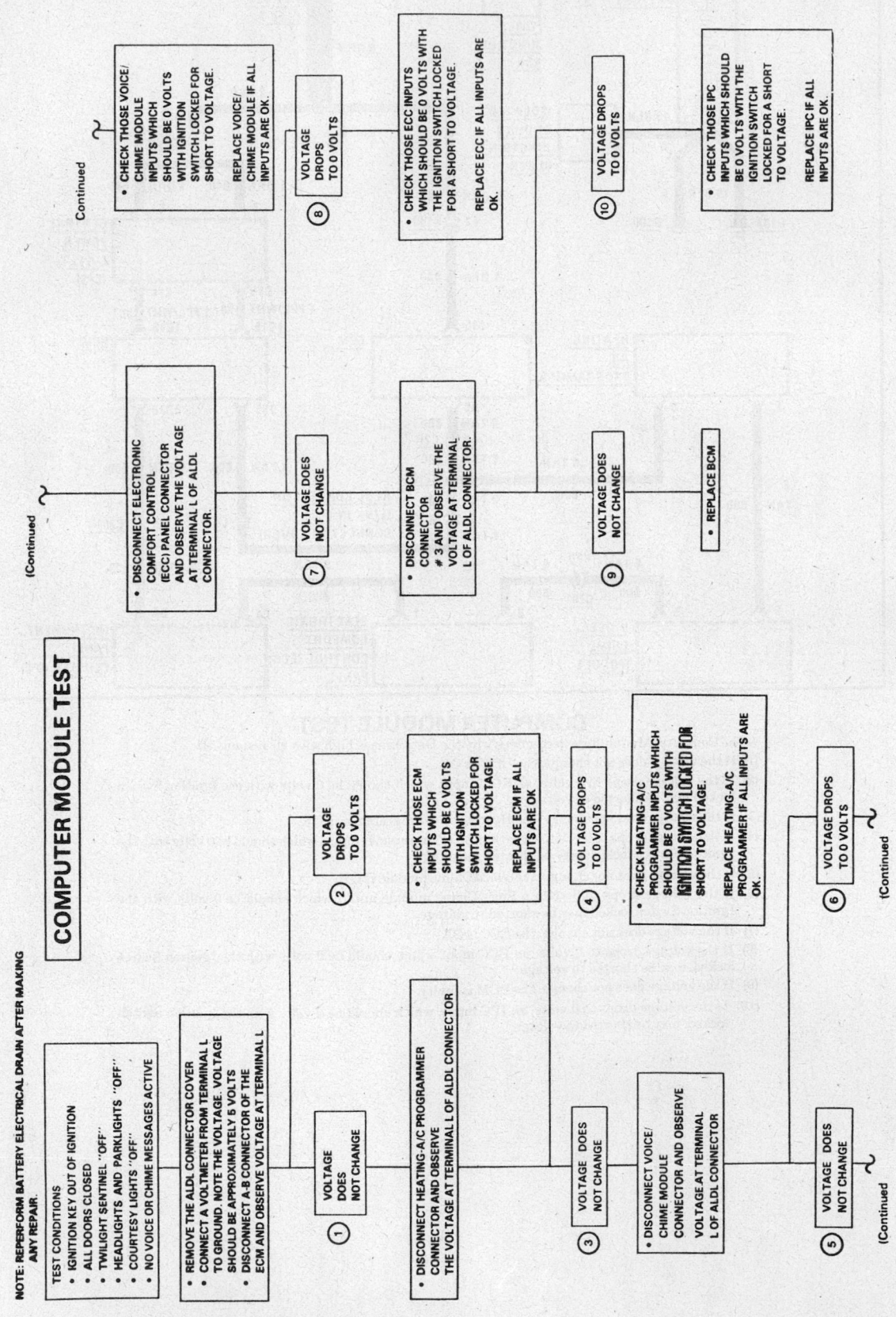

CHEVROLET SPRINT/GEO METRO ENGINE CONTROL SYSTEM

Feedback System

The purpose of the this system is to maintain a controlled air/fuel ratio, allowing the catalytic converter to reduce the tailpipe emissions and to improve fuel economy simultaneously.

The Electronic Control Module (ECM) and the oxygen sensor are the major components of the system. The oxygen sensor is mounted on the exhaust manifold and monitors the exhaust air/fuel ratio and sends signals to the ECM as to the air/fuel mixture having either a lean, correct or rich ratio by sampling the exhaust gases as they pass through the exhaust manifold.

The Electronic Control Module (ECM) processes the oxygen sensor signal and controls the operation of the mixture control solenoid in the carburetor to provide the proper air/fuel ratio to the engine.

ELECTRONIC CONTROL MODULE (ECM)

The ECM controls the pulse air control system, the fuel cut system, the idle up system and the bowl vent system, as well as the carburetor feed back system. The ECM is located behind the instrument panel. The ECM sensed parameters are as follows:

1. The exhaust oxygen concentration is sensed by the oxygen sensor installed in the exhaust manifold.

2. Engine coolant temperature is sensed by the thermal switch, installed in the intake manifold.

3. Throttle position is sensed by micro switches (wide open throttle and idle switches), mounted on the carburetor.

4. The engine speed is computed by the ECM from electrical signals received from the ignition system.

5. When equipped with a manual transaxle, the clutch switch ON signal, is sensed when the clutch pedal is depressed.

6. The ECM senses electrical loads on manual transaxle equipped vehicles to provide idle up speed compensations when the head lamps are on, the engine cooling fan is on, the heater fan is on and/or when the rear defogger is on.

7. An altitude compensation system is used when the vehicle is operated at high altitude, with the feed back system not functioning. To compensate for the richer air/fuel mixture, due to the low air density, the high altitude compensator is ON by sensing the barometric pressure and sending a signal to the ECM. Following the signal, the ECM controls the mixture solenoid in the carburetor, thus compensating for the air/fuel mixture.

8. A thermal switch senses the engine compartment temperature and sends a signal to the ECM to compensate the air/fuel ratio of the fuel mixture. When the air temperature in the engine compartment is low, the switch signals the ECM to make the mixture richer. When the air temperature in the engine compartment is high, the switch stops operating, which means the air/fuel ratio of the mixture is not controlled by the switch signals.

CHECKING SYSTEM

1. Turn on the cancel switch for the sensor light, located along the side of the fuse panel box.

2. Turn the ignition switch to the **ON** position without operating the engine. The sensor light should light, but not flash.

NOTE: If the sensor light does not illuminate, check the electrical circuit for the sensor lamp for a burned out bulb, a disconnected wire, or damage to the circuitry.

3. After the operation of the sensor lamp is confirmed, start the engine and operate it until normal operating temperature is reached.

4. With the engine at normal operating temperature, operate

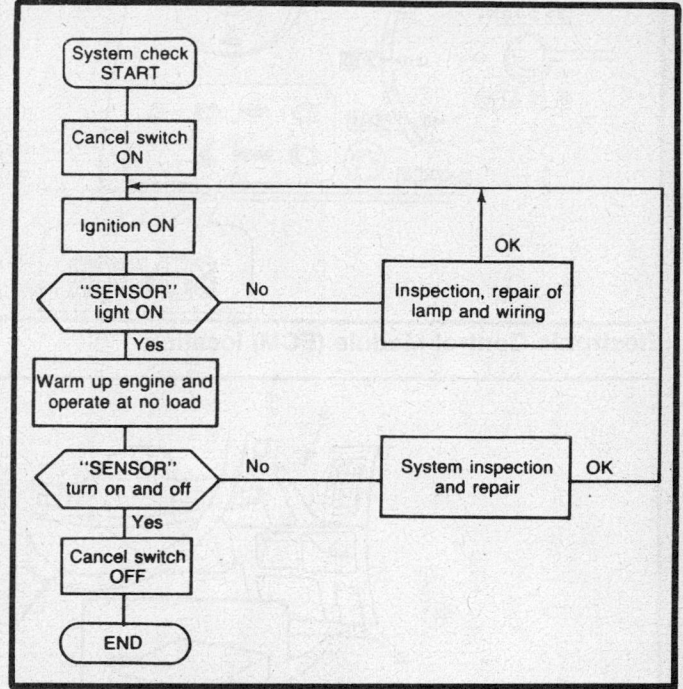

Sensor light system diagnostic flow chart

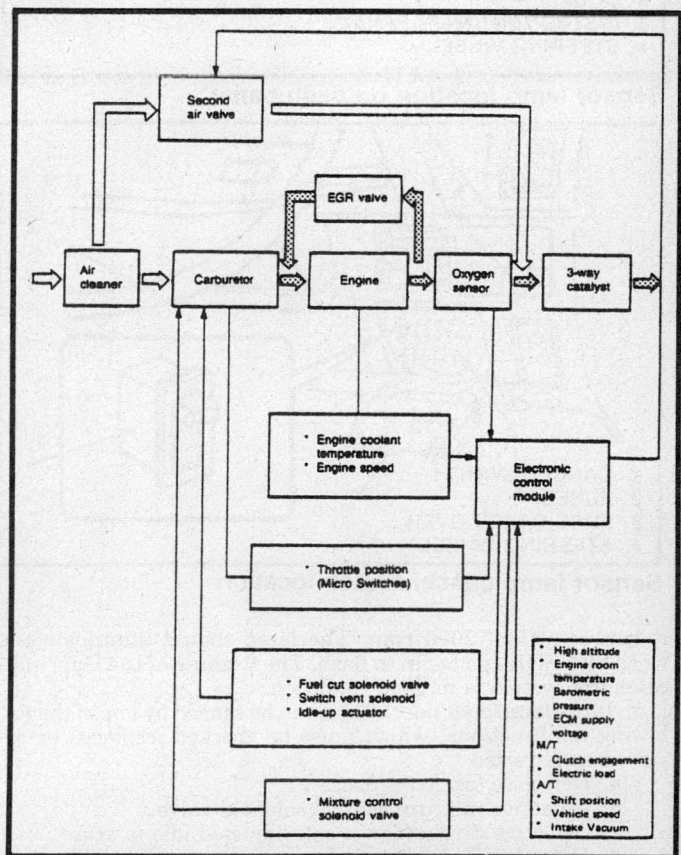

Computer Controlled Feedback system

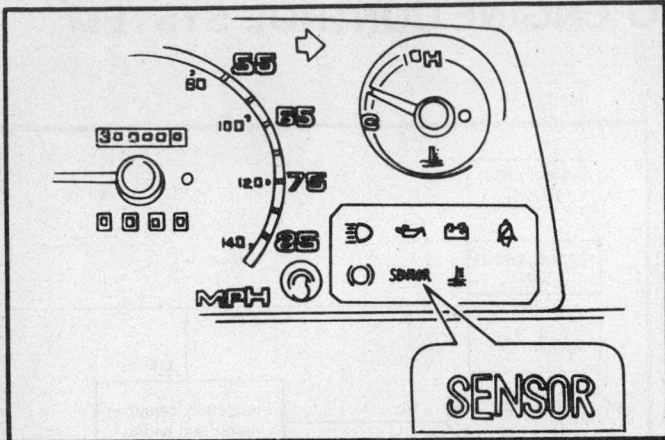

Electronic Control Module (ECM) location

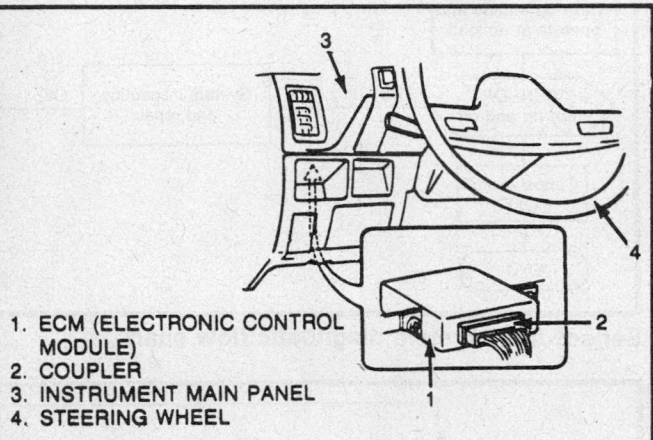

1. ECM (ELECTRONIC CONTROL MODULE)
2. COUPLER
3. INSTRUMENT MAIN PANEL
4. STEERING WHEEL

Sensor lamp location on dash panel

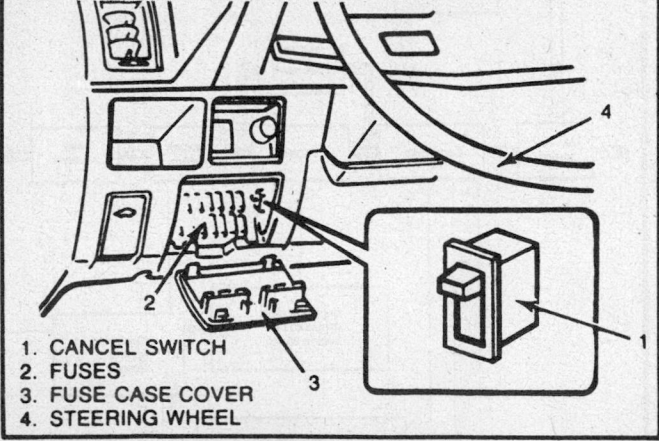

1. CANCEL SWITCH
2. FUSES
3. FUSE CASE COVER
4. STEERING WHEEL

Sensor lamp cancel switch location

it between 1500–2000 rpm. The lamp should illuminate the word SENSOR and begin to flash. The flashing of the lamp indicates the system is in good condition.

5. If the lamp does not flash, it can be caused by one of the following malfunctions, which must be checked, replaced or repaired as required.

    a. Defective oxygen sensor.
    b. Defective mixture control solenoid valve.
    c. Defective carburetor or mis-adjusted idle mixture.
    d. Defective thermal switch.
    e. Disconnected or loosely connected electrical wires for the emission control system.
    f. Defective electronic control module.
    g. Defective micro switches (idle and WOT).

6. After making sure the sensor lamp flashes, turn the cancel switch off. The lamp should go out.

7. Stop the engine and replace necessary components.

ECM GROUND CIRCUITS

Inspection

The ECM is grounded at the left side of the instrument panel to body and the top of the transaxle. If either grounding is not secure, the feedback system will not operate properly. Therefore, visually check to insure proper grounding is accomplished at these 2 points before proceeding with the following inspection.

1. Have the ignition switch in the **OFF** position.
2. Disconnect the coupler from the ECM.
3. Using an ohmmeter, the measured resistance between terminals 1, 19 and the body ground, should be 0. This indicates the ground is correct at both points.
4. If the resistance is not 0 ohm, the possibility exists that the grounds are not correct. Recheck the grounding at these points.

ECM POWER CIRCUITS

Inspection

If a disconnection or a failure of contact occurs within a power circuit including the ignition coil, solenoids, or solenoid valves, signals will not be sent to the ECM and as a result, the feedback system will not function properly. Therefore, check all power circuits in the following manner.

1. With the ignition switch in the **OFF** position, disconnect the ECM connector.
2. Turn the ignition switch to the **ON** position, but do not start the engine.
3. Connect a voltmeter between terminal 2, harness side of the disconnected connector and to the body ground. Measure the voltage which should be approximately 12 volts.
4. Repeat the same test between terminals 3, 9, 12, 13, 16 and 18. The voltage should be approximately 12 volts.
5. After the voltage test for the terminals, connect the voltmeter to terminal 13 and depress the clutch pedal, if equipped with manual transaxle. The voltage should drop to 0 volt.

NOTE: By depressing the clutch pedal, the clutch switch is turned to the ON position and the circuit is grounded. In this position, the fuel cut solenoid does not operate.

6. If the above results are not obtained, the circuit may be disconnected or a switch not making contact.
7. After the checking, re-connect the terminal connector for the ECM.

SENSORS AND WIRE LEADS

Inspection

The sensors for the feedback system are as follows;
    Wide Open Throttle (WOT) micro switch
    Idle micro switch
    Thermal switch
    High altitude compensator switch
    Thermal engine area switch

If any of the sensors malfunction or the sensor circuits have defects, signals are not sent back to the ECM and consequently, the Feedback system will not function properly. Therefore, check each sensor and its circuit to determine the malfunctioning section in the following manner:

1. Have the ignition switch in the **OFF** position.

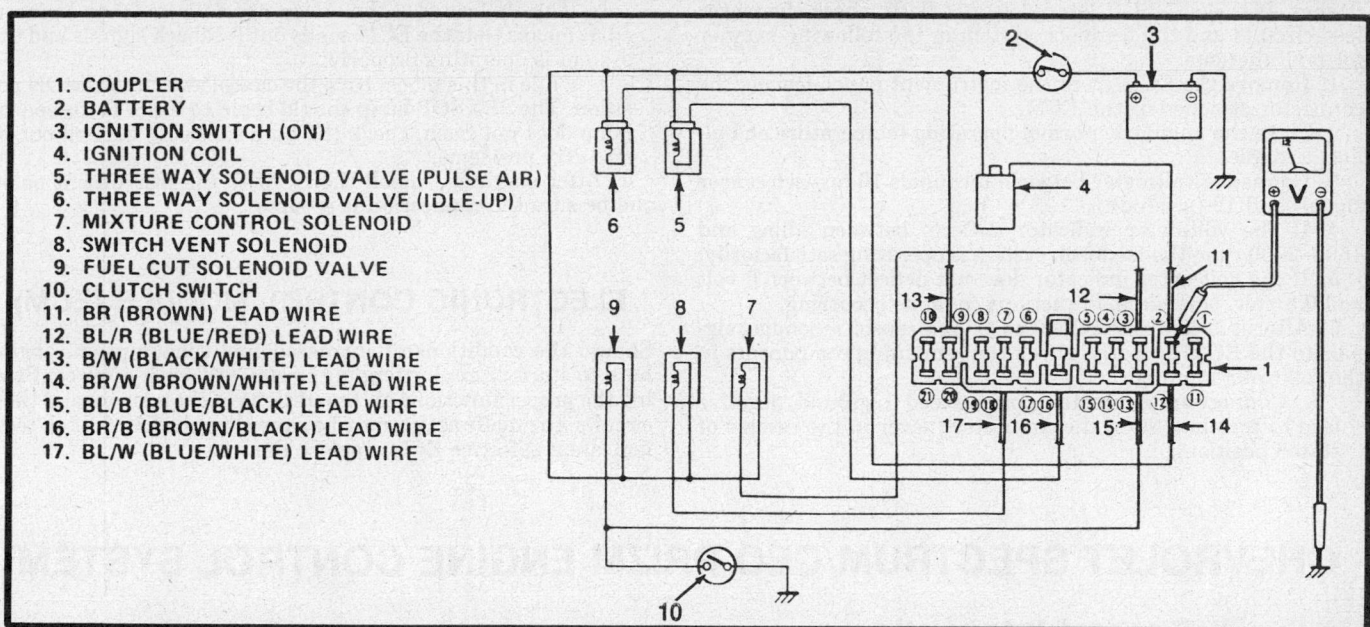

1. COUPLER
2. BATTERY
3. IGNITION SWITCH (ON)
4. IGNITION COIL
5. THREE WAY SOLENOID VALVE (PULSE AIR)
6. THREE WAY SOLENOID VALVE (IDLE-UP)
7. MIXTURE CONTROL SOLENOID
8. SWITCH VENT SOLENOID
9. FUEL CUT SOLENOID VALVE
10. CLUTCH SWITCH
11. BR (BROWN) LEAD WIRE
12. BL/R (BLUE/RED) LEAD WIRE
13. B/W (BLACK/WHITE) LEAD WIRE
14. BR/W (BROWN/WHITE) LEAD WIRE
15. BL/B (BLUE/BLACK) LEAD WIRE
16. BR/B (BROWN/BLACK) LEAD WIRE
17. BL/W (BLUE/WHITE) LEAD WIRE

Checking ECM power circuits

2. Disconnect the terminal connector from the ECM. Connect an ohmmeter between terminal 4 of the disconnected connection and terminal 19 (ground). Measure the resistance. Repeat the test with each of the following terminals, numbers 5, 6, 14 and 15.

3. If the ohmmeter readings are within specifications, the sensors and its circuits are normal. If the readings are out of specifications, the sensor or its circuit could be defective, or a connector could be disconnected within the circuit.

4. After checking, connect the connector to the ECM securely.

OXYGEN SENSOR AND FEEDBACK SYSTEM CIRCUITS

Inspection

If the oxygen sensor fails to send signals to the ECM, the feedback system does not function properly. While the feedback system is at work, the ECM sends out the carburetor feedback signal and while in this mode, when the cancel switch, located in the fuse case, is turned on or the odometer indicates 30,000 or 60,000 miles, the SENSOR lamp in the instrument cluster

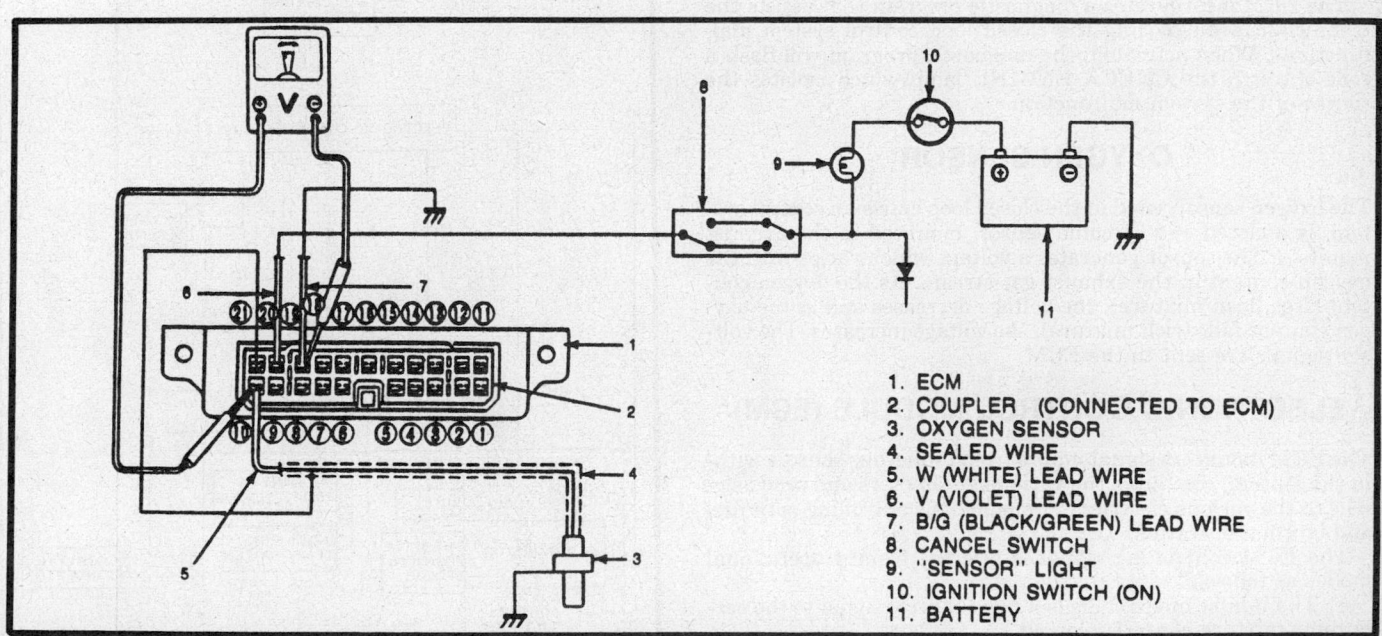

1. ECM
2. COUPLER (CONNECTED TO ECM)
3. OXYGEN SENSOR
4. SEALED WIRE
5. W (WHITE) LEAD WIRE
6. V (VIOLET) LEAD WIRE
7. B/G (BLACK/GREEN) LEAD WIRE
8. CANCEL SWITCH
9. "SENSOR" LIGHT
10. IGNITION SWITCH (ON)
11. BATTERY

Checking oxygen sensor signal

flashes. If the SENSOR lamp does not flash, check the power feed circuits and the feedback system in the following manner for malfunctions.

1. Remove the ECM from the instrument panel, leaving the connector attached to the ECM.

2. Have the engine at normal operating temperature and allow it to idle.

3. Connect a voltmeter between terminals 10 (oxygen sensor signal) and 19 (ground).

4. If the voltmeter indicator deflects between idling and 1500–2000 rpm, the feedback system is operating satisfactorily.

5. If the voltmeter indicator does not deflect between 0 volt and 0.8 volt, possible malfunctions could be occurring.

6. After it is confirmed that the oxygen sensor is sending signals to the ECM properly, check the remaining components in the following manner.

   a. Connect an ohmmeter, positive lead to ground, negative lead to terminal 20 of the connector (never in the reverse of stated position).

   b. If the indicator of the ohmmeter deflects when connected, it means that the ECM sends out feedback signals and the system is operating properly.

   c. While in this mode, turn the cancel switch to the ON position. The SENSOR lamp should begin to flash. If the sensor lamp does not flash, check the bulb for being burned out or circuitry problems.

7. After checking, install the ECM to the instrument panel and be sure the connection is secure.

ELECTRONIC CONTROL MODULE (ECM)

Should the conditions of increased fuel consumption, engine hard to start, or engine tending to stall still exist after confirming the proper functions and conditions of the sensors and their circuits, the malfunction may be caused by the ECM. If all tests indicate a defective ECM, replace the unit.

CHEVROLET SPECTRUM/GEO PRIZM ENGINE CONTROL SYSTEM

General Information

The closed loop emission control system is designed to precisely control the air/fuel mixture, allowing the use of a 3-way catalyst converter to reduce the emissions of hydrocarbons (HC), carbon monoxide (CO) and nitrogen oxides (NOx) through the exhaust system.

The major components of the system are the oxygen sensor, electronic control module (ECM), an electronically controlled air/fuel ratio carburetor and the 3-way catalytic converter.

The system also utilizes a dashboard mounted indicator lamp that indicates a malfunction in one or more of the electronic operating mode systems and alerts the operator for the need of unscheduled maintenance or repairs. In the event of a system malfunction, the CHECK ENGINE lamp will come on and remain on as long as the malfunction is recognized by the ECM and the engine is operating.

The ECM incorporates a diagnostic program that assists the technician in diagnosing the closed loop control system malfunctions. When activated, the diagnostic program will flash a code through the CHECK ENGINE lamp which isolates the source of the system malfunction.

OXYGEN SENSOR

The oxygen sensor, used in the closed loop emission control system, is a closed end Zirconia sensor, mounted in the exhaust manifold. The sensor generates a voltage which varies with the oxygen content in the exhaust gas stream. As the oxygen content rises (lean mixture), the voltage decreases and as the oxygen content falls (rich mixture), the voltage increases. The voltage signals are sent to the ECM.

ELECTRONIC CONTROL MODULE (ECM)

The ECM monitiors signal inputs from numerous sensors within the system, computes the various parameters and sends signals to the various electronic components, controlling both fuel and ignition operation.

The ECM controlling signal is selected from 4 operational modes as follows.

1. The inhibit mode: This is a fixed control signal to the carburetor mixture control solenoid.

2. Pre-WOT and WOT mode: This is a pre-selected duty cycle, selected and generated, based on the engine rpm.

3. Open loop mode: A pre-selected duty cycle mode, based on various parameters, inputed through the sensor system.

4. Closed loop mode: A caluated duty cycle, generated by the sensor inputs and voltage received from the oxygen sensor.

During the closed loop operation, the ECM measures the signal output of the varied sensors and the voltage generated by the oxygen sensor. As the sensor signals or voltage increases or decreases and passes into the ECM, the duty cycle of the output signal is immediately changed by the ECM to react to these changes and constantly sends different signals to the controlling electronic components to maintain a stoichiometric operation.

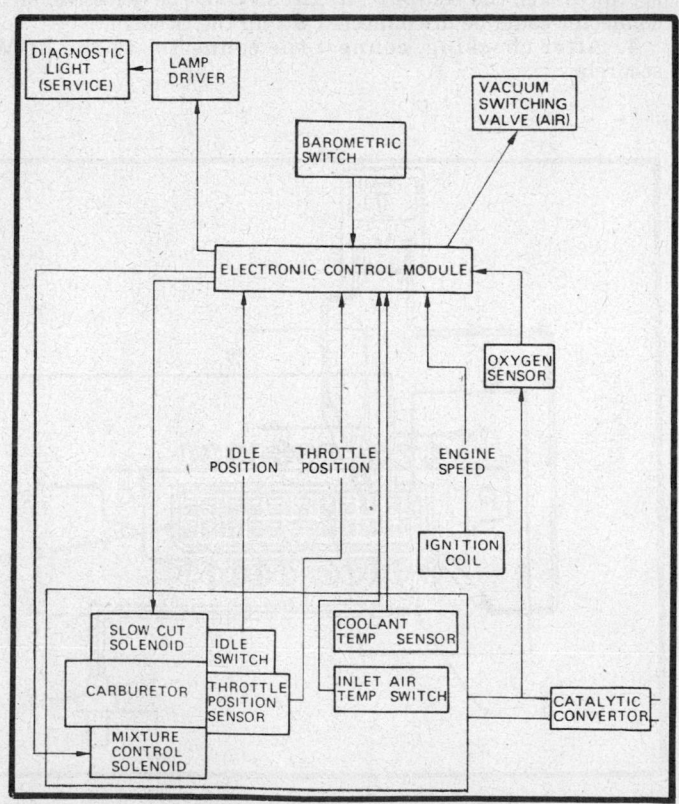

Computer Controlled Closed Loop system

CARBURETOR

The controlled air/fuel ratio carburetor incorporates a duty solenoid to carefully maintain the air/fuel ratio, in accordance with the control of the ECM.

The main metering system supplies fuel to the engine during off-idle to wide open throttle operation. The fuel is drawn from the float chamber and metered by the main jet fixed orifice and solenoid controlled fuel orifice. The fuel is then mixed with the air coming through the main air bleed and jetted into the venturi by the main nozzle. The duty solenoid changes the air/fuel ratio and is operated by the electronic control module in the closed loop system.

DIAGNOSIS

The diagnosis circuit check makes sure that the self diagnostic system operates determines that the trouble codes will display and guides the diagnosis to other trouble areas. When the enginer is operating and a malfunction occurs in the system, the CHECK ENGINE lamp will illuminate and a trouble code will be stored in the ECM trouble code memory. The lamp will remain ON with the engine operating as long as there is a problem. If the malfunction is intermittant, the CHECK ENGINE lamp will go out, but the malfunction will be stored in the ECM trouble code memory.

With the ignition in the **ON** position and the engine not operating, the CHECK ENGINE lamp should be on. This is a bulb check to indicate that the lamp is operating.

A 3 terminal connector, located near the ECM connector, is used to actuate the trouble code system in the ECM. This connector is also known as Assembly Line Diagnostic Link (ALDL) or Assembly Line Communication Link (ALCL).

To activate the trouble code system in the ECM, place the ignition switch in the **ON** position and place a jumper wire between terminal A and terminal C. The CHECK ENGINE light will begin to flash a trouble code 12. Code 12 consists of 1 flash, a short pause, then 2 flashes. There will be a longer pause and the code 12 will repeat its self 2 more times. This check indicates that the self diagnostic system is operating properly. The cycle will then repeat its self until the engine is started or the ignition switch is placed in the **OFF** position. In most cases, codes will be checked with the engine running since no codes other than code 12 or 51 will be present with the intial key **ON**.

NOTE: Remove the jumper wire from the test terminal before starting the engine.

A trouble code indicates a problem, in a given circuit and its components.

When the engine is started, the CHECK ENGINE lamp will go off. If the lamp remains on, the self-diagnostic system has a fault.

If a trouble code is stored in the ECM memory and the CHECK ENGINE lamp is off with the engine running, the trouble may be intermittant or may only occur at certain operating conditions.

Faults indicated by trouble codes 13, 44 and 45 require engine operation at part throttle for up to 5 minutes of engine operation before the CHECK ENGINE lamp will come on.

The fault indicated by trouble code 15 takes 5 minutes of engine operation before it will display.

CLEARING THE TROUBLE CODE MEMORY

The trouble code memory has a constant 12 volts applied, even when the ignition switch is in the **OFF** position. After a fault has been corrected, it will be necessary to remove the ECM fuse from the fuse block for a period of ten seconds, to clear any stored codes from the memory.

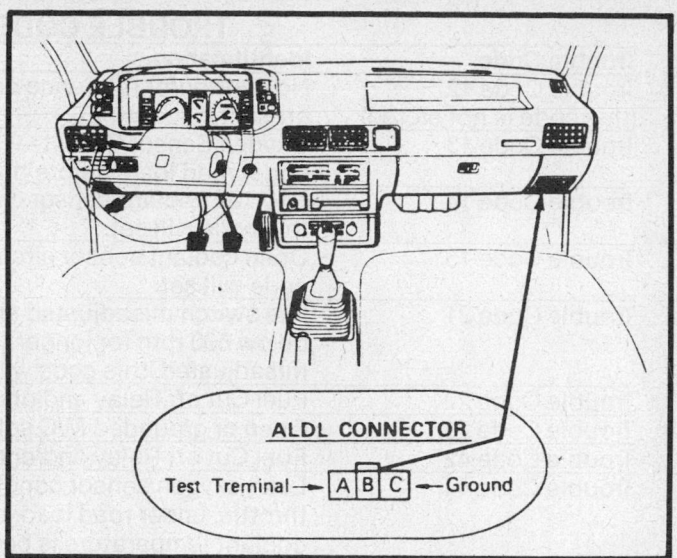

ALDL location

PIN	FUNCTION
1	Ground
2	Ground
3	Oxygen Sensor Input
4	System Malfunction Lamp Driver
5	Throttle Position Sensor Input
6	Battery + (Memory Back-Up)
7	Throttle Position Reference Voltage
8	Idle Switch Input
9	Inlet Air Temperature Switch
10	EFE Heater Relay
11	+ 12V To Ignition
12	+ 12V To Ignition
13	Not Used
14	Fuel Cut-Off Relay
15	Shift Indicator Lamp Driver
16	Diagnose Decode
17	Coolant Temperature Sensor Input
18	Barometric Switch
19	Ignition Coil Tach Input
20	Oxygen Sensor Ground
21	Carburetor Mixture Control Solenoid
22	Analog Ground

ECM connections

TROUBLE CODE IDENTIFICATION

The CHECK ENGINE light will only be on if the malfunction exists under certain conditions. It takes up to 5 seconds minimum for the light to come on when a problem occurs. If the malfunction clears, the light will go out and trouble code will be set in the ECM.

NOTE: Code 12 does not store in the ECM memory.

Any codes stored will be erased if no problem reoccurs within 50 engine starts.

TROUBLE CODE IDENTIFICATION

Trouble Code	Identification
Trouble Code 12 (this code is not stored)	No distributor reference pulses to the ECM and will only flash while the fault is present.
Trouble Code 13	Oxygen Sensor Circuit—The engine must run up to two minutes at part throttle, under road load, before this code will set.
Trouble Code 14	Shorted coolant sensor circuit—The engine must run up to two minutes before this code will set.
Trouble Code 15	Open coolant sensor circuit—The engine must run up to five minutes before this code will set.
Trouble Code 21	Idle switch misadjusted and/or circuit open. This code will set if engine speed falls below 600 rpm for longer than 32 seconds. If TPS and Idle Switch are faulty or misadjusted, this code will set.
Trouble Code 22	Fuel Cut off Relay and/or circuit open.
Trouble Code 23	Open or grounded M/C solenoid circuit.
Trouble Code 42	Fuel Cut off Relay and/or circuit shorted.
Trouble Code 44	Lean oxygen sensor condition—The engine must run up to 2 minutes at part throttle, under road load, before this code will set. This code will not set when the coolant temperature is below 70°C and/or the air temperature in air cleaner is below 0°C, in a "low altitude" condition. This code will not set in a "high altitude" condition.
Trouble Code 45	Rich system indication—The engine must run up to 2 minutes at part throttle, under road load, before this code will set. This code will not set when the engine is not between 1500 to 2500 rpm, and/or the coolant temperature is below 70°C and/or at "high altitude" condition.
Trouble Code 51	Faulty calibration unit (PROM) or installation. It takes up to 30 seconds before this code will set.
Trouble Code 54	Shorted M/C solenoid circuit and/or faulty ECM.
Trouble Code 55	Faulty ECM-problem in A/D converter in ECM.

Trouble code identification

CLOSED LOOP EMISSION CONTROL SYSTEM

Component	Sensed Parameter	Controlled Parameter	Specification
Coolant temp. sensor	Engine coolant temp.	Electrical signal to ECM	Resistance 2.1–2.9 kΩ at coolant temp 20°C
Oxygen sensor	Oxygen content in exhaust gas stream	Voltage to ECM	"Rich" ≥ 800mv "Lean" ≤ 250mv at 371°C & 450mv BIAS (699.8°F)
Altitude switch	Atmospheric Pressure	Electrical signal to ECM	"ON" ≤ 89.0 ± 0.9 kPa (Q) "OFF" ≥ Q $^{+4.4}_{+1.1}$ kPa
Inlet air temperature switch	Inlet air temp.	Electrical signal to EDM	"ON" 0 + 4°C(32 ± 39.2°F) "OFF" 15°C (59°F)
Throttle position switch	Carburetor throttle position	(Iole Sw) Electrical signal to ECM (T.P.S.) Voltage to ECM	8°–10° (M/T) 10°–12° (A/T) Voltage Ratio/Angle 75–85%/9° (M/T and A/T)

Closed loop emission control system

ELECTRONIC IGNITION SYSTEMS

General Service Precautions

1. Always turn the ignition switch **OFF** when disconnecting or connecting any electrical connectors or components.

2. Never reverse the battery polarity or disconnect the battery with the engine running.

3. Do not pierce spark plug or wiring harness wires with test probes for any reason. Due to their more pliable construction, it is important to route spark plug wires properly to avoid chafing or cutting.

4. Disconnect the ignition switch feed wire at the distributor when making compression tests to avoid arcing that may damage components, especially on computer-based ignition systems.

5. Do not remove grease or dielectric compound from components or connectors when installing. Some manufacturers use grease to prevent corrosion and dielectric compound to dissipate heat generated during normal module operation.

6. Check all replacement part numbers carefully. Installing the wrong components for a specific application can damage the system.

7. All manufacturers' instructions included with any testing equipment must be read carefully to insure accuracy of the test results. Inaccurate readings and/or damage to ignition system components may result due to the use of improper test equipment.

ELECTRONIC IGNITION QUICK CHECK CHART
(Non-computer controlled systems only)

Condition	Possible Cause	Correction
Abrupt backfire	Control unit or ignition module malfunction. Incorrect timing. Bad cap or rotor	Check ignition timing. Replace control unit or module. Replace cap or rotor
Intermittent running	Magnetic pick-up or stator malfunction. Bad trigger wheel, reluctor or armature. Control unit or ignition module failure	Replace defective components after testing as described under appropriate system in this unit repair section
Does not fire on one or more cylinders	Defective pick-up, stator, trigger wheel, reluctor or armature. Bad spark plugs or ignition wires	Replace components as necessary
Cuts off suddenly	Malfunction in control unit of module. Damaged pick-up or stator	Check operation of pick-up and stator. Replace control unit or module
Won't start	Control unit or module failure. Defective cap, rotor, pick-up or stator ①	Replace control unit or module after testing. Replace distributor components as necessary
Poor performance, no power under load	Defective pick-up, stator, or ignition coil. Worn or fouled spark plugs. Bad plug wires	Check distributor components for signs of wear or damage. Replace spark plugs and wires
Arcing or excessive burning on rotor or distributor cap	Worn or fouled spark plugs. Bad plug wires	Replace spark plugs and wires

NOTE: This chart assumes the described conditions are problems in the electronic ignition system and not the result of another malfunction. Always perform basic checks for fuel, spark and compression first. See the individual system sections for all test procedures.
① Check ballast resistor on Chrysler models

AMC/JEEP-EAGLE
Solid State Ignition (SSI) System

General Information

EAGLE AND PREMIER

The Solid State Ignition (SSI) is standard equipment on 6 cylinder and 4 cylinder engines and is of the Ford Motor Company design.

The system consists of a sensor and toothed trigger wheel inside the distributor, a permanently sealed electronic control unit which determines dwell, the ignition coil, ignition wires and spark plugs.

The trigger wheel rotates on the distributor shaft. As a tooth nears the sensor magnet, the magnetic field shifts toward the tooth. When the tooth and sensor are aligned, the magnetic field is shifted to its maximum, signaling the electronic control unit to switch off the coil primary current. This starts an electronic timer inside the control unit, which allows the primary current to remain off only long enough for the spark plug to fire. The timer adjusts the amount of time primary current is off according to conditions, thus automatically adjusting dwell. There is also a special circuit within the control unit to detect and ignore false signals. Spark timing is adjusted by both mechanical (centrifugal) and vacuum advance.

A wire of 1.35 ohms resistance is spliced into the ignition feed to reduce voltage to the coil during running conditions. The resistance wire is by-passed when the engine is being started so that full battery voltage may be supplied to the coil. Bypass is accomplished by the I-terminal on the solenoid.

The remainder of the system includes a pointless distributor, standard construction ignition coil, ignition switch, resistance wire and bypass, secondary spark plug wires and spark plugs. The electronic control unit (module) is a solid state, nonserviceable, sealed unit. This unit has reverse polarity and

voltage surge circuit protection built in. A pair of weatherproof connectors attach the control unit to the ignition circuit.

NOTE: All system electrical connectors use lock tabs that must be released to disconnect the various components.

MEDALLION AND PREMIER WITH 3.0L ENGINE

The Medallion and Premier models use a fully computer controlled eletronic ignition and fuel injection system. The distributor rotor is directly driven from the camshaft. These distributors contain no electronic components. The computer receives it rpm and timing signal from the crank sensor. The ignition power module (including the coil) is checked and receives it signals from the ECU. Timing is non-adjustable and controlled by the ECU. The 3.0L engine ignition system testing also involve ECM testing, except for checking secondary voltage wires.

SUMMIT

When the ignition switch is turned to the **ON** position, battery voltage is applied to the ignition coil primary winding. As the distributor (1.5L engine) or crank angle sensor (1.6L engine) shaft turns, the multi-port injection control unit sends signals to the power transistor. These signals activate the power transistor which causes ignition current primary winding current to flow from the ignition coil negative terminal through the power transistor to ground or be interrupted. The flow of current in the primary winding induces a high voltage in the secondary winding. This voltage flows through the distributor and spark plugs to ground completing the ignition circuit for each cylinder.

System Troubleshooting

CRANK SENSOR

Testing
MEDALLION

1. Disconnect the connector at sensor.

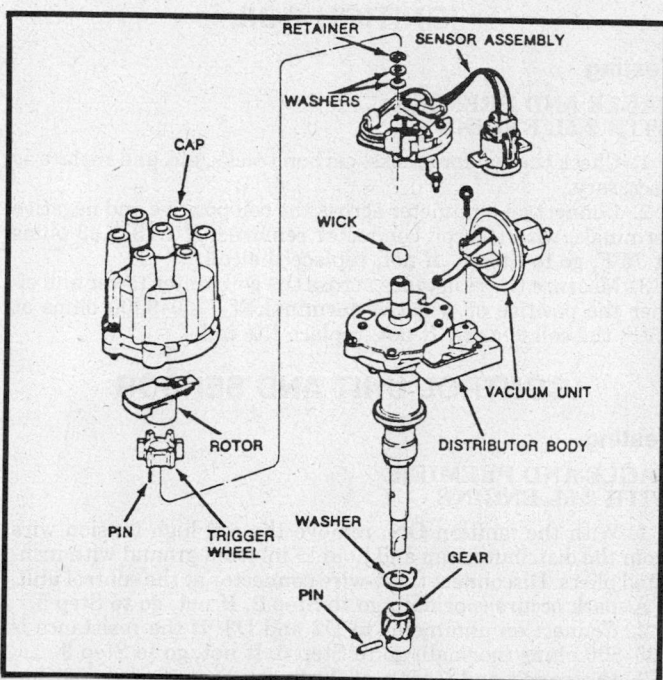

Six cylinder SSI distributor

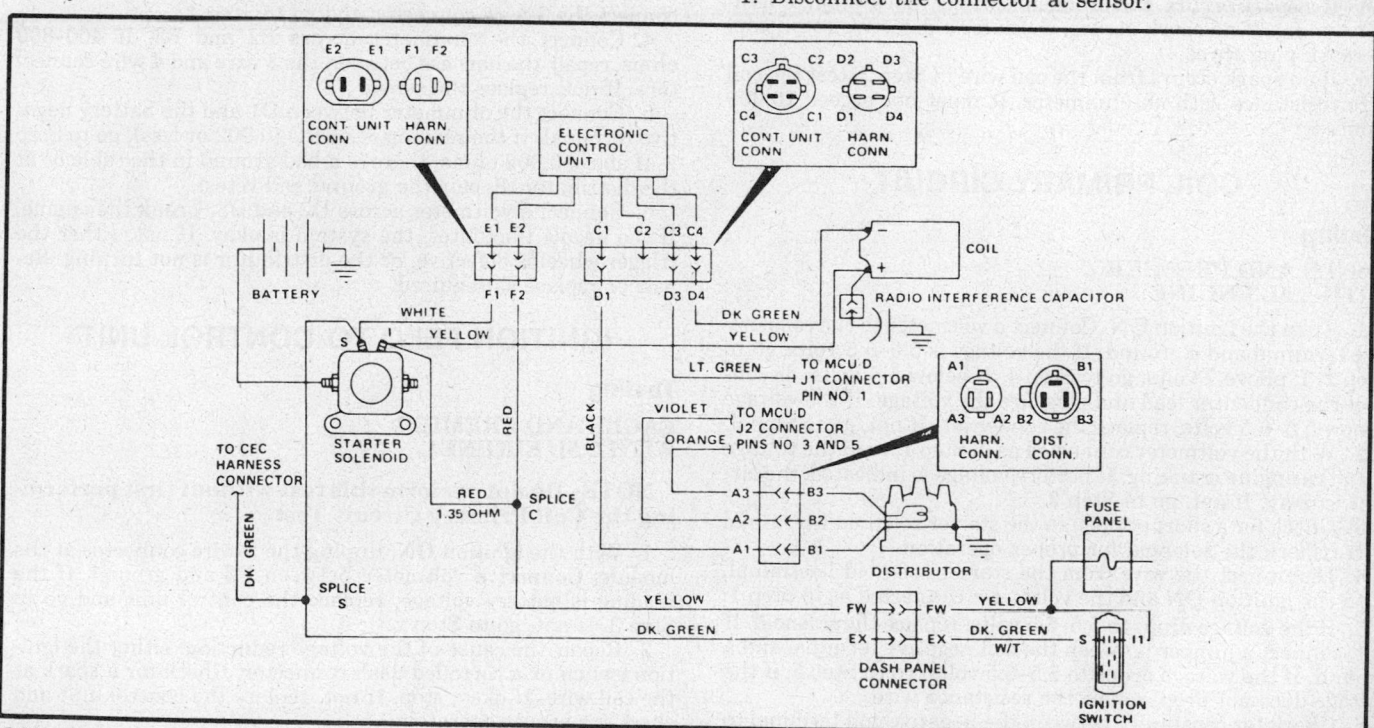

SSI system schematic

2. Check resistance between sensor terminals with engine hot.

3. Resistance should be 125–275 ohms, if not replace sensor.

COOLANT TEMPERATURE SENSOR

Testing

MEDALLION

1. Check coolant sensor resistance at 67–69°F, resistance should be 283–297 ohms.

2. Check coolant sensor resistance at 175–179°F, resistance should be 383–397 ohms.

3. Check coolant sensor resistance at 193–195°F, resistance should be 403–417 ohms.

4. If resistance varies from these specification, replace sensor.

SECONDARY CIRCUIT

Testing

**EAGLE AND PREMIER
WITH 2.5L ENGINE**

1. Disconnect the coil wire from the center of the distributor cap.

NOTE: Twist the rubber boot slightly in either direction, then grasp the boot and pull straight up. Do not pull on the wire and do not use pliers.

2. Hold the wire ½ in. from a ground with a pair of insulated pliers and a heavy glove. As the engine is cranked, watch for a spark.

3. If a spark appears, reconnect the coil wire. Remove the wire from a spark plug and test for a spark as above.

NOTE: Do not remove the spark plug wires from cylinder 1 or 5 on a 6 cylinder engine when performing this test, as sensor damage could occur.

4. If a spark occurs, the problem is in the fuel system or ignition timing. If no spark occurs, check for a defective rotor, cap, or spark plug wires.

5. If no spark occurs from the coil wire in Step 2, test the coil wire resistance with an ohmmeter. It must not exceed 10,000 ohms.

COIL PRIMARY CIRCUIT

Testing

**EAGLE AND PREMIER
WITH 2.5L ENGINE**

1. Turn the ignition **ON**. Connect a voltmeter to the coil positive terminal and a ground. If the voltage is 5.5–6.5 volts, go to Step 2. If above 7 volts, go to Step 4. If below 5.5 volts, disconnect the condenser lead and measure the voltage. If the voltage is now 5.5–6.5 volts, replace the condenser. If not, go to Step 6.

2. With the voltmeter connected as in Step 1, read the voltage with the engine cranking. If battery voltage is indicated, the circuit is okay. If not, go to Step 3.

3. Check for a short or open in the starter solenoid I-terminal wire. Check the solenoid for proper operation.

4. Disconnect the wire from the starter solenoid I-terminal, with the ignition **ON** and the voltmeter connected as in Step 1.

5. If the voltage drops to 5.5–6.5 volts, replace the solenoid. If not, connect a jumper between the coil negative terminal and a ground. If the voltage drops to 5.5–6.5 volts, go to Step 5, if the voltage does not drop, repair the resistance wire.

6. Check for continuity between the negative coil terminal to D4, also for continuity between D1 to ground. If the continuity

is okay, replace the control unit. If not, check for an open wire and go back to Step 2 to re-check.

7. Turn ignition **OFF**. Connect an ohmmeter between the coil terminal and dash connector AV. If above 1.40 ohms, repair the resistance wire.

8. With the ignition **OFF**, connect the ohmmeter between connector AV and ignition switch terminal 11. If less than 0.1 ohm, replace the ignition switch or repair the wire, whichever is the cause. If above 0.1 ohm, check connections and check for defective wiring.

IGNITION COIL

Testing

**EAGLE AND PREMIER
WITH 2.5L ENGINE**

1. Check the coil for cracks, carbon tracks, etc. and replace as necessary.

2. Connect an ohmmeter across the coil positive and negative terminals, with the coil connector removed. If 1.13–1.23 ohms at 75°F, go to Step 3. If not, replace the coil.

3. Measure the resistance across the coil center tower and either the positive or negative terminal. If 7700–9300 ohms at 75°F, the coil is okay. If not, replace the coil.

CONTROL UNIT AND SENSOR

Testing

**EAGLE AND PREMIER
WITH 2.5L ENGINE**

1. With the ignition **ON**, remove the coil high tension wire from the distributor cap and hold ½ in. from ground with insulated pliers. Disconnect the 4-wire connector at the control unit. If a spark occurs (normal), go to Step 2. If not, go to Step 5.

2. Connect an ohmmeter to D2 and D3. If the resistance is 400–800 ohms (normal), go to Step 6. If not, go to Step 3.

3. Disconnect and reconnect the 3-wire connector at distributor. If the reading is now 400–800 ohms, go to Step 6. If not, disconnect the 3-wire connector and go to Step 4.

4. Connect the ohmmeter across B2 and B3. If 400–800 ohms, repair the harness between the 3 wire and 4 wire connectors. If not, replace the sensor.

5. Connect the ohmmeter between D1 and the battery negative terminal. If the reading is ZERO (0.002 or less), go to Step 2. If above 0.002 ohms, there is a bad ground in the cable or at the distributor. Repair the ground and retest.

6. Connect a voltmeter across D2 and D3. Crank the engine. If the needle fluctuates, the system is okay. If not, either the trigger wheel is defective, or the distributor is not turning. Repair or replace as required.

IGNITION FEED TO CONTROL UNIT

Testing

**EAGLE AND PREMIER
WITH 2.5L ENGINE**

NOTE: Do not perform this test without first performing the Coil Primary Circuit Test.

1. With the ignition **ON**, unplug the 2-wire connector at the module. Connect a voltmeter between F2 and ground. If the reading is battery voltage, replace the control unit and go to Step 3. If not, go to Step 2.

2. Repair the cause of the voltage reduction: either the ignition switch or a corroded dash connector. Check for a spark at the coil wire. If okay, stop. If not, replace the control unit and check for proper operation.

3. Reconnect the 2-wire connector at the control unit and un-

plug the 4-wire connector at the control unit. Connect an ammeter between C1 and ground. If it reads 0.9–1.1 amps, the system is okay. If not, replace the module.

CONTROL UNIT CURRENT DRAW

Testing

EAGLE AND PREMIER
WITH 2.5L ENGINE

If 11 volts or more were present at the connector's F2 terminal, measure the current draw of control unit with an ammeter. Disconnect 4-wire connector and connect ammeter between the connector terminal C1 and ground. With the ignition **ON**, current draw should be 0.9–1.1 amps; if it is not, replace the control unit.

CONTROL UNIT VOLTAGE

Testing

EAGLE AND PREMIER
WITH 2.5L ENGINE

Disconnect the 2-wire connector at the control unit and measure the voltage between the connector terminal F2 and ground, with the ignition **ON**. The voltage should be above 11 volts. If it is not, check the ignition switch and the wiring for an open circuit, or a loose or corroded connector. If, after obtaining the proper voltage at F2 terminal, a spark is not produced at the coil wire when the engine is cranked and the coil and sensor check are OK, replace the control unit.

SENSOR

Testing

EAGLE AND PREMIER
WITH 2.5L ENGINE

1. Connect an ohmmeter (x100 scale) to D2 and D3 connector terminals. The resistance should be 400–800 ohms.
2. If the resistance is not within 400–800 ohms, check the voltage output of the sensor. Connect a voltmeter, 2–3 volt scale, to D2 and D3 connector terminals. Crank the engine and observe the voltmeter. A fluctuating voltmeter indicates proper sensor and trigger wheel operation. If not fluctuations are noted, check for a defective trigger wheel, distributor not turning, or a missing trigger wheel pin.
3. If the resistance in Step 1 was not 400–800 ohms, disconnect and reconnect 3-wire connector at the distributor. If the resistance is now 400–800 ohms, check sensor voltage output, Step 2.
4. If the sensor circuit resistance is still not within specification, disconnect 3-wire connector at the distributor and connect an ohmmeter to B2 and B3 terminals. If the resistance is 400–800 ohms, repair or replace the harness between 3 wire and 4 wire connector. If the resistance is still incorrect, replace the sensor.

ROTOR

Testing

EAGLE AND PREMIER
WITH 2.5L ENGINE

The rotor has silicone dielectric compound applied to the blade to reduce the radio interference. After a few thousand miles, the dielectric compound will become charred by the high voltage, which is normal. Do not scrape the residue off. When installing

a new rotor, apply a thin coat (0.030–0.120 in.) of silicone ielectric compound to the rotor blade.

IGNITION COIL

Testing Primary and Secondary Resistance
SUMMIT
1.5L Engine

1. Measure the primary coil resistance across the positive and negative terminals of the ignition coil. The resistance should be 0.72–0.88 ohms.
2. Set the ohmmeter the x1000 scale and measure the secondary coil resistance across the ignition coil positive terminal and the high voltage terminal. The resistance should be 10.3–13.9 kilo-ohms.
3. If the resisance is not as specified, replace the coil.

1.6L Engine

1. To measure the primary coil resistance, place the ohmmeter probes across the No. 4 (No. 1 cylinder) and No. 2 (No. 4 cylinder) terminals of the ignition terminal. Then place the ohmmeter probes across the No. 1 (No. 2 cylinder) and No. 3 (No. 2 cylinder). The resistance should be between 0.77–0.95 ohms.
2. To measure secondary coil resistance, first disconect the coil multi-connector. Then, place the ohmmeter probes betwen the high voltage terminals for the the No. 1 and No. 4 cylinders and between the high voltage terminals for the No. 2 and No. 3 cylinders. The resistance should be 10.3–13.9 kilo-ohms.

NOTE: Remember, the ignition coil multi-connector must be disconnected before measuring the secondary coil resistance.

3. If the resisance is not as specified, replace the coil.

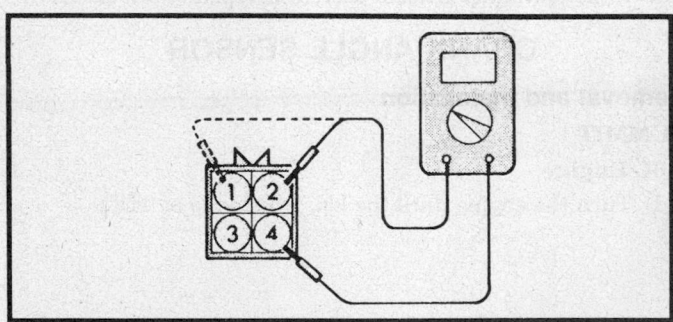

Checking ignition coil primary resistance on 1.6L engine Summit

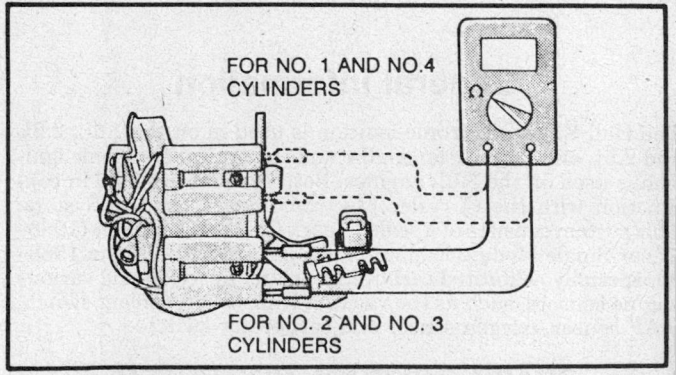

FOR NO. 1 AND NO.4 CYLINDERS

FOR NO. 2 AND NO. 3 CYLINDERS

Checking ignition coil secondary resistance on 1.6L engine Summit

POWER TRANSISTOR

Testing
SUMMIT

NOTE: When testing the power transistor, the use of an analog type circuit tester is recommended.

1.5L Engine

NOTE: This test requires the use a 1.5 volt dry cell.

1. Connect the negative terminal of the dry cell to the terminal 2 of the transistor and check for continuity across terminals 2 and 3 by alternately conecting the postive terminal of the battery to terminal 1 of the transistor. When power is applied to terminal 1 there should be continuity and there should be no continuity when power is disconnected.
2. If the continuity is not as desribed, replace the transisitor.

1.6L Engine

NOTE: This test requires the use a 1.5 volt dry cell.

To check the power coil for No. 1 and No. 4 cylinders:
1. Connect the negative terminal of the dry cell to the terminal 3 of the transistor and check for continuity across terminals 1 and 3 by alternately connecting the postive terminal of the power source to terminal 1 of the transistor. When power is applied to terminal 2 there should be continuity and there should be no continuity when power is removed.
To check the power coil for No. 2 and No. 3 cylinders:
2. Connect the negative terminal of the 1.5 volt power source to the terminal 3 of the transistor and check for continuity across terminals 6 and 5 by alternately connecting the postive terminal of the power source to terminal 5 of the transistor. When power is applied to terminal 2 there should be continuity and there should be no continuity when power is disconnected.
3. If the continuity is not as described, replace the transisitor.

CRANK ANGLE SENSOR

Removal and Installation
SUMMIT
1.6L Engine

1. Turn the engine until the No. 1 piston is at TDC.

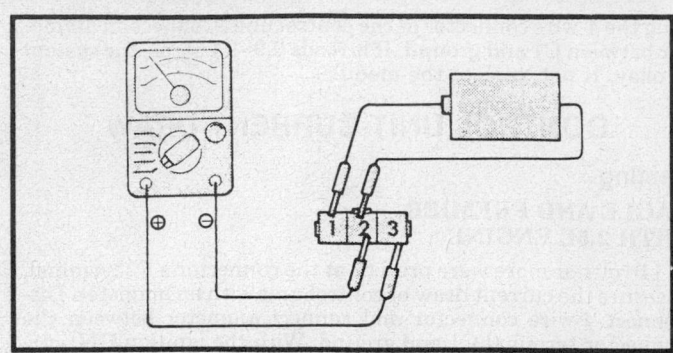

Checking power resistor continuity on 1.5L engine Summit

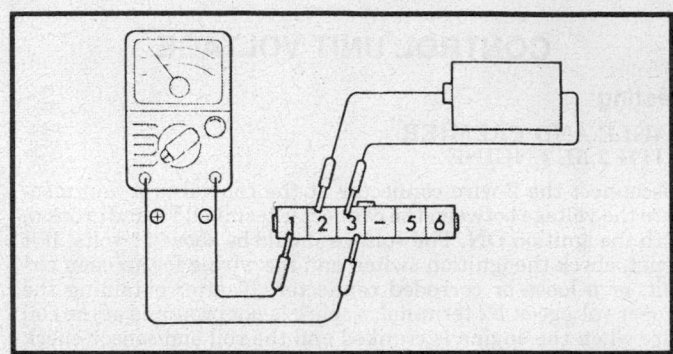

Checking No. 2 and No. 3 cylinder continuity on 1.6L engine Summit (No. 1 and No. 4 cylinders similar)

2. Disconnect the negative battrey cable.
3. Disconnect the wiring multi-connector from the crankangle sensor.
4. Remove the retaining screws and withdraw the sensor from the cylinder head.
5. To install, take the new sensor and align the notch on the plate of the sesnor with the punchmark on the sensor housing.
6. Install the sensor into the cylinder head and secure with the retaining screws.

CHRYSLER CORPORATION
HALL EFFECT AND OPTICAL ELECTRONIC IGNITION

General Information

The Hall Effect electronic ignition is used in on the 1.6L, 2.2L and 2.5L and 2.5L turbo engine and the optical electronic ignition is used on the 3.0L engines. Both systems are used in conjunction with the Chrysler Electronic Spark Control System. This system consists of a sealed Spark Control Computer (1986–87) or Single Module Engine Controller (SMEC) used in 1988–90, specially calibrated carburetor or fuel injection and various engine sensors, such as the vacuum transducer, coolant switch, MAP sensor, oxygen sensor and carburetor switch.

SPARK CONTROL COMPUTER

The Single Module Engine Controller (SMEC) replaced the Spark Control Computer (SSC) in 1988 except on 3.0L engines which were equipped with Single Engine Board Controller (SBEC). The SMEC is distinguished from the SBEC by an additional 14 pin connector located below the 60 pin connector. The SMEC and SBEC controls the entire ignition system, however both systems use the same input information and operate the same way.

During cranking, an electrical signal is sent from the distributor to the computer. The signal contains information on engine speed, fuel injection synchronization (turbo engine only) and ignition timing. This signal will cause the computer to fire the spark plugs at a fixed amount of advance. Once the engine starts, the timing will then be controlled by the computer based on the information received from the various sensors.

There are essentially 2 modes of operation of the spark control computer: the start mode and the run mode. The start mode is only used during engine cranking. During cranking, only the Hall Effect or optical pickup signals the computer. These signals are interrupted to provide a fixed number of degrees of spark advance.

After the engine starts and during normal engine operation, the computer functions in the run mode. In this mode, the Hall Effect pickup serves as only 1 of the signals to the computer. It is a reference signal of maximum possible spark advance. The computer then determines, from information provided by the other engine sensors, how much of this advance is necessary and delays the coil saturation accordingly, to fire the spark plug at the exact moment when this advance (crankshaft position) is reached.

There is a third mode of operation which only becomes functional when the computer fails. This is the limp-in mode. This mode functions on signals from the pickup only and results in very poor engine performance. However, it does allow the car to be driven to a repair shop. If a failure occurs in the pickup assembly or the start mode of the computer, the engine will neither start nor run.

On the 3.0L engine, the SBEC receives its engine speed and crankshaft position signals from an optical sensor distributor. This distributor contains a photo optic sensing unit and slotted disk assembly. The signals are used to regulate fuel injection rate, ignition timimg and the engine idle speed. The timing element consists of a thin disc which rotates at half the engine speed from the forward (left) bank camshaft.

HALL EFFECT SWITCH

The distributor contains the Hall Effect pickup assembly. The pickup assembly supplies the computer with the basic information on engine speed and crankshaft position.

COOLANT SENSOR

The coolant sensor supplies a signal to the computer to assist it in controlling the air/fuel ratio and the spark advance during periods of warm-up. A coolant sensor malfunction can cause many performance problems and should be the first sensor checked.

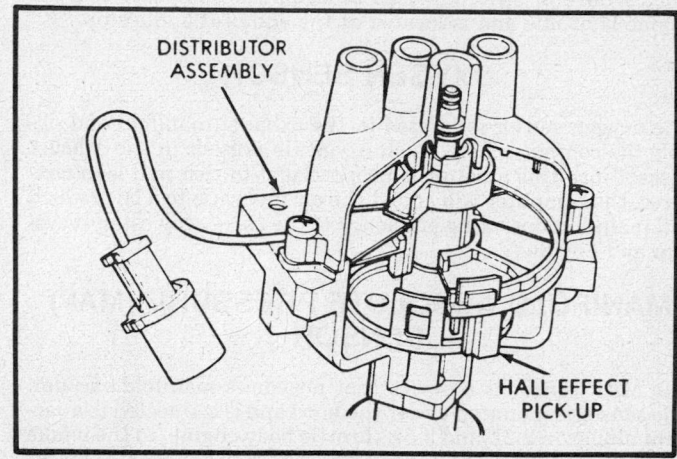

Hall Effect distributor for EFI/Carbureted models

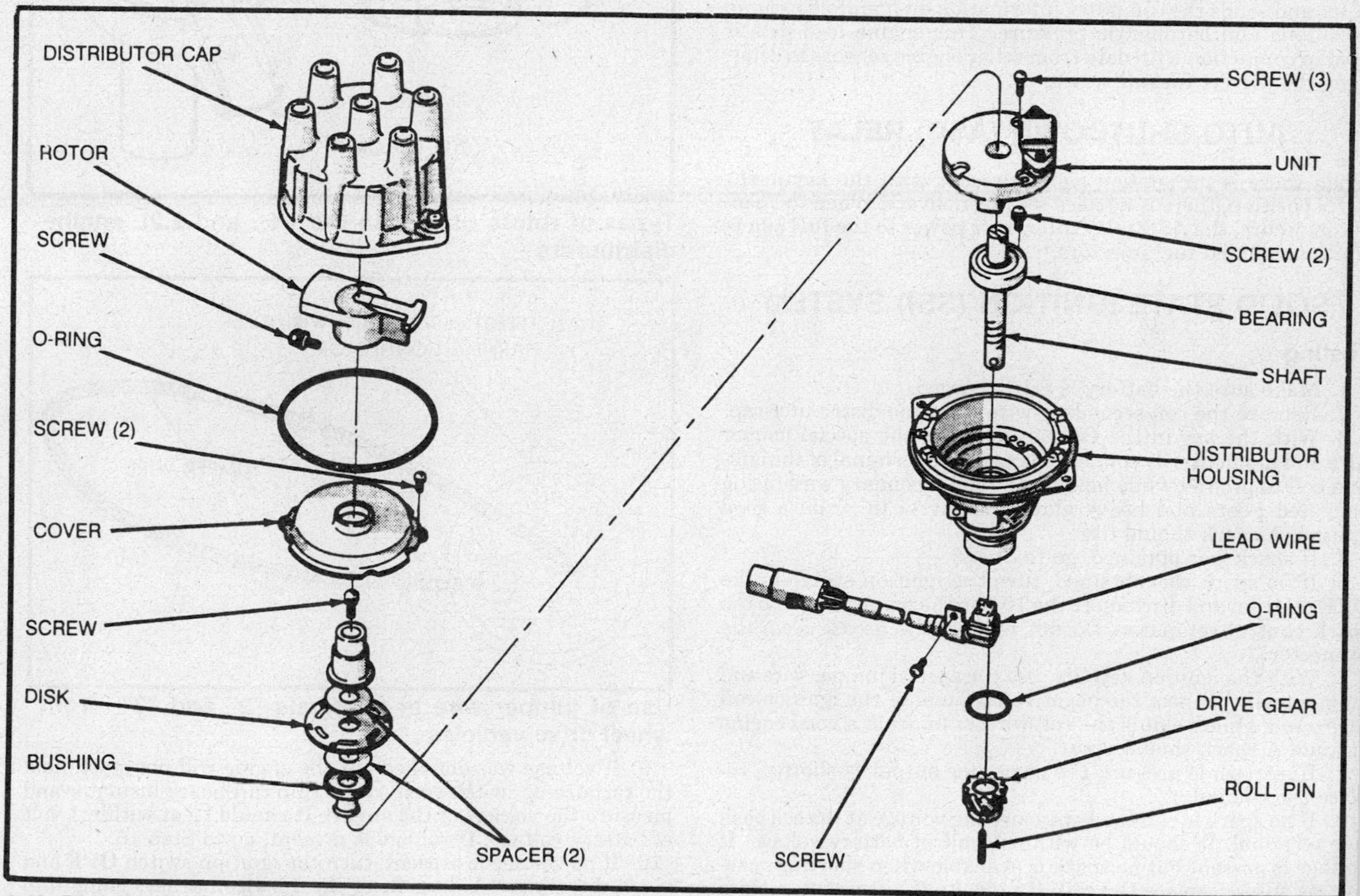

3.0L Distributor—exploded view

VACUUM SENSOR

The vacuum transducer is located on the spark control computer and it informs the computer as to the vacuum condition of the engine as it is operating. The engine vacuum is a factor that will determine how the computer will advance/retard ignition timing and with the feedback carburetor, how the air/fuel ratio will be changed.

CARBURETOR SWITCH

The carburetor switch is used to signal the computer that the engine is at idle and is located at the end of the idle stop.

OXYGEN SENSOR

The oxygen sensor is located in the exhaust manifold and signals the computer how much oxygen is present in the exhaust gases. Since this amount is proportional to rich and lean mixtures, the computer will adjust the air/fuel ratio to a level which will maintain operating efficiency of the three-way catalyst system and engine

MANIFOLD ABSOLUTE PRESSURE (MAP) SENSOR

The MAP sensor is a device that measures manifold vacuum. The sensor is mounted under the hood and is connected to a vacuum nipple on 2.2L and 2.5L throttle body engine, to the intake manifold nipple on 2.5L turbo engine or on the alternator bracket for 3.0L engine. The MAP sensor is wired directly to the computer and sends the computer information on manifold vacuum variations and barometric pressure. This engine load data is used in conjuction with data from other engine sensors to determine the correct fuel/air ratio.

AUTO SHUTDOWN (ASD) RELAY

When there is no ignition signal present with the key in the **RUN** position, there is no need for fuel delivery. When this condition occurs, the ASD relay interrupts power to the fuel pump, ignition coil and fuel injectors.

SOLID STATE IGNITION (SSI) SYSTEM

Testing

1. Make sure the battery is fully charged.
2. Remove the coil secondary wire from the distributor cap.
3. With the key in the **ON** position, use the special jumper wire and momentarily connect the negative terminal of the ignition coil to ground while holding the coil secondary wire (using insulated pliers and heavy gloves) about ¼ in. from a good ground. A spark should fire.
4. If spark was obtained, go to Step 9.
5. If no spark was obtained, turn the ignition switch to the **OFF** position and disconnect the 10-wire harness going into the spark control computer. Do not remove the grease from the connector.
6. With the ignition key **ON**, use the special jumper wire and momentarily connect the negative terminal of the ignition coil to ground while holding the coil wire ¼ in. from a good engine ground. A spark should occur.
7. If a spark is present, the computer output is shorted; replace the computer.
8. If no spark is obtained, measure the voltage at the coil positive terminal. It should be within 1 volt of battery voltage. If voltage is present but no spark is available when shorting negative terminal, replace the coil. If no voltage is present, replace the coil or check primary wiring.

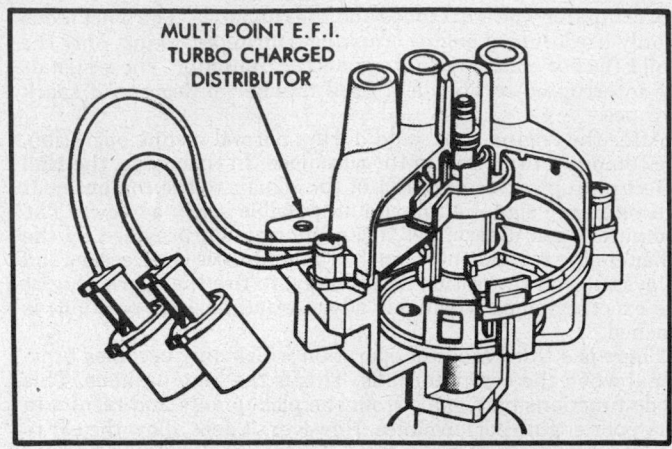

Hall Effect distributor for Turbo Multi-point EFI models

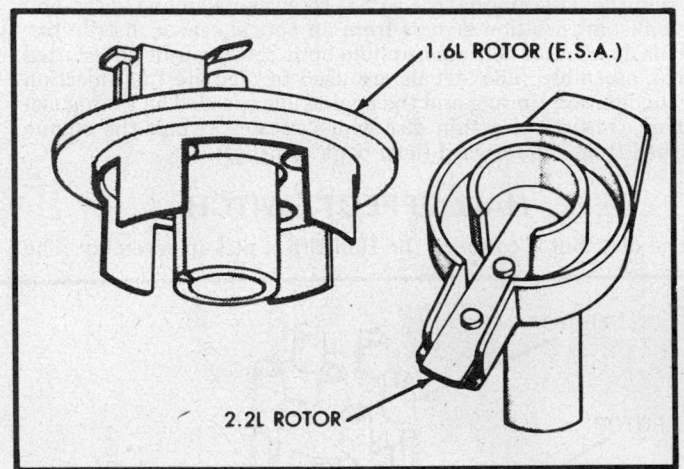

Types of rotors used with the 1.6L and 2.2L engine distributors

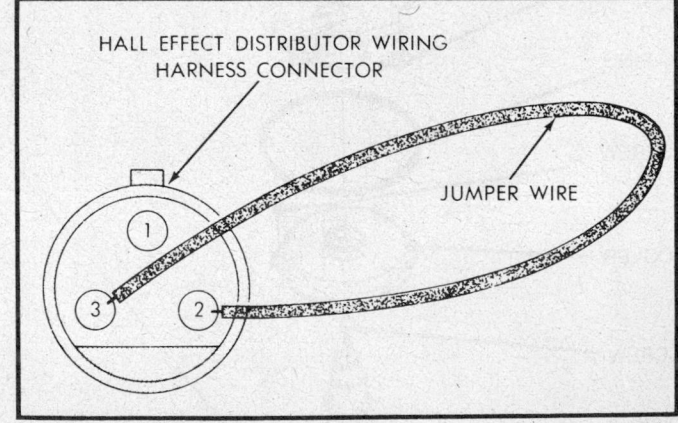

Use of jumper wire at terminals "2" and "3"—front wheel drive vehicles

9. If voltage was obtained but the engine will not start, hold the carburetor switch open with a thin cardboard insulator and measure the voltage at the switch. It should be at within 1 volt of battery voltage. If voltage is present, go to Step 16.
10. If no voltage is present, turn the ignition switch **OFF** and if not disconnected, disconnect the 10-wire harness going into the computer.

11. Turn the ignition switch **ON** and measure the voltage at terminal 2 of the connector. It should be within 1 volt of battery voltage.

12. If no battery voltage is present, check for continuity between the battery and terminal 2 of the connector. If no continuity, repair fault and repeat Step 11.

13. If voltage is present turn ignition switch **OFF** and check for continuity between the carburetor switch and terminal 7 on the connector. If no continuity is present, check for open wire between terminal 7 and the carburetor switch.

14. If continuity is present, check continuity between terminal 10 and ground. If continuity is present here, replace the computer. (Correct voltage is going in, but not coming out). Repeat Step 9.

15. If no continuity is present, check for an open wire. If wiring is OK, but the engine still won't start, go to next step.

16. Plug the 10 terminal dual connector back into the computer and turn the ignition switch **ON**, hold the secondary coil wire near a good ground and disconnect the distributor harness connector. Using a regular jumper wire, jumper terminal 2 and terminal 3, making and breaking the connection at either terminal of the connector and a spark should fire at the coil wire.

17. If spark is present at the coil wire but is not present when the when the distributor lead is re-connected, replace the Hall Effect pick-up.

NOTE: When replacing a pick-up, always make sure rotor blades are grounded using an ohmmeter.

18. If no spark is present at the coil wire, measure the voltage at terminal 1 of the distributor harness connector; it should be within 1 volt of battery voltage.

19. If correct, turn the ignition switch to the **OFF** position. Disconnect the dual connector from the computer and check for continuity between terminal 2 of distributor harness and terminal 9 of the dual connector. Repeat test on terminal 3 of distributor harness and terminal 5 of dual connector. If no continuity, repair the harness. If continuity is present, replace the computer and repeat Step 16.

20. If no battery voltage is present in Step 18, turn **OFF** the ignition switch, disconnect the 10 terminal dual connector from the computer and check for continuity between terminal 1 of distributor harness and terminal 3 of dual connector. If no continuity, repair wire and repeat Step 16.

21. If continuity is present, turn the ignition switch **ON** and check for battery voltage between terminal 2 and terminal 10 of the dual connector. If voltage is present, replace the computer and repeat Step 16. If no battery voltage is present, the computer is not grounded. Check and repair the ground wire and repeat Step 16.

SINGLE MODULE ENGINE CONTROLLER (SMEC) SYSTEM

Testing

1. Remove a spark plug wire from any spark plug.

2. Crank the engine, while holding the plug wire (using insulated pliers and heavy gloves) about ¼ in. from a good ground. A spark should fire.

NOTE: Fault code erase and SMEC damage may occur if the spark plug wire is held more than ¼ in. from ground.

3. If there was a good spark, testing of the SMEC system using Chrysler DRB II test equipment or equivalent will be necessary.

4. If there was no spark, disconnect coil secondary wire from cap and perform same test. If there is a good spark repair cap, rotor or plug wires as needed. If there was no spark procede.

5. Crank the engine for 5 seconds, check voltage at the posi-

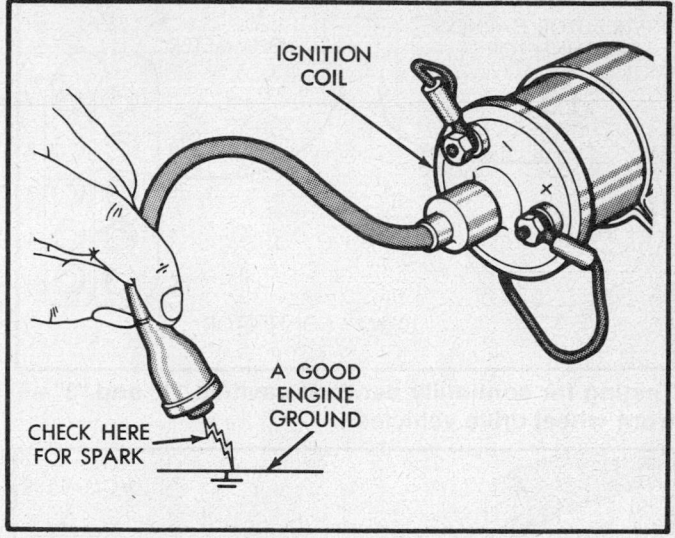

Testing for spark during engine cranking. Use insulated pliers and heavy gloves to handle coil wire

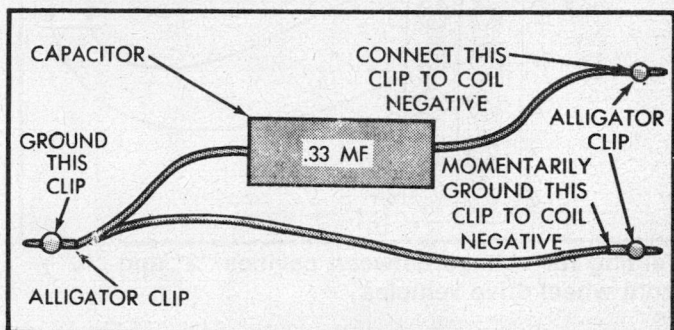

Special jumper wire from coil negative terminal to ground—front wheel drive vehicles.

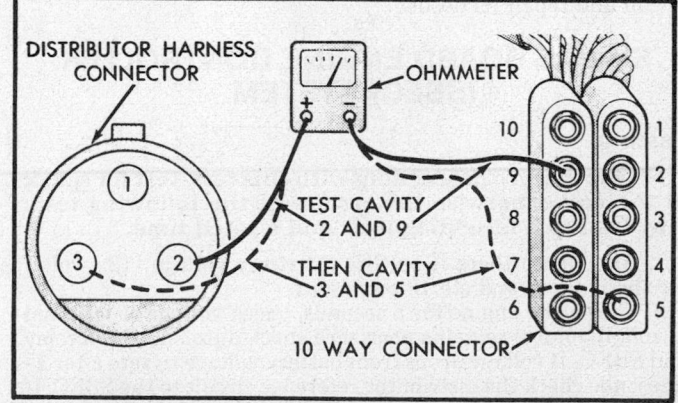

Testing cavities "2" and "9" and then cavities "3" and "5" for continuity—front wheel drive vehicles

tive terminal of coil, if voltage remains near 0 check auto shutdown relay and SEMC. If voltage drops from battery voltage to 0 after 2 seconds check SMEC system. If voltage remains near battery voltage continue.

6. With key **OFF**, remove 14-way connector from SMEC and check for bent terminals.

7. Remove positive lead to coil.

8. Using special jumper wire with 0.330 MF capacitor, momentarily touch ground terminal 12 on 14-way connector.

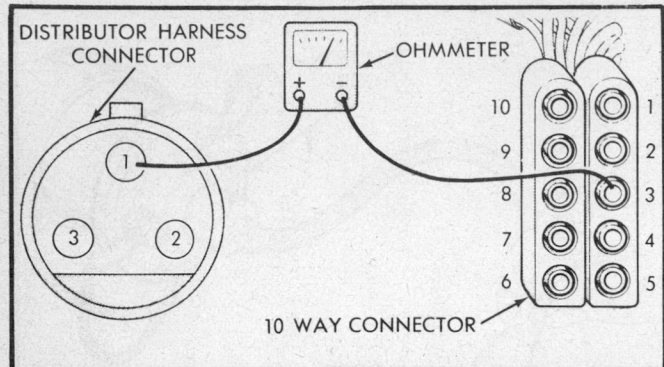

Testing for continuity between cavities "1" and "3"—front wheel drive vehicles

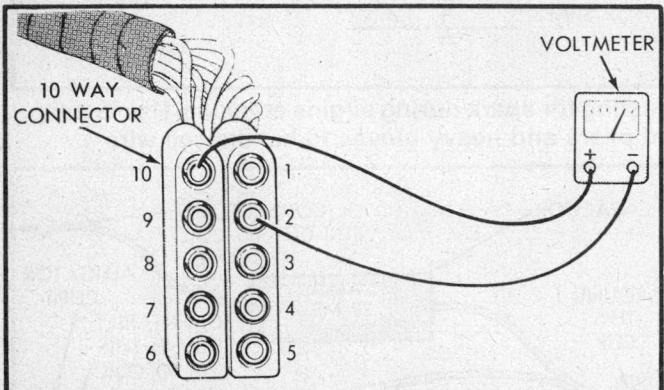

Testing for voltage between cavities "2" and "10"—front wheel drive vehicles

9. If a spark occurs, replace the SMEC.
10. If no spark, use special jumper to ground the coil negative terminal directly. If no spark replace coil. If spark check wiring to coil and repair as needed.

SINGLE BOARD ENGINE CONTROLLER (SBEC) SYSTEM

Testing

NOTE: Before proceeding with this test, test for spark at the coil otherwise the results of the following tests may lead to a false diagnosis and wasted time.

1. Make sure there is sufficient battery voltage (12.4 volts) for the ignition and starting systems.
2. Crank the engine for 5 seconds, check voltage at terminal of coil, if voltage remains near zero check auto shutdown relay and SBEC. If voltage drops from battery voltage to zero after 1–2 seconds check the distributor reference circuit to the SBEC. If voltage remains near battery voltage continue with the remainder of the procedure.
3. With key **OFF**, remove 60-way connector from the SBEC and check for bent terminals.
4. Remove positive lead to the coil and connect a special jumper wire with 0.330 MF capacitor across the postive battery terminal and the positive coil terminal.
5. Using the jumper wire, momentarily touch ground terminal 19 on 60-way connector. When the ground is removed, a spark should occur. If a spark is generated, replace the SBEC.
6. If no spark, use special jumper to ground the coil negative terminal directly. If no spark replace coil. If a spark occurs, repair the wiring harness for an open condition.

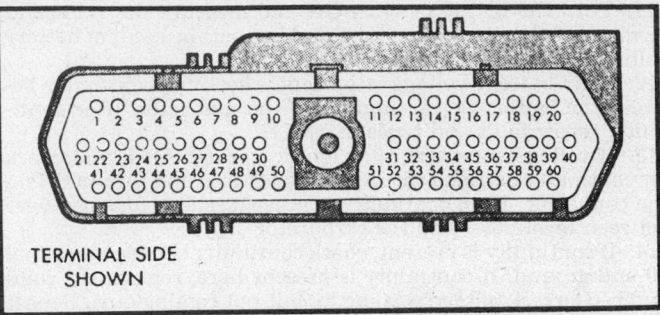

View of the 60-way connector used on Single Board Engine Controller (SBEC) systems

7. If no spark is produced, replace the ignition coil.

POOR ENGINE PERFORMANCE

Testing

Correct basic engine timing is essential for optimum vehicle performance and must be checked before any of the following testing procedures are performed. Refer to the individual vehicle section for ignition timing procedures and/or refer to the Vehicle Information label, located in the engine compartment.

CARBURETOR SWITCH

Testing

NOTE: Grounding the carburetor switch on most systems with a feedback carburetor will give a fixed air/fuel ratio.

1. With the key **OFF**, disconnect the dual connector from the computer.
2. With the throttle completely closed, check the continuity between terminal 7 of the connector and a good ground. If there is no continuity, check the wire and the carburetor switch.
3. With the throttle open, check the continuity between terminal 7 of the connector and a good ground. There should be no continuity.

COOLANT SWITCH

Testing

1. With the key in the **OFF** position, disconnect the wire connector from the coolant sensor.
2. Connect a lead of the ohmmeter to a terminal of the coolant sensor.
3. Connect the other lead of the ohmmeter to the remaining connector of the coolant sensor.
4. With the engine and coolant switch sensor at room temperature around 70°F, the reading should be 5000–6000 ohms with SSC and 7000–13000 ohms with SMEC and SBEC.

SSC DETONATION SENSOR

Testing

1. Connect an adjustable timing light to the engine.
2. Place the fast idle screw on the second highest step of the fast idle cam. Start the engine and allow it to idle. The engine should be running at 1200 rpm or more.
3. Use an open end wrench to tap lightly on the intake manifold next to the detonation sensor. As this is done, watch the timing marks; a decrease in timing advance should be seen. The amount of decrease should be directly proportional to the

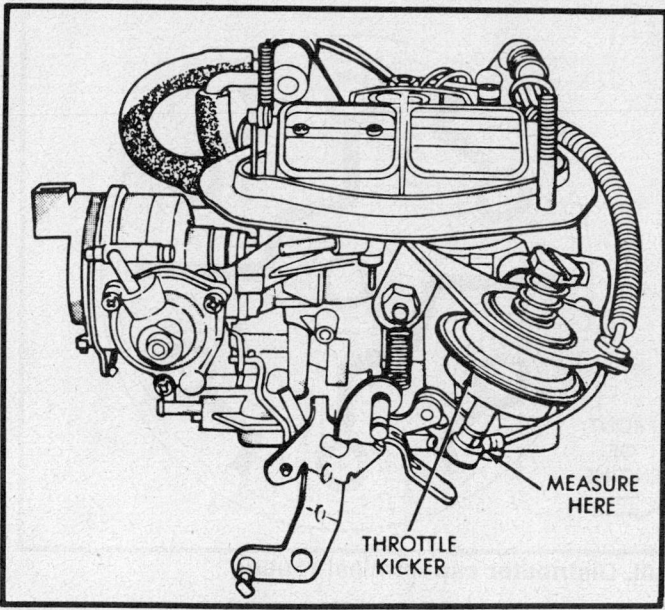

Measuring points for carburetor switch

strength and frequency of tapping. Maximum retard is 11 degrees.

4. If the sensor is not working correctly, install a new sensor and retest.

SSC ELECTRONIC THROTTLE CONTROL SYSTEM

Incorporated within the spark control computer is the electronic throttle system. A solenoid, which regulates a vacuum dashpot is energized when the air conditioner or electronic timers are activated. The 2 timers which are incorporated within the ignition electronics operate when the throttle is closed, plus a time delay of 2 seconds or after an engine start condition.

Testing

1. Connect a tachometer to the engine.
2. Start the engine and bring to normal operating temperature.
3. Depress the accelerator and release it. A higher than curb engine idle should be seen for a brief time.
4. If so equipped, turn the air conditioning unit **ON**. A slight decrease in the idle speed will be noted. Turning **OFF** the air conditioner will produce the normal idle speed.

NOTE: The air conditioning clutch will cycle ON and OFF as the system is in operation. This should not be mistaken as part of the electronic control system.

5. As the air conditioner compressor clutch cycles **ON** and **OFF**, the solenoid plunger should extend and retract.
6. If the plunger does not move with the air conditioning clutch cycling or after a start-up, check the kicker system for vacuum leaks.
7. If the speed increases do not occur, disconnect the 6-way connector at the carburetor.
8. Check the solenoid with an ohmmeter by measuring the resistance across the terminal that contains the black wire to ground. The resistance should be 20–100 ohms. If not within specifications, replace the solenoid.
9. Start the vehicle and before the time delay has timed out, measure the voltage across vacuum solenoid terminals. The

voltage should be within 2 volts of charging system voltage. If not within specifications, replace the computer.

10. Turing the air conditioner **ON** should also produce charging system voltage after the time delay has timed out. If not, check the wiring back to the instrument panel for an open circuit.

SPARK CONTROL COMPUTER ADVANCE

Incorporated in the digital microprocessor electronics are some unique spark advance schedules, which occur during cold weather operation. These commands have been added to reduce engine emissions and improve driveability. Because they will be changing at different engine operating temperatures during the engine warm-up, all spark advance testing should be done with the engine at normal operating temperature.

Testing

1. Adjust the basic timing to specifications.
2. Have the engine at normal operating temperature and the temperature sensor operating correctly.
3. Remove and plug the vacuum hose athe the vacuum transducer.
4. Connect an auxillary vacuum supply to the vacuum transducer and adjust the vacuum to 16 in. Hg.
5. Start and raise the engine speed to 2000 rpm. Wait about a minute and check the specifications.
6. The advance specifications are in addition to basic advance.

HALL EFFECT PICK-UP

Removal and Installation

1. Disconnect the negative battery cable.

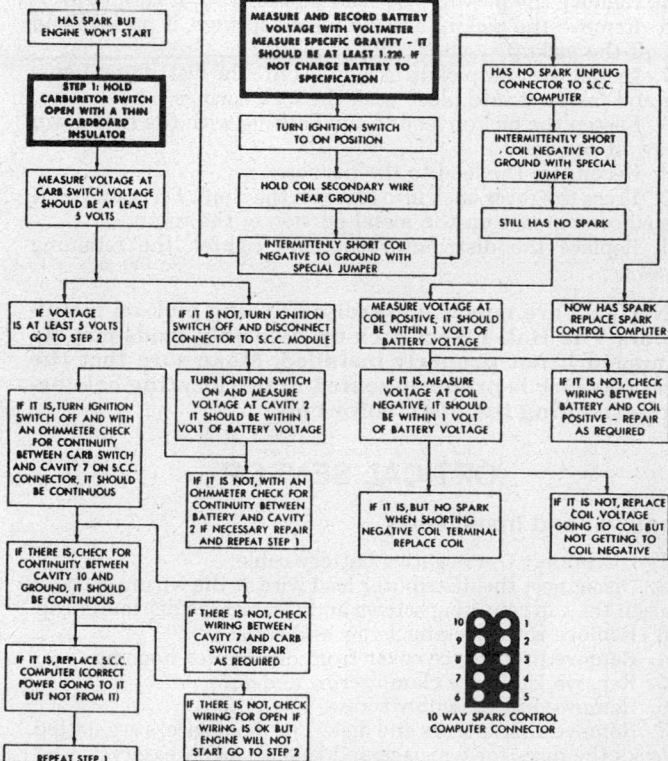

Hall Effect Electronic Spark Advance system diagnosis

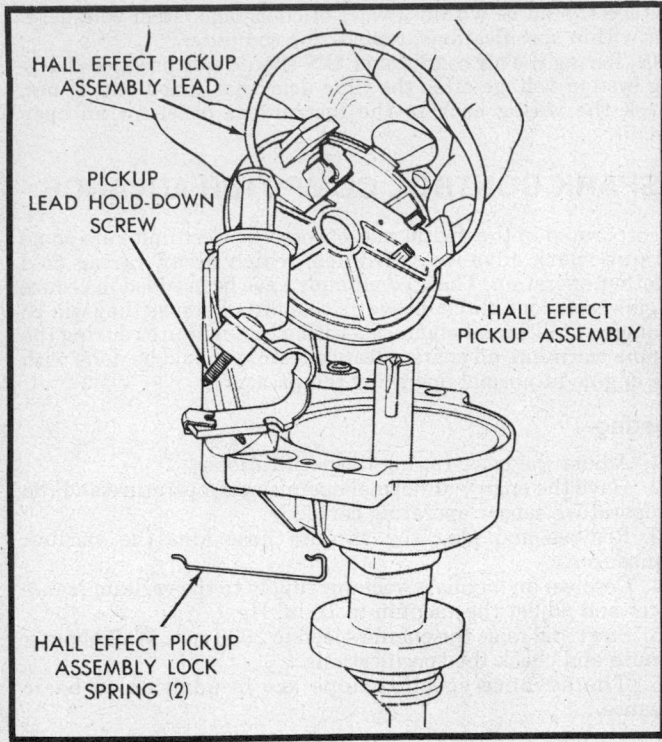

Hall Effect pickup installation

2. Loosen the distributor cap retaining screws and remove the cap.
3. Pull straight up on the rotor and remove it from the shaft.
4. Disconnect the pickup assembly lead.
5. Remove the pickup lead hold down screw, if equipped.
6. Remove the pickup assembly lock springs, if present and lift off the pickup.
7. Install the new pickup assembly onto the distributor housing and fasten it into place with the lock springs.
8. Fasten the pickup lead to the housing with the hold down screw, if equipped.
9. Reconnect the lead to the harness.
10. Press the rotor back into place on the shaft. Do not wipe off the silicone grease on the metal portion of the rotor.
11. Replace the distributor cap and tighten the retaining screws.

NOTE: Care must be exercised during pick-up installation. The Hall Effect pick-up assembly leads may be damaged if not properly installed. Make sure that the lead retainer is properly seated in the locating hole before attaching the distributor cap.

OPTICAL SENSOR

Removal and Installation

1. Disconnect the negative battery cable.
2. Disconnect the distributor lead wire at the wiring harness. Loosen the cap retaining screws and remove the disributor cap.
3. Remove rotor locking screw and rotor.
4. Remove protectivce cover from distributor housing.
5. Remove lead wire clamp screw and wire.
6. Remove disk assembly screw.
7. Remove disk spacers and disk. The disc spacers are slotted. Checks the discs for warpage and replace as necessary.
8. Remove photo optic sensor unit.
9. Installation is the reverse order of the removal procedure.

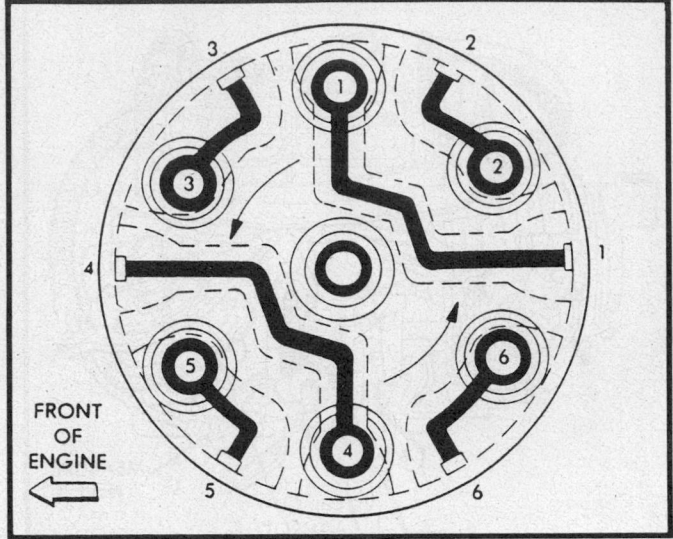

3.0L Distributor cap terminal routing

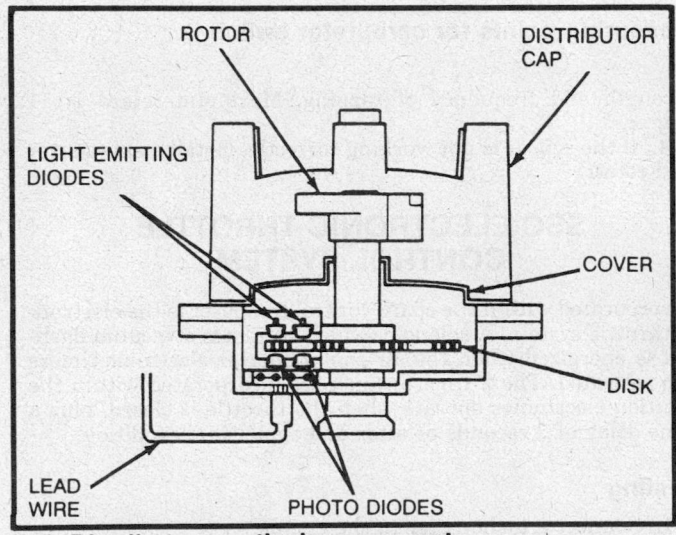

3.0L Distributor – optical components

SINGLE MODULE AND SINGLE BOARD ENGINE CONTROLLERS

Removal and Installation

1. Remove air cleaner duct.
2. Remove battery.
3. Remove module mounting screws.
4. Remove 14-way and/or 60-way connectors. SBEC units are not equipped with the 14-way connector.
5. Installation is the reverse order of the removal procedure.

NOTE: There should be at least ⅛ in. of multi-purpose grease on 60 and 14-way connectors, to prevent moisture from corroding the terminals.

SPARK PLUG WIRES

The spark plug wires do not pull from the distributor cap, but are retained with positive locking terminal electrodes and must be released from inside the distributor cap. The coil secondary lead is retained in the cap in the conventional manner.

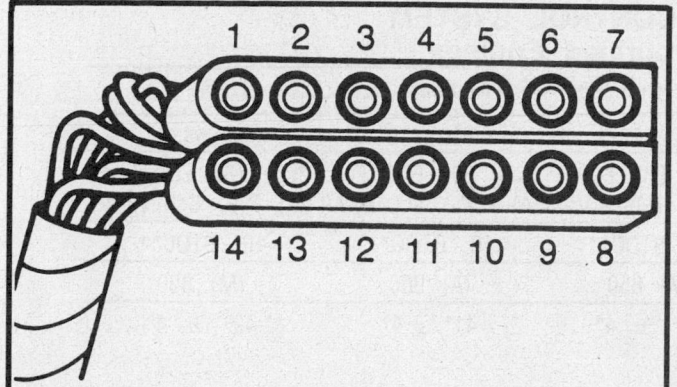

CAV.	COLOR	FUNCTION
1	N6 OR	8-VOLT OUTPUT
2	K5 BK/WT	GROUND
3	K14 DB/WT	FUSED J2
4	J2 DB	12-VOLT INPUT
5	Y13 YL/WT	INJECTOR CONTROL - BANK #3
6	J9 BK	GROUND
7	J9 BK	GROUND
8	K16 VT/YL	INJECTOR INTERFACE - BANK #1
9	Y11 WT	INJECTOR CONTROL - BANK #1
10	Y12 TN	INJECTOR CONTROL - BANK #2
11	R31 DG/OR	ALTERNATOR FIELD INTERFACE
12	J5 BK/YL	IGNITION CONTROL
13	K15 YL	IGNITION INTERFACE
14	R3 DG	ALTERNATOR FIELD CONTROL

Single module engine controller (SMEC) connector

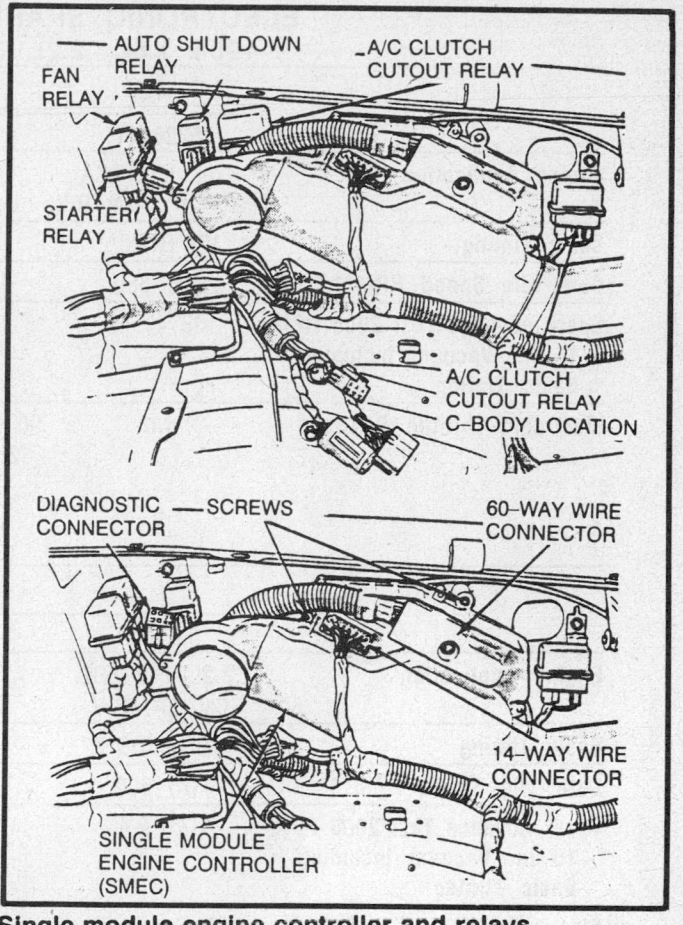

Single module engine controller and relays

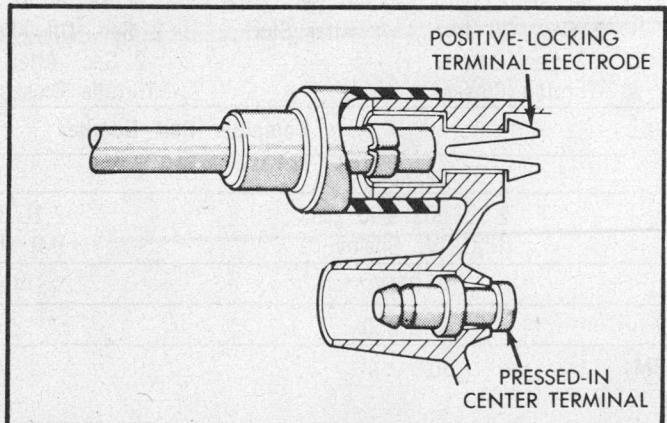

Positive locking secondary ignition wire terminal. To remove, press lock together and push wire out of distributor cap—front wheel drive vehicles

ELECTRONIC SPARK CONTROL SYSTEM
1986 1.6L, 2.2L Carbureted Engines

	Computer Part Number			
	5226411	5226429	5226433	5226439
Engine Application	1.6L E82 ECA Fed., Cal., (M) P.V.	1.6L E82 ECA Can., (M) P.V.	2.2L E62 EDE Fed. (A) P.V. Cal., Hi-Alt	2.2L E62 EDE Fed. (M) P.V. Cal. Hi-Alt
Basic Timing	12° BTDC**	12° BTDC**	10° BTDC**	10° BTDC**
Curb Idle Speed RPM***	(M) 850	(M) 850	(A) 900	(M) 800
Spark Advance Test 2000 RPM 16 in. Vacuum Including Basic Timing	33° ± 4°	33° ± 4°	41° ± 4°	42° ± 4°
Electronic Throttle Control	No	90 Sec. After Start 2 Sec. Off Idle 1 Sec. After Throttle Closes Throttle Closes	30 Sec. Hot. 30 Sec. Cold 2 Sec. Off Idle 2 Sec. After Throttle Closes	30 Sec. Hot 300 Sec. Cold After Start

	Computer Part Number			
	5226451	5226455	5226505	5226507
Engine Application	2.2L E62 EDE Cal. (A) P.V.	2.2L E62 EDE Cal. (M) P.V.	2.2L E62 EDE Can. (A) Can.	2.2L E62 EDE Can. (M) P.V.
Basic Timing	10° BTDC**	10° BTDC**	10° BTDC**	10° BTDC**
Curb Idle Speed RPM***	(A) 900	(M) 800	(A) 900	(M) 900
Spark Advance Test 2000 RPM 16 in. Vacuum Including Basic Timing	37° ± 4°	42° ± 4°	41° ± 4°	41° ± 4°
Electronic Throttle Control	30 Sec. Hot. 30 Sec. Cold 2 Sec. Off Idle 2 Sec. After Throttle Closes	30 Sec. Hot 300 Sec. Cold After Start	120 Sec. Hot. 2 Sec Cold 2 Sec. Off Idle 2 Sec. After Throttle Closes	90 Sec. Hot After Start 300 Sec. Cold After Start

	Computer Part Number	
	5226645	5227097
Engine Application	2.2L E68 EDJ Cal. (M) P.V. Shelby ①	2.2L E68 EDJ Fed. (M) P.V. Shelby ①
Basic Timing	15° BTDC**	15° BTDC**
Curb Idle Speed RPM***	(M) 850	(M) 850
Spark Advance Test 2000 RPM 16 in. Vacuum Including Basic Timing	36° ± 4°	43° ± 4°
Electronic Throttle Control	30 Sec. Hot After Start 300 Sec. Cold After Start	30 Sec. Hot 300 Sec. Cold After Start

Should the listed specifications differ from those on the Emission Control Information Label, use the specifications on the label

(A) — Automatic Transmission
(M) — Manual Transmission
Can. — Canada
Fed. — Federal
Cal. — California
BTDC — Before Top Dead Center
P.V. — Passenger Vehicle

TR — Truck
* High Altitude
**Basic Timing set with vacuum line disconnected. Do not readjust curb idle
*** Curb Idle set with vacuum line connected
① Has denotation suppression

ELECTRONIC SPARK CONTROL SYSTEM
1987 2.2L Carbureted Engines

	Computer Part Number		
	5227614	**5227608**	**5227612**
Engine Application	2.2L EDA Can. & Cal. (A)	2.2L EDE (A) exc. Cal.	2.2L EDE (M)
Basic Timing**	10° BTDC	10° BTDC	10° BTDC
Curb Idle Speed RPM***	900	900	800
Spark Advance Test 2000 RPM 16 in. Vacuum Including Basic Timing	36° ± 4°	40° ± 4	40° ± 4
Electronic Throttle Control	60 Hot 535 Cold 2 sec. off idle 2 sec. after throttle closes	60 Hot 535 Cold 2 sec. off idle 2 sec. after throttle closes	60 Sec Hot 535 Cold after start

Should the listed specifications differ from those on the Emission Control Information Label, use the specifications on the label
(A)—Automatic Transmission
(M)—Manual Transmission
Can. Canada
Cal. California
BTDC—Before Top Dead Center
**Basic Timing set with vacuum line disconnected. Do not readjust curb idle
*** Curb Idle set with vacuum line connected

ELECTRONIC SPARK CONTROL SYSTEM
1988 2.2L, 2.5L & 3.0L Engines

	Distributor Part Number		
	5226575	**5226525**	**MD116211**
Engine Application	2.2L & 2.5L	2.2L	3.0L
Basic Timing	12° BTDC	12° BTDC	12° BTDC
Curb Idle Speed RPM***	850	900	700
Spark Advance Test 2000 RPM 16 in. Vacuum Including Basic Timing	2.2L 26°M 33°A 2.5L 28°M 30°A	Turbo I 33°M 25°A Turbo II 40°M	38°A

Should the listed specifications differ from those on the Emission Control Information Label, use the specifications on the label
(A)—Automatic Transmission
(M)—Manual Transmission
BTDC—Before Top Dead Center
**Basic Timing set with vacuum line disconnected. Do not readjust curb idle
*** Curb Idle set with vacuum line connected

CHRYSLER/MITSUBISHI
ELECTRONIC IGNITION (EIS) SYSTEM

General Information

EXCEPT 2.6L ENGINE

When the ignition switch is turned to the **ON** position, battery voltage is applied to the ignition coil primary winding. As the distributor (1.8L engine) or crank angle sensor (2.0L, 2.0L turbo engine) shaft turns, the multi-port injection control unit sends signals to the power transistor. These signals activate the power transistor which causes ignition current primary winding current to flow from the ignition coil negative terminal through the power transistor to ground or be interrupted. The flow of current in the primary winding induces a high voltage in the secondary winding. This voltage flows through the distributor and spark plugs to ground completing the ignition circuit for each cylinder.

2.6L ENGINE

This system consists of the battery, ignition coil, IC igniter (electronic control unit) which is built into the distributor, spark plugs, primary and secondary wiring. Primary current to the coil is switched **ON** and **OFF** by the IC igniter in response to timing signals produced by the distributor magnetic pick-up.

The distributor consists of a power distributing section, IC igniter, advance mechanism, drive section and the signal generator. The signal generator, which houses a small magneto, produces a signal for driving the IC igniter. The signal is produced in exact synchronism with distributor shaft rotation. It is produced at equal intervals 4 times distributor shaft rotation. The distributor uses this signal as an ignition timing signal during its operation. The distributor is equipped with vacuum and centrifugal advance mechanisms.

The centrifugal advance mechanism is located below the rotor assembly. It is equipped with governor weights that move outward and inward depending on engine speed. As engine speed increases, the weights move outward which causes the reluctor to rotate ahead of the distributor shaft. This causes the ignition timing to advance:

The vacuum advance incorporates a spring loaded diaphragm which is connected to the breaker assembly. The diaphragm moves against the spring pressure by carburetor vacuum pressure. When the vacuum increases, the diaphragm causes the movable breaker assembly to pivot in direction opposite to distributor rotation. This action advances the ignition timing.

System Troubleshooting

IGNITION COIL

Testing Primary and Secondary Resistance

EXCEPT 2.6L ENGINE

1. To measure the primary coil resistance, place the ohmmeter probes across the No. 4 (No. 1 cylinder) and No. 2 (No. 4 cylinder) terminals of the ignition terminal. Then place the ohmmeter probes across the No. 1 (No. 2 cylinder) and No. 3 (No. 2 cylinder). The resistance should be between 0.77–0.95 ohms.

2. To measure secondary coil resistance, first disconect the coil multi-connector. Then, place the ohmmeter probes betwen the high voltage terminals for the the No. 1 and No. 4 cylinders and between the high voltage terminals for the No. 2 and No. 3 cylinders. The resistance should be 10.3–13.9 kilo-ohms.

NOTE: Remember, the ignition coil multi-connector must be disconnected before measuring the secondary coil resistance.

1990 LAZER

	Distributor Part Number	
	MD119306	MD119306
Engine application	1.8L	2.0L, 2.0L Turbo
Basic timing	5° BTDC	5° BTDC
Actual timing at curb idle	8° BTDC	8° BTDC
Curb idle speed rpm	800–850	650–850
Mechanical advance	Computer controlled	Computer controlled

3. If the resistance is not as specified, replace the coil.

POWER TRANSISTOR

Testing

EXCEPT 2.6L ENGINE

NOTE: When testing the power transistor, the use of an analog type circuit tester is recommended. This test requires the use a 1.5 volt dry cell battery or similar power source.

To check the power coil for No. 1 and No. 4 cylinders:

1. Connect a suitable analog circuit tester (set to Ohms range) between terminals 1 and 3 of the power transistor connector.

2. Connect a 1.5 volt dry cell between terminals 2 and 3 so that the postive side of the dry cell goes to terminal 2 and the negative side to terminal 3.

3. Check for continuity across terminals 1 and 3 by alternately connecting the postive terminal of the power source to terminal 1 of the transistor. When power is applied to terminal 2 there should be continuity and there should be no continuity when power is disconnected.

To check the power coil for No. 2 and No. 3 cylinders:

4. Connect the negative terminal of the dry cell to the terminal 3 of the transistor and check for continuity across terminals 5 and 6 by alternately connecting the postive terminal of the dry cell to terminal 5 of the transistor. When power is applied to terminal 5 there should be continuity and there should be no continuity when power is removed.

5. If continuity is not as desribed, replace the transisitor.

CRANK ANGLE SENSOR

Removal and Installation

2.0L ENGINE

1. Turn the engine until the No. 1 piston is at TDC.

2. Disconnect the wiring multi-connector from the crankangle sensor.

3. Remove the retaining screws and withdraw the sensor from the cylinder head.

4. To install, take the new sensor and align the notch on the plate of the sesnor with the punchmark on the sensor housing.

5. Install the sensor into the cylinder head and secure with the retaining screws.

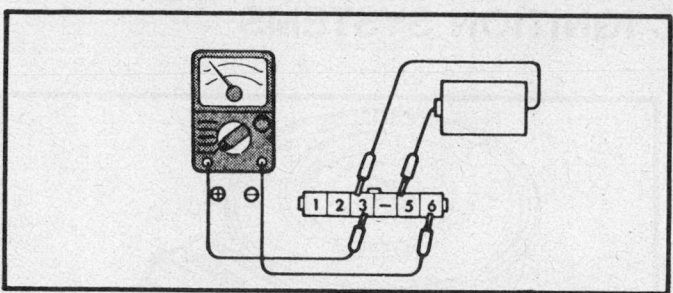

Checking No. 2 and No.4 coil side continuity on Lazer

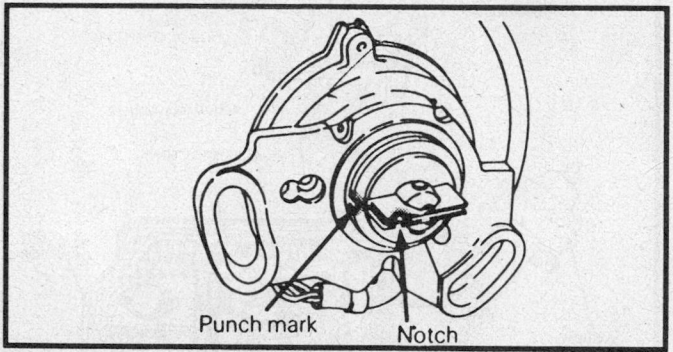

Punch mark   Notch

Align the punchmark on the housing with the notch on the plate when installing the crankangle sensor

COIL SPARK

Testing

2.6L ENGINE

1. Remove the coil wire from the center of the distributor cap.
2. Using heavy gloves and insulated pliers, hold the end of the wire $3/16-3/8$ in. away from a good engine ground and crank the engine.

NOTE: Make sure there are no fuel leaks before performing this test.

3. If there is a spark at the coil wire, it must be bright blue in color and fire consistently. If it is, continue to crank the engine while slowly moving the coil wire away from ground. Look for arcing at the coil tower. If arcing occurs, replace the coil. If there is no spark, or spark is weak or not consistent, proceed to the next step.
4. If a good spark is present, check the condition of the distributor cap, rotor, plug wires and spark plugs. If these check out, the ignition system is working; check the fuel system and engine mechanical systems.
5. With the ignition **ON**, measure the voltage at the negative coil terminal. It should be the same as battery voltage. If it is 3 volts or less, the IC distributor is defective. If there is no voltage, check for an open circuit in the coil or wiring.
6. With the ignition **ON**, hold the coil wire as instructed in Step 2 and using a jumper wire, momentarily connect the negative coil terminal to ground. There should be a spark at the coil wire.
7. If there is no spark, check for voltage at the positive coil terminal with the key on. Voltage should be at least 9 volts. If proper voltage is obtained, the coil is defective and should be replaced. If proper voltage is not obtained, check the wiring and connections.

CENTRIFUGAL ADVANCE

Testing

2.6L ENGINE

1. Run the engine at idle and remove the vacuum hose from the vacuum controller.
2. Slowly accelerate the engine to check for advance.
3. Excessive advance indicates a damaged governor spring (a broken spring will result in abrupt advance).
4. Insufficient advance is usually caused by a broken governor weight or a malfunction in cam operation. Correct as needed.

VACUUM ADVANCE

Test

2.6L ENGINE

1. Connect a timing light and adjust the engine speed to 2500 rpm.
2. Check for advance by disconnecting and then reconnecting the vacuum hose at the distributor and watching the advance or retard at the crankshaft indicator.
3. For a more accurate determination of whether the vacuum advance mechanism is operating properly, remove the vacuum hose from the distributor and connect a hand vacuum pump.
4. Run the engine at idle and slowly apply vacuum pressure to check for advance.
5. If excessive advance is noted, look for a deteriorated vacuum controller spring.
6. If insufficient advance or no advance is noted, this could be caused by linkages problems or a ruptured vacuum diaphragm. Correct as necessary.

IGNITION COIL

Testing

2.6L ENGINE

1. Clean the ignition coil.
2. Check the coil terminals for cleanliness and exterior of body for cracks. Replace if necessary.
3. Check for carbon deposit or corrosion in the high tension cable inserting hole. Repair or replace if necessary.
4. Measure the resistance of the primary coil, secondary coil and external resistor.
5. If the reading is not within 1.3–1.8 ohms on the primary coil and 9000–12000 ohms on the secondary coil windings, replace the coil.

IGNITION WIRE RESISTANCE

Testing

2.6L ENGINE

NOTE: When removing the high voltage cable at the ignition coil, grasp the cable rubber cap. Twist and pull slowly. Do not bend the cable. This could result in breaking the conductor.

1. Check the cable terminals.
2. A corroded terminal should be cleaned or replaced.
3. A broken or severely distorted cable should be replaced.
4. Check the resistance of each cable between both ends. If it exceeds 22 kilo-ohms, replace the wire.
5. Use silicone lubricant when installing wires on spark plugs.

CHRYSLER ELECTRONIC IGNITION SYSTEMS

General Information

5.0L ENGINE WITH DUAL PICK-UP DISTRIBUTOR

The computer provides the engine with ignition spark control during starting and during engine operation, providing an infinitely variable spark advance curve. Input data is fed instantaneously to the computer by a series of sensors located in the engine compartment which monitor timing, water temperature, air temperature, idle/off-idle operation and intake manifold vacuum. The program schedule module of the spark control computer receives the information from the sensors, processes it and then directs the ignition control module to advance or retard the timing as necessary. This whole process is going on continuously as the engine is running, taking only milliseconds to complete a circuit from sensor to distributor. The main components of the system are a modified carburetor and spark control computer, which is responsible for translating input data and which transmits data to the distributor to advance or retard the timing.

There are 2 functional modes of the computer, start and run. The start mode will only function during engine cranking and starting. The run mode only functions after the engine start and during engine operation. Both modes will never operate together.

Should a failure of the run mode of the computer occur, the system will go into a limp-in mode. This will enable the operator to continue to drive the vehicle until it can be repaired. However, while in this mode, very poor engine operation will result. Should failure of the pick-up coils or the start mode of the computer occur, the engine will not start.

The pick-up coil signal is a reference signal. When the signal is received by the computer the maximum amount of timing advance is made available. Based on the data from all the sensors,

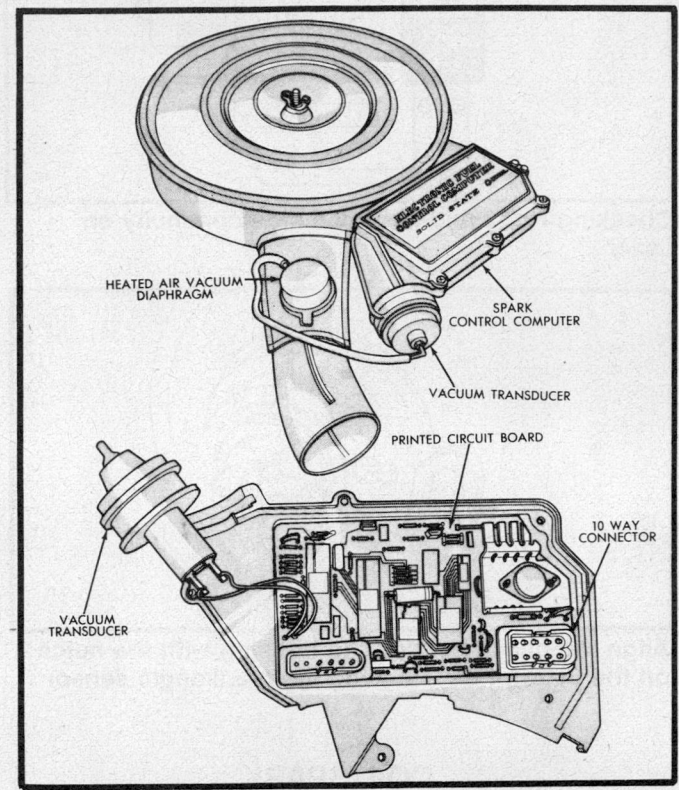

Combustion Computer assembly—typical

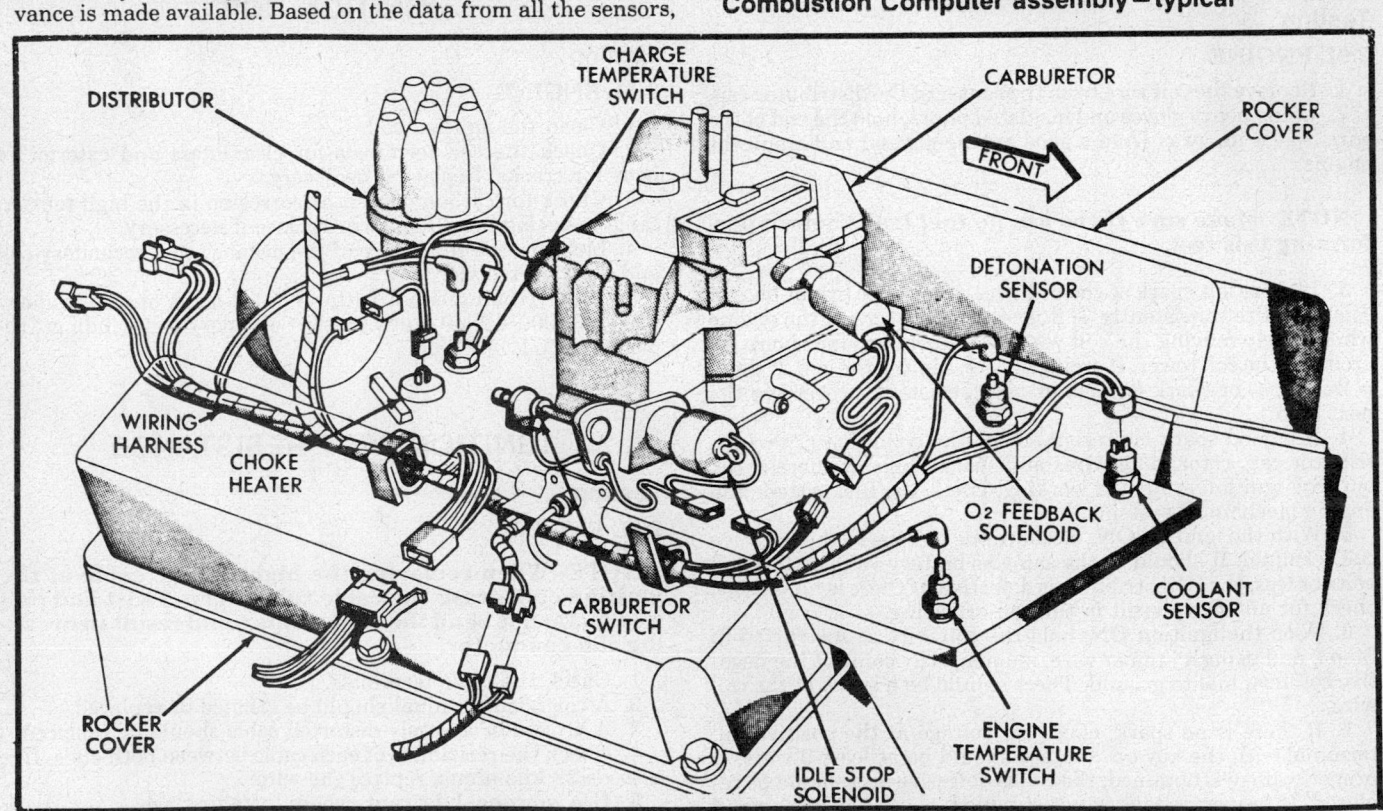

Location of V8 engine sensors and switches, Electronic Spark Control system

the computer determines how much of this maximum advance is needed at that instant.

The amount of spark advance is determined by 2 factors, enginbe speed and engine vacuum. However, when it happens depends on the following conditions:

1. Advance from the vacuum will be given by the computer when the carbutetor switch is open. The amount is programmed into the computer and is proportional to the amount of vacuum and engine rpm.

2. Advance from speed is given by the computer when the carburetor switch is open and is programmed to engine rpm.

IGNITION COMPUTER

The computer consists of an electronic printed circuit board which simultaneously receives signals from all the sensors and within milliseconds, analyzes them to determine how the engine is operating and then advances or retards the ignition timing by signaling the ignition coil to produce the electrical impulses to fire the spark plugs at the exact instant when ignition is required

MICROPROCESSOR ELECTRONIC SPARK CONTROL

The microprocessor is an electronic module located within the computer that processes the signals from the engine sensor for accurate engine spark timing. Its digital electronic circuitry offers more operating precision and programming flexibility than the voltage dependent analog system used previously.

MAGNETIC PICK-UP ASSEMBLIES

The start and the run pick-up sensors are located inside the distributor, suppling a signal to the computer to provide a fixed timing point that is used for starting (start pick-up) and the second for normal engine operation (run pick-up). The start pick-up also has a back-up function of taking over engine timing in case the run pick-up fails. Since the timing in this pick-up is at a fixed, the car will be able to run, but not very well. The run pick-up sensor also monitors engine speed and helps the computer decide when the piston is reaching the top of its compression stroke.

NOTE: The systems will not operate at the same time.

COOLANT SENSOR

The coolant temperature sensor, located in the intake manifold, informs the computer when the coolant temperature reaches a predetermined operating level. This information is required when the engine is equipped with a feedback carburetor, to prevent changing of the air/fuel ratio with the engine in a non-operating temperature mode. Its signals to the computer also help to control the amount of spark advance with a cold engine.

CARBURETOR SWITCH

The carburetor switch sensor is located on the end of the idle stop solenoid and tells the computer when the engine is at idle or off-idle. With the carburetor switch grounding out at idle, the computer cancels the spark advance and the idle control of the air/fuel ratio at the carburetor.

VACUUM TRANSDUCER

The vacuum transducer, located on the computer, monitors the amount of intake manifold vacuum present in the engine.The

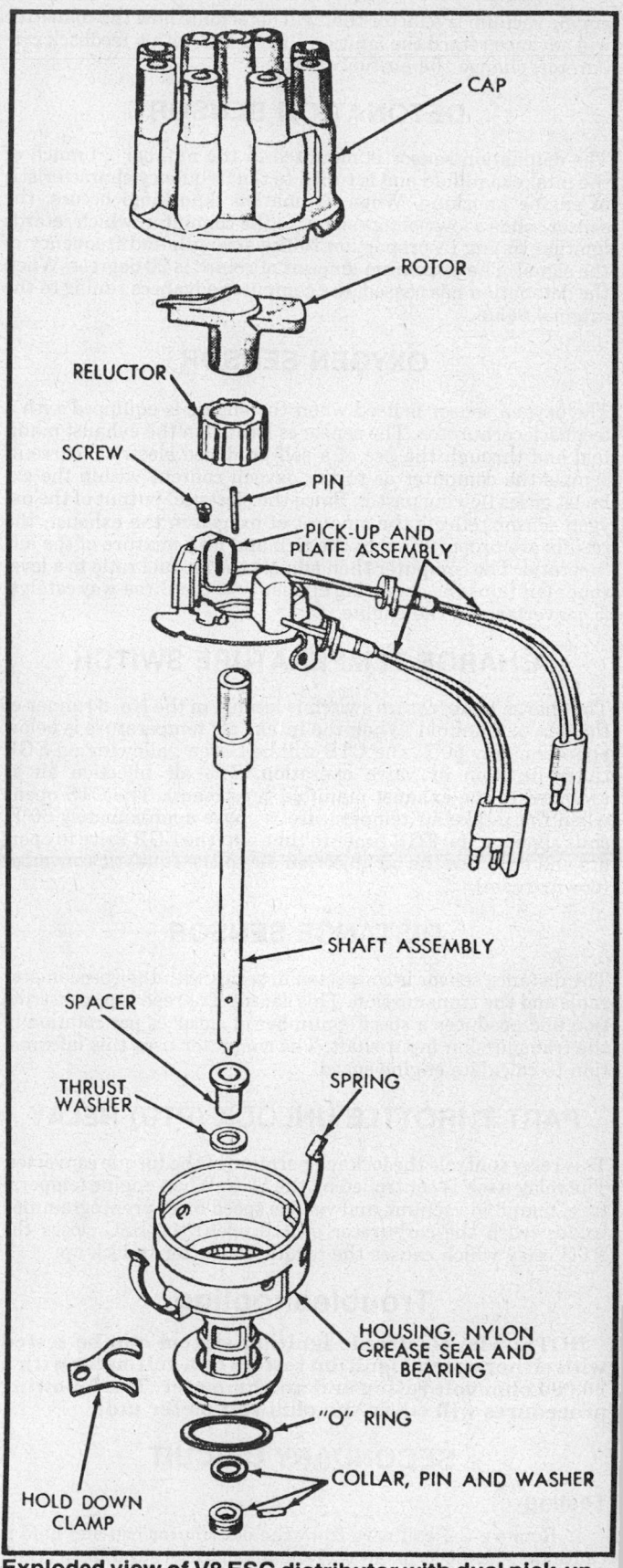

Exploded view of V8 ESC distributor with dual pick-up

engine vacuum is a factor that will determine how the computer will advance/retard the ignition timing and with a feedback carburetor, change the air/fuel ratio.

DETONATION SENSOR

The detonation sensor is mounted in the number 2 branch of the intake manifold and is tuned to the frequency characteristic of engine knocking. When detonation (knocking) occurs, the sensor sends a low voltage signal to the computer, which retards ignition timing in proportion to the strength and frequency of the signal. The maximum amount of retard is 20 degrees. When the detonation has ceased, the computer advances timing to the original value.

OXYGEN SENSOR

The oxygen sensor is used when the engine is equipped with a feedback carburetor. The sensor is located in the exhaust manifold and through the use of a self-produced electrical current, signals the computer as to the oxygen content within the exhaust gases flowing past it. Since the electrical output of the oxygen sensor reflects the amount of oxygen in the exhaust, the results are proportional to the rich and lean mixture of the air/fuel ratio. The computer then adjusts the air/fuel ratio to a level that maintains the operating efficiency of the three-way catalytic converter and the engine.

CHARGE TEMPERATURE SWITCH

The charge temperature switch is located in the No. 8 runner of the intake manifold. When the intake air temperature is below approximately 60°F, the CTS will be closed , allowing no EGR timer function or valve operation. The air injection air is switched to the exhaust manifold (upstream). The CTS opens when the intake air temperature is above approximately 60°F, thus allowing the EGR timer to time out, the EGR valve to operate and switches the air injection air to the catalytic converter (downstream).

DISTANCE SENSOR

The distance sensor is connected in series with the speedometer cable and the transmission. This sensor if of reed type construction and produces a specific number of closures per rotation of the transmission input shaft. The computer uses this information to calculate engine speed.

PART THROTTLE UNLOCK (PTU) RELAY

This relay controls the lockup operation of the torque converter. The relay itself is controlled by the SCC. When engine temperature, manifold vacuum, and vehicle speed meet preprogrammed values (with the carburetor switch open) the SSC closes the PTU relay which causes the torque converter to lock up.

Troubleshooting

NOTE: The electronic ignition system can be tested with either special ignition testers or a voltmeter with a 20,000 ohm/volt rating and an ohmmeter. The following procedures will cover the ohm/volt meter unit.

SECONDARY CIRCUIT

Testing

1. Remove the coil wire from the distributor cap and hold it cautiously about ¼ in. away from an engine ground, then crank the engine while checking for spark.

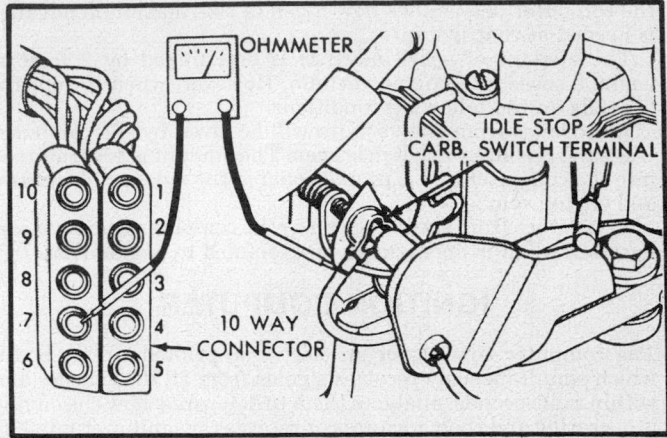

Checking continuity

2. If a good spark is present, slowly move the coil wire away from the engine and check for arcing at the coil while cranking.

3. If good spark is present and it is not arcing at the coil, check the rest of the parts of the ignition system.

IGNITION SYSTEM STARTING

Testing

1. Visually inspect all secondary cables at the coil, distributor and spark plugs for cracks and tightness.

2. Check the primary wire at the coil and ballast resistor for tightness.

NOTE: Whenever removing or installing the wiring harness connector to the control unit, the ignition switch must be in the OFF position.

3. Make sure the battery is charged properly.

4. Remove the coil secondary wire from the distributor cap.

5. With the key on, use a jumper wire and momentarily touch the negative terminal of the coil to ground while holding the coil secondary wire approximately ¼ in. from a good engine ground. A spark should be observed.

6. Verify the the spark is getting to the spark plugs. If the spark plugs are being fired, the ignition system is not responsibile for the engine not starting.

7. If no spark is observed at the ignition coil wire, turn the ignition switch to the **OFF** position and disconnect the 10-way connector from the bottom of the spark control computer. Turn the ignition switch to the **ON** position and hold the ignition coil wire approximately ¼ in. away from a good engine ground.

8. With battery current to the coil negative terminal, intermittantly short the terminal to ground. If spark now occurs, replace the spark control computer.

9. If the voltage is incorrect, check the continuity of the wiring between the battery and the coil positive terminal. Repair the wiring as required and retest.

10. Should battery voltage (within 1 volt) not be present at the coil negative terminal with the ignition key **ON**, replace the ignition coil.

11. Should battery voltage (within 1 volt) be present, but no spark is obtained when shorting the negative terminal, replace the ignition coil.

12. If spark is obrtained, but the engine will still not start, turn the ignition switch to the **RUN** positon and with the positive lead of the voltmeter, measure the voltage from cavity No. 1 to the ground lead of the disconnecxted lead from the computer. The voltage should be within 1 volt of the battery voltage noted earlier.

13. If battery voltage is not present, check the wire for an open circuit and repair. Retest as required.

14. Place a thin insulator between the curb idle adjusting screw and the carburetor switch or, make sure the curb idle adjusting screw is not touching the carburetor switch.

15. Connect the negative voltmeter lead to a good engine ground. Turn the ignition switch to the **RUN** position and measure the voltage at the carburetor switch terminal. The voltage should be approximately 5 volts.

16. If the voltage is not 5 volts, turn the ignition switch to the **OFF** position and disconnect the 10-way connector from the bottom of the spark control computer. Turn the ignition switch back to the **RUN** position and measure the voltage at terminal 2 of the connector.

17. Voltage should be within 1 volt of battery voltage. If the correct voltage is not present, check the wiring between terminal 2 of the connector and the ignition switch for open or shorted circuits or poor connections.

18. Turn the ignition switch to the **OFF** position and disconnect the connector from the bottom of the spark computer, if not already done. With an ohmmeter, check the continuity between terminal 7 of the connector and the carburetor switch terminal. Continuity should exist between these points. If not, check for opens or poor connections.

19. Check for continuity between terminal 10 of the connector and engine ground. If continuity exists, replace the spark control computer assembly. If continuity does not exist, check the wiring for open circuits or poor connections. Repeat Step 18.

20. If the engine still fails to start, turn the ignition switch to the **OFF** position and with an ohmmeter, measure the resistance between terminal 5 and terminal 9 for the start pick-up coil of the 10-way connector. The resistance should be between 150-900 ohms.

21. If the resistance is not within the specified range, disconnect the Pick-up coil leads from the distributor. Measure the resistance at the lead going into the distributor. If the reading is now between 150-900 ohms, an open circuit or faulty connections exists between the distributor connector and terminals 5 and terminal 9 of of the 10-way connector. If the resistance is not within specifications, the pick-up coil is bad. Replace it and set the air gap to specifications.

22. Connect a lead of the ohmmeter to the engine ground and with the other lead, check for continuity at each terminal of the leads going to the distributor. There should be no continuity.

23. If there is continuity, replace the pick-up coils. Adjust the air gap to specifications.

24. Attempt to start the engine. If it fails to start, repeat the tests. If the engine still fails to start, replace the spark control computer.

POOR ENGINE PERFORMANCE

BASIC TIMING

Correct basic timing is essential for optimum engine performance. Before any testing and service is begun on a poor performance complaint, the basic timing must be checked and adjusted as required. Refer to the underhood specifications label and to the vehicle section for timing adjustment procedures.

SPARK CONTROL COMPUTER ADVANCE

Testing

Incorporated within the digital microprocessor electronics are programmed spark advance schedules which occur during cold engine operation. These programmed advance schedules have been added to reduce engine emissions and improve driveability. Because they will be changing at different engine operating temperatures during warm-up, all spark advance testing should be done with the engine at normal operating temperature and a temperature sensor that is connected and operating correctly.

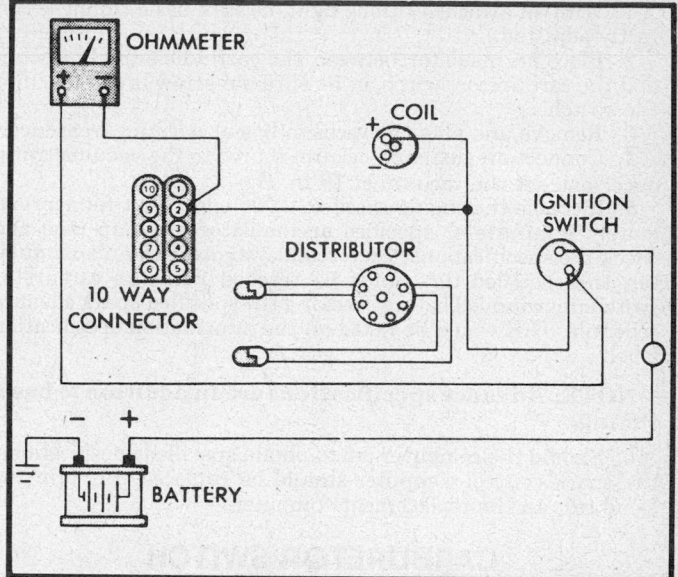

Checking continuity between terminal two and ignition switch

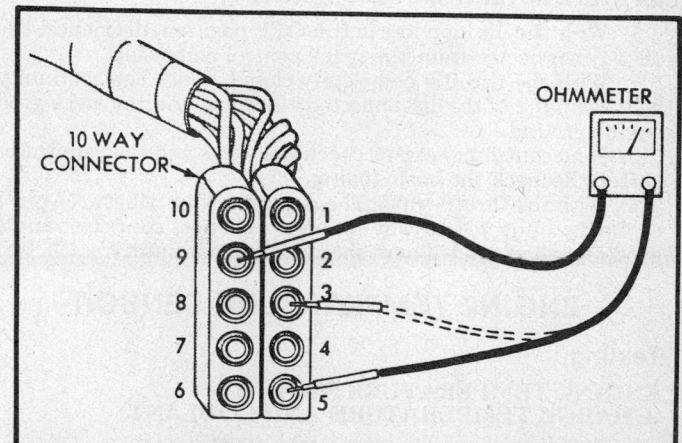

Checking resistance between terminal five and nine, then three and nine

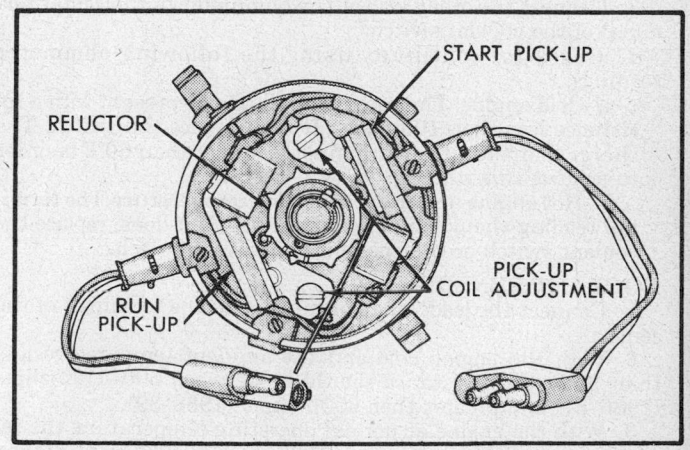

Air gap adjustment locations, dual pick-up illustrated

1. With an attached timing light, be sure basic timing is correctly adjusted.

2. Place an insulator between the curb idle adjusting screw and the carburetor switch, or be sure the screw is not touching the switch.

3. Remove and plug the vacuum line at vacuum transducer.

4. Connect an auxiliary vacuum source to the vacuum transducer and set the vacuum at 16 in. Hg.

5. Increase the engine speed to 2,000 rpm. Wait for approximately 1 minute or specified accumulator clock-up time and check the specifications. On certain systems with an accumulator, the specified time must be reached with the carburetor switch ungrounded before checking the specified spark advance schedule. This would be noted on the information specification label.

NOTE: Advance specifications are in addition to basic timing.

6. Should the computer fail to obtain specified specifications, the spark control computer should be replaced. Perform the same test on the replacement computer.

CARBURETOR SWITCH

Testing

NOTE: Grounding the carburetor switch eliminates all spark advance on most systems.

1. With the ignition key in the **OFF** position, disconnect the 10-way connector from the spark control computer.

2. With the throttle completely closed, check the continuity between pin 7 of the disconnected 10-way connector and a good engine ground.

3. If no continuity exists, check the wires and the carburetor switch. Recheck the basic timing.

4. With the throttle open, check the continuity between pin 7 of the disconnected 10-way connector harness connector and a good engine ground. There should be no continuity.

ENGINE TEMPERATURE SENSOR

Testing

ENGINE TEMPERATURE SWITCH (CHARGE TEMPERATURE AND COOLANT)

1. Turn the ignition switch to the **OFF** position and disconnect the wire from the temperature switch.

2. Connect a lead of an ohmmeter to a good ground on the engine, or in the case of the charge temperature switch, to its ground terminal.

3. Connect the other lead of the ohmmeter to the center terminal of the coolant switch.

4. Check for continuity using the following ohmmeter readings:

   a. Cold engine: The continuity should be present with a resistance less than 100 ohms. If not, replace the switch. The charge temperature switch must be cooler than 60°F in order to achieve this reading.

   b. Hot engine at normal operating temperature: The terminal reading should show no continuity. If it does, replace the coolant switch or the charge temperature switch.

COOLANT SENSOR

1. Connect the leads of an ohmmeter to the terminals of the sensor.

2. With the engine cold and the ambient temperature less than 90°F, the resistance should be between 500–1100 ohms (1986–87) and greater then 6000 ohms (1988–89).

3. With the engine at normal operating temperature, the resistance should be greater than 1300 ohms to 1987 and less than 2500 ohms (1988–89).

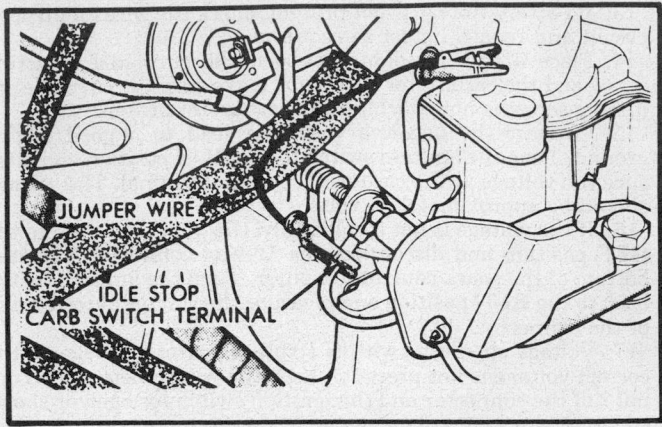

Grounding carburetor switch

4. If the resistance is not within the specified range, replace the sensor. The sensor will continually change its resistance with a change in engine operating temperature.

DETONATION SENSOR

Testing

1. Connect an adjustable timing light to the engine.

2. Start the enmgine and run it on the second highest step of the fast idle cam (at least 1200 rpm).

3. Connect an auxiliary vacuum supply to the vacuum transducer and set on 16 in. Hg.

4. Tap lightly on the intake manifold near the sensor with a small metal object.

5. Using the timing light, look for a decrease in the spark advance. The amount of decrease in the timing is directly proportional to the strength and frequency of the tapping. The most decrease in timing will be 20 degrees.

6. Turn the ignition switch to the **OFF** position. With the engine stopped, disconnect the timing light.

ELECTRONIC EXHAUST GAS RECIRCULATION SYSTEM

Testing

NOTE: The Electronic EGR control is located within the electronic circuitry of the spark control computer and its testing procedure is outlined.

1. All the engine temperature sensors must be operating properly before the tests can be done.

2. With the engine temperature cold and the ignition switch turned to the **OFF** position, connect a voltmeter lead to the gray wire on the EGR solenoid and the second to a good engine ground.

3. Start the engine. The voltage should be less than 1 volt. It will remain at this level until the engine has reached its normal operating temperature range and the electronic EGR schedule has timed out. The solenoid will then de-energize and the voltmeter will read charging system voltage.

4. If the charging system voltage is not obtained, replace the solenoid and repeat the test.

5. If the voltmeter indicates charging system voltage before the EGR schedule is complete, replace the computer or the externally mounted timer.

NOTE: The 318-2 Federal engines have no thermal delay below 60°F ambient temperature. It will follow the EGR time delay schedule only.

6. If an engine is started with the temperature hot, the EGR solenoid will be energized for the length of the time delay schedule only. It will then de-energize.

ELECTRONIC THROTTLE CONTROL SYSTEM

Incorporated within the Spark Control Computer is the electronic throttle system. A carburetor mounted solenoid is energized when the air conditioner, electric back light or the electric timers are activated. The 2 timers which are incorporated in the ignition electronics, operate when the throttle is closed, plus a time delay (2 seconds), or after an engine start condition.

Testing

1. Connect a tachometer to the engine.
2. Start the engine and run it until normal operating temperature is reached.
3. Depress the accelerator and release it. A higher than curb idle speed should be seen on the tachometer for the length of the EGR schedule.
4. On vehicles equipped with/and turning on the air conditioner or the back light, depressing the accelerator for a moment should give a higher than curb idle speed. Turning the air conditioner and back light off will produce the normal idle speed.

NOTE: With the air conditioning system on, the compressor clutch will cycle ON and OFF. This should not be mistaken as a part of the electronic control system.

5. If the speed increases do not occur, disconnect the 3-way connector at the carburetor.
6. Check the solenoid with an ohmmeter by measuring the resistance from the terminal that contains the black wire to ground. The resistance should be between 15–35 ohms. If not within specifications, replace the solenoid.
7. Start the engine and before the delay has timed out, measure the voltage of the black wire of the 3-way connector, The voltmeter should read charging system voltage. If it does not, replace the computer.
8. Turning the air conditioner or the back light on should also produce charging system voltage after the time delay has timed out. If not, check the wiring back to the instrument panel for open circuits.

DUAL PICK-UP START/RUN RELAY TEST

Testing

1. Remove the 2-way connector from pins No. 4 and No. 5 of the dual pick-up start/run relay.
2. Using an ohmmeter, touch pins No. 4 and No. 5. The meter should read 20–30 ohms. If not, replace the relay.

PICK-UP COIL AIR GAP

Adjustment

In the dual pick-up distributor, the start pick-up is identified by a 2 prong male connector and the run pick-up is identified by a male and female plug.

START PICK-UP

1. Align a reluctor tooth with the pick-up coil tooth.
2. Loosen the pick-up coil holddown screw.
3. Insert a 0.006 in. non-magnetic feeler gauge between the reluctor tooth and the pick-up coil tooth.
4. Adjust the air gap so that contact is made between the reluctor tooth, the feeler gauge and the pick-up tooth.
5. Carefully tighten the holddown screw.
6. Remove the feeler gauge. There should be no force needed to remove the gauge.
7. A 0.008 in. feeler gauge should not pass through the gap. Do not force the gauge in the air gap.

RUN PICK-UP

1. Align on reluctor tooth with the pick-up coil tooth.
2. Loosen the pick-up coil holddown screw.
3. Insert a 0.012 in. non-magnetic feeler gauge beteeen the reluctor tooth and the pick-up tooth.
4. Adjust the air gap so that contact is made between the reluctor tooth, feeler gauge and the pick-up coil tooth.
5. Carefully tighten the holddown screw.
6. Remove the feeler gauge. There should be no force required to remove it.
7. A 0.014 in. feeler gauge should not pass through the gap. Do not force the gauge in the air gap.

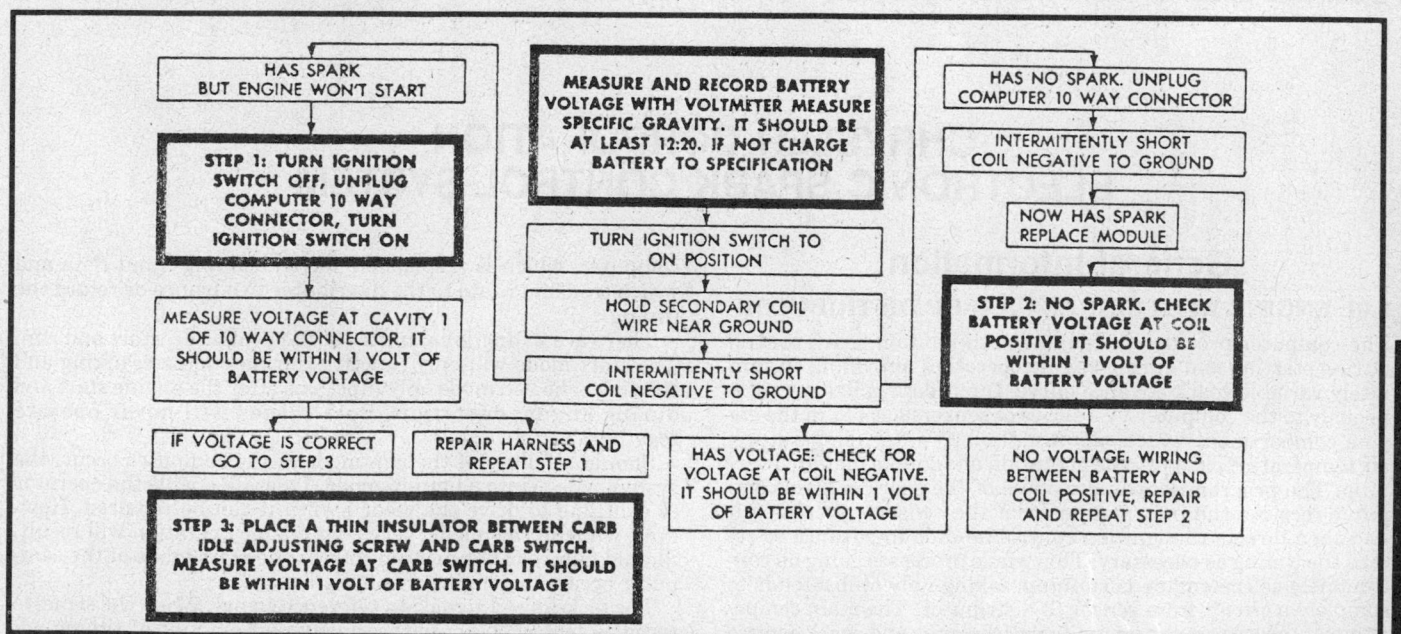

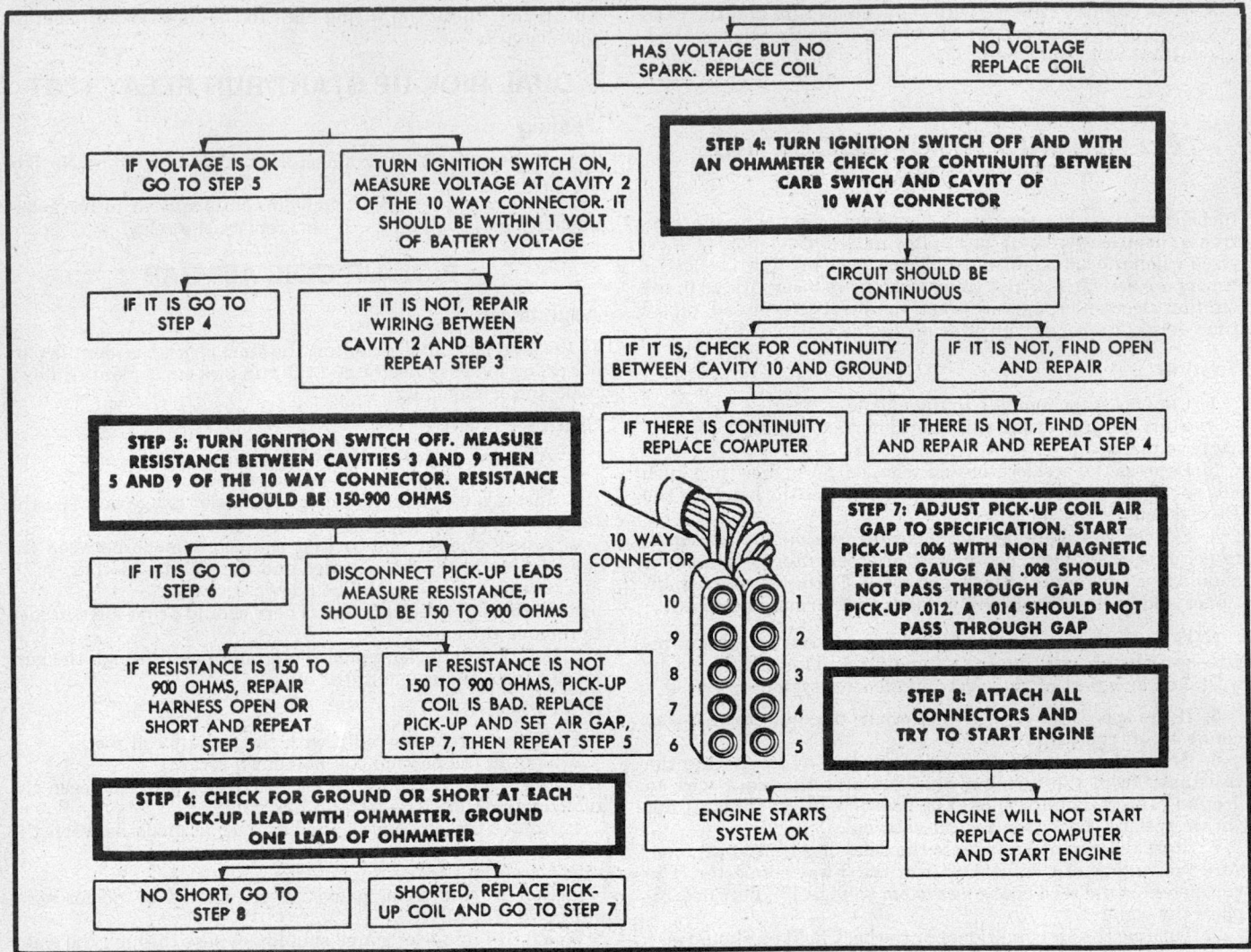

Electronic Spark Control system diagnosis, with dual pick-up distributors

CHRYSLER CORPORATION
ELECTRONIC SPARK CONTROL SYSTEM

General Information

5.0L ENGINE WITH SINGLE PICK-UP DISTRIBUTOR

The computer provides the engine with ignition spark control during starting and during engine operation, providing an infinitely variable spark advance curve. Input data is fed instantaneously to the computer by a series of sensors located in the engine compartment which monitor timing, water temperature, air temperature, idle/off-idle operation and intake manifold vacuum. The program schedule module of the spark control computer receives the information from the sensors, processes it and then directs the ignition control module to advance or retard the timing as necessary. This whole process is going on continuously as the engine is running, taking only milliseconds to complete a circuit from sensor to distributor. The main components of the system are a modified carburetor and spark control

computer, which is responsible for translating input data and which transmits data to the distributor to advance or retard the timing.

There are 2 functional modes of the computer, start and run. The start mode will only function during engine cranking and starting. The run mode only functions after the engine start and during engine operation. Both modes will never operate together.

Should a failure of the run mode of the computer occur, the system will go into a limp-in mode. This will enable the operator to continue to drive the vehicle until it can be repaired. However, while in this mode, very poor engine operation will result. Should failure of the pick-up coils or the start mode of the computer occur, the engine will not start.

The pick-up coil signal is a reference signal. When the signal is received by the computer the maximum amount of timing ad-

vance is made available. Based on the data from all the sensors, the computer determines how much of this maximum advance is needed at that instant.

The amount of spark advance is determined by 2 factors, engine speed and engine vacuum. However, when it happens depends on the following conditions:

1. Advance from the vacuum will be given by the computer when the carburetor switch is open. The amount is programmed into the computer and is proportional to the amount of vacuum and engine rpm.

2. Advance from speed is given by the computer when the carburetor switch is open and is programmed to engine rpm.

IGNITION COMPUTER

The computer consists of an electronic printed circuit board which simultaneously receives signals from all the sensors and within milliseconds, analyzes them to determine how the engine is operating and then advances or retards the ignition timing by signaling the ignition coil to produce the electrical impulses to fire the spark plugs at the exact instant when ignition is required

MICROPROCESSOR ELECTRONIC SPARK CONTROL

The microprocessor is an electronic module located within the computer that processes the signals from the engine sensor for accurate engine spark timing. Its digital electronic circuitry offers more operating precision and programming flexibility than the voltage dependent analog system used previously.

MAGNETIC PICK-UP ASSEMBLY

The pick-up sensor is located inside the distributor, supplying a signal to the computer to provide a fixed timing point that is used for starting and the second for normal engine operation. The computer also has a back-up function of fixing the engine timing in the start-up mode in case the run mode fails. Since the timing in the start-up mode is at a fixed point, the car will be able to run, but not very well. The pick-up sensor also monitors engine speed and helps the computer decide when the piston is reaching the top of its compression stroke.

NOTE: The start-up and run modes will not operate at the same time.

COOLANT SENSOR

The coolant temperature sensor, located in the intake manifold, informs the computer when the coolant temperature reaches a predetermined operating level. This information is required when the engine is equipped with a feedback carburetor, to prevent changing of the air/fuel ratio with the engine in a non-operating temperature mode. Its signals to the computer also help to control the amount of spark advance with a cold engine.

CARBURETOR SWITCH

The carburetor switch sensor is located on the end of the idle stop solenoid and tells the computer when the engine is at idle or off-idle. With the carburetor switch grounding out at idle, the computer cancels the spark advance and the idle control of the air/fuel ratio at the carburetor.

VACUUM TRANSDUCER

The vacuum transducer, located on the computer, monitors the amount of intake manifold vacuum present in the engine. The

engine vacuum is a of the factors that will determine how the computer will advance/retard the ignition timing and with a feedback carburetor, change the air/fuel ratio.

DETONATION SENSOR

The detonation sensor is mounted in the number 2 branch of the intake manifold and is tuned to the frequency characteristic of engine knocking. When detonation (knocking) occurs, the sensor sends a low voltage signal to the computer, which retards ignition timing in proportion to the strength and frequency of the signal. The maximum amount of retard is 20 degrees. When the detonation has ceased, the computer advances timing to the original value.

OXYGEN SENSOR

The oxygen sensor is used when the engine is equipped with a feedback carburetor. The sensor is located in the exhaust manifold and through the use of a self-produced electrical current, signals the computer as to the oxygen content within the exhaust gases flowing past it. Since the electrical output of the oxygen sensor reflects the amount of oxygen in the exhaust, the results are proportional to the rich and lean mixture of the air/fuel ratio. The computer then adjusts the air/fuel ratio to a level that maintains the operating efficiency of the three-way catalytic converter and the engine.

CHARGE TEMPERATURE SWITCH

The charge temperature switch is located in the No. 8 runner of the intake manifold. When the intake air temperature is below approximately 60°F, the CTS will be closed , allowing no EGR timer function or valve operation. The air injection air is switched to the exhaust manifold (upstream). The CTS opens when the intake air temperature is above approximately 60°F, thus allowing the EGR timer to time out, the EGR valve to operate and switches the air injection air to the catalytic converter (downstream).

DISTANCE SENSOR

The distance sensor is connected in series with the speedometer cable and the transmission. This sensor if of reed type construction and produces a specific number of closures per rotation of the transmission input shaft. The computer uses this information to calculate engine speed.

PART THROTTLE UNLOCK (PTU) RELAY

This relay controls the lock-up operation of the torque converter. The relay itself is controlled by the SCC. When engine temperature, manifold vacuum, and vehicle speed meet preprogrammed values (with the carburetor switch open) the SSC closes the PTU relay which causes the torque converter to lock up.

Troubleshooting

NOTE: The electronic ignition system can be tested with either special ignition testers or a voltmeter with a 20,000 ohm/volt rating and an ohmmeter. The following procedure will cover the ohm/volt meter unit.

SECONDARY CIRCUIT

Testing

1. Remove the coil wire from the distributor cap and hold it cautiously about ¼ in. away from an engine ground, then crank the engine while checking for spark.

2. If a good spark is present, slowly move the coil wire away from the engine and check for arcing at the coil while cranking.

3. If good spark is present and it is not arcing at the coil, check the rest of the parts of the ignition system.

IGNITION SYSTEM STARTING

Testing

1. Visually inspect all secondary cables at the coil, distributor and spark plugs for cracks and tightness.

2. Check the primary wire at the coil and ballast resistor for tightness.

NOTE: Whenever removing or installing the wiring harness connector to the control unit, the ignition switch must be in the OFF position.

3. With a voltmeter, make sure the battery is charged properly.

4. Remove the coil secondary wire from the distributor cap.

5. With the key on, use a jumper wire and momentarily touch the negative terminal of the coil to ground while holding the coil secondary wire approximately ¼ in. from a good engine ground. A spark should be observed.

6. Verify the the spark is getting to the spark plugs. If the spark plugs are being fired, the ignition system is not responsibile for the engine not starting.

7. If no spark is observed at the ignition coil wire, turn the ignition switch to the **OFF** position and disconnect the 10-way connector from the bottom of the spark control computer. Turn the ignition switch to the **ON** position and hold the ignition coil wire approximately ¼ in. away from a good engine ground.

8. With battery current to the coil negative terminal, intermittantly short the terminal to ground. If spark now occurs, replace the spark control computer.

9. If the voltage is incorrect, check the continuity of the wiring between the battery and the coil positive terminal. Repair the wiring as required and retest.

10. Should battery voltage (within 1 volt) not be present at the coil negative terminal with the ignition key on, replace the ignition coil.

11. Should battery voltage (within 1 volt) be present, but no spark is obtained when shorting the negative terminal, replace the ignition coil.

12. If spark is obtained, but the engine will still not start, turn the ignition switch to the **RUN** positon and with the positive lead of the voltmeter, measure the voltage from cavity No. 1 to the ground lead of the disconnected lead from the computer. The voltage should be within 1 volt of the battery voltage noted earlier.

13. If battery voltage is not present, check the wire for an open circuit and repair. Retest as required.

14. Place a thin insulator between the curb idle adjusting screw and the carburetor switch or, make sure the curb idle adjusting screw is not touching the carburetor switch.

15. Connect the negative voltmeter lead to a good engine ground. Turn the ignition switch to the **RUN** position and measure the voltage at the carburetor switch terminal. The voltage should be approximately 5 volts.

16. If the voltage is not 5 volts, turn the ignition switch to the **OFF** position and disconnect the 10-way connector from the bottom of the spark control computer. Turn the ignition switch back to the **RUN** position and measure the voltage at terminal 2 of the connector.

17. Voltage should be within 1 volt of battery voltage. If the correct voltage is not present, check the wiring between terminal 2 of the connector and the ignition switch for open or shorted circuits or poor connections.

18. Turn the ignition switch to the **OFF** position and disconnect the connector from the bottom of the spark computer, if not already done. With an ohmmeter, check the continuity be-

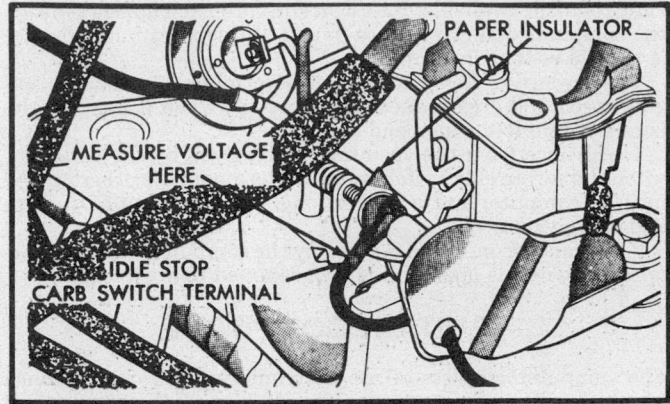

Checking voltage at carburetor switch

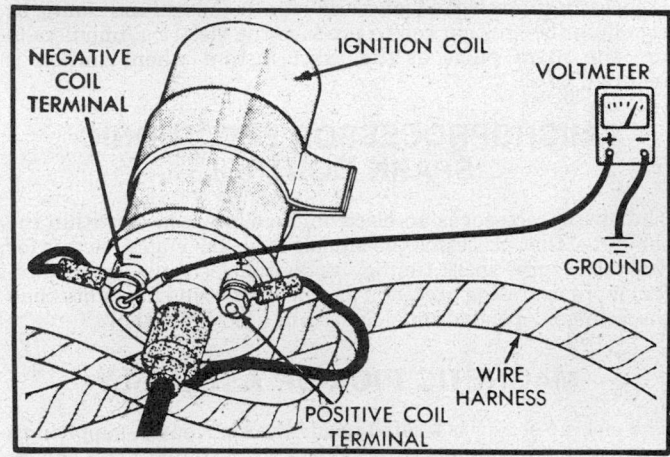

Checking resistance of coil windings

tween terminal 7 of the connector and the carburetor switch terminal. Continuity should exist between these points. If not, check for opens or poor connections.

19. Check for continuity between terminal 10 of the connector and engine ground. If continuity exists, replace the spark control computer assembly. If continuity does not exist, check the wiring for open circuits or poor connections. Repeat Step 18.

20. If the engine still fails to start, turn the ignition switch to the **OFF** position and with an ohmmeter, measure the resistance between terminal 5 and terminal 9 for the pick-up coil of the 10-way connector. The resistance should be between 150–900 ohms.

21. If the resistance is not within the specified range, disconnect the Pick-up coil leads from the distributor. Measure the resistance at the lead going into the distributor. If the reading is now between 150–900 ohms, an open circuit or faulty connections exists between the distributor connector and terminals 5 and terminal 9 of of the 10-way connector. If the resistance is not within specifications, the pick-up coil is bad. Replace it and set the air gap to specifications.

22. Connect a lead of the ohmmeter to the engine ground and with the other lead, check for continuity at each terminal of the leads going to the distributor. There should be no continuity.

23. If there is continuity, replace the pick-up coil. Adjust the air gap to specifications.

24. Attempt to start the engine. If the engine fails to start, repeat the tests. If the engine still fails to start, replace the spark control computer.

PICKUP COIL AIR GAP

Adjustment

1. Align a reluctor tooth with the pick-up coil tooth.

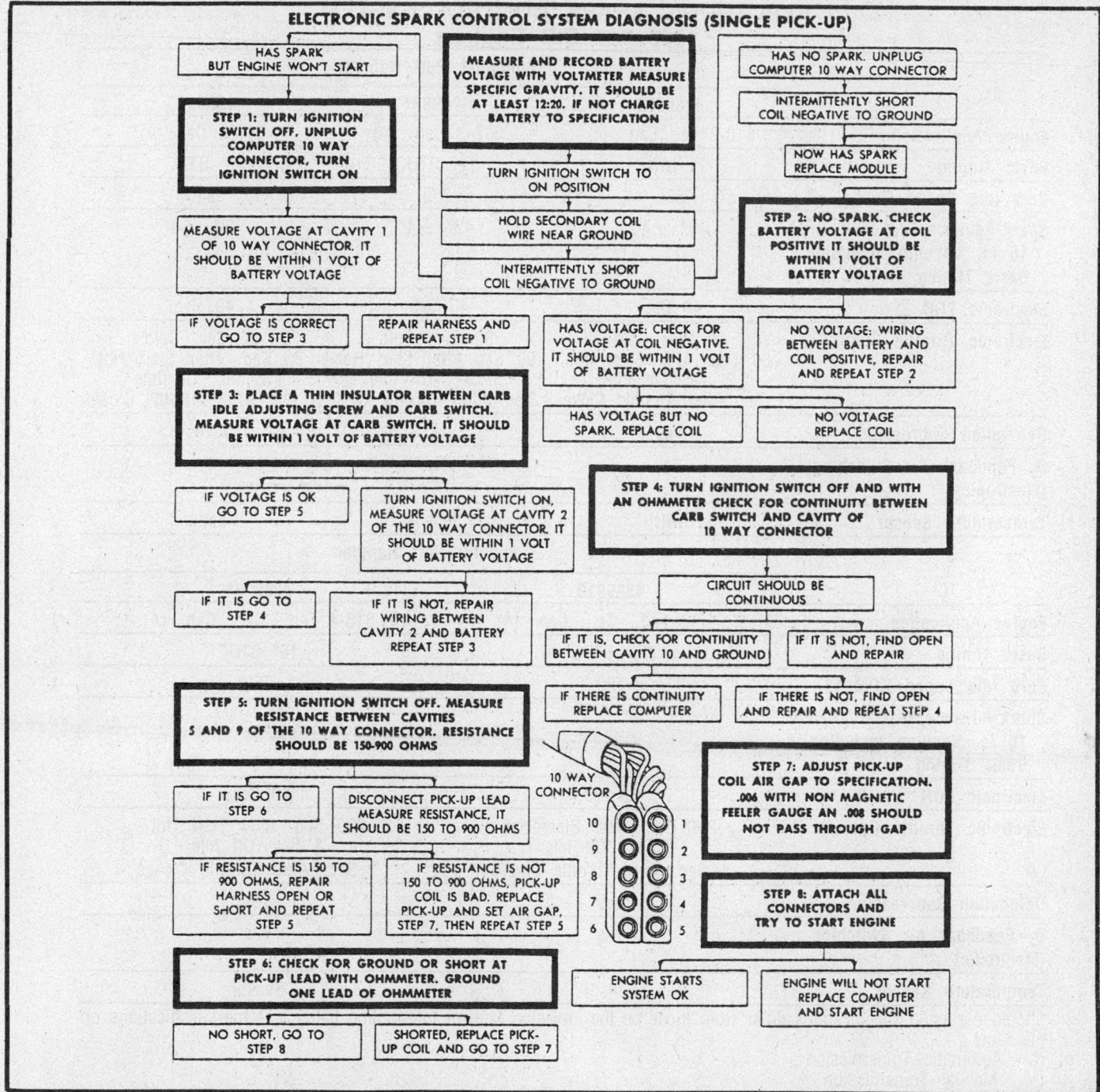

Electronic Spark Control system diagnosis with single pick-up distributor

2. Loosen the pick-up coil holddown screw.

3. Insert a 0.006 in. non-magnetic feeler gauge between the reluctor tooth and the pick-up coil tooth.

4. Adjust the air gap so that contact is made between the reluctor tooth, the feeler gauge and the pick-up tooth.

5. Carefully tighten the holddown screw.

6. Remove the feeler gauge. There should be no force needed to remove the gauge.

7. A 0.008 in. feeler gauge should not pass through the gap. Do not force the gauge in the air gap.

POOR ENGINE PERFORMANCE

NOTE: When testing for poor engine performance, refer to the electronic spark control system with dual pick-up distributor.

ELECTRONIC SPARK CONTROL SYSTEM
1986 318 CID Engines

	Computer Part Number		
	4289813	4289881	4289913
Engine Application	318-2 Fed.,Can. (A)	318-2 Can. (A)	318-2 Cal. (A)
Basic Timing	7° BTDC	12° BTDC	7° BTDC
Curb Idle Speed RPM▲	630	730	630
Spark Advance Test 2000 RPM 16 in. Vacuum including Basic Timing	46° ±4°	42° ±4°	46° ±4°
Electronic EGR	40 Sec.	40 Sec.	40 Sec.
Electronic Throttle Control	20 Sec. Cold 60 Sec. After Start Hot 2 Sec. Off Idle 1 Sec After Throttle Closes	90 Sec. Cold 90 Sec After Start Hot 5 Sec. Off Idle 3 Sec. After Throttle Closes	20 Sec. Cold 60 Sec. After Start Hot 2 Sec. Off Idle 1 Sec. After Throttle Closes
Detonation Supression	Yes	No	Yes
O_2 Feedback Air Switching (Electronic)	Yes	No	Yes
Temperature Sensor	Switch	Sensor	Sensor

	Computer Part Number	
	4289919	4289921
Engine Application	318-2 Fed., Cal., Can. (A)	318-4 Fed., Cal., Can. (A)
Basic Timing	16° BTDC	16° BTDC
Curb Idle Speed RPM***	750	750
Spark Advance Test 2000 RPM 16 in. Vacuum Including Basic Timing	38° ±4°	38° ±4°
Electronic EGR	40 Sec.	40 Sec.
Electronic Throttle Control	200 Sec. After Start Hot 3 Sec. Off Idle 1 Sec. After Throttle Closes	200 Sec. After Start Hot 3 Sec. Off Idle 1 Sec. After Throttle Closes
Detonation Suppression	Yes	Yes
O_2 Feedback Air Switching (Electronic)	Yes	Yes
Temperature Sensor	Sensor	Sensor

Should the listed specifications differ from those on the Emission Control Information Label, use the specifications on the label

(A) — Automatic Transmission
(M) — Manual Transmission
(OD) — Overdrive
Can. — Canada
Fed. — Federal
Cal. — California
BTDC — Before Top Dead Center
P.V. — Passenger Vehicle
TR — Truck
* High Altitude

**Basic Timing set with vacuum line disconnected. Do not readjust curb idle
▲Curb Idle RPM ±100 RPM, set with vacuum line connected

ELECTRONIC SPARK CONTROL SYSTEM
1987 318 CID Engines

	Computer Part Number		
	4289813	**4289881**	**4289913**
Engine Application	318-2 Fed., Can. (A)	318-2 Can. (A)	318-2 Cal. (A)
Basic Timing	7° BTDC	12° BTDC	7° BTDC
Curb Idle Speed RPM▲	630	730	630
Spark Advance Test 2000 RPM 16 in. Vacuum including Basic Timing	46° ±4°	42° ±4°	46° ±4°
Electronic EGR	40 Sec.	40 Sec.	40 Sec.
Electronic Throttle Control	20 Sec. Cold 60 Sec. After Start Hot 2 Sec. Off Idle 1 Sec After Throttle Closes	90 Sec. Cold 90 Sec After Start Hot 5 Sec. Off Idle 3 Sec. After Throttle Closes	20 Sec. Cold 60 Sec. After Start Hot 2 Sec. Off Idle 1 Sec. After Throttle Closes
Detonation Supression	Yes	No	Yes
O$_2$ Feedback Air Switching (Electronic)	Yes	No	Yes
Temperature Sensor	Switch	Sensor	Sensor

	Computer Part Number	
	4379228	**4379228**
Engine Application	318-4 Fed., Cal., Can. (A)	318-4 Fed., Cal., Can. (A)
Basic Timing	16° BTDC	16° BTDC
Curb Idle Speed RPM▲	750	750
Spark Advance Test 2000 RPM 16 in. Vacuum Including Basic Timing	38° ±4°	38° ±4°
Electronic EGR	40 Sec.	40 Sec.
Electronic Throttle Control	200 Sec. After Start Hot 3 Sec. Off Idle 1 Sec. After Throttle Closes	200 Sec. After Start Hot 3 Sec. Off Idle 1 Sec. After Throttle Closes
Detonation Suppression	Yes	Yes
O$_2$ Feedback Air Switching (Electronic)	Yes	Yes
Temperature Sensor	Sensor	Sensor

Should the listed specifications differ from those on the Emission Control Information Label, use the specifications on the label
(A)—Automatic Transmission
(M)—Manual Transmission
(OD)—Overdrive
Can.—Canada
Fed.—Federal
Cal.—California
BTDC—Before Top Dead Center
P.V.—Passenger Vehicle
TR—Truck
* High Altitude
**Basic Timing set with vacuum line disconnected. Do not readjust curb idle

ELECTRONIC SPARK CONTROL SYSTEM
1988 5.2L Engine

	Computer Part Number		
	4289813	4379167	4289913
Engine Application	318-2 Federal, California (A)	318-2 Canada (A)	318-2 California (A)
Basic Timing*	7° BTDC	7° BTDC	7° BTDC
Curb Idle Speed rpm▲	630	630	630
Spark Advance Test @ 2000 RPM 16 in. Vacuum Including Basic Timing	46° ± 4°	42° ± 4°	46° ± 4°
Electronic EGR	40 sec.	40 sec.	40 sec.
Electronic Throttle Control	20 sec. cold / 60 sec. after start hot / 2 sec. off idle / 1 sec. after throttle closes	90 sec. cold / 90 sec. after start hot / 5 sec. off idle / 3 sec. after throttle closes	20 sec. cold / 60 sec. after start hot / 2 sec. off idle / 1 sec. after throttle closes
Detonation Suppression	Yes	No	Yes
O₂ Feedback Air Switching (Electronic)	Yes	No	Yes
Charge Temperature Sensor	5226374	5226374	5226374

	Computer Part Number	
	4379228	4379228
Engine Application	318-4 Federal, California, Canada (A)	318-4 Federal, California, Canada (A)
Basic Timing*	16° BTDC	16° BTDC
Curb Idle Speed rpm ▲	750	750
Spark Advance Test @ 2000 RPM 16 in. Vacuum Including Basic Timing	38° ± 4°	38° ± 4°
Electronic EGR	40 sec.	40 sec.
Electronic Throttle Control	200 sec. after start hot / 3 sec. off idle / 1 sec. after throttle closes	200 sec. after start hot / 3 sec. off idle / 1 sec. after throttle closes
Detonation Suppression	Yes	Yes
O₂ Feedback Air Switching (Electronic)	Yes	Yes
Temperature Sensor	Sensor	Sensor

Should the listed specifications differ from those on the Emission Control Information Label, use the specifications on the label
(A)—Automatic Transmission
BTDC Before Top Dead Center
▲ Curb Idle RPM ± 100 rpm—Curb Idle set with vacuum line connected.
*Basic Timing Set With Vacuum Line Disconnected—do not readjust curb idle.

ELECTRONIC SPARK CONTROL SYSTEM
1989 5.2L Engine

	Computer Part Number	
	4379484	4379682
Engine Application	318-2 (A)	318-2 (A)
Basic Timing*	7° BTDC	7° BTDC
Curb Idle Speed rpm▲	630	630

ELECTRONIC SPARK CONTROL SYSTEM
1989 5.2L Engine

	Computer Part Number	
	4379484	4379682
Spark Advance Test @ 2000 rpm 16 in. Vacuum Including Basic Timing	46° ± 4°	46° ± 4°
Electronic EGR	40 sec.	40 sec.
Electronic Throttle Control	535 sec. cold 120 sec. after start hot 2 sec. off idle 1 sec. after throttle closes	535 sec. cold 120 sec. after start hot 2 sec. off idle 1 sec. after throttle closes
Detonation Suppression	Yes	Yes
O₂ Feedback Air Switching (Electronic)	Yes	Yes
Charge Temperature Sensor	5226374	5226374

	Computer Part Number	
	4379226	4379228
Engine Application	318-4 Federal, California, Canada (A)	318-4 Federal, California, Canada (A)
Basic Timing*	16° BTDC	16° BTDC
Curb Idle Speed ▲	750	750
Spark Advance Test @ 2000 rpm 16 in. Vacuum Including Basic Timing	38° ± 4°	38° ± 4°
Electronic EGR	40 sec.	40 sec.
Electronic Throttle Control	200 sec. after start hot 3 sec. off idle 1 sec. after throttle closes	200 sec. after start hot 3 sec. off idle 1 sec. after throttle closes
Detonation Suppression	Yes	Yes
O₂ Feedback Air Switching (Electronic)	Yes	Yes
Temperature Sensor	Sensor	Sensor

Should the listed specifications differ from those on the Emission Control Information Label, use the specifications on the label
(A)—Automatic Transmission
BTDC Before Top Dead Center
▲ Curb Idle rpm ± 100 rpm—Curb Idle set with vacuum line connected.
*Basic Timing Set With Vacuum Line Disconnected. Do not readjust curb idle.

FORD MOTOR COMPANY
SOLID STATE IGNITION SYSTEMS

General Information

There are 5 basic electronic ignition systems are being used in the Ford Motor Company vehicles.
1. Dura Spark II
2. TFI-I and TFI-IV (Thick Film Integrated)
3. Festiva and Tracer Electronic Ignition
4. Probe Electronic Ignition
5. Distributorless Ignition System (DIS)

Diagnosis of Electronic Ignition Systems

Many times a quick test can locate the cause of a problem without going into full system checkout. Included are tests which may isolate the cause of the problem. The first step is to verify that a problem exists and then to make some preliminary tests to determine if the problem is in the ignition system, a related

FORD MOTOR COMPANY ENGINE CONTROLS SYSTEMS, IGNITION SYSTEMS AND FUEL SYSTEMS
1986 Passenger Cars—50 States & Canada

Engine	Vehicle Application	Ignition System	Electronic Engine Control	Fuel System Mfg.	Fuel System Type
1.9L	Escort, Lynx, EXP	TFI-I	None	Holley	740-2V Carburetor
		TFI-IV	EEC-IV	Bosch/Ford	EFI
2.3L OHC	Mustang, Capri, LTD, Marquis	TFI-IV	EEC-IV	Carter	YFA-1V, FBC Carb.
2.3L OHC Turbo	Thunderbird, Cougar, S.V.O., Mustang, Merkur	TFI-IV	EEC-IV	Bosch/Ford	EFI
2.3L HSC 50 States	Tempo, Topaz	TFI-IV	EEC-IV	Ford	CFI
2.3L HSC Canada	Tempo, Topaz	DS-II	None	Holley	1949-IV
2.5L HSC	Taurus, Sable	TFI-IV	EEC-IV	Ford	CFI
3.0L	Taurus, Sable	TFI-IV	EEC-IV	Bosch/Ford	EFI
3.8L 50 States	Thunderbird, Cougar, LTD, Marquis, Mustang, Capri Mustang, Capri (Canada)	TFI-IV	EEC-IV	Ford	CFI
3.8L Canada	Thunderbird, Cougar, LTD, Marquis	DS-II	None	Ford	2150A-2V NFB Carburetor
5.0L	Continental, Mark VII, Thunderbird, Cougar	TFI-IV	EEC-IV	—	SEFI
	Ford, Mercury, Lincoln	TFI-IV	EEC-IV	—	SEFI
5.0L HO	Mustang, Capri Mark VII	TFI-IV	EEC-IV	—	SEFI
5.8L	Ford/ Mercury (Police) Canada Trailer Tow	UIC	MCU	Ford	7200-VV FBC Carburetor

S.V.O.—Special Vehicle Operation
EEC-IV—Electronic Engine Control (System IV)
FBC—Feedback Carburetor
EFI—Electronic Fuel Injection
MCU—Microprocessor Control Unit
M/T—Manual Transmission
A/T—Automatic Transmission
Mfg.—Manufacturer
DS-II—Duraspark II
TFI—Thick Integrated Film

UIC—Universal Integrated Circuit
HO—High Output
ATX—Automatic Transaxle
MTX—Manual Transaxle
NFB—Non-Feedback Carburetor
SEFI—Sequential Feedback Carburetor
OHC—Overhead Cam
HSC—High Swirl Combustion
CFI—Central Fuel Injection

FORD MOTOR COMPANY ENGINE CONTROLS SYSTEMS, IGNITION SYSTEMS AND FUEL SYSTEMS
1987 Passenger Cars—50 States & Canada

Engine	Vehicle Application	Ignition System	Electronic Engine Control	Fuel System Mfg.	Fuel System Type
1.9L	Escort, Lynx, EXP	TFI-IV	EEC-IV	Ford	CFI
		TFI-IV	EEC-IV	Bosch/Ford	EFI
2.3L OHC	Mustang	TFI-IV	EEC-IV	Bosch/Ford	EFI
2.3L OHC Turbo	Thunderbird, Merkur	TFI-IV	EEC-IV	Bosch/Ford	EFI
2.3L HSC 50 States	Tempo, Topaz	TFI-IV	EEC-IV	Ford	CFI
2.3L HSC Canada	Tempo, Topaz	DS-II	None	Holley	1949-IV
2.3L HSC Canada	Tempo, Topaz	TFI-IV	EEC-IV	Ford	CFI
2.5L HSC	Taurus, Sable	TFI-IV	EEC-IV	Ford	CFI
3.0L	Taurus, Sable	TFI-IV	EEC-IV	Bosch/Ford	EFI
3.8L 50 States	Thunderbird, Cougar,	TFI-IV	EEC-IV	Ford	CFI
3.8L	Thunderbird, Cougar, Taurus (Police)	TFI-N	EEC-IV	Ford	EFI
5.0L	Continental, Mark VII, Thunderbird, Cougar	TFI-IV	EEC-IV	—	SEFI
	Ford, Mercury, Lincoln	TFI-IV	EEC-IV	—	SEFI
5.0L HO	Mustang, Capri Mark VII	TFI-IV	EEC-IV	—	SEFI
5.8L	Ford/ Mercury (Police) Canada	UIC	MCU	Ford	7200-VV FBC Carburetor

EEC-IV—Electronic Engine Control (System IV)
FBC—Feedback Carburetor
EFI—Electronic Fuel Injection
MCU—Microprocessor Control Unit
Mfg.—Manufacturer
DS-II—Duraspark II
TFI—Thick Integrated Film

UIC—Universal Integrated Circuit
HO—High Output
SEFI—Sequential Feedback Carburetor
OHC—Overhead Cam
HSC—High Swirl Combustion
CFI—Central Fuel Injection

FORD MOTOR COMPANY ENGINE CONTROLS SYSTEMS, IGNITION SYSTEMS AND FUEL SYSTEMS
1988 Passenger Cars—50 States & Canada

Engine	Vehicle Application	Ignition System	Electronic Engine Control	Fuel System Mfg.	Fuel System Type
1.9L	Escort	TFI-IV	EEC-IV	Ford	CFI
		TFI-IV	EEC-IV	Bosch/Ford	EFI
2.3L OHC	Mustang	TFI-IV	EEC-IV	Bosch/Ford	EFI
2.3L OHC Turbo	Thunderbird, Merkur	TFI-IV	EEC-IV	Bosch/Ford	EFI

FORD MOTOR COMPANY ENGINE CONTROLS SYSTEMS, IGNITION SYSTEMS AND FUEL SYSTEMS
1988 Passenger Cars—50 States & Canada

Engine	Vehicle Application	Ignition System	Electronic Engine Control	Fuel System Mfg.	Fuel System Type
2.3L HSC 50 States	Tempo, Topaz	TFI-IV	EEC-IV	Bosch/Ford	EFI
2.3L HSC Plus	Tempo, Topaz	TFI-IV	EEC-IV	Bosch/Ford	EFI
2.3L HSC Canada	Tempo, Topaz	TFI-IV	EEC-IV	Ford	CFI
2.5L HSC	Taurus, Sable	TFI-IV	EEC-IV	Ford	CFI
3.0L	Taurus, Sable	TFI-IV	EEC-IV	Bosch/Ford	EFI
3.8L 50 States	Thunderbird, Cougar, LTD, Marquis, Mustang, Capri, Continental	TFI-IV	EEC-IV	Bosch/Ford	EFI
3.8L Canada	Thunderbird, Cougar, LTD, Marquis	DS-II	None	Ford	2150A-2V NFB Carburetor
5.0L	Mark VII, Thunderbird, Cougar	TFI-IV	EEC-IV	—	SEFI
	Ford, Mercury, Mustang, Town Car	TFI-IV	EEC-IV	—	SEFI
5.0L HO	Mustang, Mark VII	TFI-IV	EEC-IV	—	SEFI
5.8L	Ford/ Mercury (Police) Canada	UIC	MCU	Ford	7200-VV FBC Carburetor

EEC-IV—Electronic Engine Control (System IV)
FBC—Feedback Carburetor
EFI—Electronic Fuel Injection
MCU—Microprocessor Control Unit
Mfg.—Manufacturer
DS-II—Duraspark II
TFI—Thick Integrated Film

UIC—Universal Integrated Circuit
HO—High Output
SEFI—Sequential Feedback Carburetor
OHC—Overhead Cam
HSC—High Swirl Combustion
CFI—Central Fuel Injection

FORD MOTOR COMPANY ENGINE CONTROLS SYSTEMS, IGNITION SYSTEMS AND FUEL SYSTEMS
1989-90 Passenger Cars—50 States & Canada

Engine	Vehicle Application	Ignition System	Electronic Engine Control	Fuel System Mfg.	Fuel System Type
1.9L	Escort	TFI-IV	EEC-IV	Ford	CFI
1.9L HO	Escort	TFI-IV	EEC-IV	Bosch/Ford	EFI
2.3L OHC	Mustang	TFI-IV	EEC-IV	Bosch/Ford	EFI
2.3L OHC Turbo	Merkur	TFI-IV	EEC-IV	Bosch/Ford	EFI
2.3L HSC 50 States	Tempo, Topaz	TFI-IV	EEC-IV	Bosch/Ford	EFI
2.3L HSC Plus	Tempo, Topaz	TFI-IV	EEC-IV	Bosch/Ford	EFI
2.3L HSC Canada	Tempo, Topaz	TFI-IV	EEC-IV	Ford	CFI

FORD MOTOR COMPANY ENGINE CONTROLS SYSTEMS, IGNITION SYSTEMS AND FUEL SYSTEMS
1989–90 Passenger Cars—50 States & Canada

Engine	Vehicle Application	Ignition System	Electronic Engine Control	Fuel System Mfg.	Type
2.5L HSC	Taurus	TFI-IV	EEC-IV	Ford	CFI
3.0L	Taurus	TFI-IV	EEC-IV	Bosch/Ford	EFI
3.0L SHO	Taurus, Sable	DIS	EEC-IV	—	SEFI-MA
3.8L SC	Thunderbird, Cougar	DIS	EEC-IV	—	SEFI-MA
3.8L	Thunderbird, Cougar Continental Taurus, Sable	TFI-IV/ CBD	EEC-IV	—	SEFI
5.0L	Crown Victoria, Grand Marquis, Ford Police, Town Car	TFI-IV	EEC-IV	—	SEFI
5.0L HO	Mustang	TFI-IV	EEC-IV	—	SEFI-MA
	Mark VII	TFI-IV	EEC-IV	—	SEFI
5.8L	Crown Victoria Grand Marquis (Canada) Ford Police	DS II	MCU	Ford	7200 VV, FBC

EEC-IV Electronic Engine Control (System IV)
FBC Feedback Carburetor
EFI Electronic Fuel Injection
MCU Microprocessor Control Unit
Mfg. Manufacturer
DS-II Duraspark II
TFI Thick Integrated Film
DIS Distributorless Ignition System

MA Mass Air
CBD Closed Bowl Distributor
UIC Universal Integrated Circuit
HO High Output
SEFI Sequential Feedback Carburetor
OHC Overhead Cam
HSC High Swirl Combustion
CFI Central Fuel Injection

system or a completely unrelated system. The following procedures are intended to provide tests to identify and locate some of the more frequently encountered problems.

Intermittant faults may be the result of corroded terminals, cracked or broken wires, voltage leakage, heat related failures, etc. Verify the mode of the ignition system and engine when the malfunction occurs and relate to this mode for failure indications. (examples = engine hot or cold, acceleration or deceleration, etc).

PRELIMINARY CHECKS

NOTE: Turn ignition key OFF, before disconnecting any wiring on a computer controlled ignition system.

1. Check battery for state of charge and for clean, tight battery terminal connections.
2. Inspect all wires and connectors for breaks, cuts, abrasions or burned spots. Repair or replace as necessary. Make sure all wires are connected correctly.
3. Unplug all connectors and inspect for corroded or burned contacts. Repair as necessary and plug connectors back together. Do not remove the lubricant compound in connectors.
4. Check for loose or damaged spark plug or coil wires. If boots or nipples are removed on 8mm ignition wires, reline inside of each with new silicone dielectric compound.

SPARK PLUG WIRE RESISTANCE

Testing

1. Remove the distributor cap from the distributor assembly.
2. Inspect the spark plug wires to insure that they are firmly seated on the distributor cap.
3. Disconnect the spark plug wire(s) thought to be defective at the spark plug.
4. Using an ohmmeter, measure the resistance between the distributor cap terminal and the spark plug terminal.

NOTE: Make certain that a good connection is made between the distributor cap and the spark terminal. Never, under any circumstances, measure resistance by puncturing the spark plug wire.

5. If the measured resistance is less than 7000 ohms per foot of wire, the wire is good. If the measured resistance is greater than 7000 ohms per foot, the wire is defective and should be replaced.

NOTE: The following outline is a general explanation of the electronic ignition systems and the tests that can be performed when the engine will not start, should the fault be determined to be in the electronic ignition system of the Dura Spark II, TFI-I or TFI-IV systems.

DURA SPARK II SYSTEM

The Dura Spark II ignition system consists of the typical electronic primary and conventional secondary circuits, designed to carry higher voltages. The primary and secondary circuits consists of the following components:

PRIMARY CIRCUIT

Battery
Ignition switch
Ballast resistor start bypass (wire)
Ignition coil primary winding
Ignition module
Distributor stator assembly.

SECONDARY CIRCUIT

Battery
Ignition coil secondary winding
Distributor rotor
Distributor cap
Ignition wires
Spark plugs.

Operation

With the ignition switch in the **RUN** position, the primary circuit current is directed from the battery, through the ignition switch, the ballast resistor, the ignition coil (in the positive side, out the negative side), the ignition module and back to the battery through the ignition system ground in the distributor. This current flow causes a magnetic field to be built up in the ignition coil. When the poles on the armature and the stator assembly align, the ignition module turns the primary current flow off, collapsing the magnetic field in the ignition coil. The collapsing field induces a high voltage in the ignition coil secondary windings. The ignition coil wire then conducts the high voltage to the distributor where the cap and rotor distributes it to the appropriate spark plug.

A timing device in the ignition module turns the primary current back on after a very short period of time. High voltage is produced each time the magnetic field is built up and collapsed.

The Dura Spark II system has had several versions of control modules since its conception. They are as follows:

1. The dual mode module.
2. The universal ignition module.

DUAL MODE, CRANKING RETARD AND UNIVERSAL IGNITION MODULES

The dual mode and the universal ignition module are still being used with the Dura Spark II system, with continual updating from year to year, as required.

The dual mode ignition control module is equipped with an altitude sensor, an economy modulator, or pressure switches (turbocharged engines only). This module, when combined with the additional switches and sensor, varies the base engine timing according to altitude and engine load conditions. The dual mode ignition control modules use 3 wiring harness connectors.

Both ignition modules perform the function of turning off current flow through the ignition coil in response to a control signal. In the Dura Spark II ignition system, this signal comes from the distributor stator assembly. Additionally, the universal ignition module (UIM) can respond to another control signal from either an ignition barometeric pressure switch or the microprocessor control unit (MCU), depending upon the engine's calibration. In responding to this second control signal, the UIM provides additional spark timing control for certain operating conditions by turning off the ignition coil current flow at a different time than what would happen from just the distributor signal.

The universal ignition module has a programmable run/retard feature in a smaller, more compact module. This programmable run/retard function can be programmed as a step change by an external programming switch/resistor combination for altitude and some economy calibrations or as a variable controlled element in the closed loop system, such as with the spark control mode system. The switch/resistor combinations change resistance inside the module to determine the amount of compensation the module will make.

CENTRIFUGAL SPARK ADVANCE MECHANISM

The movement of the centrifugal weights change the initial relationship of the armature to the stator assembly ahead of its static position on the distributor shaft. This results in spark advance. The rate of movement of the centrifugal weights is controlled by calibrated springs.

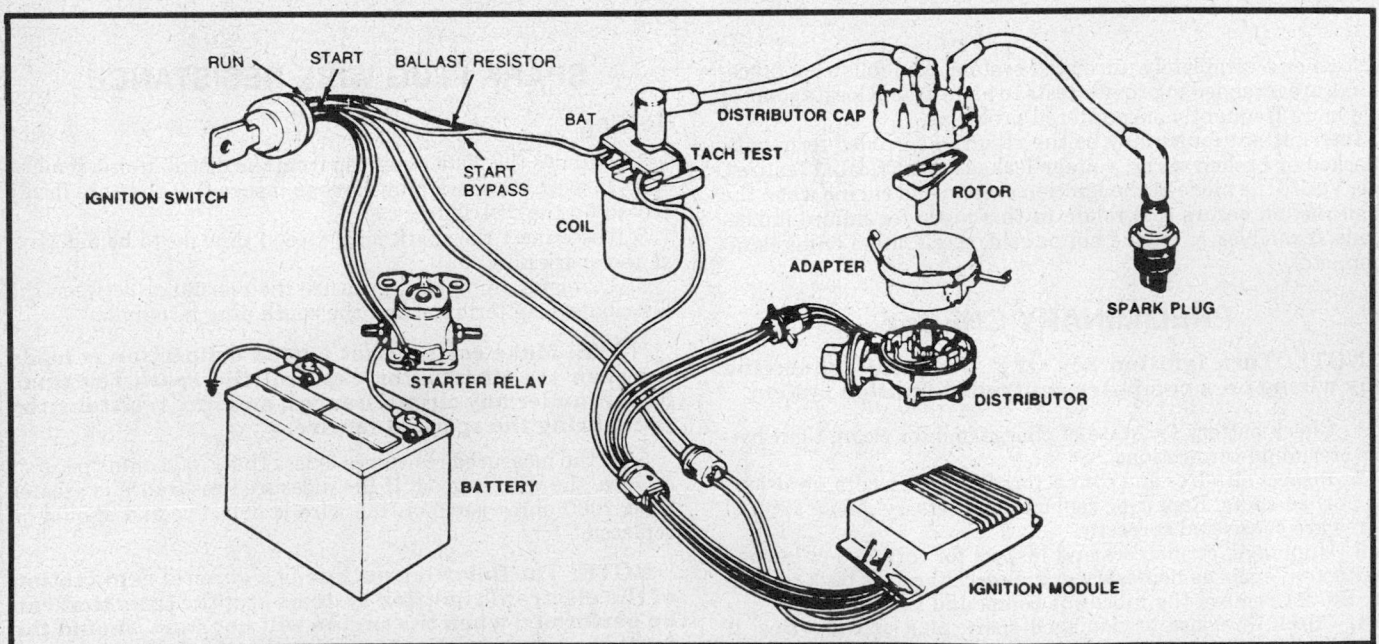

Dura Spark II component arrangement

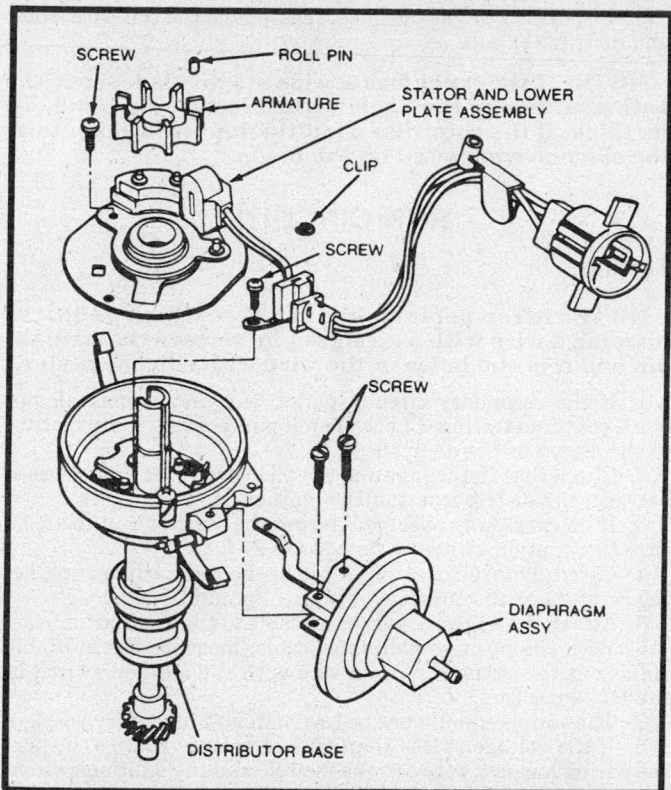

Exploded view of V8 Dura Spark II distributor

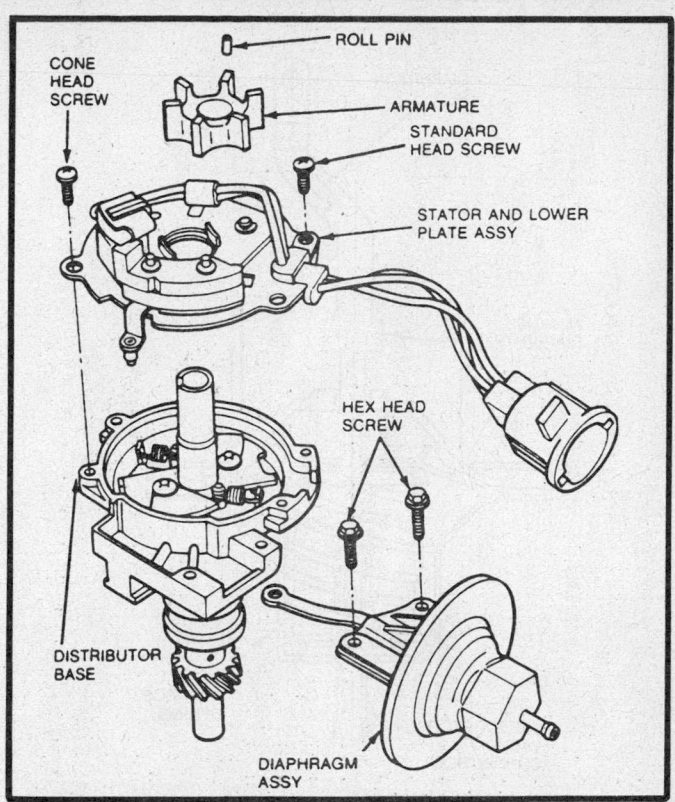

Exploded view of V6 Dura Spark II distributor

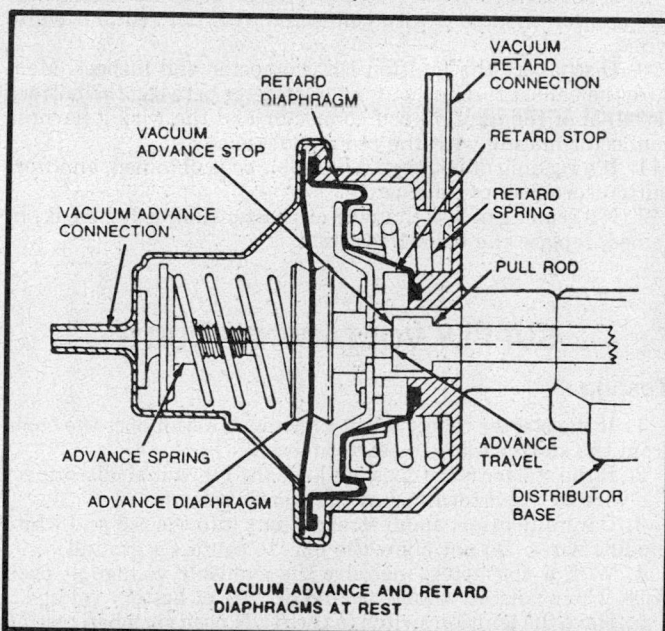

Cross section of dual diaphragm vacuum advance/retard assembly

VACUUM SPARK ADVANCE

The vacuum advance is controlled by either a single diaphragm or a dual diaphragm assembly, the use of which is controlled by engine operating and emission calibrations. The dual vacuum advance unit is an advance/retard unit. It should be noted that vacuum applied to the advance port of the assembly overrides any spark retard caused by the application of vacuum to the retard port.

NOTE:The Dura Spark II coil is energized when the ignition switch is in the ON position. When servicing the Dura Spark II system, the ignition system could inadvertently "fire" while performing ignition system services (such as distributor cap removal or rotor movement) if the ignition is in the ON position.

Adjustment

The ignition system adjustments are limited to initial timing and spark plug gap. Refer to the Vehicle Emission Information label for initial timing and spark plug specifications.

DISTRIBUTOR AND MODULE START CIRCUITS

Testing

NOTE: When testing circuits with a voltmeter, ensure that a good ground circuit exists between the distributor and the engine block or an erroneous reading could occur.

1. Remove distributor cap and rotor from distributor.
2. Crank engine to align a tooth of armature with magnet in pick-up coil (ignition **OFF**).
3. Remove coil wire from distributor cap, install a modified spark tester in the coil wire terminal and ground the spark tester shell against the engine block.
4. Turn the ignition switch to **START** and crank the engine. There should be a spark at the spark tester.
5. If there is a spark, the primary circuit is okay in the cranking mode.
6. Turn the ignition switch from the **OFF** to **RUN** to **OFF** positions several times.
7. Spark should occur each time the ignition switch goes from the **RUN** position to the **OFF** position.

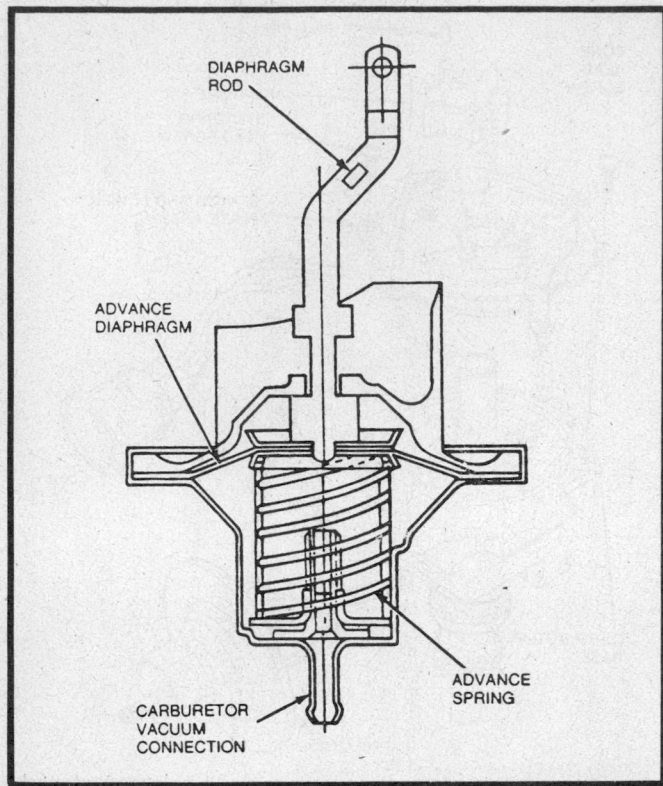

Cross section of single diaphragm vacuum advance assembly

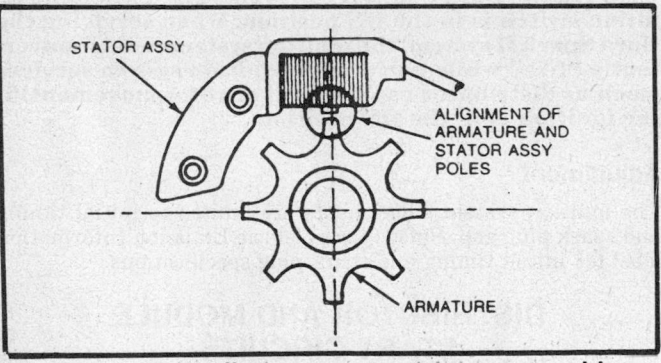

Alignment of distributor armature/stator assembly

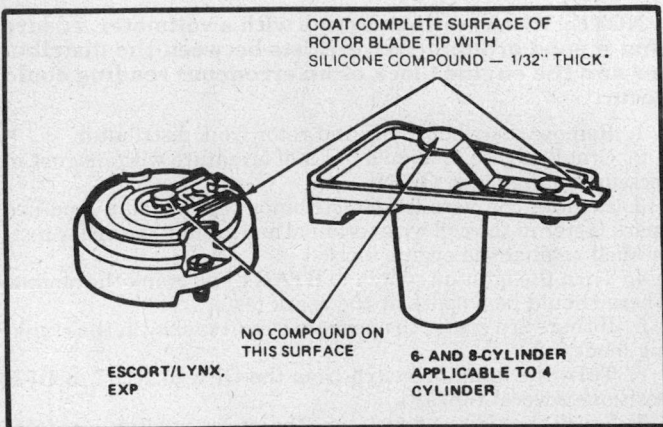

Coating of single blade rotor with silicone compound

8. If spark occurs as outlined, reassemble the coil wire, rotor and distributor cap.

NOTE: If the rotor has a wide single blade, coat the entire surface of the blade with silicone compound, ¹/₃₂ in. thick. If the rotor has a multipoint blade, do not use the silicone compound on the blade.

RUN CIRCUITS

Testing

NOTE: After performing any test which requires piercing a wire with a straight pin, remove the straight pin and seal the holes in the wire with silicone sealer.

1. If the secondary circuit sparks, but the engine will not start, continue testing. Check for roll pin securing the armature to the sleeve in the distributor.
2. Check that the orange and the purple wires are not crossed between the distributor and the ignition module.
3. If no spark was observed during the start or run tests, be sure the ignition switch is turned **OFF**.
4. Carefully insert a straight pin in the red module wire, being careful not to contact an electrical ground.
5. Attach the negative voltmeter cable to the distributor base.
6. With the positive voltmeter cable, measure the available voltage at the straight pin/red wire with the ignition switch in the **RUN** position.
7. The voltage should not be less than 90% of battery voltage.
8. If the voltage is less than 90% of battery voltage, inspect the wiring harness between the module and the ignition switch. Inspect the ignition switch for being worn or defective.
9. If the voltage is within the OK range, separate and inspect the ignition module 2-wire connector with the red and white wires.
10. Disconnect the ignition coil connector and inspect. Measure the ballast resistor with an ohmmeter between the battery terminal of the ignition coil connector and the wiring harness connector mating with the red module wire.
11. If a reading of between 0.8–1.6 ohms is obtained, an intermittent problem could exist.
12. If a reading of less than 0.8 or greater than 1.6 ohms is obtained, replace the ballast resistor

SUPPLY VOLTAGE CIRCUITS

Testing

1. If the starter relay has an **I** terminal, disconnect the cable from the starter relay to starter motor.
2. If the starter relay does not have the **I** terminal, disconnect the wire to the **S** terminal of the starter relay.
3. Carefully insert small straight pins into the red and white module wires. Do not allow the pins to contact a ground.
4. With a voltmeter, measure the available voltage at each wire. The available voltage should be 90% of battery voltage.
5. Have the ignition switch in the **RUN** position when testing the voltage at the red wire.
6. Have the ignition switch in the **START** position when testing the white wire and the **BAT** terminal of the ignition coil.
7. While the voltmeter is attached to each circuit, wiggle each wire in the wiring harness while observing the voltmeter scale.
8. If the available voltage is less than 90% of battery voltage, inspect the wiring harness and connectors in the faulty circuits. Check for a defective or worn ignition switch.

NOTE: If the circuits and connections are good, check the radio interference capacitor mounted on the ignition coil.

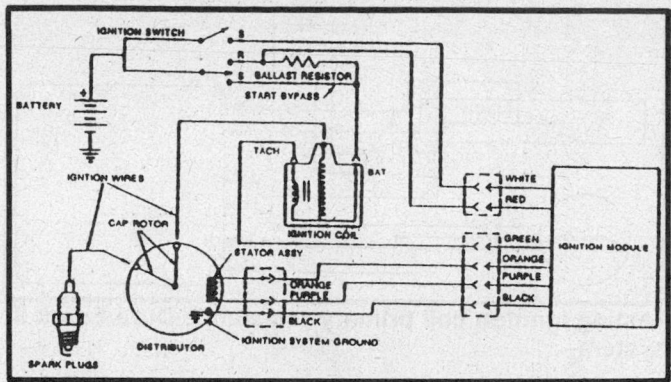

Wiring schematic of Dura Spark II Electronic Ignition system

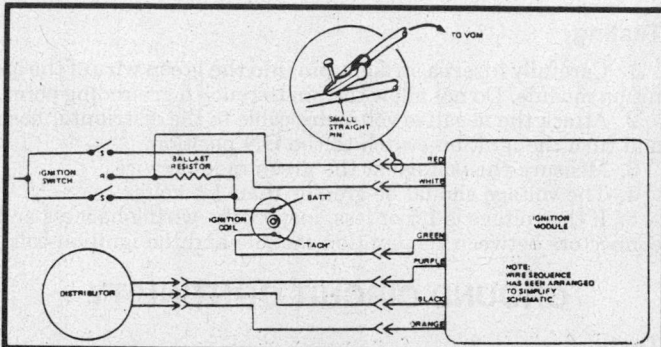

Testing module voltage-Dura Spark II system

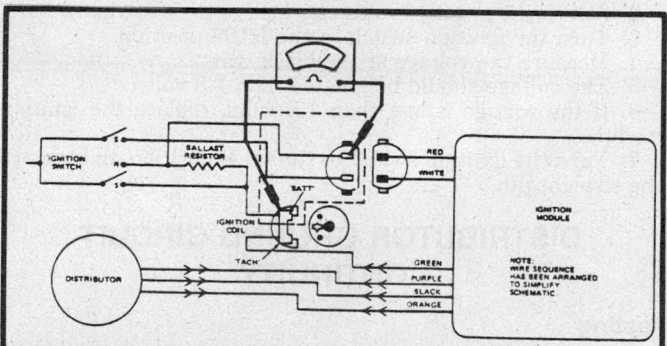

Testing ballast resistor-Dura Spark II system

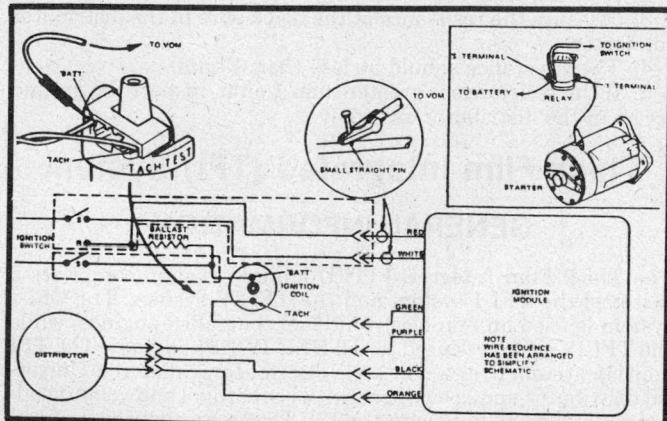

Testing Dura Spark II voltage supply circuits

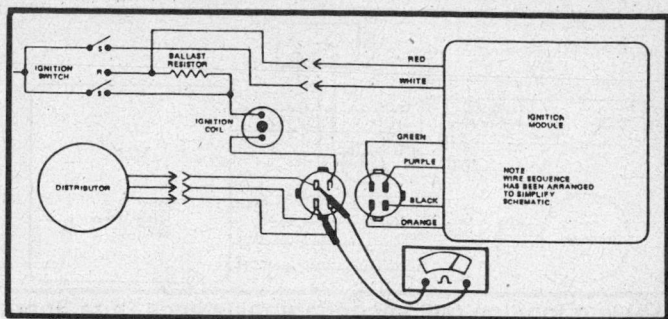

Testing Dura Spark II distributor stator assembly and wiring harness

9. Turn the ignition switch to the **OFF** position, remove the straight pins and reconnect any disconnected cables.

IGNITION COIL SUPPLY VOLTAGE

Testing

1. Attach the negative lead of the voltmeter to the distributor base.
2. Turn the ignition switch to the **RUN** position.
3. Measure the voltage at the **BAT** terminal of the ignition coil.
4. The voltage should be 6–8 volts. If less than 6 volts or more than 8 volts, test the ignition coil.
5. Turn the ignition switch to the **OFF** position.

DISTRIBUTOR STATOR ASSEMBLY AND WIRING HARNESS

Testing

1. Separate the ignition module 4-wire connector. Examine it for dirt, corrosion and damage.
2. Measure the stator assembly and wiring harness resistance between the wiring harness terminals mating with the orange and purple module wires.
3. The resistance should be 400–1300 ohms. Wiggle the wires in the wiring harness when taking the resistance reading.
4. If the reading is less than 400 ohms or greater than 1300 ohms, test the distributor stator assembly.

IGNITION MODULE TO DISTRIBUTOR STATOR ASSEMBLY WIRING HARNESS

Testing

1. Attach a lead of the ohmmeter to the distributor base.
2. Alternately measure the resistance between the wiring harness terminals mating with the orange and purple module wires and ground.
3. The resistance reading should be greater than 70,000 ohms.
4. If the resistance reading is less than 70,000 ohms, inspect the wiring harness between the module connector and distributor, including the distributor grommet.

IGNITION COIL SECONDARY RESISTANCE

Testing

1. Disconnect and inspect the ignition coil connector and the coil wire.
2. Measure the secondary resistance from the **BAT** terminal to the high voltage terminal.
3. The resistance should be 7700–10,500 ohms.

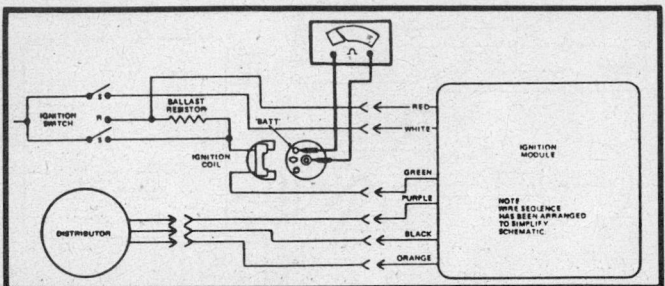

Testing ignition coil secondary resistance-Dura Spark II system

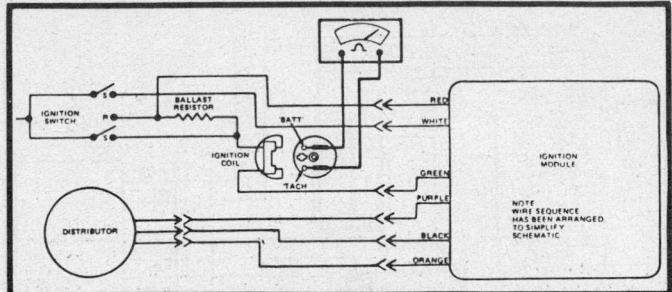

Testing ignition coil primary resistance-Dura Spark II system

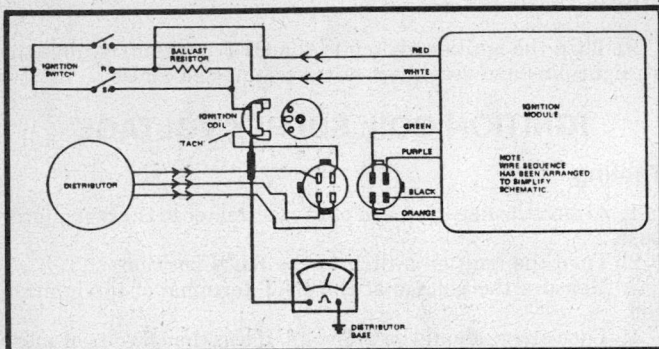

Testing module to ignition coil primary wire-Dura Spark II system

4. If the resistance reading is less than 7700 ohms or greater than 10,500 ohms, replace the ignition coil.

MODULE TO COIL WIRE

Testing

1. Separate and inspect the ignition module 4 wire connector and the ignition coil connector from the ignition coil.
2. Connect a lead of the ohmmeter to the distributor base.
3. Measure the resistance between the **TACH** terminal of the ignition coil connector and ground.
4. The resistance should be greater than 100 ohms.
5. If the resistance is less than 100 ohms, inspect the wiring harness between the ignition module and the ignition coil.

DISTRIBUTOR STATOR ASSEMBLY

Testing

1. Separate the distributor connector from the wiring harness. Inspect the connector for dirt, corrosion and damage.
2. Measure the stator assembly resistance across the orange and purple wires at the distributor connector.
3. The resistance should be 400–1000 ohms.
4. If the resistance is less than 400 ohms or greater than 1000 ohms, replace the stator assembly.
5. Reconnect the distributor and module connectors.

IGNITION COIL PRIMARY RESISTANCE

Testing

1. Disconnect the ignition coil connector.
2. Measure the primary resistance from the **BAT** to the **TACH** terminal.
3. The resistance should be 0.8–1.6 ohms.
4. If the resistance is less than 0.8 ohm or greater than 1.6 ohms, replace the ignition coil.

5. Reconnect the ignition coil connector.

PRIMARY CIRCUIT CONTINUITY

Testing

1. Carefully insert a straight pin into the green wire of the ignition module. Do not allow the pin to touch a grounding point.
2. Attach the negative voltmeter cable to the distributor base and turn the ignition switch to the **ON** position.
3. Measure the voltage at the green module wire.
4. The voltage should be greater than 1.5 volts.
5. If the voltage is 1.5 or less, inspect the wiring harness and connectors between the ignition module and the ignition coil.

GROUND CIRCUIT CONTINUITY

Testing

1. Carefully insert a straight pin in the module black wire.
2. Attach the negative voltmeter lead to the distributor base.
3. Turn the ignition switch to the **RUN** position.
4. Measure the voltage at the black wire.
5. The voltage should be greater than 1.5 volts.
6. If the voltage is less than 1.5 volts, replace the ignition module.
7. Turn the ignition switch to the **OFF** position and remove the straight pin.

DISTRIBUTOR GROUND CIRCUIT CONTINUITY

Testing

1. Separate the distributor connector from the harness. Inspect for dirt, corrosion and damage.
2. Attach a lead of the ohmmeter to the distributor base.
3. Measure the resistance at the black wire in the distributor connector.
4. The resistance should be less than 1 ohm.
5. If the resistance is greater than 1 ohm, inspect the ground screw in the distributor assembly.

Thick Film Integrated (TFI) System

GENERAL INFORMATION

The Thick Film Integrated (TFI) ignition system comprises 2 systems, the TFI-I system and the TFI-IV system. The TFI-I system is used on non-electronic fuel controlled engines, while the TFI-IV system is used for all EEC-IV/EFI engines. The TFI ignition system uses a new style distributor, called the Universal distributor and is equipped with centrifugal and vacuum advance units when used with the TFI-I system and no centrifugal and vacuum advance units when used with the TFI-IV system.

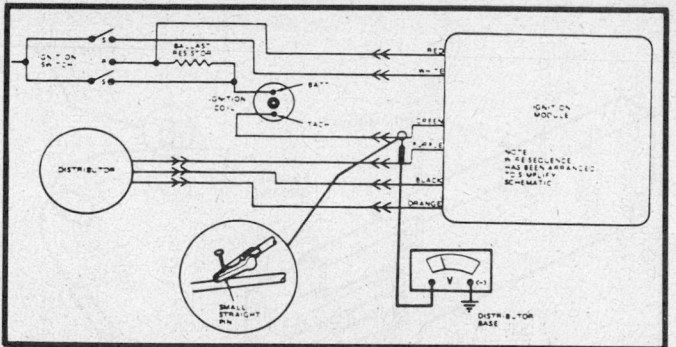

Testing Primary circuit continuity-Dura Spark II system

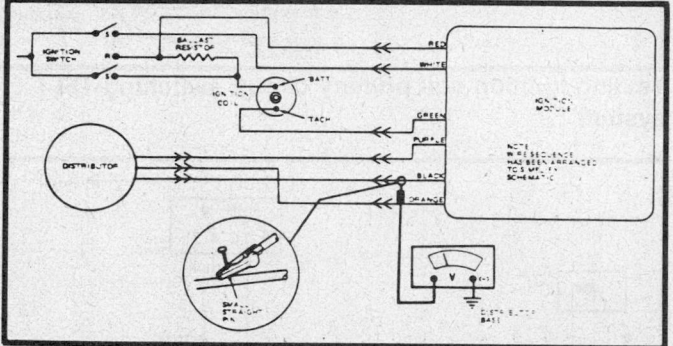

Testing ground circuit continuity-Dura Spark II system

It has a distributor base mounted TFI ignition module, which is self-contained in a moulded thermo-plastic unit. The TFI-I system module can be identified by having 3 pins, while the TFI-IV system module has 6 pins. Also, both TFI systems use an E-Core ignition coil, named after the shape of the laminations making up the core.

The universal distributor used with the TFI-IV system, contains a provision to change the basic distributor calibration with the use of a replaceable octane rod, from the standard of zero degrees to either 3 or 6 degree retard rods. No other calibration changes are possible or necessary.

NOTE: Do not change the ignition timing by the use of a different octane rod without having the proper authority to do so as Federal Emission requirements will be effected.

The TFI system was designed for use with non-EFI systems and is known as the TFI-I system. The second design is used for all EEC-IV/EFI systems and is known as the TFI-IV system.

TFI-I Ignition System

The basic operation of the distributor is the same as that of the Dura Spark system with the separate module. The rotating armature induces a signal in the stator assembly causing the ignition module to turn the ignition coil current on and off, generating the high voltage to fire the spark plugs.

The TFI-I distributor contains vacuum and centrifugal advance units

IGNITION COIL SECONDARY VOLTAGE

Testing

NOTE: After performing any test which requires piercing a wire with a straight pin, remove the straight pin and seal the holes in the wire with silicone sealer.

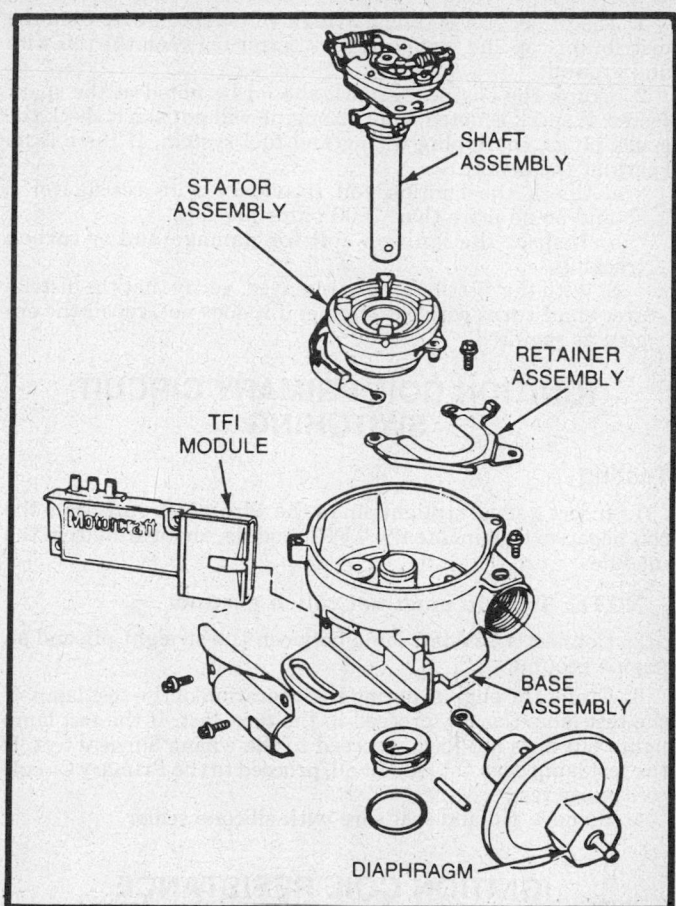

Exploded view of TFI-I Universal type distributor

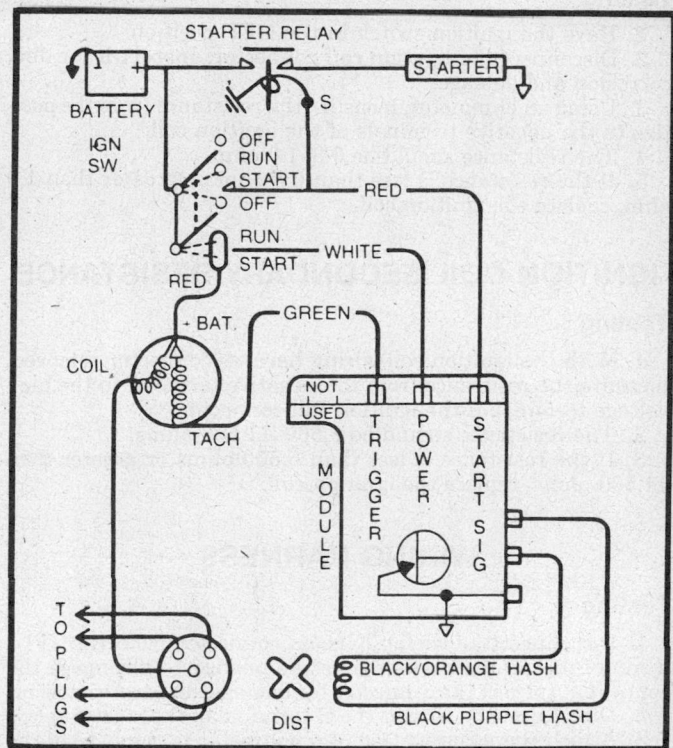

Typical electrical schematic for TFI-I Electronic Ignition system

1. Disconnect the secondary (high voltage) coil wire from the distributor cap and install a spark tester between the coil wire and ground.
2. Crank the engine. A spark should be noted at the spark tester. If spark is noted, but the engine will not start, check the spark plugs, spark plug wiring and fuel system. If there is no spark at the tester:
   a. Check the ignition coil secondary wire resistance; it should be no more than 7000 ohms per foot.
   b. Inspect the ignition coil for damage and/or carbon tracking.
   c. With the distributor cap removed, verify that the distributor shaft turns with the engine; if it does not, repair the engine as required.

IGNITION COIL PRIMARY CIRCUIT SWITCHING

Testing

1. Insert a small straight pin in the wire which runs from the coil negative terminal to the TFI-I module, about 1 in. from the module.

NOTE: The pin must not touch ground.

2. Connect a 12V test lamp between the straight pin and an engine ground.
3. Crank the engine, noting the operation of the test lamp. If the test lamp flashes, proceed to the next test. If the test lamp lights but does not flash, proceed to the wiring harness test. If the test lamp does not light at all, proceed to the Primary Circuit continuity test.
4. Remove pin and seal wire with silicone sealer.

IGNITION COIL RESISTANCE

Testing

1. Have the ignition switch in the **OFF** position.
2. Disconnect the ignition coil connector. Inspect it for dirt, corrosion and damage.
3. Using an ohmmeter, measure the resistance from the positive to the negative terminals of the ignition coil.
4. The resistance should be 0.3–1.0 ohm.
5. If the resistance is less than 0.3 ohm or greater than 1.0 ohm, replace the ignition coil.

IGNITION COIL SECONDARY RESISTANCE

Testing

1. With the ignition coil wiring harness connector removed, measure the resistance from the negative terminal to the high voltage terminal of the ignition coil connector.
2. The resistance should be 6,500–11,500 ohms.
3. If the resistance is less than 6,500 ohms or greater than 11,500 ohms, replace the ignition coil.

WIRING HARNESS

Testing

1. Disconnect the wiring harness connector from the TFI-I module; the connector tabs must be pushed to disengage the connector. Inspect the connector for damage, dirt and corrosion.
2. Disconnect the wire at the **S** terminal of the starter relay.
3. Attach the negative lead of a voltmeter to the base of the distributor. Attach the other voltmeter lead to a small straight pin and perform the follwoing:

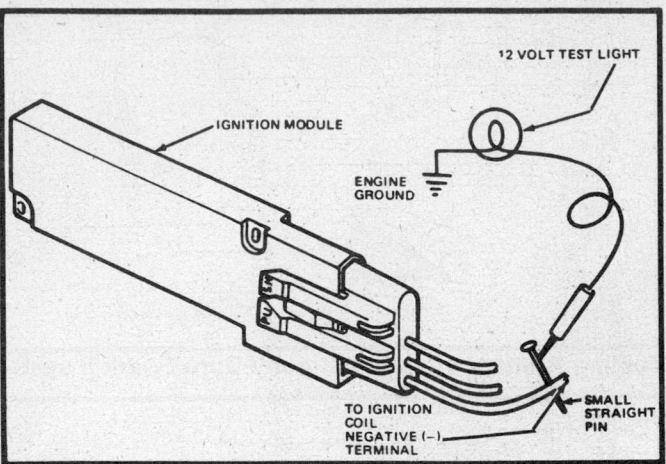

Testing ignition coil primary circuit switching-TFI-I system

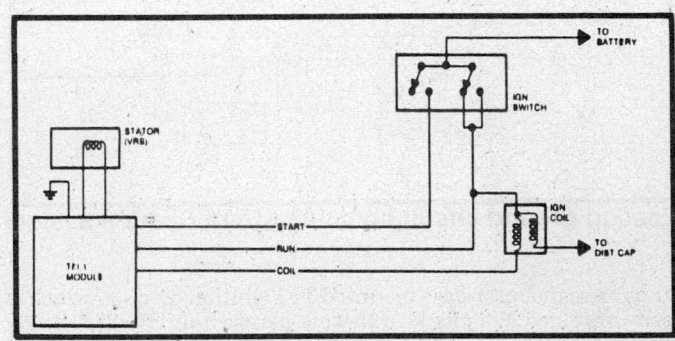

TFI-I system primary wire schematic for testing purposes

   a. With the ignition switch in the **RUN** position, insert the straight pin into the No. 1 terminal of the TFI-I module connector. Note the voltage reading, which should be 90% of battery voltage.
   b. With the ignition switch in the **RUN** position, move the straight pin to the No. 2 connector terminal. Again, note the voltage reading, which should be 90% of battery voltage.
   c. Move the straight pin to the No. 3 connector terminal, then turn the ignition switch to the **START** position. Note the voltage reading, which should be 90% of battery voltage.
4. If any reading is less than 90% of the battery voltage, inspect the wiring, connectors and/or ignition switch for defects.
5. Turn the ignition switch to the **OFF** position. Remove the straight pin and reconnect the wire at the starter relay.

STATOR ASSEMBLY AND MODULE

Testing

1. Remove the distributor.
2. Remove the TFI-I module from the distributor.
3. Inspect the distributor terminals, ground screw and stator wiring for damage. Repair as necessary.
4. Measure the resistance of the stator assembly, using an ohmmeter. If the ohmmeter reading is 650–1,300 ohms, the stator is okay, but the TFI-I module should be replaced. If the ohmmeter reading is less than 650 ohms or more than 1,300 ohms, the TFI-I module is okay, but the stator assembly should be replaced.
5. Reinstall the TFI-I module and the distributor.

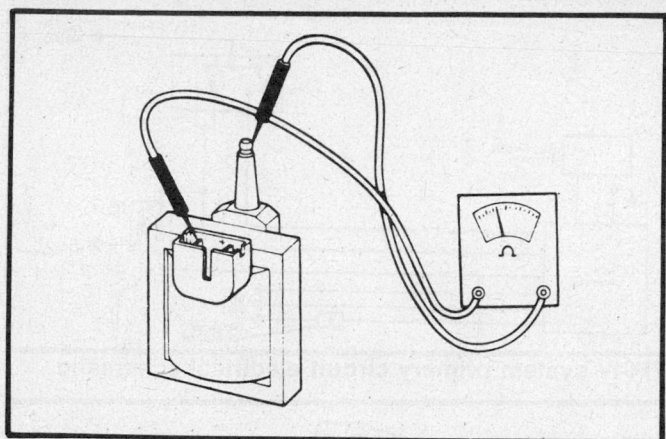

Testing ignition coil secondary resistance-TFI-I system

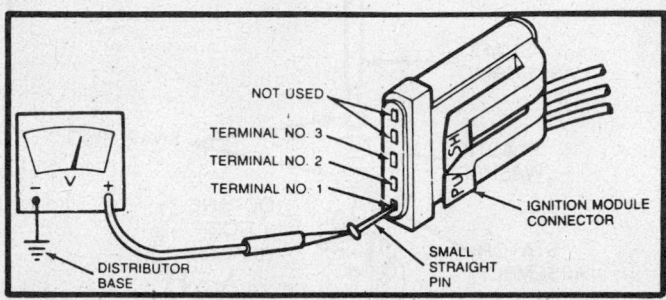

Testing wiring harness-TFI-I system

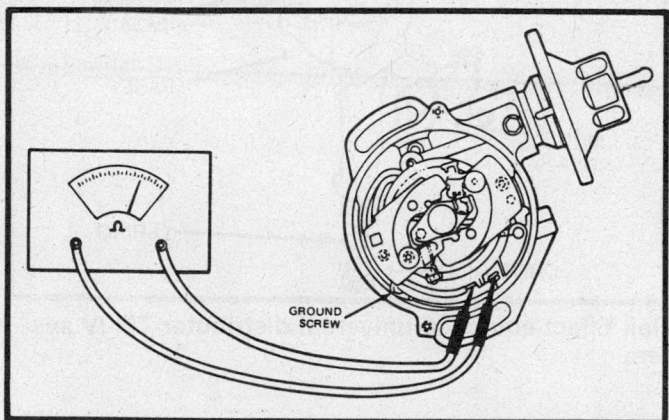

Testing module and stator assembly-TFI-I system

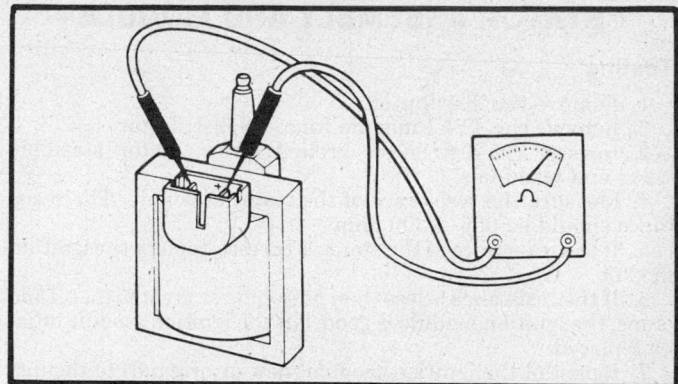

Testing ignition coil primary resistance-TFI-I system

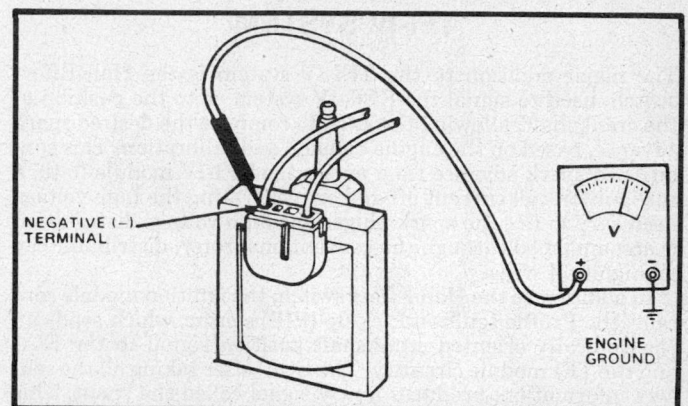

Testing ignition coil primary voltage-TFI-I system

PRIMARY CIRCUIT CONTINUITY

Testing

1. Separate the wiring harness from the ignition module by pushing the connector tabs to remove the connector.
2. Attach the negative voltmeter cable to the distributor base and measure the battery voltage.
3. Attach the positive voltmeter cable to a straight pin, inserted into the connector terminal No. 1.
4. Turn the ignition switch to the **RUN** position and measure the voltage at terminal No. 1.
5. The voltage should not be less then 90% of battery voltage.
6. If the voltage is less than 90% of battery voltage, proceed to the Ignition Coil Primary Voltage test.
7. Turn the ignition switch to the **OFF** position and remove the straight pin.

IGNITION COIL PRIMARY VOLTAGE

Testing

1. Attach the negative lead of a voltmeter to the distributor base and measure the battery voltage.
2. Turn the ignition switch to the **RUN** position and connect the positive voltmeter lead to the negative ignition coil terminal. Note the voltage reading and turn the ignition to the **OFF** position.
3. If the voltmeter reading is less than 90% of the available battery voltage, inspect the wiring between the ignition module and the negative coil terminal.

IGNITION COIL SUPPLY VOLTAGE

Testing

1. Attach the negative lead of a voltmeter to the distributor base.
2. Turn the ignition switch to the **ON** position and connect the positive voltmeter lead to the positive ignition coil terminal. Note the voltage reading, then turn the ignition to the **OFF** position.
3. If the voltage reading is at least 90% of the battery voltage, yet the engine will still not run; first, check the ignition coil connector and terminals for corrosion, dirt and/or damage; second, replace the ignition switch if the connectors and terminals are damaged or corroded.
4. If the voltage reading is less than 90% of battery voltage, inspect and repair as necessary, the wiring between the ignition coil and the ignition switch. Check for a worn or damaged ignition switch.
5. Reconnect the ignition module connector.

STATOR ASSEMBLY AND MODULE

Testing

1. Remove the distributor.
2. Remove the TFI-I module from the distributor.
3. Inspect the distributor ground screw, stator assembly wires and terminals.
4. Measure the resistance of the stator assembly. The resistance should be 650–1,300 ohms.
5. If the resistance of the stator is correct, replace the ignition module.
6. If the resistance is less than 650 ohms or greater than 1300 ohms, the ignition module is good, but the ignition module must be replaced.
7. Reinstall the ignition module (new or original) to the distributor and re-install the distributor in the engine.

TFI-IV SYSTEM

The major addition to the TFI-IV system is the Hall Effect switch, used to signal the EEC-IV system as to the position of the crankshaft, allowing the ECA to compute the desired spark advance, based on the engine demand and calibration. This conditioned spark advance then pulses the TFI-IV module to turn the ignition coil current off and on, generating the high voltage necessary to fire the spark plugs. The high voltage distribution is accomplished through the conventional rotor, distributor cap and ignition wires.

In addition to the Hall Effect switch, the ignition module contains the Profile Ignition Pick-up (PIP) sensor, which sends an electronically oriented crankshaft position signal to the ECA and the TFI module circuitry. The ECA, after taking all the sensors information, produces a new signal called the spout. This spout signal is then sent back to the TFI module for comparison with the PIP signal. The TFI-IV module then uses both of these signals to fire the ignition coil at the proper timing interval.

A modification to the circuitry allows for a push-start mode for manual transmission equipped vehicles.

The distributor has a die cast base which incorporates this integrally mounted TFI-IV ignition module and Hall effect stator assembly. No distributor calibration is required and initial timing adjustment is not normally required unless the distributor has been removed from the engine

The TFI-IV distributor contains no vacuum or centrifugal advance components, with all adjustment of timing and dwell adjusted electronically.

IGNITION COIL SECONDARY VOLTAGE

Testing

NOTE: After performing any test which requires piercing a wire with a straight pin, remove the straight pin and seal the holes in the wire with silicone sealer.

1. Disconnect the secondary (high voltage) coil wire from the distributor cap and install a spark tester between the coil wire and ground.
2. Crank the engine. A spark should be noted at the spark tester. If spark is noted, but the engine will not start, check the spark plugs, spark plug wiring and fuel system.
3. If there is no spark at the tester:
   a. Check the ignition coil secondary wire resistance; it should be no more than 7000 ohms per foot.
   b. Inspect the ignition coil for damage and/or carbon tracking.
   c. With the distributor cap removed, verify that the distributor shaft turns with the engine; if it does not, repair the engine as required.
   d. Be sure the rotor single blade is coated with silicone com-

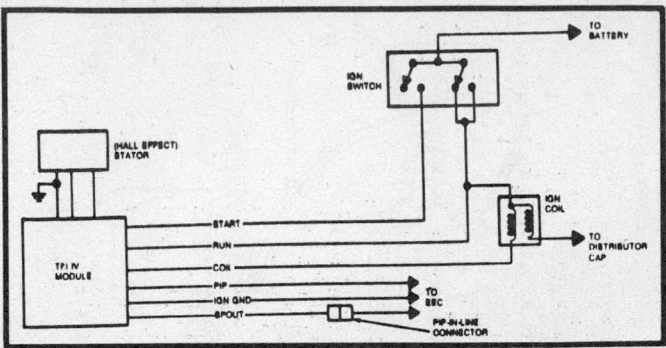

TFI-IV system primary circuit electrical schematic

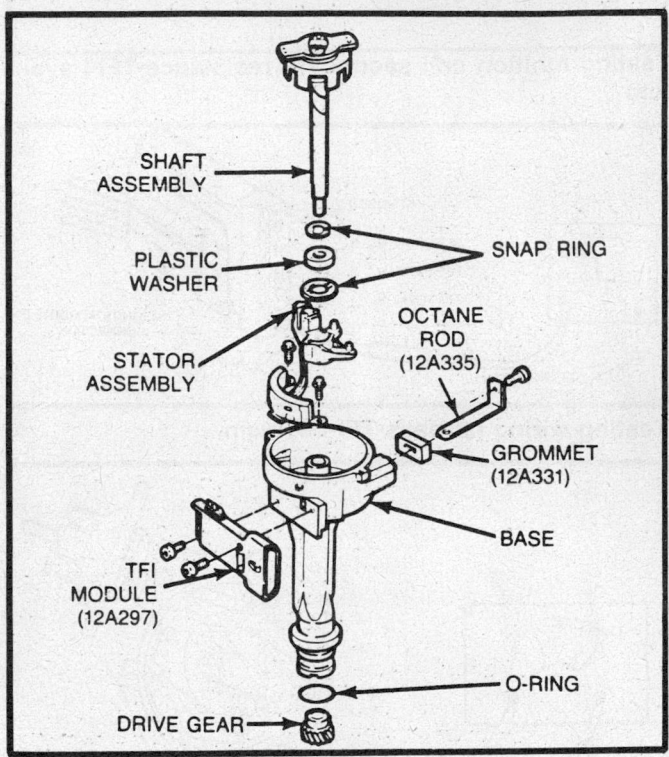

Hall Effect equipped universal distributor-TFI-IV system

pound, approximately $1/32$ in. thick. Do not coat the multipoint rotor.

IGNITION COIL PRIMARY CIRCUIT SWITCHING

Testing

1. Separate the wiring harness connector from the ignition module. Inspect for dirt, corrosion and damage. Re-connect the harness connector.
2. Attach a 12V test lamp between the ignition coil tach terminal and engine ground.
3. Crank the engine and observe the light.
4. If the lamp flashes or lights but will not flash, proceed to the ignition coil primary resistance test.
5. If the lamp does not light or is very dim, go to the primary circuit continuity test.

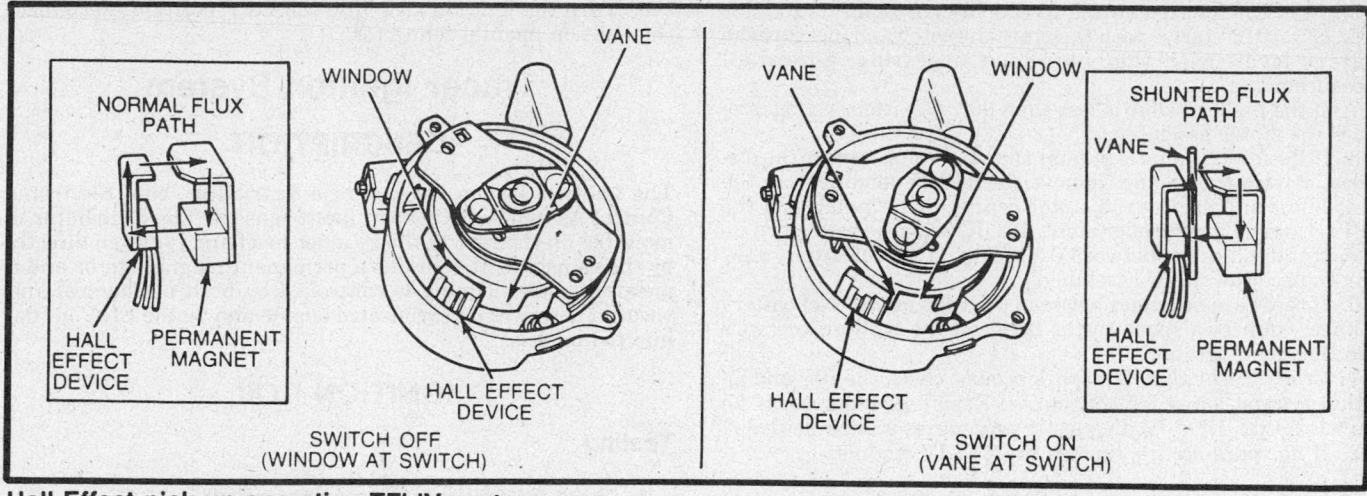

Hall Effect pick-up operation TFI-IV system

IGNITION COIL PRIMARY RESISTANCE

Testing

1. Have the ignition switch in the **OFF** position.
2. Disconnect the ignition coil connector. Inspect it for dirt, corrosion and damage.
3. Using an ohmmeter, measure the resistance from the positive to the negative terminals of the ignition coil.
4. The resistance should be 0.3–1.0 ohm.
5. If the resistance is less than 0.3 ohm or greater than 1.0 ohm, replace the ignition coil.

IGNITION COIL SECONDARY RESISTANCE

Testing

1. With the ignition coil wiring harness connector off, measure the resistance from the negative terminal to the high voltage terminal of the ignition coil connector.
2. The resistance should be 6,500–11,500 ohms.
3. If the resistance is less than 6,500 ohms or greater than 11,500 ohms, replace the ignition coil.

WIRING HARNESS

Testing

1. Disconnect the wiring harness connector from the TFI-IV module; the connector tabs must be pushed to disengage the connector. Inspect the connector for damage, dirt and corrosion.
2. Disconnect the wire at the **S** terminal of the starter relay.
3. Attach the negative lead of a voltmeter to the base of the distributor. Attach the other voltmeter lead to a small straight pin.
  a. With the ignition switch in the **RUN** position, insert the straight pin into the No. 2 terminal of the TFI-IV module connector. Note the voltage reading, which should be 90% of battery voltage.
  b. With the ignition switch in the **RUN** position, move the straight pin to the No. 3 connector terminal. Again, note the voltage reading, which should be 90% of battery voltage.
  c. Move the straight pin to the No. 4 connector terminal, then turn the ignition switch to the **START** position. Note the voltage reading, which should be 90% of battery voltage.
4. If any reading is less than 90% of the battery voltage, inspect the wiring, connectors and/or ignition switch for defects.
5. Turn the ignition switch to the **OFF** position. Remove the straight pin and reconnect the wire at the starter relay.

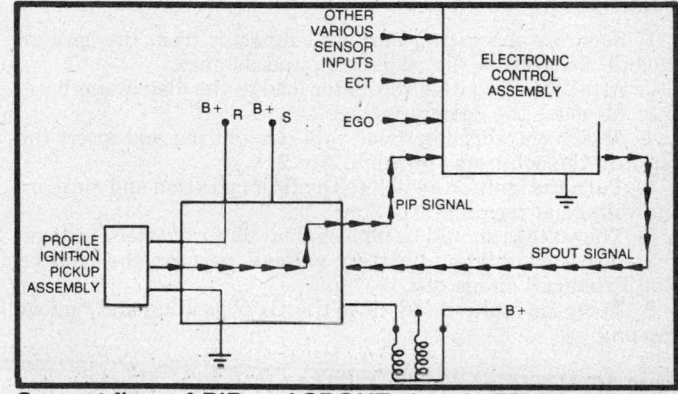

Current flow of PIP and SPOUT signals-TFI-IV system

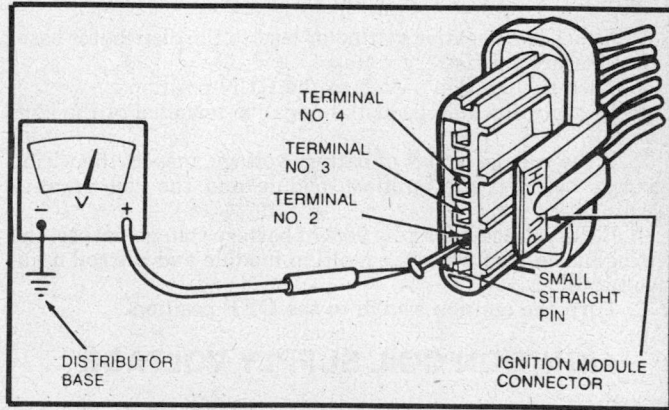

Testing wiring harness-TFI-IV system

STATOR

Testing

1. Turn the ignition switch to the **OFF** position.
2. Remove the coil wire and ground it.
3. Attach the negative voltmeter lead to the distributor base.
4. Disconnect the pin-in-line connector near the distributor and attach the positive voltmeter lead to the TFI-IV module side of the connector.

5. Turn the ignition switch to the **ON** position.

6. Bump the starter with the ignition switch and measure the voltage levels with the engine not operating. Record all measurements.

7. If the highest value is less than 90% of battery voltage, replace the stator assembly.

8. If the lowest value is greater than 0.5 volts, remove the distributor from the engine, remove the TFI-IV module from the distributor and inspect the stator connector terminals and the TFI terminals for misalignment. If OK, replace the stator.

9. If the values are between 0.5 volts and 90% of battery voltage, replace the stator assembly.

10. If there are no values between 0.5 volts and 90% of battery voltage, connect a spark tester between the ignition coil wire and the engine ground.

11. Crank the engine. If a spark occurs, check the PIP and ignition ground wires for continuity. Repair as required. If no fault is found, EEC-IV diagnostic procedures will be needed.

12. If no spark occurs, replace the TFI-IV module.

PRIMARY CIRCUIT CONTINUITY

Testing

1. Separate the wiring harness connector from the ignition module. Inspect for dirt, corrosion and damage.

2. Attach the negative voltmeter lead to the distributor base.

3. Measure the battery voltage.

4. Attach the voltmeter lead to a straight pin and insert the pin into the connector terminal No. 2.

5. Turn the ignition switch to the **RUN** position and measure the voltage at terminal No. 2.

6. The voltage should be no less than 90% of battery voltage.

7. If less than 90% of battery voltage, perform the Ignition Coil Primary Voltage test.

8. Turn the ignition switch to the **OFF** position and remove the pin.

IGNITION COIL PRIMARY VOLTAGE

Testing

1. Attach the negative voltmeter lead to the distributor base.

2. Measure the battery voltage.

3. Turn the ignition switch to the **RUN** position.

4. Measure the voltage at the negative terminal of the ignition coil.

5. If the voltage is 90% of battery voltage, inspect the wiring harness between the ignition module and the coil negative terminal.

6. If the voltage is less the 90% of battery voltage, inspect the wiring harness between the ignition module and the coil negative terminal.

7. Turn the ignition switch to the **OFF** position.

IGNITION COIL SUPPLY VOLTAGE

Testing

1. Remove the coil connector.

2. Attach the negative voltmeter lead to the distributor base.

3. Measure the battery voltage.

4. Turn the ignition switch to the **RUN** position.

5. Measure the voltage at the positive terminal of the ignition coil.

6. The voltage should be 90% of battery voltage. Inspect the ignition coil and connector for dirt, corrosion and damage. If required, replace the ignition coil.

7. If the voltage is less than 90% of battery voltage, inspect and repair, as required, the wiring between the ignition coil and the ignition switch. Check for a worn or damaged ignition switch.

8. Turn the ignition switch to the **OFF** position. Reconnect the ignition module connector.

Tracer Ignition System

DESCRIPTION

The ignition system consists of a distributor, coil, Electronic Control Assembly (ECA) and input sensors. The distributor is mounted on the rear of the cylinder head and is driven directly by the camshaft. It contains a permanent magnet stator and a pickup module. Timing is controlled by both mechanical and vacuum advances on carbureted engine and by the ECA on fuel injected models.

IGNITION COIL

Testing

1. Check for continuity in primary circuit.

2. Check resistance of secondary coil circuit. Resistance should be 8000–30,000 ohms.

3. Check resistance between primary terminal and case. Resistance should be greater than 10,000,000 ohms.

4. If not within specification, replace the coil.

SECONDARY WIRE

Testing

If resistance is greater than 5000 ohms per ft., replace wire.

CARBURETED ENGINE IGNITER MODULE

Testing

1. Disconnect the igniter wiring.

2. Check for continuity across igniter module.

3. If no continuity, replace igniter.

INJECTED ENGINE PICKUP COIL

Testing

1. Remove distributor cap, rotor and cover.

2. Check resistance between black/white terminal and white/blue terminal. Resistance should be 900–1200 ohms.

3. If resistance is not within specifications, replace pickup coil.

CENTRIFUGAL ADVANCE

Testing

FUEL INJECTED ENGINE

1. Disconnect vacuum advance hoses from distributor.

2. Connect timing light.

3. Start engine, increase engine speed to 3600 rpm, timing should gradually increase to approximately 18 degrees.

4. Repair or replace the vacuum control unit or distributor as required.

CARBURETED

1. Disconnect vacuum advance hose from distributor.

2. Connect timing light.

3. Start engine, increase engine speed to 3000 rpm, timing should gradually increase to approximately 20 degrees, increase speed to 5500 rpm and timing should be approximately 27 degrees.

4. Repair or replace the vacuum control unit or distributor as required.

VACUUM ADVANCE

Testing

FUEL INJECTED ENGINE

1. Disconnect and plug vacuum hoses at distributor.
2. Connect timing light.
3. With engine warm, apply vacuum to outer chamber.
4. Timing should gradually increase with vacuum, to approximately 28 degrees at 16 in. Hg.
5. Apply vacuum to inter chamber, timing should increase to 5 degrees at 6 in. Hg.
6. 4Repair or replace the vacuum control unit or distributor as required.

CARBURETED ENGINE

1. Disconnect and plug vacuum hose at distributor.
2. Connect timing light.
3. With engine warm, apply vacuum to chamber.
4. Timing should gradually increase with vacuum, to approximately 18 degrees at 10 in. Hg.

AIR GAP

Adjustment

Center the stator plate to achieve and even gap on both sides of the armature.

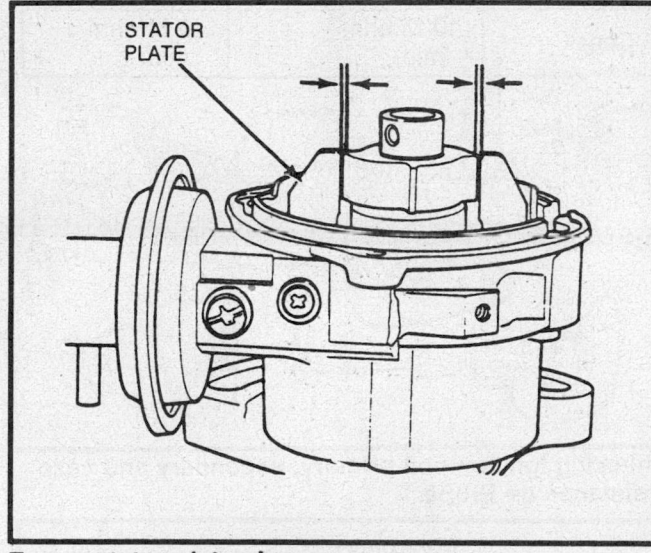

Tracer stator plate air gap

Festiva Ignition System

DESCRIPTION

The ignition system consists of a distributor, coil, Electronic Control Assembly (ECA) and input sensors. The distributor which mounts on the rear of the cylinder head and is driven directly by the camshaft. It contains a permanent magnet stator and a pickup module. Timing is controlled by both mechanical and vacuum advances and modified by ECA.

IGNITION COIL

Testing

1. Check for continuity in primary circuit.
2. Check resistance of secondary coil circuit. Resistance should be 6000-30,000 ohms.

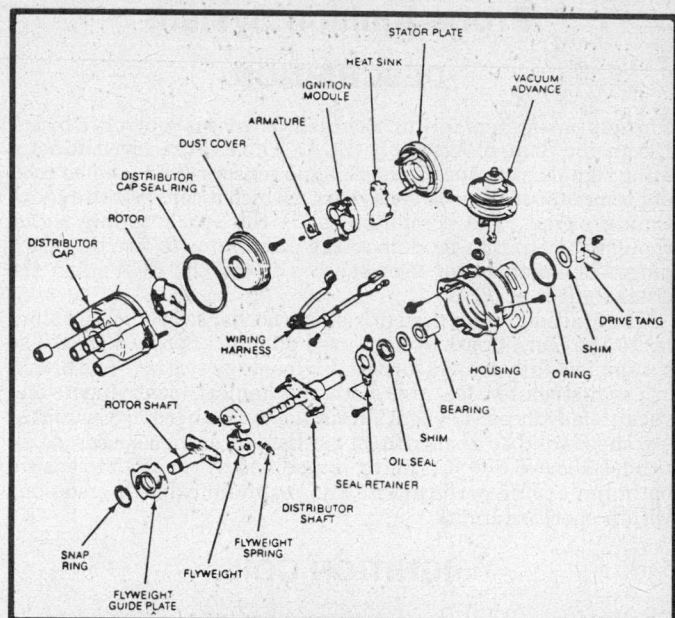

Festiva distributor—exploded view

3. Check resistance between primary terminal and case. Resistance should be greater than 10,000,000 ohms.
4. If not within specifications replace coil.

SECONDARY WIRE

Testing

If resistance is greater than 5000 ohms per ft., replace wire.

PICKUP COIL

Testing

1. Remove distributor cap, rotor and cover.
2. Check for continuity black/white and blue leads.
3. If there is no continuity, replace pickup coil.

CENTRIFUGAL ADVANCE

Testing

1. Disconnect vacuum advance hose from distributor.
2. Connect timing light.
3. Start engine, increase engine speed to 3200 rpm, timing should gradually increase to approximately 13 degrees, increase speed to 5000 rpm and timing should be approximately 17 degrees.
4. Replace the vacuum control unit or distributor as required.

VACUUM ADVANCE

Testing

1. Disconnect and plug vacuum hoses at distributor.
2. Connect timing light.
3. With engine warm, apply vacuum to **A** chamber.
4. Timing should gradually increase with vacuum, to approximately 10 degrees at 7 in. Hg.
5. Apply vacuum to **B** chamber, timing should increase to 14 degrees at 11 in. Hg.
6. Replace the vacuum control unit or distributor as required.

Probe Ignition System

DESCRIPTION

The ignition system for turbochrged vehicles is controlled by the Electronic Control Assembly (ECA). The ECA receives its actuating signals from the various engine sensors (TPS, engine coolant temperature, knock sensor, ect.) which it converts to a spark timing signal. The computer sends the spark timing signal though the ignition module to the distributor to fire the spark plugs. The distributor uses sensors to tell the ECA when the crankshaft it at TDC.

The ignition sytem used on non-turbocharged vehicles is similar to the Dura Spark system used on other Ford vehicles. The system is a fully transistorized, high energy system. The breakerless distributor features both mechanical (centrifugal) and vacuum advances. The ignition timing is advanced by vacuum at low speeds and by a centrifugal mechanism at high speeds. At altitudes above 6,500 ft., timing is modified by the ECA to ensure optimum engine performance and maintain exhaust emissions within specified limits.

IGNITION COIL

Testing

1. Check resistance in primary circuit, between terminals negative and positive. Primary resistance should be 0.720–0.880 ohms for turbocharged engines and 1.0–1.3 ohms for non-turbocharged engines.
2. Check resistance of secondary coil circuit. Resistance should be 10300–13900 ohms for turbo models and 7100–9700 ohms for non-turbocharged engines.
3. Check resistance between primary terminal and case. Resistance should be greater than 10,000,000 ohms.
4. If not within specification, replace the coil.

SECONDARY WIRE

Testing

If resistance is greater than 5000 ohms per ft., replace wire.

CENTRIFUGAL ADVANCE

Testing

1. Disconnect vacuum advance hose from distributor.
2. Connect timing light.

3. Start engine, increase engine speed to 2400 rpm, timing should gradually increase to approximately 14 degrees, increase speed to 4500 rpm and timing should be approximately 18 degrees.

VACUUM ADVANCE

Testing

TURBOCHARGED ENGINE

1. Warm up the engine until normal operating temperature is reached.
2. Adjust the ignition timing and the idle speed as required.
3. Connect a tachometer and timining light to the engine.
4. Disconnect and plug the vacuum control unit hose.
5. Gradually raise the engine speed. At 4500 rpm there should be a 22.0 degree advance (6.6 degrees at 1200).
6. If the advance is not within specifications, inspect the gov-

System	Resistance @ 20°C (68°F)	
	Turbo	Non-Turbo
Primary	0.72 to 0.88 ohm	1.04 to 1.27 ohm
Secondary	10.3 to 13.9 K ohm	7.1 to 9.7 K ohm
Case	10 M ohm min.	10 M ohm min.

Checking ignition coil primary, secondary and case resistance on Probe

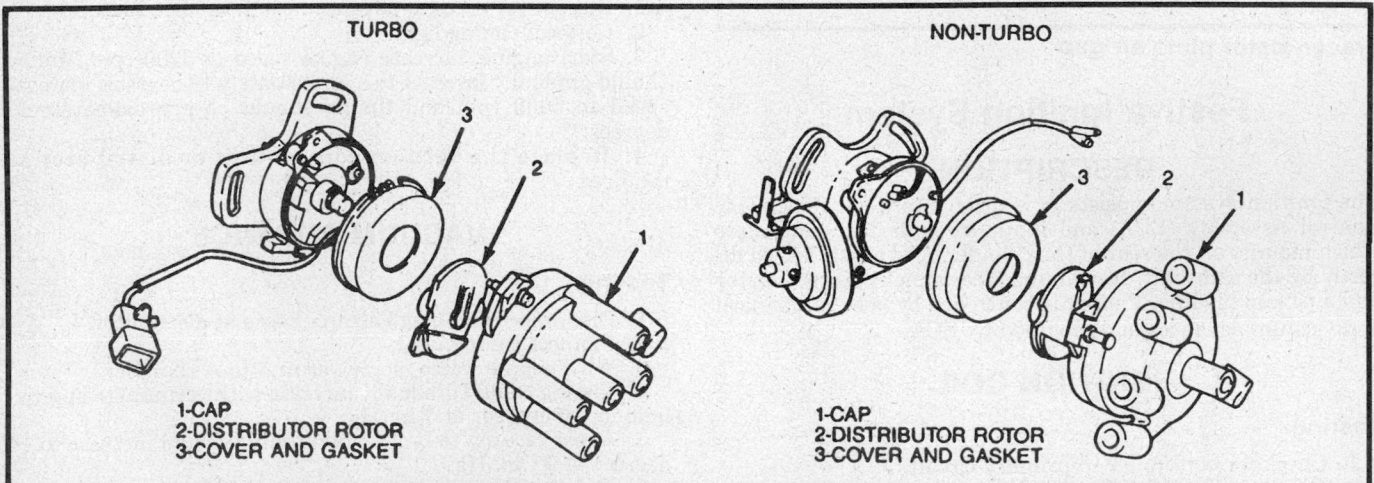

1-CAP
2-DISTRIBUTOR ROTOR
3-COVER AND GASKET

1-CAP
2-DISTRIBUTOR ROTOR
3-COVER AND GASKET

Probe distributor (turbo and non-turbo)

ernor components for wear or damage and repair/replace as necessary.

NON-TURBOCHARGED ENGINE

1. Disconnect and plug vacuum hoses at distributor.
2. Connect timing light.
3. With engine warm, apply vacuum to outer chamber.
4. Timing should gradually increase with vacuum, to approximately 20 degrees at 11 in. Hg.
5. Apply vacuum to inner chamber, timing should decrease to -6 degrees at 8 in. Hg.
6. If the vacuum advance is not as specified, replace the vacuum control unit or distributor as required.

PICKUP COIL

Testing

NON-TURBOCHARGED ENGINE

1. Remove distributor cap, rotor and cover.
2. Disconnect distributor wires.
3. Check resistance across pick-up coil. Resistance should be 900–1200 ohms.
4. If resistance is not within specification replace pick-up.

TURBOCHARGED ENGINE

1. Disconnect the distributor connector.
2. Check resistance of terminals **A** and **B**, **C** and **D**, **E** and **F** of the distributor connector.
3. Resistance should be 210–260 ohms across each pair of terminals.
4. If any terminal resistance is not within specification, replace distributor.

Ford Distributorless Ignition System (DIS)

DESCRIPTION

The distibutorless ignition system (DIS) was introduced in 1989 on the Taurus 3.0L SHO and Thunderbird 3.8L SC.

In the DIS, all engine timing and spark distribution is performed electronically with no moving parts. During basic operation, the EEC-IV determines the ignition timing required by the engine and a DIS module determines which ignition coil to fire.

The purpose of the DIS module is to deliver a full energy spark at a crank angle targeted by the EEC-IV and to provide the EEC-IV module with speed and position information. An Ignition Diagnostic Monitor (IDM) Clean Tach Out (CTO) line is also provided. The DIS inputs and outputs are listed below:

Inputs – Variable Reluctance Sensor Input (VRS) and Spark Advance Word (SAW)

Outputs – Coil drivers, one for every 2 cylinders. Profile Ignition Pickup (PIP) and Ignition Diagnostic Monitor (IDM) Clean Tach Out (CTO) line.

The distributorless ignition system consists of the following components.

a. Crankshaft timing sensor
b. Camshaft sensor
c. DIS module
d. Ignition coil pack(s)
e. Spark angle portion of the EEC-IV control module.
f. Related wiring.

Crankshaft Timing Sensor

The crankshaft timing sensor is a single hall effect magnetic switch, which is actuated by a 3 vanes on the crankshaft damper and pulley assembly. This sensor generates a Profile Ignition Pick-up (PIP) signal. The PIP signal provides base timing and

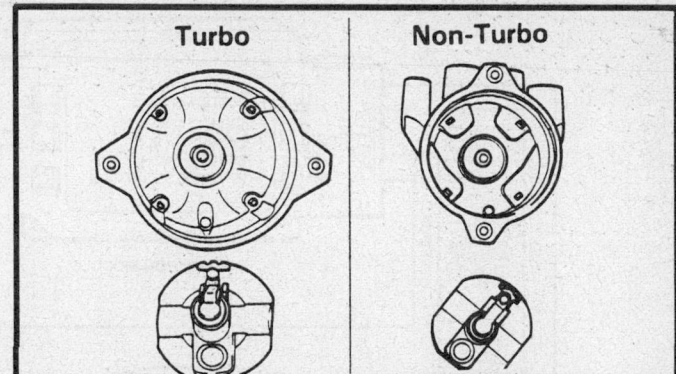

Probe distributor cap and rotor configuration

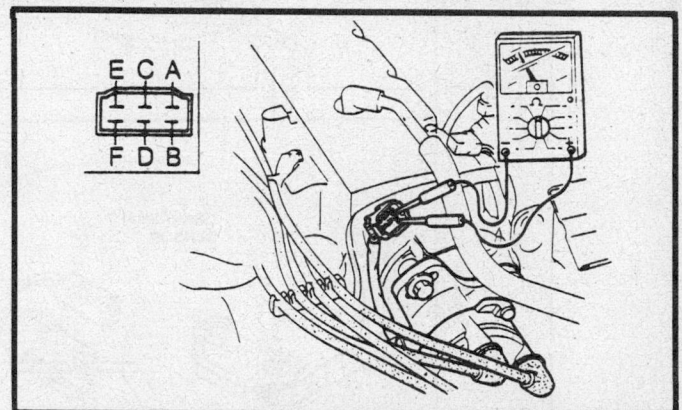

Probe turbo distributor – connector terminal locations

rpm information to the DIS module and the EEC-IV control module.

Camshaft Sensor

The camshaft sensor is a single hall effect switch magnetic switch, activated by a single vane which is driven by the camshaft. This sensor provides Cylinder Identification (CID) information for the ignition coil and fuel synchronization.

The camshaft and crankshaft sensors are digital hall effect devices. The 3.0L SHO engine camshaft sensor is located on the right end of the rear cylinder head close to the No.1 cylinder. On the 3.8L SC engine the camshaft sensor is located in the normally used portion of the engine where the distributor would sit. The camshaft sensor in both cases are the same except for the mounting bracketry.

Ignition Coil Pack

The ignition coil pack contains 3 separate ignition coils which are controlled by the DIS module through 3 coil leads. Each ignition coil fires 2 spark plugs simultaneously, one spark plug on the compression stroke and one on the exhaust stroke. The spark plug fired on the exhaust stroke uses very little of the ignition coils stored energy and the majority of the ignition coils energy is used by the spark plug on the compression stroke. Since these 2 spark plugs are are connected in series, the firing voltage of one of the spark plugs will be negative with respect to ground, while the other one will be positive with respect to ground.

DIS Module

The DIS ignition module receives the PIP signal from the crankshaft sensor, the CID signals from the camshaft sensor and the spout (spark out) signal is from the EEC-IV control module. During normal operation the PIP signal is sent to the EEC-IV

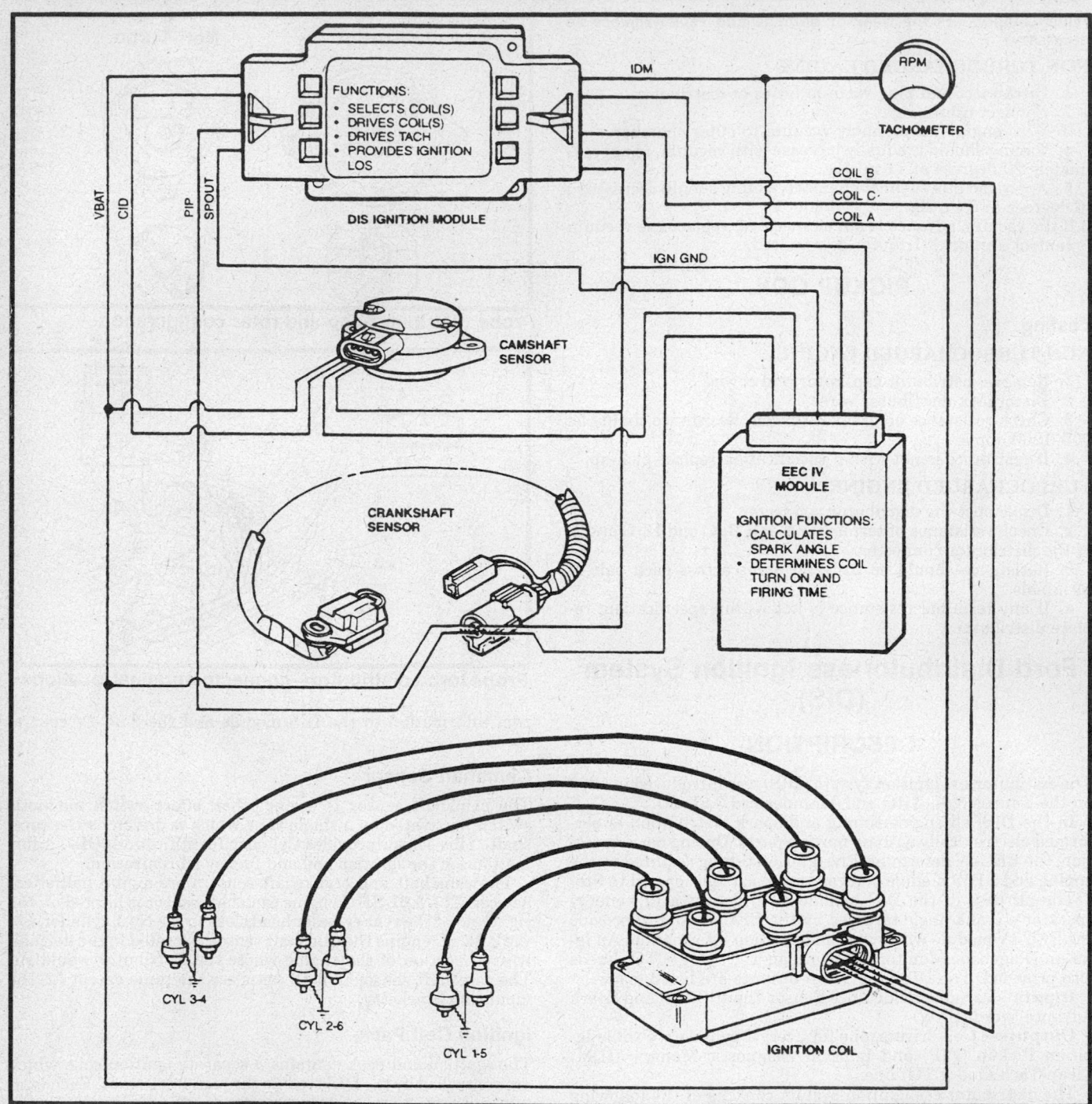

FUNCTIONS:
- SELECTS COIL(S)
- DRIVES COIL(S)
- DRIVES TACH
- PROVIDES IGNITION LOS

DIS IGNITION MODULE

VBAT / CID / PIP / SPOUT

IDM

RPM
TACHOMETER

COIL B
COIL C
COIL A

IGN GND

CAMSHAFT SENSOR

CRANKSHAFT SENSOR

EEC IV MODULE

IGNITION FUNCTIONS:
- CALCULATES SPARK ANGLE
- DETERMINES COIL TURN ON AND FIRING TIME

CYL 3-4
CYL 2-6
CYL 1-5

IGNITION COIL

Distributorless Ignition System (DIS) schematic

control module from the crankshaft timing sensor and provides base timing and rpm information. The CID signal provides the DIS module with the information required to synchronize the ignition coils so that they are fired in the proper sequence. The spout signal contains the optimum spark timing and dwell time information. The Spark angle is determined by the rising edge of the Spout while the falling edge of the spout controls the coil current **ON** or **DWELL** time. The dwell time is controlled or varied by varying the duty cycle of the spout signal.

This feature is called Computer Controlled Dwell (CCD). With the proper inputs of the PIP, CID and spout the DIS mod-

ule turns the ignition coils on and off in the proper sequence for spark control.

Ignition Diagnostic Connector

The ignition diagnostic monitor (IDM) is a function of the DIS module. The DIS module sends information on system failures to the EEC-IV control module which stores the information for diagnostic self test. The IDM signal is also used to drive the vehicle instrument tachometer and test tachometer for system diagnosis.

Failure Mode Effects Management

During some DIS faults, the failure mode effects management (FMEM) portion of the DIS module will maintain vehicle operation. If the DIS module does not receive the spout input, it will automatically turn the ignition coils on and off using the PIP signal. However, this condition will result in fixed spark timing (10° BTDC) and fixed dwell timing (no CCD). If the DIS module does not receive the CID input, random coil synchronization will be attempted by the module. Therefore, several attempts may be required to start the engine when the DIS module is in this mode.

DIAGNOSIS AND TESTING

Preliminary Checks

1. Visually inspect the engine compartment to ensure that all vacuum lines and spark plug wires are properly routed and securely connected.
2. Examine all wiring harnesses and connectors for insulation damage, burned, overheated, loose or broken conditions. Check the sensor shield connector. Check that the DIS module mounting screws are tight.
3. Be certain that the battery is fully charged and that all accessories should be **OFF** during the diagnosis.
4. The tools needed during this diagnosis procedure will be as follows:

DIS diagnostic cable Hickok HK100–306 or equivalent
Spark plug firing indicator, neon type; Champion CT–436 or equivalent
Spark plug firing indicator, gap type, D81P–6666–A or equivalent
Suitable volt/ohmmeter
A 12–14 volt test lamp
Remote starter switch
EEC-IV breakout box Rotunda T83L–50-EEC-IV or equivalent
Inductive timing light.

NOTE: It is also recommended that the DIS module tester Hickok Model 600 be used. This tester includes 12 LEDs, 12 test jacks and a built in interface cable, that allows the tester to monitor all DIS module signals. Also the DIS coil/sensor tester Hickok Model 601. This tester is similar to the 600 model except it allows monitoring of signals at the sensor and coils.

A spark plug with a broken side electrode is not sufficient to check for spark and may lead to incorrect results. When instructed to inspect a wiring harness, both visual inspection and a continuity test should be performed. Inspect the connector pins for damage (corrosion, bent or spread pins, etc.) when directed to remove a connector. When making measurements on a wiring harness or connector, it is good practice to wiggle the wires while measuring. When making voltage checks, a GROUND reading means any value within a range of 0–1 volt. Also VBAT (battery voltage) readings mean any value that falls within a range of VBAT to 2 volts less than VBAT. When using a spark plug indicator, place the grooved end as close as possible to the plug boot. Very weak flashing may be caused by a fouled plug.

DELCO-REMY HIGH ENERGY IGNITION (HEI)

General Description

The high energy ignition distributor is still used on some engines. The ignition coil is either mounted to the top of the distributor cap or is externally mounted on the engine, having a secondary circuit high tension wire connecting the coil to the distributor cap and interconnecting primary wiring as part of the engine harness.

The high energy ignition distributor is equipped to aid in spark timing changes, necessary for emissions, economy and performance. This system is called the Electronic Spark Timing Control (EST). The HEI distributors use a magnetic pick-up assembly, located inside the distributor containing a permanent magnet, a pole piece with internal timer teeth and a pick-up coil. When the teeth of the rotating timer core and pole piece align, an induced voltage in the pick-up coil signals the electronic module to open the coil primary circuit. As the primary current decreases, a high voltage is induced in the secondary windings of the ignition coil, directing a spark through the rotor and high voltage leads to fire the spark plugs. The dwell period is automatically controlled by the electronic module and is increased with increasing engine rpm. The HEI system features a longer spark duration which is instrumental in firing lean and EGR diluted fuel/air mixtures. The condenser (capacitor) located within the HEI distributor is provided for noise (static) suppression purposes only and is not a regularly replaced ignition system component.

All spark timing changes in the HEI/EST distributors are done electronically by the Electronic Control Module (ECM), which monitors information from the various engine sensors, computes the desired spark timing and signals the distributor to change the timing accordingly. With this distributor, no vacuum or centrifugal advances are used.

Troubleshooting

NOTE: An accurate diagnosis is the first step to problem solution and repair. For several of the following steps, a HEI spark tester, tool ST 125, which has a spring clip to attach it to ground. Use of this tool is recommended, as there is more control of the high energy spark and less chance of being shocked. If a tachometer is connected to the TACH terminal on the distributor, disconnect it before proceeding with this test.

SECONDARY CIRCUIT SPARK

Testing

1. Check for spark at the spark plugs by attaching the HEI spark tester, tool ST 125, to any of the plug wires, grounding the HEI spark tester on the engine and cranking the starter.
2. If no spark occurs at this wire, check a second. If spark is present, the HEI system is good.
3. Check fuel system, plug wires and spark plugs.
4. If no spark occurs from EST distributor, disconnect the 4 terminal EST connector and recheck for spark. If spark is present, EST system service check should be performed.

NOTE: Before making any circuit checks with test meters, be sure that all primary circuit connectors are properly installed and that spark plug cables are tight at the distributor and at the plugs.

Distributor with Internal Coil

IGNITION COIL

Testing

1. Remove the cap from the distributor.
2. With coil attached to cap, Connect an ohmmeter to the distributor cap terminals C and Ground. The reading should be zero ohms or nearly zero ohms. If not, replace the ignition coil.
3. Position the ohmmeter leads to terminal B+ and the high tension rotor contact in the center of the cap.
4. Using the ohmmeter high scale, measure the resistance. Reverse the ohmmeter leads and again measure the resistance.
5. Replace the coil only if both readings are infinite.

PICK-UP COIL

Testing

1. Disconnect the rotor and pick-up coil leads from the module.
2. Using an ohmmeter, connect a lead to the distributor houing and the second lead to any of the pick-up terminals in the connector.
3. The reading should be infinite.

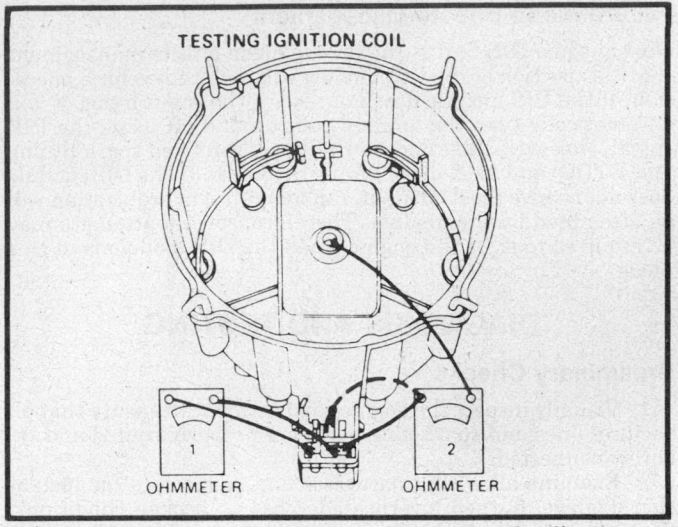

Testing ignition coil used in coil-in-cap distributor

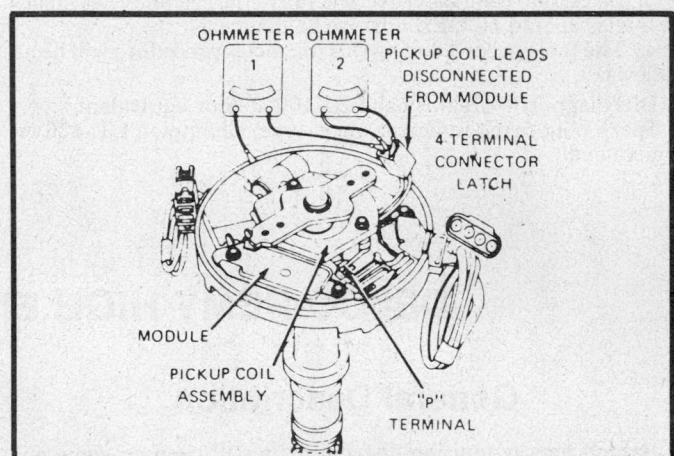

Testing pick-up coil used in coil-in-cap distributor

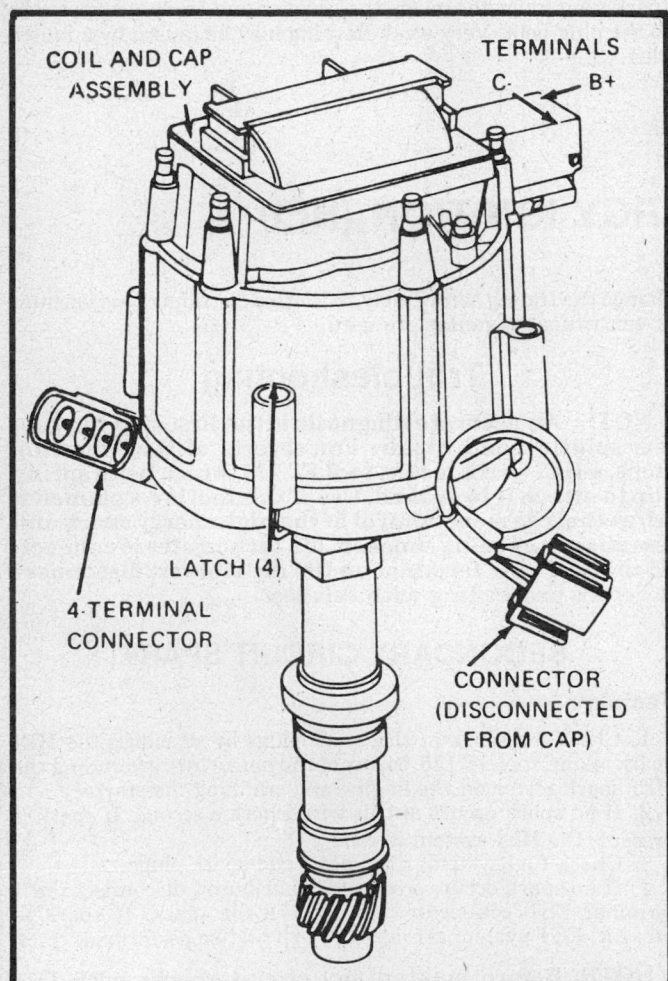

V6 engine coil-in-cap distributor, typical of V8 engine distributors

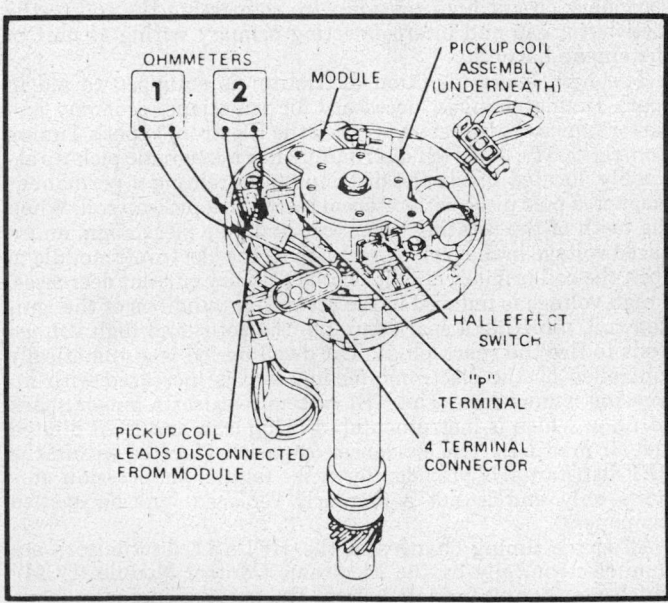

Testing coil-in-cap distributor with Hall Effect switch

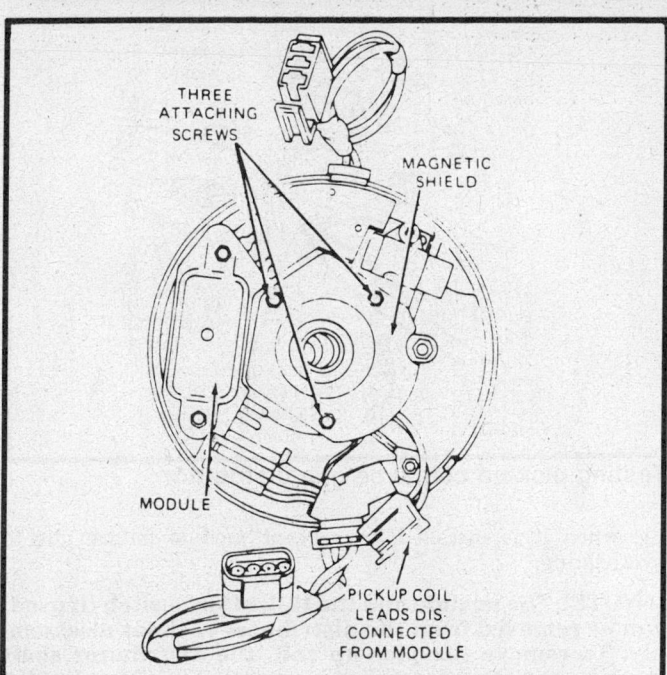

Magnetic shield used on selected coil-in-cap distributors

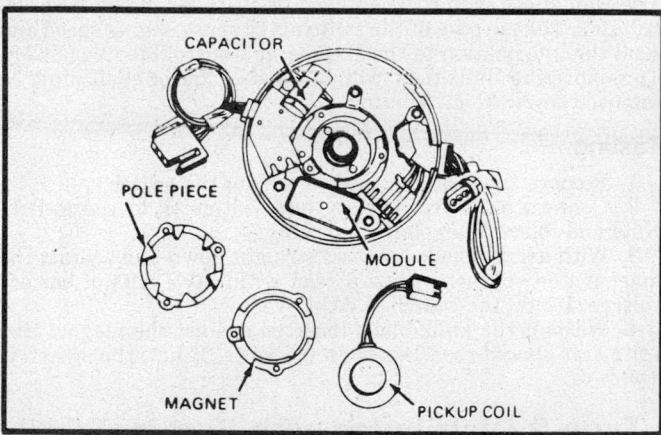

Pick-up coil components, coil-in-cap distributor

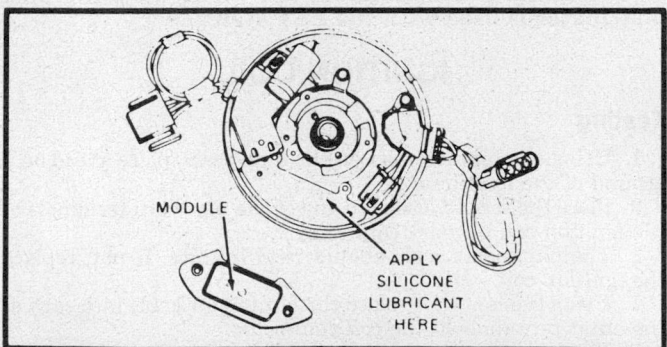

Module replacement and use of silicone lubricant, coil-in-cap distributor

NOTE: While testing, flex the leads to determine if wire breaks are present under the wiring insulation.

4. Place the ohmmeter leads into both the pick-up terminals of the connector and measure the resistance.

5. The reading should be steady at any value between 500-1500 ohms.

IGNITION MODULE

Testing

Because of the complexity of the internal circuitry of the HEI/EST module, it is recommended the module be tested with an accurate module tester.

It is necessary that silicone lubricant be used under the module when it is installed, to prevent module failure due to overheating.

NOTE: The module can be replaced without distributor disassembly. However, the distributor must be disassembled to replace the pick-up coil, magnet and pole piece

Type 1 Distributor with External Coil

NOTE: This type distributor has no vacuum or centrifugal advance mechanism and has the pick-up coil mounted above the module. This distributor is used with the EST system.

IGNITION COIL

Testing

1. Disconnect the primary wiring connectors and secondary coil wire from the ignition coil.

2. Using an ohmmeter on the high scale, connect a lead to a grounding screw and the second lead to either of the primary coil terminals.

3. The reading should be infinite. If not, replace the ignition coil.

4. Using the low scale, place the ohmmeter leads on both the primary coil terminals.

5. The reading should be very low or zero ohms. If not, replace the signition coil.

6. Using the high scale, place an ohmmeter lead on the high tension output terminal and the other lead on a primary coil terminal.

7. The reading should not be infinite. If it is, replace the ignition coil.

PICK-UP COIL

Testing

1. Remove the rotor and pick-up coil leads from the module.

2. Using an ohmmeter, attach a lead to the distributor base and the second lead to any of the pick-up coil terminals of the connector.

3. The reading should be infinite at all times.

4. Position both leads of the ohmmeter to the pick-up terminal ends of the connector.

5. The reading should be a steady value between 500–1500 ohms.

6. If not within the specification value, the pick-up coil is defective.

NOTE: While testing, flex the leads to determine if wire breaks are present under the wiring insulation.

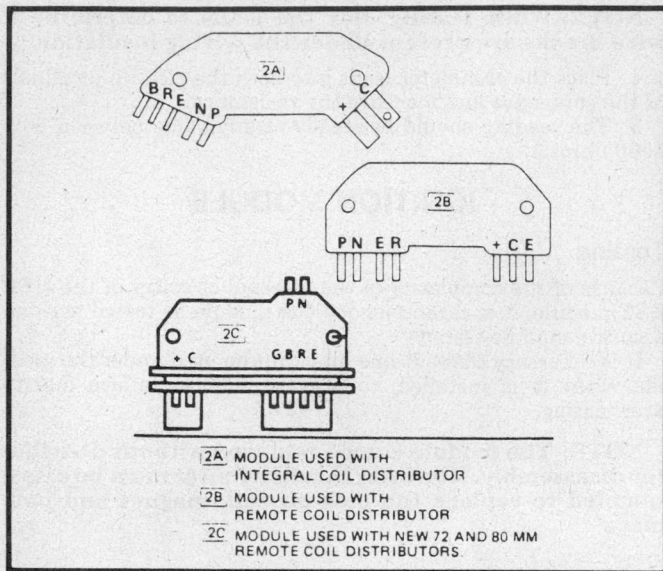

2A MODULE USED WITH INTEGRAL COIL DISTRIBUTOR
2B MODULE USED WITH REMOTE COIL DISTRIBUTOR
2C MODULE USED WITH NEW 72 AND 80 MM REMOTE COIL DISTRIBUTORS

Electronic distributor modules used with General Motors Electronic Ignition systems

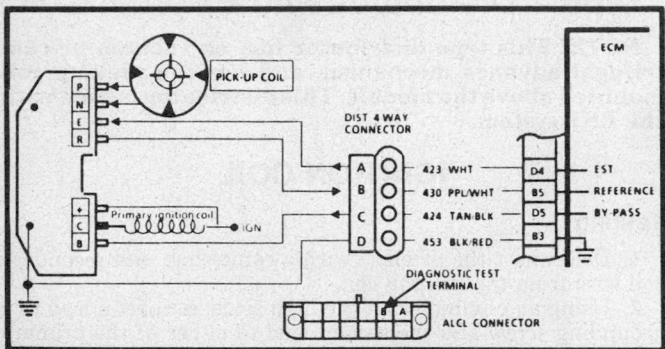

Typical wiring schematic for electronic ignition system using remote ignition coil

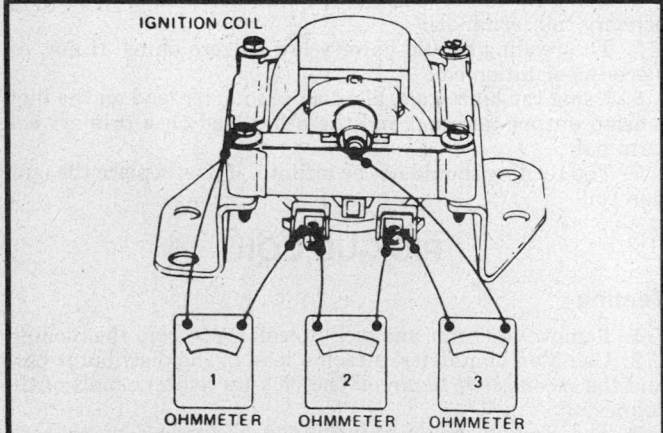

Testing ignition coil, type one distributor

IGNITION MODULE

Because of the complexity of the internal circuitry of the HEI/EST module, it is recommended the module be tested with an accurate module tester.

It is necessary that silicone lubricant be used under the mod-

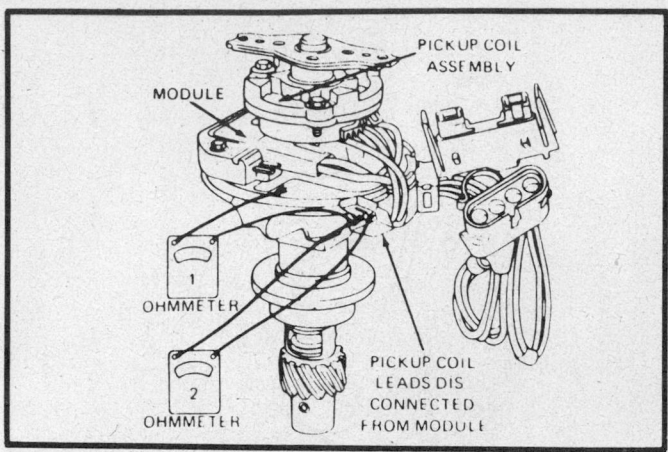

Testing pick-up coil, type one distributor

ule when it is installed, to prevent module failure due to overheating.

NOTE: The module and the Hall effect switch (if used) can be removed from the distributor without disassembly. To remove the pick-up coil, the distributor shaft must be removed to expose a waved retaining ring (C-washer) holding the pick-up coil in place.

HALL EFFECT SWITCH

The Hall effect switch, when used, is installed in the HEI distributor. The purpose of the switch is to sense engine speed and send the information to the Electronic Control Module (ECM). To remove the Hall effect switch, the distributor shaft must be removed from the distributor.

Testing

1. Remove the switch connectors from the switch.
2. Connect a 12 volt battery and voltmeter to the switch. Note and follow the polarity markings.
3. With a knife blade inserted straight down and against the magnet, the voltmeter should read within 0.5 volts of battery voltage. If not, the switch is defective.
4. Without the knife blade inserted against the magnet, the voltmeter should read less than 0.5 volts. If not, the switch is defective.

Type 2 Distributor with External Coil

NOTE: This type distributor has no vacuum or centrifugal advance mechanisms and the module has 2 outside terminal connections for the wiring harness. This distributor is used with the EST system.

IGNITION COIL

Testing

1. Using an ohmmeter set on the high scale, place a lead on a ground of the ignition coil.
2. Place the second lead into any of the rearward terminals of the ignition coil primary connector.
3. The ohmmeter scale should read infinite. If not, replace the ignition coil.
4. Using the low scale, place the ohmmeter leads into each of the outer terminals of the coil connector.
5. The reading should be zero ohms or very low. If not, replace the ignition coil.
6. Using the high scale, place an ohmmeter lead on the coil

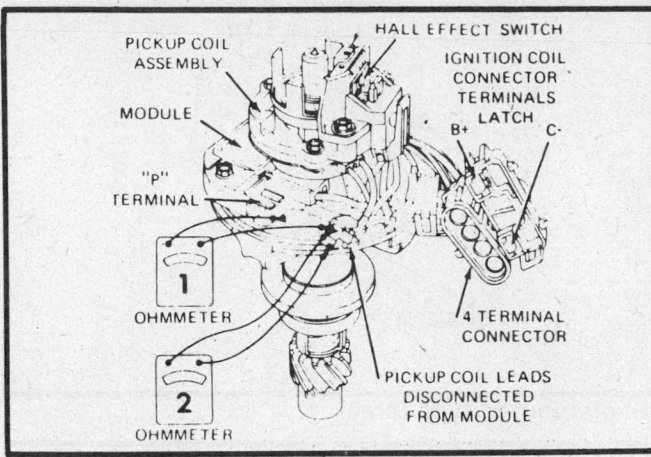

Testing Hall Effect switch, type one distributor

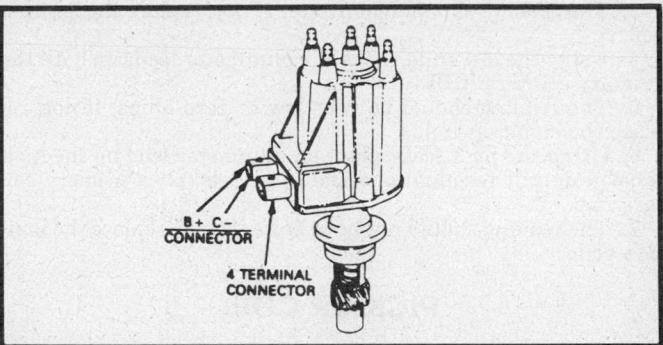

HEI/EST distributor, type two

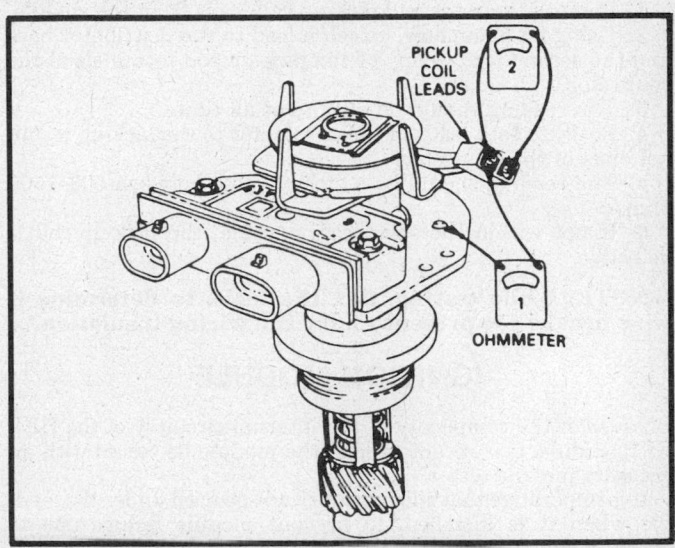

Testing pick-up coil, type two distributor

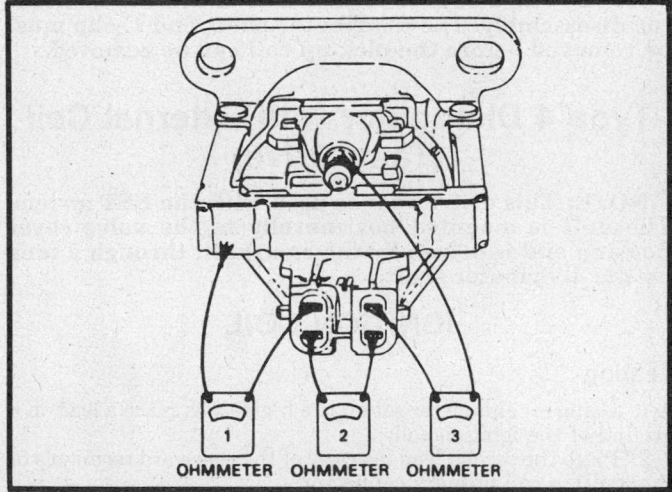

Testing ignition coil, type two distributor

secondary terminal and the second lead into the rearward terminal of the ignition coil primary connector.

7. The reading should not be infinite. If so, replace the ignition coil.

PICK-UP COIL

Testing

1. Remove the rotor and pick-up leads from the module.
2. Using an ohmmeter, connect either of the leads to the distributor base.
3. Connect the second lead to any of the pick-up coil lead terminals
4. The reading should be infinite. If not, the pick-up coil is defective.

NOTE: During the ohmmeter tests, flex the leads by hand to check for intermediate opens in the wiring.

5. Connect both ohmmeter lead to the pick-up coil terminals at the connector.
6. The reading should be at a steady value, between 500–1500 ohms.
7. If the reading is not within specifications, the pick-up coil must is defective.

IGNITION MODULE

Testing

Because of the complexity of the internal circuitry of the HEI/EST module, it is recommended the module be tested with an accurate module tester.

It is imperative that silicone lubricant be used under the module when it is installed, to prevent module failure due to overheating.

NOTE: The module can be removed without distributor disassembly. To remove the pick-up coil, the distributor shaft must be removed. A retainer can then be removed from the top of the pole piece and the pick-up coil removed.

Type 3 Distributor with External Coil

NOTE: This distributor uses vacuum and centrifugal advance units and does not have the EST system.

IGNITION COIL

Testing

1. Disconnect the primary wiring connectors and secondary coil wire from the ignition coil.
2. Using an ohmmeter on the high scale, connect a lead to a grounding screw and the second lead to any of the primary coil terminals.

3. The reading should be infinite. If not, replace the ignition coil.

4. Using the low scale, place the ohmmeter leads on both the primary coil terminals.

5. The reading should be very low or zero ohms. If not, replace the signition coil.

6. Using the high scale, place an ohmmeter lead on the high tension output terminal and the other lead on a primary coil terminal.

7. The reading should not be infinite. If it is, replace the ignition coil.

PICK-UP COIL

Testing

1. Remove the rotor and pick-up coil leads from the module.

2. Using an ohmmeter, attach a lead to the distributor base and the second lead to any of the pick-up coil terminals of the connector.

3. The reading should be infinite at all times.

4. Position both leads of the ohmmeter to the pick-up terminal ends of the connector.

5. The reading should be a steady value between 500–1500 ohms.

6. If not within the specification value, the pick-up coil is defective.

NOTE: While testing, flex the leads to determine if wire breaks are present under the wiring insulation.

IGNITION MODULE

Because of the complexity of the internal circuitry of the HEI/EST module, it is recommended the module be tested with an accurate module tester.

It is imperative that silicone lubricant be used under the module when it is installed, to prevent module failure due to overheating.

NOTE: The module can be removed without distributor disassembly. The distributor shaft and C-clip must be removed before the pick-up coil can be removed.

Type 4 Distributor with External Coil (Tang Drive)

NOTE: This distributor is used with the EST system. The unit is mounted horizontally to the valve cover housing and is driven by the camshaft, through a tang on the distributor shaft.

IGNITION COIL

Testing

1. Using an ohmmeter set on the high scale, place a lead on a ground of the ignition coil.

2. Place the second lead into any of the rearward terminals of the ignition coil primary connector.

3. The ohmmeter scale should read infinite. If not, replace the ignition coil.

4. Using the low scale, place the ohmmeter leads into each of the outer terminals of the coil connector.

5. The reading should be 0 ohms or very low. If not, replace the ignition coil.

6. Using the high scale, place an ohmmeter lead on the coil secondary terminal and the second lead into the rearward terminal of the ignition coil primary connector.

7. The reading should not be infinite. If so, replace the ignition coil.

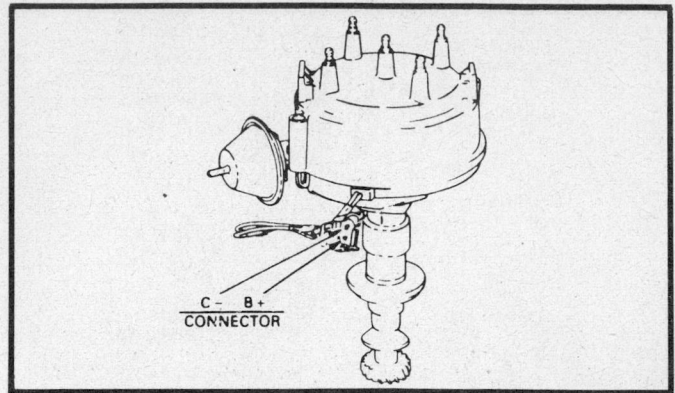

HEI distributor, type three

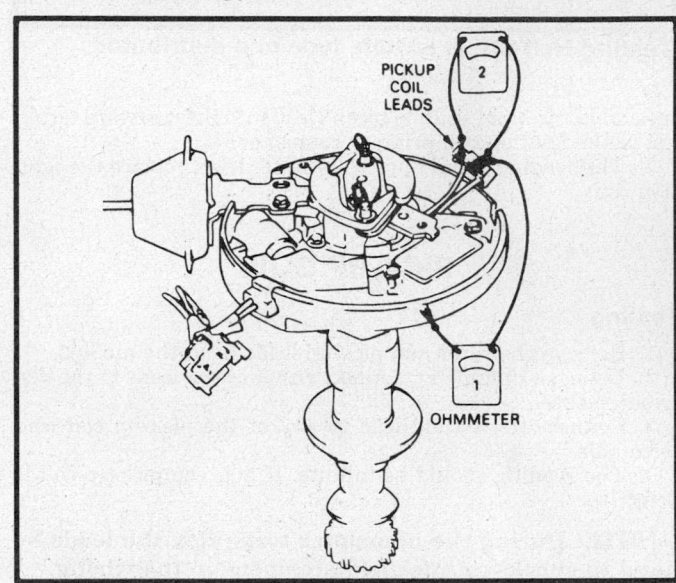

Testing pick-up coil, type three distributor

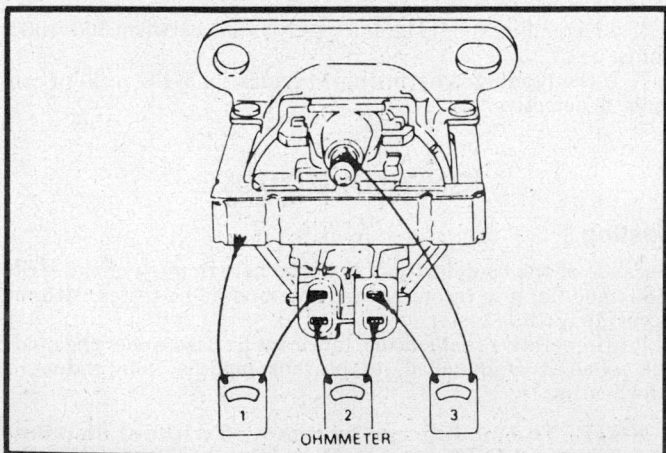

Testing ignition coil, type three distributor

PICK-UP COIL

Testing

1. Remove the rotor and pick-up leads from the module.

2. Using an ohmmeter, connect either of the leads to the distributor base.

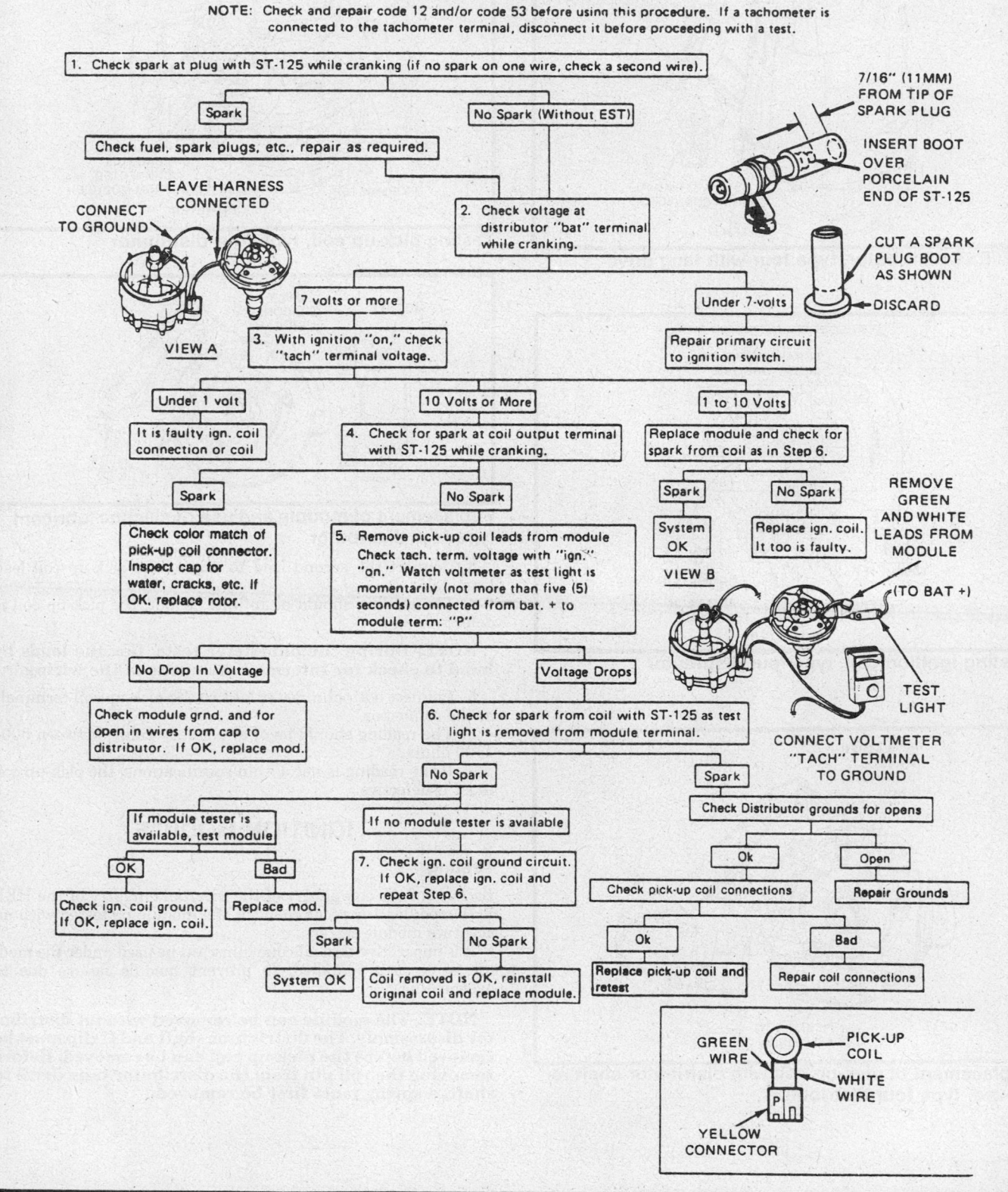

ENGINE CRANKS, BUT WILL NOT RUN
(WITH INTEGRAL IGNITION COIL)

NOTE: Check and repair code 12 and/or code 53 before using this procedure. If a tachometer is connected to the tachometer terminal, disconnect it before proceeding with a test.

1. Check spark at plug with ST-125 while cranking (if no spark on one wire, check a second wire).

Spark → Check fuel, spark plugs, etc., repair as required.

No Spark (Without EST)

7/16" (11MM) FROM TIP OF SPARK PLUG

INSERT BOOT OVER PORCELAIN END OF ST-125

CUT A SPARK PLUG BOOT AS SHOWN — DISCARD

LEAVE HARNESS CONNECTED

CONNECT TO GROUND

VIEW A

2. Check voltage at distributor "bat" terminal while cranking.

7 volts or more

Under 7-volts → Repair primary circuit to ignition switch.

3. With ignition "on," check "tach" terminal voltage.

Under 1 volt → It is faulty ign. coil connection or coil

10 Volts or More → 4. Check for spark at coil output terminal with ST-125 while cranking.

1 to 10 Volts → Replace module and check for spark from coil as in Step 6.

Spark → Check color match of pick-up coil connector. Inspect cap for water, cracks, etc. If OK, replace rotor.

No Spark → 5. Remove pick-up coil leads from module Check tach. term. voltage with "ign." "on." Watch voltmeter as test light is momentarily (not more than five (5) seconds) connected from bat. + to module term: "P"

Spark → System OK

No Spark → Replace ign. coil. It too is faulty.

VIEW B

REMOVE GREEN AND WHITE LEADS FROM MODULE

(TO BAT +)

TEST LIGHT

CONNECT VOLTMETER "TACH" TERMINAL TO GROUND

No Drop In Voltage → Check module grnd. and for open in wires from cap to distributor. If OK, replace mod.

Voltage Drops → 6. Check for spark from coil with ST-125 as test light is removed from module terminal.

No Spark

If module tester is available, test module

OK → Check ign. coil ground. If OK, replace ign. coil.

Bad → Replace mod.

If no module tester is available

7. Check ign. coil ground circuit. If OK, replace ign. coil and repeat Step 6.

Spark → System OK

No Spark → Coil removed is OK, reinstall original coil and replace module.

Spark → Check Distributor grounds for opens

Ok → Check pick-up coil connections

Open → Repair Grounds

Ok → Replace pick-up coil and retest

Bad → Repair coil connections

GREEN WIRE

PICK-UP COIL

WHITE WIRE

P

YELLOW CONNECTOR

HEI diagnosis chart

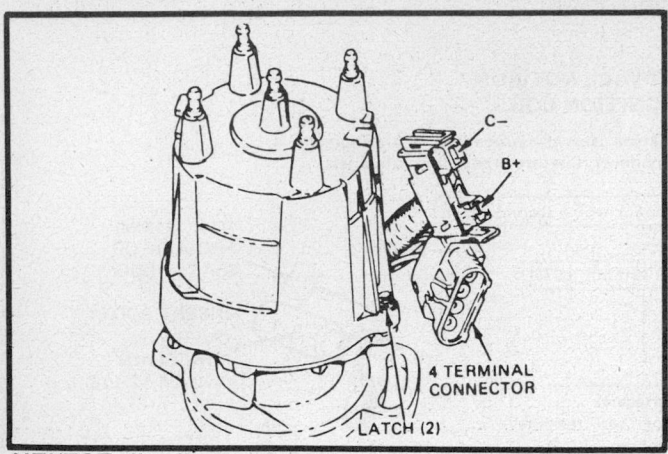

HEI/EST distributor, type four with tang drive

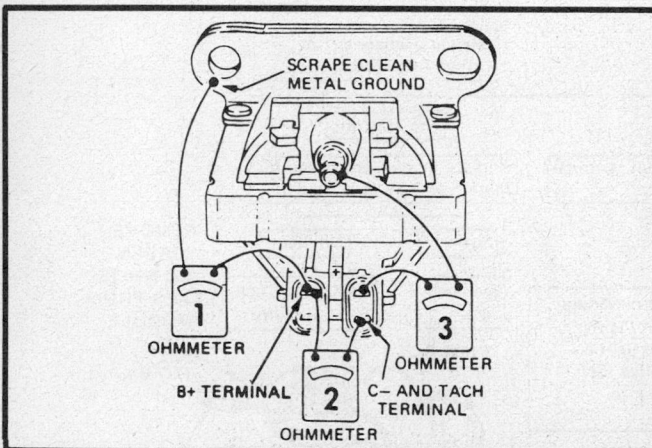

Testing ignition coil, type four distributor

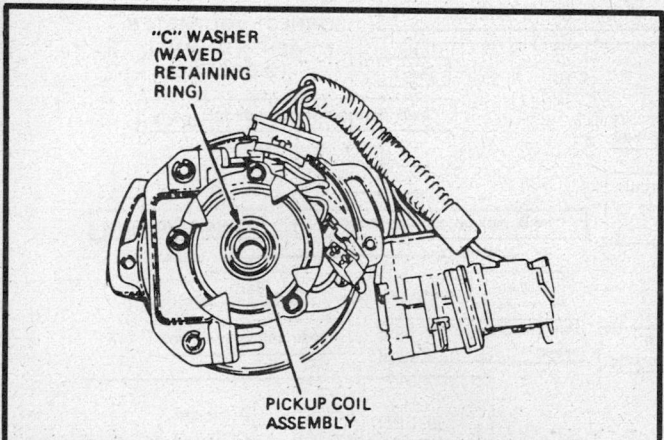

Replacement of pick-up coil with distributor shaft removed, type four distributor

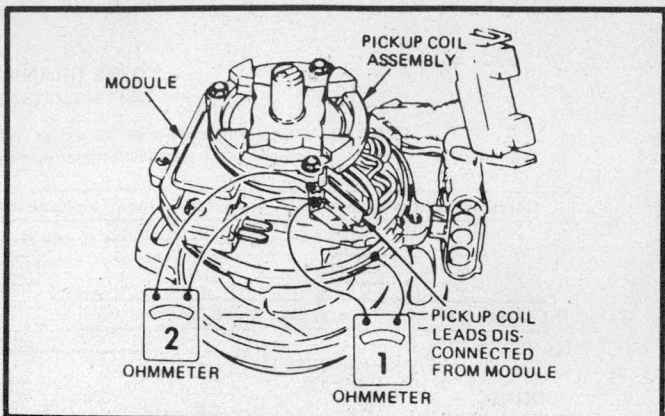

Testing pick-up coil, type four distributor

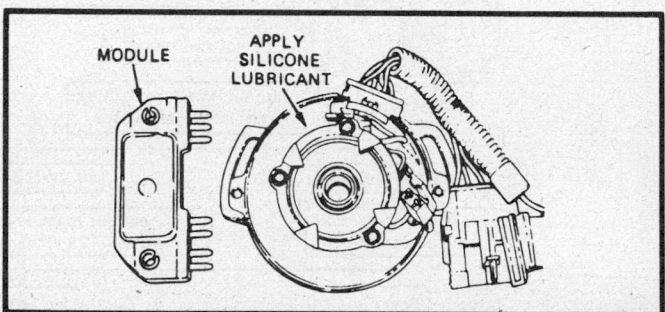

Replacement of module and use of silicone lubricant, type four distributor

3. Connect the second lead to any of the pick-up coil lead terminals

4. The reading should be infinite. If not, the pick-up coil is defective.

NOTE: During the ohmmeter tests, flex the leads by hand to check for intermediate opens in the wiring.

5. Connect both ohmmeter lead to the pick-up coil terminals at the connector.

6. The reading should be of at a steady value, between 500–1500 ohms.

7. If the reading is not within specifications, the pick-up coil must is defective.

IGNITION MODULE

Testing

Because of the complexity of the internal circuitry of the HEI/EST module, it is recommended the module be tested with an accurate module tester.

It is imperative that silicone lubricant be used under the module when it is installed, to prevent module failure due to overheating.

NOTE: The module can be removed without distributor disassembly. The distributor shaft and C clip must be removed before the pick-up coil can be removed. Before removing the roll pin from the distributor tang drive to shaft, a spring must first be removed.

COMPUTER CONTROLLED COIL IGNITION (C³I) SYSTEM DIRECT IGNITION SYSTEM (DIS)/ ELECTRONIC SPARK TIMING (EST)

General Information

The C³I System and Direct Ignition System (DIS) do not use the conventional distributor and ignition coil. These systems consist of separate ignition coils, C³I or DIS ignition module, crankshaft sensor or combination sensor, camshaft sensor (C³I), along with the related connecting wires and Electronic Spark Timing (EST) portion of the Electronic Control Module (ECM).

The C³I and DIS systems use a waste spark method of spark distribution. Companion cylinders are paired and the spark occurs simultaneously in the cylinder with the piston coming up on the compression stroke and in the companion cylinder with the piston coming up on the exhaust stroke.

1. Example of firing order and companion cylinders–1–2–3–4–5–6: 1/4, 2/5, 3/6.

2. Example of firing order and companion cylinders–1–6–5–4–3–2: 1/4, 6/3, 5/2.

3. Example of firing order and companion cylinders–1–3–4–2: 1/4, 2/3

NOTE: The companion cylinders in the V6 engine firing order remain the same, but the cylinder firing order sequence differs.

The cylinder on the exhaust stroke requires very little of the available voltage to arc, so the remaining high voltage is used by the cylinder in the firing position (TDC compression). This same process is repeated when the companion cylinders reverse roles.

It is possible in an engine no-load condition, for a plug to fire, even though the spark plug lead from the same coil is disconnected from the other spark plug. The disconnected spark plug lead acts as a plate of a capacitor, with the engine being the other plate. These 2 capacitors plates are charged as a current surge (spark) jumps across the gap of the connected spark plug.

These plates are then discharged as the secondary energy is dissipated in an oscillating current across the gap of the spark plug still connected. Because of the direction of current flow in the primary windings and thus in the secondary windings, 1 spark plug will fire from the center electrode to the side electrode, while the other will fire from the side electrode to the center electrode.

These systems utilize the EST signal from the ECM, as do the convention distributor type ignition systems equipped with the EST system to control timing.

DIRECT IGNITION SYSTEM

In the direct ignition system and while under 400 rpm, the DIS ignition module controls the spark timing through a module timing mode. Over 400 rpm, the ECM controls the spark timing through the EST mode and in the C³I system, the injectors operate in the Sequential Fuel Injection mode (SFI). In the Direct Ignition system, to properly control the ignition timing, the ECM relies on the the following information from the various sensors.

1. Engine load (manifold pressure or vacuum)
2. Atmospheric (barometric) pressure
3. Engine temperature
4. Manifold air temperature
5. Crankshaft position
6. Engine speed (rpm)

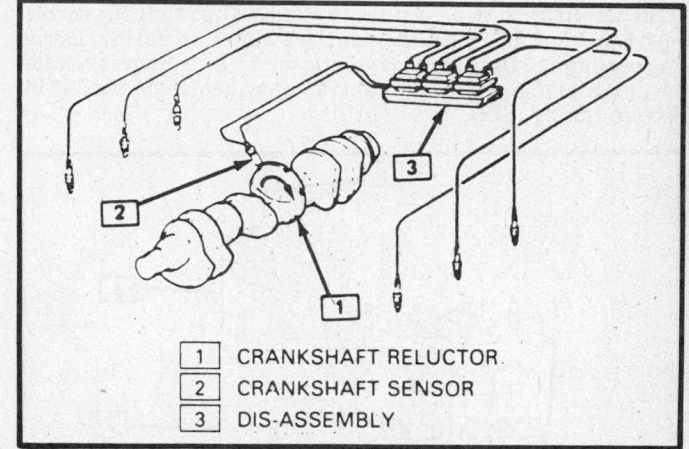

1	CRANKSHAFT RELUCTOR
2	CRANKSHAFT SENSOR
3	DIS-ASSEMBLY

Crankshaft sensor to crankshaft reluctor relationship

C³I SYSTEM

In the C³I system, to properly control the ignition timing, the ECM relies on the following information from the various sensors.

1. Crankshaft position
2. Camshaft position
3. Engine speed (rpm)
4. Engine coolant sensor (CTS) and induction air temperature (MAT)
5. Amount of air entering the throttle body (MAF)
6. Throttle position sensor (TPS)
7. ESC signal (knock retard)
8. Park/Neutral position (P/N)
9. Vehicle speed

C³I System Components

NOTE: The C³I system is used with the Sequential Fuel Injection system on Buick manufactured engines. Currently there are 3 type of C³I systems: Type I, Type II and Type III (Fast Start).

IGNITION COILS

There are 3 separate coils are mounted to the module assembly. Each coil provides spark for a pair of plugs simultaneously, called waste sprak distribution.

The ignition coils on Type I ignition coil and module assembly cannot be serviced separately, but must have the entire assembly replaced, should a coil become defective. Type II provides separate servicing of the coils or module by individual replacement, if required.

The third sytem, known as the Type III (Fast Start), is similar in appearance to the Type I. In fact the coil packs are interchangable; however, the modules are not as the harness connector plugs are not compatable. There are also notable differences in the wiring harness, crankshaft sensor and harmonic balancer. The Type III system is used on the 1988–90 3800 Buick engine.

The system uses EST and C³I control wires from the ECM like the distributor type systems. The Fast Start system used on the LN3 (3.8L multiport fuel injection) engine has 18 windows on the outer ring and 3 windows on the inner ring. This enables spark to begin sequencing before the first cam sensor pulse. The LG3 (3.8L sequential fuel injection) engine is a carryover and has a single ring on the balancer with 3 windows.

C³I MODULE

The ignition module monitors the cam and crankshaft signals. This information is passed on to the ECM so that the correct spark and fuel injector timing can be maintained during all driving conditions. During the cranking mode, it monitors the camshaft signal to begin the ignition firing sequence and the fuel injection timing (SFI).

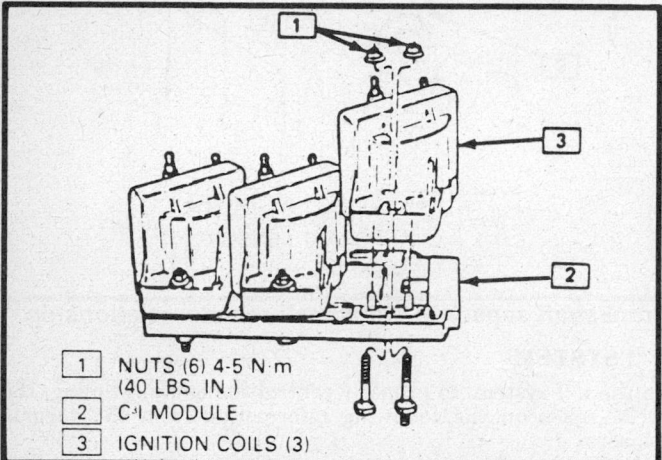

1	NUTS (6) 4-5 N·m (40 LBS. IN.)
2	C³I MODULE
3	IGNITION COILS (3)

Type II separate ignition coils and module

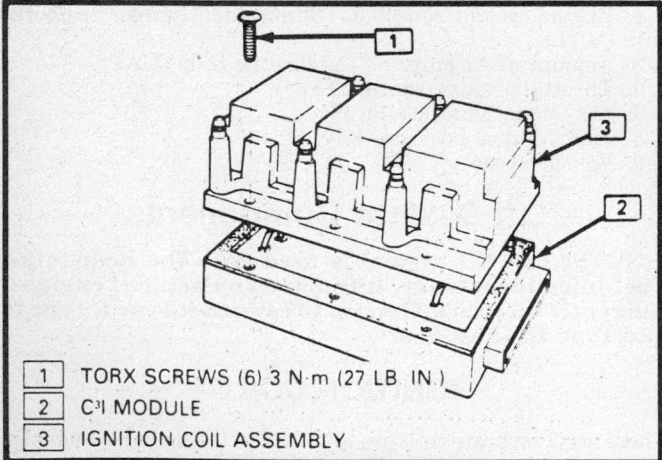

1	TORX SCREWS (6) 3 N·m (27 LB. IN.)
2	C³I MODULE
3	IGNITION COIL ASSEMBLY

Type I ignition coil assembly and module

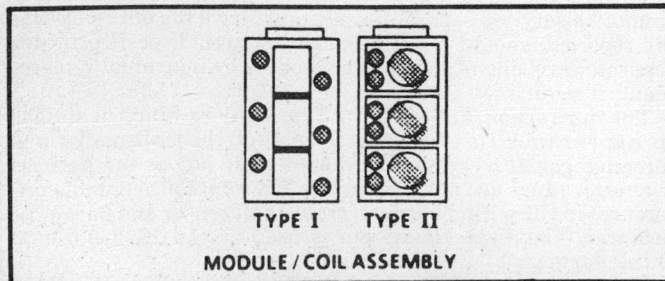

TYPE I   TYPE II

MODULE / COIL ASSEMBLY

Type I and Type II coil/module identification

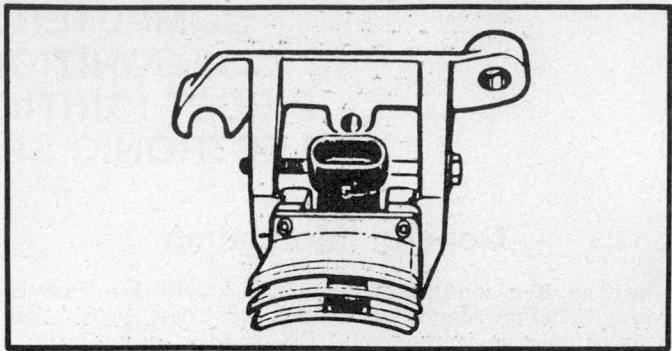

Crankshaft sensor

Camshaft sensor

Below 400 rpm, the module controls the spark advance by triggering each of the coils at a predetermined interval, based on engine speed only. Above 400 rpm, the C³I module relays the crankshaft signal to the ECM as a reference signal. The ECM then controls the spark timing and compensates for all driving conditions. The C³I module must receive a camshaft and then a crankshaft signal, in that order, to enable the engine to start.

The C³I module is not repairable. When a module is replaced, the 3 coils must be transferred to the new module. Remember that Type III modules cannot be used in Type I and Type II systems.

CAMSHAFT SENSOR

The camshaft sensor is located on the timing cover, behind the water pump, near the camshaft sprocket. As the camshaft sprocket turns, a magnet mounted on it, activates the Hall effect switch in the cam sensor. This grounds the signal line to the C³I module, pulling the crankshaft signal line's applied voltage low. This is interpreted as a cam signal (Sync. Pulse). Because the way the signal is created by the crankshaft sensor, the signal circuit is always either at a high or a low voltage, known as a square voltage signal. While the camshaft sprocket continues to turn, the Hall effect switch turns off as the magnetic field passes the cam sensor, resulting in a signal each time the camshaft makes a revolution. The cam signal is created as piston No.1 and No.4 reach approximately 25 degrees after top dead center. It is then used by the C³I module to begin the ignition coil firing sequence, starting with the No.3/6 ignition coil because the No.6 piston is now at the correct position in its compression stroke for the spark plug to be fired.

This camshaft signal, which actually represents camshaft position due to the sensors mounting location, is also used by the ECM to properly time its sequential fuel injection operation.

Both the crankshaft and camshaft sensor signals must be received by the ignition module for the engine to start. When the cam signal is not received by the ECM, such as during cranking, fuel injection is simultaneous, rather than sequenstially timed and a code (E041) will be set.

If the code (E041) is set and the engine will start and run, the fault is in circuit for the cam signal (cirk.630), the C³I module or the ECM. Under these conditions, the C³I module will determine the ignition timing.

If the fault is in the camshaft sensor circuit, the cam sensor or the cam signal portion of the C³I module, code E041 may also be present, but the engine will not start, since the C³I module can not determine the position of the No. 1 piston.

CRANKSHAFT SENSOR

A magnetic crankshaft sensor (Hall effect switch) is used and is mounted in a pedestal on the front of the engine near the harmonic balancer. The sensor is a Hall effect switch which depends on a metal intrrupter ring, mounted on the balancer, to activate it. Windows in the interrupter activates the Hall effect switch as they provide a a path for the magnetic field between the switch's transducer and its magnet.

When the Hall effect switch is activated, it grounds the signal line to the C³I module, pulling the crankshaft signal line's applied voltage low, which is interperted as a crankshaft signal. Because of the way the signal by the crank sensor is created, the signal circuit is always either at a high or low voltage (square wave signal) and 3 signal pulses are created during each crankshaft revolution. This signal is used by the C³I module to create a reference signal, which is also a square wave signal, similar to the crank signal. The reference signal is used to calculate engine rpm and crankshaft position by the ECM. A misadjusted sensor or bent interrupter ring could cause rubbing of the sensor resulting in potential driveability problems, such as rough idle, poor engine performance, or a no-start condition.

NOTE: Failure to have the correct clearance between the sensor and the interrupter ring could damage the sensor.

The crankshaft sensor is not adjustable for ignition timing, but positioning of the interrupter ring is very important. A clearance of 0.025 in. is required on either side of the interrupter ring.

A crankshaft sensor that is damaged due to mispositioning, or a bent interrupter ring can result in an engine hesitation, sag stumble or dieseling condition. To determine if the crankshaft sensor is at fault, observe the diagnostic display ECM data, ED11 (engine rpm), while driving the vehicle. An erratic display indicates that a proper reference pulse has not been received by the ECM, which may be the result of a malfunctioning crankshaft sensor.

COMBINATION SENSOR

On certain engine applications, such as the 3.0L engine, the crankshaft and camshaft functions are combined into a dual sensor, called a combination sensor, which is mounted at the harmonic balancer. It functions the same as though both camshaft and crankshaft sensors are used.

The reason this type of sensor can be used is the fact that the 3.0L engine is a simultaneously injected engine, which does not require the actual camshaft signal. Instead, it uses a sync Pulse signal from the combination sensor, at the rate of 1 per each revolution of the crankshaft. The combination sensor is activated and controls its signal lines in the same way the crankshaft sensor does on the other engines. The only difference is the sync Pulse portion of the sensor, which serves the same purpose as the cam sensor on the other engines, relative to ignition operation. That is, it starts the ignition coil firing sequence, starting with the 3–6 ignition coil.

ELECTRONIC CONTROL MODULE (ECM)

The ECM is responsible for maintaining the proper spark and fuel injection timing for all driving conditions.

To provide optimum driveability and emissions, the ECM

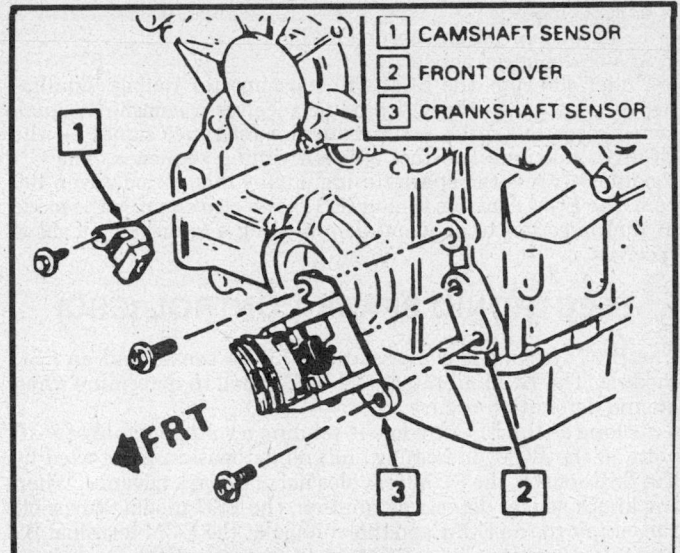

Crankshaft and camshaft sensor locations

1	CAMSHAFT SENSOR
2	FRONT COVER
3	CRANKSHAFT SENSOR

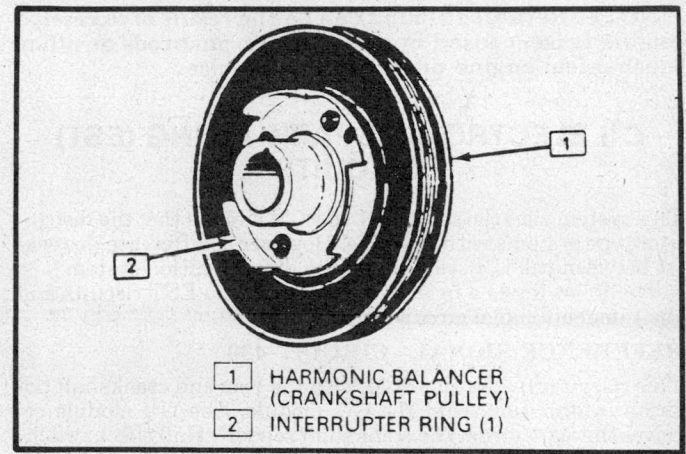

Harmonic balancer and interrupter ring

| 1 | HARMONIC BALANCER (CRANKSHAFT PULLEY) |
| 2 | INTERRUPTER RING (1) |

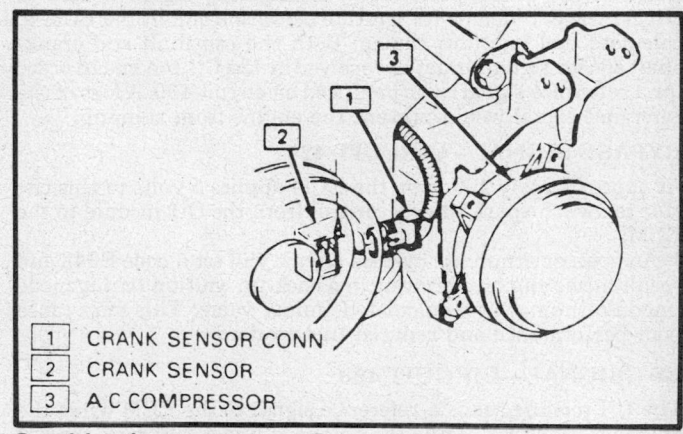

Combination sensor

1	CRANK SENSOR CONN
2	CRANK SENSOR
3	A C COMPRESSOR

monitors input signals from the following components in calculating Electronic Spark Timing (EST).
1. Ignition module
2. Coolant temperature
3. Manifold air temperature sensor
4. Mass air flow sensor
5. Park/neutral switch

6. ESC module
7. Throttle position sensor (TPS)
8. Vehicle speed sensor

Under 400 rpm, the ECM will start injector timing (simultaneous) as soon as the C³I module receives a camshaft signal, syncronizes the spark and produces a reference signal for the ECM to calculate the fuel ignition timing sequence. The C³I module controls the spark timing during this period. Over 400 rpm, the ECM controls timing (EST) and also changes the mode of fuel injection to sequential, providing a camshaft signal is received.

ELECTRONIC SPARK CONTROL (ESC)

The ESC systems is comprised of a knock sensor and an ESC module. The ECM monitors the ESC signal to determine when engine detonation occurs.

As long as the ESC module is sending a voltage signal of 8–10 volts to the ECM, indicating that no detonation is detected by the ESC sensor, the ECM provides normal spark advance. When the knock sensor detects detonation, the ESC module turns off the circuit to the ECM and the voltage at the ECM terminal B7 drops to 0 volts. The ECM then retards EST to reduce detonation.

NOTE: Retarded timing can be the result of excessive engine noise, caused by valve lifters, pushrods or other mechanical engine or transmission noise.

C³I ELECTRONIC SPARK TIMING (EST) CIRCUITS

This system uses the same EST to ECM circuits that the distributor type systems with EST use. However, a difference does exist between the C³I system and the direct ignition system.

The following is a brief description for the EST circuits and the camshaft signal circuit (CIRK 630).

REFERENCE SIGNAL – CIRCUIT 430

This circuit provides the ECM with the rpm and crankshaft position information from the C³I module. The C³I module receives the signal from the crankshaft sensor's Hall effect switch.

This signal will either be high or low, depending upon the position of the interrupter ring. This high-low signal is used to trigger the C³I module for ignition operation and by the ECM to calculate fuel injection timing. Both the camshaft and crankshaft sensor signals must be received by the C³I module in order for a reference signal to be produced on circuit 430. A loss of the reference signal would prevent the engine from running.

BYPASS SIGNAL – CIRCUIT 424

At approximately 400 rpm, the ECM applies 5 volts to this circuit to switch spark timing control from the C³I module to the ECM.

An open or grounded by-pass circuit will set a code E042 and result in the engine operating in a back-up ignition timing mode (module timing) at a calculated timing value. This may cause poor performance and reduced fuel economy.

EST SIGNAL – CIRCUIT 423

The C³I module sends a reference signal to the ECM when the engine is cranking. While the engine is under 400 rpm, the C³I module controls the ignition timing. When the engine speed exceeds 400 rpm, the ECM applies 5 volts to the by-pass line to switch the timing to the ECM control (EST).

An open or ground in the EST circuit will stall the engine and set a code E042. The engine can be restarted, but will operate in a back-up ignition timing mode (module timing) at a calculated timing value. This may cause poor performance and reduced fuel economy.

CAM SIGNAL – CIRCUIT 630

The ECM uses this signal to determine the position of the No. 1 piston in its compression stroke. This signal is used by the ECM to calculate the sequential fuel injection (SFI) mode of operation. A loss of this signal will set a Code E041. If the cam signal is lost while the engine is running, the fuel injection system will shift to the simultaneous injection mode of operation and the engine will continue to operate. The engine can be re-started, but will continue to run in the simultaneous mode as long as the fault is present.

C³I System Diagnosis

C³I IGNITION SYSTEM/EST

NOTE: Verification of Type I or Type II systems is very important, because the diagnostics are not the same for both types.

If the engine cranks, but will not operate, or starts and immediately stalls, further diagnosis must be made to determine if the failure is in the ignition system or the fuel system.

A code E041 or E042 maybe set in the computers memory and must be deleted.

Direct Ignition System Components

NOTE: The direct ignition system/EST is used with TBI and Ported fuel injection systems.

CRANKSHAFT SENSOR

A magnetic crankshaft sensor (Hall effect switch) is used and is remotely mounted on the opposite side of the engine from the "DIS" module. The sensor extends into the engine block, within 0.050 in. of the crankshaft reluctor.

The reluctor is a special wheel cast into the crankshaft with 7 slots machined into it, 6 of them being evenly spaced at 60 degrees apart. A seventh slot is spaced 10 degrees from another slot and serves as a generator of a sync-pulse. As the reluctor rotates as part of the crankshaft, the slots change the magnetic field of the sensor, creating an induced voltage pulse.

Based on the crankshaft sensor pulses, the DIS module sends reference signals to the ECM, which are used to indicate crankshaft position and engine speed. The DIS module will continue to send these reference pulses to the ECM at a rate of 1 per each 120 degrees of crankshaft rotation. The ECM actvates the fuel injectors, based on the recognition of every other reaference pulse, beginning at a crankshaft position 120 degrees after piston top dead center (TDC). By comparing the time between the pulses, the DIS module can recognize the pulse representing the seventh slot (sync pulse) which starts the calculation of ignition coil sequencing. The second crankshaft pulse following the sync pulse signals the DIS module to fire the No.2-5 ignition coil, the fourth crankshaft pulse signals the module to fire No.3-6 ignition coil and the sixth crankshaft pulse signals the module to fire the No. 1-4 ignition coil.

IGNITION COILS

There are 2 separate coils for 4 cylinder engine and 3 separate coils for the V6 engine, mounted to the coil/module assembly. Spark distribution is synchronized by a signal from the crankshaft sensor which the ignition module uses to trigger each coil at the proper time. Each coil provides the spark for a pair of spark plugs.

There are 3 types of ignition coil assemblies used: Type I, Type II and Type III. During the diagnosis of the systems, the correct type of ignition coil assembly must be identified and the diagnosis directed to that system.

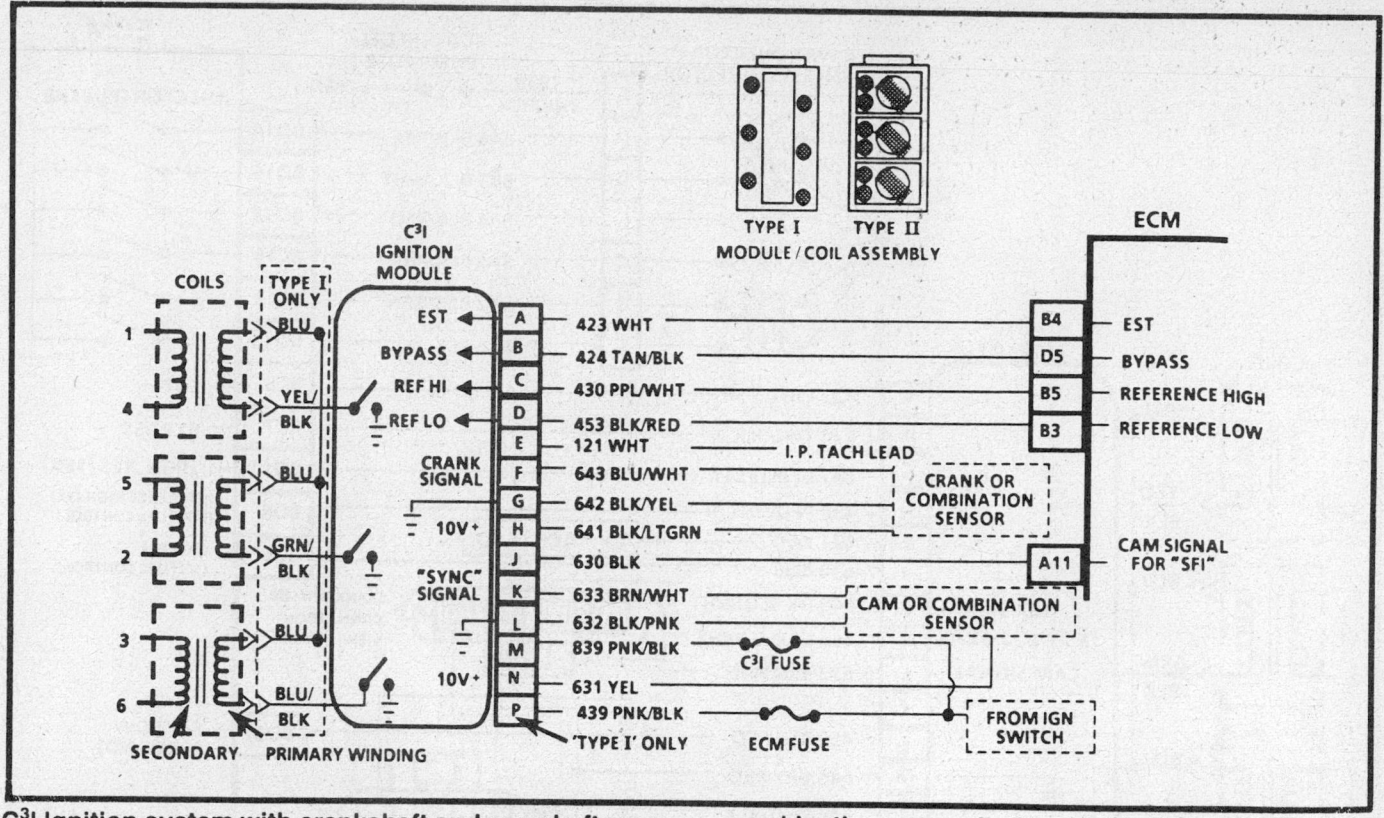

C³I Ignition system with crankshaft and camshaft sensor or combination sensor in the electrical system

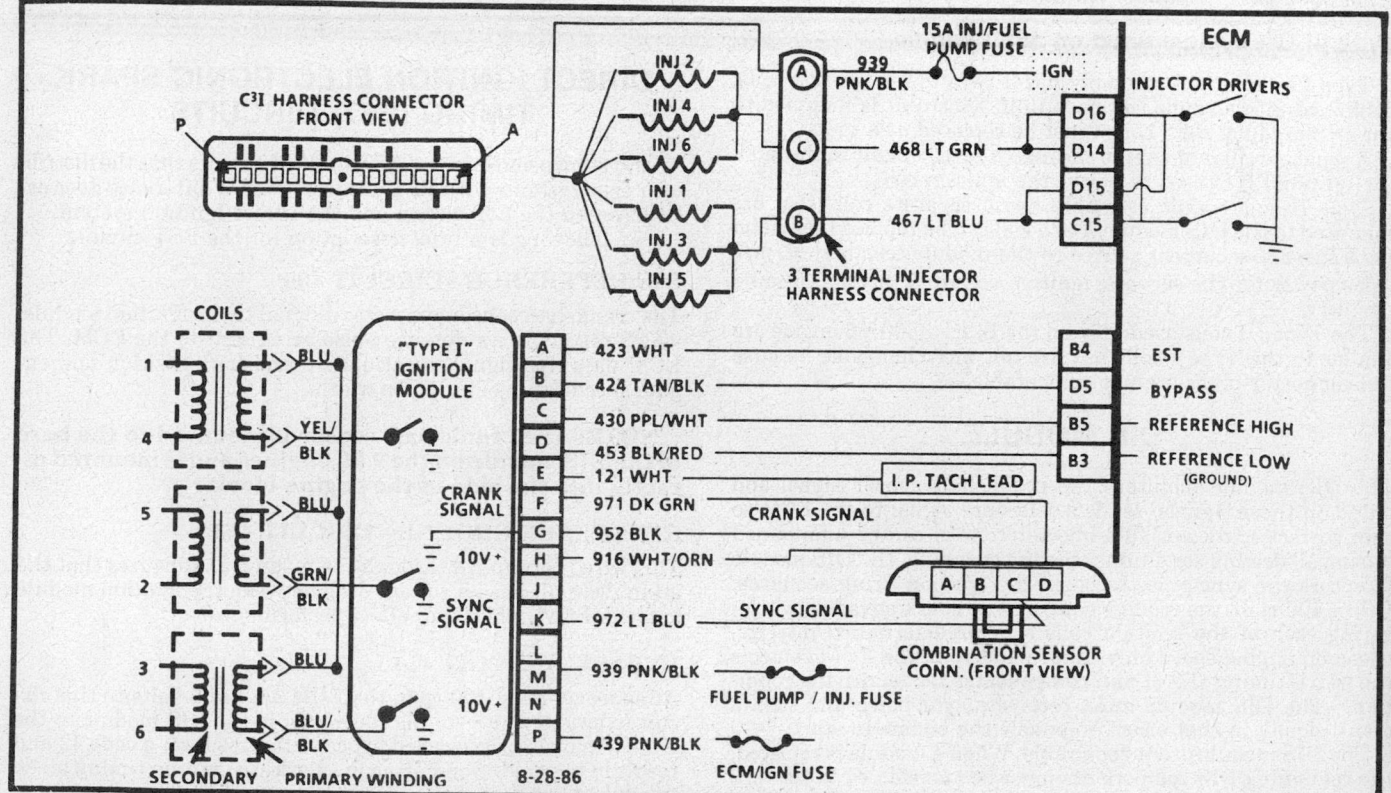

Type I C³I Ignition system with only combination sensor

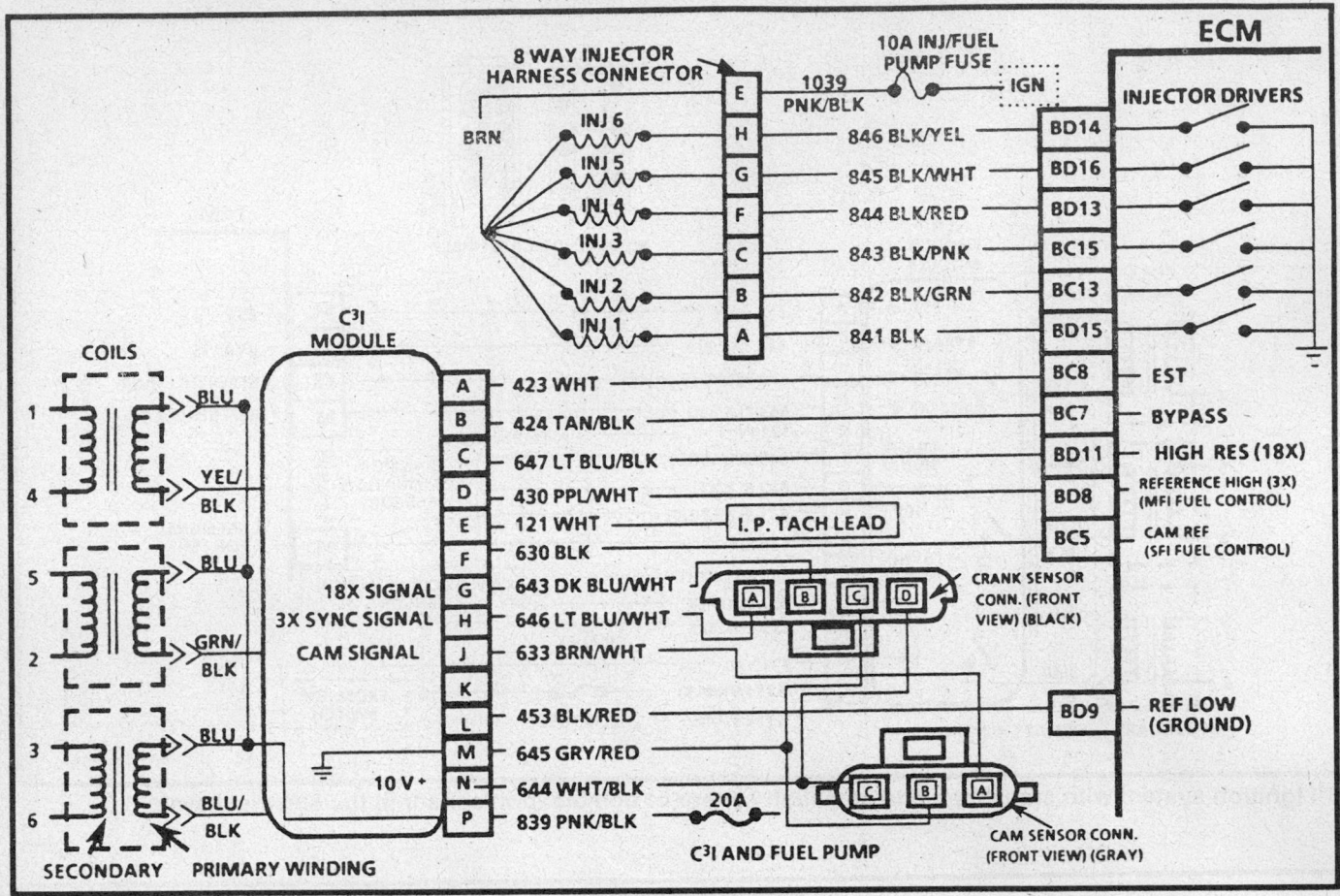

Type III C³I system used on 3800 engine

Type I module/coil assembly has 3 twin tower ignition coils, combined into a single coil pack unit. This unit is mounted to the DIS module. All 3 coils must be replaced as a unit.

A separate current source through a fused circuit to the module terminal P is used to power the ignition coils.

Type II coil/module assembly has 3 separate coils that are mounted to the DIS module. Each coil can be replaced separately. A fused low current source to the module terminal M, provides power for the sensors, ignition coils and internal module circuitry.

The Type III coils used only on the Buick 3800 V6 engine are similar to the Type I coils but are not interchangable because the connector plugs are not compatable.

DIS MODULE

The DIS module monitors the crankshaft sensor signal and based on these signals, sends a reference signal to the ECM so that correct spark and fuel injector control can be maintained during all driving conditions. During cranking, the DIS module monitors the sync-pulse to begin the ignition firing sequence. Below 400 rpm, the module controls the spark advance by triggering each of the ignition coils at a predetermined interval, based on engine speed only. Above 400 rpm, the ECM controls the spark timing (EST) and compensates for all driving conditions. The DIS module must receive a sync-pulse and then a crank signal, in that order, to enable the engine to start.

The DIS module is not repairable. When a module is replaced, the remaining DIS components must be transferred to the new module. Type III modules cannot be used with Type I and Type II systems.

DIRECT IGNITION ELECTRONIC SPARK TIMING (EST) CIRCUITS

This system uses the same EST to ECM circuits that the distributor type systems with EST use. However, a difference does exist between the C³I system and the Direct Ignition system.

The following is a brief description for the EST circuits.

DIS REFERENCE – CIRCUIT 430

The crankshaft sensor generates a signal to the ignition module, which results in a reference pulse being sent to the ECM. The ECM uses this signal to calculate crankshaft position and engine speed for injector pulse width.

NOTE: The crankshaft sensor is mounted to the base of the DIS module on the 2.5L engines and is mounted directly into the side of the engine block.

REFERENCE GROUND – CIRCUIT 453

This wire is grounded through the module and insures that the ground circuit has no voltage drop between the ignition module and the ECM, which can affect performance.

BYPASS – CIRCUIT 424

At approximately 400 rpm, the ECM applies 5 volts to this circuit to switch spark timing control from the DIS module to the ECM. An open or grounded bypass circuit will set a code 42 and result in the engine operating in a back-up ignition timing mode (module timing) at a calculated timing value. This may cause poor performance and reduced fuel economy.

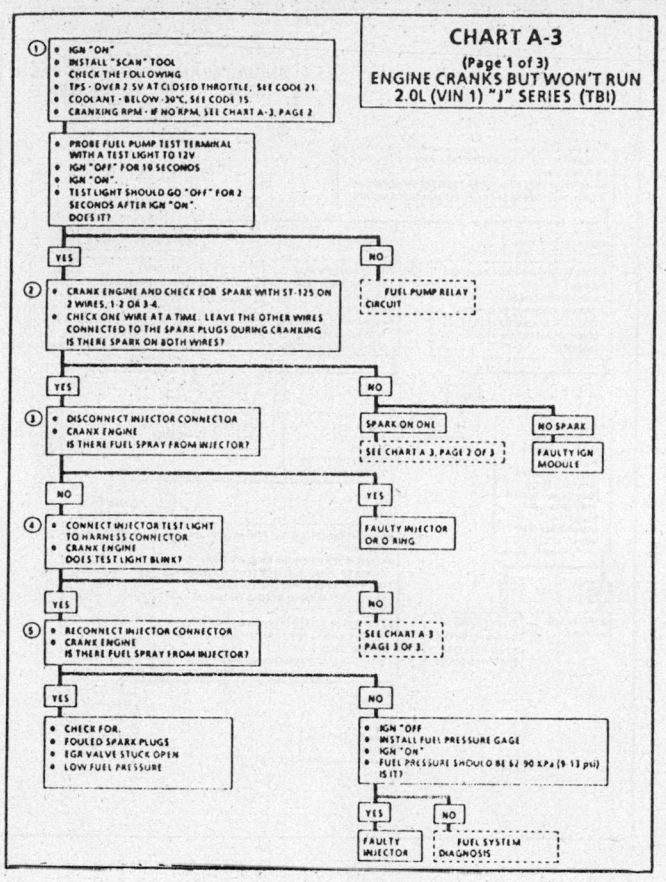

CHART A-3
(Page 1 of 3)
ENGINE CRANKS BUT WON'T RUN
2.0L (VIN 1) "J" SERIES (TBI)

(1)
- IGN "ON"
- INSTALL "SCAN" TOOL
- CHECK THE FOLLOWING:
- TPS - OVER 2.5V AT CLOSED THROTTLE, SEE CODE 21.
- COOLANT - BELOW -30°C, SEE CODE 15.
- CRANKING RPM - IF NO RPM, SEE CHART A-3, PAGE 2.

- PROBE FUEL PUMP TEST TERMINAL WITH A TEST LIGHT TO 12V
- IGN "OFF" FOR 10 SECONDS
- IGN "ON"
- TEST LIGHT SHOULD GO "OFF" FOR 2 SECONDS AFTER IGN "ON".
  DOES IT?

YES / **NO** → FUEL PUMP RELAY CIRCUIT

(2)
- CRANK ENGINE AND CHECK FOR SPARK WITH ST-125 ON 2 WIRES, 1-2 OR 3-4.
- CHECK ONE WIRE AT A TIME. LEAVE THE OTHER WIRES CONNECTED TO THE SPARK PLUGS DURING CRANKING
- IS THERE SPARK ON BOTH WIRES?

YES / **NO**

SPARK ON ONE → SEE CHART A-3, PAGE 2 OF 3
NO SPARK → FAULTY IGN MODULE

(3)
- DISCONNECT INJECTOR CONNECTOR
- CRANK ENGINE
- IS THERE FUEL SPRAY FROM INJECTOR?

NO / **YES** → FAULTY INJECTOR OR O RING

(4)
- CONNECT INJECTOR TEST LIGHT TO HARNESS CONNECTOR
- CRANK ENGINE
- DOES TEST LIGHT BLINK?

YES / **NO** → SEE CHART A-3 PAGE 3 OF 3.

(5)
- RECONNECT INJECTOR CONNECTOR
- CRANK ENGINE
- IS THERE FUEL SPRAY FROM INJECTOR?

YES / **NO**

CHECK FOR:
- FOULED SPARK PLUGS
- EGR VALVE STUCK OPEN
- LOW FUEL PRESSURE

- IGN "OFF"
- INSTALL FUEL PRESSURE GAGE
- IGN "ON"
- FUEL PRESSURE SHOULD BE 62-90 kPa (9-13 psi). IS IT?

YES → FAULTY INJECTOR / **NO** → FUEL SYSTEM DIAGNOSIS

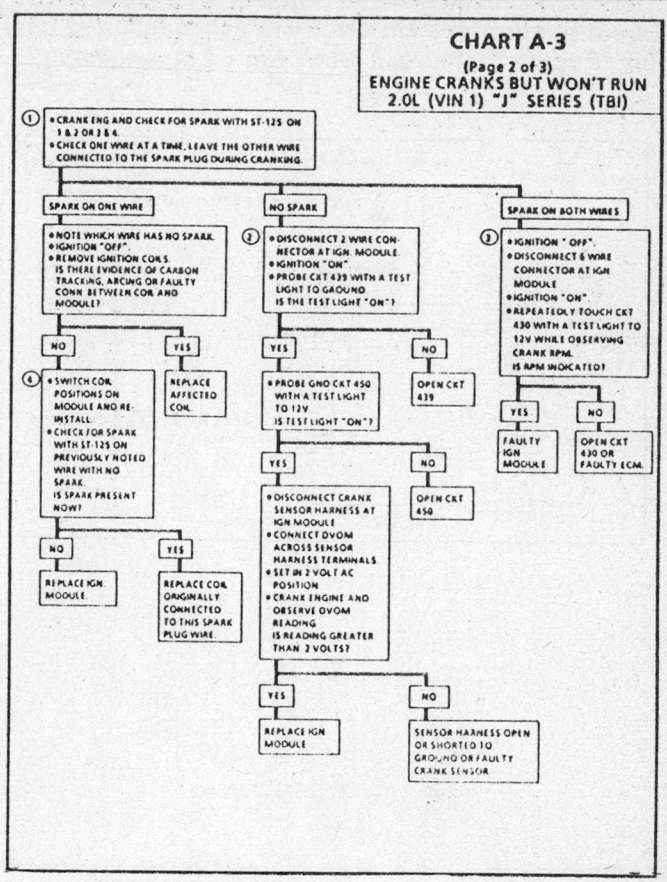

CHART A-3
(Page 2 of 3)
ENGINE CRANKS BUT WON'T RUN
2.0L (VIN 1) "J" SERIES (TBI)

(1)
- CRANK ENG AND CHECK FOR SPARK WITH ST-125 ON 1 & 2 OR 3 & 4.
- CHECK ONE WIRE AT A TIME. LEAVE THE OTHER WIRE CONNECTED TO THE SPARK PLUG DURING CRANKING.

SPARK ON ONE WIRE | NO SPARK | SPARK ON BOTH WIRES

SPARK ON ONE WIRE:
- NOTE WHICH WIRE HAS NO SPARK.
- IGNITION "OFF".
- REMOVE IGNITION COILS. IS THERE EVIDENCE OF CARBON TRACKING, ARCING OR FAULTY CONN BETWEEN COIL AND MODULE?

NO / **YES** → REPLACE AFFECTED COIL

(4)
- SWITCH COIL POSITIONS ON MODULE AND RE-INSTALL.
- CHECK FOR SPARK WITH ST-125 ON PREVIOUSLY NOTED WIRE WITH NO SPARK. IS SPARK PRESENT NOW?

NO → REPLACE IGN. MODULE / **YES** → REPLACE COIL ORIGINALLY CONNECTED TO THIS SPARK PLUG WIRE

NO SPARK:
(2)
- DISCONNECT 2 WIRE CONNECTOR AT IGN. MODULE.
- IGNITION "ON".
- PROBE CKT 439 WITH A TEST LIGHT TO GROUND. IS THE TEST LIGHT "ON"?

YES / **NO** → OPEN CKT 439

- PROBE GND CKT 450 WITH A TEST LIGHT TO 12V. IS TEST LIGHT "ON"?

YES / **NO** → OPEN CKT 450

- DISCONNECT CRANK SENSOR HARNESS AT IGN MODULE
- CONNECT DVOM ACROSS SENSOR HARNESS TERMINALS.
- SET IN 2 VOLT AC POSITION
- CRANK ENGINE AND OBSERVE DVOM READING. IS READING GREATER THAN 2 VOLTS?

YES → REPLACE IGN MODULE / **NO** → SENSOR HARNESS OPEN OR SHORTED TO GROUND OR FAULTY CRANK SENSOR

SPARK ON BOTH WIRES:
(3)
- IGNITION "OFF".
- DISCONNECT 6 WIRE CONNECTOR AT IGN MODULE
- IGNITION "ON".
- REPEATEDLY TOUCH CKT 430 WITH A TEST LIGHT TO 12V WHILE OBSERVING CRANK RPM. IS RPM INDICATED?

YES → FAULTY IGN MODULE / **NO** → OPEN CKT 430 OR FAULTY ECM.

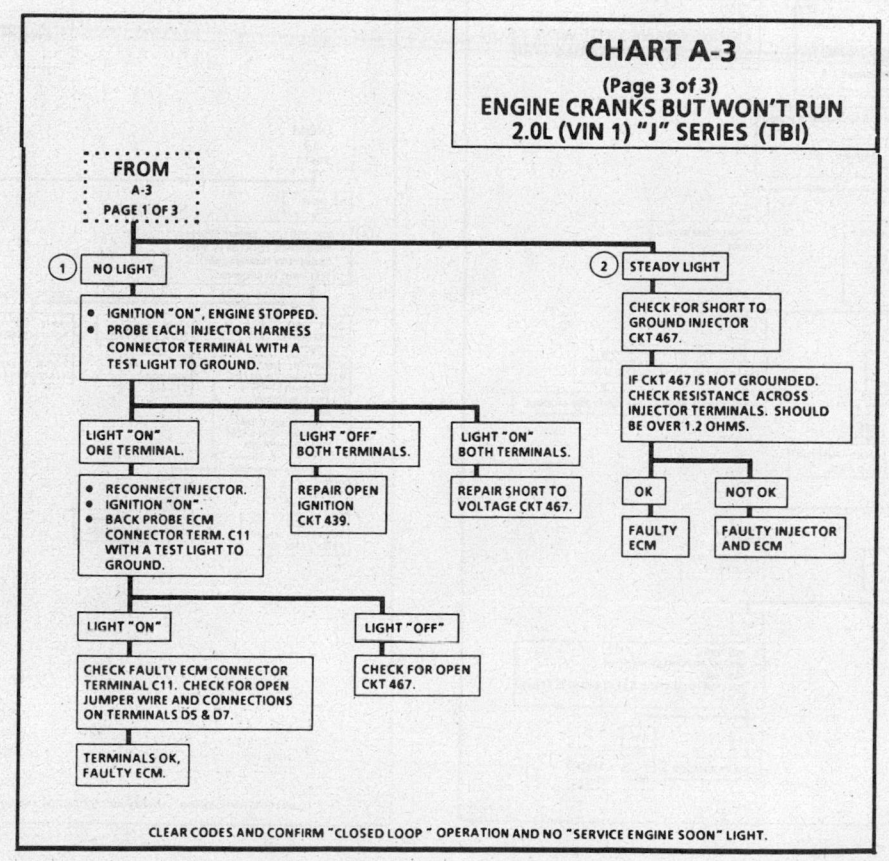

CHART A-3
(Page 3 of 3)
ENGINE CRANKS BUT WON'T RUN
2.0L (VIN 1) "J" SERIES (TBI)

FROM A-3 PAGE 1 OF 3

(1) **NO LIGHT**
- IGNITION "ON", ENGINE STOPPED.
- PROBE EACH INJECTOR HARNESS CONNECTOR TERMINAL WITH A TEST LIGHT TO GROUND.

LIGHT "ON" ONE TERMINAL. | LIGHT "OFF" BOTH TERMINALS. | LIGHT "ON" BOTH TERMINALS.

LIGHT "ON" ONE TERMINAL:
- RECONNECT INJECTOR.
- IGNITION "ON".
- BACK PROBE ECM CONNECTOR TERM. C11 WITH A TEST LIGHT TO GROUND.

LIGHT "OFF" BOTH TERMINALS → REPAIR OPEN IGNITION CKT 439.
LIGHT "ON" BOTH TERMINALS → REPAIR SHORT TO VOLTAGE CKT 467.

LIGHT "ON" | LIGHT "OFF"

LIGHT "ON" → CHECK FAULTY ECM CONNECTOR TERMINAL C11. CHECK FOR OPEN JUMPER WIRE AND CONNECTIONS ON TERMINALS D5 & D7.
→ TERMINALS OK, FAULTY ECM.

LIGHT "OFF" → CHECK FOR OPEN CKT 467.

(2) **STEADY LIGHT**
CHECK FOR SHORT TO GROUND INJECTOR CKT 467.

IF CKT 467 IS NOT GROUNDED. CHECK RESISTANCE ACROSS INJECTOR TERMINALS. SHOULD BE OVER 1.2 OHMS.

OK → FAULTY ECM / NOT OK → FAULTY INJECTOR AND ECM

CLEAR CODES AND CONFIRM "CLOSED LOOP" OPERATION AND NO "SERVICE ENGINE SOON" LIGHT.

Direct Ignition system electrical schematic and charts
for "Engine cranks but won't run", 2.5L engine

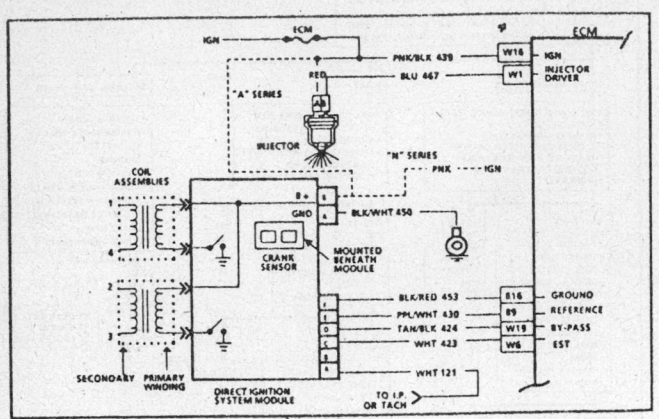

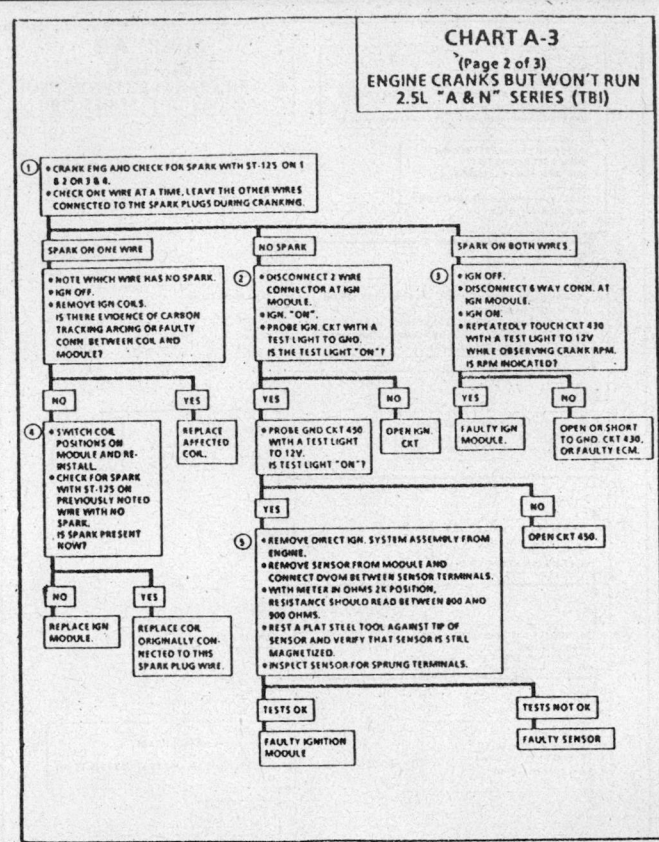

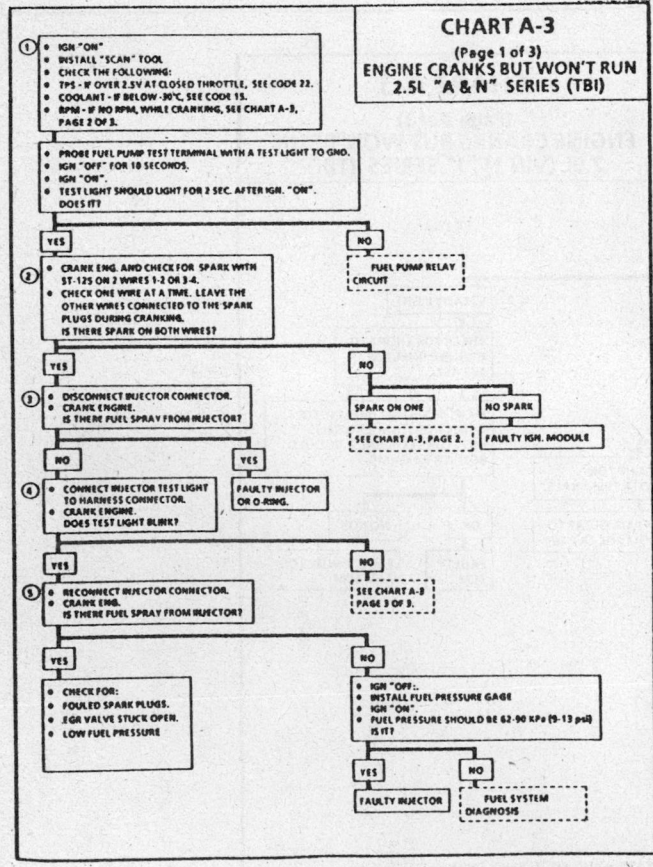

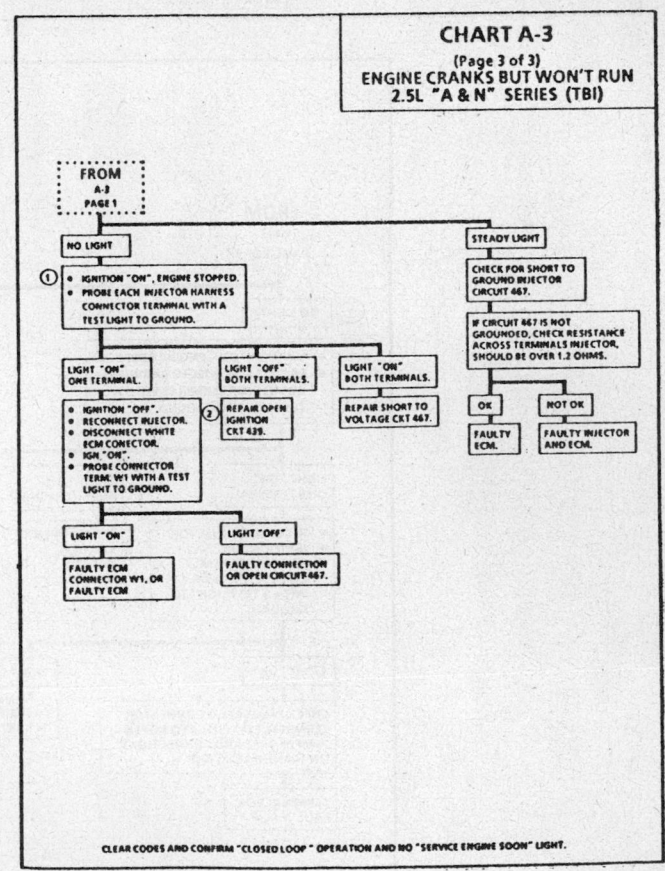

Direct Ignition system electrical schematic and charts for "Engine cranks but won't run", 2.8L engine

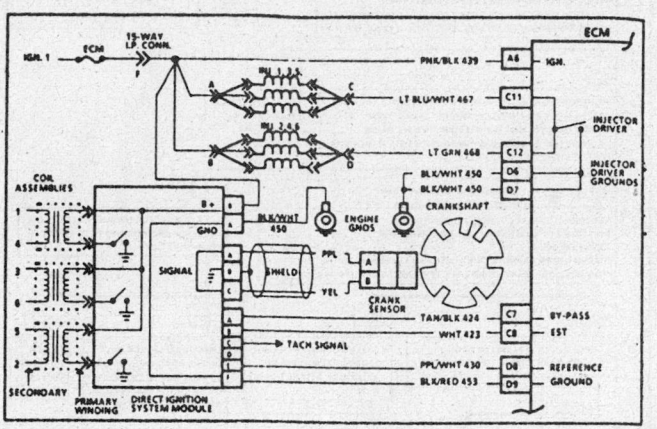

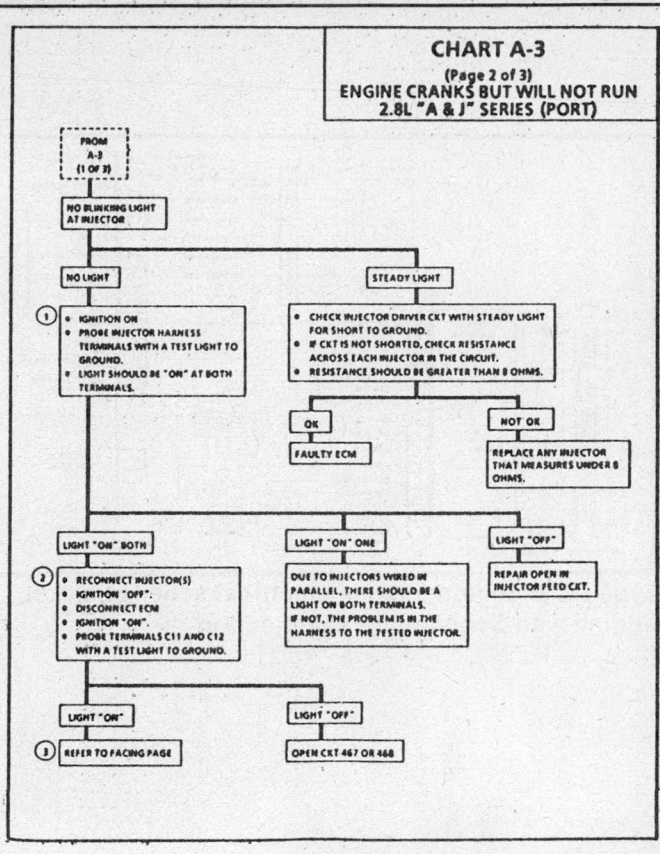

CHART A-3
(Page 2 of 3)
ENGINE CRANKS BUT WILL NOT RUN
2.8L "A & J" SERIES (PORT)

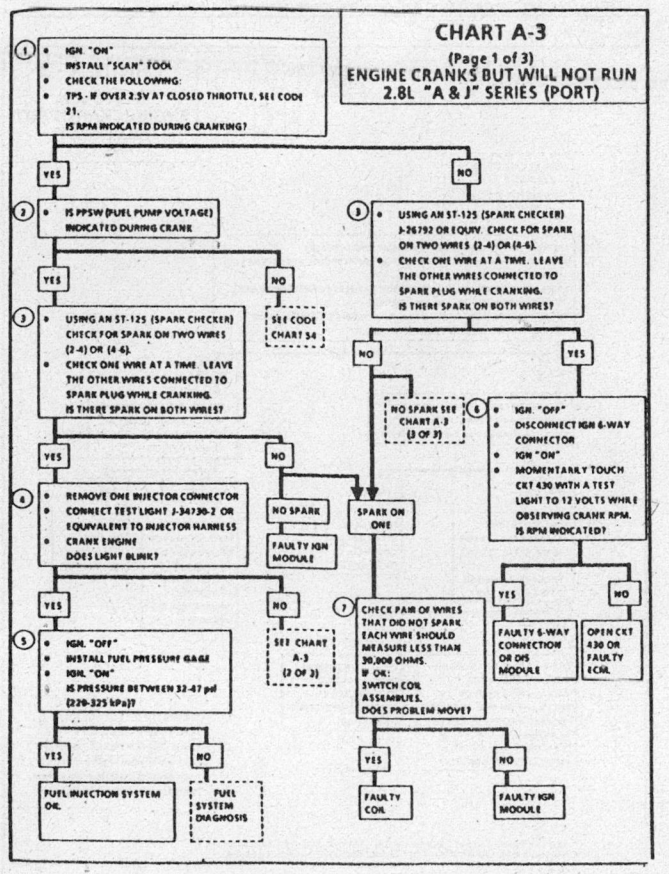

CHART A-3
(Page 1 of 3)
ENGINE CRANKS BUT WILL NOT RUN
2.8L "A & J" SERIES (PORT)

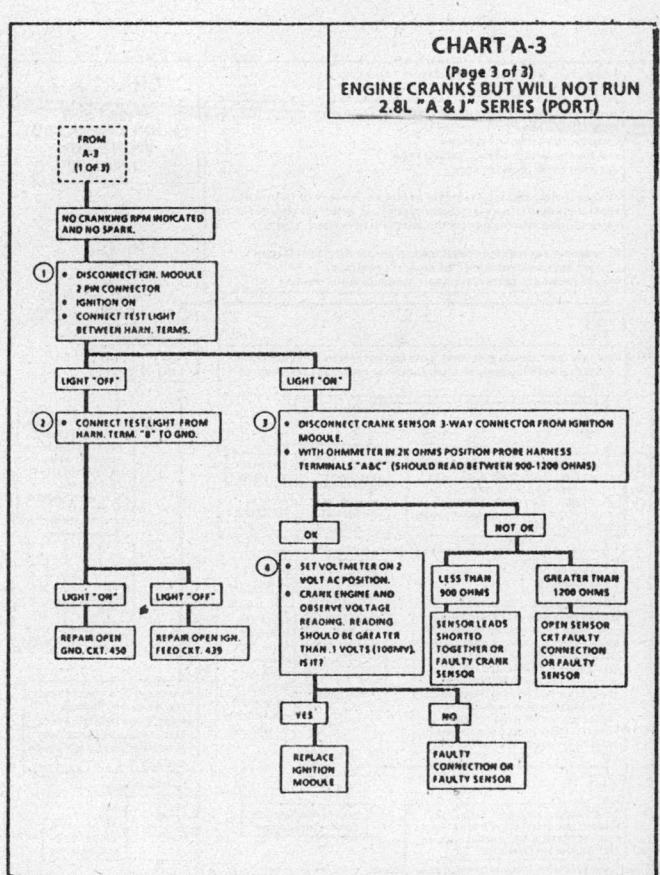

CHART A-3
(Page 3 of 3)
ENGINE CRANKS BUT WILL NOT RUN
2.8L "A & J" SERIES (PORT)

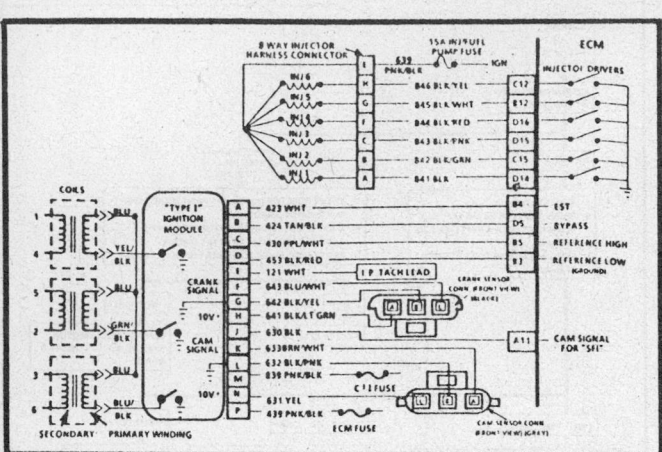

Type I C³I Ignition system electrical schematic, 3.8L engine with Sequential Fuel Injection

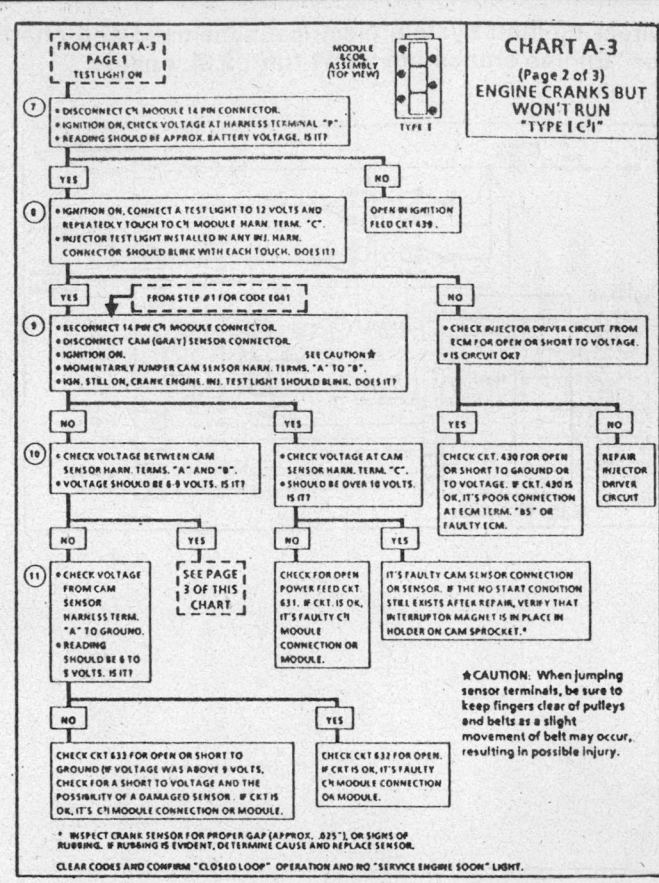

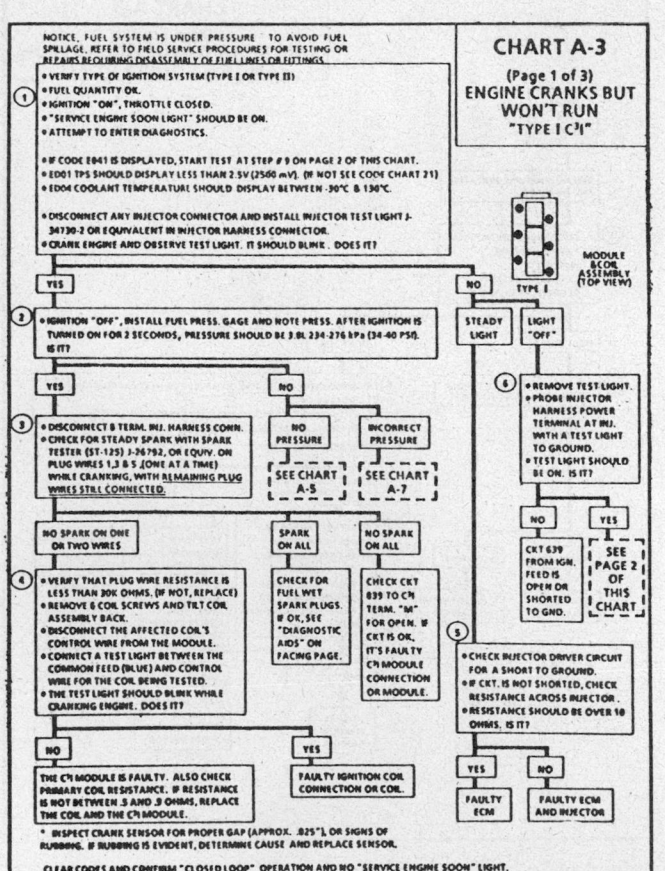

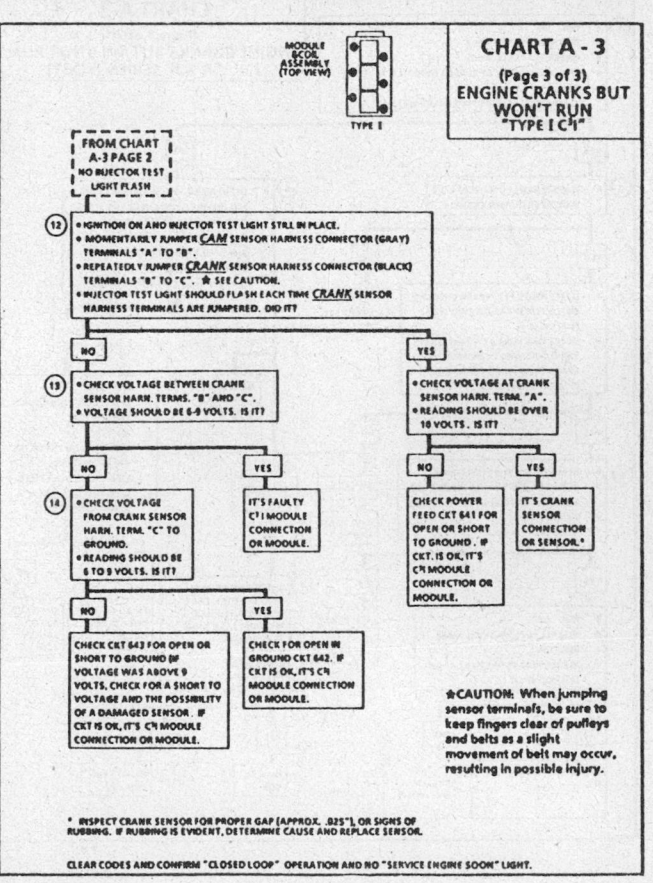

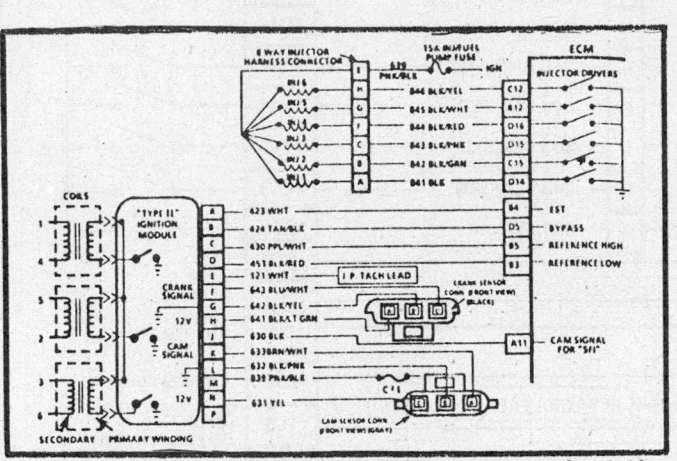

Type II C³I Ignition system electrical schematic, 3.8L engine with Sequential Fuel Injection

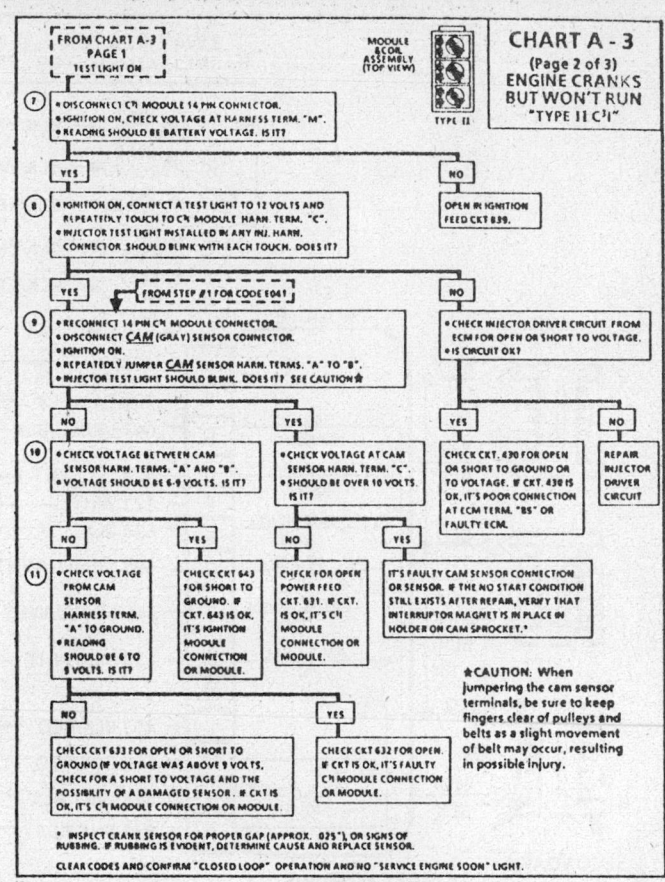

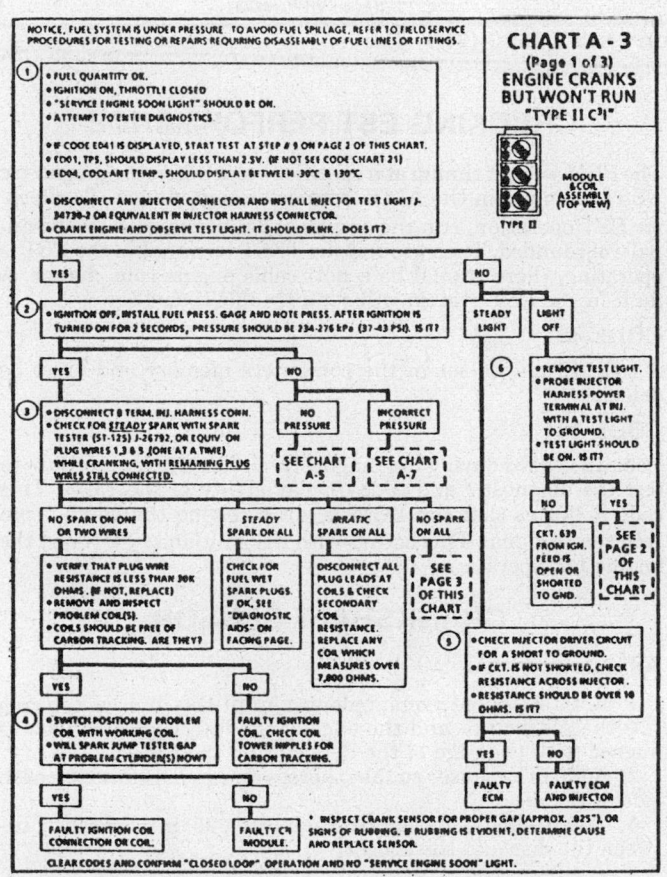

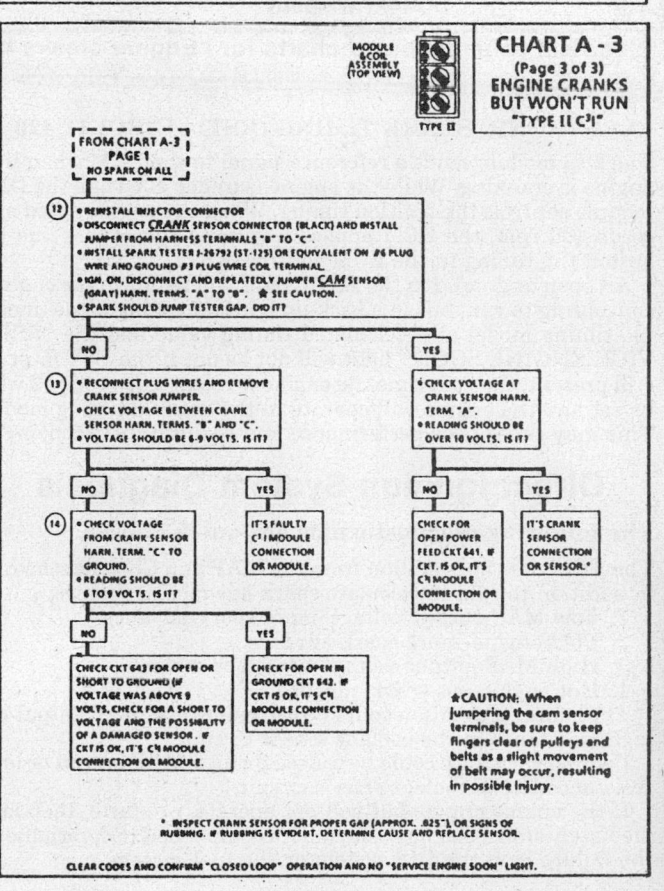

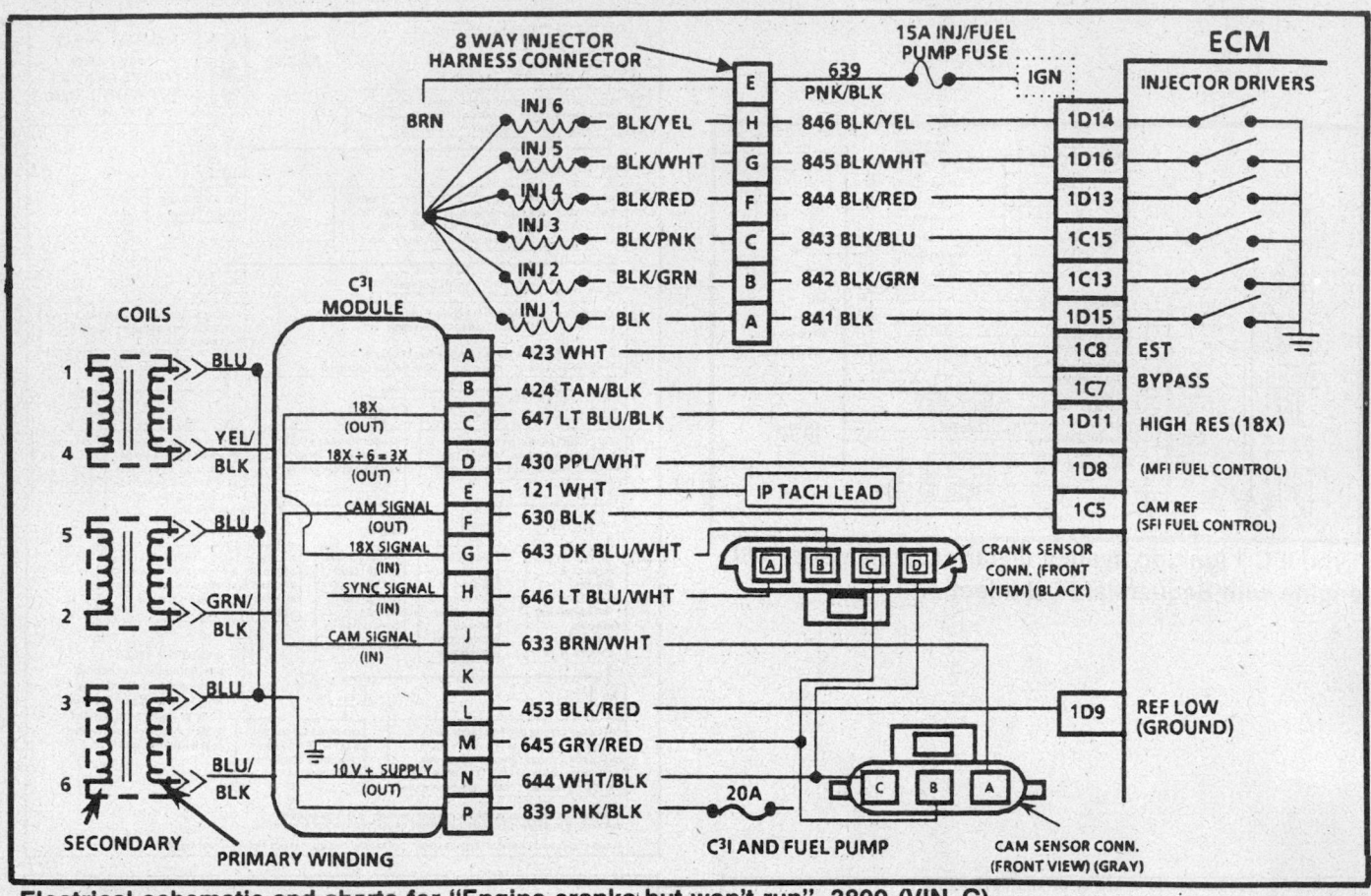

Electrical schematic and charts for "Engine cranks but won't run", 3800 (VIN–C)

ELECTRONIC SPARK TIMING (EST) – CIRCUIT 423

The DIS module sends a reference signal to the ECM when the engine is cranking. While the engine is under 400 rpm, the DIS module controls the ignition timing. When the engine speed exceeds 400 rpm, the ECM applies 5 volts to the bypass line to switch the timing to the ECM control (EST).

An open or ground in the EST circuit will result in the engine continuing to run, but in a back-up ignition timing mode (module timing mode) at a calculated timing value and the "SERVICE ENGINE SOON" light will not be on. If the EST fault is still present, the next time the engine is restarted, a code 42 will be set and the engine will operate in the module timing mode. This may cause poor performance and reduced fuel economy.

Direct Ignition System Diagnosis

The following diagnostic aids are quick checks.

The ECM uses information from the MAP and Coolant sensors, in addition to rpm to calculate spark advance as follows;
1. Low MAP output voltage–more spark advance.
2. Cold engine–more spark advance.
3. High MAP output voltage–ess spark advance.
4. Hot engine–ess spark advance.
Therefore, detonation could be caused by low MAP output or high resistance in the coolant sensor circuit.

Poor performance could be caused by high MAP output or low resistance in the coolant sensor circuit.

If the engine cranks but will not operate, or starts, then immediately stalls, diagnosis must be accomplished to determine if the failure is in the DIS system or the fuel system.

CHECKING EST PERFORMANCE

The ECM will set timing at a specified value when the diagnostic TEST terminal in the ALDL connector is grounded. To check for EST operation, run the engine at 1500 rpm with the terminal ungrounded. Then ground the TEST terminal. If the EST is operating, there should be a noticeable engine rpm change. A fault in the EST system will set a trouble code 42.

CODE 42

A code 42 maybe set in the computers memory and must be deleted.

CODE 12

Code 12 is used during the diagnostic circuit check procedure to test the diagnostic and code display ability of the ECM. This code indicates that the ECM is not receiving the engine rpm (reference) signal. This occurs with the ignition key **ON** and the engine not operating.

CRANKSHAFT SENSOR

Adjustment

1. Rotate the harmonic balancer until the interrupter ring fills the sensor slot and the edge of the interrupter window is aligned with the edge of the deflector on the pedestal.
2. Adjust the sensor so that there is an equal distance on each side of the disc.
3. There should be approximately 0.025 in. clearance between the disc and the sensor.

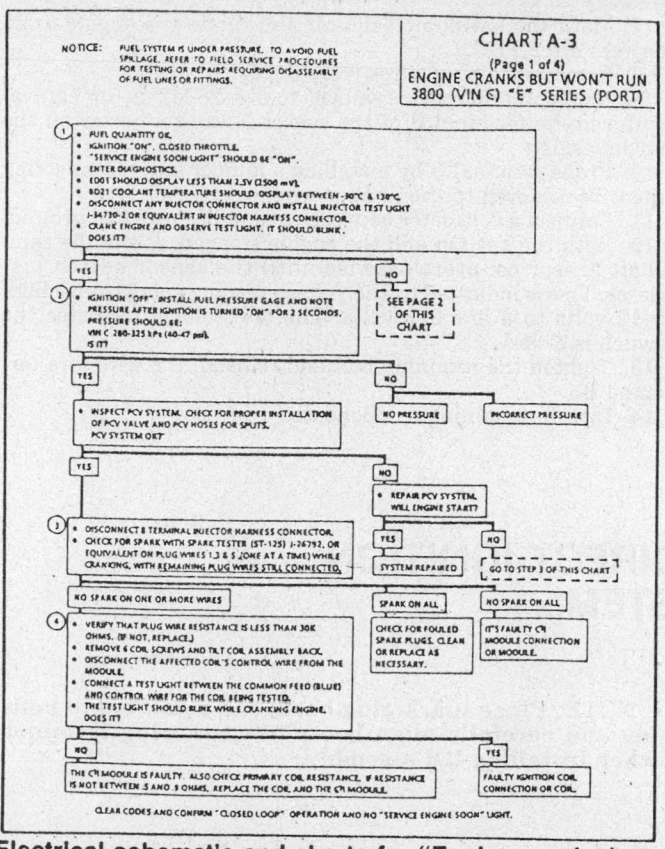

Electrical schematic and charts for "Engine cranks but won't run", 3800 (VIN–C)

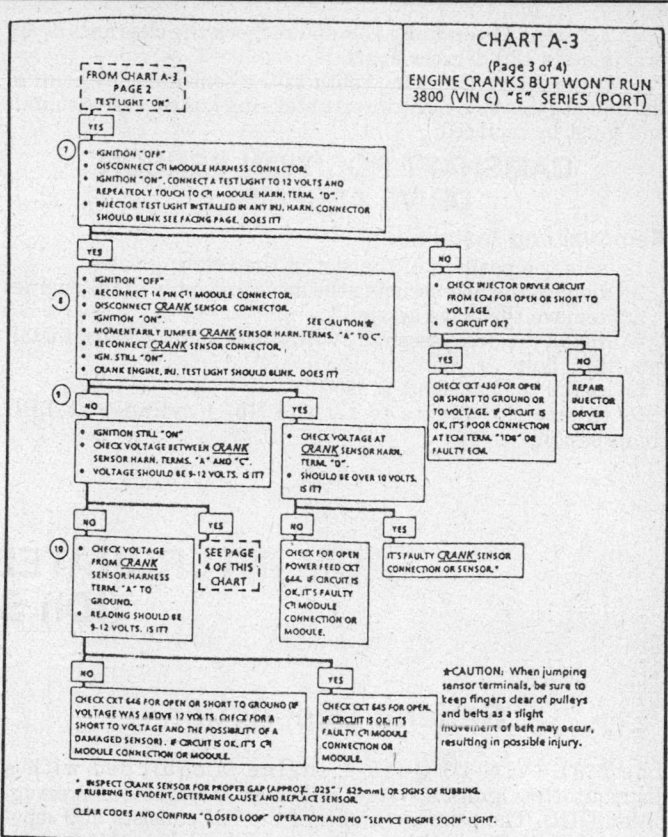

Electrical schematic and charts for "Engine cranks but won't run", 3800 (VIN–C)

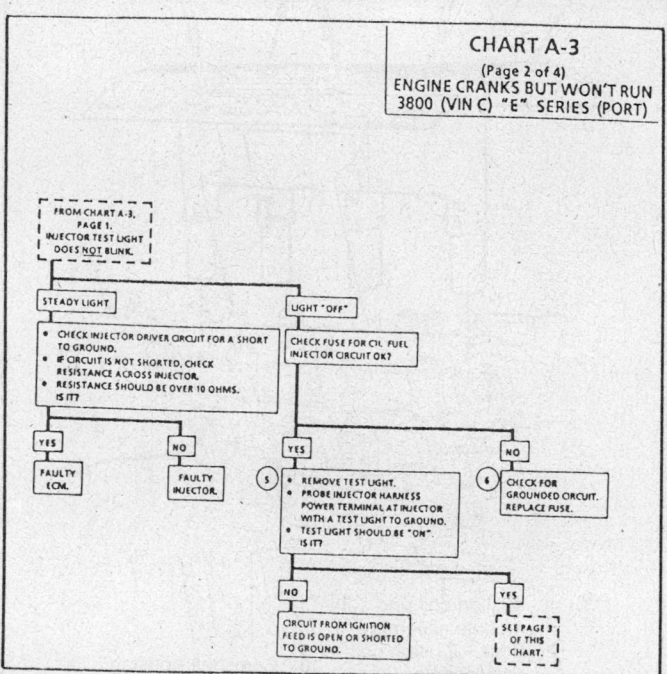

Electrical schematic and charts for "Engine cranks but won't run", 3800 (VIN–C)

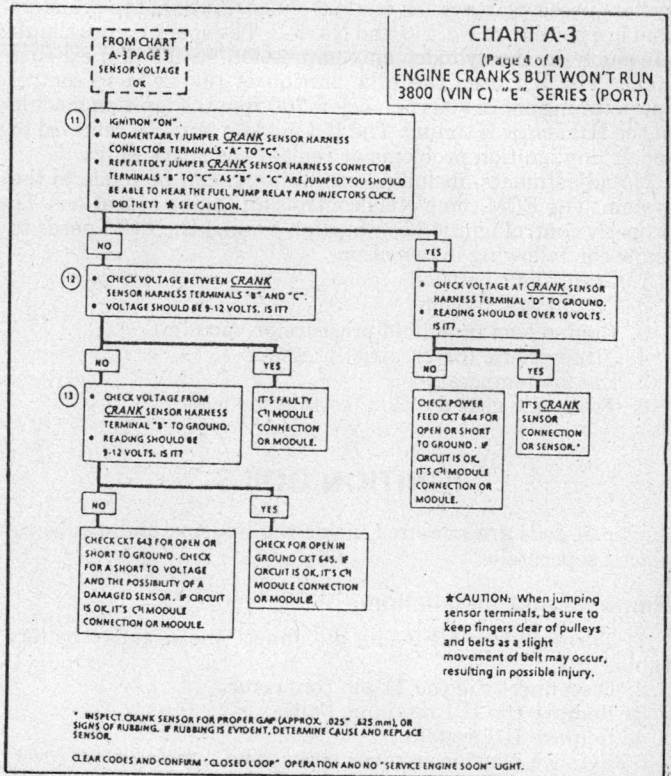

Electrical schematic and charts for "Engine cranks but won't run", 3800 (VIN–C)

4. Tighten the retaining bolt and recheck the clearance at approximately 120 degrees apart.

5. If the interrupter ring contacts the sensor at any point of the 360 degrees circle, the interrupter ring has excessive runout and must be replaced.

CAMSHAFT POSITION SENSOR DRIVE ASSEMBLY

Removal and Installation

1. Note the position of the slot in the rotating vane.
2. Remove the bolt securing the drive assembly to the engine.
3. Remove the drive assembly.
4. Install the drive assembly with the slot in the vane. Install mounting bolt.
5. Install the camshaft sensor.
6. Rotate the engine to set the No. 1 cylinder at TDC compression.

7. Mark the harmonic balancer and rotate the engine to 25 degrees after TDC.
8. Remove the plug wires from the coil assembly.
9. Using weatherpack removal tool J-28742-A, or equivalent, remove terminal B of the sensor 3-way connector on the module side.
10. Probe terminal B by installing a jumper and reconnecting the wire removed to the jumper wire.
11. Connect a voltmeter between the jumper wire and ground.
12. With the key On and the engine stopped, rotate the camshaft sensor counterclockwise until the sensor switch just closes. This is indicated by the voltage reading going from a high 5–12 volts to a low 0–2 volts. The low voltage indicates the switch is closed.
13. Tighten the retaining bolt and reinstall the wire into terminal B.
14. Install remaining components.

GM INTERGRATED DIRECT IGNITION (IDI) SYSTEM

General Description

The 2.3L (VIN D) Quad-4 engine is equipped with a distributorless ignition system called the Intergrated Direct Ignition (IDI). The primary circuit of the IDI consists of 2 separate ignition coils, an IDI (ignition) module and crankshaft sensor as well as related components, wires and electronic spark timing (EST) portion of the ECM. This distributorless ignition system uses a waste spark method of distribution, the cylinders that are paired are No. 1–4 and No. 2–3. The spark occurs simultaneously in the cylinder on compression stroke and exhaust stoke. The IDI used the EST portion of the ECM to control spark timing above 700 rpm, below 700 rpm the ignition module in the IDI controls timing. The IDI module must be removed to repair any ignition problems or replace the spark plugs.

No adjustments, including base timing, can be made to the system. The ECM completely controls all engine operations. To properly control ignition/combustion timing, the ECM needs to know the following information:
1. Crankshaft position
2. Engine speed (rpm)
3. Engine load (manifold pressure or vacuum)
4. Atmospheric (barometric) pressure
5. Engine temperature
6. Transaxle gear position (certain models)

IGNITION COILS

A pair of coils are mounted inside the housing and can be replaced separately.

Removal and Installation

1. Turn ignition **OFF** and disconnect the negative battery cable.
2. Disconnect the the 11-pin connector.
3. Remove the IDI retaining bolts.
4. Remove IDI system.
5. Remove housing to cover screws and housing from cover.
6. Remove coil harness connectors.
7. Remove coils, contacts and seals.
8. Installation is the reverse order of the removal procedure.

NOTE: Place spark plug boots and retainers to housing and carefully align boots to spark plug terminals when installing IDI assembly.

1. Ignition coil and module assembly
2. Bolts – Ignition coil and module assembly to camshaft housings
3. Camshaft housing cover
4. Spark plug

Intergrated Direct Ignition (IDI) coil and module assembly

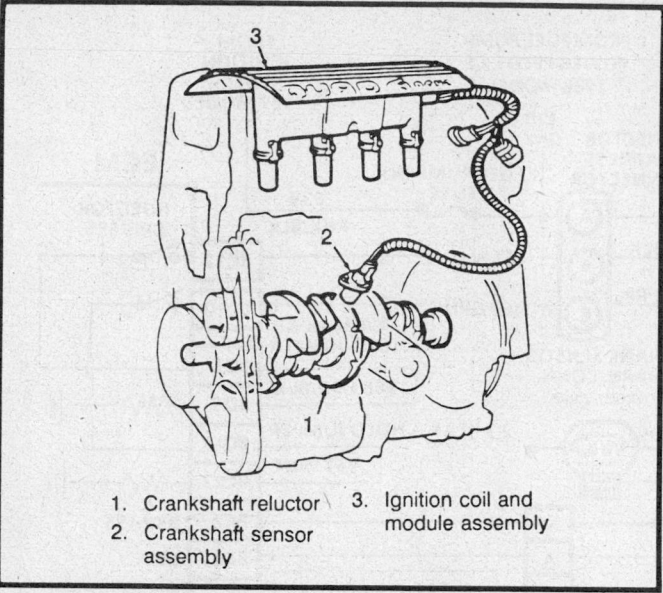

1. Crankshaft reluctor
2. Crankshaft sensor assembly
3. Ignition coil and module assembly

Intergrated Direct Ignition components

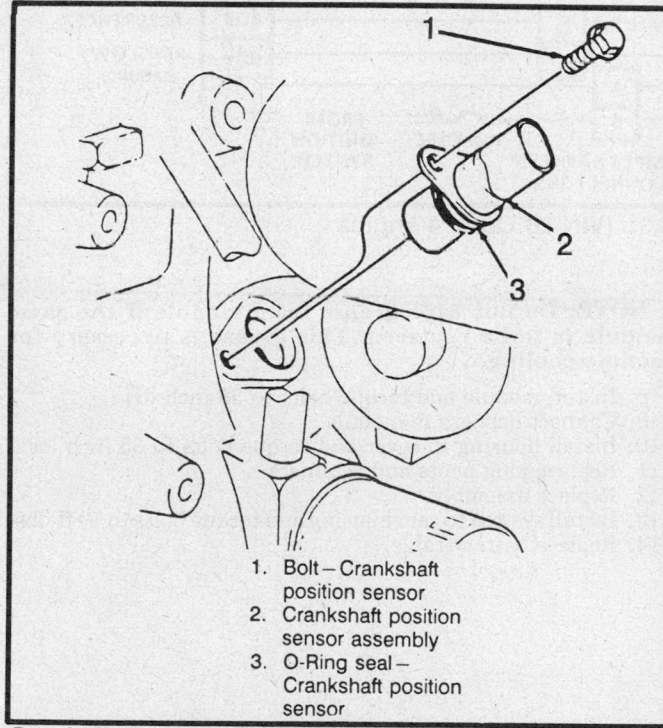

1. Bolt—Crankshaft position sensor
2. Crankshaft position sensor assembly
3. O-Ring seal—Crankshaft position sensor

Crankshaft sensor location

CRANKSHAFT SENSOR

The system uses a magnetic crankshaft sensor, which protrudes into the block within 0.050 in. of the crankshaft reluctor.

Removal and Installation

1. Disconnect harness and connector.
2. Remove retaining bolt.
3. Remove sensor.
4. Inspect O-ring for cracks or damage.
5. Lube O-ring with engine oil and install.
6. Install sensor.

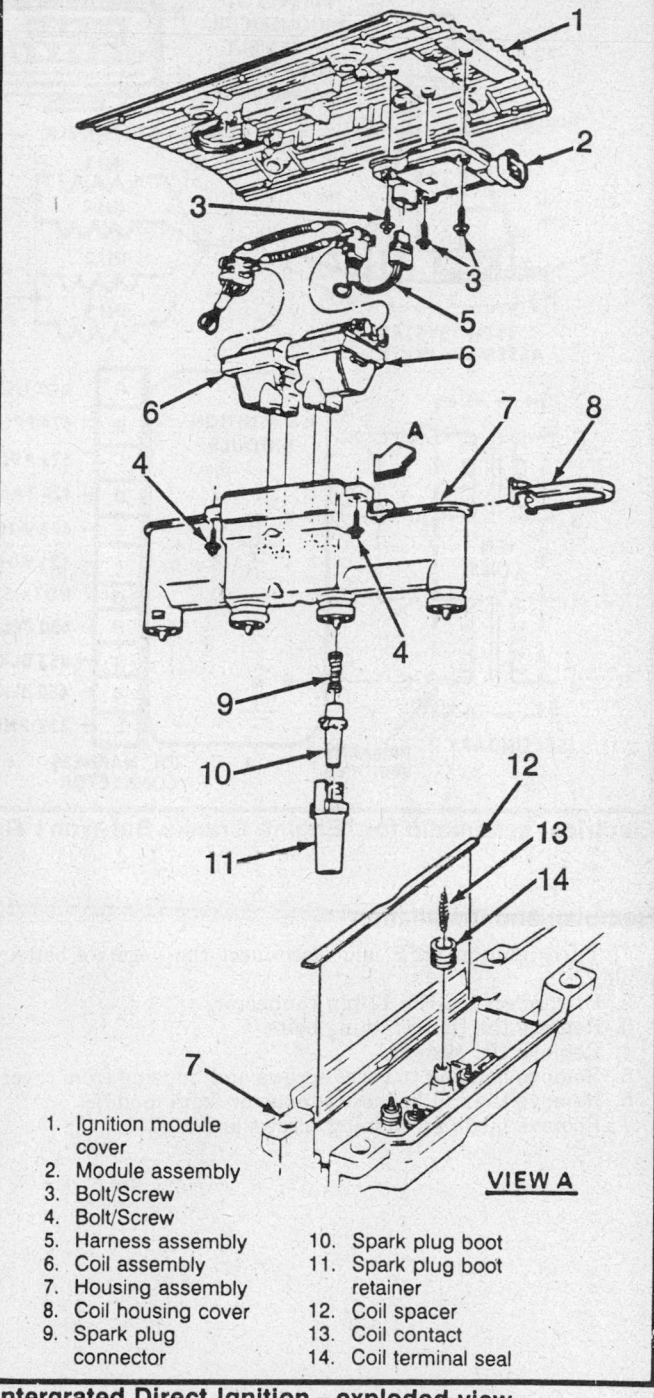

1. Ignition module cover
2. Module assembly
3. Bolt/Screw
4. Bolt/Screw
5. Harness assembly
6. Coil assembly
7. Housing assembly
8. Coil housing cover
9. Spark plug connector
10. Spark plug boot
11. Spark plug boot retainer
12. Coil spacer
13. Coil contact
14. Coil terminal seal

Intergrated Direct Ignition—exploded view

7. Install bolt and torque to 88 inch lbs.
8. Connect wiring harness.

IGNITION MODULE

The ignition module monitors the crank sensor and based on these signals sends a reference to the ECM. Below 700 rpm the module controls timing above 700 rpm the ECM controls timing. The module is not repairable and is only serviced as a unit.

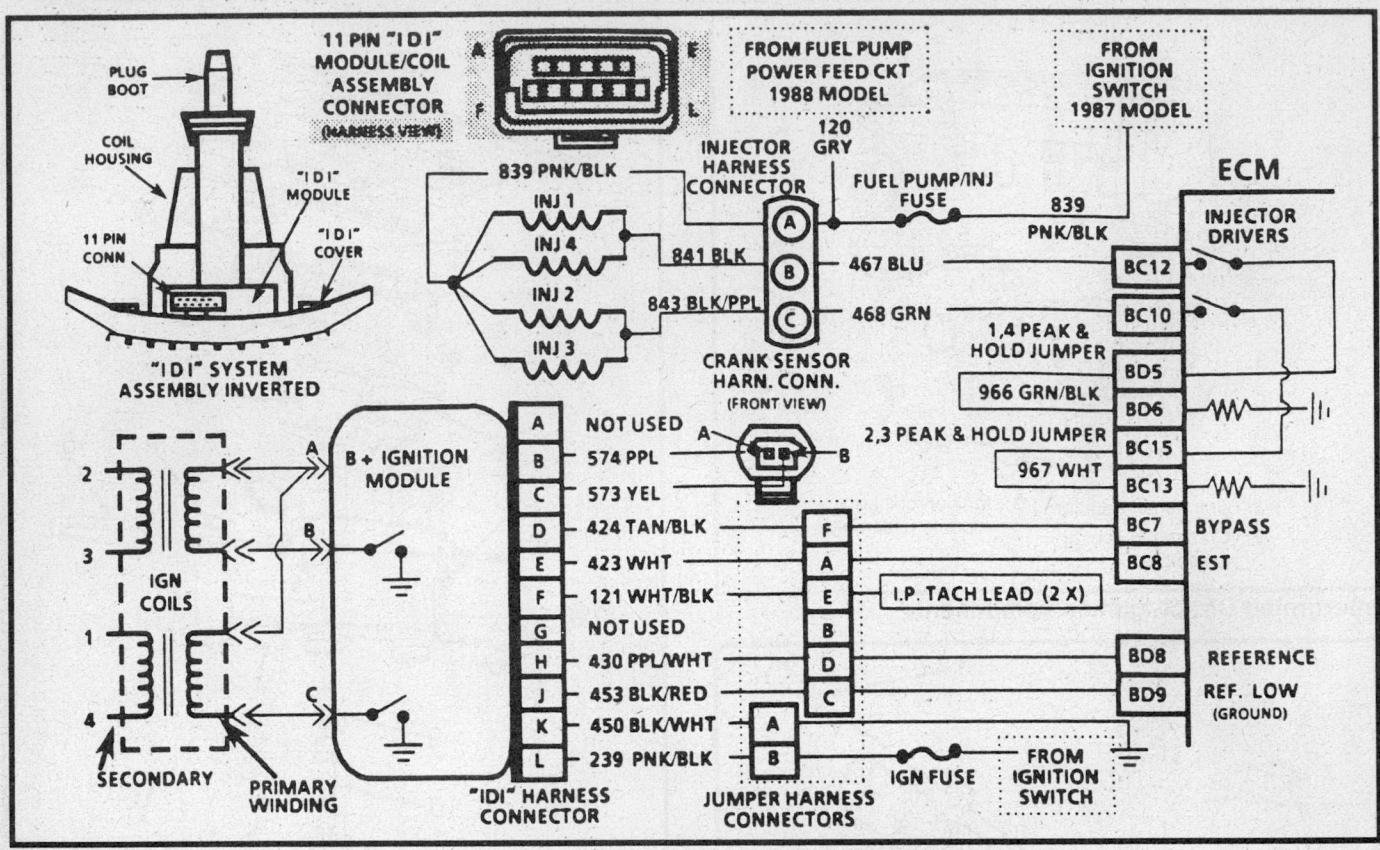

Electrical schematic for "Engine Cranks But Won't Run", 2.3L (VIN D) Quad 4 engine

Removal and Installation

1. Turn ignition **OFF** and disconnect the negative battery cable.
2. Disconnect the the 11-pin connector.
3. Remove the IDI retaining bolts.
4. Remove IDI system.
5. Remove housing to cover screws and housing from cover.
6. Remove the coil harness connector from module.
7. Reomve module retaining screws and module.

NOTE: Do not wipe grease from module if the same module is to be replaced. This grease is necessary for module cooling.

8. Install module and torque bolts to 35 inch lbs.
9. Connect harness to module.
10. Install housing to cover and torque bolts to 35 inch lbs.
11. Replace plug boots and retainers.
12. Replace assembly.
13. Install system to cam housing and torque bolts to 19 ft. lbs.
14. Replace battery cable.

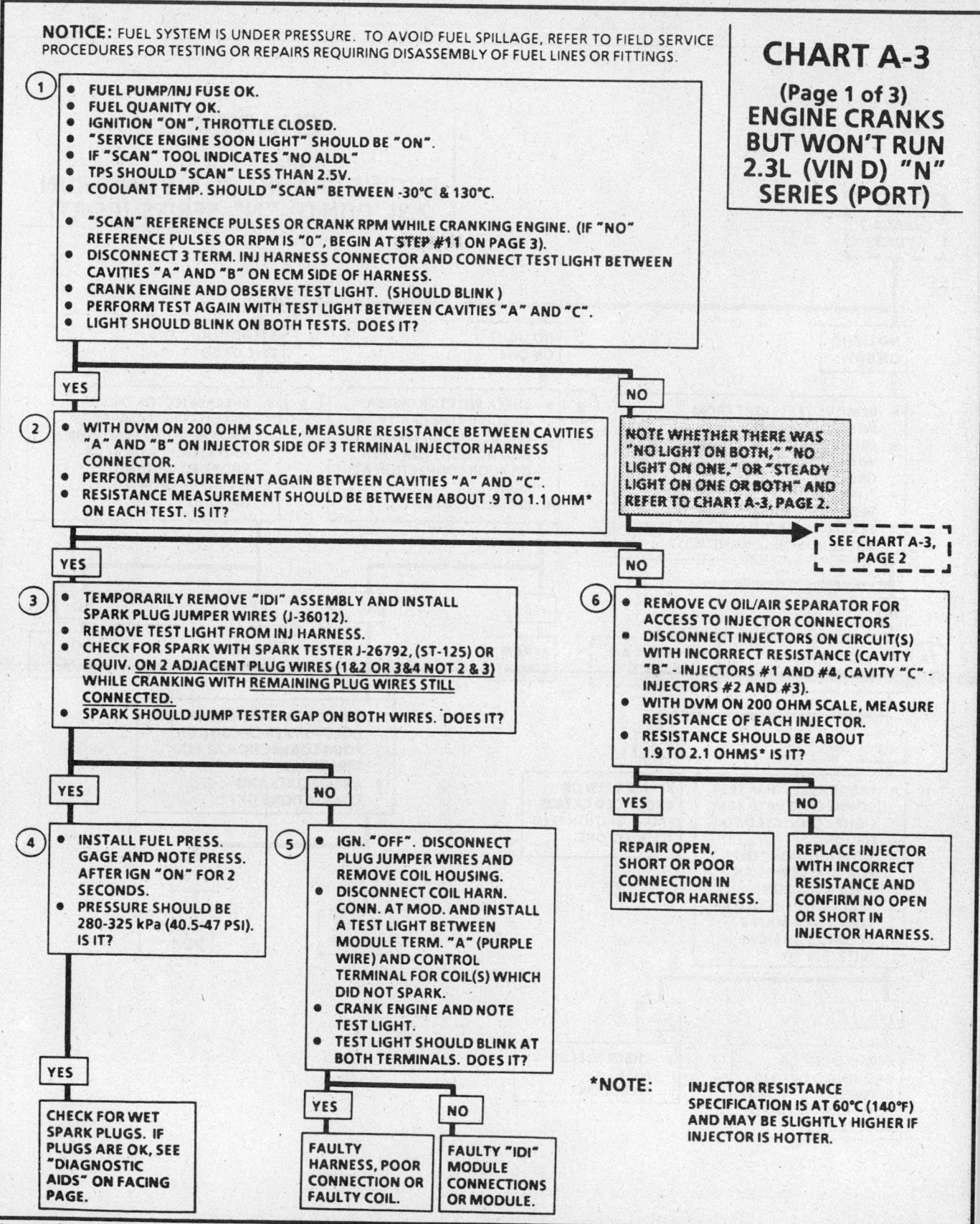

NOTICE: FUEL SYSTEM IS UNDER PRESSURE. TO AVOID FUEL SPILLAGE, REFER TO FIELD SERVICE PROCEDURES FOR TESTING OR REPAIRS REQUIRING DISASSEMBLY OF FUEL LINES OR FITTINGS.

CHART A-3

(Page 1 of 3)
ENGINE CRANKS
BUT WON'T RUN
2.3L (VIN D) "N"
SERIES (PORT)

1
- FUEL PUMP/INJ FUSE OK.
- FUEL QUANITY OK.
- IGNITION "ON", THROTTLE CLOSED.
- "SERVICE ENGINE SOON LIGHT" SHOULD BE "ON".
- IF "SCAN" TOOL INDICATES "NO ALDL"
- TPS SHOULD "SCAN" LESS THAN 2.5V.
- COOLANT TEMP. SHOULD "SCAN" BETWEEN -30°C & 130°C.

- "SCAN" REFERENCE PULSES OR CRANK RPM WHILE CRANKING ENGINE. (IF "NO" REFERENCE PULSES OR RPM IS "0", BEGIN AT STEP #11 ON PAGE 3).
- DISCONNECT 3 TERM. INJ HARNESS CONNECTOR AND CONNECT TEST LIGHT BETWEEN CAVITIES "A" AND "B" ON ECM SIDE OF HARNESS.
- CRANK ENGINE AND OBSERVE TEST LIGHT. (SHOULD BLINK)
- PERFORM TEST AGAIN WITH TEST LIGHT BETWEEN CAVITIES "A" AND "C".
- LIGHT SHOULD BLINK ON BOTH TESTS. DOES IT?

YES

NO

2
- WITH DVM ON 200 OHM SCALE, MEASURE RESISTANCE BETWEEN CAVITIES "A" AND "B" ON INJECTOR SIDE OF 3 TERMINAL INJECTOR HARNESS CONNECTOR.
- PERFORM MEASUREMENT AGAIN BETWEEN CAVITIES "A" AND "C".
- RESISTANCE MEASUREMENT SHOULD BE BETWEEN ABOUT .9 TO 1.1 OHM* ON EACH TEST. IS IT?

NOTE WHETHER THERE WAS "NO LIGHT ON BOTH," "NO LIGHT ON ONE," OR "STEADY LIGHT ON ONE OR BOTH" AND REFER TO CHART A-3, PAGE 2.

SEE CHART A-3, PAGE 2

YES

NO

3
- TEMPORARILY REMOVE "IDI" ASSEMBLY AND INSTALL SPARK PLUG JUMPER WIRES (J-36012).
- REMOVE TEST LIGHT FROM INJ HARNESS.
- CHECK FOR SPARK WITH SPARK TESTER J-26792, (ST-125) OR EQUIV. ON 2 ADJACENT PLUG WIRES (1&2 OR 3&4 NOT 2 & 3) WHILE CRANKING WITH REMAINING PLUG WIRES STILL CONNECTED.
- SPARK SHOULD JUMP TESTER GAP ON BOTH WIRES. DOES IT?

6
- REMOVE CV OIL/AIR SEPARATOR FOR ACCESS TO INJECTOR CONNECTORS
- DISCONNECT INJECTORS ON CIRCUIT(S) WITH INCORRECT RESISTANCE (CAVITY "B" - INJECTORS #1 AND #4, CAVITY "C" - INJECTORS #2 AND #3).
- WITH DVM ON 200 OHM SCALE, MEASURE RESISTANCE OF EACH INJECTOR.
- RESISTANCE SHOULD BE ABOUT 1.9 TO 2.1 OHMS* IS IT?

YES

NO

YES

NO

4
- INSTALL FUEL PRESS. GAGE AND NOTE PRESS. AFTER IGN "ON" FOR 2 SECONDS.
- PRESSURE SHOULD BE 280-325 kPa (40.5-47 PSI). IS IT?

5
- IGN. "OFF". DISCONNECT PLUG JUMPER WIRES AND REMOVE COIL HOUSING.
- DISCONNECT COIL HARN. CONN. AT MOD. AND INSTALL A TEST LIGHT BETWEEN MODULE TERM. "A" (PURPLE WIRE) AND CONTROL TERMINAL FOR COIL(S) WHICH DID NOT SPARK.
- CRANK ENGINE AND NOTE TEST LIGHT.
- TEST LIGHT SHOULD BLINK AT BOTH TERMINALS. DOES IT?

REPAIR OPEN, SHORT OR POOR CONNECTION IN INJECTOR HARNESS.

REPLACE INJECTOR WITH INCORRECT RESISTANCE AND CONFIRM NO OPEN OR SHORT IN INJECTOR HARNESS.

YES

CHECK FOR WET SPARK PLUGS. IF PLUGS ARE OK, SEE "DIAGNOSTIC AIDS" ON FACING PAGE.

YES

FAULTY HARNESS, POOR CONNECTION OR FAULTY COIL.

NO

FAULTY "IDI" MODULE CONNECTIONS OR MODULE.

*NOTE: INJECTOR RESISTANCE SPECIFICATION IS AT 60°C (140°F) AND MAY BE SLIGHTLY HIGHER IF INJECTOR IS HOTTER.

Diagnosis charts for "Engine Cranks But Won't Run", 2.3L (VIN D) Quad 4 engine

CHART A-3
(Page 2 of 3)
ENGINE CRANKS BUT WON'T RUN
2.3L (VIN D) "N" SERIES (PORT)

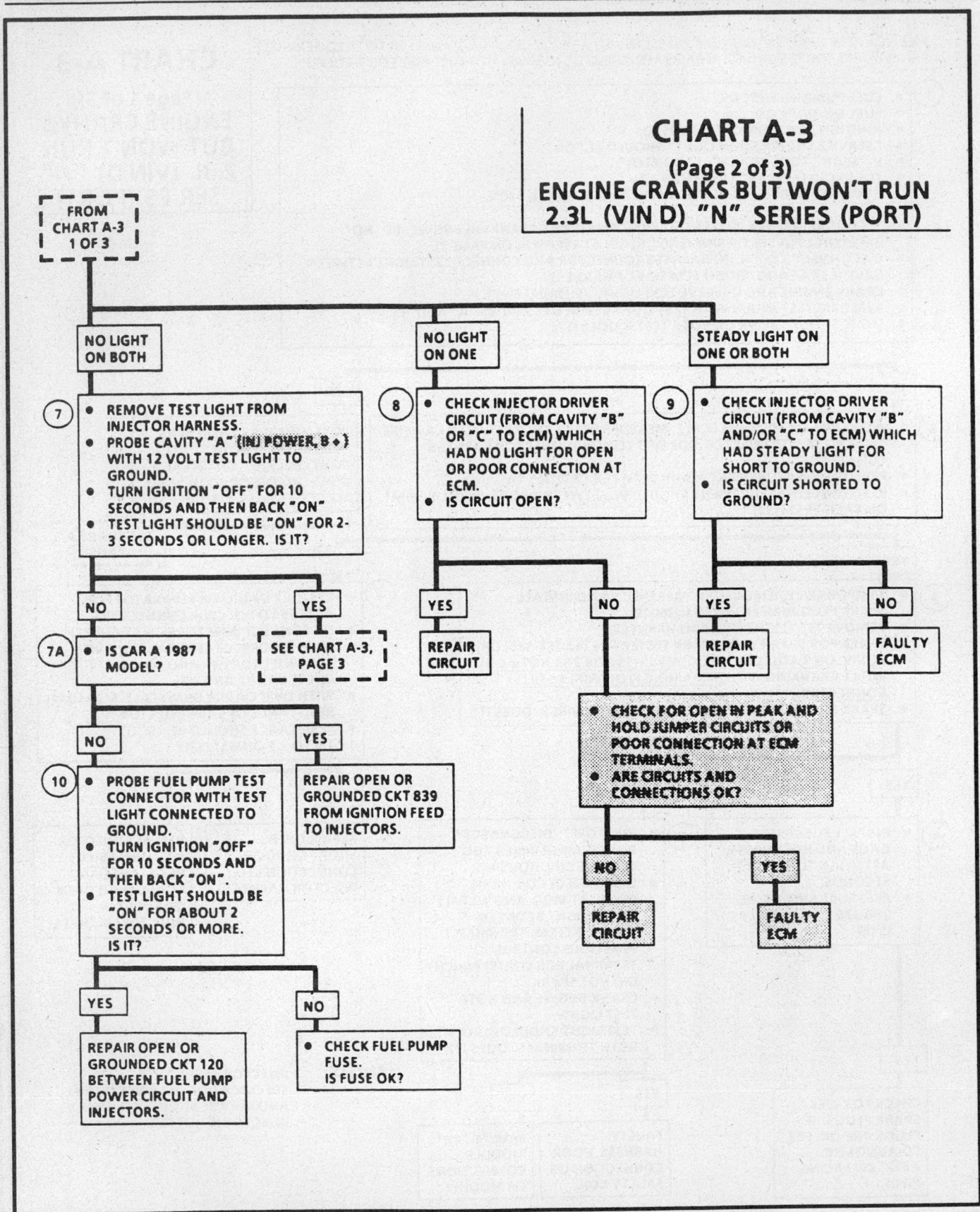

FROM CHART A-3 1 OF 3

NO LIGHT ON BOTH

⑦
- REMOVE TEST LIGHT FROM INJECTOR HARNESS.
- PROBE CAVITY "A" (INJ POWER, B +) WITH 12 VOLT TEST LIGHT TO GROUND.
- TURN IGNITION "OFF" FOR 10 SECONDS AND THEN BACK "ON"
- TEST LIGHT SHOULD BE "ON" FOR 2-3 SECONDS OR LONGER. IS IT?

NO → ⑦A IS CAR A 1987 MODEL?

YES → SEE CHART A-3, PAGE 3

⑦A NO → ⑩
⑦A YES → REPAIR OPEN OR GROUNDED CKT 839 FROM IGNITION FEED TO INJECTORS.

⑩
- PROBE FUEL PUMP TEST CONNECTOR WITH TEST LIGHT CONNECTED TO GROUND.
- TURN IGNITION "OFF" FOR 10 SECONDS AND THEN BACK "ON".
- TEST LIGHT SHOULD BE "ON" FOR ABOUT 2 SECONDS OR MORE. IS IT?

YES → REPAIR OPEN OR GROUNDED CKT 120 BETWEEN FUEL PUMP POWER CIRCUIT AND INJECTORS.

NO → • CHECK FUEL PUMP FUSE. IS FUSE OK?

NO LIGHT ON ONE

⑧
- CHECK INJECTOR DRIVER CIRCUIT (FROM CAVITY "B" OR "C" TO ECM) WHICH HAD NO LIGHT FOR OPEN OR POOR CONNECTION AT ECM.
- IS CIRCUIT OPEN?

YES → REPAIR CIRCUIT

NO → • CHECK FOR OPEN IN PEAK AND HOLD JUMPER CIRCUITS OR POOR CONNECTION AT ECM TERMINALS. • ARE CIRCUITS AND CONNECTIONS OK?

NO → REPAIR CIRCUIT

YES → FAULTY ECM

STEADY LIGHT ON ONE OR BOTH

⑨
- CHECK INJECTOR DRIVER CIRCUIT (FROM CAVITY "B" AND/OR "C" TO ECM) WHICH HAD STEADY LIGHT FOR SHORT TO GROUND.
- IS CIRCUIT SHORTED TO GROUND?

YES → REPAIR CIRCUIT

NO → FAULTY ECM

Diagnosis charts for "Engine Cranks But Won't Run", 2.3L (VIN D) Quad 4 engine (con't)

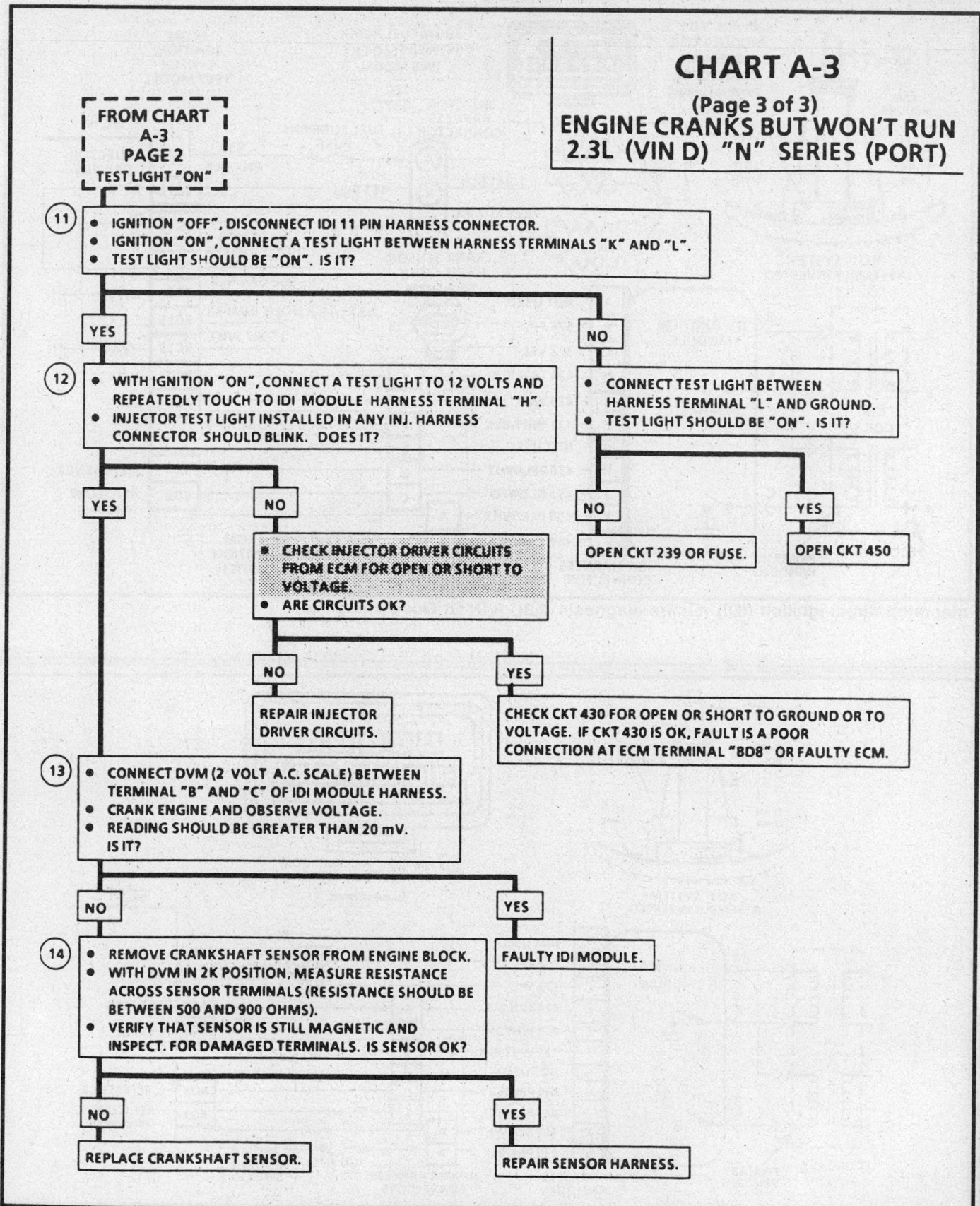

CHART A-3

(Page 3 of 3)
**ENGINE CRANKS BUT WON'T RUN
2.3L (VIN D) "N" SERIES (PORT)**

FROM CHART
A-3
PAGE 2
TEST LIGHT "ON"

11
- IGNITION "OFF", DISCONNECT IDI 11 PIN HARNESS CONNECTOR.
- IGNITION "ON", CONNECT A TEST LIGHT BETWEEN HARNESS TERMINALS "K" AND "L".
- TEST LIGHT SHOULD BE "ON". IS IT?

YES

NO

12
- WITH IGNITION "ON", CONNECT A TEST LIGHT TO 12 VOLTS AND REPEATEDLY TOUCH TO IDI MODULE HARNESS TERMINAL "H".
- INJECTOR TEST LIGHT INSTALLED IN ANY INJ. HARNESS CONNECTOR SHOULD BLINK. DOES IT?

- CONNECT TEST LIGHT BETWEEN HARNESS TERMINAL "L" AND GROUND.
- TEST LIGHT SHOULD BE "ON". IS IT?

YES

NO

NO

YES

- CHECK INJECTOR DRIVER CIRCUITS FROM ECM FOR OPEN OR SHORT TO VOLTAGE.
- ARE CIRCUITS OK?

OPEN CKT 239 OR FUSE.

OPEN CKT 450

NO

YES

REPAIR INJECTOR DRIVER CIRCUITS.

CHECK CKT 430 FOR OPEN OR SHORT TO GROUND OR TO VOLTAGE. IF CKT 430 IS OK, FAULT IS A POOR CONNECTION AT ECM TERMINAL "BD8" OR FAULTY ECM.

13
- CONNECT DVM (2 VOLT A.C. SCALE) BETWEEN TERMINAL "B" AND "C" OF IDI MODULE HARNESS.
- CRANK ENGINE AND OBSERVE VOLTAGE.
- READING SHOULD BE GREATER THAN 20 mV. IS IT?

NO

YES

14
- REMOVE CRANKSHAFT SENSOR FROM ENGINE BLOCK.
- WITH DVM IN 2K POSITION, MEASURE RESISTANCE ACROSS SENSOR TERMINALS (RESISTANCE SHOULD BE BETWEEN 500 AND 900 OHMS).
- VERIFY THAT SENSOR IS STILL MAGNETIC AND INSPECT. FOR DAMAGED TERMINALS. IS SENSOR OK?

FAULTY IDI MODULE.

NO

YES

REPLACE CRANKSHAFT SENSOR.

REPAIR SENSOR HARNESS.

Diagnosis charts for "Engine Cranks But Won't Run", 2.3L (VIN D) Quad 4 engine (con't)

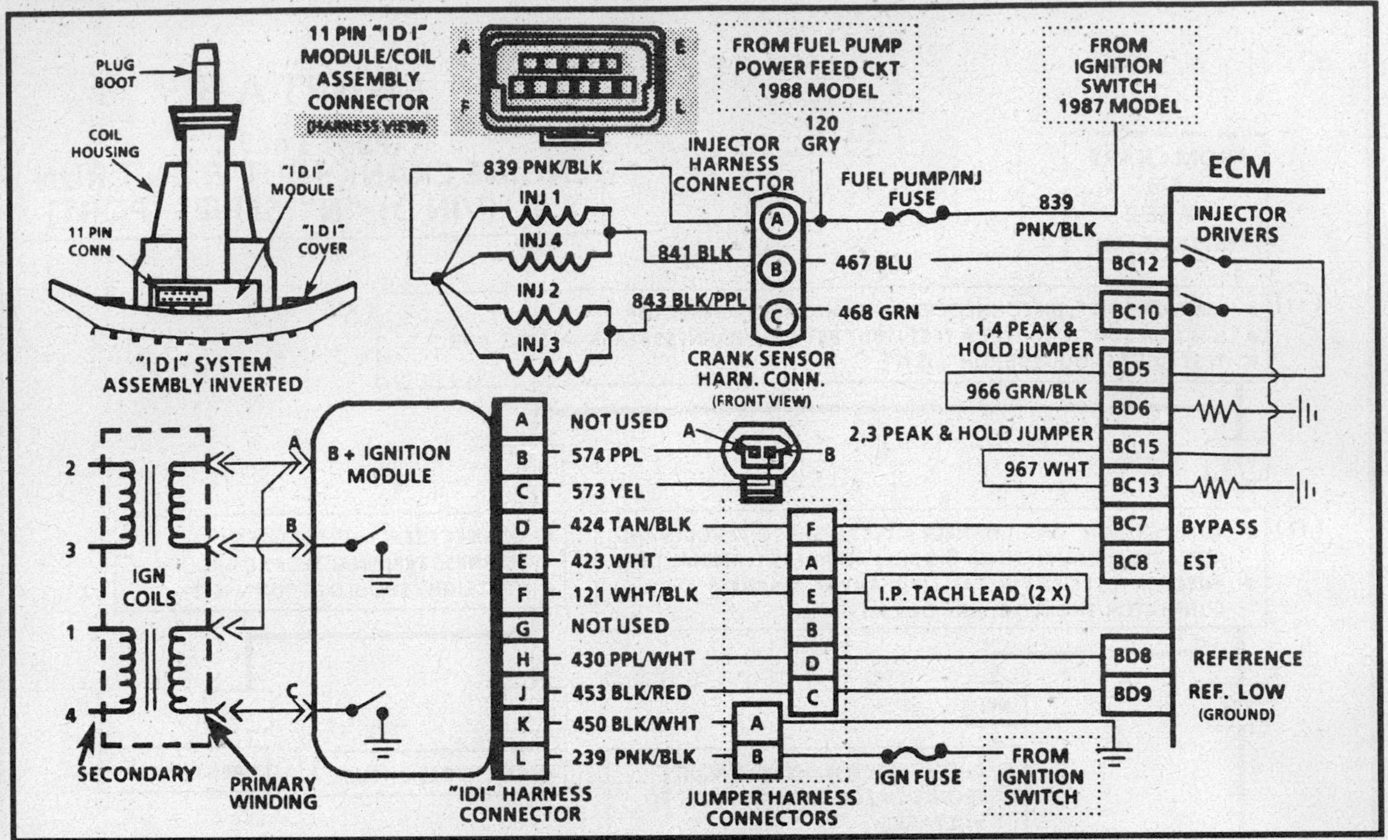

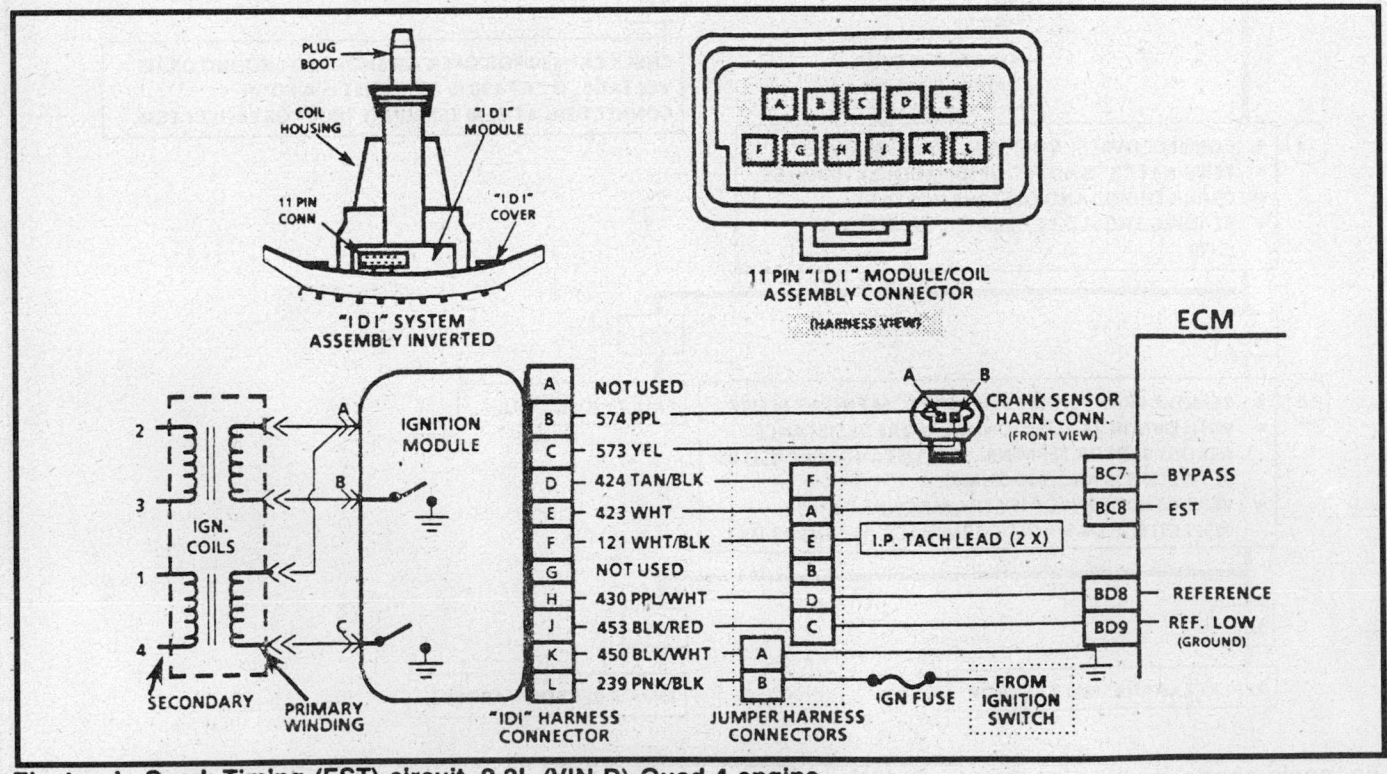

Integrated direct ignition (IDI) misfire diagnosis, 2.3L (VIN D) Quad 4 engine

Electronic Spark Timing (EST) circuit, 2.3L (VIN D) Quad 4 engine

GM ELECTRONIC SPARK TIMING (EST) SYSTEM

General Description

The High Energy Ignition (HEI) system controls fuel combustion by providing the spark to ignite the compressed air/fuel mixture, in the combustiuon chamber, at the correct time. To provide improved engine performance, fuel economy and control of the exhaust emissions, the ECM controls distributor spark advance (timing) with the Electronic Spark Timing (EST) system.

The standard High Energy Ignition (HEI) system has a modified distributor module which is used in conjunction with the EST system. The module has 7 terminals instead of the 4 used without EST. Different terminal arrangements are used, depending upon the distributor used with a particular engine application.

To properly control ignition/combustion timing, the ECM needs to know the following information:
1. Crankshaft position
2. Engine speed (rpm)
3. Engine load (manifold pressure or vacuum)
4. Atmospheric (barometric) pressure
5. Engine temperature
6. Transmission gear position (certain models)

EST SYSTEM

The EST system consists of the distributor module, ECM and its connecting wires. The distributor has 4 wires from the HEI module connected to a 4–terminal connector, which mates with a 4-wire connector from the ECM.

These circuits perform the following functions:
1. Distributor reference at terminal B – This provides the ECM with rpm and crankshaft position information.
2. Reference ground at terminal D – This wire is grounded in the distributor and makes sure the ground circuit has no voltage drop, which could affect performance. If this circusit is open, it could cause poor performance.
3. Bypass at terminal C at approximately 400 rpm, the ECM applies 5 volts to this circuit to switch the spark timing control from the HEI module to the ECM. An open or grounded bypass circuit will set a Code 42 and the engine will run at base timing, plus a small amount of advance built into the HEI module.
4. EST at terminal A, this triggers the HEI module. The ECM does not know what the actual timing is, but it does know when it gets its reference signal. It then advances or retards the spark timing from that point. Therefore, if the base timing is set incorrectly, the entire spark curve will be incorrect.
5. An open circuit in the EST circuit will set a Code 42 and cause the engine to run on the HEI module timing. This will cause poor performance and poor fuel economy. A ground may set a Code 42, but the engine will not run.

ECM SYSTEM

The ECM uses information from the MAP or VAC and coolant sensors, in addition to rpm, in order to calulate spark advance as follows:

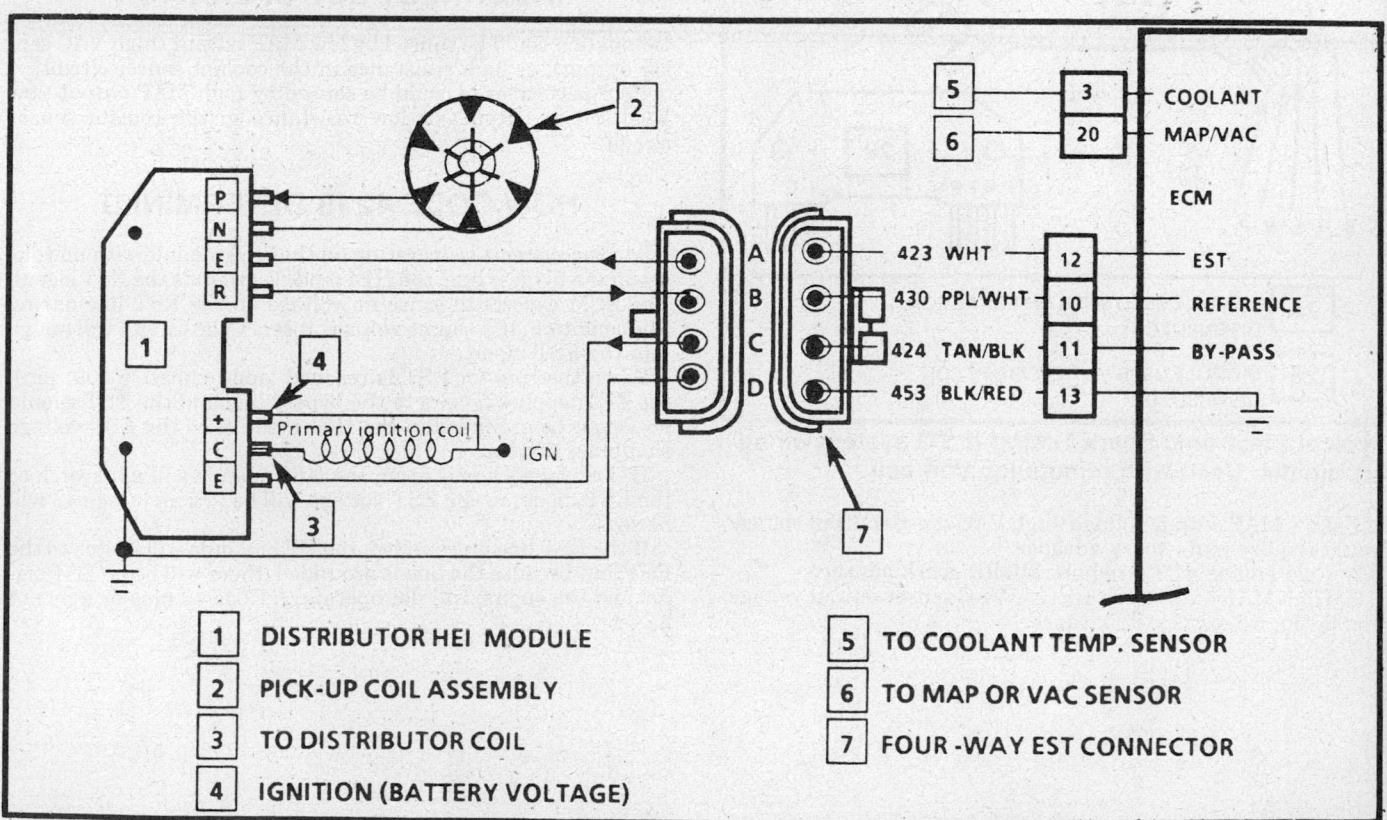

1 DISTRIBUTOR HEI MODULE	5 TO COOLANT TEMP. SENSOR
2 PICK-UP COIL ASSEMBLY	6 TO MAP OR VAC SENSOR
3 TO DISTRIBUTOR COIL	7 FOUR-WAY EST CONNECTOR
4 IGNITION (BATTERY VOLTAGE)	

Electronic Spark Timing (EST) distributor modules

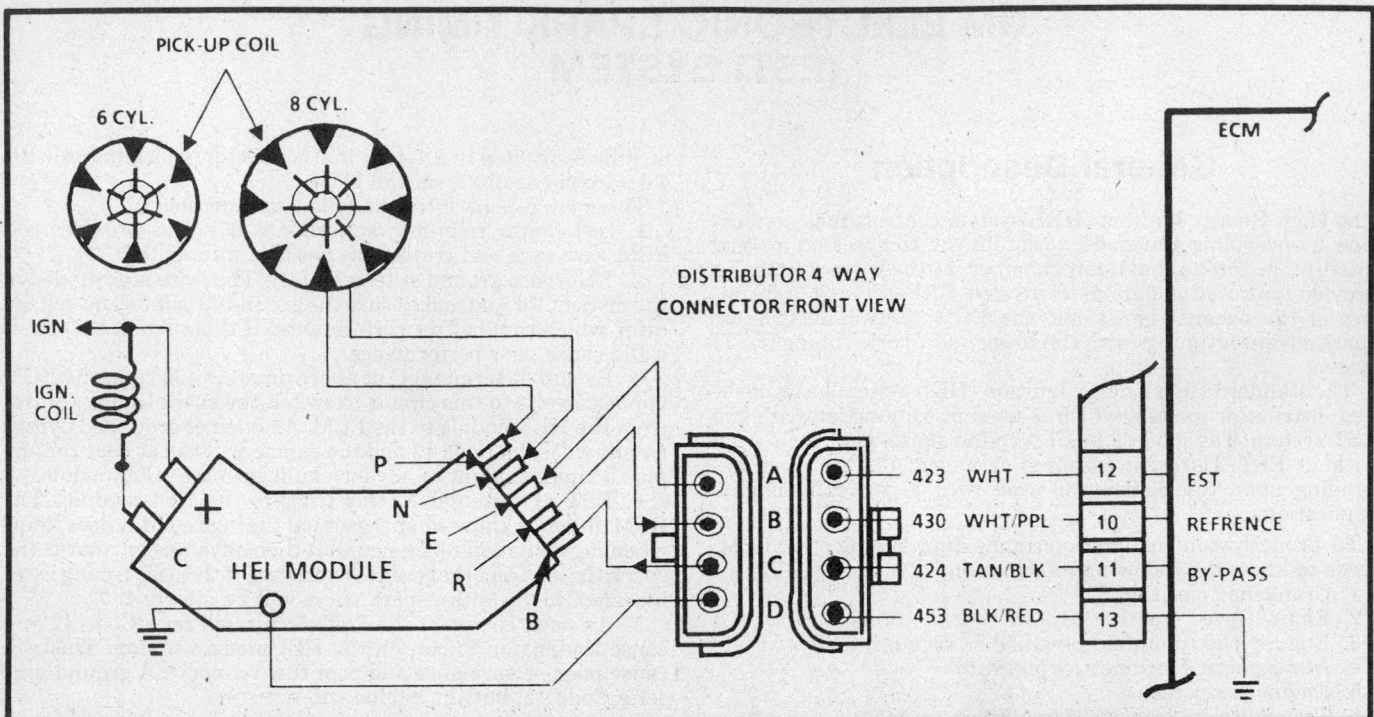

Typical Electronic Spark Timing (EST) system wiring schematic. Used with coil-in-cap distributor

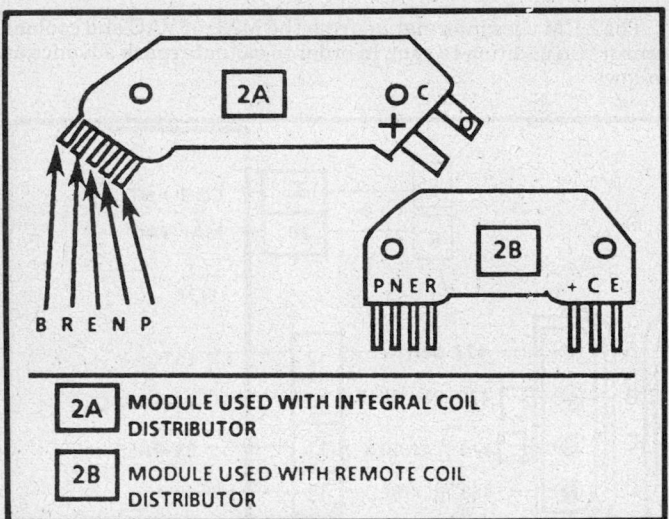

2A MODULE USED WITH INTEGRAL COIL DISTRIBUTOR

2B MODULE USED WITH REMOTE COIL DISTRIBUTOR

Typical Electronic Spark Timing (EST) system wiring schematic. Used with remote ignition coil

1. Low MAP output voltage (high VAC sensor output voltage) would require more spark advance.
2. Cold engine would require MORE spark advance.
3. High MAP output voltage (low VAC sensor output voltage) would require less spark advance.

4. Hot engine would require less spark advance.

INCORRECT EST OPERATION

Detonation could be caused by low MAP output (high VAC sensor output), or high resistance in the coolant sensor circuit.

Poor performance could be caused by high MAP output (low VAC sensor output) or low resistance in the coolant sensor circuit.

HOW CODE 42 IS DETERMINED

When the systems is operating on the HEI module with no voltage in the by-pass line, the HEI module grounds the EST signal. The ECM expects to sense no voltage on the EST line during this condition. If it senses voltage, it sets Code 42 and will not go into the EST mode.

When the rpm for EST is reached (approximately 400 rpm), the ECM applies 5 volts to the bypass line and the EST should no longer be grounded in the HEI module, so the EST voltage should be varying.

If the by-pass line is open, the HEI module will not switch to the EST mode, so the EST voltage will be low and Code 42 will be set.

If the EST line is grounded, the HEI module will switch to the EST, but because the line is grounded, there will be no EST signal and the engine will not operate. A Code 42 may or may not be set.

GENERAL MOTORS
ELECTRONIC SPARK CONTROL (ESC) SYSTEM

General Description

The Electronic Spark Control (ESC) operates in conjunction with the Electronic Spark Timing (EST) system and modifies (retards) the spark advance when detonation occurs. The retard mode is held for approximately 20 seconds after which the spark control will again revert to the Electronic Spark Timing (EST) system. There are 3 basic components of the Electronic Spark Control (ESC) system.

SENSOR

The Electronic Spark Control (ESC) sensor detects the presence (or absence) and intensity of the detonation by the vibration characteristics of the engine. The output is an electrical signal that goes to the controller. A sensor failure would allow no spark retard.

DISTRIBUTOR

The distributor is an HEI/EST unit with an electronic module, modified so it can respond to the ESC controller signal. This command is delayed when detonation is occurring, thus providing the level of spark retard required. The amount of spark retard is a function of the degree of detonation.

CONTROLLER

The Electronic Spark Control (ESC) controller processes the sensor signal into a command signal to the distributor, to adjust the spark timing. The process is continuous, so that the presence of detonation is monitored and controlled. The controller is a hard wired signal processor and amplifier which operates from 6-16 volts. Controller failure would be no ignition, no retard or full retard. The controller has no memory storage.

CODE 43

Should Code 43 be set in the ECM memory, it would indicate that the ESC system retard signal has been sensed by the ECM for too long a period of time. When voltage at terminal L of the ECM is low, spark timing is retarded. Normal voltage in the non-retarded mode is approximately 7.5 volts or more.

BASIC IGNITION TIMING

Basic ignition timing is critical to the proper operation of the ESC system. Always follow the vehicle emission control information label procedures when adjusting ignition timing.

Some engines will incorporate a magnetic timing probe hole for use with special electronic timing equipment. Consult the manufacturer's instructions for the use of this electronic timing equipment.

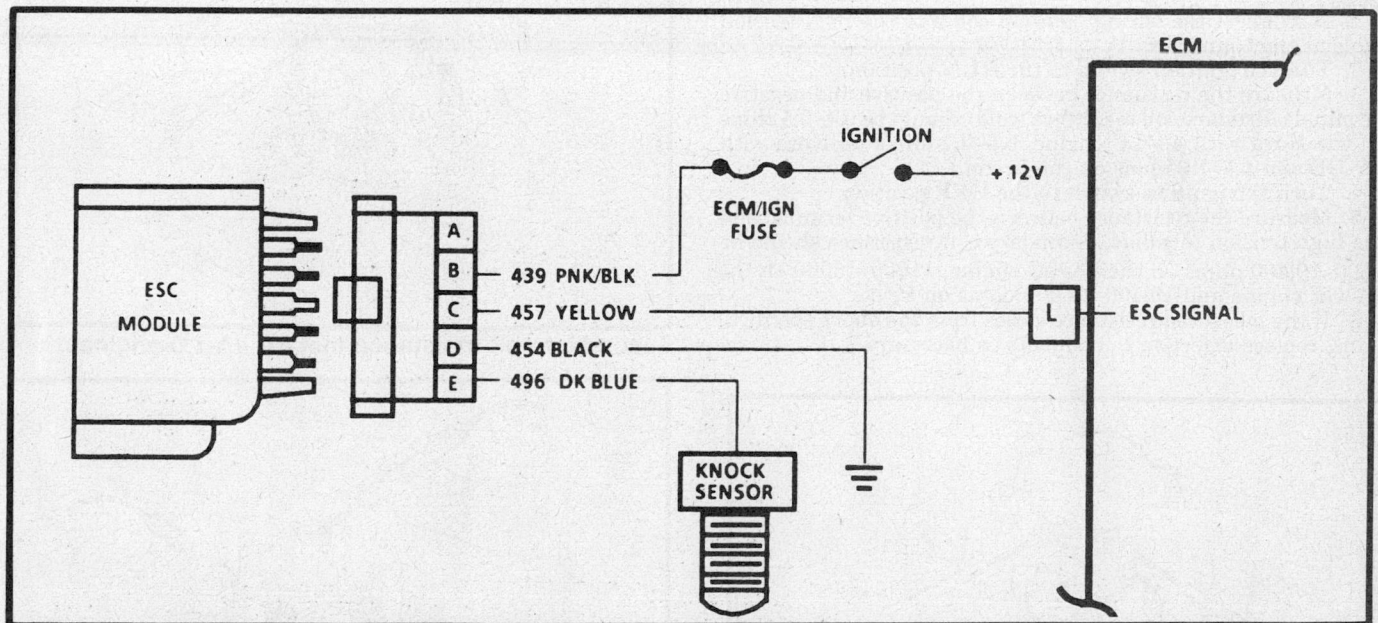

Typical wiring schematic for Electronic Spark Control (ESC) system

GENERAL MOTORS
SOLID STATE IGNITION SYSTEM

Chevrolet Nova and GEO Prizm

GENERAL DESCRIPTION

The principal components of the ignition system are the ignition coil, spark plugs and ignition coil. The distributor has a rotor, pole piece, module, centrifugal advance and vacuum advance.

The signal generator (pick-up coil) is used to generate the ignition signal and consists of a signal rotor, signal generator and a magnet. The pole piece is attached to the distributor shaft and the magnet and the pick-up coil are attached to the pick-up coil base plate.

As the distributor shaft rotates, the magnetic flux passing through the pick-up coil varies due to the change of the air gap between the pick-up coil and the pole piece. Due to this action, the alternating current voltage is induced in the pick-up coil. The induced voltage turns the module on and off which in turn switches off the ignition coil primary voltage. The high voltage is induced in the secondary winding of the ignition coil and ignition sparks are generated at the spark plugs.

Troubleshooting

IGNITION COIL

Testing

1. Disconnect the wiring, ignition coil and the high tension cable at the connector.
2. Tun the ignition switch to the **RUN** position.
3. Measure the resistance between the positive and negative terminals. Primary coil resistance (cold) should be 0.4–0.5 ohms on the Nova with 4A-LC engine, 0.5–0.7 ohms on Nova with 4A–GE and 1.3–1.6 ohms on the Prizm.
4. Turn the ignition switch to the **OFF** position.
5. Measure the resistance between the positive terminal and the high tension terminal. Secondary coil resistance should be 7500–10,400 ohms on the 4A–LC engine, 11000–16000 on the 4A–GE engine and 10,400–14,000 ohms on Prism.
6. If the measured resistance varies from the above specifications, replace defective components as necessary.

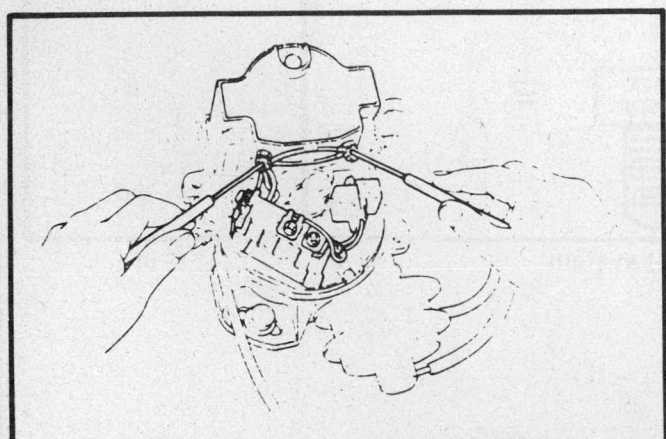

Primary coil resistance test for 4A–LC engine

PICK-UP COIL

Testing

1. Place the ignition switch in the **OFF** position.

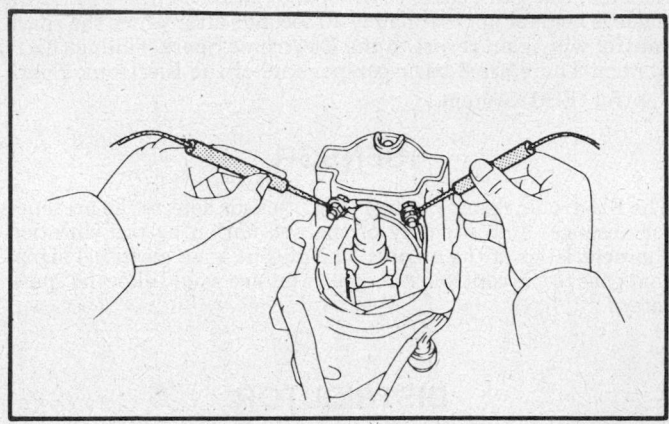

Checking primary ignition coil resistance on Prizm

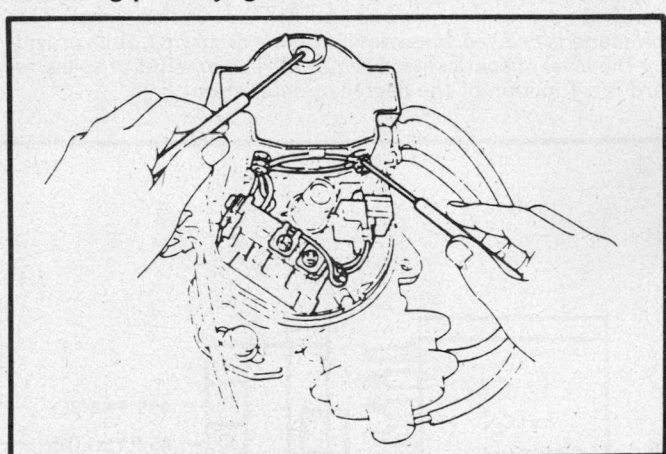

Secondary coil resistance test for 4A–LC engine

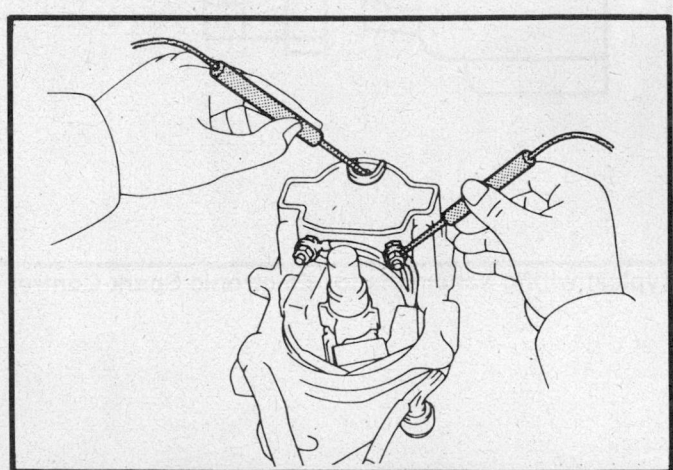

Checking secondary ignition coil resistance on Prizm

2. Remove the distributor cap.

3. Disconnect the pick-up wire from the module.

4. Measure the resistance with an ohmmeter across the pick-up coil.

5. The resistance should be 140–180 ohms.

AIR GAP

Adjustment

1. With the distributor cap off, position a reluctor lobe next to the pick-up coil projection.

2. Using a feeler gauge, measure the gap between the reluctor lobe and the pick-up coil projection.

3. The air gap should be 0.008–0.016 in.(0.2–0.4mm).

NOTE: On Nova with 4A–GE engine, this gap is non-adjustable. If not within specification, replace the distributor.

POWER SOURCE LINE VOLTAGE

Testing

1. Using a voltmeter, connect the positive probe to the ignition coil positive terminal and the negative probe to the body ground.

2. The voltage reading should be approximately 12 volts.

MODULE UNIT

Testing

1. Remove the distributor cap and turn the ignition switch to the **ON** position.

2. Using a voltmeter, connect the positive probe to the ignition coil negative terminal. Connect the negative probe to the body ground.

3. The voltage reading should be 12 volts.

4. Using a dry cell battery (1.5 volts), connect the positive pole of the battery to the pink wire terminal and the negative pole to the white wire terminal.

5. Using a voltmeter, connect the positive probe to the ignition coil negativce terminal and the negative probe to the body ground.

6. The voltage should be approximately 0–3 volts.

7. If the voltage is out of specifications, replace the module.

NOTE: Do not apply voltage for more than 5 seconds to avoid destroying the power transistor in the module.

Chevrolet/GEO Spectrum

GENERAL DESCRIPTION

The Chevrolet/GEO Spectrum uses a solid state ignition system. It consists of the spark plugs, ignition coil and distributor. The distributor has a rotor, module, pole piece, vacuum advance, centrifical advance. The ignition coil is not separate, but mounted to the side of the distributor, with internal secondary current routings.

The signal generator is used to generate the ignition signal and consists of a pole piece, a magnet and a pick-up coil. The pole piece is attached to the distributor shaft and the magnet. The pick-up coil are attached to the pick-up coil base plate.

When the distributor shaft rotates, the magnetic flux passing through the pick up coil varies due to the change in the air gap between the pick-up coil and the pole piece. Because of this, the alternating current voltage is induced in the pick-up coil. The induced voltage turns the module on and off which switches off the ignition coil primary current. The high voltage is induced in

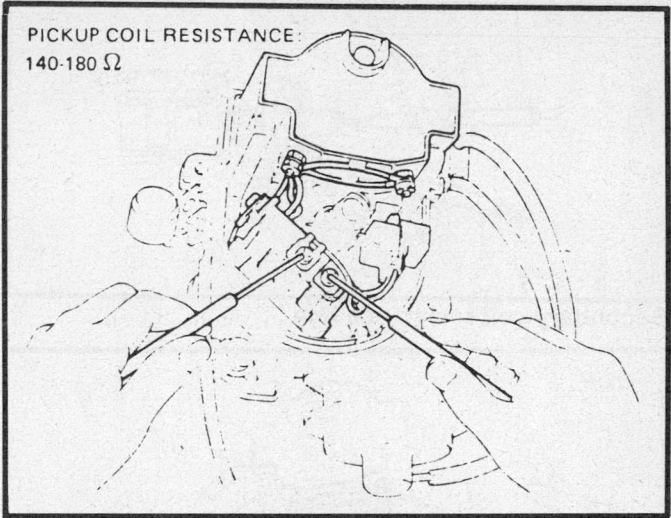

PICKUP COIL RESISTANCE: 140-180 Ω

Measuring pick-up coil resistance

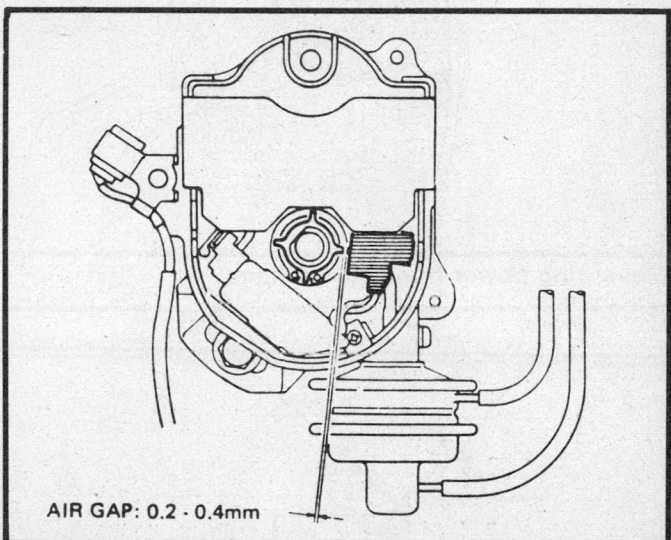

AIR GAP: 0.2 - 0.4mm

Measuring air gap

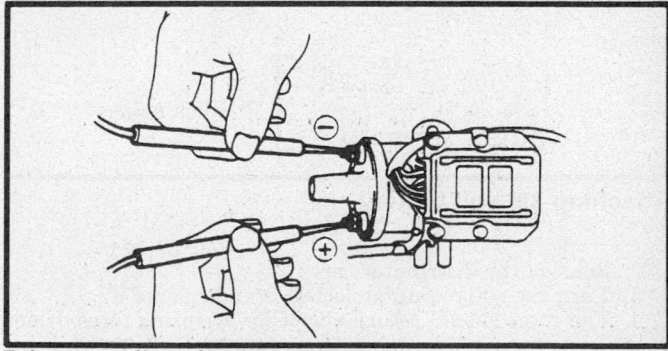

Primary coil resistance test

the secondary winding of the ignition coil and ignition sparks are generated at the spark plugs.

CENTRIFUGAL ADVANCE

Testing

1. Disconnect the negative battery cable.

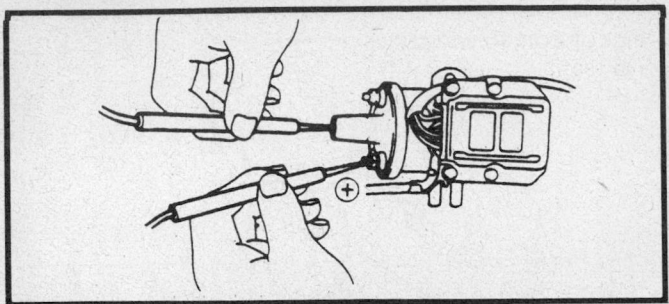

Secondary coil resistance test

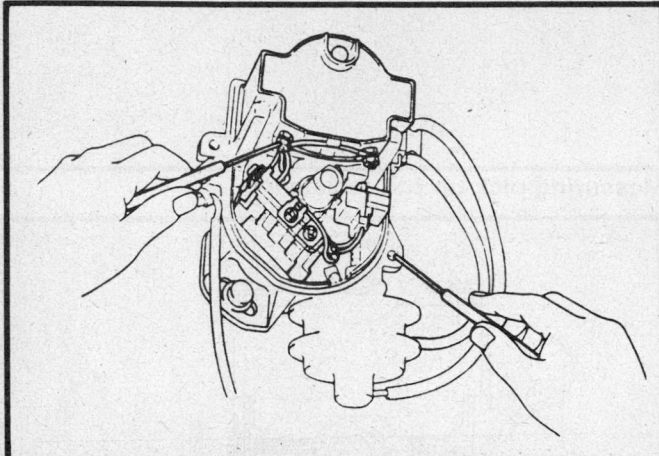

Measuring power transistor voltage

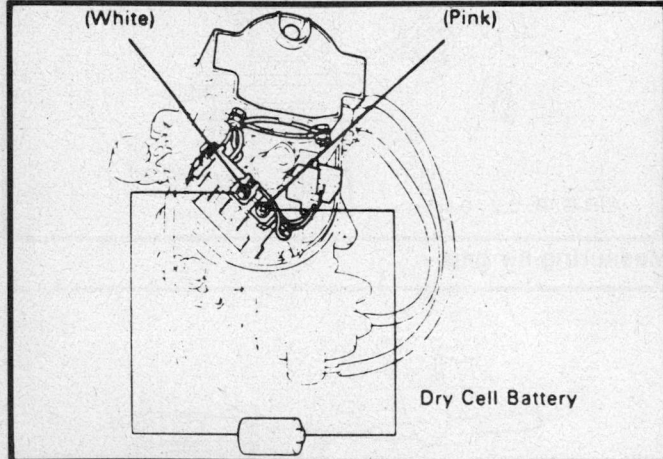

(White) (Pink)

Dry Cell Battery

Attaching 1.5 volt battery

2. Remove the distributor cap.
3. Turn the rotor counterclockwise and release it.
4. The rotor should return smoothly by spring force. If not, replace the defective components as required.

VACUUM ADVANCE

The vacuum advance unit is controlled by vacuum from the vacuum advance port on the 2 barrel carburetor. During normal operation, vacuum exerted on the A section of the advance unit from the carburetor port is sufficient to regulate the vacuum advance.

When the vehicle is idling, the advance unit B will operate

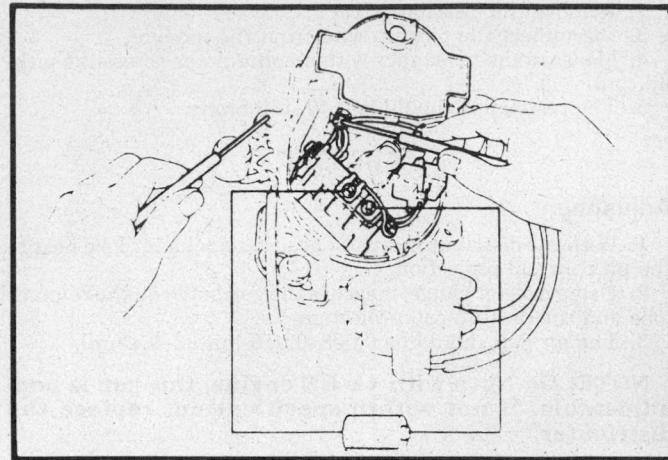

Measuring module voltage with 1.5 volt battery attached

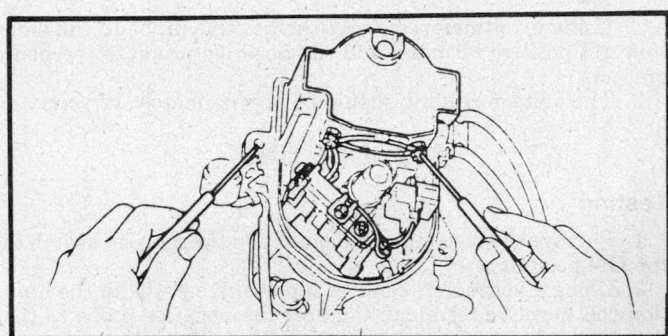

Measuring ignition voltage

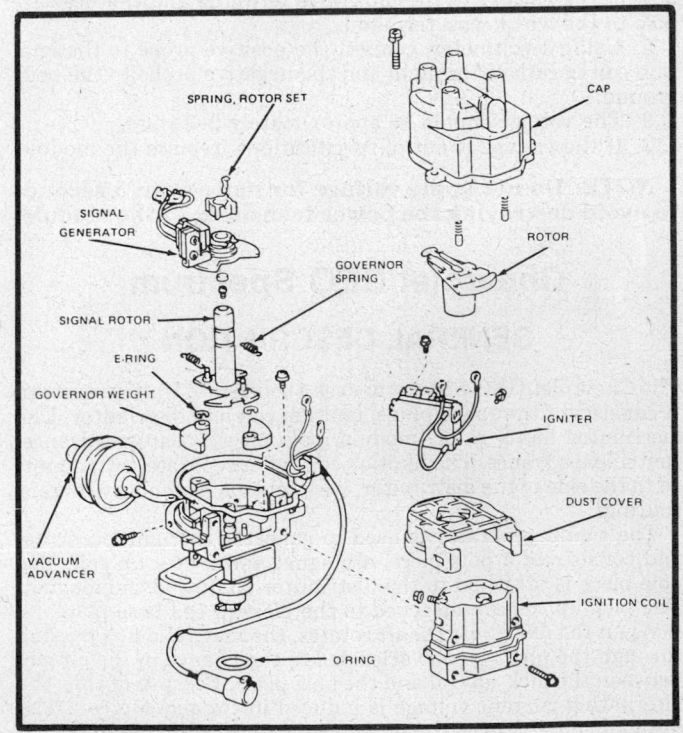

SPRING, ROTOR SET

CAP

SIGNAL GENERATOR

ROTOR

GOVERNOR SPRING

SIGNAL ROTOR

E-RING

IGNITER

GOVERNOR WEIGHT

DUST COVER

VACUUM ADVANCER

IGNITION COIL

O-RING

Distributor exploded view

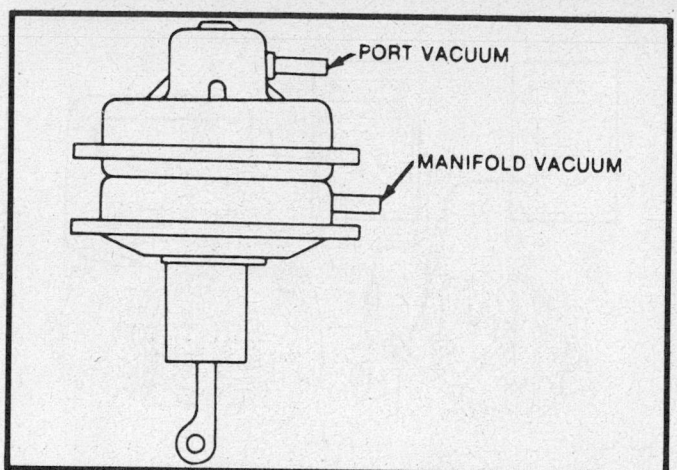

Vacuum nipple identification on vacuum advance unit

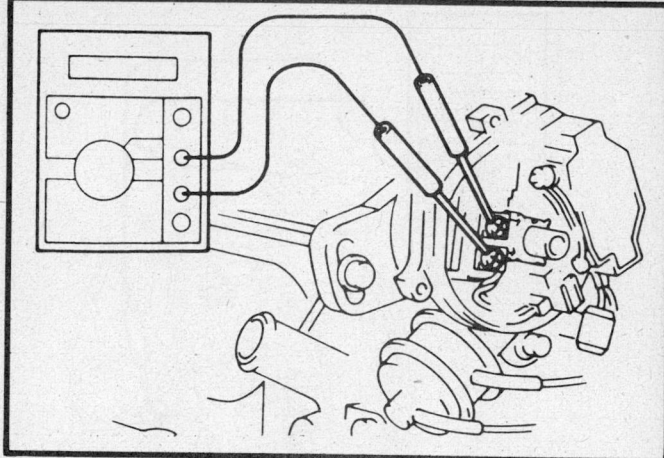

Measuring pick-up coil resistance

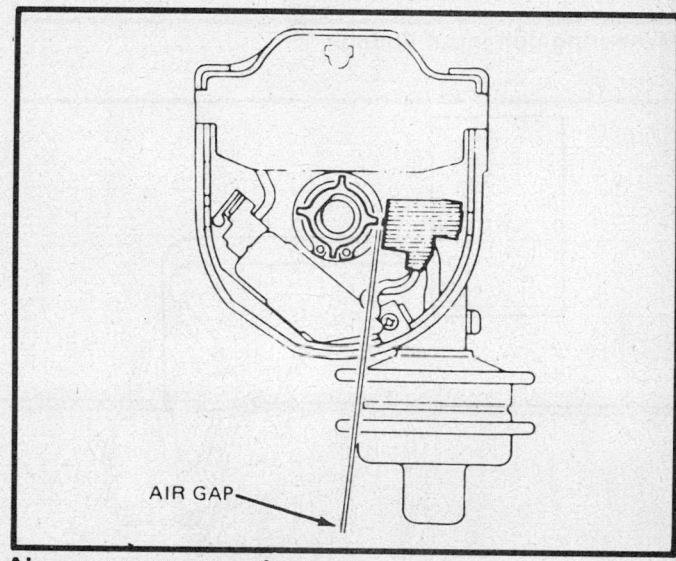

Air gap measurement

with vacuum from the intake manifold. When the carburetor throttle is again opened, the A advance will return to its operating position.

Testing

1. Disconnect the negative battery cable. Remove the distributor cap.
2. Disconnect the vacuum hose from the vacuum advance unit.
3. Connect a vacuum tester to the advance unit.
4. Apply approximately 16 in. Hg. of vacuum and release it. Check that the pick-up base plate moves smoothly. Check both A and B sides.
5. If the base plate does not move smoothly, inspect the plate and vacuum advance unit. Repair or replace as required.

PICK-UP COIL

Testing

1. Measure the resistance of the pick-up coil by connecting the probes of the ohmmeter on each terminal.
2. The resistance should be 140–180 ohms. If not, replace the coil.

AIR GAP

Adjustment

1. Use a non-magnetic feeler gauge to measure the air gap.
2. If the measurement is out of specifications of 0.008–0.016 in., adjustment of the air gap is required.

NOTE: It is recommended that a new signal generator be installed if the air gap is out of specifications.

3. If the siganl generator assembly magnet holding screw is loosened for adjustment or replacement of the signal generator, it must be cleaned of all oil or grease with a solvent.
4. A sealing agent must be installed on the screw and after the air gap adjustment is made, the sealing agent must be allowed to properly cure before engine start-up is attempted.

NOTE: Replace the rotor spring set with new springs if the signal generator assembly is replaced.

IGNITION COIL

Testing
INPUT VOLTAGE

1. With the ignition switch in the **ON** position, measure the voltage between the positive terminal of the ignition coil and ground.
2. The voltage should equal battery voltage.

PRIMARY COIL RESISTANCE

1. The ignition switch must be in the **OFF** position.
2. Disconnect the terminal of the ignition coil.
3. Measure the resistance between the positive and the negative terminals of the ignition coil.
4. The resistance should be 1.2-1.5 ohms. If not, replace the coil.

SECONDARY COIL RESISTANCE

1. The ignition switch must be in the **OFF** position.
2. Disconnect the positive terminal of the ignition coil.
3. Measure the resistance between the primary positive terminal and the high voltage terminal.
4. The resistance value should be 10.2-13.8 ohms. If not, replace the coil.

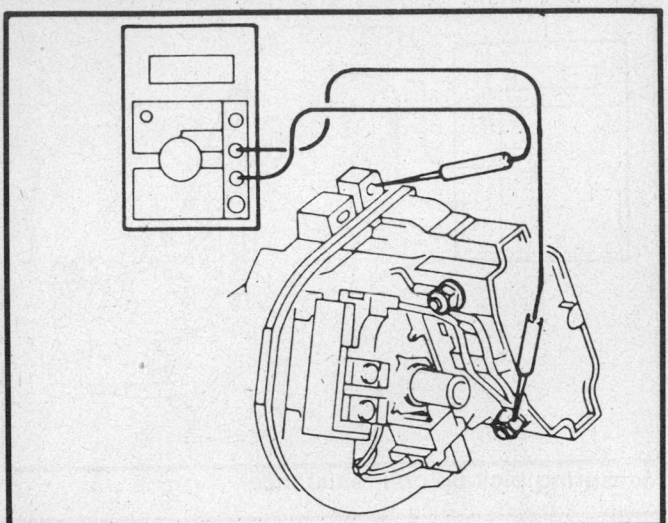

Measuring coil input voltage

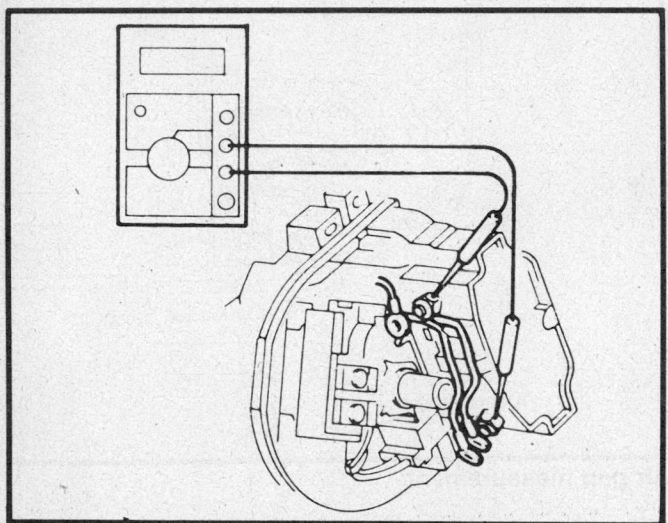

Measuring primary resistance of ignition coil

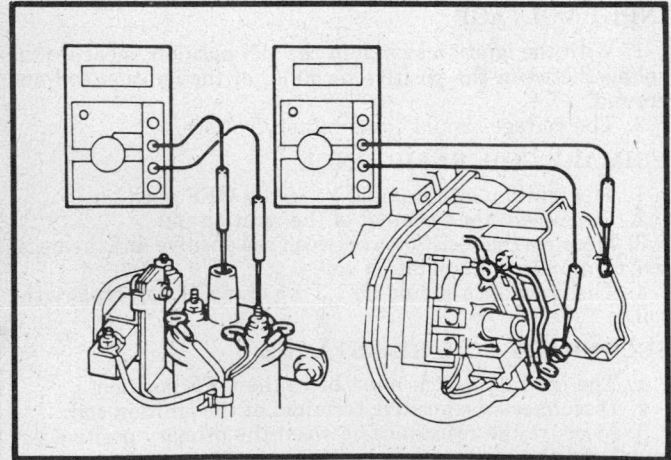

Measuring secondary coil resistance of remote and on-distributor coils

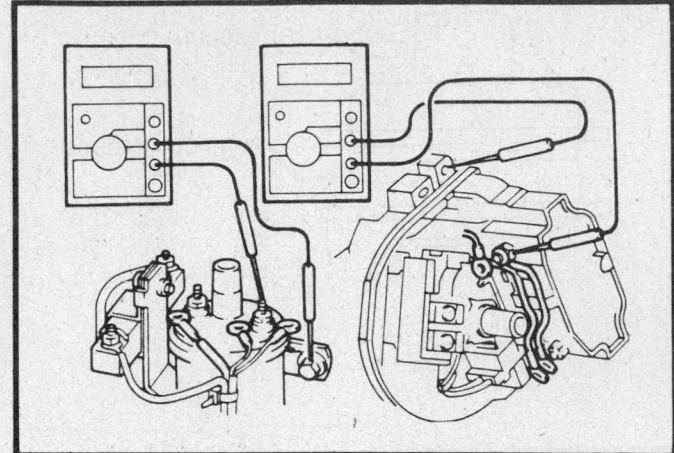

Measuring insulation resistance of remote and on-distributor coils

INSULATION RESISTANCE

Testing

1. Have the ignition switch in the **OFF** position.
2. Disconnect the positive terminal of the ignition switch.
3. Measure the resistance between the positive terminal of the coil and ground.
4. The resistance should be more than 10 ohms.

RESISTOR RESISTANCE

Testing

1. Disconnect the terminal of the resistor.
2. Measure the resistance of the resistor.
3. The resistance value should be 1.3–1.5 ohms.

Chevrolet Sprint

GENERAL DESCRIPTION

The Chevrolet Sprint 3 cylinder engine uses a solid state ignition system. It is comprised of the spark plugs, ignition coil and distributor. The distributor has a rotor, module, pole piece, vacuum advance and centrifugal advance.

The signal generator is used to generate the ignition signal and consists of a pole piece, a magnet and a pick-up coil. The pole piece is attached to the distributor shaft. The magnet and pick-up coil are attached to the pick-up coil base plate.

When the distributor shaft rotates, the magnetic flux passing through the pick-up coil varies due to the change in the air gap between the pick-up coil and the pole piece. Because of this, the alternating current voltage is induced in the pick-up coil. The induced voltage turns the module on and off which switches off the ignition coil primary current. The high voltage is induced in the secondary winding of the ignition coil and ignition sparks are generated at the spark plugs.

NOTE: The engine firing order is 1–3–2 with No. 1 cylinder at the front of the engine (right side of vehicle).

CENTRIFUGAL ADVANCE

Testing

1. Disconnect the negative battery cable.
2. Remove the distributor cap.

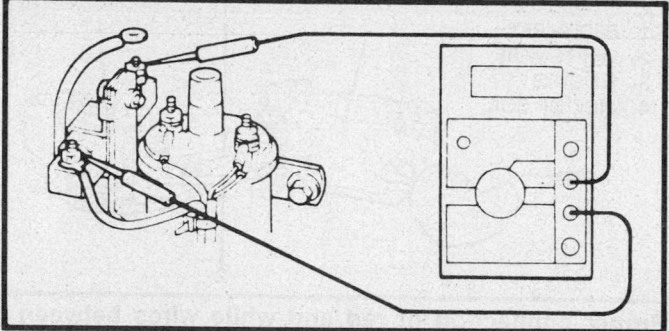

Measuring resistance of resistor unit

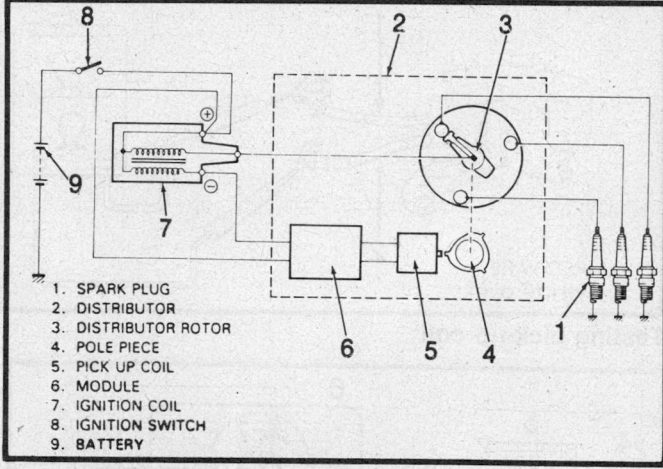

1. SPARK PLUG
2. DISTRIBUTOR
3. DISTRIBUTOR ROTOR
4. POLE PIECE
5. PICK UP COIL
6. MODULE
7. IGNITION COIL
8. IGNITION SWITCH
9. BATTERY

Sprint ignition system circuit

3. Turn the rotor counterclockwise and release it.
4. The rotor should return smoothly by spring force. If not, replace the defective components as required.

VACUUM ADVANCE

Testing

1. Disconnect the negative battery cable. Remove the distributor cap.
2. Disconnect the vacuum hose from the vacuum advance unit.
3. Connect a vacuum tester to the advance unit.
4. Apply approximately 16 in. Hg. of vacuum and release it. Check that the pick-up base plate moves smoothly.
5. If the plate does not move smoothly, inspect the plate and vacuum advance unit. Repair or replace as required.

MODULE

Testing

1. Remove the dust cover from the module. Tag and disconnect the white and red wires from the module.
2. Connect a light bulb, an ohmmeter and a 12 volt battery to the module.
3. Set the ohmmeter to the 1–10 ohm range. Allow the ohmmeter negative probe to touch the red wire terminal of the module and the positive lead to touch the white wire terminal.
4. If the light bulb begins to light, the module is good. If not, replace the module. Repair or replace as required.

NOTE: Failure to connect the ohmmeter in the described manner can result in damage to the ohmmeter and/or module.

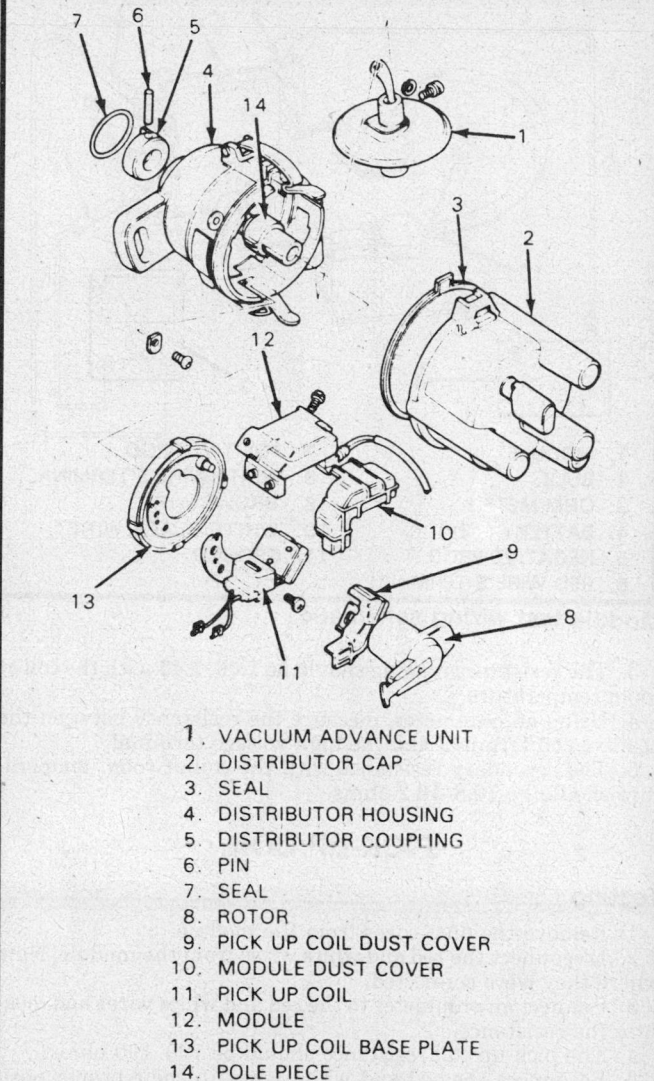

1. VACUUM ADVANCE UNIT
2. DISTRIBUTOR CAP
3. SEAL
4. DISTRIBUTOR HOUSING
5. DISTRIBUTOR COUPLING
6. PIN
7. SEAL
8. ROTOR
9. PICK UP COIL DUST COVER
10. MODULE DUST COVER
11. PICK UP COIL
12. MODULE
13. PICK UP COIL BASE PLATE
14. POLE PIECE

Exploded view of Sprint distributor

RELUCTOR AIR GAP

Testing

NOTE: The reluctor is also known as the pole piece.

1. Using a non-magnetic feeler gauge, measure the air gap between the reluctor tooth and the pick-up coil.
2. The air gap should be 0.008–0.015 in.
3. If the air gap is out of specifications, adjust it by loosening screws securing the pick-up coil.
4. Move the pick-up coil and adjust the gap to specifications.
5. After making the correct adjustment, tighten the screws and recheck the air gap.

IGNITION COIL

Testing

1. Disconnect the negative battery cable and the coil primary/secondary leads.
2. Using an ohmmeter, measure the resistance between the positive and negative terminals.

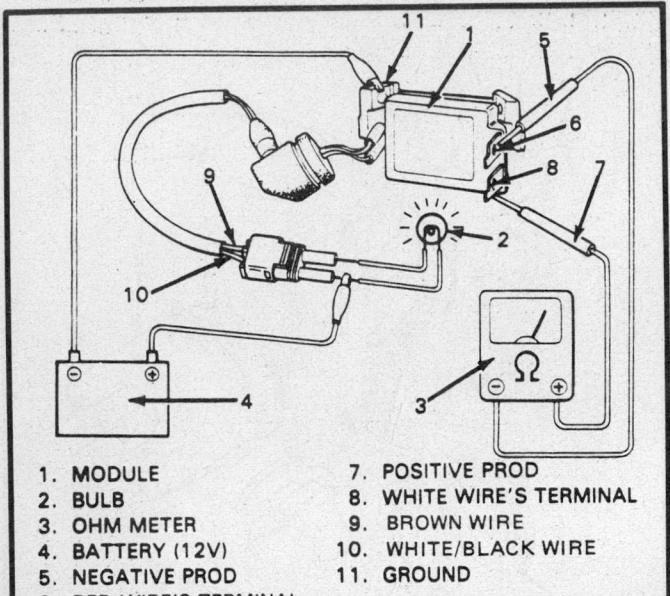

1. MODULE
2. BULB
3. OHM METER
4. BATTERY (12V)
5. NEGATIVE PROD
6. RED WIRE'S TERMINAL
7. POSITIVE PROD
8. WHITE WIRE'S TERMINAL
9. BROWN WIRE
10. WHITE/BLACK WIRE
11. GROUND

Module test wiring schematic

3. The resistance reading should be 1.06–1.43 with the coil at room temperature.
4. Using an ohmmeter, measure the resistance between the positive coil terminal and the high voltage terminal.
5. The secondary resistance with the coil at room temperature should be 10.8–16.2 ohms.

PICK-UP COIL

Testing

1. Remove the dust cover from the module.
2. Disconnect the red and white wires from the module. Note where they were connected.
3. Connect an ohmmeter to the red and white wires and measure the resistance.
4. The pick-up coil resistance should be 130–190 ohms.
5. Reconnect the red and white wires in their proper positions on the module.

NOTE: Never connect the red and white wires in a reverse position. Damage to the pick-up coil and module may occur.

GEO METRO IGNITION SYSTEM

General Description

The GEO Metro 3 cylinder engine uses 2 types of ignition systems used depending on the type of the vehicle. The Metro LSi uses a conventional solid state ignition system with vacuum/centrifugal spark control. All other models use an electronic spark control system which is controlled and monitored by the electronic control module (ECM).

The basic components of the conventional system are the spark plugs, ignition coil and distributor. The distributor has a rotor, module, pole piece, vacuum advance and centrifugal advance. Spark timing is mechanically controlled by a vacuum advance system which uses engine manifold vacuum and a centrifugal advance mechanism.

On the electronic spark control system, all spark timing changes are made electronically by the ECM. The ECM recieves

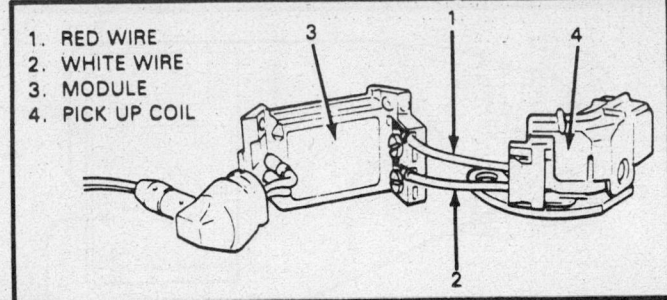

1. RED WIRE
2. WHITE WIRE
3. MODULE
4. PICK UP COIL

Proper connection of red and white wires between module and pick-up coil

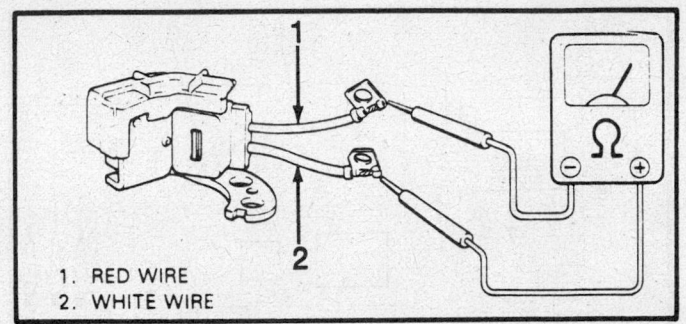

1. RED WIRE
2. WHITE WIRE

Testing pick-up coil

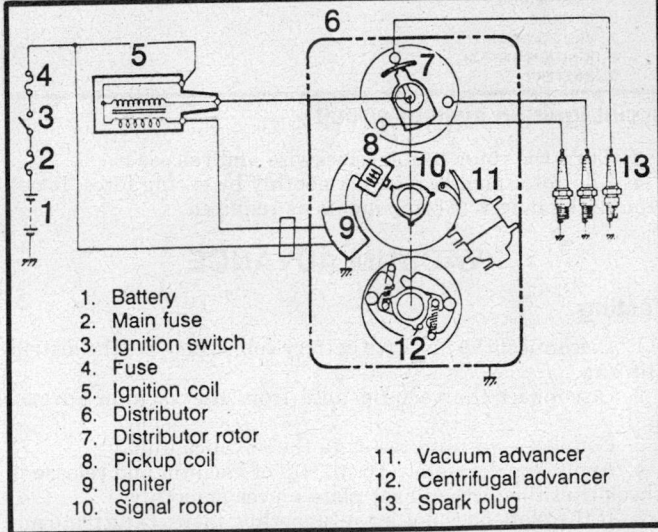

1. Battery
2. Main fuse
3. Ignition switch
4. Fuse
5. Ignition coil
6. Distributor
7. Distributor rotor
8. Pickup coil
9. Igniter
10. Signal rotor
11. Vacuum advancer
12. Centrifugal advancer
13. Spark plug

Metro conventional ignition system

input from various engine sensors, calculates the proper timing and tells the distributor to change the timing as required. There are no mechanical or vacuum advance mechanisms involved in the process.

Troubleshooting

IGNITION COIL

Testing

1. Remove the cap from the ignition coil.
2. With the ignition switch in the **ON** position, measure the voltage between the positive terminal of the ignition coil and ground. The voltage should equal battery voltage.

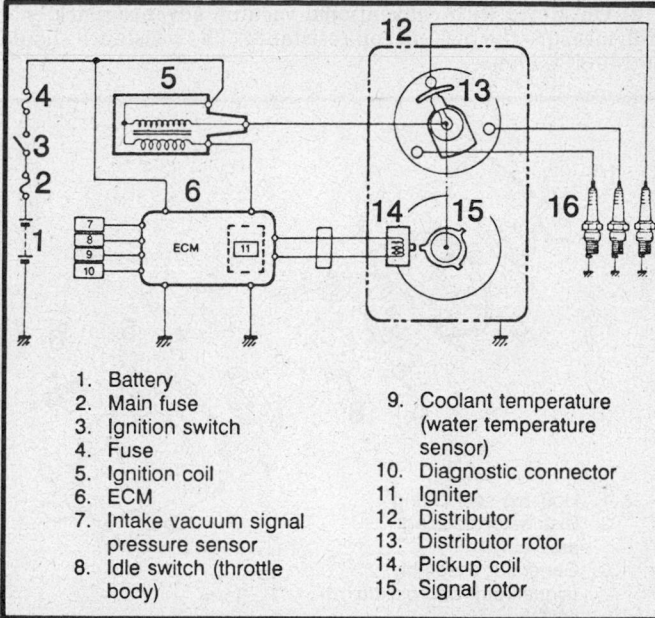

1. Battery
2. Main fuse
3. Ignition switch
4. Fuse
5. Ignition coil
6. ECM
7. Intake vacuum signal pressure sensor
8. Idle switch (throttle body)
9. Coolant temperature (water temperature sensor)
10. Diagnostic connector
11. Igniter
12. Distributor
13. Distributor rotor
14. Pickup coil
15. Signal rotor

Metro electronic spark control ignition system

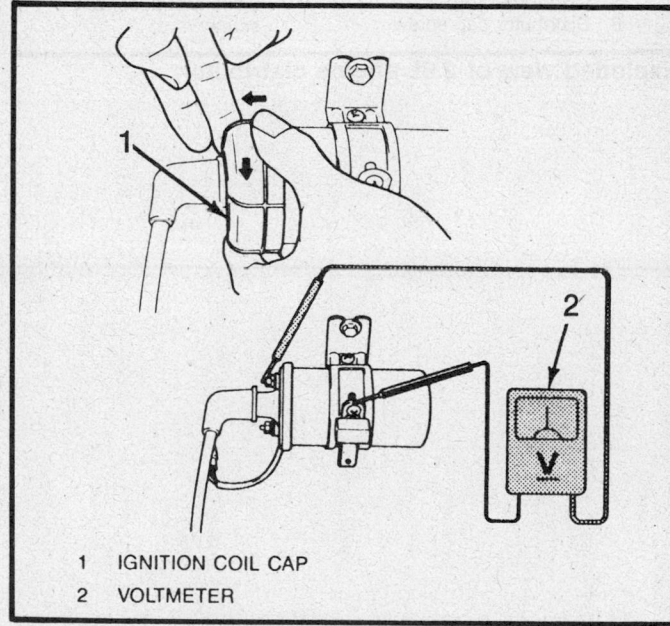

1 IGNITION COIL CAP
2 VOLTMETER

Checking ignition coil input voltage on Metro

3. Disconnect the ignition coil multi-connector and turn the ignition switch to the **OFF** position.

4. Measure the resistance between the positive and the negative terminals of the ignition coil primary winding. The resistance should be 1.33-1.55 ohms.

5. Measure the resistance of the secondary coil winding. The resistance value should be 10,700–14,500 ohms.

6. If the input voltage or primary or secondary resistances are not as specified, replace the coil.

NOISE FILTER AND CONDENSOR

Testing

The noise filter and condenser are primarily used radio noise

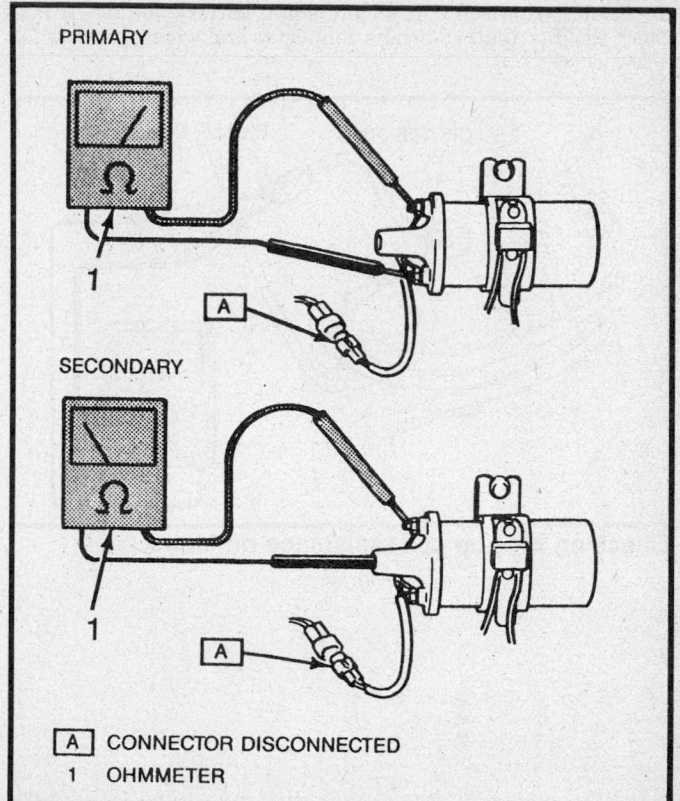

PRIMARY

SECONDARY

A CONNECTOR DISCONNECTED
1 OHMMETER

Measuring ignition coil resistance on Metro

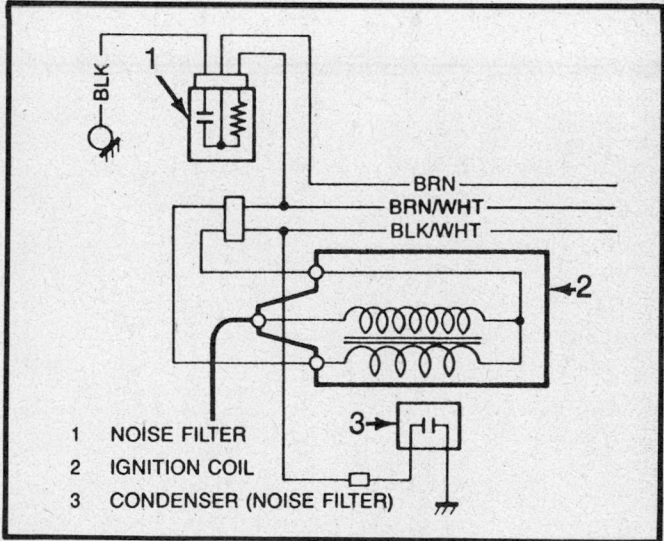

1 NOISE FILTER
2 IGNITION COIL
3 CONDENSER (NOISE FILTER)

Noise suppression circuit on Metro

supression and seldom require replacement. To test, measure the resistance of the filter and condensor with an ohmmeter. If the resistance of either unit is not 2.0–2.5 ohms, replace the affected component as required.

PICK-UP COIL

Testing

1. On Metro LSi vehicles, measure the voltage at the distribu-

tor harness connector. It should equal battery voltage. If not, check the distributor harness connector and wiring harness for

2. On Metro with conventional vacuum advance/spark control, measure the pick-up coil resistance. The resistance should be 140–180 ohms.

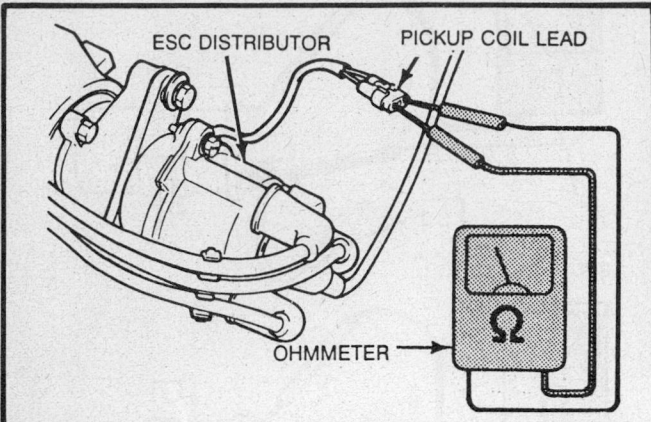

Checking pick-up coil resistance on Metro

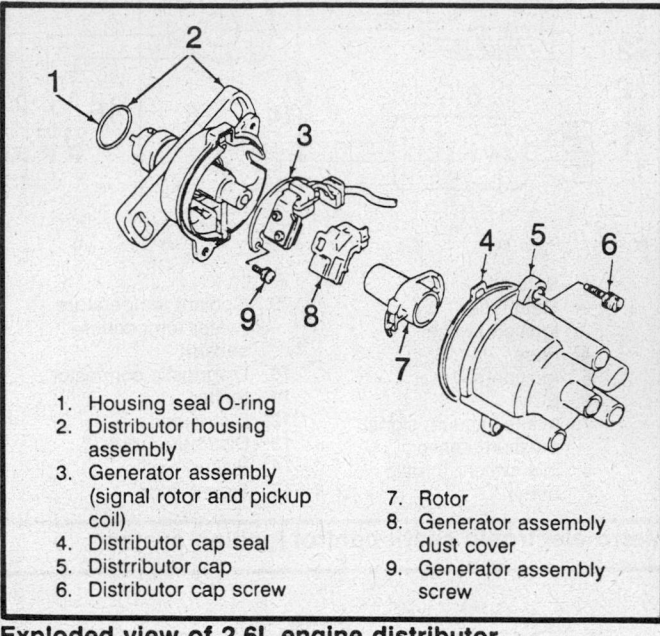

1. Housing seal O-ring
2. Distributor housing assembly
3. Generator assembly (signal rotor and pickup coil)
4. Distributor cap seal
5. Distrributor cap
6. Distributor cap screw
7. Rotor
8. Generator assembly dust cover
9. Generator assembly screw

Exploded view of 2.6L engine distributor

GENERAL MOTORS
FUEL INJECTION SYSTEMS

Digital Fuel Injection (DFI)

The Digital Fuel Injection (DFI) system, is a speed density fuel system that accurately controls the air/fuel mixture into the engine in order to achieve desired performance and emission goals. The Manifold Absolute Pressure Sensor (MAP), Manifold Air Temperature (MAT) and the Barometric Pressure Sensor (BARO) are used to determine the density (amount) of air entering the engine.

The HEI distributor provides the engine with speed (rpm) information. All of this information is then fed to the Electronic Control Module (ECM) and the ECM performs a high speed digital computations to determine the proper amount of fuel necessary to achieve the desired air/fuel mixture.

Once the ECM has calculated how much fuel to deliver, it signals the fuel injectors to meter the fuel into the throttle body. When the combustion process has been completed, some Hydrocarbons (HC), Carbon Monoxide (CO) and Nitrous Oxides (NOx) result, therefore, each DFI engine has an emission system to reduce the amount of these gases into the exhaust stream.

The catalytic converter converts these gases into a more inert gases, however, the conversion process is most efficient (lower emission levels) at an air fuel/mixture of 14.7:1.

Once the engine is warmed, the ECM uses the input from the oxygen sensor to more precisely control the air/fuel mixture to 14.7:1. This correction process is known as Closed Loop operation. Because a vehicle is driven under a wide range of operating conditions, the ECM must provide the correct quantity of fuel under all operating conditions. Therefore, additional sensors and switches are necessary to determine what operating conditions exist so that the ECM can provide an acceptable level of engine control and driveability under all operating conditions. So the closed loop DFI operation provides the acceptable level of driveability and fuel economy while improving emission levels.

The following subsystems combine to form the DFI closed loop system:

  a. Fuel delivery
  b. Air induction
  c. Data sensors
  d. Electronic control module
  e. Body control module
  f. Electric spark timing
  g. Idle speed control
  h. Emission controls
  i. Closed loop fuel control
  j. System diagnosis
  k. Cruise control
  l. Torque converter clutch

The vehicles are also equipped with a Body Control Module (BCM) that is used to control various vehicle body functions based upon data sensors and switch inputs. The ECM and BCM exchange information to maintain efficient operation of all vehicle functions. This transfer of information gives the BCM control over the ECM's self-diagnostic capabilities as well as its own.

Both the ECM and the BCM have the capability to diagnose faults with the various inputs and systems they control. When the ECM recognizes a problem, it activates a "Service Soon" telltale lamp on the instrument panel to alert the driver that a malfunction has occurred.

The digital fuel injection system consists of a pair of electronically actuated fuel metering valves, which, when actuated, spray a calculated quantity of fuel into the engine intake manifold. These valves or injectors are mounted on the throttle body above the throttle blades with the metering tip pointed into the throttle throats. The injectors are normally actuated alternately.

Fuel is supplied to the inlet of the injectors through the fuel lines and is maintained at a constant pressure across the injector inlets. When the solenoid-operated valves are energized, the injector ball valve moves to the **FULL OPEN** position. Since the pressure differential across the valve is constant, the fuel quantity is changed by varying the time that the injector is held open.

The amount of air entering the engine is measured by monitoring the intake Manifold Absolute Pressure (MAP), the intake Manifold Air Temperature (MAT) and the engine speed (rpm). This information allows the computer to compute the flow rate of air being inducted into the engine and, consequently, the flow rate of fuel required to achieve the desired air/fuel mixture for the particular engine operating condition.

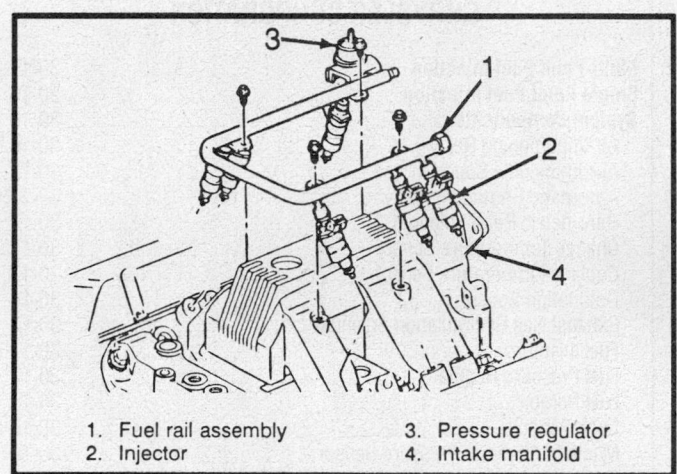

1. Fuel rail assembly
2. Injector
3. Pressure regulator
4. Intake manifold

Fuel rail and injectors, MPI system — Typical

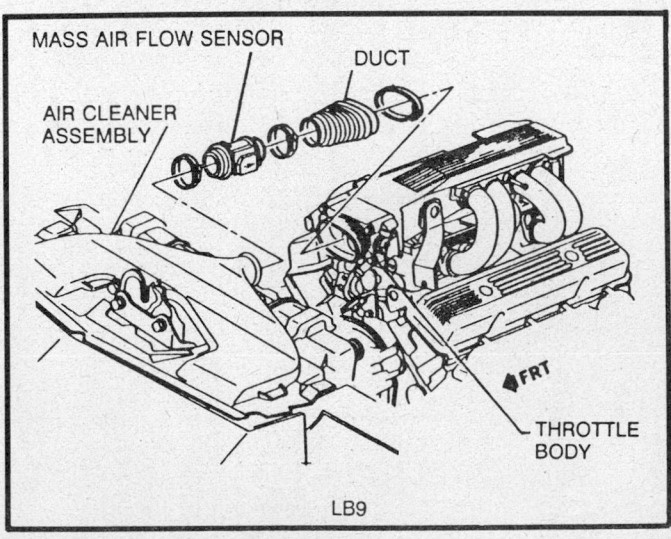

MASS AIR FLOW SENSOR

DUCT

AIR CLEANER ASSEMBLY

FRT

THROTTLE BODY

LB9

Air intake system, PFI system

	FUEL METERING PARTS
1.	FUEL METER ASSEMBLY
2.	GASKET - FUEL METER BODY
3.	SCREW - FUEL METER BODY (3)
4.	FUEL INJECTOR ASSEMBLY
5.	FILTER - INJECTOR NOZZLE
6.	SEAL - SMALL "O" RING (2)
7.	SEAL - LARGE "O" RING (2)
8.	BACK UP WASHER - INJECTOR (2)
9.	GASKET FUEL METER COVER
10.	DUST SEAL - REGULATOR
11.	GASKET - FUEL METER OUTLET
12.	SCREW - LONG (3)
13.	SCREW - SHORT (5)
14.	FUEL INLET NUT
15.	GASKET - FUEL INLET NUT
16.	FUEL OUTLET NUT
17.	GASKET - FUEL OUTLET NUT

	THROTTLE BODY PARTS
18.	THROTTLE BODY ASSEMBLY
19.	SCREW - IDLE STOP
20.	SPRING - IDLE STOP SCREW
21.	FITTING - POWER BREAK LINE
22.	LEVER - T.P.S.
23.	SCREW - T.P.S. LEVER
24.	THROTTLE POSITION SENSOR ASSEMBLY (T.P.S.)
25.	PLATE - T.P.S. RETAINER (2)
26.	SCREW - T.P.S. ATTACHING (2)
27.	WASHER - T.P.S. SCREW
28.	IDLE SPEED CONTROL ASSEMBLY (ISC)
29.	BRACKET - ISC
30.	SCREW - ISC BRACKET ATTACHING
31.	IDLE SPEED CONTROL/BRACKET ASSEMBLY
32.	GASKET - FLANGE MOUNTING

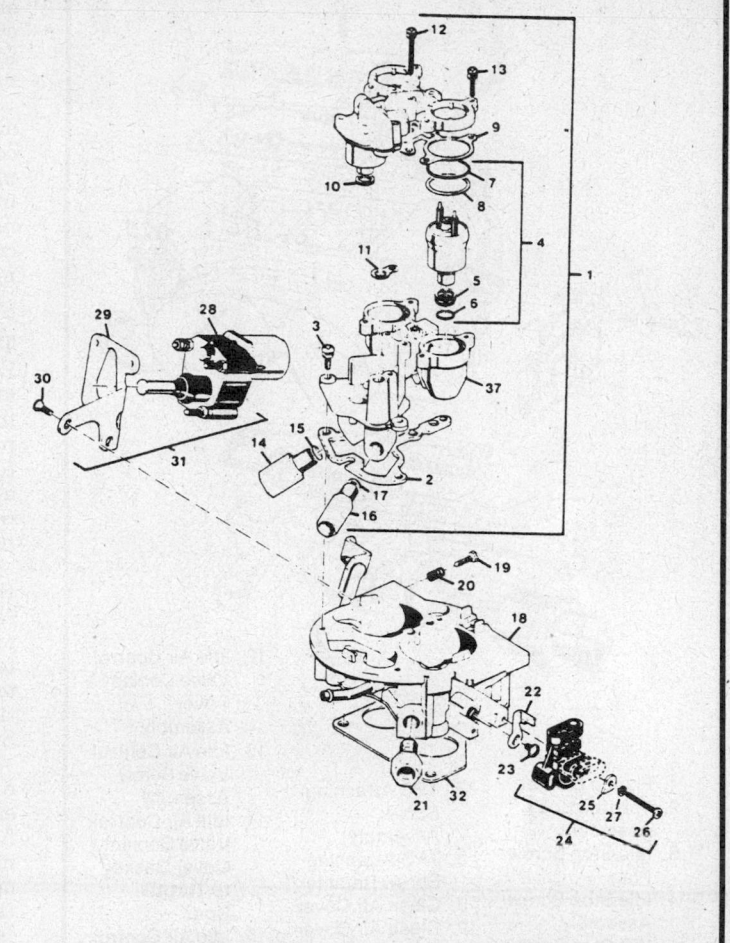

Throttle body components-DFI

Port Fuel Injection

MULTI-PORT FUEL INJECTION (MFI)

The Multi-Port Fuel Injection (MFI) system is controlled by an Electronic Control Module (ECM) which monitors engine operations and generates output signals to provide the correct air/fuel mixture, ignition timing and engine idle speed control. Input to the control unit is provided by an oxygen sensor, coolant temperature sensor, detonation sensor, hot file mass sensor and throttle position sensor. The ECM also receives information concerning engine rpm, road speed, transmission gear position, power steering and air conditioning.

The intake manifold functions like that of a diesel. It is used only to let air into the engine. The fuel is injected by separate injectors that are mounted over the intake valve.

With the port injection system, there is no need for a Thermac, EFE, map sensor or baro sensor. This system provides better cold driveability, less exhaust emissions as well as a better throttle response.

The injectors are located, one at each intake port, rather than the single injector found on the throttle body system. The injectors are mounted on a fuel rail and are activated by a signal from the electronic control module. The injector is a solenoid-operated valve which remains open depending on the width of the electronic pulses (length of the signal) from the ECM; the longer the open time, the more fuel is injected. In this manner, the air/fuel mixture can be precisely controlled for maximum performance with minimum emissions.

TUNED PORT FUEL INJECTION (TPI)

The Tuned Port Fuel Injection (TPI) system consists of individual intake and exhaust ports for each cylinder. The introduction of the TPI system has improved the torque and horse power for those engines utilizing this system.

The induction system for the TPI is made up of large forward mounted air cleaners, a new mass airflow sensor, a cast aluminum throttle body assembly with dual throttle blades, a large extended cast aluminum plenum, individual aluminum tuned runners and a protruding dual fuel rail assembly with computer controlled injectors. The base plate is cast aluminum and incorporated the crossover portion of the tuned runners. The base plate also serves as a mounting for the fuel injectors. The individual aluminum runners are designed to provide the best tuning or frequency of air pulses within the runners and for the optimum throttle response throughout the driving range, thus the name TPI. The runners are selected by length and size to take advantage of the air pulses set up by the opening and closing of the intake valves. The high pressure pulses result in denser air at each intake valve. Timing the pressure pulses to occur during the valve open period forces more air into the combustion chamber, which results in a more efficient cylinder charging and improved volumetric efficiency.

The fuel injectors fire at the same time, once each crankshaft revolution. During the 1st injection, fuel is sprayed at the base of the closed intake valve, during the 2nd injection, fuel is sprayed into the air stream entering the combustion chamber. The fuel from the first injection vaporizes from the heat of the

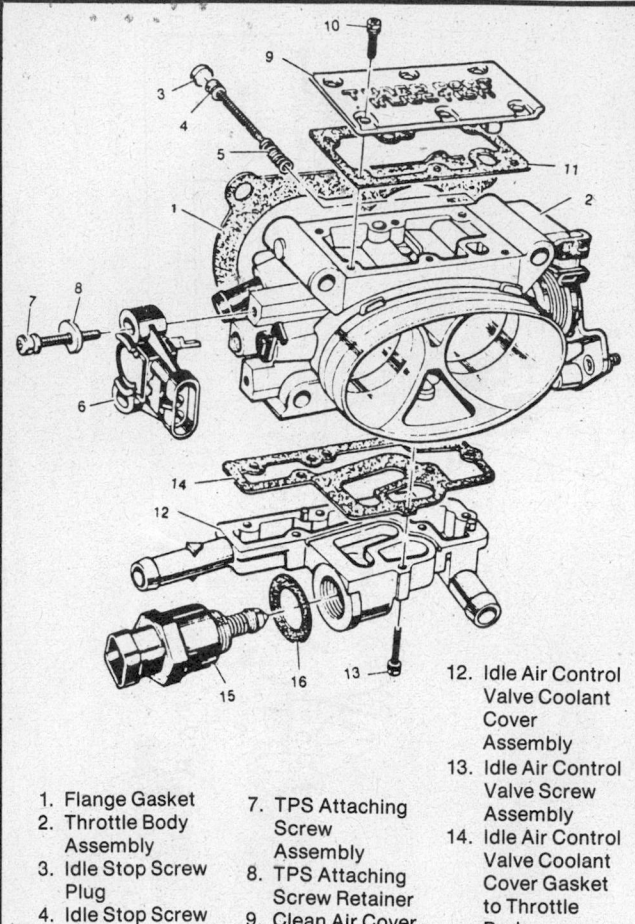

1. Flange Gasket
2. Throttle Body Assembly
3. Idle Stop Screw Plug
4. Idle Stop Screw Assembly
5. Idle Stop Screw Spring
6. Throttle Position Sensor (TPS)
7. TPS Attaching Screw Assembly
8. TPS Attaching Screw Retainer
9. Clean Air Cover
10. Clean Air Cover Screw Assembly
11. Clean Air Cover Gasket
12. Idle Air Control Valve Coolant Cover Assembly
13. Idle Air Control Valve Screw Assembly
14. Idle Air Control Valve Coolant Cover Gasket to Throttle Body
15. Idle Air Control Valve Assembly
16. Idle Air Control Valve Assembly Gasket

Exploded view of the TPI throttle body

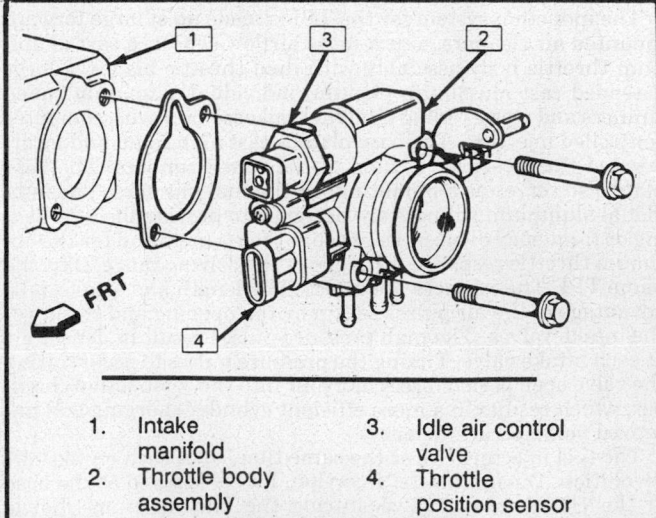

1. Intake manifold
2. Throttle body assembly
3. Idle air control valve
4. Throttle position sensor

Throttle position sensor – 3.8L turbocharged engine

intake valve and the fuel vapors are drawn into the combustion chamber along with the air when the valve opens to charge the cylinder. The fuel pressure is regulated constantly; as the manifold vacuum changes, the regulator adjusts the fuel pressure to maintain a constant drop in pressure across the injectors.

When the signals are received by the computer from the mass airflow sensor and the engine coolant temperature sensor, the computer will search its pre-programmed information to determine the pulse width of the fuel injectors required to match the input signals. The computer now, based on the engine rpm, signals the injectors to release the required amount of fuel. The computer makes mass airflow sensor readings and fuel requirement calculations every 12.5 milliseconds.

SEQUENTIAL FUEL INJECTION (SFI)

The Sequential Fuel Injection (SFI) system is controlled by an Electronic Control Module (ECM) which monitors engine operations and generates output signals to provide the correct air/fuel mixture, ignition timing and engine idle speed control. Input to the control unit is provided by an oxygen sensor, coolant temperature sensor, detonation sensor, hot film air mass sensor and throttle position sensor. The ECM also receives information concerning engine rpm, road speed, transmission gear position, power steering and air conditioning.

With SFI, metered fuel is timed and injected sequentially through 6 injectors into individual cylinder ports. Each cylinder receives 1 injection per working cycle (every 2 revolutions), just prior to the opening of the intake valve. In addition, the SFI system incorporates a Computer Controlled Coil Ignition (C^3I) system which uses an electronic coil module to replace the conventional distributor and coil used on most engines. An Electronic Spark Control (ESC) is used to adjust the spark timing.

The injection system uses solenoid-type fuel injectors, 1 at each intake port, rather than the single injector found on the earlier throttle body system. The injectors are mounted on a fuel rail and are activated by a signal from the electronic control module. The injector is a solenoid-operated valve which remains open depending on the width of the electronic pulses (length of the signal) from the ECM; the longer the open time, the more fuel is injected. In this manner, the air/fuel mixture can be precisely controlled for maximum performance with minimum emissions.

Throttle Body Injection (TBI)

The electronic fuel injection systems are fuel metering systems with the amount of fuel delivered by the Throttle Body Injector(s) (TBI) determined by an electronic signal supplied by the Electronic Control Module (ECM). The ECM monitors various engine and vehicle conditions to calculate the fuel delivery time (pulse width) of the injector(s). The fuel pulse may be modified by the ECM to account for special operating conditions, such as cranking, cold starting, altitude, acceleration and deceleration.

The ECM controls the exhaust emissions by modifying fuel delivery to achieve an air/fuel ratio of 14.7:1. The injector **ON** time is determined by various inputs to the ECM. By increasing the injector pulse, more fuel is delivered, enriching the air/fuel ratio. Decreasing the injector pulse, leans the air/fuel ratio. Pulses are sent to the injector in 2 different modes: synchronized and nonsynchronized.

SYNCHRONIZED MODE

In synchronized mode operation, the injector is pulsed once for each distributor reference pulse. In dual throttle body systems, the injectors are pulse alternately.

NON-SYNCHRONIZED MODE

In non-synchronized mode operation, the injector is pulsed once every 12.5 milliseconds or 6.25 milliseconds depending on calibration. This pulse time is totally independent of distributor reference pulses.

Non-synchronized mode results only under the following conditions:

1. The fuel pulse width is too small to be delivered accurately by the injector (approximately 1.5 milliseconds).

2. During the delivery of prime pulses (prime pulses charge the intake manifold with fuel during or just prior to engine starting).

3. During acceleration enrichment.

4. During deceleration leanout.

The basic TBI unit is made up of 2 major casting assemblies: (1) a throttle body with a valve to control airflow and (2) a fuel body assembly with an integral pressure regulator and fuel injector to supply the required fuel. An electronically operated device to control the idle speed and a device to provide information regarding throttle valve position are included as part of the TBI unit.

The Throttle Body Injection (TBI) systems provide a means of fuel distribution for controlling exhaust emissions within legislated limits by precisely controlling the air/fuel mixture and under all operating conditions for, as near as possible, complete combustion.

This is accomplished by using an Electronic Control Module (ECM), a small on-board microcomputer, that receives electrical inputs from various sensors about engine operating conditions. An oxygen sensor in the main exhaust stream functions to provide feedback information to the ECM as to the oxygen content, lean or rich, in the exhaust. The ECM uses this information from the oxygen sensor and other sensors, to modify fuel delivery to achieve an ideal air/fuel ratio of 14.7:1. This air/fuel ratio allows the 3-way catalytic converter to be more efficient in the conversion process of reducing exhaust emissions while at the same time providing acceptable levels of driveability and fuel economy.

The ECM program electronically signals the fuel injector in the TBI assembly to provide the correct quantity of fuel for a wide range of operating conditions. Several sensors are used to determine existing operating conditions and the ECM then signals the injector to provide the precise amount of fuel required.

With the EFI system the TBI assembly is centrally located on the intake manifold where air and fuel are distributed through a single bore in the throttle body, similar to a carbureted engine. Air for combustion is controlled by a single throttle valve which is connected to the accelerator pedal linkage by a throttle shaft

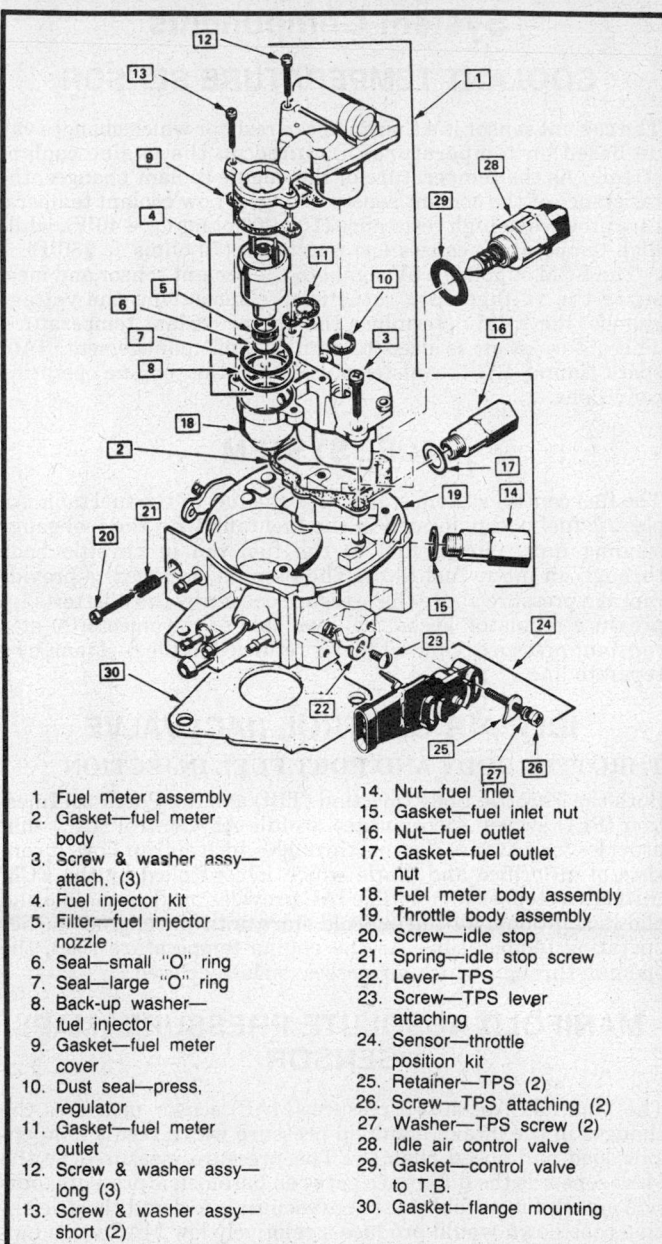

1. Fuel meter assembly
2. Gasket—fuel meter body
3. Screw & washer assy—attach. (3)
4. Fuel injector kit
5. Filter—fuel injector nozzle
6. Seal—small "O" ring
7. Seal—large "O" ring
8. Back-up washer—fuel injector
9. Gasket—fuel meter cover
10. Dust seal—press. regulator
11. Gasket—fuel meter outlet
12. Screw & washer assy—long (3)
13. Screw & washer assy—short (2)
14. Nut—fuel inlet
15. Gasket—fuel inlet nut
16. Nut—fuel outlet
17. Gasket—fuel outlet nut
18. Fuel meter body assembly
19. Throttle body assembly
20. Screw—idle stop
21. Spring—idle stop screw
22. Lever—TPS
23. Screw—TPS lever attaching
24. Sensor—throttle position kit
25. Retainer—TPS (2)
26. Screw—TPS attaching (2)
27. Washer—TPS screw (2)
28. Idle air control valve
29. Gasket—control valve to T.B.
30. Gasket—flange mounting

Exploded view of GM single throttle body injection unit.

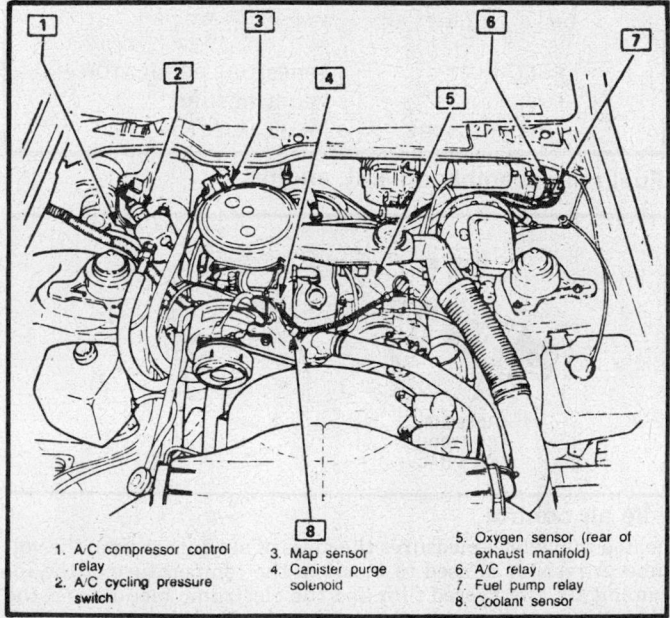

1. A/C compressor control relay
2. A/C cycling pressure switch
3. Map sensor
4. Canister purge solenoid
5. Oxygen sensor (rear of exhaust manifold)
6. A/C relay
7. Fuel pump relay
8. Coolant sensor

Engine component locations—4 cyl. 151 cu. in. engine

and lever assembly. A special plate is located directly beneath the throttle valve to aid in mixture distribution.

Fuel for combustion is supplied by a single fuel injector, mounted on the TBI assembly, whose metering tip is located directly above the throttle valve. The injector is "pulsed" or "timed" open or closed by an electronic output signal received from the ECM. The ECM receives inputs concerning engine operating conditions from the various sensors (coolant temperature sensor, oxygen sensor, etc.). The ECM, using this information, performs highspeed calculations of engine fuel requirements and "pulses" or "times" the injector, open or closed, thereby controlling fuel and air mixtures to achieve, as near as possible, ideal air/fuel mixture ratios.

System Components

COOLANT TEMPERATURE SENSOR

The coolant sensor is a thermister (a resistor which changes value based on temperature) mounted on the engine coolant stream. As the temperature of the engine coolant changes, the resistance of the coolant sensor changes. Low coolant temperature produces a high resistance (100,000 ohms @ −40°F), while high temperature causes low resistance (70 ohms @ 266°F).

The ECM supplies a 5V signal to the coolant sensor and measures the voltage that returns. By measuring the voltage change, the ECM determines the engine coolant temperature. This information is used to control fuel management, IAC, spark timing, EGR, canister purge and other engine operating conditions.

FUEL SYSTEM

The fuel control system starts with the fuel in the fuel tank. An electric fuel pump, located in the fuel tank with the fuel gauge sending unit, pumps fuel to the fuel rail or throttle body through an inline fuel filter. The pump is designed to provide fuel at a pressure above the pressure needed by the injector(s). A pressure regulator keeps fuel available to the injector(s) at a constant pressure. Unused fuel is returned to the fuel tank by a separate line.

IDLE AIR CONTROL (IAC) VALVE

THROTTLE BODY AND PORT FUEL INJECTION

Both the Throttle Body Injection (TBI) and the Port Fuel Injection (PFI) system incorporates an Idle Air Control (IAC) that provides for a bypass channel through which air can flow. It consists of an orifice and pintle which is controlled by the ECM through a stepper motor. The IAC provides air flow for idle and allows additional air during cold start until the engine reaches operating temperature. As the engine temperature rises, the opening through which air passes is slowly closed.

MANIFOLD ABSOLUTE PRESSURE (MAP) SENSOR

The Manifold Absolute Pressure (MAP) sensor measures the changes in the intake manifold pressure which result from engine load and speed changes. The pressure measured by the MAP sensor is the difference between barometric pressure (outside air) and manifold pressure (vacuum). A closed throttle engine coastdown would produce a relatively low MAP value (approximately 20–35 kPa), while wide-open throttle would produce a high value (100 kPa). This high value is produced when the pressure inside the manifold is the same as outside the manifold and 100% of outside air (100 kPa) is being measured. This MAP output is the opposite of what would be measured on a vacuum gauge. The use of this sensor also allows the ECM to adjust automatically for different altitude.

The ECM sends a 5V reference signal to the MAP sensor. As the MAP changes, the electrical resistance of the sensor also changes. By monitoring the sensor output voltage the ECM can determine the manifold pressure. A higher pressure, lower vacuum (high voltage) requires more fuel, while a lower pressure, higher vacuum (low voltage) requires less fuel.

MASS AIR FLOW SENSOR

PORT FUEL INJECTION

The Mass Air Flow Sensor (MAF) is used to measure the mass of air that is drawn into the engine cylinders. It is located just ahead of the air throttle in the intake system and consists of a

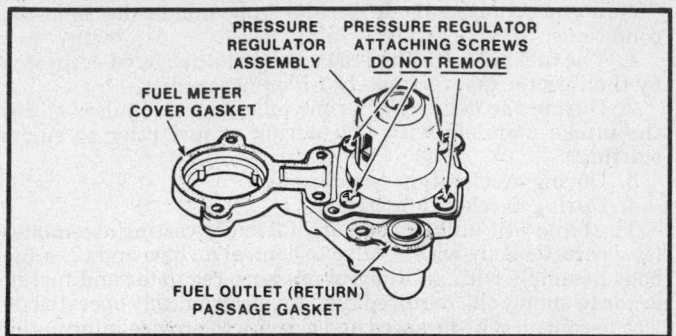

Fuel pressure regulator

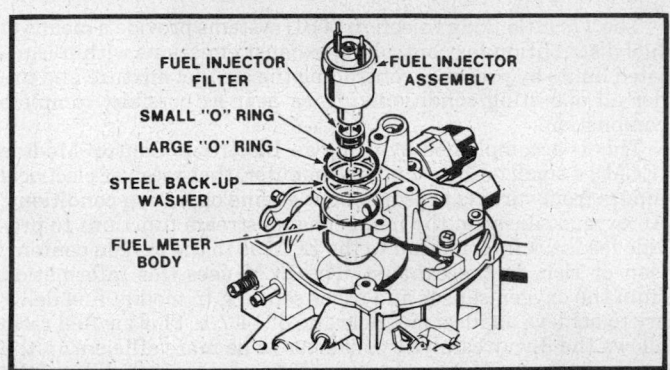

Fuel injector components

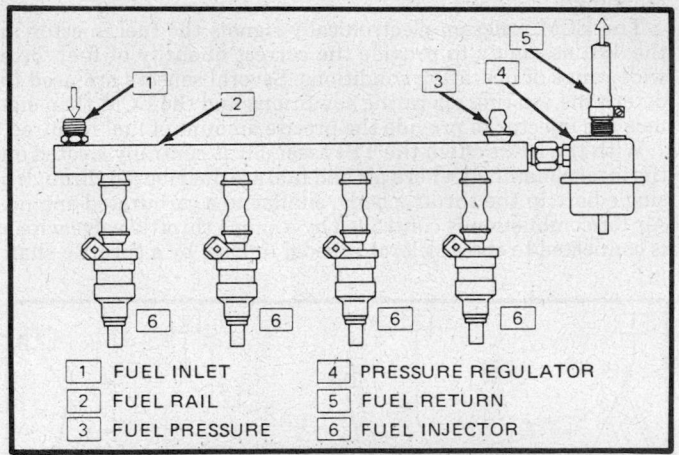

1 FUEL INLET	4 PRESSURE REGULATOR
2 FUEL RAIL	5 FUEL RETURN
3 FUEL PRESSURE	6 FUEL INJECTOR

Fuel rail assembly on 1.8L engine

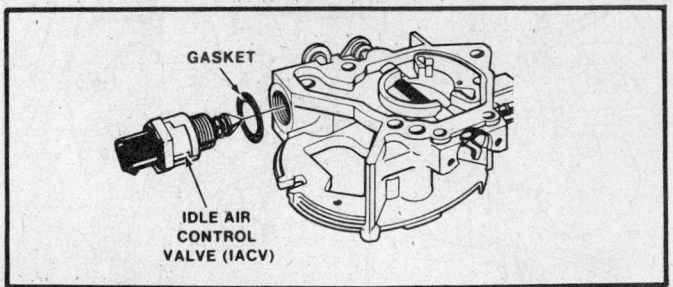

Idle air control

heated film which measures the mass of air, rather than the volume. A resistor is used to measure the temperature of the incoming air, the heated film and the electronic module and the MAF sensor maintains the temperature of the film at 75°F above ambient temperature. As the ambient (outside) air temperature rises, more energy is required to maintain the heated film at the higher temperature and the control unit uses this difference in required energy to calculate the mass of the incoming air. The control unit uses this information to determine the duration of fuel injection pulse, timing and EGR.

OXYGEN SENSOR

The exhaust oxygen sensor is mounted in the exhaust system where it can monitor the oxygen content of the exhaust gas stream. The oxygen content in the exhaust reacts with the oxygen sensor to produce a voltage output. This voltage ranges from approximately 100 millivolts (high oxygen—lean mixture) to 900 millivolts (low oxygen—rich mixture).

By monitoring the voltage output of the oxygen sensor, the ECM will determine what fuel mixture command to give to the injector (lean mixture—low voltage—rich command, rich mixture—high voltage—lean command).

Remember that oxygen sensor indicates to the ECM what is happening in the exhaust. It does not cause things to happen. It is a type of gauge: high oxygen content = lean mixture; low oxygen content = rich mixture. The ECM adjust fuel to keep the system working.

THROTTLE POSITION SENSOR (TPS)

The Throttle Position Sensor (TPS) provides the control unit with information on throttle position, in order to determine injector pulse width and hence correct mixture. The TPS is connected to the throttle shaft on the throttle body and consists of a potentiometer with one end connected to a 5V source from the ECM and the other to ground. A 3rd wire is connected to the ECM to measure the voltage output from the TPS which changes as the throttle valve angle is changed (accelerator pedal moves). At the closed throttle position, the output is low (approximately 0.4V); as the throttle valve opens, the output increases to a maximum 5V at Wide Open Throttle (WOT). The TPS can be misadjusted, open, shorted or loose; if it is out of adjustment, the idle quality of WOT performance may be poor. A loose TPS can cause intermittent bursts of fuel from the injectors and an unstable idle because the ECM thinks the throttle is moving; this should cause a trouble code to be set. Once a trouble code is set, the ECM will use a preset value for TPS and some vehicle performance may return. A small amount of engine coolant is routed through the throttle assembly to prevent freezing inside the throttle bore during cold operation.

VEHICLE SPEED SENSOR (VSS)

The Vehicle Speed Sensor (VSS) is mounted behind the speedometer in the instrument cluster. It provides electrical pulses to the ECM from the speedometer head. The pulses indicate the road speed. The ECM uses this information to operate the IAC, canister purge and TCC.

Some vehicles equipped with digital instrument clusters use a Permanent Magnet (PM) generator to provide the VSS signal. The PM generator is located in the transmission and replaces the speedometer cable. The signal from the PM generator drives a stepper motor which drives the odometer.

Modes of Operation

The ECM looks at voltage from several sensors to determine how much fuel to give the engine. The fuel is delivered under one of several conditions, called modes.

STARTING MODE

When the engine is first turned **ON**, the ECM will energize the fuel pump relay for 2 seconds and the the fuel pump will build up pressure. The ECM checks the coolant temperature sensor, throttle position sensor and crank sensor, then it determines

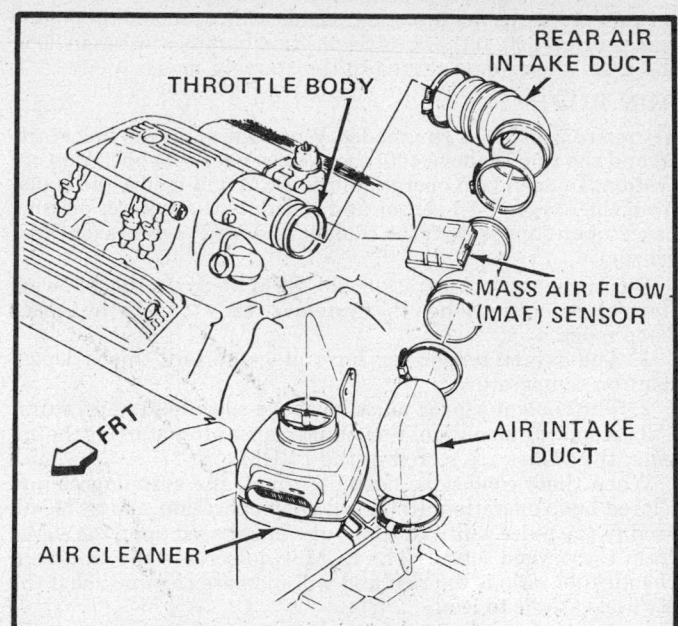

Mass air flow sensor installation—3.8L V6 shown

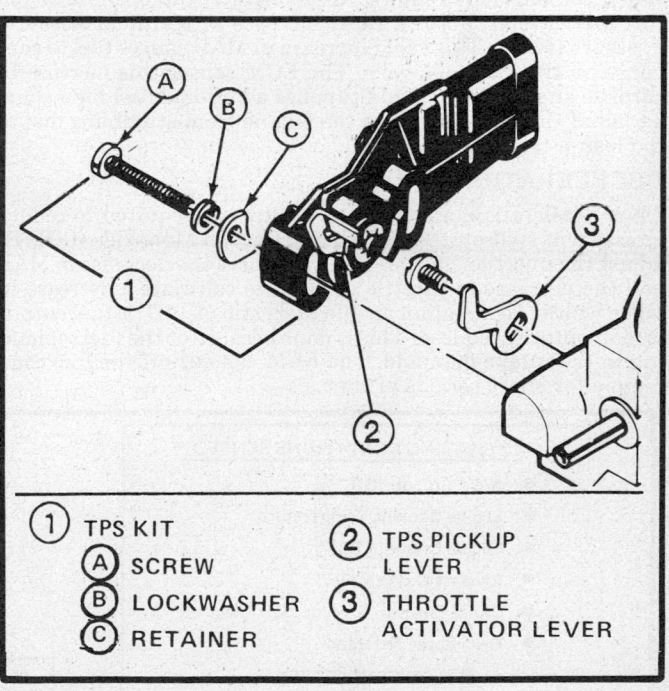

①	TPS KIT	②	TPS PICKUP LEVER
Ⓐ	SCREW	③	THROTTLE ACTIVATOR LEVER
Ⓑ	LOCKWASHER		
Ⓒ	RETAINER		

Typical TPS sensor

the proper air/fuel ratio for starting; this ranges from 1.5:1 @ −33°F to 14.7:1 @ 201°F.

The ECM controls the amount of fuel that is delivered in the starting mode by changing how long the injectors are turned **ON** and **OFF**. This is done by pulsing the injectors for very short periods.

CLEAR FLOOD MODE

If for some reason the engine should become flooded, provisions have been made to clear this condition. To clear the flood, depress the accelerator pedal to the wide-open throttle position. The ECM then issues injector pulses at a rate that would be equal to an air/fuel ratio of 20:1. The ECM maintains this injector rate as long as the throttle remains wide open and the engine rpm is below 600. If the throttle position becomes less than 80%, the ECM then would return to the starting mode.

RUN MODE

There are 2 different run modes. When the engine is first started and the rpm is above 400, the system goes into open loop operation. In open loop operation, the ECM will ignore the signal from the oxygen (O_2) sensor and calculate the injector on-time based upon inputs from the coolant and MAP sensors (or MAF sensor).

During open loop operation, the ECM analyzes the following items to determine when the system is ready to go to the Closed Loop mode.

1. The oxygen sensor varying voltage output; this is dependent on temperature.
2. The coolant sensor must be above specified temperature.
3. A specific amount of time must elapse after starting the engine; the values are stored in the PROM.

When these conditions have been met, the system goes into Closed Loop operation. In Closed Loop operation, the ECM will modify the pulse width (injector on-time) based upon the signal from the oxygen sensor. The ECM will decrease the on-time if the air/fuel ratio is too rich and will increase the on-time if the air/fuel ratio is to lean.

ACCELERATION MODE

When the engine is required to accelerate, the opening of the throttle valve(s) causes a rapid increase in Manifold Absolute Pressure (MAP). This rapid increase in MAP causes fuel to condense on the manifold walls. The ECM senses this increase in throttle angle and MAP and supplies additional fuel for a short period of time; this prevents the engine from stumbling due to too lean a mixture.

DECELERATION MODE

Upon deceleration, a leaner fuel mixture is required to reduce emission of Hydrocarbons (HC) and Carbon Monoxide (CO). To adjust the injection on-time, the ECM uses the decrease in MAP and the decrease in throttle position to calculate a decrease in pulse width. To maintain an idle fuel ratio of 14.7:1, fuel output is momentarily reduced. This is done because of the fuel remaining in the intake manifold. The ECM can cut off the fuel completely for short periods of time.

BATTERY VOLTAGE CORRECTION MODE

The purpose of battery voltage correction is to compensate for variations in battery voltage to fuel pump and injector response. The ECM modifies the pulse width by a correction factor in the PROM. When battery voltage decreases, pulse width increases.

Battery voltage correction takes place in all operating modes. When battery voltage is low, the spark delivered by the distributor may be low. To correct this low battery voltage problem, the ECM can do any or all of the following:

a. Increase injector pulse width (increase fuel)
b. Increase idle RPM
c. Increase ignition dwell time

FUEL CUT-OFF MODE

When the ignition is **OFF**, the ECM will not energize the injector. Fuel will also be cut off if the ECM does not receive a reference pulse from the distributor. To prevent dieseling, fuel delivery is completely stopped as soon as the engine is stopped. The ECM will not allow any fuel supply until it receives distributor reference pulses which prevents flooding.

System Services

IDLE SPEED

Adjustment

DIGITAL FUEL INJECTION (DFI)

1. Remove the air cleaner and plug the Thermac vacuum tap. Start the engine.
2. Enter diagnostics; select ECM parameter P.O.4, coolant temperature. Operate the engine until the engine coolant temperature is greater than 185°F.
3. Retract the idle speed control motor until the throttle lever is clear of the ISC plunger. Use the idle speed control motor tester tool J–34025 or equivalent, or use the jumper harness procedure as outlined in this section.
4. Make sure that the throttle lever is resting on the minimum air screw.

NOTE: To prevent damage to the ISC, apply finger pressure to the ISC plunger while retracting. Retracting the ISC plunger without pressure on the plunger may cause the internal gears to clash and bind. Do not leave

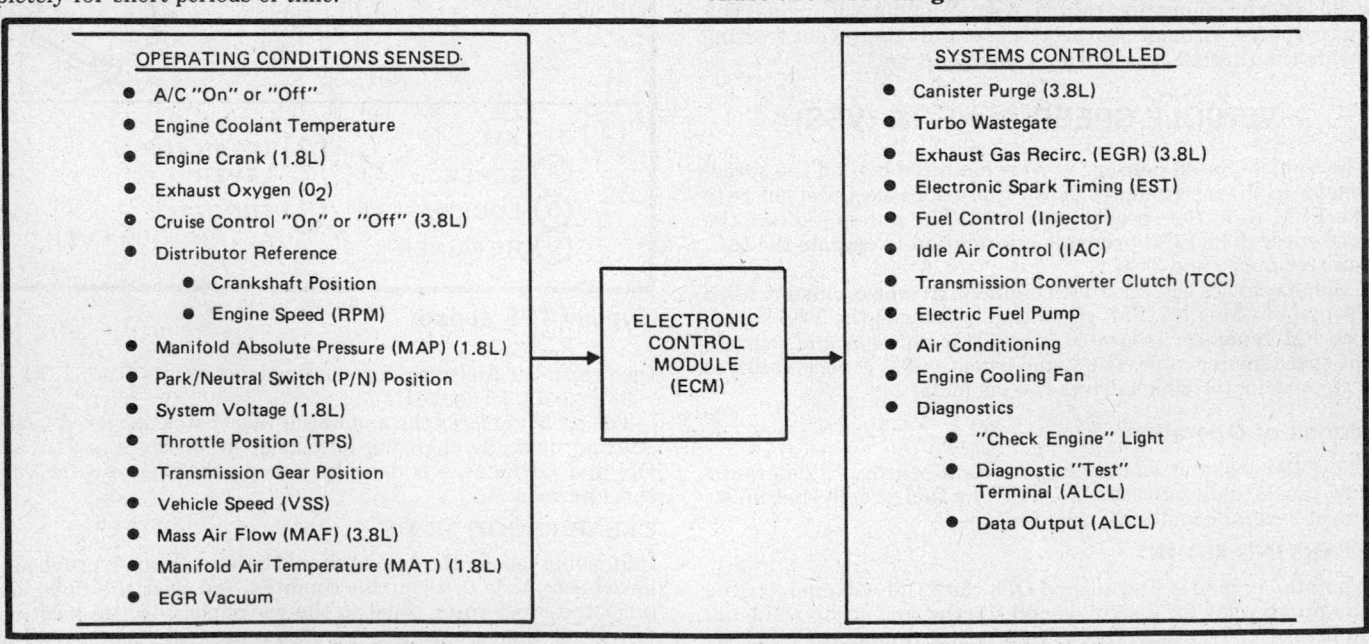

OPERATING CONDITIONS SENSED		SYSTEMS CONTROLLED
• A/C "On" or "Off"		• Canister Purge (3.8L)
• Engine Coolant Temperature		• Turbo Wastegate
• Engine Crank (1.8L)		• Exhaust Gas Recirc. (EGR) (3.8L)
• Exhaust Oxygen (O_2)	ELECTRONIC CONTROL MODULE (ECM)	• Electronic Spark Timing (EST)
• Cruise Control "On" or "Off" (3.8L)		• Fuel Control (Injector)
• Distributor Reference		• Idle Air Control (IAC)
• Crankshaft Position		• Transmission Converter Clutch (TCC)
• Engine Speed (RPM)		• Electric Fuel Pump
• Manifold Absolute Pressure (MAP) (1.8L)		• Air Conditioning
• Park/Neutral Switch (P/N) Position		• Engine Cooling Fan
• System Voltage (1.8L)		• Diagnostics
• Throttle Position (TPS)		• "Check Engine" Light
• Transmission Gear Position		• Diagnostic "Test" Terminal (ALCL)
• Vehicle Speed (VSS)		• Data Output (ALCL)
• Mass Air Flow (MAF) (3.8L)		
• Manifold Air Temperature (MAT) (1.8L)		
• EGR Vacuum		

Schematic of GM MFI annd SFI injection system operation. Not all systems are used on all engines external power applied to the ISC for longer than neces-sary to cause the plunger to clear the throttle lever. If the motor is stalled retracted for prolonged periods, damage to the ISC motor may result. Never connect a voltage source to the ISC motor terminals A and B as damage to the internal throttle switch contacts will result.

5. With the ISC plunger fully retracted the plunger should not be touching the throttle lever. If contact is noted, adjust the ISC plunger (turn in) with a pair of pliers so that it is not touch-ing the throttle lever.

6. Make sure the throttle lever is not being bound by the throttle, cruise or TV cables. The throttle lever must be resting on the minimum air screw.

7. Disable the alternator by grounding the green test connec-tor under the hood near the alternator. The alternator NO CHARGE telltale light will illuminate.

8. Check the minimum idle speed; it should be 475–550 rpm. If the minimum idle speed is not within specifications, go on to Step 9. If the minimum idle speed is within specifications, no further adjustment is necessary.

NOTE: If the engine speed in not within specifica-tions, check for a vacuum leak at the throttle body, in-take manifold vacuum fittings, tees and hoses. If the minimum air setting is made with a vacuum leak present, fuel control can be adversely affected through-out the driving range.

9. Make sure that the alternator is disabled; the No Charge telltale light will be illuminated.

10. If the minimum idle speed is out of specifications, connect a tachometer to the engine and adjust the minimum idle screw to obtain 525 rpm.

PORT FUEL INJECTION (PFI)

The throttle stop screw that is used to adjust the idle speed of the vehicle, is adjusted to specifications at the factory and cov-ered with a steel plug to prevent the unnecessary readjustment in the field. If it is necessary to gain access to the throttle stop screw, the following procedure will allow access to the throttle stop screw without removing the throttle body unit from the manifold.

1. Apply the parking brake and block the drive wheels. Re-move the plug from the idle stop screw by piercing it first with a suitable tool and applying leverage to the tool to lift the plug out.

2. Leave the Idle Air Control (IAC) valve connected and ground the diagnostic terminal (ALDL connector).

3. Turn the ignition switch **ON**. Do not start the engine. Wait for at least 30 seconds; this allows the IAC valve pintle to extend and seat in the throttle body.

4. With the ignition switch in the **ON** position, disconnect IAC electrical connector.

5. Remove the ground from the diagnostic terminal. Start the engine and allow it to reach normal operating temperatures.

6. Place the transmission in the **D** position and adjust the idle stop screw to obtain the correct specifications.

THROTTLE BODY INJECTION (TBI)

1.8L and 2.5L Engines

The throttle stop screw, used to adjust the idle speed, is adjusted to specifications at the factory and covered with a steel plug to prevent the unnecessary readjustment in the field. If necessary to gain access to the throttle stop screw, the following procedure will allow access to the screw without removing the TBI unit from the manifold.

1. Using a small punch or equivalent, mark over the center line of the throttle stop screw. Drill a $5/32$ in. diameter hole through the casting of the hardened steel plug.

2. Using a $1/16$ in. diameter punch or equivalent punch out the steel plug.

3. With the vehicle in the **P** position, the parking brake ap-plied and the drive wheels blocked, remove the air cleaner and

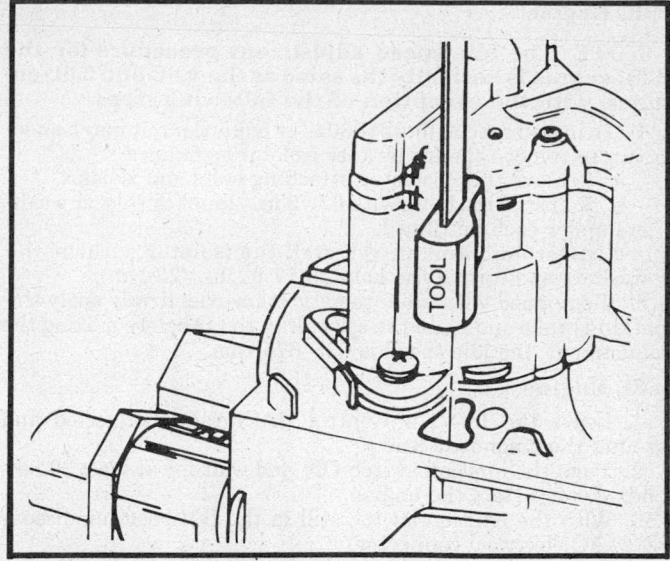

Special tool installation

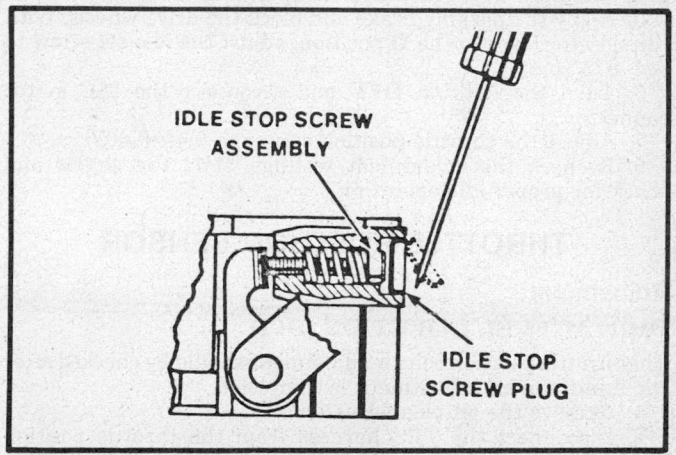

Idle stop screw plug removal

plug the Thermac vacuum port.

4. Remove the TV cable from the throttle control bracket in order to gain access to the minimum air adjustment screw (au-tomatic transaxle only).

5. Connect a tachometer to the engine and disconnect the idle air control motor connector.

6. Start the engine. Allow the engine to reach normal operat-ing temperatures and the rpm to stabilize.

7. Install the special tool J–33047 or equivalent, in the idle air passage of the throttle body. Be sure to seat the tool in the air passage until it is bottomed out and no air leaks exist.

8. Using a No. 20 Torx® head bit or equivalent, turn the throttle stop screw until the rpm is 675–725 rpm (1.8L engine) or 475–525 rpm (2.5L engine) with an automatic transaxle. On vehicles equipped with a manual transaxle, turn the throttle stop screw until the rpm is 775–825 rpm (1.8L engine) or 750–800 rpm (2.5L engine).

9. Reinstall the transaxle TV cable into the throttle control bracket (automatic transaxle only).

10. Turn the engine **OFF** and remove the special tool or equiv-alent, from the throttle body.

11. Reconnect the idle air control motor connector. Using sili-cone sealant, seal the hole drilled through the throttle body housing.

12. Check the throttle position sensor voltage. Reinstall the air cleaner and Thermac vacuum line.

2.0L Engine

NOTE: The idle speed adjustment procedure for the 2.0L engine is basically the same as the 1.8L and 2.5L engines, with the exception of the following steps.

1. To install special tool J–33047 or equivalent, it may be necessary to remove the air cleaner isolator as follows:
   a. Remove the 2 isolator attaching bolts and isolator.
   b. Reinstall the bolts with 0.079 in. (2mm) or thicker washers under each bolt head.
   c. After adjustment, reinstall the isolator without the washers and torque the bolts to 17 ft. lbs. (23 Nm).
2. If equipped with an automatic transaxle, firmly apply the parking brake and place the selector in the **D** before making the adjustment, the idle speed is 625–675 rpm.

4.3L Engine

1. Leave the Idle Air Control (IAC) valve connected and ground the diagnostic lead.
2. Turn the ignition switch **ON** and wait for at least 30 seconds. Do not start the engine.
3. With the ignition switch still in the **ON** position, disconnect IAC electrical connector.
4. Remove the ground from the diagnostic lead. Start the engine and allow it to reach normal operating temperatures.
5. Apply the parking brake and block the drive wheels. With the selector lever in the **D** position, adjust the idle set screw to 525–575 rpm.
6. Turn the ignition **OFF** and reconnect the IAC motor connector.
7. Adjust the throttle position sensor to 0.45–0.60V.
8. Recheck the adjustment settings, start the engine and check for proper idle operation.

THROTTLE POSITION SENSOR

Adjustment

DIGITAL FUEL INJECTION (DFI)

The throttle position sensor adjustment should be checked after the minimum air adjustment is completed.

1. Remove the air cleaner assembly.
2. Disconnect the TPS harness from the throttle position sensor.
3. Using 3 jumper wires, connect the TPS harness to throttle position sensor.
4. With the ignition **ON** and the engine **OFF**. Using a high impedance digital voltmeter, measure the TPS reference voltage at circuit No. 474 (gray wire) and No. 476 (black/white wire). The reference should be as follows:
   a. If the reference voltage is less than 4.90 volts—set the TPS voltage to 0.48 volt.
   b. If the reference voltage is 4.90–5.10 volts—set the TPS voltage to 0.50 volt.
   c. If the reference voltage is 5.11–5.30 volts—set the TPS voltage to 0.52 volt.
   d. If the reference voltage is more than 5.30 volts—set the TPS voltage to 0.54 volt.
5. After measuring the reference voltage, connect the digital voltmeter positive (+) probe to the TPS harness test point A which connects to circuit No. 417 (dark blue wire).
6. Connect the digital voltmeter negative (−) probe to the TPS harness test point B which connects to circuit No. 476 (black/white wire).
7. Set the digital voltmeter on the 2 volts DC scale. With the throttle fully closed against the throttle stop screw, check the voltmeter reading.
8. If the TPS voltage is within 0.05 volt of the specified voltage, no adjustment is necessary.
9. If the TPS voltage does not fall within specifications, adjust the TPS as follows:

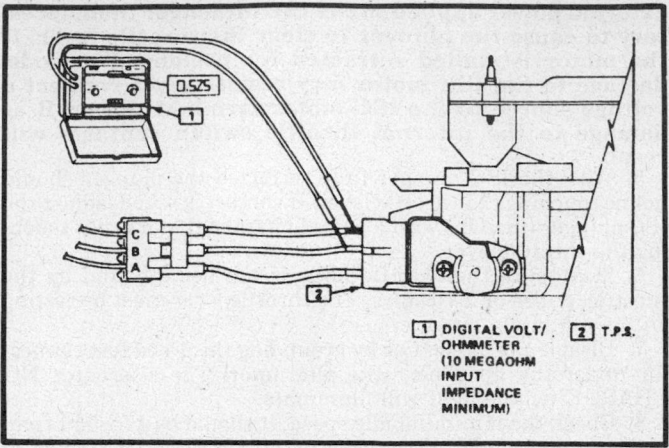

① DIGITAL VOLT/ OHMMETER (10 MEGAOHM INPUT IMPEDANCE MINIMUM)   ② T.P.S.

Throttle position sensor adjustment

   a. Loosen the TPS retaining screws enough to permit rotation of the TPS.
   b. With the throttle fully closed against the throttle stop screw, turn the TPS left or right until the voltmeter falls within specifications.
   c. Tighten the TPS mounting screws with the sensor in this position.
10. Recheck the voltmeter reading to make sure the adjustment remains within 0.05 volt of the specified voltage.
11. Turn the ignition **OFF** and reconnect the TPS harness to the throttle position sensor. Remove all test equipment.

PORT FUEL INJECTION (PFI)

Multi-Port Fuel Injection

NOTE: The throttle position sensor on some models is not adjustable. If the sensor is found out of specifications (approximately 0.450–1.25V @ idle) and the sensor is at fault, it cannot be adjusted and should be replaced.

1. Install 3 jumper wires between the throttle position sensor and the harness connector.
2. Turn the ignition switch **ON** and connect a digital voltmeter to the correct TPS terminals (a suitable ALDL scanner can also be used to read the TPS output voltage):
   a. Terminals A and B (except 1986 3.8L engine with MPI).
   b. Terminals C and B (1986 3.8L engine with MPI).
3. If the TPS is out of specifications, loosen the 2 TPS attaching screws and rotate throttle position sensor to obtain a correct voltage reading.
4. Tighten the mounting screws and recheck the reading to insure the adjustment has not changed.
5. Turn the ignition **OFF**, remove jumper wires and reconnect harness to throttle position switch.

Sequential Fuel Injection (SFI)

1. Loosen the TPS attaching screws. Install 3 jumper wires between the TPS and harness connector.
2. Turn the ignition switch **ON**. Connect a digital voltmeter to terminals B and C and adjust TPS to obtain 0.35–0.45V.

NOTE: On the 1986–90 Riviera, Toronado and Eldorado, ED01 can be used in place of a digital voltmeter. A suitable scanner can also be used on all other models.

3. Remove screws, add thread locking compound (Loctite® or equivalent) and reinstall them. Tighten the attaching screws and recheck reading to insure the adjustment has not changed.
4. Turn the ignition switch **OFF**, remove the jumper wires and connect the harness to the TPS.

THROTTLE BODY INJECTION (TBI)

NOTE: The throttle position sensor on some models is not adjustable. If the sensor is out of specifications (ap-

proximately 0.450–1.25V @ idle) and the sensor is at fault, it cannot be adjusted and should be replaced.

1. After installing the TPS to the throttle body, install throttle body unit to engine.
2. Remove the EGR valve and heat shield from engine.
3. Disconnect the TPS harness from the TPS. Using 3–6 in. jumper wires, connect the TPS harness to the TPS.
4. Turn the ignition **ON**. Do not start the engine. Using a digital voltmeter, measure the voltage between the TPS terminals as follows:
   a. Terminals A and B (except 1.8L and 2.0L engines with TBI 500 system)
   b. Terminals C and B (1.8L and 2.0L engines with TBI 500 system)
5. Loosen the 2 TPS attaching screws and rotate throttle position sensor to obtain a voltage reading of 0.45–0.60V.
6. Turn the ignition **OFF**, remove jumpers and reconnect TPS harness to TPS.
7. Install the EGR valve and heat shield to engine, using new gasket as necessary.
8. Install air cleaner gasket and air cleaner to throttle body unit.

TPS MINIMUM IDLE ADJUSTMENT SPECIFICATIONS

Year	Manufacturer	Model	Engine (liters)	VIN	Fuel Injection System	TPS Adjustment Voltage	Minimum Idle (rpm)
1986	Cadillac	Cimarron	2.0	P	TBI	NA	650 ±25②
			2.8	W	MPI	0.55 ±0.050	600 ±50②⑤
		DeVille	4.1	8	DFI	0.50 ±0.050	⑥
		Eldorado	4.1	8	DFI	0.50 ±0.050	⑥
		Seville	4.1	8	DFI	0.50 ±0.050	⑥
		Fleetwood	4.1	8	DFI	0.50 ±0.050	⑥
	Buick	Century	2.5	R	TBI	NA	500 ±25①③
			3.8	3	SFI	0.40 ±0.050	500 ±50②
			3.8	B	SFI	0.40 ±0.050	500 ±50②
		Electra	3.8	B	SFI	0.40 ±0.050	500 ±50②
		LeSabre	3.0	L	MPI	0.55 ±0.050	500 ±50②
			3.8	3	SFI	0.40 ±0.050	⑥
			3.8	B	SFI	0.40 ±0.050	500 ±50②
		Regal	3.8 T	9	SFI	0.40 ±0.050	500 ±50②
		Riviera	3.8	B	SFI	0.40 ±0.050	500 ±50②
		Skyhawk	1.8	0	TBI	NA	700 ±25③⑤
			2.0	P	TBI	NA	650 ±25②
			1.8 T	J	MPI	NA	700 ±25③⑤
		Skylark	2.5	U	TBI	NA	500 ±25①③
			3.0	L	MPI	0.55 ±0.050	500 ±50②
		Somerset Regal	2.5	U	TBI	NA	500 ±25③⑥
			3.0	L	MPI	0.55 ±0.050	500 ±50②
	Chevrolet	Camaro	2.5	2	TBI	NA	500 ±25①③
			2.8	S	MPI	0.55 ±0.050	600 ±50②⑤
			5.0	F	TPI	0.54 ±0.075	400②
		Caprice	4.3	Z	TBI	NA	425 ±25②
		Cavalier	2.0	P	TBI	NA	650 ±25②
			2.8	W	MPI	0.55 ±0.050	600 ±50②⑤
		Celebrity	2.5	R	TBI	NA	500 ±25①③
			2.8	W	MPI	0.55 ±0.050	600 ±50②⑤
		Corvette	5.7	Y	TPI	0.54 ±0.075	400②⑤
		El Camino	4.3	Z	TBI	NA	425 ±25②
		Monte Carlo	4.3	Z	TBI	NA	425 ±25②
	Oldsmobile	Calais	2.5	U	TBI	NA	500 ±25①③
			3.0	L	MPI	0.55 ±0.050	500 ±50②

TPS MINIMUM IDLE ADJUSTMENT SPECIFICATIONS

Year	Manufacturer	Model	Engine (liters)	VIN	Fuel Injection System	TPS Adjustment Voltage	Minimum Idle (rpm)
1986		Cutlass Ciera	2.5	R	TPI	NA	500 ± 25①③
			2.8	W	MPI	0.55 ± 0.050	600 ± 50②⑤
			3.8	B	SFI	0.40 ± 0.050	500 ± 50②
			3.8	3	SFI	0.40 ± 0.050	⑥
		Delta 88	3.0	L	MPI	0.55 ± 0.050	500 ± 50②
			3.8	B	SFI	0.40 ± 0.050	500 ± 50②
			3.8	3	SFI	0.40 ± 0.050	⑥
		Firenza	1.8	0	TBI	NA	700 ± 25③⑤
			2.0	P	TBI	NA	650 ± 25②
			2.8	W	MPI	0.55 ± 0.050	600 ± 50②⑤
		98 Regency	3.8	B	SFI	0.40 ± 0.050	500 ± 50②
			3.8	3	SFI	0.40 ± 0.050	⑥
		Toronado	3.8	B	SFI	0.40 ± 0.050	500 ± 50②
	Pontiac	6000	2.5	R	TBI	NA	500 ± 25①③
			2.8	W	MPI	0.55 ± 0.050	600 ± 50②⑤
		Bonneville	4.3	Z	TBI	NA	425 ± 25②
		Fiero	2.5	R	TBI	NA	500 ± 25①③
			2.8	9	MPI	—	—
		Firebird	2.5	2	TBI	NA	500 ± 25①③
			2.8	S	MPI	0.55 ± 0.050	600 ± 50②⑤
			5.0	F	TPI	0.54 ± 0.075	400②
			5.7	8	MPI	0.54 ± 0.075	400②⑤
		Grand Am	2.5	U	TBI	NA	500 ± 25③⑥
			3.0	L	MPI	0.55 ± 0.050	500 ± 50②
		Grand Prix	4.3	Z	TBI	NA	425 ± 25②
		Parisienne	4.3	Z	TBI	NA	425 ± 25②
		Sunbird	1.8	0	TBI	NA	700 ± 25③⑤
			1.8 T	J	MPI	NA	700 ± 25③⑤
1987	**Cadillac**	Cimarron	2.8	W	MPI	0.55 ± 0.075	550 ± 50②⑤
		Allante	4.1	7	MPI	0.50 ± 0.025	⑥
		DeVille	4.1	8	DFI	0.50 ± 0.050	⑥
		Eldorado	4.1	8	DFI	0.50 ± 0.050	⑥
		Seville	4.1	8	DFI	0.50 ± 0.050	⑥
		Fleetwood	4.1	8	DFI	0.50 ± 0.050	⑥
	Buick	Century	2.8	W	MPI	0.49–0.61	650②⑤
			2.5	R	TBI	NA	600 ± 25②
			3.8	3	SFI	0.36–0.44	⑥
		Electra	3.8	3	SFI	0.36–0.44	⑥
		LeSabre	3.8	3	SFI	0.36–0.44	⑥
		Regal	3.8	7	SFI	0.36–0.44	500 ± 50②
		Riviera	3.8	3	SFI	0.36–0.44	⑥
		Skyhawk	2.0	K	TBI	NA	600 ± 20②

TPS MINIMUM IDLE ADJUSTMENT SPECIFICATIONS

Year	Manufacturer	Model	Engine (liters)	VIN	Fuel Injection System	TPS Adjustment Voltage	Minimum Idle (rpm)
1987	Buick		2.0 HO	1	TBI	NA	600 ±25②
			2.0	M	MPI	NA	600 ±25②
		Skylark	2.5	U	TBI	NA	600 ±25②
			3.0	L	MPI	0.55 ±0.050	500 ±50②
	Chevrolet	Beretta	2.0	1	TBI	NA	600 ±25②
			2.8	W	MPI	0.55 ±0.10	650②⑤
		Camaro	2.8	S	MPI	0.55 ±0.060	500②⑤
			5.0	F	TPI	0.54 ±0.080	400③
			5.7	8	TPI	0.54 ±0.080	450③
		Caprice	4.3	Z	TBI	NA	425 ±25②
		Cavalier	2.0	1	TBI	NA	600 ±25②
			2.8	W	MPI	0.55 ±0.10	650②⑤
		Celebrity	2.5	R	TBI	NA	600 ±25②
			2.8	W	MPI	0.55 ±0.10	650②⑤
		Corsica	2.0	1	TBI	NA	600 ±25②
			2.8	W	MPI	0.55 ±0.10	650
		Corvette	5.7	8	TPI	0.54 ±0.080	450③
		El Camino	4.3	Z	TBI	NA	425 ±25②
		Monte Carlo	4.3	Z	TBI	NA	425 ±25②
	Oldsmobile	Calais	2.5	U	TBI	NA	600 ±25②
			3.0	L	MPI	0.55 ±0.050	500 ±50②
		Cutlass Ciera	2.5	R	TBI	NA	600 ±25②
			2.8	W	MPI	0.55 ±0.10	650②⑤
			3.8	3	SFI	0.36-0.44	⑥
		Delta 88	3.8	3	SFI	0.36-0.44	⑥
		Firenza	2.0 HO	1	TBI	NA	600 ±25②
			2.0	K	TBI	NA	600 ±25②
			2.8	W	MPI	0.55 ±0.10	650②⑤
		98 Regency	3.8	3	SFI	0.36-0.44	⑥
		Toronado	3.8	3	SFI	0.36-0.44	⑥
	Pontiac	6000	2.5	R	TBI	NA	600 ±25②
			2.8	W	MPI	0.55 ±0.10	650②⑤
		Bonneville	3.8	3	SFI	0.36-0.44	⑥
		Fiero	2.5	R	TBI	NA	600 ±25②
			2.8	9	MPI	—	—
		Firebird	2.8	S	MPI	0.55 ±0.060	600 ±50②⑤
			5.0	F	TPI	0.54 ±0.080	400③
			5.7	8	TPI	0.54 ±0.080	450③
		Grand Am	2.0	M	MPI	NA	600 ±25②
			2.5	U	TBI	NA	600 ±25②
		Grand Prix	4.3	Z	TBI	NA	425 ±25②
		Sunbird	2.0	K	TBI	NA	600 ±25②

TPS MINIMUM IDLE ADJUSTMENT SPECIFICATIONS

Year	Manufacturer	Model	Engine (liters)	VIN	Fuel Injection System	TPS Adjustment Voltage	Minimum Idle (rpm)
1987	Pontiac		2.0 T	M	MPI	NA	600 ±25②
1989-90	Cadillac	Allante	4.1	7	MPI	0.475–0.525	⑥
		Cimmaron	2.8	W	MPI	0.48–0.62	550 ± 50②⑤
		DeVille	4.5	5	DFI	0.45–0.55	⑥
		Eldorado	4.5	5	DFI	0.45–0.55	⑥
		Seville	4.5	5	DFI	0.45–0.55	⑥
		Fleetwood	4.5	5	DFI	0.45–0.55	⑥
	Buick	Century	2.8	W	MPI	0.45–0.65	650②⑤
			2.5	R	TBI	NA	600 ±2②
			3.8	3	SFI	0.36–0.44	500 ±50②
		Electra,	3.8	3	SFI	0.36–0.44	500 ±50②
		LeSabre	3.8	C	SFI	0.38–0.42	⑥
		Reatta	3.8	C	SFI	0.38–0.42	⑥
		Regal	2.8	W	MFI	0.45–0.65	500 ±50②
		Rivera	3.8	C	SFI	0.38–0.42	⑥
		Skyhawk,	2.0	K	TBI	NA	⑥
		Skylark	2.0	1	TBI	NA	⑥
			2.3	D	MPI	0.50–0.59	⑥
			2.5	U	TBI	NA	⑥
			3.0	L	MPI	0.50–0.59	⑥
	Chevrolet	Beretta	2.0	1	TBI	NA	600 ±25②
			2.8	W	MPI	0.55 ±0.10	650②⑤
		Camaro	2.8	S	MPI	0.55 ±0.10	500②⑤
			5.0	E	TBI	0.46–0.72	400③
			5.0	F	TPI	0.54 ±0.080	400③
			5.7	8	TPI	0.54 ±0.080	450③
		Caprice	4.3	Z	TBI	NA	425 ±25②
		Cavalier	2.0	1	TBI	NA	600 ±25②
			2.8	W	MPI	0.55 ±0.10	650②⑤
		Celebrity	2.5	R	TBI	NA	600 ±25②
			2.8	W	MPI	0.55 ±0.10	650②⑤
		Corsica	2.0	1	TBI	NA	600 ±25②
			2.8	W	MPI	0.55 ±0.10	650②⑤
		Corvette	5.7	8	TPI	0.54 ±0.080	450③
		Monte Carlo	4.3	Z	TBI	NA	425 ±25②
		Sprint	1.0	M	MPI	NA	NA
		Spectrum	1.5	R	MPI	0.310–0.390	900
		Nova	1.6	S	MPI	NA	⑦
	Oldsmobile	Calais	2.5	U	TBI	NA	600 ±25②
			3.0	L	MPI	0.55 ±0.050	500 ±50②
		Cutlass Ciera	2.5	R.5	TBI	NA	600 ±25②
			2.8	W	MPI	0.55 ±0.10	650②⑤

TPS MINIMUM IDLE ADJUSTMENT SPECIFICATIONS

Year	Manufacturer	Model	Engine (liters)	VIN	Fuel Injection System	TPS Adjustment Voltage	Minimum Idle (rpm)
1989-90			3.8	3	MPI	0.36–0.44	500 ±50②
		Cutlass Supreme	2.8	W	MPI	0.45–0.46	450–550②
		Delta 88	3.8	3	MPI	0.36–0.44	500 ±50②
			3.8	C	SFI	0.38–0.42	⑥
		Firenza	2.0 HO	1	TBI	NA	600 ±25②
			2.0	K	TBI	NA	600 ±25 ②
			2.8	W	MPI	0.55 ±0.10	650②⑤
		98 Regency	3.8	C	SFI	0.36–0.44	⑥
		Tornado	3.8	C	SFI	0.36–0.44	⑥
	Pontiac	6000	2.5	R	TBI	NA	600 ±25②
			2.8	W	MPI	0.55 ±0.10	650②⑤
		Bonneville	3.8	3	SFI	0.36–0.44	500 ±50②
			3.8	C	SFI	0.38–042	⑥
		Fiero	2.5	R	TBI	NA	600 ±25②
			2.8	9	MPI	—	—
		Firebird	2.8	S	MPI	0.55 ±0.060	600 ±50②⑤
			3.8	C	SFI	0.38–0.42	⑤
			5.0	F	TPI	0.54 ±0.080	600 ±50②⑤
			5.7	8	TPI	0.54 ±0.080	450③
		Grand Am	2.0T	M	MPI	NA	600 ±25②
			2.3	D	MPI	0.50–0.59	⑥
			2.5	U	TBI	NA	600 ±25②
		Grand Prix	2.8	W	MPI	0.45–0.65	450–550②
			4.3	Z	TBI	NA	425 ±25②
		Sunbird	2.0	K	TBI	NA	600 ±25②
			2.0T	M	MPI	NA	600 ±25②

T   Turbo
HO   High Output
SFI   Sequential Fuel Injection
TBI   Throttle Body Injection
MPI   Multi-Port Injection
TPI   Tuned Port Injection
DFI   Digital Fuel Injection
NA   Not Adjustable

① Manual transmission: 775 ±25 rpm
② Place gear selector in DRIVE for automatic transmission
③ Place gear selector in NEUTRAL for automatic or manual transmission
④ Manual transmission; add 50 rpm
⑤ Manual transmission; add 100 rpm
⑥ Controlled by ECM
⑦ Manual Transmission—800 rpm
   Automatic Transmission—800 rpm

CHRYSLER CORPORATION FUEL INJECTION SYSTEMS

Multi-Point Fuel Injection

The turbocharged and non-turbocharged multi-point electronic fuel injection system combines an electronic fuel and spark advance control system with a turbocharged intake system, if equipped. At the center of this system is a digital pre-programmed computer known as a Logic Module or (on 1987½–90 vehicles) a Single Module Engine Controller (SMEC) that regulates ignition timing, air/fuel ratio, emission control devices, idle speed, cooling fan, charging system, turbocharger wastegate (on turbocharge vehicles) and (on 1987½–90) speed control. This component has the ability to update and revise its programming to meet changing operating conditions.

Various sensors provide the input necessary for the Logic Module or SMEC to correctly regulate fuel flow at the fuel injectors. These include the manifold absolute pressure, throttle position, oxygen feedback, coolant temperature, charge temperature, vehicle speed (distance) sensors and throttle body temper-

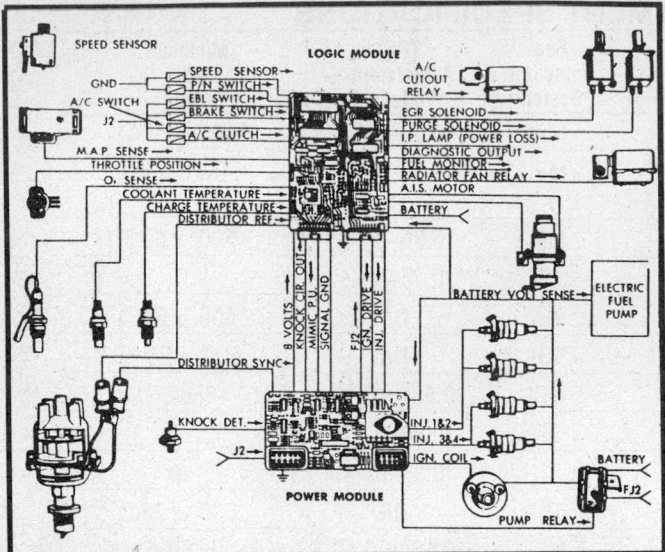

Chrysler multi-point fuel injection system schematic

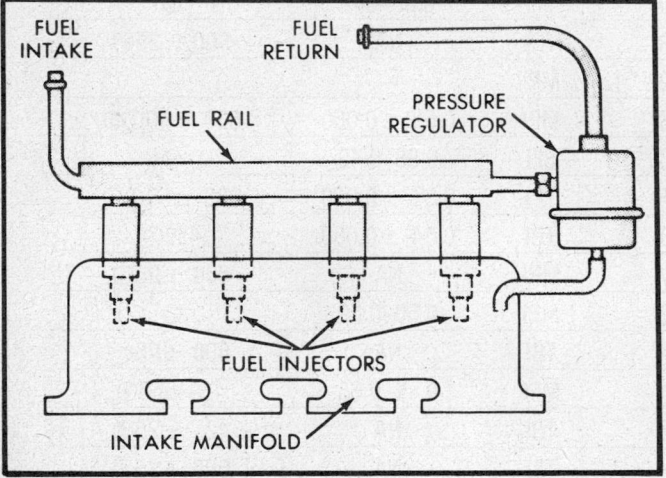

Multi-port fuel supply system

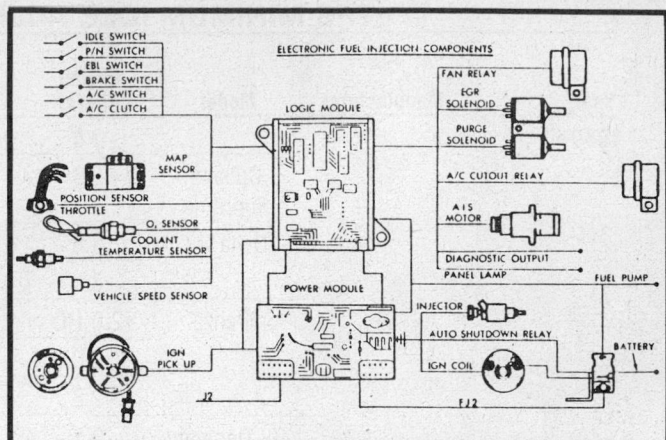

Chrysler throttle body injection system components

(SMEC) that regulates ignition timing, air/fuel ratio, emission control devices, idle speed, cooling fan and charging system. This component has the ability to update and revise its programming to meet changing operating conditions.

Various sensors provide the input necessary for the logic module or SMEC to correctly regulate the fuel flow at the fuel injector. These include the manifold absolute pressure, throttle position, oxygen sensor, coolant temperature, charge temperature, vehicle speed (distance) sensors and throttle body temperature. In addition to the sensors, various switches also provide important information. These include the neutral/safety, heated backlite, air conditioning, air conditioning clutch switches and an electronic idle switch.

All inputs to the logic module or SMEC are converted into signals sent to the power module. These signals cause the power module to change either the fuel flow at the injector or ignition timing or both.

The logic module or SMEC tests many of its own input and output circuits. If a fault is found in a major system this information is stored in the logic module or SMEC. Information on this fault can be displayed to a technician by means of the instrument panel power loss (check engine) lamp or by connecting a diagnostic read out and reading a numbered display code which directly relates to a specific fault.

System Components

AIR CONDITIONING CUTOUT RELAY

The air conditioning cutout relay is electrically connected in series with the cycling clutch switch and low pressure cut out switch. This relay is in the normally closed position during engine operation. When the Logic Module sense wide open throttle through the throttle position sensor, it will energize the relay, open its contacts and prevent air conditioning clutch engagement.

AUTOMATIC IDLE SPEED (AIS) MOTOR

The Automatic Idle Speed Motor (AIS) is operated by the Logic Module or SMEC. Data from the throttle position sensor, speed sensor, coolant temperature sensor and various switch operations, (neutral/safety and stop light switch) are used by the module to adjust engine idle to an optimum during all idle conditions. The AIS adjust the air portion of the air/fuel mixture through an air bypass in the throttle body. Basic (no load) idle is determined by the minimum air flow through the throttle body. The AIS opens or closes off the air bypass as an increase or decrease is needed due to engine loads or ambient conditions. The

ature. In addition to the sensors, various switches also provide important information. These include the transmission neutral/safety, air conditioning clutch switch, brake switch and speed control switch (on 1987½–90).

Inputs to the Logic Module or SMEC are converted into signals sent to the power module. These signals cause the power module to change either the fuel flow at the injector or ignition timing or both.

The Logic Module or SMEC tests many of its own input and output circuits. If a fault is found in a major circuit, this information is stored in the Logic Module or SMEC. Information on this fault can be displayed to a technician by means of the instrument panel power loss (check engine) lamp or by connecting a diagnostic readout and observing a numbered display code which directly relates to a specific fault.

Single Point Fuel Injection (SPFI)

The Electronic Fuel Injection System is a computer regulated single point fuel injection system that provides precise air/fuel ratio for all driving conditions. At the center of this system is a digital pre-programmed computer known as a logic module or (on 1987½–89 vehicles) a Single Module Engine Controller

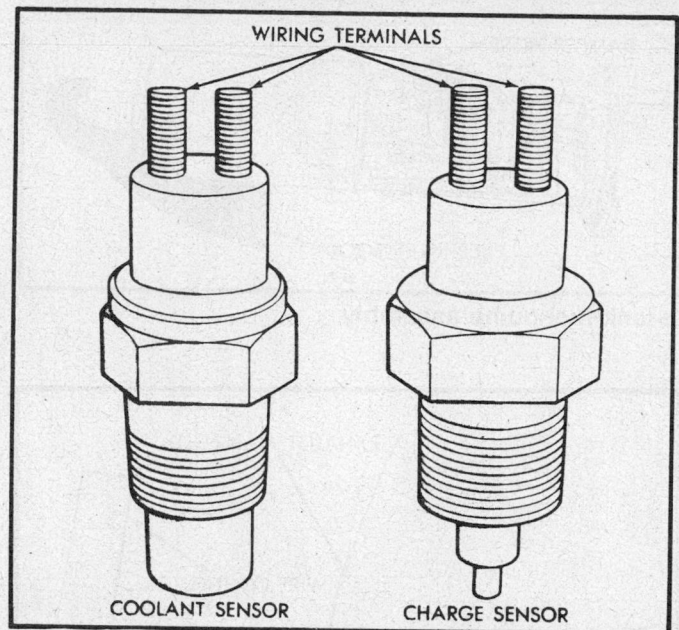

View of the charge and coolant sensors—turbocharged models

module senses an air/fuel change and increases or decreases fuel proportionally to change engine idle. Deceleration die out is also prevented by increasing engine idle when the throttle is closed quickly after a driving (speed) condition.

AUTOMATIC SHUTDOWN (ASD) RELAY

The Automatic Shutdown Relay (ASD) is powered and controlled through the power module. When the power module senses a distributor signal during cranking, it grounds the ASD closing its contacts. This completes the circuit for the electric fuel pump, power module and ignition coil. If the distributor signal is lost for any reason, the ASD interrupts this circuit in less than 1 second preventing fuel, spark and engine operations; the fast shut down serves as a safety feature in the event of an accident.

BAROMETRIC READ SOLENOID

TURBOCHARGE ENGINE

The barometric read solenoid is controlled by the logic module. The solenoid is in the MAP sensor vacuum line. The solenoid controls whether manifold pressure or atmospheric pressure is supplied to the MAP sensor. Atmospheric pressure is periodically supplied to the MAP sensor to measure barometric pressure. This occurs at closed throttle, once per throttle closure but no more often than once every 30 seconds (3 minutes on 1987-90) and below a specified rpm. The barometric information is used primarily for boost control.

CHARGE TEMPERATURE SENSOR

TURBOCHARGE ENGINE

The charge temperature sensor is a device mounted in the intake manifold which measures the temperature of the air/fuel mixture. This information is used by the logic module or SMEC to determine engine operating temperature and engine warmup cycles in the event of a coolant temperature sensor failure.

COOLANT TEMPERATURE SENSOR

The coolant temperature sensor is a device which monitors coolant temperature and functions the same as engine operating

temperature switch. It is mounted on the thermostat housing. This sensor provides data on engine operating temperature to the logic module or SMEC. This data along with data provided by the charge temperature switch, if equipped, allows the logic module or SMEC to demand slightly richer air/fuel mixtures and higher idle speeds until normal operating temperatures are reached. The sensor is a variable resistor with a range of 60°F–300°F; it is also used for cooling fan control.

DETONATION (KNOCK) SENSOR

TURBOCHARGE ENGINE

The detonation sensor is a device that generates a signal when spark knock occurs in the combustion chamber(s). It is mounted at a position on the intake manifold where detonation in each cylinder can be detected. The sensor provides information used by the logic module to modify spark advance and boost schedules in order to eliminate detonation.

EXHAUST GAS RECIRCULATION SOLENOID

The EGR solenoid is operated by the logic module. When engine temperature is below 70°F (21°C), the logic module energizes the solenoid by grounding it. This closes the solenoid and prevents ported vacuum from reaching the EGR valve. When the prescribed temperature is reached, the logic module will turn **OFF** the ground for the solenoid de-energizing it. Once the solenoid is de-energized, ported vacuum from the throttle body will pass through to the EGR valve. At idle and wide open throttle, the solenoid is energized which prevents EGR operation.

FUEL INJECTOR

MULTI-POINT FUEL INJECTION (MFI)

The fuel injector is an electric solenoid powered by the power module but controlled by the logic module. On 1987½-90 vehicles, the injectors are controlled by the Single Module Engine Controller (SMEC). The module determines when and how long the injector should operate. When an electric current is supplied to the injector, the armature and pintle move a short distance against a spring, opening a small orifice. Fuel is supplied to the injector inlet by the fuel pump, passes through the injector, around the pintle and out the orifice. Since the fuel is under high pressure, a fine spray is developed in the shape of a hollow cone. The injector, through this spraying action, atomizes the fuel and distributes it into the air entering the combustion chamber.

SINGLE POINT FUEL INJECTION (SPI)

The fuel injector is an electric solenoid driven by the power module but controlled by the logic module. The logic module, based on ambient, mechanical, and sensor input, determines when and how long the power module should operate the injector. When an electric current is supplied to the injector, a spring loaded ball is lifted from its seat. This allows fuel to flow through 6 spray orifices and deflects off the sharp edge of the injector nozzle. This action causes the fuel to form a 45 degree cone shaped spray pattern before entering the air stream in the throttle body.

NOTE: If equipped with a Single Module Engine Controller (SMEC), the fuel injector is controlled and driven solely by the SMEC.

FUEL PRESSURE REGULATOR

The pressure regulator is a mechanical device located downstream of the fuel injector on the throttle body. Its function is to maintain constant fuel pressure across the fuel injector tip. The regulator uses a spring loaded rubber diaphragm to uncover a fuel return port. When the fuel pump becomes operational, fuel

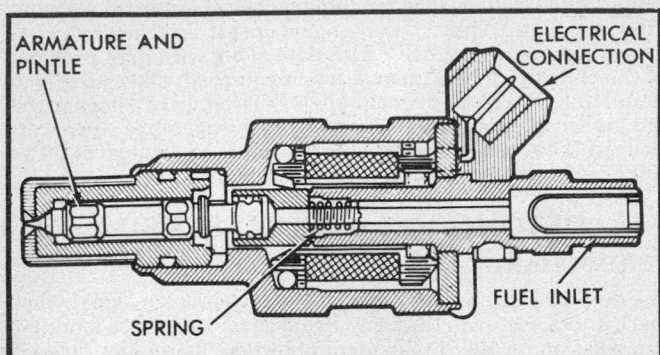

Cross-sectional view of the fuel injection nozzle—multi-point fuel injection

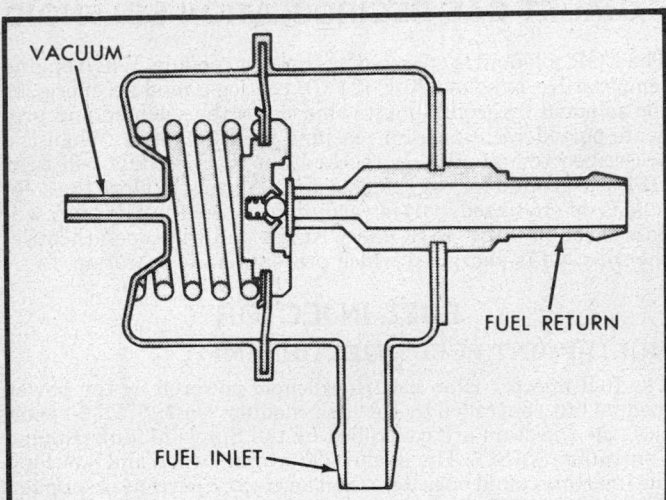

Cross section of typical fuel pressure regulator

In-tank fuel pump assembly

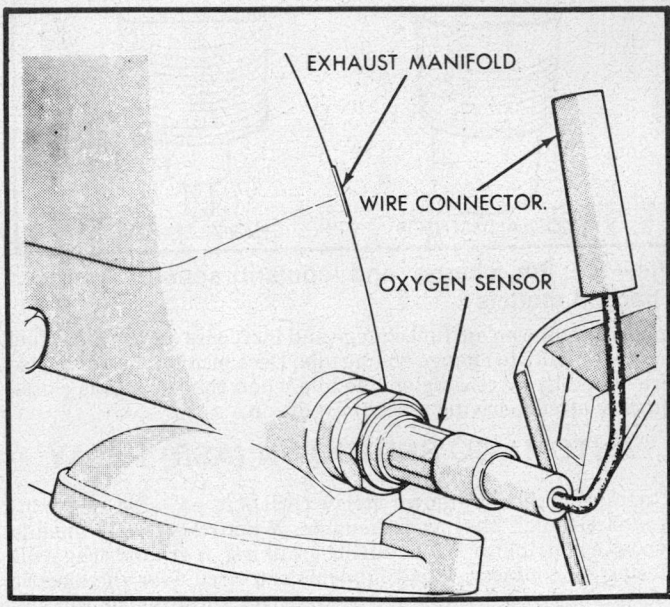

Oxygen sensor mounted in exhaust manifold

flows past the injector into the regulator and is restricted from flowing any further by the blocked return port. When the specified operating fuel pressure is reached, it pushes on the diaphragm, compressing the spring and uncovers the fuel return port. The diaphragm and spring will constantly move from an open to closed position to keep the fuel pressure constant. An assist to the spring loaded diaphragm comes from vacuum in the throttle body above the throttle blade. As venturi vacuum increases less pressure is required to supply the same amount of fuel into the air flow. The vacuum assists in opening the fuel port during high vacuum conditions. This fine tunes the fuel pressure for all operating conditions.

FUEL PUMP

The fuel pump used in this system is a positive displacement, roller vane, immersible pump with a permanent magnet electric motor. Fuel is drawn through a filter sock and pushed through the electric motor to the outlet. The pump contains 2 check valves. One valve is used to relieve internal fuel pump pressure and regulate maximum pump output. The other check valve, located near the pump outlet, restricts fuel movement in either direction when the pump is not operational. Voltage to operate the pump is supplied through the Auto Shutdown (ASD) relay.

Some turbocharged vehicles feature 2 electric fuel pumps. The secondary pump is mounted in the fuel tank. The primary pump is mounted outside the tank.

LOGIC MODULE

The logic module is a digital computer containing a microprocessor. The module receives input signals from various switches, sensors and components. It computes the fuel injector pulse width, spark advance, ignition coil dwell, idle speed, purge and EGR solenoid cycles and cooling fan and alternator.

The logic module tests many of its own input and output circuits. If a fault is found in a major system, this information is stored in the logic module. Information on this fault can be displayed to a technician by means of flashing lamp on the instrument panel or by connecting a diagnostic readout tool and reading a numbered display code which relates to a general fault.

MANIFOLD ABSOLUTE PRESSURE (MAP) SENSOR

The Manifold Absolute Pressure (MAP) sensor is a device which monitors manifold vacuum. It is connected to a vacuum nipple on the throttle body and electrically to the logic module or SMEC. The sensor transmits information on manifold vacuum conditions and barometric pressure to the logic module or SMEC. The MAP sensor data on engine load is used with data from other sensors to determine the correct air/fuel mixture.

OXYGEN SENSOR

The oxygen sensor is a device which produces an electrical voltage when exposed to the oxygen present in the exhaust gases. The sensor is mounted in the exhaust manifold and must be heated by the exhaust gases before producing the voltage. On most 1987–90 vehicles, the oxygen sensor is electrically heated internally for faster switching when the engine is running. When there is a large amount of oxygen present (lean mixture), the sensor produces a low voltage. When there is a lesser amount present (rich mixture) it produces a higher voltage. By monitoring the oxygen content and converting it to electrical voltage, the sensor acts as a rich-lean switch. The voltage is transmitted to the logic module. The logic module signals the power module to trigger the fuel injector. The injector changes the mixture.

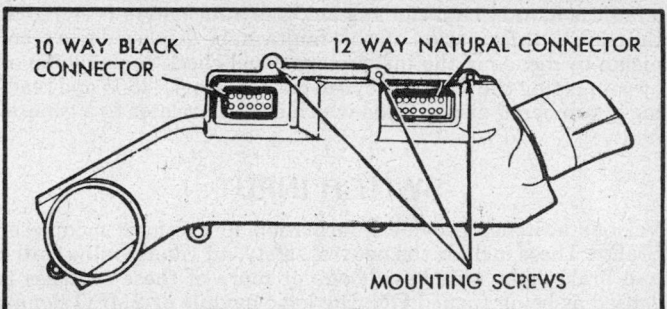

Power module—typical

POWER LOSS LAMP (CHECK ENGINE)

The power loss (check engine) lamp turns on each time the ignition is turned **ON** and stays on for a few seconds as a bulb test. If the logic module or SMEC receives an incorrect signal or no signal from either the coolant temperature sensor, manifold absolute pressure sensor or the throttle position sensor, the lamp on the instrument panel is illuminated. This is a warning that the logic module or SMEC has gone into Limp In Mode in an attempt to keep the system operational.

The lamp can also be used to display fault codes. Cycle the ignition switch **ON, OFF, ON, OFF, ON** within 5 seconds and any fault codes stored in the memory will be displayed.

Limp In Mode is the attempt by the logic module or SMEC to compensate for the failure of certain components by substituting information from other sources. If the module senses incorrect data or not data at all from the MAP sensor, throttle position sensor, charge temperature sensor (if equipped), coolant temperature sensor or (on 1987½–90 models) the system is placed into Limp In Mode and lamp on the instrument panel is activated.

POWER MODULE

The power module contains the circuits necessary to power the ignition coil and the fuel injector. These are high current devices and their power supply has been isolated to minimize any electrical noise reaching the logic module. The power module also energizes the Automatic Shut Down (ASD) Relay which activates the fuel pump, ignition coil and the power module itself. The module also receives a signal from the distributor and sends this signal to the logic module. In the event of no distributor signal, the ASD relay is not activated and power is turned **OFF** from the fuel pump and ignition coil. The power module contains a voltage converter which reduces battery voltage to a regulated 8.0 volts output. This 8.0 volts output powers the distributor and also powers the logic module.

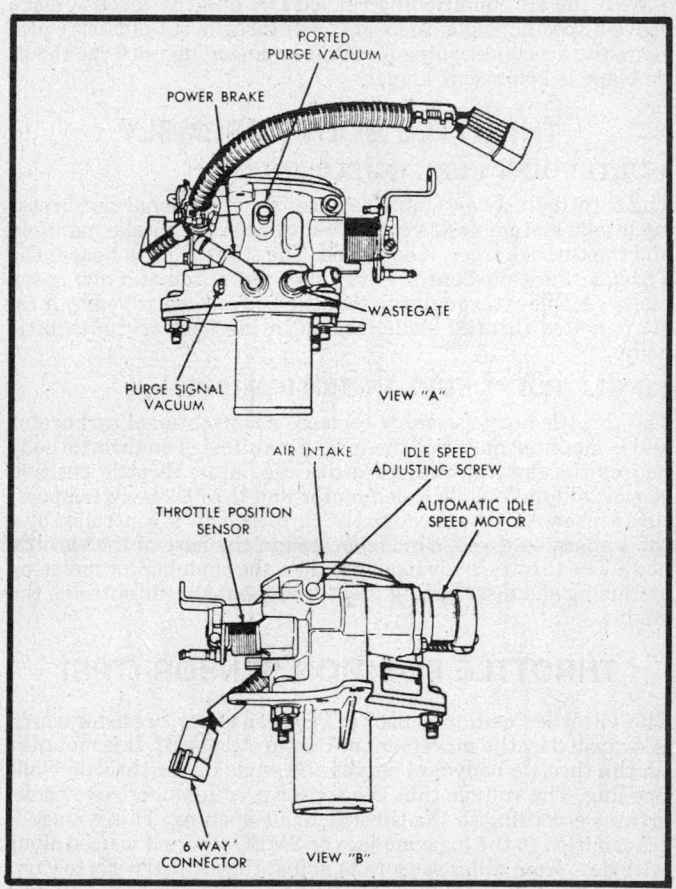

Throttle body used on multi-port injection system

PURGE SOLENOID

The purge solenoid works in the same fashion as the EGR solenoid. When engine temperature is below 145°F (61°C) the logic module energize the purge solenoid. This prevents vacuum from reaching the charcoal canister valve. When the temperature is reached, the logic module de-energizes the solenoid. Once this occurs, vacuum will flow to the canister purge valve and purge fuel vapors through the throttle body.

SINGLE MODULE ENGINE CONTROLLER (SMEC)

On 1987½–90 models, the SMEC contains the circuits necessary to drive the ignition coil, fuel injector and the alternator field. These are high current devices and have been isolated to minimize any electrical noise in the passenger compartment.

The Automatic Shut Down (ASD) relay is mounted externally, but is turned **ON** and **OFF** by the SMEC. Distributor pick-up signal goes to the SMEC. In the event of no distributor signal, the ASD relay is not activated and power is turned off from the fuel injector and ignition coil. The SMEC contains a voltage convertor which converts battery voltage to a regulated 8.0 volts output. This 8.0 volts output powers the distributor pick-up. The internal 5 volts supply which, in turn, powers the MAP sensor and TPS.

The SMEC is a digital computer containing a microprocessor. The module receives input signals from various switches and sensors. It computes the fuel injector pulse width, spark advance, ignition coil dwell, idle speed, charging system rate, activates the purge solenoid and turns the cooling fan **ON**.

The SMEC tests many of its own input and output circuits. If a fault is found in a major system, this information is stored in the SMEC. Information on this fault can be displayed to a technician by means of the instrument panel check engine lamp or by connecting the diagnostic read out tool No. C–4805 and reading a numbered display code which directly relates to a general fault.

SWITCH INPUT

Various switches provide information to the logic module or SMEC. These include the neutral safety, air conditioning clutch and brake light switches. If one or more of these switches is sensed as being turned **ON**, the logic module or SMEC signals the automatic idle speed motor to increase idle speed to a scheduled rpm.

With the air conditioning turned **ON** and the throttle blade above a specific angle, the wide open throttle cut-out relay prevents the air conditioning clutch from engaging until the throttle blade is below this angle.

THROTTLE BODY ASSEMBLY

MULTI-POINT FUEL INJECTION (MFI)

The throttle body assembly replaces a conventional carburetor air intake system and is connected to both the intake manifold and the turbocharger, if equipped. The throttle body houses the Throttle Position Sensor (TPS) and the automatic idle speed motor. Air flow through the throttle body is controlled by a cable operated throttle blade located in the base of the throttle body.

SINGLE POINT FUEL INJECTION (SPI)

The throttle body assembly replaces a conventional carburetor and is mounted on top of the intake manifold. The throttle body houses the fuel injector, pressure regulator, throttle position sensor, automatic idle speed motor and throttle body temperature sensor. Air flow through the throttle body is controlled by a cable operated throttle blade located in the base of the throttle body. The throttle body itself provides the chamber for metering atomizing and distributing fuel throughout the air entering the engine.

THROTTLE POSITION SENSOR (TPS)

The Throttle Position Sensor (TPS) is an electric resistor which is activated by the movement of the throttle shaft. It is mounted on the throttle body and senses the angle of the throttle blade opening. The voltage that the sensor produces increases or decreases according to the throttle blade opening. This voltage is transmitted to the logic module or SMEC where it is used along with data from other sensors to adjust the air/fuel ratio to varying conditions and during acceleration, deceleration, idle and wide open throttle operations.

WASTEGATE CONTROL SOLENOID

TURBOCHARGE ENGINE

The wastegate control solenoid is controlled by the logic module. The module adjusts maximum boost to varying engine conditions by varying the duty cycle of the wastegate solenoid.

System Services

MINIMUM IDLE SPEED

Adjustment

NOTE: Normal idle speed is controlled by the logic module or SMEC. This adjustment is the minimum idle speed with the Automatic Idle Speed (AIS) closed.

1. Before adjusting the idle on an electronic fuel injected vehicle the following items must be checked.
   a. AIS motor has been checked for operation.
   b. Engine has been checked for vacuum or EGR leaks.
   c. Engine timing has been checked and set to specifications.
   d. Coolant temperature sensor has been checked for operation.
2. Connect a tachometer and timing light to engine.
3. Close the AIS by using the ATM tester tool C–4805 or equivalent, ATM test code 03.
4. Connect a jumper wire to the radiator fan so it will **RUN** continuously.
5. Operate the engine for 3 minutes to allow the idle speed to stabilize.
6. Check engine rpm and compare the result with the specifications listed on the underhood emission control sticker.
7. If the idle rpm is not within specifications, use tool C–4804 or equivalent, to turn the idle speed adjusting screw to obtain specified rpm. If the underhood emission sticker specifications are different, use those values for adjustment.

NOTE: If idle will not adjust down check for binding linkage, speed control servo cable adjustment or throttle shaft binding.

8. Turn the engine **OFF**, disconnect tachometer, reinstall AIS wire and remove jumper wire from fan motor.

THROTTLE POSITION SENSOR

Adjustment

The throttle position sensor is not adjustable. If the TPS is out of voltage specification or found to be faulty, the TPS must be replaced.

FORD MOTOR COMPANY
FUEL INJECTION SYSTEMS

CENTRAL FUEL INJECTION (CFI)

The central fuel injection system is a single point, pulse time modulated injection system. Fuel is metered into the air intake stream according to engine demands by 2 solenoid injection valves mounted in a throttle body on the intake manifold.

Fuel is supplied by a high pressure, electric fuel pump (either by itself or in addition to a low-pressure pump) on all except 2.3L HSC engines, which uses a single low-pressure pump. The fuel is filtered and sent to the air throttle body where a regulator keeps the fuel delivery pressure at a constant 39 psi (high pressure system) or 14.5 psi (low pressure system). The 1 or 2 injector nozzles are mounted vertically above the throttle plates and connected in parallel with the fuel pressure regulator. Excess fuel supplied by the pump but not needed by the engine, is returned to the fuel tank by a steel fuel return line.

The fuel charging assembly is comprised of 6 individual components which perform the fuel and air metering function to the engine. The throttle body assembly mounts to the conventional

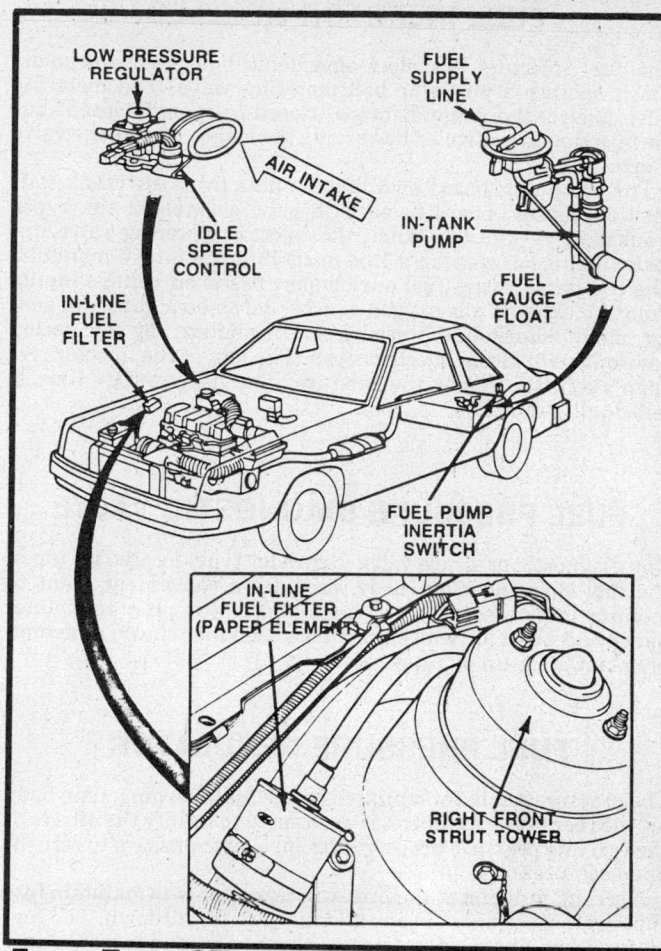

Tempo/Topaz CFI components

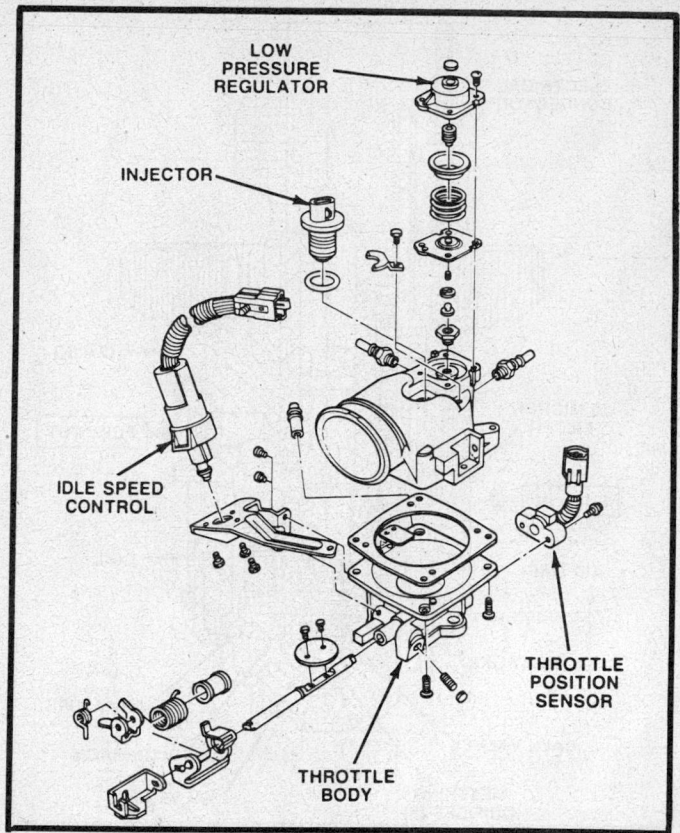

Tempo/Topaz CFI fuel charging assembly

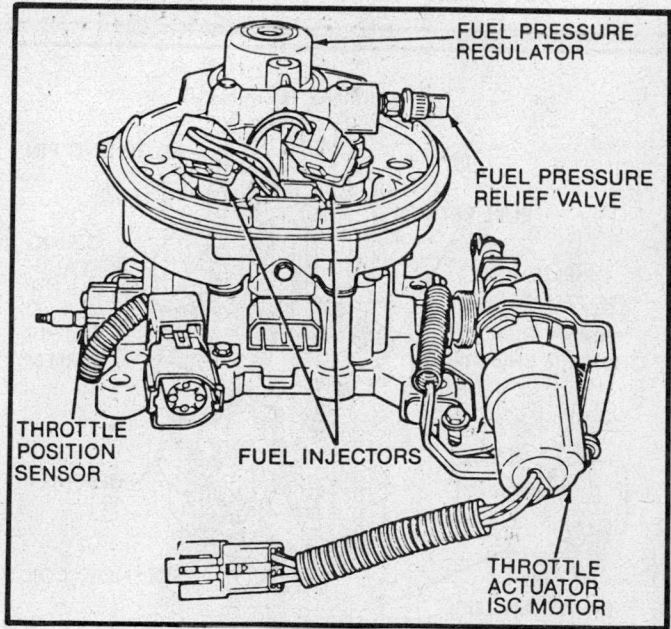

CFI fuel charging assembly—right side view

carburetor pad of the intake manifold and provides for packaging of:

Air control
Fuel injector nozzles
Fuel pressure regulator
Fuel pressure diagnostic valve
Cold engine speed control
Throttle position sensor

System Components

AIR CONTROL

Airflow is controlled by 2 butterfly valves mounting in a 2 piece, die cast aluminum housing called the throttle body. The butterfly valves are identical in design to the throttle plates of a conventional carburetor; they are actuated by a similar pedal cable and linkage arrangements.

COLD ENGINE SPEED CONTROL

The additional engine speed required during cold idle is accomplished by the ISC control motor.
The Electronic Engine Control (EEC) system monitors input signals from the various sensors, output signal to the injectors, Idle Speed Control (ISC) motor control, fuel flow and engine speed, respectively. This combination produces a good cold drive with acceptable emissions.

FUEL CHARGING ASSEMBLY

The fuel charging assembly controls air/fuel ratio. It consists of a typical carburetor throttle body and has 2 bores without venturis. The throttle shaft and valves control engine air flow based on driver demand. The throttle body attaches to the intake manifold mounting pad.

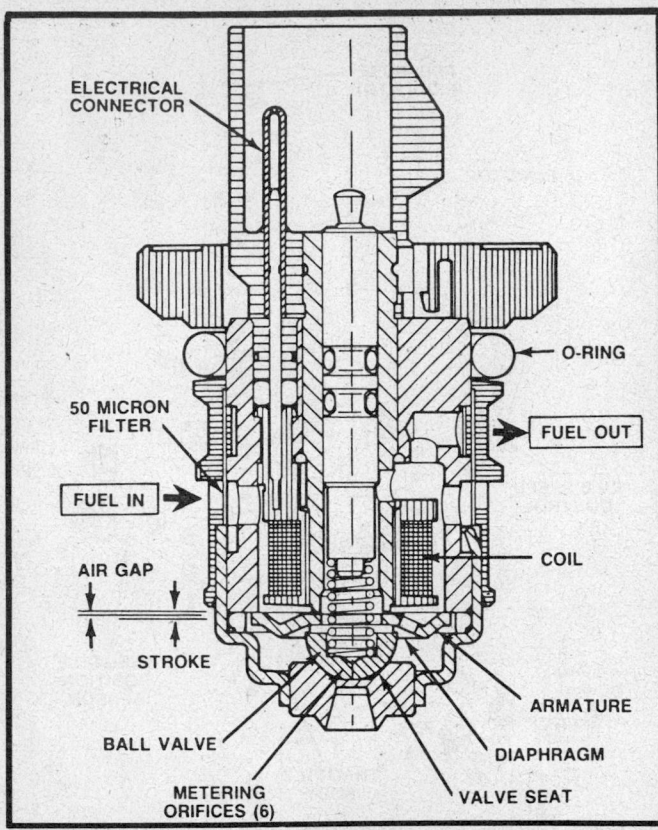

Tempo/Topaz CFI fuel injector

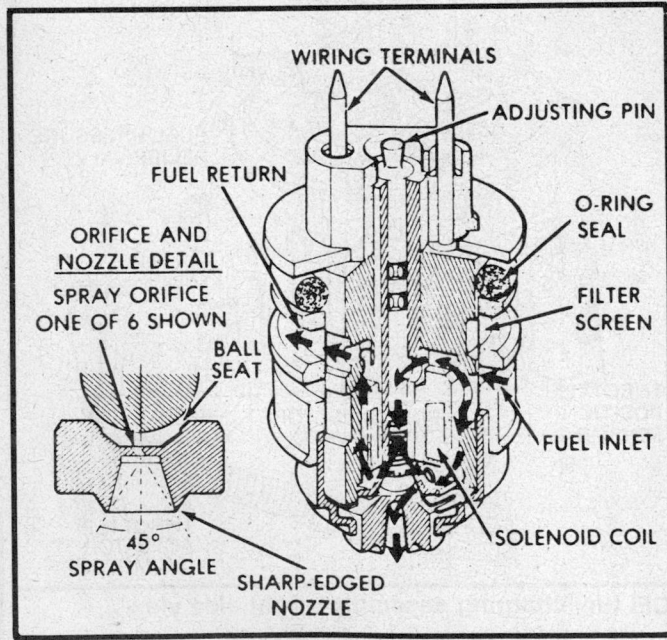

Cross-sectional view of the fuel injection nozzle — single point fuel injection

Rich or lean conditions on acceleration and other driving modes may be caused by the presence of dirt, water or other foreign material in the fuel charging assembly.

FUEL INJECTOR NOZZLES

The fuel injectors are electromechanical devices (solenoids) which operate a pintle or ball metering valve. The metering valve travels the same distance (closed-to-open-to-closed) but the injection is controlled by varying the length of time the valve is open.

The computer, based on voltage inputs from the crankshaft position sensor, operates each injector solenoid 2 times per crankshaft revolution. When the injector metering valve unseats, fuel is sprayed (in a fine mist) into the intake manifold. The computer varies fuel enrichment based on voltage inputs from the exhaust gas oxygen sensor, barometric pressure sensor, manifold absolute pressure sensor and etc., by calculating how long to hold the injectors open. The longer the injectors remain open, the richer the mixture. The injector **ON** time is called pulse duration.

FUEL PRESSURE DIAGNOSTIC VALVE

The diagnostic pressure valve (Schrader type) located on top of the fuel charging main body, provides a convenient point to monitor fuel pressure, bleed the fuel pressure prior to maintenance and bleed air which may have been introduced at assembly plant start-up or filter servicing.

FUEL PRESSURE REGULATOR

The pressure regulator mounted on the fuel charging main body (at the rear of the air horn), is positioned to nullify the effects of the fuel line pressure drops; its design is not sensitive to return-line back-pressure.

A second function of the pressure regulator is to maintain fuel supply pressure upon engine and fuel pump shutdown. The regulator functions as a downstream check valve and traps the fuel between itself and the fuel pump. The maintenance of fuel pressure upon engine shutdown precludes fuel line vapor formation and allow for rapid restarts and allows for stable idle operation immediately thereafter. It regulates the fuel pressure to the injector nozzles at 39 psi (high pressure system) or 14.5 psi (low pressure system).

THROTTLE IDLE SPEED CONTROL (ISC) DC MOTOR ACTUATOR

The DC motor actuator controls idle speed by modulating the throttle lever for the required airflow to maintain the desired engine speed for both warm engine and the additional engine speed required during cold engine idle.

An Idle Tracking Switch (ITS), integral to the DC motor, is utilized to determine when the throttle lever has contacted the actuator, thereby, signaling the need to control engine rpm.

The DC motor extends or retracts a linear shaft through a gear reduction system. The motor direction is determined by the polarity of the applied voltage.

THROTTLE POSITION (TP) SENSOR

This sensor (non-adjustable) is mounted to the throttle shaft on the choke side of the fuel charging assembly and is used to supply a voltage output proportional to the change in the throttle plate position. The sensor is used by the computer (EEC) to determine all operating modes for selection of the proper fuel mixture, spark and EGR at selected driving conditions.

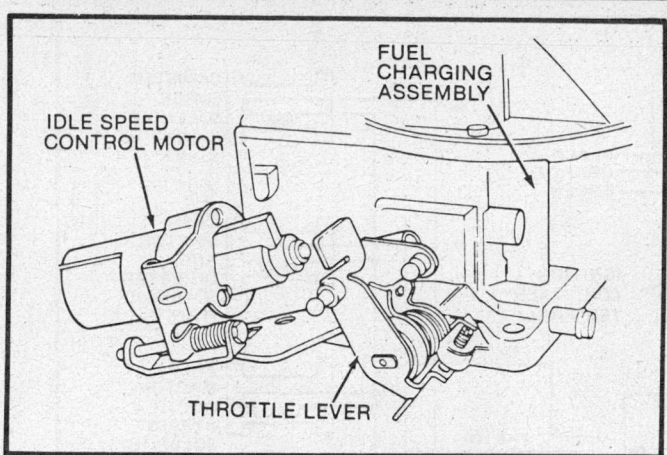

Idle speed control actuator—3.8L engine

System Services

IDLE SPEED

Adjustment
2.3L AND 2.5L ENGINES

NOTE: If for any reason the battery is disconnected or the vehicle has to be jump started, it may be necessary to perform the following procedure.

1. Apply the parking brake, block the drive wheels and place the vehicle in **N**.

2. Start the engine and allow it to reach normal operating temperatures. Then, turn it **OFF**. Connect a suitable tachometer.

3. Re-start the engine and place the transmission in **D** for automatic transmission/transaxle or **N** for manual transmission/transaxle and allow the engine to idle for 2 minutes.

NOTE: The idle rpm should now return to the the specified idle speed. The idle specifications can be found on the emission sticker located under the hood.

4. Place the transmission/transaxle in **N** or **P** and the engine rpm should increase by approximately 100 rpm. Now lightly step on and off the accelerator. The engine rpm should return to the specified idle speed. If the rpm remains high, repeat the sequence. Remember it may take the system 2 minutes to adjust.

NOTE: If the vehicle does not function as outlined, perform the following adjustment.

5. Turn the engine **OFF** and remove the air cleaner. Locate the self-test connector and self-test input connector in the engine compartment.

6. Connect a jumper wire between the self-test input connector and the signal return pin (top right terminal) on the self-test connector.

7. Place the ignition key in the **RUN** position, but be careful not to start the engine. The ISC plunger will retract. Wait approximately 10–15 seconds until the ISC plunger is fully retracted. Turn the ignition switch **OFF** and wait 10–15 seconds.

8. Remove the jumper wire and unplug the ISC motor from the wire harness. Now perform the throttle stop adjustment as follows:

   a. Remove the CFI assembly from the vehicle.

   b. Using a small punch or equivalent, punch through and remove the aluminum plug which covers the throttle stop adjusting screw.

   c. Remove and replace the throttle stop screw.

9. Reinstall the CFI assembly on the vehicle, stabilize the engine and set the idle rpm to the specifications using the throttle stop adjusting screw.

10. Turn the engine **OFF**. Reconnect the ISC motor wire harness, remove all test equipment and reinstall the air cleaner assembly.

3.8L ENGINE

1. Apply the parking brake, block the drive wheels and place the vehicle in **N**.

2. Start the engine and allow it to reach normal operating temperatures. Then, turn the engine **OFF** and connect a tachometer to the engine.

3. Turn **OFF** all accessories and place the selector in **D**. Allow the engine to run at idle for 60 seconds. The idle rpm should now return to the the specified idle speed listed on the underhood emission sticker.

4. Place the transmission/transaxle in **N** or **P**; the engine rpm should increase by approximately 100 rpm. Now lightly step on and off the accelerator. The engine rpm should return to the specified idle speed. If the rpm remains high, repeat the sequence. Remember it may take the system 2 minutes to adjust.

NOTE: If the vehicle does not function as outlined, perform the following adjustment.

5. Turn the engine **OFF** and remove the air cleaner. Locate the self-test connector and self-test input connector in the engine compartment.

6. Connect a jumper wire between the self-test input connector and the signal return pin (top right terminal) on the self-test connector.

7. Place the ignition switch in the **RUN** position, but be careful not to start the engine. Wait approximately 10–15 seconds until the ISC plunger is fully retracted. Turn the ignition switch **OFF** and wait 10–15 seconds.

NOTE: If the ISC plunger does not retract, the problem is with the EEC–IV system and the diagnostic check of the system should be made.

8. Remove the jumper wire and perform the throttle stop adjustment as follows:

   a. Using an appropriate tool, grasp the throttle stop adjusting screw threads and turn the screw until it is removed from the CFI assembly.

   b. Install a new screw.

   c. With the throttle plates closed, turn the new screw inward until there is a 0.005 in. gap between the screw tip and the throttle lever surface in which it contacts.

   d. Turn the screw inward an additional 1½ turns.

9. Remove all test equipment and reinstall the air cleaner.

Electronic Fuel Injection (EFI)

The multi point (EFI) system, is a pulse timed, speed density controlled (mass air flow) fuel injected system. Fuel is metered into the air intake stream in accordance with engine demand through the injectors mounted on a tuned intake manifold.

The Sequential Electronic Fuel Injection (SEFI) system meters fuel into each intake port in sequence with the engine firing order in accordance with engine demand.

If equipped with a turbocharger, a blow-through turbocharger system is utilized to reduce fuel delivery time, increase turbine energy available and eliminate compressor throttling.

An Electronic Engine Control (EEC–IV) computer accepts inputs from various engine sensors to compute the required fuel flow rate necessary to maintain a prescribed air/fuel ratio throughout the entire engine operational range. The computer outputs a command to the fuel injectors to meter the proper quantity of fuel. It also determines and compensates for the age of the vehicle and its uniqueness. The system will automatically sense and compensate for changes in altitude (i.e. from sea level

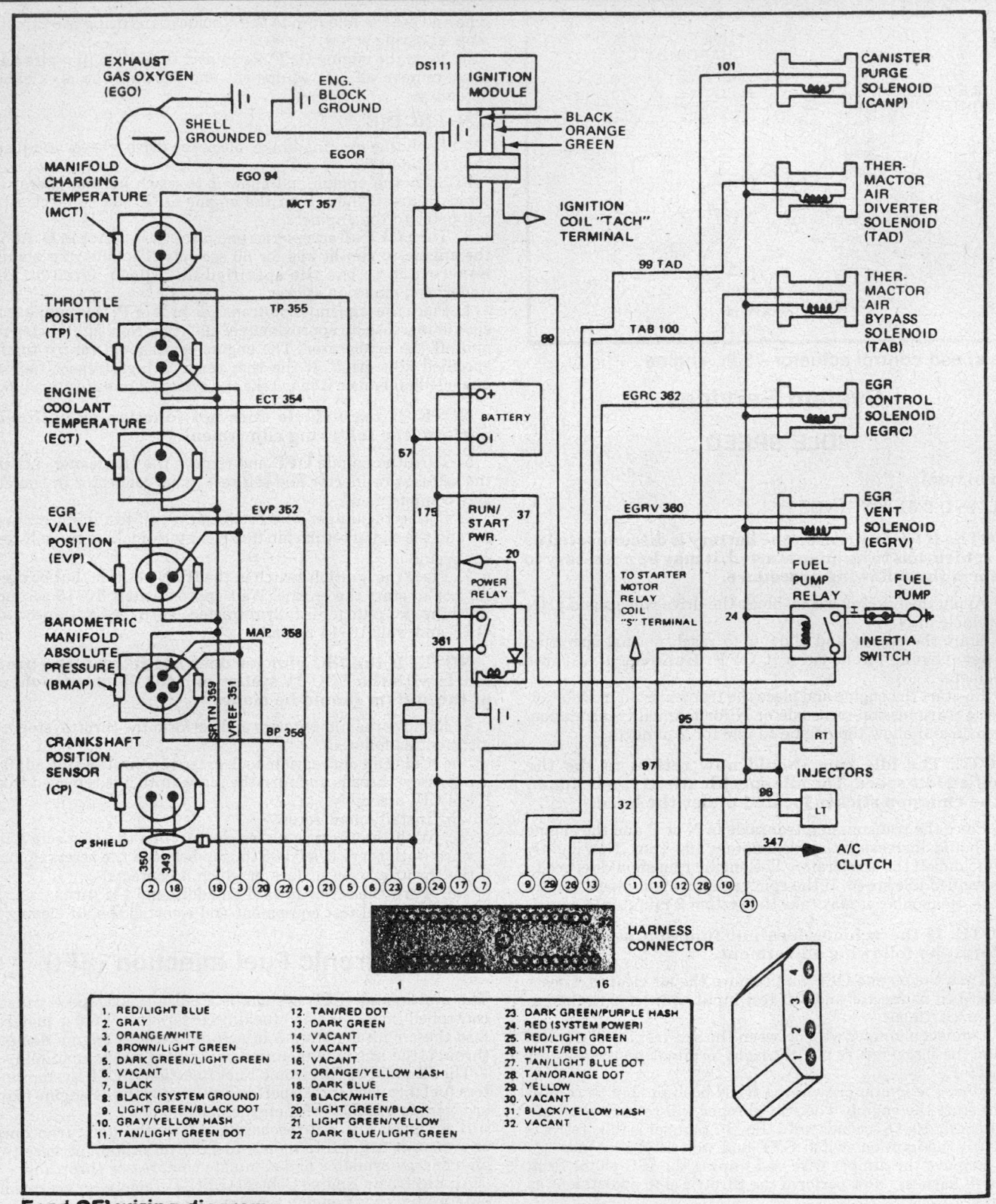

Ford CFI wiring diagram

to mountains) and will also permit push-starting the vehicle should it become necessary (manual transmission only).

The fuel delivery subsystem consists of a low pressure in-tank mounted fuel pump, a fuel filter/reservoir and a high pressure, electric fuel pump, delivering fuel from the fuel tank through a 20 micron fuel filter a fuel charging manifold assembly.

The fuel charging manifold assembly incorporates electrically actuated fuel injectors directly above each intake ports. The injectors, when energized, spray a metered quantity of fuel into the intake air stream.

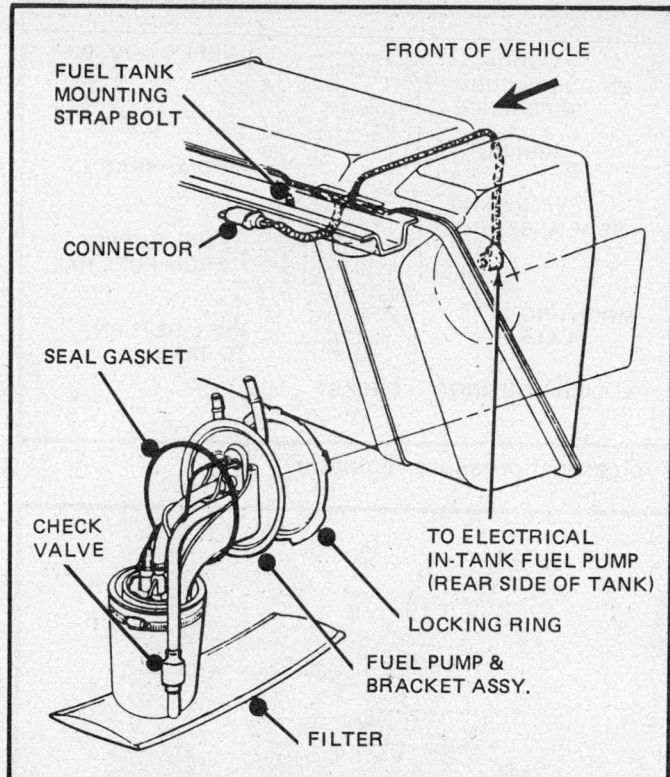

Electric fuel pump installation

A constant fuel pressure drop is maintained across the injector nozzles by a pressure regulator. The regulator is connected in series with the fuel injectors and is positioned downstream from them. Excess fuel supplied by the pump but not required by the engine, passes through the regulator and returns to the fuel tank through a fuel return line.

The injectors are energized simultaneously, once every crankshaft revolution. The period of time the injectors are energized (on time or pulse width) is controlled by the EEC computer. Air entering the engine is measured by a vane airflow meter located between the air cleaner and the turbocharger, if equipped. The airflow is compressed by the turbocharger before introduction into the fuel charging manifold. The airflow information, along with input from various engine sensors, is used to compute the required fuel flow rate necessary to maintain a prescribed air/fuel ratio for the given engine operation. The computer determines the needed injector pulse width and outputs a command to the injector to meter the exact quantity of fuel.

On the Sequential Electronic Fuel Injection (SEFI) system, each injector is energized once every crankshaft revolution in sequence with engine firing order. The period of time that the injectors are energized is controlled by the EEC computer. Air entering the engine is sensed by speed, pressure and temperature sensors. The sensors outputs are processed by the EEC–IV computer which determines the needed injector pulse width and outputs a command to the injector to meter the exact quantity of fuel.

The air intake manifold is a 2 piece (upper and lower intake manifold) aluminum casting. Runner lengths are tuned to optimize engine torque and power output. The manifold provides mounting flanges for the throttle body assembly, fuel supply manifold, accelerator control bracketry and the EGR valve. Vacuum taps are provided to support various engine accessories. Pockets for the fuel injectors are machined to prevent both air and fuel leakage. The pockets in which the injectors are mounted are positioned to direct the injector fuel spray immediately in front of each engine intake valve.

System Components
AIR VANE METER ASSEMBLY

The air vane meter assembly is located between the air cleaner or the turbocharger, if equipped, and is mounted on a bracket immediately below the air cleaner in the lower right hand corner of the engine compartment. The vane air meter contains 2 sensors (an airflow sensor and a vane air temperature sensor)

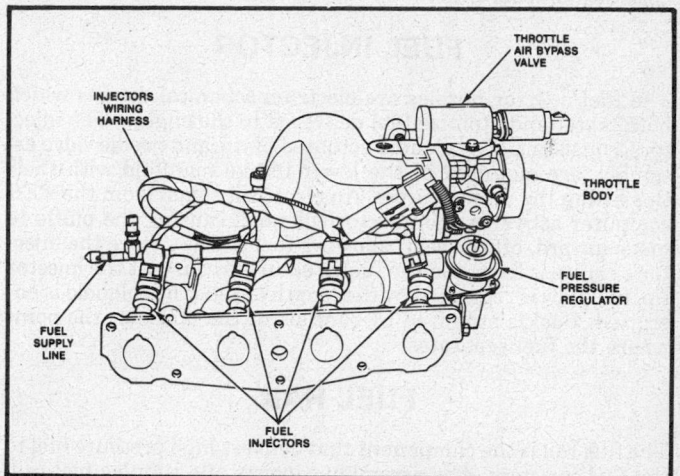

Components of EFI-EEC IV fuel system

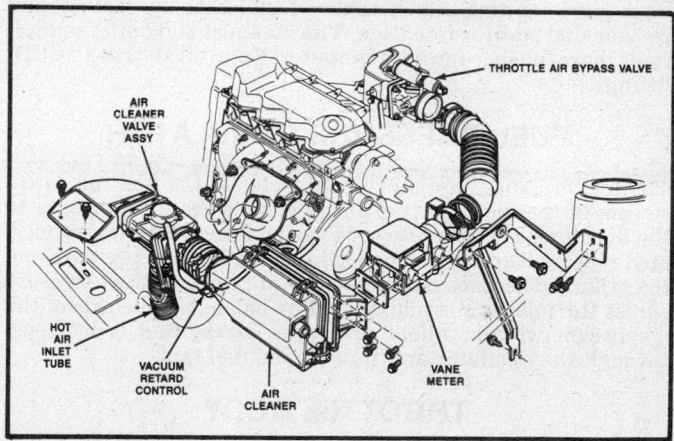

Components of EFI-EEC IV air intake system

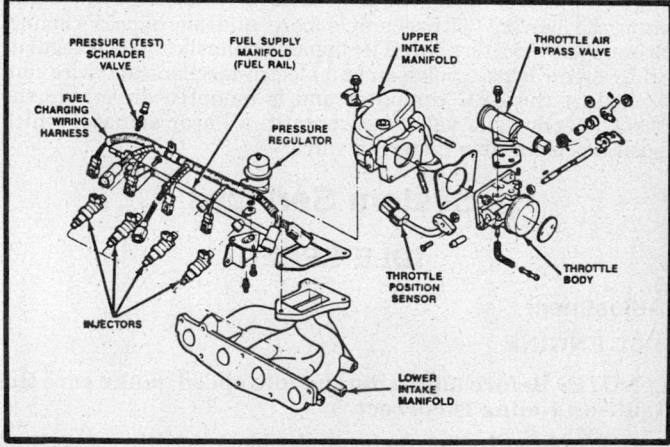

Exploded view of a 4 cylinder fuel charging manifold assembly

which furnish input to the electronic control assembly.. The air vane meter measures the volume of airflow to the engine. Airflow through the body moves a vane mounted on a pivot pin and is connected to a variable resistor which in turn is connected to a 5 volts reference voltage. The output of this variable resistor varies depending upon the volume of air flow. The temperature sensor in the air vane meter measures the incoming air temperature. The air volume and temperature inputs are used by the EEC to compute the injector pulse duration necessary for the optimum air/fuel ratio.

FUEL INJECTOR

The fuel injector nozzles are electro-mechanical devices which both meter and atomize fuel delivered to the engine. The injectors, consisting of a solenoid actuated pintle and needle valve assembly, are mounted in the lower intake manifold with their tips facing the intake valves. An electrical signal from the EEC computer activates the injector solenoid, causing the pintle to move inward, off the seat, allowing fuel to flow. Since the injector's orifice is fixed and the fuel pressure is constant the injector tip, fuel flow is regulated by the length of time the solenoid is energized. Fuel is atomized by contour of the pintle at the point where the fuel separates.

FUEL RAIL

The fuel rail is the component that delivers high pressure fuel to the fuel injectors. The assembly consists of a tubular fuel rail, injector connectors, a mounting flange to the fuel pressure regulator and mounting attachments which locate the fuel rail and provide fuel injector retention. The fuel inlet and outlet connections have push connect Computer Controlled Dwell (CCD) fittings.

FUEL PRESSURE REGULATOR

The fuel pressure regulator is connected to the fuel rail downstream of the fuel injectors and regulates the fuel pressure to the injectors. The regulator is a spring loaded diaphragm operated relief valve in which one side senses the fuel pressure and the other side senses manifold vacuum; constant fuel pressure across the injectors is maintained by balancing one side of the diaphragm with manifold pressure. Excess fuel is bypassed through the regulator and returns the fuel tank.

THROTTLE BODY

The throttle body assembly controls airflow to the engine utilizing a single lever or cable linkage. The body consists of an aluminum die casting with a single bore and air bypass channel around the throttle plate. The bypass channel control is regulated by an air bypass valve and an electro-mechanical device controlled by the EEC computer and is mounted directly to the throttle body. The valve incorporates a linear actuator which positions a variable metering valve.

System Services

IDLE SPEED

Adjustment

1.6L ENGINE

NOTE: **Before adjusting the idle speed, make sure the ignition timing is correct.**

1. Firmly apply the parking brake, block the drive wheels and place the transaxle in **N** for manual transaxle or **P** for automatic transaxle.

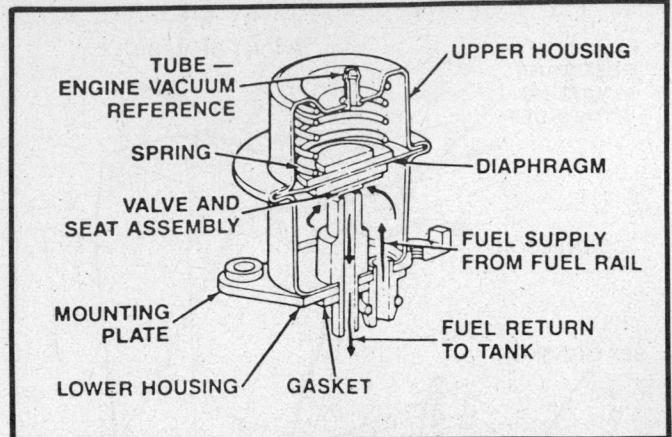

Typical fuel pressure regulator

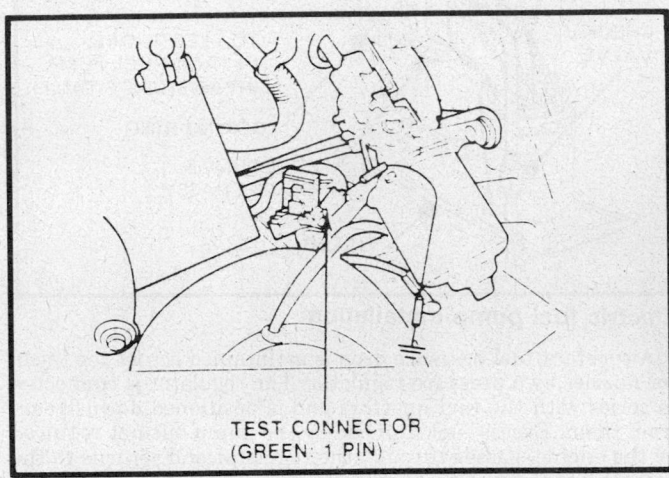

Connecting a jumper wire to the test connector green pin—1.6L engine

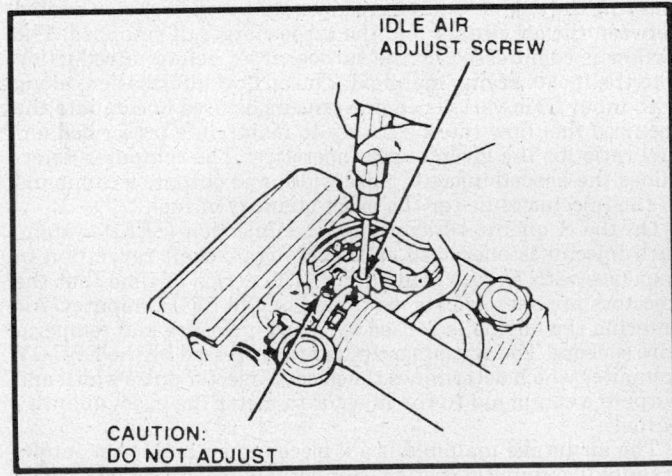

Adjusting the idle speed—1.6L engine

2. Turn **OFF** all of the accessories.
3. Start the engine and run it at 2500–3000 rpm for 3 minutes until normal operating temperatures are reached. Then, allow it to idle.
4. Using a Rotunda tachometer tool 059-00004 or equiva-

lent, connect it to test connector (white pin) and check the idle speed; it should be 800–900 rpm.

5. If necessary, connect a jumper wire to the test connector green pin.

6. If the idle speed is not within specifications, turn the idle air adjusting screw to obtain the correct idle speed.

7. After adjustment, remove the test equipment.

1.9L ENGINE

NOTE: Curb idle rpm is controlled by the EEC–IV processor and the Idle Speed Control (ISC) device.

The purpose of this procedure is to provide a means by verifying the initial engine rpm setting with the ISC disconnected. If engine idle rpm is not within specification after performing this procedure, it will be necessary to perform the appropriate EFI EEC–IV diagnostics.

1. Place the transmission in **N** or **P**.

2. Run the engine until normal operating temperature is reached. Then, turn the engine **OFF**.

3. Disconnect the vacuum connector at EGR solenoid and plug both lines.

4. Disconnect the Idle Speed Control (ISC) power lead.

5. Electric cooling fan must be **ON** during idle speed set procedure.

6. Start the engine and run it at 2000 rpm for 60 seconds.

7. Set the hand brake, block the drive wheels and place the transmission in **N** for manual transmission or **D** for automatic transmission. Check and if necessary, adjust the initial engine rpm within 2 minutes by adjusting throttle plate screw.

8. If idle adjustment is not completed within 2 minute time limit, turn the engine **OFF**, restart and repeat Steps 6 and 7.

9. If the vehicle is equipped with an automatic transmission and the initial engine rpm adjustment is more than 50 rpm or is decreased by any amount, adjust the transmission linkage.

10. Turn the engine **OFF** and remove plugs from EGR vacuum lines from the EGR solenoid and reconnect.

11. Reconnect the Idle Speed Control (ISC) power lead.

2.3L ENGINE

1. Apply the parking brake, block the drive wheels and place the transaxle in **N**.

2. Start the engine and allow it to reach normal operating temperature. Then, turn the engine **OFF**. Connect a tachometer to the engine.

3. Disconnect the idle speed control air bypass valve power lead. Start the engine and run it at 2000 rpm for 2 minutes.

NOTE: If the electric cooling fan turns ON during the idle speed adjusting procedures, wait for the fan to turn OFF before proceeding.

4. Allow the engine to idle and check the base idle, it should be at 700–800 rpm.; if it is not within specifications, adjust as necessary.

5. Adjust the engine rpm to 825–975 rpm for manual transaxle or 925–1075 rpm for automatic transaxle by adjusting the throttle stop screw.

6. Turn the engine **OFF** and reconnect the power lead to the idle speed control air bypass valve. Disconnect all test equipment.

3.0L ENGINE

NOTE: The curb idle speed rpm is controlled by the EEC–IV processor and the idle speed control air bypass valve assembly. The throttle stop screw is factory set and does not directly control the idle speed. Adjustment to this setting should be performed only as part of a full EEC–IV diagnosis of irregular idle conditions or idle speeds. Failure to accurately set the throttle plate stop position as described in the following procedure could result in false idle speed control.

1. Apply the parking brake, block the drive wheels and place the vehicle in **N**.

2. Start the engine and allow it run until normal operating temperature is reached. Then, turn the engine **OFF**. Connect a tachometer and an inductive timing light.

3. Unplug the spout line and verify the ignition timing is at 8–12 degrees BTDC. If the timing is not set to specifications, readjust as necessary.

4. Turn the engine **OFF** and disconnect the air bypass valve assembly connector. Remove the PCV entry line at the PCV line. Install the orifice tool T86P–9600–A or equivalent, in the PCV entry line (0.200 in. orifice diameter).

5. Start the engine and place the selector in **D** for automatic transmission/transaxle or **N** for manual transmission/transaxle. Unplug the electric cooling fan.

6. If the idle speed is not 595–655 rpm, adjust the throttle plate stop screw. After the idle has been adjusted to specifications, turn the engine **OFF**.

7. Start the engine and reconfirm that the idle speed is now adjusted to specifications, if not, adjust as necessary.

8. Turn the engine **OFF**, remove all test equipment, remove the orifice and reconnect the PCV entry line. Reconnect the spout line, the ISC motor and the electric cooling fan.

9. Check that the throttle plate is not stuck in the bore and the throttle plate stop screw is setting on the rest pad with the throttle closed. Correct any condition that will not allow the throttle to close to the stop set position.

10. Start the engine and after 3–5 minutes of operation, the engine idle speed should be to specifications.

5.0L ENGINE WITH SEQUENTIAL FUEL INJECTION (SFI)

1. Apply the parking brake, block the drive wheels and place the vehicle in **N**.

2. Operate the engine until normal operating temperature is reached. Then turn the engine **OFF**. Connect a tachometer to the engine.

3. Turn **OFF** all accessories and place the transmission in **P** for automatic transmission or **N** for manual transmission. Check the throttle linkage for freedom of movement and correct if necessary.

4. Check for vacuum leaks. Place the transmission in **N** and operate the engine at 1800 rpm for at least 30 seconds. Place the transmission in **D** for automatic transmission or **N** for manual transmission and allow the engine to stabilize.

5. Check the idle speed. If the curb idle speed does not meet specifications, turn the engine **OFF**. Disconnect the positive terminal of the battery for 5 minutes and reconnect it. Repeat Steps 4 and 5.

6. If the curb idle speed is still out of specifications, further diagnosis of the EEC–IV system should be made.

7. If the curb idle speed is still out specifications, back out the throttle screw until the idle speed reaches 555–595 rpm (base 5.0L automatic transmission), 605–645 rpm (5.0L H.O. automatic transmission) or 680–720 rpm (5.0L H.O. manual transmission) then back out the throttle plate stop screw an additional ½ turn to bring the throttle plate linkage into the normal operating range of the ISC system.

8. Turn the engine **OFF** and remove all test equipment.

THROTTLE POSITION SENSOR

Adjustment
NOTE: Not all throttle position sensor are adjustable. Before adjusting the throttle position sensor, be sure the idle speed and ignition timing are correct. Do not adjust the throttle stop screw at the throttle lever; doing so may damage the throttle body. The throttle stop screw is adjusted at the factory. If the non-adjustable TPS is out of voltage specification or found to be faulty, the TPS must be replaced.

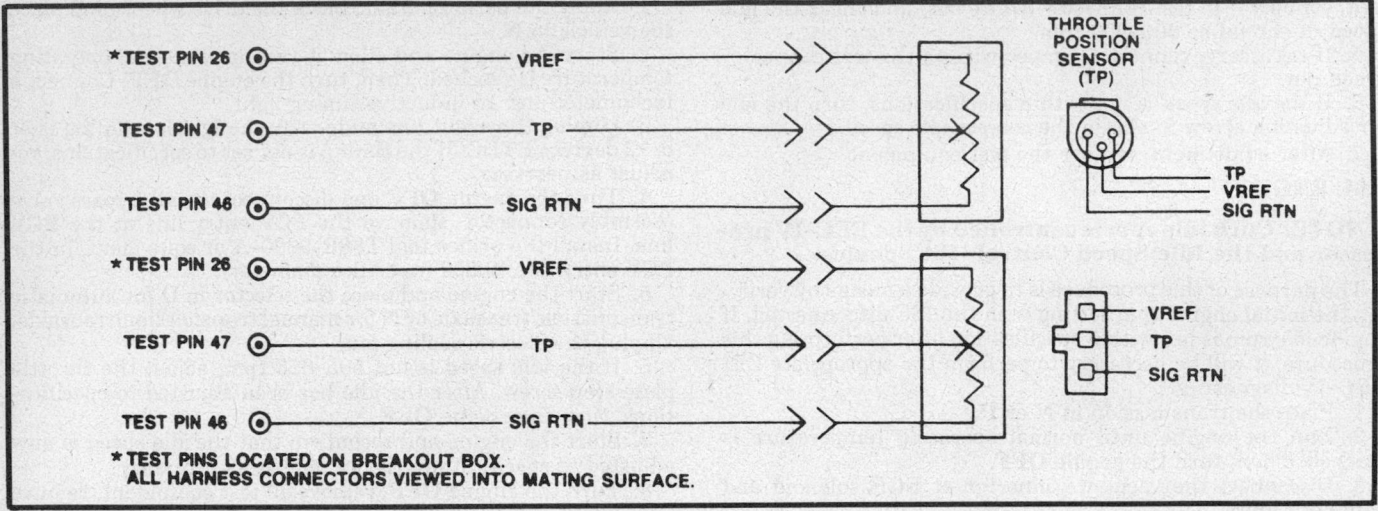

Breakout Box test pin identification

Using an ohmmeter to test the throttle position sensor—1.6L engine

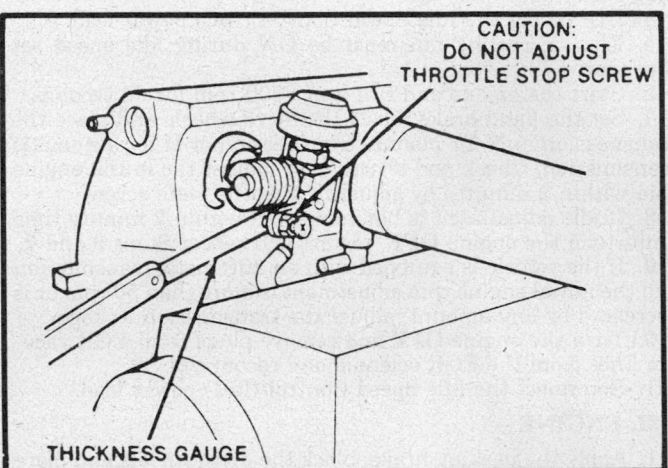

Using a feeler gauge to test the throttle position sensor—1.6L engine

1.6L ENGINE

1. Disconnect the negative battery cable.
2. Disconnect the elecrical connector from the throttle position sensor.
3. To check the throttle position sensor, perform the following checks:

   a. Position a 0.020 in. feeler gauge between the throttle and the throttle stop screw. Using an ohmmeter, check for continuity between the throttle position sensor terminals TL and IDL only.

   b. Position a 0.027 in. feeler gauge between the throttle and the throttle stop screw. Using an ohmmeter, check for continuity between the throttle position sensor terminals; there should be no continuity.

   c. Turn the throttle lever to the fully open position. Using an ohmmeter, check for continuity between the throttle position sensor terminals TL and PSW only.

4. If the throttle position sensor does not meet these tests, loosen the throttle position sensor the throttle body hold-down screws, move the sensor and retest it.

5. If the throttle positon sensor cannot be adjusted to specifications, replace it.

EXCEPT 1.6L ENGINE

1. Install the Rotunda breakout box tool T83L–50 EEC–IV or equivalent, to throttle position sensor harness.
2. Attach a DVOM Rotunda tool No. 014–00407 or equivalent and set to 20 volts scale. Connect the positive (+) lead to test pin 47 and the negative (−) lead to test pin 46.
3. Turn the ignition switch to **RUN** position, engine stopped.
4. Adjust throttle position sensor until DVOM reading reads 0.9–1.1 volt by rotating sensor.
5. Tighten the TPS attaching screws to 13 ft. lbs. (1.5 Nm).
6. While watching the DVOM, move throttle to the Wide Open position then back to idle position. For proper operation, the DVOM should move from 1.0 volt to at least 4.0 volts then back to 1.0 volt.
7. Turn the ignition switch **OFF**, remove breakout box and DVOM.

STARTER MOTORS

Ducellier and Paris-Rhone Starter

AMC MEDALLION

Disassembly and Assembly

1. Support the starter in a soft jawed vise.
2. Remove the rear mounting bracket-to-starter nuts, the bracket and the plastic cap.
3. Disconnect the field wire from the solenoid.
4. Remove the solenoid-to-starter nuts and the solenoid.
5. From the end cover, remove the nuts, the through bolts and the end cover.
6. Using a pin punch at the drive end housing, drive the yoke axle pin from the housing.
7. At the positive brushes, move the brush spring clips to the side of the brushes and pull the brushes away from the armature. Carefully pull the field housing from the drive end housing.
8. Remove the pinion yoke and armature from the drive end housing.
9. Using a deep socket which fits over the armature shaft, tap the stop collar (driving it toward the armature) to expose the snapring. Remove the snapring from the groove and slide it from the shaft.

NOTE: When removing the snapring, be careful not to bend or distort it.

10. Remove the stop collar, the drive pinion and the support plate.
11. Using compressed air or a brush, clean the drive pinion, the drive end frame, the armature, the field coils and the starter frame; all other parts can be cleaned in solvent.
12. Inspect the condition of the starter parts, perform the following procedures:
    a. Check for broken wires or badly soldered connections.
    b. Replace any bushings which are scored or badly worn.
    c. If the armature's commutator more than 0.005 in. out of round, reface it on a lathe.

NOTE: Never use emery cloth to clean a commutator.

    d. The drive pinion should be free of excessive wear or damage.
    e. If the brushes are cracked, broken, distorted or worn to less than 0.314 in., replace them.
    f. Using a growler and a hacksaw blade (placed on top of the armature), rotate the armature and check it for a shorted condition. If the hacksaw blade vibrates, a short exists; replace the armature.
    g. Using a test light, place a lead on the armature's core and the other on each commutator segment, inspect the armature for a grounded condition. If a ground exists, the test light will turn **ON**; replace the armature.
    h. Using a test light, check for continuity between the positive brushes; if no continuity exists, replace the winding. Repeat this test for the negative windings.
    i. Using a test light, place a lead on the coil housing and the other on each coil lead, make sure there is NO continuity; if continuity exists, replace the winding(s).

Assembly:

13. Lubricate the necessary parts and place the support plate onto the armature, followed by the drive pinion and the stop collar. Carefully slide the snapring into the armature groove. Slide the stop collar over the snapring until it locks.
14. Position the armature and pinion yoke into the drive end housing. Install the pinion yoke axle pin.
15. Install the coil housing over the armature and onto the

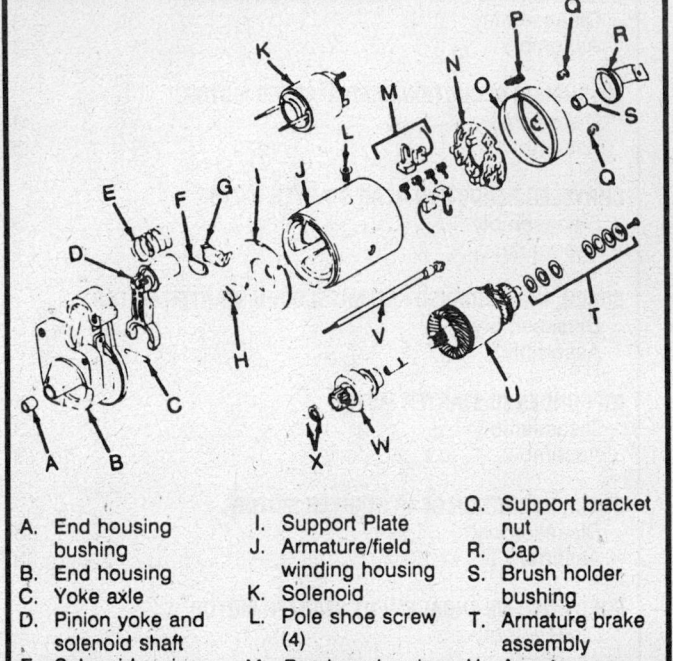

A. End housing bushing	I. Support Plate	Q. Support bracket nut
B. End housing	J. Armature/field winding housing	R. Cap
C. Yoke axle	K. Solenoid	S. Brush holder bushing
D. Pinion yoke and solenoid shaft	L. Pole shoe screw (4)	T. Armature brake assembly
E. Solenoid spring	M. Brush and spring assembly (4)	U. Armature
F. Spacer	N. Brush holder	V. Through bolts (2)
G. Pad	O. End cover	W. Drive pinion
H. Support Plate Bushing	P. Grommet	X. Collar and snap ring

Exploded view of the Ducellier and Paris-Rhone starter—AMC Alliance, Encore and Medallion

drive end housing. Position the brush holder onto the coil housing. Install the brushes and secure the brush springs.
16. Install the solenoid to the drive end housing. Position the field wire grommet to the coil housing and connect field wire to the solenoid.
17. Install the end cover to the coil housing and the install the through bolts/nuts. Install the armature brake assembly, the plastic cover and the mounting bracket.

Mitsubishi Reduction Gear Starter

AMC EAGLE PREMIER 3.0L
CHRYSLER LASER 2.0L

Disassembly and Assembly

NOTE: **Do not place the stator frame in a vise or strike it with a hammer for damage to the permanent magnets could occur.**

1. Disconnect the coil wire from the solenoid.
2. Remove the solenoid-to-front end frame screws and the solenoid.
3. Loosen, do not remove the commutator shield-to-brush holder screws.
4. Remove the through bolts, the rubber retainer (under solenoid) and the coin washer.

NOTE: **When removing the output shaft assembly, do not loose the armature shaft ball.**

5. Remove the stator frame, the commutator shield and output shaft assembly as a unit. Separate the clutch fork from the output shaft assembly.

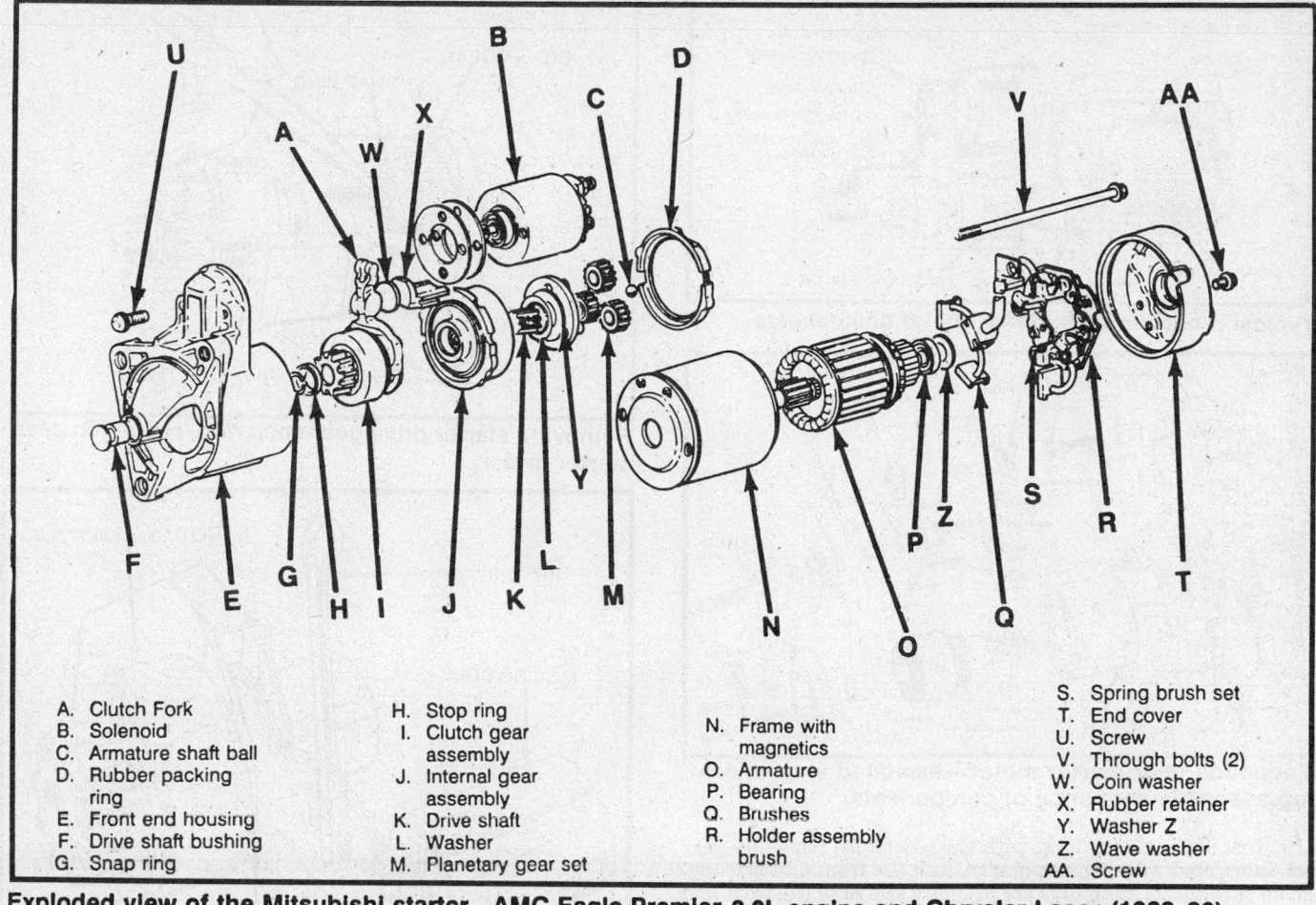

A. Clutch Fork
B. Solenoid
C. Armature shaft ball
D. Rubber packing ring
E. Front end housing
F. Drive shaft bushing
G. Snap ring

H. Stop ring
I. Clutch gear assembly
J. Internal gear assembly
K. Drive shaft
L. Washer
M. Planetary gear set

N. Frame with magnetics
O. Armature
P. Bearing
Q. Brushes
R. Holder assembly brush

S. Spring brush set
T. End cover
U. Screw
V. Through bolts (2)
W. Coin washer
X. Rubber retainer
Y. Washer Z
Z. Wave washer
AA. Screw

Exploded view of the Mitsubishi starter—AMC Eagle Premier 3.0L engine and Chrysler Laser (1989–90) 2.0L engine

6. From the stator frame, pull the output shaft assembly forward, then, push the armature and commutator shield to the rearward.

7. Remove the commutator shield-to-brush holder plate screws and the shield; do not remove the brush holder assembly.

8. Using a 22mm socket, slide it up against the commutator, slide the brush holder assembly onto the socket and position the socket/brush holder assembly aside.

9. To disassemble the output shaft assembly, perform the following procedures:

  a. Remove the rubber packing ring and the gears.

  b. Using a 17mm socket, position it into the armature end of the driveshaft and position the assembly in the vertical position, resting on the socket.

  c. Using a 12 point 14mm socket, position it against the stopring (on the clutch end). Using a hammer, strike the socket to unseat the stopring and expose the snapring.

  d. Remove the socket, the snapring and the stopring from the driveshaft.

  e. Using fine sandpaper, remove any burrs from the driveshaft. Remove the overruning clutch.

10. Using compressed air or dry cloths, clean the armature, the stator frame, the overrunning clutch, the solenoid and the brush holder. Using mineral spirits, clean all other components.

11. Inspect the following parts for damage and replace, if necessary:

  a. The stator frame and permanent magnets

  b. The driveshaft bushing (armature side)

  c. The planetary gear set and driveshaft

  d. The starter motor bushing and bearing

  e. The carbon brushes for cracks, distortion and wear below 0.354 in.

NOTE: When inspecting the brushes, do not remove the socket from the brush holder.

12. Using a growler and a hacksaw blade (placed on top of the armature), rotate the armature and check it for a shorted condition. If the hacksaw blade vibrates, a short exists; replace the armature.

13. Using a test light, place a lead on the armature's core and the other on each commutator segment, inspect the armature for a grounded condition. If a ground exists, the test light will turn **ON**; replace the armature.

14. Using a test light, place the leads on the adjacent commutator segments. If the test light turns **ON** between any 2 segments, the armature is shorted and must be replaced.

15. Inspect the commutator out-of-round, if it is more than 0.001 in., reface it on a lathe.

Assembly:

16. Using motor oil, lubricate the driveshaft and the overrunning clutch bushing. Using Lubriplate®, lubricate the overrunning clutch spiral cut splines.

17. Install the overrunning clutch on the driveshaft/planetary gear assembly, followed by the stopring and the snapring; sure to seat the snapring in the shaft groove and crimp the it with a pair of pliers.

18. Using a battery terminal puller, attach it to the driveshaft tip and press the stopring over the snapring.

NOTE: When installing the stopring, be careful not to scratch the driveshaft.

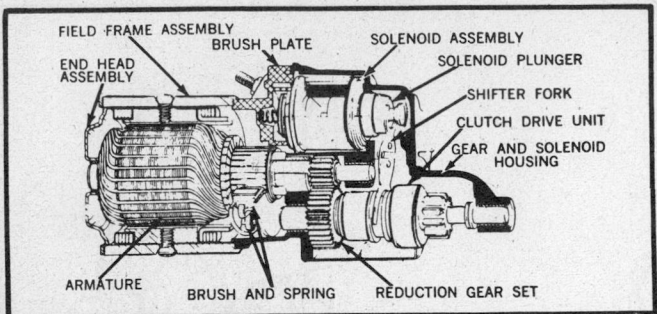

Typical reduction gear starter motor components

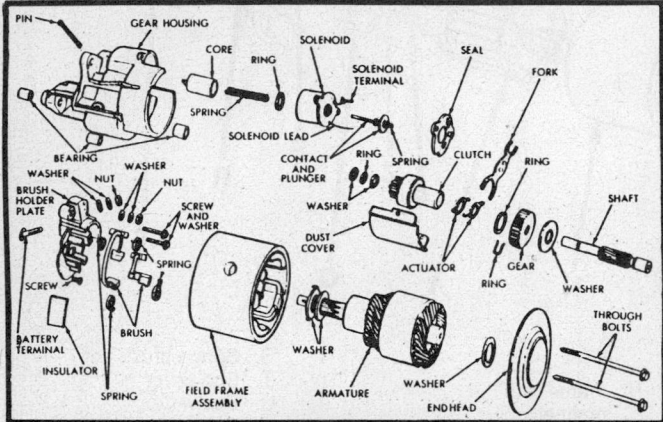

Reduction gear starter motor—exploded view showing assembly sequence of components

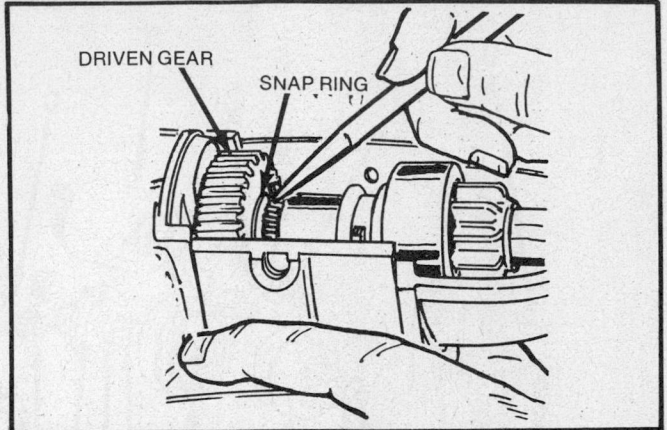

Removing starter drive gear snap ring, reduction gear starter motor

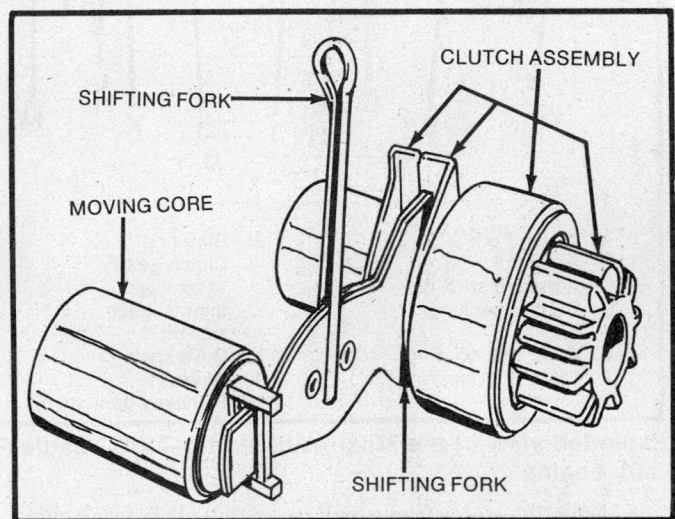

Shift fork and clutch arrangement—reduction gear starter motor

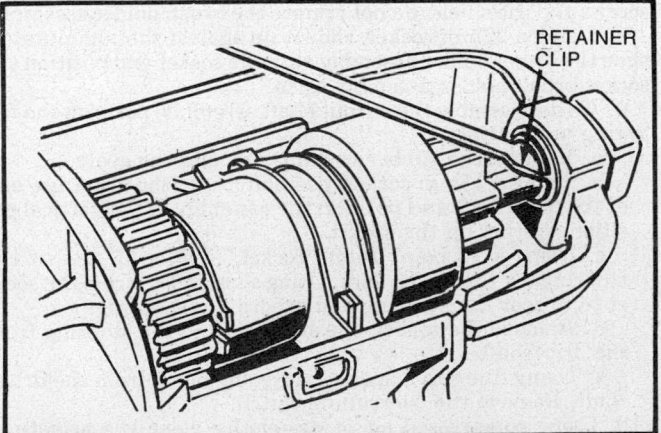

Removing the starter drive gear retaining ring—reduction gear starter motor

19. Install the clutch fork, with the assembled planetary gear set, lubricated with lithium grease, into the front end housing; make sure the locating lugs are properly seated in the front end housing.

20. Install the coin washer and the rubber fork retainer.

21. Install the rubber backing ring by placing the largest rubber lug at the top.

22. Install the brush holder onto the armature's commutator; make sure the brushes and brush holders are seated in the holder. Inspect the flex washer and install the commutator shield onto the armature. Install the brush holder screws but do not tighten them.

23. Install the armature assembly into the stator frame and seat the wire grommet into the frame.

24. Be sure the armature spline gear is seated in the planetary gear seat with the armature shaft ball in place. Seat the armature shaft in the shaft bushing bore; rotate the stator frame to align the tabs on the drive housing frame.

25. Install the through bolts and torque to 28 inch lbs. Torque the brush holder screws to 18 inch lbs.

26. To complete the assembly, reverse the disassembly procedures.

Chrysler Reduction Gear Starter

Disassembly and Assembly

1. Support assembly in a soft jawed vise; be careful not to distort or damage the die cast aluminum.

2. Remove the through bolts and the end housing.

3. To disassemble the starter motor, perform the following procedures:

   a. Carefully pull the armature up and out of the gear housing and the starter frame and field assembly.

   b. Remove the steel and fiber thrust washer.

   c. Carefully pull the frame and field assembly up enough to expose the terminal screw and the solder connection of the shunt field at the brush terminal.

   d. Place 2 wood blocks between the starter frame and starter gear housing to facilitate removal of the terminal screw.

   e. Unsolder the shunt field wire at the brush terminal.

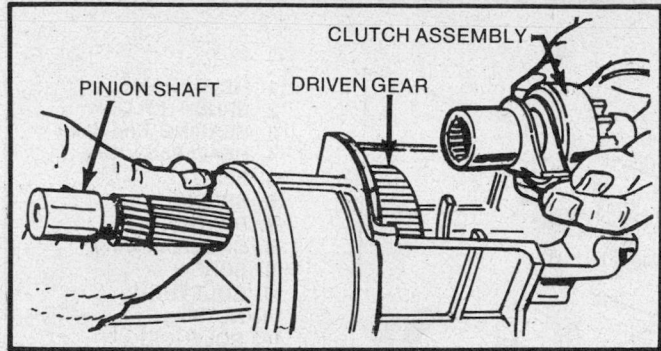

Removing the clutch assembly

NOTE: The starting motors have the wire of the shunt field coil soldered to the brush terminal. A pair of brushes are connected to this terminal. Another pair of brushes are attached to the series field coils by means of a terminal screw.

4. Support the brush terminal with a finger behind terminal and remove the screw. Unsolder the shunt field coil lead from the brush terminal and housing.

5. The brush holder plate (with terminal contact) and brushes are serviced as an assembly. Clean all old sealer from around plate and housing.

6. Remove the brush holder screw. On the shunt type, unsolder the solenoid winding from the brush terminal.

7. Remove the $^{11}/_{32}$ in. nut, washer and insulator from solenoid terminal. Remove the brush holder plate with brushes as an assembly and the gear housing ground screw.

8. The solenoid assembly can be removed from the well. Remove the nut, washer and seal from starter battery terminal and the terminal from the plate.

9. Remove the solenoid contact and plunger from solenoid and the coil sleeve. Remove the solenoid return spring, coil retaining washer, retainer and the dust cover from the gear housing.

10. Release the snapring that locates the driven gear on pinion shaft. Release the front retaining ring.

11. Push the pinion shaft rearward and remove the snapring, thrust washers, clutch/pinion and the 2 nylon shift fork actuators.

12. Remove the driven gear and friction washer. Pull the shifting fork forward and remove the moving core.

13. Remove the fork retaining pin and shifting fork assembly. The gear housing with bushings is serviced as an assembly.

Assembly:

14. Brushes that are worn to ½ the length of new brushes or oil soaked, should be replaced.

15. When resoldering the shunt field and solenoid lead, make a strong low resistance connection using a high temperature solder and resin flux; do not use acid or acid core solder. Be careful not to break the shunt field wire units when removing and installing the brushes.

16. Do not immerse the starter clutch unit in a cleaning solvent. The outside of the clutch and pinion must be cleaned with a cloth so the lubricant is not washed from inside the clutch.

17. Rotate the pinion. The pinion gear should rotate smoothly and in 1 direction only. If the starter clutch unit does not function properly or the pinion is worn, chipped or burred, replace the starter clutch unit.

18. Inspect the commutator and the surface contacted by the brushes when the starter is assembled, for flat spots, out of roundness or excessive wear.

19. Reface the commutator, if necessary, removing only a sufficient amount of metal to provide a smooth even surface.

20. Using light pressure scrape the commutator grooves with a broken hacksaw blade; do not remove any metal or expand the grooves.

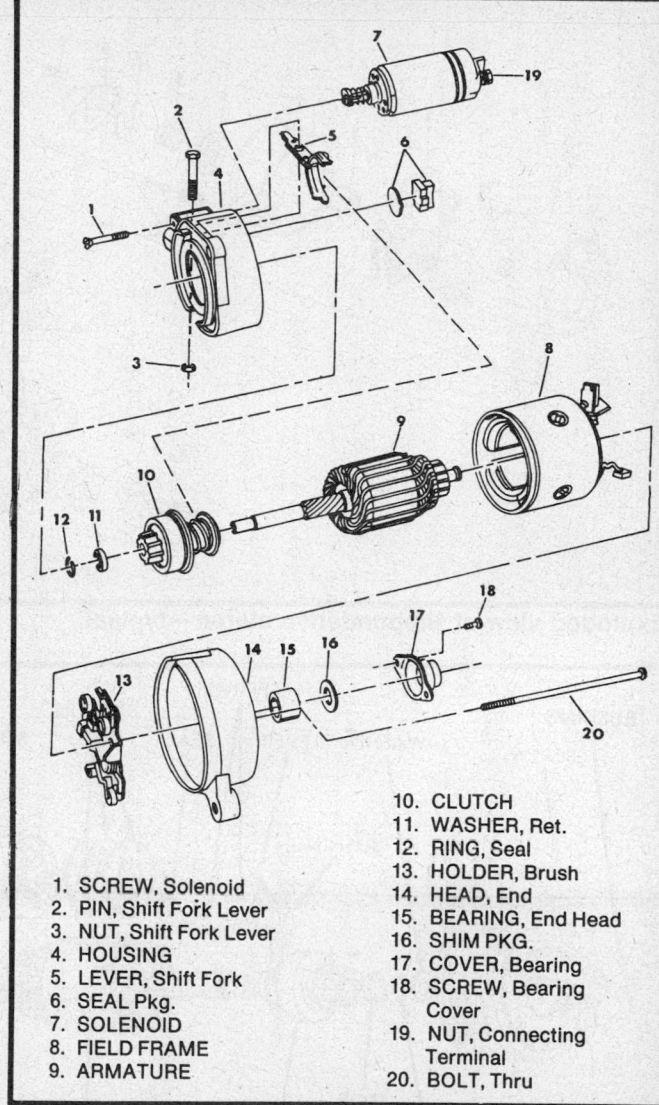

1. SCREW, Solenoid
2. PIN, Shift Fork Lever
3. NUT, Shift Fork Lever
4. HOUSING
5. LEVER, Shift Fork
6. SEAL Pkg.
7. SOLENOID
8. FIELD FRAME
9. ARMATURE
10. CLUTCH
11. WASHER, Ret.
12. RING, Seal
13. HOLDER, Brush
14. HEAD, End
15. BEARING, End Head
16. SHIM PKG.
17. COVER, Bearing
18. SCREW, Bearing Cover
19. NUT, Connecting Terminal
20. BOLT, Thru

Exploded view of the Bosch starter

21. To assemble, lubricate the bushings and reverse the disassembly procedures. The shifter fork consists of 2 spring steel plates held together by 2 rivets. Before assembling the starter check the plates for side movement. After lubricating between the plates with a small amount of SAE 10 engine oil they should have about $^1/_{16}$ in. side movement to insure proper pinion gear engagement.

1986 Nippondenso, 1986 Mitsubishi and Bosch Starters

Disassembly and Assembly

1. Position the assembly in the soft jawed vise. Disconnect the field coil wire from the solenoid terminal.

2. Remove the solenoid-to-starter screws and the solenoid (Bosch, automatic transmission) and work the solenoid plunger (Bosch, automatic transmission) from the shifting fork.

3. On Nippondenso units, remove the bearing cover, armature shaft lock, washer, spring, and seal.

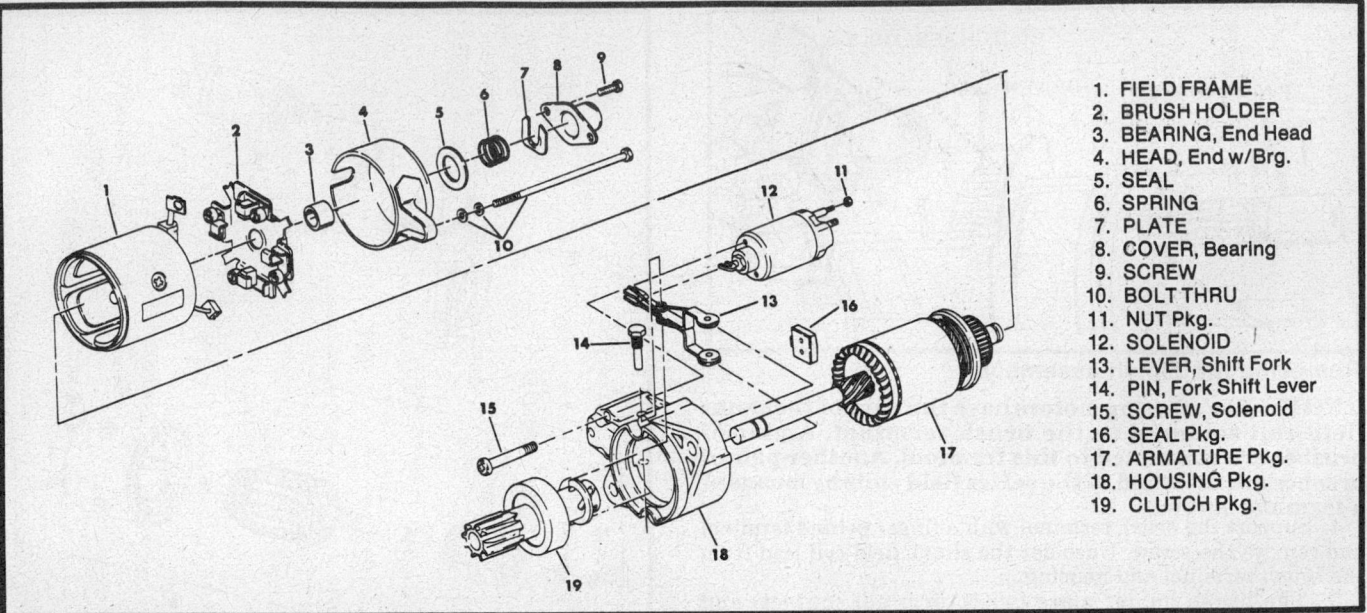

Exploded view of Nippondenso starter—typical

1. FIELD FRAME
2. BRUSH HOLDER
3. BEARING, End Head
4. HEAD, End w/Brg.
5. SEAL
6. SPRING
7. PLATE
8. COVER, Bearing
9. SCREW
10. BOLT THRU
11. NUT Pkg.
12. SOLENOID
13. LEVER, Shift Fork
14. PIN, Fork Shift Lever
15. SCREW, Solenoid
16. SEAL Pkg.
17. ARMATURE Pkg.
18. HOUSING Pkg.
19. CLUTCH Pkg.

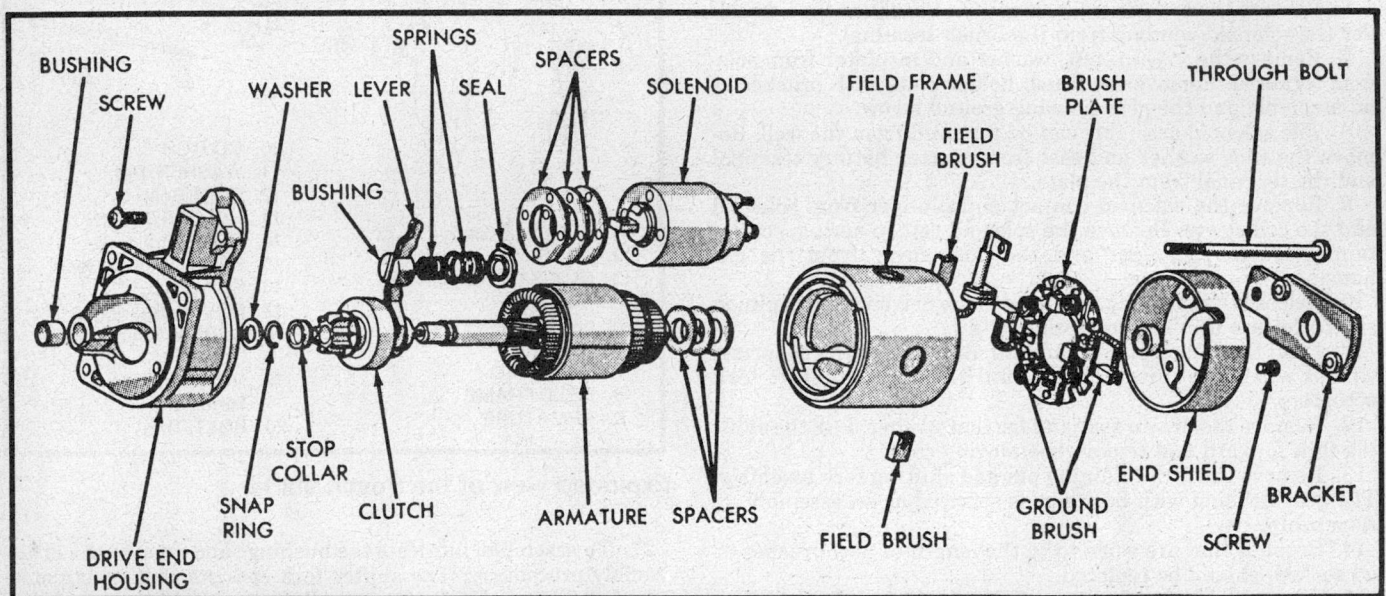

Exploded view of the Mitsubishi starter—1986 Chrysler 1.6L engine

4. On Bosch units, remove the end shield bearing cap screws, the cap and washers.

5. Remove the through bolts and the commutator end frame cover. Remove the 2 brushes and the brush plate. Slide the field frame from the armature.

6. Remove the shift lever pivot bolt, the rubber gasket and plate.

7. For the Bosch (automatic transmission) and all Nippondenso units, remove the armature assembly and shift lever from the drive end housing. For the Bosch (manual transmission) press the stop collar from the snapring. Remove the snapring, the clutch assembly and the drive end housing from the armature.

8. For all (except Bosch, manual transmission), press the stop collar from the snapring and remove the snapring, stop collar and clutch.

9. Brushes that are worn less than ½ the length of new brushes or oil soaked should be replaced; new brushes are $^{11}/_{16}$ in. long.

Assembly:

10. Do not immerse the starter clutch unit in cleaning solvent; lubricant will be washed from inside the clutch.

11. Place the drive unit on the armature shaft and while holding the armature, rotate the pinion. The drive pinion should rotate smoothly in 1 direction only. The pinion may not rotate easily but as long as it rotates smoothly it is in good condition. If the clutch unit does not function properly or if the pinion is worn, chipped or burred replace the unit.

12. To assemble, lubricate the bushings/splines and reverse the disassembly procedures.

13. On all (except Bosch—manual transmission), install the clutch, stop collar, lock ring and shaft fork on the armature. On

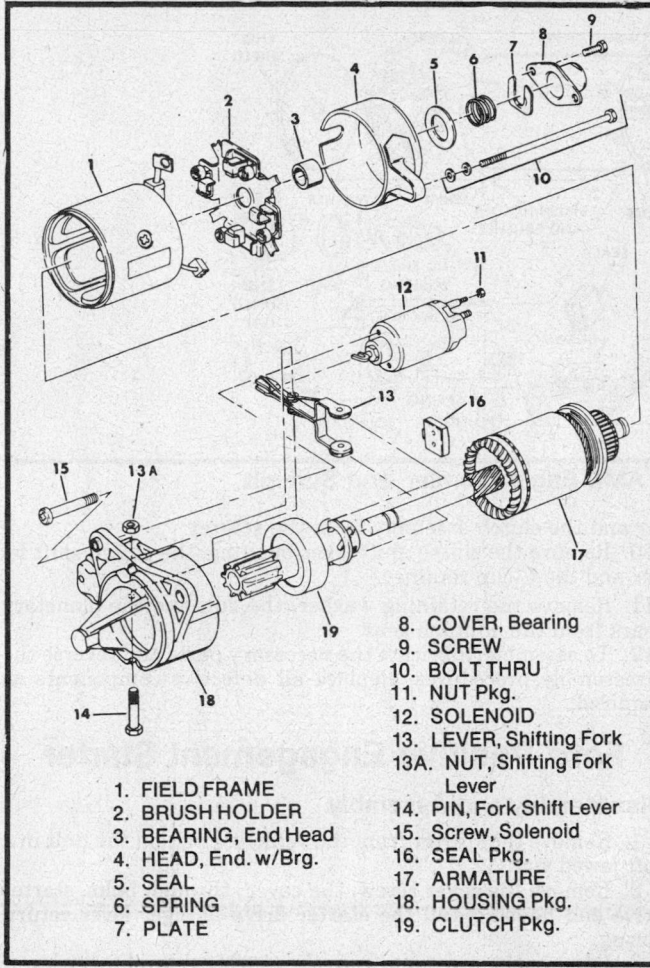

8. COVER, Bearing
9. SCREW
10. BOLT THRU
11. NUT Pkg.
12. SOLENOID
13. LEVER, Shifting Fork
13A. NUT, Shifting Fork Lever
14. PIN, Fork Shift Lever
15. Screw, Solenoid
16. SEAL Pkg.
17. ARMATURE
18. HOUSING Pkg.
19. CLUTCH Pkg.

1. FIELD FRAME
2. BRUSH HOLDER
3. BEARING, End Head
4. HEAD, End. w/Brg.
5. SEAL
6. SPRING
7. PLATE

Exploded view of the Nippondenso starter—1986 Chrysler

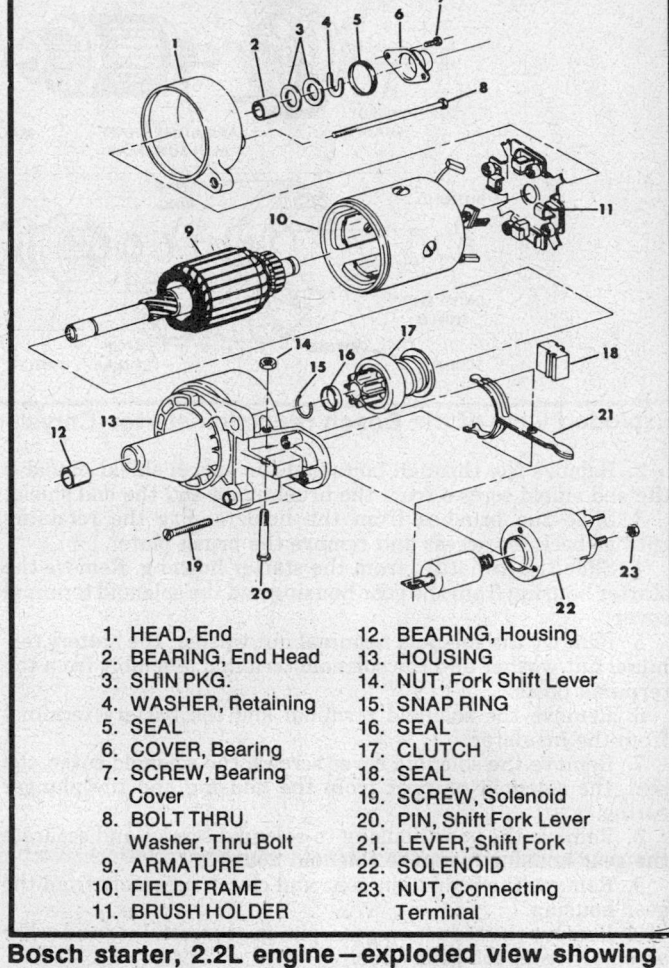

1. HEAD, End
2. BEARING, End Head
3. SHIN PKG.
4. WASHER, Retaining
5. SEAL
6. COVER, Bearing
7. SCREW, Bearing Cover
8. BOLT THRU Washer, Thru Bolt
9. ARMATURE
10. FIELD FRAME
11. BRUSH HOLDER
12. BEARING, Housing
13. HOUSING
14. NUT, Fork Shift Lever
15. SNAP RING
16. SEAL
17. CLUTCH
18. SEAL
19. SCREW, Solenoid
20. PIN, Shift Fork Lever
21. LEVER, Shift Fork
22. SOLENOID
23. NUT, Connecting Terminal

Bosch starter, 2.2L engine—exploded view showing assembly sequence of components

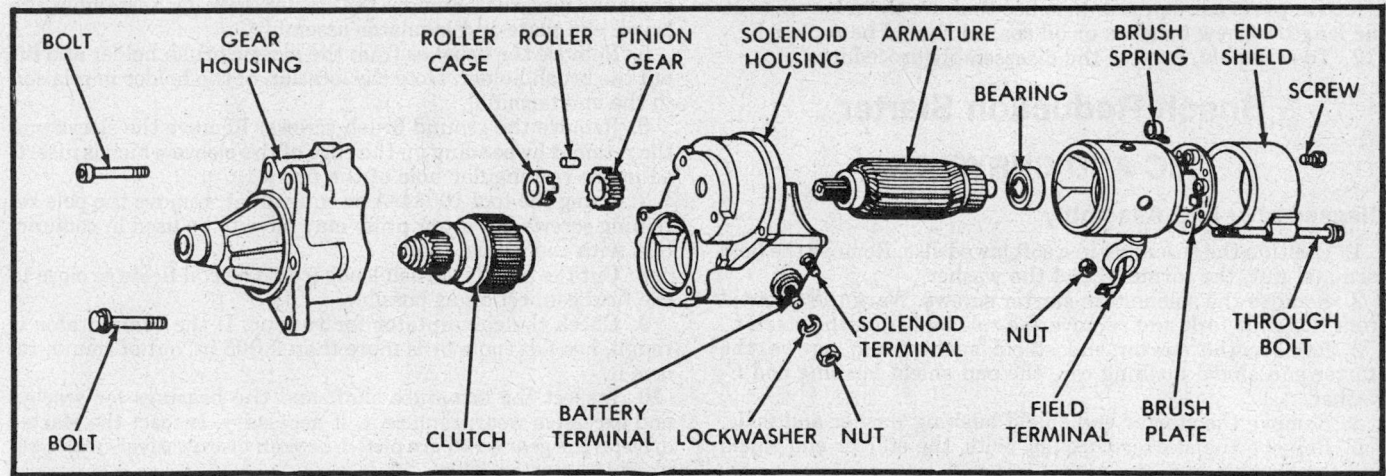

Exploded view of the Nippondenso starter—1987–90 Chrysler

the Bosch (manual transmission), install the drive end housing on the armature, the clutch, stop collar and snapring on the armature.

14. On all (except Bosch, manual transmission), install the armature assembly and shift fork in the drive end housing. On Bosch units, install the shim and armature shaft lock. Check the endplay, it should be 0.002–0.021 in.

1987–90 Nippondenso Starter

Disassembly and Assembly

1. Position the assembly in a soft jawed vise. Remove the rubber boot from the field coil terminal, the nut from the field coil terminal stud and the field coil terminal from the stud.

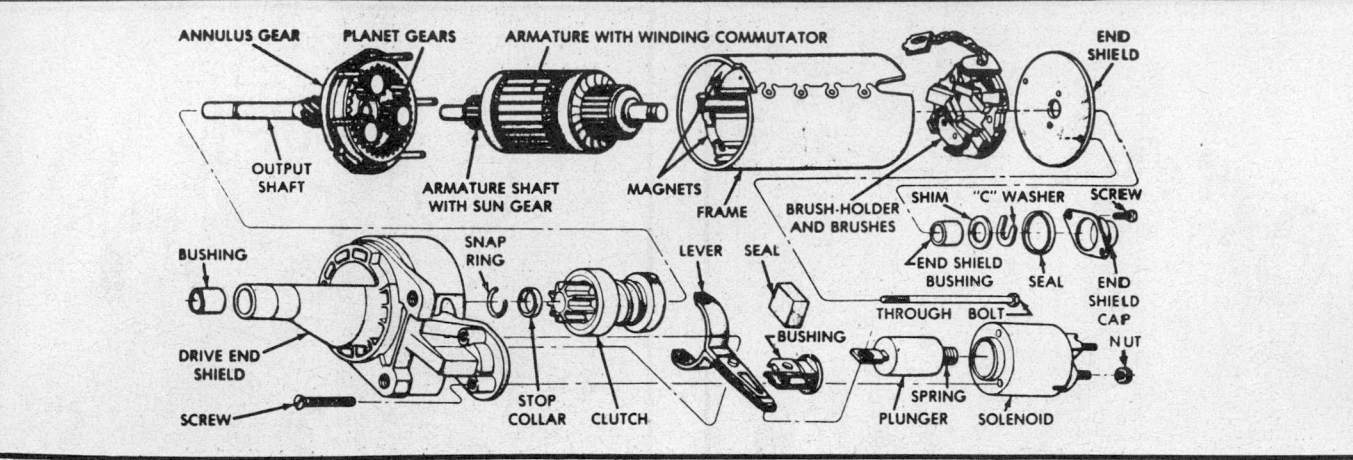

Exploded view of the Bosch reduction starter–Chrysler and AMC Eagle Premier and Summit

2. Remove the through bolts and the splash shield. Remove the end shield screws from the brush plate and the end shield.

3. Slide the brushes from the holders. Pry the retaining springs back for access and remove the brush plate.

4. Slide the armature from the starter housing. Remove the starter housing from the gear housing and the solenoid terminal cover.

5. Remove the solenoid terminal nut/washer, the battery terminal nut/washer and the solenoid terminal assembly from the terminal posts.

6. Remove the solenoid terminal and the battery terminal from the insulator.

7. Remove the solenoid cover screws, the solenoid cover, the seal, the solenoid plunger from the housing and the plunger spring.

8. Remove the gear housing-to-solenoid screws and separate the gear housing from the solenoid housing.

9. Remove the reduction gear and clutch assembly from the gear housing.

10. Remove the reduction gear, pinion gear, retainer and roller assembly from the gear housing.

11. Inspect and clean all parts, as required. Repair or replace defective parts as required. Brushes that are worn less than ½ the length of new brushes or oil soaked should be replaced.

12. To assemble, reverse the disassembly procedures.

Bosch Reduction Starter

AMC AND CHRYSLER

Disassembly and Assembly

1. Position the assembly in a soft jawed vise. Remove the field terminal nut, the terminal and the washer.

2. Remove the solenoid-to-starter screws. Work the solenoid from the shift fork and remove the solenoid from the starter.

3. Remove the starter end shield bushing cap screws, the starter end shield bushing cap, the end shield bushing and C-washer.

4. Remove the starter end shield bushing washer and seal.

5. Remove the starter through bolts, the starter end shield and the brush plate.

6. Slide the field frame from the starter and over the armature. Remove the armature assembly from the drive end housing.

7. Remove the rubber seal from the drive end housing. Remove the starter drive gear train.

8. Remove the dust plate. Press the stop collar from the snapring. Using snapring pliers, loosen the snapring.

9. Remove the output shaft snapring, the clutch stopring col-

lar and the clutch assembly from the starter.

10. Remove the clutch shift lever bushing, the clutch shift lever and the C-clip retainer.

11. Remove the retaining washer, the sun and the planetary gears from the annulus gear.

12. To assemble, lubricate the necessary parts and reverse the disassembly procedures. Replace all defective components as required.

Ford Positive Engagement Starter

Disassembly and Assembly

1. Remove the starter from the vehicle. Position the unit in a soft jawed vise.

2. Remove the cover screw, the cover, through bolts, starter drive end housing and the starter drive plunger lever return spring.

3. Remove the pivot pin from the starter gear plunger lever, the lever and the armature. Remove the stopring retainer and the thrust washer from the armature shaft.

4. Remove the stopring from the groove in the armature shaft and discard it. Remove the starter drive gear assembly, the brush end plate and insulator assembly.

5. Remove the brushes from the plastic brush holder and lift out the brush holder. Note the location of the holder in relation to the end terminal.

6. Remove the ground brush screws. Remove the sleeve and the retainer by bending up the edge of the sleeve which is inserted in the rectangular hole of the frame.

7. Using the tool 10044–A or equivalent, remove the pole retaining screws. An arbor press may have to be used in conjunction with the special tool.

8. Cut the positive brush leads from the coil fields as close to the field connection as possible.

9. Check the commutator for runout. If the commutator is rough, has flat spots or is more than 0.005 in. out of round, reface it.

10. Inspect the armature shaft and the bearings for scoring and excessive wear; replace it, if necessary. Inspect the starter drive; if the gear teeth are pitted, broken or excessively worn, replace the starter drive.

Assembly:

11. Lubricate the necessary parts and reverse the disassembly procedures.

12. Solder the field coil-to-starter switch terminal posts. Check for continuity and grounds in the assembled coils.

13. Position the ground brushes-to-starter frame and rivet securely.

14. Install the starter motor drive gear assembly onto the ar-

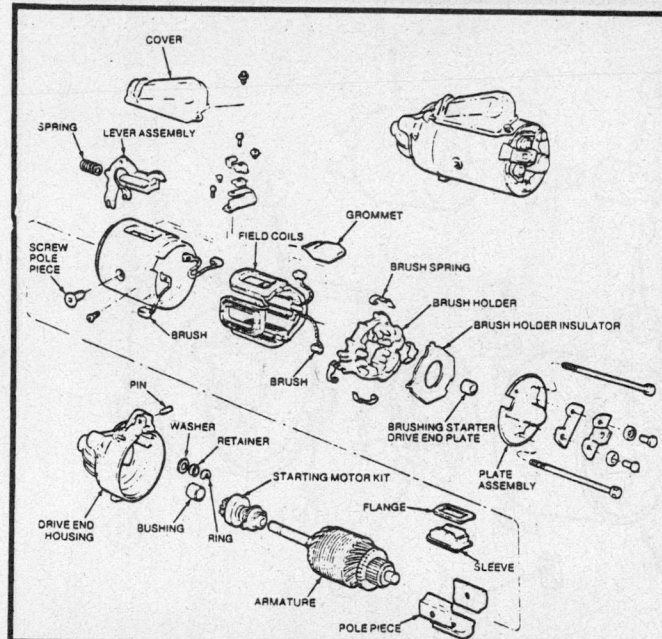

Ford positive engagement starter—exploded view (4 in. plunger pole) showing assembly sequence of components

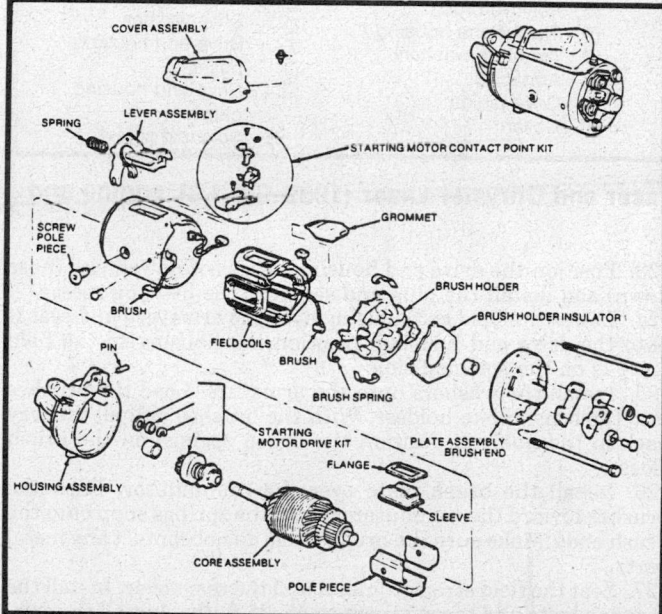

Ford positive engagement starter—exploded view (4.5 in. plunger pole) showing assembly sequence of components

mature shaft. Install a new stopring, a new stopring retainer and thrust washer.

15. Install the armature.

16. Position the drive gear plunger lever to the frame and starter drive assembly. Fill the end housing bearing bore a ¼ full or grease. Position the drive end housing onto the frame and make sure the return spring engages the lever tang. Install the pivot pin.

17. Install the brush holder, the brushes and the brush springs; make sure the brushes are positioned properly to avoid grounding.

18. Install the brush end plate; be sure the end plate insulator is positioned correctly on the end plate.

19. Install the through bolts and torque to 55–80 inch lbs. (6–9 Nm).

20. Install the starter drive plunger ever cover and tighten the screw.

21. Check the starter no-load current draw; it should be 80 amps.

Ford Direct Drive Starter

FORD FESTIVA AND TRACER CHRYSLER LASER 1.8L AND EAGLE SUMMIT

Disassembly and Assembly

1. Position the starter in a soft jawed vice.

2. Remove the field strap-to-solenoid nut and the field strap.

3. Remove the solenoid-to-drive end housing screws. Remove the solenoid from the housing by guiding it away from the drive end housing and the plunger.

4. Disconnect the plunger from the drive yoke. If shims are present between the solenoid and the starter, save them for reinstallation; the shims determine the starter pinion depth clearance.

5. Remove the starter housing through bolts. Separate the starter housing from the drive end housing.

6. Remove the rear cover-to-field frame screws, separate the strap grommet from the rear cover and remove the rear cover.

7. Using a small pry bar, lift the retaining springs and remove the brushes from their channels.

NOTE: Before removing the brush plate, remove the brushes from the plate; this will prevent possible damage to the brushes.

8. Note the position of the yoke and separate it from the drive pinion. Remove the armature and the drive pinion from the drive housing.

9. From the drive housing, remove the yoke, seal and washer.

NOTE: When removing the drive pinion, do not clamp it in a vise, for damage to the internal parts may occur.

10. Using a deep socket or equivalent, drive the armature collar towards the armature to expose the snapring. Remove the snapring from the armature's groove and slide the drive pinion from the armature.

11. Using an ohmmeter, check the each commutator-to-armature core for grounds; there should be no movement of the ohmmeter indicator. If the ohmmeter indicates a ground, replace the armature.

12. Inspect the commutator burn spots, scored surface and/or dirt. Using a set of V-blocks and a dial indicator, check the commutator runout. If the runout is greater than 0.002 in., refinish the commutator or replace the armature.

13. Using a micrometer, check the commutator's outer diameter; if it is less than 1.220 in., replace the armature.

NOTE: Never use emery cloth to clean the commutator face.

14. Inspect the depth of the insulating material between the commutator segments; it should be greater than 0.008 in. If necessary to undercut the insulating material, use a broken hacksaw blade and scrap the material to a depth of 0.020–0.031 in.

15. If the armature core shows signs of scuffing, the bushings are probably worn and need replacement.

16. Inspect the field coil for corrosion, insulation burnt/bare

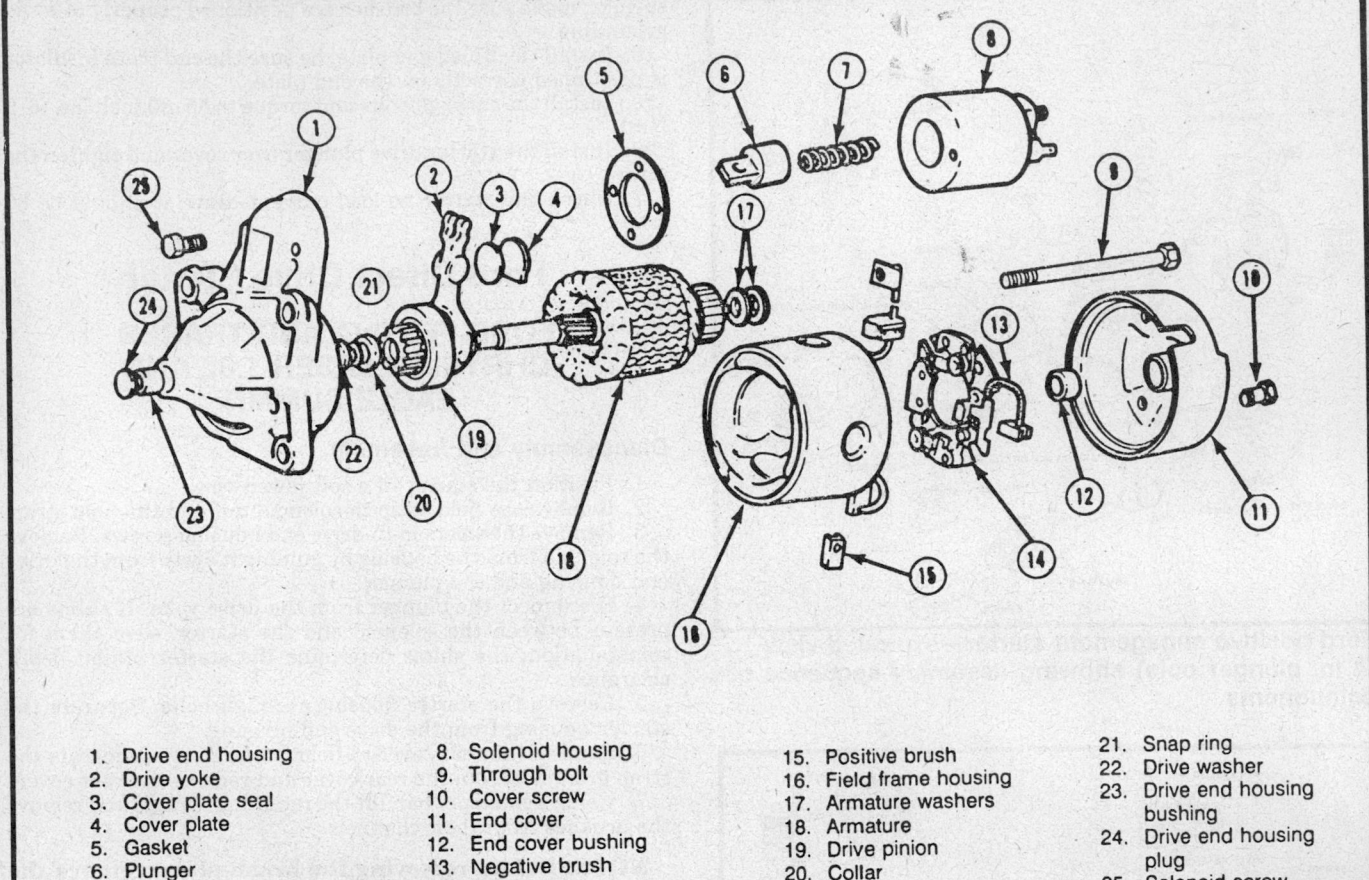

1. Drive end housing	8. Solenoid housing	15. Positive brush	21. Snap ring
2. Drive yoke	9. Through bolt	16. Field frame housing	22. Drive washer
3. Cover plate seal	10. Cover screw	17. Armature washers	23. Drive end housing
4. Cover plate	11. End cover	18. Armature	bushing
5. Gasket	12. End cover bushing	19. Drive pinion	24. Drive end housing
6. Plunger	13. Negative brush	20. Collar	plug
7. Plunger spring	14. Brush plate		25. Solenoid screw

Exploded view of the Ford direct drive starter — Festiva, Tracer and Chrysler Laser (1989–90) 1.8L engine and Eagle Summit

spots and/or deterioration; if necessary, replace the field coil housing assembly.

17. Using an ohmmeter, check the field strap connector-to-brushes for continuity; if there is no continuity, replace the field coil housing assembly.

18. Using an ohmmeter, check for continuity between the field strap connector and the field coil housing; if there is continuity, replace the field coil housing assembly. When performing this test, be certain the brushes and wires are not touching the housing.

19. Measure the brush lengths for wear, if they are near or beyond 0.453 in., replace the brushes.

20. To inspect the drive pinion, perform the following procedures:

    a. Inspect the drive pinion teeth for excessive wear or milling. If either condition exists, the drive pinion and flywheel (manual) or flexplate (automatic) must be replaced.

    b. To check the one-way clutch, try to turn the drive pinion in both directions; it should turn freely one-way and lock up the other way.

Assembly:

21. Lubricate the armature splines with Lubriplate® 777 or equivalent. Install the drive pinion and the locking collar on the armature. Install the snapring and pull the collar over the snapring to secure it.

22. Using Lubriplate® 777 or equivalent, lubricate the shift fork and install it into the drive end housing. Engage the armature assembly into the drive end housing and couple the shift fork with the drive pinion.

23. Position the drive end housing into a soft jawed vise (nose down) and install the plug and seal into the housing recess.

24. Lower the field coil housing over the armature and seat it onto the drive end housing; position the housing so the field strap is on the solenoid side.

25. Install the washers onto the armature. Load the brushes into the brush plate holders. With the brushes pull all the way back in the holders, position the brush springs on the brush sides.

26. Install the brush plate over the commutator. Push the brushes toward the commutator until the springs snap onto the brush ends. Make sure the brush wires do not contact any metal parts.

27. Seat the field strap grommet and the rear cover. Install the through bolts and torque them to 55–75 ft. lbs. Install the solenoid and shims, if equipped.

28. To check the pinion depth, perform the following procedures:

    a. If the field strap was connected to the solenoid terminal, disconnect it.

    b. Using a 12V battery, attach the negative (−) terminal to the solenoid's M-terminal and the positive (+) terminal to the solenoid's S-terminal; this will energize the solenoid.

NOTE: When energizing the solenoid, do not engage it for more than 20 seconds. Between each engagement, allow it to cool for at least 3 minutes.

    c. Using a feeler gauge and the solenoid energized, check the drive pinion-to-collar gap; it should be 0.020–0.080 in. If

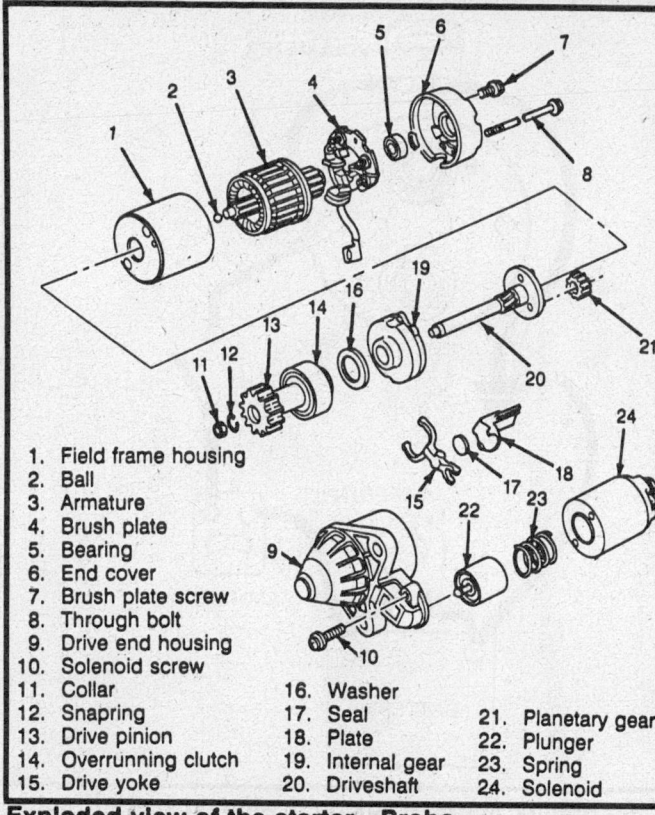

1. Field frame housing
2. Ball
3. Armature
4. Brush plate
5. Bearing
6. End cover
7. Brush plate screw
8. Through bolt
9. Drive end housing
10. Solenoid screw
11. Collar
12. Snapring
13. Drive pinion
14. Overrunning clutch
15. Drive yoke
16. Washer
17. Seal
18. Plate
19. Internal gear
20. Driveshaft
21. Planetary gear
22. Plunger
23. Spring
24. Solenoid

Exploded view of the starter—Probe

necessary, add or subtract shims between the solenoid and drive end housing until the desired depth is achieved.

Ford Probe Starter

Disassembly and Assembly

1. Secure the starter in a soft jawed vise.
2. Remove the field wire from the solenoid's M-terminal Remove the solenoid-to-starter screws and pull the solenoid from the starter; if there are any shims, save them for reinstallation purposes.
3. Disconnect the plunger and spring from the drive yoke.
4. Matchmark the end cover-to-field frame housing position. Remove the brush plate screws, the starter housing through bolts, the end cover, washer and brush holder assembly.
5. Remove the armature and the field frame housing; be careful not to lose the gear assembly ball.
6. Remove the internal gear gasket, the 3 planetary gears, the solenoid cover plate and seal and pull the gear assembly from the drive end housing.
7. Remove the gear assembly ball. Note the direction of the drive yoke faces and remove it from the gear assembly.
8. Using a deep socket, drive the collar from the snapring. From the driveshaft, remove the snapring. the collar, the drive pinion the internal gear and washer.
9. Using a small prybar, remove the brushes from the brush plate.
10. To inspect the armature, perform the following procedures:
    a. Using digital volt-ohmmeter, check for continuity between the commutator's segments and core; if there is continuity, replace the armature. Check for continuity between the commutator's segments and the shaft; it there is continuity, replace the armature.
    b. Using a set of V-blocks and a dial micrometer, measure the commutator's runout; if the runout is more than 0.002 in.

(0.05mm), lightly turn the commutator on a lathe. If the commutator's runout is excessive, replace the armature.
    c. Using a micrometer, check the commutator's outer diameter; if it is less than 1.13 in. (28.8mm), replace the armature.
    d. Using commutator sand paper, clean the commutator's face of burnt spots and/or scoring; do not use emery cloth.
    e. If the depth between the commutator segments is less than 0.008 in. (0.2mm), use a broken hacksaw blade to undercut the insulating material to 0.020–0.031 in. (0.5–0.8mm).
11. Inspect the armature bearing for looseness, binding or abnormal noise; if necessary, replace it.
12. Inspect the drive pinion and flywheel ring gear for wear, milling and/or chipping; if necessary, replace the drive pinion and/or ring gear.
13. Inspect the internal and planetary gears for wear and/or damage; replace the gears if, necessary.
14. Inspect the brushes for wear by measuring the amount of useable brush remaining; the new brush is 0.69 in. (17.5mm) and the wear limit is 0.39 in. (10.0mm). Check the brushes for free movement in the brush holder; if necessary, clean the brush channels.

Assembly:

15. Using Lubriplate® 777 or equivalent, lubricate the necessary parts.
16. Onto the armature, install the washer, the internal gear, the drive pinion and collar.
17. Install the snapring into the driveshaft groove and press the collar over the snapring.
18. Install the drive yoke onto the gear assembly; be sure the drive yoke faces the correct direction.
19. Install the gasket onto the internal gear. Slide the gear assembly into the drive end housing. Install the solenoid cover plate seal and cover plate.
20. Install the planetary gears and ball. Align the matchmarks and install the field frame housing onto the drive end housing.
21. Position the brushes into the brush holder and secure the brushes by positioning the brush springs on the side of the brushes.
22. Position the brush holder over the armature's commutator and adjust the brush springs so they press the brushes onto the commutator.
23. Slide the armature/brush holder assembly into the field frame housing and align the matchmarks. Install the through bolts and the brush holder screws.
24. Connect the plunger and spring into the drive yoke. Install the solenoid onto the drive end housing; be sure to replace any shims that were removed.
25. Using a 12V battery, connect the negative (−) lead to the starter frame and the positive (+) lead to the solenoid's "S" terminal; the solenoid should kick out the pinion.

NOTE: Do not engage the solenoid for more than 20 seconds at a time and allow 3 minutes for the solenoid to cool before attempting to energize it again.

26. With the solenoid activated, use a feeler gauge, measure the gap between the pinion and the collar; the gap should be 0.02–0.08 in. (0.5–2.0mm). If the gap is outside the measurement range, add or subtract shims until it is within specifications.
27. Install the field strap to the M-terminal on the solenoid and torque the nut to 90–110 inch lbs. (10–12 Nm).

Delco 5MT, 10MT and 27MT Starters

NOTE: In 1989, the identification for the 5MT starter was converted to the SD200 and SD250 starters.

Disassembly and Assembly

1. Remove the starter from the vehicle. Position the unit in a soft jawed vise.

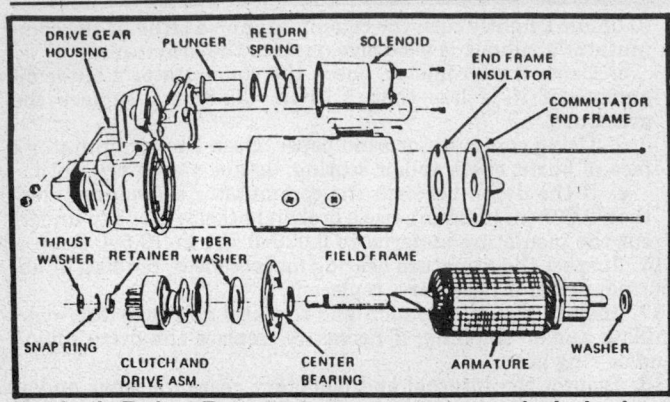

Typical Delco-Remy starter motor—exploded view showing assembly sequence of components

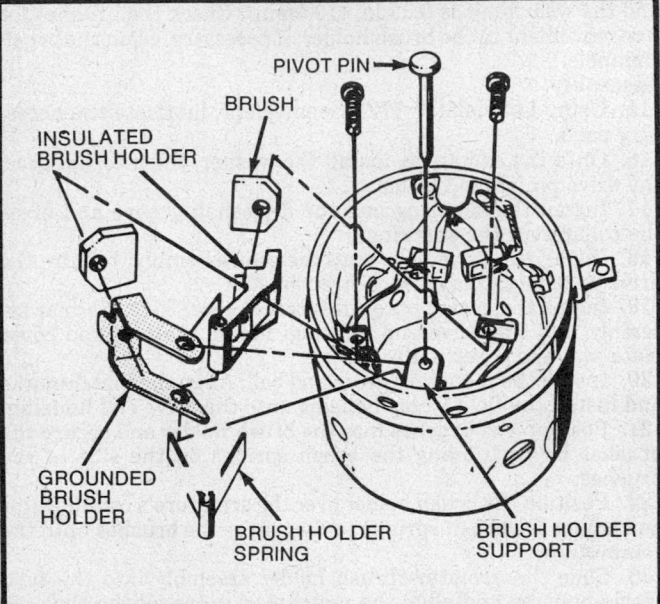

Delco-Remy starter brush replacement—all except 5 MT starter

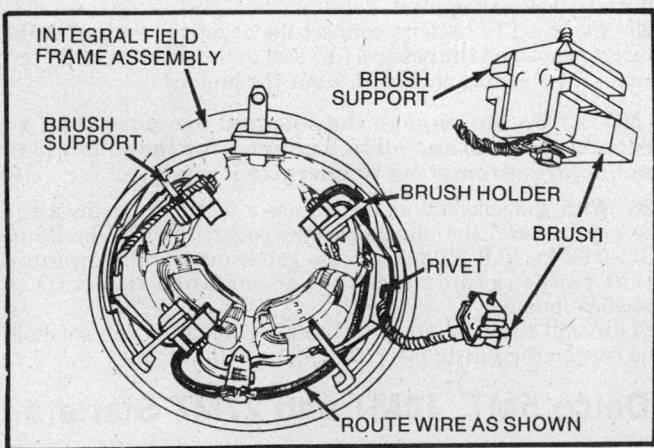

Delco-Remy 5 MT starter—Brush replacement

2. Remove the field coil connector screw and the solenoid-to-starter screws. Rotate the solenoid 90 degrees and remove it along with the plunger return spring.

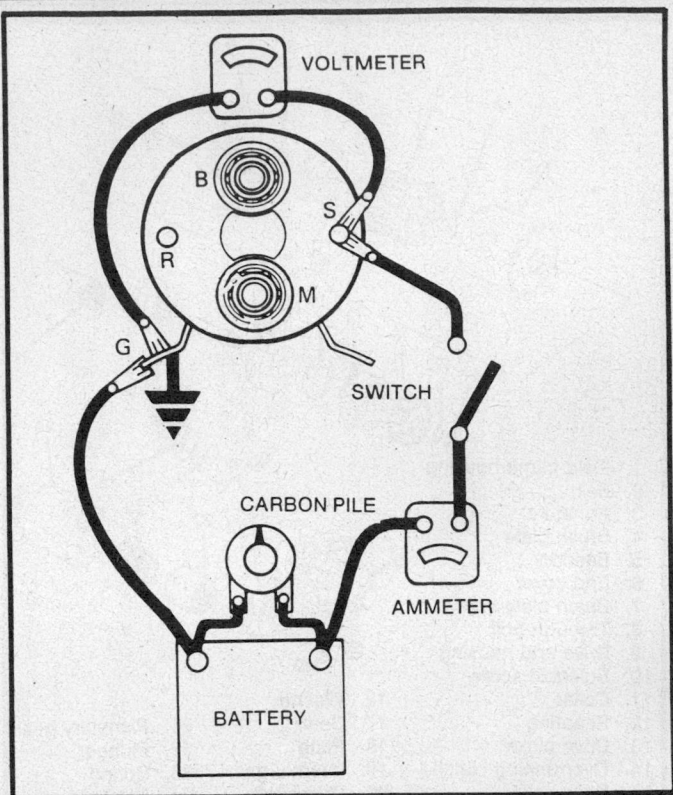

Delco-Remy starter—solenoid winding test—if solenoid is on car, the connector strap must be removed before making tests

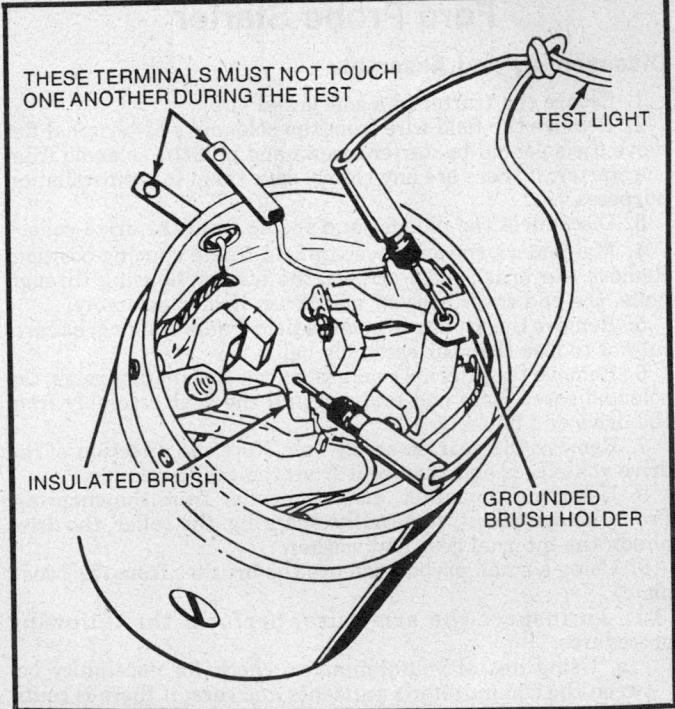

Delco-Remy starter—shunt coil test—using a test light do not let strap terminals touch case or other ground

3. Remove the starter through bolts, the commutator end frame and washer.

4. Remove the field frame assembly from the drive gear housing.

5. If equipped, remove the center bearing screws. Remove the drive gear housing from the armature shaft.

6. To remove the overrunning clutch from the armature shaft, perform the following procedures:

    a. Remove the washer or collar from the armature shaft.

    b. Using a ⅝ in. deep socket, slide it over the shaft and against the retainer. Using the socket as a driving tool, tap it with a hammer to move the retainer of the snapring.

    c. Remove the snapring from the groove in the shaft; if the snapring is distorted, replace it.

    d. Remove the retainer and the clutch assembly from the armature shaft.

7. If required, the shaft lever and the plunger can be disassembled by removing the roll pin.

8. To replace the starter brushes, remove the brush holder pivot pin which positions the insulated and the ground brushes. Remove the brush spring.

9. On 5MT starters, to replace the brushes remove the screw from the brush holder and separate the brushes from the holder.

10. Inspect armature commutator, shaft and bushings, overrunning clutch pinion, brushes and springs for discoloration, damage or wear; replace the damaged parts.

11. Check fit of armature shaft in bushing in drive housing. The shaft should fit snugly in the bushing; if it is worn, replace it.

12. Inspect armature commutator. If commutator is rough, it should be refinished on a lathe. Do not undercut or turn to less than 1.650 in. O.D. Inspect the points where the armature conductors join the commutator bars to make sure they have a good connection. A burned commutator bar is usually evidence of a poor connection.

13. Using a growler and holding hacksaw blade over armature core while armature is rotated, inspect the armature for short circuits. If saw blade vibrates, armature is shorted.

14. Using a test lamp place a lead on the shunt coil terminal and connect the other lead to a ground brush. The test should be made using both ground brushes to insure continuity through the brushes and leads. If the lamp fails to light, the field coil is open and will require replacement.

15. Using a test lamp place a lead on the series coil terminal and the other on the insulated brush. If the lamp fails to light the series coil is open and will require repair or replacement. The test should be made from each insulated brush to check brush and lead continuity.

16. If equipped with a shunt coil separate the series and shunt coil strap terminals during the test. Do not allow the strap terminals to touch case or other ground. Using a test lamp place a lead on the grounded brush holder and the other lead on either insulated brush. If the lamp lights a grounded series coil is indicated and must be repaired or replaced.

NOTE: If the solenoid has not been removed from the starter, the connector strap terminals must be removed before making the following tests. Complete the tests as fast as possible in order to prevent overheating the solenoid.

17. To check the starter winding, connect an ammeter in series with 12V battery and the switch terminal on the solenoid. Connect a voltmeter to the switch terminal and to ground. Connect a carbon pile across battery. Adjust the voltage to 10V and note the ammeter reading; it should be 14.5–16.5 amperes.

18. To check both windings, connect as for previous test and ground the solenoid motor terminal. Adjust the voltage to 10V and note the ammeter reading; it should be 41–47 amperes.

19. Current draw readings over specifications indicate shorted turns on a ground in the windings of the solenoid; the solenoid

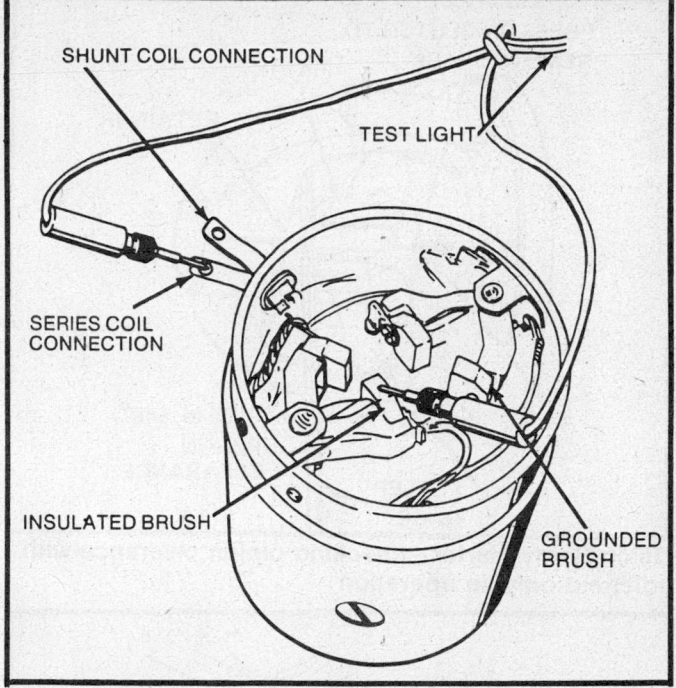

Delco-Remy starter—coil test—using a test light If lamp fails to light the series coil is open and must be repaired or replaced

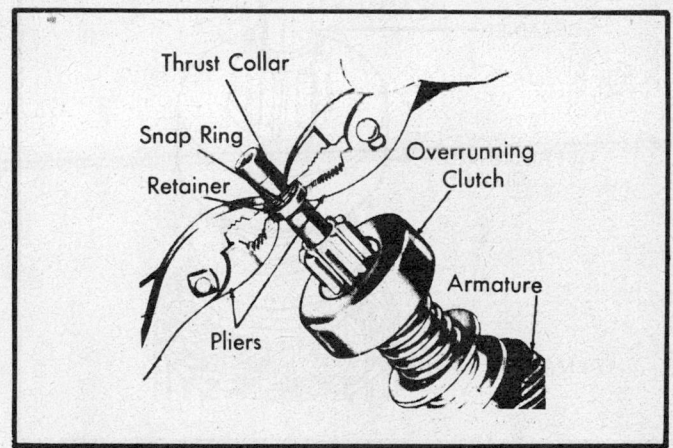

Delco-Remy starter—installing overrunning clutch thrust collar onto armature shaft

should be replaced. Current draw readings under specifications indicate excessive resistance. No reading indicates an open circuit. Check the connections and replace the solenoid (if necessary). Current readings will decrease as the windings heat up.
Assembly:

20. To assemble, reverse the disassembly procedures. Be sure to replace or repair all defective components as required.

NOTE: When the starter has been disassembled or the solenoid replaced, it is necessary to check the pinion clearance. Pinion clearance must be checked in order to prevent the buttons on the shift lever yoke from rubbing on the clutch collar during engine cranking.

21. To check the pinion clearance, perform the following procedures:

    a. Disconnect the motor field coil connector from the solenoid motor terminal and insulate the terminal.

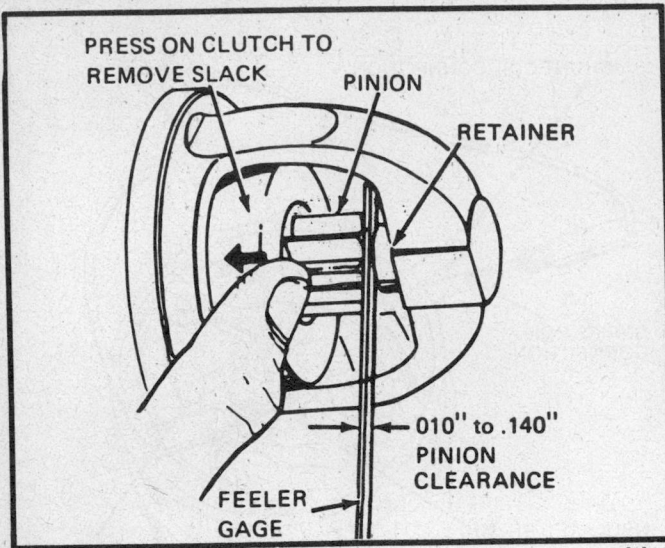

Delco-Remy starter—checking pinion clearance-with solenoid only, in operation

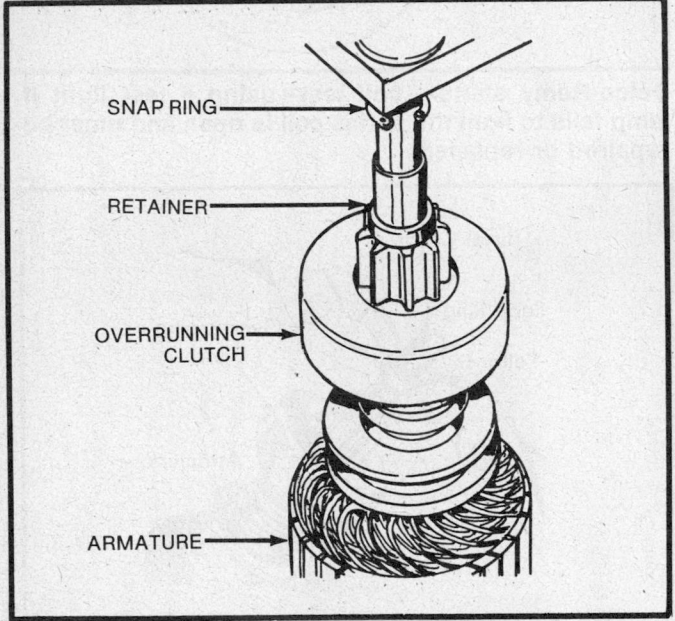

Delco-Remy starter—installing overrunning clutch thrust collar snap ring onto armature shaft

b. Connect the positive 12V battery lead to the solenoid switch terminal and the negative lead to the starter frame.

c. Touch a jumper lead momentarily from the solenoid motor terminal to the starter frame; this will shift the pinion into cranking position and remain there until the battery is disconnected.

d. Using a feeler gauge, push the pinion back as far as possible and check the clearance; the clearance should be 0.010–0.140 in.

e. Pinion clearance adjustment is not provided on the starter motor. If the clearance does not fall within limits check for improper installation and replace all worn parts.

Delco 15MT/GR Starter

Disassembly and Assembly

1. Remove the starter from the vehicle. Position the unit in a soft jawed vise.

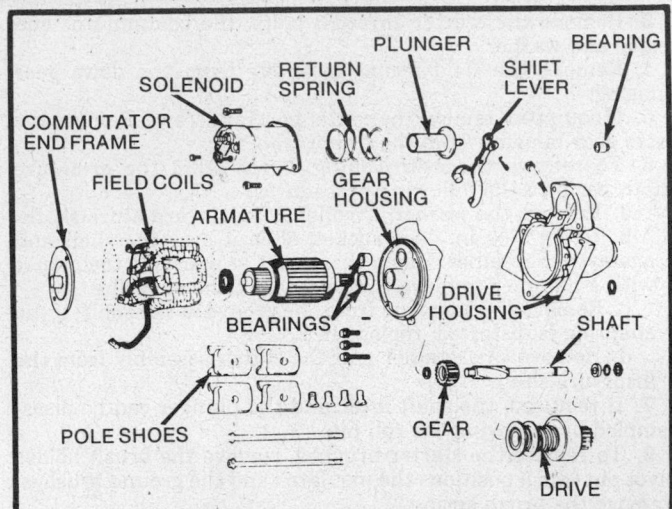

Delco-Remy 15 MT/GR starter—exploded view showing assembly sequence of components

2. Remove the field coil screw, the field frame through bolts and separate the field frame assembly from the drive gear assembly. Separate the armature and the commutator end frame from the field frame.

3. Remove the solenoid screws and the solenoid from the drive housing.

4. Remove the retaining ring, shift lever shaft and housing through bolts. Separate the drive assembly, drive housing and gear assembly.

5. To remove the overrunning clutch from the armature shaft, perform the following procedures:

a. Remove the washer or collar from the armature shaft.

b. Using a 5/8 in. deep socket, slide it over the shaft and against the retainer. Use the socket as a driving tool, tap the socket with a hammer to move the retainer off of the snapring.

c. Remove the snapring from the groove in the shaft; if the snapring is distorted, replace it.

d. Remove the retainer and the clutch assembly from the armature shaft.

6. To replace the starter brushes, remove the brush holder pivot pin which positions the insulated and the ground brushes. Remove the brush spring.

7. Inspect armature commutator, shaft and bushings, overrunning clutch pinion, brushes and springs for discoloration, damage or wear; replace the damaged parts (if necessary). Check the armature shaft fit in drive housing bushing; the shaft should fit snugly in the bushing. If the bushing is worn, it should be replaced.

8. Inspect armature commutator. If commutator is rough, it should be refinished on a lathe; do not undercut or turn to less than 1.650 in. O.D. Inspect the points where the armature conductors join the commutator bars to make sure they have a good connection. A burned commutator is usually evidence of a poor connection.

9. Using a growler and holding hacksaw blade over armature core while armature is rotated, check the armature for short circuits; if the saw blade vibrates, the armature is shorted.

10. Using a test lamp, place a lead on the shunt coil terminal and the other lead to a ground brush. The test should be made from both ground brushes to insure continuity through both brushes and leads. If the lamp fails to light, the field coil is open and will require replacement.

11. Using a test lamp, place a lead on the series coil terminal and the other lead on the insulated brush. If the lamp fails to light, the series coil is open and will require repair or replace-

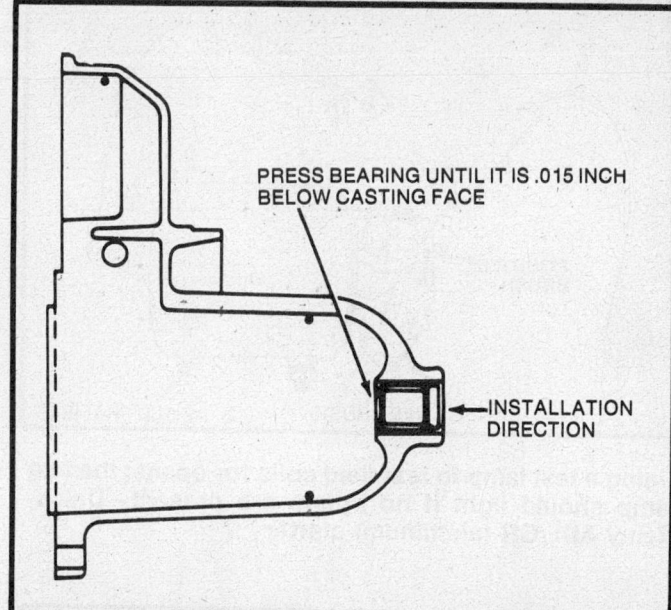

Replacing the gear housing bearing—Delco-Remy 15MT/GR

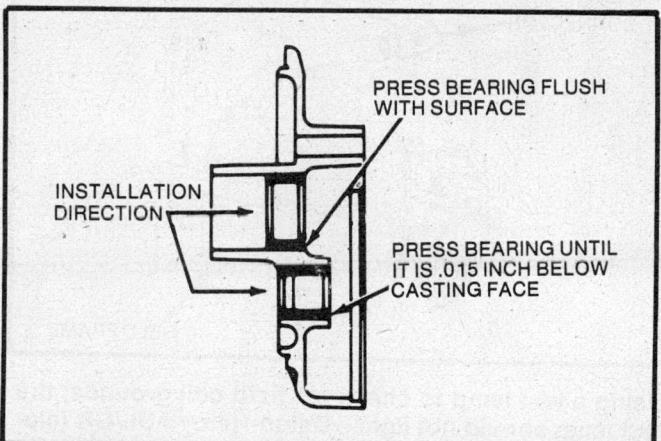

Delco-Remy 15 MT/GR starter—drive housing bearing replacement

ment. The test should be made from each insulated brush to check brush and lead continuity.

12. If equipped with a shunt coil, separate the series and shunt coil strap terminals during this test; do not allow the strap terminals to touch the case or other ground. Using a test lamp, place a lead on the grounded brush holder and the other lead on either insulated brush. If the lamp lights, a grounded series coil is indicated and must be repaired or replaced.

NOTE: If the solenoid has not been removed from the starter, the connector strap terminals must be removed before making the following tests. Complete the tests as fast as possible in order to prevent overheating the solenoid.

13. To check the starter winding, connect an ammeter in series with a 12V battery, the switch terminal and to ground. Connect a carbon pile across the battery. Adjust the voltage to 10V and note the ammeter reading; it should be 14.5–16.5 amperes.

14. To check both windings, connect as for previous test. Ground the solenoid motor terminal, adjust the voltage to 10V and note the ammeter reading; it should be 41–47 amperes.

Exploded view of the Delco-Remy AUL/GR (aluminum) starter

15. Current draw readings above specifications indicate shorted turns or a ground in the windings of the solenoid; the solenoid should be replaced. Current draw readings under specifications indicate excessive resistance. No reading indicates an open circuit. Check the connections and replace solenoid (if necessary). Current readings will decrease as windings heat up.

Assembly:

16. The roller bearing in the drive housing and the roller bearings in the gear housing must be replaced (if they are dry); do not lubricate or reuse the bearings.

17. To replace the gear housing bearing, use a tube or solid cylinder that just fits inside the housing to push bearing toward the armature side. In the opposite direction, use the tube or cylinder to press bearing flush with housing.

18. To replace the gear housing driveshaft bearing, use a tube or collar that just fits inside the housing and press bearing out; press against the open end of bearing. To install a new bearing, press against the closed end, using a thin wall tube or collar that fits in space between bearing and housing. Do not press against the flat end of the bearing; this will bend the thin metal of the bearing. As required, replace the drive housing bearing.

19. To assemble, reverse the disassembly procedures. Be sure to replace or repair all defective components as required.

NOTE: When the starter has been disassembled or the solenoid replaced, it is necessary to check the pinion clearance. The pinion clearance must be checked in order to prevent the buttons on the shift lever yoke from rubbing on the clutch collar during engine cranking.

20. To check the pinion clearance, perform the following procedures:

  a. Disconnect the motor field coil connector from the solenoid motor terminal and insulate the terminal.

  b. Connect the positive (+) 12V battery lead to the solenoid switch terminal and the other to the starter frame.

  c. Touch a jumper lead momentarily from the solenoid motor terminal to the starter frame; this will shift the pinion into cranking position and retain it until the battery is disconnected.

d. Using a feeler gauge, push the pinion back as far as possible, to take up any movement, and check the clearance; the clearance should be 0.010–0.140 in.

e. Means for adjusting pinion clearance is not provided on the starter motor. If the clearance does not fall within limits, check for improper installation and replace worn parts.

Delco ALU/GR Aluminum Starter

Disassembly and Assembly

1. Remove the starter from the vehicle. Position the unit in a soft jawed vise.

2. Remove the field connector nut, the solenoid switch screws and the solenoid.

3. If equipped with shims between the solenoid and the drive end housing, retain these for installation purposes.

4. Remove the starter through bolts and the brush holder bolts. Remove the commutator end frame from the armature and bearing assembly. Remove the field frame assembly and the armature from the center housing.

5. Pry back each brush spring so that each brush can be backed away from the armature about ¼ in. Release the spring to hold the brushes in the backed out position, then remove the armature from the field frame and brush holder.

6. Remove the shaft cover-to-center housing screws and the shaft cover. Remove the C-shaped washer and plate. Remove the center housing bolts, the center housing shim and thrust washers.

7. Remove the reduction gear, the spring holder and the lever springs.

8. To remove the drive pinion, perform the following procedures:

a. Using a ⅝ in. socket, slide it over the shaft against the stopper.

b. Using the socket as a driving tool, tap it with a hammer to move the stopper off the ring.

c. Remove the stopper and the drive pinion.

9. Remove the pinion shaft and the lever assembly. Note the direction of the lever and the lever holders.

10. Clean all parts in the proper cleaning solution. Inspect all parts for wear and damage; replace or repair defective components as required. Inspect all bearings for wear, roughness or dryness; replace damaged bearings with new ones.

11. Inspect the armature commutator. If the commutator is rough, it should be refinished on a lathe; do not turn the commutator to less than 1.480 in. outside diameter.

12. With the brush holder assembly still attached to the field frame, test the field coils for open. Using a test lamp, place a test lead on the field coil connector and the other test lead on the positive (+) brush.

13. The test light should turn **ON**. If the test light fails to light, the field coil is open; the field coil must be replaced. Repeat the test on the other positive brush.

14. To test the field coil for ground, place a test light lead on the field coil connector and the other lead on the field frame; the test light should stay **OFF**. If the test light turns **ON**, the field coils are grounded to the field frame assembly; the field frame must be replaced.

Assembly:

15. To replace the brushes, remove the positive brushes from the brush holder, the brush holder and the negative brush assembly from the field frame.

16. Cut the old brush leads off of their mountings as close to brush connection point as possible. Solder the new brushes as required. Careful installation of the positive side is necessary to prevent grounding of the brush connection point having no insulation.

17. Reinstall the positive and negative brushes in the brush holder assembly and position the assembly in the starter housing.

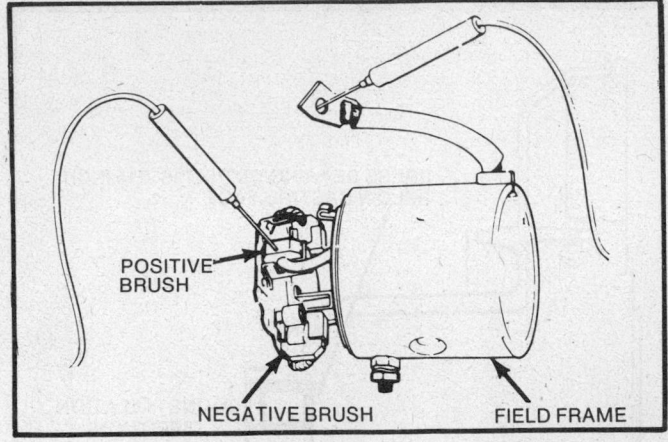

Using a test lamp to test field coils for opens; the test lamp should light if no opens are present—Delco-Remy AUL/GR (aluminum) starter

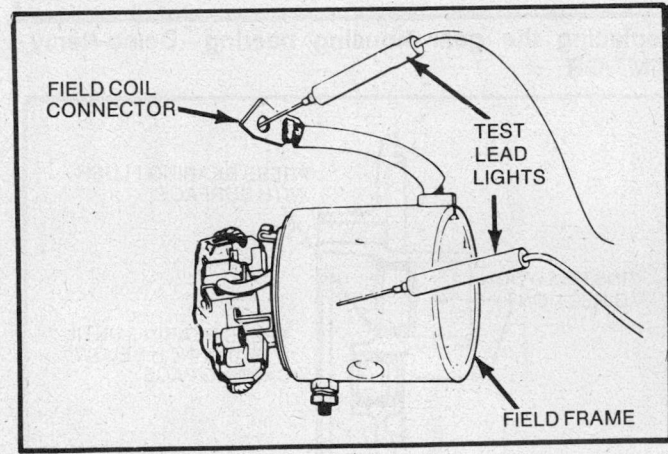

Using a test lamp to check for field coil grounds; the test lamp should not light—Delco-Remy AUL/GR (aluminum) starter

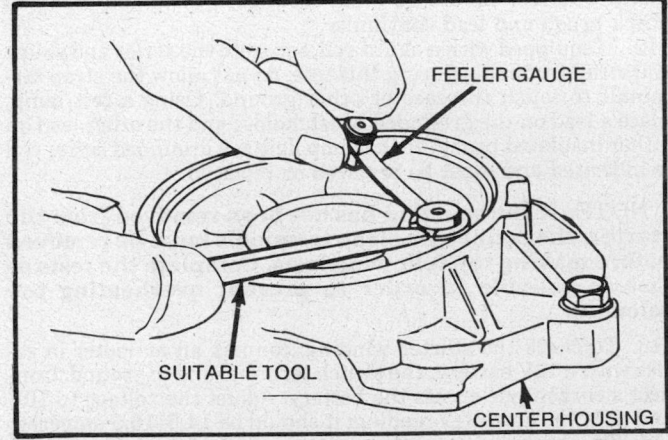

Checking the pinion shaft end play—Delco-Remy AUL/GR (aluminum) starter

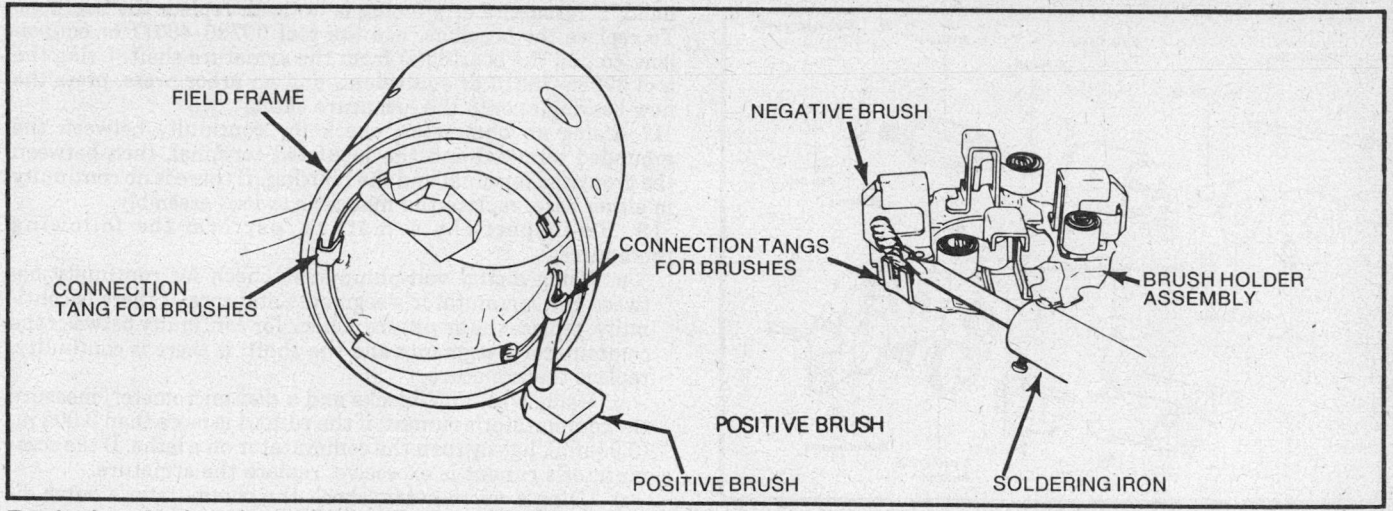

Replacing the brushes—Delco-Remy AUL/GR (aluminum) starter

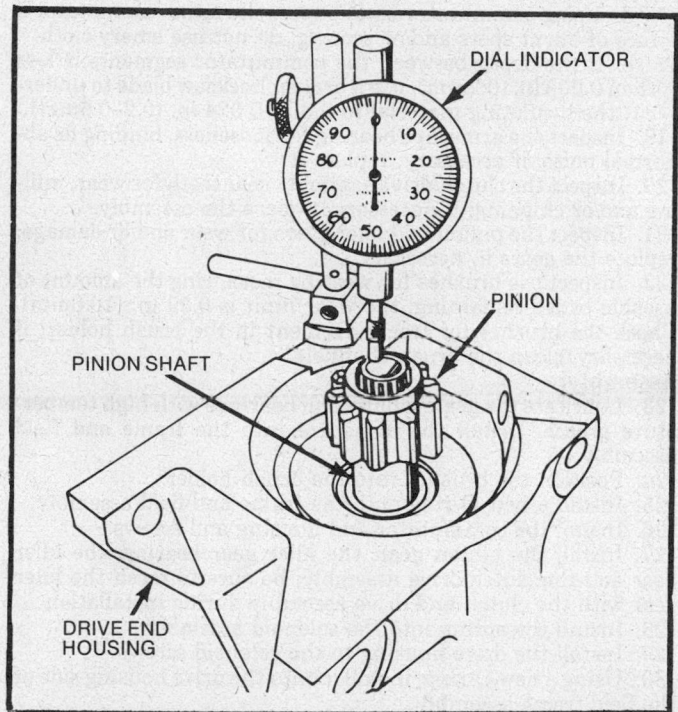

Using a dial indicator to check the drive pinion end play—it should be 0.20–0.80 in.—Delco-Remy AUL/ GR (aluminum) starter

18. In order to replace the drive end bearing, it will be necessary to press the bearing out of the drive end housing using a press. Replace the armature commutator end bearing and the armature drive end bearing.

19. To assemble, reverse the disassembly procedures. Be sure to check all parts for wear and damage; repair or replace defective parts.

20. If either the drive end housing, pinion shaft, reduction gear, shim washers or center housing were replaced, it will be necessary to check the endplay for the pinion shaft. Install the plate and C-shaped washer onto the end of the pinion shaft.

21. With the drive end housing mounted in a soft jawed vise, measure the endplay. Insert feeler gauge between C-washer and cover plate, pry the pinion shaft in the axial direction to check the endplay; it should be 0.004–0.020 in.

22. If the endplay is not correct, remove the plate, C-shaped washer, center bracket and add or remove the shim thrust washers to adjust the endplay and recheck.

NOTE: Shim thrust washers are available in 2 thicknesses 0.010 in. and 0.020 in.

23. When the starter has been disassembled or the solenoid switch has been replaced, it is necessary to check the pinion position. Pinion position must be correct to prevent the top of the lever from rubbing on the clutch collar during cranking.

24. Connect the positive lead of a 12V battery to the "S" terminal on the switch and momentarily connect the other to the starter frame. This will shift the pinion into cranking position and will retain it until the battery is disconnected. Do not leave engaged more than 30 seconds at a time.

25. Using a dial indicator (with pinion engaged), push the pinion shaft back by hand and measure the amount of pinion shaft movement; the clearance should be 0.020–0.080 in.

26. If the amount does not fall within limits, adjust it by adding or removing the shims which are located between the switch and the front bracket; adding shims decreases the amount of the movement. Solenoid switch shims are available in 2 thicknesses 0.020 in. and 0.010 in.

Chevrolet Nova and Geo Prism Starter

Disassembly and Assembly

1. Position the assembly in a soft jawed vise. Remove the nut and disconnect the motor wire from the magnetic switch terminal.

2. Remove the through bolts and pull the field frame (with the armature) from the magnetic switch assembly.

3. On the 1.0 KW type, remove the felt seal from the armature shaft; on the 1.4 KW type, remove the field frame to magnetic switch assembly O-ring.

4. Remove the starter housing to magnetic switch assembly bolts and separate the housing from the assembly.

5. On the 1.0 KW type, remove the idler gear and the clutch assembly. On the 1.4 KW type, remove the pinion gear, the idler gear and the clutch assembly.

6. Using a magnetic finger, remove the spring and the steel ball from the hole in the clutch assembly shaft.

7. Remove the field frame end cover. On the 1.4 KW type, remove the large O-ring.

8. Using a small pry bar, separate the brush springs, remove

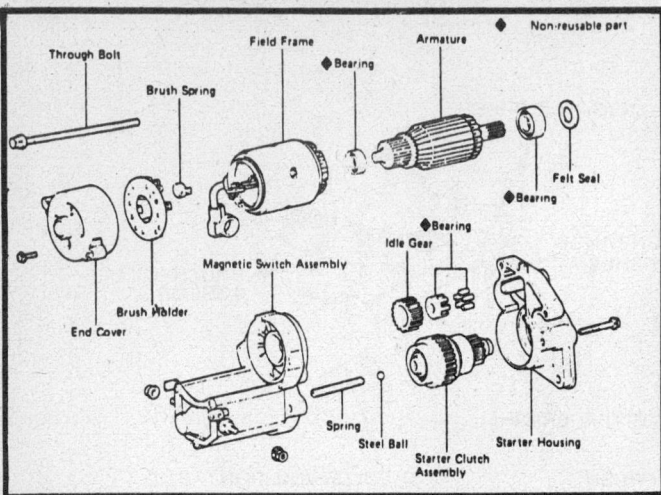

Exploded view of the 1.0 KW Nippondenso starter—GM Nova

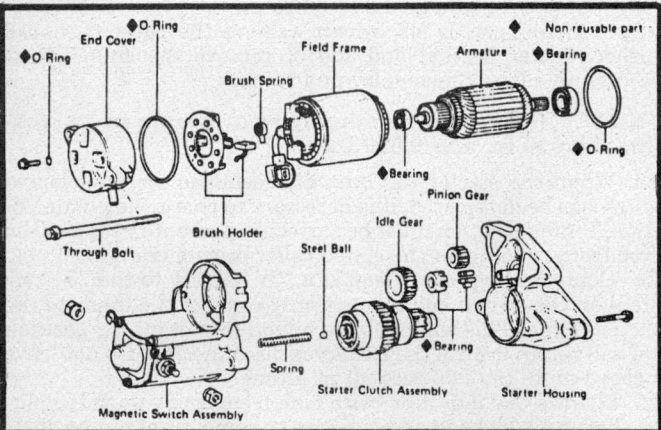

Exploded view of the 1.4 KW Nipondenso starter—Chevrolet Nova (1986–88)—Geo Prism (1989–90) similar

the brushes from the brush holder and pull the brush holder from the field frame. Remove the armature from the field frame.

9. Using an ohmmeter, make sure there is no continuity between the commutator and the armature coil core; if there is continuity, replace the armature.

10. Using an ohmmeter, check for continuity between the commutator segments. If there is no continuity between any of the segments, replace the armature.

11. If the commutator is dirty, burnt or the runout exceeds 0.0020 in., use a lathe to clean the surface; do not machine the diameter to less than 1.14 in. diameter.

12. Using an ohmmeter, make sure there is continuity between the lead wire and the brush lead of the field coil; if there is no continuity, replace the field frame.

13. Using an ohmmeter, make sure there is no continuity between the field coil and the field frame; if there is continuity, replace the field frame.

14. If the brush length is less than 0.335 in. (1.0 KW) or 0.394 in. (1.4 KW), replace the brush and dress with emery cloth.

15. Check the gear teeth for wear or damage, if damaged, replace them. Turn the clutch assembly pinion clockwise and make sure that it rotates freely, try to turn the pinion counterclockwise and make sure that it locks. If the pinion does not respond correctly, replace it.

16. While applying inward force on the bearings, turn each by hand; if resistance or sticking is noticed, replace the bearings. To replace the bearings, use the tool 09286–46011 or equivalent, to pull the bearing(s) from the armature shaft. Using the tool 09285–76010 or equivalent, and an arbor press, press the new bearing(s) onto the armature shaft.

17. Using an ohmmeter, check for continuity between the grounded terminal and the insulated terminal, then between the grounded terminal and the housing. If there is no continuity in either case, replace the magnetic switch assembly.

18. To inspect the armature, perform the following procedures:

  a. Using digital volt-ohmmeter, check for continuity between the commutator's segments and core; if there is continuity, replace the armature. Check for continuity between the commutator's segments and the shaft; it there is continuity, replace the armature.

  b. Using a set of V-blocks and a dial micrometer, measure the commutator's runout; if the runout is more than 0.002 in. (0.05mm), lightly turn the commutator on a lathe. If the commutator's runout is excessive, replace the armature.

  c. Using a micrometer, check the commutator's outer diameter; if it is less than 1.14 in. (29mm), replace the armature.

  d. Using commutator sand paper, clean the commutator's face of burnt spots and/or scoring; do not use emery cloth.

  e. If the depth between the commutator segments is less than 0.008 in. (0.2mm), use a broken hacksaw blade to undercut the insulating material to 0.008–0.024 in. (0.2–0.6mm).

19. Inspect the armature bearing for looseness, binding or abnormal noise; if necessary, replace it.

20. Inspect the clutch/drive assembly gear teeth for wear, milling and/or chipping; if necessary, replace the assembly.

21. Inspect the pinion and idler gears for wear and/or damage; replace the gears if, necessary.

22. Inspect the brushes for wear by measuring the amount of useable brush remaining; the wear limit is 0.39 in. (10.0mm). Check the brushes for free movement in the brush holder; if necessary, clean the brush channels.

Assembly:

23. Lubricate the gears, shafts and bearings with high temperature grease. Install the armature into the frame and field assembly.

24. Position the brushes into the brush holder.

25. Install a new O-ring onto the frame and field assembly.

26. Install the commutator end housing and screws.

27. Install the pinion gear, the idler gear bearing, the idler gear and the clutch/drive assembly; be sure to mesh the idler gear with the clutch and drive assembly during installation.

28. Install the spring into the solenoid assembly.

29. Install the drive housing to the solenoid screws.

30. Using a new O-ring, install it onto the drive housing side of the field frame assembly.

31. Align the matchmarks and install the field frame assembly onto the drive housing. Install and torque the through bolts to 33 ft. lbs. (45 Nm).

32. Install the lead wire to the starter solenoid terminal and torque the nut to 26 ft. lbs. (35 Nm).

Chevrolet Sprint Starter

Disassembly and Assembly

AUTOMATIC TRANSAXLE

1. Position the starter in a soft jawed vise. Remove the nut and disconnect the motor wire from the magnetic switch terminal.

2. Remove the through bolts and pull the field frame (with the armature) from the magnetic switch assembly.

3. Remove the starter housing to magnetic switch assembly bolts and separate the housing from the assembly. Remove the

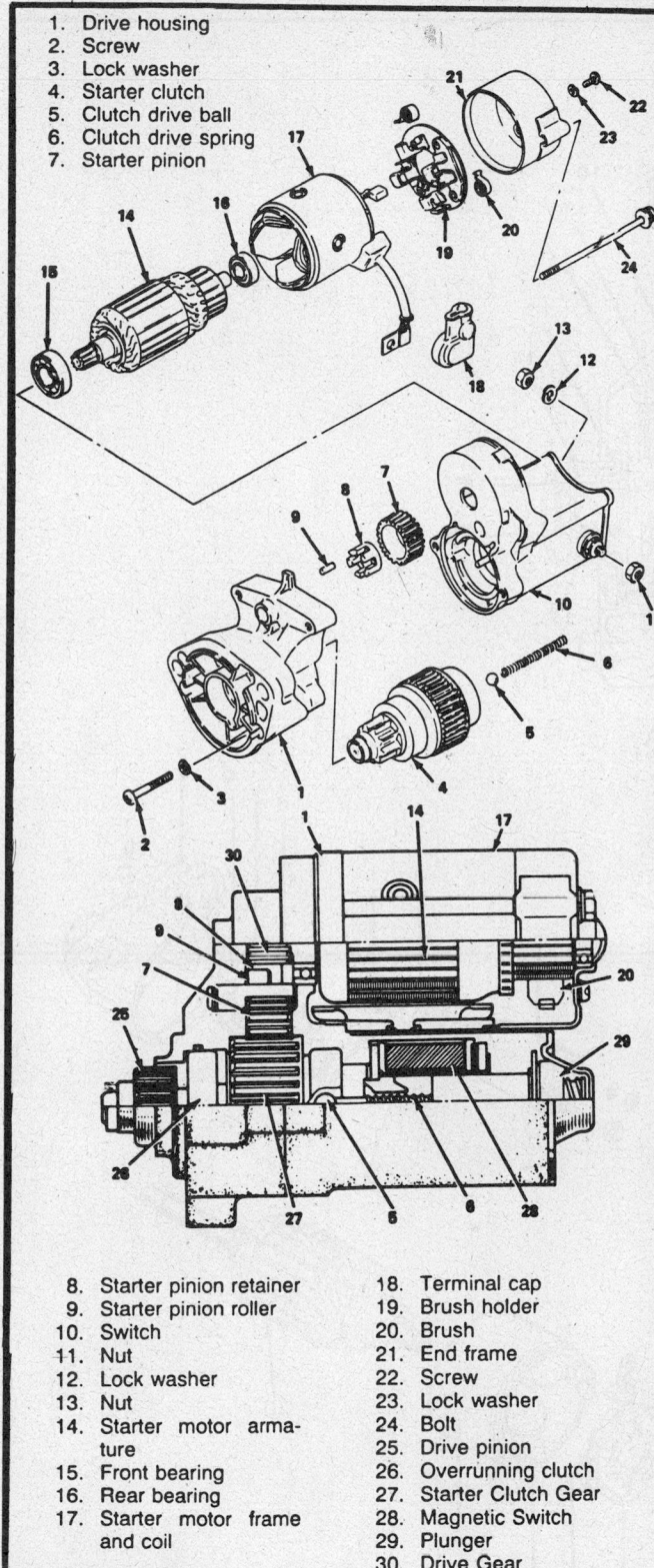

1. Drive housing
2. Screw
3. Lock washer
4. Starter clutch
5. Clutch drive ball
6. Clutch drive spring
7. Starter pinion

8. Starter pinion retainer	18.	Terminal cap
9. Starter pinion roller	19.	Brush holder
10. Switch	20.	Brush
11. Nut	21.	End frame
12. Lock washer	22.	Screw
13. Nut	23.	Lock washer
14. Starter motor arma- ture	24.	Bolt
	25.	Drive pinion
15. Front bearing	26.	Overrunning clutch
16. Rear bearing	27.	Starter Clutch Gear
17. Starter motor frame and coil	28.	Magnetic Switch
	29.	Plunger
	30.	Drive Gear

Exploded view of the automatic transaxle starter—Chevrolte Sprint (1986–88).

pinion gear, the pinion retainer/bearings and the clutch assembly.

4. Using a magnetic finger, remove the spring and the steel ball from the hole in the clutch assembly shaft. Remove the field frame end cover.

5. Using a small pry bar, separate the brush springs, then remove the brushes from the brush holder and pull the brush holder from the field frame.

6. Remove the armature from the field frame. Using an ohmmeter, make sure there is no continuity between the commutator and the armature coil core. If there is continuity, replace the armature.

7. Using an ohmmeter, check for continuity between the commutator segments. If there is no continuity between any of the segments, replace the armature.

8. If the commutator is dirty, burnt or the runout exceeds 0.002 in., use a lathe to reface the surface; do not machine the diameter to less than 1.140 in. diameter.

9. Using an ohmmeter, make sure there is continuity between the lead wire and the brush lead of the field coil. If there is no continuity, replace the field frame.

10. Using an ohmmeter, make sure there is no continuity between the field coil and the field frame. If there is continuity, replace the field frame.

11. If the brush length is less than 0.394 in., replace the brush and dress with emery cloth.

12. Check the gear teeth for wear or damage, if damaged, replace them. Turn the clutch assembly pinion clockwise and make sure it rotates freely, try to turn the pinion counterclockwise and make sure it locks. If the pinion does not respond correctly, replace it.

13. While applying inward force on the bearings, turn each by hand; if resistance or sticking is noticed, replace the bearings. To replace the bearings, use the tool 09286–46011 or equivalent, to pull the bearing(s) from the armature shaft. Using the tool 09285–76010 or equivalent, and an arbor press, press the new bearing(s) onto the armature shaft.

14. Using an ohmmeter, check for continuity between the grounded terminal and the insulated terminal, then between the grounded terminal and the housing. If there is no continuity in either case, replace the magnetic switch assembly.

Assembly:

15. Lubricate the gears, the shafts and bearings with high temperature grease.

16. Install the over-running clutch, the pinion and the retainers with the rollers into the housing.

17. Install the spring to the magnetic switch and assembly the housing and the magnetic switch.

18. Install the brushes into the brush holder; make sure the positive brush leads are not grounded.

19. Install the rear end frame to the yoke, engage the tab with the wire grommet and install the cover.

20. Install the yoke to the magnetic switch, engage the tab on the yoke with the magnetic switch notch.

21. To complete the installation, reverse the removal procedures.

Chevrolet Sprint and Geo Metro Starter

Disassembly and Assembly

MANUAL TRANSAXLE

1. Position the starter in a soft jawed. Disconnect the field coil wire from the solenoid terminal.

2. Remove the solenoid mounting screws and work the solenoid from the shift fork. Remove the bearing cover, the armature shaft lock, the washer, the spring and the seal.

3. Remove the commutator end frame cover through bolts, the cover, the brushes and the brush plate.

4. Slide the field frame from over the armature. Remove the shift lever pivot bolt, the rubber gasket and the metal plate.

5. Remove the armature assembly and the shift lever from

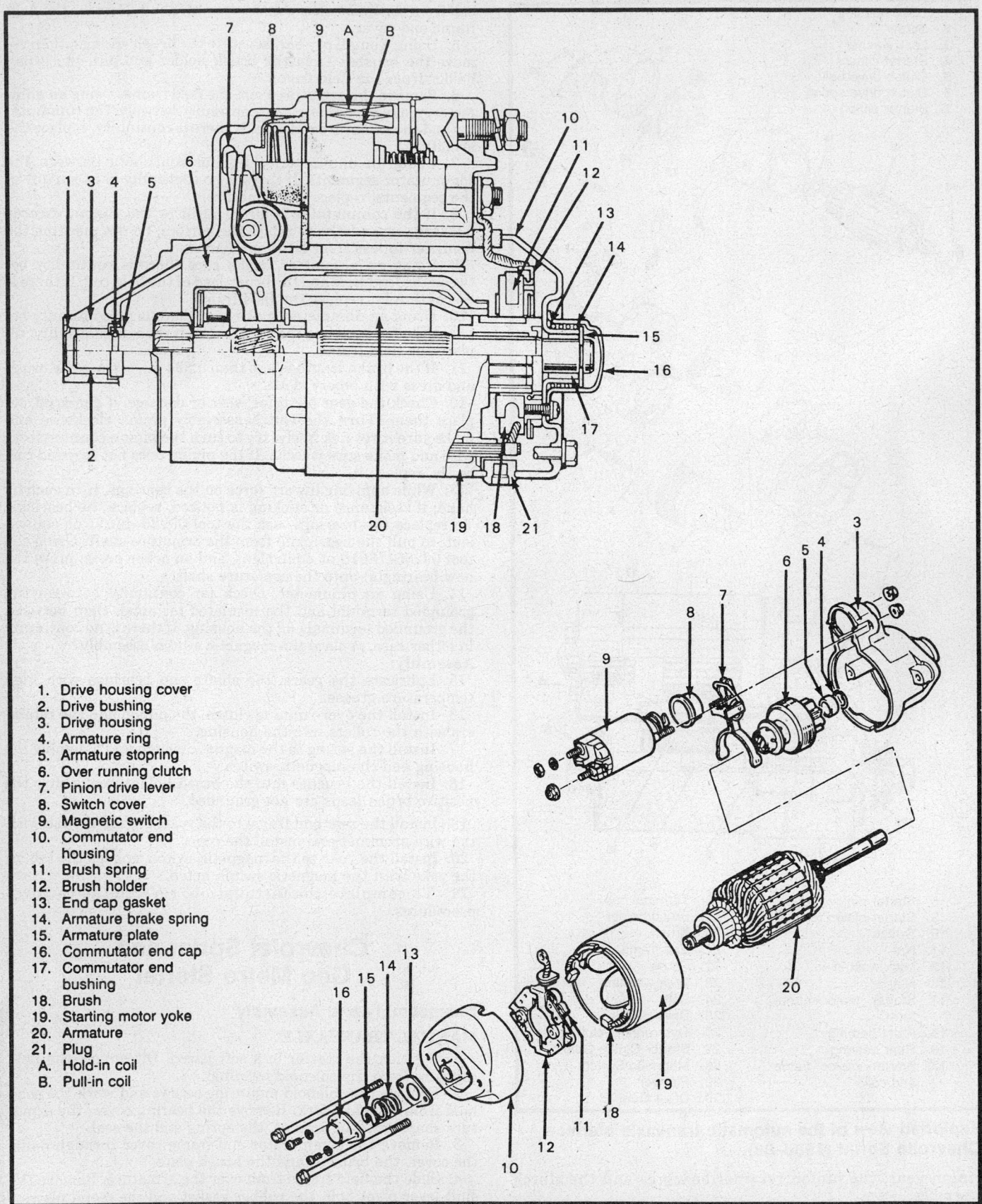

1. Drive housing cover
2. Drive bushing
3. Drive housing
4. Armature ring
5. Armature stopring
6. Over running clutch
7. Pinion drive lever
8. Switch cover
9. Magnetic switch
10. Commutator end housing
11. Brush spring
12. Brush holder
13. End cap gasket
14. Armature brake spring
15. Armature plate
16. Commutator end cap
17. Commutator end bushing
18. Brush
19. Starting motor yoke
20. Armature
21. Plug
A. Hold-in coil
B. Pull-in coil

Exploded view of the manual transaxle starter — Chevrolet Sprint (1986–88) and Geo Metro (1989–90)

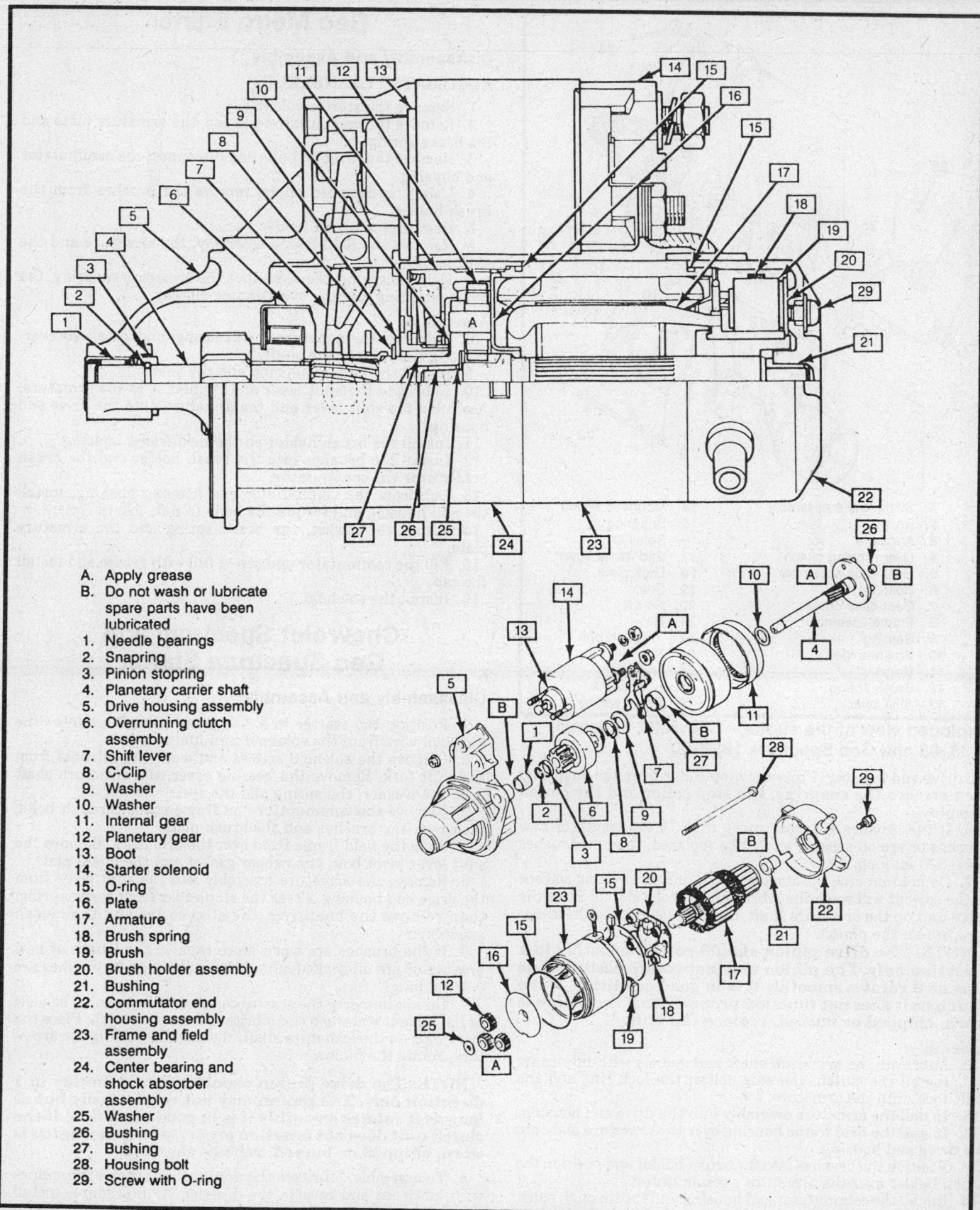

A. Apply grease
B. Do not wash or lubricate spare parts have been lubricated
1. Needle bearings
2. Snapring
3. Pinion stopring
4. Planetary carrier shaft
5. Drive housing assembly
6. Overrunning clutch assembly
7. Shift lever
8. C-Clip
9. Washer
10. Washer
11. Internal gear
12. Planetary gear
13. Boot
14. Starter solenoid
15. O-ring
16. Plate
17. Armature
18. Brush spring
19. Brush
20. Brush holder assembly
21. Bushing
22. Commutator end housing assembly
23. Frame and field assembly
24. Center bearing and shock absorber assembly
25. Washer
26. Bushing
27. Bushing
28. Housing bolt
29. Screw with O-ring

Exploded view of the manual transaxle starter—Geo Metro 1989–90

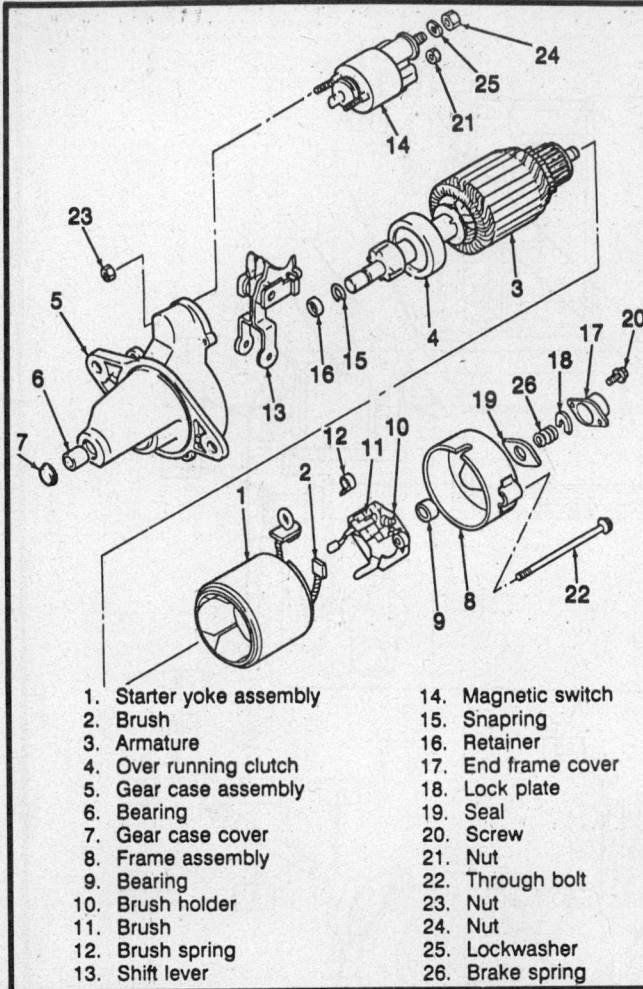

1. Starter yoke assembly	14. Magnetic switch
2. Brush	15. Snapring
3. Armature	16. Retainer
4. Over running clutch	17. End frame cover
5. Gear case assembly	18. Lock plate
6. Bearing	19. Seal
7. Gear case cover	20. Screw
8. Frame assembly	21. Nut
9. Bearing	22. Through bolt
10. Brush holder	23. Nut
11. Brush	24. Nut
12. Brush spring	25. Lockwasher
13. Shift lever	26. Brake spring

Exploded view of the starter—Chevrolet Spectrum 1986–88 and Geo Spectrum 1989–90

the drive end housing. Press the stop collar from the snapring, then remove the snapring, the stop collar and the clutch assembly.

6. If the brushes are worn more than ½ the length of new brushes or are oil-soaked, should be replaced; the new brushes are 0.630 in. long.

7. Do not immerse the starter clutch unit in cleaning solvent as the solvent will wash the lubricant from the clutch. Place the drive unit on the armature shaft, then, while holding the armature, rotate the pinion.

NOTE: The drive pinion should rotate smoothly in 1 direction only. The pinion may not rotate easily but as long as it rotates smoothly it is in good condition. If the clutch unit does not function properly or if the pinion is worn, chipped or burred, replace the unit.

Assembly:
8. Lubricate the armature shaft and splines with lubricant.
9. Install the clutch, the stop collar, the lock ring and the shift fork onto the armature.
10. Install the armature assembly into the drive end housing.
11. Install the field frame housing over the armature and onto the drive end housing.
12. Position the brushes into the brush holder and position the brush holder over the armature's commutator.
13. Install the commutator end housing and the through bolts.
14. Install the cap end gasket, the armature brake spring, the armature plate and the commutator end cap.

Geo Metro Starter

Disassembly and Assembly
AUTOMATIC TRANSAXLE
1. Remove the starter solenoid.
2. Remove the commutator end cap, the armature plate and the brake spring.
3. Remove the through bolts and disconnect the commutator end housing.
4. Using needle nose pliers, remove the brushes from the brush holder.
5. Remove the brush holder.
6. Remove the field frame assembly, the armature and the shift lever.
7. Using snapring pliers, remove the armature snapring, the pinion stopring and the overrunning clutch.

Assembly:
8. Lubricate the armature shaft bearings and install the overrunning clutch onto the shaft.
9. Install the pinion stopring and the snapring.
10. Lubricate the shift lever and connect it to the armature. Assemble the shift lever and the armature onto the drive end housing.
11. Install the brush holder on the field frame housing.
12. Install the brushes into the brush holder and the brush holder over the commutator.
13. Lubricate the commutator end housing bushing, install the end housing and torque the bolts to 6 ft. lbs. (8 Nm).
14. Install the gasket, the brake spring and the armature plate.
15. Fill the commutator end cap ½ full with grease and install the cap.
16. Install the solenoid.

Chevrolet Spectrum and Geo Spectrum Starter

Disassembly and Assembly

1. Position the starter in a soft jawed vise. Disconnect the field coil wire from the solenoid terminal.
2. Remove the solenoid screws and work the solenoid from the shift fork. Remove the bearing cover, the armature shaft lock, the washer, the spring and the seal.
3. Remove the commutator end frame cover through bolts, the cover, the brushes and the brush plate.
4. Slide the field frame from over the armature. Remove the shift lever pivot bolt, the rubber gasket and the metal plate.
5. Remove the armature assembly and the shift lever from the drive end housing. Press the stop collar from the snapring, then remove the snapring, the stop collar and the clutch assembly.
6. If the brushes are worn more than ½ the length of new brushes or are oil-soaked, should be replaced; new brushes are 0.63 in. long.
7. Do not immerse the starter clutch unit in cleaning solvent as the solvent will wash the lubricant from the clutch. Place the drive unit on the armature shaft, then, while holding the armature, rotate the pinion.

NOTE: The drive pinion should rotate smoothly in 1 direction only. The pinion may not rotate easily but as long as it rotates smoothly it is in good condition. If the clutch unit does not function properly or if the pinion is worn, chipped or burred, replace the unit.

8. To assemble, lubricate the armature shaft and the splines with lubricant and reverse the disassembly procedure. Install the clutch, the stop collar, the lock ring and the shift fork onto the armature.

AMERICAN MOTORS

Front Suspension

FRONT WHEEL ALIGNMENT

Front wheel alignment refers to the various angles formed by the components that control the front wheel turning mechanism. There are 3 adjustable alignment angles which are caster, camber and toe-in.

Caster describes the forward or rearward tilt of the steering knuckle. Tilting the top of the knuckle rearward provides positive caster. Tilting the top of the knuckle forward provides negative caster. Caster is directional stability angle which enables the front wheels to return to a straight ahead position after turns.

Adjust caster by loosening the strut rod jamnut and turning the rod adjusting nuts in or out to move the lower control arm forward or rearward to obtain the desired caster angle.

Camber describes the inward and outward tilt of the wheel relative to the center of the automobile. An inward tilt of the top of the wheel produces negative camber. An outward tilt produces positive camber. Camber greatly affects tire wear. Incorrect camber will cause abnormal wear of the tire outside or inside edge. Adjust camber by turning the lower control arm inner pivot bolt eccentric.

NOTE: On the Medallion, Premier and Summit, the caster and camber are built-in angles that are non-adjustable. If either angle is incorrect, it will be necessary to identify the suspension or steering component contributing to the incorrect angle and repair or replace as required.

Toe-in is a condition that exists when the measured distance at the front of each tire is less than the distance at the rear of the tires. When the distance at the front is less than the rear, the tires are toed-in. Toe-in compensates for normal steering play and causes the tires to roll in a straight ahead manner. Incorrect toe-in will wear the tires in a feathered edged pattern. Adjust toe-in by turning tie rod adjuster tubes in or out to shorten or lengthen tie rods to obtain desired toe-in. Position the front wheels in the straight ahead position and center the steering wheel and gear. Turn the tie rod adjusting tubes equally in opposite directions to obtain the desired toe-in setting. If the steering wheel spoke position was disturbed during the toe-in adjustment, correct the spoke position by turning the tie rod tubes equally in the same direction until the desired position is obtained.

The front suspension on the Medallion, Premier and Summit is designed for front wheel toe-out. The toe setting is adjusted only after the steering gear has been secured in a center position. Toe adjustment is accomplished by turning the steering tie rods in or out as required.

NOTE: Do not use the tie rod adjusting sleeves to recenter the steering wheel on Premier and Medallion vehicles. The proper method of recentering the steering wheel on these vehicles is to remove the steering wheel and recenter on the steering shaft as necessary. After the steering wheel is properly positioned, torque the steering wheel retaining nut to 30 ft. lbs.

FRONT WHEEL BEARINGS

Adjustment

These vehicles have a unique front axle hub and bearing assembly. The assembly is sealed and does not require lubrication, periodic maintenance, or adjustment. The hub has ball bearings

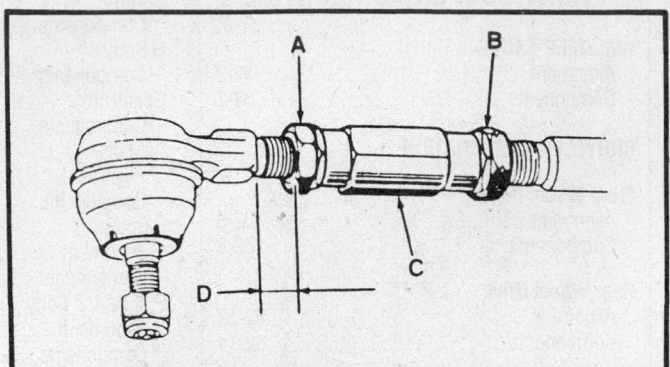

Toe-out adjustment on Medallion and Premier. Locknut "A" has right hand threads and locknut "B" has left hand threads

which seat in races machined directly into the hub. There are darkened areas surrounding the bearing race areas of the hub. These darkened areas are from a heat treatment process and are to be considered normal and therefore should not be mistaken for a problem condition.

Removal and Installation

EXCEPT MEDALLION, PREMIER AND SUMMIT

1. Raise and safely support the vehicle.
2. Remove the wheel assembly. Remove the caliper and position it aside. Secure the brake caliper to the chassis with a piece of wire. Remove the rotor.
3. Remove the bolts attaching the axle shaft flange to the halfshaft.
4. Remove the cotter pin, locknut and axle hub nut from the assembly.
5. Remove the halfshaft.
6. Remove the steering arm from the steering knuckle.
7. Remove the caliper anchor plate from the steering knuckle.
8. Remove the Torx© head bolts retaining the hub assembly.
9. Remove the hub assembly from the steering knuckle pin. Remove any grease remaining in the steering knuckle cavity.
10. Remove and set the front hub spacer aside. During removal, it may be lodged on the end of the halfshaft or on the hub shaft. If a replacement hub is to be used, the hub spacer must be installed on the new hub assembly.

To install:

11. Partially fill the hub cavity of the steering knuckle with chassis lubricant. Install the hub assembly; make sure the hub spacer is installed on the hub shaft.
12. Install the inner seal in the steering knuckle pin. Install the splash seal on the hub and bearing carrier. Install the O-ring on the hub and bearing carrier.
13. Install the carrier attaching bolts and torque to 75 ft. lbs. Install the caliper anchor plate and plate retaining bolts. Torque the retaining bolts to 100 ft. lbs.
14. Install the steering arm bolts and torque to 100 ft. lbs. Install the halfshaft. Install the axle flange-to-shaft bolts and torque to 45 ft. lbs.
15. Install the hub washer and hub nut. Torque the hub nut to 175 ft. lbs. Install the locknut and new cotter pin. Install the rotor, caliper and wheel.

MEDALLION AND PREMIER

1. Raise and safely support the vehicle.

2. Remove the wheel assembly.

3. Remove the brake caliper and attach to the chassis with a piece of twine or wire. Do not disconnect the brake lines or support the caliper by the brake line.

4. Push the driveshaft from the hub.

5. Remove the hub and wheel bearing as an assembly.

6. Remove the brake rotor safety nuts and pull the brake rotor from the hub. Replace all damaged rotor safety nuts with new.

7. Remove the bolts attaching the bearing assembly to the steering knuckle and remove the bearing assembly. If the bearing assembly is to be replaced, remove the outer bearing race with a shop press.

To install:

8. If the original bearing assembly is being replaced, lubricate the bearing and races with grease. If a new bearing is being installed perform the following:

    a. Remove both bearing races.

    b. Pack the bearing with grease.

    c. Install a bearing race and press the remaining bearing race onto the front hub.

9. Install the bearing assembly into the steering knuckle.

10. Install and tighten the bearing attaching bolts to 11 ft. lbs.

11. Position the wheel hub onto the driveshaft and insert the hub into the wheel bearing.

12. Install the driveshaft retaining nut and secure the wheel hub with a holding tool. Torque the driveshaft retaining nut to 181–184 ft. lbs.

13. Install the brake rotor and the caliper.

14. Install the wheel and lower the vehicle.

SUMMIT

1. Using an assistant, firmly, apply the brakes and loosen the halfshaft nut with the vehicle on the ground.

2. Raise and safely support the vehicle. Remove the wheel.

3. Remove the brake caliper-to-steering knuckle bolts, the caliper and suspend it on a wire.

4. Remove the lower control arm-to-steering knuckle ball joint cotter pin and nut. Using a ball joint separator tool, separate the ball joint from the steering knuckle.

5. Remove the tie rod end-to-steering knuckle cotter pin and nut. Using a ball joint separator tool, separate the tie rod end from the steering knuckle.

6. Using a wheel puller tool, press the halfshaft from the hub.

7. Remove the steering knuckle-to-strut bolts and the steering knuckle from the vehicle.

8. Using a shop press, press the hub from the steering knuckle.

9. Using a wheel puller tool, press the outer bearing inner race from the hub.

10. Using a brass rod and a hammer, drive the outer bearing races from the steering knuckle.

To install:

11. Clean and inspect the parts; if necessary, replace the damaged parts.

12. Using multi-purpose grease lubricate the bearings and races.

13. Using a shop press, press the outer bearing races into the steering knuckle until they seat. Position the bearings into the steering knuckle.

14. Using a new outer grease seal, lubricate it and position it into the hub side of the steering knuckle. Using a seal driver tool and a hammer, drive the grease seal into the hub until it is flush with the housing.

15. Using a hub installation nut/bolt tool, press the hub into the steering knuckle.

16. Using an inch lb. torque wrench, check the hub's turning torque; it should be 11 inch lbs. (1.3 Nm) or less. Using a dial indicator, check the hub endplay; it should be 0.008 in. (0.20mm) or less.

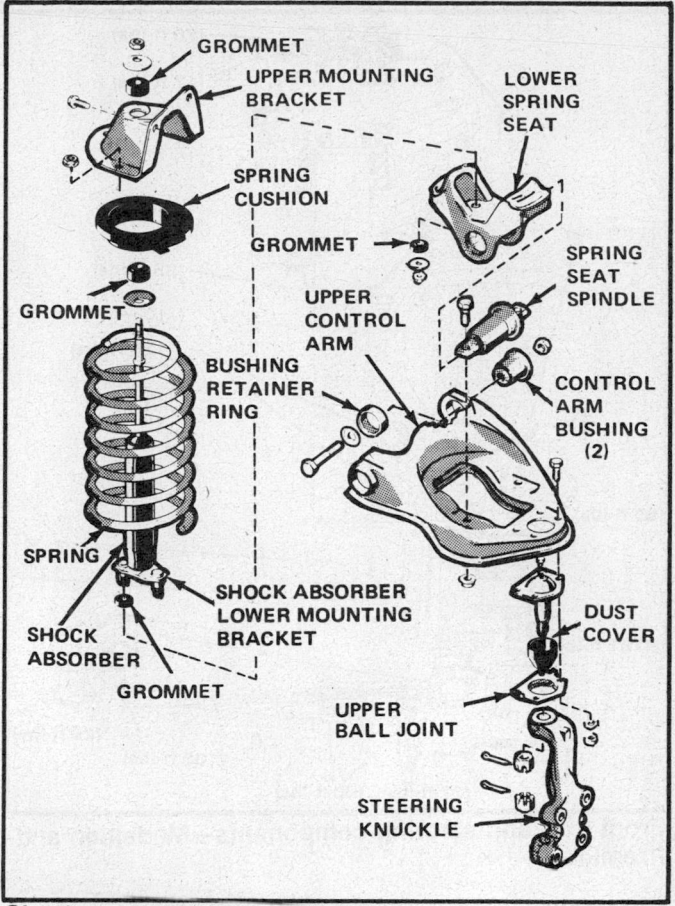

Shock absorber assembly

17. Using a new inner grease seal, lubricate it and insert it into the steering knuckle. Using an oil seal driver tool and a hammer, drive the seal into the knuckle until it is flush.

18. To complete the installation, reverse the removal procedures. Torque the:

    a. Steering knuckle-to-strut bolts to 80–94 ft. lbs. (110–130 Nm).

    b. Lower ball joint-to-steering knuckle nut to 43–52 ft. lbs. (60–72 Nm).

    c. Tie rod end-to-steering knuckle nut to 11–25 ft. lbs. (15–34 Nm).

    d. Brake caliper-to-steering knuckle bolts to 58–72 ft. lbs. (80–100 Nm).

19. Install the wheel and lower the vehicle. Using an assistant, firmly apply the brakes and torque the hub nut to 144–188 ft. lbs. (200–260 Nm).

20. Install the cotter pins. Check and/or adjust the wheel alignment.

SHOCK ABSORBER

Removal and Installation

1. Raise and safely support the vehicle.

2. Remove the lower retaining nuts, washer and grommets.

3. Remove upper mounting bracket bolts/nuts from wheelhouse panel.

4. Remove upper bracket and shock absorber from wheelhouse panel.

5. Remove upper retaining nut from shock absorber. Remove the upper bracket from shock absorber. Remove the component from the vehicle.

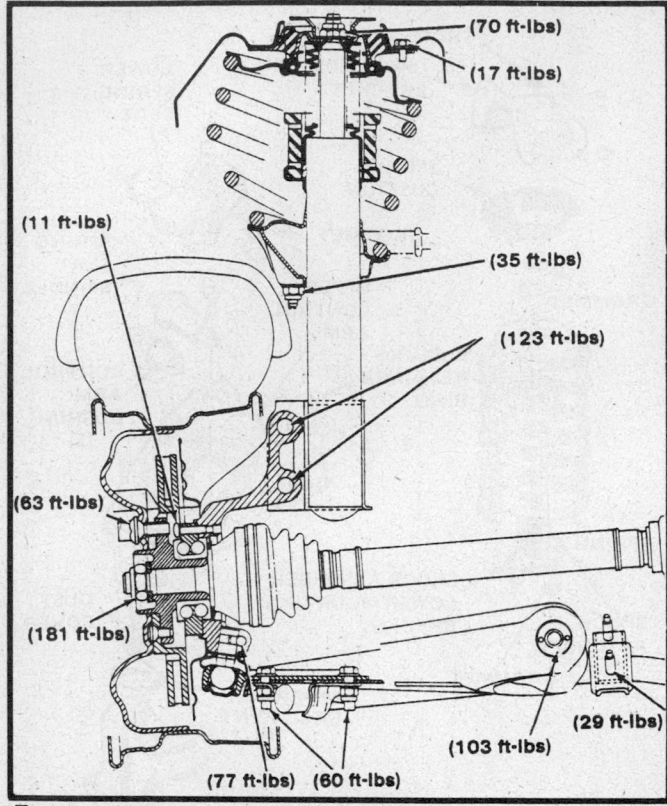

(70 ft-lbs)
(17 ft-lbs)
(11 ft-lbs)
(35 ft-lbs)
(123 ft-lbs)
(63 ft-lbs)
(181 ft-lbs)
(29 ft-lbs)
(103 ft-lbs)
(77 ft-lbs) (60 ft-lbs)

Front axle and steering components — Medallion and Premier

To install:

6. Reverse of the removal procedure. If installing adjustable shocks, adjust the shock by compressing the piston completely.

7. Holding the upper part of the shock, turn the shock until the lower arrow is aligned with the desired setting. A click will be heard when the desired setting is reached.

MACPHERSON STRUT

Removal and Installation
EXCEPT SUMMIT

1. Raise and safely support the vehicle.
2. Remove the wheel assembly. Remove the outer tie rod.
3. Remove the upper strut retaining bolts.

─────────────── **CAUTION** ───────────────

Do not remove the center strut retaining nut. The coil spring is under extreme pressure. Removal of this nut could allow the coil spring to release possibly causing serious injury.

4. Remove the steering knuckle retaining nuts. Remove the strut and spring assembly.

5. Complete the installation of the strut assembly by reversing the removal procedure. Torque the lower strut mounting bolts to 123 ft. lbs., upper strut plate retaining bolts to 17 ft. lbs and the tie rod bolt to 27 ft. lbs.

SUMMIT

1. Raise and safely support the vehicle. Remove the wheel.
2. Remove the brake line-to-strut bolts and separate the brake line from the strut.
3. Using a floor jack, support the lower control arm.
4. Remove the strut-to-chassis nuts, the strut-to-steering knuckle bolts and the strut.

5. To install, reverse the removal procedures. Torque the strut-to-steering knuckle bolts to 80–94 ft. lbs. (110–130 Nm) and the strut-to-chassis nuts to 25–33 ft. lbs. (35–45 Nm).

6. Check and/or adjust the wheel alignment.

UPPER BALL JOINT

Inspection

1. Remove upper ball joint lubrication plug and install a dial indicator gauge through the lubrication hole. Measure the up and down movement of the ball joint socket.

2. Place a pry bar under tire to load the ball joint. Raise the tire several times to seat the gauge tool pin.

3. Pry the tire upward to load the ball joint and record gauge reading. Release the tire to unload the ball joint and record gauge reading. Perform this operation several times to ensure accuracy.

4. The difference between load and no load readings represents ball joint clearance. If clearance is more than 0.080 in., the ball joint should be replaced.

Removal and Installation

If a ball joint is worn, the complete arm assembly must be replaced. Do not attempt to service the ball joint separately.

LOWER BALL JOINT

Inspection

1. Remove the ball joint lubrication plug and install a dial indicator gauge through the lubrication hole. Measure the up and down movement of the ball joint socket.

2. Place a pry bar under tire to load the ball joint. Raise the tire several times to seat the gauge tool pin.

3. Pry the tire upward to load the ball joint and record gauge reading. Release the tire to unload the ball joint and record gauge reading. Perform this operation several times to ensure accuracy.

4. The difference between load and no load readings represents ball joint clearance. If clearance is more than 0.080 in., the ball joint should be replaced.

Removal and Installation

EXCEPT MEDALLION AND PREMIER

If a ball joint is worn the complete arm assembly must be replaced. Do not attempt to service the ball joint separately.

MEDALLION AND PREMIER

1. Raise the safely support the vehicle. Remove the wheel assembly. Place a protective cloth around the driveshaft boot.

2. Loosen, but do not remove, the inner stabilizer bar bracket bolts (Premier only).

3. Remove the nuts from the outboard stabilizer bar bracket and slide the bracket off the bolts (Premier only).

4. Move the stabilizer bar away from the lower control arm. Remove the ball joint key bolt.

5. Loosen, but do not remove, the lower control arm bolts. On the Premier, remove the plastic washer installed on the ball joint stud and set aside. Remove the ball joint by tapping in an upward direction.

To install:

6. Position the lower ball joint in the lower control arm and install, but do not tighten, the retaining bolts.

7. On the Premier, install the plastic washer on the ball joint stud.

8. Intall the ball joint stud in the steering knuckle and install the key bolt, torque the key bolt to 77 ft. lbs. Make certain the key bolt is seated in the groove of the ball joint stud.

9. Connect the stabilizer bar brackets to the control arm but do not tighten the bolts. Install the wheel and lower the vehicle. Remove the protective cloth.

10. Torque the lower control arm bolts to 103 ft. lbs., the ball joint bolts to 60 ft. lbs. and stabilizer bar bolts to 29 ft. lbs.

COIL SPRING

Removal and Installation

1. Raise and safely support the vehicle. Remove the shock absorber and mounting bracket.
2. Install the spring compressor tool and compress the spring about 1 in.
3. Remove the lower spring seat pivot bolt and retaining nuts.
4. Remove the wheel assembly.
5. Pull the lower spring seat away from the vehicle and guide the lower spring seat out and over the upper control arm.
6. Remove the spring compressor tool. Remove the lower retainer, spring seat and spring.
7. To install, reverse the removal procedures.

NOTE: One side of the lower spring seat has a formed shoulder to help locate the spring properly. Position the spring on the seat so the cut off end of the spring bottom coil seats against this shoulder. If the spring seat was removed for service, be sure the shouldered end of the spring seat and cut off end of the spring bottom coil are installed so they face the engine compartment.

UPPER CONTROL ARM

Removal and Installation

1. Raise and safely support the vehicle. Remove the shock absorber and mounting bracket. Install the spring compressor tool.
2. Remove lower spring seat pivot retaining nuts and turn compressor tool until spring is compressed about 2 in.
3. Remove the wheel assembly.
4. Remove the upper ball joint stud cotter pin and retaining nut.
5. Remove the upper ball joint stud from the steering knuckle.
6. Remove the control arm inner pivot bolts. Remove the control arm from the vehicle.
7. To install, reverse the removal procedures. Do not tighten the pivot bolts until the vehicle is resting on the wheels as ride height may be affected.

LOWER CONTROL ARM

Removal and Installation
EXCEPT MEDALLION, PREMIER AND SUMMIT

1. Raise and safely support the vehicle. Remove cotter pin, locknut and hub nut.
2. Remove the wheel assembly. Remove the caliper and rotor.
3. Remove the lower ball joint cotter pin and retaining nut.
4. Remove the ball joint from the steering knuckle.
5. Remove halfshaft flange bolts and the halfshaft.
6. Remove the strut rod-to-control arm bolts.
7. Disconnect the stabilizer bar from control arm.
8. Remove the inner pivot bolt. Remove the control arm from the vehicle.
9. To install, reverse the removal procedures. Do not tighten the inner pivot bolt until the vehicle weight is supported by the wheels as ride height may be affected.

MEDALLION AND PREMIER

1. Raise and safely support the vehicle.

2. Remove the wheel. Tape a piece of protective cloth around the driveshaft boot.
3. Loosen, but do not remove the inner stabilizer bar bracket bolts, remove the the outboard stabilizer bracket bolts and and slide the bracket off the bolts. Move the stabilizer bar away from the control arm.
4. Remove the ball joint key bolt and remove the ball joint from the knuckle.
5. Remove the bolts and nuts attaching the control arm and remove the control arm. On the Premier, remove the plastic washer from the ball joint stud and set aside.

To install:
6. Position the lower control arm to the cradle and install the mounting bolts, but do not tighten the mounting bolts at this time. Install the plastic washer, if removed.
7. Install the ball joint into the steering knuckle. Install the key bolt and nut. Torque the bolt to 77 ft. lbs.
8. Connect the stabilizer bar brackets and bolts to the control arm but do not tighten the bolts at this time. Install the wheel and lower the vehicle.
9. Torque the lower control arm bolts to 103 ft. lbs. and the stabilizer bar bolts to 29 ft. lbs.

SUMMIT

1. Raise and safely support the vehicle. Remove the wheel.
2. Remove the lower control arm-to-steering knuckle ball joint cotter pin and nut. Using a ball joint separator tool, separate the ball joint from the steering knuckle.
3. Remove the stabilizer link-to-lower control arm nut and separate it from the arm.
4. Remove the lower control arm bracket-to-chassis bolts, the lower control arm-to-chassis nut/bolt and the lower control arm.

To install:
5. Clean and inspect the parts; if necessary, replace the damaged parts.
6. Install the lower control arm-to-chassis nut/bolt, the lower control arm bracket-to-chassis bolts and the lower control arm ball joint-to-steering knuckle nut but do not tighten.
7. Install the stabilizer link-to-lower control arm nut and torque to 40–51 ft. lbs. (55–70 Nm).
8. To complete the installation, reverse the removal procedures. Torque the:
   a. Lower ball joint-to-steering knuckle nut to 43–52 ft. lbs. (60–72 Nm).
   b. Lower control arm-to-chassis nut/bolt to 69–87 ft. lbs. (95–120 Nm).
   c. Lower control arm bracket-to-chassis bolts to 43–58 ft. lbs. (60–80 Nm).
9. Install the wheel and lower the vehicle.
10. Install the cotter pin. Check and/or adjust the wheel alignment.

STEERING KNUCKLE AND SPINDLE

Removal and Installation
EXCEPT MEDALLION, PREMIER AND SUMMIT

1. Raise and safely support the vehicle. Remove cotter pin, locknut and hub nut.
2. Remove the wheel assembly. Remove the caliper and rotor.
3. Remove halfshaft-to-axle flange bolts and the halfshaft.
4. Remove steering arm from the steering knuckle. Remove the caliper anchor plate from the steering knuckle.
5. Remove the Torx® head attaching bolts retaining the front wheel hub assembly. Remove the hub assembly from the knuckle.
6. Remove the rear hub seal from the steering knuckle using the proper tools.
7. Remove the upper and lower ball joint stud cotter pins and retaining nuts.

8. Separate the upper and lower ball joints from steering knuckle. Remove the steering knuckle from the vehicle.

9. To install, reverse the removal procedures.

MEDALLION AND PREMIER

1. Raise and safely support the vehicle.
2. Remove the wheel assembly.
3. Remove the brake caliper.
4. Push the driveshaft from the hub.
5. Remove the brake rotor from the hub.
6. Remove the bearing assembly-to-the steering knuckle bolts. Remove the hub and wheel bearing as an assembly with a puller tool.
7. Remove the ball joint key bolt and disengage the ball joint from the steering knuckle.
8. Both strut-to-steering knuckle bolts are splined to the strut and should be removed as follows:
   a. Loosen the strut bolt nuts until they are almost off the bolts.
   b. Tap the nuts with a hammer to loosen the bolts.
   c. Remove the nuts completely and slide the bolts from the strut and steering knuckle.
9. Remove the steering knuckle.
10. To install, reverse the removal procedures. Torque the wheel bearing-to-steering knuckle bolts to 11 ft. lbs. and driveshaft retaining nut to 181 ft. lbs.

SUMMIT

1. Using an assistant, firmly apply the brakes and loosen the halfshaft nut with the vehicle on the ground.
2. Raise and safely support the vehicle. Remove the wheel.
3. Remove the brake caliper-to-steering knuckle bolts, the caliper and suspend it on a wire.

4. Remove the lower control arm-to-steering knuckle ball joint cotter pin and nut. Using a ball joint separator tool, separate the ball joint from the steering knuckle.

5. Remove the tie rod end-to-steering knuckle cotter pin and nut. Using a ball joint separator tool, separate the tie rod end from the steering knuckle.

6. Remove the steering knuckle-to-strut bolts and the steering knuckle from the vehicle.

To install:

7. Clean and inspect the parts; if necessary, replace the damaged parts.

8. To complete the installation, reverse the removal procedures. Torque the:
   a. Steering knuckle-to-strut bolts to 80–94 ft. lbs. (110–130 Nm).
   b. Lower ball joint-to-steering knuckle nut to 43–52 ft. lbs. (60–72 Nm).
   c. Tie rod end-to-steering knuckle nut to 11–25 ft. lbs. (15–34 Nm).
   d. Brake caliper-to-steering knuckle bolts to 58–72 ft. lbs. (80–100 Nm).

9. Install the wheel and lower the vehicle. Using an assistant, firmly apply the brakes and torque the hub nut to 144–188 ft. lbs. (200–260 Nm).

10. Install the cotter pins. Check and/or adjust the wheel alignment.

STRUT ROD AND BUSHING

Removal and Installation

1. Raise and safely support the vehicle.
2. Remove the jamnut and caster adjustment nut from the strut rod.

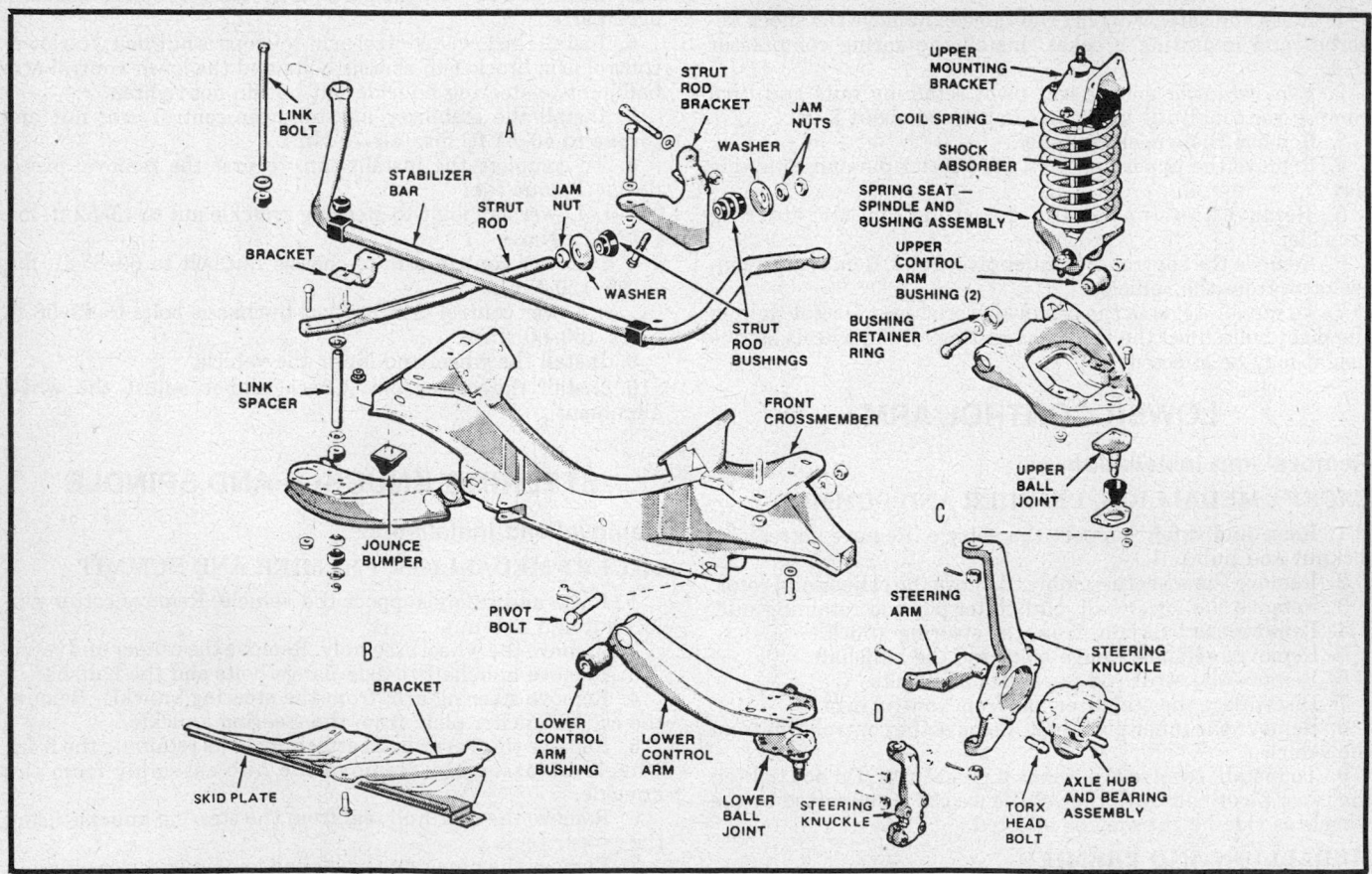

Four wheel drive suspension

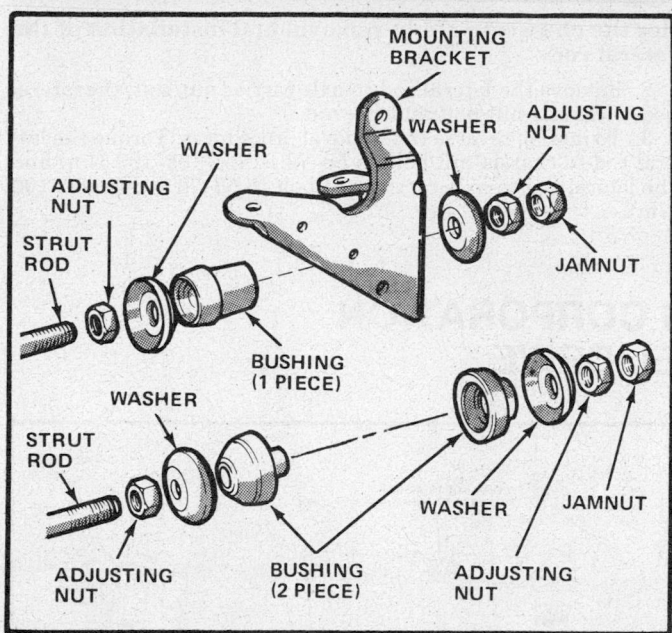

Strut rod bushings

3. Disconnect the strut rod from the lower control arm. Remove the strut rod, bushings and washers.

4. To install, reverse the removal procedures. If equipped with a 1 piece bushing, lubricate the bushing with soapy water and install. A special tool is required to press the bushing in and from the mounting bracket.

Rear Suspension

SHOCK ABSORBER

Removal and Installation

EXCEPT MEDALLION AND PREMIER

1. Raise and safely support the vehicle. Properly support the rear axle assembly.

2. Remove the locknut, retainer and grommet which retain the shock absorber lower mounting stud-to-spring plate.

3. If the vehicle is equipped with air adjustable shock absorbers, disconnect the air line.

4. Compress the shock absorber and disengage the lower mounting stud from the spring plate.

5. Remove the bolts and lockwashers attaching the shock absorber upper mounting bracket to the underbody panel. Remove the shock absorber from the vehicle.

6. To install, reverse the removal procedures.

MEDALLION AND PREMIER

NOTE: Never raise the vehicle from under the V-shaped channel on the rear axle.

1. Raise and safely support the rear corner of the vehicle.

2. Raise the bottom of the control arm from the bottom to relieve shock absorber tension.

3. Mark the upper and lower shock absorber mounting bolts prior to removal. These bolts are not interchangable.

4. Remove the upper and lower shock absorber mounting bolts and remove the shock absorber and/or coil spring from the vehicle.

5. Prime the new shock absorber and complete the installation by reversing the removal procedure. Torque the lower mounting bolt to 59 ft. lbs. and the upper mounting bolt to 59 ft. lbs.

MACPHERSON STRUT

Removal and Installation
SUMMIT

1. Raise and safely support the rear of the vehicle. Remove the wheel.

2. Using a floor jack, support the rear axle carrier to take the load off the strut.

3. Front the upper strut, remove the protective cap.

4. Remove the strut-to-chassis nuts, the strut-to-axle carrier nut/bolt and the strut.

5. Inspect the parts for damage and/or wear; if necessary, replace the worn parts.

6. To install, reverse the removal procedures. Torque the strut-to-chassis nuts to 18–25 ft. lbs. (25–35 Nm) and the strut-to-axle carrier nut/bolt to 58–72 ft. lbs. (80–100 Nm).

LEAF SPRING

Removal and Installation

1. Raise and safely support the vehicle. Properly support the rear axle assembly.

2. Remove the shock absorber lower mounting locknut, retainer and grommet.

3. Remove the U-bolts, spring clamps and clamp bracket.

4. Remove pivot bolt and nut from spring front eye.

5. Remove the shackle retaining nuts, shackle plate and shackle at rear spring eye.

6. Remove the spring assembly from the vehicle.

7. To install, reverse the removal procedures.

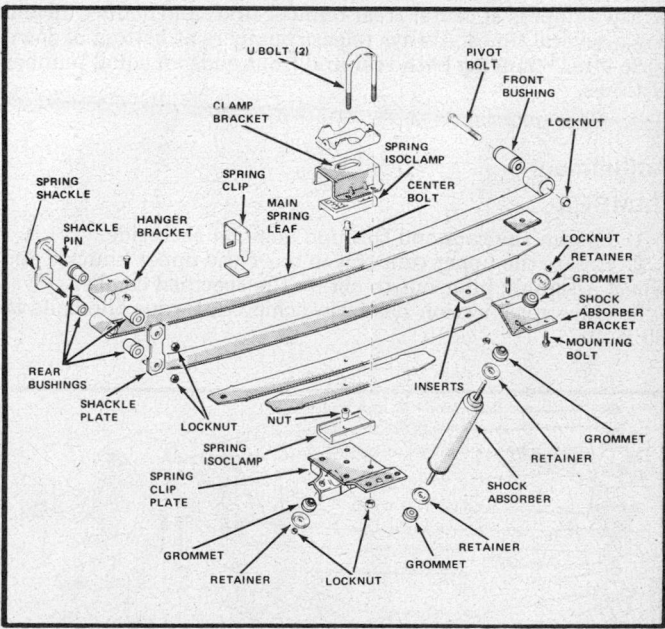

Rear suspension components

STABILIZER BAR

Removal and Installation

1. Raise and safely support the vehicle.

2. Remove the stabilizer bar-to-connecting links nuts and grommets.

3. Remove the stabilizer bar mounting clamps-to-spring clip plates bolts.

4. Remove the stabilizer bar from the vehicle.

5. To install, reverse the removal procedures.

LATERAL ROD

Removal and Installation
SUMMIT

1. Raise and safely support the rear of the vehicle. If necessary, remove the rear right wheel.

NOTE: If may be necessary to position a floor jack under the chassis to aid in removal and installation of the lateral rod.

2. Remove the lateral rod-to-axle carrier nut/bolt, the lateral rod-to-chassis nut/bolt and the rod.

3. To install, reverse the removal procedures. Torque the lateral rod-to-chassis nut/bolt to 58–72 ft. lbs. (80–100 Nm) and the lateral rod-to-axle carrier nut/bolt to 58–72 ft. lbs. (80–100 Nm).

CHRYLSER MOTORS CORPORATION
FRONT WHEEL DRIVE

Front Suspension

FRONT WHEEL ALIGNMENT

Before any attempt is made to change or correct the wheel alignment, inspection and necessary corrections must be made on those parts which influence the steering of the vehicle. Check and inflate tires to recommended pressures. Check front wheel assembly for radial runout. Check struts for proper operation.

The front suspension should be checked only after the vehicle has the recommended tire pressures, full tank of fuel, no passenger or luggage compartment load and is on a level floor or alignment rack.

To obtain an accurate reading, the vehicle should be bounced in the following manner just prior to taking a measurement. Grasp bumpers at center (rear bumper first) and bounce up and down several times. Always release bumpers at bottom of down cycle after bouncing both rear and front ends an equal number of times.

Adjustment
CAMBER

1. Loosen the cam and through bolts on each side.
2. Rotate the upper cam bolt to move the upper knuckle and wheel assembly in or out to obtain the specified camber.
3. Once specification has been achieved, torque the bolts to 85 ft. lbs.

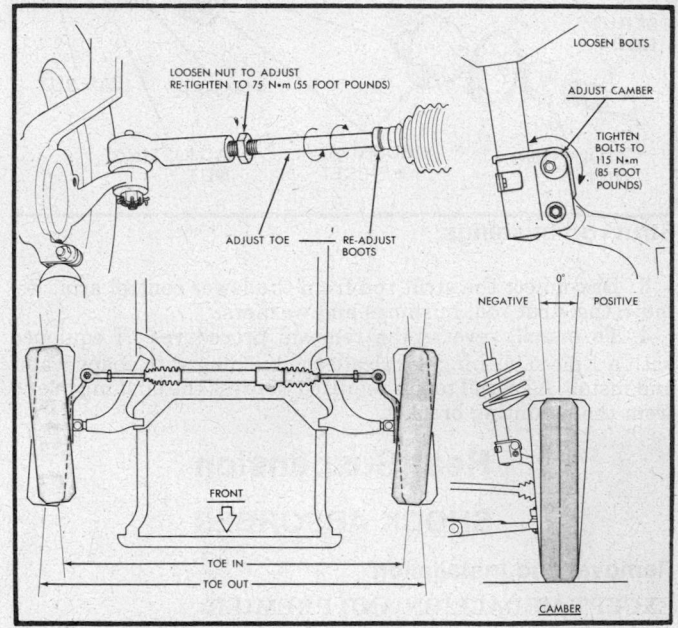

Front suspension

TOE

1. Center the steering wheel and hold it in place using a steering wheel clamp.
2. Loosen the tie rod locknuts. Rotate the tie rods to align the toe to specification.

FRONT WHEEL BEARINGS

All vehicles are equipped with permanently sealed front wheel bearings. There is no periodic lubrication, maintenance, or adjustment recommended for these units. Service repair or replacement of front drive bearing, hub, brake dust shield or knuckle will require removal from the vehicle.

STRUT ASSEMBLY

Removal and Installation

1. Raise and safely support the vehicle. Remove wheel assembly.
2. Remove cam adjusting bolt, through bolt and brake hose-to-damper bracket retaining screw. If the original strut is to be reinstalled with the original steering knuckle, mark the cam adjusting bolt before removal.
3. Remove strut damper-to-fender shield mounting nut washer assemblies. Remove the component from the vehicle.

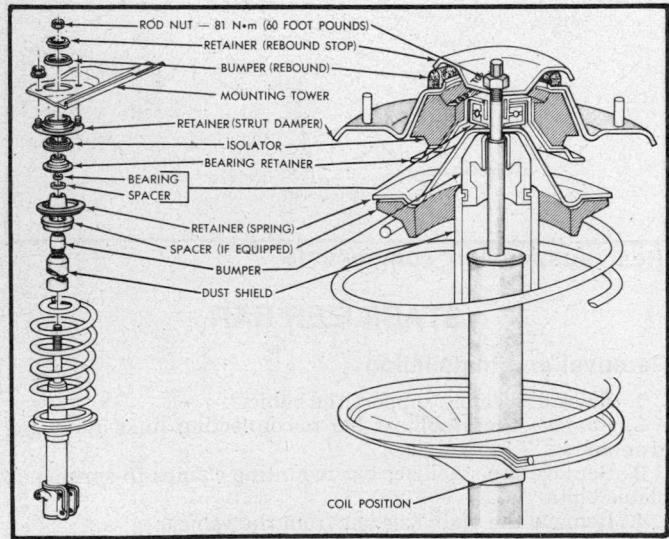

Upper spring retainer assembly

4. To disassemble, compress the coil with a spring compressor tool. Hold the strut rod while loosening the strut rod nut. Remove the nut. Remove the retainers and bushings. Remove the coil spring. Mark the spring for replacement in its original position.

To install:

5. Check the retainers for cracks and distortion. Check the bearings for binding. Be sure the bearings contain an adequate supply of lubricant.

6. Upon assembly of the spring to strut damper, be sure the coil end is seated in strut damper spring seat recess.

7. To complete the installation, reverse the removal procedures. Align the cam bolt with the matchmarks, as required. Torque the:

    a. Strut-to-body nuts to 20 ft. lbs.

    b. Wheel nuts to 80–95 ft. lbs.

    c. Brake hose bracket screw to 10 ft. lbs.

    d. Cam/steering knuckle bolts to 45 ft. lbs.—Omni and Horizon.

    e. Cam/steering knuckle bolts to 75 ft. lbs., with an additional ¼ turn—except Omni and Horizon.

LOWER BALL JOINT

Inspection

The lower ball joint is checked at the lube fitting. Try to turn the lube fitting. If it turns or wobbles, the ball joint is worn and should be replaced.

Removal and Installation

NOTE: On some vehicles, the front ball joints are welded to the control arms and are not to be pressed out. The welded ones must be serviced by complete replacement of the control arm and ball joint assembly.

1. Raise and safely support the vehicle. Pry off the seal.

2. Position receiving cup tool, to support the lower control arm.

3. Place a 1¹⁄₁₆ in. deep wall socket over the stud and against the ball joint upper housing.

4. Press the ball joint assembly from the control arm.

To install:

5. Position the ball joint housing into the control arm cavity.

6. Position the assembly in a press using installer tool, to support the control arm.

7. Align the ball joint assembly, then press it in until the housing ledge stops against the control arm cavity down flange.

8. To install a new seal, support the ball joint housing with installing tool C–4699–2 or equivalent, and position a new seal over the stud against the housing.

9. Using a 1½ in. socket, press the seal onto the joint housing with the seat against the control arm.

10. Complete the installation in the reverse order of the removal procedure. Torque the control arm pivot bolt to 105 ft. lbs. and the ball joint-to-steering knuckle bolt to 70 ft. lbs.

LOWER CONTROL ARM

Removal and Installation

1. Raise and safely support the vehicle. Remove the front inner pivot bolt.

2. Remove the rear stub strut nut, retainer and bushing.

3. Remove the ball joint-to-steering knuckle clamp bolt.

4. Separate the ball joint stud from the steering knuckle using the proper tools.

To install:

5. Install the retainer, bushing and sleeve on stub strut. Position the control arm over the sway bar and install the rear stub strut and the front pivot into the crossmember.

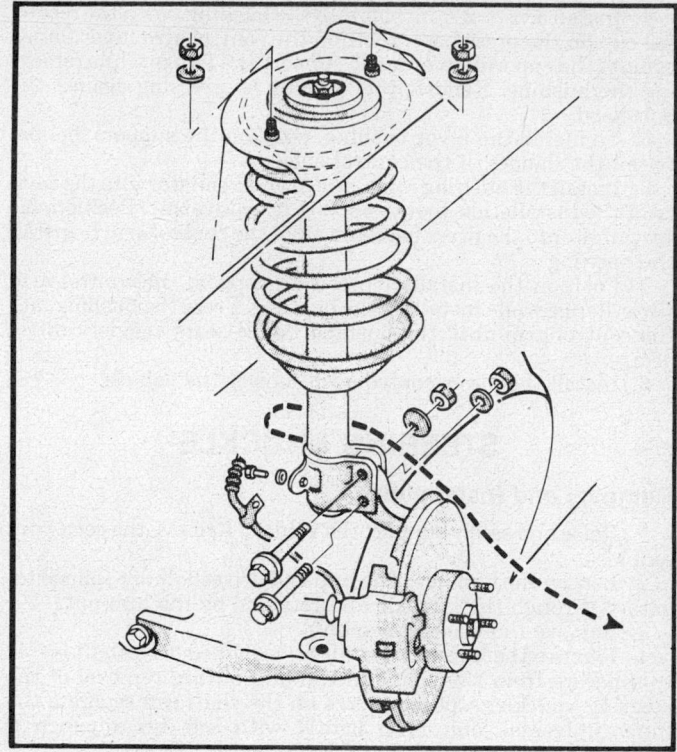

Strut assembly

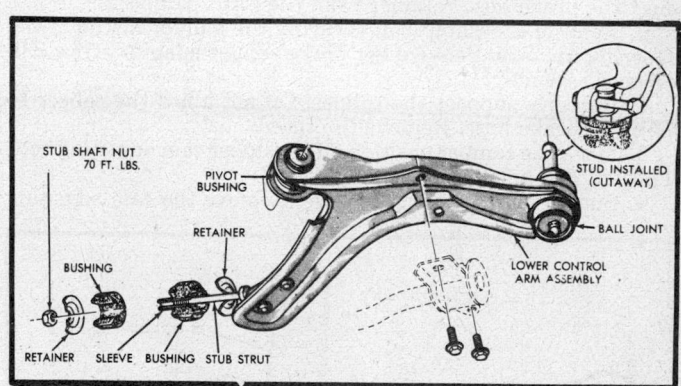

Lower control arm

6. Install the front pivot bolt and install the nut but do not tighten at this time. Install the stub strut bushing and retainer and loosely assemble nut.

7. Install the ball joint stud into the steering knuckle and install the clamp bolt. Torque the clamp bolt to 50 ft. lbs.

8. Position the sway bar end bushing retainer to the control arm. Install the retainer bolts and torque the nuts to 22 ft. lbs.

9. Lower the vehicle. With the control arm at design height torque the front pivot bolt to 100 ft. lbs. and stub strut nut to 70 ft. lbs.

LOWER CONTROL ARM PIVOT BUSHING

Removal and Installation

1. Raise and safely support the vehicle.

2. Remove the lower control arm from the vehicle.

To install:

3. To replace the pivot bushing, position a support tool between the flanges of the lower control arm and around the bushing in order to prevent the control arm from distorting.

4. Install a ½ × 2½ in. bolt into the bushing. With the receiving cup on the press base, position the control arm inner flange against the cup wall in order to support the flange while removing the bushing. Remove the bushing by pressing against the bolt head.

5. To install the pivot bushing, position the support tool between the flanges of the control arm.

6. Install the bushing inner sleeve and insulator into the cavity of the installation tool C-4699-1 or equivalent. Position the assembly onto the press base and align the control arm to install the bushing.

7. Position the installation tool to support the control arm outer flange while installing the bushing. Press the bushing into the control arm until the bushing flange seats against control arm.

8. Install the lower control arm. Lower the vehicle.

STEERING KNUCKLE

Removal and Installation

1. Raise and safely support the vehicle. Remove the cotter pin and lock.

2. Loosen the hub nut. The hub and driveshaft are splined together through the knuckle and retained by the hub nut.

3. Remove the wheel assembly.

4. Remove the hub nut. Be sure the splined driveshaft is free to separate from the spline in the hub during removal of the steering knuckle. A pulling force on the shaft can separate the inner universal joint. Tap lightly with soft brass punch if required.

5. Disconnect the tie rod end from the steering arm. Disconnect the brake hose retainer from the strut damper.

6. Remove the clamp bolt securing the ball joint stud to the steering knuckle. Remove the brake caliper adaptor screw and washer assembly.

7. Properly support the caliper. Do not allow the caliper to hang by brake hose. Remove the rotor.

8. Mark the camber position on the upper cam adjusting bolt. Loosen both bolts.

9. Support the steering knuckle. Remove the cam adjusting

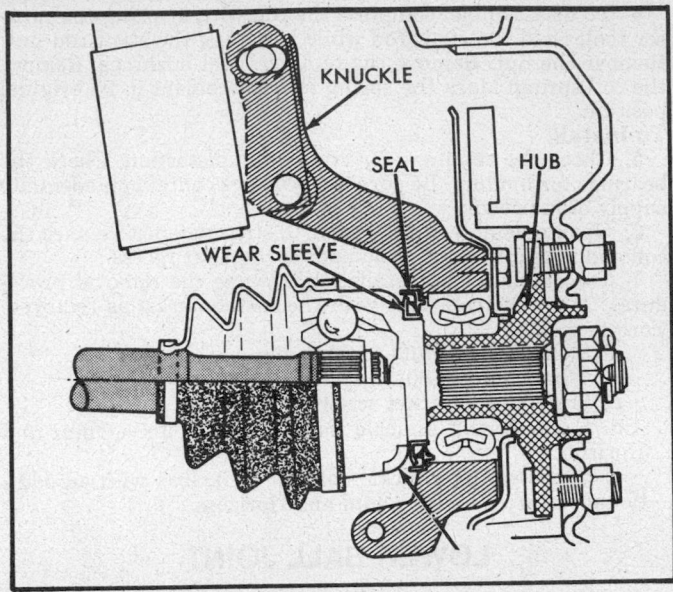

Steering knuckle and bearing

and through bolts. Move the upper knuckle leg from the strut damper bracket. Lift the steering knuckle off of the ball joint stud and remove it from the vehicle.

NOTE: Be sure to support the driveshaft during knuckle removal. Do not allow the driveshaft to hang after separating the steering knuckle from the vehicle as damage to the inboard universal joint boot will occur.

10. To install, reverse the removal procedures. Torque the:
   a. Ball joint-to-steering knuckle clamp bolt to 70 ft. lbs.
   b. Tie rod nut to 35 ft. lbs.
   c. Adapter-to-knuckle bolts to 160 ft. lbs.
   d. Hub nut to 180 ft. lbs.

HUB ASSEMBLY

Removal and Installation

1. Raise and safely support the vehicle. Remove the hub bearing using hub bearing removal tool. The bearing inner races will separate and the outboard race will stay on hub.

2. Remove the bearing outer race from hub with the thrust button from the tool and puller assembly.

3. Remove the brake dust shield and bearing retainer.

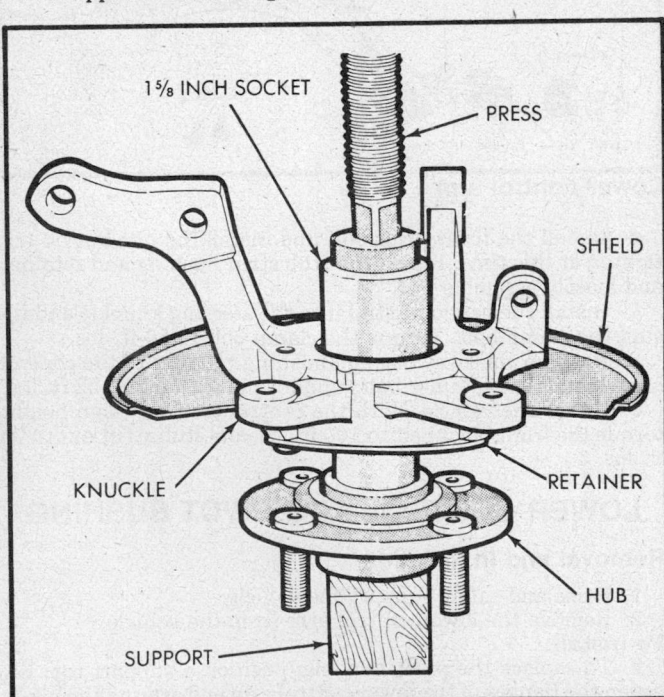

Pressing hub into knuckle bearing

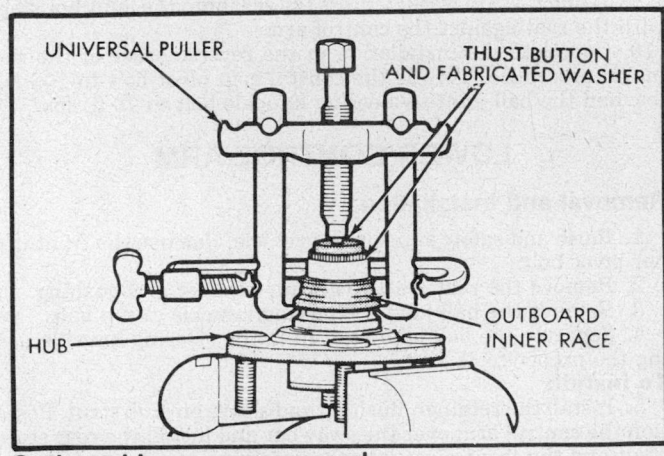

Outboard inner race removal

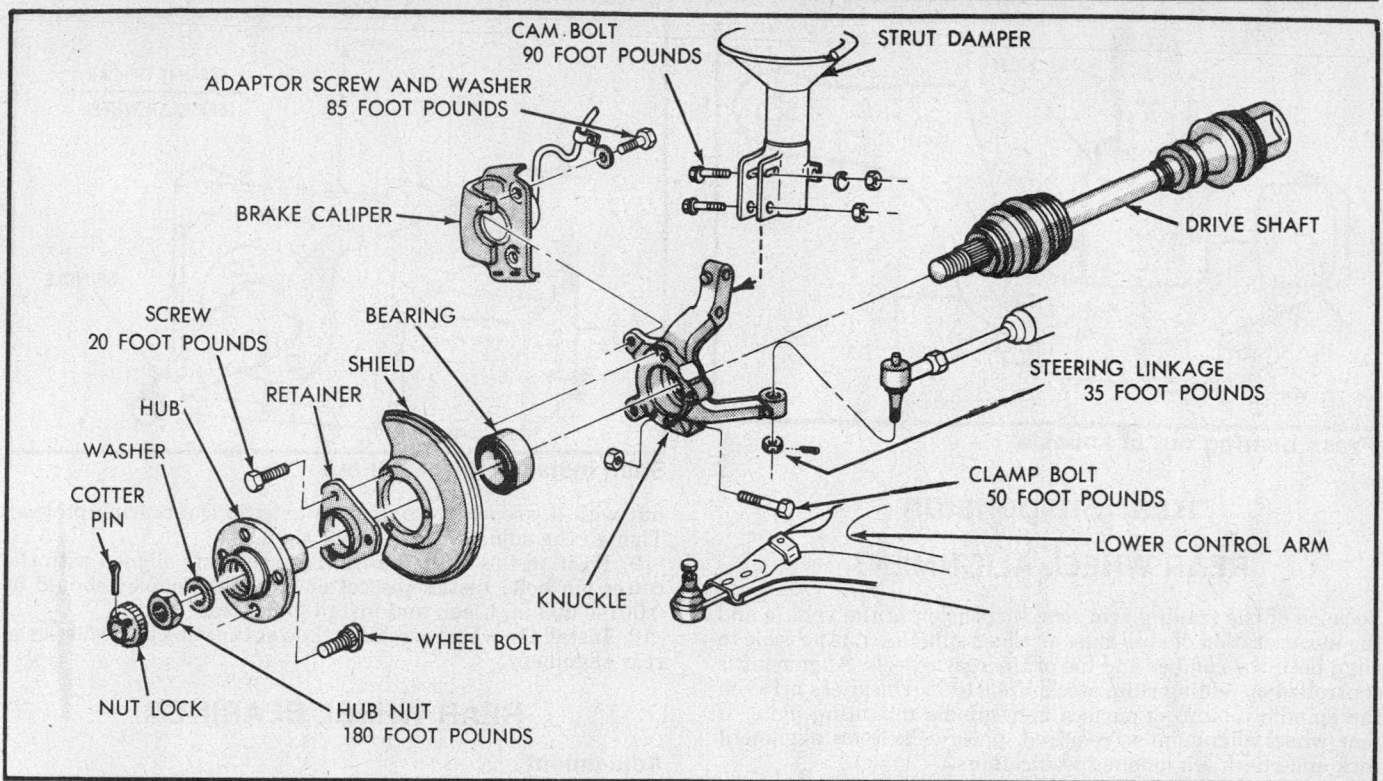

Front suspension knuckle

4. To install, reverse the removal procedures. Torque the bearing retainer screws to 20 ft. lbs. Be sure to use a new bearing. Clean and lubricate the seal and wear sleeve.

SWAY BAR

Removal and Installation

1. Raise and safely support the vehicle.

2. Remove the nuts, bolts and fasteners at the control arm assemblies.

3. Remove the crossmember clamp retaining bolts. Remove the sway bar from the vehicle.

4. To install, reverse the removal procedures.

Hub removal

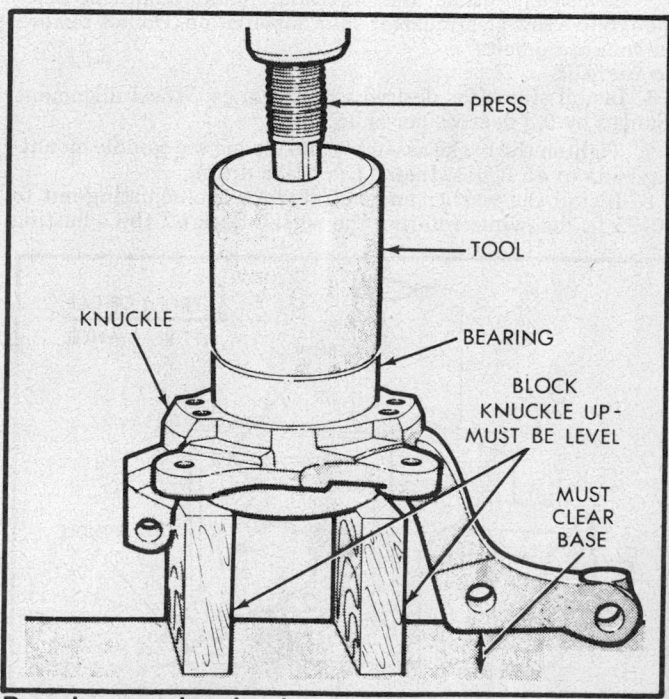

Pressing new bearing into knuckle

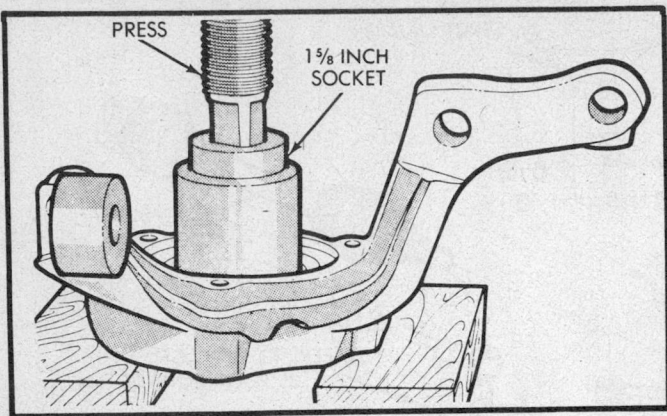

Press bearing out of knuckle

Rear Suspension

REAR WHEEL ALIGNMENT

Because of the trailing arm rear suspension of the vehicle and the incorporation of stub axles or wheel spindles, it is possible to align both the camber and toe of the rear wheels. Alignment is controlled by adding shim stock of 0.010 in. thickness between the spindle mounting surface and spindle mounting plate. If rear wheel alignment is required, place vehicle on alignment rack and check alignment specifications.

ALIGNMENT SHIMS

Removal and Installation

1. Raise and safely support the vehicle.
2. Remove the wheel assembly.
3. Remove the grease cap. Remove the cotter pin and castle lock.
4. Remove the adjusting nut. Remove the brake drum.
5. Loosen the brake assembly and spindle mounting bolts enough to allow clearance for shim installation. Do not remove the mounting bolts.

To install:

6. Install shims for desired wheel change. Wheel alignment changes by 0.3 degrees per shim.
7. Tighten the brake assembly and torque the spindle mounting bolts to 45 ft. lbs. Install the brake drum.
8. Install the washer and nut. Torque the adjusting nut to 20–25 ft. lbs. while rotating the wheel. Back off the adjusting

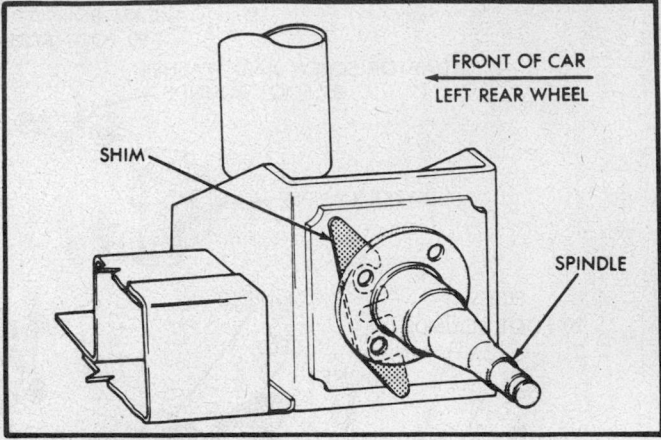

Shim installation for toe out

nut with a wrench to completely release the bearing preload. Tighten the adjusting nut finger tight.
9. Position the locknut with a pair of slots aligned with the cotter pin hole. Install the cotter pin. The endplay should be 0.001–0.003 in. Clean and install grease cap.
10. Install the wheel assembly. Lower the vehicle. Recheck the rear alignment.

REAR WHEEL BEARINGS

Adjustment

OMNI, HORIZON, CHARGER AND TURISMO

1. Raise and safely support the vehicle. Install the hub assembly on the spindle.
2. Install the outer bearing, thrust washer and nut.
3. Torque the wheel bearing adjusting nut to 20–25 ft. lbs. while rotating the hub.
4. Back off the adjusting nut to release all preload, then tighten adjusting nut finger tight.
5. Position the lock on the nut with 1 pair of slots in line with cotter pin hole. Install the cotter pin.
6. Install the grease cap. Install the wheel assembly.

EXCEPT OMNI, HORIZON, CHARGER AND TURISMO

1. Raise and safely support the vehicle. Torque the adjusting nut 20–25 ft. lbs., while rotating the wheel.
2. Stop rotating the wheel and back off the adjusting nut with a wrench to completely release the bearing preload.
3. Finger tighten adjusting nut.

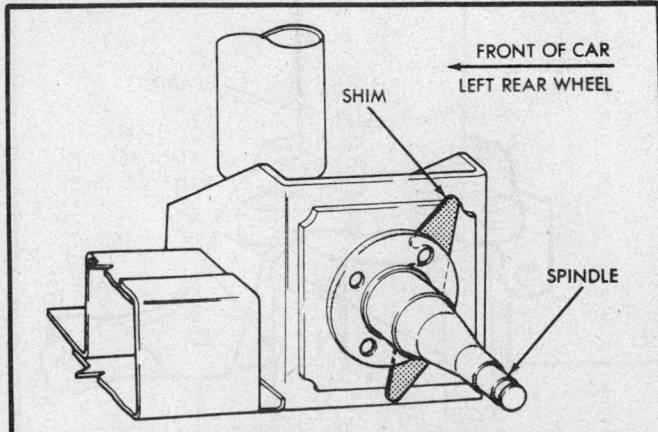

Shim installation for toe in

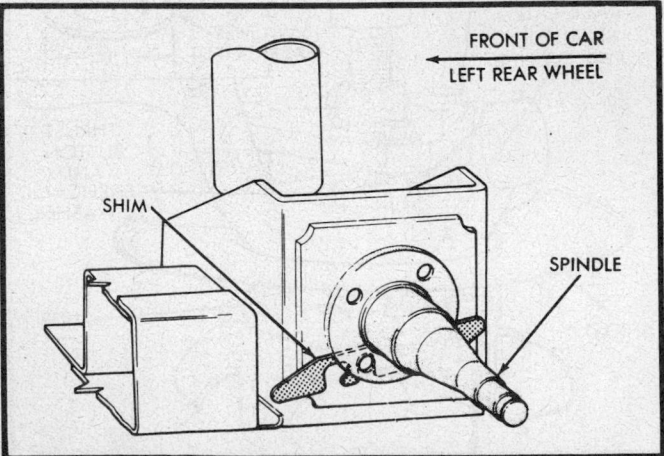

Shim installation for negative camber

4. Position the locknut with 1 pair of slots in line with the cotter pin hole. Install the cotter pin.

5. The endplay should be 0.0012–0.003 in. Clean and install the grease cap.

SHOCK ABSORBER

Removal and Installation

OMNI, HORIZON, CHARGER AND TURISMO

1. Locate the upper shock absorber mounting nut protective cap inside the vehicle at the upper rear wheel well area. If the vehicle is a 2 door, remove the lower rear quarter trim panel.

2. Unsnap the cap. Use care to retain the sound insulation material inside the cap. Remove the upper shock absorber mounting nut, isolator retainer and upper isolater.

3. Raise and safely support the vehicle. Remove the lower shock absorber mounting bolt.

4. Remove the shock absorber and coil spring assembly from the trailing arm bracket. Remove the assembly from the vehicle.

5. Using a spring compressor tool, position the tool and the component in a vise. Grip 4–5 coils of spring in the retaining nut.

CAUTION

If the coil spring is not compressed enough, serious injury could occur when retaining nut is loosened.

---

6. Remove the lower isolator, shock rod sleeve and upper spring seat. Remove the shock absorber from coil spring.

7. To install, reverse the removal procedures.

EXCEPT OMNI, HORIZON, CHARGER AND TURISMO

1. Raise and safely support the vehicle. Properly support the rear axle. Remove the wheel assembly.

2. Remove the upper and lower shock absorber retaining bolts. Remove the shock absorber from the vehicle.

3. To install, reverse the removal procedures.

COIL SPRING

Removal and Installation

EXCEPT OMNI, HORIZON, CHARGER AND TURISMO

1. Raise and safely support the vehicle.

2. Support the rear axle assembly. Remove both lower shock absorber attaching bolts.

3. Lower axle assembly until the spring assembly can be removed. Do not stretch the brake hose.

4. Remove the screws holding the bumper assembly to the rail. Remove the bumper assembly.

5. To install, reverse the removal procedures.

CHRYSLER MOTORS CORPORATION
REAR WHEEL DRIVE

Front Suspension

WHEEL ALIGNMENT

All adjustments and checks should be made in the following sequence. Front suspension height, caster and camber, toe-in, steering axis inclination check and toe-out on turns.

Adjustment

HEIGHT

Front suspension heights must be measured with the recommended tire pressures and with no passenger or luggage compartment load. The vehicle should have a full tank of gasoline or equivalent weight compensation. It must be on a level surface.

Rock the vehicle at the center of the front and rear bumpers at least 6 times to eliminate friction effects before making the vehicle height measurements. Allow the vehicle to settle on its own weight.

For Gran Fury, measure from the bottom of the front frame rail, between the radiator yoke and the forward edge of the front suspension crossmember, to the ground. For all other torsion bar front suspension vehicles, measure from the head of the front suspension crossmember front isolator bolt to the ground.

Adjust the height by turning the torsion bar adjusting bolt clockwise to raise or counterclockwise to lower. The height should not vary more than ⅛ in. from side-to-side.

CAMBER AND CASTER

1. Prepare the vehicle for measuring wheel alignment.

2. Determine the initial camber and caster readings to confirm variance to specifications before loosening the pivot bar bolts.

3. Remove all foreign material from the exposed threads of pivot bar bolts.

4. Loosen the nuts slightly and hold the pivot (caster/camber) bar. Slightly loosening the pivot bar nuts will allow the upper control arm to be repositioned without slipping to end of the adjustment slots.

5. Position the claw of the tool on the pivot bar and the pin of the tool into the holes provided in the tower. Make the adjustments by moving the pivot bar in or out.

6. To adjust the camber, move both ends of the upper control arm in or out in equal amounts. Camber settings should be held as close as possible to the preferred vehicle settings.

7. To adjust the caster, moving one end of the bar will change caster and camber. To preserve camber while adjusting caster, move each end of the upper control arm pivot bar the same amount in opposite directions. For example, to increase positive caster, move the front of the pivot bar away from the engine, then move the rear of the pivot bar towards the engine in an equal amount. Caster should be as equal as possible on both wheels.

TOE

The toe setting should be the final operation of the front wheel alignment adjustments. In all cases, follow equipment manufacturers procedure.

1. Position the steering wheel straight ahead. On vehicles equipped with power steering, start the engine before centering wheel. The engine should be kept running while adjusting toe.

2. Loosen the tie rod clamp bolts.

3. Adjust the toe by turning the tie rod sleeves. To avoid a binding condition in either tie rod assembly, rotate both tie rod ends in the direction of sleeve travel during adjustment. This will ensure that both ends will be in the center of their travel when tightening their sleeve clamps.

4. Turn the engine **OFF**.

5. Position the sleeve clamps so the ends do not locate in the sleeve slot. Tighten the clamp bolts. Be sure the clamp bolts are

indexed at or near bottom to avoid possible interference with the torsion bars.

FRONT WHEEL BEARINGS

Adjustment

1. Raise and safely support the vehicle. Torque the adjusting nut 20–25 ft. lbs., while rotating the wheel. Stop rotation and back off adjusting nut to completely release bearing preload.

2. Finger tighten the adjusting nut. Position the locknut with 1 pair of slots in line with the cotter pin hole. Install the cotter pin.

3. The adjustment should be 0.0001–0.0003 in. endplay. Clean and install the grease cap.

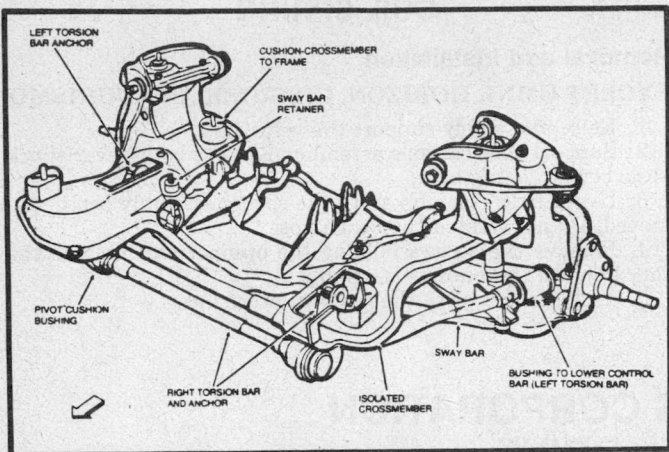

Transverse torsion bar suspension

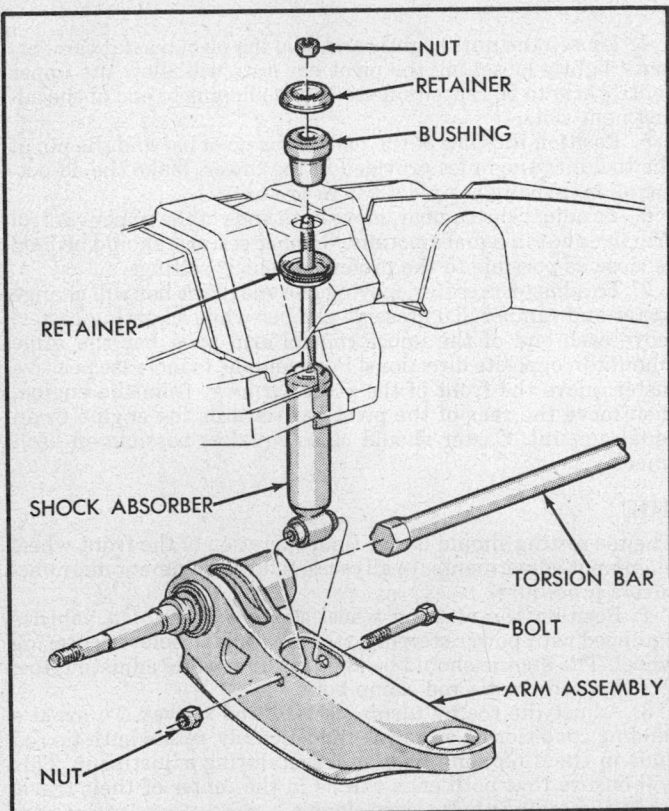

Front shock absorber—conventional torsion bar suspension

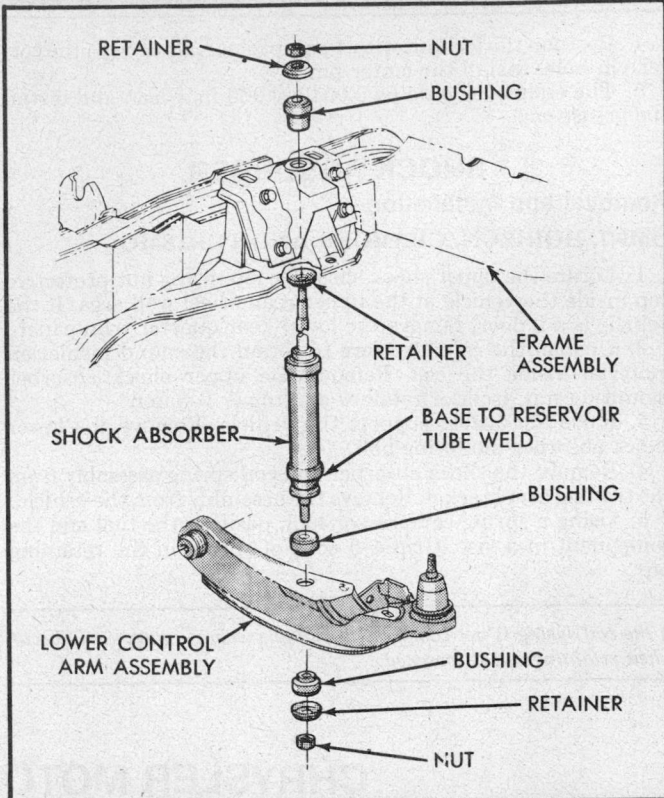

Front shock absorbers—transverse torsion bar suspension

Removal and Installation

1. Raise and safely support the vehicle.

2. Remove the caliper retaining clips and springs. Remove the caliper assembly from the caliper support housing or steering knuckle arm. Properly position the caliper aside.

3. Remove the grease cap, cotter pin, locknut and bearing adjusting nut.

4. Remove thrust washer and outer bearing. Remove the rotor.

5. Carefully drive out the inner seal from the back of the rotor. Remove the inner wheel bearing.

6. Remove the inner and outer bearing cones from the rotor using the proper removal tools.

7. To install, reverse the removal procedures. Be sure to use new seals as required. Repack the wheel bearings using the proper type lubricant.

SHOCK ABSORBER

Removal and Installation

1. Raise and safely support the vehicle. Remove the nut and retainer from the upper end of shock absorber.

2. Remove the lower shock absorber retaining nuts.

3. Compress shock absorber and remove it from the vehicle.

4. To install, reverse the removal procedures. Torque the retaining nut to 25 ft. lbs.

UPPER BALL JOINT

Inspection

1. Position a jack under the lower control arm and raise the wheel clear of the floor. Remove the wheel cover, grease cap and cotter pin.

2. Tighten the bearing adjusting nut enough to remove all play between the hub, bearings and the spindle.

3. Lower the jack to allow the tire to lightly contact the floor. It is important that the tire have contact with the floor.

4. Grasp the top of the tire and apply force inward and outward. While this force is being applied, have an observer check for any movement at the ball joints between the upper control arm and the knuckle.

5. If any lateral movement is evident, replace the ball joint.

Removal and Installation

1. Raise and safely support the vehicle.

2. Position a jackstand under the lower control arm as close to the wheel as possible. Be sure the jackstand is not in contact with the brake splash shield. The rubber rebound bumper must not contact frame.

3. Remove the wheel assembly.

4. Remove the cotter pins and nuts from the upper and lower ball joints to facilitate use of the ball joint removal tool.

5. Slide the tool on the lower ball joint stud and allow the tool to rest on the knuckle arm. Position the tool securely against the upper stud.

6. Tighten the tool to apply pressure to the upper stud and strike knuckle sharply with hammer to loosen stud. Do not attempt to force the stud out using only the tool.

7. After removing the tool, disengage the upper ball joint from the knuckle. Properly support the knuckle and brake assembly to prevent damage to the brake hose and lower ball joint.

8. Remove the upper ball joint from the vehicle.

9. To install, reverse the removal procedures.

LOWER BALL JOINT

Inspection

1. Raise the front of the vehicle and install jackstands under both lower control arms as far outboard as possible. The upper control arms must not contact the rubber rebound bumpers.

2. With the weight of vehicle on the control arm, install a dial indicator and clamp the assembly to lower control arm.

3. Position the dial indicator plunger tip against the knuckle arm. Zero the dial indicator gauge.

4. Measure the axial travel of the knuckle arm with respect to the control arm, by raising and lowering the wheel using a pry bar under the center of the tire.

5. During measurement, if the axial travel of the control arm is 0.030 in. or more, relative to the knuckle arm, the ball joint should be replaced.

Removal and Installation

1. Raise and safely support the vehicle. Remove the wheel assembly.

2. Remove brake caliper. Do not allow the caliper to hang, properly support it.

3. Remove the hub and rotor assembly and splash shield. Dis-

connect the shock absorber at the lower control arm. Unwind torsion bar.

4. Remove the upper and lower ball joint stud cotter pins and nuts. Slide the ball joint removal tool over the upper stud until the tool rests on the steering knuckle.

5. Turn the threaded portion of the tool locking it securely against the lower stud. Tighten the tool enough to place the lower ball joint stud under pressure, then strike the steering knuckle arm sharply with a hammer to loosen stud. Do not attempt to force stud from knuckle with tool alone.

6. Use the tool to press the ball joint from the lower control arm.

7. To install, reverse the removal procedures.

TORSION BARS

Removal and Installation

LONGITUDINAL TYPE

Longitudinal torsion bars have a hex formed on each end. One hex end is installed in the lower control arm anchor, the opposite end is anchored in the frame or body crossmember.

1. Raise and safely support the vehicle.

2. Release the vehicle load from the torsion bar by turning the anchor adjusting bolt in the lower control arm counterclockwise.

3. Remove the lock ring from the anchor at the rear of the torsion bar. Install the torsion bar removal tool. If necessary, remove the transmission torque shaft to provide clearance. Position the tool toward the rear of the torsion bar in order to allow sufficient room for striking the pad of the tool. Do not apply heat to the torsion bar, front anchor or rear anchor.

4. Remove tool and slide the torsion bar out through the rear anchor. Do not damage the balloon seal when removing the torsion bar.

5. To install, reverse the removal procedures. If the torsion bar hex opening does not index with the lower control arm hex opening, loosen the lower control arm pivot shaft nut, rotate the pivot shaft to index with torsion bar. Install the torsion bar. Do not tighten the pivot shaft nut while the suspension is in the rebound position.

6. Adjust front suspension height.

TRANSVERSE TYPE

Transverse torsion bars are formed with an angle for transverse mounting. Each bar is hex shaped on the anchor end with a replaceable torsion bar-to-lower control arm bushing on the opposite end and a pivot cushion bushing midway on the torsion bar.

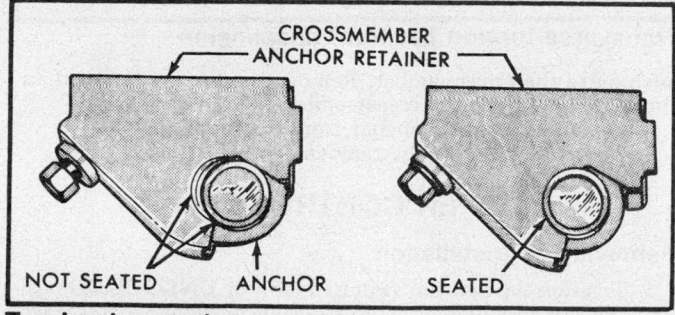

Torsion bar anchor assembly

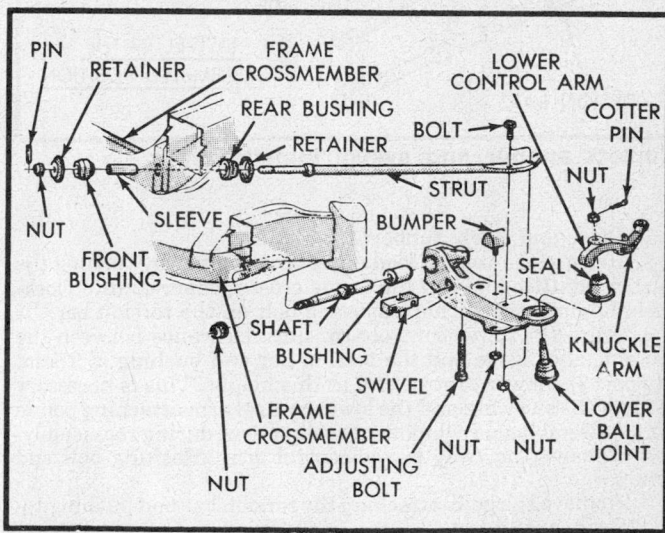

Lower control arm and ball joint

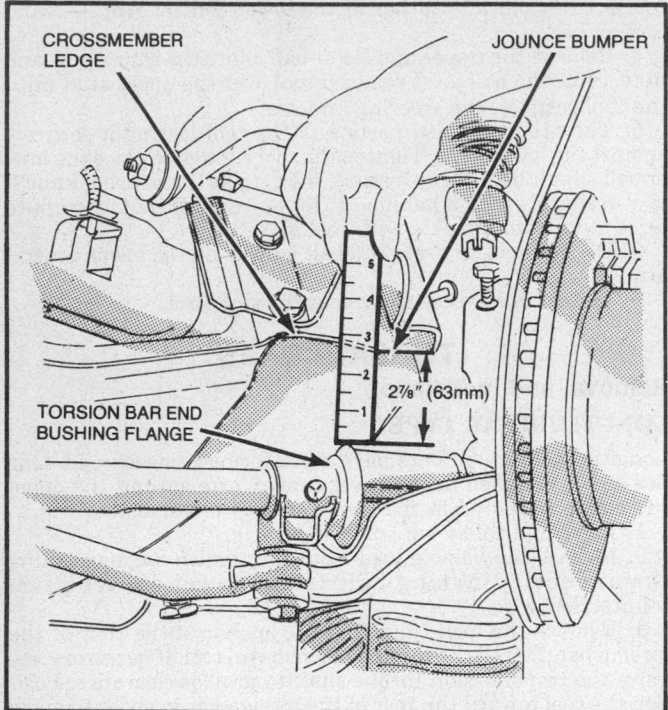

Measuring design height

CROSSMEMBER LEDGE

JOUNCE BUMPER

2⅞" (63mm)

TORSION BAR END BUSHING FLANGE

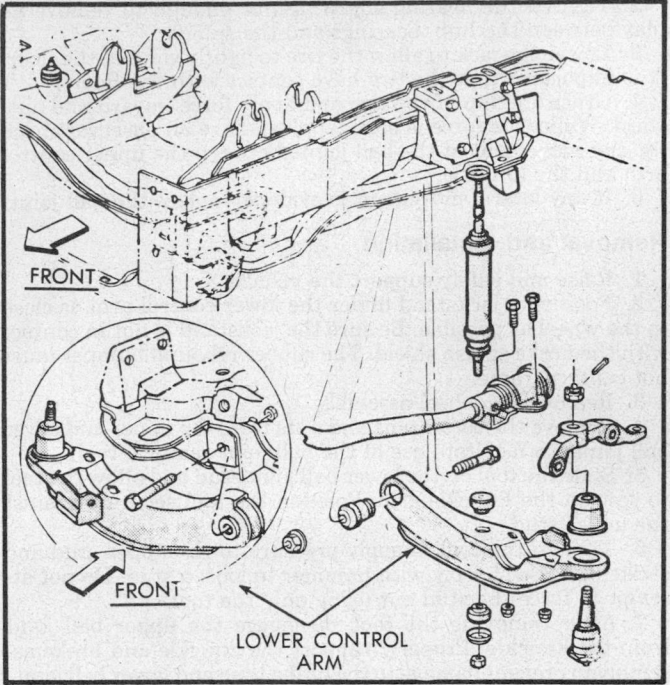

Lower control arm with transverse torsion bar suspension

FRONT

FRONT

LOWER CONTROL ARM

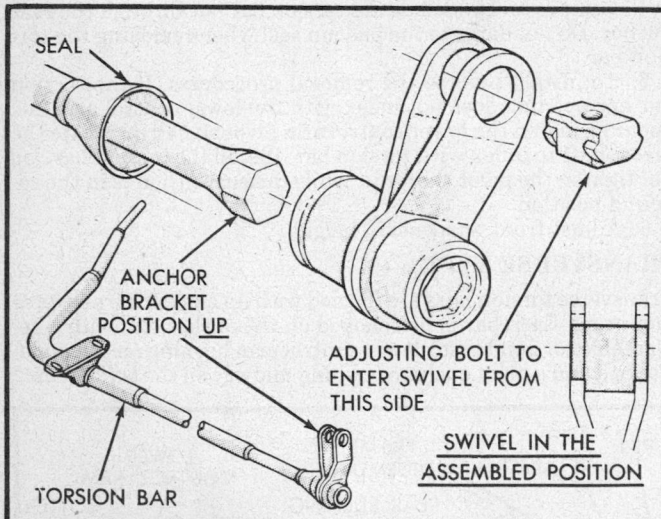

Correct anchor and swivel installation

SEAL

ANCHOR BRACKET POSITION UP

TORSION BAR

ADJUSTING BOLT TO ENTER SWIVEL FROM THIS SIDE

SWIVEL IN THE ASSEMBLED POSITION

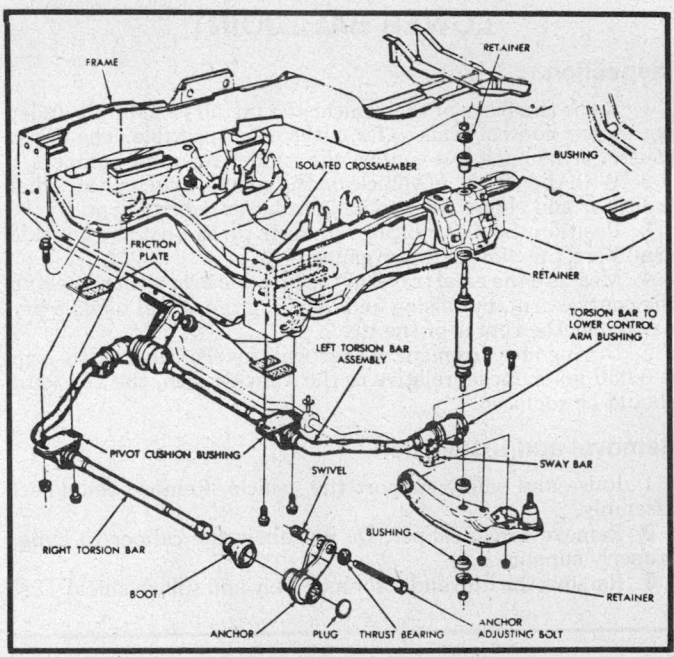

Transverse torsion bar front suspension

FRAME

RETAINER

ISOLATED CROSSMEMBER

BUSHING

FRICTION PLATE

RETAINER

LEFT TORSION BAR ASSEMBLY

TORSION BAR TO LOWER CONTROL ARM BUSHING

PIVOT CUSHION BUSHING

SWIVEL

SWAY BAR

RIGHT TORSION BAR

BUSHING

BOOT

ANCHOR

PLUG

THRUST BEARING

ANCHOR ADJUSTING BOLT

RETAINER

1. Raise and safely support the vehicle.

2. Release the vehicle load on the torsion bar by turning the anchor adjusting bolt in the frame crossmember counterclockwise. Remove the anchor adjusting bolt on the torsion bar.

3. Raise the lower control arm until clearance between the crossmember ledge and the torsion bar end bushing is 2⅞ in. Support the lower control arm at this height. This is necessary to align the sway bar and the lower control arm attaching points for disassembly and component realignment during reassembly.

4. Remove the sway bar-to-control arm attaching bolt and retainers.

5. Remove the bolts attaching the torsion bar end bushing-to-the lower control arm.

6. Remove the bolts attaching the torsion bar pivot cushion

bushing to the crossmember. Remove the torsion bar and anchor assembly from the crossmember.

7. Carefully separate anchor from the torsion bar.

8. To install, reverse the removal procedures.

UPPER CONTROL ARM

Removal and Installation

1. Position the ignition switch in **OFF** or **UNLOCKED** position. Raise and safely support the vehicle. Remove the wheel assembly.

2. Position a jackstand under the lower control arm near the splash shield. Be sure the jackstand does not contact the shield and the rebound bumpers are not under vehicle load.

3. On some vehicles, it will be necessary to remove the caliper to provide clearance for the ball joint removal tool.

4. Remove the cotter pin and nut from the upper and lower ball joints in order to facilitate use of the removal tool.

5. Slide the tool over lower ball joint stud and allow it to rest on the steering knuckle arm. Tigthen the tool in order to apply pressure to the upper ball joint stud. Strike the steering knuckle boss sharply with hammer to loosen the stud. Do not attempt to force the stud from the knuckle with only the tool.

6. After removing the tool, support the brake and knuckle assembly in order to prevent damage to the brake hose or lower ball joint. Disengage the upper ball joint from the knuckle.

7. From under the hood, remove the engine splash shield in order to expose the upper control arm pivot bar.

8. Scribe a line on the support bracket along the inboard edge of the pivot bar in order to establish suspension alignment during reassembly.

9. Remove pivot bolts and lift the upper control arm with ball joint and pivot bar assembly from the bracket.

10. To install, reverse the removal procedures.

LOWER CONTROL ARM

Removal and Installation

LONGITUDINAL TYPE TORSION BAR

1. Position the ignition switch in the **OFF** or **UNLOCKED** position. Remove the rebound bumper.

2. Raise and safely support the vehicle. Remove the wheel assembly.

3. Remove the caliper. Remove the lower shock absorber mounting bolt.

4. Remove the hub and rotor assembly. Remove the splash shield.

5. Remove the strut bar retaining bolts from the lower control arm.

6. Remove the automatic transmission gear shift torque shaft assembly if required for tool clearance.

7. Measure and record the torsion bar anchor bolt depth into the lower control arm before unwinding the torsion bar. Unwind the torsion bar. Remove the torsion bar.

8. Separate the lower ball joint from the steering knuckle arm.

9. Remove the lower control arm shaft nut from the control arm shaft and push out the shaft from frame crossmember. Strike the threaded end of the shaft with a soft hammer to loosen if necessary. Remove the lower control arm and shaft as an assembly from the vehicle.

10. To install, reverse the removal procedures. Adjust the wheel alignment.

TRANSVERSE TYPE TORSION BAR

1. Raise and safely support the vehicle. Remove the wheel assembly.

2. Remove the caliper from the vehicle.

3. Remove the hub and rotor assembly. Remove the splash shield.

4. Remove shock absorber lower nut, retainer and insulator.

5. Release the load on both torsion bars by turning the anchor adjusting bolts counterclockwise. Releasing both torsion bars is required because of the sway bar reaction from the opposite torsion bar.

6. Raise the lower control arm until clearance between the crossmember ledge and torsion bar-to-lower control arm bushing is 2⅞ in. Support the control arm at this design height. Remove the bolts retaining the torsion bar end bushing to the lower control arm.

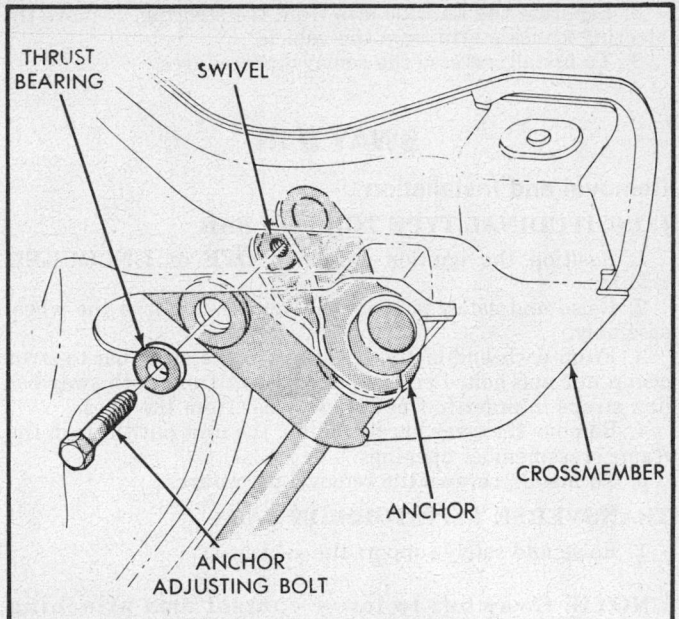

Transverse torsion bar anchor bolt

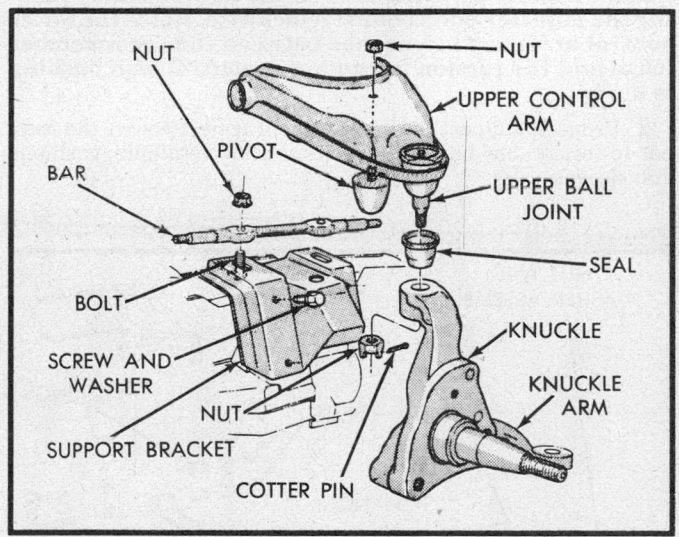

Knuckle control arm and ball joint

7. Separate lower ball joint from knuckle arm. Remove lower control arm pivot bolt. Remove the lower control arm.

8. To install, reverse the removal procedures. Check wheel alignment.

STEERING KNUCKLE ARM

Removal and Installation

1. Position the ignition switch in **OFF** or **UNLOCKED** position. Remove rebound bumper.

2. Raise and safely support the vehicle. Remove the wheel assembly.

3. Remove the caliper. Remove the hub and brake assembly.

4. Remove the brake splash shield from steering knuckle.

5. Unload the torsion bars, by turning the anchor adjusting bolt counterclockwise.

6. Disconnect tie rod from the steering knuckle arm. Use care as not to damage the seals.

7. Remove the lower ball joint stud from the knuckle arm.

8. Separate the knuckle arm from the steering. Remove the steering knuckle arm from the vehicle.

9. To install, reverse the removal procedures.

SWAY BAR

Removal and Installation

LONGITUDINAL TYPE TORSION BAR

1. Position the ignition switch in **OFF** or **UNLOCKED** position.

2. Raise and safely support the vehicle. Remove the wheel assembly.

3. From each end of the bar, remove the sway bar-to-strut clamp nut and bolt. Remove nut and bolt from both sway bar link straps in order to free the sway bar from the lines.

4. Remove the sway bar by pulling the unit out through the frame crossmember openings.

5. To install, reverse the removal procedures.

TRANSVERSE TYPE TORSION BAR

1. Raise and safely support the vehicle.

NOTE: **Sway bar to lower control arm attaching points are only aligned when the lower control arms are at the designed height. If frame contact or a twin post hoist is used, release the load on the torsion bar by turning the adjuster bolts counterclockwise. Raise the lower control arms until clearance between the crossmember ledge and the torsion bar-to-lower control arm bushing is 2⅞ in.**

2. Properly support the lower control arms. Remove the sway bar-to-torsion bar bushing attaching bolts, retainers, cushions and sleeves.

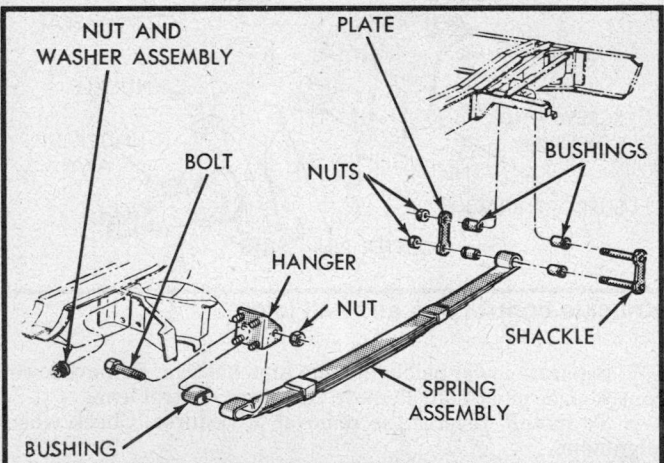

Rear suspension models with longitudinal torsion bar suspension

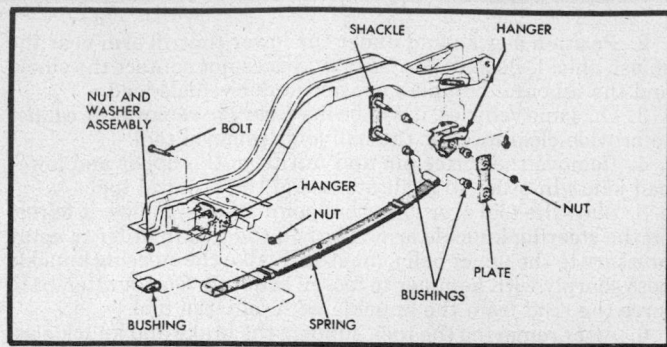

Rear suspension cars with transverse front suspension

3. Remove the retainer assembly strap bolts and retainer straps. Remove the sway bar from the vehicle.

4. To install, reverse the removal procedures.

Rear Suspension

SHOCK ABSORBER

Removal and Installation

1. Raise and safely support the vehicle. Raise the axle to relieve the load on the shock absorbers.

2. Remove the shock absorber lower end as follows. Loosen and remove the nut, retainer and bushing from the spring plate. When loosening the retaining nut, grip the shock absorber at the base to avoid reservoir damage.

3. Loosen and remove the nut and bolt from the upper shock absorber mounting. Remove the shock absorber from the vehicle.

4. To install, reverse the removal procedures.

LEAF SPRING

Removal and Installation

1. Raise and safely support the vehicle.

2. Disconnect the shock absorber at the spring plate. Lower the axle assembly, permitting rear springs to hang free. If equipped, disconnect the rear sway bar links.

3. Loosen and remove the U-bolt nuts and remove the U-bolts and spring plate.

4. Loosen and remove the nuts holding from the spring hanger to the body mounting bracket.

5. Loosen and remove the rear spring hanger bolts and let spring drop far enough to pull the front spring hanger bolts from the body mounting bracket holes.

6. Loosen and remove the pivot bolt from the front spring hanger.

7. Loosen and remove the shackle nuts and remove the shackle from the rear spring.

8. To install, reverse the removal procedures.

FORD/LINCOLN/MERCURY FRONT WHEEL DRIVE

Front Suspension

FRONT WHEEL ALIGNMENT

Adjustment

TOE

1. If equipped with power steering, start the engine and move the steering wheel left-to-right several times until it is in the straight ahead or centered position.

2. If equipped with power steering, turn the engine **OFF** and lock the steering wheel in place using a steering wheel holder. Loosen and slide off small outer clamp of the front boot prior to starting the toe adjustment. This is done in order to prevent the boot from twisting.

3. Adjust the left and right tie rods until each wheel has ½ the desired total toe specification.

4. When the jam nuts are loosened they nuts must be retightened to specification. Attach the boot clamp after adjustment and make sure the boot is not twisted.

CASTER AND CAMBER

Caster and camber angles of this suspension system are preset at the factory and cannot be adjusted. Caster measurements must be checked on the left side by turning the left wheel through the prescribed angle of sweep and on the right side by turning the right wheel through the prescribed angle of sweep.

When the inside wheel is turned 20 degrees, the turning angle of the outside wheel should be specified. The turning angle cannot be adjusted directly, because it is a result of the combination of caster, camber and toe adjustments and should, therefore, be measured only after the toe adjustment has been made. If the turning angle does not meet specification, check the knuckle or other suspension or steering parts for defect.

FRONT WHEEL BEARINGS

The wheel bearings are located in the front knuckle. These bearings do not require adjustment. The bearings are protected by inner and outer grease seals and an additional inner grease shield immediately inboard of the inner grease seal. The wheel hub is installed with an interference fit to the constant velocity universal joint outer race shaft. The hub nut and washer are installed and tightened to 180–200 ft. lbs.

STRUT ASSEMBLY

Removal and Installation

EXCEPT CONTINENTAL, FESTIVA AND TRACER

1. Raise and safely support the vehicle.

NOTE: Do not raise the Taurus or Sable by the lower control arms.

2. Remove the wheel assembly.

3. Remove brake line flex hose clip from the strut. If necessary, remove the brake rotor in order to gain working clearance.

4. Raise strut as far as possible without lifting the vehicle.

5. Install the spring compressor tool by placing the top jaw on the 2nd coil from the top and bottom jaw so as to grip a total of 5 coils . Compress the spring until there is about ⅛ in. between any 2 coils. With a medium pry bar, slightly spread the knuckle-to-strut pinch joint.

6. Place a 2 × 4 × 7½ in. long piece of wood against the shoulder on the knuckle. Using a short pry bar between the

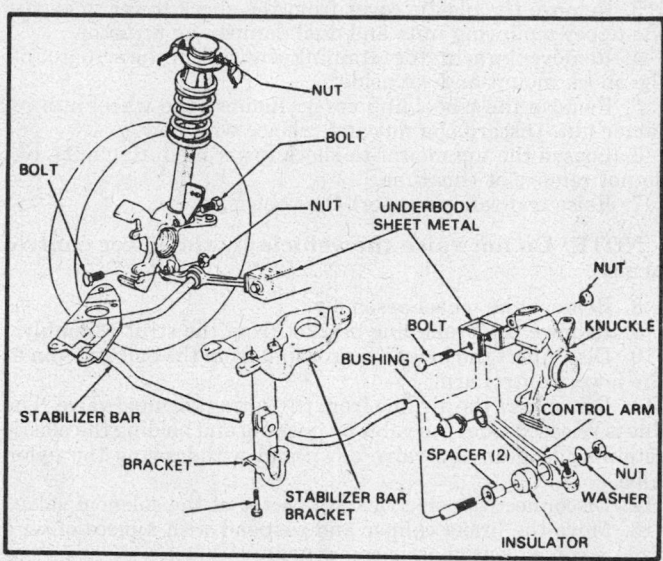

Front suspension fasteners. Bolts must be installed in direction shown

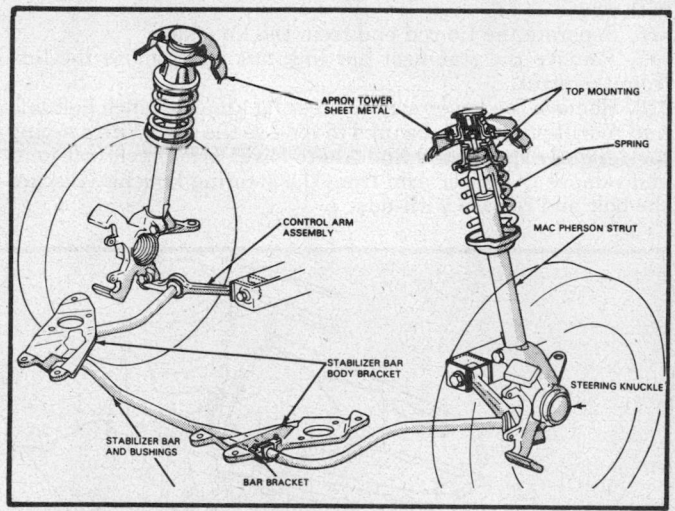

Front wheel drive suspension

wood block and the lower spring seat, separate the strut from the knuckle.

7. Remove the upper mounting nuts.

8. Remove the strut, spring and top mount assembly from the vehicle.

9. Position a 18mm deep socket on the strut shaft nut. Insert a 6mm Allen wrench into the shaft end and the clamp mount into a vise. Remove the top shaft mounting nut from the shaft while holding the Allen wrench with vise grips or a extension.

10. Remove strut top mount components and spring.

11. To install, reverse the removal procedures.

CONTINENTAL

The front suspension utilizes MacPherson struts with integral air springs and dual dampening mechanisms. The front struts are mounted to the body by means of a high percision ball bearing and rubber mount system.

1. Turn **OFF** the air suspension switch located in the left side luggage compartment. Loosen the wheel nuts.

2. Turn the ignition switch to the **OFF** position to unlock the steering wheel.

3. Remove the plastic cover from the shock tower to expose the upper mounting nuts and dual dampening actuator.

4. Remove the actuator retaining screws. Lift the actuator off the shock mount and set aside.

5. Remove the wheel/hub cover. Remove the wheel hub retainer nut. Discard the nut and replace with new.

6. Loosen the top mount-to-shock tower mounting nuts, but do not remove at this time.

7. Raise and safely support the vehicle.

NOTE: Do not raise the vehicle by the lower control arms.

8. Remove the wheel assembly.

9. Remove the brake line bracket from the strut assembly.

10. Disconnect the height sensor link from the ball stud pin at the lower control arm.

11. Disconnect the air line from the spring solenoid valve. The line is released from the valve by pushing and holding the plastic retaining ring on the valve down and withdrawing the nylon tube.

12. Disconnect the electrical connector at the solenoid valve.

13. Move the brake caliper and suspend with a piece of wire from a convenient chassis component.

14. Remove the brake rotor.

15. Remove the cotter pin from the tie rod end stud and remove the slotted nut. Discard the cotter pin and nut and replace with new.

16. Separate the tie rod end from the knuckle.

17. Remove the stabilizer bar link nut and remove the link from the strut.

18. Remove the lower arm-to-steering knuckle pinch bolt and nut. A drift punch may be used to remove the bolt. With a prying tool, slightly spread the knuckle-to-lower arm pinch bolt joint and remove the lower arm from the steering knuckle. Discard the bolt and replace with new.

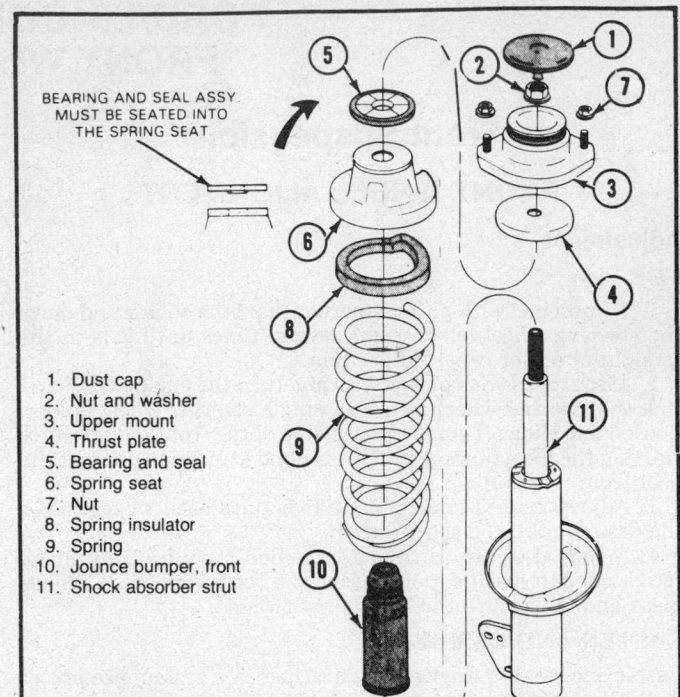

BEARING AND SEAL ASSY.
MUST BE SEATED INTO
THE SPRING SEAT

1. Dust cap
2. Nut and washer
3. Upper mount
4. Thrust plate
5. Bearing and seal
6. Spring seat
7. Nut
8. Spring insulator
9. Spring
10. Jounce bumper, front
11. Shock absorber strut

Top mount components

19. Press the halfshaft from the hub and wire the halfshaft to the body in a level position.

20. Remove the shock absorber-to-steering knuckle pinch bolt. Spread the knuckle-to-strut pinch joint as required to assist in the removal of the bolt.

21. Remove the steering knuckle and hub assembly from the shock absorber strut.

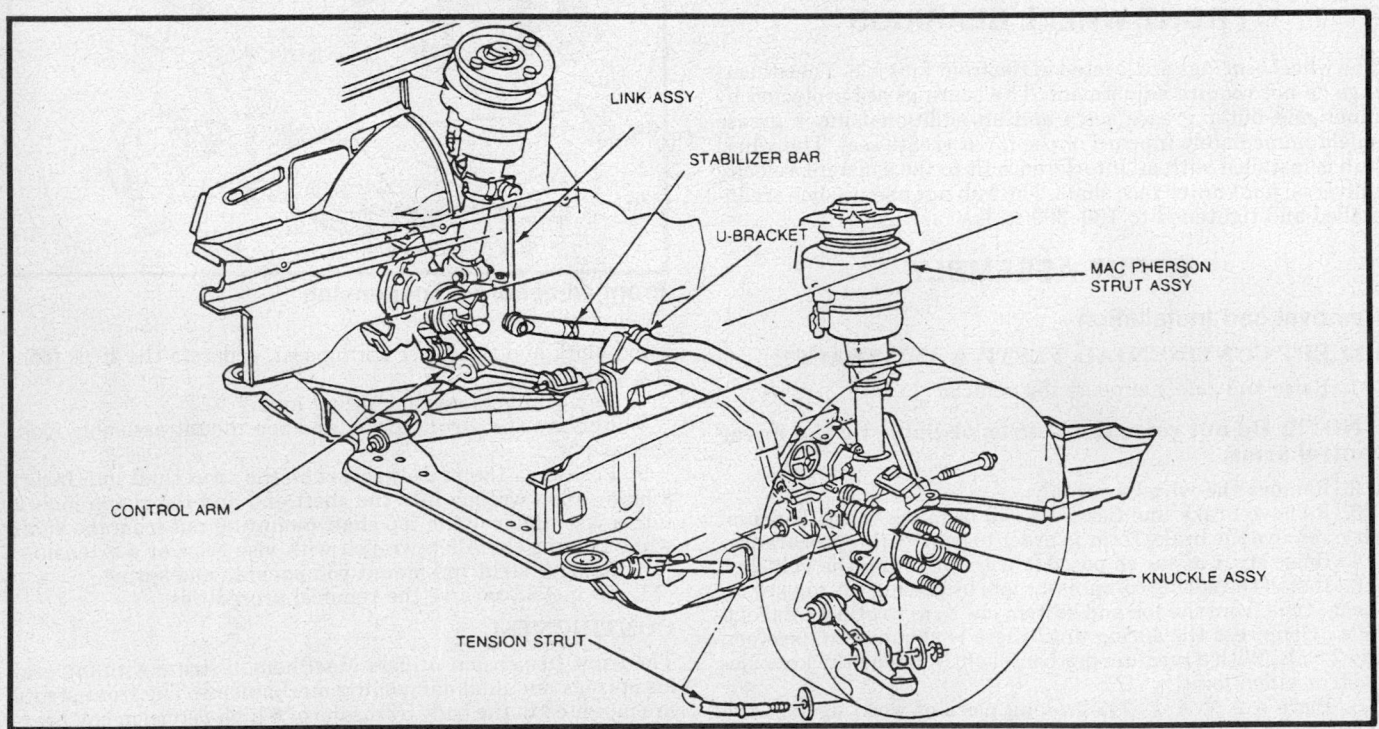

LINK ASSY
STABILIZER BAR
U-BRACKET
MAC PHERSON STRUT ASSY
CONTROL ARM
KNUCKLE ASSY
TENSION STRUT

Front suspension components—Continental

22. Remove the top mount-to-shock tower nuts and remove the strut and spring assembly from the vehicle.

23. To install, reverse the removal procedures. Torque the tie rod end nut to 23–35 ft. lbs., top mount-to-shock tower nuts to 22–32 ft. lbs. and hub nut to 180–200 ft. lbs.

FESTIVA

1. Disconnect the negative battery cable.
2. Raise and safely support the front of the vehicle until the struts are fully extended.
3. Remove the wheel assembly.
4. Remove the brake line clip from the strut lower mounting bracket cutout and disengage the brake line.
5. Remove the nuts and bolts securing the strut lower bracket to the steering knuckle.
6. In the engine compartment, remove the nuts securing the strut mounting block to the strut tower mounting studs.
7. Disengage the strut lower bracket from the steering knuckle and lower the strut assembly and spacer plate clear of the wheel well.

To install:

8. Place the strut assembly with spacer plate onto the strut tower with the white alignment mark facing outward.
9. Install the upper mounting block stud nuts and torque to 32–45 ft. lbs.
10. Engage the steering knuckle in the strut tower lower bracket and install the mounting bolts. Torque the bolts to 69–86 ft. lbs.
11. Position the brake line into the strut lower mounting bracket cutout and install the retaining clip.
12. Install the wheel assembly.

TRACER

1. Raise and safely support the front of the vehicle.
2. Remove the wheel assembly.
3. Remove the brake caliper-to-steering knuckle bolts and suspend the caliper with a piece of wire. Leave the brake hose connected.
4. Place an alignment mark on the inside of the strut mounting block.
5. Remove the strut-to-steering knuckle bolts. Remove the brake line U-clip and the brake line from its bracket.
6. Remove the upper strut-to-body nuts and the strut assembly from the vehicle.
7. To install, align the reference marks and reverse the removal procedures. Torque the strut-to-steering knuckle bolts to 69–72 ft. lbs. Check and/or adjust the front wheel alignment.

LOWER BALL JOINT

Inspection

1. Raise and safely support the vehicle. Position a jack beneath the underbody until wheel falls to the full down position.
2. Grasp the lower edge of the tire and move the tire assembly in and out.
3. As wheel is being moved in and out, observe the lower end of the knuckle and the lower control arm. Any movement between the lower end of the knuckle and lower arm indicates abnormal ball joint wear.

Removal and Installation

NOTE: The lower ball joint is not replaceable separately on all vehicles except the Tracer. The ball joint is integral with and must be removed along with the lower control arm assembly.

TRACER

1. Raise and safely support the front of the vehicle. Remove the wheel assembly.

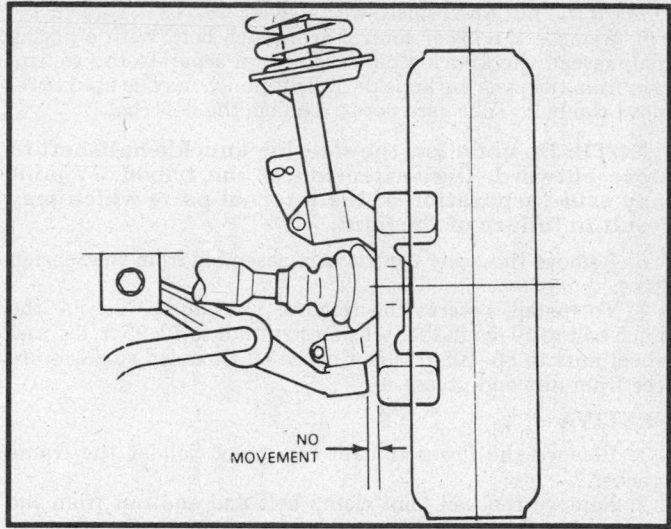

NO MOVEMENT

As wheel is being moved in and out, observe the lower end of the knuckle and the lower control arm. Any movement between lower end of knuckle and the lower arm indicates abnormal ball joint wear

2. Remove the caliper-to-steering knuckle bolts and the caliper. Suspend the caliper with a piece of wire.
3. Remove the stabilizer bar-to-lower control arm nuts/bolts and separate the stabilizer bar.
4. Remove the tie rod end cotter pin and nut. Separate the tie rod from the steering knuckle. Discard the nut and cotter pin and replace with new.
5. Remove the ball joint-to-steering knuckle clamp bolt. Separate the lower control arm from the steering knuckle.
6. Remove the ball joint-to-steering knuckle nuts and the ball joint.
7. To install, reverse the removal procedures. Torque the:
   a. Ball joint-to-steering knuckle clamp bolt to 32–40 ft. lbs.
   b. Tie rod end-to-steering knuckle nut to 22–33 ft. lbs.
   c. Caliper-to-steering knuckle bolts to 29–36 ft. lbs.

LOWER CONTROL ARM

Removal and Installation

EXCEPT CONTINENTAL, FESTIVA AND TRACER

1. Raise and safely support the vehicle. Remove the wheel assembly.
2. Remove the nut from the stabilizer bar. Pull off large dished washer.
3. Remove the lower control arm inner pivot bolt and nut.
4. Remove the lower control arm ball joint pinch bolt. Slightly spread the knuckle pinch joint and separate the control arm from the steering knuckle. A drift punch may be used to remove the bolt. Be sure steering column is in unlocked position. Do not use a hammer to separate ball joint from knuckle.
5. Remove the lower control arm pivot bolt and nut. Remove the lower control arm assembly from the tension strut.
6. To install, reverse the removal procedures.

CONTINENTAL

1. Turn **OFF** the air suspension switch located in the left side of the luggage compartment. Loosen the wheel nuts. Place the steering wheel in the unlocked position.
2. Raise and safely support the vehicle. Remove the wheel assembly.
3. Disconnect the height sensor link from the ball stud pin.
4. Remove the nut and dished washer from the tension strut.

Discard the nut and replace with new.

5. Remove the lower control arm pinch bolt. With a prying tool, spread the knuckle pinch joint and separate the control arm from the steering knuckle. A drift punch may be used to remove the bolt. Take care not to damage the bolt seal.

NOTE: Do not allow the steering knuckle/halfshaft to move outward. Over-extension of the tripod CV-joint may cause separation of the internal parts which may result in failure of the joint.

6. Remove the lower control arm assembly from the tension strut.

7. To install, reverse the removal procedures. Torque the pinch bolt to 40–55 ft. lbs., tension strut nut to 70–95 ft. lbs. and wheel nuts to 80–105 ft. lbs. Ensure all threaded surfaces are free from dirt and grease.

FESTIVA

1. Remove the lower control arm pivot bolt at the frame bracket.

2. Remove the ball joint clamp bolt and and nut from the steering knuckle assembly.

3. Remove the stabilizer bar bushing retaining nut from the rear of the control arm and remove the rear bushing washer and bushing.

4. Lower the control arm, prying the ball joint stud from the steering knuckle, if necessary. Disengage and remove the control arm from the stabilizer end.

To install:

5. Inspect the control arm for deformation or cracks and check the pivot bushing for deterioration. Verify that the ball joint swivels freely but is not loose. If the control arm pivot bushing is to be replaced, remove the old bushing and center the new bushing in the center of the control arm eye and install. Replace the lower control arm/ball joint assembly as required.

6. If the ball joint boot is damaged or deteriorated, pry the boot off with a small cold chisel. Install the new boot onto the ball joint using a adapter such as a ¾ in. socket to properly seat the boot.

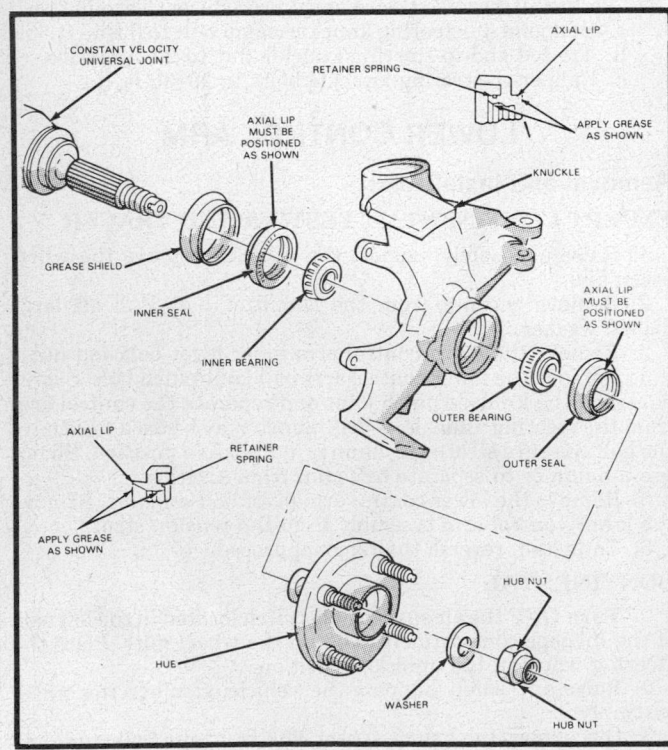

Steering knuckle

7. Complete installation of the lower control arm by reversing the removal procedure. Torque the stabilizer retaining nut to 43–52 ft. lbs., pivot bolt at the control arm frame bracket to 32–40 ft. lbs. and steering clamp nut to 32–40 ft. lbs.

TRACER

1. Raise and safely support the front of the vehicle. Remove the wheel assembly.

2. Remove the caliper-to-steering knuckle bolts and the caliper. Suspend the caliper with a piece wire.

3. Remove the stabilizer bar-to-lower control arm nuts/bolts and separate the stabilizer bar.

4. Matchmark the rear control arm bushing-to-mounting bracket and the rear control arm bushing-to-control arm.

5. Remove the ball joint-to-steering knuckle clamp bolt. Pry the lower control arm from the steering knuckle.

6. Loosen the lower control arm front bushing and rear bushing nuts.

7. Remove the lower control arm rear bushing bracket-to-chassis bolts. Remove the lower control arm front bushing bracket-to-chassis bolts.

8. Remove the lower control arm rear bushing bolt and the lower control arm.

9. Remove the lower control arm front bushing nut and the front bushing.

10. To install, reverse the removal procedures. Torque the ball joint-to-steering knuckle clamp bolt to 32–40 ft. lbs. and the caliper-to-steering knuckle bolts to 29–36 ft. lbs.

STEERING KNUCKLE

Removal and Installation

EXCEPT TRACER

1. Raise and safely support the vehicle. Remove the wheel assembly.

2. Remove the cotter pin from the tie rod end strut. Remove the fitted nut. Remove tie rod end from knuckle.

3. Remove the caliper and rotor. Remove the hub from the driveshaft.

4. Remove the lower arm-to-steering knuckle pinch bolt and nut. Using the proper tool, slightly spread the knuckle-to-lower arm pinch joint and remove lower arm from steering knuckle. Be sure steering column is in unlocked position. Do not use a hammer to separate ball joint from the knuckle.

5. Remove the shock absorber strut-to-steering knuckle pinch bolt. Using a pry bar, slightly spread the knuckle-to-strut pinch joint. Remove the steering knuckle from the shock absorber strut.

6. To install, reverse the removal procedures.

TRACER

1. Remove the halfshaft.

2. Disconnect the U-shapped clip from the center section of the caliper hose. Leave the brake hose connected to the caliper. Remove the brake caliper-to-steering knuckle bolts and support the caliper with wire.

3. Remove the tie rod-to-steering knuckle ball joint cotter pin and nut. Separate the tie rod end from the steering knuckle.

4. Mark the camber alignment cam bolt for reassembly. Remove the cam bolt and the upper attaching bolt from the strut and spindle.

5. Pull the steering knuckle assembly from the strut bracket.

6. To install, reverse the removal procedures. Torque the:
   a. Steering knuckle-to-strut bolts to 69–86 ft. lbs.
   b. Lower control arm-to-steering knuckle clamp bolt to 32–40 ft. lbs.
   c. Tie rod-to-steering knuckle nut to 22–33 ft. lbs.
   d. Caliper-to-steering knuckle bolts to 29–36 ft. lbs.

7. Lower the vehicle. Torque the hub nut to 116–174 ft. lbs. and stake the hub nut. Check and/or adjust the front wheel alignment.

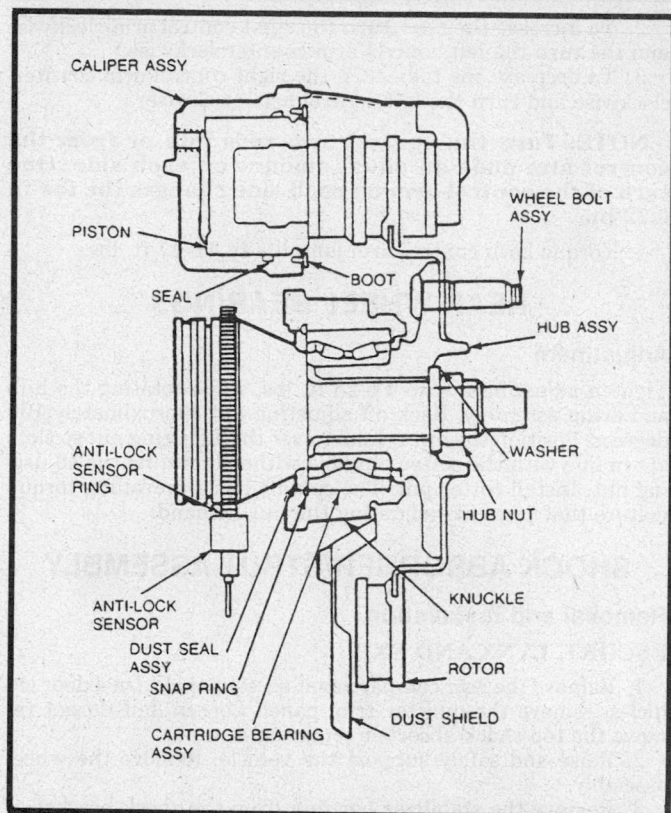

Section of the hub and bearing assembly used on Continental

HUB ASSEMBLY

Removal and Installation

EXCEPT FESTIVA

1. Remove hub retaining nut and washer by applying sufficient torque to the nut to overcome prevailing torque features of the crimp in the nut collar. The hub nut must be discarded after removal. On the Continental, remove the top strut-to-fender apron nuts.

2. Raise and safely support the vehicle. Remove the caliper. Do not remove the caliper pins from the caliper assembly. Lift caliper off the rotor and hang it free of the rotor. Properly support the caliper assembly.

3. Remove the rotor from the hub by pulling it off the hub bolts. On the Continental, remove the rotor splash shield.

4. Install hub removal tool T81P–1104–A with adaptor tools T81P–1104–C and T81P–B or equivalent, remove the hub. If the outer bearing is seized on the hub, use a puller to remove the bearing. Be careful not to damage bearing if it is being reused.

5. If bearings are being reused, carefully inspect both bearing cone and rollers, bearing cups and lubrication for any signs of damage or contamination. If damage or contamination exists, replace all bearing components including cups and seals.

6. In the event the bearings are acceptable, clean and repack bearing components. Inner and outer grease retainers and hub nut must be replaced whenever bearings are inspected.

7. Remove the steering knuckle from the vehicle.

8. To install, reverse the removal procedures. Care must be taken to prevent the hub from backing from the bearing assembly, otherwise, it will be necessary to reassemble the hub through the bearings.

FESTIVA

1. Disconnect the negative battery cable.

2. Raise and safely support the front of the vehicle.

3. Unbolt and remove front wheel from the hub assembly.

4. With a small cold chisel, straighten the staked edge of the halfshaft attaching nut. Take care not to damage the halfshaft threads.

5. Apply the brakes to prevent the rotor hub from turning. Remove the halfshaft attaching nut. Discard the nut and replace with new.

6. Remove the retaining clip securing the caliper hose to the strut bracket.

7. Remove the cotter pin and tie rod end attaching nut. Discard the cotter pin and set the nut aside. Inspect the nut for damage and replace as required.

8. Separate the tie rod end from the steering knuckle arm.

9. Support the brake caliper by hand and remove the brake caliper attaching bolts. Lift the caliper assembly from the steering knuckle. Do not allow the caliper to be suspended by the brake hose. Support the caliper with a length of rope or wire.

10. Remove the clamp bolt and nut at the point where the lower control arm ball joint connects to the steering knuckle. With a medium pry bar, separate the lower ball joint from the steering knuckle by prying downward on the lower control arm.

11. Remove the steering knuckle-to-strut bracket flanges through bolts.

12. Slide the rotor assembly from the end of the halfshaft.

13. Clean the spline end and lubricate with a coating of wheel bearing grease. Apply a thin film of clean SAE 30 weight oil to the steering knuckle/rotor hub assembly up to the point where the uppermost arm of the steering knuckle seats into the MacPherson strut bracket.

14. To install, reverse the removal procedures. Torque the:
   a. Strut-to-steering knuckle bolts to 69–86 ft. lbs.
   b. Lower control arm nut to 32–40 ft. lbs.
   c. Steering knuckle bolts to 29–36 ft. lbs.
   d. Tie rod end-to-steering knuckle nut to 22–33 ft. lbs.

STABILIZER BAR AND INSULATORS

Removal and Installation

1. Raise and safely support the vehicle.

2. Remove the nut from the stabilizer bar on each lower control arm. Remove the large dished washer.

3. Remove the stabilizer bar insulator mounting bracket bolts. Remove the stabilizer bar assembly.

4. Remove the worn insulators from the bar.

5. To install, reverse the removal procedures.

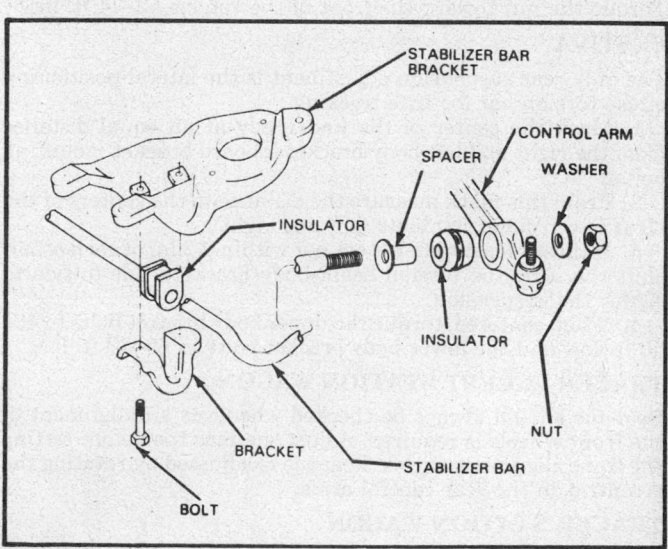

Stabilizer bar components

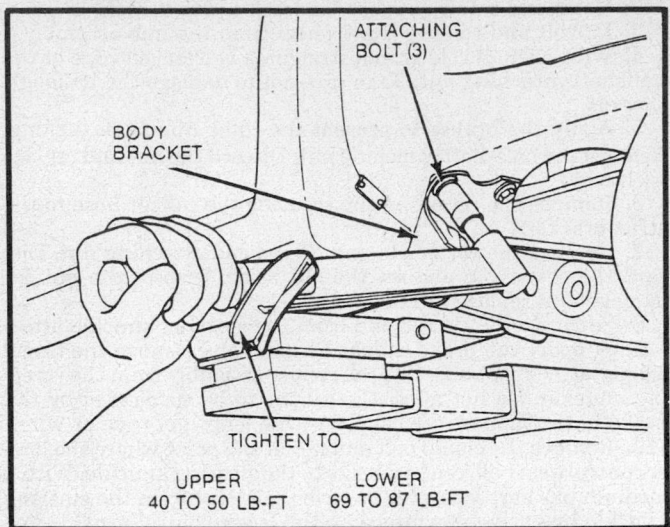

Tension bar lateral positioning—Festiva rear suspension

Rear Suspension

REAR WHEEL ALIGNMENT

Toe Adjustment

TEMPO, TOPAZ, TAURUS AND SABLE (WAGON)

1. Raise and safely support the vehicle.
2. Loosen the rear control arm-to-body retaining bolt.
3. Rotate the alignment cam until specification is obtained.
4. Torque the bolt 40–55 ft. lbs.

ESCORT, LYNX AND EXP

1. Raise and safely support the vehicle.
2. Loosen the tie rod nut, facing the front of the vehicle, and slide the tie rod rearward to increase the toe.
3. Loosen the tie rod nut, facing the rear of the vehicle, and slide the tie rod forward increase the toe.
4. After adjustment, hold the tie rod flat with a wrench and tighten the retaining nut.
5. Torque the nut toward the rear of the vehicle 6–12 ft. lbs. Torque the nut toward the front of the vehicle 52–74 ft. lbs.

FESTIVA

The only rear suspension adjustment is the lateral positioning of the torsion bar for true tracking.
1. Mark the center of the underbody at an equal distance from the right and left body bracket inboard bracket mounting bolts.
2. From this mark measure the distance to the centers of the strut lower mounting bolts (left and right).
3. If these measurements are not within 0.2 in. of each other, shift the shift the torsion beam body brackets side-to-side to center the suspension.
4. When centered, torque the upper body bracket bolts to 40–50 ft. lbs. and the lower body bracket bolts to 69–87 ft. lbs.

TRACER EXCEPT STATION WAGON

Rear toe should always be checked whenever an alignment of the front wheels is required. Adjust the rear toe before setting the front alignment angles. Rear toe is adjusted by rotating the eccentric on the rear control arms.

TRACER STATION WAGON

1. Loosen the jamnuts clockwise on the right control arm and counterclockwise on the left on the left.

2. To increase the toe—turn the right control arm clockwise and the turn the left control arm counterclockwise.
3. To decrease the toe—turn the right control arm counterclockwise and turn the left control arm clockwise.

NOTE: Turn the control arm rods into or from the control arm ends an equal amount on each side. One turn of the control arm on each side changes the toe-in 0.22 in.

4. Torque both control arm jamnuts to 41–47 ft. lbs.

REAR WHEEL BEARINGS

Adjustment

Tighten adjusting nut to 17–25 ft. lbs. while rotating the hub and drum assembly. Back off adjusting nut approximately 100 degrees. Position the nut retainer over the adjusting nut so slots are in line with the cotter pin hole without rotating the adjusting nut. Install cotter pin. The spindle has a prevailing torque feature that prevents adjusting the nut by hand.

SHOCK ABSORBER/STRUT ASSEMBLY

Removal and Installation

ESCORT, LYNX AND EXP

1. Remove the rear compartment access panels. On 4 door vehicles, remove the quarter trim panel. Loosen, but do not remove the top shock absorber retaining nut.
2. Raise and safely support the vehicle. Remove the wheel assembly.
3. Remove the stabilizer bar link from the shock bracket, if equipped. As required, remove the clip retaining the brake hose from the rear shock assembly.
4. Position a jackstand under the lower suspension arm. Loosen, but do not remove the shock-to-lower suspension arm nuts.

NOTE: The lower suspension arm must be supported before removing the upper or lower shock absorber retaining bolts.

5. Remove the upper shock retaining bolts. Remove the lower shock retaining bolts. Remove the shock absorber from the vehicle.
6. To install, reverse the removal procedures.

TEMPO AND TOPAZ

1. From inside the trunk loosen, but do not remove the nuts retaining the upper strut mount to the body.

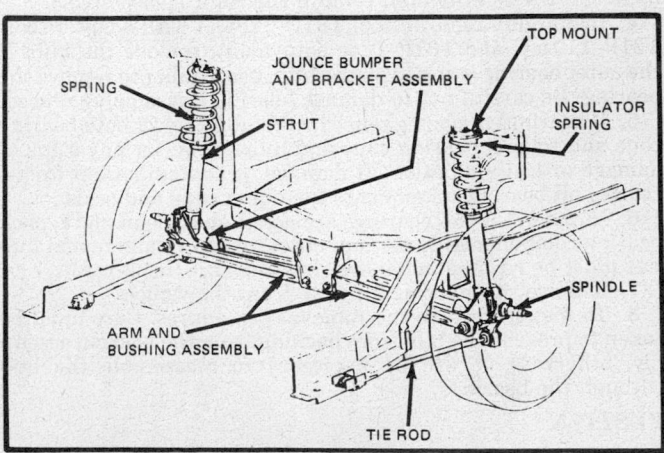

Rear suspension Tempo/Topaz

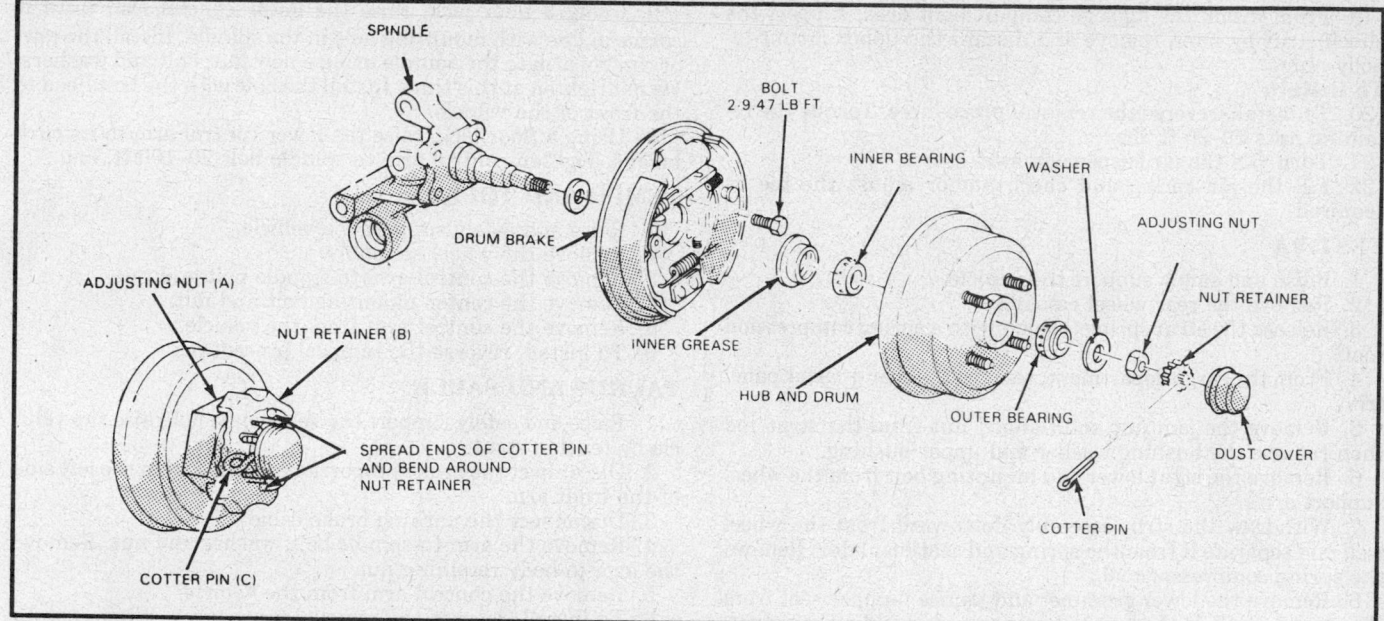

SPINDLE

BOLT
2·9.47 LB FT

INNER BEARING

WASHER

ADJUSTING NUT

NUT RETAINER

DRUM BRAKE

ADJUSTING NUT (A)

NUT RETAINER (B)

INNER GREASE

HUB AND DRUM

OUTER BEARING

DUST COVER

SPREAD ENDS OF COTTER PIN
AND BEND AROUND
NUT RETAINER

COTTER PIN

COTTER PIN (C)

Rear bearing

2. Raise and safely support the vehicle. Remove the wheel assembly.

3. Place a jackstand under the control arms to support the suspension. Care should be taken when removing the strut so the rear brake hose is not stretched or the steel brake tube is not bent.

4. Remove the bolt attaching the brake hose bracket to the strut. Carefully move the assembly aside.

5. Remove the bolts retaining the bumper bracket strut to the spindle. Remove the bumper bracket from the vehicle. Remove the shock strut from the spindle.

6. Remove the upper mount-to-body nuts. Remove the strut from the vehicle.

7. To install, reverse the removal procedures.

CONTINENTAL

1. Turn **OFF** the air suspension switch located in the luggage compartment.

2. From inside the luggage compartment, disconnect the electrical connector from the dual dampening actuator.

3. Loosen, but do not remove the strut-to-upper body nuts.

4. Raise and safely support the vehicle.

5. Disconnect the air line and electrical connector from the solenoid valve.

6. Remove the brake hose retainer at the strut bracket.

7. Disconnect the parking brake cable from the brake caliper. Remove all the wire retainers and parking brake cable retainers from the lower suspension arm.

8. Disconnect the height sensor link from the ball stud pin on the lower arm.

9. Remove the caliper assembly from the spindle and support with a piece of wire. Do not kink or place a load on the brake hose.

10. Bleed the air spring by performing the following:
   a. Remove the solenoid clip.
   b. Rotate the solenoid counterclockwise to the 1st stop.
   c. Slowly pull the solenoid straight out to the 2nd stop and bleed the air from the system.

NOTE: Do not fully release the solenoid until the air is fully bled from the spring.

   d. After the air is fully bled from the system, rotate the solenoid to the 3rd stop and remove the solenoid from the housing.

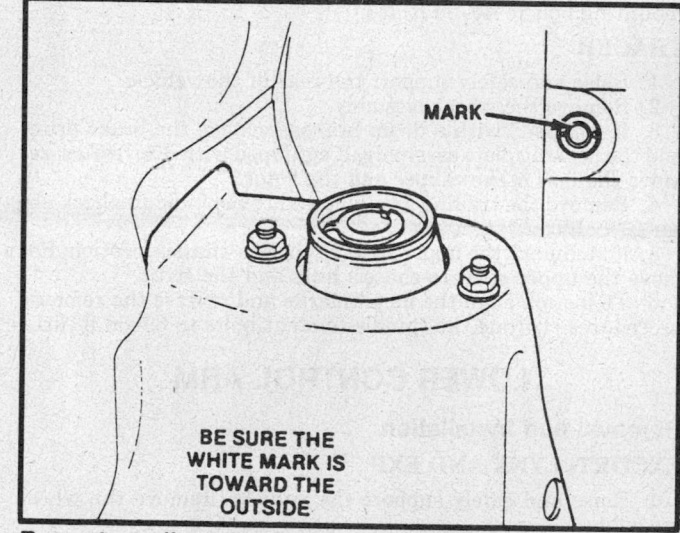

MARK

BE SURE THE
WHITE MARK IS
TOWARD THE
OUTSIDE

Rear strut alignment mark positioning—Tracer

   e. Scribe or mark the position of the notch on the toe adjustment cam.

11. Remove the nut from the inboard bushing on the suspension arm.

12. Install torsion spring remover tool, on the suspension arm. Pry up on the tool and arm using a ¾ in. drive ratchet to relieve the pressure on the pivot bolt.

13. Remove the torsion spring from the arms.

14. Remove the stabilizer U-bracket from the body.

15. Remove the nut, washer and insulator attaching the stabilizer bar to the link. Separate the stabilizer bar from the link.

16. Remove the nut washer and insulator retaining the tension strut to the spindle. Move the spindle rearward enough to separate it from the tension strut.

17. Remove and discard the shock strut-to-spindle pinch bolt. With a prying tool, spread the strut-to-spindle pinch joint as required to assist in removing the bolt.

18. Separate the spindle from the strut. Remove the spindle as an assembly with the arms attached.

19. From inside the luggage compartment area, support the shock strut by hand remove and discard the upper mount-to-body nuts.

To install:

20. To install, reverse the removal procedures. Torque the retaining nuts 19–26 ft. lbs.

21. Turn **ON** the air suspension switch.

22. Fill the air spring and check and/or adjust the toe as required.

FESTIVA

1. Raise and safely support the vehicle.
2. Remove the rear wheel assembly.
3. Release the strut spring tension with a spring compression tool.
4. From the cargo department, remove the rear quarter panel trim.
5. Remove the jam nut and flanged nut from the strut rod then remove the bushing washer and upper bushing.
6. Remove the strut lower end mounting bolt from the wheel support arm.
7. Withdraw the strut assembly downward from the wheel well and separate it from the spring and seat insulator. Remove the spring compressor tool.
8. Remove the lower grommet and jounce bumper seat from the strut rod. Slide the jounce bumper and shield off the strut.
9. To install, reverse the removal procedures. Torque the rod upper end bushing flanged nut to 12–18 ft. lbs. and lower strut mounting bolt to 40–50 ft. lbs.

TRACER

1. Raise and safely support the rear of the vehicle.
2. Remove the wheel assembly.
3. If equipped with a drum brakes, remove the brake drum and the backing plate assembly. If equipped with disc brakes, remove the disc brake caliper and the rotor.
4. Remove the trailing arm bolt and the spindle-to-shock absorber bolts.
5. Matchmark the upper strut rubber-to-chassis location. Remove the upper strut-to-chassis nuts and the strut.
6. To install, align the matchmarks and reverse the removal procedures. Torque the spindle-to-strut bolts to 69–86 ft. lbs.

LOWER CONTROL ARM

Removal and Installation

EXCORT, LYNX AND EXP

1. Raise and safely support the vehicle. Remove the wheel assembly.
2. As required, remove the brake proportioning valve from the left side of the front arm. Disconnect the parking brake cable.
3. Place a floor jack under the lower control arm between spring and spindle end mounting.
4. Remove the nuts from the control arm-to-body mount and control arm-to-spindle mount; do not remove the bolts at this time.
5. Remove the spindle end mounting bolt. Slowly lower the floor jack until the spring and spring insulator can be removed.
6. Remove the bolt from the body end. Remove the control arm from the vehicle.

To install:

7. Attach the lower control arm-to-body bracket using a new bolt and nut. Do not tighten at this time. Install this bolt with the bolt head to the front of the vehicle.
8. Place the spring in the spring pocket in the lower control arm. Be sure the spring pigtail is in the proper index in the lower control arm and the insulator is at the top of the spring, properly seated and indexed. The insulator must be replaced on the spring before the spring is placed in position.

9. Using a floor jack, raise the lower control arm until it comes in line with mounting hole in the spindle. Install the lower control arm to the spindle using a new nut, bolt and washers. Do not tighten at this time. Install the bolt with the bolt head to the front of the vehicle.
10. Using a floor jack, raise the lower control arm to its curb height. Tighten control arm to spindle bolt 90–100 ft. lbs.

TEMPO AND TOPAZ

1. Raise and safely support the vehicle.
2. Remove the wheel assembly.
3. Remove the control arm-to-spindle bolt and nut.
4. Remove the center mounting bolt and nut.
5. Remove the control arm from the vehicle.
6. To install, reverse the removal procedures.

TAURUS AND SABLE

1. Raise and safely support the vehicle; do not raise the vehicle by tension strut.
2. Disconnect the brake proportioning valve from the left side of the front arm.
3. Disconnect the parking brake cable.
4. Remove the arm-to-spindle bolt, washer and nut. Remove the arm-to-body retaining nut.
5. Remove the control arm from the vehicle.
6. To install, reverse the removal procedures. When installing new control arms, the offset on all arms must face up. The arms are stamped bottom on the lower edge. The flange edge of the right side rear arm stamping must face the front of the vehicle.

CONTINENTAL

1. Turn **OFF** the air suspension switch located in the luggage compartment.
2. Raise and safely support the vehicle.
3. Remove all wire and parking brake cable retainers from the front lower suspension arm only. Disconnect the height link sensor from the ball stud pin on the right lower arm.
4. Mark the position of the notch on the toe adjustment cam (rear arm only).
5. Remove the nut from the inboard bushing on the suspension arm.
6. Install a torsion spring remover on the suspension arm. Pry up on the tool and arm using a ¾ in. drive ratchet to relieve the pressure on the pivot bolt. Remove the bolt and lower arm.
7. Remove the nut retaining the torsion spring to the arm. Separate the spring from the arm.
8. Remove the outboard attaching bolt at the spindle.
9. Repeat the procedure for the remaining arm.

NOTE: When installing the new control arms, the offset must face up. The arms are stamped BOTTOM on the lower edge. The rear control arms have adjustment cams that fit inside the bushings at the arm-to-body attachment. These cams are installed from the front of both arms.

10. To install, reverse the removal procedures. Check and adjust the rear toe as necessary.

TENSION STRUT

Removal and Installation

TAURUS AND SABLE WAGON

1. Raise and safely support the vehicle. Place a floor jack under the rear lower suspension arm and raise the arm to normal curb height.
2. Remove the wheel assembly.
3. Remove the nut and bolt retaining the tension strut to the lower suspension arm.

4. Remove the tension strut-to-body bracket retaining nut. Remove the strut assembly.

5. To install, reverse the removal procedures. Tighten tension strut-to-body bracket bolt 40–55 ft. lbs.

TAURUS AND SABLE SEDAN

1. From inside the trunk, loosen, but do not remove the nuts retaining the upper shock strut mount to the body.

2. Raise and safely support the vehicle. Remove the wheel assembly.

3. Remove the tension strut-to-spindle retaining nut.

4. Remove the tension strut-to-body retaining nut.

5. Move the spindle rearward enough to gain working clearance in order to remove the tension strut. Remove the tension strut.

6. To install, reverse the removal procedures.

TIE ROD

Removal and Installation

TEMPO AND TOPAZ

1. Raise the vehicle enough to contact the body. From inside the trunk, loosen, but do not remove the strut top mount-to-body nuts.

2. Raise the vehicle and position a jackstand under the suspension to support it. Remove the wheel assembly.

3. Remove the top mount studs.

4. Remove the nut retaining the tie rod to the spindle. Remove the nut retaining the tie rod to the body.

5. Lower the jackstand enough so the upper strut mount studs are from the holes in the body.

6. Move the spindle rearward enough so the tie rod can be removed from the vehicle.

To install:

7. Place new washers and bushings on both ends of the tie rod. Bushings at front and rear of the tie rod are different. The rear bushings have indentations in them.

8. Insert an end into the body bracket and install a new bushing washer and nut. Do not tighten at this time.

9. Pull back on the spindle so the tie rod end can be installed in the spindle.

10. Install a new bushing, washer and nut. Do not tighten at this time.

11. Raise the jackstand enough to hold the strut mounting studs in place.

12. Install new strut-to-body mount nuts. Tighten 20–30 ft. lbs.

13. Raise the suspension to curb height and tighten the tie rod nuts 52–74 ft. lbs.

14. Remove the jackstand. Install the wheel assembly. Lower the vehicle.

FORD/LINCOLN/MERCURY
REAR WHEEL DRIVE

Front Suspension—Single Arm Design

FRONT WHEEL ALIGNMENT

Caster and camber angles of this suspension are set at the factory and cannot be adjusted in the field. Toe is adjustable.

Adjustment

TOE

Start the engine and move the steering wheel back and forth several times until it is in the straight ahead or centered position. Turn the engine **OFF** and lock the steering wheel in place using a steering wheel holder. Adjust the left and right spindle rod sleeves until each wheel has ½ the desired total toe specification. Whenever the jam nuts are loosened for toe adjustment, torque them 33–50 ft. lbs.

FRONT WHEEL BEARINGS

Adjustment

1. Raise and safely support the vehicle. Remove the wheel cover. Remove the grease cap from the hub.

2. Wipe the excess grease from the end of the spindle. Remove the cotter pin and locknut.

3. Loosen the adjusting nut 3 turns. Rock the wheel, hub and rotor assembly in and out several times to push the shoe and linings away from the rotor.

4. While rotating the wheel, hub and rotor assembly, torque the adjusting nut to 17–25 ft. lbs. to seat the bearings. Loosen the adjusting nut ½ turn, then retorque 10–15 inch lbs.

5. Place the locknut on the adjusting nut, so the castellations on the lock are in line with the cotter pin hole in the spindle. Install a new cotter pin.

6. Check the front wheel rotation. Before driving the vehicle,

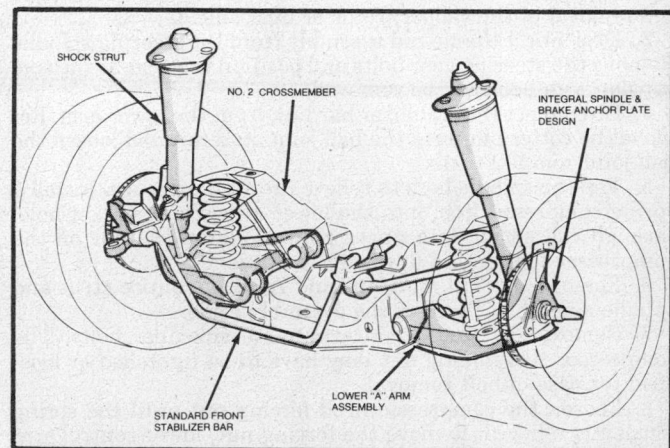

View of the single arm front suspension—Capri, Cougar, Mustang, Thunderbird and XR7

pump the brake pedal several times to restore normal brake pedal travel.

Removal and Installation

1. Raise and safely support the vehicle. Remove the wheel assembly.

2. Remove the caliper from the spindle and position it aside.

3. Remove the grease cap from the hub. Remove the cotter pin, locknut, adjusting nut and flatwasher from the spindle.

3. Remove the outer bearing cone and roller assembly. Pull the hub and rotor assembly off the spindle.

4. Using tool 1175–AC or equivalent, remove and discard the grease retainer. Remove the inner bearing cone and roller assembly from the hub.

5. To install, reverse the removal procedures. Be sure to use new grease seals as required.

STRUT ASSEMBLY

Removal and Installation

1. Place the ignition key in the unlocked position to permit free movement of front wheels. From the engine compartment, remove the 1 strut-to-upper mount attaching nut.
2. Raise and safely support the vehicle. Remove the wheel assembly. Remove the caliper and position it aside.
3. Remove the lower nuts and bolts attaching the strut to the spindle.
4. Lift the strut up from the spindle to compress the rod. Pull the assembly downward and remove it from the vehicle.
5. To install, reverse the removal procedures.

LOWER BALL JOINT

Inspection

1. Support the vehicle in normal driving position with both ball joints loaded.
2. Wipe the wear indicator and ball joint cover checking surface, so they are free of dirt and grease.
3. The checking surface should project outside the cover. If the checking surface is inside the cover, replace the defective component.

LOWER CONTROL ARM

Removal and installation

1. Raise and safely support the vehicle; allow the control arms to hang free. Remove the wheel assembly.
2. Remove the caliper and position it aside. Remove the rotor and dust shield. Some Lincoln Continentals may not require the removal of the caliper, rotor or dust shield.
3. Disconnect the tie rod assembly from the steering spindle. Remove the steering gear bolts and position the gear so the suspension arm bolt may be removed.
4. Disconnect the stabilizer bar link from the lower arm. Remove the cotter pin from the ball joint stud nut and loosen the ball joint nut 1–2 turns.
5. Tap the spindle boss to relieve the stud pressure. Install a spring compressor tool into the lower arm spring pocket hole, through coil spring into upper plate. Tighten the nut on the compressor tool until a drag on the nut is felt.
6. Remove the ball joint nut and raise the entire strut and spindle assembly. Position the assembly aside.
7. Remove the suspension arm-to-crossmember bolts. The compressor tool forcing nut may have to be tightened or loosened for ease of bolt removal.
8. Loosen the compression rod forcing nut until the spring tension is relieved. Remove the forcing nut, lower control arm and coil spring.
9. To install, reverse the removal procedures.

COIL SPRING

Removal and Installation

1. Raise and safely support the vehicle. Remove the wheel assembly.
2. Disconnect the stabilizer link bar from the lower bar. Remove the steering gear bolts and move the steering gear aside. Disconnect the tie rod from the steering spindle.
3. Using the spring compressor tool, install 1 plate with the pivot ball seat down into the coils of the spring. Rotate the plate so it is fully seated into the lower suspension arm spring seat.
4. Install the other plate with the pivot ball seat up into the coils of the spring. Insert the ball nut through the coils of the spring, so it rests in the upper plate.
5. Insert the compression rod into the opening in the lower

arm through the lower and upper plate. Install the ball nut on the rod and return the securing pin. This pin can only be inserted one way into the upper ball nut because of a stepped hole design.
6. With the upper ball nut secured, turn the upper plate, so it walks up the coil until it contacts the upper spring seat.
7. Install the lower ball nut, thrust bearing and forcing nut on the compression rod. Rotate the nut until the spring is compressed enough, so it is free in its seat.
8. Remove the lower control arm pivot bolts and nuts to disengage the lower arm from the frame crossmember. Remove the spring assembly.
9. If a new spring is to be installed, mark the position of the upper and lower plates on the spring with chalk. Measure the compressed length of the spring as well as the amount of spring curvature to assist in the compression and installation of a new spring.
10. To install, reverse the removal procedures. Be sure the lower end of the coil spring is properly positioned between both holes in the lower arm spring pocket depression.

SPINDLE

Removal and Installation

1. Raise and safely support the vehicle. Remove the wheel assembly.
2. Remove the caliper, rotor and dust shield. Remove the stabilizer link from the lower arm assembly.
3. Remove the tie rod end from the spindle. Remove the cotter pin from the ball joint stud nut and loosen the ball joint nut 1–2 turns. Do not remove the nut from the ball joint stud at this time.
4. Tap the spindle boss to relieve the stud pressure.
5. Position a floor jack under the lower arm, compress the coil spring and remove the stud nut.
6. Remove the bolts and nuts attaching the spindle to the shock strut. Compress the shock strut as required to gain working clearance.
7. Remove the spindle assembly from the vehicle.
8. To install, reverse the removal procedures.

STABILIZER BAR LINK

Removal and Installation

1. Raise and safely support the vehicle.
2. Remove the nut, washer and insulator from the upper end of the stabilizer bar attaching link bolt.
3. Remove the bolt and the remaining washers, insulators and spacer.
4. To install, reverse the removal procedures.

STABILIZER BAR

Removal and installation

1. Raise and safely support the vehicle.
2. Disconnect the stabilizer from each stabilizer link. Disconnect both stabilizer insulator attaching clamps.
3. Remove the stabilizer bar assembly.
4. To install, reverse the removal procedures.

Front Suspension—Enclosed Spring

FRONT WHEEL ALIGNMENT

Adjustment
CASTER AND CAMBER

1. Check the suspension with the front wheels in the straight

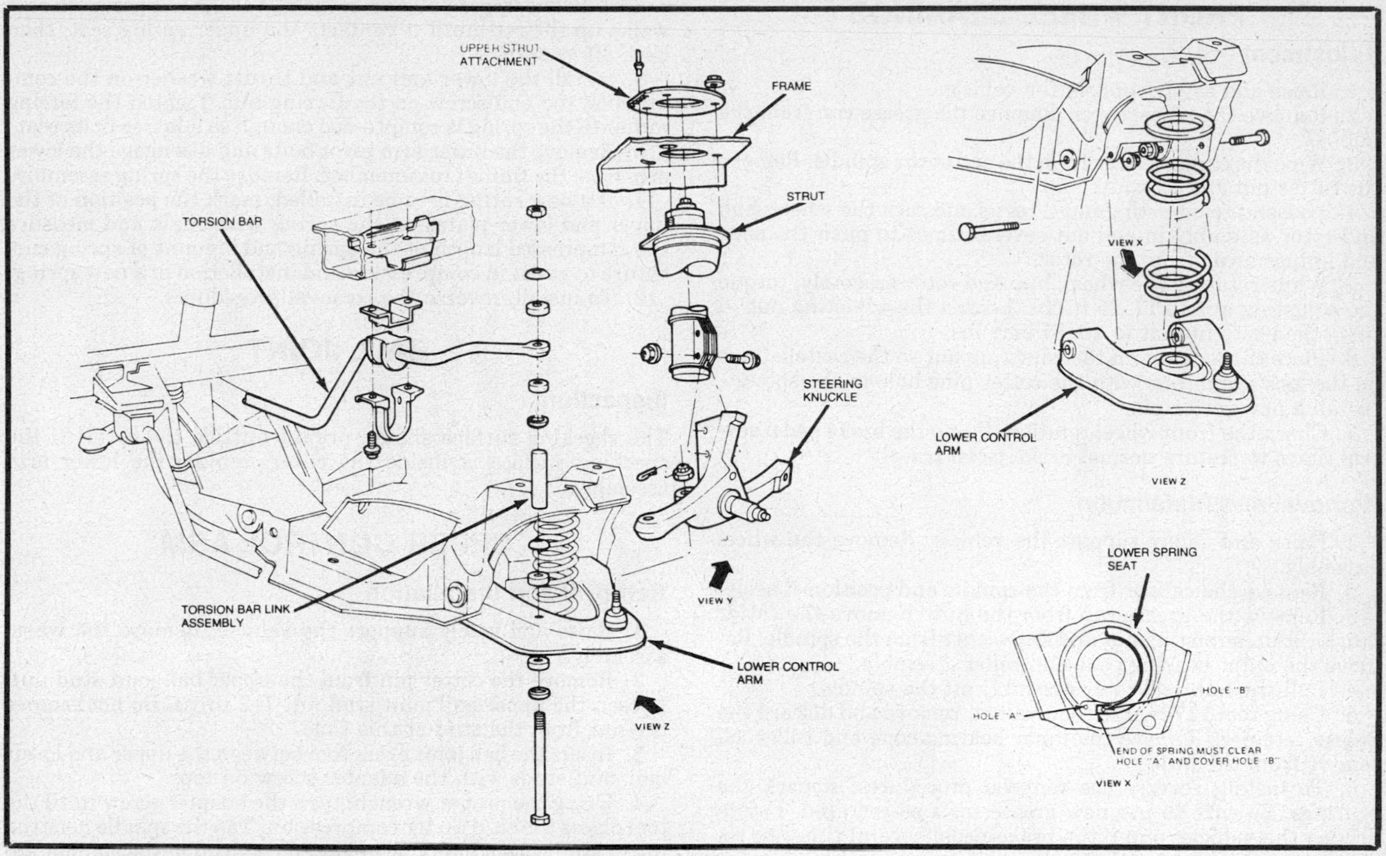

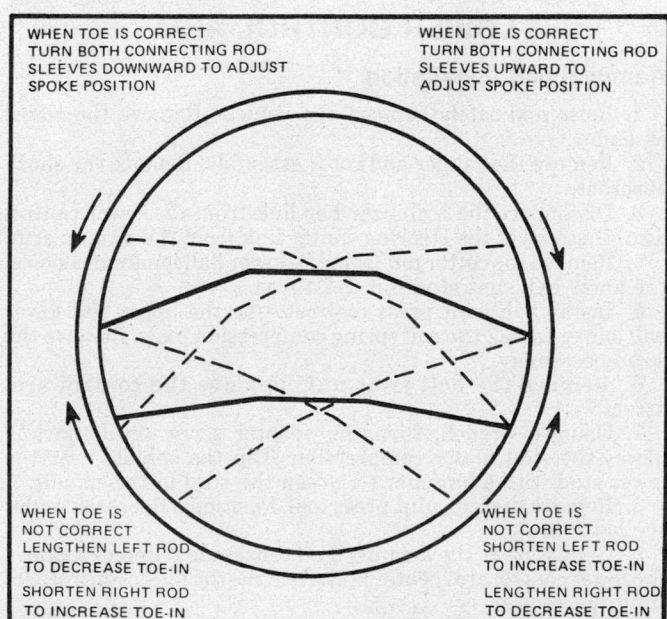

Single arm front suspension

ahead position. Run the engine so the power steering control valve will be in the center position.

2. Check the caster and camber and record the readings.

3. Compare the camber and caster readings with specification to determine if adjustment is required.

WHEN TOE IS CORRECT TURN BOTH CONNECTING ROD SLEEVES DOWNWARD TO ADJUST SPOKE POSITION

WHEN TOE IS CORRECT TURN BOTH CONNECTING ROD SLEEVES UPWARD TO ADJUST SPOKE POSITION

WHEN TOE IS NOT CORRECT LENGTHEN LEFT ROD TO DECREASE TOE-IN

SHORTEN RIGHT ROD TO INCREASE TOE-IN

WHEN TOE IS NOT CORRECT SHORTEN LEFT ROD TO INCREASE TOE-IN

LENGTHEN RIGHT ROD TO DECREASE TOE-IN

Adjust both rods equally to maintain normal spoke position

4. If adjustment is required, insert the alignment tools into the frame holes and snug the tool hooks finger tight against the upper arm inner shaft. Then tighten hex nut of each alignment tool 1 additional hex flat.

5. Loosen the upper arm inner shaft-to-frame attaching bolts so the lockwashers on bolts are unloaded. Then firmly tap the bolt heads to assure loosening of the lower assemblies.

6. Adjust camber and caster on each wheel.

7. Torque the upper arm inner shaft-to-frame attaching bolts 100–140 ft. lbs. It is not necessary to recheck caster and camber after this adjustment procedure is performed.

8. Check toe-in and steering wheel spoke position and adjust, as required.

TOE AND STEERING WHEEL SPOKE

After adjusting caster and camber, check the steering wheel spoke position with the front wheels in the straight ahead position. If the spokes are not in their normal position, they can be properly adjusted while the toe is being adjusted.

1. Loosen the clamp bolts on each spindle connecting rod sleeve.

2. Adjust the toe. If the steering wheel spokes are in their normal position, lengthen or shorten both rods equally to obtain correct toe.

3. If the steering wheel spokes are not in their normal position, make the necessary rod adjustments to obtain correct toe and steering wheel spoke alignment.

4. When toe and the steering wheel spoke position are both correct, lubricate clamp, bolts and nuts and tighten the clamp bolts on both connecting rod sleeves and specification. The sleeve position should not be changed when the clamp bolts are tightened for proper clamp bolt orientation.

FRONT WHEEL BEARINGS

Adjustment

1. Raise and safely support the vehicle.
2. Remove the wheel cover. Remove the grease cap from the hub.
3. Wipe the excess grease from the end of the spindle. Remove the cotter pin and locknut.
4. Loosen the adjusting nut 3 turns and rock the wheel, hub and rotor assembly in and out several times to push the shoe and linings away from the rotor.
5. While rotating the wheel, hub and rotor assembly, torque the adjusting nut to 17–25 ft. lbs. Loosen the adjusting nut ½ turn, then retighten it to 10–15 inch lbs.
6. Place the locknut on the adjusting nut so the castellations on the lock are in line with the cotter pine hole in the spindle. Install a new cotter pin.
7. Check the front wheel rotation. Pump the brake pedal several times to restore normal brake pedal travel.

Removal and Installation

1. Raise and safely support the vehicle. Remove the wheel assembly.
2. Remove the caliper from the spindle and position it aside.
3. Remove the grease cap from the hub. Remove the cotter pin, locknut, adjusting nut and flatwasher from the spindle. Remove the outer bearing cone and roller assembly.
4. Pull the hub and rotor assembly off the spindle.
5. Using tool 1175–AC or equivalent, remove and discard the grease retainer. Remove the inner bearing cone and roller assembly from the hub.
6. To install, reverse the removal procedures. Repack the bearings. Be sure to use new grease seals as required. Before driving the vehicle, pump the brake pedal several times to restore normal brake pedal travel.

SHOCK ABSORBER

Removal and Installation

1. Remove the nut, washer and bushing from the shock absorber upper end. Raise and safely support the vehicle.
2. Remove the screws attaching the shock absorber to the lower control arm. Remove the shock absorber from the vehicle.
3. To install, reverse the removal procedures.

COIL SPRING

Removal and Installation

1. Raise and safely support the vehicle. Remove the wheel assembly.
2. Disconnect the stabilizer bar link from the lower arm. Remove the bolts attaching the shock absorber to the lower arm assembly.
3. Remove the upper nut, retainer and grommet from the shock absorber. Remove the shock absorber.
4. Remove the steering center link from the pitman arm.
5. Using the spring compressor tool, install a plate with the pivot ball seat facing downward into the coils of the spring. Rotate the plate so it is flush with the upper surface of the lower arm.
6. Install the other plate with the pivot ball seat facing upward into the coils of the spring. Insert the upper ball nut through the coils of the spring so the nut rests in the upper plate.
7. Insert the compression rod into the opening in the lower arm through the upper and lower plate and upper ball nut. Insert the securing pin through the upper ball nut and compression rod. This pin can only be inserted one way in the upper ball nut because of a stepped hole design.

8. With the upper ball arm secured, turn the upper plate so it walks up the coil until it contacts the upper spring seat, then back off ½ turn.
9. Install the lower ball nut and thrust washer on the compression rod and screw on the forcing nut. Tighten the forcing nut until the spring is compressed enough so it is free in its seat.
10. Remove the lower arm pivot bolts and disengage the lower arm from the frame crossmember. Remove the spring assembly.
11. If a new spring is to be installed, mark the position of the upper and lower plates on the spring with chalk and measure the compressed length of the spring and amount of spring curvature to assist in compression and installation of a new spring.
12. To install, reverse the removal procedures.

BALL JOINT

Inspection

The checking surface should project outside the cover. If the checking surface is inside the cover, replace the lower arm assembly.

UPPER CONTROL ARM

Removal and Installation

1. Raise and safely support the vehicle. Remove the wheel assembly.
2. Remove the cotter pin from the upper ball joint stud nut. Loosen the upper ball joint stud nut 1–2 turns. Do not remove the nut from the stud at this time.
3. Insert the ball joint press tool between the upper and lower ball joint studs with the adapter screw on top.
4. Using the proper wrench, turn the adapter screw until the tool places the stud under compression. Tap the spindle near the upper stud with a hammer to loosen the stud in the spindle. Do not loosen the stud from the spindle with tool pressure only. Do not contract the boot seal with a hammer.
5. Remove the tool from between the joint studs. Position a floor jack under the lower control arm.
6. Remove the upper control arm attaching bolts. Remove the upper control arm assembly from the vehicle.
7. To install, reverse the removal procedures.

LOWER CONTROL ARM

Removal and Installation

1. Raise and safely support the vehicle. Remove the wheel assembly.
2. Remove the caliper and rotor assembly. Remove the shock absorber.
3. Disconnect the stabilizer bar link from the lower control arm. Disconnect the steering center link from the pitman arm.
4. Remove the cotter pin from the lower ball joint nut. Loosen the lower ball joint stud nut 1–2 turns.
5. Install ball joint press tool between the upper and lower ball joints. Install the coil spring compression tools. Remove the spring assembly.
6. Remove the ball joint nut. Remove the control arm assembly.
7. Using a wrench, turn the adapter screw until the tool places the stud under compression. Tap the spindle near the lower stud with a hammer to loosen the stud in the spindle.
8. Remove the ball joint press tool. Position a floor jack under the lower arm.
9. Gently lower the arm until all tension is relieved. Remove the lower control arm center bolt. Remove the lower control arm from the vehicle.
10. To install, reverse the removal procedures. Be sure the pigtail of the lower coil of the spring is in the proper location of the seat of the lower arm, between both holes.

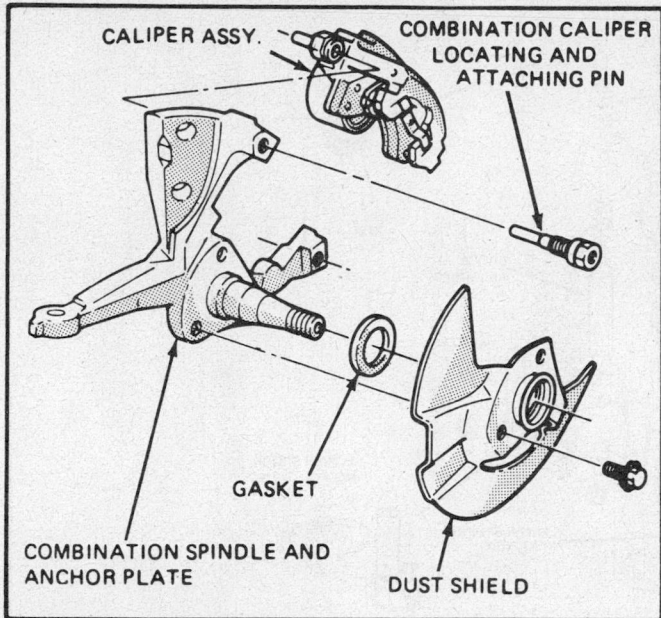

Spindle mounting

SPINDLE

Removal and Installation

1. Raise and safely support the vehicle. Remove the wheel assembly.
2. Remove the rotor and caliper assembly. Disconnect the tie rod end from the spindle.
3. Remove the cotter pins from both ball joint stud nuts and loosen the nuts 1–2 turns. Do not remove the nuts at this time.
4. Position the ball joint remover tool between the upper and lower ball joint studs. Turn the tool with a wrench until the tool places the studs under compression. With a hammer, sharply hit the spindle near the studs to break it loose in the spindle.
5. Position a floor jack under the lower control arm at the lower ball joint area.
6. Remove the upper and lower ball joint stud nuts, lower the jack carefully to and remove the spindle assembly from the vehicle.
7. To install, reverse the removal procedures.

STABILIZER BAR LINK

Removal and Installation

1. Raise and safely support the vehicle.
2. Remove the nut, washer and insulator from the lower end of the stabilizer bar attaching bolt.
3. Remove the bolt and remaining washers, insulators and the spacer.
To install:
4. Assemble a cup washer and new insulator on the bolt.
5. Insert the bolt through the stabilizer bar, then install new insulator and cup washer.
6. Install the spacer, cup washer and another new insulator on the bolt.
7. Insert the bolt through the lower arm and install a new insulator and cup washer. Install the attaching nut.

STABILIZER BAR

Removal and Installation

1. Raise and safely support the vehicle.

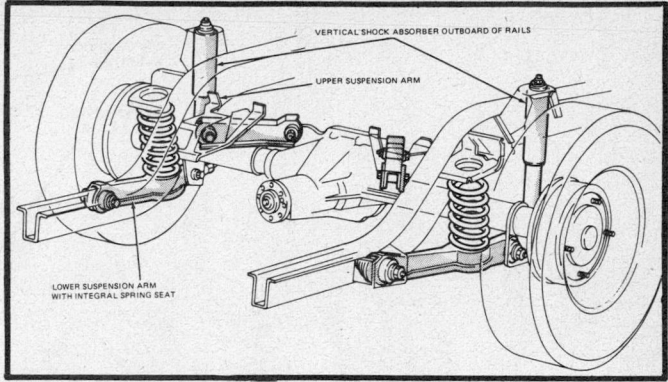

Four bar link coil rear suspension

2. Disconnect the stabilizer bar from each stabilizer link assembly. Remove both stabilizer insulator clamps. Remove the stabilizer bar assembly.
3. To install, reverse the removal procedures.

Rear Suspension—4-Bar Link Design

Adjustment

On the 1988–90 RWD vehicles, a rear toe and camber adjustment is necessary. The vehicle should be at curb height with a ½ tank of fuel.

TOE

1. Position the vehicle on an alignment rack.
2. At each rear lower control arm, inboard pivot bolt, loosen the nut to allow bolt rotation.
3. Set the toe to $\frac{1}{16}$N–$\frac{3}{16}$P.

NOTE: The toe should be divided equally, side-to-side, to prevent dog-tracking.

4. After adjustment, torque the bolt and nut to 124–170 ft. lbs. (170–230 Nm).

CAMBER

1. Position the vehicle on an alignment rack.
2. At the upper rear arm, inner pivot bolt, loosen the nut.
3. Turn the pivot bolt to adjust the camber to 1N–0.

NOTE: The camber should be divided equally, side-to-side or 0.5N.

4. After adjustment, torque the nut to 81–98 ft. lbs. (110–133 Nm).

SHOCK ABSORBER

Removal and Installation

1986–87

1. Remove the attaching nut, washer and insulator from the shock absorber upper stud.
2. Raise and safely support the vehicle. Properly support the rear axle assembly.
3. Remove the lower shock absorber bolt, washer and nut from the axle bracket.
4. Remove the shock absorber from the vehicle.
5. To install, reverse the removal procedures.

1988–90

1. Raise and safely support the rear axle.
2. Remove the shock absorber-to-upper body nut, washer and insulator.
3. Remove the shock absorber-to-lower control arm nut, bolt and shock absorber.

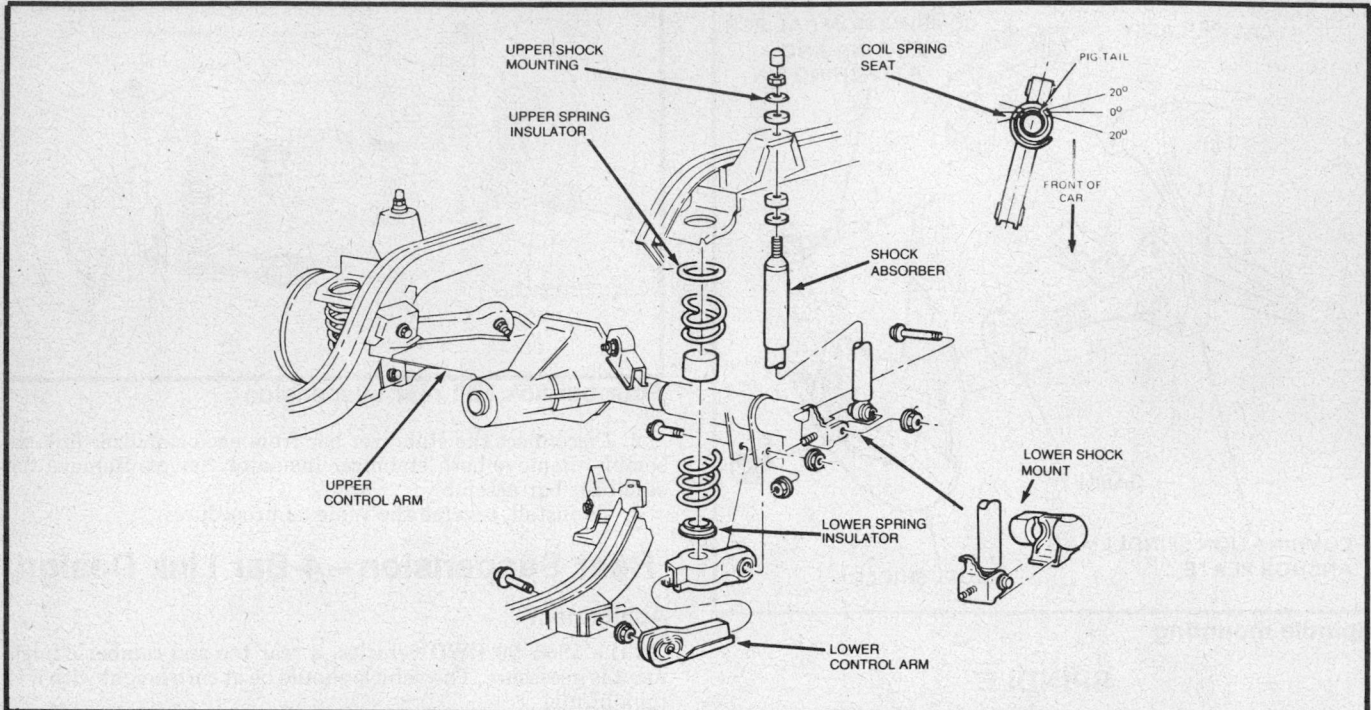

Rear suspension—Thunderbird/XR7

4. To install, reverse the removal procedures. Torque the shock absorber-to-lower control arm nut/bolt to 110–120 ft. lbs. (150–162 Nm) and the shock absorber-to-body nut to 27–35 ft. lbs. (37–47 Nm).

COIL SPRING

Removal and Installation

1986–87

1. Raise and safely support the vehicle. Properly support the rear axle assembly. If equipped, remove the rear stabilizer bar.
2. Position a jack under the lower arm axle pivot bolt. Remove the bolt and nut. Lower the jack slowly until the coil spring load is relieved. Do not stress the brake hose when lowering the rear axle.
3. Remove the coil spring and insulators from the vehicle.
4. To install, reverse the removal procedures.

1988–90

1. Raise and safely support the rear of the vehicle.
2. Remove the rear wheel.
3. At both ends of the stabilizer bar, remove the stabilizer bar link nuts; rotate the bar up and out the way.
4. From the brake caliper, disconnect the parking brake cable.
5. Using 3 spring cages, install 1, without an adjuster link, to the inboard side (innermost bend of the spring) and the others, with adjuster links, at 120 degrees to the previous link.
6. Using a floor jack, position it under the lower control arm at the extreme outside.
7. Using a wire, support the rear knuckle/caliper assembly by wiring the upper control arm to the body.
8. Remove the shock absorber-to-lower control arm bolt.
9. Mark the toe adjustment cam-to-subframe position and loosen both inboard pivot bolts on the lower control arm.

NOTE: Do not remove the plastic cap on the pivot nut nor lower the control arm until the bolts are loose.

10. Remove the lower control arm-to-knuckle nuts and bolts. Lower the control arm; be sure the spring cages properly seat on the spring as the control arm is lowered.
11. Remove the jack, lower the control arm and remove the spring.

To install:

12. Position the spring into the control arms; make sure the coils with the sleeve are facing downward, the spring is properly seated and the spring cage, without the adjuster is facing inboard.
13. Using a floor jack, raise the lower control into the knuckle bores. Install the lower control arm-to-knuckle nuts/bolts and torque to 118–148 ft. lbs. (160–220 Nm).
14. Remove the supporting wire. Install the shock absorber-to-lower control arm nut/bolt and torque to 110–120 ft. lbs. (150–162 Nm).
15. Remove the floor jack and the spring cages.
16. Connect the parking brake cable to the brake caliper. Install the stabilizer links and nuts.
17. Install the rear tire and lower the vehicle. Check and/or adjust the toe.

LOWER CONTROL ARM

Removal and Installation

1986–87

1. Raise and safely support the vehicle. Properly support the rear axle assembly. If equipped, remove the stabilizer bar.
2. Position a jack under the lower arm rear pivot bolt. Remove the bolt and nut.
3. Lower the jack slowly until the coil spring can be removed. Do not stretch the brake hose when lowering the jack.
4. Remove the lower arm assembly retaining bolts. Remove the lower arm from the vehicle.
5. To install, reverse the removal procedures.

1988–90

1. Remove the rear spring.

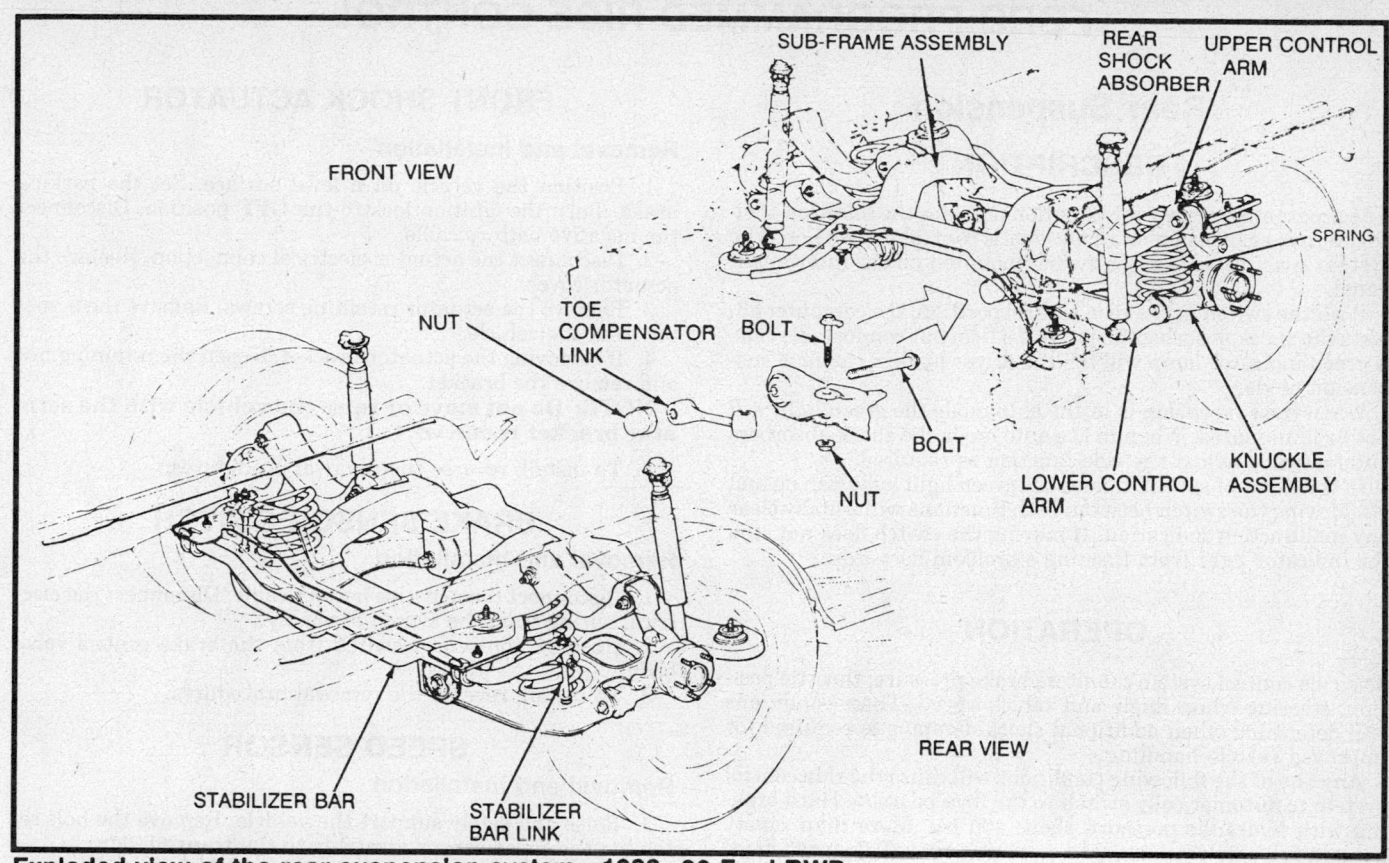

Exploded view of the rear suspension system—1988–90 Ford RWD

2. Remove the inner control arm-to-chassis nuts/bolts and the control arm.

NOTE: Do not remove the plastic cap from the front pivot nut.

3. Remove the compensating link from the control arm.
To install:
4. Install the compensating link onto the control arm.
5. Install the control arm-to-chassis and torque the toe compensating link nut to 118–148 ft. lbs. (160–200 Nm).
6. Install the spring.
7. Using a floor jack, raise the lower control into the knuckle bores. Install the lower control arm-to-knuckle nuts/bolts and torque to 118–148 ft. lbs. (160–220 Nm).
8. Install the shock absorber-to-lower control arm nut/bolt and torque to 110–120 ft. lbs. (150–162 Nm).
9. Remove the floor jack and the spring cages.
10. Connect the parking brake cable to the brake caliper. Install the stabilizer links and nuts.
11. Install the rear tire and lower the vehicle. Check and/or adjust the toe.

UPPER CONTROL ARM

Removal and Installation

1986–87
1. Raise and safely support the vehicle. Properly support the rear axle assembly. If equipped, remove the rear stabilizer bar.

2. Remove upper arm rear pivot bolt and nut. Remove front pivot bolt and nut. Remover upper arm from vehicle.
3. To install, reverse the removal procedures.

1988–90
1. Raise and safely support the rear of the vehicle.
2. Remove the rear wheel assembly.
3. Support the knuckle/hub assembly so it cannot swing outward.
4. At the upper control arm, remove the inner/outer pivot nuts and bolts.
5. Remove the upper control arm.
To install:
6. Install the upper control arm and fasteners loosely.
7. Install the rear wheel, lower the vehicle and place it on an alignment rack.
8. Torque the outboard nut to 118–148 ft. lbs. (160–200 Nm).
9. Adjust the camber and torque the inner pivot nut to 81–98 ft. lbs. (110–133 Nm).

STABILIZER BAR

Removal and Installation
1. Raise and safely support the vehicle.
2. Remove the stabilizer bar-to-brackets bolts in lower arms.
3. Remove stabilizer bar from vehicle.
4. To install, reverse the removal procedures. Make sure the bar is not installed upside down. A color code is provided on the stabilizer bar, passenger side only, as an aid for proper orientation.

FORD PROGRAMMED RIDE CONTROL

Rear Suspension

DESCRIPTION

The programmed ride control option provides the selection of either a firm suspension or an automatic control suspension. The system is activated using a switch mounted on the instrument panel.

With the switch in the firm control position, the computer adjusts the shock absorbers to provide a firm but comfortable ride. A green indicator lamp will tell the driver he is in the firm suspension mode.

When the suspension is in the auto mode the green light will not be illuminated. When in the auto mode the shock absorbers automatically adjust the ride function as required.

In the event of system failure the green light will flash on and off. Moving the switch between both functions will usually clear any malfunction indication. If moving the switch does not stop the indicator light from flashing a problem does exist.

OPERATION

The ride control system monitors brake pressure, throttle position, steering wheel angle and vehicle speed. These conditions will determine when additional shock damping is required for improved vehicle handling.

Any one of the following conditions will cause the ride control system to automatically switch to the firm position. Hard braking with hydraulic pressure above 400 psi. More than ninety percent full acceleration. Hard cornering above 0.3 gram lateral acceleration. Vehicle speed above 83 mph.

Once the condition has ceased the control system will return to the normal switch position. The system will not respond to hard turns during the first 80 seconds of hard driving. This delay allows the computer to calculate the straight ahead steering wheel position. Severe or repeated turns could lengthen the wheel position calculation by several minutes. All others features of the system will operate normally during this period.

FRONT SHOCK ACTUATOR

Removal and Installation

1. Position the vehicle on a level surface. Set the parking brake. Turn the ignition lock to the **OFF** position. Disconnect the negative battery cable.
2. Disconnect the actuator electrical connection. Remove the actuator cover.
3. Remove the actuator retaining screws. Remove the actuator from the vehicle.
4. If removing the actuator bracket, loosen the retaining nut and remove the bracket.

NOTE: Do not move or raise the vehicle with the actuator bracket removed.

5. To install, reverse the removal procedures.

BRAKE SENSOR SWITCH

Removal and Installation

1. Disconnect the negative battery cable. Disconnect the electrical wiring from the switch assembly.
2. Unscrew the sensor switch from the brake control valve body.
3. To install, reverse the removal procedures.

SPEED SENSOR

Removal and Installation

1. Raise and safely support the vehicle. Remove the bolt retaining the speed sensor assembly to the transmission.
2. Remove the speed sensor and the driven gear from the transmission assembly.
3. Disconnect the electrical connector and the speedometer cable from the sensor. Do not attempt to remove the spring retainer clip with the speedometer cable in the sensor.
4. Remove the driven gear retainer. Remove the driven gear from the speed sensor.
5. To install, reverse the removal procedures.

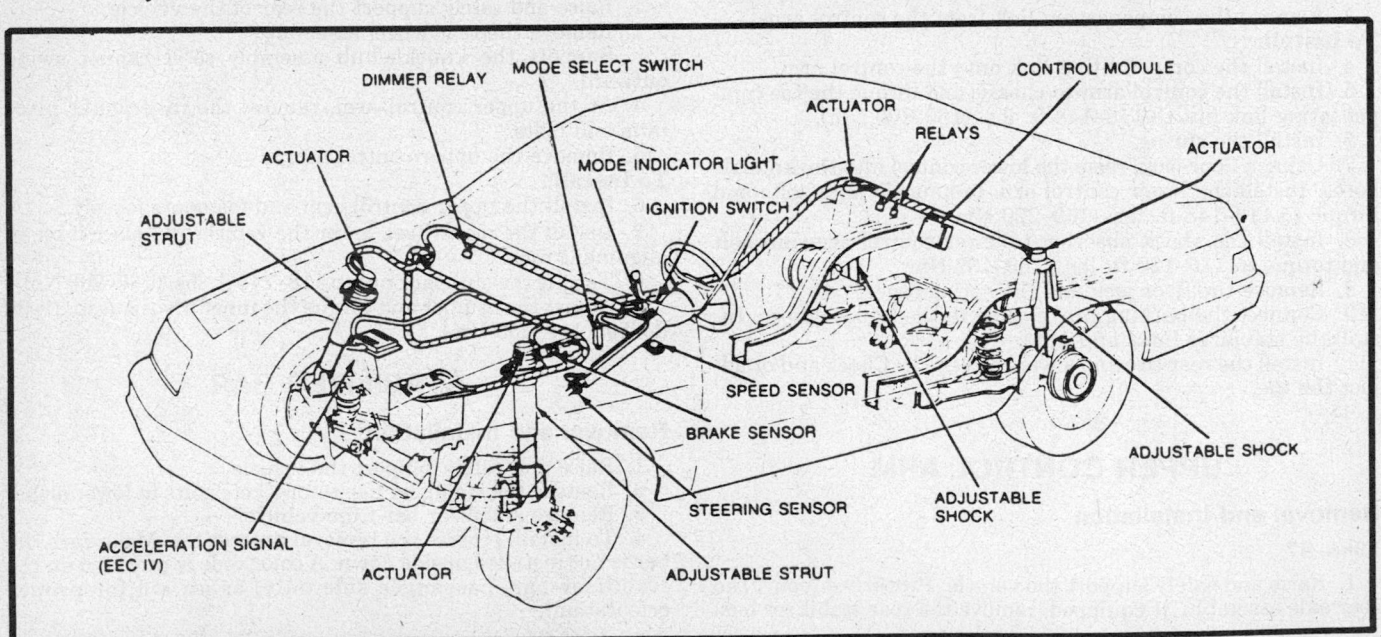

Programmed ride control component location

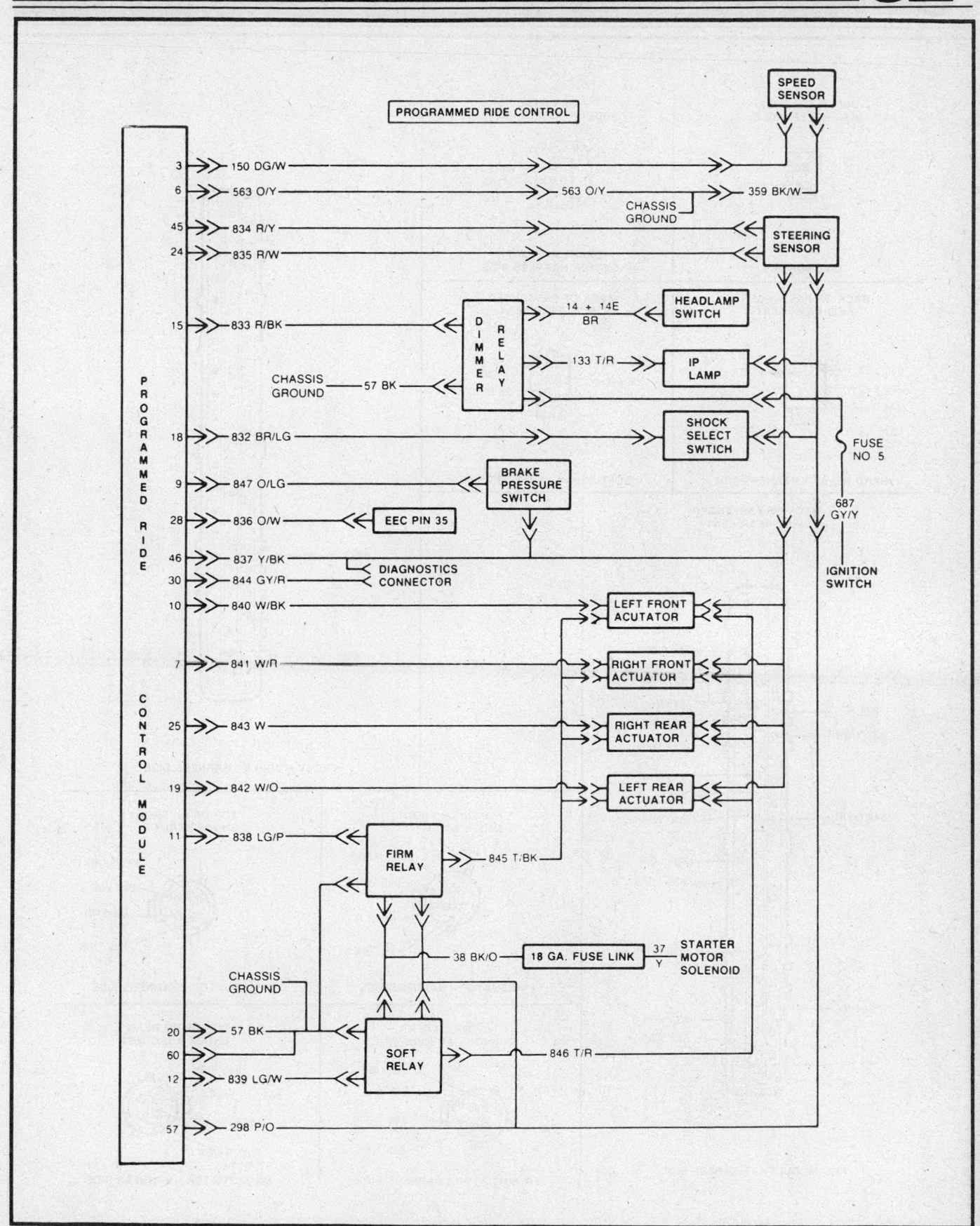

Programmed ride control electrical schematic

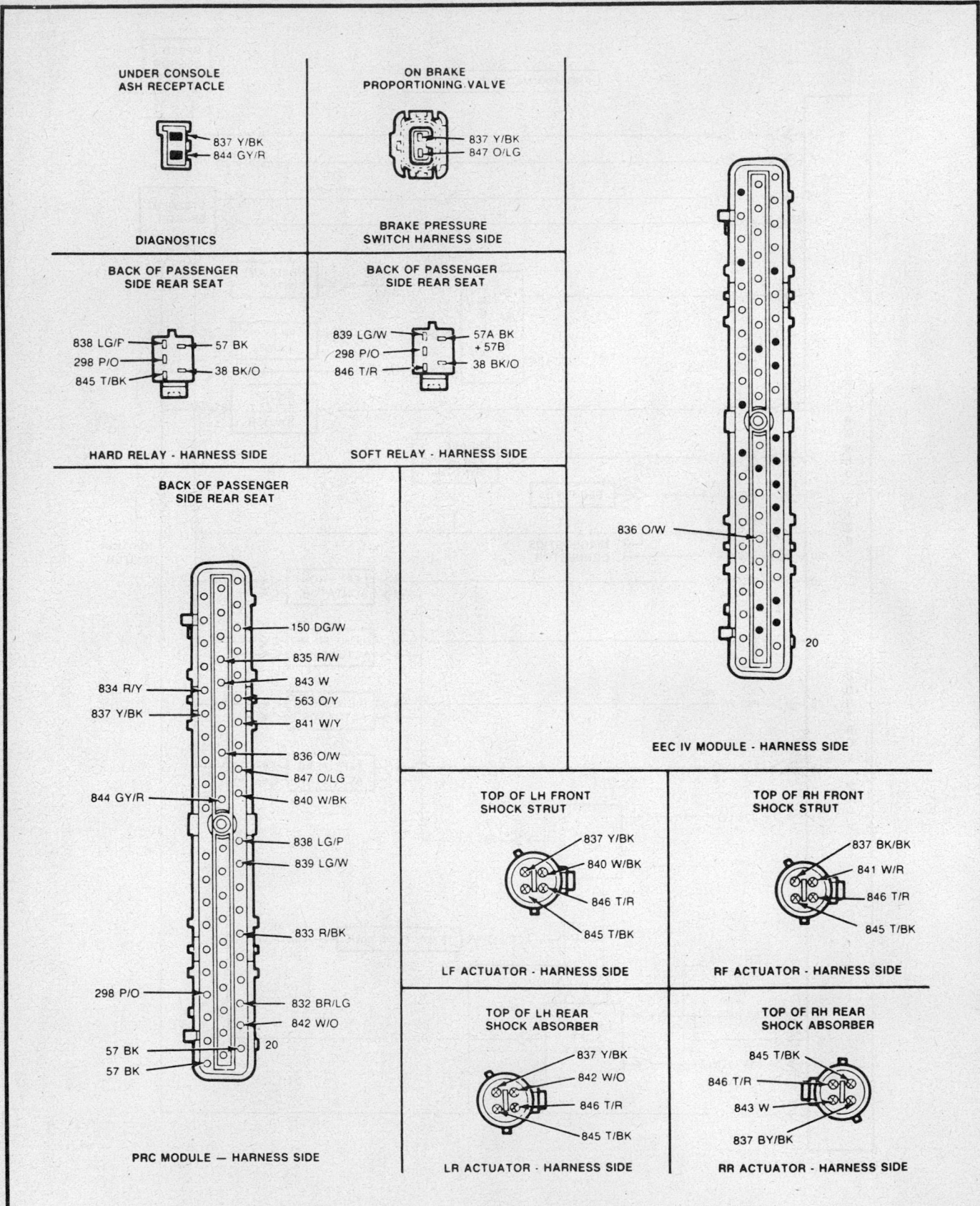

UNDER CONSOLE
ASH RECEPTACLE

837 Y/BK
844 GY/R

DIAGNOSTICS

ON BRAKE
PROPORTIONING VALVE

837 Y/BK
847 O/LG

BRAKE PRESSURE
SWITCH HARNESS SIDE

BACK OF PASSENGER
SIDE REAR SEAT

838 LG/P — 57 BK
298 P/O
845 T/BK — 38 BK/O

HARD RELAY - HARNESS SIDE

BACK OF PASSENGER
SIDE REAR SEAT

839 LG/W — 57A BK
298 P/O — + 57B
846 T/R — 38 BK/O

SOFT RELAY - HARNESS SIDE

836 O/W

20

EEC IV MODULE - HARNESS SIDE

BACK OF PASSENGER
SIDE REAR SEAT

150 DG/W
835 R/W
843 W
834 R/Y
563 O/Y
837 Y/BK
841 W/Y
836 O/W
847 O/LG
844 GY/R
840 W/BK
838 LG/P
839 LG/W
833 R/BK
298 P/O
832 BR/LG
842 W/O
57 BK
57 BK
20

PRC MODULE — HARNESS SIDE

TOP OF LH FRONT
SHOCK STRUT

837 Y/BK
840 W/BK
846 T/R
845 T/BK

LF ACTUATOR - HARNESS SIDE

TOP OF RH FRONT
SHOCK STRUT

837 BK/BK
841 W/R
846 T/R
845 T/BK

RF ACTUATOR - HARNESS SIDE

TOP OF LH REAR
SHOCK ABSORBER

837 Y/BK
842 W/O
846 T/R
845 T/BK

LR ACTUATOR - HARNESS SIDE

TOP OF RH REAR
SHOCK ABSORBER

845 T/BK
846 T/R
843 W
837 BY/BK

RR ACTUATOR - HARNESS SIDE

Programmed ride control test connector locations

CONTROL MODULE ASSEMBLY

Removal and Installation

1. Turn the ignition lock to the **OFF** position. Disconnect the negative battery cable.

2. From inside the luggage compartment, remove the screws and carefully lower the right hand panel behind the rear seat back.

3. Remove the control module and relay mounting brackets screws. Disconnect the electrical wires. Remove the assembly from the vehicle.

4. To install, reverse the removal procedures.

STEERING SENSOR ASSEMBLY

Removal and Installation

1. Disconnect the battery cable. Remove the insulator from under the steering column. Disconnect the steering sensor electrical wire.

2. Remove the steering column from the vehicle.

3. Squeeze the steering sensor plastic retainer end together in order to disengage it from the steering column bracket.

4. Wipe the lower part of the column shaft. Slide the steering sensor from the steering column. Be sure the steering column shaft is free of burrs.

5. To install, reverse the removal procedures.

REAR SHOCK ACTUATOR

Removal and Installation

1. Position the vehicle on a level surface. Set the parking brake. Turn the ignition lock to the **OFF** position. Disconnect the negative battery cable.

2. Remove the luggage compartment side trim panel. Disconnect the actuator electrical connection.

3. Squeeze the actuator retaining tabs inward and lift the assembly from its mount.

4. If removing the actuator bracket, loosen the retaining nut and remove the bracket.

NOTE: Do not move or raise the vehicle with the actuator bracket removed.

5. To install, reverse the removal procedures.

GM A-BODY AND X-BODY FRONT WHEEL DRIVE

Front Suspension

FRONT WHEEL ALIGNMENT

Front alignment consists of the camber adjustment and toe setting. The caster setting is built into the vehicle with no provisions for adjustment.

Two bolts clamp the lower end of the MacPherson strut assembly to the upper arm of the steering knuckle. The lower bolt has an eccentric washer at the head providing the camber adjustment. These special high tensile bolts with nuts are torqued to 210 ft. lbs. The camber setting is plus 0.5 degrees with a 0.5 degree tolerance.

The toe adjustment is conventional, with adjusting sleeves at the tie rod ends held in place with locking jam nuts. The toe setting is plus 0.1 degree with a tolerance of ±1 degree.

FRONT WHEEL BEARINGS

Removal and Installation

1. Loosen hub nut. Raise and safely support the vehicle. Remove the wheel assembly. Remove hub nut and discard. Remove brake caliper.

2. Remove hub and bearing attaching bolts. If old bearing is being reused, mark attaching bolts and corresponding holes for installation.

3. Install tool J-28733 or equivalent and remove bearing. If excessive corrosion is present, make sure the bearing is loose in knuckle before using tool. A boot protector should be installed whenever servicing front suspension components to prevent damage to the drive axle boot.

To install:

4. Before installation clean and inspect bearing mating surfaces and steering knuckle bore for dirt, nicks and burrs.

5. If installing steering knuckle seal, use tool J-28671 or equivalent. Apply grease to seal and knuckle bore.

6. Push bearing on axle shaft. Torque new hub until bearing is seated. Install brake caliper. Lower the vehicle. Apply final torque to hub nut.

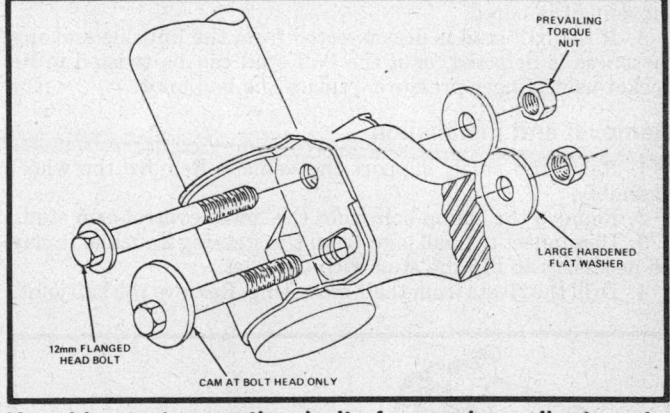

Knuckle strut mounting bolts for camber adjustment

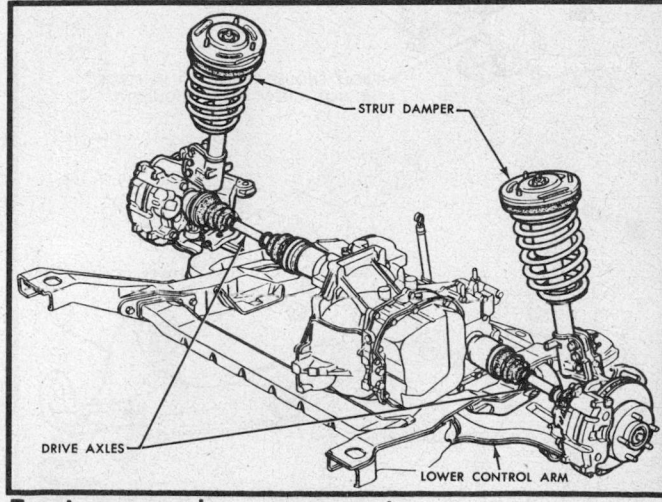

Front suspension components

STRUT ASSEMBLY

Removal and Installation

1. Support the vehicle so there is no weight on the lower control arm.
2. Remove the wheel assembly. Clean up and mark camber adjusting cam.
3. Remove the brake hose clip. Remove top bolts from the lower strut bolts. Remove the strut assembly from the vehicle.
4. To install, reverse the removal procedures.

STEERING KNUCKLE

Removal and Installation

1. Raise and safely support the vehicle. Remove wheel and wheel bearing.
2. Mark and remove the lower strut bolts. Remove tie rod end and ball joint.
3. Remove steering knuckle from the vehicle.
4. To install, reverse the removal procedures.

LOWER BALL JOINT

Inspection

1. Raise front suspension by placing jack or lift under the cradle.
2. Grasp the wheel at top and bottom and shake the wheel in an in-and-out motion. Observe for any horizontal movement of the knuckle relative to the control arm. Replace ball joint if such movement is noted.
3. If the ball stud is disconnected from the knuckle and any looseness is detected, or if the ball stud can be twisted in its socket using finger pressure, replace the ball joint.

Removal and Installation

1. Raise and safely support the vehicle. Remove the wheel assembly.
2. Remove the clamp bolt from the lower control arm stud.
3. Disconnect the ball joint from the steering knuckle. It may be necessary to tap the stud with a mallet.
4. Drill the rivets from their mounting. Remove the ball joint.

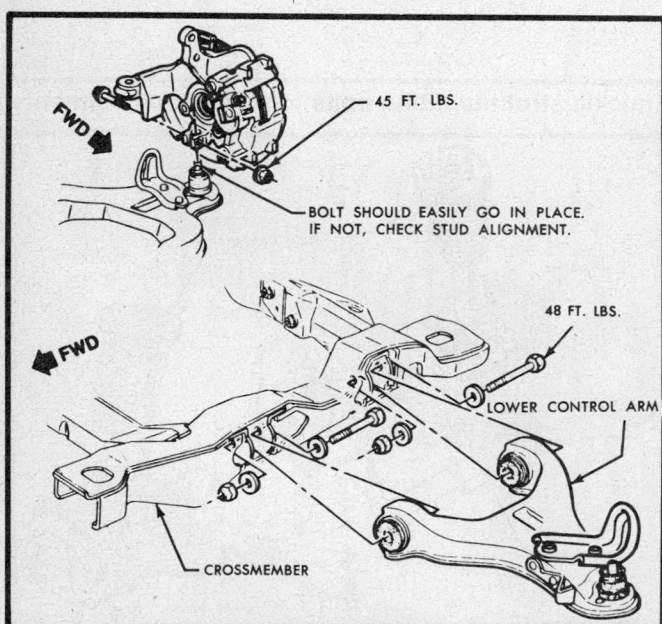

Lower control arm and/or bushings

5. To install, reverse the removal procedures. Adjust the alignment as required.

LOWER CONTROL ARM

Removal and Installation

1. Raise and safely support the vehicle. Remove the wheel assembly.
2. Remove the stabilizer bar, as required. Remove the ball joint clamping bolt.
3. Separate the ball joint from the steering knuckle. Remove the lower control arm retaining bolts. Remove the lower control arm from the vehicle.
4. To install, reverse the removal procedures. Check vehicle alignment as required.

Rear Suspension

REAR WHEEL BEARINGS

Removal and Installation

1. Raise and safely support the vehicle. Remove the wheel assembly. Remove the brake drum. Do not hammer on brake drum as damage to the bearing could result.
2. Remove the hub/bearing assembly-to-rear axle attaching bolts and remove hub and bearing assembly from axle. If studs must be removed from the hub, do not remove with a hammer as damage to bearing will result.
3. To install, reverse the removal procedures.

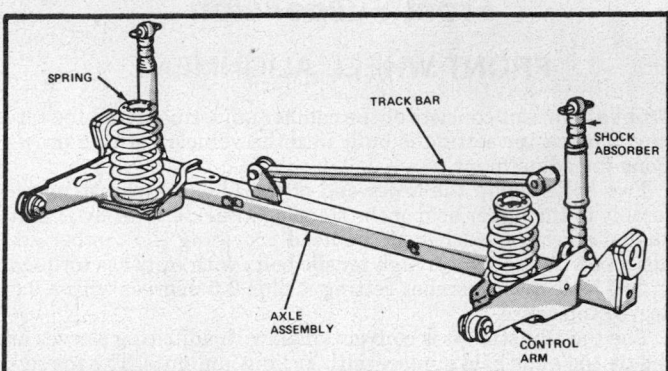

Rear suspension

SHOCK ABSORBER

Removal and Installation

1. Open the trunk. Remove the trim cover and remove upper shock attaching nut.
2. Raise and safely support the vehicle and the rear axle assembly.
3. Remove lower attaching bolt and nut. Remove the shock absorber from the verhicle.
4. To install, reverse the removal procedures.

TRACK BAR

Removal and Installation

1. Raise and safely support the vehicle and the rear axle assembly.
2. Remove nut and bolt at both the axle and body attachments and remove track bar.
3. To install position track bar in left hand reinforcement and

loosely install bolt and nut. The open side of the bar and nut must face rearward.

4. Place other end of track bar in body reinforcement and install bolt and nut (nut must be at the rear of reinforcement of both attachments). Torque nut at axle bracket to 33 ft. lbs. and torque nut at body reinforcement to 34 ft. lbs.

COIL SPRING

Removal and Installation

1. Raise and safely support the vehicle. Support the rear axle while removing the brake line brackets, the track bar and the shock absorber lower mounts.
2. Lower rear axle and remove springs.
3. To install, reverse the removal procedures. Be sure to position the springs correctly.

CONTROL ARM BUSHING

Removal and Installation

1. Raise the vehicle and support the rear axle under front side of the spring seat.
2. If removing right bushing, disconnect parking brake cable from hook guide.
3. Remove dual parking brake cables from bracket attachment and pull aside.
4. Disconnect brake line bracket attachment from frame.
5. Remove shock lower attaching nut and bolt and pull string aside.
6. Remove control arm bracket-to-underbody attaching bolts and allow control arm to rotate downward.
7. Remove nut and bolt from bracket attachment and remove bracket.
8. Press bushing from control arm.
9. To install, reverse the removal procedures.

GM C-BODY
FRONT WHEEL DRIVE

Front Suspension

FRONT WHEEL ALIGNMENT

Before adjusting caster and camber angles, the front bumper should be raised and released three times to allow the vehicle to return to its normal standing height.

Adjustment

CASTER

1. Remove the top strut mounting nuts.
2. Separate the top strut mount from the inner wheelhouse.
3. Drill $2^{11}/_{32}$ in. holes at the front and rear of the round strut mounting hole. Remove the excess metal between the existing hole and the drilled hole.

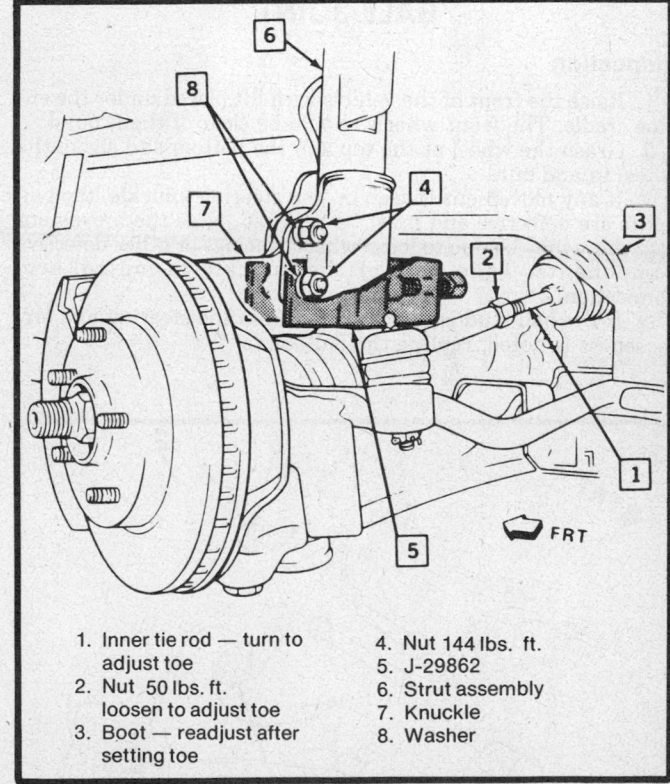

1. Inner tie rod — turn to adjust toe
2. Nut 50 lbs. ft. loosen to adjust toe
3. Boot — readjust after setting toe
4. Nut 144 lbs. ft.
5. J-29862
6. Strut assembly
7. Knuckle
8. Washer

Front camber and toe adjustmnet

4. Reinstall the strut mount in the holes. Install the washers and nuts.
5. Caster is set by moving the top of strut rearward or forward as required.
6. Tighten the strut mounting nuts.

CAMBER

1. Loosen both strut-to-knuckle nuts.
2. Install a camber adjusting tool.
3. Set camber to specification.

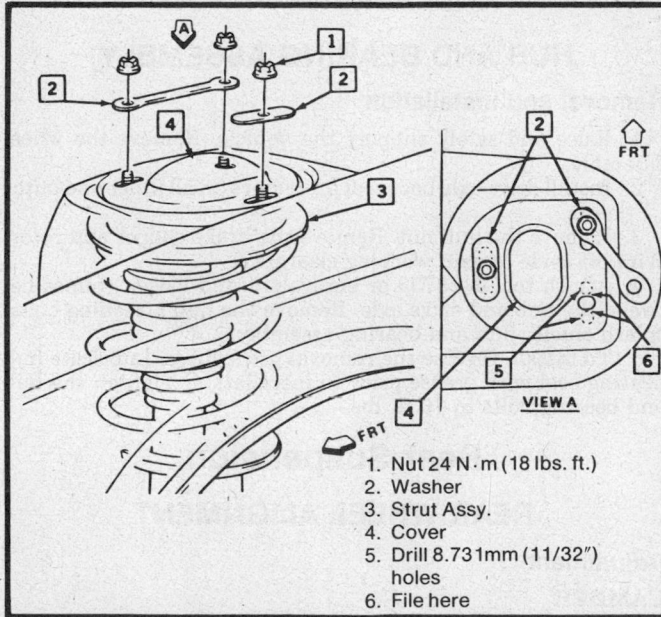

1. Nut 24 N·m (18 lbs. ft.)
2. Washer
3. Strut Assy.
4. Cover
5. Drill 8.731mm (11/32″) holes
6. File here

Front caster adjustment

TOE

1. Loosen the lock nut on both inner tie rods.
2. Set toe to specification by turning the inner tie rod accordingly.
3. Tighten the lock nuts on inner tie rods to 52 ft. lbs. (70 Nm).

STRUT ASSEMBLY

Removal and Installation

1. Remove the nuts attaching the top strut assembly to the vehicle body.
2. Raise and safely support the vehicle. Install jackstands under the vehicle cradle and lower the vehicle so the weight of the vehicle rests on the stands and not the control arm.
3. Install drive axle boot seal protectors. Care must be taken in order to prevent overextension of the inner Tri-pot joints.
4. Remove the brake line retaining bracket from the strut assembly.
5. Remove the strut-to-steering knuckle bolts.
6. Remove the strut assembly from the vehicle.
7. To install, reverse the removal procedures. Check wheel alignment. Tighten the strut-to-body bolts to 18 ft. lbs. Tighten the strut-to-steering knuckle bolts to 144 ft. lbs.

BALL JOINT

Inspection

1. Raise the front of the vehicle with lift placed under the engine cradle. The front wheels should be clear of the ground.
2. Grasp the wheel at the top and the bottom and shake the wheel in and out.
3. If any movement is seen on the steering knuckle, the ball joints are defective and must be replaced. Note the movement elsewhere may be due to loose wheel bearings or other defective components. Take note of the knuckle-to-control arm connection.
4. If the ball stud is disconnected from the steering and any looseness is noted, replace the ball joints.

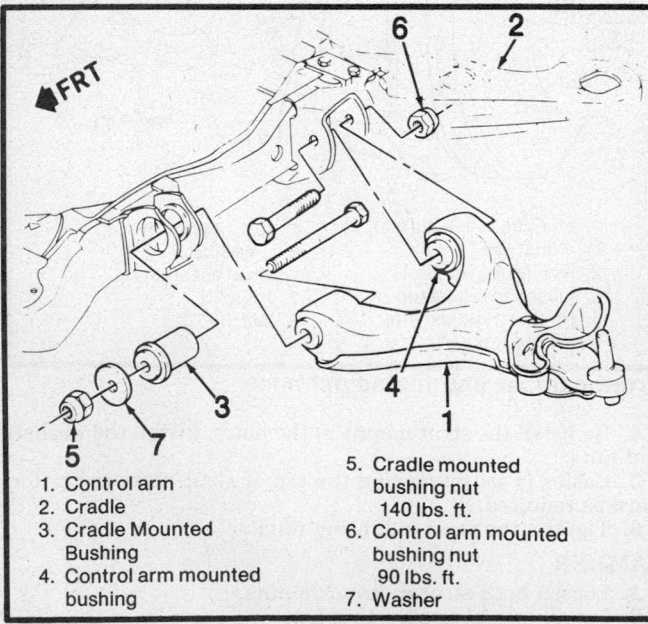

1. Control arm
2. Cradle
3. Cradle Mounted Bushing
4. Control arm mounted bushing
5. Cradle mounted bushing nut 140 lbs. ft.
6. Control arm mounted bushing nut 90 lbs. ft.
7. Washer

Control arm mounting—disassembled view

Removal and Installation

1. Raise the front of the vehicle and properly support it underneath the engine cradle. Lower the vehicle slightly so the weight rest primarily on the jackstands.
2. Remove the wheel assemblies.
3. Install drive axle covers to protect the drive axle boot seals.
4. Pull the cotter pin from the ball joint and install a ball joint separator tool. Turn the castellated nut counterclockwise to separate the ball joint from the steering knuckle.
5. Use a ⅛ in. drill bit to drill a hole approximately ¼ in. deep in the center of each of the ball joint rivets.
6. Use a ½ in. drill bit to drill off the rivet heads. Drill only enough to remove the rivet head.
7. Use a hammer and punch to remove the rivets. Drive them out from the bottom.
8. Loosen the stabilizer bar bushing assembly nut.
9. Pull down on the control arm and remove the ball joint from the steering knuckle and control arm.
To install:
10. Install the new ball joint in the steering knuckle and align the holes with those in the control arm. Install the ball joint nuts facing down and tighten the nuts to 50 ft. lbs.
11. Install the castellated nut and tighten to 81 ft. lbs. Tightening the nut for cotter pin alignment is allowed, but do not loosen it once the torque has been reached.
12. Install the cotter pin. To complete the installation, reverse the removal procedures.

STABILIZER BAR

Removal and Installation

1. Raise and safely support the vehicle. Place jackstands under the engine cradle. Lower the vehicle slightly so the weight rests on the jackstands.
2. Remove the wheel assembly. Install drive axle covers to protect the drive axle boot seals.
3. Remove the bolts from both sides connecting the stabilizer bar bushings to the control arm. Remove the stabilizer bar mounting bolts.
4. Remove the exhaust pipe between the exhaust manifold and the catalytic converter.
5. Remove the stabilizer bar from the vehicle by sliding it over the right steering knuckle.
6. To install, reverse the removal procedures.

HUB AND BEARING ASSEMBLY

Removal and Installation

1. Raise and safely support the vehicle. Remove the wheel assembly.
2. Install drive axle boot seal protectors on all inner and outer CV-joints.
3. Remove the hub nut. Remove the brake caliper and rotor. Wire off aside to gain working clearance.
4. Attach tool J-28733 or equivalent and loosen splines between the hub and drive axle. Remove the hub attaching bolts, splash shield, hub and bearing assembly.
5. To install, reverse the removal procedures. Lubricate hub bearing seal with grease prior to installation. Tighten the hub and bearing bolts to 70 ft. lbs.

Rear Suspension

REAR WHEEL ALIGNMENT

Adjustment
CAMBER

1. Raise and safely support the vehicle.

2. Loosen the strut-to-knuckle mounting nuts.

3. Install tool J–29862 and adjust the camber to specification

TOE

1. Raise and safely support the vehicle.

2. Loosen the locknut at both tie rod ends. The left and right wheel must be adjusted separately.

3. Adjust the toe to specification by turning the inner tie rod.

4. After adjustment tighten the nut at the tie rod to 48 ft. lbs.

STRUT ASSSEMBLY

Removal and Installation

1. Remove the inner side trunk cover. Remove the strut tower mounting nuts.

2. Raise and safely support the vehicle. Remove the wheel assembly.

3. Disconnect and plug the ELC air line.

4. Remove the strut anchor nuts, washers and bolts from the rear knuckle and knuckle bracket.

5. Remove the strut from the vehicle.

6. To install, reverse the removal procedures. Tighten the strut tower mounting nuts to 19 ft. lbs. Tighten the strut anchor nuts to 144 ft. lbs. Check rear wheel alignment.

COIL SPRING

Removal and Installation

1. Raise and safely support the vehicle. Remove the rear wheels.

2. Separate the rear stabilizer bar from the knuckle bracket and remove it.

3. Disconnect the ELC height sensor line and the parking brake cable retaining clip.

4. Position the tool J–23028–01 or equivalent so as to cradle the control arm bushings. Special tool J–23028–01 or equivalent, should be secured to a jack.

5. Raise the jack to remove the tension from the control arm pivot bolts. Secure a chain around the spring and through the control arm as a safety precaution.

6. Remove the rear control arm pivot bolt and nut. Move the jack so as to relieve any tension from the control arm pivot bolt. Remove the bolt and nut. Lower the jack to allow the jack to pivot downward.

7. When all pressure has been removed from the coil spring, remove the safety chain, spring and insulators.

8. To install, reverse the removal procedures. Control arm mounting nuts should not be tightened until the vehicle is unsupported and resting on its wheels at normal trim height.

BALL JOINT

Inspection

The lower ball joint is inspected for wear by visual observation alone. The vehicle must be supported by the wheels during inspection. Wear is indicated by retraction of the half-inch diameter nipple into the ball joint cover. Normal wear will be indicated by the nipple retracting slowly into the ball joint cover.

Ball stud tightness in the knuckle boss should also be checked when inspecting the ball joint. In order to accomplish this, shake the wheel and feel for movement of the stud end or castellated nut at the knuckle boss. A loose nut can also indicate a bent or damaged stud.

Removal and Installation

1. Raise and safely support the vehicle. Remove the rear wheel assemblies.

2. Disconnect the Electronic Level Control (ELC) height sensor link (right control arm) and/or the parking brake cable retaining link (left control arm).

3. Remove the cotter pin and the castellated nut from the outer suspension adjustment link.

4. Separate the outer suspension link from the knuckle.

5. Support the control arm with a jack. The lower control arm must be supported to prevent the coil spring from forcing the control arm downward.

6. Remove the ball and cotter pin.

7. Remove the castellated nut and then reinstall it with the flat side facing upward. Do not tighten.

8. Install a ball joint separator tool and separate the ball joint from the knuckle. Separate the ball joint from the control arm.

9. To install, reverse the removal procedures. Tighten the new castellated nut to 7.5 ft lbs. Tighten the nut an additional ⅔ turn.

10. Align the slot in the nut to the cotter pin hole by tightening only. Do not loosen the nut in order to align the holes.

STABILIZER BAR

Removal and Installation

1. Raise and safely support the vehicle. Remove the rear wheel assemblies.

2. Remove the stabilizer bar bolts, nuts and bar retainers.

3. Remove the bushing clip bolt.

4. Bend the open end of the support assembly downward.

5. Remove the stabilizer bar and bushings.

6. To install, reverse the removal procedures.

SUSPENSION ADJUSTMENT LINK

Removal and Installation

1. Raise and safely support the vehicle. Remove the rear wheel assemblies.

2. Remove the cotter pin and castellated nut from the knuckle.

3. Separate the outer suspension link from the knuckle.

NOTE: When separating the linkage joint, no attempt should be made to disengage the joint by driving a wedge between the joint and the attached part. Seal damage may result.

4. Remove the link assembly retaining nut and retainer. Remove the suspension adjustment link.

5. To install, reverse the removal procedures. Check rear wheel alignnment.

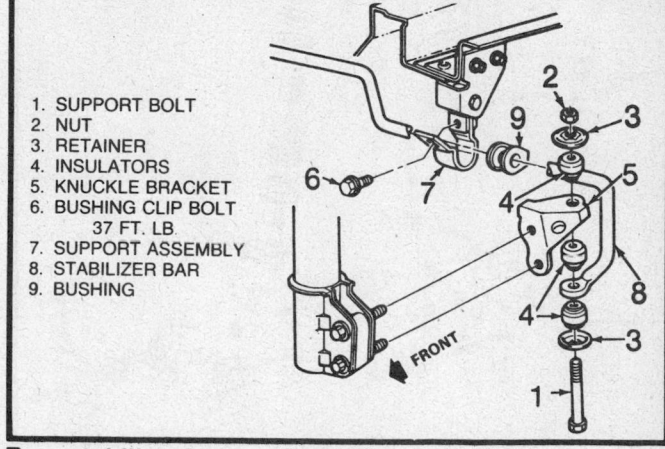

1. SUPPORT BOLT
2. NUT
3. RETAINER
4. INSULATORS
5. KNUCKLE BRACKET
6. BUSHING CLIP BOLT
   37 FT. LB.
7. SUPPORT ASSEMBLY
8. STABILIZER BAR
9. BUSHING

Rear stabilizer bar and bushing assembly

GM CORSICA AND BERETTA
FRONT WHEEL DRIVE

Front Suspension

FRONT WHEEL ALIGNMENT

Adjustment
CAMBER

1. Position vehicle on alignment equipment. Use proper tools to reach the adjustment fasteners.
2. Loosen both strut-to-knuckle bolts just enough to allow movement between the strut and the knuckle.
3. Grasp the top of the tire firmly and move it inboard or outboard until the proper camber is achieved.
4. Tighten the adjusting bolts. Be sure not to loose the alignment specification.

TOE

1. Loosen the clamp bolts at the outer tie rod.
2. Square the vehicle. Rotate the adjuster and set the toe to specification.
3. Tighten the retaining bolts to 33 ft. lbs.

STRUT ASSEMBLY

Removal and Installation

1. Disconnect the upper strut-to-body retaining bolts.
2. Raise and safely support the vehicle. Allow the suspension to hang free. Remove the wheel assembly. Install a drive axle boot protector.
3. Using tool J–24319 or equivalent, disconnect the tie rod from the strut. Support the steering knuckle to prevent tension from being applied to the brake line.
4. Remove both strut-to-knuckle retaining bolts. Remove the strut assembly from the vehicle.
5. To install, reverse the removal procedures. When installing the mounting bolts be sure to place the flats of the bolts in the horizontal position.

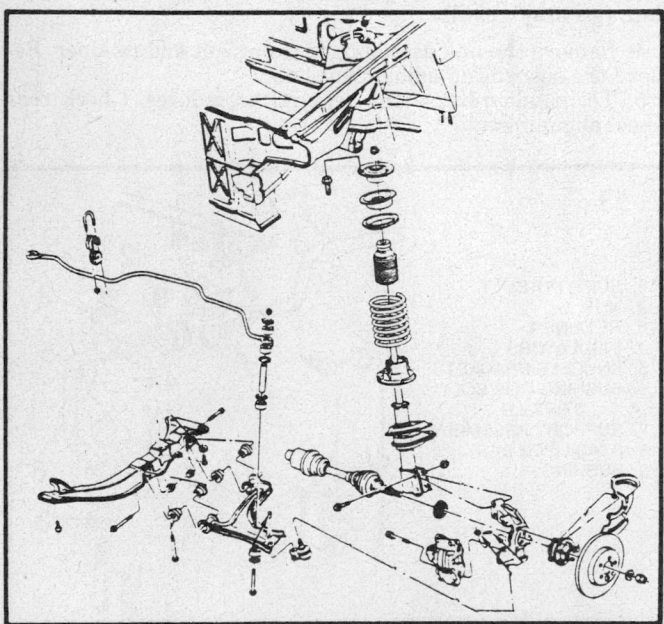

Front suspension assembly—Corsica and Beretta

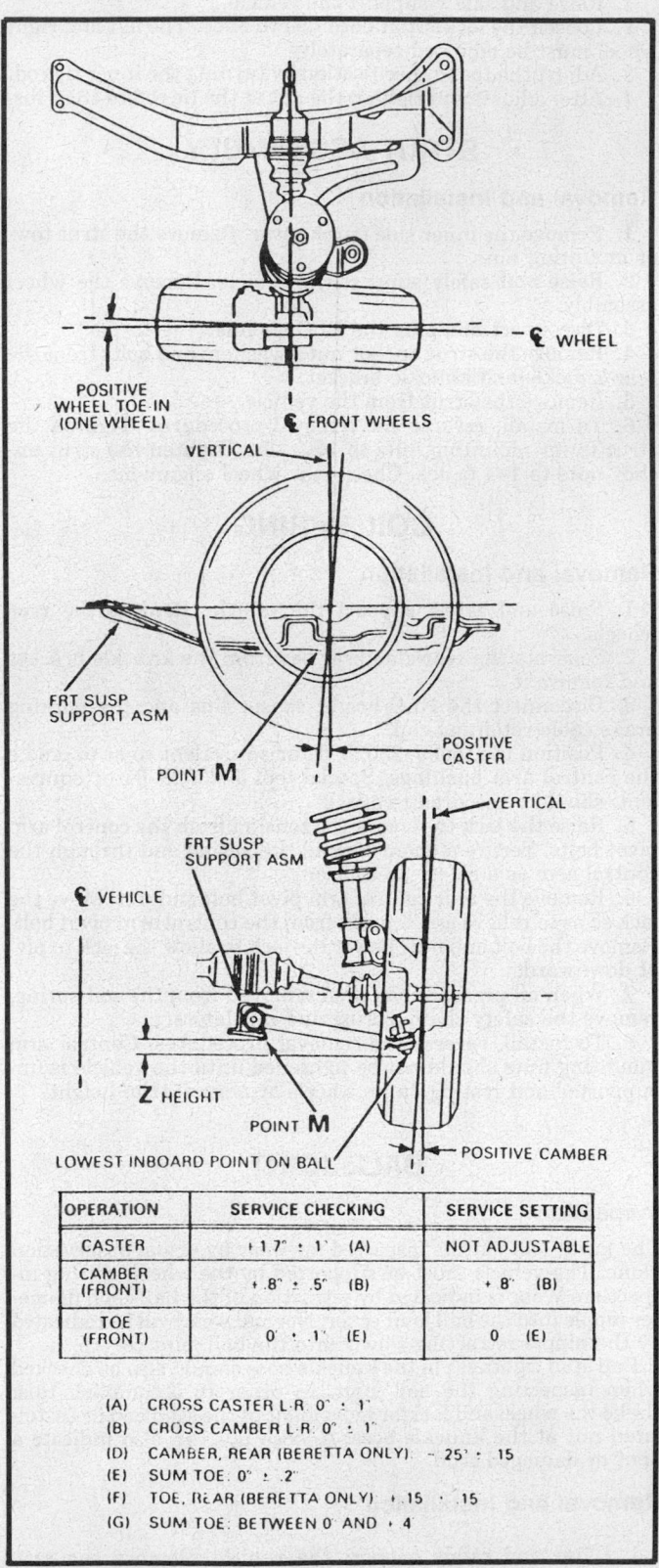

OPERATION	SERVICE CHECKING	SERVICE SETTING
CASTER	+1.7° ± 1° (A)	NOT ADJUSTABLE
CAMBER (FRONT)	+.8° ± .5° (B)	+.8° (B)
TOE (FRONT)	0° ± .1° (E)	0 (E)

(A) CROSS CASTER L-R 0° ± 1°
(B) CROSS CAMBER L-R 0° ± 1°
(D) CAMBER, REAR (BERETTA ONLY) −.25° ± .15
(E) SUM TOE 0° ± .2°
(F) TOE, REAR (BERETTA ONLY) +.15 ± .15
(G) SUM TOE: BETWEEN 0° AND +.4°

Front alignment data—Corsica and Beretta

LOWER BALL JOINT

Removal and Installation

1. Raise and safely support the vehicle and remove the wheel assembly.

2. If no countersink is found on the lower side of the rivets, carefully locate the center of the rivet body and mark it using a punch.

3. Properly drill out the rivets of the ball joint assembly. Using tool J–29330 or equivalent, separate the ball joint from the steering knuckle.

4. Disconnect the stabilizer bar from the lower control arm. Remove the ball joint from the vehicle.

5. To install, reverse the removal procedures. Align the vehicle, as required.

LOWER CONTROL ARM

Removal and Installation

1. Raise and safely support the vehicle and remove the wheel assembly.

2. Disconnect the stabilizer bar from the lower control arm assembly. Using tool J–29330 or equivalent, separate the ball joint from the steering knuckle.

3. Remove the lower control arm retaining bolts. Remove the lower control arm from the vehicle.

4. To install, reverse the removal procedures. If necessary, check the alignment.

STABILIZER BAR

Removal and Installation

1. Open the hood and install an engine support tool. Raise and safely support the vehicle; allow the suspension to hang free. Remove the left front wheel assembly.

2. Disconnect the stabilizer shaft from the control arms. Disconnect the stabilizer shaft from the support assemblies.

3. Loosen the front bolts and remove the bolts from the rear and center of the support assemblies, allowing the supports to be lowered enough to remove the stabilizer bar assembly. Remove the assembly from the vehicle.

4. To install, reverse the removal procedures. Loosely assemble all components while insuring that the stabilizer bar is centered, side-to-side.

HUB AND BEARING ASSEMBLY

Removal and Installation

1. Raise and safely support the vehicle. Remove the hub nut. Remove the wheel assembly.

2. If equipped with a 4 cylinder engine and automatic transmission, install a boot cover.

3. Remove the caliper assembly and properly position it aside. Remove the rotor.

4. Remove the hub and bearing mounting bolts. Remove the splash shield.

NOTE: If the bearing assembly is to be reused, mark the retaining bolt and corresponding hole for installation in the same position. Do not use a hammer or direct heat to remove the bearing assembly, as damage to the assembly could result.

5. Install tool J–28733 or equivalent, and turn the bolt to press the hub and bearing assembly off of the drive axle.

6. Disconnect the stabilizer link bolt at the lower control arm. Using tool J–29330 or equivalent, separate the ball joint from its mounting.

7. Remove the drive axle from the steering knuckle. Properly support the assembly.

8. To install, reverse the removal procedures.

KNUCKLE ASSEMBLY

Removal and Installation

1. Raise and safely support the vehicle. Remove the hub nut. Remove the wheel assembly.

2. If equipped with a 4 cylinder engine and automatic transmission, install a boot cover.

3. Remove the hub and bearing assembly.

4. Remove both strut-to-knuckle mounting bolts. Remove the knuckle assembly from the vehicle.

5. To install, reverse the removal procedures.

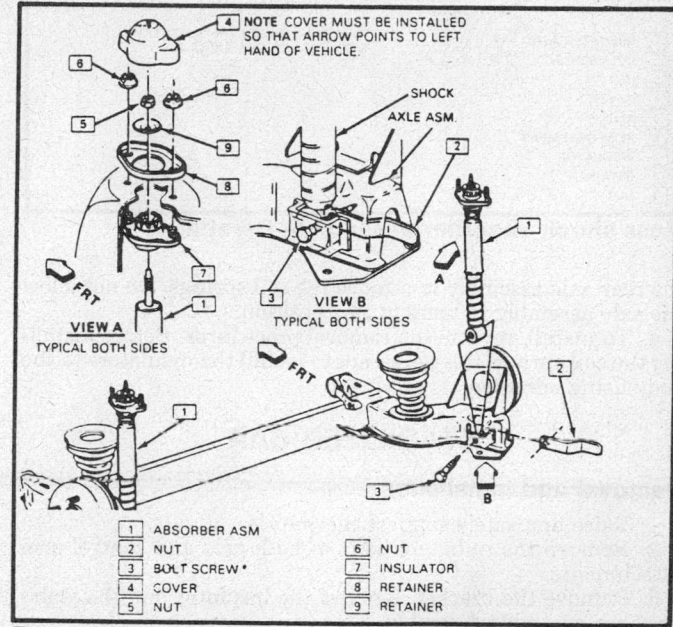

Rear shock absorber assembly—Corsica

Rear Suspension

SHOCK ABSORBER

Removal and Installation

1. Open the trunk and remove the shock absorber trim cover, if equipped. Remove the shock absorber retaining bolts. Remove each shock absorber separately when both assemblies are being replaced.

2. Raise and safely support the vehicle and the rear axle assembly.

3. Remove the lower shock retaining bolts. Remove the shock absorber from the vehicle.

4. To install, reverse the removal procedures.

COIL SPRING

Removal and Installation

1. Raise and safely support the vehicle and the rear axle assembly.

2. Remove the wheel assembly. Remove the right and left brake line bracket retaining screws from the body and allow the brake line to hang free.

3. Remove the shock absorber lower retaining bolts. Lower

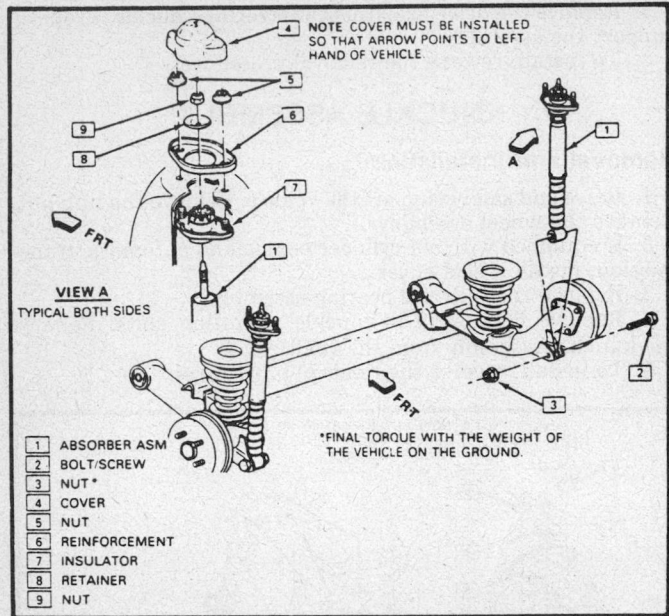

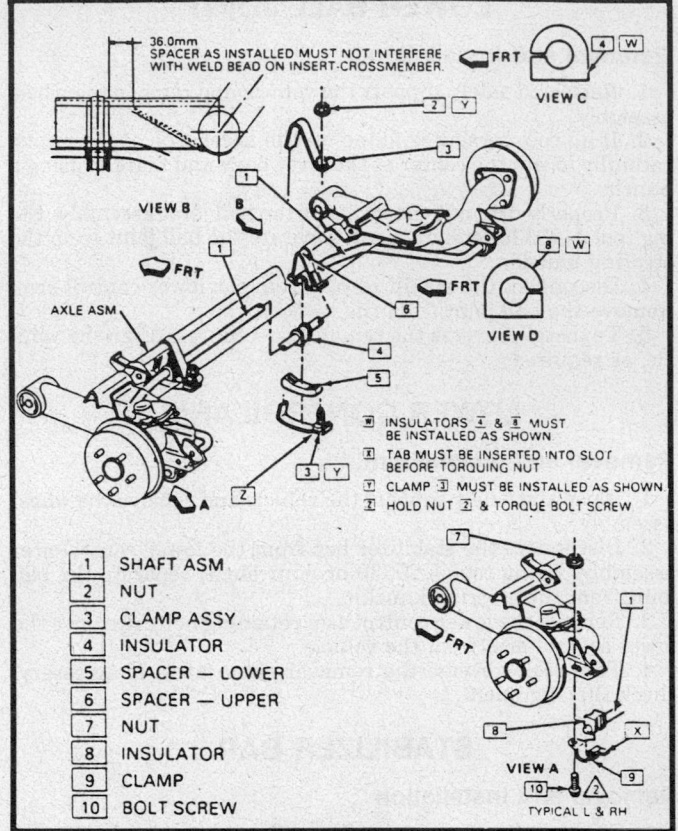

Rear shock absorber assembly—Beretta

1	ABSORBER ASM
2	BOLT/SCREW
3	NUT*
4	COVER
5	NUT
6	REINFORCEMENT
7	INSULATOR
8	RETAINER
9	NUT

*FINAL TORQUE WITH THE WEIGHT OF THE VEHICLE ON THE GROUND.

NOTE COVER MUST BE INSTALLED SO THAT ARROW POINTS TO LEFT HAND OF VEHICLE.

VIEW A
TYPICAL BOTH SIDES

the rear axle assembly to remove the coil springs. Do not allow the axle assembly to hang in this position.

4. To install, reverse the removal procedures. Before installing the coil springs it is necessary to install the insulators to the body using adhesive.

STABILIZER BAR

Removal and Installation

1. Raise and safely support the vehicle.
2. Remove the nuts and bolts at both axle and control arm attachments.
3. Remove the bracket. Remove the insulator and the stabilizer bar assembly assembly.
4. To install, reverse the removal procedures.

HUB AND BEARING ASSEMBLY

Removal and installation

1. Raise and safely support the vehicle. Remove the wheel assembly and the brake drum.
2. Remove the hub and bearing assembly-to-rear axle retaining bolts. Remove the hub and bearing assembly from the rear axle.

NOTE: The top rear retaining bolt will not clear the brake shoe when removing the hub and bearing assembly. Partially remove the assembly before removing the bolt.

3. To install, reverse the removal procedures.

Rear stabilizer assembly—Beretta

1	SHAFT ASM
2	NUT
3	CLAMP ASSY.
4	INSULATOR
5	SPACER — LOWER
6	SPACER — UPPER
7	NUT
8	INSULATOR
9	CLAMP
10	BOLT SCREW

36.0mm SPACER AS INSTALLED MUST NOT INTERFERE WITH WELD BEAD ON INSERT-CROSSMEMBER.

INSULATORS Ⅰ & Ⅱ MUST BE INSTALLED AS SHOWN.

TAB MUST BE INSERTED INTO SLOT BEFORE TORQUING NUT

CLAMP Ⅲ MUST BE INSTALLED AS SHOWN.

HOLD NUT Ⅱ & TORQUE BOLT SCREW

TYPICAL L & RH

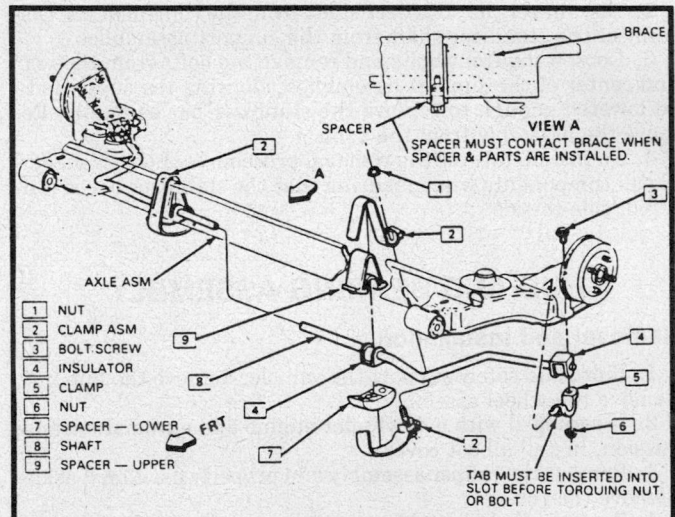

Rear stabilizer assembly—Corsica

1	NUT
2	CLAMP ASM
3	BOLT SCREW
4	INSULATOR
5	CLAMP
6	NUT
7	SPACER — LOWER
8	SHAFT
9	SPACER — UPPER

SPACER MUST CONTACT BRACE WHEN SPACER & PARTS ARE INSTALLED.

VIEW A

TAB MUST BE INSERTED INTO SLOT BEFORE TORQUING NUT OR BOLT

GM N-BODY
FRONT WHEEL DRIVE

Front Suspension

STRUT ASSEMBLY

Removal and Installation

1. Remove the strut-to-body retaining nuts. Raise and safely support the vehicle; be sure the weight of the vehicle does not rest on the lower control arm.
2. Remove the front wheel assembly. Disconnect the brake line bracket from the strut assembly. Remove the strut-to-steering knuckle bolts.
3. Remove the strut assembly from the vehicle. Care should be taken to avoid chipping or cracking the spring coating when handling the front suspension coil spring assembly.
4. To install, reverse the removal procedures.

BALL JOINT

Inspection

1. Raise and safely support the vehicle; be sure the weight of the vehicle does not rest on the lower control arm assemblies.
2. With the ball joint installed to the steering knuckle, grasp the top and bottom of the wheel, then move the wheel using an in and out shaking motion. Observe any movement between the steering knuckle and the control arm. If movement exists, replace the ball joint.

Removal and Installation

1. Raise and safely support the vehicle; be sure the weight of the vehicle does not rest on the lower control arm assemblies.
2. Remove the front wheel assembly. Remove and discard the cotter pin from the ball joint castle nut.
3. Remove the castle nut. Using the ball joint separator tool, disconnect the ball joint from the steering knuckle.
4. Using a drill, drill out the ball joint-to-steering knuckle rivets. Be careful not to damage the halfshaft boot when drilling out the ball joint rivets.
5. Loosen the stabilizer shaft bushing assembly nut. Remove the ball joint from the control arm.
6. To install, reverse the removal procedures. If necessary, check the alignment.

LOWER CONTROL ARM

Removal and Installation

1. Raise and safely support the vehicle; be sure the weight of the vehicle does not rest on the lower control arm assemblies.
2. Remove the wheel assembly. Disconnect the stabilizer shaft from the control arm and support assembly.
3. Remove the ball joint-to-steering knuckle cotter pin and nut. Using the ball joint separator tool, separate the ball joint from the steering knuckle.
4. Remove the control arm-to-support arm and the control arm.
5. To install, reverse the removal procedures.

KNUCKLE ASSEMBLY

Removal and Installation

1. Raise and safely support the vehicle; allow the wheels to hang freely. Remove the front wheel assembly.
2. Using the drive axle boot seal protector tool, on the outer

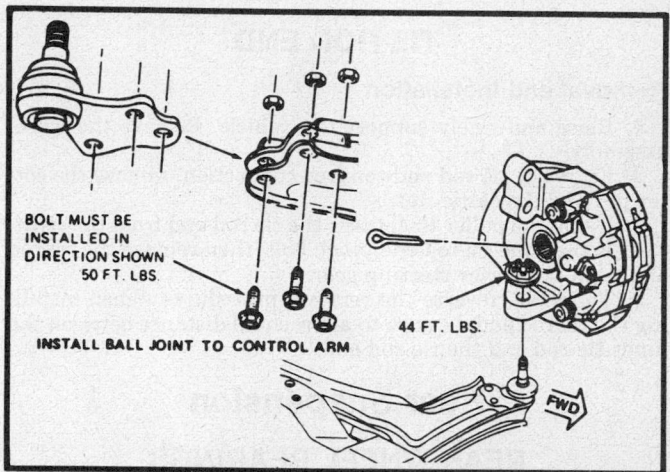

BOLT MUST BE INSTALLED IN DIRECTION SHOWN 50 FT. LBS.

INSTALL BALL JOINT TO CONTROL ARM

44 FT. LBS.

FWD

N body ball joint assembly and related components

CV-joints and the drive axle boot seal protector tool, on the inner Tri-Pot joints.

3. Insert a long punch through the caliper and into a rotor vent to keep it from turning. Clean the halfshaft threads and lubricate them with a thread lubricant.
4. Remove the hub nut and washer. Remove the caliper-to-steering knuckle bolts and position the caliper aside. Remove the rotor.
5. Using the puller tool, loosen the splined fit between the hub and shaft. Remove the hub bolts, the shield, the hub, the bearing assembly and the O-ring.
6. Remove the bearing seal from the knuckle. The hub and bearing are serviced as an assembly only.
7. At the ball joint-to-steering knuckle and the tie rod-to-steering knuckle intersections, remove the cotter pins and nuts.
8. Using the ball joint removal tool, separate the ball joint and the tie rod end from the steering knuckle.

NOTE: Before removing the steering knuckle from the strut, be sure to scribe alignment marks between them, so the installation can be easily performed.

9. While supporting the steering knuckle, remove the steering knuckle-to-strut bolts and the steering knuckle from the vehicle.

To install:

10. Using new O-rings, new bearing seals, new cotter pins and reverse the removal procedures. Lubricate the new bearing seal and the bearing with wheel bearing grease.
11. Torque the:
    a. Steering knuckle-to-strut bolts to 140 ft. lbs.
    b. Ball joint-to-steering knuckle nut 55 ft. lbs.
    c. Tie rod-to-steering knuckle nut to 35 ft. lbs.
    d. Wheel hub-to-steering knuckle bolts to 40 ft. lbs.
    e. Caliper-to-steering knuckle bolts to 28 ft. lbs.
    f. Halfshaft-to-hub nut to 185 ft. lbs.
12. Check and/or adjust the front end alignment.

STABILIZER SHAFT

Removal and Installation

1. Raise and safely support the vehicle; allow the front suspension to hang freely. Remove the wheel assembly.
2. Disconnect the stabilizer shaft-to-control arm bolts. Disconnect the stabilizer shaft from the support assemblies.

3. Loosen the front bolts, then remove the rear and center bolts from the support assemblies and lower them enough to remove the stabilizer shaft.

4. Remove the stabilizer shaft and bushings from the vehicle.

5. To install, reverse the removal procedures.

TIE ROD END

Removal and Installation

1. Raise and safely support the vehicle. Remove the wheel assembly.

2. From the tie rod end-to-strut connection, remove the cotter pin and the castle nut.

3. Using the puller tool, press the tie rod end from the strut.

4. Loosen the tie rod end pinch bolt, then remove the tie rod end from the power steering gear.

5. To install, reverse the removal procedures. When installing the tie rod end, be sure to allow equal distance between the inner tie rod and the tie rod end.

Rear Suspension

REAR WHEEL BEARINGS

Adjustment

The rear wheel bearing assembly is nonadjustable and it is serviced by replacement only.

Removal and Installation

1. Raise and safely support the vehicle. Remove the wheel assembly.

2. Remove the brake drum. Do not hammer on the brake drum during removal or damage to the assembly could result.

3. Remove the hub/bearing assembly-to-rear axle assembly bolts and the hub/bearing assembly from the axle.

NOTE: The upper rear attaching bolt will not clear the brake shoe when removing the hub and bearing assembly. Partially remove the hub prior to removing this bolt.

4. To install, reverse the removal procedures.

SHOCK ABSORBERS

Removal and Installation

1. Open the trunk and remove the trim cover, if equipped

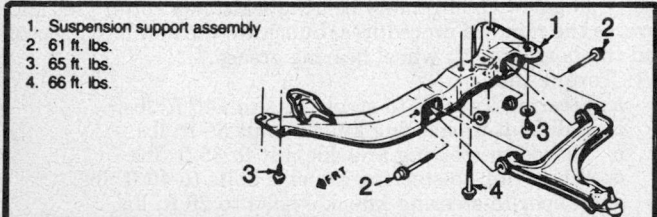

1. Suspension support assembly
2. 61 ft. lbs.
3. 65 ft. lbs.
4. 66 ft. lbs.

N body rear control arm assembly

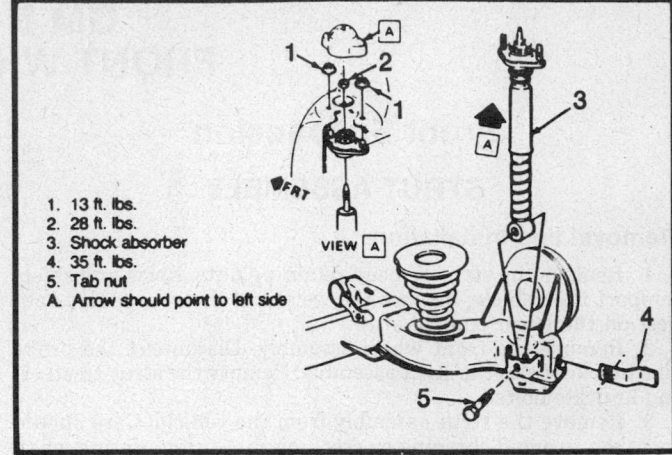

1. 13 ft. lbs.
2. 28 ft. lbs.
3. Shock absorber
4. 35 ft. lbs.
5. Tab nut
A. Arrow should point to left side

N body rear shock absorber and related components

over the shock absorber-to-body nuts. Remove the upper shock absorber attaching nut.

NOTE: Do not remove both shock absorbers at the same time as suspending the rear axle at full length could result in damage to brake lines and hoses.

2. Raise and safely support the vehicle. Remove the lower shock absorber-to-axle nut and the shock absorber.

3. To install, reverse the removal procedures.

COIL SPRING

Removal and Installation

1. Raise and safely support the vehicle and the rear axle assembly. Remove the wheel assembly.

2. Remove the right and left brake line bracket attaching screws from the body and allow the brake line to hang free.

3. Remove both lower shock absorber-to-rear axle bolts. Carefully lower the rear axle assembly and remove the springs.

NOTE: Do not suspend the rear axle by the brake hoses or damage to the hoses could result. Lower the axle just enough to remove the springs and support it during all service procedures.

4. To install, reverse the removal procedures. Position the springs and insulators in their seats and raise the axle assembly. The ends of the upper coil on the spring must be positioned in the seat of the body and within the limits.

5. Prior to installing the spring it will be necessary to install the upper insulators to the body with adhesive to keep it in position while raising the axle assembly and springs.

STABILIZER BAR

Removal and Installation

1. Raise and safely support the vehicle.

2. Remove the bolts at both the axle and control arm attachments. Remove the bracket, insulator and stabilizer bar.

3. To install, reverse the removal procedures.

GM SPRINT
FRONT WHEEL DRIVE

Front Suspension

STRUT ASSEMBLY

Removal and Installation

1. Raise and safely support the vehicle. Remove the wheel assembly.
2. Remove the brake hose securing ring and the hose from the strut. Remove the upper strut support nuts from the engine compartment.
3. Remove the strut-to-steering knuckle bolts. Remove the strut from the vehicle.
4. To install, reverse the removal procedures.

STABILIZER BAR

Removal and Installation

1. Raise and safely support the vehicle. Remove the wheel assembly and the stabilizer bar-to-body mounting bolts.
2. Remove the cotter pin, the castle nut, the washer, the bushing and the stabilizer bar from the lower control arms.

3. To install, reverse the removal procedures.

LOWER CONTROL ARM

Removal and Installation

1. Raise and safely support the vehicle. Remove the wheel assembly.
2. Remove the cotter pin, the castellated nut, the washer and the bushing from the stabilizer bar.
3. Remove the stabilizer bar-to-body mounting bracket bolts. Remove the ball stud and the control arm bolts.
4. Remove the control arm from the vehicle.
5. To install, reverse the removal procedures.

TIE ROD END

Removal and Installation

1. Raise and safely support the vehicle. Remove the wheel assembly.
2. Remove the cotter pin and the castle nut from the tie rod end.

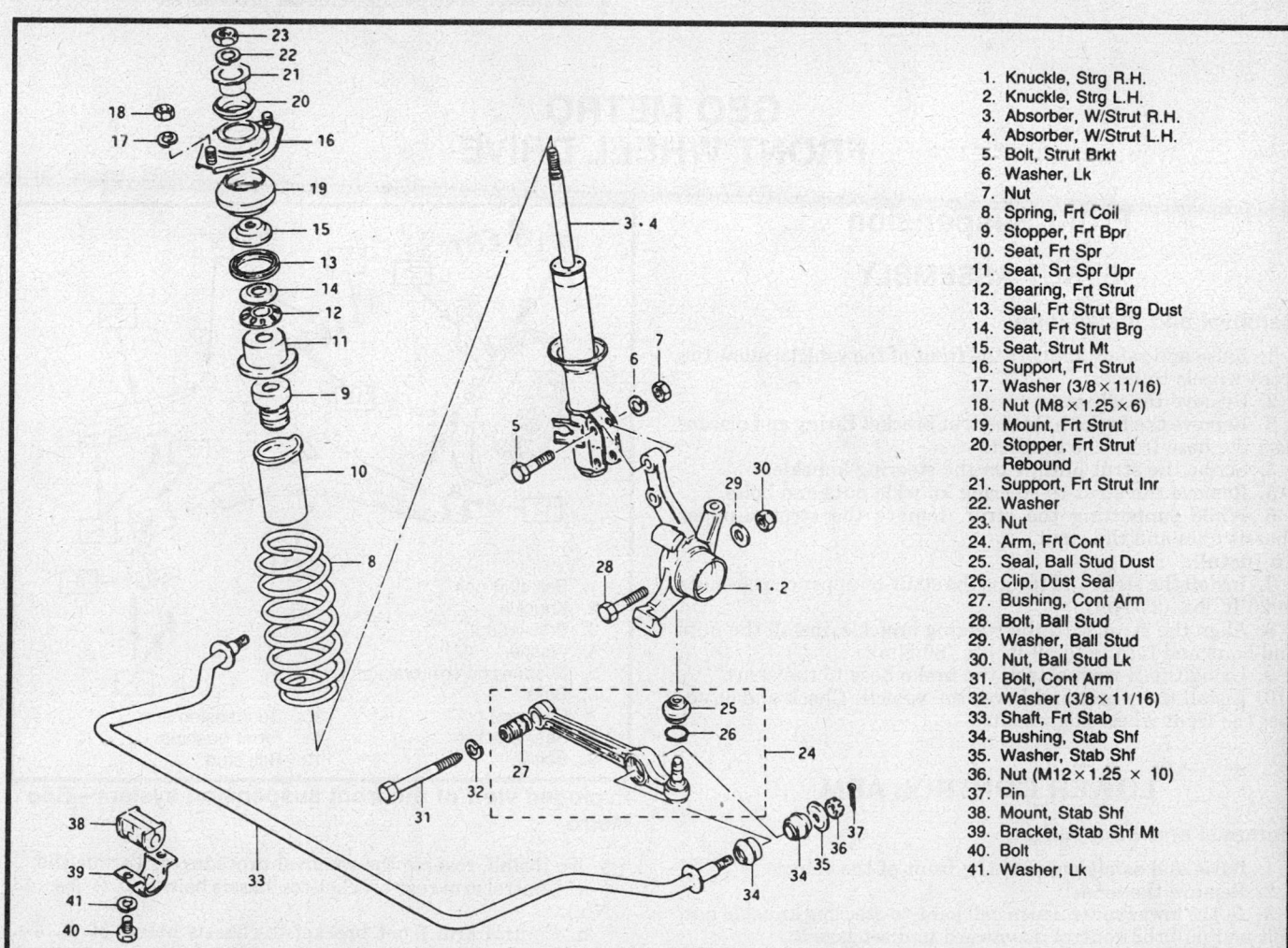

1. Knuckle, Strg R.H.
2. Knuckle, Strg L.H.
3. Absorber, W/Strut R.H.
4. Absorber, W/Strut L.H.
5. Bolt, Strut Brkt
6. Washer, Lk
7. Nut
8. Spring, Frt Coil
9. Stopper, Frt Bpr
10. Seat, Frt Spr
11. Seat, Srt Spr Upr
12. Bearing, Frt Strut
13. Seal, Frt Strut Brg Dust
14. Seat, Frt Strut Brg
15. Seat, Strut Mt
16. Support, Frt Strut
17. Washer (3/8 × 11/16)
18. Nut (M8 × 1.25 × 6)
19. Mount, Frt Strut
20. Stopper, Frt Strut Rebound
21. Support, Frt Strut Inr
22. Washer
23. Nut
24. Arm, Frt Cont
25. Seal, Ball Stud Dust
26. Clip, Dust Seal
27. Bushing, Cont Arm
28. Bolt, Ball Stud
29. Washer, Ball Stud
30. Nut, Ball Stud Lk
31. Bolt, Cont Arm
32. Washer (3/8 × 11/16)
33. Shaft, Frt Stab
34. Bushing, Stab Shf
35. Washer, Stab Shf
36. Nut (M12 × 1.25 × 10)
37. Pin
38. Mount, Stab Shf
39. Bracket, Stab Shf Mt
40. Bolt
41. Washer, Lk

Sprint front suspension assembly

3. Using the ball joint remover tool, remove the tie rod end ball joint from the steering knuckle.

4. Loosen the lock nut on the tie rod end. Unscrew the the tie rod end from the tie rod, count the number of revolutions necessary to remove the tie rod end, for installation purposes.

5. At the steering gear, remove the boot clamps and pull the boot back over the tie rod.

6. Using a pair of pliers, bend the lock washer back from the tie rod joint. Using 2 wrenches, hold the steering gear and unscrew the tie rod end.

7. Remove the tie rod and slide the boot from the tie rod.

8. To install, reverse the removal procedures.

Rear Suspension

REAR WHEEL BEARINGS

Removal and Installation

1. Raise and safely support the vehicle. Remove the wheel assembly.

2. Remove the dust cap, the cotter pin, the castle nut and the washer. Loosen the adjusting nuts of the parking brake cable.

3. Remove the plug from the rear of the backing plate. Insert a tool through the hole, making contact with the shoe hold down spring, then push the spring to release the parking brake shoe lever.

4. Using a brake drum remover tool, pull the brake drum from the axle shaft.

5. Using a brass drift and a hammer, drive the rear wheel bearings from the brake drum.

6. To install, reverse the removal procedures. When installing the wheel bearings, face the sealed sides, numbered sides, outward. Fill the wheel bearing cavity with bearing grease.

SHOCK ABSORBER

Removal and Installation

1. Raise and safely support the vehicle. Remove the wheel assembly.

2. Remove the lower mounting nut, the lock washer and and the outer washer.

3. Remove the upper mounting bolt, the lock washer and nut. Remove the shock absorber.

4. To install, reverse the removal procedures.

LEAF SPRING

Removal and Installation

1. Raise and safely support the vehicle. Remove the U-bolt nuts.

2. Remove the shackle and leaf spring front nuts. Remove the front spring bolt. Remove the spring from the vehicle.

3. To install, reverse the removal procedures.

GEO METRO
FRONT WHEEL DRIVE

Front Suspension

STRUT ASSEMBLY

Removal and Installation

1. Raise and safely support the front of the vehicle; allow the front wheels to hang.

2. Remove the wheel.

3. Remove the brake hose-to-strut bracket E-ring and disconnect the hose from the bracket.

4. Scribe the strut outline on the steering knuckle.

5. Remove the strut-to-steering knuckle nuts and bolts.

6. While supporting the strut, remove the strut-to-upper chassis nuts and the strut.

To install:

7. Install the strut and torque the strut-to-upper chassis nuts to 20 ft. lbs. (27 Nm).

8. Align the strut with the steering knuckle, install the nuts and bolts and torque to 59 ft. lbs. (80 Nm).

9. Using the E-ring, attach the brake hose to the strut.

10. Install the wheel and lower the vehicle. Check and/or adjust the front wheel alignment.

LOWER CONTROL ARM

Removal and Installation

1. Raise and safely support the front of the vehicle.

2. Remove the wheel.

3. At the lower control arm ball joint-to-steering knuckle nut/bolt and pull the control downward to disengage it.

4. Remove the control arm-to-chassis bracket nut, bolts and the control arm.

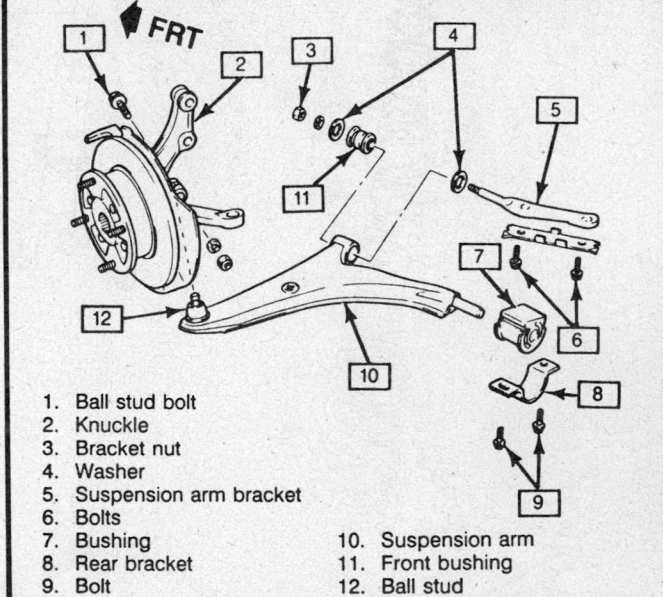

1. Ball stud bolt
2. Knuckle
3. Bracket nut
4. Washer
5. Suspension arm bracket
6. Bolts
7. Bushing
8. Rear bracket
9. Bolt
10. Suspension arm
11. Front bushing
12. Ball stud

Exploded view of the front suspension system—Geo Metro

5. To install, reverse the removal procedures. Torque the:

a. Control arm rear bracket-to-chassis bolts—32 ft. lbs. (43 Nm).

b. Control arm front bracket-to-chassis bolts—59 ft. lbs. (80 Nm).

c. Control arm-to-front bracket nut—74 ft. lbs. (100 Nm).

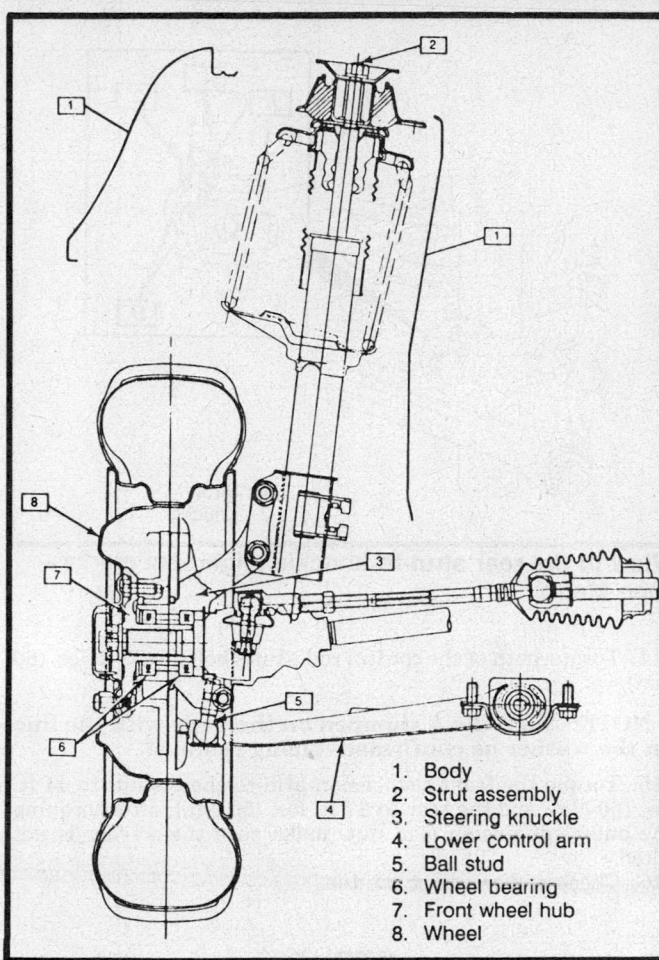

Sectional view of the front suspension system—Geo Metro

1. Body
2. Strut assembly
3. Steering knuckle
4. Lower control arm
5. Ball stud
6. Wheel bearing
7. Front wheel hub
8. Wheel

d. Ball joint-to-steering knuckle nut/bolt—44 ft. lbs. (69 Nm).

TIE ROD END

Removal and Installation

1. Raise and safely support the vehicle. Remove the wheel assembly.

2. Remove the cotter pin and the castle nut from the tie rod end.

3. Using the ball joint remover tool, remove the tie rod end ball joint from the steering knuckle.

4. Loosen the lock nut on the tie rod end. Unscrew the the tie rod end from the tie rod, count the number of revolutions necessary to remove the tie rod end, for installation purposes.

5. At the steering gear, remove the boot clamps and pull the boot back over the tie rod.

6. Using a pair of pliers, bend the lock washer back from the tie rod joint. Using 2 wrenches, hold the steering gear and unscrew the tie rod end.

7. Remove the tie rod and slide the boot from the tie rod.

8. To install, reverse the removal procedures.

Rear Suspension
CONTROL ROD

Removal and Installation

1. Raise and safely support the rear of the vehicle.

2. Remove the wheel.

3. Remove the E-ring and the brake hose from the control rod.

NOTE: Before removing the control, note the adjusting bolt line matchmarked with A for easy readjustment of the toe.

4. Remove the control rod-to-steering knuckle nut.

5. Loosen the control rod-to-body nut.

NOTE: Use another wrench to hold the inside bolt from turning while the nut is being removed.

6. Remove the control rod inside bolt and the control rod.
To install:

7. Install the control rod and the inside bolt with its cam B faced downward.

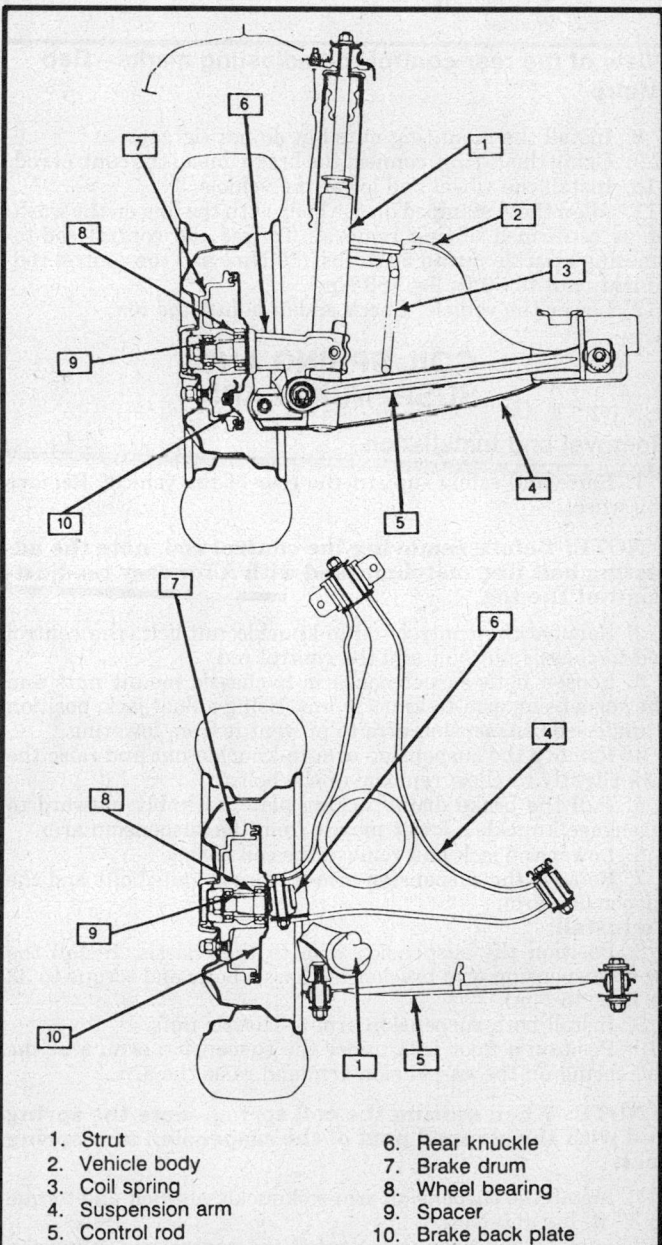

1. Strut
2. Vehicle body
3. Coil spring
4. Suspension arm
5. Control rod
6. Rear knuckle
7. Brake drum
8. Wheel bearing
9. Spacer
10. Brake back plate

Sectional view of the rear suspension system—Geo Metro

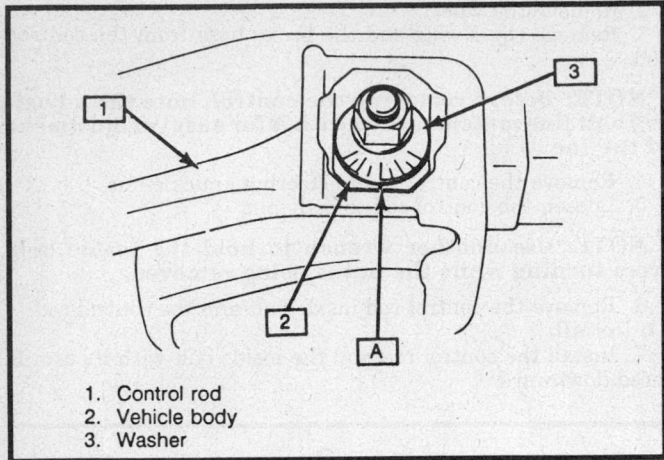

1. Control rod
2. Vehicle body
3. Washer

View of the rear control rod adjusting marks — Geo Metro

8. Install the mounting nuts but do not tighten.
9. Using the E-ring, connect the brake line to the control rod.
10. Install the wheel and lower the vehicle.
11. Align the A stamped on the body with the line on the washer as confirmed during removal. Torque the control rod-to-steering knuckle nut to 59 ft. lbs. (80 Nm) and the control rod-to-body nut to 59 ft. lbs. (80 Nm).
12. Lower the vehicle. Check and/or adjust the toe.

COIL SPRING AND SUSPENSION ARM

Removal and Installation

1. Raise and safely support the rear of the vehicle. Remove the wheel.

NOTE: **Before removing the control rod, note the adjusting bolt line matchmarked with A for easy readjustment of the toe.**

2. Remove the control rod-to-knuckle nut/bolt, the control rod-to-chassis nut/bolt and the control rod.
3. Loosen both suspension arm-to-chassis mount nuts and the suspension arm-to-knuckle nut. Using a floor jack, position it under the suspension arm to prevent it from lowering.
4. Remove the suspension arm-to-knuckle nut and raise the jack slightly to allow removal of the bolt.
5. Pull the brake drum/backing plate assembly outward to disengage knuckle's lower mount from the suspension arm.
6. Lower the jack and remove the coil spring.
7. Remove the suspension arm-to-chassis nuts/bolts and the suspension arm.
To install:
8. Position the suspension arm to the chassis. Install the front suspension arm bracket-to-chassis bolts and torque to 33 ft. lbs. (45 Nm).
9. Install both suspension arm-to-chassis nuts.
10. Position a floor jack under the suspension arm, seat the coil spring on the suspension arm and raise the arm.

NOTE: **When seating the coil spring, mate the spring end with the stepped part of the suspension arm spring seat.**

11. Install the suspension arm-to-knuckle nut/bolt and torque to 37 ft. lbs. (50 Nm).
12. Remove the floor jack. Install the control rod, align the matchmarks but do not tighten the nuts and bolts.
13. Install the wheel and lower the vehicle.

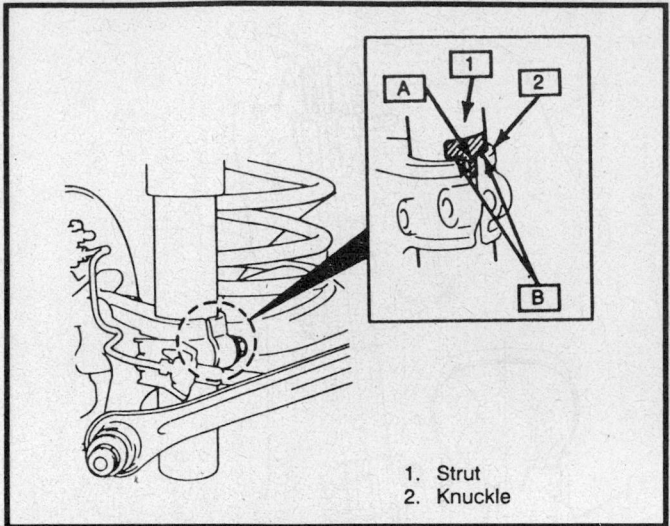

1. Strut
2. Knuckle

View of the rear strut-to-knuckle alignment marks — Geo Metro

14. Torque both of the control rod's nuts/bolts to 59 ft. lbs. (80 Nm).

NOTE: **Align the A stamped on the body with the line on the washer as confirmed during removal.**

15. Torque the front suspension arm-to-chassis nut to 44 ft. lbs. (60 Nm) and the rear to 37 ft. lbs. (50 Nm); after torquing the outer suspension arm nut, make sure the washer is not tilted.
16. Check and/or adjust the toe.

STRUT

Removal and Installation

1. Raise and safely support the rear of the vehicle. Remove the wheel.
2. Position a floor jack under the suspension arm.
3. Remove the strut-to-chassis nuts and push the strut downward to compress it.
4. Remove the strut-to-knuckle bolt and pull the strut upward from the knuckle.

NOTE: **If the strut is difficult to remove, insert a wedge into the knuckle slit but do not open the slit wider than necessary.**

——————— CAUTION ———————

Do not lower the jack lower more than necessary or the coil spring may pop out and cause personal injury.

To install:
5. Compress the strut and insert it into the knuckle; be sure to align the projection A, on the strut, with the knuckle's slit. Push the strut into the knuckle until the lips B contact the knuckle.
6. Install the strut-to-knuckle bolt and torque to 44 ft. lbs. (60 Nm).
7. Install the strut-to-chassis nuts and torque to 24 ft. lbs. (30 Nm).

NOTE: **If the strut does not reach the chassis, raise the jack.**

8. Remove the jack, install the wheel and lower the vehicle.

GM W-BODY
FRONT WHEEL DRIVE

Front Suspension

STRUT ASSEMBLY

── CAUTION ──

Do not service the strut unless the weight of the vehicle is on the suspension system, for the weight of the vehicle keeps the coil spring compressed; otherwise, personal injury may occur.

Removal and Installation

1. To asure the proper camber adjustment, scribe the strut mount cover plate-to-body position.

2. Remove the strut mount cover plate-to-body nuts and the cover plate.

3. Using a No. 50 Torx® bit and a strut rod nut remover tool, remove the strut shaft-to-body nut.

4. Using a small pry bar, pry the strut mount bushing from the upper body cavity.

5. If the vehicle is equipped with 8mm studs, use a jounce bumper retainer spanner wrench to remove the jounce bumper retainer.

6. Using a strut extension rod tool, attach it to the strut shaft, compress the shaft into the strut cartridge and remove the jounce bumper.

7. Reattach the strut extension rod tool to the strut shaft, pull the shaft upward and remove the tool. Using a strut cap nut wrench, remove the closure nut from the strut shaft.

8. Remove the strut cartridge. Using a suction device, remove the oil from the strut tube.

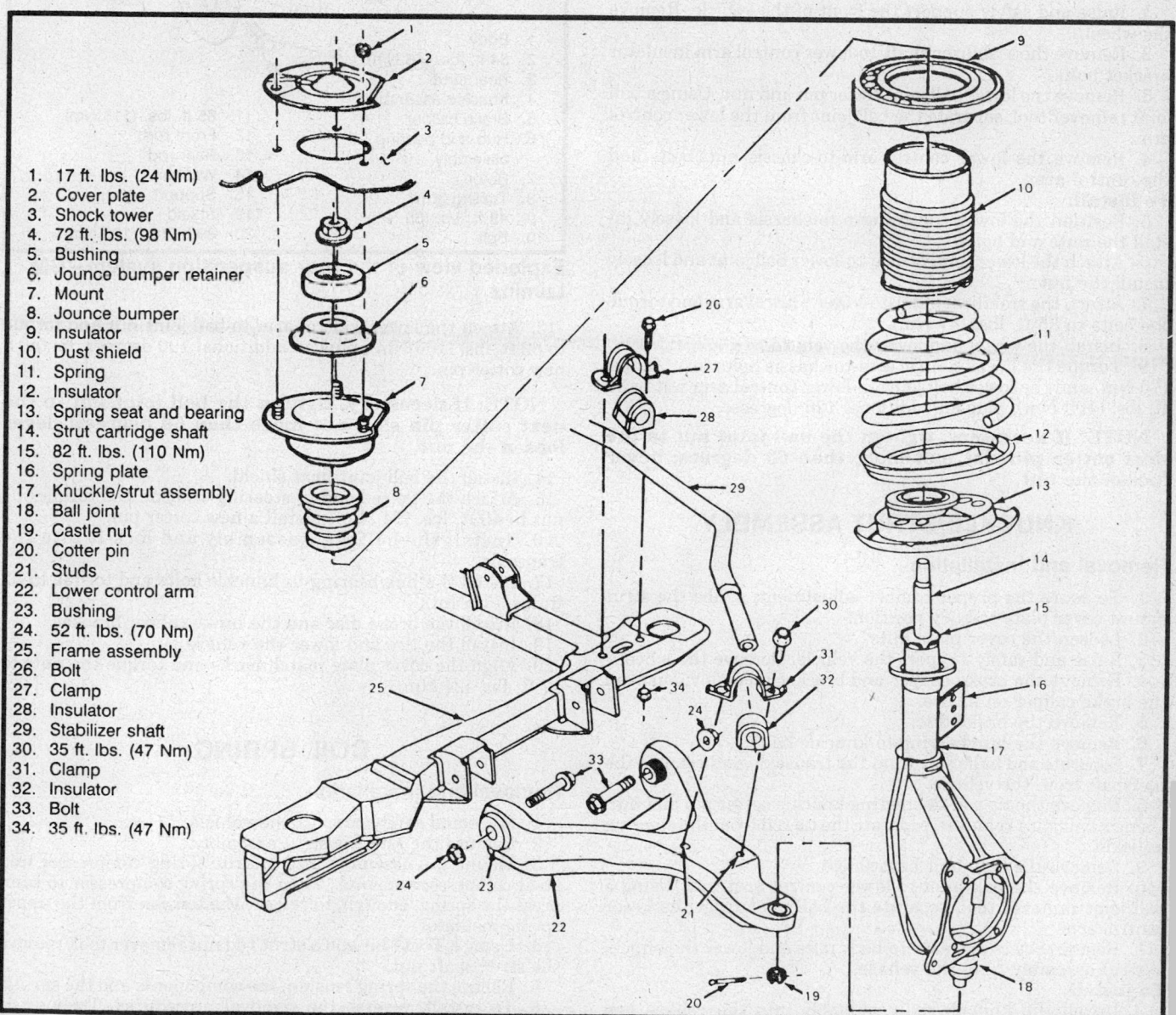

1. 17 ft. lbs. (24 Nm)
2. Cover plate
3. Shock tower
4. 72 ft. lbs. (98 Nm)
5. Bushing
6. Jounce bumper retainer
7. Mount
8. Jounce bumper
9. Insulator
10. Dust shield
11. Spring
12. Insulator
13. Spring seat and bearing
14. Strut cartridge shaft
15. 82 ft. lbs. (110 Nm)
16. Spring plate
17. Knuckle/strut assembly
18. Ball joint
19. Castle nut
20. Cotter pin
21. Studs
22. Lower control arm
23. Bushing
24. 52 ft. lbs. (70 Nm)
25. Frame assembly
26. Bolt
27. Clamp
28. Insulator
29. Stabilizer shaft
30. 35 ft. lbs. (47 Nm)
31. Clamp
32. Insulator
33. Bolt
34. 35 ft. lbs. (47 Nm)

Exploded view of the front suspension system—GM Lumina

To install:

9. Replace the oil into the strut tube and insert the strut cartridge.

10. Using a strut cap nut wrench, tighten the closure nut onto the strut.

11. Install the jounce bumper. If equipped with 8mm studs, use the jounce bumper retainer spanner wrench to install the jounce bumper retainer.

12. Lubricate the strut bushing with soap water and install it. If necessary, use the strut extension rod tool to position the strut shaft.

13. Using a No. 50 Torx® bit and a strut rod nut installer tool, torque the strut shaft-to-body nut to 72 ft. lbs. (98 Nm).

14. Install the strut mount cover and align the matchmarks.

15. Install the cover plate and torque the nuts to 17 ft. lbs. (24 Nm).

LOWER CONTROL ARM

Removal and Installation

1. Raise and safely support the front of the vehicle. Remove the wheel.

2. Remove the stabilizer shaft-to-lower control arm insulator bracket bolts.

3. Remove the lower ball joint cotter pin and nut. Using a ball joint remover tool, separate the ball joint from the lower control arm.

4. Remove the lower control arm-to-chassis nuts/bolts and the control arm.

To install:

5. Position the lower control arm-to-chassis and loosely install the nuts and bolts.

6. Attach the lower control arm-to-lower ball joint and loosely install the nut.

7. Attach the stabilizer shaft-to-lower control arm and torque the bolts to 35 ft. lbs. (47 Nm).

8. Install the wheel and lower the vehicle.

9. Torque the lower control arm-to-chassis bolts to 52 ft. lbs. (70 Nm) and the lower ball joint-to-lower control arm nut to 89 ft. lbs. (100 Nm), plus an additional 120 degrees.

NOTE: If necessary, tighten the ball joint nut to the next cotter pin slot, not more than 60 degrees; never loosen the nut.

KNUCKLE/STRUT ASSEMBLY

Removal and Installation

1. To asure the proper camber adjustment, scribe the strut mount cover plate-to-body position.

2. Loosen the cover plate nuts.

3. Raise and safely support the vehicle. Remove the wheel.

4. Remove the brake caliper and bracket assembly; suspend the brake caliper on a wire.

5. Remove the brake disc.

6. Remove the hub/bearing-to-knuckle bolts.

7. Separate the halfshaft from the transaxle and remove the halfshaft from the vehicle.

8. Remove the tie rod-to-steering knuckle cotter pin and nut. Using a ball joint remover, separate the tie rod from the steering knuckle.

9. Remove the ball joint heat shield.

10. Remove the ball joint-to-lower control arm nut. Using a ball joint remover tool, separate the ball joint from the lower control arm.

11. Remove the cover plate-to-body nuts and lower the knuckle/strut assembly from the vehicle.

To install:

12. Install the knuckle/strut assembly into the vehicle and loosely attach the cover plate-to-body nuts.

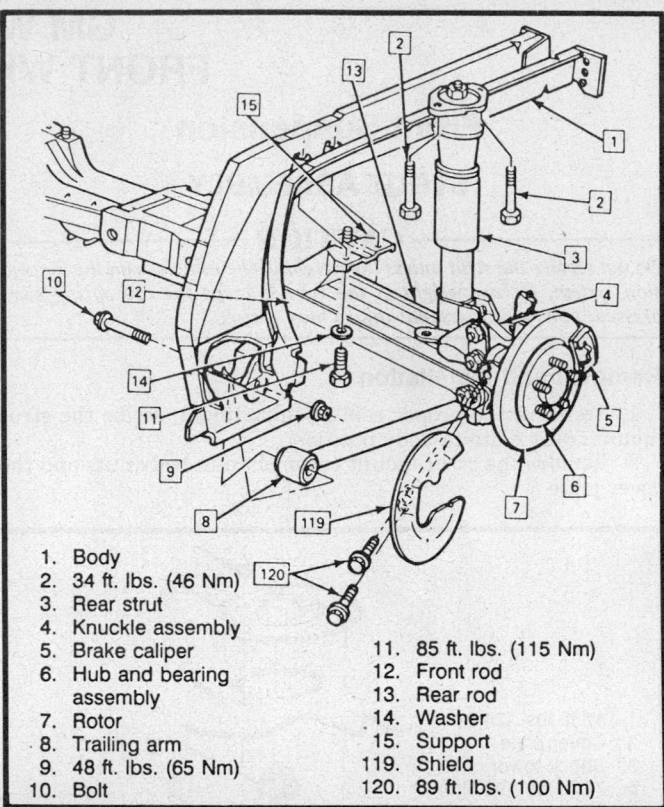

1. Body
2. 34 ft. lbs. (46 Nm)
3. Rear strut
4. Knuckle assembly
5. Brake caliper
6. Hub and bearing assembly
7. Rotor
8. Trailing arm
9. 48 ft. lbs. (65 Nm)
10. Bolt
11. 85 ft. lbs. (115 Nm)
12. Front rod
13. Rear rod
14. Washer
15. Support
119. Shield
120. 89 ft. lbs. (100 Nm)

Exploded view of the rear suspension system—GM Lumina

13. Attach the lower control arm-to-ball joint nut and torque to 89 ft. lbs. (100 Nm), plus an additional 120 degrees; install a new cotter pin.

NOTE: If necessary, tighten the ball joint nut to the next cotter pin slot, not more than 60 degrees; never loosen the nut.

14. Install the ball joint heat shield.

15. Attach the tie rod end-to-steering knuckle and torque the nut to 40 ft. lbs. (54 Nm); install a new cotter pin.

16. Install the halfshaft assembly and lock it into the transaxle.

17. Install the hub/bearing-to-knuckle bolts and torque to 52 ft. lbs. (70 Nm).

18. Install the brake disc and the brake caliper/bracket.

19. Install the tire and lower the vehicle.

20. Align the cover plate matchmarks and torque the nuts to 17 ft. lbs. (24 Nm).

COIL SPRING

Removal and Installation

1. Raise and safely support the vehicle.

2. Remove the knuckle/strut assembly.

3. Mount the assembly into a strut spring compressor and strut compressor adaptor. Turn the spring compressor to compress the spring, enough, to release the tension from the upper spring insulator.

4. Using a Torx® bit and a strut rod nut remover tool, remove the strut shaft nut.

5. Relieve the spring tension, the components and the spring.

6. To install, reverse the removal procedures. Torque the strut shaft nut to 72 ft. lbs. (98 Nm).

Rear Suspension

STRUT ASSEMBLY

Removal and Installation

1. Raise and safely support the rear of the vehicle. Remove the wheel.
2. For alignment purposes, scribe the strut-to-knuckle outline.
3. If equipped with an auxiliary spring, remove it.
4. Remove the jack pad.
5. Using a rear leaf spring compressor tool, attach it to the transverse spring and fully compress it; do not remove the spring or the retention plates.
6. Remove the strut-to-body bolts.
7. Remove the brake hose bracket from the strut.
8. Remove the strut/auxiliary spring upper bracket/stabilizer shaft bracket from the knuckle and the strut.

To install:

9. Install the strut and torque the strut-to-body bolts to 34 ft. lbs. (46 Nm).
10. Install the strut/auxiliary spring bracket/stabilizer shaft bracket-to-knuckle, align the scribe marks and torque the nuts to 133 ft. lbs. (180 Nm).
11. Attach the brake hose bracket to the strut.
12. Remove the spring compressor tool.
13. Install the jack pad and torque the bolts to 18 ft. lbs. (25 Nm).
14. If equipped with an auxiliary spring, install it.
15. Install the wheel and lower the vehicle.

CONTROL RODS

Removal and Installation
REAR ROD

1. Raise and safely support the rear of the vehicle. Remove the wheel.
2. If equipped with an auxiliary spring, remove it. If not equipped with an auxiliary spring, remove the control rod-to-knuckle bolt.
3. If equipped, remove the lower auxiliary spring bracket and the control rod.
4. Remove the rear adjusting cam and push the bolt forward to provide room for the rod removal.
5. Remove the rear control rod.

To install:

6. Install the rear control rod.
7. At the rear adjusting cam, push the bolt rearward through the rod bushing and install the rear toe adjusting cam; loosely, install the cam nut.
8. If equipped, install the lower auxiliary spring bracket to the rod and torque the nut to 133 ft. lbs. (180 Nm).
9. If not equipped with an auxiliary spring, place Loctite® on the control rod-to-knuckle bolt.
10. Install the wheel and lower the vehicle.
11. Adjust the rear toe. Torque the inboard rod-to-crossmember nut to 66 ft. lbs. (90 Nm), plus 120 degees.

FRONT ROD

1. Raise and safely support the rear of the vehicle. Remove the wheel.
2. Remove the control rod-to-knuckle bolt.
3. Remove the exhaust pipe heat shield.
4. Lower and support the fuel tank, enough, to access the rod-to-frame bolt and remove the bolt.
5. Remove the front control rod.

To install:

6. Install the front control rod.
7. Install the bolt/nut-to-frame but do not tighten.
8. Apply Loctite® to the rod-to-knuckle bolt and install the bolt. Torque the rod-to-frame bolt to 66 ft. lbs. (90 Nm), plus 120 degrees and the rod-to-knuckle bolt to 66 ft. lbs. (90 Nm), plus 120 degrees.
9. Reposition the fuel tank and the exhaust pipe heat shield.
10. Install the wheel and lower the vehicle.

TRANSVERSE SPRING

NOTE: Do not use corrosive cleaning agents, engine degreaser, solvents, silicone lubricants or etc. on or near the fiberglass transverse spring; extensive damage to the spring may occur.

Removal and Installation

1. Raise and safely support the rear of the vehicle using the chassis.
2. Remove the jack pad and spring retention plates.
3. Remove the right trailing arm from the knuckle.
4. Using a rear leaf spring compressor tool, separate it from the shank and hang the center shank of the tool at the front spring center. Connect the tool body to the center shank and spring; always center the spring on the tool rollers.
5. Using the spring compressor tool, compress the spring.
6. Slide the spring to the left side; it may be necessary to pry the spring to the left, using a pry bar against the right knuckle, tire and wheel assembly.
7. Relax the spring to provide removal clearance from the right side.
8. Remove the transverse spring.

To install:

9. Using a rear leaf spring compressor tool, attach it to the spring and compress it slightly.
10. Install the spring to the left knuckle; slide it left as far as possible and raise the right side as far as possible.
11. Compress the spring further and slide it to the right knuckle.

NOTE: The rear spring retention plates are designed with tabs on an end. The tabs must be aligned with the support assembly to prevent damaging the fuel tank.

12. Center the spring to align the spring retention plate bolt holes.
13. Install the spring retention plates and hand start the bolts.
14. Position the trailing arm, install the bolt and torque the nut to 192 ft. lbs. (260 Nm).
15. Remove the rear leaf spring compressor tool and torque the retention plate bolts to 15 ft. lbs. (20 Nm).
16. Install the jack pad and torque the bolts to 18 ft. lbs. (25 Nm).
17. Lower the vehicle.

GM H-BODY
FRONT WHEEL DRIVE

Front Suspension

STRUT ASSEMBLY

Removal and Installation

1. Remove the nuts attaching the top of the strut assembly to the body.
2. Raise and safely support the vehicle. Remove the wheel assembly.
3. Always install drive axle boot seal protectors. Care must be taken to prevent overextension of the inner Tri-pot joints.
4. Remove the brake line bracket bolt from the strut assembly. Do not disconnect the brake line from the caliper.
5. Remove the strut-to-steering knuckle bolts and then carefully remove the strut assembly.
6. To install, reverse the removal procedures. Check the wheel alignment, as required.

BALL JOINTS

Inspection

1. Raise the front of the vehicle with a lift placed under the engine cradle. The front wheel should be clear of the ground.
2. Grasp the wheel at the top and bottom and shake the wheel in and out.
3. If any movement is seen of the steering knuckle relative to the control arm, the ball joints are defective and must be replaced. Note that movement elsewhere may be due to loose wheel bearings or other troubles. Watch the knuckle-to-control arm connection.
4. If the ball stud is disconnected from the steering knuckle and any looseness is noted, often the ball joint stud can be twisted in its socket with your fingers, replace the ball joints.

Removal and Installation

1. Raise and safely support the vehicle. Remove the wheel assembly.
2. Install drive axle covers to protect the drive axle boot seals.
3. Pull the cotter pin from the ball joint and install a ball joint separator tool. Turn the castellated nut counterclockwise to separate the ball joint from the steering knuckle.
4. Use a ⅛ in. drill bit to drill a hole approximately ¼ in. deep in the center of each of the ball joint rivets.

5. Use a ½ in. drill bit to drill off the rivet heads. Drill only enough to remove the rivet head.
6. Use a hammer and punch to remove the rivets. Drive them out from the bottom.
7. Loosen the stabilizer bar bushing assembly nut. Pull down on the control arm and remove the ball joint from the steering knuckle and control arm.

To install:

8. Install the new ball joint in the steering knuckle and align the holes with those in the control arm.
9. Install the ball joint nuts facing down and tighten the nuts to 50 ft. lbs. Install the castellated nut and tighten to 81 ft. lbs. Tightening the nut for cotter pin alignment is allowed, but do not loosen it once the torque value has been reached.
10. Install the cotter pin. Installation of the remaining components is in the reverse order of removal.

LOWER CONTROL ARM

Removal and Installation

1. Raise and safely support the vehicle. Remove the wheel assembly.
2. Install drive axle covers to protect the drive axle boot seals. Remove the stabilizer bar bushing-to-control arm bolt.
3. Pull the cotter pin from the ball joint and install a ball joint separator tool. Turn the castellated nut counterclockwise to separate the ball joint from the steering knuckle.
4. Remove the remaining control arm bolts and remove the control arm from the vehicle.

To install:

5. Position the control arm and install the mounting bolts, but do not tighten.
6. Install the stabilizer bar bushing assembly. Reconnect the ball joint to the steering knuckle.
7. Raise the vehicle slightly so the weight of the vehicle is supported by the control arms. The weight of the vehicle must be supported by the control arms when tightening the mounting nuts.

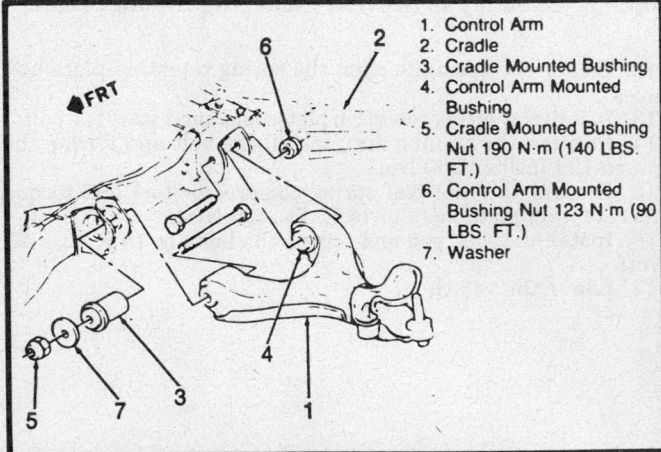

1. Control Arm
2. Cradle
3. Cradle Mounted Bushing
4. Control Arm Mounted Bushing
5. Cradle Mounted Bushing Nut 190 N·m (140 LBS. FT.)
6. Control Arm Mounted Bushing Nut 123 N·m (90 LBS. FT.)
7. Washer

H body front lower control arm assembly

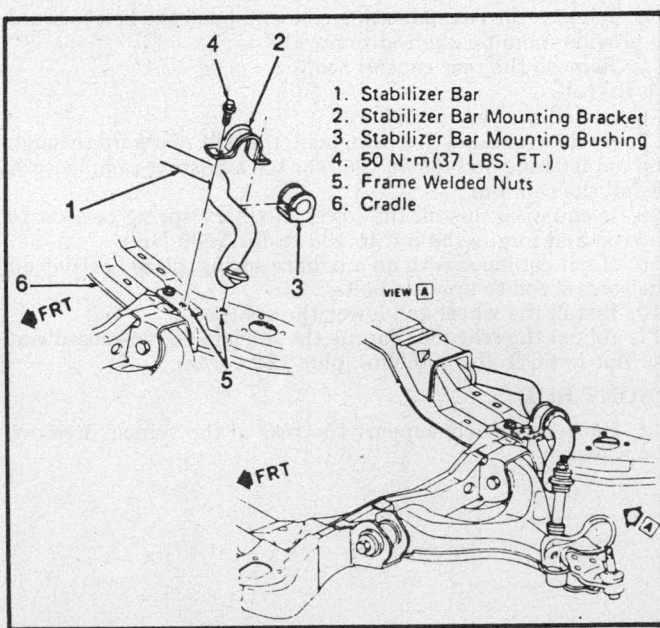

1. Stabilizer Bar
2. Stabilizer Bar Mounting Bracket
3. Stabilizer Bar Mounting Bushing
4. 50 N·m (37 LBS. FT.)
5. Frame Welded Nuts
6. Cradle

VIEW A

H body front stabilizer assembly

8. Installation of the remaining components is in the reverse order of removal.

Rear Suspension
STRUT ASSEMBLY

Removal and Installation

1. Remove the inner trunk side cover.
2. Raise and safely support the vehicle. Remove the wheel assembly.
3. Disconnect and plug the ELC air line. Remove the strut tower mounting nuts from inside the trunk.
4. Remove the strut anchor bolts, washers and nuts from the rear knuckle and knuckle bracket. Remove the strut from the vehicle.
5. To install, reverse the removal procedures.

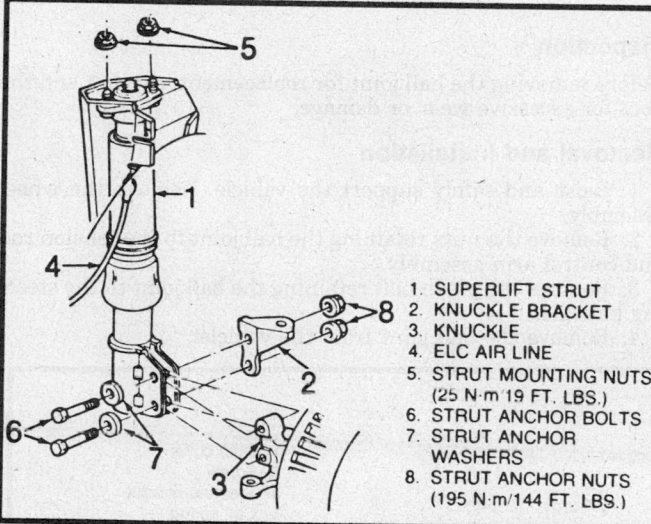

1. SUPERLIFT STRUT
2. KNUCKLE BRACKET
3. KNUCKLE
4. ELC AIR LINE
5. STRUT MOUNTING NUTS (25 N·m 19 FT. LBS.)
6. STRUT ANCHOR BOLTS
7. STRUT ANCHOR WASHERS
8. STRUT ANCHOR NUTS (195 N·m/144 FT. LBS.)

H body rear strut assembly

COIL SPRING

Removal and Installation

1. Raise and safely support the vehicle; allow the control arms to hang free. Remove the wheel assembly.
2. Separate the rear stabilizer bar from the knuckle bracket and remove it.

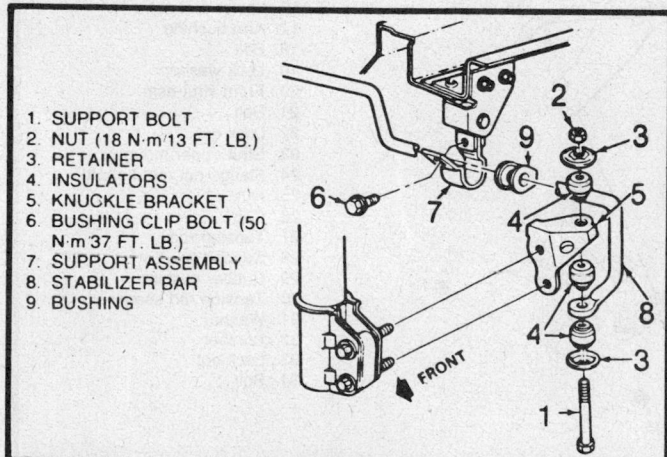

1. SUPPORT BOLT
2. NUT (18 N·m 13 FT. LB.)
3. RETAINER
4. INSULATORS
5. KNUCKLE BRACKET
6. BUSHING CLIP BOLT (50 N·m 37 FT. LB.)
7. SUPPORT ASSEMBLY
8. STABILIZER BAR
9. BUSHING

H body rear stabilizer bar assembly

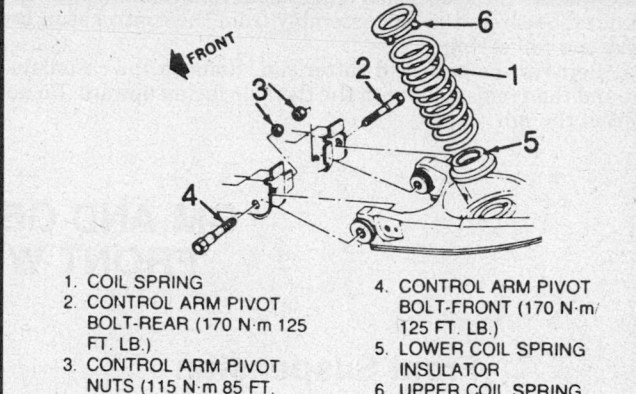

1. COIL SPRING
2. CONTROL ARM PIVOT BOLT-REAR (170 N·m 125 FT. LB.)
3. CONTROL ARM PIVOT NUTS (115 N·m 85 FT. LB.)
4. CONTROL ARM PIVOT BOLT-FRONT (170 N·m/ 125 FT. LB.)
5. LOWER COIL SPRING INSULATOR
6. UPPER COIL SPRING INSULATOR

H body rear coil spring assembly

3. Disconnect the ELC height sensor link at the right control arm and the parking brake cable retaining clip at the left control arm.
4. Position the tool J–23028–01 or its equivalent, so as to cradle the control arm bushings. Special tool J–23028–01 or equivalent, should be secured to a jack.
5. Raise the jack to remove the tension from the control arm pivot bolts. Secure a chain around the spring and through the control arm as a safety precaution.
6. Remove the rear control arm pivot bolt and nut.
7. Slowly maneuver the jack so as to relieve any tension in the front control arm pivot bolt and then remove the bolt and nut.
8. Lower the jack to allow the control arm to pivot downward.
9. When all pressure is removed from the coil spring, remove the safety chain, spring and insulators.
10. To install, reverse the removal procedures.

BALL JOINT

Removal and Installation

1. Raise and safely support the vehicle. Remove the wheel assembly.
2. Disconnect the ELC height sensor link, right control arm and the parking brake cable retaining link, left control arm.
3. Remove the cotter pin and castellated nut from the outer suspension adjustment link. Separate the outer suspension link from the knuckle.
4. Support the control arm with a jack. The lower control arm must be supported to prevent the coil spring from forcing the control arm downward.
5. Remove the ball stud cotter pin. Remove the castellated nut and then reinstall it with the flat side facing upward. Do not tighten the nut.
6. Install a ball joint separator tool and separate the knuckle from the ball stud by backing off the inverted nut against the tool.
7. Separate the ball joint from the control arm.
8. To install, reverse the removal procedures.

LOWER CONTROL ARM

Removal and Installation

1. Raise and safely support the vehicle. Remove the wheel assembly.
2. Disconnect the ELC height sensor link, right control arm and the parking brake cable retaining link, left control arm.

3. Remove the suspension adjustment link retaining nut and retainer. Separate the link assembly from the control arm. Remove the coil spring.

4. Remove the ball stud cotter pin. Remove the castellated nut and then reinstall it with the flat side facing upward. Do not tighten the nut.

5. Install a ball joint separator tool and separate the knuckle from the ball stud by backing off the inverted nut against the tool.

6. Separate the ball joint from the control arm.

7. To install, reverse the removal procedures.

GM AND GEO SPECTRUM FRONT WHEEL DRIVE

Front Suspension

STRUT ASSEMBLY

Removal and Installation

1. From the engine compartment remove the nuts retaining the strut to the body.

2. Raise and safely support the vehicle. Remove the wheel assembly.

3. Remove the brake hose clip at the strut bracket. Disconnect the brake hose at the caliper. Tape or cap the brake hose and caliper opening.

4. Pull the brake hose through the opening in the strut bracket.

5. Remove the nuts retaining the strut to the steering knuckle.

6. Remove the strut assembly.

7. To install, reverse the removal procedures. Bleed the brake system.

BALL JOINT

Inspection

Before removing the ball joint for replacement, check it and the boot for excessive wear or damage.

Removal and Installation

1. Raise and safely support the vehicle. Remove the wheel assembly.

2. Remove the nuts retaining the ball joint to the tension rod and control arm assembly.

3. Remove the pinch bolt retaining the ball joint to the steering knuckle.

4. Remove the ball joint from the vehicle.

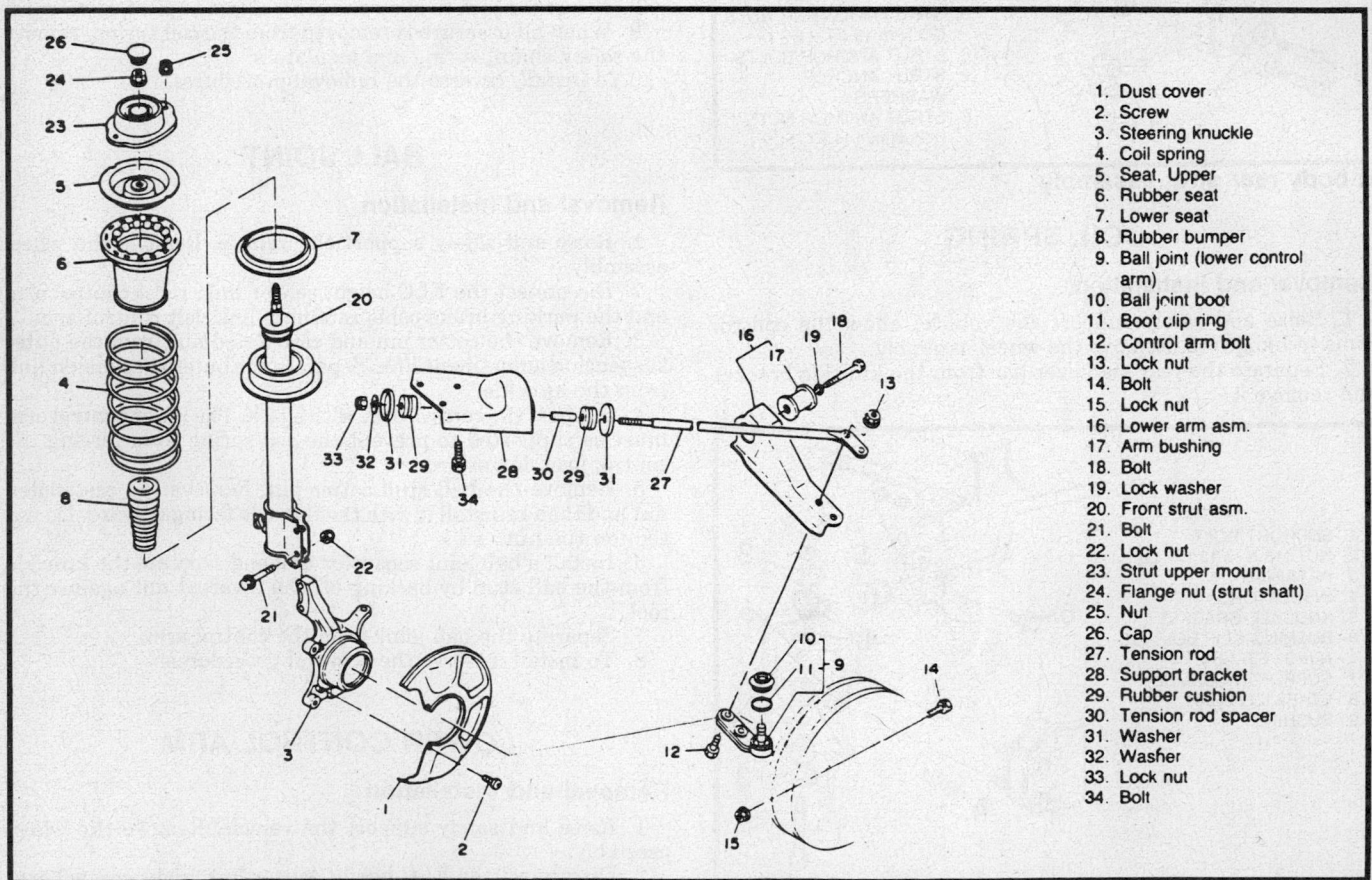

1. Dust cover
2. Screw
3. Steering knuckle
4. Coil spring
5. Seat, Upper
6. Rubber seat
7. Lower seat
8. Rubber bumper
9. Ball joint (lower control arm)
10. Ball joint boot
11. Boot clip ring
12. Control arm bolt
13. Lock nut
14. Bolt
15. Lock nut
16. Lower arm asm.
17. Arm bushing
18. Bolt
19. Lock washer
20. Front strut asm.
21. Bolt
22. Lock nut
23. Strut upper mount
24. Flange nut (strut shaft)
25. Nut
26. Cap
27. Tension rod
28. Support bracket
29. Rubber cushion
30. Tension rod spacer
31. Washer
32. Washer
33. Lock nut
34. Bolt

Spectrum front suspension assembly

5. To install, reverse the removal procedures. Align the vehicle as required.

LOWER CONTROL ARM

Removal and Installation

1. Raise and safely support the vehicle.
2. Remove the control arm-to-tension arm retaining nuts and bolts.
3. Remove the bolt securing the control arm-to-body.
4. Remove the control arm from the vehicle.
5. To install, reverse the removal procedures. Raise the control arm to a distance of 15 in. from the top of the wheel well to the center of the hub.
6. Torque the control arm-to-body bolts to 41 ft. lbs. and the control arm-to-tension rod bolts to 80 ft. lbs. This procedure aligns the bushing arm to the body.

TENSION BAR

Removal and Installation

1. Raise and safely support the vehicle.
2. If equipped with a stabilizer bar, remove the nuts, bolts and insulators retaining it to the tension rod.
3. Remove the nut and washer retaining the tension rod to the body.
4. Remove the nuts and bolts retaining the tension rod to the control rod.
5. Remove the tension rod from the vehicle.
6. To install, reverse the removal procedures.

STABILIZER BAR

Removal and Installation

1. Raise and safely support the vehicle.
2. Remove the stabilizer bar-to-tension rod nuts, bolts and insulators.
3. Remove the stabilizer bar.
4. To install, reverse the removal procedures. Align the front side of the insulator edge with the paint mark on the upper rear edge of the tension bar.

KNUCKLE AND HUB ASSEMBLY

Removal and Installation

1. Raise and safely support the vehicle. Remove the wheel assembly.
2. Remove the grease cap, cotter pin, hub nut and thrust washer. Remove the caliper and position it aside. Remove the rotor.
3. Remove the tie rod nut. Using a ball joint removal tool, separate the tie rod from the steering knuckle.
4. Remove the ball joint-to-control arm tension rod retaining nuts and bolts. Remove the strut-to-steering knuckle retaining bolts.
5. Remove the steering knuckle. When removing the axle shaft from the steering knuckle, be careful not to drop it and support it with a wire.
6. To install, reverse the removal procedures. Bleed the brake system. Align the vehicle, as required.

TIE ROD END

Removal and Installation

1. Raise and safely support the vehicle. Remove the front wheel assembly.

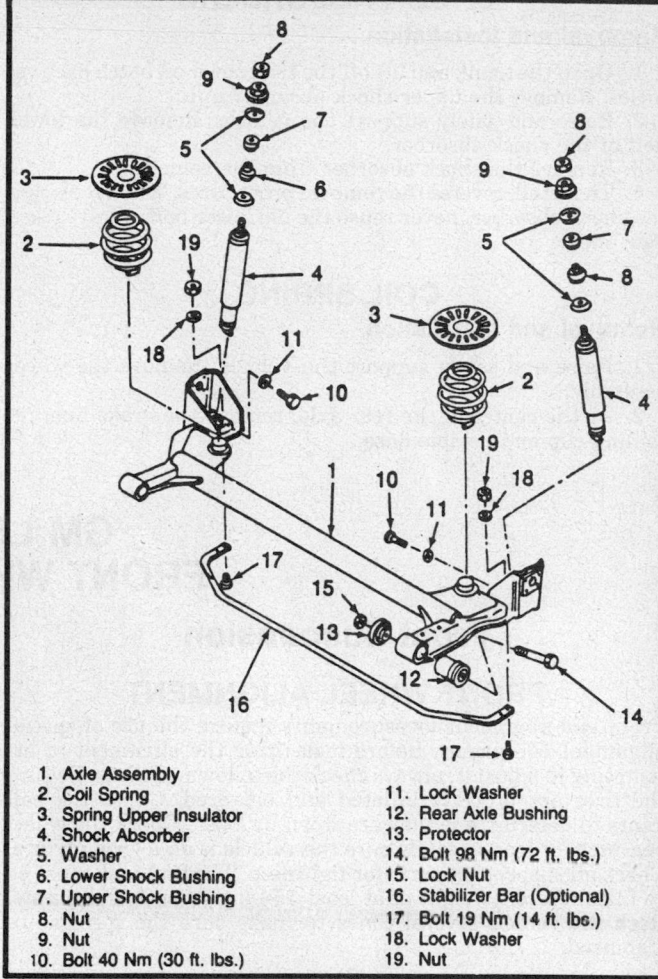

1. Axle Assembly
2. Coil Spring
3. Spring Upper Insulator
4. Shock Absorber
5. Washer
6. Lower Shock Bushing
7. Upper Shock Bushing
8. Nut
9. Nut
10. Bolt 40 Nm (30 ft. lbs.)
11. Lock Washer
12. Rear Axle Bushing
13. Protector
14. Bolt 98 Nm (72 ft. lbs.)
15. Lock Nut
16. Stabilizer Bar (Optional)
17. Bolt 19 Nm (14 ft. lbs.)
18. Lock Washer
19. Nut

Spectrum rear suspension assembly

2. Remove the castle nut from the ball joint. Using a ball joint removal tool, separate the tie rod from the steering knuckle.
3. Disconnect the retaining wire from the inner boot and pull back the boot.
4. Using a chisel, straighten the staked part of the locking washer between the tie rod and the rack.
5. Remove the tie rod from the rack.
6. To install, reverse the removal procedures.

Rear Suspension

REAR WHEEL BEARING

Removal and Installation

1. Raise and safely support the vehicle. Remove the wheel assembly.
2. Remove the hub cap, cotter pin, hub nut, washer and outer bearing. Remove the hub.
3. Using a slide hammer puller and attachment, pull the oil seal from the hub. Remove the inner bearing.
4. Using a brass drift and a hammer, drive both bearing races from the hub.
5. To install, reverse the removal procedures. Pack the bearings with grease and coat the oil seal lips with grease prior to installation.
6. If the cotter pin holes are from alignment upon reassembly, use a wrench to tighten the nut until the hole in the shaft and a slot of the nut align.

SHOCK ABSORBERS

Removal and Installation

1. Open the trunk and lift off the trim cover on hatch back vehicles. Remove the upper shock absorber nut.
2. Raise and safely support the vehicle. Remove the lower bolt of the shock absorber.
3. Remove the shock absorber from the vehicle.
4. To install, reverse the removal procedures. When replacing the shock absorber, never reuse the old lower bolt, always use a new one.

COIL SPRING

Removal and Installation

1. Raise and safely support the vehicle. Remove the wheel assembly.
2. At the center of the rear axle, remove the brake line, retaining clip and flexible hose.

3. Remove the parking brake tension spring at the rear axle. Disconnect the parking brake cable from the turn buckle and at the cable joint.
4. Properly support the axle. Remove the lower shock absorber bolt and disconnect it from the axle.
5. Lower the axle support and remove the coil spring.
6. To install, reverse the removal procedures. Raise the axle assembly to a distance of 15.2 in. from the top of the wheel well to the center of the axle hub, then torque the fasteners. Always replace the lower shock absorber bolt with a new one.

STABILIZER BAR

Removal and Installation

1. Raise and safely support the vehicle. Remove the bolts retaining the stabilizer bar to the lower ends of the axle assembly.
2. Remove the stabilizer bar from the vehicle.
3. To install, reverse the removal procedures.

GM LEMANS
FRONT WHEEL DRIVE

Front Suspension

FRONT WHEEL ALIGNMENT

Front end alignment measurements require the use of special alignment equipment. Before measuring the alignment or attempting to adjust it, always check the following points. Be sure the tires are properly inflated and balanced. Check the ball joints to determine it they are worn or loose. Check the wheel bearings for looseness. Be sure the vehicle is on a level surface. Check all suspension parts for tightness. The fuel tank must be ½ filled. Place a weight of at least 154 lbs. in both front seats. Rock the vehicle several times to make sure the springs are stabilized.

Adjustment

CASTER

Caster is the tilt of the front steering axis either forward or backward away from the front of the vehicle. When the strut is tilted rearward, the center is (+) positive. The amount of tilt is measured in degrees from vertical.

CAMBER

Camber is the slope of the front wheels from vertical when viewed from the front of the vehicle. When the wheels tilt outward (at the top), the camber is (+) positive; when the wheels tilt inward (at the top), the camber is (−) negative. The amount of tilt is measured in degrees from vertical and is called the camber angle.

TOE

Toe is the amount measured in the fraction of an inch, that the front wheels are closer together at one end than the other. Toe-in means the front wheels are closer together at the front of the tire than at the rear. The toe is (+) positive. Toe-out means the rear of the tires are closer together than the front; the toe is (−) negative.

Before performing the toe adjustment, be certain the following items are correct. The wheels must be straight ahead, the fuel tank must be full, all fluids must be at their proper level, all suspension and steering adjustments must be correct and the tires must be at their correct cold specification.

TRIM HEIGHT

1. Position the vehicle on a level surface.

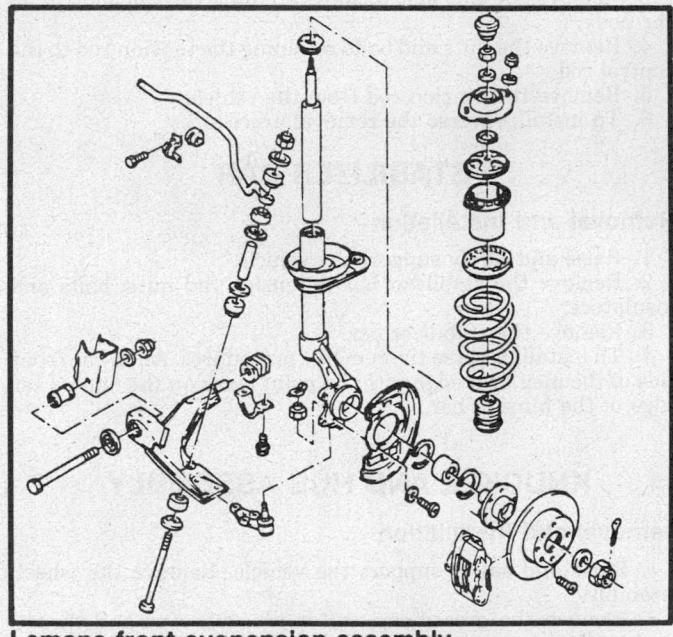

Lemans front suspension assembly

2. Using a ruler, inspect the vehicle height from the bottom of rocker panel to ground, it should be 7.7 in.

STRUT ASSEMBLY

Removal and Installation

1. Loosen the upper strut-to-body nuts and the wheel lug nuts. Remove the halfshaft-to-hub cotter pin, nut and washer.
2. Raise and safely support the vehicle; allow the wheels to hang free. Remove the wheel assembly. Using drive axle boot seal protector tools, place them on the outer CV-joints.
3. Remove the caliper-to-steering knuckle bolts. Remove the caliper and position it aside. Remove the rotor-to-wheel hub screw and the rotor.
4. Remove the outer tie rod-to-steering knuckle nut. Using tie rod remover tool, separate the outer tie rod-to-steering knuckle arm.

5. Remove the lower ball joint-to-steering knuckle retaining clip and nut. To remove the clip, lift up on the rear of the clip, while pulling outward on the loops.

6. Using ball joint separator tool, separate the lower ball joint from the steering knuckle arm.

7. Using front wheel hub remover tool, separate the halfshaft from the steering knuckle hub. Properly support the halfshaft.

8. Remove the upper strut-to-body nuts and washers. Remove the strut assembly from the vehicle.

9. To install, reverse the removal procedures. When tightening the halfshaft nut, be sure to have the vehicle resting on its wheels. If the castellated nut does not align with a shaft hole, back off the nut until it does.

BALL JOINT

Inspection

1. Raise and safely support the vehicle.
2. With the ball joint installed to the steering knuckle, Grasp the top and bottom of the wheel, then, move the wheel using an in and out shaking motion.
3. Observe any movement between the steering knuckle and the control arm. If movement exists, replace the ball joint.

Removal and Installation

1. Raise and safely support the vehicle. Lower the vehicle slightly so the weight does not rest on the control arm. Remove the wheel assembly.
2. If a silicone (gray) boot is used on the inboard axle joint, install a boot seal protector tool. If a thermoplastic (black) boot is used, no protector is necessary.
3. Remove the retaining clip from the ball joint castle nut.
4. Remove the castle nut. Using ball joint separator tool, disconnect the ball joint from the steering knuckle arm.
5. Using a drill, drill out the ball joint-to-control arm rivets. Be careful not to damage the halfshaft boot when drilling out the ball joint rivets.
6. Loosen the stabilizer shaft bushing assembly nut. Remove the ball joint from the control arm.
7. To install, reverse the removal procedures.

LOWER CONTROL ARM

Removal and Installation

1. Raise and safely support the vehicle. Lower the vehicle slightly so the weight does not rest on the control arm. Remove the wheel assembly.
2. Disconnect the stabilizer shaft from the control arm and the support assembly.
3. Remove the ball joint-to-steering knuckle cotter pin and nut. Using ball joint separator tool, separate the ball joint from the steering knuckle.
4. Remove the control arm-to-support arm bolts. Remove the control arm from the vehicle.
5. To install, reverse the removal procedures. Lower the vehicle to the floor. With the vehicle supported at curb height, torque the front control arm to support arm bolts to 140 ft. lbs. and the rear control arm-to-support arm bolts to 90 ft. lbs.

HUB AND BEARING ASSEMBLY

Removal and Installation

1. Remove the hub and steering knuckle assembly from the vehicle and position it in a holding fixture.
2. Using a halfshaft separator tool and a front wheel hub remover tool, press the hub from the steering knuckle.
3. Using a halfshaft separator tool, a front wheel hub remov-

er tool and a inner bearing race remover tool, remove the inner bearing race from the hub.

4. From inside the steering knuckle, remove the internal snaprings.

5. Using a halfshaft separator tool and a bearing remover tool, press the bearing from the steering knuckle. Whenever the wheel bearing is removed from the steering knuckle, it must be discarded and replaced with a new one.

To install:

6. Using solvent, clean all of the parts and blow dry with compressed air. Before assembling the parts, be sure to coat them with a layer of wheel bearing grease.

7. Using snapring pliers, install the outer internal snapring into the steering knuckle.

8. Using a halfshaft separator tool and a bearing installer tool, press the new wheel bearing into the steering knuckle until it butts against the snapring.

9. Using the snapring pliers, install the inner internal snapring into the steering knuckle.

10. Install the strut onto the body. Remove the seal protector from the halfshaft. Install the halfshaft into the steering knuckle assembly, then, the washer and a new halfshaft nut onto the halfshaft.

11. To complete the installation, reverse the removal procedures.

12. Torque the:
    a. Steering knuckle assembly-to-body nuts to 22 ft. lbs.
    b. Lower ball joint-to-steering knuckle nut 50 ft. lbs.
    c. Tie rod-to-steering knuckle nut to 45 ft. lbs.
    d. Rotor-to-hub screw to 3 ft. lbs.
    e. Caliper-to-steering knuckle bolts to 70 ft. lbs.
    f. Wheel lug nuts to 65 ft. lbs.

13. Tighten the halfshaft-to-hub nut to 74 ft. lbs., back off the nut, retighten to 15 ft. lbs., then, tighten another 90 degrees. When tightening the halfshaft nut, be sure to have the vehicle resting on its wheels. If the castellated nut does not align with a shaft hole, back off the nut until it does.

14. Check and adjust the front end alignment as required.

HUB AND STEERING KNUCKLE ASSEMBLY

Removal and Installation

1. Loosen the upper strut-to-body nuts and the wheel lug nuts. Remove the halfshaft-to-hub cotter pin, nut and washer.

2. Raise and safely support the vehicle; allow the wheels to hang free. Remove the wheel assembly. Using drive axle boot seal protector tools, place them on the outer CV-joints.

3. Remove the caliper-to-steering knuckle bolts. Remove the caliper and position it aside. Remove the rotor-to-wheel hub screw and the rotor.

4. Remove the outer tie rod-to-steering knuckle nut. Using a tie rod remover tool, separate the outer tie rod-to-steering knuckle arm.

5. Remove the lower ball joint-to-steering knuckle retaining clip and nut. To remove the clip, lift up on the rear of the clip, while pulling outward on the loops.

6. Using a ball joint separator tool, separate the lower ball joint from the steering knuckle arm.

7. Using a front wheel hub remover tool, separate the halfshaft from the steering knuckle hub. Properly support the halfshaft.

8. Remove the upper strut-to-body nuts and washers. Remove the strut assembly from the vehicle.

To install:

9. Reverse of the removal procedures.

10. Torque the:
    a. Steering knuckle assembly-to-body nuts to 22 ft. lbs.
    b. Lower ball joint-to-steering knuckle nut 50 ft. lbs.
    c. Tie rod-to-steering knuckle nut to 45 ft. lbs.
    d. Rotor-to-hub screw to 3 ft. lbs.

e. Caliper-to-steering knuckle bolts to 70 ft. lbs.

f. Wheel lug nuts to 65 ft. lbs.

11. Tighten the halfshaft-to-hub nut to 74 ft. lbs., back off the nut, retighten to 15 ft. lbs., then, tighten another 90 degrees. When tightening the halfshaft nut, be sure to have the vehicle resting on its wheels. If the castellated nut does not align with a shaft hole, back off the nut until it does.

12. Check and adjust the front end alignment as required.

STABILIZER BAR

Removal and Installation

1. Loosen the left front wheel lug nuts. Raise and safely support the vehicle; allow the suspension to hang free. Remove the left wheel assembly.

2. Remove the stabilizer shaft link assemblies from the control arms.

3. Remove the stabilizer shaft bushings and brackets from the body.

4. Remove the stabilizer shaft and bushings.

5. To install, reverse the removal procedures.

Rear Suspension

REAR WHEEL ALIGNMENT

Adjustment

TRIM HEIGHT

1. Position the vehicle on a level surface.

2. Using a ruler, inspect the vehicle height from the bottom of rocker panel to ground; it should be 7½ in.

REAR WHEEL BEARINGS

Adjustment

1. Raise and safely support the vehicle. Remove the grease cap from the wheel hub. Remove the cotter pin from the spindle and the spindle nut.

2. While turning the wheel, by hand, in the forward direction, tighten the spindle nut to 12 ft. lbs. The tightening procedure will remove any grease or burrs which could cause excessive wheel bearing play.

3. Back-off the nut to the just loose position. Hand tighten the spindle nut and loosen it until one of the spindle holes aligns with a slot in the nut. Install a new cotter pin and bend the ends around the nut.

4. Using a feeler gauge, measure the endplay. If it is within 0.001–0.005 in., it is properly adjusted.

Removal and Installation

1. Raise and safely support the vehicle.

2. Remove the wheel assembly.

3. Remove the brake drum detent screw and the drum. To remove the drum, it may be necessary to loosen the parking brake cable and press the parking brake lever inwards using a pry bar. Do not hammer on the drum as damage to the bearing may result.

4. Remove the hub and bearing assembly-to-axle spindle grease cap, cotter pin, hub nut, thrust washer and the outer bearing from the axle spindle.

5. Using a small pry bar, remove the grease seal from the inside of the hub. Remove the inner, outer bearing from the hub.

To install:

6. If replacing the wheel bearings, Use a hammer and a drift punch and drive both outer bearing races, in opposite directions from the wheel hub.

7. Using a cleaning solvent, not gasoline, clean the bearings, races and hub. Using compressed air, blow dry the parts. Inspect the parts for damage and wear. If necessary, replace any defective parts.

8. Using an arbor press, a rear hub inner and outer bearing race installer tool and a driver handle tool, press the outer bearing, outer race into the wheel hub until it seats. Before installing the new wheel bearings, be sure to force wheel bearing grease into the bearing.

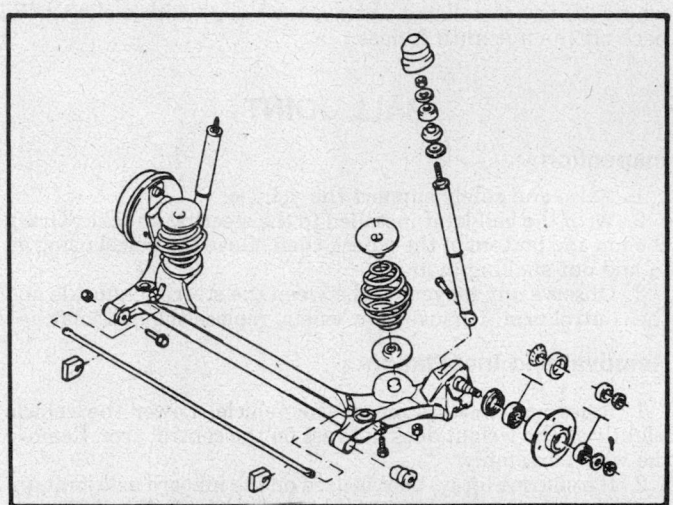

Lemans rear suspension assembly

9. Using an arbor press, a rear hub inner and outer bearing race installer tool and a driver handle tool, press the inner bearing, outer race into the wheel hub until it seats, then, install the inner bearing.

10. Lubricate the lips of the new grease seal. Using the rear hub seal installation tool, press the new seal into the hub.

11. Install the wheel bearing hub onto the axle spindle, followed by the outer, inner bearing, thrust washer and hub nut.

12. Adjust the wheel bearing play. Adjust the parking brake. Continue the installation in the reverse order of the removal procedure.

SHOCK ABSORBER

Removal and Installation

1. Open the trunk. If equipped, remove the trim cover. Remove the upper shock absorber-to-body nut.

2. Raise and safely support the vehicle and the rear axle assembly before unbolting the shock absorbers.

3. Remove the shock absorber-to-rear axle assembly bolt. Remove the shock absorber from the vehicle.

4. To install, reverse the removal procedures.

COIL SPRING

Removal and Installation

1. Raise and safely support the vehicle and the rear axle assembly. Remove the wheel assembly.

3. Remove the right and left brake line bracket attaching screws from the body and allow the brake line to hang free. Remove both lower shock absorber-to-rear axle assembly bolts.

4. Carefully lower the rear axle and remove the springs and insulators. Do not suspend the rear axle by the brake hoses or

damage to the hoses could result. Lower the axle just enough to remove the springs and support it during all service procedures.

5. To install, reverse the removal procedures. Position the springs and insulators in their seats and raise the axle assembly. The ends of the upper coil on the spring must be positioned in the seat of the body and within the limits.

6. Prior to installing the spring, it will be necessary to install the upper insulators to the body with adhesive to keep it in position while raising the axle assembly and springs.

STABILIZER BAR

Removal and Installation

1. Raise and safely support the vehicle. Remove the wheel assembly.

2. Remove the bolts at both sides of the axle assembly. Remove the insulator and stabilizer bar.

3. To install, reverse the removal procedures.

GM E, K, V AND Z-BODY
FRONT WHEEL DRIVE

Front Suspension

FRONT WHEEL ALIGNMENT

Adjustment

TORSION BAR HEIGHT

The standing height must be checked and adjusted if necessary, before performing the front end alignment procedure. The standing height is controlled by the adjustment setting of the torsion bar adjusting bolt.

Clockwise rotation of the bolt increases the front height, counterclockwise decreases the front height.

The vehicle must be on a level surface, gas tank full or a compensating weight added, front seat all the way to the rear and all tires inflated to the proper pressures. Doors, hood and trunk must be closed and no passengers or additional weight should be in vehicle or trunk.

These tolerances are production specifications on bumper height. If there is more than 1 inch difference, side-to-side, at the wheel well opening, corrective measures may need to be implemented on a case by case basis. These are curb height dimensions which include a full tank of fuel.

CAMBER AND CASTER

1. Loosen nuts on upper suspension arm front and rear cam bolts.

2. Note camber reading and rotate front bolt to correct for ½ of incorrect reading or as near as possible.

3. Rotate rear cam bolt to bring camber reading to 0 degree. Do not use a socket to adjust rear cam bolt on left side as brake pipes could be damaged. An offset box end wrench is recommended at this adjustment point.

4. Tighten front and rear bolts and check caster. If caster requires adjustment, proceed with Step 5; if not, move to Step 8.

5. Loosen front and rear cam bolt nuts.

6. Using camber scale on alignment equipment, rotate front bolt so the camber changes an amount equal to ¼ of the desired caster change. A caster-to-camber change ratio of about 2:1 is inherent to the Eldorado and Seville suspension system; when one cam is rotated sufficiently to change camber 1 degree, the caster reading will change about 2 degrees.

7. If adjusting to correct for excessive negative caster, rotate front bolt to increase positive camber. If adjusting to correct for excessive positive caster, rotate front bolt to increase negative camber. Rotate the rear bolt until camber setting returns to its corrected position according to Step 3.

8. Tighten upper suspension arm cam nuts to 95 ft. lbs. Hold head of bolt securely; any movement of the cam will affect final setting and will require a recheck of the camber and caster adjustments.

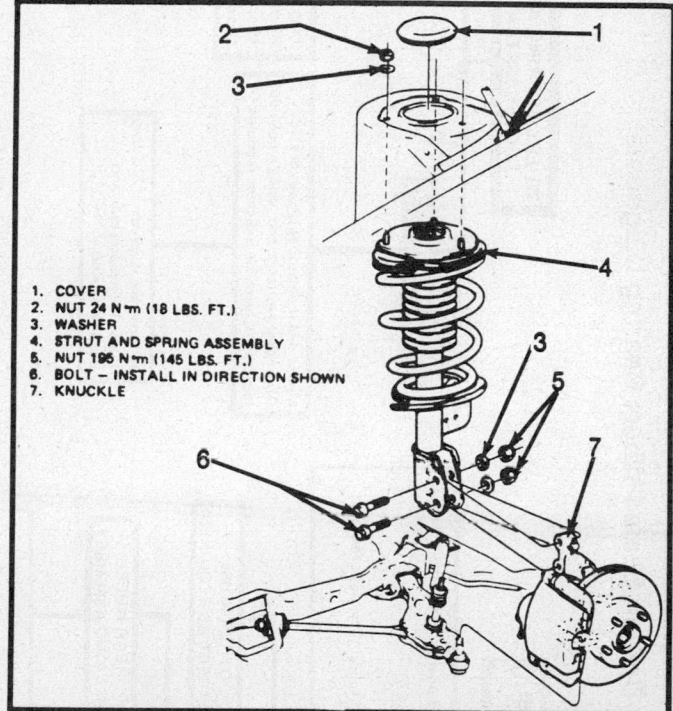

1. COVER
2. NUT 24 N·m (18 LBS. FT.)
3. WASHER
4. STRUT AND SPRING ASSEMBLY
5. NUT 195 N·m (145 LBS. FT.)
6. BOLT — INSTALL IN DIRECTION SHOWN
7. KNUCKLE

Exploded view of the front strut assembly—GM E-body and K-body

TOE

Before checking toe, make certain the intermediate rod height is correct.

Toe is adjusted by turning the tie rod adjuster tubes at the outer ends of each tie rod after loosening clamp bolts or locknuts. The readings should be taken only when the front wheels are in a straight ahead position so the steering gear is on its high spot.

1. Center steering wheel, raise and safely support the vehicle and check wheel runout.

2. Loosen tie rod adjuster nuts and adjust tie rods to obtain proper toe setting.

3. Position tie rod adjuster clamps so openings of clamps are facing up. Interference with front suspension components could occur while turning if clamps are facing down.

4. Torque the inner tie rod locknuts to 46 ft. lbs.

FRONT WHEEL BEARINGS

These vehicles have front and rear sealed wheel bearings. The bearings are preadjusted and require no lubrication mainte-

Bolt on Sealed Wheel Bearing Diagnosis

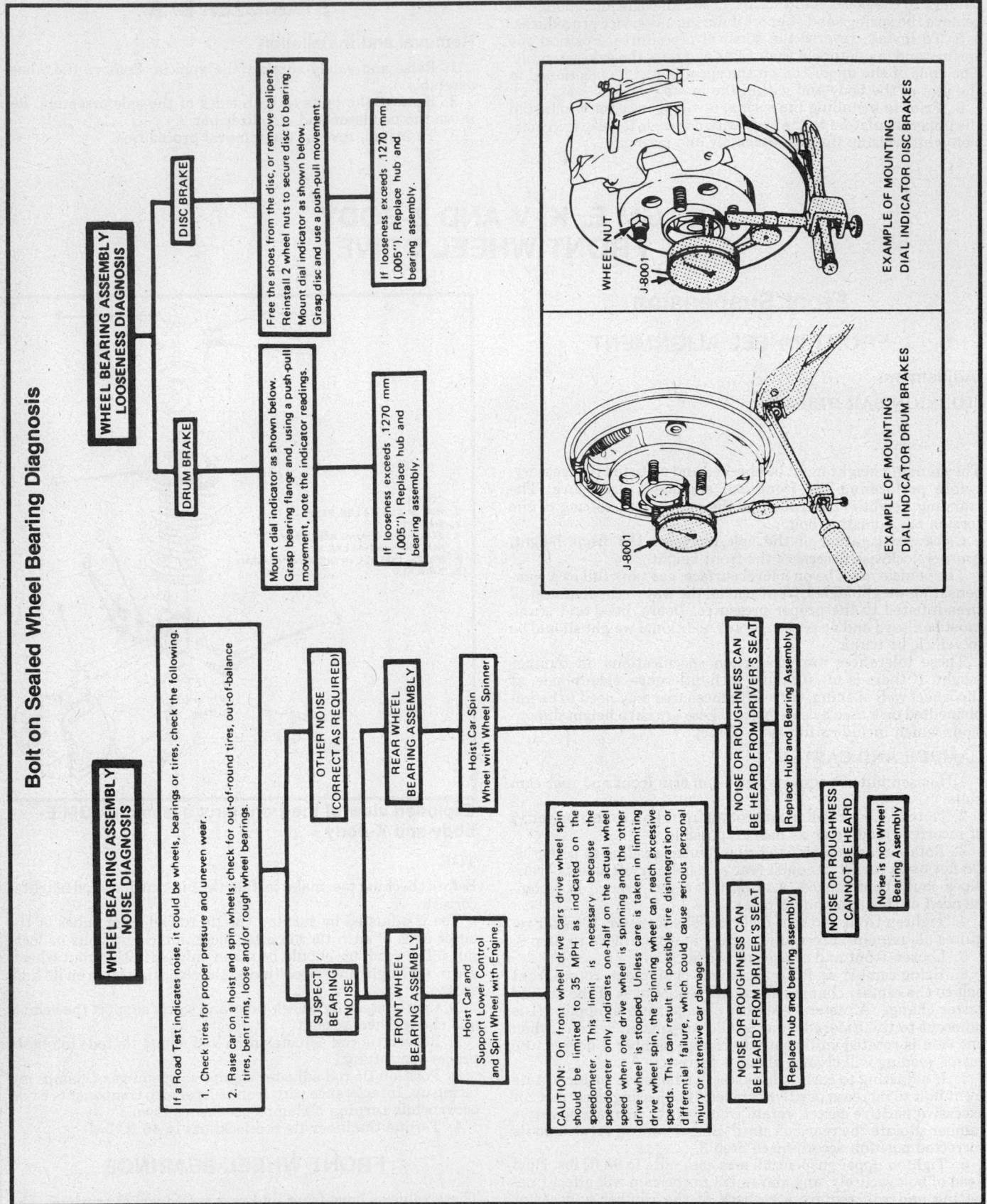

WHEEL BEARING ASSEMBLY LOOSENESS DIAGNOSIS

- **DISC BRAKE**
  - Free the shoes from the disc, or remove calipers. Reinstall 2 wheel nuts to secure disc to bearing. Mount dial indicator as shown below. Grasp disc and use a push-pull movement.
    - If looseness exceeds .1270 mm (.005"). Replace hub and bearing assembly.
- **DRUM BRAKE**
  - Mount dial indicator as shown below. Grasp bearing flange and, using a push-pull movement, note the indicator readings.
    - If looseness exceeds .1270 mm (.005"). Replace hub and bearing assembly.

EXAMPLE OF MOUNTING DIAL INDICATOR DISC BRAKES

WHEEL NUT
J-8001

EXAMPLE OF MOUNTING DIAL INDICATOR DRUM BRAKES

J-8001

WHEEL BEARING ASSEMBLY NOISE DIAGNOSIS

If a Road Test indicates noise, it could be wheels, bearings or tires, check the following.

1. Check tires for proper pressure and uneven wear.
2. Raise car on a hoist and spin wheels; check for out-of-round tires, out-of-balance tires, bent rims, loose and/or rough wheel bearings.

- **OTHER NOISE (CORRECT AS REQUIRED)**
- **SUSPECT BEARING NOISE**
  - **REAR WHEEL BEARING ASSEMBLY**
    - Hoist Car Spin Wheel with Wheel Spinner.
      - NOISE OR ROUGHNESS CAN BE HEARD FROM DRIVER'S SEAT
        - Replace Hub and Bearing Assembly
      - NOISE OR ROUGHNESS CANNOT BE HEARD
        - Noise is not Wheel Bearing Assembly
  - **FRONT WHEEL BEARING ASSEMBLY**
    - Hoist Car and Support Lower Control and Spin Wheel with Engine.
      - CAUTION: On front wheel drive cars drive wheel spin should be limited to 35 MPH as indicated on the speedometer. This limit is necessary because the speedometer only indicates one-half on the actual wheel speed when one drive wheel is spinning and the other drive wheel is stopped. Unless care is taken in limiting drive wheel spin, the spinning wheel can reach excessive speeds. This can result in possible tire disintegration or differential failure, which could cause serious personal injury or extensive car damage.
        - NOISE OR ROUGHNESS CAN BE HEARD FROM DRIVER'S SEAT
          - Replace hub and bearing assembly

Bolt on sealed wheel bearing diagnosis

nance or adjustment. There are darkened areas on the bearing assembly. These darkened areas are from a heat treatment process and do not require bearing replacement.

MACPHERSON STRUT

Removal and Installation

1. Open the hood. Remove the nuts attaching the top of the strut to the body.
2. On Reatta, Riviera and Toronado, raise and safely support the vehicle. On the Allante, Eldorado and Seville, hoist the vehicle with a twin hoist and install jackstands under the cradle. Then, lower the vehicle so it rests on the jackstands and not on the control arms.

NOTE: Support all vehicles at the rear so as components are removed, the weight will not shift, causing the vehicle to fall off the supports.

3. Remove the wheel assembly.
4. Using a sharp tool, scribe the knuckle along the lower/outboard radius of the strut. Then, scribe the strut flange on the inboard side, right along the curve of the knuckle. Finally, make a scribe mark across the strut/knuckle interface. These scribe marks will be used on reassembly to properly match the components.
5. Remove the brake line mounting bracket from the strut.

NOTE: When working near the drive axles, make sure the inner Tri-pot joints are not allowed to become overextended, as this could cause undetectible damage. Also, make sure not to scratch the spring coating, as this could result in premature failure of the spring.

6. Remove the strut-to-knuckle nuts and bolts and then carefully support the knuckle from the body with wire.
7. Remove the strut.
8. To install, reverse the removal procedures. Torque the strut-to-body nuts to 18 ft. lbs. Torque the strut-to-knuckle bolts/nuts to 145 ft. lbs. (all 1986–87 vehicles and 1987–90 Allante) or 136 ft. lbs. (all 1988–90 vehicles except Allante).

TORSION BAR

Removal and Installation

1. Raise and safely support the vehicle.
2. Install a torsion bar remover tool, remove the torsion bar adjusting bolt and nut, noting the number of turns to remove and relax the torsion bar. Do the same on the other torsion bar.
3. Remove the bolts and retainer from the torsion bar crossmember. Move the crossmember back until the bars are free and the adjusting arms can be removed. Slide the torsion bars forward, as required.
4. To install, reverse the removal procedures.

BALL JOINTS

Inspection

1. Raise the vehicle and position jackstands under the left and right lower control arm, as near as possible to each lower ball joint. The vehicle must be stable and should not rock on jack stands. The upper control arm bumper must not contact the frame. The wheel bearing must be correctly adjusted.
2. Position the dial indicator to register vertical movement at the base of the tire rim for upper ball joint and at center of hub for lower ball joint.
3. Grasp the tire at the 12 o'clock and 6 o'clock positions and rock it in and out for upper ball joint. Pry with a pry bar between the lower control arm and the outer race of the CV-joint for lower ball joint. The vertical reading must not exceed 0.125 inch in either case.

Removal and Installation

1. Raise the vehicle and support it under the cradle in a secure manner, so the control arms will hang free.
2. Remove the wheel assembly.
3. Remove the stabilizer bar insulators, retainers, spacer and bolt.
4. Using a ¼ in. drill bit for the 1st pass and a ½ in. bit for the 2nd, drill out the rivets retaining the joint. Remove the cotter pin, the nut and the ball joint.

To install:
5. Replacing the ball joint mounting rivets with bolts and torquing them to 50 ft. lbs.
6. Insert the ball joint stud into the steering knuckle and install the nut. Torque the nut to 88 inch lbs. (7 ft. lbs. on Cadillac); then turn it an additional 120 degrees (180 degrees on Cadillac vehicles and 1987–90 Allante) while watching the required torque. It must reach at least 37 ft. lbs. torque (48 ft. lbs. on all Cadillac vehicles) in the 120 degrees. The nut may be turned as much as ⅙ turn more to install the cotter pin. Install the cotter pin.
7. To complete the installation, reverse the remaining procedures.

UPPER CONTROL ARM

Removal and Installation

1. Hoist the vehicle under the lower control arm. Remove the wheel assembly.
2. Remove the upper shock attaching bolt. It is not necessary, but it does allow more working room.
3. Remove cotter pin and nut on upper ball joint.
4. Disconnect brake hose clamp from ball joint stud.
5. Separate upper ball joint stud from steering knuckle using a hammer and drift pin.

To install:
6. Guide upper control arm over shock absorber and install bushing ends into frame horns.
7. Install cam assemblies.
8. Install ball joint stud into knuckle.
9. Install brake hose clip onto ball joint stud.
10. Install ball joint nut. Torque to 55 ft. lbs. (Riviera and Toronado) and 61 ft. lbs. (Eldorado and Seville) and insert cotter pin and crimp. Cotter pin must be crimped toward upper shock attaching bolt and nut.
11. Install upper shock bolt, if removed and tighten to 95 ft. lbs.
12. Install the wheel assembly and lower the vehicle.
13. Check camber, caster and toe-in; adjust, if necessary.

LOWER CONTROL ARM

Removal and Installation

NOTE: Throughout this procedure, take care not to over extend the Tri-pot joints. Over extension could result in separation of internal components, resulting in eventual failure of the joint. The damage done would not be readily detectible.

1. Raise the vehicle and support it by the cradle on jackstands. Remove the wheel.
2. Disconnect the stabilizer shaft insulator, retainers, spacer and bolt from the control arm.
3. Disconnect the lower ball joint from the knuckle.
4. Remove the control arm bushing bolt and front nut, retainer and insulator. Then, remove the control arm from the frame.

To install:

5. Install the control arm back onto the frame with the bushing bolt and front nut, retainer and insulator.

6. Install the control arm bushing bolt and front nut, the retainer and the insulator, but do not tighten them.

7. Connect the lower ball joint to the knuckle.

8. Connect the stabilizer shaft insulator, retainers, spacer and bolt. Tighten the shaft nut/bolt to 13 ft. lbs.

9. Insert the ball joint stud into the steering knuckle and install the nut. Torque the nut to 84 inch lbs.; then, turn it an additional 120 degrees (except 1986–87 Cadillac and Allante) or 180 degrees (1986–87 Cadillac and Allante) while watching the required torque. The torque must reach at least 37 ft. lbs. (except 1986–87 Cadillac and Allante) or 48 ft. lbs. (1986-87 Cadillac and Allante) in the 120 degrees. Install the cotter pin.

10. Install the wheel and then lower the vehicle to the ground, leaving it unsupported by any jacking equipment. Torque the wheel nuts to 100 ft. lbs., then, the control arm bushing bolt to 100 ft. lbs. or nut to 91 ft. lbs. Torque the retaining nut to 52 ft. lbs.

Rear Suspension

REAR WHEEL ALIGNMENT

Rear wheel alignment should be checked and adjusted as necessary. Before alignment, check the following front and rear trim heights and electronic level control for proper operation.

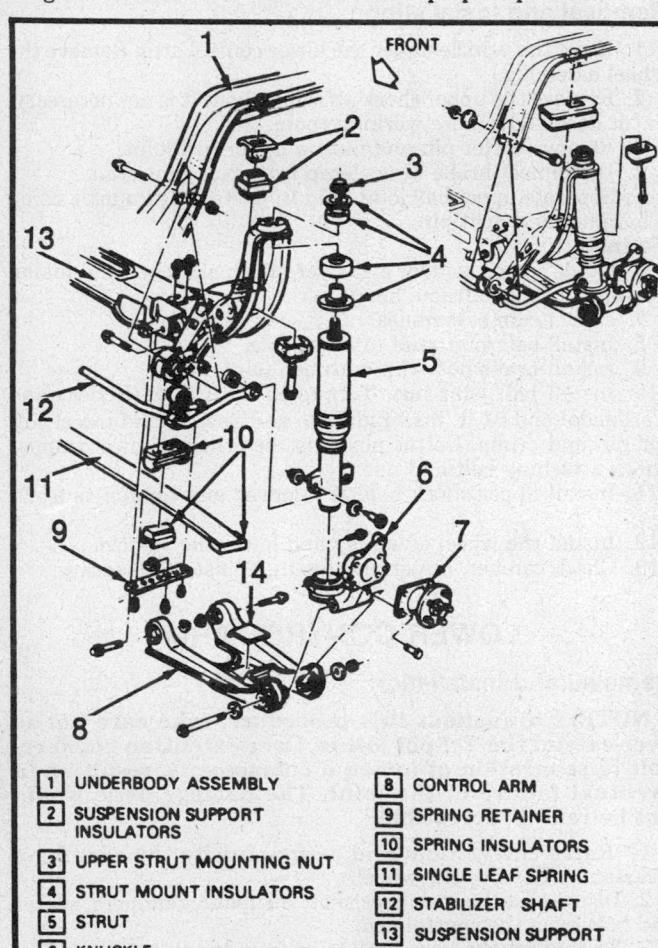

FRONT

1	UNDERBODY ASSEMBLY
2	SUSPENSION SUPPORT INSULATORS
3	UPPER STRUT MOUNTING NUT
4	STRUT MOUNT INSULATORS
5	STRUT
6	KNUCKLE
7	HUB AND BEARING ASSEMBLY
8	CONTROL ARM
9	SPRING RETAINER
10	SPRING INSULATORS
11	SINGLE LEAF SPRING
12	STABILIZER SHAFT
13	SUSPENSION SUPPORT
14	TRIM HEIGHT ADJUSTMENT SPACER (OPTIONAL)

1986–89 E and K body rear suspension components

With the vehicle backed onto alignment machine, toe-in and toe-out are reversed. Toe-in will be read as toe-out. It is very important the readings be made and understood properly.

Toe adjustments are made at the inner pivot bushings. Loosening the nut and bolt at the inner bushing will enable the toe to be moved in or out as necessary. Tighten bushing mounting nut to 97 ft. lbs. and recheck toe for correct setting. It may be necessary to use a pry bar to move the control arm. Moving the control arm rearward increases toe-in; moving it forward increases toe-out. Check camber.

MACPHERSON STRUT

Removal and Installation

1. Raise and safely support the vehicle. Remove the wheel assembly.

2. If removing the left strut assembly disconnect the height sensor link.

3. Reinstall 2 wheel lug nuts to hold the rotor and hub assembly in place.

NOTE: If equipped with Electronic Load Control (ELC), disconnect the air lines before removing shocks. Purge the new shocks of air before installing (on all models) by repeatedly extending and compressing them. On ALC equipped models, the shocks should be fully extended before installing air lines.

4. If equipped with a stabilizer bar, remove the shaft mounting bolt at the strut.

5. Remove the caliper and position it aside. Loosen but do not remove the knuckle pivot bolt on the outboard end of the assembly.

6. Remove the upper strut rod cap, mounting nut, retainer and insulator. Compress the strut and remove the lower insulator.

7. Remove the strut and knuckle assembly. Remove the knuckle pinch bolt. Remove the strut from the knuckle.

8. To install, reverse the removal procedures.

SPRINGS AND REAR CONTROL ARM

Removal and Installation

1. Raise and safely support the vehicle. Remove the wheel assembly.

2. Remove the front stabilizer bar-to-control arm bolt.

3. Remove the inner bolt and loosen the outer bolt from each side of the stabilized link.

4. Position the bottom parts of the link aside and remove the stabilizer bar.

5. Disconnect the brake line bracket from the control arm.

6. Remove about ⅔ of the fluid from the front master cylinder.

7. Loosen the parking brake tension at the cable equalizer.

8. Remove the cable from the parking brake and remove the cable bracket from the caliper or brake drum backing plate.

9. If equipped with rear disc brakes, remove the return spring, lock nut, lever and the anti-friction washer. The lever must be held while removing the nut.

10. Install and tighten a 7 in. C-clamp on the caliper at the bottom the cylinder pistons.

11. Disconnect the brake line from the brake and plug the openings to prevent the entrance of dirt.

12. If equipped with disc brakes, use a ⅜ in. Allen wrench, remove the caliper mounting bolts and remove the caliper, pads and rotor. If equipped with drum brakes, remove the hub and bearing assembly and remove the brake backing plate, along with the brake shoes.

13. If working on the left side, snap the Electronic Level Control link off the control arm.

14. Support the bottom of the control arm with a floor jack.

15. Remove the ELC line at the shock.

16. Remove the shock absorber.

17. Lower the control arm to relieve tension on the spring. Remove the spring and the insulators.

18. Remove the control arm mounting bolts and remove the control arm.

19. To install, reverse the removal procedures.

Transverse Spring

Removal and Installation

1. Raise the vehicle and support it securely by the frame. Remove the wheel.

2. If working on the left side and the vehicle is equipped with electronic level control, disconnect the ELC height sensor link.

3. If the vehicle has a stabilizer bar, disconnect the mounting bolt at the strut.

4. Reinstall 2 wheel nuts opposite each other to hold the rotor onto the hub/bearing assembly.

5. Remove and suspend the brake caliper.

6. Loosen but do not remove the knuckle pivot bolt on the outboard end of the control arm.

7. Remove the strut rod cap, mounting nut, retainer and upper insulator. Then, compress the strut by hand and remove the lower insulator.

8. Remove the inner control arm nuts. Support the knuckle and control arm with a floorjack and then remove the inner control arm bolts. Remove the control arm, knuckle, strut, hub/bearing and rotor as an assembly.

9. Suspend the outer end of the spring securely. Make sure the jackstand is square under the spring so the stand will not shift.

10. Lower the vehicle until all weight on the spring retainer is

removed. Remove the retainer mounting bolts, the retainer and the lower insulator from that side of the vehicle. Raise the vehicle slowly until the jackstand is free of downward pressure from the spring and remove it.

11. Draw the spring from the rear suspension. Remove the upper spring insulators as necessary.

To install:

12. Install any insulators that require replacement. Upper/outboard insulators must be installed so the molded arrow points toward the vehicle centerline. Torque the center and outboard insulator nuts to 21 ft. lbs.

13. Position the spring into the crossmember. Make sure the outboard and center insulator locating bands are centered on the insulators.

14. Support the outer end of the spring with a jackstand and lower the vehicle until its weight will permit easy installation of the spring retainer.

15. Install the lower insulator and spring retainer and torque the bolts to 21 ft. lbs. Raise the vehicle carefully and when the spring is clear, remove the jackstand.

16. Position the assembled control arm, knuckle, strut, hub and bearing and rotor assembly into the crossmember assembly and install the inner control arm bolts and nuts hand tight.

17. Install the lower strut insulator and position the strut rod into the suspension support assembly.

18. Install the upper strut insulator, retainer and nut. Torque the upper strut nut to 65 ft. lbs., the knuckle pivot bolt to 59 ft. lbs. and the inner control arm bolts to 66 ft. lbs.

19. Install the strut rod cap. Install the stabilizer mounting bolt if the vehicle has a stabilizer bar. Torque this bolt to 43 ft. lbs.

20. Remove the wheel nuts retaining the brake rotor. Install the remaining parts in reverse of the removal procedure. Check and adjust rear alignment, if necessary.

GM J-BODY
FRONT WHEEL DRIVE

Front Suspension

FRONT WHEEEL ALIGNMENT

Adjustment
CAMBER

1. Position the vehicle on the alignment equipment. Follow the manufacturer's instructions to obtain the camber reading.

2. Use appropriate extensions to reach around both sides of the tire. Loosen both strut-to-knuckle bolts just enough to allow movement between the strut and the knuckle. Remove tools.

3. Grasp the top of the tire firmly and move the tire inboard or outboard until the correct camber reading is obtained.

4. Carefully reach around the tire with extensions and tight-

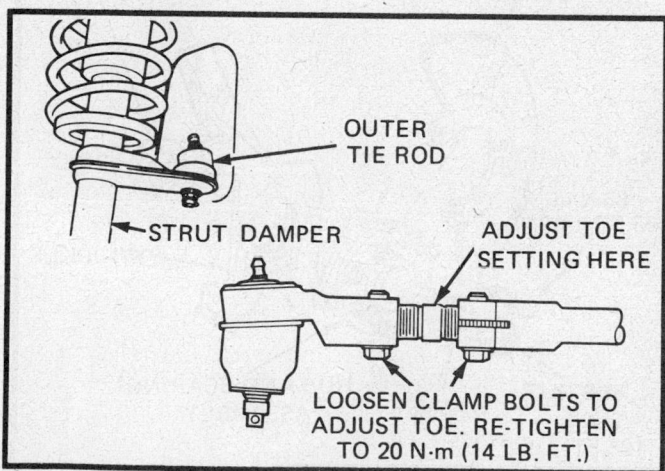

Toe adjustment

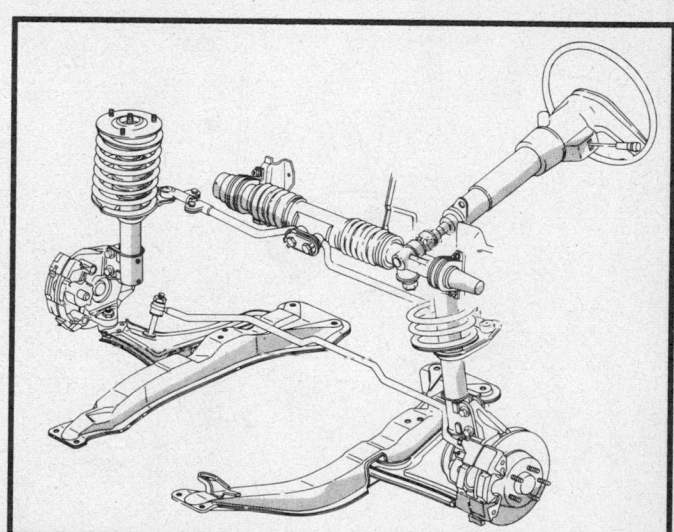

Front suspension

en both bolts enough to hold the correct camber while the wheel is removed to allow final torque.

5. With wheel removed, torque both bolts to specification. Re-install the wheel.

TOE

1. Raise and safely support the vehicle. Loosen clamp bolts at the outer tie rod.
2. Rotate adjuster to set toe to specifications.
3. Tighten clamp bolts.

STRUT ASSEMBLY

Removal and Installation

1. Raise hood and disconnect upper strut-to-body nuts.
2. Raise and safely support the vehicle; allow the front suspension to hang free.
3. Remove wheel assembly. Install drive axle boot protective cover.
4. Disconnect tie rod from strut. Remove both strut-to-knuckle bolts.
5. Remove the strut assembly from the vehicle.
6. To install, reverse the removal procedures.

BALL JOINTS

Inspection

The vehicle must be supported by the wheels so weight of the vehicle will properly load the ball joints.

The lower ball joint is inspected for wear by visual observation alone. Wear is indicated by the protrusion of the ½ in. diameter nipple into which the grease fitting is threaded. This round nipple projects 0.050 in. beyond the surface of the ball joint cover on a new, unworn joint. Normal wear will result in the surface of this nipple retreating very slowly inward.

Removal and Installation

1. Raise and safely support the vehicle. Remove the wheel assembly.
2. If no countersink is found on the lower side of the rivets, carefully locate the center of the rivet body and mark with a punch.
3. Use the proper sequence to drill out rivets.

4. Use tool J–29330 or equivalent, to separate joint from knuckle.
5. Disconnect stabilizer assembly from the control arm.
6. Remove ball joint.
7. To install, reverse the removal procedures. Check and adjust alignment as required.

LOWER CONTROL ARM

Removal and Installation

1. Raise and safely support the vehicle. Remove wheel assembly.
2. Disconnect stabilizer bar from the control arm assembly.
3. Separate the knuckle from ball joint.
4. Remove control arm assembly.
5. To install, reverse the removal procedures. Check and adjust alignment as required.

HUB AND BEARING ASSEMBLY

Removal and Installation

1. Loosen the hub nut. Raise and safely support the vehicle. Remove wheel assembly and install a boot cover tool.
2. Remove the hub nut. Remove the caliper and rotor.
3. Remove the hub and bearing mounting bolts. Remove the shield. If the bearing assembly is to be reused, mark the attaching bolt and corresponding hole for installation.
4. Install tool J–28733 or equivalent, and turn the bolt to press the hub and bearing assembly off of the driveshaft. If excessive corrosion is present, make sure the hub and bearing is loose in the knuckle before using the tool.
5. If installing a new bearing assembly, replace the steering knuckle seal, using tool J–22388.
6. To install, reverse the removal procedures. Check and adjust the alignment, as required.

STEERING KNUCKLE

Removal and Installation

1. Raise and safely support the vehicle. Remove the wheel assembly.
2. Remove the front wheel hub and bearing.

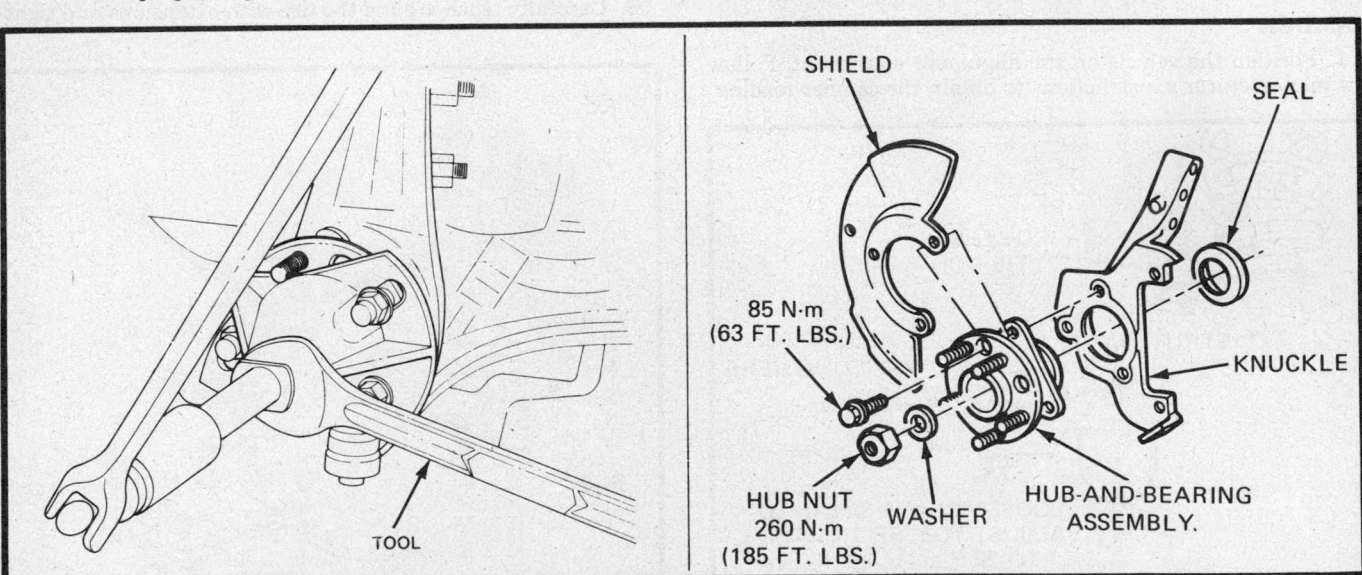

Hub and bearing assembly—removal and installation

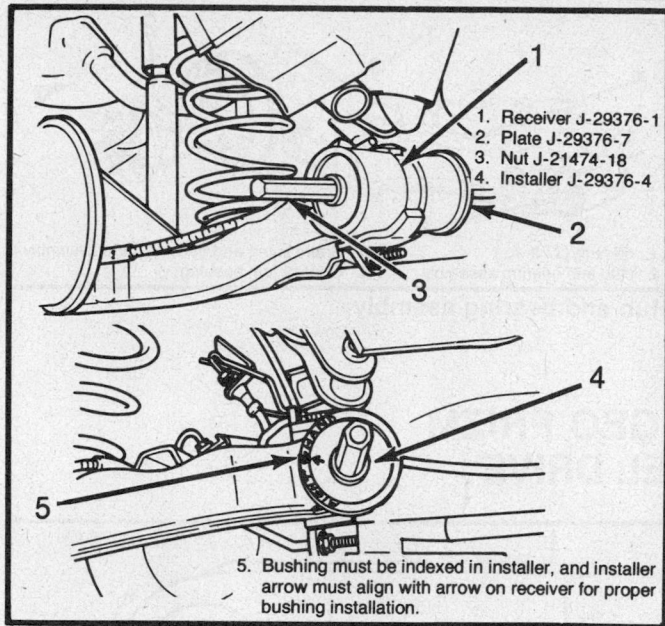

1. Receiver J-29376-1
2. Plate J-29376-7
3. Nut J-21474-18
4. Installer J-29376-4

5. Bushing must be indexed in installer, and installer arrow must align with arrow on receiver for proper bushing installation.

Control arm bushing installation

3. Disconnect the ball joint from the knuckle, using tool J–29330 or equivalent.
4. Remove both strut-to-knuckle mounting bolts. Remove the steering knuckle from the vehicle.
5. To install, reverse the removal procedures.

Rear Suspension

SHOCK ABSORBER

Removal and Installation

1. From inside the trunk, remove the trim cover. Remove the upper shock attaching nut.
2. Raise and safely support the vehicle and the rear axle assembly.
3. Remove the lower shock attaching bolt and nut. Remove the shock absorber from the vehicle.

4. To install, reverse the removal procedures.

STABILIZER BAR

Removal and Installation

1. Raise and safely support the vehicle.
2. Remove nuts and bolts at both the axle and control arm attachments.
3. Remove the bracket, insulator and stabilizer bar.
4. To install, reverse the removal procedures.

COIL SPRING

Removal and Installation

1. Raise and safely support the vehicle and the rear axle assembly. Remove the wheel assembly.
2. Remove the right and left brake line bracket attaching screws from body and allow brake line to hang free.
3. Remove right and left shock absorber lower attaching bolts.
4. Lower the rear axle assembly enough to remove the spring. Do not suspend rear axle by brake hoses as damage to hoses could result.
5. To install, reverse the removal procedures. The ends of the upper coil on the spring must be positioned in the seat of the body. Prior to installing spring it will be necessary to install upper insulators to the body with adhesive to keep it in position while raising the axle assembly and springs.

CONTROL ARM BUSHING

Removal and Installation

1. Raise and safely support the vehicle and the rear axle assembly. Remove the wheel assembly.
2. If removing right bushing, disconnect brake line from body. If left bushing is being removed, disconnect brake line bracket from body and parking brake cable from hook guide on the body. Replace only 1 bushing at a time.
3. Remove nut, bolt and washer from the control arm and bracket attachment and rotate control arm downward.
4. To remove the bushing, install bushing removal tool on control arm over bushing and tighten attaching nuts until tool is securely in place. Remove bushing from control arm by turning bolt.
5. To install, reverse the removal procedures.

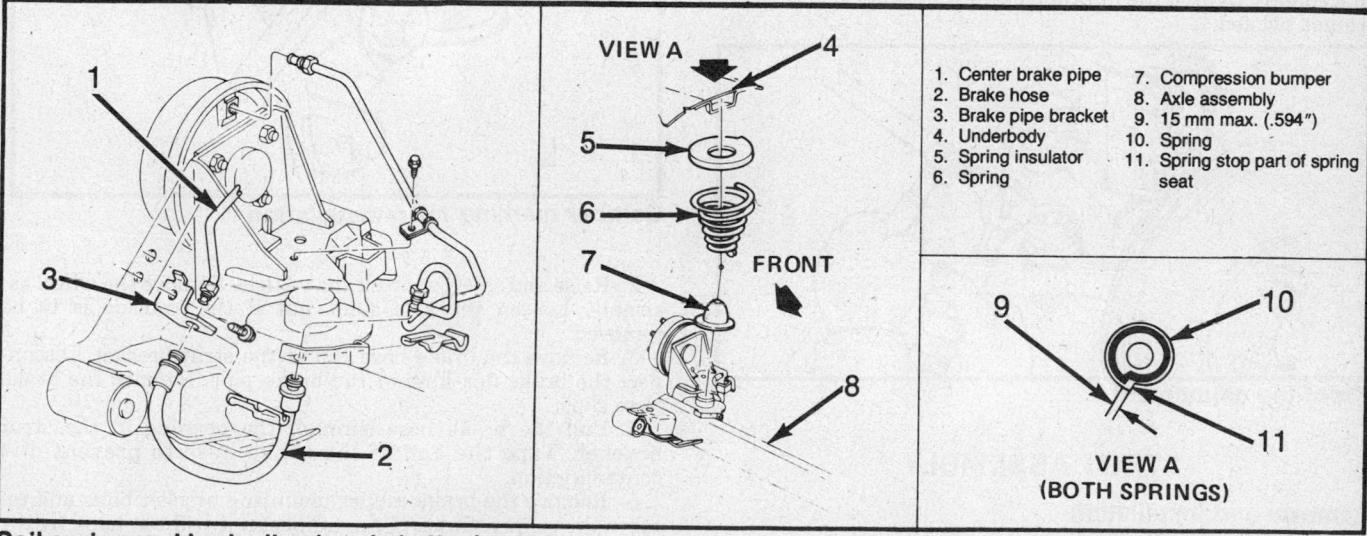

VIEW A

FRONT

1. Center brake pipe
2. Brake hose
3. Brake pipe bracket
4. Underbody
5. Spring insulator
6. Spring
7. Compression bumper
8. Axle assembly
9. 15 mm max. (.594″)
10. Spring
11. Spring stop part of spring seat

VIEW A
(BOTH SPRINGS)

Coil spring and brake line bracket attachment

HUB AND BEARING ASSEMBLY

Removal and Installation

1. Raise and safely support the vehicle. Remove the wheel assembly.

2. Remove the brake drum. Do not hammer on brake drum as damage to the assembly could result.

3. Remove hub and bearing assembly-to-rear axle attaching bolts and remove hub and bearing assembly from axle. The top rear attaching bolt will not clear the brake shoe when removing the hub and bearing assembly. Partially remove hub and bearing assembly prior to removing this bolt.

4. To install, reverse the removal procedures.

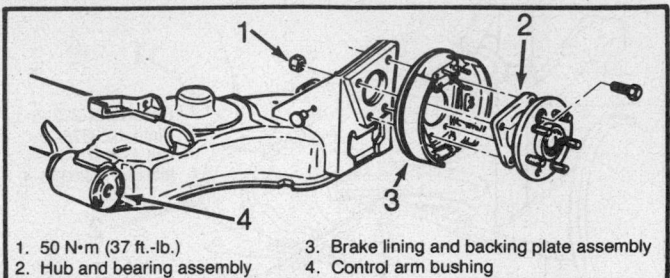

1. 50 N•m (37 ft.-lb.)
2. Hub and bearing assembly
3. Brake lining and backing plate assembly
4. Control arm bushing

Hub and bearing assmbly

GM NOVA AND GEO PRIZM FRONT WHEEL DRIVE

Front Suspension

FRONT WHEEL ALIGNMENT

Adjustment

CAMBER

Camber is adjusted by loosening the upper and lower strut-to-knuckle bolts and nuts, then rotate the cam to the correct specification. After adjustment is completed, tighten the nuts and bolts to specification. In order to prevent an incorrect reading of the caster, bounce the vehicle three times before inspection.

CASTER

Caster is not adjustable. If the caster is found to be from specification, inspect the vehicle for loose, bent or otherwise worn suspension components. Replace as necessary. In order to prevent an incorrect reading of the caster, bounce the vehicle three times before inspection.

TOE

Toe is adjusted by changing the tie rod length. Loosen the boot clamps and slide from the working area. Loosen the left and right tie rod end locknuts. Turn the left and right tie rods to specification. In this adjustment, the left and right tie rods must be equal in length. After adjustment is completed, reinstall the boot clamps, tighten the nuts and check to insure the rack boots are not twisted.

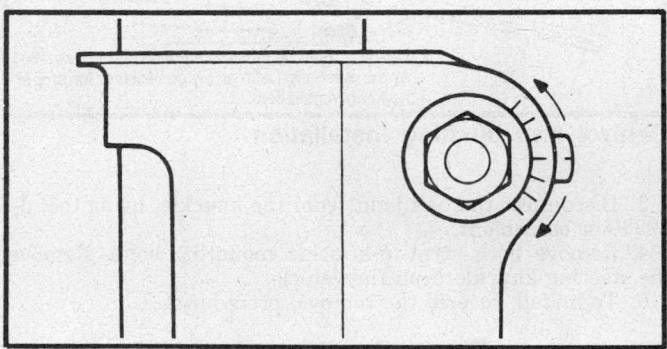

Front camber adjustment

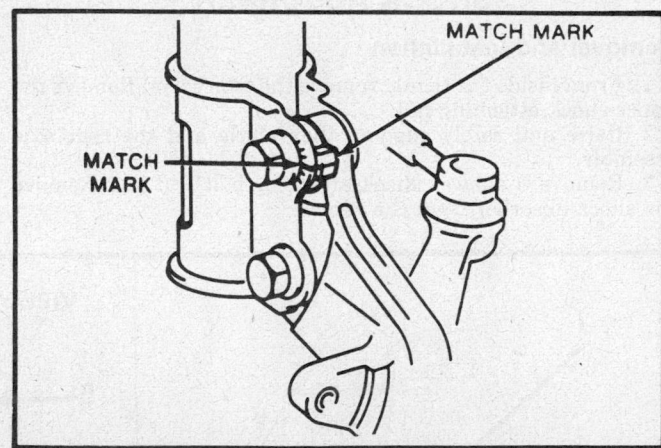

Camber marking for reinstallation

Front toe adjustment

STRUT ASSEMBLY

Removal and Installation

1. Remove the strut-to-body attaching nuts.

2. Raise and safely support the vehicle. Remove the wheel assembly. Loosen the axle shaft nut if the knuckle is to be removed.

3. Remove the brake hose clip at the strut bracket. Disconnect the brake flex hose at the brake pipe. Remove the brake hose clips.

4. Pull the brake hose through the opening in the strut bracket. Tape the end of the brake hose to prevent dirt contamination.

5. Remove the brake caliper mounting bracket bolts and remove the caliper. Support the caliper so it will not hang by the brake hose. Do not disconnect the brake hose from the caliper.

6. Mark the adjusting cam and remove both strut-to-knuckle attaching bolts.

7. Remove the strut assembly from the vehicle. Remove the camber adjusting cam from the knuckle.

8. Inspect components for signs of wear, cracks or distortion. Replace as necessary.

9. To install, reverse the removal procedures.

CONTROL ARM

Removal and Installation

1. Raise and safely support the vehicle.

2. Remove the lower control arm-to-steering knuckle attaching bolts and nuts. Remove the control arm and inspect the arm and bushing for distortion or cracking. Repair or replace as needed.

3. To remove the rear lower control arm bushing, remove the nut retainer and bushing. Torque the bushing nut to 76 ft. lbs.

4. To install, reverse the removal procedures. Always replace self locking nuts with new ones. Check wheel alignment and adjust, if necessary.

BALL JOINT

Removal and Installation

1. Raise and safely support the vehicle. Remove the wheel assembly.

2. Using tool J–35413 or equivalent, separate the ball joint from the knuckle.

3. Remove the nuts and bolts attaching the ball joint and control arm.

4. Remove the ball joint. Inspect the ball joint for excessive wear or damage to the boot seal.

5. To install, reverse the removal procedures. Torque the knuckle-to-ball joint nut to 82 ft. lbs. Torque the control arm attaching nuts to 47 ft. lbs.

6. Do not remove the hub assembly from the knuckle unless it is absolutely necessary. Should removal become necessary, the grease seals must be replaced with new ones. Never reuse a self locking nut. Always replace the self locking nut with a new one.

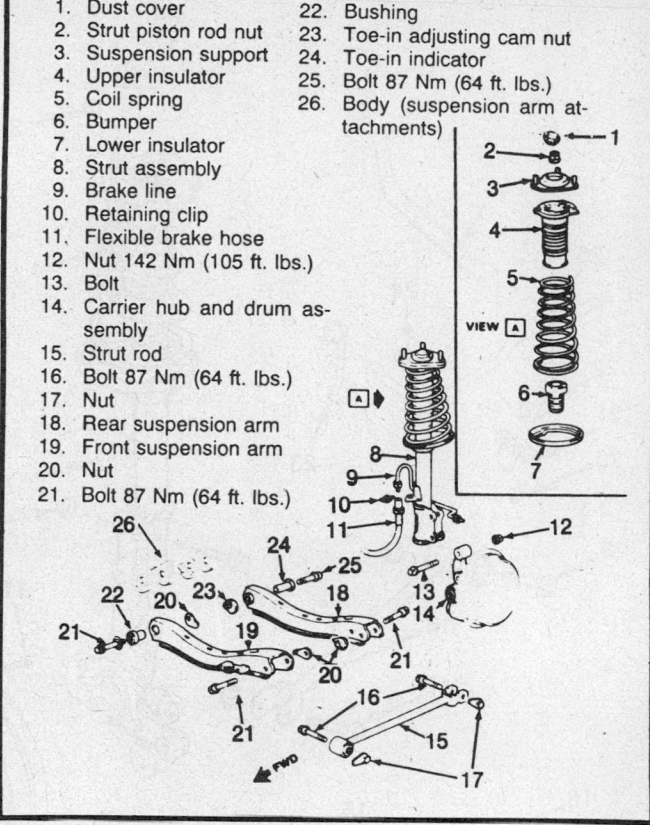

1. Dust cover
2. Strut piston rod nut
3. Suspension support
4. Upper insulator
5. Coil spring
6. Bumper
7. Lower insulator
8. Strut assembly
9. Brake line
10. Retaining clip
11. Flexible brake hose
12. Nut 142 Nm (105 ft. lbs.)
13. Bolt
14. Carrier hub and drum assembly
15. Strut rod
16. Bolt 87 Nm (64 ft. lbs.)
17. Nut
18. Rear suspension arm
19. Front suspension arm
20. Nut
21. Bolt 87 Nm (64 ft. lbs.)
22. Bushing
23. Toe-in adjusting cam nut
24. Toe-in indicator
25. Bolt 87 Nm (64 ft. lbs.)
26. Body (suspension arm attachments)

Rear suspension-exploded view

STEERING KNUCKLE

Removal and Installation

1. Raise and safely support the vehicle. Remove the wheel assembly.

2. Remove the brake hose retaining clip at the strut. Disconnect the flex hose from the brake pipe.

3. Remove the caliper bracket-to-knuckle mounting bolts. Support the caliper. Remove the disc.

4. Remove the drive axle nut. Using tool J–25287 or equivalent, push out the drive axle.

5. Remove the cotter pin. Remove the tie rod-to-knuckle attaching nut. Separate the tie rod using tool J–24319–01 or equivalent.

6. Remove the ball joint-to-control arm attaching nuts and bolts.

7. Matchmark the camber relationship and remove the strut-to-knuckle attaching bolts and nuts. Remove the knuckle.

8. To install, reverse the removal procedures.

Rear Suspension

STRUT ASSEMBLY

Removal and Installation

1. Working inside the vehicle, remove the strut cover and package tray bracket. Remove the strut retaining bolts.

2. Raise and safely support the vehicle and the rear axle assembly. Remove the wheel assembly.

3. Disconnect the brake line at the wheel cylinder and plug it. Disconnect the flexible hose from the strut.

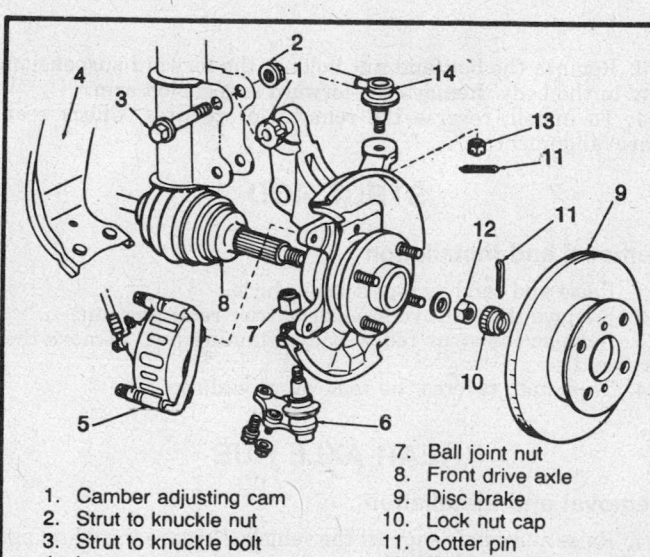

1. Camber adjusting cam
2. Strut to knuckle nut
3. Strut to knuckle bolt
4. Lower control arm
5. Brake caliper
6. Lower ball joint
7. Ball joint nut
8. Front drive axle
9. Disc brake
10. Lock nut cap
11. Cotter pin
12. Drive axle nut
13. Steering ball joint nut
14. Steering joint

Hub/knuckle-exploded view

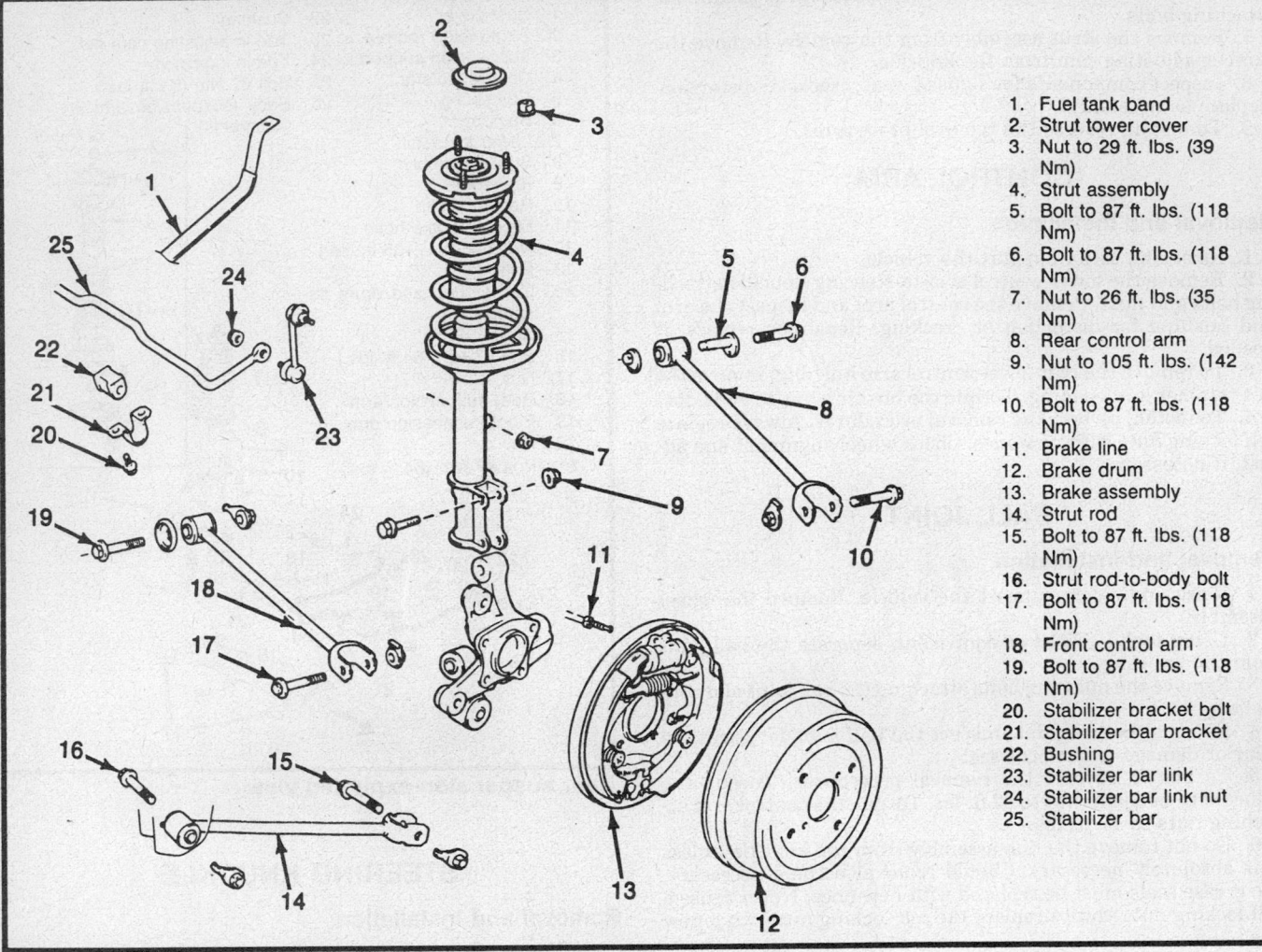

1. Fuel tank band
2. Strut tower cover
3. Nut to 29 ft. lbs. (39 Nm)
4. Strut assembly
5. Bolt to 87 ft. lbs. (118 Nm)
6. Bolt to 87 ft. lbs. (118 Nm)
7. Nut to 26 ft. lbs. (35 Nm)
8. Rear control arm
9. Nut to 105 ft. lbs. (142 Nm)
10. Bolt to 87 ft. lbs. (118 Nm)
11. Brake line
12. Brake drum
13. Brake assembly
14. Strut rod
15. Bolt to 87 ft. lbs. (118 Nm)
16. Strut rod-to-body bolt
17. Bolt to 87 ft. lbs. (118 Nm)
18. Front control arm
19. Bolt to 87 ft. lbs. (118 Nm)
20. Stabilizer bracket bolt
21. Stabilizer bar bracket
22. Bushing
23. Stabilizer bar link
24. Stabilizer bar link nut
25. Stabilizer bar

Exploded view of the rear suspension system—Geo Prizm

4. Remove the retaining bolts holding the strut-to-axle carrier. Disconnect the strut.

5. Remove the upper strut mounting nuts and remove the strut assembly.

6. To install, reverse the removal procedures. Bleed the brake system.

REAR CONTROL ARM

Removal and Installation

1. Raise and safely support the vehicle.

2. Remove the bolt and nut holding the rear suspension arm to the axle carrier.

3. Remove the cam and bolt holding the rear suspension arm to the body. Remove the suspension arm.

4. To install, reverse the removal procedures. Remember where the cam plate mark is before disassembly.

FORWARD CONTROL ARM

Removal and Installation

1. Raise and safely support the vehicle.

2. Remove the bolt and nut holding the forward suspension arm to the axle carrier.

3. Remove the bolt and nut holding the forward suspension arm to the body. Remove the forward suspension arm.

4. To install, reverse the removal procedures. Check rear wheel alignment.

STRUT ROD

Removal and Installation

1. Raise and safely support the vehicle.

2. Remove the strut rod-to-axle carrier retaining nut.

3. Remove the strut rod-to-body retaining nut. Remove the strut rod.

4. To install, reverse the removal procedures.

REAR AXLE HUB

Removal and Installation

1. Raise and safely support the vehicle. Remove the wheel assembly and the brake drum.

2. Remove the the axle hub assembly-to-axle carrier bolts.

3. Remove the axle/hub bearing assembly. Remove the O-ring.

4. To install, reverse the removal procedures.

REAR AXLE CARRIER

Removal and Installation

1. Raise and safely support the vehicle. Remove the rear axle hub.
2. Disconnect the brake line from the wheel cylinder and plug the line.

3. Remove the axle carrier-to-strut rod retaining nut. Remove the axle carrier-to-front suspension and rear suspension arm retaining nuts.
4. Remove the bolts and nuts holding the axle carrier to the strut. Remove the axle carrier.
5. To install, reverse the removal procedures. Bleed the brake system. Check the rear wheel alignment and adjust as necessary.

GM FIERO BODY
FRONT WHEEL DRIVE

Front Suspension

WHEEL ALIGNMENT

Adjustment
CASTER

1986–87

Caster angle can be changed with a realignment of washers located between the legs of the upper control arm. For adjustment, a kit containing 2 washers, 1 of 3mm thickness and 1 of 9mm thickness, must be used.

1988

Before adjusting caster angles, both the front and rear bumpers should be raised and released (jounced) 3 times each. The caster adjustment is performed by loosening the upper control arm and shaft bolts to tilt the wheel rearward of the vertical. Toe angle must be adjusted after caster/camber adjustments are performed.

NOTE: Whenever adjusting caster, it is important to always use 2 washers totalling 12mm thickness, with 1 washer at each end of locating tube.

CAMBER

1986–87

Camber angle can be increased approximately 1 degree by removing the upper ball joint, rotating it ½ turn and reinstalling it with the flat of the upper flange on the inboard side of the control arm.

1988

Before adjusting camber angles, both the front and rear bumpers should be raised and released (jounced) 3 times each. The camber adjustment is performed by loosening the upper control arm and shaft bolts to tilt the wheel forward or rearward. Toe angle must be adjusted after caster/camber adjustments are performed.

NOTE: If the upper control arm shaft bolts are removed for any reason, the paddle nut assembly must be replaced. Final torque to upper control arm shaft bolts is –52 ft. lbs., plus ¼ turn 90 degrees.

TOE

Toe is the turning in of the wheels. The actual amount of toe is normally only a fraction of a degree. The purpose of toe is to ensure parallel rolling of the rear wheels. Excessive toe-in or toe-out may increase tire wear. Toe also serves to offset the small deflections of the wheel support system which occurs when the vehicle is rolling forward. In other words, even when the wheels are set slightly to toe when the vehicle is standing still, they tend to roll parallel on the road when the vehicle is moving.

1. Follow the manufacturers instructions to obtain a toe in reading that is within specifications.
2. Loosen the jam nuts on the toe link rod.
3. Rotate the toe link rods to adjust the toe to specifications.
4. Tighten the jam nuts to 47 ft. lbs.

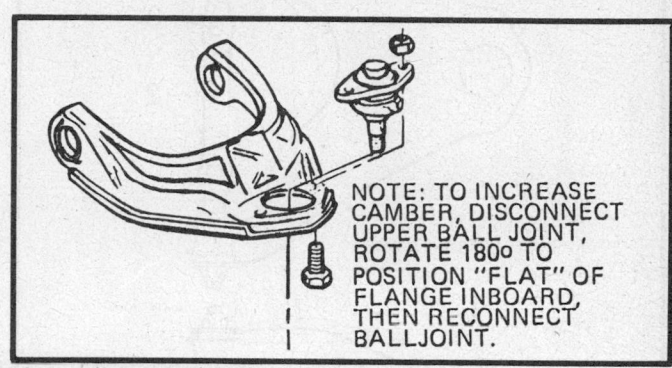

NOTE: TO INCREASE CAMBER, DISCONNECT UPPER BALL JOINT, ROTATE 180º TO POSITION "FLAT" OF FLANGE INBOARD, THEN RECONNECT BALLJOINT.

Upper ball joint/camber adjustment

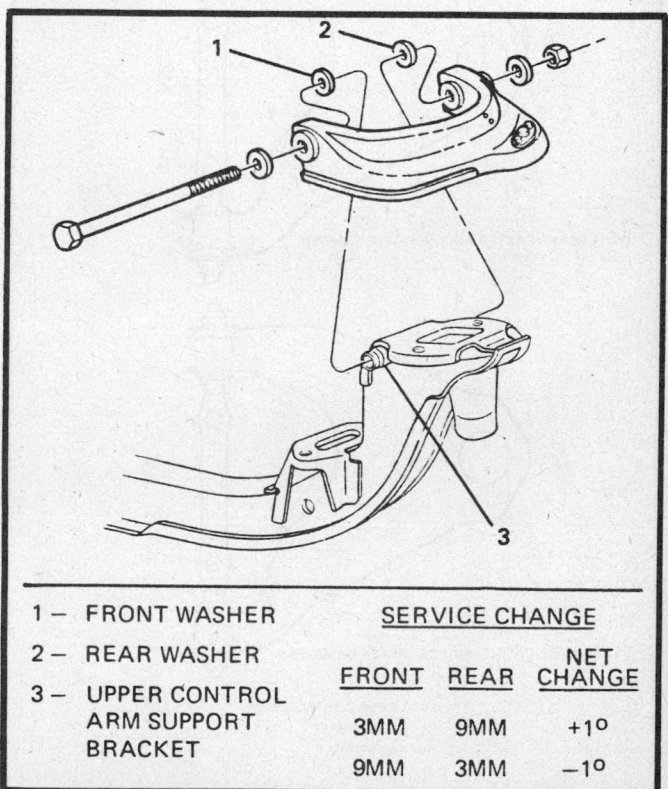

1 – FRONT WASHER	SERVICE CHANGE		
2 – REAR WASHER	FRONT	REAR	NET CHANGE
3 – UPPER CONTROL ARM SUPPORT BRACKET	3MM	9MM	+1º
	9MM	3MM	–1º

Caster adjustment

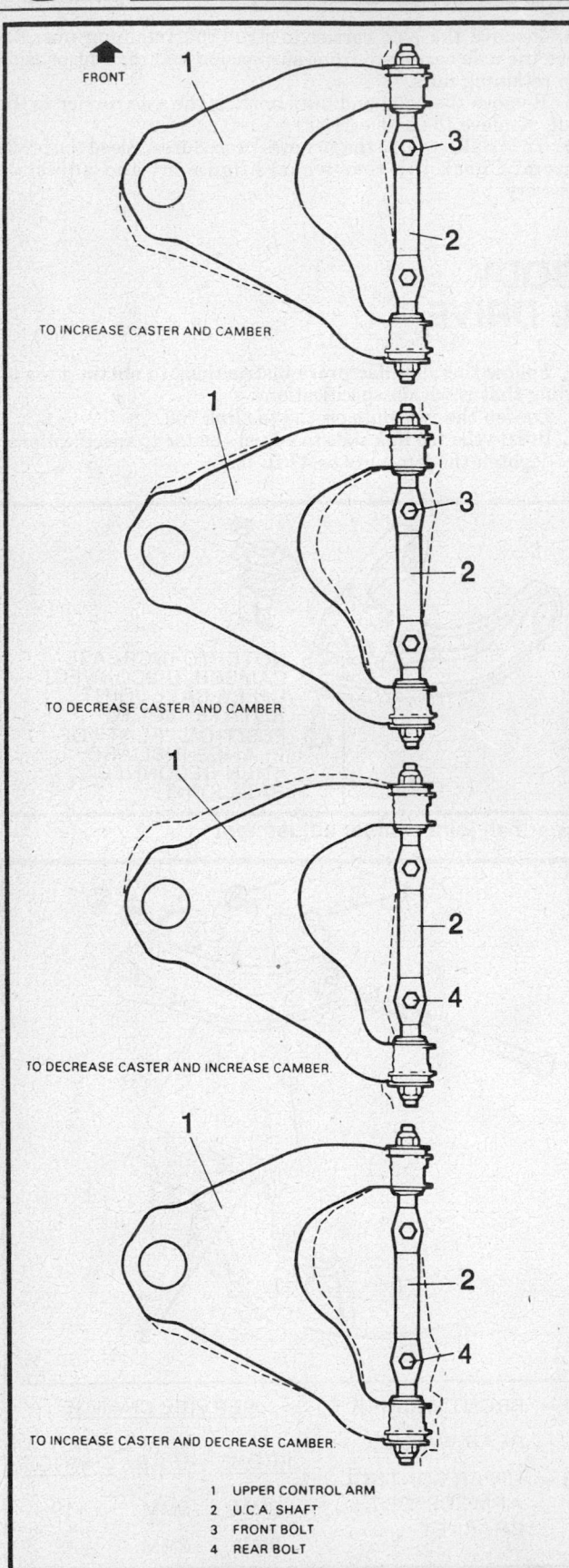

FRONT

TO INCREASE CASTER AND CAMBER.

TO DECREASE CASTER AND CAMBER.

TO DECREASE CASTER AND INCREASE CAMBER.

TO INCREASE CASTER AND DECREASE CAMBER.

1 UPPER CONTROL ARM
2 U.C.A. SHAFT
3 FRONT BOLT
4 REAR BOLT

Adjusting front caster and camber – 1988 Fiero

FRONT WHEEL BEARINGS

Adjustment

NOTE: 1988 vehicles use sealed bearings that do not require adjustment.

1. Raise and safely support the vehicle. Remove the wheel assembly.
2. Remove dust cap from hub. Remove cotter pin from spindle and spindle nut.
3. Tighten the spindle nut to 12 ft. lbs. while turning the wheel assembly forward by hand to fully seat the bearings. This will remove any grease or burrs which could cause excessive wheel bearing play later.
4. Back off the nut to the just loose position.
5. Hand tighten the spindle nut. Loosen spindle nut until either hole in the spindle aligns with a slot in the nut, not more than ½ flat.
6. Install a new cotter pin. Measure the looseness in the hub assembly. There will be from 0.001–0.005 in. endplay when properly adjusted.
7. Install the dust cap.

SHOCK ABSORBER

Removal and Installation

1. Raise and safely support the vehicle. Remove the wheel assembly.
2. Remove the upper shock absorber retaining bolts. Remove the lower shock absorber retaining bolts.
3. Remove the shock absorber from the vehicle.
4. To install, reverse the removal procedures.

UPPER BALL JOINT

Removal and Installation

1986–87

1. Raise and safely support the vehicle. Remove the wheel assembly and support the lower control arm with a jack.
2. Remove upper ball stud nut, then reinstall nut finger tight. Install tool J–26407 or equivalent with the cup end over the lower ball stud nut.

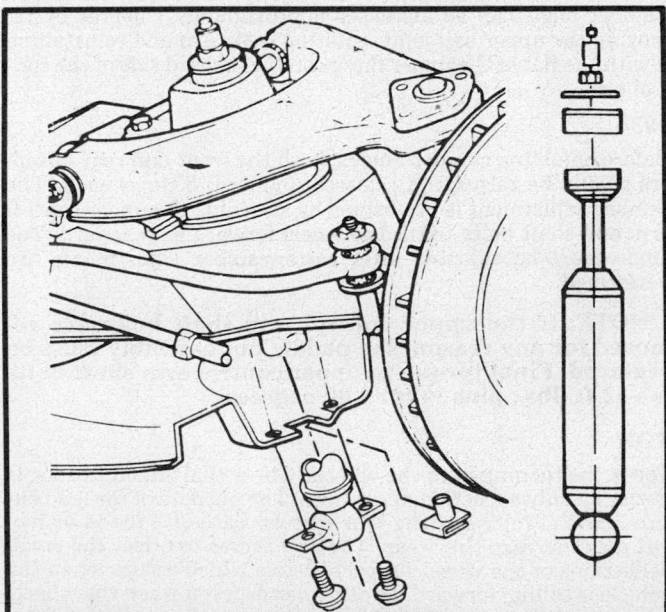

Shock absorber asembly – 1988 Fiero

3. Turn the threaded end of tool until upper ball stud is free of steering knuckle. Remove the tool. Remove the nut from the ball stud.

4. Remove nuts and bolts attaching ball joint-to-upper control arm. Note which way the flat of the ball joint is pointing before removing it. The direction of this flat on the ball joint flange should be in the same direction as the one removed unless a change in camber is desired.

5. Remove ball joint from the vehicle.

6. To install, reverse the removal procedures.

1988

1. Raise the vehicle on a hoist and support the lower control arm with a jack.

───────── CAUTION ─────────

Raising the vehicle in this manner keeps the coil spring compressed. Use care to support adequately or personal injury could result.

─────────────────────────

2. Remove the wheel assembly.

3. Remove the bolt attaching the brake line clip to the upper control arm.

4. Disconnect the tie rod end from the steering knuckle and swing the knuckle outboard.

5. Remove the nut from the upper ball joint, then use tool J-26407 or equivalent, to press the ball joint from the steering knuckle.

6. Remove the upper ball joint from the control arm by drilling out the attaching rivets.

To install:

7. Install the upper ball joint-to-the control arm with nuts and bolts.

8. Inspect the tapered hole in the steering knuckle and remove any dirt. If any out-of-roundness, deformation or damage is noted, the knuckle MUST be replaced.

9. Position the upper ball joint to the steering knuckle and install the nut.

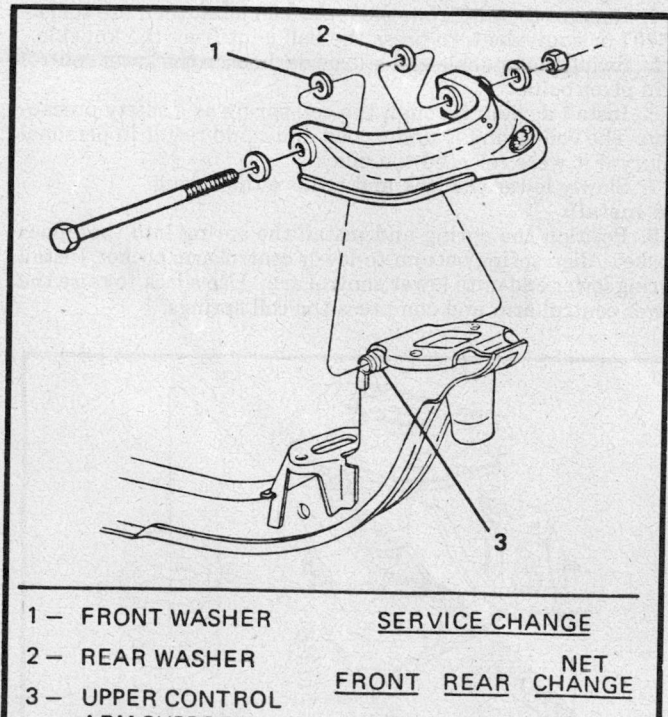

1 —	FRONT WASHER	SERVICE CHANGE		
2 —	REAR WASHER			NET
		FRONT	REAR	CHANGE
3 —	UPPER CONTROL			
	ARM SUPPORT	3MM	9MM	+1°
	BRACKET			
		9MM	3MM	−1°

Front control arm shim arrangement

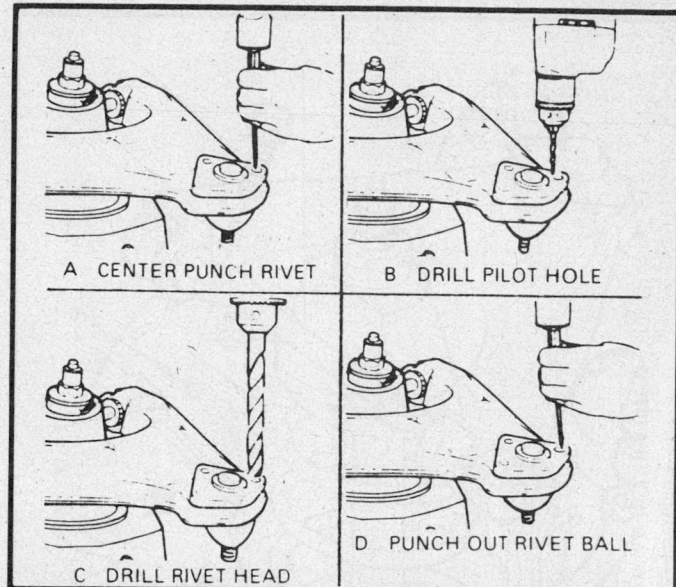

A CENTER PUNCH RIVET   B DRILL PILOT HOLE

C DRILL RIVET HEAD   D PUNCH OUT RIVET BALL

Upper ball joint removal – 1988 Fiero

10. Torque the ball joint stud nut to 30–40 ft. lbs. Rotate the nut approximately ⅙ turn to align cotter pin. Additional torque should not exceed 55 ft. lbs. Install a new cotter pin.

11. Install the brake line clip to the control arm.

12. Install the wheel assembly and lower the vehicle.

LOWER BALL JOINT

On 1986–87 vehicles, the lower ball joint is welded to the lower control arm and cannot be serviced separately. Replacement of the entire lower control arm will be necessary if the lower ball joint requires replacement.

Removal and Installation

1. Raise the vehicle and properly support the lower control arm with a jack.

2. Remove the wheel assembly.

3. Disconnect the tie rod end from the steering knuckle.

4. Remove the lower ball joint stud nut and press the ball joint stud from the steering knuckle. Position the knuckle off aside.

5. Install clamp tool J-9591-10 and bolt tool J-9519-18 with removal adapters J-37161-1 and J-37161-3 or equivalent, on the lower control arm.

6. Press the ball joint from the lower control arm.

7. To install, reverse the removal procedures. Torque the ball stud nut to 26 ft. lbs., plus a ½ turn. Torque the tie rod end nut to 15 ft. lbs., plus a ½ turn. Check the alignment and adjust as necessary.

UPPER CONTROL ARM

Removal and Installation

1986–87

1. Raise and safely support the vehicle. Remove the wheel assembly.

2. Remove the rivet holding the brake line clip to the upper control arm.

3. Properly support the lower control arm using a jack. Remove upper ball joint from the steering knuckle.

4. Remove the control arm pivot bolt. Remove control arm from vehicle.

5. To install, reverse the removal procedures.

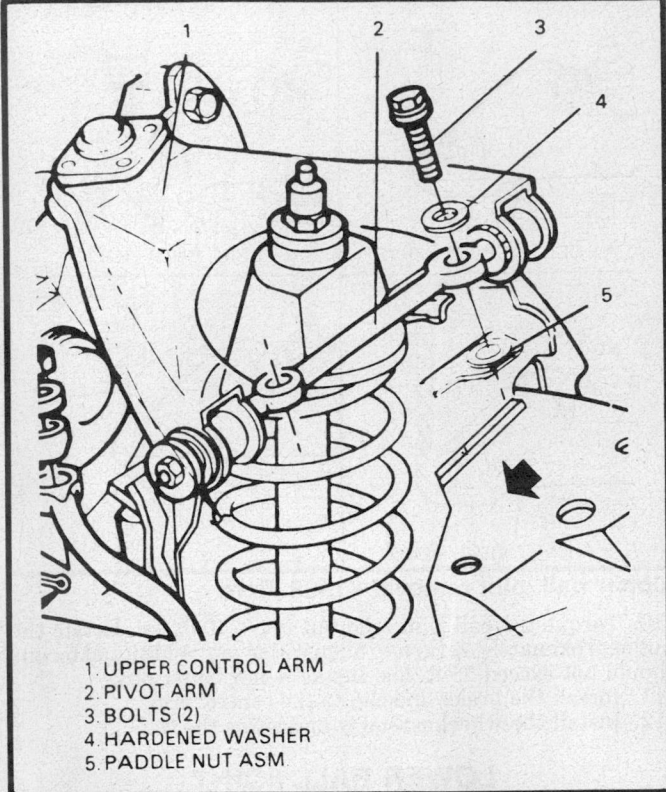

1. UPPER CONTROL ARM
2. PIVOT ARM
3. BOLTS (2)
4. HARDENED WASHER
5. PADDLE NUT ASM

Upper control arm components—1988 Fiero

1988

1. Raise the vehicle and properly support the lower control arm with a jack.
2. Remove the wheel assembly.
3. Remove the bolt attaching the brake line clip to the upper control arm.
4. Disconnect the tie rod end from the steering knuckle and swing the knuckle outboard.
5. Remove the ball joint stud nut from the ball joint and press the ball joint from the knuckle.
6. Remove the bolts and paddle nut assembly attaching the upper control arm shaft-to-crossmember and remove the control arm from the vehicle.
7. Install upper control arm shaft-to-crossmember bolts with a new paddle nut assembly. Do not apply final torque until alignment is performed.
8. To complete the installation, reversing the removal procedures. Torque the ball joint-to-steering knuckle nut to 30–40 ft. lbs. Check and and adjust the alignment as necessary.

LOWER CONTROL ARM

Removal and Installation

1. Raise and safely support the vehicle. Remove the wheel assembly.
2. Disconnect the stabilizer bar from the lower control arm. Disconnect the tie rod from the steering knuckle.
3. Disconnect the shock absorber at the lower control arm. Properly support the lower control arm with a jack.
4. Remove the nut from the lower ball joint, then use tool J–26407 or equivalent, to press the ball joint from the knuckle.
5. Swing the knuckle and hub aside. Loosen the lower control arm pivot bolts.
6. Install a chain through the coil spring as a safety precau-

tion. The coil spring is under load and could result in personal injury if it were released too quickly.
7. Slowly lower the jack and remove the spring.
8. Remove the pivot bolts at the chassis and the crossmember. Remove the lower control arm. Removal of the pivot bolt at the crossmember may require the loosening or removal of the steering assembly mounting bolts.
To install:
9. Install the lower control arm and pivot bolts at crossmember and body. Tighten slightly but do not torque.
10. Position the spring and install the spring into the upper pocket. Align spring bottom-to-lower control arm pocket. Install spring lower end onto lower control arm. Use a jack to raise the lower control arm and compress the coil springs.
11. Install the ball joint through the lower control arm and into the steering knuckle. Install nut to ball joint stud and torque to 55 ft. lbs. Install a new cotter pin.
12. Connect the stabilizer bar and torque the bolt to 16 ft. lbs. Connect the tie rod and torque to 29 ft. lbs. Install the shock absorber to the lower control arm and torque the bolt to 35 ft. lbs.
13. If the bolts were removed or loosened at the steering assembly replace with new bolts and torque to 21 ft. lbs.
14. With the suspension system in its normal standing height, torque the lower control arm-to-body bolt to 62 ft. lbs. and the lower control arm-to-crossmember nut to 52 ft. lbs. Check and set alignment as necessary.

COIL SPRING

Removal and Installation

1. Raise and safely support the vehicle. Remove the wheel assembly.
2. Disconnect the stabilizer bar from the lower control arm. Disconnect the tie rod from the steering knuckle.
3. Disconnect the shock absorber at the lower control arm. Properly support the lower control arm with a jack.
4. Remove the nut from the lower ball joint, then use tool J–26407 or equivalent, to press the ball joint from the knuckle.
5. Swing the knuckle and hub aside. Loosen the lower control arm pivot bolts.
6. Install a chain through the coil spring as a safety precaution. The coil spring is under load and could result in personal injury if it were released too quickly.
7. Slowly lower the jack and remove the spring.
To install:
8. Position the spring and install the spring into the upper pocket. Align spring bottom-to-lower control arm pocket. Install spring lower end onto lower control arm. Use a jack to raise the lower control arm and compress the coil springs.

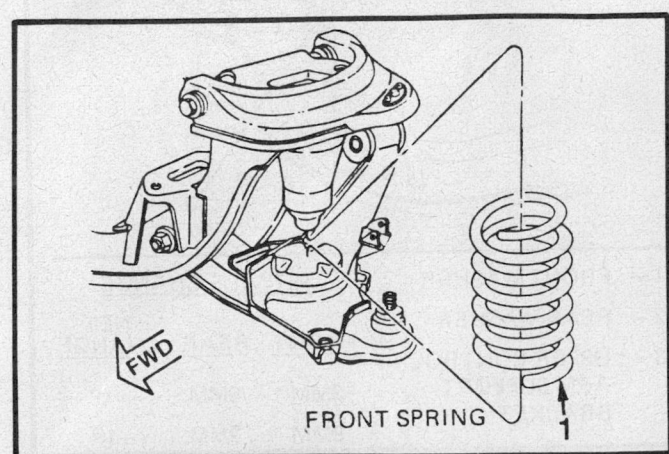

FWD

FRONT SPRING

Front coil spring positioning